BOOK AUCTION RECORDS

A PRICED AND ANNOTATED ANNUAL RECORD

OF INTERNATIONAL BOOK AUCTIONS

VOLUME 81

For the Auction Season August 1983–July 1984

Part I

Printed Books & Atlases

Part II

Printed Maps, Charts & Plans

EDITOR: Wendy Y. Heath

DAWSON

Published by Dawson Publishing

Cannon House

Folkestone, Kent CT19 5EE

© Wm Dawson & Sons Ltd., 1984

ISBN 0 7129 1033 6

Printed in Great Britain by
Unwin Brothers Limited, The Gresham Press,
Old Woking, Surrey.

Contents

Explanatory Notes

BOOK AUCTION RECORDS VOLUME 81 follows the arrangement of its predecessor. The order of description follows current bibliographical practice but with the use of dashes to ditto both Author and Title, followed where necessary by 'Anr.Copy', 'Anr.Run', or 'Anr.Edn.', to indicate another copy/set/run/volume and another edition/issue/impression. The volume as previously is in two parts, Part I, Printed Books & Atlases, Part II, Printed Maps, Charts & Plans.

The Book entries are arranged alphabetically by author (personal or corporate), or where there is no known author, by title, by private press or other obvious association. Often, official reports, directories and similar publications are listed geographically. Authors' names frequently take different forms, for instance those which are commonly Latinised, and for these we have endeavoured to use the form by which they are most generally known. Authors of pseudonymous works may be found under their real names or their pseudonymous names, but in either case are appropriately cross-referenced. An alphabetical list of pseudonyms is included in this volume. Anonymous works are indicated by enclosing the Author dash in brackets. Brackets are also used elsewhere in the usual manner to indicate notes, translations, interpolations etc., that do not appear in the original work, but have been added by the Editor or the Auctioneers' cataloguer.

Certain large categories are listed under subject headings, such as Almanacs, Albums, Atlases, Bibles, Breviaries, Costume, Haggadah, Horae, Hymnals, Magna Carta, Missals, New Testament, Prayerbooks, Psalms, Statuta, Talmud and Trials. The individual works listed under these large subject categories and under certain prolific authors such as Shakespeare and Cervantes are not always arranged alphabetically, but are often arranged chronologically or by language.

In the listings of individual works, ample bibliographical detail is given for ease of identification. After the author and title, these details include editor, translator, illustrator, place of publication, press if important, and date. Then follow details of edition/issue, number of volumes if more than one, format, description of binding and, when applicable, important ownership marks, presentation inscriptions, annotations or extraneous material such as letters, notes or other inserts. The term 'bdg. not stated' is used in entries where details of the binding has not been given by the Auctioneer. Information is also given on imperfections, damage or defects that might possibly affect the price. Where no place or date of publication appears in a work this also, if known, is given, enclosed in brackets; if not known, this fact is indicated by the usual abbreviation n.p. or n.d.

The bibliographical description is followed by the auction sale record, which gives the auction house (in code, see our 'Key to Sales'), date of sale, sale lot number, buyer's name (when given and published by the auction house) and the price made, which is the hammer price, thus not including any buyer's premium that may apply. Where known, the amount of buyer's premium charged by each Auction House is given as a percentage under 'Auction Houses with their Addresses & Buyers Premiums'. In addition cross-references are made for pseudonyms, joint authorship, nobles, important books bound together, compound names (in cases where confusion may arise) and also for the more important illustrators, editors, translators and private presses. Bibliographical abbreviations used in the records are those which appear in the list of abbreviations. Non-bibliographical abbreviations in general use are not listed.

It is not our policy to include in Book Auction Records lots of two or more unrelated works, single engravings, prints and photographs, etc., but important books bound together may appear. Volume 81 records only those lots which realised £50.00 and over (U.K.), $100.00 and over (U.S.A., Canada and Australia), or the European equivalent of £100.00 and over (see our 'Currency Conversion Rates'). For lots 'sold with all faults' (w.a.f.) only those which realised at least £100.00 and $200.00 are included.

The map entries are generally arranged alphabetically by Author or Cartographer followed by the title, place and date of publication, size, description and sale record. The description includes details of decoration, whether coloured, framed and glazed or mounted, and also any imperfections that might possibly affect the price.

Book Auction Records is compiled from the season's auction catalogues and we are constantly faced with the problem of variant, abridged, obscure and even faulty descriptions of titles, this inevitably causing much additional time to be spent on bibliographical research and checking. Therefore whilst every endeavour is made to avoid mistakes and correct faulty information, some errors will unavoidably have crept in. Certain entries in Book Auction Records may appear to be incomplete, but this is usually due to lack of information in the auction catalogue.

The more obvious value of Book Auction Records to booksellers, collectors and librarians is as a unique record of international auction prices over a long period of years, but with its vast number of incidental references to anonymous and pseudonymous authors, editors, translators, illustrators, private presses, societies and ownership, etc. it is also invaluable for general bibliographical reference.

Bibliographical References

Abbott	=	Abbott, Catalogue of Fifteenth-Century Books
BMC	=	British Museum Catalogue of Books Printed in the XVth Century
C.	=	Copinger, Supplement to Hain's Repertorium
D. & M.	=	Darlow & Moule, Historical Catalogue of the printed editions of Holy Scripture
Goff	=	Goff, Incunabula in American Libraries
H.	=	Hain, Repertorium Bibliographicum
H. & L.	=	Halkett & Laing, Dictionary of Anonymous & Pseudonymous English Literature
Sabin	=	Sabin, Dictionary of Books relating to America
STC	=	Pollard & Redgrave, Short-Title Catalogue of Books printed in England . . . 1475–1640
Wing	=	Wing, Short-Title Catalogue of Books printed in England . . . 1641–1700

Abbreviations

A.D.(s.)	= autograph document (signed)	fo.	= folio	plt(s).	= plate(s)
		fore-e. pntg.	= fore-edge painting	pol.	= polished
advt(s).	= advertisement(s)	Fr.	= French	port(s).	= portrait(s)
A.L.(s.)	= autograph letter (signed)	frontis.	= frontispiece(s)	portfo(s).	= portfolio(s)
		gt.	= gilt	pp.	= pages
Amer.	= American	hf.	= half	Pr.	= Press
A.N.(s.)	= autograph note (signed)	histor.	= historiated	prelims.	= preliminary pages
		H.M.P.	= hand-made paper	pres.	= presentation
annot(s).	= annotation(s)	ill(s).	= Illustrator/illustrated/ illustration(s)	priv. ptd.	= privately printed
anr.	= another			pt(s).	= part(s)
bd(s).	= board(s)	imp(s).	= impressions(s)	ptd.	= printed
bdg(s).	= binding(s)	impft.	= imperfect	publd.	= published
bkd.	= backed	incompl.	= incomplete	qtr.	= quarter
bkplt(s).	= bookplate(s)	inscr(s).	= inscribed/inscription(s)	rebkd.	= rebacked
bnd.	= bound	iss.	= issue/issued	rebnd.	= rebound
brkn.	= broken	Jnr.	= Junior	reprd.	= repaired
C.	= century	jnt(s).	= joint(s)	russ.	= russia leather
ca.	= circa	leath.	= leather	s.-c.('s)	= slip case(s)
card.	= cardboard	lev.	= levant	sig(s).	= signature(s)
cf.	= calf	lf.	= leaf	sigd.	= signed
chromo- litho(s).	= chromolithograph(s)	lge.	= large	sm.	= small
		liby.	= library	Soc.	= Society
cl.	= cloth	litho(s).	= lithograph(s)	spr.	= sprinkled/speckled/ spotted
col(s).	= colour(s)	ll.	= leaves		
cold.	= coloured	L.P.	= large paper	stp(s).	= stamp(s)
coll.	= collected/collection	lr. (cover)	= lower (cover)	stpd.	= stamped
compl.	= complete	Ltd.	= Limited	str.-grd.	= straight-grained
cont.	= contemporary	marb.	= marbled	supp(s).	= supplement(s)
decor(s).	= decorated/decoration(s)	mntd.	= mounted	thro.-out	= throughout
defect.	= defective	mod.	= modern	T.L.(s.)	= typed letter (signed)
detchd.	= detached	monog(s).	= monogram(s)	trans.	= Translator/translated/ translation
disbnd.	= disbound	mor.	= morocco		
doubls.	= doublures	mott.	= mottled	unbnd.	= unbound
dtd.	= dated	MS(S).	= manuscript(s)	unc.	= uncut
dupl.	= duplicate	mus. notat.	= musical notation	unif.	= uniform
d.-w.('s)	= dust wrapper(s)	n.d.	= no date	upr. (cover)	= upper (cover)
ed.	= Editor/edited	n.p.	= no place	v.d.	= various dates
edn(s).	= edition(s)	ob.	= oblong	vell.	= vellum
elab.	= elaborate/elaborately	orig.	= original	vig(s).	= vignette(s)
Engl.	= English	outl.	= outline	vol(s).	= volume(s)
engr(s).	= engraving(s)	p.	= page	v.p.	= various places
F.	= framed	panel.	= panelled	w.a.f.	= with all faults
facs.	= facsimile(s)	parch.	= parchment	wrap(s).	= wrapper(s)
F. & G.	= framed & glazed	pict.	= pictorial	wtrmkd.	= watermarked

ABBREVIATIONS FOR PLACE NAMES

Amst.	= Amsterdam	Copen.	= Copenhagen	Nuremb.	= Nuremburg
Antw.	= Antwerp	Edinb.	= Edinburgh	N.Y.	= New York
Balt.	= Baltimore	Flor.	= Florence	Phila.	= Philadelphia
Bg'ham.	= Birmingham	L.	= London	Pittsb.	= Pittsburg
Camb.	= Cambridge	L'pool.	= Liverpool	San Franc.	= San Francisco
Chic.	= Chicago	Mich.	= Michigan	St. Petersb.	= Saint Petersburg
Cinc.	= Cincinatti	N.O.	= New Orleans	Wash.	= Washington

ABBREVIATIONS FOR PRIVATE PRESSES

Ash. Pr.	= Ashendene Press	Grol. Cl.	= Grolier Club	Nones. Pr.	= Nonesuch Press
Bannat. Cl.	= Bannatyne Club	Grol. Soc.	= Grolier Society	Roxb. Cl.	= Roxburghe Club
Gold. Cock. Pr.	= Golden Cockerel Press	Kelms. Pr.	= Kelmscott Press	Shakes. Hd. Pr.	= Shakespeare Head Press
		Ltd. Edns. Cl.	= Limited Editions Club		
Gregy. Pr.	= Gregynog Press			Straw. Hill Pr.	= Strawberry Hill Press

Pseudonyms

Pseudonym.	Real Name.
A	
A	— Matthew ARNOLD
ABRAHAM A SANTA CLARA	— Johann Ulrich MEGERLE
ALAIN	— Emile Auguste CHARTIER
ALASTAIR	— Hans Henning VOIGHT
ALEPH	— W. HARVEY
ALEXIS, of Piedmont	— Girolamo RUSCELLI
ANGLO, Thoma	— Joannes THOMA
ANTONINUS, Brother	— William EVERSON
APOLLINARIS, Q.	— Walther Hermann RYFF
ARISTIDES	— W.P. van NESS
B	
BALDWIN, Edward	— William GODWIN
BALWHIDDER, Micah	— John GALT
BARKHAM, Dean	— John GUILLIM
BELL, Acton	— Anne BRONTE
BELL, Currer	— Charlotte BRONTE
BELL, Ellis	— Emily BRONTE
BICKERSTAFF, Isaac	— Sir Richard STEELE
BLACKMANTLE, Bernard	— Charles Molloy WESTMACOTT
BOBBIN, Tim	— John COLLIER
BONAVENTURA	— Aug. KLINGEMANN
BONESTOC, Venu de	— Franz von BAYROS
BORGARUCCI, Prospero	— Andreas VESALIUS
BOYD, Nancy	— Edna St. Vincent MILLAY
BOZ	— Charles DICKENS
BRASSAI	— Gyula LALSZ
BRERELEY, John	— Laurence ANDERTON
BURTON, Alfred	— John MITFORD
BURTON, Richard	— Nathaniel CROUCH
C	
CARLEGLE	— Charles Emil de EGLE
CARROLL, Lewis	— Rev. Charles Lutwidge DODGSON
CAXTON, Pisistratus	— Lord Edward George Bulwer LYTTON
CELINE, L.F.	— Louis Ferdinand DESTOUCHES
CHAM	— Comte A. NOE
CHAMPFLEURY	— Jules François FLEURY-HUSSAN
CHILIADES, Octavianus	— Georg Philip HARSDÖRFFER
CHRISTIAN, P.	— Christian PITOIS
CIPELLI, Giovanni Battista	— Joannes Baptista EGNATIUS
CLAUREN, H.	— C.G.S. HEUN
COLLODI, Carlo	— Carlo LORENZINI
COMUS	— Robert Michael BALLANTYNE
CORNEILLE	— C.G. BEVERLOO
COROLINI, Signor	— Jonathan SWIFT
CORVO, Baron	— Frederick William S. ROLFE
CRAYON, Geoffrey	— Washington IRVING
CROWQUILL, Alfred	— Alfred Henry FORRESTER
CYNICUS	— Martin ANDERSON
D	
D'ANVERS, Caleb	— General pseud. of editors of the periodical 'Craftsman Extraordinary', including:– Nicholas AMHURST Henry St. John, Visc. BOLINGBROKE William PULTENEY
DEMOCRITUS JUNIOR	— Robert BURTON
DOLEMAN, Ned	— Robert PARSONS

Pseudonym.	Real Name.
E	
EASTAWAY, Edward	— Edward THOMAS
EGERTON, William	— Edmund CURL
ELEUTHEROPHILOS	— J.J. GORRES
ELIOT, George	— Marian EVANS
ELISIUS, Ph. G.	— M. MEYER
ELUARD, Paul	— Eugene GRINDEL
EPHEMERA	— Edward FITZGIBBON
EPISCOPIUS, J.	— J. DE BISSCHOP
ETTEN, H. van	— Jean LEURECHON
F	
FARRERE, Claude	— Frederic Charles Pierre Edouard BARGON
FAVENTINUS, Didymus	— Philipp MELANCHTHON
FIELD, Michael	— Katherine Harris BRADLEY & Edith Emma COOPER
FITZADAM, Adam	— Edward MOORE
FORESTER, Frank	— Henry William HERBERT
FRANCE, Anatole	— Anatole François THIBAULT
FRAXI, Pisanus	— Henry Spencer ASHBEE
FREDERICK	— Friedrich von NEWHOFF
FURSTNERIUS, Caesarinus	— Gottfried Wilhelm LEIBNITZ
G	
GAMBADO, Geoffrey	— Henry William BUNBURY
GARRYOWEN	— Edmund FINN
GAYLL, Arthur	— Francis Joseph DONOHOE
GELATO, Ascoso	— Count Carlo Cesare MALVASIA
GLOBUS, Septimus	— Johann August APEL
GODFREY, Elizabeth	— Jessie BEDFORD
GOUGER, Robert	— Edward Gibbon WAKEFIELD
GRAND, Sarah	— Mrs. Francis E. McFALL
GRANDVILLE, Jean Jacques	— Jean Ignace Isidore GERARD
GRAY, Maxwell	— Miss. Mary Gleed TUTTIETT
GREY HAWK	— John TANNER
GRILE, Dod	— Ambrose BIERCE
GUERCINO, Il	— Giovanni F. BARBIER
H	
HANSI	— Jean Jacques WALTZ
HASOLLE, James	— Elias ASHMOLE
HAUTEVILLE, M.	— Gaspard de TENDE
HEINE, Cincinnatus	— Joaquin MILLER
HENRY, O.	— William Sydney PORTER
HEWLETT, J.	— Robert PARSONS
HEYNLIN, Johann	— Johannes de LAPIDE
HOLTING, G.	— G. WINCKELMANN
HOPE, Anthony	— Sir Anthony Hope HAWKINS
HOUDINI, Harry	— Erich WEISS
I	
IKS	— P. MASLOV
ILLO, Jose	— Jose DELGADO
INGOLDSBY, Thomas	— Rev. Richard Harris BARHAM
ION	— George Jacob HOLLYOAK
IRON, Ralph	— Mrs. Olive CRONWRIGHT, née Schreiner
J	
JEAN DES PRAIRIER	— Pierre Zacharie LACASSE
JOHNSON, Benjamin F.	— James Whitcomb RILEY
JULIEN LE BIBLIOPHILE	— Paul LACROIX

Pseudonym.	Real Name.	Pseudonym.	Real Name.
JUNIUS (Letters of Junius)	— Sir Philip FRANCIS	PINDAR, Peter	— John WOLCOT
JUVENALIS, Guido	— Guido JOUENNEAUX	PLYMLEY, Peter	— Rev. Sydney SMITH
K		PORCUPINE, Peter	— William COBBETT
KAIN, Saul	— Siegfried SASSOON	PROAVIA	— Kate HOPE
KAPPA	— John WARD	**Q**	
KLIMIUS, Nicholas	— Ludwig HOLBERG	QUERCETANUS, Joseph	— Joseph DU CHESNE
KNICKERBOCKER, Dietrich	— Washington IRVING	QUIZ	— Thomas ROWLANDSON
KRAUTERMANN, Valentin	— L. Christoph von HELLWIG	**R**	
KYD	— Joseph Clayton CLARKE	RAMAL, Walter	— Walter DE LA MARE
KYPSELER, Gottlieb	— Abraham RUCHAT	RAMIRO, Erastène	— Eugène RODRIQUES
L		RAPHAEL	— R.C. SMITH
LARA	— Robert ARMOUR, Jnr.	RAYMOND, Jean Paul	— Charles RICKETTS
LAUTREAMONT, Comte de	— Isidor-Lucien DUCASSE	RINGLENATZ, Joachim	— H. BOTTICHER
LE CORBUSIER	— Charles Edouard JEANNERET	ROSENBERG, Giacomo di	— James TUCKER
		ROSS, Martin	— Violet MARTIN
LE SAGE, A.	— Emmanuel Auguste LAS CASAS	RUTHERFORD, Mark	— William Hale WHITE
		S	
LITTLE, Thomas	— Thomas MOORE, Poet	SABRETACHE	— Albert Stewart BARRON
LOTI, Pierre	— Louis Marie Julien VIAUD	SALLWIGT, Gregorius Anglus	— Georg von WELLING
M		SAND, George	— Amandine Aurore Lucie DUPIN, Baronne Dudevant
MacDIARMID, Hugh	— Christopher Murray GRIEVE		
McDONALD, Alexander	— R.W. DICKSON	SAND, Maurice	— Maurice DUDEVANT (Son of above)
MAC ORLAN, Pierre	— Pierre DUMARCHAIS		
MASON, Stuart	— Christopher Sclater MILLARD	SAUNDERS, Richard	— Benjamin FRANKLIN
		SCOTCH MILKMAID	— Janet LITTLE
MASSARY, Isabel	— Elizabeth P. Ramsay LAYE	SCOTT, William Henry	— John LAWRENCE
MAY, Sophie	— Rebecca Sophie CLARKE	SEYMOUR, Robert	— John MOTTLEY
MERLINUS, Cocaius	— Teofilo FOLENGO	SHAW, T.E.	— Thomas Edward LAWRENCE
MERRIMAN, Henry Seton	— Hugh Stowell SCOTT		
MONCRIEFF, William G. Thomas	— William Thomas THOMAS	SIMOND, Charles	— Paul Adolphe van CLEEMPUTTE
MOORE, William V.	— John FROST	SINJOHN, John	— John GALSWORTHY
MORE, John	— John CROSS	SLEIDANUS	— Joannes PHILIPPSON
MORRELL, Charles	— James RIDLEY	SMITH, Benjamin	— Frank DAVIS
MUHLBACH, Louisa	— Clara Muller MUNDT	SMITH, Gamaliel	— Jeremy BENTHAM
N		SMITH, Johnstone	— Stephen CRANE
NADAR	— Felix TOURNACHON	SNIFT, Dean	— Benson Earle HILL
NAPULITA, Nocturno	— A. CARACCIOLO	SOLOGUB	— Fedor TETERNIKOV
NIMROD	— Charles James APPERLEY	STAHL, Pierre Jules	— Pierre Jules HETZEL
NORMYX	— Norman DOUGLAS	STENDAHL, M. de	— Marie Henri BEYLE
NOVALIS	— Friedrich Leopold von HARDENBERG	STERN, Daniel	— Marie de Flavigny, Comtesse d'AGOULT
		STRAAT, Jan van der	— Joh. STRADANUS
O		STUART, Robert	— Robert MEIKELHAM
OLD BLOCK	— Alonzo DELANO	**T**	
ORINDA	— Mrs. Katherine PHILIPS, née Fowler	T.E.	— Thomas Edward LAWRENCE
ORWELL, George	— Eric Arthur BLAIR	TEXTOR, J.	— G.E. WINCKLER
OUIDA	— Marie Louise de la RAMEE	THWACKIUS, Herman	— Jonas CLOPPER
P		TITMARSH, M.A.	— William Makepeace THACKERAY
PARLEY, Peter	— Samuel Griswold GOODRICH	TWAIN, Mark	— Samuel Langhorne CLEMENS
		U	
PASQUIN, Peter	— William Henry PYNE	URANOPHILUS, Ernestus	— Constantin Gabriel HECKER
PAUL, Jean	— Jean Paul F. RICHTER	**V**	
PERDITA	— Mrs. Mary ROBINSON	VARAMUNDUS, Ernest	— François HOTMAN
PERSE, St. John	— Marie René August Alexis SAINT-LEGER	VERONE, François de	— Jean BOUCHER
		VERSTEGAN, Richard	— Richard ROWLANDS
PERSIUS, Charles	— Charles DUNNE	VILLON, François	— François de MONTCORBIER
PHILALETHA, Irenaeus	— George STARKEY	**W**	
PHILALETHES	— Robert FELLOWES	WALKER, W.H.	— George RANKEN
PHILALETHES, Eugenius	— Robert SAMBER	WARLOCK, Peter	— Philip HESELTINE
PHILALETHES CIVIS UTOPIENSIS	— Jacobus SOBIUS	WARUNG, Price	— William ASTLEY
PHILOBIBL, J.K.	— John KERSEY	WEEGEE	— Arthur FELLIG
PHILODOSUS, Janus	— Daniel HEINSIUS	WILLINGTON, James	— Oliver GOLDSMITH
PHILOPACIFICUS	— Noah WORCESTER	WILLY	— Sidonie Gabrielle COLETTE
PHILOSARCHUS	— Daniel McLAUCHLAN	WOOD, Lambert	— Lambert van den BOS
PHIZ	— Hablot Knight BROWNE	WYN, Ellis	— George BORROW

Auction Houses

with their Addresses & Buyers Premiums

The seasons sales from each house are listed under the 'Key to Sales'.

B   J.L. BEIJERS B.V.
Achter Sint Pieter 140
3512 HT Utrecht
THE NETHERLANDS

Buyers Premium: 18%

BBA   BLOOMSBURY BOOK AUCTIONS
3 & 4 Hardwick Street
London EC1R 4RY
ENGLAND

Buyers Premium: 10%

BR   ANTIQUARIAT W. BRANDES
3300 Braunschweig 1
Postfach 1660
Wolfenbütteler Strasse 12
WEST GERMANY

Buyers Premium: 15%

BS   W. & F.C. BONHAM & SONS LTD.
Montpelier Galleries
Montpelier Street
Knightsbridge
London SW7 1HH
ENGLAND

Buyers Premium: 10%

C   CHRISTIE, MANSON & WOODS LTD.
8 King Street
St. James's
London SW1Y 6QT
ENGLAND

Buyers Premium: 8%

CA   CHRISTIE, MANSON & WOODS
(AUSTRALIA) LTD.
298 New South Head Road
Double Bay
Sydney 2028
New South Wales
AUSTRALIA

No Buyers Premium charged

CBA   CALIFORNIA BOOK AUCTION
GALLERIES INC.
358 Golden Gate Avenue
San Francisco
California 94102
U.S.A.

Buyers Premium: 10%

CE   CHRISTIE'S & EDMISTON'S LTD.
164/166 Bath Street
Glasgow G2 4TG
SCOTLAND

Buyers Premium: 8%

CH   CHRISTIE'S AMSTERDAM B.V.
Cornelis Schuytstraat 57
1071 JG Amsterdam
THE NETHERLANDS

Buyers Premium: 14%

CNY   CHRISTIE, MANSON & WOODS
INTERNATIONAL INC.
502 Park Avenue
New York
NY 10022
U.S.A.

Buyers Premium: 10%

CR   CHRISTIE'S (INTERNATIONAL) S.A.
114 Piazza Navona
00186 Roma
ITALY

Buyers Premium: 12%

CSK   CHRISTIE'S SOUTH KENSINGTON
LTD.
85 Old Brompton Road
South Kensington
London SW7 3JS
ENGLAND

No Buyers Premium charged

D   F. DÖRLING
Neuer Wall 40–42
2000 Hamburg 36
WEST GERMANY

Buyers Premium: 15%

DM   DuMOUCHELLE ART GALLERIES CO.
409 East Jefferson Avenue
Detroit
Michigan 48226
U.S.A.

Buyers Premium: 10%

DS   DURAN SUBASTAS
Serrano 12
Madrid 1
SPAIN

Buyers Premium: 10%

G   GERMANN AUKTIONHAUS
CH-8032 Zürich
Zeltweg 67
SWITZERLAND

Buyers Premium: 10–15%

GB   GALERIE GERDA BASSENGE
Erdener Strasse 5a
1000 Berlin 33
WEST GERMANY

Buyers Premium: 15%

GF   GALERIE FISHER
CH-6006 Luzern
Haldenstrasse 19
SWITZERLAND

Buyers Premium: not stated

GM   GEORGE MEALY & SONS
2 & 3 Proby's Lane
Dublin 1
EIRE

Buyers Premium: 5%

GT   GARROD TURNER
50 St. Nicholas Street
Ipswich
Suffolk
ENGLAND

No Buyers Premium charged

H   HAUSWEDELL & NOLTE
D-2000 Hamburg 13
Pöseldorfer Weg 1
WEST GERMANY

Buyers Premium: 15%

HA   HARRIS AUCTION GALLERIES
873–875 North Howard Street
Baltimore
Maryland 21201
U.S.A.

Buyers Premium: 10%

HBC   HEATHCOTE BALL & CO.
Castle Auction Rooms
78 St. Nicholas Circle
Leicester LE1 5NW
ENGLAND

Buyers Premium: 5%

HD   HOTEL DROUOT
9 Rue Drouot
75009 Paris
FRANCE

Buyers Premium: not stated

HK   HARTUNG & KARL
Karolinenplatz 5a
D-8000 München 2
WEST GERMANY

Buyers Premium: 15%

HT   DR. HELMUT TENNER KG.
Sofienstrasse 5
D-6900 Heidelberg 1
WEST GERMANY

Buyers Premium: 15%

JL   JAMES R. LAWSON PTY. LTD.
212–218 Cumberland Street
The Rocks
Sydney 2000
New South Wales
AUSTRALIA

No Buyers Premium charged

JN   JAMES (NORWICH AUCTIONS) LTD.
33 Timberhill
Norwich
Norfolk NR1 3LA
ENGLAND

No Buyers Premium charged

KH   KENNETH HINCE (BOOK AUCTIONS)
140 Greville Street
Prahan
Victoria 3181
AUSTRALIA

No Buyers Premium charged

LA   W.H. LANE & SON
The Central Auction Rooms
Morrab Road
Penzance
Cornwall
ENGLAND

The Central Auction Rooms
Kinterbury House
St. Andrew's Cross
Plymouth
Cornwall
ENGLAND

Buyers Premium: 10%

LC   LAWRENCE FINE ART
South Street
Crewkerne
Somerset TA18 8AB
ENGLAND

Buyers Premium: 10%

LH   LESLIE HINDMAN AUCTIONEERS
225 West Ohio Street
Chicago
Illinois 60610
U.S.A.

Buyers Premium: 10%

LM   LIBRAIRIE LOUIS MOORTHAMERS
Rue Lesbroussart 124
1050 Bruxelles
BELGIUM

Buyers Premium: 21%

P   PHILLIPS, SON & NEALE
Blenstock House
7 Blenheim Street
New Bond Street
London W1Y 0AS
ENGLAND

Buyers Premium: 10%

PD   PHILLIPS IN SCOTLAND
65 George Street
Edinburgh EH2 2JL
SCOTLAND

Buyers Premium: 10%

PNY   PHILLIPS, SON & NEALE INC.
406 East 79th. Street
New York
NY 10021
U.S.A.

Buyers Premium: 10%

PWC   PARSONS, WELCH & COWELL
49 London Road
Sevenoaks
Kent
ENGLAND

Buyers Premium: 10%

R   REISS & AUVERMANN
Zum Talblick 2
6246 Glashütten im Taunus 1
WEST GERMANY

Buyers Premium: 15%

RO	OINONEN BOOK AUCTIONS P.O. Box 470 Sunderland Massachusetts 01375 U.S.A. Buyers Premium: 10%		**SPB**	SOTHEBY PARKE BERNET INC. 1334 York Avenue New York NY 10021 U.S.A. Buyers Premium: 10%
RS	ROBERT W. SKINNER INC. Copley Square Gallery 585 Boylston Street Boston Massachusetts 02116 U.S.A. Buyers Premium: 10%		**SSA**	SOTHEBY PARKE BERNET SOUTH AFRICA (PTY.) LTD. P.O. Box 31010 Braamfontein 2017 Johannesburg Transvaal SOUTH AFRICA No Buyers Premium charged
S	SOTHEBY PARKE BERNET & CO. Bloomfield Place New Bond Street London W1A 2AA ENGLAND Buyers Premium: 10%		**TA**	TAVINER'S AUCTION ROOMS Prewett Street Redcliffe Bristol BS1 6PB ENGLAND Buyers Premium: 10%
SG	SWANN GALLERIES INC. 104 East 25th. Street New York NY 10010 U.S.A. Buyers Premium: 10%		**V**	VENATOR KG. St. Apernstrasse 56–62 5000 Köln 1 WEST GERMANY Buyers Premium: 15%
SI	SOTHEBY PARKE BERNET ITALIA S.R.L. Palazzo Capponi Via Gino Capponi 26 Firenze ITALY Buyers Premium: 13%		**VA**	VOLKS RARE BOOK AUCTIONS 222–224 Schubart Street Pretoria Transvaal SOUTH AFRICA No Buyers Premium charged
SKC	SOTHEBY'S WEST SUSSEX The Pulborough Salerooms Station Road Pulborough West Sussex RH20 1AJ ENGLAND Buyers Premium: 10%		**VG**	VAN GENDT BOOK AUCTIONS B.V. 96–98 Keizersgracht 1015 CV Amsterdam THE NETHERLANDS Buyers Premium: 20%
SM	SOTHEBY PARKE BERNET MONACO S.A. B.P. 45 Le Sporting d'Hiver Place du Casino Monte-Carlo MC 98000 MONACO Buyers Premium: 1í%		**VS**	VAN STOCKUM'S ANT. B.V. Prinsegracht 15 2512 EW 's-Gravenhage THE NETHERLANDS Buyers Premium: 20%
			WW	WOOLLEY & WALLIS The Castle Auction Mart Castle Street Salisbury Wiltshire ENGLAND No Buyers Premium charged

Key to Sales
August 1983–July 1984

Apr. 27	Printed Books, including Agriculture & Aviculture
May 4	Atlases, Maps & Travel Books
May 18	Printed Books
Jun. 1	Printed Books
Jun. 15	Printed Books
Jun. 29	Printed Books, including Art Reference
Jul. 6	Atlases, Maps & Travel Books
Jul. 13	Printed Books
Jul. 27	Printed Books

1983
Nov. 23–26	**D = F. DÖRLING** *(Hamburg)*
	Wertvolle Bücher, Manuskripte und Autographen, Alte und Moderne Kunst

1984
	DM = DuMOUCHELLE ART GALLERIES CO. *(Detroit)*
May 21	Books

1983
	DS = DURAN SUBASTAS *(Madrid)*
Oct. 28	Libros y Manuscritos
Nov. 25	Libros y Manuscritos
Dec. 16	Libros y Manuscritos

1984
Jan. 27	Libros y Manuscritos
Feb. 24	Libros y Manuscritos
Mar. 23	Libros y Manuscritos
Apr. 27	Libros y Manuscritos
May 25	Libros y Manuscritos

1983
	G = GERMAN AUKTIONHAUS *(Zurich)*
Sep. 15	Bucher

1983
	GB = GALERIE GERDA BASSENGE *(Berlin)*
Nov. 3–5	Bücher, Autographen und Dekorative Graphik

1984
May 3–5	Bücher, Autographen und Dekorative Graphik

1983
	GF = GALERIE FISCHER *(Lucerne)*
Nov. 11–17	Aquarelle . . . Illustrierte Bücher . . . Landkarten . . .

1983
	GM = GEORGE MEALY & SONS *(Dublin)*
Oct. 5	Antiquarian, Irish & General Interest Books
Dec. 7	The Magnificent Irish Library the Property of the Marquess of Sligo . . .

1984
	GT = GARROD TURNER *(Ipswich)*
Jun. 28–29	Furniture & Works of Art

1983
	H = HAUSWEDELL & NOLTE *(Hamburg)*
Nov. 23–24	Wertvolle Bücher, Autographen

1984
May 22–23	Wertvolle Bücher, Autographen
May 23–24	Sammlung Dr. Ernst L. Hauswedell

1983
	HA = HARRIS AUCTION GALLERIES *(Baltimore)*
Sep. 16	Civil War
Nov. 18	Books . . .
Dec. 16	Photographica

1984
Feb. 24	Books . . .
May 4	Books . . .

1984
	HBC = HEATHCOTE BALL & CO. *(Leicester)*
May 17	A Library of Books

1983
	HD = HOTEL DROUOT *(Paris)*
Sep. 21–22	Autographes . . . Livres Anciens et Modernes
Oct. 14	Livres Anciens et Modernes
Oct. 21	Bibliothèque d'un Amateur: Livres, Manuscrits, Documents sur la Corse
Nov. 9	Beaux Livres
Nov. 16	Autographes Littéraires . . . Editions Originales de Balzac . . .
Nov. 16	Incunables et Livres Anciens provenant de la Fondation Fürstenberg-Beaumesnil
Nov. 17	Livres Anciens et Modernes
Nov. 29	Autographes . . . Livres Anciens et Modernes
Dec. 1	Correspondance Autographe de Claude Monet au Professor Charles Coutela . . . Architecture–Décoration, Livres à Figures
Dec. 2	Bibliothèque d'un Manoir du Perche Paul et Julien Durand
Dec. 9	Livres Illustrés du XXe Siècle
Dec. 9	Beaux Livres Anciens et Modernes
Dec. 15	Livres Anciens d'Architecture
Dec. 16	Livres Anciens et Romantiques . . . Livres Illustrés Modernes

1984
Jan. 24	Livres Anciens, Romantiques et Modernes
Jan. 26–27	Livres Anciens et Modernes
Jan. 27	Bibliothèque Militaire de Monsieur C . . .
Jan. 30	Livres Anciens jusqu'à la fin du XIXe Siècle
Feb. 17	Beaux Livres Anciens et Modernes
Feb. 22	Livres Provenant de la Bibliothèque de Monsieur Bertrand de Jouvenel
Feb. 28	Livres Anciens, Romantiques et Modernes . . . Livres Illustrés
Feb. 29	Beaux Ouvrages Anciens à Planches
Mar. 9	Manuscrits et Autographes, Livres Illustrés
Mar. 14	Livres Anciens et Modernes
Mar. 19	Livres Anciens
Mar. 21	Livres Anciens et Modernes
Mar. 27	Livres Anciens, Romantiques et Modernes
Mar. 29	Très Beaux Livres Anciens
Mar. 30	Très Beaux Livres Anciens, Précieux Manuscrits à Peintures du XVe Siècle
Apr. 11	Livres Bien Reliés
Apr. 13	Livres Anciens et Modernes
Apr. 26	Livres Illustres Modernes
May 3–4	Bibliothèque d'un Amateur
May 11	I Bibliothèque d'un Amateur: Autour du Symbolisme. II Livres Anciens et Modernes
May 16	Livres et Documents Précieux XIXe et XXe Siècles
May 21	Livres Anciens, Romantiques et Modernes
May 25	Bibliothèque du Château des Noës
Jun. 6	Beaux Livres Anciens et Modernes
Jun. 13	Bibliothèque de Monsieur L . . .
Jun. 18	Cinquante Livres Rares
Jun. 22	Livres
Jun. 26	Livres Anciens et Romantiques, Voyages, Livres Modernes
Jun. 29	Livres Anciens et Modernes
Jul. 2	Livres Anciens et Modernes
Jul. 6	Livres

1983
	HK = HARTUNG & KARL *(Munich)*
Nov. 8–10	Wertvolle Bücher, Manuskripte, Autographen
Nov. 11–12	Literature, Bibliophilie, Kunst, des 20. Jahrhunderts
Nov. 12	Graphik

1984
May 15–17	Wertvolle Bücher, Manuskripte
May 18	Graphik

1984
	HT = DR. HELMUT TENNER KG. *(Heidelberg)*
May 8–10	Handschriften, Autographen, Wertvolle Bücher

May 23	Fine Printed & Manuscript Americana & European Historical Manuscripts	1983	**VA = VOLKS RARE BOOK AUCTIONS** *(Pretoria)*
Jun. 26	Highly Important Hebrew Printed Books & Manuscripts	Oct. 28	Valuable Africana Books, Prints, Maps & Post Cards

1983   **SSA = SOTHEBY PARKE BERNET SOUTH AFRICA (PTY.) LTD.** *(Johannesburg)*

Sep. 21   Printed Books, Africana, Prints, Maps & Manuscripts

1984
Jul. 5   Printed Books. Africana, Prints, Maps & Manuscripts

1983   **TA = TAVINER'S AUCTION ROOMS** *(Bristol)*

Aug. 18   Printed Books & Related Ephemera
Sep. 15   Printed Books & Related Ephemera
Oct. 20   Printed Books & Related Ephemera
Nov. 17   Printed Books & Related Ephemera
Dec. 15   Printed Books & Related Ephemera

1984
Jan. 19   Printed Books & Related Ephemera
Feb. 16   Printed Books & Related Ephemera
Mar. 15   Printed Books & Related Ephemera
Apr. 19   Printed Books & Related Ephemera
May 17   Printed Books & Related Ephemera
Jun. 21   Printed Books & Related Ephemera
Jul. 19   Printed Books & Related Ephemera

1983   **V = VENATOR KG.** *(Cologne)*
Sep.29–   Bücher, Graphik, Manuskripte
  Oct. 1

1984
Jan. 27   The Library of the Late Dr. Hermann Rex
Apr. 26–27   Africana, Art, Architecture, Archaeology, Anthropology

1983   **VG = VAN GENDT BOOK AUCTIONS B.V.** *(Amsterdam)*

Sep. 13–14   Interesting Books
Sep. 15   Prints, Maps & Drawings
Nov. 29–   Books, Prints
  Dec. 1

1984
Mar. 19 & 21   Books & Manuscripts
Mar. 20 & 22   Prints, Drawing, Maps & Photographs
May 3   Books from the 15th–20th Centuries

1983   **VS = VAN STOCKUM'S ANT. B.V.** *(The Hague)*

Dec. 7–9   Books, & Manuscripts

1984
Jun. 6–7   Books, including Books from the Library of the Late Count Antonind

1983   **WW = WOOLLEY & WALLIS** *(Salisbury)*
Nov. 23   Selected Books & Prints

Currency Conversion Rates

To enable readers to establish the approximate Sterling equivalent of foreign currency prices quoted in this volume we list below the exchange rates prevailing at the end of July 1984.

AUSTRALIA	Aus. $	1.57		SOUTH AFRICA	R	2.18
BELGIUM	B.Frs.	76.50		SPAIN	Pts.	213.88
FRANCE	Frs.	11.61		SWITZERLAND	Sw.Frs.	3.22
ITALY	Lire	2,321		U.S.A.	$	1.31
NETHERLANDS	Fls.	4.30		WEST GERMANY	DM	3.79

HARTUNG & KARL

Antiquariat · Auktionen

KAROLINENPLATZ 5A · D-8000 MUENCHEN 2

Telephone: (089) 284034 · Cables: Buchauktion

WEST GERMANY

Illuminated Manuscripts · Incunabulas

Books on Medicine and Natural History

Illustrated Books from the 15th to the 20th century

German Literature in First Editions

Autographs · Fine Bindings

Atlases · Decorative Prints · Maps and Views

 # AUCTIONS

as usual twice a year, May and November

Richly illustrated catalogues and lists of results

Sammleradressbuch Alte Bücher / Graphik 1984

Das Handbuch für Sammler
und Liebhaber, Antiquare und
Buchhänder ist unentbehrlich
beim An- und Verkauf, Tausch
usw. und fördert damit den
Kontakt der Sammler und Händler
miteinander und untereinander.

Aufgeführt sind:

- ca. 1500 Sammler mit ihren Interessengebieten
- ca. 800 Antiquariate bzw, Buchhandlungen mit Antiquariatsabteilung,
  meist mit Spezialgebieten, ständigen Kaufgesuchen etc.
  — 300 gekennzeichnete Antiquariate vesenden Kataloge, meist
  kostenlos
  — 180 gekennzeichnete Antiquariate bearbeiten Suchlisten
  — 160 Graphikantiquariate bzw. Antiquariate mit Graphikabteilung
- umfangreiches Register »Spezialgebiete der Antiquariate«
- umfangreiches Register »Interessengebiete der Sammler«

264 S.DIN A5. Kt. ISBN 3-923696-01-9. DM 38,-
Veröffentlichungen im Sammleradressbuch Alte Bücher/Graphik sind für
Sammler und Antiquare kostenlos und verpflichten nicht zum
Kauf des Buches. Fordern Sie für Band 3/1985 Aufnahmeformulare
beim Verlag an.

Verlag Michael Kuhle

Ottermerstraße 7 D-3300 Braunschweig Tel. (0531) 7 87 48

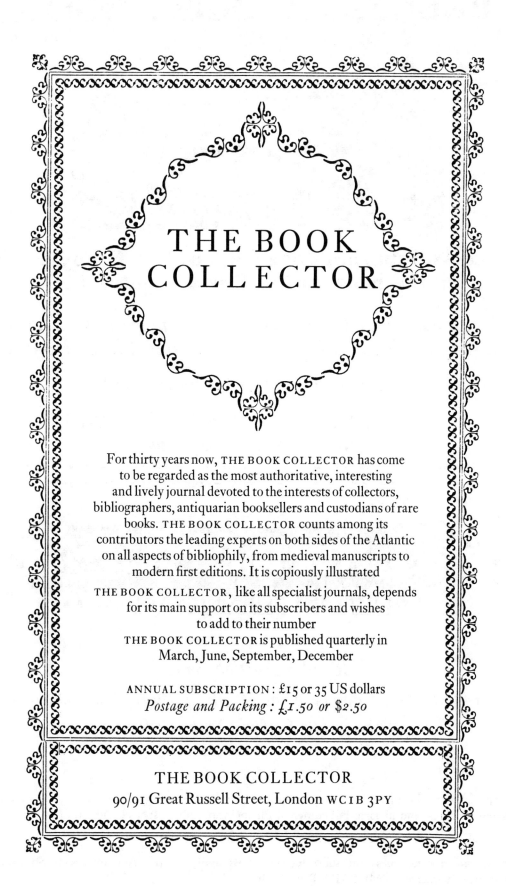

THE BOOK COLLECTOR

For thirty years now, THE BOOK COLLECTOR has come
to be regarded as the most authoritative, interesting
and lively journal devoted to the interests of collectors,
bibliographers, antiquarian booksellers and custodians of rare
books. THE BOOK COLLECTOR counts among its
contributors the leading experts on both sides of the Atlantic
on all aspects of bibliophily, from medieval manuscripts to
modern first editions. It is copiously illustrated

THE BOOK COLLECTOR, like all specialist journals, depends
for its main support on its subscribers and wishes
to add to their number
THE BOOK COLLECTOR is published quarterly in
March, June, September, December

ANNUAL SUBSCRIPTION: £15 or 35 US dollars
Postage and Packing : £1.50 or $2.50

THE BOOK COLLECTOR
90/91 Great Russell Street, London WC1B 3PY

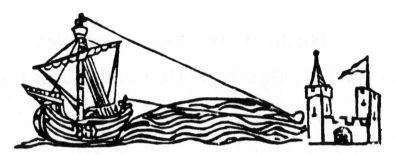

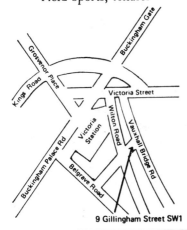

Part I

Printed Books & Atlases

A (Pseud.)
See— ARNOLD, Matthew 'A'

A B C
Ill.:– Michel Delaporte. Paris [?], ca. 1850. 135 x 1,782mm. Panorama, 24 litho. ills., orig. bds., 1 ill. repeated on upr. cover. (S. Feb.28; 296)   £240

A., L.N. & Taillard, Constant
– **Les Jeunes Voyageurs, ou Lettres sur la France.** Ill.:– Blanchard, after A.M. Perrot. Paris, 1821. 6 vols. 12mo. Spotted, cont. cf., slightly worn; van Veen coll. (S. Feb.28; 24)   £80

AA, Abraham Jacob van der
– **Aardrijkskundig Woordenboek der Nederlanden.** Zaltbommel, 1976-80. *Reprint of Gorinchem, 1839-51 Edn.* 14 vols., including Supp. Sm. 8vo. Bds. (B. Feb.8; 641)   Fls. 450
– **Biographisch Woordenboek der Nederlanden.** Haarlem, 1852-78. 21 pts. & Supp., in 19 vols. Cont. hf. cl. (VG. Sep.13; 346)   Fls. 700
– – **Anr. Edn.** Ed.:– G.D.J. Schotel. [Haarlem], ca. 1860. *New Edn.* 13 vols. only (lacks Vol. 8). Lacks all titles, mod. imitation leath., w.a.f. (VS. Dec.7; 361)   Fls. 525

AA, Pieter van der
– **La Galérie Agréable du Monde ... divisée en 66 Tomes.** Leiden, [1729]. *(100).* Vols. 2-5 in 1 vol. Le Roiaume de France. Fo. 4 engraved title vigs., engraved title border with vig. & 112 copperplts., (most double-p., some folding), 1 plt. with corner tear reprd., 1 plt. with sm. defect., cont. marb. leath. gt., gt. outer dentelle. (BR. Apr.12; 87)   DM 1,800
– **Naaukeurige Versameling der Gedenk-waardigste Zee- en Landreysen na Oost- en West-Indien, mitsg. andere Gewesten ... 1246-1698.** Leyden, [1706-]07. 122 pts. in 28 vols lacks Vol. 18 (5 pts.). Lacks 2 plts., Vol. 22 worm-holed in margin, some plts. & text-ll. loose, a few pasted together (1 slightly defect.), mod. hf. cf. [Sabin 3] (VG. Sep.14; 1070)   Fls. 3,900
– **De Voyagien der Spanjaarden na West-Indien.** Trans.:– Ant. de Herrera. Leyden, [1706]. 9 pts. in 1 vol. Fo. Some stains, mod. cl. (VG. Mar.19; 228)   Fls. 1,200
– **De Wijd-Beroemde Voyagien na Oost-en West-Indien; [De Doorlugtige Scheeps-togten der Portugysen na Oost-Indien].** Leiden, [1706]. In 2 vols. Fo. Hf.-title, engraved dedication, lacks 23 maps, cont. cf., worn, w.a.f. (CNY. May 18; 82) $300

AA, VV.
– **Venezia e la sua Laguna.** Venezia, 1847. *Ltd. numbered Edn.* 3 vols. 4to. Lacks lge. map, publishers bds., vol. 3 spine defect. (CR. Jun.6; 85)   Lire 380,000
– **Via del Corso.** Roma, 1961. *Hors Commerce.* 4to. Cl., box. (CR. Jun.6; 86)   Lire 220,000

ABARBANEL, Don Yitzhak
– **Ateret Zekeinim.** Sabionetta, 1557. *1st. Edn.* 4to. Title torn, crudely reprd. & retouched in ink, end of text rewritten in ink, slightly stained thro.-out, a few wormholes not affecting text, mor. gt. with painted pattern, 2 wormholes, worn at edges. (S. Oct.24; 3)   *Dzialowski.* £290
– **Merkevet Ha'Mishna.** Sabionetta, 1551. Fo. Repairs to a few margins, some staining, soiling,

traces of worming, mod. purple mor. gt. (SPB. Feb.1; 8) $950
– **Peirush Ha'Torah.** Venice, 1579. *1st. Edn.* Fo. Lr. outer margins of title & 1st. p. torn with loss of text, margin worming thro.-out affecting some words, some staining, inner margins of last 2 ll. strengthened, blind-tooled mor., slightly worn, rebkd. (S. Oct.24; 6)   *Stern.* £240
– – **Anr. Copy.** Fo. Slight foxing, some staining, vell., slightly rubbed, some wear. (SPB. Feb.1; 9) $750
– **Zevach Pessach [Passover Haggadah with commentary].** Venice, 1545. *2nd. Edn.* 4to. Censored but legible, slightly stained & foxed, wormhole towards beginning affecting some letters, 2 wormholes on 1st. 2 ll. reprd., mod. leath. gt.; stp. of Rabbi Friedman of Sadagura on title. (S. Oct.24; 8)   *Davis.* £2,200
– – **Anr. Edn.** Cremona, 1557. *3rd. Edn.* 4to. Censored but legible, owner's sig. on title, staining mostly in upr. margins, hf. leath., marb. paper covers. (S. Oct.24; 9)   *Durschlag.* £3,500

ABBANUS, Petrus
– **Decisiones Physionomiae ...** Venice, 1548. 16mo. Mod. cf. gt., orig. end-ll. loose in upr. cover. (LH. Sep.25; 447) $120

[ABBATE, Nicolas del] & Tulden, Theodore van
– **Les Travaux d'Ulysse, desseignez par le Sieur de Sainct Martin, de la Façon qu'ils se voyent dans la maison Royalle de Fontainebleau.** Paris, 1633. Ob. fo. 58 engraved plts., lacks engraved coat-of-arms, some soiling, some plts. dampstained, a few margin tears, mod. cf.-bkd. bds. (S. Apr.30; 150)   *Libris.* £140

ABBE, Elfriede
– **The Fern Herbal.** Manchester Center, Vt., Pr. of Elfriede Abbe, [1981]. *(150) numbered, sigd.* Sm. fo. Hf. cl., bds. (SG. May 17; 2) $100
– **Plants of Virgil's Georgics.** Ithaca (N.Y.), ca. 1975? *(50) numbered, ptd. by artist on Japanese paper from orig. blocks, each plt. captioned & sigd.* 4to. 50 wood engrs., title-lf. & plts. loose as iss. in wrap. portfo. (SG. May 17; 1) $250

ABBEVILLE, Claude d'
– **Histoire de la Mission en l'Isle de Maragnan ...** Ill.:– Léonard Gauttier. Paris, 1614. *Orig. Edn.* Cf. by Sarazin, gt. decor. & pointillé, decor. spine, inner dentelle. (HD. Dec.9; 19)   Frs. 16,000

ABBEVILLE, Pierre des Ste. Marie Magdeleine d'
– **Traitte d'Horlogiographie.** Paris, 1645. *2nd. Edn.* Slightly stained & soiled, cont. leath. (D. Nov.23; 416)   DM 400

ABBEY, Maj. John Roland
– **Catalogue of Valuable Printed Books & Fine Bindings.** 1965-67. *(4) numbered, ptd. for H.M. Nixon.* 4 vols. Cont. hf. mor.; H.M. Nixon coll., with some MS. annots., actual photos added at end Vols. 2 & 4. (BBA. Oct.6; 142)   *Maggs.* £1,000
– – **Anr. Edn.** 1965-78. 10 vols. 4to. Orig. bds. & wraps., Vol. 1 lacks spine; H.M. Nixon coll., with prices & notes added by him to Vols. 1-6. (BBA. Oct.6; 143)   *Quaritch.* £180
– – **Anr. Copy.** 10 vols. 4to. Sale catalogue, orig. bds. & wraps. (BBA. Nov.10; 18)   *Maggs.* £70
– **Life in England in Aquatint & Lithography.** 1972. *Dawson Reprint.* 1 vol. (*With:*) – **Scenery of Great**

Britain & Ireland in Aquatint & Lithography. 1972. *Dawson Reprint.* 1 vol. (*With:*) – **Travel in Aquatint & Lithography.** 1972. *Dawson Reprint.* 2 vols. Together 4 vols. 4to. Orig. cl., d.-w.'s. (TA. Dec.15; 303)   £310
– **Scenery of Great Britain & Ireland in Aquatint & Lithography.** L., 1952. *1st. Edn. (500).* 4to. Orig. cl., orig. wraps. (SI. Dec.18; 184)   Lire 240,000
– – **Anr. Edn.** Curwen Pr., 1952. *Ltd. Edn.* (*With:*) – **Life in England.** Curwen Pr., 1953. *Ltd. Edn.* (*With:*) – **Travel.** Curwen Pr., 1956-57. *Ltd. Edn.* 2 vols. Together 4 vols. Prospectus to Travel loosely inserted, d.-w.'s reprd.; 1st. vol. inscr. by author. (S. May 21; 57)   *Blackwells.* £800
– – **Anr. Edn.** 1972. *Reprint.* 4to. Cl., d.-w. (P. Sep.8; 151)   *Sanders.* £75
– **Travel in Aquatint & Lithography.** L., Curwen Pr., 1956-57. *(400).* 2 vols. 4to. Hf. mor. by Sangorski & Sutcliffe. (S. Mar.6; 1)   *Maggs.* £650

ABBOT, George
– [-] **A Briefe Description of the Whole World.** L., 1620. 4to. 1st. lf. present, blank but for sig., lr. margins of last few ll. reprd., some stains, cont. limp vell. [STC 29; Sabin 21] (BBA. May 3; 105)   *Cavendish Rare Books.* £150
– **The Reasons which Doctovr Hill hath brovght, for the Vpholding of Papistry.** Oxford, 1604. *1st. Edn.* A few ll. slightly dust soiled, cont. vell., discold., jnts. brkn., ties defect. (S. Oct.11; 477)   *Thorp.* £90

ABBOTT, Bernice (Ill.)
See— McCLAUSLAND, Elizabeth

A'BECKETT, Gilbert Abbot
– **The Comic History of England.** Ill.:– John Leech. 1846-48. *1st. Edn.* 20 orig. pts. in 19 vols. Orig. ptd. wraps., frayed at edges, mod. cl. box. (TA. Feb.16; 370)   £105
– **The Comic History of Rome.** Ill.:– John Leech. [L., 1852]. 10 hand-cold. plts., approx. 100 text wood engrs., gt.-pict. cl. (SG. Apr.19; 201) $140

ABEL, Clarke
– **Narrative of a Journey in the Interior of China.** L., 1818. *1st. Edn.* 4to. 4 engraved charts, 18 plts. (8 cold.), errata slip, some plts. slightly foxed, soiled or with margin stains, sm. tear in 2T4 without loss, later bds., unc. (S. May 22; 428)   *Asian.* £300
– – **Anr. Edn.** 1819. 4to. Cont. str.-gd. mor., covers panel. in gt. & blind, spine gt.; from liby. of Luttrellstown Castle, w.a.f. (C. Sep.28; 1725)   £480

ABEL, N.H.
– **Oeuvres Complètes.** Christiana, 1839. *Orig. Edn.* Cont. marb. cf., spine renewed. (HD. Apr.13; 67)   Frs. 2,800

ABELIN, Ph. (Ed.)
See— MERIAN, Matthaeus

ABER, Prof. Edward
– **The Term Catalogues, 1668-1709 A.D.; with a Number for Eastern Term, 1711 A.D. A Contemporary Bibliography of English Literature in the Reigns of Charles II, James II, William & Mary, & Anne.** Priv. ptd., 1903/6. 3 vols. 4to. Recent cl. (TA. Jun.21; 377)   £85

ABERCONWAY, Christobel
– **The Story of Mr. Kórah.** Ill.:– after Rex Whistler. L., 1963. 4to. Orig. cl., d.-w.; pres. copy inscr. by author to D[uncan] G[rant], August 1963. (*With:*)
– **Mr. Korah & the Monster.** Rex Whistler. L., n.d.

ABERCONWAY, Christobel -Contd.

4to. Orig. wraps., soiled; pres. copy inscr. by author 'for D. from C.' with A.L.s. from author to Duncan Grant, Oct.'63, loosely inserted. (S. Oct.30; 242)
Fas. £100

ABERCROMBY, Patrick
- **The Martial Achievements of the Scots Nation.** Edinb., 1711-15. 2 vols. Fo. Cont. spr. cf., rubbed; Sir Ivar Colquhoun, of Luss copy. (CE. Mar.22; 1)
£80
- - **Anr. Copy.** 2 vols. Fo. Slightly spotted & stained, cont. cf. (S. Apr.10; 346)
Robertshaw. £60

ABERT, James William
[-] **A Recent Report of an Expedition led by Lieutenant Abert, on the Upper Arkanses & through the Country of the Camanche Indians, in the Fall of the Year 1845.** Wash., 1846. Folding map enclosed, unbnd. & unc. as iss. in folder. (LH. Sep.25; 177)
$150
- **Report of the Secretary of War communicating ... A Report & Map of the Examination of New Mexico ...** Wash., 1848. Folding map, 24 plts., foxed, orig. ptd. wraps., unc. & unopened, lacks portion of lr. wrap. & sm. piece from upr. wrap., hf. mor. s.-c. (LH. Apr.15; 259)
$300

'ABHDISHO BAR BERIKHA ... Catalogum Librorum Chaldaeorum, tam Ecclesiasticorum, quam Profanorum.
Rome, 1653. *1st. Edn.* In Syriac & Latin, lacks 1st. lf. (blank?), old bds. (SG. Feb.9; 153) $225

ABNEY, Capt. W. de W.
- **Thebes & Its Five Greater Temples.** L., 1876. 4to. 40 Woodburytypes on numbered ptd. mounts, some foxing to mounts, orig. gt.-lettered cl., rubbed, spine faded & torn. (SG. May 10; 2) $425

ABOAB, Yitzhak
- **Menorat Ha'Maor.** Trans.:– Moshe Frankfurt. Amst., 1722. *1st. Edn. in Yiddish.* Fo. In Hebrew & Yiddish, titles mntd., owners' sigs., staining thro.-out, most in lr. margin, few lr. margins reprd. without loss of text, hf. leath. (S. Oct.24; 11)
Ludmir. £130

ABRAHAM, Patriarch, attributed to
- **Sefer Yetzirah.** Commentaries:– Abraham Ben David & others. Mantua, 1562. *1st. Edn.* 4to. Unpaginated, lacks last 2 ll. of diagrams, owner's stp. on title, some worming & staining mostly in margins, vell. (S. Oct.24; 52) *Klein.* £480

ABRAHAM ABEN EZRA
- **De Nativitatibus.** Venice, Erhard Ratdolt, 24 Dec. 1485. *1st. Edn. (Bound with:)* **FIRMIN DE BEAUVAL** – **Opuscilum Repertorii Prognosticon in Mutationes Aeris.** Venice, Erhard Ratdolt, [before 4 Nov.] 1485. *1st. Edn.* Together 2 works in 1 vol. 4to. Minor foxing & margin stains, cont. blind-stpd. cf., brass clasps, reprd., mor. box; John D. Stanitz coll. [BMC V, 291; Goff A7 & P1006] (SPB. Apr.25; 1) $4,750

ABRAHAM A SANTA CLARA [Johann Ulrich Megerle]
- **Etwas für Alle.** Würzburg, 1699. *1st. Edn.* Pt. 1 only (of 3). Frontis. mntd., lacks 4 pp. & 2 plts., slightly foxed & stained thro.-out, bds. (HK. Nov.9; 1540) DM 7,000
- - **Anr. Edn.** Ill.:– Chr. Weigel. Würzburg, 1733. Pt. 3 (of 3). Lacks engraved frontis., minimal spotting, a few plts. ptd. slightly weak, spr. vell. (HK. May 16; 1347) DM 4,100
- **De Gekheydt der Wereldt.** Amst., 1734-43. *Vol. II 2nd. Edn.* 2 vols. Sm. 8vo. Cont. cf., not unif. (VG. Sep.14; 905) Fls. 600
- **Heilsames Gemisch Gemasch.** Würzburg, 1704. *1st. Edn. 1st. Printing.* Sm. 4to. 1st. & last ll. loose, some slight soiling, cont. vell., loose, lacks spine. (HK. Nov.10; 2289) DM 750
- **Huy! und Pfuy! der Welt. Huy, oder Anfrischung zu allen Schonen Tugenden ...** Ill.:– Jan & Caspar Luyben. Würtzburg, 1707. *1st. Edn.* Fo. A few ll. with slight margin tears, last plt. torn, some slight foxing or soiling, cont. vell. (D. Nov.24; 2225)
DM 2,400

- **Iets voor Allen.** [Amst.], ca. 1717. Pt. 4. Fragment. Lacks title, cont. leath., defect., w.a.f. (R. Apr.4; 2029) DM 850
- - **Anr. Edn.** Amst., 1736. [Vol. I]. Sm. 8vo. Cf., defect. (VG. Sep.14; 1018) Fls. 2,200
- - **Anr. Edn.** Amst., 1741. [Vol. II]. Sm. 8vo. Later hf. cf., defect. (VG. Sep.14; 1019) Fls. 2,200
- - **Anr. Edn.** Amst., 1745. [Vol. III]. Sm. 8vo. Margin damp-stains, cf., defect. (VG. Sep.14; 1020) Fls. 1,350
- **Judas der Ertz-Schelm für Ehrliche Leuth ...** Salzburg, 1699 & 1702. Pts. I & II in 1 vol. Slightly browned & spotted thro.-out, title lf. Vol. I with fault mntd., title lf. Vol II torn, last ll. defect., lacks frontis. Vol. I with old MS. owners mark, cont. pig over wood bds, lr. cover brkn., roll & other stps. decor., lr. cover brkn., brsss bosses, leath. jnts., slightly rubbed. (HT. May 19; 1278) DM 650
- **De Kapelle der Dooden, of de Algemeene Dooden-spiegel.** Amst., 1737. Stained thro.-out, 2 text copper engrs. defect., some old spotting, vell., old soiling. (V. Oct.1; 3702) DM 420
- **Mercks Wienn, das ist: Des Wütenden Todts ein Umständige Beschreibung ...** Wien, 1680. *1st. Edn.* Later cf., defect., end-paper & inner cover with ex-libris & owners mark, collector stp. (H. May 22; 437) DM 1,250
- **Neu-Eröffnete Welt-Galleria.** Ill.:– Christoph Weigel after Caspar Luyken. Nuremb., 1703. *1st. Edn.* Fo. 100 engraved plts., cont. cf., spine gt.; bkplt. of Hans Sloane. (C. Dec.9; 1)
Waldersee. £1,500
- **Rheimb dich, oder ich liss dich, das ist: Allerley Materien, Discurs, Concept, und Predigen, welche bisshero in underschidlichen Tractätlen gedruckt worden ...** Ill.:– J. van den Nypoort. Salzburg, 1684. *1st. Edn.* 19 pts. in 1 vol. Light browning, some sigs. more, 2 ll. with sm. margin tear & 1 lf. with sm. fault, old MS. owners mark on title lf., cont. vell., slightly defect. (HT. May 9; 1279) DM 850

ABRAHAM ELEAZAR
- **Uraltes Chymisches Werck.** Ill.:– J.E. Boeck. Erfurt, 1735. *1st. Edn.* 3 pts. in 1 vol. F5 in pt.2 in photo facs., ptd. line on few plts. shaved, stp. on title, bds., cf. spine; from Dr. Walter Pagel liby., w.a.f. (S. Feb.7; 1) *Colombo.* £420

ABRAHAM IBN AKRA & others
- **Me'Harerei Nemeirim.** Venice, 1599. *1st. Edn.* 4to. 1 tear & hole not affecting text, title & last lf. washed, buckram. (S. Oct.24; 12) *Sol.* £220

ABRAHAM IBN DAUD
- **Sepher Ha'Kabbalah [without Seder Olam & Megillat Ta'Anit].** Mantua, 1513. *1st. Edn.* 4to. Ptd. without title, censored but legible, most ll. reprd. affecting text, some pp. badly stained, 16th. C. MS. margin glosses, mod. blind-tooled cf. (S. Oct.24; 13) *Davis.* £800

ABRAHAM SHALOM BEN YITZHAK, of Catalonia
- **Neve Shalom.** Venice, 1574. *2nd. Edn.* 4to. Censored but legible, lacks 1 lf., owners' sigs., slight staining, mostly in margins, mod. leath. gt. (S. Oct.24; 15) *Sol.* £220

ABRANCHES, J.C.
- **Album Michaelense.** Ponta Delgado, [Azores], 1869. Map, 35 col. litho. plts., cl., mor. spine, covers discold. (S. Dec.13; 174) *Coelho.* £180

ABSCHATZ, H.A. Frh. v.
- **Poetische Übersetzungen und Gedichten.** Leipzig & Breslau, 1704. *1st. Edn.* Cont. vell. (R. Oct.11; 122) DM 1,050

ACADEMIE DES DAMES
Venise [Grenoble, 1680]. Some ll. lightly yellowed, mor. gt. by Petit. (SM. Mar.7; 2363) Frs. 2,800

ACADEMIE ROYALE DES INSCRIPTIONS ET BELLES-LETTRES
- **Histoire de l'Académie Royale des Inscriptions et Belles-Lettres depuis son Etablissement (1701), jusqu'à Présent, avec les Mémoires de Littérature tirés des Registres de cette Académie.** Paris, 1717-53. Vols. 1-20 only. 4to. Cont. cf., decor. spines, spine fleurons of 1st. 6 vols. not quite unif., some turn-ins & corners defect. (HD. Sep.22; 173)
Frs. 2,100

- - **Anr. Edn.** Den Haag, Amst. & Paris, 1718-81. 102 vols. Compl. run. 1st. ll. in each vol. stpd., cont. bds., w.a.f. (HK. Nov.10; 3022) DM 500

ACCADEMIA DEL CIMENTO
- **Saggi di Naturali Esperienze fatte nell'Accademia ...** Flor., 1691. *2nd. Edn. 2nd. Iss.* Fo. Hf.-title, 2 or 3 ll. slightly browned, vell. bds.; John D. Stanitz coll. (SPB. Apr.25; 2) $450

ACCARIAS DE SERIONNE, J.
- **Les Intérêts des Nations de l'Europe, developés relativement au Commerce.** Leiden, 1766. *1st. Edn.* 2 vols. 4to. Wraps., some foxing, unc. (VG. May 3; 449) Fls. 500

ACCUM, Frederick
- **Practical Treatise on Gas-Light.** 1815. 7 hand-cold. engraved plts., 5 aquatint, 2 folding, orig. bds., soiled. (CSK. May 18; 182) £220
- - **Anr. Copy.** 7 hand-cold. plts., orig. bds., unc., s.-c. (P. Apr.12; 43) *Traylen.* £140

ACERBI, Joseph
- **Travels through Sweden, Finland, & Lapland to the North Cape.** 1802. *1st. Edn.* 2 vols. 4to. Port., folding engraved map (tear reprd.), 15 engraved plts. (5 hand-cold. of natural history subjects), engraved ll. of music, cont. pol. cf. (S. May 21; 216) *Traylen.* £350
- - **Anr. Copy.** 2 vols. 4to. Port. frontis., folding map, 15 engraved plts. (5 hand-cold.), recent hf. mor., spines gt.-decor., rubbed. (TA. Feb.16; 25) £150
- - **Anr. Copy.** 2 vols. 4to. Engraved port. frontis., lge. folding map (short tear without loss of engraved surface), 17 engraved plts. (including 6 hand-cold., 1 repeated, & additional frontis.), 1 plt. from a larger copy loosely inserted, 1 or 2 imprints shaved, some browning, cont. diced cf. gt., worn, 1 upr. cover detchd. (S. Nov.1; 66) *Rinne.* £120
- - **Anr. Copy.** 2 vols. 4to. 15 copperplts., (1 folding, 1 multi-folding copper engraved map, title verso stpd., orig. linen, slightly soiled. (HK. Nov.9; 1282) DM 650

ACHDJIAN, Albert
- **Le Tapis.** Paris, 1949. 4to. Orig. wraps. (CSK. Sep.16; 130) £50

ACKERMANN, Rudolph, Publisher
- **Fables in Action by Means of Moveable Pictures.** 1819. Comprising 18 p. pamphlet, & folder with 23 (of 24) hand-cold. figures, both in orig. s.-c., faded; inscr. by Ackermann. (CSK. Aug.19; 78) £600
- **The History of the Abbey Church of St. Peter's Westminster, its Antiquities & Monuments.** L., 1812. 2 vols. 4to. Engraved port., plan, cold. frontis. to Vol. II, 80 cold. aquatint plts., some offsetting onto text, cont. str.-grd. mor. by Charles Smith, with his ticket, covers gt.- & blind-tooled, gt. cornerpieces, spines elab. gt. in compartments, gt. dentelles, watered silk liners gt. (C. Mar.14; 21) *Traylen.* £850
- - **Anr. Copy.** 2 vols. 4to. Port., plan, 81 hand-cold. plts., offsetting, hf. mor. gt. (P. Mar.15; 182) *Cumming.* £120
- **The History of the Colleges of Winchester, Eton & Westminster.** L., 1816. *1st. Edn. 3rd. Iss.* Lge. 4to. 48 cold. engrs., subscribers' list, some staining in upr. gutter & top edges affecting plts. at corner, crushed hf. mor., gt. panel. back. (SG. Apr.26; 1) $850
- **A History of the University of Cambridge.** Ill.:– Stadler & Black, after Westall & Pugin. L., 1815. 2 vols. 4to. Engraved port., 15 hand-cold. engraved costume plts., 16 hand-cold. ports. of the Founders, 64 cold. aquatints, hf.-titles, offsetting from a few plts. onto text, cont. etruscan cf. gt.; Charles E. Dunlap bkplt. (S. Dec.1; 163) *Adains.* £2,400
- - **Anr. Copy.** 2 vols. Lge. 4to. Engraved port., 79 cold. aquatint views, lacks ports. of the founders, some offsetting onto text, cont. gt.- & blind-panel. russ., rebkd. preserving orig. spines, slightly rubbed. (C. Nov.16; 39a) *Ross.* £1,700
- **A History of the University of Oxford.** L., 1814. *1st. Edn.* 2 vols. Lge. 4to. Hf.-titles, subscribers' list & indexes, port., 81 cold. aquatint plts., 33 cold. ports., heavy offsetting thro.-out, sm. liby. stp. on

title-p., cont. red mor., spines gt., some wear. (SG. Apr.26; 2) $1,000
– – **Anr. Edn.** L., 1814. *Early Iss.* 2 vols. 4to. Engraved port. of Grenville, 17 cold. engraved plts. of costumes, 32 cold. ports. of Founders, 70 cold. aquatint views on 65 plts., str.-grd. mor. by Coverly, covers with gt.-tooled borders, spines gt. in compartments with mor. onlays. (C. Mar.14; 22) *Old Hall.* £1,500
– – **Anr. Edn.** L., 1814 [plts. wtrmkd. 1812]. 2 vols. 4to. Plts. 1, 39, 50 & 78 in 1st. state, engraved port., 17 hand-cold. engraved plts. of costumes, 70 hand-cold. aquatint views on 65 plts., without ports. of Founders & hf.-titles, cont. diced cf., rebkd. preserving orig. spines, spine ends worn. (C. Mar.14; 23) *Quaritch.* £700
– **The Microcosm of London.** Ill.:– after Rowlandson & Pugin. L., [1808-10]. 3 vols. 4to. Wood-engraved titles, engraved dedications, 104 hand-cold. aquatint plts. (wtrmkd. 1806-08), 1 neatly holed with sm. loss, cont. hf. cf., rubbed. (CSK. Dec.2; 39) £2,400
– – **Anr. Edn.** L., 1904. 3 vols. 4to. Hf. mor. gt. (S. Jun.25; 301) *Kouchak.* £170
– – **Anr. Edn.** Ill.:– Bluck, Stadler, & others, after Rowlandson & Pugin. L., n.d. 3 vols. 4to. 8 of Abbey's list of 12 plts. in 1st. state, errata uncorrected, wood-engraved titles, engraved dedications, 104 hand-cold. aquatint plts. (wtrmkd. 1807-08, text wtrmkd. 1806-07), hf.-titles, minor repair to blank margin of 1 plt., cont. diced cf., covers gt.-panel., rebkd. (C. Nov.16; 39) *Deacon.* £2,900
– **The Repository of Arts, Literature, Commerce.** 1809-20. Series 1, Vols. 1-14, Series 2, Vols. 1-10 only. 857 plts., plans & maps only (including 283 hand-cold. fashion plts., 274 hand-cold. aquatints, 115 hand-cold. engrs., & 65 plts. with mntd. cl. & paper samples), some offsetting, some light spotting, cont. cf., spines worn, w.a.f. (CSK. Aug.19; 72) £1,600
– – **Anr. Edn.** 1809-27. 18 vols. 368 hand-cold. plts., lacks some text, hf. cf., spines defect., as a coll. of plts., w.a.f. (P. Apr.12; 107) *Crossley.* £650
– – **Anr. Edn.** L., 1809-28. 40 vols., & 'General Index to the First Series'. Engraved titles, 1,491 plts. & samples of cloths, patterns, etc., including the 5 unlisted plts. & the compl. series of patterns, a few titles & plts. shaved, recent hf. mor., Index disbnd., as a periodical, w.a.f. (C. Mar.14; 25) *Baskett & Day.* £16,000
– – **Anr. Copy.** 18 vols. 442 hand-cold. plts., lacks some text, hf. cf., some spines defect., as a coll. of plts., w.a.f. (P. Apr.12; 108) *Shapiro.* £850
– – **Anr. Edn.** 1811-28. 18 vols in 17. 436 hand-cold. plts., lacks some text, hf. cf., some spines defect., as a coll. of plts., w.a.f. (P. Apr.12; 109) *Shapiro.* £800
[–] **Views of London.** L., [1809-1827.] [plts. date]. Ob. 8vo. Coll. of 3 plain & 106 cold. plts. (8 folding) from Repository of the Arts, some offsetting, some imprints shaved, cont. hf. cf., as a coll. of plts., w.a.f. (BBA. May 23; 200) *Solomons.* £580

ACKROYD, Norman & McIlvanney, William
– **Landscapes & Figures, Eight Etchings: Eight Poems.** 1973. *(125) numbered & sigd. by author & artist.* 4to. Loose in orig. portfo., s.-c. (TA. Apr.19; 288) £50

ACOSTA, Christoval
– **Trattato della Historia, Natura, et Virtu delle Droghe Medicinali ... che vengano portati dalle Indie Orientali in Europa.** Venice, 1585. *1st. Italian Edn.* 4to. Minimal browning, cont. limp vell., later renewed end-papers. [Sabin 114] (R. Oct.12; 1321) DM 1,800
– – **Anr. Copy.** 4to. Port. slightly reprd., linen vell. (DS. Dec.16; 2463) Pts. 65,000

ACOSTA, José de
– **Historie Naturael en Morael van de Westersche Indien.** Amst., 1624. *2nd. Edn.* 4to. Some browning, bds. [Sabin 127] (VG. Nov.30; 789) Fls. 700
– **Ontdekking van West-Indien.** Leyden, 1706. 12mo. Folding map, 16 engraved double-p. plts., 1 lacks blank corner, browned, some margins stained, cf.-bkd. bds., slightly rubbed. (S. Jun.25; 83) *Faupel.* £120

ACTA GENERALIS OCTAVE SYNODI SUB EUGENIO QUARTO FERRARIE INCEPTE ...
Ed.:– B. Abramo Cretensi; G. Trapezentius Cretensi. Rome, 23 May 1526. Fo. Wide woodcut title border, 3 ll. MS. in Fr. at end, 18th. C. mor., gold-tooled decor., gt. spine, gt. inner & outer dentelle, marb. end-paper. (D. Nov.23; 68) DM 1,300

ACTA LIPSIENSIA
– **Opuscula Omnia Actis Eruditorum Lipsiensibus.** Venice, 1740-43. *Early Edn.* Vols. 1-4. 4to. Staining, cont. paper wraps., mostly unopened, stitching brkn. in a few places, some soiling; John D. Stanitz coll. (SPB. Apr.25; 3) $425

ACUNA, Christoval de & others
– **Voyages & Discoveries in South America.** L., 1698. Light stains, sm. blind-stp. at foot of title, cont. panel. cf. [Sabin 152; Wing V 746] (S. Dec.1; 270) *Waggett.* £350

ADAIR, A.H
See— TOYE, Nina & Adair, A.H.

ADAIR, James
– **The History of the American Indians.** L., 1775. *1st. Edn.* 4to. Folding engraved map, crimson hf. mor. [Sabin 155] (S. May 22; 296) *Traylen.* £420
– – **Anr. Copy.** 4to. Hf.-title, cont. or early 19th. C. diced tree cf. gt., covers with central gt. coronet & Lowther Castle cypher, spine gt., upr. jnt. brkn.; the Rt. Hon. Visc. Eccles copy. [Sabin 155] (CNY. Nov.18; 1) $1,300
– – **Anr. Copy.** 4to. Folding map slightly frayed, lacks hf.-title, slightly damp-wrinkled, embossed stp. on title, pencilled annots., later hf. mor., worn. (SG. Apr.26; 3) $600

ADAM, Eugen & Roth, Abraham
– **Souvenirs Pittoresques de la Concentration des Troupes Fédérales Suisses ...** Bern, ca. 1865. Ob. fo. Litho. title with vig., 15 tinted litho. views, text & captions in Fr. & German, margin dampstain to last 2 plts., orig. blind- & gt.-stpd. cl., soiled, foot of spine torn. (C. Mar.14; 26) *Marshall.* £950

ADAM, Georg
– **Kaiserliche Russiche Armee, im Jahr 1814 in Nürenberg nach dem Leben gezeichnet ...** Augsburg, n.d. Fo. 6 mntd. plts., hf. Bradel chagrin. (HD. Jan.27; 244) Frs. 1,600

ADAM, Paul
– **Reims Dévastée.** Ill.:– Ch. Jouas. Paris, 1930. *(100) on Rives.* 4to. 71 orig. etchings, mor. by Jeanne Huch, bordeaux mor. liners, watered silk end-ll., wrap. preserved, s.-c. (HD. Jun.13; 1) Frs. 1,300
– – **Anr. Edn.** Ill.:– Charles Jouas. Paris, 1930. *(146). On Rives, numbered & sigd. by artist.* 4to. 2 orig. ills., many etchings in proof state, ptd. separately with remarks or pure etchings, mor., gt. & blind decor., mor. border, gt. decor., red wtrd. silk doubl. & end-papers, double end-papers, pict. wrap. preserved, s.-c., by La Haye. (HD. Mar.30; 26) Frs. 6,700

ADAM, Robert
– **Ruins of the Palace of the Emperor Diocletian at Spalatro in Dalmatia.** L., priv. ptd., 1764. *1st. Edn.* Fo. 61 engraved plts. on 54 ll., including 7 folding & 7 double-p., 5 trimmed to plt.-mark & 5 shaved, slight offset in places, cont. cf., gt. spine. (C. Dec.9; 2) *Phillipson.* £1,000
– – **Anr. Copy.** Atlas fo. 61 engraved plts., many double-p., badly foxed & stained, ex-liby., 7-p. subscribers list, later mott. hf. cf. (SG. May 3; 2) $1,200

ADAM, Robert & James
– **The Works in Architecture.** L., 1778 [1773-78]-86. *1st. Edn.* 2 vols. Lge. fo. Engraved frontis., 80 engraved plts., including 2 double-p. & 5 hand-çold., text in Engl. & Fr., 2 text ll. with margin tear, sm. stain to lr. blank margin of 4 uncold. plts., cont. hf. cf., worn; Emo Park Liby. bkplt. (C. Dec.9; 3) *Weinreb.* £4,000
– – **Anr. Edn.** 1900-02. 3 vols. Fo. Engraved frontis., 105 plts., text in Engl. & Fr., cl., soiled. (P. Mar.15; 69) *Woodruff.* £80
– – **Anr. Edn.** Dourdan, 1900-02. *Facs. Edn.* 3 vols.

in 1. Atlas fo. Each plt. stpd. on blank verso, not collated, ex-liby., loose in cl. folder, linen ties. (SG. May 3; 3) $425

ADAM, Robert Borthwick
– **Library Relating to Samuel Johnson & His Era.** L. & N.Y., 1929. *(500).* 3 vols. 4to. Cl., unc., some wear. (RO. Dec.11; 165) $175
– – **Anr. Edn.** Buffalo, 1929. *Ltd. Edn.* 3 vols. only (of 4). 4to. Orig. cl. (BBA. Nov.10; 20) *Howes.* £90

ADAM, William
– **Vitruvius Scoticus.** Edinb., [1810]. Lge. fo. 179 engraved plts., some double-p., list of plts., repair to fore-margin of title, text & 1st. plt., title & a few margins slightly soiled, 2 plts. reprd. at folds, a few slightly shaved, later hf. cf., rubbed, rebkd., w.a.f. (C. Dec.9; 4) *Weinreb.* £5,000

ADAMI, Giuseppe
– **Un Secolo di Scenografia alla Scala.** Milan, 1945. *1st. Edn.* 4to. 296 plts., many cold., ex-liby., gt.-pict. bds., later cl. bkd., bds. very chipped. (SG. May 3; 4) $100

ADAMS, Ansel
– **Born Free & Equal.** N.Y., 1944. 4to. Ptd. wraps., lightly rubbed. (SG. May 10; 3) $120
– **My Camera in the National Parks.** Yosemite & Boston, 1950. *1st. Edn.* Fo. Spiral bnd. bds., sigd. by Adams on 1st. lf. (PNY. Dec.1; 97) $125
– – **Anr. Copy.** Fo. Spiral-bnd. ptd. bds., d.-w. chipped; Sigd. & dtd. by author. (SG. Nov.10; 3) $120
– **Sierra Nevada: The John Muir Trail.** Berkeley, 1938. *(500) numbered.* Fo. 50 tipped in reproductions, cl., soiled. (SG. Nov.10; 4) $550
– **Taos Pueblo.** Text:– Mary Austin. Boston, 1977. *Facs. Edn. (950) numbered.* Fo. Leath.-bkd. buckram, matching buckram s.-c.; Sigd. by Adams on colophon. (SG. Nov.10; 5) $200

ADAMS, Frederick B.
– **Radical Literature in America.** N.Y., 1939. *(650).* 4to. Cl., s.-c. (SG. May 17; 3) $110

ADAMS, George
– **Astronomical & Geographical Essays.** L., 1789. *1st. Edn.* 2 pts. in 1 vol. Frontis., 21 folding engraved plts., slightly soiled, 1 torn, mod. hf. cf. (BBA. Nov.30; 85) *Walford.* £90
– – **Anr. Edn.** 1790. *2nd. Edn.* Engraved frontis., 21 folding plts., tree cf. gt., rubbed. (P. Mar.15; 65) *Quaritch.* £65
– **Micrographia Illustrata, or the Microscope Explained.** 1771. 72 engraved plts., hf.-title cut down, not affecting text, ink owners' names on title, unc., hf. cf., defect. (P. Sep.8; 315) *Nichols.* £95

ADAMS, Herbert Mayow
– **Catalogue of Books Printed on the Continent of Europe, 1501-1600 in Cambridge Libraries.** Camb., 1967. 2 vols. Lge. 8vo. Cl. (VS. Dec.7; 212) Fls. 600

ADAMS, Hannah
– **The History of the Jews from the Destruction of Jerusalem to the Nineteenth Century.** Boston, 1812. *1st. Edn.* 2 vols. 12mo. Some foxing & dampstaining, orig. bds., unc., worn, disbnd. (SG. Feb.2; 3) $150

ADAMS, Henry
– **The Education of ...** Boston, [1918]. Lev. mor., blind-& gt.-ruled, gt.-decor., by Donnelly of Chic., designed by Merle Armitage, with his bkplt. (CBA. Dec.10; 35) $200

ADAMS, John Quincy
– **The Duplicate Letters, The Fisheries & the Mississippi: Documents relating to Transactions at the Negotiation of Ghent.** Wash., 1822. 1 vol. Orig. bds., unopened, very worn. (*With:*)
– **Correspondence between ... & Several Citizens of Massachusetts ... to Dissolve the Union.** Boston, 1829. 1 vol. Unbnd. (SG. Aug.4; 3) $110
– **Oration on the Life & Character of Gilbert Motier de Lafayette.** Wash., 1835. *1st. Edn.* Cont. sheep gt., spine cracked; pres. slip to Noyes Barber. [Sabin 295] (PNY. Oct.20; 173) $350

ADAMS, Ramon F.
- **The Rampaging Herd.** Norman, 1958. (*With:*)
- **Burrs Under the Saddle.** Norman, 1964. (*With:*)
- **Six Guns & Saddle Leather.** Norman, 1969. Together 3 vols. Cl., d.-w.'s. (LH. Sep.25; 178)
$170

ADAMS, Richard
- **Watership Down.** L., 1972. *1st. Edn.* Hf.-title, orig. cl., d.-w.; inscr. by author. (S. Dec.8; 160)
Mayou. £340
– – **Anr. Copy.** Orig. cl., spine slightly bumped at head & foot, d.-w. (CSK. Apr.27; 153a) £75

ADAMS, Robert
- [–] **The Narrative of Robert Adams, a Sailor, who was Wrecked on the Western Coast of Africa, in the Year 1810, Was Detained for Three Years in Slavery ... & resided Several Months in the City of Tombuctoo.** L., 1816. 1st. Edn. 4to. Orig. 2-tone bds., untrimmed. (SG. Sep.22; 2) $150

ADAMS, William Bridges
- **English Pleasure Carriages.** L., 1837. *1st. Edn.* Frontis., plts., text ills., orig. cl. gt. (P. May 17; 228) *Quaritch.* £140
– – **Anr. Copy.** Some spotting, qtr. mod. cf. gt. (P. Sep.8; 95) *Hill.* £65
– – **Anr. Copy.** Minor spotting, orig. cl. (TA. Oct.20; 93) £56

ADAMSON, M.
- **A Voyage to Senegal, the Isle of Goree, & the River Gambia.** 1759. *1st. Engl. Edn.* Cont. cf., gt. spine. (BBA. Sep.29; 14) *Quevedo.* £90

ADAMSON, Patrick
- **Poetata Sacra cum alijs opusculis. Studio ac industria Tho., Voluseni.** 1619. 4to. Old vell., covers gt.-decor.; Sir Ivar Colquhoun, of Luss copy. [STC 148] (CE. Mar.22; 5) £280

ADAMUS, Melchior
- **Vitae Germanorum Philosophorum.–Germanorum Jurecon Sultorum et Politicorum.–Germanorum Theologorum [with Supplement].–Germanorum Medicorum ...** Heidelberg, 1615-20 (Supp. dtd. 1653). Together 4 vols. Paper discold. in places, vell. & cf., not unif.; Dr. Walter Pagel copies, as a coll., w.a.f. (S. Feb.7; 2) *Colombo.* £260

ADDISON, Joseph
- **The Works.** Bg'ham., 1761. 4 vols. 4to. Some spotting, later cf. gt.; bkplt. of Sir Henry Campbell-Bannerman. (CSK. Aug.19; 43) £75

ADDISON, Joseph & Steele, Sir Richard
- **The Spectator.** L., Mar.1, 1711-Dec. 6, 1712. Nos. I-DLV in 1 vol. Fo. Some foxing, tears reprd. in last 2 nos., panel. cf. by Sangorski & Sutcliffe, upr. cover detchd. (SPB. May 16; 1) $650
- [**The Tatler**] **The Lucubrations of Isaac Bickerstaff.** L., [1709-]11. 2 vols. in 1. Fo. No. 227 supplied in facs., some browning, early cf., rebkd., orig. spine laid down. (SG. Feb.9; 352) $375
– – **Anr. Edn.** L., 1710-11. 4 vols. Vols. 2 & 4 with hf.-titles, cont. hf. cf., spines gt. (BBA. Aug.18; 92) *Hannas.* £55
– – **Anr. Copy.** 4 vols. 9 p. subscribers list, early cf. gt., rather worn. (SG. Feb.9; 353) $100

ADDISON, Lancelot
- **West Barbary, or, A Short Narrative of the Revolutions of the Kingdoms of Fez & Morocco.** Oxford, 1671. Cont. cf., rebkd. [Wing A532] (CSK. Nov.25; 154) £85

ADE, George
- **Fables in the Slang of 1930.** [N.Y., 1929]. *Advance Printing from Jan.1930 iss. of 'Cosmopolitan'.* Sm. 8vo. Orig. silver ptd. stiff wraps., mor. solander case, inscr. to Perry Molstad. (SPB. May 16; 390) $200
- [–] **Stories of the Streets & of the Town.** Ill.:– John T. McCutcheon. Chic., 1894. *1st. Coll. Edn. Reprinted from Chicago Record.* 4to. Ills., orig. pict. wraps., soiled, spine worn; Perry Molstad copy. (SPB. May 16; 389) $550

ADELPHUS, Johannes
- **Barbarossa: ein Warhafftige Beschreibung des Lebens.** Strassburg, 1530. Fo. Collation: A in 4, B-H in 6's, I in 4, K in 8, L-M in 6's, N in 4, lacks

C3-4, light stain in corner thro.-out, 1. sig. loose wraps. (SG. Feb.9; 154) $475

ADELUNG, Johann Christian
- [–] **Geschichte der Menschlichen Narrheit oder Lebensbeschreibung berühmter Schwarzkünstler, Goldmacher ... und anderer philosophischen Unholden.** Leipzig, 1785-99. 8 vols. Some stains, hf. cf., unc.; Dr. Walter Pagel copy. (S. Feb.7; 5) *Hackhofer.* £360
- **Grammatisch-kritisches Wörterbuch der Hochdeutschen Mundart ...** Ed.:– D.W. Soltaus & F.X. Schönberger. Wien, 1808. 4 vols. Lge. 4to. Cont. hf. leath., slightly rubbed. (GB. May 4; 1569) DM 750

ADHEMAR, H
See— STERLING, C. & Adhemar, H.

ADLERFELD, Gustavus
- **The Military History of Charles XII, King of Sweden.** L., 1740. *1st. Edn. in Engl.* 3 vols. Hf. cf., needs rebdg. (SG. Feb.9; 155) $110

ADRICHOMIUS, Christiaan
- **Theatrum Terrae Sanctae et Biblicarum Historiarum.** Cologne, 1590. Fo. Engraved title, 12 engraved maps & plans, map of Holy Land with sm. holes at centre & lr. border cropped, some sm. stains, recently removed from old cf. bds., gt. Signet Liby. stp., new backstrip, bds. worn. (C. Jun.27; 1) *Shapero.* £600

ADRIEN, E.G.
- **Blüthen und Früchte.** Ed.:– Ch. v. Schmid, Hey, Auerbach & others. Gerf, 1858. Orig. bds., light old wear & soiling. (V. Oct.1; 3908) DM 400

ADVENTURER, The
Ed.:– John Hawkesworth. L., 1753-4. *1st. Edn.* 2 vols. in 1. Fo. Cont. mott. cf., spine worn. (SPB. May 16; 2) $500

AEGIDIUS, Petrus
- **Threnodia sev Lamentatio in Obitum Maximiliani ... Scholia Iac. Spiegel ...** Augsburg, 1519. 4to. Rubricated, side margin cut slightly close, some loss. to title border, some slight margin defects., no bdg. stated. (HK. May 15; 58) DM 520

AEGIDIUS SUCHTELENSIS
- **Elegantiarum Viginti Praecepta.** N.p., after 1500? 4to. Some ll. hinged, bds., lacks spine; the Walter Goldwater copy. (SG. Dec.1; 3) $300

AEMYLIUS [Oemler], Georg
- **Biblicae Historide ... Latinis Epigrammatibus ... Illustratae.** Ill.:– H.S. Beham. Frankfurt, 1539. Title with reprd. corner, some ll. with reprd. worm, slight browning, bds., ca. 1800, mod. linen s.-c. (HK. May 15; 77) DM 2,800

AEPINUS, Franz Maria Ulricus Theodorus
- **Tentamen Theoriae Electricitatis et Magnetismi.** St. Petersb., [1759]. *1st. Edn.* 4to. Several gatherings very browned, some spotting, cont. cf.-bkd. marb. bds., rebkd., orig. spine laid down, a few corners bumped; Pedro Arata & Biblioteca Arata liby. stp. thro.-out, John D. Stanitz coll. (SPB. Apr.25; 4) $1,300

AERONAUTICAL DIGEST
Ed.:– C.J. Glidden. N.Y., 1922-31. Vols. 1-19 (lacks 25 nos. in Vols. 8-14 & 16-19). Tall 4to. Vols. 1-7 & 15 binder's cl., with wraps. bnd. in, rest orig. pict. wraps., w.a.f.; most with Aero Club of Chicago stp. (SG. Oct.6; 1) $350

AEROSTATIC SPY: or, Excursions with an Air Balloon. By an Aerial Traveller
L., 1785. *1st. Edn.* 2 vols. in 1. 12mo. Engraved folding plt., cont. cf., brkn., needs rebacking. (SG. Apr.26; 4) $1,000

AESCHINES
- **Due Orationi, l'Una di Eschine contra di Tesifonte, l'Altra di Demosthene a sua Difesa.** Venice, 1554. (*Bound with:*) **DEMOSTHENES – Oratione contra la Legge di Lettine.** Venice, 1555. Together 2 vols. in 1. Sm. 8vo. Early vell. (SG. Feb.9; 158) $250

AESCHINES & Demosthenes
- **Opera Graecolatina.** Ed.:– H. Wolf. Basileae, 1572. Fo. Old cf., disbnd. (RO. Dec.11; 2) $145

AESCHYLUS
- **The Agamemnon.** Ed.:– Raymond Postgate. Camb., Rampant Lions Pr., [1969]. *(250) sigd. by ed.* Later mor. gt. by Ivor Robinson, dtd. 1979, orig. mor.-bkd. box. (CSK. Jun.15; 161) £130
- **Oresteia.** Ed.:– Robert Proctor. [L., 1904]. *(225).* 4to. Red mor., stpd. & gt., by Lakeside Pr. (LH. Sep.25; 448) $350
- **Prométhée Enchainé.** Ill.:– Fr. L. Schmied. Paris, n.d. *(150) numbered on vell. d'Arches.* 4to. Leaves, wrap., s.-c. (HD. Dec.1; 56) Frs. 2,800
- **Tragoediae VII.** [Geneva], 1557. 4to. In Greek, red ruled thro.-out, red mor., gt.-decor., panel. spine, by Roger Payne, spine darkened, a little rubbed, top section of upr. jnt. wormed; John Scott, of Halkshill bkplt. (SPB. Dec.14; 1) $600
- **Tragoediae Sex.** Venice, Feb. 1518. *1st. Edn.* In Greek, a few lr. blank margin flaws reprd., later mor. gt.; Earl of Cromer bkplt. & pres. inscr. (BBA. Nov.30; 1) *George's.* £550

AESOP
- **Esopi Leben und auserlesene Fabeln ...** Ill.:– H.S. Hack. Nuremb., 1777. 2 pts. in 1 vol. MS. owners mark on title lf. slightly browned, foxed, 2 text ll. with sm. tear, lacks 1 end-paper, cont. leath., slightly bumped & scratched. (HT. May 10; 2100) DM 720
- **The Fables.** Ed.:– John Ogilby. L., 1651. Sm. 4to. Engraved frontis. & 80 plts., some soiling & spotting, few tears reprd., lacks Ccc2 & Ccc3, some ll. cropped, old cf., worn, covers detchd., w.a.f. (S. Apr.10; 335) *Snelling.* £100
– – **Anr. Edn.** 1692. Fo. Some dampstaining, cont. cf., rebkd. [Wing A706] (CSK. Sep.30; 3) £60
– – **Anr. Edn.** Ill.:– Thomas Bewick. Newcastle, 1818. *[1st. Bewick Edn.].* Many ll. slightly soiled, hf. cf., rebkd.; inserted receipt sigd by ill. (torn & reprd.). (P. Apr.12; 287) *Dennis.* £170
– – **Anr. Copy.** Slightly soiled, mod. cl.; receipt sigd. by Bewick inserted. (BBA. Jan.19; 224) *Quaritch.* £140
– – **Anr. Copy.** Some slight spotting, bds., worn. (P. Jun.7; 274) £120
– – **Anr. Copy.** Slight spotting, cf. gt. (P. Sep.29; 45) *Wise.* £80
– – **Anr. Edn.** Ill.:– Thomas Bewick. Newcastle, 1823. *2nd. Edn.* Hf. cf., spine gt.; before title, receipt lf. with Bewick's thumb mark, numbered '105' for a Demy copy. (LC. Mar.1; 53) £140
– – **Anr. Edn.** Ill.:– Thomas Bewick. Newcastle, 1823. *2nd. Edn. (150) numbered.* Thumb-print receipt as frontis., late 19th. C. hf. cf. gt., worn. (BBA. Jun.14; 81) *Quaritch.* £220
– – **Anr. Edn.** Ill.:– Thomas Bewick. Newcastle, 1823. 'Thumb-mark' receipt, cont. cf., upr. jnt. reprd. (CSK. Nov.25; 156) £90
– – **Anr. Edn.** Trans.:– Thomas James. Ill.:– John Tenniel. L., 1848. *1st. Tenniel Edn.* Old cf., rubbed. (RO. Mar.21; 1) $120
– – **Anr. Edn.** Ill.:– Swain after Charles H. Bennett. L., [1857]. Wood engrs. hand-cold., some foxing & soiling, 2 text pp. reprd., later three-qtr. cf. & marb. bds. (CBA. Aug.21; 45) $130
– – **Anr. Edn.** Ill.:– Edward Detmold. L., 1909. *1st. Detmold Edn. (750) numbered & sigd. by artist.* 4to. Orig. pict. cl. gt., soiled. (S. Nov.22; 319) *Hirsch.* £160
– – **Anr. Copy.** 4to. 3 plts. with sm. crease mark, cl. gt., slightly worn. (P. Sep.8; 405) *Elliott.* £80
– – **Anr. Copy.** 1 plt. with sm. tear, free end-papers darkened, gt.-decor. cl. (CBA. Aug.21; 171) $700
– – **Anr. Edn.** Ill.:– Arthur Rackham. 1912. *(1450) numbered & sigd. by artist.* 4to. Orig. cl., soiled, spine faded. (CSK. Aug.19; 8) £170
– – **Anr. Copy.** 4to. Orig. cl. gt., spine faded. (P. Oct.20; 222) £150
– – **Anr. Copy.** 4to. Orig. cl., soiled, sm. chip to spine. (CSK. Dec.2; 125) £100
– – **Anr. Copy.** 4to. Elab. mor. gt. by Bayntun-Rivière, frontis. ill. inlaid in leath. on upr. cover. (SPB. Dec.13; 556) $1,600
– – **Anr. Edn.** Ill.:– Arthur Rackham. Paris, 1913. *(375) on vell., sigd. by artist.* 4to. Publisher's cl. bds. (HD. May 4; 260) Frs. 2,000
– – **Anr. Edn.** Ill.:– Arthur Rackham. 1913. *(1450) numbered & sigd. by artist.* 4to. Orig. cl. gt., soiled, spine darkened. (CSK. Jan.27; 196) £160
– – **Anr. Edn.** Ill.:– Arthur Rackham. 1913. 4to. On

vell., no bdg. stated; sigd. by artist. (HD. Jun.26; 132) Frs. 3,200
– – **Anr. Edn.** Ill.:– Arthur Rackham. L., 1916. 4to. Slightly spotted, orig. cl. gt.; pres. copy, inscr. by Rackham to Johan Briede, with pen & ink drawing on hf.-title. (S. Nov.22; 353) *Joseph.* £380
– – **Anr. Edn.** Gold. Cock. Pr., 1926. *(350) numbered.* Orig. cl.-bkd. bds., d.-w. (CSK. Oct.21; 31) £60
– – **Anr. Edn.** Trans.:– William Caxton. Ill.:– Agnes Miller Parker & William McCance. Gregy. Pr., 1931. *(250).* 4to. Number cut out of colophon, inscr. on end-lf., orig. sheep, rubbed; A.J.A. Symons bkplt. (S. Nov.22; 277) *Carlson.* £230
– – **Anr. Copy.** Sm. fo. Liby. stps. on title & at end, orig. cf., shelf mark on spine. (SG. Mar.29; 161) $250
– – **Anr. Edn.** Trans.:– Sir Roger L'Estrange. Ill.:– Alexander Calder. Paris, [1931]. *(595) numbered, designed by Monroe Wheeler.* Sm. 4to. H.M.P. over bds., brkn. box. (LH. Sep.25; 341) $120
– – **Anr. Edn.** Bibliographical Note:– Victor Scholderer. Trans.:– Samuel Croxall. Ill.:– Designer:– Bruce Rogers. Ltd. Edns. Cl., 1933. *(1500) numbered & sigd. by designer.* Lge. 8vo. Qtr. vell. & marb. bds., lacks s.-c. (SG. Mar.29; 184) $120
– – **Anr. Edn.** Trans.:– Sir Roger L'Estrange. Ill.:– Stephen Gooden. 1936. *(525) numbered & sigd. by artist.* 4to. Orig. vell. gt., lightly spotted, s.-c. (CSK. Jun.1; 58) £150
– – **Anr. Edn.** Ill.:– André Collot. Paris, 1941. *(225). (25) on imperial japan.* Fo. Orig. full-p. wash, ill., suite of engrs. in black with remarks & suite in text, ll., wrap., box. (HD. Mar.14; 118) Frs. 1,000
– **Fables; Aesopics, or a Second Collection of Fables.** L., 1668. 2 vols. in 1. Fo. Some slight staining, mostly marginal, cont. panel. cf., rather worn, rebkd. & reprd. (S. Oct.11; 478) *Lyon.* £240
– – **Anr. Copy.** 2 vols. in 1. Fo. Lack 1 port. or plt., some slight staining, cont. panel. cf., worn, covers detchd., w.a.f. (S. Mar.20; 815) *Page.* £160
– **Fables Choisies, avec le sens moral en quatre vers, et les quatrains de Benserade.** Paris, 1818. Ob. 8vo. 19th. C. cf.-bkd. bds., slightly rubbed; van Veen coll. (S. Feb.28; 26) £70
– **Les Fables d'Esope Ornées de Cent Huit Figures.** Ill.:– after Barlow. Paris, An IX [1801]. 2 vols. Ob. 4to. Hf. chagrin, corners, spines decor. (LM. Oct.22; 255) B.Frs. 10,000
– **Les Fables d'Esope Phrigien, avec Celles de Philelphe.** Amst., 1709. 2 vols. in 1. 12mo. Early cf., worn. (SG. Dec.8; 4) $110
– **Fabulae Graecae Latine Conversae.** Parma, [Bodoni], 1800. 4to. Lf. following title misbnd., cont. vell., unc., dust-soiled. (S. Oct.11; 375) *Maggs.* £150
– – **Anr. Copy.** Fo. On Bütten, cont. hf. vell., slightly worn, liby. label on spine, traces of erased ex-libris inside cover; Hauswedell coll. (H. May 24; 1227) DM 1,500
– **Le Favole di Esopo.** Epilog:– G. Mardersteig. Trans.:– Accio Zucco. Ill.:– Anna Bramanti & D. Jacomet. Verona, Bodoni Pr., 1973. *(115).* Orig. hand-bnd. hf. mor., vell. covers; Hauswedell coll. (H. May 24; 723) DM 2,000
– **The Subtyl Historyes & Fables of Esope.** Trans.:– W. Caxton. Ill.:– V. Angelo. San Franc., Grabhorn Pr., 1930. *(200) numbered & sigd. by artist.* The date 1383 in the Caxton imprint (supposedly corrected by hand after the first 25 special copies had been delivered), title-p. & 6 chapter headpieces hand-illuminated in cols. & gt., hand-drawn paragraph marks (those on the first 8 pp. in blue, rest in green), red niger, gt.-titled ribbed spine, minor scuffing to covers, s.-c. worn; the V. Angelo copy. (CBA. Oct.1; 176) $500

AETHELGIFU
See— WHITELOCK, Dorothy

AETIUS AMIDENUS
– **Contractae ex Veteribus Medicinae Tetrabiblos** ... Lyons, 1549. Fo. Closely cut, affecting some headlines, some stains, few sm. wormholes, new qtr. cf.; Dr. Federico Gomez de la Mata bkplt., Dr. Walter Pagel copy. (S. Feb.7; 6) *Poole.* £160

AGA-OGUL, Mehmet
– **Persian Bookbindings of the Fifteenth Century.** Ann Arbor, 1935. 4to. Orig. cl., partly faded; H.M.

Nixon coll., with his sig. (BBA. Oct.6; 1) *Oak Knoll Books.* £140

AGASSIZ, Prof. Jean Louis Rodolphe
– **Nomenclatoris Zoologici Index Universalis; continens, Nomina Systematica Classium, Ordinum, Familiarum et Generum Animalium Omnium, tam Viventium quam Fossilium.** Solothurn, 1848. *1st. Coll. Edn.* Sm. 8vo. Shaved, buckram. (SG. Mar.22; 12) $150

AGASSIZ, Louis Jean Rodolphe & Elizabeth Cabot
– **A Journey in Brazil.** Boston, 1868. Cl. (SG. Oct.6; 8) $100

AGATHIAS SCHOLASTICUS
– **De Bello Gotthorum et Aliis Peregrinis Historiis.** Trans.:– Christophorus Persona. Rome, 1516. *1st. Edn.* Fo. Later hf. leath., worn. (D. Nov.23; 69) DM 650

AGOSTINI, Leonardo
– **Gemmae et Sculpturae Antiquae Depictae.** Trans.:– J. Gronovius. Ill.:– A. Blooteling. Franeker, 1699. 4to. Some plts. browned, slight worming, leath., gt. decor., inner & outer dentelle, slightly rubbed & faded, lacks upr. endpaper. (D. Nov.24; 2226) DM 1,000
– **Le Gemme Antiche Figurate.** Ill.:– J.B. Galestruzzi. Rome, 1657. 4to. Some light browning, prelims. detchd., later hf. mor., worn. (CSK. Jun.29; 140) £100

AGRICOLA, Georg Andreas
– **The Experimental Husbandman & Gardener.** 1726. *2nd. Edn.* 4to. Some dampstains, cont. cf., rubbed. (BBA. Jul.27; 24) *Vine.* £60

AGRICOLA, Georgius
– **Bergwerck Buch.** Basel, 1621. *3rd. German Edn.* Fo. Some slight browning or foxing, especially in margin, some pp. with old MS. underlining & marginalia, 19th. C. hf. leath., lightly rubbed. (R. Apr.4; 1453) DM 9,000
– **De Ortu & Causis Subterraneorum.** Basel, 1546. Wide margin, author's name on title slightly altered with ink, some cont. marginalia, cont. vell., corners slightly bumped, spine pasted with old paper. (R. Oct.12; 1565) DM 5,700
– – **Anr. Edn.** Wittenberg, 1612. Paper very browned, cont. vell., lacks ties; Dr. Walter Pagel copy. (S. Feb.7; 7) *Colombo.* £140
– **De Re Metallica.** Ill.:– Hans Deutsch after Blasius Weffring. Basel, 1556. *1st. Edn.* Fo. Last 3 ll. reprd., title, final p. & few ll. slightly soiled, 17th. C. cf., rebkd., worn. (CNY. Dec.17; 526) $3,200
– – **Anr. Edn.** Trans.:– Herbert Clark Hoover & Lou Henry Hoover. L., 1912. Fo. Vell., bds. soiled. (SG. Mar.22; 13) $225
– **De Re Metallica Libri XII.** Basel, 1621. *3rd. Latin Edn.* Fo. Title with stp. & cont. owners note & ex-libris, repeated as monog. on upr. cover, several ll. very browned, some spotting, end-papers renewed, cont. vell., some spotting. (H. Nov.23; 213) DM 2,000
– **Mineralogische Schriften.** Ed.:– Ernst Lehmann. Freyberg, 1806-12. 4 vols. in 5. 1 folding plt., 9 folding tables, bds.; Dr. Walter Pagel copy. (S. Feb.7; 8) *Quaritch.* £420
– **Zwei Bücher vom Berg- und Hüttenwesen.** Trans.:– C. Schiffner, L. Darmstaedter & others. Düsseldorf, 1953. *2nd. Edn.* Orig. vell. (R. Oct.12; 1566) DM 400

AGRICOLA, Mart.
– **Musica Instrumentalis Deudsch** ... Wittenberg, 1529. *1st. Edn.* Cont. MS. entry on last p., bds. (HK. Nov.8; 72) DM 22,000

AGRICOLA [ISLEBIUS], Johann
See— MELANCHTHON, Philipp—AGRICOLA [ISLEBIUS], Johann

AGRIPPA, Camillo
– **Trattato di Scientia d'Arme.** Rome, 1553. *1st. Edn.* 4to. Port. & plt. inlaid, 2 prelims. reprd., a few lls. cropped, slight spotting, vell.; John Scott, of Halkshill bkplt. (SPB. Dec.14; 2) $600
– – **Anr. Edn.** Venezia, 1568. 4to. Some light staining, 17th. C. leath., new doubls., some worming in spine. (SI. Dec.15; 1) Lire 850,000

AGRIPPA V. NETTESHEIM, Henricus Cornelius
– **De Incertitudine & Vanitate Scientiarum & Artium.** Paris, 1531. Sm. 8vo. Apparently lacks 4 ll. between title & index, as 1st. text p. is on fo. 9, lev. gt.; gt.-lettered bkplt. of George Bentham. (SG. Feb.9; 157) $130
– – **Anr. Edn.** [Köln or Antw.], 1037 [i.e. 1537]. Light soiling, owner's entry on title, cont.-style blind-tooled leath. (V. Oct.1; 3703) DM 400
– **Die Eitelkeit und Unsicherheit der Wissenschaften.** Ed.:– Fr. Mauthner. München, 1913. *(150) De Luxe Edn. on Bütten.* 2 vols. Orig. hand-bnd. red mor. gt., by Hübel & Denck. (H. Nov.23; 870) DM 520
– – **Anr. Copy.** 2 vols. On Bütten, orig. leath., gt. spine & cover, spine slightly soiled & lightly rubbed. (R. Apr.3; 340) DM 450
– **Opera.** Lyons [Strassburg?], ca. 1630. 2 vols. Vol. 1 title defect. & reprd., browned thro.-out, bds., cf. spine; Dr. Walter Pagel copy. (S. Feb.7; 10) *Shaw.* £110
– **Three Books of Occult Philosophy** ... Trans.:– J.F. 1651. Sm. 4to. Some dampstains & minor margin defects, cont. cf., some wear. [Wing A 789] (TA. May 17; 369) £85

AGUESSEAU, H. Fr. d'
– **Oeuvres.** Paris, 1759-89. *1st. Coll. Edn.* 13 vols. 4to. Cont. spr. cf., spines gt., Vol. XIII bdg. not quite unif. (HD. May 21; 1) Frs. 1,300

A[GUIAR], V.J.
– **Viagem ao Interior da Nova Hollanda.** Lisbon, 1841. *1st. Edn.* 3 vols. in 1. Sm. 8vo. Some browning, mod. grained cf. (S. Nov.1; 8) *Thorp.* £160

AGUIRRE, D. de
– **Tratado Historico-legál del Reál Palacio Antiguo y su Quarto Nuevo de la Ciudád de Barcelona** ... Vienna, 1725. *1st. Edn.* Sm. fo. 2 pp. slightly soiled, cont. leath. (R. Oct.13; 3163) DM 700

AHAI GAON
– **She'iltot.** Venice, 1546. *1st. Edn.* Fo. Slight traces of soiling & staining, old cf., rubbed. (SPB. Feb.1; 10) $850

AHARON BERAKHYA OF MODENA
– **Ma'avar Yabbok.** Amst., 1732. *2nd. Edn.* Sm. 4to. Some browning, title remargined, recased in artless later leath. (SG. Feb.2; 140) $120

AHARON HA-COHEN OF APTA
– **Sefer Keter Shem Tov [on the Besht].** Korets, 1797. *2nd. Edn.* Sm. 8vo. Browned, some dampstaining, several ll. frayed or torn at extremities with minor loss, cont. leath., trimmed, masking tape spine label, very shabby. (SG. Feb.2; 141) $150

AHARON, of Resaro
– **Toledot Aharon.** Amst., 1652. Title soiled. *(Bound with:)* YA'AKOV SASPORTAS – **Toledot Ya'akov.** Amst., 1657. Together 2 works in 1 vol. Sm. 4to. Some browning & dampstaining, owner's stps., mod. hf. cl. (SG. Feb.2; 142) $300

AHARON SHMUEL, of Kremenitz
– **Mishnat Adam.** Hanau, 1611. *1st. Edn.* 4to. Slight staining, some foxing, bds. (SPB. Feb.1; 84) $600

AIKEN, Conrad
– **Scepticisms.** N.Y., 1919. 1 vol. Cl. *(With:)*
– **Selected Poems** N.Y. 1929. *(210)* sigd. 1 vol. cl. s.-c. *(With:)* – **The Coming Forth by Day of Osiris Jones.** N.Y., 1931. 1st. Iss. 1 vol. Cl., faded. (SG. May 24; 1) $110

AIKIN, Arthur
– **Journal of a Tour through North Wales & Part of Shropshire; with Observations in Mineralogy, & Other Branches of Natural History.** 1797. Folding frontis., spotted, old bds., leath. backstrip, untrimmed, some wear. (TA. Mar.15; 219) £62

AIKIN, John
– **A Description of the County from Thirty to Forty Miles Round Manchester.** 1795. *[1st. Edn.].* 4to. Hand-cold. folding map & folding town plan (both slightly torn), 60 plts. & maps, a few margin repairs, cf. gt., spine defect., w.a.f. (P. Feb.16; 47) £170
– – **Anr. Copy.** 4to. Extra engraved title, allegorical

AIKIN, John -*Contd.*

frontis., lge. folding plan & map (tears at folds), 69 views, plans & diagrams, little light spotting, hf. mor., partly unc., very slightly worn. (S. Mar.6; 463) *Kidd.* £160
– **England Delineated.** 1790. Cont. cf. (P. Sep.8; 237) *Georges.* £85
– – **Anr. Edn.** 1800. Mod. qtr. cf. (P. Sep.29; 229) £60
– – **Anr. Edn.** 1809. 43 maps, cont. cf. (P. Feb.16; 236) £75

AIKIN, John & others
– **The History of the Environs of London.** 1811. 4to. 14 engraved plts. (only?), 7 maps, 2 torn, some spotting, later cl., soiled, w.a.f. (CSK. Feb.10; 185) £120

AIME, J.J.J.
– **Narrative of the Deportation to Cayenne** ... L., 1800. Cont. cf. (SG. Oct.20; 2) $175

AINSLIE, Sir Robert & Mayer, Luigi
– **Interesting Views in Turkey, Selected from the Original Drawings Taken for Sir Robert Ainslie.** L., 1819 [plts. dtd. 1836]. 4to. 16 hand-cold. aquatint plts., all cut & mntd., mor.-bkd. buckram, spine gt., orig. cl. label on upr. cover. (C. Jun.27; 46a) *Martinos.* £250
– – **Anr. Copy.** 16 hand-cold. aquatints, some foxing & staining in margins, cont. hf. mor., lacks backstrip. (SKC. May 4; 1814) £150
– **Views in Egypt.** Ill.:– Milton after Mayer. L., 1801. *1st. Edn.* Fo. Tall copy, 48 hand-cold. aquatint plts., 1 or 2 margins slightly soiled, cont. cf., slightly worn. (S. May 22; 285) *Raafat.* £1,000
– – **Anr. Copy.** Fo. 45 (of 48) cold. aquatint plts., lacks port., margins thumbed with some stains, mod. hf. cf., w.a.f. (C. Nov.16; 133) *Al-Saud.* £350
– – **Anr. Edn.** 1804. Fo. 48 hand-cold. aquatint plts., a few margins lightly spotted, cont. cf., rubbed. (CSK. Jul.6; 45) £700
– – **Anr. Edn.** L., 1805. Fo. 48 col. aquatint plts. (wtrmkd. 1805, text wtrmkd. 1801), short tear to 1 plt., few sm. margin paper faults, early red hf. mor., marb. bds., armorial crest on spine. (SG. Nov.3; 138) $850
– **Views in Egypt.–Views in Palestine.–Views in the Ottoman Empire.** L., 1801-04-03. Together 3 works sewed together. Lge. fo. 96 plts. (48 cold.), on Whatman paper, most with 1801 wtrmk., lacks general title-p., disbnd. (SG. Apr.26; 138) $2,800
– – **Anr. Edn.** L., 1803-04-05. 3 pts. in 1 vol. Fo. 96 hand-cold. aquatint plts. (wtrmkd. 1805, titles & text wtrmkd. 1801), 4 titles, including an additional title in Fr., text & captions to pts. 1 & 2 in Engl. & Fr., without general title & port. of Mayer, 1 lf. slightly stained, later hf. cf., partly unc. (C. Nov.16; 134) *Irani.* £900
– – **Anr. Edn.** L., 1804. 3 vols. in 1. Fo. Engraved port., 96 hand-cold. aquatint views, general title & 4 pt. titles, including Fr. title to pt. 3, cont. red str.-grd. mor. by Staggemeier, with remnant of his ticket, covers & spine elab. gt., rubbed, corners worn. (C. Mar.14; 68) *Mathaf Gall.* £1,400

AINSWORTH, William Harrison
– **The Tower of London.** Ill.:– George Cruikshank. L., 1840. *1st. Edn.* Orig. 13/12 pts. Inserted advts. not present in pts. 1-3, orig. pict. wraps. (S. Dec.8; 67) *Maggs.* £200
– – **Anr. Edn.** Ill.:– G. Cruikshank. L., 1840. *1st. Edn. in Book Form.* A few plt. captions cropped, slightly spotted, mor. gt., red & green onlays of poppies, by Bayntun (Rivière), upr. cover inlaid with miniature hand-painted port. of ?Ainsworth, boxed. (S. Oct.4; 108) *Joseph.* £320
– **Works.** 1876. 16 vols. Red hf. mor., slightly worn. (BS. Nov.16; 74) £95

AISSE, Charlotte-Elisabeth Aïcha, dite Melle
– **Lettres à Madame C ... qui contiennent Plusieurs Anecdotes depuis 1726 jusqu'en 1733** ... Paris [Lausanne], 1787. *Orig. Edn.* Sm. 12mo. Cont. marb. cf., spine decor. (HD. Nov.9; 14) *Frs.* 2,000

AITZEMA, Lieuwe van
– **Historie of Verhael van Saken v. Staet & Oorlogh** [1621-]'69. 's-Gravenhage, 1657-71. 14 vols. in 15. 4to. 1 vols. slightly browned, some light stains, a few sm. wormholes, cf., spines gt., spine ends partly defect. (VG. May 3; 540) *Fls.* 2,000
– [–] **Verhael van de Nederl. Vreede-handeling.** 's-Grav., 1650. *Orig. Edn.* 2 pts. in 1 vol. 4to. Vell.; Is. Commelin owners entry. (VG. May 3; 538) *Fls.* 575

A'KEMPIS, Thomas
– **Imitatio Christi.** Venice, P. de Quarengliis & G.M. di Occimiano, 23 Apr. 1493. Lacks final blank, some staining, corner of last lf. torn with slight loss of text, old vell. MS. fragment over bds.; the Walter Goldwater copy. [BMC V, 511; Goff I-28] (SG. Dec.1; 186) $475

– **De Imitatione Christi. Tractatulus Joh. Gerson de Meditatione Cordis.** Milan, Leonardus Pachel, Jul. 1488. A few stains, old bds. [BMC VI, 777; Goff 118; Hain 9096] (S. May 10; 206) *Maggs.* £520
– – **Anr. Edn.** [Augsburg], E. Ratdolt. 1488. 4to. Painted woodcut initial, top of 2nd. index lf. torn off without loss, some stains & wormholes near end, old scribbling on 1st. lf. recto & last lf. verso, bds. [HC 9094; BMC 11, 382; Goff 1-16]. (VG. May 3; 492) *Fls.* 1,800
– – **Anr. Edn.** Amst., 1679. 12mo. Some old MS. underlining, (including copper engraved title), mor., gold-tooled, corner fleurons, decor. gt. spine, gt. inner & outer dentelle, mor. doubl., gold-stpd. border, vell. front free end-papers, sigd. A. & R. Maylander, s.-c., marb. covered. (D. Nov.23; 176) DM 1,500
– – **Anr. Edn.** 17th. C.?. Old cf., Mazarin arms, very worn. (LM. Mar.3; 218) B.Frs. 12,000
– **L'Imitation de Jésus-Christ.** Trans.:– [M. de Marillac]. Paris, 1643. *New Edn.* Burgundy mor. gt., sigd. by Gruel, decor., gt. decor. spine, inner & outer dentelle. (D. Nov.24; 2582) DM 1,800
– – **Anr. Edn.** Trans.:– Abbé Dassance. Ill.:– after Tony Johannot. Paris, 1836. *1st. Printing.* Some foxing, cont. long-grd. mor., gt. decor., blind cathedral, decor. spine. (HD. Mar.14; 51) Frs. 1,600
– – **Anr. Edn.** Paris, 1856-58. 2 vols., including Appendix. 4to. Unif. vell. (SG. Nov.3; 208) $400
– – **Anr. Copy.** 3 vols. Mor. gt. by Rivière. (SPB. Dec.13; 901) $325
– – **Anr. Edn.** Trans.:– P. de Lamennais. Paris, Gruel & Engelmann, ca. 1900. Fo. Followed by H. Michelant's 'Historique de l'Ornementation des Manuscrits & Explication des Planches', subscribers list, lev. gt., by Magnin, spine elab. gt., wide gt. dentelles. (SG. Nov.3; 209) $400
– – **Anr. Edn.** Foreword:– Pope Pius IX. Ill.:– Maurice Denis. Paris, 1903. *(25) on china with double suite.* 4to. Mor. by Semet & Plumelle, blind- & gt.-decor., wrap. & spine preserved, s.-c. (HD. Jun.13; 55) Frs. 4,000
– **The Imitation of Christ.** Dublin, 1822. 24mo. In Gaelic Script, orig. bds., unc., unopened. (GM. Dec.7; 370) £60
– – **Anr. Edn.** Trans.:– Richard Whitford. Ill.:– V. Angelo. Mount Vernon, Peter Pauper Pr., ca. 1940. 2 pieces of orig. artwork laid in loose, hf. cl. & decor. bds., spine slightly faded, s.-c. bumped, chipped & faded, label laid in loose; the V. Angelo copy. (CBA. Oct.1; 340) $100
– **Paraphrase in English on the Following of Christ.** 1694. A few headlines & p. numerals shaved, 19th. C. hf. mor. (C. May 30; 175) *Quaritch.* £400
– **Die Vier Buecher von der Nachfolge Christi.** Ill.:– M. Lechter. Berlin, Einhorn Pr. 1922. *Ltd. Iss. on Bütten.* numbered. Fo. Printers mark monogrammed by artist, his MS. dedication on end-paper for Stefan George, orig. blind-tooled mor., clasps, orig. box, soiled. (H. Nov.24; 1770) DM 3,800
– – **Anr. Copy.** Fo. 1st. & last ll. minimal soiled, orig. bdg. in Asiatic vegetable matter, gold & blind-tooled, slightly spotted. (HT. May 9; 1782) DM 560
– – **Anr. Copy.** Fo. Printer's mark monogrammed & numbered by Lechter, some soiling, orig. bds. bt., spine foxed, slightly worn. (GB. Nov.5; 2731) DM 450

AKERMAN, John Yonge
– **Remains of Pagan Saxondom.** 1855. 4to. Cont. hf. mor. (TA. Nov.17; 283) £50

AKIMUSHKINA, O.P
See— IVANOVA, A.A. & others

AKIYAMA, Terukazu & others
– **Arts of China.** Tokyo, [1972]. Vols. 1-3. Fo. Bdgs. not stated, d.-w.'s. (CBA. Aug.21; 690) $120
– – **Anr. Edn.** Tokyo, [1972 & 1969]. Vols. 1 & 2 only (of 3). Fo. Bdgs. not stated, d.-w.'s slightly worn, card. s.-c.'s. (CBA. Jan.29; 115) $100

AKZENTE. Zeitschrift für Dichtung
Ed.:– W. Höllerer & Hans Bender. München, 1954-76. *Orig. Edn.* Years 1-23. Orig. linen (12), orig. linen covers (8 in 42 pts.), orig. bds. (18 pts.). (GB. Nov.5; 2235) DM 500

ALABA Y VIAMONT, D. de
– **El Perfecto Capitán instruído en la Disciplina Militar, y Nueva Ciencia de la Artillería.** Madrid, 1590. Fo. Leath. (DS. Apr.27; 2007) Pts. 200,000

ALAGNA, J.G.
– **A Compleat Set of New Charts ... Containing an Accurate Survey of the Coast of Portugal & the Mediterranean Sea.** Ill.:– Maps:– Alagna of Messina & others. J. Mount & T. Page, 1764. Fo. 89 (of 93) engraved charts & sm. plans on 52 (of 53) mapsheets (16 double-p. charts surveyed by Alagna of Messina), 1st. chart incorporating title engraved by J. Larken, & including 71 (of 75: lacks nos. 17-20) sm. port. & harbour plans, with a copy of Thomas Young's chart of the coast of Tuscany publd. by Giovanni Jacopucci & 1 other of ancient Europe inserted at end, some dust-soiling & offsetting, additional charts stained & creased, hf. roan, defect., w.a.f. (S. May 21; 136) *Charles.* £850

ALAIN-FOURNIER, Henri
– **Le Grand Meaulnes.** Ill.:– Démétrius Galanis. Paris, 1927. *(15) numbered on old japan with separate suite of 64 engrs. on china.* Lge. 8vo. Sewed, s.-c. (HD. May 16; 87) Frs. 3,700
– – **Anr. Edn.** Ill.:– Berthold Mahn. Paris, [1938]. Sm. 4to. Mosaic mor. by Flammarion, watered silk doubls. & end-ll., wrap. & spine. (HD. Jun.6; 1) Frs. 1,600
– – **Anr. Edn.** Ill.:– Madeleine Melsonn. Paris, 1946. *Ltd. Edn.* 4to. Loose as iss. in orig. bd. folder, s.-c. brkn. (BBA. Jan.19; 311) *Filsell.* £85
– **Napoleon I. Eine Biographie.** Prag, Wien & Leipzig, 1889. 3 vols. Red mor. gt., by Hatchards. (R. Apr.3; 1020) DM 520

ALAMAN, D. Lucas
– **Disertaciones sobre la Historia de la Republica Megicana.** Mexico, 1844. 3 vols. Cf., rebkd. (LH. Sep.25; 180) $250

ALANUS DE INSULIS
– **Doctrinale altum seu Liber Parabolarum Metrice Descriptus cū Sententijs & Metrorum Expositionibus Vtilis Valde ad Bonorum Morum Instructionem.** Köln, Quentell, ca. 1490. 4to. Rubricated, 1 old note, no bdg. stated. [H. 377; Goff A172] (HK. Nov.8; 74) DM 2,200

ALARCON, Luis
– **Camino del Cielo.** Granada, 1550. 4to. Leath. (DS. Apr.27; 2008) Pts. 150,000

ALASHKAR, Moshe
– **Hasagot.** Ferrara, 1556. *1st. Edn.* Unpaginated, 1 hole in title not affecting text, last lf. torn & reprd. not affecting text, staining mostly in margins, some gatherings loose, blind-tooled black mor. (S. Oct.24; 17) *Herzfeld.* £700
See— SHEM TOV IBN SHEM TOV-ALASHKAR, Moshe

ALASKA
– **Alaska & the Gold Fields of Nome, Port Clarence** ... Seattle, 1900. Orig. pict. wraps., upr. wrap. chipped. (LH. Jan.15; 224) $100
– **The Official Guide to the Klondyke Country & the Gold Fields of Alaska.** Chic., 1897. Orig. wraps. (CSK. Jul.6; 16) £480

ALASTAIR (Pseud.)
See— VOIGT, Hans Henning von 'Alastair'

ALAUDA: Etudes et Notes Ornithologiques [later Revue Internationale d'Ornithologie]
Paris, 1929-83. Vols. 1-51, No.2. Plts. text ills.,

vols. 1-13 & 16-39 in 23 vols. cl.-bkd. bds., rest orig. wraps., w.a.f. (S. Apr.10; 397)
Quaritch. £240

ALBANIS DE BEAUMONT, Jean François
[–] **Select Views of the Antiquities & Harbours in the South of France.** 1794. Fo. Additional engraved title, plt. of bas-reliefs, 2 plans, 12 sepia aquatint plts., cont. hf. cf., marb. bds., spine gt., corners rubbed. (LC. Jul.5; 418) £230

ALBELDA, Moshe
– **Sha'Arei Dim'Ah.** Venice, 1586. *1st. Edn.* 4to. Some edges stained, staining mostly in margins, damp-staining in lr. margins towards end, 17th. C. Hebrew MS. note on blank lf. at beginning, mod. leath.; sig. of Simcha (Simone) Luzzatto. (S. Oct.24; 18)
Sol. £220

ALBEMARLE, George Monk, Duke of
See— MONK, George, Duke of Albemarle

ALBERS, Josef
– **Interaction of Color.** New Haven, 1963. Fo. Text plus portfo. of 80 lge. folders of 200 colours ptd. in from 2 to 22 colours each, & 48-p. Commentary in wraps., ex-liby., loose in bd. folder & cl. s.-c. (SG. May 3; 5) $1,100
– – **Anr. Copy.** Fo. 80 text pp. with portfo. of 80 lge. folders showing 200 colours, silk screen ptd. in from 2 to 22 colours each & 48-p. commentary in wraps., loose as iss. in board folder & cl. s.-c. (SG. Apr.26; 5) $1,000

ALBERTANUS CAUSIDICUS BRIXIENSIS
– **De Arte Loquendi et Tacendi.** Leipzig, [Conrad Kachelofen], 1495. 4to. Heavily wormed, some early marginalia, disbnd.; the Walter Goldwater copy. [BMC III, 627] (SG. Dec.1; 4) $275

ALBERTI, Fr. Leandro
– **Isole Appartenenti alla Italia.** Venetia, 1576. 4to. Old vell. (HD. Oct.21; 4) Frs. 3,000

ALBERTI, Giuseppe Antonio
– **I Giochi Numerici.** Bologna, 1747. *1st. Edn.* Some light foxing, few stains. (*Bound with*:).
– **Osservazioni all' Appendice de' Giuochi Numerici.** N.p., n.d. Some worming, mostly marginal. 2 works in 1 vol. Old qtr. vell. (SG. Nov.3; 1) $600

ALBERTI, Leon Battista
– **The Architecture, ... Painting, ... Statuary.** Trans.:– James Leoni. L., 1755. Fo. Engraved frontis., 74 plts., some folding, spotted, cl.-bkd. bds., soiled, new end-papers. (S. Oct.4; 123) *Hood.* £70
– **L'Architettura ...** Trans.:– C. Bartoli. Venice, 1565. Hf. vell. (HD. Dec.15; 1) Frs. 1,500
– **De Pictura ... Libri tres.** Basel, Aug. 1540. *1st. Edn.* Sm. 8vo. ll. inserted between title lf. & Bl.a2 (Epistola nuncupatoria), Vacatbll. bnd. at beginning & end, 18th. C. cf., gt. decor., gt. cover, inner & outer dentelle. marb. paper end-papers. (D. Nov.23; 70) DM 4,000
– – **Anr. Copy.** Title verso stpd., ex-libris, 18th. C. leath., slightly rubbed. (GB. Nov.3; 866) DM 950
– **Della Architettura Libri X. Della Pittura Libri III. E della Statuta Libro I.** Ed.:– G. Leoni. Trans.:– C. Bartoli. Ill.:– B. Picart. L., 1726. *1st. Engl. Edn.* 3 pts. in 1 vol. Fo. Italian/English parallel text, lacks 5 unnumbered plts. & 2 numbered plts. at end, sm. margin defects., lightly browned & slightly foxed, hf. linen. (HK. Nov.9; 1491) DM 800

ALBERTI, Leon Battista, attributed to
[–] **Ippolito e Lionara, from a Manuscript of Felice Feliciano ...** Verona, Bodoni Pr., 1970. *(200) numbered.* Orig. bds., s.-c. (S. Nov.22; 271)
Duschness. £110

ALBERTI, Rafael
– **Diez Liricografías.** Buenos Aires, 1954. *(100) numbered, sigd.* Lge. fo. All lithos. sigd. in plt., publishers cl. (DS. Apr.27; 2278) Pts. 120,000
– **Poema Dedicado a Joan Miro.** Ill.:– Renzo Romero after Alberti (lead engrs.). Rome, 1967. *(20) numbered & sigd.* Fo. Title, limitation lf. & 12 double-p. ll., loose as iss. in orig. decor. folder, s.-c. (BBA. Jan.19; 312) *Duran.* £80

ALBERTUS MAGNUS, Bp. of Ratisbon
– **Compendium Theologicae Veritatis.** Venice, Christophorus Arnoldus, 5 Apr. 1476. 4to. Wide margins, final lf. in facs. on 15th. or early 16th. C. paper, mod. vell.; the Walter Goldwater copy. [BMC V, 205-6; Goff A-232] (SG. Dec.1; 6) $300
– – **Anr. Edn.** Ulm, Johann Zainer, ca. 1478-80. Fo. 192 ll., rubricated, capitals painted in red, cont. stpd. roan over wood bds., remntd.; from Fondation Furstenberg-Beaumesnil. [H. 437; BMC II, 527] (HD. Nov.16; 59) Frs. 8,000
– – **Anr. Edn.** Ulm, Johann Zainer, not after 1481. Sm. fo. 159 ll. (of 192, lacks the 1st. 32 & 1 other lf.), cf.-bkd. bds., brkn.; the Walter Goldwater copy. [BMC II, 527; Goff A-235] (SG. Dec.1; 7) $450
– – **Anr. Edn.** Venice, Simon Bevilaqua, 10 Oct. 1492. 4to. Capital spaces with guide letters, some ll. dampstained mainly at blank margin, minor worming to some ll., mod. paper-covered bds. [H. *444; BMC V, 517; Goff A241] (C. May 30; 7)
Maggs. £280
– – **Anr. Copy.** 4to. Many margin notes & drawings in early hand (or hands), mod. vell.; the Walter Goldwater copy. [BMC V, 517; Goff A-241] (SG. Dec.1; 8) $425
– **Daraus man alle Heimligkeit dess Weiblichen Geschlechts erkennen Kan.** Frankfurt, 1581. *1st. Edn.* 4to. Lightly browned & foxed, mainly in margins, especially 1st. ll., limp vell. from old material, mod. s.-c. (R. Oct.12; 1322a) DM 3,600
– **De Anima. De Intellectu et Intellibili.** Venice, Reynaldus de Novimagio, 1481. *1st. Edn. of 1st. text.* Fo. 2 capital spaces with guide-letters, a few sm. wormholes at end, 18th. C. hf. cf., rubbed, spine defect. in 2 compartments. [BMC V, 256; Goff A221; Hain 496] (S. May 10; 207)
Maggs. £820
– **De Animalibus.** Venice, J. & G. de Gregoriis, 21 May 1495. Fo. 1st. 6 ll. in facs., final lf. (verso blank) mntd., many ll. dampstained at lr. edges, cf., covers detchd.; the Walter Goldwater copy. [BMC V, 346; Goff A-225] (SG. Dec.1; 5) $375
– **De Coelo et Mundo.** Venetia, Ioa. & Gregorius de Gregoris. 1490. Fo. Lacks 2 pp., vell. [HC 511] (CR. Jun.6; 89) Lire 750,000
– **De Duabus Sapientiis et de Recapitulatione Omnium Librorum Astronomiae.** [Nuremb., Caspar Hochfeder], ca. 1493-96. *1st. Edn.* 4to. 12 ll., capital spaces & guide letters, mod. mor.-bkd. marb. bds.; John D. Stanitz coll. [BMC II, 474; Goff A423] (SPB. Apr.25; 7) $2,600
– **[De le Virtu delle] Herbe, & Animali, & Pietre Preciose, & di Molte Maravegliose Cose del Mondo.** [Venice], 1537. Title laid down, with extensive loss, other ll. remargined, with some loss, disbnd. (SG. Oct.27; 2) $250
– **De Natura Locòrum.** Ed.:– Georg Tannstetter. Vienna, 1514. *1st. Edn.* Sm. 4to. Cont. marginalia & underlining in red ink, mod. vell.-bkd. bds.; John D. Stanitz coll. (SPB. Apr.25; 8) $1,000
– **Libellus, qui inscribitur de Formatione Hominis in vtero Materno ...** Antw., 1542. Lightly soiled thro.-out, bds. (HK. Nov.8; 75) DM 700
– **Sermones de Eucharistiae Sacramento.** [Strassburg, Printer of the Casus Breves Decretalium], ca. 1494. 4to. Mod. bds., covered with portion of a vell. music MS.; armorial bkplt. of John Jebb, Bp. of Limerick, over the upr. portion of which is pasted the label 'This book belongs to E.M. Forster', the Walter Goldwater copy. [BMC I, 161; Goff A-325] (SG. Dec.1; 9) $550
– – **Anr. Copy.** 4to. Lacks final blank, dampstained, disbnd.; the Walter Goldwater copy. [BMC I, 161; Goff A-325] (SG. Dec.1; 10) $450

ALBIN, Eleazar
– **A Natural History of English Insects.** L., 1720. *1st. Edn. 1st. Iss.* 4to. 100 hand-cold. copperplates, additional hand-cold. engraved frontis. from Albin's 'History of Spiders', 1736, subscribers list, later hf. cf., marb. bds. (SKC. Oct.26; 326) £950
– – **Anr. Edn.** Ed.:– William Derham. L., 1724. *2nd. Edn.* 4to. 100 hand-cold. engraved plts., some offsetting, a few plts. very slightly soiled, cont. cf. gt., some wear to spine, upr. jnt. split. (S. Nov.28; 1)
Katz. £780

ALBION, The: A Journal of the News, Politics, & Literature of Europe
N.Y., 4 Jan.-27 Dec. 1834. Vol. 2 nos. 1-52. Fo.

With 6 contribs. by Dickens, contents lightly foxed, three-qtr. mor. & marb. bds., marb. end-papers, covers worn, lacks portion of backstrip, remainder partly detchd. or rubbed, owner's label on upr. cover. (CBA. Mar.3; 159) $100

ALBO, Joseph
– **Ikkarim.** Soncino, [Joshua Shlomo Soncino], 31 Oct.-29 Dec. 1485. *1st. Edn.* Fo. Rabbinic Hebrew text, unpaginated, register of sigs., some ll. (including colophon) in facs., some outer margins reprd. without loss, sm. holes on 2 ll. affecting text, discold., slight staining, glosses in oriental hand on 1 p., mod. blind-tooled mor., s.-c. [H. 606; Goff Heb-64] (S. Oct.24; 1) *Stein.* £3,700
– – **Anr. Copy.** Fo. With folios 2-4 in sig. 8 (usually lacking), lacks 1st. lf., slight staining, a few repairs to margins, affecting a few letters, slight soiling to a few preliminary & final ll., notations in various early hands, old tooled panel. cf. gt. [Goff (Heb) 64; H. 606] (SPB. Feb.1; 11) $18,000
– – **Anr. Copy.** Fo. Lacks 1st. lf., 12 ll. inserted from shorter copy, some margin staining & browning, a few tears, margin repairs to 1st. & last ll., a few margins frayed, tears to 1 lf., some staining & soiling, margin glosses thro.-out in early hand, some words censored without sig., vell., worn. [H. 606; Goff Heb-64; Steinschneider 5882, 1] (SPB. Jun.26; 2) $15,000
– – **Anr. Edn.** Commentary:– Gedaliah Ben Shlomo, of Poland. Venice, 1618. *7th. Edn. [1st. Edn. of commentary].* Fo. Woodcut of birds damaged & reprd., 1 lf. with 2 holes & loss of text, stained, creased, inner margins towards end strengthened, some worming, mostly in margins, hf. leath., slightly worn. (S. Oct.24; 19)
Ludmir. £240

ALBOHAZEN, Haly, Filius Abenragel
– **Liber in Iudiciis Astrorum.** Ed.:– Bartholomaeus de Alten. Venice, Erhard Ratdolt, 4 Jul. 1485. *1st. Edn.* Fo. Sm. wormhole thro.-out most of book affecting text, anr. wormhole in margin of last few ll., some light spotting & staining, early MS. marginalia, 17th. C. vell.; deleted owners inscrs. on fly-lf., inscr. dtd. 1720 on 1st. p. of Bibliotheca (?) Buchloviensis, Bibliothèque de Peterswald armorial bkplt., John D. Stanitz coll. [BMC V, 290; Goff H4] (SPB. Apr.25; 10) $1,700

ALBRECHT (Alberti), A.
– **Zwey Bücher.** Nuremb., 1671. Fo. Endpaper & 1 lf. with sm. tear at top right (without text loss), 1 table loose, 1 p. with paste, some slight browning, cont. hf. leath., bumped & very rubbed, stained. (D. Nov.23; 1861) DM 950

ALBRECHT, E.W.
– **Morgenländische Motive.** N.p., ca. 1910. Series 1, 2, & 4 only. Fo. Some spotting, orig. hf. cl., rubbed. (S. May 1; 646) *Dennistoun.* £130

ALBRECHT, Joh. Chr.
– **Elementa Calligraphiae.** Nürmberg, [1764-65]. 4 pts. in 1 vol. Wear, cont. hf. vell., worn; Hauswedell coll. (H. May 23; 294) DM 600
– **Vollkommene Grund= und Regelmässige Anweisung zur Schön= Schreib= Kunst.** Nürnberg, [1776]. Ob. fo. Hf. leath. ca. 1880, soiled; with orig. ill. of initial W (23 cm.); coll. stp. Christian Hammer, Stockholm, Hauswedell coll. (H. May 23; 301) DM 2,400

ALBUM, L'
Ill.:– Ferdinand Bac, Caran d'Ache, Leandre, Job, A. Robida, & others. Ca. 1900-02. In 18 pts. (compl. set). 4to. Orig. wraps., some spotted & soiled. (S. Nov.21; 49) *Arts Anciens.* £110

ALBUM DE AVES AMAZONICA
Ed.:– Dr. Emilio A. Goeldi. Ill.:– Ernest Lohse. Rio de Janeiro, 1902-06. *1st. Edn.* Pts. II & III (of 3) of Atlas bnd. in 1 vol. as iss. Lge. 4to. 36 (of 48) chromolitho. plts., ptd. plt. guards, pict. title-p., no text explanations (as often), 1 plt. guard with minor tear, cont. heavy marb. bds., red mor. spine & corners; inscr. & sigd. to General Sir Desmond O'Callaghan from Athnalpa Purcell, 1926, on front end-paper. (SG. Apr.5; 205) $400

ALBUM DE LA DECORATION
Paris, ca. 1900. Vol. 3 only. Fo. 60 col. plts., loose as iss., cl.-bkd. bds. with col. plts. mntd. on cover. (SG. Aug.25; 32)   £140

ALBUM DES VOYAGES
1857. 63 cont. cold. plts., cont. hf. chagrin. (HD. Jan.24; 1)   Frs. 2,100

ALBUM DRAMATIQUE
Ill.:– after Foëch de Basle & Whirsker. Paris, 1820. Lge. 8vo. 46 engraved plts., mntd. on guards, red hf. mor., corners, spines gt., unc. (HD. Jun.22; 2)   Frs. 1,400

ALBUM GIORNALE LETTERARIO E DI BELLE ARTIS
Roma, 1835-62. Yrs. I-XXVIII. 28 vols. 4to. Hf. cf., spines gt. vols. I-X, some early spines defect., w.a.f. (CR. Jun.6; 198)   Lire 550,000

ALBUM HISTORIQUE de l'Armée et de la Marine
Paris, 1905-06. Fo. Mntd. on guards, hf. chagrin. (HD. Jan.27; 105)   Frs. 1,000

ALBUM MERVEILLEUX
Paris, ca. 1850. Lge. 4to. 5 pp. stained, lr. margin dampstained thro.-out, orig. cl.-bkd. decor. bds., ill. on upr. cover hand-cold., slightly worn; van Veer coll. (S. Feb.28; 28)   £100

ALBUM VENITIEN
Ill.:– after W. Wyld, litho. by E. Lessore. Ob. fo. 12 views on tinted ground, publishers bds. (HD. Feb.29; 47)   Frs. 1,600

ALBUMS
– [Military Expedition to Digoriya, Balkariya & Bezingi in the Central Caucasus]. [1904]. Ob. fo. 21 watercol. sketches, most sigd. 'N.' [Pogas?], 97 mntd. photographs, 1 litho. plan, 8 MS. plans, all mntd., folding plan loosely inserted, some light soiling, cont. cf. gt. (CSK. Aug.5; 53)   £280

ALCAFORADO, Marianna
– Lettres Portugaises. Ill.:– Henri Matisse. Paris, 1946. (250) numbered & sigd. by artist. 4to. Loose as iss. in orig. wraps., cl.-bkd. bd. folder, s.-c. (BBA. Jun.14; 235)   Sims, Reed & Fogg. £950

ALCARAZ Y CASTRO, Isodoro
– Breve Instruccion del Methodo, y Practica de los Quatro Juicios Criminales por el Contrabando de Reales Rentas ... Madrid, 1765. Sm. 4to. Some staining & light soiling, cont. limp vell., soiled. (CSK. May 18; 101)   £75

ALCEDO, Antonio de
– Diccionario Geogrâphico-historico de las Indias Occidentales o América ... Madrid, 1786-89. 5 vols. 4to. Leath. [Sabin 682] (D. Nov.23; 1298)   DM 1,600

ALCIATUS, Andreas
– Diverse Imprese ... Emblemi dell ... Lione, 1549. Frontis, 144 decor. pp. with emblems, vell. (DS. Feb.24; 2496)   Pts. 30,000
– Emblemata. Ill.:– P. Eskreich. Lyon, 1600. Cont. mor. gt., gold-tooled borders, lge. arms in centre. (D. Nov.23; 104)   DM 2,500
– – Anr. Edn. Padua, 1661. 4to. Copper-engraved title, 1 engraved printer's mark, 212 emblem woodcuts, some slight browning, minimal soiling, cont. hf. vell. (HK. Nov.9; 1618)   DM 440
– Les Emblèmes ... mis en Rime Francoyse. Ill.:– Mercure Jollat?. Paris, 1539. Sm. 8vo. Latin & Fr. text, minor worming at inner margin of some ll. slightly affecting a few letters, mod. mor., gt. by C. Lewis. (C. May 30; 8)   Quaritch. £1,100
– Emblemi [Latin & Italian]. Ed.:– Paulus Aemilius Cadmustus. Padua, 1626. Latin–Italian parallel text, some browning, 1st. ll. spotted, title verso, last lf. & inside cover stpd., cont. vell., slightly spotted, sm. holes. (H. May 22; 648)   DM 400

ALCOCK, Charles William
– Famous Cricketers & Cricket Grounds, 1895. Ca. 1895. Fo. Bdg. not stated, some wear. (KH. May 1; 4)   Aus. $220

ALCOCK, Sir Rutherford
– The Capital of the Tycoon, A Narrative of a Three Years' Residence in Japan. 1863. 1st. Edn. 2 vols.

Orig. cl. gt., rebkd. preserving orig. spines; pres. copy, inscr. by author. (SKC. Mar.9; 1998)   £160
– – Anr. Copy. 2 vols. Some foxing, hf. cf. gt. (P. Oct.20; 170)   £80

ALCOFORADO, Francisco
– An Historical Relation of the First Discovery of the Isle of Madera. L., 1675. 1st. Edn. Sm. 4to. Title washed, sm. hole in D2, 19th. C. pol. cf. gt. by Bedford; Sir Thomas Phillipps copy. [Wing A 888] (S. Dec.8; 8)   Lawson. £260

ALDABI, Meir
– Shvilei Emunah. Riva di Trento, 1558. 1st. Edn. 4to. Repairs to margins, with extensive repairs to 1st. 4 ll., slight staining & browning, shaved affecting some head-lines, mod. qtr. mor. gt. (SPB. Feb.1; 12) $800

ALDAM, W.H.
– A Quaint Treatise on 'Flees, & the Art a Artyfichall Flee Making'. Ill.:– after James Poole. L., 1876. 4to. 2 chromolitho. plts., 25 artificial flies with specimens of fly-tying materials in sunken mounts, some spotting & soiling, orig. decor. cl. gt., some wear. (S. Oct.4; 1)   Joseph. £400
– – Anr. Copy. 4to. 2 chromolithographed plts. & 90 (of 99?) specimens of artificial flies in 22 groups, in sunken mounts, scattered foxing, gt.-pict. cl. (SG. Mar.15; 163) $650

ALDIN, Cecil
– Old Inns. L., 1921. (380) numbered, sigd. 4to. old. plts., orig. bds., 2 corners slightly damaged. (P. May 17; 40)   Marlborough. £60
– – Anr. Edn. 1921. (460) numbered on L.P., sigd. 4to. Some light spotting, orig. vell.-bkd. bds., soiled & rubbed. (CSK. Jul.27; 149)   £140

ALDINE PRESS
– A Bibliographical Sketch ... forming a Catalogue of All Works Issued by Aldus & his successors, from 1494 to 1597. Trans.:– E. Goldsmid. Edinb., 1887. 3 pts. in 1 vol., as iss. Tall 8vo. L.P., orig. cl.; Cortlandt F. Bishop bkplt. (SG. Sep.15; 2) $110

ALDINGTON, Richard (Ed.)
See— POETS' TRANSLATION SERIES

ALDRETE, Bernard José
– Del Origen y Principio de la Lengua Castellana. Madrid, 1674. 2nd. Edn. Fo. Few repairs to prelims., some stains, later mott. cf., spine reprd. (SPB. Dec.13; 615) $150

ALDRICH, Thomas Bailey
– Friar Jerome's Beautiful Book. Ill.:– V. Angelo. Brooklyn, Valenti Angelo, 1952. (75) sigd. by Angelo. Hand-illuminated title-p. ill., initial & paragraph marks, wraps. over stiff bds., slightly darkening, ribbon tie; the V. Angelo copy. (CBA. Oct.1; 358) $130

ALDROVANDUS, Ulysses
– Quadrupedum omnium bisulcorum historia. Bologna, 1653. Fo. Lacks engraved title, some browning, last p. soiled, mod. cf. (S. Nov.28; 2)   Schuster. $200
– De Quadrupedibus Solidipedibus Volumen Integrum. Bologna, 1616. 1st. Edn. Fo. Engraved title trimmed & reprd., last imprint lf., woodcut ills., some ll. soiled, later cf., rebkd., rubbed. (BBA. May 23; 329)   Robertshaw. £180
– Serpentium et Draconu[m] Historiae Libri Duo. Bologna, 1640. 1st. Edn. Fo. 1 lf. with old liby. stp., some ll. lightly stained, slightly browned or foxed, cont. vell., spine lightly wormed. (R. Oct.12; 1788)   DM 850

ALECHINSKY, Pierre
– Crayon sur Coquille. Paris, 1971. (113). (13) not for sale. Lge. fo. 10 cold. lithos., each numbered & sigd., lacks commentary, portfo. (With:) – Serpent. Paris, 1977. (120). Lge. fo. 5 etchings, each sigd., ll. (B. Feb.8; 350)   Fls. 2,000

ALEMAN, Matheo
[–] La Vie de Guzman d'Alfarache. Amst., 1728. 3 vols. 12mo. Cont. cf. gt., decor. spines. (HD. Sep.22; 175)   Frs. 1,050
– Vida y Hechos del Picaro Guzman de Alfarache. Ill.:– Bouttats (frontis.), Lamorlet, A. Voet, &

Rentiers. Amberes, 1681. 2 vols. 12mo. Late 18th. C. tree cf., spines decor. (HD. Mar.21; 1)   Frs. 2,200
– – Anr. Copy. 4to. Leath. (DS. Apr.27; 2255)   Pts. 95,000
[–] Vitae Humanae Proscenium: in quo sub Persona Gusmani Alfaracii Virtutes & Vitia. Ed.:– Gaspar Ens. Cologne, 1623-26. 3 vols. in 1. 12mo. Lacks last (?blank) lf. to Vol. 3, browned or spotted thro.-out, cont. cf., slightly rubbed, spine slightly worn. (BBA. Nov.30; 41)   Duran. £70

ALEMBERT, Jean le Rond d'
– Essai d'une Nouvelle Théorie de la Résistance des Fluides. Paris, 1752. 1st. Edn. Sm. 4to. Cont. marb. bds., parch. spine, later label, backstrip defect.; John D. Stanitz coll. (SPB. Apr.25; 113) $300
[–] Mélanges de Litterature, d'Histoire et de Philosophie. Amst., 1773. 5 vols. 12mo. Cont. marb. cf., decor. spines. (HD. Sep.22; 176)   Frs. 1,200
– Réflexions sur la Cause Générale des Vents. Paris, 1747. 1st. Edn. 4to. Some slight spotting, 2 or 3 sm. wormholes thro.-out affecting some text, cont. mott. cf., spine gt., few corners bumped; Frères Perisse label, John D. Stanitz copy. (SPB. Apr.25; 114) $175
– Traité de Dynamique. Paris, 1743. 1st. Edn. 4to. Final privilege & errata lf., cont. Fr. mott. cf., spine gt.; John D. Stanitz coll. (SPB. Apr.25; 115) $1,900
– – Anr. Edn. Paris, 1758. 2nd. Edn. 4to. Variant imprint with pasted-on slip obscuring original, cont. mott. cf., spine gt., worn, spine ends & corners reprd.; name of J. Williamson, Paris 1846, on endpaper, later bkplt. of Philip Worsley Wood, John D. Stanitz copy. (SPB. Apr.25; 116) $200

ALEMBERT, Jean le Rond d'
See— DIDEROT, Denis & Alembert, Jean le Rond d'

ALEMBERT, Jean le Rond d' & others
– Nouvelles Expériences sur la Résistance des Fluides. Paris, 1777. 1st. Edn. Cont. mott. sheep, spine gt., sm. scar on lr. cover; John D. Stanitz coll. (SPB. Apr.25; 60) $425
– – Anr. Copy. Lge. 8vo. Title slightly dust-soiled, cont. marb. wraps., untrimmed,; inscr. on front pastedown 'M. Chauveau chez M. Izard Membre du congres a philadelphie', the Honeyman copy. (SG. Nov.3; 2) $325
See— DIDEROT, Denis & Alembert, Jean le Rond d'

ALEPH (Pseud.)
See— HARVEY, W. 'Aleph'

ALEXANDER, Aphrodisaeus
– De Anima ex Aristoteles Institutione. Trans.:– Hieronymus Donatus. Brescia, Bernardinus de Misintis, 13 Sep. 1495. 1st. Edn. 4to. Lacks initial blank, a2-b2 supplied in facs., some margin dampstains, few marginalia, qtr. vell. [BMC VII, 989; Goff A-386] (SG. Oct.27; 153) $275
– In Priora Analytica Aristotelis, Commentaria [graece]. Venice, 1520. (Bound with:) – In Sophisticos Aristotelis elenchos, commentaria [graece]. Venice, Oct. 1520. Together 2 works in 1 vol. Fo. Cont. marginalia deliberately washed away without affecting text but causing some minor margin damage, 17th. C. spr. cf., rebkd.; Wodhull copy, bought at Egerton's sale, dtd. 4 Jul. 1794; Sir Charles James Stewart bkplt. (S. May 10; 209)   Maggs. £380

ALEXANDER, D.J.
– Ausführliche Abhandlung von den Uhren überhaupt. Trans.:– Chr. Ph. Berger. Lemgo, 1763. 1 table with margin tear, plts. crumpled & with sm. margin slits, soiled at beginning, sewed, lacks spine & upr. cover. (GB. Nov.3; 1174)   DM 850

ALEXANDER, Hartley Burr
– Pueblo Indian Painting. Nice, [1932]. (500) numbered & sigd. by publisher. Fo. 50 cold. plts., loose as iss., text in Fr. & Engl., flaps & hf.-title torn, cl.-bkd. bd. folder. (SG. Aug.25; 300) $650
– – Anr. Edn. Nice, Szwedzicki, [1932]. Atlas fo. Engl. & Fr. text, 50 cold. plts., ex-liby., each plt. stpd. on blank verso, loose as iss. in orig. bd. portfo.

with lge. cold label on cover, linen ties, folder worn. (SG. May 3; 11) $1,200
- **Sioux Indian Paintings: Part I–Paintings of the Sioux & other Tribes of the Great Plains; Part II–The Art of Amos Bad Heart Buffalo.** Paris, [1938]. *(400) numbered & sigd. by publisher.* 2 vols. Fo. 50 plts., text in Fr. & Engl., cl.-bkd. bd. folder, spine of 2nd. vol. fraying. (SG. Aug.25; 347) $800

ALEXANDER, Sir James Edward
- **Excursions in Western Africa.** [1840]. *2nd. Edn.* 2 vols. Hf. cf.; Sir George Farrar bkplt. (SSA. Jul.5; 4) R 190
- **Transatlantic Sketches, comprising visits to the most interesting scenes in North & South America, & the West Indies.** Ill.:– W. Heath after Alexander. L., 1833. *1st. Edn.* 2 vols. Engraved map & 10 etched plts. on ivory paper, 12 p. publisher's catalogue at end of Vol. 1, unc., orig. bds., rebkd. with cl., new ptd. labels; the Rt. Hon. Visc. Eccles copy. [Sabin 735] (CNY. Nov.18; 3) $210

ALEXANDER, Russell George
- **Engraved Work, Etchings & Dry-Points of F.L. Griggs.** Stratford-upon-Avon, Shakes. Hd. Pr., 1928. *(325) numbered.* Sm. fo. Ex-liby., buckram. (SG. May 3; 184) $100

ALEXANDER, Sam
- **Photographic Scenery of South Africa.** 1880. 4to. Some spotting, orig. pict. mor. gt., spine heavily rubbed. (TA. Oct.20; 12) £54

ALEXANDER, William, of British Museum, 1767-1816
- **The Costume of China.** 1805. 4to. 48 hand-cold. plts., & 33 plain dupl. plts., mod. hf. mor. gt. (P. Sep.29; 247) *Shapiro.* £190
- **Picturesque Representations of the Dress & Manners of the Austrians.** L., [1813]. 50 hand-cold. aquatint plts., including backgrounds in 1st. state, cont. hf. mor., unc., rebkd., rubbed. (BBA. Dec.15; 265) *Cohen.* £60
- – **Anr. Copy.** 1 blank lf. bnd. between each copper engr. & text lf., minimal foxing, cont. red mor. gt., slightly worn. (H. Nov.23; 455) DM 480
- – **Anr. Edn.** L., 1814. 50 hand-cold. aquatint plts., some light spotting, cont. hf. mor., rebkd. in cf., rubbed. (CSK. Dec.2; 74) £85
- – **Anr. Edn.** L., ca. 1820. 50 hand-cold. plts., margin stain on final text lf., cont. maroon mor. gt., slightly rubbed. (S. Jun.25; 436) *Phelps.* £200
- **Picturesque Representations of the Dress & Manners of the Chinese.** L., 1825. Extra hand-cold. aquatint title & 50 plts., few faintly spotted, 2 extra plts. bnd. in, 1 lf. detchd. & frayed, lacks 1 lf., cf.-bkd. bds. (S. Apr.9; 1) *Fox.* £170
- **Picturesque Representations of the Dress & Manners of the English.** L., 1813. Ills. hand-cold., hf. cf., corners, crushed. (CR. Jun.6; 253) Lire 350,000
- – **Anr. Edn.** L., [1814]. 50 hand-cold. plts., some slightly soiled, cont. hf. roan, defect. (S. Mar.6; 312) *Elliott.* £90
- – **Anr. Edn.** L., n.d. 50 hand-cold. plts. (wtrmkd. 1823), slightly soiled thro.-out, hf. cf., lacks spine. (P. Jun.7; 67) £150
- **Picturesque Representations of the Dress & Manners of the Russians.** [1814]. 64 cold. engrs., few light stains, cont. hf. mor. (BBA. May 23; 202) *Bookroom.* £110
- – **Anr. Copy.** 1 blank lf. bnd. between each copper engr. & text lf., minimal foxing & light browning, cont. red mor. gt., spine slightly faded, slight wear. (H. Nov.23; 456) DM 520
- – **Anr. Edn.** Ca. 1820. 64 hand-cold. plts., cont. cf. gt., rubbed. (TA. Apr.19; 24) £120
- – **Anr. Edn.** L., ca. 1823. 64 hand-cold. plts., cont. maroon mor. gt. (S. Jun.25; 437) *Phelps.* £170
- – **Anr. Copy.** 64 hand-cold. aquatint plts., mor. (S. Apr.9; 2) *Fox.* £140
- – **Anr. Edn.** N.d. 4to. 64 hand-cold. plts., some ll. slightly soiled, cont. hf. cf., unc., rather worn. (BBA. Jan.19; 325) *Steinberg.* £80
- **Picturesque Representations of the Dress & Manners of the Turks.** L., [1814]. Reduced reprint of 'The Costume of Turkey', without Fr. text, 1 blank lf. bnd. between each engr. & text lf., some slight

foxing & slight browning, cont. red mor. gt., worn, spine slightly faded. (H. Nov.23; 457) DM 460
- – **Anr. Edn.** L., ca. 1823. 60 hand-cold. plts., cont. maroon mor., slightly rubbed. (S. Jun.25; 439) *Phelps.* £220

ALEXANDER, William, Earl of Stirling
See— STIRLING, William Alexander, Earl of

ALEXANDER (GALLUS) DE VILLA DEI
- **Doctrinale dictus cum suis Annotationibus et Exemplis in Margine Positis.** Nürnberg, 1518. 2 pts. in 1 vol. Title with sm. lr. corner tear with slight loss & slightly spotted, some ll. with sm. margin slits, stained, cont. wood bds., later wide vell. spine, end-papers renewed. (BR. Apr.12; 858) DM 650

ALEXANDER-KATZ, B.
- **Die Deutschen Patente über Flugapparate.** Berlin, 1912. Title stpd., hf. linen. (D. Nov.25; 4687) DM 400

ALEXANDRE, Arsène
- **Histoire de l'Art Décoratif du XVIe Siècle à Nos Jours.** Paris, [1891]. Fo. Hf. leath. (SPB. Nov.30; 195) $100

ALEXANDRE, Arsène & Cocteau, Jean
- **The Decorative Art of Leon Bakst.** L., 1913. Fo. 77 plts. (50 cold.), hf. vell. gt. (SG. Apr.26; 13) $1,000

ALEXANDRE, Jacques
- **Traité Général des Horloges.** Paris, 1734. *1st. Edn.* 27 folding engraved plts., 4 folding tables, slight browning & staining in upr. margins, title slightly soiled, cont. cf., worn; the Bute copy. (S. Nov.28; 104) *Henderson.* £320

ALEYN, Charles
- **The Battailes of Crescey & Poictiers ...** L., 1633. *2nd. Edn.* Few running headlines trimmed, 17th. C. sheep., worn. (SPB. Dec.13; 619) $125

ALFASI, Yitzhak
- **Rav Alfas [on Moed only].** Cracow, 1597. Fo. Some outer margins reprd. without loss of text, lightly stained, leath., spine brkn., w.a.f. (S. Jul.3; 67) £160

ALFONSO, of Zamora
- **Introductiones Artis Grammatice Hebraicae.** 1526. *1st. Compl. Edn.* Lacks blank lf. at end, owners' sigs. on fly-lf. & title, stained, orig. vell., worn. (S. Oct.24; 21) *Aldus.* £2,800

ALFONSO X, King of Leon & Castile (El Sabio)
- **Lapidario ... Codice Original.** 1881. 4to. Qtr. mor. gt. (P. Apr.12; 294) *Duran.* £50
- – **Anr. Edn.** [Madrid, 1881]. Fo. Lacks ptd. title, hf. mor., worn. (SG. Mar.22; 15) $100
- **Libros del Saber de Astronomia.** Ed.:– M. Rico y Sinobas. Madrid, 1863-66. *(200).* 4 vols. (of 5). Lge. fo. Cont. bdgs., not unif., slightly stained. (B. Jun.21; 364) Fls. 550
- **Tabulae Astronòmicae.** [Venice], Erhard Ratdolt, 4 Jul. 1483. 4to. Rubricated, some initials hand-cold., early brown & red ink annots., lacks 2 ll., 1st. lf. soiled, some light foxing & soiling thro.-out, 19th. C. blind-stpd. vell.; John D. Stanitz coll. [BMC V, 287; Goff A534] (SPB. Apr.25; 13) $1,800

ALGAZI, Shlomo
- **Halichot Eli.** Izmir, 1663. *(Bound with:)*– **Gufei Halachot.** Izmir, 1680. Pt. I only. Together 2 works in 1 vol. 4to. Slightly browned, slightly wormed not affecting text, leath., spine cracked, w.a.f. (S. Jul.3; 68) £110

ALGEMENE GESCHIEDENIS der Nederlanden
Ed.:– J.A. v. Houtte, J.F. Niermeyer, J. Romein & others. Utrecht/Antw., & c., 1949-58. 13 vols., including Index. 12 vols. cl. gt., 1 vol. unbnd. (VG. Nov.29; 347) Fls. 500

ALGER, Horatio, Jnr.
- **The Five Hundred Dollar Check.** N.Y., [1890]. Cl., 'Porter & Coates' imprint on spine blacked out (1st. state), some shelf-wear & cover soiling, rear inner jnt. brkn., slightly shaken. (RO. Jul.24; 6) $160

- **Jack's Ward; or, the Boy Guardian.** Boston, [1875]. *1st. Edn. 1st. Iss.* Cl., light wear. (RO. Jul.24; 8) $250
- **Ragged Dick; or, Street Life in New York with the Boot-Blacks.** Boston, [1868]. *1st. Edn. 1st. Iss.* Some light margin dampstains, orig. cl., shelf worn, inner jnt. brkn., lacks front end-paper. (RO. Jul.24; 10) $280
- **Sam's Chance; & How He Improved It.** Boston, [1876]. *1st. Edn. Early (1st.?) iss.* 2 advt. ll. (only 1 called for by Gardner), 4th. entry in 2nd. series of the 'Tatered Tom' advts. reads 'IV', in advts. for the 'Brave & Bold' series only the 1st. 2 titles are shown as in print (Gardner states all 3 should be), cl., light wear. (RO. Jul.24; 11) $100
- **The Young Explorer; or, Among the Sierras.** Boston, [1880]. *1st. Edn.* Some margin darkening & soiling, orig. cl., ill. spine, covers rubbed, spine ends slightly frayed. (CBA. Mar.3; 4) $100

ALHOY, Maurice
- **Le Chapitre des Accidents.** Ill.:– Victor Adam. Bruxelles, 1843. 12mo. Cont. hf. chagrin, blind- & gt.-decor. (HD. May 3; 172) Frs. 1,400

ALHOY, Maurice & Huart, L.
- **Les Cent et un Robert Macaire.** Ill.:– H. Daumier. [Paris, 1839-40]. *1st. Edn.* 2 vols. in 1. 4to. Both pts. lack ptd. title & woodcut title, plt. 78 double, lacks 77, some plts. misbnd., some slight margin tears, foxed, cont. hf. leath., rubbed. (R. Oct.12; 2189) DM 2,400
- – **Anr. Copy.** 2 vols. in 1. 4to. Slightly foxed, especially at beginning & end, cont. hf. leath. gt. (R. Oct.12; 2190) DM 2,300

ALHOY, Maurice, & others
- **Le Musée pour Rire.** Ill.:– after Daumier, Gavarni, & 'Grandville'. Paris, 1840. 4to. 49 full-p. lithos., a wood engr., a few ll. soiled, pict. bds., disbnd. (SG. Jun.7; 343) $130

ALI, A. Yusuf
- **A Monograph on Silk Fabrics produced in the North-Western Provinces & Oudh.** Allahabad, 1900. 4to. Orig. cl. (BBA. Apr.5; 235a) *Sims, Reed & Fogg.* £100

ALI BEY
- **Travels of Ali Bey in Morocco, Tripoli, Cyprus, Egypt, Arabia, Syria, & Turkey, between the Years 1803 & 1807.** 1816. 2 vols. 4to. 1 map torn, cont. tree cf.; from liby. of Luttrellstown Castle, w.a.f. (C. Sep.28; 1726) £420

ALKABEZ, Shlomo Ha'Levi
- **Manot Ha'Levi.** Venice, 1552. *1st. Edn.* 4to. Browned, creased, reprd., 1st. 4 ll. wormed with loss of few letters, staining & foxing, trimmed, hf. leath., marb. paper covers. (S. Oct.24; 24) *Sol.* £180

ALKEN, Henry
- **The Beauties & Defects in the Figure of the Horse ...** [1816]. *[1st. Edn.].* 4to. Hand-cold. title, 18 hand-cold. plts., cont. hf. cf., spine gt., rubbed; extra p. with sketch of cart-horse by Sam E. Waller inserted. (SKC. May 4; 1753) £110
- – **Anr. Copy.** 4to. Some slight spotting, cont. hf. linen, light wear, end-papers renewed. (HK. May 16; 1777) DM 440
- **Illustrations to Popular Songs.** 1822. Ob. fo. Hand-cold. title, 42 hand-cold. plts., wormhole to margin not affecting plts., hf. mor., rubbed. (P. Feb.16; 154) £300
- **The National Sports of Great Britain.** L., 1821. *1st. Edn. 1st. Iss., with frontis. dtd. 1820.* Fo. Additional hand-cold. aquatint title, 50 hand-cold. aquatint plts., some faint offsetting from text, cont. red str.-grd. mor. gt., jnts. reprd. (S. Dec.1; 165) *Joseph.* £3,400
- – **Anr. Edn.** L., 1821. Fo. Additional cold. aquatint title, 50 cold. aquatint plts., title & text in Engl. & Fr., cont. maroon str.-grd. mor., covers gt.- & blind-panel., spine gt. (C. Nov.16; 43) *Smith.* £5,500
- – **Anr. Edn.** L., 1821 [1903]. Fo. Decor. title, 46 (of 50) plts., text in Engl. & Fr., lacks ptd. title, slight margin stains, slight spotting & soiling, hf. roan, worn. (SPB. Dec.13; 768) $125

ALKEN, Henry -*Contd.*

-- **Anr. Edn.** L., 1823. Lge. fo. Title & all plts. from 1904 edn., orig. blind- & gt.-decor. mor., rebnd., slightly rubbed, corners & spine ends reprd. (VG. Mar.19; 1)　　　　　　　　　　Fls. 900
-- **Anr. Edn.** L., 1825. Lge. 8vo. 50 hand-cold. plts., slight offsetting from text, a few text ll. spotted, pres. inscr. on title & note in the same hand added in text, cont. cf. (S. Dec.1; 164)
　　　　　　　　　　　　　　　　　Burgess. £750
-- **Anr. Edn.** 1903. Fo. Chromolitho. frontis., additional title, 49 plts., parallel text in Engl. & Fr., cont. cl.-bkd. bds., rubbed & slightly faded. (CSK. Jan.27; 155)　　　　　　　　　　　£420
-- **Anr. Copy.** Fo. In Engl. & Fr., orig. buckram-bkd. cl., spine gt., partly unc. (LC. Mar.1; 435)
　　　　　　　　　　　　　　　　　　　　£380
- **Scraps from the Sketchbook of Henry Alken, Engraved by Himself.** 1823. Ob. fo. 42 hand-cold. aquatint plts., recent hf. mor. (TA. Jun.21; 383)
　　　　　　　　　　　　　　　　　　　　£260
- **Sporting Scrap Book.** L., 1824. Ob. 4to. 49 hand-cold. plts., some stains, hf. mor., upr. cover detchd., as a coll. of plts., w.a.f. (P. May 17; 214)
　　　　　　　　　　　　　　　　　Hadland. £420
- **A Touch at the Fine Arts.** 1824. Sm. fo. 12 hand-cold. aquatint plts., publishers advt. lf. bnd. in at rear, orig. bds., mor. backstrip, worn on spine. (TA. Jun.21; 574)　　　　　　　　　　　£165

ALKMAR, Heinrich von
- **Reineke der Fuchs.** Trans.:– J. Chr. Gottsched. Ill.:– A. v. Everdingen & S. Fokke. Leipzig & Amst., 1752. *1st. Edn.* 4to. Lightly browned, 1st. third very foxed & brown spotted, later bds., worn. (R. Apr.3; 109)　　　　　　　DM 1,900
-- **Anr. Copy.** 4to. Some foxing, lightly browned, cont. style bds. (GB. May 4; 1413)　　DM 1,500

ALLARD, Emile
- [-] **L'Art de Bâtir les Vaisseaux, et d'en Perfectionner la Construction.** Amst., 1719. 2 vols. in 1. 4to. 113 plts., some stains & tears, old cf., traces of wear. (HD. Mar.9; 44)　　　　　Frs. 2,500

ALLART, Johannes
- **De Republiek der Vereenigde Nederlanden, zinds de Noord-Americaansche Onlusten.** Amst., priv. ptd., 1788-1805. 35 vols. Engraved frontis., 121 engraved plts. & ports., some minor staining, Vol. XXXIV lacks directions to binder, cont. hf. cf., not quite unif. (CH. Sep.20; 16)　　　　Fls. 680
- **Tafereelen van de Staatsomwenteling in Frankrijk.** Amst., 1794-1807. 25 vols. Engraved titles, 155 engraved plts. & ports., Vol. VII lacks directions to binder, cont. hf. cf. (CH. Sep.20; 17)　　Fls. 480

ALLBUTT, Sir Thomas Clifford
- **On the Use of the Opthalmoscope in Diseases of the Nervous System and of the Kidneys.** L., 1871. *1st. Edn.* Lge. 8vo. Cl., faded, lacks hf. of spine, ex-liby. (SG. Mar.22; 16)　　　　　$110

ALLEMAGNE, Henri René d'
- **Les Accessoires du Costume et du Mobilier.** Paris, 1928. 3 vols. 4to. A few plts. loose, hf. leath. (SG. Jan.26; 167)　　　　　　　　　$300
-- **Anr. Copy.** 2 vols. 4to. Orig. cl. & bds. (CH. May 24; 109)　　　　　　　　　　Fls. 1,100
- **Les Cartes à Jouer du XIVe au XXe Siècle.** Paris, 1904. *1st. Edn.* 2 vols. 4to. Some col. plts. with gt. highlights, slight darkening to margins, orig. col. ill. bds., marb. end-papers, covers rubbed & soiled, edges worn, bkplts. (CBA. Jan.29; 3)　　$1,200
-- **Anr. Edn.** Paris, 1906. 2 vols. 4to. Hf. leath. gt., orig. wraps. bnd. in. (R. Oct.11; 947)　DM 3,600
- **Histoire des Jouets.** Paris, [1902]. *1st. Edn.* 4to. 50 col. plts., slight margin darkening, faint foxing to edges, orig. col. ill. cl., rubbing & some soiling, edges frayed. (CBA. Jan.29; 4)　　　　　$425
-- **Anr. Copy.** Lge. 4to. Orig. linen. (HK. Nov.9; 2183)　　　　　　　　　　　DM 900
- **Musée Rétrospectif. Exposition de 1900: Jeux.** Paris, 1900. 2 vols. 4to. Hf. chagrin. (HD. Feb.28; 4)　　　　　　　　　　　　Frs. 4,200
- **Récréations et Passe-temps.** Paris, [1904]. Lge. 4to. 132 plts. (30 cold.), publisher's ill. bds. (HD. Feb.28; 3)　　　　　　　　　Frs. 5,100

ALLEN, Frederick H.
- **The Great Cathedrals of the World.** Boston, [1886]. 2 vols. Some foxing, cf., edges & spine lightly nicked. (RS. Jan.17; 451)　　　　$150

ALLEN, James
- **New-Englands Choicest Blessing & the Mercy Most to be Desired by all that Wish Well to this People, Cleared in a Sermon** ... Boston, 1679. *1st. Edn.* 4to. Lacks final blank lf., very soiled & worn, bnd. with 3 other cont. works (all incompl.), stitched into old leath. covers, w.a.f. (SG. Oct.20; 5)
　　　　　　　　　　　　　　　　　　　$1,900

ALLEN, John
- **Principles of Modern Riding for Gentlemen.** 1825. Frontis., 31 plts., some light foxing, cf., rubbed. (P. Feb.16; 96)　　　　　　　　　　£90

ALLEN, John Carter & Charles Manning
See— STUART, John Sobieski Stolberg & Charles Edward [i.e. John Carter & Charles Manning Allen, afterwards John Hay & Charles Stuart Hay Allan]

ALLEN, Thomas
- **History of the County of Lincoln.** 1830-34. 2 vols. Map hand-cold., hf. cf. (LA. Nov.29; 196)　£70
- **Lancashire Illustrated.** 1839. 4to. 110 engrs. on 56 sheets, staining, lacks upr. cover, as a coll. of plts. w.a.f. (P. Apr.12; 157)　　　*Kidd.* £100
- **A New & Complete History of the County of York.** Ill.:– after N. Whittock. 1828-31. 6 vols. Some spotting, cont. hf. cf., 1 upr. cover detchd., spines worn. (TA. Apr.19; 104)　　　　£190
-- **Anr. Copy.** 6 vols. Engraved frontis.'s, title-pp., 136 plts., 1 detchd., cont. hf. cf., rubbed. (CSK. Dec.2; 146)　　　　　　　　　　£170

ALLEN PRESS
- **Four Fictions.** Ill.:– Blair Hughes-Stanton, Michele Forgeois, Joseph Low & Paolo Carasonne. Kentfield, Calif., Allen Pr., 1973. *(137) ptd. on 4 different H.M.P.* Tall fo. 4 full-p. drawings in 3 colours, bds., prospectus laid in. (SG. May 17; 6)
　　　　　　　　　　　　　　　　　　　$425

ALLERS, C.W. & Ganghofer, L.
- **Das Deutsche Jägerbuch.** Ill.:– H. Engl. Stuttgart, [1897]. *1st. Edn.* Fo. Orig. pict. linen. (GB. May 4; 1966)　　　　　　　　　　DM 600

ALLESTREE, Richard
- [-] **The Ladies Calling.** Oxford, 1673. *1st. Edn.* Title reprd., cont. panel. mor. gt., central panel decor., hinges reprd., new end-papers. (P. Sep.29; 154)
　　　　　　　　　　　　　　　　　Pearson. £70
- [-] **The Works of the learned & Pious Author of the Whole Duty of Man.** Oxford, 1695. *3rd. Imp.* Fo. Engraved frontis. creased, several sigs. browned, cont. Engl. red mor., gt. covers with centre decor., pointillé, drawhandle tools, etc., gt. spine decor., [by Robert Steele]; Sir Robert Leighton copy, H.M. Nixon coll., with his MS. purchase note on fly-lf. [Wing A1084] (BBA. Oct.6; 224)
　　　　　　　　　　　　　Oak Knoll Books. £170

ALLEZARD, J.-J.
- **Nouveau Recueil de Plans des Principaux Ports de la Mediterranée.** Livornio, Marseille, 1800. *New Edn.* Ob. 8vo. Title & 152 maps, cont. hf. cf., corners. (HD. Jun.18; 1)　　　　　　£80
- **Recueil de 163 Principaux Plans des Ports et Rades de la Mediterranée.** Livorno, 1817. Ob. 4to. Title with sm. liby. stp., slightly spotted, folding plts. pasted with linen strips, linen, ca. 1850. (HK. Nov.9; 1867)　　　　　　　　　DM 850

ALLGEMEINES HISTORISCHES LEXICON ALLER STROME UND FLUSSE IN OBER-UND NIEDER DEUTSCHLAND
Frankfurt, 1743. Cont. blind-stpd. pig over wood bds. (BBA. Jan.19; 20)　　　*Bücherkabinett.* £80

ALLGEMEINES KUNSTLER-LEXIKON
Frankfurt, 1922. 6 vols., with 2 Supps. Orig. hf. linen. (V. Sep.30; 1821)　　　　　DM 420
-- **Anr. Copy** 6 vols. Orig. hf. linen, vol. 6 not unif., slightly rubbed. (D. Nov.23; 1795)　DM 400

ALLGEMEINES TEUTSCHES GARTEN-MAGAZIN
Weimar, 1804-06. Jahrgang I-III. 4to. Many plts. hand-cold., cont. hf. cf. (C. Nov.16; 44)
　　　　　　　　　　　　　　　　　Schuster. £620

-- **Anr. Edn.** Weimar, 1804-24. 2 vols., including continuation. 4to. Plts. only: 396 (of 515) copper-engrs., all but 3 cont. hand-cold., cont. hf. leath. (B. Oct.4; 772a)　　　　　　　　Fls. 5,000

ALLIACO, Petrus de
- **Tractatus et Sermones.** Strassburg, Georg Husner, 1490. Fo. Many initials, etc. in red & blue, lacks final blank, very wormed thro.-out, sometimes with loss of text, mod. vell.; the Walter Goldwater copy. [BMC I, 141; Goff A-488] (SG. Dec.1; 11)
　　　　　　　　　　　　　　　　　　　$425
- **Vita Beatissimi Patris, D. Petri Caelestini Quinti, Pontificis Maximi** ... Paris, 1539. 4to. Title device, lge. woodcut port. on A6v, M8v & P4v, some marginal browning & early marginalia & under-scoring, cont. inscr. on title & last lf. verso, early vell., worn. (SG. Apr.19; 85)　　　　$650

ALLINGHAM, William
See— DOYLE, Richard

ALLIONIO, Carolo
- **Flora Pedemontana sive Enumeratio Methodica Stirpium Indigenarum Pedemontii.** Ill.:– J.B. Stagnon after Molinari (port.), Petrus Peiroleri, J. Merc after Piantin. Augustae Taurinorum, 1785. 3 vols., including plt. vol. Fo. 92 plts., cont. hf. roan, corners. (HD. Mar.21; 3)　　　　Frs. 9,000

ALLNUTT, Z.
- **Useful & Correct Accounts of the Navigation of the Rivers & Canals West of London** ... [1810]. *2nd. Edn.* Folding engraved map, cold. outl., strengthened along folds, orig. ptd. wraps., soiled & frayed. (TA. Apr.19; 436)　　　　　£50

ALLOM, Thomas
- **Forty-Six Views of Tyrolese Scenery.** Ca. 1836. 4to. Engraved title & map spotted, orig. embossed cl. gt., from liby. of Luttrellstown Castle, W.a.f. (C. Sep.28; 1727)　　　　　　　　£170
-- **Anr. Copy.** 4to. Folding map, 45 steel engrs., prelims. & map foxed, orig. cl. gt., rebkd. (TA. Feb.16; 28)　　　　　　　　　　£105
-- **Anr. Copy.** 4to. Engraved title, folding map, 44 engraved views, orig. cl. gt., spine slightly torn. (P. Sep.8; 30)　　　　　　　*Tzakas.* £95
-- **Anr. Copy.** 4to. Engraved title, 1 engraved folding map, 45 steel engrs., foxed, orig. linen, bumped. (R. Oct.13; 3212)　　　　DM 400
-- **Anr. Edn.** L., ca. 1840. Engraved title, 45 steel engrs., 1 folding map, all plts., with light stains in side margin, lacks 8 pp., cont. leath. (R. Apr.5; 3006)　　　　　　　　　　DM 400
- **Souvenirs des Pyrénées.** Pau, n.d. 4to. 16 hand-cold. engraved plts., cont. cf.-bkd. bds., lightly rubbed. (CSK. Jul.6; 4)　　　　　　£100

ALLOM, Thomas (Ill.)
See— BEATTIE, William
See— BRITTON, John & Brayley, Edward Wedlake
See— CARNE, John
See— NOBLE, Thomas & Rose, Thomas
See— ROSE, Thomas
See— WALSH, Rev. Robert
See— WRIGHT, Rev. George Newnham

ALMACK, Edward, F.S.A.
- **Fine old Bindings with other interesting Miscellanea in Edward Almack's library.** 1913. *(200) numbered.* Fo. Orig. cl., a little stained; H.M. Nixon coll., with his acquisition note & some annots. & corrections. (BBA. Oct.6; 24)
　　　　　　　　　　　　　Oak Knoll Books. £240

ALMAIN ARMOURER'S Album
Ed.:– Visc. Harold A. Dillon. Ill.:– W. Griggs. L., 1905. Fo. Orig. parch., soiled. (BBA. Apr.5; 190)
　　　　　　　　　　　　　　Barrie Marks. £80

ALMANACS
- **Almanach Royal.** Paris, 1744. Old marb. cf., decor. spine, fleurs-de-lys decor.; with consular Paris arms, comte Godefroy de Montgrand ex-libris. (HD. Mar.30; 1)　　　　　Frs. 4,200
- **Almanach Royal, Année Bissextile.** Paris, 1752. Cont. red mor., gt. & pointillé decor., gt. tooled centre arms, decor. spine. (HD. Mar.14; 4)
　　　　　　　　　　　　　　　　　Frs. 8,500
- **Almanach Royal.** Paris, 1757. Old red mor., decor., fleurs-de-lys, Du Buisson plaque, gouache

centre arms of Madame Adélaide, on medallion under mica, slight loss, wtrd. silk doubls. & end-papers. (HD. Mar.30; 2) Frs. 26,000
– – **Anr. Edn.** Paris, 1761. Old red mor., decor. fleur-de-lys spine, lge. rocaille plaque, centre Louis-Antoine Philippe arms, sm. inner dentelle, paper doubl. & end-papers, gt. decor. (HD. Mar.30; 4) Frs. 23,100
– – **Anr. Copy.** Old red mor., decor. & fleur-de-lys, spine, lge. gt. decor., gt. Dubuisson plaque, centre arms, decor. paper doubl. & end-papers, sm. inner dentelle. (HD. Mar.30; 3) Frs. 18,000
– **Almanach Royal, Année Bissextile 1764.** Paris, 1764. 1 vol. Decor. Marb. cf. (*With:*) – **Almanach Impérial pour l'An XIII.** Paris, [1805]. 1 vol. Hf. cf., spine decor. (LM. Oct.22; 46) B.Frs. 10,000
– **Almanach des Environs de Paris.** Paris, 1773. 12mo. Double-p. engraved title, 16 double-p. cold. engraved maps, cont. marb. cf., jnts. strengthened. (HD. Mar.19; 86) Frs. 1,400
– **Almanach Royal.** Paris, 1776. Sm. title repair, old red mor., decor., spine, gt. decor. centre Turgot arms, sm. inner dentelle, paper doubls. & end-papers. (HD. Mar.30; 5) Frs. 33,000
– **Almanach Royal Année MDCCLXXXII.** Paris, 1782. Cont. Fr. red mor., on covers plaque by Dubuisson, composed of interlacing fillets, fleurons & shells, spine fully gt. in compartments with fleur-de-lys in each compartment, gt.-embossed end-papers, as a bdg., w.a.f. (S. May 10; 210) *Loeb.* £340
– **Almanack for 1783.** [1782]. Miniature book. Inlayed cf. gt., in Georgian style. (PD. Aug.17; 302) £55
– **Almanach des Monnoies Année 1786.** [1785]. 12mo. Cont. red mor. (HD. Jun.29; 6) Frs. 1,300
– **Almanach Royal, Année MDCCLXXXVII.** [Paris, 1787]. Cont. Fr. red mor. gt. decor., Louis XV arms, silk liners, faint trace of worm at foot of spine; owners inscr. 'Cécile Madden à Versailles' on front free end-paper. (C. May 30; 66) *Hill.* £480
– **Almanach Royal.** Paris, [1788]. Mod. mor. gt., centre arms of Louise-Marie-Adélaïde de Bourbon-Penthièvre, Duchesse d'Orléans, fleurs-de-lys decor. spine, inner roll-stp. (HD. Sep.22; 177) Frs. 6,100
– **Almanach de la Garde Nationale de Lyon pour l'Année 1790.** Lyon, 1790. Cont. roan, Lyon arms, spine decor. (HD. Nov.9; 133) Frs. 1,700
– **Almanac de Gotha.** Ill.:– after Chodowiecki. Gotha, [1792]. 12mo. Orig. lacquered bds., gold decor., centre fleuron. (R. Apr.3; 110) DM 200
– **MDCCXCVI The Royal Repository or Polite Pocket Diary.** 1796. 12mo. Calendarium & cash-account pp. unused, orig. bds., orig. pict. s.-c., box; J.R. Abbey bkplt. (P. Apr.12; 80) *Quaritch.* £90
– **Polite Repository or Pocket Companion.** 1796. Cont. inlaid mor., orig. mor. s.-c. (P. Dec.8; 194) *Finch.* £75
– **Almanach de Gotha. Gothaischer Kalender.** Gotha, 1796-1944. Years 32-181, 151 vols. only (lacks Vol. 50), including 3 Supps. 12mo., sm. 8vo. & 8vo. 42 vols. orig. bds., 5 vols. cf., 104 vols. cl., some spines slightly defect., discold. or reprd. (VS. Dec.8; 717) Fls. 2,900
– **Brigg's Maryland, Pennsylvania & Virginia Almanac; or, Baltimore Ephemeris: for the Year of our Lord, 1798 ...** Balt., [1797]. 16mo. 18 unnumbered ll., few interleaved blanks, light brown stain thro.-out at top of gutter, some cont. ink notations at front blank & few interior blanks, saddle-stitched, cont. unlettered marb. wraps., worn. (HA. May 4; 339) $120
– **Almanak voor Re:zigers i.h. Koningrijk der Nederlanden.** Amst., 1819. Mod. hf. chagrin, orig. wraps. preserved; Valck Lucassen & Koch bkplts. (VS. Dec.9; 972) Fls. 475
– **Davy Crockett's Almanack [renamed The Crockett Almanac for Vol. 2].** Nashville, 1835-40. Vol. 1 nos. 1-4, Vol. 2 nos. 1-2. (*With:*) – **The Crockett Almanac.** Nashville, Berry & Tanhill, 1841. (*With:*) – **Ben Hardin's Crockett Almanac.** N.Y., Turner & Fisher, 1842. (*With:*) – **Fisher's Crockett Almanac.** N.Y., Turner & Fisher, 1843. Together 9 vols. Heavy foxing to the 1843 no., orig. pict. wraps., most with minor defects, two-thirds of lr. cover of 1837 no. lacking & supplied in facs. (SPB. May 23; 35) $6,000
– **English Bijou Almanack.** Ill.:– L.E. L[andon]. L.,

[1836]. 20 × 15mm. Miniature Book. Rather loose in orig. wraps. gt., slightly discold., similar s.-c., in orig. roan fitted case, with magnifying glass. (S. Nov.22; 422) *Bondy.* £120
– – **Anr. Copy.** 20 × 14mm. Miniature Book. Orig. wraps., top of covers lightly worn, s.-c., slightly rubbed. (S. Dec.20; 728) *Libris.* £80
– **London Almanack.** L., 1840. 57 × 33mm. Miniature book. Folding plt. mntd. as 2 ll., cont. red mor., multi-cold. onlays, ruled & tooled in gt., covers lightly rubbed affecting onlays. (CSK. Dec.2; 100) £65
– **Davy Crockett's Almanac.** Boston, 1844. Orig. pict. wraps., disbnd., folder & s.-c. (LH. Jan.15; 274) $170
– **London Almanack for the Year ... 1855.** [1855]. 58 × 16mm., Miniature Book. Engraved thro.-out, each lf. folded vertically to form 'finger' almanac, 1 lf. with sm. clean tear at fold, orig. diced mor., unif. s.-c.; pres. inscr. (CSK. May 18; 114) £70
– **London Almanack for the Year ... 1857.** [1857]. 31 × 31mm. Miniature Book. Engraved thro.-out, each lf. folded horizontally, orig. mor., unif. s.-c.; pres. inscr. (CSK. May 18; 116) £55
– **London Almanack for the Year ... 1861.** [1861]. 56 × 16mm. Miniature Book. Engraved thro.-out, each lf. folded vertically to form 'finger' almanac, orig. cf., elab. gt., unif. s.-c. (CSK. May 18; 117) £130
– **London Almanack for the Year ... 1862.** [1862]. 58 × 16mm. Miniature Book. Engraved thro.-out, each lf. folded vertically to form 'finger' almanac, 1 lf. with sm. clean tear at fold, orig. mor., vertical blind fillets, unif. s.-c. (CSK. May 18; 118) £65
– **London Almanack for 1866.** [1866]. 31 × 31mm. Miniature Book. Engraved thro.-out, each lf. folded horizontally, orig. diced mor., unif. s.-c. (CSK. May 18; 119) £60
– **Mignon Almanach auf des Jahr 1829.** Vienna, n.d. 18 × 28mm. Miniature book. Orig. glazed paper bds., covers gt.-blocked, in mother-of-pearl box, sliding cover with hand-painted town view (defect.). (CSK. Apr.6; 77) £95

ALMAZAN, Duque de
– **Historia de la Monteria en España.** Madrid, 1934. *(505) numbered.* Fo. Rag paper, MS. dedication, orig. red mor., gt. tooled, arms. (DS. Dec.16; 2074) Pts. 80,000

ALMER, Christian
– **A Facsimile of Christian Almer's Führerbuch 1856-1894. Reproduced Under the Superintendance of C.D. Cunningham & Capt. W. de W. Abney.** 1896. *(200) numbered.* Orig. cl., rubbed. (BBA. May 3; 340) *Bob Finch Books.* £160

ALMOLI, Shlomo
– **Pitron Halomot [on passages in the Talmud relating to dreams].** Amst., 1637. Sm. 8vo. Some browning & dampstaining, title & 1 other remargined, 101 restored with part of text supplied in MS., later mott. cf., extremities worn. (SG. Feb.2; 143) $950

ALMOSNINO, Moshe
– **Ma'Amatz Ko'Ach.** Venice, 1588. *1st. Edn.* 4to. Sigd. by 3 censors, Owner's stp. on title, staining mostly in margins, creased, leath. (S. Oct.24; 25) *Sol.* £300
– **Tephila Le'Moshe.** Saloniki, 1563. *1st. Edn.* 4to. Browned & stained, some worming affecting some letters towards end, vell. (S. Oct.24; 26) *Aldus.* £600

ALPHABET & IMAGE
Ed.:– Robert Harling. L., 1946-48. Nos. 1-8. Sm. 4to. Orig. ring-bkd. wraps. or orig. wraps., a few slightly soiled. (*With:*) – **IMAGE. A Quarterly of the Visual Arts.** Ed.:– Robert Harling. L., 1949-52. Nos. 1-8. Sm. 4to. Orig. wraps., a few slightly soiled. (BBA. Apr.5; 315) *Oak Knoll Books.* £90

ALPHABET DES METIER DES RUES
Epinal, 1863. 24 cold. plts., cont. bds., newly bnd. with linen, cold. orig. upr. wrap. mntd; Hauswedell coll. (H. May 23; 117) DM 420

ALPHABET PITTORESQUE-PICTURESQUE ALPHABET
Paris, Fournier, ca. 1850?. Ob. 12mo. 26 hand-cold. accordion-folding litho. plts., captions in Fr. & Engl., several plts. with sm. surface abrasions, 1 plt. with sm. tear, cl.-bkd. bds., chipped. (SG. Dec.8; 13) $110

ALPHABETUM BRAMMHANICUM SEU INDOSTANUM
Ed.:– [G.C. Amaduzzi]. Rome, 1771. *1st. Edn.* Partly browned, old patterned bds., slightly stained. (SG. Oct.27; 8) $175

ALPHABETUM DIVINI AMORIS
[Cologne, Ulrich Zel], ca. 1466-67. *1st. Edn.* Sm. 4to. Fully rubricated, later vell.; the Walter Goldwater copy. [BMC I, 179; Goff A-524] (SG. Dec.1; 12) $6,500

ALPHABETUM GRECUM
Strassburg, 1568. Sm. printers' marks on title cold. light brown, few MS. notes, slightly soiled, bds. (HK. Nov.8; 78) DM 700

ALPHAND, Adolphe
– **Les Promenades de Paris.** N.d. Atlas vol. only. Lge. fo. Engraved title, 105 plts. & plans only, orig. mor.-bkd. cl., spine chipped. (CSK. Oct.7; 28) £160

ALPHERAKY, Sergius
– **The Geese of Europe & Asia, Being the Description of Most of the Old World Species.** 1905. 4to. Orig. cl. gt., slightly rubbed. (TA. May 17; 271) £240

ALPHONSO X, King of Castille
– **Tabulae Astronomicae Alfonsi Regis.** Venetiis, Ioa. Hamman, 1492. 4to. Lacks 2 pp., including colophon, initials, no bdg. stated. [H. 869] (CR. Jun.6; 92) Lire 750,000

ALPINUS, Prosper
– **De Medicina Aegyptiorum.** Paris, 1645. 4to. Title little stained, liby. stp., cf., rebkd.; Dr. Walter Pagel copy. (S. Feb.7; 12) *Israel.* £90
– – **Anr. Edn.** Leiden, 1719, 1718 (pts. 2-4). *New Edn.* 4 pts. in 1 vol. 4to. Cont. vell., cover blind-tooled. (HK. Nov.8; 426) DM 580

ALSHEICH, Moshe
– **Chavatzelet Ha'Sharon.** Venice, 1591. *2nd. Edn.* 4to. Title torn & mntd. affecting few letters in text, owner's sig., top margins of 2 ll. reprd., staining mostly in margins, cl. (S. Oct.24; 27) *Klein.* £300
– **Dvarim Nichumim.** Venice, 1601. *1st. Edn.* 4to. Tear on title not affecting text, creased, staining mostly in margins, cl. (S. Oct.24; 28) *Klein.* £190
– **Dvarim Tovim.** Venice, 1601. *1st. Edn.* 4to. Title from anr. copy, some margins reprd. without loss of text, slightly stained & soiled, cl. (S. Oct.24; 29) *Klein.* £200
– **Einei Moshe.** Venice, 1601. *1st. Edn.* 4to. Slightly creased, slight staining mostly in margins, cl. (S. Oct.24; 30) *Klein.* £200
– **Mar'ot Ha'Zovot.** Venice, 1603-07. *1st. Edn.* Fo. Inner margin reprd. without loss of text, 2 wormholes not affecting text, slight foxing, mod. blind-tooled mor. (S. Oct.24; 32) *Klein.* £260
– **Masat Moshe.** Venice, 1601. *1st. Edn.* 4to. Margins rather frayed, last 4 ll. reprd. with loss of some letters, staining & worming mostly in margins, cl. (S. Oct.24; 33) *Sol.* £130
– **Rav Peninim.** Venice, 1601. *1st. Edn.* 4to. Staining mostly in margins, edges frayed, slightly discold., late 17th. C. owner's inscr. on last p., mod. leath. (S. Oct.24; 34) *Klein.* £280
– **Romemot El.** Venice, 1605. *1st. Edn.* 4to. Title from anr. copy, wormhole at beginning affecting some letters, stained & slightly foxed, mod. leath. (S. Oct.24; 35) *Klein.* £300
– **Shoshanat Ha'Amakim.** Venice, 1591. *1st. Edn.* 4to. Title damaged & crudely reprd., anr. lf. reprd. with loss of a few letters, edges frayed, staining, browned, cl. (S. Oct.24; 36) *Sol.* £120

ALSOP, Richard (Ed.)
See— JEWITT, John R.

ALSTEDT, Johann Heinrich
– **Scientiarum Omnium Encyclopaediae.** Lyon, 1649. 7 pts. in 2 vols. Fo. Some slight browning &

ALSTEDT, Johann Heinrich -Contd.

spotting, cont. bds., blind-tooled centre-piece, corners bumped, lightly reprd., lacks ties. (D. Nov.24; 4323)   DM 1,700

ALT, Franz
- **Aus den Alpen. Ansichten aus der Alpenwelt.** Vienna, n.d. Series 1 only. Ob. fo. 20 chromolithos., most slightly defect., spotted in margins, orig. bds., worn, as a coll. of plts., w.a.f. (P. May 17; 347)
Walford. £280

ALTERNANCE
Text:– Mauriac, Ginaudoux, Eluard, & others. Ill.:– Laboureur, Matisse, Goerg, Cocteau, Marie Laurencin, & others. Paris, 1946. 4to. Leaves, box. (HD. Nov.17; 88)   Frs. 3,250

ALTESERRA, Antonio Dadino
- **Asceticon sive Originum Rei Monasticae Libri Decem.** Paris, 1674. 4to. Cont. Fr. red mor., triple gt. border-lines, arms of Guillaume Ier de Lamoignon (1617-1677), President du Parlement de Paris, his cipher at corners & in compartments on spine, title in 2nd. compartment, shelfmark in 6th. compartment on spine, sm. ink-stain touching arms on upr. cover, sm. strip of mor. scraped, book label & bkplt. of Sir William Fitz Herbert Bart., as a bdg., w.a.f. (S. May 10; 211)   *Loeb.* £360

ALTHAMER, Andr.
- **Conciliationes Locorum Scripturae.** Nürnberg, 1553. Title with owners mark, lightly browned, cont. blind-tooled pig over wood bds., 2 clasps. (HK. May 15; 62)   DM 400
- **Von dem Hochwirtigen Sacrament ...** [Augsburg, 1526]. 4to. Title slightly soiled, old liby. stp., bds. (R. Oct.11; 7)   DM 550

ALTING, Jacob
- **Fundamenta Punctationis Linguae Sanctae.** Frankfurt, 1521. (*Bound with:*) - **Synopsis Institutionum Chaldaearum et Syrarum.** Frankfurt, 1521. (*Bound with:*) OTHO, Georgius – **Synopsis Institutionum Samaritanarum, Rabbinicarum, Arabicarum, Aethiopicarum et Persicarum.** Frankfurt, 1521. Together 3 works in 1 vol. Later vell., trimmed, soiled. (SG. Feb.2; 2) $130

ALTRAS, David
- **Sefer Tsuf Devash.** Venice, 1714. *1st. Edn.* 16mo. Soiled & dampstained, old leath.-bkd. flexible bds., worn. (SG. Feb.2; 256) $110

ALUNNO, Francesco
- **Le Osservationi.** Venice, 1550. Vell. gt. (PD. Dec.14; 340)   £50

ALVARES or ALVAREZ, Francisco
- **Noticia del Establecimiento y Poblacion de las Colonias Inglesas en la America Septentrional.** Madrid, 1778. Sm. 4to. Later pres. inscr. on 1st. text lf., cont. Spanish cf., slightly worn. [Sabin 975] (S. Dec.1; 271)   *Israel.* £250
- **Warhafftige Bericht von den Landern ... des Mechtigen Königs in Ethiopien.** Eissleben, 1566. *1st. German Edn.* Title with 2 sm. bkd. tears. (*Bound with:*) VALERIUS MAXIMUS – **Neun Bücher vom Namhafften und Wunderbaren Geschichten und Exempeln, beide der Römer und anderer ausslendischen Völcker.** Ed.:– Niclas Heiden. Trans.:– P. Selbeth. Frankfurt, 1565. Printers mark cut in lr. margin. Together 2 works in 1 vol. Some old MS. marginalia, cont. blind-tooled pig over wood bds., roll-tooled decor., 2 brass clasps. (D. Nov.23; 1226)   DM 2,700

ALVAREZ SEMEDO, F.
- **The History of ... Monarchie of China.** L., 1655. 4to. Leath. (DS. Nov.25; 2006)   Pts. 22,000

AMADOR DE LOS RIOS, José & others
- **Historia de la Villa y Corte de Madrid.** Madrid, 1861-64. 4 vols. Lge. fo. Linen, chagrin corners. (DS. Feb.24; 2081)   Pts. 120,000

AMAR DURIVIER, M.A.
- **La Gimnastica.** Madrid, 1807. Mor. (DS. Mar.23; 2009)   Pts. 50,000

AMBROSELLI, G.
- **Venise.** Paris, n.d. *(220).* Lge. 4to. Leaves, folder; 10 etchings justified & sigd. by artist. (HD. Jun.6; 3)   Frs. 1,000

AMBROSI-ROSTINI, A.
- **Histoire des Corses et de leur Civilisation.** Bastia, 1914. Sewed; A.L.s. to Capitaine France. (HD. Oct.21; 7)   Frs. 1,000

AMBROSIUS, Saint Bp. of Milan
- **Opera.** Basel, J. Amerbach, 1492. *1st. Coll. Edn.* Pt. 3 only (of 3). Fo. Some red & blue painted initials, stained in lr. margin thro.-out, & in some side margins, 10 ll. defect in lr. margins without loss, 1st. 9 ll. wormed with some loss, late gothic blind-tooled pig over wood bds., 8 corner & 2 centre bosses, with buckles & clasps, woodcut arms ex-libris in inner cover dtd. 1559 (slightly defect.). [HC. 896; BMC III, 753; GoffA-551] (R. Oct.11; 1)   DM 2,000
- **Opera Omnia.** Basle, 1527. 3 vols. in 1. Lge. fo. 1 lf. torn without loss of letters, cont. stpd. cf. over wood bds., richly decor., brass corners & clasps, jnts. reprd.; from Fondation Furstenberg-Beaumesnil. (HD. Nov.16; 83)   Frs. 4,200

AMELOT DE LA HOUSSAYE, Abraham Nicolas
[–] **Abregé du Procès fait aux Juifs de Metz.** Paris, 1670. 12mo. Early 19th. C. red mor., gt. decor., gt. spine, inner & outer dentelle, spine sigd. by Thouvenin, very rubbed. (D. Nov.24; 4212)   DM 1,000

AMERICA, Confederate States of
- **Acts & Resolutions of the First Session of the Provisional Congress of the Confederate States.** Montgomery, 1861. Early ink spots, last pp. foxed & browned, few margin ink & pencil notations, cont. cf. & marb. bds., worn & scuffed; Huston Lee (Capt. & Assistant Quartermaster, C.S.A.) copy, sigd. with rank, 'Charleston, S. Ca., August 10, 1861' at front pastedown, & sigd. at title, tipped to front end-papers is 4-p. order from Adjutant & Inspector General's Office, Richmond, Aug., 1861, sigd. in type by Samuel Cooper. (HA. Sep.16; 315) $120
- **Journal of the Congress of ... 1861-1865.** Wash., 1904-05. 7 vols. Tall 8vo. Sheep & cl., backs rubbed with some scuffing, leath. brittle. (HA. Sep.16; 350) $175
- **Regulations for the Army of the Confederate States for the Quartermaster's Department, including the Pay Branch Thereof.** Richmond, 1862. Intermittent foxing, orig. cf. & marb. bds., covers worn & scuffed at edges; Huston Lee (Major & Chief Quartermaster, Department of South Carolina, Georgia, & Florida) copy, with stpd. leath. label incorporating name, rank & duties at front cover, sigd. in ink at front end-paper, tipped to rear blank is 3-p. ptd. circular from Quartermaster General's Office, Richmond, Sep. 15, 1864, on transportation of public stores. (HA. Sep.16; 325) $150

AMERICAN BOOK COLLECTOR
Plainfield & Metuchen, 1932-35. Vols. 1-6 nos. 6 (lacks Jan. 1934 iss.), & Supp. 'The Book Fool ... '. Tall 8vo. Ptd. wraps. (SG. Sep.15; 4) $250
- - **Anr. Edn.** Ed.:– Charles F. Heartman & Harry B. Weiss. Metuchen [N.J.], 1932-35. Vols. 1-6 (all publd.), 42 pts. in 6 vols. Lge. 8vo. Binder's cl., orig. wraps. bnd. in. (SG. May 17; 11) $110

AMERICAN BOOK PRICES CURRENT
Newark & N.Y., 1895-1972. Vols. 1-57, 59-75, together 74 vols. Buckram, few d.-w.'s. (SG. May 17; 12) $800
- - **Anr. Edn.** N.Y., [1925-80]. Vols. 56-59, 62-76, 78-81, & 83-84, and Index vols. for 1916-22, 1933-40, & 1945-65. Buckram, 2 vols. soiled, 7 vols. with d.-w., 3 vols. ex-liby. (SG. Aug.4; 7) $435
- - **Anr. Edn.** 1950-74. 24 vols., lacks 1963 & 1964; & 5-year indexes 1945-50, 1960-65, & 2-vol. 1965-70. Cl., gt.-lettered, light wear, ex-liby. with some markings. (HA. May 4; 138) $350
- - **Anr. Edn.** N.Y., [1959-66]. Vols. 65-72. Buckram, last vol. without d.-w. (SG. Aug.4; 8) $100
- - **Anr. Edn.** N.Y., 1959-82. Vols, 65 & 67-87. 1979 addendum laid in, cl. (SG. Jan.5; 4) $550

- Index. 1970-1975.
N.Y., 1976. 2 vols. Cl., worn. (RO. May 29; 4) $115

AMERICAN CIVIL WAR
- **Atlas to Accompany the Official Records of the Union & Confederate Armies.** Wash., 1891-95. *1st. Edn. 1st. Iss.* 35 pts. Fo. 3 supp. maps in pt. 27, most maps & charts outl. or fully cold., lacks index, a few maps & plts. lightly chipped at side margin, orig. ptd. wraps., all chipped & detchd., some soiled. (HA. Nov.18; 96) $250
- **Official Records of the Union & Confederate Navies in the War of the Rebellion.** Wash., 1894-1927. 29 vols. only (Lacks Series II, Vol. I), & separate Index. Lge. 8vo. Some texts lightly rippled, few individual vols. with minor to moderate wear, ribbed cl., gt.-lettered. (HA. Sep.16; 395) $300.
- - **Anr. Copy.** Series I: 24 vols. only (lacks Vols. XII & XIII, dupls. of Vols. VII & XXII). Lge. 8vo. Some text affected by dampstaining, ribbed cl., gt.-lettered, lr. edges of covers with some recent dampstains. (HA. Sep.16; 396) $100
- **Photographic History of the Civil War.** Ed.:– F.T. Miller. N.Y., 1912. 10 vols. 4to. Cl. (SG. Aug.4; 250) $200

AMERICAN COAST SURVEY
- **Report of the Superintendent ... Showing the Progress of the Survey During the Year 1855.** Wash., 1856. 4to. 60 litho. plts. & maps, some slightly spotted, orig. cl., slightly rubbed. (BBA. May 3; 284)   *Haunted Bookshop.* £90

AMERICAN CONTINENTAL CONGRESS
- **Extracts from the Votes & Proceedings of the American Continental Congress, Held at Philadelphia, 10th May 1775.** N.Y., 1775. *1st. Printing.* Lacks final text lf., 2 ll. remargined, few blank corners missing, wraps., resewed, unc. (SG. Jan.19; 161) $175

AMERICAN COUNTRY HOUSES OF TODAY
N.Y., 1922, 1927, 1930. 3 vols. 4to. Cl., 2nd. vol. shaken. (SG. Aug.25; 9) $100

AMERICAN FABRICS
N.Y., 1946-51. Nos. 1-17. Tall 4to. Pict. wraps., worn, apparently compl. but uncollated, w.a.f. (RO. Mar.21; 133) $220

AMERICAN MAGAZINE
Boston, Feb. 1744. Sm. 4to. Scattered stains, side-stitched, upr. wrap. loose & frayed. (SG. Jan.19; 172) $175

AMERICAN NUMISMATIC SOCIETY
- **Museum Notes.** N.Y., 1968-81. Nos. 14-26. Orig. wraps. (S. May 1; 448)   *Spink.* £60

AMERICAN REVIEW: a Whig Journal
N.Y., Jan.-Jun. 1845. Vol. I, in 6 monthly nos. With 2 contribs. each by Poe & Whitman, some dampwrinkling, later hf. cf., spines cracked. (SG. Mar.29; 250) $130

AMERICAN TYPE FOUNDERS COMPANY
- **Specimens of Type, Ornaments & Borders ...** Chic., [1896]. Lge. 4to. Errata slip pasted in upr. cover, cl., rear inr. hinge torn. (SG. May 17; 333) $100

AMERY, L.S.
- **The Times History of the War in South Africa.** 1900-09. 7 vols., including Index vol. Orig. cl., spines gt. (some rubbed), some ll. unc. (LC. Mar.1; 436)   £60

AMES, Nathaniel
- **An Astronomical Diary, or, An Almanack ... 1734** ... Boston, 1734 [1733]. 16mo. 7 unnumbered ll. with integral title, removed, a few faint old stains, lacks part of bottom margin of title-lf., & sm. part of bottom fore-e. corner of last lf., edges worn with chips & sm. old tears, especially at corners, with loss of few text nos. in last lf., old stab holes at gutter with later hand-stitching. (HA. May 4; 338) $150

AMETHYST, Der
- **Blätter für Seltsame Litteratur und Kunst.** Ed.:– Franz Blei. Contribs.:– Verlaine, Poe, Schröder, Wilde & others. Ill.:– Behmer, Rops, Kubin, Besnaux. [Wien], 1906. *(800) numbered.* 11 (of 12)

pts. in 8. Lacks 1 ill., lacks vol. II with Beardsley ills., 2 sigs. loose, orig. wraps. (D. Nov.24; 2936)
DM 800
– – **Anr. Edn.** Ed.:– Franz Blei. Trans.:– Contribs.:– Brod, Wilde, Verlaine, Poe & others. Ill.:– Heine, Beardsley, Kubin, Behmer, Bayros & others. [Wien], 1906. *Numbered Copy for subscribers only.* Number removed, orig. linen. (D. Nov.24; 2937)
DM 600
– – **Anr. Copy.** 12 pts. in 1 vol., compl. Numbering erased in printers mark, orig. linen, very spotted, end-papers renewed. (H. May 23; 1122) DM 420

AMHURST, Lord, of Hackney & Thomson, Basil
– The Discovery of the Solomon Islands by Alvaro de Mendana in 1568, Translated from the Original Spanish Manuscripts ... 1901. *(100)* L.P. 2 vols. Lge. 8vo. Sm. defects & minor soiling, bdg. not stated, unc. (KH. May 1; 6) Aus. $380

AMICI, Domenico
– Raccolta dell Principali Vedute di Roma. Rome, 1835. Ob. fo. 42 engraved plts., mntd., slight margin spotting, prelims. loose, hf. mor., very worn. (SKC. Mar.9; 1963) £100
– – **Anr. Edn.** Rome, [1841]. Ob. fo. Engraved title & 40 views on india paper, spotted & stained in margins, minor worming in lr. margins, cont. maroon hf. mor., worn. (S. Apr.9; 3) *Fox.* £260

AMIOT, Joseph Marie
– Art Militaire des Chinois, ou Recueil d'Anciens Traités sur la Guerre composés avant l'Ere Chretienne par Différents Généraux Chinois. Paris, 1772-82. *1st. Edn.* 4to. Some sm. margin tears, cont. wraps., spine slightly defect. (HT. May 10; 2617)
DM 720

AMIS & AMILE
– Of the Friendship of Amis & Amile. Trans.:– William Morris. Kelms. Pr., 1894. *(500).* Orig. linen-bkd. bds. (P. Dec.8; 192) *J. Martin.* £75

AMMAN, Jost
– Gynaeceum. Frankfurt, 1586. *1st. Latin Edn.* Sm. 4to. Some slight browning, leath. gt., gt. spine, cover, inner & outer dentelle, in Grolier style; from C. Fairfax Murray & Sylvain S. Brunschwig coll. with ex-libris. (R. Apr.3; 13) DM 2,600

AMMAN, Jost & Boeksperger, H.
– Ein Neuw Thierbuch. Frankfurt, 1569. *1st. Edn.* Wide margin, 1 lf. verso with MS. mark, slightly spotted, cont. vell., borders, arms supralibros Kaiser Rudolf II on both covers, reprd., some wear, 4 ties. (HK. May 15; 63) DM 20,000
– Thierbuch. Frankfurt, 1579. Wide margin, a few margin repairs to title, minimal spotting, 19th. C. hf. vell.; Hausewedell coll. (H. May 24; 864)
DM 10,500

AMMON, Friedrich August von
– Klinische Darstellungen der Krankheiten des Menschlichen Auges. Berlin, 1838. Fo. Orig. bds., unc. (R. Apr.4; 1258) DM 2,000

AMOS, William
– Minutes of Agriculture & Planting ... Boston, 1810. *2nd. Edn.* 4to. 9 engraved plts., 2 hand-cold., 3 ll. with 10 mntd. specimens of grass types, later mor.-bkd. cl., faded. (CSK. May 18; 178) £160
– The Theory & Practise of the Drill – Husbandry. 1794. *1st. Edn.* 4to. Orig. bds., unc. (PD. Dec.14; 210) £135

AMPERE, André Marie
– Note sur un Mémoire lu à l'Académie Royale des Sciences dans la Séance du 4 Décembre 1820. Paris, 1820. Not bnd. (D. Nov.23; 664) DM 500

AMPHIAREO DA FERRARA, Vespasiano
– Opera. Nell quale s'insegna a scrivere varie Sorti di Lettere & massime vna Lettera Bastarda ... Cancellaresco, & Mercantesco ... Venetia, 1588. 1 sig. mispntd., some ll. with paper repairs, handbnd. red mor., gt. spine, covers, inner & outer dentelles; Hausewedell coll. (H. May 23; 217)
DM 3,800

AMSINCK, Paul
– Tunbridge Wells & Its Neighbourhood. L., 1810. 4to. Frontis., 30 plts., spotted, hf. cf. gt. (P. Nov.24; 70) *Fancycrest.* £55

– – **Anr. Copy.** 4to. Str.-grd. mor., upr. cover detchd. (P. Sep.29; 89) *Wilmot.* £50

AMSTERDAM
– Afbeeldinge van de Verscheyde Vergrootinge van Amsterdam, met der Zelver Voorn. Gebouwen ... Representation de Plusieurs Agrandissemens d'Amsterdam. Ill.:– J. Veenhuysen & S. Webbers. Amst., ca. 1670. Ob. 8vo. In Dutch & Fr., stained, cont. vell.; Six copy, Schretlen & Boekenogen bkplts. (VG. Sep.14; 1131) Fls. 550
– Verzaameling van alle de Huizen en Prachtige Gebouwen langs de Keizers en Heere-grachten der Stadt Amsterdam. Ill.:– Gaspar-Philips Jacobs. Amst., ca. 1780. Fo. Mod. marb. cf. gt., spine decor. (HD. Jun.18; 3) Frs. 10,500

AMTHOR, E.
– Der Alpenfreund. Gera, 1870-77. Vols. 1-10 only (of 11), in 5 vols. Vol. 5 lacks 3 plts., Vol. 9 lacks 1 panorama, lightly browned, some foxing, orig. gold-tooled linen. (R. Oct.13; 3182) DM 1,150

AMUNDSEN, Roald
– The South Pole. L., 1912. *1st. Engl. Edn.* 2 vols. Orig. cl. (S. Mar.6; 63) *Ryman.* £150
– – **Anr. Copy.** 2 vols. 1 folding chart detchd., cl., slightly marked. (KH. May 1; 7) Aus. $290
– – **Anr. Edn.** Trans.:– A.G. Chater. 1912. 2 vols. Cl. gt., d.-w.'s torn. (P. Jun.7; 16) £500
– – **Anr. Copy.** 2 vols. 4to. Orig. cl. gt. (TA. Sep.15; 98) £120
– Sydpolen, den norske Sydpolsfae Verd med 'Fram' 1910-1912. Kristiana, 1912. *1st. Edn.* 2 vols. Cf. gt., rebkd. (S. Jun.25; 23) *Sormani.* £60

ANACREON
– Odaria. Parma, 1785. In Greek, mod. mor.-bkd. decor. bds. (S. Dec.20; 771) *Brown.* £80
– – **Anr. Edn.** Parma, 1785. *(310). (50) on 'Carta Reale Francese'* with wtrmrk. 4to. Completely ptd. in majuscules, Grk. text, Latin commentary, cont. mor., elab. gt. decor., gt. inner & outer dentelle, cold. paper end-paper & doubl.; Hausewedell coll. (H. May 24; 1225) DM 4,000
– – **Anr. Edn.** Parma, 1785. *(250) on bluish paper.* Lge. 4to. Wide margin, in Greek, cont. red mor., gt. spine, cover, inner & outer dentelles, moire silk liners, by Derome le Jeune. (HK. Nov.10; 3024)
DM 3,600
– – **Anr. Edn.** Parma, Bodoni Pr., [1785]. *2nd. Bodoni Edn. (310).* 4to. Greek text, Latin commentaries, title vig.-port., dedication lf. vig., cont. cf. gt. (SG. Apr.19; 40) $175
– Odaria (Graece) Praefixo Commentario (Latine) que Poetae Genus traditur et Bibliotheca Anacreonteia adumbratur. Commentary:– P. Paciaudi. Parma, 17 Apr. 1785. *(250). (50) on 'carta reale francese'.* 4to. Cont. bds., bumped. (BR. Apr.12; 903) DM 1,100
– Odes. Trans.:– J.B. de Saint-Victor. Paris, 1813. *2nd. Edn.* 12mo. Greek & Fr. parallel text, red mor. gt. by Arnaud, 1847, spines decor. (HD. May 3; 173) Frs. 1,100
– – **Anr. Edn.** Ill.:– A. Deveria. Paris, n.d. Fo. 20 orig. lithos. & 17 orig. drawings, cont. hf. chagrin. (HD. May 4; 244) Frs. 2,500

ANACREON & others
– Anacreon, Sapho, Bion et Moschus. Traduction Nouvelle ... Trans.:– Moutonnet de Clairfonds. Ill.:– Eisen, engraved by Massard. Paris, 1773. Some light foxing, cont. blind-decor. cf., foot of spine rubbed. arms or cypher scratched. (HD. May 3; 2) Frs. 1,300
– – **Anr. Copy.** (*Bound with:*) THEOCRITUS
– Idylles ... précédée d'Héro et Léandre. Syracuse/Paris, 1775. *1st. Edn.* Together 2 pts. in 1 vol. Cont. marb. cf., spine gt., slightly rubbed. (VG. Mar.19; 281) Fls. 500

ANANIA, Giovanni Lorenzo d'
– L'Universale Fabrica del Mondo, overo Cosmografia. Venice, 1596. 4to. Title slightly soiled, some browning & staining, cont. vell., soiled. (S. Dec.1; 258) *Quaritch.* £300

ANANOFF, Alexandre
– François Boucher, a Catalogue Raisonné. Geneva, 1976. 2 vols. Fo. No bdg. stated. (SPB. Nov.30; 16) $275

ANATOLI, Yakov
[–] Ruach Chen. Cremona, 1566. *4th. Edn.* 4to. Staining thro.-out, browned, hf. leath. (S. Oct.24; 37) *Bragadin.* £320

ANAV, Zidkiah
[–] Tanya. Cremona, 1565. *2nd. Edn.* 4to. Margins of 1st. 2 ll. reprd. without loss of text, owner's sigs. on titles, 3 ll. with holes affecting some words, discold., some staining, cl. (S. Oct.24; 55)
Heitner. £330

ANBUREY, Thomas
– Reisen im Inneren Amerika. Trans.:– G. Forster. Berlin, 1792. *1st. German Edn.* Cont. hf. leath. gt., spine rubbed. [Sabin 1370]. (R. Oct.13; 2945)
DM 550
[–] Travels through the Interior Parts of North America. L., 1789. *1st. Edn.* 2 vols. Hf.-titles, folding map strengthened at folds, 7 plts., a few short tears, cont. cf. [Sabin 1366]. (S. May 22; 297)
Sawyer. £200
– – **Anr. Copy.** 2 vols. Partly hand-cold. folding engraved map, 6 engraved plts., including 5 folding, 1 folding lf. of facs., cont. cf., spines gt., spines & corners worn; the Rt. Hon. Visc. Eccles copy. [Sabin 1366] (CNY. Nov.18; 6) $700

ANDERSEN, Hans Christian
– Eventyr og Historier. Copen., 1862-73. *1st. Coll. Edn.* 2 vols. Cont. qtr. mor. gt. (P. Jul.5; 223) £85
– Fairy Tales. Ill.:– W. Heath Robinson. 1913. *(100) numbered & sigd. by artist.* 4to. Orig. vell., lightly soiled. (CSK. Jun.29; 159) £580
– – **Anr. Edn.** Ill.:– Kay Nielsen. L., [1924]. 4to. Orig. cl. gt., slightly rubbed. (P. Feb.16; 285)
£130
– – **Anr. Edn.** Ill.:– Kay Nielsen. L., [1924]. *(500) numbered & sigd. by artist.* 4to. Orig. cl. gt., upr. cover bowed, slightly rubbed. (S. Nov.22; 343)
Libris. £380
– – **Anr. Copy.** 4to. Slight foxing to fore-e.'s, prelims., final pp., & end-papers, elab. gt.-decor. vell., light spotting. (CBA. Aug.21; 428) $950
– – **Anr. Copy.** 4to. 12 cold. plts., gt.-pict. cl., d.-w. (SG. Apr.26; 153) $800
– – **Anr. Copy.** 4to. Gt.-pict. cl., rubbed, spine worn. (SG. Dec.8; 250) $450
– – **Anr. Edn.** Ill.:– Arthur Rackham. L., [1932]. *1st. Trade Edn.* 4to. Ink inscr. to front fly, orig. gt.-decor. cl., lightly rubbed & spotted. (CBA. Aug.21; 505) $110
– – **Anr. Edn.** Ill.:– Harry Clarke. N.Y., n.d. 4to. Inscr. dtd. 1921, orig. pict. cl. (SKC. Jan.13; 2138)
£60
– Mährchen und Erzählungen für die Kinder. Braunschweig, 1839. *1st. compl. German trans.* 4 vols. in 2. Some browning, hand-bnd. hf.-leath., wear, spine slightly faded; Hausewedell coll. (H. May 24; 1636) DM 700
– Märchen. Trans.:– J. Reuscher. Ill.:– Th. Hosemann. Berlin, [1844-49]. *1st. Edn.* 4 vols. in 2. Some slight browning & foxing, hand-bnd. hf. leath., worn, spine slightly faded; Hausewedell coll. (H. May 24; 1637) DM 1,200
– Neue Mährchen. Trans.:– Le Petit & H. Zeise. Hamburg, 1848 & 1846. *1st. Edn. vol. II, 2nd. Edn. vol. I.* 2 vols. Vol. II slightly foxed & loose, orig. bds.; Ida Schoeller ex-libris; Hausewedell coll. (H. May 24; 1643) DM 2,200
– Sein oder nicht sein. Leipzig, 1857. 3 pts. in 1 vol. Cont. linen, Romantic gt., MS. dedication sigd. on end-paper. (GB. Nov.4; 1988) DM 400
– Stories. Ill.:– Edmund Dulac. L., 1911. *1st. Trade Edn.* 4to. Frontis. detchd., some slight margin darkening, decor. cl. (CBA. Aug.21; 190) $110
– – **Anr. Edn.** Ill.:– Edmund Dulac. L., [1911]. *(750) sigd. by artist.* 4to. Orig. vell. gt., lacks ties. (SPB. Dec.13; 810) $375
– – **Anr. Edn.** Ill.:– Edmund Dulac. N.Y. & L., n.d. 4to. Later three-qtr. mor., light wear. (RO. Jul.24; 26) $105
– Wonder Stories Told for Children. Ill.:– V. Pedersen & M.L. Stone. N.Y., 1870. *Author's Edn.* Title loose, gt.-decor. cl., rubbed. (SG. Dec.8; 19)
$125
– The Complete Andersen. Trans.:– Jean Hersholt. Ill.:– Fritz Kredel. N.Y., Ltd. Edns. Cl., [1949].

ANDERSEN, Hans Christian -*Contd.*

(1500) sigd. by trans. & artist. Lge. 8vo. Ills. hand-cold., hf. cl. & decor. bds., minor wear to covers. (CBA. Nov.19; 321) $110

ANDERSON, Aeneas
- A Journal of the Forces ... under the Command of ... **General Sir Ralph Abercromby in the Mediterranean & Egypt.** L., 1802. *1st. Edn.* 4to. Folding plan crudely reprd., several plts. dampstained, sm. abrasion on title, buckram. (SG. Sep.22; 18) $175

ANDERSON, Charles John
- **The Lion & the Elephant.** 1873. Publishers catalogue bnd. in at rear, orig. cl. gt., recased. (TA. Jun.21; 45) £105

ANDERSON, David
- **Canada: or, A View of the Importance of the British American Colonies.** L., 1814. R4 inserted (possibly a cancel), folding engraved map hand-cold., map offset on title, some ll. browned, old hf. cf., spine & edges worn; the Rt. Hon. Visc. Eccles copy. [Sabin 1891] (CNY. Nov.18; 7) $160

ANDERSON, George William
- **A New, Authentic & Complete Collection of Voyages Around the World** ... Ca. 1780. Fo. Subscribers list bnd. in at end, torn without loss, cont. reversed cf., worn. (TA. Nov.17; 59) £195
- - **Anr. Edn.** L., 1784. Fo. 153 folding maps & folding plts., defect., recovered leath. (DS. Feb.24; 2186) Pts. 110,000
- - **Anr. Edn.** [1784-86]. Fo. Some staining, some maps & plts. loose, many torn, bds., crudely reprd., as a collection of plts., w.a.f. (P. Oct.20; 204) £130
- - **Anr. Copy.** Fo. 100 plts., maps & views (only 90 called for), including 1 folding (torn), lacks engraved frontis., title soiled & detchd., some browning or spotting, last few ll. defect., cont. cf., defect., lacks lr. cover, w.a.f. (S. Nov.1; 1) *Shapiro.* £120
- - **Anr. Edn.** L., ca. 1784. Lge. fo. Leath. (DS. Dec.16; 2135) Pts. 80,000

ANDERSON, J. Corbet
- **English Landscapes & Views.** Ill.:- after E. Duncan, G.H. Andrews, T. Allom, A.L. Thomas, & W. & F.J. Havell. 1883. Lge. ob. fo. 24 steel engrs. on India paper, some minor margin dampstains, not affecting engraved surface, contents completely loose, orig. cl., dampstained & soiled. (TA. May 17; 118) £260
- - **Anr. Copy.** Ob. fo. 23 (of 24) engraved views on India paper, dampstains, mainly affecting margins, mor., covers detchd., w.a.f. (P. Mar.15; 8) *Grosvenor.* £220

ANDERSON, James
- **An Account of the Present State of the Hebrides & Western Coast of Scotland** ... Edinb., 1785. Orig. bds., unc. (PD. May 16; 99) £110
- **Essays relating to Agriculture & Rural Affairs.** Edinb., 1784. *3rd. Edn.* 2 vols. Hf. cf., spines gt.; sig. & bkplt. of the Marquess of Tweeddale. (LC. Jul.5; 110) £70
- **Selectus Diplomatum & Numismatum Scotiae Thesaurus.** Ed.:- Thomas Ruddiman. Edinb., 1730. Fo. 181 numbered plts., including additional titles, facs., seals & coins, engraved cut in text, & 1 engraved plt. not called for, spr. cf., spine gt.; Sir Ivar Colquhoun, of Luss copy. (CE. Mar.22; 10) £400

ANDERSON, Johann
- **Beschryving van Island, Groenland en de Straat Davis.** Ed.:- N. Horrebow. Trans.:- J.D.H. Waar. Amst., 1756. *2nd. Edn.* 2 pts. in 1 vol. 4to. Later hf. roan., unc. (VG. Nov.30; 792) Fls. 1,400

ANDERSON, John, Bookseller & Binder
- **A Catalogue of Books ... including a Small Collection of Persian MSS., many of which are in Elegant Bindings & selling very cheap.** 1792. Title creased & slightly torn, disbnd.; H.M. Nixon coll. (BBA. Oct.6; 165) *Quaritch.* £100

ANDERSON, John, Genealogist, 1789-1832
- **Historical & Genealogical Memoirs of the House of Hamilton** ... Edinb., 1825. 4to. Cont. hf. cf. (PD. May 16; 136) £50

ANDERSON, John, Naturalist, 1833-1900
- **Anatomical & Zoological Researches: An Account of the Zoological Results of the Two Expeditions to Western Yunan in 1868 & 1875.** L., 1878. 2 vols. 4to. Cl., brkn., ex-liby. (RO. Dec.11; 362) $900
- **Zoology of Egypt: Volume First. Reptilia & Batrachia.** 1898. *(100).* 4to. Orig. cl., slightly soiled, partly untrimmed. (TA. Nov.17; 317) £54

ANDERSON, Joseph & Drummond, James
- **Ancient Scottish Weapons.** Edinb. & L., 1881. *(500)* numbered. Fo. Cold. plts., mor.-bkd. cl., slightly soiled, partly unc. (S. Apr.10; 347) *Donald.* £190
- - **Anr. Copy.** 4to. 54 plts., qtr. mor., rubbed. (P. Mar.15; 183) *Walford.* £140

ANDERSON, Robert, Mathematician
- **The Genuine Use & Effects of the Gunne ... with Tables of Projection** ... by Thomas Streete. 1674. 2 pts. in 1 vol. 4to. Lightly stained thro.-out, old cf., worn, lacks upr. cover. [Wing 3104] (CSK. Sep.30; 140) £260

ANDERSON, Robert
- **Rudiments of Tamul Grammar.** 1821. 4to. Folding table mntd. on linen hf.-title, orig. bds., rather worn, unopened. (BBA. May 23; 353) *Kossow.* £75

ANDERSON, Sherwood
See— SINSABAUGH, Art & Anderson, Sherwood

ANDERSON, William
- **The Pictorial Arts of Japan.** 1886. Fo. Orig. mor.-bkd. cl. (BBA. Sep.8; 111) *Boswell.* £75

ANDERTON, Basil & Gibson, W.H.
- **Bewick Collection Catalogue.** [Newcastle], early 20th. C. Tall 8vo. Cl., orig. ptd. wrap. mntd. to upr. cover. (SG. Aug.4; 33) $120

ANDERTON, Laurence 'John Brereley'
[-] **The Apolgie of the Romane Church.** 1604. *1st. Edn.* 4to. MS. notes on title, 19th. C. cf. [STC 3604] (P. Jan.12; 203) *Georges.* £75

ANDRADE, Alonso de
- **El Estudiante Perfecto.** Madrid, 1643. Vell. (DS. Oct.28; 2473) Pts. 25,000

ANDRADE, Manoel Carlos de
- **Luz da Liberal e Nobre Arte da Cavallaria.** Lisbon, 1790. *1st. Edn.* 2 pts. in 1 vol. Fo. Engraved port., 93 engraved plts., many folding, plt. 86 with tear in upr. left corner, reprd., gathering Z misbnd., recased in cont. cf., spine gt., covers rubbed with minor abrasions, spine ends reprd. (C. Mar.14; 153) *Old Hall.* £2,200
- - **Anr. Copy.** Pts. 1 & 2. Fo. Some sm. repairs, old leath. (DS. Nov.25; 2185) Pts. 290,000

ANDRASY, E.
- **Reise in Ostindien, Ceylon, Java, Cina und Bengalen.** Pest, 1859. *1st. Edn.* Lge. fo. Plts. slightly foxed, cont. hf. leath., bumped. (R. Oct.13; 3016) DM 1,050

ANDRE, A. & Elder, M.
- **L'Atelier de Renoir.** Paris, 1931. 2 vols. Fo. Orig. wraps. (SPB. Nov.30; 62) $2,800

ANDRE, Peter
See— CHAPMAN, John & André, Peter

ANDREA, Giovanni
- **Opera Chiamata Confusione della Setta Machumetana** ... Trans.:- Domenico da Gaztelu. Seviglia [but Italy], 1537. *1st. Edn. in Italian.* 19th. C. hf. leath. (SI. Dec.18; 2) Lire 250,000

ANDREAE, Johannes
- **Arbor Consanguinitatis, Arbor Affinitatis, Arbor Spiritualis Cognationis.** Nuremb., Friedrich Creussner, [not after 1477]. Sm. fo. 10 ll., 1 plt. folding (lightly cut by binder), initials & rubric painted in red, 19th. C. bds., spine & corners from 14th. C. liturgical MS. [H. 1026] (SM. Mar.7; 2426) Frs. 4,000

- **Chirurgiae.** Venice, 1573. Stiff bd. wraps. (DM. May 21; 80) $650
- **Fama Andreana reflorescens, sive Jacobi Andreae Waiblingensis Theol. Doctoris Vitae, Funeris, Scriptorum, Peregrinationum et Progeniei recitatio.** Strassburg, 1630. Lge. 12mo. 3 engraved ports. at end mntd. on strong paper, cont. vell. (S. May 10; 213) *Quaritch.* £480
- **Hieronymianus.** [Cologne, Conrad Winters, de Homborch], 9 Aug., 1482. *1st. Edn.* Fo. 112 ll. (of 113 lacks final blank), lge. capital 'H' in blue & red with decor. penwork, other capitals in red, few with decor. penwork, rubricated, capitals on 3 ll. rubbed with some damage, light stains on upr. margins, 18th. C. cf., spine gt.; Heber copy. [Goff A627] (SPB. May 17; 563) $2,200
- **Novella super Secundo Decretalium.** Venice, 1505. (*Bound with:*) **FRANCISCO DE ACOLTIS, de Aretio** - **Admiranda Commentaria Maximi.** Milan, 1505. Together 2 works in 1 vol. Lge. fo. Cont. stpd. cf. over wood bds., decor., clasps, chain, spine reprd.; from Fondation Furstenberg-Beaumesnil. (HD. Nov.16; 84) Frs. 7,200
- **Super Arboribus Consanguinitatis** ... Nuremb., Friedrich Creussner, 1483. Fo. Wide margins, fully rubricated, very wormed, mostly in margins, early owner's annots. in margins, bds., leath. spine; the Walter Goldwater copy. [Goff A-612] (SG. Dec.1; 15) $850

ANDREAS DE ESCOBAR, Hispanus
- **Canones Poenitentiales.** [Rome, Johann Besicken], ca. 1495. 4to. Fully rubricated, lacks initial blank, mod. bds., covered with fragment of a medieval vell. MS.; the Walter Goldwater copy. [BMC IV, 73; Goff A-659] (SG. Dec.1; 16) $400

ANDREE, K.
- **Nord-Amerika in Geographischen und Geschichtlichen Umrissen.** Braunschweig, 1851-54. Text & atlas vol. Lge. 8vo. & ob. 4to. Foxed, cont. bds. & hf. leath., slightly rubbed. [Sabin 1461] (GB. Nov.3; 51) DM 500

ANDRES, Abate D. Giovanni
- **Dell'Origine, Progressi e Stato Attuale d'Ogni Letteratura.** Parma, 1782-99. Vols. 1-7 only, (of 8). 4to. Cont. mott. cf., triple gt. borderline, fleurons, spine gt. in compartments; pres. copy to Le comte de Blacas. (S. Apr.10; 284) *Wade.* £70

ANDREWS, Dr. Arthur
- **The First Settlement of the Upper Murray, 1835 to 1845.** Sydney, 1920. A few signs of use, bdg. not stated. (KH. May 1; 8) Aus. $100

ANDREWS, Frederick Henry
- **One Hundred Carpet Designs from Various Parts of India.** L., 1905-06. Extracted from 'Journal of Indian Art'. Fo. 100 plts., 1 folding, 10pp. text, qtr. leath., lacks spine. (SG. Aug.25; 280) $170

ANDREWS, Henry C.
- **The Botanist's Repository, for New & Rare Plants.** L., 1797[-1809]. Vols. I-VIII only (of 10). 4to. Engraved titles (lacking in Vol. II), ptd. title in Vol. I, 551 (of 552) hand-cold. engraved plts., some folding, some plts. trimmed by binder, mostly in 1st. vol. (with some loss of numbers, names or imprints), some offsetting, mostly from plts. onto text, 1 plt. reprd. in fold, green hf. mor., brown mor. spines, elab. gt.; Maria Theresa Earle bkplt. (S. Nov.28; 3) *Schuster.* £3,500
- - **Anr. Edn.** L., 1797[-1814]. 10 vols. in 5. 4to. Engraved titles, 664 hand-cold. engraved plts., some folding, a few just shaved, some staining in margins, cont. spr. cf., some jnts. reprd., others weak. (C. Nov.16; 212) *Sotheran.* £5,800
- - **Anr. Edn.** Berlin, [1800-04]. 4to. Most plts. cut close & slightly foxed, cont. hf. leath., defect. (R. Oct.12; 1790) DM 2,500
- **Coloured Engravings of Heaths** ... 1802. Vol. 1 only. Sm. fo. 72 col. engraved plts., text for plts. in Latin & Engl., some light spotting & browning, mostly affecting text, hf. cf., worn. (PD. Aug.17; 303) £500
- **The Heathery.** L., 1845. *2nd. Edn.* 6 vols. Cold. pict. title, 300 hand-cold. plts., some foxing, publisher's cl., light wear, few spine tips slightly chipped, 1 spine torn. (RO. Dec.11; 8) $3,200

ANDREWS, Israel D.
- **Report on the Trade & Commerce of the British North American Colonies** ... Wash., 1853. *1st. Iss. of text*. Cont. hf. cf., marb. bds., disbnd., 4 very lge. hand-cold. folding maps unbnd. as iss., binders cl. folder, orig. cover mntd.; ex-liby., inscr. & sigd. by Andrews to the Library of Yale University in text vol. [Sabin 1498] (SG. Apr.5; 6) $120

ANDREWS, John, 1736-1809
- **History of the War with America, France, Spain, & Holland.** 1785-86. 4 vols. Engraved titles, 31 ports., 6 maps (hand-cold. in outl., 5 folding), some slight discolouration, qtr. cf. [Sabin 1501] (S. May 22; 298)   *Sawyer*. £240
- - **Anr. Copy.** 4 vols. Engraved titles, 19 ports., 7 folding maps, hand-cold. outl., some light spotting, cont. cf., worn. (CSK. Jun.1; 76)   £140
- - **Anr. Copy.** 4 vols. Subscribers list, scattered spotting, early marb. cf., spines gt., some wear, 2 hf. mor. s.-c.'s. (SG. Jan.19; 97) $500
- - **Anr. Copy.** 4 vols. 7 maps, some cold. in outl., 24 ports., tear on S8 Vol. 2, some offsetting, cont. mott. cf., spines lack most labels. (SPB. Dec.13; 429) $375

ANDREWS, John, Geographer & Dury, Andrew
- **A Map of the Country Sixty-Five Miles round London.** 1776. Fo. 20 hand-cold. maps, plus extra map 'Andrews New Travelling Map of South East England', hf. cf., covers detchd. (P. Dec.8; 403)   *Printed Page*. £380

ANDREWS, Lorrin
- **Grammar of the Hawaiian Language.** Honolulu, 1854. Some underlining in pencil, spotting, cont. qtr. roan. (S. May 22; 466)   *Maggs*. £180

ANDREWS, William Loring
- **Jean Grolier de Servier, Viscount d'Aguisy: Some Account of his Life & of his Famous Library.** N.Y., De Vinne Pr., 1892. *(140) on H.M.P.* Plts. on Japan vell., gt.-pict. cl. (SG. Sep.15; 9) $240
- **Roger Payne & his Art: A Short Account of his Life & Work as a Binder.** N.Y., De Vinne Pr., 1892. *(120) on Holland paper.* Cl. (SG. Sep.15; 10) $300

ANDRICHOMIUS, C.
- **Theatrum Terrae Sanctae et Biblicarum Historiarum.** Cologne, 1628. Fo. 10 (of 14?) double-p. engraved maps, various sizes, engraved title trimmed at lr. margin, vell., stained, upr. corner defect., as a coll. of plts., w.a.f. (P. Jan.12; 126)   *Hirschler*. £280

ANEAU, Barthelemy
- **Picta Poesis.** Lyons, 1564. Printers device on title-p. & many emblem. text woodcuts, last lf. blank but for colophon, recent mor. (BBA. May 23; 321)   *Lurie*. £150

ANGAS, George French
- **Description of the Barossa Range & its Neighbourhood in South Australia** ... Adelaide, 1979. *Facs. Edn. (1000) numbered.* 4to. Bdg. not stated. (KH. May 1; 9)   Aus. $150
- **The Kafirs Illustrated.** 1849. Fo. Frontis., 28 (of 30) uncold. plts., each mntd. on linen, plt. 5 torn in hf. & pasted down, staining to last 6 plts. & pp., hf. mor. (SSA. Jul.5; 9)   R 1,450
- **The New Zealanders Illustrated.** 1846. Fo. Hand-cold. title, 60 hand-cold. lithos., dedication, subscribers list, prospectus (loose), hand-cold. title laid down, ptd. title creased, some plts. foxed, hf. mor. gt. (P. Mar.15; 122)   *Thorp*. £1,850
- - **Anr. Edn.** L., 1847. Fo. Additional hand-finished cold. litho. title, litho. dedication, 60 hand-cold. litho. plts., subscribers list, some plts. lightly spotted, mainly in margins, mod. hf. mor. (C. Nov.16; 46)   *Foyle*. £1,700
- - **Anr. Edn.** 1967. *Facs. of 1847 edn.* Fo. Hf. mor. gt. (P. Apr.12; 213)   £90
- **Savage Life & Scenes in Australia & New Zealand** ... L., 1847. 2 vols. Lge. 12mo. Orig. cl., loosening a little, unc. short split at head of 1 backstrip. (KH. Nov.9; 529)   Aus. $270
- **South Australia Illustrated.** L., 1846-47. 10 orig.

pts. Lge. fo. Additional symbolic cold. litho. title, litho. dedication, 60 hand-finished cold. litho. plts., list of subscribers, some minor spotting, affecting some 5 plts., loose in guttapercha bdg., orig. litho. paper wraps., cl. backstrips, in gt.-lettered mor. box. (C. Jun.27; 109)   *Maggs*. £9,500
- - **Anr. Edn.** L., 1847. Fo. Additional hand-cold. litho. title, litho. dedication, list of subscribers, 54 (of 60) hand-cold. litho. plts., heightened with varnish, all letterpress present except 51, margin of title & a few plts. frayed, some plts. lightly spotted, mainly in margins, loose in cont. hf. roan guttapercha bdg., rubbed, spine ends chipped; Sir John Hindmarsh's subscribers copy. (C. Mar.14; 27)   *Jones*. £5,200
- - **Anr. Edn.** Artarmon, 1967. *Facs. Edn. (1000) numbered.* Fo. Hf. mor. (KH. May 1; 10)   Aus. $450

ANGELES, Fray Juan de los
- **Diálogos de la Conquista Espiritual.** Alcalá, 1602. Vell. (DS. Apr.27; 2012)   Pts. 37,000

ANGELO, Domenico
- **L'Ecole des Armes avec L'Explication Générale des Principales Attitudes et Positions concernant L'Escrime.** L., 1763. Ob. fo. A few margins lightly soiled, title & dedication detchd., cont. bds., worn, lacks backstrip. (CSK. Jun.1; 30)   £500
- **The School of Fencing, with a general explanation of the principal attitudes & positions.** Ill.:– Grignon, Ryland, & others, after J.W. Gwyn. L., 1765. Ob. fo. 47 engraved plts., text in Engl. & Fr., cont. mott. cf., spine & jnts. worn. (C. Nov.9; 2)   *Temperley*. £600

ANGELO, Henry Charles William
- **A Treatise on the Utility & Advantages of Fencing.** Ill.:– Rowlandson, etc. 1817. Ob. fo. Advt. slip, 1st. 9 plts. with some staining, orig. wraps. (SKC. Sep.9; 1949)   £450

ANGELO, Valenti
- **Valenti Angelo: Author-Illustrator-Printer.** Bronxville, [Pr. of Valenti Angelo], 1970. *(55) sigd.* Many trial sheets, facs., etc. hand-illuminated, hf. pig & bds., spine blind-stpd., spine just darkening, s.-c. slightly worn; the V. Angelo copy. (CBA. Oct.1; 403) $500
- - **Anr. Edn.** San Franc., Book Cl. of California, 1976. *(400) sigd.* Sm. fo. Hf. cl. & decor. bds., light soiling to covers & s.-c.; the Valenti Angelo copy, with many plts. specifically hand-cold. for this copy (sigd. & noted to that effect in colophon), some plts. with added sigs., sigd. extra sheet from Book of Job laid in loose, & with orig. announcement & broadside for an exhibition in San Franc. Public Liby. (CBA. Oct.1; 64) $900
- - **Anr. Copy.** Fo. Cl.-bkd. paper bds. (LH. Sep.25; 324) $425

ANGELONI, Francesco
- **L'Historia Augusta da Giulio Cesare a Constantino.** Rome, 1685. *2nd. Edn.* Fo. A few margin stains, cont. vell. bds., slightly soiled; Charles Bathurst bkplt. (S. May 1; 449)   *Spink*. £80

ANGLAIS PEINTS PAR EUX-MEMES
Trans.:– E. de Labédeffierre. Paris, 1840-41. Minimal foxing, cont. hf. leath. gt., rubbed. (R. Oct.12; 2186)   DM 400

ANGLES Y GORTARI, Matias
- **Muy Ilustres Sres. Inquisidores ... de Lima.** Potosi, 1731. No bdg. stated. (DS. Oct.28; 2605)   Pts. 75,000

ANGLO-SAXON REVIEW
Ed.:– R.S. Churchill. Contribs.:– A. Swinburne, M. Beerbohm, E. Gosse, G.B. Shaw, etc. L., 1899-1901. 10 vols. Vols. I-X (all publd.). Orig. cf. gt., each bdg. a replica of old bdg (Dérome etc.), 2 spines defect., 6 vols. rebkd. (BS. Jun.6; 135)   Fls. 600

ANGUS, William
- **The Seats of the Nobility & Gentry in Great Britain & Wales.** Ill.:– after Malton, Nattes, Sandby, & others. L., [Islington, the Engraver], 1787-1815. *[1st. Edn.].* Ob. 4to. Engraved title, 63

plts., cont. str.-grd. purple mor. gt., gt.- & blind-panel.; Sir Hew Dalrymple bkplt. (C. Dec.9; 5)   *Weinreb*. £220
- - **Anr. Copy.** Ob. 4to. Engraved title, 63 views, 1 slightly frayed, some spotting & offsetting, cont. red mor. (S. Mar.6; 195)   *Sanders*. £130
- - **Anr. Copy.** Ob. 4to. Engraved title, 63 plts., dampstained, affecting lr. portion of many plts., others marginally foxed, cont. qtr. roan, worn. (SG. Jun.7; 327) $120

ANHEISSER, Roland
- **Altschweizerische Baukunst.** Bern, 1906/07. Fo. 100 facs. plts. after pen ills., loose ll., cold. bd. portfo., linen strengthened. (GF. Nov.16; 1161)   Sw. Frs. 1,700

ANNALEN DER PHYSIK
Leipzig, 1900-06. 4th. Series. Vols. 1-21. Hf. linen. (R. Apr.4; 1515)   DM 4,800

ANNALS OF THE KINGDOM OF IRELAND
Trans.:– John O'Donovan. Dublin, 1848. *1st. Edn.* 3 vols. Lge. 4to. Orig. subscribers copy for Marquis of Sligo, orig. decor. cl. (GM. Dec.7; 471)   £160
- - **Anr. Edn.** Ed.:– John O'Donovan. Dublin, 1856. *2nd. Edn.* 7 vols. 4to. Orig. bds., defect., w.a.f. (GM. Oct.5; 45)   £200
- **Three Fragments ... by Dubhaltach Mac Firbisigh.** Ed.:– John O'Donovan. Dublin, 1860. 4to. Cl. (GM. Dec.7; 67)   £60

ANNALS OF SPORTING & Fancy Gazette, The
Ill.:– after Alken, Landseer, & others. L., Jan. 1822-Jun. 1828. 13 vols. Hf.-titles in Vols. 1-6, woodcut titles in Vols. 7-13, 152 (of 153) engraved plts., (49 hand-cold.), some browning & staining thro.-out, few sm. text tears, folding map in Vol. 2 torn, cont. hf. cf., unc., spines gt., Vol. 1 reprd., but brkn., qtr. red mor. gt. s.-c.'s, w.a.f. (CNY. Dec.17; 527)   £500

ANNAN, Thomas
- **The Old Closes & Streets of Glasgow.** Intro.:– William Young. Glasgow, 1900. *(100) for the Corp. of Glasgow.* Fo. 50 photogravures, cl., gt. arms, worn & spotted, spine heavily worn & holed. (SG. Nov.10; 9) $950
- **The Old Country Houses of the Old Glasgow Gentry.** Glasgow, 1878. *2nd. Edn. (225).* 4to. Cont. mor. gt. by Maclehose, 1 jnt. split. (S. Mar.6; 362)   *Weinreb*. £150

ANNENBERG, Maurice
- **Type Foundries & their Catalogs.** Balt. & Wash., 1975. *(500).* 4to. Ills., cl., d.-w. (SG. May 17; 14) $110

ANNESLEY, George, Visc. Valentia
See— VALENTIA, George Annesley, Visc.

ANNUAIRE HERALDIQUE UNIVERSEL
1901. Lge. 8vo. Publisher's chagrin. (HD. Mar.21; 105)   Frs. 1,050

ANNUAL REGISTER
1777-75-1823. *Various Edns.* Vols. 1-65 in 66, & 2 vol. indices for 1758-92. Cont. cf.-bkd. bds., spines gt., lacks 13 labels, spine ends chipped, w.a.f. (CSK. Dec.16; 31)   £180

ANNUNZIO, Gabriele d'
- **L'Oleandro.** Ill.:– G.G. Boehmer. [Verona], Bodoni Pr., 1936. *(150) on Marais-Bütten.* Sm. fo. Orig. wraps. in orig. linen cover. (H. Nov.24; 1206)   DM 1,300

ANRY, N.
- **Orthopädie.** Berlin, 1744. *1st. German Edn.* 2 pts. in 1 vol. Cont. leath., very wormed. (R. Apr.4; 1346)   DM 3,200

ANSELMUS, Saint
- **Meditaciones de ...** Xerex de la Frontera, 1784. Leath. (DS. Mar.23; 2262)   Pts. 20,000

ANSON, George, Lord
[-] **An Authentic Account of Commodore Anson's Expedition.** L., 1744. *1st. Edn.* Foxed, reprd., mod. hf. mor., medallion inlaid in upr. cover. (SPB. Dec.13; 431) $400

ANSON, George, Lord -*Contd.*

- **Voyage autour du Monde.** Trans.:– [E. de Jancourt]. Amst. & Leipzig, 1749. *1st. Fr. Edn.* 4to. Title & 2nd. lf. with slight brown mark, cont. leath. gt. [Sabin 1637] (R. Oct.13; 3063)   DM 500
- – **Anr. Copy.** Sm. 4to. 3 maps with tears (partly bkd.), some light browning & spotting, cont. cf. gt., lightly bumped, spine slightly torn. [Sabin 1637] (H. May 22; 239)   DM 400
- – **Anr. Edn.** Paris, 1764. 5 vols. (*With:*) – **Voyage à la Mer du Sud fait par Quelques Officiers Commandants le Vaisseau Le Wager: pour servir de Suite au Voyage de Georges Anson.** Lyon, 1756. 1 vol. Together 6 vols. 12mo. Cont. unif. marb. cf., spines decor. (HD. Mar.19; 2)   Frs. 2,000
- **A Voyage round the World in the Years 1740-44.** L., priv. ptd., 1748. *1st. Edn.* 4to. 42 engraved maps & plts., many folding, cont. mott. cf., spine reprd. (C. Nov.16; 47)   *Quaritch.* £350
- – **Anr. Copy.** 4to. L.P., 42 engraved plts. & charts, subscribers' list, some spotting, later hf. mor., rubbed. (BBA. Jun.28; 190)   *Rudge.* £300
- – **Anr. Copy.** 4to. Map, 42 plts., some folding, cont. cf. (PD. May 16; 199)   £220
- – **Anr. Copy.** 4to. 41 engraved plts. & maps only, some affected by offsetting, 2 maps cleanly torn, cont. mott. cf., rebkd., old spine laid down, mod. spine label. (CSK. Jan.27; 128)   £120
- – **Anr. Copy.** 4to. Some offsetting, general restorations, liby. blind stps. to plts., old bds. with recent leath. backstrip. (TA. Oct.20; 30)   £90
- – **Anr. Copy.** Lge. 4to. Cont. bds., leath. spine. (D. Nov.23; 889)   DM 1,000
- – **Anr. Edn.** 1749. *5th. Edn.* 4to. A few clean tears, some light offsetting, old cf., rubbed, rebkd. (CSK. Jul.6; 21)   £180
- – **Anr. Edn.** 1776. *15th. Edn.* 4to. Lacks 1 plt., 1 plt. duplicated, cont. spr. cf., spine ends chipped, rubbed. (TA. Apr.19; 55)   £100
- – **Anr. Copy.** 4to. 43 engraved plans & plts. (plt. 36 duplicated, lacks plt. 37), cont. spr. cf., chipped at top & bottom of spine, rubbed. (TA. Mar.15; 14)   £80
- – **Anr. Copy.** Lge. 4to. 43 folding engraved maps, charts, views & c., some staining or foxing, 1 plt. torn, sm. hole in title, title & plts. with liby. blind-stp., hf. leath., worn. (SG. Sep.22; 20) $100

ANSTICE, Robert
- **Remarks on the Comparative Advantages of Wheel Carriages.** Bridgewater, 1790. *1st. Edn.* Silhouette port., 8 folding plts., cont. cf. rebkd.; pres. copy. (P. May 17; 230)   *Quaritch.* £320

ANTES, Horst
- **Buch der Feste.** Ulm, 1964. *(48) numbered & printers mark sigd. by artist.* Cold. pictor. orig. sewed. (GB. May 5; 3249)   DM 450

ANTHOINE-LEGRAIN, Jacques & Others
- **Pierre Legrain Relieur, Repertoire Descriptif et Bibliographique.** Paris, 1965. *(600) numbered.* Fo. Unbnd. as iss. in orig. portfo., s.-c.; H.M. Nixon coll., with his MS. notes. (BBA. Oct.6; 2)   *Joseph.* £120

ANTHOLOGIA HIBERNICA – or Monthly Collections of Science, Belles-Lettres & History
Dublin, Jan. 1793-Dec. 1794. 4 vols. 4 engraved frontis., 2 folding maps, 51 engraved plts., including 2 hand-cold., Index loose Vol. 2, hf. cf., rubbed & defect.; Carton copy. (GM. Dec.7; 281)   £70

ANTHOLOGIE FRANCOISE, ou Chansons Choisies
1765. 3 vols. Later hf. mor., rubbed. (TA. Dec.15; 494)   £80

ANTIGUA
[–] **Vues des Etablissemens Missionaires Fondés par la Communauté Evangelique des Frères-Unis.** Ill.:– F. Hegi & Hurliman, after work of Stobwasser. Basle, n.d. Ob. fo. Title also in German, light spotting & browning, loose in orig. ptd. wraps., light soiling. (SPB. Dec.14; 35) $700

ANTI-JACOBIN (The)
1797-98. Nos. 1-36 (all publd.), & 2 prospectuses. Fo. Hf. cf. gt. (P. Feb.16; 237)   £90
- – **Anr. Copy.** Nos. 1-36 (all publd.) in 1 vol. 4to.

Few repairs to No. 22, roan-bkd. cl., spine worn. (S. Mar.20; 686)   *Primrose.* £65

ANTIQUITES ROMAINES EXPLIQUEES DANS LES MEMOIRES DU COMTE DE B*
La Haye, 1750. 4to. 2 plts. torn, pres. inscr. dtd. 1762 on front free end-paper, cont. mott. cf., spine gt. (BBA. Nov.30; 2)   *Snelling.* £70

ANTIQUITIES OF THE RUSSIAN EMPIRE–Drevnosti Rossiiskago Gosydarstva
Trans.:– W.S. Mirrielees & R. Harrison. L.,; Moscow, 1855; 1849-53. 6 vols. in 7 pts.; 6 vols. in 1. Plt. vols. lge. atlas fo.; text vol. 4to. Plt. vols. with plt.-lists in Engl., plts. with engraved captions in Russian, illuminated title & hf.-title, 508 chromolitho. plts., text vol. in Russian, some slight foxing, liby. stp. on each title-p., cont. red mor., wide borders, spines elab. gt., raised bands, gt. dentelles; armor. bkplt. of John Naylor of Leighton; from Haggerston Castle Liby., Northumberland. (SG. Apr.26; 7) $6,000

ANTIQUITY, a Periodical Review of Archaeology
1927-82. *Vol. 1 in Reprint.* Vols. 1-56, issue 1-218 (lacks issue no. 53 for Mar. 1940). Vols. 1-16 orig. buckram, rest in orig. wraps. (CE. Sep.1; 103)   £250
- – **Anr. Run.** L., 1927-37. Vols. 1-11 only. 4to. Orig. cl. (BBA. Apr.5; 164)   *Thorp.* £55

ANTONELLI, G.
- **Collection of Views in Rome.** Ca. 1840. Ob. 4to. 98 engrs., no title or text, hf. mor. gt. (P. Dec.8; 283)   £80
- **Nuova Raccolta delle Principali Vedute Antiche e Moderne ... di Roma.** Rome, ca. 1830. Ob. 4to. Engraved title, 48 line engrs., last 3 with margin dampstains, hf. mor. gt., stained. (P. Jul.26; 106)   £50

ANTONINI, Carlo
- **Manuale di vari Ornamenti ...** Roma, 1777. 2 vols. 4to. 100 engraved plts., hf. cf. (CR. Jun.6; 3)   Lire 250,000
- – **Anr. Edn.** Rome, 1781. 2 vols. in 1. Fo. 101 engraved plts., some spotting, cont. hf. vell., soiled, spine chipped. (CSK. May 18; 26)   £90

ANTONINUS, Brother (Pseud.)
See— EVERSON, William 'Brother Antoninus'

ANTONINUS, Saint, Archbp. of Florence
- **Chronicon.** [Basle, Nicolaus Kesler, 1491]. Pt. 2 only. Fo. Lacks 1 title-lf. & 2 blanks, 1st. & last few ll. dampstained, with margin fraying, mod. vell.; the Walter Goldwater copy. [BMC III, 769; Goff A-780] (SG. Dec.1; 22) $225
- **Confessionale in Vulgari Sermoni Editum; Sermone che fece un Fra Iordano in Pisa del Corpo de Christo ...** Flor.?, 15 Apr. 1472. 4to. Lacks 1st. 2 table ll., cont. hf. roan over wood bds.; from Fondation Furstenberg-Beaumesnil. [H. 1216] (HD. Nov.16; 25)   Frs. 7,000
- – **Anr. Edn.** Venice, Johannes de Colonia & Johannes Manthen, 1476. Sm. fo. 15 ll. with corners old extended & new extended, (quite long but without loss), 1st. blank lf. extended in lr. half with old paper, large corner of last blank lf. extended with loss of old MS. entries, 1-3 sm. wormholes, nearly thro.-out, some in margin, some sigs. lightly browned, some spotting, some old marginalia, sig. K content misbnd. [HC. 1179, BMC V226; Goff A-803] (R. Apr.3; 1a)   DM 1,600
- – **Anr. Edn.:**– Illius Habe. Flor., Francesco di Dino, 10 Jul. 1481. 4to. In Italian, last 2 ll. reprd., some browning, later vell.; the Walter Goldwater copy. [BMC VI, 633; Goff A-784] (SG. Dec.1; 23) $600
- – **Anr. Edn.** Venice, Antonius de Strata de Cremona, 6 Aug. 1481. 4to. Fully rubricated, very stained, last lf. reprd., vell.; the Walter Goldwater copy. [BMC V, 292; Goff A-808] (SG. Dec.1; 24) $400
- – **Anr. Edn.** [Rome, Eucharius Silber], 23 May 1483. 4to. An initial 'D' richly decor. in red & blue, sm. wormholes in all outer margins, some early marginalia, a few gutters dampstained, old bds., worn & loose; the Walter Goldwater copy. [Goff A-809b (the present copy only)] (SG. Dec.1; 25) $475

- – **Anr. Edn.** Venice, [Philippus Pincius], 2 Jun. 1495. 4to. Last few ll. oil-stained, 18th. C. mott. cf., spine gt.; the Walter Goldwater copy. [Goff A-828] (SG. Dec.1; 26) $425
- – **Anr. Copy.** 4to. Lacks a1, some spotting & stains, tooled cf.; the Walter Goldwater copy. [Goff A-828] (SG. Dec.1; 27) $300
- – **Anr. Edn.** Flor., Laurentius de Morgianis & Johannes Petri, for Piero Pacini, 1496. *2nd. Flor. Edn.* 4to. Lacks 2 ll., probably ptd. later, margin dampstains, jansenist mor. gt.; from Fondation Furstenberg-Beaumesnil. [H. 1211; BMC VI, 683; Goff A836] (HD. Nov.16; 27)   Frs. 3,500
- – **Anr. Edn.** Strassburg, Martin Flach, 1496. 4to. 1 sm. wormhole through most of vol., mod. bds.; the Walter Goldwater copy. [BMC I, 154; Goff A-829] (SG. Dec.1; 28) $425
- **De Censuris et De Sponsalibus et Matrimonio.** Venice, J. de Colonia & J. Manthen, 23 Sep. 1474. 4to. Fully rubricated, lacks 1st. blank, blank upr. margin of 1st. lf. supplied, mod. vell.; the Walter Goldwater copy. [BMC V, 225; Goff A-776] (SG. Dec.1; 20) $1,300
- – **Anr. Edn.** Venice, J. de Colonia & J. Manthen, 10 May 1480. 4to. Initials in red thro.-out, vell.; the Walter Goldwater copy. [BMC V, 236; Goff A-778] (SG. Dec.1; 21) $700
- **Defecerunt Scrutantes Scrutinio ...** Venice, Petrus de Quarengiis, 15 Feb. 1499. 4to. Disbnd.; the Walter Goldwater copy. [Goff A-831] (SG. Dec.1; 29) $225
- **Omnia Mortalium Cura Specchio di Coscienza.** Flor., Sanctum Jacobum de Ripoli, before 24 Oct. 1477. 1 capital in blue, paragraph marks in red thro.-out, lacks a1 & h6, & with e6, nl.8, o1.10 bnd. at end, fl loose, n8 silked, o3 torn, foxed, stained, crude marginalia, qtr. mor. on early wood bds; G.W. Davis bkplt. [Goff A847] (SG. Feb.9; 251) $350
- **Summa Confessionum. De Restitutionibus.** [Venice], Bartholomaeus Cremonensis, [not after July] 1473. Sm. fo. Initial D (5 lines) on folio lr. painted in gold & cols. & with foliate decor. extending into inner margin (somewhat shaved at head & foot), initials & paragraph marks supplied thro.-out alternatively in red & blue, capitals touched in yellow, some margins lightly spotted, mod. vell. [Goff A797] (S. May 10; 217)   *Quaritch.* £800
- **Summa Theologica, Secunda Pars.** Venice, Franciscus Renner de Heibron & Nicolaus de Frankfordia, 1474. *1st. Edn.* Fo. Rubricated, initials painted in red or blue, 1st. initial painted in pink & blue on gt. ground, scratched owner's stp. on 1st. lf., 17th. C. vell., spine old renewed; from Fondation Furstenberg-Beaumesnil. [BMC V, 192; Goff A867] (HD. Nov.16; 60)   Frs. 12,000
- – **Anr. Edn.** Venice, Leonardus Wild, 1480. Vol. 3 pt. 2 only. Fo. Lge. margins, lacks ll. d1-2 & a blank, register lf. torn, old oak bds., leath back, lacks clasps; the Walter Goldwater copy. [Goff A-873] (SG. Dec.1; 30) $250
See— AUGUSTINUS, Saint Aurelius, Bp. of Hippo–ANTONINUS FLORENTINUS–MATTHAEUS DE CRACOVIA
See— PLATEA, Franciscus de–ANTONINUS FLORENTINUS, Saint

ANTONINUS Pius, Titus A.
- **Iter Britanniarum.** Commentaries:– Thomas Gale. 1709. Sm. 4to. Folding map torn, last 5 pp. of advts., some ll. slightly browned, cont. cf., rather worn. (BBA. Jun.14; 68)   *Bennett & Kerr Books.* £50

ANTONIO DE LEBRIXA
See— NEBRISSENSIS or LEBRIXA, Aelius Antonius or Antonio de

ANTONIUS, Nebrissensis
See— NEBRISSENSIS or LEBRIXA, Aelius Antonius or Antonio de

ANTONIUS DE BITONTO
- **Sermones Dominicales per Totum Annum.** [Venice], B. Locatellus for N. de Frankfordia, 10 Oct. 1499. Mod. hf. leath.; the Walter Goldwater copy. [BMC V, 452; Goff A-894] (SG. Dec.1; 31) $350
- **Sermones Quadragesimales de Vitiis.** Venice, J.

Hamman for N. de Frankfordia, 14 Feb. 1499. Lacks sig. m, mod. marb. bds., vell. back; the Walter Goldwater copy. [BMC V, 311; Goff A-896] (SG. Dec.1; 32) $200

ANTONIUS DE VERCELLIS
– **Sermones Quadragesimale de XII Mirabilibus Christianae Fidei Excellentis.** Venice, J. & G. de Forlivio [for A. Calcedonius], 16 Feb. 1492/93. 4to. Minimal worming, very early bds. & vell. back, metal clasps defect.; portion of G. Kloss's bkplt. on rear end-paper, bkplts. of Eric Sexton, the Walter Goldwater copy. [BMC V, 343; Goff A-918] (SG. Dec.1; 33) $1,100
– – **Anr. Copy.** 4to. Lacks title, very stained, last lf. frayed, disbnd.; the Walter Goldwater copy. [BMC V, 343; Goff A-918] (SG. Dec.1; 34) $250

ANVILLE, Jean Baptiste Bourguignon d'
– **Atlas & Geography of the Antients.** L., 1813. Fo. 12 (of 13) lge. dbl.-p. or folding engraved maps, hand-cold., some slight offsetting, cont. hf. russ., gt., unc. (S. Apr.9; 75) *Berg.* £120
– **A Complete Body of Ancient Geography.** Laurie & Whittle, 1806. Fo. 14 engraved maps, hand-cold. in outl., additional map of Greece, some light spotting, cont. hf. cf. (CSK. Oct.7; 24) £70
– – **Anr. Edn.** 1808. Fo. 13 partly cold. maps, hf. cf., worn. (P. Jul.5; 389) £65
– **Nouvel Atlas de la Chine.** The Hague, 1737. Fo. 42 engraved maps (3 folding, 9 double-p. & 30 full-p.), many pict. cartouches, hf. leath., rebkd., orig. spine laid down, relined. (SG. Apr.26; 8) $1,700
– – **Anr. Copy.** Atlas fo. 42 engraved maps (10 double-p., 28 single-p., 4 folding, the 1st. 2 hand-cold. in outl., on guards, sm. gouge at extreme fore-edge of some ll., sm. margin tear to map 12, sm. holes to margins of map 15, light margin soiling to title, some slight spotting, cont. cf., rebkd., edges & corners worn. (CNY. May 18; 93) $1,200

See— HARRISON, John, Publisher

APHRODITE, a Mythical Journey in Eight Episodes
Texts:– William Blake, D.H. Lawrence, Guillaume Apollinaire, & others. Ill.:– Ann Brunskill. World's End Pr., 1970. *(75) numbered & sigd. by artist.* Fo. Each etching captioned & sigd. by artist, unsewn as iss., orig. wraps., cl. portfo., ties. (S. Nov.22; 316) *Makiya.* £110

APIANUS, Petrus
– **Astronomicum Caesareum.** Ingolstadt, priv. ptd., 1540. *1st. Edn.* Fo. 36 full-p. figures (21 with a total of 83 volvelles (compl.) & 30 with 35 (of 44) silk threads (but without the 12 seed pearls), cold. thro.-out, but for initials & full-p. woodcut arms (earlier version) of author, at end, with cancelled lf. G3 bnd. at end, a blank lf. bnd. between cancel G3 & G4, correction slip pasted to Klr (without the 2 slips sometimes found on G4r) slight browning & staining, sm. repairs to D1 & G3, latter with slight textual loss, minor graze on H2r, some wormhole in inner margin at end, 1 thread on M4r rather short, 18th. C. red-brown mor., double gt.-ruled border, gt. spine. (CSK. Feb.1; 4) *Burgess.* £25,000
– – **Anr. Edn.** Leipzig, 1967. *Facs. of Ingolstadt 1540 Edn. (750).* 2 vols. (text & commentary). Lge. fo. & lge. 4to. Orig. pig & orig. hf. linen, hf. linen box; Hauswedell coll. (H. May 23; 438a) DM 950
– – **Anr. Copy.** 2 vols. (facs. & commentary). Some ills. with moving parts, some ills. & all initials old. hand-cold., orig. pig. & orig. hf. linen, orig. hf. linen box, spine slightly defect., some slight wear. (D. Nov.23; 389) DM 900
– – **Anr. Edn.** N.Y., 1969. *Facs. Reprint of 1540 edn. (750) numbered.* 2 vols., with Commentary. Fo. & 8vo. Orig. pig- & cl.-bkd. bds., box worn. (BBA. Feb.23; 82) *Elliott.* £65
– **Cosmographia.** Ed.:– Gemma Frisius. Antw., 1540. 4to. Wide margin, 4 woodcuts with moving parts, mod. leath. (Sabin 1744) (D. Nov.23; 388) DM 1,850
– – **Anr. Edn.** [Antw., 1564]. 4to. Ptd. title with lge. woodcut globe diagram, folding woodcut cordiform world map. woodcut diagrams & other ills. in text (1 only with volvelles, inserted from anr. copy), foot

of title & folding map reprd., 1 or 2 outer margins shaved affecting ptd. surface, some faint discolouration, mod. vell., w.a.f. (S. May 21; 160) *Arkway.* £550
– – **Anr. Edn.** Ed.:– Gemma Frisio. Antw., 1575. *3rd. Spanish text Edn.* 4to. Ptd. title with lge. woodcut globe diagram, folding woodcut cordiform world map at K, woodcut ills. in text, those on C2v, D1v, I1v & P3r with volvelles, that on C3v with string & bead pointer, light browning, cont. limp vell., lettered in ink on spine, soiled. [Sabin H. 1756] (S. May 21; 159) *Northwick.* £800
– **Inscriptiones Sacrosanctae Vetustatis non illae quidem Romanae, sed Totius fere Orbis Summo Studio.** Ingolstadt, 1534. Fo. Orig. cf., arms, rubbed, reprd.; from Fondation Furstenberg-Beaumesnil. (HD. Nov.16; 86) Frs. 4,000
– **Libro de Cosmographia ...** Amberes, 1548. 4to. Vell. (DS. Nov.25; 2156) Pts. 200,000
– **Quadrans ... Astronomicus et iam Recens Inventus et nunc primum Editus.** Ingolstadt, 1532. *1st. Edn.* Fo. Minor worming, some spotting & soiling, 4 ll. short (supplied from anr. copy?), mod. mor.-bkd. marb. bds.; sig. of Carlos de Siguenze (?) Pongora, dtd. 1572, on title-p., John D. Stanitz coll. (SPB. Apr.25; 15) $3,400

APOCRYPHA
– **Ben Sira & Tobit [Hebrew & Latin].** Isny, 1542. *1st. Edn.* 4to. Wide margins, Latin glosses, lightly stained, hf. cl., sig. of Phillip Gamon, w.a.f. (S. Oct.25; 14) £420
– **Ecclesiasticus: The Wisdom of Jesus, the Son of Sirach.** Chelsea, Ash. Pr., 1932. *(353). (328) on paper.* Fo. Orig. limp vell., silk ties, s.-c. (C. Nov.9; 170) *Fletcher.* £600
– **'t Wonderlyck Evangelium van Nicodemus. Met Uyt-leggingen, begrijpende den Ouden en Nieuwen Toestandt der H. Roomsche Kerck.** Trans.:– A. Montanus. Rotterdam, 1671. *New Edn.* 2 pts. in 1 vol. Sm. 8vo. Cont. vell. (VG. Nov.30; 973) Fls. 500

APOLLINAIRE, Guillaume
– **Alcools. Poemes (1898-1913).** Ill.:– Pablo Picasso (etched frontis. port.). Paris, 1913. *1st. Edn. Approx. (600) numbered.* 12mo. Maroon hf. mor., gt.-panel. spine, partly unc., orig. ptd. wraps. (including spine) bnd. in; Frederic Dannay copy. (CNY. Dec.16; 4) $650
– **Contemporains Pittoresques.** Ill.:– Picasso (port.). Paris, [1929]. *1st. Edn. (305) numbered on Arches paper.* 12mo. Hf. mor., orig. upr. wrap. bnd. in. (SG. Jan.12; 11) $100
– **Le Poète Assassiné.** Ill.:– Raoul Dufy. Paris, 1926. *(470) numbered.* 4to. Orig. wraps., bd. folder with design by Dufy on upr. cover, slightly worn, unc. (S. Nov.21; 18) *Duran.* £300
– – **Anr. Copy.** 4to. Orig. wraps., bd. folder with ties, slightly rubbed, spine slightly torn. (BBA. Jun.14; 207) *Sims, Reed & Fogg.* £160
– **Sept Calligrammes.** Ill.:– O. Zadkine. [Paris, 1967]. *(75) on Velin d'Arches.* Fo. All etchings sigd. by artist & publisher, loose ll. in orig. wraps. & linen cover. (H. May 23; 1569) DM 3,800

APOLLINARIS, Q. (Pseud.)
See— RYFF, Walther Hermann 'Q. Apollinaris'

APOLLONIUS, of Rhodes
– **Argonautica [with the Scholia of Lucillus, Sophocles & Theon].** Flor., [Laurentius (Francisci) de Alopa, Venetus], 1496. *1st. Edn.* 4to. Lacks final blank, sm. margin repairs to 1st. lf., early 19th. C. red skiv.-grd. mor., stpd. in gt. & blind, spine dark, extremities rubbed; British Museum dupl. stp. dtd. 1804, Sir Robert D'Arcy Hildyard & John Scott, of Halkshill bkplts. [BMC VI, 667; Goff A-924; HC 1292*] (SPB. Dec.14; 4) $3,500

APOLLONIUS PERGAEUS
See— ARCHIMEDES–APOLLONIUS PERGAEUS–THEODOSIUS

APPELL, J.W.
– **Der Rhein und die Rheinlande.** Darmstadt, 1855. Pt. 1. 1 view cut into, slightly browned, cont. bds., slightly bumped. (R. Oct.12; 2447) DM 8,700
– – **Anr. Copy.** Pt. 1. Engraved title & 144 steel engraved views, cont. hf. leath. (R. Apr.4; 2269) DM 8,100

– – **Anr. Copy.** Pt. 1. Wide margin, steel engraved title, 144 steel engraved plts., some slight browning, most in margins, 5 plts. with lr. title cut, cont. hf. leath., some wear, bumped. (HT. May 10; 2958) DM 4,800

APPERLEY, Charles James 'Nimrod'
– **Hunting Reminiscences.** L., 1843. *1st. Edn.* Mod. red mor. gt., covers & spine decor., by Bayntun, Bath, orig. cl. covers & spine preserved. (S. Oct.9; 251) *Old Hall.* £140
– – **Anr. Copy.** Hf. mor. gt. (P. Dec.8; 228) *Allen.* £80
– **The Life of a Sportsman.** Ill.:– Henry Alken. L., 1842. *1st. Edn. 1st. Iss.* Additional hand-cold. engraved title, 35 cold. plts., a few plt. imprints or letterpress shaved, as usual, cont. gt.-decor. cl., corners scuffed, in chemise & mor. pull-off case by Riviere. (C. Jun.27; 3) *Ross.* £650
– – **Anr. Edn.** L., 1842. *1st. Edn. 2nd. Iss.* Hand-cold. title, 35 hand-cold. plts., orig. cl. gt., discold., cl. s.-c. (P. Feb.16; 95) £380
– – **Anr. Edn.** Ill.:– after H. Alken. L., 1874. Hand-cold. additional title, 37 plts., 4 mntd., a few ll. detchd., stitching shaken, orig. cl., rubbed, w.a.f. (CSK. Dec.2; 46) £170
– – **Anr. Edn.** Ill.:– after Henry Alken. 1901. Hand-cold. frontis., additional title, 34 plts., red mor. gt. by Zaehnsdorf. (CE. Sep.1; 6) £90
– – **Anr. Edn.** L., Alken. L., 1905. Title & 35 plts., hand-cold. (With:) – **Memoirs of the Life of the Late John Mytton.** Alken & Rawlins. L., n.d. Title & 20 hand-cold. plts. Together 2 vols. Unif. red mor. gt. (S. Oct.4; 73) *Chelsea.* £210
– – **Anr. Copy.** Tall 8vo. Orig. cl. gt., rubbed. (TA. Apr.19; 171) £54
– – **Anr. Edn.** L., n.d. Hand-cold. title, 34 hand-cold. plts. (2 mntd.), cl. gt. soiled. (P. May 17; 215a) *Way.* £140
– **Memoirs of the Life of the Late John Mytton.** 1851. *3rd. Edn.* Aquatints hand-cold., publisher's advts., orig. cl. gt. (TA. Aug.18; 25) £120
– – **Anr. Edn.** L., [1869]. *4th. Edn.* Engraved title, 18 hand-cold. plts., cl. gt. (P. May 17; 215b) *Finch.* £110
– – **Anr. Copy.** Later red mor., orig. linen upr. cover bnd. in. (R. Oct.12; 1942) DM 650
– – **Anr. Edn.** 1870. *4th. Edn.* Additional vig. title, 18 hand-cold. plts., minor spotting to text, cont. hf. cf., gt.-decor. spine. (TA. Oct.20; 101) £70
– – **Anr. Edn.** L., 1877. *4th. Edn.* Engraved title, 18 hand-cold. plts., orig. cl. gt., slightly soiled. (P. May 17; 232) *Richards.* £140
– **Sporting ... Illustrative of British Field Sports.** Ill.:– after Gainsborough, Landseer, Hancock, & others. L., [1837]. Fo. Some spotting, orig. linen, loose, light soiling. (V. Sep.29; 1474) DM 550
– – **Anr. Edn.** L., 1838. Fo. Some foxing, orig. gold & blind-tooled linen. (R. Oct.12; 1944) DM 400

APPIANUS ALEXANDRINUS
– **De Bellis Civilibus.** [Venice], Vindelinus de Spira, 1472. Tall fo. Lge. copy, lacks 1st. & last blanks, slight worming, 3 or 4 ll. smudged, later bds., vell. back; the Walter Goldwater copy. [BMC V, 160; Goff A-931] (SG. Dec.1; 35) $3,600
– **Historia Romana.** Reggio Emilia, F. de Mazalibus, 22 Oct. 1494; Scandiano, P. de Pasqualibus, 10 Jan. MCCCCLCXV [i.e. 1495]. *Mixed Edns.* Pts. 1 & 2, in 1 vol. Fo. Later vell.; the Walter Goldwater copy. [BMC VII, 1088 & 1118; Goff A-932 & 930] (SG. Dec.1; 36) $1,500
– **Romaikon Keltike ... Romanarum Historiarum.** Paris, 1551. Fo. In Greek, later hf. mor. (CSK. Aug.5; 117) £85
– **Romanarum Historiarum. Ex Bibliotheca Regia.** [Paris], 1601. Tall 8vo. Vell. (LH. Sep.25; 449) $130

APPLETON'S CYCLOPEDIA OF AMERICAN BIOGRAPHY
Ed.:– James Grant Wilson & John Fiske. N.Y., 1887-89. Lge. 8vo. Three-qtr. cf., rubbed. (RO. Jun.26; 6) $120

APRES DE MANNEVILLETTE, J.B. Nicolas Denis d'
– **Le Neptune Oriental.** Paris, 1775-81. 2 vols. Lge. fo. Lacks 1 plt. & 1 map, hf. vell., slightly rubbed. (D. Nov.23; 742) DM 7,000

APULEIUS, Lucius

- **Amor und Psyche.** Trans.:– R. Jachmann. Ill.:– M. Klinger. München, [1880]. Sm. fo. Vigs. on China, 1st. ll. slightly foxed, orig. linen, gold-tooled. (H. Nov.24; 1704) DM 2,200
- – – **Anr. Copy.** Fo. A few text pp. slightly foxed, orig. pict. linen gt. (R. Apr.3; 284) DM 1,250
- **Asinus Aureus.** Bologna, Benedictus Hectoris, 1 Aug. 1500. Fo. Lacks the 4 ll. (1 blank) between index & preface, blank lr. half of title restored, register lf. mntd., some loss of text in index, very stained, etc., old vell.; the Walter Goldwater copy. [BMC VI, 845-6; Goff A-938] (SG. Dec.1; 37) $225
- **The Golden Ass.** Trans.:– J. Lindsay. Ill.:– P. Goodman. N.Y., Ltd. Edns. Cl., 1932. *(1500), sigd. by artist.* Ills., elab. mosaic inlaid bdg. by Curtis Walters, with cold. inlays, mor.-bkd. wrap-around & open-bkd. s.-c.; Perry Molstad copy. (SPB. May 16; 410) $600
- **Metamorphose, autrement l'Asne d'Or.** Trans.:– George de la Bouthière Autunois. Lyon, 1553. 16mo. 19th. C. pink mor. gt. by Hardy. (C. May 30; 68) *Hill.* £480

AQUILA, Joh.

- **Opusculum Enchiridion appellatum ... de Omni Ludorum Genere.** Oppenheim, 1516. 4to. Light stains, cut slightly close at sides, bds. (HK. Nov.8; 85) DM 950

AQUILA PRESS

See— LERMONTOV, Mikhail Yurievitch

AQUINAS, Saint Thomas

- **Commentum in Octo Libros Physiciorum Aristotelis.** [Venice], 1480. Fo. Lacks 1st. blank, rubricated, initials supplied in red & blue with long flourishes, 1st. initials with decor. penwork in margin, some sm. margin wormholes, dampstained at fore-margin towards end, fore-margins of last 6 ll. reprd., mod. mor.-bkd. bds.; Stanitz coll. [BMC V. 584; Goff T248] (SPB. Apr.25; 421) $1,600
- **Confessionale.** Paris, ca. 1510. Lacks last lf. blank, leath. (HK. Nov.8; 358) DM 700
- **Côtra Gentiles cum Côme.** Venice, 1524. Fo. Minor worming at beginning & end very slightly affects text, cont. blind-stpd. cf. over wood bds., roll-tool borders, rebkd., lacks clasps. (S. Oct.11; 422) *Maggs.* £210
- **De Veritate Catholicae Fidei.** Venice, Franciscus Renner & Nicolaus de Frankfordia, [1476]. 4to. Rubricated in red & blue, 1st. lf. doubled, lacks last blank lf., Italian 18th. C. marb. vell., decor., Pius VI arms; from Fondation Furstenberg-Beaumesnil. [H. 1386; BMC V, 193] (HD. Nov.16; 61) Frs. 8,000
- **Enarrationes Evangeliorvm Dominicalium & Quadragesemalium per Totum Annum.** Köln, 1535. Title with stp. & owners mark, minimal spotting, cont. blind-tooled pig over wood bds., lightly rubbed, minimal worming. (HK. May 15; 247) DM 520
- **In Duodecim Metaphysicorum Libros Aristotelis, Commentaria Celeberrima.** Venice, 1588. Fo. Book-label pasted to verso of colophon lf., some ll. spotted or browned, cont. limp vell., worn. (S. Mar.20; 816) *Poole.* £75
- **Prima Pars Secunde Partis Summe Theologie.** Venecia, 1470. 4to. Lge. gt. & cold. capital, decor. red & blue initials, slight repair 1st. & last lf., cont. leath. over wood, metal clasps. [BMC V, 194; HC 1448; Goff T204] (DS. Jan.27; 2061) Pts. 200,000
- – – **Anr. Edn.** Paris, 19 Mar. 1521. With final colophon/register lf., lr. blank margin of title & a1 cut away, a few side-notes near end just trimmed, mid-16th. C. Roman red mor. by Vatican Bindery, covers elab. gt. & tooled, centre episcopal arms (shield defaced), 3 gt. spine raised bands, lacks ties; from Hans Fürstenberg coll. (S. May 10; 419) *Fletcher.* £880
- **Prima Pars Summe Sacre Theologie ... –Tertia Pars Summe ...** Venice, Johannes Rubeus, 20 Dec. 1497; Venice, Philippus Pinzius, 12 Sep. 1493. 2 works in 1 vol. Fo. Rubricated, some ll. browned, cont. leath., decor., spine old restored, worn, lacks clasps. [Goff T-202, Hain 1446; Goff T-223, Hain 1471] (GB. Nov.3; 956) DM 1,500
- **Primum Scriptum Sententiarum.** Lyon, 1520. Vol. I only. Margin cut away above title, with loss to engr., stpd. cf., by Jacques Pandelaert, decor.,

medallion representing Hope, spine reprd.; from Fondation Furstenberg-Beaumesnil. (HD. Nov.16; 160) Frs. 5,200
- **Quaestiones de XII quodlibet.** Nuremb., Johann Sensenschmidt & Andreas Frisner, 15 Apr. 1474. Lge. fo. Rubricated, painted initials, 19th. C. hf. roan, s.-c.; from Fondation Furstenberg-Beaumesnil. [HC 1402; BMC II, 406; Goff T184] (HD. Nov.16; 32) Frs. 35,100
- **Summa Theologica. Pars Secunda.** Venice, 9 Aug. 1496. Fo. 1st. 20 ll. with sm. worm-holes, some slight spotting, some old MS. underlining & margin annots., 19th. C. hf. leath., slightly worn. [Goff T218; HC 1467; BMC V, 419] (D. Nov.23; 147) DM 1,600

ARABIAN NIGHTS

- **Abendländische Tausend und eine Nacht ... – Fortsetzung ... Einhundert und eine Nacht.** Meissen, 1838-40. *1st. Edn.* 15 vols. in 5, & 4 vols. in 2. Some spotting, cont. linen & hf. linen (2), romantic gt., wear; ex-libris; Hauswedell coll. (H. May 24; 1467) DM 920
- **Alle Verhalen van 1001 Nacht.** Ed.:– J.C. Mardrus. A. Helman. Ill.:– A. Pieck. Amst., 1943-45. 16 pts. in 8 vols. 4to. Decor. cl. (B. Apr.27; 767) Fls. 700
- **Arabian Nights.** Trans.:– Sir Richard Francis Burton. L., [1885-88]. 16 vols., including 6 vols. of supplemental Nights. Orig. cl. (CSK. Dec.2; 198) £130
- **Arabian Nights Entertainment.** Trans.:– Richard F. Burton. Ill.:– Valenti Angelo. N.Y., Ltd. Edns. Cl., 1934. *(1500) numbered, sigd. by artist.* 6 vols. Lge. 8vo. Ills., hf. cf., pict. bds., orig. s.-c. (SG. May 17; 157) $110
- **The Book of the Thousand Nights & a Night.** Trans.:– Sir Richard Francis Burton. 1897. *Liby. Edn.* 12 vols. Mor. gt. (P. Feb.16; 221) £120
- **The Book of the Thousand Nights & a Night; with Supplemental Nights.** Trans.:– Sir. R.F. Burton. Benares, Kamashastra Soc., for private subscribers only, 1885-88. 16 vols. Tall 8vo. Gold- & silver-decor. cl. (SG. Mar.29; 28) $250
- – – **Anr. Edn.** Trans.:– Sir R.F. Burton. L., Burton Cl., n.d. *(1000).* 17 vols. Orig. cl., spines faded. (S. Dec.13; 171) *Edwards.* £65
- – – **Anr. Edn.** Trans.:– Sir R.F. Burton. Burton Cl., n.d. *Baroda Edn., (950) numbered.* 16 vols. Hf. cf. by Bayntun, spines gt.-decor., unopened. (SKC. Mar.9; 1767) £320
- – – **Anr. Edn.** Trans.:– Sir Richard Burton. Priv. ptd., n.d. *MS. Edn. (99) numbered with frontis. in 2 states.* 16 vols. Lge. 8vo. Lev. mor. gt. decor., some minor rubbing. (RO. Apr.23; 25) $900
- **The Book of the Thousand Nights & One Night.** Trans.:– John Payne. Ill.:– Ad. Lalauze. L., for Subscribers, 1884. *(500) numbered.* 9 vols.; with 6 supp. vols. Lge. 8vo. Red three-qtr. mor., backs gt., some covers detchd., some bdgs. worn. (SG. Mar.15; 89) $120
- **Contes des Mille Nuits et Une Nuit.** Trans.:– J.C. Mardrus. Ill.:– Jacques Touchet. [1939]. *(1500).* Sm. 4to. Hf. mor., corners, mosaic spine, wrap. preserved. (SM. Mar.7; 2099) Frs. 1,400
- – – **Anr. Edn.** Ill.:– Edmund Dulac. Paris, n.d. *(300) sigd. by artist.* 4to. Elab. stpd. & painted purple mor. by Moulhac, '1912'. (SPB. Dec.13; 523) $750
- **Die Erzählungen aus den Tausendundein Nächten.** Ed.:– F.P. Greve. Intro.:– Hugo von Hofmannsthal. Ill.:– M. Behmer. 1912-14. 12 vols. Orig. hf. leath., gt. partly lightly rubbed., some spotting. (GB. May 5; 3386) DM 680
- – – **Anr. Copy.** 12 vols. Orig. hf. leath. (HK. Nov.11; 3414) DM 480
- **Erzählungen aus Tausend und eine Nacht.** Ill.:– Ed. Dulac. Weimar, ca. 1920. *(800). (700) on japan bütten.* Orig. vell., clasps; etched ex-libris. (D. Nov.24; 3017) DM 600
- **Fairy Tales from the Arabian Nights.–More Fairy Tales.** Ed.:– E. Dixon. Ill.:– J.D. Batten. L., 1893; 1895. *Ltd., numbered Edns. on L.P., with extra set of text ills. on mntd. India proof plts.* Together 2 vols. 4to. Orig. cl., 2nd. bdg. spotted, end-papers darkened, bkplt. (SG. Dec.8; 20) $175
- **Hassan Badreddine el Bassraoui, Conte des Milles et Une Nuits.** Trans.:– J.C. Mardrus. Ill.:– Kees Van Dongen. Paris, 1918. 4to. On holland, with 4 censored ills., ll., pict. wrap., box. (HD. Dec.16; 157) Frs. 3,000

- **Die Inseln Wak Wak.** Ill.:– M. Slevogt. Berlin, [1921]. *(360) numbered.* Fo. Printers mark with MS. sig. artist, 56 orig. lithos., orig. pict. silk, minimal spotting, corners lightly bumped. (GB. May 5; 3344) DM 3,000
- – – **Anr. Copy.** 56 lithos. (not 54), orig. cold. pict. silk, soiled, bumped, printers mark sigd. by artist. (D. Nov.24; 3192) DM 720
- – – **Anr. Edn.** Trans.:– F.P. Greve. Ill.:– M. Slevogt. Berlin, [1921]. *(460) on Bütten.* Fo. Orig. pict. silk; printers mark sigd. by artist. (H. Nov.24; 2083) DM 1,600
- **Le Livre des Mille Nuits et une Nuit.** Paris, 1899-1904. 16 vols. Hf.-titles, some ll. slightly affected by damp, later hf. cf. (BBA. Feb.23; 68) *Russell.* £60
- – – **Anr. Edn.** Trans.:– J.C. Mardrus. Paris, ca. 1920. 8 vols. 156 col. plts., liby. stp. erased from frontis. verso, orig. decor. hf. cf. gt., slightly rubbed. (VS. Dec.8; 546) Fls. 450
- – – **Anr. Edn.** Trans.:– J.C. Mardrus. Ill.:– Léon Carré. Racim Mohammed (decor.). Paris, 1926-32. 12 vols. 4to. On vell., roan, blind decor., decor. spines, gt. inner dentelle, wrap., 7 vols. with upr. cover only, unc. (HD. Dec.16; 158) Frs. 5,700
- – – **Anr. Copy.** 12 vols. 4to. Numbered copy on vell., sewed, box. (HD. Jun.26; 111) Frs. 4,200
- – – **Anr. Edn.** Trans.:– J.C. Mardrus. Ill.:– Van Dongen. 1955. 3 vols. 4to. On vell., pict. bds. [after Paul Bonet]. (HD. Dec.16; 159) Frs. 2,600
- **La Mille et Deuxième Nuit.** Ed.:– T. Gautier. Ill.:– Ad. Lalauze. Paris, 1898. *(160) De Luxe Edn.* With triple series of ills. on Japan, hand-bnd. mor. gt. by Pierson, decor., gt. inner & outer dentelle, slightly rubbed. (H. Nov.23; 648a) DM 400
- **Les Mille et Une Nuits.** Trans.:– Galland. Ill.:– after Chasselat (frontis.). Paris, 1837. 3 vols. Cont. pink cf. gt., richly decor. (HD. Nov.9; 100) Frs. 3,900
- – – **Anr. Edn.** Trans.:– Galland. Ill.:– Wattier, Laville & Demoraine. Paris, [1840]. *1st. Printing of ills.* 3 vols. 1840 & 1843 subscription prospectuses, str.-grd. hf. mor., corners, by Noulhac, spines decor., unc., wraps. (HD. May 4; 336) Frs. 7,000
- – – **Anr. Edn.** Trans.:– Galland. Ill.:– after Ad. Lalauze. Paris, 1881. *(107) on Dutch paper.* 10 vols. Orig. mor. by Ramage, spines & 2 covers discold. (VG. Nov.29; 210) Fls. 480
- **Les Mille et Une Nuits, Contes Arabes.** Paris, 1822. 7 vols. No bdg. stated. (With:) **Les Mille et un Jours, Contes Orientaux.** Paris, 1826. 5 vols. Qtr. cf., bkplts. (GM. Dec.7; 702) £300
- **Persian Stories.** Trans.:– Sir Richard F. Burton. Ill.:– Michèle Forgeois. Kentfield, Calif., Allen Pr., 1980. *(140) on St. Cuthberts all-rag paper.* 3 fascicles. Thin fo. Pen-&-ink drawings, green columndividers, gt. initials, loose, ptd. wraps., cl. folding-case, prospectus laid in. (SG. May 17; 8) £300
- **[Portfolio of Plates for Burton's Arabian Nights].** Ill.:– after Albert Letchford (gravure plts.), Adolphe Lalauze (etchings). L., 1897. *(100) with the Letchford plts. sigd. by him.* 71 gravure plts., 20 etchings, index pamphlet & prospectus laid in, lacks a few tissue guards, plts. loose as iss. in cl. folding case, elab. gt. carpet design on upr. cover, slightly worn. (SG. Mar.29; 30) $200
- **Princess Badoura ...** Ed.:– Laurence Housman. Ill.:– Edmund Dulac. L., n.d. *(750) numbered & sigd. by artist.* 4to. A few ll. very slightly soiled, orig. buckram gt., worn, partly unc. (S. Dec.20; 533) *Rosenblatt.* £100
- **Sinbad the Sailor & Other Stories from the Arabian Nights.** Ill.:– Edmund Dulac. L., [1911]. 4to. Later three-qtr. mor., light wear. (RO. Jul.24; 289) $110
- **Sindbad der Seefahrer.** Ill.:– M. Slevogt. Berlin, 1908. *(300).* Fo. Orig. cold. pict. vell.; printers mark sigd. (H. Nov.24; 2090) DM 1,600
- **Stories from the Arabian Nights.** Ed.:– Laurence Housman. Ill.:– Edmund Dulac. 1907. 4to. Orig. cl. gt. (TA. Aug.18; 240) £50
- **Tales from the Thousand & One Nights.** Ill.:– Edward J. Detmold. L., [1924]. *1st. Detmold Edn.* 4to. Prelims., last pp. & end-papers foxed, elab. gt.-decor. vell., slightly warped. (CBA. Aug.21; 172) $180

See— LETCHFORD, Albert

ARAGO, Jacques

- **Narrative of a Voyage round the World, in the Uranie & Physicienne Corvettes, commanded by Captain Freycinet.** L., 1823. 4to. Some foxing, hf.

mor., corners, by Morrell, worn. (HD. Mar.14; 5)
Frs. 2,000

ARAGON, Louis
– Henri Matisse. 1971. 2 vols. 4to. Orig. cl., d.-w.'s., s.-c. (BBA. Jul.27; 238)
Sims, Reed & Fogg. £70
– Je N'ai Jamais Appris à Ecrire ou les Incipit. Ill.:– Joan Miró. Geneva, 1969. *(175) numbered with orig. cold. etching sigd. by Miró.* 4to. Loose as iss. in orig. wraps., orig. vell.-bkd. bd. folder, s.-c. (BBA. Jun.14; 237) *Barrie Marks.* £700

ARAMA, Meir Ben Yitzhak
– Meir Job. Venice, 1567. *2nd. Edn.* 4to. Margins of 1st. 4 ll. crudely reprd. not affecting text, stained, 2 holes in inner margin of last lf. affecting some letters, mod. blind-tooled mor. (S. Oct.24; 56)
Sol. £280

ARATUS SOLENSIS
– Phainomena kai Diosemeia [& other works]. Ed.:– John Fell. Oxford, 1672. Frontis. & title trimmed at upr. edge, early annots., qtr. vell. (SG. Oct.6; 14)
$100

ARBAUD, Joseph
– La Bête du Vacarrès. Ill.:– Raymond Guerrier. N.p., 1958. *(40) with suites in black & cols. & decomposition of 2 plts.* 1 vol. & album. 4to. & fo. Leaves, box, album in box. (HD. Jun.13; 2)
Frs. 1,300

ARBAUMONT, Jules d'
See— BEAUNE, Henri & Arbaumont, Jules d'

ARBOGAST, Louis François Antoine
– Du Calcul des Derivations. Strassburg, 1800. *1st. Edn.* 4to. Some foxing, liby. de-accession stp. on title, cont. roan, scuffed, rebkd.; John D. Stanitz coll. (SPB. Apr.25; 16)
$120

ARBUTHNOT, Charles
– Table of Ancient Coins, Weights & Measures, Explain'd & Exemplify'd in Several Dissertations. 1727. 1 vol. 4to. Engraved tables bnd. in at rear, disbnd. (*With:*) – Miscellaneous Works of the Late Dr. Arbuthnot. 1770. *New. Edn.* 2 vols. Cont. tree cf., worn on corners, rebkd. & recased. (TA. Jan.19; 220)
£52

ARBUTHNOT, John
– An Essay Concerning the Nature of Aliments. L., 1731-32. *1st. Edn.* 2 vols. 2nd. vol. has hf.-title & errata slip at end, scattered early underscoring & marginalia in 2nd vol., cont. cf., worn, rebkd., & early qtr. cf., worn. (SG. Mar.22; 21)
$120

ARCANGELO, Francesco
– Storia della Vita di S. Monica Madre di S. Agostino. Siena, 1757. 4to. Cont. Italian vell., richly decor., Benedict XIV arms; from Fondation Furstenberg-Beaumesnil. (HD. Nov.16; 167)
Frs. 2,300

ARCE, Manuel José
– Memoria de la Conducta Publica y Administrativa de Manuel José Arce Durante el Periodo de su Presidencia. Mexico City, 1830. Wormed, wraps. (SG. Oct.20; 15)
$150

ARCHAEOLOGIA CANTIANA
1858-1911. Vols. 1-29, plus extra vol. 1907 & 'Kent Records' 1912. Orig. cl. gt. (P. Nov.24; 65)
Parry. £75

ARCHDALL, Mervyn
– Monasticon Hibernicum; or an History of the Abbies, Priories & other Religious Houses in Ireland. L., 1786. *1st. Edn.* 4to. Cf. (GM. Dec.7; 78)
£200
– – *Anr. Edn.* Ed.:– Rt. Rev. P.F. Moran. Dublin, 1873-76. Vols. I & II only (of 3). Sm. 4to. Mor.-bkd. (GM. Dec.7; 446)
£85

ARCHDEACON, Matthew
[–] Legends of Connaught, Irish Stories, etc. etc. Dublin, 1839. *1st. Edn.* Hf. mor., armorial motif on spine. (GM. Dec.7; 407)
£110

ARCHENHOLTZ, J.W. von
– Geschichte des Siebenjährigen Krieges in Deutschland. Ill.:– Berger, Nussbiegel & others; Chodowiecki, Meil & Henne. Berlin, 1789. Kalender lacks

title lf., folding map with sm. tear, cont. bds. gt., slightly rubbed. (GB. Nov.3; 224)
DM 480

ARCHER, Sir Geoffrey & Godman, Eva M.
– The Birds of British Somaliland & the Gulf of Eden. Ill.:– A. Thorburn, H. Gronvold, & others. L., 1937-61. 4 vols. Lge. 8vo. 1 map torn in fold, liby. stps. on titles, orig. cl. gt., 1st. vol. slightly marked, last 2 vols. in d.-w. (S. Nov.28; 4)
Antik Junk. £300

ARCHER, John Wykeham
– Vestiges of Old London. 1851. 4to. 37 hand-cold. plts., 1 text lf. loose, cf. gt. (P. Sep.8; 4)
Wilmot. £50

ARCHEVOLTI, Schmuel
– Arugat Ha'Bosem. Venice, 1602. *1st. Edn.* 4to. Owner's sig. on title, creased, browned, stained thro.-out, hf. vell., marb. paper bds., slightly worn. (S. Oct.24; 60)
Sol. £200

ARCHIMEDES
– Opera ... Ed.:– Nic. Tartalea Brixianus. [Venice, Apr. 1543]. *1st. Edn.* 4to. Lengthy MS. note in German & Fr. on end-paper, title & some ll. cut slightly close at top, title slightly browned & with sm. ink spots, 2 ll. slightly spotted, bds. (HK. May 15; 65)
DM 2,800
– – *Anr. Edn.* Ed.:– [Isaac Barrow]. 1675. [Wing A3621]. (*Bound with:*) APOLLONIUS PERGAEUS – Conica. Ed.:– [Isaac Barrow]. 1675. [Wing A3536]. (*Bound with:*) THEODOSIUS – Sphaerica. Ed.:– [Isaac Barrow]. 1675. [Wing T857a]. Together 3 pts. in 1 vol. Sm. 4to. Few ll. slightly soiled, cont. cf., slightly soiled, brkn., loose. (BBA. Aug.18; 208)
Feingold. £80
– [Opera]. Cum Eutocii Ascalonitae Commentariis. Ed.:– Joseph Torelli. Oxonii, 1792. Fo. L.P., parallel Greek & Latin text, some perforation stps., old cl., worn, ex-liby. (RO. Dec.11; 10)
$120
– Quae Supersunt Omnia. Ed.:– Joseph Torelli. Oxford, 1792. Fo. L.P., parallel Latin & Greek text, light stain along top margin at beginning, frontis. offset onto title-p., 19th. C. mor.-bkd. bds., corners & jnts. rubbed; John D. Stanitz coll. (SPB. Apr.25; 18)
$850

ARCHIMEDES OF SYRACUSE & others
– Tetragonismus. Ed.:– Lucas Gauricus. Venice, 28 Aug. 1503. Sm. 4to. On thick paper, some staining & browning, sm. wormholes affecting a few letters of text in 2nd. hf. of book, washed, lev. mor. gt. by Lakeside Press; John D. Stanitz coll. (SPB. Apr.25; 17)
$3,500

ARCHITECTURES
Ill.:– L. Sue, A. Mare & others. Paris, 1921. *(500).* Vol. I (all publd.). Fo. Hf. vell., corners, wrap. & spine. (HD. Jun.6; 4)
Frs. 4,700

ARCHIV FUR BUCHGEWERBE
Leipzig, 1912-17. Vols. 49-54 in 10. Lge. 4to. Hf. cl. (VG. Sep.13; 361)
Fls. 480

ARCOS, Rene
– Medardus. Ill.:– Fr. Masereel. Leipzig, 1930. *(50) De Luxe Edn. on Japan.* Printers mark sigd. by author & artist, hand-bnd. orange mor. gt. (H. Nov.24; 1822)
DM 840

ARDEN'S SYDNEY MAGAZINE of Politics & General Literature
Sydney, 1843. Vol. 1 nos. 1 & 2 (all publd.). Some slight staining, lacks frontis. to no. 1, later bds., qtr. buckram, 3 (of 4) wraps. bnd. in. (KH. May 1; 20)
Aus. $270

ARDENNE DE TIZAC, H. d'
See— TIZAC, H. d'Ardenne de

ARENALES, Jose
– Memoria Historica sobre las Operaciones e Incidencias de la Division Libertadora ... Buenos Aires, 1832. 4to. Some worming, mostly marginal, old hf. leath., spine defect. (SG. Oct.20; 17)
$130

ARETINO, Pietro
– De Ragionamenti. 1584. 2 pts. in 1 vol. Later mott. cf., slightly worn. (TA. Nov.17; 533)
£90
– Quattro Comedie. [L.], 1588. *[1st. Engl. Edn.].* Slight browning, tear in G6, slightly affecting text, reprd., 18th. C. cf., rebkd., old spine preserved;

sig. 'Thos Bowlby, Florence, 1746' on title. [STC 19911] (S. Oct.11; 376)
Lurie. £120
– – *Anr. Copy.* Cont. vell., loose, armorial supralibros. [STC 19911] (SG. Oct.27; 258)
$225
– Les Sonnets Luxurieux. Ed.:– Isidore Liseux. Paris, 1904. (500) numbered on Hollande. Ob. 4to. Cont. hf. mor., decor., bd. s.-c. (HK. Nov.9; 2094)
DM 1,500
– La Terza, et Ultima Parte de Ragionamenti. [L.], 1589. Some slight stains, 18th. C. cf., spine gt. [STC 19913] (BBA. Mar.21; 10)
Bondy. £110

ARGENSOLA, Lupercio Leonardo & Bartolome Leonardo
– Rimas. Saragossa, 1634. *1st. Coll. Edn. 2nd. Iss.?, with engraved title, & approbation dtd. 1634.* Pages 268 & 269 misnumbered 262 & 263 (as in the 1st. iss.), 2 sm. burn holes in engraved title, old liby. stps., old vell. (SG. Oct.27; 11)
$175

ARGENTERIO, Giovanni
– Varia Opera de re Medica. Flor., 4 Feb. 1550. Fo. Cont. blind-stpd. cf., roll-tool border, orig. spine torn; Praemonstratensian Abbey at Steingaden bkplt., dupl. of Royal Liby., Munich, Dr. Walter Pagel copy. (S. Feb.7; 15)
Klingsor. £600

ARGOLI, Andrea
– Exactissimae Secundorum Mobilium Tabulae ... Padua, 1651. Some worming of title & following lf., Mm2 shaved. (*Bound with:*) – Pandosion Sphaericum in quo Singula in Elementaribus Regionibus atque Aetherea Mathematice Pertractantur. Padua, 1644. *1st. Edn.* Hf.-title, fo. 9 reprd. Together 2 works in 1 vol. 4to. Cont. cf., rebkd.; Dr. Walter Pagel copy. (S. Feb.7; 19)
Bozzo. £330

ARIEL POEMS
L., 1917-31. Nos. 2, 4, 9, 18-24, 26-29 & 33. Nos. 9 & 33 1st. edns. in envelopes, others proof copies, Eliot's 'Animula' with ill. uncold. & by 'Gertrude Hughes-Stanton', & 'Marina' with wording 'Datta Dayadhvam Damyata' in McKnight Kauffer's cold. ill., orig. pict. wraps., Lawrence's 'The Triumph of the Machine' in grey wraps., nos. 26-29 unnumbered on lr. cover, few wraps. slightly soiled. (S. Mar.20; 848)
Abbott. £100
– – *Anr. Edn.* N.Y., 1927. *1st. Amer. Edns. (27) to secure U.S. copyright.* [Nos. 1-7]. Orig. wraps. (S. Oct.11; 303)
Waterfield. £240
– – *Anr. Copy.* [Nos. 1-8]. Orig. wraps. (S. Dec.8; 162)
Mayhew. £200
– – *Anr. Edn.* [1927-31]. *Nos. 9 & 33: 1st. Edns.* Nos. 1, 3, 5, 6, 9, 18-24, 26-29, 33, together 17 vols. Nos. 9 & 33 in envelopes, some with variations from the 1st. edns., Eliot's 'Animula' with ill. uncold. & 'by Gertrude Hughes Stanton' & 'Marina' with the wording 'Datta Dayadhvam Damyata' in McKnight Kauffer's cold. ill., orig. pict. wraps., some slightly dust-soiled, Lawrence's 'The Triumph of the Machine' in greyish wraps., nos. 26-29 unnumbered on lr. cover; some nos. proof copies. (S. Oct.11; 305)
Minerva. £80
– – *Anr. Edn.* [1927-31]. *Nos. 9 & 33: 1st. Edns. No. 24 1st. Edn., 1 of (300) sigd.* Nos. 3, 6, 9, 18-24, 26-29, 33, together 15 vols. Nos. 9 & 33 in envelopes, Eliot's 'Marina' with wording 'Datta Dayadhvam Damyata' in McKnight Kauffer's cold. ill. & 'Animula' with ill. uncold. & 'by Gertrude Hughes-Stanton', no. 24 orig. bds., others orig. wraps., a few slightly dust-soiled, Lawrence's 'The Triumph of the Machine' in greyish wraps., nos. 26-29 unnumbered on lr. cover; proof copies but for nos. 9, 24, & 33. (S. Oct.11; 307)
Minerva. £50
– – *Anr. Edn.* L., [1929-30]. Nos. 18-31. Proof copies, some with variations from 1st. edns., Eliot's 'Animula' with ill. uncold. & by 'Gertude Hughes-Stanton' & 'Marina' with wording 'Datta Dayadhvam Damyata' in McKnight Kauffer's cold. ill., orig. pict. wraps., Lawrence's 'The Triumph of the Machine' in grey wraps., nos. 25-31 unnumbered on lr. cover, slight soiling, tear in upr. cover of no. 31. (S. Mar.20; 847)
Abbott. £100

ARINGHI, Paolo
– Roma Subterranea Novissima in qua post Antonium Bosium ... et Celebres alios Scriptores ... Monimenta, Epitaphia, Inscriptiones, ac Nobiliora Sanctorum Sepulchra ... illustrantur. Rome, 1651.

ARINGHI, Paolo -*Contd.*

2 vols. Fo. Some staining & browning, cont. vell., slightly loose. (SI. Dec.15; 44) Lire 450,000
-- **Anr. Edn.** Köln, 1659. *2nd. Edn.* 2 pts. in 1 vol. Lge. fo. Upr. margin stained, cont. vell., slightly soiled. (HK. Nov.8; 1070) DM 600
-- **Anr. Edn.** Paris, 1659. 2 vols. Fo. Engraved frontis., double-p. plan, title to Vol. 1 & prelims. & 2T4, Vol. 1 browned & slightly affected by damp, later bds., stitching split. (CSK. Mar.9; 186) £50

ARIOSTO, Ludovico
- **Orlando Furioso.** Venice, 1545. *2nd. 8vo. Edn.* Sm. 8vo. Cont. vell.; Louis de Rozel & Charles de Baschi's copy, ex-libris almost entirely torn away. (HD. Nov.9; 1) Frs. 3,700
-- **Anr. Edn.** Lyon, 1556. 4to. Lr. part of title with printers mark torn off, stained nearly thro.-out, some light browning, blind-tooled leath., old spotting & wear. (V. Oct.1; 3705) DM 420
-- **Anr. Edn.** Venice, 1568. 4to. Engraved title-p., 51 wood-engraved plts., title reprd., some slight spotting, slightly loose, paper-covered bds. (SKC. May 4; 1655) £100
-- **Anr. Copy.** 4to. Some ll. with sm. stain, old vell. (HD. Jan.30; 1) Frs. 1,700
-- **Anr. Edn.** Ed.:– Jeronimo Ruscelli. Lyons, 1580. 2 vols. 12mo. Later gt.-panel. crushed mor. (TA. Nov.17; 529) £125
-- **Anr. Edn.** Venice, 1580. 4to. Some margin foxing & dampstaining, old cf., rebkd. (SG. Oct.27; 13) $325
-- **Anr. Edn.** Ed.:– [G. Ruscelli]. Ill.:– Girolamo Porro. Venice, 1584. 4to. Title & almost all the cartouches & engraved initials in cols. & gold by a mod. hand, sm. hole in title-p., rust-hole in N5, headline cut away from S1, minor defect in ill. to canto 34, some browning, minor imperfections, 17th. C. vell., slightly soiled. (S. Oct.11; 377) *Simonds.* £230
-- **Anr. Edn.** 1773. 4 vol. Engraved port., 46 plts., some annots., a few ll. lightly browned, cont. russ., spines gt., top of 1 spine defect. (BBA. Dec.15; 175) *Soave.* £120
-- **Anr. Copy.** 4 vols. Port., 46 engraved plts., subscribers list, errata lf., some light foxing, mostly marginal, scarlet mor. gt. extra, spines onlaid & gt., gt. dentelles, by Kalthoeber. (SG. Nov.3; 5) $850
-- **Anr. Copy.** 4 vols. 4to. 45 plts., foxed, cont. red mor. gt., decor., turn-ins & corners slightly worn. (LM. Mar.3; 8) B.Frs. 44,000
-- **Anr. Edn.** Trans.:– John Hoole. L., 1783. *1st. Compl. Edn.* 5 vols. Prefatory notice dtd. 24 Jan. 1784, 13 p. subscribers list, cont. cf., slightly worn. (SG. Feb.16; 7) $130
-- **Anr. Edn.** Trans.:– John Hoole. 1785. *2nd. Edn.* 5 vols. Slight spotting, later str.-grd. mor. gt., spines rubbed. (TA. Dec.15; 450) £52
-- **Anr. Edn.** Paris, 1795. Wide margin, some slight foxing, cont. marb. cf. gt., decor. on gold ground, gt. inner & outer dentelle, minimal rubbed, some light wear, corners bumped. (HT. May 9; 1362) DM 1,200
-- **Anr. Edn.** Ill.:– Cipriani, Eisen, etc. Paris, 1803-04. 4 vols. 4to. Browned, gt.-tooled cf., worn. (CR. Jun.6; 4) Lire 220,000
-- **Anr. Edn.** Preface:– G. Carducci. Ill.:– G. Doré. Mailand, 1881. Fo. Orig. linen covers gt., renewed spine, linen loose in parts, gt. faded. (D. Nov.24; 2261) DM 400
- **Orlando Furioso in English Heroical Verse. ...Epigrams.** Trans.:– Sir John Harington, of Bathe, Knight. L., 1634. Sm. fo. Mor., the Club Bindery, 1906; from the libraries of Beverly Chew & Alfred Nathan. (LH. Sep.25; 451) $200
- **Orlando Furioso; Li Cinque Canti.** Venice, 1565. 2 pts. in 1 vol. Title-p. & last lf. reprd., stains, cont. vell.; bkplt. of David Garnett. (BBA. Mar.21; 6) *Snelling.* £140
-- **Anr. Edn.** Venice, 1572. (*Bound with:*) - **I Cinque Canti Di M. Lodovico Aricsto.** N.p., n.d. Together 2 works in 1 vol. Mor., gt.-stpd. unidentified arms in centre of covers, inner borders of gt.-stpd. mor., by Hering. (LH. Sep.25; 452) $300
- **Rasender Roland.** Ill.:– B.A. Dunker. Bern, 1778. Wide margin, on Dutch paper, few ll. with light staining, cont. marb. cf., gt. floral spine, slightly rubbed, owner mark & engraved ex-libris on early lf. & inside cover; Hauswedell coll. (H. May 24; 1216) DM 820
- **Rime e Satire.** Flor., 1822. Cont. red mor., gold-tooled decor., gt. decor. spine on pointillé ground, gt. inner & outer dentelle. (D. Nov.24; 2381) DM 400
- **Roland Furieux.** Trans.:– d'Ussieux. Ill.:– Cochin, Moreau &c. Paris, 1775-83. 4 vols. Cont. tree cf., decor. red mor. spines; Guy Pellion ex-libris. (HD. Sep.22; 181) Frs. 2,600
-- **Anr. Edn.** Trans.:– D'Ussieux. Ill.:– after Baskerville & Cochin. Paris, 1789. 4 vols. 93 engraved plts., name & sm. stp. on title-pp., cont. tree cf. gt., rubbed, 2 spines slightly worn, a few wormholes. (S. Dec.20; 796) *Strinati.* £185
-- **Anr. Edn.** Trans.:– A.J. du Pays. Ill.:– Gustave Doré. Paris, 1879. *1st. Printing of ills.* Fo. Publisher's decor. buckram. (HD. May 3; 174) Frs. 4,000
-- **Anr. Edn.** Trans.:– A.Y. Du Pays. Ill.:– Gustave Doré. Paris, 1879. *(50) on china.* Some foxing, mainly on frontis. & title-p., jansenist red mor. gt.; Jules Creté copy. (HD. Jun.13; 3) Frs. 6,000

ARIPOL, Samuel
- **Lev Chacham.** Constantinople, 1586. 4to. Slight browning & soiling to some ll., several margins reprd., mod. hf. mor. gt. (SPB. Feb.1; 15) $2,200

ARISTARCHUS OF SAMOS
- **De Magnitudinibus et Distantiis Solis et Lunae.** Ed.:– F. Commandinus. Pesaro, 1572. *1st. Separate Edn.* Sm. 4to. Title-p. guarded, minor damage to last 2 ll. reprd., lacks prelim. blank, mod. cf.; John D. Stanitz coll. (SPB. Apr.25; 19) $1,200

ARISTIDES, Aelius
- **Orationes [Graece].** Flor., 1517. Fo. Some offsetting at beginning & end, 18th. C. cf., corners bumped, cover loose, ex-Liby. (GB. Nov.3; 925) DM 800

ARISTOPHANES
- **Aristophanis Comoediae Novem [with the Scholia].** Ed.:– [Marcus Musurus]. Venice, Aldus Manutius, 15 Jul. 1498. *1st. Edn.* Fo. Lacks final blank lf., a few ll. browned, some slight spotting, 3 ink smudges on fo. 49, 2 sm. spots to lr. margin between folios 92 & 95, late 18th. C. Engl. diced russ. gt., rebkd., orig. backstrip laid down, corners worn, qtr. cf. s.-c.; Nicholas Vansittart & Ross Winans bkplts., Robert W. Martin & Thomas B. Stevenson copy. [BMC V, 559 (IB 24470); Goff A-958; HC 1656] (CNY. May 18; 83) $4,600
- **Comoediae Ennea Meta. Comoediae Novem.** Basle, 1547. Fo. Some staining, cont. blind-stpd. cf., rebkd., lacks clasps. (CSK. Jul.13; 78) £130
- **Comoediae Vndecim.** Leiden, 1600. 16mo. In Greek, late 18th. C. cf., worn, in a, probably, German silver bdg. over red velvet, pierced & chased with design of roses, thistles etc., the 2 clasps similarly decor., rather loose; J.H. Frere's copy, with bkplt., as a bdg., w.a.f. (S. May 10; 218) *Bruno.* £480
-- **Anr. Edn.** Ed.:– Ludolphus Kusterus. Amst., 1710. Lge. fo. L.P., in Greek & Latin, cont. cf., spine gt., hinged; armorial bkplt. of Sir John E. Swinburne, Capheaton. (SG. Feb.9; 162) $400
- **The Eleven Comedies.** L., 1912. *(600) numbered.* 2 vols. Maroon cf. gt. by Sangorski & Sutcliffe. (LH. Sep.25; 463) $130
- **Lysistrata.** Ill.:– A. Beardsley. N.p., priv. ptd., 1905. *(400) numbered.* 4to. Orig. bds., soiled. (HK. Nov.11; 3403) DM 520
-- **Anr. Edn.** Trans.:– Johannes Minckwitz. Ill.:– A. Beardsley. N.p., priv. ptd., ca. 1910. *(200) numbered.* Fo. Chagrin, gold-tooled cover vig. (GB. Nov.5; 3155) DM 500
-- **Anr. Edn.** Trans.:– Jack Lindsay. Ill.:– Norman Lindsay,. Fanfrolico Pr., 1926. *(725) numbered & sigd. by trans.* Fo. Orig. hf. mor. (BBA. Jan.19; 288) *Blackwells.* £140
-- **Anr. Copy.** Fo. Orig. hf. mor. gt., slightly worn. (S. Dec.20; 553) *Salina.* £80
-- **Anr. Copy.** Fo. Bdg. not stated; Harry F. Chaplin copy. (JL. Jul.15; 248) Aus. $220
-- **Anr. Edn.** Trans.:– Gilbert Seldes. Ill.:– Pablo Picasso. N.Y., Ltd. Edns. Cl., 1934. *(1500) sigd. by artist & trans.* 4to. 6 etchings, 40 text drawings, pict. bds., protective bds., orig. s.-c. (SG. May 17; 159) $1,000
-- **Anr. Copy.** 4to. 6 orig. etchings, orig. decor. bds., publisher's box worn. (SPB. Dec.14; 75) $900
-- **Anr. Copy.** 4to. 6 orig. etchings, orig. decor. bds., publisher's box worn. (SPB. Dec.13; 883) $750
- **Lysistrate.** Trans.:– Raoul Veze. Ill.:– Carlegle. Paris, [1928]. *(790) numbered on velin d'Arches.* Tall 4to. Watercolour drawings, hf. lev., orig. wraps. bnd. in. (SG. Feb.16; 8) $110
-- **Anr. Edn.** Trans.:– C. Poyard. Ill.:– Barta. Paris, 1932. *(20) on Montval with suite in bistre.* 4to. Vell., decor. with 2 paintings by Barta, wrap. preserved, folder, s.-c.; extra-ill. with watercol. & 2 orig. drawings by Barta. (HD. Jun.13; 4) Frs. 1,600
- **Women in Parliament.** Trans.:– Jack Lindsay. Ill.:– Norman Lindsay. Fanfrolico Pr., 1929. *(500) numbered & sigd. by trans.* Fo. Orig. hf. mor. gt., slightly rubbed. (S. Nov.22; 335) *Buzek.* £170

ARISTOPHANES, Being a Classic Collection of True Attic Wit. Containing the Jests, Gibes ... & Most Extraordinary Anecdotes of Samuel Foote Esq., ... Wherein is Given the Lively Jeux d'Esprit of the First Ladies of the Age ... Collected by a Gentleman
1778. Sm. 8vo. Cont. sheep, gt.-decor. spine. (TA. Mar.15; 516) £135

ARISTOTELES
- **Acrosaes Physicae Libri VIII. Argyropilo interprete ....** Ed.:– Joan. Eckii. Augsburg, Jun. 1518. Owners mark on title. (*Bound with:*) - **Libri de Coelo ... de Generatione ... Meteorum.** Ed.:– Ioan. Eckius. Augsburg, 15.VI.1519. (*Bound with:*) - **De Anima ... de Sensu & Sensato ... de Memoria & Reminiscentarijs** ... Augsburg, 16.IV.1520. Together 3 works in 1 vol. Fo. 1st. & last ll. soiled & wormed, slightly browned, old MS. notes, MS. owner's note on end-paper, cont. blind-tooled pig over wood bds., wormed, rubbed, lacks clasps. (HK. Nov.8; 91) DM 1,100
- **Aristotelis Summi semper Philosophi Opera.** Ed.:– Erasmus. Bâle, 1550. 2 vols. in 1. Fo. Cont. mor., lge. dentelle border on covers, centre arms, decor. spine, turn-ins renewed, restorations on covers. (HD. Sep.22; 180) Frs. 1,250
De Historia Animalium, de Partibus Animalium, de Generatione Animalium. De Communi Animalium. Trans.:– Theodoro Gaza & Petro Alcyonio. Paris, 1533. 3 pts. in 1 vol. Fo. Cont. MS. notes, title reprd. & stained, bb4 blank corner torn off, 18th. C. Italian hf. cf.; Dr. Walter Pagel copy. (S. Feb.7; 22) *Colombo.* £190
-**De Poetica Liber.** Ed.:– Thomas Tyrwhitt. Oxford, 1794. 4to. Cont. str.-grd. red mor. gt., triple-ruled borders, sm. corner ornaments, spine in 6 compartments, turn-ins gt., by Charles Kalthoeber, with his ticket, sm. abrasion on upr. cover & spine; bkplt. of Charles Hoare, Thomas B. Stevenson copy, as a bdg., w.a.f. (CNY. Dec.17; 576) $220
- **Decem Librorum Moralium tres Conversiones.** Ed.:– J. Lefevre d'Estaples. Paris, 1516. 3 pts. in 1 vol. Fo. Slightly stained, hf. vell., rebkd., unc. (B. Apr.27; 560) Fls. 600
- **Ethica, Politica et Oeconomica.** Trans.:– Leonardus Aretinus. [Strasburg, Johann Mentelin], n.d. Fo. Rubricated, apparently lacks 2 blank ll., many cont. MS. annots. in 2 different hands at beginning, cont. stpd. vell. over wood bds., traces of studs & clasps; from Fondation Furstenberg-Beaumesnil. [H. 1762; Pellechet 1238; BMC I, 53] (HD. Nov.16; 44) Frs. 92,000
- **Histoire des Animaux (Graece) avec la Trad. Françoise par Camus.** Paris, 1783. *1st. Edn.* 2 vols. 4to. 1st. ll. vol. 1 stained, cont. hf. leath. gt. (BR. Apr.12; 571) DM 500
- **Libri tres de Anima Singulorum Epitomis ... ejusdem Parva Naturalia ... ac Postillis M. Anton. Zimarae.** Pavia, 3 Jan. 1521, Oct. 1520, 30 Apr. 1521. 3 pts. in 1 vol. Last pt. under separate title, cont. blind-stpd. cf., worn & laid down, rebkd., corners reprd.; Dr. Walter Pagel copy. (S. Feb.7; 18) *Phelps.* £150
- **The Metaphysics.** Trans.:– Thomas Taylor. L., priv. ptd., 1801. *1st. Edn.* Lge. 4to. Hf.-title, unc., old cl., shabby. (SG. Nov.17; 156) $225

– Meteorologia. Nuremb., 11 Nov., 1512. 4to. 8 lge. woodcuts, slightly wormed, sm. paper fault in F6, early marginalia, vell. (SG. Apr.26; 9)　　$850
– Meteorologica. ... G. de Thiensis tractatus de Reactione et de Intentione et Remissione Formarum. Ed.:– Franciscus de Macerata. Commentary:– Gaietanus de Thiensis. Venice, Johannes & Gregorius de Gregoriis, de Forlivio. 22 Oct. 1491. Fo. Capital spaces with guide letters, some very sm. wormholes, old paper bds. [BMC V, 342; Goff A1008; Hain 1697] (S. May 10; 219)
McKiddrick. £900
– Opera [Greek]. Venice, Aldus manutivs, 1497. *1st. Edn. in Greek.* Vol. IV only. Fo. 3 texts only (of 5), lacks title, subscription & register, early 19th. C. hf. cf., spine decor.; from Fondation Furstenberg-Beaumesnil. [HC 1657; BMC V, 553; Goff A959] (HD. Nov.16; 75)　　Frs. 3,200
[–] [Opera Nonnulla]. Trans.:– [Joannes Argyropulus & others]. Venice, Joannes & Gregorius de Gregoriis, de Forlino, for Benedictus Fontana, 13 Jul. 1496. Fo. 198 ll., including 8 blanks, slight worming in inner blank margin of some ll., cont. Italian cf.-bkd. wood bds., spine blind-tooled, 2 (of 4) leath. clasps with catches, foot of spine renewed, w.a.f. [BMC V, 349; Goff A-966; HC 1659*] (C. Nov.9; 35)
Cavendish. £450
– Opera Omnia quae extant. Ed.:– A. Turnebus, I. Casaubon, J. Pacius & G. Du Val. Lutetiae Parisiorum, 1619. 2 vols. Lge. fo. In Greek & Latin, old marb. cf., spine richly decor. (LM. Oct.22; 54)
B.Frs. 17,500
– Poetica, per Alexandrum Paccium, Patritium Florentinum, ... [Venice], 1516. 16mo. In Latin & Greek, qtr. mor. (LH. Sep.25; 308)　　$250
– Problemata .... Paris, Jul.1520. Fo. Some worming, blank corners of few ll. defect., some margin stains, 110v & 111 stained, cont. blind-stpd. cf. on oak bds., rebkd., new end-papers; Dr. Walter Pagel copy. (S. Feb.7; 17)　　*Rix.* £160
– Sapientissimi Philosophi Aristotelis Stagiritae Theologiae.... Rome, 1519. *(Bound with:)*
ARISTOTELES & Muhammed Ibn Ahmad, called Ibn Rushd, or Averroes – Sententiae. N.p., 1525. Together 2 works in 1 vol. 4to. Bds.; from Fondation Furstenberg-Beaumesnil. (HD. Nov.16; 89)
Frs. 1,300
– Suessanus in Libros Metheorum. Augustini Niphi ... in Libris Aristotelis Meteorologicis Commentaria. Venice, 1531. Fo. Title stained, 2 ll. browned, a few slight wormholes, mod. vell.-bkd. bds. (S. Oct.4; 252)　　*Rhys-Jones.* £50

ARISTOTELES & others
– Auctoritates Aristotelis et Aliorum Philosophorum. Deventer, [Richard Paffraet], 27 Sep. 1489. 4to. Rubricated, woodcut heightened with red (soiled & slightly rubbed), reprd. tear to last lf. affecting a few words, lr. margin of same lf. reprd., lev. mor. by Sangorski & Sutcliffe; John D. Stanitz coll. [BMC IX, 51] (SPB. Apr.25; 24)
$2,100

ARISTOTELES & Theophrastus
– Historiae, cum de Natura Animalium tum de Plantis et earum Causis. Lyon, 1552. *(Bound with:)*
THEOPHRASTUS – De Historia Plantarum Libri X. Lyon, 1552. Together 2 pts. in 1 vol. Cont. blind-stpd. cf., decor., clasps incompl.; from Fondation Furstenberg-Beaumesnil. (HD. Nov.16; 90)
Frs. 1,800

ARIT, F. Ritter von
– Die Krankheiten des Auges. Prag, 1851-56. *1st. Edn.* Minimal foxing, cont. hf. leath. (R. Oct.12; 1329)　　DM 600

ARITHMETICAL EXERCISE ... at the Free-Writing School in Newcastle upon Tyne
1709. Some pp. browned, cont. MS. annots., orig. cf. (P. Jul.5; 318)　　£280

ARIZMENDI, A. de
– Prontuario ... de las Piezas de Madera de Construcción de Baxeles y Edificios. Madrid, 1789. Lge. fo. Vell. (DS. Oct.28; 2446)　　Pts. 30,000

ARLAND, Marcel
– Maternité. Ill.:– Marc Chagall. 1926. Sewed. (HD. Dec.9; 13)　　Frs. 2,600

ARLINGTON, Lewis Charles
– Chinese Drama from the Earliest Times until To-Day. Shanghai, 1930. *(750) numbered & sigd.* 4to. This copy unnumbered, frontis., 115 col. plts., disbnd. (SG. Nov.17; 190)　　$110

ARMENDARIZ, Michele de
– La Maniera di ben giuocare al Riversino. Rome, 1756. 12mo. Cont. cf. gt., slightly rubbed. (BBA. Feb.23; 49)　　*Parikian.* £55

ARMITAGE, Merle
– Gershwin. Contribs.:– P. Whiteman, A. Schoenberg, J. Kern, O. Hammerstein II, & others. N.Y., 1938. 4to. Two-tone cl. (SG. Nov.17; 246)
$120

ARMITAGE, Merle (Text)
See— WESTON, Edward

ARMOUR, Robert, Jr. 'Lara'
[–] The Question of the Rejection of the Speaker of the House of Assembly of Lower Canada Considered. [Montreal, 1827]. 5 ll., trimmed & inlaid, MS. title, pencil inscr. on fly-lf., crushed lev. gt. by Rivière; sigd. by author. (SG. Jan.19; 131)
$225

ARMSTRONG, Col. John
– The History of the Ancient & Present State of the Navigation of the Port of King's-Lyn, & of Cambridge. 1766. Fo. 3 plans, 4 folding engraved maps, including 2 partly hand-cold., 1 slightly torn, plans dampstained, some ll. spotted or browned, later hf. cf., slightly worn. (BBA. Oct.27; 271)
Greer. £100

ARMSTRONG, John, of Minorca
– History of the Island of Minorca. L., 1752. *1st. Edn.* Hf.-title, folding map torn in fold, cont. cf., covers detchd. (S. Mar.6; 69)　　*Shapero.* £130
– – Anr. Edn. L., 1756. *2nd. Edn.* Cont. cf. (C. Nov.16; 1)　　*Blackwells.* £160

ARMSTRONG, John, Physician & Poet, 1709-79
– Miscellanies. L., 1770. *1st. Coll. Edn.* 2 vols. Sm. tears in inr. margins of 01-4 in vol.2, cont. red mor. gt.; bkplts. of J.T.Stanley of Alderley & Graham Pollard. (SPB. May 16; 3)　　$275

ARMSTRONG, Mostyn John
– An Actual Survey of the Great Post Roads between London & Edinburgh. 1776. Some spotting, hf. cf. (P. Dec.8; 402)　　*Mallett.* £140
– – Anr. Edn. 1796. Engraved vig. title, frontis., 44 maps, some outl. col., staining, 5 ll. loose, cf., defect. (P. Jun.7; 341)　　£110
– A Scotch Atlas: or Description of the Kingdom of Scotland. 1777. 4to. Engraved title, 30 hand-cold. engraved maps, some slight foxing, cont. spr. cf.; Sir Ivar Colquhoun, of Luss copy. (CE. Mar.22; 11)　　£440

ARMY & NAZY GAZETTE
Ill.:– R. Simkin. [1897]. 32 col. plts., cl., defect., as a coll. of plts., w.a.f. (P. Apr.12; 194)
Taylor. £220

ARNALD, G.
– Picturesque Scenery on the River Meuse. Ill.:– W. Reynolds, C. Turner, W. Ward etc. L., ca. 1828. Sm. fo. Folding map, 30 plts., some yellowing, cont. hf. chagrin. (HD. Mar.14; 6)　　Frs. 5,000

ARNAS, Vicente
– Escenas Taurinas. Text:– Salvador Ferrer. Madrid, 1983. *(75) numbered, sigd. by artist.* Series of 6 etchings in col., publishers portfo. (DS. Oct.28; 2361)　　Pts. 40,000

ARNAUD, Henri
– The Glorious Recovery by the Vaudois of their Valleys. L., 1827. Folding engraved map, 12 views, blind liby. stp. on few ll., cont. cf., slightly worn. (BBA. Mar.21; 102)　　*J.Brailey.* £55

ARNAULT, Antoine Vincent
– Les Souvenirs et les Regrets du Vieil Amateur Dramatique. Ill.:– Foech de Basle & Whirsker. Paris, 1829. *1st. Edn.* Sm. 8vo. Cont. mor. finish hf. roan, corners, spine decor., unc. (HD. May 3; 175)　　Frs. 1,050

ARNDT, Ernst Moritz
– Mährchen und Jugenderinnerungen. Ill.:– Th. Hosemann.... Berlin, 1843. *1st. Edn.* Vol. 2 (of 2). Slightly foxed, unc., bds., lr. cover & spine mntd. on bds. (HK. Nov.10; 2312)　　DM 400
– Schriften für und an seine Lieben Deutschen. Leipzig, 1845. *1st. Edn.* 3 vols. Fine-grd. mor. gt., blind-stpd. decor., wide gt. inner dentelle. (V. Oct.1; 3793)　　DM 850

ARNDT, Johann
– De Vero Christianismo. Leipzig, 1704. Narrow 8vo. Cont. Dutch vell., richly decor.; from Fondation Furstenberg-Beaumesnil. (HD. Nov.16; 92)　　Frs. 1,500

ARNEMANN, J.
– Praktische Arzneimittellehre. Göttingen, 1795. 2 vols. Cont. hf. leath. gt. (HK. May 15; 311)
DM 460

ARNIM, Gisela von
[–] Drei Mährchen. Ill.:– G. & Maximiliane v. Arnim, M. v. Olfers & H. Grimm. Berlin, 1853. *1st. Coll. Edn.* Some light spotting, later bds., orig. wraps. bnd. in. (GB. May 4; 1195)　　DM 400

ARNIM, Ludwig Achim von
– Fürst Gazgott und Sänger Halbgott. Ill.:– Max Neumann. München, Marees-Gesellschaft, 1919. *(150) on Bütten.* 4to. Hand-bnd. black mor., gt. covers, inner & outer dentelle, slightly bumped, silk end-papers & doubls,. (H. Nov.23; 1156) DM 420
– Halle und Jerusalem. Studentenspiel und Pilgerabentheuer. Ill.:– L.Grimm after Holbein. Heidelberg, 1811. *1st. Edn.* Slightly foxed, cont. hf. leath. gt. (R. Oct.11; 137)　　DM 1,100
– – Anr. Copy. Title verso stpd., sm. tear in title, cont. red hf. leath. gt., slightly rubbed; Hauswedell coll. (H. May 24; 1207)　　DM 900
– – Anr. Edn. Berlin, 1846. Lacks coll. title & dedication lf., bds., marb. paper covered, gold-tooled leath., vell. strengthened ·corners. (D. Nov.24; 2384)　　DM 400
– Sämtliche Werke. Ed.:– W. Grimm. Berlin, 1839-48. *1st. Coll. Edn.* Vols. 1-3 & 5-20. Together 19 vols. With all 5 mus. supps. & litho. or engraved plts., including port., some sigd. lightly browned, cont. hf. leath., decor., lightly rubbed, corners slightly bumped. (GB. May 4; 1196)　　DM 4,400
– Vier und Zwanzig Alte Deutsche Lieder aus dem Wunderhorn .... Ed.:– [J.N. Boehl von Faber]. Heidelberg, 1810. *1st. Edn.* 4to. Wide margin, hf. leath., ca. 1900, orig. wrap. bnd. in, partly bumped; Paul Ernst ex-libris; Hauswedell coll. (H. May 24; 1212)　　DM 1,200

ARNIM, Ludwig Achim von & Brentano, Clemens
– Des Knaben Wunderhorn. Alte Deutsche Lieder... Wit Anhang: Kinderlieder. Heidelberg, 1806-08. *1st. Edn.* 3 vols. Hand-bnd. hf. mor., elab. gt., by Mercier, unc.; Hauswedell coll. (H. May 24; 1208)
DM 15,000

ARNOBIUS
– Disputationum adversus gentes libri octo. Rome, 1542. Fo. Dedication dtd. 1543, MS. note pasted to blank a4, 19th. C. cf. gt., Devonshire arms gt. on covers. (BBA. Feb.23; 3)　　*Thorp.* £190

ARNOLD, Edwin
– The Light of Asia; or, The Great Renunciation. Boston, 1880. *1st. Amer. Edn.* Tall 12mo. Orig. gt.-pict. cl., spine slightly soiled & slightly worn on ends; armorial Roosevelt bkplt. & his inscr. (SG. Mar.15; 2)　　$300

ARNOLD, G.
– Waare Afbeelding der Eerste Christenen, volgens hun Leevendig Geloof en Heylig Leeven. Trans.:– W. Sewel. Ill.:– Jan Luyken. Amst., 1700-01. 2 vols. Fo. Some corners reprd., vell., some stains. (B. Jun.21; 500)　　Fls. 460

ARNOLD, Matthew 'A'
– Alaric at Rome. Ed.:– T.J. Wise. 1893. *Facs. Edn. (30?).* Bds., a little worn. (BBA. Sep.29; 208)
Wyse. £50
– Cromwell,: a Prize Poem, Recited in the Theatre,. Oxford, 1843. *1st. Edn.* 12mo. Orig. ptd. wraps., cl. case; Frederick Dannay copy. (CNY. Dec.16; 6)　　$750

ARNOLD, Matthew 'A' -*Contd.*

- **Empedocles on Etna & other Poems. By A.** L., 1852. *1st. Edn.* Cl., rubbed; pres. copy from author. (P. Mar.15; 284) *Jarndyce.* £180
- – **Anr. Copy.** 12mo. Orig. cl.; pres. copy from author, Frederic Dannay copy. (CNY. Dec.16; 8) $130
- **The Forsaken Merman.** Ill.:– Jean C. Archer. L., 1901. *(10) on vell.* Orig. buckram, decor. end-papers, partly unc.; Frederic Dannay copy. (CNY. Dec.16; 9) $280
- **Geist's Grave.** '1881'. Hf. mor. gt. by Tout; A.N.L. Munby bkplt., W.B. Slater copy, pencil note by John Carter. (P. Apr.12; 28) *Questor.* £120
- **On Translating Homer: Three Lectures given at Oxford. – On Translating Homer: Last Words.** L., 1861;1862. *1st. Edns. 1st. work earliest iss.* 2 vols. 1st. work with 24-p. catalogue dtd. Oct. 1860, bkplt., removed, with slight damage to book-list in upr. cover, bkplt. in each vol., both orig. cl., lev. folding case. (SG. Mar.15; 90) $130
- **The Popular Education of France with Notices of that of Holland & Switzerland.** 1861. *1st. Edn.* Hf.-title, hf. cf. (P. Feb.16; 238) £75
- **The Strayed Reveller.** 1849. *1st. Edn.* Orig. cl. (BBA. Sep.29; 205) *Cox.* £50
- – **Anr. Copy.** 12mo. Early owner's name deleted from a p., orig. cl.; Frederic Dannay copy. (CNY. Dec.16; 10) $350
- **The Works** ... L., 1898. 12 vols. Hf. cf. gt., worn. (PNY. Jun.6; 446) $150

ARNOT, Hugh
- **The History of Edinburgh** .... Edinb., 1779. 4to. Folding map slightly torn, cont. panel. tree cf. (PD. May 16; 172) £75

ARNOTT, James A. & Wilson, John
- **The Petit Trianon, Versailles.** N.Y., 1907-08. 3 vols. Atlas fo. 97 plts., ex-liby., loose in ptd. bd. folders, linen ties. (SG. May 3; 18) $130

ARNOULD
- **Système Maritime et Politique des Européens pendant le XVIIIe Siècle fondé sur leurs Traités de Paix, de Commerce et de Navigation.** Paris, An v [1797]. Hf. roan. (HD. Feb.22; 4) *Frs.* 1,000

ARNOUX, Alexandre
- **La Legende du Roi Arthur et des Chevaliers de la Table Ronde d'après les Textes Anciens.** Ill.:– Arthur Rackham. [1920]. 4to. On japan, numbered, no bdg. stated. (HD. Jun.26; 134) *Frs.* 2,800

ARNOUX, Guy
- **Le Soldat Francais dans les Guerres.** 1916. 4to. Publisher's bds. (HD. Dec.9; 2a) *Frs.* 1,050

ARON BERECHYA BEN MOSHE MODENA
- **Maavar Yabek.** Mantua, 1626. *1st. Edn.* 4to. 1st. pt. ends with blank lf. & continues in 3rd. pt., lacks blank lf., some gatherings browned, stained, slight worming not affecting text, 4 ll. torn & crudely reprd. with loss of words, hf. leath. (S. Oct.24; 62) *Toporwitch.* £320

ARON IBN CHAIM
- **Korban Aron.** Venice, 1609-11. *1st. Edn.* Fo. Owners' sigs. on title, title & 1st. p. reprd. not affecting text, last p. of index in facs., 1 lf. holed with loss of a few words, stained & browned, buckram. (S. Oct.24; 65) *Stern.* £180
- **Lev Aron.** Venice, 1609. *1st. Edn.* Fo. Owners' sigs. on fly-lf. & title, staining, last 3 ll. with sm. wormholes not affecting text, orig. blind-tooled leath. mntd. on wood, worn, lacks clasps. (S. Oct.24; 64) *Davis.* £280

AROSSEV, A. (Ed.)
See— **SOVIET CINEMA**

ARP, Jean or Hans
- **Auch das ist nur eine Wolke. Aus den Jahren 1920 bis 1950.** Basel, [1951]. *1st. Edn. (100) for sale.* 4to. Printers mark sigd. by artist, orig. wraps. (H. May 23; 1127) DM 800
- **Dreams & Projects.** N.Y., 1952. *1st. Edn. (320) numbered.* 4to. Text in German Engl. & Fr., loose ll. in orig. wraps., s.-c., sm. liby. label on spine; printer's mark sigd. by artist. (GB. Nov.5; 2250) DM 1,400
- – **Anr. Edn.** Trans.:– [R. Manheim.]. Ill.:– J. Arp. N.Y., [1952]. *(295).* 4to. Engl., Fr. & German text, printers mark sigd. by artist, loose ll. in orig. wraps., spine faded. (H. May 23; 1127a) DM 1,400
- **Gedichte. Weisst du Schwarzt du.** Ill.:– M. Ernst. Zürich, 1930. *1st. Edn. (200) numbered on paper.* Orig. bds., orig. pict. wraps. (GB. Nov.5; 2422) DM 1,000
- **Onze Peintres.** Ill.:– Kandinsky. Zürich, 1949. *(200) numbered.* 1 woodcut (sigd.), 2 cold. woodcuts, (1 sigd.), orig. wraps. (HK. May 17; 2534) DM 1,600
- **Worttraeume und Schwarze Sterne: Auswahl aus den Gedichten der Jahre 1911-52.** Wiesbaden, [1953]. *(100) numbered.* 4 woodcut plts., each sigd., 4 halftone plts., mor. gt., pict. wraps. bnd. in as iss., s.-c. (SG. Apr.26; 10) $650

ARPHE Y VILLAGANE, José de
- **Varia Commesuración para la Escultura y Architectura.** Madrid, 1773. *6th. Edn.* Fo. Vell. (DS. May 25; 2201) Pts. 50,000

ARRIANUS, Flavius
- **Arrian on Coursing. The Cynegeticus of the Younger Xenophon.** Trans.:– William Dansey. 1831. *(250).* 2 vols. 4to. Lithòs. & ills. on India, unlisted plt. of author's dog, prelims. spotted, cont. mor. by C. Smith, front inner hinge brkn., spine rubbed; A.L.s. from Delabere P. Blaine to trans. (TA. Feb.16; 123) £150

ARRIGHI, A.
- **Histoire de Pascale Paoli, ou la Dernière Guerre de l'Indépendance (1755-1807).** Paris, 1843. 2 vols. Some light foxing, mod. marb. hf. roan, corners, wraps. (HD. Oct.21; 12) *Frs.* 1,900

ARRIGHI, G.M.
- **Viaggio di Licomede in Corsica.** Trans.:– Delaunay. Paris, 1806. *Orig. Edn. in Italian & Fr.* 2 vols. Cont. gt.-decor. cf., arms of Napoleon I, spines decor. (HD. Oct.21; 11) *Frs.* 30,000
- – **Anr. Copy.** 2 vols. in 1. Dampstain on title, mod. hf. chagrin, spine decor. (HD. Oct.21; 11b) *Frs.* 2,200

ARROWSMITH, Aaron
- **Atlas to Thompson's Alcedo or Dictionary of America & West Indies.** 1816. Lge. fo. 19 double-p. & folding hand-cold. maps, diced cf. gt., covers loose. (P. Jul.26; 234) £2,800
- **A New General Atlas.** L., 1817. Fo. Frontis., 103 engraved full-p. maps, linen. (DS. Dec.16; 2139) Pts. 34,000
- **Orbis Terrarum...a Comparative Atlas of Ancient & Modern Geography.** 1828. Fo. Engraved title (torn), dedication, index, 53 maps hand-cold. in outl., slightly soiled, cont. cf., rebkd. (BBA. Oct.27; 238) *Cassidy.* £90
- – **Anr. Copy.** 4to. Title, dedication, 52 maps, cold. in outl., mod. qtr. mor. (P. Nov.24; 314) *Graham.* £60

ARS HISPANIAE. Historia universal del Arte Hispanico
Madrid, [1947-77]. 22 vols. 4to. No bdg. stated. (SPB. Nov.30; 167) $800

ARS NOVA. Hervorragende Werke der Bildenden Künste des Jahres 1901
Ed.:– F. von Myrbach, M. Herzig. Wien, Leipzig & Budapest, [1902]. Lge. fo. Orig. linen, elab. silver decor., slight scratching. (HT. May 9; 1029) DM 400

ART & AUSTRALIA
Sydney, 1963-81. Vols. 1-18 & index (for vols. 1-10, covering years 1963-73, but publd. 1973). Sm. 4to. Orig. bds. (S. Apr.30; 156) *Leicester.* £150

ART ET DECORATION, Revue Mensuelle d'Art Moderne
Paris, 1902-05. Vols. 11-13, 15 & 17, 5 vols. 4to. A few ll. loose, soiled & frayed, orig. cl., soiled, 1 cover stained, as a periodical, w.a.f. (S. Apr.30; 157) *Aust. Nat. Gall.* £135

ART & L'IDEE. Revue Contemporaine du Dilettantisme Litteraire et de la Curiosité
Ill.:– E. Courboin, F. Vallotton, F. Rops, P. Vidal, L. Morin, J. Cheret, E. Grasset, A. Lunois & others. Paris, 1892. *(60) De Luxe Edn.numbered. (15) on China.* 12 pts. (all publd.). This copy unnumbered, with supp. ills., orig. ills., some slight foxing, orig. wraps. (GB. May 5; 3425) DM 5,600

ART & PRACTICE OF ENGLISH BOXING ... by a Celebrated Pugilist
Ca. 1810. *3rd. Edn.* 12mo. Folding engraved frontis. spotted, orig. wraps., slightly torn. (BBA. Feb.9; 77) *Laywood.* £70

ART & SONG
Ed.:– R. Bell. Ill.:– after J.M.W. Turner, John Martin & others. L., [Chiswick Pr.], 1867. 4to. Upr. blank margin lightly stained, orig. mor.-bkd. imitation(?) walnut papier-mache bds., upr. cover & spine gt.-blocked. (CSK. Feb.24; 98) £60
- – **Anr. Copy.** 4to. Some ll. foxed, Art Nouveau bdg., mor., decor. with mor. gt. onlays, spine in 6 compartments with mor. gt. onlays, mor. doubls. with mor. gt. onlays, vell. end-pp., by Guild of Women-Binders, inscr. 'Designed by Miss Baly. Worked by Mrs. Conner', as a bdg., w.a.f. (CNY. Dec.17; 567) $1,600

L'ART DANS LE MONDE SERIES
Paris, 1969. 46 vols. 4 to. No bdg. stated. (SPB. Nov.30; 277) $375

ART D'AUJOURD'HUI
Paris, 1925-29. 5 vols. 4to. Cl.-bkd bd. folders. (SG. Aug.25; 17) $260

ART DE FRANCE. Revue Annuelle de l'Art Ancien et Moderne
Ill.:– Villon, Ernst Masson, Soulage & others. Paris, 1961-64. 4 vols. (all publd.). 4to. Orig. wraps. & bds., slightly soiled. (BBA. Sep.8; 261) *Trocchi.* £60

ART ET DECORATION. Revue Mensuelle d'Art Moderne
1897-1975. 271 Issues. 4to. Stpd., some defects. & staining, orig. wraps., ex-libris. (D. Nov.23; 1753) DM 480

ART IN AUSTRALIA
Sydney, 1916-42. 1st., 2nd., 3rd. & 4th. Series: 100 pts. (compl. set). No bdg. stated. (JL. Nov.13; B455) Aus. $5,750
- – **Anr. Edn.** Sydney, 1919. Special no.: 'The Art of Arthur Streeton'. Bdg. not stated, d.-w. & plastic cover. (JL. Jul.15; 549) Aus. $11
See— **URE SMITH, Sydney & Stevens, Bertram**

ART IN CALIFORNIA: A Survey of American Art with Special Reference to Californian Painting, Sculpture, & Architecture...
San Franc., 1916. Lge. 4to. Linen-bkd. bds., spine worn. (SG. Aug.25; 6) $375

ART IN PHOTOGRAPHY: with Selected Examples of European & American Work
Ed.:– Charles Holme. L., 1905. Lge. 4to. Ptd. wraps., lightly chipped. (SG. Nov.10; 86) $120

ART OF ANCIENT EGYPT, The, as Displayed on & in the Pyramids, Palaces & Tombs
N.Y., ca. 1930. Fo. 32 plts., loose as iss., including 11 hand-cold., few plts. slightly chipped, bd. folder, cl. ties, spine crudely taped. (SG. Aug.25; 134) $110

ART OF SPEAKING (THE): Written in French by Messieurs de Port Royal: In Pursuance of a Former Treatise, intituled The Art of Thinking. Rendered into English. 1676. A few cont. annots., liby. stp. on recto & verso of title, recent panel. cf. (TA. Jun.21; 347) £90

ART UNION (THE)
L., 1846. 1 vol. only. 4to. Lacks title, some spotting, cont. hf. cf., rubbed. (S. Apr.30; 243) *Lennert.* £95

ARTAUD, Chevalier
See— **POUQUEVILLE, François Charles Hughes Laurent - ARTAUD, Chevalier - LASALLE, M. de**

ARTE DEL LIBRO E DELLA RIVISTA nei Paesi d'Europa e d'America [cover title]
Ed.:– C. Ratta. Bologna, 1927. *(750) numbered.* 2 vols. Sm. fo. Cl. (SG. Sep.15; 13) $220

ARTE DI SCRIVERE, L'
Padua, 1796. 4to. 15 Copperplates, many folding, leath.-bkd. bds. (SG. Dec.8; 365) $250

ARTEDI, Peter
– Ichthyolgia; sive, Opera Omnia de Piscibus; scilicet, Bibliotheca Ichthyologica; Philosophia Ichthyologica: Genera Piscium; Synonymia Specierum; Descriptiones Specierum. Ed.:– C. Linne. Leiden, 1738. *1st. Edn.* 5 pts. in 1 vol. Some liby. stps., slightly browned, buckram. (SG. Mar.22; 24) $300

ARTEMIDORUS
– Dell'Interpretatione de Sogni. Trans.:– Pietro Lauro. Venice, 1547. *Early 17th Century reprint.* Lacks last blank, early 17th. C. Italian mor., covers tooled in imitation of 16th, C. gt. entrelac bdg., spine much reprd.; from Jean Fürstenberg coll. (S. May 10; 220) *Thomas.* £280

ARTICO, Angelo
– Della Inalveazione, e del Regolamento del Fiume Brenta. Milano, 1795. 4to. Hf.-title, mod. bds., unc. (SI. Dec.15; 140) Lire 400,000

ARTIGNY, Antoine Gachet d'
– Nouveaux Mémoires d'Histoire, de Critique et de Littérature. Paris, 1749-56. 7 vols. 12mo. Cont. marb. cf., spines decor. (HD. Nov.9; 15) Frs. 3,100

ARTIS AURIFERAE QUAM Chemiam Vocant Volumina Duae, quae continent Turbam Philosophorum aliosque Antiquiss ...
Basle, 1610. *Pt. 3: 1st. Edn.* 3 vols. in 1. Very browned, limp vell.; Dr. Walter Pagel copy. (S. Feb.7; 26) *Radzowsky.* £800

ARTISTES ANCIENS ET MODERNES
Paris, ca. 1850. 5 vols. in 1. Lge. fo. 5 engraved titles with litho vigs., 120 litho plts., some on china, cont. leath, defect. (R. Apr.4; 2084) DM 1,500

ARTISTES CONTEMPORAINS
Ill.:– Delacroix, Gavarni, Nanteuil & others after Decamps, Dupré, Leroux & others. Paris, 1846-49. Yrs. 1-4 in 2 vols. Fo. Yr. 4 lacks title, slightly foxed thro.-out, hf. red leath. gt. (D. Nov.24; 2232) DM 2,000

ARTISTES DU LIVRE
Ill.:– Carlègle, Hemard, Laboureur, Dignimont. Lobel-Riche, Vertès, Marty, Bonnard, Chomit, etc. Paris, 1928-33. 21 vols. only (of 24, Lacks nos. 5,7 & 0). 4to. On vell., sewed. (HD. Dec.16; 62) Frs. 4,300

ARTOIS
– Plans et Cartes des Villes d'Artois. N.p., ca. 1700. 133 copper-engraved maps & views, engraved title-p. almost detchd., some offsetting, light foxing & staining, cont. mott. cf., elab. gt.-decor. spine. (CBA. Dec.10; 224) $120

ARTS OF CHINA
See— AKIYAMA, Terukazu & others –
AKIYAMA, Terukazu & Matsubara, Sabura –
YONEZAWA, Yoshiho & Kawakita, Michiaki

ARZEI LEVANON: Midrash Konen; Ha'Emunah Ve'Habitachon, Ha'Nikud; Ha'Chashmal; Mayan Ha'Chochma; Pirkei Heichalot
Venice,. 1600-01. *1st. Edn.* 4to. Owners' sigs. on title, slight staining in margin, hf. leath. (S. Oct.24; 39) *Sol.* £240

ARZT, Der, eine Medizinische Wochenschrift ...
Ed.:– Johann August Unzer. Lüneberg, Leipzig, Hamburg, 1769. 6 vols. Cont. hf. cf., spines gt. (C. Dec.9; 331) *Braecklein.* £190

ASAEL, Yehuda Mehatov
– Kisa'Ot Le'Vet David. Verona, 1646. *1st. Edn.* 4to. Tear in title affecting 2 words, owner's sig. on title, staining, slight worming not affecting text, few ll. trimmed, mod. mor. (S. Oct.24; 68) *Hirschler.* £140

ASBJØRNSEN, Peter Christen
– Norge Fremstillet i Tegninger. Ed.:– C. Tönsberg. Ill.:– C. Müller., E. Baerentzen & others. Christiania, 1848. 4 vols. Ob. fo. Some text browning & foxing, plts. slightly browned, Vol. 1 with slight stain thro.-out, cont. hf. leath., bumped & worn. (R. Oct. 13; 3299) DM 1,220

ASBJØRNSEN, Peter Christen & Moe, Jørgen
– A l'Est du Soleil et a l'Quest de la Lune. Trans.:– E. Pilon. Ill.:– Kay Nielsen. Paris, 1919. *(1500) numbered.* Lge. 4to. Some foxing, partly unc., hand-bnd. hf. mor. gt., gt. decor., orig. wraps. bnd in, sigd. 'SIM/KRA/REL'. (V. Oct.1; 4325) DM 500
– East of the Sun & West of the Moon. Old Tales from the North. Ill.:– Kai Nielsen. L., ca. 1920. Orig. cl., some stains. (B. Feb.8; 624) Fls. 450
– – Anr. Edn. Ill.:– Kay Nielsen. N.d. Sm. 4to. Orig. cl. (P. Sep.29; 390) *Sitwell.* £60

ASCHAM, Roger
– A Report & Discourse of the Affairs & State of Germany & the Emperour Charles His Court. [1570?]. *1st. Edn.* 4to. 3 pp. biography of author in 16th. C. hand loosely inserted, pol. cf. gt. [STC 830] (BBA. Jan.19; 118) *Pickering & Chatto.* £400

ASCHERI, Gio, Andrea
– Notizie Storiche intorno alla Riunione delle Famiglie in Alberghi in Genova. Genova, 1846. 4to. Old hf. cl. (HD. Oct.21; 16) Frs. 1,200

ASELLI, Caspare
– De Lactibus sive Lacteis Venis. Leiden, 1640. 4to. Cont. vell., rebkd. (SG. Oct.6; 18) $400

ASH, Edward C.
– Dogs: their History & Development. 1927. *1st. Edn.* 2 vols. 4to. 160 plts., frontis.'s loose, orig. cl., sm. tear in 1 spine. (SKC. May 4; 1830) £80

ASHBEE, Charles Robert
– An Endeavour Towards the Teaching of John Ruskin & William Morris. [Essex House Pr., 1901]. *(350) numbered.* Orig. vell., lightly soiled. (CSK. Nov.25; 146) £55
– Modern English Silverwock: an Essay ... Together with a Series of Designs by the author. Essex House Pr., 1909. *(200) numbered. & sigd. by arthor.* 4to. 100 litho. plts., some partially hand-cold., a few very slightly spotted, orig. cl., faded (mainly spine). (S. May 1; 674) *Sims.* £260

ASHBEE, Henry Spencer
– An Iconography of Don Quixote 1605-1895. 1895. 4to. Orig. buckram-bkd. bds.; H.M. Nixon coll. (BBA. Oct.6; 183) *Quaritch.* £100

ASHBEE, Janet E.
– The Essex House Song Book. Essex House Pr., [1905]. *(205) numbered.* Orig. vell.-bkd. bds., lightly rubbed. (CSK. Apr.6; 12) £50

ASHBERY, John
– The New Spirit. N.Y., [1970]. *(65) numbered & sigd.* 4to. Pict. wraps. (SG. Mar.1; 9) $110
– Sunrise in Suburbia. N.Y., 1968. *(26) lettered & sigd.* Ob. sm. 8vo. Wraps., patterned d.-w. (SG. Mar.1; 10) $130
– Turandot & Other Poems. Ill.:– Jane Freilicher. N.Y., 1953. *1st. Edn., (300).* Orig. decor. wraps., stitched as iss.; Marshall Clements & Frederic Dannay copy. (CNY. Dec.16; 10) $450

ASHBURNHAM, Earl of
– The Ashburnham Library. Catalogue of the Magnificent Collection of Printed Books. 1897-98. 20 cold. plts. only (of 22?), cuttings referring to sale loosely inserted, cont. hf. mor.; H.M. Nixon coll., with his MS. notes on front fly-lf. (BBA. Oct.6; 145) *Beres.* £65

ASHE, Thomas
– Travels in America, Performed in 1806, for the Purpose of Exploring the Rivers Alleghany, Monogahela, Ohio, & Mississippi. L., 1808. *1st. Edn.* 3 vols. 12mo. Some foxing, orig. bds., unc., corners worn, spines chipped; the Rt. Hon. Visc. Eccles copy. [Sabin 2180] (CNY. Nov.18; 10) $300

ASHENDENE PRESS
– A Chronological List, with Prices, of the Forty Books printed at The Ashendene Press MDCCCXCV-MCMXXXV. Chelsea, 1935. *Ltd. Edn., for private circulation.* 1 vol. Fo. Ptd. wraps. (*With:*) – A Descriptive Bibliography of the Books printed at The Ashendene Press MDCCCXCV-MCMXXXV. [By Charles Harry St. John Hornby]. [San Franc., 1976]. *Facs. of 1935 Edn., (375).* 1 vol. 4to. Cl. (SG. Sep.15; 14) $110
– A Descriptive Bibliography of the Books printed at the Ashendene Press MDCCCXCV-MCMXXXV. [By Charles Harry St. John Hornby]. Chelsea, Ash. Pr., 1935. *(390) numbered & sigd. by Hornby.* Fo. 2 errata slips tipped in, orig. mor., slightly marked. (S. Nov.22; 295) *Carlson.* £450
See— APOCRYPHA
See— CERVANTES SAAVEDRA, Miguel de
See— FRANCIS OF ASSISI, Saint
See— LONGUS
See— THUCYDIDES
See— VERGILIUS MARO, Publius

ASHER BEN YECHIEL
– She'Eilot U'Teshuvot. Venice, 1608. *3rd. Edn.* Fo. Owner's sig. on title, holes in title crudely reprd. with loss of some letters, creased, browned & stained, trimmed with loss of parts of few letters, hf. leath., marb. paper bds. (S. Oct.24; 69) *Klein.* £280

ASHKENAZI, Bezalel
– She'Eilot U'Teshuvot. Venice, 1590 or 1595?. *1st. Edn.* Fo. Tears in title affecting some decor. & 1 letter, staining mostly in inner margin, slight worming, margins of last lf. reprd. without loss of text, buckram. (S. Oct.24; 70) *Klein.* £280

ASHKENAZI, Elieser
– Peirush Megillat Esther. Cremona, 1576. *1st. Edn.* 4to. Some margins reprd. not affecting text, some staining. mod. mor. (S. Oct.24; 71) *Stern.* £320

ASHKENAZI, Shmuel Yafo
– Yefe Mar'eh. Venice, 1590. *1st. Edn.* Fo. Owner's sig. on title, 2 tears in title not affecting text, worming affecting some letters, staining, some ll. browned, slightly foxed, lacks unpaginated correction lf. (added later), bds.; M. Gasher stp. on title. (S. Oct.24; 72a) *Jansen.* £320
– Yefe To'Ar. Venice, 1596-1606. *1st. Edn.* Fo. Owner's sigs. on title, some worming & staining, last 3 ll. crudely reprd. not affecting text, lacks index (ptd. later) as usual, buckram. (S. Oct.24; 72) *Jansen.* £340

ASHLEY, John
– Memoirs & Considerations Concerning the Trade & Revenues of the British Colonies in America. L., 1740-43. *1st. Edns.* 2 pts. Panel. cf. antique; sig. of Philip Morant, the Rt. Hon. Visc. Eccles copy. [Sabin 2192 & 2193] (CNY. Nov.18; 11) $220

ASHMOLE, Elias
– The Institutions, Laws & Ceremonies of the Most Noble Order of the Garter. 1693. Fo. Old panel. cf., rebkd.; Sir Ivar Colquhoun, of Luss copy. [Wing A 3984] (CE. Mar.22; 12) £270

ASPIN, Jehoshaphat
– A Familiar Treatise on Astronomy, to Accompany Urania's Mirror. 1834. Text vol. with 4 plts. (1 torn), s.-c. with folding plt. (torn), 32 hand-cold. plts., orig. bds., defect. (P. Jan.12; 154) *Treleaver.* £80

ASPLUND, Karl
– Zorn's Engraved Work. Trans.:– Edward Adams-Ray. Stockholm, 1920-21. *(300) numbered.* 2 vols. Lge. 4to. 288 reproductions, ex-liby., hf. mor. (SG. May 3; 396) $700

ASSELINEAU, Charles
– L'Enfer du Bibliophile. Ill.:– Leon Lebegue. Paris, 1905. *(800). (100) De Luxe on japan.* 3 states of engrs., including 1 in col., mntd. on guards, red mor., by Affolter, gt.-decor. decor. spine, mor. doubls., inner dentelle, wrap. & spine preserved; K. Kettanech ex-libris. (HD. Dec.9; 93) Frs. 1,600

ASSEMBLEE NATIONALE
- **Les Enfans de Sodome à l'Assemblée Nationale, ou Dépuation de l'Arbre de la Manchette. - Fredaines Lubriques de Jxx Fxx Maury**.... Paris, 1790. 2 pts. in 1 vol. 12mo. 19th. C. hf. mor., mosaic spine. (HD. May 3; 35) Frs. 4,000

ASSIETTE AU BEURRE, L'
Ill.:– Steinlen, Cheret, Willette, Grandjouan, Hermann-Paul, & others. Paris, 1901-03. Nos. 1-104 (lacks 11 nos.), & 2 issues 'Hors Série'. 4to. Orig. wraps., some soiled or spotted. (S. Nov.21; 48) *Arts Anciens.* £140
– – **Anr. Edn.** Ill.:– Juan Gris, Fr. Kupka, J. Pissarro, K. von Dongen, T. Steinlen etc. Paris, 1901-06. Yrs. I-V in 5 vols. 4to. Includes special part 'Crimes et Chatiments' with 23 orig. lithos. by Vallotton, 1000 cold. ills., most full-p., including many orig. lithos., light margin browning, some pp. loose, 2 pp. pasted, 1 with tear, orig. linen, blind & gold-tooled in Jugendstil, relief stpd. ill. inset in upr. cover, slightly spotted. (HT. May 9; 1721) DM 3,000
– – **Anr. Edn.** Ill.:– Grandjouan, Ibels, Gris & others. Paris, 1901-10. 79 pts. (consecutive) in 5 vols. Fo. Many pts. defect. & loose, some incompl., hf. linen, bumped, w.a.f. (HK. Nov.11; 3381b) DM 460
– – **Anr. Edn.** Ill.:– Ed. Bernard, W. Crane, R. Flores, A. Kubin, Steinlen, etc. Paris, 1905 & 1907. Nos. 197-248 & 301-352 (lacks 230 & 233): 2 years in 4 vols. 4to. Hf. cl. (B. Apr.27; 609) Fls. 475

ASSMANN, R. & Berson, A.
- **Wissenschaftliche Luftfahrten ausgeführt vom Deutschen Verein zur Förderung der Luftschiffahrt un Berlin.** Braunschweig, 1899-1900. Fo. Spotted, orig. sewed. (R. Oct.12; 1609) DM 450

ASSOCIAZIONE TIPOGRAFICO-LIBRARIA ITALIANA
- **Catalogo Collettivo della Libreria Italiana.** Milan, [1881]. *New Edn.* 4 vols. including Index. Sm. 4to. Unif. qtr. leath., cl., spines & corners badly worn, orig. wraps. bnd. in. (SG. May 17; 142) $100

ASSYRIAN DICTIONARY of the Oriental Institute of the University of Chicago
Ed.:– I.J. Gelb. B. Landsberger, A.L. Oppenheim & c. Chic., 1956-73. Vols. 1-9, 16 & 21, in 12 vols. 4to. Cl. (B. Jun.21; 5) Fls. 1,600

ASTAUT, Jules Léon
- **Les Parnassiens de la Jaune Paléarctique.** Leipzig, 1889. 32 cold. plts., excerpt from letter by Edward Janson pasted in, hf. mor.; Robert H. Rippon's copy with his sig. (SKC. Oct.26; 328) £140

ASTELL, Mary
[–] **An Essay in Defence of the Female Sex**.... 1697. *3rd. Edn.* (*Bound with:*) - **Reflections Upon Marriage.** 1706. *3rd. Edn.* Together 2 works in 1 vol. Cont. panel. cf. (TA. Nov.17; 412) £110
– – **Anr. Copy.** (*Bound with:*) [–] **Reflections upon Marriage.** 1706. *3rd. Edn.* Together 2 works in 1 vol. Cont. panel. cf. (TA. May15; 492) £65
[–] **A Serious Proposal to the Ladies.** 1697 (pt. 1 dtd. 1701). *1st. coll. Edn. (pt. 1 4th Edn.).* 2 pts. in 1. 12mo. General title holed with loss & reprd., browned & spotted, cont. cf., rebkd. & cornered, rubbed, w.a.f. [Wing A4065 & A4065a] (CSK. Jun.1; 164) £120

ASTESANUS DE AST
[–] [**Summa de Casibus Conscientiae**]. Venice, J. de Colonia & J. Manthen, 18 Mar. 1478. Books 5-8, index & register only. Fo. Wide margins, lacks final blank, disbnd.; the Walter Goldwater copy. [BMC V, 233; Goff A-1165] (SG. Dec.1; 38) $375

ASTLE, Thomas
- **The Origin & Progress of Writing.** L., 1784. *1st. Edn.* 4to. 31 engraved plts. on 28 ll., including 10 folding, hf.-title, 1 plt. torn, hf. cf., slightly rubbed. (S. Dec.20; 813) *Maggs.* £50
– – **Anr. Edn.** L., 1803. *2nd. Edn.* Fo. Engraved port., 32 plts., few cold., some offsetting, cont. cf.

gt.; Lincoln's Inn Liby. stp. on upr. cover. (S. Apr.10; 384) *Marlborough.* £160
– – **Anr. Edn.** L., 1876. Some light spotting, orig. hf. leath., gt. decor., lightly worn & bumped, stains. (HK. May 17; 3401) DM 440
See— **GROSE, Francis & others**

ASTLEY, Phillip
- **The Modern Riding Master.** L., 1775. Cf. gt. by J. Larkins. (P. Sep.8; 118) *Sutherland.* £260

ASTLEY, Thomas
- **A New General Collection of Voyages & Travels.** 1745-47. *[1st. Edn.].* 4 vols. 4to. Cont. cf. (CSK. Aug.19; 21) £520
– – **Anr. Copy.** 4 vols. 4to. Lacks 2 plts., some slight browning or staining, cont. cf., worn, w.a.f. (S. Nov.1; 2) *Vine.* £180
– – **Anr. Copy.** 4 vols. 4to. Maps, plts., some browning & offsetting, cont. cf., worn, some covers loose, w.a.f. (SPB. May 17; 564) $400
– – **Anr. Edn.** L., priv. ptd., 1746. *1st. Edn.* Vol. III only. 4to. 60 full-p. & folded copperplt. maps, charts, & views, 1 plt. with ink spot in 1 margin, some browning, orig. stpd. cf., upr. cover detchd., covers worn. (HA. Feb.24; 302) $150

ASTON, Francis William
- **Isotopes.** L., 1922. *1st. Edn.* Orig. cl. (BBA. Mar.21; 37) *Heuer.* £50
– – **Anr. Copy.** Orig. cl.; John D. Stanitz coll. (SPB. Apr.25; 21) $200

ASTRANA MARIN, Luis
- **Vida Ejemplar y Heroica de Miguel de Cervantes Saavedra.** Madrid, 1948-58. 7 vols. Fo. Linen. (DS. Apr.27; 2225) Pts. 32,000

ATAR, Chaim Ibn
- **Orchot Chaim.** Venice, 1741-42. *1st. Edn.* 2 pts. in 1 vol. Fo. Some ll. reprd. without loss of text, edges frayed, discold. & stained, upr. margin trimmed with loss of parts of letters, buckram. (S. Oct.24; 73) *Davis.* £2,000

ATGET, Eugene
- **E. Atget, Lichtbilder.** Preface:– Camille Recht. Port.:– Berenice Abbott. Leipzig, [1930]. *1st. Edn. in German. (1000) numbered.* 4to. Separate pamphlet of captions tipped in lr. cover, some pencil notations to preface, cl., rubbed & soiled, spine ends & corners worn; port. sigd. in ink by Abbott. (SG. May 10; 9) $300
- **Photographe de Paris.** Preface:– 'Pierre Mac Orlan.' N.Y., [1930]. *1st. Amer. Edn.* 4to. Port., 96 full-p. reproductions, separate pamphlet of captions tipped in lr. cover, some dampstaining along lr. edges, affecting only plt. margins, gt.-lettered moiré cl., minor stains. (SG. Nov.10; 15) $130
- **20 Photographs.** Ed.:– Berenice Abbott. N.Y., 1956. *(100).* 4to. Title with editors dedication, text & 20 plts. loose in orig. linen portfo., 1 spot. (H. May 23; 1449) DM 3,600

ATHENAEUS, Clemens Alexandrinus & others
- **Ex Veterum Comicorum Fabulis, quae Integrae non extant Sententiae.** Paris, 1554. 12mo. Crimson mor. gt. (P. Apr.12; 288) *Poole.* £90

ATHENIAN LETTERS, or, The Epistolary Correspondence ...
1798. 2 vols. 4to. Mod. hf. cf. gt. (P. Jun.7; 95) £65

ATKINS, Sir Robert
- **The Ancient & Present State of Glostershire.** L., 1712. Fo. Port.-frontis., 68 plts. (62 double-p.), 1 defect., frontis. laid down, many text-pp. reprd., old cf. defect., as a collection of plts., w.a.f. (P. May 17; 13) *Gilbert.* £420

ATKINSON, Capt. George Francklin
- **The Campaign in India 1857-58.** L., 1859. Fo. Tinted litho. title, 25 plts. on 19 ll., lightly spotted thro.-out, later hf. mor. (CSK. Feb.24; 22) £120
– – **Anr. Copy.** Tinted litho. title, 25 plts. on 19 ll., most ll. torn, spotted, orig. cl., dampstained, ex-liby. (CSK. Jan.13; 101) £95
– – **Anr. Copy.** Tinted litho. title with vig., 25 views on 19 plts., text & plts. detchd., few margins slightly frayed, text spotted, plts. slightly spotted, orig. cl., worn. (S. Mar.6; 22) *Maggs.* £80

ATKINSON, Henry
- **Expedition up the Missouri.** Wash., 1826. Light foxing, three-qtr. maroon mor. (LH. Apr.15; 262) $120

ATKINSON, J.
- **The Miseries of Human Life.** 1807. Ob. 8vo. 16 hand-cold. aquatints, 1 text p. loose, orig. bds., unc., jnt. brkn., spine chipped. (SKC. May 4; 1612)£75

ATKINSON, James, of Oldbury
- **An Account of the State of Agriculture & Grazing in New South Wales.** L., 1826. *1st. Edn.* Lge. engraved folding map, hand-cold. in outl., folding hand-cold. aquatint view, 4 aquatint plts. (3 cold.), advt. lf. at end, orig. ptd. paper bds., unc. (CA. Apr.3; 136) Aus. $7,500

ATKINSON, James
See— **WAKELY, Andrew & Atkinson, James**

ATKINSON, James & Wilson, Henry
- **A Compleat System of Navigation; In Two Parts. I. Atkinson's Epitome. II. Navigation New Modell'd**.... Dublin, 1767. Extra 19th. C. diagram & mathematical verse tipped in, mor. gt. by Brian Frost & Co., Bath. (TA. Aug.18; 352) £65

ATKINSON, John Augustus
- **Sketches in Afghaunistan.** L., 1842. Fo. Tinted litho. title, 24 (of 25) tinted litho. plts., some spotting, mainly marginal, a few margins frayed, mor.-bkd. cont. cl., rebkd. preserving orig. spine. (C. Nov.16; 48) *Walford.* £240
– – **Anr. Copy.** Fo. Loose in mod. wraps., disbnd. (TA. Sep.15; 67) £190

ATKINSON, John Augustus & Walker, James
- **A Picturesque Representation of the Manners, Customs & Amusements of the Russians.** 1803-4. 3 vols. in 1. Fo. 100 hand-cold. plts., text in Engl. & Fr., lacks port., some spotting, cf. gt., defect. (P. Oct.20; 116) £220
– – **Anr. Copy.** 3 vols. in 1. Atlas fo. Port., 100 cold. plts., each with text lf. in Engl. & Fr., plts. on Whatman paper dtd. 1823, some text ll. foxed, no hf.-titles, ex-liby., cont. cf., gt.-tooled borders, spine gt. (SG. May 3; 25) $550

ATKINSON, William B.
- **The Physicians & Surgeons of the United States.** Ed.:– William B. Atkinson. Phila., 1878. *1st. Edn.* Lge. 8vo. Orig. hf. mor., spine torn. (SG. Mar.22; 206) $100

ATLAS GEOGRAPHUS: or A Compleat System of Geography.
Ill.:– Herman Moll. L., 1711-14. Vols. 1-4 only. 4to. 78 of 87 engraved plts. & maps, some torn, browned thro.-out, cont. cf., worn, some covers loose, w.a.f. (BBA. May 3; 251) *Faupel.* £210

ATLASES
- **American Military Pocket Atlas.** [1776]. 6 lge. folding maps, outl. cold., a few repairs, cont. cf.-bkd. bds.; Will. Green bkplt. (BBA. Sep.29; 128) *Goldsmith.* £1,000
- [**Atlas**]. Ill.:– Carl-Gottfried Eicher &c. Early 19th. C. Ob. 4to. 29 (of 34?) engraved plts., bds. (HD. Mar.9; 102) Frs. 1,000
- **Atlas Elemental ... Nuevo Tratado de la Esfera** .... Madrid, 1786. 22 engraved maps, cold. & folding, 2 folding cold. engrs., no bdg. stated. (DS. Mar.23; 2018) Pts. 30,000
- **Atlas en Miniature, ou Léger Aperçu de Géographie Physique et Politique, à la Jeunesse Curieuse et qui désire s'instruire.** Paris, ca. 1825. 5 pts. Ob. 8vo. Orig. bds., slightly worn, orig. pict. s.-c., slightly rubbed; van Veer coll. (S. Feb.28; 33) £500
- **Atlas Moderne ... par plusiers Auteurs.** Paris, [1762-73]. 4to. Wide margin, 2 engraved plts, 75 cold. double-p. copper engraved maps, a few maps slightly spotted, cont. hf. leath., defect. (D. Nov.23; 744) DM 3,000
– – **Anr. Copy.** Fo. 73 (of 74) double-p. outl. cold. maps, on yellowish bd.-like paper, cont. marb. leath. gt., corners bumped. (GB. Nov.3; 2) DM 2,600
- **Atlas National Illustré des 86 Départements et des Possessions de la France.** Ill.:– after V. Levasseur. Ob. fo. Engraved title, 100 engraved outl. cold. maps & 1 folding map, with tears bkd., slightly

spotted, cont. hf. leath., spine worn. (D. Nov.23; 745) DM 900
- **Atlas National Portatif de la France, Destiné à l'Instruction Publique.** Paris, 1791. Ob. Fo. Engraved title, 91 engraved maps (2 double-p.), mostly hand-cold. in wash & outl., inscr. on hf.-title, cont. vell. (S. Apr.9; 73) *Quaritch.* £250
- **Atlas Novus, das ist Abbildung vnd Beschreibung von allen Ländern des Erdreichs.** Amst., G. Blaeu, 1635. Lge. fo. Wide margin, engraved title typographically pasted in empty centre of engraved border, title bkd. in side margins & other parts, 1 tear bkd., owners entry on title, cont. orig. vell., decor., 4 ties, spine renewed with old leath., slightly spotted, corners strengthened, spine renewed. (GF. Nov.12; 680) Sw. Frs. 26,000
- **[Atlas of Plates, Plans & Maps Relating to Egypt].** Ill.:– after T. Powell. L., [T. Payne, 1810]. Atlas fo. 25 plts., maps, etc., hf. cf., as an atlas, w.a.f. (GM. Dec.7; 726) £110
- **Black's General Atlas: Comprehending Sixty-One Maps from the Latest & Most Authentic Sources.** Edinb., A. & C. Black, 1844. Fo. 61 steel-engraved maps, borders hand-tinted, some moderate soiling or foxing, some margin darkening, three-qtr. mor. & cl., covers rubbed, stained & soiled. (CBA. Mar.3; 14) $190
- **Britannia et Hibernia.** Maps:– R. Morden. 1714. Vol. 1 only. 4to. 3 plts., 16 maps, text & plts. loose, bdg. not stated. (P. Dec.8; 408) *Kentish.* £110
- **Cartes Provenant de l'Atlas Universel de Géographie Physique, Politique, Statistique et Minéralogique sur l'Echelle de Vandermaelen.** Ill.:– H. Ode. Bruxelles, 1827. 238 maps, outls. cold., lacks maps 14-17 in 'Amerique Septentrionale', 41 in 'Oceanie' & 31-33 in 'Afrique', in sheets in 2 portfos. (LM. Oct.22; 107) B.Frs. 180,000
- **Description Hydrographique et Géographique de l'Isle de Corse.** Lausanne, 1769. 2 vols., including Atlas. 12mo. & 4to. Text sewed, Atlas in ll., box. (HD. Oct.21; 17) Frs. 14,000
- **Dispatch Atlas.** 1863. Fo. Some maps outl. hand-cold., some ll. slightly soiled, a few reprd., cont. hf. roan. (BBA. Sep.29; 132) *Faupel.* £190
- **The Edinburgh Geographical & Historical Atlas.** Ca. 1830. Fo. 70 double-p. cold. engraved maps, cont. hf. cf., covers detchd. (SKC. Nov.18; 2060) £210
- **[Europe & Asia].** V.p., 18th. C. Fo. Collection of 110 double-p. engraved maps by Schenck, Visscher, Homann, Ottens, & others, most partly hand-cold., some browning & soiling, some tears, old cf., worn, as a coll. of maps, w.a.f. (SPB. Dec.13; 494) $4,500
- **Géographie Mathématique, Physique et Politique de Toutes les Parties du Monde. Atlas.** Paris, 1804. Fo. 45 cold. engraved maps, most double-p., cont. bds., unc. (HD. Mar.19; 6) Frs. 2,000
- **[Germany, & others].** V.p., v.d. (mainly mid-18th. C.). Fo. Collection of 60 engraved maps & city views by Homann, Danckerts, Schenck, Valck, & others, most double-p. maps fully or partly hand-cold., slight browning & soiling, minor tears, sheep-bkd. bds., worn, as a coll. of maps, w.a.f. (SPB. Dec.13; 495) $1,500
- **Mapas Españoles de America.** Madrid, 1951. *(312).* Pts. XV-XVII in 1 vol. Fo. 78 facs. maps, some double-p., some heightened with gold, orig. hf. mor. gt., untrimmed. (TA. Apr.19; 78) £190
- **Middle East.** 18th. C. 80 uncold. maps & plts., hf. cf., worn. (P. Dec.8; 401) £160
- **Neptune Americo-Septentrional ... depuis le Groenland inclusivement, jusques et compris le Golfe du Mexique.** Ill.:– after Holland, Southack, Des Barres, Fisher, Blamey, & others. [Paris], Depot General des Cartes, Plans et Journauz de la Marine. [1775-80]. Lge. fo. Engraved titles, 26 engraved mapsheets, most double-p., some slight offsetting or surface dirt, cont. cf. gt., slightly worn. (S. Dec.1; 233) *Burden.* £3,100
- **Nieuwe Atlas van de Provincie Friesland, bevattende Kaarten de de Dertig Gemeenten ... Alsmede van Ameland en Schiermonnikoog.** Leeuwaerden, 1849-59. *(286) for subscribers.* Lge. fo. Cont. hf. cf. (VG. Sep.14; 789) Fls. 2,700
- **Nouvel Atlas des Enfans, ou Principes Clairs pour prendre facilement en peu de Tems la Géographie.** Amst. & Leiden, 1799. *8th. Edn.* 12mo. Hf.-title, 24 hand-cold. folding engraved maps, short tear at

inner margin of 1 map & 2 text ll., orig. bds., unc. soiled., van Veen coll. (S. Feb.28; 123) £70
- **Plans of Various Lakes & Rivers between Lake Huron & the River Ottawa; to Accompany the Geological Reports for 1853-54-55-56.** Toronto, 1857. 4to. 22 folding litho. maps, some with sm. tears along folds, cont. roan-bkd. cl., worn. (CSK. Dec.16; 50) £70
- **Recueil de Cartes intéressant L'Espagne et le Portugal.** Ill.:– De L'Isle, Jaillot, Baillieul, Roussel. Early 18th. C. Lge. fo. 22 maps, double-p. or folding, outt cold., cont. bdg., lacks all but part of spine. (HD. Feb.29; 34) Frs. 3,000
- **Der Rhein von den Quellen in der Schweiz bis zur Mündung in die Nordsee. Historisch-Topographischer Damp-Schiffahats-Atlas, mit den Abstechern auf der Eisenbahn ....** Zweibrücken, 1842. Section titles pasted, ll. lightly foxed, cold. pen litho. ornament from title ll. slightly discold., orig. bd. box, orig. bd. s.-c., slightly spotted & bumped. (V. Sep.29; 112) DM 3,000
- **The Royal Engagement Pocket Atlas.** L., 1788. 12mo. Orig. engraved wraps., lightly soiled, in cont. red mor. s.-c., elab. gt., multi-col. mor. onlays. (CSK. Nov.25; 15) £160
- **The Royal Illustrated Atlas of Modern Geography.** Ca. 1860. Fo. 76 maps, plans & ills., some double-p., cont. hf. cf., rubbed. (TA. Apr.19; 43) £360
- **Sammelband aus Berghaus, Physikalischer Atlas.** Gotha, 1837-47. Ob. fo. 84 engraved & cold. maps & plts., 3 tables, many plts. Loose, foxing & staining, hf. leath., defect. (D. Nov.23; 743) DM 400
- **Tabulae Geographicae.** Ill.:– F. Bertin, J.V. Gelais, A. Recurti, & others, after or attributable to N. or G. Sanson, A. Ortelius, Pierre du Val, & others. Padua, Stamperia del Seminario, 1697. 4 pts. in 1 vol. Fo. 94 maps of the ancient world on 95 mapsheets, most double-p., lacks? 2 maps in pt. 4 (replaced by 2 dupls. of Ewich's map of the Low Countries), a few margin wormholes not affecting engraved surface, reprd., some faint browning or staining, cont. vell. bds., worn, reprd. (S. Dec.1; 196) *Burgess.* £1,800
- **– Anr. Edn.** Padova, 1699. 4 pts. in 1 vol. 4to. 1 single-p. map, 84 double-p. engraved maps, old vell., some wear. (TA. Sep.15; 63) £620
See— AMERICAN CIVIL WAR
See— UNITED STATES GEOLOGICAL SURVEY

AUBERT, Ed.
- **La Vallée d'Aoste.** Paris, 1860. 4to. Sm. stains at head of some ll., publishers hf. havanna chagrin, blind-decor., decor. spine, some grazing. (HD. Dec.9; 94) Frs. 5,500

AUBERY DU MAURIER, Louis
- **Histoire de l'Exécution de Cabrière et de Merindol et Autres Lieux de Provence....** Paris, 1645. *1st. Edn. in Fr.* 4to. Cont. cf., Michel-Etienne Turgot arms, spine decor. (HD. Nov.9; 109) Frs. 8,000

AUBIGNE, Th.-Agrippa d'
- **Les Avantures du Baron de Faeneste.** Le Dezert, 1640. Ruled, violet blind-decor. mor. by Boyet, mor. liners, gt. dentelle; from Marquis de La Baume Pluvinel liby. (HD. Mar.29; 2) Frs. 1,400
- **– Anr. Edn.** Ed.:– Pr. Mérimée. Paris, 1855. *Orig. Edn. of Preface & Notes.* Sm. 12mo. Hf. mor. gt., corners, by Cuzin, spine decor., unc. (HD. May 16; 1) Frs. 1,100
- **Mémoires.** Paris, 1731. *1st. Edn. with this title.* 2 vols. in 1. 12mo. Red mor. by Derome, spine decor.; from libys. of Pâris de Meyzieu & Destailleur. (HD. Mar.29; 1) Frs. 10,000

AUBIN, Nicolas
- **[–] Dictionnaire de Marine contenant les Termes de la Navigation et de l'Architecture Navale.** Amst., 1722. 4to. Cont. spr. cf., spine decor. (HD. Jun.18; 2) Frs. 4,500
- **– Anr. Copy.** 4to. 1st. ll. mntd. on guards, cont. cf., spine decor. (HD. Mar.9; 46) Frs. 3,600

AUBLET, Fusée
- **Histoire des Plantes de La Guiane Françoise.** Paris, 1775. 4 vols. 4to. Frontis., 392 plts., some browning, liby. stp. on titles, qtr. cf., defect. (P. Nov.24; 243) *Walford.* £700

AUBREY, John
- **The Natural History & Antiquities of the County of Surrey.** [1718]-19. 5 vols. Some margins lightly soiled, cont. cf., rubbed, 2 vols. rebkd., old spines laid down. (CSK. Jul.6; 118) £180

AUCASSIN & NICOLETTE
Ill.:– Lucien Pissarro. Hammersmith, Eragny. Pr., 1903. *(230).* Title foxed, orig. bds., corners bumped, end-papers browned. (GB. May 5; 3096) DM 1,000

AUCTORITATES NOTABILES DE CASTITATE ET MORIBUS
[Cologne, Retro Minores], after 1500. Sm. 8vo. Mod. bds.; the Walter Goldwater copy. [C. 728; Goff A-1025] (SG. Dec.1; 39) $250

AUDEBERT, Jean Baptiste & Vieillot, Louis Jean Pierre
- **Histoire Naturelle et Générale des Grimpereaux et des Oiseaux de Paradis.** Paris, 1802. Lge. fo. Wide margin, some plts slightly foxed, red hf. leath., bumped in parts. (D. Nov.23; 692) DM 9,500
- **Oiseaux Dorés ou à Reflets Metalliques.** Paris, 1800-02. *(200) with captions ptd. in gold.* 2 vols. Fo. 190 col.-ptd. plts. (1 double-p.), a few plts. spotted, cont. red hf. mor., gt. spines, reprd. (C. Jun.27; 137) *Chaponniere.* £13,000
- **– – Anr. Edn.** Paris, [1800-]02. 2 vols. Fo. 189 (of 190) hand-cold. plts., many illuminated in gold & silver, some folding, plt. 14 in watercolour, cont. hf. cf. gt., hinges reprd. (P. Mar.15; 255) *Marks.* £2,200

AUDEN, Wystan Hugh
- **Poems.** S.H.S., 1928. *1st. Edn.* 16mo. Limitation corrected from 'about 45 copies' to 'no 24 (about)', ptd. errata lf. loosely inserted, orig. ptd. paper wraps; pres. inscrs. from author & publisher to David Ayerst. (C. Nov.9; 171) *Gekoski.* £6,200
- **– – Anr. Edn.** L., [1930]. *1st. Edn.* Orig. ptd. wraps., unopened; Frederic Dannay copy. (CNY. Dec.16; 12) $450
- **– – Anr. Copy.** Orig. ptd. wraps., soiled, a little worn; sigd. by author, Frederic Dannay copy. (CNY. Dec.16; 13) $260
- **Selections from Poems.** Ill.:– Henry Moore. Petersburg Pr., 1974. *(300) roman-numbered & sigd. by artist, with 4 additional lithos. numbered & sigd. by artist in separate portfo.* Fo. Orig. linen, fitted box. (S. Nov.22; 340) *Minou.* £600
- **Three Songs for St. Cecilia's Day.** [N.Y.], priv. ptd., 1941. *1st. Edn. (250).* 12mo. Ptd. wraps., braded ribbon tie. (SG. Jan.12; 17) $300
- **Two Songs.** N.Y., 1968. *(26) lettered & sigd.* Ob. sm. 8vo. Wraps. (SG. Mar.1; 12) $275

AUDEN, Wystan Hugh & Isherwood, Christopher
- **The Ascent of F6.** 1937. Slightly soiled, orig. cl., soiled, spine worn; front free end-paper inscr. 'To Jackie with love from Wystan & Christopher'. (CSK. Apr.6; 183) £50

AUDENAERDE
- **Annales du Cercle Archéologique & Historique d'Audenaerde. Handelingen van den Oudheid– & Geschiedkundigen Kring van Audenaerde.** Audenaerde, 1906 [& later]. Vols. I-XIV, Pt. 1 (Lacks Vol. X, Pt. 1 & Vol. XII, Pt. 2). Bdg. not stated. (LM. Oct.22; 61) B.Frs. 18,000

AUDIBERTO, C.M.
- **Regiae Villae poetice Descriptae.** Turin, 1711. Sm. 4to. Lacks 1 plt., additional engraved title with upr. margin shaved, slight dampstaining, margin worming sometimes affecting text & plts., mod. cf.-bkd. bds., w.a.f. (S. Nov.1; 68) *Edistar.* £110

AUDIN, Marius
- **Histoire de l'Imprimerie par l'Image.** Paris, 1928-29. 4 vols. Sq. 4to. Red three-qtr. lev., orig. wraps. bnd. in. (SG. Feb.16; 11) $150

AUDOT
- **Roma descritta e dipinta coi suoi minori Stati Vicini ....** Cremona, 1857. Approx. 90 steel engraved plts., some double & triple, hf. vell., as a coll., w.a.f. (CR. Jun.6; 94) Lire 280,000

AUDOT, Padre
Italie, La Sicile, Les Iles Eoliennes ... La Sardaigne, La Toscane ... La Lombardo-Venetie ... Text:– after Chateaubriant, Lamartine, Saint Non & others. Ill:– C.D. de la Chavanne, Saint Germain, Leduc & others. Paris, 1834–35. Lge. 8vo. Hf. chagrin, spine decor. (SM. Mar.29; 2106) Frs. 2,600

AUDOUIT, Edmond
– L'Herbier des Demoiselles, ou Traité Complet de la Botanique Presenté sous une Forme Nouvelle. Paris, 1847. *1st. Edn.* Text ills. hand-cold., frontis. lightly foxed, mor. gt., bnd. for the Infanta Louisa Fernanda, with her crowned initials gt.-stpd. on cover in gt.- & blind-stpd. ornamental design, slightly rubbed. (SG. Dec.8; 22) $275

AUDRAN, Girard
– Les Proportions du Corps Humain Mesurées sur les plus Belles Figures de l'Antiquité. Paris, 1683. Fo. Title, advt. lf., 30 engraved plts., may lack anr. text lf., sm. hole in advt. lf., title stained in margin, short marginal tears in 3 plts., some sm. wormholes, few stains, new bds., spine cf. (S. Apr.10; 467) *Jones.* £100

AUDSLEY, George Ashdown & Bowes, James L.
– La Céramique Japonaise. Paris, 1880. 2 vols. Fo. Cont. hf. mor., rubbed. (S. May 1; 612) *Gilbert.* £60
– – Anr. Copy. 2 vols. Tall fo. 67 plts., most chromolithos., text engrs., few plts. stained on versos, ex-liby., qtr. mor., worn. (SG. May 3; 74) $225
– Keramic Art in Japan. 1875. 2 vols. Fo. Few ll. slightly spotted or soiled, orig. mor. gt. (BBA. Nov.10; 289) *Gilbert.* £170
– – Anr. Copy. 2 vols. Fo. Cont. mor. (BBA. Sep.8; 205) *Belanske.* £150

AUDSLEY, W. & G.
– Cottage, Lodge & Villa Architecture. Ca. 1860. Bdg. not stated, worn. (JL. Mar.25; 708) Aus. $250
– Polychromatic Decoration as Applied to Buildings in the Mediaeval Styles. 1882. Fo. 36 chromo-illuminated plts., liby. stps. on prelims., recent qtr. mor. gt. (TA. Jul.19; 424) £80
– – Anr. Copy. Fo. Cold. plts., some slight margin soiling, title detchd., orig. cl., rubbed & soiled. (S. May 1; 525) *Quaritch.* £50

AUDUBON, John James Laforest
– The Birds of America; from Original Drawings. Ill.:– W.H. Lizars, & Robert Havell, Jnr., after Audubon. L., priv. ptd., 1827-38. *1st. Edn.* 4 vols. Double elephant fo. As iss., without text, engraved titles, 435 hand-cold. aquatint plts., variants in legends & wtrmks.: plt. I Wild Turkey, 3rd. variant, wtrmkd. 'J Whatman 1838', plt. II Yellow-billed Cockoo, 4th. variant, wtrmkd. 'J Whatman 1838', plt. III Prothonotary Warbler, 2nd. variant, wtrmkd. 'J Whatman 1831', plt. IV Purple Finch, 3rd. variant, wtrmkd. 'J Whatman 1831', plt. V Bonaparte's Flycatcher, 2nd. variant, wtrmkd. 'J Whatman 1831', plt. VI Wild Turkey, 3rd. variant, wtrmkd. 'J Whatman 1838', plt. VII Purple Grakle, 3rd. variant, wtrmkd. 'J Whatman 1836', plt. VIII White throated Sparrow, 2nd. variant, wtrmkd. 'J Whatman 1837', plt. IX Selby's Flycatcher, 2nd. variant, wtrmkd. 'J Whatman 1837', plt. X Brown Titlark, 2nd. variant, wtrmkd. 'J Whatman 1836', superficial 'bloom' in darkest areas of some plts. in 4th. vol., plt. I bnd. close with slight concealment of foliage at lr. inner edge & ½-inch tear in outer margin, margin tears to other plts., some reprd., plt. VI with iss. & plt. no. & top of Turkey's head obscured in bdg. & 1 letter of caption shaved, plt. C creased, bkd. & stained, plt. CC creased, plt. CCLXXXI with 1st. letter of caption just shaved, plt. CCC creased, bkd. & stained, plt. CCCI slightly stained in sky, plt. CCCCXV with inking on plt.-mark, plts. CCCCXIX-CCCCXXI foxed, plt. CCCCXXXV creased & bkd. & slightly stained, sm. tears, mainly in lr. inner margins, cont. hf. russ. gt., spines in 8 compartments, gt. with palmettes, slightly worn & reprd.; Dr. John C. Marrian copy, given by him to National Academy of Sciences, placed on loan by them to Smithsonian Institution. (S. Feb.1; 1) *Berry Hill.* £1,000,000
– – Anr. Edn. N.Y. & Phila., 1840-41. Vols. 1 & 3 only. Cf., spine brkn., edges & corners scraped. (RS. Jan.17; 454) $1,400
– – Anr. Edn. N.Y. & Phila., 1840-44. *1st. 8vo. Edn.* 7 vols. 500 hand-cold. plts., subscribers lists in all vols. except Vol. IV, hf. leath. & marb. bds., spines lightly nicked & rubbed, edges lightly rubbed. (RS. Jan.17; 452) $12,500
– – Anr. Copy. 7 vols. 500 cold. litho. plts. hand-finished in colours, hf.-titles, subscribers' lists, some foxing, vol. 7 pp.33-40 bnd. inverted, cont. roan gt., few spines defect., few hinges brkn. (SG. Apr.26; 11) $10,500
– – Anr. Copy. 7 vols. 500 hand finished cold. litho. plts., 2 plts. with margin tears, badly foxed & browned, hf. cf., very worn. (SPB. Dec.13; 430) $8,500
– – Anr. Copy. 7 vols. 500 hand-finished col.-ptd. litho. plts., hf.-titles in each vol., some 15 plts. with smudges or spotting, 2 plts. shaved at upr. edge, scattered foxing to text ll. & affecting a few plts. thro.-out, some fore-margins in Vol. 1 dampstained without affecting plts., cont. hf. mor. gt. (CNY. Nov.18; 294) $7,500
– – Anr. Edn. N.Y., 1856. *2nd. 8vo. Edn.* 7 vols. Lge. 8vo. 500 col. litho. plts., hf.-titles, few minor tears, few plt. margins soiled, 1 reprd., orig. elab. blind-stpd. leath., worn. (SG. Mar.22; 25) $7,500
– – Anr. Edn. N.Y., 1859. 8 vols. Some foxing, cf., spine & edges scraped, corners rubbed. (RS. Jan.17; 453) $3,600
– – Anr. Edn. Ill.:– Bowen after Audubon. N.Y., 1861. 7 vols. 500 col. litho. plts., a few text ll. in Vol. 7 with faint dampstaining not affecting plts. (*With:*) **AUDUBON, John James Laforest & Bachman, Rev. John – The Quadrupeds of North America.** Ill.:– Bowen, after J.J. & J.W. Audubon. N.Y., [after 1861]. 3 vols. 155 col. litho. plts., text ll. in Vol. 1 slightly darkened. Together 10 vols. Royal 8vo. Orig. unif. blind-stpd. hf. mor., gt.-lettered, covers rubbed & with slight wear to extremities. (CNY. Nov.18; 295) $4,000
– – Anr. Edn. N.Y., [1871]. 8 vols. Lge. 8vo. 480 (of 500) col. litho. plts., orig. leath., extremities rubbed. (SG. Jun.7; 328) $4,400
– – Anr. Edn. N.Y. & Amst., 1971-72. *Facs. of 1827-38 edn. (250) numbered.* 4 vols. Double elephant fo. 435 cold. plts., lf. preceding list of plts. in Vol. 4 is a dupl. of that in Vol. 3, orig. hf. cf., unc.; Duke of Palmela copy. (C. Jun.27; 138) *Parkway.* £19,000
– – Anr. Edn. L., Ariel Pr., 1972. *(1000) numbered, sigd. by a director of Ariel Pr.* Vol. 1 only (of 2). Lge. fo. 20 cold. plts., orig. hf. cl. (S. Apr.10; 468) *Perham.* £520
– – Anr. Edn. L. & Leipzig, Ariel Pr. & Edn. Leipzig, [1972]. *(750) numbered. (250) sigd. by a director of the Ariel Pr.* Lge. fo. 20 cold. plts., lr. margins affected by damp, orig. hf. cl., lightly soiled & affected by damp, in publisher's box. (CSK. Mar.9; 150) £320
– The Original Water-Colour Paintings for The Birds of America. L. & N.Y., 1966. 2 vols. 4to. Orig. cl., s.-c. (BBA. Jun.28; 263) *T. Parsons.* £70
– – Anr. Copy. 2 vols. 4to. No bdg. stated. (SPB. Nov.30; 214) $100

AUDUBON, John James Laforest & Bachman, Rev. John
– The Quadrupeds of North America. N.Y., 1849-54. *1st. 8vo. Edn.* 3 vols. Lge. 8vo. 155 col. litho. plts., hf.-title in Vol. III only, some smudges, mostly marginal, few plts. & ll. sprung, cont. mor. (SG. Nov.3; 4) $2,800
– – Anr. Copy. 3 vols. Lge. 8vo. 155 col. litho. plts., hand-finished in cols., hf.-titles in Vols. 1 & 3, some foxing chiefly on tissue-guards, cont. hf. cf., worn. (SG. Mar.22; 29) $2,200
– – Anr. Copy. 3 vols. 149 (of 155) cold. litho. plts., marginal soiling on few plts., some browning, mostly to text, plt. 6 loose & worn at margins, cont. mor.-bkd. bds. (SPB. May 17; 566) $1,800
– – Anr. Copy. 3 vols. Lge. 8vo. 149 (of 155) hand-cold. litho. plts., hf. leath., lacks spines, covers detchd., ex-liby. (SG. Oct.6; 21) $1,600
– – Anr. Edn. N.Y., Victor Gifford Audubon, 1851-51-54. *1st. combined Edn. 2nd. Iss.* 3 vols. Tall 8vo. 155 full-p. col. litho. plts., some hand-finished, 1 plt. with ink spot at edge of image from stain at bottom edge of 1 guard, tissue guards partly foxed, with very slight offset to outer margins of few plts., very slight foxing at edges of few ll., plt. sequence & pagination identical with orig. fo. & 4to. edn. of plts. & text, respectively, iss. separately 1845-54, Vols. I & II bear printer's mark of H. Ludwig, Vol. III with R. Craighead, most plts. with printer's credit of J.T. Bowen, many in Vol. I credit Nagel & Weingaertner, few by W.E. Hitchcock, few with colouring credit of J. Lawrence, red turkey mor. & marb. bds., 5 raised bands, gt. lettering & plain spine rules, mild scuffing at corners & edges of spine, slight wear. (HA. May 4; 236) $3,500
– – Anr. Edn. N.Y., 1854. 3 vols. Imperial 8vo. 155 hand-cold. litho. plts., hf.-titles, cont. gt.-panel. mor., rebkd. (C. Nov.16; 214) *Schuster.* £1,200
– – Anr. Edn. Ill.:– John James Laforest Audubon & J.W. Audubon. N.Y., 1856-56-60. 3 vols. Cf., spines lightly rubbed. (RS. Jan.17; 455) $2,300
– The Viviparous Quadrupeds of North America. Ill.:– J.T. Bowen, after J.J. & J.W. Audubon. N.Y., priv. ptd., 1845-48. *1st. Edn.* 3 vols. (without the three 8vo. text vols.). Lge. fo. Engraved titles (creased in Vols. I & III), 150 cold, plts., plt. 129 misnumbered 124, plt. 1 slightly creased & with 2 short tears in margins reprd., margin repair to plt. 141, a few other sm. margin tears, some slight soiling or discolouration, cont. hf. mor. gt., rebkd., old spines laid down, covers faded. (S. Feb.1; 2) *Taylor.* £61,000
– – Anr. Copy. 3 vols. in 2 (without the three 8vo. text vols.). Lge. fo. Engraved titles (foxed & linen-bkd.), 150 cold. plts., MS. dedication lf., 1 title omitted, plt. 1 bkd., plt. 2 creased, plt. 4 a little short in lr. margin (inserted from anr. copy?), plt. 25 with lge. repair to upr. blank corner, plt. 29 with long clean tear reprd., plt. 76 creased & bkd. & with corner reprd., plt. 88 with caption just trimmed, plts. 102 & 127 with short tears touching ill., plt. 144 with long tear reprd., a few other minor margin repairs, slight soiling & discolouration, near cont. russ. gt., upr. covers lettered in gt., 'From The Loyal Citizens of New Jersey/To His Excellency/Andrew G. Curtin/The Loyal Governor of Pennsylvania' (1st. vol. with calligraphic dedication address), worn, rebkd. (S. Feb.1; 3) *Dew.* £36,000
– – Anr. Copy. 2 (of 3) text vols., & plt. vols. Royal 8vo. & atlas fo. 150 col. litho. plts., lacks litho. title to Vol. 2 & 2 contents ll., 4 inch reprd. tear to plt. 71, slight adhesion loss to plt. 38, 5 plts. stained at lr. & upr. outer margins, including 1 with sm. margin repair & anr. stained on verso, bdg. stains to extremities of 3 plts. & some minor soiling to a few margins, sm. ink liby. stps. on titles, text in orig. cl., brkn., plts. disbnd. from 5 cont. hf. sheep vols., bds. preserved, & contained in mod. folding box, w.a.f. (CNY. Nov.18; 296) $50,000

AUERBACH, B.
– Die Geschichte des Diethelm von Buchenberg. Ill.:– M. Unold. [1923]. *(100) De Luxe Edn.* 1 supp. orig. etching on japan, full-p. etchings sigd. by artist, hand-bnd. orig. pig, blind-tooled decor. (GB. May 5; 3414) DM 600
– Der Selbstmörderwettbewerb. Ill.:– Marcus Behmer. Berlin, Priv. Ptd. 1921. *(150) numbered.* 2 sigd. orig. etchings as title & frontis., orig. hf. vell. gt., spine with sm. fault. (GB. May 5; 2183) DM 750

AUGUSTINUS, Saint, Archbp. of Canterbury
– Regula B. Augustini Episcopi et Constitutiones Fratrum Ordinis Praedicatorum– Incipit Constitutiones Sororum Ordinis Praedicatorum. Lima, 1625. 2 works in 1 vol. Sm. 8vo. cropped, cont. vell. (SG. Jan.19; 305) $100

AUGUSTINUS, Saint Aurelius, Bp. of Hippo
– Confessiones. [Cologne, Bartholomaeus de Unkel], 9 Aug. 1482. 4to. Rubricated, lacks final blank (but may be a lf. before a1), cont. MS. ex-libris of the Dortmund convent, old blind-stpd. cf., rebkd., 2 metal clasps; the Walter Goldwater copy. [BMC I, 241; Goff A-1252] (SG. Dec.1; 44) $1,300
– Les Confessions. Trans.:– Arnauld d'Andilly. Paris, 1660. *8th. Edn.* 12mo. Jansenist mor. by Hardy. (HD. May 3; 7) Frs. 1,100
– – Anr. Edn. Paris, 1820. 6 vols. 12mo. Cathedral

style mor., orig. wood box, metal inlays, key, sigd. by Simier. (DS. Nov.25; 2104)   Pts. 125,000
- **The Confessions.** Ill.:– Clemence Housman, after P. Woodroffe & L. Housman. Phila., [Chiswick Pr.], 1900. *(150)*. Vell., gt.-lettered spine, many pp. unopened, covers slightly worn & darkened, fly-ll. soiled; Marymount College bkplt. (CBA. Mar.3; 136) $130
- **De Civitate Dei.** Venice, Nicolas Jenson, 2 Oct. 1475. Sm. fo. Wide margins, capitals painted in red & blue, some decor., 1st. text lf. with lge. letter elab. decor., traces of margin dampstains, lacks ll ll., old vell.; Thomas Braccioli's copy, sigd. by him several times & dtd. 1562, with his drawings & notes on 1st. & last blank ll. (HD. May. 21; 5)   Frs. 3,800
- – **Anr. Edn.** Venice, B.Locatellus for O. Scotus, 9 Feb. 1486. 4to. Some ll. lightly browned in margins, some light staining, 7 index & 8 text ll. bkd. in upr. margin, lacks last lf. blank, red & blue painted – in initials, lge. multi-cold. initials on gold ground on 1 lf., cold. & gold decor. borders with sm. painted arms, hf. leath., with old vell. covers mntd. on, probably 19th. C. [H.2055; C. 758 (R. Oct.11; 2)   DM 2,300
- – **Anr. Edn.** Venice, [B. Locatellus] for Octavianus Scotus, 18 Feb. 1489/90. Fo. Lacks title-lf., bds., covered with vell. music MS. lf.; Ink inscr. on margin of register lf., apparently by Angelus de Carletti Clavasio. the Walter Goldwater copy. [BMC V, 437; Goff A-1245] (SG. Dec.1; 41) $600
- – **Anr. Edn.** Freiburg im Breisgau, [Kilianus Piscator], 1494. Fo. 1st. few ll. remargined, some worming, many cont. MS. notes on margins of 1st. 100 ll., qtr. cf.; the Walter Goldwater copy. [BMC III, 695; Goff A-1246] (SG. Dec.1; 42) $850
- – **Anr. Copy.** [BMC III, 695 (IB 14206); Goff A-1246] *(Bound with:)* - **De Trinitate.** [Fribourg, Kilianus Piscator (Fischer)], 1494. [BMC III, 695 (IB 14207); Goff A-1346] Together 2 works in 1 vol. Rubricated, initials painted in red & blue, orig. owner's name on 1st. initial on gold ground, his MS. note at end of 2nd. work, some margin annots., two 16th. C. MS. ex-libris on title & 1st. lf., 18th. C. Spanish red mor. gt., crowned monog. 'P.R.'; from Fondation Furstenberg-Beaumesnil. (HD. Nov.16; 28)   Frs. 14,000
- – **Anr. Edn.** Ed:– C. Weymann. Ill.:– A. Simons. [München, Bremer Pr., 1924]. *(385)*. Lge. 4to. On Bütten. hand-bnd. orig. vell., gold decor. (P. Nov.23; 939)   DM 1,500
- – **Anr. Edn.** [Munich, Bremer Pr., 1925]. *(385)*. Fo. Linen-bkd. bds. (LH. Sep.25; 340) $550
- – **Anr. Copy.** Fo. Orig. gt. decor. vell., bd. s.-c., defect. (HK. May 17; 2597)   DM 1,300
- **De la Cita d'Dio.** [Venice?, Antonio di Bartolommeo], not after 1483. *1st. Edn. in Italian.* Fo. Lge. margins, table of contents at end, vell.; the Walter Goldwater copy. [BMC VII, 1136; Goff A-1248] (SG. Dec.1; 43) $2,400
- – **Anr. Copy.** Rubricated, initials painted in red & blue, decor. 1st. initial painted on gt. ground, lacks 1 blank lf., stp. in margin of 1st. lf., late 18th. C. vell., turn-in partly torn; from Fondation Furstenberg-Beaumesnil. [HC 2071; BMC VII, 1136; Goff A1248] (HD. Nov.16; 68)   Frs. 18,000
- **De Trinitate.** Venice, Paganinus de Paganinis, 12 Nov. 1489. 4to. Initials in red & blue thro.-out, lacks 1st. blank, 1st. few ll. remargined, 1st. lf. & many margins dampstained, old vell., worn; the Walter Goldwater copy. [BMC V, 455; Goff A-1344] (SG. Dec.1; 53) $650
- **De Virtute Psalmorum.** [Louvain, J. de Pederborn (Westphalia)], before 1479. 4to. Initials in red & blue, 2 ll. in facs., bds., covered with old rubricated lf.; the Walter Goldwater copy. [BMC IX, 147; Goff A-1349a (this copy)] (SG. Dec.1; 54) $375
- **Epistolae Pulcherrimae.** Venice, Bernardinus Benalius, ca. 1490. 4to. Vell.-bkd. limp bds.; the Walter Goldwater copy. [Goff A-1269] (SG. Dec.1; 45) $700
- **Explanatio Psalmorum.** Venice, Bernardinus Benalius, 4 Aug. 1493. Fo. Last lf. in the variant state, with lge. woodcut at end, beneath the register, & the Explicit beginning on line 27 of the 2nd. column, 1st. lf. mntd., next few rehinged, last few ll. also rehinged, with some loss of text (including part of imprint), disbnd.; the Walter

Goldwater copy. [BMC V, 374; Goff A-1273] (SG. Dec.1; 46) $325
- **Manuale.** [Strassburg, Printer of Henricus Ariminensis], ca. 1476. Fo. 2 initials on 1st. p. in cols. & gold, rubricated thro.-out, slight soiling, vell.; the Walter Goldwater copy. [Goff A-1284 (this copy only)] (SG. Dec.1; 47) $1,200
- **Manuell, or Little Book of the Contemplation of Christ.** L., 1586. Lacks ll. A3-8, 19th. C. cf. [STC 928] (BBA. Mar.21; 160)   *Robertshaw.* £55
- **Meditationes.** [Paris, Philippe Pigouchet], ca. 1499. Sm. 8vo. 16 ll., title-lf. supplied in photostat, mod. velvet; the Walter Goldwater copy. [Goff A-1291; GW 2983 (calling for only 14 ll.)] (SG. Dec.1; 48) $600
- **Opera.** Venice, 1550. Vol. X only. 4to. 16th. C. Italian red mor., richly decor., Pius V arms, inscrs. 'PIUS V' & 'P.O.M.', brass studs, clasps; from Fondation Furstenberg-Beaumesnil. (HD. Nov.16; 165)   Frs. 8,000
- – **Anr. Edn.** Paris, 1679-1700. *1st. Muguet Edn.* 11 vols. in 8, including Index. Fo. Some foxing or spotting, mod. buckram, orig. spine labels affixed & marb. free end-papers bnd. in. (CBA. Dec.10; 439) $200
- **Opera Omnia.** Lugduni, 1664. 11 vols. in 7. Fo. Blind-tooled vell. over wood bds., slight defects, lacks clasps. (B. Oct.4; 785)   Fls. 750
- **Opus Canonum.** Strasburg, Martin Schott, 1490. [H. 2076, BMC I, 95] *(Bound with:)* **GRUNER, Vincentius** - **Officii Missae Sacrique Canonis Expositio.** Reutlingen, Johann Otmar, 1483. [BMC II, 584] Together 2 works in 1 vol. Fo. 2nd. work lacks last (colophon) lf., some ll. dampstained, cont. stpd. cf. over wood bds., richly decor., turn-ins & jnts. reprd.; from Fondation Furstenberg-Beaumesnil. (HD. Nov.16; 50)   Frs. 18,000
- **Opus Quaestionum.** Lyons, Johannes Trechsel, 25 Apr. 1497. Fo. Qtr. cf., spine worn; the Walter Goldwater copy. [BMC VIII, 301; Goff A-1297] (SG. Dec.1; 49) $700
- **Opuscula.** Venice, Dionysius Bertochus, 25 Mar. 1491. 4to. Blind-stpd. cf.; the Walter Goldwater copy. [BMC V, 488; Goff A-1219] (SG. Dec.1; 40) $650
- **Regola del P.S. Agostino e Constituzioni della Religione di S. Gio. di Dio...coll'aggiunta di alcune Annotazioni.** Rome, 1718. 4to. Cont. Italian red mor., sides elab. gt. decor., arms of member of the Altieri family of Rome, a Bp., on sides, upr. hinge cracked, as a bdg., w.a.f. (S. Apr.10; 306)   *Tolemei.* £100
- **Sermo super Orationem Dominicam, Expositio super Symbolum, De Ebriate.** [H. 1989; BMC I, 183; Goff A1303], *(Bound with:)* **ANTONINUS FLORENTINUS** - **Summa Confessionum, cum Chrysostomi Sermone de Poenitentia.** [H. 1162; BMC I, 183; Goff A788] *(Bound with:)* **MATTHAEUS DE CRACOVIA** - **Dialogus Rationis et Conscientiae de Frequenti Usu Communionis.** [H. 5805; BMC I, 185; Goff M368] [Cologne, Ulrich Zel, not after 1470]. Together 3 works in 1 vol. Sm. 4to. Capitals, paragraph marks & foliation inserted thro.-out in red, some minor worming thro.-out, especially in last work, cont. blind-tooled cf. over wood bds., very worn, lacks spine, remains of brass clasps. (C. May 30; 10)   *Rosenthal.* £1,800
- **Sermones.** Basel, Johann Amerbach. 1494. Pts. I & II only (of 7). Fo. A few sm. stains, 1 lf. reprd. at margin, suede over bds., rubbed. [BMC III, 756; Goff A-1308; H. 2008] (SPB. Dec.14; 5) $500
- **Sermones ad Heremitas.** Strasbourg, [J. Prüss], before 1487. 4to. 1st. lf. margin defect., corner of 1 lf. reprd., tear in 1 lf., old owners inscr. on 1st. 2 ll., old vell., a little loose, stained. [HC 1997*; BMC I, 1125; Goff A-1314] (VG. May 3; 490)   Fls. 1,300
- – **Anr. Edn.** Venice, Vincentius Benalius, 26 Jan. 1492/93. Sm. 8vo. Rubricated, some stains, old deer over bds.; the Walter Goldwater copy. [BMC V, 525; Goff A-1317] (SG. Dec.1; 50) $700
- – **Anr. Edn.** Venice, Simon Bevilaqua, 4 Nov. 1495. Very stained, mainly at lr. margins, tooled cf., rebkd.; the Walter Goldwater copy. [BMC V, 520; Goff A-1319] (SG. Dec.1; 51) $250
- **Sermones ad Heremitas.-Opuscula.** Milan, 3 Jun. 1484; Venecia, 28 May 1483. 2 works in 1 vol. 4to. Slight worming in 1st. ll., linen, vell. spine. [BMC

VI, 752, Goff A 1312; BMC V, 277. Goff A 1216] (DS. Oct.28; 2327)   Pts. 140,000
- **Sermones de Verbis Apostoli [i.e. Part III of Sermones].** Basel, [Johann Amerbach], 1494. Fo. Mod. bdg. from old vell. antiphoner lf. [BMC III, 756; Goff A-1308; H. 2008*] (SPB. Dec.14; 6) $250
- **Soliloquia.** Flor., [L. Morgiani & J. Petri], 10 Nov. 1[4]91. 4to. In Italian, very stained, disbnd.; the Walter Goldwater copy. [BMC VI, 681; Goff A-1329] (SG. Dec.1; 52) $375

AUGUSTINUS, Saint Aurelius, Bp. of Hippo & Ignatius of Loyola
- **Unless the Grain die.** Worcester, Stanbrook Abbey Pr., 1961. *(200)* numbered. Fo. Orig. cf.-bkd. bds. (BBA. May 23; 183)   *Blackwell.* £55

AUGUSTINUS DE ANCONA
- **Summa de Potestate Ecclesiastica.** Rome, In Domo F. de Cinquinis, 20 Dec. 1479. 4to. 6 ll. badly torn at outer margins, with considerable loss of text, last lf. torn, cont. of. back, later bds.; the Walter Goldwater copy. [BMC IV, 76; Goff A-1365] (SG. Dec.1; 55) $250

AUGUSTUS FREDERICK, Duke of Sussex
- **Carmina Linguis Exoticis in Honorem dei Pueri a Tribus Magis Adorati ....** [Rome, 1793]. *[Ltd. pres. iss.?]*. Fo. Cont. red mor., flat gt. spine, ornate borders round sides with urn-shaped cornerpieces, arms of Augustus Frederick on covers, rather rubbed. (S. Oct.11; 379)   *Maggs.* £200

AUK, The: A Quarterly Journal of Ornithology
Lancaster, Pa.; Wash., D.C., 1953-1983. Vols. 70-100, No.1. Plts., text ills., vols.70-88 hf. cl., rest orig. wraps., w.a.f. (S. Apr.10; 401)   *Quaritch.* £180

AULDJO, John
- **Narrative of an Ascent to the Summit of Mont Blanc.** 1828. *1st. Edn.* 4to. 22 litho. plts., maps, etc. on India paper, some margins frayed & soiled, MS. note glued on hf.-title, cl., slightly worn. (BS. Nov.16; 14)   £170
- **Sketches of Vesuvius, with Short Accounts of its Principal Eruptions.** Naples, 1832. Lacks frontis., orig. wraps., unc., torn. (PD. Dec.14; 271)   £130
- – **Anr. Edn.** 1833. Hand-cold. folding map, 16 plts. (4 folding), folding map & the folding plts. linen-bkd., some stains & spotting, hf. cf. (P. Jul.5; 219)   £70

AULNOY, Marie Catherine, Comtesse d'
- **Les Contes des Fées; Nouveaux Contes des Fées.** Amst., ca. 1710. 2 vols. 12mo. 9 p. catalogue at end of 1st. vol., last few ll. of both vols. slightly wormed, affecting a few letters of text, cont. sheep; van Veen coll. (S. Feb.28; 114)   £580

AUNGERVILLE or BURY, Richard de
- **Philobiblon.** Speyer, Johann & Konrad Hist, [after 13 Jan. 1483]. 4to. Wide margin, slightly wormed at beginning, 1st. ll. with marginalia & underlining in old MS., a few red initials, some margin browning, 1st. ll. with restored margin tear, cont. wood bds., pig over spine, 1 clasp, upr. cover brkn., slightly wormed, owners mark inside cover; Hauswedell coll. [BMC II, 502] (H. May 24; 1181)   DM 74,000
- – **Anr. Edn.** Oxford, 1599. *1st. Engl. Edn.* 4to. Blank H4 & appendix present, a little margin worming, a few margin annots., some staining, cont. cf., rebkd. [STC 959] (BBA. May 3; 98)   *Quaritch.* £1,250

AUNT MAVOR'S PRESENT...comprising Aunt Mavor's Alphabet
1856. 160 hand-cold. ills., orig. cl., blind-& gt.-decor. (SKC. Mar.9; 1762)   £70

AURELIUS, Marcus Antoninus
- **The Golden Boke of Marcus Aurelius, Emperour & Eloquent Oratour.** L., 1542. 4to. Lacks 2 ll., later sheep, rebkd. (TA. Nov.17; 534)   £140
- **The Thoughts.** Ill.:– Sir W. Russell Flint. L., 1909. *(500)* numbered. 4to. Orig. limp vell., ties, partly unc. (S. Dec.20; 535)   *Wood.* £180
- – **Anr. Copy.** 4to. Orig. linen-bkd. bds., partly unc., covers slightly marked. (LC. Mar.1; 62)   £100

AURIOL, George
– Le Premier [Second, Troisième] Livre des Cachets, Marques et Monogrammes. 1901. 3 vols. 12mo. 2 vols. cont. hf. mor., mosaic spine, wrap. & spine, last vol. sewed; autograph dedication & letter to Gustave Babin. (HD. Mar.21; 131)   Frs. 2,200

AUSTELLUNG DEUTSCHER KUNST aus der Zeit von 1775-1875 in der Königlichen Nationalgalerie Berlin 1906
Ill.:– P. Behrens. München, 1906. 2 vols. 4to. Orig. linen, silver-tooled, slightly rubbed, name on endpaper & inside cover. (GB. May 4; 1849) DM 800

AUSTELLUNG   DEUTSCHER ZEITGENOSSISCHER   ARCHITEKTUR. Organisiert durch die Gesellschaft für Kulturelle Verbindung der Sowetunion mit dem Auslande 'Woks' und die Allrussische Kooperative Vereinigung der Arbeiter der Bildenden Künste 'Wsekochudoschnik'. Ed.:– A. Kuhn. Moscow, 1932. 14 plts., orig. bds. (GB. May 5; 2139)
DM 750

AUSTEN, Gabriel (Ed.)
See— HYDE, Donald

AUSTEN, Jane
– Emma. 1816. 1st. Edn. 3 vols. 12mo. Lacks hf.-titles, minor foxing & slight stain affecting about 6 ll. in Vol. I, cont. hf. cf., slightly rubbed, mod. mor.-bkd. buckram case; sig. of Charlotte Elizabeth Craven on each title. (C. May 30; 136a)
Quaritch. £800
– Letters. Ed.:– R.W. Chapman. Oxford, 1932. 2 vols. Bds., qtr. cl., slightly worn d.-w.'s. (KH. Nov.4; 12)   Aus. $160
[–] Mansfield Park. L., 1816. 1st. Edn. 3 vols. 12mo. Vol.3 with advt. lf. at end & 4 pp. advts. dtd. Apr. 1814 inserted, orig. bds., unc., Vols. 1 & 3 spines torn; from liby. of Prince & Princess Starhemberg. (S. Dec.8; 69)   Joseph. £4,200
– Novels. Edinb., 1906. Winchester Edn. 10 vols. Orig. cl., spines gt., partly unc., slightly soiled. (LC. Jul.5; 255)   £55
– – Anr. Edn. Ed.:– R.W. Chapman. Oxford, 1923. (1000) on L.P. 5 vols. (With:) – Letters. Ed.:– R.W. Chapman. Oxford, 1932. 2 vols. Together 7 vols. Unif. cl.-bkd. marb. bds. (SKC. Jan.13; 2183)
£120

AUSTEN, Ralph
– A Treatise on Fruit-Trees. Oxford, 1653. 1st. Edn. Sm. 4to. Title slightly browned, old cf., rebkd.; bkplt. of Richard Chamberlain. [Wing A4238] (BS. Nov.16; 34)   £170

AUSTIN, Gabriel
– The Library of Jean Grolier. A Preliminary Catalogue. N.Y., 1971. 4to. Orig. cl.; H.M. Nixon coll., with his sig. (BBA. Oct.6; 4) Georges. £50

AUSTIN, Mary
– The Land of Little Rain. Boston, 1903. 1st. Edn. Decor. cl. (LH. Sep.25; 183) $120

AUSTIN, Mary (Text)
See— ADAMS, Ansel

AUSTRALIA
– Aerial, Geological & Geophysical Survey of Northern Australia. Canberra, v.d. In 19 pts., as iss. Sm. fo. Not collated, wraps. (KH. May 1; 3)
Aus. $220
– Landscape Scenery illustrating Sydney, Paramatta, Richmond, Maitland, Windsor & Port Jackson. Sydney, 1855. 1st. Edn.?. 42 etchings, some detchd., orig. bdg., some minor repairs. (JL. Mar.25; 566)   Aus. $1,350
– Outline of the Plan of a Proposed Colony to be Founded in South Australia. L., 1834. Orig. wraps., unc. (P. Jul.5; 326)   £220
– Papers Relating to an Expedition recently Undertaken for the Purpose of Exploring the Northern Part of Australia. Map:– J. Arrowsmith. 1857. Fo. Folding litho. map outl. hand-cold., slightly soiled, liby. stp. on title, disbnd. (BBA. Jan.19; 77)   McCormick. £160

AUTOBIOGRAPHY OF AN IRISH TRAVELLER
L., 1835. 1st. Edn. 3 vols. 12mo. Hf. cf., gt.-tooled spine with armorial motif. (GM. Dec.7; 374) £150

AUTREFOIS OU LE BON VIEUX TEMPS. Types Français du XVIIIe Siècle
Text:– Audebrand, Roger de Beauvoir, E. de la Bedollière & others. Ill.:– after T. Johannot, Th. Fragonard, Gavarni, Ch. Jacque. Paris, [1842]. 1st. Printing of ills. Lge. 8vo. 40 plts., cold. & gommées, hf. mor. gt., corners, by Champs, spine decor., unc., wrap. (HD. Jun.22; 12)   Frs. 2,600
– – Anr. Copy. Lge. 8vo. Old str.-grd. hf. mor., corners, spine decor., wrap. (HD. May 3; 177)
Frs. 1,400

AVALANCHE (THE); or, the Old Man of the Alps, a Tale, Translated from the French
Clapham, 1829. 12mo. Litho. frontis. spotted, inscr. on hf.-title, cont. cl., rubbed. (BBA. May 3; 341)
Gastons Alpine Books. £60

AVALUN Pr.
See— BOHME, J.
See— PATER, Walter

AVEDON, Richard
– Nothing Personal. Text:– James Baldwin. [N.Y., 1964]. 1st. Edn. Fo. Silver-stpd. glossy bds., spine discold., matching bd. s.-c., rubbed & scuffed. (SG. May 10; 11) $100
– Observations. Comments:– Truman Capote. [N.Y., 1959]. 1st. Edn. Fo. Ptd. bds., matching bd. s.-c., lightly scuffed. (SG. Nov.10; 18) $130
– – Anr. Copy. Fo. Ptd. bds., orig. ptd. bd. s.-c., soiled & chipped. (SG. May 10; 12) $100

AVENARIUS, Johannes
– Sefer Ha'shoroshim. Wittenberg, 1589. Fo. Outer margins of 1st. 24 ll. frayed not affecting text, lightly stained, vell., w.a.f. (S. Jul.3; 70)   £120

AVERROES
See— MUHAMMED IBN AHMAD, called Ibn Rushd, or Averroes

AVICENNA (Pseud.)
See— HUSAIN IBN 'ABD ALLAH, Abû Alî, called Ibn Sînâ or Avicenna

AVRAHAM BEN MEIR IBN EZRA
– Peirush al HaTorah. Ed.:– Moshe ben Shem Tov Ben Chaviv of Lisbon. Naples, Yosef [ben Yakov] Ashkenazi [Gunzenhausen] & son, 36th. day of Omer 5248 [May 1488]. 1st. Edn. Fo. Lacks 1st. 2 ll., uncensored, slight margin staining, sm. trace of wormholes to a few margins, outer margins reprd. on 6 ll., a few prelim. & final ll. soiled, a few corners frayed, cf.-bkd. bds., very rubbed. [Goff Heb-1; Steinschneider 680, 4221, 1] (SPB. Jun.26; 11) $27,500

AVRAHAM DE BALMES
– Peculium Abrahamis ... / Sefer Mikne Avraham. Venice, 1523. 4to. Title & contents supplied in MS., lacks 19 ll. at beginning, 1 in middle, 5 at end, 9 ll. defect. with loss, owner's note on title verso dtd. 1829 concerning author & provenance, other old annots., later vell., soiled & worn. (SG. Feb.2; 146) $175

AVRAHAM GALLICO
– Lekah Tov. Venice, [1595]. 2nd. Edn. 16mo. Mildly dampstained, disbnd. (SG. Feb.2; 147)
$550

AVRAHAM IBN EZRA
– Sefer Tsahut be-Dikduk. Ed.:– [Eliyahu Levita]. Venice, 1546. Pt. 3 only (of 3). (Bound with:)
– Sefer Moznayim. Homburg, 1770. (Bound with:)
– Sefer Pirkei Rabbi Eliezer by Levita. Homburg, 1770. Together 3 works in 1 vol. Sm. 8vo. 1 lf. torn with slight loss, margins trimmed close with some loss to running heads & catchwords, binder's cl. (SG. Feb.2; 148) $225

AXE, J. Wortley
– The Horse: Its Treatment in Health & Disease. With a Complete Guide to Breeding, Training & Management. L., 1908. 3 vols. Sm. 4to. Gt.-ornamental mor.-bkd. cl., some rubbing. (SG. Mar.15; 266) $200

AYME, Marcel
– La Table aux Crevés. Ill.:– Maurice de Vlaminck, engraved by Pierre Bouchet. Paris, 1960. 4to. Leaves, box. (HD. Jun.13; 5)   Frs. 1,300

AYROUARD
– Recueil de Plusieirs Plans des Ports et Rades et de quelques Cartes Particulières de la Mer Méditerranné. N.p., 1736. Sm. fo. Double-p. engraved title, lge. folding map & 78 double or folding plans, old cf. gt., spine decor., upr. turn-in worn. (HD. Jul.2; 2)   Frs. 3,500

AYRTON, Michael
See— VERLAINE, Paul – AYRTON, Michael

AYSCOUGH, Samuel
– A Catalogue of the Manuscripts preserved in the British Museum .... 1782. 1st. Edn. 2 vols. 4to. Cont. tree cf., spines gt.; Sir Ivar Colquhoun, of Luss copy. (CE. Mar.22; 14)   £420

AYSMA, Joannes
– Spiegel der Sibyllen. Ill.:– J. Luyken, C. Decker & others. Amst., 1685. Engraved title cut slightly short, mntd. on later paper with tear & defect., ptd. title with MS. owners mark, some plts. slightly spotted, 2 plts. with sm. reprd. tears, some text ll. with extended margin, 1 lf. loose, wormhole, later hf. leath. (HT. May 9; 1286)   DM 420

AYTOUN, William Edmondstone
– Lays of the Scottish Cavaliers, & Other Poems. Edinb., 1872. Sm. 8vo. Blind-tooled mor., fore-e. pntg., painted continuously round all edges. (SG. Nov.17; 222) $450
– – Anr. Edn. Edinb., 1881. 4to. Cont. red mor. gt., mor. gt. inlaid border round centre device, with fore-e. pntg., as a fore-e. pntg., w.a.f. (SPB. May 17; 728) $325
– – Anr. Copy. Sm. 4to.?. Mor., upr. cover stained, 2 Indian bkplts., fore-e. pntg. (KH. May 1; 32)
Aus. $150

AYTZING, M. von
– Nova Qvaestionis Solvtio. Augsburg, 1956. Fo. Title with sm. repair, lightly foxed & stained, bds. (HK. Nov.8; 98)   DM 700

AZARA, Don Felix de
– Voyages dans l'Amérique Meridionale. Paris, 1809. 5 vols., including Atlas. 8vo. & fo. Atlas with port., 5 folding engraved maps, 19 other maps & plts., several double-p., 3 folding tables in text, light stains affecting atlas, sm. liby. stps. at foot of titles, text hf. cf., hinges brkn., atlas orig. bds., worn. (S. Dec.1; 272)   Maggs. £320

AZIKRI, Elasar
– Chareidim. Venice, 1601. 1st. Edn. 4to. Owner's sig. & stp. on title, slight staining in outer margin, mod. mor. gt. (S. Oct.24; 77)   Klein. £280
– Sefer Haredim. Constantinople, 1757. Sm. 4to. Slight margin worming, owner's stps., later qtr. leath., shabby. (SG. Feb.2; 150) $150

AZNAR CARDONA, Pedro
– Expulsion justificada de los Moriscos Españoles. Huesca, 1612. 2 pts. in 1 vol. Linen. (DS. Feb.24; 2237)   Pts. 75,000

AZULAI, Hayyim Yosef David
– Sefer Simhat ha-Regel. Livorno, 1782. 1st. Edn. Sm. 4to. Mild dampstaining, title reprd., mod. leath.; pres. inscr. in Sefardi hand from Yitshak ibn Sassoon to Hakham Ya'akov Adav. (SG. Feb.2; 151) $275

B., H. (Pseud.)
See— DOYLE, John

BAADER, Fr. von
– Sämmtliche Werke. Ed.:– Fr. Hoffmann. Leipzig, 1850-60. Title verso with stp., cont. blind-tooled linen. (HK. Nov.10; 2316)   DM 1,600

BABBAGE, Charles
See— PEACOCK, George – HERSCHEL, J.F.W. – BABBAGE, Charles

BAC, F. & Guillaume, A.
– Femmes de Théâtre. Nos Amoureuses. Les Alcôves. Nos Femmes. Etoiles de Mer. Y a des Dames. Madame est Servie. Faut Voir. Paris, ca. 1905. 8 albums in 1 vol. Fo. 1 lf. torn, reprd., hf. cf., rubbed. (VG. Mar.21; 836)   Fls. 450

BACCI, Andrea
- De Thermis libri septem .... Venice, 1571. *1st. Edn.* Fo. Bds.; Dr. Walter Pagel copy. (S. Feb.7; 31) *Heller.* £160

BACH, Johann Sebastian
- Grosse Passionsmusik nach dem Evangelium Johannis. Partitur. Berlin, 1831. *1st. Edn.* 4to. Lacks port., few pencil marks, slight wear, hf. mor. (B. Oct.4; 389) Fls. 450
- Das Wohltemperirte Clavier. Zürich, ca. 1800. Slightly foxed & stained thro.-out, 3 pp. pts. 1 with sm. tear in lr. corner, hf. leath., ca. 1840. (HK. Nov.9; 2234) DM 2,200

BACHAUMONT, Louis Petit de
- Mémoires Secrets pour Servir à l'Histoire de la République des Lettres en France, ou Journal d'un Observateur. L., 1777-89. 36 vols. 12mo. Cont. marb. cf., grotesque decor. spines. (HD. Sep.22; 182) Frs. 4,800

BACHELARD, Gaston (Text)
See— CHAGALL, Marc

BACHER
- Recherches sur les Maladies Chroniques, particulièrement sur les Hydropisies, et sur les Moyens de les guérir. Paris, 1776. *Orig. Edn.* Cont. red mor., gt. decor., gold tooled centre arms, decor. spine. (HD. Mar.14; 8) Frs. 3,800

BACHMAN, Rev. John
See— AUDUBON, John James Laforest & Bachman, Rev. John

BACHMAN, Otto
- Zwölf Zeichnungen Zu Goethes Faust. Switzerland, 1943. *Ltd. Edn., sigd. by artist.* Fo. 12 orig. black & white lithos., loose in orig. wraps. as iss. (SPB. Nov.30; 215) $125

BACHOFEN, Johann Jakob
- Versuch über die Gräbersymbolik der Alten. Basle, 1859. *1st. Edn.* Hf. cl.; Ernest Jones copy, with sig., Dr. Walter Pagel copy. (S. Feb.7; 32) *Weiner.* £90

BACKHOUSE, James
- [–] A Christian Address to the Free Inhabitants of New South Wales & Van Dieman's Land. Sydney, 1838. Sewn in plain wraps. (KH. May 1; 33) Aus. $300
- A Narrative of a Visit to the Australian Colonies. L., 1843. 3 folding hand-cold. maps, 15 plts., maps offset, some plts. foxed, rebnd. hf. mor., partly unc., sig. on front end-paper. (CA. Apr.3; 16) Aus. $300
- – Anr. Copy 1843. Frontis. a little foxed, orig. cl., unc., worn. (KH. Nov.8; 15) Aus. $160

BACKMAN, D.A.
- Med Guds Walsignande Nad ... om Nyttan ... af des Nybygge i America, fordom Nya Swerige Kalladt. Ed.:– Peter Kalm. Abo (Turku), [1754]. Sm. 4to. Sm. owner's stp. at head of title, later bds. (S. Dec.1; 273) *Israel.* £250

BACON, Edward Denny
- Catalogue of the Philatelic Library of the Earl of Crawford. L., 1911-26. 2 vols., including supp. Fo. Liby. stps. on title versos, mod. hf. mor., orig. wraps. preserved. (BBA. Mar.7; 329) *R. Bodily.* £80

BACON, Sir Francis, Baron Verulam
- De Sapientia Veterum ... Ad Inclytam Academicum Cantabrigiensem .... L., 1617. 12mo. Inscr. on title, cont. vell., worn. [STC 1128] (PNY. Dec.1; 11) $140
- The Essayes or Counsels, Civill & Morall. L., 1625. *1st. Compl. Edn. 2nd. Iss.* Sm. 4to. Lacks blank lf. A1, 2 lf. index misbnd., sm. repair to title on verso, very sm. tears to some ll., mod. cf., spine gt., trimmed. (SG. Feb.16; 12) $325
- – Anr. Edn. L., 1664. 12mo. Lacks last blank, cont. cf., rebkd. [Wing B285] (BBA. May 3; 148) *Howes Bookshop.* £55
- – Anr. Edn. Ed.:– W.C. Taylor. L., 1840. Sm. 8vo. Cf. gt., spine gt., fore-e. pntg. (SG. Feb.16; 13) $350
- – Anr. Edn. Ill.:– Anna Simons. Tölz, Bremer Pr., 1920. *(270) numbered.* 4to. Orig. vell., gt. decor., bd. s.-c. (HK. May 17; 2598) DM 650

- – Anr. Copy. 4to. Some foxing, orig. hand-bnd. vell., sigd. Brema Binderei Fr[ieda] Th[iersch], slight slits. (GB. May 5; 2240) DM 400
- – Anr. Edn. L., Cresset Pr., ptd. at the Shakes. Hd. Pr., 1928. *(250) numbered on Batchelor's Kelmscott H.M.P.* Tall fo. Gt.-lettered heavy vell., partly unc., slightly warped & slightly discold. (SG. Jan.12; 76) $175
- The Historie of Life & Death .... L., 1688 [i.e. 1638]. *Unauthorised Edn.* 12mo. Engraved title, imprimatur lf., F6 reprd., some headlines cropped, P3 soiled, some soiling & sm. margin tears, old cf., rebkd. [STC 1157] (SPB. May 16; 4) $275
- The Historie of the Reign of King Henry the VII. Ill.:– John Payne (engraved port.). L., 1622. *1st. Edn.* Sm. fo. Old spr. cf. (CE. Sep.1; 46) £80
- – Anr. Copy. Sm. fo. Stained in upr. margin, cf. gt., rubbed. [STC 1159] (P. Feb.16; 216) £50
- – Anr. Copy. Fo. Pol. cf. by Riviere. (LH. Sep.25; 454) £400
- – Anr. Copy. Fo. Iss. with errata partly corrected, engraved port., lacks first blank, some soiling, later cf., gt. lozenge on covers; bkplt. of Charles Lilburn. [STC 1159] (SPB. May 16; 5) $225
- History Naturall & Experimentall of Life & Death. Trans:– Rawley. 1638. *1st. Edn.* 12mo. Both license ll. present, 4 ll. in dupl., lacks last blank (?), piece cut from lr. margin of title, sm. hole in 1 lf. affecting 2 or 3 words, cont. cf. [STC 1158] (BBA. Jun.14; 33) *Weininger.* £90
- Instauratio Magna. [Novum Organum]. L., 1620. *1st. Edn. 2nd. Iss.* Fo. L.P., paper wtrmkd. with crowned shield, e3 excised, errata on recto of e4, lacks 1st. blank lf., colophon washed & margin reprd., sm. hole affecting 1 letter, title lightly soiled, slight dampstaining affecting a few ll., mor. gt. by Rivière, cl. s.-c.; Borowitz-Stanitz coll. [STC 1163] (SPB. Apr.25; 25) $7,750
- The Naturall & Experimentall History of Winds.... Trans:– R.G. Gent. L., 1653. *1st. Edn. in Engl.* 12mo. Lacks final blank, without catalogue (as often), some light staining, cont. unlettered sheep, rubbed, spine top worn; early owners inscr. of Richd. Davenport on end-paper, John D. Stanitz coll. [Wing B305] (SPB. Apr.25; 26) $750
- Of the Advancement & Proficiencie of Learning. 1674. Fo. Reprd. tear on f4, last few ll. dampstained, mor. gt. (CE. Sep.1; 51) £80
- De Proef-Strucken [Essays]. Trans:– P. Boener. Leiden, 1647. *1st. Edn. in Dutch. 2nd. Iss.* 4to. Errata lf., few ll. lightly spotted or soiled, cont. cf., worn. (S. Mar.20; 850) *Smallwood.* £80
- Resuscitatio. L., 1657. *1st. Edn.* Fo. Engraved port., notat. on title of Constantor 1660, cont. cf., sig. on endpaper; bkplt. of Downfield. [Wing B 319] (SPB. May 16; 6) $225
- Scripta in Naturalis et Universali Philosophia. Amst., 1653. *1st. Elzevir Edn.* 24mo. Lacks plt., early inscrs., cont. vell., hand-lettered spine. (SG. Feb.9; 163) $100
- Sylva Sylvarum: or a Naturall History. In Ten Centuries. L., 1651. Sm. 4to. Hf. cf., marb. paper bds., somewhat discold. (LH. Sep.25; 455) $150
- – Anr. Edn. L., 1670. 4 pts. only (of 5), in 1 vol. Fo. Some foxing & stains, pol. cf. antique. (SG. Feb.9; 164) $100

BACON, John
- Opus super Quattuor Sententiarum Libris. Milan, 1511. *1st. Compl. Edn.* Vol. I only. Fo. Cont. stpd. cf. over wood bds., richly decor., jnts. reprd.; from Fondation Furstenberg-Beaumesnil. (HD. Nov.16; 93) Frs. 5,800

BACON, Nathaniel
- [–] An Historical Discourse of the Uniformity of the Government of England. 1647-51. 2 vols. in 1. Sm. 4to. Browned thro.-out, mod. hf. mor. (BBA. Jul.27; 98) *Coulter.* £50

BACON, Roger
- The Cure of Old Age & Preservation of Youth. Trans:– Richard Browne. L., 1683. *1st. Engl. Edn.* 2 pts. in 1 vol. Advt. lf., few headlines touched by binder, cont. cf.; bkplts. of Shadwell Court & Robert Steele, Dr. Walter Pagel copy. [Wing B 372] (S. Feb.7; 30) *Quaritch.* £280
- Opus Majus. Ed.:– Samuel Jebb. L., 1733. *1st. Edn.* Fo. Subscribers list, some soiling, browning & spotting, some creasing along inner margins, mod.

mott. hf. cf., marb. bds.; John D. Stanitz coll. (SPB. Apr.25; 27) $1,500

BACQUEVILLE DE LA POTHERIE, Claude C.L.
- Histoire de l'Amérique Septentrionale. Paris, 1722. *1st. Edn.* 4 vols. 12mo. Engraved frontis. in Vol. 1, 3 engraved maps, 25 engraved plts., some folding, cont. spr. cf., rubbed, 1 spine chipped; the Rt. Hon. Visc. Eccles copy. [Sabin 2692] (CNY. Nov.18; 12) $2,200
- – Anr. Copy. 4 vols. 12mo. Minor staining & soiling in Vol. 4, old wax seal affixed to each title-lf., affecting few words on each, lacks? 1 plt., cont. hf. cf., light wear, w.a.f. (RO. Dec.11; 17) $430

BADDELEY, John F.
- Russia, Mongolia, China. L., 1919. *(250) numbered.* 2 vols. Fo. 6 folding maps in pocket, cont. vell., Wellington College arms gt. on upr. covers, partly unc.; pres. copy from author to Wellington College. (C. Mar.14; 130) *McDowell.* £1,000
- – Anr. Copy. 2 vols. Fo. Several maps in pocket on back of Vol. 1, orig. cl.-bkd. bds., bumped & slightly scuffed, spines discold. (CSK. Jan.27; 66) £600

BADER, J.
- Badische Volkssitten und Trachten. Karlsruhe, 1843-44. 4 pts. only (of 9?). Lge. 8vo. 2 hand-cold. aquatint plts., 14 steel-engraved views & plts., incompl., foxed, wraps., as a print coll., w.a.f. (VS. Dec.8; 782) Fls. 825

BADESLADE, T. & Toms, W.H.
- Chorographia Britanniae, or a set of Maps of all the Counties of England & Wales. 1742. *1st. Edn. 1st. Iss.* Sm. 8vo. Hand-cold. dedication lf., 46 hand-cold. maps, mott. cf. gt. (P. Jun.7; 343) £440
- – Anr. Copy. Engraved title, dedication & index ll., 46 County & regional maps (dtd. Sept. 29 1741), each with table listing market towns, title & 1 or 2 ll. slightly discold., mod. cf., w.a.f. (S. May 21; 32) *Nicholson.* £420

BADGER, Mrs. C.M.
- Floral Belles from the Green-House & Garden. N.Y., 1867. Fo. 16 cold. plts., frontis. loose, plts. stpd. on versos, minor soiling & foxing, orig. mor., ex-liby. (RO. Dec.11; 18) $325

BADGER, George Percy
- The Nestorians & Their Rituals. 1852. 2 vols. Spotting, cont. mor., rubbed. (CSK. Jan.13; 91) £190

BADMINTON LIBRARY of Sports & Pastimes
Ed.:– Duke of Beaufort & A.E.T. Watson. 1885-96. *(250) on L.P.* 28 vols. 4to. Orig. hf. mor., rubbed. (CSK. Jun.15; 157) £600
- – Anr. Edn., 1886-1902. 13 vols., various. Orig. cl., lightly soiled. (CSK. Nov.25; 98) £95
- – Anr. Edn. 1886-1903. *Various Edns.* 30 vols. Cl. (WW. Nov.23; 138) £210
- – Anr. Edn. Ca. 1890-1910. *Mixed Edns.* 30 vols. Orig. decor. cl., some little soiled. (TA. Sep.15; 454) £320

BAECK, Elias
- Atlas Geographicus oder Accuratae Darstellung der Gantzen Welt .... Augsburg, [1710]. Ob. fo. 1 map with brown stain, cont. hf. leath., rubbed & bumped. (HK. Nov.8; 884) DM 2,700

BAEDEKER, Karl
- Indien. Leipzig, 1914. *1st. Edn.* Orig. linen. (D. Nov.23; 951) DM 750
- – Anr. Copy. Orig. linen, lr. cover with sm. spot. (H. Nov.23; 339) DM 520
- – Anr. Copy. Orig. bdg., worn. (B. Feb.8; 559g) Fls. 450
- Russia; with Teheran, Port Arthur, & Peking. Handbook for Travellers. Leipzig, 1914. *1st. Edn.* Sm. 12mo. 40 maps & 78 plans, cold. & tinted, some folding, orig. cl. gt. (SG. Mar.29; 292) $275
- – Anr. Copy. 12mo. Some margin notes in pen & pencil, orig. cl., worn. (SG. Sep.22; 45) $200
- La Russie. Manuel du Voyageur. 1902. *3rd. Edn.* Sm. 8vo. Orig. cl. gt., spine rubbed. (TA. Apr.19; 71) £58

BAEDEKER, Karl -*Contd.*

- – **Anr. Copy.** Sm. 8vo. Fr. text, orig. cl. gt., rubbed on spine. (TA. Jun.21; 78)   **£52**
- **Russland. Handbuch für Reisende.** Leipzig, 1888. 1 plan with tear, 1 map loose, orig. linen. (D. Nov.23; 942)   **DM 480**

BAER, Karl Ernst von
- **Nachrichten über Leben und Schriften des Herrn Geheimrathes....** St. Petersb., 1865. Sm. Fo. Cl., hinges roughly reprd.; pres. copy from author to Prof. Hermann Wagner, with bkplt., Dr. Walter Pagel copy. (S. Feb.7; 37)   *Haas.* **£320**
- **Untersuchungen über die Gegaessverbinding Zwischen Mutter und Frucht.** Leipzig, 1828. Fo. Hf.-title, some foxing, orig. ptd. bds.; stp. of Prof. Dr. Volkmann on title, Dr. Walter Pagel copy. (S. Feb.7; 34)   *Haas.* **£340**

BAERMANN, Dr. Gustav & Eckersdorff, Dr. Otto
- **Atlas Tropischer Darmkrankeiten.** Leipzig, 1913. 4to. Orig. cl., rubbed. (TA. Dec.15; 560)   **£105**

BAESSLER, Arthur
- **Ancient Peruvian Art.** Trans.:– A.H. Keane. Leipzig, 1902-03. 4 vols. Atlas fo. 165 plts., many cold., each liby. stpd. on verso, loose in buckram folders, soiled. (SG. May 3; 28)   **$1,400**

BAFFO, Giorgio
- **Raccolta Universale delle Opere.** Côme, 1789. 4 vols. in 2. 19th. C. mor., spines decor., 1 spine slightly defect., 2nd. vol. rubbed. (SM. Mar.7; 2367)   **Frs. 2,600**

BAGLIVI, Giorgio
- **De Fibra Motrice et Morbosa ... de Circulatione Sanguinis ... Cordis Anatome.** Perugia, 1700. *1st. Ed.* (*Bound with:*) **PASCOLI, Alessandro – Il Corpo-umano o Breve Storia ...** Perugia & Venice, 1700. 20 engraved plts., hf.-title. Together 2 works in 1 vol. 4to. Vell., stained; Dr. Walter Pagel copy. (S. Feb.7; 38)   *Phillips.* **£450**

BAGSHAW, Samuel
- **History, Gazetteer & Directory of the County of Kent.** Ca. 1847. 2 vols. Orig. stpd. cl. (PWC. Jul.11; 573)   **£50**

BAIF, Jean-Antoine de
- **Mimes, Enseignemens et Proverbes.** Paris, 1576. 12mo. Compl. with 2 final blanks, 19th. C. hardgrd. mor. gt. (C. May 30; 69)   *D'Arcy.* **£1,300**

BAIF, Lazarus de
See— **BAYFIUS or BAIF, Lazarus de**

BAIGENT, William
- **A Book on Hackles for Fly Dressing.** [Newcastle upon Tyne, priv. ptd.], ca. 1941. *(40?).* 4to. Port., 4 plts., 164 hackles mntd. between perspex & framed in ll loose mounts (warped), text in mor., the whole contained in folding mor. case; included with lot a coll. of hackles in 33 sm. cellophane packets, each identified, & with note by Scott Atkinson: 'These hackles were bought from Doctor Baigent's widow ...'. (S. Oct.4; 2)   *Head.* **£1,250**

BAILEY, F. Manson
- **The Queensland Flora....** Brisbane, 1899-1902. 6 vols. (without General Index). Minor wear, bds., qtr. cl. (KH. May 1; 34)   **Aus. $140**

BAILEY, Nathan
- **Dictionarium Britannicum: Universal Etymological English Dictionary.** 1730. 4to. Cf. (PD. Dec.14; 204)   **£52**

BAILEY, William
- **One Hundred & Six Copper Plates of Mechanical Machines & Implements of Husbandry ....** Ed.:– A.M. Bailey. L., 1782. 2 vols. in 1. Fo. 106 engraved plts., some folding, cont. cf. (C. Nov.9; 3)   *Henderson.* **£720**
- [–] **Theoretisch – prakt. Werk, die Künste, Manufacturen u. Handelschaft betr. ....** München & Leipzig, 1779. 4to. Cont. hf. leath., rubbed. (HK. Nov.9; 1536)   **DM 400**

BAILLIE, Granville Hugh
- **Watchmakers & Clockmakers of the World.** 1929. *1st. Edn.* (*With:*) – **Watches, Their History,**

Decoration & Mechanism. 1929. *1st. Edn.* Together 2 vols. 4to. Orig. matching cl., gt.-decor. spines, slightly worn at ends. (TA. May 17; 456)   **£68**

BAILLIE, Robert
[–] **Ladensium Autokatakisis, the Canterburians Self-Conviction. Or an Evident Demonstrations of the Avowed Arminianisme, Poperie, & Tyrannie of that Faction.** [Edinb.], Apr. 1640. *1st. Edn.* 4to. Limp vell., s.-c.; Sir Robert Gordon sig. [STC 1205] (BBA. May 3; 122)   *Thomas.* **£55**

BAILLON, H.
- **Dictionaire de Botanique.** Ill.:– Faguet. 1876-92. 4 vols. & supp. 4to. Supp. pasted to Vol. 2, publisher's hf. chargin, corners worn. (HD. Jul.6; 3)   **Frs. 1,100**
- **Iconographie de la Flore Française.** N.d. 5 vols. Approx. 500 cold. plts., leaves, folders. (HD. Jul.6; 4)   **Frs. 1,600**

BAILLY
- **Manual de Fisica.** Madrid, 1830. Later leath., gold-tooled decor., gt. spine, gt. inner & outer dentelle. (D. Nov.23; 665)   **DM 420**

BAILLY, Jean Sylvain
- **Histoire de l'Astronomie Moderne.** Paris, 1779. *1st. Edn.* 2 vols. Lge. 4to. 18 folding engraved plts., some foxing, cont. mott. cf., spines gt., some wear. (SG. Apr.26; 12)   **$275**
- – **Anr. Edn.** 1779 (Vols. 1 & 2), 1785 (Vol. 3). 3 vols. 4to. Cont. roan. (HD. Jan.24; 3)   **Frs. 1,150**

BAILLY-HERZBERG, Janine
- **L'Eau-Forte de Peintre au Dix-Neuvième Siècle** Paris, 1972. *(500) numbered.* 2 vols. 4to. Orig. cl., d.-w. (S. Apr.30; 2)   *Brecht.* **£60**

BAINBRIDGE, George C.
- **The Fly Fisher's Guide.** L'pool., 1816. *1st. Edn.* 9 hand-cold. plts. (8 called for, plt. 9 inserted from later edn.), slight spotting & offsetting, orig. bds., unc., slightly worn. (S. Oct.4; 3)   *Banks.* **£200**

BAINBRIDGE, Henry Charles
- **Peter Carl Fabergé.** L., 1949. *(350) De Luxe.* 4to. Orig. hf. mor., s.-c. (S. May 1; 676) *Ritchie.* **£125**

BAINES, Edward
- **History of the County Palatine & Duchy of Lancaster.** L., 1836. 4 vols. 4to. Ports., maps, plts., hf. mor. (S. Apr.9; 161)   *Kohler.* **£180**
- – **Anr. Copy.** 4 vols. 4to. 123 engraved plts. & maps, including 3 folding, folding pedigrees, some foxing, cont. cf., gt. spines, rubbed, Vol. 4 spine defect. (SKC. May 4; 1769)   **£120**
- – **Anr. Edn.** Ed.:– John Harland. 1868-70. *New Edn.* 2 vols. Lge. 4to. Subscribers list, folding map (foxed), orig. cf. gt., Vol. 1 unopened. (SKC. Mar.9; 1964)   **£60**

BAIONNETTE
Ill.:– G. Bofa, Sem, C.Laborde, Falké & others. 2 Jan. 1919-22 Apr. 1920. 67 nos. (of 68) in 1 vol. Lacks no. 24. 4to. Bds., very worn, lacks spine. (HD. Mar.14; 85)   **Frs. 1,800**

BAIRD, Spencer F.
- **Birds of the Boundary, with Notes by the Naturalists of the Survey.** [Wash., 1857]. From Emory's 'United States & Mexican Boundary Survey'. 4to. 25 hand-cold. litho. plts., hf. cf., ex-liby. (SG. Oct.6; 29)   **$120**

BAIRD, Spencer F. & others
- **The Birds of North America.** Phila., 1860. 2 vols. Lge. 4to. 100 hand-cold. litho. plts., 1 plt. discold. in margin, few lightly smudged, prelims. in text vol. foxed, orig. cl., spines faded, ex-liby. (SG. Oct.6; 32)   **$700**
- **A History of North American Birds.** Boston, 1874. 3 vols. 4to. 64 hand-cold. plts., some spotted, text ills., orig. cl., spotted, spines worn. (S. Apr.10; 469)   *Quaritch.* **£120**
- – **Anr. Edn.** Boston, 1875. 3 vols. Hf. mor. & marb. paper bds., corners bumped. (LH. Jan.15; 232)   **$110**
- **The Water Birds of North America.** Boston, 1884. 2 vols. 4to. Many woodcuts hand-cold., some foxing, cl., some wear. (RO. Dec.11; 19)   **$500**

BAKER, Charles H., Jr.
- **The Gentleman's Companion. I.--Exotic Cookery Book; II--Exotic Drink Book.** 1939. *Derrydale Pr., (1250).* 2 vols. Tall 8vo. Two-toned cl. (SG. Mar.15; 207)   **$110**

BAKER, Charles Henry Collins
- **Crome.** 1921. 4to. Orig. cl. (BBA. Sep.8; 112)   *Zwemmer.* **£60**
- – **Anr. Copy.** 4to. Orig. cl., rubbed. (BBA. Jul.27; 233)   *Sims, Reed & Fogg.* **£50**
- **Lely & the Stuart Portrait Painters.** 1912. *(375) numbered on pure rag paper.* 2 vols. 4to. Cl. gt., untrimmed; Lord Lee, of Fareham bkplt. (SKC. Mar.9; 1703)   **£340**

BAKER, Charles John
- **Sydney & Melbourne, with Remarks on the Present State & Future Prospects of New South Wales....** 1845. No errata slip, bdg. not stated, unc., slight wear. (KH. May 1; 35)   **Aus. $180**

BAKER, Edward Charles Stuart
- **The Fauna of British India....** L., 1922-30. *2nd. Edn.* 8 vols. Cold. plts., orig. cl. (S. Apr.10; 403)   *Wesley.* **£120**
- **The Game Birds of India, Burma & Ceylon.** 1921-30. 3 vols. Cont. hf. mor., rubbed. (BBA. Feb.23; 128)   *Jackson.* **£80**
- **The Indian Ducks & their Allies.** Ill.:– after Gronvold, Lodge & Keulemans. L., Bombay, Calcutta & Simla, 1908. Additional title. 30 cold. litho. plts., cont. hf. mor. by R.H. Porter lightly rubbed, covers slightly bowed. (CSK. Apr.27; 76)   **£90**
- – **Anr. Copy.** 30 chromolitho. plts., some spotting, hf. mor. (S. Apr.10; 471)   *Walford.* **£80**
- **Indian Pigeons & Doves.** Ill.:– after Gronvold & Lodge. 1913. 27 cold. plts., some light spotting, cont. hf. mor., lightly soiled & scuffed. (CSK. Apr.27; 75)   **£85**
- – **Anr. Copy.** Cold. plts., spotted, hf. mor., worn. (S. Apr.10; 470)   *Evans.* **£65**

BAKER, Henry
- **The Microscope Made Easy.** L., 1742. *1st. Edn.* Title remargined, buckram, ex-liby. (SG. Mar.22; 34)   **$100**

BAKER, Humphrey
- **The Well Springe of Sciences, which Teacheth the Perfect Worke & Practice of Arithmeticke.** L., 1574. Sm. 8vo. A little, mainly marginal, worming, some later margin notes & calculations, dust stained, cont. cf., worn, lr. cover loose. [STC 1210a] (BBA. May 3; 5)   *Thomas.* **£700**

BAKER, J.
- **The Imperial Guide with Picturesque Plans of the Great Post Roads.** 1802. 32 plts., some hand-cold., some staining, cl. (P. Jun.7; 233)   **£170**

BAKER, Sir Richard
- **A Chronicle of the Kings of England....** Ill.:– W. Marshall (engraved title). 1660. *3rd. Edn.* Fo. Later hf. cf., spine gt. (SKC. Nov.18; 1861)   **£70**

BAKER, Sir Samuel White
- **Der Albert Nyanza.** Trans.:– J.E. Martin. Jena, 1867. *1st. German Edn.* 2 vols. Title lf. with old liby. stp., cont. bds., slightly rubbed. (GB. May 3; 29)   **DM 680**
- **Ismailia.** 1874. *1st. Edn.* 2 vols. Slight spotting, orig. decor. cl. gt. (SKC. Mar.9; 1999)   **£60**

BAKER, Thomas
[–] **Hampstead Heath. A Comedy.** L., 1706. *1st. Edn.* Sm. 4to. Some ll. spotted or slightly stained, some tears reprd., MS. note tipped in wraps.; bk.-label of James Tregaskis. (S. Apr.9; 237)   *Hannas.* **£80**

BAKER STREET JOURNAL: An Irregular Quarterly of Sherlockiana
Ed.:– Edgar W. Smith. N.Y., 1951-78. Vols.1-28, New Series, together 112 numbers. Ills., pict. wraps., stapled, inserted in 14 gt.-lettered plastic & metal binders. (SG. Apr.19; 251)   **$175**

BAKST, Leon
- **The Designs for The Sleeping Princess ....** Preface:– Andre Levison. 1923. *(1000) numbered.*

Fo. Port., 54 mntd. col. plts., 2 mntd. col. ills., orig. vell.-bkd. cl., spine gt., partly unc., covers slightly stained. (LC. Jul.5; 9) £300
- The Inedited Works. N.Y., 1927. (600). Lge. 4to. Phototypes hand-cold., some offset, mainly from tipped in plts., some light soiling, a few tipped in plts. lifting, hf. cl. & bds., d.-w. lightly soiled, edges chipping & tearing. (CBA. Mar.3; 18) $250

BAKST, Leon & others
- The Russian Ballet. Ill.:- Bakst, Goncharova, Matisse, Picasso. etc. L., 1921. (500) numbered. Fo. Linen; dedication copy. (DS. Oct.28; 2118) Pts. 30,000

BALASCHOFF, P. de & Herbillon, A.
- L'Armée Allemande sous l'Empereur Guillaume II. Paris, 1890. 4to. 620 engrs., & 4 chromolitho. watercols., some glue marks, mor., Egypt arms painted on upr. cover. (HD. Jan.27; 248) Frs. 5,000

BALBINO, B.A.
- Diva Wartensis, seu Origines et Miracula Magnae Dei, Hominumque Matris Mariae .... Prague, 1655. Sm. 4to. Cont. cf. (HD. Dec.2; 63) Frs. 1,000

BALCAZAR Y SABARIEGOS, José
- Hernán Peréz del Pulgar el de las Hazañas. Est. Hist. Crítico. Ciudad Real, 1898. Ltd. Iss. 4to. Wraps. (DS. Apr.27; 2472) Pts. 20,000

BALCOMB, Mary N.
- Nicolai Fechin. [Flagstaff, 1975]. 1st. Edn. 4to. Bdg. not stated, d.-w. slightly rubbed. (CBA. Jan.29; 186) $100

BALDAEUS, Philippus
- Naauwkeurige Beschryvinge van Malabar en Choromandel ...en het machtige Eyland Ceylon ... nevens afgoderye der Oost-Indische Heydenen. Amst., 1672. 1st. Edn. Fo. Additional engraved title, 2 ports., 35 engraved plts. & maps (all but 1 double-p.), 1 or 2 fore-margins shaved, wormholes in inner margins of 1st. few gatherings, cont. cf., reprd. (S. May 22; 430) Randall. £370
- Wahrhaftige Ausuführliche Beschreibung der Berühmten Ost - Indischen Kusten Malabar und Coromandel, als auch der Insel Zeylon.... Amst., 1672. 1st. German Edn. Fo. Cont. leath., slight worming. (R. Oct.13; 3017) DM 4,000

BALDJIANTZ, Fr. Agheksandr
- Vayelagruthiwn [Calligraphy]. Vienna, ca. 1840. Ob. fo. Some plts. slightly soiled, orig. wraps., worn. (BBA. Jan.19; 25) Parikian. £170

BALDUNG, Hieronymus
- Aphorismi Compunctionis Theologicales. [Strasburg], Joh. Grüninger, 1497. 4to. Rubricated, bds., from Fondation Furstenberg-Beaumesnil. [H. 2270; BMC I, 111] (HD. Nov.16; 53) Frs. 18,200

BALDUS, Edouard
- Recueil d'Ornements d'apres les Maîtres, les plus Celèbres des XV, XVI, XVII et XVIIIe Siècles. Paris, 1866. Fo. 100 heliogravure plts., loose as iss. (SG. Nov.10; 19) $130

BALDUS DE JANUA, Johannes
- Catholicon. [Strasburg, Adolf Rusch], ca. 1470. Lge. fo. Many initials painted in red or blue, 1st. lf. 19th. C. decor., margin of 1st. text lf. reprd., lacks 13 ll. (including last), cont. stpd. cf. over wood bds., brass corners & clasp, spine renewed, lr. cover separated in 2; Paul Schmidt copy. [HC 2251; BMC I, 65; Goff B23] (HD. Mar.21; 41) Frs. 8,500
- - Anr. Edn. Venice, B. Locatellus for Octavianus Scotus, 20 Nov. 1495. Fo. Final lf. supplied in early MS., blank lr. half of title lf. replaced, 1st. few ll. loose, cont. tooled leath. over oak bds., reprd., lacks spine & clasps; the Walter Goldwater copy. [BMC V, 445; Goff B-33] (SG. Dec.1; 56) $800

BALDWIN, Edward (Pseud.)
See— GODWIN, William 'Edward Baldwin'

BALDWIN, Thomas
- Airopaidia. Chester, 1786. 1st. Edn. Hf.-title, sm. margin tear in title, hf. cf. (S. Mar.6; 467) Quaritch. £360

BALDWIN, William
See— KNAPP, Andrew & Baldwin, William

BALFOUR-KINNEAR, G.P.R.
- Flying Salmon. L., 1937. 1st. Edn. 1 vol. Hf. cf. gt. by Bayntun, spine emblematically tooled. (With:) - Spinning Salmon. L., 1938.1st. Edn. 1 vol. Cf. gt. by Bayntun, spine emblematically tooled. (S. Oct.4; 4) Gmur. £90

BALLADS & BROADSIDES Chiefly of the Elizabethan Period
See— COLLMAN, Herbert L.

BALLADS & SONGS OF LOVE
Ed.:- J. Hofmiller. Ill.:- A. Simons. [München, Bremer Pr., 1930]. (280) on Bütten. Sm. 4to. Orig. hand-bnd. vell., gold decor., by Frieda Thiersch, engraved ex-libris. (H. Nov.23; 951) DM 780

BALLANTYNE, Rev. James
- Homes & Homesteads in the Land of Plenty, A Handbook of Victoria. Melbourne, 1871. Cl.-bkd. decor. bds., covers faded. (CA. Apr.3; 17) Aus. $170

BALLANTYNE, Robert Michael 'Comus'
- The Coral Island: A Tale of the Pacific Ocean. L., 1858. 1st. Edn. 1 vol. A.N. by Mrs. Ballantyne 'My dear husband's own working copy. J.D.B.'. 4 p A.L.s. (dtd. 25 Aug. 1892) to his wife, mntd. cut sig. (With:) - The Buffalo Runners: A Tale of the Red River Plains. L., 1891. 1st. Edn. 1 vol. 4 p A.L.s. (dtd. 14 Mar. 1892) to his wife. Together 2 vols. Orig. cl., 1 in folding case. (SG. Sep.22; 51) $150

BALLARD, George
- Memoirs of Several Ladies of Great Britain, who have been Celebrated for their Writings or Skill in the Learned Languages Arts & Sciences. Oxford, 1752. 1st. Edn. 4to. Few ll. spotted, cont. cf.-bkd. bds., worn. (BBA. Jun.28; 5) Lake. £55

BALLARD COLLECTION
- Illustrated Catalogue & Description of Ghiordes Rugs of the Seventeenth & Eighteenth Centuries. St. Louis, [1916]. (100) numbered, with pres. inscr. by Ballard. 4to. Prospectus laid in, three-qtr. mor., spine rubbed. T.L.s. from Ballard to Mr. & Mrs. Breckinridge Long presenting the book. (SG. Jan.26; 255) $200
- Oriental Rugs in the City Art Museum of St. Louis. Ed.:- Maurice S. Dimand. St. Louis, 1935. (1000) numbered. 4to. Port. frontis., 69 plts., cl. (SG. Jan.26; 256) $250

BALLESTEROS, Thomas de
- Tomo Primero de las Ordenanzas del Peru. Lima, 1685. Fo. Linen. (DS. Nov.25; 2040) Pts. 160,000

BALLINO, Giulio
- De' Disegni delle piu Illustri Città, & Fortezze del Mondo. Venice, 1569. Pt. 1 (all publd.). Sm. fo. Lacks 9 etchings, slightly foxed & spotted, title with erased MS. owners mark, 18th. C. hf. leath. defect. (HK. May 15; 71) DM 3,800

BALS D'ENFANTS
Ill.:- Lievre. Paris [?], ca. 1850. 152 x 1,810mm. Panorama, 16 tinted litho. ills., hand-cold., slightly spotted, orig. bds. gt., title on upr. cover; van Veen coll. (S. Feb.28; 299) £70

BALTARD, Victor & Callet, F.
- Monographie des Halles Centrales de Paris construites sous le Règne de Napoléon III. 1863. Lge. fo. Margin slit without defect to 1 plt., plt. stains, some pp. with margin stains, cont. hf. chagrin, 1 cover with paper loss. (HD. Feb.29; 1) Frs. 4,200

BALTAZAR, Jean
[-] Histoire de la Guerre de Guyenne, Commancée sur la Fin du Mois de Septembre 1651, et Continuée jusques à l'Année 1653. [Paris?, 1657?]. Minor margin dampstains to few ll., cont. vell., MS. ex-libris. (SG. Oct.27; 18) $600

BALTHASAR DE PORTA
- Expositio Canonis Missae. [Leipzig], Konrad Kachelofen, 1497. 4to. Blank portion of last lf. reprd., bds., covered with fragment from a medieval MS. missal; the Walter Goldwater copy. [Goff B-40] (SG. Dec.1; 57) $350

BALTHUS, Balthazar Klossowski, dit
- Mitsou. Preface:- Rainer Maria Rilke. Erlenbach-Zürich & Leipzig, [1921]. Sm. 4to. Sewed. (HD. May 16; 62) Frs. 7,100

BALTIMORE, Cecil Calvert, Baron
See— MARYLAND

BALTRUSAITIS, Jurgis
- Etudes sur l'Art Medieval en Georgie et Armenie. Paris, 1929. 4to. Orig. wraps., slightly soiled. (BBA. Sep.8; 267) Sims, Reed & Fogg. £55

BALZAC, Honoré de
- Béatrix ou les Amours Forcés, Scènes de la Vie Privée. Paris, 1839. Orig. Edn. 2 vols. Cont. glazed hf. cf., corners, spines gt.; Michel Bolloré coll. (HD. Nov.16; 13) Frs. 17,000
- Le Cabinet des Antiques. Scène de la Vie de Province. Paris, 1839. Orig. Edn. (With:) - Gambara. Paris, [1839]. Together 2 vols. Washed, mntd., hf. mor. gt., corners, unc., sigd. by Belz-Niedre; Eug. Richtenberger copy. (HD. Mar.19; 13) Frs. 4,000
- Les Cent Contes Drolatiques colligez es Abbaies de Touraine.... 1832-37. Orig. Edn. 3 vols. Cont. hf. chagrin. (HD. Jun.29; 12) Frs. 3,900
- César Birotteau. Paris, 1838. Orig. Edn. 2 vols. Cont. hf. roan. (HD. Jun.29; 16) Frs. 3,200
- - Anr. Copy. 2 vols. 22 pp. advts., some light foxing, sewed, ptd. wraps., sm. paper loss from 2 corners & centre of wrap. (HD. Mar.19; 12) Frs. 1,400
- Le Chef - d'oeuvre inconnu. Ill.:- P. Picasso. (65) De Luxe Edn. on Jap. Imp. Lge. 4to. With 2nd series of engravings, printers mark sigd. or monogrammed, hand-bnd. red mor., decor. inner & outer dentelles, wtrd. silk doubls. & end-papers, s.-c., orig. pictor. wraps. bnd. in, spine slightly faded & slightly rubbed; Hauswedell coll. (H. May 24; 676) DM 41,000
- Les Chouans. Ill.:- Julien Le Blantwood engraved by Léreillé. Paris, 1889. 4to. Cont. hf. mor., decor. & mosaic spine, corners, unc., wrap. & spine preserved, by Ch. Meunier. (HD. Feb.17; 49) Frs. 2,700
- Comédie Humaine. Ed.:- George Saintsbury. 1895-1905. 40 vols. Hf. mor., spines gt., partly unc. (S. Oct.11; 304) Traylen. £420
- La Conestable. Ill.:- Albert Robida. Paris, 1914. (100) with suite on china. 4to. Vell. by Levitzky, painted border, wrap. preserved; extra-ill. with 2nd. suite. (HD. Jun.13; 8) Frs. 2,000
- Les Contes Drôlatiques Colligez ez Abbayes de Touraime.... Ill.:- Gustave Doré. Paris, 1855. [5th. Edn.]. Late 19th. C. red mor, blind- & gt.-decor.; Michel Bolloré coll. (HD. Nov.16; 24) Frs. 7,500
- - Anr. Copy. Publisher's pict. bds., unc. (HD. Feb.17; 8) Frs. 3,100
- - Anr. Copy. Hf. mor., unc. (HD. Apr.11; 3) Frs. 1,200
- - Anr. Copy. Lge. 8vo. Page XX for XXI, 'Joyeulx' on p. 326, Adresse on p.425, other corrections, cont. hf. leath. gt. (H. May 22; 610) DM 1,000
- Le Curé de Village. Scène de la Vie de Campagne. Paris, 1841. Orig. Edn. 2 vols. Cont. hf. cf., spines gt., Lord Henry Seymour armorial cypher; Michel Bolloré coll. (HD. Nov.16; 16) Frs. 44,000
- - Anr. Copy. 2 vols. Cont. hf. roan. (HD. Mar.19; 17) Frs. 1,900
- David Séchard. Paris, 1843. Orig. Edn.?. 2 vols. in 1. Owner's stp. on titles, hf. roan, spine blind- & gt.-decor. (HD. Mar.19; 20) Frs. 1,250
- Le Dernier Chouan ou la Bretagne en 1800. Paris, 1829. Orig. Edn. 4 vols. Sm. 12mo. Stp. on titles, cont. hf. roan, spines gt.; Michel Bolloré coll. (HD. Nov.16; 1) Frs. 18,000
- Die Dressig Tolldreisten Geschichten. Trans.:- B. Rüttengaur. Ill.:- H. Zille. Leipzig, 1911. 2 vols. 6 ll.sigd., 1 lf. monogrammed, 1 lf. dtd. '1916', some ll. with artists MS. pen or pencil notes, private burgundy mor., blind-tooled, leath. inlaid decor. (HT. May 10; 2457) DM 41,000
- Droll Stories. Trans.:- G. Sims. Ill.:- Gustave Doré. L., ca. 1874. Orig. decor. cl., red mor.-bkd.

BALZAC, Honoré de -Contd.

s.-c.; A.N. by artist & 1 p. letter by author tipped in. (SPB. Dec.13; 806) $250
- **Etudes de Moeurs au XIXe Siècle. Scènes de la Vie Parisienne.** Paris, 1834-35. Orig. Edn. 4 vols. Cont. hf. roan, spines gt., Michel Bolloré coll. (HD. Nov.16; 7)   Frs. 8,500
- **Etudes de Moeurs au XIXe Siècle. Scènes de la Vie de Province.** Paris, 1837. Orig. Edns. Vols. III & IV only. On papier Jonquille, cont. hf. cf., spines decor.; from Ph. Burty liby., Michel Bolloré coll. (HD. Nov.16; 10)   Frs. 17,100
- **Eugénie Grandet.** Ill.:– August Leroux. Paris, 1911. Hf. mor., corners, by Blanchetière, spine decor., wrap. (HD. Jun.13; 6)   Frs. 1,300
- **La Fille aux Yeux d'Or.** Ill.:– Henri Gervex. Paris, 1898. 4to. Jansenist mor., red mor. liners, blind– & gt.-decor, wrap. preserved, spine slightly faded. (HD. Jun.13; 7)   Frs. 4,800
- **Die Frau Konnetable.** Ill.:– L. Corinth. 1922. (380) on H.M.P., sigd. by artist. 4to. 15 orig. lithos., orig. pict. hf. vell.; printer's mark sigd. by artist. (GB. Nov.5; 2360)   DM 1,500
- – **Anr. Copy.** Lge. 4to. 15 lithos., some margins slightly spotted, orig. hf. vell., cover ill. (H. Nov.24; 1452)   DM 800
- **Gesammelte Werke.** Reinbek, (1952-64) De Luxe Edn. 24 vols. (of 40). Orig. red mor. (H. May 22; 973)   DM 1,200
- **Gobseck.** Trans.:– P. Cohen-Portheim. Ill.:– F. Feigl. Berlin, 1922. De Luxe Edn., (30) numbered on Bütten, with etchings sigd. by artist. 4to. 10 orig. etchings, orig. vell. gt. (GB. Nov.5; 2460)   DM 600
- – **Anr. Copy.** Lge. 4to. 10 etchings, some foxing, orig. vell., spine lightly faded. (H. Nov.24; 1232)   DM 540
- – **Anr. Edn.** Trans.:– P. Cohen – Portheim. Ill.:– F. Feigl. Berlin, [1922]. (120) numbered. Lge. 4to. Orig. vell., upr. cover. gold-tooled. (HK May 17; 3061)   DM 400
- **Un Grand Homme de Province à Paris, Scène de la Vie de Province.** Paris, 1839. Orig. Edn. 2 vols. Cont. glazed hf. cf., spines decor.; Milal Bolloré coll. (HD. Nov.16; 14)   Frs. 7,100
- – **Anr. Copy.** 2 vols. Hf. chagrin, unc.; Marquis de Villeneuve-Butel copy. (HD. Mar.19; 15)   Frs. 1,050
- **The Hidden Treasures, or, The Adventures of Maître Cornelius.** Ill.:– Mallette Dean, illuminated & hand-cold. by D. Allen. Kentfield, 1953. (160). Two-tone bds., covers lightly rubbed, spine faded. (CBA. Nov.19; 1) $200
- **Histoire de la Grandeur et de la Décadence de César Birotteau.** Paris, 1838. Orig. Edn. 2 vols. Cont. glazed hf. cf., spine blind– & gt.-decor.; Michel Bolloré coll. (HD. Nov.16; 11)   Frs. 11,000
- **Histoire des Parens Pauvres: La Cousine Bette et les Musiciens.** Paris, [1846-47]. Orig. Edn. Bnd. from the pts. 4to. Lacks 'les grands danseurs du roi', cont. hf. cf., spine gt. (HD. Mar.19; 24)   Frs. 1,400
- **Histoire des Treize.** Bruxelles, 1833. 16mo. Cont. hf. roan, spine blind– & gt.-decor. (HD. Mar.19; 10)   Frs. 3,000
- **L'Initié.** Paris, [1848]. Orig. Edn. 2 vols. Cont. hf. chagrin, spines gt.; Tsarskoe Selo liby. stps. on hf.-titles, Michel Bolloré coll. (HD. Nov.16; 21)   Frs. 6,500
- **Une Instruction Criminelle.** Bruxelles, 1836 [for 1846]. 16mo. Sewed. (HD. Mar.19; 23) Frs. 1,100
- **Eine Leidenschaft der Wüste.** Trans.:– E. von Hollander. Ill.:– W. Geiger. 1924. (220) numbered, with etchings sigd. 4to. 8 orig. etchings, orig. pict. hf. vell. (GB. Nov.5; 2507)   DM 750
- **Le Livre Mystique: Les Proscrits; Histoire Intellectuelle de Louis Lambert; Séraphita.** Paris, 1 Dec. 1835. 1st. Coll. Edn. 2 vols. Cont. hf. roan, corners, spines decor., Michel Bolloré coll. (HD. Nov.16; 8)   Frs. 4,500
- **La Lune de Miel.** Paris, [1845]. 2 vols. Hf. cf., spines blind– & gt.-decor., wraps., sm. repair to corner of lr. cover of wrap. (HD. Mar.19; 22)   Frs. 1,750
- **Madame de la Chanterie [La Femme de Soixante Ans].** Paris, [1854]. New Edn. Cont. hf. chagrin, spine gt.; Tsarskoe Selo liby. stp. on hf.-title, from Michel Bolloré coll. (HD. Nov.16; 23) Frs. 1,800

- **Das Mädchen mit den Goldaugen.** Trans.:– E. Hardt. Ill.:– Marcus Behmer. Leipzig, 1904. (500). 4to. Orig. vell., gt. spine & upr. cover, spotted, unc. (B. Apr.27; 744)   Fls. 500
- **La Maison du Chat-qui-Pelote.** Preface:– F. Sarcey. Ill.:– L. Dunki wood engraved by Baud. Paris, 1899. (200) numbered on vell. du Marais. Jansenist Bradel mor., gt. decor., wrap. preserved, by Champs. (HD. Feb.17; 50)   Frs. 1,000
- **Maximes et Pensées.** Paris, 1852. 1st. Separate Edn. Sm. 12mo. Glazed hf. cf. by Allô, spine gt., unc.; Victor Déséglise ex-libris, Michel Bolloré coll. (HD. Nov.16; 22)   Frs. 1,500
- [–] **Le Médecin de Campagne.** Paris, Feb. & Jul. 1833. Orig. Edn. 2 vols. 4 pp. errata, 8 pp. advts., cont. cf., blind– & gt.-decor., spines slightly worn; Michel Bolloré coll. (HD. Nov.16; 6) Frs. 18,000
- – **Anr. Edn.** 1833. Orig. Edn. 2 vols. in 1. Errata at end of Vol. 1, catalogue at end of Vol. 2, cont. mor. finish hf. roan, spine decor. (minor defects). (HD. Jun.29; 13)   Frs. 5,100
- **Les Mémoires de Deux Jeunes Mariées.** Paris, 1842. Orig. Edn. 2 vols. Cont. pol. hf. roan, corners, spines decor.; Tsar Nicholas I copy, Tsarskoe Selo stp. (HD. May 16; 3)   Frs. 13,500
- **Menschliche Komödie.** Intro.:– H. von Hofmannsthal. Trans.:– F.P. Greve & others. Ill.:– E. Gill. Leipzig, 1908-11. (100) or (200) on Bütten. 16 vols. On Bütten, orig. mor. (With:) – **Physiologie der Ehe.** Trans.:– H. Conrad. Leipzig, 1908. 2nd. Edn. (100). De Luxe Edn. Orig. mor. (H. May 22; 977)   DM 2,800
- **Mystische Geschichten.** Gg. Goyert. Ill.:– A. Kubin. München, 1920. 1st. Edn. De Luxe Edn., (200) numbered on Bütten. Stp. on lr. pastedown, orig. hf. leath. (HK. Nov.11; 4122)   DM 540
- **Nouveaux Contes Philosophiques. Maître Cornélius. Madame Firmiani. L'Auberge Rouge. Louis Lambert.** Ill.:– Tony Johannot, engraved by Porret (frontis.). Paris, 1832. Orig. Edn. Cont. glazed hf. cf., spine blind– & gt.-decor.; Michel Bolloré coll. (HD. Nov.16; 5)   Frs. 3,200
- **Oeuvres.** Ill.:– T. Johannot, Stoal, Bertall, Monnier, Daumier, etc. Paris, 1867. 4 vols. 4to. Last ll. vol. IV wormed, cont. hf. roan. (HD. Mar.14; 86)   Frs. 1,150
- **Oeuvres Complètes. La Comédie Humaine....** 1853-55 (1 vol. dtd. 1846). 2nd. Edn. 20 vols. 1 port. & 149 figures (of 154), cont. hf. chagrin, Vol. 2 in imitation bdg. (spine faded). (HD. Jun.29; 17)   Frs. 4,200
- – **Anr. Edn.** Ill.:– T. Johannot, Meissonier, Gavarni etc. Paris, 1855. 20 vols. Some foxing, 1 lf. slit, maroon hf. chagrin. (HD. Dec.16; 5)   Frs. 3,400
- – **Anr. Edn.** Paris, 1874. Private hf. mor. gt., some light rubbing & defects. (HT. May 9; 1365)   DM 540
- – **Anr. Edn.** Ill.:– after Johannot, Gavarni, Nanteuil, Daumier, Bertall, etc. Paris, 1877. 20 vols. Hf. red chagrin. (HD. Apr.11; 2) Frs. 6,100
- **Oeuvres Illustrées.** Ill.:– after T. Johannot, Staal, Bortall, H. Mornet, Meissorier, Daumer, etc. [1867-79]. 8 vols. bnd. in 4. 4to. Old hf. roan, limp decor. spines, sm. defects. (HD. Dec.9; 96)   Frs. 1,100
- **Paris Marié. Philosophie de la Vie Conjugale....** Ill.:– Gavarni. Paris, 1846. 1st. Printing of ills. Sm. 8vo. Cont. hf. roan, spine decor. (HD. May 3; 179)   Frs. 1,250
- **La Peau de Chagrin.** Ill.:– Tony Johannot, engraved by Porret. Paris, 1831. Orig. Edn. 2 vols. Some foxing, traces of dampstaining, hf. cf. by Vogel, spines blind– & gt.-decor., Michel Bolloré coll. . (HD. Nov.16; 4)   Frs. 9,100
- – **Anr. Copy.** 2 vols. Hf. mor., by L. Pouillet, 1871, decor. spine, marb. covers, marb. end-papers, lightly bumped; ex-libris. (D. Nov.24; 2388)   DM 3,000
- – **Anr. Edn.** Ill.:– Gavarni, Baron Janet-Lange & others. Paris, 1838. 1st. Printing. 19th. C. hf. chagrin, spine decor. (slightly rubbed). (HD. May 3; 178)   Frs. 1,200
- **Le Péché Véniel.** Ill.:– Paul Avril. Paris, 1901. (400). (65) on japan with etchings in 3 states. Lge. 8vo. Hf. mor., corners, by Yseux, spine decor., wrap & spine, unc. (HD. May 3; 180) Frs. 1,450
- **Petites Misères de la Vie Conjugale.** Ill.:– Bertall. Paris, [1846]. Orig. Edn. 1st. Printing. Some

worming, hf. maroon chagrin, unc., wrap., reprd. (HD. Jan.30; 28)   Frs. 1,100
- [–] **Physiologie du Mariage.** Paris, 1830. Orig. Edn. 2 vols. Cont. glazed hf. cf., spines gt.-decor., Michel Bolloré coll. (HD. Nov.16; 2)   Frs. 9,000
- – **Anr. Edn.** Paris, 1830, [1829]. Orig. Edn. 2 vols. Cont. hf. cf., sm. corners, blind– & gt.-decor., unc., s.-c., minor repairs to jnts. (HD. Mar.19; 7)   Frs. 2,000
- **Romans et Contes Philosophiques.** Ill.:– Perret after Tony Johannot. Paris, 1831. Orig. Edns. (except 'La Peau de Chagrin'). 3 vols. Frontis.'s ptd. on chine, cont. hf. chagrin, corners, spines richly decor.; Tsarskoîe-Selo liby. stp. on 1st. lf. (HD. Sep.22; 184)   Frs. 10,000
- **Scènes de la Vie Privée.** Paris, 1832. Vols. III & IV: Orig. Edn., rest: 2nd. Edn. 4 vols. Cont. hf. cf., spines gt., slightly faded. (HD. Mar.19; 9)   Frs. 3,500
- **Une Ténébreuse Affaire.** Ill.:– Francois Schommer, engraved by L. Boisson. Paris, 1909. Edn. De Grand Luxe. Lge. 8vo. On vell., hf. mor., corners, by Bernard, ill. wrap. & spine preserved, unc. (HD. May 3; 181)   Frs. 1,600
- **Ursule Mirouet.** Bruxelles, 1841. 2nd. Belgian Edn. 2 vols. 18mo. Sewed; Michel Bolloré coll. (HD. Nov.16; 19)   Frs. 1,000
- – **Anr. Edn.** Paris, 1842. Orig. Edn. 2 vols. Hf. cf., spines gt., unc.; H. Destailleur ex-libris, Michel Bolloré coll. (HD. Nov.16; 17)   Frs. 8,500
- – **Anr. Copy.** 2 vols. 18mo. Cont. hf. cf., spines blind– & gt.-decor.; Michel Bolloré coll. (HD. Nov.16; 18)   Frs. 1,000
- **La Vendetta.** Ill.:– Adrien Moreau. Paris, 1904. Numbered on Japan. Etching's in 3 states including pure etching & finished state with remarks, cont. hf. red mor., decor. spine, corners, unc., wrap. preserved, by Carayon. (HD. Feb.17; 51)   Frs. 2,000

BALZAC, Honoré de (Text)
See— **FRANÇAIS PEINTS PAR EUX-MÊMES**

BALZAC, Jean-Louis Guez de
- **Le Barbon.** Paris, 1648. Orig. Edn. L.P., cont. lavallière mor., Du Seuil decor; autograph dedication to M. de Saumaise on title, from E. Daguin liby. (HD. Mar.29; 4)   Frs. 25,000
- **Lettres Choisies.** Paris, 1647. Orig. Edn. 2 vols. L.P., cont. lavallière mor., Du Seuil decor; autograph dedication to Monsieur de Saumaise on title of each vol., from E. Dagim liby. (HD. Mar.29; 3)   Frs. 32,000
- – **Anr. Edn.** Leiden, 1652. 12mo. Red mor. gt. extra by Thouvenin-Jeune, sigd. in gt. on spine, rubbed; inscr. & bkplt. of Franklin D. Roosevelt. (PNY. Jun.6; 427) $200

BALZAC, René
- **Ballade du Pauvre Macchabé mal enterré.** Ill.:– André Derain. N.d. 4to. Served in Italian style, slightly soiled. (HD. Dec.9; 115)   Frs. 1,100

BANCK, O.A.
- **Die Gallerien von München.** Leipzig & Dresden, ca. 1850. 4to. Slightly browned, cont. leath., rubbed & bumped. (R. Apr.4; 2085)   DM 520
- – **Anr. Edn.** Leipzig & Dresden, ca. 1860. 2 vols. 4to. Some foxing, cont. hf. leath., rubbed. (HK. Nov.9; 1397)   DM 440

BANCROFT, Edward, M.D.
- **Experimental Researches concerning the Philosophy of Permanent Colours, & the Best Means of Producing Them, by Dyeing, Calico Printing, &c.** Phila., 1814. 1st. Amer. Edn. 2 vols. Some stains, spotting, etc., crude hf. linen, ex-liby. (SG. Oct.6; 139) $100

BANCROFT, George
- **Memorial on the Canal de Haro as the Boundary Line of the United States of America.** [Berlin], Ca. 1872. 4to. Hf. mor.; H.O. Havemeyer Jnr. bkplt., 1895. (SG. Jan.19; 99) $175

BANCROFT, Hubert Howe
- **The Book of the Fair.** Chic., 1893. 3 vols. Fo. Three-qtr. mor., rubbed. (RO. Mar.28; 12) $150

BANDELLO, Matteo
- Le Nouvelle Del Bandello. L., 1740. 4 vols. 4to. Tooled cf.; St. John Hornby bkplt. (LH. Sep.25; 456) $150

BANDELLO DE CASTRONOVO, Vincenzo
[–] Disputatio Solemnis de Conceptione b. Virgi. [Valladolid], 1502. 4to. Lacks 1 lf. with woodcut & 2 ll. at end, some staining & soiling, minimal worming, cont. blind-tooled mor. over wood bds., corners restored, end-papers renewed, ties defect. (HK. Nov.8; 100) DM 950

BANGE, E.F.
- Die Deutschen Bronzestatuetten, des 16. Jahrhunderts. Berlin, 1949. 4to. Orig. cl.-bkd. bds. (BBA. Sep.8; 236) Leicester Art Books. £65

BANGE, J.
- Thüringische Chronick oder Geschichtbuch. Mühlhausen, 1599. 4to. Browned, some slight foxing, some underlining, title side margin bkd., 18th. C. bds., very bumped. (HK. Nov.9; 1223) DM 550

BANGS, John Kendrick
- The Pursuit of the House-Boat. Ill.:– Peter Newell. N.Y., 1897. 1st. Edn. 12mo. Pict. cl., light wear, d.-w., some fraying & chipping; Ker Leach coll. (RO. Jun.10; 379) $160

BANIER, Abbé & Le Mascrier, Abbé
- Histoire Générale des Cérémonies, Moeurs et Coutumes Religieuses de tous les Peuples du Monde. Ill.:– after Bernard Picart & Cochin. Paris, 1741. 7 vols. Fo. Lacks 1 plt., 1 plt. torn, cont. marb. cf., spines decor., worn. (HD. Jun.26; 4) Frs. 7,200

BANKES, Rev. Thomas
- A New & Authentic System of Universal Geography. [1787]. 2 vols. Fo. Vol. 1 lacks title & a few text ll., some maps slightly torn, cf. gt., 3 covers detched., as a coll. of plts., w.a.f. (P. Dec.8; 28) Burgess. £500
- – Anr. Edn. ca. 1790. Fo. Engraved frontis., 85 engraved plts. & 2 maps only, later cl., w.a.f. (CSK. Oct.7; 33) £400
- – Anr. Copy. 2 vols. Fo. Frontis., 23 engraved maps, 84 engraved plts., cont. cf., jnts. cracked & reprd. with tape, w.a.f. (S. May 21; 162) Traylen. £250
- – Anr. Edn. Ca. 1800. Fo. Rebnd., mod. panel cf. (PD. Jun.13; 126) £450
- A System of Universal Geography. L., [1787]. 2 vols. Fo. Engraved frontis., 89 plts., 22 folding maps, some torn with loss, soiled thro.-out, later hf. cf., w.a.f. (CSK. Aug.5; 9) £380
- – Anr. Edn. N.d. 2 vols. in 1. Fo. 83 engraved plts., 22 maps (some folding, several soiled or cleanly torn), title detchd., old cf., worn, w.a.f. (CSK. Jul.6; 143) £180

BANKS
- A Treatise on Mills. L. & Kendal, 1795. 1st. Edn. 4 pts. in 1 vol. Hf.-title, subscribers list, errata, slight offsetting, cont. tree cf., spine gt.; John D. Stanitz coll. (SPB. Apr.25; 28) $600

BANKS, Joseph
- The Endeavour Journal .... Ed.:– J.C. Beaglehole. Ca. 1962. 1st. Edn. 2 vols. No bdg. stated. (JL. Jun.24; 90) Aus. $130
- – Anr. Edn. Ed.:– J.C. Beaglehole. Sydney, 1963. 2nd. Edn. 2 vols. Bdg. not stated. d.-w.'s. (KH. May 1; 36) Aus. $110

BANNERMAN, David Armitage
- The Birds of the British Isles. Ill.:– George E. Lodge. 1953-63. 1st. Edn. 12 vols. 4to. Orig. cl. gt., d.-w.'s, protective cellophane; Vol. 1 sigd. by author on hf.-title. (TA. Jul.19; 249) £300
- – Anr. Copy. 12 vols. 4to. Orig. cl. gt., d.-w.'s (spines browned, some frayed at edges, 1 reprd. with cellophane). (TA. Apr.19; 138) £240
- – Anr. Copy. 12 vols. Orig. cl. gt., d.-w.'s. (P. Dec.8; 261) Tryon. £220
- – Anr. Copy. 12 vols. 4to. Orig. buckram. (SKC. Jan.13; 2302) £160
- The Birds of Tropical West Africa. 1930-51. 8 vols. 4to. Orig. cl., 6 vols. in d.-w. (SKC. May 4; 1832) £320
- The Birds of West & Equatorial Africa. Edinb. &

L., 1953. [1st. Edn.]. 2 vols. Plts., some cold., text ills., orig. cl. (S. Apr.10; 404) Sharpe. £80
- – Anr. Copy. 2 vols. Orig. cl. (LC. Mar.1; 134) £50

BANNERMAN, David Armitage & Winnifred Mary
- Birds of the Atlantic Islands. 1963-68. 4 vols. Lge. 8vo. Orig. cl., d.-w. (LC. Mar.1; 136) £250
- Birds of Cyprus. Ill.:– D.M. Reid-Henry & Roland Green. 1958. 1st. Edn. Orig. cl., d.-w. (LC. Mar.1; 137) £130
- – Anr. Copy. Orig. cl., d.-w. (BBA. May 3; 74) Grahame. £70

BANNERMAN, Helen
- The Story of Sambo & the Twins. L., [1937]. 1st. Engl. Edn. Sq. 12mo. Cl., d.-w.; A.N.s., autograph postcard sigd. & 3 p A.L.s., all from Alexander Gregory (Bannerman's companion, friend & secretary). (SG. Dec.8; 25) $150

BANNING, Kendall
- Bypaths in Arcady: A Book of Love Songs. Ill.:– after Lejaren A. Hiller. Chic., 1915. (77) numbered on Japan vell. 4to. This copy unnumbered, sewed, unopened; all photogravures sigd. by Hiller in pencil. (SG. Nov.10; 82) $200

BANSEMER, J.M. & Falkenhagen Zaleski, P.
- Atlas, containing Ten Maps of Poland. 1837. Fo. 10 double-p. engraved hand-cold. maps, orig. cl., rubbed, loose. (BBA. Feb.9; 251) Lettres Slaves. £55

BANVILLE, Théodore de
- Odes Funambulesques.... Alençon, 1857. Orig. Edn. 12mo. Minimal foxing, red mor. gt. by Lortic, spine decor., wrap.; A.L.s. by author. (HD. May 3; 183) Frs. 2,300
- – Anr. Edn. Paris, 1859. 12mo. Red hf. mor. by Lortic. (HD. Oct.14; 16) Frs. 1,000
- Oeuvres diverses. Paris, v.d. 10 vols. 12mo. Unif. 19th. C. hf. red mor. (HD. Apr.11; 4) Frs. 1,300
- Les Princesses. Ill.:– Georges Rochegrosse. Paris, 1904. (45) numbered with 3 states of engrs. including pure etching & state with remark on japan. Cont. Bradel hf. red mor., gt., blind & mosaic decor., corners, unc., wrap. & spine preserved, by Carayon, added pict. prospectus. (HD. Feb.17; 52) Frs. 1,450
- – Anr. Edn. Ill.:– G. Rochegrosse, engraved by E. Decizy. Paris, 1904. (400). (130) on japan or grand vélin d'Arches, with 2 states of ills. before the letter (1 with remarks). 4to. Bordeaux hf. mor., corners, by Yseux, wrap. & spine preserved, unc. (HD. May 3; 184) Frs. 1,200

BAPST, Germain
- Souvenir d'un Canonier de l'Armée d'Espagne (1808-1814). Paris, [1892]. Dedication preserved, hf. bradel buckram, corners, wrap. (HD. Jan.27; 4) Frs. 1,000

BARADO, Francisco
- Nuestros Soldados. Ill.:– Jose Cusachs. Barcelona, [1909]. Fo. Publishers cl. (DS. Nov.25; 2041) Pts. 22,000

BARANTE, Amable-Guillaume-Prosper Brugiere, baron de
- Histoire des Ducs de Bourgogne. 1826. 13 vols. Cont. grd. cf., limp decor. spines. (HD. Dec.9; 97) Frs 2,600

BARATTA, A.
- Constantinopoli Effigiata e Descritta .... Ill.:– T. Allom, J. Sands, & others. Turin, 1840. 4to. Frontis., 98 engraved plts., some light foxing, frontis. slightly soiled, & with blank corner torn away, 1 or 2 plts. loose & slightly frayed at edges, cont. russ.-bkd. bds., rubbed. (C. Mar.14; 28) Martinos. £150

BARATTI, Giacomo
- The Late Travels ... into the Remote Countries of the Abissins, or of Ethiopia Interior. 1670. 1st. Engl. Edn. Lacks 1st. & last (blank?) ll., browned thro.-out. repair to 1 lf., mod. bds. [Wing B677] (BBA. Sep.29; 16) Remington. £160

BARBA, A. A.
- Docimasie oder Probir- und Schmeltz-Kunst. Ed.:– M. Godar. Wien, 1749. 1st. German Edn. [Sabin 3255c]. (Bound with:) – Berg-Büchlein. Trans.:– I.L.M. [ie. J. Lange]. Frankfurt, 1739. 3rd. German Edn. 2 pts. [Sabin 3255b]. Together 2 works in 1 vol. Copper engrs. to 1st. bnd. at end. Cont. hf. vell., head of spine slightly defect. (R. Apr.4; 1456) DM 3,400
- – Anr. Copy. (Bound with:) – Berg Büchlein ... Frankfurt, 1739. Together 2 works in 1 vol. Cont. hf. vell. (HK. Nov.8; 448) DM 1,800

BARBARO, D.
- La Pratica della Perspectiva .... Venice, 1568. Sm. fo. Foxing at end of vol., cont. paper bds. (HD. Dec.15; 2) Frs. 2,500

BARBAULT, Jaae
- Nouveau Recueil de Vues des Principales Eglises, Places, Rues et Palais de Rome Moderne. Roma, 1763. Fo. Album, 45 engraved plts., frontis. & some plts. with folds, frontis. stained, lacks bdg., as a coll., w.a.f. (CR. Jun.6; 95) Lire 2,800,000
- Les Plus Beaux Monuments de Rome Ancienne. Rome, 1761. 1st. Edn. Fo. Hf.-title, 128 engraved plts., title creased, some stains, 1 plt. torn & reprd., 2 with sm. holes, mod. leath. (SG. Apr.26; 14) $550

BARBER, John W.
- History & Antiquities of New Haven (Conn.). New Haven, 1831-[32]. 1st. Edn. 12mo. 8 hand-cold. engraved plts., ptd. note tipped in, old linen, outer corners dampstained. (SG. Jan.19; 100) $200

BARBER, John W. & Howe, Henry
- Historical Collections of the State of New York. N.Y., 1841. Folding map cold. in outl., slightly spotted, cf., worn. (BBA. Jul.27; 271) Clark. £60

BARBER, Mrs. Mary
- Some Drawings of Ancient Embroidery. Ed.:– W. Butterfield. L. & Manchester, 1880. 1st. Edn. Tall fo. 30 chromolitho. plts., ex-liby., gt.-pict. cl. (SG. May 3; 31) $150

BARBER, Thomas
- Picturesque Illustrations of the Isle of Wight. N.d. Some light spotting, cont. red mor. gt. (CSK. Feb.10; 153) £55

BARBER, William
- Farm Buildings; or Rural Economy. L., 1802. 1st. Edn. 5 (of 6) sepia plts. (Bound with:) DEARN, T.D.W. – Designs for Lodges & Entrances to Parks, Paddocks & Pleasure-Grounds. L., 1811. 1st. Edn. 20 sepia plts. (Bound with:) MORRIS, Richard – Essays on Landscape Gardening. L., 1825. 1st. Edn. 3 hand-cold. plts. & 3 sepia plts. (2 with overslips). Together 3 works in 1 vol. 4to. Hf. mor., gt.-tooled spine, bkplt. (GM. Dec.7; 620) £575

BARBERINO, Francesco
- Documenti d'Amore. Ill.:– Bloemaert. Rome, 1640. 4to. Faint traces of damp in some margins, cont. vell. (C. May 30; 11) Thorp. £300

BARBEY D'AUREVILLY, Jules
- Les Bas-Bleus. Paris, 1878. Orig. Edn. Last 5 ll. frayed, not affecting text, richly decor. mor., bnd. for author by Gayler-Hirou; orig. photo. of author mntd. on bristol, bnd. opposite title. (HD. Apr.26; 16) Frs. 3,400
- Le Chevalier des Touches. Paris, 1864. Orig. Edn. 12mo. Hf. mor., corners, spine decor., wrap. & spine preserved. (With:) – Une Histoire sans Nom. Paris, 1882. Orig. Edn. 12mo. Hf. buckram, corners, wrap. (HD. May 3; 185) Frs. 2,900
- Les Diaboliques. Paris, 1874. Orig. Edn. 12mo. Bradel hf. mor., corners, by Champs, wrap. & spine preserved; extra-ill. with port. & 9 plts. by F. Rops for Lemerre edn. (HD. May 3; 186) Frs. 5,500
- – Anr. Copy. 12mo. Cont. hf. chagrin, spine gt. (HD. Mar.27; 43) Frs. 1,900
- – Anr. Edn. Ill.:– Lobel-Riche. Paris, [1910]. (300). 21 engrs., 3 plts. not used in the work at end, mor., s.-c., some wear to box. (SPB. Dec.13; 776) $600
- Littérature Epistolaire. Paris, 1892. Orig. Edn. (12) numbered on holland. Orig. bdg. (HD. Apr.26; 17) Frs. 1,050

BARBEY D'AUREVILLY, Jules -*Contd.*

- **Oeuvres Complètes.** Paris, 1926-27. *1st. Coll.
Edn., partly Orig. Edn. (200) on Arches.* 15 vols.
(of 17, lacks 'Une Vieille Maitresse'). Hf. roan,
unc. (HD. May 21; 102) Frs. 1,300
- - **Anr. Edn.** Paris, 1926-27. *1st. Coll. Edn., partly
Orig. Edn.* 17 vols. Numbered copy on vergé, sewed.
(HD. Jul.2; 39) Frs. 2,300
- **Teufelskinder.** Trans.:– A. Schurig. A. Kubin,
München, 1921. *1st. Edn. De Luxe Edn., (60)
numbered on H.M.P., sigd. by artist.* 4to. Orig.
pict. cold. vell. (HK. Nov.11; 4124) DM 620

BARBIER, Antoine Alexandre

- **Dictionnaire des Ouvrages Anonymes et Pseu-
donymes.** Paris, 1806-08. 4 vols. Cont. hf. cf. (BBA.
Nov.10; 5) *Robertshaw.* £65
- - **Anr. Edn.** Paris, 1806-09. 4 vols. Cont. cf., worn.
(BBA. Nov.10; 4) *Duran.* £50
- - **Anr. Edn.** Paris, 1872-78. *3rd. Edn.* 4 vols. in 7
pts. Lge. 8vo. Ptd. wraps., defect. (SG. Sep.15; 20)
$200

BARBIER, George

- **Casanova: Panorama Dramatique, Décors et
Costumes.** Paris, [1921]. 24 hand-cold. plts., many
heightened in gold or silver, sm. tear to title reprd.,
decor. bd. folder, lightly soiled, lacks ties. (SG.
Jan.12; 25) $600
- **Falbalas et Fanfreluches: Almanach des Modes
Presentes, Passées et Futures.** Paris, [1921-25]. 5
vols. Each vol. with title vig. & 12 plts., cold.
through stencils, unif. red hf. cf., slightly rubbed,
orig. pict. wraps. bnd. in. (S. Nov.21; 51)
Desk. £1,700
- - **Anr. Edn.** Paris, 1922, 1924-26. 4 pts. Loose in
orig. pict. wraps. (R. Oct.12; 2194) DM 7,200
- **La Guirlande des Mois.** Paris, 1917-21. 5 vols.
16mo. 31 hand-cold. plts., ills., orig. decor. silk
bdgs., decor. d.-w's., & s.-c.'s., slightly worn, 1917
vol. possibly not orig. (SPB. May 17; 567) $2,000

BARBIERI, Carlo

- **Direction pour les Voiageurs en Italie.** Bologna,
1779. *5th. Edn.* Slight dampstains, cont. hf. mor.,
slightly rubbed; Chiswick House bkplt. (BBA.
Nov.30; 71) *George's.* £75

BARBOUTAU, Pierre

- **Biographies des Artistes Japonais dont les Oeuvres
Figurent dans la Collection Pierre Barboutau:
Volume I, Peintres; Volume II, Estampes et Objets
d'Art.** Paris, 1904; Amst., 1905. *(1000) numbered.*
2 vols. Sm. fo. Decor. wraps., spines defect. (1
taped), disbnd. (SG. Aug.25; 217) $120

BARBUSSE, Henri

- **L'Enfer.** Ill.:– Edouart Chimot. Paris, [1921].
Definitive Edn. (355) numbered on velin d'Arches.
Fo. 12 etched plts., lacks 1 tissue-guard, lev. by
Renée Kieffer, lge. rings in gold & silver on both
covers, spine gt., orig. wraps. bnd. in; pict. bkplt.
of Pieter Tjebbes. (SG. Feb.16; 20) $650
- - **Anr. Edn.** Ill.:– Edouard Chimot. Paris, 1921.
Definitive Edn. 4to. Hf. mor., corners, by David,
spine decor. (slightly faded), wrap. preserved. (HD.
Jun.13; 9) Frs. 3,000

BARBUT, Jacques

- **Les Genres des Insectes de Linnée.** 1781. *[1st.
Edn.].* 4to. Plts. hand-cold., text in Engl. & Fr.,
subscribers list, cont. hf. cf., spine gt. (SKC. May
4; 1833) £130
- - **Anr. Copy.** 4to. Extra engraved title, 2 lge.
uncold. folding plts., 20 hand-cold. copperplates,
parallel Fr. & Engl. text, subscribers lf., mod. hf.
mor. (SG. Nov.3; 6) $400

BARCLAY, Rev. James

- **A Complete & Universal Dictionary.** ca. 1840.
4to. Engraved title (loose), 54 maps & town plans,
cf. gt., spine defect., w.a.f. (P. Oct.20; 3) £420
- - **Anr. Copy.** 4to. Many maps & town plans badly
foxed, hf. cf., defect. (P. Sep.8; 373)
Postaprint. £360
- - **Anr. Copy.** 4to. Some plts. hand-cold., hf.-title
defect., title spotted, slight browning, cont. hf. cf.,
rubbed. (S. Dec.20; 814) *Morris.* £60
- - **Anr. Edn.** Ill.:– Thomas Moule. L., n.d. 4to.
Engraved frontis., title, 7 plts., 53 county maps &

plans, cont. cf., lightly rubbed. (CSK. Dec.2; 10)
£480
- - **Anr. Copy.** 4to. 62 maps, including 21 cold. in
outl., 1 torn & loose, text stained, hf. cf., as a coll.
of plts., w.a.f. (P. Dec.8; 40) *Nicholson.* £380
- **Universal English Dictionary.** Ed.:– B.B.
Woodward. 1840. 4to. Hf. cf. gt. (P. Sep.8; 374)
Brown. £420
- - **Anr. Edn.** Maps & plans: T. Moule. Ca. 1840.
4to. 54 maps & plans, some staining, bdg. defect.
(P. Mar.15; 35) *Potter.* £440
- - **Anr. Copy.** 4to. 55 engraved maps & plans,
plts., lacks title, some soiling, cont. hf. mor., worn,
w.a.f. (CSK. Nov.4; 14) £350
- - **Anr. Edn.** Maps:– J. Archer. Ca. 1850. 4to.
Engraved frontis., additional vig. title, 56 engraved
county maps, 3 general maps, hand-cold. in outl.,
some margin dampstains, prelims. heavily soiled,
cont. bds., worn & brkn. (TA. Jul.19; 79) £85
- - **Anr. Copy.** 4to. Cont. hf. mor., gt.-decor. spine.
(TA. Nov.17; 155) £70
- - **Anr. Edn.** Ill.:– J. Archer. Ca. 1860. 4to.
Engraved title, 57 county maps, hand-cold. in outl.,
minor spotting, cont. hf. cf., upr. cover detchd. (TA.
Aug.18; 63) £68

BARCLAY, Robert

- **Eine Apologie oder Vertheidigungs-Schrifft, der
Recht-christlichen Gotts-Gelehrtheit....** N.p., 1684.
1st. German Edn. Sm. 4to. Lightly browned thro.-
out, cont. hf. vell., slightly spotted & rubbed, spine
defect. (HT. May 8; 76) DM 560
- **An Apology for the True Christian Divinity, Being
an Explanation & Vindication of the Principles &
Doctrines of the People called Quakers.** Bg'ham.,
Baskerville Pr. 1765. *8th. Edn. in Engl.* 4to. Some
foxing & minor stains, later three-qtr. mor. (RO.
Dec.11; 20) $155
- - **Anr. Copy.** Lge. 4to. Lacks errata lf., later hf.
mor. & cl. (SG. Apr.19; 19) $110
- **An Apology of the Quakers.** Bg'ham., 1765. *8th.
Edn.* Lge. 4to. Cont. cf. gt. (VG. Mar.21; 1064)
Fls. 550

BARCLAY-SMITH, Phyllis
See— **POLLARD, Hugh Bertie Campbell &
Barclay-Smith, Phyllis**

BARDECHE, M. & Brasillach, Robert

- **Histoire du Cinéma.** Paris, 1943. *Partly Orig.
Edn. (25) numbered on Arches.* Hf. mor. gt.,
corners. (HD. Apr.26; 20) Frs. 1,700

BARDI, Louise

- **[Views of Florence].** [Italy], ca. 1800. Ob. fo. 26
engrs., light marginal stains, hf. cf., defect. (S.
Apr.9; 23) *Mugnani.* £230

BARDSWELL, Monica
See— **TRISTRAM, Ernest William & Bardswell,
Monica**

BARDUZZI, Bernardino

- **A Letter in Praise of Verona.** Trans.:– Betty
Padice. Verona, Officina Bodoni, 1974. *(150)
numbered on H.M. Pescia paper.* Tall 8vo. Lge.
initial, vell.-bkd. patterned bds., s.-c. (SG. May 17;
278) $325

BARDWELL, Thomas

- **The Practice of Painting & Perspective made
Easy.** 1756. 4to. Dampstain to lr. verso of title-p.,
repair to margin of 1 lf., cont. cf., gt. arms.; sigd.
by author. (P. Oct.20; 41) £70

BAR[E]LETA, Gabr.

- **Sermones Quadragesimales de Sanctis.** Lyon,
1504. *3rd. Edn.* Sm. 4to. 19th. C. leath. in cont.
style, 1 centre clasp. (GB. Nov.3; 926) DM 500

BARETTI, Joseph

- **A Journey from London to Genoa through
England, Portugal, Spain & France.** 1770. 4 vols.
(With:) - **An Account of the Manners & Customs
of Italy, with Observations on the Mistakes of some
Travellers.** 1768. *1st. Edn.* 2 vols. Slight staining to
some ll. in Vol. 2. Together 6 vols. Cont. spr. cf.,
spines gt. (LC. Oct.13; 230) £200
- - **Anr. Copy.** 4 vols. in 2. No hf.-titles, cont. hf.
cf., worn. (BBA. Dec.15; 64) *Bickersteth.* £70

**BARGON, Frederick Charles Pierre Edward
'Claude Farrère'**

- **Mademoiselle Dax, Jeune Fille.** Ill.:– Pierre
Brissaud. Paris, 1926. *(625) Vergé d'Arches.* Decor.
bds., spine & edges darkening, Offset to end-papers.
(CBA. Aug.21; 457) $120
- **La Maison des Hommes Vivants. Roman.** Paris,
[1911]. *Orig. Edn. (26) on japon impérial.* 12mo.
Jansenist mor. by David, 1911, mor. liners, silk
double end-ll., wrap. & spine; autograph dedication
to Henriette Roggers, from Claude Farrère liby.
(HD. May 21; 114) Frs. 1,800
- **Les Petites Alliées.** Paris, [1910]. *Orig. Edn. (30)
on imperial japan.* 12mo. Damson mor., lavallière
mor. doubl., gt. decor., damson silk doubls., s.-c.,
by Semet & Plumelle. (HD. Mar.14; 119)
Frs. 1,500
- **Thomas l'Agnelet Gentilhomme de Fortune.** Ill.:–
Guy Arnoux. Paris, 1927. 4to. Red mor. by
Creuzevault, spine decor., imitation clasp, wrap.
preserved, s.-c. (HD. Jun.13; 29) Frs. 3,200

BARHAM, Henry

- **Hortus Americanus; containing, An Account of
the Trees Shrubs, & Other Vegetable Productions
of South-America & the West India Islands, &
Particularly of the Island of Jamaica.** Kingston,
Jamaica, 1794. *1st. Edn.* Lacks 2 prelims., title &
1st. few ll. dampstained, title & E1 reprd., some
liby stps., buckram. [Sabin 3376] (SG. Mar.22; 35)
$250

BARHAM, Rev. Richard Harris 'Thomas Ingoldsby'

- **The Ingoldsby Legends.** Ill.:– Arthur Rackham.
L., 1907. 4to. 1 plt. loose, red mor., upr. cover
with central panel of col. onlays & blind tooling
reproducing an ill. from the book, gt.-tooled cornerpieces, by Rivière. (S. Nov.22; 348) *Joseph.* £180
- - **Anr. Edn.** Ill.:– Arthur Rackham. L., 1907.
(560) numbered & sigd. by artist. 4to. Mor. gt.,
with reproduction of design from the de-luxe edn.
on upr. cover, inner borders gt., silk doubls. & end-
ll. (S. Nov.22; 347) *Joseph.* £230

BARIZIUS, Gasp.

- **Epistole.** Strassburg, Prüss, 1486. 4to. Rubricated
at beginning, title with sm. margin defects., slightly
wormed, slightly browned & stained near end, last
lf. very spotted with defects., sewed. [H. 2676;
BMC I, 120; Goff B 264] (HK. Nov.8; 102)
DM 800

BARKER, Matthew Henry

- **[-] Greenwich Hospital.** Ill.:– George Cruikshank.
1826. 4to. 12 hand-cold. engraved plts., some ll.
slightly spotted, later cf. by Morrell, rebkd., with
orig. gt. spine; bkplt. of Austin Dobson. (BBA.
Oct.27; 55) *Primrose Hill.* £140

BARKER, Nicolas

- **Bibliotheca Lindesiana.** Roxb. Cl., 1977. Orig.
qtr. mor. (S. Oct.4; 232) *Traylen.* £85
- **The Publications of the Roxburghe Club, 1814-
1962.** Roxb. Cl., 1964. Orig. qtr. mor. (S. Oct.4;
233) *Maggs.* £340

BARKER, Thomas

- **[-] The Art of Angling. ....** 1653. *2nd. Edn.* Sm.
4to. Somewhat browned & soiled, title torn in lr.
margin, 19th. C. hf. roan, worn; bkplt. of Thomas
Joy, with note of purchase at the White Knights
(Blandford) sale, 7 Jun. 1819, given to him by J.
Garle Browne. [Wing B783] (S. Oct.4; 5)
Head. £780

BARKER, Thomas, Artist, 1769-1847

- **Forty Lithographic Impressions from Drawings by
....** Bath, 1813. *1st. Edn. (200).* Fo. 40 mntd. litho.
plts., cont. bds., slightly spotted, rebkd. with mor.
(C. Mar.14; 28a) *Weston.* £320

BARLACH, Ernst

- **Der Findling.** Berlin, 1922. *[1st. Edn.].* Lge. 4to.
Printers mark sigd. by artist, without 2nd. series of
woodcuts on Japan, orig. vell., upr. concer gt. (HK.
May 17; 2556) DM 900
- - **Anr. Copy.** 4to. 20 orig. woodcuts, some
browning in parts, orig. pict. bds. (GB. Nov.5;
2262) DM 650
- **Die Wandlung Gottes.** Paris, 1922. *1st. Edn.* Ob.
fo. Slightly yellowed, orig. pict. bds., margins
slightly spotted. (GB. May 5; 2151) DM 500

BARLAEUS, Caspar
– Nederlandsch Brazillië onder het Bewind van Johan Maurits, Grave van Nassau, 1637-44. Trans.:– S.P. L'Honore Naber. 's-Gravenhage, 1923. *1st. Dutch Edn.*, *(160)* on H.M.P. Lge. fo. Cl., unc. (B. Oct.4; 714) Fls. 1,600

BARLUT, Jacques
– The Genera Vermium. 1783. 4to. Engraved frontis., 11 hand-cold. engraved plts., cont. cf. gt., worn. (SKC. Sep.9; 1981) £85

BARNARD, Fred
– A Series of Character Sketches from Dickens. L., [1879]. Tall fo. Minor edge stains & fraying, orig. ptd. bd. portfo., worn, some cover soiling & staining. (RO. Apr.23; 126) $120

BARNARD, George
– The Brunnens of Nassau & Scenery of the River Lahn. N.d. Fo. List of plts. with vig. (stained), 28 tinted litho. plts., including 4 titles (all as called for), some spotting to 7 plts., slight margin staining, plts. loose due to gutta-percha bdg., orig. mor.-bkd. cl. gt., spine rubbed. (LC. Mar.1; 444) £1,800

BARNARDUS DE GORDONIO
– Opus Lilium Medicinae Inscriptum de Morborum prope Omnium Curatione .... Lyons, 1550. Slight margin worming, blank corner of title torn, vell., very soiled; Dr. Walter Pagel copy. (S. Feb.7; 48) *Phelps.* £100

BARNEBY, W. Henry
– Life & Labour in the Far, Far West ... a Tour of the Western States .... L., 1884. *2nd. Edn.* Frontis. loosely inserted, cont. maroon mor. gt. by Zaehnsdorf; pres. copy, inscr. to Paul H. Foley, with 3 A.L.s from author to Foley laid in, the Rt. Hon. Visc. Eccles copy. (CNY. Nov.18; 14) $260

BARNES, Djuna
[–] Ladies Almanack. Paris, 1928. *(1000) numbered on Alfa paper.* Sm. 4to. Pict. wraps., unc., unopened. (SG. Mar.1; 16) $100
– – **Anr. Edn.** Paris, priv. ptd., 1929. *(1000) numbered on Alfa paper.* Sm. 4to. Pict. wraps., unlettered glassine sleeve. (SG. May 24; 6) $110
– Ryder. N.Y., 1928. Cl., d.-w. (SG. Mar.1; 18) $100
– Selected Works. N.Y., [1962]. Qtr. cl., d.-w.; inscr. (SG. Mar.1; 21) $150

BARNES, Joseph K. & others
– The Medical & Surgical History of the War of the Rebellion. Ill.:– Bell, Ward, French & others. Washington, 1870-88. 3 vols. bnd. in 6. Thick lge. 4to. Orig. cl., worn, liby stps. (SG. Apr.5; 11) $475
– – **Anr. Copy.** Pt. I Vols. 1 & 2, Pt. II Vols. 1 & 2, Pt. III Vol. 1. Lge. 4to. Cl., torn & completely loose, w.a.f. (SG. Oct.6; 34) $275

BARNES, Joshua
– Euripidis Quae Extant Omnia: Tragoediae nempe XX.... Camb., 1694. 2 pts. in 1 vol. Fo. In Greek & Latin, cont. cf. with old reback, some minor wear. [Wing E3415] (TA. Aug.18; 269) £58
– History of ... Edward III, King of England & France ... together with that of Edward, Prince of Wales ... Sirnamed the Black-Prince. Camb., 1688. *1st. Edn.* Fo. Engl. mor. gt. cover borders, gt. inner & outer dentelle, gt. spine, slightly bumped; engraved Robert Clayton ex-libris, Robert Taylor ex-libris. (D. Nov.24; 3872) DM 600

BARNES, Dame Juliana
See— BERNERS or BARNES, Dame Juliana

BARNES, William
– Poems of Rural Life, in the Dorset Dialect. Dorchester, 1844. *1st. Edn.* Orig. cl., unc.; Frederic Dannay copy. (CNY. Dec.16; 18) $320

BARNETT, P. Neville
– Australian Book-Plates, & Book-Plates of Interest to Australia. Sydney, 1950. *(200) numbered & sigd.* 4to. Bds., qtr. vell., unc., d.-w. (KH. May 1; 38) Aus. $270

BARNETT, R.D. (Ed.)
See— JEWISH MUSEUM of London

BARON & FEME: A Treatise of the Common Law Concerning Husbands & Wives
L., 1700. *1st. Edn.* Disbnd. [Wing B 899] (SG. Oct.27; 20) $130

BARONIUS, Caesar, Cardinal
– Annales Ecclesiastici. Antio., 1593. Vol. 3 (of 12). Fo. Title with owners mark, cont. blind-tooled pig over wood bds., slightly spotted, some scratches, 8 part chiselled brass bosses, 2 clasps. (HK. May 15; 72) DM 700

BAROZZI, Giacome, called Vignola
– Le Due Regole della Perspettiva Pratica. Ed.:– E. Danti. Bologne. 1682. Vell. (HD. Dec.15; 57) Frs. 1,600
– Grand et Nouveau Vignole, augmenté de l'Ordre Français avac un Traité de Géometrie de la Cour de Pierres; des Batiments et Jardins; de Charpente; de Menuiserie et Serrurerie .... Ed.:– Panseron. Ill.:– Vanmaelle. Paris, ca. 1780. Fo. Hf. cf., corners worn. (HD. Feb.22; 225) Frs. 1,100
– [The Palazzo Farnese at Caprarola]. Ill.:– Giuseppe Vasi. Rome, 1746-48. Fo. Suite of 5 engraved plans & views, comprising 3 folding & 2 double-p., recased in cont. Roman red mor., elab. gt., with arms of a Cardinal of the Orsini family, reprd., rebkd. (C. Dec.9; 164) *Henderson.* £700
[–] Règles des Cinq Ordres d'Architecture de Vignolle. Ed.:–Le Muet. Paris, n.d. Engraved title, 50 plts., cont. vell., defect. (P. Jul.5; 224) £110
– – **Anr. Edn.** Ed.:– Le Muet. Paris, early 16th. C. Cont. vell. (P. Jan.12; 170) *Kentish.* £150
– Vignola Revived. L., 1761. Sm. fo. 56 engraved plts. (3 folding), folding plts. torn & 1 holed, other defects., mainly marginal, stained, qtr. sheep, worn, ex-liby. (SG. Jan.26; 174) $400
See— LABACCO, Antonio – BAROZZI, Giacomi, called Vignola

BARPO, G.B.
See— VILLE, Antoine de – BARPO, G.B. – COCARELLA, B.

BARRA, F.X.
– Proyecto Memoria de ... sobre ia Conducción de Aguas a Madrid. Madrid, 1832. Lge. fo. Mor. (DS. Oct.28; 2493) Pts. 42,000

BARRADAS, José Perez de
– Orfebreria Prehispanica de Columbia. Madrid, 1954-65. 6 vols. 4to. Cl., d.-w. (LH. Sep.25; 185) $170

BARRATT, Thomas
[–] The Annals of Hampstead. 1912. *(550) sigd.* 3 vols. 4to. Orig. cl., d.-w.'s torn. (BBA. Jun.14;305) *Levy.* £120
– – **Anr. Copy.** 3 vols. 4to. Orig. cl., d.-w.'s; 2 A.L.s loosely inserted. (SKC. Sep.9; 2027) £100
– – **Anr. Copy.** 3 vols. 4to. Orig. cl., spines slightly faded, slightly rubbed. (S. Jun.25; 306) *Shapiro.* £70

BARRAUD, Charles Decimus
– New Zealand: Graphic & Descriptive. 1877. Fo. Additional litho. title with vig., engraved map, 24 mntd. chromolitho. views, 6 other lithos., hf. mor. (S. May 22; 467) *Nevill.* £800

BARRAUD, W. & H.
– Sketches of Figures & Animals. L., n.d. Fo. Tinted litho. title, 18 plts. (of 25), rather soiled & stained, orig. cf.-bkd. cl., worn. (BBA. May 23; 275) *Primrose Hill.* £110

BARRE, Louis
– Herculaneum et Pompei. Paris, 1861-62. 8 vols. 4to. Bds., defect. (DS. Nov.25; 2160) Pts. 28,000
– – **Anr. Copy.** 8 vols. 4to. Bds., defect. (DS. Apr.27; 2210) Pts. 25,000
– – **Anr. Edn.** Ill.:– H. Roux. Paris, 1870-72. 8 vols. Some spotting, orig. bds. (BBA. Sep.8; 302) *Marcheselli.* £55

BARRELIERO, J.
– Plantae per Galliam, Hispaniam et Italiam Observatae, Iconibus Aeneis Exhibitae.... 1714. Fo. Cont. hf. roan. (HD. Jun.29; 18) Frs. 4,200

BARRES, Maurice
– Du Sang de la Volupté et de la Mort. Ill.:– Albert Decaris. Paris, 1930. *(55) on japon impérial with extra suite.* 4to. Red mor. by Semet & Plumelle, mor. liners, blind– & gt.-decor, watered silk end-ll., wrap. preserved, s.-c. (HD. Jun.13; 10) Frs. 4,000
– Greco, ou le Secret de Tolède. Ill.:– Aug. Brouet. Paris, 1928. *(218). (40) on japon impérial with 2 states ot etchings & prospectus.* 4to. 23 orig. etchings, leaves, folder & s.-c. (HD. May 3; 187) Frs. 2,600
– Un Jardin sur l'Oronte. Ill.:– Sureda. Paris, 1927. 4to. This copy not for sale, on Japan, 1 orig. drawing, 2 sets of plts. on China & Japan, 1 set of ills. on Japan, 1 plt. in 11 states on China, leaves, box. (HD. Nov.17; 93) Frs. 1,000
– La Mort de Venise. Ill.:– Henry de Waroquier. Lyon, 1936. *(160) numbered on papier velin de Vidalon.* 4to. Art Deco bdg. of orange lev. mor. by J.K. Van West, sigd. on upr. turn-in, covers with lge. elaborate onlaid palladium-lettered domed architectural ornament design continuous across gt.- & palladium-lettered smooth spine, upr. & lr. doubls. with onlaid design of a gondola & a raven respectively, gt. or palladium-decor., silk free end-pp., marb. paper fly-ll., partly unc., orig. wraps. & spine preserved, matching hf. mor. chemise & mor.-edged s.-c., s.-c. cracked & reprd.; Dr. Georges Marchal bkplt. (CNY. May 18; 202) $19,000

BARRETT, Charles Golding
– The Lepidoptera of the British Islands. L., 1893-1907. 11 vols. Royal 8vo. L.P., orig. cl. gt., with supp. index in orig. wraps. loosely inserted. (SKC. Oct.26; 330) £480

BARRETT, Charles Leslie
– Across the Years: The Lure of Early Australian Books. Melbourne, 1948. *(650).* Orig. cl., clear wrap. spotted. (KH. Nov.8; 18) Aus. $100

BARRETT, Charles Raymond Booth
– Essex: Highways, Byways, & Waterways. 1892-93. *(120).* 2 vols. 4to. Orig. cl., soiled. (BBA. Feb,9; 340) *Mullett.* £70

BARRETT, Francis
– The Magusor Colestial Intelligencer ... & Occult Philosophy. L., 1801. *1st. Edn.* 2 vols. in 1. 4to. Frontis. port., 21 plts., 4 plts., crudely cold., three-qtr. cf., rebkd., new end-papers. (CBA. Dec.10; 355) $140

BARRI, Giraldus de
– The Itinerary of Archbishop Baldwin through Wales, A.D. 1188. Trans.:– Sir Richard Colt Hoare. 1806. 2 vols. 4to. Engraved plts. & hand-cold. folding map, orig. bds., unc., rebkd. (TA. Jun.21; 201) £70

BARRIE, Sir James Matthew
– The Admirable Crichton. Ill.:– H. Thomson. [1914]. *(500) numbered & sigd. by artist.* 4to. Orig. vell., lightly soiled, lacks ties. (CSK. Aug.19; 11) £85
– Peter Pan in Kensington Gardens. Ill.:– Arthur Rackham. 1906. *(500) numbered & sigd. by artist.* 4to. Orig. cl. gt., soiled, covers bowed, lacks ties. (CSK. Mar.9; 131) £240
– – **Anr. Copy.** 4to. 48 cold. plts. only, lightly soiled, orig. vell., soiled & rubbed, lacks ties. (CSK. Apr.6; 116) £220
– – **Anr. Edn.** Ill.:– Arthur Rackham. 1906. 4to. Orig. cl. gt., spine rubbed. (TA. Mar.15; 430) £70
– – **Anr. Copy.** 4to. Orig. cl. gt. (TA. Nov.17; 463) £62
– – **Anr. Copy.** 4to. All plts. (except frontis.) bnd. after text, ink inscr. erased from hf.-title, pol. cf., gt.-pict. upr. cover, gt.-decor. spine, gt. dentelles, marb. end-papers; Marymount College copy. (CBA. Mar.3; 458) $225
– – **Anr. Edn.** Ill.:– Arthur Rackham. 1907. *[4th. Edn.].* 4to. Orig. cl. gt. (P. Dec.8; 386) *Ayres.* £85
– – **Anr. Copy.** 4to. Contents lf. detchd. & frayed at edges, orig. gt.-decor. cl., worn & dampstained. (TA. May 17; 648) £58
– – **Anr. Edn.** Ill.:– Arthur Rackham. Ca. 1920. *New Edn.* 4to. Orig. gt.-decor. cl., d.-w. frayed. (TA. Jun.21; 592) £82
– Piter Pan dans les Jardins de Kensington. Ill.:–

BARRIE, Sir James Matthew -*Contd.*

Rackham. Paris, 1907. *(250) numbered on paper à la forme.* 4to. Publishers bds., vell. (HD. Feb.17; 113) Frs. 2,200
– – **Anr. Edn.** Ill.:– Arthur Rackham. 1907. 4to. On vell., no bdg. stated. (HD. Jun.26; 128) Frs. 3,200

BARRIE, Sir James Matthew & Doyle, Sir Arthur Conan
– **Jane Annie; or, The Good Conduct Prize.** Music:– Ernest Ford. L., 1893. *1st. Edn. 2nd. Iss.* Orig. wraps., sewed, disbnd., gt. qtr. mor. & cl. s.-c. (SG. Apr.19; 205) $110

BARRINGTON, Daines
– **Miscellanies.** L., 1781. *1st. Edn.* 4to. 2 engraved plts., 2 engraved folding maps, offset, 5 tables, cont. cf., rebkd. (S. Apr.10; 386) *Baron.* £240
– – **Anr. Copy.** 4to. Cont. cf. gt., rubbed. (BBA. Sep.29; 39) *Brook-Hitching.* £200

BARRINGTON, George
– **An Account of a Voyage to New South Wales.** L., 1803. Engraved title & 7 plts. only, all hand-cold., lacks map, soiled & browned thro.-out, cont. hf. roan, worn. (BBA. May 3; 295) *Kelly.* £65
– – **Anr. Copy.** Hand-cold. engraved title, 19 hand-cold. engraved plts., lacks port., some discolouration in lr. margins of pp. 97-107, hf. cf., covers slightly rubbed. (CA. Apr.3; 18) Aus. $550
– **The History of New Holland from its First Discovery in 1616 to the Present Time....** 1808. Some staining & dust-soiling, sm. repair to lr. corner of title-p. & next 2 ll., mod. str.-grd. mor. (KH. May 1; 41) Aus. $320
– **The History of New South Wales.** L., 1802. Engraved title with hand-cold. vig., 11 (of 14) cold. plts., lacks hf.-title. (*With:*) – **An Account of a Voyage to New South Wales.** 1803. Engraved title with hand-cold. vig., 10 cold. plts., lacks port. & 1 plts., lacks 3 prelims., soiled & browned, owners inscr. & stp. on some plt. versos & 1st. title. Together 2 vols. Cont. cf., worn. (S. Apr.9; 4) *Elliott.* £70
– – **Anr. Copy.** 1 vol. Engraved title with hand-cold. vig., 14 (of 19) hand-cold. plts., hf.-title, lacks folding map, some spotting & foxing, cont. hf. cf. (*With:*) – **A Voyage to New South Wales.** L., 1795. 1 vol. Lacks title-p., Middle Hill bds., unc., spine defect.; Phillipps copy, with press-mark. (S. Mar.6; 2) *Elliott.* £60
– – **Anr. Copy.** (*With:*) – **An Account of a Voyage to New South Wales.** L., 1803. Together 2 vols. Port., hand-cold. engraved map, 24 hand-cold. engraved plts., lacks list of plts., some slight discolouration round margins of some plts., hf. cf. (CA. Apr.3; 19) Aus. $900
– **A Sequel to Barrington's Voyage to New South Wales.** 1800. Hf.-title, mod. hf. cf., spine slightly faded. (S. Nov.1; 11) *Thorp.* £70
– **A Voyage to New South Wales.** Phila., 1796. *1st. Amer. Edn.* 12mo. Hf.-title & advt. lf., browned & stained thro.-out, cont. sheep, rebkd., slightly worn. (S. Nov.1; 10) *Thorp.* £65
– – **Anr. Edn.** N.Y., John Swain. ca. 1801. Slightly browned, mod. cl.-bkd. bds. (BBA. Jan.19; 82) *Kelly.* £140

BARRINGTON, Sir Jonah
– **Historic Memoirs of Ireland.** L., 1836. *New Edn.* 2 vols. 4to. 2 port. frontis., 6 facs., 34 other ports., list of subscribers, hf. mor., gt.-tooled spine with armorial motif. (GM. Dec.7; 325) £120

BARRIO, G.
– **De Antiqvitate et Sitv Calabriae.** Rome, 1571. *1st. Edn.* Browning, cont. vell., slightly wormed. (HK. Nov.8; 101) DM 420

BARROS, Joao de
– **Twee Ongelukigge Scheeps-Toogten na Oost-Indien, van Jorge de Mello ....** Leyden, 1706. Few repairs, some soiling, mod. cf.-bkd. bds. (SPB. Dec.13; 432) $100

BARROS, Joao & Couto, Diego de
– **Da Asia.** 1602-73. *1st. 3 vols. 2nd. Edn., rest 1st. Edn.* 10 vols. 4to. & fo. A few minor repairs affecting 1 or 2 letters only, some ll. browned or

with light stains, mod. mor., royal arms of Portugal on covers. (S. May 22; 431) *Cortes.* £7,200

BARROW, A.S.
[–] **More Shires & Provinces.** Ill.:– Lionel Edwards. L., 1928. 4to. Cold. plts., orig. cl., d.-w. defect. (P. May 17; 29) *Perham.* £140
[–] **Shires & Provinces. – More Shires & Provinces.** Ill.:– Lionel Edwards. 1927-28. 2 vols. 4to. Orig. cl., d.-w.'s. (P. Oct.20; 34) £220

BARROW, Isaac
See– EUCLID – BARROW, Isaac

BARROW, Sir John
– **The Eventful History of the Mutiny & Piratical Seizure of H.M.S. Bounty.** L., 1831. *1st. Edn.* Later bds., qtr. cl., unc. (KH. Nov.9; 538) Aus. $170
– **Some Account of the Public Life...of the Earl of Macartney.** 1807. 2 vols. 4to. Port., some offset on title, crimson str.-grd. mor. gt. (P. Sep.8; 322) *Tzakas.* £160
– **Travels in China.** 1804. *[1st. Edn.].* 4to. 4 plts. hand-cold., hf. cf. (P. Sep.8; 271) £140
– – **Anr. Copy.** 4to. 8 plts., (5 hand-cold.), marginal tear to 002, cl., ex-liby. (S. Apr.9; 5) *Remington.* £100
– – **Anr. Copy.** 4to. Hand-cold. aquatint frontis., 7 plts. (4 cold.), frontis. caption shaved, title slightly soiled, spotted, cl. (S. Jun.25; 34) *Shapiro.* £80
– – **Anr. Edn.** L., 1806. *2nd. Edn.* 4to. 8 engraved plts. (2 double-p.), a few aquatint & cold., a few spots & stains, cont. grained cf., slightly rubbed, rebkd. (S. Jun.25; 35) *Shapiro.* £90
– **Travels into the Interior of Southern Africa, in the Years 1797 & 1798....** Ill.:– Neele (folding engraved map). 1801. 4to. Folding engraved map cold. in outl., cont. tree cf., gt.-decor. spine. (TA. Aug.18; 35) £55
– – **Anr. Edn.** 1801-4. 2 vols. 4to. 8 hand-cold. engraved aquatint plts., 10 folding maps & plans only, some light staining, cont. cf., lightly rubbed, rebkd., old spine laid down, w.a.f. (CSK. May 4; 72) £110
– – **Anr. Copy.** 2 vols. Lge. 4to. 9 folding maps & plans (1 reprd.), folding aquatint view of Cape Town, hf. cf., shabby, loose. (SG. Sep.22; 3) $150
– – **Anr. Edn.** L., 1802. *2nd. Edn.* 2 vols. 4to. 9 maps & charts, 8 hand-cold. aquatint plts., some offsetting from maps, lge. map slightly dusty & reprd. along hinge, lacks hf.-title in vol. 2, hf. cf.; Hagley Hall bkplt., from M.Z. Brown liby. (VA. Apr.27; 660) R 580
– – **Anr. Edn.** L., 1806. 2 vols. 4to. 8 hand-cold. plts., 9 maps, Directions for plts. & Cadell & Davis catalogue at end of both vols., lacks hf.-titles, slight offsetting on a few maps & plts., old hf. cf. & marb. bds., cf. dry & cracked. (VA. Oct.28; 406) R 580
– – **Anr. Copy.** 2 vols. 4to. Cont. tree cf., rubbed & worn, cover loose. (SSA. Jul.5; 25) R 450
– **A Voyage to Cochinchina.** 1806. *1st. Edn.* 4to. 2 folding maps, 19 hand-cold. aquatints, no hf.-title, 19th. C. hf. cf., R. Davies of Bg'ham. ticket on front pastedown. (BBA. Sep. 29; 78) *Traylen.* £230
– – **Anr. Copy.** 4to. 20 cold. plts., map, folding panorama torn, slightly browned, cf., worn, covers loose. (SPB. May 17; 568) $200

BARTH, Henry
– **Reisen und Entdeckungen in Nord- und Central-Afrika in den Jahren 1849 bis 1855.** Gotha, 1857-58. *1st. Edn.* 5 vols. Minimal browning, Vols. III & IV slightly loose, orig. linen, slightly worn, some spotting, 1 sm. spine tear, mostly unc. (H. May 22; 242) DM 3,000
– – **Anr. Edn.** Gotha, 1859-60. 2 vols. Some margin browning, cont. hf. leath. (GB. Nov.3; 32) DM 650
– **Travels & Discoveries in North & Central Africa.** 1857-58. 5 vols. Orig. cl. (BBA. Sep.29; 1) *Traylen.* £260

BARTHELEMY, Abbé Jean Jacques
– **Atlas pour le Voyage du Jeune Anucharsis en Grèce.** Paris, 1830. Ob. 4to. 37 plans, maps & views, cont. hf. cf. (HD. Jan.26; 23) Frs. 1,400
– **Reise d. Jungen Anacharsis durch Griechenland.** Trans.:– D. Jenisch & J.E. Biester. Berlin [& Libau], 1789-93. *1st. German Edn.* 7 vols. Vols. 3 & 4 lack 1 plt., some light spotting, cont. leath.

gt., cold. paper end-ll., slightly rubbed & bumped, w.a.f. (HK. May 16; 1940) DM 420
– **Travels of Anacharsis the Younger in Greece.** L., 1806. *4th. Edn.* 8 vols., with Atlas. 8vo. & 4to. 40 engraved plts. & maps, some folding, few hand-cold. in outl., some ll. slightly spotted, cont. tree cf. & hf. cf. (BBA. Mar.21; 103) *Dimakarakos.* £100
– **Viaggio di Anacarsi il Giovine nella Grecia.** Milan, 1820-24. 14 vols. Sm. 8vo. Cont. qtr. leath. gt. (BBA. Jun.28; 113) *Demetzy Books.* £80
– **Voyage du Jeune Anacharsis en Grèce.** Paris, 1788. *1st. Edn.* 4 vols. & Atlas. 4to. 31 engraved maps & plts., some double-p., some outl. cold., all titles with cont. MS owners note, vol. 1 slightly soiled in upr. margin, 2 p. numbers omitted in pagination, cont; hf. leath., bumped. (HK. Nov.8; 1026) DM 440
– – **Anr. Edn.** Paris, 1789-98. *2nd. Edn. Atlas New Edn., (130) with supp. analysis of maps.* 8 vols., including Atlas. 8vo. & 4to. 39 maps & plts., some hand-cold. in outl., various cont. bdgs., worn. (CSK. Dec.16; 19) £70
– – **Anr. Edn.** Paris, An VII [1799]. 7 vols. & atlas. 8vo. Lacks 1 plt., lr. margin of atlas wormed, red hf. mor., corners, spines decor. (HD. Jun.26; 34) Frs. 2,100
– – **Anr. Copy.** 8 vols., including atlas. 8vo. & 4to. Bdg. not stated. (HD. Oct.14; 17) Frs. 1,900
– – **Anr. Edn.** 1822-24-25. 8 vols., including Atlas. Cf. by Simier. (HD. Jan.24; 4) Frs. 2,000

BARTHEZ, Paul Joseph
– **Nouvelle Méchanique des Mouvements de L'Homme et des Animaux.** Carcassonne, An VI [1798]. *1st. Edn.* 4to. Additional imprint slip tipped to foot of title, liby. stp. on title, scattered foxing, some ink emendations in later hand, mod. spr. qtr. cf. gt. (SG. Mar.22; 36) $175

BARTHOLINUS, Caspar
– **Institutiones Anatomicae.** Leiden, 1641. *1st. Edn.* A few folding plts. with sm. margin tears, 1 longer tear pasted on verso, some light browning or light foxing, cont. vell. (R. Oct.12; 1355) DM 500

BARTHOLINUS, Thomas
– **Anatome Ex Omnium Veterum Recentiorumque Observationibus ...Ad Circulationem Harvejanam, et Vasa Lymphatica Quartum Renovata.** Leiden, 1673. Cont. hf. vell., worn. (TA. Apr.19; 364) £50
– **Anatomia, ex Caspari Bartholini Parenios Institutionibus.** Leiden, 1651. *3rd. Edn.* Folding plts– with sm. tears, 1st & last ll. with slight browning in side margin, light stain in upr. margin, some light soiling, cont. leath. gt., rubbed. (R. Oct.12; 1357) DM 430

BARTHOLOMAEUS ANGLICUS
– **Boeck ven den Proprieteyten der Dinghen.** Haarlem, Jacob Bellaert, 1485. Fo. 19 lge. painted initials in several cols. with scroll-work extending into margin, lombards supplied in red, rubricated, 8 full-p. woodcuts (of 11), full-p. printers device at end, all in light paint. col., lacks 16 ll. (2 blanks), rest replaced by facs. ptd. on old paper, sm. hole in 1 lf., few margin repairs, 1 woodcut over half lined on blank verso, few stains, few sm. wormholes in last few ll., mod. blind-stpd. cf. over wood bds., s.-c. [BMC IX, 102; Goff B 142] (B. Apr.27; 561) Fls. 17,000
– **De Proprietatibus Rerum.** Nuremb., Anton Koberger, 20 Jun. 1492. Fo. Final blank supplied, capital spaces with guide letters, 1 or 2 sm. wormholes in margin of 1st. few ll., 17th. C. Spanish mott. cf. over wood bds., scuffed; Andre Simon-John D. Stanitz copy. [BMC II, 435; Goff B141] (SPB. Apr.25; 29) $1,100
– **Liber de Proprietatibus Rerum.** Strassburg, 1505. Fo. Some worming at beginning & end, browned, lr. margin of 1 lf. torn loose, 16th. C. blind-stpd. pig, stained, lacks clasps, later end-papers; John D. Stanitz coll. (SPB. Apr.25; 30) $200

BARTHOLOMAEUS BRIXIENSIS
– **Casus Decretorum.** Basle, Nicolas Kesler, 1489. 190 ll., rubricated in red & blue, 16th. C. stpd. vell., richly decor.; from Fondation Furstenberg-Beaumesnil. [H. 2472; BMC III, 768; Goff B151] (HD. Nov.16; 12) Frs. 5,500

BARTHOLOMAEUS DE CHAIMIS
- **Confessionale.** Milan, Christophorus Valdarfer, 29 Sep. 1474. 1st. initial in gold, rubricated thro.-out, with initials in blue & red, old vell.; the Walter Goldwater copy. [BMC VI, 725; Goff B-153] (SG. Dec.1; 58) $1,500
- – **Anr. Edn.** Venice, Reynaldus de Novimagio, 28 Sep. 1486. 4to. Wide margins, lacks initial blank, index lf. supplied by early owner, with folio nos. correponding to MS. foliation supplied thro.-out, some foxing, 19th. C. mor., wide gt. dentelles; the Walter Goldwater copy. [BMC V, 258; Goff B-162] (SG. Dec.1; 60) $750
- – **Anr. Copy.** 4to. Lacks e8, mod. vell., with medieval-style MS. title in blank, blue & red, leath. ties; the Walter Goldwater copy. [BMC V, 258; Goff B-162] (SG. Dec.1; 59) $375

BARTISCH, Georg
- **Augen-Dienst.** Salzburg, 1686. 4to. Folding copperplts. creased, bkd. tears, slightly browned & foxed thro.-out, wraps. (HK. May 15; 316) DM 3,200

BARTLET, John
- **Pharmacopoeia Hippiatrica, or the Gentleman Farrier's Repository, ... The Diseases of Horses G11.** Eton, 1764. 12mo. Cont. cf., bkplt. (GM. Dec.7; 592) £65

BARTLETT, John Russell
- **Personal Narrative of Explorations & Incidents in Texas, New Mexico, California, Sonora, & Chihuahua.** N.Y., 1854. 1st. Edn. 2 vols. Folding map (little torn), 16 tinted lithos., some folding, many full-p. & text woodcuts, 1 geyser plt. (as usual), unlisted view of Tucson, orig. cl., gt. pict. spines, Vol. II brkn. (SG. Apr.5; 12) $350
- – **Anr. Edn.** L., 1854. 1st. Engl. Edn. 2 vols. 2 folding litho. frontis. (slightly foxed), engraved folding map, 14 litho. plts., 1 lf. torn & reprd., orig. blind-stpd. cl., spines & corners worn; the Rt. Hon. Visc. Eccles copy. [Sabin 3746 (note)] (CNY. Nov.18; 15) $160

BARTLETT, Thomas
- **New Holland; Its Colonization, Productions & Resources, with Observations on the Relations subsisting with Great Britain.** 1843. Lge. 12mo. Bdg. not stated; inscr. by author. (KH. May 1; 43) Aus. $160

BARTLETT, Truman H.
- **The Art Life of William Rimmer.** Boston, 1882. 1st. Edn. Lge. 4to. 31 heliotype plts., gt.-decor. cl. (SG. Oct.13; 286) $110

BARTLETT, William Henry
- **Gleanings on the Overland Route.** 1851. Added engraved title, engraved plts., 1 folding, text ills., orig. cl., faded & slightly worn. (BS. May 2; 12) £60
- **Ireland.** Ed.:– Markinfield Addey. Ill.:– W.H. Bartlett. N.Y., [1881]. 2 vols. 4to. 120 steel-engraved plts., some light foxing, mor. (RO. Dec.11; 21) $100
- **The Nile Boat; or, Glimpses of the Land of Egypt.** N.Y., 1851. Tall 8vo. Frontis. detchd., gt.-pict. cl., spine ends chipped. (SG. Sep.22; 128) $100
See— STEBBING, Henry & Bartlett, William Henry
See— WILLIS, Nathaniel Parker & Bartlett, William Henry

BARTLETT, William Henry (Ill.)
See— BEATTIE, William

BARTLEY, G.C.T. (Trans.)
See— STIELER, Karl, Wachenhusen, K.S.H. & Hacklander, F.W.

BARTOLI, Cosimo
- **Del Modo di Misurare, le Distantie, le Superficie i Corpi...tutte le Altre Cose Terrene, che Possono Occorrera a gli Homini.** Venice, 1589. 4to. Cont. vell., hand-ptd. end-papers, slightly soiled. (TA. Oct.20; 382) £105

BARTOLI, Daniello
- **Del Suono de'Tremori Armonici e dell'Udito.** Rome, 1679. 1st. Edn. Sm. 4to. Hf.-title, final

register lf., unpressed copy, cont. vell., later label; liby. stp. of Lorenzo Puppati on title-p. (S. May 10; 4) Frers. £280

BARTOLI, Pietro Santo
- **Admirandi Romanarum Antiquitatum ac Veteris Sculpturae Vestigia.** Ed.:– J.P. Bellori. Rome, 1693. Ob. fo. 82 (of 84?) plts., including title & dedication, some light foxing, mainly marginal, 19th. C. cf. gt. super extra, slightly rubbed, etc. (SG. Jan.26; 173) $200
- – **Anr. Copy.** Ob. fo. Cf. (DS. Nov.25; 2184) Pts. 32,000
- – **Anr. Copy.** 35 x 50cm. Album, browned, orig. sewed. (CR. Jun.6; 8) Lire 280,000
- **Medailles de Grand et Moyen Bronze du Cabinet de la Reine Christine ....** Trans.:– Sigebert Havercamp. The Hague, 1742. Fo. Titles in Latin & Fr. & with Latin & Fr. double-column text, later hf. cf., slightly worn, foot of spine defect. (S. May 1; 508) Marlborough. £120
- **Museum Odescalchum Sive Thesaurus Antiquarum Gemmarum.** Rome, 1751-52. [1st. Edn.]. 2 vols. Fo. Hf.-titles, cont. vell.-bkd. bds. (SKC. Sep.9; 801) £170
- – **Anr. Copy.** 2 vols. in 1. Fo. Hf.-titles, last few ll. slightly stained & worn at outer margins, cont. stiff vell. (SG. Nov.3; 7) $325

BARTOLOZZI, Francesco & others
- **Eighty-Two Prints ... from the Original Drawings of Guercino ... - [Seventy-Three Prints ... from the Original Pictures & Drawings of Michael Angelo ...].** L., ca. 1800. Together 2 works in 1 vol. Lge. fo. 151 engraved sepia-ptd. engraved plts. (of 155, lacks 4 plts. in 2nd. work), including 1 folding, some spotting & discoloration, 1 caption cropped, cf.-bkd. bds., w.a.f. (C. Nov.9; 36) Litman. £1,900

BARTRAM, William
- **Reisen durch Nord- und Süd-Karolina, Georgien, Ost- und West-Florida ....** Trans.:– E.A.W. Zimmermann. Berlin, 1793. Cont. hf. leath., rubbed. [Sabin 3872] (R. Oct.13; 2947) DM 550
- **Travels through North & South Carolina, Georgia, East & West Florida.** 1792. Port., folding map, & 7 engraved plts., tree cf., rebkd.; Holland House copy with bkplt. & crest on upr. cover. [Sabin 3870] (S. May 22; 302) Sawyer. £360
- – **Anr. Copy.** Engraved port., folding map, 7 plts., including 1 folding, Dd2 creased before printing, but legible, 2 quires at end unopened. [Sabin 3870] (Bound with:) WANSEY, Henry – The Journal of an Excursion to the United States of North America, in the Summer of 1794. Salisbury, 1794. 1st. Edn. Port. frontis., bistre-sepia aquatint, hf.-title, fly-title lf., errata lf. & 6 1/2 p. list of books at end, some browning in sig. E. [Sabin 10124] Together 2 works in 1 vol., Cont. tree cf., slight wear to spine & corners; Sir John Smith bkplt., the Rt. Hon. Visc. Eccles copy. (CNY. Nov.18; 16) $1,400

BARTSCH, Adam
- **Le Peintre Graveur.** Vienna & Leipzig, 1803-20 & 1843. 21 vols., & Vol. 1 of Supp. (all publd.). 91 (of 92?) engraved plts., institutional stps. on titles, orig. bds., spines chipped, last vol. cl., spine reprd. with tape; dupl. from Museum Boymans. (CH. Sep.20; 68) Fls. 850
- – **Anr. Copy.** 21 vols & Vol. 1 of supp. (all publd.),. 91 (of 92?) engraved plts., stps. on titles, orig. bds. (spines chipped), last vol. cl. (spine taped); dupl. copy from Museum Boymans. (CH. May 24; 111) Fls. 650
- – **Anr. Edn.** Hildesheim, 1970. 4 vols. Orig. cl. (SI. Dec.15; 185) Lire 320,000

BARTSCH, Jacobus
See— KEPLER, Johannes & Bartsch, Jacobus

BARTSCH, R.H.
- **Vom Sterbenden Rokoko.** Ill.:– Hugo Steiner-Prag. Leipzig, 1913. (20) numbered on imperial japan. Printers mark sigd. by author, cold. lithos. sigd., orig. pold. cf. gt. (GB. May 5; 3358) DM 950

BARUCH BEN BARUCH
- **Kohelet Yakov Kedosh Israel.** Venice, 1598. 1st. Edn. Fo. Worming affecting some letters, soiled,

short tears in margin not affecting text, buckram. (S. Oct.24; 81) Loewy. £300

BARUCH BEN YITZCHAK of Worms
- **Sefer Ha'Trumah.** Venice, 1523. 1st. Edn. 4to. Title-p. laid down, some worming, mostly in margins, slight foxing, bds. [Steinschneider 4508, 1] (SPB. Jun.26; 29) $2,250

BASAN, Pierre François
- **Dictionnaire des Graveurs Anciens et Modernes depuis l'Origine de la Gravure.** Ill.:– Cochin & Pierre (frontis.), Choffard (vigs.), Aliamet & others. Paris, 1789. 2nd. Edn. 2 vols. With engr. of Comte Le Rossignol by Picart in Vol. II (often lacking), cont. spr. cf. (HD. May 3; 8) Frs. 1,600

BASCHET, Armand
- **Le Roi chez la Reine ou Histoire Secrète du Mariage du Louis XIII et d'Anne d'Autriche.** Paris, 1864. (3) on vell. Red lev. mor. gt. by Capé, covers elab. decor., spine in 6 compartments, gt.-lettered in 2, repeated dentelle panel in rest, turn-ins gt., unc., fleece-lined cl. box; Albert Pascal bkplt. (CNY. May 18; 176) $1,000

BASHDOW, H.
- **Journal of the Government North-West Expedition....** Adelaide, 1914. Wraps. (KH. May 1; 45) Aus. $150

BASEDOW, Johann Bernhard
- **Kupfersammlung zu J.B. Basedows Elementarwerke fur Jugend und ihre Freunde.** Ill.:– Schleuen, Schuster, G. Chodowiecki & others, majority after D. Chodowiecki. Berlin & Dessau, 1774. Ob. 4to. Cont. hf. sheep, rubbed; van Veer coll. (S. Feb.28; 130) £800

BASILIUS MAGNUS
- **De Poetarum Oratorŭ Historicorŭqz ac Philosophorum Legēdis Libris.** Leipzig, 1515. 4to. Some cont. MS notes, wide side & bottom margins, hf. linen. (HK. May 15; 73) DM 1,300

BASILIUS VALENTINUS
- **Triumph-Wagen Antimonii allen so den Grund der Uhralten Medicin suchen auch zu der Hermetischen Philosophie Beliebnis Tragen ... publiciret.** Nuremb., 1676. Engraved frontis. reprd., 1 index page badly inkstained, vell.; Dr. Walter Pagel copy. (S. Feb.7; 43) Colombo. £480
See— RHENANUS, Joannes – BASILIUS VALENTINUS

BASLER KONZIL
- **Libellus Apostolorum Nationis Gallicane: cum Constitutione Sacri Concilii Basilien [sis] et Arresto Curie Parlamenti super Annatis no[n] solve[n]dis.** Paris, [21 Feb. 1512]. 4to. Hf. red mor. (D. Nov.23; 72) DM 750

BASNAGE, Henry
- [–] **Histoire des Ouvrages des Savants.** Amst., 1687-1709. 24 vols. in 27. 12mo. Cont. cf., 1st. 9 vols. with gt. fillets bordering covers & arms in centre, decor. spines, inner roll-stp., slight defects; from Bullion de Bonnelles & La Rochefoucauld Bisaccia libys. (HD. Sep.22; 187) Frs. 2,600

BASNAGE, Jacques
- **Le Grand Tableau de l'Univers, ou l'Histoire des Evenements de l'Eglise ....** Amst., 1714. Fo. 1 map torn, other maps with tears & faults, lr. corner defect. in 1st. ll., slightly soiled, cont. leath. gt. spine defect., rubbed & bumped, gt. oxidised, MS. annots. on end-paper. (HK. Nov.8; 926a) DM 450
- **The History of the Jews.** Trans.:– Tho. Taylor. 1708. Fo. Engraved frontis. creased, some ll. browned, cont. cf., worn. (BBA. Sep.29; 147) Quaritch. £180

BASS, Shabbetai
- **Siftei Yesheinim.** Amst., 1680. 1st. Edn. Sm. 4to. Light dampstaining, scattered Hebrew ink marginalia, without the prayers, few gatherings starting, old dyed vell., worn. (SG. Feb.2; 153) $400
- – **Anr. Edn.** Zolkiew, 1806. 2nd. Edn. 2 pts. in 1 vol. 4to. Soiled & foxed, owners' stps., hf. sheep, shabby. (SG. Feb.2; 154) $110

BASSANO, A.F. da
- Vita e Miracoli del Gloriossimo S. Nicola di Tolentino ... di nuova ornata et ampliata dal R.P.F. Iacomo Alberici da Sarnico Berganasco. Rome, 1610. 4to. Old cf. (HD. Dec.2; 65) Frs. 1,100

BASSANTIN, J.
- Astronomique Discours. Ill.:– Denis de Sallo. Lyon, 1557. 1st. Edn. Lge. fo. Wide margin, 'De Tournes' device on title-p., anr. device on 1 f., p. 278 lacks 21 of 3) moving pts., arabesque type ornamental head-pieces, arabesque tail-pieces, criblé initials, sm. arabesque initials, 1 initial from lambda alphabet, title very spotted & restored with loss of paper & letters, slightly browned or brown spotted, cont. leath., gold tooled arms or initials, 7 gold-tooled stps. on spine. (D. Nov.23; 391)
DM 9,500

BASTER, J.
- Natuurkundige Uitspanningen, behelz. eenige Waarneemingen over Zee-planten en Zee-insecten. Ill.:– after J. Rhodius. Haarlem, 1759-65. 2 pts. (6 iss.) in 1 vol. 4to. 29 hand-cold. folding plts. (possibly cold. by Rhodius), slightly foxed, cont. hf. cf., spine gt., unc. (VG. Mar.19; 259) Fls. 800

BASTON, T[homas]
- Twenty Two Prints of several Capital Ships of his Majesties Royal Navy with Variety of other Sea Pieces. Ill.:– J. Sartor, du Bose, S. Cole, J. Harris, & E. Kirkall, after Baston. L., ca. 1721. Fo. Engraved allegorical title, 21 engraved plts., including a double-p., sm. inkstain on blank margin of title, cont. cf., rebkd. (S. Dec.1; 382) Marshall. £2,600

BATACCHI, Domenico
- Opere Complete. Ill.:– Darcourt, Deslames. Parigi, 1830. Lge. 8vo. Cont. bds., worn. (SM. Mar.7; 2388) Frs. 1,300

BATAVIA, de Hoofdstad van Neerlands O. Indien
Amst. & Harlingen, 1782-83. 2 vols. in 1. 4to. Engraved frontis., 8 folding views & maps on 6 plts. only (of 7), few sm. margin tears & wormholes, later hf. cf. (BBA. Mar.21; 73) J. Randall. £70

BATE, John
- The Mysteries of Nature & Art. [L.], 1635. 2nd. Edn. 4 pts. in 1 vol. Sm. 4to. Some soiling or staining, mod. cf., lightly rubbed; sigs. of George Ferguson (ptd. 1655), John Gordon & John Payne Collier, John D. Stanitz copy. (SPB. Apr.25; 31)
$650

BATEMAN, James
- The Orchidaceae of Mexico & Guatemala. Ill.:– George Cruikshank & others (wood-engraved vigs.); & M. Gauci after Miss S.A. Drake, Miss Jane Edwards, Samuel Holden, & Mrs. Augusta Withers. [L.], 1837-43). (125). Lge. fo. Litho. title (without imprint), 40 hand-cold. plts., 'Addenda et Corrigenda' & 'Directions to the Binder' slips at end, some foxing, lr. corner of pp. 11/12 reprd., cont. red hf. mor. by J. Mackenzie, spine richly gt., rubbed, upr. cover loose, ports. of W.J. Hooker mntd. on front pastedown. (S. Feb.1; 7)
Parker. £8,800

BATES, Alfred (Ed.)
See— DRAMA: its History, Literature ...

BATES, David Homer
- Lincoln in the Telegraph Office. N.Y., 1907. Orig. cl. gt.; inscr. by author to Gen. Henry L. Burnett. (LH. Apr.15; 265) $110

BATES, James Hale
- Notes of a Tour in Mexico & California. N.Y., for private distribution, 1887. 2 vols. 8vo., inlaid to lge. 4to. Mor. by Neumann, spines gt.; author's copy, with bkplt., a gift to his wife, with her inscr. on front fly-ll., extra-ill. with wood engrs., ephemera, approx. 160 mntd. albumen photos by A. Briquet, C.R. Savage, W.H. Jackson, & others, & some 20 mntd. A.L. from those who received complimentary copies. (SG. May 10; 13) $2,000

BATESON, Edward & others
- A History of Northumberland. Newcastle, 1893-1940. 15 vols. 4to. Cl., few spines slightly stained. (SKC. Mar.9; 1965) £120

BATESON, F.W. (Ed.)
See— CAMBRIDGE BIBLIOGRAPHY OF ENGLISH LITERATURE

BATSCH, Dr. August J.G.K.
- Der Geöffnete Blumengarten. Weimar, 1802. In German & Fr., title lf. with name or stp., 1 copper engr. & 1 lf. loose, 1 copper engr. slit without loss, some spotting or browning, cont. hf, leath., very worn & spotted, spine defect. (H. Nov.23; 255a)
DM 1,400

BATTEUX, Abbé Charles
- Les Quatre Poétiques d'Aristote, d'Horace, de Vida, de Despreaux, avec les Traductions et des Remarques.... Ill.:– Saint-Aubin after Cochin. Paris, 1771. 2 vols. L.P., frontis. in double state, cont. red mor. gt., decor, spines, inner roll-stp. (HD. Sep.22; 188) Frs. 3,300
– – Anr. Copy. 2 vols. L.P., cont. cf. gt., slight stains on covers. (HD. May 3; 10) Frs. 1,700

BATTEUX, Ch. L.-G. & others
[–] Mémoires concernant l'histoire, les Sciences, les Arts, les Moeurs et les Usages des Chinois, par les Missionaires de Pekin. Paris, 1776-91. 15 vols. 4to. 195 (of approx. 200) mostly engraved plts., cont. leath., partly slightly defect., rubbed, staining. (GB. May 3; 52) DM 2,400

BATTISS, William
- The Artists of the Rocks. Pretoria, 1948. (500). 4to. Cl., d.-w. (SSA. Sep.21; 19) R 210

BATTLE SMOKE: A Pictorial Record of the War
Melbourne, Mar.-Jul., 1900. Nos. 1-6 in 1 vol. Fo. Not collated, some wear, bdg. not stated. (KH. Nov.8; 32) Aus. $240

BATTY, Elizabeth Frances
- Italian Scenery. L., 1820. 4to. Hf.-title, engraved title with vig. & 60 engraved views, light margin stains at beginning & end, cont. mor., rubbed. (S. May 21; 217) Rebecchi. £200
– – Anr. Copy. 4to. Engraved title, 60 plts., some margins stained, cont. hf. cf. (CSK. Nov.4; 34)
£130

BATTY, Robert
- French Scenery. L., 1822. 4to. Steel-engraved title, 65 steel engraved plts, lightly browned thro.-out. (HK. May 15, 790) DM 440
- German Scenery .... L., 1823. 4to. Engraved title, full-p. vig. at end, 60 views, red hf. mor., spine gt. (C. Jun.27; 5) Maliye. £1,000
– – Anr. Copy. 4to. Engraved title with vig., frontis. (fore-margin just shaved), 60 engraved views, cont. mor., rubbed. (S. May 21; 219) Maliye. £850
– – Anr. Copy. 4to. Engraved title vig., 61 (of 62) steel engraved plts., lightly browned thro.-out, hf. leath., ca. 1900, corners bumped, upr. jnt. torn at foot. (HK. May 15; 711) DM 3,600
– – Anr. Copy. 58 (of 61) steel engraved plts., slightly foxed, cont. leath., spine renewed. (R. Oct.12; 2350a) DM 3,200
- Hanoverian & Saxon Scenery. L., 1829. Imperial 8vo. Engraved title with vig., 61 engraved plts., without dedication, some plts. spotted, mainly in margins, cont. mor., covers & spine gt., by J. MacKenzie, spine ends worn. (C. Nov.16; 49)
Schuster. £1,200
– – Anr. Edn. [L., 1829]. Lge. 8vo. On vell., wide margin, engraved dedication lacks engraved title, End. & Fr. text, 61 steel engrs. & 60 woodcut vigs., some foxing, 1 lf. with margin tear, washed, mod. cf., some light scratches, miscol. (H. May 22; 336)
DM 4,600
- Scenery of the Rhine, Belgium & Holland. L., 1826. L.P., engraved frontis., title, 60 views, all plts. on India paper, text in Engl. & Fr. (With:)
- Hanoverian & Saxon Scenery. L., 1829. L.P., Engraved title, frontis., dedication, 60 views, all plts. on India paper, text in Engl. & Fr. Together 2 vols. 4to. Unif. maroon mor. gt., spines gt. (C. Nov.16; 50) Schuster. £2,000
– – Anr. Copy. 4to. Some light browning or spotting, cont. mor. gt. (CSK. Sep.16; 202) £700
– – Anr. Copy. 4to. Engraved title with vig., frontis. & 60 engraved views, cont. mor., rubbed. (S. May 21; 218) Bailey. £620
- Select Views of some of the Principal Cities of

Europe. 1832. 4to. Engraved title & dedication, 30 engraved plts., 30 outl. plts., slight spotting, cl., worn. (P. Jul.26; 212d) £190
– – Anr. Copy. Hf. roan, upr. cover detchd. (P. Oct. 20; 146) £150
- Views on the Rhine in Belgium & Holland. L., 1824-25. Pts. 1-9 only (of 12). 4to. 45 engraved India proof plts., a few slightly foxed, orig. ptd. wraps. (C. Jun.27; 6) Rheinbuch. £450

BAUDART, Guillaume
- Les Guerres de Nassau. Amst., 1616. 2 vols. in 1. Ob. 8vo. Engraved title, 277 plts., some browning & soiling, old cf., worn, rebkd., as a coll. of plts., w.a.f. (SPB. Dec.13; 497) $2,200
– – Anr. Copy. 2 pts. in 1 vol. Ob. 8vo. Lacks 20 ll. with 14 engrs., place of 1 engr. left blank & engr. ptd. on text lf., 4 engrs badly ptd., some worming & light dampstains, bds., slight defects. (B. Oct.4; 715) Fls. 5,800

BAUDELAIRE, Charles
- Les Epaves. Amst. [Bruxelles], 1866. Partly Orig. Edn., (260). (250) numbered on papier vergé de Hollande. 12mo. Port. by Felicien Rops on china, Bradel hf. buckram bds., corners, by V. Champs, unc. (HD. May 16; 7) Frs. 2,100
- Erato, Douze Poèmes. Brussels, 1928. (112) numbered. (12) with 2 extra suites of the ills. & a sigd. & dtd. pencil drawing. Lge. 4to. Orig. wraps., unsewn as iss., unc.; all full-p. ills. sigd. & dtd. (S. Nov.21; 21) Desk. £260
- Les Fleurs du Mal. Paris, 1857. Orig. Edn. 1st. Printing. With 6 comdemned pieces, pagination error '44' for '45', 'Feurs' on pp. 31 & 108, jansenist mor. by Lortic, mor. liners, watered silk end-ll., wrap. & spine preserved, light scratch on turn-in. (HD. Jun.13; 11) Frs. 22,000
– – Anr. Edn. Paris, 1857. 1st. Edn. 1st. state, with the 6 condemned poems, misprint 'feurs' for 'fleurs' in running headlines on pp. 31 & 108, & 'Les Fleurs du Mal' not included in publisher's advts. on lr. wrap., 3 engraved ports. on papier de Chine & engraved frontis. by Felicien Rops for 'Les Epaves' inserted, crushed lev. mor. gt., upr. cover with lge. device in Art Nouveau style, elab. designs of cold. onlaid mor. on covers & spine, mor. doubls., silk liners, orig. ptd. wraps. preserved, leath.-lined paper s.-c., by De Samblancx-Weckesser; Frederic Dannay copy. (CNY. Dec.16; 19) $3,200
– – Anr. Copy. 12mo. With 6 comdemned pieces, Bradel mor. gt. by Charles Meunier, 1909, mosaic decor, unc., wrap. (3rd. state) & spine, s.-c.; 2 ports. of author on china from 'Charles Baudelaire' (Paris, 1869) bnd. at beginning. (HD. May 16; 3)
Frs. 17,500
– – Anr. Copy. 12mo. With 6 censored pieces, jansenist mor. by Noulhac, mor. doubl., gt.-decor., silk liners, without wrap. (HD. Dec.16; 66) Frs. 8,500
– – Anr. Copy. Cont. red hf. mor. (D. Nov.24; 2391)
DM 4,400
– – Anr. Edn. Paris, 1858. 1st. Edn. 2nd. Iss. Old mott. cf. gt., crudely rebkd; Frederic Dannay copy. (CNY. Dec.16; 20) $130
– – Anr. Edn. Paris, 1861. 2nd. Edn. 12mo. Lacks 6 condemned pieces, mor. gt. by Noulhac, 1919, mosaic decor, wrap. & spine, folder; with 37 unpubld. poems & several altered pieces, 3 autograph poems & 3 A.L.s. to Poulet-Malassis. (HD. May 16; 4) Frs. 255,000
– – Anr. Copy. 12mo. Lacks port. by Bracquemond, foxing, MS. names on title & hf.-title, cont. hf. roan. (HD. Jun.26; 51) Frs. 2,100
– – Anr. Edn. Ed.:– Th. Gautier. Paris, [1868]. Definitive Edn. Limp leath., ca. 1900; 18 line MS. dedication from Melchior Lechter to Maria Reichl, Berlin, Christmas 1906 on end-paper. (HK. Nov.10; 3029) DM 400
– – Anr. Edn. Ill.:– G. Rochegrosse, engraved by Decizy. Paris, 1910. (100) on japon impérial with 2 states of etchings (1 before the letter with remarks). Hf. mor., corners, by Lance, mosaic spine, wrap. & spine preserved, unc. (HD. May 3; 189) Frs. 4,800
– – Anr. Edn. Ill.:– G. Rochegrosse. Paris, 1917. De Luxe Edn., (30). 7 series of etchings in 3 states (before the letter, with the letter & cold.), supp. series of woodcuts on Japan, 2 series of etchings in 3 states without woodcuts on Japan, without cold. sketch, other etchings in 2 states, mor., decor.

spine & gt. inner dentelle, gold decor. cover & outer dentelles, silk doubls. & end-papers, orig. cold. wraps. bnd. in, by H. Blanchetière. (H. Nov.24; 1349) DM 1,000
– – **Anr. Edn.** Ill.:– M. Lydis. Paris, 1928. *(290) (text), (104) (plts.).* 2 vols. Fo. Orig. wraps. (HK. Nov.11; 3752) DM 520
– – **Anr. Edn.** Ill.:– after E. Chimot. Paris, 1941. Lge. 4to. On vella d'Arches, with 5 refused plts., leaves, wrap., box. (HD. Dec.16; 68) Frs. 1,900
– – **Anr. Edn.** Ill.:– H. Matisse, engraved by T. Schmied. Paris, 1947. *(300) numbered & sigd. by artist.* 4to. 33 orig. photo-lithos., 1 orig. etching, loose ll. in orig. pict. wrap. & hf. leath. box. (GB. Nov.5; 2795) DM 4,800
– – **Anr. Edn.** Ill.:– Henri Matisse. Paris, 1947. *(320) on Rives, sigd. by artist.* 4to. Frontis. on china, leaves, box. (HD. May 3; 190) Frs. 4,800
– **Les Paradis Artificiels. Opium et Haschisch.** Paris, 1860. *Orig. Edn.* 12mo. Mor. gt. by Rene Kieffer, spine raised bands (slightly faded), unc., wrap. & spine. (HD. May 16; 6) Frs. 1,700
[–] **Souvenirs, Correspondance. Bibliographie suivie de Pièces Inédites.** Paris, 1872. *Orig. Edn.* Hf. mor., corners, decor. spine, unc., by Smeers. (HD. Dec.16; 67) Frs. 1,700
– **Théophile Gautier.** Preface:– Victor Hugo. Paris, 1859. *Orig. Edn.* 12mo. Bradel buckram, unc., wrap. (HD. May 16; 5) Frs. 1,000
[–] **Le Tombeau de Charles Baudelaire.** Text:– Mallarmé, Coppée, Louÿs & others. Paris, 1896. *Orig. Edn., (245). (1) on papier ocre, with facs. in 2 states & port. by Nadar.* Sm. 4to. Sewed. (HD. Jun.6; 10) Frs. 3,600
– **La Vie et l'Oeuvre d'Eugène Delacroix.** Paris, 1928. *Ltd. Edn.* 4to. No bdg. stated. (SPB. Nov.30; 30) $150
– **Die Vorhölle. Eine Lyrische Nachlese.** Ill.:– P.W. Wolff. Berlin, 1911. *(200).* 4to. Vell., publisher's recovered limp bdg. (HD. Dec.1; 57) Frs. 3,500

BAUDELAIRE, Charles (Contrib.)
See— GIL BLAS ILLUSTRE

BAUDELOCQUE, Jean Louis
– **L'Art des Accouchements.** 1815. *5th. Edn.* 2 vols. Cont. decor. tree of. (HD. Mar.21; 132) Frs. 1,300

BAUDOIN, Jean
– **Histoire des Chevaliers de l'Ordre de S. Jean de Hierusalem.** Paris, 1659. Fo. Printers mark on engraved title excised & bkd., lightly browned, cont. leath., gt., jnts. worn & partly brkn. (R. Apr.5; 2974) DM 2,900

BAUDRY DE SAUNIER, Charles Louis
– **Histoire de la Locomotion Terrestre.** Paris, 1936. Fo. Cold. plts., ills., cl.-bkd. bds., worn. (P. May 17; 284) Allan. £55

BAUDRY DES LOZIERES, Louis N.
[–] **Voyage à la Louisiane et sur le Continent de L'Amérique Septentrional, Fait dans les années 1794 & 1798.** Paris, 1802. *1st. Edn.* Hf.-title, folding map very slightly foxed, cont. of. gt., corners worn; the Rt. Hon. Visc. Eccles copy. [Sabin 3979] (CNY. Nov.18; 17) $300
– – **Anr. Copy.** Title-p. mntd., 3 lines restored, bds., unc. (SG. Jan.19; 101) $200

BAUER, K.M. & Glutz von Blotzheim, U.N. & others
– **Handbuch der Vogel Mitteleuropas.** Frankfurt & Wiesbaden, 1966-82. Vols. 1-9 in 10. Cold. plts. & ills., ptd. corrections pasted into vol.1, orig. cl., all but vol. 1 in d.-w.'s. (S. Apr.10; 405) Quaritch. £200

BAUER, Max
– **Precious Stones.** Trans.:– L.J. Spencer. 1904. *1st. Engl. Edn.* 4to. Hf. mor., spine slightly scuffed & worn. (BS. May 2; 155) £50

BAUER, P.
– **Die Bürgerliche Revolution in Deutschland ....** Berlin, 1849. Browned thro.-out, cont. hf. linen. (R. Oct.11; 1171) DM 420

BAUGEAN, Jean-Jérôme
– **Recueil des Petites Marines.** Paris, 1817. Ob. 4to. 150 plts. (1 in facs., 2 mntd.), hf. bdg. (HD. Mar.9; 49) Frs. 12,500

BAUHINUS, Caspar
– **Anatomes liber primus [-secundus] Externarum**

Humani Corporis .... Basle, Mar. 1591-Mar. 1592. 2 vols. in 1. Errata & colophon ll., paper discold. & browned in places, dyed limp vell.; Dr. Walter Pagel copy. (S. Feb.7; 44) Phillips. £320
– **Theatrum Anatomicum Novis Figuris.** Frankfurt, 1600-05. Slightly browned thro.-out, some underlining & old MS. marginalia, cont. vell., spotted, 1 jnt., torn, gold-tooled supralibros. (GB. May 3; 978) DM 1,600

BAUM, Lyman Frank
– **The Army Alphabet.** Ill.:– Harry Kennedy. Chic., 1900. *1st. Edn.* 4to. 1 plt. torn, cl.-bkd. bds., rubbed, shaken; Sigd. & inscr. 'Frank Joslyn Baum from Dad to 'Our Army Boy' ... Chicago, 1900', with F.J. Baum bkplt., also sigd. by Joslyn Stanton Baum. (SG. Dec.8; 30) $2,000
– – **Anr. Copy.** 4to. 1 plt. soiled, some light margin soiling or minor tearing, owner's inscr. on title & end-paper, cl.-bkd. pict. bds., covers scratched, edges rubbed. (SG. Mar.29; 48) $300
– **Dorothy & the Wizard in Oz.** Ill.:– John R. Neill. Chic., [1908]. *1st. Edn. 1st. Iss., with publisher's full imprint at foot of spine.* 1 plt. with slight paper loss, not affecting image, cl., extremities rubbed; inscr. 'my dear son Frank Joslyn Baum L. Frank Baum·Aug. 4 1908', also sigd. by Joslyn Stanton Baum. (SG. Dec.8; 33) $1,800
– **The Emerald City of Oz.** Ill.:– John R. Neill. Chic., [1910]. *1st. Edn.* 1st. state, a few text ll. creased, cl., spine ends slightly bumped. (SG. Dec.8; 34) $300
– **The Enchanted Island of Yew.** Ill.:– Fanny Y. Cory. Indianapolis, 1903. *1st. Edn.* 1st. state, with Braunworth imprint on copyright p. & the text ill. on p. 238 ptd. inverted, a few ll. with slight margin dampstaining, owner's sig. on front pastedown, cold. pict. cl., tips & spine ends rubbed. (SG. Dec.8; 31) $175
– **The Navy Alphabet.** Ill.:– Harry Kennedy. Chic., 1900. *1st. Edn.* 4to. A few ll. with margin defects., rear end-paper reprd., cl.-bkd. pict. bds., lr. cover scraped, edges & spine ends rubbed; sigd. & inscr. 'For my son, Frank Joslyn Baum ...', with F.J. Baum bkplt., also sigd. by Joslyn Stanton Baum. (SG. Dec.8; 29) $1,600
– **The Patchwork Girl of Oz.** Ill.:– John R. Neill. Chic., [1913]. *1st. Edn.* 1st. state, with 'Chap. Three' on p. 35 overlapping text, pict. cl., rubbed & bumped. (SG. Dec.8; 35) $140
– **The Woggle-Bug.** Ill.:– Ike Morgan. Chic., 1905. *1st. Edn.* Tall 4to. Title & 3 ll. tape-reprd., a few ll. with sm. margin tears, cl.-bkd. pict. wraps., 2nd. state, with pale yellow background ptd. on upr. cover & 'Woggle-Bug Book' ptd. in yellow on lr. cover, worn & soiled. (SG. Dec.8; 32) $375
– **The Wonderful Wizard of Oz.** Ill.:– W.W. Denslow. Chic., 1900. *1st. Edn.* 4to. With publisher's name on spine in unornamented type, the 'Co.' set in ordinary fashion, single rule round advts., 'Peices' & 'low wail on ...', colophon has 11 lines, initial letter cold. in box, etc., plts., some frayed, light soiling, orig. decor. cl., soiled, spine frayed, mor.-bkd. folding box, Fred A. Berne copy. (SPB. May 16; 168) $1,300

BAUMER, J.W.
– **Medicina Forensic.** Frankgurt & Leipzig, 1778. *1st. Edn.* Ms. owners mark on title, cont. bds. (R. Apr.4; 1280) DM 630

BAUMGAERTNER, A.H.
[–] **Asiatisches Bilderbuch; Magazin über Asien.** Leipzig, [1806]. 3 pts. in 1 vol. 4to. Engraved title, 54 plts., all but 1 cont. hand-cold., lacks ptd. title(?), text partly foxed, 1 text lf. slightly defect., orig. bds., slightly defect. (VG. Nov.30; 800) Fls. 700

BAURENFEIND, Michael
– **Vollkommene Wieder-Herstellung der bisher sehr in Verfall gekommenen gründll u., zierl. Schrieb-Künst.** Nürnberg, [1716?]. Ob. fo. Spotted, wear, cont. bds. defect. (HK. May 17, 3402) DM 520

BAUSCH, J.L.
– **Schediasmata Bina Curiosa de Lapide Haematite et Aetite ....** Leipzig, 1665. *1st. Edn.* 2pts. in 1 vol. 1st. title stpd., lacks 1 plt. pt. 1 & 2 plts. pt. 2, lightly browned, cont. bds. (R. Apr.4; 1457a) DM 500

BAX, Sir Arnold
– **Summer Music for Orchestra.** L., [1933]. *1st. Edn.* Fo. Full score, no bdg. stated; pres. inscr. to Basil Cameron, annots. by Bax & others. (S. May 10; 181) Parlett. £80

BAXTER, George
– **The Pictorial Album.** L., 1837. 10 col.-ptd. plts., lacks engraved title, cont. purple mor., worn, front end-paper loose. (S. Dec.20; 600) Crete. £130
– – **Anr. Edn.** N.d. 4to. Title, 9 plts. only ptd. in oil cols., sm. section of wording of title erased, orig. mor. gt. (CSK. Feb.10; 154) £85

BAXTER, Richard
– **The Poor Man's Family Book.** 1677. *3rd. Edn.* Cont. gt.-decor. mor., rubbed. (P. Jul.5; 258) £500
– **The Saints Everlasting Rest.** 1650. *1st. Edn.* 4to. Some ll. loosening, old cf., leath. lacking from part of spine & upr. cover. (LC. Jul.5; 260) £50

BAXTER, William
– **British Phaenogamous Botany.** Oxford, 1834-43. *Vol. I: 2nd. Edn.* 6 vols. 509 hand-cold. engraved plts., slight browning, mor.-bkd. cl., spines worn. (S. Nov.28; 7) Wheldon & Wesley. £300
– – **Anr. Edn.** Oxford, 1834-43. 6 vols. 509 hand-cold., engraved plts., slight offsetting, a few plt. marks trimmed, hf. cf. (S. Nov.28; 6) Antik Junk. £380
– – **Anr. Copy.** 6 vols. 501 hand-cold. plts., hf. cf. gt., rubbed, 1 spine defect. (P. Feb.16; 80) £320
– – **Anr. Copy.** Vols. 1-3, 5 & 6 only. 428 hand-cold. plts., lacks 1 title, bdgs. not stated, but defect., as a coll. of plts., w.a.f. (P. Oct.20; 21) £240

BAYARD, M.H.
– **Etudes des Bâtiments et des Barques Napolitaines Dessinés d'après Nature.** [1832]. Ob. 4to. 20 orig. etchings, hf. roan. (HD. Mar.9; 50) Frs. 1,000

BAYER, Johann
– **Uranometria.** - **Explicatio Characterum Aeneis Uranometrias Imaginum Tabulis Insculptorum.** Ulm; Augsburg, 1723; 1654. Together 2 vols. Plt. vol. fo., text vol. 4to. Pict. engraved title, 51 double-p. engrs., both vols. foxed, plt. vol. cont. mott. cf., spine gt., jnts. very worn, text vol. loose in old vell. covers. (SG. Apr.26; 17) $1,300

BAYEUX TAPESTRY
[1819-23]. Fo. Mod. cl. (P. Apr.12; 305) Gilbert. £70

BAYFIUS or BAIF, Lazarus
– **Annotationes in Legem II. de Captius & Postliminio Reversis ... item A. Thylesius de Coloribus ....** Basel, 1541. 4to. Pagination jumps from p. 301-304, mod. bds., defect., slightly stained. (D. Nov.23; 73) DM 1,300
– – **Anr. Edn.** Paris, 1549. Sm. 4to. Upr. margin of title browned & with short bear, old vell. (S. May 21; 6) Schumann. £220
– – **Anr. Copy.** 4 metalcut initials. Slightly foxed, a little browning, 18th C. vell. gt. (HK May 15, 75) DM 1,500
– – **Anr. Copy.** 4to. Mor., gt. spine, cover, inner & outer dentelle with corner fleurons, [by Tregaskis, Caxton Head]. (HK. Nov.8; 99) DM 1,300

BAYLDON, Oliver
– **The Paper Makers Craft.** Ill.:– Rigby Graham. Leicester, Twelve by Eight Pr., 1965. *('Less than 400') numbered & sigd. by John Mason.* Sm. fo. Orig. bds. (BBA. Jun.14; 172) Maggs. £55

BAYLE, Pierre
– **The Dictionary Historical & Critical.** 1734-38. *2nd. Engl. Edn.* 5 vols. Fo. Spr. cf., spines gt.; Sir Ivar Colquhoun, of Luss copy. (CE. Mar.22; 19) £360
– – **Anr. Copy.** 5 vols. Fo. Cont. cf. (TA. Aug.18; 368) £70
– – **Anr. Copy.** 5 vols. Fo. Port., old suede, reprd., worn. (SG. Apr.19; 22) $200
– **Dictionnaire Historique et Critique.** Rotterdam/Geneva, 1702-22. 4 vols. including Supp. Fo. Blind-tooled vell., wraped, slightly browned. (VG. May 3; 475) Frs. 500
– – **Anr. Edn.** Ed.:– Prosper Marchand. Amst., 1720. *3rd. Edn.* 4 vols. Fo. Cont. decor. cf., some defects. (HD. Mar.19; 30) Frs. 2,500

BAYLE, Pierre -*Contd.*

– – **Anr. Edn.** Amst. & Leiden, 1730. 4 vols. Fo. Cf. (HD. Feb.22; 10) Frs. 4,000
– – **Anr. Edn.** Ed.:– Des Maizeaux. Amst., 1740. *5th. Edn.* 4 vols. (*With:*) CHAUFEPIE, J.F. – Nouveau Dictionnaire ... Amst., 1750-56. 4 vols. Together 8 vols. Fo. Lacks port., engraved arms ex-libris inside cover, minimal browning, cont. cf. gt., very worn & bumped, 2 repairs, 2 sm. spine tears. (H. Nov.23; 100) DM 640
– – **Anr. Edn.** Basle, 1741. 4 vols. Fo. Cont. cf., worn. (BBA. Feb.23; 47) *Subunso.* £50
– – **Anr. Edn.** Paris, 1820. *New Edn.* 16 vols. Foxing & minor stains, old marb. bds., cf. backs. (RO. Dec.11; 24) $250
– **An Historical & Critical Dictionary.** 1710. 4 vols. Fo. Hf. mor. gt. (P. Sep.8; 108) *Bickersteth.* £110
– **Oeuvres Diverses.** The Hague, 1727-31. 4 vols. Fo. Cf. (P. Nov.24; 199) *Aspin.* £80
– **Pensées Diverses Ecrites à un Docteur de Sorbonne à l'Occasion de la Comète qui parut au Mois de Décembre 1680.** Amst., 1749. 4 vols. 12mo. Cont. mor., arms of Duc de La Vallière & Jeanne-Julie-Françoise de Crussol, spine decor., watered silk liners; from libys. of Comte de Lignerolles & Bordes. (HD. Mar.29; 5) Frs. 60,000

BAYLEY, Frank W.
– **Five Colonial Artists of New England.** Boston, priv. ptd., 1929. *(500).* Tall 4to. Cl. (SG. Oct.13; 27) $175

BAYLEY, F.W.N
See— JERRARD, Paul & Bayley, F.W.N.

BAYLEY, John
– **The History & Antiquities of the Tower of London.** 1821-25. *1st. Edn.* 2 vols. Fo. 29 engraved plts., including 1 extra plt. not called for in list of plts., cont. mor., slightly rubbed. (SKC. May 4; 1770) £70

BAYLEY, Richard
– **An Account of the Epidemic Fever which Prevailed in the City of New-York during Part of the Summer & Fall of 1795.** N.Y., 1796. *1st. Edn.* Hf.-title, later cf., worn, ex-liby. (SG. Oct.6; 39) $110

BAYLIES, Francis
– **Northwest Coast of America ... Report.** Wash., 1826. No. of report changed thro.-out in cont. ink, heavily foxed, three-qtr. mor. (LH. Apr.15; 267) $110

BAYLIS, Edward
– **A New & Compleat Body of Practical Botanic Physic ....** L., 1791-93. Vol. 1 (all publd.). 4to. 48 hand-cold. engraved plts., several ll. misbnd., some spotting, lacks advt. lf. at end, mod. cf. (C. Jun.27; 139) *Dunsheath.* £320

BAYLISS, J.C.
– **Views in Shropshire.** 1884. Pt. IV only. Fo. 16 tinted litho. plts., some very spotted, orig. cl., worn. (TA. Dec.15; 102) £85

BAYREUTH BLATTER. Monatschrift d. Bayreuther Patronatvereines
Ed.:– R. Wagner & H.v. Wolzogen. [1878-89]. Years 1-12, including members lists & indexes, from 'Allgemeiner Richard Wagner-Verein', Vol. 7. Some light browning, hf. linen. (V. Sep.30;2257) DM 750

BAYROS, Franz von
– **Bayros-Mappe I und II.** München, [1911-12]. *(500) numbered.* 4to. Orig. hf. vell. portfos., ex-libris. (GB. Nov.5; 2268) DM 450
– **Bayros-Mappe I-III.** München, 1911-1913. *(500) numbered (I & II), (260) numbered (III).* 4to. Orig. hf. vell. portfo., inside portfo. slightly foxed. (GB. May 5; 2474) DM 1,200
– **Die Bonbonniere.** Ed.:– A. de la Houlette. Wien, [1907]. *(530) numbered.* Pts. 1-2 only (of 5). Lge. 4to. Some light browning & some foxing, hf. linen box. (HK. Nov.11; 3390) DM 520
– **Exlibris, die sie nicht tauschten.** L., Paris & Wien, 1908. *Ltd. Iss., numbered,.* Orig. hf. vell. (GB. Nov.5; 2434) DM 650
– **Mappe.** Preface:– H. Bartsch. Wien, n.d. *(200) numbered.* Lge. fo. Printers mark sigd. by Bayros,

with supp. MS. Hölderlin verse, orig. hf. linen portfo., worn. (HK. May 17; 2566) DM 450

BAYSIO, Guido de
– **Rosarium Decretorum.** [Venice], Johannes Herbort de Seligenstadt, for Johannes de Colonia, Nicolas Jenson et Socii, 3 Apr. 1481. Lge. fo. Rubricated, capitals painted in red or blue, several lge. initials decor. with red pen strokes, cont. stpd. cf. over wood bds., richly decor., perforated brass corners & centre on upr. cover, lge. wood studs on lr. cover, clasps; from Fondation Furstenberg-Beaumesnil. [BMC V, 301; Goff B288] (HD. Nov.16; 67) Frs. 4,900

BAZELEY, Rev. William
See— HYETT, Francis A. & Bazeley, Rev. William

BAZIN, René
– **Le Roi des Archers.** Ill.:– D. Henri Ponchon. Roubaix, 1931. *(115) numbered. (25) for pres. to foreign bibliphiles, sigd.* 4to. Watercolour sigd. by artist on hf.-title, etched plts. & text vigs., each in 2 states, armorial diced mor. gt., mor. onlays, gt. dentelles, qtr. mor. d.-w., s.-c., by Creuzevault. (SG. Apr.26; 18) $500

BAZIN-FOUCHER, Mme. E
See— FOUCHER, A. & Bazin-Foucher, Mme. E.

BEACONSFIELD, Benjamin Disraeli, Earl of
See— DISRAELI, Benjamin, Earl of Beaconsfield

BEALE, Charles William
– **The Secret of the Earth.** L. & N.Y. [but N.Y.?], [1899]. *1st. Edn.* Orig. pict. wraps., advt. on lr. cover, covers lightly worn, spine slightly chipped. (CBA. Oct.29; 68) $400

BEAN, C.E.W.
– **The Official History of Australia in the War of 1914-1918....** Sydney, 1923-42. *Various Edns.* 12 vols. Cl., slightly marked. (KH. May 1; 52) Aus. $100

BEANEY, Dr. J.G.
[–] **Lithotomy: Its Successes & Dangers; Being a Verbatim Report, from Shorthand Notes, of an Inquest....** Melbourne, 1876. Sm. stain at corner of frontis., bdg. not stated, minor marking. (KH. May 1; 53) Aus. $110

BEAR, Donald (Text)
See— WESTON, Edward

BEARD, Charles R.
– **A Catalogue of the Collection of Martinware Formed by Mr. Frederick John Nettlefold.** 1936. Fo. Orig. cl. (S. Nov.8; 493) *Thorp.* £170
– – **Anr. Copy.** Fo. Liby. stp. on verso of title only, a little dust soiled along top edge, orig. cl. gt., partly untrimmed, rubbed. (TA. Jun.21; 427) £130

BEARDSLEY, Aubrey
– **The Early Work. The Later Work.** Intro.:– H.C. Marillier. L., 1899-1901. 2 vols. 2 ports., 330 ills. on plts., orig. linen gt.; ex-libris inside cover. (GB. May 5; 2169) DM 580
– **Illustrations to Salome.** Ca. 1905. 4to. 17 engraved plts. in orig. hf. vell.-bkd. portfo., ties. (PD. Oct.19; 170) £50
– **The Morte D'Arthur Portfolio.** L., 1927. *(300) numbered.* Sm. 4to. Cf.-bkd. vell. bds. gt., boxed. (LH. Jan.15; 235) $110
– **'Salome' A Portfolio of Drawings.** [L.], ca. 1894. 17 plts., slightly darkened at margins, loose in folding three-qtr. buckram & gt.-decor. bd. portfo., lightly worn, lacks ties, some wear to folding wrap. inside bds. (CBA. Aug.21; 40) $225

BEARDSLEY, Aubrey (Ill.)
See— ARISTOPHANES
See— BRADLEY, Will
See— JONSON, Ben
See— LUCIAN, of Samosata
See— MALORY, Sir Thomas
See— POSTER, The
See—STUDIO: An Illustrated Magazine of Fine & Applied Art
See— WILDE, Oscar
See— YELLOW BOOK, The, an Illustrated Quarterly

BEASLEY, Harry G.
– **Pacific Island Records. Fish Hooks.** 1928. *(250).* 4to. Orig. cl. (CSK. Sep.16; 95) £120

BEATON, Cecil
– **Cecil Beaton, Cooling's Galleries, 92 New Bond Street, W.1.** Ed.:– Appreciation:- Osbert Sitwell. [L., 1929]. 12mo. Ptd. wraps., rubbed. (SG. May 10; 14) $110

BEATSON, Robert
– **Naval & Military Memoires of Great Britain from 1727 to 1783.** L., 1804. 6 vols. Hf. cf. gt. (SG. Sep.22; 56) $150

BEATTIE, James
– **Essays.** Edinb., 1776. *1st. Coll. Edn.* 4to. Cont. spr. cf.; Sir Ivar Colquhoun, of Luss copy. (CE. Mar.22; 20) £260
– – **Anr. Copy.** 4to. Orig. bds., unc., torn, lacks front end-paper. (PD. Jun.13; 80) £72

BEATTIE, William
– **The Danube:Its History, Scenery, & Topography.** Ill.:– W.H. Bartlett. Ca. 1840. 4to. Port. frontis, additional vig. title, 2 maps, 80 steel engrs., port. & vig. title stained, cont. hf. cf., gt.-decor. spine, rubbed. (TA. May 17; 67) £180
– – **Anr. Edn.** Ill.:– after W.H. Bartlett. L., 1844. 4to. Additional engraved title, map, 78 steel engrs., slightly spotted & stained, cont. maroon mor. gt., rubbed. (S. Jun.25; 155) *Burgess.* £190
– – **Anr. Copy.** 4to. Engraved title, 74 (of 79) engraved views, hf. mor. gt. (P. Nov.24; 182) *Schuster.* £150
– – **Anr. Copy.** 4to. Map, engraved title, port., 78 plts., hf. mor., rubbed. (SPB. Dec.13; 778) $250
– – **Anr. Copy.** Lge 4to. Steel engraved frontis, 78 steel engraved plts., 1 steel engraved map, many woodcuts, some plts. lightly foxed, cont. mor., gt. spine, cover, inner & outer dentelle. (HK. May 15; 770) DM 1,100
– – **Anr. Copy.** 4to. Engraved title with vig., engraved map, 78 steel engrs, some foxing & staining, cont. hf. leath., bumped. (R. Oct.12; 2494) DM 900
– – **Anr. Edn.** Ill.:– after W.H. Bartlett. L., [1844]. 4to. Engraved map, engraved title, 78 steel-engraved plts., plts. foxed, cont. hf. leath. gt., upr. cover loose. (HK. Nov.8; 969) DM 600
– – **Anr. Edn.** Ill.:– W.H. Bartlett. L., ca. 1844. 4to. Additional engraved title, port., 2 maps, 80 engraved views, cont. hf. cf. (C. Jun.27; 7) *Davidson.* £220
– – **Anr. Edn.** L., ca. 1850. 4to. Port., engraved title, 2 maps, 79 (of 80) steel engrs., slightly foxed, cont. hf. leath., bumped & worn. (R. Apr.4; 2317) DM 1,020
– – **Anr. Edn.** Ill.:– after William Bartlett. N.d. 4to. Steel-engraved port., additional title & 80 plts., 2 maps, some light spotting, cont. hf. mor., slightly rubbed. (CSK. Jul.6; 5) £240
– – **Anr. Copy.** 4to. Steel-engraved port., additional title & 80 plts., 2 maps, margins lightly soiled, cont. cf., worn. (CSK. May 4; 112) £210
– – **Anr. Copy.** 4to. Port. frontis., engraved title, 2 maps, 80 plts., cl. (WW. Nov.23; 13) £200
– **Scotland Illustrated. [Caledonia Illustrated].** Ill.:– after Allom, Bartlett, & others. L., 1838. *[1st. Edn.].* 2 vols. 4to. Engraved titles, map, 118 orig. plts., some light spotting, panel. hf. cf. (PD. Oct.19; 69) £62
– – **Anr. Copy.** 2 vols. 4to. Additional engraved vig. titles, folding map, 118 steel-engraved plts., slight spotting to some plts., hf. cf. gt., rubbed, lacks some spine labels. (LC. Jul.5; 179) £75
– – **Anr. Copy.** 2 vols. 4to. Vig. title to each vol., folding map, 118 steel engrs., some minor spotting, cont. gt.-decor. mor., rubbed on spines, upr. cover of Vol. 2 detchd. (TA. Mar.15; 215) £66
– – **Anr. Copy.** 2 vols. 4to. Steel-engraved additional titles, 1 folding map & 118 plts., light browning & spotting thro.-out, cont. hf. mor., worn. (CSK. Jun.1; 94) £55
– – **Anr. Copy.** 2 vols. 4to. 2 engraved titles, folding map, 118 full-p. engraved plts., some foxed in Vol. I, some ageing, some foxing, later cf. & buckram, gt.-lettering, covers slightly worn at extremities, bkplts. (HA. Nov.18; 236) $100
– – **Anr. Edn.** [1838]. 2 vols. 4to. 2 engraved vig.

titles, port., map, 167 engrs., some staining, hf. mor. gt., rubbed. (P. Jan.12; 178) *Willis.* £70
– – **Anr. Edn.** L., [1839]. 2 vols. 4to. Additional engraved titles, port., map, 161 views, some spotted, cont. mor. gt. (S. Jun.25; 307) *Haile.* £100
– – **Anr. Edn.** L. & N.Y., ca. 1840. 2 vols. 4to. 2 engraved titles, 1 steel-engraved map, 163 (of 166) steel-engraved plts., 1 supp. plt., cont. hf. leath., lightly rubbed. (R. Oct.13; 3108) DM 450
– – **Anr. Edn.** 1842. 2 vols. 4to. 2 steel-engraved additional titles, 118 plts., 4-pp. publishers advts., orig. cl. (CSK. Mar.23; 5) £70
– – **Anr. Edn.** 1847-48. 2 vols. 4to. 2 vig. titles, folding map, 118 engraved plts., some foxing, orig. cl. gt. (P. Sep.8; 21) *Edistar.* £60
– – **Anr. Edn.** L., ca. 1850. 2 vols. 4to. Additional engraved vig. titles, map, port., 167 steel-engraved views, hf. mor., slightly rubbed. (S. Dec.13; 195) *Vitale.* £80
– **La Suisse Pittoresque.** Ill.:– W.H. Bartlett. L. & Paris, 1836. 2 vols. 4to. 2 engraved title frontis. with title vig., double-p. map, 106 steel engrs., some slight foxing, cont. bdg., spine long-grd. mor., gt. decor. covers. (HD. Feb.29; 2) Frs. 6,500
– – **Anr. Copy.** 2 vols. 4to. wide margin, engraved folding map, 105 (of 106) steel-engraved plts., some foxing, especially in margin, some sigs. & 1 plt. quite browned, other margin browning, orig. decor. hf. leath. gt. (V. Sep.29; 125) DM 1,300
– – **Anr. Copy.** 2 vols. 4to. 105 steel engraved ills., orig. leath. gt. (GF. Nov.16; 1139) Sw.Frs. 1,100
– **Switzerland Illustrated.** Ill.:– after W.H. Bartlett. 1834. 2 vols. 4to. Engraved vig. titles, folding map, 106 engraved plts., slight staining to 17 plts. in Vol. 1 & title & 2 plts. in Vol. 2, hf. mor. gt. (LC. Oct.13; 232) £280
– – **Anr. Edn.** Ill.:– W.H. Bartlett. L., 1834-36. Vols. 1 & 2 (pp. 1-40) in 1 vol. 4to. 1 (of 2) engraved titles, 53 (of 106) steel engrs., some slight foxing, lacks 2 ptd. titles & pt. 2 copper engraved title, cont. hf. leath., rubbed. (R. Apr.5; 3066) DM 700
– – **Anr. Edn.** L., 1836. 2 vols. 4to. 2 additional engraved titles with cold. vigs., engraved map, 106 hand-cold. engraved views, cont. hf. mor., rubbed. (S. May 21; 220) *Serafini.* £580
– – **Anr. Copy.** 2 vols. 4to. Engraved titles & 94 plts., folding map slightly torn, some ll. slightly spotted, cont. hf. mor., rubbed. (BBA. May 3; 322) *Traylen.* £320
– – **Anr. Copy.** 2 vols. 4to. 2 engraved titles, 106 engraved views, some foxing, hf. cf., spines defect. (P. Mar.15; 2) *Marshall.* £300
– – **Anr. Copy.** 2 vols. in 1. 4to. Additional engraved titles with vigs., folding map, 106 steel-engraved views, folding map torn without loss, sm. margin stain affecting 1st. few plts., some faint browning, cont. hf. cf. gt., rubbed. (S. Dec.1; 335) *Walford.* £280
– – **Anr. Copy.** 2 vols. 4to. Folding map detchd., some spotting & dampstaining, mainly in margins, cont. cf. gt., worn, spines chipped, w.a.f. (C. Nov.16; 51) *Hart.* £240
– – **Anr. Copy.** 2 vols. in 1. 4to. 106 steel engraved views & 1 map, hf. leath., spine loose. (G. Sep.15; 2057) Sw. Frs. 1,800
– – **Anr. Copy.** 2 vols. Cl. (SSA. Jul.5; 29) R 350
– – **Anr. Edn.** Ill.:– after W.H. Bartlett. L., [1836]. 2 vols. Lge. fo. 2 steel engraved titles, 104 steel engraved plts., 1 double-p. steel engraved map, slightly foxed, blind-tooled orig. linen, gt., slight wear. (HK. May 15; 1088) DM 1,100
– – **Anr. Edn.** L., 1837. 6 vols. 4to. 2 engraved titles with vigs., 106 steel-engraved plts., upr. margin foxed, mostly stained, cont. hf. leath., spine slightly rubbed. (HK. Nov.9; 1249) DM 800
– – **Anr. Edn.** [1844]. 2 vols. 4to. 2 ports., 2 hand-cold. vig. titles, folding map, 106 hand-cold. plts., orig. cl., hinges worn. (P. Sep.8; 83) *Heald.* £780
– – **Anr. Edn.** N.d. 2 vols. 4to. 2 ports., 2 vig. titles, 1 map, 106 plts., red mor. gt. (P. Oct.20; 192) £260
– **The Waldenses.** L., 1836. 4to. 70 steel engrs. & 1 map, gold-tooled leath. (G. Sep.15; 2058) Sw. Frs. 600
– – **Anr. Copy.** 4to. Approx. 70 steel engrs., 1 plt. partly loose, browned due to quality of paper, mor. (CR. Jun.6; 98) Lire 320,000

– – **Anr. Edn.** L., 1838. 2 vols. 4to. Spotted, roan-bkd. cl., rubbed. (S. Jun.25; 154) *Sormani.* £140
– – **Anr. Copy.** 4to. Additional engraved title with vig., port., folding map, 70 plts., slight spotting, sm. margin stain, cont. cf. gt., rebkd. preserving spine. (S. Nov.1; 69) *Zanazzo.* £120
– – **Anr. Copy.** 4to. Engraved frontis., vig. title, folding map, 70 engraved plts., frontis. & title stained, 11 plts. slightly stained, margin stains to a few others, orig. decor. red leath. gt. (LC. Oct.13; 231) £90

BEATTIE, William – PARDOE, Julia
– **The Danube, its History, Scenery, & Topography.**
– **The Beauties of the Bosphorus.** Ca. 1840; [1838]. Together 2 works in 1 vol. 4to. 2 engraved titles, 2 ports., 2 maps, 166 engraved views, slight spotting in 1st. work, str.-grd. cf. gt. (P. Sep.8; 194a) *Schuster.* £220
– – **Anr. Edn.** L., ca. 1842; ca. 1839. Together 2 works in 8 pts., bnd. as 8 vols. 4to. 2 engraved additional titles with vigs., 3 ports., 3 full-p. maps, 165 engraved plts., publisher's catalogues in pts. 1 & 8, 1 or 2 plts. loose, some light spotting, publisher's unif. decor. cl. gt., spines slightly chipped, slightly soiled. (S. Dec.1; 349) *Maliye.* £240

BEATTY, Sir Alfred Chester
– **The Chester Beatty Library, a Catalogue of the Armenian Manuscripts, ...** Intro.:– Sirarpie der Nersessian. Dublin, 1958. 2 vols. Fo. Orig. cl., unc. (S. Apr.30; 369) *Azezian.* £180
– **The Chester Beatty Library. A Catalogue of the Turkish Manuscripts & Miniatures.** Fo. Orig. cl. (BBA. Sep.8; 16) *Makiya.* £60

BEATTY, C.
– **Guds Rades Werk bland Hedningarna.** Stockholm, 1772. Unnumbered advt. lf. at end, later cl.-bkd. bds., partly unc. (S. Dec.1; 276) *Israel.* £350

BEAUBOURG, Maurice
– **La Saison au Bois de Boulogne.** Ill.:– Laboureur. 1928. *Orig. Edn.* 4to. 16 orig. engrs., 4 dupl. pp., sewed. (HD. Apr.13; 150) Frs. 1,800

BEAUCHAMP, Sir Harold
– **Reminiscences & Recollections.** New Plymouth, 1937. Orig. cl.; inscr. & sigd., T.L.s from author tipped in. (KH. Nov.9; 328) Aus. $170

BEAUFORT D'AUBERVAL
– **Contes Erotico-philosophiques....** Ill.:– Amédée Lynen. 1882. Hf. mor., corners, by Durvand, spine decor., wrap. (*With:*) – **Le Combat du Père Barnabé et de Satan.** Rome, 1867. 12mo. Red mor. (HD. May 3; 191) Frs. 1,600

BEAUGRAND, Jean de
– **Paecilographie ou Diverses Escritures Propres pour l'usage Ordinaire.** [Paris, 1601]. Engraved dedication lf. [1601], ptd. dedication lf., 42 copper plts., 1 lf. dtd. 1601, 3 ptd. ll., (1598 privilege), 1 lf. blank, (*Bound with:*) – **Panchrestographie.** [Paris, 1604]. 2 engraved titles, 3 ptd. dedication ll., 2 engraved ll. with figures, arms etc., 45 engraved ll., 6 ptd. ll., 1 lf. crumpled, some repairs, sm. tears & stains. Together 2 works in 1 vol. Ob. & te., old vell., spotted, lr. cover scribbled; Hauswedell coll. (H. May 23; 221) DM 7,000

BEAUHARNAIS, Eugenie Hortense, Queen of Holland
See— HORTENSIA, Queen Consort of Louis, King of Holland

BEAUMARCHAIS, Pierre Auguste Caron de
– **La Folle Journée, ou le Mariage de Figaro, Comédie en Cinq Actes.** Ill.:– Malapeau. Paris, 1785. *Orig. Edn.* Some foxing & soiling, cont. decor. cf., spine gt. (HD. Jul.2; 3) Frs. 3,500
– **Der Lustige Tag, oder Figaro's Hochzeit.** Ill.:– St. Quentin. Kehl, 1785. *1st. definitive German Edn.* Minimal spotting, cont. cf., spine slightly torn, slightly bumped; Hauswedell coll. (H. May 24; 1219) DM 620
– **Oeuvres.** Paris, 1809. 7 vols. Bdg. not stated. (HD. Oct.14; 21) Frs. 1,000

BEAUMONT, Cyril W.
– **The Strange Adventure of a Toy Soldier.** Ill.:– Wyndham Payne. L., 1926. *(110) numbered on 'Nippon' vell., sigd. by author & artist.* Tall 8vo. Vell.-bkd. pict. bds., sm. tears to d.-w. (SG. Dec.8; 45) $100

BEAUMONT, Francis
– **Salamacis & Hermaphroditus.** Ed.:– Gwyn Jones. Ill.:– John Buckland-Wright. Gold. Cock. Pr., 1951. *(380) numbered. (50) on cream vell.-paper.* Sm. fo. Orig. bds., s.-c. (CSK. Oct.21; 34) £65

BEAUMONT, Francis & Fletcher, John
– **Collected Plays.** Ed.:– Arnold Glover & A.R. Waller. Camb., 1905-12. 10 vols. Orig. cl. gt. (LC. Jul.5; 261) £75
– **Comedies & Tragedies.** L., 1647. *1st. Edn.* Fo. Engraved frontis.-port. in 2nd state, bkd., some marginal tears & repairs, soiling, some browning, old cf., rebkd., new endpapers. (SPB. May 16; 8) $550
– **Fifty Comedies & Tragedies.** L., 1679. 2 pts. in 1 vol. Fo. Engraved port., 2 ll. remargined, a few sm. holes & tears, a few ll. slightly soiled, cont. cf., rebkd., slightly rubbed. [Wing B1582] (BBA. May 3; 160) *Rhys Jones.* £200

BEAUMONT, John
– **The Present State of the Universe.** L., 1704. 12mo. Lacks A1 (? blank), later cf. by C. Lewis. (BBA. May 30; 273) *Cavendish Rare Books.* £120

BEAUMONT, Joseph
See— SPENSER, Edmund – BEAUMONT, Joseph

BEAUMONT, W. Worby
– **Motor Vehicles & Motors: Their Design, Construction, & Working by Steam, Oil, & Electricity.** Westminster, 1900. L., 1906. *1st. Edns.* 2 vols. Lge. 8vo. Each vol. with supplementary Lippincott imprint, folding plts. linen-bkd., cl. & crude hf. linen, ex-liby. (SG. Oct.6; 23) $110

BEAUMONT, William
– **Experiments & Observations on the Gastric Juice; & the Physiology of Digestion.** Plattsburgh, 1833. *1st. Edn.* Foxed, owners' MS. ex-libris, orig. bds., worn, rebkd., hinge reprd., lacks free end-paper. (SG. Oct.6; 40) $850
– – **Anr. Edn.** Notes:– Andrew Combe. Edinb., 1838. Hf.-title, orig. cl.-bkd. bds., upr. cover stained, head of spine chipped. (C. Nov.9; 37) *Bickersteth.* £100

BEAUNE, Henri & Arbaumont, Jules d'
– **La Noblesse aux Etats de Bourgogne de 1350 à 1789.** Dijon, 1864. 4to. 100 engraved plts., hf. mor., corners, spine decor. (HD. Mar.21; 106) Frs. 1,800

BEAUSOBRE, Isaac de
– **Histoire Critique de Manichée et du Manicheisme.** Amst., 1734-39. *1st. Edn.* 2 vols. 4to. Hf. mor. gt., marb. bds., unc., cover loose. (SG. Oct.27; 25) $100

BEAUSOBRE, M.C.S. de
See— SAURIN, J. & Beausobre, M.C.S. de

BEAUTE MORALE DES JEUNES FEMMES
Paris, ca. 1830. 6 vols. 12mo. 8 hand-cold. plts., heightened with gold, spotted, orig. hand-cold. litho. decor. bds., van Veen coll. (S. Feb.28; 34) £90

BEAUTES DE L'OPERA
Text:– Théophile Gautier, Jules Janin & Philarète Chasles. Paris, 1845. *1st. Printing of ills.* 4to. Cont. hf. chagrin, spine decor. (HD. May 3; 192) Frs. 2,800

BEAUTY & THE BEAST
Ill.:– E.V. B[oyle]. L., [1875]. 4to. 2 pp. loose, orig. decor. cl. (S. Dec.20; 604) *Steenson.* £90

BEAUTY & THE BEAST: Or, A Rough Outside with a Gentle Heart ... Set to Music by Mr. Whitaker.
1813. Sq. 8vo. 8 hand-cold. engraved plts., some minor spotting, 1 lf. with slight tear, orig. red hf. mor. & ptd. bds., spine chipped at head, slightly worn. (LC. Oct.13; 97) £260

BEAUVOIR, Comte Ludovic de
– Java, Siam, Canton. Voyage autour du Monde. Ill.:– Deschamps. Paris, 1881. (*With:*) – **Australie.** Paris, 1883. (*With:*) – **Pekin, Yeddo.** San Francisco. Paris, 1884. Together 3 vols. 12mo. 7 folding maps in col., 41 plts., sm. tear to 1 map, hf. red chagrin. (HD. Dec.16; 41) Frs. 1,500

BECANUS, Joan. Goropius
– Opera. Antw., 1680. Fo. Dampstained thro.-out, cont. panel. cf., gt.-decor. spine. (TA. Sep.15; 499) £100
– Origines Antwerpianae. Antw., 1569. *1st. Edn.* Fo. Cont. stpd. cf. over wood bds., decor.; from Fondation Furstenberg-Beaumesnil. (HD. Nov.16; 94) Frs. 4,200
– – Anr. Copy. Fo. Privilege lf., slight margin worming not affecting text, blind-stpd. pig, slightly worn. (LM. Mar.3; 2b) B. Frs. 10,000

BECANUS, Martin
– Manuale Controversiarum huius Temporis, in Quinque Libros distributum.... Würzburg, 1623. *1st. Edn.* Some staining in parts, cont. blind-tooled vell. over wood bds., slits, 1 (of 2) clasps. (GB. Nov.3; 927) DM 500

BECCARI, Odoardo
– Wanderings in the Great Forests of Borneo. Ed.:– F.H.H. Guillemard. Trans.:– Dr. Enrico H. Giglioli. 1904. Orig. cl. gt., partly untrimmed, spine slightly faded. (TA. Oct.20; 20) £100

BECCARIA, Giovanni Battista
– Della Elettricita Terrestre Atmosferica a Cielo Sereno Osservazioni. [Turin, 1775]. *1st. Edn.* 4to. With 1st. blank lf. & final lf. of Imprimatur, minor margin flaw in 1 lf. without loss of text, recent sheep; John D. Stanitz coll. (SPB. Apr.25; 32) $250
– Dell'Elettricismo Artificale e Naturale. Turin, 1753. *1st. Edn.* 4to. S4 a cancel, hf.-title, 1st. few ll. stained, some browning & discoloration, new vell., unc. (S. Apr.10; 473) *Samueli.* £120

BECHAYEI BAN ASHER
– Rabbeinu Bechayei Al Ha'torah. Amst., 1726. Fo. Cl., w.a.f. (S. Jul.3; 72) £110

BECHAYEI BEN JOSEPH IBN PAKUDA
– Chovot Ha'levavot. Ed.:– Shlomo ben Perez [Bonfoi Zarfati]. Trans.:– Yehudah Ibn Tibbon. [Naples], Yosef (ben Yaacov) Ashkenazi [Gunzenhausen], 1st. day of Chanukah [25 Kislev] 5250 [19 Nov. 1490]. *1st. Edn.* 4to. Uncensored, lacks 15 text ll. & final blank, some soiling, browning & staining, a few inner margins reprd., a few other minor repairs, bds. [Steinschneider 4526, 1] (SPB. Jun.26; 4) $13,000
– – Anr. Edn. Trans.:– Yehuda Ibn Tibbon. Venice, 1548. *2nd. Edn.* 4to. Owners' sigs. on title & last p., stained thro.-out, slightly soiled, hf. vell. (S. Oct.24; 89) *Dzialowski.* £450
– – Anr. Copy. (*Bound with:*) **YEHUDA HALEVI – Kuzari.** Venice, 1547. Together 2 works in 1 vol. 4to. Marginalia in various hands, some phrases in 2nd. work censored, sigd. by Clemente Renatto & Giovanni Dominico Carreto, '1628' (i.e. 1608?), slight soiling & staining, vell., lr. cover detchd.; Hochschule für die Wissenschaft des Judenthoms stps. (SPB. Jun.26; 3) $1,600
– – Anr. Copy. 4to. Some spotting & staining, owners' sigs. on title, old vell., rubbed. (SPB. Feb.1; 19) $900

BECHER, H.C.R.
– A Trip to Mexico. Toronto, 1880. Some soiling, cl., worn, slightly shaken. (RO. Dec.11; 25) $120

BECHER, Johann Joachim
– Parnassus Medicinalis Illustratus. Ulm, 1662/63. *1st. Edn.* 4 pts. in 1 vol. Fo. Pt. 1 comprising pp. 39-50 & 59-104 only, some other pp. defect., pts. 2 & 3 with a few ll. incompl., lacks last 1 or 2 ll. from index at end of pt. 4, together approx. 900 (of some 1,200) woodcuts, some heavy browning & old spotting, hf. leath., defect., spine with pasted on leath. strips. (V. Sep.29; 1322) DM 750
– Physica Subterranea ... Specimen Beccherianum, Fundamentorum Documentorum, Experimentorum, subjunxit C.E. Stahl. Leipzig, 1738. *New Edn.* 4to. Foxed, cont. cf. gt. (SG. Oct.6; 42) $375

BECHOFFEN, Johannes
– Quadruplex Missalis Expositio. Basle, 1509. (*Bound with:*) **BIEL, Gabriel – Passionis Dominice Sermo Historialis.** [Mainz], Fr. Herman, 1509. Together 2 works in 1 vol. Lge. 8vo. Cont. blind-stpd. cf., decor., studs, clasps, spine renewed; from Fondation Furstenberg-Beaumesnil. (HD. Nov.16; 95) Frs. 7,200

BECHSTEIN, Johann Matthias
– Die Jagdwissenschaft. Gotha, 1820. *[1st. Edn.].* Vol. 1. Cont. bds., rubbed & bumped. (R. Apr.4; 1825) DM 500
– – Anr. Copy. 2 vols. Some slight foxing, 1st. ll. stained in lr. margin. cont. bds., spine pasted over. (BR. Apr.12; 1195) DM 420

BECHSTEIN, Ludwig
– Deutsches Märchenbuch. Ill.:– L. Richter. Leipzig, 1845. *1st. Edn.* Foxed, some light browning, title-lf. crumpled, cont. hf. leath., slightly worn & bumped; Hauswedell coll. (H. May 24; 1646) DM 800
– – Anr. Edn. Ill.:– G. Alboth after K.W. Schurig. Leipzig, 1846. *1st. Ill. Edn.* Slightly spotted & soiled, orig. cl., slightly faded & stained, recased, van Veen coll. (S. Feb.28; 133) £120
– Märchenbilder und Erzählungen, der Reiferen Jugend geweiht. Leipzig, [1829]. *1st. Edn.* Sm. 4to. Engraved frontis. & 5 plts. hand-cold., 3 pp. advts. at end, cont. hf. cf.; prize certificate to Carel August Nairac, Kampen, 1830, van Veen coll. (S. Feb.28; 132) £340
– Märchenbuch. Ill.:– L. Richter. Leipzig, 1857. *2nd. pictor. Edn.* Margins lightly browned, minimal spotting, orig. linen, blind tooled, spine torn, corners bumped; Hauswedell coll. (H. May 24; 1649) DM 680
– Der Sonntag. Ill.:– Ferd. Berthold. Leipzig, [1832]. Ob. fo. Sm. stain at beginning outside plt. margin, cont. marb. bds., lightly bumped. (GB. May 4; 1197) DM 400

BECICHEMUS, Marinus
– Elegans et Docta in C. Plinium Praelectio [with other commentaries]. Paris, 10 Aug. 1519. Fo. New bds. (S. Dec.20; 772) *Brown.* £90

BECIUS, J.
– Het Ghesette Exemplaer der Godloosen: ofte Historie Sodomae ende Gomorrae. Arnhem, 1638. 5 pts. in 1 vol. 4to. Frontis. (dtd. 1639) mntd., 1 quire double, slightly stained, cont. vell., ties, new end-papers. (VG. Nov.30; 967) Fls. 660

BECK, J.J.
– Tractatus de eo, quod justum est circa Stuprum. Von Schwäch- u. Schwängerung der Jungfern u. Ehrlichen Witwen .... Nuremb., 1743. 4to. Some ll. slightly wormed in upr. corner, cont. leath. (HK. Nov.9; 2044) DM 420
– Tractatus de Juribus Judaeorum. Nuremb., 1741. 4to. Cont. hf. leath., gt. decor. spine, slightly bumped. (D. Nov.24; 4213) DM 800

BECKER, Dr. Felix
– Handzeichnungen Holländischer Meister aus der Sammlung D. C. Hofstede de Groot im Haag. Leipzig, 1923. 2 vols. Fo. Loose as iss., with text, in orig. hf. parch. portfos. (BBA. Sep.8; 30) *Sims, Reed & Fogg.* £80
See— **THIEME, Dr. Ulrich & Becker, Dr. Felix**

BECKER, G.W.
[–] Gemälde von Leipzig und seiner Umgebung ... Schlachten bei dieser Stadt. Ill.:– G. Baettger. Leipzig, 1823. Lacks folding plan, plts. slightly foxed, orig. bds., worn & soiled. (R. Oct.13; 2772) DM 460
– Neue Haus- u. Reise-Apotheke. Leipzig, 1815. 2 pts. in 1 vol. Foot of title stpd., some offsetting, cont. hf. leath gt. (HK. Nov.8; 446) DM 440

BECKER, Robert H.
– Designs on the Land: Diseños of California Ranchos & their Makers. San Franc., 1969. *(500).* Ob. fo. Sm. tear to 1 folding sheet, hf. suede & cl. (CBA. Nov.19; 259) $150

BECKER, Wilhelm Gottlieb
– Taschenbuch zum Geselligen Vergnügen. Ed.:– Fr. Kind. Leipzig, [1819 & 1826]. Years 1820 & 1827 in 2 vols. Minimal browning & spotting, orig. pict. bds., slightly spotted. (H. May 22; 576) DM 900

BECKETT, Samuel
– En Attendant Godot. Paris, 1952. *1st. Edn.* Slightly browned, orig. wraps. (BBA. Nov.30; 269) *Johnson & O'Donnell.* £210
– Molloy. Paris, 1951. 1 vol. Orig. wraps. (*With:*) **– Malone meurt.** Paris, 1951. 1 vol. Inscr. on hf.-title, orig. wraps. (*With:*) **– Waiting for Godot.** 1956. *1st. Engl. Edn.* 1 vol. Publisher's slip, orig. cl., d.-w. (*With:*) **BECKETT, Samuel & others – Our Exagmanination round his Factification for Incamination of Work in Progress.** N.d. *2nd. Edn.* 1 vol. Orig. cl., d.-w. (BBA. Nov. 30; 270) *Johnson & O'Donnell.* £190
– More Pricks than Kicks. L., 1934. *1st. Edn.* Orig. cl., some spine letters rubbed. (C. Nov.9; 188) *Rota.* £200
– – Anr. Copy. Orig. cl., rubbed & soiled, lacks fly-lf. (BBA. May 23; 59) *Blackwell.* £130
– Murphy. L., 1938. *1st. Edn.* Orig. cl., slightly rubbed. (BBA. May 23; 60) *Rota.* £260
– No's Knife. L., [1967]. *1st. Edn. De Luxe Edn., (100) not for sale.* Orig. hf. leath.; printer's mark sigd. by author. (H. Nov.24; 1358) DM 400
– Proust. L., 1931. *1st. Edn.* Orig. pict. bds., d.-w. slightly soiled. (S. Dec.13; 320). *Shapero.* £55
– Whoroscope. Paris, Hours Pr., 1930. *1st. Edn., (300). (100) sigd.* Orig. ptd. wraps., stapled as iss.; inscr. by author to Harry Sinclair, correction apparently in Beckett's hand, Frederic Dannay copy. (CNY. Dec.16; 21) $1,400

BECKETT, Samuel & others
– Our Exagmination round his Factification for Incamination of Work in Progress. 1929. Orig. wraps.; bkplt. inscr. by Beckett. (P. Jul.5; 116) £100

BECKFORD, Peter
– Thoughts upon Hare & Fox Hunting. L., 1796. Some very slight spotting, later cf. gt., partly unc. (S. Mar.20; 688) *J. Allen.* £90
– – Anr. Edn. Dublin, 1797. Later hf. vell. (GB. Nov.4; 1534) DM 520
– Thoughts on Hunting. 1810. Mod. mor. gt. by Bayntun. (CSK. Jun.1; 3) £60

BECKLER, Peter
[–] Illustre Stemma Ruthenicum. Schleitz, 1684. Fo. 2 folding letterpress tables cleanly torn, browned, last lf. shaved with a little loss, cont. vell., soiled. (CSK. Nov.4; 178) £60

BECKMANN, Johann
– Beyträge zur Geschichte der Erfindungen. Leipzig, 1782-1805. 5 vols. Cont. hf. leath. & 1 cont. bds. (R. Apr.4; 1578) DM 900
– – Anr. Edn. Leipzig, [1783]-99. Vols. 1-4 only (of 5). Cont. hf. leath. gt., rubbed. (R. Oct.12; 1729) DM 1,100

BECKMANN, Max
– Apokalypse. Frankfurt, priv. ptd., 1943. Fo. Unnumbered copy, rough ll. in orig. bd. cover. (HK. Nov.11; 3410) DM 7,500
– Die Hölle. Berlin, [1919]. *Ltd. Iss.* Fo. Orig. wraps., title ill. pasted on, faded & stained. (H. Nov.24; 1359) DM 520
– Jahrmarkt. München, 1922. *(75) De Luxe Edn. on Japan.* Lge. fo. 10 orig. etchings, all ll. sigd. & stpd., margins under guards slightly darkened as usual, loose ll. in orig. hf. vell. portfo., slightly defect; Hauswedell coll. (H. May 24; 578) DM 26,000
– – Anr. Edn. München, 1922. *(125) numbered on Bütten.* Fo. 12 sigd. etchings, all ll. with artists MS sig, & under guards, orig. hf. lines portfo. (HK. May 17; 2570) DM 22,000
– Lili von Braunbehrens. Stadtnacht. München, 1921. *1st. Edn. (500).* Sm. 4to;. Orig. hf. vell.; printers mark sigd. (H. Nov.24; 2451) DM 2,400

BECON, Thomas
– The Reliques of Rome. 1563. Qtr. cf., rubbed. (P. Jun.7; 319) £170

BECOURT, A. de
– Art de Fabriquer toutes sortes d'Ouvrages en Pâpier. Paris, 1828. *2nd. Edn.* Hand-cold. frontis., 21 folding plts., hf.-title. (*Bound with:*) **– Art de**

Construire en Cartonage. Paris, 1828. *2nd. Edn.* 8 folding plts. Together 2 works in 1 vol. 12mo. A few ll. slightly spotted, cont. bds., slightly rubbed. (BBA. Mar.7; 165) *Blackwells.* £110

BECQUEREL, Edmond
- **Traité Experimental de L'electricité et du Magnétisme.** Paris, 1834-40. 7 vols. & Atlas. 8 vo. & 4to. Atlas of 28 plts., cont. hf. damson chagrin, decor. spine. (HD. Jan.26; 26) Frs. 2,480

BECQUEREL, Henri
- **Recherches sur une Propriété Nouvelle de la Matiére. Activité Radiante Spontanée ou Radioactivité de la Matière.** Paris, 1903. *1st. Edn.* 4to. Errata lf., orig. ptd. wraps., unc. & unopened, spine & part of upr. cover faded, folding box; John D. Stanitz coll. (SPB. Apr.25; 33) $600
- - **Anr. Copy.** 4to. Orig. wraps., boxed, covers lightly stained. (LH. Sep.25; 459) $170

BECQUET, Etienne
- **Marie ou le Mouchoir Bleu.** Paris, 1884. *(1200). (200) on 'grand papier vélin'.* 16mo. 4 engraved plts. & 2 vigs., all in 3 states, cont. mor. gt. by Chambolle-Duru, richly decor., silk damask doubls. & free end-papers, orig. wraps. bnd. in. (CSK. Jan.13; 112) £200

BEDARSCHI, Yedaiah Penini ben Avraham
- **Bechinat Olam.** Soncino, [Joshua Solomon Soncino], 24 Kislev 5245 [12 Dec. 1484]. 4to. 20 ll., compl., slight staining & soiling, minor margin repair, 1 phrase on final p. censored, cl.; traces of Hochschule für die Wissenschaft des Judenthums stps. [Steinschneider 5670, 2] (SPB. Jun.26; 5) $18,000

BEDDOME, R.H.
- **Icones Plantarum Indiae Orientalis.** L., 1874. 4to. 300 plts., orig. cl.-bkd. bds., worn & shaken; Royal Commonwealth Soc. copy. (P. Nov.24; 286) *Weldon & Wesley.* £80

BEDE, the Venerable
- **De Natura Rerum et Temporum Ratione Libri Duo.** Basel, 1529. Fo. Cont. annots., some browning, mod. vell.; John D. Stanitz coll. (SPB. Apr.25; 34) $1,500
- **History of the Church of Englande.** Shakes. Hd. Pr., 1930. *(475).* 4to. Orig. cf.-bkd. bds., unopened, slightly faded. (CSK. Jun.1; 57) £50

BEDFORD, Francis
- **Catalogue of the Choice Library of the late Mr. Francis Bedford, the eminent Bookbinder.** 1884. MS. prices & buyers' names, cont. cl.-bkd. bds.; H.M. Nixon coll. (BBA. Oct.6; 147) *Maggs.* £180

BEDIER, Joseph
- **Le Roman de Tristan et Iseut.** Ill.:– Robert Engels. Paris, [1933]. 4to. Three-qtr. lev. by Levitzky, spine gt. with silver inlays, orig. wraps. bnd. in. (SG. Feb.16; 28) $325

BEDOS DE CELLES, François
- **La Gnomonique Pratique, ou l'Art de Tracer les Cadrans Solaires.** Paris, 1760. 2 plts. with blank margins reprd., 1 with sm. clean tear, cont. mott. cf., spine gt., head very slightly chipped. (CSK. Dec.16; 10) £110

BEE, John
- **Sportsman's Slang.** 1835. 12mo. Folding frontis. hand-cold., torn at fold & laid down, cont. gt.- & blind-tooled str.-grd. mor., spine gt., rebkd., later end-papers, double fore-e. pntg., later box. (CSK. Jul.27; 31) £320

BEEBE, Charles William
- **A Monograph of the Pheasants.** Ill.:– after A. Thorburn, H. Gronvold, G.E. Lodge, & others. L., 1918-22. *[1st. Edn.]. (600).* 4 vols. Fo. Mod. maroon hf. mor. gt. (C. Jun.27; 140) *Barclay.* £1,200
- - **Anr. Copy.** 4 vols. Fo. 90 cold. plts., photogravure plts., orig. cl.; R. Meinertzhagen bkplt. (C. Mar.14; 154) *Wheldon & Wesley.* £700
- - **Anr. Copy.** 4 vols. Fo. Worming to Vols. 2 & 3 affecting some plts. & ll., orig. cl., Vols. 2 & 3 reprd. & rebkd. preserving orig. spines. (C. Mar.14; 101) *Senior.* £280
- - **Anr. Copy.** 4 vols. Fo. 20 distribution maps, 88

photogravure plts., 90 cold. plts., orig. gt.-lettered cl., some covers rubbed. (CNY. May 18; 133) $900
- - **Anr. Copy.** 4 vols. Fo. 20 maps, 88 photogravures, 90 col. plts., cl. gt., Vol. 1 worn & faded. (PNY. Jun.6; 441) $800

BEECHEY, Capt. Frederick William
- **Narrative of a Voyage to the Pacific & Beering's Strait, to Cooperate with the Polar Expeditions.** L., 1831. *1st. Edn.* 2 vols. 4to. 3 engraved maps, including 2 folding, 23 full-p. plts., hf.-titles, errata slip tipped in Vol. 1 (lacks that in Vol. 2), advt. lf. at end Vol. 2, orig. paper bds., unc., spines & covers with inked titles added, spines chipped & worn; the Rt. Hon Visc. Eccles copy. [Sabin 4347] (CNY. Nov.18; 18) $1,500
- - **Anr. Copy.** 2 vols. 4to. 3 maps, 23 pits., plts. foxed, hf. cf., marb. paper bds., rehinged & rebnd. [Sabin 4347] (LH. Sep.25; 188) $400
- - **Anr. Copy.** 2 vols. 3 engraved charts, 23 engraved plts., sm. tears in 2 charts, many plts. foxed & shaved, title & charts foxed, hf. cf., covers slightly rubbed. (CA. Apr.3; 20) Aus. $200
- **A Voyage of Discovery Towards the North Pole, Performed in His Majesty's Ships Dorothea & Trent, Under the Command of Captain David Buchan, R.N., 1818.** 1843. Orig. cl. (LC. Mar.1; 197) £160

BEECKMAN, Isaac
- **Journal Tenu de 1604 à 1634.** Ed.:– C. de Waard. La Haye, 1939-53. 4 vols. 4to. Cl. (B. Jun.21; 365) Fls. 475

BEER, A.
- **Einleitung un die Höhere Optik.** Braunschweig, 1853. *1st. Edn.* Cont. bds. (R. Oct.12; 1646) DM 440

BEER, Georg Joseph
- **Lehre von den Augenkrankheiten.** Wien, 1813-17. 2 vols. Cont. hf. leath. (R. Oct.12; 1332) DM 2,100
- **Pflege Gesunder und Geschwächter Augen ....** Wien & Leipzig, 1800. *1st. Edn.* Cont. bds., slightly rubbed. (GB. May 3; 980) DM 600

BEER, J.C.
- [–] **Beschreibung der Gefürsteten und sehr Mächtigen Graffschaft Tyrol.** Augsburg, 1703. *1st. Edn.* 1 lf. stpd., title with sm. excision without loss, cont. hf. leath. (GB. Nov.3; 93) DM 2,400
- [–] **Das Neu-Beharnischte Gross-Britannien.** Nuremb., 1690. 4to. Engraved frontis., 3 folding outl.-cold. copper-engraved maps, 31(of 42) copper plts., cont. bds., lacks spine, old pasted with paper. (R. Oct.13; 3110) DM 600

BEERBOHM, Sir Max
- **A Book of Caricatures.** L., 1907. *1st. Edn.* Fo. Cold. frontis., 48 plts., hf.-title & frontis. loose, orig. buckram-bkd. cl., slightly marked, spine faded. (S. Dec.13; 321) *Peck.* £80
- **Caricatures of Twenty-Five Gentlemen.** L., 1896. *1st. Edn. 2nd. Iss., with reading 'and Co.' on spine.* 4to. Hf.-title, orig. cl. gt., slightly marked. (S. Dec.13; 325) *Perkins.* £120
- **The Happy Hypocrite.** New Fairfield, Bruce Rogers, 1955. *(600).* Orig. cl.-bkd. decor. bds.; pres. copy from Rogers to Sir Sydney Cockerell, inscr. by Rogers & note by Cockerell on fly-lf. (S. Dec.13; 331) *Rota.* £110
- **Heroes & Heroines of Bitter Sweet.** L., [1931]. *1st. Edn. (900) numbered.* Fo. Facs. letter & 5 cold. plts. mntd. in card. folders, title & contents list ptd. on recto of card., loose as iss., orig. vell.-bkd. bd. portfo. (S. Dec.13; 328) *Blackwell.* £60
- **A Peep into the Past.** U.S.A., priv. ptd., 1923. *(300) on Japanese vell.* Orig. cl.-bkd. bds., orig. s.-c. slightly damaged. (LC. Mar.1; 52) £50
- **The Poets' Corner.** L., 1904. *1st. Edn.* Fo. 20 chromolitho. plts., a few spots & stains, cl., orig. pict. bds. preserved; title blind-stpd. 'Presentation copy', fly-lf. with pencilled inscr. 'A.E. Manning Foster from M.B.' (not in Beerbohm's hand). (S. Dec.13; 332) *Peck.* £75
- **A Survey.** L., 1921. *1st. Edn. (275) numbered & sigd., specially bnd.* 4to. Cold. frontis., title with lge. ill. (not in ordinary edn.), 51 plts., hf.-title, orig. bds., d.-w. (S. Dec.13; 322) *Blackwell.* £140

- **The Works.** N.Y., [6 Jun.] 1896. *1st. Edn.* Hf.-title, slight spotting, orig. decor. cl. gt., partly unc., slightly marked. (S. Dec.13; 333) *Perkins.* £120
- **The Works ... with a Bibliography by John Lane.** L., [10 Jun.] 1896. *1st. Engl. Edn. 1st. Printing of Lane's 'Bibliography'.* Hf.-title, 16 pp. of inserted advts. at end, orig. cl., slightly soiled. (S. Dec.13; 334) *Perkins.* £55

BEERS, F.W.
- **Atlas of the Hudson River Valley from New York City to Troy, Including a Section of about 8 Miles in Width.** N.Y., Watson & Co., 1891. Fo. 40 double-p. hand-cold. litho. maps, gt.-lettered cl., rebkd. (SG. Jun.7; 31) $200
- **County Atlas of Berkshire, Massachusetts, from Actual Surveys.** N.Y., 1876. Tall fo. Full & double-p. maps in full col. of towns & villages, 20 litho. plts. of many residences, mills, business houses, etc., orig. cl., rubbed. (SG. Jun.7; 23) $175
- **State Atlas of New Jersey.** N.Y., 1872. Lge. 4to. Litho. vig., many full-p. or double-p. col. litho. maps & plans, inserted advert. ll., few stains, repairs, orig. cl., rebkd. & recornered; ex-liby. (SG. Apr.5; 136) $275

BEERS, S.N. & D.G.
- **New Topographical Atlas of Saratoga Co., New York, from Actual Surveys.** Phila., Stone & Stewart, 1866. Fo. 32 full & double-p. maps in col., 2 litho. views on 1 plt., bds., crudely rebkd. (SG. Jun.7; 32) $175

BEETHOVEN, Ludwig van
- **Fifth Symphony, Opus 67.** Leipzig, [1826]. *1st. Edn.* Some spotting, title-p. stained, cont. marb. bds., worn; bkplt. & sig. of Charles Salaman. (S. Nov.17; 85) *Brody.* £450
- **First Symphony Opus 21.** L., [1809]. *1st. Edn.* Sm. 4to. Title-p. with 1 sm. alteration: the no. 'II' appears in MS. instead of 'XXVI, 1st. p. of music bears heading 'Beethoven's Symph: II', overall browning, mod. bds. (S. Nov.17; 83) *Brody.* £400
- **Fourth Symphony, Opus 60.** Bonn & Cologne, [1823]. *1st. Edn.* A little spotted & stained, orig. wraps., marb. bds., unc., slightly worn. (S. Nov.17; 84) *MacNutt.* £450
- **Neunte Symphonie.** Leipzig, 1924. Lge. fo. A few sm. tears, orig. linen box. (HK. Nov.9; 2236) DM 700
- **Ninth Symphony, Opus 125.** Mainz & Paris, [1826]. *1st. Edn. 1st. Iss.* Fo. Subscribers' list, some foxing & spotting, cont. annots. in blue & black pencil, cont. cl.-bkd. bds.; from Gesellschaft der Musikfreunde, Vienna, release stp. on 1 end-paper. (S. Nov.17; 88) *MacNutt.* £1,450
- **Seventh Symphony, Opus 92.** Vienna, [1816]. *1st. Edn.* 4to. Some spotting, cf.-bkd. cont. marb. bds., worn; sigd. on fly-lf. 'Moritz Parthey'. (S. Nov.17; 87) *MacNutt.* £750
- **Sixth Symphony, Opus 68.** Leipzig, [1826]. *1st. Edn.* A few 19th. C. pencil annots., mod. bds. with orig. wrap. affixed. (S. Nov.17; 86) *Brody.* £500
- - **Anr. Copy.** Plt. no. 4311, litho. title-p., without orig. wrap., some spotting & foxing, mod. bds., rebkd. (S. May 10; 7) *Macnutt.* £240

BEETON, Mrs. Isabella
- **The Book of Household Management.** L., 1861. *1st. Edn.* Slight spotting, cut down, cont. hf. cf. (S. Mar.20; 689) *Witeson.* £160
- - **Anr. Copy.** Additional cold. title, 12 cold. plts., lacks frontis., orig. cl. gt.; sigd. pres. copy from author. (SKC. Jan.13; 2276) £100
- - **Anr. Copy.** Frontis. in facs., cl. gt., rebkd. (PNY. Dec.1; 43) $150
- - **Anr. Copy.** Sm. 8vo. Bnd. without advts., lacks a single lf. of text, rebnd. preserving much of cl. from backstrip & upr. bd. (KH. Nov.9; 541) Aus. $100

BEEVERELL, James
- **Les Délices de la Grande Bretagne.** Leyden, 1727. *2nd. Edn.* 7 vols. only (lacks Vol.4). Engraved folding titles, 4 folding plts., 186 folding plts., margin of 1 plt. reprd. with sellotape, cont. mott. cf., gt. spines. (C. Dec.9; 6) *Burgess.* £120
- - **Anr. Copy.** 8 vols. 12mo. 250 folding plts., some stains, cont. marb. cf., spines decor. (HD. Mar.19; 32) Frs. 2,500

BEGER, Loranz
– **Regum et Imperatorum Romanorum Numismata.** Brandenburg, 1700. Fo. Engraved vig. on title & 68 engraved plts., hf.-title with owner's inscrs., slight browning, cont. vell. bds., soiled, foot of spine reprd. (S. May 1; 451) *Spink.* £80
– **Spicilegium Antiquitatis.** Brandenburg, 1692. Fo. 1st. lf. stained, some light spotting, cont. vell. (BBA. Nov.30; 55) *Matthews.* £70
– **Thesauri Regii et Electoralis Brandenburgici; Antiquorum Numismatum et Gemmarum.** Berlin, ca. 1700. Lge. fo. 41 (of 44) engraved plts., text engrs., title-p. reprd. & mntd. with publisher & date cut away, badly foxed, later vell., spine gt. (SG. Apr.19; 134) $110

BEGIN, Emile Auguste
– **Voyage Pittoresque en Espayne et en Portugal.** Ill.:– Rouargue frères. Paris, [1852]. 4to. 10 engraved cold. costume plts. & 26 steel engraved views, slightly foxed, cont. hf. leath. gt., slightly bumped. (R. Apr.5, 2960) DM 700
– – **Anr. Copy.** Ill.:– Rouargue Frères. [1852]. Lge. 8vo. 36 copper engrs. (10 hand-cold.), publisher's buckram bds. (HD. Mar.21; 133) Frs. 2,200
– – **Anr. Copy.** Publisher's decor. buckram. (HD. May 3; 194) Frs. 1,250
– **Voyage Pittoresque en Suisse, en Savoie et sur les Alpes.** Ill.:– Rouargues. Paris, 1852. *1st. Edn.* 8 cold. plts., 14 (of 16) steel engrs., slightly foxed, cont. hf. leath., rubbed. (R. Oct.13; 3248) DM 750

BEGUILLET, Edme
– **Manuel du Meunier et du Charpentier de Moulins.** Paris, 1775. *1st. Edn.* Slight spotting, owners inscr. partly erased from hf.-title, cont. mott. cf., spine gt., leath chipped along edges; John D. Stanitz coll. (SPB. Apr.25; 35) $475

BEHMER, Max
– **Niemand kann wider sein Schicksal.** Weimar, 1905. Fo. Folded sigs. (H. Nov.24; 1369) DM 460

BEHN, Aphra & others
– **Miscellany, being a Collection of Poems by Several Hands, Together with Reflections on Morality, or Seneca Unmasqued.** L., 1685. *1st. Edn.* Lacks a4 blank, slight browning, cont. cf., worn, upr. cover detchd.; front free end-paper inscr. 'Katherine Blount/Given my by Sr Thomas Pope Blount/July ye 10th/1696', later bkplt. of James Rimington. [Wing M2230] (S. Oct.11; 308) *Pickering & Chatto.* £220

BEHRENS, P.
– **Feste des Lebens und der Kunst Eine Betrachtung des Theaters als Höchsten Kultur symbols.** Leipzig, 1900. 4to. Slightly browned, orig. bds. (HK. May 17; 2580) DM 600
– – **Anr. Copy.** Orig. bds. (HK. Nov.11; 3421) DM 420

BEHRING, Emil von
– **Die Geschichte der Diptherie.** Leipzig, 1893. *1st. Edn.* Title stpd., cont. hf. linen. (R. Oct.12; 1360) DM 450

BEISSEL, Joh. Cont.
– [–] **Urständliche u. Erfahrung-volle Hohe Zeugüsse Wie man zum Geistlichen Leben und dessen Vollkommenheit gelangen möge ....** Ephrata, 1745. 4to. Title stpd., browned & stained, sm. margin defects., cont. hf. linen, corners bumped. (HK. Nov.9; 1504) DM 1,050

BEIT, Otto
– **Catalogue of the Collection of Pottery & Porcelain in [his] Possession.** Ed.:– Van de Put & Bernard Rackham. L., priv. ptd. at the Chiswick Pr., 1916. *(70) numbered.* Fo. 29 plts., qtr. mor., rubbed. (SG. Jan.26; 66) $175

BEJOT, Eugène
– **Du 1er au XXe. Les Arrondissements de Paris.** Preface:– Jules Claretie. Paris, 1903. *Ltd. Edn.* 4to. Leaves, publishers portfo. (HD. Feb.17; 53) Frs. 2,500

BEKANNTNUSS DER THEOLOGEN und Kirchendiener zu Heidelberg.
Heidelberg, 1575. *2nd. Edn.* 4to. Some old

underlining & sm. marginalia on a few pp., hf. vell. (R. Oct.11; 47) DM 500

BEKE, Charles T.
– **The Sources of the Nile: Being a General Survey of the Basin of that River, & of its Head-Streams; with the History of Nilotic Discovery.** 1860. Orig. cl., rubbed, spine faded. (TA. Feb.16; 7) £65

BEKKER, Balthasar
– **Le Monde Enchanté.** Amst., 1694. 4 vols. 16mo. Bdg. not stated. (HD. Oct.14; 23) Frs. 1,200

BELCH, W.
See— LANGLEY, E. & Belch, W.

BELCHER, Charles F.
– **The Birds of ... Geelong.** Geelong, n.d. No bdg. stated. (JL. Jun.24; 138) Aus. $160

BELCHER, Sir Edward
– **Narrative of a Voyage Round the World.** L., 1843. *1st. Edn.* 2 vols. 19 engraved plts. including frontispieces (some foxing), 3 folding maps in pocket at beginning of Vol. 1, orig. cl. [Sabin 4390] (S. May 21; 163) *Cavendish.* £480
– – **Anr. Copy.** 2 vols. Lacks maps, liby. stp. on each plt., hf. mor. (SKC. May 4; 1804) £55

BELCHER, J. & Macarthy, M.E.
– **Later Renaissance Architecture in England.** [1897]-1901. 6 pts. Fo. Unbnd. as iss. in orig. portfo., soiled. (CSK. Jun.29; 190) £80

BELDEN, Frank A.
See— HAVEN, Charles T. & Belden, Frank A.

BELGIUM
– **Vues Pittoresques de la Belgigue et de ses Monuments les plus Remarquables.** Bruxelles, n.d. Lge. 4to. Publisher's bds., spine strengthened. (LM. Mar.3; 21) B.Frs. 18,000

BELIDOR, Bernard Forest de
– **Architecture Hydralique ou l'Art de Conduire, d'Eléver et de Ménager les Eaux pour les Différens Besoins de la Vie.** Paris, 1737-53. *1st. Edn.* 2 pts. in 4 vols. 4to. Some light browning, cont. cf., spines gt., spine ends chipped; John D. Stanitz coll. (SPB. Apr.25; 36) $2,600
– – **Anr. Edn.** Paris, 1782-90. 2 pts. in 4 vols. 4to. Some slight browning, cont. hf. linen, unc. (GB. May 3; 1136) DM 1,500
– **La Science des Ingeniers dans la Conduite des Travaux de Fortification et d'Architecture Civile.** Paris, 1739. Cf., worn. (RS. Jan.17; 458) $100

BELIN, Mme. Th.
–**Bibliothèque.** Paris, 1936-37. 3 vols. 4to. Ptd. price lists inserted, orig. wraps., spines worn or brkn.; H.M. Nixon coll., with some MS. notes. (BBA. Oct.6; 148) *Laywood.* £90

BELKNAP, Jeremy
[–] **The Foresters.** Boston, 1793. *1st. Edn.* Sigs. on title-p., some browning, sm. stains, cont. cf., covers detchd. [Sabin 4333] (SPB. Dec.13; 434) $125

BELL, Acton (Pseud.)
See— BRONTE, Anne 'Actor Bell'

BELL, Sir Charles
– **Essays on the Anatomy of Expression in Painting.** L., 1806. *1st. Edn.* 4to. Wide margins, lacks final blank, plts. slightly foxed, mod. leath. gt. (SG. Mar.22; 38) $300
– **A Series of Engravings, explaining the Course of the Nerves.** L., 1803. *1st. Edn.* Lge. 4to. Some foxing & offsets, mod. marb. wraps. (SG. Oct.6; 44) $250

BELL, Clive
– **The Legend of Monte della Sibilla.** Ill.:– Duncan Grant, & Vanessa Bell. Hogarth Pr., 1923. *1st. Edn.* 4to. Orig. pict. bds., d.-w. torn. (S. Apr.30; 247) *Henderson.* £50

BELL, Currer (Pseud.)
See— BRONTE, Charlotte 'Currer Bell'

BELL, Ellis (Pseud.)
See— BRONTE, Emily 'Ellis Bell'

BELL, Gertrude
– **The Arab War.** Gold. Cock. Pr., 1940. *(30) numbered, specially bnd.* 4to. With facs. supp., orig. niger mor., s.-c.; from D. Bolton liby. (BBA. Oct.27; 126) *Hossain.* £280

BELL, James
– **A System of Geography.** Glasgow, 1838-36. 6 vols. 57 engraved plts. & maps including 1 dupl., most spotted, folding table, bkplt. on verso of titles, orig. cl., rubbed. (BBA. May 3; 253) *Franks.* £85

BELL, James Stanislaus
– **Journal of a Residence in Circassia.** 1840. *1st. Edn.* Cold. frontis., map, 11 hand-cold. & tinted litho. plts., non-unif. cl. (P. Dec.8; 305) *Bookroom.* £50

BELL, John, of Antermony
– **Travels from St. Petersburg in Russia, to diverse Parts of Asia.** Glasgow, priv. ptd., 1763. 2 vols. 4to. Last advt. lf. Vol. 1 & errata Vol. 2, lacks 1st. lf. (blank?) in Vol. 2, cont. cf. (BBA. Sep.29; 87) *Morrell.* £200

BELL, John, Publisher
– **British Theatre.** 1791-96. 34 vols. 12mo. Lacks general titles, cont. cf., 1 cover detchd. (CSK. Aug.19; 15) £160

BELL, John, Surgeon
– **Engravings Explaining the Anatomy of The Bones, Muscles and Joints.** Edinb., 1794. *1st. Edn.* 4to. Title, 2 plts. & several ll. defaced with crayon, some (mainly margin) worming, other defects, qtr. cf., worn. (SG. Mar.22; 39) $120

BELL, Robert
See— ART & SONG

BELL, Solomon (Pseud.)
See— SNELLING, William J. 'Solomon Bell'

BELL, Thomas
– **The Anatomy, Physiology, and Diseases of the Teeth.** Trans.:– F. Kearny. Phila., 1830. *1st. Amer. Edn.* Foxed, old cf., needs rebdg. (SG. Mar.22; 88) $100

BELL, Rev. William
– **Hints to Emigrants; in a Series of Letters from Upper Canada.** Edinb., 1824. *1st. Edn.* Sm. 8vo. Folding frontis. map with 2 slight fold tears reprd. on verso, maroon hf. mor., partly unc.; 3 letters from A. Bell (the author's son) in Appendix, the Rt. Hon. Visc. Eccles copy. [Sabin 4483] (CNY. Nov.18; 19) $260

BELLAMY, Edward
– **Looking Backward, 2000-1887.** Boston, 1888. *1st. Edn. 1st. Iss.* With printer's slug on copyright-p., 'wore' for 'were' on p.210, orig. cl. gt., cl. s.-c.; Perry Molstad copy. (SPB. May 16; 397) $300

BELLANGE, Hippolyte
– **Uniformes de l'Armée Francaise depuis 1815 jusquià nos Jours.** Paris, n.d. 4to. 105 (of 110) litho. plts., all but 4 mntd. on guards, late 19th. C. hf. chagrin, corners. (HD. Jan.27; 250) Frs. 8,500

BELLANGER, Stanislas
– **La Touraine Ancienne et Moderne.** Preface:– Abbé Orsini. Ill.:– Th. Frère, Brévière, Lacoste & others. Paris, 1845. Lge. 8vo. Cont. cf. gt., spine decor. (HD. May 3; 195) Frs. 1,850

BELLARMINO, Roberto
– **De Aeterna Felicitate Sanctorum.** Antw., 1617. *2nd. Edn.* Cont. Dutch roan, silver-decor., from Fondation Furstenberg-Beaumesnil. (HD. Nov.16; 96) Frs. 1,300

BELLASIS, G.H.
– **Views of Saint Helena.** 1815. Ob. fo. 6 hand-cold. plts., wraps., hf. mor. portfo. (P. Feb.16; 126) £310

BELLE ASSEMBLEE, La
L., Jun. 1806-Dec. 1815. 18 vols. Some engraved titles bnd. in, 448 plts. (161 hand-cold.), some folding, advts., some plts. & text cropped, a few loose, some slight spotting & offsetting, some staining in Vol.17, cont. mott. cf. gt. (S. Mar.20; 690) *Shapero.* £500
– – **Anr. Edn.** 1807-28. 28 vols. 19 plain plts., 298 hand-cold. plts., lacks a few title, some text loose, hf. cf., many covers detchd., as a coll. of plts., w.a.f. (P. Dec.8; 98) *Walford.* £550
– – **Anr. Edn.** 1828-30. Vols. 7-12. 80 hand-cold. plts., hf. cf. gt. (P. Jul.26; 187) £190

BELLEAU, Remy
– **Les Oeuvres Poétiques.** Paris, 1578. *1st. Coll. Edn.* 2 vols. in 1. 12mo. 19th. C. mor. gt. (C. May 30; 70) *Lyon.* £900

BELLEGARDE, Jean Baptiste Movan de
[–] **A General History of all voyages & Travels throughout the Old & New World...by Monsr. Du Perier.** L., 1708. Cont. panel. cf., rebkd. (S. Jun.25; 84) *Traylen.* £180

BELLEVAL, Richier de
– **Demonstrations Elementaires de Botanique.** Lyon, 1796. Text vol. (Series 1 & 2) & atlas, together 2 vols., incompl. 4to. 324 engraved plts., 19th. C. cf., sm. loss from spine. (HD. Jul.6; 6) Frs. 1,150

BELLI, Silvio
– **Libro del misurar con la Vista.** Venezia, 1566. Sm. 4to. 2 frontis. edges reprd., stained, cont. vell., discold., loose. (SI. Dec.15; 141) Lire 380,000

BELLIN, Jacques Nicolas
– **Description Geographique et Historique de l'Isle de Corse.** Paris, 1769. 4to. Lacks maps, cont. hf. vell. (HD. Oct.21; 19) Frs. 3,500
– **Essai Géographique sur les Iles Britanniques.** Paris, 1770. 2 vols. 12mo. Cont. roan, spines decor. (HD. Mar.19; 33) Frs. 8,500

BELLINGSHAUSEN, Capt. T.
– **The Voyage of ... to the Antarctic Seas 1819-21.** Ed.:– F. Debenham. 1945. 2 vols. Cl., d.-w.'s. (P. Jun.7; 18) £150

BELLINI, Vincenzo
– **De Monetis Italiae Medii Aevi.** Ferrera, 1755-79. 4 vols. 4to. Some plts. loose, non-unif. cont. vell., some worming. (S. Dec.20; 773) *Brown.* £170

BELLMER, Hans
– **Les Dessins.** Preface:– Constantin Jelenski. [Paris,], 1966. *(30) hors commerce.* 4to. 1 sigd. copper engr., loose ll. in orig. linen & s.-c., spotted & slightly bumped; Hauswedell coll. (H. May 24; 583) DM 900
– **La Poupée.** Trans.:– Robert Valencay. Paris, 1936. *(100) numbered.* Sm. 4to. 10 mntd. photographs, a postcard with further ill. in series loosely inserted, orig. wraps. (S. Nov.21; 53) *Baum.* £1,150

BELLOC, Hilaire
– **The Dramatic Works of Hilaire Belloc. I: The Fall of Man.** [Kensington, Cayme Pr.], 1925. *(1) sigd.* 4to. 8 ll., ptd. on 1 side only, interleaved with blanks, hf. cl. & bds., moderate soiling & fading to covers, wear to extremities; inscr. '... from the Unhappy Author, HB. August 18, 1925' to Lady Howard de Walden. (CBA. Mar.3; 23) $300
– **The Highway & its Vehicles.** 1926. *(1,250) numbered.* Lge. 4to. Plts., some mntd. & cold., orig. cl., d.-w. (CSK. Jul.13; 173) £55
– **Marie Antoinette.** L., 1909. Extra-ill. with 11 engraved plts., a few hand-cold., very slightly spotted, red mor. gt. by Bayntun (Rivière), upr. cover inlaid with miniature hand-painted port. of Marie Antoinette, boxed. (S. Oct.4; 109) *Bender.* £420
– **Milton.** L., 1935. Extra-ill. with 12 engraved plts., a few hand-cold., slightly spotted, mor. gt. by Bayntun (Rivière), upr. cover inlaid with miniature hand-painted port. of Milton. (S. Oct.4; 110) *Joseph.* £200
– **Verses & Sonnets.** L., 1896. *1st. Edn.* 12mo. Orig. cl., unopened, orig. d.-w.; Frederic Dannay copy. (CNY. Dec.16; 23) $340

BELLORI, Giovanni Pietro
– **Colonna Traiana.** Ill.:– P.S. Bartoli. [Rome, 1673]. Ob. fo. 126 engraved plts., cont. reverse cf., worn. (SKC. May 4; 1803) £60
– – **Anr. Edn.** Ed.:– A. Ciacone. Trans.:– G.P. Bellori. Rome, ca. 1680. *1st. Edn.* Ob. fo. Lacks 14pp. typographic text, cont. leath., slightly rubbed, worn. (GB. Nov.3; 868) DM 600
– – **Anr. Edn.** Ill.:– P.S. Bartoli. Roma, [1700?]. 35 × 45cm. Album, browned, cont. hf. cf. (CR. Jun.6; 9) Lire 300,000
– **Columna Antoniniana.** Ill.:– P.S. Bartoli. Rome, ca. 1700. 1 vol. Fo. Engraved title, 75 (of 77) plts., cont. cf. (*With:*) – **Colonna Traiana.** Rome, ca. 1700. 1 vol. Fo. Engraved title & dedication. 126 engraved plts., 2 plts. inverted, dampstain mainly to blank corner of plts., cont. diced russ., covers elab. gt.-panel., spine ends worn. (C. Dec.9; 176) *Gilbert.* £120
– **Columna Cochlis M. Aurelio Antonino Augusto dicata.** Ill.:– P.S. Bartoli. Rome, 1704. Ob. fo. Engraved title, dedication, 80 plts., slight margin dampstaining, not affecting plt. surfaces, cont. hf. roan, worn. (S. Oct.11; 380) *Tosi.* £100
– **Picturae Antiquae Cryptarum Romanorum et Sepulcri Nasonum ...** Ed.:– M.A. Causseo. Ill.:– P.S.Bartoli. Rome, 1738. *1st. Edn.* Tall fo. Later bds., vell. back. (SG. Nov.3; 8) $550
– **Le Pitture Antiche del Sepolcro de Nasonii nella Via Flaminia.** Ill.:– P.S. Bartoli. Roma, 1680. Fo. Lacks 2 plts., cont. vell., defect., w.a.f. (CR. Jun.6; 10) Lire 220,000
– **Le Pitture Antiche delle Grotte di Roma.** Ill.:– P.S. & F. Bartoli. Rome, 1706. 2 pts. in 1 vol. Fo. Some light spotting, later mor.-bkd. cl. (CSK. Aug.19; 90) £90
– – **Anr. Copy.** Fo. 19th. C. hf. leath., slightly rubbed & gt. (GB. May 3; 881) DM 500
– **Recueil de Peintures Antiques trouvées à Rome; imitées Fidelement, pour les Couleurs et le Trait, d'Après les Dessins Coloriés par Pietro-Sante Bartoli.** Ill.:– P.S. Bartoli. Paris, 1783-87. *2nd Edn.* (100) on L.P. 3 vols. Fo. Wide margins, 54 engraved plts. in 2 states, plain & hand-cold., 1 plain plt. in Vol. I, 6 plts. (in 2 states) in Vol. III being dupls. of those in Vol. II, pp. 67/68 in Vol. III present in both cancelled & uncancelled state, hf.-titles, cont. Engl. str.-grd. red mor., spines gt. between raised bands, Greek key pattern round covers, arms of Louis XVIII, inner gt. dentelles, minor repair to upr. cover of Vol. I; the Abdy-Peyrefitte copy. (S. May 10; 222) *Koch.* £6,000
– **Veteres Arcus Augustorum Triumphis Insignes.** Ill.:– P.S. Bartoli & others. Rome, 1690. *1st. Edn.* Fo. 49 plts. (numbered 1, 3-6, 6, 7, 7-15, 20-52) on 47 ll., including 26 double-p., some foxing, mostly marginal, 19th. C. cf. gt. super extra, cover stained. (SG. Nov.3; 11) $225
– – **Anr. Copy.** Fo. Some light stains, cont. vell. (SI. Dec.15; 45) Lire 450,000

BELLOT, Mosen Pedro
– **Anales de Orihuela. Siglos XIV-XVI.** Ed.:– Juan Torres Fontes. Orihuela, 1954. 2 vols. 4to. Pict. wraps. (DS. Feb.24; 2239) Pts. 25,000

BELLOW, Saul
– **Dangling Man.** N.Y., 1944. *1st. Edn.* Orig. cl., d.-w. slightly worn. (S. Mar.20; 853) *Hawthorn.* £100

BELLOWS, A.F. (Ill.)
See— NEW YORK CITY – Description of the New York Central Park

BELLOWS, George
– **The Paintings.** N.Y., 1929. *1st. Edn. (2000) numbered.* Sm. fo. Cold. frontis., port., 143 plts., ex-liby., vell.-bkd. bds. (SG. May 3; 37) $150

BELMONTE, Mosseh de Joseph
See— PRAYER BOOKS [Hebrew] – BELMONTE, Mosseh de Joseph

BELON DU MANS, Pierre
– **Livres de Plusieurs Singularités et Choses Mémorables Observées en Divers Pays Estrangers.** Paris, 1555. 3 books in 1 vol. Lge. 8vo. Lacks title of 1st. book & map of Sinai, mod. hf. cf. (LM. Mar.3; 234) B.Frs. 16,000
[–] **[La Nature & Diversité des Poissons].** [Paris, 1555]. *1st. Edn.* Ob. 8vo. Title in pen facs., a few headlines & p. numerals trimmed, piece torn from margin of c6, repair to E8, slight soiling, 19th. C. red hf. mor. (S. Nov.28; 8) *Antik Junk.* £460
– **Les Observations de Plusieurs Singularitez et Choses Mémorables, trouvées en Grèce, Asie....** Paris, 1553. 3 pts. in 1 vol. 4to. Bordeaux hf. mor. by Malet. (HD. Jun.29; 78) Frs. 6,300
– – **Anr. Edn.** Paris, 1588. Sm. 4to. 1 folding plt. only (of 2), woodcut ills., lacks ff. 2G1-4 & 3N4 (?blank), soiled & stained thro.-out, some ll. trimmed, some head-lines & ills. affected, early 20th. C. hf. cf., slightly rubbed. (BBA. May 23; 325) *Rix.* £100
– – **Anr. Copy.** 4to. Lacks 2 folding woodcut maps & 1 view, a number of ll. at end loose, slight staining, old limp vell., soiled. (S. Oct.4; 253) *Rix.* £60

BELTRAMI, Giacomo Constantino
– **La Decouverte des Sources du Mississippi et de la Riviere Sanglante ....** N.O., 1824. *1st. Edn.* Errata slip, sm. rubber stp. on title-p., cont. qtr. cf. & marb. bds., head of spine chipped; the Rt. Hon. Visc. Eccles copy. [Sabin 4604] (CNY. Nov.18; 20) $350

BELVISI, F.
– **Elogi d'Illustri Bolognesi.** Parma, 1791. Lge. 4to. L.P., cont. red hf. mor. (VG. Sep.13; 385) Fls. 625

BELZONI, Giovanni Battista
– **Narrative of the Operations & Recent Discoveries... in Egypt & Nubia.** 1820. 2 vols. including atlas vol. 4to & fo. Text vol. with litho. port. & 1 plt., both with lr. margins trimmed, lacks map, atlas vol. with 44 plts. (40 hand-cold.) on 34 ll., some light spotting, title torn & laid down, cont. hf. mor. & mod. hf. mor. (CSK. Jul.6; 44) £900
– – **Anr. Edn.** L., 1821-20. *2nd. Edn.* 2 text vols. & atlas of plts. 4to. & fo. Text vols. with litho. mor. frontis. & folding map (both slightly spotted), atlas with 44 etched or litho. plts. & plans on 34 ll. (2 folding), all but 2 hand-cold., title with vertical crease & tear reprd. & piece cut from upr. outer corner, 1 plt. with margin tear reprd., orig. bds., unc. (C. Jun.27; 8) *Campbell.* £1,400
– **Places Illustrative of the Researches & Operations in Egypt & Nubia.** 1820. Fo. 40 (of 44) litho. & engraved plts. on 33 (of 34) ll., including 2 folding, many hand-cold., orig. bds., spine torn. (C. Dec.9; 178) *Schuster.* £550

BEMBO, Pietro, Cardinal
– **Gli Asolani.** Venice, Mar. 1505. *1st. Edn.* Dedication to Lucrezia Borgia on verso of title & a2 (later suppressed & cancelled & only present in some copies), errata lf. at end, capital spaces with guide letters, 4 sm. wormholes to 1st. 5 ll., paper restoration to a2 affecting 6 letters, 1st. ll. faintly stained, some slight margin soiling, mod. mor., gt. anchor device on covers, spine gt.-lettered, qtr. mor. box; Newton Hall, Camb. bkplt., Thomas B. Stevenson copy. (CNY. May 18; 87) $1,100
– – **Anr. Edn.** Venice, 1554. Some slight browning, mod. hf. vell. (HT. May 8; 79) DM 480
– **Delle Lettere.** Venice, 1597. 2 vols. in 1. Sm. hole in title & 2nd. lf., Vol. 1 stained, title marked, later spr. cf., spine richly gt., rubbed. (BBA. Jul.27; 72) *Quaritch.* £80
– **Opere.** Venice, 1729. [*1st. Compl. Edn.*] 4 vols. in 2. Lge. fo. Latin & Italian text, 2 title-pp. reprd., cont. vell. (CBA. Dec.10; 33) $130
– – **Anr. Copy.** Fo. Later hf. cf., spine slightly bumped. (SI. Dec.15; 60) Lire 360,000
– **Le Prose.** Venice, 1557. 12mo. 2 final blanks, cont. Italian red mor., gt.-panel. covers, outer gt. border of intertwined branches & an ornamental central device, fleurons at corners with decors. formed of sm. circles, spine with 3 raised bands plain but for 4 gt. lines, reprd. at top & bottom. (S. May 10; 223) *Crete.* £350

BEMBO, Pietro & others
- Carmina Quinque Illustrium Poetarum. Flor., 1552. 2 pts. in 1 vol. 16mo. Later cf., lightly rubbed. (CSK. Jul.13; 70) £80

BEMROSE, William
- Longton Hall Porcelain .... L., 1906. Sm. stain on lr. bd. (KH. Nov.9; 542) Aus. $150

BENAVIDES, Fray Alonso
- The Memorial. Trans.:– Mrs. Edward E. Ayer. Chic., 1916. Cl.; inscr, by Edward A. Ayer. (LH. Sep.25; 189) $140

BENDER, E. & Muller, W.Y.
- Die Kunst Ferdinand Hodlers. Zürich, 1923-41. 2 vols. 4to. Orig. hf. leath. & orig. hf. linen. (GB. May 5; 2693) DM 420

BENEDICTUS, Edmond
- Nouvelles Variations. Paris, [1928]. Tall fo. 20 cold. plts., ex-liby., each plt. on blank verso, loose in ptd. bds., lge. cold. design mntd. on cover, linen ties., covers soiled. (SG. May 3; 20) $500
- - Anr. Edn. Paris, 1920's. New Edn. Fo. 20 pochoir-cold. plts., loose as iss., cl.-bkd. bds., soiled, cl. ties. (SG. Aug.25; 51) $275
- Relais 1930. Ill.:– J. Saude. Paris, 1930. Tall fo. 15 pochoir-cold. plts., ex-liby., each plt. stpd. on blank verso, loose in cold. pict.-bds., covers soiled, linen ties. (SG. May 3; 21) $550
- Variations. Ill.:– J. Saude. Paris, [1928]. Tall fo. 20 pochoir-cold. plts., ex-liby., each plt. stpd. on blank verso, bds., linen ties defect. (SG. May 3; 19) $550
- - Anr. Edn. Paris, 1920's. New Edn. Fo. 20 plts., pochoir-cold. by Saude, loose as iss., cl.-bkd. bd. folder, cl. ties partially lacking. (SG. Aug.25; 52) $300

BENESCH, Otto
- The Drawings of Rembrandt. 1954-57. 6 vols. 4to. Orig. cl., d.-w.'s. (S. Nov.8; 494) Zwemmer. £100

BENET, Stephen Vincent
- Five Men & Pompey. Boston, 1915. 1st. Edn. 1st. state, orig. bds., hf. mor. s.-c.; sigd. by author, bkplt. of Montgomery Evans II, Frederic Dannay copy. (CNY. Dec.16; 24) $220
- John Brown's Body. Garden City, 1928. 1st. Edn. (201) numbered on L.P., sigd. Orig. ptd. bds., unopened, d.-w., publisher's box, hf.-mor. s.-c.; Frederic Dannay copy. (CNY. Dec.16; 25) $300

BENEVENT, Ierome de
- Paraphrase sur les Huit Livres de la Politique d'Aristote. Paris, 1621. 4to. Vell. (HD. Feb.22; 13) Frs. 1,000

BENEVIENI, Hieronymo
- Opere ... con una Canzona dello Amor Celeste & Divino. Commentary:– P. della Mirandola. [Venice, 12 Apr. 1522]. Few margin stains, later pol. tree sheep gt.; Wilmerding bkplt. (SG. Oct.27; 305) $425

BENEZIT, Emmanuel
- Dictionnaire Critique et Documentaire des Peintres, Sculpteurs, Dessinateurs et Graveurs. Paris, 1948-55. 8 vols. Orig. cl., slightly soiled, ex-liby. (BBA. Nov.10; 155) Temperley. £65
- - Anr. Copy. 8 vols. Cl. (P. Jun.7; 279) £50
- - Anr. Copy. 8 vols. Publisher's cl. (LM. Mar.3; 57) B. Frs. 8,000
- - Anr. Edn. Paris, 1960. 8 vols. orig. cl., recovered. (S. Nov.8; 495) Knight. £140
- - Anr. Copy. 8 vols. Orig. cl. gt. (P. Jun.7; 143) £110
- - Anr. Copy. 8 vols. No bdg. stated. (SPB. Nov.30; 216) $350
- - Anr. Edn. Paris, 1960-69. 8 vols. Orig. cl., spines worn, ex-liby. (BBA. Nov.10; 156) Scott. £110
- - Anr. Edn. 1966. 8 vols. Cl. (BS. May 2; 143) £240
- - Anr. Copy. 8 vols. Orig. cl., all but 1 vol. in cellophane wraps. (SKC. May 4; 1563) $220
- - Anr. Copy. 8 vols. Orig. cl. (CSK. Jun.29; 97) £190
- - Anr. Copy. 8 vols. Orig. cl. (CSK. Nov.4; 70) £140
- - Anr. Copy. 8 vols. Cl. (P. Jan.12; 116) Newall. £110

- - Anr. Copy. 8 vols. Cl., acetate wraps. (CBA. Jan.29; 53) $350
- - Anr. Edn. 1976. 10 vols. Plts., cl. (P. May 17; 321) Duran. £150
- - Anr. Edn. Paris, n.d. 3 vols. 4to. Hf. mor., gt. spine. (SPB. Nov.30; 217) $350

BENGOR, E.
See— MONTGOMERY, James & others

BENINGA, E.
- Volledige Chronyk van Oostfriesland, Behelsende ook Alle Nabuirige Volkeren. Ed.:– E.F. Harkenroht. Emden, 1723. 4to. Cont. vell. (VG. Nov.30; 802) Fls. 750

BENIOWSKI, Maurice Auguste, Comte de
- Reisen durch Sibirien und Kamtschatka über Japan und China nach Europa. Trans.:– J.R. Forster. Berlin, 1790. Cont. hf. leath. gt. (R. Oct.13; 3051) DM 550

BENJAMIN, of Tudela
- Masaot. Amst., 1698. 5th. Edn. 16mo. Ptd. without title, browned, mod. leath., w.a.f. (S. Oct.25; 15) £120
See— MENASSEH BEN ISRAEL – BENJAMIN, of Tudela

BENJAMIN, S.G.W.
- A Group of Etchers. Ill.:– Whistler & others. N.Y., [1882]. Fo. 20 etchings, orig. gt.-pict. cl., worn, ex-liby. (SG. Dec.15; 131) $450

BENJAMIN KAZES
- Megillat Sepher. Constantinople, 1755. 2 pts. in 1 vol. Fo. Lightly stained, cl.; autograph dedication, w.a.f. (S. Jul.3; 75) £140

BENN, Gottfried
- Morgue und andere Gedichte. Berlin, 1912. 1st. Edn. De Luxe Edn., (5) on vell. Mor., gold-tooled decor., red cold. points, gt. inner dentelle, marb. end-papers, sm. scratch on lr. cover. (HK. Nov.11; 3424) DM 5,000
- Söhne. Neue Gedichte. Ill.:– Ludw. Meidner. Berlin, [1913]. 1st. Edn. Sewed. (BR. Apr.13; 1639) DM 440

BENNET, George
See— TYERMAN, Rev. Daniel & Bennet, George

BENNET, Robert Ames
- Thyra: A Romance of the Polar Pit. Ill.:– E.L. Blumenschein. N.Y., 1901. 1st. Edn.,. 1st. state, cl., spine a little darkened. (CBA. Oct.29; 86) $140

BENNETT, Geoffrey D.S.
- Famous Harness Horses. L., 1926-32. (600) numbered. 2 vols. Plts., 1 loose, orig. cl. gt. (P. May 17; 234) Allan. £170

BENNETT, George
- Gatherings of a Naturalist in Australasia. L., 1860. 8 litho. plts., mostly hand-cold., title slightly foxed, orig. blind-stpd. cl., unc., spine & covers stained & faded. (CA. Apr.3; 22) Aus. $160
- Wanderings in New South Wales.... 1834. 2 vols. Bnd. without advts., 2nd. errata slip & lf. of binder's directions, pol. cf., Signet arms, some rubbing. (KH. May 1; 57) $180
- - Anr. Copy. 2 vols. 10 pp. of book advts. only at end of Vol. 1, frontis.'s & many ll. foxed, orig. cl.-bkd. bds., unc., covers worn. (CA. Apr.3; 21) Aus. $200

BENNETT, James F.
- Historical & Descriptive Account of South Australia .... L., 1843. 12mo. Secondary bdg. cf. salmon cl. (KH. Nov.9; 543) Aus. $160
- The South Australian Almanac & General Directory for 1841.... Adelaide, Ca. 1841. Mod. cf. (KH. May 1; 58) Aus. $160

BENNETT, Richard & Elton, John
- History of Corn Milling. L. & L'pool., 1898-1904. 1st. Edn. 4 vols. Slight staining & spotting, orig. cl., lightly rubbed & stained; John D. Stanitz coll. (SPB. Apr.25; 37) $400

BENNETT, William
- John Baskerville. Bg'ham., 1939. 2 vols. Orig. cl. (BBA. Mar.7; 168) Maggs. £110

BENNISON, T.T.
- A Collection of Original Country Dances, ... L., between 1802 & 1811. 1st. Edn. Paper wrap.; hrs. sigd. by composer. (S. Nov.17; 95) Maggs. £150

BENOIST, Felix
[-] Album de l'Ile de Jersey avec Coup d'Oeil sur Guernsey et les Côtes de la Manche de Cherbourg au Cap Fréhel. Text:– L. Petit & Ropartz. Paris, Nantes, 1870. Fo. Fr. & Engl. text, some foxing, publisher's bds., worn. (HD. Jul.2; 5) Frs. 4,700
- La Bretagne Contemporaine. Paris, 1865. 3 vols. Fo. Some foxing, 1 plt. disbnd., publisher's hf. chagrin gt., spines decor., dampstain to bds. (HD. Jul.2; 4) Frs. 11,000

BENOIST, Philippe & Felix
- Rome dans sa Grandeur. Paris, 1870. 3 vols. Lge. fo. Cold. map, 99 full-p. tinted litho. plts., some minor offsetting, old qtr. mor. gt.; Thomas B. Stevenson copy. (CNY. Dec.17; 537) $380

BENOIT, Pierre, 1886-1962
- L'Atlantide. Paris, 1919. Orig. Edn. (50) on Japon. numbered. 12mo. Hf. mor., corners, unc., wrap. (HD. Dec.16; 71) Frs 1,100
- Koenigsmark. Paris, 1918. Orig. Edn. (60) numbered on holland. Red mor., gt. & cold. mor. decor., watered silk doubls. & end-papers, wrap. & spine, red hf. mor. s.-c., by G.H. Lillaz. (HD. Dec.16; 70) Frs. 1,300
- Oeuvres Romanesques...Oeuvres Diverses. Ill.:– J. Thevenet & others. Paris, 1966-70. Definitive Edn. 7 vols. Bradel, leath. (HD. Jul.2; 41) Frs. 1,600

BENOIT, Pierre Jacques, 1782-1854
- Voyage à Surinam. Brussels, 1839. 1st. Edn. Lge. fo. Slightly foxed, mostly in plt. margins, cont. hf. leath, worn, spine burst. (R. Apr.5; 2793) DM 1,800
- - Anr. Copy. Lge. fo. Litho. frontis. on 49 litho plts., list of plts. loose in portfo., text slightly foxed (as usual), bds., ties. [Sabin 4737] (VG. Nov.30; 503) Fls. 1,600
- - Anr. Copy. Fo. Wide margin, minimal browning, cont. hf. leath., worn, corners slightly bumped. [Sabin 4737] (H. Nov.23; 329a) DM 850

BEN-SHAAUL, David
- Nudes. Israel, 20th. C. (50). Sq. fo. Portfo. of 8 (of 10) matted lithos. of compositions of 3 or more nudes, each approx. 21 × 26cm., lacks sheet of preface, cl.-bkd. art vell. bds., rubbed; each litho. sigd. & numbered in pencil by artist. (SG. Feb.2; 49) $100

BENSON, Sir Arthur Christopher & others
- The Book of the Queen's Dolls' House. 1924. 1st. Edn. (1500) numbered. 2 vols. Orig. linen-bkd. bds. gt., unc. (LC. Jul.5; 12) £110
- - Anr. Copy. 2 vols. 4to. Orig. holland-bkd. bds. (BBA. Apr.5; 194) Thorp. £90
- - Anr. Copy. 2 vols. 4to. Qtr. linen, unc. & unopened, spine ends slightly torn, s.-c. (SG. Dec.8; 292) $275
- - Anr. Copy. 2 vols. 4to. 116 plts. (32 cold.), some foxing, mainly on verscs of plts., red three-qtr. mor., spines gt., jnts. very worn. (SG. Jan.5; 271) $200

BENSON, Robert
- Sketches of Corsica. L., 1825. 5 cold. aquatint plts. (only 1 plt. in the Abbey copy cold.), errata slip tipped in, without final errata lf. & directions to binder, pol. hf. cf. by Root, spine gt., slightly rubbed; pres. copy from author. (C. Jun.27; 9) Houle. £180
- - Anr. Copy. Unc., mod. hf. chagrin. (HD. Oct.21; 22) Frs. 2,200

BENSON, Robert & Evelyn
- Catalogue of Italian Pictures at 16 South Street, Park Lane, London & Buckhurst in Sussex. Priv. ptd., 1914. (125). 4to. Orig. vell.-bkd. bds.; pres. copy from R. Benson. (BBA. Nov.10; 157) Marlborough Rare Books. £55

BENSON, Robert & Hatcher, Henry
- Old & New Sarum or Salisbury. 1843. From Sir Richard C. Hoare's 'The History of Modern Wiltshire'. Fo. 10 holograph pp. inserted & some annots. by Hatcher, hf. mor. (SKC. Sep.9; 2029) £80

BENTHAM, G. & Mueller, Baron F. von
- Flora Australiensis: A Description of the Plants of the Australian Territory. L., 1863-78. 7 vols. Cl., worn; Royal Commonwealth Soc. copy. (P. Nov.24; 275) *Weldon & Wesley.* £65

BENTHAM, Jeremy
- Defence of Usury .... L., 1787. *1st. Edn.* Sm. 8vo. Cont. cf.-bkd. bds., minor worming at hinge. (C. Nov.9; 38) *Quaritch.* £650
- Papers relative to Codification & Public Instruction including Correspondence with the Russian Emperor & Divers Constituted Authorities in the American United States. 1817-22. 3 pts. in 1 vol. Some light spotting, orig. bds., worn, lacks backstrip, upr. cover detchd. (CSK. May 18; 94) £380

BENTLEY, Harry
- A Correct Account of all the Cricket Matches which have been Played by the Mary-le-bone Club & all other Principal Matches from the Year 1786 to 1822 Inclusive. 1823. Hf.-title, some spotting & staining, cont. cf., rebkd., new end. papers. (SKC. Jan.13; 2304) £100

BENTLEY, Richard
- A Dissertation upon the Epistles of Phalaris. L., 1699. Cont. mott. cf., worn. (SG. Apr.19; 25) $200

BENZONI, Girolamo
- Le Historia del Mondo Nuovo. [Venice, 1565] (Colophon). Y2-6 & part of H supplied in facs., without final blank, some spotting, mod. cf. (CSK. May 18; 111) £75
- - **Anr. Edn.** Trans.:– Urbain Chauveton. [Paris], 1579. Leter three-qtr. scored cf., gt.-ruled ribbed spine, later fly-ll. (CBA. Dec.10; 10) $140

BEOWULF
- The Tale of Beowulf. Trans.:– William Morris & A.J. Wyatt. [Hammersmith, Kelms. Pr., 1895]. *(308). (300) on paper.* 4to. Vell., ribbon ties. (LH. Sep.25; 404) $400
- - **Anr. Copy.** Lge. 4to. Orig. vell. gt., ties. (GB. Nov.5; 2659) DM 2,400

BERAIN, Jean
- Ornemens Inventez par J. Berain; Desseins de Cheminées. Paris, ca. 1712. 2 pts. in 1 vol. Ob. fo. Pt. 1: engraved ornamental title, frontis. port., 68 engraved plts. on 64 ll., Pt. 2: engraved architectural title, 39 engraved plts.; 2 plts. slightly browned, cont. mott. cf., rebkd. preserving orig. spine, corners reprd., w.a.f. (C. Dec.9; 7) *Sims, Reed & Fogg.* £800
- Sammelband mit Ornamentstichen. Augsburg, ca. 1690. Ob. fo. Most wide margin. 1 plt. with bkd. tear, 1 plt. loose & 1 margin torn & slightly frayed some light crumpling, upr. margin slightly stained in parts, slightly foxed. cont. hf. vell., rubbed, bumped, paper partly loose. (HK. Nov.9; 1987) DM 1,150

BERALDI, Henri
- La Reliure du XIXème Siècle. Paris, 1895-97. *(295).* 4 vols. 4to. Red hf. mor., corners, by Thierry, unc., wraps. & spines. (HD. Jun.6; 13) Frs. 7,500
- - **Anr. Edn.** Paris, 1897. Pt. 4. Lge. 4to. L.P., 101 heliogravure plts. of bdgs., hf. mor., very scuffed, liby. bkplt. (SG. Sep.15; 49) $240
See— PORTALIS, Baron Roger & Beraldi, Henri

BERANGER, Pierre Jean de
- Oeuvres Complètes. Ill.:– Dutillois (port), Johannot, Monnier & others. Paris, 1834. 5 vols. including supp. On vell., 120 wood engraved figures bnd at end for 1836 Edn., with A.L.s. from author, Passy, Nov. 1843, 4pp. 4to. bdg. by Champs, ca. 1900, decor. (HD. Apr.11; 5) Frs. 3,200
- - **Anr. Edn.** Ill.:– Grandville & Raffet. Paris, 1836. *1st. Printing of ills.* 3 vols. Hf. cf., corners, by Dewatine, spines decor.; extra-ill. with 2nd. port. of author. (HD. May 3; 197) Frs. 1,950
- - **Anr. Edn.** Paris, n.d. Foxing, red hf. mor. by Villetard, spine decor. (SM. Mar.7; 2390) Frs. 1,500

BERAUD, Henri
- La Gerbe d'Or. Paris, 1928. *Orig. Edn. (35) numbered on japon impérial.* 12mo. Mor. by Lavigne-Gayon, blind- & gt.-decor., unc., wrap. & spine, spine faded; sigd. autograph dedication (1928), author's autograph MS. lf. bnd. in, with corrections & erasures. (HD. Mar.27; 48) Frs. 1,550
- Le Martyre de l'Obèse. Ill.:– Gus Bofa. 1927. Separate suite of 25 plts., sewed, sm. stain on cover. (HD. Dec.9; 71) Frs. 1,050

BERBERIUS, Johannes
- Viatorium Utriusque Iuris. [Lyon, Guillaume Balsarin], ca. 1487-90. *Orig. Edn.* Sm. 4to. Lacks 8 ll., initials & rubrics painted in red, some stains, several corners defect., 16th. C. vell., worn, some repairs. [C. 948] (SM. Mar.7; 2428) Frs. 2,600

BERENSON, Bernard
- I Disegni dei Pittori Fiorentini. Milan, 1961. 3 vols. Lge. 4to. Qtr. leath. (SG. Oct.13; 29) $200
- The Drawings of the Florentine Painters. 1938. 3 vols. Lge. 4to. Orig. hf. cl. (SI. Dec.18; 187) Lire 480,000
- The Italian Painters of the Renaissance. [L., 1952]. 1 vol. Tall 4to. Cl., d.-w. (*With:*) – Italian Pictures of the Renaissance. [L., 1963]. 2 vols. Tall 4to. Cl., d.-w.'s. (SG. Oct.13; 30) $200
- Italian Pictures of the Renaissance. Central & North Italian Schools. 1968. 3 vols. 4to. Orig. cl., d.-w.'s. (BBA. Sep.8; 114) *Sims, Reed & Fogg.* £140
- Italian Pictures of the Renaissance: Venetian School; Florentine School; Central Italian & North Italian Schools. L., [1957; 1963]; 1968. 2 vols.; 2 vols.; 3 vols. 4to. Orig. cl., d.-w's. (S. Apr.30; 3) *Quaritch.* £700
- - **Anr. Copy.** Together 3 pts. in 7 vols. Sm. 4to. No bdg. stated. (SPB. Nov.30; 79) $800

BERENSON, Bernard (Contrib.)
See— MINER, Dorothy

BERENSON, B. & Valentiner, W.R.
- Catalogue of a Collection of Paintings & some Art Objects. Phila., 1913-14. *(300) for private distribution.* 3 vols. 4to. Orig. hf. mor., lightly rubbed; a quantity of related correspondence from J. Johnson to William Roberts loosely inserted. (CSK. Mar.23; 93) £90

BERESFORD, James
- [-] Bibliosophia; or, Book-wisdom. L., 1810. Hf.-title, later hf. mor. (BBA. Mar.7; 169) *C. Cox.* £75

BERG, Albert
- Die Insel Rhodus. Braundschweig, 1862. 2 vols. Fo. Minimal foxing, hf. leath. gt. (HK. Nov.8; 1028) DM 750

BERGE, Friedrick
- Schmetterlingsbuch. Stuttgart, 1842. *1st. Edn.* 4to. Some plts. loose, foxed or worn, cont. linen, spotted, spine renewed. (HK. May 15; 517) DM 650
- - **Anr. Copy.** 4to. Text browned & spotted, plts. soiled, cont. linen, defect. & spotted. (H. May 22; 178) DM 400
- - **Anr. Edn.** Ed.:–H. v. Heinemann & W. Steudel. Stuttgart, 1876. 4to. Margin lightly stained, some sigs. loose & with margin defects., cont. linen, slightly cockled & stained. (HK. Nov.8; 713) DM 520
- - **Anr. Edn.** Ed.:– H. v. Heinemann. W. Steudel. Stuttgart, 1889. 4to. Slightly soiled, orig. pict. linen. (BR. Apr.12; 804) DM 550
- - **Anr. Copy.** 4to. Orig. hf. linen. (HK. Nov.8; 714) DM 520

BERGE, Friedrich & Riecke, V.A.
- Giftpflanzenbuch .... Stuttgart, 1850. Sm. 4to. Plts. with MS. trans. of Latin names, text lightly browned, later hf. leath. gt. (GB. May 3; 1095) DM 600
- - **Anr. Edn.** Stuttgart, 1855. *New Edn.* 4to. Text slightly stained or soiled, cont. hf. linen. (GB. Nov.3; 1117) DM 400

BERGE, K.F.W.
- Käferbuch. Stuttgart, 1844. 4to. 36 plts., including 34 hand-cold., some browning & margin staining of text, cl., worn, inside hinges brkn. (S. Nov.1; 264) *Wedekind.* £80

BERGE, P. v.d.
- Theatrum Hispaniae. Amst., ca. 1710. Ob. fo. Some bkd. tears, cont. hf. vell., slightly soiled & bumped. (HK. Nov.9; 1289) DM 2,100

BERGERET, Gaston
- Les Evenements de Pontax. Ill.:– after Henriot. Paris, 1899. *(200) On vell. du Marais, numbered.* Cont. Bradel hf. mor., mosaic decor. spine, corners, uncc., pict. wrap. preserved, by Carayon. (HD. Feb.17; 54) Frs. 1,600

BERGGRUEN, O. (Ed.)
See— GRAPHISCHEN KUNSTE

BERGHAUS, Heinrich
- Physikalischer Atlas. Gotha, 1852. 2 vols. Fo. 83 (of 93) engraved & cold. maps, plts. & tables, later hf. leath. (D. Nov.23; 747) DM 580

BERGHUIS, S.
- De Nederlandsche Boomgaard I-II: Appels; Peren en Steenvruchten. Ill.:– Severijns after Berghuis. Groningen, 1868. 2 vols. Lge. 8vo. Chromolitho. frontis. & port., 112 cont. hand-cold. litho. plts., several advts., lacks last 3 fascicules (with 12 plts.), loose as iss. in orig. decor. cl. binders. (VS. Dec.8; 638) Fls. 1,200

BERGIER, Nicolas
- Apologie de la Religion Chrétienne. Paris, 1769. *1st. Edn.* 2 vols. 12mo. Cont. red mor. gt., Christophe de Beaumont arms, spines decor. (HD. Nov.9; 16) Frs. 3,200

BERGK, J.A.
[-] Tirol und die Tiroler, im Jahre 1809. Nuremb., 1810. Lightly browned, especially at beginning, orig. wraps., with engraved vig., spine & turn ins pasted with strips, half of spine torn. (R. Oct.13; 3213) DM 400

BERGOMENSIS FORESTUS, Jacobus Philippus
- Confessionale seu Interrogatorium Aliorum Omnium Novissimus. Venezia, ca. 1500. Last p. detchd., with slight loss of text, lightly browned, later bds., bumped. (SI. Dec.15; 17) Lire 300,000
- Supplementum Chronicarum. Venice, Bernardinus Benalius, 23 Aug. 1483. *1st Edn.* Fo. Capital spaces with guide letters, sm. hole in 1st. 2 ll. reprd. with slight loss of text, inner blank margin of 1st. lf. reprd., a few sm. wormholes, mod. cf., blind-stpd. in antique style. [BMC V, 370; Goff J208; H. 2805] (S. May 10; 310) *Thomas.* £480
- - **Anr. Edn.** Venice, Bernardino Benagli, 15 Dec. 1486. *3rd. [1st. Ill.] Edn.* Fo. Several lr. margins slit, 1 lf. torn without loss, hole in 1st. lf. with loss of some words in table, early 19th. C. vell.; from Fondation Furstenberg-Beaumesnil. [BMC V, 371; Goff J210] (HD. Nov.16; 71) Frs. 14,000
- - **Anr. Edn.** Venice, Bernardinus Rizus, 15 Feb. 1492/93. Fo. Cont. owner's note on title-p. 'ad annum 1490', writing on a2 scored through, vell.; the Walter Goldwater copy. [BMC V, 404; Goff J-212; H. 2809] (SG. Dec.1; 197) $2,800
- - **Anr. Copy.** Fo. Frontis. & title rehinged, with woodcut ornaments at lr. edges supplied in pen facs., some spotting & dampstains, vell., from early MS. with initials in red & blue, defect.; the Walter Goldwater copy. [BMC V, 404; Goff J-212; H. 2809] (SG. Dec.1; 198) $1,100
- - **Anr. Edn.** Paris, 1535. Fo. Lacks prelim. gathering [c]² (as often), title soiled & holed with slight loss to verso, old bevelled bds., rebkd. [Sabin 25088] (SG. Jan.19; 198) $200
- Supplementum. Supplementi de la Chroniche.... Venice, 1520. Fo. N3 torn & reprd., some dampstains, few margin repairs, old vell., rebkd. (TA. Sep.15; 419) £300
- - **Anr. Edn.** Venice, 1535. Fo. Title bkd. & reprd. at margins, a few ll. shaved, 2 with headlines cropped, title & a few ll. rehinged, minor worming to title & a few ll. of Table, a few minor tears, mod. vell. (C. May 30; 35) *Snelling.* £320

BERGONIER
- Le Guide Maternel. Paris, 1842. MS. 4 line dedication from author, cont. velvet, gold metal bosses, corner-pieces, 3 decor. bosses on spine, decor. clasps, silk doubl. & end-papers, ex-libris. (D. Nov.23; 529) DM 1,600

BERGSTROM, I.
- Dutch Still Life Paintings in the Seventeenth Century. N.Y., 1956. *1st. Amer. Edn.* 4to. Cl. (BS. Nov.16; 57) £100

BERKELEY, George, Bp. of Cloyne
[-] Alciphron, or, the Minute Philosopher. L., 1732. *1st. Edn.* 2 vols. Vigs. on titles, cont. cf., rebkd., worn, upr. covers detchd.; pres. copy. (SPB. May 16; 9) $700
[-] The Analyst; or a Discourse Addressed to an Infidel Mathematician. L., 1734. *1st. Edn.* Final lf. blank but for 2-line errata, 2 MS. corrections not in ptd. errata, as usual, on p. 85, cont. cf., spine gt., rubbed, spine worn; E.N. da C. Andrade-John D. Stanitz copy. (SPB. Apr.25; 38) $1,100
- The Querist. Dublin, 1735-37. *1st. Edns. of Orig. pts.* 3 pts. in 1 vol. Advt. lf., few light stains, cont. cf., rebkd., relined. (SG. Apr.26; 19) $750
[-] Siris: a Chain of Philosophical Reflexions .... Dublin, 1744. *1st. Edn.* Errata lf., slight worming in few lr. margins, cont. of., spine gt., rebkd. retaining orig. spine, slightly worn, pres. copy. (SPB. May 16; 10) $600
-- Anr. Copy. Cont. MS. verse on fly-ll., cont. cf., rebkd. (SG. Nov.3; 12) $175

BERKELEY, George Monck
- Poems. Ed.:- Mrs. Berkeley. L., 1797. 4to. Title brown, some spotting, cf., rubbed, cover detchd.; inscr. by Mrs. Berkeley (Ed. & mother of George Monck). (BBA. Jun.28; 9) *Hannas.* £55

BERKOWITZ, David Sandler
- In Remembrance of Creation: Evolution of Art & Scholarship in the Medieval & Renaissance Bible. Waltham, Mass., [1968]. 4to. Pict. leatherette. (SG. Sep.15; 24) $200

BERLAGE (Ill.)
See— KRONIEK

BERLEPSH-VALENDAS, H. E.
- Dekorative Anregungen. Leipzig, [1899]. Fo. 30 (of 33) mntd. col. plts., loose as iss., minor chipping not affecting plts., decor. cl. folder, spine worn, cover detchd. (SG. Aug.25; 40) $160

BERLIN
- Die Bauwerke und Kunstdenkmäler von Berlin. Berlin, 1955-80. 4 vols. & Atlas, in 7 pts. Lge. 8vo. & lge. 4to. Orig. linen & orig. leatherette portfo. (GB. Nov.3; 229) DM 500
- Berlin und seine Bauten. Berlin, 1877. *1st. Edn.* 2 pts. in 1 vol. Margins lightly browned, orig. linen, corners bumped, end-papers renewed. (GB. Nov.3; 231) DM 900
- Die Königliche Museen in Berlin. Dresden, ca. 1850. 4to. A few text ll. slightly foxed, cont. Prussian blind-tooled linen. (GB. Nov.3; 291) DM 1,700

BERLINER, Rudolf
- Die Bildwerke in Elfenbein, Knochen, Hirsch - u. Steinbockhorn. Augsburg, 1926. Fo. Orig. Linen. (R. Apr.3; 710) DM 470

BERLINER KALENDER auf das Gemein Jahr 1834, 1835 und 1836
Berlin, 1834-36. 3 vols. Orig. bds., 1 spine defect., 2 orig. s.-c.'s. (GB. Nov.3; 236) DM 500

BERLINISCHE MONATSSCHRIFT
Ed.:- F. Gedike & J.E. Biester. Berlin, 1786-87. Vols. 7-10 in 4 vols. All titles with bkd. excision & sig., cont. hf. leath. gt. (GB. May 4; 1571) DM 850

BERLINISCHER TASCHEN-KALENDER auf das Schalt-Jahr 1820
Ill.:- F. Meyer after L. Wolf. [Berlin, 1819]. 12mo. Some slight browning, cont. linen, rubbed. (HT. May 9; 1337) DM 580

BERLINISCHER TASCHEN-KALENDAR auf das Schalt-Jahr 1820 und das Gemein Jahr 1821
Berlin, [1819-20]. 2 vols. Sm. 8vo. Some light browning, cont. red mor., slightly worn. (H. May 22; 577) DM 600

BERNAL, Arias
- Album Historico la II Guerra Mundial. N.P., 1946. *(250) numbered, sigd. & dtd.* Fo. 56 col. reproductions, loose as iss. in ptd. bd. portfo., worn; 1st. cartoon sigd. & dtd. by Bernal. (SG. Jun.7; 329) $150

BERNARD, Claude
- Leçons sur la Physiologie et la Pathologie du Système Nerveux. Paris, 1858. 2 vols. Hf.-title, 4 pp. advt., stps. on titles, 19th. C. bds.; Dr. Walter Pagel copy. (S. Feb.7; 47) *Goodrich.* £180
- Leçons sur les Propriétés Physiologiques et les Alterations Pathologiques des Liquides de l'Organisme. Paris, 1859. *1st. Edn.* 2 vols. Ptd. wraps., unc. & unopened, lacks 1 upr. wrap., 1 spine reprd., ex-liby. (SG. Oct.6; 45) $110
- Sur Une Nouvelle Fonction du Foie Chez l'Homme et Les Animaux. Paris, 1850. In: 'Comptes Rendus, Acad. Des Sciences', Vol. 31. Lge. 4to. Orig. paper wraps., unopened. (LH. Sep.25; 461) $375

BERNARD, Jacques
[-] The Acts & Negotiations ... of the General Peace .... L., 1698. Some browning, panel. cf., rubbed. [Wing B 1994] (P. Mar.15; 287) £55

BERNARD, Pierre & others
- Le Jardin des Plantes .... Paris, 1842-43. 2 vols. Frontis., 14 litho. ports., 169 plts. (33 hand-cold.), p. 407 in Vol. 1 torn & reprd., cont. hf. mor. gt., slightly scuffed. (C. Jun.27; 113) *Cavendish.* £220

BERNARD, Pierre Joseph, dit Gentil-Bernard
- Oeuvres. Ill.:- Roger after Prud'hon. 1823. Cf. by Ed. Vivet, richly blind- & gt.-decor. (HD. Apr.13; 79) Frs. 2,500
- Oeuvres Ornées de Gravures. Ill.:- Prudhon, engraved by Beisson & Copia. Paris, 1797, An V. *1st. Printing of ills.* Sm. fo. Red mor. gt. decor. by Lebrun, 1838, unc.; J. de Nouvion ex-libris, engraved by G. Barbier. (HD. May 3; 13) Frs. 3,400

BERNARD, Tristan
- Tableau de la Boxe. Ill.:- A.D. de Segonzac. Paris, 1922. *Ltd. Edn.* Sm. 4to. Some spotting, orig. wraps., slightly soiled. (BBA. Jun.14; 203) *Makiya.* £180
-- Anr. Edn. Ill.:- A. Dunoyer de Sagonzac. Paris, 1922. *(315).* Sm. 4to. On Lafuma, sewed. (HD. May 3; 198) Frs. 2,700
-- Anr. Edn. Ill.:- A. Dunoyer de Sagonzac. Paris, 1922. *On vell. Lafuma.* 4to. With lge. orig. pen ill sigd., mor., blind & platine decor., buckram mosaic, inner mor. border, buckram doubls. & end-papers, wrap., spine, s.-c., by Geuzevault. (HD. Mar.14; 91) Frs. 18,000

BERNARD, W.D.
- Narrative of the Voyages & Services of the Nemesis. L., 1844. *1st. Edn.* 2 vols. 7 engraved plts., 3 folding maps, some spotting, orig. cl., spotted. (S. Apr.9; 6) *Asian.* £140

BERNARDINUS SENENSIS
- De Contractibus et Usuris. [Strassburg], Printer of Henricus Arimi. before 1474. *1st. Edn.* Fo. Wide margin, rubricated, many painted red initials, approx. last 12 ll. reprd. or bkd., suede. [HC 2835; BMC 1,78; Goff B-345] (R. Apr.3; 1) DM 5,400

BERNARDUS CLARAVALLENSIS ABBATIS, Saint
- Flores. Venice, 1503. Woodcut device on title, full-p. woodcut, woodcut initials, some floriated, s6 torn & reprd., minor worming, early inscr. on title, 19th. C. panel. & tooled in blind, worn. (SG. Apr.29; 26) $450
- Melliflui Devotique Doctoris Sancti Bernardi ... Opus Preclarum suos Complectens Sermones. [Lyon, 1515]. 4 pts. in 1 vol. Fo. Cont. vell., lacks ties. (S. Feb.9; 170) $300
- Modus Bene Vivendi. Flor., L. Morgiani & J. Petri for Pietro Pacini, 27 Jan. 1495/6. 4to. Lacks prelims. *1-4, some stains, last 3 ll. wormed & holed, with slight loss, vell.; N.C. Starr bkplt. [BMC VI, 683; Goff B-418] (SG. Oct.27; 155) $300
- Opuscula. Ed.:- [Philotheus de Brixia]. Venice, Simon Bevilaqua, 17 Oct. 1495. Capital spaces with guide letters, sm. stain on 2 ll., cont. Venetian mor., covers tooled in blind to conventional design, spine & corners reprd.; from Jean Fürstenberg coll. [BMC V, 520; Goff B365; Hain 2922] (S. May 10; 224) *Fletcher.* £700

-- Anr. Copy. 12mo. Lacks most of 1st. map except 2 title lines on white lf., recent vell. (CR. Jun.6; 100) Lire 800,000
- Sermones de Tempore et de Sanctis; una cum Homiliis et Epistolis. Venice, J. Emiricus de Spira for L. Giunta, 12 Mar. 1495. 4to. Last 25 ll. wormed in text, some dampstains, old vell., leath. ties defect.; the Walter Goldwater copy. [BMC V, 540; Goff B-440] (SG. Dec.1; 62) $550
- Sermones de Tempore et de Sanctis et de Diversis. Basel, N. Kessler, 1495. Fo. Old owners mark on title, printers mark painted with ink & ill. by same old hand, 1st. ll. with sm. wormhole at side, last qtr. wormed, some light stains, most in margins, some heavier nearing end, cont. wood bds., wide pig spine, 1 clasp. [HC. 2848; H 2847; BMC III 771; Goff B-439] (R. Apr.3; 1c) DM 3,300
- Sermones super Cantica Canticorum. Brescia, Angelus Britannicus, 28 Jan. 1500. 4to. Title lf. reprd. & strengthened, last lf. stained, some early marginalia, later bds., vell. back; the Walter Goldwater copy. [BMC VII, 981; Goff B-431] (SG. Dec.1; 63) $350
- Speculum de Honestate Vitae. [Rome, Stephan Plannck], ca. 1490-95. 4to. Disbnd.; the Walter Goldwater copy. [Goff B-446] (SG. Dec.1; 64) $125

BERNARDUS TREVISANUS, Count della Maria di Treviso
- Chemische Schriften. Trans.:- Caspar Horn. Nuremb., 1643. g7-8 blank, title bkd. & defect. with date missing, new panel. cf.; Dr. Walter Pagel copy. (S. Feb.7; 49) *Janssen.* £350

BERNATZ, John Martin
- Album des Heiligen Landes. Text:- G.H. v. Schubert & J.R. Roth. Stuttgart, [1839]. Ob. 4to. Foxed, hf. linen, rubbed. (D. Nov.23; 1387) DM 450
-- Anr. Edn. Text:- G. v. Schubert & J. Roth. Stuttgart, [1855]. Lge. ob. 8vo. Folding map, 50 tinted litho. views, including 1 double-p., text in Engl., German & Fr., cont. hf. roan, slightly rubbed. (VG. Nov.30; 504) Fls. 1,000
- Scenes in Ethiopia. München & L., 1852. *1st. Edn.* 2 vols. in 1. Lge. ob. fo. Wide margin, 2 litho. titles, 1 litho. map & 48 tinted or cold. litho. plts., cont. red leath. gt., spine reprd. (R. Apr.5; 2664) DM 2,300

BERND, Chr. S. Th.
- Wappenbuch der Proussischen Rheinprovinz. Bonn, 1835. 2 vols. in 1. 2 litho. titles, 1 litho. dedication, 193 litho. arms plts., lightly browned, some slight spotting, a few plts. with light spots, newer hf. linen, slightly spotted. (H. May 22; 372) DM 400

BERNER BAUTEN Herausgegeben vom Ingenieur- & Architekten-Verein
Ill.:- after H. Voellger. Bern, [1895]. Fo. 56 plts., loose in gt.-lettered cl. folder, worn. (SG. Oct.13; 340) $150

BERNERS or BARNES, Dame Juliana
- Boke of St. Albans. 1881. *Facs. Edn.* 4to. Orig. parch., soiled, covers torn, the lr. with loss. (CSK. Jan.13; 105) £50
- The Treatyse of Fysshynge with an Angle, from the Book of St. Albans. Intro. Essay:- William Loring Andrews. N.Y., 1903. *(150) on H.M.P..* Sm. 8vo. Gt.-lettered vell., partly unc., linen ties scale frayed. (SG. Mar.15; 176) $100
-- Anr. Edn. L. [Chelsea], Ash. Pr., 1903. *(150). (125) for sale.* Sm. 4to. Orig. vell. (D. Nov.24; 2948) DM 700

BERNHARD V. LUXEMBURG
- Sermones de Symbolica Colluctatione Septe[m] Vitio[num] Capitalium et Vitutum Spiritualiu[m]. Köln, 1516. 4to. Wide margin, slightly spotted, 18th. C. sewed, wraps. (stained) with MS. ex-libris. (HK. May 15; 80) DM 750

BERNHARDT, Sarah
- Memoires of My Life. N.Y., 1907. *(250) numbered & sigd.* This copy unnumbered, cl. gt., slightly soiled. (SG. Nov.17; 165) $175

BERNHART, J. (Ed.)
See— LIEDER DER DEUTSCHEN MYSTIK

BERNINO, Domenico
– Memorie Historiche Dicio, che hanno operato li Sommi Pontefici dal Primo Passagio in Europa fino all'Anno 1684. Rome, 1685. 4to. Cont. vell. gt., Innocent XI arms, spine decor.; from Fondation Furstenberg-Beaumesnil. (HD. Nov.16; 98)
Frs. 1,500

BERNOUILLI, Daniel
– Hydrodynamica, sive de Viribus et Motibus Fluidorum Commentarii. Strassburg, 1738. *1st. Edn.* 4to. Slight browning, cont. cf., rebkd., spine gt.; Earl of Bute armorial bkplt., John D. Stanitz coll. (SPB. Apr.25; 41)
$1,900
– Recherches sur la Manière la plus Avantageuse de Supléer à l'Action au Vent sur les Grands Vaisseaux.... [Paris, 1753], 1769. *1st. Separate Edn.* 4to. Mod. vell.-bkd. marb. bds.; John D. Stanitz coll. (SPB. Apr.25; 42)
$325

BERNOULLI, or Bernouilli, Jacob
– Ars Conjectandi, Opus Posthumum. Basel, 1713. *1st. Edn.* Sm. 4to. Some slight browning, last few ll. slightly stained, lr. blank margin of 1 lf. reprd., cont. vell.; John D. Stanitz coll. (SPB. Apr.25; 39)
$1,500
– – Anr. Copy. 4to. Some early 19th. C. marginalia & underlining, 2 pp. with sm. inkstain in lr. margin, some slight foxing & some ll. slightly browned, cont. leath. gt., worn & bumped. (HK. Nov.8; 459)
DM 3,300
– Opera. Geneva, 1744. 2 vols. 4to. 3 plts. shaved affecting blank. area, some dampstaining, cont. mott. cf., Vol. 1 rebkd., old spine laid down. (CSK. Nov.4; 132)
£85
– Opera Omnia. Lausanne & Geneva, 1742. *1st. Compl. Edn.* 4 vols. 4to. Hf.-title in Vol. I only, lacks ports. (as often), browned & spotted, some staining in Vol. I, cont. vell., some spotting or staining; John D. Stanitz coll. (SPB. Apr.25; 40)
$550
See— LEIBNITZ, Gottfried Wilhelm von & Bernouilli, Jacob

BERNT, Walther
– The Netherlandish Painters of the Seventeenth Century. Trans:– P.S. Falla. [N.Y., 1970]. *1st. Edn. in Engl.* 3 vols. Tall 4to. Cl. gt., d.-w.'s. (SG. Oct.13; 34)
$300
– Die Niederländischen Maler des 17. Jahrhunderts. Munich, [1960-62]. 4 vols. 4to. Orig. cl., cardboard boxes. (S. Apr.30; 4)
Starmer. £320
– – Anr. Edn. München, [1960-62]. *2nd. Iss.* 4 vols., including Supp. Lge. 8vo. Cl. (VS. Dec.7; 13)
Fls. 475

BERNUS, A. von
– Maria im Rosenhag. Ill:– Thylmann. München, 1909. *1st. Edn. (500).* 4to. Hand-bnd. orig. cf. gt., lightly bumped & with sm. scratches, spine discold.; MS. dedication of author on end-paper. (H. Nov.24; 2138)
DM 450

BEROALDE DE VERVILLE, François
[–] Le Moyen de Parvenir. Mid. 17th. C. 12mo. Mor. gt. (P. Jan.12; 199)
Shapiro. £65
– – Anr. Edn. Dissertation:– La Monnaye. Nulle part [Holland, 1734]. *Latest Edn.* 2 vols. in 1. 18mo. Mor. gt. by Amand, mosaic decor. (HD. Mar.27; 2)
Frs. 2,800
– – Anr. Edn. Ed:– Bern. de La Monnoye. Ill:– Martinet. [Paris], 1757. 2 vols. 12mo. On holland paper, ruled copy, La Vallière mor., gt. decor., decor. spine, mor. doubl., gt. dentelle, by Trautz-Bauzonnet. (HD. Mar.14; 10)
Frs. 4,100

BEROALDUS, Philippus
See— CICERO, Marous Tullius – BEROALDUS, Philippus

BERQUEN, Robert de
– Les Merveilles des Indes Orientales et Occidentales, ou Nouveau Traitté des Pierres Precieuses & Perles. Paris, 1661. *Orig. Edn.* 4to. Hf. cf. (HD. Dec.1; 80)
Frs. 40,000

BERQUIN, Arnaud
– L'Ami des Enfans. Ill:– DeLaunay, Maillet, Delignon & others after A. Borel. Paris, 1803. 7

vols. 12mo. Vol. 1 dampstained, cont marb. cf.-bkd. bds. gt., unc., slightly rubbed; von Veen coll. (S. Feb.28; 35)
£120
– Idylles, Romances et autres Poésies.... Ill:– Borel, Marillier, Le Barbier & others. Paris, 1803. 12mo. On vell., ills. before the letter & on pink paper, str.-grd. mor. gt. by Bozérian Jeune, spine decor. (slightly faded). (HD. May 3; 199)
Frs. 1,300
– Oeuvres Complètes. Ill:– after Borel, Le Barbier, Marillier, Monsau, & Morean. Paris, 1803. 17 vols. (compl., Cohen/De Ricci incorrectly stating 18 vols.). 12mo. Cont. tree cf., 5 vols. rebkd., including 4 preserving orig. spines. (C. Nov.9; 39)
Snelling. £280
– Oeuvres: Figures. Ill:– after Borel & others. [Paris], 1803. 2 pts. in 2 vols. Sm. 8vo. Proofs ptd. before the letter on thick vell., mntd. on guards, red Bradel hf. mor., corners, by Pagnant, unc. (HD. Jun.22; 15)
Frs. 2,000

BERRIN, Emille & Savin, Jacque
– Neueste Englische und Französische Muster zu aller Art der Stickerei für Damen wie auch für Fabrikanten. Leipzig, [1800]. Ob. fo. Lacks 3 copperplts., 1 plt. torn, some slight soiling, especially plts., cont. style hf. leath., mntd. upr. title of orig. wraps. (GB. Nov.3; 871)
DM 900

BERRY, William
– Atlas. Ill:– after N. Sanson. 1684. Lge. fo. 20 hand-cold. maps after N. Sanson, no title, old sheep, covers loose. (P. Jan.12; 328)
Burgess. £560
– The History of the Island of Guernsey. 1815. 4to. 29 engraved aquatint plts., folding map, some light spotting, later hf. mor. gt., extremities lightly rubbed. (CSK. May 4; 108)
£140

BERRYMAN, John
– The Dispossessed. N.Y., [1948]. *1st. Edn.* Orig. cl., d.-w.; Frederic Dannay copy. (CNY. Dec.16; 26)
$160

BERSON, A.
See— ASSMANN, R. & Berson, A.

BERSTEIN, Eduard
– Die Geschichte der Berliner Arbeiter-Bewegung. Berlin, 1907-10. 3 vols. Orig. cl., slightly rubbed. (BBA. Feb.9; 113).
Maggs. £70

BERTACHINUS, Johannes
– Repertorium Juris Utriusque. [Lyons, Johannes Siber], 1499. Pts. 1 & 3 only. Lge. fo. Lacks blanks, lr. blank margins soiled, hf. pig; the Walter Goldwater copy. [Goff B-501 (this incompl. set only)] (SG. Dec.1; 66)
$750

BERTALL, Charles Albert d'Arnoux
– La Vigne. Paris, 1878. *Orig. Edn. 1st. Printing.* 4to. Cont. maroon hf. chagrin, wrap. (HD. Mar.14; 92)
Frs. 14,000

BERTARELLI, A. & Prior, H.
– Il Biglietto da Visita Italiano. Bergamo, [1920?]. *Ltd. Edn.* 4to. Publishers cl. (CR. Jun.6; 101)
Lire 400,000

BERTELLI, Francesco
– Il Carnevale Italiano Mascherato oue si Veggono in Figura Vari e Inuentione [sic] di Capritii. N.p., 1642. Sm. 8vo. Engraved title with author's name partially hidden by 1 of the characters, 23 plts., top fore-corner of 21st. plt. torn away with very slight loss of engraved area, mod. bds. (S. May 10; 225)
James. £1,700

BERTELLI, Pietro
– Vite degli' Imperatori de Turchi. Vicenza, 1599. Fo. Engraved title, 15 full-p. engraved ports., colophon lf. at end, sm. liby. stp. on verso of title, vell. bds., spine defect. (S. May 22; 270)
Samiramis. £750

BERTHIER, Louis Alexandre, Maréchal de l'Empire
– Relation de la Bataille de Marengo gagnée le 25 Prairial An 8 par Napoléon Bonaparte. Paris, 1806. 4to. Some traces of damp, 1 map reprd. along fold, cont. tree cf. gt., imperial arms of Napoleon, edges slightly scuffed; MS. pres. note of Maréchal Prince Alexandre tipped in. (C. May 30; 71)
D'Arcy. £220

BERTHOLLET, Comte Claude Louis
– Elements de l'Art de la Teinture. Paris, 1791. *Edn. with smaller type.* 2 vols. Hf.-titles, cont. qtr. pol. sheep, marb. bds., spine gt., rubbed. (SG. Oct.6; 46)
$300
– Uber die Gesetze der Verwandtschaft in der Chemie. Trans:– E.G. Fischer. Berlin, 1802. *1st. German Edn.* Cont. sewed, unc.,. (R. Oct.12; 1648)
DM 460

BERTHORIUS, Petrus
– Morale Reductorium Super Totã Bibliam. Basle, Jun. 1517. Final blank, p. 2-5 inserted from a smaller copy, sm. wormhole at beginning slightly affects text. (*Bound with:*) NAUSEA, Fredericus –Sermones Adventuales. Cologne, 1536. Pt. 1 only (of 4). Light spotting. (*Bound with:*) GREGORIUS NYSSANUS –Libri Octo. Strasbourg, 1512. Title woodcut border shaved at outer & upr. margins, wormhole in outer margins at end affecting some sidenotes, a few stains; long inscr. on 12v by Georgius Piesensis. Together 3 works in 1 vol. Fo. 16th. C. blind-stpd. vell.-bkd. wood bds., clasps. (S. Nov.17; 2)
Tzakas. £190

BERTHOUD, Ferdinand
– L'Art de Conduire et de regler les Pendules et les Montres. Den Haag, 1761. Cont. sewed, unc., upr. cover loose. (R. Apr.4; 1646)
DM 410
– Essai sur l'horlogerie. Paris, 1763. *1st. Edn.* 2 vols. 4to. Cf., flat spines. (DS. Feb.24; 2013)
Pts. 55,000

BERTIUS, Petrus
– Commentariorum Rerum Germanicarum Libri Tres. Amst., 1616. *1st. Edn.* Ob. 4to. 1st. 5 ll. with wormhole in lr. margin, part of 1st. book lightly stained, 2 views with short outer margins, old MS. owners mark & notes on end-paper, cont. vell., slightly cockled & spotted. (HT. May 10; 2897)
DM 17,500

BERTOL-GRAIVIL, E.
– Voyage de M. Carnot, Président de la République dans le Midi et la Corse. Ill:– Paul Boyer. Paris, 1890. 4to. Light foxing, mod. marb. hf. roan, corners. (HD. Oct.21; 25)
Frs. 1,000

BERTOLI, Giandomenico
– Le Antichità d'Aquileia Profane e Sacre. Venezia, 1739. Fo. Some slight stains, cont. hf. leath., bumped. (SI. Dec.15; 62)
Lire 350,000

BERTOTTI-SCAMOZZI, Ottavio
– Il Forestiere Istruito delle Cose piu Rare di Architectura ... della Citta di Vicenza. Ill:– Cristoforo Dall'Acqua. Vicenza, 1761. *[1st. Edn.].* 4to. Engraved vig. title, engraved frontis. port., 36 plts., most folding, 1 plt. with repair at blank corner, cl.-bkd. cont. bds. (C. Jun.27; 10)
Nercato. £400
– – Anr. Copy. Engraved port. frontis., 36 plts., most double-p., 2 plts. reinserted on stubs with repairs in inner margins, cont. cf., rebkd. (C. Dec.9; 8)
Mediolanum. £350

BERTRAN DE LIS, V.
– R. Empresa Isabel II. Esposición ... al ... Secretarie de Estado. Madrid, 1835. 4to. Cl. (DS. Apr.27; 2025)
Pts. 35,000

BERTRAND, L.
– Gaspard de la Nuit. Ill:– Armand Guérin. Paris, 1904. *(230) numbered on vell.* 4to. Foxing, leath. sigd. by E.A. Séguy, cut & painted, gt. & mosaic decor., painted silk liners, unc., ill. wrap. & spine. (HD. Jul.2; 42)
Frs. 21,000

BERTRAND DE MOLEVILLE, Antoine François
– Costume des Etats Hereditaires de la Maison d'Autriche. L., 1804. 4to. Engrs. hand-cold., cont. cf., gt.-tooled. (CR. Jun.6; 150)
Lire 1,300,000
– Histoire de la Révolution de France, pendant les Dernières Années du Règne de Louis XVI. Paris, 1801-03. 14 vols. Some repairs, cont. marb. cf., decor. spine, gt.-decor. (HD. Jan.26; 35)
Frs. 1,600

BERTUCH, Friedrich Justus
– Bilderbuch für Kinder. Weimar, [1790-]95. Vols. I & II only (of 12). 4to. 186 (of 200) hand-cold. engraved plts., a few trimmed, some browning of text, cont. cl., rebkd. preserving old spines, w.a.f. (S. Nov.28; 9)
Schuster. £300
– – Anr. Edn. Weimar, [1792]. Vol. 1. 100 old cold. copperplts, text in German, Fr., Latin & Engl.,

BERTUCH, Friedrich Justus *-Contd.*

slightly foxed or soiled, cont. leath. gt., slightly bumped. (R. Oct.12; 2136) DM 1,350
– – **Anr. Edn.** Weimar, 1798-1803. *Vols. I & II 2nd. Edn., Vol. III 1st. Edn.* Vols. I-III. Sm. 4to. German & Fr. text, lacks 1 plt. & text lf. in vol. II., 2 text ll. vol. II with lge. excision & margin tear with loss, several sm. margin tears, some slight margin tears, some spotting or browning, cont. hf. leath., very worn & bumped. (H. May 22; 944) DM 1,600
– – **Anr. Edn.** 1803. Vol. 2. 100 old cold. copperplts., slightly foxed, cont. hf. leath., bumped. (R. Oct.12, 2137) DM 1,050
– – **Anr. Edn.** Rumburg, 1807. Vol. 2. 4to. 32 cold. copperplts., interim sewed. (GB. May 4; 1501) DM 750
– – **Anr. Edn.** [Weimar], ca. 1810. Vols. 3 & 4 only (of 22). 4to. 102 hand-cold. plts., German, Fr., Engl. & partly Italian text, some foxing & browning to text, orig. hf. cf., rubbed. (VG. Sep.13; 726) Fls. 750
– – **Anr. Edn.** Weimar, 1810 u. 1860. Vols. 7 & 9. Foxed & soiled thro.-out, some staining, some plts. loose, cont. leath. & hf. leath., defect. (D. Nov.23; 2108) DM 1,000
– **Bilderbuch zum Nutzen und Vergnügen der Jugend.** Wien, 1809. 48 cold. copper engrs., hf. leath. (G. Sep.15; 2064) Sw. Frs. 800

BERTY, Adolphe
– **La Renaissance Monumentale en France.** Ill.:– after author & C. Salard. Paris, 1864. 2 vols. Fo. 100 engraved plts., ex-liby., later hf. mor. (SG. May 3; 38) $100

BERZELIUS, Jons Jacob
– **Essai sur la Théorie des Proportions Chimiques et sur l'Influence Chimique de l'Electricité.** Trans.:– Suedois. Paris, 1819. Hf.-title, spotted, new cl. (S. Dec.13; 248) *Bicker.* £110
– **A View of the Progress & Present State of Animal Chemistry.** Trans.:– G. Brunnmarck. 1813. *1st. Edn.* Hf.-title, lib–. stp. on title, orig. bds., backstrip defect. (BBA. Jul.27; 3) *Maggs.* £200

BESANT, Walter
– **South London.** L., 1899. Crushed crimson panel. lev., spine gt. with fleurons, by Fazakerley, fore-e. pntg. (SG. Nov.17; 223) $200

BESLER, Basilius
[–] **Hortvs Eystettensis.** [Ingolstadt], 1640. Lge. fo. 1 plt. with pasted tear, 2 with sm. hole in margin, 1st. 13 ll. lightly margin stained, cont. blind tooled leath., corners bumped, spine slightly defect & reprd., Hauswedell coll. (H. May 24; 855) DM 120,000

BESOLD, C.
– **Historia Constantinopolitana.** Strassburg, 1634. 2 pts. in 1 vol. Slightly browned thro.-out, cont. vell., clasps, 1 loose. (R. Oct.11; 992) DM 410

BESSA, Pancrace
– **Flore des Jardiniers** .... Paris, 1836. In 1 vol. 4to. 270 (of 390) engraved hand-cold. plts., no title or text, cont. mor.-bkd. bds., as a coll. of plts., w.a.f. (C. Nov.16; 218) *Burden.* £1,600

BEST & EASIEST METHOD OF PRESERVING UNINTERRUPTED HEALTH TO EXTREME OLD AGE
L., 1752. *2nd. Edn.* 12mo. Cont. cf. gt. (P. Feb.16; 240) £65

BESTERMANN, Theodore
– **Old Art Books.** 1975. *(300) numbered & sigd.* Lge. 4to. Orig. cl. gt. (TA. Dec.15; 311) £60
– **The Pilgrim Fathers.** Ill.:– G. Wales. Golden Cockerell Pr., 1939. *(300) numbered.* Orig. mor.-bkd. cl. (BBA. May 23; 184) *Thorpe.* £70
– **A World Bibliography of Bibliographies.** L., Priv. ptd., 1950. *2nd. Edn.* 3 vols. including Index. 4to. Cl. (P. May 17; 117) *Elliott.* £65
– – **Anr. Edn.** Lausanne, 1965-66. *4th. Edn.* 5 vols. 4to. Orig. cl., ex-liby. (BBA. Sep.8; 1) *Wise.* £130
– – **Anr. Edn.** N.Y., Scarecrow Pr., n.d. *3rd. Edn.* 2 vols. 4to. Buckram. (SG. Jan.5; 27) $150
See— **POPE, Arthur Upham** – **BESTERMAN, Theodore**

BETANCOURT (or **BETHENCOURT**) **Y MOLINA, Augustin de**
– **Mémoire sur la Force Expansive de la Vapeur de l'Eau, lu à l'Academie Royale des Sciences.** Paris, [1790]. *1st. Edn.* 4to. Slight spotting, cont. cf.-bkd. bds., spine gt., slightly rubbed; John D. Stanitz coll. (SPB. Apr.25; 45) $225
See— **LANZ, Philippe Louis & Betancourt y Molina, Augustin de**

BETHGE, H.
– **Das Lied von der Erde.** Ill.:– R. Genin. Berlin, 1923. *De Luxe Edn., (50) sigd. by author & artist, with supp. etching before title.* 4to. Orig. vell., cold. cover ill.; all full-p. etchings sigd. by artist. (H. Nov.24; 1521) DM 620

BETJEMAN, John
– **A Few Late Chrysanthemums.** L., 1954. *1st. Edn. (50) numbered & sigd.* 12mo. Orig. cl., d.-w. torn; Frederic Dannay copy. (CNY. Dec.16; 29) $140
– **Ghastly Good Taste.** 1933. *1st. Edn.* 8vo. Errata slip pasted on p. [xii], mod. mor., s.-c. (*With:*) – **An Oxford University Chest.** 1938. *1st. Edn.* 4to. Mod. mor.-bkd. bds., s.-c. (BBA. Jun.28; 10) *T. Parsons.* £50
– – **Anr. Copy.** Ill.:– Peter Fleetwood-Hesketh. L., 1933. *1st. Edn.* 12mo. Qtr. cl., ptd. bds., glassine jacket. (SG. May 24; 265) $110
– **Mount Zion or in Touch with the Infinite.** L., James Pr., [1931]. *1st. Edn.* Orig. decor. bds.; Frederic Dannay copy. (CNY. Dec.16; 28) $210

BETTANGE
– **Traité des Monnoyes.** Avignon, 1760. 2 vols. 12mo. Cont. roan. (HD. Feb.22; 17) Frs. 1,300

BETTERMANN, Gerh.
– **Fünf Minuten nach Zwölf.** Flensburg, [1947]. *(25).* Lge. fo. Limitation on MS. L. from artist dtd. 16.5.1938, Loose in orig. hf. linen portfo. (BR. Apr.13; 1641) DM 750

BETTS, John
– **The Family Atlas.** 1848. Fo. Maps, hand-cold., hf. mor. gt., worn. (P. Sep.29; 433) *Sweet.* £120

BEULAY, Honoré
– **Mémoires d'un Grenadier de la Grande Armée. 1808-1815.** Paris, 1907. Hf. chagrin. (HD. Jan.27; 6) Frs. 1,450

BEUQUE, Emile
– **Platine, Or & Argent: Dictionnaire des Poinçons Officiels Français & Etrangers, Anciens & Modernes, XIVe Siécle à nos Jours.** Paris, [1962]. 2 vols. 4to. Mor., orig. ptd. wraps. bnd. in. (*With:*) – **Dictionnaire des Poinçons de Maitres-Orfèvres Français du XIVe Siécle à 1838.** Paris, 1964. 1 vol. 4to. Unif. mor., orig. ptd. wraps. bnd. in. (SG. Oct.13; 310) $150

BEURDELEY, Michel
– **Porcelaine de la Compagnie des Indes.** Fribourg, 1969. 4to. Publisher's bds. (HD. Jun.26; 54) Frs. 1,300

BEVERLEY, Pidgie
[–] **Hurrah for New England!; or The Virginia Boy's Vacation.** Boston, 1850. *5th. Edn.* Lge. 16mo. Engraved frontis., partially & crudely hand-cold., frontis. & title-p. foxed & a little soiled, orig. blind-stpd. cl., cont. inscrs. on upr. & lr. end-papers; from liby. of F.D. Roosevelt, inscr. (as President) by him. (SG. Mar.15; 4) $150

BEVERLOO, C.G. 'Corneille'
– **Histoire des Etat et Empire de la Lune et du Soleil.** Paris, 1967. *(65).* Lge. fo. 5 lithos., leaves, portfo. cl.; each litho. & colophon sigd. (B. Feb.8; 362) Fls. 550

BEVERWYCK, Johan van
– **Alle de Wercken, soo in de Medecyne als Chirurgye.** Amst., 1652. *2nd. Coll. Edn.* 8 pts. in 1 vol. 4to. A little soiled & frayed at beginning & end, cont. vell., loose. (VS. Jun.7; 921) Fls. 725
– – **Anr. Edn.** Amst., [1656]. 5 pts. in 1 vol. 4to. Engraved general title, emblematic text engrs. thro.-out, owner's stp. & 18th. C. inscr. on title, some marginalia & underscoring, cont. vell., loose. (SG. Apr.19; 27) $325

– **Epistolicae Quaestiones, cum Doctorum Responsis** .... Rotterdam, 1644. 2 pts. in 1 vol. A few stains, cont. cf., worn, spine torn; Dr. Walter Pagel copy. (S. Feb.7; 160) *Maggs.* £220
– **Exercitatio in Hippocratis Aphorismum de Calculo ad. Cl.Salmasium. – De Calculo Renum et Vesicae.** Leiden, 1641-38. Together 2 works in 1 vol. 12mo. Vell.; Dr. Walter Pagel copy. (S. Feb.7; 159) *Goldschmidt.* £260
– **Wercken der Genees-Konst.** Ed.:– J. Cats. Amst., 1663-64. 4 pts. in 1 vol. 4to. 3 engraved titles, 74 text plts., hf. cf. gt. (P. Dec.8; 124) *Shapero.* £130

BEWICK, Thomas
– **Bewick Gleanings: Being Impressions from Copper Plates & Wood Blocks.** Ed.:– Julia Boyd. 1886. 4to. Sm. paper, mor.; 'pres. copy'. (CE. Sep.1; 14) £50
– – **Anr. Copy.** 2 pts. in 1 vol. 4to. L.P., frontis., 2 ports., 53 plts., hf. mor., spine worn; sigd. by ed. (SG. Aug.25; 53) $175
– **A General History of Quadrupeds,** .... Newcastle, 1792. *3rd. Edn. Royal 8vo. Iss.* Old mor., trimmed, some mild discolouration. (KH. Nov.9; 544) Aus. $220
– – **Anr. Edn.** Newcastle, 1820. *7th. Edn.* Cont. hf. mor., rebkd., orig. gt.-decor. spine relaid. (TA. Feb.16; 126) £50
– – **Anr. Edn.** Newcastle, 1824. *8th. Edn.* Bds., unc., rebkd., orig. label ('Demy Paper') preserved. (BBA. Jun.14; 82) *Bondy.* £60
– **History of British Birds.** Newcastle, 1797-1804. *1st. Edn.* 2 vols. (without Supp.). Woodcut vigs., slight soiling, 19th. C. hf. cf. gt. (S. Apr.10; 407) *Evans.* £170
– – **Anr. Copy.** 2 vols. Hf. cf. (P. Sep.8; 293) *Ayres.* £95
– – **Anr. Edn.** 1804. 2 vols. Some light spotting, cont. hf. cf., lightly rubbed. (CSK. Jan.13; 4) £120
– – **Anr. Copy.** 2 vols. Wood engraved ills., browned, cont. hf. cf., worn. (CSK. May 18; 75) £75
– – **Anr. Edn.** Newcastle, 1804[-05]. *(150).* 2 vols. Cont. tree cf., spines gt., slightly worn. (BBA. Jun.14; 78) *T. Scott.* £150
– – **Anr. Edn.** 1804 [1805-]1821. *Vol. 1: 3rd. Edn., Vol. 2: 1st. Edn. [Roscoe's variant A], Supps.: 1st. Edn.* 4 vols., including Supps., in 2. Demy and Royal 8vo. Later hf. mor., rubbed. (CSK. Jul.27; 162e) £120
– – **Anr. Edn.** Newcastle, 1804, 1821. 2 vols., including 2 pt. Supp. Hf. mor., marb. bds. (SKC. Sep.9; 1983) £100
– – **Anr. Edn.** Newcastle, 1805. 2 vols. Vig. titles, woodcuts, bdg. defect. (P. May 17; 316) *Cavendish.* £80
– – **Anr. Edn.** Newcastle, 1809. 2 vols. in 1. Some ll. spotted, cont. cf., rebkd., slightly rubbed. (BBA. Feb.23; 84) *The Bookroom.* £75
– – **Anr. Copy.** 2 vols. in 1. Some spotting, cont. tree cf. (TA. Dec.15; 128) £50
– – **Anr. Edn.** Newcastle, 1821. 2 vols. Crushed maroon mor. by Leighton, gt.-decor. spines, spines slightly faded. (TA. May 17; 279) £240
– – **Anr. Copy.** 2 vols. Orig. cf. (P. Oct.20; 198) £70
– – **Anr. Edn.** Newcastle, 1826. *6th. Edn.* 2 vols. Cont. diced cf. gt., spines slightly worn. (TA. Apr.19; 156) £60
– – **Anr. Edn.** Newcastle, 1832. 2 vols. Some foxing, orig. hf. cl. & bds. (nearly detchd. Vol. 1). (CBA. Aug.21; 49) $110
– – **Anr. Edn.** Newcastle, 1847. 2 vols. Orig. blind-stpd. cl., spines slightly faded & rubbed. (TA. May 17; 280) £70
– – **Anr. Copy.** 2 vols. Hf. cf. gt. (P. Jul.26; 201) £50
– **History of British Birds. – A General History of Quadrupeds.** 1797-1804; 1807. 2 vols.; 1 vol. Unif. mor. gt. (P. Oct.20; 26) £170
– – **Anr. Edn.** Newcastle, 1809; 1807. *2nd. work:* 5th. Edn. 2 vols. in 1; 1 vol. Unif. cont. cf. gt., slightly rubbed, jnts. reprd. (SKC. Jan.13; 2305) £110
– – **Anr. Edn.** Newcastle, 1809-11. *1st. work: 6th. Edn.* 2 vols. in 1; 1 vol. 1st. work lacks pp. XXI-XXIV, 2nd. work lacks fo. 301, rather soiled & spotted, mod. cf.-bkd. cl. (BBA. Nov.30; 89) *London Liby.* £70

- Works. Newcastle, 1885-87. *Memorial Edn.,* (750) sigd. by publisher B. Quaritch. Hf. mor. gt. (P. Dec.8; 92) *Joseph.* £170

BEWICK, Thomas (Ill.)
See— AESOP
See— COLLECTION OF RIGHT MERRIE GARLANDS for North Country Anglers
See— CONSETT, Matthew
See— LE GRAND D'AUSSY, Pierre Jean Baptiste
See— RITSON, Joseph
See— SOMERVILLE, William
See— THOMSON, James, Poet
See— THORNTON, Robert John

BEWICK, Thomas & John
- Select Fables. Newcastle, 1820. [*1st. Edn.*] Hf. mor. by Bayntun. (S. Oct.11; 447)
Bookroom. £110
- - Anr. Copy. Slight offset, cf. gt. (P. Sep.29; 44)
Wise. £60
- - Anr. Copy. Orig. cl., light wear, some chipping at spine edges; A.N.s by author tipped to front end-paper. (RO. Mar.21; 9) $700

BEY, Hamdy & Launay, Marie de
- Les Costumes Populaires de la Turquie en 1873. Ill.:– after Pascal Sebah. Constantinople, 1873. Fo. 74 toned phototype plts., captions in Turkish & Fr., title foxed & stained, orig. ptd. wraps., cl. spine, worn & chipped, partly disbnd. (SG. Nov.10; 142) $850

BEYER, Johann Hartmann
- Eine Newe und Schoene Art der Volkommenen Visier-Kunst, Derengleichen Hiebevor Neimaln in Keiner Spreach Gesehen Worden. Frankfurt, 1603. *1st. Edn.* 4to. Light dampstaining, etc., mod. hf. lev. (SG. Nov.3; 14) $500

BEYLE, Marie Henri 'Stendhal'
L'Abbesse de Castro. Ill.:– Eugène Courdoin. Paris, 1890. Numbered, mor. gt. by David, spine decor. (faded), wrap.; Paul Arbaud copy. (HD. Jun.13; 102) Frs. 3,500
- Die Abtissin von Castro. Ill.:– Alois Kolb. Hellerau, 1924. *(300) De Luxe Edn.* (150) numbered. 4to. Full-etching sigd., mor., decor. spine, cover & inner dentelle, bd. s-c. (HK. May 17; 2550)
DM 550
- La Chartreuse de Parme. Preface:– Francisque Sarcey. Ill.:– V. Foulquier. Paris, 1883. *Textual Reprint of Orig. Edn.* 2 vols. On vell., red hf. mor., corners, spines decor., unc., wrap. (HD. May 21; 150) Frs. 2,700
- - Anr. Copy. 2 vols. Hf. mor., corners, by Durvand, spine decor., unc. (HD. May 4; 429)
Frs. 2,500
- Rome, Naples et Florence. Paris, 1826. 2 vols. in 1. Cont. red hf. mor., spine blind- & gt.-decor. (HD. Mar.19; 154) Frs. 2,000
- Le Rouge et le Noir. Preface:– Léon Chapron. Ill.:– H. Dubouchet. Paris, 1884. *Textual Reprint of Orig. Edn.* (150) on japan. 3 vols. Red mor. by Gruel, blind- & gt.-decor., red mor. liners, wrap. preserved, s.-c. (HD. Jun.13; 101) Frs. 5,200
- - Anr. Copy. 3 vols. Lge. 8vo. On japan, port. in triple bradel, pink bradel hf. mor., corners, by Marius Magnin, spines decor., wraps. & spines preserved. (HD. May 4; 430) Frs. 2,600
- Vie de Rossini. 1824. *Orig. Edn.* 2 vols. Hf. mor., corners, by Champs, spine decor, wrap. & spine, unc., wrap. reprd. (HD. Apr.13; 120) Frs. 3,600

BEYNON, E.
- Barmhertziger Samariter. Nuremb., 1690. 3 pts. in 1 vol. 12mo. Frontis. slightly frayed, lightly browned, cont. vell., 4 ties, 2 defect. (HK. Nov.8; 463) DM 700

BEYTRAGE ZUR GESCHICHTE DER ERFINDUNGEN
See— BECKMANN, J.

BEZAE, Theodore de
- Poemata Varia. [Genf], 1614. Title stpd., slightly browned, cont. blind-tooled vell., lacks front free end-paper. (HK. Nov.10; 3033) DM 400
See— MAROT, Clément & Bèze, Théodore de

BEZALEL DARSHAN, of Slutzk
- Amudeha Shiv'ah. Prague, 1674. *2nd. Edn.* 4to. Unpaginated, owners' sigs. on title, margins of 1st. 2 ll. reprd. not affecting text, soiled, some staining, cl., trimmed. (S. Oct.24; 94) *Hirschler.* £100

BEZOUT, Etienne
- Cours de Mathématiques, à l'Usage des Gardes du Pavillon et de la Marine. Algebre, Mécanique. Paris, 1766-67. 3 vols. Cont. red mor. gt., decor. spines, inner roll-stp. (HD. Sep.22; 189) Frs. 1,800

BHAGUAT GEETA, or Dialogues of Kreeshna & Arjoon
Trans.:– Charles Wilkins. 1787. 4to. Cont. cf. gt., worn. (PD. Feb.15; 71) £75

BIAL, Col.
- Les Carnets, Souvenirs des Guerres de Révolution et de l'Empire.... Paris, 1928. Hf. cf. (HD. Jan.27; 7) Frs. 1,400

BIANCHI, S.
- Les Cinquante deux Tableaux ... du Vieux et du Noveau Testament. Ill.:– after Raphael. Rome, 1788. Ob. 4to. Engraved title & dedication, port., 50 (of 52) plts., torn, all soiled, hf. cf., worn. (P. Dec.8; 88) *Duran.* £60

BIANCHINI, Francesco
- Del Palazzo de Cesari. Verona, 1738. Fo. In Latin & Italian, mod. hf. leath. (SI. Dec.15; 64)
Lire 550,000

BIANCHINI, Giuseppe
- Dei Gran Duchi di Toscani della Reale Casa de Medici. Ill.:– A. Halwech & others. Venice, 1741. *1st. Edn.* Tall fo. Wide margins, hf.-title & errata lf., most ll. lightly dampstained at outer margins, cont. mott. cf., worn. (SG. Nov.3; 15) $350

BIANCO, Pamela
- Flora. With Verses by Walter de la Mare. Ill.:– after Bianco. L., [1919]. 4to. Slight margin darkening, bdg. not stated, cover edges darkening, jacket soiled & chipped; inscr. & sigd. by Bianco to Valenti Angelo, dtd. 1950, 7 A.N.s. (including 3 C'mas. cards) laid in, card for 1923 Bianco exhibit laid on rear end-papers. (CBA. Oct.1; 49) $120

BIANCONI, F.
- Cartes Commerciales et Minières des Pays Sud-Africaines. Paris, 1896. Cl.-bkd. bds., rubbed. (VA. Apr.27; 718) R 280

BIBELOT, The
Ed.:– T.B. Mosher. N.Y., [1925]. *Testimonial Edn. (500) numbered sets.* 21 vols., including index. 16mo. Three-qtr. mor., spines gt. (SG. Feb.16; 30) $100

BIBESCO, Princess
- Alexandre Asiatique, ou l'Histoire du Plus Grand Bonheur Possible. Ill.:– Léon Toublanc. Paris, 1927. *(300) numbered on velin d'Arches.* 4to. Hf. lev., slight wear, orig. wraps. bnd. in. (SG. Mar.29; 15) $150

BIBIENA, Ferdinando Galli
- L'Architettura Civile preparata su la Geometria, e ridotta alle prospettive, Considerazione Pratiche. Parma, 1711. *1st. Edn.* Fo. Lge. copy, engraved medallion port., 72 engraved unnumbered plts., lf. Q2 torn & reprd., dampstain affecting outer edges towards end, margin ink stain to plt. 66, some spotting, 19th. C. Italian red mor. gt., lge. gt. arms on covers of Pope Gregory XVI with blue & white mor. gt. onlaid shield, smooth spine gt., new spine label, unc., edges worn. (CNY. May 18; 96) $4,000

BIBIENA, Guiseppe Galli
- Architetture e Prospettive.... Ill.:– J.A. Pfeffel, Salomon Kleiner, L. Zucchi & others. Augsburg, 1740. Fo. Engraved title, frontis., port. of Emperor, engraved lf. of dedication, 1 lf. of ptd. text, 50 plts. of theatrical scenery, decors. for festivities, etc., cont. paper bds.; bkplt. of Marchese Joseph Pepoli. (S. May 10; 228) *Ungers.* £3,200

BIBLES (*Arranged alphabetically by Language, each Language chronologically*)

BIBLES [Dutch]
- Den Bibel. Tgeheele Oude ende Nyeuwe Testame[n]t. Antw., 1541. 2 pts. in 1 vol. Fo. Lacks 1st. title, 2 prelim. ll., 1 index & 1 text lf., map defect., cont. cf., rubbed & rebkd., lacks clasps. (VG. May 3; 704) Fls. 950
- Den Bibel, Inh. dat Oude & Nieuwe Testament. [Emden], 1560. 3 pts. in 1 vol. Lge. 8vo. Title & last lf. mntd., stained thro.-out, title & last pp. slightly soiled, 17th. C. vell. (VS. Dec.9; 1339)
Fls. 2,000
- - Anr. Edn. [Antw.], 1564. 4 pts. in 1 vol. Dampstained thro.-out, last lf. slightly defect. & reprd., tear in 1 lf., some wormholes in inner margins towards end, sm. stp. on title, old cf., 19th. C. spine, new end-papers. (VG. Mar.19; 200)
Fls. 1,100
- - Anr. Edn. Antw., 1566. Fo. Title soiled, some margin repairs & dampstains, cont. blind-stpd. cf., rebkd., lacks clasps. (TA. Feb.16; 281) £100
- Biblia Dat is de Gantsche Heylighe Schriftuere. Arnhem, 1616. 3 pts. in 1 vol. Fo. Title in engraved border, woodcut ills., lacks 0008, PPP1 & last lf. blank [?], FF6 torn, other sm. tears, stained & spotted, slight worming, cont. cf., lacks clasps. (S. Apr.10; 312) *Tile.* £280
- - Anr. Edn. Leyden, [1637]. *1st. Edn. States Version.* 3 pts. in 1 vol. Fo. Warranted by Barent Langenes & dtd. 1637, no sig. of Langenes on 2nd. title verso & no colophon at end of O.T., many cont. underlinings & annots, some margin staining, some repairs, 1 p. misbnd., a little short, cont. blind-stpd. cf. over wood bds., clasps brkn., corner & centre pieces missing, jnts. partly split. (VS. Jun.7; 939) Fls. 1,300
- - Anr. Edn. Leyden, 1641. *Early Edn. of States-Version.* 3 pts. in 1 vol. Fo. A few margin stains, 2 ll. loose, cont. blind-stpd. russ. over wood. later? brass clasps & catches, foot of spine defect., slightly rubbed; sigd. & dtd. on title verso by B. Langenes, 1642. (VG. Nov.30; 914) Fls. 1,150
- Bible. Haarlem, 1643. Fo. Lacks Old Testament title-p. & maps, cont. blind-tooled cf., 2 metal clasps, worn. [D. & M. 3307] (SG. Feb.9; 10)
$140
- Biblia, dat is: da gantsche H. Schrifture. The Hague, [1649]. 4 pts. in 1 vol. Fo. Engraved title (slightly defect. & mntd.), 58 (of 61) double-p. plts., many mntd., lacks maps, 19th. C. cf., slightly worn. (S. Nov.17; 4) *Tzakas.* £380
- Biblia Sacra: dat is de Geheele Heylighe Schrifture ... oversien en verbetert na den Roomschen text. Ill.:– C. v. Sichem after Dürer. Antw., 1657. 2 vols. in 1. Fo. Edges of title frayed, margin of 3V4 torn, 1 or 2 other minor tears, cont. cf. over wood bds., worn, jnts. brkn., lacks clasps. (CH. Sep.20; 19)
Fls. 1,200
- Biblia Sacra. Dat is de Gehele Heylighe Schrifture bedeylt in't Oud en Nieu Testament. Ed.:– Henricus van Leemputte. Antw., 1657. Lge. fo. Cont. cf., reprd., spine renewed. (LM. Mar.3; 110)
B.Frs. 40,000
- - Anr. Edn. Ill.:– after Christophe van Sichem. Antw., 1657; 1645. In 1 vol. Fo. Some ll. remargined, cont. cf. over wood bds., decor., chiselled bronze clasps, renewed. (HD. Jan.30; 30)
Frs. 2,500
- - Anr. Edn. Ill.:– Christoffel Van Sichem. [Amst., 1657, 1646]. 2 vols. Fo. Lacks part of imprint on engraved title, old suede & old cf., needs rebdg. [D. & M. 3314] (SG. Feb.9; 12) $400
- - Anr. Copy. 2 vols. Sm. fo. Extra engraved title, many woodcut text ills., vigs. & historiated initials, lacks general title, some ll. loose, other minor defects, early pol. cf. gt., worn, mildly damp-wrinkled, sold for ills. only. [D. & M. 3314] (SG. Apr.19; 28) $200
- Biblia, dat is De gantsche H. Schrifture. Maps:– Plancius & Baptista van Deutecom. Amst., 1661. *States-General version.* Fo. Engraved title, licence verso dtd. Dec. 15, 1656, 7 double-p. engraved maps & plans, Plancius's 'Orbis Terrarum Typus' in State 2, other maps bear imprint of Jan Evertsz Cloppenburg, 1 or 2 short tears or repairs touching engraved surface, some faint stains, cont. cf. over wood bds., rebkd., brass corner- & centre-pieces, clasps & 1 (of 2) catches, spine defect. (S. May 21; 109) *Golden.* £1,400

BIBLES [Dutch] *-Contd.*
– – **Anr. Edn.** Leiden, 1663. *Bible des Etats.* 3 pts. in 2 vols. Lge. fo. L.P., 1 map defect. with loss, 1 slightly torn, 2 cut at side, Vol. 2 stained, slightly browned & foxed, cont. vell. gt., Vol. 1 spine loose. (R. Oct.12; 2227) DM 2,200
– – **Anr. Edn.** Ill.:– N. Visscher. Amst., 1664. *States General Edn.* 3 pts. in 1 vol. Fo. 1st. & last ll. lightly stained in margin, minimal defect. in outer lr. corner, 1 lf. of O.T. defect., with loss, cont. vell. over wood bds., very spotted, some defects. (HK. May 16; 1368) DM 1,000
– – **Anr. Edn.** Ill.:– Sluiter & others, after Hoet. Amst., 1687. 3 pts. in 1 vol. Fo. Lacks maps(?), partly stained, cont. russ. over wood bds., brass clasps, & corner pieces, lr. cover brkn., spine slightly defect., 1 clasp loose. (VS. Dec.9; 1340) Fls. 800
– – **Anr. Edn.** Dordrecht, 1690. *States General version.* 3 pts. in 1 vol. Fo. Title stained & weak at edges with tiny loss of text & edges reprd., cont. blind-stpd. cf. over wood bds., brass cornerpieces & clasps, recased. (CH. Sep.20; 20) Fls. 950
– – **Anr. Edn.** Dordrecht & Amst., 1700. Fo. Cont. leath. over wood bds., lightly stained, brass corner bosses brkn., lacks clasps. (D. Nov.23; 82) DM 550
– **Biblia, dat is de Gantsche H. Schriftuure...Nu van nieuws uijt Luthers Hoogd. Bybel...overgezet.** Amst., 1701-02. 4 pts. in 1 vol. Fo. Lacks engraved title, maps frayed, some defects, some foxing, slight staining, some margin wormholes, cont. russ. gt. over wood, port. of Luther, orig. brass clasps & corner-pieces preserved, spine renewed. (VG. Nov.30; 915) Fls. 1,500
– **Biblia, dat is de Gantsche H. Schrifure.** Dordrecht & Amst., 1702. *States General Version.* Fo. Cont diced russ. over wood bds., later brass corners & clasps, spine torn, rubbed. (CH. May 24; 5) Fls. 1,500
– – **Anr. Copy.** 2 pts. in 1 vol. Fo. Lacks title & 1st. index & 4 maps, several ll. defect. &/or reprd., cont. blind-stpd. russ. over wood bds., brass corners & clasps, top of spine defect., w.a.f. (VS. Jun.7; 940) Fls. 575
– – **Anr. Edn.** Ill.:– Stoopendaal. Dordrecht & Amst., 1714. 3 pts. Engraved title & 6 double-p. engraved maps, all in cont hand-col. & gold heightened. (*Interleaved with:*) **BASNAGE. J. – 't Groot Waerelds Tafereël. Waar in de Heilige & Waereldsche Geschiedenissen & Veranderingen zedert de Schepping des Waerelds.** Trans.:– A. Alewyn. Amst., 1715. 2 pts. 2 cont. hand-cold. engraved titles, 1 etched plt. & 166 etched plts. on 83 ll., most by Rom. de Hooghe, possibly lacks 3 plts., rather browned. Together 2 works in 5 pts. in 1 vol. Fo. A little stained at beginning, cont. russ., gt. Atlas & owners name 'Jan de Burlett 1717', over woods bds., upr. cover brkn., spine defect., later brass clasps & corner pieces, 1 clasp brkn. (VS. Jun.7; 941) Fls. 1,900
– – **Anr. Edn.** Ill.:– D. Stoopendael (maps), D. Jonkman. Dordrecht & Amst., 1716. *Keur Edn.* 3 pts. in 1 vol. Fo. Extensive margin annots., 1st. map margin defect., some margins a little frayed, a little browned thro.-out, cont. russ. with blind-stpd. centre piece in double borders over wood bds., foot of spine defect., brass clasps & corners. (VS. Jun.7; 942) Fls. 1,100
– **Biblia ofte inhoud des O. en N. Testamts.** The Hague, 1719. 32mo. Upr. margins of plts. trimmed, edges sometimes a little shaved, plts. pasted at inner margins, cont. spr. cf., silver cornerpieces, & clasps. (CH. Sep.20; 34) Fls. 850
– **Biblia, Dat is de Gantsche H. Schrifture verv. alle de Canonijcke Boecken des O. & N. Testaments. De Boecken genaemt Apocryphe.** Ill.:– D. Stoopendaal (maps), J. v. Visnne, C. Huiberts & others after Hout, Houbraken & Picart (plts.). Dordrecht, 1729. *Keur Bible.* 3 pts. in 2 vols. Fo. Margin annots., probably lacks 1 map, cont. hf. cf., corners a little defect., jnts. vol. 1 slightly split. (VS. Jun.7; 943) Fls. 1,100
– – **Anr. Edn.** Ill.:– Stoopendaal. Dordrecht, 1730. *Keur Bible.* 3 pts. in 1 vol. Fo. Extensive margin annots., maps frayed, a little loose & stained in places, cont. blind-stpd. russ. over wood bds., top of spine reprd., brass corners & clasps. (VS. Jun.7; 944) Fls. 775
– **Geestelyke Natuurkunde.** Ed.:– J.J. Scheuchzer. Amst., 1735. 15 pts. in 4 vols. Fo. 4 plts. with bkd. & reprd. tears, slightly browned thro.-out, some spotting, vol. 1 stained near end slightly, some staining to 1st. approx. 50 ll. vol. 2, vol. 4 approx. 30 ll. near end slightly stained, cont. vell. (HT. May 8; 94) DM 5,200
– **Biblia.** Dordrecht, 1736. 4 pts. in 1 vol. Fo. Foxed, maps frayed, 18th. C. inscrs., cont. cf., elab. blind-tooled on covers, jnts. badly worn, lacks clasps, cl. folding case. (SG. Feb.9; 22) $130
– – **Anr. Edn.** Dordrecht, 1741-44. *States General Version.* 3 vols. in 1. Fo. 1 map slightly torn at fold, 2 torn at corners, 1 lf. torn, some browning, cont. diced russ. over wood bds., brass corners & clasps, upr. jnt. a little cracked, spine slightly worn. (CH. May 24; 7) Fls. 1,100
– – **Anr. Edn.** Dordrecht, 1752. *States-General Version.* O.T. only: 1 vol. Sm. 8vo. 1 plt. mntd., cont. red mor. with black onlays, elab. gt.-decor., gt. spine. (CH. Sep.20; 21) Fls. 800
– – **Anr. Edn.** Ill.:– Scheits, Jonkman, Folkema, & others, after A. Houbraken & others. Haarlem, 1782. 4 vols. in 2. 4to. Hand-cold. title, 2 frontis., 5 double-p. engraved maps, 164 engraved plts., including 14 double-p., some minor foxing, cont. mott. cf. gt., richly decor. (VS. Dec.9; 1341) Fls. 1,900
– – **Anr. Edn.** Haarlem, 1791. *States-General Version.* O.T. only: 1 vol. 12mo. Cont. Dutch mor. gt. extra, spine elab. tooled. (SG. Nov.17; 166) $110
– **Bijbel, bevattende de Verhalen des Ouden en Nieuwen Verbonds.** Ill.:– Rembrandt. Amst., [1906-10]. 2 vols. Lge. fo. Cf., richly gt., designed by T. Nieuwenhuis, slightly rubbed. (VG. Nov.29; 185) Fls. 600

BIBLES [English]
– **The Byble in Englyshe.** Ill.:– Holbein?. 1541. *6th. Great Bible.* 5 pts. in 1 vol. Fo. General title defect. with margin loss of engraved border (supplied in pen & ink facs.), margins of 1 Calendar lf. reprd., margins of 1st. 2 ll. & colophon lf. reprd. with parts of headlines supplied in facs., repairs to 8 ll. slightly affecting text, some headlines shaved, a few cropped, a few other minor margin repairs, mod. crushed mor. gt. by Rivière; Wellington College copy, w.a.f. [STC 2075; D. & M. (H.) 62] (C. May 30; 2) *Aspin.* £2,600
– – **Anr. Edn.** Ill.:– Holbein?. [1541]. *4th. Great Bible.* 5 pts. in 1 vol. Fo. Lacks general title, titles to pts. II, III & IV, 5 ll. Calendar/Prologue & 1 lf. in pt. II, fore-margins of 1st. 17 ll. in pt. I frayed or shaved affecting some text & side-notes, 2 ll. in pt. I with sm. wormholes affecting a few words, New Testament has short tear to 1 lf, anr. lf. bkd. with loss of table on verso, lacks 1 lf. but fragment including colophon mntd. at end, some ll. in pt. I misbnd., some headlines shaved, a few cropped, a few ll. loose, 18th. C. cf., rebkd., brkn.; Wellington College copy, w.a.f. [STC 2072; D. & M. (Herbert) 60] (C. May 30; 1) *Aspin.* £650
– **The Bible: that is the Holy Scriptures conteined in the Old & New Testament.** L., 1599. 4to. Book of Psalms, no imprint, bnd. in, early mor., gt.-stpd.; inscr. 'James Boswell of Auchinlek, Anno Dom. 1600'. (SG. Feb.9; 5) $275
– **The Bible, that is, The Holy Scriptures Conteined in the Olde & Newe Testament. – Whole Book of Psalms.** L., 1599. 4to. Extra wood-engraved titles, text woodcuts, 1st. engraved title & final lf. of O.T. mntd., title-p. of 'Psalms' mntd., old tree cf., disbnd.; armorial bkplt. [STC 2179] (SG. Apr.19; 31) $175
– **The Bible.** 1603. 4 pts. in 1 vol. 4to. 1st. engraved title torn with some text loss, lacks 2 prelims., soiled & dampstained thro.-out, some tears, some text loss, later cf., worn. [STC 2189] (BBA. Oct.27; 10) *Byatt.* £60
– **The Holy Bible... College of Doway.** Doway, 1609; [Rouen], 1635. *1st. Edn.; 2nd. Edn.* 2 vols. 4to. Woodcut initials, some slight staining & soiling vol. 1, lacks engraved additional title vol.2 (?), some outer margins shaved with slight loss, later hf. cf., rubbed; ex-liby. [STC 2207; 232] (CSK. May 18; 141) £90
– **The Holy Bible.** L., 1611. *Earlier iss., with 'He' in Ruth III 15.* 2 vols. in 1. Fo. Lacks engraved title, folios A1-4, Z1, 3R1, 3-4 & N.T. Y4-2A6, without map & folios A1-2 of Genealogies, some ll. loose, some torn, with some loss of text, soiled thro.-out, cont. cf., worn. [D. & M. 240; STC 2216] (BBA. Mar.21; 167) *Holdstock.* £260
– **The Bible.** N.T. dtd. 1611 [but 1613]. Fo. Lacks general title & some ll., some other ll. loosely inserted, cont. cf., worn, w.a.f. (CSK. Jul.27; 67) £190
– **The Holy Bible.** 1613. *Authorised Version.* Fo. Reading 'He' in Ruth III.15, general title defect., printed part within cut-out & trimmed woodcut architectural border probably from anr. copy & rebkd., 72 ll. cut round & remargined to size, New Testament title margins reprd., Genealogies lack 2 ll. & map, sm. rust-hole at A3 affecting a few letters, 3U2 reprd. affecting a few words, other minor margin repairs, 19th. C. blind-stpd. mor. by Tuckett, marb. paper doubls. & end-papers, rubbed; Wellington College copy, w.a.f. [STC 2226; D. & M. (H.) 322] (C. May 30; 3) *Smith.* £350
– – **Anr. Edn.** L., 1613-14. 4to. 1st. title relaid with loss of lr. part, prelims. dampstained, cont. panel. mor., worn, covers detchd. (TA. Apr.19; 413) £52
– – **Anr. Edn.** Camb., 1629. *1st. Camb. printing of Authorised Version.* 2 pts. in 1 vol. Fo. Ruled in red thro.-out; engraved title & next lf. very slightly defect. at inner margin, cont. dark mor., worn, lacks clasps. [D. & M. 424; STC 2285] (BBA. Nov.30; 194) *Primrose Hill.* £70
– – **Anr. Edn.** Trans.:– Engl. College of Dovvay. [Rouen], 1635. *2nd. Edn.* 2 vols. 4to. Errata & royal privilege lf., early 19th. C. russ., rebkd.; armorial bkplts. of Henry White & C.E.H. St. John. (SG. Feb.9; 9) $225
– **The Holy Bible. – Whole Book of Psalms.** 1641. Book of Common Prayer bnd. at beginning, impft., cont. Engl. cf., gt., all over tooled decor., initials ML on both covers, some wear; H.M. Nixon coll. [Wing B2200; Wing B2381] (BBA. Oct.6; 231) *Quaritch.* £95
– **The Holy Bible.** Oxford, 1688. Sm. fo. Woodcut Royal arms on titles, 231 engraved plts., all hand-cold., a few repairs, later reversed cf., slightly rubbed. (BBA. Feb.23; 164) *Smith.* £450
– **Holy Bible, containing the Old Testament & the New. – Book of Common Prayer & Psalter.** L., 1716, 1717. 4to. Many unsigd. copperplts., port., 3 copperplts., cont. red mor. gt.-tooled. (SG. Feb.9; 19) $200
– **The Holy Bible.** Oxford, 1717-16. *Authorised Version.* Fo. Browned & spotted, cont. black mor., upr. cover soiled. (S. Mar.20; 692) *Thorp.* £110
– – **Anr. Edn.** Edinb., 1722. Fo. Cont. panel. cf. (PD. Dec.14; 195) £300
– – **Anr. Edn.** Oxford, 1759. 2 vols. Apparently lacks ptd. title for O.T., some ll. torn, cont. Scottish cf., elab. gt.-tooled, gt.-panel. spine, gt. dentelles. (SG. Feb.9; 23) $225
– – **Anr. Copy.** 2 vols. Slightly browned & foxed, cont. mor., gt. cover, inner & outer dentelle, centre-pieces, 10 pt. silver bosses, rubbed & slightly bumped, Vol. 1 cover nearly detchd., 2 clasps. (R. Nov.9; 1552) DM 500
– – **Anr. Edn.** Camb., 1763. *1st Baskerville Edn. 1st. Iss., with subscribers list ending with 'Winwood'.* Lge. fo. Strip (name?) cut from blank upr. margin of title, cont. red gt.-panel. mor., 'Rd. & Eliz. Johnson 1763' gt.-stpd. on upr. cover (purchased from W. Stuart, a bookseller of Preston, the orig. subscriber), rebkd. preserving orig. gt. spine. (C. Nov.9; 41) *Franklin.* £800
– – **Anr. Copy.** Lge. fo. Subscribers' list in 3rd. state (ending with the Hon. Charles York), cont. russ., spine gt.; bkplt. of Thomas Boswall, of Blackadder. (S. Dec.8; 34) *Sotheran.* £260
– **The Christian's Family Bible.** Ed.:– Rev. W. Rider. 1767-70. 3 vols. Fo. Some staining, cf., spines reprd. (P. Mar.15; 116) *Cavendish.* £60
– **Practical Family Bible.** Ed.:– Francis Willoughby & Joseph Wise. Ill.:– Grignion & others. L., 1775, 1773. *O.T.: 2nd. Edn., N.T.: 1st. Edn.* Lge. fo. Cont. suede, brkn. (SG. Feb.9; 29) $130
– **The Holy Bible.** Bg'ham., 1782. Fo. Cont. cf., cover detchd. (SKC. Nov.18; 1891) £65
– **Complete British Family Bible.** Ed.:– Paul Wright. Ill.:– Pollard, Picart, & others. L., ca. 1782. Lge. fo. Date removed from title, old suede, worn. (SG. Feb.9; 31) $100
– **The Holy Bible.** Oxford, 1786. (*Bound with:*) **BIBLIANA [English] – Historical Part of the Holy**

Bible. Ill.:– John Stuart. N.d. Together 2 works in 1 vol. 4to. Cont. red mor. (SG. Feb.9; 33) $225
– – **Anr. Edn.** Ill.:– James Fittler after Durer & others. L., 1795. *1st. Edn.* 2 vols. 4to. Approx. 60 plts., cont. russ., covers detchd. (SG. Feb.9; 38) $100
– – **Anr. Edn.** Ill.:– after Corbould. L., 1795. 2 vols. Lge. fo. 2 extra engraved titles, about 20 copperplts., cont. str.-grd. crimson mor., wide gt. borders, very worn. (SG. Feb.9; 39) $200
– – **Anr. Edn.** 1796. 12mo. Margins of 1st. & last few ll. lightly wormed, watered silk end-papers, cont. black str.-grd. gt.-decor. mor., inset centre vell. ovals on covers, ovals soiled & slightly creased, spine ends rubbed & chipped, fore-e. pntg. of cathedral; inscr. 'Margaret Roscoe ... from her affectionate father W. Roscoe', other family inscrs. (CSK. Oct.21; 48) £100
– – **Anr. Edn.** Ill.:– after Loutherbourg & others. L., 1800. 6 vols. Lge. fo. Hf.-titles, 8 p. subscribers list, without Apocrypha, cont. cf., elab. gt.-tooled, worn, all covers detchd. (SG. Feb.9; 41) $225
– **The Illuminated Bible, Containing the Old & New Testaments...also the Apocrypha.** Ill.:– J.A. Adams. N.Y., 1846. 4to. Elab. gt.-stpd. mor., head of spine slightly torn, inner jnt. reprd. (RO. Dec.11; 150) $100
– **The Holy Bible containing the Old & New Testaments.** 1851. Velvet, pierced gt. brass mounts & clasp, in mor. box. (PD. Dec.14; 341) £55
– **The English Bible.** Hammersmith, Doves Pr., 1903-05. *(500).* 5 vols. Fo. Few ll. foxed, mor. gt., triple ruled gt. borders, flat spines in 6 compartments, gt.-decor., turn-ins gt., sigd. 'The Doves Bindery 19 C-S 06', slightly worn, Vol.3 lr. cover with 2¾ inch score; bkplts. of Warren B. Clark, as bdg., w.a.f. (CNY. Dec.17; 553) $3,200
– – **Anr. Copy.** 5 vols. Fo. 5 ll. in Vol.1 foxed, orig. limp vell., 2 leath.-bkd. folding boxes. (CNY. Dec.17; 554) $1,500
– **The Holy Bible.** Boston, Merrymount Pr., ca. 1910. *(488) numbered.* 14 vols. Orig. undyed pig., stpd. & lettered in blind, partly unc., unopened. (SG. Feb.16; 31) $250
– – **Anr. Edn.** Ill.:– Stephen Gooden. Nones, Pr., 1924-27. *(1075) numbered, 'Apocrypha' 1 of (1325) numbered.* 5 vols. Fo. Unc., unopened, orig. parch. gt., slightly worn. (S. Nov.22; 260) *Forsyth.* £100
– – **Anr. Edn.** L., Nones. Pr., 1924-27. *(75) numbered on Arnold unbleached rag paper.* 5 vols. Fo. 1 vol. with minor staining in upr. margin, limp vell., gt.-lettered spines, light wear & cover soiling. (RO. Dec.11; 253) $900
– – **Anr. Edn.** Ill.:– Stephen Gooden. Nones. Pr., 1924-27. *(1000) on Japon vell.* 5 vols. Sm. fo. Owner's sig. on front free end-papers, gt.-decor. vell. bds., slight wear. (SG. Jan.12; 277) $175
– – **Anr. Edn.** Nones. Pr., 1924-27. *(1000) & (1250).* 5 vols., including Apocrypha. 4to. Orig. bds., spines stained. (CSK. Jan.27; 69) £50
– – **Anr. Edn.** Boston, ca. 1934. *(488) on H.M.P.* 14 vols. 1 plt. foxed, 2 ll. with sm. fore-edge tear, hf. pig & wood bds., blind-stpd. spine, partly unopened, some rubbing to spines, a few spine heads slightly chipped, minor offsetting from covers to end-papers, bkplts. (CBA. Nov.19; 430) $750
– **The Holy Bible, containing the Old & New Testaments [the Lectern Bible, designed by Bruce Rogers].** 1935. *[200].* In 1 vol. Fo. Some ll. soiled, pig, upr. cover blind– & gt.-tooled, by Rivière, rubbed, s.-c. worn; pres. inscr. from Mrs. Cecil Curwen to the Rev. S. Gay. (S. Nov.22; 301) *Carlson.* £2,600
– **Holy Bible.** N.Y., Ltd. Edns. Cl., 1935-36. *King James Version. (1500) numbered.* 5 vols. Gt.-pict. cl., 2 gt. s.-c.'s. (SG. May 17; 160) $100
– **Bible in English.** Ill.:– Paul G. Winkler. Berlin, 1949. The only copy completed, being copy no. 1, ptd. for President Truman (but never presented), with 5 of the full-p. litho. engrs. sigd. by artist, untrimmed, 1st. & last blanks pasted down, catalogue clipping on rear pastedown, pict. bds., s.-c. (SG. Jan.12; 44) $850
– **The Holy Bible.** Cleveland, ca. 1960?. *Facs. of 1611 1st. Edn. of King James' Bible. (1500).* Fo. Gt.-decor. mor. (CBA. Dec.10; 444) $100
– – **Anr. Edn.** Boston, n.d. 14 vols. Ruled mor., stpd. spines. (CBA. Dec.10; 442) $110

BIBLES [Esquimaux]
– **Biblia de Esquimaux Indians de Labrador.** L., 1813. Bdg. (DS. Mar.23; 2027) Pts. 100,000

BIBLES [French]
– **La Saincte Bible contenant le Vieil et Nouveau Testament conduicte de Latin en Français.** Anvers, 1578. Traces of old dampstains, old cf., spine mod. renewed. (LM. Mar.3; 111) B.Frs. 33,000
– **La Sainte Bible.** Ed.:– S. & H. Des Marets. Amst., 1669. *New Edn.* 2 vols. Fo. Some plts. with slits with loss, 18th. C. marb. roan. (HD. Mar.14; 11) Frs. 1,700
– **Biblia Gallica. La Sainte Bible ....** Amst., 1707. 3 pts. in 2 vols. Fo. A few pp. misbnd., some ll. with margin bkd., maps mostly bkd. in fold & margin, cont. leath. gt., worn & partly defect. [D. & M.II, 3784] (HK. May 16; 1353) DM 900
– **La Sainte Bible.** Trans.:– Maistre de Sacy. Ill.:– Marillier. Paris, 1789-An XII [1804]. *1st. Edn.* 12 vols. Hf.-titles, folding map, 300 copperplts., foxed, cont. bds., unc., very worn. (SG. Feb.9; 35) $250
– – **Anr. Edn.** Trans.:– Maistre de Sacy. Ill.:– after Raphael & others. Paris, 1851. Sm. fo. Some foxing, hf. mor. (SG. Feb.9; 81) $150
– – **Anr. Edn.** Ill.:– Gustave Doré. Tours, 1866. 2 vols. Fo. Cont. black mor., spines rubbed. (CSK. Jun.1; 137) £100
– – **Anr. Copy.** 2 vols. Fo. Plts., text decors., crushed hf. mor., gt.-panel. backs, partly unc. (SG. Apr.19; 216) $325
– – **Anr. Copy.** 2 vols. Fo. Cont. red mor. gt., spines decor. (HD. May 4; 420) Frs. 4,100
– – **Anr. Copy.** 2 vols. Fo. Buckram, unc., spine slightly faded. (HD. Feb.17; 9) Frs. 1,200
– – **Anr. Copy.** 2 vols. Lge. fo. Publisher's cl. (DS. Nov.25; 2044) Pts. 50,000
– – **Anr. Edn.** Ill.:– Gustave Doré. Page decors. by Giacomelli. Tours, [1866?]. 2 vols. Fo. Cont. red mor., gold-decor. (SKC. Jan.13; 2142) £55

BIBLES [German]
– **Bible.** Nuremb., Anton Koberger, 17 Feb. 1483. *9th. German Bible.* Fo. Fo. 1 with 9 line capital B illuminated in cols. on gauffred & burnished gold ground, fo. 5 with 7 line capital I & fo. 296 with two 8 line capitals, all illuminated in similar style, some lge. capitals supplied in blue & red, others in red only, paragraph marks & initial strokes in red, all woodcuts cold. by cont. hand, Creation woodcut at fo. 5 heightened with burnished gold, lacks the 2 blanks between folios 295 & 296 & last blank, slight dampstains to extreme upr. edge of some 24 ll., sm. area at lr. margin of fo. CXII renewed, 3 ll. with minor patches at extreme lr. margin, fo. CCXCV with strip at fore-margin reinforced, 1 illuminated capital at fo. 296 slightly rubbed, early to mid 19th. C. Engl. dark purple str.-grd. mor. over wood bds., richly blind-panel., spine gt.-lettered, broad blind-tooled turn-ins, vell. doubls. & end-ll., edges gt. & gauffred from a 16th. C. German bdg., with legend 'Biblia' & date '1580', orig. sm. leath. index tabs present, extremities slightly shelfworn, fleece-lined s.-c.; Charles Butler bkplt. [BMC V, 424 (IC 7283); Goff B-632; H. 3137*] (CNY. May 18; 97) $24,000
– – **Anr. Copy.** 2 vols. Fo. 10 line capital 'B' illuminated in cols. with gold ground, 2 other capitals illuminated with gold, capitals thro.-out in red or blue, paragraph marks & some initial strokes in red, 21 woodcuts with cont. hand-colouring, lacks 1st. blank in Vol. 1 & 1st. & last blanks in Vol. 2, some 15 ll. with minor margin tears reprd., fo. 34 with repairs to gutter margin, fo. 162 with sm. puncture affecting 4 letters, fo. 469 torn & reprd., few stains, early blind-stpd. cf. on bds., covers panel. with concentric rolls, spines diapered, some corners worn. (CNY. Dec.17; 538) $12,000
– **Die Gantze Bibel.** Zürich, Froschauer, 1530. 1 lf. & 2 last numbered ll. (index & printer's mark) present in photocopy, minimal old spotting, pig, roll & stp. pict. decor., blind-tooling on upr. cover faint, slightly bumped & rubbed, lacks clasps. (V. Oct.1; 3710) DM 2,600
– **Biblia beider Allt unnd Newen Testamenten.** Trans.:– D. Johann Dietenberger. Ill.:– H.S. Beham & A. Woensam. Mainz, 1534. *1st. Edn.* Fo. Title with crudely reprd. tear, 1st. 12 ll. bkd. in margin, some loss, 3 ll. with longer tears, slightly browned, stained, some spotting, lacks last 4 numbered ll. with index, mod. leath. over wood bds., clasps, (from old material). (HT. May 8; 81) DM 2,900
– **Biblia Germanica.** Augsburg, 1537. *1st. Edn.* Fo. Lacks Moses & Prophets, lacks 1 blank & 6 unnumbered ll. at end, some early ll. slightly soiled with some notes or margin repairs, minimal spotting, cont. blind-tooled pig over wood bds., 2 clasps, end-papers include 2 ll. from old Hebrew vell. MS., some wear, inner cover & end-papers slightly wormed, lacks ties. (HK. Nov.8; 108) DM 1,600
– **Biblia beider Allt und Newen Testamenten....** Ed.:– Johann Dietenberger. [Cologne], Aug. 1540. 2 pts. in 1 vol. Fo. 61 woodcuts in Old Testament, 4 in New Testament, no ills. in Apocalypse, lacks last lf., (?blank or colophon), 2 holes in title, 1 causing loss of letters & affecting woodcut border, sm. hole in following lf., upr. corner of 3V4 reprd., sm. tears or holes, some marginal, some just affecting letters in gl, nl, Oo5 3S6, AA6, GG3-5, a few stains, some Ms. notes, cont. blind-stpd. vell. over bds., 1 clasp loose. (S. May 10; 226) *Bruno.* £300
– **Biblia: dat ist: dia gantze Heilige Schrifft.** Trans.:– Martin Luther. Wittenberg, 1541. 2 pts. in 1 vol. Fo. The 6 prelims. differ from those in British & Foreign Bible Soc. copy, lacks final blank in each pt. & title-p. of pt. 2, title-p. slightly defect. & reprd., severe tears & defects (reprd., slight loss of text) in 2nd. P5 & Y6, some other margin defects & short tears, some stains, 19th. C. cf. over wood bds., clasps, black mor. pull-off box; label on spine asserting book to be Luther's copy. (S. Nov.17; 5) *Bender.* £2,800
– – **Anr. Copy.** 2 pts. in 1 vol. Fo. Pt. 1 lacks title & 1 lf., last 4 ll. with lge. bkd. margin repairs, last 7 ll. partly bkd. at margins & corners, other sm. faults or tears, some bkd. or extended, browned, slightly soiled, cont. blind-tooled pig over wood bds., 2 clasps, worn, slightly bumped, spine defect., end-papers renewed, 1 tie loose. (HK. Nov.8; 109) DM 7,500
– **Bibel.** Trans.:– Johann von Eck. Ingolstadt, 1550. 2 pts. in 1 vol. Fo. Sm. copy, lacks title-p., lr. fore-corner of Y5 torn away with missing text in facs., some short tears, stains, loose ll. & other minor imperfections, cont. blind-stpd. pig over wood bds., clasps, w.a.f. (S. Oct.11; 382) *Snelling.* £160
– **Bibell, Das ist, Alle Bücher Alts und News Testaments.** Ed.:– Johan Dietenberger. Ill.:– A. Woensam & Hans Sebald Beham. Köln, 1556. Sm. fo. Light browning or old soiling & staining, some paper defects in margin & sm. excisions with some loss, 2 ink stains in lr. margin reaching text in approx 6 ll., pig, blind-tooled roll-stp. decor., 2 chiselled brass clasps. (V. Oct.1; 3708) DM 4,100
– – **Anr. Edn.** Trans.:– J. Dietenberger. Köln, 1567. 2 pts. in 1 vol. Fo. Some underlining & old annots., some slight spotting, last ll. lightly wormed, cont. blind-tooled pig over wood bds., 10 part brass bosses, 2 clasps, lacks ties. (HK. May 15; 86) DM 2,600
– **Catholische Bibell.** Ed.:– J. Dietenberger. Ill.:– Virgil Solis & others. Cologne, 1575. Fo. All woodcuts cold. by early hand, about 40 of the lge. histor. initials ornamented in cols. & gold, N.T. title-p. defect., some tape repairs & other defects, very foxed & stained, etc., heavy vell. over wood bds., elab. blind-stpd., & dtd. 1599, metal corner– & centrepieces, 2 metal clasps intact. (SG. Nov.3; 34) $1,200
– **Biblia, das ist die Gantze Heilige Schrifft.** Trans.:– Luther. Ill.:– H. Brosamer, G. Lemberger & others. Wittenberg, 1589-90. *Reprint of 1558-61 Edn.* 2 pts. in 1 vol. Fo. Ll. 229-240 misbnd., lacks Pt. 1, ll. 199, 235 & Pt. II, ll. 85, 90, 430-? & part of Index, margins short, repairs, margin stains, 19th. C. chagrin, brass corners & catches, 1 brkn., w.a.f. (VS. Jun.7; 938) Fls. 1,100
– **Biblia Germanica.** Ed.:– G. Schönfelt. Trans.:– M. Luther. Kassel, 1601. Fo. Lightly browned, old MS. marginalia on a few pp., cont. vell. gt., slightly soiled & cockled, light spine defect. (R. Oct.11; 10) DM 1,600
– **Biblia Germanica. Bibell.** Trans.:– J. Dietenberger. Köln, 1604. Fo. Lacks end-lf., browned, slightly foxed & stained, cut slightly close at margin & some text annots slightly excised, 19th.

BIBLES [German] *-Contd.*

C. hf. leath., rubbed. (HK. May 16; 1355) DM 520
– **Biblia** .... Wittenberg, 1606. Lge. fo. Imprint on 2nd. title lf. includes earlier date of 1601, separate title lf. for Prophets & New Testament section, lacks front title lf. (& some other prelims.?), many ll. later reprd. with loss of portion of text or engrs., browning thro.-out, later diced cf. with black stamping. (HA. Feb.24; 384) $200
– **Biblia, das ist: Die Gantze Heilige Schrifft.** Trans.:– M. Luther. Hanau, 1615. 4 pts. in 1 vol. Slight worming with slight loss, later cf., w.a.f. (CSK. Aug.19; 105) £150
– **Bibell, das ist, Alle Bücher Alts vnd News Testaments.** Trans.:– Joh. Dietenberger. Köln, 1618. 2 pts. in 1 vol. Fo. Pt. 1 title defect. & mntd., lacks 2 ll. preface, 1st. ll. with margin defects. & loose, 1 lf. N.T. very defect., browned, some staining, last ll. very soiled in margins, last lf. very defect., cont. blind-tooled pig over wood bds., very worn, lacks clasps. (HK. Nov.9; 1557) DM 700
– **Biblia das ist : Die Gantze Heilige Schrifft.** Trans.:– M. Luther. Wittenberg, 1621. Cont. vell., soiled, lacks spine. (GB. Nov.3; 929) DM 950
– **Sacra Biblia, das ist, die Gantze H. Schrifft Alten und Newen Testament.** Trans.:– Casparum Ulenbergium. Cologne, 1630. *1st. Ulenberg Edn.* Lge. fo. Hf.-title, errata list, leath. on old wood bds., bdg. brkn., lacks clasps. [D. & M. 4217] (SG. Feb.9; 7) $325
– – **Anr. Copy.** Fo. Lacks 1 prelim lf., 1 lf. with corner tear reprd., MS. entries on 3 ll. end-papers, cont. blind-tooled pig over wood bds., 2 (of 8) corner brass bosses, 2 brass clasps, 1 defect, 3 defects in cover, foot of spine torn. [D & M 4217] (R. Apr.4; 2071) DM 2,500
– – **Anr. Copy.** Fo. 8 ll. near end half torn out, browning, stain, sm. worm traces, woodcuts faint, blind-tooled decor. pig, lacks clasps. (V. Oct.1; 3713) DM 1,300
– – **Anr. Edn.** Trans.:– M. Luther. Lüneburg, 1654. *Stern Bibel.* Sm. 8vo. Some spotting & browning, 18th. C. red mor., elab. gt. decor., metal stylised clasps, leath. ties with gt. ornament, 2 sm. metal rosettes on covers, spine & lr. cover with 3 sm. defects., slightly spotted. (H. May 22; 655) DM 1,700
– – **Anr. Edn.** Trans.:– M. Luther. Chapter-headings:– L. Hütter. Wittenberg/Frankfurt, 1660. 3 pts. in 1 vol. 4to. Lr. corner of prelims. defect., some margins reprd. & stained, 1st. pt. wormholed, cont.blind-stpd. & panel. pig, defect., jnts. brkn., old brass corner-pieces & catches, lacks clasps. [D. & M. 4215, note] (VG. Mar.19; 202) Fls. 600
– – **Anr. Edn.** Trans.:– M. Luther. Nuremb, 1662. 2 pts. in 1 vol. Lge. fo. Some sm. margin slits reprd., O.T. copper engraved & ptd. title with light margin slits, cont. leath over wood bds., 8 brass bosses, 1 (of 2) centre-pieces, 4 brkn. clasps., spine reprd. (R. Apr.4; 2072) DM 4,500
– – **Anr. Edn.** Mainz, 1662. 3 pts. in 1 vol. Lge. 4to. Copper-engraved title with several pasted tears, lacks port. & 1 copper engr., a few ll. with sm. tears, most in margin, 2 pp. pt. 3 very defect. & taped, 1st. 30 ll. slightly frayed, lightly browned. cont. blind-tooled pig over wood bds., lacks 2 clasps. (HK. Nov.9; 1558) DM 1,600
– **Catholische Mayntzische Bibel.** Ill.:– after M. Merian. Mayntz, 1662. 2 vols. Fo. Some copper engrs. ptd. weakly, old MS. owners entries on title & end-papers, some ll. slightly stained, cont. marb. leath. gt., spine renewed with old material. [D. & M. II, 1,4236] (D. Nov.23; 79) DM 1,800
– **Biblia, Das ist: Die Gantze H. Schrifft.** Trans.:– M. Luther. Lüneburg, 1663-64. 3 pts. in 1 vol. 4to. 2 copper engrs. with corner tear, maps slightly crumpled, some browning & soiling, heavier at beginning, pig over wood bds., decor. tooled, 10 metal bosses & leath. bands, rubbed. (H. Nov.23; 613) DM 4,400
– – **Anr. Edn.** Wittenberg, 1665. *Lutheran Version.* Fo. Some browning & staining thro.-out, cont. blind-stpd. pig over wood bds., brass centre- & corner-pieces, 1 (of 2) clasps, a few wormholes, w.a.f. (S. Jun.25; 13) *Hildebrandt.* £220
– – **Anr. Edn.** Trans.:– Luther. Wittenberg, 1670. 3 pts. in 1 vol. 1 double-p. map detchd., laid down & cleanly torn, some soiling, cont. cf., rubbed, a few gatherings sprung, gt. metal clasps with sections lacking, w.a.f. (CSK. Mar.9; 98) £240
– – **Anr. Edn.** Trans.:– Luther. Lüneburg, 1672. Fo. Lacks all copperplts. except title, both title ll. completely bkd., beginning & end margins slightly torn, lightly browned & soiled, cont. blind-tooled leath. over wood bds., spine renewed or rebnd., lacks ties. (HK. Nov.9; 1559) DM 1,000
– – **Anr. Edn.** Trans.:– Martin Luther. Wittenberg, 1686. 3 pts. in 1 vol. Fo. 1st. 5 ll. detchd. with blank margins frayed, old mor., spine worn, w.a.f. (CSK. Apr.6; 68) £150
– – **Anr. Edn.** Trans.:– M. Luther. Ulm, 1688. Fo. 1st. & last ll. defect., some loose, lacks 1 lf. N.T., woodcut excised on 2 pp., stained & slightly soiled, cont. blind-tooled pig over wood bds., very defect., slightly wormed, lacks clasps. (HK. Nov.9; 1560) DM 460
– – **Anr. Edn.** Trans.:– M. Luther. Nürnberg, 1692. Fo. Several copper engrs., & ll. with sm. margin tears & spotting, 3 ll. with lge tears, 1 copper engr. torn & defect, last lf. with sm. defect., some light browning, prelim. lf. with MS. owners mark, cont. pig over wood bds., blind-tooled, metal clasps, slightly worn, some sm. spots. (H. May 22; 615) DM 5,800
– – **Anr. Edn.** Ed.:– P. Tossani. Frankfurt, 1693. Fo. 1 plan with margin slits, cont. leath. gt., gold-tooled cover borders, bumped & rubbed. lr. cover & spine with stains at top, spine defect., 2 clasps. (D. Nov.23; 80) DM 1,680
– – **Anr. Edn.** Preface:– J. Dieckmann. Trans.:– M. Luther. Stade, 1702 & 1701. 3 vols. in 1. Fo. Some copper engrs. bkd. in margin, several text ll. with sm. margin repairs, some sm. wormholes in III in lr. margin, some reprd., lightly browned thro.-out, several sigs. with heavy brown mark in upr. margin, in II in side margin, 19th. C. cf., slightly worn, some worming, sm. scratches. (H. Nov.23; 614) DM 1,600
– – **Anr. Edn.** Trans.:– M. Luther. Leipzig, 1707. Fo. Rubricated title, some wear & ageing, cont. black cf. over stiff wood bds., raised bands, 2 brass clasps on leath. straps, hand-marb. end-papers, covers detchd., scuffed, some ageing & chips at corners of jnts. (HA. Feb.24; 385) $210
– – **Anr. Copy.** Fo. Lightly browned, cont. leath. over wood bds., cover loose, rubbed, 2 clasps. (HK. May 16; 1362b) DM 800
– – **Anr. Edn.** Ed.:– N. Haas. Trans.:– M. Luther. Leipzig, 1710. 4to. Cont. leath., rubbed, especially spine. (R. Apr.4; 2073) DM 600
– **Biblia, mit der Ausslegung.** Ed.:– Luther; Ossiandri.... Lüneburg, 1711. Lge. fo. 19th. C. leath., Romantic gt. decor., lightly rubbed. (HK. May 16; 1356) DM 2,400
– **Biblia das ist Die gantze Heil Schrift.** Trans.:– M. Luther. Basel, 1712. Fo. Separate titles for Prophets, Apocrypha, & New Testament, last 5 ll. severely wormed with loss of text to last 2 ll., browned thro.-out, orig. black pig over wood bds., brass corner & centre fittings, lacks cf. for brass fore-edge clasps. (HA. Feb.24; 386) $120
– – **Anr. Edn.** Trans.:– M. Luther. Ulm, 1714. 3 pts. in 1 vol. Cont. leath., silvered outer dentelles, 2 silver clasps, monogrammed 'S.M.C.' & dtd. 1736. (BR. Apr.12; 1227) DM 420
– – **Anr. Edn.** Trans.:– M. Luther. Nuremb., 1720. Fo. Few margins lightly wormed, old cf., worn, upr. cover detchd. (CSK. Sep.30; 51) £65
– – **Anr. Edn.** Berleburg, 1726-39. Vols. I-VII (of 8). Fo. Includes 2 Apocrypha (Wisdom of Solomon & Jesus Sirach), & proverb supp. Vol. 1 title bkd. in margin, some browning, some margin tears sm. worm traces with some slight loss, some spotting or staining, cont. vell., spotted & partly rubbed. (HT. May 8; 83) DM 2,800
– – **Anr. Edn.** Tübingen, 1729. 2 pts. in 1 vol. Fo. Title to pt. 1 detchd., tear in 2nd. lf., a few stains, cont. blind-stpd. pig over wood bds., metal clasps, 3 (of 8) metal cornerpieces, w.a.f. (S. Oct.11; 383) *Simonds.* £210
– – **Anr. Edn.** Basel, 1729. Fo. Lacks 2 text ll. & end-lf. (?with printers mark), folding map with some margin defects., some old spotting & wear, blind-tooled pig over wood bds., 5(of 8) chiselled brass corner bosses, 2 central bosses, spine torn, soiled, clasps defect. (V. Oct.1; 3714) DM 800
– – **Anr. Edn.** Ed.:– Christoph Matthaei Pfaffen. Trans.:– Martin Luther. Tübingen, 1730. 2 vols. in 3. Lge. fo. All copper plts. clipped & tipped in, cont. cf., brkn., not collated, w.a.f. [D. & M. 4231] (SG. Feb.9; 21) $300
– – **Anr. Edn.** Trans.:– Johannis Piscatoris. Bern, 1736. 3 pts. & supp. in 1 vol. Fo. Pt. 1 lightly stained at beginning, 1 p. with tear, pt. 2 lacks ll. F1-F3, pt. 3 pagination jumps 1 p., 1 p. with sm. tear, a few pp. wormed with slight loss, some ll. slightly browned or foxed, cont. leath. over wood bds., reprd., 10 part bosses, 2 clasps, jnts., bosses & clasps reprd. (HK. May 16; 1358) DM 900
– – **Anr. Edn.** Trans.:– Luther. Ill.:– E. Porzel after J. v. Sandrart. Nurnberg, 1736. *Kurfürstenbibel.* Fo. Plts. weak, 1st. ll. torn & creased with loss, lacks title copper engr., browned & spotted thro.-out, cont. blind-tooled pig over wood bds., split in upr. cover pasted, wormed, torn & worn, 5 (of 10) part bosses, lacks clasps. (HK. May 16; 1359) DM 700
– **Die Gantze Heil. Schrifft.** Ed.:– F. Battier & T. Gernler. Trans.:– Martin Luther. Basel, 1736. Fo. 2nd. double-p. map inserted in N.T., cont. late Renaissance style blind-tooled pig over wood bds., 8 corner bosses, 2 centrepieces, clasps completed in cont. style. (GF. Nov.16; 1155) Sw. Frs. 2,200
– **Biblia Parallelo-Harmonico-Exegetica, Das ist: Die mit sich selbst wohl uverinstimmende, und sich selbst erklärende, ganze Heilige Schrift. Alten und Neuen Testaments ... des Seligen D. Martin Luthers** .... Freyberg, 1739, 1742. 2 vols. in 1. Lge. fo. Rubricated titles, marginal ptd. annots. in German & Hebrew, some text cracks, cont. cf. over paper bds., raised bands, covers with cf. peeling & well worn. (HA. Feb.24; 387) $120
– **Catholisch Mayntzische Bibel.** Frankfurt, 1740. Fo. 19th. C.(?)blind-tooled pig over wood bds., slightly rubbed, 5 (of 8) corner bosses & 2 metal clasps. (GB. Nov.3; 931) DM 2,200
– **Biblia, das ist: Die gantze Heilige Schrifft detz Alten und Neuen Testaments. Wie Solche von Hern Doctor Martin Luther Teel.** Ill.:– Claussner. Nurnberg, 1747. Fo. Browned thro.-out, some pp. creased, light stains, last lf. reprd., worn, text trimmed at lr. edge, with date lost from title-lf., cont. cf. (HA. Feb.24; 388) $225
– – **Anr. Copy.** Fo. Many ll. detchd. or severely chipped (especially port. plts.), orig. pig over wood bds., covers very worn with portions of leath. lacking. (HA. Feb.24; 389) $175
– – **Anr. Edn.** Trans.:– M. Luther. Ill.:– J. Wangner & J.G. Pintz after G. Eichler. [Regensburg], 1756. Fo. 1st. ll. soiled, light stains in margins thro.-out, cont. leath., spine with tear & sm. defect., end-papers with tears & defects. (D. Nov.23; 81) DM 800
– – **Anr. Edn.** Preface:– Joh. Mich. Dilherrn. Trans.:– Luther. Nürnberg, 1764. Fo. Lightly browned, frontis. very browned & mntd., some sm. defects. reprd., lacks free end-papers, cont. blind-tooled pig over wood bds., defect., 1 (of 8) corner bosses, 2 clasps, lacks ties. (HK. May 16; 1360a) DM 1,100
– – **Anr. Edn.** Ed.:– A. Rehberger. Preface:–J.M. Dillherr. Trans.:– M. Luther. Nuremb., 1765. 2 pts. in 1 vol. Fo. Some slight browning or foxing, cont. pig over wood bds., 7 (of 8) corner bosses, clasps. (R. Apr.4; 2075) DM 3,000
– – **Anr. Edn.** Ed.:– J. Sauberti & Joh. M. Dilherrn. Ill.:– Seligmann (frontis.) & J.C. Klaussner. Nuremb., 1765. Fo. Some light browning, slightly soiled thro.-out, 1st. ll. very browned in lr. margin, cont. blind-tooled pig over wood bds., 2 clasps, 1 defect. (HK. Nov.9; 1562a) DM 1,600
– – **Anr. Edn.** Nürnberg, [1765?]. Fo. Cut close at foot, title lacks date, lightly browned & slightly stained, especially at beginning & end, 1st. frontis. creased, last lf. lightly defect., verso of port. with owners mark 1768, leath., ca. 1800, very bumped & rubbed, jnts. brittle, 2 clasps, 1 defect. (HK. May 16; 1360B) DM 480
– – **Anr. Edn.** Trans.:– Martin Luther. Nuremb., 1768. Lge. fo. Cont. cf. gt. over wood bds., spine decor., gt. clasps incompl., very worn; from Fondation Furstenberg-Beaumesnil. (HD. Nov.16; 100) Frs. 3,700
– – **Anr. Edn.** Preface:– Joh. Chr. Klemm. Trans.:– M. Luther. Ill.:– Matth. Schultes. Tübingen, 1769.

Fo. Lacks last 3 index ll., foxed, stained in margin, some ll. at beginning & end loose, cont. blind-tooled pig over wood bds., upr. jnt. torn, loose, 2 clasps, lacks ties, w.a.f. (HK. May 16; 1361) DM 550

-- **Anr. Edn.** Trans.:- Luther. Nurnberg, 1770. Lge. fo. Ageing, some very old dampstains intermittently thro.-out, 1st. few ll. wrinkled & creased, cont. tooled pig over interior bevelled thick wood bds., brass clasps & corner shields, raised bands, tooling worn, lacks 2 brass tooled corner shields. (HA. Feb.24; 390) $225

-- **Anr. Copy.** Fo. Copper engraved title loose & frayed, 1st. 100 ll. very soiled in lr. corner, minimal spotting, 1st. sigs. slightly loose, cont. blind-tooled pig over wood bds., leath. re-nailed in parts, worn, end-papers renewed, 2 clasps, lacks upr. clasp. (HK. May 16; 1362) DM 1,000

-- **Anr. Edn.** Ed.:- J.M. Dilherrn. Trans.:- M. Luther. Ill.:- E. Porzel after Sandrart. Nuremb., 1773. Fo. Several ll. loose or frayed, browned & some staining thro.-out, old MS. annots. & lining, cont. blind-tooled pig over wood bds., wormed, worn, 8 pt. brass bosses (lacks 4), 2 clasps, lacks ties. (HK. Nov.9; 1561) DM 850

-- **Anr. Edn.** Trans.:- M. Luther. Germantown, 1776. *Gun-Wad Bible.* Thick 4to. Title-p. mntd. & lacks part at top, foxing, some stains, cont. cf. over wood bds., leath. & metal clasps, worn. (SG. Apr.5; 14) $250

-- **Anr. Edn.** Nuremb., 1788. Some foxing, blind-stpd. leath. on bevelled wood bds., metal corner bosses, leath. & metal clasps. (CBA. Dec.10; 443) $200

-- **Anr. Copy.** Fo. 2 port. copper engrs. with sm. pasted tears in lr. margin, some light browning or foxing, cont blind-tooled pig over wood bds., 8 corner bosses, clasps, 1 tie slightly defect. (R. Oct.12; 2222) DM 2,700

- **Die Heiligen Schriften des Alten [Neuen] Testaments.** Freiburg, ca. 1810. 2 vols. Some slight browning, O.T. lacks plt. 18, later hf. leath., some wear. (HT. May 8; 96) DM 480

-- **Anr. Edn.** Trans.:- M. Luther. Ill.:- G. Doré. Stuttgart, ca. 1870. 2 vols. Fo. 3rd. 1st. 4 ll. 'Familien-Chronik' with margin decor. in woodcut, vacant place for entries, cont. red leath. gt., blind-tooled cover decor. (BR. Apr.12; 1229) DM 1,100

-- **Anr. Edn.** Trans.:- M. Luther. Ill.:- after G. Doré. Stuttgart, ca. 1875. 2 vols. Fo. Some slight foxing, orig. leath. gt. (R. Oct.12; 2229) DM 420

- **Biblia. Das ist : Die Gantze Heilige Schrifft.** Trans.:- M. Luther. Ill.:- A. Simons. [München, Bremer Pr., 1926-28]. *(365) on Bütten.* 5 vols. Lge. 4to. Hand-bnd. orig. mor., gold decor. spine, covers, inner & outer dentelle, by Frieda Theirsch. (H. Nov.23; 944) DM 5,400

-- **Anr. Copy.** 5 vols. Fo. Orig. gt. decor. mor., by Frèda Thiersch, slight traces of an ex-libris, s.-c. partly bumped. (HK. May 17; 2599) DM 4,600

-- **Anr. Edn.** Trans.:- M. Luther. [Leipzig, 1935]. *Facs. of Wittenberg 1534 Edn.* Orig. leath. over wood bds. by H. Fikentscher, Leipzig. (GB. Nov.4; 1229) DM 750

BIBLES [Low German]

- **Biblia Dudesch.** Halberstadt, 8 Jul. 1522. *4th. Low German Bible.* 2 vols. Fo. Vol. I: sm. rusthole running through some ll. reprd. but with loss of letters, sm. repairs with some loss of text & woodcut, 2 paper flaws affecting letters, slight worming scattered through text after sig. h; Vol. II: sm. section (name?) cut from blank inner panel of title, sm. hole reprd. affecting 3 words, sm. rust hole, lge. piece torn from 1 lf. with partial loss of woodcut & some text, anr. tear reprd. slightly affecting text on verso, scattered minor worming from 07 to end, cont. blind-stpd. pig over wood bds., 4 brass cornerpieces on each cover, centre bosses, 2 brass clasps on each vol., restored, buckram boxes. [D. & M. 4185] (C. May 30; 12) *Bender.* £6,500

- **Biblia: Dat ys: De Gantze Hillige Schrifft.** Ed.:- J. Bugenhagen & V. Theoder. Trans.:- M. Luther. Magdeburg, 1545. Fo. Margins stained, 1st. 19 ll. with extended margins & corners (without loss), old entries on last blank lf. & lr. doubl., cont. blind-tooled leath. over wood bds, 6 (of 8) chiselled brass corner bosses, spine renewed, lacks clasps, upr. end-paper renewed; 1 old end-paper with dedication from 1560 mntd. (HK. May 15; 87) DM 4,400

BIBLES [Greek, Latin & German]

- **Biblia Sacra.** Hamburg, 1596. 5 pts. in 2 vols. Fo. Cont. vell. gt. (P. Oct.20; 50) £260

BIBLES [Hebrew]

- **Torah, Chamesh Megillot & Haftarot.** Brescia, Gershom Ben Moshe Soncino [Menzelan Soncin], 15 Kislev [5] 254 [24 Nov. 1493]. *6th. Printing of Pentateuch in Hebrew.* Unpaginated, catchwords & chapter nos., blank spaces left for woodcut head-pieces at openings of 5 books of Pentateuch, 1st. 3 & last 2 ll. blank, lacks register, blank part cut away after colophon, light dampstains thro.-out, fly-ll. from 14th. C. Hebrew MSS. on vell. (1 with commentary on Passover Haggadah), cont. (North Italian?) blind-tooled sheep over wood bds., sewn on 2 double bands, ruled in panel & diaper design stpd. with sm. crescent & floral tools, metal catches & stubs of clasps, leath. defect. on cover & part of spine, other wear, later name on fly-lf. crossed out. [H. 12572] (S. Oct.25; 457) *J.T.S.* £64,000

- **Neviim Rishonim Ve'Achronim.** Venice, 1521. 2 vols. 4to. 2 hf.-titles, slight staining, mod. hf. mor., marb. paper bds. (S. Oct.24; 110) *Alex.* £550

- **[Perush ha'Torah le-rav Rabeinu Moshe bar Nachman]. Pentateuch [with commentaries of Rashi, Ramban & Ibn Ezra], Megillot [with commentaries of Rashi & Ibn Ezra], Haftarot [with commentaries of Rashi & Kimchi].** Constantinople, 1522 [from colophon at end of Megillot]. In 2 vols. Fo. 1st. 3 pts. of Pentateuch (only), 308 ll. & 2 facs., a few ll. fragments only, loss of text to some ll., extensive repairs to worming thro.-out, staining & browning, mod. spr. hf. cf. gt. (SPB. Feb.1; 21) $3,000

- **Magna Biblia Rabbinica [with Targum & commentaries].** Commentaries:- Rashi & others. Venice, 1524-26. 4 vols. Fo. Vol. I: unpaginated, some passages censored, title margin torn & crudely reprd. not affecting text, some holes affecting some letters, staining, browned, 1 lf. towards end reprd., owners' sigs. on title & anr. p., Vol. II: unpaginated, some margins including title crudely reprd. without loss of text, stained thro.-out, Vol. III: unpaginated, title & 1st. p. in facs., some worming affecting some letters crudely reprd., some staining, trimmed thro.-out, Vol. IV: unpaginated, title reprd. without loss of text, edges frayed, last index lf. torn with loss of 4 words, slightly wormed & soiled; hf. leath., marb. paper bds. [D. & M. 5085] (S. Oct.24; 96) *Halprin.* £2,400

- **Magna Biblia Rabbinica [Former & Latter Prophets].** Commentaries:- Rashi, David Kimchi. Venice, 1547. 2 vols. Fo. Lr. margins reprd. in a few ll. without loss of text, lr. margins shaved, lightly stained, leath. & hf. leath., w.a.f. (S. Oct.25; 18) £800

- **Bible.** Antw., 1566. 8 vols. 12mo. Wide margins, compl. title & 3 hf. titles, lightly stained, 18th. C. cf., w.a.f. (S. Oct.25; 19) £1,100

- **Hamisha Humshei Tora; Tis Kenis Thiathikis Apanda [Hebrew Bible & New Testament].** Antw., 1573. Together 2 works in 1 vol. Sm. 8vo. 2nd. work lacks separate title-p., some stains, margins trimmed very close, with some loss to verse nos., later russ., slightly worn, crudely rebkd. (SG. Feb.9; 4) $500

- **Bible.** Antw., 1573-74. 16mo. Without Nikud, title & 3 hf.-titles, indexing tabs, cont. cf. over wood bds., clasps defect., worn, cont. notes on fly-ll.; from liby. of St. Lawrence of Brindisi 1559-1619, with his ownership note, & later inscrs. of friar Dominic of Padua & others, w.a.f. (S. Oct.25; 21) £850

- **[Bible. Mikra'ot Gedolot].** Venice, 1617-18. *5th. Edn. of the Rabbinic Bible.* 3 (of 4) pts. in 3 vols. Fo. Lacks the Torah, scattered dampstaining & margin worming, later tree cf., worn, crudely rebkd., loose. (SG. Feb.2; 158) $550

- **[Mikra'ot Gedolot].** Ed.:- Johannes Buxtorf, the Elder. Basel, 1620. *6th. Edn. of the Rabbinic Bible.* Pt. 4 only (of 4). Fo. Ketuvim only. (*Bound with:*) **BUXTORF, Johannes, the Elder - Tiberias Sive Commentarius Masorethicus Triplex.** [Basel, 1665]. Together 2 works in 1 vol. Fo. Some mild browning, cont. vell., soiled & shabby. (SG. Feb.2; 159) $175

- **[Bible with nikud].** Amst., 1635. 4to. 3 hf.-titles, 1st. title & last p. in facs., 1st. title torn & crudely reprd. without loss of text, browned & soiled, leath. gt. (S. Oct.24; 101) *Moriah.* £200

-- **Anr. Edn.** Amst., 1639. Slightly discold., loose, vell., worn. (S. Oct.24; 100) *Griner.* £750

- **Biblia Hebraica.** Amst., 1639. *3rd. Edn. by Menasseh ben Israel.* Cont. mor. gt., rubbed. (BBA. Jun.28; 115) *Landau.* £130

-- **Anr. Edn.** Ed.:- D.E. Jablonski. Berlin, 1699. 4to. L.P., wide margin, cont. leath., dtd. 1705 on lr. cover, remains of cont. gold tooling, owners monog. (I.D.L.S.P.) on upr. cover, 2 leath. clasps, 2 (of 4) brass bosses, clasps reprd. with old material. (BR. Apr.12; 1231) DM 1,000

-- **Anr. Edn.** Ed.:- Everado van der Hooght. Amst. & Utrecht, 1705. Slight soiling, a few ll. loose, cont. gt.-stpd. vell., rubbed. [D. & M. (Hebrew) 5141] (SPB. Feb.1; 23) $400

-- **Anr. Edn.** Ed.:- H. Opitz. Kiel, 1709. 4to. Some sigs. loose, bds., very spotted. (V. Oct.1; 3797) DM 650

- **Cinco Libros de la Ley Divina con las Aphtaroth.** Amst., 1724. Slight foxing, mod. leath. (S. Oct.24; 105) *Stein.* £680

- **Torah & Haftorot [with treatise on the Calendar by Selomoh de Olivera].** Ill.:- B. Picart &c. (titles). Amst., 1726. Hebrew text with Spanish treatise, short tear in margin of 1st. title not affecting engrs. or text, slightly discold., some foxing, mod. mor. (S. Oct.24; 106) *Alex.* £550

- **Bible.** Venice, 1739. 4to. With the Griselini plts. (not always present), slight traces of staining & worming, minor losses to a few ll., a few ll. detchd., contents loose in bdg., old panel. cf., very rubbed. (SPB. Feb.1; 25) $2,000

- **[Bible with treatise on grammar by Simcha Calimani].** Venice, 1739-41. 4 vols. 4to. Hebrew text with Italian explanations, title & 1st. p. in Vol. I reprd. with loss of part of column & 4 words, some staining, edges frayed, slight worming mostly in margins, a few ll. in Vol IV reprd. with loss of some letters, discold., trimmed with some loss of parts of letters, mod. mor. (S. Oct.24; 102) *Bragadin.* £180

- **Torah, 5 Megillot & Haftarot.** Venice, 1784. Verses of Pentateuch numbered in ink, slightly creased, orig. blind-tooled mor., slightly worn. (S. Oct.24; 107) *Gubbay.* £400

- **Karaite Bible.** Gozluv, 1840. 4to. Slight traces of browning & soiling, later velvet, slightly rubbed. (SPB. Feb.1; 26) $850

- **Biblia Hebräisch.** Berlin, 1931. *(850) on Bütten, for members of Soncino Soc.* Fo. Cold. title with removed owners stp., some slight spotting., orig. hf. leath., corners bumped. (HK. Nov.11; 3839) DM 800

- **Chamisha Chumshei Torah.** Berlin, 1933. *(850) on van Gelder paper.* Fo. Orig. vell., slightly soiled. (BBA. Oct.27; 341) *Quaritch.* £130

BIBLES [Hebrew & Latin]

- **Hebraica Biblia.** Trans.:- Sebastian Munster. Basel, 1546. *2nd. Edn.* Fo. Pagination uncertain, title multi stpd. & with MS. owners mark, slightly spotted & stained thro.-out, especially lr. margin, last 2 lr. corners defect., end-papers loose & defect., cont. pig over wood bds., roll-stp. blind-tooled decor., 2 brass clasps. (HT. May 8; 88) DM 3,200

BIBLES [Italian]

- **La Bibbia.** Trans.:- Giovanni Diodati. Geneva, 1607. *1st. Edn. of this trans.* Lge. 4to. Ink underlinings on some pp., cont. blind-stpd. decor. vell. [D. & M. 5598] (SG. Feb.9; 6) $425

BIBLES [Latin]

- **Biblia Latina.** [Cologne, Conrad Winter of Homborch], ca. 1469 (?). Vol. 1 (of 2). Fo. Wide margins, initials rubricated in blue & red, sometimes with margin extensions (especially on 1st. lf.), lacks table lf., worming, cont. blind-decor. cf., spine renewed & worn, traces of clasps. (HD. Jun.26; 7) Frs. 7,500

-- **Anr. Edn.** Rome, after 15 Mar. 1471. Pt. 2 only (of 2). Fo. Wide margin, lge. hand-painted cold. letters, lacks 1st. lf., 3 other ll., & table, lacks corner of 1 lf., extended with old paper & text

BIBLES [Latin] *-Contd.*

supplied in MS., sm. MS. inscrs. on some pp., 1st. 30 ll. remargined, recovered with lf. of 15th. C. gradual with mus. notat. [HC 3051; Goff B-535] (HD. Jan.30; 2) Frs. 7,200
– – **Anr. Edn.** Venice, Reynaldus de Novimagio & Theodorus de Reynburch, 1478. Fo. 2 lge. & 2 smaller historiated initials & approximately 175 other initials supplied in cols. & gold, a few with floral extenders into margin, other initials supplied is red or blue, lacks final blank, paper losses reprd. at inner margins of 1st. 2 quires, a few letters of text affected on fo. a2, brown stain affecting 1st. few ll., some light staining & spotting elsewhere, sm. liby. stps. at beginning & end, mod. blind-stpd. cf., rubbed. [BMC V, 254; Goff B-556; HC 3070*] (SPB. Dec.14; 7) $4,200
– – **Anr. Edn.** Nuremb., Anton Koberger, 6 Aug. 1479. *3rd. Koberger Edn.* Lge. fo. Rubricated in red & blue, lge. 1st. initial painted in gold on blue ground, various cold. leaves & fruit in margin, table lf. cut out & pasted to front end-paper, cont. stpd. pig over wood bds., traces of clasps; from Fondation Furstenberg-Beaumesnil. [HC 3072; BMC II, 417; Goff B564] (HD. Nov.16; 34) Frs. 40,000
– – **Anr. Edn.** Venice, Octavianus Scotus, 31 May 1480. 4to. Initials painted in blue or red, 2 1st. initials painted in various cols. & gt., 2 medallions with painted scenes, lacks blank 1st. lf., cont. blind-stpd. cf. over wood bds., spine painted in red, traces of clasps; from Fondation Furstenberg-Beaumesnil. [BMC V, 276; Goff B570] (HD. Nov.16; 65) Frs. 8,500
– **Biblia Latina (cum Postillis Nicolai de Lyra).** [Venice, J. Herbort de Seligenstadt for Colonia, Jenson et Socii, 31 Jul. 1481]. Fo. Lge. copy, 'Proverbs' to 'Malachi' only, last lf. mntd., with some loss of text, last 3 ll. reprd., later bds., vell. back; the Walter Goldwater copy. [BMC V, 301; Goff B-611] (SG. Dec.1; 70) $475
– **Biblia Latina.** Nuremb., Koberger, 31.XII.1482. Fo. Rubricated, many initials in red or blue pen & some multi-cold., lacks 1 blank at beginning & end & 1st. 1 text ll. mispaginated, last sigs. defect. with loss, 10 text ll. with sm. margin tears, 1 lf. with corner tear & loss, slightly stained, 16th. C. blind-tooled pig over wood bds., defect. [H. 3084; BMC II, 424; Goff B575] (HK. Nov.8; 112) DM 1,600
– – **Anr. Edn.** Venice, J. Herbort de Seligenstadt, 30 Apr. 1484. 4to. Lacks a1, register & list of Hebrew names heavily stained, with some tears very slightly affecting text, some dampstaining, str.-grd. russ.; the Walter Goldwater copy. [BMC V, 304; Goff B-580] (SG. Dec.1; 68) $600
– – **Anr. Copy.** 4to. N.T. rubricated thro.-out, 1st. 2 ll. & lf. a8 in photostat, last lf. of 'Interpretationes' badly frayed at margins, many headlines cropped, some dampstains, entirely disbnd.; the Walter Goldwater copy. [BMC V, 304; Goff B-580] (SG. Dec.1; 67) $550
– – **Anr. Copy.** 4to. Rubricated, initials painted in red or blue, lacks 1st. lf., 2 ll. torn without loss of text, 2 ll. stained, 1st. & last ll. remntd. [HC 3091; BMC V, 304; Goff B580] (HD. Mar.21; 42) Frs. 7,500
– – **Anr. Edn.** Basle, Nicolaus Kesler, 9 Jan. 1491. Fo. N.T. rubricated, thumb-tabs, last lf. torn & reprd. with loss of a few letters, blank piece torn from title-p., some worning at beginning affecting text slightly, a few stains, some quires sprung, cont. blind-stpd. pig over wood bds., lacks clasps, worn. [Goff B591] (S. Nov.17; 7) *Tzakas.* £500
– **Bible.** Strassburg, [Johann (Reinhard) Grueninger], 26 Apr. 1497. Fo. Rubricated, lacks title & last 20 ll., table defect., stained, bnd. at end 16 additional ll. sigd. JJ6 & LL4 'Tabula Auctoritatum biblie', old vell. over wood bds., very worn, w.a.f. (SPB. Dec.13; 631) $650
– **Bible [with the Postilla of Nicolaus de Lyra, etc.].** Nuremb., Anton Koberger, 6 Sep. 1497. Pt. 2 only (of 4). Fo. Capitals, initial-strokes, paragraph marks, & underscores supplied in red, Do4 reprd., corner off Do5, some stains, early marginalia, old vell. [BMC II, 443; Goff B-618] (SG. Oct.27; 157) $600
– **Biblia Latina.** Ed.:– Petrus Angelus de Monte Ulmi. Venice, Hieronymous de Paganinis, 7 Sep. 1497. Lacks 1st. 12 ll., but with F8 blank, many sm. capital letters illuminated in gt. & cols., other capitals supplied in red or blue thro.-out, ruled in red, 1st. lf. rather defect. with some text missing, outer upr. blank corner of last lf. reprd., 19th. C. vell., antique-style, sm. damage to upr. cover, 2 clasps. [BMC V 459; Goff B601; Hain 3123] (S. May 10; 230) *Watson.* £540
– – **Anr. Copy.** Lacks register & 2 or 3 other ll., minor tears to a few ll., early wood bds., covered with elab. panel. cf., 1 metal clasp impft.; the Walter Goldwater copy, w.a.f. [BMC V, 459; Goff B-601] (SG. Dec.1; 69) $500
– **Biblia Latina. Secunda par Lyre [Esdras-Ecclesiasticus].** [Nuremb., Anton Koberger, 1497]. Lge. fo. Wide margins, some foxing, some oil-stains along top margins, cont. pig. on heavy wood bds., elab. blind-stpd., 2 metal clasps. [Goff B619] (SG. Feb.9; 2) $1,000
– **Biblia....** Venice, Hieronymus de Paganinis, 1497. Title-p. reprd., mod. vell. (HD. Jun.29; 24) Frs. 3,000
– **Biblia cum Concordantijs Veteris et Novi Testamenti.** Ed.:– Albertus Castellanus. [Venice, 15 Oct. 1519]. Pagination jumps ll. 424-445, cut slightly close, 1st. & last ll. with heavy old spotting, sm. worm trace at end, title corner stpd., 17th. C. pig over wood bds., decor. roll-stp., gold-tooled, 2 clasps, episcopal supralibros. (V. Oct.1; 3709) DM 800
– **Biblia cum Concordantijs Veteris et Noui Testamenti et Sacrorum Canonum.** Lyon, 3 Mar. 1525. Fo. Lacks final blank, a few light margin stains, bds., covered with fragment of late 15th. C. liturgical MS. (S. Nov.17; 8) *Tzakas.* £650
– **Biblia Sacra.** Paris, 1528. Cont.-style stpd. cf. by Petit; from Fondation Furstenberg-Beaumesnil. (HD. Nov.16; 99) Frs. 1,900
– **Bibliorum Opus Sacrosanctum Vulgatis.** Ill.:– G. Leroy & others. Lyon, 1532. Fo. Title with a few wormholes, Solomon woodcut with ink marks, some worming occasionally affecting a few words of text, short tear in 1 lf., a few words inked out, mod. vell. (C. May 30; 13) *Snelling.* £520
– **Bibliorvm Opvs Sacrosanctvm Vvlgatis quide[m] Characteribus ....** Lyon, 1536. Fo. Lacks unnumbered ll. 3-6 at beginning, title verso & last ll. with notes & sigd., some notes & underlining, 1st. ll. slightly soiled, browned near end in upr. corner, last ll. slightly wormed, cont limp vell., lacks ties. (HK. Nov.8; 113) DM 400
– **Vtriusque Testamenti iuxta Vvlgatam Translationem ....** Ill.:– after H. Holbein. Lyon, 1538. *1st. Edn.* Fo. Title soiled, stpd. & with owner's mark, lightly browned thro.-out, some foxing or staining, some slight margin defects., some repairs, parch., ca. 1600, cover slightly soiled & bumped, spine & end-papers renewed. (HK. Nov.8; 114) DM 9,000
– **Biblia Sacrosancta Testamenti Veteris & Novi....** Ill.:– after Holbein. Lugduni, 1544. Fo. Margin dampstained, 1 p. reprd., 18th. C. marb. roan, spine decor. (HD. Mar.21; 10) Frs. 2,700
– **Biblia.** Paris, 1545. O.T. only. 16th. C. cf., polychrome mosaic decor, spine renewed, very rubbed; from Fondation Furstenberg-Beaumesnil. (HD. Nov.16; 161) Frs. 4,200
– – **Anr. Copy.** 2 vols. Faint red ink ruling thro.-out, lightly browned & with some slight spotting, 1st. lf. of 2nd. vol. with extended lr. corner, last lf. verso mntd., cont. cf., blind-tooled decor., corner fleurons, gold-tooled centre-piece, gt. spine, reprd., slightly spotted & worn. (HT. May 8; 89) DM 1,400
– **Biblia Sacra.** 1549. *2nd. Edn.* Fo. Ruled, margins decor., 17th. C. spr. cf. (HD. Jun.29; 25) Frs. 1,250
– **Biblia Sacrosancta.** Lyon, 1551. Fo. Title soiled & cleanly torn, margin of last lf. torn away, old cf., worn. (CSK. Nov.4; 92) £75
– – **Anr. Copy.** Title soiled & cleanly torn, margin of last lf. torn away, old cf., worn. (CSK. Oct.7; 49) £70
– **Biblia Sacrosancta ad Hebraicam ....** Basel, 1551. Title with tear in lr. margin, 1st. 2 ll. with old entries, some slight spotting at beginning, cont. blind-tooled pig over wood bds., defect. (HK. May 15; 83) DM 400
– **Biblia Sacra.** Ill.:– Bernard Salomon. Lyon, 1554. Lacks last lf. blank & next last with ornament, Jansenist mor., gt. inner & outer dentelle, sigd. by Chambolle-Duru, marb. end-papers. (D. Nov.23; 77) DM 4,000
– – **Anr. Edn.** Ed.:– R. Estienne. Ill.:– Bernard Salomon. Lyons, 1556. *2nd. De Tournes Edn.* Fo. Title with minor wormholes & sm. repair, anr. lf. reprd., a few ll. at front & end rehinged, a few blank margins wormed, mod. decor. cf., spine rubbed. [D. & M. 6138] (C. May 30; 14) *Snelling.* £260
– – **Anr. Edn.** Ill.:– after P. Vase. Lyon, 1562. Lacks title lf., some old lining, lightly browned, slightly foxed, some margins strengthened, late 17th. C. leath., slightly wormed & rubbed, spine renewed, 1 (of 2) brass clasps. (HK. Nov.8; 115) DM 480
– – **Anr. Edn.** Ill.:– J. Annan. [Frankfurt], 1585. Vol. 2. Lacks last lf. with printers mark, 1 woodcut cold. in, some old MS. underlining, 18th. C. leath., bumped & rubbed, upr. cover brkn. at jnt., lr. cover jnt. defect. (D. Nov.23; 78) DM 350
– **Biblia Sacra Vulgatae Editionis Sixti V. & Clementis VIII. pont. max Auctoritate recognita.** Paris, 1666-65. *New Edn.* 2 vols. in 1. 4to. Cont. black leath., gt. 'à La Du Seuil', gold decor., gt. arms supralibros spine slightly defect. (R. Oct.12; 2225) DM 1,000
– **Biblia Sacrae.** Venice, 1697. *Vulgate Edn.* 4to. (in 8's). Cont. vell., wrinkled, partly loose in bdg. (SG. Feb.9; 17) $100
– **Biblia Latina.** Ed.:– Schwenke. Leipzig, 1913-14 & 1923. *Facs. Reproduction of 42 line Gutenberg Bible 1455-56. (287) on Bütten.* 2 vols. & supp. vol. Fo. Painted initials, cover, end-papers & doubl. slightly spotted, in supp. vol. end-paper, title & hf.-title with paper defect. in margin, hand-bnd. orig. pig, blind-tooled, by O. Dorfner Weimar & hf. vell.; Hauswedell coll. (H. May 23; 439) DM 8,000
– – **Anr. Edn.** New Jersey & N.Y., 1961. *The 'Cooper Square Gutenberg Bible', (1000).* 2 vols. Lge. fo. Hf. mor. (B. Oct.4; 268) Fls. 1,900
– **Biblia Latina. [Gutenberg Bible].** N.Y. & Brussels, 1968. *Facs. Reprint of [Mainz], ca. 1455-56 Edn.* Sm. fo. 8 cold. reproductions from MS. books of Hours in vol.3, cl., s.-c. (S. Apr.9; 195) *Kubicek.* £120

BIBLES [Latin & French]
– **La Sainte Bible.** Notes:– Dom Calmet. Paris, 1748. 14 vols. 4to. Cont. marb. cf., spines decor., slight defects; from Château des Noës Liby. (HD. May 25; 4) Frs. 2,700

BIBLES [Latin & German]
– **Biblia Sacra Vulgatae Editionis. Bible oder Heilige Schrift.** Ed.:– T.A. Erhard. Augsburg, 1726. *2nd. Edn.* 2 pts. in 1 vol. Fo. Cont. blind-tooled pig. over wood, 1 brass clasp (of 2). [D. & M. 4229 & 6259] (VG. Nov.30; 913) Fls. 500
– – **Anr. Edn.** Constance, 1763. *Vulgate Edns.* 4 vols. in 2. Fo. Some foxing, elab. blind-stpd. leath. on boards, mor. & metal clasps, each vol. lacking metal for 1 clasp. (CBA. Dec.10; 440) $200
– **Biblia Germanico-Latina. – Biblia Sacra Vulgatae ed. jussu Sixti V. Pontif. Max. recognita.** Ed.:– P. Germani Cartier. Konstanz, 1763. Fo. German-Latin parallel text, lacks 65 copperplts., some mispagination, some light foxing, some slight worming, cont. marb. leath. gt. decor., rubbed. (HK. May 16; 1365) DM 620

BIBLES [Polyglot]
– **[Biblia 1. Hebraica, 2. Samaritana ... 7. Arabica, quibus textus originales totius Scripturae Sacrae ... exhibentur].** Paris, 1635. Vol. VIII only: 'Esdras-Ecclesiasticus' (of 10). Fo. Some minor discolouration, cont. Parisian red mor., spine gt. in compartments, 2 borders à la Du Seuil on covers, decor., arms of Henri-Auguste de Lorenie, comte de Brienne, rubbed & marked; 18th. C. bkplt. of Inner Library, the bequest of Thos. Eyre. [D. & M. 1442] (S. Nov.17; 6) *Tzakas.* £150
–**Biblia Sacra Polyglotta.** Ed.:– Brian Walton. L., 1657. 6 vols. Fo. Old cf., worn, ex-liby. [Wing B2797] (CSK. Jan.13; 107) £380
– **Biblia, dat is de Gantsche H. Schrifture.** Ill.:– after Picart & others. Amst., 1664. Lge. fo. In Hebrew (Greek in N.T.), Engl., German, Latin, Fr. & Dutch, copperplts. apparently inserted from early 18th. C. source, first few ll. badly chewed,

outer top margins stained thro.-out, disbnd., w.a.f. (SG. Feb.9; 13) $200
- **Biblia Sacra Quadrilinguia Veteris Testamenti Hebraici** .... Trans.:– Chr. Reineccio. Preface:– S. Deylingii. Leipzig, 1750. Fo. Hebrew-Grk.-Latin-German parallel text, title with old owners mark, 1st. ll. lightly frayed in margin & dog-eared, lightly spotted, cont. vell., lr. outer corner of upr. cover defect. (HK. May 16; 1369) DM 540

BIBLES [Romansch]
- **La Sacra Bibla.** Scuol [Lower Engadine], 1679; 1678. Sm. fo. (in 6s). N.T. title in historiated border, browned, few marginal repairs, lacks general title & last 4-pp. of Apocrytha, cont. blind-tooled & panel. cf., worn, headband loose, metal centre & cornerpieces, clasps. [D. & M. 7688] (SG. Apr.19; 35) $175
- **La Sacra Biblia quai ais tout la Sonchia Scrittura: dal Velg et Nouf Testament cun l'aguinta dall'Apocrifa.** Trans.:– J.A. Vulpio & J. Dorta. Scuol, 1743. *2nd. Edn.* 4 pts. in 1 vol. Fo. Some light spotting, minimal soiling, some light staining in upr. margin in middle, cont. leath. over wood bds., 8 corner & 2 centre brass bosses, clasps brkn., end.lf. & following end-paper with 19th. C. rhaetoromanisch entries. [D. & M. 7689] (R. Oct.12; 2228) DM 1,600
- **Biblia o vero la Soinchia Scritüra del Velg Testamaint.** Trans.:– J.A. Vulpius. Chur, 1815. Some slight spotting, cont. owners entry in Ladino, cont. leath., clasps, 1 jnt. & clasps reprd. & partly renewed. (HT. May 8; 93) DM 560

BIBLES [Russian]
- **Bible [Gospels, with Calender etc.].** N.p., [dedication dtd. 1809.]. Fo. Impft., brass on wood bds., spine with 5 chased repousse emblems in compartments, each cover with chased repousse silver centrepiece & 4 chased repousse cornerpieces, 1 (of 2) cast silver clasps, with pewter hinge, silver fittings dtd. 1822, upr. centrepiece defect., lr. cornerpiece defect., other lesser defects. (SG. Feb.9; 46) $700

BIBLES [Spanish]
- **Biblia. Que es, los Sacros Libros del Vieio y Nuevo Testamento.** Ed.:– Cypriano de Valera. Amst., 1602. *2nd. Edn.* 3 pts. in 1 vol. Fo. Inserted extra lf. 2S3, without lf. of address sometimes inserted after title, sm. hole or tear affecting letters in folios 2-7, short tear in margin of folio 8 & S1, tiny rusthole in P3, cont. Dutch vell., blind-stpd. central ornament on covers, upr. cover loose & worn. [D. & M. 8475] (S. May 10; 227) *Sawyer.* £420
- **Biblia en Lengua Española. Traduzida Palabra por Palabra de la Verdad Hebrayca ... Vista y examinada por el Officio de la Inquisicion ... y ahora de nuevo corregida ....** Amst., 5421 [1661]. *1st. 8vo. Edn.* 3 vols. Some browning & dampstaining, early mott. cf., chafed, 2 spines badly worn, margins trimmed. [D. & M. 8481] (SG. Feb.2; 21) $800
- **Antiguo Testamento [&] Neuvo Testamento.** Valencia, 1791-98. 10 vols. Fo. Cont. mott. cf. (SPB. Dec.13; 630) $550

BIBLES [Tatar]
- **Sefer Tirgum Nevi'im [Yehoshua, Shofetim, Shmuel, & Melakhim].** Goslov [Yevpatoria], 1841. 4to. Title in Hebrew text in Tatar in vocalized Hebrew characters, some mild browning or dampstaining, cont. blind-tooled pol. cf., owner's name (in Russian) blind-stpd. on upr. cover, worn. (SG. Feb.2; 160) $300

BIBLIANA *(Chronologically by Language)*

BIBLIANA [Dualla]
- **Iyala Ya Bwam. E. Tatilabe na Mattiyn. Boambu bo Dualla.** Bethel, Cameroons, 1848. Hf. cf. (S. Dec.13; 160) *Edwards.* £160

BIBLIANA [Dutch]
- **Der Zielen Lusthof, Inh. I Het Leven ende Lijden onses Heeren Iesv Christi. M. Meditatien daer op uyt L. de Ponte. II De Wercken der Apostelen. III De Openbaringe van St. Jan.** Ill.:– C. v. Sichem. Loven, 1629. Browned, title defect., slightly stained at beginning, partly loose, cont. vell., soiled. (VS. Dec.9; 1353) Fls. 550
- **Historie des Ouden en Nieuwen Testaments.** Ill.:– after Elliger. Amst., 1700. 2 vols. Fo. Wide margin,

cont. blind-stpd. vell. [1st. bdg.], centre medal, decor. (HD. Dec.16; 2) Frs. 2,000
- - **Anr. Copy.** 2 vols. Fo. Hf. cf., slight defects. (B. Jun.21; 513) Fls. 1,400
- - **Anr. Copy.** 2 vols. in 1. Fo. Some stains, cont. cf., spine gt., covers rubbed, hinges weak. (VS. Jun.7; 948) Fls. 850
- **Taferelen der voornaamste Geschiedenissen van het Oude en Nieuwe Testament.** Ill.:– Hoet, Houbraken, Picart. The Hague, 1728. Vols. I-II (of 3). Fo. Engraved title-vigs., frontis., dedication lf. & 142 engraved plts., cont. catspaw cf., gt. panels, borders & centre decor., jnts. weak. (CH. May 24; 27) Fls. 900
- **Kern des Bibels.** The Hague, 1750. 42 x 29mm., miniature book. Cont. red mor. gt., cont. fitted case, recovered with plain paper & inscr. by owner in 1882; van Veen coll. (S. Feb.28; 184) £500
- - **Anr. Copy.** 41 x 27mm., miniature book. Cont. red mor. gt., van Veen coll. (S. Feb.28; 185) £320
- - **Anr. Copy.** 45 x 30mm. Miniature Book. Cont. gt.-decor. cf., spine gt., slightly defect., silver clasp. (VG. Sep.14; 980) Fls. 1,300
- - **Anr. Copy.** 45 x 30mm. Miniature Book. Cont. red mor., richly gt. (VG. Nov.30; 635) Fls. 1,100
- - **Anr. Edn.** 's-Gravenhage, 1751. 47 x 30mm. Miniature Book. Cont. str.-grd. mor. (VG. Sep.14; 981) Fls. 1,500

BIBLIANA [English]
- **The Bible in Miniature; or a Concise History of the Old & New Testaments.** 1778. 45 x 30mm. Miniature Book. 1 plt. soiled, lacks Q1, A1 torn, orig. red mor. gt., covers with scared monog. blocked onto mor. inlays, rubbed. (CSK. Jan.13; 175) £50
- **A Curious Hieroglyphick Bible; or, Select Passages in the Old & New Testaments.** L., 1788. *6th. Edn.* 12mo. Orig. pict. bds., hole in front end-paper. (SG. Dec.8; 195) $275
- **Evangelical Expositor.** Ed.:– Thomas Haweis. L., 1821. 2 vols. in 20. Tall fo. Over 1,800 18th. C. copperplts. & 19th. C. steel & wood engrs. mntd. on blank interleaves, qtr. mor., scuffed. (SG. Feb.9; 112) $175
- **History of the Bible.** Ill.:– L.E. L[andon]. L., 1831. 49 x 42mm. Miniature Book. Orig. roan, fitted folder & hf. mor. case. (S. Dec.20; 621) *Fletcher.* £120
- **Illustrations of the Old & New Testaments.** Ed.:– Hobart Caunter. Ill.:– Westall & Martin. L., 1837. L.P.?, 144 wood engrs., some foxing, hf. mor., very worn. (SG. Feb.9; 151) $100
- **Genesis.** Ill.:– Paul Nash. Nones. Pr., 1924. *(375) numbered.* 4to. Orig. bds., unc., unopened. (S. Nov.21; 201) *Blackwells.* £220
- **The Book of Jonah.** Ill.:– David Jones. Gold. Cock. Pr., 1926. *(175) numbered.* 4to. Orig. cl., unc., spine slightly discold., d.-w. lacks backstrip. (S. Nov.21; 217) *Blackwells.* £250
- - **Anr. Copy.** 4to. Orig. cl., unopened, d.-w. torn, with label 'Ex Libris Golden Cockeral Press M.G., R.G.'. (S. Nov.21; 218) *Joseph.* £220
- **The Book of Job.** Ill.:– V. Angelo. [San Franc., Grabhorn Pr., 1926]. *(210) sigd. by artist.* Fo. Hf. cl. & decor. bds., s.-c. worn; the V. Angelo copy, frontis. sigd., titled & dtd. 1926 by Angelo, a sigd. pull of the frontis. laid in loose, the verso having a double-p. with ills. to the Book of Ruth, both with ptd. titles not present in the book version, 2 xerox copies of a British Museum letter inserted. (CBA. Oct.1; 147) $180
- **The Book of Ruth.** Ill.:– V. Angelo. [San Franc., Grabhorn Pr., 1926]. *(150) sigd. by artist.* Hand-drawn initials & borders, specially bnd. in decor. & gt.-ruled mor., spine faded, s.-c. slightly darkened; the V. Angelo copy. (CBA. Oct.1; 150) $400
- **The Lamentations of Jeremiah.** Ill.:– Blair Hughes-Stanton. Gregy. Pr., 1933. *(250) numbered.* Sm. fo. Blind-stpd. lev., slightly rubbed. (SG. Jan.12; 145) $400
- **The Book of Esther.** Ill.:– V. Angelo. N.Y., Golden Cross Pr., 1935. *(135) sigd. by artist.* Hand-illuminated in gold, Duchnes announcement laid in loose, blind-stpd. niger, slightly darkened, s.-c.; the V. Angelo copy, 6 fo. trial ll. laid in. (CBA. Oct.1; 136) $225
- **The Book of Job. – The Book of Ruth.** Prefaces:– Mary Ellen Chase. Ill.:– Arthur Szyk. N.Y., Ltd. Edns. Cl., 1946; 1947. *(1950) numbered, sigd. by*

artist. Together 2 vols. Tall 4to. 8 mntd. cold. plts. in each vol., mor., gt.-pict. bds., unc., unopened, 1 spine with sm. tears, orig. s.-c.'s. (SG. May 17; 162) $150
- **The Book of Ruth.** Preface:– Mary Ellen Chase. Ill.:– Arthur Szyk. N.Y., Ltd. Edns. Cl., 1947. *(1950) numbered & sigd. by artist.* 4to. Hf. mor., gt.-pict. white bds., cellotape repairs to s.-c. (SG. Feb.2; 115) $175
- **Book of Job.** Ill.:– Frank Brangwyn. Leigh-on-Sea, 1948. *(110) on H.M.P.* 4to. 33 orig. etched plts., each sigd. by artist, hf. vell. gt., s.-c. (P. May 17; 333) *Marks.* £150
- **The Book of Ruth & Boaz according to the King James Version of the Holy Bible.** Ill.:– V. Angelo. N.Y., Pr. of Valenti Angelo, 1949. *(150) sigd. by Angelo.* Crease to rear pastedown, slight soiling to bds.; the V. Angelo copy. (CBA. Oct.1; 365) $120
- **The Holkham Bible Picture Book.** Intro. & Commentary:– W.O. Hassall. Dropmore Pr., 1954. Orig. hf. mor. (CSK. Sep.30; 13) £65
- - **Anr. Copy.** (S. May 1; 399) *Bennet & Kerr.* £50
- - **Anr. Copy.** Three-qtr. red niger mor. & vell., slight discoloration to vell., scuffing at extreme top edge of upr. cover; Marymount College copy. (CBA. Mar.3; 244) $150
- **The Bookes of Genesis to Deuteronomie, King James Version. Printed by Robert Barker. London, 1611.** Preface:– Charles Hamilton. 1958. Fo. Mor. gt. (LH. Sep.25; 462) $100
- **The Book of Jonah.** Ill.:– V. Angelo. N.p., Hammer Creek Pr., 1960. *(40) on Japanese fancy paper.* Decor. wraps. over bds., slight wear, d.-w.; the V. Angelo copy. (CBA. Oct.1; 214) $190
- **The Book of Ruth.** N.p., [Hammer Creek Pr.], 1960. *(35) hand-ptd.* Japanese-style bnd. wraps.; inscr. by John Fass to V. Angelo. (CBA. Oct.1; 215) $160
- **The Book of Proverbs.** Ill.:– V. Angelo. N.Y., Ltd. Edns. Cl., 1963. *(1500) sigd. by artist.* Monthly Letter laid in loose, gt.-decor. cf., spine slightly darkening, ends lightly scuffed; the V. Angelo copy, with note & pres. blind-stp. on colophon, T.L.s. from Helen Macy with excerpt from anr. laid in loose. (CBA. Oct.1; 258) $150
- **The Book of Jonah.** Ill.:– David Jones. Clover Hill Edns., 1979. *(410) roman-numbered. (100) on H.M.P. with a set of the wood engrs. on japon.* Prospectus loosely inserted, the extra set of ills. in pocket in lr. cover, orig. mor.-bkd. bds., s.-c.; 3 letters & a receipt from Douglas Cleverdon loosely inserted. (S. Nov.21; 187) £160
See— BIBLES [English] – BIBLIANA [English]

BIBLIANA [French]
- **Histoire du Vieux et du Nouveau Testament.** Amst., 1700. 2 vols. Fo. Some slight browning & foxing, cont. spr. leath., gt. spine, inner & outer dentelle, slightly worn, corners reprd. (HK. Nov.9; 1554) DM 1,000
- **[Les Figures de la Bible].** Ill.:– L.A. de Marne. [Paris, ca. 1750]. 3 vols. Lge. ob. fo. 481 (of 500) plts., some cut to margin & mntd., cont. hf. cf., spines gt., some defects. (VG. Nov.30; 926) Fls. 500
- **Sainte Bible, mise en Vers par J.P.J. du Bois.** The Hague, 1762. 52 x 33mm., miniature book. Cont. cf. gt., slightly worn; van Veen coll. (S. Feb.28; 204) £340
- **L'Ancien et le Nouveau Testament représentés en Cinq Cens Tableaux gravés d'après les Desseins de Raphael et autres Grands Maîtres.** Ill.:– L.A. de Marne. Paris, 1763. Fo. Very soiled at beginning, cont. marb. leath. gt. (BR. Apr.12; 1234) DM 2,100
- **Bible en Estampes, à l'Usage de la Jeunesse.** Paris, 1817. Ob. 8vo. Engraved frontis., pict. title-p. & 18 plts., hand-cold., orig. ptd. bds., spine slightly rubbed; van Veen coll. (S. Feb.28; 39) £90

BIBLIANA [French & Hebrew]
- **Le Livre d'Esther.** Ill.:– Arthur Szyk. Paris, [1925]. *(775) numbered.* Sm. 4to. Ptd. wraps., unc. (SG. Feb.2; 117) $425

BIBLIANA [German]
- **Die Bergpredigt Jesu Christ.** Text:– G. Hewitt. Trans.:– M. Luther. [Leipzig, 1908]. *De Luxe Edn., (25) on vell.* Orig. hand-bnd. suede. (H. Nov.23; 906a) DM 5,200

BIBLIANA [German] -*Contd.*

- **Das Buch Judith.** Trans.:– M. Luther. Ill.:– L. Corinth. Berlin, Pan Pr., 1910. *De Luxe Edn., (60) on Japan, sigd. by artist.* Fo. Orig. black hand-bnd. mor., gold-tooled, gold decor. inner dentelles, by Carl Sonntag jun., Leipzig, scratched. (H. Nov.24; 1454) DM 6,200
- **Ruth.** Trans.:– M. Luther. Ill.:– Luise Kleukens. [Darmstadt, Ernst Ludwig Pr.], 1914. *(50) on vell.* Orig. hand-bnd. mor. gt., wear, light stain. (H. Nov.23; 1038) DM 4,000
- **Das Evangelium S. Johannis.** Trans.:– M. Luther. Ill.:– Kay H. Nebel. Frankfurt, 1920. *(50) De Luxe Edn. on Japan.* Hand-cold. woodcuts, vell., gold decor., silk end-papers, by Ernst Rehbein, Darmstadt. (R. Apr.3; 281) DM 550
- **Ecclesiastes oder der Prediger Salomo.** Ill.:– M. Behmer. [Berlin, 1920]. *De Luxe Edn., (250) on Zanders-Bütten, sigd. by artist.* 4to. Gold-heightened initials, lightly browned, hand-bnd. orig. vell., gold decor., by Bruno Scheer, Berlin; Franz Goldstein ex-libris. (H. Nov.24; 1365) DM 2,200
- **Die Heiligen Bücher des Alten Bundes.** Trans.:– L. Goldschmidt. [Berlin, 1921-25]. *De Luxe Edn., (12).* 3 vols. Lge. 4to. Hand-bnd. orig. mor., gold-tooled, leath. onlay, gt. inner & outer dentelles, by Schnabel, Berlin. (H. Nov.23; 909) DM 2,600
- **Das Buch Judith.** Ill.:– Doris Homann. Berlin, 1922. Fo. On Zanders-Bütten, hand-bnd. orig. vell., by Reinhold Maetzke, Berlin; Lazarus Goldschmidt ex-libris inside cover. (GB. May 5; 2255) DM 2,400
- **Saul und David. Die Beiden Bücher Samuelis.** Ill.:– L. Corinth. 1923. *(300) numbered. This one of (50) numbered De Luxe Edn.* Fo. Without supp. suite & sigd. etching on Japan, printers mark sigd. by artist, 28 orig. lithos. (23 full-p.), orig. red mor. gt. (GB. May 5; 2289) DM 1,700
- – **Anr. Copy.** 1st. Series only. Fo. Lacks sigd. etching, orig. red mor., s.-c. (HK. Nov.11; 3480) DM 850
- **Das Buch Ruth.** Ill.:– M. Liebermann. 1924. *(200) on Bütten. (150) numbered on Bütten.* Fo. This copy unnumbered, 9 orig. lithos., including 5 full-p. lithos. sigd. by artist, slightly foxed, orig. linen, gt. cover vig. (GB. May 5; 2882) DM 2,700

BIBLIANA [Greek]
- **Biblioglyphae Sive Icones Biblicae, Arte Calcographica, et Poetica ... Biblische Figuren/darinnen ...–Zweyter Theil. – Dritter Theil.** Heidelberg, 19 Mar. 1671. 3 pts. in 1 vol. Cont. marb. leath., gt. spine & outer dentelle, flowered end-paper, black & gold on burgundy ground, orig. leath. s.-c., lined with patterned paper, decor. (GF. Nov.12; 686) Sw. Frs. 3,800
- **Die Wiener Genesis. Cod. Vindob. Theol. Graec. 31.** Ed.:– H. Gerstinger. Wien, [1931]. *Facs. Edn.* Text & facs. vol. Sm. fo. Hf. vell., 1 loose. (H. May 22; 35) DM 500

BIBLIANA [Hebrew]
- **Neviim Rishonim.** Commentary:– David ben Joseph Kimchi. Soncino, [Joshua Solomon Soncino], 6 Heshvan 5246 [15 Oct. 1485]. *1st. Edn.* Fo. Lacks 1st. lf., sigd. by censors 'Laurentia Frangella, 1575 (?)' & 2 others, without censorship of text, a few prelim. & final ll. soiled & slightly browned, traces of stps. on 1 lf., cf.-bkd. bds, rubbed. [Steinschneider 3; Goff Heb-22] (SPB. Jun.26; 6) $25,000
- **Neviim Achronim.** Commentary:– David ben Joseph Kimchi. [Soncino, Joshua Solomon Soncino], ca. 1486. *1st. Edn.* Fo. Lacks 3 ll., uncensored, space left at beginning of all books for 1st. words to be written in by hand, many margin additions in early hand from Ibn Ezra commentary, some chapter & verse nos., vowel-points & accents, opening words of books & other marginalia, made from 2 copies at early date (?), some soiling & staining, a few minor margin repairs, no bdg. stated; Hochschule für die Wissenschaft des Judenthums stps. [Steinschneider 4; Goff Heb-24] (SPB. Jun.26; 7) £22,500
- **Yona ha-Navi Meforash / Id est: Jonas Vates Expositus [with Targum Jonathan, greater & lesser Masora, & various commentaries].** Frankfurt, 1697. Sm. 4to. Browned & dampstained, cellotape repair to title, last lf, remargined, mod. cl.-bkd. bds., worn. (SG. Feb.2; 161) $120
- **Yad Kol Bo.** Ed.:– Perachya Ben David Lida. Frankfurt, 1727. Fo. A few ll. detchd. with frayed margins, some browning & slight staining, minor repairs, cont. diced cf., worn. (SPB. Feb.1; 75) $850

BIBLIANA [Hebrew & Latin]
- **Pentateuchus Hebraicus Latinus.** Venecia, 1551. 4to. Vell. (DS. Mar.23; 2129) Pts. 150,000

BIBLIANA [Kalispel]
- **Lu Tel Kaimintis Kolinzueten Kuitlt Smiimi: Some Narratives from the Holy Bible in Kalispel ....** Montana, 1879. Lge. 8vo. Mod. qtr. mor., unc. (LH. Apr.15; 344) $100

BIBLIANA [Latin]
- **Concordantiae Maiores Bibliae.** Strassb, 1530. 2 pts. in 1 vol. Fo. Title with owners mark, lacks last lf. blank, 1st. sigs. defect. in side margin, lightly browned, margins partly foxed & stained, some sm. defects., cont. blind-tooled pig over wood bds., rubbed & bumped, spine with tears, brass corner bosses, most defect., 2 clasps, lacks ties. (HK. May 15; 85) DM 700
- **Historiae Biblicae Veteris et Novi Testamenti.** Augsburg, n.d. Ob. fo. Bdg. not stated. (HD. Oct.14; 25) Frs. 2,900

BIBLIANA [Latin & German]
- **Biblia Veteris Testamenti Historie ... Biblische Historien ....** Ill.:– Hans Sebold Beham. Frankfurt, [1557]. 16mo. 1st. 4 ll. badly wormed, 5 ll. rimmed, 1st. few ll. lightly & partly cold., crude later bds. (SG. Feb.9; 97) $550

BIBLIANA [Polyglot]
- **Icones Biblicae Praecipuas Sacrae Scripturae Historias eleganter & graphicè Representantes.** Ill.:– after Merian. Amst., 1659. 3 pts. in 1 vol. Ob. 8vo. In Latin, Engl., German, Dutch & Fr., slightly soiled, foxing, some margin stains & repairs, cont. vell. (VS. Dec.9; 1351) Fls. 675

BIBLIOGRAPHICA
L., 1895-97. 12 pts. in 3 vols. 4to. Facs. plts., some cold., text ills., hf. leath., spines worn, orig. wraps. bnd. in. (SG. May 17; 31) $175

BIBLIOGRAPHICAL NOTES & QUERIES ...
Ed.:– P.H. Muir. L., Jan. 1935-May 1939. Vol. I pts. 1-4 & Vol. 2, pts. 1-12, together 15 iss. Inserted in binder. (S. May 1; 372) *Quaritch.* £70

BIBLIOGRAPHICAL SOCIETY of the University of Virginia
- **Papers [later Studies in Bibliography].** Charlottesville, Virginia, 1948-81. Vols. 1-34. Orig. wraps., bds. & cl. (BBA. Nov.10; 8) *Maggs.* £170

BIBLIOGRAPHY OF STATE PARTICIPATION IN THE CIVIL WAR, 1861-1866. War Department Library, Subject Catalogue No. 6
Wash., 1913. *3rd. Edn.* Tall 8vo. Maroon roan cf. & cl., gt.-lettered, moderate wear, light scuffing. (HA. Sep.16; 302) $175

BIBLIOPHILE FANTAISISTE
Turin, 1869. *(50) numbered on China.* 12mo. Red mor., oval mor. onlay centrepiece, sm. floral gold stp. in centre, gt. decor., gt. inner & outer dentelle, marb. papers; henri Bonnasse ex-libris. (D. Nov.23; 348) DM 770

BIBLIOPHILE'S LIBRARY of Literature, Art & Rare Manuscripts
1916. *(1000).* 30 vols. Three-qtr. leath. gt. (DM. May 21; 110) $130

BIBLIOTECA AMBROSIANA, Milan
- **Hebraica Ambrosiana. I Catalogue of Undescribed Hebrew Manuscripts in the Ambrosiana Library, by A. Luzzatto; II Description of Decorated & Illuminated Hebrew Manuscripts in the Ambrosiana Library, by L.M. Ottolenghi.** [Milan], 1972. *(650).* Lge. 4to. Cl., d.-w. (SG. Feb.2; 22) $100

BIBLIOTHECA ORIENTALIS. Uitgeg. d.h. Nederl. Instituut v.h. Nabije Oosten
Ed.:– F.M.Th. Böhl, A. de Buck, A.A. Kampman & others. Leiden, 1943-77. Years I-XXXIV, lacks XXV 5/6 & XXXIII contents table. 4to. Years I-XXVI bnd. in 14 vols., rest in pts. (B. Jun.21; 10) Fls. 600

BIBLIOTHEK WARBURG
- **Vorträge der Bibliothek Warburg.** Ed.:– F. Saxl. Leipzig & Berlin, 1923-32. 7 vols. (lacks Vols. II & V). Lge. 8vo. Margins partly browned, some underlining, orig. wraps., unc. (H. May 22; 126) DM 420

BIBLIOTHEQUE BLEUE
Ill.:– Desrais. Paris, 1776-83. 7 pts. in 2 vols. Cont. spr. cf., arms of Rochechouart, Duc de Mortemart, spines decor., upr. turn-ins worn. (HD. May 3; 16) Frs. 2,400

BIBLIOTHEQUE JANSENISTE
Bruxelles, 1739. *3rd. Edn.* 2 vols. 12mo. Cont. cf. (HD. Feb.22; 101) Frs. 1,600

BIBLIOTHEQUE PORTATIVE DES VOYAGES
Paris, An VII-1810. 49 vols. 16mo. Glazed cf., spines decor., some turn-ins weak, Vol. 24 spine torn. (SM. Mar.7; 2004) Frs. 8,000

BICHAT, Xavier
- **General Anatomy, applied to Physiology & Medicine.** Trans.:– G. Hayward. Boston, 1822. *1st. Edn. in Engl.* 3 vols. 1st. vol. disbnd., rest cont. mott. cf., very worn. (SG. Oct.6; 48) $140

BICKHAM, George
- **The British Monarchy.** 1743 [plts. dtd. 1743-49]. Engraved title, 2 pp. subscribers list & 188 ll. only, including 5 general maps, lacks 2 engraved alphabets, some ll. torn, margins browned, mod. cf. (CSK. Jan.13; 34) £85
- **Musical Entertainer.** L., [plts. dtd. 1737-8]. 2 vols. in 1. Fo. 132 engraved plts. only, several lightly soiled, lacks titles & tables, cont. hf. cf., worn, w.a.f. (CSK. Dec.2; 48) £450
- **The Universal Penman.** L., 1741. *1st. Edn.* 2 pts. in 1 vol. Title with bkd. margin tear, approx 3 ll. cut to margin, cont. hf. leath., slightly rubbed & defect. (D. Nov.24; 2355) DM 2,500
- – **Anr. Edn.** L., [1741]. Lge. fo. Frontis., 212 plts., some light foxing, 2 minor tears reprd., later qtr. roan, very worn, marb. bds. (SG. May 17; 34) $500
- – **Anr. Edn.** Ill.:– after Gravelot. L., 1743. Fo. Cont. style hand-bnd. mor., gt., decor covers & outer dentelles; Hauswedell coll. (H. May 23; 279) DM 4,200

BICKNELL, Clarence
- **Flowering Plants & Ferns of the Riviera.** L., 1885. *[1st. Edn.].* 82 cold. plts., title & 2 ll. loose, qtr. mor. gt. (P. May 17; 37) *Lloyd.* £90
- – **Anr. Copy.** 82 col. plts., spotting, qtr. mor., rubbed. (P. Mar.15; 84) *Walford.* £75
- – **Anr. Copy.** 82 col. plts., qtr. cf. gt. (P. Jun.7; 238) £55

BICKNELL, W.I.
- **Illustrated London.** [1847]. 2 vols. 2 vig. titles, 185 views on 112 sheets, cl. gt. (P. Dec.8; 5) *Finney.* £75
- – **Anr. Edn.** Ca. 1860. 2 vols. Some foxing & margin stains, cont. hf. cf. gt. (TA. Nov.17; 167) £74

BICYCLE. Illustrated Weekly Newspaper
Feb. 1936-Jan. 1939. Vol. 1 no.1-Vol.7 no. 151, in 5 vols. 4to. Advts., cl., rubbed. (TA. May 17; 560) £85

BIDDELL, Herman
- **The Suffolk Stud Book ....** Diss, 1880. 14 litho. plts., hf. cf., rubbed; from the Farmers' Club Liby. (P. Jul.5; 3) £55

BIDERMANN, J.
- **Operum Comicorum Pars Altera ....** München, 1666. *1st. Edn.* Minimal spotting, cont. leath., gt. spine, cover & outer dentelle, rubbed, gt. oxidised, lacks ties. (HK. Nov.10; 3034) DM 540

BIDET, N.
- **Traité sur la Nature et sur la Culture de la Vigne....** Ed.:– Duhamel du Monceau. Ill.:– P.P. Choffard after Maugein. Paris, 1759. *2nd. Edn.* 2 vols. Title

stpd., folding copper engrs. slightly crumpled, cont. leath. gt. (R. Oct.12; 2123)   DM 670

BIE, Corn. de
– **Het Gulden Cabinet vande ... Schilder-Const ... vande Vermarste Schilders, Architecte, Beldthowers end Plaetsnyders ....** [Antw., 1662]. 4to. 2 ll. cold. in, lacks 18 pp. & the end of the book, 1 lf. torn, some staining & foxing, slightly frayed at end, cont. leath., bumped & slightly defect. (HK. Nov.9; 2032)   DM 520

BIE, Oskar
– **Holländisches Skizzenbuch.** Ill.:– M. Liebermann. Berlin, 1911. *(450).* Lge. ob. 4to. Orig. pict. linen. (H. Nov.24; 1782)   DM 560
– **Musik auf der Wolga.** Ill.:– R. Sterl. Leipzig, 1914. *1st. Edn. (200) numbered on Zanders-Bütten.* Lge. 4to. Orig. bds., gold-tooled upr. cover, orig. bd. box, slightly rubbed, unc. (HK. May 17; 3164)   DM 420
– **Das Theater. Bühnenbilder und. Kostüme.** Ill.:– Karl Walser. Berlin, ca. 1911. Lge. 4to. On van gelder Bütten, some light spotting, orig. pictor. lf. linen, slightly spotted; ex-libris & pencil dedication on end-paper. (HK. May 17; 3210)   DM 520

BIE, O. (Ed.)
See– NEUE RUNDSCHAU

BIEDENFELD, F. Frh. v.
– **Geschichte und Verfassung aller Geistlichen und Weltlichen und Blühenden Ritterorden.** Weimar, 1841. 2 pts. & Atlas, in 1 vol. 4to. Title lf. mntd., some foxing in parts, cont. bds. (GB. Nov.3; 959)   DM 950

BIEL, Gabriel
– **Sacri Canonis Misse Expositio, in Alma Universitate Tüwingensi Ordinarie Lecta.** Tübingen, Johann Otmar for Frederic Meynberger, 29 Nov. 1499. *2nd. Edn.* Fo. Beginning rubricated, MS. annots. in margins, last lf. disbnd., cont. German stpd. pig over wood bds., traces of clasps; 1631 Bamberg Jesuit College ex-libris on title, from Fondation Furstenberg-Beaumesnil. [BMC III, 703; Goff B660] (HD. Nov.16; 58)   Frs. 8,200
– – **Anr. Copy.** Fo. Wide margin, partly rubricated, some old marginalia, title with 2 old MS owners marks, last lf. slightly stained, cont. blind-tooled pig over wood bds.; Hans Fürstenberg ex-libris. [Hain 3179, BMC III 703; Goff B 660] (HK. May 15; 88)   DM 5,200
– **Sermones Gabrielis de Festivitatibus Gloriose Virginis Marie; Sermones de Sanctis.** [Tübingen, Otmar, 14]99. 2 pts. in 1 vol. 4to. (in 8's). 8 lf. 'Annotatio Titulorum' of 2nd. pt. bnd. in error before text of 1st. pt., sm. worming thro.-out, cont. blind-stpd. pig. on wood bds., 2 metal clasps; Vollbehr bkplt. [Goff B662] (SG. Feb.9; 171) $1,300
– – **Anr. Copy.** Vol. I only (of 4). 4to. Rubricated initials, following final blank is an 8 lf. quire headed 'Annotatio titulorum de sanctis p. anni circulum ...' & ending 'Finis Registri' (not noted in the BMC collation), some worming thro.-out, old hf. cf., spine worn; the Walter Goldwater copy. [BMC III, 703; Goff B-662] (SG. Dec.1; 71) $175
See– BECHOFFEN, Johannes – BIEL, Gabriel

BIER, Justus (Contrib.)
See– MEISS, Millard

BIERBAUM, Otto Julius
– **Gesammelte Werke.** Ed.:– M.G. Conrad & H. Brandenburg. München, [1912-17]. *1st. Coll. Edn. (200) numbered De Luxe Edn. on Bütten.* Vol. 1 & 4-7 (all publd.) in 5 vols. Red. mor. gt. (BR. Apr.13; 1642)   DM 560
– **Gugeline.** Ill.:– E.R. Weiss. Berlin, [1899]. *1st. Edn. (5) numbered & sigd. by artist.* Ills. hand-cold., orig. pict. bds., cold. pict. end-papers & doubls., slightly spotted. (H. Nov.24; 1379)   DM 5,000
– **Samalio Pardulus.** Ill.:– A. Kubin. München, 1911. 1st. Edn. *De Luxe Edn., (100).* 4to. Orig. red mor. gt. (HK. Nov.11; 427)   DM 420
– **Das Schoene Maedchen von Pao.** Ill.:– Bayros. München, [1910]. *De Luxe Edn. (600).* 4to. Hand-bnd. mor. gt., elab. decor. inner covers, by Hübel &

Denck, Leipzig, slightly discold & rubbed, Hauswedel coll. (H. May 24; 575)   DM 1,400
– – **Anr. Copy.** 4to. Orig. mor. gt., gt. inner dentelle. (D. Nov.24; 2943)   DM 1,000
– – **Anr. Edn.** Ill.:– F. von Bayros. 1919. *(600)* on Enschede Bütten in 4 old types. Orig. gold-decor. chagrin by Paul Renner, decor. free end-papers, corners slightly bumped. (GB. Nov.5; 3154)   DM 1,800

BIERCE, Ambrose
– **Black Beetles in Amber.** San Franc. & N.Y., 1892. *1st. Edn.* Frontis.-port. sigd., slight stains in margins, orig. cl., soiled; Perry Molstad copy. (SPB. May 16; 409) $175

BIERKOWSKI, L.J. von
– **Anatomisch-chirurgische Abbildungen nebst Darstellung und Beschreibung der Chirurgischen Operationen nach den Methoden von v. Graefe, Kluge und Rust.** Berlin, 1827. *De Luxe Edn. on vell.* Plt. vol. without text. Lge. fo. Some plts. slightly browned or stained, hf. linen, defect. (HT. May 8; 518)   DM 1,200

BIERMANN, Georg
– **Der Zeichner Lovis Corinth.** Dresden, 1924. *(200) De Luxe Edn. with etching sigd. by artist.* Sm. 4to. Orig. hf. leath., spine. faded & slightly worn; ex-libris Thomas Corinth, etched & sigd. by Charlotte Berend-Corinth inside cover. (H. May 23; 1185)   DM 1,400

BIERMANN, G. (Ed.)
See– JAHRBUCH DER JUNGEN KUNST

BIESTER, J.E. (Ed.)
See– BERLINISCHE MONATSSCHRIFT

BIGELOW, Jacob
– **American Medical Botany, Being a Collection of the Native Medicinal Plants of the United States....** Boston, 1817. *1st. Edn.* Vol. 1 (pts. I & II) only. Tall 8vo. 20 full-p. hand-cold. copperplts., tissue guards, moderate foxing, some light margin foxing to some plts., ex-liby., few internal minor markings at beginning of text, oval perforation stp. at title (through publisher's credit) & last lf. of text, cont. marb. bds. recently rebkd. with leath., fore-edge corners of covers worn. (HA. May 4; 239) $325
– **Florula Bostoniensis; A Collection of Plants of Boston and its Vicinity.** Boston, 1824. *2nd. Edn.* Lge. 8vo. Title reinforced, shaved, buckram. (SG. Mar.22; 41) $110
– **Nature in Disease, Illustrated in Various Discourses & Essays.** Boston, 1854. *1st. Edn.* Sm. 8vo. Cl., spine ends chipped; pres. copy from author to J.H. Abbot. (SG. Oct.6; 49) $100

BIGGE, J.T.
– **Report of the Commissioner of Inquiry into the State of the Colony of New South Wales.** 1822. Fo. Qtr. cf. (S. Nov.1; 14)   *McCormick.* £280

BIGSBY, J.J.
– **The Shoe & Canoe or Pictures of Travel in the Canadas.** 1850. *1st. Edn.* 2 vols. 20 engraved plts., 4 maps & a plan, orig. cl. [Sabin 5360] (S. May 22; 303)   *Quaritch.* £350
– – **Anr. Copy.** 2 vols. Orig. cl., lightly rubbed. (CSK. Jul.6; 99)   £320
– – **Anr. Copy.** 2 vols. 4 maps, including 2 folding, 21 engraved plts., a few foxed, orig. cl., jnts. & corners worn; the Rt. Hon. Visc. Eccles copy. [Sabin 5360 (misdating it 1851)] (CNY. Nov.18; 22) $400

BIGSBY, Robert
– **Historical & Topographical Description of Repton.** L., 1854. 4to. Litho, title, port. on India paper, & 12 plts., ills., slightly soiled thro.-out, cont. hf. roan, worn. (BBA. May 3; 311)   *Chesters.* £50

BILBAO
– **Ordenanzas de la ... Universidád y Cása de Contratación de ... Bilbao.** Ill.:– Paret. Madrid, 1819. Fo. Cf. (DS. Mar. 23; 2197)   Pts. 25,000

BILCHES, Francisco de
– **Santos y Santuarios del Obispado de Jaen y Baeza.** Madrid, 1653. Fo. Vell. (DS. Mar. 23; 2028)   Pts. 50,000

BILDER-CONVERSATION-LEXIKON für das Deutsche Volk
Leipzig, 1837-41. 4 vols. 4to. Title double stpd., some browning, vol. 4 with staining at beginning, cont. hf. leath., slightly rubbed. (HK. May 16; 1382)   DM 650

BILDNISSE BERUHMTER DEUTSCHEN
Leipzig, ca.1850. Fo. Some light margin foxing, cont. hf. leath. (R. Oct.12; 2260)   DM 580

BILGUER, J.U.
– **Chirurgischer Wahrnehmungen.** Berlin, 1763. Foxed, cont. bds., spine leath. renewed. (GB. Nov.3; 1004)   DM 500

BILIBIN, I.J.
– **Das Märchen von Iwan, dem Zarensohn, dem Feuervogel umd dem Grauen Wolf.** St. Petersb., 1901. Lge. 4to. Cold. pict. orig. wraps., spine slightly bumped. (HK. Nov.11; 3429)   DM 750
– **Wassilissa, die Wunderschöne.** St. Petersb., 1901. 4to. Cold. pict. wraps. (GB. May 5; 2210)   DM 800

BILLINGS, Robert William
– **The Baronial & Ecclesiastical Antiquities of Scotland ....** Edinb., 1845-52. 4 vols. 4to. Engraved titles, 240 engraved plts., mor. gt. (PD. May 16; 171)   £155
– – **Anr. Copy.** 4 vols. 4to. Cont. embossed cf. gt. (PD. Feb.15; 222)   £78
– – **Anr. Copy.** 4 vols. 4to. Cont. mor. gt. (PD. Jun.13; 68)   £60
– – **Anr. Edn.** Ca. 1855. 4 vols. 4to. Minor spotting, cont. hf. cf. (TA. Oct.20; 66)   £80
– – **Anr. Copy.** 4 vols. 4to. Minor spotting, cont. hf. cf. (TA. Sep.15; 130)   £64
– – **Anr. Edn.** N.d. 4 vols. Lge. 4to. Engraved plts. in 2 states, on India paper mntd., some spotting, cont. crimson mor. gt. by Maclehose, scuffed; bkplt. of Sir Henry Campbell-Bannerman. (CSK. Aug.19; 50)   £160
– **Illustrations of the Architectural Antiquities of the County of Durham.** Durham, 1846. 4to. 64 engraved plts., hf. mor. gt., upr. cover detchd. (P. Feb.16; 49)   £50

BILLMARK, Carl Johan
– **Aquarell-Lithographier och Tontryck Teckningar efter Naturen Sverige [Gripsholm; Skokloster; Uppsala Sigtuna].** Stockholm, ca. 1860. 3 pts. only (of 4?). Fo. 36 litho. plts., with details supplied by hand, sm. owner's stp. on contents lf. or wraps., cont. roan-bkd. cl., ptd. wraps. bnd. in. (S. Dec.1; 313)   *Marks.* £220

BILSON, Thomas
– **The True Difference between Christian Subjection & Unchristian Rebellion....** Oxford, 1585. *1st. Edn.* Sm. 4to. Cont. limp vell., slightly soiled, lacks ties. (GB. Nov.3; 934)   DM 750

BILTON, William
[–] **The Angler in Ireland; or An Englishman's Ramble through Connaught & Munster ... 1833.** L., 1834. *1st. Edn.* 2 vols. Sm. 8vo. Hf. cf., armorial motif on spine, bkplt. (GM. Dec.7; 359)   £160

BING, Samuel
– **Artistic Japan.** L., 1888-91. Nos. 1-36 in 6 vols. Sm. fo. Pict. cl., or hf. cl., slightly rubbed & soiled, orig. wraps. bnd. in, some cropped. (S. May 1; 585)   *Katzoff.* £200
– – **Anr. Copy.** 36 pts. in 6 vols. Sm. fo. Plts., many cold., text ills., ex-liby., cold. pict. cl., orig. wraps. bnd. in. (SG. May 3; 41) $400
– **Collection.** Paris, 1906. 6 pts. Fo. Sale catalogue, orig. wraps., in orig. portfo. (CSK. Dec.16; 145)   £90

BINGHAM, Hiram
– **A Residence of Twenty-One Years in the Sandwich Islands; or the Civil, Religious, & Political History of Those Islands.** Hartford & N.Y., 1847. *1st. Edn.* Cl., worn, spine edge torn. (RO. May 29; 33) $135

BINGLEY, Thomas
– **Tales of Shipwrecks & Other Disasters at Sea.** Boston, 1851. *1st. Amer. Edn.* Sm. 12mo. Orig. cl., gt. floral spine (ends slightly nicked), covers spotted;

BINGLEY, Thomas -Contd.

from liby. of F.D. Roosevelt, inscr. by him (as President). (SG. Mar.15; 5) $350

BINGLEY, Rev. William

- **North Wales.** 1804. 2 vols. Cont. cf. gt. (P. Jun.7; 179) £60

BINION, Samuel Augustus

- **Ancient Egypt, or Mizraim.** N.Y. & Buffalo, [1887]. *De Luxe Edn., (2000).* Vols. II & III only. Atlas fo. Pict. titles, 72 plts., slight fraying at a few plt. margins, Vol. II in liby. hf. buckram, Vol. III loose as iss. in 2 bd. folders, brkn. (SG. Nov.3; 16) $575

BINYAMIN HA-COHEN

- **Eit ha-Zamir.** Mantua, 1753. 12mo. Leatherette. (SG. Feb.2; 278) $150

BINYON, Robert Lawrence

- **The Drawings & Engravings of William Blake.** 1922. *(200) numbered.* Fo. Orig. vell., contained in cl. portfo., lacks ties. (CSK. Mar.23; 26) £70
- **– Anr. Edn.** L., 1922. *(200) numbered, out-of-series copy.* Lge. 4to. 16 col. & 90 monochrome plts., partly untrimmed, orig. vell. gt., cl. folding case. (SG. Oct.13; 36) $150
- **– Anr. Edn.** L., 1922. 4to. orig. vell.-bkd. bds. (BBA. Apr.5; 98) *Subun-So.* £50
- **The Followers of William Blake.** 1925. 4to. Cl. gt. (P. Sep.29; 1) *Toynbee Clark.* £60
- **– Anr. Edn.** L. & N.Y., 1925. Tall 4to. 80 plts. including 8 cold. & mntd., ex-liby., cl. (SG. May 3; 48) $130
- **The Poems of Nizami described.** 1928. *(55) numbered, with additional set of 16 plts.* 2 vols. Fo. Orig. vell., additional plts. on card. Loose in portfo. (BBA. Jan.19; 299) *Trotter.* £95

BINYON, Robert Lawrence & Sexton, J.J. O'Brien

- **Japanese Colour Prints.** 1923. *(100) numbered & sigd., with extra set of 16 mntd. col. plts. loose in folder.* 4to. Orig. mor., partly untrimmed, head of spine slightly worn, orig. folder with ties. (TA. Aug.18; 298) £100
- **– Anr. Copy.** 4to. Partly untrimmed, orig. mor., head of spine worn, orig. folder with ties. (TA. Sep.15; 362) £90
- **– Anr. Edn.** N.Y., 1923. 4to. 46 plts., cl. (SG. Aug.25; 221) $110

BINYON, Robert Lawrence, Wilkinson, James Vere S. & Gray, Basil

- **Persian Miniature Painting. Including a Critical & Descriptive Catalogue of the Miniatures Exhibited at Burlington House.** L., 1933. Fo. No bdg. stated. (SPB. Nov.30; 219) $425

BIOGRAPHIE UNIVERSELLE ANCIENNE ET MODERNE

Paris, 1811-62. 85 vols. Cont. qtr. cf., spines gt. (S. Apr.10; 287) *Wade.* £380
- **– Anr. Edn.** Paris, 1811-28. 51 vols. only (lacks vol.30). Cont. cf., gt., spines gt., w.a.f. (S. Apr.10; 286) *Wade.* £320
- **– Anr. Edn.** Intro.:– Ch. Nodier. Paris, Leipzig, [1842-65]. *New Edn.* 45 vols. 4to. Several sigs. in 2 vols. misbnd., pol. hf. leath. gt., gt. monog. on spine, ex-libris. (V. Sep.30; 2292) DM 1,900

BIOLOGIA CENTRALI-AMERICANA

- **Insecta [containing Godman & Salvin's Lepidoptera-Rhopalocera & Druce & Gray's Lepidoptera-Heterocera].** Ill.:– after R.H.F. Rippon, W. Purkiss, F.W. Frohawk, & A.J.J. Wendel. 1879-1901, 1881-1915. [Vols. 36-42]. 4to. 224 cold. litho. plts., edges of plts. slightly darkened, mod. buckram, partly unc. (CNY. May 18; 134) $1,500

BION, Nicolas

- **Traité de la Construction et des Principaux Usages des Instrumens de Mathématique.** La Haye, 1723. *New Edn.* 4to. Mod. antique-style mott. cf., spine gt. (VG. Sep.14; 1223) Fls. 1,200
- **– Anr. Edn.** Paris, 1752. *4th. Edn.* 4to. Light stain in lr. margin nearly thro.-out, cont. leath. gt., very rubbed & bumped, spine defect. (R. Apr.4; 1579) DM 920

BIONDI, Giovanni Francesco

- **Donzella Desterrada, or the Banished Virgin.** Trans.:– James Hayward. L., 1635. *1st. Edn. in Engl.* Fo. Title trimmed & remntd. with sm. tear slightly affecting text, old cf., rubbed, jnt. reprd. [STC. 3074] (RO. Apr.23; 11) $250

BIRAGO, Franciscus Mediobarbus

- **Imperatorum Romanorum Numismata.** Mediolani, 1683. Fo. Title slightly stained & with liby. stp., cont. mott. cf., gt. coats-of-arms on covers, slightly rubbed. (S. May 1; 509) *Drury.* £90
- **– Anr. Copy.** Fo. Mott. cf., spine gt., some slight scuffing. (LC. Oct.13; 14) £60

BIRCH, Thomas

- **The Heads of Illustrious Persons of Great Britain.** 1756. Fo. Some light spotting, cont. cf., rubbed. (CSK. Jun.1; 27) £150
- **– Anr. Edn.** Ill.:– Houbraken & Vertue. L., 1813. *New Edn.* Lge. fo. Lge. title vig., 108 engraved ports., cont. russ., gt. borders, rebkd. (SG. Jun.7; 372) $250

BIRCH, Walter de Gray

- **Catalogue of Seals in the Department of Manuscripts in the British Museum.** 1887-1900. 6 vols. Liby. stps., orig. cl., rubbed. (BBA. Jul.27; 245) *Maggs.* £60

BIRD, Charles

- **Picturesque Old Bristol.** 1885-89. 2 vols. 4to. 52 etched plts., orig. mor. gt., scuffed. (TA. Dec.15; 105) £90

BIRD, Paul

- **Fifty Paintings by Walt Kuhn.** N.Y., 1940. 4to. Cl., d.-w.; pres. copy from Kuhn, portion of an A.L.s. & Christmas card laid in. (PNY. Dec.1; 26) $150

BIRD & BULL PRESS

See— TAYLOR, W. Thomas & Morris, Henry

BIRGITTA, Saint

- **Revelationes.** Nuremb., Anton Koberger, 21 Sep. 1500. *2nd. Edn. in Latin.* Fo. Fully rubricated, initials in blue & red, lacks 1 woodcut & final blank, lf. d3 supplied in facs., some staining, etc., old wood bds., covered with paper, worn; the Walter Goldwater copy. [BMC II, 445; Goff B-688] (SG. Dec.1; 72) $1,600

BIRINGUCCIO, Vannuccio

- **La Pyrotechnie, ou Art du feu ....** Trans.:– Iaques Vincent. Paris, 1572. *2nd. Fr. Edn.* Sm. 4to. Some browning & slight margin staining, minor margin repairs, sig. on K1 cropped, med. vell. (S. Nov.28; 107) *Gurney.* £420

BIRKBECK, Morris

- **Notes on a Journey in America, from the Coast of Virginia to the Territory of Illinois.** L., 1818. *2nd. Edn.* Folding map laid in, 16 pp. advts. (dtd. 1 Jan 1818), some foxing, buckram. (SG. Jan.19; 104) $130

BIRKEN, Sigmund von

- **Spiegel der Ehren des Hochlöblichsten Kayser-und Königlichen Erzhauses Oesterreich ....** Ed.:– J.J. Fugger. Ill.:– Ph. Kilian, C.N. Sturtz, & others. Nuremb., 1669. *1st. Edn.* Fo. 8 blank ll. old paper, a few ll. slightly browned or foxed, 2 sm. corner tears, without loss, 26 ll. cont. MS. 'Nota ex Jure Publico' bnd. at end, cont. blind-tooled pig over wood bds., clasps. (R. Oct.13; 3184) DM 2,400

BIRTWHISTLE, John

- **The Vision of Wat Tyler.** Ill.:– Graham Clarke. Boughton Monchelsea, Ebenezer Pr., 1972. *[75] sigd. by author.* Lge. fo. 33 etched plts. on 16 sheets, each mntd. between 2 pp. of calligraphic text, loose as iss., orig. rough cf., unc., orig. hessian wrap. with ties; each sheet marked 'Artists proof' & sigd., inscr. by artist to Mr. & Mrs. Ronald Kinsey. (S. Nov.21; 181) *Gerrard.* £170

BISBEE, Eugène Shade

- **The Treasure of the Ice.** N.Y., [1898]. *1st. Edn.* No bdg. stated. (CBA. Oct.29; 102) $160

BISCHOFF, James

- **Sketch of the History of Van Diemen's Land ....** L., 1832. Sm. repair to folding map, bds., qtr. cl., unc. (KH. Nov.9; 546) Aus. $350
- **– Anr. Copy.** Plts. slightly stained, sm. tear in map, title offset, orig. cl.-bkd. bds., unc., cover worn. (CA. Apr.3; 23) Aus. $160

BISCIONIO, A.M.

- **Bibliothecae Mediceo-laurentianae Catalogus ....** Flor., 1752. 2 pts. in 1 vol. Fo. Cont. cf. (HD. Dec.2; 68) Frs. 1,100

BISHOP, Elizabeth

- **North & South.** [Boston, 1946]. *1st. Edn.* Orig. wraps., upr. corners creased thro.-out; advance proof copy, Frederic Dannay copy. (CNY. Dec.16; 34) $400

BISHOP, J.G.

- **'A Peep into the Past:' Brighton in the Olden Time.** Brighton, 1880. 4to. Extra-ill. with many engrs. & old advts., some spotting, last lf. detchd. & frayed, red hf. mor., worn, covers loose or detchd. (S. Dec.13; 196) *Haddon.* £85

BISHOP, Richard E.

- **Bishop's Birds. Etchings of Water-Fowl & Upland Game Birds.** L., 1936. *(250).* 4to. Orig. cl., soiled, stp. on end-paper. (SPB. Dec.13; 577) $150
- **– Anr. Edn.** Intro.:– H.P. Sheldon. Phila., 1936. *1st. Edn. (1000) sigd. by Bishop & Sheldon.* 4to. Pict. cl., some rubbing & light foxing to covers. (HA. Feb. 24; 161) $130

BISMARCK, Fr. W. Graf von

- **Vierundzwanzig Plane zur Ideen-Taktik der Reuterey.** Karlsruhe, 1829. Fo. Cont. bds. (D. Nov.25; 4478) DM 600

BISSCHOP, J de 'J. Episcopius'

- **Paradigmata Graphices Variorum Artificium.** Ill.:– after Corregio, Zuccaro, Raphael, Michelangelo, & others. Amst., [1671]. Engraved title & 57 etched & engraved plts. *(Bound with:)* – **Signorum Veterum Icones.** N.p., ca. 1670. Engraved title & 100 etched & engraved plts., Together 2 works in 1 vol. Fo. Old hf. leath., disbnd. (SG. Jun.7; 346) $150

BISSING, F.W. von

- **Die Mastaba des Gem-ni-kai.** Berlin, 1905-11. 2 vols. 4to. Hf. mor., unc. (B. Jun.21; 61) Fls. 550

BISTOLFI, Leonardo

- **Alla Pascoliano, Canti di Giovanni Pascoli.** Ill.:– Vico Vigano. 1911. *(500).* 4to. Publishers bdg. (CR. Jul.6; 102) Lire 280,000

BITAUBE, Paul-Jérémie

- **Joseph.** Ill.:– Cochin, engraved by St Aubin (port.); Marillier, engraved by Née. Paris, 1786. *4th. Edn.* Cont. red mor. gt. (HD. May 3; 17) Frs. 1,200

BITONTO, Antonius de

- **Expositiones Evangeliorum Dominicalium.** Venice, J. Hagmann for Niklaus von Frankfurt, [15 Aug.] 1496. Owners mark on title, minimal spotting, cont. hf. leath. over wood bds., decor., brass clasps, spine restored. [HC. 3222; BMC V. 427; Goff A 889] (HT. May 8; 37) DM 2,300
- **Sermones in Epistolas Dominicales et Quadragesimales.** Venice, Johannes Hammam for Nicolaus de Frankfordia, 17 Jun.-1 Jul. 1496. *1st. Edn.* Variant, with 'impensis spectabilis viri.n.de frank' in 2nd. colophon, & v2 foliated '15', a1 & 8 supplied in facs., 2 lines on a2r & 1 on v4v inked through, sm. margin hole in v4, light margin dampstains, old vell. [BMC V, 427; Goff A-895] (SG. Oct.27; 154) $225

BIVERO, P. de

- **Sacrum Sanctuariun Crucis et Patientia Crucifixorum et Cruciferorum, Emblematicis Imaginibus.** Ill.:– C. Galle. Antw., 1634. 4to. Slightly foxed & browned thro.-out, some worming, mainly in margins, cont. vell,, some sm. defects. (VG. Nov.30; 595) Fls. 550

BIZARO, Petro

- **Rerum Persicarum Historia, Initia Gentis, Mores, Instituta.** Francofurti, 1601. Fo. Unif. browning,

18th. C. cf., later German arms, spine decor.; from Fondation Furstenberg-Beaumesnil. (HD. Nov.16; 101) Frs. 2,000

BIZOT, [Pierre]

– **Histoire Metallique de la République de Hollande.** Paris, 1687. *1st. Edn.* Fo. Some spotting & staining, DD2 worn to hole in lr. margin, cont. cf., rubbed. (S. May 1; 510) *Marlborough.* £120

– – **Anr. Edn.** Amst., 1688. *New Edn.* 2 vols. & supp. Vell. (HD. Feb.22; 18) Frs. 1,600

– **Senatus Populi Genuensis Rerum Domi Forisque Gestarum Historiae.** Antw., 1579. Fo. Some foxing, cont. gt.-decor. cf., spine renewed. (HD. Oct.21; 26) Frs. 2,900

BLACK, Adam & Charles

– **General Atlas.** Edinb., 1844. Fo. 55 partly col. maps, hf. mor., rubbed. (P. Jul.5; 388) £55

– – **Anr. Edn.** Edinb., 1853. Fo. Cont. hf. mor. (BBA. Mar.21; 130) *M. Cassidy.* £75

– – **Anr. Edn.** L., 1867. Fo. Hf. mor., worn. (P. Nov.24; 308) *Haddon.* £65

BLACK SUN PRESS

See— **LACLOS, Pierre Ambroise François Choderlos de**

BLACKBURNE, E.L.

– **Sketches Graphic & Descriptive for a History of the Decorative Painting Applied to English Architecture During the Middle Ages.** L., 1847. Fo. Chromolitho, title & plts., spotted, orig. cl., gt., rubbed & stained. (S. May 1; 528) *Quaritch.* £60

– – **Anr. Copy.** 24 col. litho. plts. (1 double-p.), orig. cl. gt., extremities rubbed, spine mostly worn away, ex-liby. (SG. Jan.26; 178) $225

BLACKER, William

– **Catechism of Fly Making, Angling & Dyeing.** [L.], 1843. 2 titles (1st. dtd. 8 Dec. 1843, 2nd. engraved & dtd. Mar. 1842), 6 plts., 14 artificial flies & fly-tying specimens mntd. on 4 plts., some spotting, russ. gt., Blacker's advt. slip mntd. on upr. pastedown, orig. roan case worn. (S. Oct.4; 6) *Simpson.* £820

BLACKMORE, Sir Richard

– **Prince Arthur.** L., 1695. Fo. Cont. cf. (CSK. Feb.24; 179) £60

BLACKMORE, Richard Doddridge, 1825-1900

– **Fringilla. Some Tales in Verse.** Ill.:– Lovis Fairfax Wuckley & James Linton. L., 1895. *(25) De Luxe Edn. numbered on Spalting-Bütten.* Orig. vell. gt., lge. cover ill., decor., lf cover vig. (GB. May 5; 2215) DM 900

– – **Anr. Edn.** Ill.:– Will H. Bradley. Cleveland, 1895. *(600) numbered.* Somewhat spotted, orig. linen-bkd. bds., rather soiled; pencil note 'From collection of G.W. Jones 1936'. (S. Nov.22; 311) *Wade.* £110

– – **Anr. Copy.** Linen-bkd. decor. bds., bkplt. (PNY. Oct.20; 191) $250

BLACKSTONE, Sir William

– **An Analysis of the Laws of England.** 1758. *3rd. Edn.* 2 pts. in 1 vol. Cont. pol. cf., slightly rubbed. (TA. Dec.15; 458) £66

– **Commentaries on the Laws of England.** Oxford, 1765-69. *1st. Edn.* 4 vols. 4to. Some light spotting, cont. hf. cf., spines gt. (CSK. Aug.19; 44) £2,700

– – **Anr. Edn.** Oxford, 1765-69. *Vols. 1, 3 & 4: 1st. Edns., Vol. 2: 2nd. Edn.* 4 vols. 4to. 4 ll. inserted in Vol. 1, little browning & staining, 19th. 'Supplement to the First Edition' C. hf. cf.; sig. of Sir Norman Moore in Vol. 1. (S. Dec.8; 370) *Blackwood.* £1,100

– – **Anr. Edn.** Oxford, 1766-66-68-69. *2nd. Edn. vol. 1, 1st. Edns. vols. 2-3.* 4 vols. 4to. 2 plts., errata ll., some foxing & browning, vol. 4 title reprd., sig. on titles, cont. cf.-bkd. marb. bds., worn, one upr. cover detchd.; bkplts. of B. George Ulizio. (SPB. May 16; 11) $1,200

– – **Anr. Edn.** Oxford, 1766-69. *Vols. 1 & 2: 2nd. Edns., Vols. 3 & 4: 1st. Edns.* 4 vols. Lge. 4to. Cont. cf., spines elab. gt., slightly worn. (SG. Nov.3; 18) $1,100

– – **Anr. Edn.** Oxford, 1770. *4th. Edn.* 4 vols. Some spotting, cont. cf., spines worn. (CSK. Aug.19; 148) £130

– – **Anr. Edn.** L., 1793-95. *12th. Edn.* 4 vols. Some foxing, staining & darkening, cont. cf., covers worn, upr. cover of Vol. 1 & both covers of Vol. 4 detchd. (CBA. Mar.3; 330) $150

– – **Anr. Edn.** Ed.:– Edward Christian. L., 1809. *15th. Edn.* 4 vols. Diced cf.; early armorial bkplt. of Abraham Wildey Robarts. (SG. Feb.16; 33) $225

– – **Anr. Edn.** Ed.:– Edward Christian, & [Richard Price]. L., 1830. 4 vols. Lge. 8vo. Orig. two-tone bds., unc. & unopened. (SG. Nov.17; 176) $200

BLACKWALL, John

– **A History of Spiders of Great Britain & Ireland.** L., [1859-]60-64. 2 pts. in 1 vol. Fo. 29 hand-cold. litho. plts., a few plts. spotted, 2 plts. with tear, cont. tree cf. gt., rebkd. preserving orig. spine, rubbed. (C. Mar.14; 131) *Wheldon & Wesley.* £130

BLACKWELL, Elizabeth

– **Herbarium Blackwellianum.** Preface:– D. Chr. J. Trew. Nuremb., 1754. Fo. Ptd. title verso with stp. excision, M.S. Latin names in upr. & lr. margins, 1 plt. oxidised, copper engraved & ptd. title & 1 lf. & 6 plts. with tears partly reprd., (1 lf. with slight loss), some margin repairs, margin soiling, cont. leath. gt., faded. (HK. May 15; 337) DM 3,500

– – **Anr. Edn.** Preface:– C.J. Trews. Ill.:– N.F. Eisenberger. Nürnberg, 1754-73. 6 vols. Fo. Cont. cf., gt. spine; monog. stp. of Kaiser Franz I. von Osterreich & of Fidei-Commiss liby., Vienna on verso of title ll., Hauswedell coll. (H. May 24; 856) DM 52,000

– – **Anr. Edn.** Preface:– C.J. Trew. Nürnberg, 1767-65. Centuria I-III & V only (of 6). Fo. Lacks 1 plt. Vol. II, 1 plt. Vol. III numbered twice, Vol. V with 102 plts., plts. with old (19th. C.?) MS. in Polish, 3 plts. with sm. slits, slightly foxed, cont. leath. gt., heavily rubbed & worn. (GB. Nov.3; 1119) DM 7,600

BLACKWOOD, Adam

[–] **Martyre de la Royne D'Escosse, Dovarière de France.** Edinb. [Paris], 1587. *1st. Edn.* Cont. vell., defect. [STC 3107] (P. Apr.12; 277) *Thorp.* £250

– – **Anr. Copy.** With penultimate Epitaph lf. but lacks (?blank), few ll. slightly soiled, upr. margin trimmed sometimes affecting pagination, cont. vell., slightly worn, lacks ties. [STC 3107] (BBA. Oct.27; 9) *Robertshaw.* £55

BLACKWOOD, Lady Alicia

– **Scutari, The Bosphorus & Crimea.** Ventnor, 1857. 2 vols. Fo. 2 litho. titles, 19 litho. plts., 2 torn, orig. wraps. (P. Oct.20; 8) £340

– – **Anr. Copy.** 2 vols. Fo. Litho. titles, 19 litho. views, including 4 folding, sm. hole affecting last view in Vol. 1, orig. ptd. wraps., slightly worn or defect. (S. Dec.1; 353) *Martinos.* £250

BLACKWOOD, William & Sons

– **The Atlas of Scotland containing Maps of each County.** Edinb., n.d. *Re-iss. of Thomson Edn.* Fo. Index map, 2 folding engraved plts. & 58 engraved col. maps, hf. cf. gt., slightly worn. (PD. Jun.13; 191) £200

BLADES, William

– **The Life & Typography of William Caxton.** 1861-63. 2 vols. 4to. Cont. roan-bkd. cl. (BBA. Nov.10; 10) *Rix.* £110

BLAES, Gerardus

See— **BLASIUS or BLAES, Gerardus**

BLAEU, Johannes or Jan

– **Atlas Major, sive Cosmographia Blaviana.** Amst., Joannes Blaeu, 1662. *1st. Compl. Edn.* 11 vols. Fo. In Latin, 9 engraved frontis. (comprising 2 in Vol. 4 & none in Vols. 2, 3 & 11), sub-title to Vol. 10 pt. 2, 11 ptd. titles with vigs., 597 engraved maps, plans, views & plts., most maps double-p., 3 folding, some full-p. or in text, including 9 plts. of Brahe's astronomical instruments (1 with his port.) in Vol. 1, views of Stonehenge & Avebury in Vol. 5, 7 plts. of the Escorial, including 3 folding, in Vol. 9, cont. hand-cold. thro.-out, including fully cold. frontis.'s, & sub-title (heightened with gold), title vigs., & all cartouches, arms, costumes, views, etc. on maps, on guards thro.-out, index lf. at end of each vol., Vol. 1: with 2 additional dedication ll. not called for by Koeman, lacks 'Blaeu to the reader', 4 pp., sm. surface flew to 1 map, Vol. 2: without Phillips map no. 34 (not in index or called for by Koeman), worming of inner margins at end, slightly affecting maps 27-39, Vol. 3: Koeman includes a map 'Terrotii Lindaviensis' (no. 94) omitted by Phillips, who numbers the last map as 2 to give same total, Vol. 4: last 2 maps slightly browned, Vol. 5: 58 maps (Phillips includes the view of Stonehenge to give a total of 59) & 3 views, repair to lr. blank fore-corner of 3L1-2 & 3M1, minor staining to a few lr. margins, Vol. 6: 7 maps slightly stained or discold., Vol. 7: with the map 'La Bresse Chalomnoise' not listed by Phillips, sm. repair to margin of 1 map, some maps a trifle discold., frontis. creased, Vol. 8: without maps of 'Veneti Ducatus' & Padua called for by index, without the 4 extra maps of the Ticino in the Liby. of Congress copy (but not called for by index), lacks dedication lf. cited by Koeman, ptd. title mntd., sm. hole in blank surface of 1 map, anr. map creased, Vol. 9: with dedication lf. not called for by Koeman, Vol. 11: collation differs from Koeman, old mott. cf. gt., 2 spines defect. (S. Dec.1; 193) *Schuster.* £50,000

– [**Atlas of Scotland**]. Ca. 1662. Fo. 46 engraved maps, Fr. text on versos, soiled, damp-damaged thro.-out, w.a.f. (CSK. Aug.5; 19) £320

– **Le Grand Atlas, ou Cosmographie Blaviane.** Amst., 1967-68. *Facs. of 1663 Edn.* 12 vols. Lge. fo. Imitation cf. (VG. Sep.13; 54) Fls. 1,200

– – **Anr. Edn.** Amst., [1967-68]. *Facs. of 1663 Edn. (1000) numbered.* 12 vols. Atlas fo. Ex-liby., gt.-panel. & ornamented vell. bds. (SG. Apr.26; 21) $1,000

– **Novum Italiae Theatrum.** The Hague, Rutgert Alberts, 1724. Vol. 3. Fo. Engraved additional title in Fr., ptd. title in red & black, 37 engraved plans, panoramas, maps & views, faint margin stain at end, cont. gt.-panel. vell., slightly soiled, w.a.f. (S. May 21; 172) *Giunta.* £1,100

– – **Anr. Copy.** Vol. 1-3 (of 4). Lge. fo. 3 engraved titles, 3 double-p. engraved maps, 192 most double-p. copperplts., vol. II lacks 8 maps mentioned in index, vol. 1 sig. nos. jump & pagination also, cont. leath. gt., worn & bumped, spines partly defect. (HK. May 15; 886) DM 85,000

– **Russia.** Amst., ca. 1650. Fo. 2 town plans, 6 hand-cold. maps, mod. bds. (P. Oct.20; 263) £320

– **Théâtre des Etats de Son Altesse Royale le Duc de Savoye ....** The Hague, 1700. 2 vols. Lge. fo. Titles with lge. engraved vigs., 2 engraved frontis., 3 ports., plt. of arms, 131 engraved plts., comprising 12 folding, 109 double-p. & 10 single-p., double-p. genealogical table, mntd. on guards thro.-out, no port. in Vol. 2, cont. cf., spines gt. (C. Dec.9; 9) *Bemberg.* £5,800

– – **Anr. Copy.** 2 vols. Lge. fo. Titles with engraved vigs., 143 engraved plts., comprising 2 allegorical frontis., 5 ports. (1 additional, not called for by Koeman), 3 double-p maps, plt. of arms, double-p. genealogical table, 121 double-p. plans & views (some also folding), 10 single-p. plts., outer margins of 1 double-p. plt. shaved, early 19th. C. red hf. mor., corners rubbed. (C. Mar.14; 30) *Marshall.* £5,600

– **Theatrum Statuum Regiae Celsitudinis Sabaudiae Ducis [Piedmont & Savoy].** Amst., Johannes Blaeu's Heirs, 1682. *1st. Edn.* 2 vols. Fo. Engraved allegorical titles, 138 (of 140) engraved plts. (including 111 double-p. maps, plans, views & a gencalogical table, 12 lge. folding panoramas, 13 full-p. plts. showing ports. & architectural elevations, & 4 ills. in text), lacks 1 port. & 1 architectural elevation, some browning, 1 or 2 tears reprd. without loss of engraved surface, 1 plt. shaved to neatline, cont. vell. gt., slightly soiled, lacks ties, w.a.f. (S. May 21; 174) *King.* £5,400

– **Vierde Stuck der Aerdrycks-beschryving, welck vervat Engelandt, Theatrum.** Amst., 1648. Vol. IV [England & Wales]. Fo. Dutch text, engraved title with ptd. label, 57 engraved mapsheets (of 58, lacks Cheshire), title & mapsheets hand-cold. in outl., all embellishments fully illuminated & heightened with gold in manner of van Santen, staining affecting text & maps, cont. Dutch red mor., gt.-panel in roll borders, slightly worn, w.a.f. (S. May 21; 25) *Welbeck.* £5,000

BLAEU, Willem or Giulielmus Janszoon
- Tweede Deel des Groote Zee Spiegel...Derde Deel der Groote Zee Spiegel.... Amst., 1658. Sm. fo. 105 maps, 26 pp. from 1st. pt. bnd. at beginning, foxing & tears, parch., worn, disbnd., traces of worming. (SM. Mar.7; 2429) Frs. 35,500

BLAEU, Willem or Giulielmus Janszoon & Johannes or Jan
- Le Grand Atlas ou Cosmographie Blaviane. Amst., 1963. (1000) numbered. 12 vols. Fo. Decor. leath. in old style. (SI. Dec.15; 188) Lire 950,000
- Le Théâtre du Monde. Amst., 1638-48. Vols. 1-4 (of 6), Vols. 1 & 2 in 2 pts. Together 4 vols. 6 cold. engraved titles & 332 cold. copper engraved maps (double-p. or folding, 2 full-p., 3 half-p.), 4 hf.-p. text copper engrs., many text woodcuts, 1 lf. misbnd., 2 mispaginations in vol. 4, some margin tears, world map wormed in upr. & lr. margin, 5 maps crumpled, 10 maps with reprd. tears, some soiling, MS. owners note on vols. 1-3 end-papers, cont. vell., gold tooled, vol. 1 spine restored, slightly rubbed & bumped, partly defect. (D. Nov.23; 749) DM 105,000
- - **Anr. Edn.** Amst., J. Blaeu, 1645. Fr. Edn. Pt. 3 [Italy]. Fo. Engraved architectural title with ptd. overslip, 66 engraved maps, comprising 62 double-p., 1 full-p. & 3 hf.-p., all hand-cold., mntd. on guards thro.-out, cont. vell., covers gt.-panel. & with gt. centrepiece & corner ornaments. (C. Mar.14; 29) La Fenice. £2,300
- - **Anr. Edn.** Amst., 1646-50. 4 vols. Fo. Fr. text, Vol. 1-3 in 2 pts., 5 architectural engraved titles with ptd. title slips, 332 mostly double-p. engraved maps (of 334, lacks 2 maps of British Isles), 2 ptd. hf.-titles, index lf. at end of each vol., maps cont. hand-cold. thro.-out, titles & all embellishments fully so, in Vol. I map of Europe loosely inserted & map 'Circuli Westphaliae' mntd. on copy of map 'Westphalia Ducatus', in Vol. III last few maps detchd., 1 or 2 folding maps torn at additional folds, some short tears or minor creases at centrefolds, a few maps slightly browned, cont. vell. gt.-panel., slightly worn & soiled, w.a.f. (S. May 21; 105) Maggs. £18,000
- - **Anr. Edn.** Amst., 1647. Vol. 1 in 2 pts. Lge. fo. 2 engraved titles, partly gold-heightened, 118(of 120) double-p. cold. copper engraved maps. cont. vell. gt., slightly faded, lacks ties. (D. Nov.23; 750) DM 32,500
- - **Anr. Copy.** Pt. 3. Lge. fo. Engraved & cold. title, 62 double-p. cold. copper engraved maps, cont. vell. gt., slightly faded. (D. Nov.23; 751) DM 12,500
- Theatrum Orbis Terrarum, sive Atlas Novus. Pars quarta, Theatrum. Amst., 1646. Vol. 4 [England & Wales]. Fo. Latin text, engraved allegorical title with paste-on slip, heightened with gold, & 58 engraved regional & Country maps (57 double-p., Isle of Man full-p.), engraved & woodcut ills. in text, maps hand-cold. in outl., title & embellishments fully so, slight damage by adhesion affecting title, some browning or slight discolouration, cont. vell., gt.-panel, soiled, w.a.f. (S. May 21; 23) Hughests. £3,800
- Theatrum Orbis Terrarum; sive, Novus Atlas. Amst., Jan Blaeu, 1654. 1st. Edn. in Latin. Vol. V only: 'Scotland & Ireland'. Fo. Cold. & gt. engraved passepartout title with letterpress overslip, 1 single- & 54 double-p. engraved maps, all cold. by early hand, some ll. & about 10 maps browned, some other browning or foxing, few margin defects, cont. vell. gt. extra. (SC. Nov.3; 19) $2,400
- Theatrum Statutuum Regiae Celsitudinis Sabaudiae Ducis. Pedemontii Principis, Cypri Regis. Amst., 1682. 2 vols. Fo. Vol. 1: frontis, arms plt., 2 ports., engraved double-p. genealogical table double-p. map, 64 double-or triple-p. plts., Vol. 2: frontis., 2 ports., 2 double-p. maps, 67 double-or triple-p. plts., slight defects., 1 title remntd., margin repairs to 4 plts., foxing, some plts. heartily, cont. parch., gt.-decor., angle fleurons, lge. centre motif, decor. spine. (HD. Feb.29; 3) Frs. 60,000

BLAGDON, Francis William
- A Brief History of Ancient & Modern India. L., 1805 [text wtrmkd. 1820-22, plts. wtrmkd. 1831-34]. 3 pts. in 1 vol. Lge. fo. Additional hand-cold. engraved title, 2 hand-cold. engraved plts., handcold. aquatint title to 'Twenty-Four Views in Hin-

doostan', 64 hand-cold. aquatint views, 1 plt. creased in margin, engraved title slightly spotted in margin, 1 plt. slightly stained in margin, mod. purple hf. mor., orig. gt.-lettered mor. label in gt. scroll border. (C. Nov.16; 53) Hart. £950
- Graphic History of the Life, Exploits, & Death of Horatio Nelson ... Memoirs. L., 1806. 1st. Edn. Fo. On J. Whatman 1804 wtrmkd. laid paper, 4 full-p. or folding engraved plts. with orig. hand colouring, without 1 partial p. view (never ptd. on p.), 1 partial engr. trimmed at fore-edge, text lightly browned, a few sm. liby. hand-stps. at margin corners, orig. cl. over bds., lacks backstrip, covers very worn. (HA. Nov.18; 291) $220
See— WILLIAMSON, Capt. Thomas & Blagdon, Francis William

BLAIR, David
- The History of Australasia .... Glasgow, &c., 1879. 4to. Publisher's roan gt. (rubbed). (KH. Nov.8; 30) Aus. $120

BLAIR, Eric Arthur 'George Orwell'
- Animal Farm, a Fairy Story. 1945. 1st. Edn. Orig. cl., grey/green d.-w. (BBA. Jun.28; 66) T. Parsons. £160
- - **Anr. Copy.** Orig. cl., partially faded, d.-w. slightly frayed. (TA. Jan.19; 317) £95
- Burmese Days. L., 1935. 1st. Edn. Orig. cl., rubbed. (BBA. Nov.30; 319) Words etc. £60
- Critical Essays. L., 1946. 1st. Edn. Orig. cl., d.-w. (BBA. Nov.30; 321) Walton. £50
- Down & Out in Paris & London. L., 1933. 1st. Edn. Spotted, orig. cl., rubbed. (BBA. May 23; 121) Walton. £180
- - **Anr. Copy.** Orig. cl. (S. Mar.20; 948) Gekoski. £100
- Nineteen Eighty-Four. 1949. 1st. Edn. Orig. cl., red d.-w. (BBA. Jun.28; 67) T. Parsons. £110
- - **Anr. Copy.** Orig. cl., d.-w. slightly torn. (S. Mar.20; 949) Hildebrandt. £50
- - **Anr. Copy.** Burgundy mor. gt. (SPB. Dec.13; 552) $300
- - **Anr. Copy.** Orig. linen. (R. Oct.11; 370) DM 440

BLAIR, Hugh
- Sermons. Edinb., 1777-1801. 1st. Edns. 5 vols. Cont. cf., spines gt.; Sir Ivar Colquhoun, of Luss copy. (CE. Mar.22; 24) £230

BLAIR, Rev. John
- The Chronology & History of the World. 1754-68. 2 pts. in 1 vol. Fo. Engraved title, dedication, 114 tables & 15 double-p. maps, mod. cl., w.a.f. (CSK. May 4; 30) £150
- The Chronology & History of the World ... to ... 1779. L., 1779. Fo. Cont. cf. (GM. Dec.7; 723) £70

BLAIR, Robert
- The Grave. 1808. Fo. Slight spotting, tree cf., spine defect. (P. Jan.12; 125) Bickersteth. £180
- - **Anr. Edn.** Ill.:- after William Blake. 1813. 4to. Some light spotting, mod. cl.-bkd. bds., orig. label mntd. (CSM. Jun.1; 60) £95
- - **Anr. Copy.** 4to. Engraved extra title, engraved port., 11 plts., cont. cl., rebkd., old spine laid down. (CSK. Feb.24; 2) £50
- - **Anr. Copy.** 4to. Some spotting, mostly of text., port., title & final plt. stained, orig. cl., worn. (SPB. Dec.13; 781) $150

BLAIZOT, Claude & Gautrot, Jean-Edouard
- Chahine Illustrateur 1874-1947, Catalogue Raisonné. Preface:- Roger Marx. Paris, 1974. (365) numbered. 2 vols. Lge. 4to. 7 etched plts. in separate cl. folder, orig. cl. (S. Dec.20; 490) Leicester. £80

BLAKE, William
- The Book of Ahania. Paris, Trianon Pr., 1973. (32) for Trustees of the Blake Trust, with set of plts. showing progressive states of collotype & hand-stencil process & guide sheet, stencil & copper-plt. 4to. Mor., s.-c. (SPB. Dec.13; 905) $300
- A Cradle Song: The Divine Image: A Dream: Night. Ill.:- V. Angelo. N.Y., Valenti Angelo, 1949. (125) sigd. by Angelo. Hand-illuminated, bdg. not stated, slight adhesion damage to lr. cover, spine

darkening; the V. Angelo copy. (CBA. Oct.1; 361) $150
- Illustrations of the Book of Job, being all the Water-Colour Designs, Pencil Drawings & Engravings, reproduced in Facsimile. Ed.:– L. Binyon & Geoffrey Keynes. N.Y., 1935. 6 pts. Fo. Orig. wraps., unc., buckram fitted box worn; with several sigs. including that of Nigel Nicolson. (S. Nov.22; 313) Carlson. £360
- Jerusalem. L., Trianon Pr., [1974]. (32) with set of plts. showing progressive states of collotype & hand-stencil process & guide sheet & stencil. Lge. 4to. Mor., s.-c. (SPB. Dec.13; 906) $550
- Marriage of Heaven & Hell. [L., 1868]. 1st. Facs. Edn., [150?]. 4to. 27 hand-finished litho. facs. ll., some foxing, orig. mor.-bkd. cl., some soiling. (SPB. Dec.13; 780) $300
- - **Anr. Edn.** [1868]. 4to. Title & 26 ll., all handcold., spotted, orig. cf.-bkd. cl., slightly rubbed. (BBA. Feb.23; 214). Subunso. £85
- Pencil Drawings. Ed.:- Geoffrey Keynes. Nones. Pr., 1927. (1550) numbered. 4to. Cl.-bkd. bds., d.-w., soiled. (P. Mar.15; 247) Joseph. £55
- - **Anr. Edn.** Ed.:– Geoffrey Keynes. L., Nones. Pr., 1927-56. Ltd. Edns. [1st. &] 2nd. Series: 2 vols. 4to. Orig. hf. cl., & orig. cl., d.-w. (BBA. Apr.5; 105) Thorp. £80
- - **Anr. Copy.** 2 vols. 4to. Orig. hf. cl. & cl., Vol. 1 slightly soiled, Vol. 2 with d.-w. (BBA. Sep.8; 71) Leicester Art Books. £60
- Poetical Sketches. 1868. 1st. Reprint. Hf.-title, 1st. advt. lf., orig. cl. (BBA. Sep.29; 199) Pickering & Chatto. £56
- Silver Drops, or Serious Things. Ca. 1670. Cont. red mor., gt.-stpd. 'To the Lady de la Mere' on upr. cover, slightly worn, in mod. s.-c. (BS. Nov.16; 50) £190
- Songs of Innocence. Oxford, 1893. (100) numbered. Sm. 8vo. Orig. ptd. wraps., trifle worn. (BBA. Nov.30; 264) Quaritch. £110
- Songs of Innocence & Experience. 1839. 1st. Typographic Reprint. Orig. cl.,. (BBA. Sep.29; 198) Pickering & Chatto. £160
- - **Anr. Edn.** [L., Trianon Pr., 1955]. Facs. Edn. (526) numbered on Arches pure rag paper. 54 handcold. & illuminated plts., reprd. mor., gt.-lettered spine (darkened), boxed; the A.A. Houghton, Jnr. copy. (SG. Sep.15; 37) £650
- Vala or the Four Zoas. Ed.:– G.E. Bently. Oxford, 1963. Fo. Orig. cl., d.-w. (BBA. Apr.5; 120) Subun-So. £55
- Visions of the Daughters of Albion. 1959. (20) numbered. 4to. Set of hand-cold. plts. showing progressive stages, col. proofs & orig. guide sheet & stencil, cf., s.-c. (SSA. Jul.5; 37) R 410
- Works. Ed.:- E.J. Ellis & W.B. Yeats. L., 1893. 3 vols. Tall 8vo. Advt. lf., orig. pict. cl. gt. (SKC. Mar.9; 1713) £130
- - **Anr. Copy.** 3 vols. 3 ports., hf. mor., unc., ex libris. (P. May 17; 83) Bickersteth. £110
- The Writings. Ed.:– Geoffrey Keynes. Nones. Pr., 1925. (1500) numbered. 3 vols. Sm. fo. Orig. marb. bds., parch. backstrips, untrimmed. (TA. Nov.17; 558) £110
- - **Anr. Copy.** 3 vols. (With:) WILSON, Mona - The Life of William Blake. Nones. Pr., 1927. (1480) numbered. 1 vol. Together 4 vols. 4to. Unif. parch.-bkd. bds., lightly soiled. (CSK. Jul.27; 22) £85
- - **Anr. Edn.** Ed.:- Geoffrey Keynes. Nones. Pr., 1925. 3 vols. Soiled, title-pp. reprd., mod. cf., exliby. (CSK. Mar.23; 119) £65

BLAKSTON, W.A. & others
- The Illustrated Book of Canaries & Cage-Birds. [1877-80]. 4to. Chromolitho. frontis., 55 plts., title reprd. & slightly soiled, margins of 2 plts. browned, later hf. mor., lightly rubbed. (CSK. Jan.27; 152) £75
- - **Anr. Copy.** 55 col. plts., 1 loose, orig. cl. gt. (P. Feb.16; 25) £60

BLANC, Ch.
- Histoire des Peintres de Toutes les Ecoles. Paris, [1861]-76. 14 vols. Lge. 4to. Wide margin, Some slight browning & spotting, hf. leath., slightly worn. (H. May 22; 101a) DM 1,200

BLANC, François, dit LA GOUTTE
- Poésies en Patois du Dauphiné Grenoblo Malhérou. Preface:- George Sand. Ill.:- Rahoult, Dardelet. Grenoble, 1864. Lge. 80. At end: 'Copie

de la Lettre (Coupi de la Lettra)', Grenoble, 1874, 'Jacquety de le Comare', Grenoble, 1874, glossary at end hf. Ravanna chagrin, corners, decor. spine. (HD. Feb.29; 4) Frs. 1,700

BLANCARD or BLANKAART, Stephen
– Nauwkerige Verand. v.d. Scheur-buik en des Selfs Toevallen. Amst., 1684. 2 pts. in 1 vol. Sm. 8vo. Some stains, cont. vell., spine soiled. (VG. Nov.30; 745) Fls. 500

BLANCH, Antonio Puig
– La Inquisición sin Máscara. Cadiz, 1811. 16 issues. 4to. Leath. (DS. Mar.23; 2234) Pts. 75,000

BLANCHARD, P.
– Le Buffon de la Jeunesse. Zoologie, Botanique, Minéralogie. Ed.:– Chenu. Paris, ca. 1850. Lge. 8vo. Lithos, hand-cold., some foxing, cont. hf. mor. (VG. Sep.14; 794) Fls. 650
– Cours Elémentaire d'Histoire Naturelle: Le Buffon de la Jeunesse; Zoologie, Botanique, Mineralogie. Ed.:– M. Chenu. Paris, 1858. Sm. 4to. 91 hand-cold. woodcut plts., buckram. (SG. Mar.22; 52) $100

BLANCHETON, André Antonine
– Vues Pittoresques des Châteaux. Paris, [1826-30]. 2 vols. Lge 80. Wide margin, 2 litho. titles with vig., litho. port., 130 litho plts., titles & plt. verses with liby. stp., some light foxing, cont. hf. leath. gt., unc., rubbed & bumped. (R. Oct.13; 3087) DM 2,900

BLANCK, Jacob
– Bibliography of American Literature. New Haven & L., 1955-73. 6 vols. 4to. Orig. cl.; Fred A. Berne copy. (SPB. May 16; 186) $210
– – Anr. Edn. New Haven, [1955-73]. Vols.1-6. Lge. 8vo. Cl. (SG. Jan.5; 43) $225

BLANCUS, Marcus Antonius
– Practica Criminalis. Venice, 1583. Some foxing, some fore-edges reprd., cont. vell. (CBA. Dec. 10; 68) $100

BLAND, Humphrey
– A Treatise of Military Discipline. L., 1740. *4th. Edn.* Cont. cf. (SG. Sep.22; 58) $175

BLANDFORD, George Spencer, Marquis of
– White Knights Library, Catalogue. L., 1819. 2 pts. in 1 vol. Ruled in red thro.-out, prices & purchasers neatly marked in MS., title spotted, cont. cf., slightly rubbed. (S. May 1; 373)
Georges. £140
– – Anr. Copy. 2 pts. in 1. Buyers & prices marked in MS., title spotted, cont. cf. (S. Oct.11; 458)
Quaritch. £100

BLANDIN, P.F.
See– LEFOULON, P.J.– BLANDIN, P.F.

BLANE, William N.
[–] An Excursion Through the United States & Canada During the Years 1822-23. L., 1824. *1st. Edn.* Lacks errata lf., sm. tear to map reprd., cont. hf. mor., spine gt.; the Rt. Hon. Visc. Eccles copy. [Sabin 5872] (CNY. Nov.18; 24) $230

BLANKAART, Stephen
See– BLANCARD or BLANKAART, Stephen

BLANOT, E., Editor
– [Exposition Universelle Vues de Paris]. Paris, n.d. Ob. 4to. 30 hand-cold. tinted litho. plts, only, some light soiling, some upr. margins stained, orig. pict. cl., rubbed & soiled. (CSK. Jan.27; 222) £170

BLANQUET, J.P.
– A Series of Lithographic Drawings Illustrative of the Relation Between the Human Physiognomy & that of the Brute Creation from Designs by Charles le Brun. 1827. Lge. fo. Engraved port. frontis. (loose), 37 plts., some sm. margin tears, cl.-bkd. bds., worn, end-papers loose. (SKC. Jan.13; 2128) £85

BLASE, E.
– Le Chasseur au Chien Courant. Paris, 1838. *Orig. Edn.* 2 vols. Cont. lf. chagrin, corners, decor. spines, slightly faded. (HD. Dec.9; 100) Frs 1,400

BLASIS, Carlo
– Manuel Complet de la Danse. Trans.:– Paul Vergnaud. Paris, 1830. *1st. Fr. Edn.* 18mo. 86 figures on 5 engraved plts. (4 folding), 24-pp. mus. notat., orig. woodcut-pict. wraps., upr. wrap. & 1st. 2 gatherings loosening, unc. (SG. Apr.26; 23) $325
– Traité Elementaire, Théorique et Pratique de l'Art de la Danse. Milan, 1820. *1st. Edn.* 14 engraved plts., foxed, orig. wraps., brkn., hand-stp. on upr. wrap., unc., sigd. (SG. Apr.26; 22) $550

BLASIUS, Ernst
– Akiurgische Abb. od. Darst. d. Blutigen Chirurg. Operationen u. der f. dieselben erfundenen Werkzeuge. Berlin, 1844. Lge. fo. Last plt. with sm. bkd. side tear, slightly browned & soiled, cont. hf. leath. (HK. Nov.8; 466) DM 560

BLASIUS (or BLAES), Gerardus
– Anatome Animalium, Terrestrium Variorum, Volatilium, Aquatilium, Serpertium, Insectorum.... Ill.:– J. Luytuns. Amst., 1681. *1st. Edn.* 4to. Lightly browned & slightly brown spotted, cont. leath, gt., bumped. corners worn. (R. Apr.4; 1283) DM 1,350
– Observata Anatomica in Homine, Simia, Equo, Vitulo, Ove, Testudine, Echino, Glire, Serpente, Ardea .... Leiden & Amst., 1674. Sm. 8vo. Additional engraved pict. title, 18 copperplates, mod. buckram-bkd. bds. (SG. Oct.6; 54) $175

BLAST
1914-15. 2 vols. 4to. Orig. wraps. (P. Oct.20; 48) £220

BLAYDES, R.O.
– Lady Eve. San Franc., 1899. *1st. Edn.* No bdg. stated. (CBA. Oct.29; 123) $200

BLEI, Franz (Ed.)
See– AMETHYST, Der

BLESSINGTON, Countess of
– Heath's Book of Beauty, for 1834, 1835 & 1836. L., 1834-36. 3 vols. Mor. gt. (GM. Dec.7; 667) £85

BLEW, William C.A.
– Brighton & its Coaches. L., 1894. 20 hand-cold. plts., cl. gt. (P. May 17; 235) *Marlborough.* £65
– A History of Steeple-Chasing. Ill.:– after Henry Alken. 1901. Tall 8vo. 12 hand-cold. plts. & ills. to text. orig. cl. gt., partly untrimmed, slightly rubbed. *(With:)* – Famous Sporting Prints, IV - Coaching. 1927. Slim 4to. 8 col. plts., orig. wraps., rubbed. (TA. Jun.21; 254) £62
– The Quorn Hunt & its Masters. 1899. Double-p. map, 12 hand-finished col. plts.,cont. hf. mor. gt. by Hatchards, Piccadilly, partly untrimmed. (TA. Sep.15; 334) £70

BLIGH, William
– The Log of the Bounty. Ill.:– Lynton Lamb. Gold. Cook. Pr., 1937. *(300) numbered.* 2 vols. Sm. fo. Orig. cl., unc. (S. Nov.21; 225) *Buzek.* £280
– – Anr. Edn. Foreword:– Earl Mountbatten. [Guildford], 1975. *Facs. Edn., (500) numbered.* Fo. Three-qtr. cf. gt. (SG. Sep.22; 60) $550
– The Log of H.M.S. Providence 1791-93. L., 1976. *Facs. of MS. (500) numbered.* Sm. fo. Orig. hf. cf., s.-c. (BBA. Mar.21; 81) *The Bookroom.* £60
– – Anr. Copy. Fo. Three-qtr. cf. gt. (SG. Sep.22; 60a) $200
– – Anr. Copy. Hf. cf., s.-c. (JL. Nov.13; B80) Aus. $200
– A Narrative of the Mutiny on Board His Majesty's Ship Bounty .... L., 1790. *1st. Edn.* 4to. Plt. & 1 chart creased, chart with tears to margins & cut close at 2 borders, a few sm. stains & repairs to margins, mod. mor. (C. Jun.27; 80) *Morris.* £350
– – Anr. Copy. 4to. Maps & plt. all laid down on linen, title foxed, paper loss at head of title reprd., diced cf. gt., rebkd. (CA. Apr.3; 128) Aus. $900
Voyage in the Resource from Coupang to Batavia.... Gold. Cock. Pr., 1937. *(350) numbered.* Sm. fo. Bdg. not stated. (KH. May 1; 76) Aus. $230
– A Voyage to the South Seas...in his Majesty's Ship the Bounty ... Including an Account of the Mutiny on Board .... L., 1792. *1st. Edn.* Tall 4to. Inner margins of port.,title & 4 prelim. ll. reset on margin stubs when rebnd., port. dampsoiled &

reprd. on top inner margin, title with short blank fore-e. tear, last plt. rather foxed & bnd. in after final text lf., 1 coner defect., minor foxing on blank extremities of some ll., mod. qtr. leath. & marb. bds. [Sabin 5910] (SG. Sep.22; 59) $2,000
– – Anr. Copy. 4to. Port., 7 engraved maps & charts (4 folding or double-p), port. offset, some browning & foxing, final chart foxed, some margin soiling & spotting, cont. tree cf., Grantham bkplt. [Sabin 5910] (SPB. May 16; 12) $1,500
– – Anr. Copy. 4to. Slight foxing & offsetting, early cf., rebkd., corners rubbed. (KH. May 1; 74) Aus. $2,100
– – Anr. Copy. 4to. Most plts. laid down, title & most charts offset or foxed, 1 plt. margin torn off, hf. cf., rebkd., covers rubbed. (CA. Apr.3; 24) Aus. $1,100

BLISS, Robert Woods
– Robert Woods Bliss Collection: Pre-Columbian Art. Ed.:– S.K. Lothrop & others. L., 1957. Fo. No bdg. stated. (SPB. Nov.30; 130) $275

BLOCH, Jean-Richard
– Dix Filles dans un Pré. Ballet. Ill.:– Marie Laurencin. 1926. *Orig. Edn. (35) on japon impérial with double set of engrs.* 4 etchings, 2 suites, in leaves, sewed. (HD. Apr.13; 151) Frs. 9,200

BLOCH, Marcus Elieser
– Allgemeine Naturgeschichte der Fische. Berlin, 1783-87. 5 vols. only (of 12). Titles with wood-engraved vigs., 216 hand-cold. engraved plts., some heightened with silver & varnish, a few ptd. in red, non-unif. cont. hf. russ. (C. Jun.27; 141) *Koch.* £1,200
– Ichthyologie, ou Histoire Naturelle, Générale et Particulière des Poissons. Trans.:– J.C. Thibault de Laveaux. Berlin, 1795-85-97. 12 pts. in 6 vols. Fo. Engraved vigs. on titles, 432 hand-cold. engraved plts., some heightened in silver, lacks dedication lf. in Vol. I, a few stains in margins at beginning of pt. V & at end of pt. XII, sm. flaw affecting text on Nl pt. III, margin repair to C2 Pt. VIII, hf. mor. gt. by Zaehnsdorf, spines emblematically tooled in compartments. (S. Feb.1; 8) *Tulkens.* £15,000
– Oeconomische Naturgeschichte der Fische Deutschlandes. [Berlin, 1782-85]. Plt. vol. Ob. fo. Title lf. stpd., prelim. if. with owener's note, 4 sm. margin tears, l pasted, some sm. spots, lightly soiled thro.-out, cont. hf. leath., very defect. (H. Nov.23; 226) DM 12,500

BLOCH, (Contribs.)
See– GENIUS

BLOEMART, Abraham
– Eerste Beginseln der Tekenkunst. Amst., ca. 1720. Sm. fo. Etched frontis., 140 numbered engraved & etched plts., including 7 titles, a little stained at end & some slight soiling, 1 plt. tape reprd., cont. marb. cf. gt., spine & corners slightly defect. (VS. Jun.7; 864) Fls. 475

BLOIS, John T.
– Gazetteer of the State of Michigan, in Three Parts, ... with a Succint History of the State. Detroit, 1838. *1st. Edn.* Lge. 12mo. Foxed, lacks errata slip, cont. gift bndg. gt. decor. cf., inscr. on front fly-lf to Hon. William Woodbridge (Governor of Michigan). (SG. Apr.5; 126) $140

BLOK, Alexander
– Dvenacat. Ill.:– Larionov & Gontscharowa. Paris, 1920. Orig. sewed, owner's mark on end-paper. (GB. Nov.5; 2302) DM 800
– The Twelve. Trans.:– Babette Deutsch & Avrahm Yarmolinsky. Ill.:– George Biddle. N.Y., 1931. *(100) with lithos. by Biddle, 1 sigd.* 4to. Leath.-bkd. patterned bds., s.-c. spotted & faded. (SG. Jan.12; 45) $250

BLOK, P.J.
See– MOLHUYSEN, P.C., Blok, P.J. & others

BLOME, Richard
– Britannia or, a Geographical Description of the Kingdoms of England, Scotland, & Ireland. L., 1673. *1st. Edn.* Fo. 50 double-p. engraved maps, Kent torn, Scotland loose, cont. cf., rebkd. (P. Nov.24; 310) *Burgess.* £1,400
– – Anr. Copy. Sm. fo. Engraved plan, 49 folding

BLOME, Richard -*Contd.*

or double-p. maps, 12 engraved ll. of arms, sm.wormhole in upr. margin prelims., cont. cf. gt. (BBA. Sep.29; 127) *Angle Books.* £1,250
- **The Fanatick History; or an Exact Relation & Account of the Old Anabaptists & New Quakers.** L., 1660. *1st. Edn.* 1 margin reprd. affecting side note. 19th. C. mor. [Wing B3212] (BBA. May 3; 144) *Howes Bookshop.* £120
- **The Gentleman's Recreation.** Ill.:– Gribelin, Soly, & others. L., by S. Roycroft for Richard Blome, 1686. *1st. Edn.* 2 pts. in 1 vol. Fo. Engraved frontis., 85 plts., 1 plt. laid down, 3 plts. roughly cut down, 8 ll. wormed in 1r. margin, including 6 plts., hole in 1 text lf., old hf. russ., worn, covers detchd., w.a.f. [Wing B3213] (C. Mar.14; 120) *Douwma.* £850
- **The present State of His Majesties Isles & Territories in America... with New Maps of every Place.** Ill.:– Robert Morden. L., 1687. *1st. Edn.* Lacks map of Jamaica, perforated liby stp. &c. on title, three-qtr. lev. by Stikeman. (SG. Jan.19; 107) $1,300
See— **COX, Nicholas & Blome, Richard**

BLOMFIELD, Francis
- **An Essay Towards a Topographical History of the County of Norfolk.** 1805-10. *2nd. Edn.* 11 vols. 4to. Some browning in a few vols., cont. russ. gt., some hinges strengthened. (SKC. Mar.9; 1967) £280

BLOMFIELD, Sir Reginald T.
- **A History of French Architecture, 1494-1774.** L., 1911-21. *1st. Edn.* 4 vols. 4to. 378 plts., cl. (SG. Oct.13; 38) $150

BLONDEL, François, 1618-86
- **Cours d'Architecture.** Paris, 1683. *Orig. Edn.* Pts. 2-5 in 2 vols. Fo. Cont. cf. (HD. Dec.15; 3) Frs. 1,200

BLONDEL, Jacques Francois 1705-74
- **Architecture Françoise.** Paris, 1752-56. *1st. Edn.* 4 vols. Fo. 500 engraved plts. on 499 ll., many double-p. or folding, few plts. & text ll. wormed, few ll. discold., some spotting, few minor fold tears, 1 plt. reprd., 1 plt. shaved, a few others trimmed to plt. mark, cont. mott. cf., spines gt., many repairs to some covers. (C. Dec.9; 10) *Weinreb.* £3,000
- **Cours d'Architecture ou Traité de la Decoration, Distribution & Construction des Batiments.** Paris, 1771-77. 9 vols., including 3 plt. vols. Cont. marb. cf., decor. spines, plt. vols. not unif. with others, some slight wear. (HD. Dec.1; 62) Frs. 2,000
- **De la Distribution des maisons de plaisance ....** Ill.:– Cochin. Paris, 1737-38. *1st. Edn. 1st. Iss.* 2 vols. 4to. Engraved frontis., 155 plts., many double-p. or folding, errata lf. & hf.-title to Vol. 1 only, some fore-edges of plts. strengthened, cont. cf., spines gt. (C. Dec.9; 11) *Waldersee.* £500
- **Décorations Extérieures & Intérieures des XVIIe & XVIIIe Siècles.** Bruxelles, ca. 1910. Fo. 225 full-p. gravure plts., some extremities of plts. slightly darkened, loose in hf. cl. & decor. bd. portfo., slightly worn & lightly soiled, ties. (CBA. Jan.29; 154) $180

BLONDUS, Flavius
- **Historiarum ab Inclinatione Romanorum Imperii Decades.** Venice, Octavianus Scotus, 16 Jul. 1483. Fo. Lacks 1st. blank, hf. cf.; the Walter Goldwater copy. [BMC V, 277; Goff B-698] (SG. Dec.1; 73) $550
- **Roma Instaurata. De Gestiis Venetorum.** Verona, Boninus de Boniniis, 1481. Fo. 52 (of 60) numbered pp., lacks 6 pp. table at beginning & 2 blank pp., light staining, mod. bds. [HC 3243] (CR. Jun.6; 103) Lire 750,000

BLOODSTOCK BREEDER'S REVIEW, The
1912-76. Vols. 1-65. Hf. cf. & cl. gt. (P. Dec.8; 201) *Allen.* £900

BLOOMFIELD, Robert
- **The Fakenham Ghost, a True Tale.** L., William Darton, n.d. 16mo. Ills. hand-cold., 1 lf. lacks corner slightly affecting text, soiled, inscr. dtd. 1810, orig. wraps., with engraved title on upr. cover & the last

ill. & verse on lr. cover, worn, backstrip worn & crudely restitched. (S. Nov.22; 369) *Hirsch.* £80

BLOSSFELDT, Karl
- **Art Forms in Nature.** N.Y., 1929-32. 1st. & 2nd. Series: 2 vols. 4to. 240 photogravure plts., 1st. vol. with 1 plt. detched & some light dampwrinkling, orig. gt.-pict. cl., the 1st. loose. (SG. Nov.10; 28) $150

BLOUNT, Sir Henry
- **A Voyage into the Levant.** L., 1638. *3rd. Edn.* 4to. Recased in mod. vell. [STC 3138] (C. Nov.16; 54) *Martinos.* £100

BLOUNT, Sir Thomas Pope
- **Censura Celebriorum Authorum.** 1690. *1st. Edn.* Fo. Hf.-title, bdg. not stated, rebkd. & reprd., slightly rubbed. [Wing B3346] (BBA. Sep.29; 146) *Mackitterick.* £90

BLOW, John
- **Amphion Anglicus. A Work of Many Compositions, For One, Two, Three & Four Voices: With serveral Accompangments of Instrumental Musick....** L., priv. ptd., 1700. *1st. Edn.* Fo. Without the engraved frontis. of Blow, orig. panel. cf., a little scuffed, stained & foxed. (S. Nov.17; 89) *MacNutt.* £250

BLOXAM, R.W.
- **Sketches of Cottage & Farmhouse Windows.** Ca. 1840. 4to. Engraved title, 17 plts., mor. gt. (P. Jul.26; 142) £100

BLUETT, Thomas
- **Some Memoirs of the Life of Job ... Who was a Slave about two Years in Maryland.** L., 1734. *1st. Edn.* Without the folding port. (found in some copies), margin tear in [A3] reprd., just touching a few letters, maroon hf. mor.; the Rt. Hon. Visc. Eccles copy. [Sabin 6011] (CNY. Nov.18; 25) $420

BLUM, A. & Laure, P.
- **La Miniature Française aux XVe et XVIe Siècles.** Paris & Brussels, 1930. 4to. Cont. hf. cf., orig. upr. wrap. bnd. in. (S. Apr.30; 118) *Gerino.* £90

BLUME, Karl Ludwig
- **Rumphia.** Brussels & Leiden, 1836-48. Vols.1, 3 & 4. Fo. 2 ports., 143 cold. lithos., some spotting, loose in orig. ptd. bds., spines brkn. (SPB. May 17; 571) $900

BLUMENBACH, Johann Friedrich
- **Abbildungen Naturhistorischer Gegenstände.** Göttingen, 1810. Hf.-title, 100 plts. (11 cold.), cont. hf. cf.; Dr. Walter Pagel copy. (S. Feb.7; 54) *Quaritch.* £170
- **Handbuch der Vergleichenden Anatomie.** Göttingen, 1805. *1st. Edn.* Cont. hf. leath. (R. Oct.12; 1366) DM 950

BLUMENHAGEN, W.
- **Wanderungen durch den Harz.** Ill.:– after Ludwig Richter. Leipzig, [1838]. 30 steel engrs., slightly foxed thro.-out, cont. hf. leath., jnts. sprung, inner jnt. brkn., rubbed. (GB. May 3; 154) DM 400

BLUMEN-LIEDER FUR KNABEN UND MADCHEN
Ill.:– F.von Pocci. [München, 1832]. Ob. 4to. Loose 11. with corded wraps. (GB. Nov.4; 1869) DM 750

BLUNDEN, Edmund
- **The Poems, 1914-30.** 1930. *1st. Edn.* Orig. cl., slightly soiled; pres. inscr. & 6 lines of verse by author on front free end-paper, & A.N.s. pasted in upr. cover. (BBA. Feb.23; 322) *Fletcher.* £60

BLUNDEVILLE, Thomas
- **The Foure Chiefest Offices belonging to Horsemanship.** L., 1609. 4 pts. in 1 vol. Sm. 4to. (in 8's). Dampstained, some sigs. & catchwords cropped, mostly at end, last lf. rehinged, some slight margin worming at end, lev. mor. by Sangorski & Sutcliffe, spine gt.-lettered; Thomas B. Stevenson copy. [STC 3157] (CNY. May 18; 135) $750
- **M. Blundeville His Exercises ....** L., 1594. *1st. Edn.* 6 pts. in 1 vol. Sm. 4to. Woodcut ills. on fo. 145r & fo. 350r with woodcut movable parts for

their volvelles untrimmed as iss. & bnd. in, diagram on fo. 338v with woodcut volvelle parts bnd. in between folios 342 & 343, no volvelle on U7 (as in B.L. copy), diagram reprd. at fold, slight flaws to folios 13, 14 & 210, minor margin defects, 19th. C. vell., due to possible lack of movable parts, w.a.f. [Sabin 6023; STC 3146] (C. Nov.9; 42) *Quaritch.* £1,400
- - **Anr. Edn.** L., 1606-05. *3rd. Edn.* 8 pts. in 1 vol. Sm. 4to. Lacks preliminary blank & folios 337 & 348-9, fo. 147 & folding table torn, last lf. reprd., headlines in latter portion trimmed, annots. to title & some other pp., cont. of., worn. [STC 3148] (PNY. Mar.27; 149) $525

BLUNT, Sir Anthony
- **Nicholas Poussin.** N.Y., 1967. 3 vols. No bdg. stated. (SPB. Nov.30; 60) $225

BLUNT, Sir Anthony (Ed.)
See— **ROTHSCHILD, James A. de**

BLUNT, Charles
- **An Essay on Mechanical Drawing, comprising an Elementary Course of Practice in the Perspective Delination of Machinery.** L., 1811. *1st. Edn.* 4to. 63 plts., many partly in aquatint, disbnd. (SG. Oct.6; 55) $200

BLUNT, John (Pseud.)
See— **FORES, Samuel William 'John Blunt'**

BLUNT, Wilfred Jaspar Walter
- **Flora Magnifica.** Ill.:– Paul Jones. L., 1976. *(506)* sigd. by artist. Fo. Orig. hf. vell. by Zaehnsdorf, cl. s.-c. (C. Nov.16; 220) *Windlesham.* £80
- **Flora Superba.** Ill.:– Paul Jones. [1971]. *(406)* numbered & sigd. by artist. Fo. Orig. hf. vell., s.-c. (CSK. Mar.23; 121) £130
See— **SITWELL, Sacheverell & others**

BLUNTSCHLI, J.C.
[-] **Die Kommunisten in der Schweiz.** Zürich, 1843. *1st. Edn.* Title-lf. with faded stamp, orig. hf. linen, slightly soiled. (GB. Nov.4; 1514) DM 560

BOADEN, James
- **Memoirs of Mrs. Siddons.** L., 1893. Extra-ill. with 45 ports. & views, lev. mor. decor. tool cornerpieces, upr. cover set with oval miniature port. of Mrs. Siddons after Sir Joshua Reynolds, gt. spine in 6 compartments, turn-ins gt., silk marker, fleece-lined folding cl. box, by W. Root & son, w.a.f. (CNY. Dec.17; 597) $1,600

BOARD OF AGRICULTURE & INTERNAL IMPROVEMENT
- **Agricultural Reports, Drawn up for the Consideration of the Board of Agriculture & Internal Improvement.** L. or Edinb., 1793-95. Comprising a series of 77 reports (49 for England & Wales, & 28 for Scotland), bond. in 9 vols. 4to. Cont. cf., as a coll., w.a.f. (C. Nov.9; 125) *Traylen.* £2,400

BOASE, G.C. & Courtney, William Prideaux
- **Bibliotheca Cornubiensis.** L., 1874-82. 3 vols., including Supp. Orig. cl. (BBA. Apr.5; 270) *Dawson.* £140

BOATE, Gerard
[-] **A Natural History of Ireland, in Three Parts.** Dublin, 1726. 4to. Some dampstains, cf. (GM. Dec.7; 458) £180

BOBBIN, Tim (Pseud.)
See— **COLLIER, John**

BOBERG, Folke
- **Mongolian-English Dictionary.** Stockholm & Copen., 1954-55. 3 vols. 4to. Orig. cf.-bkd. cl., d.-wis. (BBA. Mar.7; 28) *Ad Orientem.* £110

BOBRIK, E.
- **Handb. der Praktischen Seefahrtskunde.** Leipzig, 1848. 4 vols., including atlas. Lacks 1 plt., few plts. torn & reprd., text slightly foxed, orig. hf. cf., slightly worn, 1 spine reprd. (VG. Sep.13; 136) Fls. 450

BOCCACCIO, Giovanni
- **Affrican & Mensola.** Oxford, Roxb. Cl. 1946. Hf. mor., unc. (S. Oct.11; 588) *Maggs.* £90
- **L'Amorosa Fiammetta.** Venice, Gabriel Giolito

de Ferrari, 1545. Cont. limp vell. (BBA. Mar.21; 4) *Thorp.* £55
- **The Decameron. [English].** Ill.:– Thomas Derrick. L., 1924. Cf., 2 metal clasps in medieval style. (SG. Feb.16; 34) $100
- – **Anr. Edn.** Ill.:– Fritz Kredel. N.Y., Ltd. Edns. Cl., [1940]. *(530) numbered, designed by George Macy, sigd. by artist.* 2 vols. 4to. Qtr. cf., gt.-patterned cl. (SG. May 17; 161) $100
- – **Anr. Edn.** Trans.:– Richard Aldington. Ill.:– Rockwell Kent. Garden City, 1949. *(1500) sigd. by artist.* 2 vols. Lge. 8vo. Cl., spines slightly rubbed at foot, s.-c. chafed. (SG. Mar.29; 177) $175
- **Le Décameron [French].** Ill.:– after Gravelot, Eisen, & Cochin fils. 'Londres' [i.e. Paris], 1757-61. 5 vols. L.P., engraved titles, port., 110 plts., 2 sm. paperfaults, 1 blank fore-edge remargined, short tear in blank margin of anr. lf. reprd., cont. Fr. red mor. gt., spines gt., slight chipping at head or foot of 3 spines, spines slightly rubbed; Duke of Hamilton bkplt. (C. Nov.9; 43) *Chaponniere.* £1,600
- – **Anr. Copy.** 5 vols. Extra-ill with erotic engraved plts., some browning & spotting, affecting some plts., cont. Spanish red mor. gt., gt. spine, some rubbing, scuff mark on spine & lr. cover of Vol. 5, inner hinges reinforced. (SPB. Dec.14; 40) $2,400
- – **Anr. Copy.** 5 vols. Free suite by Gravelot (frontis. & 20 figures in 1st. printing) bnd. in, early 19th. C. red mor. gt., sigd. by Hering. (HD. Mar.19; 34) Frs. 28,000
- – **Anr. Copy.** 5 vols. Frontis. added from suite 'Estampes galantes des contes de Boccace', Vol. IV washed, margin tear in 2 ll., cont. str.-grd. red mor. gt., decor. spines. (HD. Sep.22; 192) Frs. 6,300
- – **Anr. Copy.** 5 vols. Wide margin, on Dutch paper, 1st. & last ll. lightly browned or brown spotted, 2 engraved ex-libris inside cover, cont. cf., gt. spine, rubbed, spine torn in jnts. (H. May 22; 616) DM 1,800
- **Das Dekameron. [German].** Ill.:– [A. Wesselski]. [Leipzig, 1912]. *Jubiläumsausgabe. (825) numbered on Bütten.* 4to. Orig. leath., gt., spine, & corners slightly worn. (HK. May 16; 1944a) DM 400
- **Il Decamerone, [Italian].** Trans.:– Leonardo Salviati. Flor., 1587. *4th. Edn.* 4to. Vell. (DS. Nov.25; 2142) Pts. 38,000
- – **Anr. Edn.** Trans.:– Luigi Groto Cieco d'Adria, Gir. Ruscelli. Venice, 1590. 4to. Staining, cont. vell., slightly disbnd., spotted. (GB. May 4; 302) DM 400
- – **Anr. Edn.** Amst., 1665. 12mo. 18th. C. mor., decor. spine, inner foll-stp. (HD. Sep.22; 191) Frs. 2,200
- – **Anr. Copy.** 12mo. I lf. with slight tear, some pencil underlining, red-black mor., in Bozérian style, France, ca. 1810, gold decor., stps., at inner & outer dentelle, red-brown silb doubl. & endpapers, s.-c.; from Jean Fürstenberg liby. (D. Nov.23; 157) DM 1,550
- – **Anr. Edn.** [Venice, 1729]. *Facs. of the Flor., 1527 edn.* Cont. Vell., soiled. (BBA. Feb.23; 40) *Maggs.* £85
- – **Anr. Copy.** 19th. C. hf. cf., gt. spine, rubbed. (BBA. Nov.30; 62) *Quaritch.* £65
- – **Anr. Copy.** 4to. L.P. leath.; Sir Edward Sullivan ex-libris. (DS. Nov.25; 2144) Pts. 36,000
- – **Anr. Copy.** 4to. L.P. 19th. C. leath. (DS. Apr.27; 2301) Pts. 30,000
- – **Anr. Edn.** Ill.:– Aliamet, Baquoy, & others, after Gravelot, Boucher, Cochin, & Eisen. L. [Paris], 1757. *1st. Iss., with paraphe.* 5 vols. Engraved title, port., 110 plts., H4 & 5 in Vol. 5 with margin tear reprd., glue discold., cont. red mor., spine gt., rubbed (especially Vol. 3). (SPB. Dec.13; 782) $1,200
- – **Anr. Copy.** 5 vols. Cont. cf. gt. (HD. May 3; 18) Frs. 10,000
- **Les Dix Journées.** Ed.:– Paul Lacroix. Trans.:– Le Macon. Ill.:– Léopold Flameng. Paris, 1873. *(600) on Holland H.M.P.* 4 vols. Sm. 8vo. 11 etched plts., crimson crushed lev. gt. by Cuzin, spines & dentelles gt. (SG. Feb.16; 35) $140
- **Genealogiae ... eiusdè de Motibus & Syluis, de Fontibus ....** Venezia, 15 Nov. 1511. Sm. fo. Some worming with light loss of text, later bds. (SI. Dec.15; 5) Lire 250,000
- **Gesammelte Werke.** Ed.:– B. Wolffram. Ill.:–

Ludwig Kainer. Potsdam, 1921. *De Luxe Edn., (100) numbered, with etchings sigd.* 3 vols. 25 orig. etchings, orig. hand-bnd. vell., gold-decor. & cold. centre-piece, by Otto Dorfner, Weimar, ex-libris. (GB. Nov.5; 2304) DM 1,000
- **Opera Volgari....** Firenze, 1828. Crimson hf. mor., bkplt. (GM. Dec.7; 685) £95
- **Il Philocopo.** Venice, 1538. Some foxing, early vell., wrinkled. (SG. Oct.27; 30) $200
- **Le Plaisant Livre aquel il traicte des Faictz & Gestes des Illustres & Clères Dames.** Trans.:– [Laurent de Premierfait]. Paris, 4 Mar. 1538. *2nd. Edn.* 19th. C. mor., blind-tooled decor., gold-tooled corner fleurons & lge. orientalised centre-piece, gt. spine, gt. inner & outer dentelle, sigd. by Lortic. (D. Nov.23; 91) DM 2,800

BOCCACCIO the Younger
- **Recueil des plus Jolis Contes en Vers....** Paris, [1786]. 24mo. Cont. red mor. gt. (HD. May 3; 19) Frs. 1,200

BOCCHIUS, Achilles
- **Symbolicarum Quaestionum de Universo Genere.** Ill.:– Giulio Bonasone. Bologna, 1555. Sm. 4to. Engraved port., 146 ills. only, 1 holed, anr. cleanly torn, lacks title, 1st. 3 prelims. & all after 2V2 dampstained, cont . marginalia, stitched. (CSK. Feb.24; 97) £65
- – **Anr. Edn.** Ill.:– Giulio Bonasone, retouched by Agostino Caracci. Bologna, 1574. *2nd. Edn.* Sm. 4to. 150 full-p. copperplts., erratically numbered, lacks 3 plts., some light foxing, 18th. C. mott. cf. (SG. Feb.9; 218) $250

BOCHART, Samuel
- **Opera Omnia.** Leiden & Utrecht, 1692. 3 vols. Fo. 4 titles with engraved vig., engraved frontis. & port., 13 engraved maps (4 double-p.), cont. blind-panel. vell., 1 spine chipped. (C. Mar.14; 132) *Tooleys.* £240

BOCHIUS, Joannes
- **Descriptio Publicae Gratulationis.** Antw., 1595. Fo. Lacks all after L6, some margins dampstained, cont. vell., soiled, w.a.f. (CSK. Jun.15; 100) £100
- – **Anr. Copy.** Fo. 19th. C. hf. cf. (LM. Mar.3; 2) B.Frs. 38,000
- – **Anr. Copy.** Fo. Lightly browned, 1 title lf. & some ll. with ink stains & sm. margin creases, 1 copper engr with sm. bkd. defect. & 1 with tear, cont. vell., defect. (HT. May 10; 2322) DM 1,900
- **Historica Narratio Profectionis et Inavgvrationis... Belgii Principvm Alberti et Isabellae, Avstriae Archidvcvm.** Ill.:– P. van der Borcht after O. van Veen. Antw., 1602. Fo. Some margins with sm. tears with slight loss, 2 title ll. & last lf. with owners mark, mod. lf. vell. (H. May 22; 360) DM 1,200

BOCK, A.
- **Der Flurschütz.** Mainz, Ernst Ludwig Pr., 1929. *(135) numbered.* Orig. vell. gt., orig. bd. s.-c. (GB. Nov.5; 2425) DM 450

BOCK, C.E.
- **Atlas der Pathologischen Anatomie.** Leipzig, 1855. *1st. Edn.* Text ll. foxed, cont. hf. linen, slightly rubbed. (R. Apr.4; 1284) DM 480

BOCK, Hieronymous
- **Kräuterbuch.** Ed.:–Sebizius. Strassb., 1630. Fo. Lacks ptd. title & 1 lf. preface, Copper engraved title reprd. with paper strips in outer margin & 1r. corner, some old notes, some soiling or foxing, 2 ll. with tears, later (18th. c.?) leath. (D. Nov.23; 426) DM 5,300
- **Kreuter Buch.** Strassburg, 1546. *2nd. Edn.* 3 vols. in 1. Fo. Title lf. bkd. Pt. III with separate title lf., pt. III lacks 23 ll. & 14 index ll., some woodcuts with monog. DK, many ll. reprd. with pasted tears, some with much loss, approx. 20 ll. covered with vell. Paper on both sides, spotted & browned, many MS annots., old cf. over wood bds., reprd., clasps renowed. (H. May 22; 196) DM 2,000
- [–] **New Kreuter Buch.** Ed.:– M. Sebizius. Ill.:– D. Kandel. [Strassbourg], ca. 1577-87. Fo. Lacks 1st. 15 ll. & 23 ll. index at end, lightly browned, slightly wormed, several reprd. defects., some foxing & staining, 19th. C. hf. vell. from old 17th. C. vell. bdg., bumped. (HK. Nov.8; 468) DM 1,100

BOCKLER, Georg Andreas
- **Architectura Curiosa Nova.** Nuremb., 1664. 4 pts. in 1 vol. Fo. Engraved frontis., 231 plts. on 200 ll., including 1 folding, short fold-tear, sm. paper fault in plt. 66, cont. cf.; the Sir Andrew Balfour copy. (C. Dec.9; 12) *Waldersee.* £700
- – **Anr. Edn.** Trans.:– J. Ch. Sturn. Nuremb., 1701. *2nd. Edn. of Sturn's trans.* Fo. 230 plts., cont. marb. roan, spine decor. (HD. Mar.21; 11) Frs. 5,500
- **Theatrum Machinarum Novum, das ist, Neu-vermehrter Schauplatz der Mechanischen Künsten.** Nuremb., 1661. *1st. Edn.* Fo. Sm. wormhole in inner margin at front, engraved title hinged with wear to inner margins, some light spotting, vell. bds.; John D. Stanitz coll. (SPB. Apr.25; 46) $2,200
- – **Anr. Edn.** Nuremb., 1673. *[2nd. Edn.].* Fo. A few short margin tears, engraved title loosening, cont. cf., spine gt., slightly rubbed, head of spine worn; John D. Stanitz coll. (SPB. Apr.25; 47) $800
- – **Anr. Copy.** Fo. Extra engraved title, 154 plts., engraved title reinforced on verso of blank edges, approx. 50 plts. have fore-edges replaced on verso with 18th. C. paper, mod. qtr. mor. (SG. Apr.19; 41) $600
- **Anr. Copy.** *2nd. Edn.* Fo. Plt. section slightly stained near end in upr. margin, 1 plt. bnd. inverted, cont. vell. (R. Apr.4; 1621) DM 3,000
- – **Anr. Edn.** Nürnberg, 1703. Fo. Title copper engr. with some loss, 15 copperplts. with bkd. defects., some staining, foot of spine defect., 1r. cover very rubbed, cont. leath. gt., supralibros on upr. cover. (BR. Apr.12; 600) DM 2,200

BOCKSPERGER, Hans
See— **AMMAN, Jost & Bocksperger, Hans**

BODE, Johann Elert
- **Kurzgefasste Erläuterang der Sternkunde....** Berlin, 1778. *1st. Edn.* 2 vols. Cont. leath. gt. (R. Apr.4; 1506) DM 430
- **Vorstellung der Gestirne; Representation des Astres....** Berlin & Stralsund, 1805. *2nd. Edn.* 2 vols. including Atlas. 4to. & ob. 4to. Text in German & Fr., atlas with engraved title & 34 maps, later hf. mor. (SG. Apr.26; 25) $300

BODE, Dr. Wilhelm von
- **Frans Hals: Sein Leben und Seine Werke.** Ed.:– M.J. Binder. Berlin, 1914. *(200) numbered, on Van Gelder H.M.P.* 2 vols. Fo. 194 gravure plts., lettered tissue-guards, ex-liby., three- qtr. leather. (SG. May 3; 196) $250
- **Die Gemäldegalerie des Herrn A. de Ridder.** Berlin, 1910. *(100) numbered.* Some ll. slightly spotted, mor.-bkd. cl., partly unc., a little wear. *(With:)* - **Die Gemäldesammlung Marcus Kappel.** Berlin, 1914. *(150) numbered.* Cont. cf., rubbed. (S. Apr.30; 273) *Zwemmer.* £50

BODE, W. (Ed.)
See— **JAHRBUCH DER KONIGLICH PREUS-SISCH KUNSTSAMMLUNGEN**

BODE, Dr. Wilhelm & Hofstede de Groot, Cornelis
- **Complete Work of Rembrandt.** Trans.:– Florence Simmonds. Paris, 1897-1906. 8 vols. Lge. fo. 595 plts., each with title-lf. & tissue-guard, ills., ex-liby., orig. buckram. (SG. May 3; 303) $750

BODENEHR, Gabriel
- [–] **Atlas Curieux oder Neuer und Compendieuser Atlas.** Augsburg, ca. 1720-30. Engraved title, 102 engraved maps & tables, folding index, with supp. title & 20 (of 25) additional maps, most partly hand-cold., few tears & repairs, slight soiling, old cf., rubbed. (SPB. Dec.13; 498) $2,300
- **Europens Pracht und Macht in 200 Kupfer-Stucken....** Augsburg, ca. 1720. Ob. 4to. Engraved title, dedication, register, 200 engraved views, some on 2 sheets & folding, 2 additional plts. bnd. in, text & index in Latin (misbnd.), outer margin of 2 plts. slightly shaved, margin tear in plt. 28, slight worming in lr. margin of a few plts., affecting text in about 8 plts., 19th. c. hf. vell. (C. Jun.27; 11) *Rheinbuch.* £9,000
- **Force d'Europe.** Augsburg, ca. 1720. Sm. ob. fo. Engraved title, 181 (of 200) plans & views, including 20 folding, with 1 additional double view

BODENEHR, Gabriel -*Contd.*

of Lisbon before & after the 1755 earthquake by David Herrliberger, 1756, title & last plt. slightly creased, 1 or 2 outer margins slightly frayed, cont. qtr. parch., paper bds., worn. (S. Dec.1; 204)
Shapero. £2,050

BODENSCHATZ, Johann Christoph Georg
– **Kirchliche Verfassung der heutigen Juden sonderlich derer in Deutschland in IV Haupt-Theile abgefasst.** Erlangen, 1748; Frankfurt & Leipzig, Coburg, 1749. 4 pts. in 1 vol. 4to. 2 title-pp., engraved frontis. & 29 plts., errata lf. at end, cont. hf. vell. (S. May 10; 232)   *Steinberg.* £580

BODIN, Jean
– **De La Démonomanie des Sorciers.** Paris, 1580. *Orig. Edn.* 4to. Sm. hole in title–p., Old MS. margin notes, slight foxing on title & some ll., a little short at head. old hf. havanna roan, limp decor. spine. (HD. Dec.9; 3)   Frs. 4,000
– **De Magorum Daemonomania Libri IV.** Trans.:– Lotarius Philoponus (ie. Fr. Junius). Basel, 1581. *1st. Latin Edn.* 4to. Slightly browned, 1 lf. very spotted, title with old name & stpd., cont. limp vell., spine slightly defect. (R. Apr.3; 17) DM 640
– – **Anr. Copy.** Title with old stp. & deleted name, prelims. with light stain, some light browning, cont. blind-tooled leath., gt. piece centre, corners bumped, spine pasted with old leath. (R. Oct.11; 13)   DM 900
– **Les Six Livres de la République....** Paris, 1578. *3rd. Edn.* Fo. Old marb. roan. (HD. Jun.29; 28)   Frs. 2,600
– – **Anr. Edn.** Paris, 1580. 1 or 2 margin repairs, some light staining, cont. vell. (CH. May 24; 74)   Frs. 750

BODMER, Joh. J. & Breitinger, Joh. J.
– **Fabeln aus den Zeiten der Minnesinger.** Zürich, 1757. *1st. Edn.* On fine ribbed Bütten, cont. bds., bumped; Hauswedell coll. (H. May 24; 1223)   DM 500

BODONI PRESS
– **Das Werkbuch einer Handpresse in den ersten 6 Jahren ihres Wirkens.** Ill.:– Fr. Masereel. Paris, 1929. *(350).* Fo. Slightly foxed, orig. linen, spotted & bumped. (HK. Nov.11; 3836) DM 900

BOECKLIN, Arnold
– **Arnold Boecklin: Eine Auswahl der Hervorragendsten Werke des Kuenstlers.** Munich, ca. 1895. 3 vols. Tall fo. 120 heliogravure plts., some foxing & dampstaining to 1r. edges of 2 vols. & upr. edges of the other, gt.-lettered mor., very worn. (SG. Jan.26; 179) $175

BOEKSPERGER, H.
See— **AMMAN, Jost & Boeksperger, H.**

BOEMUS, Johannes
– **The Manners, Lawes, & Customes of All Nations.** Trans.:– E. Aston. L., 1611. *1st. Engl. Edn.* 4to. Some stains & annots., sm. margin worm-hole, some ll. creased, a few corners defect., cont. limp vell., loose & soiled. [Sabin 6120] (VG. Sep.14; 1078)   Fls. 450

BOERHAAVE, Hermann
– **Elementa Chemiae.** Basel, 1745. 4to. Some slight foxing or staining, cont. bds., bumped & rubbed. (D. Nov.23; 462)   DM 600
– **Institutiones Medicae in Usus Annuae Exercitationis Domesticos.** Venice, 1723. Slightly browned with light staining, 1 lf. with tear pasted over, inner doubl. & end-paper with sm. tears & owners mark or notes, cont. vell. (HT. May 8; 522a) DM 640
– **A New Method of Chemistry.** Trans.:– P. Shaw. 1741. *2nd. Edn.* 2 vols. Some spotting, cf., rubbed. (P. Jan.12; 200)   *Phelps.* £120
– **Praelectiones Publicae de Morbis Oculorum.** Ed.:– [A. V. Haller]. Göttingen, 1746. *1st. Edn.* Slightly foxed, worn, cont. bds. (HK. Nov.8; 430) DM 850

BOETHIUS, Anicius Manilius Torquatus Severinus
– **De Consolatione Philosophiae.** [Cologne], Johann Koelhoff, the Elder, 27 Jan. 1488. Fo. Fully rubricated, lacks final blank, old cf., needs rebdg.; the Walter Goldwater copy. [Goff B-783] (SG. Dec.1; 74) $950

– – **Anr. Edn.** Deventer, Jacobus de Breda, 19 Mar. 1491. 4to. Wide margins, rubricated, 17th. C. cf., spine gt., jnts. worn, 1 clasp defect.; bkplt. 'ex Bibliotheca Renessiana', the Walter Goldwater copy. [Goff B-794] (SG. Dec.1; 75) $1,700
– – **Anr. Edn.** Rennes, 1515. End-papers of 2 defect. copies of Indulgence iss. to raise funds for Hospital of St. James at Compostela 1503, Cont. Engl. cf. over wood bds., blind-stpd., upr. cover decor., with figures of saints, lr. cover with acorn panel, end-papers of 2 defect. copies of on Indulgence, lacks clasps, jnts. reprd., as a bdg., w.a.f. (P. Oct.20; 59)   £320
– **De Disciplina Scholarum.** Deventer, Jacobus de Breda, 3 Feb. 1492. 4to. Rubricated, 1st. initial in blue & red, new bds., covered with lf. from a vell. antiphonal, leath. clasps; the Walter Goldwater copy. [Goff B-823] (SG. Dec.1; 76) $1,700
– **De Institutione Arithmetica.** Augsburg, Erhard Ratdolt, 20 May 1488. *1st. Edn.* 4to. A few scattered wormholes affecting text, most at end, last few ll. lightly stained in places, mod. bdg. from ptd. missal parch. lf.; John D. Stanitz coll. [BMC II, 381; Goff B828] (SPB. Apr.25; 48) $5,250
– **De Philosophiae Consolatione, Eiusdem de Scholastica Disciplina.** Ed.:– [Nic. Crescius]. [Venice, 1515?]. Title with 18th. C. owners mark, & leg. arms stp., 1st. ll. slightly spotted, last ll. with sm. worm trace, later vell. (HT. May 5; 100) DM 460
– **De Philosophico Consolatu sive de Consolatione Philosophiae.** Strassburg, 1501. Fo. Upr. outer blank corners of 1st. 9 ll. reprd., cont. Ms. notes, cf. by Winstanley. (P. Oct.20; 60)   £360
– **Vande Vertroosting der Wysheyd.** Trans.:– D. V. Coornhert. Ill.:– van Sichem (port.). Amst., 1616. *2nd. Edn. of Coornhert's 2nd. trans.* Sm. 8vo. Loosening, old hf. cf., M. Buisman J. Fz. sig. (VS. Dec.9; 1360)   Fls. 700

BOETIUS, Anselmus de Boot
See— **BOOT, Anselmus Boetius de**

BOETTGER, A.
– **Die Pilgerfahrt der Blumengeister.** Ill.:– after J.J. Granville. Leipzig, 1857. 36 hand-cold. plts., browned & spotted, orig. mor., worn. (CSK. Mar.23; 88)   £55

BOETTICHER, Friedrich von
– **Malerwerke des Neunzehnten Jahrhunderts.** Hofheim im Taunus, [1969]. 4 vols. Sm. 4to. Cl., d.-w.'s. (SG. Oct.13; 40) $150

BOFA, Gus
– **Le Cirque.** Preface:– Mac Orlan. N.d. *Orig. Edn., (448). (8) on japon imperial.* Sm. 4to. Hf. mor., corners, mosaic spine. (HD. Jul.6; 100) Frs. 1,500
– **Déblais.** 1951. 2 vols. 4to. Orig. etchings, separate suite of 11 engrs. on Japan, separate suite of 7 refused etchings, 3 trial proofs, including 1 for cover, with supp. vol. of 200 engrs., proofs, refused plts., states, remarks, printings on different papers, leaves, warp. & s.-c. s; orig. sigd. ill., [J.G. Daragnès copy. (HD. Dec.9; 7y)   Frs. 3,100
– **Malaises....** Paris, 1930. *Ltd. Edn. with orig. etching in 2 states.* 4to. Orig. wraps., s.-c. (BBA. Jun.14; 189)   *Makiya.* £110
– – **Anr. Copy.** 4to. Etching in 2 states, sewed, s.-c.; lge. orig. ill. on end-paper sigd. & dedicated by Bofa, J.G. Doragnès copy. (HD. Dec.9; 7n)   Frs. 1,300
– **La Symphonie de La Peur.** Paris, 1937. *(125) numbered.* 4to. Orig. wraps., s.-c. (BBA. Jun.14; 188)   *Makiya.* £95

BOFFRAND, G.
– **De Architectura Liber. Livre d'Architecture...**
– **Description de ce qui a été practiqué pour fondre la Statue Equestre de Louis XIV....** Ill.:– Badel, Blondel & C. Lucas; Boucher. 1745-43. 2 vols. in 1. Fo. Cont. marb. roan. (HD. Jun.29; 29)   Frs. 6,000
– **Description de ce qui a été pratiqué pour fondre en bronze d'un Seul Jet la Figure Equestre de Louis XIV elevée par la Ville de Paris dans la Place de Louis le Grand....** Paris, 1743. *1st. Printing.* Fo. Cont. cf., spine decor. (HD. May 21; 11)   Frs. 3,300

BOGDANOVITCH, Gen. E.
– **La Bataille de Navarin (1827).** Paris, n.d. Red mor. by Ch. Meunier, 'Hommage de l'auteur à Monsieur André...' stpd. on upr. cover, watered silk liners, s.-c.; pres. copy. (HD. Jan.27; 10)   Frs. 1,500

BOHME, Jacob
– **Mysterium Magnum order Erklärung über das erste Buch Mosis von der Offenbarung Goettlichen Worts....** [Amst.], 1640. *1st. Edn.* 2 pts. in 1 vol. 4to. Lacks engraved title, vell.; Dr. Walter Pagel copy. (S. Feb.7; 56)   *Ritman.* £420
– **Theosophia revelata.** Ed.:– J.G. Gichtel. [Leiden?], 1730. Vols. 1-12 (of 14 or 16) in 4 vols. Vol. 1 slightly loose, cont. vell., slightly spotted. (R. Apr.3; 138)   DM 1,400
– **Vom übersinnlichen Leben.** Wien & Leipzig, Avalun Pr., 1921. *(243) on Bütten.* Lge. 4to. Orig. hand-bnd. mor., decor., by P.A. Demeter, Hellerau. (H. Nov.23; 883)   DM 420
– **[Collected Works].** Ed.:– [George Gichtel]. Amst., 1682. 9 works only (of 15) in 3 vols. 12mo. Cont. mor., each vol. with 2 brass clasps, 2 defect. (C. Dec.9; 303)   *Hesselink.* £300

BOHN, Henry C.
– **A Catalogue of Books.** 1841. Cont. cf., worn. (SKC. May 4; 1714)   £70

BOHN, Johan
– **Circulus Anatomico-Physiologicus seu Oeconomia Corporis Animalis.** Leipzig, 1697. 4to. Browned, vell. (S. Apr.10; 479)   *Phillips.* £110

BOHNY, Niklaus
– **Neues Bilderbuch. Anleitung zum Anschauen, Denken, Rechnen und Sprechen.** Stuttgart & Esslingen, [1848]. *1st. Edn.* Ob. fo. 37 litho. plts., all but last hand-cold., short tears in last plt., counting exercises reprd., text slightly spotted, orig. cl., rebkd.; van Veen coll. (S. Feb.28; 137)   £520
– – **Anr. Edn.** Stuttgart & Esslingen, ca. 1850. Ob. fo. 36 hand-cold. litho plts., lacks last uncold. pl., title & foreword, plt. 36 & text creased, plts. soiled, mainly in lr. margins, orig. cl.-bkd. bds., covers loose & worn, lacks spine; van Veen coll. (S. Feb.28; 138)   £360
– – **Anr. Edn.** Esslingen bei Stuttgart, [1885]. *12th. Edn.* Ob. fo. 36 cold. litho. plts., 4 pp. advts. at end, short tear in 1 reprd., sm. part of inner margin of last plt. torn away, orig. cl.-bkd. pict. bds.; van Veen coll. (S. Feb.28; 139)   £60

BOHR, Niels
– **On the Constitution of Atoms & Molecules.** L., 1913. *1st. Edn.* 'Philosophical Magazine', Vol. 26, Nos. 151, 153 & 155. Orig. ptd. wraps., spines slightly chipped, Stanitz coll. (SPB. Apr.25; 49) $475
– **Studien over Metallernes Elektrontheorie.** Copen., 1911. *1st. Edn.* 4to. Slight margin browning, orig. ptd. wraps., some fading, mor. -bkd. folding box; owners inscr. of Martin Ljostrom, Upsala, 1911 on wraps. & title, John D. Stanitz coll. (SPB. Apr.25; 51) $450

BOHRINGER, C.
– **Ueber die Zucker-Eizeugung aus dem Safte des Ahornbaumes in den Kais. Osterreichischen Staaten.** Wien, 1810. Lr. corner of title extended, slightly browned, bds. (D. Nov.24; 4133)   DM 400

BOHTLINGK, O.V.
– **Sanskrit Wörterbuch in Kürzerer Fassung.** Ed.:– R. Schmidt (Supp. vol.). Leipzig, 1923-25. *Reprint of St. Petersburg, 1879-89 Edn.* 7 vols. in 3 & 1 supp. bd. 4to. Orig. linen d hf. linen. (D. Nov.25; 4746)   DM 720

BOHUN, Ralph
– **A Discourse Concerning the Origine & Properties of Wind.** Oxford, 1671. *1st. Edn.* Lf. A1 present, pres. inscr. on 1st. lf., later cf. [Sabin 6146; Wing B3463] (BBA. May 3; 10)   *Ximenes.* £170

BOIARDO, Matteo Maria
– **Orlando Innamorato.** Venice, 1655. 4to. Light browning, upr. margins shaved with some slight loss of text, sm. tear to title, cont. vell., slightly soiled. (CSK. Jul.27; 138)   £70

BOILEAU-DESPREAUX, Nicolas Edme
- Oeuvres. Amst., 1718. 2 vols. 4to. Cf. (DS. Feb.24; 2019) Pts. 30,000
- - Anr. Edn. Ill.:– Keller (port.), Picart le Romain. La Haye, 1729. *Reprint of 1718 Edn.* 2 vols. Fo. Cont. marb. cf. gt. (HD. May 3; 22) Frs. 1,150
- - Anr. Edn. Ed.:–Brossette. Ill.:– Rigaud, engraved by Daulle (port.), C. Eisen, Mathey, Cochin & others. Paris, 1747. *New Edn.* 5 vols. Cont. marb. cf. (HD. May 3; 23) Frs. 3,900
- - Anr. Edn. Ill.:– Picart & De Meer. Paris, 1772. 5 vols. Cf. gt., spine decor. (HD. Nov.17; 5) Frs. 1,600
- Les Oeuvres...avec des Eclaircissements Historiques. Ill.:– after Rigaud (frontis.). Paris, 1740. 2 vols. 4to. Cont. cf. gt., centre arms of University of Paris, decor. spines. (HD. Sep.22; 194) Frs. 1,450
- Oeuvres Diverses du Sieur D***: Avec le Traité du Sublime ou du Merveilleux dans le Discours. Paris, 1674. *Partly Orig. Edn.* 2 pts. in 1 vol. 4to. Cont. Engl. red mor., Duke of Buckingham arms, spine decor. (HD. Mar.29; 7) Frs. 18,000
- - Anr. Edn. Paris, 1694. *New Edn., partly Orig. Edn.* 2 vols. 12mo. Cont. red mor., arms of Jean de la Vieuville, spine decor. (HD. Mar.29; 8) Frs. 34,000
- Recueil contenant plusieurs Discours Libres et Moraux ez Vers.... N.p., 1666. *Orig. Edn.* 12mo. Mor. by Lortic; from E. Daguin liby. (HD. Mar.29; 6) Frs. 14,000
- [-] Satires du Sieur D. Paris, 1667. *2nd. Edn.* 12mo. Crimson lev., gt. dentelles, by Cape; Charles Lormier bkplt. (SG. Oct.27; 32) $140

BOILLOT, Joseph
- Artifices Defeu & Dieurs Instruments du Guerre. Ill.:– Joh. Brantzius Jnr. Strassburg, 1603. *(Bound with:)* LORINI, Bonaiuti – Fünff Bücher von Vestungs Bauwen. Frankfurt, 1607. Lacks copper engrs. *(Bound with:)* PERRET, Jacob – Etlicher Festungen, Städt, Kirchen, Schlösser un Häuser... Trans.:– Dietrich de Bry & others. Frankfurt, 1602. Lacks 5 ll. & 9 copperplts. Together 3 works in 1 vol. Fo. Cont. blind-tooled pig, re-cased. (GB. Nov.3; 985) DM 2,000

BOILLY
- Recueil de Croquis dessinés à Rome. Paris, 1830. Fo. Frontis. & 8 engraved plts., hf. cf. (CR. Jun.6; 105) Lire 200,000

BOIS, D.
- Atlas des Plantes de Jardins et d'Appartements. Paris, 1896. 4 vols. Three-qtr. mor. (CBA. Dec.10; 341) $250

BOIS, Jules
- Prière, Poème. 1895. *Orig. Edn.* Ill. wrap. by Filiger. *(With:)* - Les Petites Religions de Paris. 1894. *Orig. Edn.* No bdg. stated; author's dedication. (HD. May 11; 5) Frs. 1,300

BOISARD, Jean-Jacques Francois Marin
- Fables. Paris, 1779. 2 vols. L.P., early 19th. C. tree cf., sigd. by Bozerian Lefebvre, covers decor., spines gt. in compartments with animal stps., a little rubbed, spines faded, wormhole in jnt. of Vol. II, open-bkd. s.-c.'s; Schiff-Abbey bkplts. (SPB. Dec.14; 41) $300

BOISGELIN DE KERDU, P.M. Louis de
- Ancient & Modern Malta. L., 1804-05. 3 pts. in 2 vols. 4to. Lge. engraved linen-bkd. folding map, key, 12 engraved ports. & plts., 11 aquatint views, hf.-title to Vol. 1, minor dampstain to some plts., cont. bds., unc. (C. Mar.14; 1) *Blackwell.* £400
- Travels through Denmark & Sweden. L., 1810. Vol. 1 only. 4to. 10 aquatint plts., including frontis., offsetting, unc., trs. orig. bds., spine defect. (GM. Dec.7; 642) £70

BOISSARD, Jean Jacques
- Emblematum Liber. Ill.:– Th. de Bry. Frankfurt, 1593. 4to. Lacks 1lf. preface with port., side of title lf. slightly cut & old re-margined, cont. leath., corners bumped, upr. cover loose, spine slightly restored. (D. Nov.23; 105) DM 1,000
- [-] Pannoniae Historia Chronologica: Res per Vngariam, Transylvaniam...a Constitutione Regnorum illorum ... maxime vere hoc Bello gestae.... Frankfurt, 1596. Title copper engr. very slit in upr. margin

with erased owners entries, last lf. with fault, printers mark with loss, some old soiling, cont. vell., spotted, spine with fault, lacks ties. (HT. May 8; 101) DM 1,000
- Theatrum Vitae Humanae. [Metz], 1596. Sm. 4to. Lacks last lf. (blank?), text slightly defect. in last 2 ll., inner margins of 1st. 2 gatherings reinforced, a few light stains, mod. hf. mor. (S. Nov.17; 9) *Snelling.* £350
- Topographia Romae. Ill.:– Bry & others. Frankfurt, 1627. 6 pts. in 2 vols. Fo. Pt. 1 with engraved title, engraved architectural titles to pts. 2-6, 4 engraved ports., double-p. folding map, 2 double-p. maps, about 518 engraved plts., several double-p., some text ll. in pt. 1 browned, pt. 4 without plt. 125 (as usual), cont. cf., rebkd. (C. Jun.27; 12) *Weinreb.* £350
- Topographia Urbis Romae. Frankfurt, 1681 [ca. 1700]. Fo. Minimal foxing, cont. bds., bumped. (GB. Nov.3; 97) DM 800
- Vitae et Icones Sultanorum Turcicorum, Principum Persarum...ab Osmane Usque ad Mahometem II. Ill.:– J.J. Boissard. Frankfurt, 1596. *(Bound with:)* LONICER, Joh. Adam – Pannoniae Historia Chronologica. Ill.:– J.J. Boissard. Frankfurt, 1596. Lacks engraved map. Together 2 works in 1 vol. Vell., light wear. (V. Oct.1; 3717) DM 900

BOISSARD, Jean Jacques & others
- Topographia Romae. Frankfurt, 1627-1597-1602. 6 pts. in 1 vol. Fo. Lacks 2 ills., text & some ills. very browned, late 17th. C. red mor., some slight worming in spine, w.a.f. (SI. Dec.15; 52) Lire 500,000

BOISSEREE, Sulpiz
- Denkmale der Baukunst vom 7ten bis zum 13ten Jahrhundert am Nieder-Rhein. München, 1844. Lge. fo. Some old soiling, especially in margin, a few plts. of sketches quite foxed, orig. linen. (V. Sep.29; 36) DM 7,300

BOITARD, Louis-Philippe
- The Cries of London in Six Parts. L., 1821. 4to. Title lf. sigd. by Boitard & Simon François Ravenet, 72 etchings, most with tri-lingual captions, 3 plts. loose, jnts. brkn., browned & foxed, hf. leath., slightly rubbed; ex-libris; Hauswedell coll. (H. May 23; 59) DM 2,000

BOITARD, Pierre
- Le Jardin des Plantes. Ill.:– Girardet, Francais, Marville, Traviés & others. Paris, 1842. *1st. Printing.* Lge. 8vo. Hf. mor., corners, by Salviac, spine decor. (HD. May 3; 205) Frs. 2,100
- Traité de la Composition et de l'Ornement des Jardins.... Paris, 1825. *3rd. Edn.* Ob. 4to. 97 engraved plts., errata lf. at beginning & publisher's advts . at end, cont. pict. wraps. mntd. on cont. bds., spine label chipped. (C. Dec.9; 13) *Henderson.* £240

BOITET, R.
- [-] Beschrijving der Stadt Delft. Delft, 1729. Fo. Cont. vell., slightly soiled. (VG. Sep.14; 1137) Fls. 1,500

BOLETIN JUVENTUD CATOLICA MADRID
Madrid, 1872-73. 46 issues (all publd.). Fo. Linen. (DS. Apr.27; 2026) Pts. 36,000

BOLINGBROKE, Henry St. John, Visc.
- Dissertation upon Parties in Several Letters to Caleb Denver. L., 1735. *2nd. Edn.* Cf. (HD. Feb.22; 20) Frs. 1,000
- Lettres sur l'Histoire. Trans.:– J. Barbeu du Bourg. L., 1735. Cf. (HD. Feb.22; 19) Frs. 1,100
- Works. 1753-77. 11 vols. various. Cont. cf., rubbed. (CSK. Mar.23; 32) £50

BOLIVIA
- Proyecto de Constitucion para la Republica de Bolivia, y Discurso del Libertador. Buenos Aires, 1826. 2 pts. in 1 vol. Slightly dampstained, later wraps. (BBA. Mar.21; 92) *Baldwin.* £70

BOLLER, Henry
- Among the Indians. Eight Years in the Far West: 1858-1866. Phila., 1868. *1st. Edn.* Folding map (not issued in all copies), orig. cl., mostly unopened, rebkd. preserving orig. spine & label (chipped),

corners worn; the Rt. Hon. Visc. Eccles copy. [Sabin 6221] (CNY. Nov.18; 26) $380

BOLLINGEN FOUNDATION
- The Tomb of Ramesses VI. N.Y., 1948. 2 vols. 4to. Loose as iss. in orig. cl. portfo., orig. cl. s.-c. (S. Dec.13; 430) *Loman.* £60

BOLSWERT, Boece de
- Voyage des Deux Soeurs Colombelle Volontairette vers leur Bien-Aimé en la Cité de Jérusalem. Liège, 1734. *New Edn.* Sm. 8vo. Mod. cf. (LM. Mar.3; 162) B. Frs. 9,000

BOLTON, Arthur T.
- The Architecture of Robert & James Adam. L., 1922. 2 vols. Fo. Orig. cl., slightly soiled. (BBA. Apr.5; 178) *Weinreb.* £180
- - Anr. Copy. 2 vols. Fo. Orig. cl. gt. (P. Sep.29; 303) £140
- - Anr. Copy. 2 vols. Fo. Ills., ex-liby., cl., gt. medallion on covers. (SG. May 3; 51) $475

BOLTON, Edmund
- The Elements of Armories. 1610. Sm. 4to. 1 woodcut ill. with moveable overslips, 18th. C. cf.-bkd. bds. (BBA. Mar.21; 166) *R. Rouse.* £140

BOLTON, James
- Geschichte der Merkwürdigsten Pilze. Ed.:– Ch. G. & Th. Fr. L. Nees von Esenbeck. Trans.:– C.L. Wildenow. Berlin, 1795-1820. 4 vols. On heavy Bütten, 86 (of 182) cold. copperplts., sewed & folded ll., unc. (GB. Nov.3; 1121) DM 560

BOLTZMANN, Ludwig
- Vorlesungen über Gastheorie. Leipzig, 1896[-98]. *1st. Edn.* 2 vols. Hf.-titles, browning, mostly to endpapers, orig. cl., extremities rubbed; John D. Stanitz coll. (SPB. Apr.25; 52) $425

BOLUS, H.
- Icones Orchidearum Austro-Africanarum Extra-Tropicarum. L., 1896-1913. 3 vols. in 4. 296 plts., including 4 double-p., mostly partly cold., plts. in Vol. 1 loose, cl; Vol. 1 pres. copy from author, Royal Commonwealth Soc. copy. (P. Nov.24; 269) *Quaritch.* £680
- The Orchids of the Cape Peninsula. Cape Town, 1888. Offprint from the 'Transactions of the South-African Philosophical Soc.', Vol. 5 pt. 1. 36 plts., mostly partly cold., some pp. loose, orig. cl.; Royal Commonwealth Soc. copy. (P. Nov.24; 270) *Weldon & Wesley.* £55

BOLZANO, B.
- Beyträge zu e. begründeteren Darstellung d. Mathematik. Prag, 1810. Pt. 1 (all publd.). Slight foxing, cont. bds. (HK. May 15; 468) DM 480

BOLZANO URBANO
See— URBANUS BELLUNENSIS

BOMBAST, Comte de, Nephew of Paracelsus?
- [-] Le Miroir des Alchimistes .... 1609. 12mo. Sigs. run from G-I (but compl. in itself), bds.; Albert Poisson bkplt., Dr. Walter Pagel copy, w.a.f. (S. Feb.7; 59) *Weiner.* £150

BOMBERG, David
- Russian Ballet. L., Hendersons The Bomb Shop, 1919. Orig. stiff paper wraps., foxed. (C. Nov.9; 172) *Henderson.* £1,100

BON GENRE (Le): Réimpression du Recueil de 1827
Preface:– Léon Moussinac. Paris, [1931]. *(760) numbered.* Fo. This copy unnumbered, 115 engraved plts., cold. by Saude, includes 24-p. 'Observations...', Loose as iss., bds., lacks spine. (SG. Aug.25; 94) $650
- - Anr. Edn. Paris, [1931]. *(750) numbered.* Fo. 115 plts., cold. by Saude, with the 24 text pp. 'Observations sur les Modes et les Usages de Paris, pour servir d'Explication aux 115 Caricatures Publiées sous le Titre de Bon Genre', loose as iss. in cl.-bkd. ptd. bd. folder. (SG. Oct.13; 41) $550

BONACINI, A.
- Bibliografid delle Arti Scrittorie & della Calligrafia. Flor., 1953. *(666).* MS. dedication to Dr. Hauswedell in inner cover, lf. vell., calligraphic spine title, orig. wraps. bnd. in Hauswedell coll. (H. May 23; 346) DM 400

BONALD
- Oeuvres Complètes. Paris, 1864. 3 vols. 4to. Title-p. defect., hf. chagrin. (HD. Feb.22; 21)
Frs. 1,800

BONAMICO, J.F.
- Laureae Cotoneriae. Lyon, 1672. 4to. Margin worming, cont. vell., soiled. (CSK. Sep.16; 186)
£50

BONANNI, Filippo
- Descrizione degl'Istromenti Armonici d'Ogni Genere. Ill.:– Wanwesterout. Rome, 1776. 2nd. Edn. 4to. Double-p. engraved title (in Italian & Fr., text also in Italian & Fr.), 144 engraved plts. (only 140 called for on title-p.), 1 folding, final errata lf., orig. pre-bdg. bds., unc. (S. May 10; 233)
Hillman. £1,250
- Numismata Pontificum Romanorum quae a Tempore Martini V. Rome, 1699. 2 vols. Ownership inscr. & liby. stps. on titles, some staining in Vol. 2, cont. vell. bds., slightly soiled. (S. May 1; 452)
Drury. £280
- Numismata Summorum Pontificum Romanorum quae Tempore Martini V. Rome, 1699-1799. 2nd. Edn. Fo. Slight worming in lr. margin, cont. leath., spine defect., some worming & wear. (HK. Nov.9; 1934)
DM 1,100
- Numismata Summorum Pontificum Templi Vaticani Fabricam Indicantia. Rome, 1696. 1st. Edn. Fo. Lge. title vig., 86 full-p. & folding engraved plts., some margin stains & age-browning, disbnd., unc. (SG. Apr.19; 43)
$400
- Verzeichnüss der Geistlichen Ordens-Personen in der Streitenden Kirchen. Nuremb., 1724,1720 (Vol. 3). 1st. German Edn. (Vol. 3). 3 vols. 4to. 1 plt. lightly defect., cont. leath. gt., very worn, spine defect., lr. cover vol. 1 loose. (HK. Nov.9; 1830)
DM 420

BONAPARTE, Prince Charles Lucien
- Iconographie des Pigeons. Ill.:– Lemercier, after Oudart, Willy, & Blanchard. Paris, 1857. Fo. 55 hand-cold. litho. plts., hf.-titles, a few plts. slightly soiled or spotted, 1 browned at margins, 1 lf. reprd. at corner, final lf. reprd. at margins, some minor spotting, later cl. (C. Nov.16; 221)
Lyon. £1,400
- - Anr. Edn. Ill.:– Paul Louis Oudart, F. Willy, & E. Blanchard, ptd. by Lemercier. Paris, 1857[-58]. Lge. fo. 55 hand-cold. litho. plts., some spotting, mostly marginal, unbnd. in orig. ptd. wrap. to livraison 3e, preserved in mod. cf.-bkd. portfo., s.-c. (S. Feb.1; 9)
Park. £2,000
- - Anr. Copy. Fo. 55 cold. litho. plts., text & plts. loose as iss. in ptd. wraps., spine worn, mod. cl. folding case. (SG. Nov.3; 20)
$1,500
See— WILSON, Alexander & Bonaparte, Charles Lucien

BONAPARTE, Prince Charles Lucien & Schlegel, Hermann
- Monographie des Loxiens. Leiden & Dusseldorf, 1850. 4to. 54 hand-cold. litho. plts. on guards, title & a few ll. browned & reinforced at hinge, red hf. mor.; sigd. pres. copy, inscr. from author to 'Mr. le Comte Wladimir Komar'. (C. Mar.14; 156)
Wheldon & Wesley. £900
- - Anr. Copy. 54 litho. plts., cold. & gommées, Bonaparte's 'Note sur lez Tangaras' bnd. at end, cont. hf. chagrin gt.; autograph dedication by Bonaparte, sigd. & dtd. (HD. Jun.26; 8)
Frs. 8,100

BONAPARTE, Prince Roland
- Une Excursion en Corse. Paris, priv. ptd., 1891. 4to. Hf. chagrin, corners. (HD. Oct.21; 32)
Frs. 1,250
- Les Habitants de Suriname. Paris, 1884. Fo. Litho. frontis., 2 double-p. maps, 13 chromolitho. & 62 photo plts., orig. cl., rebkd. preserving orig. spine. (C. Mar.14; 31)
Thorp. £260

BONATERRE, Abbé
- Tableau Encyclopédique et Méthodique... Ophiologie. Paris, 1790. 4to. Cont. hf. leath., slightly loose. (SI. Dec.15; 142)
Lire 280,000

BONATUS DE FORLIVIO, Guido
- Decem Tractatus Astronomiae. Augsburg, Erhard Ratdolt, 26 Mar. 1491. 4to. Lacks register (added later?), ink stain on 1 lf., some light stains, sm. stab

hole through last few ll., cont. limp vell., reprd., folding box; John D. Stanitz coll. (SPB. Apr.25; 54)
$2,600
- Liber Astronomicus. Augsburg, Erhard Ratdolt, 26 Mar. 1491. 1st. Edn. 4to. 19th. C. Italian hf. cf.; from Fondation Furstenberg-Beaumesnil. [HC 3461; BMC II, 384; Goff B845] (HD. Nov.16; 6)
Frs. 14,000

BONAVENTURA, Saint Giovanni Fidenzo, Bp. of Albano
- Commentarius in Secundum Librum Sententiarum Petri Lombardi. Venice, R. de Novimagio & T. de Reynsburch, 1477. Fo. Lge. copy, 1st. ptd. lf. with lge. illuminated initials & illuminated arms at foot, other initials in red & blue, 1st. blank defect., 1st. & last few ll. dampstained & browned, ll. wrinkled thro.-out, cont. stpd. cf. over wood bds., reprd., lacks clasps; the Walter Goldwater copy. [BMC V, 254; Goff B-873] (SG. Dec.1; 77) $650
- Dieta Salutis. Cologne, Johannes Koelhoff the Elder, 1474. Fo. Rubricated, initials painted in red & blue, Lacks 1st. 8 ll. (7 table ll. & 1 blank), mod. blind-stpd. cf. over wood bds., unc., old brass clasps; Berlin Liby. stp. in lr. margin of 1st. lf., from Fondation Furstenberg-Beaumesnil. [BMC I, 219; Goff B874] (HD. Nov.16; 20) Frs. 4,600
- - Anr. Edn. Venice, J. de Quarengiis, 1 Feb. 1497/98. Sm. 8vo. Rather stained, numerous early marginalia, mor.-bkd. bds., spine worn; the Walter Goldwater copy. [BMC V, 513; Goff B-879] (SG. Dec.1; 78) $375
- Meditationes Vitae Christi. [Romen, Le Talleur, ca. 1487]. 4to. Many old MS. marginalia stained thro.-out in lr. part, 1st ll. browned, 19th C. vell., slightly soiled. (R. Oct.11; 6) DM 3,600
- - Anr. Edn. Venice, [A. de Zanchis], after 1500?. 4to. In Italian, lacks title lf., headlines partly shaved thro.-out , mod. bds.; the Walter Goldwater copy. [Goff (Supp.) 903a (this copy only)] (SG. Dec.1; 79) $425
See— KLINGEMANN, Aug.

BOND, W.H.
- The Houghton Library 1942-1967. Camb., Mass., 1967. Fo. Orig. buckram; H.M. Nixon coll., with his & John Carter's sigs . on fly-lf., & typescript & cutting of Carter's review for T.L.S. loosely inserted. (BBA. Oct.6; 59) Oak Knoll Books. £50

BONDY, G.
- Zur Geschichte der Juden in Böhmen, Mähren und Schlesien von 906 bis 1620 Ed.:– F. Dworsky. Prag, 1906. 2 vols. in 1. Orig. hf. leath., rubbed. (R. Oct.11; 1075) DM 650

BONE, Sir Muirhead & Lady Gertrude
- Old Spain. 1936. (265) numbered & sigd. 2 vols. Fo. With portfo. containing 2 sigd. drypoints, orig. pig gt. (P. Sep.8; 229) £240
- - Anr. Edn. Ill.:– Muirhead Bone. L., 1936. (205) numbered & sigd. by author & artist, with 2 sigd, orig. drypoints. 2 vols. Fo. Orig. pig, unc.; bkplt. of S.L. Courtauld (by Stephen Gooden). (S. Mar.6; 86) Frame. £200

BONELLI, E.
- Sabara. Madrid, 1887. 4to. Linen, by Menard. (DS. Mar.23; 2035) Pts. 25,000

BONELLI, Georgio
- Hortus Romanus. Rome, 1772. Vol. I only. Fo. Title with hand-cold. vig., engraved port. ptd. in blue, double-p. plan 'Prospectus Horti Romani' ptd. in green, 100 hand-cold. plts., each with cold. wash border, 1 plt. with stain in lr. blank margin, cont. hf. vell. (C. Nov.16; 223) Walford. £2,900

BONESTOC, Venu de (Pseud.)
See— BAYROS, Franz von 'Venu de Bonestoc'

BONFINIS, Matthaeus
- Annotationes in Horatianis Operibus. Roma, ca. 1514. 4to. 18th. C. red mor. gt., spine decor.; from Fondation Furstenberg-Beaumesnil. (HD. Nov.16; 102) Frs. 1,500

BONIFACIUS VIII, Pope
- Liber Sextus Decretalium. Nuremb., Anton Koberger, 12 Mar. 1482. [Goff B-993] (Bound

with:) CLEMENS V. Pope – Constitutiones. Nuremb., Anton Koberger, 15 Jan. 1482. [Goff C-725] Together 2 works in 1 vol. Fo. Fully rubricated, initials in red & blue, cont. stpd. of. over wood, covers detchd., lacks part of spine, metal clasps; the Walter Goldwater copy. (SG. Dec.1; 81) $2,600
- - Anr. Copy. Wide margin, rubricated, painted red & blue initials, 1multi-cold. miniature, Cont. MS. contents index on upr. end-paper. [HC3603; BMC11,422; goff B-993]. (Bound With:-) CLEMENS, V. – Constitutiones [cum Apparatu Joannis Andreae]. Nuremb., A. Koberger, 15 Jan. 1482. Rubric., painted red & blue initials, 1 multi-cold. miniature, cont. MS. contents index on blank 1st lf. verso, [HC.5427; BMC11, 421, Goff C-725]. Together 2 works in 1 vol. Fo. old MS. marginalia, slight stain in lr. inner corner thro. out, especially 1st. ll, end-paper & ll.1-8 reprd., cont. Flemish leath. over wood bds., clasps brkn., decor. stps., spine & endpapers renewed. (R. Apr.3; 3)
DM 1,200
- - Anr. Edn. Venice, Bernardino Benalius, 1484. 4th. (3rd. dtd.) Imp. [H. 3608; BMC V, 371; Goff B998] (Bound with:) CLEMENS V. Pope – Constitutiones; Extravagantes Decretales, cum Apparatu Joh. Andreae. Venice, Bernardino Benalius, 1484. 3rd. (2nd. dtd.) Imp. [H. 5432; BMC V, 370; Goff C731] Together 2 works in 1 vol. 4to. Cont. stpd. cf. over wood bds., decor., traces of clasps; from Fondation Furstenberg-Beaumesnil. (HD. Nov.16; 69) Frs. 5,500

BONNARD, Camille & Mercuri, Paolo
- Costumes Historiques des XIIe, XIIIe, XIVe et XVe Siècles. 1860-61. 3 vols. 4to. Publisher's hf. cl. (HD. Apr.13; 99) Frs. 1,550
- Costumes Historiques des XIIe, XIIIe, XIVe et XVIIIe Siècles.– Costumes Historiques des XVIe, XVIIe et XVIIIe Siècles. Ill.:– Paul Mercuri & others. Paris, 1860-67. 3 vols. & 2 vols. Lge. 4to. 200 & 150 hand-cold. plts. respectively, some foxing, most plts. not affected, unif. bnd. in hf. leath., spines gt. (SG. Apr.26; 26) $550

BONNAT, Léon
- Album National de la Guerre. Ill.:– after Baschet & others. Paris, [1915]. (50) sigd. on japan. 4to. Red mor. by Kieffer, monog. 'F.D.A.' stpd. on upr. cover. (SM. Mar.7; 2068) Frs. 2,200

BONNE, Rigobert
[-] Atlas de toutes les parties connues du Globe Terrestre. [Geneva, 1780]. 4to. 50 folding engraved maps, 22 ptd. tables, most folding, some slightly torn, some ll. slightly soiled, cont. cf., rebkd., rather worn. [Sabin 68081] (BBA. Sep.29; 129)
Spivey. £220
- - Anr. Copy. Atlas vol. to Raynal's 'Histoire'. 4to. 50 double-p. & folding copper-engraved maps, map versos multi stpd., cont. hf. leath. (R. Oct.13; 2868)
DM 800
- Atlas Maritime. Paris, Lattre, 1778. Sm. 12mo. 37 double-p. cold. maps, cont. red mor., spine decor. (HD. Jun.18; 5) Frs. 12,500
- Petit Tableau de la France. – Description Géographique de la France. Paris, 1764. 2 works in 1 vol. Sm. 12mo. Cold. engraved frontis. & 28 double-p. cold. maps, cont. red mor., spine decor. (HD. Jun.18; 6) Frs. 8,800

BONNE, Rigobert & Desmarest, Jean
[-] Atlas Encyclopédique. [Paris, 1788]. Vol. 2 only (of 2). 4to. 50 double-p. engraved map-sheets, title & front end-paper soiled, some faint spotting, cont. vell., worn. (S. Nov.1; 180)
Marlboro Rare Bks. £130

BONNEFOY, Yves
- Pierre Ecrite. Ill.:– Racul Ubac. Paris, 1958. (125) numbered & sigd. by author & artist. Fo. Unsewn in orig. wraps., unc., folder & s.-c. (S. Nov.21; 122)
Makiya. £120

BONNET, Charles
- Oeuvres d'Histoire Naturelle et de Philosophie.... Neuchatel, 1779/81. Vols. I-V only in 7. 4to. Port. frontis. to Vol. 1, 58 engraved plts., cont. tree cf., Vol. 1 upr. cover detchd. (TA. Jun.21; 365) £60

– – Anr. Copy. Vols. I-V only in 7. 4to. Cont. tree cf., vol. 1 upr. cover detchd. (TA. Apr.19; 189) £55

– **La Paligénésie Philosophique.** Genève, 1769. 2 vols. Cont. marb roan, decor. spines. (HD. Jan.26; 47) Frs. 1,200

BONNEY, T.G.
See— WALTON, Elijah & Bonney, T.G.

BONNIER, Gaston
– **Flore Complète Illustrée en Couleurs de France, Suisse et Belgique.** Neuchâtel, Paris, Bruxelles, n.d. 2 text vols. & 4 plt. vols. 4to. 721 plts., mntd. on guards, hf. roan. (HD. Jul.6; 12) Frs. 4,800

BONOLI, P.
– **Istorie della Citta di Forli, intrecciate di Varii Accidenti della Romagna, e dell'Italia.** Forli, 1661. Sm. 4to. Some stains to 1st. ll., cont. vell. (HD. Dec.2; 72) Frs. 1,700

BONPLAND, Aimé
See— HUMBOLDT, Alexander von & Bonpland, Aimé

BONSTETTEN, K.V. von
– **Briefe an Friederike Brun.** Ed.:– Fr. v. Matthisson. Frankfurt, 1829. 2 pts. in 1 vol. Cont. bds., rubbed & bumped. (D. Nov.24; 2397) DM 400

BONTEKOE, C.
– **Alle de Philosophische, Medicinale en Chymische Werken.** Amst., 1689. 5pts. in 1 vol. 4to. Part of ll. reprd. in fold, with loss on last ll., some sm. tears, some heavy browning, mod. pig over wood bds., blind- tooled, metal clasps, slightly worn, ex-libris inside cover. (H. May 22; 186) DM 620

BONWICK, James
– **The Bushrangers, Illustrating the Early Days of Van Diemen's Land.** Melbourne, 1856. 12mo. Several ll. with sm. defect in lr. margin, mod. hf. cf., unc. (KH. May 1; 77) Aus. $110
– **Daily Life & Origin of the Tasmanians.** 1870. *1st. Edn.* Lacks plt. at p. 135, bnd. without hf.-title & advts., margin stain to a few ll., early hf. cf., slightly rubbed. (KH. May 1; 78) Aus. $110
– – **Anr. Edn.** L., 1898. *2nd. Edn.* Orig. cl., unc. (KH. Nov.9; 551) Aus. $120
– **John Batman, the Founder of Victoria....** 1868. *2nd. Edn.* Bdg. not stated. (KH. May 1; 79) Aus. $120
– **The Last of the Tasmanians, or, The Black War of Van Diemen's Land.** 1870. With final advts. not called for by Ferguson, bdg. not stated, unc. (KH. May 1; 80) Aus. $240
– **Port Philip Settlement.** 1883. *1st. Edn.* Bdg. not stated, few marks; sig. of Will Sowden. (KH. May 1; 84) Aus. $300
– **Wesleyan Methodism in South Australia....** Adelaide, ca. 1851. With advt, lf., but without 'slip' mentioned by Ferguson (7189), rather stained, cl. bds., roan backstrip defect., detchd. (KH. Nov.8; 42) Aus. $190

BOOK AUCTION RECORDS
1903-75. Vols. 1-2, 5-6, 8-16, 19, 22, 27-35 (in pts.), 49-71, & 1st. & 8th. Indexes. Orig. cl., & wraps. (BBA. Sep.8; 3) *Wise.* £160
– – **Anr. Edn.** 1903-81. Vols. 1-77 in 78. 8vo. & 4to. Orig. cl., some spines faded. (TA. Jul.19; 459) £320
– – **Anr. Edn.** 1903-82. Vols. 1-79 & 1st.-3rd. Indexes, in 83 vols. 8vo. & 4to. Vol. 1 hf. cl., Vols. 2-8 wraps., rest orig. cl., some rubbed. (BBA. Feb.9; 212) *Folchi Vici d'Arcevia.* £250
– – **Anr. Edn.** L., 1923-24; 1967-68. Vols. 21-37; 39-62; 64-65, together 43 vols. Cl. (SG. May 17; 43) £450
– – **Anr. Edn.** L., 1924-73. Vols. [20-21, 24-57, 59, 62-67 & 69, & dupl. [of Vol. 47, together 45 vols. Orig. cl. (BBA. Mar.7; 175) *Ong.* £100
– – **Anr. Edn.** L. & Folkestone, 1940-73. Vols. 37-69 (dupl. of Vol. 66) & 4th.-7th. General Indexes, together 38 vols. 8vo. Orig. cl., a few slightly worn. (S. Mar.20; 697) *Martin.* £160
– – **Anr. Edn.** L. & Folkestone, 1960-82. Vols. 56-79, & 6th.-8th. Indexes. 8vo. & 4to. Orig. cl. (BBA. Apr.5; 264) *Ayres.* £260
– – **Anr. Edn.** 1968-82. Vols. 66-79. 8vo. & 4to. Orig. cl. (CSK. Feb.10; 170) £360

– – **Anr. Edn.** L., 1970-77. Vols. 66-73, & Index for Vols. 61-65, together 9 vols. 4to. or 8vo. Buckram. (SG. Jan.5; 47) $150
– – **Anr. Edn.** Folkestone, 1970-80. Vols. 66 & 69-76. 8vo. 4to. Orig. cl. (S. Mar.20; 696) *Elliott.* £140
– – **Anr. Edn.** 1970-82. Vols. 68-79. 8vo. & 4to. Orig. cl., rubbed. (TA. May 17; 403) £250
– – **Anr. Edn.** Folkestone & L., 1973-81. Vols. 69-78,. 8vo. & lge. 8vo. No bdg. stated. (VS. Dec.7; 226) Fls. 850

BOOK COLLECTOR (The)
L., 1951-81. Vols. 1-30, 26 vols. & 11 pts., including index 1952-61 (lacks 1952, pts. 2-4, 1954, pts. 1 & 4, & 1955, pts. 1 & 2). Cl. & wraps. (VG. Mar. 21; 775) Fls. 650
– – **Anr. Edn.** Ed.:– Ian Fleming, John Hayward, & P.H. Muir. L., Spring 1952-Summer 1981. Vol. 1 no. 1-Vol. 30 no. 2, & Index for 1952-61. Ptd. wraps., some wear. (RO. Dec.11; 37) $525
– – **Anr. Edn.** 1952-82. Vols. 1-31 & Index to Vols. 1-10, in 125 pts. Orig. wraps., some slightly soiled, a few torn & loose; H.M. Nixon coll. (BBA. Oct.6; 9) *Maggs.* £240
– – **Anr. Edn.** 1961-82. Vol.10 no.4-Vol.31 no.1, & 18 Indexes. Orig. wraps. (BBA. Feb.9; 214) *Sims, Reed & Fogg.* £80

BOOK COLLECTOR'S QUARTERLY
Ed.:– Desmond Flower & A.J.A. Symons. L., 1930-32. *Special Edn. (100) & (75) on H.M.P.* Vols. 1-8. Ills. thro-out, orig. cl.; Perry Molstead copy. (SPB. May16; 403) $175

BOOK-LOVER'S LIBRARY, The
Ed.:– Henry B. Wheatley. L., 1887-1910. 15 vols. only,. Orig. cl. (BBA. Mar.7; 177) *Biblio-Archiv.* £55

BOOK OF COMMON PRAYER [English]
See— PRAYERBOOKS [English]

BOOK OF DURROW
– **Codex Dumarchensis.** Olten, Lausanne & Freiburg, 1960. *(650) numbered.* 2 vols. Fo. Orig. ornamental cf., Celtic design, & hf. cf. (GM. Dec.7; 494) £460
– **Evangeliorum Quattuor Codex Durmachensis.** Olten, [1960]. *(650) numbered.* 2 vols. Fo. Text ills., leather, upr. over embossed, & qtr. leath. (SG. Apr.26; 27) $425
– – **Anr. Edn.** Ed.:– A.A. Luce. [Lausanne & Freiburg, 1960]. *(650).* 2 vols. Fo. Vol. 1 in niger, stpd. in Celtic design, a few sm. scratches to lr. cover, Vol. 2 hf. niger & bds., covers slightly soiled, together in orig. packing box; Marymount College copy. (CBA. Mar.3; 50) $325

BOOK OF ENGLISH TRADES, & Library of the Useful Arts
L., 1818. 68 (of 73?) plts., some foxing, slightly browned, cont. leath., bumped. (R. Apr.4; 2033) DM 750
– – **Anr. Edn.** L., 1823. *New Edn.* 86 plts., some light browning, mod. hf. leath. (H. May 22; 358) DM 1,000

BOCK OF GEMS
Ed.:– Samuel Carter Hall. L., 1863. 3 vols. maroon crushed lev. mor., covers with elab. gt. & onlaid design in Art Nouveau style, spines in 6 compartments, 5 raised bands, similarly gt.-tooled, turn-ins gt., watered silk linings, each vol. with different fore-e. pntg., turn-ing sigd silk-lined cl. folding boxes, 'Fazakerely, Liverpool', as a bdg., w.a.f. (CMY. Dec.17; 557) $4,600

BOOK OF KELLS
– **Celtic Ornaments from the Book of Kells.** Dublin & L., 1895. 4to. Orig. cl. gt. (S. Oct.11; 467) *Nolan.* £50

BOOK OF SPORT
Ed.:– William Patten. Contributions:– Ruth Underhill, Foxhall Keene & others. N.Y., 1901. *Edn. de Grande Luxe. (450) numbered.* Sm. fo. Plts., including hand-cold. frontis. on Japan vell., hf.-title loose, somwhat shaken, cont. gt. hf. mor., cl. cover; inscr. to Racquet & Tennis Cl. by R.H. Williams. (SG. Mar.15; 180) $100

BOOK OF THE BENCH
Ill.:– after 'Spy' & others. 1909. *1st. Edn.* 4to. Minor spotting, orig. parch. gt., spine soiled. (TA. Oct.20; 179) £180

BOOK OF THE DEAD
Trans.:– Sir Ernest Alfred Thompson Wallis Budge. 1890. Fo. Title & a few ll. restored on outer edge, recent qtr. mor. (TA. May 17; 26) £85
– **Book of the Dead: The Papyrus of Ani in the British Museum.** Trans.:– Sir E.A. Wallis Budge. L., 1895. Sm. fo. Three-qtr. mor., scuffed, ex-liby. (SG. Mar.29; 20) $100

BOOK OF THE OLD EDINBURGH CLUB
Edinb., 1908-72. Vols. I-XXXIII, with general index for Vols. I-XX, & dupl. copies Vols. XX-XXII, together 35 vols. & 3 pamphlets. Orig. gt. cl., Vol. XXXIII unbnd. – in 3 pts. as iss. (PD. Aug.17; 82) £135
– – **Anr. Edn.** Edinb., 1908-56. Vols. I-XXIX, & General Index for Vols. I-XX. 4to. Orig. cl. gt. (PD. Feb.15; 88) £105

BOOK OF TRADES, The
L., 1830's. 12mo. 24 hand-cold. engrs. on 12 plts., ptd. wraps. (SG. Dec.8; 69) $100

BOOK PRICES CURRENT
L., 1887-1919; 1887-1916. 32 vols. (lacks 1918 vol.) & 3 index vols., together 35 vols. Lge. 8vo. Cl. (SG. May 17; 46) $200

BOOKBINDER, The, An Illustrated Journal for Binders, Librarians & all Lovers of Books [later The British Bookmaker]
1888-89. Vols. 1 & 2 only. Orig. cl., worn. (P. Sep.8; 257) *Ralph.* £120
– – **Anr. Edn.** 1888-94. Vols. I-7 in 4. 4to. Advts., Vol. 1 hf. mor., rubbed, Vols. 2 - 4 cl., 1 a little worn; H.M. Nixon coll., with his MS. notes, as a periodical, w.a.f. (BBA. Oct.6; 7) *Quaritch.* £750

BOOKBINDING TRADES JOURNAL, The
Ed.:– W. Mellor. [Manchester], 1904-14. Vol. 1 nos. 1-24 & Vol. 2 nos. 1-16 (all publd.), in 1 vol. Title to Vol. 1, mor.-bkd. cl., as a periodical, w.a.f. (S. Oct.4; 130) *Blackwells.* £350

BOOLE, George
– **An Investigation of the Laws of Thought.** 1854. Orig. cl., rubbed; pres. copy, inscr. by author. (CSK. Jan.27; 119) £380

BOORDE, J.
– **The Breviarie of Health.** 1575. 2 vols. in 1. Some margins slightly frayed, mod. cf. (BS. Nov.16; 25) £820

BOOT, Anselmus Boetius de
– **Gemmarum et Lapidum Historia.** Ed.:– Adrianus Toll. Leiden, 1636. Sm. 8vo. Some foxing, cont. vell., metal clasp. (SG. Feb.9; 175) $200

BOOTH, Edwin Carton
– **Australia.** Ill.:– after Skinner Prout, N. Chevalier, & others. L., [1873-76?]. *1st. Edn.* 2 vols. 4to. 8 cold. engraved maps, 111 steel-engraved plts., including 13 additional plts. & 2 additional maps not in list, a few plts. slightly spotted in margins, sm. hole in blank margin of Vol. 2 ptd. title, cont. hf. mor., jnts. rubbed, corner slightly wormed. (C. Jun.27; 81) *Remington.* £300
– – **Anr. Copy.** 8 orig. pts. 4to. 2 engraved titles, 8 col. maps, 109 engraved views, text & plts. loose, orig. cl., worn. (P. Oct.20; 11) £250
– – **Anr. Edn.** L., 1875? 8 vols. Pages loose, orig. bdg., very worn. (JL. Jul.15; 363) Aus. $750
– – **Anr. Edn.** N.d 2 vols. 4to. 2 maps & some ll plts. more than called for, some foxing & soiling, old hf. roan. (KH. Nov.8; 47) Aus. $700
– – **Anr. Copy.** Orig. 8 divisions. Lacks 4 engraved plts. & a few text ll., several plts. stained (2 badly), loose, as a coll. of plts., w.a.f. (KH. May 1; 87) Aus. $650
– – **Anr. Copy.** 2 vols. 4to. 6 plts. more than called for, & 1 plt. not corresponding with caption in list, 1 engraved title stained, some foxing or soiling, non-unif. mor. & hf. mor., rubbed & brkn. (KH. Nov.9; 555) Aus. $620

BOOTH, Edwin Carton -*Contd.*

BOOTH, John
- The Battle of Waterloo. Ill.:– Capt. George Jones, engraved by S. Mitan (etchings). N.d. 3 vols. 3 hand-cold. folding maps in Vol. 1, port. frontis., engraved title & 2 hand-cold. folding maps in Vol. 2, 34 etchings in Vol. 3, unif. hf. cf., spines gt. (SKC. Mar.9; 1736) £150
See— **GODDARD, T. & Booth, John**

BOPPE, Commandant P.
- La Croatie Militaire (1809-1813). Les Régiments Croates à la Grande Armée. Paris, Nancy, 1900. Hf. chagrin. (HD. Jan.27; 111) Frs. 1,300
- La Légion Portugaise 1807-1813. Paris, Nancy, 1897. On holland, hf. chagrin. (HD. Jan.27; 112) Frs. 1,700

BOR, Pieter
- Oorssprongk, Begin & Vervolgh der Nederlandsche Oorlogen. Ill.:– J. Luiken & C. Decker. Amst., 1679-84. 4 vols. Fo. Engraved frontis. (with sm. owner's stp.), 39 (of 40) engraved ports., 39 (of 40) engraved plts., including 38 double-p., 1 or 2 sm. tears, cont. vell., spine of Vol. IV reprd. (CH. Sep.20; 22) Fls. 1,800

BORCHERT, W.
- Lanterne, Nacht und Sterne. Gedichte um Hanburg. Hamburg, 1946. *1st. Edn.* Slightly yellowed, orig. sewed. (GB. Nov.5; 2307) DM 650

BORDELON, Laurent
- L'Histoire des Imaginations Extravagantes de Monsieur Oufle. Paris, 1754. 5 vols. in 2. 12mo. 10 engraved plts. (1 folding), cont. tree cf., spines very worn. (SG. Apr.19; 197) $100

BORDEN, W.W.
- Borden's Leadville. A Treatise on Leadville, Colorado .... New Albany, Indiana, [1879]. 16mo. 10 pp. of ill. advts., orig. ptd. wraps. (LH. Apr.15; 272) $275

BORDEU, Théophile de
- Recherches sur le Tissu Muqueux. Paris, 1767. Hf.-title, cont. cf. gt. (SG. Oct.6; 59) $110

BORDONA, J.D.
- Die Spanische Buchmalerei v. 7.-17. Jhdt. Leipzig, 1930. Lge. 4to. Orig. linen. (HK. Nov. 11; 4313) DM 500

BORDONE, Benedetto
- Isolario. Venice, Nicolo d'Aristotile, detto Zoppino, 1534. *3rd. Edn.* Sm. fo. Ptd. title in red & black in woodcut border, 7 double-p. maps (including a world map), 104 maps in text, 1 diagram, all woodcut, title slightly soiled, 1 or 2 neatlines shaved, last lf. reprd., a few MS. sidenotes in ink, marb. paper bds. [Sabin 6419] (S. May 21; 140) Cope. £2,600
- Libro...nel qual si ragiona de tutte l'Isole del mondo (Isolario). Venice, Nicolo d'Aristotile, detto Zoppino, 1528. *1st. Edn.* Sm. fo. Title in red & black in woodcut border, 7 double-p. maps, including the World map on the oval projection, title slightly soiled, some staining, dampstain affecting last 4 ll., strengthened with slight text loss on last lf., a few margin inkstains & underlinings in text, mod. red mor. gt. [Sabin 6147] (S. Dec.1; 177) Burgess. £2,400

BOREGK, M.
- Behmische Chronica. Wittenberg, 1587. 2 pts. in 1 vol. Fo. Lightly browned, some ll. with reprd. margin slits, 2 pp. defect. with loss & reprd., some old marginalia, some slight excisions, title with old owners mark, cont. blind-tooled pig over wood bds, clasps. (R. Apr.3; 18) DM 1,300

BOREL, Pierre
- Bibliotheca Chimica. Paris, 1654. *1st. Edn.* 12mo. Cont. vell., spine darkened. (SG. Oct.6; 60) $850

BORGARUCCI, Prosper (Pseud.)
See— **VESALIUS, Andreas**

BORGSTEDE, A.H.
[–] Statistisch-Topographische Beschreibung der Kurmark Brandenburg. Berlin, 1788. 4to. Cont. hf.

leath., slightly rubbed. gt. decor. (GB. May 3; 246) DM 500

BORIA, J. de
- De Moralische Sinn-Bilder. Trans.:– F. Scharff. Berlin, 1698. *1st. German Edn.* Lightly spotted or stained, 2 pp. with cont. marginalia. cont. vell., slightly spotted, lr. cover very defect. (HT. May 9; 1292) DM 420

BORKHAUSEN, Moritz Balthasar & others
- Teutsche Ornithologie oder Naturgeschichte aller Vögel Teutschlands in Naturgetreven Abbildungen und Beschrelbungen. Ill.:– H. Curtmann, J.C. Susemihl, E.F. Lichthammer, J.T. Susemihl, & E.E. Susemihl, Darmstadt,. [1800-11]. 21 pts. in 1 vol. Fo. 126 hand-cold. etched plts., some slight spotting or soiling in margins, cont. German cf. gt., rebkd., old spine laid down. (S. Feb.1; 10)
Quaritch. £13,000

BORLASE, Edmund
[–] The History of the Execrable Irish Rebellion. L., 1680. *1st. Edn.* Fo. Lacks folding table, cont. cf. (GM. Dec.7; 487) £125
– – **Anr. Copy.** Fo. Cf., rubbed. (GM. Dec.7; 98) £95

BORLASE, William
- Antiquities, Historical & Monumental of the County of Cornwall. L., 1769. *2nd. Edn.* Fo. Folding engraved map, 26 plts., slight offsetting & spotting, cont. cf., spine worn. (S. Mar.6; 203) Scott. £130
– – **Anr. Copy.** Fo. 27 engraved plts. & maps. engraved ills., rather browned, cont. cf., worn. (BBA. May 3; 312) Elliott. £70
- The Natural History of Cornwall. 1758. *1st. Edn.* Fo. Newly rebnd. in panel. cf. (LA. Nov.29; 91) £113
– – **Anr. Copy.** Fo. Engraved folding map, 29 plts., map & 1 plt. with tears, cont. cf., worn. (S. Mar.6; 204) Ambra. £110
- Observations on the Ancient & Present State of the Islands of Scilly. Oxford, 1756. *[1st. Edn.].* 4to. Hf.-title, some faint margin staining, cont. bds., unc., rebkd., worn. (S. Nov.1; 100) Scott. £180
– – **Anr. Copy.** Mott. cf. (LA. Nov.29; 95) £100
- Observations on the Antiquities...of the the County of Cornwall. Oxford, 1754. *1st. Edn.* Fo. 31 maps & plts., orig. mott. cf. (P. Jun.7; 119) £120
– – **Anr. Copy.** Fo. 24 engraved plts., subscribers list, a few plts. frayed on margins & loose, old cf., sides paper-covered, worn, a few covers stained. (SKC. May 4; 1774) £65
– – **Anr. Edn.** 1769. *2nd. Edn.* Fo. Folding engraved map, 25 engraved plts. (1 folding), cont. pol . cf., spine gt.-decor., slightly worn, cover detchd. (SKC. May 4; 1773) £130

BORN, I. de
- Méthode d'extraire des Métaux Parfais des Minérals et Autres Substances Métalliques par le Mercure. Wien, 1788. Stp. on title, some slight spotting, cont. hf. leath. (D. Nov.25; 4617) DM 400

BORNE, Ludwig
- Gesammelte Schriften. Hamburg & Frankfurt, 1862. 12 vols. Minimal foxing, cont. hf. leath. gt. (GB. Nov.4; 2002) DM 480

BORONAT Y BARRACHINAS, Pascual
- Los Moriscos Españoles: y su Expulsión. Intro.:– Manual Danvilla y Collado. Valencia, 1901. 2 vols. 4to. Linen. (DS. Feb.24; 2236) Pts. 42,000
– – **Anr. Copy.** 2 vols. 4to. Leath. (DS. Mar.23; 2503) Pts. 22,000

BORROW, George
- The Bible in Spain. L., 1843. *1st. Edn.* 3 vols. 12mo. Hf.-titles, advt. slip in Vol. 1, slightly spotted, owner's inscr. on each title, 1 gathering loose, orig. cl., unc., worn. (S. Mar.20; 856) Brook. £70

BORULAWSKI, Joseph
- Memoirs of the Celebrated Dwarf,.... Trans.:– M. des Carrières (Engl. trans.). 1788. *1st. Edn.* In Fr. & Engl., subscribers list, engraved frontis. stained, cl. (LC. Mar.1; 453) £80

BORUP, Th. L.
- Det Menneskelige Livs Flugt eller Dode-Dands.... Copen., 1814. *3rd. Edn.* Sm. 4to. Foxed & lightly

browned, cont. hf. vell., spine torn, inner cover with coll stp, cont. hf. liners, spine torn. (H. May 22; 439) DM 640

BORUSSIA. Museum für Preussische Vaterlandskunde
[Dresden, 1838-42]. 3 vols. 4to. Vol. 1 end-paper slightly worn, 1 text lf. holed, 1 plt. with tear, some slight browning, orig. bds., wear. (HT. May 10; 2898) DM 18,200

BORY DE SAINT-VINCENT, J.B.G.M.
- Voyages dans les Quatre Principales Iles des Mers d'Afrique. Paris, 1804-05. Atlas vol. only. 4to. 58 plts. & folding maps, old bds., unc. (SG. Sep.22; 62) $225

BOSA, E.
- Gridatori ed Altri Costumi Popolari del Trieste. Ill.:– E. Bosa. Mailand & Venice, 1835. 4to. Fragment, 26 etchings from both series, lacks orig. title lf., replacement title lf. 'Sketch-book by an American in Venice 1860', sm. stain in lr. margin in 5 early ll., cont. hf. linen , bumped. (R. Oct.12; 2188) DM 1,100

BOSC, Claude du
- The Military History of his Serene Highness Prince Eugene of Savoy, as also...the Duke of Marlborough .... L., 1735-37. 2 vols. Fo. Cont. stpd. cf., slightly worn. (VA. Apr.26; 209) R 540

BOSCHETTI, A.
[–] Il Mar Baltico e sue Coste. Triest, 1854. *2nd. Edn.* Lge. 4to. Cont. hf. leath. (R. Oct.13; 3308) DM 600

BOSCHINI, Marco
- La Carta del Navegar Pitoresco. Dialogo tra un Senator Venetian Deletante, e un Professor de Pitura, soto none d'Ecelenza, e de Compare. Venice, 1660. Sm. 4to. Engraved frontis. & 25 full-p. engrs. in text, hf.-title, some light staining & spotting. 19th. C. red mor. gt., slightly worn. (S. May 10; 237) Parikian. £800
- Il Regno Tutto di Candia Delineato a Parte et Intagliato. Venice, 1651. 4to. Engraved title, ptd. dedication, engraved birds eye view & 59 views & plans only (of 61) (lacks nos. 20 & 44), several folding, mod. mor., old cf. trimmed & laid downoon bds. & 5 panels of spine. (CSK. May 4; 200) £1,200

BOSCOVICH, Roger Joseph
- De Solis ac Lunae Defectibus. L., 1760. *1st. Edn.* 4to. Lacks hf.-title, mod. qtr. cf. (SG. Oct.6; 61) $300
- Philosophiae Naturalis Theoric Redacta ad Unicam Legern Virium in Natura Existentium. Wien, 1759. *2nd. Edn.* 4to. Slightly foxed, some light margin staining, cont. leath., spine defect. (R. Oct.12; 1651) DM 850
- A Theory of Natural Philosophy. Trans.:– J.M. Child. Chic., 1922. *1st. Edn. in Engl.* Sm. fo. Cl. gt. (SG. Mar.22; 42) £130
– – **Anr. Copy.** Fo. Latin & Engl. text, orig. cl.; John D. Stanitz coll. (SPB. Apr.25; 56) $110

BOSMAN, Willem
- A New & Accurate Description of the Coast of Guinea. L., 1721. A few light margin stains, cont. cf. (S. May 22; 413) Norwich. £200
- Voyage de Guinée. Utrecht, 1705. *1st. Fr. Edn.* Plts. with some creasing, slightly foxed & stained, cont. leath. gt. very worn. (HK. Nov.8; 798) DM 400

BOSQUET, A.
- A Series of Essay on Several Most Important New Systems & Inventions, Particularly Interesting to the Mercantile & Maritime World. 1818. Orig. bds., partly unopened, upr. part of spine torn; inscr. by author. (P. Jan.12; 201) Cavendish. £85

BOSQUET, Alain & others
- Le Livre d'Eros. Ill.:– Pierre Yves Trémois. Paris, 1970. Square 4to. On vélin d'Arches, orig. cf., cf. box; sigd. engr. by Trémois, set of ills. in box corresponding to those of book, most orig., drawing in ink & wash, sigd. & dtd. 1970, & wash drawing annotated by artist, 1971. (SM. Mar.7; 2353)
Frs. 17,000

BOSSCHE, G. van den
- **Historica Medica.** Brüssel, 1639. *1st. Edn.* 4to. Some slight staining, cont. vell., lightly cockled, lr. end-paper partly loose. (D. Nov.23; 532) DM 500

BOSSCHERE, Jean de
- **12 Occupations.** L., 1916. Lge. sq. 12mo. In Fr. & Engl., pict. wraps. (SG. Mar.1; 27) $325

BOSSE, Abraham
- **La Pratique du Trait à Preuves, de Mr Desargues Lyonnois, pour la Coupe des Pierres en l'Architecture.** Paris, 1643. *1st. Edn.* Lge. 8vo. L.P., 2 additional engraved titles, 1st. p. of dedication engraved, 114 engraved plts. on 58ll., line after 'FIN' on last lf. erased, 18th. C. cf. gt. (SG. Oct.13; 42) $275
- **Recueil de Figures, pour apprendre a dessiner sans Maître le Portrait, la Figure, l'Histoire et le Paysage.** Paris, 1736-37. 4 pts. in 1 vol. 4to. 2 engraved titles & 120 copperplts., 36 ll from various works (including 2 costume plts., 4 element allegories, some slight foxing, cont. cf. gt., slightly rubbed. (H. May 22; 129) DM 1,300
- **Traité des Manières de Dessiner les Ordres d'Architecture Antique....** N.d. Engraved title plus dedication, 66 engraved plts. (*Bound with:*)
- **Representations Géometrales.** Paris, 1688. Engraved title, 22 engraved plts. Together 2 works in 1 vol. Fo. Cont. cf. (P. Oct.20; 44) £220
- **Traité des Manières, de Graver en Taille Douce sur L'Airan.** Paris, 1701. 1 plt. torn, cont. sheep, worn. (BBA. Nov.10; 199) *Blackwell.* £100
- **Traité des Pratiques Géometrales et Perspectives.** Paris, 1665. *1st. Edn.* Engraved dedication, additional engraved title, 69 plts., including 1 double-p., A2-3 transposed with A1, early red mor. gt. extra. (SG. Oct.27; 36) $350
- - **Anr. Copy.** Cont. leath., bumped, lr. cover slightly torn at top & bottom. (D. Nov.23; 1869) DM 700

See— LAIRESSE, G. de - BOSSE, A.

BOSSERT, Helmuth Theodor
- **Geschichte d. Kunstgewerbes aller Zeiten u. Völker.** Berlin, 1928-35. 6 vols. 4to. Orig. hf. leath., owners mark on upr. doubl. (HK. May 17; 3427) DM 600
- - **Anr. Copy.** Orig. hf. leath. (HK. Nov.12; 4623) DM 550
- - **Anr. Edn.** Berlin, 1928 to 1935. Lightly browned, slightly spotted, orig. hf. leath., partly worn, 1 jnt. sprung. (HT. May 9; 1058) DM 500
[-] - **Anr. Copy.** 6 vols. Orig. hf. leath. gt. (R. Apr.3; 718) DM 450
- **Ornament.** 1924. Fo. Orig. cl., d.- w. (CSK. Aug.5; 50) £70
- **Ornament in Applied Art.** N.Y., 1924. Fo. 122 cold. plts., ex-liby., buckram. (SG. May 3; 53) $225
- **Peasant Art in Europe.** L., 1927. Fo. Orig. cl. (S. Dec.13; 432) *Traylen.* £55

BOSSERT, Helmuth Theodor & Guttmann, Heinrich
- **Aus der Fruehzeit der Photographic, 1840-70.** Ill.:– after Talbot, Nadar, Cameron, Daguerre, & others. Frankfurt, 1930. *1st. Edn.* Foxed, orig. cl., spine torn. (SG. May 10; 18) $125

BOSSHART, J.
- **Neben der Heerstrasse.** Ill.:– E.L. Kirchner. Zürich, 1919. 24 orig. woodcuts, some light yellowing, orig. hf. linen, covers slightly faded. (GB. Nov.5; 2663) DM 1,000
- - **Anr. Edn.** Ill.:– E.L. Kirchner. Zürich, 1923. *1st. Edn.* 24 orig. woodcuts, some light yellowing, orig. pict. hf. linen name on end-paper. (GB. May 5; 2772) DM 950
- - **Anr. Edn.** Ill.:– E.L. Kirchner. Zürich & Leipzig, [1923]. Slightly browned, orig. hf. linen. (HK. Nov.11; 3688) DM 460

BOSSI, Benigno
- **Opere Varie....** Milan, ca. 1790. 4 pts. in 1 vol. Fo. 4 engraved titles, 69 engraved ll., many with 2 or more plts., some ptd. in sepia, cont. roan-bkd. bds., w.a.f. (C. Nov.9; 45) *Erlini.* £800

BOSSOLI, Carlo
- **The War in Italy.** [1859-60]. 4to. 2 maps, litho. title, 39 plts. (loose), some text & plts. frayed &

stained in margins, orig. cl. gt., spine torn. (P. Sep.8; 190) *Edistar.* £240
- - **Anr. Copy.** 2 vols. Hf.-titles, folding engraved map slightly torn, mod. cf. [Sabin 6466] (BBA. Sep.29; 41) *Morrell.* £190
- - **Anr. Copy.** 2 vols. Hf.-titles, cont. cf.; the Rt. Hon. Visc. Eccles copy. [Sabin 6466] (CNY. Nov.18; 28) $750

BOSSU, N.
- **Nieuwe Reizen naer Noord-Amerika.** Amst., 1769. 2 vols. Sm. 8vo. Some stains, mod. hf. vell., unc. [Sabin 6467] (VG. Nov.30; 804) Fls. 450
- **Nouveaux Voyages aux Indes Occidentales....** Ill.:– after G. de St. Aubin. Paris, 1768. *1st. Edn.* 2 pts. in 1 vol. Sm. 8vo. Cont. mott. cf., spine gt., 1 spine end slightly defect. (VG. Nov.30; 803) Fls. 600

BOSSUET, Jacques Benigne
- **Defensio Declarationis Celeberrimae, quam de Potestate Ecclesiastica sanxit Clerus Gallicanus XIX Martii MDCL XXXII.** Luxembourg, 1730. *Orig. Edn.* 2 vols. in 1. 4to. Errata lf. at end of each vol., lacks port., lightly browned, cont. red mor. gt. decor., Armand Gaston de Rohan-Soubise arms ; old initials 'A.A.' & no. 60 on title. (SM. Mar.7; 2430) Frs. 3,300
- **Divers Ecrita.** Paris, 1598. *Orig. Edn.* Cont. red mor. gt., Duc du Maine arms, spine decor.; from Daguin liby. (HD. Mar.29; 13) Frs. 72,000
- - **Anr. Edn.** Paris, 1698. *1st. Edn.* 4 ll. of Avertissement inserted, bnd. for author in cont. Fr. red mor. gt., author's arms on sides, sm. scratches on upr. cover reprd.; Edouard Rahir & Lucien-Graux bkplts. (C. May 30; 72) *Henner.* £2,700
- **Oraison Funèbre de très Haut et très Puissant Prince Louis de Bourbon, Prince de Condé....** Paris, 1687. *Orig. Edn.* 4to. L.P., cont. black mor., arms of Louis XIV & Bouthillier family spine decor.; from Baron de Franchetti liby. (HD. Mar.29; 12) Frs. 60,000
- **Oraisons Funèbres.** Paris, 1680. *3rd. Edn.* 12mo. Cont. red mor., Du Seuil border, spine decor.; from Comte de Lignerolles liby. (HD. Mar.29; 10) Frs. 14,000
- - **Anr. Edn.** Paris, 1939. Sewed. (HD. Jun.13; 117) Frs. 1,000
- **Réglement du Séminaire des Filles de la Propagation de la Foy, établies en la Ville de Mets.** Paris, 1672. 16mo. Cont. cf., spine decor.; cont. MS. note 'de la propagation de la foy de Sedan', from Guyot de Villeneuve liby. (HD. Mar.29; 9) Frs. 30,000
- **Sermon Presché à l'Ouverture de l'Assemblée Générale du Clergé de France, le 9 Novembre 1681.** Paris, 1682. *Orig. Edn.* 4to. 'Ordonnance et Instruction Pastorale de Monseigneur l'Evesque de Meaux, sur les Etats d'Oraison', 1695, at end, cont. red mor., spine decor.; Bossuet's copy with 2-line note in his hand, from Baron de Claye liby. (HD. Mar.29; 11) Frs. 22,000
- **Traité du libre-arbitre et de la Concupiscence.** Paris, 1731. *Orig. Edn.* 12mo. Cont. cf., sm. defects. (HD. Feb.22; 22) Frs. 1,000

BOSSUS, Mathaeus
- **De Instituendo Sapientia Animo.** Bologna, F. [Plato] de Benedictis, 6 Nov. 1495. 4to. Early 19th. C. bds., vell. back; the Walter Goldwater copy. [BMC VI, 828; Goff, B-1045] (SG. Dec.1; 82) $850
- **Dialogus de Veris et Salutaribus Animi Gaudiis.** Additions:– A. Politianus & T. Veronensis. Flor., Francesco Bonaccorsi, 8 Feb. 1491. *1st. Edn.* 4to. 1 capital printed in blue, paragraph marks & initial-strokes supplied in green, all on a5r, lacks the 2 blanks, a2-4 supplied in facs., a5-b1 stained, wormed, & reprd., 16-8 remargined & 19 laid down, few old marginalia, hf. sheep, slightly wormed. [BMC VI, 674; Goff B-1041] (SG. Oct.27; 158) $225
- **Recuperationes Faesulanae.** Bologna, Franciscus (Plato) de Benedictis, 10 Jul. 1943. Fo. Lacks all prelims., 72 ll. in all, 1 lf. torn, 1 lf. stained on verso, later cf. gt., rehinged. [Goff B1045] (SG. Feb.9; 252) $200

BOSSUT, Charles
- **Histoire Générale des Mathématiques depuis leur Origine jusqu'á l'Année 1808.** 1810. 2 vols. Cont.

spr. roan, Collège Royal de Tours superlibris. (HD. Apr.13; 69) Frs. 1,600
- **Traité Elémentaire d'Hydrodynamique....** Paris, 1771. *1st. Edn.* 2 vols. Hf.-title, some browning, mostly of end-papers, sm. wormholes in 1st. vol. inner margin, cont. mott. sheep, initial 'EMB' on spimes; John D. Stanitz Coll. (SPB. Apr.25; 58) $225
- **Traité Théorique et Experimental d'Hydrodynamique.** Paris, 1786. *1st. Edn.* 2 vols. Some spotting & browning, cont. hf. vell., marb. bds., rubbed, stp. & label of Société de Lecture on titles & spines, sig. of Pierre François Bellot, John D. Stanitz copy. (SPB. Apr.25; 59) $350

BOSSUT & Viallet
See— SILBERSCHLAG- BOSSUT & Viallet

BOSWELL, Henry
- **The Antiquities of England & Wales.** Ill.:– T. Kitchen & others. Ca. 1780. Pt. 2. Fo. 125 plts., including 39 maps, subscribers list, cont. hf. mor., rather worn. (SKC. Mar.9; 1968) £300
- **Historical Descriptions of New & Elegant Picturesque Views of the Antiquities of England & Wales....** 1786. Fo. Lacks maps, cont. reversed cf. (TA. Apr.19; 114) £130
- - **Anr. Edn.** [1786]. Fo. Frontis., 48 maps, 193 engraved plts., hf. cf., upr. cover detchd., w.a.f. (P. Oct.20; 5) £440
- - **Anr. Edn.** Ill.:– T. Kitchen. L., for Alex. Hogg, ca. 1790. Fo. Engraved frontis., 50 engraved county maps, many engraved plts ., views & plans on 191 ll., cont. hf. cf., worn, w.a.f. (C. Mar.14; 102) *Kidd.* £420
- **Picturesque Views of the Antiquities of England & Wales.** [1786]. Fo. Engraved frontis., 50 maps, 191 plts., several hand-cold., cont. hf. cf., cover detchd. (CSK. Sep.16; 217) £180
- - **Anr. Edn.** Ill.:– Kitchin (county maps). N.d. Fo. Engraved frontis., 153 plts. only, 50 county maps, cont. cf., lightly rubbed, rebkd., covers reprd., w.a.f. (CSK. May 4; 26) £420

BOSWELL, James
- **British Essays in Favour of the Brave Corsicans, by several hands.** L., 1769. *1st. Edn.* 12mo. Hf.-title, cont. hf. cf. (C. Nov.9; 129) *Quaritch.* £1,100
- **The Journal of a tour to the Hebrides.** 1785. *1st. Edn.* Lacks hf.-title, errata lf., cf., covers detchd. (P. Apr.12; 281) *Argyll Etkin.* £60
- **The Journal of a Tour to the Hebrides with Samuel Johnson.** 1785. *1st. Edn. 1st. Iss.* Last errata lf. with advt. for Boswell's 'Life of Johnson', lacks hf.-title & last (?blank) lf., few ll. slightly soiled, mod. cf.-bkd. bds. (BBA. Oct.27; 272) *Bloomsbury Rare Books.* £55
- - **Anr. Edn.** 1785. *2nd. Edn.* Hf.-title, advt. lf., cont. tree cf., spine gt.; Sir Ivar Colquhoun, of Luss copy. (CE. Mar.22; 28) £280
- **The Life of Samuel Johnson.** L., 1791. *1st. Edn.* 2 vols. 4to. 1st. state of Vol. I, S4r, line 10 with misprint 'gve' for 'give', all 7 cancels as listed by Rothschild, cont. cf., spines gt. (C. Nov.9; 130) *Brooke-Hitching.* £2,600
- - **Anr. Copy.** 2 vols. 4to. Page 135 line 10 of Vol. 1 with reading 'gve', Vol. 1 with cancels 2M4 & 2N1, Vol.2 with cancels E3, 204, 2Q3 & 2Z1, Vol. 2 lacks 1st. blank, cont. mott. cf., spines gt.; bkplt. of Thomas Boswall, of Blackadder. (S. Dec.8; 35) *Marlborough.* £1,200
- - **Anr. Copy.** 2 vols. 4to. S4r in 2nd. state with 'give' on line 10, with 7 cancels, without 1st. blank in Vol. II, Vol. I with cancels 2M4 & 2N1 misbnd., sm. hole at 3C2 in Vol. I & L2 in Vol. II affecting a few letters, 2 plts. with numerals shaved, cont. tree cf., rebkd., orig. spines preserved; Lord Birkenhead bkplt., early 19th. C. owners inscr. of William Cribb with his pencil marginalia. (C. May 30; 137) *Pickering.* £600
- - **Anr. Copy.** 2 vols. Lge. 4to. 1st. state, 'Gve' reading on p. 135 vol. 1, 2 engraved plts., new marb. bds., lev. spines. (SG. Apr.26; 28) $1,500
- - **Anr. Copy.** 2 vols. 4to. Reading 'GVE' on Vol. I p. 135, port. laid onto verso of free end-paper, title-lf. strengthened on verso, some minor stains or foxing & c., later marb. bds., cf. spines & corners, rubbed. (RO. Apr.23; 14) $400

BOSWELL, James -*Contd.*

- - **Anr. Edn.** L., 1793. *2nd. Edn.* 3 vols. Tree cf. gt., rebkd. (P. Sep.8; 336) £120
- - **Anr. Copy.** 3 vols. Cont. tree cf. gt. (P. Sep.29; 134) *Spake.* £100
- - **Anr. Copy.** 3 vols. Extra-ill. by A.W. Waters of Leamington Spa with some 150 inserted views, ports. & facs., three-qtr. lev. gt. by Bayntun. (SG. Nov.3; 23) $475
- - **Anr. Copy.** 3 vols. Frontis. offset on title, cont. cf., rebkd. (LH. Sep.25; 499) £120
- - **Anr. Edn.** Boston, 1807. *1st. Amer. Edn.* 3 vols. Some foxing, cont. cf., rubbed & slightly dried. (RO. Apr.23; 15) $165
- - **Anr. Edn.** L., 1820. *New Edn.* 4 vols. Cont. cf., rebkd. (SG. Feb.16; 39) £140
- - **Anr. Edn.** Oxford, 1887. 6 vols. Cf. gt. (P. Sep.8; 91) *Wolfson.* £65
- - **Anr. Edn.** Ed.:– Glover. L., 1901. 3 vols. in 6. Extra-ill. with numerous additional engraved plts., many inlaid, a few hand-cold., a little light spotting, 1 lf. reprd., cont. spr. panel. cf. gt. by Sangorski & Sutcliffe, slight wear to 1 vol. (S. Oct.4; 76) *Cavendish.* £360
- - **Anr. Edn.** Ed.:– G.B. Hill, & L.F. Powell. Oxford, 1934-50. 6 vols. Cl. gt. (*With:*) - **Letters, 29 July 1758 to 19 May 1795.** Ed.:– C.B. Tinker. Oxford, 1924. 2 vols. Cl. gt. (SG. Sep.15; 64) $175
- **The Life of Samuel Johnson. - Principal Corrections & Additions to....** L., 1791; 1793. Together 2 vols. 4to. 'Gve' reading in vol.1, usual cancels, engraved port. & 2 plts. of facs., early marginal annots., some foxing, cont. of., spines worn, jnts. reprd., 2 jnts. cracked, anr. brkn. (SPB. May 17; 572a) $1,300
- **Private Papers.** L., 1951-60. *Yale Edn. (350-1050).* 6 vols. Vell.-bkd. cl., s.-c.'s. (LH. Sep.25; 500) $210
- **Relation de l'Isle de Corse.** Trans.:– J.P.I. Du Bois. Ill.:– Map:-Polak. La Haye, 1769. *1st. Ill. Fr. Edn.* Cont. hf. roan. (HD. Oct.21; 40) Frs. 3,200
- - **Anr. Copy.** Cont. leath. gt. (R. Oct.13; 3088) DM 460
- **Relazione della Corsica.** L., 1769. Lacks 'giornale del Viaggio', old hf. chevrette, corners. (HD. Oct.21; 38) Frs. 1,800
- - **Anr. Copy.** (*Bound with:*) **GIUSTINIANI, P.M.** [-]Riposta ad un Libello Famoso Intitolato Desinganno intorno alla Guerra di Corsica. Friburgo, 1737. Together 2 works in 1 vol. Old marb. hf. roan, corners; Auria ex-libris. (HD. Oct.21; 39) Frs. 2,800

BOSWORTH, N.A.

- **A Treatise on the Rifle, Musket, Pistol, & Fowling- Piece.** N.Y., 1846. *1st. Edn.* 12mo. 3 ll. advts., orig. cl., worn. some soiling & minor stains &c. (RO. May 29; 41) $100

BOSWORTH, Newton

- **Hochelaga Depicta: The Early History & Present State of the City & Island of Montreal.** Ill.:– Christie after J. Duncan. Montreal, 1839. *1st. Edn.* Engraved title vig., 2 folding engraved maps, 20 engraved plts., a few light dampstains. (*Bound with:*) - **Hochelaga Depicta: Or, A New Picture of Montreal ...with an Addenda.** Montreal, 1846. *1st. Edn.* Scattered light spotting. Together 2 works in 1 vol. Later cl.; the Rt. Hon. Visc. Eccles copy. (CNY. Nov.18; 29) $240

BOSWORTH, Newton

See— GOOD, John Mason & others

BOTERO, Giovanni

[-]**An Historicall Description of the Most Famous Kingdomes & Common-Neales in the Worlde.** Trans.:– [Robert Johnson]. L., 1603. 4to. Wormhole in upr. margin of 13 ll. touching a few letters, natural flaw in 1 lf., later hf. mor. [STC 3400] (BBA. May 3; 255) *Riley-Smith.* £170
- **Le Relationi Universali.** Venice, 1605. 4 engraved double-p. maps, browned & soiled, mod. hf. mor. (BBA. Jun.28; 118) *Lake.* £200
- - **Anr. Edn.** Venice, 1617-18. *1st. Vecchi Edn.* 8 pts. in 2 vols. 4to. Title Vol. 1 with MS. owner's note, 1 lf. with sm. paper fault with loss, 1 lf. with upr. corner torn with some loss, lr. corner Vol. 1 &

Vol. 2 increasingly browned to end, cut slightly short at head, cont. vell. [Sabin 6807] (HK. Nov.8; 822) DM 2,400

BOTTA, Paul Emile & FLANDIN

- **Monument de Ninive.** 1849. 1 text vol. & 4 plt. vols. Fo. 455 plts., mod. hf. mor., vell. covers. (HD. Apr.13; 81) Frs. 7,100

BOTTARI, G.G.

- **Musei Capitolini.** Ill.:– after Campiglio. Rome, 1750-55. Vols. I-III. Fo. Engraved title Vol. I dtd. 1748, ptd. title dtd. 1750, slightly browned, cont. cf., slightly bumped & worn, 1 upr. cover holed, 2 loose. (H. Nov.23; 419) DM 620

BOTTET, Maurice

- **Vétérans, Frères d'Armes de l'Empire Français, Débris et Médailles de Saint-Hélène. (1792-1815).** Paris, 1906. Sewed. (HD. Jan.27; 113) Frs. 1,000

BOTTICHER, H.

See— RINGELNATZ, Joachim (ie H. Bötticher)

BOTTIGLIONI, Gino

- **Atlante Linguistico Etnografico Italiano della Corsica.** Ill.:– Guido Colussi. Pisa, 1933-41/42. 10 vols. Lge. fo. Gt.-decor. chagrin, Victor Emmanuel arms. spines decor., silk liners, clasps. (HD. Oct.21; 42) Frs. 30,000
- **L'Ortografia delle Parlate Corse nell'Uso degli scrittori.** 1931. (*With:*) - **Vita Corsa.** Cagliara, 1932. (*With:*) - **Attente Linguistico Entographico Italiano della Corsica.** Pisa, 1932. (*With:*) - **Le Parlate Corse nella Classificazione dei Dialetti Italiani.** Cagliari, 1935. (*With:*) - **Caratteri Etnicolinguistici della Corsica.** Rome, 1941. (*With:*) - **Le Parlate Corse nella loro Storica Formazione.** Bologna, 1942. Together 6 pamphlets. Sewed. (HD. Oct.21; 41) Frs. 2,400

BOUCHE, Henri

See— DOLLFUS, Charles & Bouché, Henri

BOUCHER, Lucy

- **Un Conte de Merlin.** Ill.:– J. Gradassi (frontis) & Lucy Boucher. Nice, 1966. 4to. On velin de Lama, this copy numbered, blind- & gt.-decor. leath., unc., s.-c.; orig. watercold. drawing sigd. L. Boucher. (HD. Jun.26; 56) Frs. 1,300

BOUCHER DE PERTHES, J.

- **Antiquités Celtiques et Antediluviennes.** Paris, 1847 [1849-]64. *1st. Edn.* 3 vols. 118 litho. plts., text slightly foxed, cont. hf. cf., rubbed; Lord Avebury bkplt. (S. Dec.13; 179) *Rota.* £340

BOUCHET, André de

- **Sur le Pas.** Ill.:– Pierre Tal-Coat. Paris, 1959. (*200*) numbered & sigd. by author & artist. 4to. Unsewn in orig. pict. wraps., unc., folder & s.-c. (S. Nov.21; 120) *Makiya.* £250

BOUCHET, Jean

- **Les Anciennes et Modernes Genéalogies des Royes de France et mesmement du Roy Pharamond, avec leurs Epitaphes et Effigies.** Poitiers, [1535], Sm. 4to. Tear in 1 lf. reprd., slightly affecting text, 19th. C. hard- grd. mor. gt. by Bauzonnet-Trautz. (C. May 30; 74) *Snelling.* £380
- **Le Panegyric du Chevallier sans Reproche.** Poitiers, 28 Mar. 1527. 4to. Errors in foliation, compl. with blank *4, a few headlines shaved, 19th. C. mor. gt. (C. May 30; 73) *Fletcher.* £880
- **Sensuyt le Labyrinth de Fortune et Séjour des Troys Nobles Dames....** Paris, n.d. 4to. 19th. C. str.-grd. mor. gt. (C. May 30; 75) *Rosenthal.* £600

BOUCHETTE, Joseph

- **The British Dominions in North America....** L., 1831. *1st. Edn. 1st. Iss., with this date.* 2 vols. in 1. 4to. Engraved port., 10 maps & plans, including 1 folding, 15 litho & 5 aquatint plts., 3 engraved tables, some spotting, hf. cf. (S. Dec.1; 274) *Liberty.* £500
- - **Anr. Copy.** 2 vols. 4to. 3 engraved charts, 11 engraved maps & plans, 20 uncold, plts., including port., hf.-title in Vol. 2, orig. bds., unc., spines & edges worn; publisher's prospectus lf. sigd. by author, the Rt. Hon. Visc. Eccles copy. (CNY. Nov.18; 30) $1,300
- - **Anr. Edn.** L., 1832. *2nd. Iss.* 2 vols. 4to. Hf.-title in Vol. 2, port., 29 engraved maps, plans &

views, including folding map & double-p. view of Montreal, 3 engraved tables, advt. lf., cont. tree cf., rejointed. [Sabin 6828] (S. May 22; 304) *Maggs.* £400
- - **Anr. Copy.** 2 vols. 4to. Some soiling, cont. hf. mor. (CSK. Sep. 30; 113) £320
- - **Anr. Copy.** 2 vols. Port. frontis. to Vol. 1, vig. titles to each, uncold. litho. plts. (*With:*) - **A Topographical Dictionary of the Province of Lower Canada.** 1832. Some spotting. Together 3 vols. 4to. Recent unif. qtr. cf. gt., ex-liby. copies with stp. on titles only. (TA. Jun. 21; 53) £170

BOUCHOT, Henri

- **Catherine de Medicis.** Paris, 1899. *(1000). A numbered limitation (unstated) of the Edn. de Luxe.* Lge. 4to. Plts. & vigs. in 2 states, some cold., cont. mor. by Ruban, red mor. doubls, tooled in gt. & blind, silk free end-papers, orig. wraps. bnd. in, s.-c. (CSK. Nov.4; 144) £80
- - **Anr. Edn.** Paris, 1899. *(200) numbered on japon impérial.* 4to. Plts. in double state, red mor. gt. decor. by Durvand, wrap. & spine, unc., s.-c. (HD. May 21; 104) Frs. 2,100
- **La Miniature Francaise, 1750-1825.** Paris, 1907. *(200) numbered.* Tall 4to. 74 mntd. gravure plts., some hand-cold., cont. brocade cl., unc. (SG. Oct.13; 240) $300
- **Les Reliures d'Art à la Bibliothèque Nationale.** Paris, 1888. *(1000) numbered.* Cont. hf. mor., spine decor. with mor. onlays, orig. wraps. bnd. in, by Babin; H.M. Nixon coll. (BBA. Oct.6; 11) *Quaritch.* £280

BOUCHU, P.

See— COURTIVRON, Gaspard le Compasseur, Marquis de & Bouchu, P.

BOUDAILLE, George

See— DAIX, Pierre & Boudaille, George

BOUDRIOT, Jean

- **Le Vaisseau de 74 Canons. Traité Pratique d'Art Naval.** Grenoble, 1973-77. Vols 1,2 & 4 only (of 4). 4to. Publisher's bdgs. (HD. Jan.27; 114) Frs. 1,300

BOUFFLERS, Stanislas Jean, Marquis de

- **Aline, Reine de Golconde.** Ill.:– E. Gaujean after Al. Lynch. Paris, 1887. *Ltd. Edn., for members of Société des Amis des Livres.* 18th. C. style mor. gt. by Chambolle-Duru, spine decor.; 'bons à tirer' of 10 plts. sigd. by Octava Uzanne. (HD. Mar.27; 50) Frs. 2,100

BOUGAINVILLE, Baron H.Y.Ph. de

- **Journal de la Navigation autour du Globe de la Frégate la Thétis et de la Corvette l'Espérance pendant les Années 1824-1826.** Paris, 1837. Fo. 42 plts. (of 56), including 11 watercold., cont. hf. roan. (HD. Jun.22; 17) Frs. 10,500

BOUGAINVILLE, Louis Antoine de

- **Reis rondom de Weereldt....** Trans.:– P. Leuter. Dordrecht, 1772. 4to. L.P., mod. hf. cf., unc. [Sabin 6872] (VG. Nov.30; 805) Fls. 550
- **Voyage autour du Monde.** Paris, 1771. *1st. Edn.* 4to. 23 engraved maps & plts., most folding, hf.-title, cont. cf., slightly worn. [Sabin 6863] (S. Dec.1; 260) *Boon.* £800
- - **Anr. Copy.** 4to. Cont. cf. (CSK. Aug.19; 18) £550
- - **Anr. Edn.** Paris, 1772. *2nd. Edn.* 2 vols. 1 (of 3) folding plts., 21 engraved folding maps & charts, hf. -titles, 1 title & 1 map washed, last 12 ll. of Vol. II with sm. nick on fore-e., few prelims. in Vol. I misbnd., 19th. C. red qtr. mor., unc. [Sabin 6855] (SG. Sep.22; 63) $375
- **A Voyage round the World.** L., 1772. *1st. Engl. Edn.* 4to. 1 engraved plt., 5 folding engraved maps, some slight discoloration, a few neatlines on maps shaved, cont. cf., rebkd. (S. Dec.1; 261) *Traylen.* £550
- - **Anr. Copy.** 4to. 5 (of 6) folding plts. & charts, cont. hf. russ. gt. [Sabin 6869] (S. Dec.1; 262) *Backer.* £240
- - **Anr. Copy.** 4to. Advts. at end, title & plts. linenbkd., foxed, some stains, few margin defects, old liby. stp. on title, cont. cf., shabby, covers detchd. (SG. Sep.22; 64) $500
- - **Anr. Copy.** 4to. Some foxing, early pol. cf.,

rebkd. & recornered. (KH. May 1; 211)
Aus. $1,700
– – **Anr. Copy.** 4to. Title slightly foxed, some charts offset, a few ll. with slight foxing, cf. gt. (CA. Apr.3; 25) Aus. $1,000

BOUGARD, R.
– **Le Petit Flambeau de la Mer ou le Véritable Guide des Pilotes Cotiers....** Havre de Grace, 1763. Sm. 4to. Dampstains in upr. margin, cont. vell. (HD. Jul.2; 6) Frs. 1,800
– – **Anr. Edn.** Le Havre-de-Grâce, 1789. Sm. 4to. Hf. vell. (HD. Mar.9; 53) Frs. 1,600

BOUGUER, Jeanne Pierre
– **Traité Complet de la Navigation.** Paris, priv. ptd., 1706. 4to. Cont. spr. roan, spine decor; from Château des Noés Liby. (HD. May 25; 5) Frs. 2,100
– **Traité du Navire.** Paris, 1746. *1st. Edn.* 4to. Privilege lf., 12 folding plts., dampstained, cont. cf., worn. (SG. Oct.6; 62) $200
– – **Anr. Copy.** 4to. Owner's stp. & sigs. on title, hf. roan. (HD. Mar.9; 56) Frs. 1,100

BOULAESE, J.
– **Le Thrésor et Entière Histoire de la Triomphante Victoire du Corps de Dieu sur l'Esprit Maling Beelzebub, obtenue à Laon l'An Mil Cinq Cens Soixante Six.** Paris, 1578. *Orig. Edn.* Sm. 4to. Mod. hf. chagrin; inscr. 'Bibliothecae Colbertinae' on title. (HD. Dec.2; 73) Frs. 2,200

BOULAINVILLIERS, Comte Henri de
– **Etat de la France.** L., 1737. 6 vols. 12mo. Cf., roc d'echiquier & inscr. on spine each vol., corners worn. (HD. Feb.22; 24) Frs. 1,900
– **Histoire de l'Ancien Gouvernement de la France avec XIV Lettres Historiques sur les Parlemens ou Etats-Généraux.** La Haye & Amst., 1727. *Orig. Edn.?* 3 vols. 12mo. Cont. cf., spines decor. (HD. Nov.9; 115) Frs. 2,700
– **Histoire de la Pairie de France et du Parlement de Paris.** L., 1753. 2 vols. in 1. 12mo. Cf., corners worn. (HD. Feb.22; 25) Frs. 1,100
– **Lettres sur les Anciens Parlements de France que l'on nomme Etats-Généraux.** L., 1753. 3 vols. in 1. 12mo. Cf., corners worn. (HD. Feb.22; 26)
Frs. 1,000

BOULART, Raoul A.
– **Ornithologie du Salon ... Oiseaux de Volière Européens et Exotiques.** Paris, 1878. 4to. 40 hand-cold. plts., cl., ex-liby. (SG. Oct.6; 63) $150

BOULENGER, Jules César
– **De Theatro, Ludisque Scenicis Tricassibus, Ex Typis Petri Chevillot.** 1603. Cont. limp vell., lightly soiled. (CSK. Jul.27; 26) £130
– – **Anr. Copy.** Cont. limp vell., lightly soiled. (CSK. Apr.27; 111) £50

BOULGER, Prof. George S. & Perrin, Mrs. Henri or Ida S.
– **British Flowering Plants ....** 1914. *(1000) numbered.* 4 vols. 4to. Orig. buckram & d.-w.'s. (PD. Aug.17; 139) £65
– – **Anr. Copy.** 4 vols. Lge. 4to. Some light spotting, orig. buckram, lightly soiled. (CSK. Apr.27; 109) £60
– – **Anr. Copy.** 4to. 300 cold. plts., orig. cl. gt., partly untrimmed, soiled,. (TA. Dec.15; 147) £54

BOURASSE, Abbé Jean Jacques
– **La Touraine. Histoire et Monuments.** Ill.:– Karl Girardet & Français. Tours, 1855. *1st. Printing.* Fo. Foxing, cont. mor., richly blind– & gt.-decor., mor. doubls. (HD. Mar.27; 3) Frs. 4,500
– – **Anr. Edn.** Ill.:– K. Girardet, Français, Daubigny, & others. Tours, 1856. Fo. Publisher's chagrin, centre arms, spine decor. (HD. Mar.21; 134) Frs. 2,800
– – **Anr. Copy.** Fo. Cont. chagrin, gt. decor., centre arms, some sm. slits. (HD. Dec.9; 102) Frs. 1,800

BOURDALOUE, Louis
– **Oeuvres Complètes.** Paris, 1707-21. 14 vols. Cont. spr. cf. gt., spine decor. (LM. Mar.3; 118)
B.Frs. 24,000
– **Oraison Funèbre de Trés-haut et Très-puissant Prince Louis de Bourbon, Prince de Condé ....** Paris, 1687. *Orig. Edn.* Lge. 4to. L.P., cont. black mor.,

---

arms of Colbert, Marquis de Torcy; from Comte de Lignerolles liby. (HD. Mar.29; 14) Frs. 31,000
– **Pensées.** Paris, 1746. 3 vols. *(With:)* – **Sermons.** 1716. 3 vols. Together 6 vols. 12mo. Mor., Madame Victoire arms, spines decor. (SM. Mar.7; 2005a)
Frs. 8,000

BOURDE DE VILLEHUET, J.
– **Manuel des Marins.** L'Orient, 1773. 2 vols. in 1. Cont. marb. cf., spine decor.; from Château des Noës liby. (HD. May 25; 6) Frs. 1,500

BOURDET, Bernard
– **Soins Faciles pour la Propreté de la Bouche.** Paris, 1771. *2nd. Edn.* Cont. leath. gt. (R. Oct.12; 1502)
DM 530

BOURDIGNE, Jean de
– **Hystoire Agregative des Annalles et Croniques Daniou Contenant le Commencement et Origine Avecques Partie des Chevaleureux et Marciaulx Gestes des Magnanimes Princes, Consulz, Contes et Ducs Daniou.** Paris, Jan. 1529. *1st. Edn.* Fo. Sm. hole in title-p., piece of old paper pasted above it, lr. margins at beginning vary affected by worming, a few other margin wormholes, late 18th./early 19th. C. marginalia, cont. Fr. blind-stpd. cf., very worn & defect. (S. Nov.17; 10) *Tzakas.* £500

BOUREAU-DESLANDES, André Francois
– **Essai sur la Marine des Anciens et Particulièrement sur leurs Vaisseaux de Guerre.** Paris, 1756. 12mo. Cont. roan, spine decor. (HD. Nov.9; 167)
Frs. 1,600
[–] **Essay sur la Marine et sur le Commerce.** N.p., 1743. *Orig. Edn.* Cont. marb. cf. gt., spine decor. (HD. Nov.9; 166) Frs. 1,300

BOURGEOIS, Constant
– **Recueil de Vues et Fabriques Pittoresques d'Italie.** Ill.:– Guyot, Lameau, & others, after Bourgeois. Paris, ca. 1810. Fo. 175 engraved views on 96 ll., cont. mor.-bkd. pebbled cl. gt., orig. ptd. paper wraps. bnd. in, rebkd. (C. Jun.27; 13)
Marlborough. £420

BOURGEOIS, J.
– **Leven, Lyden ende Doodt ons Heeren Iesv Christi in Virige Meditatien ende Vytstortinge des Geests Begrepen.** Ill.:– Boetius a Bolswert. Hantwerpen, 1623. *1st. Edn. in Dutch.* Engraved title, 76 engraved plts., some minor margin stains, cont. overlapping vell., lacks ties. (VS. Dec.9; 1363)
Fls. 500

BOURGET, Paul
– **Une Idylle Tragique (Moeurs Cosmopolites).** Ill.:– Dillon. Paris, 1896. *(100) on Hollande.* 12mo. Havanna mor., decor. & mosaic spine, gt., blind & mosaic decor., mor. doubl., gt. decor., unc., wrap. & spine preserved, s.-c., by Kieffer. (HD. Feb.17; 55)
Frs. 5,500
– **Pastels.** Ill.:– Robaudi & Giraldon. Paris, 1895. *(200) on Japan.* Mor. gt. by Chambolle-Duru. (S. Nov.8; 497) *Greenwood.* £70
– – **Anr. Edn.** Ill.:– A. Robaudi. Paris, Société des Beaux Arts. ca. 1900. *Edn. des Deux Mondes. (20) lettered on Japan vell.* 4to. Plts. & text engrs. in 3 states (plain, India-proof & cold.), all (excepting 1 state of the text engrs.) with vig. remarque, orig. lev. gt., cold. mor. inlays, dentelles elab. gt.-decor., lev. doubls., upr. doubl. with inlaid oval hand-cold. engraved vig. ptd. on vell., moire grosgrain cl. liners, partly unc. (SG. Feb.16; 282) $475

BOURGOGNE
– **Coutume Générale des Pays et Duché de Bourgogne.** Commentary:– Taisand. Dijon, 1698. Fo. 18th. C. marb. roan, spine decor. (HD. Mar.21; 11b) Frs. 1,250

BOURGOING, Baron Jean François
– **Nouveau Voyage en Espagne, ou Tableau de l'Etat Actuel de cette Monarchie....** Paris, 1789. *Orig. Edn.* 3 vols. Cont. hf. roan, spines decor. (HD. Jun.26; 35) Frs. 1,300
– **Tableau de l'Espagne Moderne.** Paris, 1797. *2nd. Edn.* 3 vols. folding copper-engraved map, 10 folding copper-plts., cont. hf. leath. gt. (R. Oct.13; 3164) DM 1,500

BOURIGNON, A.
– **Afbeeldingen van 's Menschen Leven....** Ill.:– D. Bosboom. Utrecht, 1699. Sm. 8vo. Cont. cf., spine gt. (VS. Dec.9; 1364) Fls. 600
– **Das Heilige Persectiv.** Amst., 1684. Sm. 8vo. Some foxing, 19th. C. bds.; B. Luza bkplt. (VS. Dec.9; 1365) Fls. 650

BOURKE, Comte Ed. de
– **Notice sur les Ruines les plus Remarquables de Naples et de ses Environs.** Ill.:– Langlume. Paris, 1823. Cont. paper Bradel bds. (HD. May 21; 80)
Frs. 1,100

BOURKE, Ulick, Marquis of Clanricarde
See— CLANRICARDE, Ulick Bourke, Marquis of

BOURNE, John
– **A Treatise of the Screw Propeller, with Various Suggestions of Improvement.** L., 1852. *1st. Edn.* 4to. Errata lf., some foxing & soiling, cont. cf., worn; John D. Stanitz coll. (SPB. Apr.25; 61)
$125

BOURNE, John C.
– **The History & Description of the Great Western Railway.** L., 1846. Fo. Litho. title, 1 chart, 2 col. maps, 43 (of 47) lithos. on 28 (of 33) sheets, stained, text & plts. loose, orig. bds., worn, spine defect., as a coll. of plts., w.a.f. (P. Mar.15; 249)
Burgess. £520

BOURNE, William
– **Inuentions or Deuises. Very Necessary for all Generalls & Captaines, or Leaders of Men, as wel by Sea as by Land.** L., 1578. *1st. Edn.* 4to. Title creased, rubbed creating sm. hole, margin repairs. 3 ll. reprd. in margins, sm. stain in upr. inner corner, stitch marks, light browning, later hf. cf., worn; bkplt. of John Scott, of Halkshill. [STC 3421] (SPB. Dec.14; 8) $2,300

BOUTET, Frédéric
– **Tableau de l'Au-delà.** Ill.:– Ed. Goerg. Paris, 1927. *Numbered on velin Lafuma.* 4to. 14 orig. etchings, orig. bdg. (HD. Apr.26; 129) Frs. 1,000

BOUTET, Henri
– **Pointes Sèches.** Paris, 1898. 4to. 100 plts. (some cold.) & orig. dry-point frontis., sewed; autograph dedication to Georges Deschamps. *(With:)* – **Le Petit Café Blanc.** Paris, 1913. Square 12mo. On papier vergé à la forme, 66 drawings & orig. cold. etching, sewed. (HD. Jun.22; 19) Frs. 1,300
– – **Anr. Edn.** Paris, 1898. *(550).* 1 vol. With orig.? drypoints. *(With:)* MAILLARD, Léon – **Henry Boutet, Graveur et Pastelliste; Catalogue Raisonné.** Paris, 1895. *Ltd. Edns.* 2 vols. 2nd. vol. inscr. & sigd. by Maillard to Baron de Claye, sigd. & inscr. cold. crayon drawing bnd. in 1st. vol., pencil drawing in 2nd. vol. Together 3 vols. 4to. Threeqtr. lev., spines inlaid, by Meunier, orig. pict. wraps. bnd. in. (SG. Nov.3; 26) $1,500

BOUVY, Eugène
– **Daumier. L'Oeuvre gravé du Maître.** Paris, 1933. *(550).* 2 vols. 4to. Orig. wraps., unopened. (BBA. Sep.8; 34) *Leicester Art Books.* £60
– – **Anr. Copy.** 2 vols. 4to. Orig. wraps., unopened. (BBA. Nov.10; 200) *Duran.* £55

BOVE, Giacomo
– **Expedición austral Argentina.** Buenos Aires, 1883. 8 maps (5 folding), 46 plts. & diagrams, a few margins stained or defect., sm. liby. stp. on title-p., orig. mor.-bkd. cl., slightly rubbed. (BBA. Feb.9; 289) *Burton-Garbett.* £65

BOVER, Joaquim Maria
– **Biblioteca de Escritores Baleares.** Palma, 1868. 2 vols. Hf.-titles, few ll. slightly soiled, cont. wraps., worn. (BBA. Mar.7; 180) *Duran.* £60

BOVILLE, Père P.
– **Dame de la Foy. Histoire de la Descouverte et Merveilles de l'Image Nostre Dame de Goy trouvée en un Chesne près la Ville de Dinan, Pays de Liège. l'An 1609.** Toul, 1628. 12mo. Cont. vell. (HD. Dec.2; 74) Frs. 1,200

BOWDICH, Thomas Edward
– **Excursions dans les Isles de Madère et de Porto Santo.** [Paris & Strasbourg, 1826]. Atlas only. 4to.

BOWDICH, Thomas Edward -*Contd.*

22 plts., including 3 folding, bds., cf. spine. (S. Dec.13; 175) *Brockhaus.* £80

BOWDITCH, Nathaniel
– **The New American Practical Navigator.** Newburyport., 1802. *1st. Edn.* Pages 96 & 561 correctly numbered, frontis., 7 plts. (*Bound with:*) – **An Appendix...containing Tables for Clearing the Apparent Distance of the Sun & Moon...** Newburyport, 1804. Together 2 works in 1 vol. Cont. sheep, upr. cover loose; inscr. 'Jonathan P. Felt Salem Mass' & 'Barque Eliza 1832'. (PNY. Mar.27; 124) $1,800
– – **Anr. Copy.** 7 engraved plts., folding engraved map, woodcut diagrams, tables, 3-pp. errata, 4-pp. advts., foxed, few plts. soiled, 1 reinforced, map with sm. separation on fold, sig. L2 reprd., sig. Jj2 with tear, cont. inscr., cont. tree cf., spine split, upr. jnt. badly worn, cont. inscr. & bk.-label of Amasa Churchill. (SG. Apr.26; 30) $950
– – **Anr. Copy.** Pages 96 & 561 correctly numbered, 7 plts., frontis. map in facs., worn, cont. sheep, front & back end-sheets replaced. (PNY. Mar.27; 123) $475

BOWDITCH, Nathaniel & Kirby, Thomas
– **The Improved Practical Navigator.** Newburyport, 1807. *2nd. Edn.* Folding chart, 10 plts., chart stengthened, signals for vessels pasted in lr. cover, cont. cf., label replaced, label of Cushing & Appleton pasted in upr. cover. (PNY. Mar.27; 127) $325

BOWEN, Clarence W.
– **The History of the Centennial Celebration of the Inauguration of George Washington.** Contribs.:- P.L. Ford, A.B. Gardiner, B. Ives, R.W. Gilder, & others. N.Y., 1892. Lge. 4to. Orig. gt.-stpd. mor., corners scraped. (SG. Aug.4; 327) $110

BOWEN, Emmanuel
– **A Complete System of Geography.** L., W. Innys, etc., 1747. 2 vols. Fo. 70 engraved mapsheets, including 42 folding, a few short tears without loss of engraved surface, slight creasing, some faint browning, 1 or 2 margins slightly frayed, titles & index ll. soiled, cont. cf., defect. (S. Dec.1; 264) *Map House.* £1,800
– – **Anr. Copy.** Vol. 2 only. Fo. 40 engraved maps, including 34 folding, some light browning, cont. cf., worn, w.a.f. (CSK. Oct.21; 100) £1,700
– – **Anr. Copy.** 2 vols. Fo. 74 engraved mapsheets (only 70 called for), including 46 double-p. or folding, a few tears with some slight loss of engraved surface, 1 or 2 margins frayed, some creasing, text generally browned, index ll. defect., cont. cf., very worn. (S. Dec.1; 197) *Nicholson.* £1,600
– **The Maps & Charts to the Modern Part of the Universal History.** 1766. Fo. 39 folding engraved maps (list of maps calls for only 37, but maps of Italy, & Kingdoms of Naples & Sicily each on 2 plts.), numbered in ink, cont. hf. roan gt., marb. bds., rubbed. (LC. Mar.1; 455) £760
– – **Anr. Edn.** Ill.:– E. Brown & T. Kitchen. L., [1767]. Fo. State II of the twin-hemispherical world map, showing 'Holy Ghost Land' & 'Tierra de Espiritu Santo' off the Australian coast, also the 'Supposed Straits of Anian' off northwestern America, 39 double-p. or folding maps (only 37 called for), a few minor tears & repairs at additional folds without loss of engraved surface, some dust soiling, cont. hf. cf., slightly worn. (S. Dec.1; 207) *Cox.* £800
See— OGILBY, John & Bowen, Emmanuel

BOWEN, Emmanuel & Kitchen or Kitchin, Thomas
– **The Large English Atlas: or, a New Set of Maps of all the Counties in England & Wales.** Ill.:– by or after Bowen, Kitchen, C. Bowles, & R.W. Seale. L., Carington Bowles, 1767 [1780 or later?]. Fo. 47 lge. double-p. or folding engraved maps, handcold. in outl., some faint offsetting, sm. liby. stp. removed from foot of title, cont. hf. cf., covers detchd. (S. Dec.1; 155) *Burgess.* £3,100
– – **Anr. Edn.** Ill.:– Maps:– Bowen, Kitchin, C. Bowles, R.W. Seale, J. Dorret & J. Corbridge. L., R. Sayer, [1780]. Lge. fo. Title (incorporating list of contents) ptd. in red & black, 47 lge. double-p. engraved regional & county maps, all but 1 (Shropshire) hand-cold. in outl., Bowen's map of

Suffolk replaced by 'An Actual Survey of the County of Suffolk', unsigd. but attributable to James Corbridge [1765], some faint offsetting or browning, 1 or 2 light creases, some maps loose, cont. bds., defect., w.a.f. (S. May 21; 31) *Mizon.* £2,600
– – **Anr. Edn.** L., 1780 or later. Fo. 47 lge. double-p. maps, hand-cold. in outl., sm. inscrs. on title, some browning & creasing, cont. hf. moc., worn, upr. cover detchd. (S. Dec.8; 292) *Burgess.* £1,200

BOWEN, Frank C.
– **The Golden Age of Sail.** L., 1925. *(1500) numbered.* 4to. Orig. cl., d.-w. (BBA. Apr.5; 196) *Thorp.* £55
– **The Sea, its History & Romance.** L., [1924-26]. 4 vols. 4to. Orig. cl. gt. (S. Mar.20; 698) *Thorp.* £50
See— PARKER, Capt. H. & Bowen, Frank C.

BOWER, Alexander
– **An Account of the Life of James Beattie** .... 1804. 2 vols. Orig. bds., unc.; Sir Ivar Colquhoun, of Luss copy. (CE. Mar.22; 29) £190

BOWES, James Lord
See— AUDSLEY, George Ashdown & Bowes, James Lord

BOWES, Mary Eleanor, Countess of Strathmore
– **The Confessions of the Countess of Strathmore.** 1793. 19th. C. spr. cf., gt.-decor. spine. (TA. Nov.17; 407) £70

BOWKER, J.H.
See— TRIMEN, R. & Bowker, J.H.

BOWLER, Thomas William & Thomson, W.R.
– **Pictorial Album of Cape Town with Views of Simon's Town, Port Elizabeth, & Graham's Town.** Cape Town, 1866. Ob. fo. 12 tinted litho. plts., including 1 folding, lightly spotted, title browned, orig. cl., rebkd., lightly soiled, inner hinges reprd. (CSK. Dec.2; 41) £2,600

BOWLES'S DRAWING BOOK FOR LADIES; or Complete Florist
L., ca. 1780. Ob. 4to. Some light spotting, sm. tear nearly thro.-out, cont. wraps. (R. Oct.12; 1794) DM 1,000

BOWLES, Carrington
– **Bowles' Universal Display of the Naval Flags of all Nations of the World.** N.d. 16mo. Engraved title (in Engl. & Fr.), 19 double-p. hand-cold. plts., plts. cropped close at outer margin, qtr. cf., rubbed. (P. Mar.15; 291) *Cavendish.* £70

BOWLES, Thomas & John
– **Scotland Delineated.** 1745. Ob. 4to. 36 uncold. maps, wraps. (P. Jul.26; 232) £400

BOWLKER, Richard
– **The Art of Angling Improved, in all its Parts, Especially Fly-Fishing.** Worcester, [1746]. *1st. Edn.* 12mo. Some ll. stained, M4 reprd. at inner margin slightly affecting text, 19th. C. cf. (S. Oct.4; 8) *Head.* £260

BOWMAN, H. & Crowther, J.S.
– **The Churches of the Middle Ages.** L., ca. 1850. 2 vols. Fo. Some litho. plts. spotted, cont. red hf. mor., rubbed. (S. May 1; 531) *Weinreb.* £50

BOWYER, Robert
– **An Impartial Narrative of those Momentous Events...1816 to 1823.** 1823. Lge. tall 4to. Aquatints marked 'proof' or 'proof impression', facs. sig. plts. foxed, some slight spotting & faint offsetting from plts. hf. cf. (S. Nov.1; 71) *Thorp.* £70

BOWYER, William
See— NICHOLS, John & Bowyer, William

BOXHORN, Marcus Zuerius
– **Monumenta Illustrium Virorum et Elogia.** Amst., 1638. Fo. Cont. cf., spine decor.; from Fondation Furstenberg-Beaumesnil. (HD. Nov.16; 103) Frs. 3,000

BOY'S BOOK OF SPORTS & GAMES ... By Uncle John
Phila., 1851. 16mo. 16 p. catalogue of publisher's

advts., tear in 1 text lf., orig. gt.-pict. cl., corners & spine frayed, shaken. (SG. Dec.8; 73) $150

BOYD, James
– **Drums.** Ill.:– N.C. Wyeth. N.Y., 1928. *2nd. Edn. (525) sigd. by author & artist, with note 'One of 25 Presentation Copies'.* 4to. Orig. cl., lge. cold. pict. label on cover, remains of glassine d.-w., publisher's box. (SPB. May 17; 718) $450

BOYD, Julian P.
– **Indian Treaties.** Phila., 1938. *(500) numbered.* Fo. Cl., unc., some wear, s.-c. (worn & tape-reprd.). (RO. Dec.11; 38) $230

BOYDELL, John
– **Heads of Illustrious & Celebrated Persons.** 1811. Fo. Engraved frontis. & 27 mezzotints, slight snotting, later hf. mor., covers detchd., worn. (BBA. Jun.28; 12) *Lake.* £120

BOYDELL, John & Josiah
– **A Collection of Prints...Illustrating the Dramatic Works of Shakespeare.** 1803. 2 vols. in 1. Lge. fo. Light soiling, cont. mor. gt. (CSK. Sep.16; 149) £550
– – **Anr. Copy.** 2 vols. Lge. fo. 2 frontis., 2 vig. titles, 92 engraved plts., 3 additional plts. inserted, title & list of plts. in 1 vol. loose, mor. gt., covers detchi., spines defect. (P. Oct.20; 200) £340
– – **Anr. Copy.** 2 vols. Fo. 2 engraved ports., vig. titles, 96 engraved plts., some mntd., some foxing, mostly marginal, cont. gt.-& blind-tooled red str.-grd. mor., gt. dentelles, rehinged, extremities worn; Stephen Williamson bkplts. (SG. Nov.3; 27) $1,100
– **Graphic Illustrations of the Dramatic Works of Shakespeare.** 1791-1801. Sm. fo. 100 engraved plts., some spotting, disbnd. (TA. May 17; 378) £85
– – **Anr. Edn.** Ill.:– Blake, Bartolozzi & others. [1802]. Fo. 100 plts., rather spotted, cont. hf. mor. (BBA. Aug.18; 227) *Demetzy.* £160
See— COMBE, William & Boydell, John & Josiah

BOYLE, Mr.
– **Art of Drawing & Painting in Water-Colours – Manuscript of the Great Mr. Boyle.** 1731. Unc., sewn. (BBA. Nov.10; 194) *Traylon.* £55

BOYLE, Robert
– **A Continuation of New Experiments Physico-Mechanical Touching the Spring & Weight of the Air; & their Effects.** Oxford, 1669. *1st. Edn.* 4to. Imprimatur lf. at end, some browning & soiling of plts., some soiling of title-p., light margin browning, mod. mott. hf. cf., John D. Stanitz coll. [Wing B3934] (SPB. Apr.25; 62) $1,200
– **A Defence of the Doctrine touching the Spring & Weight of the Air...against the Objections of Franciscus Linus... – An Examen of Mr. T. Hobbes his Dialogus Physicus De Natura Aëris As far as it concerns Mr. R. Boyle's Book of New Experiments....** L., 1662. Sm. 4to. Margin soiling, mod. mor.; cont. sig. of Jonathan Grundy on title, monog. stp. on title, John D. Stanitz coll. [Wing B3941] (SPB. Apr.25; 63) $850
– **Essays of the Strange Subtilty Determinate Nature Great Efficacy of Effluviums.** L., 1673. *1st. Edn. 2nd. Iss.* Cont. MS. note on 1 lf., 4-pp. catalogue at end, sm. hole in 1 lf. affecting 2 or 3 letters, cont. cf. [Wing B3951] (BBA. May 3; 13) *Lawson.* £140
– **Exercitationes de Atmosphaeris Corporum Consistentium.** L., 1673. *1st. Latin Edn.* 6 pts. in 1 vol. 12mo. A little light staining, cont. vell. [Wing B3957] (BBA. May 3; 14) *Traylen.* £150
– **Experimentum Novorum Physico-Mechanorum....** Geneva, 1682. 4to. Some browning & spotting, cont. cf., rebkd., worn. (CSK. Jul.27; 116) £65
– **A Free Discourse against Customary Swearing, & a Dissuasive from Cursing.** 1695. 2 pts. in 1 vol. 2 pp. advts., 2nd. pt. lacks X3 (?), a few upr. margins slightly wormed, later cf. [Wing B3978] (CSK. Jun.1; 36) £65
– **General Heads for the Natural History of a Country.** L., 1692. *1st. Edn.* 12mo. Cont. cf.; the Pembroke copy. [Sabin 7139] (SG. Nov.3; 28) $550
– **Hydrostatical Paradoxes, Made Out by New Experiments, (For the Most Part Physical & Easie).** Oxford, 1666. *1st. Edn.* Some ll. slightly soiled or

dampstained, cont. cf., worn, upr. cover detchd.
[Wing B3985] (BBA. May 3; 11) *Thomas*. £650
- **Medicinal Experiments: or, a Collection of Choice Remedies.** 1692. 3 pts. in 1 vol. 12mo. Dampstaining, some margins torn, old cf., worn. [Wing B3989] (CSK. Sep.16; 160) £160
- **New Experiments Physico-Mechanical Touching the Spring of the Air, & its Effects.** Oxford, 1662. *2nd. Edn.* 3 pts. in 1 vol. Sm. 4to. 2 engraved plts., (1 folding torn & reprd.), light stain thro.-out upr. margin, sm. hole in 24, lacks last blank, hf, cf. (P. May 17; 165) *Rota*. £750
- – **Anr. Copy.** 4to. Lacks folding plt. & final blank, margin tears, browning, liby. blind-stp., liby. cl. (SPB. Dec.13; 643) $175
- **Nova Experiments Physicomechanica de Viaeris Elastica – in Nova Machina Pneumatica.** The Hague, 1661. 12mo. Plt. slightly torn in folds, lr. corner of Q4 torn affecting catchword, limp vell. (S. Dec.13; 250) *Finch*. £50
- [–] **Occasional Reflections.** L., 1665. *1st. Edn.* 2 pts. in 1 vol. Few headlines shaved, recent bds.; Dean Sage copy, his engraved piscatorial bkplt. remntd. (SG. Mar.15; 184) $400
- **The Sceptical Chymist: or Chymico-Physical Doubts & Paradoxes ... To Which in this Edition are Subjoyn'd Divers Experiments & Notes About the Producibleness of Chymical Principles.** Oxford, 1680. *2nd. Edn.* 2 pts. in 1 vol. Advt. lf. in facs., sm. rust hole in 1 lf., cont. cf., slightly rubbed. [Wing B4022] (BBA. May 3; 16) *Quaritch*. £1,500
- **Some Considerations Touching The Usefulnesse of Experimental Naturall Philosophy.** 1664. *2nd. Edn.* 2 pts. in 1 vol. Sm. 4to. Inner margin of title reprd., mod. panel. cf. gt. (P. Sep.8; 8) £95
- – **Anr. Copy.** 2 pts. in 1 vol. 4to. Lacks 2nd. vol., publd. in 1671, longitudinal title-lf., cont. cf., worn. [Wing B4030] (BBA. May 3; 10a) *Thomas*. £80
- **Tractatus de Qualitatibus Rerum Cosmicis. Suspicionibus Cosmicis. Temperie Regionum Sub-Marinarum ....** L., 1672. [Wing B4050] (*Bound with:*) - **Paradoxa Hydrostatica.** Oxford, 1669. *1st. Latin Edn.* Longitudinal title present. [Wing B4017]. Together 2 works in 1 vol. 12mo. Cont. cf., top of spine defect.; Thomas Stonor 18th. C. bkplt. (BBA. May 3; 12) *Thomas*. £60
- **Tracts Consisting of Observations About the Saltness of the Sea.** L., 1674. *1st. Edn.* 9 pts. in 1 vol. A little staining, lacks 1st. blank lf., cont. sheep, rebkd. [Wing B4053] (BBA. May 3; 15) *Thomas*. £460
- **The Works ....** Ed.:- Richard Boulton. 1699-1700. *1st. Coll. Edn. in Engl.* 4 vols. Engraved port. frontis. to Vol. 1, 20 engraved plts., cont. panel. cf., all vols. brkn., 1 bd. detchd., spines worn. (LC. Mar.1; 456) £320

BOYLE, Roger, Earl of Orrery
See– ORRERY, Roger Boyle, Earl of

BOYLESVE, René
- **La Leçon d'Amour dans un Parc. - Nouvelles Leçons d'Amour dans un Parc.** Ill.:- René Lelong. Paris, 1923-30. *Edition De Grand Luxe. (150) numbered on vell.* Together 2 vols. 4to. Orig. bds., d.-w.'s, s.-c. (HD. Apr.26; 41) Frs. 1,600

BOYS, John
- **A General View of the Agriculture of the County of Kent.** l., 1796. *2nd. Edn.* Errata lf., lacks hf.-title?, slightly spotted, cont. cf., slightly worn; Kelso Liby. copy, inscr. 'The Gift of His Grace the Duke of Roxburgh'. (S. Mar.6; 409) *Marrin*. £80

BOYS, Thomas Shotter
- **Original Views of London as it is.** 1954. *Facs. of 1842 edn.* 2 vols. Fo. Qtr. mor. gt., s.-c. (P. Apr.12; 62). *Woodruff*. £65

BOYS, William
- **Collections for an History of Sandwich in Kent.** 1892 [1792]. 4to. Cf. gt., unc., rebkd. (P. Sep.8; 368) *Frankland*. £150

BOZ (Pseud.)
See– DICKENS, Charles

BOZE, C.G. de
- **Catalogue des Livres du Cabinet.** Paris, 1753. Some MS. prices, cont. cf. (BBA. Mar.7; 284) *W. Forster*. £80

- – **Anr. Copy.** Mod. cl., unc., unopened, orig. marb. wraps. bnd. in. (P. May 17; 95) *Maggs*. £60

BRAAK, M. Ter
See– FILMLIGA

BRACELLUS, J. & Pontanus, J. Jovianus
- **Ein Schöne Cronica vom Königreich Hispania.** Augsbourg, 18 Aug. 1543. Fo. Some ll. remargined, vell. (HD. Jan.30; 3) Frs. 8,000

BRACKEN, Henry
- **Farriery Improv'd, or a Complete Treatise upon the Art of Farriery ....** 1738. *2nd. Edn.* Cont. cf. (PD. Aug.17; 129) £105

BRACKENBURY, H. & Huyshe, G.L.
- **Fanti & Ashanti Three Papers Read on Board the S.S Ambriz on the Voyage to the Gold Coast.** 1873. Sm. 8vo. Cont. red mor. gt. by Leighton, satin doubls. & free end-papers. (CSK. Jan.13; 113) £90

BRACKENRIDGE, Henry Marie
- **Views of Louisiana....** Pittsb., 1814. *1st. Edn.* Old mott. cf. (LH. Apr.15; 274) $400

BRADBURY, John
- **Travels in the Interior of America, in the Years 1809, 1810, & 1811.** L'pool., priv. ptd., 1817. *1st. Edn.* Errata slip, cont. cf. gt., spine faded; the Rt. Hon. Visc. Eccles copy. [Sabin 7207] (CNY. Nov.18; 32) $750

BRADBURY, Ray
- **The Illustrated Man.** Garden City, 1951. *1st. Edn.* No bdg. stated, jacket lightly soiled & creased, spine fading, slight wear; sigd., & with 5 line inscr. from author, dtd. 1951. (CBA. Oct.29; 144a) $225

BRADFORD, G.
- **Esquisse du Pays, du Caractère et du Costume, en Portugal et en Espagne...en 1808 et 1809.** L., 1812. Fo. Fr. & Engl. text, 55 cold. litho. plts., cont. hf. cf., worn. (HD. Jun.6; 19) Frs. 5,300

BRADFORD, Thomas Gamaliel
- **A Comprehensive Atlas, Geographical, Historical & Commercial.** Boston, 1835. 4to. Engraved maps & charts, most hand-cold. in outl., minor foxing age-darkening, gt.-lettered cl., leath. back & tips, worn. (SC. Jun.7; 3) $425
- – **Anr. Edn.** Boston, [1835]. Fo. 58 engraved maps, cold. in outl., lacks frontis., orig. three-qtr. leath., brkn., lacks part of backstrip. (RO. Dec.11; 39) $275

BRADFORD, Rev. William
- **Sketches of the Country, Character & Costume in Portugal & Spain.** L., 1809-10. 2 pts. in 1 vol., including supp. 'Sketches of Military Costume in Portugal & Spain'. Fo. L.P., 1 engraved plt., 53 hand-cold. aquatints, including 13 of military uniforms, early 19th. C. hf. mor. (C. Mar.14; 33) *Traylen*. £800
- – **Anr. Edn.** 1812-13. 2 pts. in 1 vol. Fo. 55 hand-cold. plts., text in Engl. & Fr., very slight offsetting, red str.-grd. mor., rubbed. (P. Feb.16; 143) £460
- – **Anr. Edn.** L., [1813?]. 3 pts. in 1 vol., including the 2 Supps. Fo. 54 hand-cold. aquatint plts., without the plt. 'Monument at Corunna' (usually found in earlier issues), but with additional plt. 'Toro from the River Douro' not listed by Abbey, text in Engl. & Fr., some offsetting, lacks title to last Supp., cont. str.-grd. mor. gt., gt. spine, rubbed. (C. Jun.27; 14) *Zanzotto*. £550
- – **Anr. Edn.** L., [plts. wtrmkd. 1824]. 3 pts. in 1 vol. Fo. 54 hand-cold. aquatint plts., without frontis. & plt. 19 in Abbey's list, but with 2 unlisted plts., some offsetting, a few margin tears, minor spotting & soiling to a few margins, cont. hf. mor. (C. Nov.16; 56) *Orssich*. £320

BRADLEY, Richard
- **A Complete Body of Husbandry.** 1727. 4 pp. advts., cont. cf., rubbed. (P. Feb.16; 241) £70
- **A Philosophical Account of the Works of Nature.** L., 1721. *1st. Edn.* 4to. 28 hand-cold. engraved plts., advt. lf., a few slight stains, tear reprd., cont. of., spine gt., lacks label. (S. Mar.20; 758) *Page*. £100
- – **Anr. Copy.** 4to. 28 engraved hand-cold. plts.,

advt. lf., cont. cf. gt., upr. bd. detchd. (PD. Oct.19; 70) £95
See– FURBER, Robert & Bradley, Richard

BRADLEY, Will
- **Bradley his Book.** Ill.:- Bradley, Parish, Penfield, Beardsley, & others. Springfield, Mass., May-Nov. 1896. Vol. 1 nos. 1-4, Vol. 2 no. 1. Tall 8vo. & 4to. Orig. decor. wraps. (*With:*) - **Happenings Here & There along the Trail.** Pasadena, 1949. *(500)*. 1 vol. Wraps. (PNY. Oct.20; 190) $450

BRADLOW, R.F. & Kenmuir, D.
- **The Art of Edmund Caldwell.** Mazoe, 1982. *(250)* sigd. by publisher. Vol. 2. Fo. Qtr. leath. (VA. Apr.27; 661) R 460

BRADSHAW, George
- **General Railway & Steam Navigation Guide.** Sep. 1874. No. 494. Orig. wraps.; the Eighth Earl Poulett copy. (LC. Oct.13; 456) £50
- **Railway Time Tables, & Assistant to Railway Travelling No. 3.** L., 1839. 16mo. Folding litho. map, 8 double-p. maps & plans, slightly spotted, orig. cl., upr. hinge split. (S. Mar.6; 207) *Ash*. £50

BRADSHAW, Percy V.
- **The Art of the Illustrator.** Ill.:- H.M. Bateman, W. Russell Flint, & others. N.d. 20 pts. Fo. Orig. wraps., publisher's box; T.L.s. loosely inserted. (CSK. Oct.21; 51) £60

BRADSHAW, T. & Rider, W.
- **Views in the Mauritius, or Isle of France.** 1832. Fo. 40 litho. plts., some foxed, hf. cf., rubbed. (P. Mar.15; 101) £580
- – **Anr. Copy.** Fo. Some margin dampstains & foxing, hardly affecting plts., cont. panel. cf. gt., heavily rubbed. (TA. Nov.17; 25) £300

BRADWARDINE, Thomas
- **Geometria Specualtive...De Quadratura Circuli.** Paris, 6 Mar. 1511. *2nd. Edn.?* Sm. fo. Lr. margins slightly cropped, short reprd. tear to title-p., reprd. wormholes thro.-out, MS. annots., disbnd.; John D. Stanitz coll. (SPB. Apr.25; 65) $500

BRAHE, Tycho
- **Astronomiae Instaurate Mechanica.** Stockholm, 1901. *Facs. of Wandesbeck Edn. (1598).* Fo. Orig. ptd. wraps., unc. & unopened; John D. Staintz coll. (SPB. Apr.25; 66) $175
- **Epistolarum Astronomicarum Libri Quorum Primus ... Principis Gulielmi Hassiae Landgravij ....** Uranieborg, Frankfurt, 1610 [1596 at end]. 4to. 2 sm. slits in title (from name & stp.), 2 pp. with sm. margin slits, from paper fault, 2 pp. with sm. restored margin tear, 2 pp. with sm. corner tear at foot, some browning or slight foxing, cont. limp. vell. (R. Apr.4; 1508) DM 3,500

BRAIM, Thomas Henry
- **A History of New South Wales.** L., 1846. 2 vols. Titles & frontis.'s foxed, diced cf. gt., spine labels to Vol. 1 detchd.; Lord Derby bkplt. (CA. Apr.3; 26) Aus. $300

BRAINERD, David
- **An Abridgment of Mr. David Brainerd's Journal Among the Indians.** L., 1748. *1st. Engl. Edn.* 12mo. Old cf. (RO. Dec.11; 58) $170

BRAITHWAIT, Richard
See– BRATHWAITE or BRAITHWAIT, Richard

BRAMAH, Ernest
- **Kai Lung's Golden Hours.** L., 1924. *(250)* sigd. Light foxing to edges, hf. cl. & bds., end-papers irregularly darkening, jacket very lightly soiled, spine darkening. (CBA. Oct.29; 147) $140

BRAMHALL, Rev. John, D.D.
- **The Works ....** Dublin, 1677. *1st. Edn.* Fo. Some soiling, reprd., cf. (GM. Dec.7; 91) £75

BRANCA, Giovanni
- **Le Machine.** Rome, 1629. *1st. Edn.* 4to. Slightly browned & foxed, later limp vell.; John D. Stanitz coll. (SPB. Apr.25; 67) $3,250

BRAND, Adam
- **Relation du Voyage de Mr. Evert Isbrand ... à l'Empereur de la Chine.** Amst., 1699. *1st. Edn.*

BRAND, Adam *-Contd.*

Engraved frontis., folding map, lacks last lf. (blank), cont. vell. (BBA. May 23; 343)
Ennison. £120

BRAND BOOK
- **The Big Four Brand Book...for the Spring Work of 1897.** Kansas City, Mo., [1897]. 12mo. Advts., orig. leath., shabby. (SG. Jan.19; 115) $300

BRAND, John
- **The History & Antiquities of the Town & County of the Town of Newcastle Upon Tyne.** 1789. *[1st. Edn.].* 2 vols. 4to. 2 additional plts. & anr. loosely inserted, Index by William Dodd (1881) bnd. in at end, 19th. C. cf. gt., hinges reprd. (SKC. Mar.9; 1969) £130
- - **Anr. Copy.** 2 vols. 4to. Engraved titles, 32 engraved plts., some folding or double-p., list of subscribers, lacks frontis. port. & plan of Newcastle, a few plts. loose, hf. cf., spines gt., inner hinge of Vol. 1 brkn. (LC. Jul.5; 183) £60

BRANDES, R. & Krüger, F.
- **Neue Physikalisch-Chemische Beschreibung der Mineralquellen zu Pyrmont.** Pyrmont, 1826. Cont. hf. linen. (R. Oct.13; 2668) DM 850

BRANDON, Isaac
- [-] **Fragments: In the Manner of Sterne.** L., 1797. *1st. Edn.* Device on title, 3 engraved plts., with proof of plt. for Anna: A Fragment mntd. on G8v, cont. red str.-grd. mor., spine gt.; inscr. to author's wife with her sig., author's bkplt. (SG. Apr.19; 45) $150

BRANDT, Caspar & Cattenburgh, A. van
- **Historie van het Leven des Herren Huig de Groot.** Ill.:– J. Houbraken (ports.). Dordrecht & Amst., 1727. 3 pts. in 1 vol. Fo. Blind-tooled vell., slightly soiled. (B. Oct.4; 720) Fls. 500

BRANDT, Gerard
- **Historie der Reformatie en Andere Kerkelyke Geschiedenissen, in en omtrent de Nederlanden.** Ill.:– R. de Hooghe (frontis.), & others. Amst., 1671-1704. *1st. Edn.* 4 vols. 4to. Few light stains, cont. cf., spines gt., some defects. (VG. Sep.14; 1303) Fls. 460
- [-] **Historie der Vermaerde Zee- en Koop-stadt Enkhuisen.** Enkhuisen, 1666. *1st. Edn.* 2 pts. in 1 vol. 4to. Folding plan cut to plt. & mntd., some staining, tear in plan, cont. vell., gt. arms on sides, lacks ties. (VG. Sep.14; 1140) Fls. 850
- **Het Leven en Bedryf van den heere Michiel de Ruiter.** Amst., 1687. Fo. Engraved frontis., port., 8 plts., including 7 double-p. ('Voorede' disbnd.), some staining, fore-edge of port. a little frayed, 19th. C. hf. cf., worn. (CH. Sep.20; 23) Fls. 550
- - **Anr. Edn.** Amst., 1691. Fo. Cont. blind-stpd. vell. (CH. May 24; 12) Fls. 1,000
- - **Anr. Edn.** Ill.:– Stopendaal. Amst./'s-Graven-hage, &c., 1732. *3rd. Printing.* Fo. Cont. cf., spine ends slightly defect. (VG. Sep.14; 1002) Fls. 825
- - **Anr. Copy.** Fo. Cont. hf. roan, lacks part of chintz on covers, unc. (VS. Jun.7; 1033) Fls. 575
- - **Anr. Edn.** Ill.:– D. Vrydag, G. Brouwer, & others. Dordrecht, 1835-37. 5 vols. Hand-cold. port. frontis., 7 folding hand-cold. engraved plts., 1 other plt., cont. hf. chagrin. (VS. Dec.8; 821) Fls. 450

BRANDT or BRANT, Sebastian
- **De Origine et Conversatione Bonorum Regum et Laude Civitatis Hierosolymae.** Basle, Joh. Bergman de Olpe, 1495. 4to. 2 engrs., including 1 cold., lacks last lf. with colophon & printer's mark, cont stpd. hf. pig over wood bds.; from Fondation Fursten-berg-Beaumesnil. [H. 3735; BMC III, 794; Goff B1097] (HD. Nov.16; 15) Frs. 23,500
- **Expositiones siue Declaratiões omnium Titulorum Juris tam Ciuilis qu[am] Canonici.** Ill.:– Urs. Graf. Basel, 1514. 4to. 1st ll with sm. margin defects, 1st & last ll. slightly stained, slightly wormed, cont. blind-tooled leath. over wood bds., spine, corners & end-papers renewed, 2 clasps, lacks ties. (HK. Nov.8; 123) DM 420
- **Stutifera Navis.** Trans.:– [Jacobus Locher Philo-musus]. Strassburg, Johann [Reinhard] Gruen-inger, 1 Jun. 1497. 4to. Initials & decor. border

supplied in cols. on fo. lv, col. seeping & staining title-p., sm. margin tape repair on same lf., stained & wormed thro.-out, 16th. C. blind-stpd. panel. cf. over wood bds., brass clasps & corner-pieces, rebkd. [BMC I, 112; Goff B-1089; H. 3749] (SPB. Dec.14; 9) $2,200
- - **Anr. Edn.** Paris, [Georg Wolf, for] Geoffroy de Marnef, 8 Mar. 1498. *Reprint of Bergmann de Olpe Edn., Basle, 1 Aug. 1497.* 4to. 1st. 3 ll. discold with wormhole affecting a few letters & sm. hole affecting woodcut, probably inserted from anr. copy, pagination of 1 p. shaved, 19th. C. cf. [BMC VIII, 150; Goff B1092; HC 3753] (C. May 30; 16) *Rosenthal.* £1,000
- [-] **Stultifera Nauis ... The Ship of Fooles ....** Trans.:– Alexander Barclay. L., 1570. *2nd. Edn.* 3 pts. in 1 vol. Fo. Lacks sig. P (6 ll.), inner margin of 1 lf. reprd., short tear in G1 & G2, some staining, cont. mott. cf., gt. medallion on covers with Byde arms & name of Edward Byde, rebkd. [STC 3546] (S. Dec.8; 2) *Rix.* £600
- **Welt Spiegel/oder Narren Schiff.** Trans.:– Nico-laus Höniger von Tauber Königshoffen. Basel, [1574]. 10 pp. pagination defect., 1st. ll. slightly wormed, slight stains & some browning thro.-out, cont. owners mark on title, cont. vell.; monog. IMH dtd. 1603 on upr. cover; Hauswedell coll. (H. May 24; 1130) DM 4,000

BRANGWYN, Frank
- **British Empire Panels Designed for the House of Lords.** 1933. *(200) numbered & sigd., with sigd. etching.* 4to. Some light spotting, orig. cl., lightly soiled. (CSK. Aug.5; 38) £80
- **Illustrations to the Arabian Nights.** L., 1897. *(100) numbered & initialled.* 36 monochrome plt. proofs on Japanese vell., hf.-title lightly foxed, loose in folding cl. box, slightly worn, lacks ties. (CBA. Aug.21; 63) $140

BRANNEN, Noah & Elliot, William
- **Festive Wine: Ancient Japanese Poems from the Kinkafu.** Ill.:– Haku Mari. N.Y., 1969. *1st. Edn. (150) on Kokyushi H.M.P.,* with each print sigd. by artist. Announcement for separate sale of the prints laid in, gt.-stpd. hf. goat & buckram, decor. in silver & gt., Japanese paper wrap., wood box. (CBA. Aug.21; 731) $400

BRANNON, George
- **Vectis Scenery.** Southampton, 1825. Ob. 4to. Engraved map, 25 plts., spotted & stained, some text ll. torn, publisher's roan-bkd. bds., worn. (S. Mar.6; 208) *Robinson.* £70
- - **Anr. Edn.** Wotton Common, 1828. Ob. 4to. 26 engraved plt., 1 map, hand-cold. outl., some light spotting, cont. mor.-bkd. bds., rubbed. (CSK. Jul.6; 91) £70
- - **Anr. Edn.** Wootton, I.O.W., [1837]. Ob. 8vo. Some spotting, hf. cf. (S. Mar.6; 209) *Young.* £120
- - **Anr. Edn.** 1854. 4to. Spotting, orig. cl., crudely rebkd. (P. Sep.29; 201) *Wright.* £100

BRANT, Sebastian
See– BRANDT or BRANT, Sebastian

BRANTEGHEM, G.
- [-] **La Vie de Nostre Seigneur Jesuchrist selon le texte des Quatre Evangelistes et les Evangiles. Epistres et Prophéties de toute l'année chantées en la Messe.** N.p., 1543. 16 inc. Mor., gt.- & blind-decor., decor. spine, inner dentelle, s.-c., by Cham-bolle-Duru; from J. Renard Liby. (HD. Dec.9; 5) Frs. 4,500

BRANTOME, Pierre de Bourdeille, Seigneur de
- **Mémoires.** Leyde, 1666. *Orig. Edn.* 2 vols. 12mo. MS. table bnd. at end of 1st. vol., cont. red mor.; from Edward Vernon Utterson liby. (HD. Mar.29; 15) Frs. 21,000
- - **Anr. Edn.** Leyden, 1722. 10 vols. 16mo. Cont. spr. cf., decor. spine, some defects. (HD. Dec.9; 6) Frs. 1,300
- **Oeuvres.** Remarks:– le Duchat, Lancelot & Pro-sper Marchand. Ill.:– J.V. Schley (frontis.). La Haye [Rouen], 1740. *New Edn.* 15 vols. Sm. 12mo. Cont. roan gt., spine decor.; from liby. of Charles de Baschi, Marquis d'Aubais. (HD. Nov.9; 116) Frs. 5,000

- - **Anr. Edn.** L. [Maestricht], 1779. *Reprint of 1740 Edn.* 15 vols. 12mo. Lacks 1 folding table (?), cf. gt., ca. 1860, spines decor. (HD. Jun.6; 20) Frs. 1,500
- **La Vie des Dames Galantes.** Ill.:– Malassis. Paris, 1930-31. 2 vols. 4to. Unnumbered on vell. with suite in cols., leaves, wrap., box. (HD. Mar.14; 95) Frs. 1,000

BRANTZKY, F.
- **Architektur.** Köln, [1906]. 4to. 2 sigd. orig. etch-ings, title slightly soiled, orig. linen. (R. Apr.3; 723) DM 550

BRAQUE, Georges
- **Cahier de Georges Braque 1917-1947.** Paris, [1948]. *Ltd. Iss.* Sm. fo. 94 ills., loose ll. in orig. col. litho. wraps., linen cover. (H. Nov.24; 1396) DM 400
- **Les Facheux.** Paris, 1924. *(75) hors commerce.* 2 vols. 4to. Orig. pict. wraps., s.-c.; bkplt., defect. (BS. May 2; 71) £380

BRASCIANUS, J.A.
- **Caesar Libellus.** Augsburg, 1519. 4to. Sm. stain in lr. wide margin, bds., unc. (HK. Nov.8; 124) DM 580

BRASHER, Rex
- **Birds & Trees of North America.** Kent, CT., 1929-32. *(100).* 12 vols. Ob. fo. 867 hand-cold. plts., 11 vols. in orig. hf. mor. gt.; 2 vols. sigd. (SPB. Dec.13; 578) $7,500
- - **Anr. Edn.** Kent, CT., 1932. 3 vols. (of 12). Hand-cold. plts., orig. hf. pig. (SPB. May 17; 573) $650

BRASILLACH, Robert
See– BARDECHE, M. & Brasillach, Robert

BRASSAC, René de Bearn, Marquis de
- **L'Empire De L'Amour, Ballet Héroique, Repré-senté Pour La Première Fois, Par L'Académie Royale De Musique, Le quatorzième d'Avril 1733 ....** Paris, 1733. *1st. Edn.* Ob. 4to. Full score, ptd. note on contents p.: 'Nous Soussignez, avons Vû & Lû, Le Prologue & les Entrées Des Mortels & Des Génies, du Ballet de L'Empire De L'Amour, Imprimez en Musique. A Paris, le 13 d'Avril 1733', each of 4 pts. separately paginated, Prologue, 80 pp., 'Les Mortels', 72 pp., 'Les Dieux', 86 pp. & 'Les Génies Du Feu', 72 pp., type-set music, text & contents, cont. pol. cf., gt. spine, gt. arms of Comte de Toulouse in triple gt. fillets on covers, foot of spine & 1 corner reprd., a little rubbed. (S. May 10; 22) *Macnutt.* £600
- **Léandre Et Héro, Tragédie, Mise en Musique Par L'Auteur du Ballet de l'Empire de l'Amour.** Paris, 1750. *1st. Edn.* Fo. Full score, cont. pol. cf., gt. ornamental spine, & corners reprd. gt. arms of Louis-Auguste de Bourbon, Duc du Maine & his wife Anne-Louise-Benedicte de Bourbon-Condé, duchesse du Maine, in triple gt. fillets, a little rubbed & worn; stp. of Bibliothèque Du Roi Palais Royal on title-p. (S. May 10; 23) *Macnutt.* £600

BRASSAI [i.e. Gyula Lalsz]
- **Voluptés de Paris.** Paris, ca. 1930. 4to. 38 photos. with titles, ring bnd. with orange cold. orig. wraps. (GB. May 5; 2516) DM 800
- - **Anr. Edn.** [Paris], ca. 1940. Sm. 4to. Loose, orig. wraps., slightly discold. (H. May 23; 1452) DM 600

BRASSAI [i.e. Gyula Lalsz] (Ill.)
See– MORAND, Paul

BRASSINGTON, W. Salt
- **Historic Bindings in the Bodleian Library, Oxford.** 1891. 4to. Orig. mor.-bkd. cl.; H.M. Nixon coll., with his sig., acquisition note & some MS. notes. (BBA. Oct.6; 14) *Goldschmidt.* £380
- **A History of the Art of Bookbinding.** 1894. Orig. pict. cl., spine ends slightly worn; H.M. Nixon coll., with his sig. (BBA. Oct.6; 15) *Maggs.* £280
- - **Anr. Copy.** 4to. Orig. decor. cl. (BBA. Nov.10; 40) *Solomons.* £170
- - **Anr. Copy.** 4to. Orig. pict. cl., partly untrimmed, rubbed. (TA. May 17; 443) £100

BRATHWAITE or BRAITHWAIT, Richard
[–] Drunken Barnaby's Four Journeys to the North of England. L., 1723. *3rd. Edn.* Sm. 8vo. Engraved frontis., 5 plts., all partly hand-cold., frontis. torn & reprd., few ll. slightly browned, late 19th. C. mor. (BBA. Mar.21; 206) *Coupe.* £65
- The English Gentleman. L., 1633. *2nd. Edn.* Sm. 4to. Engraved frontis., few marginal repairs, 19th. C. cf. gt., rebkd. [STC 3564] (P. May 17; 197) *Weininger.* £520
- A Survey of History. L., 1638. *2nd. Edn.* Sm. 4to. Engraved frontis., some light spotting, mod. cf. gt. [STC 358a] (P. May 17; 198) *George.* £340

BRAUER, H. & Wittkower, R.
- Die Zeichnungen des G. Bernini. Berlin, 1931. 2 vols. (text & plts.). 4to. Orig. linen. (GB. May 4; 1871) DM 600

BRAUN, G. & Hogenberg, F.
- Beschreibung und Contrafactur der Vornembster Stät der Welt. Ed.:– M. Schefold. Plochingen, 1965. *Facs. of 1574-1618 Edn.* 6 vols. Fo. German text, upwards of 360 cold. double-p. maps, plans & views, publisher's vell., s.-c.'s, w.a.f. (S. May 21; 94) *Wiegund.* £450
- Civitates Orbis Terrarum. Cologne, [1575-81 or later]. *Latin Edn.* 5 vols. Fo. 5 elab. engraved titles, 304 (of 305) double-p. engraved plts. (many with 2 or more subjects on each) showing detailed perspective town plans, views, & a double-p. map of Denmark, many embellished with coats of arms & figures in cont. local costume, without lge. folding plan of Antw., a few plts. partly hand-cold., some worming affecting some centre-folds, a few plts. & ll. faintly browned, cont. purple vell., gt.-ruled, sm. centre-& corner ornaments, spines numbered in ink, slightly faded, 1 cover defect., w.a.f. (S. May 21; 91) *Burgess.* £22,000
- – Anr. Edn. Ca. 1600. Pt. 2. Fo. 34 full-p. cont. hand-cold. town plans only, 6 loose hf.-p. town plans from anr. edn. inserted, text cut down with loss of text, no title, 2 plans with tears, 5 defect. (3 beyond repair), cont. cf., defect. (P. Mar.15; 383) *Burgess.* £1,700
- – Anr. Edn. Cologne, 1612 [preface dtd. 1572]. Fo. Engraved emblematic title, 57 (of 58) double-p. views & plans, all fully cold., 1st. few ll. on later guards, upr. corner torn from title with slight loss of engraved area, split in fold of 1 map, cont. vell. gt., w.a.f. (C. Jun.27; 14a) *Rheinbuch.* £6,000
- – Anr. Edn. Cologne, 1612. Pt. 1. Fo. Hand-cold. title, 29 cont. hand-cold. full-p. & 1 hf.-p. plt. only, & 7 plts. defect. but repairable, 3 plts. badly defect., 4 plts. lacking part of image, text cut down with loss of text, cont. cf., defect. (P. Mar.15; 382) *Burgess.* £2,100
- – Anr. Edn. Cologne, 1616. Pt. 3. Fo. Col. frontis., 45 cont. hand-cold. full-p. & 2 hf.-p. plts. only, 4 with tears, text cut down with loss of text, cont. cf., defect. (P. Mar.15; 384) *Burgess.* £2,200
- – Anr. Edn. Intro.:– R.A. Skelton. Cleveland & N.Y., 1966. 3 vols. Atlas fo. Cl., d.-w.s. (SG. Dec.15; 2) $175

BRAUN, Jean
[–] Vorweisung verschiedener Teutsch = u. Französischer Schriften. Mülhausen, [1774]. Ob. 4to. Wide margin, title slightly spotted, 1 plt. with full name dtd. 1774, hf. mor.; Hauswedell coll. (H. May 23; 298) DM 500

BRAUN, Johannes
- Bigdei Kohanim / id est, Vestitus Sacerdotum Hebraeorum. Amst., 1680. *1st. Edn.* 2 pts. in 1 vol. 4to. Additional engraved title, 15 engraved plts., release stp. on title, cont. vell., soiled, shelf label removed from spine. (SG. Feb.2; 32) $200

BRAUN, Louis
See— MULLER, Karl & Braun, Louis
BRAUN, Thomas
- L'An. Poèmes. Ill.:– Franz Melchers. Lyon & Brüssel, 1897. *Ltd. Iss. numbered.* Fo. MS. dedication from artist on hf.-title, orig. sewed. (GB. May 5; 2962) DM 3,400

BRAUNBEHRENS, Lili von
- Stadtnacht. Ill.:– M. Beckmann. München, 1921. *1st. Edn. Ltd. Iss.* 4to. Printers mark sigd. by artist,

orig. hf. linen, spine slightly faded. (H. May 23; 1142) DM 3,500

BRAUNE & LEVY
- Souvenir of Pretoria, Transvaal. Johannesburg, [1907?]. Ob. 8vo. 36 views, cl. gt., little faded, inner hinge loose. (VA. Jan.27; 367) R. 150

BRAUNER, J. J.
- Thesaurus Sanitatis. Frankfurt, 1725. Browning & foxing, cont. leath., spine with sm. wormholes & covered with paper strips. (D. Nov.23; 533) DM 1,400
- – Anr. Edn. Frankfurt, 1725-32. 4 vols. Cont. leath., lightly rubbed, spine slightly faded, old MS owners mark on upr. doubl. (HK. May 15; 345) DM 4,400

BRAUNFELS, L.
- Die Mainufer und ihre Nächsten Umgebungen. Ill.:– after H. Bamberger. Würzburg, [1844-47]. Folding map, 54 steel angrs., map torn, some browning & foxing. (R. Oct.12; 2502) DM 9,000

BRAUNFELS, Otto
- Kreüterbuch contrafayt, beyde Teyl. Ill.:– after H. Weiditz. Strassburg, 1539-40. *2nd. German Edn.* 4to. Lacks title lf., 2 ll. defect. with text loss, 1 lf. with text & ill. loss, old MS. notes & descriptions, cut close in top margin, private vell. (D. Nov.23; 429) DM 1,700

BRAVO, Francisco
- The Opera Medicinalia. Intro.:– Francisco Guerra. [L.], 1970. *Facs. of Mexico, 1570 edn.* (250) numbered on H.M.P. 2 vols. 16mo. Vell. by Zaehnsdorf, unopened. (SG. Mar.22; 44) $140

BRAY, Mrs. Anna Eliza Stothard
- Life of Thomas Stothard, R.A. with Personal Reminiscences. L., 1851. 1 vol. expanded to 3. Fo. Expanded with approx. 566 engraved plts. & ills., most after Stothard, red lev. mor. by Tout, spines & corners lavishly gt., inner gt. dentelles; A.L.s. from Stothard tipped in, 1 p., 8vo., dtd. 21st. Nov. 1815, to Miss Jermyn, concerning a motif. (BBA. Dec.15; 291) *Snelling.* £400

BRAY, William
See— MANNING, Rev. Owen & Bray, William

BRAYBROOKE, Lord Richard Cornwallis Neville
- The History of Audley End. L., 1836. 4to. Extra engraved title, 18 plts., some faint spotting, cont. red mor. by Leighton. (S. Mar.6; 210) *Marlborough.* £90

BRAYLEY, Edward Wedlake
- Ancient Castles of England & Wales. 1825. 2 vols. Hf. cf. gt. (P. Sep.8; 342) *Brayley.* £55
- History of Surrey. Ed.:– E. Walford. [1878-81]. 4 vols. Cl., worn. (P. Jan.12; 175) *Hadden.* £120
- – Anr. Edn. Ed.:– E. Walford. n.d. 4 vols. 4to. Orig. decor. cl. gt. (SKC. Mar.9; 1970) £150
- A Topographical History of Surrey. L., 1850. 5 vols. 4to. Some plts. & ll. spotted, cont. hf. russ., defect. (S. Mar.6; 212) *Hayden.* £110
- Topographical Sketches of Brighthelmston & its Neighbourhood. Ill.:– R. Havell. [1824]. Hand-cold. engraved aquatint title & 12 plts., all marked proof, margins lightly soiled, 1 corner cleanly torn with loss, lacks text, window mntd. thro-out in later mor. album. (CSK. May 4; 91) £150
- – Anr. Copy. 4to. Engraved title, 12 proof plts., all hand-cold., slightly soiled, 1 torn & reprd., mntd. on card, cont. mor.-bkd. bds., gt., Spanish Royal arms on covers, rubbed. (BBA. Dec.15; 78) *Snelling.* £130
See— BRITTON, John & Brayley, Edward Wedlake

BRAYTON, M.
- The Indian Captive. A Narrative of the Adventures & Sufferings of Matthew Brayton. Cleveland, Ohio, 1860. *1st. Edn.* Some ll. slightly soiled or with sm. stains, cf. (S. May 22; 305) *Quaritch.* £380

BREADLOAF ANTHOLOGY
Preface:– Robert Frost. Middlebury, Vt., 1939. Lge. 8vo. Qtr. cl., sigd., Kenneth Roberts bkplt. (SG. Mar.1; 166) $175

BREBEUF, Father Jean de
- The Travels & Sufferings...among the Hurons of Canada. Ill.:– Eric Gill. Gold. Cock. Pr., 1938. (300) numbered. Fo. Orig. cl., d.-w., torn; from D. Bolton liby. (BBA. Oct.27; 127) *Maggs.* £200
- – Anr. Copy. Fo. Orig. cl. (SPB. Dec.13; 828) $150

BRECHT, Bertold
- Baal. Potsdam, 1922. *1st. Edn. 1st. Printing. Ltd. Iss.* Orig. pict. linen, spine faded, 1 end-paper creased. (H. Nov.24; 1403) DM 460
- Svendborger Gedichte. L., 1939. *1st. Edn. De Luxe Edn., numbered & sigd.* Margins lightly browned & crumpled, orig. wraps., browned & lightly rubbed. (H. Nov.24; 1412) DM 1,600

BRECHT, Berthold (Contrib.)
See— NEUE RUNDSCHAU

BREDIUS, A.
- Künstler-Inventare. Urkunden zur Gesch. der Holl. Kunst des 16.-18. Jhdts. Nachträge. Register. 's-Grav., 1915-22. 8 vols. Plts. & facs., cl. (VG. May 3; 270) Fls. 1,100

BREE, Charles Robert
- A History of the Birds of Europe, not observed in the British Isles. 1859-63. 4 vols. 238 hand-cold. plts., some spotting, a few loose, hf. cf., rubbed. (P. Jun.7; 9) £200
- – Anr. Edn. L., 1860-63 [1859-67]. *1st. Edn.* 4 vols., bnd. from orig. pts. Sm. 4to. 237 (of 238) wood-engraved cold. plts., most bird plts. partly hand-cold., tissue guards, crushed hf. mor., marb. bds., gt.-panel. spines, some wear. (SG. Apr.26; 32) $700
- – Anr. Edn. L., 1863-64 [1859-67]. *1st. Edn.* 4 vols., bnd. from orig. pts. Sm. 4to. 238 wood-engraved plts., most bird plts. partly hand-cold., few plts. lightly foxed, hf. mor. gt., cl. covers, by Bickers & Son. (SG. Mar.22; 45) $400
- – Anr. Edn. L., 1863-64. 4 vols. 238 hand-cold. plts., some spotting, orig. cl. gt., spines slightly worn & faded. (S. Nov.28; 10) *Antik Junk.* £340
- – Anr. Copy. 4 vols. 238 cold. plts., some spotting, cont. hf. mor. gt. (C. Jun.27; 143) *Milner.* £280
- – Anr. Edn. L., 1863. Vols. 1, 2 & 4 only (of 4). Plts. hand-cold., some slight spotting, orig. cl., decor. gt. (SKC. Jan.13; 2306) £80
- – Anr. Copy. 4 vols. Litho. plts. hand-cold., orig. decor. cl., unc. (SI. Dec.15; 144) Lire 750,000
- – Anr. Copy. 4 vols. Lacks 6 lithos., publishers cl., as a collection of plts., w.a.f. (CR. Jun.6; 111) Lire 700,000
- – Anr. Edn. 1866-67. 4 vols. 227 hand-cold. plts. only, Vol. 2 lacks G1-6, light dampstaining thro.-out, orig. cl., worn, Vols. 1 & 2 warped by damp, w.a.f. (CSK. Oct.21; 128) £220
- – Anr. Edn. L., 1875. *2nd. Edn.* Vols. 1-4 only (of 5). 207 (of 253) cold. engraved plts., tree cf., rebkd., Vol. 3 without spine. (C. Mar.14; 134) *Harris.* £200

BREEN, H.H.
- St. Lucia. L., 1844. *1st. Edn.* Hf.-title, one gathering loose, some discoloration, orig. cl.; author's bkplt. (S. Mar.6; 56) *Villiers.* £150

BREES, Samuel Charles
- Pictorial Illustrations of New Zealand. 1847. 4to. Engraved title, 21 plts., orig. cl. gt. (P. Mar.15; 59) *Thorp.* £220
- – Anr. Edn. L., 1849. Fo. Additional engraved title (dtd. 1847), 65 steel-engraved views on 21 plts. (1 double-p.), 2 folding engraved maps, maps with short tear at hinge reprd., 2 ll. & 1 plt. loose, orig. cl. gt., soiled. (C. Jun.27; 82) *Walford.* £150

BREHM, Dr. Alfred Edmund
- Cassell's Book of Birds. Ed.:– T.R. Jones. L., 1869-73. 4 vols. 4to. 40 col. litho. plts., gt.-decor. cl., spines worn, ex-liby. (SG. Oct.6; 83) $110
- – Anr. Edn. Ed.:– Thomas Rupert Jones. L., n.d. 4 vols. in 2. Cold. plts., ills., some light offsets, few spots, cont. hf. mor. (S. Apr.10; 533) *Haddon.* £150
- – Anr. Copy. 4 vols. in 2. 4to. 40 col. plts., hf. cf., rubbed. (P. Feb.16; 128) £130
- Reiseskizzen aus Nord-Ost-Afrika. Jena, 1855.

BREHM, Dr. Alfred Edmund -Contd.

1st. Edn. 3 vols. Slightly foxed, later hf. leath., slightly bumped. (H. May 22; 243) DM 520
- **Thier Leben.** Leipzig, 1891. *3rd. Edn.* 8 vols. Three-qtr. leath. & pressed fabric bds. (DM. May 21; 101) $100
- - **Anr. Copy.** 4to. Orig. hf. leath., spine slightly faded, w.a.f. (HK. May 15, 346) DM 500
- **La Vita degli Animali.** Torino, 1893-98. 5 vols. 4to. Hf. vell. (CR. Jun.6; 112) Lire 260,000

BREHM, Christian Ludwig
- **Handbuch der Naturgeschichte aller Vögel Deutschlands.** Ill.:– W. Müller & Schwäniz. Ilmenau, 1821. Some copper engrs. cut close in upr. margin, minimal foxing, cont. hf. leath. gt. (GB. Nov.3; 1123) DM 850

BREITINGER, Joh. J.
See— BODMER, Joh. J. & Breitinger, Joh. J.

BREITKOPF, Joh. G. Imm.
- **Einige Deutsche Lieder für Lebensfreuden.** Leipzig, 1793. Title lightly foxed, cold. paper covered bds. (HK. Nov.10; 2328) DM 400
- **Versuch d. Ursprung d. Spielkarten.** Leipzig, 1784. 2 vols. 4to. Cont. cold. paper wraps., worn. (HK. Nov.9; 2178) DM 2,100

BREMER PRESS
See— AUGUSTINUS, Saint Aurelius, Bp. of Hippo
See— BALLADS & SONGS OF LOVE
See— BIBLES [German]
See— DANTE ALIGHIERI
See— EMERSON, Ralph Waldo
See— GOETHE, Johann Wolfgang von
See— GOSSAERT, G.
See— HOFMANNSTHAL, Hugo von
See— KANT, Immanuel
See— KLEIST, Heinrich von
See— LEAR, Edward
See— LIEDER DER DEUTSCHEN MYSTIK
See— PSALMS, PSALTERS & PSEUMES [German]
See— SAPPHO
See— SCHRODER, Rudolf Alex
See— SIMONS, Anna
See— TACITUS, Publius or Gaius Cornelius
See— TIBULLUS, Albius
See— VERFASSUNG DES DEUTSCHEN REICHS
See— VESALIUS, Andreas

BREMOND, Abbé Henri
- **Histoire Littéraire du Sentiment Religieux en France depuis la Fin des Guerres de Religion jusqu'à nos Jours.** Paris, 1916-28. *Partly Orig. Edn.* 8 vols. Lge. 8vo. Hf. chagrin, corners, by Bernasconi, unc., wraps. & spines preserved. (HD. May 3; 207) Frs. 1,200

BREMOND
See— MICHELOT & Brémond

BRENCHLEY, Julius L.
- **Jottings during the Cruise of H.M.S. Curacoa among the South Sea Islands in 1865.** L., 1873. Some spotting & foxing, orig. bdg., spine detchd. (JL. Jul.15; 369) Aus. $300

BRENNAN, Christopher J.
- **The Burden of Tyre.** Ill.:– Lionel Lindsay. Priv. ptd. by Harry F. Chaplin. 1953. *(50) numbered on parch.* 2 orig. etchings, qtr. mor.; Harry F. Chaplin copy. (JL. Jul.15; 270) Aus. $260
- - **Anr. Copy.** 2 orig. etchings, qtr. leath.; Harry F. Chaplin copy. (JL. Jul.15; 271) Aus. $220

BRENNER, Sebastian
[–] **Das Grosse Planeten Buch** .... Erfurt, 1669. Browned thro.-out, cont. MS. vell., slightly soiled. (GB. Nov.3; 908) DM 650

BRENTANO, Clemens
- **Die Chronik des Fahrenden Schülers.** Ill.:– after F. v. Pocci. Leipzig, 1923. *(100) De Luxe Edn. on Bütten.* Orig. cf., gt. spine, cover & outer dentelle, decor. inner dentelle, orig. wraps. by Fischer f. Sperling, Leipzig. (HK. May 16; 1951) DM 580
- **Gesammelte Schriften. - Gesammelte Briefe.** Ed.:– Chr. Brentano: Emilie Brentano, J. Merckel & Joh.

Fr. Böhmer. Frankfurt, 1852-55. *1st. Coll. Edn.* 7 vols. & 2 vols. Some spotting, 1 title with completed margin tear, inside cover with staining, cont. hf. leath. gt., cover slightly rubbed; Hauswedell coll. (H. May 24; 1235) DM 3,800
- **Gockel, Hinkel, Gakeleia.** Frankfurt, 1838. *1st. Edn.* Some foxing, especially in margins, 1 plt. with short tear, cont. bds., bumped; Hauswedell coll. (H. May 24; 1238) DM 6,800
- **Der Goldfaden.** Ill.:– L.E. Grimm. Heidelberg, 1809. *1st. Edn.* Title verso stpd., foxing, later linen, supralibros, spine faded; Hauswedell coll. (H. May 24; 1237) DM 1,000
- **Die Märchen.** Ed.:– Guido Görres. Stuttgart & Tübingen, 1846-47. *1st. Edn.* Minimal spotting, hf. vell.; Hauswedell coll. (H. May 24; 1240) DM 1,200
- **Viktoria u. ihre Geschwister, mit Fliegenden Fahnen u. Brennender Lunte.** Berlin, 1817. *1st. Edn.* Minimal spotting, sewed, unc. (HK. Nov.10; 2330) DM 500
See— ARNIM, Ludwig Achim von & Brentano, Clemens

BREQUIGNY, Louis Oudart Fendrix de
- **Histoire des Revolutions de Gênes.** Preface:– Bellin. Paris, 1750. *1st. Edn.* 2 vols. 12mo. Cont. marb. cf., spines decor. (HD. Oct.21; 44) Frs. 1,200

BRERELEY, John (Pseud.)
See— ANDERTON, Laurence 'John Brereley'

BRÈS, Jean Pierre
- **Les Jeudis dans le Château de ma Tante.** Paris, Ca. 1830. 6 vols. (lacks Vols. 3 & 7). 12mo. 6 hand-cold. engraved plts., former owner's pencil scribbling in 1 vol., orig. hand-cold. litho. pict. wraps., slightly rubbed, 1 backstrip torn at foot; van Veen coll. (S. Feb.28; 48) £50
- **Simples Histoires Trouvées dans un Pot au Lait.** Paris, 1825. 8 vols. 12mo. 8 hand-cold. engraved plts., a few ll. slightly spotted, orig. litho. decor. wraps., orig. box, worn, lacks side of lid; van Veen coll. (S. Feb.28; 46) £270
- - **Anr. Copy.** 6 vols. (of 8). 12mo. 6 hand-cold. engraved plts., orig. hand-cold. litho. decor. wraps.; van Veen coll. (S. Feb.28; 47) £60

BRETEZ, Louis
- **La Perspective Pratique de l'Architecture.** Paris, 1751. Cont. cf. (HD. Dec.15; 4) Frs. 2,400
- **Plan [de Turgot] en Perspective de la Ville de Paris.** Ill.:– J. Lucas. 1759. Last lf. slightly loose, cont. red mor. gt. decor., Paris arms on covers, spine decor., lr. cover stained. (LM. Oct.22; 146) B.Frs. 90,000

BRETIN, Abbé Claude
[–] **Contes en Vers.** Ill.:– Legrand. Paris, 1797 [An V]. Sm. 8vo. Glazed cf. gt. by Hardy. (HD. May 3; 24) Frs. 1,900

BRETON, André
- **Au Regard des Divinités.** Ill.:– Slavko Kopac. 1949. *Orig. Edn. (100) sigd. by author & artist.* 12mo. Sewed, stitched, recovered bds. with engraved frontis. (HD. Apr.13; 152) Frs. 2,500
- **Martinique Charmeuse de Serpents.** Ill.:– André Masson. Orig. Edn, 1948. *Orig. Edn. (15) on holland with orig. litho ptd. in red.* Sewed. (HD. Apr.13; 153) Frs. 3,100
- **Ode à Charles Fourier.** Ill.:– F.J. Kiesler. Paris, 1947,. *Ltd. Iss. numbered.* Orig. wraps., slightly spotted. (GB. May 5; 2253) DM 420
- **Les Pas Perdus.** [Paris, 1933]. 12 mo. MS. dedication on hf.-title, dtd. 5 Apr. 1935, orig. sewed. (D. Nov.24; 2639) DM 700
- **Qu'est-ce que le Surréalisme?.** Brüssel, 1934. *1st. Edn. (1000).* 4to. Orig. wraps. (HK. Nov.11; 3454) DM 400
- **Second Manifeste du Surréalisme.** Ill.:– S. Dali. Paris, 1930. *1st. Book Edn. (50) numbered, for Jose Corti.* 4to. Wide margin, orig. bds., spine defect. (HK. Nov.11; 3455) DM 650
- **Le Surréalisme et la Peinture.** Ill.:– after Ernst, De Chirico, Braque, Picasso, Man & others. Paris, 1928. *Ltd. Edn. numbered.* 4to. Orig. wraps., backstrip slightly worn; sig. of Quentin Bell. (S. Apr.30; 250) *Libris.* £80

- - **Anr. Copy.** 4to. Orig. wraps., slightly torn & loose. (BBA. Nov.10; 161) *Ahnert.* £65
- **Les Vases Communicants.** Paris, 1932. *Orig. Edn.* Sm. 8vo. On vélin omnia, sewed, ill. wrap. by Max Ernst; dedication by Valentine Hugo. (SM. Mar.7; 2070) Frs. 1,600

BRETON, André (Ed.)
See— DICTIONNAIRE ABREGE DU SURRE-ALISME

BRETON, André (Text)
See— RAY, Man

BRETON, Lieut. William Henry
- **Excursions in New South Wales, Western Australia & Van Diemen's Land....** 1833. *1st. Edn.* Bnd. without errata slip, some foxing, later hf. cf. (KH. May 1; 96) Aus. $300
- - **Anr. Edn.** L., 1834. *1st. Edn.* Plts. foxed, title & some ll. slightly foxed, 2nd. plt. & last section loose, orig. cl.-bkd. bds., unc. (CA. Apr.3; 28) Aus. $400
- - **Anr. Copy.** Title & some ll. foxed, old sig. on title, hf. cf. (CA. Apr.3; 27) Aus. $260

BRETON DE LA MARTINIERE, Jean Baptiste Joseph
- **China; Its Costume, Arts, Manufactures, & c.** L., 1812. *1st. Edn.* 4 vols. in 2. Sm. 8vo. 80 hand-cold. plts., lacks hf.-titles, some offsetting of text on most plts. (occuring before insertion of plt. guards), mod. hf. mor., gt.-floral decor., edges rubbed, spines slightly faded; George T. Ramsden armorial bkplts. (SG. Mar.29; 299) $300
- - **Anr. Edn.** L., 1813. 4 vols. 80 cold. copperplts., some slight browning & foxing, cont. long-grd. mor., gt. spine, inner & outer dentelle, spine slightly rubbed, corners slightly defect. (HK. May 16; 1632) DM 800
- **Le Japon.** Paris, 1818. 4 vols. 12mo. Cont. cf. gt., gold-tooled decor., gt. inner & outer dentelle. (D. Nov.23; 1400) DM 3,500

BRETSCHNEIDER, E.
- **Botanicon-Sinicum: Notes on Chinese Botany from Native and Western Sources.** L., 1882, Shanghai, 1892-95. *1st. Edn.* 3 vols. Sm. 4to. Buckram, partly unc. (SG. Mar.22; 46) $600

BRETTINGHAM, Matthew
- **Plans, Elevations & Sections of Holkham in Norfolk.** 1773. Lge. fo. 69 engraved plts., including 8 double-p., some browning & spotting to a few plts., mainly marginal, 1 plt. inverted, final plt. reprd., mod. hf. mor. (C. Dec.9; 14) *Walter.* £450

BREVAL, John Durant
- **Remarks on Several Parts of Europe.** L., 1726. 2 vols. Fo. Cont. panel. cf., worn. (S. Mar.6; 75) *Scott.* £190
- - **Anr. Edn.** L., 1726-38. 4 vols. in 2. Fo. 1 lf. torn & reprd., some margin annots., cont. cf., rubbed & slightly defect. (VG. Mar.19; 229) Fls. 1,000

BREVAL, Roger
- **20 Dessins de Roger Breval, pour Illustrer les Chansons de Bilitis.** 1930. *(200) numbered.* Fo. Unbnd. as iss. in orig. cl.-bkd. portfo., lightly soiled, ties. (CSK. Jun.15; 164) £65

BREVIARIES
- *(Arranged chronologically irrespective of use).*
- **Breriarium Magdeburgense.** Georgio Stuchs, [20 Jun. 1491]. Fo. Unsigd. cahier at beginning of vol. 8 ll., (not 6) cahier C 6 ll (not 8), lacks 1st. lf. (wood engraved arms verse, blank recto), 3 15th. C. MS. ll. bnd. at end, some defects, old cf. over wood bds., blind-stp., worn, clasps. [HC. 3856] (HD. Mar.30; 8) Frs. 17,000
- **Breviarium Constantiense.** Augsburg, Ratdolt, 1499. 2 vols. Fo. 32 cold. decor. woodcut initials, lacks calendar (8 ll.). & ll. 1 & 4 (blank?) of Tabula, other pt. lacks 6 ll. of calendar, last blank lf. at end of officium, 1st & 4th (blank?) lf. of Tabula, slightly spotted, several ll. with tears & reprd. margin defects, 30 ll. with burn defects, slight loss, notes & underlining, later blind-tooled pig over wood bds., very bumped & worn, some staining, some jnts. brittle, 2 clasps , lacks ties. [H 3830; Golf 131157] (HK. May 15; 90) DM 2,500

– **Breviarium Secundum Ritum alme Ecclesie Arosiensis.** [Basle, 3 Feb. 1513]. *2nd. Edn.* Lacks 1st. 17 ll. (title-p. present in facs.), x4, 2nd. a1 & 8, b5, g2 & 7, i4, A1, 2nd. A2 & C6-8, many defects, some reprd., with loss of text, especially M4, 2nd. a2 & 3, a8, b5, h8, many other ll. with minor margin repairs, some with loss of sig., many ll. slit, bds., covered with part of a 17th. C. liturgical lf. (S. Nov.17; 11) *Hannas.* £700

– **Breviarium Carthusiense.** Paris, 1521. Title stpd., 1st. ll. slightly wormed, some soiling, some old annots., last p. with slight offset from old annots. removed, 16th. C. vell. from 15th. C. MS., 3 (of 4) ties. (HK. Nov.8; 125) DM 420

– **Breviarium Romanum.** Venice, 10.1.1524. Lacks 1st. 8 ll., early lf.with sm. repair, last ll. slightly wormed, lf. vell. (HK. Nov.8; 126) DM 600

– **Breviarium Secundum Ritum Monachorum Nigrorum Observantium Ordinis D. Benedicti, Congregationis Casinensis, alias Sancte Justine [etc.].** Venice, 1562. Some foxing, cont. hf. vell., slightly rubbed. (GB. Nov.3; 935) DM 750

– – **Anr. Edn.** Antw., 1704. 4to. Engraved & ptd. titles, engraved plts., contents rubricated thro.-out, cont. leath., brass clasps, rubbed. (TA. Jun.21; 389) £54

– **Breviarium Parisiense.** Ill.:– Thomassin. Paris, 1714. Ruled, old red mor., mosaic dentelle, gt. & mosaic centre motif, inner dentelle, gt. paper doubl. & end-papers, Firmin-Didot ox-libris, mod. ex-libris pasted on end-paper. (HD. Mar.30; 20) Frs. 5,500

– **Le Breviaire Romain: Partie d'Eté et Partie d'Hiver.** Paris, 1742. 2 vols. Decor. red mor. gt., arms. (LM. Mar.3; 217) B.Frs. 11,000

– – **Anr. Edn.** Paris, 1756. 4 vols. 4to. Cont. red mot., limp decor. spines. wide gt. dentelle, inner roulette, engraved centre arms, watered silk liners. (HD. Jan.26; 56) Frs. 2,100

– **Breviarium ad Usum Laicorum. Novo Ordine Dispositum.** [France, 18th. C.]. 4 vols. 12mo. 18th. C. mor., decor., centre arms, red mor. doubls., decor., gt. paper end-papers, ex-libris Cartland Bishop. (HD. Mar.30; 18) Frs. 25,100

BREWER, James Norris
– **The Beauties of Ireland.** L., 1825. 2 vols. (all publd.). 24 engraved views, etc., cl.-bkd. bds. (GM. Dec.7; 48) £65
See— STORER, James Sargent & Henry Sargent & Brewer, James Norris

BREWER, Luther A.
– **My Leigh Hunt Library Collected & Described.** Cedar Rapids, Iowa, priv. ptd., 1932. Orig. cl. (CSK. Feb.24; 85) £70

BREWER, T.M
See— BAIRD, Spencer F. & others

BREWINGTON, M.V. & D.
– **Marine Paintings & Drawings in the Peabody Museum.** Salem., Mass., 1968. 4to. Orig. cl., d.-w. (BBA. Apr.5; 12) *Burnett.* £60

BREWSTER, Sir David
– **Letters on Natural Magic, addressed to Sir Walter Scott.** L., 1832. Cont. 16mo. f. cf., corners, spine richly decor. (HD. Feb.28; 15) Frs. 1,300

BRIAN, Thomas
– **Der Englische Wahrsager aus dem Urin, oder Gawisse Wahrsagungen aus dem Wasser-Glase.** Trans.:– [J.A. Stdberg]. Frankgurt & Leipzig, 1760. *3rd. German Edn.* (*Bound with:*) **MAIUS, Th. - Urin-Buchlein. Samt des Apollinaris Tractatlein vom Urin und Pulse.** Frankfurt & Leipzig, 1760. Together 2 works in 1 vol. cont. hf. vell. (R. Apr.4; 1287) DM 500

BRIANO, G.
– **La Sina & l'Asia Minore.** Turin, 1841. 4to. Foxing, cont. hf. leath., defect. (D. Nov.23; 859) DM 480

BRICE, Germain
– **Description Nouvelle de la Ville de Paris.** Ill.:– N. de Fer. Paris, 1698. *3rd. Edn.?* 2 vols. 12mo. Cont. cf., spines decor. (HD. Mar.19; 88) Frs. 1,100
[–] **A New Description of Paris.** 1687. *1st. Engl. Edn.* 12mo. Some staining, cont. cf., rebkd. [Wing B4440] (BBA. Jan.19; 169) *Lomax.* £50

BRIDGES, Robert
– **Poems.** L., 1873. *1st. Edn.* Orig. cl., partly unopened, free end-papers browned, few faint stains on upr. cover, h.f. mor. s.-c.; Frederic Dannay copy. (CNY. Dec.16; 41) $400
– – **Anr. Edn.** Oxford, Daniel Pr., 1884. *(150)* numbered. 4to. Mor., spine gt., partly unc. (LC. Mar.; 55) £60
– **The Testament of Beauty.** Oxford, 1929. *1st. Publd. Edn., (250). (50)* numbered & sigd. 4to. Orig. cl., d.-w. slightly frayed; Frederic Dannay copy. (CNY. Dec.16; 42) $180

BRIDGEWATER TREATISES (THE)
L., 1833-40. 8 works in 12 vols. Some ll. soiled or spotted, orig. cl., slightly worn. (BBA. May 3; 17) *The Bookroom.* £75

BRIETIO, Philippo
– **Parallela Geographiae Veteris et Novae.** Paris, 1648. 3 vols. 4to. Hf. leath. (DS. Jan.27; 2415) Pts. 150,000

BRIGGS, William
– **Opthalmographia, sive Oculi ejusque Partium Descriptio Anatomica. Cui Accessit Nova Visionis Theoria.** L., 1685. 2 pts. in 1 vol. Lacks A3 in 1st. pt. & A2 in 2nd., printing flaw on l.p., cont. cf., covers detchd.; 'ex dono authoris' inscr. on front free end-paper. [Wing B4668A] (BBA. May 3; 18) *I.S. Levy.* £70
– – **Anr. Edn.** Leyden, 1686. *Orig. Edn.* 12mo. Lacks hf.-title, cont. cf. (HD. Mar.19; 82) Frs. 1,600

BRIGHT, P.M. & Leeds, H.A.
– **A monograph of the British Aberrations of the Chalk-Hill Butterfly.** L., 1938. 4to. 18 plts., with supp. on sm. copper butterfly aberrations, orig. leath. gt. (SKC. Oct.26; 333) £70

BRIGHT, Richard
– **Travels from Vienna through Lower Hungary.** Edinb., 1818. *1st. Edn.* 4to. Lacks hf.-title or initial blank, foxed, old. cl., untrimmed & partly unopened, loose. (SG. Sep.22; 65) $275

BRILLAT-SAVARIN, Jean Anthelme
– **Physiologie des Geschmacks od. Physiol. Anleitung z. Studium d. Tafelgenüsse.** Trans.:– C. Vogt. Braunschweig, 1865. *1st. German Edn.* Hf. leath. (HK. Nov.9; 1662) DM 440
– **Physiologie du Goût ou Méditations de Gastronomie Transcendante.** 1826. *Orig. Edn.* 2 vols. Some foxing, hf. cf., sigd. by Thouvenin, spine decor.; A.N. (HD. Mar.21; 135) Frs. 15,100
– – **Anr. Copy.** 2 vols. Hf.title with faded entry, some spotting, cont. bds., bumped, partly split; Hauswedell coll. (H. May 24; 780) DM 1,200
– – **Anr. Edn.** Contribs.:– Baron Richerand & Honoré de Balzac. Paris, 1839. *Orig. Edn. of Balzac's treatise.* 12mo. Cont. hf. cf., gt.-decor., decor.; Michel Bolloré coll. (HD. Nov.16; 15) Frs. 3,600
– – **Anr. Edn.** Preface:– Ch. Mouselet. Ill.:– Ad. Lalauze. Paris, 1879. 2 vols. 12 mo. Hf havanna mor., corners, decor. spines, wraps. preserved, by canape. (HD. Dec.9; 103) Frs. 1,600
– – **Anr. Copy.** 2 vols. 12mo. On vergé, hf. mor., corners, unc. wrap. & spine. (HD. Dec.16; 78) Frs. 1,300
– – **Anr. Copy.** 2 vols. 12mo. Hf. mor., corners, by Yseux, unc., spines unif. faded. (HD. May 3; 208) Frs. 1,100

BRINCK, C.F.
[– **Neue Kurzgefasste Beschreibung des Vorgebirges der Guten Hoffnung ....** Leipzig, 1779. 2 pts. in 1 vol. Some slight browning, cont. hf. leath. gt. (D. Nov.23; 1229) DM 410

BRINCKMANN, A. E.
– **Barock-Bozzetti: Volumes I & II – Italian Sculptors; Volume III – Netherlandish & French Sculptors; Volume IV – German Sculptors.** Frankfurt, 1923-24. *Engl. - German Edn.* 4 vols. Sm. fo. Linen-bkd. bds., slightly shaken. (SG. Aug.25; 67) $2,400

BRINCKMAN, A.E. (Ed.)
See— HANDBUCH DER KUNSTWISSENSCHAFT

BRINKLEY, Capt. Frank
– **Japan & China.** Boston & Tokyo, [1901-02]. *'Viceroy' Edn. (50)* numbered on Japan paper. 12 vols. This copy with blue star in lieu of no., many ills. on silk, mor., covers with gt. borders & lge. panel. ornaments, spines in 3 compartments, turn-ins gt., silk doubls., silk markers, partly unc. (CNY. Dec.17; 539) $900
– **Japan Described & Illustrated by the Japanese. Written by Eminent Japanese Authorities & Scholars.** Boston, [1897]. *1st. Edn. Orient Edn., (500).* 10 vols. Fo. 10 colotypes, 30 mntd. hand-cold. albumen photos, brocaded cloths, bnd. in the Japanese manner, spines lightly faded. (HA. Dec.16; 161) $400
– – **Anr. Edn.** Boston, [1897-98]. *De Luxe Edn., (750)* numbered. 10 vols. Fo. 10 collotypes of Japanese flowers, 60 hand-cold. albumen photos, matted, nearly 200 hand-cold. albumen photos mntd. thro.-out, text, 4 (of 10) 'xylograph' reproductions of Japanese paintings, lacks 1 text photo, some foxing thro.-out, affecting a few photos, bds., each vol. covered with different col. pict. crepe paper, bnd. in the Japanese manner, laced, Vol. 2 defect. (SG. May 10; 70) $550
– **Oriental Series: Japan & China.** Boston & Tokyo, [1901-02]. 15 vols. Monograph copy ptd. on japan, ill. & bnd. by Keller-Farmer Co. for Elizabeth S. Moore, extra-ill. with orig. watercolour paintings on silk, photos, many orig. watercolor margin decors., elab. purple mor. gt., gt. panel., mor. gt. inlays each corner of panels, red mor. gt. inlays surrounding panel, mor. doubls., silk endpapers. (SPB. May 17; 721) $4,500
– – **Anr. Edn.** Boston & Tokyo, [1902]. *Imperial Edn. (26) lettered.* 12 vols. Tall 8vo. Orig. unsigd. watercols. on silk matted frontis. in each vol. hand-cold. or toned reproduced photographs, few mntd. facs of cont. woodblock prints, lettered tissue guards, limitation lf. in each vol., unif. brick-red mor., elab. gt.-stpd. decors. on all covers & backstrips, mor. continuous onto all pastedowns, identical stream & tree design gt.-stpd. mor. panels mntd. at inside of all covers, watered silk end-ll., untrimmed Japan vell. (HA. May 4; 240) $475

BRINKMAN, Carel Leonhard
– **Catalogus der Boeken, 1951-75.** Leiden/Alphen, 1958-82. 10 cumulative vols & 5 repertoria. Hf. chagrin & cl. (VG. Mar.21; 777) Fls. 1,400

BRINON, Pierre de
[–] **La Triomphe des Dames.** Rouen, 1599. Sm. 12mo. 18th. C. marb. cf., spine decor. (HD. Nov.9; 30) Frs. 3,900

BRION, Marcel
– **La Reine Jeanne.** Ill.:– Barta. N.p., 1936. 4to. Recovered vell. by Lavaux, decor. with 2 paintings by Barta, wrap. preserved, folder, s.-c.; artist's copy, extra-ill. with suite on china, drawing & orig. watercol. (HD. Jun.13; 13) Frs. 1,050

BRION DE LA TOUR, Louis
– **Atlas Général, Civil et Ecclesiastique ... faites par Thirikcow et de l'Isle.** Paris, 1767. Vol. 1 only (of 6). Lge. 4to. Copper-engraved title & contents lf. slightly stained, some plts. with sm. tears, some slight soiling, cont. leath., decor., worn. (HK. Nov.8; 885) DM 800
– **Recueil des Côtes Maritimes de la France.** Paris, 1766. 4to. Title, folding general map & 51 cold. plts., cont. hf. roan, spine decor., worn; from Château des Noës liby. (HD. May 25; 7) Frs. 3,500

BRIQUET, Charles Moise
– **Les Filigranes.** Leipzig, 1923. *2nd. Edn.* 4 vols. 4to. Orig. hf. cl. (BBA. Nov.10; 41) *Blackwell.* £300
– – **Anr. Edn.** Hildesheim & N.Y., 1977. 4 vols. Orig. cl. (SI. Dec.15; 189) Lire 420,000

BRIQUET ET FILS
[–] [**Souvenir de la Suisse.**]. [Geneva], n.d. Ob. 4to. 26 titled litho. plts., 1 detchd. & torn, lightly soiled, orig. cl., worn. (CSK. Oct.21; 110) £550

BRISBANE, Sir Thomas Makdougall
– **Reminiscences....** Edinb., ptd. for private circulation, 1860. 4to. Hf.-title slightly discold., mod. hf. mor.; sigd. & inscr. (KH. May 1; 98) Aus. $280

BRISEUX, Charles Etienne
- L'Art de bâtir des Maisons de Campagne. Ill.:– Moreau & others after Briseux. Paris, 1743. *1st. Edn.* 2 vols. 4to. Lacks 2 text ll. in vol. 1, 253(of 260) copperplts., cont. hf. leath. gt., very worn. (HT. May 9; 863)   DM 520
- – **Anr. Edn.** Paris, 1761. 2 vols. 4to. A few plts. lightly browned, cont. leath. gt., lightly worn & slightly bumped. (HK. Nov.9; 1579)   DM 700

BRISSON, Mathurin Jacques
- Ornithologie. Ill.:– Martinet. Paris, 1760. *1st. Edn.* 6 vols. 4to. Additonal engraved/Latin titles, 261 engraved plts., folding tables, little browned, supp. bnd. at end vol.6, cont. cf. gt. (SG. Apr.26; 33) $1,300
- Traité Elementaire ou Principes de Physique. Paris, 1789. 3 vols. 46 folding plts., cont. cf., arms of Ruolz family on sides. (S. Apr.10; 483)
          Kurzer. £70

BRISSOT DE WARVILLE, Jacques-Pierre
- Nouveau Voyage dans les Etats-Unis de l'Amérique Septentrionale, fait en 1788. Paris, 1791. *1st. Edn.* 3 vols. Hf.-titles in Vols. 1 & 2 (not required in Vol. 3), cont. qtr. cf. & paper bds., bds. rubbed, light wear to corners & heads of spines; the Rt. Hon. Visc. Eccles copy. [Sabin 8035] (CNY. Nov.18; 33) $260
See— CLAVIERE, Etienne & Brissot de Warville, Jacques P.

BRISTOL & GLOUCESTERSHIRE ARCHAEO-LOGICAL SOCIETY
- Transactions. 1876-1967. Vols. 1-86 (lacks Vols. 79-81), & Indexes. 23 vols. in cont. cl., rest orig. ptd. wraps., some little worn on spines. (TA. Nov.17; 307)   £130
- – **Anr. Copy.** Vols. 1-86 (lacks Vols. 79-81), & Indexes. 23 vols. in cont. cl., rest in orig. ptd. wraps., some slightly worn on spines. (TA. Sep.15; 144)
          £110

BRITANNICUS, Gregorius
- Sermones Funebres et Nuptiales. Brescia, Jacobus Britannicus, 5 Sep. 1500. Sm. 8vo. Mod. cf., chipped; the Walter Goldwater copy. [Goff B-1212] (SG. Dec.1; 83) $350

BRITISH ALMANAC, The
L., 1880. Cont. red mor. gt., with fore-e.pntg., as a fore-e.pntg., w.a.f. (SPB. May 17; 731) $225

BRITISH AMERICAN GUIDE BOOK: being a Condensed Gazetteer, Directory & Guide to Canada, the Western States, & Principal Cities of the Seaboard
N.Y., [1859]. *1st. Edn.* 4 Pts. Many woodcuts, many full-p., many unnumbered ll. of merchants' advts., bnd. thro.-out, orig. blind decor. cl; cont. sig. on upr. end-papers. (SG. Apr.5; 24) $325

BRITISH BOOK MAKER, The
L., 1892-93. Vols. 5-7 in 2. 4to. Various cont. bdgs., spines worn. (CSK. Feb.24; 195)   £190

BRITISH COMPENDIUM, or, Rudiments of Honour
1723-22. *5th. Edn.* 3 vols. Plts. partly hand-cold., some ink staining in Vol. 3, mod. cf. gt. (P. Jun.7; 83)   £60

BRITISH CYCLOPAEDIA, The
Ed.:– C.F. Partington. 1835-38. 10 vols. Hf. cf. (P. Dec.8; 253)   £90

BRITISH ENCYCLOPAEDIA
Manchester & L., 1806. 5 vols. 4to. Title to Vol. 1 cleanly torn, cont. cf., rubbed. (CSK. Jun.1; 182)
          £50

BRITISH ESSAYISTS, The
Ed.:– A. Chalmers. 1817. 45 vols. 12mo. Cont. cf. gt., some spines chipped, a few covers scuffed. (LC. Jul.5; 270)   £85
- – **Anr. Edn.** Ed.:– James Ferguson. 1819. 44 vols. only (of 45, lacks Index vol.?). 12mo. Cont. tree cf. gt. (LC. Jul.5; 313)   £100
- – **Anr. Edn.** Ed.:– James Ferguson. 1823. *2nd. Edn.* 40 vols. 12mo. Cont. mor. gt. (CSK. Jan.27; 1)   £340
- – **Anr. Copy.** 40 vols. 12mo. Cont. cf., spines gt. (CSK. Aug.19; 16)   £220

BRITISH HUNTS & HUNTSMEN
1908-11. 4 vols. Fo. Hf. mor. gt. (P. Dec.8; 239)
          Ackermann. £65

BRITISH MUSEUM
- Assyrian Sculpture in the British Museum, from Shalmaneser III to Sennacherib. L., 1938. Sm. fo. 69 plts., buckram. (SG. Oct.13; 22) $140
- British Antarctic ('Terra Nova') Expedition, 1910; Natural History Reports.... 1914-64. 11 vols. in 63 pts. 4to. Several prelims. (slightly frayed) for collective vols. loosely inserted, not collated, wraps. (KH. May 1; 99)   Aus. $480
- Catalogue of the Birds. L., 1874-95. 27 vols. Some browning, liby. stps. & cancels, most in orig. cl., some repairs, rebdgs., as a periodical, w.a.f. (SPB. Dec.13; 579) $1,000
- – **Anr. Edn.** Ill.:– J.G. Keulemans & J. Smit. L., 1890-94. Vols. 15, 16, 18, 19 & 23. 71 cold. plts., orig. cl. (S. Apr.10; 410)   *Grahame.* £200
- Catalogue of the Books, Manuscripts, Maps & Drawings (Natural History). 1903-40. 8 vols., including 3 Supps. 4to. Orig. cl. gt. (LC. Jul.5; 15)   £200
- Catalogue of Books Printed in the XVth Century. L., 1962-63. 11 vols. in 12. Fo. Orig. cl.-bkd. bds. (BBA. Apr.5; 271)   *Quaritch.* £420
- – **Anr. Edn.** L., 1962-71. 12 vols., including 2 facs. Fo. Publishers bds.,. (DS. Dec.16; 2365)
          Pts. 80,000
- – **Anr. Edn.** L., 1963-71. 12 vols., including 2 plt. vols. Fo. Orig. cl.-bkd. bds. (CSK. Feb.24; 197)
          £420
- – **Anr. Copy.** Vols. 1-9 & 2 vols. of facsimiles (for Vols. 1-7). Fo. Orig. cl.-bkd. bds. (S. May 1; 375)
          Dawson. £370
- Catalogue of Engraved British Portraits. Ed.:– Freeman O'Donoghue & Henry M. Hake. 1908-25. 5 vols., including supp. & indexes. Orig. cl., slightly soiled. (S. Apr.30; 164)   *Sims.* £80
- Catalogue of Western Manuscripts in the Old Royal & King's Collection. 1921. 4 vols. 4to. Orig. cl. (S. Nov.8; 500)   *Sims.* £210
- Schools of Illumination: Reproductions from Manuscripts. L., 1914-30. Pts. 1-6 in 1 vol. Tall fo. Pt.1 with 16 plts., others 15 plts. each, some cold., ex-liby., each plt. stpd. on blank verso, loose in ptd. bds., cl.-bkd., linen ties. (SG. May 3; 61) $350
See— HOBSON, Robert Lockhart

BRITISH NOVELISTS
1820. *New Edn.* 50 vols. Cont. diced cf. gt. (PD. Oct.19; 58)   £310

BRITISH NUMISMATIC JOURNAL (THE)
L., 1904-28. 1st. Series Vols. 1-10, 2nd. Series Vols. 1-9. 4to. Orig. cl., spines faded. (S. May 1; 454)
          Dreesman. £350

BRITISH SPORTS & SPORTSMEN
L., 1911. 2 vols. only: 'Racing Course & Steeple Chase'. Cl. (JL. Mar.25; 892)   Aus. $175
- – **Anr. Edn.** N.d. *(1000) numbered.* 15 vols. 4to. Orig. red mor. gt. (BS. Nov.16; 60)   £340
- Shooting & Deerstalking. – Yachting & Rowing. 1913, 1916. *(1000) numbered.* 2 vols. Fo. Crimson mor. gt., 1st. vol. scuffed on rear cover. (TA. Jun.21; 400)   £56

BRITO FREIRE, Francisco de
- Nova Lusitania, Historia da Guerre Brasilica; [Viagem da Armada da Compahnia do Commercio, e frotas do Estado do Brazil. Lisbon, 1675. 2 pts. in 1 vol. Fo. Tear to 1 prelim., 1 lf. of index to 1st. pt. with repair to paper prior to printing, later mott. cf., spine gt. [Sabin 8130-31] (S. Dec.1; 280)
          Maggs. £950

BRITTEN, Benjamin
- Children's Crusade, Kinderkreuzzug. Op. 82. A Ballad for children's voices & orchestra, words by Bertolt Brecht. Ill.:– Sidney Nolan. 1973. *(1000) numbered & sigd. by composer & artist.* Fo. Orig. qtr. mor., s.-c. (TA. Jul.19; 508)   £80

BRITTON, John
- The Architectural Antiquities of Great Britain. L., 1806-14. Vols. 1-4 only (of 5). 4to. 5 engraved titles & 274 plts., 2 ll. of text in Vol. 4 defect., rather spotted thro.-out, cont. cf., rubbed, most

covers detchd. (BBA. May 3; 313)
          Ingol Maps. £50
- – **Anr. Edn.** L., 1835. 5 vols. 4to. Some slight offsetting, cont. hf. mor., slightly rubbed. (S. Dec.13; 436)   *Price.* £170
- Bath & Bristol ... in a Series of Views. 1829. 4to. Vig. title, 48 views on 24 sheets, hf. cf. gt. (P. Oct.20; 114)   £140
- Cathedral Antiquities. L., 1836. 5 vols. 4to. Cont. hf. mor., slightly rubbed. (S. Dec.13; 435)
          Price. £90
- Graphical & Literary Illustrations of Fonthill Abbey. L., 1823. 4to. Extra engraved title, 10 plts. (2 hand-cold.), spotted, orig. bds., unc., soiled. (S. Mar.6; 214)   *Quaritch.* £90
- Picturesque Antiquities of the English Cities. 1830. 4to. Engraved vig. title, 60 plts., some spotting, cl., hinges reprd. (P. Mar.15; 245)   £250
- – **Anr. Copy.** 4to. 59 (of 60) plts., some staining, cl. (P. Sep.29; 202)   £220
- – **Anr. Edn.** Ill.:– after W.H. Bartlett. L., 1836. 4to. 60 engraved plts., engraved title cut round & mntd., some spotting, cont. hf. cf., rubbed, upr. cover detchd. (S. Jun.25; 310)   *Price.* £220

BRITTON, John & Brayley, Edward Wedlake
- The Beauties of England & Wales. 1801-15. 18 vols. in 25. Hf. mor. gt. (P. Jun.7; 158) £440
- – **Anr. Copy.** 18 vols. in 25. Engraved titles with vigs., steel-engraved plts., some discolouration, cont. hf. cf., 1 hung & brkn. (S. May 21; 58)
          Traylen. £400
- – **Anr. Copy.** 16 vols. Cont. hf. russ., a few spines worn. (S. Dec.13; 199)   *Haddon.* £260
- – **Anr. Edn.** L., 1801-16. 18 vols. in 25. Cont. cf. gt., 1 spine slightly torn at head, w.a.f. (LC. Oct.13; 240)   £320
- – **Anr. Edn.** 1801-18. 19 vols. in 31. Cf. gt., rebkd., 1 spine defect.; extra-ill. with 3,919 hand-cold. maps & plts., w.a.f. (P. Apr.12; 136)
          Crossley. £1,450
- – **Anr. Copy.** 18 vols. only (lacks intro. vol.), in 23 vols. Engraved plts. & maps, some hand-cold. in outl., some light soiling, cont. hf. cf., w.a.f. (CSK. Dec.16; 115)   £360
- Cornwall Illustrated. Ill.:– T. Allom. L., 1831. 4to. Engraved map, title, 44 views on 22 plts., spotted, cf., worn. (S. Jun.25; 302) *Kouchak.* £90
- Devonshire & Cornwall Illustrated. 1829. 2 vols. in 1. 4to. 2 engraved vig. titles, 2 maps, 138 engrs. on 69 sheets, spotting, hf. mor., scuffed. (P. Jun.7; 215)   £190
- – **Anr. Copy.** 2 pts. in 1 vol. 4to. Engraved title, 92 views on 46 plts. only, no ptd. titles., spotted & soiled, cont. hf. cf., rubbed. (BBA. Jan.19; 115)
          Goodey. £110
- – **Anr. Edn.** 1829-32. 2 vols. in 1. 4to. Additional engraved titles with vig., 2 hand-cold. engraved maps, 69 plts. on India paper, some spotting, cont. cf. gt., spine defect. (S. Nov.1; 104) *Vine.* £120
- – **Anr. Edn.** 1831. 2 pts. in 1 vol. 4to. 1 additional engraved title only, 1 full-p. map only, 69 plts., few text ll. defect., some browning or staining, mod. hf. cl. (S. Nov.1; 103)   *Burgess.* £130
- – **Anr. Edn.** Ill.:– after Bartlett, Allom & others. 1832. 2 pts. in 1 vol. 4to. 2 steel-engraved additional titles, 138 views on 69 plts., 2 maps, cont. mor.-bkd. bds. (CSK. May 4; 51)   £180
- – **Anr. Copy.** 2 pts. in 1 vol. 4to. A few light margin stains, roan-bkd. cl. (S. Dec.13; 200)
          Burgess. £130

BRITTON, John & Pugin, Augustus Charles
- Illustrations of the Public Buildings of London. L., 1825-28. 2 vols. 2 additional engraved titles, engraved plan, 143 engraved plts., hf. titles, cont. diced cf., rebkd. (C. Dec.9; 15) *Quaritch.* £240

BRO, Gen.
- Mémoires Recueillis. Paris, 1914. On japan, hf. chagrin by Lavaux, wrap. (HD. Jan.27; 14)
          Frs. 1,800

BROCKEDON, William
- The Hand-book for Travellers in Italy from London to Naples. Ill.:– W. & E. Finden after Stanfield, Prout & Brockedon. L., [1835]. Fo. Wide

margin, engraved title with vig., 5 engraved maps, 24 steel-engraved views on China, plts. stained in margins, mod. hf. linen. (R. Oct.13; 3135) DM 400
- **Illustrations of the Passes of the Alps.** L., 1828-29. 12 pts. in 2 vols. Fo. L.P., engraved titles, engraved general map, 12 other maps, 84 engraved plts., titles & plts. on India paper, some spotting, mainly affecting margins, red mor. gt. by Bank, of Edinb., rubbed; pres. copy to the Duke of Sussex, inscr. on blank before title. (C. Jun.27; 15) *Lovatt.* £460
- – **Anr. Copy.** 2 vols. Fo. L.P., 108 engraved maps & plts. on India paper, some foxing, some text discold., not affecting plts., str.-grd. mor. gt. (P. Mar.15; 260) *Marshall.* £400
- – **Anr. Copy.** 2 vols. 4to. Double-p. map, 108 plts. & maps, spotting, mor. gt., rubbed. (P. Jun.7; 219) £220
- – **Anr. Copy.** 2 vols. 4to. 13 maps, 95 engraved plts. (foxed), diced cf., defect., w.a.f. (P. Sep.8; 137) *Edistar.* £170
- – **Anr. Copy.** 2 vols. Fo. Wide margin, minimal soiling, cont. mor., gt. cover, inner & outer dentelle, end-papers & some corners renewed, spine browned, cover slightly soiled & worn. (HK. Nov.8; 819) DM 900
- – **Anr. Edn.** 1829. Vol. 2 only (of 2). 4to. 53 engraved maps & plts, slight spotting, mor. gt. (P. Apr.12; 134) *Richards.* £120
- – **Anr. Copy.** Vol. 2 only. 4to. 7 maps, 48 engraved views, mor. gt. (P. Sep.8; 57) *Edistar.* £75
- – **Anr. Edn.** Ca. 1877. 2 vols. 1 double-p. map, 12 maps, 96 plts., orig. cl. gt. (P. Oct.20; 193) £260
- – **Anr. Edn.** L., n.d. 2 vols. Hf. leath. & marb. bds., spines & edges rubbed. (RS. Jan.17; 460) $175
- **Italy, Classical, Historical, & Picturesque.** L., Ca. 1847. Fo. Engraved title, 60 steel-engraved views, some plts. foxed, cont. cf., rebkd. & rubbed. (S. May 21; 222) *Liberia.* £320
- – **Anr. Copy.** Fo. Engraved title, 60 plts., many spotted, hf. mor., rubbed, bdg. detchd. (S. Jun.25; 156) *L'Acquaforte.* £280
- **Road-Book from London to Naples.** L., 1835. Vig. title, 5 maps, 24 engraved views, spotting, orig. cl., worn. (P. Nov.24; 205) *Rossi.* £50

BROCKES, B.H.
- **Irdisches Vergnügen in Gott.** Hamburg, 1734-48. *1st. Edn. (Vols. 5-10).* 9 Pts. in 9 vols. & supp. Vol. 10. Cont. leath., rubbed. (GB. May 4; 1210) DM 2,700
- – **Anr. Edn.** Hamburg & Tübingen, 1739-48, 1750. Vols. 1-2 & 4-9 (of 9) in 8 vols. Some light browning or foxing, cont. leath., rubbed & bumped. (R. Apr.3; 144) DM 1,400

BROCKHAUS, Albert
- **Netsuke.** Leipzig, 1909. *Orig. Edn.* Orig. leath. (V. Sep.30; 1936) DM 2,400

BROCKHAUS, F.A.
- **Allgemeine Deutsche Real-Encyclopädia für die Gebildeten Stände [Conversations-Lexicon].** Leipzig, 1819-20. *5th. Orig. Edn.* 10 vols. Cont. hf. leath., slightly rubbed, not collated. (R. Apr.3; 653) DM 580
- – **Anr. Edn.** Leipzig, 1820-24. Orig. Series: 10 vols., New Series: 2 vols. in 4, & Supp. vol. Hf. leath., 1 spine with sm. fault. (V. Sep.30; 2028) DM 650
- – **Anr. Edn.** Leipzig, 1830. 12 vols. Some foxing, cont hf. leath. gt., some corners bumped. (GB. Nov.3; 969) DM 600
- **Enzyklopädie.** Wiesbaden, 1966-76. 20 vols. & 4 supp. vols. Orig. hf. leath., orig. wraps. (D. Nov.24; 4324) DM 2,000
- **Der Grosse Brockhaus. Handbuch des Wissens.** Leipzig, 1928-35. 21 vols. Hf. linen, corners slightly bumped, vol. 1 spine torn. (D. Nov.24; 4325) DM 700
- **Konversations-Lexikon.** Leipzig, 1898. *14th. Edn. Jubilee Edn.* 16 vols. & supp. vol. in 17 vols. Orig. hf. leath. gt., decor., slightly rubbed. (R. Apr.3; 655) DM 800
- – **Anr. Copy.** 16 vols. & supp. vol. Some cold. plts. with paste or col. traces. 4 plts. loose, orig. hf. leath. (GB. May 3; 946) DM 450
- – **Anr. Edn.** Leipzig, 1901-04. 17 vols. with Supp.

Plts., some folding, ills., orig. hf. roan, rubbed, most spines worn. (BBA. May 23; 355) *Loose.* £50
- **Lexikon.** 1893. 17 vols. 4to. Hf. leath. (G. Sep.15; 2249) Sw. Frs. 600

BROCKLEHURST, Capt. H.C.
- **Game Animals of the Sudan.** 1931. *1st. Edn.* Orig. cl. gt., rubbed. (TA. Jul.19; 12) £85

BROD, Max (Contribs.)
See — GENIUS

BRODRICK, Thomas
- **A Compleat History of the late War in the Netherlands.** L., 1713. 2 vols. Cont. panel. cf., slightly worn. (S. Mar.6; 76) *Scott.* £80

BRODRICK, William
See — SALVIN, Francis Henry & Brodrick, William

BROEBES, Jean Baptiste
- **Vues des Palais et Maisons de Plaisance de sa Majesté le Roy de Prusse.** Augsburg, 1733. Fo. Double-p. engraved title/preface, 68 engraved plts. on 47 double-p. ll., minor worming at blank margin of a few plts., cont. cf., rubbed, corners worn. (C. Dec.9; 16) *Goldschmidt.* £5,500

BROEKHUIZEN, G. van
See — MELTON, Edward [G. van Broekhuizen?]

BROGLIE, Louis Victor de
- **Ondes et Mouvements.** Paris, 1926. *1st. Edn.* Fascicle I in 'Collection de Physique Mathématique'. Lge. 8vo. Light browning, orig. wraps., faded, light soiling, spine reprd., mor. folding box; John D. Stanitz coll. (SPB. Apr.25; 69) $700
- **Recherches sur la Théorie des Quanta.** Paris, 1924. *1st. Edn.* Orig. ptd. wraps., unopened, reprd., slight soiling, mor.-bkd. folding box; pres. copy, Stanitz coll. (SPB. Apr.25; 70) $900

BROINOWSKI, Gracius Joseph
- **The Birds of Australia.** Melbourne, 1890. Vols. I & II. Fo. Lacks 8 plts., no bdg. stated. (JL. Nov.13; B523) Aus. $580
- – **Anr. Edn.** Melbourne, 1890-91. 6 vols. Fo. 303 chromolitho. plts., tears to 2 plts. & accompanying text lf., 1 other text lf. torn, 1 plt. with ink stain in upr. margin, a few plts. with tissue guards adhering, a few ll. & plts. with sm. margin tears, some slight spotting or soiling, roan gt., worn, crude repair to 1 spine. (S. Nov.28; 11) *Vischer.* £900
- **The Cockatoos & Nestors of Australia & New Zealand.** 1888. Sm. fo. Publisher's roan or mor., gt., some chipping; inscr. (KH. May 1; 101) Aus. $1,650

BROME, Richard
- **Five New Playes.** L., 1653. Lacks blank?, cf. gt., rebkd. (P. Nov.24; 50) *Rix.* £60

BROMME, Traugott
- **Gemälde von Nord-Amerika in allen Beziehungen von der Entdeckung an bis die Neueste Zeit.** Stuttgart, 1842. 2 vols. Engraved title & port., 87 steel engrs., browned & spotted thro.-out, cont. hf. leath., slightly bumped. [Sabin 8204] (H. May 22; 269) DM 500
- **Hand-und Reisebuch für Aus-Wanderer und Reisende nach Nord– Mittel- und Süd-Amerika.** Ed.:– G. Struke. Bamberg, 1867. Slightly foxed, map mntd. on linen, 2 sm. tears, cont. hf. leath. (R. Oct.13; 2957) DM 750
- **Illustrirter Hand-Atlas der Geographie und Statistik.** Stuttgart, 1862. Sm. fo. 48 litho. double-p. maps outl. cold., 1 map loose, 7 cold. litho. arms plts., 1 torn, 7 cold. litho. flag plts., 218 text woodcuts, cont. hf. leath., rubbed. (GB. May 3; 2) DM 950

BROMWELL, William J.
See — LESTER, W.W. & Bromwell, William J.

BRONTE, Anne 'Acton Bell'
- **Self-Communion.** Ed.:– T.J. Wise. L., priv. ptd., 1900. *(30).* Bds.; O. Brett bkplt. (P. Mar.15; 66) *Jarndyce.* £75
- **The Tenant of Wildfell Hall.** 1848. *2nd. Edn.* 3 vols. Some text slightly spotted, qtr. mor. gt. (P. Jan.12; 138) *Jarndyce.* £95

BRONTE, Charlotte 'Currer Bell'
- **The Professor.** 1857. *1st. Edn.* 2 vols. in 1. 2 hf.-titles, 2 pp. advts. at end of Vol. 1, mod. cf. gt.; from Norman Tarbolton liby. (P. Apr.12; 17) *Wolf.* £170
- – **Anr. Copy.** 2 vols. in I. 24 pp. advts., few ll. lightly spotted, orig. cl., rebkd., old spine laid down. (CSK. Jan.13; 217) £70
- – **Anr. Copy.** 2 vols. Hf.-titles, advts., red hf. mor. gt. (P. Jan.12; 137) *Morris.* £55
- – **Anr. Copy.** 2 vols. Hf.-titles, 16-pp. advts. dtd. June 1857 in vol.2, advt. lf. in vol. 1, orig. cl. with binder's label of Westleys & Co. in vol. 1; Fred A. Berne copy. (SPB. May 16; 187) $475
- **Shirley.** 1849. *1st. Edn.* 3 vols. Advts., some foxing, orig. cl., rebkd., orig. spine preserved, fleece-lined cl. s.-c.; Lady Diana Duff Cooper bkplt. in each vol., from Norman Tarbolton Liby. (P. Apr.12; 16) £170
- **Villette.** 1853. *1st. Edn.* 3 vols. 12 pp. advts. at end of Vol. 1, red mor. gt. (P. Jan.12; 136) *Scott.* £95
- – **Anr. Copy.** 3 vols. Advts. dtd. Jan. 1853, orig. cl., binder's label of Westleys & Co., some fraying, little discold., tear on spine jnt. in vol. 3; Fred A. Berne copy. (SPB. May 16; 188) $500

BRONTE, Emily 'Ellis Bell'
- [–] **Wuthering Heights.** N.Y., 1848. *1st. Amer. Edn.* 2 vols. 8vo. (in 12's). Early text ll. slightly stained, some foxing thro.-cut, unc., orig. wraps., Vol. 1 lacks lr. wrap. & part of spine, other wraps. frayed & soiled, spines cocked, owner's sig. on upr. wraps. (SG. Nov.17; 16) $325
- – **Anr. Copy.** Some foxing, cont. three-qtr. leath., rubbed. (RO. Apr.23; 19) $110
- – **Anr. Edn.** Ill.:– Clare Leighton. N.Y., Lakeside Pr., 1931. *(450)* numbered & sigd. by artist. 4to. Cl. (LH. Sep.25; 501) $100

BRONTE, Emily, Charlotte & Anne 'Ellis, Currer & Acton Bell'
- **The Novels.** Ill.:– Edmund Dulac. L., 1905. 10 vols. 12mo. Hf. mor. gt., wood-veneer covers & end-papers. (SG. Mar.29; 134) $300
- – **Anr. Edn.** L., 1911. *Thornton Edn.* 12 vols. with Life. Orig. cl., spines gt., very slightly rubbed. (BBA. May 3; 242) *Roberts.* £140
- – **Anr. Edn.** Ed.:– Temple Scott. Edinb., 1924. *Thorton Edn.* 11 vols. (without Mrs. Gaskell's Life of Charlotte Bronte). Orig. cl. (KH. Nov.8; 53) Aus. $190
- **Poems.** 1846. *1st. Edn. 2nd. Iss.* Sm. 8vo. No errata slip, advt. at end, orig. blind-stpd. cl., gt. spine. (SKC. Jan.13; 2192) £180
- – **Anr. Edn.** L., 1846. *1st. Edn. 2nd. Iss.* 12mo. Errata slip, 16 p. catalogue of advts. dtd. May 1848, cont. inscr., orig. cl. [Carter's bdg. 'A(ii)'], shaken, cl. folding box; T.L.s. from John Carter laid in; Frederic Dannay copy. (CNY. Dec.16; 44) $400
- **Life & Works ....** L., 1891. 7 vols. Hf. mor. (GM. Dec.7; 684) £85
- **The Works.** 1893. *(150)* numbered on L.P. 12 vols. Orig. buckram gt., unc., spines darkened. (SKC. Sep.9; 1898) £80
- **Life & Works.** Ed.:– Mrs. H. Ward & Clement K. Shorter. L., 1899-1900. *Haworth Edn.* 7 vols. Red three-qtr. of. by Bayntun, spines gt. (SG. Feb.16; 45) $425
- **Works.** 1905. 12 vols. Orig. cl. gt. (P. Apr.12; 225) *Thorp.* £85
- – **Anr. Edn.** L., 1920. *Haworth Edn.* 7 vols. Hf. cf., spines faded. (S. Oct.11; 311) *Booth.* £90
- – **Anr. Edn.** Oxford, Shakes. Hd. Pr., 1932-38. 8 vols. Orig. cl. (KH. Nov.8; 54) Aus. $220
- **Works. With the Life of Charlotte Bronte by Mrs. Gaskell.** L., 1899-1900. 7 vols. Slight darkening, owner's blind-stp. on prelims., three-qtr. mor. & cl., gt.-ruled & decor., marb. end-papers, by Morrell, edges slightly rubbed, some spine ends slightly chipped. (CBA. Dec.10; 39) $150

BROOKE, Sir Arthur de Capell
- **Travels through Sweden, Norway & Finmark to the North Cape.** 1823. 4to. 22 litho. plts. (2 hand-cold.), some spotting, cont. hf. cf., slightly worn, upr. cover detchd. (TA. Dec.15; 55) £65
- **A Winter in Lapland & Sweden.** 1826. *1st. Edn.*

BROOKE, Sir Arthur de Capell -*Contd.*

4to. Lacks advt. lf., inscr. on title, 1 map strengthened at folds, some faint browning, cont. hf. cf. gt. (S. Nov.1; 72) *Hannas.* £130
– – **Anr. Edn.** 1827. *1st. Edn.* 4to. 1 litho. plt. on India paper (not called for by Abbey), advt. lf. at end, 1 folding plt. slightly worn without loss at folds, inscr. on title, some faint spotting or browning, cont. hf. cf., worn. (S. Nov.1; 73) *Hannas.* £110

BROOKE, Lord Fulke Greville
– Caelica. Ed.:– U. Ellis-Fermor. Gregy. Pr., 1936. *(255).* Qtr. mor. gt., partly unc. (P. Mar.15; 89) *Quaritch.* £75
See— HODDESDON, John – BROOKE, Lord Fulke Greville

BROOKE, Sir James
– Narrative of Events in Borneo & Celebes, down to the Occupation of Labaun. L., 1848. *1st. Edn.* 2 vols. Some foxing, orig. cl. gt., spine ends torn. (S. Oct.11; 431) *Cavendish.* £160
– – **Anr. Edn.** Notes:– Capt. R. Mundy. 1848. *2nd. Edn.* 2 vols. Portfo., prize gt. cf. (PD. Jun.13; 158) £135

BROOKE, T.H.
– A History of the Island of St. Helena. 1808. Publisher's advts. bnd. in at end, cont. hf. cf., rubbed. (TA. Jul.19; 35) £50

BROOKES, Richard, M.D.
– The Art of Angling, Rock & Sea-Fishing. L., 1740. *1st. Edn.* 12mo. 5 pp. advts., 19th. C. cf. gt. (S. Oct.4; 10) *Blackwells.* £200
– The General Gazzetteer: Or, Compendious Geographical Dictionary .... 1786. *6th. Edn.* 9 uncold. folding engraved maps, margins a little browned, cont. spr. cf., rebkd. (TA. Mar.15; 54) £54

BROOKS, H.C.
– Compendiosa Bibliografia di Edizioni Bodoniae. Firenze, 1927. *(700) numbered on H.M.P.* Orig. bds., unc., ptd. wraps. (SI. Dec.15; 227) Lire 350,000

BROOKSHAW, George
– Pomona Britannica. L., priv. ptd., 1812. *1st. Edn.* Lge. fo. 90 cold. hand-finished aquatint plts., numbered to 93, slip at p. 30 explaining that 3 of the pineapple plts. were never publd., title with vertical crease, cont. crimson str.-grd. mor., covers elab. blind– & gt.-tooled; Sir Thomas Swinnerton bkplt. (C. Mar.14; 157) *Davidson.* £31,000
– – **Anr. Copy.** Lge. fo. 90 col. plts. finished by hand, red str.-grd. mor. gt., upr. cover detchd. (P. Nov.24; 244) *Heald.* £17,000
– Six Birds. L., 1817. *1st. Edn.* 4to. 6 stipple-engraved plts., each in cold. & plain state, some light browning, cont. red str.-grd, mor, lge. gt. design on covers in gt.-tooled borders, worn. (SG. Apr.26; 34) $800

BROSSA, Joan
– Pas D'Amors, poèmes que son ... compostos l'any 1959. Ill.:– Antoni Tapies. [Barcelona, 1983]. *(612).* Out-of-series copy. Ptd. decor. wraps., with sm. litho.; pres. copy. (PNY. Jun.6; 483) $110

BROSSES, Charles de
– L'Italie il yaa Cent Ans ou Lettres Ecrites d'Italie à Quelques Amis en 1739 et 1740. Paris, 1836. *2nd.* *[1st. Compl.] Edn.* 2 vols. Hf. cf., spines decor. (HD. Mar.19; 37) *Frs.* 1,300
– [–] Terra Australis Cognita: or, Voyages to the Terra Australia .... Ed:– [John Callander]. Edinb., 1766-68. 3 vols. Cont. cf. (C. Nov.16; 5) *Quaritch.* £2,400
– Vollständige Geschichte des Schiffahrten nach dem noch gröstentheils Unbekannten Südländern aus dem Französ .... Ed.:– J. Chr. Adelung. Halle, 1767. *1st. German Edn.* 2 vols. 4to. Cont. bds., lightly spotted & bumped. [Sabin 8389] (HK. May 15; 674) DM 1,400

BROTOFFER, Ratichs [i.e. Christopher Rotbarth?]
– Aut hic aut Nusquam. Elucidarius major oder Erleuchtung über die Reformation .... Vienna, 1752.

2 pts. in 1 vol. New cf.; Dr. Walter Pagel copy. (S. Feb. 7; 65) *Ritman.* £500
– Elucidarius Chymicus oder Erleuchtung ... Chymische Secreta da Lapide Philosophorum .... Luneburg, 1616. *1st. Edn.* Colophon lf., very browned, title margin out into, some worming, new bds.; Dr. Walter Pagel copy. (S. Feb.7; 64) *Quaritch.* £850

BROUER VAN NIEDEK, Mathias
– Het Verheerlykt Watergraefs- of Diemer-Meer by ... Amsterdam. Ill.:– Daniel Stopendael. Amst., 1725. *1st. Edn.* Fo. Engraved frontis., 2 folding plans, 60 plts. on 30 ll., cont. hf. vell. (C. Dec.9; 37) *Goldschmidt.* £750
– Het Zegenpralent Kennemerlant .... Ill.:– Hendrik de Leth. Amst., ca. 1728. 2 pts. in 1 vol. Fo. 2 engraved frontis., folding map, 100 plts. on 50 ll., map laid down & tear reprd., gt.-panel. mor. by Zaehnsdorf, unc. (C. Dec.9; 38) *Weinreb.* £400
– – **Anr. Edn.** Ill.:– H. de Leth. Amst., ca. 1730. Fo. Hf. cf., slight defects. (B. Oct.4; 731) Fls. 1,200

BROUERIUS VAN NIDEK, Mathaius
See— HALMA, Francois & Brouer van Niedek, Mathias

BROUGHTON, Rhoda
– Second Thoughts. 1880. *1st. Edn.* 2 vols. Hf.-titles, advts., orig. floral chintz. (P. Jan.12; 144) *Jarndyce,.* £120

BROUGHTON, Urban Huttleston Rogers
– The Dress of the First Regiment of Life Guards in Three Centuries. 1925. *(300) numbered.* 4to. Plts., some cold. & mntd., orig. pig. d.-w., orig. box. (CSK. May 18; 84) £110
– – **Anr. Copy.** 4to. Orig. pig. (P. Sep.8; 201) *Georges.* £80

BROWN, A.
– The Poster Stamp. N.Y., ca. 1928. 29 plts., loose as iss., 12-p. pamphlet laid in, bd. folder. (SG. Aug.25; 290) $170

BROWN, Carleton
– Register of Middle English Religious & Didactic Verse. 1916-20. 2 vols. Sm. 4to. Orig. buckram-bkd. bds.; H.M. Nixon coll. (BBA. Oct.6; 202) *Quaritch.* £65

BROWN or BROWNE, Edward, 1644-1708, Physician & Traveller
– A Brief Account of some Travels in Divers parts of Europe. L., 1685. *2nd. Edn.* Fo. 16 engraved plts. (6 folding), advt. lf., title browned & discold., 1 plt. shaved, cont. panel. cf., rebkd.; Dr. Walter Pagel copy. [Wing B 5111] (S. Feb.7; 66) *Bickersteth.* £220
– Durch Niederland, Teutschland, Hungarn, Servien ... Oesterreich ...gethane gantz sonderbare Reisen etc. Nuremb., 1686. *1st. German Edn.* 4to. Frontis. & 10 copper engrs. with sm. bkd. parts & repairs, some text ll. with margin repairs, sm. tears, some spotting & staining, linen. (H. Nov.23; 322) DM 440
– Reysen door Nederland, Duytsland, Hongaryen, Servien, Bulgarien, Macedonien, Oostenrijk, Stiermark, enz. Ill.:– Luyken. Amst., 1682. 3 pts. in 1 vol. 4to. 4 plts. reprd., 3 mntd., cont. hf. vell. (VG. Sep.14; 1080) Fls. 650

BROWN, Frank
– Frost's Drawings of Ipswich & Sketches in Suffolk. Ipswich, 1895. *(105) numbered & sigd. by author.* Lge. 4to. Col. frontis., 27 monochrome plts., subscribers list, orig. cl.-bkd. watered silk bds., cl. soiled, silk fraying. (LC. Mar.1; 200) £50

BROWN, Glenn
– History of the United States Capitol. Wash., 1900-03. 2 vols. sm. fo. 324 plts., ex-liby., gt.-decor. cl. (SG. May 3; 63) $375

BROWN, John Ednie
– The Forest Flora of South Australia. Adelaide, 1882-90. 9 pts. Fo. 4 or 5 ll. with sm. margin stains, pt. 8 with margin tears & a few repairs, wraps., some slightly chipped. (KH. May 1; 106) Aus. $1,700

BROWN, J.H., of Brighton
– [–] Spectropia: Or, Suprising Spectral Illusions .... N.Y., 1864. *1st. Amer. Edn.* 4to. Ills. hand-cold., pict. bds., spine defect., slight dampstaining at upr. corner, covers loose. (SG. Dec.8; 328) $100
– – **Anr. Edn.** L., 1865. *4th. Edn.* 4to. Ills. hand-cold., pict. bds., disbnd. (SG. Dec.8; 329) $100

BROWN, John Carter
– Bibliotheca Americana: Catalogue of the John Carter Brown Library in Brown University. N.Y., 1975-63, Providence, 1973. 8 vols. 4to. & lge. 8vo. Cl., slight wear. (RO. May 22; 19) $260
– – **Anr. Edn.** Millwood, N.Y., 1973-75. *Kraus Reprint (2 vols. supplied from orig. printing).* 6 vols., & vol. of Additions. Tall 8vo. Cl. (SG. Sep.15; 36) $375

BROWN, Louise Norton
– Block Printing & Book Illustration in Japan. L., 1924. *1st. Edn.* Fo. 43 plts. (18 cold), hf. cl. (PNY. Jun.6; 463) $160
– – **Anr. Copy.** 4to. Cl. (SSA. Jul.5; 51) R 230

BROWN, Richard, Architect
– The Principles of Practical Perspective. L., 1815. 4to. Cont. style hf. leath. (D. Nov.23; 1871) DM 600

BROWN, Robert, Botanist
– The Miscellaneous Botanical Works. 1868. Atlas vol. only. 4to. Bds., some wear. (KH. May 1; 111) Aus. $190

BROWN, Robert, Farmer
– General View of the Agriculture of the West Riding of Yorkshire. 1799. Vell.-bkd. bds.; from the Farmers' Club Liby. (P. Jul.5; 7) £65
– Strictures & Remarks on the Earl of Selkirk's Observations on the Present State of the Highlands of Scotland .... Edinb., Ptd. by Abernethy & Walker, 1806. *1st. Edn.* Lacks hf.-title, foxed, maroon hf. mor. by Sangorski & Sutcliffe; the Rt. Hon. Visc. Eccles copy. [Sabin 69460 (variant imprint)] (CNY. Nov.18; 34) $380

BROWN, Samuel R.
– The Western Gazetteer. Auburn, N.Y., 1817. *1st. Edn. 1st. Iss.* Some foxing, margin tears to title & front free end-paper, with the errata slip, cont. tree sheep, extremities slightly worn. (SG. Apr.5; 27) $110

BROWN, Solyman
– Dentologia: A Poem on the Diseases of the Teeth, & their Proper Remedies. Notes:– Eleazar Parmly. N.Y., 1833. *1st. Edn.* Some ll. dampstained in margin, orig. cl. gt., rebkd., tips restored, slightly spotted & discold.; Milton Asbell bkplt. (SG. Oct.6; 70) $140

BROWN, T. Julian
– The Stonyhurst Gospel of Saint John. Oxford, Roxb. Cl., 1969. Typescript of G.D. Hobson's 'The Binding of Manuscripts. The Manuscript of St. John's Gospel in the Library of Stonyhurst College', 1940, loosely inserted, orig. mor.-bkd., H.M. Nixon coll., with his sig. (BBA. Oct.6; 117) *Quaritch.* £120
– – **Anr. Copy.** Facs. plts., qtr. mor. gt. (P. May 17; 64) *Georges.* £85

BROWN, Capt. Thomas
– Illustrations of the American Ornithology of Alexander Wilson & Charles Lucien Bonaparte. Edinb., [1831–]35. *Early iss.* Lge. fo. Engraved title & dedication, 124 hand-cold. etched plts., accords with Ellis copy & Faxon's no. 4, having plts. XLIV & LXI in states before inclusion of additional figures, with plts. with uncorrected misnumbering, some slight discolouration, a few spots or stains, hf. mor., Duke of Sutherland's arms gt. on upr. cover, rebkd. (S. Feb.1; 11) *Taylor.* £25,000
– Illustrations of the Fossil Conchology. 1849. 4to. 117 litho. plts., a few hand-cold., some ll. spotted, cont. roan-bkd. cl., worn. (BBA. Jun.28; 265) *Bookroom Cambridge.* £65
– Illustrations of the Genera of Birds. 1845-47. 5 orig. pts. only. 4to. 2 plain & 24 hand-cold. plts., orig. wraps., torn, as a coll. of plts., w.a.f. (P. Oct.20; 25) £190

BROWN, William
See— JAMIESON, John & Brown, William

BROWN, William H.
- Portrait Gallery of Distinguished American Citizens. [N.Y., 1931]. *(600).* Tall fo. 27 ports., each with facs. letter, gt.-decor. buckram. (SG. Dec.15; 133) $125

BROWNE, Hablot Knight 'Phiz'
- How Pippins enjoyed a Day with the Fox Hounds; A Run with the Stag-Hounds. L., 1863. 2 vols. Ob. fo. 24 hand-cold. litho. plts., rather stained, in margins of 1st. vol., 2 plts. loose, orig. hf. roan, worn. (BBA. May 23; 204) *Clay.* £100

BROWNE, Dr. John, 1642-1700.
- Verteutschte Neue Beschreibung derer in den Menschlichen Cörper befindlichen Musculen. Ed.:– Chr. Maxim. Spener. Berlin, 1704. Sm. fo. Title verso stpd., cont. hf. leath., slightly rubbed, spine reprd. (GB. May 3; 984) DM 1,800

BROWNE, John Ross
- Adventures in the Apache Country: A Tour through Arizona & Sonora, with Notes on the Silver Regions of Nevada. N.Y., 1869. *1st. Edn.* 12mo. Orig. cl., corners slightly frayed. (SG. Jan.19; 117) $150
- Reisen u. Abenteuer im Apachenlande. Trans.:– H. Hertz. Gera, 1877. Cont. hf. linen gt., slightly rubbed. (HK. May 15; 598) DM 520

BROWNNE, J.S.
See— HUNTINGTON, A.T. & Brownne, J.S.

BROWNE, James
- A History of the Highlands & of the Highland Clans. Glasgow, 1838. *1st. Edn.* 4 vols. Lge. 8vo. Red three-qtr. mor., spines gt.; armorial Rangemore bkplt. (SG. Feb.16; 266) $150

BROWNE, Sir Thomas
- Christian Morals...The Second Edition. With a Life of the Author by Samuel Johnson. 1756. *2nd. Edn.* Hf.-title, a few ll. browned, cont. cf., worn. (BBA. Jan.19; 195) *Lawson.* £130
- - Anr. Copy. Hf.-title cropped & reprd., slightly browned, cont. sheep, rebkd. (BBA. May 3; 205) *Maggs.* £65
- Hydriotaphia, Urne-Buriall. 1658. Sm. 8vo. Advt. lf. & longitudinal hf.-title to 'The Garden of Cyrus', sm. hole in 1 lf. affecting a few words, minor worming to blank margin touching 1 catchword, without errata, cont. sheep, rubbed; Laurence Strangman bkplt. [Wing B5154] (C. May 30; 138) *Maggs.* £350
- [-] A Key to the King's Cabinet. Oxford, 1645. *1st. Edn.* 17th. C. note on title & verso of 1st. lf., corner of title-p. clipped; Robert Harley bkplt. [Wing 5181a] *(Bound with:)* - Considerations touching the Late Treaty for a Peace held at Uxbridge. Oxford, 1645. *1st. Edn. [Wing C5920]* Together 2 works in 1 vol. 4to. Cont. cf. (BBA. Jun.14; 46) *Sanders of Oxford.* £65
- Posthumous Works. 1712. *1st. Edn.* Engraved frontis. port., 21 engraved plts. (4 folding), cont. cf., gt.-decor. spine; Sir Ivar Colquhoun, of Luss copy. (CE. Mar.22; 36) £400
- - Anr. Copy. Panel cf., re-bkd. (BS. May 2; 53) £90
- Pseudodoxia Epidemica. 1646. *1st. Edn.* Sm. fo. Sm. piece torn from margins of 2 ll., cont. cf., rebkd., orig. spine preserved, corners reprd. [Wing B5159] (C. May 30; 139) *Traylen.* £100
- - Anr. Copy. Sm. fo. A3 torn, A6 detchd., burnholes in 2A1 & 2A2, lacks last blank, spotted, stained, cont. cf., worn, rebkd. [Wing B5159] (S. Apr.10; 337) *Smallwood.* £90
- - Anr. Edn. L., 1650. *2nd. Edn.* Fo. 1 margin torn, later hf. cf. [Wing B5160] (BBA. Mar.21; 185) *John Andrew.* £65
- - Anr. Copy. Fo. Cf., worn, gt.-panel. spine crudely reprd. (CBA. Dec.10; 117) $110
- Works. 1686. *1st. Edn.* Sm. fo. Sm. hole in 2 ll. slightly affecting a few words, cont. blind-panel. cf., rebkd. [Wing B5150] (C. May 30; 140) *Traylen.* £110
- - Anr. Copy. Fo. Lacks last 2 ll., little slight browning, cont. cf.; bkplts. of Earl of Lonsdale & J. Lowe. [Wing B5150] (S. Oct.11; 312) *Rhys-Jones.* £80

BROWNE, William George
- Travels in Africa, Egypt & Syria from the year 1792 to 1798. 1799. *1st. Edn.* 4to. Cont. patterned cf. gt., rebkd., new end-papers. (SKC. Mar.9; 2000) £120
- - Anr. Copy. 4to. Some light offsetting, cont. cf., rebkd. (CSK. Nov.25; 67) £95
- - Anr. Edn. 1806. *2nd. Edn.* 4to. Minor spotting, cont. cf., old reback, some wear. (TA. Sep.15; 40) £80

BROWNE, William of Tavistock
[-] Britannia's Pastorals. The First (Second) Book. L., 1625. 2 pts. in 1 vol. Notes & inscrs. in a number of 17th. C. hands on verso of last lf. & rear free end-paper, lacks K8, some staining, cont. cf [STC 3916] (BBA. May 3; 106) *Hannas.* £110

BROWNHILL, W.R.
- The History of Geelong & Corio Bay. Melbourne, 1955. 4to. 1 sm. margin repair, owner's inscr., orig. cl. (KH. Nov.8; 57) Aus. $320

BROWNING, Elizabeth Barrett
- Aurora Leigh. L., 1857. *1st. Edn.* P.106 in early state & pp.133 & 144 corrected, orig. blindstpd. cl., spine gt.; inscr. by John Kenyon (Dedicatee), bkplt. of Amelia Henry, Fred A. Berne copy. (SPB. May 16; 189) $150
- An Essay on Mind. L., 1826. *1st. Edn.* Orig. bds., unc., hf. mor. folding box; fragment of A.L.s. laid in, 4-line holograph in Robert Browning's hand on verso, Frederic Dannay copy. (CNY. Dec.16; 46) $800
- Poems. L., 1844. *1st. Edn. 1st. Iss.,* with reading *'let the flood/Of your salt scorn dash on me'* at p. 141 in Vol. 1. 2 vols. Sm. 8vo. 8 pp. of inserted advts. dtd. 1 Jan. 1846 in Vol. 1, a few ll. carelessly opened, orig. green cl. [Carter's 'B' bdg.], worn, especially at spine ends; inscr. on 1st. title-p. 'Emily Burton (?) from her ever affectionate Ba.', O.O. Fisher bkplt. (SG. Nov.3; 30) $850
- - Anr. Copy. 2 vols. Sm. 8vo. No inserted advts., & no lf. following p. 250 Vol. 1, mod. red str.-grd. three-qtr. mor., spines gt., gift inscr. on blank fly-lf. of each vol. (SG. Nov.17; 17) $275
- Poetical Works. L., 1886. 5 vols. Sm. 8vo. Hf. cf., spines gt., slightly worn. (SG. Feb.16; 46) $130
[-] The Seraphim, & other Poems. 1838. *1st. Edn.* 12mo. Hf.-title, 1st. blank lf. with MS. verses after Frances Thompson, orig. cl., faded. (BBA. Sep.29; 194) *Swales.* £100
- Sonnets from the Portuguese. Intro.:– Louis Untermeyer. Ill.:– V. Angelo. N.Y., Ltd. Edns. Cl., 1948. *(1500)* sigd. by artist. *(15) pres. copies from the publishers.* Fo. Gt.-decor. cl., spine & s.-c. slightly faded; the V. Angelo copy, with his initials. (CBA. Oct.1; 263) $100

BROWNING, Robert
- Bells & Pomegranates. L., 1841, 1843. *1st. Edns.* Nos. 1 & 3 in 1 vol. Orig. ptd. wraps.; pres. copy from author to Mrs. Basil Montagu of No. 3, 2 corrections in ?Browning's hand, Frederic Dannay copy. (CNY. Dec.16; 51) $420
- - Anr. Edn. L., 1841[-46]. *1st. Edns.* Nos. 1[-8] in 1 vol. 4 pp. advts., orig. cl., blind-stpd., corners & spine reprd.; Frederic Dannay copy. (CNY. Dec.16; 50) $400
- Complete Works. N.Y., 1910. *'Asolo' Edn. (50)* numbered. 12 vols. Plts. in 2 states, cold. & uncold., crushed lev. mor., covers with gt.-ruled borders, onlaid mor. gt. ornaments, gt. spines in 6 compartments, turn-ins gt., crushed lev. mor. doubls., watered silk free end-pp., partly unc. (CNY. Dec.17; 540) $800
- - Anr. Edn. Intro.:– W.L. Phelps. N.Y., [1910]. *Florentine Edn. (1000) numbered sets.* 12 vols. Lge. 8vo. Gravure plts. on Japan vell., crimson three-qtr. mor., spines gt. with fleurons, partly unc., partly unopened. (SG. Feb.16; 47) $425
- Dramatis Personae. 1864. *1st. Edn.* Hf.-title, last advt. lf., orig. cl.; loosely inserted A.L.s. from author, 19 Warwick Crescent, 3rd. Nov. 1886, to Lady Sophia Palmer, 1 p., 12mo. (BBA. Sep.29; 203) *Bauman.* £200
- Gold Hair. '1864'. Unbnd., cl. folder; Oliver Brett bkplt. (P. Apr.12; 29) *Jarndyce.* £130
- Men & Women. L., 1855. *1st. Edn.* 2 vols. 12mo.

Orig. cl. [Carter's bdg.'A']; bkplt. of A. Bethune Baker, Frederic Dannay copy. (CNY. Dec.16; 52) $420
- The Ring & the Book. 1868-69. *1st. Edn.* 4 vols. Later mor. by Zaehnsdorf, gt.-decor. spine & corners. (BBA. Sep.29; 204) *Maggs.* £130

BRUCCOLI, Matthew J.
- First Printings of American Authors. Contributions Toward Descriptive Checklists. Detroit, [1977-79]. 4 vols. 4to. Cl., light wear. (RO. May 29; 47) $180

BRUCE, Sir James of Kinnaird
- Carte et Figures du Voyage en Nubie et en Abyssinie. Paris, 1792. Fo. 88 engrs., linen. (DS. Mar.23; 2037) Pts. 100,000
- Reisen zur Entdeckung der Quellen des Nils. Ed.:– Joh. Fr. Blumenbach. Trans.:– J.J. Volkmann. Leipzig, 1790-91. *1st. German Edn.* 5 vols. Some slight foxing, cont. hf. leath., corners lightly rubbed. (GB. May 3; 30) DM 2,000
- - Anr. Copy. 5 vols. Title & lf. & endpapers in 1 vol. with slight worming, cont. hf. leath., rubbed & bumped, 1 spine with sm. fault, jnts. brkn. in 1 vol. (D. Nov.23; 1230) DM 1,500
- - Anr. Copy. 5 vols. Title with owner's note, excised & bkd., Vol. 5 lacks both maps, cont. marb. leath. gt., bumped & rubbed, Vol. 1 & 2 spines defect. (HK. Nov.8; 799) DM 1,200
- Travels to Discover the Source of the Nile. Edinb., 1790. *1st. Edn.* 5 vols. 4to. Cont. tree cf., spines gt. (C. Nov.16; 6) *Kossow.* £1,000
- - Anr. Copy. 5 vols. 4to. Orig. bds., unc. (PD. Dec.14; 200) £490
- - Anr. Copy. 5 vols. 4to. 3 folding engraved maps, 59 plts., cont. russ. gt., slightly rubbed. (SKC. Mar.9; 2001) £420
- - Anr. Copy. 5 vols. 4to. Titles with engraved ill., 15 engraved plts. & plans, 3 folding engraved maps, 43 natural history plts., 8 pp. of specimen script, lacks port., a few imprints & 1 plan shaved, some spotting & fold tears to maps, tear in 1 text lf., cont. tree cf., 1 cover detchd. (C. Mar.14; 103) *Blairman.* £380
- - Anr. Edn. 1808. *2nd. Edn.* 8 vols., including plt. vol. 8vo. & 4to. 79 plts. & maps, mott. cf., spines gt. (BBA. Sep.29; 2) *Sawyer.* £200
- Voyage aux Sources du Nil, en Nubie et en Abyssinie. Pendant les Années 1768...1772. Trans.:– J.H. Castera. Paris, 1790-92. *1st. Fr. Edn.* 10 text vols. & atlas. 8vo. & 4to. Some light text browning or spotting, cont. cf. gt., 1 cont. hf. leath., slightly worn & bumped, 1 sm. spine tear, 1 corner defect. (H. May 22; 244) DM 1,400

BRÜCKE, E.
- Anatomische Beschreibung des Menschlichen Augapfels. Berlin, 1847. *1st. Edn.* 4to. Stpd., cont. hf. leath., rubbed. (R. Oct.12; 1333) DM 400

BRUCKER, J.
- Ehren-Tempel der Deutschen Gelehrsamkeit. Ill.:– J.J. Haid. Augsburg, 1747. 4to. 1st. 2 ll. stpd., slightly stained near end, cont. hf. leath. gt., bumped & worn, spine slightly defect. (HK. Nov.9; 2034) DM 2,200

BRUCKNER, Albert (Ed.)
See— CHARTERS

BRUCKNER, G.
- Handbuch der Neuesten Erdbeschreibung. Hildburghausen, 1837. *1st. Edn.* Some slight foxing, later hf. linen, loose. (BR. Apr.12; 75) DM 450

BRUCKNER, John
[-] A Philosophical Survey of the Animal Creation, An Essay .... Dublin, 1770. *1st. Dublin Edn.* 12mo. Hf.-title spotted, cont. cf., gt. spine, slightly rubbed; the James Madison copy, with inscr. on title-p. (CNY. Nov.18; 322) $2,800

BRUELE, W.
- Praxis Medicinae Theorica et Empirica Familiarissima. Lyon, 1589. Title with erased owner's note, foxed & stained, cont. vell., spine defect., lacks endpapers & ties. (HK. Nov.8; 473) DM 500

BRUGEL, W.
- Männer der Rakete. Leipzig, [1933]. Orig. sewed, foot of spine wormed & slightly defect. (R. Oct.12; 1612) DM 530

BRUGMANS, A.
- Tentamina Philosophica de Materia Magnetica, ejusque Actione in Ferrum et Magnetem. 1765. 4to. L.P., orig. limp bds., spine slightly defect. (VG. Sep.14; 1229) Fls. 450

BRUGUIERE, Francis
- Beyond This Point. Text:– Lance Sieveking. L., [1929]. 1st. Edn. 4to. Cl., rubbed & soiled, corners worn, owner's inscr. on front free end-paper. (SG. May 10; 19) $100

BRUHL, Graf Carl & Spiker, S.H.
- Lalla Rukh, ein Festspiel mit Gesang und Tanz .... Berlin, 1822. 4to. 23 hand-cold. aquatint plts., including a lge. folding plt., orig. bds., spine & stitching brkn. (C. Nov.16; 57) Kossow. £340

BRUIN, Claas
- Aanmerkingen op O. van Veens Zinnebeelden der Goddelyke Liefde. Ill.:– J. Folkema. Amst., 1726. Slightly soiled & browned, cont. leath., decor., bumped. (HK. Nov.9; 1620) DM 420

BRUIN or BRUYN, Cornelis de
- Reizen door de Vermaardste Deelen van Klein Asia, de Eylanden Scio, Rhodus, Cyprus...mitsg. Egypten, Syrien en Palestina. Delft, 1698. [1st. Edn.] Fo. Lacks map (publd. later), 1 folding plt. incompl., some repairs, some staining, vell., rebkd. & rebnd. (VG. Sep.14; 1081) Fls. 1,650
- – Anr. Copy. Engraved port. frontis., 1 folding map, 210 numbered engraved plts. & views on single, double & folding ll. & in text, several plts. reprd., a little soiled & margin stained, mod. hf. cf. (VS. Jun.7; 996) Fls. 1,600
- Reizen over Moskovie, door Persie en Indie. Amst., 1714. Fo. Additional engraved title, engraved port., folding map, 260 numbered figures on 108 sheets, many double-p. or folding, frontis. torn, short tear to lf. T2, plt. nos. 115/116 & 2 following text ll. torn, ink sig. on title, orig. Dutch publisher's blind-stpd. vell. (CNY. May 18; 124) $480

BRUIN, Georg
See— BRAUN or BRUIN, Georg & Hogenberg, Franz

BRUMOY, Pierre
- Théâtre des Grecs. Ill.:– Borel, Defraine, Le Barbier, & others. Paris, 1785-89. New Edn. 13 vols. 4to. On vell., cont. marb. cf., spines decor., partly rubbed. (HD. Nov.9; 19) Frs. 2,750
- – Anr. Copy. 13 vols. Cont. tree sheep, decor. spine. (HD. Sep.22; 199) Frs. 1,850

BRUNE, Johann de
- Emblemata of Zinne-Werck. Middleburg, 1624. 1st. Edn. 4to. Lightly browned, some slight staining, cont. vell., lacks ties. (HK. May 16; 1424) DM 900
- – Anr. Edn. Ill.:– J. Folkema. Amst., 1661. 3rd. Edn. 4to. Title with owner's note, 2 ll. bkd. in side margin, upr. corner slightly stained, cont. vell. (HK. Nov.9; 1621) DM 1,600
- – Anr. Edn. Ill.:– J. Galle, W. v.d. Pas & others after A. v.d. Venne. Amst., [1688]. 2nd. [i.e. 4th.] Printing. 4to. Cont. vell. (VG. Mar.19; 135) Fls. 700

BRUNET, Gustave
- La Reliure Ancienne et Moderne. Paris, 1878. Fo. 111 (of 116) plts., some margins lightly stained, loose as iss. in orig. buckram portfo., worn, lacks ties; H.M. Nixon coll., with some MS. annots. (BBA. Oct.6; 17) Quaritch. £130

BRUNET, Jacques Charles
- Manuel du Libraire et de l'Amateur de Livres. Paris, 1842. 5 vols. 4to. Linen, wraps. (DS. Oct.28; 2306) Pts. 110,000
- – Anr. Edn. Paris, 1842-44. 4th. Edn. 5 vols. Lge. 8vo. Cont. hf. russ., corners, spine raised bands. (HD. May 16; 10) Frs. 1,000
- – Anr. Edn. Paris, 1842-89. 6 vols., with Supp. Spotted, later cl.-bkd. bds. & cl. (BBA. Nov.10; 43) Duran. £90

- – Anr. Edn. Paris, 1860, n.d. 5th. Edn. 6 vols., with 2 vols Supp. in 1. Lge. 8vo. Hf. mor., corners, by David, supp. vol. spine faded. (HD. May 3; 210) Frs. 3,700
- – Anr. Edn. Paris, 1860-65, 1878. 5th. Edn. 6 vols. in 12, with supp. in 2 vols. Lacks' Dictionnarie de Gréographie; Cl. bds. (HD. Jun.6; 21) Frs. 2,600
- – Anr. Edn. Paris, 1860-78. 8 vols. in 7, including Supp. Cont. vell.-bkd. cl. (BBA. Apr.5; 272) Maggs. £190
- – Anr. Copy. 7 vols. Cont. hf. chagrin. (HD. Jan.26; 59) Frs. 2,200
- – Anr. Edn. Paris, 1860-80. 8 vols., including 2 Supps. Later hf. mor. (BBA. Sep.8; 4) Sawyer. £170
- – Anr. Edn. Paris, ca. 1920. (With:) DESCHAMPS, P. & Brunet, G. – Supplément. Together 8 vols. Cont. bds., unc. (HD. Jan.30; 31) Frs. 2,900
- – Anr. Edn. Berlin, 1922. 5th. Edn. 6 vols. Hf. mor., marb. paper. (D. Nov.23; 234) DM 760
- – Anr. Edn. Copenhagen, 1966-68. Reprint of Paris 1860-80 Edn. 9 vols. Orig. linen. (R. Apr.3; 602) DM 850
- – Anr. Copy. 9 vols., including Indexes & Supps. Cl. (VS. Dec.7; 233) Fls. 575

BRUNFELS, Otto
- Herbarum Vivae Eicones. Adiecta Appendix Isagogica. – Novi Herbarii Tomus II-Tomus Herbarii III. Strassburg, 1532-36. Pt. 3: 1st. Edn. Fo. Pt. 1 Appendix dtd. 1532 at end, name stp. on 1st title lf. verso, old 17th. C. vell. (R. Oct.11; 16) DM 22,000

BRUNHOFF, Jean de
- The Story of Babar, the Little Elephant. – Babar the King. – Zephir's Vacation. – Babar & his Children. Trans.:– Merle Hass. N.Y, 1933; 1935; [1937; 1938]. 1st. Edns. in Engl. Together 4 vols. Fo. Cl.-bkd. pict. bds. (SG. Dec.8; 77) $375

BRUNI, Leonardo
- The History of Leonard Aretine, Concering the Warres Between the Imperialles & the Gothes for the Possession of Italy. Trans.:– Arthur Golding. L., 1563. Sm. 8vo. Lacks last prelim. lf., lr. blank margin of last lf. defect., title-p. dust-stained, cont. limp vell. [STC 3933] (BBA. May 3; 93) Maggs. £200

BRUNNER, A.A.
- Einleitung zur Nöthigen Wissenschaft eines Zahnarztes. Wien, 1766. Cont. hf. leath. gt. (D. Nov.23; 536) DM 600

BRUNO, Saint
- Opera & Vita. [Paris, 1524]. Fo. Title with printer's device dtd. 1820, in architectural border, 6 text ills., initials thro-out, some historiated, light stains at lr. margins, early owner's sig. on title deleted, 16th. C. panel. pol. cf., roll-tooled borders, brass clasps & corners. (SG. Apr.19; 46) $450
- Psalterium ex Doctorum Dictis Collectum. [Würzburg, Georg Reyser], ca. 1485. Fo. Lacks 2 blank ll., cont. stpd. pig, traces of clasps; from Fondation Furstenberg-Beaumesnil. [H. 40ll; BMC II, 571; Goff P1046] (HD. Nov.16; 81) Frs. 21,100

BRUNSCHWIG, Hieronymus
- Das Buch zu distillieren die zusamen gethonen Ding Composita genant, durch die eintzige [n] Ding, und das Buch Thesaurus Pauperu [m], für die Armen. Strassburg, J. Grüninger, 28 Aug. 1519. 2nd. Edn. Fo. Minimal browning, later leath. over wood bds., blind-tooled, clasps, corners & spine cont. renewed, spine leath. split, free end-papers vell. with old Calligraphic owners entry, vell. MS. leaf in upr. cover, in lr. cover double lf. of 16th. C. printing with astronomical Woodcut pasted in, many gold, red or green vell. index tabs. (R. Apr.3; 20) DM 18,000
- Distillierbuch. Frankfurt, 1555. 4to. Old MS. Latin names for plants (described in German), cont. style mod. leath. (R. Apr.3; 21) DM 3,800
- Liber de Arte Distillandi de Compositis. Strassburg, 1512. 1st. Edn. Fo. Title facs., some browning, mostly in margins, some slight spotting, some cont. underlining in red & black & brown ink margin annots., MS. extension on last lf. dtd. 1543, 1 lf. with tear in lr. margin & last 4 lines reprd. without

loss, 1 sm. margin hole, index tabs, blind-tooled pig, ca 1600, worn, scratched, jnts. brittle, upr. jnts. split. (HK. May 15; 92) DM 7,500

BRUSCAMBILLE
- Oeuvres. Rouen, 1622. Revised Edn. 12mo. Cont. cf.; from libys. of Parison, Comte de Lignerolles & Edouard Rahir. (HD. Mar.29; 17) Frs. 9,000

BRUSLE DE MONTPLEINCHAMP, Abbé J.C.
[–] Esope en Belle Humeur ou Dernière Traduction ... de ses Fables en Prose et en vers. Ill.:– Harrewyn. Brussels, 1700. 2 vols. Frontis., 163 hf.-p. engrs., privilege lf., few stains, cont. cf., worn, spines slightly defect. (S. Apr.10; 289) Marshall. £100

BRUSSEL, Isidor Rosenbaum
- Anglo-American First Editions, 1826-1900: East to West. Intro.:– G. Pollard. L., 1935. (500). Tall 8vo. Orig. bds. (SG. Sep.15; 74) $100
- Anglo-American First Editions 1826-1900. East to West. West to East. L. & N.Y., 1935-36. (500). 2 vols. Orig. bds., unc.; Comte Alain de Suzannet bkplt. (S. May 1; 377) Forster. £100
- – Anr. Copy. 2 vols. Bds., paper parch. backs, unc., worn. (RO. Jun.26; 23) $160

BRUST, M.
- Prakt. Darstellung wichtiger Gegenstände der Zimmerbaukunst. Prag, 1800. Fo. 2 plts. lightly creased, some slight foxing or staining, cont. hf. leath., worn & slightly bumped. (HK. May 16; 1394) DM 600

BRUUN, Johan Adolf
- An Enquiry into the Art of the Illuminated Manuscripts of the Middle Ages, Part I, Celtic Illuminated Manuscripts. Stockholm, 1897. All publd. 4to. Cont. hf. mor., gt.-decor. spine, partly untrimmed. (TA. Jun.21; 440) £65

BRUYN, Cornelis de
See— BRUIN or BRUYN, Cornelis de

BRUYS, François
[–] Histoire des Papes depuis St. Pierre jusqu'à Benoit XIII inclusivement. La Haye, 1732-34. Orig. Edn. 5 vols. 4to. Vol. III title replaced with hf.-title from 4-vol. edn., cont. red mor. gt., spines decor. (HD. May 21; 15) Frs. 3,500
- – Anr. Copy. 5 vols. 4to. Cont. marb. cf.; Conte d'Heliand ex-libris. (SI. Dec.18; 65) Lire 250,000

BRUZEN DE LA MARTINIERE, Antoine Augustine
- Le Grand Dictionnaire Géographique Historique et Critique. Paris, 1768. 6 vols. Fo. Some staining vol. III, cont. marb. cf., decor. spines, defects. (HD. Jan.27; 198) Frs. 2,100
- Introduction à l'Histoire de l'Asie, de l'Afrique, et de L'Amérique. Amst., 1735. 1st. Edn. 2 vols. 12mo. Cont. mott. cf., jnts. & extremities worn, 1 upr. cover loosening. [Sabin 8783] (SG. Oct.20; 33) $140

BRY, Theodor de
- Major Voyages. [Virginia & Florida]. Frankfurt am Main, 1590-91. Pts. 1 & 2, together 2 vols. Fo. Engraved titles, plts., lacks folding maps, few ll. cropped, disbnd., w.a.f. (S. Apr.9; 19) Burden. £600
- Voyages. Frankfurt, 1613. Pt. 10 only. Sm. fo. Engraved title, 2 plts. only, some light spotting, mod. bds.(CSK. Jul.6; 1340) £220

BRY, Theodor de & Johann Theodor de
- Collectiones Peregrinationum un Indiam Orientalcm. Frankfurt, 1598-1607. 1st. Latin Edn. Fo. Most unnumbered plts. misbnd., 5 maps & 1 plan with old partly bkd. defects., with loss, 1 cut close, 1 map in pt. 3 & 2 copper engrs. in pt. 2 supplied in facs., 1 map from German edn. bnd. in pt. 6, some light browning or foxing, cont. vell. (R. Oct.13; 2808) DM 7,000
- Zehender theil der Orientalischen Indien Begreiffende .... Frankfurt, 1613. Sm. fo. Early 19th. C. mor. gt. by Pratt; sigd. letter from Henry Stevens certifying the correctness of this iss. tipped in, a copy of Carlos Sanz's 4 p. check-list of edns of the Quiros Memorial loosely inserted. (KH. May 1; 212) Aus. $3,500

BRYAN, Michael
- Dictionary of Painters & Engravers. L., 1903. 5 vols. Hf. mor., spines unif. faded. (SPB. Nov.30; 221) $375
- – Anr. Copy. 5 vols. 4to. Two-tone cl., covers lightly soiled. (CBA. Jan.29; 76) $325
- – Anr. Edn. Ed.:– George C. Williamson. L., 1903-05. 5 vols. 4to. Orig. cl. (S. Oct.4; 134) *Dempster.* £80
- – Anr. Copy. 5 vols. 4to. Orig. cl. gt. (SKC. Nov.18; 1803) £50
- – Anr. Edn. 1918-19. 5 vols. 4to. Slight browning, orig. cl., slightly rubbed & soiled. (S. Apr.30; 165) *Simpson.* £100
- – Anr. Edn. 1918-19-15. 5 vols. 4to. Orig. cl., lightly soiled. (CSK. Jan.27; 25) £120
- – Anr. Edn. Ed.:– George C. Williamson. 1926-34. 5 vols. Lge. 8vo. Cl., spines faded. (LC. Mar.1; 35) £80
- – Anr. Edn. 1964. 5 vols. Buckram. (BS. May 2; 142) £85

BRYANT, Gilbert Ernest
- The Chelsea Porcelain Toys. L., 1925. *1st. Edn. (650) numbered & sigd.* Very tall 4to. 47 col. plts., cl., head of spine frayed, d.-w. worn. (SG. Oct.13; 58) $175
- – Anr. Copy. 4to. 47 col. plts., cl., extremities rubbed. (SG. Jan.26; 68) $100

BRYANT, Jacob
- A New System, or, an Analysis of Ancient Mythology. 1775-76. *Vols. 1 & 2: 2nd. Edn., Vol. 3: 1st. Edn.* 3 vols. 4to. Cont. cf. (CSK. Aug.19; 59) £60
- Observations & Inquiries Relating to ... Ancient History. Camb., 1767. 4to. Tree cf. gt. (P. Feb.16; 115) £80

BRYANT, William Cullen
- Picturesque America. [1872]. *[1st. Edn.].* Vol. 1 only. 4to. Engraved title loose, some spotting, qtr. mor. gt. (P. Sep.29; 193) *Willis.* £75
- – Anr. Edn. N.Y., [1872-74]. *[1st. Edn.].* 2 vols. 2 steel-engraved frontis., 2 extra titles, 45 plts., some light spotting, orig. mor. gt., 1 bd. detchd. (CSK. Feb.24; 107) £120
- – Anr. Copy. 2 vols. 4to. Some foxing, hf. mor. gt. (PD. Aug.17; 41) £100
- – Anr. Copy. 2 vols. Lge. 4to. Orig. mor. (SG. Oct.20; 283) $200
- – Anr. Copy. 2 vols. Lge. 4to. Orig. three-qtr. mor., worn & partly loose. (SG. Aug.4; 251) $160
- – Anr. Copy. 2 vols. Lge. 4to. Engraved titles, 47 full-p. steel engrs., engraved titles & 1 frontis. foxed, orig. publisher's gt.– & blind-decor. pebbled mor., extremities rubbed; the Rt. Hon. Visc. Eccles copy. [Sabin 62692] (CNY. Nov.18; 225) $110
- – Anr. Edn. Ca. 1875. 4 vols. 4to. Mor. gt., covers detchd. (P. Mar.15; 52) *Martin.* £100
- – Anr. Edn. 1894-97. 4 vols. 4to. Orig. cl. gt. (P. Sep.29; 305) *Pederson.* £190
- – Anr. Edn. N.Y., n.d. 2 vols. 4to. Engraved titles, 47 plts., a few ll. slightly spotted, cont. mor., gt. spines, worn. (BBA. Dec.15; 39) *Kassis.* £70
- – Anr. Copy. 4 vols. 4to. Orig. cl. gt., spine faded. (LC. Mar.1; 201) £55
- Poems. Camb., 1821. Foxed, orig. bds., unc., rebkd., hf. mor. case; 2 A.Ls. tipped in, 1 from author, 1 from John Howard Bryant, Frederic Dannay copy. (CNY. Dec.16; 55) $600

BRYANT, William Cullen
See– CENTURY ASSOCIATION

BRYDALL, John
- Jus Imaginis apud Anglos or the Law of England relating to the Nobility & Gentry. 1675. 1 p. of publisher's advts. at end, old sheep. [Wing B 5261] (P. Mar.15; 292) *Thorp.* £95

BRYDGES, Sir Samuel Egerton
- The Sylvan Wanderer. 1813-15-17. *(100).* 2 vols. in 1. Cont. mor. gt., spine gt. in compartments, armorial bkplt. (SKC. May 4; 1616) £180

BRYDONE, Patrick
- A Tour through Sicily & Malta. 1775. 2 vols. 4to. Hf.-titles, advts., cont. tree cf.gt., silk doubls.gt., corners worn, fore-e.pntg. in each vol. (BBA. Feb.9; 321) *Edgar Backus.* £80

BRYNE, W.
See– HEARNE, Thomas & Bryne, W.

BRYSON, C.L.
See– GILBERT, Paul & Bryson, C.L.

BUBER, Martin
- Luis Camnitzer Illustrates Martin Buber. Ill.:– Luis Camnitzer. N.Y., [1970]. *(100) sigd. by artist.* Fo. Woodcuts on Arches, loose as iss. in ptd. cl. portfo. & matching box-type case; woodcuts sigd. by artist. (SG. Feb.2; 50) $800

BUCCELLA, N.
- Confutatio Responsi Simonis Simonii Lucensis ad Epistolam Georgii Chiakor .... Krakau, 1588. 4to. Old name on title & sm. red ink stain, cont. limp vell. (R. Oct.12; 1370) DM 650

BUCELINUS, Gabriel
- Nuciei Historiae Universalis. Augsburg [& Ulm], 1664. 3 pts. in 1 vol. Some light foxing, cont. vell., clasps. (R. Oct.13; 2838) DM 1,100

BUCH, M.
- Bilder aus Griechenland. Ill.:– after A. Löffler. Triest, ca. 1880. Fo. Woodcut title vig., 6 woodcuts, 18 steel engrs., slightly foxed or wormed, orig. linen, stained & lightly bumped. (HK. May 15; 840) DM 420

BUCHAN, John
- A Lost Lady of Old Years...a Romance. 1899. *1st. Edn.* Orig. cl.; author's bkplt. (PD. Oct.19; 192) £100
- Musa Piscatrix – the Bodley Head Anthologies. 1896. *1st. Edn.* Orig. cl. gt., unc.; author;s bkplt. (PD. Oct.19; 193) £85

BUCHANAN, A.W.G.
- [-] Journal of Three Months in Italy & the East. Glasgow, 1878. *(Bound with:)* [-] Forty Thousand Miles of Travel round the World: A.W.G.B.'s Journal ... Glasgow, 1880. Together 2 works in 1 vol. Old hf. cf., rubbed; author's bkplt. (KH. May 1; 115) *Aus.* $270

BUCHANAN, Francis H.
- A Journey from Madrid through the Countries of Mysore, Canara & Malabar. L., 1807. *1st. Edn.* 3 vols. 4to. 39 engraved plts. (1 cold.), lacks folding map, some plts. spotted, cont. cf., hinges split, 1 cover detchd. (S. Mar.6; 26) *Shapero.* £130

BUCHANAN, George
- [-] De Maria Scotorum Regina ... Historia. N.p., [1571]. *1st. Edn.* A few 17th. C. annots., piece torn from lr. blank margin of last lf., cont. limp vell. [STC 3978] (BBA. May 3; 95) *Howes Bookshop.* £180
- The History of Scotland. Trans.:– J. Fraser. 1690. 4to. Cf. (PD. May 16; 191) £95

BUCHANAN, H.
See– SITWELL, Sacheverell & others

BUCHANAN, Robert
- North Coast & other Poems. 1868. Spotted, orig. decor. cl., rubbed; inscr. by Robert Browning to Mrs. Binzon, Christmas Eve 1867. (BBA. Feb.23; 213) *Cox.* £80

BUCHANAN, Robertson
- Illustrations of Mill Work & other Machinery, together with Tools of Modern Invention. L., 1841. Atlas vol. Fo. Margin dampstain affecting few plts. towards end, cont. mor. gt., Rennie family arms, watered silk end-ll., some rubbing, corners & head of spine bumped; pres. copy from publisher, John Weale, to George Rennie, Rennie's sig. on end-paper, pres. letter from Weale, John D. Stanitz coll. (SPB. Apr.25; 73) $800
- Practical & Descriptive Essays on the Economy of Fuel, & Management of Heat. Glasgow, 1810. *1st. Edn.* Plts. lightly spotted, 1 folding, later hf. cf., lightly rubbed, re-bkd., old spine preserved. (CSK. May 18; 186) £160
- Practical Essays on Mill Work & other Machinery. Ed.:– Thomas Tredgold. L., 1823. *2nd. Edn.* 2 vols. Errata, advts., 'To Subscribers' lf., some spotting, mostly at end of Vol. 2, 19th. C. hf. cf. gt., light rubbing, John D. Stanitz coll. (SPB. Apr.25; 71) $175

- – Anr. Edn. Ed.:– Thomas Tredgold & George Rennie. L., 1841. *3rd. Edn.* 2 vols. Preface & advts. in 2nd. vol., light browning, hf. vell., marb. bds., slight soiling; John D. Stanitz coll. (SPB. Apr.25; 72) $400
- Praktische Beiträge zur Mühlen- und Maschinen-Baukunst. Trans.:– M.H. Jacobi. Berlin, 1825. *1st. German Edn.* Title stpd., cont. bds. (R. Oct.12; 1763) DM 450

BUCH DER ERFINDUNGEN, GEWERBE U. INDUSTRIEN
Leipzig & Berlin, 1872-74. 6 vols. Some light browning, orig. hf. linen, 5 vols. with orig. wraps., w.a.f. (HK. Nov.8; 475) DM 400
- – Anr. Edn. Ed.:– F. Reuleaux. Leipzig & Berlin, 1884-88. 8 vols. Orig. gold-tooled hf. leath. (GB. May 3; 1139) DM 400
- – Anr. Edn. Ed.:– F. Reuleaux. Leipzig & Berlin, 1884-93. 8 vols. & supp. vol. in 9 vols. Orig. hf. leath., some slight bumping. (R. Apr.4; 1581) DM 550

BUCH DER FABELN
Ed.:– C.H. Kleukens. Intro.:– O. Crusius. Ill.:– F.W. Kleukens. Leipzig, Ernst Ludwig Pr., 1913. *De Luxe Edn., (100) on Bütten.* Hand-bnd. orig. mor. gt., spine & upr. margin slightly faded. (H. Nov.23; 1037) DM 760

BUCH DER TOTEN
Ed.:– W. Przygode. Trans.:– Contribs.:– H. Kasack & M. Merrmann (Neisse). Ill.:– Frz. Marz & W. Gramatte. München, 1919. *1st. separate printing. (125) numbered on Bütten, with sigd. & numbered etching.* Lge. 4to. Orig. hf. leath., slightly rubbed & bumped. (HK. Nov.11; 3460) DM 1,050

BUCH DER WELT
Stuttgart, 1847. Litho. title, 12 steel engraved plts., 36 cold. litho. plts., some foxing, later hf. linen, spotted. (R. Apr.4; 1970) DM 400
- – Anr. Edn. Stuttgart, 1851. Litho. title, 12 steel engraved plts., 36 cold. litho. plts., lightly foxed, cont. hf. leath. gt. (R. Apr.4; 1971) DM 620
- – Anr. Edn. Stuttgart, 1854. Litho. title, 12 steel engraved plts., 36 cold. litho. plts., slightly browned & foxed, orig. linen, gold tooled, slightly bumped. (R. Apr.4; 1972) DM 500
- – Anr. Edn. Stuttgart, 1859-64. 6 vols. Sm. 4to. 6 engraved titles, 216 cold. wood engraved plts., 72 steel engraved plts., some browning or foxing, some slight staining in lr. margin, cont. linen gt., slightly bumped. (GB. May 3; 3) DM 1,400
- – Anr. Edn. Stuttgart, 1860. Litho. title, 12 steel engraved plts., 36 cold. litho. plts., browned & foxed, slightly soiled at beginning, cont. hf. leath., rubbed & bumped, end-papers renewed. (R. Apr.4; 1975) DM 420
- – Anr. Edn. Stuttgart, 1862. 4to. Litho. title, 12 steel engraved plts., 34 (of 36) cold. litho. plts., foxed, orig. hf. linen, defect & loose. (R. Apr.4; 1976) DM 400
- – Anr. Edn. Stuttgart, 1864. Litho. title, 11 (of 12) steel engraved plts., 36 cold. litho. plts., foxed, cont. hf. linen, orig. wraps pasted on. (R. Apr.4; 1977) DM 450

BUCHENAU, S. (Ed.)
See– IMPRIMATUR

BUCHERSTUBE, Die. Blätter für Freunde des Buches und der Zeichnenden Künste
Ed.:– E. Schulte-Strathaus & others. München, 1920[-27]. Years I-V (all publd.). Bds., 1 upr. wrap. bnd. in. (H. Nov.23; 56) DM 420

BUCHHEIT, H. & Oldenbourg, R.
- Das Miniaturenkabinett der Münchener Residenz. Munich, 1921. 4to. Cl., rubbed. (P. Mar.15; 174) *Tzakas.* £50

BUCHNER, Georg
- Danton's Tod, Dramatische Bilder aus Frankreichs Schreckensherrschaft. Frankfurt, 1835. *1st. Edn.* Sm. 8vo. 4 ll. advts. at end, some foxing thro-out, cont. cl. (C. Dec.9; 205) *Quaritch.* £1,400
- Lenz, Ein Fragment. Ill.:– W. Gramatte. Hamburg, 1925. *(150) on Bütten.* Fo. Hand-bnd. orig. bds. (H. Nov.23; 1085) DM 700
- Sämtliche Werke u. Handschriftlicher Nachlass.

BUCHNER, Georg -Contd.

Ed.:– K.E. Franzos. Frankfurt, 1879. *1st. Coll. Edn.* Cont. hf. linen, orig. upr. wrap. excised & mntd. (HK. Nov.10; 2331) **DM 950**

BUCHON, Jean Alexandre C.
- **Choix d'Ouvrages Mystiques.** Paris, 1860. 4to. Hf. cl., worn. (HD. Feb.22; 29) **Frs. 1,600**
- **Collection des Chroniques Nationales et Françaises ecrites en Langue Vulgaire du 13e au 16e Siècle.** Paris, 1826-28. 47 vols. Hf. cf., decor. spines. (HD. Feb.22; 27) **Frs. 5,500**

BUCHOZ, Pierre Joseph
- **Centuries de Planches.** Paris & Amst., [1775?-]81. 'Première Centurie' & 'Seconde Centurie': 2 vols. in 4. Fo. Engraved thro.-out, with 20 series of 10 plts., all plts. in 2 states, uncold. & with cont. hand-colouring, each series with title & explanatory text lf., some titles col.-ptd., wormhole in lr. blank margin of 1st. title & 18 plts. in Vol. 3, not affecting ptd. area, last 4 plts. & text lf. dampstained, cont. cf.-bkd. bds., rubbed & worn, in 2 mod. mor.-bkd. boxes. (C. Mar.14; 158) *Lyon.* **£2,800**
- **Collection coloriée des plus Belles Variétés de Tulipes ....** Paris, 1781. Fo. Wide margin, 11 nos. erased with thin places & 2 sm. holes, mod. hf. leath., Hauswedell coll. (H. May 24; 857) **DM 11,000**
- **Les Dons Merveilleux et Diversement Coloriés de la Nature dans le Regne Végétal.** Paris, priv. ptd., [1779-83]. 2 vols. in 1. Fo. Engraved titles, 200 hand-cold. engraved plts., 2 pp. list of plts. at end, some plt. numerals partly supplied in MS., a few minor stains at some margins, cont. cf., worn, upr. cover detchd. (C. Nov.16; 225) *Bucherkabinett.* **£4,600**
- **Histoire Universelle du Regne Vegetal ....** Ill.:– Fessard, Robert, & others. Paris, 1775-76. 12 pts. vols. in 6 portfos. Fo. 9 ptd. titles, 9 hf.-titles, 1,160 (of 1,200) engraved botanical plts., including frontis., lacks all text & the 1st. 40 plts. in Vol. 4, some minor discoloration, mainly in margins, unstitched & loose in cl.-bkd. portfos., with ties, w.a.f. (C. Jun.27; 145) *Gordon.* **£2,800**

BUCK, Samuel & Nathaniel
- **Castles & Abbeys of England ....** [1813]. Ob. fo. 157 plts., hf. vell., worn, as a coll. of plts., w.a.f. (P. Jul.26; 27) **£520**
- **Views of Ruined Abbeys & Castles in England & Wales.** [1732/33?]. 3 contents pp. & 23 plts. only, mostly West Country, dtd. 1732 & 1733, ?later facs., loose in old folder. (SKC. Jan.13; 2367) **£70**

BUCKEN, E. (Ed.)
See— HANDBUCH DER MUSIKWISSENSCHAFT

BUCKING, J.J.H.
- **Vollständige Anweisung zum Zahnausziehen.** Stendal, 1782. *1st. Edn.* Plts. slightly crumpled, cont. bds., bumped. (R. Oct.12; 1503) **DM 850**

BUCKINGHAM, G. Williams, Duke of
See— ROHAN, Henri, Duc de – BUCKINGHAM, G. Williams, Duke of – LEICESTER, R. Dudley, Earl of

BUCKINGHAM, James Silk
- **The Eastern & Western States of America.** Ill.:– after W.H. Bartlett. L., [1842]. 3 vols. 15 double-p. engraved plts., 12 pp. prospectus & subscribers list for author's series on America followed by 12 p. index to his work 'The Slave States', all bnd. at end of Vol. 3, plts. slightly foxed, orig. blind-stpd. cl., spines gt.; William Brodie bkplts., the Rt. Hon. Visc. Eccles copy. [Sabin 8896] (CNY. Nov.18; 35) **$160**
- **The Slave States of America.** L. & Paris, [1842]. 2 vols. Slightly spotted, orig. cl., spines worn. (BBA. Jul.27; 280) *Kaplan.* **£65**

BUCKINGHAM, L.F.A.
See— WRIGHT, Rev. George Newnham & Buckingham, L.F.A.

BUCKINGHAM, Nash
- **Mark Right! Tales of Shooting & Fishing.** N.Y., Derrydale Pr., [1936]. *1st. Edn. (1250).* Slight

margin darkening, light wear, inscr., cl. (CBA. Nov.19; 123) **$130**
- - **Anr. Copy.** Hf.-title, a few top-e.'s slightly damp-spotted, leatherette, cold. medallion by Dr. Edgar Burke on upr. cover; inscr. of Harry M. Carpenter. (SG. Mar.15; 208) **$120**
- **Ole Miss'.** Foreword:– Paul A. Curtis. N.Y., Derrydale Pr., [1937]. *1st. Edn. (1250).* Light ageing, cl. (CBA. Nov.19; 124) **$130**

BUCKLAND, Rev. William
- **Reliquiae Diluvianae; Or, Observations on the Organic Remains Contained in Caves, Fissures, & Diluvian Gravel, & on Other Geological Phenomena, Attesting the Action of an Universal Deluge.** 1823. 4to. 27 engraved or litho. plts., including 3 cold. & 1 folding, orig. bds., unc., spine worn. (TA. Jun.21; 364) **£80**

BUCKLER, John Chessel
- **Sixty Views of Endowed Grammar Schools.** 1827. 4to. Spotted, orig. cl.-bkd. bds., rubbed. (BBA. Jun.28; 200) *Euston.* **£120**

BUCKLER, John & John Chessel
- **Views of Eaton Hall in Cheshire.** L., 1826. Fo. Engraved port., 20 litho. plts. on India paper, spotted, cont. mor. (S. Mar.6; 469) *Marlborough.* **£130**

BUCKLER, William
- **The Larvae of British Butterflies & Moths.** Ed.:– H.G. Stainton. L., 1885-99. 9 vols. 154 cold. plts., orig. cl. gt. (SKC. Oct.25; 337) **£420**
- - **Anr. Edn.** L., 1886-1901. 9 vols. 164 hand-cold. & chromolitho. plts., 1 plt. detchd., tree cf., spines gt., 3 vols. rebkd., 2 covers detchd. (C. Mar.14; 135) *Wheldon & Wesley.* **£340**

BUCKLEY, Francis
- **History of English Glass.** 1925. 4to. Orig. cl. (BBA. Sep.8; 239) *Hill.* **£70**

BUCKLEY, T.E.
See— EVANS, A.H. & Buckley, T.E.
See— HARVIE-BROWN, J.A. & Buckley, T.E.

BUCKNALL, Thomas Skip Dyot
- **The Orchardist: or, a System of close Pruning & Medication, for Establishing the Science of Orcharding.** L., 1797. *1st. Separate Edn.* Errata lf. at end, cont. tree cf., rebkd. (S. Oct.11; 496) *Thorp.* **£60**

BUCQUOI, J. de
- **Aanmerkelyke Ontmoetingen i.d. 16-jaarige Reize naa de Indiën.** Haarlem, 1744. *1st. Edn.* 4to. Some margin stains in text & on 1 plt., mod. hf. vell. (VG. Sep.14; 1082) **Fls. 880**

BUCQUOY, Commandant Eugene Louis
- **Fanfares et Musiques des Troupes à Cheval, 1640-1690.** Paris, [1948]. *(450).* 6 series. 4to. Leaves, box. (HD. Jan.27; 125) **Frs. 1,500**
- **Les Gardes d'Honneur du Premier Empire.** Nancy, 1908. *(885).* Sewed. (HD. Jan.27; 123) **Frs. 1,100**

BUDAEUS, G.
- **De Transitu Hellenismi ad Christianismum, Libri Tres.** Paris, 1535. *1st. Edn.* Sm. fo. 4 lge., metal cut initials, 1st. & last ll. lightly foxed in margins, title with 2 stps. & 1 liby. sig., 1 lf. with sm. margin tear at top, later old interim bds. (R. Apr.3; 22) **DM 1,100**

BUDAPEST MUSEUM of Fine Arts
- **Master Drawings from the Collection of ....** L., 1957. 4to. Plts., mor. gt., panel. spine, by Zaehnsdorf, s.-c. (P. May 17; 146) *Way.* **£75**

BUDGE, Sir Ernest Alfred Thompson Wallis
- **The Life of Takla Hâymânôt....** L., priv. ptd., 1906. *(250).* 1 vol. in 2. Lge. 4to. Orig. cl. (BBA. Apr.5; 166) *Marks.* **£120**
- - **Anr. Copy.** 2 vols. Lge. 4to. Orig. cl. (BBA. Sep.8; 5) *Belanske.* **£80**
- **The Miracles of the Blessed Virgin Mary, (Lady Meux Manuscripts Nos. 2-5).** L., 1900. 4to. Title slightly spotted, cont. mor., rubbed. (S. Dec.13; 437) *Kerr.* **£75**
- **Osiris & the Egyptian Resurrection.** 1911. 2 vols. (With:) - **Babylonian Life & History.** 1925. *2nd. Edn.* 1 vol. (With:) - **Cleopatra's Needles & Other**

Egyptian Obelisks. 1926. 1 vol. Together 4 vols. Orig. cl. gt., a little rubbed. (TA. Jun.21; 2) **£58**

BUDGEN, L.M.
- [-] **Episodes of Insect Life by Acheta Domestica.** L., 1849-51. *[1st. Edn.].* 3 vols. Orig. pict. cl. gt., soiled. (P. Mar.15; 113) *Thorp.* **£70**
- - **Anr. Copy.** 3 vols. Orig. cl., elab. gt.-decor., recased, new end-papers. (SKC. May 4; 1838) **£55**

BUEK, Friedrich Georg
- **Hamburg u. seine Umgebungen im 19. Jhdt.** Hamburg, 1844-48. 2 pts. in 1 vol. Some side margins cut slightly close, plan with sm. tear, cont. hf. leath., spine rubbed, end-papers renewed. (HK. Nov.8; 1046) **DM 7,200**
- **Wegweiser durch Hamburg und die Umliegende Gegend.** Ill.:– O. Speckter, I.L. Sommelrahn. Hamburg, 1836. *1st. Edn.* 1st. sigs. stained, browned, mod. hf. linen. (H. Nov.23; 371) **DM 500**
- - **Anr. Copy.** 35 lithos. on 10 plts., lacks folding plan, lightly browned & foxed thro.-out, mod. bds., old linen covered, spine faded. (H. May 22; 319) **DM 400**

BUEL, Clarence C.
See— JOHNSON, Robert U. & Buel, Clarence C.

BUENIUS, G.
- **Generosissimi ... Ludovico de Bils ... Specimina Anatomica.** Rotterdam, 1661. *(Bound with:)* - **Epistola Apologetica ad Magnum Th. Bartholinum ... de Calumniis Nobiliss Ludovico Bilsio.** Rotterdam, 1661. Together 2 works in 1 vol. 4to. Mod. hf. cf. (SG. Oct.6; 50) **$120**

BUENTING, Heinrich
- **Itinerarium Sacrae Scripturae, oder. Reise-Buch über die Gantze Heilige Schrifft.** Erfurt, 1754. *2nd. Edn.* 5 pts. in 1 vol. 4to. Some pts. slightly stained, foxed & browned, cont. cf. (VG. Sep.14; 1083) **Fls. 550**

BUFFON, George Louis Leclerc, Comte de
- **The Book of Birds.** Ed.:– M. Achille, Comte. Trans.:– Benjamin Clarke. 1841. Tall. 8vo. Additional vig. title, 38 hand-cold. plts., cont. panel. mor. gt., rubbed. (TA. May 17; 297) **£70**
- **Buffon in Miniatuur, of Natuurlijke Historie voor de Jeugd.** Amst., ca. 1830. 5 vols. 99 x 63 mm., miniature book. Orig. ptd. bds., box, top with inset glass, lacks part of gt. border; van Veen coll. (S. Feb.28; 180) **£210**
- **Histoire Naturelle, classée par Ordres ... d'après ... Linné; Avec les Charactères Génériques ... Linnéennes.** Ed.:– R.R. Castel. Paris, 1802. 26 vols. 204 cold. copperplts., cont. bds., faded, very worn & defect., 2 spines loose. (HK. Nov.8; 478) **DM 500**
- **Histoire Naturelle de Buffon Mise en Ordre d'après le Plan Tracé par lui-même.** Ill.:– Drouais (port.), Blakey (figures), & after de Sève (plts.). Paris, 1804. *New Edn.* 10 vols. Lge. 8vo. Port., 2 figures, 2 cold. folding maps, 84 copper-engraved plts., on indigo paper & cont. cold., cont. tree cf. gt.-decor. spines, inner roll-stp. (HD. Sep.22; 200) **Frs. 14,000**
- [-] **Histoire Naturelle Des Oiseaux.** Paris, 1775-85. Vols. 5 & 7-18. 12mo. Nearly 200 plts., cont. mott. cf. gt., spines slightly worn. (SG. Mar.22; 49) **$225**
- [-] **Histoire Naturelle Générale et Particulière, avec La Description du Cabinet du Roi.** Paris, 1749-67. *1st. Edn.* Vols. I-XV only. Lge. 4to. 2 engraved folding maps, 572 plts., some browning, foxing & soiling, some liby. stps., buckram. (SG. Mar.22; 50) **$250**
- **Histoire Naturelle, Générale et Particulière.** Paris, 1750-61. *Vols. I & II: 2nd. Edn. rest: 1st. Edn.* Vols. 1-2, 4-5 & 7-9 only (of 15). 4to. Wide margin, a few ll. with light stains, cont. marb. leath., gt. decor., some worming & rubbing, ex-libris. (H. Nov.23; 221) **DM 600**
- - **Anr. Edn.** Paris, 1752. 53 vols. 12mo. Bdg. not stated. (HD. Oct.14; 30) **Frs. 2,000**
- - **Anr. Edn.** Paris, 1770-89. 52 (of 56) vols. Approx. 620 (of 700) plts., cont. cf., gt.-tooled spines, many vols. slightly defect., w.a.f. (CR. Jun.6; 114) **Lire 800,000**
- - **Anr. Copy.** 25 vols. only, including 15 vols. 'Histoire Naturelle des Oiseaux'. 12mo. Cont.

marb. sheep, decor. spines. (HD. Sep.21; 110)
Frs. 2,000
- - **Anr. Edn.** Paris, 1771-75. Vols. 2 & 18 only. 4to. Cont. mott. cf. gt. (PD. Jun.13; 90) £82
- - **Anr. Edn.** 1785. 6 vols. only. 43 hand-cold. plts., cf., defect., as a coll. of plts., w.a.f. (P. Mar.15; 137) £120
- - **Anr. Edn.** Zweibrücken, 1785-91. 54 vols. 328 copperplts., 1 uncold., orig. bds., unc. (HK. Nov.8; 476) DM 2,600
- - **Anr. Edn.** Paris, An VII [1799-1807]. 125 vols., lacks Vols. 1 & 20. Spr. cf., spines decor., some bdgs. torn. (SM. Mar.7; 2006) Frs. 15,000
- - **Anr. Edn.** Ed.:- C.S. Sonnini. Paris, 1799-1808. *New Edn.* 129 vols. Orig. marb. bds., unc., some spines slightly defect. (BR. Apr.12; 611) DM 5,500
- **Histoire Naturelle, Générale et Particulière des Mollusques, Animaux sans Vertèbres et à Sang Blanc.** Paris, 1805. 6 vols. 72 col.-ptd. plts., light stains, crudely sewn, cont. bds., 1 lacking, untrimmed. (TA. Nov.17; 339) £85
- **Histoire Naturelle, Oeuvres Complètes.** Paris, 1855. 12 vols. Hf. leath. (G. Sep.15; 2082)
Sw. Frs. 1,200
- **Historia Naturál, General y Particulár.** Madrid, 1791-1805. 21 vols. 4to. Cf. (DS. Mar.23; 2627)
Pts. 225,000
- **Natural History, General & Particular.** Trans.:- William Smellie. Edinb., 1780-85. 9 vols. Engraved frontis., port., 313 plts., some folding, cont. cf., spines gt.; Sir Ivar Colquhoun, of Luss copy. (CE. Mar.22; 41) £580
- - **Anr. Edn.** 1785. '2nd. Edn.'. 9 vols. Port., folding map, 300 copper engrs., cont. tree cf. gt., lacks some vol. spine labels. (SKC. May 4; 1839) £70
- - **Anr. Edn.** Trans.:- William Smellie. 1812. *New Edn.* 20 vols. Port. frontis. to Vol. 1, 680 copperplt. engrs., cont. diced cf., gt.-decor. spines, worn at top & bottom of spines. (TA. Jun.21; 550) £180
- - **Anr. Copy.** 20 vols. Some spotting & offsetting, cont. hf. russ., spines tooled, 1 spine defect., jnts. to last vol. crudely reprd., w.a.f. (S. Dec.13; 253)
McKiernan. £140
- - **Anr. Copy.** 20 vols. Some light soiling, cont. cf. (CSK. Aug.19; 27) £75
- - **Anr. Copy.** 20 vols. Browning due to quality of paper, hf. cf., 1st. vol. spine defect. (CR. Jun.6; 115) Lire 650,000
- - **Anr. Edn.** Ed.:- H.A. Chambers. Trans.:- W. Smellie. L., 1817. 2 vols. 4to. Some ll. with sm. tears, some spotting, cont. leath. (D. Nov.23; 370) DM 600
- - **Anr. Edn.** Ed.:- Rev. W. Hutton. 1821. 100 hand-cold. engrs., including frontis. & title-pp., 1 gathering loose, pol. cf. gt. (SKC. Sep.9; 1986) £70
- **The Natural History of Birds.** 1792-93. 9 vols. Cont. pol. cf., spines gt.-decor. (SKC. Nov.18; 1961) £160
- - **Anr. Copy.** 9 vols. 292 copperplt. engrs., cont. tree cf., rubbed, Vol. 9 spine split. (TA. Apr.19; 144) £80
- **Naturgeschichte der Vögel.** Ed.:- F.H.W. Martini & (from Vol. 7) B.C. Otto. Berlin, 1772-98. Vols. 1-28 only (of 37),. Lacks 4 plts. in Vol. 5, 2 plts. in Vol. 23 & 1 plt. in Vol. 24, some text ll. in Vols. 9 & 10 slightly stained, hf. leath. gt., bumped. (R. Oct.12; 1797) DM 13,000
- - **Anr. Edn.** [Hamburg, 1772 ff.]. 1 plt. loose, cont. leath. gt., slightly rubbed. (R. Apr.9; 1678) DM 2,000
- - **Anr. Edn.** Berlin, 1782. Vol. 8. Slightly browned & some light foxing, cont. leath., worn. (R. Oct.12; 1798) DM 750
- - **Anr. Edn.** 1786. Vol. 1. Cont. bds. (R. Apr.4; 1668) DM 400
- - **Anr. Edn.** 1787. Vol. 5. Cont. bds. (R. Apr.4; 1672) DM 700
- - **Anr. Copy.** Vol. 4. Cont. bds. (R. Apr.4; 1671) DM 400
- - **Anr. Edn.** Brünn, 1788. Vol. 6. Cont. bds. (R. Apr.4; 1673) DM 700
- - **Anr. Edn.** Berlin, 1789. Vol. 15. Cont. leath., worn. (R. Oct.12; 1799) DM 400
- - **Anr. Edn.** Berlin, 1797. Vol. 26. Cont. leath., worn. (R. Oct.12; 1800) DM 700
- - **Anr. Edn.** 1800. Vol. 32. Cont. leath. (HK. Nov.8; 765) DM 500

- **Le Nouveau Buffon de la Jeunesse.** Paris, 1817. *3rd. Edn.* 4 vols. 42 engrs., tree cf.; Kenneth H. Oldaker copy. (P. Jan.12; 299) *Cavendish.* £60
- **Oeuvres.** Paris, 1774 & later. 57 vols. (of 90). 12mo. Cont. marb. cf., spines decor., slight defects; from Chateau des Noës liby. (HD. May 25; 8)
Frs. 5,000
- - **Anr. Edn.** Paris, 1835-6. 9 vols. Cont. cf.-bkd. bds., rubbed. (BBA. Jun.28; 267) *Dilua.* £90
- **Oeuvres Complètes.** Paris, 1774, 1790. 58 vols. 12mo. Many hand-cold. plts., mor., spines decor. (SM. Mar.7; 2432) Frs. 20,000
- - **Anr. Edn.** Ed.:- M.F. Cuvier. Paris, 1829. 24 vols. 4 maps & 196 plts. (91 cold.), old hf. roan, rubbed. (SM. Mar.7; 2073) Frs. 2,500
- - **Anr. Copy.** 26 vols. Lacks 2 engrs., some light foxing, publisher's bds. (HD. Jun.29; 33)
Frs. 2,000
- - **Anr. Edn.** Ed.:- [A. Comte] (suites). Ill.:- after V. Adam. Paris, 1835-36. *New Edn.* Vols. 4-6 (of 6). 4to. Some staining or foxing, some worming, cont. hf. leath., spine slightly defect., vol. 6 spine loose, bumped & rubbed. (D. Nov.23; 698)
DM 750
- - **Anr. Edn.** Ed.:- M. Flourens. Paris, 1853-55. 12 vols. 4to. Lightly browned thro.-out, cont. hf. leath., spine lightly faded. (HT. May 8; 224)
DM 1,000
- - **Anr. Edn.** Ed.:- M. Flourens. Paris, [1855?]. 12 vols. Lge. 8vo. Engraved frontis., port., 157 engraved plts., most hand-cold., some light foxing, a few ll. loose, cont. mor.-bkd. bds., slightly soiled & faded, 1 or 2 corners & spines chipped, Vol. VII with lr. cover stained. (CH. Sep.20; 4) Fls. 480
- - **Anr. Edn.** Paris, 1856. 6 vols. including plt. vol. Lge. 8vo. Cont. hf. roan, spines decor. (HD. Jun.6; 22) Frs. 2,200
- **Oeuvres Complètes, suivies de ses Continuateurs Daubenton, Lacépède, Cuvier, Dumeril, Poiret, Lesson et Geoffroy-St.-Hilaire.** Brüssel, 1828-33. *1st. Belgian Coll. Edn.* 14 vols & 6 plt. vols. Some foxing, especially plt. vols. 1-4, cont. hf. leath. gt., bumped, 3 spines lightly torn. (R. Apr.5; 1667a)
DM 3,000

BUFFON, Georges Louis Leclerc, Comte de (Text.)
See— KEEPSAKE D'HISTOIRE NATURELLE. Description des Mammifères

BUFFON, George Louis Leclerc, Comte de & D'Aubenton, Jean Louis Marie
- **De Algemeene on Byzondere Naturlyke Historie** .... Ill.:- Schley & Vinkeles. Amst., 1773. 4to. All plts., maps, vigs., etc. hand-cold., cont. mott. cf. gt., gt.-decor. spine, piece detchd. from spine & laid in loose. (CBA. Dec.10; 342) $225

BUGDELL, E.
- **A Letter to the Merchants & Tradesmen of Great Britain Particularly to those of London & Bristol.** L., 1733. 1 lf. of advts., lacks (?) blanks, hf. cf. (P. Nov.24; 188) *Quaritch.* £60

BUGENHAGEN, J.
- **Jonas Propheta Expositus.** Wittenberg, 1550. Lightly browned, title stpd., 19th. C. bds. (R. Apr.3; 23) DM 800

BUHLE, Christian Adam Adolph
[-] **Die Naturgeschichte in Getreuen Abbildungen** ... **Vögel.** Halberstadt, ca. 1831-40. Plt. vol. only. Engraved title, 182 hand-cold. engraved plts., some defaced by scribbling, some with nos. cut away by binder, some soiling & minor stains, disbnd., w.a.f. (RO. Dec.11; 63) $350

BUILDER'S PRACTICAL DIRECTORY (The)
[1855-57]. 4to. Litho. title, 179 plts. (many col.), tree cf. gt. (P. Feb.16; 222) £55

BUKOWSKI, Charles
- **At Terror Street & Agony Way.** Los Angeles, Black Sparrow Pr., 1968. *(75) numbered & sigd., with sigd. watercolor mntd. on 2nd. fly-lf. Out-of-series copy.* Cl., acetate d.-w.; marked 'for presentation'. (SG. Mar.1; 30) $200
- **It Catches my Heart in its Hands.** [New Orleans, 1963]. *[Ca. 20] sigd.* Lge. 8vo. Ptd. bds., d.-w.; poet's sig. dtd. 3 Aug. 1963, about 2 months earlier than 'First Printing, October 1963' on copyright p. (SG. May 24; 14) $110

BULKELEY, John & Cummings, John
- **A Voyage to the South-Seas in the Years 1740-1** .... L., 1743. *1st. Edn.* Cont. cf., rebkd. [Sabin 9108] (C. Nov.16; 58) *Brooke-Hitching.* £240

BULL, John Wrathall
- **Early Experiences of Life in South Australia** .... Adelaide, 1884. Orig. cl., unc. & unopened. (KH. Nov.9; 561) Aus. $110

BULLART, Isaac
- **Académie des Sciences et des Arts, contenant les Vies et les Eloges Historiques des Hommes Illustres.** Ill.:- E. de Bouloncis & N. de Larmessin. Bruxelles, 1682. 2 vols. Fo. Some stains & worming at foot, cont. cf., decor. spines, some defects. (HD. Jan.30; 35) Frs. 1,600

BULLEID, Arthur & St. George Gray, Harold
- **The Glastonbury Lake Village.** Glastonbury, 1911-17. 2 vols. 4to. Orig. cl. gt. (BBA. Nov.10; 316) *Museum Bookshop.* £90
- - **Anr. Copy.** 2 vols. 4to. Orig. cl. gt. (TA. Nov.17; 295) £66

BULLER, Walter L.
- **A History of the Birds of New Zealand.** Ill.:- Keulemans. L., [1887-]88. *2nd. Edn.* 2 vols. Lge. 4to. 2 litho. plts. of bones, 48 col. litho. plts., fore-edges foxed, hf. mor., orig. upr. wraps. bnd. in, ex-liby. (SG. Oct.6; 73) $900

BULLET, Pierre
- **Traité de L'Usage du Pantometre, Instrument Géometrique, Nouvellement Inventé par le Sr. Bullet.** Paris, 1675. *1st. Edn.* 12mo. Hf.-title, errata lf., cont. red mor. gt. (SG. Mar.22; 53) $325

BULLETIN MORGAND
Paris, 1883-1904, 1904-14. 15 vols. Hf. chagrin. (HD. Jun.6; 24) Frs. 6,200

BULLIARD, Pierre
- **Dictionnaire Elémentaire de Botanique.** Paris, 1783. *Orig. Edn.* Fo. Cont. bds., worn, spine torn. (HD. Dec.9; 7) Frs 1,400
- - **Anr. Copy.** 4to. Later vell. (G. Sep.15; 2083)
Sw. Frs. 600
- **Herbier de la France.** Paris, 1780. Fo. Hand-cold. title (stained), 308 hand-cold. plts., 6 ll. of table, hf. roan, covers detchd., as a coll. of plts., w.a.f. (P. Feb.16; 83) £800

BULLOCK, William
- **Six Months' Residence & Travels in Mexico; Containing Remarks on the Present State of New Spain.** L., 1824. Hf. mor. (LH. Sep.25; 192) $225

BULWER, John
[-] **Anthropometamorphosis; Man Transform'd; or, The Artificial Changeling by J.B. Sirnamed The Christopher.** 1650. *1st. Edn.* 12mo. Errata p. & 2 pp. advts. at end, mor. gt. by Rivière. (SKC. Mar.9; 1825) £380
- - **Anr. Edn.** L., [1653]. 4to. Plt. present at S2, lacks port., frontis., title-p., 3Z4 & 4F2-4G4, margin repairs, some staining, cont. cf., rebkd. [Wing B5461] (BBA. May 3; 19) *Rix.* £70
[-] **Chirologia ... whereunto is added Chironomia** .... L., 1644. *1st. Edn. of Pt. 2.* 2 pts. in 1 vol. Final errata lf. to each pt., tear in 1 ill., cont. sheep, spine defect. [Wing B 5462 & 5466] (C. Nov.9; 46)
Lawson. £330

BUNBURY, Henry William 'Geoffrey Gambado'
- **An Academy for Grown Horseman by Geoffrey Gambado.** L., 1787. *1st. Edn.* Fo. Frontis., 9 hand-cold. plts., text browned, dampstain to frontis., cont. mott. cf., worn. (PNY. Oct.20; 193) $200
- - **Anr. Edn.** 1812. *4th. Edn.* 4to. Col. frontis., ll col. plts., mod. hf. cf. gt. (P. Feb.16; 97) £75
- **An Academy for Grown Horsemen. - Annals of Horsemanship.** 1787, 1791. *1st. Edns.* 2 vols. 4to. 12 engraved plts. (1st. vol.), 17 engraved plts. (2nd. vol.), frontis. cropped, cont. cf.-bkd. marb. bds; Sir Ivar Colquhoun, of Luss, copies. (C.E. Mar.22; 42) £480
- - **Anr. Copy.** 2 vols. in 1. Fo. A few engraved plts. cropped, some spotting, mostly in 2nd. vol., cont. cf., rebkd. & reprd., preserving most of orig. spine. (S. Oct.4; 258) *Rhys-Jones.* £80
- - **Anr. Edn.** Ill.:- Rowlandson after Bunbury. L.,

BUNBURY, Henry William 'Geoffrey Gambado' - *Contd.*

1808. *3rd. Edn. (1st. work).* Together 2 vols. in l. Sm. fo. 29 stipple copperplts. in sepia, slightly foxed, bottom blank inner corner of 1 plt. neatly reprd., mod. gt. crushed hf. mor. & cl. (SG. Mar.15; 289) $130

– – **Anr. Edn.** 1812; [1791]. *4th. Edn., 1st. Edn.* 2 works in 1 vol. 4to. Corner of lp. missing (no loss to text), some margins with slight stains, cont. hf. cf. (SKC. Mar.9; 1766)   £110

– **Twenty-two Plates, Illustrative of ... The Plays of Shakespeare.** 1793-96. Lge. fo. Stipple engravings, some slight foxing thr.-out, hf. cf., brkn. (BS. May 2; 62)   £150

BUNCE, Daniel

– **Language of the Aborigines of the Colony of Victoria ....** Geelong, 1859. *'2nd. Edn.' [i.e. 3rd. Edn.].* Bds. (KH. May 1; 118)   Aus. $110

BUNDETO, Carlos

– **El Espejo de la Muerte.** Ill.:– Romain de Hooghe. Antw., 1700. 4to. Mor. (DS. Oct.28; 2269)
                                            Pts. 65,000

BUNON, R.

– **Expériencès et Démonstrations faites à l'Hôtel de la Salpêtrière & à S. Côme en Presence de l'Académie Royale de Chirurgie ... les Malédies des Dents.** Paris, 1746 [1747 at end]. *1st. Edn.* Approbation dtd. 31 Dec. 1745, Privilege 5 Apr. 1746, lp. with margin excision at foot, some slight foxing, cont. leath., bumped, spine defect. (R. Oct.12; 1504)
                                            DM 800

BUNSEN, Robert Wilhelm

– **Gasometrische Methoden.** Braunschweig, 1857. *1st. Edn.* Hf.-title, some foxing, cont. hf. cl. (SG. Oct.6; 74) $150

– – **Anr. Copy.** Some slight foxing, stp., cont. hf. linen. (D. Nov.23; 464)   DM 400

BUNTING, Heinrich

– **Itinerarium Sacrae Scripturae Das ist, Ein Reisebuch über die Gantze Heilige Schrifft.** Wittenberg, 1588. 4 pts. in 1 vol. Fo. Ptd. title in red & black, woodcut devices on sectional titles, 12 woodcut maps & plans (10 double-p.), some browning, some faint stains & underlinings in text, 1 or 2 minor tears without loss of ptd. surface, cont. blind-stpd. pig over wood bds., soiled. brass clasps (1 loose). (S. May 22; 273)   *Norwich.* £2,800

BUNYAN, John

– **The Acceptable Sacrifice.** L., 1689. *1st. Edn.* 12mo. Browned, some upr. margins shaved close, stitched with remains of old spine adhering, stitching brkn. [Wing B5480] (CSK. Dec.2; 184)
                                            £480

– **Den Heyligen Oorlogh.** Ill.:– Jan Luiken. Amst., 1685. *1st. Edn. in Dutch & 1st. Ill. Edn. 1st. Iss.* 12mo. Cont. vell. (VG. Nov.30; 932)   Fls. 525

– **The Jerusalem-Sinner Saved: or, Good News for the Vilest of Men ....** L., 1715. *9th. Edn.* 12mo. Ptd. advt. on recto of engraved port., browned, cont. spr. sheep, head of spine chipped. (S. Dec.13; 340)
                                       Veilbrief. £80

– **The Pilgrims Progress.** Ed.:– G.B. Harrison. Ill.:– after William Blake. N.Y., Ltd. Edns. Cl., 1941. *(1500).* 4to. Bdg. not stated, spine slightly darkening, extremities with light wear. (CBA. Nov.19; 330)   £110

[–] **Pilgrim's Progress, Masihi Musafir Ka Ahwal.** Lahore, 1880. In transliterated Urdu, 22 cold. plts., orig. cl.-bkd. bds. (BBA. Mar.7; 74a)
                                       Quaritch. £75

BUOCHENBACH, H.J. Breuning von und zu

– **Orientalische Reyss.** [Strassburg, 1612]. *1st. Edn.* Fo. Lacks engraved title's border, port. & folding. plt., 1st. ill. stained, several sm. margin tears, 3 ll. with margin repairs, last lf. with sm. hole, some slight browning & spotting, 4 ll. with lge. stain, cont. hf. leath., stained. (H. May 22; 296)
                                            DM 1,000

BUONAIUTI, B. S.

– **Italian Scenery.** Ill.:– J. Godley. L., 1806. *1st. Edn.* Fo. 30 (of 32) plts. in col. etching, light browning, some text ll. slightly foxed, 2 text ll.

defect in margins, mod. hf. linen, engraved title. wraps. pasted on, unc. (R. Apr.5; 2964)   DM 550

BUONAMICI, G.

– **Metropolitana di Ravenna Architettura.** Bologne, 1748. 2 vols. in 1. Fo. 1 plt. cut with loss, cont. vell. (HD. Dec.2; 75)   Frs. 1,700

BUONARRUOTI, F.

– **Osservazioni sopra Alcuni Frammenti di Vasi Antichi di vetro ornati di Figure trovati ne' Cimiteri di Roma.** Flor., 1716. 4to. 19th. C. hf. red mor. (D. Nov.23; 1971)   DM 700

BURBANK, Luther

– **His Methods & Discoveries & their Practical Application.** N.Y., 1914. 12 vols. Elab. blind-stpd. mott. sheep, sigd. (SPB. Dec.13; 515) $175

– – **Anr. Edn.** Ed.:– John Whitson & others. N.Y. & L., Luther Burbank Pr., 1914-15. *(250) numbered.* 12 vols. Mor., covers with double gt. rule & onlaid ornaments, gt.-tooled spines in 6 compartments, turn-ins gt., watered silk end-pp., red mor. gt. doubls., partly unc. (CNY. Dec.17; 541) $950

BURCKHARDT, J.

– **Der Cicerone. Eine Anleitung zum Genuss der Kunstwerke Italiens.** Basel, 1855. *1st. Edn.* Some light spotting, slightly loose in fold, cont. hf. leath., slightly rubbed. (H. May 22; 623)   DM 400

BURCKHARDT, Jakob

– **Weltgeschichtliche Betrachtungen.** München, Ruprecht Pr., 1928-29. *(150) numbered on Zandersbütten.* 4to. Hf. mor., cold. paper cover, gt. spine; Prinz Rupprecht ex-libris. (GB. May 5; 3189)
                                            DM 500

BURCKHARDT, John Lewis

– **Travels in Nubia.** L., 1819. *1st. Edn.* Tall 4to. Cont. marb. bds., cf. tips, rebkd. with new cl., ex-Liby; Sir Edward Synge armorial bkplt. (SG. Sep.22; 69) $175

– – **Anr. Edn.** 1822. *2nd. Edn.* 4to. Port. frontis., single-p. map, 2 folding linen-bkd. maps, some spotting, mainly to margins, cont. cf., rebkd. (TA. Mar.15; 21)   £145

– **Travels in Syria & the Holy Land; Published by the Association for Promoting the Discovery of the Interior Parts of Africa.** 1822. *[1st. Edn.].* 4to. Port. frontis., 2 folding linen-bkd. maps, 4 single-p. maps, some minor spotting, cont. cf., rebkd. (TA. Mar.15; 20)   £230

– – **Anr. Copy.** 4to. Lacks 1 map, slight spotting, hf. cf. (P. Sep.8; 199)   *Wood.* £130

– – **Anr. Copy.** 4to. Lacks 1 map, plts. & title foxed, offsetting, hf. cf. cover loose. (SG. Sep.22; 71)
                                            $200

BURCKHARDT, Rudolf F.

– **Gewirkte Bildteppiche des XV & XVI Jahrhunderts im Historiches Museum zu Basel.** Leipzig, 1923. Fo. Orig. cl. (BBA. Nov.10; 339)
                                       Schwarz. £70

– – **Anr. Copy.** Atlas fo. 25 cold. mntd. plts., ex-liby., pict. cl. (SG. May 3; 65) $250

BURDELL, Harvey & John

– **Observations on the Structure, Physiology, Anatomy, & Diseases of the Teeth.** N.Y., 1838. *1st. [& only] Edn.* 2 pts. in 1 vol. 1st. state(?), with woodcut on p. 78 unnumbered, some foxing, title & few other ll. stpd., orig. cl., worn; Milton Asbell bkplt. (SG. Oct.6; 75) $175

BURDSALL, Richard L. & Emmons, Arthur B.

– **Men Against the Clouds. The Conquest of Minya Konka.** L., 1935. *1st. Engl. Edn.* Orig. cl., faded. (BBA. May 3; 342)   *Losain's Books.* £50

BURE, Guillaume-François de

– **Bibliographie Instructive ou Traité de la Connaissance des Livres Rares et Singuliers. Supplément à la Bibliographie Instructive ou Catalogue des Livres de M. Gaignat.** Paris, 1763-69; 1782. 10 vols. Cont. cf. gt., decor. spines. (HD. Sep.22; 201) Frs. 2,500

– **Catalogue des Livres Provenans de la Bibliothèque ... Duc de la Vallière.** Paris, 1767. 2 vols. Sm. 4to. Sale catalogue, priced, mod. cl. (BBA. Mar.7; 289)
                                      W. Forster. £60

– **Catalogue des Livres Rares et Precieux de M.*** Paris, 1780. 2 pts. in 1 vol. Priced in ink, slightly

browned, mod. wraps. (BBA. Mar.7; 288)
                                 Questor Books. £60

BUREAU OF AMERICAN ETHNOLOGY

– **Annual Reports.** Wash., 1883-1930/31. 2nd.-48th. Years: 53 vols. Cl., last 4 vols. in new buckram, ex-liby. (SG. Aug.4; 60) $950

BURGER, F. (Ed.)

See— HANDBUCH DER

BURGER, Gottfried August

– **Gedichte.** Ill.:– D. Chodowiecki. Göttingen, 1778. *1st. Edn.* Slightly foxed, cont. hf. leath. gt., slightly bumped; ex-libris; Hauswedell coll. (H. May 24; 1242)   DM 1,200

– – **Anr. Copy.** Some copper engrs. slightly weak, 1 copper engr. in dupl., some slight foxing, red mor. gt., ca. 1800. (D. Nov.24; 2239)   DM 460

– – **Anr. Edn.** Ill.:– Joh. H. Meil & Riepenhausen after D. Chodowiecki. Göttingen, 1789. Some ll. pt. 2 completed in lr. margin, foxing & soiling, cont. hf. leath. gt., reprd.; Hauswedell coll. (H. May 24; 1243)   DM 750

– – **Anr. Edn.** Ed.:– K. von Reinhard. Berlin, 1823. *De Luxe Edn. on L.P. vell.* 2 vols. Some sigs. washed, cont. red mor., elab. gt. spine, cover, inner & outer dentelles, cold. end-papers & doubl., slightly rubbed, foxing cont.; Paul Hirsch ex-libris; Hanswedell coll. (H. May 24; 1244)   DM 3,600

– **Leonora.** Trans.:– W.R. Spencer. Ill.:– after Lady Diana Beauclerc. 1796. Fo. In German & Engl., hf. cf.; Sir Ivar Colquhoun, of Luss copy. (CE. Mar.22; 42a)   £140

– **Sämmtliche Schriften.** Ed.:– K. Reinhard. Ill.:– Kohl after Kininger & Fiorillo. Wien, 1796-98 (Ptd. title VI 1799). 6 vols. Vol. VI with supp. Lenore. Wien, 1798, minimal foxing, cont. mor., elab. gt., gt. inner & outer dentelles, cold. paper end-ll. & doubls.; Hauswedell coll. (H. May 24; 1241)   DM 3,800

– **Wunderbare Reisen zu Wasser und Lande, Feldzüge und Lustige Abenteuer des Freiherrn von Münchhausen.** Ill.:– W. Klemm. Weimar, 1923. *Numbered Iss. This copy unnumbered.* 4to. 52 orig. woodcuts monogrammed by artist, orig. hf. mor., gt. cover vig. (GB. May 5; 2799)   DM 500

BURGER, L.

– **Die Königl. Preussische Armee in Ihrer Neuesten Uniformierung.** Berlin, ca. 1865. Title lf. slightly foxed, 'Orig. portfo., in s.-c. (HK. Nov.9; 1880)
                                            DM 850

BURGERMEISTER, J.S.

– **Bibliotheca Equestris.** Ulm, 1720. *1st. Edn.* 2 vols. 4to. Cont. vell. (R. Apr.3; 1054)   DM 1,000

BURGGRAV, Johann Ernst

[–] **Introductio in Vitalem Philosophiam cui Cohaeret Omnium Morborum Astralium et Materialium ....** Frankfurt, 1623. 4to. Title border shaved, some marginalia touched by binder, bds., roan spine; Radcliffe liby. stp., Dr. Walger Pagel copy. (S. Feb.7; 68)   *Gurney.* £420

BURGHER, Ed.

– **Zehn Aquatinta-Radierungen zur Antigone.** N.p., n.d. *(75) numbered, with etchings sigd. & numbered.* Fo. 10 aquatint etchings, Lacks text, orig. silk portfo. (HK. Nov.11; 3383)   DM 1,100

BURGHEIM, Julius

– **Sammlung leicht auszuführender Grab-Monumente aufgenommen auf den vorzüglichsten Kirchhöfen Deutschlands und Frankreichs.** Bielefeld, 1837. Pts. 1-2 (all publd.). 4to. Old liby. stp., cont. hf. leath., spine slightly defect., orig. wraps. bnd. in. (GB. Nov.3; 873)   DM 450

BURGKMAIR, Hans

– **Images de Saints et Saintes issus de la Famille de l'Empereur Maximilien I.** Vienna, 1799. Fo. Lacks 7 plts., upr. margin stained, light foxing, 19th. C. vell. (HK. Nov.8; 131a)   DM 2,500

– **Kaiser Maximilians I. Triumph. Triomphe de l' Empereur Maximilien.** Vienna, 1796. *1st. Edn.* Fo. 135 woodcut plts., title-p. & folios A & B slightly damaged & reprd. but with minor loss of text on folio A, folios K-Q misbnd. before folios A-I, 19th. C. hf. cf. cf., slightly worn; bkplt. of Merry of Waterford & Seville. (S. May 10; 238)   *Erlini.* £2,800

See— **VOGTHERR, Heinrich & Burgkmair, Hans**

BURGOYNE, Lieut.-Gen. John
- **A State of the Expedition from Canada, as laid before the House of Commons.** Ill.:– W. Faden. L., 1780. *1st. Edn.* 4to. Lge. folding engraved map, 5 folding battle plans, 2 with overslips, all with hand-cold. details, some slight spotting to text, cont. spr. cf. gt. by C. Kalthoeber, with his ticket, head of spine just chipped; Chillingham Castle bkplt., the Rt. Hon. Visc. Eccles copy. [Sabin 9255] (CNY. Nov.18; 37) $1,400
– – **Anr. Copy.** Lge. 4to. Tall copy, 2 maps with overlays, 5 maps partly hand-cold. in outl., orig. two-tone bds., unc., some spotting on covers, spine chipped, mor. gt. & cl. s.-c. [Sabin 9255] (SG. Nov.3; 31) $1,100
– – **Anr. Copy.** 4to. 4 (of 6?) maps, each partly hand-cold., 2 with overlays, early cf., worn, cover detchd. [Sabin 9255] (SG. Jan.19; 121) $225
– – **Anr. Copy.** Lge. 4to. folding engraved map, 5 folding battle plans, 2 with overslips (detchd.), all with hand-cold. details, offsetting to 1st. map, some slight spotting to text. [Sabin 9255] *(Bound with:)* HOWE, Visc. William – **The Narrative of Lieut. Gen. Sir William Howe ... relative to His Conduct, during his late command of the King's Troops in North America.** L., 1780. *1st. Edn.* 1st. 2 ll. with slight tears at inner margin, last lf. dustsoiled on verso & with sm. hole causing loss of 8 letters, stabbed. [Sabin 33342] *(Folded & bound in:)* SAYER, Robert & Bennett, John, Publishers – **The Theatre of War in North America ...** L., 20 Nov. 1776. Sheet size 725 x 515mm. (map measuring 420 x 513mm.). Engraved map, hand-cold. in outl., 2 inset panels, below a 3 column panel of text 'A Compendious Account of the British Colonies in North America', sm. inset table at foot, 1½ inch tear at foot of centrefold. [Sabin 15040] Together 3 works in 1 vol. 4to. Near-cont. hf. cf. gt., mor. spine label lettered 'American Campaigns', upr. jnt. brkn., extremities worn; owner's inscrs. on titles of both books of members of the Bence family, the Rt. Hon. Visc. Eccles copy. (CNY. Nov.18; 5) $2,500

BURGUES DE MISSIESSY, Edouard
- **Arrimage des Vaisseaux.** Paris, 1789. 4to. Sm. stain to 1 plt., old roan, spine decor. (HD. Mar.9; 59) Frs. 1,800
- **Installation des Vaisseaux.** Paris, 1798. 4to. Old hf. roan, spine decor. (HD. Mar.9; 58) Frs. 3,200

BURGUNDIA, Antonius a
- **Mundi Lapis Lydius sive Vanitas per Veritatem Falsi Accusata & Convicta.** Antw., 1639. *1st. Edn.* 4to. Engraved title, 50 engrs., all hand-cold., a few underlinings, some ll. slightly stained, later hf. vell. (VG. Nov.30; 598) Fls. 660

BURGY, A. de
- **Catalogus van de Weergalooze en Eenigste Volkoome Verzameling der Printkunst van Rembrandt.** Den Hang, 1755. Cont. leath. (R. Apr.3; 893) DM 850

BURK, John
- **The History of Virginia.** Petersburg, 1804-05-16. *1st. Edn.* 4 vols. Folding table in Vol. 3 (not called for by Sabin or Howes), errata lf. at end Vol. 4, browning in Vol. 4, Vols. 1 & 2 cont. cf., Vols. 3 & 4 cont. sheep (spine ends chipped); the Rt. Hon. Visc. Eccles copy. [Sabin 9273] (CNY. Nov.18; 38) $320

BURKE, Edmund
- [-] **A Philosophical Enquiry into the Origin of Our Ideas of the Sublime & Beautiful.** L., 1757. *1st. Edn.* Hf.-title, cont. cf., worn, cover detchd.; R.B. Adam bkplt. (SG. Oct.27; 45) $175
- **Reflections on the Revolution in France.** 1790. *1st. Edn.* 1st. ll. annotated, cont. cf., gt. spine, rubbed, hinges reprd., s.-c. (BBA. Jun.28; 16)
R. Parsons. £220
– – **Anr. Copy.** Floral ornament on p. iv. facing right, & catchword 'of' on p. 103, some early penned notes in margins, lacks hf.-title, later three-qtr. mor. (RO. Dec.11; 64) $275
– – **Anr. Copy.** Some light foxing, hf. mor. (SG. Feb.9; 178) $225
– – **Anr. Edn.** 1790. *1st. Edn. 1st. Iss.* 4 cancel ll.,

few ll. slightly spotted, cont. hf. cl., rebkd. & reprd., author's sig. inserted. (BBA. Oct.27; 35)
Spencer. £140
– – **Anr. Edn.** Dublin, 1790. *1st. Dublin Edn.* Cont. tree cf., bkplt. (GM. Dec.7; 206) $50
– – **Anr. Edn.** L., 1790; 1796. *1st. Edns. 1st. Iss. (2nd. work).* 2 works in 1 vol. 2nd. work, hf.-title, sig. on title, little spotting, cont. mott. cf., rebkd.; bkplt. of William John Darby. (S. Apr.10; 349)
Thoemmes. £80
- **The Speeches of ....** L., 1816. 4to. Hf. cf., armorial motif on spine. (GM. Dec.7; 411) £85
[-] **Storia degli Stabilimente Europei in America.** Venice, 1763. 2 vols. Cont. cf.-bkd. bds., slightly rubbed. (S. Jun.25; 158) *Scott.* £50
- **Two Letters Addressed to a Member of the Present Parliament ....** L., 1796. *1st. Edn.* 1 vol. Wraps., frayed. *(With:)* - **A Third Letter to a Member of the Present Parliament ...** L., 1797. *1st. Edn.* 1 vol. Hf. leath., very worn. (SG. Feb.9; 180) $110
- **The Works ....** 1801. 8 vols. Cont. mott. cf.; Sir Ivar Colquhoun, of Luss copy. (CE. Mar.22; 44) £270

See— **BURNABY, Rev. A.** – **BURKE, Edmund**

BURKE, H. Farnham
- **The Coronation of Their Majesties King Edward VII & Queen Alexandra in 1902.** L., priv. ptd., 1904. Plts. hand-cold., three-qtr. red Morrocan leath., gt.-embossed, boxed. (DM. May 21; 60) $175
- **The Historical Record of the Coronation etc.** Priv. ptd., 1902. 24 x 18 inches. No bdg. stated. (JN. Mar.3; 223) £120
– – **Anr. Edn.** Ill.:– A. Pearse. L., [1911]. Fo. Port. frontis., 20 mntd. plts., maroon lev., gt. fillet borders with 2 crowned monogs., spine & dentelles gt., moire satin doubls. & end-ll. (SG. Feb.16; 68) $100

BURKE, Rev. William P.
- **History of Clonmel.** Waterford, 1907. *1st. Edn.* 4to. Vell. (GM. Dec.7; 444) £340

BURKEL, Heinrich
- **Ein Mahlerleben der Biedermeierzeit von Luigi v. Buerkel.** München, 1940. 4to. Orig. linen, orig. wraps. (GB. Nov.4; 1410) DM 480

BURLEIGH, Walter
- **Expositio in Artem Veterem Porphyrii et Aristotelis.** Venice, B. Locatellus for O. Scotus, 8 Jul. 1488. Sm. fo. Lacks 1st. & last blanks, holes in 1st. 3 ll. reprd. with some loss of text, some smaller repairs, some stains, old margin annots., old Cistercian liby stp. in lr. margin of 1st. 2 ll., mod. blind-stpd. cf., cl. box. (VG. Mar.19; 149)
Fls. 750

BURLEUS, G.
- **Expositiones super Decem Libros....** 18 Jul. 1521. Fo. 16th. C. blind-stpd. vell., spine worn. (HD. Jun.29; 34) Frs. 1,000

BURLEY, Walter
- **Expositio in Aristotelis Physica.** Padua, Bonus (Gallus) de Francia & Thomas ex Capitaneis de Aaula, 18 Jul. 1476. *1st. Edn.* Fo. Tall copy, capital spaces, lr. margins damp damaged thro.-out, especially at beginning & end, lr. margins of 31 ll. renewed, 1 lf. reprd. at upr. margin, sm. wormhole in inner margin of last few ll., 18th. C. vell., foot of spine torn; John D. Stanitz coll. [BMC VII, 918; Goff B1302] (SPB. Apr.25; 74) $2,900
- **Expositio in Octo Libros Aristotelis Physica.** Ed.:– Nicoletus Vernia. Venice, Bonetus Locatellus for Octavianus Scotus, 2 Dec. 1491. Fo. Slight worming at front, some stains mostly at end, a few ll. browned, new hf. leath. over cont. bds., folding box; Paolo Giovio's copy, owners inscr. dtd. 1506 on fly-lf., John D. Stanitz coll. [Goff B1305] (SPB. Apr.25; 75) $1,500

BURLINGTON, C. & others
- **The Modern Universal British Traveller.** 1779. Fo. Map, 96 engraved views, many torn & crudely reprd., map, title & some text defect., bdg. not stated, as a coll. of plts., w.a.f. (P. Jul.5; 230) £130
– – **Anr. Edn.** [1779]. Fo. 2 plts. torn, some stains, cont. cf. (P. Sep.29; 197) *Hadden.* £200

BURLINGTON FINE ARTS CLUB
- **Catalogue of a Collection of European Enamels ... to the End of the XVII Century.** 1897. Lge. 4to. Orig. cl., slightly rubbed & faded. (S. Apr.30; 168)
Acanthus. £70
– – **Anr. Copy.** Fo. 72 plts., buckram gt., soiled, lr. cover loose. (SG. Oct.13; 149) $100
- **Catalogue of an Exhibition of Carvings in Ivory.** 1923. 4to. Orig. cl., lightly soiled. (CSK. Jan.27; 15) £110
- **Exhibition of a Collection of Silversmiths' Work of European Origin.** L., 1901. Fo. 120 plts., buckram gt., worn & soiled. (SG. Oct.13; 314) $110
- **Exhibition of English Mezzotint Portraits Circa 1750 to Circa 1830.** 1902. Fo. 30 plts., orig. buckram gt., unc., unopened. (SKC. Jan.13; 2104) £50
- **Exhibition of the Faience of Persia & the Nearer East.** Intro.:– C.H. Read. L., 1908. Fo. 27 plts., gt.-lettered cl., bumped. (SG. Jan.26; 142) $220
- **Exhibition of Illuminated Manuscripts.** L., 1908. Fo. Some ll. spotted, liby. stp. on title, orig. cl. (BBA. Apr.5; 273) *Hartley.* £90
- **Illustrated Catalogue of Bookbindings.** 1891. Fo. Orig. buckram, rebkd. with mor.; H.M. Nixon coll., with his sig., MS. annots. & corrections. (BBA. Oct.6; 18) *Lyon.* £420

BURMEISTER, Hermann
- **Erläuterungen zur Fauna Brasiliens.** Berlin, 1856. Lge. fo. Few text ll. lightly foxed, not sewed, unc. (R. Oct.12; 1805) DM 460

BURNABY, Rev. Andrew
- **Travels through the Middle Settlements in North America.** 1775. *[2nd. Edn.].* 4to. Errata lf., mod. hf. cf. [Sabin 9359] (P. Dec.8; 354)
Walford. £170
– – **Anr. Copy.** Hf.-title, errata lf. at end, cont. cf. gt., a little rubbed on spine. (LC. Mar.1; 458) £60

BURNE-JONES, Sir Edward
- **The Beginning of the World. Twenty-Five Pictures ....** Intro.:–Georgiana Burne-Jones. 1902. *Ltd. Edn.* Fo. Orig. bds., linen backstrip, untrimmed, a little soiled & rubbed. (TA. Jun.21; 544) £55
– – **Anr. Edn.** Ill.:– after Burne-Jones. L., 1902. 4to. Orig. hf. cl. & bds., unopened. (CBA. Aug.21; 74) $100
- **The Flower Book.** 1905. *(300) numbered.* 4to. Orig. mor. gt., spine faded, end-papers lightly spotted. (CSK. Aug.5; 113) £500
– – **Anr. Copy.** 4to. 38 cold. plts., mor. gt., partly unc., cl. folding-case, little worn. (SG. Apr.26; 36) $1,100

BURNE-JONES, Sir Edward (Ill.)
See— **CHAUCER, Geoffrey**
See— **MORRIS, William**
See— **PAGEANT, The**
See— **STUDIO: An Illustrated Magazine of Fine & Applied Art**

BURNES, Alexander
- **Cabool.** 1842. Some light soiling, cont. hf. mor.; inscr. on behalf of author. (CSK. Sep.30; 36) £85

BURNET, Bp. Gilbert
- **History of His Own Time.** 1724-34. *1st. Edn.* 2 vols. Fo. Subscribers list in each vol., MS. note on verso of Vol. 2 title, cont. cf.; Sir Samuel Hoare bkplt. (SKC. May 4; 1582) £80
– – **Anr. Copy.** 2 vols. Fo. Without list of subscribers, slightly dampstained thro.-out, cont. cf., spines gt., slightly rubbed. (BBA. Nov.30; 210) *Matthews.* £55
- **The History of the Reformation of the Church of England.** 1681-1715. *2nd. Edn.* 3 vols. including supp. Sm. fo. Cont. cf., rebkd. (BBA. Jul.27; 108) *Howes.* £75
- **Some Letters Containing an Account of ... Switzerland, Italy, & c.** N.p., 1687. 12mo. A10 reprd., few margins browned & frayed, cont. cf., worn. [Wing B 5917] (SG. Oct.27; 46) $120

BURNET, Jacob
- **Notes on the Early Settlement of the North-Western Territory.** Cincinnati, 1847. *1st. Edn.* With the errata slip before the Appendix & 14 p. publishers catalogue, port., some foxing, orig. cl., slightly worn & spotted; inscr. & sigd. on front free

BURNET, Jacob -*Contd.*

end-paper 'the Hon. William Woodbridge (Governor of Michigan) with the regards of his friend, J. Burnet'. (SG. Apr.5; 29) $130

BURNET, John & others
[-] **Engravings from the Pictures of the National Gallery.** L., 1840. Fo. 29 mntd. engraved plts. on India paper, most spotted, mor. gt. by Rivière, slightly rubbed; bkplt. of Sydney Courtauld. (S. Oct.4; 135) *Nolan.* £160

BURNET, Thomas
– **The Theory of the Earth; Containing an Account of the Origin of the Earth, & of All the General Changes which it hath already undergone.** L., 1697. *3rd. Edn.* 2 pts. in 1 vol. Fo. Cont. cf., lightly worn; Duke of Kent & Earl de Grey bkplts. [Wing B5953] (PNY. Oct.20; 194) $125

BURNETT, Frances Hodgson
– **The Secret Garden.** Ill.:– Charles Robinson. L., 1911. *1st. Robinson Trade Edn.* Some slight darkening & soiling, gt.-decor. cl., owner's stp. on front free end-paper. (CBA. Aug.21; 548) $100

BURNETT, James, Lord Monboddo
[–] **Of the Origin & Progress of Language.** Edinb., 1773. *1st. Edn.* 3 vols. Cont. cf., spines gt.; Sir Ivar Colquhoun, of Luss copy. (CE. Mar.22; 48) £200

BURNETT, W.
See— **DUGDALE, Thomas & Burnett, W.**

BURNETT, William Hickling
– **Views of Cintra.** Ca. 1835. Fo. 14 litho. plts., 1 plt. slightly foxed, a few spotted in margins, 19th. C. hf. mor. (SKC. Nov.18; 2001) £110
– – **Anr. Edn.** Ill.:– Hullmandel after Burnett. L., [1836]. Fo. Dedication & 14 hand-cold. litho. views on India paper, mor. gt., orig. ptd. wraps. bnd. in, cl. s.-c. (C. Jun.27; 16) *Maggs.* £1,200

BURNEY, Dr. Charles
– **A General History of Music, from the Earliest Ages to the Present Period.** 1776-89. *[1st. Edn.].* 4 vols. 4to. Cont. spr. cf., spine ends reprd., new labels. (TA. May 17; 602) £370
– – **Anr. Copy.** 4 vols. 4to. 13 engraved & woodcut plts., engraved & woodcut music, subscribers list, errata-lf. at end of Vol. I, II, & IV, slight browning, 19th. C. pol. cf., gt.; bkplt. recording in Latin gift of books to (Sir) Walter Morley Fletcher from M.R. James in 1904. (S. May 10; 27) *Maggs.* £300
– – **Anr. Copy.** 4 vols. 4to. 13 engraved & woodcut plts. (lacks plt. III in Vol. I, but with dupl. of frontis. in vol. II inserted in Vol. III), list of subscribers, errata-lf, at end Vol. I, II & IV, folding ptd. table 'Des douze termes du Yang et du Yn' (with pencil inscr. 'Journal des Scavans Juillet 1789') inserted at end of Vol. I, a few cont. MS. notes in Vol. I, slight browning, 19th. C. panel. cf. gt., slightly rubbed. (S. May 10; 26) *Scott.* £260
– – **Anr. Copy.** 4 vols. 4to. Frontis., margins spotted, 19th. C. hf. cf., slightly rubbed. (C. May 30; 142) *Maggs.* £200
– **The Present State of Music in France & Italy.** 1771. *1st. Edn.* Advt. lf., cont. cf., spine gt.; Sir Ivar Colquhoun, of Luss copy. (CE. Mar.22; 48a) £260
– **The Present State of Music in Germany. The Netherlands & United Provinces.** 1773. *1st. Edn.* 2 vols. Proposals, errata & advt. pp., bookseller's stp. on title-pp., anr. stp. on fly-ll., cont. hf. cf., worn, hinges brkn. (SKC. Mar.9; 1886) £75

BURNEY, Fanny (Pseud.)
See— **D'ARBLAY, Frances 'Fanny Burney'**

BURNEY, James
– **A Chronological History of the Discoveries in the South Seas.** L., 1808-13. Vols. 1-3 only (of 5). 4to. 34 engraved plts. & maps, many folding, liby. stp. on recto of frontis. in Vol. 1 & all plts. in Vol. 3, some ll. soiled, cont. hf. roan, unc., worn, covers detchd., 1 lacking. (BBA. Mar.21; 78) *Simper.* £85
– **History of the Buccaneers of America.** L., 1816. 4to. Title slightly soiled, 1 folding map with sm.

holes & tears, laid down, hf. mor., unc., worn. (S. Jun.25; 86) *Scott.* £110

BURNEY, Sarah Harriet
– **Traits of Nature.** 1812. *1st. Edn.* 5 vols. Hf.-titles, slightly spotted, cont. hf. cf., spine gt., slightly rubbed. (BBA. Jun.28; 18) *T. Scott.* £90

BURNOUF, Eugene & Jacquet, E.
– **L'Inde Française ....** Ill.:– Marlet, after Bardel, Geringer, & others. Paris, 1827-35. 17 pts. only (of 25), in 1 vol. Fo. 100 (of 102) Hand-cold. litho. plts., lacks title & introductory ll., cont. red mor.-bkd. bds., w.a.f. (C. Nov.16; 59) *Shapero.* £290

BURNS, Edward
– **The Coinage of Scotland ....** Edinb., 1887. *(500).* 3 vols. 4to. 78 plts. in Vol. 3, hf. mor. gt. (PD. May 16; 167) £280
– – **Anr. Copy.** 3 vols. 4to. Cont. hf. mor.; compliments slip from family of Mr. Coats tipped in at front end-paper. (CSK. Jun.1; 43) £190

BURNS, Robert
– **Poems, chiefly in the Scottish Dialect.** Edinb., 1787. *2nd. (1st. Edinb.) Edn.* Hf.-title, subscribers list, 'Boxburgh' & 'skinking' readings, mod. mott. cf. by Riviere; Diocese of Southwark copy. (C. May 30; 130) *Traylen.* £140
– – **Anr. Copy.** 1st Iss. Subscribers list, cont. tree cf., spine rubbed. (TA. Feb.16; 206) £90
– – **Anr. Copy.** Iss. with reading 'Duke of Boxburgh' on p. xxxvii & 'stinking' on p. 263. Minor foxing, cf., defect. (PD. Aug.17; 157) £60
– – **Anr. Copy.** 1st. Iss. With 'Boxburgh' in subscribers' list & 'stinking' p.263, port., hf.-title, later mott. cf., spine gt., jnts. worn. (SG. Apr.19; 47) £200
– – **Anr. Edn.** L., 1787. *3rd. Edn. 1st. Iss.* Subscribers list, cont. mott. cf. gt., spine rubbed. (TA. Feb.16; 207) £50
– **Poems. – Poems Chiefly in the Scottish Dialect.** Edinb., 1787. *1st. Edinb. Edn.; 3rd. Edn.* Together 2 vols. 1st. work, with 'stinking' & 'Boxburgh', subscribers'list, engraved port.-frontis., hf.-title soiled, some spotting, old cf., unc., rebkd., 2nd. work, frontis.-port., hf.-title, subscribers' list, few ll. spotted, cf. gt. by Morrell. (SPB. May 16; 18) £250
– **Works.** L'pool., 1800. *1st. Coll. Edn.* 4 vols. Ink inscrs. on title & frontis., foxed, later diced cf., blind-& gt.-decor., gt. & blind dentelles. (CBA. Dec.10; 123) $160
– **Complete Works.** Phila., 1896. *'Ellisland' Edn., (50).* 6 vols. in 12. Gt.-decor. mor., trs. silk doubls. (PNY. Oct.20; 181) $400
– **The Complete Writings.** Boston & N.Y., 1926. *(750) on L.P. for America.* 10 vols. Hf. mor. gt. by Riverside Pr., gt. design on spines. (SPB. May 17; 722) $450

BURNS, Rev. Thomas
– **Old Scottish Communion Plate ....** Edinb., 1892. *(175) numbered.* 4to. Hf. mor. gt. (PD. May 16; 181) £90

BURR, Mrs. A.W.
[–] **Sketches.** Ca. 1850. Lge. fo. List of plts. (foxed & lr. margin defect.), 14 hand-cold. litho. plts. mntd. on 12 sheets, mounts foxed but plts. generally clean, lacks ptd. title, loose in orig. portfo., covers detchd. (S. May 22; 271) *Rostron.* £1,400

BURR, Aaron
– **The Private Journal. Reprinted in Full from the Original Manuscript in the Library of William K. Bixby. of St. Louis, Mo. ....** Rochester, 1903. *1st. Unexpurgated Edn. (250) numbered & initialled by Bixby.* 2 vols. 4to. Orig. qtr. cl., bds.; both vols. inscr. & sigd. by Bixby to Frederic A. Delano; Delano bkplt. in 1 vol.; from liby of F.D. Roosevelt, inscr. 'To my distinguished nephew--The President (Franklin D. Roosevelt)--from Frederic A. Delano, Jan. 12/41'. (SG. Mar.15; 6) $400

BURR, Thomas Benge
– **The History of Tunbridge Wells.** 1766. Qtr. cf. (PWC. Jul.11; 579) £76

BURRARD, Gerald
– **The Modern Shotgun.** N.Y., 1931-32. *1st. Amer. Edn.* 3 vols. Cl., ex-liby. (SG. Mar.15; 253) $100

BURRIEL, Andres Marco
[–] **Paleografia Española ... [por] Estevan Terreros y Pando.** Madrid, 1758. *1st. Edn.* 4to. Lge. copy, errata lf., title rehinged, old vell. (SG. Nov.3; 194) $375

BURROUGHS, Edgar Rice
– **Tarzan of the Apes.** Chic., 1914. *1st. Edn.,. 2nd. Printing.* Bdg. not stated, covers very lightly soiled, spine fading & leaning slightly, label residue to spine foot, liby. bkplt., card, pocket & due slip on end-papers with no other markings, circulated; sigd. pres. copy from author to R.H. Davies. (CBA. Oct.29; 170) $2,000
– – **Anr. Edn.** Chic., 1914. *1st. Edn.* With Old Engl. Type on copyright p., without acorn on spine, slight browning, orig. cl., light soiling, Fred A. Berne copy. (SPB. May 16; 193) $750
– **Tarzan the Untamed.** Ill.:– J. Allen St. John. Chic., 1920. *1st. Edn.* Bdg. not stated, jacket rubbed, clawed, chipped & soiled, few spots to covers, tiny tear to front outer joint. (CBA. Oct.29; 174) $425

BURROUGHS, John
– **Works.** Boston, 1905-13. 23 vols. only (of 27). Three-qtr. mor., spines gt. (PNY. Oct.20; 182) $350
– **The Writings.** Boston & N.Y., 1904. *'Autograph' Edn.,. (750) numbered & sigd. by author & publisher.* 15 vols. Lev. mor., gt.-decor., onlaid mor. ornament, spines in 5 compartments, gt.-decor., turn-ins gt., lev. mor. doubls., silk markers, watered silk linings, partly unc. (CNY. Dec.17; 542) $850

BURROUGHS, John (Text)
See— **HARRIMAN ALASKA EXPEDITION**

BURROW, J.C. and Thomas, W.
– **'Mongst mines & miners; or Underground Scenes by Flashlight a series of Photographs.** L. and Camborne, 1893. Lge. 4to. Mntd. photo frontis., folding plan, 26 mntd. photos on 13 ll., some light spotting, orig. cl., lightly soiled. (CSK. Jul.27; 153) £360

BURROWS, George Man
– **Commentaries on the Causes, Forms, Symptoms, & Treatment, Moral & Medical, of Insanity.** L., 1828. *1st. Edn.* Lacks front free end-paper & hf.-title, orig. qtr. cl.; Dr. S. E. Lawton bkplt. (SG. Mar.22; 54) $200

BURRUS, Ernest J.
– **Kino & the Cartography of Northwestern New Spain.** Tuscon, 1965. *(750).* Fo. Cl. (LH. Sep.25; 193) $130
– – **Anr. Edn.** Tucson, 1965. *1st. Edn. (750), sigd. by author on title-p.* Sm. fo. Gt. pictor. rose cl., sm. scratch on upr. cover. (SG. Apr.5; 9) $110

BURTHOGGE, Richard
– **An Essay upon Reason & the Nature of Spirits.** 1694. *1st. Edn.* 1st. 10 ll. frayed, fly-lf. defect., dampstained, old cf., worn. [Wing B6150] (BBA. Jul.27; 111) *Waterfield.* £150

BURTIN, François Xavier
– **Oryctographie de Bruxelles ou Description des Fossiles.** Brussels, 1784. Fo. Engraved title, 32 cold. plts., slight spotting & soiling, cont. bds., rebkd. with cf., unc. (S. Nov.28; 12) *Quaritch.* £240

BURTON, A. (Pseud.)
See— **MITFORD, John 'A. Burton'**

BURTON, Lady Isabel
– **The Life of Captain Sir Richard F. Burton.** [1st. Edn.], 1893. 2 vols. Recent cl. (TA. Apr.19; 12) £52
– – **Anr. Copy.** 2 vols. Orig. cl. gt., slightly worn. (S. Dec.13; 172) *Jongsma.* £50
– **The Passion-Play at Ober-Ammergau.** Ed.:– W.H. Wilkins. L., 1900. Orig. cl., spine faded & chipped, liby. bkplt. on front pastedown. (SG. Sep.22; 73) $225

BURTON, Rev. John, 1696-1771
– **The Duty & Reward of Propagating Principles of Religion & Virtue in the History of Abraham. A Sermon ....** L., Ptd. by J. March & Sold by Mount & Page, 1733. *1st. Edn.* 4to. Lacks final blank, fore-margin of last lf. cut close, maroon hf. mor. by

Sangorski & Sutcliffe; the Rt. Hon. Visc. Eccles copy. [Sabin 9492 (with different printer in imprint)] (CNY. Nov.18; 41) $420

BURTON, John
- **Landschafts Maler nach der Natur.** Leipzig, ca. 1790. Ob. fo. 1st. lf. loose, lightly soiled, some slight foxing, loose, cont. wraps., lacks spine. (HK. Nov.9; 1583) DM 400

BURTON, John Hill
- **History of Scotland.** Edinb., [1873]. *New Edn.* 9 vols., including index. Sm. 8vo. Cf. gt. by Seton & Mackenzie. (SG. Feb.16; 50) $225

BURTON, Sir Richard Francis
- **The Book of the Sword.** L., 1884. *1st. Edn.* Ills., few light spots, orig. cl., slightly worn. (S. Apr.9; 7) *Trophy.* £120
- **The City of the Saints & Across the Rocky Mountains to California.** 1861. *1st. Edn.* Hf.-title, slight spotting, orig. cl. gt. (SKC. Mar.9; 2002) £120
- **Explorations of the Highlands of Brazil.** L., 1867. 2 vols. Folding map reprd., some spotting, mod. hf. cf., ex-liby. (CSK. Nov.25; 65) £90
- **Falconry in the Valley of the Indus.** 1852. 12mo. Hf.-title, last 4 advt. ll., orig. cl., faded. (BBA. Aug.18; 182) *F. Edwards.* £190
- **First Footsteps in East Africa.** 1856. *1st. Edn. 2nd. Iss.* Orig. cl., slightly soiled, unc. (S. Dec.13; 161) *Morrell.* £235
- **– Anr. Edn.** L., 1856. *1st. Edn.* Cont. cf. (S. Jun.25; 63) *Loman.* £250
- **A Glance at the 'Passion Play'.** 1881. *1st. Edn.* Hf.-title, orig. red cl. gt. by Smith Bros., with their ticket, spine faded. (LC. Mar.1; 298) £130
- **The Gold-Mines of Midian & the Ruined Midianite Cities.** L., 1878. *1st. Ein.* 1st. gathering spotted, orig. cl., spine faded. (S. Dec.13; 167) *Traylen.* £140
- **The Guide Book. A Pictorial Pilgrimage to Mecca & Medina.** L., 1865. *1st. Edn.* Frontis. port., orig. pict. wraps., preserved in fold-over cl. box. (S. May 22; 272) *Mantoura.* £1,100
- **The Lake Regions of Central Africa.** L., 1860. *1st. Edn.* 2 vols. Hf.-titles, folding engraved map cold. in outl., 12 'chromoxylograph' plts., orig. cl. (S. May 22; 414) *Maggs.* £400
- **– Anr. Copy.** 2 vols. Folding engraved map, cold. in outl., 12 'chromoxylograph' plts., hf.-titles, cont. cf. (S. Jun.25; 64) *Maggs.* £290
- **– Anr. Edn.** 1860. *1st. Edn. 1st. Iss.* 2 vols. Folding map in Vol. 1, 12 tinted plts., later cf., gt. spines. (BBA. Sep.29; 17) *Rothman.* £266
- **– Anr. Edn.** L., 1860. *1st. Edn. 2nd. Iss.* 2 vols. Engraved folding map, 12 tinted plts., some spotting, orig. cl., unc., spines darkened. (S. Dec.13; 162) *Raylen.* £240
- **– Anr. Copy.** 2 vols. Lacks 2 wood engrs., titles cropped, ink stps. on titles & elsewhere, cl., worn. (SG. Sep.22; 75) $175
- **The Land of Midian (Revisited).** L., 1879. *1st. Edn.* 2 vols. Folding map, 16 litho. plts., 1 gathering loose, orig. cl., slightly worn, unopened. (S. Dec.13; 168) *Traylen.* £180
- **– Anr. Copy.** 2 vols. in 1. 1 plt. loose, cf. gt., rubbed. (P. Jul.5; 133) £75
- **The Lands of Cazembe. Lacerda's Journey to Cazembe in 1798.** 1873. Orig. cl. (BBA. Sep.29; 3) *Trocchi.* $60
- **A Mission to Gelele. – Personal Narrative of a Pilgrimage to Al-Madinah & Meccah.** L., Memorial Edn. 1893. 2 vols. & 2 vols. Maps, plts., orig. cl., gt. (S. Apr.9; 8) *Hosains.* £70
- **Personal Narrative of a Pilgrimage to El-Medinah & Meccah.** L., 1855-56. *1st. Edn.* 3 vols. Without hf.-titles to Vols. I & II, frontis. to Vol. I detchd., cont. cl. (C. Nov.16; 60) *Wood.* £520
- **– Anr. Copy.** 3 vols. 4 maps & plans, 14 plts., the errata lf. in Vol. I, plt. list in Vol. I only, 24 p. catalogues (dtd. Sep. 1854 & Nov. 1855) in Vols. I & III, orig. cl., 1st. bdg. torn & partly loose; A.N.s. from Burton to Stirling-Maxwell tipped in. (SG. Nov.3; 32) $1,400
- **– Anr. Copy.** 3 vols. 4 maps or plans, 14 plts., including frontis.'s, three-qtr. lev. (SG. Mar.29; 295) $425
- **– Anr. Copy.** 3 vols. 4 full-p. maps & plans (3 folding), 14 plts. (5 fold.), hf.-title in vol. 3 only,

cont. hf. vell. gt., soiled, edges of vell. backs sprung or starting on vols. 2 & 3. (SG. Apr.26; 38) $350
- **– Anr. Edn.** L., 1857. *2nd. Edn.* 2 vols. in 1. 4 maps & plans (3 folding), 14 plts., cl. gt., backstrip separating. (PNY. Jun.6; 465) $110
- **– Anr. Edn.** L., 1879. *3rd. Edn.* 2 or 3 points of variation from Penzer's collation, orig. cl., sewing weak in part. (KH. Nov.8; 58) Aus. $120
- **– Anr. Edn.** 1893. *Memorial Edn.* 2 vols. Publisher's cl. gt., spines slightly chipped. (S. Nov.1; 51) *Burgess.* £75
- **Scinde; or, The Unhappy Valley.** L., 1851. *2nd. Edn.* 2 vols. Slight spotting, blind-stpd. cl., spine ends slightly bumped. (SG. Sep.22; 74) $275
- **Two Trips to Gorilla Land & the Cataracts of the Congo.** 1876. *1st. Edn.* 2 vols. 40 pp. of advts. in Vol. 1 dtd. Feb. 1875, orig. gt.-decor. cl. (SKC. May 4; 1805) £400
- **Ultima Thule.** L., 1875. *1st. Edn.* 2 vols. 2 folding maps, 7 litho. plts., plts. spotted, orig. cl. gt., spines slightly darkened. (S. Dec.13; 165) *Traylen.* £150
- **Vikram & the Vampire or Tales of Hindu Devilry.** Ill.:– Ernest Griset. L., 1870 [1869]. *1st. Edn. 1st. Iss.* Some ll. rather spotted, orig. cl., rather rubbed. (BBA. May 23; 64) *Thorpe.* £130
- **Wanderings in West Africa.** L., 1863. *1st. Edn.* 2 vols. in 1. Decor. cl. (S. Dec.13; 164) *Scott.* £75
- **– Anr. Copy.** 2 vols. Orig. cl., partly unopened. (SG. Sep.22; 76) $650
- **Zanzibar.** 1872. *1st. Edn.* 2 vols. Hf. mor., hinges reprd. (P. Oct.20; 165) £100
- **The Works.** L., 1893-94. *Memorial Edn.* 6 vols. only (lacks Vol. 5). Orig. cl. gt., 2 spines worn. (S. Dec.13; 170) *Primrose.* £60

BURTON, Robert 'Democritus Junior'
- **The Anatomy of Melancholy.** 1632. *4th. Edn.* 4to. 1 p. torn, old cf., worn; bkplt. of E. Chatterton-Orpen. (BS. Nov.16; 30) £320
- **– Anr. Edn.** L., 1660. Fo.,. Pict. engraved title remargined, some foxing, mor. gt., cover detchd. [Wing B 6183] (SG. Feb.9; 188) $175
- **– Anr. Edn.** L., 1676. *8th. Edn.* Fo. Engraved title, last advt. lf., hf.-title & M1 torn & reprd. affecting text, some ll. slightly soiled, mod. cf. [Wing B6184] (BBA. May 3; 158) *Howes Bookshop.* £210
- **– Anr. Edn.** Ill.:– E. McKnight Kauffer. Nones. Pr., 1925. *(750) numbered.* 2 vols. Fo. Orig. parch.-bkd. bds., unc., unopened. (S. Nov.22; 261) *Joseph.* £120
- **– Anr. Copy.** 2 vols. Vell.-bkd. bds., slightly soiled. (P. Mar.15; 177) *Joseph.* £85
- **– Anr. Copy.** 2 vols. Sm. fo. Qtr. vell., slightly soiled. (SG. Oct.6; 78) $120

BURTON, W.K.
See— **MILNE, John & Burton, W.K.**

BURTON, William, Antiquary 1609-57
- **A Commentary on Antoninus: His Itinerary in Britain.** L., 1658. *1st. Edn.* 4to. Lacks frontis., hf. lev. mor. & qtr.-sawn oak, silver(?) corner guards, chain closures, rebnd. by Dr. Charles Hadden Parker, 1906, with holograph note on front free end-paper, new fly-ll. foxed. (CBA. Dec.10; 86) $100

BURTON, Wm., Topographer
- **The Description of Leicestershire.** L., 1622. 4to. Red mor. gt. (HBC. May 17; 337) £190
- **– Anr. Edn.** 1777. 4to. Cont. cf. (HBC. May 17; 337c) £100

BURTON, Sir William Westbrooke
- **The State of Religion & Education in New South Wales.** L., 1840. Slightly soiled, bdg. not stated; 'Signet Library' inscr. (JL. Nov.13; B7) Aus. $240
- **– Anr. Copy.** 1 errata slip only, some foxing & discolouration, bdg. not stated, unc., recased. (KH. May 1; 122) Aus. $100

BURY, Adrian
- **Syon House.** Ill.:– John Buckland Wright. 1955. *(175) numbered.* 4to. Mor. by Hiscox, gt. armorials, case. (HBC. May 17; 236) £105

BURY, Lady Charlotte
- **Diary Illustrative of the Times of George the Fourth.** L., 1839. 4 vols. Tall 8vo. Gf. gt. by Riviere, gt. spines & dentelles. (SG. Feb.16; 51) $200

BURY, Rev. E.
- **The Three Great Sanctuaries of Tuscany.** 1833. Ob. 4to. Port., 6 aquatint plts., some spotting, cl. (P. Dec.8; 65) *Queveda.* £60

BURY, Richard de Aungerville
See— **AUNGERVILLE or BURY, Richard de**

BURY, Thomas Talbot
- **Coloured Views on the Liverpool & Manchester Railway, A Facsimile of the Original Edition published in 1831, by R. Ackermann.** 1977. *(250) numbered.* 4to. Orig. maroon cf. gt. by Zaehnsdorf, s.-c. (TA. Jun.21; 580) £54

BUSBECQ, Ogier Ghiselin de
- **Legationis Turc. Epistolae IV.** Munich, 1620. *1st. Ill. Edn.* 12mo. Title reprd., few margin defects with loss of few letters, few dampstains, old cf. gt., little stained, spine holed; Earl of Essex bkplt. on title verso. (SG. Sep.22; 78) $200
- **Omnia Quae Extant.** Ill.:– Duysend (engraved title). Leiden, 1633. *1st. Edn.* 24mo. Cont. vell.; from Bibliotheca Elzeviriana of E. Heron-Allan. (SG. Sep.22; 79) $150

BUSBY, Thomas Lord
- **Costume of the Lower Orders of London.** L., [1820]. *[1st. Edn.].* 1st. Iss. 4to. Frontis., 23 hand-cold. engraved plts., some minor spotting, mainly in margins, mod. hf. mor. (C. Jun.27; 17) *Levy.* £420
- **– Anr. Edn.** L., [1820]. *1st. Edn. 2nd. Printing.* 4to. 24 cold. etchings, including frontis., hand-bnd. mor., gt. spine, covers, inner & outer dentelles, by Birdsall, Northampton & L., little wear, lr. cover with print marks; hauswedel coll. (H. May 23; 58) DM 2,600

See— **CRIES OF LONDON**

BUSCH, G.C.B. & Trommsdoff, J.B.
- **Almanach der Fortschrittle in Wissenschaften, Künsten, Manufakturen und Handwerken.** Erfurt, 1797-1812. 38 (of 39) folding copperplts., cont. bds., slightly rubbed. (R. Oct.12; 1732) DM 1,900

BUSCH, Wilhelm
- **Abenteuer u. Junggesellen.** Heidelberg, 1875. *1st. Edn.* Hf. leath., orig. wraps. with woodcut bnd. in, upr. wrap. lightly spotted. (HK. Nov.10; 2335) DM 400
- **Bilder zur Jobsiade.** Heidelberg, [1872]. *1st. Edn.* Title & last p. with lime traces, some slight foxing, cont. linen, slightly bumped. (HK. Nov.10; 2336) DM 520

BUSCHING, A.F. Anton Friedrich
- **Grosse Erdbeschreibung.** Troppau & Brünn, 1784-87. 24 vols. Lacks 4 index vols., some vols. ink spotted, title with owners mark, cont. hf. leath. gt., slightly bumped & lightly wormed, w.a.f. (HK. May 15; 754) DM 1,000
- **A New System of Geography.** Ill.:– Thomas Kitchen. 1762. 6 vols. 4to. 42 folding engraved maps, some ll. spotted, cont. hf. cf., slightly worn, 1 cover loose. (BBA. Oct.27; 240) *Jeffery.* £90

BUSHELL, Stephen W.
- **Chinese Art.** L., 1904-06. 2 vols. 12mo. Ptd. wraps., loose & reprd.; sigs. & margin notes of Herbert A. Giles, with A.L.s. from Bushell to Giles (dtd. Peking, 1884) tipped in. (SG. Oct.13; 88) $110

See— **WALTERS, William T.**

BUSSE, Joachim
- **Internationales Handbuch aller Maler und Bildhauer des 19. Jhs.** Wiesbaden, 1977. Fo. Orig. leatherette, wraps., s.-c. (V. Sep.30; 1605) DM 410

BUSTI, Bernardinus de
- **Mariale: de Singulis Festivitatibus Beate Virginis per Modum Sermonum Tractans.** Strasburg, Martin Flach, 1496. *1st. Flach Edn.* Fo. Initials painted in red, cont. stpd. pig over wood bds., clasps incompl.; from Fondation Furstenberg-Beaumesnil. [BMC I, 154: Goff B1334] (HD. Nov.16; 52) Frs. 8,000
- **– Anr. Edn.** Strassburg, Martin Flach, 15 Aug. 1498. Sm. fo. Fully rubricated, title & final lf. mntd., later bds., leath. back, cover detchd.; the

BUSTI, Bernardinus de -*Contd.*

Walter Goldwater copy. [BMC I, 155; Goff B-1335] (SG. Dec.1; 84) $800
– **Rosarium Sermonum.** Venice, Georgius Arrivabenus, 31 May & 16 Aug. 1498. 2 vols. 4to. Each title-p. inscr. 'Iste liber est ad usu fr'is geraphini surdi forliviensis ...', old vell., rebkd.; the Walter Goldwater copy. [BMC V, 387; Goff B-1336] (SG. Dec.1; 85) $650

BUTIGELLA, Hieronymus
– **Oratic pro Joanne Philippo Gambaloita Habita.** [Pavia], after 13 Dec. 1494. 4to. Some early marginalia, mod. bds.; the Walter Goldwater copy. [BMC VII, 1020; Goff B-1339] (SG. Dec.1; 87) $325

BUTINI, Pierre
– **Nouvelles Observations et Recherches Analytiques aur la Magnesie du sel d'Epsom.** Geneva, 1781. *1st. Edn.* Orig. bds., unc. (S. Dec.13; 254)
Phelps. £100

BUTLER, Dr. Arthur Gardiner
– **Birds of Great Britain & Ireland.** (Order Passeres). Ill.:– H. Gronwold & F.W. Frohawk. [1904-08]. 2 vols. 4to. 115 cold. plts., orig. cl., slightly worn & stained. (S. Nov.1; 267)
Elliott. £50
– – **Anr. Edn.** Ill.:– H. Gronvold & F.W. Frohawk. [1907-08]. 4to. Hf. leath. gt. (SKC. Nov.18; 1962) £120
– – **Anr. Edn.** Ill.:– after H. Gronvold & F.W. Frohawk. N.d. 2 vols. 4to. 115 chromolitho. plts., 2 sm. tears to 1 plt., 1 plt. detchd., some margins lightly soiled, cont. cl., scuffed. (CSK. Apr.6; 126) £130
– **Foreign Finches in Captivity.** Ill.:– F.W. Frohawk. L., 1894[-96]. *1st. Edn.* 4to. 60 hand-cold. litho. plts., lacks hf.-title(?), slight margin spotting, hf. mor., rubbed. (S. Nov.28; 13) *Gregory.* £780
– – **Anr. Edn.** Ill.:– F.W. Frohawk. 1899. *[2nd. Edn].* Lge. 8vo. Orig. cl. (LC. Mar.1; 138) £70
– – **Anr. Copy.** 4to. 60 chromolitho. plts., two-tone cl., shaken, ex-liby. (SG. Oct.6; 79) $110
– **Lepidoptera Exotica.** L., 1874. 4to. 64 cold. plts., orig. cl. (SKC. Oct.26; 340) £300

BUTLER, Arthur Joshua
– **Islamic Pottery: a Study Mainly Historical.** L., 1926. *1st. Edn.* Fo. 92 plts., some cold., lettered tissue-guards, ex-liby., cl. (SG. May 3; 75) $300

BUTLER, Charles
– **The Feminin' Monarchi', or the Histori of Bee's.** Oxford, 1634. *3rd. (1st. Phonetic) Edn.* Sm. 4to. Some dampstaining, 19th. C. hf. cf., spine gt. [STC 4194] (S. Nov.28; 14) *Lawson.* £250

BUTLER, Capt. Henry
– **South African Sketches.** L., 1841. Fo. Pict. litho. title, 15 plts., partly hand-cold., mod. cl. (BBA. Mar.21; 82) *Clarkes Bookshop.* £180

BUTLER, Joseph
– **The Analogy of Religion, Natural & Revealed.** L., 1736. *1st. Edn.* 4to. Hf.-title, minor dampstains, cont. panel. cf., rebkd. & restored. (SG. Oct.27; 49) $130
– – **Anr. Copy.** 4to. Lacks hf.-title, cont. panel. cf., rebkd. (SG. Feb.9; 189) $110

BUTLER, Martin & Joll, Evelyn
– **The Paintings of J.M.W. Turner.** 1977. 2 vols. 4to. Orig. cl., d.-w.'s. (CSK. Sep.30; 82) £70

BUTLER, Richard
– **An Essay Concerning Blood-Letting.** 1734. Old cf. gt., rubbed. (P. Jan.12; 205) *Bickersteth.* £140

BUTLER, Rohan (Ed.)
See– DOCUMENTS OF BRITISH FOREIGN POLICY ...

BUTLER, Samuel, Philosopher
– **Erewhon.** Intro.:– Aldous Huxley. Ill.:– Rockwell Kent. Ltd. Edns. Cl., 1934. *(1500) numbered & sigd. by artist.* Lge. 8vo. Cl., bkplt. removed from inside of upr. cover. (SG. Mar.29; 192) $150
– **Seven Sonnets & a Psalm of Montreal.** Camb., Oriv. ptd., 1904. Cont. mor. by Bramhall &

Menzies, slightly faded, orig. wraps. preserved. (BBA. Sep.29; 218) *Jarndyce.* £60
– **Works.** 1923-26. *Shrewsbury Edn. (750) numbered.* 20 vols. Qtr. vell. gt. (P. Jun.7; 259) £150
– – **Anr. Copy.** 20 vols. Orig. vell.-bkd. buckram, spines soiled. (CSK. Jun.15; 178) £70

BUTLER, Samuel, Satirist
[–] **Hudibras.** L., 1663. 12mo. Imprimatur lf., sm. marginal wormholes, sig. on title, browning from bdg., cont. sheep, slight wear, sm. wormholes in spine. [Wing B 6302] (SPB. May 16; 19) $100
– – **Anr. Edn.** Ill.:– William Hogarth. L., 1726. Some foxing & darkening, cont. diced cf., rebkd., title & date gt. on spine, corners defect., inked name to front free end-paper. (CBA. Aug.21; 307) $180
– – **Anr. Edn.** Ed.:– Z. Grey. Ill.:– Vertue (port.), J. Mynde after W. Hogarth (plts.). Camb., 1744. 2 vols. Port. & some 10 ll. dampstained, cont. spr. cf., covers panel. (SG. Oct.27; 50) $100
– – **Anr. Edn.** Ill.:– W. Hogarth, Ross, & Ross after Lely (port.). 1793. 4 pts. in 3 vols. 4to. Last errata ll., cont. str.-grd. mor., slightly faded. (BBA. Aug.18; 122) *F. Edwards.* £300
– – **Anr. Edn.** Ill.:– J. Clark. L., 1822. 2 vols. 12 hand-cold. plts., offset, some slight spotting, owners' inscrs. erased from title of Vol. 1 & from A2 Vol. 2, cont. str.-grd. mor. gt. (S. Oct.4; 77) *Soloman.* £50

BUTLER, Samuel, Settler in Australia
– **The Hand-Book for Australian Emigrants...New South Wales, South Australia, & Swan River Settlement....** Glasgow, 1839. *7th. Thousand.* 12mo. Cl., unc., slightly rubbed. (KH. May 1; 123) Aus. $120

BUTLER, Sir Walter Lawry
– **A History of the Birds of New Zealand.** L., 1888; 1905. Vols. I & II, with Supp. Fo. Leath., Supp. in cl. (JL. Nov.13; B509) Aus. $2,200

BUTLIN, Martin
– **The Paintings & Drawings of William Blake.** 1981. 2 vols. 4to. Orig. cl., d.-w.'s. (CSK. Sep.30; 81) £75

BUTOR, Michel
– **Les Mots dans la Peinture.** Geneva, 1969. *(175) numbered.* 4to. Lacks orig. aquatint by Matta, loose as iss. in orig. wraps., orig. vell.-bkd. bd. folder, s.-c. (BBA. Jun.14; 194) *Makiya.* £80
– **Le Rêve de l'Ombre.** Ill.:– Cesar Peverelli. 1976. *(150) numbered on vélin de Rives. (20) with numbered suite of plts., all sigd. by artist, on Auvergne.* Lge. 4to. Subscriber's name deleted, leaves, ill. wrap., box. (HD. May 21; 106) Frs. 1,100

BUTT, Isaac
[–] **Irish Life in the Castle, the Courts, & the Country.** L., 1840. *1st. Edn.* 3 vols. Hf.-titles, Vol. 1 lacks front blank, cl.-bkd. bds. (GM. Dec.7; 120) £55

BUTTERFLY, The
Ill.:– S.H. Sime, Max Beerbohm, Joseph Pennell, & others. Mar. 1899-Feb. 1900. Nos. 1-12 (all publd.), in 2 vols. Advts., recent hf. mor., orig. wraps. bnd. in. (TA. Jul.19; 340) £52

BUTTERWORTH, Benjamin
– **The Growth of Industrial Art.** Wash., 1892. Some foxing, edges nicked, no bdg. stated. (RS. Jan.17; 461) $225

BUXTON, Thomas Fowell
– **The African Slave Trade.** L., 1839. *2nd. Edn.* Slightly spotted towards end, orig. cl., faded & slightly stained. (S. Jun.25; 65) *Scott.* £60
– **Letter on the Slave Trade.** 1838. *1st. Edn.* Orig. cl.; inscr. by author. (P. Mar.15; 91) *Jarndyce.* £150

BUXTORF, Joannes
– **Grammaticae Chaldaicae et Syriacae Libri III.** Basileae, 1615. *1st. Edn.* Some foxing, cont. vell., with wallet-flaps, gt.-stpd. centre panels, some wear. (RO. Dec.11; 67) $125
– **Institutio Epistoleris Hebraica ... cum Epistolarum**

Hebraicarum ... **Accessit Appendix Variarum Epistolarum R. Maiemonis ....** Basel, 1629. In Hebrew & Latin, browning thro.-out. *(Bound with:)* LIPSIUS, Justus – Epistolica Institutio. Amst., 1591. Together 2 works in 1 vol. 12mo. Cont. vell. (PNY. Dec.1; 40) $100

BUXTORF, Johannes, the Elder
See– BIBLES [Hebrew] – BUXTORF, Johannes, the Elder

BUXTORF, Johannes, the Elder & Younger
– **Lexicon Chaldaicum, Talmudicum et Rabbinicum.** Basel, 1640. *1st. Edn.* Fo. Additional engraved title dtd. 1639, some browning, early vell., sprung, soiled, bowed, end-paper defect. at upr. cover fore-edge. (SG. Feb.2; 33) $130

BUYS DE MORNAS, Claude
– **Atlas Méthodique et Elémentaire de Géographie et de l'Histoire.** Paris, 1761-62. 4 vols. Fo. 4 engraved titles, 1 engraved dedication, 257 copperplts., most cold., some foxing or browning, cont. bds., vols. 1 & 2 defect. (D. Nov.23; 752) DM 7,500

BYAM, Lydia
– **A Collection of Fruits from the West Indies ....** L., at the Oriental Pr. ... for the author, 1800. Fo. 9 hand-cold. engraved plts., last plt. slightly spotted, pres. inscr. on title, cont. bds., lacks backstrip. (C. Nov.16; 227) *Burton-Garbett.* £1,600

BYBLIS. Miroir des Arts du Livre et de l'Estampe
Ill.:– E. Legrand, Berthold Mahn, Hémard, Mariette Lydis, Chas-Laborde, & others. Paris, 1922-31. *(600). (500) on velin pur fil.* 10 vols. 4to. Leaves, loose in folder. (HD. Sep.22; 202) Frs. 3,900

BYERLEY, Frederick J.
– **Narrative of the Overland Expedition of the Messrs. Jardine from Rockhampton to Cape York, Northern Queensland.** Brisbane, 1867. Tear in map, plts. stained in margins, orig. cl. gt., spine torn & partly lacking; inscr. by author in upr. cover. (CA. Apr.3; 137) Aus. $1,500

BYLANDT, H. Ade
– **Dogs of All Nations. Their Varieties, Characteristics, Points &c.** L., 1905. 2 vols. Sm. fo. Orig. decor. cl. gt. (VS. Dec.8; 646) Fls. 475
– **Les Races de Chiens.** Bruxelles, 1897. Fo. Lr. margin slightly stained in places, orig. hf. mor., slightly impft. (VG. Mar.21; 534) Fls. 650

BYNE, Arthur & Stapley, Mildred
– **Provincial Houses in Spain. – Majorcan Houses & Gardens.** N.Y., 1925; 1928. Together 2 vols. Fo. 190 & 188 plts. from photos., ex-liby., cl. (SG. May 3; 69) $120

BYNG, Admiral John
– **The Trial of ....** 1757. Fo. Slight browning, later cl. (SKC. Jan.13; 2194) £60

BYRD, Adm. Richard E.
– **Skyward.** N.Y., 1928. *(500) numbered & sigd., with 2 pieces of cl. from wings of plane Josephine Ford mntd. in upr. cover.* Lge. 8vo. Sm. liby. stp., hf. cl., unc. (SG. Sep.22; 81) $110

BYRES, James
– **Hypogaei or Sepulchral Caverns of Tarquinia.** [1842]. Fo. 41 Engraved plts., few margins lightly stained, mod. hf. mor., orig. wraps. bnd. in. (CSK. Feb.10; 146) £110

BYRNE, Julia Clara
– **Twelve Years' Wanderings in the British Colonies....** 1848. 2 vols. Map in pocket at end of each vol., 1 slightly defect., mod. hf. mor., partly unc. (KH. May 1; 124) Aus. $420

BYRON, Lord George Gordon Noel
– **Childe Harold's Pilgrimage.** L., 1812-16-18. *1st. Edns.* [Cantos I-IV], in 3 vols. 4to. & 8vo. Various bdgs., 1 vol. untrimmed. (SG. Nov.17; 22) $225
– – **Anr. Edn.** L., 1812-16-18. *1st. Edns., Cantos. 1-3 2nd. Iss., Canto 4, 3rd. Iss.* Cantos. 1,2,3 & 4, together 4 vols. 4to. & 8vo. Cantos. 1-2, facs. plt., advt. lf., some spotting, old bds., drab spine, unc., worn, Canto 3, hf.-title, 2 ll. inserted ll. advts., browned, orig. drab wraps., worn & chipped, Canto

4, advt. lf., orig. drab bds., worn, brkn. (SPB. May 16; 21) $150
– – **Anr. Edn.** L., 1816. *1st. Edn. 2nd. Iss.* Canto III: 1 vol. Hf.-title, last 2 advt. ll., orig. wraps., slightly worn. (*With:*) – **Mazeppa.** L., 1819. *1st. Edn. 1st. Iss.* 1 vol. Hf.-title, last 5 advt. ll., orig. wraps., slightly worn. (*With:*) – **Marino Faliero.** L., 1821. *1st. Edn. 1st. Iss.* 1 vol. Hf.-title & 1st. blank lf., last advt. lf., orig. bds., slightly worn. (BBA. Nov.30; 253) *Jarndyce.* £160
– – **Anr. Edn.** L., 1816-18. *1st. Edn. 2nd. Iss.* Cantos III & [IV]: 2 vols. Hf.-title & 1st. 2 advt. ll. in 1st. vol., last advt. lf. in 2nd., orig. wraps. & bds., rubbed. (*With:*) – **The Corsair.** L., 1814. *1st. Edn. 2nd. Iss.* 1 vol. Variant, hf.-title, last 2 advt. ll. dtd. Feb. 1814, orig. wraps., spine slightly torn. (BBA. Nov.30; 250) *Jarndyce.* £85
– – **Anr. Edn.** L., 1859. Cont. mor. gt., jnts. reprd., fore-e. pntg., w.a.f. (SPB. May 17; 732) $350
– **Don Juan.** 1819-23. *Cantos I & II 2nd. Edns., rest 1st. Edns.* 3 vols. Hf.-title to Vol. I, errata slip, without advt. ll. N2 & I2 at end of Cantos VIII & XVI, cont., cf. by Riviere, spines gt.; Diocese of Southwark copy. (C. May 30; 131) *Bennett.* £70
– – **Anr. Edn.** L., 1819-24. *1st. Edns.* Cantos 1-16 in 6 vols. 4to. & 8vo. Hf.-titles in 1st. & 2nd. vols., erratum slip in last vol., Cantos 1 & 2 in 1 4to. vol., orig. bds., recased, back & corners renewed with new label, Cantos 3-16 in 3 8vo. vols., orig. bds., some slight repairs to extremities of 2 vols., 1 label chipped, all uncl., cl. box; the 8vo. vols. with Isabel Clayton bkplts., Frederic Dannay coll. (CNY. Dec.16; 60) $1,000
– – **Anr. Copy.** 6 vols. 4to. (1 vol.) & 8vo. Vol. 1 has hf.-titles for both books, vol.2 has hf.-title & imprint lf. at end, other vols. iss. without hf.-titles, advts. in 3 vols., tipped-in erratum slip in vol.6, mott. cf. gt., gt. dentelles, partly uncl., by Riviere, vol.1 covers detchd., others worn. (SG. Apr.26; 39) $800
– – **Anr. Edn.** L., 1819 & 1821, 1823-24. *1st. Edn.* 6 vols. Unif. three-qtr. mor. by Sangorski & Surcliffe, spines gt., folding box. (CBA. Dec.10; 134) $650
[–] **English Bards; & Scotch Reviewers. A Satire.** L., [1809]. *1st. Edn.* 12mo. Lacks hf.-title, slight soiling, cont. russ., reprd., covers detchd. (S. Oct.11; 314) *Wise.* £85
– – **Anr. Edn.** L., [1809]. *1st. Edn., with preface; wtrmkd. '1805'.* 12mo. Lacks hf.-title, cont. cf., rather worn,. (SG. Mar.15; 95) $110
– – **Anr. Edn.** 1809. *2nd. Edn.* Lacks hf.-title & final advt. lf., cont. hf. cf., worn; inscr. 'with Byron's Complts.'. (CSK. Sep.16; 61) £55
– **Hebrew Melodies.** L., 1815. *1st. Separate Edn. 1st. Iss.* Advts., hf.-title slightly soiled, some minor spotting, orig. wraps., uncl., backstrip slightly worn; Frederic Dannay copy. (CNY. Dec.16; 59) $360
– **Hours of Idleness.** Newark, 1807. *1st. Edn.* Hf.-title, D3 a cancel & the 3 unlisted errata, cont. hf. mor., spine gt., bd. sides rubbed & slightly soiled; cont. sig. of Joshua Wilson at title. (C. May 30; 143) *Jarndyce.* £400
– – **Anr. Copy.** D3 a cancel, hf.-title, 6 ll. rehinged, prelims. & some other ll. washed, cleaned lev. mor. gt.; bkplts. of Viscount Esher & Charles Whibley, Frederic Dannay copy. (CNY. Dec.16; 58) $260
– **Lara, a Tale. Jacqueline, a Tale [by Samuel Rogers].** 1814,. *1st. Edn.* Hf.-title, Last 2 ll. of Murray's catalogue, cont. cf., spine gt., slightly rubbed. (BBA. Feb.9; 59) *Wise.* £90
– **Letters & Journals.** Ed.:– Leslie A. Marchand. 1974-82. 12 vols. Orig. cl., d.-w.'s. (BBA. Oct.27; 124) *Simon.* £60
– **Manfred.** Trans.:– W. Starke. Müchen, 1912. *De Luxe Edn., (7) on vell.* Sm. 4to. Orig. vell., by Carl Sonntag jun., Leipzig, end-papers & doubls. slightly spotted. (H. Nov.23; 1111) DM 920
– **Marino Faliero. Doge of Venice.** Ill.:– S. Frank. Wien & Leipzig, (1922). *De Luxe Edn., (50) sigd. by artist, with 2nd. series of sigd. col. etchings.* 40. Orig. vell., gold decor. & orig. sik box, 1 corner slightly bumped. (H. Nov.24; 1506) DM 650
– **Poems.** L., 1816. *1st. Edn. 1st. Iss.?.* Lacks 2 pp. of advts., text slightly darkened, three-qtr. gt.-decor. mor. & cl., 2 Greek postage stps. commemorating Bryon on front fly-lf., pencil notes erased from verso of front free end-paper; A.L.s. from Augusta Leigh (Byron's half-sister) to the

publisher John Murray tipped onto front free end-paper with tape (soiled, worn at central crease, sm. chips, remnants of sealing wax, pencil notes erased, tape darkened), dtd. 5 Apr. 1816 by later hand in pencil below. (CBA. Mar.3; 63) $275
– **The Poetical Works.** 1839. 8 vols. 4to. L.P., a few ll. spotted, later cf. gt. by F. Bedford, 2 vols. rebkd. with orig. spines, slightly rubbed. (BBA. Feb.23; 205) *Dennistoun.* £170
– – **Anr. Copy.** 8 vols. Profusely extra-ill., str.-grd. mor., gt. extra, by Morrell. (PNY. Dec.1; 13) $250
– – **Anr. Edn.** Ill.:– Finden, after J.M.W. Turner & others. L., 1866. 10 vols. 16mo. Crimson three-qtr. mor., spines gt. with fleurons. (SG. Feb.16; 52) $350
– **The Prisoner of Chillon & other Poems.** L., 1816. *1st. Edn. 1st. Iss.* Hf.-title, last advt. lf., mod. bds. (BBA. Nov.30; 251) *Pickering & Chatto.* £55
– **Werner, a Tragedy.** 1823. *1st. Edn.* Dampstain to upr. hf.-title & title, orig. wraps., uncl. (P. Feb.16; 242) £65
– **Works.** 1810-23. 12 vols. Extra-ill. with views & ports., neat annots. with poems & notes, mor. gt., as a coll. of plts., w.a.f. (P. Sep.29; 139) *Wise.* £300
– – **Anr. Edn.** L., 1832-33. 17 vols. Sm. 8vo. Hf. cf. gt. (PNY. Dec.1; 14) $200
– **Works; with Letters & Journals & Life.** Ed.:– Thomas Moore. L., 1832-33. 17 vols. 16mo. Three-qtr. mor., spines gt., by Bumpus; lge. armorial bkplt. of Sir W.D. Pearson, Visc. Cowdray. (SG. Feb.16; 53) $600
– – **Anr. Edn.** Ill.:– W.E. Finden after Turner, Cattermole, Stanfield, & others. L., 1832-34. *1st. Edns. (but for Vol. 3, dtd. 1834).* 17 vols. Sm. 8vo. 17 frontis., 17 engraved titles, plt. in Vol. 6, folding facs. in Vols. 7 & 9, hf.-titles, some light foxing, hf. mor. gt., little worn & discold. (SG. Mar.15; 96) $200
– – **Anr. Edn.** Ed.:– Thomas Moore. L., 1847. 17 vols. Sm. 8vo. Hf. mor. (SPB. May 17; 723) $350

BYRON, Lord George Gordon Noel & others
– **The Liberal, Verse & Prose from the South.** L., 1822-23. *1st. Edn.* 2 vols. Cont. cf. gt., rebkd. (P. Nov.24; 223) *Scott.* £80

BYRON, Hon. Adm. John
– **The Narrative ... Containing an Account of the Great Distresses ... on the Coast of Patagonia.** 1768. *1st. Edn.* Hf.-title, cont. spr. cf.; Sir Ivar Colquhoun, of Luss copy. (CE. Mar.22; 51) £290
– – **Anr. Copy.** Cont. cf.; A.L.s. from author (Pirbright, 29 Jun. 1784) loosely inserted, Earl Fitzwilliam bkplt. (BBA. Sep.29; 54) *Wyse.* £100
– – **Anr. Copy.** Frontis. offset on title, sm. glue stain on M5 with loss of a few letters on M4v, cont. cf. gt., upr. cover detchd.; the Rt. Hon. Visc. Eccles copy. [Sabin 9730] (CNY. Nov.18; 43) $160
– – **Anr. Copy.** Mod. hf. cf. [Sabin 9730] (KH. May 1; 125) Aus. $140
– – **Anr. Copy.** Cont. leath. gt. spine & outer dentelle. [Sabin 9730]. (D. Nov.23; 893) DM 1,000
[–] **A Voyage Round the World, in H.M.S. Dolphin.** L., 1767. *1st. Edn.* Advt. lf. loose, cont. cf., covers betchd. [Sabin 9732] (S. Mar.6; 3) *Quaritch.* £100
– – **Anr. Copy.** Advt. lf. at end, cont. cf., extremities slightly worn; the Rt. Hon. Visc. Eccles copy. [Sabin 9732] (CNY. Nov.18; 44) $240

BYRON, May
– **Cecil Aldin's Happy Family.** Ill.:– Cecil Aldin. L., 1912. *1st. Edn.* 4to. Hf. cl. & bds., lightly worn. (CBA. Aug.21; 5) $180
– – **Anr. Copy.** Minor foxing, hf. cl. & bds., slightly soiled. (CBA. Aug.21; 6) $150

BYVANCK, Alexandre William & Hoogewerff, Godefridus Joannes
– **La Miniature Hollandaise dans les Manuscrits des XIVe XVe et XVIe Siècles.** La Haye, 1922-26. *(300) numbered.* 3 vols. Fo. 240 plts. in 2 portfos., hf. cl. (B. Oct.4; 556) Fls. 2,200

CABECA DE VACA, Alvar Nunez
– **Relation that Alvar Nunez Cabeca de Vaca gave ....** Intro.:– Oscar Lewis. Ill.:– V. Angelo. San Franc., Grabhorn Pr., 1929. *(300) sigd. by artist.*

4to. Decors. hand-illuminated in cols. & gt., specially bnd. in gt.-ruled pig., leath. onlays, gt. crest on upr. cover, spine slightly faded, s.-c. lightly worn; the V. Angelo copy. (CBA. Oct.1; 169) $550

CABELL, James Branch
– **Jurgen, a Comedy of Justice.** Ill.:– John Buckland-Wright. Gold. Cock. Pr., 1949. *(100) numbered, with extra engr., sigd. by artist, specially bnd.* Orig. mor. gt., s.-c.; from D. Bolton liby. (BBA. Oct.27; 128) *Joseph.* £160
– **The King was in his Counting House.** Ill.:– Charles Child. N.Y., [1938]. *1st. Edn. (125) sigd.* Imitation mor., gt. cover vig., light rubbing, long inscr. on front end-paper. (CBA. Oct.29; 178) $225

CABEZA, Bernabe Josef
– **Memoria Interesante de las Persecuciones de la Iglesia Catolica y sus Ministros en España en los Últimos Tiempos de Cautividad de ... Bernando VII ....** Madrid, 1814. Fo. Leath. (DS. Dec.16; 2320) Pts. 22,000

CABINET OF GENIUS, The
L., 1787. 2 vols. Sm. 4to. Engraved titles & plts., 1 title torn, spotted, slight offsetting, few slight tears, cont. cf.-bkd. bds., lacks 1 label. (S. Apr.9; 200) *Barker.* £70

CABINET OF LILLIPUT: Instructive Stories
L., 1802. 12 vols. 60 x 60mm. Miniature Book. Frontis.'s & several covers loose or detchd., orig. bds., all but 1 rebkd., 1 spine defect., orig. wood box, chipped & rubbed. (SG. Dec.8; 83) $750

CABINET-MAKERS ASSISTANT, The
L., 1853. Fo. Engraved frontis., additional title, 100 engraved plts., spotting, 1 plt. reprd., later hf. mor. (CSK. Nov.4; 62) £70

CABINET DES PIERRES GRAVEES contenant les Bagues Antiques [Tome I] et les Pierres Antiques [Tome II]
Paris, 1778. 2 vols. 4to. Lacks port., foxing, cont. cf. gt., spines decor., worn. (HD. May 21; 17) Frs. 1,500

CABINET OF NATURAL HISTORY & American Rural Sports.
Phila., 1830-32. Vols. 1 & 2 only (of 3). 4to. 44 (of 47) cold. litho. or engraved plts., 5 engraved plts. uncold., lacks 3P-3U in Vol. 2, M2 torn, 1 plt. torn with margin loss, scattered stains mostly minor, other defects, cont. cl., rebkd. & recornered. (SG. Mar.22; 55) $450

CABINET SATYRIQUE
[Holland], ca. 1710. 2 vols. 12mo. Some gatherings yellowed, cont. marb. cf. (HD. May 3; 25) Frs. 1,100

CABRERA, Paul Felix
See– DEL RIO, Capt. Don Antonio & Cabrera, Paul Felix

CADELL, W.A.
– **A Journey in Carniola, Italy & France.** Edinb., 1820. 2 vols. Folding engraved map, 32 engraved plts., some folding, some spotting, cont. hf. cf., slightly worn. (TA. Dec.15; 62) £50

CADIZ
– **Constitucion Política de la Monarquía Española, promulgada en Cádiz a 19 de marzo de 1812.** Cadiz, [19 Mar. 1812]. *1st. Edn.* Cf. (DS. Nov.25; 2120) Pts. 34,000
– **El Cordero de Cadiz.** Cádiz, 1795. Nos. 1-94 in 1 vol. 4to. Cf. (DS. Mar.23; 2072) Pts. 46,000
– **Guia de Cadiz para 1845.** Cadiz, 1844. Sm. tear in port., cf. (DS. Dec.16; 2273) Pts. 34,000

CADIZ ALEGRE
1906-07. Nos. 1-34. 4to. Linen. (DS. Dec.16; 2261) Pts. 36,000

CADIZ UNIVERSIDAD DE CARGADORES DE INDIAS
– **Ordenanzas para el Prior y Consules de la Universidad.** Cadiz, 1803. Fo. Sewed. (DS. Oct.28; 2549) Pts. 26,000

CADRATUS, Petrus
- **Oratio ad Innocentium VIII Habita.** [Rome, Stephan Plannck], after 11 Feb. 1485. 4to. Later bds.; the Walter Goldwater copy. [BMC TV, 85; Goff C-15] (SG. Dec.1; 88) $150

CAESAR, Gaius Julius
- **Les Commentaires de César, des Guerres de la Gaule.** Trans.:– Blaise de Vigenère. Paris, 1576. *1st. Edn.* 4to. Sm. repair to title margin (cont. lined), 17th. C. red mor., arms of Prince Eugène de Savoie, spine decor.; stp. of Bibliothèque Impériale de Vienne, from Comte de Lignerolles liby. (HD. Mar.29; 18) Frs. 280,500
- **Commentaria.** Flor., 1508. Later qtr. cf. gt., spine little worn at head. (TA. Nov.17; 532) £100
- **Commentaries.** Trans.:– Somerset de Chair. Ill.:– Clifford Webb. Gold. Cook. Pr., 1951. *(320) numbered.* Orig. buckram gt.; from D. Bolton liby. (BBA. Oct.27; 129) *Primrose Hill.* £55
- **I Commentari ....** Trans.:– Francesco Baldelli. Venice, 1557. Sm. 8vo. Headpiece & device on title, 2 double-p. maps, 3 double-p. views, many histor. initials, lge. printer's device on final blank verso, early owner's sig. & scrawls on title, old mott. cf., rebkd. (SG. Apr.19; 49) $150
- – **Anr. Edn.** Ill.:– after A. Palladio. Venice, 1619. 4to. 2 engraved maps, 40 double-p. etched plts., some foxing, old hf. vell., worn. (SG. Oct.27; 51) $225
- **Commentarii.** Venice, Nicolaus Jenson, 1471. *2nd. Edn.* Fo. Ornamental capital at beginning with decor. in cols. & gold extending into 3 margins, space for coat-of-arms in lr. margin, 14 similar decor. capitals thro.-out, lacks 1st. & last blanks, MS. marginalia erased, a few gatherings in centre loosening, 18th. C. Fr. mor. gt., gt.-panel. spine (darkened), gouge in upr. cover, some scuffing; bkplt. of John Scott, of Halkshill. [BMC V, 169; Goff C-17; H. 4213] (SPB. Dec.14; 10) $9,000
- – **Anr. Edn.** Ed.:– Philippus Beroaldus. [Lyon, Baltharat de Gabiano, 20 Jun. 1508]. *Counterfeit of Flor. Guinta Edn.* Cont. cf., blind-decor., spine old renewed; cont. MS. ex-libris of Vendôme Benedictine Liby. (HD. Jan.30; 5) Frs. 2,100
- – **Anr. Edn.** Ed.:– Jos. Scaligeri. Leiden, 1635. 12mo. Title with reprd. tear at head, 1 map cleanly bkd. in fold, some slight browning. cf. gt. ca. 1790. gold-tooled & blind-tooled decor., gt. inner & outer dentelle, sigd. 'Rel. P. Lefebve', part lightly rubbed. (HT. May 9; 1413) DM 800
- **De Bello Gallico Commentarii VII ....** Lugduni, 1574. Fo. Cf., gold-tooled. (CR. Jun.6; 173) Lire 280,000
- **The Egypt Bookes ... Conteyning his Martiall Exploytes in the Realme of Gallia.** Trans.:– Arthur Golding. L., 1565. *1st. Compl. Edn. in Engl.* Sm. 8vo. Title in woodcut border, woodcut initials & ornaments, 10 extra ll. of exposition at end, sm. margin wormholes, old sheep rebkd., cover detchd. (SG. Apr.19; 50) $650
- [–] **Julius der erst Römisch Keiser.** [Strassburg, 1507]. *1st. Edn.* Fo. Lacks last 15 ll, slightly wormed, more near end, slightly foxed & soiled, title soiled & torn in lr. margin, no bdg. (HK. May 15; 93) DM 900
- **[Opera] Quae Extant.** Ed.:– Joseph Scaligeri. Leyden, 1635. 12mo. Old red mor., gt.-decor. spine worn. (CBA. Dec.10; 202) $190
- **[Works].** Ed.:– Samuel Clarke. L., 1712. Fo. Double-p. pict. title, 2 ports., 6 double-p. maps, 78 plts. (54 double-p.), sm, hole in title, few sm. tears or repairs, mostly marginal, pict. title & 1 vig. bkd., early mor. gt.; bkplt. of Earl of Roden. (SG. Feb.9; 192) $350

CAESAR, Caius Julius
See— DU PRAISSAC, Sieur – CAESAR, Caius Julius

CAESAR, Th.
- **Alchimy Spiegel.** Frankfurt, 1613. Title with 2 sm. old stps., lightly browned, cont. style leath. (R. Apr.4; 1427) DM 2,200

CAESARINUS FURSTNERIUS (Pseud.)
See— LEIBNITZ, Gottfried Wilhelm. 'Caesarinus Fürstnerius'

CAESARIUS, J.
See— RHEEDE VAN DRAAKESTEIN, Hendrik Adrian van & Caesarius, J.

CAHAN, Abraham
- **Yekl. A Tale of the New York Ghetto.** N.Y., 1896. *1st. Edn.* Decor. cl., light wear, light foxing & spotting of covers, d.-w., some fraying; Ken Leach coll. (RO. Jun.10; 335) $380

CAHIER, Charles & Martin, Arthur
- **Mélanges d'Archéologie, d'Histoire, et de Littérature.** Paris, 1847/49-56. Vols. 1[-4]. Lge. 4to. Qtr. mor. (SG. Jan.26; 169) $150

CAHIER, Le P. Ch.
- **Nouveaux Melanges d'Archéologie, d'Histoire et de Littérature sur le Moyen-Age: Décoration d'Eglises; Curiosités Mystérieuses; Bibliothèques; Ivoires, Miniatures, Emaux.** Paris, 1875. 4 vols. Lge. 4to. Hf. chagrin, unc. (LM. Oct.22; 53) B. Frs. 10,000

CAHIERS D'ART
Paris, 1935-60. Vols. 3, 4 & 7, 10-35, bnd. in 16 vols. 4to. Ills., some cold., ex-liby., vols. 3, 4 & 7 in cl., 5 years in orig. pict. wraps. rest in cl. or leath. (SG. May 3; 70) $3,000
- – **Anr. Edn.** Ill.:– Picasso, Matisse, Klee. Paris, 1940-48. 4to. No bdg. stated. (SM. Mar.7; 2074) Frs. 1,200

CAHIERS DE LA CERAMIQUE ET DES ARTS DU FEU
Sevres, 1955-66. Years 1-10, 40 fascicules. 4to. S.-c. (SM. Mar.7; 2075) Frs. 4,800

CAHILL, Holger
- **Max Weber.** N.Y., 1930. *(250) sigd. by Weber.* Sm. 4to. Silver-lettered cl.; frontis. sigd. (SG. Jan.12; 349) $325

CAHOON, Herbert
- **Overbrook Press Bibliography, 1934-1959.** Foreword:– F. Altschul. Ill.:– M.B. Evans (design). Stamford, Overbrook Pr., [1963]. *1st. Edn. (150).* 4to. Cl., glassine d.-w. (SG. Sep.15; 254) $240

CAHUSAC, Louis de
- **La Danse Ancienne et Moderne ....** 1754. *Orig. Edn.* 3 vols. 16mo. Cont. cf. (HD. Jan.24; 6) Frs. 3,400

CAILLE, René
- **Travels through Central Africa to Timbuctoo.** 1830. 2 vols. Foxed, orig. bds. (BBA. Sep.29; 4) *Price.* £80

CAILLER, P.
See— LIORE, A. & Cailler, P.

CAILLEUX, A. de
See— TAYLOR, Bon J., Nodier, Ch. & Cailleux, A. de

CALASCIBETTA, M.
- **Vida de ... San Cayetano.** Madrid, 1653. 4to. Linen. (DS. Apr.27; 2032) Pts. 25,000

CALCOTT, W.
- **A Candid Disquisition of the Principals & Practices... of Free & Accepted Masons.** L., 1772. Cf., rubbed. (P. Jan.12; 208) *Georges.* £120

CALDECOTT, Randolph
- **The Complete Collection of ... Contributions to the 'Graphic'.** L., 1888. *(1250) numbered.* Fo. L.P., orig. cl. defect. (GM. Dec.7; 656) £65
- **The Complete Collection of Pictures & Songs ....** [1887]. *(800) numbered on L.P.* Orig. cl. (GM. Dec.7; 655) £85
- – **Anr. Copy.** Lge. 4to. Two-toned cl. (SKC. Sep.9; 1860) £50
- **Graphic Pictures.** 1891. *Ltd. Edn.* Ob. 4to. Orig. cl. gt. (P. Jul.5; 241) £130
- **Picture Books.** L., ca. 1878-84. Compl. set of 16 titles in 2 vols. 4to. & ob. 4to. 8 titles in each vol., unif. either 32 pp. with integral title, or 24 pp. plus upr. title wrap., lacks lr. wraps, containing advts., light wear, upr. wraps. & some ll. reinforced with linen hinges, 2 ll. in 1 title slightly misbnd., with additional vertical fold at right edge of ll., matching ca. 1920 mor. & marb. bds. by Rivière, raised bands, gt.-lettering. (HA. Feb.24; 224) $300

CALDER, Alexander
- **Gouaches et Totems.** [Paris, 1966]. *(150) numbered on velin de Rives paper.* Special no. of 'Der-*rière Le Miroir'. Sm. fo. Unbnd. in col.-pict. wraps., heavy bd. s.-c.; sigd. in pencil by Calder. (SG. Mar.29; 33) $250

CALDERINUS, Johannes
- **Repertorium Iuris.** [Basel, Michael Wensler], 12 Dec. 1474. Pt. II only (of 2). Fo. Capitals supplied in red or blue, lacks final black, worming at front & back, 16th. C. pig over wood bds., rubbed, lacks clasps. [BMC II, 721; Goff C-51; HC 4248*] (SPB. Dec.14; 11) $600

CALDERWOOD, W.L.
- **The Salmon Rivers & Lochs of Scotland.** L., 1909. *(250) numbered.* 4to. Orig. cl., partly unc., sm. stain on lr. cover. (S. Oct.4; 15) *Chelsea.* £90

CALDWELL, Charles
- **Medical & Physical Memoirs, Containing ... a Particular Enquiry into the Origin & Nature of the Late Pestilential Epidemics of the United States.** Phila., 1801. *1st. Edn.* Some foxing, cont. sheep, worn. (SG. Oct.6; 80) $110

CALDWELL, Erskine
- **The Bastard.** N.Y., Heron Pr., [1929]. *(200) numbered & sigd. by author & artist. Out-of-series copy?.* Lge. 8vo. Cl.; inscr. by author. (SG. Mar.1; 37) $400

CALENDARIO SARDO PER LA REAL CORTE 1774
N.p., 1775. 32mo. Decor. red mor., bdg. inscr. 'mad. cha. Rocca'. (SM. Mar.7; 2008) Frs. 1,400

CALENDRIER DE LA COUR
[1823]. 24mo. Cont. red long-grd. mor., blind-& gt.-decor., centre arms, limp decor. spine, (HD. Dec.9; 105) Frs. 2,400
- – **Anr. Edn.** [1825]. 24mo. Cont. long-grd. red mor., gt.-decor., centre arms, limp decor. spine. (HD. Dec.9; 106) Frs. 2,300

CALEPINUS, Ambrosius
- **Dictionarium.** Reggio Emilia, 1502. *1st. Edn.* Fo. A few capital spaces with guide letters, 1st. lf. & colophon lf. reprd. with some loss, a few ll. with minor repairs to margins & hinges, sm. tear in 2 ll., mod. parch.-bkd. bds., w.a.f. (C. May 30; 17) *Quaritch.* £300

CALIFORNIA
- **Junta de Fomento de Californias, Colección de los Principales Trabajos ....** [Mexico], 1827. 8 pts. in 1 vol. Mod. mor. (LH. Apr.15; 276) $850

CALLANDER, John
- [–] **Terra Australis Cognita, or Voyages to the Terra Australis, or Southern Hemisphere.** L., 1766-68. *1st. Edn.* 3 vols. Maps offset, sm. tears in maps, some reprd., old cf., covers rubbed. [Sabin 10053] (CA. Apr.3; 29) Aus. $2,800

CALLAWAY, Henry
- **Nursery Tales, Traditions & Histories of the Zulus ....** Springfield, Natal, 1868. Vol. 1 (all publd.). Some foxing thro.-out, cl., stained. (VA. Oct.28; 52) R 170

CALLENBERG, J.H.
See— SELIG, G. – CALLENBERG, J.H.

CALLET, F.
See— BALTARD, Victor & Callet, F.

CALLIGRAPHIA NOVA
See— RUTLINGER, Casper – CALLIGRAPHIA NOVA

CALLIMACHUS or CALLIMACO
- **Hymni, Epigrammata, et Fragmenta.** Utrecht, 1697. 2 vols. I.P., some spotting & offsetting, 18th. C. stained cf., spines gt., with monogs. of Duke Albert of Sachsen Teschen, corners worn; Lucius Wilmerding bkplts., Thomas B. Stevenson copy. (CNY. Dec.17; 543) $300
- **Hymni & Epigrammata.** [Parma, 1792.] *(100).* Fo. In Greek, without vigs., last lf. blank with erased stp., cont. bds., bumped. (HK. Nov.10; 3068) DM 420

CALLIOPE, or English Harmony, A Collection
N.d. Vol. 2. Mod. hf. cf. (SKC. May 4; 1641) £80

CALLISEN, H.
- Principia Systematis Chirugiae Hodernae. Kopenhagen, 1788-90. *1st. Edn.* Cont. bds., spine lightly spotted. (R. Oct.12; 1372) DM 450

CALLISTENIA O GINNASTICA per le Giovani o sia Trattato Elementare dei Differenti Esercizi atti a Rafforzare il Corpo, Mantenere la Salute e Preparare una Buona Complessione
Milan, 1829. 24mo. 25 engraved plts., 1 folding, orig, wraps. (S. May 10; 239) *Goldschmidt.* £220

CALLON, J.
- Lectures on Mining Delivered at the School of Mines, Paris. Trans.:– C. Le Nève Foster & W. Galloway. L. & Paris, 1876-86. 6 vols. 8vo. & 4to. Orig. cl./bds., linen backstrips, rubbed. (TA. Feb.16; 450) £75

CALLOT, Jacques
[-] Capricci di Varie Figure. Nancy, [1623]. Ob. 8vo. Ills. cut to the line & fixed on papier vergé de Rives, mod. vell. gt. spine decor.; MS. note 'Cette suite vient de la collection de Cherubini. ler état 2e planche.'. (HD. May 21; 18) Frs. 4,200
- De Droeve Ellendigheden van den Oorlogh seer Aerdigh em Konstigh Afgebeeldt. N.p., ca. 1720. Ob. 8vo. Lacks 1 plt., hf. cf. (B. Oct.4; 602) Fls. 650
- – Anr. Edn. Ed.:– Loreyns Elderman. Ill.:– Leon Schenk after Callot. Ca. 1750. Sm. ob. fo. Hf. cf. (CE. Sep.1; 66) £60
- Les Misères et les Malheurs de la Guerre. Paris, 1633. Title slightly soiled, 2 – 4 line old MS. entries in upr. & lr. margin, old entry at head of plt. 5 verso, light margin soiling, cont. vell., gt. centrepiece, restored, re-cased. (R. Apr.4; 1979) DM 4,700
- [-] Vita Beatae Mariae Virginis Matris Del...Vie de la Bienheureuse Vierge Marie, Mère de Dieu. Paris, 1646. *2nd. Edn.* 4to. Lacks 1 plt., hole in 1 plt. affecting enr., traces of dampstain, bds. (HD. May 21; 19) Frs. 1,600

CALLWELL, Maj.-Gen. Sir C.
- The History of the Royal Artillery. Woolwich, 1931-40. 3 vols. & folder of maps. Cl. (P. Jul.5; 197) £55

CALMET, Augustin
- Het Algemeen Groot Historisch ... Naam- en Woordboek van den Gantschen H. Bybel. - Byvoegzel .... Trans.:– M. Gargon; J. v. Ostade & A.H. Westerhovius. Leiden, Amst. & Leiden, 1725-27; 1731. *1st. Dutch Trans.* 2 vols. & 2 vols. Fo. Vol. 3 lacks 2 engraved plts., 1 plt. reprd., foxing or some browning, cont. hf. roan. a little rubbed, unc. (VS. Jun.7; 951) Fls. 875
- Dictionary of the Holy Bible. 1732. 3 vols. 4to. Soiled, cont. panel. cf., rebkd., rubbed. (BBA. Jun.28; 20) *G. Jeffrey.* £80
- Dictionnaire Historique ... de la Bible. Paris, 1722-28. 4 vols. Fo. Frontis., 208 maps & plts., hf. cf. gt. (P. Oct.20; 107) £220
- Gelehrte Verhandlung der Materi, von Erscheinung der Geisteren .... Augsburg, 1751. *1st. German Edn.* 2 vols. in 1. Title & a few text ll. stpd., ptd. text slightly offset to opposite pp., slightly foxed, cont. vell., spine slightly defect. (R. Apr.4; 1428) DM 480

CALONNE, Charles Alexandre de
[-] Mémoire Justificatif en Forme de Requête adressée au Roi. N.p., 1787. (*Bound with:*)
- Developpements...pour Faire Suite au Mémoire. 1787. (*Bound with:*) - Mémoire en Réponse de M. de Calonne à l'Ecrit de M. Necker Publié en Avril 1787, Contenant l'Examen des Comptes... (*Bound with:*) - Pièces Essentielles et Indispensables. Tableaux de Régie, Appendix qui font Suite au Mémoire de M. de Calonne. Feb. 1788. Together 4 pts. in 1 vol. Cont. roan, spine decor. (HD. Nov.9; 119) Frs. 1,300

CALVERT, Albert F.
- The Aborigines of Western Australia. 1894. Bdg. not stated. (KH. May 1; 153) Aus. $110
- Journal of the Calvert Scientific Exploring Expedition, 1896-7.... Perth, 1902. Sm. fo. The lge. folding

map (all called for?) detchd., stapled, no wraps. (KH. May 1; 154) Aus. $200
- Spain. L., 1911. 2 vols. Fo. Orig. stpd. cl. (DS. Apr.27; 2379) Pts. 26,000

CALVERT, Cecil, Baron Baltimore
See— MARYLAND

CALVERT, F. & Roberts, P.
- Isle of Wight Illustrated, in a Series of Coloured Views. L., 1846. 4to. Hf.-title, tinted litho. frontis., cold. engraved map, & 20 hand-cold. aquatinted views, very slight damage by adhesion on final plt., orig. cl. gt. (S. May 21; 67) *Young.* £460

CALVERT, George Chambers
- A Defense of the Dilettante. Ill.:– Frederic Goudy. [Indianapolis, Grabhorn Pr.], 1919. *(200).* 4to. Light soiling to lr. margins, bds., darkening at edges, spine slightly chipping, no cover label. (CBA. Nov.19; 164) $100

CALVI, François de
[-] Histori of Pracktycke der Dieven. Utrecht, n.d. 12mo. Cont. vell. (VG. Nov.30; 581) Fls. 500

CALVIN, John
- Catechisme c'est à dire le Formulaire d'instruire les Enfans en la Chrestienté.... [Geneva], 1553. Lacks pp. 61-64, title with owner's mark, some sm. defects, partly repaired, very stained, incunable paper covered bds. (HK. Nov.8; 132) DM 520
- Commentarii in Isaaim Prophetam. Ad Edvardum VI. Anglia Regem. Geneva, 1551. *1st. Edn.* Fo. Dedication dtd. 8 Jan. 1551, some staining, 18th. C. bds., defect. (GB. Nov.3; 938) DM 860
- Institutio Christianae Religionis. Lausanne, 1576. Cont. stpd. pig over wood bds. [by Hans Cantzer of Wittenberg?], decor., cont. painted ports. in centre, initials S.G. & date 1582 blind-stpd., corners sigd. H.P. with studs, lacks 2 corners, clasps; from Fondation Furstenberg-Beaumeanil. (HD. Nov.16; 105) Frs. 8,000
- The Institution of Christian Religion. 1634. Fo. Title & last lf. cleanly torn & soiled, some staining, old cf., crudely rebkd. [STC 4425] (CSK. May 18; 106) £50
- Praelectiones in XII Prophetas (quon vocant) Minores. Genevae, 1559. Fo. Owners' inscrs. on title, some stains, vell. (B. Feb.8; 514) Fls. 600

CALWER, C.G.
- Deutschlands Obst - und Beerenfrüchte. Stuttgart, 1854. Text foxed & browned, orig. hf. linen, bumped, spine defect. (R. Apr.4; 1712) DM 800

CAMBI, Bartolomeo
[-] Vita dell'Anima Desiderosa di Cavar Frutto Grande Dalla Santma. Passione di Giesu Christo .... Ed.:– R.P.F. Bartolomeo Saluthio. Rome, 1614. Engraved title, 35 engraved plts., woodcut on final lf. recto, few plts. reprd. on verso, damp-wrinkled, some spots, owner's stp. on title, early vell. (SG. Apr.19; 53) $225

CAMBRIDGE ANCIENT HISTORY (The)
Camb., 1923-39. 12 vols., compl. Cl., d.-w.'s. (LH. Sep.25; 505) $375
- – Anr. Edn. Camb., 1924-54. *Various Edns.* 12 vols. text, 5 vols. plts. Orig. cl., d.-w.'s. (S. Oct.4; 78) *Georges.* £170

CAMBRIDGE BIBLIOGRAPHICAL SOCIETY
- Transactions; Monographs. Camb., 1949-81. Vols. 1-8 pt. 1; Nos. 1-9; together in 42 pts. Orig. wraps., some slightly soiled; H.M. Nixon coll. (BBA. Oct.6; 19) *Oak Knoll Books.* £100

CAMBRIDGE BIBLIOGRAPHY OF ENGLISH LITERATURE
Ed.:– F.W. Bateson. Camb., 1940-57. 5 vols. 4to. Orig. cl., d.-w.'s. (BBA. Aug.18; 6) *Traylen.* £55
- – Anr. Edn. Ed.:– F.W. Bateson. Camb., 1940-66. 5 vols., including Supp. Orig. cl. (BBA. Aug.18; 248) *Traylen.* £60
- – Anr. Edn. Ed.:– F.W. Bateson. N.Y., 1941. 4 vols. Cl., d.-w. (LH. Sep.25; 458) $100
- – Anr. Edn. N.Y. & Camb., 1941-57. 5 vols., including Supp. Cl., light wear, some tears & fraying to d.-w.'s. (RO. May 22; 34) $180

- – Anr. Edn. Ed.:– F.W. Bateson. Camb., 1957-66. 5 vols. Orig. cl., 1 vol. in d.-w. (BBA. Aug.18; 249) *Bell, Book & Radmall.* £60
- – Anr. Edn. Ed.:– G. Watson & F.W. Bateson. 1969. 5 vols., including Index & Supp. Cl., d.-w.'s. (P. Jul.5; 291) £50

CAMBRIDGE MEDIEVAL HISTORY, The
Camb., 1911-36. 8 vols., & 8 portfos. of maps. Orig. cl., d.-w.'s. (BBA. Feb.23; 224) *Quaritch.* £110
- – Anr. Copy. 8 vols., & 7 portfos. of maps only (lacks no. 6). Orig. cl., rubbed. (BBA. Feb.23; 229) *Bennett & Kerr.* £60
- – Anr. Edn. Ed.:– H.M. Gwatkin & J.P. Whitney. N.Y. & Camb., 1924-36. 8 vols. Cl., worn. (RO. Mar.28; 31) $200

CAMBRIDGE MODERN HISTORY, The
Camb., 1904-12. 14 vols., with Index & Atlas vol., & the prospectus. Orig. cl., some vols. slightly rubbed. (BBA. Feb.23; 223) *Quaritch.* £70

CAMDEN, William
- Anglica, Normannica, Hibernica, Cambrica, a Veteribus Scripta. Frankfurt, 1603. *1st. Edn.* Fo. Title-p. & last lf. dust-stained, cont. spr. cf., corners worn; Fortescue Turville bkplt. (BBA. Nov.30; 34) *Stewart.* £60
- Britain, Or A Chorographical Description of the Most Flourishing Kingdomes, England, Scotland, & Ireland, & the Ilands Adioyning .... Trans.:– Philamon Holland. 1610. *1st. Edn. in Engl.* Fo. 53 (of 57) maps, most with plt. nos., & 8 full-up. engraved ills. of coins, engraved ill. of Stonehenge (lacks part of lf.), lacks, engraved title, dedication lf., last 2 ll. of 'Table of Ireland', ll. B2, F6, G5, P6 & 3N6, staining to some maps, Cornwall frayed at edges & laid down, Scotland, Ireland, Devon & Kent frayed at edges, sides of Dorset & Somerset cropped, lacks portions of margins from Westmorland & Montgomery, edge of Anglesey strengthened, Rutland cut away a portion missing at head, tears & parts of corners missing to 1st. 6 ll., ink annots., parts of which cut off when book was rebnd., 19th. C. hf. leath., spine gt. (LC. Mar.1; 203) £950
- – Anr. Edn. Trans.:– Philemon Holland. L., 1637. *2nd. Holland Edn.* Fo. Engraved title with map, 8 plts. of coins, 56 (of 57) engraved maps, all but 2 double-p., a few mapsheets shaved at outer margin (1 or 2 strengthened), 1 or 2 others slightly frayed, some margin staining or sm. rust holes affecting text, 18th. C. cf. gt., worn. [STC 4510] (S. Dec.1; 151) *Burden.* £1,200
- – Anr. Copy. Fo. 8 plts., 57 engraved maps, engraved & ptd. titles & 1st. few text ll. detchd., engraved title cut round & mntd., some staining, cont. cf., rebkd., very worn. (S. Dec.8; 293) *Burgess.* £440
- – Anr. Edn. Trans.:– Edmund Gibson. L., 1695. *1st. Gibson Edn.* Fo. Wide margins, engraved frontis. port., plt. of coins, without the Morden maps, replaced with 39 maps from C. Saxton's 'The Shires of England & Wales...', ca. 1693, 4 county maps by Jansson, Blaeu's 'Scotia Regnum cum insulis adjacentibus' & Moxon's map of Ireland, lacks the general intro. & the descriptions of Scotland & Ireland, old cf. gt., worn, some leath. on covers torn; John Anderson bkplt., as an atlas, w.a.f. (LC. Jul.5; 419) £6,000
- – Anr. Copy. Fo. Engraved frontis. port., 10 engraved plts., 50 double-p. maps, 3 sm. maps from 'Antoninus Itinerary' tipped in, 2 maps with tear to centrefold, anr. trimmed to outer border, cont. reverse cf., with 18th. C. reback; inscr. of Elias Mason 1694 on title, the William Stukeley copy, annotated by him thro.-out in ink (including several pasted in slips & long notes & some additions to maps), Charles Eve bkplt. & MS. note dtd. 1 Sep. 1767, as an atlas, w.a.f. [Wing C 359] (C. Nov.9; 48) *Quaritch.* £2,200
- – Anr. Copy. Fo. Engraved hand-cold. port., uncold. plts. of coins, 50 double-p. hand-cold. maps, old cf., rebkd.; Edward, Duke of Norfolk bkplt. (C. Nov.16; 62) *Walford.* £1,200
- – Anr. Copy. Fo. Engraved Port., 50 double-p. or folding engraved maps, 9 full-p. plts. showing coins or antiquities, engraved or woodcut ills in text, 1 or 2 maps just shaved at neatlines, some offsetting in text, cont. blind-ruled cf., rebkd., w.a.f. (S. May 21; 28) *Henly.* £900

CAMDEN, William -*Contd.*

- - **Anr. Copy.** Fo. Engraved frontis. port., 9 plts. of coins, 50 double-p. engraved maps, port. laid down, final lf. rehinged, printing defect to 1 map, anr. map reprd. at fold, dampstain to some ll. & maps, liby. stp. on title verso, mod. cl., w.a.f. (C. Mar.14; 136) *Walford.* £700

- - **Anr. Copy.** Fo. Port., 48 (of 50) folding or double-p. maps, lacks Staffordshire & the West Riding, 8 plts., few text engrs., port. & last few ll. wrinkled, Scotland map frayed without loss, cont. panel. cf. gt. extra, worn. (SG. Jun.7; 4) $850

- - **Anr. Edn.** L., 1695. Fo. Engraved port. (margins reprd.), 8 plts., 50 folding maps, last errata lf., slight dampstain thro.-out, a few sm. tears & holes, mostly marginal, mod. hf. cf. [Wing C359] (BBA. Dec.15; 112) *Postaprint.* £660

- - **Anr. Copy.** Fo. 43 (of 50) maps, old cf., lacks upr. cover. (P. Oct.20; 256b) £540

- - **Anr. Edn.** Trans.:- Edmund Gibson. 1722. *2nd. Gibson Edn.* 2 vols. Fo. Frontis. port., 10 plts., 51 double-p. engraved maps, cont. cf., rebkd. (PD. May 16; 261) £720

- - **Anr. Copy.** 2 vols. Fo. Engraved port., plts. of coins, 50 double-p. engraved maps, a few maps torn at fold, dampstained thro.-out, old cf., rubbed & worn, w.a.f. (C. Mar.14; 36) *Shapiro.* £600

- - **Anr. Copy.** Vol. 2 only. Fo. 15 double-p. engraved maps, some soiling, cont. panel. cf. gt., worn. (S. Mar.6; 221) *Deane.* £220

- - **Anr. Copy.** 2 vols. Fo. Port., 10 numismatic plts., 51 double-p. maps, liby. stp. in margin of title-pp., cont. cf., worn, rebkd. (SG. Nov.3; 33) $1,200

- - **Anr. Edn.** Trans.:- Edmund Gibson. L., 1753. *3rd. Gibson Edn.* 2 vols. Fo. Engraved port., plts. of coins, 51 double-p. maps, cont. cf., spines gt., slightly rubbed. (C. Nov.16; 7) *Burden.* £850

- - **Anr. Edn.** Trans.:- Richard Gough. L., 1789. *1st. Gough Edn.* 3 vols. Fo. Slight offsetting on some maps, diced russ., some covers detchd., w.a.f. (C. Nov.16; 63) *D'Arcy.* £300

- - **Anr. Copy.** Vol. 1 only. Fo. Engraved port., 21 plts., 19 double-p. maps, 2 cleanly torn at fold, cont. reversed cf. (CSK. Dec.16; 166) £170

- - **Anr. Copy.** Vol. 1 only. Fo. Engraved port., 21 plts., 19 double-p. maps, 2 cleanly torn at fold, cont. reversed cf. (CSK. Sep.16; 18) £130

- - **Anr. Edn.** Trans.:- Richard Gough. 1806. *2nd. Gough Edn.* 4 vols. Fo. Engraved port., 160 plts. & maps, some offsetting, slightly browned & spotted thro.-out, cont. cf. gt., rebkd. (BBA. Feb.9; 250) *Intercol London,.* £400

- - **Anr. Copy.** 4 vols. Fo. Engraved port., plts., views, 60 maps, mostly double-p. & folding, cont. tree cf., covers detchd., as a atlas, w.a.f. (C. Jun.27; 18) *Shapero.* £280

- - **Anr. Copy.** 4 vols. Fo. Flts., 61 col. maps, qtr. roan. (P. Mar.15; 389) *Walford.* £240

- - **Anr. Copy.** Vol. 2 only. Fo. 16 engraved plts., 19 double-p. maps, mod. cf., w.a.f. (CSK. Sep.16; 215) £130

- **Britannia Abridged.** 1701. Vol. 2. Port., 33 maps, cont. cf. (P. Oct.20; 256e) £150

- **Britannia sive Florentissimorum Regnorum Angliae, Scotiae, Hiberniae....** Ill.:- Maps:- William Kip & William Hole. 1607. Fo. 57 engraved maps, including 1 folding & 55 double-p., cont. cf., 1 cover detchd. (SKC. Nov.18; 2057) £1,800

- - **Anr. Edn.** Maps:- Pieter van den Keere. Amst., 1617. Ptd. title incorporating woodcut device, 44 (of 46) miniature full-p. county & regional maps, without Port. of Camden, all maps detchd., dark impressions thro.-out, some faint browning, cont. cf., worn, w.a.f. (S. May 21; 21) *Marsden.* £700

- **The History of the Most Renowned & Victorious Princess Elizabeth.** 1688. *'4th. Edn.'.* Fo. Some light browning, 2 ll. cleanly torn, cont. cf., rubbed, upr. cover detchd.; bkplt. of John Duke of Rutland. [Wing C363a] (CSK. Jun.15; 141) £50

CAMERA WORK

Ill.:- after Steichen. N.Y., 1903. No. 2. 4to. Wraps., partly unopened, worn, lacks portion of upr. wrap. (SG. Nov.10; 35) $325

- - **Anr. Edn.** Ill.:- after the Hofmeisters, Demachy, Puyo, Steichen, Le Bergue, & others. N.Y., 1904, 1906. Nos. 7 & 16. 4to. Wraps., lacks spines, heavily chipped, disbnd. (SG. Nov.10; 36) $275

CAMERARIUS, Joachim

- **De Philippi Melanchthonis Ortu, totius Vitae Curriculo et Morte.** Leipzig, 1566. *1st. Edn.* Old liby stp. on title, lightly stained at end, blind-tooled pig. dtd. 1566, margins slightly stained. (R. Apr.3; 24) DM 700

- - **Anr. Copy.** Cont. blind-tooled vell., old MS. on end-papers. (GB. Nov.3; 949) DM 400

- **Elementa Rhetoricae.** Leipzig, 1564. Cont. marginalia & underlining, cont. limp vell. (R. Oct.11; 19) DM 400

- **Symbolorum & Emblematum ex Re Herbaria Desumtorum Centuria ... - ex Animalibus Quadrupedus ... - ex Volatibus et Insectis ... - ex Aquatilibus et Reptilibus....** Nuremb., 1590 [sic, for 1593], 1595, 1596, 1604. *1st. Edns.* 4 centuries in 1 vol. Sm. 4to. Sm. margin stain to some ll., cont. mor., spine & corners reprd. (HD. Jan.30; 4) Frs. 2,300

- - **Anr. Edn.** Ill.:- Hans Siebmacher. Frankfurt, 1661-64. 4 pts. in 1 vol. 4to. Pt. 3 lacks 7 ll., pt. 4 lacks 1 lf. & last lf. blank, 1 copper engr. cold. in, cont. vell., end-paper crumpled. (HK. Nov.9; 1622) DM 1,300

- **Uber die Mondfinsternis.** Leipzig, 1554. Fo. 1 MS. correction, lightly browned, minimal foxing, no bdg. stated. (HK. Nov.8; 134) DM 800

CAMERARIUS, Philippus

- **The Living Library.** L., 1625. *2nd. Edn. in Engl.* Sm. fo. Slightly browned, cont. cf., rubbed. [STC 4530] (BBA. Feb.23; 143) *Fletcher.* £60

- **Operae Horarum Succisivarum sive Meditationes Historicae Auctiones quam Antea Edita.** Nuremb., 1599. 4to. Paper discold. & browned, vell. (S. Dec.20; 775) *Brown.* £120

CAMERON, John

- **Our Tropical Possessions in Malayan India: Being a Descriptive Account of Singapore, Penang, Province Wellesley, & Malacca ....** 1865. 7 cold. & tinted litho. plts. (1 double-p.), cont. hf. cf., rebkd. (TA. Mar.15; 22) £120

CAMERON, Julia Margaret & H.H. Hay

- **Alfred, Lord Tennyson & His Friends.** Reminiscences:- Anne T. Ritchie. L., 1893. *1st. Edn. (400).* Lge. fo. Some lge. dampstains in last p. & plt. margins, not affecting images, some foxing to text, orig. gt.-pict. cl., later recased with buckram spine, orig. backstrip laid down, new end-papers, covers rubbed & worn. (HA. Dec.16; 165) $225

CAMERON, Cdr. Verney Lovatt

- **Across Africa.** 1877. *1st. Edn.* 2 vols. 2 frontis., 31 plts., folding map in pocket, cl. gt. (P. Jun.7; 5) £85

- - **Anr. Copy.** 2 vols. Folding map in pocket, orig. cl. (S. Mar.6; 4) *Morrell.* £55

- **Quer durch Afrika.** Leipzig, 1877. *1st. German Edn.* 2 vols. Lacks litho. map, some margins slightly browned, some light spotting, mod. linen. (H. May 22; 245) DM 400

CAMILLI, Camillo

- **Impresse Illustri di Diversi, Coi Discorai ....** Ill.:- Girolamo Porro. Venice, 1586. *1st. Edn.* 3 pts. in 1 vol. Sm. 4to. Vell. (LH. Sep.25; 506) $225

CAMOCIO, G.F.

- **Isole Famose, Porti, Fortezze et Terre Maritime ....** Venice, [maps dtd. 1570-75]. Ob. 4to. 50 engraved maps, plans & bird's-eye views (29 fully or partly crudely hand-cold.), 17th. C. MS. index preceding 1st. map, lacks title, maps 43-50 defect. in upr. margin, 2 with slight loss of ptd. area, 5 plts. with sm. wormholes, 2 reprd., late 17th. C. mott. cf., w.a.f. (C. Jun.27; 19) *Franks.* £1,600

CAMOENS, Luis de

- **The Lusiad.** L., 1655. *1st. Edn.* 4to. Lacks 2 engrs., hf. mor. (DS. Jan.27; 2412) Pts. 20,000

CAMPANELLA, Thomas

- **De Sensv Rervm et Magia, Libri Quatour.** Frankfurt, 1620. *1st. Edn.* 4to. Foxed, some red pen underlining, cont. vell., lacks ties. (HK. Nov.8; 482) DM 1,800

- **De Sensu Rerum et Magia, Libri Quatuor. - Prodromus Philosophiae Instaurandae, id est, Discertatione de Natura Rerum Compendium.** Frankfurt, 1620. *1st. Edns.* 2 books in 1 vol. 4to. Slightly browned, old Jewish entry on title-p., liby stp. on title lf. verso 2nd work, cont. vell. (D. Nov.23; 93) DM 3,200

CAMPANUS, Joannes Antonius

- **Opera.** Ed.:- [Michael Fernus]. Rome, Eucharius Silber for Michael Fernus, 31 Oct. 1495. *1st. Coll. Edn.* Fo. White-on-black initials, folios 124 & 127 from slightly smaller copy, some browning & spotting, several 16th. C. marginalia, 18th. C. vell.; 16th. C. owner's inscr. of Scipione Fortiguerra, 18th. C. inscr. of Francesco Albizzi. [Goff C73] (S. Nov.17; 13) *A. Thomas.* £850

CAMPARDON, Emile

- **Les Comédiens du Roi de la Troupe Italienne.** 1880. *(335) numbered.* 2 vols. Orig. wraps. (P. Sep.29; 157) £50

CAMPBELL, Albert H. & others

- **Report upon the Pacific Wagon Roads ....** Wash., 1859. 6 lge. folding maps at end, red three-qtr. mor. (LH. Apr.15; 278) $300

CAMPBELL, Alexander

- **The Grampians Desolate: A Poem.** 1804. *1st. Edn.* Hf.-title, 4 pp. advts., orig. paper-bkd. marb. bds., unc., slightly chipped at top; Sir Ivar Colquhoun, of Luss copy. (CE. Mar.22; 54) £190

- **A Journey from Edinburgh through Parts of North Britain.** 1802. 2 vols. 4to. 2 frontis., 42 sepia aquatint plts., hf.-title in Vol. 1, errata ll. & lists of plts., ink stains on Vol. 1 title, str.-grd. mor., spines gt. (LC. Oct.13; 243) £150

CAMPBELL, Archibald

- **A Voyage Round the World.** Edinb., 1816. *1st. Edn.* Hf.-title, folding engraved map, liby. stp. on verso of title & at end, cont. cf., rebkd. [Sabin 10210] (S. May 22; 468) *Bonham.* £380

- - **Anr. Copy.** Folding engraved map with journey hand-cold., hf.-title, mod. str.-grd. red mor. gt., upr. cover detchd., unc.; the Rt. Hon. Visc. Eccles copy. [Sabin 10210] (CNY. Nov.18; 49) $700

CAMPBELL, Archibald & Twining, W.J.

- **Reports upon the Survey of the Boundary Between the Territory of the United States & the Possessions of Great Britain ....** Wash., 1878. *1st. Edn.* Lge. 4to. 3 folding maps, 14 tinted litho. plts., mod. pol. hf. cf.; the Rt. Hon. Visc. Eccles copy. (CNY. Nov.18; 50) $240

CAMPBELL, Colen & others

- **Vitruvius Britannicus.** L., [1715-25?]. Vols. 1-3 in 1. Lge. fo. 3 engraved titles, engraved dedications to Vols. 1 & 3, 230 (of 231) engraved plts., including 54 folding, engraved titles & text in Engl. & Fr., without subscribers list, privilege & Vol. 3 ptd. title, 1 plt. torn at fold, cont. cf., worn, brkn., w.a.f. (C. Dec.9; 179) *Stair.* £1,000

- - **Anr. Edn.** L., 1715-71. 5 vols., including Supp. Lge. fo. 4 engraved titles, engraved dedications to Vols. 1, 4 & 5, 385 engraved plts., several double-p., ptd. title & dedication to Vol. 3, privilege (dtd. 1715), subscribers list in each vol., 2 plts. torn at fold, 1 plt. defect., sm. hole in blank area of plt. 93 in Vol. 4, a few plts. browned, a few margin tears, cont. panel. cf., ends of spines worn. (C. Dec.9; 17) *Weinreb.* £4,200

- - **Anr. Edn.** [L., 1715-]71. *Early Edn.* 5 vols. Lge. fo. A few ll. torn in fold, some light browning & spotting, sm. wormholes in IV & 1 text lf. extended at upr. margin, cont. cf., slightly rubbed, spine renewed, various engraved ex-libris inside cover. (H. May 22; 59) DM 4,000

- - **Anr. Edn.** 1717. Vols. 1 & 2 only (of 5). Lge. fo. 2 engraved titles in Engl. & Fr., engraved dedication, 158 engraved plts., some folding, spr. cf., spines gt.; Sir Ivar Colquhoun, of Luss copy. (CE. Mar.22; 55) £520

- - **Anr. Edn.** L., 1717?-31. 3 vols. in 2. Fo. Titles, text & captions in Engl. & Fr., 295 engraved plts., few folding plts. partly separated at crease, some tape repairs, scattered browning or stains, disbnd. (SG. Apr.19; 54) $500

CAMPBELL, Donald

- **A Journey Over Land to India ....** 1795. *1st. Edn.* 4to. Some minor spotting, cont. tree cf., upr. cover detchd. (TA. Jul.19; 4) £62

CAMPBELL, George, of Marischal College, Aberdeen
– The Philosophy of Rhetoric. 1776. *1st. Edn.* 2 vols. Cf. (PD. Dec.14; 234) £100

CAMPBELL, John, LL.D. 1708-75
[–] A Compleat History of Spanish America. L., 1742. Cont. cf., rebkd. (S. Jun.25; 87) *Ash.* £100
[–] A Concise History of the Spanish America. L., 1741. *1st. Edn.* Cont. cf., gt. spine, worn, bkplt. removed. (BBA. Dec.15; 51) *Waggett.* £130
– The Political Survey of Britain .... 1774. *1st. Edn.* 2 vols. 4to. Hf.-titles, cont. spr. cf., spines gt.; Sir Ivar Colquhoun, of Luss copy. (CE. Mar.22; 56) £200
[–] The Present State of Europe; Explaining the Interests, Connections, Political & Commercial Views of its Several Powers. Dublin, 1750. Early cf. (SG. Jan.19; 130) £100
[–] The Spanish Empire in America. By an English Merchant. L., 1747. *1st. Edn.* Cont. cf., worn, corners restored, neatly rebkd. (SG. Apr.5; 39) $200

CAMPBELL, John, Lord
– Leben u. Thaten d. Admirale u. anderer Berühmter Britannischer Seeleute. Leipzig [& Göttingen], 1755. *1st. German Edn.* 4to. Title verso & 1 end-paper stpd., minimal spotting, cont. hf. leath., floral gt., slightly rubbed. (HK. Nov.9; 1868) DM 600
– Lives of the Admirals. 1761. *3rd. Edn.* 4 vols. Cont. cf. gt.; armorial bkplt. of Adm. Visc. Nelson in Vol. 1. (LC. Oct.13; 311) £60

CAMPBELL, Rev. John, 1766-1840
– Travels in South Africa.... L., 1815. 1 vol. Some foxing & staining thro-out, lacks hf.-title, sm. burn hole in middle of 1 plt. (*With:*) – Travels in South Africa...A Narrative of a Second Journey... L., 1822. 2 vols. 12 hand-cold. aquatint plts., hf.-titles, some foxing & offsetting, unc. Together 3 vols. Unif. hf. cf., corners of 1 vol. worn. (VA. Apr.27; 666) R 400
– Travels in South Africa... (A Narrative of a Second Journey ...). 1822. 2 vols. 2 hand-cold. frontis., folding map, 10 col. plts., cont. cf. gt. (P. Sep.8; 272) £210
– – Anr. Copy. 2 vols. Partly hand-cold. folding map (mntd. on linen), 12 hand-cold plts., hf.-titles, last blank & 2 preceding advt. ll. in Vol. 1, a few ll. slightly spotted, blind liby. stp. on a few ll., cont. hf. cf., rebkd. (BBA. Sep.29; 18) *Morrell.* £150
– – Anr. Copy. 2 vols. Hf. cf.; Sir George Farrar bkplt. (SSA. Jul.5; 63) R 520
– – Anr. Copy. 2 vols. Hf. cf. (SSA. Sep.21; 69) R 370

CAMPBELL, Roy
– Taurine Provence. L., 1932. (100) sigd. by author. 4to. Orig. cl., d.-w., slightly soiled. (BBA. May 23; 65) *Jolliffe.* £95

CAMPBELL, Thomas, 1777-1844
– The Pleasures of Hope. Ill.:– Mitchell & others, after J. Graham. Edinb., 1799. *1st. Edn.* Errata lf., engraved port. frontis. inserted, slight foxing to plts. with some offsetting, some browning, cont. tree cf. gt.; bkplt. of Robert Dalrymple Steuart Muirhead, Frederic Dannay copy. (CNY. Dec.16; 63) $170
– Poetical Works. 1837. Engraved port. & engraved vigs. in text, gt. pold. cf., by Zaehnsdorf, spine faded. (BS. May 2; 16) £65

CAMPBELL, Dr. Thomas
[–] A Philosophical Survey of the South of Ireland. Dublin, 1777. *1st. Dublin Edn.* Piece torn from top of title-p., 1 lf. loose, cont. cf. (GM. Dec.7; 139) £50

CAMPBELL, Thomasina
– Southward ho! Notes sur la Corse en 1868. Ajaccio, 1872. 12mo. Sewed. (HD. Oct.21; 48) Frs. 1,700

CAMPBELL, W.
– My Indian Journal. 1864. 7 litho. plts., some spotting thro-out, hf. mor. gt., slightly scuffed, by Zaehnsdorf. (BS. May 2; 14) £50

CAMPBELL, William W.
– An Historical Sketch of Robin Hood & Captain Kidd. N.Y., 1853. *1st. Edn.* Sm. 8vo. Orig. blind &

gt.-stpd. cl., spine shelf-darkened & slightly nicked on ends; from liby of F.D. Roosevelt, inscr. by him (as President). (SG. Mar.15; 8) $350

CAMPE, Joachim Heinrich
– Bibliothèque Géographique et Instructive des Jeunes Gens.... Paris & Amst., 1802-07. 70 vols. in 35, lacks III. année Vol. 9-10. 12mo. 1 map torn, cont. hf. cf., slightly rubbed; van Veen coll. (S. Feb.28; 53) £80
– Le Nouveau Robinson, pour servir à l'Amusement et à l'Instruction des Enfans de l'Un et de l'Autre Sexe. Amst., 1790. 2 vols. in 1. 12mo. Cont. cf. gt.; van Veen coll. (S. Feb.28; 49) £100
– – Anr. Edn. Ill.:– Desrais. Paris, 1800. 2 vols. 12mo. Orig. wraps., unc.; van Veen coll. (S. Feb.28; 50) £60
– Sammlung Interessanter Reisebeschreibungen für die Jugend. Wien, 1812. 12 vols. 12mo. Cont. hf. leath. gt., 3 vols. with slight worming in jnt., corners slightly bumped. (D. Nov.23; 2112) DM 4,000

CAMPEN, Jacob van
– Afbeelding van't Stadt-huys van Amsterdam. Amst., 1661. Fo. Foxed, mainly at beginning, cont. hf. cf., defect. (VG. Sep.14; 1143) Fls. 450

CAMPENDONK, H.
– Programm zur Tagung des Deutschen Werkbundes am 25. Juni 1926 in Krefeld. [Krefeld, 25 Jun. 1926]. Slightly spotted or discold., orig. wraps., a little wear. (GB. Nov.5; 2327) DM 400

CAMPER, P.
– Vorlesungen, gehalten in der Amsterdamer Zeichen-Akademie.... Trans.:– G. Schaz. Berlin, 1793. *1st. German Edn.* 4to. Title with old owners mark, margins lightly browned, later hf. linen, worn. (H. May 22; 132) DM 520

CAMPILLO, J
See— CASTRO, C. & Campillo, J.

CAMPO, Antonio
– Cremona, Fedelissima Citta et Nobilissima Colonia de Romane. Milan, 1645. *1st. Edn.* 4to. 21 p. MS. index by early owner, later vell.-bkd. marb. bds. (SG. Feb.9; 197) $150

CAMPO Y RIVAS, M.A.
– Compendio Historico ... de la Ciudad de Cartago. Guadalajara, 1703. 4to. Folding plt. torn, cont. pol. sheep gt. (SG. Oct.20; 69) $225

CAMPOS, G.
– Sylva de Varias Questiones Naturales y Morales.... Valencia, 1587. *2nd. Edn.* Light worming, restored, linen by Menard, corners. (DS. Apr.27; 2034) Pts. 100,000

CAMPOS, Joao Correia Aires de
[–] Catalogo da Notavel e Preciosa Livraria do Conde do Ameal. Ed.:– José Dos Santos. Porto, 1924. (*500*). Thick 4to. Cont. hf. mor. & cl., orig. ptd. wraps. bnd. in; Costa Ferreira bkplt. (SG. Apr.5; 211) $120

CAMPWELL, Capt. Robert
– La Caza en todos los Países y a través de los Siglos. Barcelona, 1885. 2 vols. in 1. Lge. fo. Publishers stpd. cl. (DS. Apr.27; 2480) Pts. 24,000

CAMUSET, Dr. Georges
[–] Les Sonnets du Docteur. Preface:– A. Silvestre. Ill.:– F. Rops. Paris, 1893. *3rd. Edn.* (*1st. Compl. Edn.*). (*500*) on vell. Hf. mor., corners, by Stroobants, unc., wrap. & spine preserved; added proof on japan of 2 compositions by Rops. (HD. May 3; 211) Frs. 2,400

CANADA
– Canadian Portfolio. 1837. Wraps., unopened. (P. Jun.7; 312) £130
– Picturesque Canada. A Pictorial Delineation .... L., Cassell, [1890-1900?]. 6 vols. 4to. Orig. gt.-decor. cl.; the Rt. Hon. Visc. Eccles copy. (CNY. Nov.18; 226) $120

CANALETTO or CANALE, Antonio
– Prospectuum Aedium, Viarumque Insigniorum Urbis Venetiarum .... Ill.:– Brustolon, after Canaletto & Moretti. Venice, 1763. Lge. ob. fo. Engraved title, etched port., lge. folding plan, 21

plts., followed by suite of 12 plts. showing the festivities &c. at the installation of the Doge, cont. bds., reverse cf. spine; Edmond Fatio bkplt. (C. Dec.9; 18) *Hammond.* £10,000
– Urbis Venetiarun Prospectus Celebriores. Venice, 1742. 3 pts. in 1 vol. Ob. fo. Engraved title vigs., plt. of ports., 38 etched views. cont. cf., sides covered with marb. paper, rebkd.; early stp. of Lord Milford. (C. Dec.9; 19) *Giunta.* £4,000

CANARO, Antonius de
– De Insinuationibus. Pescia, Laurentius & Franciscus de Cennis, for Bastianus de Orlandis. 7 Mar. 1485. Fo. Final blank, 1 or 2 16th. C. marginalia, early bdg. from fragment of medieval MS. with illuminated initial E, rebkd., somewhat torn. [Goff C87; Hain 4304*] (S. May 10; 240) *James.* £1,200

CANAVILLES, A.J.
– Observaciones sobre la Historia Natural, Geografia, Agricultura, Población y Frutos del Reyno de Valencia. Madrid, 1795. 2 vols. Lge. fo. Cont. bdg. (DS. Mar.23; 2047) Pts. 150,000

CANDID REMARKS ON DR. WITHERSPOON'S ADDRESS TO THE INHABITANTS OF JAMAICA...
Phila., 1772. *1st. Edn.* Title-p. slightly chipped at edges, title & 1st. few ll. dampstained on outer corners, final lf. with short tear at top edge, unbnd., unc. (SG. Jan.19; 347) $325

CANEPARIUS, Petrus Maria
– De Atramentis .... L., 1660. *1st. Engl. Edn.* 4to. Foxed, cont. limp vell. [Wing C 425b] (SG. Sep.15; 81) $350

CANETTI, E.
– Die Blendung. Ill.:– A. Kubin. Wien, 1936. *1st. Edn.* Orig. pict. linen, browned & slightly bumped. (H. May 23; 1174a) DM 640

CANINA, Luigi
– Descrizione dell'Antico Tuscolo. Rome, 1841. *1st. Edn.* Fo. 53 plts., including litho. views on India paper, 5 cold., slightly spotted, cont. cf., worn. (S. May 1; 534) *Sims.* £220
– Gli Edifizi di Roma Antica. Rome, 1848-51. Vols. I-IV only (of 6), including 2 plt. vols. Lge. fo. Engraved map of Rome on 15 double-p. sheets, 304 engraved views & plts., many double-p., cont. hf. vell., spines gt., rubbed. (C. Jun.27; 26) *Weinreb.* £180
– Ricerche sull'Architettura piu propria dei Tempi Cristiani .... Roma, 1846. *2nd. Edn.* Fo. Cl., spine loose. (CR. Jul.6; 120) Lire 380,000

CANINI, Giovanni Angelo
– Iconografia. Cioe Disegni d'Imagini de Famosissimi Monarchi .... Rome, 1669. *1st. Edn.* Fo. 116 engraved plts., 2 slightly torn, old vell. (SKC. May 4; 1715) £150

CANISIUS, Petrus
– Notae in Evangelicas Lectiones .... Freiburg, 1591. *1st. Edn.* 4to. Title with owner's mark, cont. blindtooled cf. over wood bds., slightly bumped, 2 clasps, lacks ties. (HK. Nov.8; 135) DM 700

CANPANTON, Yitzhak
– Darchei Ha'Gemara. Mantua, 1593. *3rd. Edn.* Browned, some wormholes without loss of text, some margins reprd. not affecting text, mod. blindtooled mor. (S. Oct.24; 122) *Sol.* £220

CANTEMIR, Demetrius
– The History of the Growth & Decay of the Othman Empire. 1734. 2 pts. in 1 vol. Fo. Additional engraved title (tipped in), folding map, 23 ports., sm. hole in title, cf. gt., rebkd. (P. Sep.8; 355) £170
– – Anr. Edn. Trans.:– N. Tindal. L., 1756. Fo. Engraved port., folding map, 22 port. plts., cont. cf. gt. (SG. Oct.27; 55) $250

CANTENER, L.P.
– Histoire Naturelle des Lépidoptères Rhopalogères on Papillons Diurnes, des Départemens des Haut et Bas-Rhin, de la Moselle, de la Meurthe et des Vosges. Paris, 1834. Pt. 1. Explanatory plt. & 38 cold. plts., cont. hf. roan, spine decor., unc. (HD. May 21; 81) Frs. 2,000

CANTILLON, M. de
- **Vermakelykheden van Brabant.** Amst., 1768-70. 4 vols. in 2. Engraved frontis. to Vol. 1, 190 folding plts., 4 other plts., cont. cf. gt. (P. Nov.24; 241) *Traylen.* £360

CANTON RIVER
- **Correspondence Relative to the Operations in the Canton River. April, 1847.** Brighton, 1847. Sm. fo. Lge. hand-cold. folding map, cont. hf. mor., spine defect.; 2 or 3 corrections in text with initials G.D.A. (BBA. Jun.14; 292) *Browning.* £130

CANTONE, G.
- **Nvovo, e Facil Modo di fare Horologi Solari, Orizontali, e Verticali a tutte l'eleuationi di Polo.** Turin, 1688. *2nd. Edn.* Lge. 4to. Pt. 2 lacks title, most corners reprd., leath. (HK. Nov.8; 732) DM 1,000

CANTU, C.
- **Historie des Italiens.** Trans.:- A. Lacombe. Paris, 1859-62. 12 vols. Hf. roan. (HD. Feb.22; 34) Frs. 4,300

CAPE BRETON
- **The Importance of Cape Breton Consider'd.** L., 1746. *1st. Edn.* Sigd. in print 'Massachusettensis' on last p., hf. mor. by Sangorski & Sutcliffe; the Rt. Hon. Visc. Eccles copy. [Sabin 10731] (CNY. Nov.18; 52) $700

CAPE CYCLOPAEDIA, The
Cape Town, 1835. Vol. 1 only. Cl., label of B. de Roos, bookbinder. (SSA. Jul.5; 66) R 165

CAPE OF GOOD HOPE ASSOCIATION FOR EXPLORING CENTRAL AFRICA
- **A Catalogue of the South African Museum now Exhibiting in the Egyptian Hall....** L., 1837. Mod. paper bds., inscr. to Prof. Van Breda of Leyden Museum by W.H. Fitton. (VA. Oct.28; 435) R 310

CAPEL, R.
- **Norden, oder zu Wasser und Lande im Els und Schnee, mit Verlust Blutes und Gutes ....** Hamburg, 1678 [1676(supp.)]. *1st. Edn.* 4to. Prelims. worned in lr. margin, mod. wraps. (R. Oct.13; 3302) DM 1,050

CAPELL, Edward
[-] **Notes & Various Readings to Shakespeare.** N.d. 3 vols. 4to. Some ll. slightly spotted, cont. cf., worn, ex-liby. (BBA. Aug.18; 8) *Quaritch.* £190

CAPITALES DU MONDE
Paris, 1892. *(25) De Luxe Edn. on China paper.* 4to. Mor., gold-tooled decor., gt. spine, inner & outer dentelle, sigd. by Chambolle & Duru. (D. Nov.24; 2244) DM 1,800

CAPORALI, G.
- **Architettura.** [Perugia, 1536]. Fo. Stained & slightly foxed, later bds., defect. (D. Nov.23; 1877) DM 1,400

CAPOTE, Truman
- **In Cold Blood.** N.Y., [1965]. *1st. Edn. (500) numbered & sigd.* 8vo. *(With:)* - **A Christmas Memory.** N.Y., [1966]. *1st. Edn. (600) numbered & sigd.* Lge. 8vo. Together 2 vols. Cl., plastic d.-w.'s, s.-c.'s. (SG. Jan.12; 56) $150

CAPPER, James
- **The Bodensee.** L., 1881. Linen. (G. Sep.15; 2088) Sw. Frs. 900

CAPRA, Domenico
- **Il Vero Riparo il Facile, il Naturale per ovviare o rimediare ogni Corrosione, e Ruina di Fiume, e Torrente, ebbenche giudicata irremediabile. Dottrina Prattica ... esposta a Beneficio di Tutti i Simili Danneggiati, e Massime della Città di Cremona.** Bologna, 1685. Sm. 4to. 1 plt. torn, some stains, rustic bds., bumped. (SI. Dec.18; 145) Lire 300,000

CAPREOLUS, Johannes
- **Quaestiones in IV Libros Sententiarum, seu Libri IV Defensionum Theologiae Thomas Aquinatis.** Venice, Octavianus Scotus, 1483. Pt. II only. Fo. Lge. margins, lacks the 4 prelims. before the blank

preceding a2, sm. wormhole thro.-out, disbnd.; the Walter Goldwater copy. [BHC V, 278-9; Goff C-129] (SG. Dec.1; 91) $375
- - **Anr. Edn.** Venice, Octavianus Scotus, 1484. Pt. IV only (of 4). Fo. Capitals supplied in red & blue, a few with margin tracery, lge. initial C on fo. 6 painted in grey, green & gold on burnished gold background, lr. margin with painted floral border in gold & cols. with port. of Christ on blue shield, lacks folios 1 & 5 (both blank), some slight dampstaining to lr. portions of a few ll., some cropping at extremities of some cont. MS. margin annots., cont. (ca. 1500) north-west German monastic bdg. of cf. over wood bds., covers elab. decor., brass catches (lacks clasps), rebkd. preserving most of orig. spine, upr. inner jnt. brkn., some repairs to edges, end-papers renewed at early date; Bibliothek Oberherrlingen bkplt. [Goff C-129; HC 4410] (CNY. May 18; 98) $2,000

CAPRICE (Le)
Paris, 1844. Vol. VIII. 4to. 42 cont. watercold. plts., hf. roan. (HD. Jun.22; 27) Frs. 1,100

CARACCI, Annibale
- **Diverse Figure Al Numero do Ottanta, Disegnate di Penna Nell'hore di Ricreatione da Annibale Carracci ... E cavate dagli Originali da Simone Guilino Parigino.** Rome, 1646. Tall fo. Title & 80 etched plts., trimmed to plt. mark & mntd. or double-mntd., lacks text & plt.-list, some plt. nos. altered by an early owner, few plts rubbed, later qtr. cf., reprd. (SG. Jun.7; 331) $900
- **Livre du Portraiture.** Flor., ca. 1690. Ob. fo. Some foxing & brown spotting, later hf. vell. (H. May 22; 133) DM 480

CARACCIOLUS, Robertus
- **Opera Varia.** Venice, Franciscus Renner de Heilbronn, 1479. Pt. 1 only. 216 (of 239) ll., decor. initial M in blue, green & red on a3r, initials, initial strokes & paragraph marks in red thro.-out, caption on a3r ptd. in red, light stains & minor worming, mainly marginal, some early marginalia, foliated in early hand, 16th. C. vell., worn; J.F. Hurst copy. [Goff C131] (SG. Apr.19; 107) $450
- - **Anr. Edn.** Venice, J. & G. de Gregoriis de Forlivio, 15 Mar. 1490. 4to. Lacks the 1 line title-lf., final lf. (register) mntd., with loss of some 7 words, old vell.; the Walter Goldwater copy. [BMC V, 341; Goff C-134] (SG. Dec.1; 92) $350
- **Sermones de Laudibus Sanctorum.** Naples, Mathias Moravus et Socii, 31 Jan. 1489. 4to. Lacks the 2 blanks, last 3 ll. reprd., with loss of a few words, vell.; the Walter Goldwater copy. [BMC VI, 864; Goff C-143] (SG. Dec.1; 93) $800
- - **Anr. Edn.** Venice, Georgius Arrivabenus, 7 Jul. 1489. 4to. Lacks final blank, ll. 198-9 in facs., a few outer margins reprd., some staining, old bds., vell. back; Michael Chasles bkplt., the Walter Goldwater copy. [BMC V, 383; Goff C-144] (SG. Dec.1; 94) $175
- - **Anr. Edn.** Venice, Bernardinus Benalius, 1 Oct. 1490. 4to. Lacks final blank, last few ll. stained & trifle defect., mod. vell., many fore-edges unc.; the Walter Goldwater copy. [BMC V, 373; Goff C-150] (SG. Dec.1; 95) $350
- **Sermones Quadragesimales de Peccatis.** Venice, J. & G. de Gregoriis de Forlivio, 11 May 1490. 4to. Lacks final blank, last few ll. heavily stained, vell. bds.; the Walter Goldwater copy. [Goff C-162] (SG. Dec.1; 96) $225
- **Sermones Quadragesimales de Poenitentia.** Venice, Franciscus Renner de Heilbronn, 1472. Fo. Fully rubricated, initials in red & blue, some foxing & stains, qtr. cf., no fly-ll.; the Walter Goldwater copy. [BMC V, 191; Goff C-167] (SG. Dec.1; 97) $1,000
- - **Anr. Edn.** Cologne, Ulrich Zel, 17 Jan. 1473. Fo. Lge. margins, rubricated thro.-out, lacks 1st. blank & last lf. of table, wood bds., cf. back, 2 metal clasps; from the Bruce Coll., the Walter Goldwater copy. [BMC I, 191; Goff C-171] (SG. Dec.1; 98) $1,100

CARACCIOLUS, Robertus
See— **TURRECREMATA, Johannes** – **CARACCIOLUS, Robertus**

CARACTERES DE LA FAMILLE ROYALE, des Ministres d'Etat et des Principales Personnes de la Cour de France...Traduit de l'Anglais
Villefranche, 1703. *Orig. Edn.* 12mo. 19th. C. red mor. gt. (HD. Mar.27; 5) Frs. 1,000

CARACTERES ET ALPHABETS de Langues Mortes et Vivantes
[Paris], ca. 1765. Extracted from Diderot & Alembert's 'Encyclopédie'. Fo. 25 copperplts., disbnd. (SG. Jan.5; 84) $175

CARADOC, of Llancarfan
- **The Histoire of Cambria, now called Wales.** Trans.:- H. Lhoyd. L., 1584. *1st. Edn.* Title & 1st. few ll. defect., lge. piece torn from B4 (blank), MS. annots. in 17th.C. hand, some staining, 17th. C. cf., rebkd., worn. [STC 4606] (S. Mar.6; 222) *Thomas.* £160

CARAFFA, Tito de
- **Les Poissons de Mer et la Pêche sur les Côtes de la Corse.** Preface:- Louis Roule. Paris, 1929. *2nd. Edn.* Hf. chagrin, wrap. (HD. Oct.21; 50) Frs. 1,300

CARATHEODORY, C.
- **Vorlesungen über Reelle Funktionen.** Leipzig & Berlin, 1918. *1st. Edn.* Cont. hf. leath., orig. wraps. bnd. in; author's ex-libris. (HT. May 8; 348) DM 500

CARAVAN (The)
[Presno, Calif., 1931]. Vol. V, no. 1, Dec. 1931. 4to. Ptd. Wraps. (SG. May 24; 39) $250

CARAVANSERAIL ou Recueil de Contes Orientaux
Trans.:- Adrien de Sarrazin. Paris, 1811. 3 vols. in 2. 16mo. Cont. mor. gt., spines decor. (HD. May 21; 20) Frs. 1,400

CARBURI DE CEFFALONIE, Conte Marin
- **Monument Elevé à la Gloire de Pierre le Grand....** Ill.:- Delvaux & Sellier after Blarenbergh & Fossier. Paris, 1777. Fo. Pp. 17-20 misbnd., cont. bds., mod. label on spine, unc. (HD. Jun.18; 7) Frs. 4,500

CARCANO, Michel de
- **Sermoniarim de Peccatis per Adventum et per duas quadragesimas.** Basel, M. Wenssler, 29 May 1479. 2 pts. in 1 vol. Fo. Wide margin, some ll. at beginning lightly stained, some sm. wormholes near end in lr. margin, pt. 1 sig. e 3 ll. removed & bnd. in new order, pt. 1 lacks 1 blank & 1 table, pt. 2 lacks last lf.blank, a few index tabs torn out with sm. margin slits, 2 new ll. bnd. at beginning between cover & book, MS. owners entry from 1623 in upr. margin lf 1, cont. pig over wood bds., decor., 10 lge. metal bosses, 2 clasps, many vell. index tabs., worned. [HC. 4509; BMC III 726; Goff C-195] (R. Apr.3; 3a) DM 5,000

CARCO, Francis [i.e. François Carcopino Tusoli]
- **L'Amour Vénal.** Ill.:- Vertès. Paris, 1926. *(95). (69) on Holland, with 2 suites of plts. on Holland & Chine.* 4to. Orange mor., silk end-papers, s.-c. (HD. Nov.17; 96) Frs. 2,200
- **Dignimont.** Monte-Carlo, 1946. *(385) on vélin de Rives.* Fo. Leaves, wrap., folder, box; frontis. numbered & sigd. by artist. (HD. Jul.2; 46) Frs. 1,000
- **L'Equipe.** Paris, 1919. *Orig. Edn. (10) 'n japan.* 12mo. Sewed; sigd. autograph dedication to Henri Martineau. (HD. Dec.16; 83) Frs. 1,300
- - **Anr. Edn.** Ill.:- Dignimont. Paris, 1925. *(274) numbered on pur fil Lafuma.* Mor., sigd. by P. Bonet, art deco, red & mor. inlays, red wtrd. silk end-papers & doubls., hf. mor. wrap., orig. s.-c. with mor. borders. (D. Nov.23; 158) DM 7.000
- **L'Homme Traqué.** Ill.:- Chas Laborde. Paris, 1929. *Edition De Grand Luxe, (149). (15) on japon impérial.* 4to. This copy ptd. for Louis Barthou, suite in bistre on vell., 1 suite in 1st. state, 1 in 2nd. state on japan with remarks; author's sigd. autograph copy of 1st. paragraph on 1st. blank lf. before title, rejected etching in 3 states (2 with remarks). (HD. Apr.26; 60) Frs. 2,400
- - **Anr. Edn.** Ill.:- Chas Laborde. 1929. 4to. 3 separate suites of etchings in proof state, in bistre,

etc., leaves, wrap. & s.-c. (HD. Dec.9; 35p)
Frs. 1,450
- **Images Cachées.** Ill.:– Luc-Albert Moreau. Paris, 1928. *Orig. Edn. (145).* 4to. On Hollande, with suite of lithos in 2 states, mor., watered silk liners, s.-c. (HD. Jan.26; 64) Frs. 1,100
- **Montmartre Vécu par Utrillo.** 1947. *Orig. Edn., (240).* 4to. Light foxing, leaves, box. (HD. Jun.29; 37) Frs. 8,000
- **Quelques-unes.** Ill.:– Louis Legrand. 1931. *(130). (126) on Arches.* 4to. Mor., silk end-papers, s.-c. (HD. Nov.17; 99) Frs. 1,100
- - **Anr. Edn.** Ill.:– Louis Legrand. 1931. 4to. Mor. gt. by Semet & Plumelle, spine decor. (slightly faded), wrap. preserved, s.-c. (HD. Jun.13; 15)
Frs. 12,000
- **Tableau de l'Amour Venal.** Ill.:– Luc-Albert Moreau. Paris, 1924. *Orig. Edn.* 4to. On vell., some foxing, sewed. (HD. Dec.16; 84) Frs. 1,100

CARDANUS (or Cardan or Cardano), Hieronymus or Girolamo or Jérome
- **Commentaria in Septem Aphorismorum Hippocratis... De Venerorum Differentiis, Viribus, & adversus ea Remediorum Praesidiis ... De Providentia Temporum Liber.** Basle, 1564. Fo. 17th. C. roan, worn. (HD. Mar.21; 13) Frs. 1,800
- **De Rerum Varietate Libri XVII.** Basel, 1557. *1st. Edn.* Fo. Margin worming at beginning affecting pagination on a few ll., some light foxing & staining, 18th. C. sheep gt., slightly rubbed; John D. Stanitz coll. (SPB. Apr.25; 77) $1,800
- - **Anr. Edn.** Basle, 1581. Cont. vell.; Dr. Walter Pagel copy. (S. Feb.7; 72) *Jahncke.* £120
- **De Subtilitate Libri XXI.** Basel, Mar. 1560. Early 18th. C. inscr., cont. blind & stpd. pig., roll borders & panel with ports., clasps, 4 brkn., some soiling; Honeyman copy. (SPB. Dec.13; 645) $275
- - **Anr. Copy.** Fo. Lightly stained, slight wormholes thro.-out, especially last lf., 1 lf. bkd. in lr. margin, lacks both blanks, old bds., bumped, lacks spine, upr. cover loose. (R. Oct.12; 1657) DM 500
- - **Anr. Edn.** Basel, 1582?. Fo. Title-p. soiled, few ll. with sm. wormholes, light stain to lr. corners at beginning, lacks last lf. (blank or colophon?), later cf., rebkd.; early owners inscr. on title, Rouen Seminary liby. stp., John D. Stanitz copy. (SPB. Apr.25; 78) $400
- **In Hippocratis Coi Prognostica.** Basel, 1568. Fo. Foxed, few margin stains & wormholes, old suede, rebkd., shabby, covers detchd. (SG. Apr.19; 55)
$140
- **Offenbarung der Natur unnd Natürlicher Dingen.** Trans.:– Pantaleon. Basel, 1559. *1st. German Edn.* Light worming at beginning & end of vol., some old MS. underlining, cont. decor. blind-tooled of over wood bds., 8 corner & 2 centre brass bosses, buckles, ties defect., some sm. wormhole spine old renewed. (R. Oct.11; 21) DM 6,700
- **Opus Novum de Proportionibus Numerorum ... Praeterea Artis Magni, sive de Regulis Algebraicis...Item. De Aliza Regùla Liber, hoc est, Algebraicae.** Basel, 1570. *1st. & 3rd pts. 1st. Edns., 2nd pt. 2nd. Edn.* 3 pts. in 1 vol. Fo. Sm. wormhole in lr. margin thro.-out 2nd. hf. of book, tear in 1 lf., near-cont. bdg. from early vell. antiphoner lf., soiled; name of Stephan Spleiss on verso of front free end-paper, several margin notes & calculations in same hand, David P. Wheatland bkplt., John D. Stanitz copy. (SPB. Apr.25; 76) $1,300
- **Somniorum Synesiorum.** Basle, Sept., 1585. 2 pts. in 1 vol. 4to. Colophon lf., some pp. browned, Vol. 1 1st. pp. stained, cont. pol. cf. gt., gt.centrepiece; Dr. Walter Pagel copy. (S. Feb.7; 73)
Klingsor. £140

CARDERERA Y SOLANO, Valentin
- **Iconografía Española.** Madrid, 1855. *(275).* 2 vols. Lge. fo. Spanish & Fr. descriptions, chagrin, blind-tooled. (DS. May 25; 2322b) Pts. 135,000

CARDILUCIUS, Johann Hiskias
- **Antrum Naturae et Artis Reclusum ... Bruederschafft des Ordens Goeldenen und Rosen-Creutzes.** [Nuremb.], 1710. Vell.; Nordkirchen & Dr. Walter Pagel copy. (S. Feb.7; 75) *Ritman.* £560

CARDONNEL, Adam de
- **Numismata Scotiae, or a Series of the Scottish Coinage....** Edinb., 1786. 4to. 20 engraved plts.,

with 2 additional plts. tipped in, hf. cf., defect. (CE. Sep.1; 2) £50
- **Oratio in Funere Cardinalis Ardicini de La Porta [with Epistola Cardinalis de La Porta ad Innocentium VIII].** [Rome, Andreas Freitag]. after 4 Mar. 1493. 4to. Limp vell. [BMC IV, 135; Goff C-199; HC (Add) 4511*] (SPB. Dec.14; 12) $250
- - **Anr. Copy.** 4to. Last lf. reprd., with slight loss of text, mod. wraps.; the Walter Goldwater copy. [BMC IV, 135; Goff C-199] (SG. Dec.1; 99) $150

CAREME, Antonin
- **Le Maître d'Hôtel Français. Traité des Menus.** Paris, 1854. *New Edn.* 2 vols. Cont. hf. roan, spines decor. (HD. Mar.19; 53) Frs. 4,000

CAREW, George
- **A Retrospect into the Kings Certain Revenue annexed to the Crown, under the Survey of His Majesties Cort of Exchequer.** 1661. Fo. Additional unsigd. 5 ll.(?), ruled in red thro.-out, sm. area of worming through lr. margins, affecting ruled borders, cont. mott. cf., worn, spine defect. [Wing C550; Sabin 10823] (C. May 30; 144)
Drury. £550

CAREW, Richard
- **The Survey of Cornwall.** 1602. *1st. Edn.* Orig. vell. (LA. Nov.29; 114) £220
- - **Anr. Edn.** 1811. *[3rd. Edn.].* 4to. Cont. cf., jnts. strengthened. (SKC. Nov.18; 2002) £50

CAREW, Thomas
- **Poems.** L., 1640. *1st. Edn.* 7-line errata, G7 cancelled, separate title to 'Coelum Brittanioum' dtd. 1640, engraved port. inserted from a 1794 work, tear on B1 reprd., E6 catchword cropped, K1 supplied, paper flaw in K2&3, some worming, 18th. C. cf., jnts. worn; sig. of Thomas Park, the John Hayward copy. (SPB. May 16; 22) $500

CAREY, David
- **Life in Paris.** Ill.:– George Cruikshank. 1822. Hand-cold. aquatint frontis., 20 plts., recent panel. cf. gt. by Bookends Bindery. (TA. Feb.16; 369)
£200

CAREY, Henry
- **Poems on Several Occasions.** L., 1729. *3rd. Edn.* 4to. Mezzotint port., subscribers' list, P1 a cancel for 04, browned, later hf. red mor., spine gt., worn, new title label. (SPB. May 16; 23) $200
- **Songs & Poems.** Ill.:– Robert Gibbings. [Gold. Cock. Pr., 1924]. *(380) numbered.* Orig. vell.-bkd. bds. (CSK. Oct.21; 32) £60

CAREY, Henry Charles & Lea, Isaac
- **A Complete Historical, Chronological, & Geographical American Atlas.** Phila., L., 1823. Fo. 46 double-p. hand-cold. maps, double-p. hand-cold. tables & charts, maps of the principal rivers & mountains of the world, mntd. on guards thro.-out, mod. hf. cf. (C. Mar.14; 121) *Traylen.* £1,250

CARICATURE [POLITIQUE], Morale, Religieuse, Litteraire et Scénique
Ed.:– Ch. Philipon. Paris, 4 Nov. 1830-27 Aug. 1835. Nos. 1-251 in 5 vols. 4to. 526 litho. plts. (numbered to 524), including 91 hand-cold., some double-p., several on India paper, mntd., 5 plts. with overslips, without plt. 19 'Un ami du peuple' (as iss.), without preliminary prospectus containing 2 plts., lacks plt. 231 'Plan d'Anvers', cont. purple hf. mor., unc., orig. wraps. for 'Première Année-Tome Premier' bnd. at end of Vol. 1, as a periodical, w.a.f. (C. Jun.27; 21) *Fiduciary.* £9,000

CARION, Johannes
- **Chronica.** Ed.:– P. Melancthon & Caspar Pevcervs. Ill.:– L. Cranach. Wittenberg, 1588. Fo. Woodcut port. dtd. 1561, cont. pig-bkd. wood bds., blind-tooled, lacks 1 clasp; Graf Christoph Wenzel von Nostitz ex-libris in cover. (H. Nov.23; 582)
DM 780

CARLETON, Capt. George, fl. 1728
- **Memoirs.** Edinb., 1808. In 2 vols. Extra-ill., engraved port., maps & views, some folding, cut out & remntd., some offsetting, slight margin spotting, cont. cf. gt., rebkd. & reprd. (S. Oct.11; 501)
Nolan. £240

CARLETON, George, Bp. of Chichester, 1559-1628
- **A Thankfull Rememberance of Gods Mercie.** L., 1630. *4th. Edn.* Sm. 4to. (extended). Extra-ill. with over 140 inserted 17th. to 19th. C. prints, mostly ports., a few views, a little spotting, early 19th. C. russ., rebkd., old spine preserved. [STC 4634] (S. Oct.11; 502) *Rhys-Jones.* £100

CARLETON, William
- [-] **Traits & Stories of the Irish Poasantry.** Dublin, 1833. 2nd. Series: 3 vols. 12mo. Hf. mor., armorial motif on spine. (GM. Dec.7; 371) £100

CARLETTI, Nic.
- **Topografia Universale della Citta di Napoli.** Naples, 1776. 4to. Cont. hf. cf. (HD. Mar.9; 114)
Frs. 1,150

CARLEVARIUS, Luca
- **Le Fabriche, e Vedute di Venetia.** Venice, [1703]. Ob. fo. Engraved title, dedication, 103 etchings, title with crease & MS. index on verso, cont. cf., rebkd., corners reprd.; bkplt. of William Michel Sale. (C. Dec.9; 20) *Litman.* £4,200

CARLI, Conte Giovanni Rinaldo
- [-] **Le Lettere Americane.** Cremona, 1781-83. *New [1st. Enlarged] Edn.* 3 vols. Sm. 8vo. Cont. vell., gt. spines. [Sabin 10911] (SG. Oct.20; 74) $130

CARLIER DE LANTSHEERE, A.
- **Trésor de l'Art Dentellier ... de Tous les Pays ....** Pref.:– A. Lefebure. Brussels & Paris, 1922. *1st. Edn.* Lge. 4to. 96 photo. plts., lettered tissue-guards, ex-liby., liby. buckram. (SG. May 3; 72)
$250

CARLILE, Lieut. & Martindale, Lieut.-Col.
- **Recollections of Canada ... Quebec.** L., 1873. *1st. Edn.* Ob. fo. 25 full-p. litho. views, orig. gt.-decor. cl., slightly faded, slight wear to edges & corners; the Rt. Hon. Visc. Eccles copy. (CNY. Nov.18; 53)
$100

CARLSCROON, Jean Dumont, Baron de
See— DUMONT, Jean, Baron de Carlscroon

CARLYLE, G.
See— MAPEL, Carrillo & Carlyle, G.

CARLYLE, Joseph Dacre
- **Specimens of Arabian Poetry.** Camb., 1796. *1st. Edn.* 4to. Text in Engl. & Arabic, engraved mus. frontis., errata lf., cont. cf., spine & jnts. very worn. (SG. Apr.19; 12) $110

CARLYLE, Thomas
- **The French Revolution: a History.** L., 1837. *1st. Edn.* 3 vols. Special author's bdg. of maroon mor., spines gt., mod. maroon lev. mor.-bkd. buckram box; pres. copy from author to Mrs. John Welsh, part of a lf. of the orig. MS. inserted in Vol. 1. (S. Dec.8; 83) *John Howell.* £3,400
- **Latter-Day Pamphlets.** Boston, 1850. *1st. Amer. Edn.* Orig. 8 pts. Sewed, ptd. wraps., 1 lr. wrap. partially torn away, pt. VIII unbnd., mor.-bkd. cl. folding case. (SG. Nov.17; 24) $100
- - **Anr. Edn.** 1850. *(Bound With:)* – **Chartism.** 1842. Together 2 vols. in 1. Mod. hf. mor. (BBA. Jul.27; 144) *Howes.* £50
- [**Collected Works**]. 1850; 1858-65; 1867; 1843; 1851; 1882; 1881. *1st. Edns.* 14 vols. hf. cf., orig. cl. gt., orig. cl., unbnd., unbnd., wraps., cl. gt. (PD. Aug.17; 153) £125
- - **Anr. Edn.** 1870-71. 23 vols. only (of 30). Hf. cf. (SSA. Jul.5; 68) R 205
- **The Works.** 1896-99. *Centenary Edn.* 30 vols. Cl. gt. (PD. Oct.19; 56) £50
- **Collected Works.** L., n.d. 34 vols. Cont. hf. cf. by Bickers & Son, spines gt. (S. Mar.20; 759)
Booth. £150

CARMAN, Bliss
- **Low Tide on Grand Pré: a Book of Lyrics.** L., 1893. *1st. Engl. Edn.* Sq. 8vo. Sheets folded, orig. cl., mostly unopened or untrimmed; probably an advance, trial or proof copy, Frederic Dannay copy. (CNY. Dec.16; 64) $240

CARMICHAEL, Mrs. A.C.
- **Domestic Manners & Social Conditions of the White, Coloured & Negro Population of the West**

CARMICHAEL, Mrs. A.C. -*Contd.*

Indies. L., 1833. *1st. Edn.* 2 vols. Orig. bds., unc., vol.1 spine defect. (P. May 17; 2)   *Drewett.* £80

CARMICHAEL, John
– A Self-Defensive War Lawful. Phila., 1775. Dampstained, bds. (SG. Oct.20; 76) $100

CARNARVON, Earl of
[–] Catalogue of Books selected from the Library of An English Amateur. Priv. ptd., 1893-97. *(153).* 2 pts. in 1 vol. Fo. Buckram; book label & pres. inscr. of F.S. Ferguson to H.M. Nixon, H.M. Nixon coll. (BBA. Oct.6; 176)   *Kokoro.* £100

CARNE, John
– Syria, The Holy Land, Asia Minor, & c. Illustrated. 1836-38. 3 vols. 4to. Additional engraved titles, 2 maps, 117 steel-engraved plts., some spotted, cont. russ., rubbed. (S. Nov.1; 52)   *Clegg.* £150
– – Anr. Copy. 3 vols. 4to. 3 engraved titles, 2 maps, 117 engraved views, some spotting, hf. cf. gt. (P. Sep.8; 3)   *Map House.* £95
– – Anr. Edn. L., [1836-38]. 3 vols. 4to. Engraved titles, 2 maps, 117 views, some spotting, cont. cf. (S. Mar.6; 14)   *Havenfirst.* £140
– – Anr. Copy. 3 vols. 4to. Steel-engraved additional titles & 115 plts., 2 maps, some light spotting, cont. cf., spines rubbed. (CSK. Jul.6; 81)   £110
– – Anr. Copy. 3 vols. in 2. 4to. Engraved vig. titles, 2 maps, 117 engraved plts., some light foxing in pt. 3, cont. panel. cf. gt. (PD. Oct.19; 104)   £92
– – Anr. Edn. Ill.:– after Bartlett, Purser & others. L., [1837]. Vol. II only. Lge. 4to. Additional pict. title, 36 steel-engraved plts., orig. cl., richly embossed in blind, lge. gt. design in centre of covers, gt.-pict. back. (SG. Sep.22; 83) $100
– – Anr. Edn. Ca. 1838. 3 vols. 4to. 3 engraved titles, 2 maps, 117 plts., some foxed, hf. mor. gt. (P. Jul.26; 46)   £170
– – Anr. Edn. Ill.:– after Bartlett & Allom. L., [1861-63]. 2 vols. in 1. Lge. 4to. 2 frontis., 2 pict. titles, 114 plts., mor. gt. (SG. Sep.22; 84) $200
– – Anr. Edn. N.d. 3 pts. in 1. 4to. 3 additional steel-engraved title, 2 maps, 115 plts. only, cont. hf. cf., lightly rubbed, jnts. reprd. (CSK. Apr.6; 185)   £85
– – Anr. Copy. 4 vol. in 2. 4to. Engraved vig. titles, 3 maps, 123 plts., some spotting, cont. hf. mor., rubbed. (BBA. Dec.15; 60)   *Trotter.* £65
– – Anr. Copy. Hf. mor. (SSA. Jul.5; 71)   R 170

CARNELL, P.P.
– A Treatise on Family Wine Making: Calculated for Making Excellent Wines from the Various Fruits of this United Country .... 1814. Some spotting, orig. bds., untrimmed, some wear, crudely rebkd. (TA. Mar.15; 384)   £52

CARNOT, Lazare N.M.
– Essai sur les Machines en Général. Dijon, 1786. *2nd. Edn.* Errata lf., cont. wraps., unc.; John D. Stanitz coll. (SPB. Apr.25; 79) $380
– Principes Fondamenteaux de l'Equilibre et du Mouvement. Paris, 1803. *1st. Edn.* Hf.-title, errata lf., cont. paper wraps (lined with ptd. astronomical tables for Feb. 1823), unc., sm. losses to spine & label, ct. box; John D. Stanitz coll. (SPB. Apr.25; 80) $800
– Réflexions sur la Métaphysique du Calcul Infinitésimal. Paris, 1797. *1st. Edn.* Title-p. lightly soiled, traces of bkplt. on verso, few ll. ink-spattered, plt. stained, unbnd., stitched; John D. Stanitz coll. (SPB. Apr.25; 81) $200
– – Anr. Edn. Paris, 1813. *2nd. Edn.* Hf.-title, prelims. lightly foxed, hf.-title partly stuck to fly-lf., 19th. C. hf. cf., slightly rubbed, sm. liby label on spine; John D. Stanitz coll. (SPB. Apr.25; 82) $100

CARNOT, Nicolas Leonard Sadi
– Réflexions sur la Puissance Motrice du Feu et sur les Machines Propres à Developper cette Puissance. Paris, 1824. *1st. Edn.* Hf.-title (guarded & with ink-stain), foxed, lr. margin of 2 ll. defect. without affecting text, cf.-bkd. bds., mor. solander case; John D. Stanitz coll. (SPB. Apr.25; 83) $5,750

CARO, Annibal
– De la Rettorica d'Aristotile. Venice, 1570. (*Bound with:*) MURET, Marc-Antoine – Oratio. Rome, 1571. Together 2 works in 1 vol. 2nd. work incompl., 16th. C. Venetian mor., richly decor.; from Fondation Furstemberg-Beaumesnil. (HD. Nov.16; 163)   Frs. 5,500

CARO, Joseph
– Bedek Ha'Bayit. Venice, 1606. 4to. With the 2 special ll. of approbation (often lacking), slight staining & soiling, 1 lf. misbnd., cl.-bkd. bds., rubbed. (SPB. Feb.1; 28) $400

CARON DE BEAUMARCHAIS, Pierre Auguste
See— BEAUMARCHAIS, Pierre Auguste Caron de

CARPENTER, James
See— NASMYTH, James & Carpenter, James

CARPENTER, Nathanael
– Geography Delineated. Oxford, 1625. *1st. Edn.* 2 vols. in 1. Sm. 4to. 1st. & last blank ll., dampstained & soiled thro.-out, A1-4 in Vol. 2 torn affecting text, cont. cf., worn. [STC 4676] (BBA. May 3; 256)   *Fleming.* £50

CARR, John
– Caledonian Sketches, or a Tour through Scotland in 1807. L., 1809. *1st. Edn.* 4to. Folding aquatint frontis., 11 aquatint views, cont. bds., unc., spine ends frayed. (C. Mar.14; 3)   *Foyle.* £170
– – Anr. Copy. 4to. 1 plt. lightly soiled, cont. hf. cf., lightly rubbed. (CSK. Jul.6; 32)   £110
– Descriptive Travels in the Southern & Eastern parts of Spain & the Balearic Isles in the year 1809. L., 1811. 4to. Title & a few ll. spotted, cont. bds., unc., rebkd. (S. Jun.25; 160)   *Orssich.* £140
– A Northern Summer; or Travels round the Baltic. 1805. 4to. 11 aquatint plts., 1 reprd., cont. cf., rebkd. (CSK. Dec.16; 45)   £110
– – Anr. Copy. 4to. Tree of. gt. (P. Dec.8; 329)   *Hildebrandt.* £80
– The Stranger in Ireland, or a Tour in ... 1805. L., 1806. *1st. Edn.* 4to. Folding aquatint frontis., cold. map, 15 aquatint plts., diced cf. gt. (GM. Dec.7; 448)   £240
– – Anr. Copy. 4to. Folding tinted frontis., 16 aquatint plts., including 4 folding, cancelled liby. stp., hf. cf., w.a.f. (GM. Oct.5; 260)   £220
– – Anr. Copy. Folding litho. frontis., 15 (of 16) litho. plts., some folding, 1 loose, hf. mor., w.a.f. (GM. Oct.5; 459)   £170
– A Tour through Holland, along the Right & Left Banks of the Rhine, to the South of Germany. L., 1807. 4to. Engraved map & 20 tinted aquatint views, title & prelims. discold., cont. cf. (S. May 21; 223)   *Schwedi.* £220
– – Anr. Copy. 4to. Cont. style hf. leath. (R. Apr.4; 2185)   DM 1,300

CARRACCI, Agostino
[–] L'Aretin d'Augustin Carrache, ou Receuil de Postures Erotiques. [Paris,. 1798]. 4to. 20 engraved plts., some spotting, some tears strengthened, cont. red mor. gt. by P. Lefebvre. (SPB. Dec.13; 817) $550

CARRACCI, Annibale
See— CARACCI, Annibale

CARRANZA, Jeronimo
– Libro de ... que trata de la Philosophia de las Armas. Sanlucar de Barrameda, 1582. 4to. Leath.; Marqués de Jerez de los Cabaleros copy with his supralibros. (DS. Mar.23; 2042)   Pts. 200,000

CARRE DE CHAMBON, Barthelemy
– Voyages des Indes Orientales, Mêlé de Plusieurs Histories Curieuses. Paris, 1699. 2 vols. 12mo. Cont. cf. gt. (SG. Sep.22; 86) $150

CARRE DE MONTGERON, L.B.
– La Vérité des Miracles .... Utrecht, 1737. *Orig. Edn.* 4to. Some slight browning & foxing, cont. leath. gt., slightly spotted & rubbed, defect. at jnts. (HT. May 8; 527)   DM 420

CARRIAGE BUILDERS' & HARNESS MAKERS' Art Journal
L., July 1859-June 1860. Vol. 1. 59 plts., including

14 hand-cold. under coach varnish, some spotting, hf. cf., worn, as a periodical, w.a.f. (P. May 17; 241)   *Henderson.* £240
– – Anr. Edn. L., Jul. 1859-Jun. 1862; n.d. Vols. 1-3. 4to. 38 hand-cold. plts., 128 plain plts., vol.3 lacks plt. no. 19, some spotting, qtr. mor., 2 spines misnumbered, as a periodical, w.a.f. (P. May 17; 240)   *Henderson.* £1,350

CARRIAZO, Juan de Mata
– Colección de Cronicas Españolas. Madrid, 1940-46. 9 vols. Orig. wraps., few spines torn, 1 cover detchd. (BBA. Aug.18; 152)   *Duran.* £50
– – Anr. Copy. 9 vols. 4to. Orig. wraps. (DS. Feb.24; 2146)   Pts. 20,000

CARRICHTER, Bartholomeus
– Practia. I. Von Allerhand Leibs Krankheiten. II. Von Ursprung der offenen Schaeden und irer Heylung. Strassburg, 1575. Blank strip cut from title, 170 pp. MS. notes in near-cont. hand at end, limp vell., lacks 2 ties; Dr. Walter Pagel copy. (S. Feb.7; 77)   *Quaritch.* £380

CARRIERE, Jean
– L'Univers de Jean Carrière. Ill.:– Bernard Loué-'din. Trebeurden, 1975. *Orig. Edn. (12)* on vell. de Rives, sigd. by author & artist. Fo. Cold. suite on japan nacré, suite black on Auvergne, suite black on vell. of. copper engrs. & cancelled copper engr., leaves, pict. wrap., box with inset plexi-glass. (HD. Dec.16; 88)   Frs. 1,500

CARRINGTON, John B. & Hughes, George R.
– The Plate of the Worshipful Company of Goldsmiths. Oxford, 1926. *1st. Edn.* Tall 4to. 85 photographic plts., gt.-armorial cl., spine slightly stained. (SG. Oct.13; 179) $425

CARROLL, F.S.
– The New Counties, Hundreds, & District Atlas of South Australia & Northern Territory.... Adelaide, 1876. Fo. Lacks the map of Adelaide County, folding general map of South Australia badly torn with slight loss, a few ll. detchd., bdg. not stated, worn & brkn. (KH. May 1; 157)   Aus. $420

CARROLL, Lewis (Pseud.)
See— DODGSON, Rev. Charles Lutwidge 'Lewis Carroll'

CARSWELL, Robert
– Pathological Anatomy. 1838. 4to. Some spotting, cont. hf. mor., rubbed. (BBA. Jul.27; 5)   *Phillips.* £1,400

CARTARI, Vincenzo
– Imagines Deorum. Mainz, 1687. *1st. Edn.* Some slight browning, cont. leath., bumped & worn. (GT. May 8; 106)   DM 480
– Le Imagini de i Dei de gli Antichi. Venice, 1571. Sm. 4to. Lacks last blank, a few ills. slightly cropped at fore-edge, slight soiling & staining, cont. cf., worn. (S. Dec.20; 753)   *Fenton.* £130
– – Anr. Edn. Venice, 1674. Lge. 8vo. 1 corner stained thro.-out, cont. vell. (SG. Feb.9; 198) $110

CARTER, Charles
– The Compleat City & Country Cook: or, Accomplish'd Housewife. L., 1732. *1st. Edn.* Tears in 2 plts., some browning, dampstain in lr. margins of plts., cont. reverse cf., upr. cover detchd. (S. Oct.4; 296)   *Hoppen.* £290
– The Complete Practical Cook .... L., 1730. *1st. Edn.* 4to. 59 engraved plts., some folding, engraved folding table, cont. blind-panel. cf. (C. Nov.9; 132)   *Traylen.* £620

CARTER, Harry
See— MORISON, Stanley & Carter, Harry

CARTER, John
– Specimen of the Ancient Sculpture & Painting now remaining in England. 1838. 2 vols. in 1. Fo. Etched titles, 117 plts. (3 folding), some hand-cold., some offsetting & spotting, cont. red mor. gt. (BBA. Sep.8; 274)   *Lenton.* £75
– – Anr. Copy. 2 pts. in 1 vol. Fo. Engraved titles, frontis.'s, 115 plts., some hand-cold., a few folding, few ll. slightly spotted, cont. hf. mor. (BBA. Apr.5; 199)   *Clarke.* £70
– – Anr. Edn. 1887. 2 vols. in 1. Fo. Litho. frontis.'s,

additional titles, 115 plts., some cold. & hand-finished, a few folding or double-p., some soiling, cont. hf. mor., rubbed. (CSK. Jul.27; 125) £100

CARTER, John Waynflete
- **Binding Variants in English Publishing, 1820-1900.** L., 1932. *[1st. Edn.]. (500).* Orig. bds. (SG. Sep.15; 83) $250
- - **Anr. Copy.** 1 vol. 8vo. Orig. qtr. art vell. *(With:).*
- **More Binding Variants.** L., [1938]. *1st. Edn.* 1 vol. Sm. 8vo. Orig. wraps. (SG. Jan.5; 85) $225
- - **Anr. Edn.** L. & N.Y., 1932. *(500).* Orig. parch.-bkd. bds., Esher bkplt., MS. notes (apparently by Esher), H.M. Nixon coll., with his sig. & acquisition note. (BBA. Oct.6; 20) *Segal.* £190
- - **Anr. Copy.** *(With:).* –**More Binding Variants.** L., 1938. Interleaved. Together 2 Vols. Orig. lodgs.; Fred A. Berne Copy. (SPB. May 16; 170) $225

CARTER, John Waynfleet & Muir, Percy H.
- **Printing & the Mind of Man.** L., 1967. *1st. Edn.* Fo. Orig. cl.; 2 ll. with ptd. pres. to Robert Birley loosely inserted. (S. Oct.4; 216) *Heuer.* £180
- - **Anr. Copy.** 4to. Orig. cl. gt. (P. Sep.8; 219) *Georges.* £75
- - **Anr. Copy.** Orig. cl., d.-w. Paris, (TA. Nov.17; 511) £62
- - **Anr. Copy.** Orig. cl., d.-w. Paris, (TA. Jul.19; 429) £58
- - **Anr. Copy.** 1 vol. in 2. Sm. fo. Interleaved, orig. cl., cl. s.-c.; inscr. by Muir to Laurie. 1648. Deval. (SC. Apr.26; 41) $375
- - **Anr. Copy.** Bdg. not stated, some minor offsetting from d.-w. (CBA. Nov.19; 671) $300
- - **Anr. Copy.** Tall 4to. Cl., d.-w. (SG. Sep.15; 271) $225
- - **Anr. Copy.** Sm. fo. Facs. ills., cl., d.-w. (SG. May 17; 299) $150
- - **Anr. Copy.** Sm. fo. Bdg. not stated. (KH. May 1; 158) Aus. $100
- - **Anr. Copy.** 4to. Cl. (VG. May 3; 144) Fls. 480

CARTER, John Waynflete & Pollard, Graham
- **An Enquiry into the Nature of Certain Nineteenth Century Pamphlets.** L., 1934. *1st. Edn.* Orig. cl., d.-w.; inscr. by Carter to Ralph Straus. (SG. Jan.5; 86) $165
- - **Anr. Copy.** Cl., covers spotted. (SG. Sep.15; 85) $100

CARTERET, Léopold
- **Le Trésor du Bibliophile. Epoque Romantique 1801-1875. Livres Illustrés du XIXe Siècle.** Paris, 1927. 4to. Chagrin, gt. fleuron on covers, inner roll-stp., by Seguin. (HD. Sep.22; 203) Frs. 1,200
- **Le Trésor du Bibliophile Romantique et Moderne....** Paris, 1924-28. 4 vols. Lge. 8vo. Hf. mor., corners, by Randeynes et fils, spines decor., wraps. & spines preserved. (HD. May 3; 212) Frs. 2,800
- - **Anr. Copy.** 4 vols. Hf. mor., corners, by Randeynes et fils, wraps. & spines preserved. (HD. Jun.29; 38) Frs. 2,200
- - **Anr. Copy.** 4 vols. Cl. (LM. Oct.22; 172) B.Frs. 10,000
- **Le Trésor du Bibliophile.** Paris, 1946-48. 5 vols. Orig. wraps. (BBA. Mar.7; 186) *Quaritch.* £120
- - **Anr. Copy.** 5 vols. Tall 8vo. Ptd. wraps., unc. (SG. May 17; 55) $275
- **Le Trésor du Bibliophile. Livres Illustrés Modernes 1875 à 1945.** Paris, 1946-48. 5 vols. On vell., sewed. (HD. Jul.2; 47) Frs. 2,400
- - **Anr. Edn.** Paris, 1946-48. *(150)* numbered. 5 vols. 4to. Orig. wraps., slightly faded. (BBA. Sep.8; 6) *Duran.* £90
- - **Anr. Copy.** 5 vols. No bdg. stated. (DS. Feb.24; 2411) Pts. 38,000

CARTIER, J.B.
- **L'Art du Violon ou Collection choisie dans les Sonates des Ecoles Itallienne; Françoise et Allemande, Precedée d'un Abregé de Principes pour cet Instrument....** Paris, Dec. [1798]. *1st. Edn.* Fo. Cont. vell. (S. May 10; 169) *Macnutt.* £450

CARTIER-BRESSON, Henri
- **Beautiful Jaipur.** Intro.:– Max J. Oliver. [Bombay], ca. 1948. *1st. Edn.* 4to. Piot. cl., lr. edges of covers nicked, partly sprung. (SG. Nov.10; 39) $110
- **The Decisive Moment.** N.Y., [1952]. Fo. 2 copies

of the separate pamphlet of captions laid in, pict. bds., with design by Matisse, lr. cover dented at top edge, lightly rubbed, foot of spine cracked, pict. d.-w. worn & reprd. (SG. Nov.10; 40) $300
- - **Anr. Copy.** Fo. Separate pamphlet of captions laid in, pict. bds., with design by Matisse, warped, matching pict. d.-w., rubbed & chipped. (SG. May 10; 27) $200
- - **Anr. Copy.** Fo. Separate pamphlet of captions tipped to title-p., pict. bds., with design by Matisse, laminated, spine age-darkened & reinforced at ends with cl. (SG. Nov.10; 41) $150
- **The Europeans.** N.Y., [1955]. Fo. Pamphlet of captions laid in, pict. bds., with design by Miro, lightly rubbed, corners of spine slightly chipped. (SG. May 10; 29) $150
- **Les Européens.** Paris, [1955]. *1st. Edn.* Fo. Pict. bds., with design by Miro. (SG. May 10; 28) $400
- **Les Européens. Photographies. - Images à la Sauvette. Photographies.** Paris, 1950, 1952. Together 2 vols. 4to. On vell., ill. bds. by Joan Miró & H. Matisse. (HD. May 21; 163) Frs. 2,500
- **Images à la Sauvette.** Paris, [1952]. *1st. Edn.* Fo. Pict. bds., with design by Matisse, lightly rubbed, spine discold., a few minor chips. (SG. May 10; 26) $350

CARTWRIGHT, George
- **A Journal of Transactions & Events During a Residence of Nearly Sixteen Years on the Coast of Labrador.** Newark, 1792. *1st. Edn.* 3 vols. 4to. Engraved frontis. port., 2 lge. folding engraved maps, 14 p. 'Labrador: A Poetical Epistle' in Vol. 3, subscribers list in Vol. 1, frontis. lightly browned, cont. hf. cf., spines gt., Vol. 1 rebkd. preserving orig. spine, rubbed; the Rt. Hon. Visc. Eccles copy. [Sabin 11150 (calling incorrectly? for plts. & 5 maps)] (CNY. Nov.18; 56) $2,200

CARTWRIGHT, William
- **Comedies, Tragi-Comedies, with other Poems.** L., 1651. *1st. Coll. Edn.* Engraved port., fore-e. frayed, **7 cancelled, with dupl. ll. pp. 301-6, with f4 blank, gathering H possibly from anr. copy, slight soiling, cont. sheep., some scuffing, some cracking of spine; sig. of Isaac Baylis & bkplt. of Thomas Beale Cooper. [Wing C709] (SPB. May 16; 24) $250
- - **Anr. Copy.** Same collation as the Hayward catalogue copy in cont. sheep, but with the addition of 2 extra ll.: a variant [a7], 1 state sigd. on verso 'T.P. Baronet', the other sigd. with 2 coronets, & a variant [M5], each with different type sizes, reprint of Lombart's port. inserted, some staining to a few ll., port., title & dedication ll. darkened & probably inserted from a shorter copy, port. rehinged, red mor. by Zaehnsdorf, tightly bnd.; Frederic Dannay copy. (CNY. Dec.16; 65) $220

CARUS, Carl Gustav
- **Erfahrungsresultate aus Arztlichen Studien und Arzlichen Wirken während eines Halben Jahrhunderts.** Leipzig, 1859. *1st. Edn.* Some slight foxing, newer bds. (H. May 22; 186a) DM 420
- **Vorlesungen Uber Psychologie.** Leipzig, 1831. *1st. Edn.* Cont. hf. leath. gt. (R. Oct.12, 1457) DM 450

CARUSO, Enrico
- **Caricatures.** N.Y., 1914. *New Edn.* Fo. Orig. pict. cl. covers soiled; on blank p. opposite title-p. is Caruso's pen-&-ink caricature drawing of E.M. Gattle, inscr. & sigd. (SG. Sep.29; 52) $500

CARVER, Jonathan
- **Travels throught the Interior Parts of North-America.** L., 1778. *1st. Edn.* 2 folding maps hand-cold. in outl., 4 engraved plts., orig. bds., unc., without paper covering. [Sabin 11184] (S. May 22; 308) *Hammond.* £320
- - **Anr. Copy.** Folding maps hand-cold., title & a few ll. slightly browned, old of. gt., rebkd., upr. cover detchd.; the Rt. Hon. Visc. Eccles copy. [Sabin 11184]. (CNY. Nov.18; 57) $800
- - **Anr. Edn.** L., 1779. *2nd. Edn.* 2 engraved folding maps, 5 plts., including tobacco plant engr. (not called for), a few ll. slightly spotted, cont. cf., rebkd. (S. Jun.25; 88) *Faupel.* £300
- - **Anr. Copy.** 2 folding maps, 5 engraved plts.

(including the tobacco plant, not called for but sometimes present), some foxing, tree cf., rebkd. [Sabin 11184] (S. May 22; 307) *Crete.* £260
- - **Anr. Edn.** 1781. *3rd. Edn. 2nd. Iss.* Mezzotint port. of Carver, 2 folding maps (hand-cold. in outl.), 5 engraved plts. (4 cold. including the tobacco plant), hf. cf. [Sabin 11184] (S. May 22; 309) *Sawyer.* £550
- - **Anr. Copy.** Folding maps & all but 1 plt. hand-cold., slight tear to inner margin of title, outer edge of 1 plt. dampstained, cont. tree cf. gt., smooth spine gt.-tooled, recased & restored; the Rt. Hon. Visc. Eccles copy. (CNY. Nov.18; 58) $1,000
- - **Anr. Copy.** Foxing, mott. cf., spine worn, upr. cover detchd.; Bibliotheca Heberiana stp. on end-paper. [Sabin 11184] (SPB. Dec.13; 437) $400
- **Voyage dans les parties intérieures de l'Amérique Septentrionale.** Paris, 1784. *1st. Fr. Edn.* Cf., spine slightly rubbed. (S. Jun.25; 89) £130

CARY, John
- **Actual Survey of the Country Fifteen Miles Round London.** 1786. Engraved title, explanation, 50 hand-cold. maps, 1 double-p. general map, some light offsetting, cont. cf., rebkd. (CSK. May 4; 32) £300
- - **Anr. Copy.** Title, advt. lf., explanation lf., double-p. general map, 50 maps, slightly soiled thro.-out, cont. cf., rebkd., corner worn. (BBA. Dec.15; 121) *Postaprint.* £120
- - **Anr. Copy.** Double-p. frontis. key map (loose), engraved title, 50 single-p. maps, cont. tree cf. (GM. Dec.7; 575) £85
- **Improved Map of England & Wales.** L., 1832. Lge. ob. fo. Engraved title, index map, engraved map in 63 (of 75) sections, each hand-cold. in outl. & with wash border, minor stain to some lr. margins old hf. cf., covers detchd. (C. Nov.16; 69) *Shapero.* £90
- **New & Correct English Atlas.** 1787. 4to. 47 maps, hand-cold. in outl., subscribers list, mod. mor., gt. spine. (SKC. May 4; 1552) £260
- - **Anr. Copy.** 4to. General map, 46 partly cold. maps, hf. roan, reprd. (P. Dec.8; 412) *Nicholson.* £200
- - **Anr. Copy.** 4to. 47 engraved maps, cold. outl., hf. russ., worn. (BBA. Jun.14; 255) *C. Smith.* £170
- - **Anr. Edn.** 1793. 47 outl. cold. maps, 18 pp. road directions, orig. limp leath., flap. (P. Jan.12; 323) £280
- - **Anr. Copy.** 4to. Engraved title & plt. list, general map, 46 partly cold. maps, hf. cf., upr. cover detchd. (P. Dec.8; 410) *P. Martin.* £240
- - **Anr. Copy.** Sm. 4to. 45 (of 47) sm. double-p. engraved mapsheets, mntd. on guards thro.-out, uncold. & without text, few short splits at centre-folds, some slight dust-soiling, cont. fold-over limp cf., worn. (S. Nov.8; 137) *Burgess.* £110
- - **Anr. Copy.** 4to. Engraved title & dedications, 33 (of 47) engraved maps, hand-cold. in outl., slightly browned, some loose, blind liby. stp. on title, cont. cf., worn, covers detchd. (BBA. Dec.15; 122) *Jeffery.* £55
- - **Anr. Edn.** 1809. 4to. Engraved title, 47 hand-cold. maps, orig. limp leath., flap reprd. (BBA. Sep.29; 130) *Mullett.* £240
- **New English Atlas.** L., 1809. Lge. ob. fo. Engraved title, 42 hand-cold. maps on 46 sheets, 40 pp. index bnd. before title, cont. hf. russ., upr. cover detchd. (C. Nov.16; 70) *Quaritch.* £750
- - **Anr. Copy.** Lge. ob. fo. Engraved title, 46 hand-cold. maps, index bnd. in at end, hf. mor., worn. (P. Oct.20; 256) £440
- - **Anr. Copy.** Fo. 46 hand-cold. double-p. engraved maps, separate contents lf. at beginning & indexes at end, cont. russ. gt., 2 brass clasps, jnts. brkn. (C. Nov.16; 68) *Smith.* £420
- - **Anr. Copy.** 4to. 40 pp. index at end, title-p. detchd. & creased, 3 maps detchd. at hinge, 1 with minor margin chipping, 1 soiled on verso & slightly creased, paper slightly darkening, with some darkening from colouring, three-qtr. gt.-ruled cf. & marb. bds., table of contents & a sm. plt. laid on front fixed end-paper, covers worn, upr. cover & free end-paper detchd. (CBA. Mar.3; 15) $650
- - **Anr. Edn.** L., 1811. Fo. Engraved title, 42 regional & county maps on 44 double-p. engraved mapsheets, hand-cold. in wash & outl., with the

CARY, John -Contd.

exception of map of Cornwall (dtd. 1806) the title & imprint dates altered to 1811, index & tables at end, some slight offsetting, cont. hf. russ. gt., rubbed. (S. Dec.1; 160) *Potter.* £420
– **New Map of England & Wales, with Part of Scotland.** 1794. 4to. Key map, engraved map on 81 ll. (including title), hand-cold. in outl., cont. hf. cf., marb. bds. (SKC. Nov.18; 2058) £120
– – **Anr. Copy.** 4to. Engraved map on 81 ll., hand-cold. in outl., cont. cf., rebkd., ex-liby. (CSK. May 4; 39) £70
– – **Anr. Edn.** 1824. *2nd. Edn.* 4to. Double-p. general map, plus key, 78 single-p. maps, hand-cold. in outl., (nos. 67, 71, 72 & 80 are blank sheets, not present), orig. wallet-style mor., worn. (TA. Jun.21; 211) £55
– **New Universal Atlas.** 1808. Fo. 60 double-p. maps, 1st. 10 with tears, many soiled, hf. cf., worn. (P. Oct.20; 270) £580
– – **Anr. Edn.** 1811. Fo. Engraved title, 55 folding hand-cold. engraved maps on 60 sheets, spotted & offset, 5 slightly torn in fold, cont. hf. cf., rebkd., worn. (BBA. Oct.27; 241) *Jeffery.* £400
– – **Anr. Copy.** Fo. Double-p. engraved title, 39 (of 60) double-p. engraved maps on 42 sheets, fully hand-cold. in wash & outl., discold., staining & worming, upr. blank margins frayed, disbnd. (S. Nov.1; 178) *Burgess.* £140
– **Survey of the High Roads from London.** L., 1801. Tall narrow 4to. Double-p. engraved title, explanation, general map, plan, 80 strip road maps on 40 plts., hand-cold. thro.-out, cont. str.-grd. mor. gt., slightly worm. (S. Dec.1; 159) *Tooley's.* £230
– **Traveller's Companion, Or, a Delineation of the Turnpike Roads of England & Wales....** 1790. *[1st. Edn.].* Sm. 8vo. 42 maps (1 folding), all hand-cold. in outl., cont. hf. cf. (TA. Apr.19; 120) £95
– – **Anr. Copy.** Sm. 8vo. General map of England & Wales, 43 county maps on 22 ll., (1 folding), hand-cold. in outl., cont. tree cf., rebkd. (TA. Mar.15; 245) £90
– – **Anr. Copy.** Sm.8vo. 22 maps (1 folding), all hand-cold. in outl., orig. hf. cf., spine slightly worn. (TA. Dec.15; 90) £65
– – **Anr. Edn.** 1791. Engraved title, folding map, 42 hand-cold. engraved maps (dtd. 1792), cont. tree cf. gt.; the Hinton House copy. (LC. Oct.13; 422) £110
– – **Anr. Edn.** L., 1806. Engraved title, advt. & contents lf., 43 maps, (1 folding), hand-cold. in outl., gazetteer at end, cont. cf., rebkd. preserving spine. (S. Apr.9; 142) *Flavel.* £110
– – **Anr. Copy.** Sm. 8vo. 42 (of 43) county maps, hand-cold. in outl., some foxing, cont. hf. cf., lr. cover defect. (TA. Jul.19; 62) £105
– – **Anr. Edn.** L., 1810. Engraved title, 43 maps (1 folding), hand-cold. in outl., contents & advt. ll., cont. cf., worn. (S. Jun.25; 427) *Burgess.* £90
– – **Anr. Edn.** L., 1812. 35 partly cold. maps, ink marks on title, qtr. cf. (P. Nov.24; 309) *Burgess.* £70
– – **Anr. Edn.** 1828. 2 works in 1 vol., as iss.?. 48 col. maps, mod. cl. (P. Jul.5; 378) £110

CARY, John & Stockdale, John
[–] **New British Atlas.** L., 1805. Fo. Engraved title, contents list, 49 double-p. or folding maps, hand-cold. in outl., some slight creasing & soiling, later 19th. C. hf. roan, worn. (S. Mar.6; 226) *Burgess.* £400

CASANOVA, Santu
– **Primavera Corsa.** Bastia, 1927. 12mo. Sewed; visiting card & A.L.S. to J.D. Guelfi. (HD. Oct.21; 53) Frs. 1,250

CASANOVA DE SEINGALT, Giacomo
– **Erinnerungen.** Trans.:– Heinrich Conrad. München & Leipzig, 1907-13. *(100) numbered.* 15 vols. Vell. gt. (D. Nov.24; 2645) DM 1,000
– – **Anr. Copy.** 15 vols. Orig. hf. vell. gt. (R. Apr.3; 343) DM 530
– **Mémoires.** Paris, 1924-31. 10 vols. Cont. hf. mor., spines gt., some faded, orig. wraps. bnd. in. (CSK. May 18; 217) £65
– – **Anr. Edn.** Ill.:– Auguste Leroux. Paris, 1931. *Ltd. Edn.* 10 vols. 4to. 2 plts. from 'Mémories de

Casenove' (Paris, 1932. (470)) bnd. at end of each vol., mor.-bkd. bds. (SPB. Dec.13; 516) $225
– **Mémoires...Suivis de Fragments des Mémoires du Prince de Ligne.** Paris, [1900]. 8 vols. Later red hf. mor. (PNY. Oct.20; 183) $175
– **The Memoirs.** Trans.:– [Arthur Machen]. [L.], priv. ptd., 1894. *(1000) numbered.* 12 vols. Art vell. gt., lightly soiled, spine ends bumped, some pencil notations on end-papers. (SG. Mar.25; 34) $100

CASATI, Major Gaetano
– **Ten Years in Equatoria & the Return with Emim Pasha.** 1891. *2nd. Edn.* 2 vols. Folding map in rear pocket at end of each vol., orig. decor. cl., some minor wear to top & bottom of spines. (TA. May 17; 39) £64

CASCALES MUNOZ, José
See– LEON SANCHEZ, Manuel & Cascales Muñoz, José

CASE, Arthur E.
– **A Bibliography of English Poetical Miscellanies, 1521-1750.** 1935. *[1st. Edn.].* 4to. Orig. hf. cl. (CSK. Oct.7; 53) £50
– – **Anr. Copy.** Sm. 4to. Linen-bkd. bds., unopened. (SG. Sep.15; 86) $110

CASEMENT, Roger
– **Passages Taken from the Manuscript Written by Roger Casement in the Condemned Cell at Pentonvill Prison.** Preface:– H.O. Mackey. [Dublin], for private circulation, [1950]. Sm. 8vo. Orig. ptd. wraps. (GM. Dec.7; 344) £55

CASH, John
See– POOL, Robert & Cash, John

CASORATI, F.
– **Teorica delle Funzioni di Variabili Complesse.** Paris, 1868. *1st. Edn.* Dedication on upr. orig. wrap., wraps. with sm. defects., later hf. linen, orig. wraps. bnd. in. (HT. May 8; 491) DM 440

CASPAR, Karl
– **Passion.** Munich, early 20th. C. *(132) numbered.* Fo. Portfo. of 10 lithos., loose as iss., orig. pict. bds., worn; each plt. sigd. in pencil. (SG. Dec.15; 134) $125

CASSAS, Louis François
– **Voyage Pittoresque de la Syrie, de la Phoenicie, de la Palestine et de la Basse Egypte.** Paris, an VII [1799]. 3 vols. Fo. 176 plts., lacks title-p. & text, cont. hf. red mor. roan, corners, limp decor. spines. (HD. Dec.9; 10) Frs. 14,000

CASSERIUS, Julio
– **Pentaestheseion.** Frankfurt, 1610. *2nd. Edn.* Fo. Sm. stp. in lr. corner of copper-engraved title, some light browning, cont. vell., slightly spotted. (R. Oct.12; 1374a) DM 1,700

CASSIANUS, Johannes
– **De Institutis Coenobiorum.** [Venice, eponymous pr. (Paganinus de Paganinis?)], 1491. Fo. Lacks 1st. blank & sig. L, some margin worming, some margins with brown ink drawings, mod. patterned bds., vell. back; the Walter Goldwater copy. [BMC V, 586; Goff C-234] (SG. Dec.1; 100) $125

CASSIEN & Debelle
– **Album du Dauphiné.** Grenoble, 1835-39. 4 vols. 4to. 188 (of 192) lithos., 1 text p. with margin slit, 1 plt. disbnd., cont. hf. red chagrin. (HD. Feb.29; 7) Frs. 11,300

CASSIN, John
– **Illustrations of the Birds of California, Texas, Oregon, British & Russian America ....** Ill.:– G.G. White & W.E. Hitchcock. Phila., 1862. 4to. 49 (of 50) col. litho. plts., some minor staining in gutter, not affecting plts., orig. cl., cover detchd., spine worn, ex-liby. (SG. Oct.6; 84) $550

CASSIN, John
See– BAIRD, Spencer F. & others

CASSINI, Jacques
– **De La grandeur et de la Figure de la Terre. (Suite des Mémoires de l'Académie Royale des Sciences).** Paris, 1720. *Orig. Edn.* 4to. Cont. marb. cf., spine decor.; from Château des Noës liby. (HD. May 25; 10) Frs. 2,000
– **Nuova Raccolta Delle Megliori Vedute Antiche, e Moderne di Roma.** 1775. Ob. 4to. Engraved title & dedication, 79 (of 80) engraved plts., & 33 additional plts., including ll hand-cold., all plts. laid down, hf. cf., upr. cover detchd. (P. Sep.8; 191) *Erlini.* £220
– **Tables Astronomiques du Soleil, de la Lune, des Planètes; Additions aux Tables Astronomiques.** Paris, 1740-56. *1st. Edns.* Together 2 vols. in 1. 4to. 26 folding engraved plts. bnd. at end, ptd. tables, some folding, liby. stp. on a few pp., 19th. C. hf. mor., rubbed. (BBA. Feb.23; 86) *Rousseau-Girard.* £110
– – **Anr. Copy.** 2 works in 1 vol. 4to. Cont. leath. gt. (D. Nov.23; 394) DM 500

CASSINI de THURY, César François, dit Cassini III
– **La Méridienne de L'Observatoire Royal de Paris.** Ill.:– Moreau. Paris, 1744. 4to. Cont. marb. cf., decor. spine. (HD. Mar.14; 14) Frs. 3,000

CASSIODORUS, Flavus Marcus Aurelius
– **Oper Omnia quae extant.** Genf, 1650. 4to. Some margin staining, some old MS. notes in 2nd. half, cont. vell. (D. Nov.23; 94) DM 650

CASTELBOLOGNESI, Eliezer Yona
– **Darkhei Shehita u-Vedika.** Reggio, 1822. Mildly dampstained, mod. crushed mor., orig. wraps. (remarginated) bnd. in. (SG. Feb.2; 166) $150

CASTELL, Robert
– **The Villas of the Antients Illustrated.** 1728. Fo. A few margins lightly stained, mod. mor.-bkd. cl. (CSK. Jun.15; 84) £170
– – **Anr. Copy.** Fo. 13 engraved plts. (9 double-p.), lacks subscribers list, E2 with 2 sm. tears, fore-margins of a few ll. lightly dampstained, mod. mor.-bkd. cl. (CSK. Apr.6; 41) £65

CASTELLAN, Antoine Laurent
– **Lettres sur la Grèce, l'Hellespont et Constantinople.** Paris, 1811. 2 vols. in 1. Hf.-title, 20 engraved plts., 2 folding maps, cont. sheep-bkd. paper bds., rubbed. (BBA. Jun.28; 203) *Martinos.* £400
– **Lettres sur l'Italie, faisant Suite aux Lettres sur la Morée, l'Hellespont et Constantinople.** Paris, 1819. 3 vols. 50 plts., cont. tree roan, spines decor. (HD. Mar.9; 87) Frs. 2,000

CASTELLANO
Madrid, 1839. 22 issues (complete). 4to. Bds. (DS. Apr.27; 2041) Pts. 45,000

CASTELLI, Benedetto
– **Delle Misure dell'Acque Correnti.** Rome, 1628. *1st. Edn.* Sm. 4to. Errata ptd. on verso of last lf., ptd. slip pasted to foot of p. 48 adding line of text, slight browning, tear in title reprd. without loss, cont. limp vell. gt., bee device from Barberini arms, possibly pres. bdg. to Pope Urban VII (dedicatee), cl. folder & s.-c., minor wear to spine; illegible early inscr. at foot of title, name on end-paper & foot of title of Richard Towneley, Rome, 3 Jul. 1650, John D. Stanitz copy. (SPB. Apr.25; 84) $900
– – **Anr. Edn.** Bologna, 1660. *3rd. Edn.* 4to. Margin staining, some browning, cont. vell. over bds., cont. liby. tag on spine, sm. gouge at head of spine; Piccola Biblioteca Biancheri & Antonio Biancheri bkplts., John D. Stanitz copy. (SPB. Apr.25; 85) $400
– – **Anr. Copy.** 4to. A little torn, cont. vell. (SI. Dec.15; 147) Lire 260,000

CASTELLI, Benedetto
See– GALILEI, Galileo & Castelli, Benedetto

CASTELLI, Ignace Friedrich
– **Erzählungen von allen Farben.** Wien, 1839-40. *1st. Edn.* 6 vols. Minimal foxing, orig. cold. pict. wraps., 2 slightly defect., 3 hf. leath. boxes gt.;

Eduard Hoffmann ex-libris. Hauswedell coll. (H. May 24; 1250) DM 500
– **Memoiren meines Lebens.** Ed.:– J. Bindtner. [1913]. *(150) numbered De Luxe Edn. on holländischem Bütten.* 2 vols. Orig. mor., gt., gold-tooled borders & centre-pieces on covers, slightly rubbed. (GB. May 5; 2263) DM 420

CASTELLIO, Sebastian
– **Cort Verhael van Vijff Beletselen waer door der Mensuchen Herten end' Oogen vande Kennisse der Waerheyt inde Goddelicike Dinghen Affgeleydet worden.** Trans:– Coornhert?. N.p., 1604. Sm. 4to. Disbnd., Loose. (VG. Sep.14; 1308) Fls. 1,000

CASTELLIONAEI, J.A.
– **Mediolanenses Antiquitates.** Ill.:– Blancus. Milan, 1625. 4to. 1 lf. lacks corner, cont. cf., gt.-decor., decor. spine; inscr. 'Bibliothecae Colbertinae' on title. (HD. Dec.2; 79) Frs. 1,500

CASTIEAU, William
See– PROCTOR, Percival & others

CASTIGLIONE, Baldassare
– **Il Libro del Cortegiano.** Venice, Apr. 1528. *1st. Edn.* Fo. Some margin worming at front & back with repairs to blank areas of 1st. & last ll., some ll. stained, washed, cont. Venetian blind-tooled mor., covers & most of backstrip laid down on 19th. C. cf., covers elab. decor., qtr. mor. box; Thomas B. Stevenson copy. (CNY. May 18; 90) $2,400
– – **Anr. Edn.** Venice, May 1533. Title a little stained, cont. blind-stpd. cf., reprd. & rebkd. (BBA. Nov.30; 4) Poole. £120
– – **Anr. Edn.** Flor., 1537. Cont. vell. (C. May 30; 18) Maggs. £120
– – **Anr. Edn.** 1552. Some slight spotting, cf., worn; inscr. Biblioth. Rawlinsoniana in upr. cover. (P. Mar.15; 295) Duran. £50

CASTIGLIONE, Giuseppe
– **Palais, Pavillons et Jardins construits par Giuseppe Castiglione dans le Domaine Impérial du Yuan Ming Yuan, au palais d'Eté de Pékin.** 1783-86. 20 plts. on thin china, pasted on papier vergé, in sheets, buckram s.-c. (HD. Jun.18; 9) Frs. 215,000

CASTIGLIONE, Fra. Sabba da
– **Rivordi overo Ammaestramenti ....** Venice, 1575. Title & some early ll. partly reprd. with japan paper, light stain at head near end, old MS. underlining, later hf. vell. (D. Nov.23; 95) DM 200

CASTILLO, Bernal Diaz del
– **The Discovery & Conquest of Mexico, 1517-1521.** Ed.:– Harry Block. Trans.:– A.P. Maudslay. Ill.:– Miguel Covarrubias. Mexico [City], Ltd. Edns. Cl., 1942. *Ltd. Edn., sigd. by ed., artist & printer.* 4to. Tree cf., extremities lightly rubbed, spine ends rubbed & chipped, end-papers darkening at leath. overlay, lacks box. (CBA. Nov.19; 336) $110

CASTILLO, Pedro Agustin del
– **Descripción Histórica y Geografica de las Islas Canarias.** Preface:– Menendez Pidal. Madrid, 1948-60. 5 vols. 4to. Wraps. (DS. Feb.24; 2288) Pts. 22,000

CASTLEHAVEN, Earl of
– **Review of the ... Irish Wars.** Dublin, 1815. Cont. str.-grd. mor., gt.-tooled borders & spine, by Mullins?. (GM. Dec.7; 361) £75

CASTRO, C. & Campillo, J.
– **Mexico y sus Alrededores.** Ed.:– V. Debray. Mexico, [1859-69]. Fo. 39 chromolitho. plts., cl., s.-c., lightly foxed. (LH. Sep.25; 196) $2,100

CASTRO, David Henriques de
– **Auswahl von Grabsteinen auf dem Niederl.-Portug.-Israel. Begraebnissplatze zu Ouderkerk an den Amstel ....** Leiden, 1883. Erste Sammlung (all publd.). Fo. Additional title in Dutch, text in Dutch & German, 1 plt. loose, orig. bds., rubbed, extremities worn. (SG. Feb.2; 38) $275

CASTRO, Rod. de
– **De Universa Mulierum Medicina ....** Hamburg, 1603-04. *1st. Edn.* 2 pts. in 1 vol. Fo. Some slight soiling, cont. vell. (HK. Nov.8; 484) DM 600

CASTRO Y ASCARRAGA, Pedro de
– **Construcción, y Uso des Compas de Proporción.** Madrid, 1758. Sm. 8vo. Cont. vell. (SG. Mar.22; 72) $120

CASUS PAPALES
– **Episcopales, et Abbatiales.** [Antw., Mathias van der Goes], ca. 1488-91. 4to. Lge. copy, rubricated initials, qtr. cf.; the Walter Goldwater copy. [C. 1493] (SG. Dec.1; 101) $1,150

CASWALL, Edward
[–] **The Grand Master, or Adventures of Qui Hi? in Hindostan.** 1816. *1st. Edn.* Hand-cold. aquatint title, 27 hand-cold. plts., including 1 folding, errata slip at end, title & folding plt. cropped at outer edge, some slight spotting, cont. cf. gt. (S. Nov.1; 53) Wolfe. £200

CASWELL, John
See– WALLIS, John – DEN CASWELL, John

CATALOGUE DE LA BIBLIOTHEQUE IMPERIALE – l'Histoire de France
Paris, 1855-95. 12 vols. 4to. One title reprd., cl. (S. Apr.10; 388) Greenwood. £85

CATALOGUE OF BOOKS OF ALL SORTS...to be sold by Way of Auction, upon [Monday Decemb. Second 1695]
Edinb., 1695. Sm. 8vo. Sale date on title left blank & inserted in ink, outer margin of title frayed with loss of 1 letter, lr. corner of 1 lf. torn & reprd., sm. piece torn from upr. corner of last lf., verso of last lf. slightly stained & rubbed, some stains thro.-out, headlines sometimes shaved, antique-style mor. (C. May 30; 136) Hill. £4,000

CATALOGUE OF A COLLECTION OF EUROPEAN ENAMELS from the Earliest Date to the End of the XVII Century
L., 1897. Fo. 72 plts. (including tryptich folding frontis.), cl., faded, spine ends worn. (SG. Aug.25; 135) $250

CATALOGUE OF GREEK COINS IN THE BRITISH MUSEUM
– Italy. – Sicily. – Seleucid Kings of Syria. – Crete & Aegean Islands. – Troas, Aeolis & Lesbos. 1873; 1876; 1878; 1886; 1894. 5 vols. All orig. cl. gt., a little rubbed on spines. (TA. Jun.21; 502) £150

CATALOGUE DES LIVRES Imprimez de la Bibliothèque du Roy
See– CATALOGUS Codicum Maunscriptorum Bibliothecae Regiae – CATALOGUE des Livres Imprimez de la Bibliothèque du Roy

CATALOGUE D'UNE RICHE COLLECTION DE TABLEAUX...de Monseigneur le Prince de Conti
Paris, 1777. Priced in cont. hand, some light browning, cont. hf. cf., worn, upr. cover detchd. (CSK. Jun.29; 84) £75

CATALOGUS BIBLIOTHECAE HUNGARICAE Francisci com. Széchényi
Pesth, 1799-1807. 7 pts. in 5 vols. Sm. name stp. on title lf. badly erased, orig. decor. hf. leath. gt., slightly bumped. (D. Nov.23; 239) DM 750

CATALOGUS Codicum Manuscriptorum Bibliothecae Regiae
Parisiis, 1739-44. Vols. I-III only (of 4). (*With:*) **CATALOGUE DES LIVRES IMPRIMEZ de la Bibliothèque du Roy** Paris, 1739-50. Vols. I-III only (of 6). Together 2 works in 6 vols. Fo. Cont. marb. cf. gt., Louis XV arms, cypher on spines; from Fondation Furstenberg-Beaumesnil. (HD. Nov.16; 107) Frs. 3,200

CATANEO, Pietro
– **L'Architettura.** Venice, 1567. Fo. Old cf. (HD. Dec.15; 8) Frs. 1,800

CATECHISMO PARA LA INSTRUCCION DE LOS NUEVAMENTE CONVERTIDOS DE MOROS
Valencia, 1599. 4to. Leath. (DS. Mar.23; 2045) Pts. 75,000

CATECHISMUS EX DECRETO Sacro Sancti Concilli Tridentini
Venice, 1601. Slightly soiled & stained thro.-out, some tears & wormholes, mod. cl. (BBA. Mar.21; 13) Snelling. £55

CATECHISMUS oder Kinder Predig
Berlin, 1540. (*Bound with:*) **VON DER GEBRAUCH der Heiligen Hochwirdigen Sacramenten** [Berlin.], n.d. (*Bound with:*) **KIRCHEN ORDNUNG im Churfurstenthum der Marcken zu Brandenburg** Berlin, 1540. Together 3 works in 1 vol. Sm. 4to. Cont. German stpd. pig, decor., arms of Johann Friedrich, Elector of Saxony, spine old renewed, traces of clasps; from Fondation Furstenberg-Beaumesnil. (HD. Nov.16; 108) Frs. 11,800

CATERUS, J.
– **Virtutes Cardinales Ethico Emblemata Expressae.** Ill.:– Galle. Antw., 1645. 4to. 19th. C. red hf. mor. (VG. Nov.30; 604) Fls. 700

CATESBY, Mark
– **The Natural History of Carolina, Florida & the Bahama Islands.** 1731-43?. Fo. Coll. of 24 hand-cold. engraved plts., 2 plts. with sm. margin tears, 1 reprd., 19th. C. hf. roan, as a coll. of plts., w.a.f. (C. Jun.27; 146) Symonds. £1,350
– – **Anr. Edn.** Ed.:– George Edwards. Ill.:– Mostly by & after author, 3 by G.D. Ehret. L., 1754 [1748-56]. *2nd. Edn.* 2 vols. Fo. Double-p. cold. map, 220 hand-cold. etched plts., some offsetting, mainly onto text, cont. red mor., gt.-decor., spines with vertical design & dotted lines gt. in compartments, slightly rubbed; Tatton Park-Plesch copy. (S. Feb.1; 13) Taylor. £40,000

CATHER, Willa
– **April Twilights.** Boston, 1903. *1st. Edn.* 12mo. Orig. bds., mor.-bkd. s.-c.; Perry Molstad copy. (SPB. May 16; 416) $650
– **Death Comes for the Archbishop.** Ill.:– Harold Von Schmidt. N.Y., 1929. *(175) numbered & sigd.* Vell. (LH. Sep.25; 508) $170
– **Obscure Destinies.** N.Y., 1932. Publisher's dummy, with 15 ll. from book & blank fillers, cl., paper cover & spine labels, some wear, covers slightly soiled & spotted; pres. copy, inscr. 'For my dear Elizabeth – Willa Cather – Boston – 9-6-33', & with pencilled caricature by Cather on front end-paper. (RO. Dec.11; 70) $650

CATHERWOOD, Frederick
– **Views of Ancient Monuments in Central America, Chiapas, & Yucatan.** Text:– J.L. Stephens. Ill.:– Owen Jones (title), A. Picken, H. Warren, & others (plts.). L., priv. ptd., 1844. *(300).* Fo. Chromolitho. title in red, blue & gold, uncold. map, 25 tinted litho. plts. on thick paper, title laid down, sm. area of border slightly rubbed & defect., 1 plt. with tear in blank margin reprd., orig. mor.-bkd. moiré bds., corners & inner jnts. reprd., new labels. [Sabin 11520] (C. Jun.27; 22) Quaritch. £5,000

CATLETT, James M
See– WARDER, T.B. & Catlett, James M.

CATLIN, George
– **Catalogue of Catlin's Indian Gallery of Portraits, Landscapes, Manners & Customs.** N.Y., 1838. 12mo. Cf.-bkd. marb. bds. [Sabin 11531] (LH. Jan.15; 249) $180
– **Illustrations of the Manners, Customs, & Condition of the North American Indians.** Ill.:– after Catlin. L., 1857. *9th. Edn.* 2 vols. Lge. 8vo. Hf. cf., rubbed, cover detchd. (SG. Jan.19; 144) $130
– – **Anr. Edn.** 1876. 2 vols. Orig. cl., lightly soiled. (CSK. Jul.6; 31) £240
– – **Anr. Copy.** 2 vols. Some plts. detchd., stitching shaken, orig. cl. (CSK. Sep.30; 150) £95
– – **Anr. Copy.** 2 vols. Royal 8vo. 3 maps, 177 col.-ptd. plts., orig. cl. gt., worn, inner bdg. of Vol. 1 brkn.; the Rt. Hon. Visc. Eccles copy. (CNY. Nov.18; 59) $650
– **Die Indianer Nord-Amerikas.** Trans:– H. Berghaus. Brüssel, 1851. 1 added chromolitho., text slightly browned, orig. pict. linen, lacks front end-paper. (V. Sep.29; 4) DM 400
– **Manners, Customs & Condition of the North American Indians.** N.Y., 1841. *1st. American Edn.* 2 vols. With errata slip Vol. 1, plts. slightly foxed, a few plts. stained on outer part, cont. gt. hf. mor., cl., jnts. very worn. (SG. Apr.5; 48) $400
– – **Anr. Edn.** L., 1841. 2 vols. Last 4 ll. vol. 2

CATLIN, George -*Contd.*

stained, orig. linen, vol. 2 jnts. & lr. cover reprd. (R. Apr.5; 2756) DM 850

-- **Anr. Edn.** L., 1841 [but ca. 1892]. 2 vols. Folding map, 179 cold. plts., a few detchd., some inner margins strengthened, few margin repairs, hf. mor., worn, ex-liby. (S. Mar.6; 57)
Brockhams. £110

-- **Anr. Edn.** L., 1842. *3rd. Edn.* 2 vols. Lge. 8vo. Frontis. & title detchd., gt.-lettered cl., spine ends chipped; ex-liby., plts. unstpd. (SG. Jan.19; 143)
$175

-- **Anr. Edn.** 1844. *4th. Edn.* 2 vols. 4to. Orig. cl., worn & reprd., jnt. brkn. in Vol. 1. (LC. Mar.1; 462) £70

-- **Anr. Edn.** Ill.:– after Catlin. L., 1880. 2 vols. Lge. 8vo. Orig. gt.-pict. cl., spine ends bumped. (SG. Jan.19; 145) $425

-- **Anr. Edn.** 1892. *Facs. Reprint of 1st. Edn.* 2 vols. Orig. cl., spine reprd. (BBA. Oct.27; 293)
Sons of Liberty Books. £80

-- **Anr. Edn.** Phila., 1913. 2 vols. Orig. pict. cl. (S. Mar.6; 58) *Thorpe.* £100

- **North American Indian Portfolio.** L., 1844. *[1st. Edn.].* Lge. fo. 25 hand-cold. litho. plts. mntd. on card, some slight spotting or soiling to mounts, traces of tissue adhering to plt. 13, 20 pp. text (short tear in last), cont. red hf. roan, binder's ticket of Phillip Giles, St. Austell (Cornwall). (S. May 22; 299) *Prince.* £24,000

-- **Anr. Copy.** Lge. fo. 31 hand-cold, (colouring later?) litho. plts. (25 numbered & a further 6 unnumbered), 1 full-p. litho. map of Valley of Mexico (not called for), contents list, some faint margin discolouration, mod. red mor. gt. (S. Feb.1; 14) *Schuster.* £7,200

-- **Anr. Copy.** Atlas fo. 25 hand-finished cold. litho. plts., each mntd. on stiff board, sm. thumbprints on mount margins, loose in hf. mor. folder, orig.? leath. lettering-piece on upr. cover. (SG. Nov.3; 35)
$34,000

CATO, Dionysius

- **Cato: Disticha de Moribus, etc.** Basel, [Johann Amerbach], 14 Jun. 1486. 4to. Lacks final blank, some stains & margin worning, vell. over bds., from a rubricated old MS. lf.; the Walter Goldwater copy. [BMC III, 748; Goff C-297] (SG. Dec.1; 102) $1,300

- **Disticha de Moribus ad Filium.** Ill.:– Jan Fokke. Amst., 1759. In Latin, Greek, Engl., German, Dutch, & Fr., later mor.; Robert Hoe bkplt. (SG. Oct.27; 56) $140

CATO, Marcus Porcius

- **Libri De Re Rustica.** Venice, Aldine Pr., May, 1514. Aldine device on 1st. & 2nd. titles & on final lf. verso. woodcut text diagrams, 1st. title lightly soiled, few marginal worn-holes, some early marginalia & underscoring, qtr. russ., spine badly worn. (SG. Apr.19; 4) $130

CATS, Jacob

- **Alle de Wercken.** Amst., 1658. Fo. Lr. margins 1st. ll. cropped & frayed, some foxing & short tears, vell., reprd., new spine; pres. copy from Cats to Margareta Heydanus, wife of Casp. Commelin, 1661, name of M.H. on upr. cover, inscr. dtd. 1661 on lr. cover, 3 ll. notes re Commelin family in 17th. & early 19th. C. MS. & annot. stating Cats' pres. lf. cut out. (VG. May 3; 744) Fls. 1,100

-- **Anr. Edn.** Dordrecht, 1659. 3 vols. 4to. Slightly browned, a few sm. tears, cont. hf. cf., slight defects. (B. Apr.27; 853) Fls. 550

-- **Anr. Edn.** Amst. & Utrecht, 1700. Fo. Some dampstaining towards end, 1 or 2 minor tears, cont. vell., rebkd. (CH. Sep.20; 24) Fls. 1,000

-- **Anr. Copy.** 2 vols. in 1. Fo. Lacks 1 port. & double-p. plts., a little margin staining, cont. blind-stpd. vell., soiled & defect., w.a.f. (VS. Jun.7; 885) Fls. 600

-- **Anr. Edn.** Ill.:– Matnam, Van Bremden & others after A. v.d. Venne. Amst., 1712. *4th. Fo. Edn.* 2 vols. in 1. Fo. Some foxing, cont. blind-stpd. Russ. over wood bds., brass clasps & corner pieces, foot & top of spine a little defect. (VS. Jun.7; 886) Fls. 1,600

-- **Anr. Copy.** 2 pts. in 1 vol. Fo. Some foxing, 1st. quire loosening, cont. panel. blind-stpd. russ. over

wood, orig. brass corner– & centre-pieces, clasps & catches, lacks 1 catch, spine slightly defect. (VG. Sep.14; 1029) Fls. 1,200

-- **Anr. Copy.** 2 vols. in 1. Fo. 1 plt. torn at fold, margin stains & tears, early 19th. C. pol. cf. (VS. Jun.7; 887) Fls. 1,050

-- **Anr. Copy.** 2 vols. Fo. 3 quires slightly stained, cont. marb. cf., spine gt., rubbed, some defects. (VG. Mar.19; 285) Fls. 850

-- **Anr. Copy.** 2 vols. Fo. Lacks 1 double-p. engraved plt., foxing, some pp. torn, cont. cf., spines defect. (VS. Jun.7; 888) Fls. 775

-- **Anr. Edn.** Ill.:– Matham, Van Bremden, & others, after A. v.d. Venne. Amst. & 's-Gravenhage, 1726. *5th. Fo. Edn. [9th Printing].* 2 vols. Fo. Cont. pol. cf., spines gt., foot of spine Vol. 1 slightly defect. (VS. Dec.9; 1022) Fls. 1,300

-- **Anr. Copy.** 2 vols. Fo. Lacks ptd. title & hf.-titles, hf. leath., defect., lacks spines. (VG. Mar.19; 287) Fls. 1,050

- **Houwelyck. Dat is De Gansche Gelegentheyt des Echten Staets.** Middleburg, 1625. *1st. Edn.* 4to. 1 lf. with margin tear, cont. vell., rebkd., rubbed; Robert Hoe bkplt. (BBA. Sep.29; 98)
Jeudwyne. £280

-- **Anr. Edn.** Pordrecht, 1634. 6 pts. in 1 vols,. 12mo. Title lf. with slight tear, 18th. C. hf. leath. over cont. vell., slightly loose. (D. Nov.23; 106)
DM 500

- **Spiegel van den Ouden ende Nieuwen Tydt.** Amst., 1689. Frontis., 78 hf.-p. copperplts., some worming, faint margin stain, vell. (SG. Feb.9; 220)
$110

CATTAN, Christophe de

- **La Géomance.** Ed.:– Gabriel du Préau. Paris, 1558. *Orig. Edn.* Sm. 4to. Ruled copy, some foxing & worming in upr. margin of 8 ll., mod. bradel vell. (HD. Mar.14; 15) Frs. 1,800

- **The Geomancie of Maister Christopher Cattan Gentleman ....** Trans.:– [Francis Sparry]. L., 1591. *1st. Edn. in Engl.* Sm. 4to. Lacks final blank lf., short reprd. tear in R1 slightly affecting headline, 1 sentence on 2B3 crossed out, 19th. C. str.-grd. blind-stpd. mor. [STC 4864] (C. Nov.9; 50)
Howes. £580

CATTANEUS, S.

- **Enchiridion Eorum Quae in Controversiam Vocantur.** Ingolstadt, 1589. Cont. German blind-stpd. vell., figures of Justice (upr. cover) & St. Catherine (lr. cover), former sigd. MA, minor worming & abrasion. (BBA. Nov.30; 5)
Maggs. £75

CATTENBURGH, A. van
See— **BRANDT, Caspar & Cattenburgh, A. van**

CATTON, Charles

- **Animals Drawn from Nature.** L., 1788. *1st. Edn.* Ob. 4to. Lacks title-lf., some pp. chipped, foxing & old stains thro.-out, text shaken, some ll. detchd., cont. red cf. & marb. bds., covers very worn & partly brkn. (HA. Feb.24; 225) $330

CATULLUS, Gains Valerius

- **[Gedichte].** Trans.:– E. Hohenemser. Ill.:– Marcus Behmer. Berlin, 1920. *(120) numbered on Hahne Bütten, sigd.* 4to. 8 supp. col. maps mntd. on plts., long-grd hand-bnd leath., unc., s.-c. (V. Oct.1; 3995) DM 430

CATULLUS, Caius Valerius, Tibullus, Albius & Propertius, Sextus Aurelius

- **[Carmina].** Ed.:– [Benedictus Ricardinus Philologus]. Flor., Filippo Giunta, 5 Aug. 1503. *Counterfeit Edn.* Capital spaces with guide letters, some dampstaining at end, some other ll. soiled at front, mostly marginal, full-p. 17th. or 18th. C. pen & ink port. on blank verso of ee2, old ex-libris pasted on title-p., cont. limp vell., covers stained. (CNY. May 18; 92) $1,000

- **[Opera].** Ed.:– B. Gyllenius, Partenius, & P. Beroaldus. Venetiis, Symone Bernilaqua Papiensem, 26 Jun. 1493. Fo. Hf. cf. [H. 4764] (LM. Oct.22; 239) B. Frs. 24,000

-- **Anr. Edn.** Venice, Aldine Pr., Jan., 1502. *1st. Aldine Edn., 1st. state.* Capitals in red or blue, end-title 18 lacking, title thumbed, few marginalia, some underscoring, 19th. C. vell. gt., defect.; MS.

bkplt. of Carnerius Daniel of Ingolstadt (1503) & others. (SG. Apr.19; 5) $325

-- **Anr. Edn.** Venice, Mar. 1515. Lacks last lf. with anchor, cont. Venetian mor. by the Master of Andrea Gritti, covers panel. in gt. & blind, fleurons at corners, names of Catullus & Tibullus on upr. cover in gt., spine decor. in blind, slightly torn at top & bottom, front fly-lf. torn out. (S. May 10; 247) *Burda.* £720

-- **Anr. Edn.** Venice, 1562. Title-p. restored, str. grd. mor., gt. tooled spine & covers, by Bozerian Jeune, slightly stained, jnts. slightly weak. (BS. May 2; 33) £180

-- **Anr. Edn.** B'gham., 1772. *1st. Baskerville Edn.* Lge. 4to. Variant, with reading 'Charbydis', & A2 canceled but H3 uncanceled, few margins slightly stained, qtr. vell., bds. (SG. Oct.27; 21) $300

-- **Anr. Copy.** 12mo. Red mor. gt. (LH. Sep.25; 322) $160

CAUCHY, Augustin-Louis

- **Exercices de Mathématiques.** Paris, 1826-30. *1st. Edn.* 5 vols. in 4. 4to. Some foxing, 19th. C. hf. vell. over marb. bds., spines gt., extremities slightly worn; John D. Stanitz coll. (SPB. Apr.25; 86)
$1,100

- **Exercises d'Analyse et de Physique Mathématique.** Paris, 1840-47. *1st. Edn.* 4 vols. in 2. 4to. Lacks hf.-titles (?), some light foxing & browning, 19th. C. hf. mor., extremities rubbed; G.H. Hardy's sig. on fly-lf. of each vol., John D. Stanitz copy. (SPB. Apr.25; 87) $700

CAUER, W.

- **Betrieb und Verkehr der Preussischen Staatsbahnen. (Bd. 2: Personen und Güterverkehr der Vereinigten Preussischen und Hessischen Staatsbahnen).** Berlin, 1897-1903. 2 vols. Orig. linen. (GB. Nov.3; 1203) DM 500

CAULFIELD, James

- **Cromwelliana: A Chronological Detail of Events in which Oliver Cromwell was Engaged.** Westminster, 1810. Sm. fo. Hf.-title, extra ill. with approx. 132 engraved plts., some double-p., mostly inlaid, 19th. C. red hf. mor. & marb. bds., gt.-panel. spine, by Kaufmann. (SG. Feb.16; 73) $130

CAUNTER, Hobart (Ed.)
See— **BIBLIANA [English]**

CAUS, Isaac de

- **Nouvelle Invention de Lever l'Eau plus haut que sa Source avec Quelques Machines Mouantes par le Moyen de l'Eau et un Discours de la Conduite d'ycelle.** L., 1644. *1st. Edn.* Fo. Text unc., plts. larger, margin tear in 1 plt., cont. mott cf., rebkd.; John D. Stanitz coll. [Wing C1528] (SPB. Apr.25; 90) $2,900

CAUS, Salomon de

- **Eusatz von Allerhand Mühl-Wasser und Grotten-Wercken.** [Frankfurt, 1688]. Sm. 4to. Lacks last lf. (blank or colophon?), some foxing, sm. repair to 1 plt., mod. cf., upr. cover detchd.; Kenney-Stanitz copy. (SPB. Apr.25; 91) $550

CAVAFY, C.P.

- **Fourteen Poems.** Trans.:– Nikos Stangos & Stephen Spender. Ill.:– David Hockney. Edns. Alecto, 1967. *(500) numbered & sigd. by artist. (250) with additional sigd. etching.* Fo. Prospectus loosely inserted, orig. cl., s.-c. (S. Nov.21; 192)
Desk. £1,650

CAVALIERI, Bonaventura

- **Geometria Indivisibilibvs Continvorvm Noua Quadam Ratione Promota.** Bologna, 1653. *2nd. Edn.* 4to. Title soiled & partly bkd., blank corner torn from 1 prelim. lf., some margin repairs, some lr. outer corners dampstained, cont. spr. cf., spine gt., slight wear; John D. Stanitz coll. (SPB. Apr.25; 92) $325

CAVALLO, Tiberius

- **A Complete Treatise of Electricity in Theory & Practice, with Original Experiments.** 1777. Errata & advt. ll., short split to 1 plt. fold, cont. paper-bkd. bds., unc. & unopened. (C. May 30; 110) *Hill.* £350

- **The History & Practice of Aerostation.** L., priv. ptd., 1785. *1st. Edn.* Sig. on title, orig. bds., unc.,

spine defect., stitching loose. (S. Nov.28; 109)
Brooke-Hitching. £420

CAVAZZI, J.A.
– Historische Beschreibung der in dem Occidentalischen Mohrenland legenden drey Königreichen Congo, Matamba, und Angola und der jenigen Apolstolischen Missionen denes PP. Capucinern .... Ed.:– F. Alamandini. München, 1694. *1st. German Edn.* 4to. Some blue pencil underlining, map with sm. bkd. tear, some plts. slightly cut in lr. margin, some slight browning, slight spotting in upr. margin, some slight worming, cont. lf. leath, bumped, spine defect. (R. Oct.13; 2895) DM 3,000

CAVE, Col. Francis O. & Macdonald, James D.
– Birds of the Sudan. Their Identification & Distribution. Ill.:– D.M. Reid Henry. 1955. *1st. Edn.* Orig. cl., d.-w. (LC. Mar.1; 140) £90

CAVE, R. & Wakeman, G.
– Typographia Naturalis. Wymondham (Leicestershire), Brewhouse Private Pr., 1967. *(333).* 4to. Orig. lf. leath.; Hauswedell coll. (H. May 3; 508) DM 400

CAVE, William
– Scriptorum Ecclesiasticorum Historia Literaria. Oxford, 1740-43. 2 vols. Fo. Lacks 2nd. hf.-title, cont. cf., rebkd. (SG. Sep.15; 87) $150

CAVENDISH, William, Duke of Newcastle
See– NEWCASTLE, William Cavendish, Duke of

CAXTON, Pisistratus (Pseud.)
See– LYTTON, Lord Edward George Bulwer 'Pisistratus Caxton'

CAYET, P.V.P.
– Histoire Prodigieuse et Lamentable de Jean Fauste. Cologne, 1712. 16mo. Engraved frontis. reinforced in lr. margin, cont. red mor., gt.-decor., decor. spine; from Franchetti liby. (HD. Dec.16; 12) Frs. 2,500

CAYLEY, Neville W.
– Australian Parrots.... Sydney, 1938. Bdg. not stated. (KH. May 1; 160) Aus.$120

CAYLUS, Anne Claude Philippe, Comte de
– Oeuvres Badines Complètes. Ill.:– Cochin (port.) & Marillier. Amst., Paris, 1787. 12 vols. Cont. spr. roan gt.; A.L.s. to Pigalle, 15 Mar. 1756. (HD. Jun.6; 28) Frs. 2,600
[–] Recueil d'amtiquités Egyptiennes, Etrusques, Grecques et Romaines. Paris, 1752-67. 7 vols. 4to. Titles with owners marks, vol. 6 slightly stained, slight wear, cont. blind-tooled calf. (HK. May 16; 1294) DM 3,000
– – Anr. Edn. Paris, 1761-56-67. *Vol. 1:New Edn.* 7 vols., including Supp. 4to. Cont. cf., rebkd., some covers detchd., w.a.f. (CSK. Feb.10; 67) £160

CAYLUS, Marthe-Marguerite, Marquise de
– Souvenirs. Preface:– Voltaire. Ill.:– L. Péraux. Paris, 1908. *New Edn. (150).* On Japon, suite before the letter & remarks by Péraux, red mor. gt. by Rivière, spine decor., wrap. & spine, box. (HD. Nov.29; 128) Frs. 2,600

CAZENAVE, Alphee
– Traité des Syphilides, ou Maladies Veneriennes de la Peau. Paris, 1843. Tall fo. 12 col. litho. plts., col. litho. port. of a sufferer laid in, some foxing, ptd. bds., spine torn. (SG. Oct.6; 87) $150

CAZOTTE, Jacques
– Ollivier. Ill.:– Lefevre, engraved by Godefroy. Paris, An VI, 1798. 2 vols. in 1. 18mo. Red mor. gt. decor. by Petit-Simier. (HD. May 3; 27) Frs. 2,400

CECCALDI
See– BERTHELOT & CECCALDI

CECCHINI, G.B. & others
– Vedute dei Principali Monumenti di Venezia. Ill.:– Lefevre, after Cecchini, Pividor, & Viola. Venice, ca. 1840. Ob. fo. Title, 12 litho. views, all cold., orig. ptd. bds., slightly soiled. (S. Dec.1; 342)
Crete. £440
– – Anr. Edn. Venice, n.d. Fo. Hand-cold. litho. title & 12 plts., 1 with tissue guard adhering on

plt., lr. corners stained thro.-out, orig. cl.-bkd. bds., soiled. (CSK. Jul.6; 85) £220

CECIL, Robert, Earl of Salisbury
[–] An Answere to Certaine Scandalous Papers, Scattered Abroad Under Colour of a Catholicke Admonition. L., 1606. Sm. 4to. 1st. lf. blank but for sig., slightly dust-soiled at beginning & end, 19th. C. hf. cf. [STC 4895] (S. Oct.11; 388)
Georges. £60

CECILIAN GIFT: or, Romances of the Musicians, A Christmas, New Year, & Birthday Gift
N.Y., n.d. Lge. 12mo. Col. litho. pres. plt. & 5 steel-engraved port. plts., lacks additional engraved title, orig. gt.-floral red mor., spine & corners very worn; from liby. of F.D. Roosevelt, inscr. by him. (SG. Mar.15; 21) $120

CELAKOVSKY, F.L.
– Ohlas Pjsnj Ruskych. Prague, 1829. *1st. Edn.* 12mo. Foxed, qtr. mor.; Bibliotheca Lindesiana bkplt. (SG. Nov.17; 186) $110

CELAN, Paul
– Edgar Jene. Der Traum vom Traum. Preface:– Otto Basil. Ill.:– Edgar Jené. Wien, 1948. *1st. Edn. (700) numbered.* 8 orig. lithos., orig. sewed. (GB. May 5; 2264) DM 460
– Schwarzmaut. Ill.:– G. Celan-Lestrange. Vaduz, 1969. *(70) numbered on lge. vell. de Rives.* Fo. Printer's mark sigd. by author & artist, orig. etchings, loose ll. in orig. hf. linen portfo., orig. s.-c. (GB. Nov.5; 2331) DM 800

CELAN-LESTRANGE, Gisèle
– Six Gravures à l'eau-forte. Paris, 1967. Fo. Series of 6 ll. numbered & sigd., loose in orig. linen portfo. (BR. Apr.13; 1661) DM 700

CELINE, Louis Ferdinand (Pseud.)
See– DESTOUCHES, Louis Ferdinand 'Louis Ferdinand Céline'

CELLA, P.D.
– Narrative of an Expedition from Tripoli in Barbary to the Western Frontier of Egypt .... 1822. Cont. cf.; Sir George Farrar bkplt. (SSA. Jul.5; 75)
R 170

CELLARIUS, Andreas
– Architectura Militaris oder Gruendtliche Underweissung der ... Gebraeuchlichen Fortificationen. Amst., 1656. *2nd. Edn.* Fo. 1 plt. cleanly torn, 1 letterpress table shaved with loss, margins wormed, affecting plts. & a few characters of text, A1 cleanly torn & reprd., later hf. vell. (CSK. Nov.4; 130) £280
– Harmonia Macrocosmica seu Atlas Universalis et Novus. Amst., Johannes Jansson. 1661. *1st. Edn. 2nd. Iss.* Fo. Engraved allegorical title, 29 double-p. engraved cosmographical charts, hand-cold. thro.-out in cont. hand, title & several charts pointed with gold, 1 or 2 short splits at centrefolds reprd. without loss of engraved surface, sm. piece torn from lr. blank margin of title, some light creasing, browning mostly affecting text, cont. gt.-panel. vell., slightly soiled, w.a.f. (S. May 21; 107)
Serafini. £7,500
– – Anr. Edn. Amst., 1708. Fo. Engraved frontis. & 29 hand-cold. double-p. celestial charts, 7 with clean tears affecting plt. surface, 3 torn with loss along fold, margins soiled thro.-out with some loss, old bds., disbnd., w.a.f. (CSK. Jul.6; 96) £1,600

CELLARIUS, Christophorus
– Geographia Antiqua. Ed.:– Samuel Patrick. L., 1745. Cont. cf. gt. (BBA. May 3; 277)
Maggs. £80
– – Anr. Edn. Ill.:– Maps:– R.W. Seale & W.H. Toms. L., 1799. 4to. 32 (of 33) double-p. engraved maps, some browning, cont. bds., defect. (S. Mar.6; 105) *Diba.* £75
– Notitia Orbis Antiqui, sive Geographia Plenior. Leipzig, 1731-32. 2 vols. 4to. Engraved port., 34 engraved folding maps, text ills., some faint browning, cont. vell., slightly soiled. (S. Apr.9; 74)
Quaritch. £280
– – Anr. Copy. 2 vols. 4to. Vell. (P. Sep.29; 321)
Tooley. £120

CELLINI, Benvenuto
– Life, written by Himself. Intro.:– Thomas Craven. Trans.:– J.A. Symonds. Ill.:– Fritz Kredel. Verona, Officina Bodoni for Ltd. Edns. Cl., 1937. *(1550) numbered, sigd. by artist.* Sm. fo. Patterned linen, s.-c. reprd. (SG. May 17; 279) $100
– Selbstbiographie. Trans.:– Goethe. Ill.:– M. Slevogt. Berlin, 1913. Orig. hf. vell. gt. (HK. May 17; 3135) DM 400
– La Vie de B...écrite par lui-même. Ed.:– M. Franco. Trans.:– Leopold Leclanchée. Ill.:– F. Laguillermie. Paris, 1881. *(80) on Whatman.* 2 vols. Bradel hf. mor., corners, wrap. preserved. (HD. Jun.13; 19) Frs. 1,200

CELSIUS, Anders
– Dissertatio Astronomico-Physica, de Luna non Habitabili. Ed.:– Ericus Engman. Uppsala, 1740. Sm. 4to. Title with margin paper loss, disbnd. (SG. Mar.22; 60) $175

CELSUS, Aurelius Cornelius
– De Arte Medica Libri Octo. Ed.:– G. Pantinus. Basel, 1552. Stained nearly thro.-out, 17th/18th. C. bds., loose, slightly bumped & spotted. (R. Oct.12, 1375) DM 450
– De Re Medica. Solingen, 1538. *(Bound with:)* SAMMONICUS. Q. Serenus – De Medicina. Solingen, 1538. Together 2 works in 1 vol. Some browning & soiling, some ll. stained, owners note & ex-libris, cont. vell., spotted. (H. Nov.23; 239)
DM 450
– Medicinae Libri. VIII. Venice, 1528. 4to. Wide margin, title lf. with sm. repair some slight browning & staining, new hf. leath. (H. May 22; 548) DM 540
– Of Medicine. In Eight Books. Trans.:– James Greive, M.D. L., 1756. *1st. Edn. of Greive's trans.* Early owners stp. on title, lacks hf.-title & endpapers, old cf., rubbed, some soiling, lacks spine label. (RO. Jun.26; 32) $100

CENDRARS, Blaise
– La Fin du Monde. Ill.:– Fernand Léger. Paris, 1919. *1st. Edn. Ltd. Iss.* 4to. MS. dedication on hf.-title & sig of artist, orig. pict. bds., some light fading, Hauswedell coll. (H. May 24; 660)
DM 4,800
– – Anr. Copy. 4to. Hf. mor., orig. pict. wraps. bnd. in. (GB. Nov.5; 2738) DM 3,400
– – Anr. Copy. 4to. Orig. bds., slightly faded. (H. Nov.24; 1773) DM 2,200
– – Anr. Edn. Ill.:– Ferrand Leger. Paris, 1919. *(1225).* Fo. Some browning, orig. wraps., ptd. after Leger's design, some soiling & rubbing. (SPB. Dec.14; 63) $550
– Kodak (Documentaire). 1924. *(77) on Holland Van Gelder.* Square 8vo. Wrap. by Francis Picabia. *(With:)* – Rhum. Paris, 1930. *Orig. Edn. (46) on vell.* 12mo. No bdg. stated. (SM. Mar.7; 2092)
Frs. 1,200

CENSO DE LA POBLACION DE ESPAÑA ... 1797 ...
1801. Double fo. Linen. (DS. Mar.23; 2051)
Pts. 150,000

CENT ANS OU QUELQUES REFLEXIONS sur la Collection Particulière de M. H*
Paris, 1928. *Ltd. Edn., numbered.* Sm. 4to. Bds. d.-w. torn. (SG. Jan.26; 171) $110

CENT NOUVELLES NOUVELLES
Ill.:– R. de Hooghe. Cologne, 1701. 2 vols. Sm. 8vo. Cont. red mor. gt., spines decor., inner hinges reprd. (HD. May 3; 92) Frs. 3,400

CENTAUR, The, & the Bacchante
Ill.:– T.S. Moore. Vale Pr., 1899. *(150).* Orig. buckran, untrimmed, slightly rubbed. (TA. Jun.21; 603) £54

CENTURY ASSOCIATION
– The Bryant Festival at 'The Century'. N.Y., 1865. *Ill. Edn. (150) numbered.* 4to. Liby. stp. on plt. versos, qtr. leath., worn. (SG. Nov.10; 34) $110

CEOLDO, Pietro
– Albero della Famiglia Papafava, Nobile di Padova. Venezia, 1801. Fo. Lge. genealogical table at end, cont. marb. leath., spine slightly bumped. (SI. Dec.18; 100) Lire 240,000

CEPEDA Y GUZMAN, Carlos
- Descripcion de una Fiesta de Toros y Cañas. Sevilla, 1671. *(100)*. 4to. Leath. (DS. Mar.23; 2052) Pts. 30,000

CERCEAU, Jacques Androuet de
- Livre d'Architecture. Paris, 1615. Fo. Cont. cf. (HD. Dec.1; 59) Frs. 2,100
- Le Premier [Second] Volume des plus Excellents Bastiments de France. Paris, 1607. *2nd. Edn.* 2 vols. in 1. Fo. Wide margin, 19th. C. Engl. hand-bnd. red mor., gt. decor., wide inner dentelle border., by F. Bedford, sigd., corners slightly bumped. (H. May 22; 58) DM 5,000

CEREDI, Giuseppe
- Tre Discorsi sopra il modo d'Alzar Acque da' Luoghi Bassi. Parma, 1567. *1st. Edn.* Sm. 4to. 1 plt. reprd. at folds & slightly stained, stained towards end, parch.-bkd. marb. bds.; John D. Stanitz coll. (SPB. Apr.25; 94) $350

CERILLO, E.
- Dipinti Murali di Pompei. Naples, n.d. Fo. 20 col. plts., text in Italian & some Fr., dampstaining & tears, mor. gt., spine damaged. (P. Feb.16; 164) £95

CERMISONUS, Antonius
- Consilia contra Omnes Fere Egritudines a Capite usque ad Pedes. Brescia, Henricus de Colonia, 4 Sep. 1476. *1st. Edn.* Fo. 1st. lf. blank, lacks last blank lf., capital spaces, upr. outer blank corner reprd. with new paper thro.-out the book, a few sm. wormholes at end, old paper bds. [BMC VII, 965; Goff C402; H. 4885] (S. May 10; 249) *Maggs.* £650

CERRUTI, Père
- [-] Apologie Générale de l'Institut et de la Doctrine des Jésuites. Lausanne, 1763. 4to. L.P., cont. red mor. gt., richly decor., slight dampstain on 1 cover; from Mac Carthy-Reagh liby. (HD. Nov.17; 9) Frs. 2,100

CERTAIN NECESSARY DIRECTIONS AS WELL FOR THE CASE OF THE PLAGUE
1665. *1st. Edn.* Imprimatur lf., mod. hf. cf. gt. [Wing C1708] (P. Apr.12; 52) *Thorp.* £150

CERVANTES SAAVEDRA, Miguel de
- The Dialogue of the Dogs. Ill.:– Mallette Dean. Kentfield, Calif., Allen Pr., 1969. *(140) handset on all-rag Wookey Hole Mill paper.* 4to. Text in columns of initials & decors., cl., prospectus laid in. (SG. May 17; 5) $250
- Don Quixote *(Arranged under Languages)*.
- [Dutch] Don Quichot. Trans.:– J.C. Weyerman. Ill.:– B. Picart & others, after Coypel, Boucher, Cochin, & others. 's-Gravenhage, 1746. Fo. L.P., some foxing, corners slightly defect., cont. hf. cf. gt., unc., slightly defect. (VS. Dec.9; 1026) Fls. 600
- – Anr. Copy. 4to. Hf. cf., covers re-covered with mod. paper. (LM. Mar.3; 123) B. Frs. 13,000
- [-] [Engl.] Don Quixote. Trans.:– John Phillips. L., 1687. *1st. Edn.* Sm. fo. Engraved frontis., 16 engraved plts., later mott. cf. gt., worn, covers detchd. [Wing C1774] (SG. Apr.19; 59) $350
- – Anr. Copy. 2 pts. Fo. Leath. (DS. Feb.24; 2036) Pts. 60,000
- – Anr. Edn. Trans.:– Charles Jarvis. Ill.:– Van der Gucht after Vanderbank. L., 1742. 2 vols. Lge. 4to. Engraved port., 69 engraved plts., lacks hf.-titles, old mott. hf. cf., marb. bds., jnts., spines & corners badly worn. (SG. Apr.19; 57) $140
- – Anr. Edn. Trans.:– T. Smollett. Ill.:– Hayman. L., 1755. *1st. Edn.* 2 vols. 4to. Some foxing, cont. cf., rubbed, spines slightly dried & lacking labels, 1 jnt. brkn. (RO. Apr.23; 35) $170
- – Anr. Edn. Trans.:– T. Smollett. Dublin, 1796. 4 vols. Early cf. (SG. Feb.9; 202) $120
- – Anr. Edn. Trans.:– Charles Jarvis. L., 1801. 4 vols. Extra-ill. with 51 plts., (27 cold.), crushed lev. mor., elab. decor. in gt. & blind, turn-ins gt., by Bayntun. (CNY. Dec.17; 544) $600
- – Anr. Copy. 4 vols. All plts. stained on lr. margins, cont. diced cf., rebkd. (SG. Feb.16; 57) $130
- – Anr. Edn. Ill.:– Pisan after Gustave Doré. L.,

ca. 1865. 4to. Slight darkening & soiling, three-qtr. mor. & cl., marb. end-papers, covers rubbed, cl. tearing on lr. cover, corners & edges bumped, inner jnts. reprd. with tape, covers & contents separated at front hinge. (CBA. Mar.3; 178) $130
- – Anr. Edn. Trans.:– P.A. Motteux. Ill.:– Ad. Lalauze. Edinb., 1879-84. 4 vols. Lge. 8vo. Cf., tooled in gt. & blind, gt. vigs. on spines. (SG. Feb.16; 56) $425
- – Anr. Edn. Trans.:– Thomas Shelton. Chelsea, Ash. Pr., 1927. 2 vols. Fo. Mor. (SM. Mar.7; 2469) Frs. 1,100
- – Anr. Edn. Trans.:– Thomas Shelton. Ill.:– W.M. Quick after Louise Powell. Chelsea, Ash. Pr., 1927-28. *(245). (225) on paper.* 2 vols. Fo. Cl.-bkd. bds., unc., spines slightly worn & darkened, spine tips frayed, labels slightly chipped. (RO. Dec.11; 14) $850
- [French] Don Quichette. Ill.:– Coypel, Picart, & others. La Haye, 1746. *1st. Printing.* 4to. Some foxing & yellowing cont. marb. cf., gt.-decor., decor. spine, sm. defects. (HD. Dec.9; 12) Frs. 5,700
- – Anr. Copy. Lge. 4to. Figures in 2 states, including 1st. proofs with numbers, mor. by De Samblanx & Weckesser, Du Seuil decor., spine decor. (HD. Mar.21; 14) Frs. 4,000
- – Anr. Copy. 4to. Ills. before the number, cont. marb. cf. gt. cracked. (HD. May 3; 28) Frs. 3,800
- – Anr. Copy. Fo. L.P., copper engrs. in 1st. state, before numbering, some slight spotting, cont. leath. gt., corners bumped. (HK. May 17; 2413) DM 900
- – Anr. Edn. Ill.:– Cochin, Coypel, Picart, & others. Paris, 1752. *New Edn.* 6 vols. 12mo. 1st. ll. of Vol. VI dampstained, cont. cf. gt., spines decor., reprd. (HD. Nov.29; 52) Frs. 1,500
- – Anr. Edn. Ill.:– Coypel, Picart le Romain, & others. Liége, 1776. Lge. 4to. Cont. bds. (LM. Oct.22; 111) B.Frs. 11,000
- – Anr. Edn. Ill.:– Florian. Paris, 1799. *Orig. Edn.* 3 vols. Cf., gold-tooled. (CR. Jun.6; 124) Lire 380,000
- – Anr. Edn. Trans.:– H. Bouchon Dubournal. Ill.:– Vernet & Lami engraved by Lignon, Prevost, Leroux & Caron. Paris, 1822. 4 vols. in 8. On L.P. vell., 11 ills. in 2 states, 517 other ills. including 41 orig. ills. & 1 orig. aqua., 20 series of engrs. from various Edns. (Series on L.P. japan included, some sigd. by Brunet), 14 ports. in various states, with map, some slight foxing & staining. (D. Nov.24; 2245) DM 22,000
- – Anr. Edn. Trans.:– Louis Viardot. Ill.:– after T. Johannot. Paris, 1836-37. *1st. Edn.* 2 vols. Lge. 8vo. Lge. copy, some foxing, cont. mor. gt., spines gt. (SG. Nov.3; 110) $375
- – Anr. Copy. 2 vols. Lge. 8vo. 2 frontis. on china, hf.-titles on vell., some gatherings yellowed, cont. hf. cf., spines decor. (unif. faded). (HD. May 3; 218) Frs. 1,500
- – Anr. Edn. Trans.:– Louis Viardot. Ill.:– after Tony Johannot. Paris, 1836-40. 2 vols. Lge. 8vo. Cont. chagrin, richly gt.– & blind-decor. (HD. Nov.9; 90) Frs. 3,000
- – Anr. Edn. Paris, 1838. Ob. 8vo. 34 cont. cold. litho. plts., publisher's ill. bds., disbnd. (HD. May 3; 219) Frs. 1,300
- – Anr. Edn. Trans.:– Louis Viardot. Ill.:– Gustave Doré, engraved by Pisan. Paris, 1869. 2 vols. Fo. Some minimal worming, gt.-lettered buckram covers, spines decor. (HD. May 3; 217) Frs. 2,600
- – Anr. Edn. Ill.:– Daniel Vierge. Paris, 1909. *(360).* 4 vols. 4to. On vell., spines decor. (unif. faded), wraps. & spines preserved. (HD. May 3; 220) Frs. 1,200
- – Anr. Edn. Ill.:– Gus Bofa. 1927. 4 vols. 4to. On Holland paper, separate suite, sewed, wraps. & s.-c.'s. (HD. Dec.9; 7j) Frs. 3,750
- – Anr. Edn. Ill.:– Louis Jou. 1948-50. 4 vols. 4to. Leaves, wraps. & box. (HD. Jan.24; 57) Frs. 1,450
- – Anr. Edn. Ill.:– H. Lemarie. Paris, 1960. 4 vols. Sm. 4to. On velin de Rives, vermillion hf. mor., corners, by J. Etienne, unc., wrap. & spine. (HD. Jun.26; 64) Frs. 3,800

- [German] Don Qvixote Von Mancha, Abentheurliche Geschichte. Basel & Frankfurt, 1682. *1st. compl. German Trans.* 2 vols. Cont. vell. (HK. May 16; 1965) DM 5,500
- [Spanish] Don Quixote. Madrid, por Iuan de Cuesta, 1608. *3rd. Cuesta Edn.* Sm. hole in X2 affecting 3 letters, minor staining to some ll. in sig. kk, cont. cf., spine gt., worn, spine & hinges defect. (C. Nov.9; 49) *Quaritch.* £4,000
- – Anr. Edn. Brussels & Lisbon, 1617. 2 vols. 4to. 1st. pt.: a few headlines shaved, browned in places, 19th. C. mor. gt., spine head chipped; 2nd. pt.: browned, lightly dampstained thro.-out, upr. outer corner of last few ll. rotted with slight loss of text, 2 short tears in title reprd., cont. limp vell., lacks ties, lr. cover very stained. (C. May 30; 19) *Duran.* £300
- – Anr. Edn. Madrid, 1647. 4to. Vell. (DS. Oct.28; 2250) Pts. 140,000
- – Anr. Edn. Amberes, 1697. 2 vols. 4to. Vell. (DS. Dec.16; 2494) Pts. 130,000
- – Anr. Copy. 2 vols. Cf. (DS. Oct.28; 2266) Pts. 70,000
- – Anr. Edn. Madrid, 1714. 2 vols. 4to. Vell. (DS. Oct.28; 2251) Pts. 45,000
- – Anr. Edn. Amberes, 1719. 2 vols. 4to. Cf., covers loose. (DS. Jan.27; 2575) Pts. 44,000
- – Anr. Edn. Madrid, 1750. 2 vols. 4to. Vell. (DS. Apr.27; 2272) Pts. 60,000
- – Anr. Edn. Ed.:– Juan Bole. L. & Salisbury, 1781. 3 vols. 4to. Later hf. cf. gt., spines rubbed. (TA. May 17; 341) £100
- – Anr. Copy. 6 vols. in 3. 4to. Cont. cf., most covers detchd. (TA. Feb.16; 212) £95
- – Anr. Edn. Madrid, 1808. Cf. (DS. Jan.27; 2078) Pts. 25,000
- – Anr. Edn. Ill.:– G. Stalker. Paris, 1832. *'Segunda Edicion'.* 2 vols. 32mo. Miniature Book. Vell., gt.-tooled, spines gt., orig. wraps. bnd. in. (SG. Feb.16; 55) $225
- – Anr. Edn. Ed.:– Vicente de los Rios. Trans.:– Biography:– Jeronimo Moran. Madrid, 1862-63. *5th. Academy Edn.* 3 vols. in 1. Fo. Stpd. leath. (DS. Oct.28; 2346) Pts. 75,000
- – Anr. Edn. Barcelona, 1871-79. *Facs. of 1st. Edn.* 4 vols. 4to. 2 vols. with facs., 3rd. with 'Las 1683 notas puesta por...J.E. Hartzenbusch a la edic. del ...' reprod. by Francisco Lopez Fabra, 4th. with 'Iconografia de D. Quijote', publishers gt.-stpd. bdg. (DS. Nov.25; 2311) DM 34,000
- – Anr. Edn. Madrid, 1880. 2 vols. 32mo. Vell., covers hand-painted by Losilla, vell. clasps. (SG. Feb.16; 228) $225
- – Anr. Edn. Ed.:– Rodriguez Marin. Ill.:– Ricardo Marin. Madrid, 1916-17. *(125).* Vols. 1 & 2 only (of 4). Lge. fo. Rag paper, wraps. (DS. Nov.25; 2310) Pts. 42,000
- Galatea, dividida en seys Libros. Paris, 1611. Leath.; Duke of Devonshire ex-libris. (DS. Nov.25; 2141) Pts. 190,000
- – Anr. Edn. Ill.:– O. Hettner. Wien & Leipzig, 1922. *(50) numbered Deluxe Edn.* Fo. Separate series of 65 sigd. lithos. on Japan & 9 further, orig. pict. vell., bd. s.-c., orig. pict. bd. box, foot of spine slightly crumpled, upr. jnt. slightly split. (HK. May 17; 2539) DM 700
- Leben und Thaten des Weisen Junkers Don Quixote von la Mancha. Ill.:– D. Berger after D. Chodowiecki. Leipzig, 1780-81. *2nd. Ill. Edn.* Lightly browned, later marb. bds. gt., some slight bumping, Hauswedell coll. (H. May 24; 1251) DM 1,600
- Los Trabajos de Persiles y Sigismunda. Brussels, 1618. 19th. C. linen, corners. (DS. Dec.16; 2399) Pts. 125,000
- – Anr. Edn. N.Y., 1827. Cont. red mor. gt. spine & cover borders, slightly spotted. (D. Nov.24; 2413) DM 400

CESAIRE, Aimé
- Soleil Cou-Coupé. Ill.:– Hans Hartung. Paris, 1948. *1st. Edn. (10) hors commerce on chiffon du Marais.* Cf., cold inlays, sigd. by Leroux, 1960, hf. leath. wrap., s.-c. (D. Nov.24; 3070) DM 4,500

CESCINSKY, Herbert
- English Furniture of the Eighteenth Century. L., 1909 & n.d. 3 vols. 4to. Orig. hf. mor., worn. (S. May 1; 700) *Dennistoun.* £100
- – Anr. Edn. L., [1909-11 & n.d.]. 3 vols. 2 vols.

in orig. hf. mor., hinges reprd., rubbed, other vol. nearly unif. mor. (S. May 1; 699)   *Kapusi.* £70
– – **Anr. Edn.** 1911. 3 vols. 4to. Hf. mor. gt. (P. Dec.8; 137)   *Joseph.* £120
– – **Anr. Edn.** N.d.-1911. 3 vols. 4to. Hf. mor. gt., slight wear. (P. Jul.5; 187)   £140
– – **Anr. Edn.** N.d. 3 vols. 4to. Hf. cf., worn. (BS. May 2; 113)   £130
– – **Anr. Copy.** 3 vols. 4to. Titles slightly spotted, orig. hf. mor. (S. Oct.4; 138)   *Woodruff.* £90
– – **Anr. Copy.** 3 vols. 4to. Few pp. lightly dust-soiled, orig. hf. mor., slightly worn. (S. Nov.8; 506)   *Stodart.* £65

CESCINSKY, Herbert & Gribble, E.R.
– **Early English Furniture & Woodwork.** 1922. *[1st. Edn.].* 2 vols. 4to. Orig. mor.-bkd. cl., publisher's boxes. (CSK. Apr.6; 61)   £160
– – **Anr. Copy.** 2 vols. in 1. 4to. Orig. cl. gt., slightly rubbed. (TA. May 17; 418)   £62
– – **Anr. Copy.** 2 vols. in 1. Fo. Hf. mor. (BS. May 2; 118)   £55
– – **Anr. Copy.** 2 vols. in 1. Lge. 4to. Hf. buckram & cl., some light soiling to covers, corner bumped, lacks fly-lf. (CBA. Jan.29; 198) $140
– – **Anr. Copy.** 2 vols. Sm. fo. Two-tone cl. (SG. Oct.13; 82) $110

CESCINSKY, Herbert & Webster, Malcolm R.
– **English Domestic Clocks.** 1914. *2nd. Edn.* Lge. 4to. Cont. hf. mor., extremities rubbed. (CSK. Oct.21; 167)   £55

CESNOLA, Alexander Palma di
– **Salaminia.** L., 1882. 4to. Orig. cl., rubbed. (BBA. May 3; 327)   *Martino.* £60

CESSART, Louis Alexandre de
– **Description des Travaux Hydrauliques.** Paris, 1806-08. *1st. Edn.* 2 vols. Lge. 4to. Mod. hf. mor. gt., unc. (GB. May 3; 1140)   DM 800

CESTI, Pietro
– **Il Pomo d'Oro ....** Ill.:– Kusel after L. Burnacini. Wien, 1668. 4to. 12 copperplates (only), all loose, old spotting, sm. faults & crumples, vell., restored. (V. Oct.1; 3726)   DM 1,500

CHABERT, Joseph Bernard, Marquis de
– **Voyage fait par Ordre du Roi en 1750 et 1751, dane l'Amérique Septentrionale ....** Paris, 1753. *1st. Edn.* 4to. Title-p. browned, cont. cf. gt., spine & edges worn; the Rt. Hon. Visc. Eccles copy. [Sabin 11723] (CNY. Nov.18; 60) $600
– – **Anr. Copy.** 4to. Some slight foxing, cont. leath., gold-tooled heraldic supralibros on both covers, slightly bumped. (D. Nov.23; 1261)   DM 2,050

CHABERT, Philibert
– **Traité du Charbon ou Anthrax dans les Animaux. Traité de la Gale et des Dantres des Animaux.** Paris, 1786-87. 2 vols. bnd. in 1. Sm. fascicule 'Instruction adressée aux Artistes Vetérinaires', Paris 1785, bnd. at end, cont. red long-grd. mor., gt.-decor., limp decor. spine., from J.B. Howard liby. (HD. Dec.9; 13)   Frs. 2,400

CHABOT, M. de
[–] **Abrégé des Commentaires de M. de Folard, sur l'Histoire de Polybe.** Paris, 1754. *Orig. Edn.* 3 vols. 4to. Cont. marb. cf., spines decor. (HD. May 21; 21)   Frs. 1,700

CHABOT, Auguste Jean François
– **La Chasse à travers les Ages ...** Paris, 1898. 4to. Hf. mor., corners, wrap.; from Château des Noës liby. (HD. May 25; 11)   Frs. 2,000

CHACON Y ORTA, F.
– **Breve Ideá de las Maquinas de Vapór y su Applicación a la Navegación.** Cadiz, 1850. 4to. Sewed. (DS. Mar.23; 2079)   Pts. 20,000

CHADWICK, Sir Edwin
[–] **Report to Her Majesty's Principal Secretary of State ... from the Poor Law Commissioners ... Sanitary Condition of ... Great Britain.—A Supplementary Report.** L., 1842. *1st. Edn.* 2 vols. 1 map spotted & torn at fold in 1st. vol., cont. cl. (S. Mar.20; 704)   *Drury.* £190

CHADWYCK HEALEY, Charles E.H.
– **The History of the Part of West Somerset Comprising the Parishes of Luccombe, Selworthy ...** 1901. *(60) numbered on L.P.* 4to. Orig. buckram, unc. & unopened. (SKC. Mar.9; 1972)   £75

CHAFFERS, W. & Markham, C.A.
– **Hallmarks on Gold & Silver Plate.** L., 1922. No bdg. stated. (JL. Jun.24; 198)   Aus. $100

CHAGALL, Marc
– **Bible.** Paris, 1956. Verve no. 33/34. Fo. Orig. pict. bds. (S. Nov.21; 8)   *Maurer.* £1,600
– – **Anr. Copy.** Verve no. 33/34. 4to. 16 orig. cold. lithos., orig. bds. (SPB. Dec.14; 43) $1,800
– – **Anr. Copy.** Verve 33/34. Fo. 28 orig. lithos. (16 cold.), orig. cold. pict. bds. (GB. May 5; 2267)   DM 7,400
– – **Anr. Copy.** Verve no. 33/34. Fo. 28 orig. lithos., including 16 cold., orig. cold. litho. bds., 2 corners worn; Chagall's MS. dedication on hypographic title. lf. (GB. Nov.5; 2336)   DM 6,800
– – **Anr. Copy.** Verve Vol. VII, Nos. 33 & 34. Fo. 18 cold. orig. lithos., orig. pict. bds. (HT. May 9; 1760)   DM 6,000
– **Derrière le Miroir.** Paris, [1962 & 1979]. No. 132 & 235. Fo. 4 cold. orig. lithos., orig. wraps. (D. Nov.24; 2992)   DM 450
– – **Anr. Edn.** Paris, 1964. No. 147. Fo. 3 orig. lithos., orig. wraps. (D. Nov.24; 2993)   DM 420
– **Dessins et Aquarelles pour le Ballet.** Text:– Jacques Lassaigne. Paris, [1969]. Lge. 4to. 1 cold. litho & many partly cold. plts. & ills., orig. linen. (H. Nov.24; 1445)   DM 450
– **Dessins et Lavis.** Text:– Marcel Arland. [Paris], 1964. *(150) numbered on velin de Rives paper.* Special no. of 'Derrière Le Miroir'. Sm. fo. Unbnd. in col.-pict. wraps., heavy bd. s.-c. (SG. Mar.29; 37) $140
– **Dessins pour la Bible.** Paris, 1960. Verve no. 37/38. Fo. Orig. pict. bds. (S. Nov.21; 9)   *Quaritch.* £1,400
– – **Anr. Copy.** Verve no. 37/38. Lge. 4to. 24 col. lithos., orig. pict. bds. (P. Feb.16; 218)   £1,000
– – **Anr. Copy.** Verve no. 37/38. 4to. 24 orig. cold. lithos., orig. bds. (SPB. Dec.14; 44) $1,600
– – **Anr. Copy.** Verve no. 37/38. 4to. 24 orig. cold. lithos., some with sm. tears & creasing, orig. bds., bumped. (SPB. Dec.13; 787) $1,500
– – **Anr. Copy.** Verve no. 37/38. Fo. Cold orig. lithos., each with sm. black & white litho on verso, orig. pict. bds. (R. Oct.11; 816)   DM 6,000
– – **Anr. Copy.** Verve 37/38. Fo. Orig. bds. (HK. May 17; 2646)   DM 4,500
– – **Anr. Copy.** Verve 37/38. Fo. Orig. bds., minimal bumping. (HT. May 9; 1761)   DM 3,700
– – **Anr. Copy.** Verve no. 37/38. Fo. 24 cold. litho. plts., orig. decor. bds. (VS. Dec.7; 32)   Fls. 4,300
– – **Anr. Edn.** Paris, [1960]. Verve no. 37/38. Sm. fo. 24 col. lithos., 96 black & white plts., col.-pict. bds. (SG. Mar.29; 35) $1,300
– **Drawings for the Bible.** Text:– Gaston Bachelard. N.Y., 1960. Fo. Pict. title, 25 col. lithos. (including covers), bds., d.-w. frayed. (SG. Nov.3; 36) $1,400
– **Drawings & Water Colors for the Ballet.** Text:– Jacques Lassaigne. N.Y., [1969]. Fo. Cl., col.-pict. d.-w. (SG. Mar.29; 38) $120
– **Glasmalereien für Jerusalem.** Text:– J. Leymarie. Monte Carlo, 1962. 4to. 2 orig. cold. lithos., orig. linen, wraps. (GB. Nov.5; 2339)   DM 750
– **Illustrations for the Bible.** [N.Y.,], 1956. Verve no. 33/34. Fo. Orig. pict. bds. (S. Nov.21; 59)   *Koch.* £950
– – **Anr. Copy.** Fo. Orig. cold. pict. bds. (R. Oct.11; 819)   DM 8,000
– – **Anr. Copy.** Fo. Orig. bds., with col. litho., orig. wraps., some wear. (HK. Nov.11; 3465)   DM 6,200
– – **Anr. Edn.** N.Y., [1956]. Lge. 4to. 28 lithos. (16 cold.), 105 full-p. heliogravures, cold. pict. bds., worn, pict. d.-w. (SG. Apr.26; 42) $1,700
– **The Jerusalem Windows.** Ed.:– J. Leymarie. Ill.:– Sorlier. Monte Carlo, 1962. Fo. Orig. linen, orig. cold. litho. wraps, s.-c. (HK. May 17; 2648)   DM 620
– – **Anr. Edn.** Text:– Jean Leymarie. Monte Carlo, [1962]. Fo. 2 orig. lithos., bdg. not stated, d.-w. (CBA. Jan.29; 105) $200
– – **Anr. Copy.** 4to. Orig. linen. (H. Nov.24; 2460)   DM 580
– – **Anr. Edn.** Text:– Jean Leymarie. [N.Y.], 1962].

1st. Amer. Edn. Fo. 2 orig. lithos., bdg. not stated, covers lightly rubbed. (CBA. Jan.29; 106) $150
– – **Anr. Copy.** Sm. fo. Cl., col.-pict. d.-w. (SG. Mar.29; 36) $110
– **XXe Siècle.** Ill.:– Chagall & Fautrier. Paris, 1957. New Series No.9. 4to. Orig. bds. (D. Nov.24; 2974)   DM 1,400
– – **Anr. Edn.** Ill.:– Chagall, Alechinsky & Fiedler. Paris, 1960. New Series XXII. Année. No.14. 4to. 3 cold. orig. lithos., orig. bds. (D. Nov.24; 2975)   DM 400
– **Vitraux pour Jérusalem.** Intro.:– Jean Leymarie. Monte Carlo, 1962. Fo. 2 orig. cold. lithos., orig. linen, cold. orig. wrap. (GB. May 5; 2268)   DM 650
– – **Anr. Copy.** Fo. Orig. linen, slightly soiled, cold. pict. wraps. (R. Oct.11; 820)   DM 600
– – **Anr. Edn.** Ed.:– J. Leymarie. Ill.:– Chagall, & Sorlier after Chagall. [Monte Carlo, 1962]. 4to. 38 cold. lithos. & many partly cold. plts., orig. linen. (H. Nov.24; 1443)   DM 620

CHAGALL, Marc (Ill.)
See— ARLAND, Marcel
See— GOGOL, N.
See— GOLL, Claire
See— GOLL, Claire & Ivan
See— LASSAIGNE, Jacques
See— MOURLOT, Fernand
See— SENGNOR, L.S.
See— STRELETZ [The Archer]
See— STURM, Der
See— TRIOLET, Elsa
See— VERVE, Revue Artistique et Literaire

CHAGIZ, Shmuel
– **Dvar Shmuel.** Venice, 1596. *[1st. Edn.].* 4to. Stained & browned, margins of title reprd. not affecting text, owner's sig. on title, edges frayed, discold., 1 lf. rubbed with loss of some letters, buckram. (S. Oct.24; 126)   *Sol.* £200
– **Dvar Shmuel.—Mevakesh Ha'Shem.** Venice, 1596. *1st. Edns.* 2 vols. 4to. A few repairs, mainly to margins, slight traces of worming, slight soiling & staining, mod. hf. cf. gt. (SPB. Feb.1; 31) $850
– **Mevakesh Ha'Shem.** Venice, 1596. *1st. Edn.* 4to. Wormholes affecting some letters, owner's sig. on title, creased, staining mostly in margins, buckram. (S. Oct.24; 127)   *Sol.* £190

CHAGIZ, Yakov
– **Halachot Ketanot.** Ed.:– Moshe Chagiz. Venice, 1704. *1st. Edn.* Stained & reprd., owner's sig. on title. *(Bound with:)* GALANTE, Moshe
– **Korban Chagigah.** Ed.:– Moshe Chagiz. Venice, 1704. Owner's stp. on title, staining mostly in margins, creased. Together 2 pts. in 1 vol. 4to. Buckram. (S. Oct.24; 128)   *Sol.* £100

CHAIR, Somerset de
– **The First Crusade.** Ill.:– Clifford Webb. Gold. Cock. Pr., 1945. *(100) numbered, specially bnd.* Sm. fo. Orig. vell. gt., s.-c.; from D. Bolton liby. (BBA. Oct.27; 132)   *Maggs.* £190

CHALKHILL, John
– **Thealma & Clearchus.** L., 1683. *1st. Edn.* Cancel title-p., some staining, lacks 1st. blank lf., old pol. cf., rebkd. with port of old backstrip; bkplt. & inscr. of William Cole, Hagley Hall bkplt., Frederic Dannay copy. [Wing C 1795] (CNY. Dec.16; 66) $150

CHALLAMEL, A. & Tenint, W.
– **Les Français sous la Révolution.** Ill.:– Massard after Wattier & others. Paris, [1843]. *Orig. Edn. 1st. Printing.* 49 plts. cold. & gommées, some foxing, cont. hf. chagrin, spine decor. (HD. May 21; 83)   Frs. 1,800

CHALMERS, Alexander
– **A History of the Colleges, Halls, & Public Buildings, Attached to the University of Oxford, including the Lives of the Founders.** Oxford, 1810. 2 vols. Minor spotting, cont. hf. cf., worn. (TA. Sep.15; 133)   £50

CHALMERS, Alexander (Ed.)
See— BRITISH ESSAYISTS, The

CHALMERS, George
✝ **Political Annals of the Present United colonies, from their Settlement to the Peace of 1763.** L., priv.

CHALMERS, George -*Contd.*

ptd., 1780. *1st. Edn.* Book I (all publd.). 4to. Crude hf. linen, ex-liby. (SG. Aug.4; 68) $140

CHALON, A.E.
- Recollections of the Italian Opera, 1835. Ill.:– R.J. Lane. L. & Paris, 1836. Fo. Litho. title/wrap., 7 hand-cold. litho. plts., ptd. plt. list, sm. tears in most fore-margins, orig. wraps. (C. Nov.16; 71) *Marks.* £400

CHALON, J. & J.
- Twenty Four Subjects Exhibiting the Costume of Paris. L., 1821. 4to. 24 col. litho. plts., orig. hf. cf. gt., rubbed. (P. Nov.24; 59) *Shapero.* £480

CHALYBS, Petr.
- Diue Catherine Virgins ... Heroica Vital. Nuremb., 1515. 4to. Some MS. annots. & sm. MS. owner's mark on title, 1st. 3 ll. slightly wormed, some slight spotting, bds. (HK. Nov.8; 140) DM 1,700

CHAM (Pseud.)
See— NOE, Comte Amédée-Charles-Henri 'Cham'

CHAMBERLAIN, Henry
- Vistas e Costumes de Cidade e Arredores do Rio de Janiero. Trans.:– R. Borba de Moraes. Rio de Janeiro, San Paulo, 1943. *Orig. Edn.* Ob. fo. Orig. leath., bumped. (D. Oct.23; 1312) DM 800

CHAMBERLAINE, John
- Imitations of Original Drawings by Hans Holbein, in the Collection of His Majesty. L., 1792[-1800]. Lge. fo. 91 col.-ptd. stipple plts., including 8 inserted plts., 18 mntd., little browning, early 19th. C. red hf. mor., spine gt. (S. Dec.8; 387) *Joseph.* £900

CHAMBERS, Ephraim
- Cyclopaedia or, an Universal Dictionary of Arts & Sciences. 1741, 1753. *5th. Edn.* 2 vols. & 2 vol. Supp. Fo. Near-unif. cont. cf., spines gt.-decor.; Sir Ivar Colquhoun, of Luss copy. (CE. Mar.22; 60) £580
- – Anr. Copy. 2 vols & 2 vol. Supp. Fo. A few plts. a little worn, cont. cf., worn. (S. Oct.11; 503) *Rhys-Jones.* £80
- – Anr. Edn. L., 1781-86. 5 vols., including plt. vol. Fo. Without title to plt. vol., cont. tree cf., w.a.f. (C. Nov.9; 51) *Traylen.* £320
- – Anr. Edn. 1786-79-83. 4 vols. Fo. Cont. cf. (CSK. Dec.16; 215) £120
- – Anr. Edn. 1788-83-78. 5 vols., including plt. vol. Fo. 143 engraved plts., including 2 folding, torn & reprd., cont. cf., worn. (CSK. Sep.16; 56) £100

CHAMBERS, Sir William
- Plans, Elevations, Sections & Perspective Views of the Gardens & Buildings at Kew. 1763. Lge. fo. 43 engraved plts., including 3 folding, cont. hf. cf., unc., rebkd., engraved armorial bkplt. of John Spencer. (C. Dec.9; 21) *Weinreb.* £850
- Treatise on Civil Architecture. 1759. *1st. Edn.* Fo. 49 (of 50) engraved plts., later cf., rebkd., spine gt. (BBA. Feb.9; 185) *Clarke.* £120
- A Treatise on the Decorative Part of Civil Architecture ... With Illustrations, Notes ... J. Gwilt. L., 1825. *4th. Edn.* Royal 8vo. Subscribers list, slight offsetting on title, red hf. mor., spine gt., unc. (VA. Apr.26; 211) R 350

CHAMBERS, W. & R.
- Golfing, A Handbook to the Royal & Ancient Game. 1887. Bdg. not stated. (PD. Jul.13; 65) £90

CHAMISSO, Adalbert von
- L'Homme qui a perdu son Ombre. Ill.:– Bernard Naudin. Paris, 1913. *(100). (75) on papier vergé de Hollande.* 4to. Str.-grd. mor. by G. Schroeder, blind- & gt.-decor, spine faded, unc. upr. cover wrap., s.-c. (HD. Jul.2; 48) Frs. 2,700
- Peter Schlemihl from the German of Lamotte Fouque. Ill.:– G. Cruikshank. L., 1824. *1st. Engl. Edn.* Mor. ca. 1920, decor., gt. spine, inner & outer dentelle, inner dentelle with corner fleurons, sigd. by Rivière. (GB. May 4; 1223) DM 900
- Werke. Ill.:– A. Schrödter. Leipzig, 1836-39. *1st. Coll. Edn.* 6 vols. in 5. Slightly spotted, cont. hf. leath., gt. decor. spines, vols. V/VI slightly

different, 2 covers split in jnts.; Joh. Prinz ex-libris, cont. owners mark Otto Morgenbesser, Hauswedell coll. (H. May 24; 252) DM 2,200

CHAMBRAY, R.F. de
[–] Parallèle de l'Architecture Antique et de la Moderne. Paris, 1689. Fo. Title slightly creased, some soiling & dampstaining, cont. bds., worn. (CSK. Jun.15; 77) £70
- Peter Schlemihls Wundersame Geschichte. Ed.:– Fr. Baron de la Motte Fouqué. Nuremb., 1814. *1st. Edn.* Cont. bds., very bumped, spine loose & partly missing. (D. Nov.24; 2414) DM 1,200
- – Anr. Copy. Cont. marb. bds. (GB. Nov.4; 2011) DM 600

CHAMOUIN, J.B.
- Collection de 28 Vues de Paris prises au Daguerreotype. [Paris], ca. 1845. Ob. fo. Engraved title, 28 steel engrs., some spotting, publisher's qtr. roan. (S. Mar.6; 79) *Symonds.* £100
- – Anr. Edn. [Paris], n.d. Ob. 4to. 25 engraved plts., cont. mor.-bkd., worn, upr. cover detchd. (CSK. May 4; 61) £70

CHAMPAGNAC, Jean Baptiste Joseph & Olivier, Guillaume Antoine
- Voyage autour du Monde. Ill.:– Frères Rouargue. Paris, 1858. Lge. 8vo. Cont. hf. chagrin, spine decor., from Château des Noës liby. (HD. May 25; 12) Frs. 1,500

CHAMPFLEURY, Jules François Felix Husson
- Les Chats. Paris, 1870. *Edn. de Luxe: 5th. Edn.* Mor. gt. by Chambolle-Duru, covers with overall pattern of repeated cat ornament, spine in 6 compartments, gt.-lettered in 2, cat ornament in rest, turn-ins gt., red floral brocade linings, marb. end-pp., spine discold.; extra-ill. with 27 inserted pieces, including an A.L.s. from author, Robert Hoe bkplt., w.a.f. (CNY. May 18; 177) $400
- – Anr. Copy. Square 8vo. Cont. chagrin, corners, wrap. (HD. Mar.21; 137) Frs. 1,400

CHAMPIER, Symphorien
- La Nef des Princes et des Batailles de Noblesse ... Lyon, Guillaume Balsarin, 1502. *1st. Edn. in Fr.* 2 pts. in 1 vol. 4to. Mispaginated, washed & remntd., red mor. by Lortic, richly decor., doubls.; from P. Desq & J. Renard libys. (HD. Nov.9; 2) Frs. 72,200

CHAMPLAIN, Samuel de
- Les Voyages de la Nouvelle France Occidentale, dite Canada ... Paris, 1640. *1632 Edn.* 4to. Title renewed, map in old printing, worming, cont. spr. cf., spine decor., worn; from Château des Noës liby. (HD. May 25; 13) Frs. 72,000
- The Works ... Toronto, Champlain Soc., 1922-36. *(550).* Vols. I-VI & s.-c. of plts. & maps, compl. Cl. (LH. Sep.25; 200) $250

CHAMPLAIN SOCIETY
- Hudson Bay Record Society Series. Toronto, L. & Winnipeg, 1938-77. Vols. I-XXXI, compl. Cl., later copies with d.-w.'s. (LH. Sep.25; 197) $900
- The Ontario Series. Toronto, 1957-77. *(600-1250).* Vols. I-X, compl. Cl. (LH. Sep.25; 198) $325
- Publications. Toronto, 1907-78. *(520-1750).* Vols. I-L, compl. Cl. (LH. Sep.25; 199) $2,000

CHAMPLIN, John Denison & Perkins, Charles C.
- Cyclopedia of Painters & Paintings. N.Y., 1887. 4 vols. 4to. Blind-stpd. mor. (SPB. Nov.30; 227) $300
- – Anr. Copy. 4 vols. 4to. Three-qtr. mor., lightly rubbed. (RO. Sep.13; 35) $115

CHAMPOLLION, Jean François
- L'Egypte sous les Pharaons. Paris, 1814. 2 vols. Cont. tree cf., decor. spines. (HD. Sep.22; 206) Frs. 1,600
- Précis du Systeme Hieroglyphique des Anciens Egyptiens. Paris, 1824. *1st. Edn.* Text & plt. vol. Lge. 8vo. Title lf. loose, with 'Avis au Relieur' in plt. vol., 16 plts. in text vol., plt. vol. with light margin browning, slightly foxed thro-out, cont. bds., slightly spotted & bumped, & later bds., unc. (H. May 22; 253) DM 3,600

CHANCELLOR, E. Beresford
- The Pleasure Haunts of London. L., 1925. 17 plts., extra-ill. with 16 plts., a few hand-cold., a few ll. spotted, mor., elab. gt., by Bayntun (Rivière), upr. cover inlaid with miniature hand-painted port. of Peg Woffington, boxed. (S. Oct.4; 111) *Joseph.* £270

CHANDLER, Raymond
- The Big Sleep. N.Y., 1939. *1st. Edn.* Orig. cl., some soiling, endpapers slightly browned, d.-w. as ill. in Bruccoli; Fred A. Berne copy. (SPB. May 16; 212) $600

CHANDLER, Richard
- Travels in Asia Minor. 1775. 4to. 1st. & last few ll. spotted, later bds., mor. backstrip, untrimmed. (TA. Nov.17; 57) £62

CHANDLESS, William
- A Visit to Salt Lake; being a Journey Across the Plains. L., 1857. *1st. Edn.* Lacks advts., hf. cf. & marb. bds. (LH. Jan.15; 251) $120

CHANG-FOO, Yau
See— HACKNEY, Louise Wallace & Chang-Foo, Yau

CHANLAIRE, Pierre Gregoire
See— DUMEZ & Chanlaire, Pierre Gregoire

CHANNEVELLE, Jacques
- Accurata Totius Philosophiae Institutio Juxta Principia Aristotelis. Paris, 1667. 2 vols. The dedication copy. *(With:)* - Physica Universalis. Paris, 1669. 2 vols. The dedication copy. *(With:)* - Metaphysica Generalis. Paris, 1677. 2 vols. Together 6 vols. 12mo. Cont. Fr. red mor., not unif., gt. spines, triple gt. fillet à la Du Seuil, arms of Jean-Baptiste Colbert, foot of 1 spine chipped, a few other minor faults. (S. Nov.17; 14) *Chapponiere.* £900

CHANSONS D'AMOUR
Ed.:– J. Hofmiller. Ill.:– Anna Simons. [München, Bremer Pr., 1921]. *(270) on Bütten.* 4to. Hand-bnd. orig. mor., gt. spine, covers, inner & outer dentelles, silk doubls. & end-papers, by Bremer Binderei Frieda Thiersch; Houswedell coll. (H. May 24; 725) DM 2,800

CHANSONS MADECASSES
Trans.:– Evariste Parny. Ill.:– Jean-Emile Laboureur. Paris, 1920. *(412). (400) numbered.* Sm. 8vo. Pink crushed lev. mor., spine in 6 compartments, gt.-lettered, bd. edges with double gt. fillet, turn-ins gt.-decor., gt. poudré marb. end-papers, partly unc., orig. ptd. wraps. & spine preserved at end, matching mor.-edged fleece-lined s.-c.; Raphael Esmerian bkplt. (CNY. May 18; 183) $500

CHANTS & CHANSONS Populaire de la France
Ed.:– H.L. Delloye. [Paris], 1843. 3 vols. Three-qtr. mor. (CBA. Dec.10; 335) $200
- – Anr. Copy. Vols. 2 & 3 only (of 3). Lge. 8vo. Some minor foxing, gt.-decor. mor. by Rivière, panel. spines elab. tooled & lettered in gt., gt. dentelles, marb. end-papers & fly-ll., light wear. (CBA. Mar.3; 38) $160
- – Anr. Copy. 3 vols. Lge. 8vo. Contains most remarks of 1st. printing, cont. hf. chagrin, spine decor. (HD. Mar.21; 138) Frs. 1,900
- – Anr. Edn. Ed.:– H.L. Delloye. Paris, 1843-44. 3 vols. Slight discoloration, mod. cl., orig. decor. wraps. laid down, in glassine wraps. (SPB. Dec.13; 871) $250
- – Anr. Edn. Ed.:– H.L. Delloye. [Paris], 1843[-45]. 3 vols. 4to. Light spotting, orig. bds., rubbed, rebkd. (CSK. Nov.25; 47) £50
- – Anr. Edn. Ed.:– Du Mersan. Ill.:– Mm. E. de Beaumont, Boilly, Daubigny, etc. Paris, [1848?]. 3 vols. Fo. Mod. hf. mor., orig. wraps. bnd. in Vols. I & III. (CH. Sep.20; 5) Fls. 750

CHANUTE, Octave
- Progress in Flying Machines. N.Y., [1894]. *1st. Edn.* Margin staining towards end, orig. cl. gt., some soiling & rubbing; John D. Stanitz coll. (SPB. Apr.25; 95) $400

CHANVALON, Jean Baptiste Thibault de
[-] **Voyage à la Martinique.** Paris, 1763. *1st. Edn.*
4to. 2 errata ll. at end, a few ll. trimmed close just
affecting a few side-notes, some dampstaining, cont.
roan-bkd. bds., spine wormed, slightly rubbed. (S.
Jun.25; 91) *Maggs.* £150

CHAPELAIN, Jean
- **La Pucelle ou la France Délivrée.** Paris, 1656.
12mo. 19th. C. str.-grd. red hf. mor. gt., arms
of Marie-Caroline de Bourbon-Sicile, Duchesse de
Berry (1798-1870), spine decor. (HD. May 21; 22)
Frs. 1,500

CHAPMAN, Abel
- **Savage Sudan.** 1921. *1st. Edn.* (*With:*) - **The
Borders & Beyond.** 1924. *1st. Edn.* (*With:*)
- **Retrospect.** 1928. *1st. Edn.* (*With:*) - **Memories.**
1930. *1st. Edn.* Frontis. loose. Together 4 vols.
Unif. ribbed cl. gt. (SKC. Jan.13; 2369) £180

CHAPMAN, Edmund
- **An Essay on the Improvement of Midwifery;
chiefly with regard to the Operation.** L., 1733. *1st.
Edn.* Browned & stained, cont. cf., very worn. (S.
Dec.13; 256) *Phillips.* £130

CHAPMAN, Frederik Henrik af
- **Architectura Navalis Mercatoria.** Holmiae
[Stockholm], 1768. *1st. Edn.* Lge. fo. Fr., Engl. &
Swedish index bnd. at end, mod. cf., gt. title on
upr. cover, spine decor.; added Engl. index in cont.
MS., sig. of W. Wallis, 1793, on title. (HD. Jun.18;
10) *Frs.* 90,000
- **Traité de la Construction des Vaisseaux.** Paris,
1779. Fo. 11 engraved plts., 2 additional folding
tables at end, mod. hf. cf., Signet Liby. arms on
covers. (C. Nov.9; 52) *Lawson.* £260
-- **Anr. Edn.** Ed.:– Vial du Clairbois. Ill.:– de La
Guardette. Brest, Paris, 1781. 4to. Cont. marb. cf.,
spine decor., 1 turn-in torn. (HD. Jun.18; 11)
Frs. 4,800
-- **Anr. Copy.** 4to. On 'papier azuré', lacks preface
lf. & 1 plt. (both supplied in old MS.), cont. marb.
cf., some traces of wear. (HD. Mar.9; 65)
Frs. 1,600

CHAPMAN, George
- **Caesar & Pompey: a Roman Tragedy.** L., 1631.
1st. Edn. 1st. Iss. Sm. 4to. Lacks A1 blank, rust
holes in F3 & G3, short tear in F1, stained, 19th.
C. red hf. mor.; Sir Edmund Gosse bkplt. [STC
4993] (S. Dec.8; 12) *Quaritch.* £350
See— **MARLOWE, Christopher & Chapman,
George**

CHAPMAN, John & André, Peter
- **A Map of the County of Essex from an Actual
Survey taken in MDCCLXXII: LXXIII &
MDCCLXXIV.** 1 Oct. 1777. *1st. Edn.* Ob. fo.
(520 × 680mm.). 25 engraved sheets, with index
map, inset plans showing Colchester & Harwich,
outl. hand-cold., title-sheet slightly dust-soiled (sm.
puncture affecting outer neatline), few slight stains
or short tears, cont. cf.-bkd. bds., defect. (S. Nov.1;
156) *Quaritch.* £220
-- **Anr. Edn.** Colchester, W. Keymer, Jun. 1785.
2nd. Edn. Lge. ob. fo. Lge. scale (2": 1 mile) county
map in 25 engraved mapsheets (without index),
some slight dust-soiling, 19th. C. hf. roan, rubbed,
w.a.f. (S. May 21; 44) *Roberts.* £200

CHAPMAN, Kenneth M.
- **Pueblo Indian Pottery.** Nice, 1933-36. (*750*)
numbered & sigd. by publisher. 2 vols. Tall 4to.
100 col. plts., loose as iss., intro. & notes in Fr. &
Engl., pict. bd. portfos., worn, spines defect. (SG.
Jan.26; 145) $425

CHAPMAN, Nathaniel
- **Discourses on the Elements of Therapeutics and
Materia Medica.** Phila., 1817. *1st. Edn.* 2 vols.
Slight browning, owner's sig., few liby. stps., mod.
hf. cf. (SG. Mar.22; 62) $130

CHAPMAN, Robert William
- **Cancels.** L., 1930. [*1st. Edn.*] (*500*). Few ll.
slightly spotted, orig. vell.-bkd. bds. (BBA. Mar.7;
187) *Dawson.* £95
-- **Anr. Copy.** Orig. qtr. vell., marb. bds., unc. (SG.
Jan.5; 91) $130

CHAPMAN, William
- **A Treatise ... on the Preservation of Timber from
Premature Decay ... in Ships & Buildings.** L., 1817.
1st. Edn. Hf. cf., bkplt. (GM. Dec.7; 689) £80

CHAPPE D'AUTEROCHE, Jean
- **Voyage en Californie pour l'Observation du
Passage de Venus ...** Paris, 1772. *1st. Edn.* 4to. Plan
lightly discold. at edges, pp. 83-88 discold., hf. mor.;
the Rt. Hon. Visc. Eccles copy. [Sabin 12003]
(CNY. Nov.18; 61) $600

CHAPPELL, Lieut. Edward
- **Narrative of a Voyage to Hudson's Bay in His
Magesty's Ship Rosamond ...** 1817. [*1st. Edn.*].
Folding map spotted, cont. tree cf., rebkd. (TA.
Feb.16; 36) £170
-- **Anr. Copy.** Folding engraved map, 4 full-p.
engraved plts., 2 engraved text ills., advts. at end,
orig. paper bds., unc., rebkd. preserving old spine
label; the Rt. Hon. Visc. Eccles copy. [Sabin 12003
(incorrectly calling for 9 plts., rather than 9 subjects
as listed] (CNY. Nov.18; 63) $380

CHAPPUYS, G.
[-] **Figures de la Bible, declarées par stances. par
G.C.T.** Lyon, 1582. Hf. havana mor., corners, decor.
spines, by Rivière & Sons. (HD. Dec.9; 14)
Frs. 1,600

CHAPTAL, Jean-Antoine comte de Chanteloup
- **L'Art de faire le Vin.** Ill.:– Thierry. Paris, 1819.
Cont. spr. cf., limp decor. spine, gt. roulette. (HD.
Jan.26; 73) *Frs.* 4,000

CHAPUIS, Alfred
- **Montres et Emaux de Genève. Louis XIV, Louis
IV, Louis XVI et Empire. Collection H. Wilsdorf.**
Genf, 1944. (*600*). 4to. Orig. linen; hf.-title with
dedication from Wilsdorf. (HK. Nov.12; 4633)
DM 400

CHAR, René
- **Dent Prompte.** Ill.:– Max Ernst. Paris, 1969. (*290*)
numbered. Fo. This copy hors commerce, printers
mark sigd. by author & artist, portfo. with 10 cold.
lithos. 10 poems & 1 cold. litho. on wrap., loose
double ll. in orig. pict. wrap, in orig. linen box.
(GB. May 5; 2455) DM 3,800
-- **Anr. Copy.** Printers mark sigd. by author &
artist, ll. in orig. wraps. with cold. sigd. litho., orig.
linen box. (HK. May 17; 2707) DM 1,800
- **L'Inclémence Lointaine.** Ill.:– Vieira da Silva.
Paris, 1961. (*130*) numbered on Japan, sigd. by
author & artist. Fo. Leaves, wrap., box. (HD.
Dec.16; 94) *Frs.* 6,000
- **Le Marteau sans Maître.** Ill.:– Joan Miro. Paris,
20 Apr. 1976. (*175*) numbered & sigd. by author &
artist. (*50*) with 23 orig. col. lithos. Lge. fo. On
lge. velin d'Arches pur fil, lacks plts. on japan & 3
unpubld. plts., leaves, ill. wrap. & box. (LM. Mar.3;
23) B.Frs. 31,000
- **Le Soleil des Eaux, Spectacle pour une Toile des
Pêcheurs.** Ill.:– Georges Braque. Paris, 1949. (*200*)
numbered & sigd. by author & artist. 4to. Unsewn
in orig. wraps., unc., folder & s.-c. (S. Nov.21; 4)
Makiya. £460

CHARCOT, Jean Baptiste, 1867-1936
- **The Voyage of the 'Why Not?' in the Antarctic.**
[1911]. Cl. gt. (P. Jun.7; 21) £150

CHARCOT, Jean Martin
- **Klinische Vorträge über Krankheiten des
Nervensystems.** Trans.:– B. Fetzer. Stuttgart, 1874-
78. *1st. German Edn.* 2 vols. Cont. hf. leath. (R.
Oct.12; 1376) DM 610

CHARCOT, Jean Martin & others
- **Traité de Médecine.** Paris, 1891-94. 6 vols. Lge.
8vo. Some minor spotting, cont. crimson qtr. mor.
gt. (TA. Feb.16; 261) £90

CHARCOT, Jean Martin & Richer, Paul
- **Les Difformes et les Malades dans l'Art.** Paris,
1889. *1st. Edn.* Sm. fo. Later buckram, ex-liby.
(SG. Oct.6; 91) $110

CHARDIN, John
- **Travels into Persia & the East Indies.** Ill.:– D.
Loggan. L., 1686. [*1st. Edn.*]. Vol. 1 (all publd.).
Fo. Extra engraved title, port., 17 plts., including
folding map & 9 views, some in 2 plts., 1 plt. reprd.,
few headlines shaved, 18th. C. cf. [Wing C 2043]
(S. Mar.6; 27) *Thorpe.* £280
-- **Anr. Copy.** 2 pts. in 1 vol. Vol. 1 (all publd.).
Fo. Light browning, cf., defect. (CR. Jun.6; 18)
Lire 650,000
-- **Anr. Edn.** L., 1691. Fo. Additional engraved
title, port., folding map, 14 (of 15) plts., 2 short
tears, cont. cf., rubbed, rebkd. (S. Jun.25; 36)
Maggs. £120
-- **Anr. Copy.** Fo. Frontis. from 1686 edn., cont.
cf., chipped. (LH. Sep.25; 514) $250
- **Voyages en Perse et autres Lieux de l'Orient.**
Amst., 1711. 10 vols. Few plts. with sm. tears, cont.
marb. leath. gt., slightly rubbed. (HK. Nov.8; 867)
DM 1,400
-- **Anr. Copy.** 10 pts. in 5 vols. Old MS. notes on
plt. versos, slightly foxed, cont. bds. (HK. May 15;
633) DM 1,200
-- **Anr. Edn.** Amst., 1735. *New Edn.* 4 vols. 4to.
Old str.-grd. mor. gt., spines decor. (HD. May 21;
23) *Frs.* 32,000
-- **Anr. Edn.** Ed.:– Louis-Mathieu Langlès. Paris,
1811. Atlas vol. only. Fo. Engraved port. frontis.,
64 engraved plts. (10 folding), including lge. general
map, views & elevations, hand-cold. thro.-out, hf.-
title, title faintly spotted, some margin browning,
mod. maroon panel. cf. (S. Feb.1; 15)
Hatch. £3,500
-- **Anr. Copy.** 10 vols. & atlas. 8vo. & fo. Port., 2
maps & 82 plts. (several folding), cont. tree roan,
spines decor., atlas bdg. not unif. (HD. Jun.26; 36)
Frs. 10,500

CHARIVARI
Paris, Jan.-Dec. 1866. 2 vols. Fo. Internal losses &
defects, cont. hf. chagrin, worn. (HD. Jun.6; 30)
Frs. 2,400
-- **Anr. Edn.** Ill.:– Honoré Daumier & others.
Paris, 26 Jan.-31 May 1868. 4to. 23 orig. lithos. in
1st. printing, hf. buckram. (HD. Jun.22; 32)
Frs. 1,400

CHARLES I, King of England
[-] **Eikon Basilike.** 1648. *2nd. Iss.* Some light
offsetting, lightly wormed with loss of a few
characters, upr. margins shaved, with loss of a few
headlines, later mor., lightly rubbed. [Wing E271]
(CSK. Oct.21; 162) £70
- **A Large Declaration Concerning the Late Tumults
in Scotland, from their First Originalls ...** 1639.
Fo. Some cont. marginalia, cont. cf., rebkd. (TA.
Jun.21; 369) £65
- **Reliquiae Sacrae Carolinae or the Works.** Hague,
1651. Cont. panel. cf. (P. Jan.12; 173)
Cavendish. £85

CHARLES II, King of England
- **His Majesties Gracious Patent to the Goldsmiths,
for Payment & Satisfaction of their Debt.** L., 1677.
Sm. fo. Margins of title mntd., slightly browned,
mod. cf. by Sangorski & Sutcliffe. [Wing C3039]
(BBA. May 3; 159) *Coupe.* £60

CHARLES, William, publisher
- **Pug's Visit to Mr. Punch.** Phila., 1815. Square
16mo. Some pencil scribblings, orig. ptd. wraps.,
worn, some cover staining & soiling, worn; Kane
family copy, many sigs. (RO. Mar.21; 99) $550

CHARLES D'ORLEANS
See— **ORLEANS, Charles d'**

CHARLET, Gaston
- **Decoration Moderne dans le Textile.** Paris, 1920's.
Fo. 20 pochoir-cold. plts., loose as iss., cl.-bkd. bds.
(SG. Aug.25; 370) $110

CHARLET, Nicolas-Toussaint
- **Recueil de Costumes de l'Ex-Garde.** Paris, [1819-
20]. Lge. 4to. 30 orig. lithos., mntd. on guards, str.-
grd. hf. mor., corners, spine decor., unc., wrap. in
place of title. (HD. Jun.22; 24) *Frs.* 1,800

CHARLETON, Walter
- **Exercitationes de Differentiis & Nominibus
Animalium.** Oxford, 1677. Sm. fo. Cont. spr. cf.,
rebkd., lacks front free end-paper; Sir R. Grosvenor,
of Eaton bkplt. (BBA. Feb.23; 156) *Thorp.* £160
-- **Anr. Copy.** Fo. Title soiled, cont. cf. worn,
rebkd., reprd.; Dr. Walter Pagel copy. [Wing C
3672] (S. Feb.7; 76) *Heller.* £130

CHARLEVOIX, Pierre François Xavier de
– Histoire de l'Etablissement ... du Christianisme dans l'empire du Japon. Rouen, 1715. *1st. Edn.* 3 vols. 12mo. 2 marginal tears, flaw in D5 vol.3, slightly spotted, cont. cf., head of 2 spines lacking; ex-liby. (S. Apr.9; 10) *McKiernan.* £110
– Histoire de l'Isle Espagnole ou de S. Domingue ... Ill.:– Baquoy (vigs.). Paris, 1730-31. *Orig. Edn.* 2 vols. 4to. Lacks 4 maps or plts., cont. spr. cf., spine decor., worn; from Château des Noës liby. (HD. May 25; 14) Frs. 3,200
– – **Anr. Edn.** Amst., 1733. 4 vols. Leath. (DS. Apr.27; 2638) Pts. 150,000
– Histoire du Paraguay. Ill.:– Maps:– Bellin. Paris, 1756. *1st. Edn.* 3 vols. 4to. Hf.-titles, 7 folding engraved maps, sm. liby. stps. on title, cont. Fr. mott. cf. [Sabin 12129] (S. May 22; 392) *Frers.* £600
– – **Anr. Copy.** 3 vols. 4to. hf.-titles, liby. stps. at foot of titles, cont. Fr. mott. cf., slightly worn. [Sabin 12129] (S. Dec.1; 275) *Baker.* £480
– – **Anr. Copy.** 3 vols. 4to. Cont. marb. cf., spines decor. (HD. Jul.2; 8) Frs. 4,000
– Histoire et Description Genérale du Japon. Paris, 1736. *1st. Edn.* 2 vols. 4to. 27 engraved plts. & maps only, 15 folding, 1 defect. & loose, engraved vigs., last privilege lf. in Vol. 2, lacks hf.-titles & pp. 713-744 of 'Table des Matières', slight stains on some ll., mostly marginal, cont. cf., rubbed. (BBA. May 3; 274) *Vine.* £80
– – **Anr. Copy.** 9 vols. 8 maps & plans & 48 plts., cont. cf., rubbed, some stains. (VG. May 3; 647) Fls. 1,350
– Histoire et Description Genérale de la Nouvelle France, avec Le Journal Historique d'un Voyage ... dans l'Anérique Septemtrionale. Paris, 1744. *1st. Edn.* 3 vols. 4to. Vig. titles, 28 engraved maps & plans, most folding, 96 numbered figures on 22 folding engraved plts., hf.-titles, sm. tears to 2 maps, 1 lf. in Vol. 3 slightly torn, cont. tree cf., spines gt., heads of 2 spines chipped, corners rubbed; the Holdernesse & Rt. Hon. Visc. Eccles copy. [Sabin 12135] (CNY. Nov.18; 64) $2,400
– – **Anr. Copy.** 3 vols. 4to. 50 folding maps & plts., cf.-bkd. marb. paper bds. (LH. Sep.25; 201) $1,900
– History & General Description of New France. Trans.:– John Gilmary Shea. N.Y., 1866-72. 6 vols. 4to. Three-qtr. mor., rubbed; ex-liby. (SG. Jan.19; 132) $100
– Journal of a Voyage to North America. L., 1761. *1st. Engl. Edn.* 2 vols. Hf.-titles, folding engraved map, cont. cf., slightly rubbed. [Sabin 12139] (S. May 22; 310) *Sawyer.* £340
– – **Anr. Copy.** 2 vols. Hf.-titles, lge. folding map, hf. mor., partly unc. [Sabin 12139] (S. May 22; 311) *Watt.* £320
– – **Anr. Copy.** 2 vols. Hf.-titles, cont. pol. cf., gt. spines; the Rt. Hon. Visc. Eccles copy. [Sabin 12139] (CNY. Nov.18; 65) $550
– – **Anr. Edn.** Ed.:– Louis Phelps Kellogg. Chic., Caxton Cl., 1923. 2 vols. Cl., s.-c. (LH. Sep.25; 342) $100
[–] La Vie de la Mère Marie de l'incàrnation. Paris, 1724. *1st. Edn.* Cont. leath., 2 sm. wormholes in spine. [Sabin 12141] (R. Oct.13; 2976) DM 650

CHARMETON, Georges
– Livre d'Ornement, gravé par Ducerceau. [1670?]. Ob. 4to. New marb. bds. (S. May 10; 248) *Bruno.* £240

CHARNAY, Desiré
– Les Anciennes Villes du Nouveau Monde. Paris, 1885. 4to. Publishers decor. red buckram, limp decor. spine. (HD. Dec.9; 107) Frs. 1,400

CHARNOCK, John
– An History of Marine Architecture. L., 1800-02. 3 vols. 4to. Additional engraved title slightly foxed, 99 aquarinted & line-engraved plts., with plt. of Flying Proa of the Ladrone Islands, minor damage by adhesion to plt. of chinese Junk in Vol. 3, a few unprints shaved, cont. hf. cf. (S. May 21; 7) *Cavendish.* £1,300
– – **Anr. Copy.** 3 vols. 4to. Lacks 1 plt., cont. Engl. cf., spine decor., worn; 1 cover detchd. (HD. Jun.18; 12) Frs. 5,800
– – **Anr. Copy.** 3 vols. 4to. 90 plts., old cf., spines

renewed, corners worn. (HD. Mar.9; 66) Frs. 5,000

CHARPENTIER, Johann
– Essia sur la Constitution Géognostique des Pyrénées. Paris, 1923. Cont. hf. leath. gt. (HK. May 15; 792) DM 400

CHARRON, Pierre
– De la Sagesse. Bordeaux, 1601. *Orig. Edn.* L.P., ruled, port. from 1607 edn. added as frontis., cont. red mor.; from libys. of Robert S. Turner & Noilly. (HD. Mar.29; 19) Frs. 13,000
– – **Anr. Edn.** Leiden, [1659]. 12mo. Long-grd mor., gt. roulette, decor spines. inner roulette, attributed to Roger Payne; Francis Kettaneh ex-libris. (HD. Dec.9; 15) Frs. 1,700

CHARTERS
– Chartae Latinae Antiquiores: Facsimile-Editions of the Latin Charters prior to the Ninth Century. Ed.:– A. Bruckner & R. Marichal. Olten & Lausanne, 1954-63. Pts. I-III only (of 10?). Fo. Qtr. vell., d.-w.'s. (SG. Oct.27; 63) $100
– The Charter Granted by their Majesties King William & Queen Mary ... Boston, 1742. Some foxing, possibly lacks some edges at end, cf., spine & edges rubbed. (RS. Jan.17; 479) $175

CHASDAI BEN AVRAHAM CRESCAS
– Or Hashem. Ferrara, 1555. *1st. Edn.* 4 pts. in 1 vol. 4to. Uncensored, marginalia in early hand thro.-out, owners sigs., some staining & soiling, cf.-bkd. bds., worn; Hochschule für die Wissenschaft des Judenthums stps. [Steinschneider 4739, 1]. (SPB. Jun.26; 8) $1,800

CHASE, Thomas & others
– Narratives of the Wreck of the Whale-Ship Essex. Ill.:– Robert Gibbings. Gold. Cock. Pr., 1935. *(275)* numbered. Fo. Orig. cl., soiled; pres. inscr. from Gibbings to W.T. Hooper, & with an A.L.s. from Gibbings to Hooper. (BBA. Feb.23; 241) *Sawyer.* £200

CHASLES, M.
– Apercu Historique sur l'origine et le Developpement de Méthodes en Géometrie ... Paris, 1889. *3rd. Edn.* 4to. Cont. hf. leath, slightly bumped. (HT. May 8; 387) DM 500

CHASSANT, A. & Tausin, H.
– Dictionnaire des Devises Historiques et Héraldiques ... Avec une Table Alphabétique des Noms. Paris, 1878. 3 vols. Cont. hf. chagrin, unc., wraps. (HD. Mar.27; 132) Frs. 1,000

CHASSENEUS, Bartholomeus de
– Tertia Recognitio Commentarii in Consuetudines Ducatus Burgundiae ac totius Gallie. Lyon, 1528. 4to. Some ll. restored, light browning, newer cont-style leath, 2 clasps. (V. Oct.1; 3723) DM 850

CHASSEPOL, François de
[–] The History of the Grand Viziers, Mahomet, & Achmet Coprogli, ... with the most Secret intrigues of the Seraglio. Trans.:– John Evelyn, Jnr. 1677. *1st. Engl. Edn.* 8vo. License lf., cont. cf., spine gt., slightly rubbed. top of spine defect.; Rolle bkplt. [Wing, C3728] (BBA. Jan.19; 162) *O'Neill.* £80

CHASTEL
– Nicholas Poussin. Paris, 1960. 2 vols. 4to. No bdg. stated. (SPB. Nov.30; 61) $125

CHASTELLUX
– De la Félicité Publique. Amst., 1772. *Orig. Edn.* 2 vols. in 1. Cont. roan, spine faded. (HD. Feb.22; 36) Frs. 1,900

CHASTELLUX, François Jean, Marquis de
– Travels in North-America, In the Years 1780, 1781, & 1782. Dublin, 1787. 2 vols. A few ll. slightly dust soiled, cont. cf., rebkd. with orig. backstrip laid down, corners reprd.; the Rt. Hon. Visc. Eccles copy. [Sabin 12229] (CNY. Nov.18; 66) $170
– Voyages ... dans l'Amérique. Paris, 1786. *1st. Compl. Authorised Edn.* 2 vols. Hf.-titles, 2 folding maps, 3 folding plts., cont. mott. cf. gt., little worn, early bk-label of Trambly de Laissardière. (SG. Apr.26; 43) $375

CHASTENET DE PUYSEGUR, Jacques François de
– Art de la Guerre, par Principes et par Règles. Paris, 1748. *[1st. Edn.].* 2 vols. Fo. 41 folding engraved plts., slightly spotted, some wormholes affecting text & plts., some reprd., mor.-bkd. bds. (S. Dec.20; 785) *Greenwood.* £150
– – **Anr. Copy.** 2 vols. Fo. Engraved title to Vol.2, engraved port., 41 plts., many double-p, some margin staining, cf., defect. (S. Mar.20; 741) *Shapero.* £100
– – **Anr. Edn.** Paris, 1749. 2 vols. 4to. Hf.-title to Vol.2, some plts. of maps cropped, cont. mott. cf., spines gt. (S. Mar.20; 789) *Blanko.* £150
– – **Anr. Copy.** 2 vols. 4to. Cont. marb. cf. (HD. Apr.13; 41) Frs. 3,100

CHATEAUBRIAND, François Auguste-René, Vicomte de
– Atala. René. Ill.:– J.B. Garnier. Paris, 1805. 2 pts. in 1 vol. 12mo. Minimal foxing, cont. spr. roan gt., spine decor. (HD. May 3; 222) Frs. 1,200
– La Brière. Ill.:– Meheut. Paris, 1924. *(31)* on Holland Van Gelder with suite on japan. Square 8vo. Hf. mor. by Klein, unc., wrap. & spine preserved. (HD. May 3; 225) Frs. 1,500
– Combourg. Ill.:– Decaris. Paris, 1928. 4to. Leaves, box. (HD. Jun.13; 17) Frs. 1,500
– Itineraire de Paris à Jérusalem et de Jérusalem à Paris, en allant par la Grèce, et revenant par l'Egypte la Barbarie et l'Espagne. Paris, 1811. *Orig. Edn.* 3 vols. Cont. sheep, decor. spines. (HD. Sep.22; 211) Frs. 1,300
– Les Martyrs, ou le Triomphe de la Religion Chrétienne. Paris, 1809. *Orig. Edn.* 2 vols. Cont. tree cf. gt., decor. spines. (HD. Sep.22; 209) Frs. 1,100
– Mémoires d'Outre-Tombe. Paris, 1849-50. *Orig. Edn.* 12 vols. With subscribers list, sewed, sm. libraire Dion-Lambert label on cover of each vol., s.-c.'s; letter from author to Delloye. (HD. Sep.22; 212) Frs. 18,000
– – **Anr. Edn.** Paris, 1860. 6 vols. Hf. roam. (HD. Feb.22; 37) Frs. 2,500
– – **Anr. Edn.** Ill.:– Staal, de Moraine & Ganglet. Paris, n.d. *New Edn.* 6 vols. Lge. 8vo. 30 vigs. on chine collé, some foxing, hf. chagrin, corners, by Bernasconi, unc., wraps. & spines preserved, wraps. slightly soiled. (HD. May 3; 224) Frs. 2,300
– Les Natchez. 1826. *Orig. Edn.* 2 vols. Sewed, hf. mor. folder & s.-c. (HD. Apr.13; 83) Frs. 1,500
– Oeuvres. Paris, 1861. 20 vols. in 10. Lge. 8vo. Cont. hf. mor. (HD. Mar.9; 67) Frs. 1,000
– Oeuvres Complètes. Ill.:– Thompson (frontis.), A. & T. Johannot & others. Paris, 1826-31. *1st. Edn.* 20 vols. in 31. Cont. glazed hf. cf., spines decor. (HD. Nov.29; 84) Frs. 24,000
– – **Anr. Copy.** 31 vols. Some foxing, cont. hf. cf., spines gt. (HD. May 21; 85) Frs. 2,700
– – **Anr. Copy.** 28 vols. in 31. Vols. IX & XIII without woodcut title, later hf. leath. gt., slightly bumped & worn. (H. May 22; 629) DM 620
– Travels in Greece, Palestine, Egypt, & Barbary. Trans.:– Frederic Schoberl. L., 1811. *1st. Edn. in Engl.* 2 vols. Cont. spr. cf., extremities worn; Richard Strachey armorial bkplt. (SG. Sep.22; 88) $175

CHATEAUBRIAND, François August René, Vicomte de & Gessner, Salomon
– Atala, from the French of Chateaubriand; Death of Abel, Idyls, & First Navigator, from the German of Gessner. L., 1825. Sm. 12mo. Pol. cf., spine elab. gt., fore-e. pntg. (SG. Nov.17; 221) $275

CHATEAUBRIANT, Alphonse de
– Monsieur des Lourdines. Ill.:– Henri Jourdain. Paris, 1929. *Ltd. Edn., numbered, on Vélin de Rives.* 4to. Decor. mor. by Blanchetière, lined endpapers, s.-c. (SM. Mar.7; 2095) Frs. 3,600

CHATELAIN, Emile
– Paléographie des Classiques Latins. Paris, 1884-1900. 2 vols. Fo. Perforation stps. in title, plts. hand-stpd. on rectos. in Vol. I, on versos in Vol. II, hf. mor., ex-liby. (RO. Dec.11; 267) $175

CHATELAIN, Henri Abraham
[–] Atlas Historique. Amst., 1705-14. Vols. 1-4 (of 7). Fo. 3 engraved allegorical titles in vols. 1, 2 & 4, 133 copper engraved maps & plts. & 29 text

plts., cont. leath. gt., some wear. (D. Nov.23; 753) DM 2,400
– – **Anr. Edn.** Amst., 1721-20-20-14-19-19-20. *Various Edns.* 7 vols. Fo. 4 engraved additional titles, 267 plts., tables & maps only, but with 2 additional maps not called for, 2 maps with different numbering, & map numbered 30 in Vol. 6 is on 2 separate folding sheets, not 1 as listed, lacks 4 maps in Vol. 1 & A-F inclusive, some maps, tables & plts. cleanly torn at folds, some browning, cont. cf., spines chipped. (CSK. Dec.16; 2) £3,600

CHATTERTON, E. Keble
– **Sailing Ships. The Story of their Development** ... 1909. (*With:*) –**Fore & Aft. The Story of the Fore & Aft Rig from Earliest Times.** 1912. Together 2 vols. 4to. Orig. decor. cl. gt., rubbed on spines. (TA. Jun.21; 285) £50
– **Ship Models.** L., 1923. *(1000) numbered.* 4to. Plts., some cold., some text ll. slightly spotted, orig. buckram, gt. (S. Apr.9; 203) *Libris.* £70
– **Old Ship Prints.** 1927. *(125) numbered on H.M.P., with 3 extra ills. in photogravure hand-ptd. in col.* 4to. Buckram gt., unc. & unopened. (SKC. Sep.9; 2015) £70
– **Steamship Models.** 1924. *(1000) numbered & sigd.* 4to. Slight spotting on text, buckram gt., d.-w. (SKC. Sep.9; 2014) £60

CHATTERTON, Lady H.G.M.
– **The Pyrenees with Excursions Into Spain.** L., 1843. 2 vols. 16 tinted litho. plts., slight spotting, hf. cf. gt. (P. Feb.16; 213) £85

CHATTERTON, Thomas
– **Miscellanies in Prose & Verse.** 1778. *1st. Edn.* Hf.-title, advt. lf. bnd. in at end, cont. cf., rebkd. (TA. Feb.16; 201) £54
[–] Poems, Supposed to have been Written at Bristol, by Thomas Rowley ... L., 1777. *1st. Edn.* C4 cancelled, b1 torn, browned, cont. cf., corners worn, jnts. reprd., spine split, qtr. mor. gt. s.-c.; bkplt. of Horace Walpole, Frederic Dannay copy. (CNY. Dec.16; 67) $100
– **The Revenge, A Burletta.** L., 1795. *1st. Edn.* Slight foxing & darkening, three-qtr. mor. & marb. bds., covers rubbed, corners bumped, catalogue entry & adhesion stain to front pastedown. (CBA. Mar.3; 129) $100

CHAUCER, Geoffrey
[–] The Canterbury Tales. Westminster, William Caxton ca. 1476/77. *1st. Edn.* Sm. fo. 1 lf. [Y3] only. 2 sm. tears, 2 pieces of gummed tape on verso; Frederic Dannay copy. (CNY. Dec.16; 69) $850
– – **Anr. Edn.** Ed.:– T. Tyrwhitt. 1822. *New Edn.* 5 vols. Red mor. gt. by Henderson, Bissett. (PD. Dec.14; 330) £120
– – **Anr. Edn.** Ill.:– William Russell Flint. Medici Soc., 1913. *(500).* 3 vols. 4to. Orig. vell. gt., box. (P. Jul.26; 33) £240
– – **Anr. Copy.** 3 vols. 4to. Orig. limp vell., lightly soiled, ties. (CSK. Mar.9; 135) £170
– – **Anr. Copy.** 3 vols. 4to. Linen-bkd. paper bds. (LH. Sep.25; 565) $190
– – **Anr. Edn.** Ill.:– Eric Gill. Waltham St. Lawrence, Gold. Cock. Fr., 1929. *(485).* 4 vols. 4to. Folded in sigs., unbnd., paper chemises of folders; sigd. pres. copy from Gill to William B. Wootten. (CBA. Nov.19; 151) $1,300
– – **Anr. Edn.** Ill.:– Eric Gill. Waltham St. Lawrence, Gold. Cock. Pr., 1929-31. *(485) numbered on H.M.P.* 4 vols. Fo. Orig. mor.-bkd. decor. bds.; inscr. by Robert Gibbings in Vol. I. (C. May 30; 187) *Henderson.* £1,100
– – **Anr. Edn.** Trans.:– William Van Wyck. Ill.:– Rockwell Kent. N.Y., 1930. *(75) numbered & sigd. by artist, with sigd. proof sheets of the full-p. plts. laid in.* 2 vols. Fo. Pig, spines darkened & brittle, cl.-covered s.-c. (SG. Mar.29; 178) $550
– – **Anr. Edn.** Intro. & Trans.:–Nevill Coghill. Ill.:– Elizabeth Frink. [L.], 1972. *(175) numbered & sigd. by artist.* Double elephant fo. Wtrmkd. cotton paper sized with gelatine, unsewn folded sheets, untrimmed, laid into cl.-covered fold-down portfo. by F. & J. Randall. (HA. Feb.24; 226) $375
– **The Workes.** [L.], 1542. *2nd. Coll. Edn.* Fo. 1 woodcut cold., about 50 ll. supplied from other copies, last lf. in facs., TT2 reprd. with loss, title cropped & laid down, several repairs, mostly marginal, partly wormed, early MS. recipe for ink on 1 fly-title, blind-stpd. sheep antique by Bernard Middleton. [STC 5070] (SG. Nov.3; 38) $2,300
– – **Anr. Edn.** L., ca. 1551. *4th. Edn.* Fo. 5 headlines shaved, title slightly soiled & with 3 early inscrs., few ll. stained, sm. tears to Cc5 & Qq6. lacks final blank, 17th. C. cf., gt.-panel., central gt. ornaments on covers, spine reprd., cl. s.-c.; bkplts. of Ham Court & Hannah D. Rabinowitz, Frederic Dannay copy. [STC 5071] (CNY. Dec.16; 70) $4,500
– – **Anr. Edn.** 1602. *5th. Edn.* Fo. Few sm. holes in title & port., old cf., rebkd.; bkplts. of M.M. Sykes & W. Combes. (BS. Nov.16; 40) £400
– – **Anr. Edn.** L., 1602. *7th. Edn.* Fo. 2R1 & 2R6 repeated, 2R2, 2R5 & errata lf. inserted from anr. copy, sm. holes in title, port. & few text ll., some staining, cont. blind-stpd. cf., rebkd., lacks clasps. [STC 5080] (S. Dec.8; 13) *Sotheran.* £280
– – **Anr. Copy.** Fo. Lacks frontis., prelims., catalogue of translations, & glossary, 4 ll. impft. & reprd., M6 reprd. without loss, corner off 3D5, other minor defects, 19th. C. pol. roan gt. extra, extremities worn. [STC 5080 or 5081] (SG. Oct.27; 64) $200
– – **Anr. Copy.** Fo. Sm. Errata lf. at ind., wormholes in outer margins of 1st. & last 5 ll. reprd., mod. vell. (R. Apr.3; 155) DM 1,250
– – **Anr. Edn.** L., 1687. Sm. fo. Slightly browned & spotted, cont. cf., arms of the Earl of Coningsby on covers, head of spine worn. (S. Dec.13; 347) *Finch.* £180
– – **Anr. Copy.** Fo. Engraved frontis. with later hand-colouring, lacks 2 ll., 1 lf. torn with some loss & reprd., some light spotting, mod. hf. mor., lightly rubbed. [Wing C3736] (CSK. Jun.15; 74) £65
– – **Anr. Edn.** Ed.:– John Urry. L., 1721. Fo. Old cf., needs rebdg. (SG. Oct.27; 65) $175
– – **Anr. Edn.** L., 1845. 6 vols. Cf. gt. extra by Zaehnsdorf. (PNY. Oct.20; 184) $300
– – **Anr. Edn.** Ed.:– F.S. Ellis. Ill.:– after E. Burne-Jones & William Morris. Hammersmith, Kelms. Pr., 1896. *(438). (425) on paper.* Lge. fo. Pig, spine gt.-lettered, unc., edges & corners with slight wear, fleece-lined cl. box. (CNY. May 18; 112) $6,500
– – **Anr. Edn.** Ill.:– Hugh Chesterton & Lynton H. Lamb. Oxford, Blackwell [at the Shakes. Hd. Pr.], 1928. *(350).* 8 vols. 4to. Hf. cl. & bds., light soiling to covers, some bkplts. removed; Marymount College copy, with a few stps. (CBA. Mar.3; 131) $550
– – **Anr. Edn.** Basilisk Pr., 1974. *[Facs. of Kelmscott Edn.]. (515) numbered.* 2 vols. Fo. Orig. cl., s.-c. (CSK. Sep.16; 148) £190

CHAUCER, Geoffrey (Trans.)
See— **LORRIS, Guillaume de & Meung, Jean de**

CHAUCHARD, Jean Baptiste Hippolyte
– **A General Map of the Empire of Germany, Holland, the Netherlands, Switzerland, the Grisons, Italy, Sicily, Corsica, & Sardinia.** L., J. Stockdale, 1800. Fo. Engraved dedication, 3 index maps, engraved map on 23 sheets, most double-p., cont. russ.-bkd. bds., spine rubbed & chipped. (C. Mar.14; 37) *Jeffries.* £120
– – **Anr. Copy.** Lge. fo. Engraved dedication, index map, 25 engraved mapsheets, mostly double-p., some light creasing, publisher's bds., defect. (S. Mar.6; 121) *Klingsor.* £80
– – **Anr. Copy.** fo. 24 uncold. maps, most double-p., bds., crudely rebkd. (P. Jan.12; 325) £65
– – **Anr. Copy.** Imperial fo. 2 maps lightly frayed, some creased, some foxing, some maps with offsetting, cont. hf. leath., lacks spine, very defect. (HK. Nov.8; 886) DM 650
– – **Anr. Copy.** Fo. Engraved hf.-title, 3 engraved index maps, 22 double-p. copper-engraved maps, cont. hf. leath., worn & rubbed. (GB. Nov.3; 6) DM 500

CHAUFEPIE, J.F.
See— **BAYLE, Pierre & Chaufepie, J.F.**

CHAULNES, Duc de
– **Nouvelle Methode pour Diviser les Instruments de Mathématique et d'Astronomie.—Description d'un Microscope, et le Differents Micrometers.** [Paris], 1768. From the 'Description des Arts et Metiers' series: 2 works in 1 vol. Tall fo. Cont. bds., spine defect. (SG. Oct.6; 92) $200
– – **Anr. Copy.** 2 works in 1 vol. Fo. Outer ll. slightly soiled, disbnd. (SG. Mar.22; 66) $120

CHAUMETON, Fr. P. & Poiret
– **Flore Medicale.** Paris, 1814-20. *1st. Edn.* 7 vols. in 8. Vol. VII with separate title, some light staining & foxing, cont. marb. leath. gt. (H. Nov.23; 256) DM 3,600
– – **Anr. Copy.** 8 vols. Some slight foxing, cont. hf. leath. gt., slightly rubbed. (HT. May 8; 281) DM 3,000

CHAUVEAU, L.
– **Les Histoires du Petit Renaud.** Ill.:– Pierre Bonnard. Paris, [1927]. *(322) numbered.* 4to. 50 pochoir cold. ills., orig. sewed, unc.; ex-libris. (HT. May 9; 1744) DM 640

CHAUVETON, Urbain
– **Brief Discours et Histoire d'un Voyage de Quelques François en la Floride.** N.p., 1579. Natural paper flaw in 2A8 with loss of approx. 30 letters, hf. mor. (SG. Apr.26; 44) $1,000
– – **Anr. Copy.** Sm. 8vo. Mod. hf. mor. (SG. Nov.3; 39) $800

CHAVANNES, Edouard
– **Documents sur les Tou-Kiue (Turcs) Occidentaux.** Paris, ca. 1900. 4to. Slightly affected by damp, mod. cl. (BBA. Mar.7; 59) *D. Loman.* £60
– **Mission Archeologique dans la Chine Septentrionale.** Paris, 1909-15. Vol. 1 in 2 pts. & 2 atlas vols. Together 4 vols. Lge. 8vo. & lge. 4to. 488 plts. in 2 atlas vols., 149 additional plts. numbered 489-637 in text vols., text vols. buckram, plts. loose in ptd. bds., linen ties. (SG. May 3; 92) $900

CHAVES, Jeronimo de
– **Chronographia o Repertorio de los Tiempos, el mas Copioso y Preciso que Hasta Ahora ha Salido à Luz.** Seville, 1548. *1st. Edn.* Sm. 4to. Sm. loss to blank margin of C4, lacks final blank, washed, margin annots. in early hand (a few shaved), mod. mor., fully gt., s.-c.; inscr. 'W. Patten, 1551'. (S. May 21; 161) *Quaritch.* £5,500

CHAYUN, Nechemia
– **Hatzad Tzvi.** Amst., 1714. (*With:*). **ERGAS, Joseph – Tochacha Megula V'Hatzad Nachash.** L., 1715. (*With:*). **SCHOLEM, Gershon – Chalomatav shel Hashabtai R. Mordecai Ashkenazi.** Schocken, 1938. *(150).* Together 3 vols. Various sizes. Some slight staining & soiling, various bdgs., some wear. (SPB. Feb.1; 32) $1,500

CHEADLE, W.B.
See— **MILTON, Visc. William W. Fitzwilliam & Cheadle, W.B.**

CHEESEMAN, Thomas Frederick & Hemsley, W.B.
– **Illustrations of the New Zealand Flora.** L., 1914. 2 vols. 4to. Orig. cl., slightly worn, soiled; Royal Commonwealth Soc. copy. (P. Nov.24; 290) *Weldon & Wesley.* £100

CHEEVER, John
– **Homage to Shakespeare.** Stevenson, Conn., [1968]. *(150) numbered & sigd.* Cl., d.-w. (SG. Mar.1; 40) $130

CHEFETZ, [Gentile] Moshe
– **Melchet Machshevet.** Ill.:– Giose Valeriani (title) & c. Venice, 1710. *1st. Edn.* Fo. Port. (often missing), slightly creased, buckram. (S. Oct.24; 131) *Moriah.* £500

CHEFS-D'OEUVRE du Roman Contemporain, Realists-Romancists
Phila., [1897-1901]. *Ltd. Edn. on Japan paper, for subscribers only.* 16 books in 20 vols. Ills. in 4 forms: on Chine, in bistre, in black, & hand-cold., 16 different bdgs. of various cols. & designs, covers with gt. borders or panels, mor. gt. doubls., some with flower-painted silk panels, all elab. decor. & gt.-tooled, various brocaded, corded & patterned silk end-pp.; ptd. statement on verso of hf.-titles 'This special copy ... prepared & bnd. for James T. Maxwell'. (CNY. Dec.17; 545) $3,600

CHEIA INTELESULUI [The Key of Intelligence]
Bucharest, 1678. *1st. Rumanian Edition.* Sm. fo.
Ptd. in Cyrillic, woodcut arms round title, woodcut
arms on verso, woodcut head pieces, lacks lf. []4
with woodcut ill. & Gospel quotation, & last blank
lf., 1st. 4ll. & last 5 crudely reprd., with loss of text
on 1st. 3, boiled thro.-out, some marginalia, liby.
stps. on a few pp., later cf., worn, clasps. (BBA.
May 23; 337) *Bloomsbury Rare Bks.* £80

CHEKE, Sir John
- De Pronuntiatione Graecae Potisimum Linguae
Disputationes. Basle, 1555. Title tipped in, mott.
cf. (P. Jan.12; 210) *Poole.* £100

CHELMINSKI, Jan V.
- L'Armée du Duché de Varsovie. Text:-
Commandant A. Malibran. Paris, 1913. Fo. Hf.
chagrin, wrap. preserved. (HD. Jan.27; 131)
Frs. 2,000

CHEMNITZ, Martin
- Examinis Concilii Tridentini ... Frankfurt, 1590.
Stpd. pig over wood bds., decor., ports. on covers,
title & date of bdg. (1593) stpd. in gold, clasps; from
Fondation Furstenberg-Beaumesnil. (HD. Nov.16;
111) Frs. 3,500

CHENAVARD, Antoine-Marie
- Voyage en Grèce et dans le Levant fait en 1842 et
1844. Lyons, 1858. *(200).* Fo. 2 maps, 77 engraved
plts., cont. cl.-bkd.; bds.; inscr. 'A Monsieur Dardel
Architecte, hommage affectieux de l'auteur à
Chenavard'. (C. Mar.14; 38) *Hantzis.* £1,300

CHENESSEAU, G.
- L'Abbaye de Fleury à Saint Benoit sur Loire.
1931. 4to. Sewed; A.L.s. by author. (HD. Apr.13;
83b) Frs. 1,150

CHENIER, André
- Les Bucoliques. Ill.:- Henri Fantin-Latour & G.
Simoes da Fonseca. Paris, 1905. *(177). (150)*
numbered on velin du Marais. 4to. Lithos. & culs-
de-lampe, etc. in 3 states, unc., marb. cf. by Denis
Puech, with bronze plaque, unc., s.-c. (S. Nov.21;
23) *Desk.* £620
- Oeuvres ... Intro. & Notices:- Henri Clouard.
Paris, 1927. *(1070). (1000) numbered on Vergé à
la forme des papeteries d'Arches.* 3 vols. Art Deco
series bdg. of hf. mor & marb. paper covers by Paul
Bonet, sigd. at upr. turn-in of each vol., cover plain
but for author's surname gt.-lettered at foot with
vol. no., smooth spines silver-lettered horizontally
across the 3, lettering enclosed in onlaid mor.
strapwork panel with 4 impressed silver squares &
2 triple silver line tools, marb. paper linings, partly
unc., spines slightly discold., silver slightly discold.,
silver slightly tarnished. (CNY. May 18; 172)
$600

CHENIER, Marie Joseph
- Charles IX ou l'Ecole des Rois, Tragédie. Ill.:-
Lefèvre (port.) & Borel. Paris, Nantes, 1790. On
vell., figures before the letter, cont. mor. gt. (HD.
May 3; 30) Frs. 1,000

CHENU, J.C.
- Manuel de Conchyliologie. Paris, 1859-62. 2 vols.
Tall 8vo. Three-qtr. leath., rubbed, Vol. I brkn.
(RO. Jun.26; 34) $150

CHERBUIN, L.
See— KALKEISEN, J.J. & Cherbuin, L.

CHERBULIEZ, Victor
- Oeuvres Diverses. Paris, v.d. 15 vols. 12mo. Hf.
red mor., corners. (HD. Apr.11; 10) Frs. 1,000

CHERBURY, Lord Edward Herbert
See— HERBERT, Lord Edward, of Cherbury

CHERET-MARX, R.
- La Décoration et l'Art Industriel à l'Exposition
Universelle de 1889. Ill.:- Jules Cheret. Paris, 1890.
(400). (30) on japan. 4to. Preface from Kongress of
Societé Centrale des Architectes Français, 17 Jun.
1890, authors dedication on end-paper, 2 supp. pulls
of title litho., 1 sigd. lf. bnd before text, orig. sewed.
(D. Nov.24; 2249) DM 800

CHERONNET, Louis
- Extra-muros, Lithographies Originales ... Ill.:- G.
Annankoff. Paris, 1929. 4to. Hf. mor., corners. red.
(CR. Jun.6; 127) Lire 380,000

CHERPONTIUS, J.
- Aliqvot Formandis tum Iuuentutis Moribus, tum
Linguae Graccae, Latinae, Gallicae & Germanicae
Vtilissime. [Geneva], 1581. Slightly browned, some
underlining, cont. vell. gt., soiled, gt. mostly
oxidised, lacks ties. (HK. Nov.8; 142) DM 900

CHERRY-GARRARD, Apsley
- The Worst Journey in the World, Antarctic 1910-
1913. 1922. *1st. Edn. 1st. Iss.* 2 vols. Orig. cl.-bkd.
bds., d.-w.'s. (P. Jun.7; 22) £580
- - **Anr. Edn.** [1922]. *1st. Edn.* 2 vols. Slight foxing,
bds., qtr. linen, unc., spare labels tipped in. (KH.
Nov.8; 68) Aus. $500
- - **Anr. Edn.** 1924. 2 vols. Bdg. not stated; inscr.
(JL. Mar.25; 627) Aus. $110

CHERRY-GARRARD, Apsley (Ed.)
See— SOUTH POLAR TIMES, The

CHERTABLON, N. de
- La Manière de se bien préparer à la Mort, par des
Considérations sur la Cène, la Passion et la Mort
de Jésus-Christ ... Ill.:- Romain de Hooghe. Antw.,
1700. *[1st. Fr. Edn.].* 4to. Jansenist mor., mor.
doubl., sm. tools. by Bebz-Niédrée. (HD. Mar.14;
17) Frs. 4,650
- - **Anr. Copy.** 4to. Some sm. stains, 19th. C. cf.,
spine decor. (HD. Mar.19; 40) Frs. 3,000
- - **Anr. Copy.** 4to. Frontis., 41 plts., defects &
dampstains, cont. cf., spine decor. (HD. Mar.21;
14b) Frs. 1,700

CHESELDEN, William
- Anatomie des Menschlichen Körpers. Preface:-
J.F. Blumenbach. Trans.:- H.F. Wolff. Ill.:-
Riepenhausen after van Gucht. Göttingen, 1790.
1st. German Edn. Title stpd., some browning &
foxing, sm. stain in upr. margin, cont. hf. leath.,
rubbed, spine slightly defect. (R. Oct.12; 1379)
DM 500
- The Anatomy of the Human Body. 1713. *1st. Edn.*
Lacks blank before title, sm. tear to folding plts.,
cont. cf. gt. (P. Oct.20; 88) £250
- Osteography, or the Anatomy of the Bones. L.,
1733. Fo. Engraved vig. title, frontis., 56
numbered & 10 unnumbered plts., vigs., browned,
some stains, cont. hf. cf., crudely rebkd. (BBA.
May 3; 20a) *Phillips.* £280

CHESNEAU, Augustinus
- Orpheus Eucharisticus sive Deus Absconditus
Humanitatis ... Opus Novum, ... Tomus Primus.
Ill.:- Albert Flamen. Paris, 1657. *1st. Edn.* Vol. 1
only (all pubd.). Some lr. margins dampstained,
tiny rust-hole in Ss2, cont. red mor., gt.-panel.
covers, decors. at corners, emblem of Sacred Heart
in centre, spine fully gt. (S. May 10; 251)
Watson. £170

CHESNUTT, Charles W.
- The Conjure Woman. N.Y., 1899. *1st. Edn.* Orig.
pict. cl., spine ends bumped. (SG. Nov.17; 26)
$130

CHESTER PLAY OF THE DELUGE, The
Ill.:- David Jones. Gold. Cock. Pr., 1927. *(275)*
numbered. 4to. Orig. buckram, unc., slightly damp-
affected, d.-w. faded & slightly torn; T.L.s from
Robert Gibbings to Henry Bergen together with 5
Gold. Cock. labels & invoices. (S. Nov.21; 219)
Marks. £420
- - **Anr. Copy.** Lge. 4to. Buckram, covers spotted,
spine faded. (SG. Jan.12; 123) $200
- - **Anr. Edn.** Ill.:- David Jones. Clover Hill Edns.
1977. *(337) roman-numbered. (80) on H.M.P. with
a set of the wood-engrs. on japon.* 4to. Prospectus
(1 of 50 numbered copies), orig. mor.-bkd. bds., cl.
folder & s.-c.; with a letter from Douglas Cleverdon.
(S. Nov.21; 186) *Appleton.* £220

**CHESTERFIELD, Philip Dormer Stanhope, Earl
of**
- Letters Written ... to his Son. L., 1774. *1st. Edn.*
2 vols. Fo. Hf.-titles, 'Qui auroit' spelling on p.55,
line 16, vol.1, frontis.-port., errata, cancels, some
MS. marginalia, tear in vol.1 hf.-title, browning &

spotting, cont. mott. cf., 1 cover detchd. from each
vol., later endpapers. (SPB. May 16; 26) $275
- - **Anr. Copy.** 2 vols. 4to. Misprint on p.55 vol.1
corrected, hf.-titles, engraved port., errata lf., some
spotting & browning, cont. cf., spines gt., slightly
worn, mor.-bkd. folding box; bkplts. of Richard
Hippisley Coxe, Perry Molstad copy. (SPB. May
16; 418) $200
- - **Anr. Edn.** 1774. 4 vols. Cont. cf., gt.-decor.
spines; Sir Ivar Colquhoun, of Luss copy. (CE.
Mar.22; 62a) £230
- - **Anr. Edn.** 1932. *King's Printer's Edn. (900)*
numbered. 6 vols. Orig. cl., soiled. (CSK. Apr.27;
139) £70
- - **Anr. Copy.** 6 vols. Buckram, slight fading &
spotting. (KH. Nov.8; 69) Aus.$120
- Miscellaneous Works. L., 1777. *1st. Edn.* 2 vols.
Lge. 4to. L.P., hf.-titles, 8 engraved ports., spotting,
orig. marb. bds., unc., rebkd., corners worn. (SPB.
May 16; 27) $200
- The Poetical Works. Montagnola, Bodoni Pr.,
1927. *(250) numbered.* 4to. Orig. patterned bds.,
spine & corners slightly worn. (BBA. Oct.27; 194)
Duschnes. £230
- Supplement to the Letters. L., 1787. *1st. Edn.* 4to.
Hf.-title, H4 cancelled, spotting & browning, cont.
cf. (SPB. May 16; 28) $200

CHETHAM, James
- The Angler's Vade Mecum. L., 1681. *1st. Edn.*
Without last 4 ll. of appendix & errata, some
browning & spotting, old owners' inscrs. on title,
sm. hole in Kl, cont. sheep, spine worn. [Wing
C3788] (S. Oct.4; 17) *Way.* £70

CHETWOOD, William Rufus, attributed to
[-] The Voyages, Dangerous Adventures &
Imminent Escapes of Captain Richard Falconer ...
Written by Himself ... L., 1720. *1st. Edn.* Cont. spr.
sheep gt., upr. cover detchd., corners worn; Henry,
Duke of Kent & Wrest Park bkplts., the Rt. Hon.
Visc. Eccles copy. [Sabin 23723] (CNY. Nov.18;
68) $100

CHEVALIER, Guillaume Sulpice
See— GAVARNI, Paul [ie. Guillaume Sulpice
Chevalier]

CHEVALIER, P.
- Souvenir de Venise. Ill.:- after Canaletto.
[Venice], ca. 1840. Ob. 4to. Hand-cold. litho. title,
20 plts., slight margin spotting, mor.-bkd. bds. (S.
Nov.1; 70) *Quaritch.* £260

CHEVRERIUS, Philippus
- Oratio ad Innocentium VIII. Rome, Stephan
Plannck, after 4 Feb. 1485. 4to. Unbnd.; the Walter
Goldwater copy. [BMC IV, 85; Goff C-447] (SG.
Dec.1; 104) $200

CHEVRILLON, André
- La Mer dans les Bois. Ill.:- André Dauchez. Paris,
1928. *(183).* 4to. On vell., leaves, pict. wrap., box;
orig. ill. (washed), sigd. by artist, 3 A.L. from
author. (HD. Dec.16; 96) Frs. 2,900

CHEYNE, George
- The English Malady; or a Treatise of Newons
Diseases of all Kinds. 1734. *4th. Edn.* Cf. (PD.
Dec.14; 238) £50
- An Essay of Health & Long Life. L., 1724. *1st.
Edn.* Cont. panel. cf. (SG. Mar.22; 67) $130
- The Natural Method of Cureing the Diseases of
the Body, and the Disorders of the Mind Depending
on the Body. L., 1742. *1st. Edn.* Cont. cf.,
extremities worn, covers chafed, early MS. ex-libris.
(SG. Mar.22; 68) $140

CHIARI, J. & others
- Klinik der Geburtshilfe und Gynaekologie.
Erlangen, 1855. *1st. Edn.* Some light foxing, hf.
leath. (R. Apr.4; 1292) DM 400

CHICAGO
- An Act to Incorporate the City of Chicago. Passed
March 4, 1837. Chic., 1837. *1st. Edn.* Foxed, sig.
on title, red mor. gt.; Thomas W. Streater bkplt.
(LH. Jan.15; 252) $8,000

CHIDOSH YARE'ACH
Pisa, 1818. Inner margin of last lf. reprd. without
loss of text, dampstained, 1 line of text erased &

retraced in ink, buckram. (S. Oct.24; 133)
Maggs. £150

CHIEREGATUS, Leonellus
- Oratio in Funere Innocentii VIII. Rome, Stephan
Plannck, after 28 Jul. 1492. 4to. later vell.; the
Walter Goldwater copy. [Goff C-452] (SG. Dec.1;
105) $200
- Propositio Coram Carolo VIII Facta. [Rome,
Stephan Plannck], after 20 Jan. 1488. 4to. Later
stiff wraps.; the Walter Goldwater copy. [BMC IV,
91; Goff C-454] (SG. Dec.1; 106) $225
- Sermo in Publicatione Confoederationis inter
Alexandrum VI et Romanorum Reges. [Rome,
Johann Besicken], after 12 Apr. 1495. 4to. Mod.
decor. wraps.; the Walter Goldwater copy. [BMC
IV, 140; Goff C-640] (SG. Dec.1; 107) $250

CHILD, Sir Josiah
- A New Discourse of Trade. L., 1698. *3rd. Edn.*
Slight browning, a little dampstaining at beginning,
cont. cf. [Wing C3862] (S. Oct.11; 505)
Drury. £80
- - Anr. Edn. [1740]. *4th. Edn.* 12mo. Last advt.
lf., some ll. spotted, cont. cf., rubbed. (BBA. Feb.23;
177) *Thorp.* £55

**CHILD'S INSTRUCTOR (The), or Picture
Alphabet**
Ill.:– after Bewick. Glasgow, Lumsden & Son,
[wtrmkd. 1813]. 16mo. Leath.-bkd. bds. (SG.
Dec.8; 12) $110

**CHINESCHE SCHIMMEN, Geheel op Nieuw
Bewerkt tot Vermaak en Leering der Jeugd**
Leyden, [1864]. 4to. Moving picture book, ills. with
tissue paper screens, all but figures hand-cold., orig.
cl.-bkd. pict. bds.; van Veen coll. (S. Feb.28; 266)
£230

CHINESE ART SOCIETY of America
- Archives. [N.Y., 1946-54]. Nos. I-VIII. Tall 4to.
Ptd. wraps. (SG. Oct.13; 91) $175

CHIPIEZ, Charles
See— PERROT, Georges & Chipiez, Charles

CHIPPENDALE, Thomas
- The Gentleman & Cabinet-Maker's Directory.
L., [1754]. *1st. Edn.* Fo. Title, hf.-title, engraved
dedication-lf., list of subscribers, 160 engraved plts.,
the last creased, torn & reprd., some stains, a few
plts. lightly spotted, slight margin soiling, al & 2
loose (preface), owner's inscr. on verso of hf.-title,
cont. cf., worm, rebkd. & reprd., new end-papers,
s.-c. (S. May 1; 535) *Kapusi.* £500
- - Anr. Edn. L., 1762. *3rd. Edn.* Fo. Engraved
dedication & 200 plts., margin repairs to title,
dedication & 4 plts., tear in plt. 25 reprd., 2
wormholes affecting outer margins at head of some
plts., some slight spotting, cont. cf., rebkd., rubbed.
(S. May 1; 702) *Acanthus.* £780
- - Anr. Copy. Fo. Sm. repair to title & lr. margin
of plt. XVI, contents little browned, cont. cf. (TA.
Sep.15; 366) £640
- - Anr. Copy. Fo. Engraved dedication, 200
engraved plts., title slightly stained, some
dampstaining, some margins soiled, antique-style
cf. (C. Nov.9; 53) *Henderson.* £600
- - Anr. Edn. L., [1762?]. *[3rd. Edn.?].* Fo.
Engraved dedication lf., 199 (of 200) engraved
plts., spotted, slightly browned, margins stained, 2
torn, 1 creased & reprd., 3 ll. torn & reprd. with
slight loss of text, lacks title & all before Al, qtr.
mor., w.a.f. (S. Oct.4; 139) *Weinreb.* £280

**CHIROMANCIE UNIVERSELLE (La),
Representée en Plusieurs Centaines de Figures ...**
Paris, 1682. 4to. 90 woodcut plts., dampstain, last
lf. restored, margin worming in some 15 ll., mod.
18th. C. style spr. sheep, decor. spine. (HD. Sep.22;
216) Frs. 2,100

CHISHOLM, Caroline
- Mrs. Chisholm's Advice to Emigrants. L'pool.,
1853. Lightly soiled, orig. wraps., soiled. (CSK.
Sep.16; 205) £65

CHISHOLM, Marquis
- The Adventures of a Traveling Musician in
Australia, China, & Japan. 1865. 8vo. Orig. blind-
stpd. cl., slightly rubbed. (BBA. Jan.19; 75)
Arnold. £120

CHLADNI, E.Fl. Fr.
- Entdeckungen über die Theorie des Klanges.
Leipzig, 1787. Some spotting, some ll. slightly
wormed in margin, plt. margins lightly stained,
cont. bds., slightly spotted. (H. Nov.23; 267)
DM 2,000

CHOCANO, José Santos
- Alma America. Ill.:– Juan Gris. Madrid, 1906.
Orig. decor. wraps., some tears. (SPB. Dec.13; 831)
$100

**CHODERLOS DE LACLOS, Pierre Ambroise
François**
See— LACLOS, Pierre Ambroise François
Choderlos de

CHODOWIECKI, Daniel
- Images pour la Jeunesse. N.p., n.d. Ob. 4to. 2
frontis. & 52 plts. mntd. on guards, mod. bradel
bds., unc. (HD. May 3; 227) Frs. 1,500

CHOISEUL, Duc de
[-] Memoires de Divers Emplois et des Principales
Actions du Maréchal du Plessy. Paris, 1676. 4to.
Cont. marb. cf., arms of Le Fèvre de Caumartin,
Marquis de Saint-Ange, spine decor. (HD. Jun.6;
32) Frs. 1,450

CHOISEUL-GOUFFIER, M.G.F.A. de.
- Reise des Grafen v. Choiseul-Gouffier, durch
Griechenland. Gotha, 1780-82. Vol. 1, pts. 1 & 2(all
publd). Title foxed, vol. 1 with MS. owners mark,
cont. hf. leath., gt. slightly worn. (HK. May 15;
840a) DM 550
[-] Voyage Pittoresque de la Grèce. 1782. Vol. 1
only. Fo. Engraved vig. title, 4 folding maps & 73
sheets of plts., only, some loose, cf., defect., as a
coll. of plts., w.a.f. (P. Oct.20; 117) £360
- - Anr. Edn. Ill.:– Berthaut, Choffard, Delignon,
Dequevauviller, & others. Paris, 1782-1809-22. *1st.
Edn. Vol. 1: 1st. Printing.* 2 vols. in 3. Fo. Port. of
author bnd. in Vol. 2 pt. 2, pol. cf. gt., 2 spines
defect. (C. Mar.14; 122) *Hantzis.* £1,700
- - Anr. Copy. 2 vols. in 3. Fo. Port. of author bnd.
in Vol. 2 pt. 2, bnd. without publisher's advt., list
of plts. & 'Notice sur la vie de M. le Comte de
Choiseul-Gouffier ... ', sometimes found in 2nd. vol.,
Vol. 1 slightly discold. with some spotting, Vol. 1
cont. cf., rubbed & worn, Vols. 2 & 3 19th. C.
roan-bkd. bds. (C. Mar.14; 39)
Demakarakos. £1,200
- - Anr. Copy. 2 vols. in 3. Fo. 168 plts., cont. bds.,
marb. paper, unc. (HD. May 21; 24) Frs. 12,500
- - Anr. Edn. 1782-1822. *1st. Printing.* 3 vols. Fo.
Cont. bds., some defects, Vol. 1 disbnd. (HD.
Jun.29; 82) Frs. 14,000
- - Anr. Copy. 3 vols in 2. Fo. Some plts. Vol. II
disbnd., much staining, old hf. red mor., l corner of
upr. cover torn off. (HD. Dec.9; 17) Frs. 9,000

CHOISY, Auguste
- L'Art de Batir chez les Byzantins. Ill.:– J. Sulpis.
Paris, 1883. Tall fo. 25 engraved plts., each plt.
liby.-stpd. on blank verso, loose in ptd. bd. folder,
linen ties. (SG. May 3; 94) $200
- L'Art de Batir chez les Romains. Paris, 1873. Sm.
fo. 24 plts., few double-p., each plt. stpd. on blank
verso, disbnd., in ptd. bd. folder, linen ties. (SG.
May 3; 93) $130

CHOISY, Francois-Timoléon, Abbé de
- Histoire de Charles V.—Histoire de Charles VI.
Paris, 1695. Together 2 vols. 4to. Cont. cf., spines
decor.; stp. of Le Tellier, Marquis de Courtanvaux,
on each title. (HD. Nov.9; 121) Frs. 1,200
- Journal du Voyage de Siam fait en 1685 et 1686.
Paris, 1687. *1st. Edn.* 4to. Cont. diced cf., spine
decor. (HD. Nov.9; 22) Frs. 1,900
- La Vie de Madame de Miramion. Paris, 1706. 4to.
Cont. marb. cf., Callenberg arms, spine decor. (HD.
Jun.6; 33) Frs. 1,000

CHOISY, Abbé de & Dangeau, Abbé de
- Quatre Dialogues. Ill.:– Sebastien Le Clerc. Paris,
1684. *Orig. Edn.* 12mo. Cont. red mor.; from libys.
of J.-J. de Bure & Chartener. (HD. Mar.29; 20)
Frs. 4,800

**CHOIX DE GRAVURES à l'eau forte d'après les
peintures originales et les marbres de la Galerie de
Lucien Bonaparte**

1812. Fo. 140 engraved plts., most spotted, plts, at
end marginally stained, cont. red str.-grd. mor. gt.,
slightly rubbed. (S. Apr.30; 14) *Sims.* £110

CHOLIERES, Nicolas de
- Les Contes, et Discours Bigarrez Deduits en Neuf
Matimées. Paris, 1610. 18mo. Sm. repair to upr.
margin of title, glazed cf. gt. by Bauzonnet. (HD.
Mar.27; 6) Frs. 1,050

CHOMEL, Noel
- Dictionnaire Economique contenant Divers
Moyens d'augmenter son Bien et de conserver sa
Santé ... Lyon, 1718. 2 vols. Lge. fo. Old
dampstains, Lacks title to Vol. I, old cf., spine
decor., worn. (LM. Mar.3; 125) B.Frs. 8,500
- Dictionaire Oeconomique: or, The Family
Dictionary. Ed.:– R. Bradley. 1725. 2 vols. in 1. Fo.
Lacks title to Vol. 2, spr. cf., spine gt.; Sir Ivar
Colquhoun, of Luss copy. (CE. Mar.22; 64) £210
- Huishoudelyk Woordboek, verv. Vele Middelen om
zyn Geod te vermeerderen en zyne Gezondheid te
behouden. Ill.:– F. de Bakker. Leyden & Amst.,
1743. *1st. Dutch Edn.* 2 vols. 4to. Engraved frontis.,
79 (of 80) engraved plts., most folding, corners
defect., slightly stained, cont. hf. cf., defect., chintz
partly gone. (VS. Dec.9; 1311) Fls. 450

CHOMPRET, Dr. J.
- Faïences Françaises Primitives. Paris, 1946. 4to.
Publisher's bds., ill. d.-w. (HD. Jun.29; 41)
Frs. 1,550
- Répertoire de la Majolique Italienne. Paris, 1949.
2 vols. 4to. Publisher's decor. bds. (HD. Jun.29;
42) Frs. 4,000
- - Anr. Edn. Paris, [1949]. *(1500) numbered.* 2
vols. Sm. fo. Bds., with circular col. plt. (SG. Jan.26;
77) $300

CHORIER, Nicolas 'Johannes Meursius'
See— MEURSIUS, Joannes, i.e. Nicolas Chorier

CHORIS, Louis
- Voyage Pittoresque Autour du Monde ... Paris,
1822. Fo. 100 (of 104) hand-cold. litho. plts., lacks
port. & 2 maps, list of subscribers & list of plts.
supplied in facs. at end, some spotting, mod. hf.
mor. gt., w.a.f. [Sabin 12884] (C. Mar.14; 40)
Davidson. £1,800
- Vues et Paysages des Regions Equinoxiales,
recueillis dans un Voyage autour du Monde. Paris,
1826. Fo. 24 cold. lithos., some foxing, cont. bds.,
worn. (HD. Jun.26; 37) Frs. 18,500

CHOULANT, Ludwig
- History & Bibliography of Anatomic Illustration.
Trans.:– Mortimer Frank. Chic., [1920]. Lge. 8vo.
Cl. (SG. Oct.6; 100) $125

CHRIST, Joh. L.
- Naturgesch., Klassification u. Nomenclatur der
Insekten vom Bienen, Wespen u. Ameisengeschlecht
... Hymenoptera. Mit häutigen Flügeln. Frankfurt,
1791. 2 vols. (text & plts.). 4to. Copper engraved
title, title & 1 plt. stpd. on verso, cont. leath. gt.,
some wear & slightly bumped. (HK. Nov.8; 541)
DM 3,400

CHRISTIAN, Arthur
- Origines de l'Imprimerie en France. Paris, 1900.
Fo. L.P., cont. hf. mor., rebkd. with orig. spine.
(BBA. Mar.7; 188) *Questor Books.* £55
- - Anr. Copy. Tall fo. Loose as iss. in ptd. bd.
folder with ties. (SG. Sep.15; 93) $120

CHRISTIAN, Gerard Joseph
- Traité de Mecanique Industrielle ...
Principalement à l'Usage des Manufacturiers et des
Artistes. Paris, 1822-25. 4 vols., including Atlas.
4to. Atlas with 60 double-p. plts., hf.-titles, liby.
stps., cl., mor. spine, 1 cover loose. (S. Dec.13; 257)
Phelps. £60

**CHRISTIAN MAN, A Necessary Doctrine &
Erudition for any Christen Man, set furthe by the
Kynges Maiestie of England & c**
L., 29 May 1543. 4to. Woodcut title-border shaved

CHRISTIAN MAN, A Necessary Doctrine & Erudition for any Christen Man, set furthe by the Kynges Maiestie of England & c
L., 29 May 1543. 4to. Woodcut title-border shaved at foot, inner corners of 1st. few ll. stained a little, mainly margin, worming, mod. cf.; A.L.s. from Albert Erham loosely inserted. [STC 5170a] (BBA. Dec.15; 154) *News Today.* £170

CHRISTIE, Agatha
- The Murder of Roger Ackroyd. L., [1926]. *1st. Edn.* Few ll. slightly spotted, orig. cl.; Fred A. Berne copy. (SPB. May 16; 213) $250

CHRISTIE'S
- Catalogue of the Choice & Valuable Collection of Ancient & Modern Prints, the Property of John Woodhouse. 1801. *(Bound with:)* - Catalogue of Engravings by Bartalozzi, the Property of Andrew Tuer. 1881. Together 2 vols. in 1. Sale catalogues, priced thro.-out, mod. mor. gt. (BBA. Jul.27; 242) *Maggs.* £75

CHRISTMAS BLOSSOMS, & New Year's Wreath, for 1847
Ill.:– John Sartain. Boston, 1847. Sm. 8vo. Additional engraved title-p. & 5 other mezzotint plts., orig. gt.-pict. cl., corners nicked, spine lightly chipped, with A.L.s. from Sartain to W.P. Garrison, & A.L.s. from Sartain's son to W.P. Garrison, both mntd. on front fly-ll.; from liby of F.D. Roosevelt, inscr. by him (as Governor). (SG. Mar.15; 22) $350

CHRISTMAS BLOSSOMS, & New Year's Wreath, for 1848. By Uncle Thomas.– ... for 1851
Ill.:– John Sartain. Boston; Phila., 1848; 1851. 2 vols. Lge. 12mo. Gt.-floral orig. cl., outer corners nicked, spine ends very worn on 1st. vol.; from liby of F.D. Roosevelt, both vols. inscr. by him. (SG. Mar.15; 23) $225

CHRISTOPH V. STADION, Bp. of Augsburg
- Statuta Diocesana ... in Celebratione Sinodi ... Augsburg, 10. xi.1517. Fo. Title with MS. note, title & Last lf., soiled, some staining & foxing, lightly browned, 19th C. hf. leath., rubbed. (HK. Nov.8; 143) DM 600

CHROMOLITHOGRAPH, The: A Journal of Art, Literature, Decoration & the Accomplishments
L., 1867-68. Vol.1 nos.1-12, in 1 vol. 4to. Title-p. to No.10 bnd. at start of vol., three-qtr. mor., worn. (SG. Jan.5; 97) $100

CHRYSOSTOMUS, Saint Johannes, Archbp. of Constantinople
- Ausslegung über die Euangelia Sancti Matthei, vnnd Sancti Johannis ... über das Haupt Euangelion Sanct Johanns ... Trans.:– D. Casp. Hedius. Strassburg, 1540. 2 pts. in 1 vol. Fo. Some margins lightly stained & with sm. defects., some ll. with tears, cont. blind-tooled pig-bkd. wood bds., slightly rubbed & soiled, corners slightly worn, 2 clasps, lacks ties. (HK. Nov.8; 234) DM 950
- De Compunctione Cordis. [Basel, Michael Furter], ca. 1500. Sm. 8vo. Vell.; the Walter Goldwater copy. [BMC II, 786; Goff J-279; H. 5046] (SG. Dec.1; 201) $275
- The Golden Book ... concerning the Education of Children. Trans.:– John Evelyn. L., 1659. *1st. Edn. 1st. Iss.?.* 12mo. Lacks blanks A1-2, upr. corners torn from B9-12 with loss 2 p. numerals on B11, blank portion torn from E9 margin, mod. red mor. gt. by Elizabeth Greenhill. [Wing C3978] (S. Dec.8; 19) *Quaritch.* £1,000
- Opera Graecè. Eton, 1612. 8 vols. Fo. Engraved title-p. detchd., some vols. with new end-papers, cont. Engl. (probably Oxford) blind-stpd. cf., some spines defect., some repairs. [STC 14629c] (S. Nov.17; 15) *Marlboro' Bks.* £250
- Opera Omnia. Lyon, 1687. *1st. Edn.* 5 pts. in 4 vols. Fo. Titles with owners mark, slightly foxed & browned, stained, minimal worming, cont. blind-tooled pig, some light spotting, w.a.f. (HK. May 16; 160?) DM 600
- Sermones de Patientia in Job. [Esslingen, Conrad Fyner], not after 1475. Fo. Rubricated, 1st. lf. soiled, some sm. worming thro.-out, later vell.; the Walter Goldwater copy. [BMC II, 514; Goff J-306; H. 5025] (SG. Dec.1; 202) $750

See— **GERARDUS DE ZUTPHANIA- CHRYSOSTOMUS, Saint Johannes, Archbp. of Constantinople**

CHRYSTIN, Jean Baptiste
[-] Histoire Générale des Pais-Bas. Brussels, 1720. *New Edn.* 4 vols. 6 copper engrs. with creased margin's, several sm. margin tears, folding plt. index torn, some light browning & spotting, cont. marb cf. gt., slightly worn. (H. May 22; 298) DM 1,300

CHRYSTIN, Jean Baptiste & Foppens, F. & Pierre
- Les Délices des Pays-Bas.—Dictionnaire Historique.—Atlas. Paris, 1786. 5 vols; 2 vols.; 1 vol. 12 mo. & 4to. Cont. grd. roan, limp decor. spines (text), cont. hf. roan, corners (atlas). (HD. Dec.9; 18) Frs. 3,800

CHRYTAEUS, David
- Chronicon Saxoniae & Vicinarum. Aliquot Gentium: Ab Anno Christi 1500 usque ad 1593. Leipzig, 1593. 30 pts. in 1 vol. Fo. Slightly browned or old soiling, a few ll. stained, upr. fly-lf. slightly defect., renaissance pig. decor. roll stps., 2 brass clasps, some old wear. (V. Oct.1; 3724) DM 2,000

CHUBB, Ralph
- Songs Pastoral & Paradisal. Brockweir, Gloucester, Tintern Pr., 1935. *(100) numbered & sigd.* Sm. fo. Orig. hf. mor., rubbed. (TA. Jul.19; 499) £55

CHUN, Woon-Young
See— **HU, Hsen-Hsu & Chun, Woon-Young**

CHURCH, A.H. & others
- Some Minor Arts as practised in England. 1894. Fo. 2 margins cracked, orig. cl. gt., a little rubbed; lady Mount-Stephen bkplt., H.M. Nixon coll., with his MS. annots. (BBA. Oct.6; 24) *Oak Knoll Books.* £60

CHURCH, John
- A Cabinet of Quadrupeds. Ill.:– James Tookey after Jules Ibbetson. L., 1805. *1st. Edn. of Vol. II.* 2 vols. Sm. fo. Additional engraved titles, 84 plts., most plts. & some early text ll. in Vol. II partly dampstained, buckram. (SG. Mar.22; 70) $110
- - Anr. Edn. Ill.:– James Tookey after J. Ibbetson. L., 1805. *1st. Printing.* 2 vols. 4to. Cont. Engl. long-grd. mor., gt.-& blind-decor., decor. spines. (HD. Dec.9; 110) Frs 5,500
- - Anr. Edn. L., 1805. 2 vols. 4to. Light browning & stains, hf. cf., spines remade. (CR. Jun.6; 128) Lire 380,000

CHURCH, Willis H.
See— **HOAK, Edward W. & Church, Willis H.**

CHURCHILL, Charles
- Poems. L., 1763; 1765. *1st. Coll. Edn.* 2 vols. 4to. L. & thick P., marginal tear in 2C3 vol. 1, cont. nott. cf. gt., spines worn; bkplt. of John Smith Budgen. (SPB. May 16; 29) $100

CHURCHILL, J.A.
- Goldsmiths of Italy: Some Account of their Guilds, Statutes, & Work. Ed.:– Cyril G. E. Blunt. L., 1926. Lge. 4to. Col. frontis., 20 plts., cl. (SG. Aug.25; 167) $170

CHURCHILL, James Morss
See— **STEPHENSON, John & Churchill, James Morss**

CHURCHILL, William Algernon
- Watermarks in Paper in Holland, England, France, etc. in the XVII & XVIII Centuries & their Interconnection. Amst., 1935. *1st. Edn.* Fo. Orig. cl. (BBA. Apr.5; 277) *Dawson.* £150

CHURCHILL, Sir Winston Leonard Spencer
- London to Ladysmith via Pretoria. L., 1900. *1st. Edn.* Inscr. on blank 'To B.T.B. [Lord Basil Blackwood] ... from his patient disciple Winston S. Churchill', inscr. in anr. hand 'Blackwood's? '1/7/[19]00 Capetown', advt. lf. & 32 pp. inserted advts. dtd. Oct. 1899 at end, lacks hf.-title, a few spots & stains, later owner's inscrs. on blank margin of frontis. map & front free end-paper, orig. pict. cl., rubbed & soiled. (S. Dec.8; 167) *F.A.S.* £920
- - Anr. Copy. Last 17 advt. ll., orig. cl., spine slightly faded. (BBA. Sep.29; 20) *Howell.* £140
- - Anr. Copy. Inscr. by author in 1947, publisher's catalogue at end, orig. cl., slightly stained. (BBA. Oct.27; 86) *Sawyer.* £120
- - Anr. Copy. Advts. at end, orig. pict. cl., slightly worn; from Norman Tarbolton liby. (P. Apr.12; 22) *Hatchards.* £50
- Marlborough: His Life & Times. L., [1933-38]. *(155) numbered & sigd.* Lge. 8vo. Orig. mor. gt., orig. s.-c.'s. (CSK. Dec.2; 114) £300
- - Anr. Copy. 4 vols. Hf. mor., spines gt., by Bayntun (Rivière), very slightly worn. (S. Oct.4; 79) *Cavendish.* £260
- Prison & Prisoners. 1910. 1 vol. Orig. wraps., soiled. *(With:)* - Naval Estimates in the Great War. 1915. 1 vol. Wraps. *(With:)* - The Liberal Government & Naval Policy. 1912. 1 vol. Wraps., in cl. folder. (P. Feb.16; 244) £160
- The Second World War. N.d. *'Chartwell' Edn.* 106 pp. publishers specimen, title & various text & plt. ll., 1 lf. holed, orig. cl., folding cl. pastedowns formed from 2 proposed upr. cover & spine designs; inscr. 'For John on your birthday W S Churchill 1961'. (CSK. Jun.29; 184) £240
- The Story of the Malakand Field Force. An Episode in Frontier War. 1898. *1st. Edn.* Errata slip present, publisher's catalogue bnd. in at rear, some spotting, orig. cl. gt., a little soiled. (TA. Jun.21; 281) £210
- The War Speeches ... Ed.:– Charles Eade. L., 1951-52. 3 vols. Orig. cl., d.-w.'s. a little chipped, 1 torn. (KH. Nov.8; 78) Aus. $120
- The World Crisis. L., 1923-31. *Various Edns.* 6 vols. 1st. 4 vols. cf. gt., rest hf. cf., unif. spines gt. (S. Oct.4; 80) *Cavendish.* £180
See— **ROOSEVELT, Franklin D. & Churchill, Sir Winston Leonard Spencer**

CHURCHYARD, Thomas
[-] The Right, Pleasant, & Delightful History of Fortunatus & His Two Sons. Ca. 1700. *12th. Edn.* 12mo. Later str.-grd. mor. gt. (SKC. Mar.9; 1770) £140

CHYTRAEUS, D.
See— **SCHUTZ, C.**

CHYTRAEUS, Nathan
- Variorum in Europa Itinerum Delicaciae seu ex Variis Manuscriptis Selectiora tantum Inscriptionum maxime Recentium Monumenta ... Herborn, 1594. *1st. Edn.* Lacks cont. front blanks, lr. edge of title-p. replaced, cont. monastic bdg. of pig, covers pict. blind-stpd., & dtd. on upr. cover '1597'; mor. gt. bkplt. of Bernardo Mendel. [Sabin 13037] (SG. Nov.3; 40) $1,300

CIAMPINI, Giovanni Giustino
- De Sacris Aedificiis a Constantino Magno Constructis. Romae, 1693. Fo. Hf. cf., slight defects. (B. Jun.21; 428) Fls. 650

CIBBER, Colley
- An Apology for the Life of Mr Colley Cibber ... 1740. *2nd. Edn.* Some light spotting, cont. gt.-panel. mor. (CSK. Jan.27; 46) £90

CICERI, E.
- Les Pyrénées d'après Nature. Luchon, n.d. 1st. pt. Ob. Fo. Publisher's buckram. (HD. Dec.9; 111) Frs. 2,000

CICERO, Marcus Tullius
- Cato Major or the Book of Old Age. 1648. 12mo. Later cf., lightly soiled. [Wing C4288] (CSK. Jun.15; 98) £100
- De Officiis. De Amicitia. Venecia, 13 Mar. 1484. Fo. Slight worming, slight fault in lr. margin, linen. (DS. Oct.28; 2337) Pts. 125,000
- De Oratore. Ed.:– J. Proust. Oxford, 1714. Engraved frontis.-port., some spotting & browning, red-str. grd. mor., gt. tooled spine, gt. & blind rules on covers, in style of Roger Payne, mor.-bkd. s.-c.: Stanley-Beckford- Houghton copy with bkplts., as a bdg., w.a.f. (SPB. May 16; 30) $225
- De Paradoxa, ad Marcum Brutum. 1551. *(Bound with:)* - Officiorum, Lib. III. 1550. *(Bound with:)* - De Senectute Dialogus, ad T. Pomponium Atticum. 1549. Together 3 works in 1 vol. 4to. Red mor., ca. 1610-20, fanfare decor., arms of France, some repairs, mainly to central medallion, s.-c. (HD. Mar.21; 78) Frs. 3,600
- De Philosophia. Lyon, 1574. 2 vols. in 1. Cont.

mor. gt., arms (of Abbé Genesse?), spine decor.; from Château des Noës liby. (HD. May 25; 16)
Frs. 1,800
– **Epistolae ad Brutum, ad Quintum fratrem, ad Atticum, & c.** Ed.:– [Joannes Andreae, Bp. of Aleria]. Rome, Conradus Sweynheym & Arnoldus Pannartz, [before 30 Aug.] 1470. *1st. Edn.* Fo. Capitals supplied in blue thro.-out, lacks final blank lf., fo. 2 supplied in 18th. C. typographic facs. (without capital), some upr. margins dampstained in middle, some staining to earlier ll., sm. hole at fo. 17 with partial loss of 2 letters, a few early margin ink annots., some cropped, folios 10 & 1 misbnd. after fo. 5, late 18th. C. str.-grd. red mor. gt., jnts., edges & corners worn, some wear to covers, qtr. leath. s.-c.; Otto Vollbehr, Joseph Onderwyzer & Thomas B. Stevenson copy. [BMC IV, 9 (IB 17152); Goff C-499; HC 5213] (CNY. May 18; 99) $2,000
– – **Anr. Edn.** Venice, [Philippus Pincius], 12 Jun. 1499. Tear to lr. margin a4, marginalia & some dampstaining thro.-out, vell.-bkd. bds. [BMC V, 499; Goff C-503; HC 5217*] (PNY. Dec.1; 42) $325
– **Epistolarum ad Atticum, ad Brutam, ad Quintum Fratmen.** Venice, Aldus, June 1513. *1st. Aldine Edn.* Device in title & at end, some light spotting & staining, old cf., mor. back & corners; Fred A. Berne copy. (SPB. May 17; 582) $300
– **Les Epitres Familières en Seize Livres.** Trans.:– Jean Bachou. Paris, 1656. 2 vols. in 1. 12 mo. Cont. mor., fleurs-de-lys, gt. centre arms, monogs., slightly soiled. (HD. Jan.30; 36) Frs. 1,600
– **In omnes Epistolas ...** Basel, 1540. Title slightly soiled, upr. margin stained, some marginalia & underlining in old MS. at beginning cont. blind tooled pig over wood bds., slightly rubbed & bumped, 2 clasps. (HK. May 15; 100) DM 440
– **Officia.** Trans.:– J. Neubers. Ill.:– H. Weiditz. Augsburg, 29 Apr. 1531. *1st. Edn. 2nd. Printing.* Fo. Title slightly spotted & with owners note, soiled, many ll. stained in margins, some ll. with sm. wormhole, 1 lf. with restored tear, some woodcuts repeated, 18th. C. bds., defect. (H. Nov.23; 583)
DM 3,000
– – **Anr. Edn.** Ill.:– Hans Burgkmair. Augsburg, 3 Nov. 1545. Sm. Fo. Lacks title-p., repairs to 1st. 2 ll. & at end, tear with loss to 3rd. engr., anr. tear, without loss, lge. dampstain at end, late 18th. C. bds. (HD. Mar.21; 16) Frs. 2,800
– **Oper Rhetorica, Oratoria & Forensica.–Opera Philosophica.** Paris, [1527]. 2 works in 1 vol. Fo. Some light browning, slightly stained in margins, more near end, cont. style. mod. leath. gt. (R. Apr.3; 27a) DM 380
– **Opera.** Ed.:– J. Olivetus. Geneva, 1758. 9 vols. 4to. Cont. spr. cf., spines gt. (LC. Oct.13; 314)
£100
– **Opera. Ex Petri Victorii Codicibus Maxima ex Parte Descripta.** Paris, 1539-38. 4 vols. in 2. Fo. 17th. C. cf., rebkd. with most of orig. spines preserved. (S. Oct.11; 389) *Lurie.* £160
– **Opera Quae Supersunt Omnia.** Ed.:– Isaacus Verburgius. Amst., 1724. 16 vols. Titles in red & black, hf.-titles & frontis. vols. 4,6,8.10 & 12 titles black only & without hf.-titles & frontis cont. pol. cf., spines gt., vol. 1 spine slightly wormed. (S. Apr.10; 290) *Boyle.* £200
– **Orationum ...** Ed.:– P. Manutius. Venice, 1554. 3 vols. 3rd. title reprd., without loss, few stains, some worming, mostly marginal, some early marginalia, old vell., soiled. (SG. Oct.27; 3) $250
– **Rhetoricorum ad C. Herennium. Lib. IIII.** Venice, 1521. *2nd. Aldine Edn.* Lge. 8vo. Washed, end-papers renewed, mid-16th. C. Venetian mor., blind- & gt.-decor., turn-ins reprd.; Marquis de Morante liby., from Fondation Furstenberg-Beaumesnil. (HD. Nov.16; 109) Frs. 10,300
– **Rhetoricorum Libri Quatuor ad Herrenium, Item M. Tullii Ciceronis de Inuentione libri duo.** Paris, 1524. Red mor. gt., rubbed on bd. edges & spine; sig. of P. Ramssant. (LC. Mar.1; 307) £65
– **Rhetoricorum ad C. Herennium libri III. incerto auctore. Ciceronis De Inventione libri II. Topica ad Trebatium, Oratoriae partitiones ... ; [De Oratore libri III, Orator. De Claris Oratoribus].** Venice, 1559. 2 vols. in 1. Capital spaces with guide letters, sm. restorations to lr. blank margins of C5, H3 & X1 & 2 in 1st. vol., a few slight stains, early 19th.

C. Engl. russet mor., anchor device gt. -stpd. on covers, spine gt.-lettered, corners slightly bruised; inscr. of John Lainson, William Ewart Gladstone bkplt., Thomas B. Stevenson copy. (CNY. May 18; 91) $100
– **Der Teütsch Cicero.** Trans.:– J. Schwarzenberg., Augsburg, 4 Mar. 1535. *2nd. Edn.* Fo. Lacks 4 ll. (woodcuts), 1. lf. numbered double, title-lf. defect. with slight loss, 1 hf. torn, some spotting especially 1st ll., cont. vell., soiled, spine wormed. (HK. Nov.8; 147) DM 2,100
– **Tullius Cicero Manucciorum Commentariis illustratus.** Venezia, 1582-83. 10 vols. Fo. Some slight staining, cont. vell., 2 spines lightly bumped. (SI. Dec.15; 8) Lire 1,000,000
– **Tusculanae Disputationes.** Commentary:– Philippus Beroaldus. Bologna, Benedictus Hectoris, 27 Jul. 1496. Fo. 8 lf. 'Tabula Vocabulorum in Tusculanis Questionibus' after title (not called for in register, & not in BMC, but required?), lacks final blank. [BMC VI, 843; Goff C-640] (*Bound with:*) BEROALDUS, Philippus – **Commentarii Philippicarum.** Bologna, Benedictus Hectoris, 23 Dec. 1501. 2 works in 1 vol. Fo. Vell.; the Walter Goldwatr copy. (SG. Dec.1; 108) $1,100
– **Tusculanarum Quaestionum Libri V.** Paris, 1549. 4to. Some outer margins lightly stained, cont. Parisian cf. gt., rebkd. with orig. spine preserved, a few other repairs. (S. Oct.11; 390) *Maggs.* £80
See– **TITELMAN, Fr.—CICERO, Marcus Tullius**

CICOGNA, E.
– **Saggio de Bibliografia Veneziana.** Venice, 1847. 4to. Cont. sheep. (BBA. Mar.7; 189) *Jenner.* £100

CICOGNARA, Conte Leopoldo
– **Antonio Diedo e Giannantonio Selva.** Venezia, 1838-40. 2 vols. Fo. Cont. hf. leath., decor. spines. (SI. Dec.15; 194) Lire 1,000,000

CILLIERS—BARNARD, B.
– **Simbole.** 1969. *(100).* Lge. fo. 11 plts. & 2 text ll., loose in portfo. (VA. Oct.28; 439) R 330

CIMBER & Danjou
– **Archives Curieuses de l'Histoire de France depuis Louis XI jusqu'à nos Jours.** Paris, 1834-40. 27 vols. Hf. cf. (HD. Feb.22; 40) Frs. 6,800

CIMITARRA DEL SOLDADO MUSULMAN
Valencia, 1822. 8 nos. Leath. (DS. Apr.27; 2663)
Pts. 25,000

CINGRIA, Charles Albert
– **Les Limbes.** Ill.:– Jean Lurcat. Paris, 1930. *(130) numbered.* 4to. Ptd. wraps., spine end chipped. (SG. Jan.12; 245) $200

CIRNEO, P.
– **Istoria di Corsica Divisa in Quatro Libri ...** Parigi, 1834. In Latin & Corsican, quires yellowed, mod. hf. roan, wrap. (HD. Oct.21; 58) Frs. 1,300

CIRUELO, Pedro
– **Expositio Libri Missalis Peregregia.** Alcala de Hemares, 1528. *1st. Edn.* Fo. Some browning, few tears, old vell. (SPB. Dec.13; 651) $225

CLADEL, Judith
– **Auguste Rodin L'Oeuvre et L'Homme.** Brussels, 1908. *Ltd. Edn.* Fo. Vell. gt., soiled. (P. Feb.16; 119) £60

CLAIRAC, L.A. de la M. de
– **The Field Engineer.** Trans.:– John Miller. 1773. *2nd. Edn.* A few plts. creased, cont. spr. cf., slightly rubbed. (BBA. Jul.27; 6) *Blackwell's.* £70

CLAIRAUT, Alexis-Claude. – Elémens de Géométrie. Paris, 1741. *1st. Edn.* Hf.-title, light soiling, cont. mott. cf., spine slightly worn; John D. Stanitz coll. (SPB. Apr.25; 96) $175
See– **EULER, Leonard—CLAIRAUT, Alexis-Claude**

CLAMART, S.A.
– **Chasse.** Ill.:– Jean Commère. Paris, 1964. *(50) on vell. with suite of double plts. in cols.* 4to. Leaves, box. (HD. Jun.13; 20) Frs. 1,800

CLANRICARDE, Ulick Bourke, Marquis of
– **Memoirs of the Rt Hon. The Marquis of Clanricarde, Lord Deputy General of Ireland. To which is Prefix'd a Dissertation ... [by Thomas**

Sullivan]. Dublin, 1744. Lacks front blanks, some stains, cf., rubbed, bkplt. (GM. Dec.7; 392) £90

CLAPPERTON, Capt. Hugh
– **Journal of a Second Expedition into the Interior of Africa, from the Bight of Benin to Soccatoo.** 1829. 4to. Cont. cf., gt.-decor. spine, upr. cover detchd. (TA. Nov.17; 20) £105
See– **DENHAM, Maj. Dixon & Clapperton, Capt. Hugh**

CLARE, John
– **Poems descriptive of Rural Life & Scenery.** L., 1820. *1st. Edn.* 12mo. Errata slip, 8 ll. of advts., slightly spotted, orig. bds., unc., soiled, spine rubbed. (S. Dec.13; 348) *Quaritch.* £160
– – **Anr. Copy.** Sm. 8vo. 2 ll. advts. dtd. Oct. 1819 inserted, initial blank lf. before hf.-title not bnd. in, without errata slip, orig. bds., unc.; Frederic Dannay copy. (CNY. Dec.16; 72) $320
– **The Shepherd's Calendar.** L., 1827. *1st. Edn.* 12mo. Hf.-title, final advt. lf., frontis. foxed & offset to title, some spotting, orig. bds., unc., partly unopened, qtr. mor. gt, s.-c.; bkplt. of George Mason Lamonte, Frederic Dannay copy. (CNY. Dec.16; 74) $420
– **The Village Minstrel, & other Poems.** 1821. *1st. Edn.* 2 vols. 12mo. Lacks hf.-titles & last 2 advt. ll. Vol. 2, cont. cf., gt. spines,. (BBA. Sep.29; 172) *Traylen.* £150
– – **Anr. Copy.** 2 vols. in 1. 12mo. Lacks hf.-titles & 2 ll. advts. at end Vol. 2, cf., back defect. (P. Sep.29; 176) *Spake.* £55
– – **Anr. Copy.** 2 vols. Frontis. in each vol., 2 inserted advts. ll., orig. bds. [Carter's bdg. 'A'], unc.; Frederic Dannay copy. (CNY. Dec.16; 73) $1,600

CLARENDON, Edward Hyde, Earl of
– **Brief View & Survey of ... Mr. Hobbes's ... Leviathan.** [Oxford], 1676. 4to. Engraved title vig., ills. & initials, some ll. slightly creased. cont. cf., rubbed. [Wing C4420] (CSK. May 18; 147) £70
– **The History of the Rebellion & Civil Wars of England.** Oxford, 1704. 3 vols. Fo. & lge. title vig. in each vol., hf.-titles, 1 vol. slightly damp-wrinkled, cont. panel. cf., rebkd. (SG. Apr.19; 61) $130
– – **Anr. Edn.** 1732. Fo. Cont. cf., rebkd. (BBA. Jul.27; 115) *Bloomsbury Rare Books.* £130
– – **Anr. Copy.** 3 pts. in 1 vol. Fo. Cont. pol. leath. gt., gold-tooled, slightly rubbed. 1 jnt. torn. (HT. May 10; 2505a) DM 400
– – **Anr. Edn.** Oxford, 1807. *New Edn.* 6 vols. Hf.-titles, cont. pol. cf., spines gt., East India College arms. (SKC. Mar.9; 1740) £65
– – **Anr. Edn.** Oxford, 1826. Cf. (HD. Feb.22; 41) Frs. 1,100
– **The History of the Rebellion & Civil Wars in England.—The Miscellaneous Works ...** 1732; 1751. *2nd. Edn. (2nd. work).* 2 vols. Fo. 1st. work: engraved frontis. port. shaved, old spr. cf., 2nd. work: cont. tree cf.; Sir Ivar Colquhoun of Luss copies. (CE. Mar.22; 65) £180

CLARETIE, Jules
– **Le Drapeau.** Ill.:– A. de Neuville (plts.) & Ed. Morin (text-ills.). 1879. 4to. Unnumbered, on japan, mosaic mor. by Lortic, wrap. (HD. Jan.24; 58) Frs. 2,100
– **Les Jouets.** Paris, [1893]. 4to. Buckram, col.- & gt.-decor. (HD. Feb.28; 24) Frs. 1,500

CLARIANA, Bernardo
– **Rendezvous with Spain: A Poem.** Trans.:– Dudley Fitts. Ill.:– Julio de Diego. N.Y., Gemor Pr., 1946. *(20) numbered & sigd. by artist.* Lge. 8vo. 3 full-p. ills.,& pict. wraps. cold. by artist. (SG. Mar,1; 394) $120

CLARK, Daniel Kinnair
– **Railway Machinery; a treatise on the Mechanical Engineering of Railways.** L., 1855. *1st. Edn.* 2 vols. Lge. 4to. Some faint spotting, cont. hf. cf., rubbed. (S. Dec.13; 231) *Quaritch.* £80

CLARK, Edwin
– **The Britannia & Conway Tubular Bridges.** Ed.:– R. Stephenson. L., 1850. 2 text vols. & atlas, compl. 8vo. & lge. fo. Plts. partly loose & foxed, orig. cl., atlas spine slightly defect. (VG. Mar.19; 23)
Pls. 690

CLARK, J.O.M.
See— NOEL, E.B. & Clark, J.O.M.

CLARK, J.W.
See— WILLIS, Robert & Clark, J.W.

CLARK, O.S.
- Clay Allison of the Washita. Recollections of Colorado, New Mexico & the Texas Panhandle. N.p., priv. ptd., 1922. Wraps., boxed, spine chipped. (LH. Sep.25; 202) $130

CLARK, R. & R.
- Golf, a Royal & Ancient Game. [Edinb.], 1875. *1st. Edn.* Bdg. not stated. (PD. Jul.13; 25) £600
-- **Anr. Copy.** Sm. 4to. Orig. cl. gt. (PD. Oct.19; 27) £260
-- **Anr. Edn.** 1893. *2nd. Edn.* Bdg. not stated. (PD. Jul.13; 32) £150
-- **Anr. Edn.** 1899. *3rd. Edn.* Bdg. not stated. (PD. Jul.13; 26) £170

CLARK, Roland
- Etchings. N.Y., Derrydale Pr., 1938. *(800).* Some soiling, a plt. sliced out, orig. cl., soiled, worn; orig. sigd. etching, w.a.f. (SPB. Dec.13; 582) $200
-- **Anr. Edn.** [1938]. *Derrydale Pr.,. (800)* numbered. Fo. Etched frontis. (The Morning Flight) sigd. in pencil by Clark, hf. buckram, linen covers. (SG. Mar.15; 209) $475
-- **Anr. Copy.** Fo. 69 plts., two-tone cl., glassine wrap. darkening & edges tearing, box. (CBA. Nov.19; 130a) $350

CLARK, William
See— LEWIS, Meriwether & Clark, William

CLARKE, Asa B.
- Travels in Mexico & California ... Boston, 1852. *1st. Edn.* Orig. ptd. wraps. [Sabin 13393] (LH. Apr.15; 287) $275

CLARKE, Rev. Edward
- Letters concerning the Spanish Nation. L., 1763. Fo. Leath. (DS. Mar.23; 2057) Pts. 40,000

CLARKE, Edward Daniel
- Travels in Various Countries of Europe, Asia & Africa. L., 1810-19. *1st. Edn.* 5 vols. (of 6). 4to. 148 engraved plts., 19 maps, some folding, offset, foxed, cont. cf., rebkd. (S. Apr.9; 12) *Rinne.* £120
-- **Anr. Edn.** 1810-23. 6 vols. 4to. Some light soiling, cont. cf. (CSK. Feb.10; 207) £240
-- **Anr. Copy.** 6 vols. 4to. 28 maps & plans, some folding, 156 plts., some folding, a few captions shaved, cont. cf. gt. (BBA. Feb.9; 267) *Remington.* £230
-- **Anr. Edn.** 1811-12. *2nd. Edn.* Pts. 1 & 2 only: 2 vols. 4to. 70 engraved plts. & Maps, some folding, some ll. rather spotted or browned, few margin tears, cont. cf., rebkd., orig. gt. spines. (BBA. Sep.29; 27) *Baumann.* £50
-- **Anr. Edn.** 1811-19. *Vol. 1: 2nd. Edn.* Vols. 1-5 only (of 6). 4to. 166 engraved plts. (12 folding, 5 double-p.), some offsetting, cont. tree gt., some covers detchd. (SKC. May 4; 1806) £120
-- **Anr. Edn.** 1813-16. *3rd. Edn.* Vols. I-IV only. 4to. Cont. cf., spines worn, some covers detchd. (TA. Oct.20; 60) £54
-- **Anr. Edn.** 1813-23. 3 pts. in 6 vols. 4to. Slight staining to a few plts., sm. tear in 2 folding maps, cont. diced cf., 1 cover detchd. (LC. Oct.13; 247) £120
-- **Anr. Edn.** L., 1816-24. 11 vols. Some spotting, cont. cf., hinges reprd. (S. Mar.6; 5) *Cumming.* £120

CLARKE, Graham
- Balyn & Balan. [1971]. *(25) artist's proof copies. (6) especially bnd.* Fo. Orig. cf.-bkd. sycamore bds., unbnd. as iss. (CSK. Jun.15; 160) £60
- The Goose Man & Other Poems. Boughton Monchelsea, Ebenezer Pr., 1974. *(80). (5) artist's proofs.* Sm. ob. 4to. Ills. initialled & hand-cold., orig. mor. over wood bds., orig. linen s.-c.; inscr. by author to Mr. & Mrs. Ronald Kinsey. (S. Nov.21; 182) *Gerrard.* £130

CLARKE, Harold George
- Baxter Colour Prints Pictorially Presented. 1920. 4to. Mod. hf. mor. (BBA. Nov.10; 202) *Blackwell.* £70

-- **Anr. Edn.** L., 1920-21. 4to. Publisher's qtr. mor., worn. (KH. Nov.9; 566) Aus. $190

CLARKE, Hermann F.
- John Coney, Silversmith, 1655-1722. Intro.:– Hollis French. Boston, 1932. *(365) numbered.* 4to. Gt.-pict. cl. (SG. Oct.13; 316) $100
- John Hull: A builder of the Bay Colony. Portland, 1940. *(500) numbered.* 4to. Cl., box worn. (SG. Oct.13; 317) $110

CLARKE, I.
[–] Scotland Sixty Years ago. Paisley, 1882. *(150) numbered & sigd. by publisher.* Lge. fo. 32 aquatint plts., a few margins lightly soiled, cont. mor.-bkd. cl., worn. (CSK. Dec.2; 43) £1,600

CLARKE, James
- Plans of the Lakes in Cumberland, Westmorland, & Lancashire. 1793. 4to. Some margins browned, mod. cl.-bkd. bds. (CSK. Jul.6; 54) £220

CLARKE, James Stanier & McArthur, John
- The Life & Service of Horatio Nelson. L., n.d. 3 vols. Some slight spotting & offsetting, orig. cl. (S. Mar. 20; 706) *Edwards.* £55

CLARKE, John Willis
See— WILLIS, Prof. Robert & Clarke, John Willis

CLARKE, Joseph T. & others
- Investigations at Assos: Drawings & Photographs of the Buildings & Objects Discovered during the Excavations of 1881-83. Ed.:– Francis H. Bacon. L., Camb., Leipzig, 1902-[21]. *(525).* Atlas fo. Ex-liby., stp. on verso of all separate plts., loose in ptd. bd. folder. (SG. May 3; 95) $350

CLARKE, Samuel
- The Works. L., 1738. *1st. Edn.* 4 vols. Fo. Some spots & stains, cont. spr. cf.; bkplt. of Thomas Boswall of Blackadder. (S. Dec.8; 39) *Finch.* £100
See— LEIBNITZ, Gottfried Wilhelm von & Clarke, Samuel

CLARKSON, Thomas
[–] An Essay on the Slavery & Commerce of the Human Species. L., 1786. *1st. Edn.* Slightly soiled, cont. sheep, rebkd., slightly rubbed. (BBA. May 3; 220) *Thomas.* £190

CLASSIQUES DE LA TABLE
Intro.:– Justin Améro. Paris, 1855. *New Edn.* 2 vols. 12mo. Hf. mor. by David, spines decor. (slightly faded), unc. (HD. Jun.22; 44) Frs. 1,100

CLAUDE LE LORRAIN [i.e. Claude Gelée]
- Beauties of Claude Lorraine. L., 1825. Fo. Additional engraved title, 24 engraved plts., loose as iss., some slight spotting, mostly marginal, orig. cl.-bkd. bds., rubbed, rebkd., lacks ties. (S. Dec.13; 441) *Hutton.* £110
- Liber Veritatis: Or, a Collection of Prints, after the Original Designs of ... Ill.:– Richard Earlom. L., 1777 & 1819. *1st. Edns.* Vols. 2 & 3 only (of 3). Fo. 2 mezzotint ports., 98 (of 100) & 96 (of 100) bistre mezzotint engrs., some peripheral foxing, not affecting images, early roan-bkd. bds., disbnd. (SG. Nov.3; 41) $2,200
-- **Anr. Copy.** 3 vols. Fo. 3 port. frontis., 300 plts., red hf. mor. by Wright, sigd. in upr. cover, spines gt. (PNY. Jun.6; 467) $2,000
-- **Anr. Edn.** Ill.:– Richard Earlom,. L., [1777-1819?]. 3 vols. 3 engraved ports., 300 plts., 3 with minor tears, spotted, mainly in margins, hf. russ., rebkd., worn. (S. Oct.4; 140) *Burgess.* £2,200
-- **Anr. Copy.** 3 vols. Fo. 3 engraved ports. & 300 plts., some spotting or soiling, mostly marginal, cont. hf. mor., spines gt., slightly worn. (S. Apr.30; 16) *Haynes.* £1,800
-- **Anr. Edn.** L., 1814-19. 3 vols. Fo. 3 ports., 300 engraved plts., hf. red mor. gt. (SPB. May 17; 583) $1,700

CLAUDEL, Paul
- L'Annonce faite à Marie. Ill.:– Michel Ciry. Paris, 1964. *(55) on Auvergne.* 1 vol. & album. 4to. Mor. gt., mosaic decor., folder, s.-c., hf. mor. album;

extra- ill. with suite on japon nacré & suite on Rives. (HD. Jun.13; 22) Frs. 6,000
- Cette Heure qui est entre le Printemps et l'Eté. Paris, 1913. *1st. Edn. (300).* 4to. Hand-bnd. cherry red mor., gold decor. covers, inner & outer dentelles, by E. Ludwig, Frankfurt, orig. wrap. bnd. in; MS. dedication from author. (H. Nov.24; 1451) DM 680
- L'Oiseau Noir dans le Soleil Levant. Ill.:– Foujita. Paris, 1927. *(425) on vergé d'Arches.* 4to. Red hf. mor., orig. pict. wraps. bnd. in. (HK. Nov.11; 3550) DM 850
[–] Tête d'Or. [Paris, Nov. 1890]. Orig. Edn., *(100)* on vell. Red Bradel hf. mor., corners, by Alfred Farez, unc., wrap. & spine; sigd. (HD. May 16; 66) Frs. 2,100
[–] La Ville. Paris, 1893. *Orig. Edn. (200) numbered on white vell.* Sm. 4to. Cont. Bradel hf. chagrin, unc., wrap.; author's autograph dedication to Paul Morand, Brussels, 15 Apr. 1935. (HD. Mar.27; 55) Frs. 1,250

CLAUDEL, P. (Text)
See— MUNCHNER BLATTER FUR DICHTUNG UND GRAPHIK

CLAUDIANUS, Claudius
- Opera. Parma, Angelus Ugoletus, 23 Apr. 1493. 4to. Lacks a1, some light staining, etc., old stiff vell.; the Walter Goldwater copy. [BMC VII, 1945; Goff C-702] (SG. Dec.1; 109) $400

CLAUDIN, Anatole
- The First Paris Press. 1898. 4to. Orig. buckram-bkd. bds.; H.M. Nixon coll., with his sig. (BBA. Oct.6; 186) *Traylen.* £50

CLAUDIUS, M.
- Werke. Ill.:– after Chodowiecki. Hamburg, 1829. 4 vols. in 2. Contents lf. bnd. at end, 2 ll. loose, some ll. spotted, cont. hf. leath., gt. spine decor. end-papers with old owners entries; Hauswedell coll. (H. May 24; 1254) DM 1,800

CLAUSIUS, Rudolf
- Abhandlungen über die Mechanische Wärmetheorie ... Braunschweig, 1864-67. *1st. Edn.* 2 vols. in 1. Hf.-titles, some foxing & slight browning, recent qtr. cf.; John D. Stanitz coll. (SPB. Apr.25; 97) $450

CLAVASIO, Angelus Clarette de
- Summa Angelica de Casibus Conscientiae. Chivasso, Jacobinus Suigus de Suico, 13 May 1486. *1st. Edn.* Sm. 4to. Many initials & paragraph marks in red & blue, lacks last lf. of table, cont. blind-stpd. cf. over wood bds., worn, wormed, reprd., lacks clasps; the Walter Goldwater copy. [BMC VII, 1111; Goff A-713] (SG. Dec.1; 17) $900
-- **Anr. Edn.** Nuremb., Anton Koberger, 10 Feb. 1492. Fo. Lge. copy, lacks qq2-6, cont. wood bds., shabby, lacks clasps; the Walter Goldwater copy. [BMC II, 434; Goff A-722] (SG. Dec.1; 18) $275
-- **Anr. Edn.** Venice, Georgius Arrivabenus, 2 May 1495. Without the 12 lf. supp., stained & browned at front & back, later vell.; the Walter Goldwater copy. [Goff A-726] (SG. Dec.1; 19) $225

CLAVE, J.A. (Ed.)
See— METRONOMO

CLAVEL, F.T.B.
- Historia de la Franc-Masoneria y de las Sociedades Secretas ... Madrid, 1847. 4to. Leath. (DS. Mar.23; 2058) Prs. 20,000

CLAVIERE, Etienne & Brissot de Warville, Jacques P.
- De La France et des Etats-Unis. L., 1787. *1st. Edn.* Title-p. slightly soiled, cont. tree cf., upr. jnt. split. (SG. Apr.5; 56) $175

CLAVIJERO, Padre Francisco Javier
- Historia de la Antigua o Baja California. Mexico, 1852. Qtr. cf. (LH. Sep.25; 203) $170
- The History of Mexico. Trans.:– Charles Cullen. 1787. *1st. Engl. Edn.* 2 vols. 4to. 2 folding maps, 25 engraved plts., 1 map loose, cont. tree cf., spine gt.; Samuel Enderby bkplt. (LC. Oct.13; 248) £280

CLAVIO BAMBERGENSE, P. Christoforo
– Aritmetica Prattica. Rome, 1586. Vell. (DS. Mar.23; 2059)   Pts. 50,000

CLAWSON, John
– A Catalogue of Early English Books in the Library of ... Ed.:– Seymour De Ricci. Phila., 1924. *1st. Edn. (200) numbered on Strathmore paper.* Tall 4to. Prices pencilled in margins thro.-out, cl. (SG. Sep.15; 105) $110

CLAY, John
– The Sheep Herder's Grave. [Chic.], n.d. Orig. ptd. wraps. (LH. Jan.15; 263) $100
– The Tragedy of Squaw Mountain. [Chic.], n.d. Orig. ptd. wraps. (LH. Jan.15; 264) $120

CLAYTON, Ellen C.
– Queens of Song: Memoirs of Some of the Most Celebrated Female Vocalists. Ill.:– Armytage. L., 1863. 2 vols. Lge. 8vo. Three-qtr. cf., spines gt. (SG. Feb.16; 218) $100

CLEAVER, Arthur H.
See— HATTON, Thomas & Cleaver, Arthur H.

CLEEMPUTTE, Paul Adolphe van 'Charles Simond'
– La Vie Parisienne à travers le XIXe Siècle. Paris de 1800 à 1900 d'après les Mémoires et les Estampes du Temps.—Les Centennales Parisiennes ... Paris, 1900-02. 4 vols. 4to. Hf. roan, spines decor. (HD. Mar.19; 127)   Frs. 1,600

CLEIRAC, Estienne
[–] Us et Coustume de la Mer. Bordeaux, 1647. 4to. With separately paginated 'Explication des Termes de Marine', title vig. with sm. tear, later qtr. cf. (SG. Feb.9; 280) $200

CLELAND, Elizabeth
– A New & Easy Method of Cookery. Edinb., 1770. *3rd. Edn.* Some ll. slightly soiled, cont. sheep, rather worn. (BBA. May 3; 211)   *Quaritch.* £210

CLEMEN, Paul
– Die Romanischen Wandmalereien d. Rheinlande. Düsseldorf, 1905. Plt. vol. only. Fo. 64 partly cold. plts., light old spotting, loose in orig. linen portfo. (V. Sep.30; 1611)   DM 600

CLEMENS, Samuel Langhorne 'Mark Twain'
– The American Claimant. Ill.:– Dan Beard. N.Y., 1892. *1st. Edn.* Cl., hf. mor. case, worn; A. McCowan-Merle Johnson copy, sigd. by McCowan, inscr. by Johnson on front pastedown, frontis. sigd. & inscr. by ill., A.L.s from McCowan to Johnson. (RO. Apr.23; 293) $550
– The Celebrated Jumping Frog of Calavaras County. N.Y., 1867. *1st. Edn. 1st. Printing.* 12mo. Some foxing, few stains, orig. cl. gt. (a variant, with the frog emblem on upr. cover facing up), spine cocked. (SG. Nov.17; 138) $600
– English as She is Taught. Boston, [1900]. *1st. Edn. 1st. Iss., with 'the five' on p. 16.* Cl., hf. mor. case, worn; Merle Johnson copy, bibliographical note sigd. by him on front pastedown. (RO. Apr.23; 302) $150
– Following the Equator. A Journey Around the World. Hartford, 1897. *1st. Edn. Single-imprint iss.* Orig. three-qtr. mor., lightly rubbed. (RO. Apr.23; 307) $240
– Huckleberry Finn. L., 1884. *1st. Edn. Blanck's Iss. A.* Inserted publisher's catalogue at end, few tears & clippings removed, pict. cl., gatherings sewn in thread, worn. (RO. Apr.23; 286) $110
– – Anr. Edn. Ill.:– E.W. Kemble. N.Y., 1885. *1st. Amer. Edn.* Square 8vo. Early Iss., title a cancel, 'was' for 'saw' on p.57, plt. listed at p.88, state 3 of pagination on folio 155, frontis. in 1st. state, p.283 on a stub, final lf. blank, orig. pict. cl., hf.-mor. s.-c.; Frederic Dannay copy, inscr. 'Barnaby Ross'/'Ellery Queen'. (CNY. Dec.16; 76) $3,000
– – Anr. Copy. 4to. Title & p.283 cancelled, port. bust cf Heliotype Printing Co., p.155 with last numeral missing, pp.13 & 57 in early states, orig. cl., mor.-bkd. s.-c.; Perry Molstad copy. (SPB. May 16; 419) $700
– – Anr. Copy. 4to. With 1884 copyright date, 'Him and another Man' on p. 88, lacks final '5' in pagination of p. 155, 'was' for 'saw' on p. 57, 1st. state of p. 283, light browning, later sheep, spine &

corners worn; A.N. by artist relating to the plt. on p. 283. (SPB. Dec.13; 653) $450
– – Anr. Copy. 4to. Early state, with 'was' for 'saw' at line 23 p. 57 & the ill. 'Him & another Man' listed at p. 88, orig. pict. cl., rubbed at foot, cover loose, hf. mor. s.-c.; inscr. by Kemble 'To Ralph', pencil drawing by Kemble pasted on front fly-lf., K.O. Foltz & Ralph C. Runyon bkplts. (LH. Jan.15; 407) $325
– – Anr. Copy. Title-lf. cancel, gt.-pict. cl., worn, slightly shaken, some fraying of spine ends. (RO. Apr.23; 284) $220
– – Anr. Copy. Sq. 8vo. Late iss., with all corrections as noted in BAL, gt. pict. cl. (SG. Dec.8; 349) $140
– Tom Sawyer. Hartford, 1876. *1st. Amer. Edn. 1st. Iss.* Lge. square 8vo. Versos of hf.-title & frontis. blank, 4 pp. of advts. marked 'Revised December 1st, 1876', a few ll. soiled, gt. decor. cl., tips & spine ends worn, owner's sig. & bkplt. on front end-paper, leath.-bkd. folding box. (SG. Dec.8; 350) $350
– – Anr. Edn. Hartford, 1876. *1st. Amer. Edn. Blanck's 1st. Printing.* Fly-title on p. (I), p. (III) blank, some ll. loose or frayed, cont. sheep, peach end-paper, brkn., lacks most of spine, some staining &c. (RO. Apr.23; 289) $180
– – Anr. Copy. On wove paper, p. (III) blank, lacks fly-title lf., some ll. loose, frayed, soiled, creased & c., cont. sheep, peach end-papers, disbnd., lacks spine. (RO. Apr.23; 288) $160
– – Anr. Edn. Hartford, 1876. *1st. Amer. Edn. 2nd. Printing [Iss. 'A'].* Square 8vo. Orig. cl., hf. mor. s.-c.; Frederic Dannay copy, inscr. 'Barnaby Ross'/'Ellery Queen'. (CNY. Dec.16; 75) $1,100
– – Anr. Copy. Orig. sheep, rubbed, inner jnt. reprd. (RO. Apr.23; 290) $130
– Life on the Mississippi. Boston, 1883. *1st. Edn.* Blanck's lst. State, Intermediate B(A1). no tail-piece on p. 441, caption on p. 443 'The St. Louis Hotel', gt. pict. cl., light wear. (Ro. Apr.23; 230) $185
– – Anr. Copy. Tall 8vo. 1st. state, intermediate 'B' ('A'?), no tailpiece on p. 441, caption on p. 443 'The St. Louis Hotel', gt.-pict. cl., spine ends slightly frayed, nick on 1 cover. (SG. Dec.8; 351) $125
– Mark Twain: San Francisco Correspondent. Selections from his Letters to the Territorial Enterprise: 1865-6. Ed.:– Henry Nash Smith & Frederick Anderson. San Franc., [Allen Pr.], 1957. *(400).* With prospectus, cl.-bkd. decor. paper covers. (LH. Sep.25; 334) $130
– Queen Victoria's Jubilee: the Great Procession of June 22, 1897, in the Queen's Honor ... [N.Y.?], priv. ptd., [1910?]. *1st. Edn. in Book Form. (195) numbered & sigd.* Cl.-bdk. pict. bds.; also sigd. by Merle Johnson. (SG. Dec.8; 352) $550
– Roughing It. Hartford, 1876. cl., worn, slightly shaken; pres. copy inscr. by author on front free end-paper to C.W. Stoddard, Oct. 1877. (RO. Apr.23; 339) $675
– A Social Fireside Conversation in the Time of the Tudors. N.p., Gander Pr., n.d. *(150) numbered.* Tall 12mo. This copy unnumbered, pict. & ptd. wraps., tied, bottom edge of wraps. chipped; with about 22 pp. of autograph correspondence from A.M. Traubel to Mr. Lion, sm. 8vo., mostly on letterhead of Contemporary Cl. of Phila., 'Horace Traubel, Treasurer'; inscr. & sigd. on 1st. p. by Horace Traubel, 'Given to me by Laurens Maynard ... '. (SG. Mar.15; 158) $120
– The Tragedy of Pudd'nhead Wilson & the Comedy Those Extraordinary Twins. Hartford, 1894. *1st. Edn. Blanck's 1st. State.* Title-lf. conjugate, frontis. Blanck's state 'A', orig. cl., worn. (RO. Apr.23; 349) $110
– A Tramp Abroad. Hartford, 1880. *1st. Edn.* Port. Blanck's state 'B', frontis. 1st. state, sheets state 'A', publisher's three-qtr. mor., worn. (RO. Apr.23; 352) $225
– – Anr. Copy. Port. in Blanck's state 'A', frontis. Blanck's 2nd. state, sheets state 'B', cl., cover stp. state 'B', worn, spine ends slightly frayed. (RO. Apr.23; 350) $110
– The Works. 1899-1907. *Author's De Luxe Edn. (620) numbered & sigd.* 25 vols. Orig. cl. bds., unc. (PD. Feb.15; 58)   £225
[–] Writings of Mark Twain. N.Y., 1922. *Definitive*

Edn. (1024) sigd. 35 vols. Hf. mor., gt. spine inlaid. (SPB. May 17; 724) $3,100
– – Anr. Edn. N.Y., 1929. *Stormfield Edn., (1024).* 37 vols. Gt.-lettered cl., portly unc. & unopened spines midly cockled, several d.-w.'s slightly chipped; A.L. s. From Clemens to Miss. Mary H. Beale (strengthed with tape at folds). (SG. Nov.3; 214) $1,500

CLEMENS, Samuel Langhorne 'Mark Twain' & Warner, Charles Dudley
– The Gilded Age, a Tale of Today. Hartford, 1873. *1st. Edn. Early Iss.* Most 1st. state points noted by Blanck, title-p. in 2nd., 'forged', state, advts., folding plt. torn, cl., slightly worn & shaken, inner jnts. brkn. (RO. Apr.23; 309) $220
– – Anr. Edn. N.Y., [1901]. 2 vols. in 1. Cl., light wear; sigd. by author on front pastedown. (RO. Apr.23; 311) $220

CLEMENS ALEXANDRINUS
– Omnia quae quidem extant Opera. Flor., 1551-Oct. 1550. 2 vols. Fo. Vol. 1 in Latin, Vol. 2 in Greek sections 2 & 3 in Vol. 1 under separate title-p., vell., not quite unif.; Lord Vernon & Dr. Walter Pagel copy. (S. Feb.7; 82)   *Van Aorst.* £240

CLEMENS V, Pope
See— BONIFACIUS VIII, Pope—CLEMENS V, Pope

CLEMENS VIII, Pope
– Caeremoniale Episcoporum Jussu Clementis VIII. Pont. Max ... Venice, 1600. Lge. 8vo. Cont. gt.-decor. mor., spine gt., monog. repeated in compartments, by De Thou, with his gt. supralibros. (VG. Sep.14; 848)   Fls. 1,900

CLEMENS XIV, Pope
– Lettres Intéressantes. Ill.:– Bille, engraved by Queverdo (frontis.). Lyon, Rouen, 1776. 2 vols. Cont. red mor., spine decor. (HD. Mar.21; 17)   Frs. 1,200

CLEMENT, David
– Bibliothèque Curieuse, Historique et Critique. Göttingen & Hanover, 1750-54. Vols. 1-5 only (of 9). 4to. Some ll. browned, lr. margins Vol. 2 dampstained, cont. cf. (BBA. Nov.10; 48)   *Maggs.* £50

CLENARDUS, Nicolaus
– Institutiones Linguae Graecae. Venice, 1570. *1st. Aldine Edn.* Sm. 8vo. Light margin stains, cont. vell., wrinkled. (SG. Feb.9; 160) $200

CLERK, John
– An Essay on Naval Tactics. 1790. 4 pts. in 1 vol. 4to. 52 plts., orig. str.-grd. mor. (P. Jun.7; 166)   £90
– – Anr. Edn. Edinb., 1804. *2nd. Edn.* 4to. Most plts. with sm. sections hand-cold., very spotted, 1 plt. with part of outer blank margin excised, cont. cf., spine gt., rubbed. (CSK. Jun.15; 39)   £65

CLERKE, Charles
[–] A Journal of a Voyage round the World in His Majesty's ship the Dolphin, commanded by the Honourable Commodore Byron ... L., 1767. *[2nd. Edn.].* Mod. hf. mor.; Clement K. Shorter bkplt. (C. Jun.27; 83)   *Brooke-Hitching.* £220
– – Anr. Copy. Cont. tree cf., slightly rubbed. [Sabin 9732] (S. Jun.25; 277)   *Traylen.* £90

CLIFFORD, Isidore E. & R.E.
– Crown, Bar, & Bridge-work. 1885. Orig. cl. (P. Apr.12; 56)   *Henderson.* £55

CLIFFORD, J.
– The Tunbridge Wells Guide. 1837. Vig. title, dedication, 2 folding hand-cold. maps (1 loose, linen-bkd.), 2 plans, 21 plts. (7 hand-cold.), cf., rubbed. (P. Apr.12; 160)   *Davidson-Merritt.* £70

CLIO & EUTERPE, or British Harmony
1759-62. 3 vols. Lacks folding advts., slightly worn, hf. cf. (BS. Nov.16; 3)   £320
– – Anr. Edn. L., 1762. 3rd. vol. only with engraved headings, orig. bds., worn, spine brkn. (S. May 10; 156)   *Maggs.* £160
– – Anr. Copy. 3 vols. Engraved advt. mntd. on verso of each frontis., some age-browning & margin

CLIO & EUTERPE, or British Harmony -*Contd.*

fraying, mod. two-tone buckram. (SG. Nov.3; 42)
$650

CLIVE, R.
- **A Series of Lithographic Drawings from Sketches ... Lying Principally Between the Persian Gulf & the Black Sea.** L., [1852]. 2 pts. (of 3) only in 1 vol. Fo. 17 subjects on 16 hand-cold. litho. plts., folding plt. torn, some margin spotting, publisher's ptd. wraps., frayed. (S. May 22; 274)
Samiramis. £700

CLONNARD, Teniente Gral. Conde de
- **Album de la Infantería Española.** Madrid, 1861. Lge. fo. Linen, covers loose. (DS. Jan.27; 2201)
Frs. 90,000

CLOQUET, J.G.C.
- **Anatomie de l'Homme.** Paris, 1821-31. Fo. Cont. style red hf. leath. gt. (D. Nov.23; 541) DM 6,500
- - **Anr. Edn.** Bruxelles, 1828. 2 pts. in 1 vol. Lge. fo. 300 litho. plts., slightly foxed, few margin repairs, sm. margin stains, cont. hf. vell., rebnd., slightly soiled. (VG. Sep.14; 1234) Fls. 880
- **Manuel d'Anatomie Descriptive du Corps Humain.** Paris, 1825[-31]. 3 vols. 1st. plts. slightly stained, some plts. lightly browned, 3 plts. with tears, 5 with sm. margin slits, some light foxing, cont. hf. leath., slightly rubbed & bumped. (R. Oct.12; 1381)
DM 410

CLOUET, J.B.L.
- **Géographie Moderne avec une Introduction.** Paris, 1793. Lge. fo. Lacks 1 map, slightly stained, cont. hf. leath., very rubbed & bumped. (HK. Nov.8; 887) DM 850

CLOUZOT, Henri
- **La Ferronnerie Moderne.** Paris, 1920's. 2nd.-4th. Series: 3 vols. 4to. 100 plts., cl.-bkd. decor. bd. folder. (SG. Aug.25; 31) $280

CLOUZOT, H. & Follot, Ch.
- **Historie du Papier Peint en France.** Paris, 1935. 4to. Orig. wraps., unc., roan-bkd. folder, s.-c. (S. Apr.30; 171) *Potterton.* £140
- - **Anr. Copy.** Sm. fo. 27 mntd. col. plts., ptd. wraps. (SG. Aug.25; 89) $140

CLOWES, William Laird
- **The Royal Navy, a History.** L., 1897-1903. 7 vols. 4to. Lacks 2 plts., orig. cl., Caledonian United Service Club stp. on upr. covers, spine ends worn. (S. Dec.20; 822) *Maggs.* £280
- - **Anr. Copy.** 7 vols. Lge. 8vo. Orig. cl. gt., slightly soiled,. (SKC. Jan.13; 2356) £260

CLUB FRANÇAIS DE MEDAILLE (LE)
Paris, 1963-78. Nos. 1-58 in 13 vols. Cont. mor.-bkd. cl., orig. wraps. bnd. in. (S. May 1; 457)
Spink. £220

CLUMBER LIBRARY
- **The Catalogue of the Magnificent Library the Property of the late Seventh Duke of Newcastle.** 1937-38. 4 pts. in 2 vols. 4to. Cl.; H.M. Nixon coll., with some prices & buyers' names added by him in MS. (BBA. Oct.6; 150) *Montagliari.* £70

CLUNY
- **Milénaire. (Congrès d'Histoire et d'Archéologie tenu à Cluny les 10, 11, 12 sept. 1910).** Macon, 1910. 2 vols. Hf. vell. à la bradd, wraps. & spine preserved. (HD. Dec.9; 113) Frs. 2,000

CLUNY, Alexander
[-] **The American Traveller.** L., 1769. 1st. Edn. 4to. Sm. tear in fold of map, disbnd. [Sabin 13796] (C. Jun.27; 23) *Quaritch.* £650
- - **Anr. Copy.** [Sabin 13796] (*Bound with:*)
ANONYMOUS - **The Case of the Late Election for the County of Middlesex.** L., 1769. Together 2 works in 1 vol. 4to. Cont. spr. sheep, rebkd. in period style; the Rt. Hon. Visc. Eccles copy. (CNY. Nov.18; 69) $1,700

CLUSIUS, Charles
- **Rariorum aliquot Stirpium per Hispanias observatorum Historia, Libris duobus expresa ...** Amberes, 1576. Upr. margin slightly short, old leath. (DS. Apr.27; 2380) Pts. 110,000

CLUTTERBUCK, James Bennett
- **Port Phillip in 1849** ... 1850. Hf.-title (not called for by Ferguson), bdg. not stated, sm. snag at foot of backstrip. (KH. May 1; 171) Aus. $300
- **The History & Antiquities of the County of Hertford.** 1815-27. 1st. Edn. 3 vols. Fo. Folding map, 52 plts. & maps, including 2 hand-cold., hf. mor. gt. (P. Jun.7; 157) £220

CLUVERIUS, Philippus
- **Germania Antiquae.** Leiden, 1616. 1st. Edn. 4 pts. in 1 vol. Fo. Engraved title, 11 maps, 26 plts., vell. (P. Dec.8; 71) £150
- - **Anr. Copy.** Fo. Engraved title, 11 double-p. maps, 24 (of 26?) engraved plts., many double-p., cont. vell., spine frayed. (C. Nov.16; 204)
Burgess. £100
- **Introductionis in Universam Geographiam Libri VI.** Braunschwerg, 1641. [1st. German Edn.]. Sm. 4to. Some ll. lightly wormed in lr. margin, cont. vell. (R. Oct.13, 2840) DM 700
- - **Anr. Copy.** 4to. Lacks ptd. title, cont. vell. (BR. Apr.12; 77) DM 650
- - **Anr. Edn.** Amst., 1661. 4to. Folding plt., 45 folding maps, plt. & 3 maps torn, cont. cf. (BBA. May 3; 260) *Martino.* £320
- - **Anr. Edn.** Amst., 1672. 12mo. Engraved title-p., 2 engraved folding plts., 35 engraved folding maps only, cont. cf. (PD. Dec.14; 289) £105
- - **Anr. Copy.** 2 pts. in 1 vol. 12mo. Engraved title, 20 folding engraved maps, folding table, later str.-grd. mor., very slightly worn. (SG. Apr.19; 63)
$275
- - **Anr. Edn.** [Amst.], 1682 or later. Atlas only. Fo. 45 engraved maps & plts. (39 double-p.), 1 or 2 detchd., cont. cf., defect. (S. Jun.25; 287)
Leycester Maps. £260
- - **Anr. Edn.** Amst., 1697. 4to. Additional engraved title-p., 2 folding tables, 46 plts. & folding maps, vig. on title-p., X3 & 4 & 1 map stained, cont. cf., a little worn; ptd. overslip on title-p. reads 'Amstelaedami, Typis Joannis Wolters. Londini, Prostant apud Sam. Smith & Benj. Walford, in Coemeterio D. Pauli. MDCXCVII.'. (BBA. May 3; 261) *Ingol Maps.* £220
- - **Anr. Edn.** Amst., 1729. 4to. Frontis., 4 plts., 1 folding table, 47 folding maps, cont. vell. gt. (P. May 17; 422) *Faupel.* £270

CLYMER, W.B.S. & Green, Charles R.
- **Robert Frost: A Bibliography.** Amherst, Mass., 1937. (150) numbered & sigd. by Frost. Qtr. mor., partly unc., s.-c. (SG. Mar.1; 167) $350

COACHBUILDER, The
L., May 15, 1885-Jan.25, 1887. Bnd. in 1 vol. 4to. 35 plts., some folding, cl. worn, as a periodical, w.a.f. (P. May 17; 242) *Quaritch.* £100

COACH BUILDERS HARNESS MAKERS & Sadlers Art Journal
L., Sep. 1886-Mar. 1890. 121 plts., most cold., 1 loose, qtr. mor., as a collection of plts., w.a.f. (P. May 17; 243) *Schuster.* £280

COACH BUILDERS, WHEELWRIGHTS' & Motor Car Manufacturers' Art Journal
L., 1905. Vol. 26. 4to. Plts., ills., folding diagrams, cl., as a periodical, w.a.f. (P. May 17; 244)
Quaritch. £150

COACHMAKERS' Journal, The
L., Dec. 1885-Nov. 1887. Vols. 1 & 2. 4to. Advts., 80 (of 83) plts., cl., as a periodical, w.a.f. (P. May 17; 245) *Quaritch.* £130

COATEN, Arthur W. & Rouch, W.A.
- **Famous Horses of the British Turf.** L., n.d. (600). 10 vols. 4to. Orig. cl. gt.; review copy. (P. Dec.8; 219) *Allen.* £65

COATES, Charles
- **The History & Antiquities of Reading.** 1802. 4to. Folding engraved plan, 7 aquatint plts. only, including 1 folding, some light spotting, cont. hf. cf., rebkd. (CSK. Nov.4; 61) £55

COATES, D. & others
- **Christianity the Means of Civilization, Shown in the Evidence Given Before a Committee of the House of Commons on Aborigines ...** 1837. 12mo. Mod.

bds., qtr. mor., partly unc. (KH. May 1; 172)
Aus. $100

COBBETT, William 'Peter Porcupine'
- **The English Gardener.** L., 1829. 1st. Edn. Qtr. cf. (HBC. May 17; 425) £85
- **A History of the Protestant 'Reformation' in England & Ireland.** L., 1824-27. 2 vols. Some spotting, bds., unc.; Chillingham Castle bkplt. (P. Mar.15; 296) *Scott.* £75
- **Rural Rides in the Counties of Surrey, Kent, Sussex ...** L., 1830. 1st. Edn. 12mo. Pages 45* to 124* present, cont. cf., rebkd. (BBA. Dec.15; 194)
Snelling. £100
- - **Anr. Copy.** 12 pp. advts., some foxing, hf. cl., stp. to pastedown. (CBA. Dec.10; 172) $160
- **A Treatise on Cobbett's Corn.** L., 1828. 1st. Edn. 6 advt. ll., 3 plts., some staining & spotting, orig. bds., unc. (S. Apr.10; 351) *Drury.* £60
- **Works.** 1801. 12 vols. Cont. cf., rubbed. (CSK. Jul.6; 136) £95

COBBOLD, Rev. Richard
[-] **The History of Margaret Catchpole, A Suffolk Lady.** L., 1845. 3 vols. Lacks advts., hf. cf., covers slightly rubbed. (CA. Apr.3; 31) Aus. $200

COBDEN-SANDERSON, Thomas James
- **Das Idealbuch oder das Schöne Buch.** Trans.:- Richard Stettiner. Berlin, 1921. (30) De Luke Edn. on Zanders Bütten. Hand-bnd. orig. cf. by Hübel & Denck; Hauswedell coll. (H. May 23; 432)
DM 420

COBURN, Alvin Langdon
- **London.** Intro.:- Hilaire Belloc. L., N.Y., [1909]. Fo. 20 tipped in photogravure plts., orig. gt.-lettered bds., worn, leath. spine renewed, later box. (SG. Nov.10; 45) $1,500
- **Men of Mark.** L., 1913. 4to. 33 plts., few minor spots, orig. cl., slightly soiled; pres. copy, short A.N. loosely inserted. (S. Apr.9; 206) *Bennett.* £190
- **More Men of Mark.** L., [1922]. 1st. Edn. 4to. 33 tipped in collotype reproductions, some plt. mounts lightly stained from tissue guards, two-tone gt.-lettered cl., rubbed & soiled. (SG. Nov.10; 46)
$175

COCARELLA. B.
See- **VILLE, Antoine de—BARPO, G.B.— COCARELLA. B.**

COCHIN, Charles Nicolas
See- **GRAVELOT, Hubert François Bourguignon & Cochin, Charles Nicolas**

COCHLAEUS [DOBNECK], Johannes
- **Specvlvm Antiqvae Devotionis circa Missam ...** Mainz, Feb. 1549. 1st. Edn. Fo. Bds. (HK. Nov.8; 148a) DM 400

COCHRANE, Archibald, Ninth Earl of Dundonald
See- **DUNDONALD, Archibald Cochrane, Ninth Earl of**

COCHRANE, Basil
[-] **An Improvement in the Mode of Administering the Vapour Bath.** L., 1809. 1st. Edn. 4to. 11 engraved plts., some slight spotting, orig. bds., spine worn; title inscr. 'Alexander Boswell Esq with the Author's Compliments'. (S. Dec.20; 893)
Henderson. £140

COCK, S.
- **The Narrative of Robert Adams ... who was Wrecked on the Western Coast of Africa.** 1816. 4to. Bds., unc., defect. (P. Feb.16; 113) £50

COCKAYNE, Sir Edward
- **The Complete Peerage.** Ed.:- Vicary Gibbs. L., 1910-53. 2nd. Edn. 13 vols. only (of 14, lacks Vol. XII pt. 2). 4to. Orig. buckram gt., partly unc. (C. Nov.9; 54) *Laywood.* £550

COCKBURN, Lieut.-Gen. Sir George
- **A Voyage to Cadiz & Gibralter.** L., 1815. 1st. Edn. 2 vols. Engraved titles, 6 maps or plans, 23 hand-cold. aquatint plts., captions cropped, spotted, Vol.2 stained, cf. gt. by Asprey, stain on 1 cover. spines discold. (S. Mar.20; 760) *Whiteson.* £95
- - **Anr. Copy.** 2 vols. Spotted, orig. cl.-bkd. bds., rubbed. (BBA. Jun.14; 310) *Orssich.* £90
- - **Anr. Copy.** 2 vols. 2 engraved titles, 6 maps &

plans, 23 aquatint plts. only (lacks plt. 8, but with dupl. of plt. 22), most hand-cold., some light spotting, cont. cl.-bkd. bds. (CSK. Sep.30; 70) £75

COCKBURN, Maj. James Pattison
– Swiss Scenery. L., 1820. Lge. 8vo. Engraved title with vig., 60 engraved views, 1st. plt. creased & torn in inner margin, a few plts. with imprints shaved, cont. russ., jnts. brkn. (S. Dec.1; 331)
Walford. £280
– – Anr. Copy. 4to. Steel engraved title with vig., end vig., 60 steel-engraved plts., some pp. with offset, 1 plt. torn & loose, cont. linen gt., covers loose, slightly rubbed & bumped, upr. end-paper loose. (HK. May 15; 1090) DM 1,500
– Views to illustrate the Route of Mont Cenis. Ill.:– C. Hullmandel after Cockburn. L., 1822. Fo. 38 (of 50) & 7 supp. litho. plts., lr. margin at beginning stained, orig. bds., hf. leath. spine, defect., upr. cover loose. (R. Oct.13; 3136) DM 2,200

COCKS, Ch. & Feret, Edouard
– Bordeaux & its Wines. Paris & Bordeaux, 1883. 1 map torn, rather browned, orig. cl., worn, spine detchd.; inscf. by Feret to Sir Joseph Renals. (BBA. Aug.18; 118) *Price.* £65
– Bordeaux und seine Weine nach Ihren Lagen und Klasson geordnet. Trans.:– P. Wendt. Stettin-Bordeaux, 1893. *1st. German Edn.* Orig. linen. (D. Nov.24; 4127) DM 1,000

COCKX-INDESTEGE, E. & Glorieux, G.
– Belgica Typographica 1541-1600. Catalogus Librorum Impressorum ab Anno 1541-1600 in Regionibus quae nunc Regni Belgarum Partes sunt. Nieuwkoop, 1968-80. 2 vols. 4to. Cl. (VS. Dec.7; 246) Fls. 550

COCLES, Bart. della Rocca
[–] Phisonomei. [Strassburg?], 1541. 4to. Title verso with old MS. note, some old MS. marginalia, slightly browned & spotted thro.-out, last 2, ll. with defects. reprd., mod. mor., blind- & gold-tooled, s.-c. (D. Nov.23; 542) DM 2,600

COCTEAU, Jean
– L'Ange Heurtebise. Paris, 1925. *(350) with a Rayograph & 12 orig. watercolours by H. Mohr. (250) on velin d'Arches à la cuve.* Fo. Col. onlays, mor. doubls. & end-papers, by Myria, some scuffing; pres. copy from Mohr to Comtesse Barbey de Jumilhoc, with bkplt. (SPB. Dec.13; 795) $425
– – Anr. Copy. Fo. Minor dampstain in lr. margin of gravure, unsewn as iss. in orig. ptd. wraps., soiled & stained. (SG. May 10; 87) $375
– Dessins. Paris, 1923. *Orig. Edn. 1st. Printing. (50) on vell. pur fil, hors commerce.* 4to. Orig. ill., autograph dedication sigd. by author, sewed, wrap. a little worn. (HD. Mar.14; 97) Frs. 3,500
– – Anr. Edn. 1923. *Orig. Edn. 1st. Printing of ills. (100) on Madagascar with drawing & author's annot. on end-paper.* 4to. Sewed. (HD. May 3; 230) Frs. 1,100
– Le Livre Blanc. Paris, 1930. *Orig. Edn. 1st. Ill. Edn. (22) hors-commerce, lettered, on vell. d'Arches.* 4to. Autograph dedication sigd. from author, lge. orig. pen ill. & 17 ills., sewed, box. (HD. Mar.14; 98) Frs. 10,100
– – Anr. Edn. Paris, 1930. *(380) on Arches.* 4to. Hand-cold., some spotting, orig. wraps., cl.-bkd. bd. folder, s.-c. defect. (BBA. Jun.14; 197)
Sims, Reed & Fogg. £300
– Le Mystère de Jean l'Oiseleur. Monologue. Paris, 1925. *Orig. Edn. (142) numbered & with paraph by author.* 4to. This copy not for sale, 31 drawings, leaves, ill. corrugated card. box. (HD. Nov.29; 130t) Frs. 3,000
– Le Mystère Laic. Ill.:– G. Chirico. Paris, 1927. *(10) on Japan Imperial.* 4to. 2 separate sigd. orig. etchings, orig. sewed; 1 orig. ill. on hf.-title with author's MS. dedication to Maurice Sachs & sig. of author & artist (Paris, Juin 1928). (GB. Nov.5; 2345) DM 10,000
– – Anr. Edn. Ill.:– Giorgio de Chirico. Paris, 1928. Sm. 8vo. On Rives, sewed. (SM. Mar.7; 2102) Frs. 1,500
– – Anr. Edn. Ill.:– Giorgio de Chirico. Paris, [1928]. *1st. Edn. Ltd. Iss.* Orig. wraps. (GB. May 5; 2279) DM 4000
– Renaud et Armide, Tragédie. Paris, 1943. *Orig. Edn. (121) numbered, not for sale, on chestnut*

wood. 12mo. Sewed; hf.-title decor. with drawing by author & dedication to 'Hubert', 1943. (SM. Mar.7; 2103) Frs. 1,000
– – Anr. Edn. Ill.:– C. Bérard. Paris, 1945. *(355) on vell. de Rives.* 4to. Sewed, box. (HD. Jan.26; 80) Frs. 1,100

See– ALEXANDRE, Arsène & Cocteau, Jean
See– LHOTE, André & Cocteau, Jean

CODDING, I.
– A Republican Manual for the Campaign ... Princeton, n.d. *1st. Edn.* Orig. ptd. wraps., minor chipping, light soiling of upr. wrap., hf. mor. box; William Harrison Lambert copy. (LH. Apr.15; 337) $3,100

CODE D'INSTRUCTION CRIMINELLE
Paris, 1810. *Orig. Edn.* 4to. Cf. gt. by Meslant, spine decor. (HD. May 4; 231) Frs. 10,200

CODE PENAL
Paris, 1810. *Orig. Edn.* 4to. Cf. gt. by Meslant, spine decor. (HD. May 4; 232) Frs. 11,100

CODET, Louis
– La Petite Chiquette. Ill.:– Henri Mirande. 1932. *(175) numbered on vell.* Sigd. by artist, wrap., box, with 4 orig. pencil ills. (HD. Mar.14; 99) Frs. 1,300

CODEX BARBERINI
– The Badianus Manuscript. Trans.:– E.W. Emmart. Balt., 1940. 4to. Orig. cl. (BBA. Mar.7; 344) *K. Gregory.* £65

CODEX SINAITICUS PETROPOLITANUS
Ed.:– Kirsopp Lake. Oxford, 1911. Lge. 4to. Cont. hf. mor. (S. May 1; 383) *Smith.* £500

CODICE DE DRESDEN: Manuscrito Pictorico Ritual Maya
Mexico, 1947. *(50) numbered & initialled by publisher.* Tall 8vo. Hand-cold. thro.-out, accordion-folding into leath. covers, hf. leath. s.-c. (SG. Oct.20; 216) $700

CODRINGTON, Kenneth de Burgh
– Ancient India, from the Earliest Times to the Gupta. Preface:– William Pothenstein. L., 1926. Tall fo. 76 photo. plts., ex-liby., cl. (SG. May 3; 97) $140

COEHORN, M. V.
– Neuer Vestungs-Ball. Wesel, 1705. *1st. German Edn.* 4to. Lightly browned, cont. bds. (R. Oct.12; 2276) DM 1,000

COELUM PHILOSOPHORUM, seu Secreta Naturae ...
Paris, 1544. Wormed thro.-out, minor repairs, later cf. gt. (TA. Sep.15; 423) £130

COFFEY, Brian
– Death of Hektor. Ill.:– Stanley W. Hayter. [Guildford], Circle Pr., 1979. *1st. Edn. (300) numbered sigd. by author & artist.* Fo. Each print numbered & sigd. in pencil by artist, unsewn loose folded sheets, as iss., untrimmed, in orig. cl.-covered interlocking fold-down box, & orig. cl.-covered s.-c., all in orig. card. shipping box. (HA. Feb.24; 227) $225

COGLER, Joh.
– Imagines Elegantissimae qvae Mvltvm Lvcis ad Intelligendos Doctrinae Christianae Locos adferre possunt, Collectae, partim ex Praelectronibus D. Ph. Melanthonis, partim ex Scriptis Patrum . Trans.:– Preface:– D.G. Maioris. Wittenbreg, 1560. Title stpd. & lightly browned, lack ll. with sm. repair, 19th. C. bds. (HK. Nov.8; 143) DM 420

COHEN, Abraham
– Kehunat Abraham. Venice, 1719. *1st. Edn.* 5 pts. in 1 vol. 4to. 5 hf.-titles, lacks port., 2nd. title mntd., inner margins of 1st. 3 ll. strengthened, owners' sigs. on fly-lf. & title, vell., slightly worn. (S. Oct.24; 135) *Agassi.* £200

COHEN, Henry
– Guide de l'Amateur de livres à Gravures du XVIIe Siècle. Paris, 1886. *Ltd. Edn.* Hf.-title, last 4 advt. ll., cont. cl., soiled. (BBA. Mar.7; 316) *D. Lomax.* £50

COHEN, Mordecai, of Safed
– Siftei Cohen. Venice, 1603. *1st. Edn.* Fo. Mispaginated, stained & soiled, creased, old blind-tooled leath., slightly worn, lacks clasps. (S. Oct.24; 138) *Ludmir.* £320

COHEN, Tuvia
– Maase Tuvia. Venice, 1708. *1st. Edn.* 3 pts. in 1 vol. 4to. With 'Noi Reformatori' (often missing), 2nd. lf. from anr. copy, 1 lf. stained & reprd., some other staining, cl. (S. Oct.24; 139) *Jansen.* £1,200
– – Anr. Copy. 3 pts. in 1 vol. 4to. 'Noi Reformatori' at end as called for, slight staining to a few ll., roan-bkd. bds., rubbed. (SPB. Feb.1; 36) $3,250
– – Anr. Copy. 3 pts. in 1 vol. 4to. Title remargined without loss, 2 ll. supplied from anr. copy, minor staining & margin worning not affecting text, early cf., worn, loose, lacks spine. (SG. Feb.2; 167) $2,000

COHN, Albert M.
– George Cruikshank, A Catalogue Raisonné. Ill.:– George Cruikshank. L., 1924. *(500) numbered.* Lge. 4to. Orig. cl., lightly soiled. (CSK. Feb.24; 63) £160

COI, Giovanni
[–] Ragionamento intorno ai fiumi del Veronese, Polesine, e Padovano. Padova, 1777. 4to. 1 map with sm. reprd. tear, some light staining, cont. bds. (SI. Dec.15; 149) Lire 250,000

COIGNET, Capt.
– Cahiers (1776-1850) Publiés d'après le Manuscrit Original par Loredan Larchey. Ill.:– J. Le Blant. Paris, 1896. *(10) on japan, with orig. watercolour & suite of plts.* 4to. Mod. hf. chagrin. (HD. Jan.27; 17) Frs. 1,550

COKAYNE, Sir Edward
See– COCKAYNE, Sir Edward

COKE, Edward
– The First Part of the Institutes of the Laws of England. L., 1664. *6th. Edn.* Fo. Portion of title margin torn off, table torn, few margin dampstains, margin ink notes, cf., covers peeling. (SG. Oct.27; 183) $200
– The First [Second; Third; Fourth] Parts of the Institutes of the Lawes of England. L., 1629-69. *1st. Edn. of Vol. 1, 3rd. Edn. of Vol. 2, 4th. Edn. of Vols. 3 & 4.* 4 vols. in 3. Fo. Engraved port. in Vol. 2 & 3 only, Vol. 1 with last errata ll., but lacks 1st. (? blank), Vol. 2 with blank f. 524 but lacks 1st. (? blank), last blank lf. in Vol. 3, but lacking in Vol. 4, many ll. browned & soiled, some sm. tears in text, with loss on f. 324 in Vol. 2 & B1 in Vol. 3, some marginalia, 19th. C. pig. worn, covers detchd., lacks 2. [STC 15784; Wing C4950; 4963; 4931] (BBA. May 3; 108) *White.* £400

COKE, Henry J.
– A Ride over the Rocky Mountains to Oregon & California. 1852. *1st. Edn.* Hf. cf., soiled. (P. Dec.8; 330) *Kentish.* £70

COKE, Thomas
– A History of the West Indies ... L'pool., 1808, L., 1810-11. *1st. Edns.* 3 vols. Orig. two-tone bds., unc., brkn. (SG. Nov.3; 43) $600
– – Anr. Edn. L'pool., 1808-11. 3 vols. Folding map hand-cold., orig. bds., untrimmed, soiled, some wear to spines. (TA. Jul.19; 14) £125

COLANGE, Leo de
– The Picturesque World. Boston, 1878. 2 vols. Fo. Browned & lightly foxed, orig. hf. leath. gt., very bumped & worn. (HK. Nov.8; 959) DM 1,000
– Voyages & travels or Scenes in Many Lands. Boston, 1887. 2 vols. Lge. 4to. Orig. linen, col. & gold-tooled, lightly bumped. (HK. Nov.8; 960) DM 850
– – Anr. Edn. Boston, [1887]. 4to. 73 views on 52 steel-engraved plts., 6 plts. in heliogravure, some foxing, cont. hf. leath., very rubbed. (R. Oct.12; 2355) DM 800
– – Anr. Copy. 2 vols. 4to. Hf. leath., very rubbed. (R. Apr.4; 2186) DM 650

COLAS, René
- Bibliographie Générale du Costume et de la Mode. Paris, 1933. (1000) numbered. 2 vols. Lge. 8vo. Unopened, disbnd. (SG. Jan.5; 102) $130
- - Anr. Edn. N.Y., 1969. Reprint. 2 vols. Tall 8vo. Orig. cl. (TA. Dec.15; 392)   £70

COLDEN, Cadwallader, 1688-1776
- The History of the Five Indian Nations of Canada, which are dependent on the Province of New York. L., 1747. 1st. Engl. Edn. 2 pts. in 1 vol. Folding engraved map, cont. cf., rebkd.; Kimbolton Castle copy with shelf-label. [Sabin 14273] (S. May 22; 312)   Sawyer. £280
- - Anr. Copy. 2 pts. Cont. cf., light wear at extremities; the Rt. Hon. Visc. Eccles copy. [Sabin 14273] (CNY. Nov.18; 71) $300
- - Anr. Edn. 1750. 2 pts. in 1 vol. Folding engraved map, advt. lf. facing title, some slight discolouration, cont. cf., rebkd. (S. May 22; 313)   Quaritch. £160

COLE, Sir Christopher
[-] Illustrative Account of ... the Capture of the Island of Banda. [L., 1811]. Ob. fo. 1 lf. ptd. text & 2 plts., margin wear, loose (as iss.?). (SG. Sep.22; 97) $425

COLE, George Watson
- A Catalogue of Books Relating to the Discovery & Early History of North & South America Forming a Part of the Library of E.D. Church. N.Y., 1951. 5 vols. Cl., light wear. (RO. Dec.11; 78) $275

COLEBROOK, Henry Thomas
[-] Remarks on the Present State of the Husbandry & Commerce of Bengal. Calcutta, 1795. 1st. Edn. 4to. 3 letters on title rubbed, cont. hf. cf.; Northwick Liby. bkplt. (C. Nov.9; 55)   Ad Orientem. £550

COLECCIÓN DE CRONICAS ESPAÑOLAS
See— CARRIAZO, Juan de Mata

COLEMAN, Charles
- A Series of Subjects Peculiar to the Campagna of Rome & Pontine Marshes. Rome, 1850. Fo. 53 etched plts., cont. hf. vell.; inscr. by E.J. Sartoris. (SKC. Nov.18; 2004)   £200

COLEMAN, Edward
- Observations on the Structure, Oeconomy, & Diseases of the Foot of the Horse. L., 1798-1802. Vol. 1; 2nd. Edn. 2 vols. 4to. 38 engraved plts., including 15 hand-cold., hf.-title in Vol. I, lacking in Vol. II, errata slip pasted on last lf., some ll. browned, cont. hf. cf., rebkd. & reprd., rubbed; James Lidderdale bkplt. (BBA. Nov.30; 94)   Comben. £130

COLERIDGE, Samuel Taylor
- La Chanson du Vieux Marin. Trans.:– Auguste Barbier. Ill.:– G. Doré. Paris, 1877. Fo. Publisher's buckram, special tool decor. (HD. Dec.1; 45)   Frs. 2,000
- - Anr. Copy. Publisher's deocr. buckram. (HD. Dec.1; 66)   Frs. 1,100
- Christabel: Kubla Khan, a Vision: The Pains of Sleep. L., 1816. 1st. Edn. Hf.-title, pol. cf. gt., by Riviere; Frederic Dannay copy. (CNY. Dec.16; 78) $500
- Kubla Khan. Ill.:– Jessica Mycroft. 1978. (50) numbered. Fo. Orig. cl. portfo., unbnd. as iss. (CSK. Jun.15; 158)   £55
- The Literary Remains. Ed.:– Henry Nelson Coleridge. L., 1836-39. 1st. Edn. 4 vols. Lacks hf.-titles, cont. hf. cf. gt., rubbed. (SG. Mar.15; 98) $100
- On the Constitution of the Church & State, according to the Idea of Each; with Aids toward a Right Judgement on the Late Catholic Bill. L., 1930. 1st. Edn. On laid paper, orig. paper-bkd. bds., untrimmed, some rubbing, spine ends chipped with some chipping to label, in mor. & cl. case, cl. inner protective sleeve, later bkplt. (HA. Feb.24; 188) $120
- The Plot Discovered. Bristol, 1795. 1st. Edn. Some spots & stains, orig. ptd. wraps., unopened, unc., slightly dust soiled, mod. red lev. mor.-bkd. box. (S. Dec.8; 40)   Quaritch. £1,050
- Poems Chosen out of the Works of ... L., Kelms. Pr., 1896. (300). Woodcut title, initials &

decoration, vell., ties, s.-c. (P. May 17; 58)   Henderson. £270
- - Anr. Copy. Orig. limp vell., unc., soiled, silk ties. (S. Nov.22; 292a)   Quaritch. £240
- Poems on Various Subjects. L., 1796. 1st. Edn. Hf.-title & advt. lf. at end in ptd. facs., late 19th. C. lev. mor. by Rivière; bkplt. of T.J. Wise. (S. Dec.8; 41)   Sotheran. £340
- - Anr. Copy. Hf.-title, 2 ll. errata & advts. [With:] COLERIDGE, Samuel Taylor, Lamb, Charles & Lloyd, Charles – Poems. Bristol & L., 1797. 2nd. Edn. Together 2 vols. Sm. 8vo. Unif. spr. cf. gt. by F. Bedford; inscr. of George Daniel stating vols. had belonged to Charles Lamb, Frederic Dannay copies, w.a.f. (CNA. Dec.16; 77) $1,300
- The Rime of the Ancient Mariner. Ill.:– Gustave Doré. N.Y., 1877. 1st. Amer. Edn. Tall fo. Gold-stpd. cl., minor wear, publisher's box, worn; Ken Leach coll. (RO. Jun.10; 9) $400
- - Anr. Edn. L., Essex House Pr., 1903. (150) on vell. Vell., blind-stpd. on upr. cover, spine gt., minor wear. (SG. Nov.3; 45) $300
- - Anr. Edn. Ill.:– Willy Pogany. L., ca. 1910. 4to. Some light soiling, orig. gt.- & col.-stpd. cl., corners bumped, 1 showing, spine darkening, sm. spots & ink inscr. to decor. front free end-paper. (CBA. Aug.21; 460) $170
- Sibylline Leaves. 1817. 1st. Edn. Lacks hf.-title, some ll. slightly spotted, cont. cf. by F. Thomas, Truro, with his ticket, rebkd. (BBA. Oct.27; 47)   Quaritch. £100
- Poetical & Dramatic Works. L., ca. 1855. 12mo. Cont. red gt.-tooled mor., fore-e. pntg. (SG. Nov.17; 225) $175
See— WORDSWORTH, William & Coleridge, Samuel Taylor

COLERIDGE, Samuel Taylor & Southey, Robert
- Omniana or Horae Otiosores. L., 1812. 1st. Edn. 2 vols. Hf.-title in Vol. 1, hf. cf., worn, 1 cover loose; Dr. Walter Pagel copy. (S. Feb.7; 83)   Bickersteth. £60

COLERERUS or COLER, Johannes, of Parchina
- Oeconomia oder Haussbuch ... Wittenb., 1610-12. Pts. 1-3 (of 6) in 1 vol. 4to. 1st. 4 ll. part 1 creased, 2 pp. pt. 2 with bkd. tear, browned & slightly foxed thro.-out, cont. vell., partly defect., upr. cover vell. removed, lacks 4 ties. (HK. May 16; 1528)   DM 1,100
- Oeconomia Ruralis et Domestica. [Deutsch]. Mainz, 1651. 2 pts. in 1 vol. Fo. 1st. pt. lacks title & 18 pp., pt. 2 lacks 13 pp., browned & stained, some reprd. margin defects. with some text loss, 19th. C. hf. leath., bumped, cover defect. (HK. Nov.9; 1739)   DM 620

COLETTE, Sidonie Gabrielle
- Claudine à l'Ecole; Claudine à Paris; Claudine en Menage; Claudine s'en va. Ill.:– Grau Sala. Paris, 1947. (10) numbered on vell. de Rives. Together 4 vols. Sm. 4to. Sewed, pict. wraps., box; 4 orig. aquatints sigd. by artist. (HD. Dec.16; 103)   Frs. 4,800
- - Anr. Edn. Ill.:– Charles Laborde. Paris, 1924-25. Ltd. Edns., numbered. Together 4 vols. 4to. Ills. cold. through stencils, cont. hf. mor., orig. wraps. bnd. in. (S. Dec.20; 499)   Greenwood. £80
- L'Envers du Music-Hall. Ill.:– Louis Macard after Edouard Chimot. Paris, 1937. (20) on japon nacré with suite in black & orig. drawing. Without copper plt., pink mor. by Semet & Plumelle, richly decor., silk end-ll., wrap. preserved, spine slightly faded, s.-c.; 7 trial plts. added. (HD. Jun.13; 23)   Frs. 7,500
- Flore et Pomone. Ill.:– Pierre Laprade. Paris, 1943. Orig. Edn. (41) on vergé. 4to. Orig. ill. ink heightened, suite in black of ills., hf. mor., mosaic decor., wrap. & spine, unc., by Marot-Rodde. (HD. Dec.16; 104)   Frs. 3,200
- Gigi. Ill.:– Mariette Lydis. Paris, 1948. (315). (100) on Arches. Fo. Leaves, box. (HD. Nov.17; 102)   Frs. 2,800
- L'Ingénue Libertine. Ill.:– Louis Icart. Paris, 1926. (15) on Hollande hors commerce. 4to. Sewed. (HD. Mar.14; 101)   Frs. 4,100
- La Paix chez les Bêtes. Ill.:– A. Roubille. Paris, 1926. (39) on japan with suite on old japan & suite in cols. on japon impérial. Sm. 4to. Sewed. (HD. Jun.13; 118)   Frs. 1,000

- Paradis Terrestes. Ill.:– Jouve. Lausanne, 1932. Orig. Edn. 2 vols. 4to. 51 plts. only, leaves, box; artist's pres. copy to René Guy, extra-ill. with 2 suites (1 in black & 1 in cols.). (HD. Jun.13; 24)   Frs. 7,000
- Pour un Herbier. Ill.:– Raoul Dufy. Paris, 1951. (241). (7) numbered with orig. watercol. by Dufy. 4to. Loose as iss. in orig. wraps., orig. bd. folder, s.-c. (BBA. Jun.14; 209)   Quaritch. £1,000
- La Treille Muscate. Ill.:– Terechkovitch. Paris, 1961. 4to. 14 orig. lithos., leaves, box (faded); with prospectus. (HD. Jun.13; 24)   Frs. 2,500
- La Vagabonde. Ill.:– Vertès. Paris, 1927. (305). (15) on japon impérial with 3 suites of ills. & 1 proof of rejected plts. 4to. Sewed, box. (HD. May 4; 233)   Frs. 5,500

COLETTI, Luigi
- La Camera degli Sposi del Mantegna a Mantova. Milano, 1959. Fo. 92 figures & 30 cold. plts., publishers cl. (CR. Jun.6; 131)   Lire 200,000

COLIN, Paul
- La Peinture Belge depuis 1830. Bruxelles, 1930. (1000), not for sale. 4to. Publisher's cl. (LM. Mar.3; 61)   B. Frs. 14,000

COLLECTIO PISAURENSIS Omnium Poematum, Carminum, Fragmentorum Latinorum
1766. 6 vols. 4to. Cont. marb. cf., decor. spines. (HD. Sep.22; 221)   Frs. 1,150

COLLECTION COMPLETE DES TABLEAUX HISTORIQUES DE LA REVOLUTION FRANCAISE
Ill.:– after Ozanne, Sweebach, & Duplessis-Berteaux (plts.); after Mme Vigée-Lebrun, Gérard, & others (ports.). Paris, 1798-1804. 3 vols. Fo. 3 frontis., 144 plts., cont. bds. (HD. Mar.9; 130)   Frs. 5,800

COLLECTION DES MORALISTES ANCIENS
Paris, 1782-95. 20 vols. in 16. 16mo. On vell., lacks the 'La Morale de Jesus-Christ', but completed by F. Noel's 2 vol. 'Livres Classiques de l'Empire de la Chine', 1784, cont. red mor. gt., decor. spines, inner roll-stp. (HD. Sep.22; 222)   Frs. 4,000

COLLECTION OF RIGHT MERRIE GARLANDS for North Country Anglers
Ill.:– Thomas Bewick & others. Newcastle, 1836. Cont. cl., unc.; sig. of John Carr, of Newcastle, bkplts. of Rev. Thomas Hugo, Rev. John Bigge & Edward E. Bigge. (C. Mar.14; 152)   Cavendish. £180

COLLECTION UNIVERSELLE DES MEMOIRES Particuliers Relatifs à 'Histoire de France
L. & Paris, 1785-1807. 70 vols. Cont. cf., rubbed. (CSK. Jun.1; 191)   £260

COLLECTOR, The: a Monthly Journal devoted to Autographs
Ed.:– W.R. Benjamin. N.Y., Sep. 1887-Aug. 1888. Vol. I. Tall 8vo. Hf. leath. (SG. Aug.4; 26) $100

COLLEY, Richard, Marquis Wellesley
See— WELLESLEY, Richard Colley, Marquis

COLLIER, J.
See— FENNING, Daniel & Collier, J.

COLLIER, Jane
[-] An Essay on the Art of Ingeniously Tormenting. 1753. 1st. Edn. Orig. cf. gt. (P. Jul.5; 228)   £55

COLLIER, Jeremy
- A Short View of the Immorality & Profaneness of the English Stage ... L., 1698. 2nd. Edn. 1 gathering misbnd., title & last lf. a little stained, cont. cf., spine gt. [Wing C5264] (BBA. May 3; 178)   Armstrong. £60

COLLIER, John 'Tim Bobbin'
- The Passions, humourously delineated. L., 1846. Cut to plt. margin at sides in places, 2 plts. with slight margin slits, loose, some offsetting from plts. to facing text p., light browning, cont. hf. leath. (R. Oct.12; 2143)   DM 3,400

COLLIER, John Payne
[-] **Punch & Judy.** Ill.:– George Cruikshank. L., 1828. *1st. Edn.* Frontis., 23 etched plts., all hand-cold., some spotting, 1 text lf. torn & reprd., a few sm. margin repairs, cf. gt. (SG. Dec.8; 128) $300

COLLIER, V.W.F.
– **Dogs of China & Japan in Nature & Art.** 1921. Fo. No bdg. stated; inscr. by author. (WW. Nov.23; 114) £75

COLLIER'S ENCYCLOPAEDIA
1980. 24 vols. & yearbook for 1981. 4to. Orig. imitation mor. gt. (TA. May 17; 537) £80

COLLINGNON, Maxine
– **Le Parthenon: l'Histoire l'Architecture et la Sculpture.** Ill.:– Frederic Boissonnas & W.A. Mansell & Co. Paris, [1912]. 2 vols. Atlas fo. 136 photo. plts., ex-liby., mor. spines & tips. (SG. May 3; 98) $325

COLLINGRIDGE, George
– **The Discovery of Australia** ... Sydney, 1895. A little staining, liby. stp. on title-p., recased in orig. cl. (KH. Nov.9; 568) Aus. $350
– – **Anr. Copy.** Orig. cl., some slight wear; sig. of W.B. Alexander. (JL. Mar.25; 575) Aus. $250

COLLINS, Arthur
– **The Peerage of England.** 1735. 4 vols. Cont. cf. gt., lacks spine labels; the Hinton House copy. (LC. Oct.13; 424) £90
– – **Anr. Edn.** 1779-84. 9 vols., including Supp. Cf. gt., hinges reprd. (P. Jun.7; 80) £70

COLLINS, David
– **An Account of the English Colony in New South Wales ... to which are added some particulars of New Zealand.** Ill.:– J. Heath, W. Lowry, & J. Neagle. L., 1798. *1st. Edn.* 4to. Engraved frontis. map, folding engraved chart, 18 engraved plts., short tear at corner of folding map, frontis. map slightly affected in blank area by sig. on verse, cont. spr. cf., rebkd. preserving orig. spine. (C. Jun.27; 84) *Remington.* £400
– – **Anr. Edn.** L., 1798-1802. *1st. Edn.* 2 vols. 4to. 2 charts, folding map, 23 engraved plts., hf.-titles, list of engrs. at end of each vol., top edge of 2 plts. very slightly cropped, staining to 1 plt., A1 in Vol. 1 with slight margin tear, not affecting text, cont. spr. cf., spines rubbed; Samuel Enderby bkplt. (LC. Oct.13; 251) £4,200
– – **Anr. Copy.** 2 vols. 4to. Bnd. without lf.-title Vol. II, slight foxing or offsetting, early mott. cf., rebkd. (KH. Nov.9; 569) Aus.$4,800
– – **Anr. Copy.** 2 vols. 4to. 26 engraved charts & plts., plts. in Vol. 1 trimmed on 1 margin, 1 in Vol. 2 trimmed & laid down, 2 plts. reinforced along 1 margin, title to Vol. 2 offset, sig. at head of titles, tree cf., 1 spine reinforced. (CA. Apr.3; 33) Aus. $4,000
– – **Anr. Edn.** L., 1804. *2nd. Edn.* 4to. Port.-frontis., 2 maps (1 folding), 23 engraved plts., text ill., 19th. C. owner's sig. on title, early pol. hf. cf. gt., covers detchd. (SG. Apr.26; 46) $800
– – **Anr. Copy.** 4to. 2 folding maps, 24 engraved plts., title soiled, some slight foxing on some plts., pol. cf. gt., rebkd. (CA. Apr.3; 32) Aus. $1,200
– – **Anr. Edn.** 1971. 2 vols. No bdg. stated. (JL. Jun.24; 52) Aus. $150
– – **Anr. Copy.** 2 vols. 4to. Bdg. not stated. (KH. May 1; 173) Aus. $100

COLLINS, Capt. Greenville
– **Great Britain's Coasting Pilot.** 1744. Fo. Engraved frontis., 49 charts & plts. (2 folding), 1 with sm. tears, cl., defect. (P. Jan.12; 324) *Burgess.* £1,750
– – **Anr. Edn.** 1753. 2 pts. in 1 vol. Fo. Engraved frontis., 45 (of 49) engraved charts (most double., 4 folding), slight stains, cont. cf., worn. (SKC. Nov.18; 2059) £1,320

COLLINS, Maurice
– **Quest for Sita.** Ill.:– Mervyn Peake. 1946. *(500).* 4to. Orig. cl., partly untrimmed, d.-w. torn. (TA. Aug.18; 252) £50

COLLINS, Samuel, 1619-70
[-] **Relation Curieuse de L'Estat Présent de la Russia.** Paris, 1679. A few tears, some spotting, cf., rubbed. (P. Jan.12; 211) *Anderson.* £65

COLLINS, William
– **Odes on Several Descriptive & Allegoric Subjects.** L., 1747. *1st. Edn.* Engraved vig. on title, errata, mor. gt. by Bedford; bkplt. of Anne, Countess Dowager of Galloway. (SPB. May 16; 33) $2,000

COLLINS, William Wilkie
– **After Dark.** 1856. *1st. Edn.* 2 vols. in 1. Hf.-titles, hf. mor. gt.; from Norman Tarbolton liby. (P. Apr.12; 18) *Jarndyce.* £130
– **Antonina; or, the Fall of Rome.** L., 1850. *1st. Edn.* 3 vols. Orig. embossed cl., spines discold., corners bumped. (LH. Sep.25; 516) $280
– **The Queen of Hearts.** L., 1859. *1st. Edn.* 3 vols. Lacks advts., a few sigs. sprung, orig. cl. by Leighton, Son & Hodge (ticket in Vol. 1), worn. (RO. Apr.23; 38) $900
– **The Woman in White.** 1860. *1st. Engl. Edn.* 3 vols. Sadleir 605a, but without inserted publisher's catalogue, cont. hf. cf. gt. (BBA. Sep.29; 209) *Jarndyce.* £150
– – **Anr. Copy.** 3 vols. Pol. cf. gt., by Riviere, Fred A. Berne copy. (SPB. May 16; 203) $375
See— DICKENS, Charles & Collins, William Wilkie

COLLINSON, Rev. John
– **The History & Antiquities of the County of Somerset.** Bath, 1791. *[1st. Edn.].* 3 vols. 4to. Cont. pol. cf. gt., 1 cover detchd. (SKC. Mar.9; 1973) £160
– – **Anr. Copy.** 3 vols. 4to. Folding map (repairs in folds), 40 engraved plts. & letterpress ill. of Frome School, some ll. spotted, cf. gt., some spines chipped, 1 cover detchd. (LC. Mar.1; 207) £80
– – **Anr. Edn.** Bath, 1791, 1898. 3 vols. & Index vol. 4to. Folding map, 40 plts., list of subscribers, 2 tears to folding map, hf. mor. gt., Index in cl., worn. (P. Jun.7; 289) £90

COLLIVER, E.J. & Richardson, B.H.
– **The Forty-Third: The Story & Official History of the 43rd Battalion, A.I.F.** Adelaide, 1920. Orig. cl., d.-w. (KH. Nov.9; 571) Aus. $130

COLLMAN, Herbert L.
– **Ballads & Broadsides Chiefly of the Elizabethan Period.** Roxb. Cl., 1912. Fo. Orig. hf. mor. (BBA. Nov.10; 50) *Maggs.* £120
– – **Anr. Copy.** Fo. Orig. mor.-bkd. cl. (BBA. Aug.18; 251) *Forster.* £110
– – **Anr. Edn.** Oxford, Roxb. Cl., 1912. *(40).* Sm. Fo. 2 ll. loose, hf. mor., worn. (SG. Jan.5; 277) $150

COLLN, G. Fr. W. v.
[-] **Vertraute Briefe über die Inneren Verhsltnisse am Preussischen Hofe seit dem Tode Friedrichs II.** Amst. & Cölln [i.e. Leipzig], 1807-09. 6 vols. Cont. bds. (GB. Nov.3; 245) DM 1,500

COLLYER, J.J.
– **The Campaign in German South-West Africa.** Pretoria, 1937. Cl. (SSA. Sep.21; 100) R 210

COLLYER, Joseph
See— FENNING, Daniel & Collyer, Joseph

COLMENARES, Diego
– **Historia de ... Segovia ...** Madrid, 1640. *2nd. Edn.* Fo. Cf. (DS. Mar.23; 2065) Pts. 75,000

COLNETT, James
– **A Voyage to the South Atlantic & round Cape Horn into the Pacific Ocean ...** L., priv. ptd., 1798. *1st. Edn.* 4to. Engraved port., 3 plts., 6 engraved maps, 1 p. subscribers list, 2 maps with minor tears at fold, 1 with slight offsetting from text, cont. tree cf., slightly worn. [Sabin 14346] (C. Jun.27; 85) *Remington.* £1,500

COLOM, Jacob Aertz
– **De Groote Lichtende ofte Vijrighe Colom over de Zee-kusten van't Wester, Ooster, en Noorder Vaerwater.** Amst., priv. ptd., 1661. 5 pts. in 1 vol. Fo. Ptd. title with lge. engraved allegoric vig., 5 sectional titles with lge. woodcut devices (dtd.

1653), 60 engraved sea-& coastal charts covering northern & western Europe (including folding general chart, 38 double-p. sheets showing 51 subjects, & 9 full-p.), woodcut diagrams, coastal profiles & additional inset diagrammatic charts in text, 2 (1 engraved) with volvelles, at b2v & d2r respectively cont. hand-cold. thro.-out, title vig. heightened with gold, 1 or 2 minor tears without loss of engraved surface, cont. gt.-panel. vell., lge. central & corner arabesques on covers, w.a.f. (S. May 21; 142) *Traylen.* £7,800
– **Zee-Atlas ofte Werelts Water-Deel.** Amst., 1668. Engraved title, 44 folding or double-p. maps (compl. according to index), including 1 cont. outl. cold., 10 (of 12) pp. text, lr. margins of title, prelims. & 13 maps defect. & reprd., slightly affecting engraved surface of 2 maps & title, some maps without margins, folding maps partly slightly worn, some light browning & foxing. (*Bound with:*) – **Atlas ou Colom Ardante.** 1668. Engraved title & 6 pp. only. Together 2 works in 1 vol. Fo. Later hf. vell. (VG. Nov.30; 796) Fls. 15,000

COLOMBANI, P.
– **Saggio Storico del Regno di Corsica dalla Sollevazion del 1729 fino alla meta del 1768.** Venezia, 1768. 12mo. old hf. roan with mor. finish. (HD. Oct.21; 61) Frs. 3,300

COLOMBO, F.
– **Noticia hist. del Origen de la Milagross Imagen de N. Señora de los Remedios.** Madrid, 1698. Linen. (DS. Apr.27; 2053) Pts. 26,000

COLONIAL MAGAZINE & COMMERCIAL MARITIME JOURNAL
Ed.:– R. Montgomery Martin. L., 1840-41. Vols. 1-4. Old hf. cf., 1 vol. not unif. (KH. Nov.9; 653) Aus. $160

COLONNA, F.
– **Minus Cognitarum Plantarum Prima, & Secunda Pars Purpura.** Rome, 1616. *2nd. Edn.* 4to. Lightly browned, some slight foxing & staining, 18th. C. red cf., gt., slightly spotted, spine restored; Hauswedell coll. (H. May 24; 858) DM 1,500
[-] **Le Tableau des Riches Inventions couvertes du Voile des Feintes Amoureuses, qui sont representeés dans le songe de Poliphile.** Ed.:– Beroalde de Verville. Paris, 1600[= after 1610]. *1st. Edn. 3rd. printing.* 4to. Copper engraved title slightly slit at foot, slightly browned thro.-out, few sm. wormholes in 2nd. hf., 1 text lf. with reprd. tear (paper fault), cont. leath., cont. style spine, corners restored. (R. Apr.3; 28) DM 1,600

COLONNA DE CESARI-ROCCA
– **Les Seigneurs d'Ornano et leurs Descendants d'après les Documents Conservés dans les Dépôts Publics et Privés de Gênes, Ajaccio, Paris, Barcelone, Pise, Venise, Rome, Vérone.** Paris, 1899. 4to. Sewed. (HD. Oct.21; 62) Frs. 3,500

COLOPHON, The
N.Y., 1930-31. *(3000).* Nos. 1-8. 4to. Decor. bds., covers to no. 1 soiled & darkening, rest soiled & darkening at edges, all but pt. 1 with orig. glassine d.-w., darkened & severely chipped. (CBA. Nov.19; 702) $225
– – **Anr. Run.** N.Y., 1930-37. Orig. Series 20 pts., New Series, 12 pts., Index Orig. Series, together 33 vols. 4to. & 8vo. Pict. bds. & cl. (SG. May 17; 65) $225
– – **Anr. Run.** N.Y., Metuchen, 1930-50; 1968. 1st. Series 20 pts., New Series 12 pts., New Graphic Series, 4 pts., The New colophon 8 pts. & vol. 3, Annual of Book-making, Index to the Original Series, Index to Later Series, together 48 vols. (Compl.run). 4to. & 8vo. Orig. decor. bds. & cl. linen; bkplts. of Lester Douglas (designed by Bruce Rogers), several letters from Elmer Adler to Douglas tipped in, & nearly compl. file of flyers, subscription notices, trial-pp. etc. (SG. Apr.26; 47) $700
– – **Anr. Run.** N.Y., [1931-]50. Orig. series: nos. 5-16, New Graphic Series: 4 pts., New Colophon: pt. 8, together 17 pts. 4to. Pict. bds. (SG. Jan.5; 103) $200
– – **Anr. Run.** N.Y., 1935-38. New Series, vols. 1-3, together 12 numbers. Tall 8vo. Pict. bds. & cl., some covers soiled. (SG. May 17; 66) $150

COLQUHOUN, Patrick
- A Treatise on the Wealth, Power, & Resources of the British Empire. 1814. *1st. Edn.* 4to. Cont. paper-bkd. bds., unc., head of spine slightly torn. (C. May 30; 145) *Jarndyce.* £420

COLTMANN, Nathaniel
See— LAURIE, Robert & Whittle, James

COLTON, George Woolworth
- Colton's General Atlas, Containing One Hundred & Eighty Steel Plate Maps & Plans. N.Y., 1860. Fo. 180 cold. engraved maps, some foxing, staining, minor tears thro.-out, ex-liby., maps unstpd., hf. leath., partially disbnd., shabby, w.a.f. (SG. Jun.7; 7) $300
-- **Anr. Edn.** N.Y., G.W. & C.B. Colton, 1871. Fo. 180 cold. engraved maps, on 119 sheets, gt.-lettered cl., leath. back, shabby. (SG. Jun.7; 6) $325

COLTON, George Woolworth & Fisher, R.S.
- Atlas of the World. N.Y., 1857. 2 vols. Fo. Litho. additional titles, 100 hand-cold. maps including 57 of the Americas, 5 double-p., 1 table, lacks map of Niagara falls, orig. mor.-bkd. cl., worn, 1 cover detchd., w.a.f. (CSK. May 4; 139a) £420

COLTON, Joseph H., Publisher
- Colton's Traveler & Tourist's Guide-Book through the United States of America & the Canadas. N.Y., 1850. *1st. Edn.* 12mo. Title-p. foxed, orig. cl. gt., spine faded; the Rt. Hon. Visc. Eccles copy. (CNY. Nov.18; 72) $280
- The Western Tourist & Emigrant's Guide. N.Y., 1850. 12mo. Folding map at end & text lightly foxed, orig. cl. gt., faded. (LH. Jan.15; 267) $150
See— JOHNSON, Alvin Jewett & Colton, Joseph H.

COLUMBO, Realdo
- De Re Anatomica libri XV. Frankfurt, 1593. Vell.; Dr. Walter Pagel copy. (S. Feb.7; 80) *Phillips.* £280

COLUMELLA, Lucius Junius Moderatus
- Les Douze Livres des Choses Rustiques. Trans.:- Claude Cotereau. Paris, 1555. *1st. Fr. Trans.* 4to. Sm. stain on 1st. 4 ll., 18th. C. cf., spine decor.; P. Guiraud ex-libris. (HD. Nov.9; 3) Frs. 5,000
- Of Husbandry. In Twelve Books: & his Book concerning Trees. 1745. *1st. Edn. in Engl.* 4to. Mott. cf., rebkd.; Dr. G.E. Fussell copy. (P. Jul.5; 54) £120
-- **Anr. Copy.** 4to. Minor worming, cont. bds., rebkd. (BBA. Jan.19; 191)
Primrose Hill Books. £65
-- **Anr. Copy.** 4to. Cont. panel. cf. (PD. May 16; 259) £58

COLUMNA, Franciscus
- Hypnerotomachia Poliphili. Venice, Aldus Manutius, Dec. 1499. Fo. Lf. m6 supplied from anr. copy?, last 1st. 4 & last 4 ll., later vell.; the Walter Goldwater copy. [BMC V, 561-2; Goff C-767] (SG. Dec.1; 111) $7,250

COLVIN, Sidney
- Early Engraving & Engravers in England. L., 1905. Fo. Orig. mor.-bkd. bds., very slightly rubbed & soiled. (S. Oct.11; 461)
Bennett & Kerr. £60

COMBE, Charles
- Nummorum Veterum Populorum et Urbium qui in Museo Gulielmi Hunter. 1782. 4to. 68 engraved plts., cont. russ. gt.; Sir Ivar Colquhoun, of Luss copy. (CE. Mar.22; 66) £120
-- **Anr. Copy.** 4to. 68 engraved plts., some ll. slightly spotted or browned, cont. russ., slightly rubbed, rebkd., preserving orig. spine. (S. May 1; 458) *Drury.* £90

COMBE, William
- The Dance of Life, a Poem. Ill.:- Thomas Rowlandson. 1817. *[1st. Edn.].* Hand-cold. aquatint frontis., additional title & 24 plts., cont. cf., rebkd. (CSK. Jul.13; 149) £240
-- **Anr. Copy.** Lge. 8vo. Later hf. lincs, lightly rubbed; collector stp. inside cover, later hf. leath., lightly rubbed. (H. May 22; 442) DM 1,500
[-] The English Dance of Death. L., 1815-16. *1st.*

Edn. in Book Form. 2 vols. Hand-cold. aquatint title, 72 plts. (*With:*) [-] **The Dance of Life.** L., 1817. *1st. Edn. in Book Form.* 1 vol. Hand-cold. aquatint title, 25 plts. Together 3 vols. Some plts. & ll. reprd., unif. later mor. gt. (S. Oct.11; 506)
Pashby. £460
-- **Anr. Edn.** Ill.:- Th. Rowlandson. L., 1815-16. *1st. Edn.* 2 vols. Lge. 8vo. Some light text browning, engraved title with old owners mark; later hf. leath., spine slightly rubbed; coll. stp. inside cover. (H. May 22; 443) DM 3,000
-- **Anr. Edn.** Ill.:- Thomas Rowlandson. L., 1815-16 [i.e. 1814-16]. *1st. Edn. 1st. Iss.*, plts. wtrmkd. *1813-14, text 1813-15.* 24 orig. pts. in 2 vols. 74 cold. aquatint plts., very light foxing & offsetting, bkplts. removed, lev. gt., gt. dentelles, by Riviere. (SG. Apr.26; 48) $850
[-] **The History of Johnny Quae Genus.** Ill.:- T. Rowlandson. L., 1822. *1st. Edn.* Text with slight offset from plts., cont. hf. leath. gt., jnts. strengthened inside & out, spine slightly split, rubbed & bumped, end-papers renewed. (HK. May 17; 2421) DM 950
[-] **A History of Madeira.** L., 1821. 4to. Title with cold. aquatint vig., 27 cold. aquatint plts., cont. embossed ribbed cl., partly unc., spine torn. (C. Mar.14; 41) *Dupont.* £320
- Journal of Sentimental Travels in the Southern Provinces of France. Ill.:- T. Rowlandson. L., 1821. *1st. Edn.* 18 cold. aquatints, cont. leath., upr. cover loose, defect. (HK. May 15; 817) DM 600
[-] **The Life, Adventures, & Opinions of George Hanger.** L., 1801. *1st. Edn.* 2 vols. Hf.-titles, advts., cont. tree cf., corners nicked. (SG. Jan.19; 155) $130
[-] **The Tour of Doctor Prosody after William Combe.** L., 1821. 20 hand-cold. engraved plts., some ll. slightly spotted or soiled, cont. cf., spine gt., rubbed. (BBA. May 23; 209) *Solomons.* £75
[-] **Tour of Doctor Syntax [1st].** 1813. 30 hand-cold. plts., some text ll. torn & soiled, cf., defect., as a coll. of plts., w.a.f. (P. Dec.8; 114) *Tzakas.* £100
-- **Anr. Edn.** Ill.:- T. Rowlandson. L., [1813]. *2nd. Edn.* Some plts. dtd. 1813, some light browning, plts. soiled & some spotting, 1 with bkd. tear, some plt. captions cut at foot, cont. leath., bumped, spine restored. (R. Oct.12; 2174) DM 450
- Tours of Doctor Syntax [1st. & 2nd.]. Ill.:- after Thomas Rowlandson. L., n.d. & 1821. 2 vols. Engraved title, 55 cold. aquatint plts., some light spotting, cont. cf., worn, w.a.f. (CSK. Feb.24; 116) £110
[-] **Tours of Doctor Syntax [1st., 2nd. & 3rd.].** Ill.:- T. Rowlandson. L., 1812-20[-21],. *1st. Edns. 1st. Issues in Book Form.* 3 vols. Cold. aquatint title in Vols. I & III, 78 aquatint plts., cold. aquatint vig. at end of Vol. III followed by 4 pp. of publisher's advts., some slight offsetting onto text, 2 ll. of Vols. II & III detchd., orig. bds., unc., 2 paper labels present, covers detchd., each vol. in lev. mor. box. (C. Nov.16; 72) *Foyles.* £1,000
-- **Anr. Edn.** Ill.:- Thomas Rowlandson. L., [1812-]20[-21]. *1st. Edns.* Together 3 vols. 2 hand-cold. aquatint titles, tail-piece & 78 plts., some light spotting & offsetting, cont. cf., gt., rebkd., corners reprd., 1 vol. with slightly variant bdg. (S. Apr.9; 207) *Dallas.* £300
-- **Anr. Edn.** Ill.:- Thomas Rowlandson. 1812-20[-21]. *2nd. Edn., 1st. Edn., 1st. Edn.* Together 3 vols. 81 hand-cold. plts., a few in Vol. 1 spotted, str.-grd. mor. gt. by Kaufmann, slightly rubbed. (SKC. Mar.9; 1813) £340
-- **Anr. Edn.** Ill.:- Rowlandson. L., 1813-20-[21]. *Vol. I: 4th. Edn., rest: 1st. Edns.* 3 vols. 2 hand-cold. aquatint titles, 78 plts., a few with slight offsetting from text, corner of 1 plt. reprd., 20th. C. hf. mor., spines gt. (S. Oct.4; 81) *Chelsea.* £360
-- **Anr. Edn.** Ill.:- Thomas Rowlandson. L., 1819-20. 3 vols. Lge. 8vo. Publisher's decor. buckram, unc. (HD. Jun.22; 71) Frs. 3,100
-- **Anr. Edn.** Ill.:- Thomas Rowlandson. [1819-]20-21. *Vol. 1: 8th. Edn., Vol. 2: 2nd. Edn., Vol. 3: 1st. Edn.* 3 vols. in 1. 80 hand-cold. plts., 1 hand-cold. vig., 19th. C. mor., gt.-decor. (SKC. Nov.18; 1830) £280
-- **Anr. Edn.** Ill.:- T. Rowlandson. L., 1820-21. *Vols. 2 & 3: 1st. Edns.* 3 vols. Slightly foxed & spotted, red leath., ca. 1860, gt. spine, cover,

inner & outer dentelle. (HK. Nov.10; 3040)
DM 900
-- **Anr. Edn.** Ill.:- Thomas Rowlandson. L., 1823-28. *4th. Edn.* 3 vols. Cont. blind-tooled linen, slightly spotted. (GB. May 4; 1227) DM 1,150
-- **Anr. Edn.** Ill.:- after Th. Rowlandson. L., 1823 [1828 vol. II]. 3 vols. 12mo. Later cf. gt., gold-tooled decor., corner fleurons, gt. inner & outer dentelle. (D. Nov.24; 2342) DM 850
-- **Anr. Edn.** Ill.:- Th. Rowlandson. L., ca. 1825. *9th. Edn.* 3 vols. Wide margin, slightly spotted, 2 plts. with sm. margin defects., 1st. plt. verso with owner's notes, linen with old cover material. (HK. Nov.10; 3041) DM 550
-- **Anr. Edn.** L., 1855. *9th. Edn.* 3 vols. 2 hand-cold. aquatint titles, 78 plts., some spotting or offsetting onto text, orig. cl., worn. (S. Dec.20; 898)
Elliot. £120
-- **Anr. Copy.** 3 vols. Tall 8vo. Vig. titles to Vols. 1 & 3, 78 hand-cold. plts., some margin spotting, orig. cl. gt., spines faded & with some wear. (TA. May 17; 646) £82
-- **Anr. Copy.** 3 vols. Minimal foxing, cont. linen gt., spine lightly faded. (GB. Nov.4; 1925)
DM 1,500
-- **Anr. Edn.** Ill.:- T. Rowlandson. L., [late 1850's]. 3 vols. Tall 8vo. 2 additional pict. titles, 78 cold. aquatint plts. (title-p. calling for 80 plts.), 2 frontis. loose, hf. cf. gt. (SG. Nov.17; 30) $110
-- **Anr. Edn.** Ill.:- Thomas Rowlandson. L., 1820-21. *5th. Edn., 2nd. Edn., 1st. Edn.* Together 3 vols. 81 hand-cold. plts., including 2 vigs., slightly soiled, a few pp. in 1st. vol. loose & torn, a few pp. in 3rd. vol. loose & 1 plt. slightly torn, cont. hf. cf., spines defect. (SKC. Mar.9; 1814) £120
-- **Anr. Edn.** N.d.-1820-21. 3 vols. 2 hand-cold. titles, 78 hand-cold. plts., cont. mor. gt., Vol. 3 upr. cover & 1st. few ll. punctured. (CSK. Aug.19; 17)
£220
-- **Anr. Edn.** Ill.:- after Rowlandson. N.d. *Vol. 1: 9th. Edn.* 3 vols. Hand-cold. additional titles to Vols. 1 & 3, 78 col. plts., panel. hf. cf. (PD. Dec.14; 327) £200
[-] **Tours of Doctor Syntax [2nd. & 3rd.].** L., 1855. *9th. Edn.* 2 vols. Hand-cold. aquatint title, 48 plts., slightly spotted & offset, orig. cl., worn. (S. Dec.20; 895) *Davidson.* £65
[-] **Tour of Doctor Syntax through London, or the Pleasures & Miseries of the Metropolis.** 1820. *1st. Edn.* Hand-cold. vig. & 19 hand-cold. plts., little spotting, hf. cf. (BBA. Jun.28; 313) *Lake.* £55
-- **Anr. Edn.** 1820. Col. frontis., vig. title, 18 col. plts., mod. qtr. mor. gt. (P. Sep.8; 269) £65

COMBE, William & Boydell, John & Josiah
- An History of the River Thames. L., 1794-96. *1st. Edn.* 2 vols. 4to. L.P., early imps. of the plts. in aquatint borders, engraved frontis. 'Tamesis', 2 double-p. engraved maps, 76 hand-cold. aquatint views, including 3 double-p. views of L. & Rochester, wtrmkd. 1794, with general titles 'An History of the Principal Rivers', dedications to Orford & the King, tables, lists of plts., cont. tree cf., covers with foliate roll-tool in greek key borders, spines similarly gt., all but 1 jnt. reprd. (C. Mar.14; 32) *Quaritch.* £5,200
-- **Anr. Copy.** 2 vols. Lge. 4to. Engraved plt. 'Tamesis', 2 double-p. maps, 76 hand-cold. aquatint plts., with general titles 'An History of the Principal Rivers', cont. hf. russ., spines gt. (C. Nov.16; 3)
Maggs. £3,200
-- **Anr. Copy.** 2 vols. Fo. L.P., general titles, particular title in Vol. 1 only, dedication to Walpole (but not that to George III), lists of plts., frontis. Mask of Tame, folding engraved map (Lond. as 2 separate sheets), 76 hand-cold. aquarints, (3 double-p., some with aquatinted borders), some slight spotting to a few ll. of text, hf. mor. (S. May 21; 65) *Traylen.* £2,000
-- **Anr. Copy.** 2 vols. Lge. 4to. Engraved plt. 'Tamesis', 2 double-p. maps, 76 hand-cold. aquatint plts., with general titles 'An History of the Principal Rivers', 2 plts. & a few text ll. slightly spotted, cont. hf. cf., upr. cover detchd. (C. Nov.16; 55)
Davidson. £1,700
-- **Anr. Copy.** 2 vols. in 3. Fo. Wide margin, on vell. engraved frontis., 1 engraved map in 2 pts., 76 cold. aquatint etchings, (3 double-p.), without main title, dedication lf. for George III & 2 contents ll.,

title verso stpd., some slight browning, later red mor., gt. & blind-tooled spine, covers, inner & outer dentelles, very worn; Hauswedell coll. (H. May 24; 881) DM 5,000

COMBER, Thomas
– A Companion to the Temple. Part I. 1679. *3rd. Edn.* [Wing C5454] *(With:)*– ... Part II. 1679. *2nd. Edn. (With:)*– A Companion to the Altar. 1681. *3rd. Edn.* [Wing C5450B]. Together 3 vols. Unif. cont. mor., richly tooled in blind, rubbed; each vol. with inscr. of Thomas Tomlins, 1683. (BBA. Jun.28; 24) *Maggs.* £240

COMBRUNE, M.
– An Essay on Brewing. 1758. Blanks loose, cf., covers detchd. (P. Jul.26; 52) £160

COMEIRAS
[–] Abrégé de l'Histoire Générale des Voyages Faits en Europe. Paris, 1803-05. 12 vols. Cont. marb. cf., decor. spines. (HD. Sep.22; 224) Frs. 1,950

COMENIUS or KOMENSKY, John Amos
– Janua Linguae Latinae. Schaffhaus, 1656. Engraved title-p., 13 engraved plts. (2 double-p.), mor. (BBA. Mar.21; 17) *Quaritch.* £220
[–] Lux e Tenebris, novis Radiis Aucta, hoc est Solemnissimae Divinae Revelationes in usum Seculi Nostri Factae. L., 1665-66. Lacks 1st. lf. of section II, cont. vell.; Bridgwater bkplt., Dr. Walter Pagel copy. (S. Feb.7; 87) *Ritman.* £800
– Neuer Orbis Pictus für die Jugend. Ed.:– J.E. Gailer. Reutlingen, 1832. In German, Latin & Fr., some old soiling & wear, 1 text lf. incompl., many sm. margin tears bkd., hf. leath. gt. (V. Oct.1; 3922) DM 900
– – Anr. Edn. Reutlingen, 1838. Engl.-German-Fr.-Latin parallel text, lightly browned or soiled, cont. hf. linen, defect. (HT. May 10; 2124) DM 1,300
– Orbis Pictus. Koniggrätz/Krakow, 1833. Latin, German, Czech, Polish & Fr. text, lightly foxed, cont. hf. leath. gt. (GB. May 4; 1510) DM 800
– – Anr. Copy. Latin-German-Czech-Polish-Fr. paralel text, title ll. with sm. bkd. defects., 2 ll. with margin tears, slightly browned & foxed, later bds. (HT. May 10; 2113) DM 540
– – Anr. Edn. Ed.:– Adelbert Müller. Nürnberg, 1835. 2 vols. Ob. 8vo. Orig. ptd. bds., slightly soiled & stained, van Veen coll. (S. Feb.28; 142) £280
– Orbis Sensualis Pictus. Nürnberg, 1698. Title lf. with reprd. margin slit, some spotting, cont. vell. (GB. Nov.4; 2013) DM 1,700
– Orbis Sensualium Pictus Quadrilinguis ... Nuremb., 1679. Cont. vell. (HK. Nov.10; 2828) DM 1,300
– – Anr. Copy. German, Italian, Latin & Fr. text. Lacks title lf. & 1st. 3 preface ll., 1 title stpd., lightly foxed, dog-eared at beginning cont. vell., defect. (GB. May 4; 1509) DM 750

COMERFORD, Rev. M.
– Collections Relating to the Dioceses of Kildare & Leighlin. Dublin, n.d. 3 vols. Cl. (GM. Dec.7; 15) £50

COMESTOR, Petrus
– Scolastica Historica Sacre Scripture. Strasburg, Georg Husner, 1485. Fo. Rubricated, 2 initials in red & blue, lge. 1st. initial painted in blue with margin extension, 2 ex-libris on title-p., many cont. MS. notes & drawings on 1st. pp., 1 lf. reprd., cont. stpd. cf. over wood bds., richly decor., spine end-papers renewed; from Fondation Furstenberg-Beaumesnil. [H. 55333; BMC I, 132] (HD. Nov.16; 47) Frs. 8,500

COMITIVA REGIA en el Casamiento de S.M. el Rey de España Don Alfonso ... Archiduquesa ... Maria Christina de Austria
L., 1877. Ob. fo. Title, table, 63 chromo. litho. plts., orig. portfo., as a collection of plts., w.a.f. (P. May 17; 246) *Allan.* £180

COMITUM, Natalis
– Mythologia. Frankfurt, 1584. *2nd. Edn.* Cont. stpd. pig over wood bds. [by Hans Crantzer of Wittenberg?], decor., port. & arms of Johann Friedrich, Elector of Saxony, initials 'MPXSP' & date 1587 blind-stpd. on upr. cover, initials 'IPS' & date 1613 over-written in black, clasps incompl.;

from Fondation Furstenberg-Beaumesnil. (HD. Nov.16; 110) Frs. 2,500
– – Anr. Edn. Ed.:– Antonii Tritonii. Padua, 1615-16. 4to. Few sm. wormholes, vell.; Dr. Walter Pagel copy. (S. Feb.7; 84) *Colombo.* £150

COMMANDINO, Federico
– Liber de Centro Gravitatis Solidorum. Bologna, 1565. Sm. 4to. Spotting, mostly at end, stp. removed from title, leaving hole bkd. with paper (not affecting letterpress), red mor.-bkd. bds., wormholes, light rubbing; John D. Stanitz coll. (SPB. Apr.25; 98) $650

COMMELIN, Caspar
– Beschrijving van Amsterdam. Amst., 1693. 2 vols. Fo. L.P., frontis., 52 plans, views & plts., most double-p., over 75 text ills., short tear in 2 text ll. reprd., a few margin stains, cont. blind-stpd. vell. (VG. May 3; 545) Fls. 2,200
– – Anr. Edn. Amst., 1694. 2 vols. Fo. Lacks 6 plts., some staining, tears in some plts. & text ll., other defects, cont. hf. vell., not unif., w.a.f. (VG. Sep.14; 1145) Fls. 1,000
– – Anr. Edn. Amst., 1726. *2nd. Printing.* Vol. 1 only (of 2). Fo. Cf., defect. (VG. Sep.14; 1146) Fls. 750

COMMELYN, Jan
– Frederick Hendrick van Nassauw Prince van Orangien. Zyn Leven en Bedryf. Amst., 1651. 2 vols. in 1. Fo. Lacks 5 engrs., cont. vell. (VS. Dec.9; 1200) Fls. 1,600

COMMINES, Philippe de
– De Rebus Gestis Lvdovici, eivs Nominis Vndecimi, Galliarum Regis, & Caroli, Burgundine Ducis. Trans.:– I. Sleidanus. Strassburg, 1545. *1st. Latin Edn.* 4to. Wide margin, title with later owner's mark, cont. limp vell., slight wear; author's MS. dedication on end-paper. (HK. Nov.8; 150) DM 1,500
– Mémoires. Leide, 1648. *1st. Elzevir Edn.* Red mor. gt. by E. Pouget; Victorien Sardou ex-libris. (HD. Mar.27; 7) Frs. 1,750
– – Anr. Edn. Ill.:– Vermeulen. Bruxelles, 1706. 3 vols. Sm. 8vo. Cont. cf., decor. spines, slightly defect. (HD. Sep.21; 115) Frs. 1,100
– – Anr. Edn. Ill.:– Picart (frontis.). L. & Paris, 1747. 4 vols. 4to. Cont. marb. cf. gt., decor. spines, inner roll-stp., some defects. (HD. Sep.22; 223) Frs. 2,100
– Las Memorias. Antw., 1643. *1st. Edn. in Spanish.* 2 vols. in 1. Fo. Hf.-title in Vol. 1, some ll. browned, some worming on a few ll., affecting some letters, cont. blind-stpd. cf., worn, upr. cover detchd. (BBA. Feb.23; 18) *Baldwin.* £130

COMMINES DE MARSILLY, L.J.A. de & others
– Catalogue des Plantes Vasculaires Indigènes ou Généralement Cultivées en Corse. Paris, 1872. Sewed. (HD. Oct.21; 63) Frs. 1,600

COMMITTEE FOR CHRISTIAN GERMAN REFUGEES
– Rare Books Auction [Catalogue]. Dedication:– A.S.W. Rosenbach. Preface:– A. Einstein. Foreword:– T. Mann. [N.Y., 1938]. Pict. wraps., sigd. by Einstein & Mann beneath their ptd. sigs. (SG. Nov.3; 70) $500

COMNENE, Stéphanopoli de
– Précis Historiques de la Maison Impériale des Comnenes où l'on trouve l'Origine, les Moeurs et les Usages des Maniotes. Amst., 1784. Mod. hf. cl. (HD. Oct.21; 64) Frs. 1,600

COMOLLI, Angelo
See— SANZIO, Raffaello

COMPARATIVE VIEW of the Form & Character of the English Racer & Saddle-horse
L., 1836. 4to. 18 litho. plts. on India, many lightly stained, cl. (P. Jan.12; 9b) *Orde.* £200

COMPENDIEUSES SACK- UND FUTERAL-CALENDERLEIN samt einer Poetischen Blumenlese auf das Jahr Christi 1805
Basel, [1804]. 83 x 51 mm., miniature book. Orig. bds., s.-c.; van Veen coll. (S. Feb.28; 181) £110

COMPENDIUM DEPRECATIONUM
Venice, Antonius de Zanchis, 14 Jul. 1498. Few margin defects., pol. mott. sheep gt., satin doubls.; Quaritch collation note, William Littleton & O.O. Fisher bkplts. [Goff C-790] (SG. Nov.3; 47) $1,600

COMPENDIUM PRIVILEGIORUM FRATRUM MINORUM ... Regulum Fratrum ...
Salamanca, 1532. 1 vol. Vell. (DS. Mar.23; 2067) Pts. 100,000

COMPLEAT GUIDE to all Persons who have any Trade or Concern with the City of London & Parts Adjacent
1740. Title stained, contents browned, old sheep, worn. (TA. Sep.15; 143) £52

COMPLEAT WIZZARD (The)
1770. Slightly soiled, cont. cf., rubbed. (P. Feb.16; 247) £170

COMPLETE FARMER (THE): or, A General Dictionary of Husbandry ... By a Society Gentleman
1777. *3rd. Edn.* 4to. Engraved frontis. & 27 folding plts., cont. spr. cf., spine gt., extremities bumped. (CSK. Apr.27; 51) £170

COMPONIMENTI POETICI per l'Ingresso Solenne ... di Proccuratore di San Marco ... Lodovico Manin
Venice, [1764]. Sm. fo. Thick paper, orig. Broccato d'Oro paper wraps., buckram case. (C. Dec.9; 159) *Lyon.* £400

COMPONIMENTI POETICI VOLGARI, LATINI ET GRECI di Diversi sopra la S. Imagine della Beata Vergine dipinto da San Luca ... con la Sua Historia in dette tre Lingui scritta da Ascanio Persius
Bologne, 1601. 16mo. In Italian, Greek & Latin, red chagrin, inner dentelle, by Delaunay. (HD. Dec.2; 149) Frs. 1,020

COMTE, Auguste
– Cours de Philosophie Positive. 1830-42. *[1st. Edn.].* 6 vols. Spotting, liby-stp. on title, recent hf. cf. (TA. Dec.15; 568) £270
– – Anr. Copy. 6 vols. Some ll. spotted, mod. cf.-bkd. bds., slightly soiled. (BBA. Feb.23; 62) *Quaritch.* £200
– – Anr. Edn. Paris, 1864. *2nd. Edn.* 6 vols. A few ll. slightly soiled, orig. wraps., torn, some vols. brkn. (BBA. Feb.23; 63) *Edwards.* £80
– Système de Politique Positive, ou Traité de Sociologie, instituant la Religion de l'Humanité. Paris, 1851-54. *1st. Edn.* 4 vols. 3 title ll. with owners marks, many-pencil annots. & linings, Some foxing or browning, cont. linen, spotted, spine browned & with sm. tears. (H. May 22; 424) DM 1,800

CONABERE, Betty
See— GARNET, J.R. & Conabere, Betty

CONCEPCION, Geronimo de la
– Emporio del Orbe. Cadiz ilustrada, Investigación de Sus Antiguas Grandezas ... Amst., 1690. Lge. fo. Genealogical tree, cf. (DS. Oct.28; 2653) Pts. 75,000

CONCORDANTIAE UTRIUSQUE JURIS
Speier, [printer of Gesta Christi], ca. 1475. Fo. 4 ll. (of 6, lacks 1st. & last ll.), mod. mor., blind-decor., unc., s.-c.; from Fondation Furstenberg-Beaumesnil. (HD. Nov.16; 43) Frs. 2,100

CONDE, Louis de Bourbon, Prince
[–] Mémoires de Condé ou Recueil pour Servir à l'Histoire de France ... L. & Paris, The Hague (Supp.), 1743. 6 Vols., including Supp. 4to. Cont. marb. cf., minor defects., spines decor. (HD. Nov.17; 15) Frs. 2,100
[–] Sommaire Recuil des Choses Mémorables que le, Seigneur Prince de Condé a Protestées ... N.p., 1564. 16mo. Red mor., gt.-decor., decor. spine, inner roulette, s.-c., by Asper frères. (HD. Dec.9; 20) Frs. 1,700

CONDILLAC, l'abbé Etienne Bonnet de
– Cours d'étude pour l'instruction du Prince de Parme. Genève, 1780. 12 vols. Cont. marb. cf.,

CONDILLAC, l'abbé Etienne Bonnet de -*Contd.*

decor. spines; Margins de Flamarens ex-libris. (HD. Jan.26; 86) Frs. 1,350
- **Traité des Sistèmes.** La Haye, 1749. *Orig. Edn.* 2 pts. in 1 vol. 12mo. Cont. red mor. by Anguerrand, spine decor. (HD. Mar.29; 21) Frs. 18,000

CONDIVI, A.
- **Vita di Michelangelo Buonarroti;.** Rome, 16 Jul. 1552. *1st. Edn.* 4to. Minimal foxing, 18th. C. vell. (D. Nov.23; 1838) DM 5,000

CONDORCET, Marie Jean Antoine Nicolas de Caritat, Marquis de
- **Esquisse d'un Tableau Historique des Progrès de l'Esprit Humain.** Paris, [1794-95]. *1st. Edn.* Some slight foxing, 2pp. with sm. tear without loss, cont. leath. gt., corners bumped. (D. Nov.24; 2423) DM 950
- - **Anr. Edn.** Paris, [1795]. *2nd. Edn.* Cont. hf. vell., folding cl. case; MS. annots. by Sainte-Beuve in pen & pencil thro.-out, Sainte-Beuve's father's name inscr. at head of title (cropped by binder). (C. May 30; 77) *Drury.* £650
- **Essai sur l'Application de l'Analyse à la Probalité des Decisions rendues a la Pluralité des Voix.** Paris, 1785. *Orig. Edn.* 4to. Mod. hf. chagrin. (HD. Feb.22; 42) Frs. 8,500

CONEY, John
- **Beauties of Continental Architecture.** 1843. Fo. 29 plts. (2 double-p.). slight split at fold, mor. gt., rubbed. (P. Feb.16; 158) £60
- **Engravings of Ancient Cathedrals, Hotels de Ville & other Public Buildings.** 1832. Fo. 32 plts. on India paper, spotting, hf. cf., rubbed. (P. Apr.12; 203) *Shapiro.* £70
- - **Anr. Edn.** 1842. Fo. 31 double-p. engraved plts. only, reprd., some soiling, cont. hf. mor., worn. (CSK. Apr.6; 162) £100
- **A Series of Fifty-Six Etchings, consisting of Architectural Sketches, Civil & Ecclesiastical, in France, the Low Countries, Germany, & Italy.** L., 1833. *1st. Edn.* Sm. 4to. Engraved title, 55 mntd. India-proof plts., orig. cl., soiled, spine very worn. (SG. Oct.13; 125) $110

CONFUCIUS
- **The Analects.** Trans.:– Lionel Giles. Ltd. Edns. Cl., 1933. *(1500) numbered.* Tall 8vo. Brocaded wraps., stabbed & sewed in Chinese manner, two-part wood box. (SG. Mar.29; 194) $110
- **Confucius Sinarum Philosophus ...** Paris, 1687. *1st. Edn. publd. outside China.* Fo. Cont. cf. (C. Nov.9; 6) *Quaritch.* £220
- **The Morals.** Ed.:– J. Frazer. 1691. Some spotting, tree cf. gt. (P. Jan.12; 212) *Cavendish.* £170

CONGREVE, William
- **The Way of the World.** L., 1700. *1st. Edn.* 4to. Hf.-title reprd., some spotting, wormhole on fore-e., stab-holes, soiling, mor.-bkd. cl. [Wing C 5878] (SPB. May 16; 34) $500
- **Works.** Bg'ham., 1756. 3 vols. Some light soiling, cont. mor. gt., lightly rubbed. (CSK. Jun.15; 90) £160
- - **Anr. Edn.** Bg'ham., 1761. 3 vols. Mor. (LH. Sep.25; 320) $100
- **The Complete Works.** Ed.:– Montague Summers. Nones. Pr., 1923. *Ltd. Edn.* 4 vols. 4to. Buckram-bkd. bds., unc.; from liby. of Luttrellstown castle, w.a.f. (C. Sep.28; 1834) £100

CONNAISSANCE DES ARTS
Mar. 1952-Dec. 1956. Nos. 1-58 in 5 vols. 4to. Publisher's bdgs. (SM. Mar.7; 2114) Frs. 1,700

CONNER, Bernard
- **History of Poland, in Several Letters to Persons of Quality.** 1698. *1st. Edn.* 2 vols. 1 port. in dupl., cont. cf., spines gt. [Wing C5888 & 5889] (BBA. Jan.19; 176) *Spring.* £100

CONNETT, Eugene V.
- **American Big Game Fishing.** Derrydale Pr., [1935]. *(850).* 4to. Gt.-decor cl., partly untrimmed, unopened, d.-w. slightly worn. (SG. Mar.15; 211) $350
- **Feathered Game: from a Sporting Journal.** Ill.:– Edgar Burke. Derrydale Pr., 1929. *(500) numbered.*

4to. Owner's inscr. on fly-lf., hf. cl., unc. & unopened, quite rubbed. (SG. Mar.15; 210) $150
- **Random Casts.** Ill.:– Ralph L. Boyer & Milton C. Weiler. Derrydale Pr., [1939]. *(1075) numbered.* Tall 8vo. Gt.-decor. patterned cl., unopened. (SG. Mar.15; 212) $130

CONNOISSEUR (THE)
1901-13. Vols. 1-35, & 2 vol. index for Vols. 1-24. 4to. Orig. cl., rubbed. (S. Apr.30; 173) *Kapusi.* £100
- - **Anr. Run.** L., Sep. 1901-14. Vols. 1-38 in 19, No bdg. stated. (R. Nov.24; 107) *Walford.* £65
- - **Anr. Run.** 1901-19. Vols. 1-55, & index to Vols. 1-12, in 27 vols. 4to. Cont. hf. mor. & cl. (BBA. Sep.8; 277) *Makiya.* £120
- - **Anr. Run.** L., Sep. 1901-Aug. 1928. Vols. 1-81. 4to. Cl. gt. (P. Nov.24; 106) *Walford.* £280
- - **Anr. Run.** 1906-17. Vols. 16-25, 27-34 & 46-48. 4to. Cl. (S. Dec.13; 442) *Daveney.* £70

CONNOLLY, Cyril
- **The Rock Pool.** Paris, 1936. *1st. Edn.* Orig. wraps., slightly soiled. (BBA. Nov.30; 273) *Belanske.* £120

CONNOLLY, Cyril (Ed.)
See— **HORIZON**

CONNOP, J.
[-] [Views in Yorkshire & Derbyshire]. Ill.:– T. Cartwright after Connop. L., ca. 1810. Ob. 4to. 10 (of 22) cold. aquatint views, last plt. cold. & mntd. (this plt. uncold. in Abbey's copy), without text lf. to 1 plt., text ll. slightly spotted, mod. hf. mor. gt., w.a.f. (C. Mar.14; 42) *Harley-Mason.* £300

CONRAD, Joseph
- **Almayer's Folly.** L., 1895. *1st. Edn. 1st. Iss.* With 'e' missing in 'generosity' on p.110 & 'of' lacking, orig. cl., partly unc., some staning, endpapers slightly spotted; Fred A. Berne copy. (SPB. May 16; 204) $425
- - **Anr. Edn.** L., 1895. *1st. Edn.* Orig. cl., partly unc., spine discold. (S. Mar.20; 860) *Gekoski.* £130
- - **Anr. Copy.** Stained, a few ll. worn at outer margin, cl., stained. (P. Mar.15; 167) *Marlborough.* £50
- - **Anr. Copy.** Misprints on p.110, orig. cl., spine slightly worn, cl. s.-c.; Perry Molstad copy. (SPB. May 16; 421) $475
- - **Anr. Copy.** Sm. 8vo. 1st. state, with letters missing in last 2 lines of p.110, hf.-title, lev., spine gt., gt. dentelles, by Bayntun. (SG. Feb.16; 63) $375
- **Almayer's Folly—Nostromo.** 1895, 1904. *1st. Edn.* 2 vols. 1st. vol.: hf.-title, 'e' missing from generosity & 'of' missing from bottom line on p. 110, orig. cl.; bkplt. of E. Thornton-Smith. 2nd. vol.: hf.-title, some spotting, orig. cl. (LC. Mar.1; 313) £120
- **The Arrow of Gold.** L., 1919. *1st. Engl. Edn.* Light margin browning, cf. gt. by Bayntun; pres. copy to Lady Millais, Perry Molstad copy. (SPB. May 16; 422) $500
- **Chance.** L., [1913]. *1st. Edn. 1st. Iss.* With 1913 date on title verso, 8-pp. advts. dtd. 1913, orig. cl., orig. pict. d.-w. slightly worn & reinforced, mor.-bkd. s.c.; bkplt. of E.E.Taylor, Lilly Liby. label, Perry Molstad copy. (SPB. May 16; 423) $3,100
- **Geography & Some Explorers.** L., 1924. *(30) sigd.* Orig. ptd. wraps.; Perry Molstad copy. (SPB. May 16; 425) $700
- **The Nigger of the 'Narcissus'.** L., 1898. *1st. Publd. Engl. Edn.* Publisher's imprint on spine in lge. capitals with larger initial, 16-p. cat. for 1897, title embossed 'pres. copy', orig. cl.; Perry Molstad copy. (SPB. May 16; 429) $150
[-] **Preface to The Nigger of the 'Narcissus'.** [Hythe, Kent, Priv. ptd. 1902]. *1st. Edn. (100).* Wire-stitched as iss., very slight rust mark, mor.-bkd. s.-c.; Perry Molstad copy. (SPB. May 16; 430) $1,100
[-] **Preface to 'Simple Cooking Precepts for a Little House' by Jessie Conrad.** [L., 1921]. *1st. Separate Edn. (100).* Marginal browning, wraps., sigd., with Jessie Conrad's 'A Handbook of Cookery', L. 1923, orig. bdg.; Perry Molstad copies. (SPB. May 16; 431) $350
- **Recits du Congo.** Ill.:– Auguste Mambour. Liege,

1934. *(75) numbered.* Lge. 4to. Loose as iss, in orig. wraps., folder, s.-c. defect. (S. Dec.20; 503) *Browning.* £60
- **The Rover.** Garden City, N.Y., 1923. *1st. Edn. (377) L.P., sigd.* Etched port., orig. decor. parch., glassine wrap. & ptd. d.-w., unc., mor.-bkd. s.-c.; bkplt. of E.E.Taylor, Perry Molstad copy. (SPB. May 16; 432) $275
- **The Secret Agent.** L., 1923. *(1000) sigd.* Orig. parch.-bkd. bds., partly unopened. (S. Mar.20; 862) *Reuter.* £75
- - **Anr. Copy.** Bds., unc. & unopened, slightly worn, d.-w. (P. Mar.15; 168) *Quaritch.* £55
- - **Anr. Copy.** Tall 8vo. Paper-bkd. bds., slightly cocked, d.-w., spine darkened & edges torn. (SG. Jan.12; 69) $140
- **Some Reminiscences.** L., 1912. *1st. Edn.* Orig. cl., pres. copy to James B. Pinker. (SPB. May 17; 588) $1,000
- **Suspense.** Garden City, 1925. *1st. Edn. L.P. Iss. (377) numbered.* Lge. 8vo. Gt.-pict. bds., partly unc., unopened, d.-w., s.-c. (SG. May 24; 272) $130
- **The Warrior's Soul.** L., 1920. *(25) for Private Circulation.* 4to. Orig. ptd. wraps., unopened, cl. folder. (SPB. May 17; 589) $600
- **Youth: a Narrative.** 1902. *1st. Edn. (With:)*
- **Under Western Eyes.** 1911. *1st. Edn.* Together 2 vols. Orig. cl. (BBA. Aug.18; 66) *Sumner & Stillman.* £55
- **Works.** 1920-21. *(780) numbered & sigd.* 18 vols. Orig. buckram-bkd. bds., slightly soiled. (BS. Nov.16; 73) £100
- - **Anr. Edn.** L., 1921-27. *(780) numbered & sigd.* 20 vols. Orig. cl.-bkd. bds., 1st. vol. with d.-w. (S. Dec.13; 349) *Traylen.* £300
- - **Anr. Copy.** 20 vols. Cl.-bkd. bds., slightly soiled & worn. (P. Mar.15; 170) *Walford.* £150
- - **Anr. Edn.** 1925. *Medallion Edn.* 20 vols. Orig. cl. gt. (P. Jul.26; 29) £130
- - **Anr. Copy.** 20 vols. Orig. cl., lightly rubbed. (CSK. Mar.23; 27) £80

CONRAD, Joseph & Hueffer or Ford, Ford Madox
- **The Inheritors.** N.Y., 1901. *1st. Edn. 1st. Iss.* With dedication in uncorrected state with misprint 'Boys' for 'Borys', orig. pict. cl., soiled, cl. case; Lilly liby. label, Perry Molsted copy. (SPB. May 16; 434) $800

CONRAD DE ALEMANNIA
- **Concordantiae Maiores Biblie.** *(Bound with:)* **JOHANNES DE SEGOVIA** - **Concordantiae Partium sive Dictionum Indeclinabilium Totius Biblie.** Basle, 1521. Together 2 works in 1 vol. Fo. Cont. German stpd. marb. roan over wood bds., richly decor., lacks metal pieces; from Fondation Furstenberg-Beaumesnil. (HD. Nov.16; 112) Frs. 5,800

CONRADUS, Abbot of Aversperg [Liechtenaw]
- **Chronicum usque ad Tempora Friderici II.** Ed.:– Melancthon & Mylius. Basle, 1569. *(Bound with:)* **OTTO FRISINGENSIS, Bp.** - **Chronicon ad sua usque Tempora [1146] Gestarum.** Basle, 1569. Together 2 works in 1 vol. Fo. Few light margin stains, blind-stpd. decor. pig over wood, initials N.C. & date 1569 on upr. cover, clasps preserved, slightly worn, corners slightly defect., few sm. wormholes in covers. (VG. Sep.14; 1087) Fls. 650

CONSETT, Matthew
- **A Tour Through Sweden, Swedish-Lapland, Finland & Denmark.** Ill.:– Thomas Bewick. Stockton, priv. ptd., 1789. *1st. Edn.* 4to. Wide margins, 8 engraved & wood-engraved plts., including additional imp. of the 'Entrance to Upsal', a proof before letters, subscribers list, lacks hf,-title & frontis., offsetting from some plts., some slight spotting, cont. tree cf. gt. by C. Kalthofber, rubbed. (LC. Mar.1; 208) £130
- - **Anr. Edn.** Ill.:– Thomas Bewick. L. & Stockton, 1789. 4to. 7 engraved plts., hf.-title, cont. paper-bkd. bds., unc. (C. Mar.14; 5) *Hannas.* £360

CONSPIRACY DISCOVERED ... of the Conspirators & others in the late Treason, June 17, 1641
1641. Woodcut frontis., title & 4 pp. text, mod. mor. (P. Feb.16; 181) £60

CONSTABLE, John
[–] A Catalogue of the Valuable Finished Works, Studies & Sketches ... which will be Sold by Auction by Messrs. Foster & Sons. L., 1838. 4to. 1st. part priced in MS., orig. wraps., portion torn away from upr. cover. (S. Apr.30; 18)   *Leicester*. £420
– **English Landscape Scenery**. Ill.:– D. Lucas. 1855. Fo. 40 mezzotints, spotting, hf. mor., rubbed. (P. Jan.12; 108)   *Kidd*. £190

CONSTANT DE REBECQUE, Benjamin
– **Adolphe; Anecdote trouvée dans les Papiers d'un Inconnu**. L. & Paris, 1816. *1st. Edn. L. Iss.* Iss. without hf.-title, advt. lf. at end, cont. hf. cf., marb. paper sides, in upr. compartment of spine crest with motto 'Rinasce piu gloriosa'. (S. May 10; 256)   *Quaritch*. £2,600
– **Journaux Intimes**. Paris, 1952. *(80) on velin pur fil*. Chagrin, wrap. preserved, s.-c. (HD. Nov.9; 92)   Frs. 1,000
– **Principes de Politique Applicable à tous les Gouvernements representatifs** ... Paris, 1815. *Orig. Edn*. Sewed, wrap. (HD. Feb.22; 43)   Frs. 1,300

CONSTITUCION Y LAS LEYES
[Cadiz, 1822-23]. 2 vols. 4to. Linen. (DS. Dec.16; 2592)   Pts. 140,000

CONSTITUTIO CRIMINALIS THERESIANA oder der ... Majestät Mariä Theresiä ... Peinliche Gerichtsordnung
Wien, 1769. 2 pts. & 2 supps. in 1 vol. Fo. Folding copper engrs. slightly creased, 1 tear, all copper engrs & 1 text cf. with stain, some browning, MS. name & date on supp. Ruddphi & llten Martii [1] 1774a, cont. cf., very defect. (H. May 22; 412)   DM 1,300

CONTANT D'IVRY, Pierre
– **Les Oeuvres d'Architecture**. Paris, 1769. Fo. Engraved port., title, 79 plts. on 70 ll. (numbered 2-72), 2 overslips on plt. 62, cont. cf.-bkd. bds. (C. Dec.9; 23)   *Weinreb*. £1,000

CONTARENUS, Pietre Giovanni
– **Historiae de Bello nvper Venetis a Selimo II. Tvrcarvm Imperatore illato, Liber vnvs**. Trans.:– I.N. Stvpanus. Basel, 1573. 4to. MS. note & extended corner on title, title & last p. stpd., some browning, leath. (HK. Nov.8; 154)   DM 750
– **Historia delle Cose Successe dal. Principio della Guerra Mossa da Sellum Ottomano a'Venetiani**. Venice, 1572. Sm. 4to. Later cf.-bkd. bds. (PNY. Oct.20; 204) $100

CONTES ORIENTAUX, Tirés des Manuscrits de la Bibliothèque du Roy de France
La Haye, 1743. 2 vols. 12mo. Cont. cf. gt.; 2 added figures by Marillier from 'Nouveaux Contes Orientaux'. (HD. May3; 32)   Frs. 1,500

CONTET, Frederic
– **Interieurs: Directoire et Empire**. Ill.:– after Belanger & others. Paris, 1932. Tall fo. 24 cold. plts., ex-liby., each plt. stpd. on blank verso, liby. buckram. (SG. May3; 102) $130
– **Les Vieux Hôtels de Paris**. Paris, 1913-34. 21 vols. Tall fo. Ex-liby., many plts. stpd. on blank versos, loose in marb. bd. folders, cl.-bkd., linen ties. (SG. May3; 101) $1,000

CONTI, Pietro Paolo
– **Della Inalveazione de'Fiumi del Bolognese, e della Romagna**. Roma, 1766. 4to. 3 maps torn, frontis. with defect. reprd., cont. vell. (SI. Dec.15; 150)   Lire 380,000

CONTINENTAL CONGRESS
– **Journals of Congress, Containing the Proceedings from January 1st, 1777, to January 1st, 1778**. Phila., [1778]. Vol. III. 1st. 210 pp. wormed, some margin stains, browned thro.-out, recent buckram-bkd. early plain bds., bds. worn, backstrip with few sm. tape repairs. [Sabin 15545] (HA. Nov.18; 109) $110

CONTINENTAL TOURIST, The
– **Belgium & Nassau**. L., ca. 1830. Engraved title, 61 plts., lacks 2 maps, orig. cl. worn. (P. May 17; 309)   *Gill*. £220
– – **Anr. Edn**. Ca. 1850. L.P., engraved title, folding map, 61 proof plts., cf. gt. (P. Oct.20; 7)   £85

CONVENCAO ENTRE OS MUITO ALTOS E MUITO MODEROSOS SENHORES O PRINCIPE REGENTE DE PORTUGAL E EL REY DO REINO UNIDO da Grande Bretanha e Irlanda, para as Questoes e Indemnizar as Perdas dos Vassallos Portuguezes no Trafico de Esclavos de Africa ...
Rio de Janeiro, 1815. Sm. fo. Portuguese & Engl. text, 4 pp., top edge of both ll. neatly reprd., cont. ptd. vell., vell. ties, red silk end-papers, unc. (SG. Apr.5; 328) $300

CONWAY, Sir William Martin
– **The Bolivian Andes**. L., 1901. Orig. cl., slightly rubbed. (BBA. May 3; 343)
          Cavendish Rare Books. £95
– **Climbing & Exploration in the Karakoram-Himalayas**. L., 1894. *1st. Edn*. 2 lge. folding maps in pockets, orig. cl., slightly soiled. (S. Jun.25; 37)   *Kossow*. £150

COOK, Arthur Bernard
– **Zeus, a Study in Ancient Religion**. Camb., 1914-40. 3 vols. in 5. Orig. cl., d.-w.'s. (S. Mar.20; 709)   *Thorp*. £190

COOK, Capt. James
– **An Abridgement of Captain Cook's Last Voyage**. Ed.:– Capt. James King. 1784. Tree cf. gt. (P. Jan.12; 239)   £160
– **Cartes et Figures du Troisième Voyage de Cook**. Paris, 1785. Lacks 1 plt., bdg. not stated, lacks spine. (JL. Mar.25; 323)   Aus. $450
– – **Anr. Copy**. 7 maps, 13 plans, ports., lightly foxed, some soiling, lge. general map (plt. 1) with reprd. tears. margins slightly crumpled, 3 plts. with sm. margin wormhole, cont. hf. leath., slightly defect. [Sabin 16261] (HT. May 10; 2749)   DM 900
[–] **James Cook, Surveyor of New Foundland, being a Collection of Charts of the Coasts of Newfoundland & Labradore ... Reproduced in Facsimile ...** San Franc., Grabhorn Pr., 1965. *(365)*. 2 vols. including 1 vol. of folding charts. Fo. Orig. wraps., orig. buckram box. (CSK. May.4; 125)   £160
– **Journal During his Voyage Round the World made in H.M. Bark 'Endeavour' ...** Ed.:– Capt. W.J.L. Wharton. L., 1893. 1 short margin tear, Unc., orig. cl., unc. (KH. Nov.9; 573)   Aus. $140
– **The Journal of H.M.S. Resolution 1772-75**. L., 1981. *(500)*. Fo. Orig. hf. mor., s.-c. (CSK. Feb.24; 40)   £55
– **The Journals ... on his Voyages of Discovery ...** Ed.:– J.C. Beaglehole. Camb., Hakluyt Soc., 1955-67. *1st. Edn*. 3 vols. in 4 (with folder of charts & views). Orig. cl., 1d.-w. reprd.; 1st. vol. sigd. & inscr. by Beaglehole & with two l p. letters from him loosely inserted. (KH. Nov.8; 100); Aus. $230
– – **Anr. Edn**. Ed.:– J.C. Beaglehole. Camb., 1968-69,. 5 vol. in 6, including portfo. 8vo. & fo. Charts loose as iss., orig. cl., d.-w.'s. (BBA. Dec.15; 24)
          Sons of Liberty Books. £190
– – **Anr. Edn**. Ed.:– J.C. Beaglehole. Camb., &c, 1968-74. 5 vols. in 6, including portfo. Fo. & 8vo. Gt.-pict. cl., d.-w.'s. (SG. Sep.22; 99) $300
– **Premier [Deuxième et Troisième] Voyages autour du Monde fait en 1768 ... 1780, précédés des Relations de MM. Byron, Carteret et Wallis**. Trans.:– J.B.J. Breton. Ill.:– Brion. Paris, 1804. 15 vols., including 3 atlas vols. 16mo. & 12mo. 3 lge. folding maps, 73 plts., cont. tree cf., spines decor. (HD. Nov.29; 85)   Frs. 4,300
– **Relation des Voyages entrepris par Ordre de sa Majesté Britannique ...** Paris, 1774. *1st. Edn. in Fr*. 8 vols. in 4. (without Atlas) Cont. marb cf., spine, sm. defects, slight foxing. (HD. Dec.9; 21)   Frs. 1,300
– – **Anr. Copy**. 4 vols. only (lacks Atlas); 4 vols. only (lacks Vol. I); 4 vols. 4to. 1st. work: 43 (of 52) engraved plts. & maps; 2nd. work: 46 (of 65) engraved plts. & maps; 3rd. work: 39 (of 88) engraved plts. & maps; some slight staining & fraying, 19th. C. hf. cf. [Sabin 30940; 16249; 16261] (VS. Dec.9; 1274)   Fls. 650
– **Troisième Voyage ou Voyage à l'Océan Pacifique**. Paris, 1785. 4to. 88 folding engraved maps & plts., many folding, lge. map of the Pacific cold. & with short tears in folds, sm. flaw in 1 plt., cont.

mott. cf., slightly worn. (S. Dec.1; 267)
          Bowes. £240
– – **Anr. Copy**. 4 vols. 4to. 86 engraved maps & plts. (81 only called for), most folding, some short tears at folds, few shaved, lacks folding map, a few spots, cont. mott. cf., spines gt. (S. Mar.20; 761)
          Haddon. £210
– – **Anr. Copy**. 4 vols. 4to. 88 engraved plts. (including maps & charts, views, & ports.), many folding or double-p., 1st. map torn, cont. cat's paw full cf. gt. extra. (SG. Sep.22; 102) $900
– – **Anr. Copy**. 5 vols. including Atlas. 4to. Cont. cf., decor. spines, worn. (HD. Mar.14; 18)   Frs. 4,600
– – **Anr. Edn**. [1785]. Atlas only. Fo. 88 plts. (slight tears & stains), cont. red mor. gt., spine blind-decor. (HD. Jul.2; 9)   Frs. 4,100
– **Voyage dans l'Hémisphère Austral, et autour du Monde**. Paris, 1778. *1st. Fr. Trans*. 5 vols. 4to. 65 engraved folding plts. (of 66), folding table split, 1 plt. disbnd., dampstains & foxing, cont. marb. cf. gt., spines decor., slightly worn. (HD. May 21; 25)   Frs. 5,500
– **A Voyage to the Pacific Ocean. [3rd. Voyage]**. 1784. *[1st. Edn.]*. 4 vols., including Atlas. Frontis. to Vol. 1, 28 plts. in text vols., Atlas with 2 folding charts, 61 plts., dampstains & foxing, sm. tear to title Vol. 3, 2 pp. torn, 1 with loss of text, cf. & hf. cf., defect., w.a.f. (P. Feb.16; 78)   £880
– – **Anr. Copy**. Atlas vol. only. Fo. 63 engraved plts. only (including folding chart & double-p. chart), interleaved thro.-out with extracts from ptd. text in cont. hand, some tears, all but one short & reprd., hf. cf., covers detchd. (S. Apr.9; 13) *Palmer*. £700
– – **Anr. Copy**. 3 vols. only (without Atlas vol.). 4to. 24 engraved plts. & charts, some folding, contrary to directions on plt. list no. XXIII is not bnd. in Vol. I but plt. LXXXVII included in Vol. II, cont. tree cf., spines gt. (C. Nov.16; 8)
          Brooke-Hitching. £550
– – **Anr. Copy**. 4 vols. 42 engraved ports. & plts., cont. diced cf., worn. (CE. Sep.1; 18)   £240
– – **Anr. Copy**. 4 vols. Cf. gt. (P. Sep.8; 323) £220
– – **Anr. Edn**. Dublin, 1784. *1st. Irish Edn*. 3 vols. Cont. tree cf., spines worn. (SG. Sep.22; 101) $500
– – **Anr. Edn**. [1784]. Atlas vol. only. Fo. 56 (of 63) engraved plts., 1 plt. stained, hf. cf., covers detchd. (P. Jul.26; 189)   £750
– – **Anr. Edn**. L., 1784 or later. Atlas vol. only. Lge. fo. 63 engraved plts., including 2 folding charts, margins of 1 plt. slightly spotted, cont. hf. cf., rubbed & worn, covers detchd. (C. Jun.27; 86)
          Lindh. £1,200
– – **Anr. Edn**. 1785. *2nd. Edn*. 3 vols. only (lacks atlas vol.). 4to. Lacks port. frontis. to Vol. 1, orig. marb. bds., unc.; bkplt. of Thomas Boswell, of Blackadder. (PD. Dec.14; 272)   £220
– – **Anr. Edn**. Ed.:– James King. N.Y., 1796. Vols. II-IV only. Browned with light foxing & wear, orig. mott. cf., covers worn & scuffed. (HA. Nov.18; 342) $100
– – **Anr. Edn**. L., n.d. Atlas vol. only. Fo. 2 folding engraved charts, 61 plts., some light spotting, orig. bds., worn, w.a.f. (CSK. Feb.24; 30)   £850
– **A Voyage Towards the South Pole & Round the world [2nd. Voyage]**. L., 1777. *2nd. Edn*. 2 vols. Lge. 4to. 63 (of 64) plts., many folding, including several maps & charts, title-p. & 4 plts. partly dampstained, cont. mott. cf., disbnd. [Sabin 16245] (SG. Mar.29; 303) $450
– – **Anr. Edn**. Dublin, 1784. *1st. Irish Edn*. 2 vols. Hf.-titles, cont. tree cf. (SG. Sep.22; 100) $275
– – **Anr. Copy**. 2 vols. Orig. leath. (JL. Jul.15; 372)   Aus. $450

COOK, Capt. James & Hawkesworth, John
– **Voyages round the world.[1st., 2nd. & 3rd.]**. L., 1773; 1777; 1784. *1st. Edns*. 3 vols.; 2 vols.; 3 vols.; with Atlas vol.; together 9 vols. 4to. & fo. A few ll., mostly in text of 1st. work, with browning, slight foxing & offsetting, some Atlas plts. with pale foxing, mostly in blank margins, a little col. (probably pencil) added to a few maps & plts., some repairs & strengthtenings with tape, a few early ll. in 1 vol. slightly worned, sm. section cut away at intersection of folds in 1 map, some 3 or 4 plts. lightly shaved, text non-unif. early cf., rebkd., Atlas later hf. mor. (KH. Nov.8; 98) Aus. $4,800

COOK, Capt. James & Hawkesworth, John -Contd.

- – Anr. Edn. 1773; 1777; 1785. *1st. Edn.; 1st. Edn.; 2nd. Edn. 1st. Iss. of 1st. work, without the chart of the Straight of Magellan.* 3 vols.; 2 vols.; 3 vols., without Atlas vol.; together 8 vols. 4to. 1st. work: 23 engraved plts., 28 charts & profiles, some folding; 2nd. work: engraved frontis. port., 63 charts & plts.; 3rd. work: 24 charts & plts; margin tear to 1 folding chart, some slight staining to a few ll. & plts., unif. tree cf. gt.; Samuel Enderby bkplts. (with 'William Enderby' superimposed in most vols.). (LC. Oct.13; 252) £2,200
- – Anr. Edn. L., 1773; 1777; 1784. *2nd. Edn.; 1st. Edn.; 1st. Edn.* 3 vols.; 2 vols. & Atlas; 3 vols. & Atlas. 4to. & fo. 1st. work: 52 engraved maps, charts & plts., some folding, tear in 2 charts, 1 reprd.; 2nd. work: 63 engraved maps, charts & plts., some margins discold.; 3rd.: 24 engraved maps & charts in text vols., 63 engraved maps & plts. in atlas, 1 plt. loose, some margins slightly discold., some offsetting; text vols. unif. tree cf., rebkd., covers slightly rubbed, atlases hf. cf., covers rubbed, corners reinforced. (CA. Apr.3; 34)
Aus. $5,200
- – Anr. Edn. L., 1773; 1779; 1785. *1st. Edn.; 3rd. Edn.; 2nd. Edn.* 3 vols.; 2 vols. & Atlas; 3 vols. & Atlas. 4to. & fo. 1st. work: 52 engraved maps, charts & plts., some folding, sm. tears in 3 maps, some offsetting, Vol. 3 title lightly foxed; 2nd. work: 63 engraved maps, charts & plts.; 3rd. work: 24 engraved maps & charts in text vols., 62 (of 63) engraved maps & plts. in atlas, some light foxing in margins of some plts., 1 plt. with tear in margin reprd., margins of titles slightly stained; text vols. unif. blind-stpd. cf. gt., rebkd., atlases hf. cf. gt. (CA. Apr.3; 129) Aus. $4,500
- – Anr. Edn. L., 1777-84. *2nd. Edn. (1st. Voyage), 1st. Edns. (2nd. & 3rd. Voyages).* 3 vols., 2 vols., 3 vols. & Atlas. Lge. 4to. & fo. Many full-p. & folding maps, engraved plts. etc., some foxing & minor repairs, old liby. stp. on titles, atlas vol. with 2 lge. folding charts, 61 engrs. with tissue guards, few plts. badly foxed, cont. tree cf., spines gt., atlas vol. cont. hf. cf., marb. bds., disbnd. (SG. Apr.26; 49) $4,000
- – Anr. Edn. Paris, ca. 1780. Atlases only: 3 vols. 4to. 178 plts., 1st. 2 vols. incompl., 3rd. vol. compl. with 88 plts., cont. cf. or hf. cf., 2 vols. worn. (HD. Mar.9; 71b) Frs. 5,800
- – Anr. Edn. Ill.:– Bewick, Beilby, &c. Newcastle, 1790. 2 vols. in 4. 50 plts., including port., folding chart & folding plt., advt. lf., lacks 2 quires, sm. hole in 1 plt. affecting engraved surface, margin worming at beginning of Vol. 1, some slight browning, cont. cf., slightly worn, w.a.f. (S. Nov.1; 22) Mulden. £240
- – Anr. Edn. Glasgow, 1807-09. 3 vols. Engraved port. frontis., folding map, 18 plts., few tears reprd., map creased, some browning, cont. qtr. cf. (With:) - Illustrations to Captain Cook's Voyages. Ca. 1780. Engraved port., 115 plts., few margins trimmed, some slight spotting, mod. hf. cf. gt. (S. Nov.1; 20) Brockhaus. £140
- – Anr. Edn. N.d. Fo. 151 maps, charts & plts., Lacks title & some text, hf. mor., as a coll. of plts., w.a.f. (P. Sep.29; 63) Peterson. £380
- – Anr. Copy. Plt. vol. only. 67 engraved maps & plts., many folding & double-p., titles in Fr., cf. gt., lacks lr. cover, as a coll. of plts., w.a.f. (P. Mar.15; 18) Walford. £280

COOK, Sir Theodore Andrea

- A History of the English Turf. 1901[-04]. 3 vols. in 6. 4to. Orig. cl. gt. (P. Dec.8; 221) Mar. £60
- – Anr. Edn. [1901-04]. 3 vols. 4to. Orig. cl. gt. (P. Jun.7; 132) £70

COOK, Walter (Contrib.)
See— MEISS, Millard

COOK & CO., Parisian Mantle Saloon

- New Designs in Cloaks ... [1833-49]. 4to. 158 plts., including 151 hand-cold., a few torn & trimmed in margins, some reprd., hf. cf. gt. (P. Dec.8; 30)
Welford. £100

COOKE, Edward William

- Leaves from my Sketch-Book. 1876. Ob. 4to. 26 lithos. on 25 sheets, cl. gt. (P. Jun.7; 278) £65

- Shipping & Craft. L., 1829. 4to. 49 (of 50) etched plts., including title & plt. list, foxed & spotted, loose in defect. cl. folder. (S. Mar.6; 229)
Ash. £440
- Sixty-Five Plates of Shipping & Craft. 1829. 4to. Vig. title, 63 plts., list of plts. lf., plts. lightly foxed, disbnd. (P. Mar.15; 5) Brown. £550

COOKE, George Alexander

- Topography of Great Britain ... Ca. 1806-22. 44 vols. only (of 46), in 13 vols. 12mo. 46 folding maps, 190 plts. on 95 sheets, some staining, hf. cf., rebkd., as a coll. of plts., w.a.f. (P. Jun.7; 234) £220

COOKE, J.C.

- Cookery & Confectionary ... 1824. Cont. cf. (PD. Aug.17; 145) £60

COOKE, William

- The Medallic History of Imperial Rome. L., 1781. 2 vols. 4to. 61 engraved plts., cont. spr. cf., spines gt., slightly worn. (S. May 1; 460) Drury. £130

COOKE, W.E.

- Views in Leicestershire. Loughborough, ca. 1900. [1st. Series]. Ob. fo. Bdg. not stated. (HBC. May 17; 316) £85
- – Anr. Edn. N.d. 2nd. Series. Fo. Bdg. not stated. (HBC. May 17; 319) £85

COOKE, W.J.
See— ROHBOCK, Ludwig & Cooke, W.J.

COOKE, William Bernard

- Picturesque Views (mostly Devon, Cornwall & the South Coast of England). Ill.:– after J.M.W. Turner. Ca. 1825. 4to. 45 engraved plts., Lacks title, margins browned, cont. str.-grd. mor. (TA. Nov.17; 156) £200

COOKE, William Bernard & Owen, Samuel

- The Thames. L., 1811. 2 vols. 4to. 84 engraved views, 1 lf. reprd. in margin, cont. russ., rebkd., rubbed. (S. Jun.25; 311) Young. £260
- Views on the Thames. L., ca. 1819. Fo. L.P., frontis., 74 engraved plts., cont. hf. mor., w.a.f. (S. Mar.6; 383) Sanders. £280
- – Anr. Edn. Ill.:– after S. Owen, W. Havell, & others. L., 1822. Atlas vol. only. Fo. 74 (of 75) plts., with 2 additional plts. not called for in plt. list, some spotting, cont. hf. mor., spine gt., head of spine chipped. 15(C. Jun.27; 25). Harris. £300

COOLIDGE, Calvin

- Have Faith in Massachusetts. Boston, 1919. Cl., slightly rubbed; inscr. by author to Mrs. Henry F. Osborn, with her bkplt. (LH. Jan.15; 39) $140

COOMARASWAMY, Ananda

- Rajput Painting: Hindu Paintings of Rajasthan & the Panjab Himalayas. L., 1916. *(525).* 2 vols. Fo. 77 mntd. plts., some cold., ex-liby., buckram, slightly soiled. (SG. May 3; 103) $350

COOPER, Anthony Ashley, Earl of Shaftesbury
See— SHAFTESBURY, Anthony Ashley Cooper, Earl of

COOPER, Betty M.

- Catalogue of the Scott Collection of Books, Manuscripts, Prints & Drawings. L., 1954. 4to. Cl. (SG. Sep.15; 241) $100

COOPER, Duff

- Translations & Verses. 1949. *(600) numbered. (50) sigd. & specially bnd.* Lge. 8vo. Red mor., unc., d.-w., case. (HBC. May 17; 209) £60

COOPER, James Fenimore

- [–] Afloat & Ashore; or the Adventures of Miles Wallingford. Phila., priv. ptd., 1844. *1st. Amer. Edns.* [1st. & 2nd. Series:] 4 vols. in 2. 12mo. Some foxing, hf. cf. (SG. Nov.17; 31) $150
- [–] The Headsman; or, the Abbaye des Vignerons. Phila., 1833. *1st. Amer. Edn.* 2 vols. 12mo. Old marb. bds., cf. spines & corners, hf. mor. s.-c., rubbed. (RO. Apr.23; 59) $100
- The History of the Navy of the United States of America. Phila., 1839. *1st. Edn.* 2 vols. Hf.-titles, slight foxing, later two-toned cl. (SG. Mar.15; 99) $120
- Lederstrumpf-Erzählungen. Trans.:– K. Federn. Ill.:– M. Slevogt. Berlin, 1909. *De Luxe Edn.* Fo.

Lacks lf. with printers mark, supp. series of 89 lithos., all sigd. by artist, most designated 'Probedrucke', some ll. designated by artist 1st. (2nd.) state, or 'Abdruck', dtd. Oct 1908-Mar. 1910, 6 ll. with initials, with nos. in lr. margin all ll. under guards, some loose of browned, several foxed, on varius paper, orig. red mor., gt., by C. Sonntag jun., slightly bumped, light scratches, spine faded, 2 mor. boxes cold. & gt. arms, slightly worn. & bumped. (H. May 23; 1505) DM 40,000
- – Anr. Edn. Trans.:– K. Feder. Ill.:– Max Slevogt. Berlin, 1909. *(250).* Orig. linen, gt. spine & upr. cover minimal wear. (HK. May 14; 3136)
DM 4,000
- – Anr. Edn. Trans.:– K. Feder. Ill.:– Slevogt. Berlin, 1922. *De Luxe Edn., (150) numbered.* 5 vols. 4to. On paper, orig. vell., gt.-decor., gt.-stpd. centre-piece on upr. cover, unc. (GB. Nov.5; 3017)
DM 1,900
- Novels. N.Y., 1871-72. 32 vols. Cont. pol. cf., spines richly gt. in compartments, inner dentelles, 1 or 2 labels slightly chipped. (RO. Dec.11; 80)
$250
- [–] The Redskins; or, Indian & Injin. N.Y., 1846. *1st. Amer. Edn.* 2 vols. in 1. 12mo. Cont. three-qtr. leath., rubbed, some childish drawings on blank end-ll. (RO. Apr.23; 74) $100
- Satanstoe, or, The Family of Littlepage. A Tale of the Colony. L., 1845. *1st. Edn.* 3 vols. Some light foxing, cf., extremities worn. (With:) - The Chain-Bearer, or, The Littlepage Manuscripts. L., 1845. *1st. Edn.* 3 vols. Final quotation marks present on Vol. 1 title-p., some light foxing, cf., to match preceding 3 vols., extremities worn. (SG. Mar.15; 100) $150
- Complete Works. N.Y., n.d. *Leather-Stocking Edn. (1000).* 32 vols. Ill., hf. mor. (SPB. May 17; 725) $600

COOPER, Samuel, Surgeon

- Neuestes Handbuch der Chirurgie. Ed.:– L.F. von Froriep. Weimar, 1819-21. *1st. German Edn.* 3 vols. Cont. bds., very rubbed. (HT. May 8; 530)
DM 420

COOPER, Rev. Samuel

- A Sermon Preached before His Excellency Thomas Pownall ... October 16th, 1759 ... Boston, [1759]. *1st. Edn.* Lacks A1 (hf.-title?), mor. gt.; the Rt. Hon. Visc. Eccles copy. [Sabin 16601] (CNY. Nov.18; 73) $200

COOPER, Bp. Thomas

- Thesaurus Linguae Romanae et Britannicae. 1584. 2 pts. in 1 vol. Fo. Last lf. from anr. edn., some tears, sometimes affecting text, some ll. soiled & stained, later cf., rebkd., worn. [STC 5689] (BBA. Jan.19; 119) Bloomsbury Rare Books. £50

COOPER, Thomas, M.D.

- Renseignemens sur l'Amérique. Hamburg, 1795. Cont. hf. cf., lightly rubbed. (CSK. Feb.24; 39)
£50
- Some Information respecting America. L., 1794. *1st. Edn.* Cf. [Sabin 16615] (P. Dec.8; 331)
Lawson. £95
- – Anr. Copy. Errata lf. at end, folding map torn in 2 places & bkd. with linen, 1st. & last ll. washed, tree cf. gt. by Sangorski & Sutcliffe, spine slightly worn; the Rt. Hon. Visc. Eccles copy. [Sabin 16615] (CNY. Nov.18; 74) $150

COOPER, Thomas Sidney

- [–] Drawing Book of Animals. N.d. 4to. Lacks title, 32 litho. plts., several spotted, orig. cl., lightly soiled. (CSK. May 18; 198) £60
- Groups of Cattle. L., 1839. Fo. Tinted litho. title, frontis., 24 (of 25) plts., some lightly spotted, orig. mor.-bkd. cl. (CSK. Feb.24; 21) £380
- – Anr. Edn. L., [1839]. Fo. Litho. title & 22 (of 25) cold. tinted lithos., trimmed to image & mntd. on card as iss., lacks frontis. & 3 plts., some foxing, orig. portfo. with title on upr. covers. (SPB. May 17; 590) $2,500
- New Drawing Book of Animals & Rustic Groups. 1837. Ob. 4to. 32 plts., some foxing, cl. gt. (P. Dec.8; 325) Sims, Reed & Fogg. £60
- Studies of Cattle, Drawn from Nature. Ca. 1840. *New Series.* Pts. 6, 9, & 10 only. Ob. fo. 12 cold. litho. plts., loosely contained in orig. ptd. wraps. (TA. Jun.21; 491) £65

COOPER, William
- A Guide in the Wilderness: or, the History of the First Settlements in the Western Counties of New York ... Dublin, 1810. *1st. Edn.* Lacks [A1] (blank?), sm. hole in [C4] affecting a few letters, cont. (Irish?) str.-grd. red mor. gt., slight wear to extremities; the Rt. Hon. Visc. Eccles copy. (CNY. Nov.18; 75) $2,400

COOPER, William T.
See— FORSHAW, Joseph M. & Cooper, William T.

COOTE, Sir Charles
- General View of the Agriculture & Manufacture of the Queen's County ... Dublin, 1801. *1st. Edn.* Hf.-title, lacks map, cl. (GM. Dec.7; 13) £100
- Statistical Survey of the County of Cavan. Dublin, 1801. *1st. Edn.* Red hf. mor. (GM. Dec.7; 426) £180

COPELAND, R. Morris
- Country Life: A Handbook of Agriculture, Horticulture, & Landscape Gardening. Boston, 1859. *1st. Edn.* Tall 8vo. Orig. cl., soiled. (SG. Oct.13; 127) $110

COPERNICUS, Nicholas de
- De Revolutionibus Orbium Coelestium Libri VI. Nuremb., 1543. *1st. Edn.* Sm. fo. Leath., ca. 1700. (R. Oct.12; 1659) DM 75,000
- - **Anr. Edn.** Basel, 1566. *2nd. Edn.* Fo. Title-p. guarded, reprd. tear not affecting letters or device, sm. paper loss at top corner, slightly discold. thro.-out, a few ll. with minor margin stains, 17th. C. Engl. blind-stpd. cf., rebkd., part of orig. spine preserved; Anthony Linton's owners inscr. dtd 1585, scattered annots. in his hand & underlining, British Museum stp. on verso of title-p., 2 Coward College bkplts., New College, London, General Liby. bkplt., Thomas Henry Court-John D. Stanitz copy. (SPB. Apr.25; 99) $5,750

COPLAND, Samuel
- Agriculture, Ancient & Modern: A Historical Account of its Principles & Practice. 1866. 2 vols. Lge. 8vo. Engraved frontis., 2 engraved titles, 41 plts., slight staining, hf. cf. gt., spines gt., rubbed; Dr. G.E. Fussell copy. (P. Jul.5; 55) £60

COPPARD, Alfred Edgar
- The Higgler. N.Y., Chocorua Pr., [1930]. *1st. Separate Edn.* (39) with page of orig. MS. Lge. 4to. Orig. canvas-bkd. bds., s.-c. worn; Perry Molstad copy. (SPB. May 16; 438) $100

COPPER PLATE MAGAZINE, or Monthly Treasure for the Admirers of the Imitative Arts
Ill.:– after P. Sandby & others. L., 1778. 4to. Engraved title, 124 engraved ports. & plts., cont. cf., w.a.f. (C. Nov.16; 9) *Maggs.* £190
- - **Anr. Edn.** L., [1792-1802]. 5 vols. Ob. 4to. Engraved titles, 250 engraved views, some very slight spotting, Vol. 3 stained, cont. cf.-bkd. marb. bds., worn. (S. Dec.1; 175) *Nicholson.* £650
- - **Anr. Copy.** 4 vols. only in 2. Ob. 4to. 4 engraved titles, 200 plts., some light spotting, mod. cl., 1 cover soiled. (CSK. Dec.2; 30) £480
- - **Anr. Edn.** N.d. 4 vols. in 2. Ob. 4to. 4 engraved titles, 200 plts. (dtd. 1792-1800), some light spotting, lacks 2 text ll. from Vol. 3, mod. cl., 1 cover soiled. (CSK. Feb.10; 18) £400

COPPER-ROYER, J.
- La Marqueterie de Paille. Paris, 1954. 4to. Sewed. (HD. May 4; 234) Frs. 1,050

COPPIER, André Charles
- Les Eaux Fortes Authentiques de Rembrandt. Paris, 1929. 2 vols. 4to. Plts. in Vol. 1 loose as iss., Vol. 2 hf. mor. (SPB. Nov.30; 146) $225

COQUIOT, Gustave
- Les Pantins de Paris. Ill.:– after Jean L. Forain. Paris, 1920. *(250) roman-numbered. (50) with a suite of the ills. on Chine.* 4to. Mor. by R. Laurent, spine & outer corners with mor. onlays & gt. line tooling, orig. wraps. bnd. in, s.-c., spine faded. (S. Nov.21; 22) *Marks.* £250
- Poupées de Paris: Bibelots de Luxe. Ill.:– Lobel-Riche. Paris, [1912]. *(300)* numbered. 4to. 1 plt. loose, three-qtr. lev., spine with gt. & leath. inlay

designs, ptd. wraps. bnd. in. (SG. Mar.29; 102) $110
- - **Anr. Edn.** Ill.:– Lobel-Riche. Paris, [1912]. *(300). (110) on vell. with state on japan with remarks in black & definitive state.* 4to. 40 orig. etchings, red hf. mor., corners, by Yseux, unc., wrap. & spine preserved. (HD. May 4; 235) Frs. 3,000
- Suite Provinciale. Ill.:– after M. Chagall. Paris, 1927. *(500) on velin de Rives.* 4to. Orig. wraps., unc. (HK. Nov.11; 3466a) DM 1,100

CORBET, Richard
- Certain Elegant Poems. L., 1647. *1st. Edn.* Lacks A1 (?blank) & blank E4, title soiled, ink scrawls on verso, red mor. gt. by Wallis, mor.-bkd. case; Harold Greenhill-Borowitz copy. (SPB. May 16; 36) $500

CORBIERE, Tristan
- Les Amours Jaunes. Paris, 1873. *Orig. Edn., (490) numbered.* Lge. 12mo. On papier de Hollande, Bradel hf. mor., corners, by Alfred Farez, unc., wrap. (HD. May 16; 12) Frs. 3,800
- La Rapsodé Foraine et le Pardon de Sainte-Anne. Ill.:– Maurice Asselin. Paris, 1929. *(100).* 4to. On velin de Rives, hf. mor., unc. wrap. & spine. (HD. May 21; 109) Frs. 1,000

CORDA, A.C.J.
- Pracht-Flora Europaeischer Schimmelbildungen. Leipzig/Dresden, 1839. *(100).* Fo. 25 lithos., including 24 hand-cold., orig. bds., worn. (VG. Sep.14; 1235) Fls. 1,800

CORDECCIUS, A.
- Nova Gigantomachia, contra Sacram Imaginem Deiparae Virginis a Sancto Luca depictam et in Monte Claro Czestochoviensi ... Cracovie, 1655. Sm. 4to. Wormholes, cont. vell. (HD. Dec.2; 83) Frs. 1,000

CORDIER, F.S.
- Les Champignons. 1876. *4th. Edn.* Lge. 8vo. 60 chromolithos., hf. chagrin, spine raised bands, 2 corners worn. (HD. Jul.6; 19) Frs. 1,300

CORDINER, Rev. Charles
- Antiquities & Scenery of the North of Scotland, in a Series of Letters to Thomas Pennant ... L., 1780. Sm. 4to. Engraved title & 2 or 3 ll. with minor foxing, a little offsetting, 19th. C.(?) hf. cf. (KH. Nov.9; 575) Aus. $110
- Remarkable Ruins, & Romantic Prospects, of North Britain, with Ancient Monuments, & Singular Subjects of Natural History. 1788-95. 2 vols. 4to. 2 engraved titles, frontis., 97 plts., cont. tree cf. gt., spines gt.-decor.; Sir Ivar Colquhoun, of Luss copy. (CE. Mar.22; 69) £620
- - **Anr. Edn.** Ill.:– after Mazell. 1795. 4to. 2 engraved frontis. & titles, 97 plts., cont. gt.-panel. cf. (PD. Aug.17; 91) £130

CORDOVERO, Moshe
- Sefer Pardes Rimmonim. Korets, 1780. *[2nd. Edn. according to Tauber, 3rd. Edn. according to Friedberg].* Sm. fo. Some dampstaining & margin worming, 1st. gathering loose, edges frayed, old pol. cf., defect. (SG. Feb.2; 169) $110

CORFIELD, Prof. William Henry
- Catalogue of the Collection of Books in Valuable Bindings. 1904. Sm. 4to. Sale catalogue, 5 cold. plts. defect., 1 lf. loose, later cl.; H.M. Nixon coll. with some MS. annots. (BBA. Oct.6; 151) *Ralph.* £120
- - **Anr. Copy.** 4to. Sale catalogue, a few plts. slightly defect., title torn & reprd., mod. hf. mor. (BBA. Nov.10; 25) *Lyon.* £90

CORINTH: Results of Excavations conducted by the American School of Classical Studies at Athens
1930-61. Vols. 1-16 in 29. 4to. & lge. fo. Many plts. & text ills., ex-liby., lacks pt. 2 of vol. 7, cl. (SG. May 3; 105) $1,800

CORINTH, Lovis
- Eli. Ed.:– M.J. bin Gorion. Trans.:– Rahel Ramberg. Leipzig, 1919. Sm. 4to. On Bütten, title litho. sigd. by artist, hand-bnd. orig. vell.; ex-libris cf. Thomas Corinth inside cover, etched & sigd. by

Charlotte Berend-Corinth. (H. May 23; 1183a) DM 740
- Gesammelte Schriften. Berlin, 1920. 4to. Orig. hf. linen. (R. Oct.11; 825) DM 520
- Das Leben Walter Leistikows. Berlin, 1910. Lge. 8vo. Orig. bds. (H. May 23; 1184a) DM 750
- - **Anr. Copy.** Sm. 4to. 2 orig. etchings, orig. bds., spine slightly torn. (R. Oct.11; 887) DM 520
- - **Anr. Copy.** Title with MS. owner's mark, orig. bds., end-papers renewed. (HK. Nov.11; 3733) DM 440
- - **Anr. Edn.** Berlin, 1910. *(100) De Luxe Edn.* 4to. 2 orig. etchings & 12 text vigs., orig. bds. (BR. Apr.13; 1805) DM 450
- Selbstbiographie. Ed.:– [Charlotte Berend-Corinth]. Leipzig, 1926. *1st. Edn. (150) De Luxe Edn.* Sm. 4to. Hand-bnd. orig. mor., gt. spine, cover, inner & outer dentelle, Spamersche Buchbinderei, Leipzig; ex-libris etched & sigd. by C. Berend-Corinth on end-paper. (H. May 23; 1183) DM 1,150

CORINTH, Lovis (Ill.)
See— BIBLIANA [German]

CORINTH, L. & Hausenstein, W.
- Von Corinth und über Corinth (binder's title). Leipzig, [1920]. *1st. Edn. (100) De Luxe Edn. with etching sigd. by artist.* Sm. 4to. On Bütten, 2 ill. with sm. brown spot, last p. margin browned, hand-bnd. cf., spine & margins lightly discold., lr. cover worn; ex-libris Thomas Corinth inside cover, etched & sigd. by Charlotte Berend-Corinth. (H. May 23; 1186) DM 540

CORIOLIS, Gaspard Gustave de
- Du Calcul de l'Effet des Machines. Paris, 1829. *1st. Edn.* 4to. Hf.-title, final errata lf., some spotting, cont. mor.-bkd. bds., spine rubbed; John D. Stanitz coll. (SPB. Apr.25; 100) $375
- Théorie Mathématique des Effets du Jeu de Billard. Paris, 1835. *1st. Edn.* Hf.-title, spotted, light stain in upr. margins, many pencil notes in margins, cf.-bkd. marb. bds., light rubbing; John D. Stanitz coll. (SPB. Apr.25; 101) $200

CORN COMMITTEE
- Report from Corn Committee. On the Prohibition of Distillation from Grain. 1810. Fo. Orig. wraps. (P. Jan.12; 275) *Phelps.* £70

CORNAZZANO, Antonio
- De Re Militari. Venice, 1536. Partly dampstained, old vell., loose. (SG. Oct.27; 219) $100

CORNEILLE (Pseud.)
See— BEVERLOO, C.G. 'Corneille'

CORNEILLE, Jean-Baptiste & Le Clere, Sebastien
- Les Premiers Elemens de la Peinture Pratique. Paris, 1684. Engraved vig. title, appendix with engraved title, 51 plts., bdg. not stated; Sir Ivar Colquhoun, of Luss copy. (CE. Mar.22; 70) £250

CORNEILLE, Pierre
- L'Imitation de Jésus-Christ Traduite et Paraphrasée en Vers Francois. Ill.:– Campion, Chauveau &c. Rouen, 1656. 2 vols. 12mo. Old str.-grd. mor., spines decor. (HD. May 3; 33) Frs. 1,300
- - **Anr. Edn.** Ill.:– L. Simonneau. Paris, 1665. Ruled copy, cont. red mor., Du Seuil decor., decor. spine, inner dentelle, hf. mor. box, corners. (HD. Mar.14; 19) Frs. 4,000
- Oeuvres. Rouen & Paris, 1644. *1st. Orig. Coll. Edn.* Pt. 1 (all publd.). Sm. 12mo. Cont. cf., spine decor.; from Jules Lemaître Liby. (HD. Mar.29; 22) Frs. 52,000
- - **Anr. Edn.** Paris, 1830-31. 12 vols. Cont. roan-bkd. bds., spines gt., spines slightly worn; bkplt. of Gustav & Anna Florsheim. (S. Mar.20; 762) *Blanko.* £90
- Remerciement au Roy. Paris, 1663. *Orig. Edn.* 4to. Jansenist red mor. by Trautz-Bauzonnet, 1859, Baron de Lurde cypher; from Baron de Ruble liby. (HD. Mar.29; 24) Frs. 65,000
- Le Théâtre de P. Corneille. Paris, 1682. *Revised Edn. 1st. Printing.* 4 vols. 12mo. With Vol. IV frontis. (often lacking), cont. red mor., spines decor. (HD. Mar.29; 23) Frs. 75,000
- - **Anr. Edn.** Commentaires. Voltaire. Ill.:– Pierre, engraved by Watelet (frontis.), Gravelot.

CORNEILLE, Pierre -Contd.

[Genève], 1764. *1st. Printing of ills.* 12 vols. Cont. cf., spine decor., later arms of Turinetti, Marquis de Prié. (HD. Apr.13; 12) Frs. 6,500
– – **Anr. Edn.** Ill.:– Gravelot. Genève, 1774. 8 vols. Stains, some foxing & yellowed ll., cont. spr. cf., gt.-decor., sm. defects. (HD. Dec.9; 22) Frs. 5,500
– – **Anr. Copy.** 4to. Cont. marb. cf., spines decor. (HD. May 3; 34) Frs. 4,800
– – **Anr. Edn.** N.p., 1776. 10 vols. Old str.-grd. mor. gt., spines blind-decor., labels detchd. (HD. Nov.17; 16) Frs. 1,500
– – **Anr. Edn.** Commentaries:– Voltaire. Paris, 1795. *(250) on vell.* 10 vols. Lge. 4to. Cont. hf. sheep, decor. spines. (HD. Sep.22; 225) Frs. 2,200
– – **Anr. Edn.** Paris, 1877-79. 5 vols. 12mo. Cont. hf. havanna mor. (HD. Apr.11; 14) Frs. 1,500

CORNELIUS, Brother

– **Keith: Old Master of California.** N.Y., [1942]. *1st. Edn.* Bdg. not stated, covers lightly darkened, label removed from front fly-lf. (CBA. Jan.29; 280) $200

CORNELIUS, Mary A.

– **The White Flame.** Chic., [1900]. *1st. Edn.* No bdg. stated, covers lightly soiled, upr. cover perforated near bottom through prelims. (CBA. Oct.29; 224) $120

CORNELIUS, W.

See— **KOBBE, Th. von & Cornelius, W.**

CORNIDE, José

– **Observaciones sobre la Pesca llamada de Bou ... en el Golfo de Valencia.** Valencia, 1821. Fo. Bds. (DS. Apr.27; 2059) Pts. 24,000

CORNWALL, Barry (Pseud.)

See— **PROCTER, Bryan Waller 'Barry Cornwall'**

CORNWALLIS, Sir William

– **Essays.** [L.], 1600. *1st. Edn. of Pt.1.* 12mo. Faint stain on N gathering, lacks final blanks, slight worming, later sheep., bkplts. of Marquis Cornwallis & Lord Braybrooke. [STC 5775] (SPB. May 16; 37) $150

CORONA BEATAE MARIAE VIRGINIS

See— **TURRECREMATA, Johannes de**— **CORONA BEATAE MARIAE VIRGINIS**

CORONATIONS

– **Services for Coronations of 1902 & 1911.** L., 1902; 1911, *(500) on Japan vell. (1st. vol.).* 2 vols. 4to. Vell. gt., covers slightly bowed, gt. emblems, 2nd. vol. with silk endll.; each inscr. by Joseph Chamberlain to his wife. (SG. Apr.19; 211) $100

CORONELLI, Vincenzo Maria

– **Atlante Veneto.** Ill.:– Maps:– G.G. de Rossi & others. Venice, 1695 [colophon 1691]. 2 vols. Fo. Engraved hf.-title & title, 3 'gli argonauti' plts., 3 engraved frontis. (2 double-p.), 2 ports., engraved dedication lf., ptd. title to Corso geografico in Vol. II, 312 engraved plts. showing maps, plans, cosmographical diagrams, panoramic views, naval subjects (158 double-p., 80 full-p., many showing several subjects), & including 4 maps & plans by G.G. de Rossi, MS. plan of Livorno in ink & cols., unsigd., & 10 ll. of MS. notes on cosmography & geography (1 lf. with moveable volvelle) compiled by Giovanni Battista Vitolini dtd. 1736, ptd. index ll. at end of both vols. listing 190 subjects only, some staining or faint discolouration, a few light creases, 1 or 2 margins frayed without loss of engraved surface, vell.-bkd. bds., worn, w.a.f. (S. May 21; 117) *Hillman.* £19,000
– **Corso Geografico Universale.** Venice, 1692. Fo. Engraved frontis., 118 engraved mapsheets (114 double-p., some showing 2 or more subjects), index lf. at end, 1 or 2 short tears without loss of engraved surface, cont. cf., worn, w.a.f. (S. May 21; 144) *Hillman.* £9,000
– **Epitome Cosmographica.** Cologne, 1693. Engraved title, 22 (of 37) folding plts., 1 with volvelles, a few ll. slightly spotted, cont. vell., rperd., soiled. (BBA. Feb.23; 29) *Callea.* £65
– **Globi Del P. Coronelli.** Venice, [1693 but later (one plate dated 1691)]. MS. title in engraved border, 3 engraved 'gli argonauti' plts., double-p. dedication, port. of Coronelli, 2 plts. showing globe diagrams, 152 full-p. plts. showing gore sections for the 2″, 4″, 1 foot & 3 foot terrestrial & celestial globes, together with equatorial ring plts., 1st. 'argonauti' plt. reprd., sm. erasure on title, some light margin soiling, hf. cf. gt., w.a.f. (S. May 21; 114) *Schuster.* £17,500
– **Isolario Descrittione Geografico-Historica ... dell' Atlante Veneto.** Venice, [1691-97]. Fo. Double-p. engraved view, 2 double-p. engraved plans, 110 engraved maps on 99 double-p. sheets, mntd. on guards thro.-out, lacks titles & all text, 1 plan slightly defect. at head of fold, Pelloponese holed affecting a few letters, Azores with short tear at foot of fold, a few maps slightly dampstained, a few bkd., 2 maps creased, a few margin repairs, mod. hf. vell., as an atlas, w.a.f. (C. Jun.27; 26) *Faupel.* £4,000
– **Libro dei Globi.** Ca. 1688. Card ll. to make 2 globes (1 terrestrial & 1 celestial), 48 plts., 4 caps & 8 plts. for equators, in sheets, cl. bds. (HD. Jun.18; 13) Frs. 160,000
– **Mémoires Historiques et Géographiques du Royaume de la Morée.** Amst., 1686. 12mo. Cont. cf. (HD. Jun.29; 84) Frs. 4,300
– **Memoire Istoriografiche de Regni della Morea, Negroponte e Littorali sin' a Salonichi.** [Venice, 1686]. *2nd. Edn.* Engraved title, 42 plts., maps & plans (only 37, including title, called for in plt.-list), hf.-title, 1 or 2 tears without loss of engraved or ptd. surface, some slight soiling, cont. vell. bds., soiled. (S. Dec.1; 345) *Hansis.* £840
– **Theatro della Guerra. Partie Corse.** [Vinezia, 1700.]. Ob. 4to. Sewed. (HD. Oct.21; 65) Frs. 6,800
– – **Anr. Edn.** Naples, 1706. Ob. 4to. Engraved title, sub.-title, 2 ptd. titles, 2 ports., 117 plts. & part titles, margins stained or defaced, cont. limp vell., rubbed & soiled. (BBA. May 23; 344) *Nolan.* £550

CORONER'S GUIDE: or The Office & Duty of a Coroner

1756. *2nd. Edn.* Interleaved thro.-out with MS. notes in cont. hand, cont. reversed cf., rubbed. (CSK. Jul.13; 89) £220

CORREO LITERARIO Y ECONOMICO DE SEVILLA

Seville, 1804-06. Vols. 1, 3, 4, 5 & 8. 4to. Sewed. (DS. Dec.16; 2013) Pts. 90,000

CORRI, Domenico

– **A Complete Musical Grammar, With a Concise Dictionary Comprehending all the Signs, Marks & Terms Necessary to the Practice of Music ...** Edinb. & L., ca. 1787. Engraved thro.-out, in folding sections, designed to be opened out to a width of approx 80cm., cf. bds. (S. May 10; 67) *Quaritch.* £400

CORROZET, Gilles

– **Les Antiquités, Croniques et Singularitéz de Paris ...** Ill.:– Jean Rabel. Paris, 1586-88. *1st. Printing of woodcuts.* 2 pts. in 1 vol. Title doubled, cont. limp vell. (HD. Mar.19; 89) Frs. 1,600

CORRY, John & Evans, John

– **The History of Bristol.** Bristol, 1816. 2 vols. Vol. 1 title cleanly torn & reprd., cont. cf. (CSK. Sep.16; 161) £75

CORSICA

– **Code Corse, ou Receuil des Edits, Déclarations, Lettres Patentes, Arrêts & Règlemens, Publiés dans l'Isle de Corse depuis sa Soumission à l'Obéissance.** Paris, 1778, Bastia, 1778-92. 3 vols., 11 vols. 4to. In Fr. & Italian, cont. vell., spines restored. (HD. Oct.21; 59) Frs. 28,000
– **Stato Attuale degl'Affari Presenti in Corsica.** Venezia, 1767. 12mo. Sewed. (HD. Oct.21; 165) Frs. 1,100

CORSO, Gregory

– [**Ankh.**]. N.Y., 1971. *(26) lettered, sigd.* Ob. 8vo. Ptd. wraps. (SG. May 24; 25) $110
– **The Vestal Lady on Brattle, & Other Poems.** Camb., Mass., [1955]. *(500).* Ptd. wraps., trifle discold. (SG. May 24; 20) $140

CORTES, Hernando

– **Correspondence de Fernand Cortes avec l'Empereur Charles-Quint, sur la Conquête du Mexique.** Trans.:– Vicomte de Flavigny. Switzerland, 1779. Cont. crushed mor., spine faded, slightly worn. (TA. Feb.16; 363) £70
– **Historia de la Nueva España ...** Ed.:– [Francisco Antonio Lorenzana]. Mexico City, 1770. *1st. Edn.* Sm. fo. Vig. title, 2 folding maps, 34 engraved plts., title & a few other ll. lightly spotted, reprd. wormholes to extreme inner margin of some 40 ll., cont. vell., rebkd.; the Rt. Hon. Visc. Eccles copy. [Sabin 16938] (CNY. Nov.18; 76) $1,600
– – **Anr. Copy.** Fo. Mor.-bkd. bds. [Sabin 16938] (LH. Sep.25; 207) $950

CORTES DE ALBACAR, Martin

– **Breve Compendio de la Sphaera y de la Arte de Navegar.** Seville, 1551. *1st. Edn.* Fo. Lacks volvelles, title & margins of many pp. restored affecting side-notes & sometimes text, antique-style elab. blind-tooled mor. over bds., brass clasps, w.a.f. [Sabin 1551] (C. May 30; 21) *Arkway.* £650

CORTES SOCIETY

– **Documents & Narratives Concerning the Discovery & Conquest of Latin America.** N.Y., 1917-22. *(250) numbered.* 5 vols. in 7. Cl.-bkd. paper bds. (LH. Sep.25; 205) $200
– [**Publications**]. Berkeley & Alburquerque, 1942-67. New Series: Vols. I-V. 4to. & 8vo. Cl. (LH. Sep.25; 206) $275

CORTESAO, Armando

– **History of Portuguese Cartography.** Cimbra, 1969 & 71. *(1000).* 2 vols. 4to. Title lf. with MS. dedication, orig. linen. (D. Nov.23; 877) DM 450

CORTESIUS, Alexander

– **Oratio Habita in Aede D. Petri in Epiphania.** [Rome, S. Plannck], after 25 Jan. 1483. 4to. Lge. copy, disbnd.; the Walter Goldwater copy. [BMC IV, 82; Goff C-940] (SG. Dec.1; 112) $200
– – **Anr. Copy.** 4to. Lacks final blank, mod. bds; the Walter Goldwater copy. [BMC IV, 82; Goff C-940] (SG. Dec.1; 113) $125

CORTISSOZ, Royal

– **The Architecture of John Russell Pope.** N.Y., [1925-30]. 3 vols. Tall fo. 302 photo. plts., ex-liby., buckram. (SG. May 3; 285) $550

CORTOT, Alfred

– **La Musique Française du Piano.** Paris, 1930-32. *1st. Edn.* 2 vols. in 1. Mod. marb. bds.; sigd. & inscr. (S. May 10; 40) *Crete.* £180

CORVISART, Jean Nicolas

– **Essai sur les Maladies et les Lésions Organiques du Coeur et des Gros Vaisseaux.** Paris, 1806. *1st. Edn.* Cont. marb. leath, gt., decor., worming on covers reprd. (HK. Nov.8; 487) DM 450
– – **Anr. Edn.** Paris, 1818. *3rd. Edn.* Some browning, marginal stains, cont. hf. cf., worn. (S. Apr.10; 489) *Phelps.* £70

CORVO, Baron (Pseud.)

See— **ROLFE, Frederick W.S. 'Baron Corvo'**

CORY, Charles B.

– **Birds of the Bahama Islands.** Boston, 1880. *1st. Edn.* 4to. 8 hand-cold. litho. plts., gt.-decor. cl., spine ends worm, ex-liby. (SG. Oct.6; 108) $225
– **The Birds of Haiti & San Domingo.** Boston, [1884-]85. *(300).* 4 pts. in 4 vols. 4to. Map, 22 hand-cold. litho. plts., some light foxing, orig. pict. wraps., chipped, disbnd., ex-liby. (SG. Oct.6; 109) $300

COSSIO, M.B. & Soteras, J. Pijoan y

– **Summa Artis; historia general del arte.** Madrid, 1931-77. 25 vols. 4to. No bdg. stated. (SPB. Nov.30; 235) $450

COSTA, Gianfrancesco

– **Les Délices de la Brenta.** Venice, [1730-56]. 2 vols. Fo. 3 engraved titles, 139 plts. (numbered 2-70 & 1-70), possibly lacking an additional title in Italian in Vol. 1, cont. bds., MS. labels on upr. covers, spine extremities reprd. (C. Dec.9; 24) *Weinreb.* £18,500

COSTA, Micer Juan
- Gobierno del Ciudadano. Zaragoza, 1584. 4to. Linen, subralibros. (DS. Mar.23; 2074)
Pts. 80,000

COSTA DE BASTELICA, F.M.
- La Corse et son Recrutement. Paris, 1873. Some light foxing, mod. hf. roan. From 'Recueil des mémoires de medecine, de chirurgie et de pharmacie militaires'. (HD. Oct.21; 69) Frs. 1,100
- Sampiero Corso. Ajaccio, 1905. Hf. chagrin, wrap. (HD. Oct.21; 70) Frs. 1,200

COSTELLO, Dudley
- Piedmont & Italy. L., 1861. 2 vols. in 1. 4to. Additional engraved titles with vigs., 6 double-p. maps, 130 steel-engraved plts., cont. hf. cf. gt. (S. Dec.1; 340) King. £280
- – Anr. Edn. L., 1862. 2 vols. in 1. 4to. 2 Engraved titles, 6 double-p. maps, 129 (of 130) engraved plts., some spotting, cont. hf. cf., worn, covers detchd. (BBA. Dec.15; 67) Erlini. £140

COSTUME
- Chinese Costumes. Foreword:– Hardy Jowett. Peking, [1932]. Sm. fo. 24 hand-cold. plts., orig. silk. (BBA. Nov.10; 291) Han Shan Tang. £80
- 50 Costumes des Pyrénées. Paris, ca. 1850. Leporello album with 50 cold. lithos., orig. linen, spine faded. (HK. Nov.9; 1832) DM 520
- The Civil Costume of England, from the Conquest to the Present Time ... Ill.:– L. Martin after C. Martin. L., 1842. 4to. Hand-cold. additional etched title, 60 hand-cold. etchings, mor. gt. (SG. Sep.22; 106) $350
- Collection de Costumes de Tous les Ordres Monastiques, Supprimés à Différentes Epoques dans la Ci-Devant Belgique. Brussels, [after 1797]. 4to. Engraved title, 106 hand-cold. engraved plts., thumbed, few smudges, early marginalia, cont. cf. (SG. Nov.3; 46) $350
- Collection de Cris et Costumes de Paysans et Paysannes de St. Petersbourg. Ill.:– Alexandre Pluchart. St. Petersb., 1823. Fo. Wide margin, title with wide typographic border, with defects., 16 cold. lithos. & 1 added litho. port., plts. with sm. hole thro-out, defect. in lr. margin (? from defect. in lr. cover?), old hf. leath., defects., loose; Hauswedell coll. (H. May 23; 165) DM 3,800
- A Collection of Fashion Plates. [Paris, 1862-68]. 4 vols. 4to. 1 litho. & 486 engraved plts., including 14 folding, most hand-cold., cont. hf. mor., w.a.f. (CSK. Aug.19; 57) £800
- Conjunto (Racolta di Costumes dello Stato Romano) de 43 Láms. grabs. de Figuras Religiosas y Militares., Color. 1822. Linen. (DS. Apr.27; 2560) Pts. 75,000
- Conseiller des Dames et des Demoiselles: Journal d'Economie Domestique et de Travaux à l'Aiguille. Paris, 1848-57. Vols. II, V, VII, VIII, X & XI. Tall 8vo. Plts. hand-cold., cont. qtr. cf. gt. (SG. Sep.22; 98) $190
- Costume of all Nations, disegned by the First Munich Artist. L., [1900?]. Lge. 4to. Publishers cl. (CR. Jun.6; 100) Lire 320,000
- Costume of the Russian Empire. L., 1803. 1st. Edn. Early Iss., with text & plts. wtrmkd. 1796. 4to. 73 hand-cold. engraved plts., title & text in Engl. & Fr., cont. red str.-grd. mor., covers with gt. roll-tool frame enclosing gt. Spencer arms in the Russian eagle, lr. cover slightly stained. (C. Mar.14; 44) Bifolco. £220
- – Anr. Edn. 1803. Fo. Fr. & Engl. title & text, 73 hand-cold. engraved plts., cont. hf. cf., rubbed. (CSK. Jul.6; 27) £240
- – Anr. Copy. Fo. 73 hand-cold. engraved plts. (wtrmkd. 1823), Fr. title, text in Engl. & Fr., without Engl. title, 1 plt. with margin tears, 1 margin strengthened, mod. cl. (C. Mar.14; 137) Bifolco. £160
- – Anr. Copy. 4to. 72 (of 73) hand-cold. plts., few slightly soiled, str.-grd. mor. gt. (P. Sep.29; 248) £110
- – Anr. Copy. Fo. Extra engraved cold. title, 72 hand-cold. engraved plts., each with tissue guard & text lf. in Engl. & Fr., cont. gt.-tooled russ., rebkd.; armorial bkplt. of Sir Gore Ouseley. (SG. Apr.26; 50) $550
- – Anr. Copy. Sm. fo. 73 hand-cold. engrs.

(wtrmkd. 1807), leath., worn, covers detchd. (SG. Sep.22; 107) $225
- – Anr. Edn. L., [1803]. 4to. Engraved title with lge. hand-cold. vig., 72 hand-cold. plts., some slightly soiled, cont. red mor., rebkd. (S. Mar.6; 80) Export. £140
- – Anr. Edn. L., 1804. Fo. 73 hand-cold. engraved plts. (wtrmkd. 1819-20, text wtrmkd. 1818), titles & text in Engl. & Fr., cont. purple hf. mor., spine gt., slightly rubbed. (C. Nov.16; 74) Bifolco. £150
- – Anr. Copy. 4to. Fr. & Engl. text, 73 engraved hand-cold. plts., hf. cf., corners, gt.-tooled spine. (CR. Jun.6; 299) Lire 850,000
- – Anr. Edn. L., 1811. 4to. Text in Engl. & Fr., extra engraved title with lge. cold. vig., 72 hand-cold. engraved plts., some slight spotting, cont. mor.; bkplt. of Duke of Sussex. (S. Apr.9; 14) Traylen. £160
- – Anr. Copy. Fo. Additional hand-cold. engraved title, 70 hand-cold. engraved plts., some slight margin soiling, cont. russ., rubbed, covers detchd., lacks most of spine. (S. Dec.13; 184) Schuster. £130
- – Anr. Copy. Fo. Text in Engl. & Fr., 73 hand-cold. engraved plts., ex-liby., some foxing, cont. str.-grd. mor., gt. borders & spine. (SG. May 3; 110) $300
- – Anr. Copy. Lge. 4to. Engl. & Fr. text, 1 plt. misbnd. & without text lf., a few plts. lightly foxed, cont. red mor. gt., slightly worn. (H. Nov.23; 458) DM 600
- – Anr. Copy. Fo. Frontis., 69 (of 72) engrs. in col., text in Engl. & Fr., red chagrin, rubbed. (DS. Jan.27; 2486) Pts. 30,000
- Costumes de l'Empire Russe. L., 1803. Lge. 4to. Engl. & Fr. text, 73 cold. plts., some foxing, str.-grd. mor. by Carpenter, blind- & gt.-decor., rubbed. (HD. May 4; 236) Frs. 2,800
- Les Costumes des Peuples de la Russie. Berne, 1791. 4to. Plt. list in Fr. & German, engraved title vig., 28 engraved plts., plt. list reprd., marginal tear in title, cl.-bkd. bds. (SG. Apr.26; 173) $225
- Costumes Européens du XVIIe au XIXe Siècle. Ill.:– Job & Herouard. Paris, ca. 1910. Lge. fo. 59 (of 60) aquarelles, all laid on cartridge-paper, liby. blind- & rubber-stp. on verso of each plt., mod. buckram. (CBA. Dec.10; 178) $110
- Costumes Français depuis Clovis jusqu'à nos Jours. Paris, 1836-38. 4 vols. 639 (of 640) hand-cold. plts., foxed & browned, cf.-bkd. bds. (SPB. Dec.13; 799) $550
- – Anr. Copy. Vols. I-III (of 4). 480 col. plts., slight foxing, cont. hf. cf., corners, spines decor.; S.A.R. Mgr le Duc d'Orléans liby. stp. (HD. May 4; 237) Frs. 2,200
- Costumes Historiques des XVIe, XVIIe et XVIIIe Siècles. Text:– Georges Duplessis. Ill.:– after E. Lechevallier-Chevignard. Paris, 1867. 2 vols. Fo. 150 hand-cold. engraved plts., few plts. in Vol. I lightly foxed, hf. mor., rather worn. (SG. Aug.25; 97) $260
- Les Costumes Regionaux de la France. Text:– Henry Royère. Preface:– Princesse Bibesco. Ill.:– G. de Gardilanne & E.W. Moffat. Paris, 1929 [1930]. 4 vols. Fo. Numbered copy, plts. in leaves, text in cl. fascicle, box. (HD. May 21; 110) Frs. 5,100
- Costumes Suisses. L., ca. 1870. 22 mntd. photos. in concertina form, split along folds into 3 pts., orig. cl., slightly worn. (S. Apr.9; 15) Locker. £50
- Die Costuymen Ubettē eñ Statuyten vande Seale eñ Casselrie vā Ypre. [Ypern], 1571. Sm. 4to. Preface dtd. 18 Jun. 1535, lacks 2 ll. after title, last lf. torn, cut close in upr. margin, some soiling, cont. vell., slightly defect. (H. Nov.23; 595) DM 3,200
- Etat de tous les Uniformes des Regimentes et Corps de'Armée Imperiale et Royal. Vienna, 1786. Engraved title, 135 hand-cold. engraved plts., some titled in ink, cont. diced cf. gt.; the Hinton House copy. (LC. Oct.13; 415) £500
- Fourth Year of the French Republic. 1795. Dresses of the Representatives of the People, Members of the Two Councils, & of the Executive Directory ... 1796. Additional engraved title, 15 hand-cold. engraved plts., cf., spine gt.; the Hinton House copy. (LC. Oct.13; 439) £110
- Galerie des Femmes Célèbres de l'Ancienne France. Ill.:– Gatine after Lante. Paris, n.d. Sm. fo.

70 hand-cold. plts., same as those in 1827 'Galerie Française de Ferres Calèbres', bds., disbnd. (SG. Aug.25; 99) $140
- Gallerie des Modes et Costumes Français ... Ill.:– Bacquoy, Leroy, Voysard, & others, after Desrais, Leclerc, & others. Paris, 1778-81. Vols. I & II only (of 4). Fo. Engraved title, 192 hand-cold. engraved plts., plt. 141 with reprd. tear, 3 plts. with sm. tears in lr. blank margins, cont. cf., worn. (C. Nov.16; 91) Ginsburg. £10,000
- – Anr. Edn. N.d. Pt. 3. 20 cold. reproductions of hand-cold. plts., loose as iss. in portfo., with ties. (SKC. Mar.9; 1776) £85
- Journal des Jeunes Personnes. Paris, 1835-46. Vols. III, V-IX, & XIV. Many plts. hand-cold., some foxing, &c., cont. qtr. mor. (SG. Sep.22; 110) $100
- Katalog der Lipperheideschen Kostümbibliothek. Ed.:– E. Nienholott & G. Wagner-Neumann. Berlin, 1965. 2 vols. 4to. Orig. linen. (R. Apr.3; 661) DM 480
- Le Keepsake de Costumes ... Album offert aux abonnés du Journal Les Modes Parisiennes. Ill.:– Gavarni, etc. Paris, 1853. 4to. 52 cold. plts., hf. leath. gt. (SKC. Sep.9; 1874) £160
- Military Costume of Europe. L., 1822. 2 vols. Tall fo. 97 hand-cold. engraved plts., each with text lf., liby. stp. on titles, 1st. title-p. soiled, some light stains, mod. cl. (SG. Apr.26; 141) $1,100
- The Military Costume of Turkey. L., 1818. Fo. Text ll. with offset from plts., cont. restored mor., gt.- & blind-tooled, slightly worn. (H. Nov.23; 460) DM 900
- Modes de Paris. Ca. 1830. 53 hand-cold. plts., hf. mor. (P. Mar.15; 95) Thorp. £160
- Musée Cosmopolite. Paris, [1850-63]. 2 pts. only (of 11), in 1 vol. 27 & 37 hand-cold. plts., slight spotting, cont. red mor., gt.-& blind-stpd., slight rubbing, as a coll. of plts., w.a.f. (SPB. Dec.13; 800) $275
- Nouvelle Suite de Costumes des Pyrénées. Ill.:– Ferogio after Lagarrigne. Paris, ca. 1850. Fo. 16 cold. litho. plts., 2 additional cold. plts. bnd. in, a few plts. foxed, cont. hf. mor., gt.-decor. (SKC. Nov.18; 1831) £140
- Preussische Armee-Uniformen unter der Regierung Friedrich Wilhelm II. Konigs von Preussen. Potsdam, 1789. 136 cold. engraved plts. (Bound with:) - Nachtrag zu den Preussichen Armee-Uniformen oder Vierzehnte Lieferung von Vierzehn Blattern Worinnen die Campagne Uniformen. Potsdam, 1791. 14 hand-cold. plts. (Bound with:) - Preussische Armee-Uniformen Anhang von sechs Blattern. Potsdam, 1789. 6 hand-cold. plts. Together 3 works in 1 vol. Cont. diced cf. gt.; the Hinton House copy. (LC. Oct.13; 414) £1,600
- Raccolta di 30 Costumi con Altretante Vedute le piu Interessanti della Citta di Milano. Milan, [1810-15]. On vell., etched title, 1 lf. intro., 30 numbered aquatint engrs., alternating with 1 text lf., minimal spotting, loose, cont. bds., spine defect; Hauswedell coll. (H. May 23; 124) DM 3,400
- Recueil des Habillements Différentes Nations, Anciens et Modernes. 1757. Vols. 1 & 2 only (of 4). Vig. titles, 237 engraved plts., text in Fr. & Engl., 1 vig. title loose, disbnd., as a coll. of plts., w.a.f. (P. Sep.8; 50) Frankel. £110
- Standard Uniforms & Patterns of the Army, Navy, Militia, Volunteers, Civil Service, Court Dress & c. L., W. Jones & Co., ca. 1856. Fo. Cold. & plain litho. plts., 12 loose plts. inserted at beginning, some frayed, some slight margin soiling, orig. cl. gt., rubbed & soiled. (S. Dec.20; 549) Power. £880
- The World of Fashion. 1846. Sm. 4to. 72 plts. (60 cold.), cont. hf. cf. (SKC. Mar.9; 1928) £100
- Zur Geschichte der Kostüme. Ill.:– after W. Diez, C. Fröhlich, C. Häberlin & others. München, ca. 1885. Fo. Ll. 1-95 each with 4 cold. ills., hf. linen. (GB. May 3; 936) DM 400
- Zur Geschichte der Kostueme. Ill.:– after Braun, Diez, Froelich, Gehrts, Haeberlin, Heil, Mueller, Rothbart, & others. Munich, late 19th C. Sm. 4to. 125 hand-cold. double-p. plts., typed contents list in Engl. added, cl., disbnd. (SG. Aug.25; 115) $110
- Zweihundert Historische Kostüme–und Volkstrachten Bilder. Berlin, ca. 1885. 191 (of 200)

COSTUME -*Contd.*

woodcut or steel engrs., plts. dtd. between 1875 & 1884 in lr. margin, loose in lf. linen portfo., spine defect. (R. Oct.12; 2219) DM 800
See— **UNITED STATES ARMY**

COTERIE
Ill.:– after Sickert, H. Gaudier Brzeska & others. 1919-21. Pts. 1-7 in 6 (all publd.). 4to. Orig. pict. wraps., mostly lightly soiled, a few with backstrip cleanly torn. (CSK. Jul.13; 164) £60
– – **Anr. Copy.** 7 numbers (all published). 4to. Browned, orig. ptd. wraps. (SPB. May 16; 439) $175

COTES, Roger
– **Harmonia Mensurarum** ... Ed.:– Robert Smith. Camb., 1772. *1st. Edn.* 4to. Hf.-title, slight browning, mostly of end-papers, cont. cf., rebkd., orig. label laid down, corners rubbed; 76 pp. cont. MS. notes by William Morgan bnd. at end, John D. Stanitz copy. (SPB. Apr.25; 102) $250

COTMAN, John Sell
– **Architectural Antiquities of Normandy.** L., 1822. 2 vols. Fo. 96 etched plts., some spotting, cont. cf. (S. Mar.6; 82) *Sanders.* £270
– **Engravings of Sepulchral Brasses in Norfolk & Suffolk.** 1839. *2nd. Edn.* 2 vols. Fo. 171 plts., cont. hf. mor., lightly rubbed. (CSK. Mar.23; 14) £110
– **A Series of Etchings Illustrative of the Architectural Antiquities of Norfolk.** L., 1818. 2 pts. in 1 vol. Fo. 110 etched plts., pt. 2 without title or text, a few plts. spotted, mainly at margins, later hf. mor., spine rubbed. (C. Mar.14; 105) *Craddock.* £220
– **Specimens of the Architectural Antiquities of Norfolk.** Yarmouth, 1812. Pts. 1-6 & 8 only. Fo. 42 (of 60) plts., numbered 1-36 & 43-48, spotted, 6 dampstained, orig. wraps., torn & loose, 1 lacking. (BBA. Feb.23; 111) *Craddock & Barnard.* £150

COTOVICUS, Joannes
– **Itinerarium Hierosolymitanum et Syriacum.** Antw., 1619. *1st. Edn.* 4to. 1 folding table torn, errata-slip for pp. 344-518 & prelims. laid in, cont. vell.; J.W. Ingraham MS. ex-libris. (SG. Sep.22; 114) $700

COTTEAU
See— **LOCARD & COTTEAU**

COTTON, Charles
[–] **The Complete Gamester.** [L., 1680]. *2nd. Edn.* Lacks ptd. title & 2 following ll., 16 MS. ll. transcribing title-pp. of the first 5 edns. & containing bibliographical information bnd. in, 19th. C. three-qtr. mor., scuffed. (SG. Oct.27; 75) $150
– **Memoirs of the Sieur de Pontis; Who Served in the Army Six & Fifty Years.** 1694. Fo. Liby. stp. on title verso, cont. panel. cf., some wear. (TA. Jul.19; 377) £54
– **The Planters Manual.** L., 1675. Come spotting, cont. cf., worn. [Wing C6388] (CSK. Nov.4; 164) £240
– **Poems on Several Occasions.** L., 1689. *1st. Edn.* Slight printing flaws on 2G3 verso & 2G6 recto, slight spotting, inscr. on title, cont. cf., spine very worn. [Wing C6390] (S. Dec.8; 14) *Quevedo.* £100
– **The Wonders of the Peake.** L., 1681. *1st. Edn.* Lacks final blank, a little spotting, cont. cf.; sig. of R. Greene. (S. Oct.11; 508) *Hannas.* £160

COTTON, Charles
See— **WALTON, Isaac & Cotton, Charles**

COTTON, John
– **Beautiful Birds Described.** Ed.:– Robert Tyas. Ill.:– J. Andrews. L., 1868. 2 vols. 12mo. 36 hand-cold. plts., 1 plt. creased at inner edge, orig. gt.-pict. cl., slightly shaken. (SG. Oct.6; 41) $120
– **The Song Birds of Great Britain [comprising] The Resident Song Birds, The Summer Migrant Song Birds.** 1935. 2 pts. in 1 vol. 33 hand-cold. plts., pencil captions, red hf. mor., spine emblematically gt., unc. (SKC. May 4; 1844) £750

COTTON, Nathaniel
– **Poetical Works.** 1812. (*Bound with:*) **FALCONER, William** – **Poetical Works.** 1809. Together 2 works in vol. 16mo. Cf. gt., lightly rubbed, fore-e. pntg. (CSK. Jul.13; 101) £90

COTTREAU, G.
– **Illustration de Job. Tenues des Troupes de France.** Paris, [1904]. 3 vols. 4to. Hf. mor., spine richly decor.; Henri Marcus copy. (HD. Jan.27; 132) Frs. 7,500

COTUGNO, Domenico
– **De Ischiade Nervosa Commentarius.** Napoli, 1764. *1st. Edn.* Some stains, cont. hf. leath., slightly bumped & wormed. (SI. Dec.15; 151) Lire 550,000

COUCH, Jonathan
– **A History of the Fishes of the British Islands.** L., 1862-65. [1860-65]. *1st. Edn.* 4 vols. 252 wood-engraved hand-finished cold. plts., some minor spotting, mod. hf. mor. gt. (C. Jun.27; 148) *Ross.* £480
– – **Anr. Copy.** 4 vols. 252 cold. plts., a few ll. loose, cont. hf. mor., spines gt., inner hinge of Vol. 4 brkn. (C. Jun.27; 114) *Parkway.* £280
– – **Anr. Copy.** 4 vols. Orig. cl. (CSK. Dec.16; 226) £150
– – **Anr. Copy.** 4 vols. Orig. cl., worn, last vol. in hf. mor., all with same cont. inscr. on titles. (BBA. Jul.27; 8) *R.V. Elliott.* £110
– – **Anr. Copy.** 4 vols. Lithos. hand-cold., publishers cl., gt. (CR. Jun.6; 142) Lire 850,000
– – **Anr. Edn.** [L., ca. 1860]. 3 vols. Sm. ob. 4to. Mntd. on guards, hf. red mor., corners, unc. (HD. Dec.1; 83) Frs. 2,700
– – **Anr. Edn.** L., 1862-66. 4 vols. Slightly foxed, orig. gold-tooled linen. (R. Apr.4; 1709) DM 1,300
– – **Anr. Copy.** 4 vols. Plts. hand-cold., hf. mor., corners. (CR. Jun.6; 141) Lire 900,000
– – **Anr. Edn.** L., 1862-67. 4 vols. 252 cold. plts., hf. mor., spines gt. in compartments, orig. wraps. bnd. in at end of each vol. (C. Mar.14; 144) *Traylen.* £360
– – **Anr. Edn.** L., 1864-65. 4 vols. Some slight spotting, hf. mor., spines gt., by C.J. Andrews. (S. Mar.20; 763) *Dearing.* £200
– – **Anr. Edn.** L., 1867-68. 4 vols. Cont. hf. leath. (R. Oct.12; 1835) DM 1,200
– – **Anr. Edn.** 1877. 4 vols. 4to. 252 col. plts., 1 vol. plts. loose, cl. gt. (PD. Aug.17; 260) £165
– – **Anr. Edn.** 1877-78. 4 vols. 252 col. plts., orig. cl. gt., rubbed. (TA. Feb.16; 110) £200
– – **Anr. Copy.** 4 vols. 4to. 219 (of 249) chromolitho. plts., orig. gt.-decor. cl., moderate wear to covers, spine ends chipped, lacks portion on Vol. 1. (CBA. Mar.3; 412) $225
– – **Anr. Edn.** L., n.d. 4 vols. Hf. leath., spine & edges worn. (RS. Jan.17; 463) $200

COUCHE, Jacques
– **Galerie du Palais Royal, Gravée d'après les Tableaux des Differentes Ecoles qui la Composent** ... Ed.:– Abbé de Fontenai. Ill.:– J. Couche & others. Paris, 1786. Vol. 1 only (of 3). Fo. 169 plts., light foxing, some stains & tears, mainly in margin, hf. leath., spine defect. (SG. Oct.13; 163) $140
– – **Anr. Edn.** Paris, 1786-1808. *[1st. Edn.].* 3 vols. Fo. Engraved title, dedication, 343 (of 355) plts., 2 plts. torn, cont. red mor.-bkd. bds., unc., w.a.f. (C. Nov.9; 56) *Teresi.* £650
– – **Anr. Copy.** 3 vols. Fo. Some foxing, some margin tears, some tissue guards torn or lacking, cl., leath. backs & tips, tips little chipped. (RO. Dec.11; 82) $500
– – **Anr. Copy.** 3 vols. Lge. Fo. Engraved title, engraved dedication, 352 copperpts., some margin foxing, cont. mor. gt. (D. Nov.23; 785) DM 3,000
– – **Anr. Copy.** Fo. Lacks 5 copperplts., slightly foxed, cont. hf. leath. (R. Apr.4; 2086) DM 2,800

COULOMB, Charles Augustin
– **Observations Théoriques et Experimentals sur l'Effet des Moulins à Vent, & sur la Figure de leurs Ailes.** [Paris, 1781]. *1st. Edn.* 4to. Extract from 'Mémoires de l'Academie Royale des Sciences', mod. mor.; John D. Stanitz coll. (SPB. Apr.25; 106) $200
– **Théorie des Machines Simples, en ayant Egard au** **Frottement de leurs Parties et à la Roideur des Cordages** ... Paris, 1821. *New Edn.* 4to. Some worming, mostly marginal, affecting a few lines of text in gatherings 11 & 12, lacks hf.-title, soiling, slight spotting, cont. hf. cf., spine worn, rubbed; John D. Stanitz coll. (SPB. Apr.25; 107) $400

COULTER, Henry
– **The West of Ireland, its Existing Conditions & Prospects.** Dublin, 1862. *1st. Edn.* Hf.-title, folding map, 36 litho. plts., including 11 hand-cold., cl. (GM. Dec.7; 409) £120

COUNCIL OF TRENT
– **Canones et Decreta Sacrosancti Oecumenici, et Generalis Concilii Tridentini** ... Rome, Aldine Pr., 1564. 4to. Sm. cont. ink note, later red mor. gt., spine gt.-panel., gt. inner dentelles, silk marker; Syston Park Liby. bkplt. (CBA. Dec.20; 8) $850

COURBEILLE DE FLEURS [Panier de Fruits]
Ill.:– Maradan after Prêtre. Paris, 1807. 2 vols. Each vol. with 24 hand-finished col.-ptd. plts., unif. cont. tree cf. gt., spine ends scuffed & reprd. (C. Nov.16; 265) *Walford.* £320

COURBOIN, Francois
– **Histoire Illustrée de la Gravure en France.** Paris, 1923-28. *(750) numbered.* Together 7 vols. (4 text 3 plts.). Fo. & lge. fo. 1392 reproductions, lettered tissue guards, each plt. liby.-stpd. on verso, loose in bd. folders with ties. (SG. May 3; 122) $200

COURIER, Paul Louis
– **Collection Complète des Pamphlets Politiques et Opuscules Littérures.** Brukelles, 1826. *1st. Coll. Edn.* Some light foxing, cont. hf. cf., decor. spine. (HD. Dec.9; 1116) Frs. 1,000

COURMESVIN, L. Des Hayes de
– **Voiage de Levant ... en l'année 1621.** Paris, 1624. *1st. Edn.* 4to. Some staining, some foxing, 4 ill. loose, light browning, cont. vell., slightly defect. & darkened. (H. May 22; 297) DM 1,300

COURNOT, Antoine Augustin
– **Traité Elementaire de la Théorie des Fonctions et du Calcul Infinitesimal.** Paris, 1841. *Orig. Edn.* 2 vols. Hf. roan. (HD. Feb.22; 44) Frs. 1,900

COURS DE DANSE FIN DE SIECLE
Ill.:– Louis Legrand. Paris, 1892. *(350) numbered.* Etched frontis., 10 plts., dampstained, orig. wraps., slightly worn. (S. Dec.20; 502) *Erlini.* £80

COURT, P. de la & Witt, John de
[–] **Interest v. Holland, ofte Gronden van Hollands Welvaren ... — Hist. der Gravelike Regering in Holland — Stadthouderl. Regeeringe in Hollandt. — Naeuwk. Consideratie van Staet, wegens de Vrye en Geheymen Staetsregeering.** Amst. [Leyden], 1662. *1st. Edns. 2nd. Issues.* Together 4 works in 1 vol. Sm. 8vo. Cont. vell. (VG. Sep.14; 948) Fls. 475

COURTALON, Abbé
– **Atlas Elementaire ... de l'Empire d'Alemagne.** Paris, 1774. 4to. Wide margin, double-p. engraved title, 13 cold. copper engraved maps, (10 double-p.), 24 double-p. partly cold. tables, cont. red mor., gt. arms. supralibris on both covers, gt. decor., gt. inner & outer dentelle, gt. decor. spine. (D. Nov.23; 754) DM 11,000

COURT DE GEBELIN, Antoine
– **Histoire Naturelle de la Parole; ou Précis de l'Origine de Langage & de la Grammaire Universelle; Extrait du Monde Primitif.** Paris, priv. ptd., 1776. *1st. Edn.* Hf.-title, cont. stained cf. gt. (SG. Oct.27; 77) $250
– – **Anr. Copy.** Hf.-title, marb. bds. (SG. Oct.6; 111) $150
– **Monde Primitif.** Paris, priv. ptd., 1775. *1st. Edn.* 4to. Engraved frontis., 22 engraved plts., most folding, hf.-title, old qtr. cf. (SG. Oct.27; 78) $275

COURTE DE LA BLANCHARDIERE, Abbé
[– **A Voyage to Peru.** L., 1753. 12mo. 3 pp. advts., title-p. soiled, unbnd., wraps. [Sabin 17177] (P. Dec.8; 332) *Remington.* £140

COURTIERS & FAVOURITES of Royalty
Ed.:– Leon Valley. Paris, ca. 1900. *(1000)*. 20 vols.
Orig. three-qtr. red mor., 1 cover a little stained.
(CBA. Dec.10; 179) $180

COURTIVRON, Gaspard le Compasseur, Marquis de & Bouchu, F.
– Nauka o Gatunkach i Szukaniu Rudy Zelazney.
Ed.:– H.N. Malachowskiego. Warsaw, 1782. 4to.
34 plts., some staining, 2 ll. cropped, cont. bds., lr.
inside hinge brkn. (S. Apr.10; 490)
Henderson. £100

COURTNEY, William Prideaux
See— BOASE, G.C. & Courtney, William Prideaux

COURTNEY, William Prideaux & Smith, David Nichol
– Samuel Johnson: A Bibliography. Oxford, 1925.
Reissue of the 1915 Edn. (350). Cl. (SG. Sep.15;
189) $190

COUSINERY, E.M.
– Voyage Dans La Macédoine. Paris, 1831. 2 vols.
4to. Folding map, 23 plts., some hand-cold., 1
torn & reprd., hf. cf. gt. (P. Sep.8; 6) *Wood.* £220

COUSTEAU, Pierre
– Le Pegme, avec les Narrations Philosophiques.
Trans.:– Lanteaume de Romieu. Lyon, 1560. *2nd.
Edn. in Fr.* Sm. 8vo. Gt.-decor. red mor. by Allô.
(VG. Sep.14; 910) Fls. 1,800

COUSTUMES du Pais de Normandie, Anciens Ressors, et Enclaves d'Iceluy
Paris, 1586. *1st. Edn.* 4to. L.P., ruled, pasted-in slip
with copy of 1861 exhibition catalogue description,
cont. mor. gt., corners reprd.; from Fondation Furstenberg-Beaumesnil. (HD. Nov.16; 113)
Frs. 5,500

COUSTUMIER DE NORMENDIE, la Chartre des Previlèges & Libertés de Normendie ...
Rouen, 1552. *1st. Round Letter Edn.* Sm. 8vo.
With tree of consanguinity (oftn lacking), cont. cf.,
very worn; from Château des Noës liby. (HD. May
25; 18) Frs. 1,350

COUTO, Diego de
See— BARROS, Joao & Couto, Diego de

COUTS, Joseph
– A Practical Guide for the Tailor's Cutting-Room;
Being a Treatise on Measuring & Cutting Clothing
in all Styles. Ca. 1850. 4to. 27 engraved costume
plts., including 13 hand-cold., 18 line-engrs., some
minor margin dampstains, cont. hf. cf., recased.
(TA. Jun.21; 496) £105

COUZIJN, Wessel
– Il. Text:– B. Daneau. La Haye, 1966. *(83).* Lge.
ob. fo. 12 hand-ptd. ll. loosley inserted, decor. cl.,
unc. (B. Feb.8; 370) Fls. 1,000

COVIAN, Antonio
– Los Triunfos del Sacramento. Idea con que ...
**Granada adornó la Plaza en la Solemnidad del ...
Corpus ...** 1815. [Granada, 1815]. 4to. Leath. (DS.
Mar.23; 2378) Pts. 19,000

COWAN, Robert Ernest & Robert Granniss
– A Bibliography of the History of California. San
Franc., [1st Edn.] 1933. 3 vols. Tall 4to. Linen-
bkd. bds., unc., mostly unopened. (SG. Apr.26; 51)
$225
– – **Anr. Copy.** 3 vols. 4to. Prospectus, dtd. 1932,
laid in, orig. cl.-bkd. paper bds., slight soiling to
spines, box brkn.; the Rt. Hon. Visc. Eccles copy.
(CNY. Nov.18; 77) $170
– – **Anr. Copy.** 3 vols. 4to. Cl. (LH. Sep.25; 210)
$120

COWARD, Noel
– 'I'll leave it to You'. 1920. Orig. cl.; inscr. on
front free end-paper 'I feel rather Promising, Noel
Coward 26/5/21'. (CSK. Sep.30; 105) £100
– To night at 8.30. L. & Toronto, 1937. (With:)– To
step aside. Seven Stories N.Y., 1939. Together 2
works, each vol. with autograph dedication from
author, publishers bds. (HD. Mar.14; 109)
Frs. 2,000

COWART, Jack
– Roy Lichtenstein 1970-1980. N.Y., [1981]. *1st.
Edn.* Sm. fo. Pict. cl., s.-c.; sigd. by Cowart &
Lichtenstein. (SG. Jan.12; 224) $325

COWELL, John
– The Interpreter. 1637. *1st. Edn.* Cf. gt., rubbed.
[STC 5901] (P. Feb.16; 248) £110

COWLEY, Abraham
– Poemata Latina. L., 1678. *2nd. Edn.* 12mo.
Engraved port., cont. cf.; John Evelyn's copy with
pressmark N.48 in his hand. [Wing C6681] (SPB.
May 16; 39) $125
– Poems. L., 1656. *1st. Edn.* Fo. Few ll. slightly
spotted, cont. sheep., spine & corners reprd., worn,
qtr. mor. s.-c.; Charles C. Kalbfleisch & Frederic
Dannay copy. [Wing C 6682] (CNY. Dec.16; 84)
$180
– The Works of ... Ill.:– W. Faithorne (engraved
port.). 1668. *1st. Coll. Edn.* Fo. Cont. cf. (CE.
Sep.1; 42) £50
– – **Anr. Edn.** L., 1669. Fo. Slightly stained, slightly
soiled, cont. cf., worn, lacks upr. end-lf. (S. Oct.11;
320) *Heighton.* £50

COWLEY, Malcolm
– Blue Juaniata, Poems. N.Y., [1929]. *1st. Edn.*
Orig. cl.; pres. copy from author to Weldon Kees,
Frederic Dannay copy. (CNY. Dec.16; 85) $240

COWPER, William
– Poems. L., 1782. E6 & I6 cancels, N8 & O3 with
slight tears, few ll. little browned, without 'Preface',
cont. qtr. cf. gt., vell. corners, board edges slightly
worn; Frederic Dannay copy. (CNY. Dec.16; 86)
$420
– – **Anr. Edn.** L., 1782-85. *1st. Edn. 1st. Iss., with
E6 & I6 uncancelled.* 2 vols. Without John Newton's Preface (not called for but found in a few
copies), very few margin stains, pol. tree gt.
extra. (SG. Nov.3; 48) $950
– – **Anr. Edn.** L., 1782-85. *1st. Edn.* 2 vols. Hf.-
title in vol.2, advt. ll., errata, without John Newton's
'Preface', mor. gt. by Riviere. (SPB. May 16; 41)
$150
– – **Anr. Edn.** 1811-15. 3 vols. 2 engraved frontis.,
5 plts., lightly spotted, cont. mor. gt., gt. inner
dentelles, lightly rubbed. (CSK. Jan.27; 6) £140
– Poetical Works. L., 1853. 2 vols. Crushed lev. gt.
by J. Wright, spines & dentelles gt. (SG. Feb.16;
70) $175
– – **Anr. Edn.** L., 1870. *Globe Edn.* Sm. 8vo. Mor.
gt., fore-e. pntg. (SG. Nov.17; 226) $150
– The Works. L., 1836-37. 15 vols. Most extra
engraved titles & frontis.'s stained, cont. cf. (S.
Mar.20; 764) *Booth.* £80

COWPER, William & Newton, John
[–] Olney Hymns. L., 1779. *1st. Edn.* 12mo. Hf.-
title, slight browning & soiling, cont. cf. (S. Oct.11;
321) *Waterfields.* £80
– – **Anr. Copy.** 12mo. Thick paper, hf.-title, errata,
advt. lf., cont. inscr. cm hf.-title, cont. cf., rebkd.;
Robert-Hoe-John Drinkwater bkplts. (SPB. May
16; 40) $750

COWPER, William, Surgeon
– Anatomia Corporum Humanorum Centum et Qua-
tuordecim Tabulis ... Leiden, 1739. Fo. Short tear
to blank margin of 2 plts. not affecting engraved
area, 2 plt. numerals shaved, cont. mott. cf. gt.,
rubbed, short tear at foot of spine. (C. May 30;
111) *Traylen.* £480

COX, David
– A Series of Progressive Lessons ... the Art of
Landscape Painting in Water Colours. 1823. Ob.
4to. 10 plain & 8 hand-cold. plts., hf. mor., defect.
(P. Jun.7; 277) £110

COX, Ed. G.
– A Reference Guide to the Literature of Travel.
N.Y., 1969. *Reprint of 1935-49 Edn.* 3 vols. Orig.
linen. (GB. May 4; 1811) DM 400
– – **Anr. Edn.** N.Y., [1969]. *Reprint of Seattle
1935-49 Edn.* 3 vols. Orig. linen. (R. Apr.3; 609)
DM 550

COX, James
– A Descriptive Catalogue of the Several Superb &
Magnificent Pieces of Mechanism & Jewellery
Exhibited in Mr. Cox's Museum. L., 1772. Last lf.
laid down, wraps. (P. Jan.12; 214)
Sims, Reed & Fogg. £110

COX, Nicholas & Blome, Richard
[–] The Gentleman's Recreation. L., 1697. 4 pts. in
1 vol. Spotted & stained, cont. panel. cf., rebkd.
[Wing C 6706] (S. Mar.20; 710) *Thorp.* £80

COX, Raymond
– Les Soieries d'Art depuis les Origines Jusqu'à nos
Jours. Paris, 1914. 4to. Col. frontis., 100 plts.,
some foxing, three-qtr. mor., spine slightly stained,
extremities rubbed. (SG. Jan.26; 292) $140

COX, Richard
– Hibernia Anglicana; or the History of Ireland ...
L., 1689-90. *1st. Edn.* 2 vols. Fo. Cont. mott. cf.
(GM. Dec.7; 468) £140

COX, Ross
– Adventures on the Colombia River. L., 1831. *1st.
Edn.* 2 vols. No hf.-titles, cont. hf. cf. [Sabin 17267]
(S. May 22; 315) *Sawyer.* £300
– – **Anr. Copy.** 2 vols. Cont. cf. gt., slight wear at
jnts.; the Rt. Hon. Visc. Eccles copy. [Sabin 17267]
(CNY. Nov.18; 78) $650
– – **Anr. Edn.** 1832. *2nd. Edn.* 2 vols. Cont. hf. cf.,
extremities slightly scuffed. (CSK. May 4; 117)
£160
– – **Anr. Edn.** N.Y., 1832. *1st. Amer. Edn.* Lacks
advt. lf., some foxing, cont. hf. cf., marb. bds. (SG.
Jan.19; 163) $150

COXE, William, Archd., 1747-1828
– Account of the Russian Discoveries between
Asia & America. 1780. 4to. Sm. repair to title,
cont. tree cf. (P. Sep.8; 273) £100
– – **Anr. Edn.** L., 1787. *3rd. Edn.* Spotted thro.-out,
cont. cf. (BBA. Dec.15; 17) *Quaritch.* £140
– – **Anr. Edn.** 1803. Tree cf. gt., upr. cover loose.
(P. Dec.8; 58) *Bowes.* £70
– Memoirs of John Duke of Marlborough. L., 1820.
2nd. Edn. 7 vols. Various sizes. Slight browning,
cont. cf. (S. Oct.11; 509) *Edwards.* £80
– Travels into Poland, Russia, Sweden & Denmark.
L., 1784-90. *1st. Edn.* 3 vols. 4to. 26 engraved
plts. & maps, some folding, last advt. lf. in Vol. 3,
cont. cf., rubbed. (BBA. Dec.15; 68) *Hannas.* £85
– – **Anr. Edn.** 1802. 5 vols. 13 plts., 15 maps &
plans, 3 tables, many folding orig. bds. (BBA.
Feb.9; 326) *Spring.* £70
– Travels in Switzerland & in the Country of the
Grisons in a Series of Letters to William Melmoth
Esq. Ill.:– after I. Smith & others. L., 1794. *3rd.
Edn.* 2 vols. 4to. L.P., lge. engraved folding hand-
cold. map, 3 plans, including 1 folding, 23 plts., sm.
tear at fold of map, some spotting & discoloration,
cont. spr. cf. gt. (C. Nov.16; 10) *Hart.* £550
– – **Anr. Edn.** L., 1801. *4th. Edn.* 3 vols. 4 engraved
maps & plans (of 5), 1 reprd. at folds, 23 plts.,
some slightly spotted, cf., defect. (S. Apr.9; 16)
Traylen. £160
– – **Anr. Copy.** 3 vols. Lge. 8vo. L.P., 2 plans, 3
folding maps, 2 natural history plts., 21 plts. of
views, advt. lf. e2 in Vol. 1, some foxing, mostly
marginal, hf. cf., unc. (SG. Nov.3; 49) $275
– Voyage en Pologne, Russie, Suède, Danmark, etc.
Trans.:– M.P.H. Mallet. Genève, 1786. 2 vols. 4to.
Cont. marb. cf., gt.-decor., angle fleurons, centre
arms, decor. spines. (HD. Dec.9; 24) Frs. 2,000
– L'Espagne sous les Rois de la Maison de Bourbon
ou Mémoires rélatifs à l'Historie de Cette Nation.
Paris, 1827. 6 vols. 4to. Mor.; Maria Luisa superlibris on all vols. (DS. Jan.27; 2121) PTs. 34,000

COYNE, Joseph Stirling
See— WILLIS, Nathaniel Parker & Coyne, Joseph
Stirling

COYPEL, C.A.
– Bilder zum Don Quixote. Wien, [1844]. Slightly
foxed in margin, orig. bds., soiled. (R. Apr.3; 159)
DM 420

COZENS, Z.
[–] A Tour through the Isle of Thanet. L., 1793. *1st.
Edn.* 4to. 8 engraved plts., some slight spotting or
offsetting, cont. cf., slightly worn. (S. Mar.6; 415)
Frankland. £170

CRAAN, W.B.
- An Historical Account of the Battle of Waterloo. L., 1817. Orig. bds., rebkd. (CSK. Aug.5; 17) £70

CRAANDIJK, J. & Schipperús, P.A.
- Wandelingen door Nederland met Pen en Potlood. Ill.:– Lankhout after Schipperus. Haarlem, 1875-82. *1st. Edn.* Pt; 1, 4-6 in 4 (of 8) vols. Lacks vols. 2-3, 7-8 & atlas. 65 tinted lithos., some foxing, orig. decor. cl. gt., a little loose. (VS. Jun.7; 624) Fls. 500
- – Anr. Edn. Haarlem, 1875-84. 7 vols. (lacks Supp. & Atlas). Lge. 8vo. 112 lithos., cl. (B. Feb.8; 649) Fls. 2,000
- – Anr. Edn. Haarlem, 1882-88. *2nd. Printing.* 9 vols., including Supp. 20 maps, 123 plts., a few plts. & 1 bdg. loose, cl. (B. Feb.8; 650) Fls. 900
- – Anr. Edn. Haarlem, 1883-88. *2nd.-3rd. Printing.* 8 vols. only (of 9, lacks 'North Holland'), including Supp. 127 litho. maps & views, decor. cl. (B. Feb.8; 651) Fls. 625
- Wandelingen door Nederland.—Nieuwe Wandelingen door Nederland. Haarlem, 1875-88; 1888. 6 vols. & Atlas; 1 vol. Lge. 8vo. Several plts. foxed or stained in margin, orig. cl. (2 vols.) & hf. cl. orig. wraps. (VG. Sep.14; 798) Fls. 850

CRABBE, George
- The Village. L., 1783. *1st. Edn.* 4to. Hf.-title, some slight spotting mod. qtr. cf.; Frederic Dannay copy. (CNY. Dec.16; 87) $240

CRACE, Frederick
- A Catalogue of Maps, Plans & Views of London, Westminster & Southwark. Ed.:– J.G. Crace. L., 1878. Some spotting, orig. cl.; Editor's copy, with additions & corrections. (BBA. Apr.5; 281) *Maggs.* £60

CRADOCK, Mrs. E. Grove
- The Calendar of Nature; or, The Seasons of England. Ed.:– Lord John Russell. [L.], 1849-50. Fo. Additional col. litho. title, 21 (of 24) col. litho. plts., 23 (of 24) uncold. plts., lacks 1 text lf., some light foxing, rarely affecting col. plts., buckram. (SG. Mar.22; 56) $175

CRAFTY [ie Victor Gerusez]
- La Chasse à tir. Paris, [1888]. *Orig. Edn.* Publishers decor. buckram. (HD. Dec.9; 112) Frs. 2,000

CRAIG, Clifford
- The Engravers of Van Diemen's Land. 1961. *(1000) numbered & sigd.* No bdg. stated. (JL. Jun.24; 177) Aus. $220
- Old Tasmanian Prints ... Launceston, 1964. *(1000) numbered & sigd.* Bdg. not stated. (KH. May 1; 182) Aus. $210
- – Anr. Copy. No bdg. stated. (JL. Jun.24; 178) Aus. $180

CRAIG, C. & others
- Early Colonial Furniture in N.S.W.—Van Diemen's Land. Melbourne, 1972. No bdg. stated. (JL. Jun.24; 120) Aus. $120

CRAIG, Edith N.
See— ROBERTSON, Edward Graeme & Craig, Edith N.

CRAIG, Edward Gordon
- Henry Irving. 1930. *(75) numbered, with 2 additional plts., sigd. by author.* Orig. pig-bkd. cl., spine slightly soiled. (CSK. Nov.25; 214) £95
- Nothing: or, the Bookplate. L., 1924. *(280) numbered.* Sm. 4to. 50 mntd. plts., & 1 cut pulled by hand from orig. wood, sigd. by Craig, cl., slightly stained. (SG. Jan.5; 108) $225
- On the Art of Theatre. L., 1911. *(150) sigd.* 4to. Limp cl.; pres. inscr. to Waldo R. Browne, T.L.s. from Craig to Browne laid in. (PNY. Dec.1; 109) $225
- A Production 1926—being Designs Projects or Realised for The Pretenders', Henrik Ibsen ... Oxford, 1930. *(605).* Fo. Orig. gt. cl., unc. (PD. Feb.15; 240) £75
- A Production: being Thirty-Two Collotype Plates ... for the Pretenders of Henrik Ibsen ... L., 1930. *(105) numbered on H.M.P., sigd.* Atlas fo. 32 plts.,

some cold., lettered tissue-guards, ex-liby., cl. (SG. May 3; 124) $225

CRAIG, John
- De Calculo Fluentium. Libri Duo. Quibus subjuguntur Libri Duo. De Optica Analytica. L., 1718. *1st. Edn.* 4to. Cont. blind-stpd. cf., slight rubbing; John D. Stanitz coll. (SPB. Apr.25; 108) $375
- Methodus Figurarum Lineis Rectis & Curvis Comprehensarum Quadratures Determinandi. L., 1685. *1st. Edn.* 4to. Errata, margin stain, sm. wormholes affecting some letters, old mott. cf., rebkd.; John D. Stanitz coll. [Wing C6797] (SPB. Apr.25; 109) $250

CRAIG, Maurice
- Irish Bookbindings, 1600-1800. 1954. 4to. Orig. cl., d.-w., a little torn; H.M. Nixon coll., with his sig. & some MS. notes. Craig's 'Irish Bookbindings' from the Irish Heritage Series loosely inserted, cuttings, rubbings, & other notes by Nixon loosely inserted. (BBA. Oct.6; 25) *Howell.* £160
- – Anr. Copy. 4to. Orig. cl., d.-w. a little torn. (BBA. Mar.7; 306) *De Burca.* £110

CRAKES, Sylvester, Jnr.
- Five Years a Captive among the Black-Feet Indians ... Columbus, 1858. *1st. Edn.* Old cf., rebkd. (LH. Apr.15; 290) $225

CRAMER, Joh. A.
- Anfangsgründe der Metallurgie. Blankenb. & Quedlinb., 1774. 3 pts. in 1 vol. Fo. Preface & contents stpd., sm. tears in title margin bkd., slightly foxed thro.-out, leath., blind-tooled decor., unc. (HK. Nov.8; 451) DM 2,400
- Elements of the Art of Assaying Metals. 1741. Cont. cf., rebkd., rubbed, cover detchd. (BBA. Jul.27; 9) *Bickersteth.* £100

CRAMER, Pieter & Stoll, Caspar
- De Uitlandsche Kapellen voorkomende in de drie Waereld-deelen Asia, Africa en America. Ill.:– after G.W. Lambertz. Amst. & Utrecht, [1775-]79-82[-84], Supp.: Amst., [1787-]91. 5 vols., including Supp. 4to. Hand-cold. engraved allegorical title, 442 hand-cold. engraved plts., a few plt. numerals trimmed or bnd. in, some soiling & minor staining, verso of plt. 19 stained, several margin pencil annots., recent qtr. mor., cont. cf. gt. backstrips laid down. (CNY. May 18; 137) $2,000
- – Anr. Edn. Amst., 1779-82, Supp.: Amst., 1791. 6 vols., including Supp. 4to. Additional hand-cold. engraved title, 2 engraved frontis., 442 hand-cold. engraved plts., unif. cont. hf. mor., spines gt., unc. (C. Nov.16; 229) *Neidhart.* £4,800

CRANACH PRESS
See— HOMER
See— RILKE, Rainer Maria
See— SHAKESPEARE, William
See— SOLOMON, King of Israel
See— VALERY, Paul
See— VERGILIUS MARO, Publius

CRANBROOK PAPERS
[Detroit], Cranbrook Pr., 1900-01. Nos. 1-10 (all publd.). 4to. On H.M.P., hand-illuminated initials thro.-out, ptd. wraps., mod. buckram folding case. (SG. Jan.5; 109) $325

CRANDALL, M.L.
- Confederate Imprints. [Boston], 1955. 2 vols. *(With:)* HARWELL, R. - More Confederate Imprints. Richmond, 1957. 2 vols. Together 4 vols. Cl. & ptd. wraps. (SG. Apr.5; 64) $100

CRANE, Hart
- The Bridge. Ill.:– after Walker Evans. Paris, Black Sun Pr., 1930. *1st. Edn., (283). (200) numbered on Holland paper.* 4to. Orig. wraps., some soiling at spine, glassine overlay d.-w., publisher's box defect.; Frederic Dannay copy. (CNY. Dec.16; 90) $550
- White Buildings: Poems ... Foreward: Allan Tate. N.Y., 1926. *1st. Edn. 1st. Iss.* Orig. cl.-bkd. batik bds., light wear; Frederic Dannay copy. (CNY. Dec.16; 89) $1,100

CRANE, Stephen
- The Black Riders. Boston, 1895. *1st. Edn.* 12mo. Slight foxing, orig. ptd. bds., bkplt. of Clifton Waller Barrett; Perry Molstad copy. (SPB. May 16; 440) $350
- The Little Regiment & Other Episodes of the American Civil War. N.Y., 1896. *1st. Edn. Blanck's 1st. Printing.* Decor. cl., light wear, upr. cover slightly spotted. d.-w., some minor fraying; Ker Leach coll. (RO. Jun.10; 339) $350
- The Monster & Other Stories. N.Y., 1899. *1st. Edn.* Black- & gold-stpd. cl., light wear, slight spotting of covers, several owner stps. on end-paper, d.-w., advts. on back, some chipping; Ken Leach coll. (RO. Jun.10; 505) $440
- The Red Badge of Courage. N.Y., 1895. *1st. Edn. 1st. Printing.* With perfect type on last line of p.225, advts., light marginal browning, orig. cl., some soiling; Barton Currie bkplt. & pencilled note, Fred A. Berne copy. (SPB. May 16; 210) $550
- – Anr. Edn. N.Y., 1895. *1st. Edn.* Perfect type in 'congratulated' on p.225, top edge stained yellow, 1st. advt. page headed 'Gibert Parker's Best Books', orig. decor. cl., inr. hinge reprd., ptd. d.-w., lightly soiled, red mor.-bkd. s.-c.; Perry Molstad copy. (SPB. May 16; 441) $1,700
- – Anr. Edn. Ed.:– Fredson Bowers. Wash., [1973]. *MS. Facs. Edn. (1000) numbered.* 2 vols. Sm. fo. Cl., cl. s.-c. (SG. Mar.1; 42) $100
- The Third Violet. N.Y., 1897. *1st. Edn.* Decor. cl., light wear. d.-w. (light fraying, spine-tip slightly chipped); Ken Leach coll. (RO. Jun.10; 388) $350
- War is Kind. Ill.:– Will Bradley. N.Y., 1899. *1st. Edn.* Orig. pict. bds., designed by Bradley, unopened, spine & lr. corners slightly worn; Frederic Dannay copy. (CNY. Dec.16; 92) $420
- – Anr. Edn. Ill.:– Will Bradley. N.Y., 1899. Decor. paper over bds., unc., tape offset to endpapers. (PNY. Oct.20; 192) $325

CRANE, Walter
- The Bluebeard Picture Book. L., [1875]. *1st. Edn.* 4to. Gt.-pict. cl. (SG. Dec.8; 121) $130
- 8 Illustrations to Shakespeare's Tempest. 1893. *(600) numbered & sigd. by artist & printer.* 4to. Spotted, orig. cl. case. (P. Jan.12; 67) *Bookroom.* £60
- The First of May: A Fairy Masque. L., 1881. *(200).* Mntd. India proofs, some foxing, mostly on mounts, gt.-ruled mor., ribbed spine, gt.-ruled inner dentelles, decor. end-papers, some scuffing, corners defect., sigd. by artist. (CBA. Aug.21; 119) $125
- Renascence. A Book of Verse. L., 1891. *(500). (350) for England.* Sm. 4to. Erratum slip, crushed lev. mor. gt., elab. gt.-decor., mor. gt. onlays, rounded spine in 6 compartments, gt. decor., turnins gt., sigd. 'Fazakerley, Liverpool': M.C.D. Borden bkplt., as a bdg., w.a.f. (CNY. Dec.17; 556) $500

CRANE, Walter
See— GREENAWAY, Kate & Crane, Walter

CRANE, Walter (Ill.)
See— SPENSER, Edmund
See— STUDIO: An Illustrated Magazine of Fine & Applied Art
See— WILDE, Oscar

CRANMER, Thomas
- A Defence of the True & Catholike Doctrine of the Sacrament of the Body & Bloud of our Saviour Christ. L., 1550. 4to. Some staining, particularly at end, cont. limp vell. [STC 6002] (BBA. May 3; 91) *Thomas.* £225

CRANZ or CRANTZ, David
- Historie v. Groenland. Ill.:– J. Swertner. Amst., 1779. 3 vols. 4to. slightly browned in part, mod. hf. vell. (VG. Sep.14; 1088) Fls. 650
- The History of Greenland: Containing a Description of the Country & its Inhabitants. 1767. *1st. Engl. Edn.* 2 vols. Cont. cf. gt., jnts. & heads & tails of spines reprd. (LC. Mar.1; 210) £130
- – Anr. Copy. 2 vols. Cont. cf., covers detchd. (SG. Mar.29; 304) $200

CRANTZ, H.J.N.
- Stirpium Austriacarum. Wien, 1769. 6 pts. in 2 vols. 4to. Cont. bds. (BR. Apr.12; 769) DM 400

CRASSET, J. (S.J.)
- Aussführliche Geschicht der in dem äussersten Welt-Theil gelegenen Japonesischen Kirch ... Augsburg, 1738. *1st. German Edn.* 2 pts. in 1 vol. Fo. Prelims. lack 4 ll. dedications as often, title with sm. lr. corner tear, some slight foxing, cont. leath. (BR. Apr.12; 34)   DM 800

CRAUZAT, E. de
- L'Oeuvre Gravé et Lithographié de Steinlen. Paris, 1913. *(575) roman-numbered. (50) on vélin d'Arches, with the plts. & lithos. in 2 states.* Fo. With the litho. 'Le Chant de la Pluie' in 1st. state, unsewn in orig. wraps., unc., folder & s.-c., the latter defect. (S. Nov.21; 119)   *Sims.* £580

CRAVEN, Lady Elizabeth
- A Journey through the Crimea to Constantinople. 1789. 4to. Hf.-title folding engraved map slightly torn, cont. hf. mor., slightly rubbed. (BBA. Sep.29; 88)   *Martinos.* £80

CRAWFORD, John
- History of the Indian Archipelago. Edinb., 1820. *1st. Edn.* 3 vols. Folding map, hand-cold. in outl., 34 plts. (1 cold.), some offsetting & spotting, lacks hf.-titles, hf. cf., rebkd. (S. Jun.25; 38) *Ran.* £170
- - **Anr. Copy.** 3 vols. 1 copperplt. engr. cont. hand-cold., lge. folded map hand-cold. in outl., cont. pol. gt. cf., bkplts. (HA. Nov.18; 372) $170

CRAWFURD, George
- A Genealogical History of the Royal & Illustrious Family of the Stewarts ... Edinb., 1710. *1st. Edn.* Fo. Cont. panel. cf., worn; inscr. on 1st. end-paper 'Gifted by the Author To David Crawford Secretary to the Dutches of Hamilton 1 May 1710', Sir Ivar Colquhoun, of Luss copy. (CE. Mar.22; 73)   £140

CRAWFURD, John
- History of the Indian Archipelago. Edinb., 1820. *1st. Edn.* 3 vols. Folding map, hand-cold. in outl., 34 plts. (1 cold.), some offsetting & spotting, lacks hf.-titles, hf. cf., rebkd. (S. Jun.25; 38) *Ran.* £170
- - **Anr. Copy.** 3 vols. 1 copperplt. engr. cont. hand-cold., lge. folded map hand-cold. in outl., cont. pol. gt. cf., bkplts. (HA. Nov.18; 372) $170
- Journal of an Embassy ... to the Court of Ava. 1834. *2nd. Edn.* 2 vols. Folding engraved map slightly torn, lacks 5 fossil plts. in Vol. 2, a few ll. in Vol. 2 slightly stained, cont. cf., spines gt., slightly rubbed. (BBA. Jan.19; 95)   *Bertram Rota.* £80
See— RAFFLES, Sir Thomas Stamford & Crawfurd, John

CRAWHALL, Joseph
- Chap-Book Chaplets ... 1883. 8 pts. in 1 vol. 4to. Ills. hand-cold., advt. lf., orig. paper-covered decor. bds., unc. orig. pt. wraps. bnd. in. (PD. Apr.18; 209)   £50
- Chaplets from Coquet-side. 1873. *(100).* Hand-cold. decor., slightly spotted, orig. bds., rebkd. in mor. (BBA. Jun.14; 88)   *Cavendish.* £100
- [-] The Compleatest Angling Booke that ever was writ ... L., priv. ptd., 1859. *1st. Edn. [40].* Sm. 4to. Hand-cold. initials, some ills. hand-cold., a few water-colour drawings on blank versos of text ll., title & front free end-paper detchd., cont. maroon hf. mor.; pres. copy, inscr. by author to Rev. John F. Bigge, & with 2 A.L.s from author to Bigge dtd. 1870 & 1882 pasted to title verso & front free end-paper, Edward E. Bigge bkplt. (C. Mar.14; 150)   *Marks.* £1,650
- - **Anr. Edn.** Newcastle, priv. ptd., 1881. *2nd. Edn. (100).* 4to. Some ills. hand-cold., cont. cf., pres. copy, inscr. by author to Rev. John F. Bigge, Edward E. Bigge bkplt. (C. Mar.14; 151)   *D'Arcy.* £600
- [-] Grouse Shooting made Quite Easy ... 1827. 4to. Litho. port., title & 6 pp. of text, litho. plts., some in 2 states, 4 orig. sketches by Crawhall, Snr., hf. mor. (P. Jun.7; 327)   £750
- Olde Ffrendes wyth Newe Faces. Leadenhall Pr., 1883. 4to. Ills. hand-cold., orig. bds., unc., worn. (S. Dec.20; 525)   *Cavendish.* £60

CRAWSHAY, Capt. Richard
- The Birds of Tierra del Fuego. 1907. *(300) numbered.* 4to. Cold. map, 21 hand-touched cold. plts., landscape photos (1 loose), lacks 1 cover & spine, other cover detchd. (SKC. May 4; 1845)   £240

CREALOCK, Henry Hope
- Among the Red Deer; Sketches from Nature in the Forest. ... [Sketches dtd. 1869-70]. 80 mntd. photographic ills., with ptd. captions, loose, as iss., in orig. pict. folder, as a coll., w.a.f. (LC. Mar.1; 470)   £190
- Deer-Stalking in the Highlands of Scotland. 1892. *(250) numbered.* Fo. Some light spotting, orig. cl. (CSK. Sep.30; 148)   £260

CREBILLON, Claude Prosper Jolyot de
- Electre, Tragédie. 1709. *Orig. Edn.* 12mo. Cont. marb. cf., s.-c.; autograph dedication from author to Abbé Martin, from libys. of Dr. A Ripault, Dr. Lucien-Graux & Jacques Millot. (HD. Apr.13; 13)   Frs. 1,400
- La Nuit et le Moment. Ill.:– Louis Icart. Paris, 1946. *(15) artist's copies.* 4to. On japan, 20 orig. cold. etchings, leaves, box; extra-ill. with copper plt., 1 suite of plts. in sanguine, 1 in black, 1 loose suite of 5 plts. & 1 orig. drawing sigd. by ill. (HD. Jun.13; 26)   Frs. 4,300
- - **Anr. Edn.** Ill.:– Louis Icart. Paris, 1946. *(100) numbered on Rives with orig. cold. drawing sigd. by artist.* 4to. Lacks suite of ills. in sanguine, leaves, wrap., box. (HD. Jun.26; 68)   Frs. 3,000
- - **Anr. Edn.** Londres (Paris), 1755. *Orig. Edn.* 16mo. Mor. gt. by Charles Meunier, Ed. & Jules de Gomcourt monog. on covers, sewed silk doubls. & end-ll. with cold. floral motifs. (HD. Mar.27; 8)   Frs. 2,300

CREDO
Hammersmith, Doves Pr., 1908. Some slight spotting, orig. mor. gt. by the Doves Bindery, with their stp. on the turndown. (LC. Oct.13; 20)   £140

CREIGHTON, J.N.
- Narrative of the Siege & Capture of Bhurtpore. 1830. 4to. Light spotting, cont. cf. (CSK. Sep.30; 67)   £190

CRELLIUS, Johann, 1590-1633.
- Beschr., van Godt en zijne Eyghenschappen. Trans.:– F. Socini. Rakow [Amst.], ca. 1670?. 2 pts. in 1 vol. 4to. Some scribbling & stains on title, cont. vell. (VG. Sep.14; 1312)   Fls. 450
- De Uno Deo Patre. Rakow, 1631. *1st. Edn.* Final errata lf., some browning, inscr. partly erased from title, 18th. C. Fr. red mor. gt. (S. Mar.20; 801)   *Blanko.* £110

CREPY FILE
- Nouveau Livre d'Ecriture. 1773. Double fo. No bdg. stated. (DS. Mar.23; 2076)   Pts. 50,000

CRESCENZIO, Pietro
- De Agricultura vulgare. Venezia, 6 Sep. 1511. *1st. Edn. in Italian.* 4to. Some slight staining, 18th. C. š. leath., some worming. (SI. Dec.18; 10)   Lire 1,500,000
- - **Anr. Copy.** Lacks 1st. 6 ll. & 2 others, Venetian blind-decor. mor., bands; from Fondation Furstenberg-Beaumesnil. (HD. Nov.16; 159)   Frs. 5,300
- Crescentio ... Trans.:– Francesco Sansovino. Venezia, 1561. 4to. Stain on frontis., 18th. C. vell. (SI. Dec.15; 152)   Lire 750,000
- Opera d'Agricoltura. Venice, 1538. Vell., spine defect.; Dr. Walter Pagel copy. (S. Feb.7; 86)   *Gorini.* £160

CRESOLLIUS, Ludovicus
- Theatrum Veterum Phetorum, Oratorum, Declamatorum, ques in Graecia Nominabant [Sophistas, graecè], Expositum. Paris, 1620. *1st. Edn.* Mid 17th. C. Fr. mor., spine & covers decor., arms of Louis II de Bourbon-Condé, 'le Grand Condé'; sig. of Pierre Foucault. (S. Nov.17; 16)   *Chapponiere.* £400

CRESPET, Pierre
- [-] Le Jardin de Plaisir et Recréation Spirituelle. Paris, 1602. *2nd. Edn.?.* 2 vols. in 1. Cont. vell., soiled. (SG. Oct.27; 80) $100

CRESPIN, J. & Goulart, S.
- [-] Das Grosse Martyr-Buch, und Kirchen-Historien ... Trans.:– P. Crocius. Bremen, 1682. *3rd. Edn.* Fo. Slightly browned, some sm. wormholes in upr. margin in last part, cont. vell., slightly spotted, corners slightly defect. (R. Oct.11; 1132)   DM 1,100

CRESWELL, K.A.C.
- The Mosques of Egypt. Giza, 1949[-51]. 2 vols. Fo. Cold. titles & frontispieces, plts. (several cold.),
2 folding maps & Index in pocket at end of 1st. vol., orig. cl. (S. May 22; 275)   *Hague.* £760
- - **Anr. Copy.** 2 vols. Fo. 2 folding maps & Index in pocket at end Vol. 1, orig. roan. (S. Mar.6; 15)   *Browning.* £420

CRESY, Edward & Taylor, G.L.
- The Architectural Antiquities of Rome, Measured & Delineated. L., 1821-22. *1st. Edn.* 2 vols. Atlas fo. 130 engraved plts., ex-liby., much foxing & offsetting, later hf. mor., very worn. (SG. May 3; 125) $250

CRETSER, G. de
- Beschryvinge van 'sGravenhage. Mitsg. de Oude Coustumen, Bygevoegt de Zeestraat op Scheveninge. Ill.:– C. Huygens. Amst., 1711. 2 pts. in 1 vol. 4to. Slightly browned, cont. vell. (VG. Nov.30; 1020)   Fls. 650

CREUZER, Fr.
- Symbolik und Mythologie der Alten Völker, besonders der Griechen. Leipzig & Darmstadt, 1810-12. *1st. Edn.* 4 vols. Some foxing, cont. hf. leath. gt. (R. Oct.11; 162)   DM 700
- - **Anr. Copy.** 4 vols. Some soiling & browning, cont. hf. leath. gt., slightly bumped & rubbed, ex-libris. (HK. Nov.9; 1588)   DM 440

CREVECOEUR or CREVECIEYR, Michel Guillaume St. Jean de
- Letters from an American Farmer. L., 1782. *1st. Edn.* Lacks hf.-title & X8, some browning & spotting, later hf. cf., corners renewed. [Sabin 17496] (SPB. Dec.13; 438) $750
- - **Anr. Copy.** Some browning, hf. mor. [Sabin 17496] (SPB. Dec.13; 438a) $650
- [-] Voyage dans la Haute Pensylvanie et dans l'Etat de New York. Paris, 1801 [An IX]. *1st. Edn.* 3 vols. 4 engraved folding maps & plans, 7 plts., 4 folding tables, 1 map reprd., few spots, cont. cf., slight wear. (S. Apr.9; 17)   *Blackwell.* £140
- - **Anr. Copy.** 3 vols. With hf.-titles, 11 full-p. & folding maps & plts., 4 folding tables, cont. mott. cf., gt. backs, worn, jnts. brkn. (SG. Apr.5; 65) $275

CREVEL, René
- Mr. Knife, Miss Fork. Trans.:– Kay Boyle. Ill.:– Max Ernst. Paris, Black Sun Pr., 1931. *(200) on 'finest bristol paper'.* 12mo. 19 photograms, gt.-pict. bds. (SG. Nov.3; 50) $1,800

CRICKET: A Weekly Record of the Game
28 Jan. 1892-23 Sep. 1911. Vol. XI no. 290-Vol. XXX no. 886 (lacks Vol. XXVII & some individual nos.), in 19 vols. 4to. Liby. hf. roan, worn, 2 or 3 covers detchd. or loose. (KH. May 1; 185)   Aus. $620

CRIES OF LONDON
Ill.:– after T.L. Busby. L., 1823. Engraved frontis., 23 cold. etchings, minimal spotting, cont. hf. leath., slightly defect.; Hauswedell coll. (H. May 23; 63)   DM 900

CRIES OF LONDON EMBELLISHED
L., William Darton, ca. 1805. 32mo. Ills. hand-cold., slightly soiled, a few owner's pencil marks, orig. pict. wraps., worn, upr. cover detchd. (S. Nov.22; 374)   *Maggs.* £100

CRIPPLE CREEK
- The Official Manual of the Cripple Creek District. Colorado Springs, 1900. *1st. Edn.* Vol. 1 (all publd.). 4to. Lge. map torn at folds, cl., shaken, hinges brkn. (LH. Jan.15; 273) $100

CRISP, Sir Frederick Arthur
- Armorial China: Chinese Porcelain with Coats of Arms. N.p., priv. ptd., 1907. *(150) numbered.* (*With:*) - Lowestoft China. N.p., priv. ptd., 1907. *(150) numbered.* Together 2 vols. 4to. Hf. vell., bumped, 2nd. with slightly defect. cl., leath. labels worn, end-papers browned. (SG. Jan.26; 79) $225
- Catalogue of Lowestoft China. Priv. ptd., 1907. *(150) numbered.* Sm. fo. Port., 14 cold. plts., ex-liby., hf. vell., slightly worn. (SG. May 3; 77) $110

CRISTOVAL, Henrique
- Codigo Formado por los Negros de la Isla de Santo Domingo de la Parte Francesa hoi Estado de Hayti. Trans.:– Juan Lopez Candelada. Cadiz, 1810. Sm.

CRISTOVAL, Henrique -*Contd.*

4to. Sm. stp. on title verso, later hf. mor. gt., cont. patterned wraps. bnd. in, unc., lr. wrap. clipped on top corner. (SG. Jan.19; 180) $250

CROESE, G.
– **Quäker-Historie.** Berlin, 1696. *1st. German Edn.* Browned, title with 2 sm. holes without loss, last 6ll. with wormhole in text, mod. cold. paper wraps. (R. Apr.3; 1115) DM 630

CROFF, G.B.
– **Model Suburban Architecture.** N.Y., 1870. *1st. Edn.* 1 vol. Sm. fo. 37 litho. plts., orig. cl. (*With:*)
– **Progressive American Architecture.** N.Y., 1875. *1st. Edn.* 1 vol. Sm. fo. 98 litho. plts., orig. cl. (SG. Oct.13; 129) $550

CROFTS, Thomas
– **Bibliotheca Croftsiana.** L., n.d. Priced in MS. thro.-out, old hf. cf., worn. (CSK. Feb.24; 217) £75

CROKER, J. Wilson T.C.D.
[–] **Familiar Epistles to Frederick E. Jones, Esq on the Present State of the Irish Stage.** Dublin, 1805. *4th. Edn.* 1 vol. Sm. 8vo. Errata lf. at end, cont. str.-grd. mor., bkplt.; inscr. by author to Marchioness of Sligo. (*With:*) – **Familiar Discourses.** N.p., n.d. 1 vol. Hf. cf. (GM. Dec.7; 199) £55

CROKER, Thomas Crofton
– **Memoirs of Joseph Holt, General of the Irish Rebels, in 1798** ... 1838. 2 vols. Sm. ink-spot on 1 plt., orig. bds., unc., recased, new backstrips & end-papers, orig. title labels. (KH. May 1; 186) Aus. $200
– **A Walk from London to Fulham.** L., 1860. 1 vol. in 2. Extra-ill. with 75 plts., mostly engraved ports., mod. mor. by Morell; initialled A.L. by author & A.L. from C. Bathurst Woodman to author loosely inserted. (BBA. Mar.21; 118) *Woodruff.* £120

CROLL or CROLLIUS, Oswald
– **Basilica Chymica.** Frankfurt, ca. 1610. 4to. Browned & discold., cont. inscrs., cont. cf.; dupl. of Yale Univ., Dr. Walter Pagel copy. (S. Feb.7; 90) *Heller.* £120

CROMBIE, Benjamin William
– **Modern Athenians ... a Series of Original Portraits of Memorable Citizens of Edinburgh** ... Notes:– W.S. Douglas. Edinb., 1882. 4to. 49 col. plts., red mor.-bkd. (PD. May 16; 169) £85
– – **Anr. Edn.** 1882. *(1040).* 4to. Hand-cold. litho. frontis, 48 folding plts., orig. cl., soiled. (CSK. Feb.10; 111) £50

CROMBIE, Charles
– **Laws of Cricket.** Ca. 1915. Ob. fo. Copyright of 'Perrier' Water, 12 cold. cartoons, each with advt. pasted to verso, plus single advt. lf. bnd. in at rear, orig. ptd. bds., soiled, some wear. (TA. Jun.21; 553) £100
– – **Anr. Edn.** N.d. Ob. 4to. A few margins dampstained, orig. cl.-bkd. bds., soiled, w.a.f. (CSK. Jun.15; 187) £120
– **The Rules of Golf Illustrated.** N.d. Ob. 4to. 1 ill. torn & with part lacking, 2 with defect. margins, cl. (PWC. May 3; 665) £100

CROMMELIN, May
– **In the West Countrie.** 1883. *1st. Edn.* 3 vols. Hf.-titles, 18 pp. advts. at end, some spotting. (*With:*)
– **Joy or the Light of Cold-Home Ford.** 1884. *1st. Edn.* 3 vols. Hf.-titles, 24 pp. advts. at end. Together 6 vols. Orig. cl. (LC. Jul.5; 292) £110

CROMMELYNCK, F.
– **Le Cocu Magnifique.** Ill.:– Pablo Picasso. Paris, priv. ptd., [1968]. *(180)* on Velin de Rives. Ob. fo. Printers mark sigd. by author & artist, loose ll. in orig. vell. wraps & hand-bnd. red orig. leath. box, by J. Duval. (H. May 23; 1457) DM 12,000

CROMWELL, Thomas Kitson
[–] **Excursions in the County of Norfolk.** 1818-19. 2 vols. Extra engraved titles, folding map & plan, 97 views, cont. hf. russ., unc. (S. Mar.6; 233) *Besley.* £80
– **Excursions through Ireland.** L., 1820. Vols. I &

II: 'Province of Leinster'. 12mo. 92 engraved plts., bds., w.a.f. (GM. Oct.5; 214) £105
– **Walks through Islington.** 1835. *1st. Edn.* Hf. cf., rubbed. (P. Apr.12; 161) *Argyll Etkin.* £80
– – **Anr. Edn.** 1835. Mod. mor. gt. (BBA. Jul.27; 327) *Ralph.* £50

CRONICA BREVE DE I FATTI DE' RE DI FRANCIA
Venice, 1588. *1st. Edn.* 4to. Dampstain to lr. blank margins, 17th. C. vell. (C. May 30; 22) *Van Den Abbeel.* £200

CRONICA DEL ESCLARESCIDO REY DON ALSONSO ONZENO
Medina del Campo, 1563 (colophon '1551'). *2nd. Edn.* Fo. Some browning, a few later MS. notes, old limp vell., soiled, tears in spine. (S. May 10; 252) *Duran.* £240

CRONICA VAN DER HILLIGER STAT COELLEN
Köln, T. Kiethoff. 23 Aug. 1499. *1st. Edn.* Wide margin, index bnd. at end, cont. MS. date on colophon, stained, mostly in upr. & lr. margin, especially at beginning & end & some tears reprd., sm. hole with slight loss in 1 lf. bkd., last ll. wormed, lacks 2 blank end-ll., 18th. C. vell. [HC. 4349. BMCI, 299; Goff C-476] (R. Oct.11; 3) DM 18,000

CRONIN, William Vine
See– **GRAVES, Algernon & Cronin, William Vine**

CRONNELLY, R.F.
– **Irish Family History.** Dublin, 1865. *1st. Edn.* Rebnd. hf. cf. (GM. Dec.7; 245) £85

CROOKE, Helkiah
– **Microcosmographia, A Description of the Body of Man.** 1631. 2 pts. in 1 vol. Fo. Engraved & ptd. titles frayed & reprd., many ll. dampstained, mod. cf. (P. Sep.8; 344) *Bickersteth.* £140

CROOKES, William
– **On Radiant Matter. A Lecture Delivered to the British Association for the Advancement of Science, Friday August 22, 1879.** L., 1879. *1st. Edn.* Tear on title, orig. wraps., spine worn, tear in corner of upr. cover, some soiling; John D. Stanitz coll. (SPB. Apr.25; 110) $250

CROSBY, Harry
– **Red Skeletons.** Ill.:– 'Alastair'. Paris, 1927. *(366)* numbered. 4to. Ptd. wraps., unc. (SG. Mar.29; 3) $325
– **Transit of Venus.** Paris, Black Sun Pr., 1929. *(200)* numbered. 12mo. Ptd. wraps., unc., unopened, glassine d.-w., s.-c., silver bands worn away. (SG. Mar.1; 49) $175

CROSS, Maj. Osborne
– **Report in the Form of a Journal ... the March of the Regiment of Mounted Riflemen to Oregon** ... [Wash., 1850]. Comprising pp. 125-244 of government document 587, 35 plts., some folding, later three-qtr. mor. (LH. Apr.15; 294) $160

CROSS, Thomas
– **The Autobiography of a Stage-Coachman.** L., 1861. *1st. Edn.* 3 vols. 3 frontis, orig. cl. gt., soiled. (P. May 17; 248) *Allan.* £65
– – **Anr. Edn.** 1904. *(500).* 2 vols. 4to. 42 plts., including 41 hand-cold., mod. hf. mor. (CSK. Dec.2; 31) £240
– – **Anr. Copy.** 2 vols. Port., 41 hand-cold. plts., cl. gt. (P. Jun.7; 230) £180
– – **Anr. Copy.** 2 vols. 1 plain & 41 hand-cold. plts., slight spotting, orig. cl. gt. (P. Sep.8; 97) *Solomon.* £140
– – **Anr. Copy.** 2 vols. 4to. 42 plts., including 41 hand-cold., 2 detchd., cont. cl., lightly faded. (CSK. Nov.25; 64) £110

CROTCH, William
– **Specimens of Various Styles of Music.** [1808]. 3 vols. 4to. Later hf. mor. gt. by Roger de Coverly. (BBA. Feb.23; 192) *Quaritch.* £130

CROWLEY, Aleister 'The Master Therion'
– **Magick in Theory & Practice ... being part III of Book 4.** Paris, [1929?]. All publd. Sm. fo. Wraps., worn & soiled; Israel Regardie's copy, his sig. in

green ink & some annot., partly in Hebrew. (BBA. Jun.28; 29) *Bloomsbury Rare Books.* £100
– **Moonchild.** L., 1929. *1st. Edn.* Bdg. not stated, jacket darkening slightly. (CBA. Oct.29; 240) $180
– **The Spirit of Solitude.** L., Mandrake Pr., 1929. *1st. Edn.* 2 vols. 4to. On Japan vell., pict. cl., lightly soiled. (SG. Jan.12; 79) $150

CROWNE, John
– **Thyestes a Tragedy.** 1681. *1st. Edn.* 4to. Lacks A1 (blank), title-p. & following lf. reprd., slightly browned, mod. mor. gt. [Wing C7408] (BBA. Jan.19; 138) *Sutherland.* £75

CROWQUILL, Alfred (Pseud.)
See– **FORRESTER, Alfred Henry 'Alfred Crowquill'**

CROWTHER, J.S.
See– **BOWMAN, H. & Crowther, J.S.**

CROXTONSMITH, A.
See– **EARL, M. & Croxtonsmith, A.**

CROY, Ch. A. de
– **Mémoires Guerriers de ce qu'y c'est passé aux Pays Bas, 1600-06.** Antw., 1642. *2nd. Edn.* 4to. Lacks plans 1 (not iss.?), 5, 21 & 35, cont. cf. (VG. Sep.14; 1148) Fls. 1,900

CROZE-MAGNAN, S.C.
– **Le Musée Francais.** Paris, 1803-05. 5 vols. Lge. Fo. Lacks 7 plts., hf. cf., corners, gt. spine, as a collection of engrs., w.a.f. (CR. Jun.6; 23) Lire 3,800,000

CROZET
– **Voyage to Tasmania, New Zealand, the Ladrone Island, & the Philippines.** Trans.:– H. Ling Roth. L., 1891. *(500)* numbered. Folding map with sm. tear reprd., lines down margins & underlining to some ll., stp. on title, cl. (CA. Apr.3; 100) Aus. $170

CRUIKSHANK, George
– **The Bachelor's Own Book, being the Progress of Mr. Lambkin, (Gent.) in the Persuit of Pleasure & Amusement.** L., 1844. *1st. Edn.* Ob. 8vo. Pict. title, 12 plts., each in 2 panels, some foxing, later hf. mor.; inscr. to Alfred Forrester. (SG. Jun.7; 339) $550
– **The Comic Almanack.** L., for 1835-49. *1st. Edns.* 7 vols. Gt.-decor. mor., spines panel., dentelles, marb. end-papers, slight wear to covers; Joe E. Brown & Marymount College bkplts. in a few vols. (CBA. Mar.3; 147) $250
[–] **The Cries of London.** L., ca. 1830. 26 woodcuts, 20 sm. woodcuts on 6 numbered pp., each p. with woodcut decor. border, some spotting, orig. pict. bds., spotted, spine torn; Hauswedell coll. (H. May 23; 67) DM 780
– **London Characters** ... 1827. 24 plts., later hf. cf. by Morell. (PD. Aug.17; 35) £130
– **My Sketch Book** ... L., [1834-36]. Long 8vo. 37 hand-cold. plts., later mor. by Rivière, upr. wrap. bnd. in, wrap. inscr. no. 4 of the cold. copies. (PNY. Dec.1; 44) $190
– **Points of Humour.** L., 1823-24. 2 pts. in 1 vol. Tall 8vo. 20 cold. plts., crushed mor. gt. by Riviere, jnts. slightly rubbed. (SG. Jun.7; 340) $175
– **Punch & Judy.** 1828. Spotted, cont. hf. cf. (BBA. Aug.18; 129) *Quaritch.* £65

CRUIKSHANK, George (Ill.)
See– **AINSWORTH, William Harrison**
See– **BARKER, Matthew Henry**
See– **BATEMAN, James**
See– **CAREY, David**
See– **COHN, Albert M.**
See– **COLLIER, J.P.**
See– **DEFOE, Daniel**
See– **DICKENS, Charles**
See– **EGAN, Pierce**
See– **GRIMM, Jakob Ludwig Karl & Wilhelm Karl**
See– **IRELAND, William Henry**
See– **MAYHEW, H.**
See– **MUDFORD, William**
See– **NEVILL, Ralph**
See– **PETTIGREW, Thomas Joseph**
See– **SPENSER, Edmund**

See— STOWE, Harriet Beecher
See— WIGHT, John

CRUIKSHANK, Isaac Robert
– **Lessons of Thrift.** L., 1820. Engraved title, 12 hand-cold. aquatint plts., cont. hf. roan, slightly rubbed. (S. Dec.20; 828) *Cavendish.* £70
– – **Anr. Copy.** Engraved title, 12 plts., all hand-cold., some ll. slightly soiled, cont. cf., rebkd., slightly rubbed. (BBA. Dec.15; 276)
Solomons. £60

CRUNDEN, John
– **Convenient & Ornamental Architecture.** L., 1788. *3rd. Edn.* 4to. 57 engraved plts. (numbered 1-70), including 11 folding, few trimmed, 4 cropped, cont. cf. (C. Dec.9; 25) *Lyon.* £200

CRUSIUS, Martinus
– **Schwäbische Chronick.** Frankfurt, 1733. 2 vols. Fo. Some slight foxing, cont. vell. (HK. Nov.8; 899)
DM 2,400
– **Turco-Graeciae Libri Octo utraque Lingua edita** ... Basilae, n.d. *1st. Edn.* Fo. Parallel Greek & Latin text, cont. blind-stpd. pig. (HD. Jun.29; 86)
Frs. 4,800

CRUSIUS, O. (Intro.)
See— BUCH DER FABELN

CRUTCHLEY, Brooke
– **Bridges on their Backs.** Intro.:– P. Eden. Ill.:– David Gentleman. Camb., Christmas 1961. 4to. Orig. cl. folder, s.-c. (BBA. Nov.10; 53)
Blackwell. £55

CRUTTWELL, Clement
– **A Tour Through the Whole Island of Great Britain.** 1801. 6 vols. Folding map. hand-cold., slight foxing, cont. cl.-bkd. bds. (SKC. Jan.13; 2373) £50
– – **Anr. Edn.** L., 1806. 6 vols. 6 engraved titles, 2 folding cold. copper engraved maps, 128 steel-engraved views, some light foxing, cont. leath. gt., lightly bumped. (R. Oct.13; 3111) DM 820
– **Universal Gazetteer.** [1808]. Atlas only. Fo. 28 double-p. maps, col. in outl., hf. cf. gt. (P. Jul.26; 230b) £140

CRUTTWELL, W.C.
– [–] **Sir Richard's Daughter, a Christmas Tale of the Olden Times.** Frome, 1852. Sm. 4to. Orig. blue ptd. wraps. (BBA. Nov.30; 259) *Blackwell.* £90

CRYSTAL PALACE EXHIBITION
– **Exhibition of the Works of Industry of All Nations, 1851.** L., 1852. Sm. 4to. Elab. gt.-decor. & blind-stpd. cl., slightly worn; 'pres. copy'. (SG. Jan.26; 191) $150

CUALA PRESS
See— YEATS, William Butler

CUBA
– **Guía de Forasteros de ... Cuba para el Año 1866.** Habana, 1865. Leath. (DS. Nov.25; 2395)
Pts. 25,000

CUBBIN, Thomas
– **The Wreck of the Serica, A Narrative of 1868 by Thomas Cubbin, Master Mariner of Liverpool.** Ill.:– John Worsley. 1950. *(300) numbered. (30) sigd. by artist & writer of intro.,* specially bnd. 4to. Mor., unc., d.-w. (HBC. May 17; 194) £62

CUCCIONI, Tommaso
– **Numero Cento Vedute di Roma.** Roma, [1830?]. Album, 1st. map browned, vell. (CR. Jun.6; 144)
Lire 350,000
– [–] **Vedute Antiche e Moderne della Citta di Roma e sue Vicinanze.** Rome, n.d. Ob. 4to. Engraved title & 100 plts., cont. hf. cf., worn. (CSK. Jul.6; 116) £70

CUEVA, Luis de la
– **Dialogos de las Cosas Notàbles de Granada y Lengua Española** ... Sevilla, 1603. 4to. Leath., Marqués de la Fuensanta del Valle supralibros. (DS. Mar.23; 2078) Pts. 150,000

CUITT, George
– **Wanderings & Pencillings amongst Ruins of the Olden Time.** 1848. Fo. Hf. mor., worn. (P. Apr.12; 300) *Erlini.* £65

CULLEN, William
– **Anfangsgründe der Praktischen Arzneywissenschaft.** Leipzig, 1778-85. *1st. German Edn.* 4 pts in 4 vols. Cont. bds., slightly spotted. (GB. May 3; 989) DM 450

CULPEPER, Nicholas
– **Complete Herbal.** 1818. 4to. Port., 40 hand-cold, plts., staining, sheep, rebkd. (P. Feb.16; 160) £100
– – **Anr. Edn.** L., 1835. 4to. Engraved port., 20 hand-cold. plts., cont. cf., spine gt. (SKC. Nov.18; 1963) £70
– – **Anr. Copy.** Lge. 4to. Frontis., 180 hand-cold. engrs. on 20 copperplates, frontis. dampstained, early tree cf., jnts. torn. (SG. Oct.6; 112) $100
– **A Directory for Midwives: Or a Guide for Women** ... 1671. 2 vols. in 1. Lacks plt., cont. cf. [Wing C7942] (TA. Nov.17; 376) £70
– **English Physician & Complete Herbal.** Ed.:– E. Sibley. 1790. 2 vols. in 1. 4to. Mod. hf. cf., spine gt.-decor. (SKC. Nov.18; 1964) £75
– – **Anr. Copy.** 2 vols. in 1. 4to. Engraved port. & 29 hand-cold. plts. in Vol. 1, 13 anatomical plts. in Vol. 2, slight spotting, cont. tree cf. (SKC. Jan.13; 2308) £65
– **A Physical Directory of & Translation of the Dispensatory made by the Colledge of Physitians of London.** L., 1650. *2nd. Edn.* Fo. Without sigs. Ss-Vv (but compl.), advt. lf. at end, some worming in margins, some reprd., affecting text & ptd. lines, upr. outer corner of Xx2 defect, with loss, some stains, qtr. cf., very worm, dpr. cover loose. [Wing C 7541] (S. Dec.13; 259) *Thomas.* £95
– **Semeiotica Uranica.** [L.], 1671. *4th. Edn.* Sm. 8vo. Advts., 2 copperplate horoscopes tipped in, port. trimmed & inlaid, some foxing & soiling, disbnd. [Wing C 7548A] (SG. Oct.6; 113) $175

CUMMING, A.
– **The Elements of Clock & Watch-Work.** L., 1766. *1st. Edn.* 4to. Light browning & spotting, cont. cf., slightly worn. lr. cover spotted. (H. Nov.23; 290)
DM 2,800

CUMMING, Roualeyn George Gordon
– **A Hunter's Life in South Africa.** 1850. 2 vols. Hf. mor. (BS. Nov.16; 101) £65

CUMMINGS, Edward Estlin
– **Eimi.** N.Y., Grove Pr., [1933]. *1st. Edn. (26) lettered & initialled, specially bnd.* Hf. cl. (SG. Jan.12; 81) $175
– – **Anr. Edn.** N.Y., Grove Pr., [1958?]. *(26) lettered & sigd.* Qtr. cl. (SG. Mar.1; 55) $350

CUMMINGS, John
See— BULKELEY, John & Cummings, John

CUNDALL, Herbert Minton
– **Birket Foster R.W.S.** 1906. *Edn. de Luxe. (500) numbered & sigd. by publishers.* 4to. Orig. decor. cl., partly untrimmed, heavily rubbed, rebkd., old spine relaid. (TA. Jan.19; 280) £62

CUNDALL, Joseph
– **On Bookbindings Ancient & Modern.** L., 1881. 4to. 2 plts. loose, orig. cl.; H.M. Nixon coll., with his sig., 2 MS. notes & acquisition note. (BBA. Oct.6; 28) *Solomons.* £140
– – **Anr. Copy.** 4to. 1 plt. loose, slightly spotted, orig. cl., sm. hole in spine. (S. Oct.4; 144)
Bennett & Kerr. £90

CUNITIA, Maria
– **Urania Propitia sive Tabulae Astronomicae mire Faciles.** 1650. Fo. Hf.-title, contents browned, cont. marginalia, cont. bds., spine worn, end-papers wormed. (TA. Sep.15; 422) £55

CUNNINGHAM, Joseph Davey
– **A History of the Sikhs, from the Origin of the Nation to the Battles of the Sutlej.** 1849. *1st. Edn.* Publishers cat. bnd. in at rear, orig. cl., untrimmed, faded on spine, rubbed. (TA. Jun.21; 33) £90

CUNNINGHAM, Peter Miller, Surgeon
– **Two Years in New South Wales.** L., 1827. *1st. Edn.* 2 vols. Cont. cf. gt. (HK. Nov.8; 897)
DM 550
– – **Anr. Edn.** L., 1827. *2nd. Edn.* 2 vols. Cf. gt. (CA. Apr.3; 35) Aus. $420
– – **Anr. Copy.** 2 vols. Some spots, sm. tear in

folding chart, hf. leath., covers worn. (JL. Mar.25; 327) Aus. $280

CUNNINGHAM, Peter
– **The Story of Nell Gwyn & the Sayings of Charles II.** L., 1892. *(250).* Extra-ill. with 20 plts., a few hand-cold., mor., elab. gt., by Bayntun (Rivière), upr. cover inlaid with miniature hand-painted port. of Nell Gwyn, boxed. (S. Oct.4; 112)
Sawyer. £300

CURAEUS, Joa.
– **Exegesis.** Heidelb., 1575. *1st. German Edn.* 4to. Upr. margin slightly stained, sm. margin tear on last lf. bkd. neatly, hf. vell. (HK. May 15; 106)
DM 400

CUREL, P.P.-N.
– [–] **Memorie Storiche sopra le Missioni dell'Indie Orientale.** Nuremb., 1754. 4 vols. in 3. Vell. bds. (S. Dec.1; 371) *Gilbert.* £280

CURICKE, Reinhold
– **Der Stadt Dantzig historische Beschreibung.** Ed. Ill.:– G.R. Curicke. Amst. & Danzig, 1687. *1st. Edn.* Lacks 2 plts., approx. 15 text ll. & plts. from anr. edn., 1 folding copper engr. defect. with loss, some other margin defects, staining & browning. (*Bound with:*) – **Freuden Bezeugung der Stadt Danzig über die höchst-erwünschte Königliche Wahl u. Krönung Augusti des Andern, Königes in Pohlen etc.** Danzig, 1698. A few ll. from anr. edn., some old soiling, some plts. strengthened. Together 2 works in 1 vol. Fo. Linen. (V. Sep.29; 40)
DM 2,600

CURIE, Marie
– **Recherches sur les Substances Radioactives** ... Paris, 1904. *2nd. Edn.* Some light spotting, few pencil marginalia, cl.; John D. Stanitz coll. (SPB. Apr.25; 111) $175
– **Traité de Radioactivité.** Paris, 1910. *1st. Edn.* 2 vols. Lge. 8vo. Liby. stps. on titles, hf. cl., covers & spine of orig. wraps. laid down, unc. & partly unopened, slight score mark on Vol. II, cl. s.-c.'s; John D. Stanitz coll. (SPB. Apr.25; 112) $500
– – **Anr. Copy.** 2 vols. Lge. 8vo. Hf.-titles, 7 plts., text figures, hf. mor., jnts. very worn. (SG. Apr.26; 53) $325
– – **Anr. Copy.** 2 vols. Orig. sewed, unc., wraps. defect., paper partly browned. (V. Sep.29; 1346)
DM 650

CURIEUSE NEUE HAUSS-APOTHEKE
Frankfurt, 1699. 1 supp. vol. removed from bdg., some browning in parts, cont. hf. vell., bumped. (GB. Nov.3; 1017) DM 550

CURIO, C.S.
– **Thesavrvs Lingvae Latinae.** Ed.:– [A. Burer]. Basel, 1576-78. *2nd. Edn.* 3 vols. (all publd.). Fo. 15 ll. including title with margin defects., some mis-pagination, some corners defect. & approx 240 ll. wormed, lightly foxed, unif. cont. pig over wood bds., blind-tooled, brass clasps, lacks some; ex-libris. (HT. May 8; 116) DM 660

CURIOSE SCHREIBER ... SAMBT DEM CURIOSEN MAHLER ...
Dresden, 1695. *2nd. Authorised Edn.* 2 pts. in 1 vol. In 2nd. pt. 1 p. paginated double, lightly browned thro.-out, some spotting, cont. vell., slightly soiled, margin tear. (H. May 22; 164)
DM 920

CURIOSITÉS ET MERVEILLES DE LA NATURE
Text:– Munerelle. Ill.:– Lemaître. Paris, 1869. 4to. 28 lithos. in col. & cont. gommé, together 37 plts., cont. hf. red chagrin. (HD. Jan.30; 42) Frs. 1,200

CURLL, Edmund 'William Egerton'
– **Faithful Memoirs of the Life, Amours & Performances, of ... Mrs. Anne Oldfield.** L., 1731. *1st. Edn.* Folding port., extra-ill. with 51 ports., many laid down, hf. cf., as an extra-ill. copy, w.a.f. (P. Mar.15; 298) *Hannas.* £240

CURLO, Girolamo
– **Esposizione di Fatto Concernente la Missione del Vescowo di Segni nell'Isola di Corsica.** N.p., n.d. (*Bound with:*) – **Osservazioni di uno de Nobili del**

CURLO, Girolamo -*Contd.*

Regno di Corsica sopra le Lettere Patenti Attribuite alla Corte di Torino. [2 Oct. 1745]. (*Bound with:*) GASTALDI, Girolamo – Discorso Teologico, Canonico, Politico riguardante la Missione de Monsignore Cesare Crescenzio de Angelis in Corsica un Qualità di Visitatore Apostolico. ca. 1760. Together 3 works in 1 vol. 4to. Old vell.; D. de Auria ex-libris. (HD. Oct.21; 72) Frs. 3,800

CURNOW, H.
- **The Life & Art of William Strutt.** Wellington, 1980. *(1500) numbered.* Hf. cf. & cl., boxed. (JL. Mar.25; 725) Aus. $260

CURR, Edward
- **An Account of the Colony of Van Dieman's Land.** L., 1824. *1st. Edn.* 12mo. Errata lf., some spotting, faint margin staining, orig. bds., unc., slightly soiled, spine worn. (S. Mar.6; 6a) *Elders.* £280
- – **Anr. Copy.** 12mo. Sm burnhole in 1 lf. with slight loss of text, cont. hf. cf. (S. Nov.1; 23) *Maggs.* £200
- – **Anr. Copy.** 12mo. Some foxing, 1 tear reprd., family inscr. & sig., early bds., qtr. cl., unc. (KH. May 1; 190) Aus. $180
- **The Australian Race ...** Melbourne, 1886-87. 4 vols., including fo. of language tables. Later hf. cf., fo. with 1 bd. spotted & minor staining. (KH. Nov.8; 115) Aus. $220
- – **Anr. Copy.** 3 vols., with the vol. of language tables. 8vo. & fo. 1 frontis. with margin defects., mod. buckram. (KH. May 1; 191) Aus. $190

CURTIS, Aza
- **Flowers, a series of short poems ...** Priv. ptd., 1827. *Ltd. Edn.* Sm. 4to. 14 hand-cold. litho. plts., orig. hf. vell. gt., soiled. (C. Jun.27; 149) *Maggs.* £450

CURTIS, Edward S.
- **In the Land of the Headhunter.** Yonkers, 1915. Cl.-bkd. decor. bds.; sigd. (PNY. Jun.6; 474) $130

CURTIS, Henry
- **Beauties of the Rose.** Bristol, 1853. Vol. II only. 4to. Some minor margin dampstains, orig. gt.-decor. cl., worn. (TA. Apr.19; 190) £220

CURTIS, John
- **British Entomology ...** L., 1823-40. *1st. Edn.* 8 vols. 770 hand-cold. engraved plts., without hf.-titles, cont. hf. mor., partly unc. (C. Jun.27; 150) *Wheldon & Wesley.* £1,800
- – **Anr. Edn.** L., 1824-39 [1823-40]. 16 vols. 770 hand-cold. plts., including plt. 205*, some title-pp. browned, with dupl. Vol. XVI, but containing new title-pp., preface, subscribers list & index for the work to be arranged in 8 vols., bds., slightly worn & stained. (S. Nov.28; 15) *Robinson.* £1,650
- **The Genera of British Lepidoptera.** L., 1858. 4to. 35 cold. plts., loose, leath. backing, covers detchd. (SKC. Oct.26; 348) £110
- – **Anr. Copy.** 4to. 35 hand-cold. plts., orig. bds., recent mor. backstrip. (TA. May 17; 315) £70

CURTIS, Natalie
- **Indians' Book: An Offering by the American Indians of Indian Lore, Musical & Narrative.** N.Y., 1907. *1st. Edn.* 4to. Col.-patterned cl., unopened. (SG. Jan.19; 191) $130
- – **Anr. Copy.** 4to. Decor. buckram, spine rubbed & scraped. (SG. Mar.29; 63) $100

CURTIS, Paul A.
- **Sportsmen All.** Foreword:– Freeman Lloyd. Ill.:– Marguerite Kirmse. Derrydale Pr., [1938]. *(950) numbered.* Gt.-decor. cl. (SG. Mar.15; 213) $110

CURTIS, William
- **The Botanical Magazine.** 1787. Vol. I only. 69 hand-cold. engraved plts., cont. hf. cf., rubbed. (S. Nov.1; 268) *Ash.* £160
- – **Anr. Copy.** Vol. 1. Lacks 1 cold. copper engr., cont. leath., rubbed & bumped. (R. Oct.12; 1809) DM 920
- – **Anr. Run.** L., 1787-88. Vols. I & II in 1 vol. 72 numbered old cold. copperplts., some slight browning, cont. hf. leath. (HT. May 8; 284) DM 1,300
- – **Anr. Run.** 1787-91. Vols. 1-4. 1 plain & 287 hand-cold. plts., slight spotting, cf. gt. (P. Oct.20; 18) £560
- – **Anr. Run.** Ill.:– after James Sowerby, Sydenham Edwards & others. L., 1787-98. Vols. I-II & V-XII, in 2 vols. 354 (of 358) cold. plts., lacks title & index-lf. for Vol. X & a few text ll., 5 plts. defect., few scattered stains, some light foxing, other minor defects., old hf. cf. gt., rubbed. (SG. Mar.22; 75) $1,500
- – **Anr. Run.** 1787-1814. Vols. 1-39 in 17 vols. 1,635 hand-cold. plts., some folding, cont. cf. & hf. cf. gt., worn. (P. Jul.5; 255) £3,800
- – **Anr. Run.** 1788-94. Vols. 1-8, in 6 vols. 300 hand-cold. plts., including 12 from Vol. 9, indexes for Vols. 1-8, title-pp. (not corresponding with contents), some slight browning, cont. red hf. leath., marb. bds., gt. spines. (SKC. Sep.9; 1987) £750
- – **Anr. Copy.** Vols. 2 & 7-8, in 2 vols. 1 plain & 133 hand-cold. plts., mod. hf. cf. gt., as a coll. of plts. w.a.f. (P. Oct.20; 20) £320
- – **Anr. Run.** 1790-91. Vols. 3 & 4 in 2 vols. Cont. leath. gt., bumped. (R. Apr.4; 1683) DM 1,400
- – **Anr. Run.** 1790-1807. Vols. 3-6, 25 & 26, in 3 vols. 236 hand-cold. engraved plts., cont. cf., very worn, 1 cover detchd., w.a.f. (S. Oct.4; 262) *Burdon.* £500
- – **Anr. Run.** L., 1793-1800. Vols. 1, 2 & 9-14, in 4 vols. 288 hand-cold. engraved plts., some offsetting, some stains, 1st. vol. in mod. qtr. cf., rest in hf. russ., worn, 1 spine brkn., w.a.f. (S. Dec.13; 260) *Beisler.* £620
- – **Anr. Run.** L., 1793-1801. Vols. 1-12 in 6 vols. 432 hand-cold. engraved plts., some browning & spotting, mainly affecting text, hf. roan, spines defect., w.a.f. (S. Nov.28; 18) *Schuster.* £1,000
- – **Anr. Run.** L., 1793-1810. Vols. 1-32 in 16 vols. 1,325 (of 1,328) hand-cold. engraved plts., some folding, lacks title & index lf. to Vol. 16, a few plts. spotted & some offsetting, mostly onto text, 1 plt. & facing text p. damaged by adhesion, cont. tree cf., recently rebkd., w.a.f. (S. Nov.28; 17) *Robinson.* £3,200
- – **Anr. Run.** 1794. Vols. 7 & 8, in 1 vol. 72 hand-cold. plts., slight spotting at beginning & end, hf. cf. (S. Nov.1; 269) *Gilbert.* £180
- – **Anr. Copy.** Vols. 7 & 8 in 1 vol. Some foxing, cont. hf. leath., bumped & worn. (R. Oct.12; 1810) DM 1,500
- – **Anr. Run.** L., 1795-96. Vols. 9-10 only in vol. 72 hand-cold. plts., a few ll. slightly spotted, cont. cf., worn, covers detchd. (BBA. May 3; 76) *Toolay.* £190
- – **Anr. Copy.** Vols. 9 & 10 in 1 vol. Cont. hf. leath., bumped. (R. Oct.12; 1811) DM 1,500
- – **Anr. Run.** 1797. Vols. 9-15, in 4 vols. 284 hand-cold. plts., slight spotting, cf. gt., 1 cover detchd. (P. Oct.20; 19) £460
- – **Anr. Run.** L., 1804. Vols. 19 & 20. Cont. hf. leath., bumped. (R. Oct.12; 1813) DM 1,300
- – **Anr. Run.** 1805. Vols. 21 & 22 in 1 vol. 94 hand-cold. plts., hf. cf. gt., rubbed. (P. Mar.15; 14) *Cumming.* £230
- – **Anr. Run.** L., 1807. Vol. 25. Lightly browned at beginning, cont. hf. leath., spine renewed. (R. Oct.12; 1814) DM 1,050
- – **Anr. Run.** 1811. Vols. 33 & 34 in 1 vol. Cont. hf. leath., bumped. (R. Apr.4; 1690) DM 1,200
- – **Anr. Run.** L., 1812. Vols. 35 & 36 in 1 vol. 83 engraved hand-cold. plts., cont. hf. cf., rubbed. (BBA. Nov.30; 95) *Heuer.* £190
- – **Anr. Run.** 1817. Vol. 44. Cont. hf. leath., bumped. (R. Apr.4; 1691) DM 1,200
- – **Anr. Run.** L., 1818. Vol. 45. Cont. marb. cf. gt. (BR. Apr.12; 614) DM 880
- **Flora Londinensis.** Ill.:– after S. Edwards, J. Sowerby, W. Kilburn, & others. L., priv. ptd., 1777-98. *1st. Edn. (300) cold. by William Graves.* 6 fascicules in 3 vols. Fo. Title to Vol. 1 with engraved vig., 434 hand-cold. engraved plts., arranged alphabetically, 6 p. 'Catalogue of certain plants growing ... in the environs of Settle', plt. 268 torn & reprd., cont. russ. gt. by Staggemeier(?). (C. Mar.14; 159) *Currey.* £4,200
- – **Anr. Edn.** Ill.:– after S. Edwards, James Sowerby, W. Kilburn, & others. L., priv. ptd., 1777-98. *1st. Edn.* 6 fascicules in 2 vols. Fo. 2 ptd. titles, title to Vol. 1 with engraved vig., 426 (of 434)

engraved plts. (196 hand-cold.), lacks 1st. dedication lf., 4 pp. subscribers list, 4 pp. 'General Observations ... ', 6 pp. 'A Catalogue of certain Plants' & 10 pp. general indexes, sm. hole in letterpress to 5th. plt. in fascicule 1, with loss of 5 letters of text, mod. hf. cf., w.a.f. (C. Jun.27; 151) *Burgess.* £2,200
- – **Anr. Edn.** Ill.:– after Sydenham Edwards & others. L., [1775-]77[-98]. *1st. Edn.* 6 pts. in 2 vols. Fo. Title to Vol. 1 with engraved vig., 432 engraved plts., uncold. except for 4 plts. in last pt., 1 subscribers list, lacks title & dedication to Vol. 2, without the 'Catalogue of Plants around Settle or Observations on Grasses', some plts. slightly browned, some lr. corners stained in Vol. 1, offsetting on text, 1 plt. mntd., 19th. C. hf. cf., very worn, covers detchd. (S. Nov.28; 16) *Schuster.* £920
- – **Anr. Edn.** Ed.:– George Graves. 1817. *New Edn.* Vol. 1 only (of 2). 228 hand-cold. plts., disbnd., lacks covers, w.a.f. (LA. Jul.20; 166) £1,100
- **Lectures on Botany.** L., 1804. *1st. Edn.* Vols. II & III (of 3). 72 numbered old cold. copperplts., some slight browning, cont. gold-tooled leath., worn, jnt. brittle, 1 cover loose. (HT. May 8; 283) DM 600

CURTIUS RUFUS, Quintus
- **De Rebus Gestis Alexandri Magni.** Ed.:– [Pomponius Laetus]. [Rome], Georgius Lauer, not after Jan. 1472. *1st. or 2nd. Edn.* 4to. 1st. p. with initial I supplied in gold on red & blue ground gold descender & three-qtr. p. border of leaves & flowers with gold dots & penwork tracery, cold. coat-of-arms of orig. owner (probably Michaelis de Lucerna, see below) in lr. margin, 6 other lge. initials at book headings in blue, red, green, purple, yellow & white with cold. & decor. margin ascenders & descenders, rubricated, upr. corner of final blank lf. defect., some slight margin soiling, some cont. margin annots., lev. mor. by Riviere, spine gt.-lettered, 1 corner slightly bruised, qtr. mor. box; inscr. below colophon 'Generossi secundum epistolas domini Michaelis de Lucerna vero presens oppus', the sense conveyed by this when joined to colophon suggests a relationship between Lauer & Michaelis (possibly as a subscriber or financial supporter), Charles W. Clark & Thomas B. Stevenson copy. [BMC IV, 37 (IB 17457); Goff C-999] (CNY. May 18; 101) $3,400
- – **Anr. Edn.** Commentary:– S. Pitiscus. Utrecht, 1685. 2 vols. Minimal browning & light stains, late 17th. C. vell., gt. elab. decor., corner fleurons, gt. centre Utrecht arms. (H. May 22; 652) DM 500

CURWEN, John Christian
- **Hints on the Economy of Feeding Stock & bettering the Condition of the Poor.** 1808. Cont. cf. gt. (P. Feb.16; 250) £75
- **Observations on the State of Ireland.** L., 1818. 2 vols. Crimson hf. mor., bkplt. (GM. Dec.7; 389) £130

CURWEN PRESS
- **A Specimen Book of Pattern Papers.** Intro.:– Paul Nash. L., 1928. *(220) numbered.* 4to. Orig. cl. (BBA. Mar.7; 195) *S. Fogg.* £420

CURZON, Hon. Robert
- **Vists to Monasteries in the Levant.** 1849. *1st. Edn.* 8vo. Cont. hf. vell., spine gt. (BBA. Jan.19; 103) *Quaritch.* £80

CUSHING, Harvey
- **From A Surgeon's Journal, 1915-18.** Boston, 1936. *Later Edn.* Cont. limp mor., single gt. cover rule, inner gt. dentelles, silk end-ll.; pres. bdg. to Baltimore doctor by Maryland Pedic Association; lengthy sigd. ink pres. inscr. by Cushing. (HA. May 4; 464) $150
- **The Pituitary Body & its Disorders.** Phila. & L., 1912. *1st. Edn.* Cold. frontis., folding plt., ills., orig. cl. (S. Apr.10; 491) *Phillips.* £95
- – **Anr. Edn.** Phila., [1912]. *1st. Edn.* 1 vol. Lge. 8vo. Liby. Buckram. (*With:*) - **Tumors of the Nervus Acusticus.** Phila., 1917. *1st. Edn.* 1 vol. Lge. 8vo. Orig. cl., ex-liby. (SG. Mar.22; 76) $325

CUSPINIAN, Joannes
- **Ein ausserlesne Chronicka von C. Julio Caesare biss auff Carolum Quintum ... auch von allen Orientischen oder Griechischen und Türckischen Keysern.** Preface:– Ph. Melanchthon. Trans.:– C. Hedion.

Strassburg, 1541. *1st. German Edn.* 2 pts. in 1 vol. Fo. Stained, foxed, lightly wormed, especially at beginning & end, lacks last text lf. pt. 2 & end-lf. with printers mark, mod. leatherette. (R. Apr.3; 30) **DM 400**

CUST, Lionel
– **British Museum Catalogue of the Collection of Fans & Fan-Leaves presented ... by the Lady Charlotte Schreiber.** 1893. Liby. stp. on title, orig. cl. (BBA. Sep.8; 238) *Sawyer.* £65

CUTBUSH, James
– **A System of Pyrotechny.** Phila., 1825. Foxed, cont. sheep, extremities rubbed. (SG Mar.22; 77) $110

CUVIER, Baron Georges Leopold Chretien
– **The Animal Kingdom arranged in Conformity with its Organization ...** Additional Descriptions:– Edward Griffith. L., 1827-35. 16 vols. 755 (of 801) plts., some spotting & offsetting, cont. red mor. gt. by Townsend, partly unc., spine ends slightly rubbed. (S. Nov.28; 19) *Traylen.* £640
– – **Anr. Copy.** 16 vols. 773 engraved plts. only (645 hand-cold. or partially hand-cold.), cont. mor. gt., w.a.f. (CSK. Jan.27; 57) £380
– – **Anr. Copy.** 16 vols., with Index. Hf. mor. (P. Dec.8; 248) *Bowes.* £130
– – **Anr. Copy.** 16 vols. Lge. 8vo. Offsetting, some foxing & margin staining to 8 vols., hf. cf., several vols. loose or with hinges crudely reinforced with tape, ex-liby. (SG. Oct.6; 115) $400
– – **Anr. Copy.** 16 vols. Lge. 8vo. Offsetting, foxing & some margin stains in mammal & bird vols., hf. cf., several vols. loose or with hinges crudely reinforced, ex-liby., plts. unmarked. (SG. Mar.22; 78) $275
– – **Anr. Edn.** [1833]-34-37. 8 vols., including 4 plt. vols. 39 plain & 678 hand-cold. plts., hf. cf. gt. (P. Feb.16; 215) £260
– – **Anr. Edn.** L., 1834. 4 vols. Most engrs. hand-cold., hf. cf., corners. (CR. Jun.6; 146) Lire 320,000
– – **Anr. Edn.** Ill.:– Latreille. L., 1834-37. 4 vols. text, 4 vols. plts. Hand-cold. lithos., some foxing, hf. leath. & marb. bds., spines reprd., edges rubbed, end-papers torn. (RS. Jan.17; 487) $160
– – **Anr. Edn.** 1837-36-37. 8 vols., including 4 plt. vols. Many plts. partly hand-cold., cf., rubbed, some staining. (P. Feb.16; 136) £210
– **The Class Reptilia.** Descriptions:– Edward Griffith & Edward Pidgeon. L., 1831. *1st. Engl. Edn.* Vol. III of 'The Animal Kingdom'. Sm. 4to. 55 engraved plts., most cold., a few plts. damp-soiled at top corners, buckram, unc. (SG. Mar.22; 79) $150
– **Leçons d'Anatomie Comparée.** Ed.:– C. Dumeril & G.L. Duvernoy. Paris, 1835-46. *2nd. Edn. (mixed set).* 8 vols. in 9. Buckram, ex-liby. (SG. Mar.22; 80) $125
– – **Anr. Copy.** 8 pts. in 9 vols. All titles multi-stpd., cont. hf. leath., w.a.f. (HK. Nov.8; 490) DM 420
– **Le Règne Animal.** Paris, [1836-49]. 10 text & 10 plt. vols. 4to. Some slight foxing, cont. red hf. leath. (R. Oct.12; 1818) DM 7,200
See— GEOFFROY SAINT-HILAIRE, Etienne & Cuvier, Baron Georges Leopold Chretien
See— LACEPEDE, Comte Bernard Germaine Etienne de & Cuvier, Baron Georges Léopold Chretien

CUVILLIES François
– **Oeuvres.** Paris, 1738-73. Fo. Coll. of 205 engraved plts., 6 slightly browned, cont. cf., spine tooled in blind, spine extremities & lr. corners reprd. (C. Dec.9; 26) *Weinreb.* £3,500

CYPRIAN, E.S.
– **Catalogus Codicum Manuscriptorum Bibliothecae Gothanae.—Clarorum Virorum Epistolae. CX VII e Bibliothecae Gothanae Autographis.** Leipzig, 1714. 2 pts. in 1 vol. Sm. 4to. Cont. bds., rubbed & bumped. (R. Apr.3; 610) DM 450

CYPRIANUS, Saint
– **Opera.** Venice, Lucas Dominicus F., 4 Dec. 1483. Fo. Lacks 2 blanks, cf.-bkd. bds.; the Walter Goldwater copy. [BMC V, 281; Goff C-1013] (SG. Dec.1; 114) $650

CYRANO DE BERGERAC, Sevirien
– **Les Oeuvres Diverses.** Ill.:– Schern. Amst. [Rouen], 1710. 2 vols. Sm. 8vo. Cont. cf. gt., decor. spines, inner roll-stp. (HD. Sep.22; 228) Frs. 7,100

CYRILLUS, Saint, Archbp. of Alexandria
– **Opus Insigne in Evangelium Ioannis.—Preclarum Opus Thesaurus.—Commentarium in Leviticum Sexdecem Libris Digesti.** Paris, 1521. *2nd. Edn.* 3 works in 1 vol. Fo. Cont. stpd. pig over wood bds., clasps; from Fondation Furstenberg-Beaumesnil. (HD. Nov.16; 114) Frs. 3,800

CYRILLUS (pseudo-Cyrillus)
– **Speculum Sapientiae.** [Paris], Georg Mittelhus, ca. 1497. Lacks sig. e, title-lf. reprd. & mntd., some margin stains, later vell.; the Walter Goldwater copy. [BMC VIII, 129; Goff C-1020] (SG. Dec.1; 115) $225
– – **Anr. Edn.** [Paris], Jean Petit, after 1500?. Sm. 8vo. Cf., gt. borders enclosing blind-stpd. arms of William Stirling, by J. MacKenzie & Son; Keir bkplt., the Walter Goldwater copy. [BMC VIII, 200; Goff C-1021] (SG. Dec.1; 116) $375

CZECH, Fr. H.
– **Versinnlichte Denk- u. Sprachlehre, mit Anwendung auf die Religions- u. Sittenlehre u. auf d. Leben.** Wien, 1836. *1st. Edn.* 4to. Title slightly soiled, minimal foxing, cont. hf. leath. gt., slightly bumped. (HK. Nov.9; 1590) DM 500

CZESCHKA, C.O.
– **Kalender 1904.** N.p., 1904. Sm. 4to. Orig. litho. sewed, orig. wraps. (GB. May 5; 2306) DM 750

D.C.A.
– **Melzinga: A Souvenir.** N.Y., 1845. 12mo. Old bds., worn, spine tips chipped; inscr. & sigd. by Millard Fillmore on front free end-paper. (RO. Jun.26; 120) $110

D., R.
– **The Footman's Friendly Advice To his Brethren of the Livery; & to all Servants in General.** N.d. 2 pp. of advts. at end, cont. cf. gt., slightly worn; the Hinton House copy. (LC. Oct.13; 427) £200

D'ABRERA, B.
– **Birdwing Butterflies of the World.** Melbourne, 1975. Lge. 4to. Cl., d.-w., orig. s.-c. (*With:*) – **Butterflies of the Neo-Tropical Region.** Melbourne, 1981. Pt. 1: 'Papilionidae & Pieridae'. Lge. 4to. Cl., d.-w. (SKC. Oct.26; 349) £75
– **Butterflies of the Afrotropical Region.** Melbourne, 1980. Lge. 4to. Cl., d.-w. (SKC. Oct.26; 351) £60
– **Butterflies of the Australian Region.** Melbourne, 1977. Lge. 4to. Cl., d.-w. (SKC. Oct.26; 352) £75

DABRY DE THIERSANT, C.P.
– **La Pisiculture et la Pêche en Chine.** Intro.:– J.L. Souberain. Paris, 1872. Fo. Some light foxing, cost. hf. leath., worn, slightly bumped. (HK. May 16; 1443) DM 850

DACIER, Emile
– **Les Plus Belles Reliures de la Réunion des Bibliothèques Nationales.** Paris, 1929. *(600) numbered.* Fo. Loose as iss. in orig. ptd. bds., a little rubbed; H.M. Nixon coll., with 1 or 2 MS. notes. (BBA. Oct.6; 29) *Maggs.* £130

DADA ALMANACH
Ed.:– Aich. Huelsenbeck. Berlin, 1920. Margin slightly browned, orig. pict. sewed, spine browned. (CB. May 5; 2314) DM 800

D'AGINCOURT, Jean Baptist Louis George
– **Sammlung Denkmaeler der Architectur Vorzugsweise.** Ed.:– A.F. von Quast. Frankfurt, ca. 1850. 4 pts. in 1 vol. Fo. 328 plts., cl., worn. (F. Mar.15; 53) £65

DAGLISH, Eric Fitch
– **Birds of the British Isles.** 1948. *1st. Edn. (1500).* No bdg. stated. (JL. Jun.24; 13) Aus. $240.

DAGLISH, John
– **Practical Observations on Vaccine Inoculation ... Small-Pox in the Neighbourhood of Newcastle.** Newcastle, 1825. Orig. bds. (P. Jul.5; 322) £100

DAGUERRE, Louis Jacques Monde
– **Das Daguerrestyp und das Diorama.** Stuttgart, 1839. Cont. bds. (R. Apr.4, 1631) DM 2,600
– **Historique et Description des Procedés du Daguerreotype et du Diorama.** Paris, 1839. *New Edn. 1st. Iss., before the addition of printer's imprint on last p.* Orig. mauve ptd. wraps., unopened, soiled & frayed. (BBA. Mar.21; 40) *Museion.* £350

DAHL, Roald
– **Someone Like You.** L., 1954. *1st. Edn.* 1 vol. Orig. cl., d.-w.; sigd. by author. (*With:*) – **Kiss Kiss.** L., 1960. *1st. Edn.* 1 vol. Orig. cl., d.-w.; sigd. by author. (BBA. Nov.30; 328) *Words etc.* £50

DAHLBERG, Count Eric Jonsson
– **Suecia Antiqua et Hodierna.** Stockholm, 1690-1714. *1st. Edn.* 3 vols. Fo. 3 engraved titles, 3 ports., 2 double-p. maps, 346 plts., many double-p. & folding, cont. hf. cf., covers scuffed, unc. (C. Dec.9; 27) *Lyon.* £2,000
– – **Anr. Copy.** 3 vols. 4to. Cont. cf., Du Seuil decor. (HD. Jun.18; 14) Frs. 31,000
– – **Anr. Edn.** Ill.:– Adam, Percelle, Marot, & others. Stockholm, [1693-1715]. 3 pts. in 2 vols. Lge. 4to. Some plts. mntd. & sm. tears restored, 1 plt. inverted, cf., tooled. (D. Nov.23; 852) DM 7,500

DAILY EXPRESS
– **Children's Annual, No. 3.** Ed.:– S. Louis Giraud. L., ca. 1925. 7 double-p. col. pop-up plts., pict. bds., spine worn. (SG. Dec.8; 275) $125

DAIX, Pierre & Boudaille, George
– **Picasso: The Blue & Rose Periods: A Catalogue Raisonné of the Paintings, 1900-1906.** Greenwich, [1967]. Lge. 4to. 61 tipped-in col. plts., bdg. not stated, edges slightly bumped & soiled, acetate wraps. slightly chipped. (CBA. Jan.29; 343) $140

DALBERG, K.T.A.M. von
[–] **Perikles. Ueber den Einfluss der Schönen Künste auf das Offentliche Glück.** Gotha, 1806. *1st. Edn.* Cont. hf. leath. (GB. Nov.4; 2016) DM 800

DALE, Samuel
See— [TAYLOR, Silas] & Dale, Samuel

DALECHAMPS, Jacques
[–] **Historia Generalis Plantarum.** Lyon, 1586. *1st. Edn.* Fo. Browned, mod. vell. (R. Apr.4; 1694) DM 2,500

DALENCE, Joachim
– **Traité de l'Aiman.** Amst., 1687. *1st. Edn.* 2 pts. in 1 vol. Copper engraved title cut & with bkd. tear, slightly browned, some ll. with sm. stains, cont. vell., slightly soiled & bumped, end-papers 17th. C. renewed, ex-libris. (HK. Nov.8; 492) DM 600

DALEY, Charles
– **The History of South Melbourne.** Melbourne, 1940. Orig. cl., d.-w. slightly worn; pres. slip tipped in. (KH. Nov.8; 117) Aus. $110

DALI, Salvador
– **Cent Aquarelles pour la Divine Comédie.** Text:– R. Cogniat, C. Roger-Marx, M. Brion, J.P. Crespelle. [Paris, 1960]. 4to. Sewed; orig. pencil drawing by Dali on hf.-title, dedicated, dtd. 1960 & sigd. twice. (HD. Jun.22; 31) Frs. 9,500
[–] **Les Chevaux de Dali.** Preface:– Yves Saint-Martin. Text:– Alain Decaux & Leon Zitrone. Paris, 1983. *(1000) numbered on velin d'Arches.* Lge. fo. Ills. sigd. in the plt., lacks the 2 sigd. lithos., leaves, wrap., velvet box. (HD. Mar.27; 56) Frs. 1,750
– **Our Historical Heritage.** N.Y. & Paris, [1975]. *(400) numbered on Arches, with plts. sigd. & numbered.* Fo. 11 lge. hand-cold. dry-points, loose as iss. in cl. folder, s.-c. with bronze medallion mntd. on upr. cover. (SG. Apr.26; 54) $1,400
– **Verborgene Gesichter.** Trans.:– R. Hermstein. Frankfurt, 1973. *1st. German Edn.* Orig. coarse linen, orig. cork s.-c., sigd. by author. on end-paper. (R. Apr.3; 162) DM 850

DALI, Salvador –*Contd.*
See— MALRAUX, A. & Dali, Salvador

DALIZE, René
– **Ballade du Pauvre Macchabé mal Enterré.** Ill.:–
André Derain,. Paris, 1919. *(110) numbered on
Arches.* Ob. 4to. 6 orig. woodcuts, later hf. lev.
mor., partly unc., orig. wraps. (spotted) preserved.
(BBA. Jan.19; 314)   *Marks,.* £200

D'ALLAIS, V.
– **Histoire des Sevarambes, Peuples qui habitent
une Partie du Troisiéme Continent, communement
appellé La Terre Australe** ... Amst., 1702. 2 vols. in
1. 12mo. Sm. section cut from 1st. title-p., later qtr.
cf. (KH. May 1; 194)   Aus. $110

DALLAWAY, James
– **Constantinople.** 1797. *1st. Edn.* 4to. Cont. cf.,
covers detchd. (P. Dec.8; 288)   *Martinos.* £120
– **Inquiries into the Origin & Progress of the Science
of Heraldry in England.** Gloucester, 1793. 4to. Plts.
hand-cold., some offsetting of plts. to text, cont.
mott. cf. gt. (TA. Oct.20; 140)   £58

DALLIMORE, William
– **Poisonous Plants, Deadly, Dangerous & Suspect.**
Ed.:– Dr. A.W. Hill. Ill.:– John Nash. Haslewood
Books, 1927. *(350) numbered.* Fo. Orig. cl. gt., d.-
w. slightly worn. (S. Nov.21; 204)   *Campus.* £170

DALLINGTON, Sir Robert
[–] **Aphorismes Ciuill & Militarie ... out of the First
Quarterne of Fr. Guicciardine.** L., 1613. *1st. Edn.*
2 pts. in 1 vol. Fo. Lacks 1st. blank, slight browning,
a little worming, scarcely affecting text, cont. cf.,
gt. arms of Signet Liby. on covers, spine worn.
[STC 6197] (S. Oct.11; 514)   *Quaritch.* £70
– – **Anr. Copy.** 2 pts. in 1 vol. Fo. Cont. marginalia,
19th. C. cf., worn, covers detchd. (S. Oct.11; 391)
                                          Georges. £60

DALLY, N.
See— WAHLEN, A.

DALRYMPLE, Alexander
– **A Collection of Voyages Chiefly in the Southern
Atlantick Ocean. Published from Original Mss.** Priv.
ptd., 1775. *1st. Edn.* 4to. Hf.-title, lacks lf. of
contents & 3 folding engraved charts, disbnd.
[Sabin 18336] (TA. Mar.15; 13)   £60
– **The Spanish Pretensions Fairly Discussed.** L.,
1790. *1st. Edn.* Title-p. dust soiled, with sm. margin
tear reprd., hf. cf.; the Rt. Hon. Visc. Eccles copy.
[Sabin 18343] (CNY. Nov.18; 79) $1,800

DALRYMPLE, Sir David
– **Annals of Scotland.** Edinb., 1776-79. *1st. Edn.* 2
vols. 4to. Hf.-titles, cont. spr. cf., faded; Sir Ivar
Colquhoun, of Luss copy. (CE. Mar.22; 75) £100

DALRYMPLE, Sir James, Earl of Stair
See— STAIR, Sir James Dalrymple, Earl of

DALRYMPLE, Sir John
– **Memoirs of Great Britain & Ireland.** Edinb.,
1771-73-88. *1st. Edn.* 3 vols. 4to. Cont. spr. cf.,
spines gt.; Sir Ivar Colquhoun, of Luss copy. (CE.
Mar.22; 79)   £140

DALRYMPLE, W.
– **Golfing Guide to the United Kingdom.** 1895. Bdg.
not stated. (PD. Jul.13; 66)   £220

D'ALTON, John
– **King James's Irish Army List, [1689].** Dublin,
1855. *1st. Edn.* Cl. (GM. Dec.7; 37)   £55

DALTON, John Call
– **Topographical Anatomy of the Brain.** Phila., 1885.
1st. Edn. (250). 3 vols. Fo. 48 heliotype plts., few
margin dampstains, orig. cl., ex-liby. (SG. Mar.22;
81) $450

DALTON, Michael
– **The Countrey Justice.** L., 1630. Title frayed.
(Bound with:) – **Officium Vicecomitum, the
Office & Authoritie of Sherifs.** L., 1623. Together
2 works in 1 vol. Fo. Slight browning, mod. cf.-bkd.
bds. (S. Mar.20; 820)   *Boswell.* £200
– – **Anr. Edn.** L., 1635. *6th. Edn.* Fo. Some ll.
slightly soiled & browned, mod. cf. [STC 6211]
(BBA. Mar.21; 176)   *Bowers.* £150

DALTON, Ormonde Maddock
– **Catalogue of Early Christian Antiquities &
Objects from the Christian East in the Bristish
Museum.** L., 1901. 4to. 35 plts., cl. (SG. Aug.25;
118) $200
– **Catalogue of the Ivory Carvings of the Christian
Era ... [in] the British Museum.** L., 1909. 4to. 125
plts., cl. (SG. Aug.25; 208) $450

DALTON, Ormonde Maddock
See— READ, Charles Hercules & Dalton,
Ormonde Maddock

DALTON, Philip (Ed.)
See— SHERLOCK HOLMES JOURNAL

DALTON, William H.
– **The New & Complete English Traveller.** L., 1794.
Fo. Engraved frontis., 18 (of 23) engraved mapsheets, mostly full-p., some slight spotting, cont. cf.,
worn, w.a.f. (S. Mar.6; 235)   *Whiteson.* £260

DALVIMART, Octavien
[–] **The Costume of Turkey.** L., 1802. Fo. In Engl. &
Fr., red mor., blind- & gold-tooled decor., blind-
tooled corner fleurons, gt. spine, gt. inner & outer
dentelle. (D. Nov.23; 1390)   DM 1,150
– – **Anr. Edn.** L., 1804. Fo. Engraved title, 60 plts.
(wtrmkd. 1823), all hand-cold., text in Engl. & Fr.
(wtrmkd. 1818), some slight offsetting, cont. purple
str.-grd. mor. gt. (BBA. Mar.21; 322)
                                          Thorp. £280
– – **Anr. Copy.** Sm. fo. Title vig., 60 hand-cold.
engrs. (wtrmkd. 1817-19), mor., disbnd. (SG.
Sep.22; 108) $400

DALY, M. Caesar
– **Bibliothèque de la Architecte. L'Architecture
Privée aux XIX Siècle. Nouvelles Maisons de Paris
et des Environs.** Paris, 1870-72. 1st. & 2nd. Series:
6 vols. Fo. Some spotting, liby. stps. on titles, unif.
cont. qtr. mor. gt., some wear. (TA. Jul.19; 422)
                                                  £100
– – **Anr. Edn.** Paris, 1870-77. 1st. & 2nd. Series: 6
vols. Tall fo. Engraved plts., each liby.-stpd. on
blank verso, loose in bds., linen ties, portfos. loose &
shabby. (SG. May 3; 127) $550
– **Décorations Intérieures Peints.** Paris, 1877. 2 vols.
Tall fo. 119 chromolitho. plts., each liby.-stpd. on
blank verso, loose in later bd. folders, orig. cover
labels. (SG. May 3; 128) $600
– **Motifs Historiques d'Architecture et de Sculpture
d'Ornement.** Paris, 1869, 1880. 1st. & 2nd. Series:
4 vols. Tall fo. Engraved plts., ex-liby., hf. mor.,
worn. (SG. May 3; 126) $200

DALY, Mrs. Dominic D.
– **Digging, Squatting & Pioneering Life in the Northern Territory** ... 1887. *1st. Edn.* Light foxing to
2 or 3 ll., outer edge of folding map slightly frayed,
early hf. cf., some rubbing. (KH. May 1; 195)
                                          Aus. $380

DALZEL, Alexander
– **The History of Dahomy.** 1793. 4to. Title, folding
map & plts. tipped in, margin soiling, text spotted,
cont. bds., soiled. (CSK. Sep.30; 112)   £130

DALZIEL, G. & E.
– **The Brothers Dalziel, a Record of Fifty Years'
Work.** L., 1901. 4to. Orig. cl. (S. Apr.30; 135)
                                          Quaritch. £55

DALZIEL, H.
– **British Dogs.** L., 1889. *2nd. Edn.* 2 vols. 15 cold.
plts., hf. cf. gt. (P. May 17; 153)   *Forsmen.* £95

DAMAS, Jan de
See— HIPPOCRATES—DAMAS, Jan de

DAME TRUELOVE'S TALES
1817 [wtrmkd. 1815-16]. *1st. Edn.* 16mo. Engraved
frontis., title-p., 21 plts., all but title-p. hand-cold.,
soiled & worn, a few ll. lack sm. parts of outer
margin, orig. roan-bkd. bds., worn; van Veen coll.
(S. Feb.28; 4)   £100

**DAME WIGGINS OF LEE, & her Seven Won-
derful Cats**
Ed.:– John Ruskin. Ill.:– Kate Greenaway & others.
Sunnyside, Orpington, 1885. L.P., gt.-pict. cl., spine
ends slightly rubbed, lightly soiled. (SG. Mar.29;
70) $100

DAMHOUDER, J. de
– **Praxis Rerum Criminalium.** Antw., 1570. *6th.
Latin Edn.* 4to. Lightly browned & slightly spotted,
title lf. with MS. owner's mark, lacks 4 pp., cont.
pig, blind-tooled, spotted & rubbed, spine defect.
(HT. May 10; 2684a)   DM 1,300

DAMIANO DE ODEMIRA
– **Libro da imparare Giochare a Scachi** ... N.p., ca.
1540.?. Cont. MS. acquisition note, a few other
annots., 2pp. MS. with ills. at end, a few stains,
cont. vell. (BBA. May 23; 316)
                                  Macdonald Ross. £400

DAMIANUS, Petrus, Saint
– **Vita ... Romualdi.** Forli, 1641. 4to. Cont. limp
vell., stained. (SG. Oct.27; 254) $125

DAMPIER, William
– **A New Voyage round the World.** L., 1698-99-
1703. *Vol. 1: 3rd. Edn., rest: 1st. Edn.* 3 vols. 24
maps & plts., piece torn from 1 margin, non-unif.
cont. cf., Vol. 1 covers very worn, sig. on front end-
paper of Vol. 1. (CA. Apr.3; 36)   Aus. $1,100
– – **Anr. Edn.** L., n.d.-1705-03. 3 vols. 23 maps &
plts. only, Vol. 1 lacks title & 1 chart, 1 map torn,
most pp. offset, cont. cf., rebkd., covers worn, upr.
covers to Vols. 1 & 3 detchd. (CA. Apr.3; 131)
                                          Aus. $450
– – **Anr. Edn.** Argonaut Pr., 1927. *(With:)*
– **Voyages & Discoveries.** Argonaut Pr., 1931.
Together 2 vols. 4to. vell.-bkd. cl. gt., spines darkened, untrimmed. (SKC. Jan.13; 2374)   £60

DANA, Charles A. (Trans.)
See— NUTCRACKER & SUGARDOLLY: A
Fairy Tale

DANA, Richard Henry, Jnr.
– **The Seaman's Friend.** Boston, [1841]. *1st. Edn.*
12mo. Light foxing, cont. cf., light wear. (RO.
Dec.11; 85) $400
– – **Anr. Copy.** Sm. 8vo. Foxed, orig. cf., worn &
slightly shaken; from liby. of F.D. Roosevelt, inscr.
by him & a cont. owner. (SG. Mar.15; 12) $275
– **Two Years Before the Mast.** N.Y., 1840. *1st. Edn.
3rd. Iss.* 16mo. Impft. type on copyright notice &
on running head of p. 9, ink sig. clipped from blank
top edge of title-p., mod. gt. hf. mor., partly unc.
(SG. Mar.15; 101) $100
– – **Anr. Edn.** N.Y., 1840. *1st. Edn.* 12mo. With
dotted 'i' in copyright notice & perfect type in
running headline on p.9, some foxing, orig. ptd.
muslin 1st. state, with 105 titles listed in Harper's
Family Liby., soiled, spine worn, jnts. reprd., hole
in cl. of lr. cover, mor.-bkd. s.-c.; Perry Molstad
copy. (SPB. May 16; 442) $1,100
– – **Anr. Edn.** Ill.:– E.A. Wilson. Chic., Lakeside
Pr., 1930. *(100).* 4to. Gt.-pict. cl.,boxed; sigd. col.
drawing by Wilson on front free end-paper. (SG.
Jan.12; 190) $200

D'ANCORA, Gaetano
– **Guide du Voyageur pour les Antiquités ... de
Pouzel.** Naples, 1792. Slight margin staining of
early ll., cont. hf. cf., spine slightly worn. (S. Nov.1;
76)   *Erlini.* £100

DANDINI, Girolamo
– **Voyage du Mont Liban.** Trans.:– R[ichard]
S[imon]. Paris, 1684. *New Edn.* 12mo. Hf.-title,
folding map with sm. repair, lacks fly-ll., old cf.,
very worn. (SG. Sep.22; 116) $275

DANDIRAN, F.
See— MIALHE, Francisco & Dandiran, F.

DANDOLO, Count
– **The Art of Rearing Silk-Worms.** 1825. Orig. bds.
(PD. Dec.14; 260)   £75

DANDULO, Fantinus
– **Compendium Catholicae Fidei.** [Venice, Reynaldus de Novimagio], ca. 1486-88. 4to. Fully
rubricated, some margin repairs & stains, mod.
blind-tooled mor.; the Walter Goldwater copy.
[BMC V, 258; Goff D-4] (SG. Dec.1; 117) $250

DANEAU, Lambert
– **Deux Traitez Nouveaux très Utiles pour ce Temps.**
Geneva?, 1579. *2nd. or 3rd. Edn.* Sm. 8vo. Cont.
vell. (HD. Nov.9; 4)   Frs. 4,000

DANES, John
– Paralipomena Orthographiae, Etymologiae, Prosodiae. 1638. *1st. Edn.* Sm. 4to. Slight browning, last 6 ll. inlaid, cont. elab. gt. purple mor., spine tooled in compartments, rubbed & faded, lacks ties; Viscountess Scudamore bkplt. [STC 6233] (S. Oct.11; 515) *Maggs.* £120

DANET, Guillaume
– L'art des Armes. Ill.:– Taraval after Vaxillère. Paris, 1788. 2 vols. Cont. marb. roan, limp decor. spines. (HD. Jan.26; 90) Frs. 2,000

DANGEAU, Abbé de
See— **CHOISY, Abbé de & Dangeau, Abbé de**

DANGEAU, Abbé L. Coureillon de
[–] Les Principes du Blazon où l'on explique Toutes les Règles de cete Siance. 1715. 4to. Cont. bds., lacks spine. (HD. Mar.21; 110) Frs. 1,000

DANGEAU, Ph. de Courcillon de
– Journal. Paris, 1854-60. *1st. Compl. Edn.* 19 vols. Later hf. leath., slightly rubbed. (H. May 22; 500) DM 620

DANGERVILLE, Moutle
[–] Vie Privée de Louis XV. Londres, 1781. *Orig. Edn.* 4 vols. 12mo. Cont. marb. cf., spine decor. (HD. Mar.21; 21) Frs. 2,500

D'ANGLEBERT, Jean Henry
– Pieces de Clavecin ... avec la Manière de les jouer, Diverses Chaconnes, Ouvertures, et Autres Airs de Monsieur Lully mis sur cet Instrument, quelques Fugues pour l'Orgue, et les Principles de l'Accompagnement, Livre Premier. Paris, priv. ptd. [1689]. *1st. Edn.* Ob. fo. Engraved music, privilege & preface, engraved port. of composer, title-p., rust-mark on p. 25, a little stained in places, a few pencil annots., cont. mott. cf., spine gt., tooled in compartments, cont. cold. decor. end-papers, rubbed; Julian Marshall/Thomas Taphouse copy. (S. May 10; 42) *Fenyves.* £2,400

DANIEL, Gabriel
– Histoire de France. Paris, 1729. 10 vols. Some ll. browned, cont. cf., gt. spines, a little worn. (S. Mar.20; 765) *Booth.* £120
– Histoire de la Milice Françoise ... Paris, 1721. 2 vols. 4to. Some stains, cont. roan, decor. spines, slightly rubbed. (HD. Feb.22; 46) Frs. 2,500

DANIEL, Samuel
– The Civile Wares betweene the Howses of Lancaster & Yorke. Ill.:– Thomas Cockson (title). 1609. E4 a cancel, lacks A4 (blank). title-p. laid down, str-grd. red mor. by Hering, blind- & gt.-decor.; Winston H. Hagen bkplt. & label, Richard Heber's copy, with his note on front free end-paper & anr. note in his hand inserted. [STC 6345] (BBA. Jan.19; 120) *Bennett.* £250

DANIEL, Rev. William Barker
– Rural Sports. L., 1801-02. 2 vols. 4to. 2 engraved titles, 3 tables, 61 plts., most spotted, cont. red mor. (S. Apr.9; 211) *Sanders.* £120
– – **Anr. Edn.** L., 1801, 1807, 1807, 1813. 4 vols., including Supp. Sm. 4to. 74 engraved plts., including an engraved title-p. in each vol., 1 text lf. loose in Vol. IV, some foxing, affecting some plts., cont. mott. cf., rebkd. with gt.-pict. mor., 1 mor. spine label brittle; armorial bkplt. of Rufus Ter Bush in each vol. (SG. Mar.15; 205) $170
– – **Anr. Edn.** [1801-]n.d. 3 vols. Engraved titles, 70 plts., cf. gt., spines defect., as a coll. of plts., w.a.f. (P. Mar.15; 41) £110
– – **Anr. Edn.** [1805]. 2 vols. 4to. 1 engraved plt. loose, slight spotting, mor. gt. (P. Sep.8; 259) *Ayres.* £120
– – **Anr. Edn.** L., 1805-13. 3 vols. & Supp. 4to. 4 engraved titles, 72 (of 74) copper engrs. (1 cold.), slightly foxed, cont. decor. leath., spine renewed. (D. Nov.24; 4196) DM 2,400
– – **Anr. Edn.** L., 1807. 3 vols. 4to. 3 engraved additional titles, & 70 copperplts., light foxing, cont. diced cf., backs gt. with decors. (SG. Mar.15; 206) $120
– – **Anr. Edn.** 1807, & 1813 (Supp.). 3 vols. & Supp. 4to. 66 col. plts. (plus 65 dupls. in black & white), some foxing & loose pp. in Vol. III, unif. mor. gt., slightly worn, Supp. tooled leath. spine (bd. loose). (JN. Mar.3; 224) £135
– – **Anr. Edn.** L., 1812. 3 vols. 4to. Foxed, cont. russ. gt., spines worn & reprd., 1 cover detchd. (S. Dec.13; 314) *Quaritch.* £130

DANIEL PRESS
See— **BRIDGES, Robert**

DANIELL, Samuel
– African Scenery & Animals. [1804-05]. *1st. Edn.* 2 pts. in 1 vol. Lge. ob. fo. Uncold. aquatint titles, 30 hand-cold. aquatint plts., 10 ll. of text, diagonal repair to corner of 1st. p. of text, not affecting text, minor foxing to tissue ll., not affecting plts. or text, appears to lack 1 additional front free end-paper, cont. panel. cf. gt. (PD. Aug.17; 305) £15,200
– – **Anr. Edn.** 1976. *(550) numbered & sigd. by Frank R. Bradlow.* Lge. fo. Hf. cf. (BS. May 2; 67) £100

DANIELL, Thomas & William
– Oriental Scenery. 1812-16. 6 pts. in 2 vols. 4to. Each pt. with vig. title & 24 aquatint plts., last pt. with 8 extra ground plans, some staining to 3 plts. & 1 vig. title, slight margin staining to a few other plts., cont. maroon hf. mor. gt. (LC. Oct.13; 256) £480
– – **Anr. Edn.** 1813-16. Pts. III-VI only, in 2 vols. Fo. Engraved pt. titles, 96 uncold. aquatint views, 8 ground plans in pt. VI, a few plts. spotted, cont. hf. mor., rubbed. (TA. Apr.19; 52) £240
– A Picturesque Voyage to India; by the Way of China. L., 1810. Fo. 50 hand-cold. aquatints on card. & mntd. to guards, hf. mor. (S. May 22; 437) *Nevill.* £1,050
– – **Anr. Copy.** Ob. fo. 50 hand-cold. aquatint-engraved plts., stain affecting inner margin of 1st. 30 plts. & text ll., some slightly spotted in margins, cont. hf. russ., worn, defect. (S. Dec.1; 367) *Asian Collectors.* £750

DANIELL, William
[–] [Interesting Selections from Animated Nature]. L., [Plts. dtd. 1807-12]. 1 vol. only (of 2). Ob. 4to. 70 aquatint plts., lacks title, cont. bds., poorly rebkd., upr. cover detchd.; pres. inscr. on fly-lf. (torn) 'to Emma Daniell from her affectionate father Dec. 25, 1828'; w.a.f. (C. Jun.27; 152) *Mellen.* £150
– – **Anr. Edn.** [1809]. 4to. 50 uncold. aquatints, a few with margin stains, cont. hf. mor. gt. (LC. Oct.13; 180) £110
– – **Anr. Edn.** [1809-11]. 1 vol. only. Ob. 4to. Diced cf. gt., covers detchd. (P. Sep.8; 321) *Ayres.* £55
– Sketches of Natives, Animals & Scenery of Southern Africa. [plts. dtd. 1820]. Ob. 4to. 48 litho. plts., a few slightly foxed, cl. (P. Mar.15; 6) *Schrire.* £380
See— **MOORE, Lieut. Joseph—KERSHAW, Capt. James & Daniell, William**

DANJOU
See— **CIMBER & Danjou**

DANNEBERG, C.W.
– Harmlose Betrachtungen gesammelt auf einer Reise von Hamburg nach Griechenland, Constantinopel und dem Schwarzen Meere. Hamburg, 1823. Cont. hf. leath., spine defect. (R. Oct.13; 3143) DM 560

D'ANNUNZIO, Gabriele
– L'Oleandro. Ill.:– G.G. Boehmer [Verona], Bodoni Pr., 1936. *(150) on Marais-Bütten.* Sm. fo. Orig. wraps. in orig. linen cover. (H. Nov.24; 1206) DM 1,300
– Francesca da Rimini: Tragedia ... Milan, 1902. *1st. Edn.* 4to. Orig. gt.-decor. limp cl., worn & spotted, ties; laid in proof sheet for an earlier setting of pp. 24 & 25 (numbered 32 & 33), with holograph corrections by author in outer margin of 1 p. (SG. Nov.17; 34) $100

DANREITER, Franz Anton
– Die Garten Prospect von Hellbrun. Augsburg, ca. 1730. Ob. fo. Engraved title, 19 plts., some light margin dampstaining, mod. bds., unc. (C. Dec.9; 28) *Weinreb.* £1,900
– Lust-Stück der Gärten. Augsburg, ca. 1740. 2 vols. in 1. Ob. 4to. Engraved titles, 22 & 20 engraved plts., cont. hf. pig. (C. Dec.9; 29) *Weinreb.* £700
– [Suite of Views of the Gardens & Palace of Mirabell in Salzburg]. Ill.:– I.A. Corvinus after Danreiter. N.p., ca. 1740. Ob. fo. 14 engraved plts. (5 unnumbered), mod. bds. (C. Dec.9; 31) *Weinreb.* £1,200

DANSDORF, Chrysilla von
– Heart's Desire. Ill.:– John Buckland Wright. 'Paris', [Gold. Cock. Pr.], n.d. *(70) numbered, for private circulation.* Additional set of engraved plts. in pocket in lr. cover, & paste-up proofs for 5 of the ills. hand-cold. by Wright, with autograph notes in margins, & with 2 other engraved ills. (1 in 2 states) not in book, mor.-bkd. bds. (S. Nov.22; 314) *Downithorne.* £650

DANTE Alighieri
– Comedia [German]. Trans.:– Rudoff Borchardt. Ill.:– Anna Simons. München, Bremer Pr., 1922. *(153) numbered on Zanders Bütten.* Fo. Orig. vell., gt.-decor., bd. s.-c. (HK. May 17; 2602) DM 700
– – **Anr. Edn.** Trans.:– R. Borchardt. Ill.:– A. Simons. [München, Bremer Pr., 1922]. *(120).* Lge. 4to. Hand-bnd. orig. vell., by Frieda Thiersch. (H. Nov.23; 932) DM 1,600
– Dante con l'Espositione di C. Landino e di A. Vellutello. Venice, 1564. Fo. Leath. (DS. Oct.28; 2319) Pts. 70,000
– Divina Commedia [Italian]. Commentary:– Cristoforo Landino. Brescia, Boninus de Boninis, 31 May 1487. *1st. Edn.* Fo. 62 (of 68) woodcuts, traces of col., lacks 1st. lf. & 14 ll., including last 4, 4 ll. reprd. with much loss of text, 1st. 2 ll. reprd. without loss of text, unsewn, 19th. C. Italian hf. roan, spine decor.; from Fondation Furstenberg-Beaumesnil. [HC 5948; BMC VII, 971; Goff B31] (HD. Nov.16; 18) Frs. 20,000
– – **Anr. Edn.** Vinegia, Aug. 1504. Cont. entry on title, 1 lf. with erased stp., some light staining in margins, cont. gold & blind-tooled cf., oval centre-piece, decor. (H. Nov.23; 585) DM 2,200
– – **Anr. Edn.** Venice, 1529. Fo. Lacks prelims. & AA, staining & wormhole to L4-7, affecting few letters, cf., defect., w.a.f. (P. Sep.8; 75) *Edmunds.* £120
– – **Anr. Copy.** Fo. Some light staining & soiling, old corrections, leath. gt., ca. 1700, bumped, spine wormed. (HK. May 15; 107) DM 5,400
– – **Anr. Edn.** Ed.:– Alexandro Vellutello. [Venice, 1544]. *1st. Vellutello Edn.* 4to. 87 lge. woodcuts, 3 lines omitted in Canto II stpd. in place at foot of V7 recto, final lf. has blank lr. hf. restored, mod. lev., decor. gt. borders surrounding 5 sm. designs, spine gt., some wear. (SG. Apr.19; 66) $700
– – **Anr. Copy.** Some staining, ink notes, three-qtr. gt.-decor. vell., Vatican Liby. stps. (CBA. Dec.10; 182) $500
– – **Anr. Edn.** Venice, 1554. Some staining, mor., defect. (P. Sep.8; 73) *Aspin.* £75
– – **Anr. Edn.** Paris, 1758. 2 vols. 12mo. Cont. mor. gt., slightly rubbed; Maurice Baring bkplt. (BBA. Jul.27; 82) *Maggs.* £60
– – **Anr. Edn.** Turin, 1911. *Facs. of 1st. Edn., Foligno, 1472. (200) numbered.* Fo. Orig. vell. (BBA. Dec.15; 148) *Quaritch.* £50
– – **Anr. Edn.** Ed.:– B. Wiese. Ill.:– A. Simons. [Müchen, Bremer Pr., 1921]. *(300).* 4to. Hand-bnd. orig. mor., gt. decor. spine, cover, inner & outer dentelle, silk doubls. & end-papers, by Frieda Thiersch. (H. Nov.23; 931) DM 2,800
– – **Anr. Edn.** Ill.:– Amos Nattini. Milan, 1923-36-41. 3 vols. Lge. fo. With several of the col. plts. rolled in a tube, 2 vols. brown mor., 1 vol. black mor., 1 cover detchd., rubbed, w.a.f. (SPB. Dec.13; 803) $500
– – **Anr. Edn.** Ed.:– P. Friedländer. Ill.:– after S. Botticelli, B. Rollitz. [Berlin], Serpentis Pr., 1925. *De Luxe Edn., (25).* Fo. Initials col. painted, hand-bnd. mor., gt. spine, covers, inner & outer dentelles, by Rudolf Lang, München. (H. Nov.24; 1211) DM 7,400
– – **Anr. Edn.** Ill.:– after S. Botticelli, B. Rollitz. [Berlin], Serpentis Pr., 1925[-40]. *(200) on Bütten.* Lge. fo. 1st. 2 ll. slightly cockled in margins, orig. bds., lightly spotted. (HK. Nov.11; 3840) DM 420
– La Divina Commedia [Italian & English]. Ed.:– M. Casella & H.F. Cary. Ill.:– after S. Botticelli. Nones. Pr., 1928. *Ltd. Edn.* 4to. Orig. parch. gt., spine faded. (P. Mar.15; 140) *Thorp.* £65
– La Divina Commedia [Italian & German]. Ill.:– F. von Bayros. Zurich, Leipsig & Vienna, [colophon:

DANTE Alighieri -Contd.

1921]. *(1100) numbered.* 3 vols. 4to. Orig. vell.-bkd. bds., s.-c.'s. (CSK. Apr.6; 90) £220

- La Divine Comédie. Paris, 1878. 2 vols. 12mo. Cont. decor. mor., watered silk doubls., unc. (SM. Mar.7; 2474) Frs. 1,200

- - **Anr. Edn.** Trans.:– J. Brizeux. Ill.:– Salvador Dali. 1959-63. 6 vols. Fo. On vélin de Rives, numbered, leaves, wrap., box. (HD. Jun.26; 70) Frs. 3,800

- - **Anr. Edn.** Ill.:– Dali. Paris, 1963. *(350) numbered on vell. de Rives.* 6 vols. 4to. With suite of decomposition of cols., leaves, wrap., s.-c. (HD. Mar.30; 27) Frs. 7,000

- L'Enfer, le Purgatoire (et le Paradis). Ill.:– after Gustave Doré. Paris, 1865-68. 2 vols. Fo. Some light foxing, publisher's decor. buckram, sm. defects. to bdg. of 1st. vol. (HD. May 4; 238) Frs. 1,700

- Die Goettliche Komoedie. Intro.:– Max v. Boehn. Trans.:– Karl Witte. Berlin, 1921. *De Luxe Edn., (250) numbered.* 4to. On Japan, orig. pict. vell. (GB. Nov.5; 2368) DM 450

- Die Hoelle. Ill.:– Willy Jaeckel. Berlin, 1923. *(200) numbered. (80) specially bnd.* Lge. fo. 35 ills., 10 as plts., each sigd. in pencil by artist, gt.-lettered pig, partly unc., covers bowed, spine ends very worn. (SG. Mar.29; 168) $110

- Opere. Ill.:– Giampiccolo, Magnini, Rizzi, & others. Venice, 1757-58. 4 vols. in 5 pts., in 5 vols. 4to. 115 engraved plts., hf.-title, subscribers lists, cont. mott. cf. gt., gt. dentelles, rebkd. (SG. Nov.3; 54) $1,100

- Il Purgatorio e il Paradiso. Ill.:– G. Doré. Paris, 1868. *1st. Edn.* 2 pts. in 1 vol. Fo. Orig. linen, slightly loose, spine slightly torn. (GB. Nov.4; 1743) DM 500

- Le Terze Rime [Lo Inferno e'l Purgatorio e'l Paradiso]. Venice, Aug. 1502. *1st. Aldine Edn., 1st 8 vo. Edn.* Wide margin, printer's mark Ædibus for Aedibus, 1st. lf. in facs. 19th. C. long-grd. mor. (possibly by Bozérian), gt.- decor. of sm. stps., gt. inner & outer dentelle, silk end-papers, linen wrap., hf. mor., s.c. (D. Nov.23; 100) DM 7,500

- - **Anr. Edn.** Venice, Aug. 1515. *2nd. Aldine Edn.* Sm. 8vo. Old vell. (HD. Nov.17; 20) Frs. 5,500

- The Vision: or Hell, Purgatory & Paradise. Trans.:– H.F. Cary. L., 1819. *2nd. Edn.* 3 vols. Hf.-titles, cf., spines gt. (SG. Feb.16; 82) $100

- Vita Nuova. Flor., 1576. Sm. 8vo. Foxed thro.-out, later cf., 1 cover detchd. (SG. Feb.9; 207) $140

- - **Anr. Edn.** Trans.:– Henri Cochin. Ill.:– Jacques Camille & Georges Beltrand, after Maurice Denis. Paris, 1907. *(130) numbered. Ltd. Iss. with extra suite of 68 sheets on chine & japon of cold. progressions for ills.* 4to. Crushed lev. mor. by Robert Joly, sigd. on upr. turn-in, covers with 2 double gt. fillet borders enclosing elab. panel in 16th. C. style of central rectangle with deeply incurved corners, interwoven by 4 lge. interlocking cornerpieces, all in gt. strapwork design, stylized leaf corner ornaments, spine in 6 compartments, gt.-lettered in 1, repeated design of strapwork panel with sm. tools in rest, bd. edges with double gt. fillet, mor. doubls. with single & 2 double gt. fillet borders, corded silk free end-pp., marb. paper fly-ll., partly unc., orig. wraps. preserved, matching hf. mor. gt. chemise & mor.-edged s.-c. (CNY. May 18; 182) $5,000

- - **Anr. Edn.** Ed.:– Benedetto Croce. Montagnola, 1925. *(225) On Vell. di Fabriano.* Fo. Orig. linen, gold-tooled colophon. (GB. May 5; 3039) DM 2,200

DA PONTE, L.

- Don Juan. Ill.:– M. Slevogt. engraved by R. Hoberg. Berlin, 1921. *De Luxe Edn. A, (20).* Lge. 4to. Ills. sigd., Hand-bnd. orig. red mor., by H. Sperling, slightly rubbed & scratched, upr. cover loose & torn. (H. Nov.24; 2088) DM 3,600

DAPPER, Olfert

- Asia. Amst., 1672. *1st. Edn.* 2 pts. in 1 vol. Fo. Cont. leath., spine very defect. (R. Oct.13; 3009) DM 800

- - **Anr. Edn.** Nuremb., 1688-89. *1st. German Edn.* 2 pts. in 1 vol. Fo. Ptd. & copper-engraved title slightly defect. at side & bkd., cont. vell., upr. cover spotted. (R. Oct.13; 3008) DM 2,200

- Description de l'Afrique. Amst., 1686. Fo. Cont.

cf., edges worn; Sir George Farrar bkplt. (SSA. Jul.5; 96) R. 1,200

- Description Exacte des Isles de l'Archipel et de quelques autres Adjacentes ... Amst., 1703. Fo. Cont. marb. cf. (HD. Jun.29; 88) Frs. 8,500

- Description Exacte des Iles de l'Archipel, et de Quelques Autres Adjacentes. Traduit du Flamand. The Hague, 1730. Lge. fo. Hf.-title, plt.-list, 4 inserted plts., perhaps from Dutch-text edn. (variants of Rhodes & Cyprus plts., 1 botanic plt., & 1 of a bird), cont. cf., quite worn. (SG. Sep.22; 118) $1,600

- Historische Beschryving der Stadt Amsterdam [by] O.D. Amst., 1663. Fo. Engraved frontis., coat of arms, 6 double-p. maps & plans, 66 double-p. engraved views, 1 defect., other repairs, all but 1 in margins, 1 map or plan cut close, a few light stains, sm. burnhole in 3C2, hf. cf. (S. Dec.1; 327) *Israel.* £320

- - **Anr. Copy.** Fo. Lacks 1 plt. & 1 plan, some minor imperfections, folding plt. slightly defect., some blank lr. margins wormholed, cont. cf., back gt. (VG. Sep.14; 1149) Fls. 2,200

- - **Anr. Copy.** Fo. Lacks engraved arms & 9 views, a few plts. torn or loose, some staining, cont. cf., very defect., loosening, w.a.f. (VG. Nov.30; 1021) Fls. 1,650

- Naukeurige Beschryving der Eilanden in de Archipel de Middelantsche Zee. Amst., 1688. *[1st. Edn.].* Fo. Additional engraved title, 27 engraved maps & plts., 5 further plts. showing coinage, ills. in text, 1 or 2 short tears, cont. vell. (S. May 21; 224) *Martinos.* £800

- - **Anr. Copy.** Fo. 2 plts. loose, cont. cf., rubbed, slightly defect. (VG. Mar.19; 237) Fls. 2,250

- Naukeurige Beschryving van Gantsch Syrie en Palestyn of Heilige Lant ... Amst., 1677. 2 pts. in 1 vol. Fo. Engraved title (slightly defect.), 8 double-p. maps, 21 (of 30) plts., most double-p., lacks last lf., 1 plt. reprd., a few stains, cf., spine gt. (B. Feb.8; 561) Fls. 525

D'APRES DE MANNEVILLETTE, Jean-Baptiste Nicolas Denis

- Le Neptune Orientale. Paris, Demonville, & Brest, Malassis, 1775. *2nd. Edn.* Lge. fo. Engraved allegorical frontis., dedication lf. with vig., 63 sea & coastal charts (32 double-p.), including the 22 charts from the edn. of 1745, frontis. slightly soiled, some faint offsetting, cont. cf. gt., gt. arms of Croppet de Varissan on covers, rebkd. preserving spine; cont. owner's inscr. dtd. 4 Jul. 1775 acknowledging pres. of the atlas by d'Apres de Mannevillette. (S. Dec.1; 205) *Baker.* £900

D'ARBLAY, Frances 'Fanny Burney'

- Camilla. 1796. *1st. Edn.* 5 vols. List of subscribers, advt. lf. at end of Vol. 1, some spotting, cont. red hf. leath. gt., marb. bds.; the Hinton House copy. (LC. Oct.13; 429) £150

- - **Anr. Copy.** 5 vols. 12mo. Hole in N12 Vol. 5 affecting 2 words, few other slight tears, cont. red qtr. mor. gt. (P. Sep.8; 56) *Scott.* £70

DARBOUX, G.

- Leçons sur la Théorie Générale des Surfaces et les Application Géometriques du Calcul Infinitesiual. Paris, 1887-96. Cont. hf. leath. (HT. May 8; 388) DM 840

DARBY, William

- The Emigrant's Guide to the Western & South-Western States & Territories. N.Y., 1818. *1st. Edn.* Folding frontis. map with 4 inch tear, foxing, cont. hf. roan, edges slightly worn; the Rt. Hon. Visc. Eccles copy. [Sabin 18527] (CNY. Nov.18; 80) $220

- A Tour from the City of New-York, to Detroit, in ... 1818. N.Y., 1819. *1st. Edn.* 3 maps, errata slip, foxed, few short margin tears, orig. bds., crudely rebkd., unc. (SG. Jan.19; 164) $175

DARCEL, Alfred

See— ROUYER, Eugène & Darcel, Alfred

DARCY, G.

- Or et Couleurs: Recueil de 60 Dessins ... dans le Gout Nouveau. Paris, ca. 1925. Tall fo. 20 pochoir-cold. plts. on gray art paper, ex-liby., each plt. stpd. on blank verso, loose in orig. gt.-pict. bd. folder, cl.-bkd., linen ties. (SG. May 3; 22) $425

DARCY, Henry

- Recherches Expérimentales relatives au Mouvement de l'Eau dans les Tuyaux. Paris, 1857. *1st. Edn.* 2 vols. 4to. & atlas fo. Hf.-title, errata, light soiling, orig. wraps., rebkd., corners reprd.; John D. Stanitz coll. (SPB. Apr.25; 130) $350

DARELL, Rev. William

- The History of Dover Castle. L., 1786. 4to. L.P., engraved title with vig., folding plan, 9 plts., title & frontis. spotted & with sm. stains, little spotting elsewhere, cont. diced russ. gt., slightly worn. (S. Mar.6; 416) *Sanders.* £70

D'ARGENVILLE, Antoine Joseph Dezallier

[-] Abrégé de la Vie des Plus Fameux Peintres. Paris, 1745. 2 vols. Title-pp. soiled, mott. cf., armorial stpd. on upr. covers, spine defect. (BS. Nov.16; 100) £50

[-] L'Histoire Naturelle ... Paris, 1742. Without Supp. 4to. Engraved frontis., 32 plts., old cf., spine ends chipped. (C. Nov.16; 231) *Henderson.* £130

- - **Anr. Edn.** Paris, 1757. 2 vols. in 1. 4to. Engraved frontis., 40 engraved plts., a few ll. of index browned, cont. mott. cf., gt. spine, rubbed. (C. Jun.27; 116) *Shapiro.* £160

- L'Histoire Naturelle ... Lithologie ... Conchyliologie. Paris, 1742. 4to. Cont. cf., worn. (BBA. May 3; 25) *Korn.* £60

[-] L'Histoire Naturelle eclaircie dans une de ses Parties Principales, l'oryctologie. Paris, 1755. 4to. MS. cold. pencil notes on 3 plts. & some text, staining in some sigs., some slight discoloring, cont. vell. (R. Apr.4; 1454) DM 450

- La Théorie et la Pratique du Jardinage. Paris, 1713. *2nd. Edn.* 4to. 37 engraved folding plts., cont. cf. gt., arms of Comte d'Hoym on sides, upr. cover stained. (C. Dec.9; 35) *Thomas-Scheler.* £400

- - **Anr. Copy.** 4to. Cont. cf. (HD. Dec.1; 65) Frs. 1,250

- - **Anr. Edn.** Paris, 1760. *4th. Edn.* 4to. Cont. marb. roan, spine decor. (HD. Nov.9; 171) Frs. 4,000

[-] The Theory & Practice of Gardening. Trans.:– J. James. 1712. 4to. Cont. cf., a little worn. (BBA. Sep.29; 148) *Steedman.* £310

D'ARGENVILLE, Antoine Nicolas Dezallier, fils

- Voyage Pittoresque de Paris. Ill.:– J. Robert. Paris, 1752. *2nd. Edn.* 12mo. Cont. marb. cf. (HD. Mar.19; 91) Frs. 1,400

DARISTE, A.-J.

- Mémoire sur la Non-contagion de la Fièvre Jaune, suivi de Conseils aux Européens qui passent dans les Pays Chauds, et notamment aux Antilles. Bordeaux, 1824. *(With:)* - Recherches Pratiques sur la Fièvre Jaune. Bordeaux, 1825. Together 2 vols. Cont. leath. (HD. Mar.27; 166) Frs. 1,050

DARIUS, Phrygins

See— DICTYS CRETENSIS & Darius, Phrygius.

DARLEY, F.O.C.

- Six Illustrations of Rip Van Winkle. N.p., 1848. Ob. fo. 6 mntd. India-proof plts., stiff pict. ptd. wraps., light wear, d.-w. with 'India Proof Copy' at top left corner (some edge wear & chipping): Ken Leach coll. (RO. Jun.10; 1) $600

DARLOW, T.H. & Moule, H.F.

- Historical Catalogue of the Printed Editions of Holy Scripture in the Library of the British & Foreign Bible Society. N.Y., 1963. 4 vols. 4to. Cl. (BBA. Jan.19; 337) *Dawson.* £120

DARRELL, John

- A True Narration of the Strange & Grevous Vexation by the Devil of Seven Persons in Lancashire ... 1600. Errata lf. at end, 8 headlines shaved, mor. gt. [STC 6288] (P. Jul.5; 250) £220

DART, Rev. John

- The History & Antiquities of the Cathedral Church of Canterbury. 1726. *[1st. Edn.].* Fo. L.P., 41 plts., 9 engraved pp. of subscribers, cont. panel. cf., spine decor., rubbed; Sir Ivar Colquhoun, of Luss copy. (CE. Mar.22; 81) £160

- - **Anr. Copy.** Fo. Cf., rebkd. & reprd. (P. Sep.29; 93) *Fancycrest.* £50

- Westmonasterium, or the History & Antiquities of the Abbey Church of St. Peters, Westminster.

Ca. 1723. 2 vols. Fo. Cont. red mor. gt., spine gt. (P. Mar.15; 186) *Cavendish.* £160

DARTON, F.J. Harvey
See— SAWYER, Charles J. & Darton, F.J. Harvey

DARWIN, Bernard & Elinor
- The Tale of Mr. Tootleoo. L., Nones. Pr., ca. 1920. 1 vol. Some light soiling, Limp bds., upr. cover embossed medallion. (*With:*) – Tootleoo Two. L., Nones, Pr., ca. 1920. 1 vol. Very light soiling, Limp bds. (CBA. Aug.21; 158) $140

DARWIN, Charles
- The Descent of Man. L., 1871. *1st. Edn.* 2 vols. Marginal tear in 1st. hf.-title, pencil marginalia, orig. cl., qtr. lev. s.-c.; Stephen A. McClellan copy. (SG. Apr.26; 61) $475
- The Different Forms of Flowers on Plants of the Same Species. L., 1877. *1st. Edn.* Advts., orig. cl., qtr. lev. s.-c.; Stephen A. McClellan copy. (SG. Apr.26; 64) $250
- The Effects of Cross & Self Fertilisation in the Vegetable Kingdom. L., 1876. *1st. Edn.* Errata slip, orig. cl., loose, qtr. lev. s.-c.; Stephen A. McClellan copy. (SG. Apr.26; 63) $300
- – Anr. Copy. Sm. 8vo. Errata lf., Cl. (SG. Oct.6; 117) $130
- – Anr. Copy. Cl., unc., covers slightly soiled. (CA. Apr.3; 11) Aus. $110
- The Expression of the Emotions in Man & Animals. L., 1872. *1st. Edn. 2nd. Iss.* 7 heliotype plts. (3 folding), in 1st state, 1 laid down, crig. cl., worn, qtr. lev. s.-c.; Stephen A. McClellan copy. (SG. Apr.26; 62) $300
- – Anr. Edn. 1872. *1st. Edn.* Prize cf. gt. (SKC. Jan.13; 2309) £50
- The Formation of Vegetable Mould, through the Action of Worms, with Observations on thier Habits. 1881. *1st. Edn. 1st. Iss.* Advt. lf. bnd. in at end, orig. cl., spine slightly rubbed. (TA. May 17;278) £54
- – Anr. Edn. L., 1881. *1st. Edn.* Orig. cl., qtr. lev. s.-c.; Stephen A. McClellan copy. (SG. Apr.26; 66) $325
- Gesammelte Werks. Trans.:– J. V. Carus. Stuttgart, 1875-78. Vols. 1-12 only (of 16), in 6 vols. Some foxing, hf. linen. (D. Nov.23; 372) DM 400
- Insectivorous Plants. L., 1875. *1st. Edn.* Cl., unc. (CA. Apr.3; 12) Aus. $120
- Journal of Researches into the Geology & Natural History of the Various Countries Visited by H.M.S. Beagle. L., 1839. *1st. Edn. 1st. Separate Iss.* Lge. 8vo. Orig. cl. [Freeman's variant a], loose, qtr. lev. s.-c.; from Stephen A. McClellan Collection. (SG. Apr.26; 56) $1,000
- – Anr. Edn. Ill.:– Robert Gibbings. N.Y., Ltd. Edns. Cl., 1956. *(1500)* numbered. 4to. Orig. cl., s.-c.; sigd. by artist. (CSK. Mar.23; 106) £70
- – Anr. Copy. Sm. fo. Decor. cl., orig. s.-c. (SG. May17; 179) $110
- [Letters on Geology]. [Camb. Univ. Pr., 1835]. *1st. Edn.* Drophead title, disbnd., lacks (plain) wraps. (BBA. Nov.30; 99) Korn. £2,800
- Life & Letters. Ed.:– Francis Darwin. L., 1887. *1st. Edn.* 3 vols. Lge. 8vo. Three-qtr. cf., spines gt. (SG. Feb.16; 84) $110
- The Movements & Habits of Climbing Plants. L., 1875. Spotting, mainly to end-pp., orig. bdg. (JL. Jul.15; 616) Aus. $100
- The Movements & Habits of Climbing Plants.— Insectivorous Plants. L., 1875; 1875. *1st. Edns.* Together 2 vols. Lacks hf.-titles, cont. hf. cf. & orig. cl., qtr. lev. s.-c's.; Stephen A. McClellan copy. (SG. Apr.26; 59) $350
- On the Origin of Species by Means of Natural Selection. L., 1859. *1st. Edn.* Hf.-title, advts. at end dtd. Jun. 1859, a few light pencil annots., title few ll. detchd. from bdg., publisher's cl. [state A], spine ends worn, tear in front end-paper; bkplt. of Henry Baker Tristram, his owner's inscr. dtd. Dec. 1859 on front end-paper, A.L.s from Darwin to Tristram, Beckenham, 26 Feb. 1874, mntd. on front end-paper, with envelope. (C. May30; 112) *Wheldon & Wesley.* £1,700
- – Anr. Copy. Advts., hf.-title loose, orig. cl. [Freeman's variant a], qtr. lev. s.-c.; from Stephen A. McClellan Collection. (SG. Apr.26; 57) $4,000
- – Anr. Copy. Lacks all before title, title stained,

some ll. with margin foxing, rebnd. hf. cf. (CA. Apr.3; 15) Aus. $1,000
- – Anr. Edn. 1860. *5th. Thousand.* Publishers' advts., orig. cl., slight wear. (P. Oct.20; 227) £60
- – Anr. Edn. N.Y., 1860. *1st. Amer. Edn.* Orig. cl., rebkd. preserving most of spine, some wear. (RO. Dec.11; 86) $130
- On the Various Contrivances by which British & Foreign Orchids are Fertilised by Insects. L., 1862. *1st. Edn.* Folding plt., ills., title with stp. partly erased & slightly soiled, orig. cl. gt., jnts. & spine partly torn, unc. (S. Apr.10; 493) *Cox.* £100
- – Anr. Copy. Folding plt., 33 wood engrs., advts., orig. cl. [1st. bdg.], qtr. lev. s.-c.; Stephen A. McClellan copy. (SG. Apr.26; 58) $350
- – Anr. Copy. Gt.-decor. cl. (CBA. Dec.10; 343) $250
- – Anr. Copy. No inserted advts., cl. [apparently Freeman's bdg. variant b, without vertical lines], some wear. (RO. Dec.11; 87) $160
- The Power of Movement in Plants. L., 1880. *1st. Edn.* Orig. cl., qtr. lev. s.-c.; Stephen A. McClellan copy. (SG. Apr.26; 65) $325
- The Variation of Animals & Plants under Domestication. L., 1868. *1st. Edn. 1st. Iss.* 2 vols. 32 pp. advts. dtd. Apr. 1867 in Vol. 1, 1 lf. advts. in Vol. 2, orig. cl., slightly worn. (S. Oct.4; 264) *Porter.* £110
- – Anr. Copy. 2 vols. Lge. 8vo. Orig. cl., Vol.2 loose, qtr. lev. s.-c.; Stephen A. McClellan copy. (SG. Apr.26; 60) $500
- – Anr. Edn. 1868. *1st. Edn.* 2 vols. Orig. cl., slightly soiled. (BBA. Jul.27; 10) *Korn.* £85
See— FITZROY, Capt. Robert, King, Adm. P.P. & Darwin, Charles

DARWIN, Erasmus
[-] The Botanic Garden. Ill.:– William Blake, Fuseli, & others. L., 1791, Lichfield, 1789. *1st. Edns.* 2 vols. in 1. 4to. 2 engraved frontis., 16 engraved plts. (1 folding), errata lf. in Vol.1 & errata slip pasted to final lf., lacks hf.-titles, 1st. frontis. offset on title, 1st. ll. of both vols. spotted, cont. cf. gt., bdg. extensively reprd. by Stoakley of Camb.; Frederic Dannay copy. (CNY. Dec.16; 94) $180
- – Anr. Edn. 1791. 4to. Cont. diced cf., rebkd. (BBA. Jul.27; 125) *Cox.* £80
- – Anr. Edn. Ill.:– W. Blake & others. 1795-94. *Pt. 1: 3rd. Edn., Pt. 2: 4th. Edn.* 2 pts. in 1 vol. 4to. With added lf. between pp. 174 & 175, slightly stained, cont. cf., spines gt., rubbed, jnts. cracked. (CSK. May 18; 171) £110
- Phytologia; or the Philosophy of Agriculture & Gardening. L., 1800. *1st. Edn.* 12 plts., some spotting, cf. (P. Jan.12; 217) *Cole.* £120
- – Anr. Copy. 4to. Cont. diced cf., rebkd. (BBA. Jul.27; 13) *Cox.* £100
- – Anr. Copy. 4to. 12 engraved plts., slight spotting, unc., orig. bds., spine worn; bkplt. of Thomas Boswall, of Blackadder. (S. Dec.13; 262) *Quaritch.* £70
- Zoonomia; or the Laws of Organic Life. 1794-96. 2 vols. 4to. Cont. diced cf., rebkd. (BBA. Jul.27; 12) *Bickersteth.* £170

DA SILVA, I.F.
- Diccionario Bibliographico Portugués. Lisbon, 1973. 25 vols. Bds., d.-w.'s. (SG. Jan.5; 113) $120

DASSIE, F.
- L'Architecture Navale, contenant la Manière de Construire les Navires ... Paris, 1677. *Orig. Edn.* (*Bound with:*) – Le Routier des Indes Orientales et Occidentales ... Paris, 1677. Together 2 works in 1 vol. 4to. 1st. ll. stained in corner, slight margin worming at beginning, cont. cf., spine renewed. (HD. Mar.9; 74) Frs. 2,200

DATUS, Augustinus
- Elegantiolae. [Venice, Printer of Duns Scotus ...], ca. 1474. 4to. 1st. 22 ll. with margin guides in early hand, later bds., leath. back, worn; armorial bkplt. of Robert W. Webb, the Walter Goldwater copy. [BMC V, 204; Goff D-59] (SG. Dec.1; 118) $900

D'AUBENTON, Jean Louis Marie
See— BUFFON, George Louis Leclerc, Comte de & D'Aubenton, Jean Louis Marie

DAUDET, Alphonse
- La Mort du Dauphin. Ill.:– O.D.V. Guillonnet. Paris, 1907. *(25)* numbered on japan à la forme. Sm. 4to. Orig. etching, 3 states of engrs., cont. mor., gt.-decor., inner dentelle, by Stroobants, wrap. preserved. (HD. Feb.17; 60) Frs. 2,500
- Oeuvres Complètes. Ill.:– Dignimont, Henri Beraud, Bagarry, Edy Legrand, & others. Paris, 1930-31. *5th. Coll. Edn.* 20 vols. 4to. Hf. chagrin, corners, wraps. preserved. (HD. Nov.17; 106) Frs. 2,500
- Sapho. Moeurs Parisiennes. Ill.:– E. Abot & A. Duvivier, after Rejchan (plts.), G. Montaigut (text vigs.). [Paris], 1888. *(50)* on papier du Japon, with plts. in 2 states. Lge. 8vo. Edn. no. scratched away from limitation p., purple mor. by Yvert & Cie, of Amiens, sigd. on upr. turn-in, also sigd. on verso of free end-paper 'A. Cabochette Rel. d'Art M, O, F', upr. cover with onlaid mor. lettering of 'Sapho', 1st. letter decor, with 2 col. onlaid mor. & blind-tooled roses & grapes, decor. three-qtr. border of onlaid mor. outlined in gt., lr. cover with 3 gt. line ornaments, those at corners heart shaped enclosing red roses, spine in 5 compartments, gt.-lettered & with decor. mor. onlays outlined in gt., gt. cupid at centre, bd. edges with dotted gt. rule, turn-ins gt. with rose border & onlaid mor. leaf corner ornaments, watered silk linings, partly unc., orig. upr. ptd. wrap. preserved. (CNY. May 18; 203) $400
- Tartatin sur les Alpes. Ill.:– Aranda, Beaumont, Montenard, Myrberch, Rossi. Paris, 1885. *Orig. Edn. 1st. Printing of ills.* *(100)* on japan. Hf. mor., corners, mosaic spine, unc., wrap.; with specimen. (HD. May 21; 111) Frs. 1,700
- The Works. Boston, 1898-1900. *'Champrosay'* Edn. *(100)* numbered. 24 vols. Elab. gt. decor., mor., red mor. onlays. sm. gt. armorial stp. on upr. covers, watered silk end-pp., mor. doubls., partly unc. (CNY. Dec.17; 548) $1,200

DAUDET, Alphonse (Text)
See— TYPES DE PARIS

DAUDIN, F.M.
- Traité Elémentaire et Complet d'Ornithologie, ou Histoire Naturelle des Oiseaux. Ill.:– Duval after Barraband. Paris, An VIII [1800]. *1st. Edn.* 2 vols. 4to. Hf.-titles, some stains, mainly marginal, qtr. mor., worn, lacks part of 1 spine. (SG. Mar.22nd; 84) $450

DAULBY, Daniel
- A Descriptive Catalogue of the Works of Rembrandt ... L'pool., 1796. 4to. Errata lf., cont. tree cf. gt., spine gt.-decor.; Sir Ivar Colquhoun, of Luss copy. (CE. Mar.22; 82) £210

DAUMIER, Honoré
[-] Les Representans Represented. [Paris], mid-19th. C. 4to. 36 hand-cold. lithos., some minor foxing, minor damage to 1st. plt., hf. leath., worn, spine partly lacking. (SG. Jun.7; 342) $900
- Les Robert Macaire. Paris, [1830-38]. Sm. fo. Some light restorations, margins unequal, some worming & staining, long-grd. hf. mor., limp decor spine, by Mercier. (HD. Dec.9; 117) Frs 45,000
- – Anr. Edn. Paris, 1836-38. *1st. Printing of ills.* 4to. 100 lithos., cont. cold. & gommées, lacks table (as often), cont. lf. roan, spine decor, slightly rubbed. (HD. Nov.29; 87) Frs 73,000
- Voyage en Chine ... 1843-45. 4to. Traces of folds in some plts., light foxing, old bradel hf. buckram. (HD. May 4; 239) Frs. 8,200

D'AUNAY, Alfred
- Les Ruines de Paris et de ses Environs, 1870-1871: Cent Photographies. Paris, 1872. Vol. 1 only (of 2). Ob. 4to. 50 albumen photographs, plts. with minimal edge fading, leath., worn. (SG. Nov.10; 104) $750

DAUNCEY, John
- A Compendious Chronicle of the Kingdom of Portugal ... Together with a Cosmographical Description. L., 1661. *1st. Edn.* 3 ll. advts. at end, mod. cf. gt. [Wing D289] (S. Oct.11; 516) *Quaritch.* £90

DAUTHENDRY, Max
- **Schwarze Sonne.** Leipzig, 1910. *1st. German Edn.*
4to. Orig. leath., ex-libris. (HK. Nov.11; 3503)
DM 480

DAVENANT, Charles
[-] **A Discourse upon Grants & Resumptions ...**
1700. *1st. Edn.* Cont. panel. cf., worn; Sir Ivar
Colquhoun, of Luss copy. [Wing D 304] (CE.
Mar.22; 83) £130

DAVENANT, Sir William
- **The Cruell Brother.** L., 1630. *1st. Edn.* Sm. 4to.
Portion torn from lr. outer corner of A1 (blank),
slight browning, a little margin dampstaining, some
MS. underlinings & 2 sm. corrections, disbnd.
[STC 6302] (S. Oct.11; 323) *Maggs.* £110
- **Gondibert: an Heroick Poem.** L., 1651. *1st. Edn.*
4to. Some rust-holes, cont. sig. on 1st. Blank recto,
cont. cf., rebkd.; 40 corrections by author, a few in
other hands. [Wing D 324] (S. Dec.8; 16)
Finch. £270
- **The Witts. A Comedie.** 1636. *1st. Edn.* 4to. Lacks
A1 (with license?), last lf. laid down, a few lr.
margins shaved, later cf.; Bridegwater-Clawson
copy. [STC 6309] (BBA. Jan.19; 122)
Maggs. £160
- **The Works.** L., 1673. *1st. Coll. Edn.* Fo. Cont.
cf. [Wing D 320] (C. Nov.9; 7) *Traylen.* £160
- - **Anr. Copy.** Fo. Few sm. holes, short tears in
Xx1-2 (no loss), some marginal stains, cont. red
mor. gt., spine gt., jnts. & corners reprd.; bkplts. of
John Kettle, Visc. Mersey & Graham Pollard.
(SPB. May 16; 42) $425

DAVENPORT, Cyril
- **Cameo Book-Stamps.** 1911. Orig. decor.
buckram, spine a little faded; H.M. Nixon coll,
with his sig. (BBA. Oct.6; 34) *Knuf.* £80
- **English Embroidered Bookbindings.** N.Y., 1899.
Sm. 4to. Lev. gt., beaded panels on covers, ex-liby.
(SG. Feb.16; 112) $175
- **English Heraldic Book-Stamps.** 1909. Orig.
buckram, a little rubbed; H. M. Nixon coll., with
his sigs., note on front free end-paper, & many
annots. (BBA. Oct.6; 33) *Beres.* £550
- **Roger Payne, English Bookbinder of the Eight-**
eenth Century. Chic., Caxton Cl., 1929. *(250).* Orig.
cl. gt., partly unc., spine slightly faded, s.-c.; Hugh
Tregaskis bkplt. (S. May 1; 386) *Stables.* £340
- - **Anr. Copy.** 4to. Orig. cl. gt., spine a little faded;
H. M. Nixon coll., with his sig. & a few MS. notes.
(BBA. Oct.6; 35) *Goldschmidt.* £280
- - **Anr. Edn.** Chic., Caxton Cl., 1929. 4to. Gt.-
decor. cl., light wear. (RO. Dec.11; 89) $300
- **Samuel Mearne, Binder to King Charles II.** Chic.,
Caxton Cl., 1906. *(255).* 4to. Some light foxing,
orig. cl.-bkd. bds.; H. M. Nixon coll., with his MS.
notes. (BBA. Oct.6; 32) *Goldschmidt.* £350
- - **Anr. Copy.** 4to. Some ll. spotted, orig. cl.-bkd.
bds., unc., slightly rubbed. (S. May 1; 387)
Stables. £240
- **Thomas Berthelet. Royal Printer & Bookbinder**
to Henry VIII, King of England. Chic., Caxton Cl.,
1901. *(255).* 4to. Orig. cl.-bkd. bds.; H. M. Nixon
coll., with his sig. & acquisition note. (BBA. Oct.6;
31) *Blackwell.* £280
See— YOUNGHUSBAND, George & Davenport,
Cyril

DAVENPORT, H.
See— LAMPE, M.A. & Davenport, H.

DAVENPORT, W.
- **Historical Portraiture of Leading Events in the**
Life of Ali Pacha. L., 1823. Fo. 6 hand-cold. aquatints, some offsetting from plts., advt. lf. at end,
orig. cl. wrap. with label bnd. in, qtr. mor. (S. May
22; 276) *Hague.* £1,350

DAVID
- **Naissance du Génie d'un Peintre.** Preface:- Jean
Cassou. Paris, 1933. *(289) numbered on purfil paper*
à la forme de chez Johannot. Lge. 4to. Leaves,
wrap., box with bronze medal. (HD. Mar.30; 28)
Frs. 4,400

DAVID, Abbé Armand & Oustalet, M.E.
- **Les Oiseaux de la Chine.** Ill.:- Arnoul. Paris,
1877. 2 vols. 124 hand-cold. litho. plts., orig. decor.
cl., slight wear. (SKC. Nov.18; 1965) **$**1,800

DAVID, François Anne
- **Le Museum de Florence ou Collection des Pierres**
Gravées, Statues et Medailles ... 1787-96. 6 vols.
4to. 477 (of 479) plts., cont. cf. (HD. Jan.24; 10)
Frs. 1,100

DAVID IBN HIN
See— GERSHON, Yitzhak & David Ibn Hin

DAVIDSON, Maj. H.
- **History & Services of the 78th Highlanders.**
Edinb. & L., 1901. 2 vols. 4to. Frontis., 16 maps &
plans (1 folding), 40 plts., 2 ll. detchd., some light
spotting, cont. hf. cf. (CSK. Feb.24; 60) £100

DAVIES, G.C.
- **Norfolk Broads & Rivers.** 1883. Frontis., 11 photogravure plts., cf. gt. (P. Jul.5; 181) £60

DAVIES, Hugh William (Ed.)
See— MURRAY, Charles Fairfax

DAVIES, Nina M. & Gardiner, Alan H.
- **Ancient Egyptian Paintings.** Chic., 1936. 3 vols.
Atlas fo. & tall 8vo. 104 cold. plts., buckram, ex-
liby. (SG. May 3; 130) $1,300
- - **Anr. Copy.** 3 vols. Lge. fo. & tall 8vo. Cl. (B.
Jun.21; 72) Fls. 2,200

DAVIES, Norman de Garis
- **The Rock Tombs of El Amarna.** L., 1903-08. 6
vols. 4to. Hf. cl. (B. Jun.21; 77) Fls. 600

DAVIES, William H.
- **Selected Poems.** Gregy. Pr., 1928. *(310)* numbered. Orig. decor. bds., linen backstrip & outer
edge, slightly rubbed. (TA. Jun.21; 601) £70
- **The Soul's Destroyer & other Poems.** [L., 1905].
1st. Edn. Orig. ptd. wraps., lightly worn, mor.-bkd.
s.-c.; Perry Molstad copy. (SPB. May 16; 443)
$700
- - **Anr. Copy.** 12mo. Orig. ptd. wraps., author's
name inked in on spine; Frederic Dannay copy. (C.
Dec.16; 96) $160
- **True Travellers.** Ill.:- William Nicholson. 1923.
(100) numbered & sigd. by author & artist. Sm.
4to. orig. cl.-bkd. marb. bds., unc., fitted box. (SKC.
Jan.13; 2169) £90

DAVILER, Augustin Charles
- **Cours d'Architecture.** La Haye, 1730. *3rd. Edn.*
3 vols., including Supp. Sm. 4to. 2 frontis., 130
plts., cont. marb. cf., lightly worn. (LM. Mar.3; 6)
B.Frs. 8,500

DAVILLIER, Baron Charles
- **L'Espagne.** Ill.:- after Gustave Doré. 1874. *1st.*
Edn. in Book Form. 4to. Contents detchd. from
bdg., publisher's decor. hf. chagrin. (HD. Mar.21;
143) Frs. 1,300
- **Recherches sur l'Orfevrerie en Espagne du Moyen**
Age à la Renaissance. Paris, 1879. *(500).* Lge. fo.
Mor. (DS. Mar.23; 2641) Pts. 125,000

DAVIS, A.
- **The Velocipide; Its History & Practical Hints**
How to Use it. L., 1869. 12mo. Hf. cf., wraps. bnd.
in; Sir David Salomons bkplt. (PNY. Dec.1; 45)
$100

DAVIS, James Richard Ainsworth
- **The Natural History of Animals.** 1903-04. 8 vols.
Imperial 8vo. Some plts. & ills. cold., orig. pict. cl.
gt., spines slightly faded; from liby. of Luttrellstown
Castle, w.a.f. (C. Sep.28; 1770) £180

DAVIS, John
- **Tracks of MacKinlay & Party across Australia.**
Ed.:- William Westgarth. L., 1863. 14 tinted litho.
plts., pres. inscr. on title & front end-paper, blind-
stpd. cl. gt., unc., covers rubbed. (CA. Apr.3; 38)
Aus. $480
- - **Anr. Copy.** Map in end pocket, repairs to 1 plt.,
a few sm. defects, bdg. not stated, unc., rebkd. &
recased. (KH. May 1; 202) Aus. $400
- - **Anr. Copy.** 14 tinted litho. plts., frontis. & title
soiled, pp. 81-96 misbnd., hf. cf., covers rubbed.
(CA. Apr.3; 37) Aus. $120

DAVIS, John King
- **The Sailor's Companion.** N.Y., 1849. Foxed, text
stained on bottom of inner margins, self-wraps.,

sewed, loose in later wraps.; from liby. of F.D.
Roosevelt, inscr. by him. (SG. Mar.15; 13) $150
- **With the 'Aurora' in the Antarctic, 1911-1914.**
L., ca. 1919. 1 blank prelim. lightly foxed, orig. cl.;
inscr. & sigd., 3 short A.L. & 2 sigd. cards loosely
inserted. (KH. Nov.8; 119) Aus. $320
- - **Anr. Copy.** Bdg. not stated. (KH. May 1; 206)
Aus. $210

DAVIS, Richard Harding & others
- **The Great Streets of the World.** Ill.:- A.B. Frost &
others. N.Y., 1892. *1st. Edn.* 4to. Gt.-decor. blue
cl. [Blanck's 1st. bdg.]. light wear. d.-w., some
chipping & fraying; Ker Leach coll. (RO. Jun.10;
191) $130

DAVIS, Solomon
- **A Prayer Book in the Language of the Six Nations**
of Indians. N.Y., 1837. *1st. Edn.* Sm. 8vo. Orig.
blind-stpd. floral cl., ex-liby. [Sabin 18885] (SG.
Oct.20; 192) $120

DAVIS, William Heath
- **Seventy-Five Years in California.** San Franc.,
1929. *Argonaut Edn. (100) sigd. by ed. & publisher,*
with p. of orig. MS. Linen-bkd. bds., d.-w. (LH.
Sep.25; 214) $130
- - **Anr. Copy.** Linen-bkd. paper bds. (LH. Apr.15;
296) $110

DAVIS, William John
- **The Nineteenth Century Token Coinage of Great**
Britain ... 1904. *(258) numbered.* 4to. Orig. mor.-
bkd. cl., rubbed. (BBA. Jul.27; 246) *Peters.* £65

DAVIS, William W.H.
- **The Spanish Conquest.** Doylestown, 1869. Cl.
(LH. Sep.25; 213) $130

DAVY, Sir Humphrey
- **On the Safety Lamp for Coal Miners, with some**
researches on flame ... 1818. *1st. Edn.* Orig. bds.
(PD. May 16; 75) £420
- **Six Discourses delivered before the Royal Society.**
L., 1827. *1st. Edn.* 4to. Cont. wraps., unc. & partly
unopened, spine defect. (SG. Mar.22; 85) $100
- **The Collected Works.** Ed.:- John Davy. 1839-40.
9 vols. Some staining, orig.[cl., soiled & slightly
worn. (TA. Dec.15; 514) £85

DAVY, J. & Sons
See— DRYDEN PRESS

DAVY, John
- **An Account of the Interior of Ceylon, & of its**
Inhabitants ... L., 1821. *1st. Edn.* 4to. Folding map,
13 plts., mod. qtr. mor. (SG. Mar.29; 305) $225

DAWSON, G.P.
- **Observations on the Walchern Diseases Which**
Affected The British Soldiers in the Expedition to
the Scheldt. Baltely, Ipswich, 1810. Errata lf., orig.
bds., unc., worn. (P. Jan.12; 215) *Cole.* £150

DAWSON, Robert
- **The Present State of Australia ...** L., 1830. Minor
soiling, mainly to fore-e.'s 3 or 4 sm. margin repairs,
no final advts., orig. bds., some wear, later backstrip,
unc. (KH. Nov.9; 580) Aus. $100
- - **Anr. Edn.** 1831. *2nd. Edn.* Lacks 1 of the final
ironmongery advt. ll., hf. cf., slightly marked. (KH.
May 1; 208) Aus. $170

DAWSON, Simon James
- **Report on the Exploration of the Country Between**
Lake Superior & the Red River Settlement ...
Toronto, 1859. *1st. Edn.* Fo. 1 map reprd. at fold,
recent hf. mor. & cl. bds., orig. ptd. label on
upr. cover; the Rt. Hon. Visc. Eccles copy. (CNY.
Nov.18; 82) $160

DAWSON, Thomas F. & Skiff, F.J.V.
- **The Ute War: a History of the White River Mass-**
acre ... Denver, 1879. *1st. Edn.* 8 pp. of advts., cont.
name in light ink on title, orig. ptd. wraps., cl. s.-
c. (LH. Apr.15; 297) $900
- - **Anr. Copy.** Orig. paper wraps., boxed; Littell
bkplt. (LH. Sep.25; 215) $800

DAWSON, Warren R.
See— SMITH, G. Elliot & Dawson, Warren R.

DAY, Cyrus Lawrence
- The Music & Musical Instruments of Southern India & & the Deccan. 1891. *(700).* 4to. Orig. cl. gt., soiled. (TA. May 17; 17) £85

DAY, Cyrus Lawrence & Murrie, Eleanore Boswell
- English Song-Books 1651-1702. A Bibliography with a first-line index of Songs. 1940. Sm. 4to. Buckram-bkd. bds.; H.M. Nixon coll. (BBA. Oct.6; 218) *Morton-Smith.* £70
- - **Anr. Copy.** Sm. 4to. Orig. holland-bkd. bds., slightly soiled. (BBA. Nov.10; 55) *May & May.* £65

DAY, J., Mechanic
- The History of the Scheme & Construction of the Diving Vessel. [1774]. Sm. 4to. Hf. cf. gt. (P. Jan.12; 216) *Quevedo.* £100

DAY, Thomas
[-] The History of Sandford & Merton, a Work Intended for the Use of Children. 1783-86-89. *1st. Edns.* 3 vols. 8vo. & 12mo. Vol. II: 4 pp. advts., slight margin hole in F5, sm. portions lacking from margins of L5-8, Vol. III: 4 pp. advts. at end (slightly stained), engraved frontis. stained, some offsetting on title, unif. cont. hf. roan, marb. bds., spines gt. (rubbed). (LC. Mar.1; 111) £700

DAY-LEWIS, Cecil
See— LEWIS, Cecil Day

DAYOT, Armand
- Les Animaux vus par les Meilleurs Animaliers: Animaux Decoratifs; Stylisés (Plumes); Stylisés (Poils); D'après Nature; Etudes. Paris, 1920's. 5 vols. Sm. fo. 256 plts. (loose as iss.), cl.-bkd. lettered bds., some wear. (SG. Aug.25; 11) *Sanders.* £120
- Louis XIV. De La Règence á la Révolution. Les Journées Révolutionnaires. Napoléon. La Restauration. Histoire Contemporaine. Paris, [1906]. 6 vols. Ob. fo. Cont. red hf. chagrins, corners, decor. spines. (HD. Dec.9; 118) *Frs. 1,800*

DE AMICIS, Ed.
- Holland & its People. N.Y., 1885. *Zuyder Zee Edn. (600) numbered & sigd. by publishers.* Royal 8vo. Cl. gt., defect. (GM. Dec.7; 643) £50

DEAN & SON
- New Book of Dissolving Views. L., ca. 1890. 4to. 6 plts. with moving pts., orig. pict. bds. (P. May 17; 394) *Glendale.* £80

DEARBORN, Nathaniel
- Boston Notions; Being an Authentic & Concise Account of 'That Village' from 1630 to 1847. Boston, Priv. ptd., 1848. *1st. Edn.* 16mo. 32 full-p. & folded engraved maps, charts, facs., scenes. & ports., very slight offsetting from plts., later str.-grd. crimson mor. by Bayntun, raised bands, gt. panels & ornamented borders, light wear, some rubbing at extremities. (HA. May 4; 364) $130

DEARN, Thomas Downes Wilmot
- An Historical, Topographical & Descriptive Account of the Weald of Kent. Ill.:– M. Dubourg after Dearn. Cranbrook, 1814. *1st. Edn.* Etched map, 8 aquatints, offset onto text, cont. hf. mor., partly unc., spine slightly worn. (S. Mar.6; 419) *Sanders.* £100
- - **Anr. Copy.** Mod. hf. mott. cf. (P. Sep.29; 94) *Owen.* £80

See— BARBER, William—DEARN, T.D.W.— MORRIS, Richard

DEBELLE
See— CASSIEN & Debelle

DE BLAMONT
See— FUSELIER & DE BLAMONT

DE BOTON, Abraham
- Lechem Mishneh. Venice, 1604. *1st. Edn.* 2 pts. in 1 vol. Fo. Some browning & staining, contents loose in bdg., old reverse cf., very rubbed. (SPB. Feb.1; 37) $950

DE BOURCARD, Francesco
- Usi e Costumi di Napoli e Contorni. Napoli, 1965. *Ltd. Edn. Reprint of Naples 1853 Edn.* 2 vols. Cf., gt.-tooled. (CR. Jun.6; 147) Lire 280,000

DE BOURRIENNE, F.
- Memoirs of Napoleon Bonaparte. 1836. 4 vols. Hf. cf. by Morrell, spines gt.-decor., 2 spines chipped at head. (SKC. Mar.9; 1743) £60

DE BURE, Guillaume-François
- Bibliographie Instructive. L., 1763-68. 7 vols. (Lacks Supp.). Cont. cf., worn. (BBA. May 23; 244) *Maggs.* £55
- - **Anr. Edn.** 1763-69. 9 vols. Mott. cf., lightly rubbed, spines gt. (CSK. Jun.1; 102) £260

DECAISNE, Joseph
- Le Jardin Fruitier du Muséum ou Iconographie de Toutes les Espèces et Variétés d'Arbres Fruitiers. Paris, 1858-64. 6 vols. (only, of 9). Sm. fo. 288 engraved plts., partly hand-cold., cont. hf. cf., most covers detchd., rubbed, w.a.f. (C. Jun.27; 153) *Burden.* £950

DE CARAFFA & LUCCIANA
- Pratica delli Capi Ribelli Corsi. Bastia, 1885. Cont. hf. chagrin, spine decor. (HD. Oct.21; 143) Frs. 4,800

DE CASTELLA, Hubert
- John Bull's Vineyard; Australian Sketches. Melbourne, 1886. Lacks lr. wrap., upr. wrap. slightly chipped, backstrip defect. (KH. May 1; 214) Aus. $260

DECHELETTE, Joseph
- Manuel d'Archeologie. Préhistorique, Celtique et Gallo-Romaine. Paris, 1908-14. 4 vols. Later cl. (TA. Nov.17; 233) £64
- - **Anr. Edn.** Paris, 1924-34. 6 vols. in 7. Orig. ptd. wraps., unc. & partly unopened, spines slightly worn. (TA. Nov.17; 234) £66

DE CHERTABLON
See— LA VIGNE, D.—DE CHERTABLON

DECISIONES ROTAE ROMANAE
Venice, J. & G. de Gregoriis for B. Fontana, 19 Jul. 1496. Tall fo. Many margins stained, some wormed, last 2 ll. reprd., with some loss of text, vell.; the Walter Goldwater copy. [BMC V, 349; Goff D-111] (SG. Dec.1; 119) $500

DECISIONES ROTE NOVE & ANTIQUE
Lyon, 1509. Sm. fo. Sm. wormhole in last few ll. with very slight damage to text, cont. blind-stpd. pig-bkd. wood bds., clasps, crack in lr. cover. (S. Nov.17; 17) *Harper.* £480

DECKER, Paul
- Ausfürliche Anleitung zur Civil Bau-Kunst. Nuremb., ca. 1730. 3 vols. in 1. Fo. 60 engraved plts., including 3 titles & dedication lf., some faint margin foxing, pencil annots. on a few plts., cont. cf., 1 corner reprd. (C. Dec.9; 32) *Weinreb.* £700
- Fürstlicher Baumeister, oder Architectura Civilis. Ill.:– Bodenehr, Bocklin, Corvinus, Engelbrecht, & others. Augsburg, 1711-16. *1st. Edn.* Pts. 1 & 2, & Supp. Fo. Engraved frontis., 133 plts., including 33 plts. in pt. 2 (as opposed to 39 in the Fowler copy), with address lf. from publisher to the reader (not recorded in Fowler), 4 plts. shaved, edges of 1 plt. frayed, sm. area of worming in Supp. & pt. 2, slightly affecting a few plts. in pt. 2, a few light stains, cont. sheep; inscr. of Johann Gottfried Aschenborn on titles. (C. Dec.9; 33) *Lyon.* £1,700
- - **Anr. Copy.** Pts. 1 & 2, & Supp., in 2 vols. Fo. Some plts pt. 1 slightly stained in lr. margin, lacks last plt., some maps with sm. tears, cont. hf. leath. (R. Oct.11; 792) DM 9,200
- - **Anr. Copy.** Pts. 1 & 2, & Supp., in 1 vol. Lge. ob. fo. Pt. II lacks title, minimal browning & spotting, 2 ll. extended in margin, some bkd. tears, later hf. leath., slightly rubbed. (H. May 22; 61) DM 6,400
- Gothic Architecture Decorated, Consisting of a Large Collection of Temples, Banqueting, Summer & Green Houses, Gazebo's, Alcoves, & c. L., 1759. Ob. 4to. 12 engraved plts. (slight spotting & discolouration), mod. hf. mor. (C. Jun.27; 27) *Weinreb.* £280

DECLARATION OF OFFICERS OF THE GARRISON OF HULL
1649. Qtr. mor. gt. (P. Feb.16; 183) £65

DECOR FLORAL
Paris, ca. 1900. Sm. fo. 50 tinted photographic plts., most with liby. stp. on verso, loose as iss. in marb. bd. portfo., lacks spine. (SG. Nov.10; 52) $200

DECORATION EGYPTIENNE
Paris, ca. 1930. 4to. 36 mntd. col. plts., loose as iss., some minor chipping not affecting images, cl.-bkd. bd. folder, spine ends frayed. (SG. Aug.25; 133) $110

DECORATION PICTURALE AU XXme SIECLE (Le)
Ill.:– after Moreau-Neret, Picard, & others. Paris, n.d. 60 cold. plts., some hand-finished, some light spotting, unbnd. as iss. in orig. cl.-bkd. bds., soiled. (CSK. Mar.23; 128) £160

DECORATIONS FOR PARKS & GARDENS, Designs for Gates, Garden seats, Alcoves, Temples, Baths, etc.
L., Ca. 1800. Engraved title, 55 plts., 16 pp. advts. tipped in, orig. wraps., stabbed as iss., unc. (C. Dec.9; 34) *Henderson.* £280

DE COSTER, Charles Théodore Henri
- Die Geschichte von Ulenspiegel und Lamme Goedzak. Trans:– Karl Wolfskehl. Ill.:– F. Masereel. 1926. *Ltd. 1st. German Edn.* 2 vols. 150 orig. woodcuts, orig. linen. (GB. Nov.5; 2780) DM 600
- La Legende et les Aventures Heroîques, Joyeuses et Glorieuses d'Ulenspiegel et de Lamme Goedzak au Pays de Flandres et Ailleurs. Ill.:– C. Montald. Bruxelles, 1929. *(360). (320) numbered on holland.* 2 vols. 4to. Publisher's boxes. (LM. Oct.22; 118) B.Frs. 13,000
- - **Anr. Edn.** Ill.:– F. Masereel. Antw., 1937. *1st. Belgian Edn. (500) numbered.* 2 vols. 4to. Orig. pict. wraps., unc. (BR. Apr.13; 1815) DM 4000

DE COUTIVRON
- Traité Complet de Natation. Essai sur son Application à l'Art de la Guerre. Ill.:– Gudin. Paris, 1836. Some foxing, hf. chagrin. (HD. Sep.22; 226) Frs. 1,000

DECREMPS, Henri
[-] The Conjurer Unmasked ... Ed.:– Denton & others. L., 1790. *3rd. Edn.* Hf.-title, last 2 advt. ll., partly unopened, orig. wraps., soiled. (BBA. Nov.30; 238) *Sutherland.* £220
- La Magie Blanche devoilée. Paris, 1784. *1st. Edn.* Some foxing, cont. marb. leath., gt. spine & outer destelle. (HK. Nov.9; 1947) DM 900
- - **Anr. Edn.** Paris, 1784-85. 2 vols. in 1, including Supp. 1st. vol. lacks lf. with logograph. (*Bound with:*) PINETTI DE WILLEDAL, Joseph - Amusemens Physiques et Differentes. Paris, 1785. *New Edn.* Hf.-title, 1 plt. loose. Together 3 vols. in 1. Cont. cf.-bkd. bds., spine gt., rubbed. (BBA. Nov.30; 75) *Dylan's.* £200
- - **Anr. Edn.** Paris, 1789. 3 pts. in 2 vols. Some spotting, some sm. margin defects, cont. hf. leath. gt., lightly bumped. (HK. Nov.9; 1948) DM 700
- - **Anr. Edn.** Paris, 1792. 2 vols., including Supp. (*With:*) - Testament de Jérôme Sharp, Professeur de Physique Amusante. Pour Servir de Complément à la Magie Blanche Dévoilée. Paris, priv. ptd., 1783. (*With:*) - Les Petites Aventures De Jérôme Sharp. Liège, 1793. (*With:*) - La Science Sanculotisée. Premier Essai, sur les Moyens de Faciliter l'Etude de l'Astronomie. Paris, priv. ptd. 1794. Together 6 vols. Hf. cf., 1st. 5 vols. by Gruel, blind-decor. spines. (HD. Sep.22; 229) Frs. 4,700

DEERING, Charles
- Historical Account of the Town of Nottingham. Nottingham, 1751. 4to. Cont. cf. (HBC. May 17; 349) £55

DEFECTA IN MISSA OCCURRENTES
[Rome, Johann Besicken], ca. 1493-94. 4to. Later vell.; the Walter Goldwater copy. [Goff D-132] (SG. Dec.1; 120) $125

DEFER, Nicolas
- Les Forces de l'Europe Recueil de 181 Figures et Plans. Paris, 1695. Ob. 4to. Cont. grd. cf., decor. spine. (HD. Mar.14; 22)   Frs. 12,100

DEFINITIVE TREATY (The) ... Concluded at Paris, the 10th Day of February, 1763
See— PRELIMINARY ARTICLES OF PEACE between His Britannick Majesty, the Most Christian King, & the Catholick King—DEFINITIVE TREATY (The) ... Concluded at Paris, the 10th Day of February, 1763

DEFOE, Daniel
[–] Les Avantures, ou, la Vie et les Voyages de l'ancien Robinson, surnommé Crusoe ... Frankfurt, Den Haag & Leipzig, 1769. 2 pts. in 1 vol. Some slight browning, bds. unc. (HK. May 17; 2423)   DM 450
– – Anr. Edn. Ill.:– 'Grandville' & Francais. Paris, 1840. New Trans. 1st. Printing. Hf. mor., corners, by R. Raparlier, spine decor., unc. (HD. May 4; 270)   Frs. 2,200
– – Anr. Edn. Paris, ca. 1860. Publisher's hf. chagrin & buckram, spine decor. (HD. Nov.29; 89)   Frs. 1,300
[–] An Essay on the History & Reality of Apparitions. 1727. Cont. cf., rebkd. (CSK. Sep.30; 119)   £95
[–] The Farther Adventures of Robinson Crusoe. 1719. 1st. Edn. Publisher's advts. at end, Map incompl., cont. panel. cf. (TA. Oct.20; 270) £58
– The History of the Union between England & Scotland. 1786. 4to. Cont. tree cf. gt. (PD. Jun.13; 148)   £62
– The History of the Union of Great Britain. Edinb., 1709. 1st. Edn. Fo. Cont. panel. cf., rubbed; Sir Ivar Colquhoun, of Luss copy. (CE. Mar.22; 85)   £180
– – Anr. Copy. Fo. 4-lf. dedication to Queen inserted after title, cont. cf., rebkd. (BBA. Oct.27; 2)   Snelling. £170
[–] The History of the Wars, Charles XII King of Sweden. 1720. 2nd. Edn. Publisher's advts. at end, cont. cf. gt. (P. Jul.5; 137)   £55
– A Journal of the Plague Year. Ill.:– Davenport after George Cruikshank. L., 1835. Sm. 8vo. 4 engraved plts., facing each plt. is drawing, wash over pencil, sigd. by Cruikshank, lev. gt. extra, gt. dentelles, by Riviere. (SG. Apr.26; 52) $1,600
[–] Jure Divino: a Satyr. L., 1706. 1st. Edn. Fo. Some light foxing, cont. cf. (P. Feb.16; 251) £85
– – Anr. Copy. Fo. Some browning or light soiling, early cf., worn, covers loose. (SG. Feb.9; 210) $130
– Das Leben ... des Weltberühmten Engelländers Robinson Crusoe. Ill.:– W. Klemm. Leipzig, 1919. (300) numbered. Fo. 10 sigd. orig. [lithos., orig. hf. vell., sigd. by Hübel & Denck, Leipzig. (GB. May 5; 2801)   DM 550
– – Anr. Edn. Ill.:–R. Janthur. 1922. (800) on Japan paper. 4to. 31 cold. orig. lithos., orig. pict. vell. (GB. May 5; 2736)   DM 1,100
– – Anr. Copy. Fo. Orig. pict. hf. vell. (GB. Nov.5; 2633)   DM 500
– – Anr. Edn. Ill.:– F. Heubner. München, [1922]. (100) on Bütten. 4to. Etched title & 20 etchings sigd. by artist, titel & last ll. slightly browned, hand-bnd. orig. mor. gt., by P.A. Demeter, Hellerau, faded & discold. (H. Nov.23; 987)   DM 540
– – Anr. Copy. Lge. 4to. 20 sigd. etchings, orig. bd portfo. (HK. May 17; 2637)   DM 420
[–] Levengeschiedenis en Lotgevallen. Amst. & Rotterdam, 1791. New Edn. 3 vols. Corners slightly defect., cont. pol. hf. cf., unc. (VS. Dec.9; 1034)   Fls. 460
– The Novels of ... Edinb., 1810. 11 vols. 16mo. Hf. cf., bkplt. (GM. Dec.7; 377)   £100
– A Plan of the English Commerce ... L., 1728. 1st. Edn. Title & some ll. spotted in blank margins, later cf., gt. Signet Liby. arms on covers, jnts. & head of spine worn. (C. Nov.9; 59)   Quaritch. £260
[–] Robinson Crusoe. Boston, Fowle & Draper. [1757-62]. Pamphlet, 10pp., A4-B4, browned, sewn in orig. wraps., child's inscr. on lr. cover. (SPB. Oct.26; 21) $8,500
– – Anr. Edn. 1785. 2 vols. Hf. cf. gt. (P. Sep.8; 276)   £70
– – Anr. Edn. Ill.:– after Stothard. 1790. 2 vols.

Some foxing, cont. russ., spines gt.; Sir Ivar Colquhoun, of Luss copy. (CE. Mar.22; 86) £400
– – Anr. Edn. N.Y., 1815. 12mo. Some foxing, early cf. (SG. Dec.8; 130) $100
– – Anr. Edn. Ill.:– Heath after Thomas Stothard. L., 1820. 2 vols. 2 vig. titles, 20 engraved plts., gt., lacks 1 label. (P. Nov.24; 206) Heighton. £50
– – Anr. Copy. 2 vols. Lge. 8vo. L.P., 22 plts., each in 2 states, lev. gt. by Riviere, spines gt. with fleurons, gt. dentelles. (SG. Feb.16; 86) $400
[–] Robinson Crusoe.—The Farther Adventures of Robinson Crusoe. L., 1726. 7th. Edn.; 5th. Edn. Together 2 vols. 12mo. Cont. cf., extremities worn, hinges strengthened. (SG. Apr.19; 68) $175
[–] The Secret History of the White-Staff. L., 1714-15. 2nd. Edn. Pts. 1-3 in 1 vol. Hf. mod. cf. (P. Dec.8; 51)   Rota. £70
[–] The Secrets of the Invisible World Disclos'd. 1735. 2nd. Edn. Upr. margin trimmed, spotted, later panel cf., spine gt; inscr. & sigd. on title-p. by A. Conan Doyle. (BBA. Jun.14; 6)   Bertram Rota. £110
[–] The Shortest-Way with the Dissenters. L., 1702. 1st. Edn. 4to. Three-qtr. cf. (SG. Feb.9; 209)$425
– La Vie et les Aventures Surprenantes de Robinson Crusoe. Ill.:– B. Picart, engraved by J.L.B. Chatelain. Londres [Paris], 1784. 4 vols. 18mo. Cont. marb. cf., spine decor. (HD. Mar.21; 22)   Frs. 1,050
– – Anr. Edn. Trans.:– Pétrus Borel. 1836. 2 vols. Vigs. foxed, str.-grd. hf. mor., spines decor. (HD. Jul.6; 104b)   Frs. 1,650
– Works. N.Y., 1905. 'Hand-Made' Edn. (150) numbered. 16 vols. Frontis.'s cold. & uncold. (Vol. 1 uncold. only), engraved plts. in 2 forms, mor., gt.-stpd. panels, red mor. onlays, turn-ins gt., red mor. doubls., watered silk free end-pp., partly unc. (CNY. Dec.17; 549) $2,400

DE FOREST, Lee
- Television Today & Tomorrow. N.Y., 1942. Cl., d.-w. torn; inscr. by author,. (LH. Jan.15; 280) $110

DE FRÉVILLE, M.
- Histoire des Nouvelles Découvertes faites dans la Mer du Sud en 1767, 1768, 1769 & 1770 ... 6. Paris, 1774. 2 vols. Early mott. cf. (KH. May 1; 215)   Aus. $220

DE GAULLE, M.J.
- Nouvelle Histoire de Paris et de ses Environs. Ed.:– Charles Nodier. Paris, 1839. 5 vols. in 10. Plan, map, 49 steel-engraved plts., foxed, cont. sheep, decor. spines, slightly faded. (HD. Sep.21; 121)   Frs. 1,750

DEGENHARDT, W.
- Wie Kijkt Er Meê? Leerzaam Prentenboek. Amst., [inscr. dtd. 1871]. 4to. Moving picture book, 8 ills. hand-cold., stitching week, orig. cl.-bkd. pict. bds., hand-cold. ill. on upr. cover; van Veen coll. (S. Feb.28; 269) $80

DEGENHART, B. & Schmitt, A.
- Corpus der Italienischen Zeichnungen. Berlin, 1968. 4 vols. Lge. 4to. Orig. cl. (SI. Dec.15; 196)   Lire 900,000
– – Anr. Edn. Berlin, 1980. 4 vols. Lge. 4to. Orig. cl. (SI. Dec.15; 197)   Lire 550,000

DE GOLYER, E.
- The Journey of Three Englishmen Across Texas in 1568. El Paso, 1947. (465). Paper bds., d.-w. (LH. Sep.25; 401) $170

DE GOUY, L.P.
- The Derrydale Cook Book of Fish & Game. Derrydale Pr., 1937. (1250) numbered. 2 vols. Cl. gt., box worn. (DM. May 21; 18) $115
– – Anr. Edn. Derrydale Pr., [1937]. (1250). 2 vols. Gt.-decor. leatherette, s.-c. (SG. Mar.15; 217) $225

DEGREVAUNT
- Sire Degrevaunt. [Hammersmith, Kelms. Pr., 1896]. (358). (350) on paper. Linen-bkd. paper bds., unc. (LH. Sep.25; 407) $200

DE GUERIN, Maurice
- Poèmes en Prose, Précédés d'une Petite Lettre sur les Mythes par Paul Valéry. Ill.:– George Barbier.

[Paris, 1928]. (150). 4to. Loose in orig. decor. wraps. as iss., folder, box rubbed.; pres. copy from Barbier to Violette Gath. (SPB. Dec.14; 39) $1,400

DEGUIGNES, Joseph
- Histoire General des Huns, des Turcs, des Mongols et des autres Tartares Occidentaux, & c. Paris, 1756-58. 4 vols. in 5. 4to. Hf.-titles, cont. cf., decor. spines. (SI. Dec.15; 69)   Lire 480,000

DEHIO, George
- Geschichte der Deutschen Kunst. Berlin, 1921-26. 3 text & 3 plt. vols. Orig. bds. & orig. linen. (D. Nov.23; 1757)   DM 400
– – Anr. Edn. Berlin & Leipzig, 1930-34. 4 vols. in 8. 4to. Orig. cl., 1 d.-w. torn. (S. Dec.13; 444)   Leicester. £55
– – Anr. Copy. 4 text & 4 plt. vols., in 8 vols. 4to. Orig. linen. (GB. May 4; 1851)   DM 560

DEHMEL, Richard
- Aber die Liebe. Ill.:– Willi Jaeckel. Berlin, 1921. (340). De Luxe Edn., (25) numbered on Japan vell., with full-p. etchings sigd. by artist. 4to. With supp. etching of hf.-title in state before the letter, sigd. by artist, orig. red mor., sigd. by Bruno Scheer, gt.-decor. (GB. May 5; 2729)   DM 2,100
– – Anr. Copy. Lge. 4to. With supp. proof pull of an etching before letter, hand-bnd. mor. by Br. Scheer, Berlin. (H. Nov.24; 1663)   DM 1,850
- Der Buntscheck. Ill.:– P. & R. Dehmel & others. Köln, [after 1904]. 2nd. Edn. 4to. Orig. bds., spine slightly worn, paper covered. (GB. May 5; 2320)   DM 700
- Die Verwandlungen der Venus. Ill.:– W. Geiger. München, 1909. (150). Lge. fo. Printer's mark sigd. by author & artist, some margins lightly browned, orig. raw silk. (H. May 23; 1229a)   DM 2,000

DE JONG, Dirk & Sallieth, M.
- Atlas van alle de Zee-havens der Bataafsche Republiek. Amst., 1802. Fo. Wide margins, engraved title, 28 double-p. engraved plts., mntd. on guards, 1 or 2 minor tears at folds, reprd., cont. hf. cf., slightly rubbed. (CH. May 24; 49)   Fls. 12,000

DE KAY, James E.
- Zoology of New York. Albany, 1844. Pt. 2: 'Birds'. 4to. 141 cold. plts., few plts. browned or spotted, 1 loose with edges frayed, orig. gt.-pict. cl., extremities worn, lacks backstrip. (SG. Mar.22; 86) $500

DE KERCHOVE DE DENTERGHEM, Comte
- Le Livre des Orchidées. Paris, 1894. Hf. cf., corners. (CR. Jun.6; 149)   Lire 280,000

DELABARRE, C.F.
- Traité de la Seconde Dentition ... Paris, 1819. 1st. Edn. Title facs., on old paper, lacks hf. title, some light foxing, 2 sm. margin tears reprd., new hf. leath. (R. Apr.4; 1405)   DM 1,150

DELACHENAL
- Histoire de Charles V. Paris, 1909-31. 5 vols. Hf. chagrin, some stains Vol. 1. (HD. Feb.22; 47)   Frs. 2,200

DELACOUR, Jean
- The Waterfowl of the World. Ill.:– Peter Scott. 1954-64. 1st. Edn. 4 vols. 4to. Orig. cl. gt., rubbed. (TA. Apr.19; 142)   £75

DE LA CREQUINIERE
- The Agreement of the Customs of the East-Indians with those of the Jews & other Ancient People. Trans.:– John Toland. L., 1705. 1st. Edn. in Engl. 6 plts., cont. cf. (SG. Apr.19; 65) $150

DELACROIX, Eugène
- Album mit den Illustrationen zu Goethes Faust. Paris, ca. 1850. Last state. Lge. fo. On vell., all plts. mntd. on silk, slight stain in upr. margin nearly thro-out, light foxing, lacks woodcut title, cont. hf. leath. (R. Apr.3; 164)   DM 3,200
- Hamlet. Seize Sujets dessinés et lithographiées. Paris, 1864. 2nd. Edn. Lge. fo. Some light margin foxing, some lithos. sigd. in stone & dtd. between 1834 & 1843, orig. hf. linen, slightly bumped, spine defect, upr. cover loose. (R. Apr.3; 165)   DM 3,200
- Trente-et-un Dessins et Aquarelles du Maroc

reproduites en Facsimile. Paris, 1928. *(300)*. Ob. fo. Leaves. (HD. Jun.6; 41) Frs. 2,100

DE LA FOSSE, Jean Charles
- **Algemeen Kunstenaars Handboek.** Ill.:– Jan de Witt. Amst., ca. 1775. Fo. Wide margin. some margin foxing & soiling, cont. hf. leath. gt., slightly rubbed & bumped, unc. (HT. May 9; 944) DM 450
- **Recueil des Fontaines ... Pyramides, etc ...** Amst., 1720. 2 vols. in 1. Fo. 103 engraved plts., mod. vell. (CR. Jun.6; 25) Lire 300,000

DE LA MARE, Walter
- **Behold, This Dreamer.** 1939. *1st. Edn. (50)* numbered & sigd. Orig. parch. bds., unc., s.-c.; 2 p. A.L. inserted. (P. Apr.12; 280) *O'Neill.* £95
- – – **Anr. Copy.** 2 ll. torn, vell. gt. (P. Jan.12; 23) *Georges.* £70
- **Crossings.** Music:– C. Armstrong Gibbs. Ill.:– Randolph Schwabe. [L., Beaumont Pr., 1921]. *(10)* on vell., sigd. by author, artist & composer. Orig. vell., mor.-bkd. s.-c.; bkplt. of W. Van R. Whitall, Perry Molstad copy. (SPB. May 16; 444) $500
- **Early One Morning.** 1935. *(50)* sigd. Orig. parch. bds., unc., s.-c.; 6 line inscr. by author, 2 p. A.L. inserted. (P. Apr.12; 279) *O'Neill.* £85
- **Lispet, Lispett & Vaine.** Vine Books, 1923. *(200)* sigd. Vell. (P. Jan.12; 27) *Joseph.* £50
- **The Listeners & Other Poems.** L., 1912. *1st. Edn.* 12mo. Orig. cl., orig. glassine d.-w., mor. s.-c.; sigd. by author in 1924, Frederic Dannay copy. (CNY. Dec.16; 99) $100
- [–] **Songs of Childhood.** L., 1902. *1st. Edn.* 12mo. Orig. cl., parch. spine a little soiled, orig. ptd. d.-w., cl. s.-c.; Frederic Dannay copy. (CNY. Dec.16; 98) $680
- – – **Anr. Copy.** 12mo. Orig. cl., parch. spine slightly spiled, mor.-bkd. s.-c.; inscr., Perry Molstad copy. (SPB. May 16; 446) $400
See— BIANCO, Pamela

DELAMOTTE, William
- **Twenty Etchings.** Sandhurst, 1817. *(Bound with:)*
- **Ten Etchings.** Sandhurst, 1817. Together 2 works in 1 vol. 4to. Slight spotting to some plts., hf. mor. gt., slightly rubbed. (LC. Oct.13; 19) £50

DELANEY, Patrick
- **Observations upon Lord Orrery's Remarks on the Life & Writings of Dr. Jonathan Swift.** L., 1772. Cont. mott. cf., bkplt. (GM. Dec.7; 394) £50

DELAPORTE, Yves
- **Les Vitraux de la Cathédrale de Chartres.** Ill.:– after Etienne Houvet. Chartres, 1926. 4 vols. 4to. Cold. frontis., text. ills., 284 plts., some cold., each plt. liby.-stpd. on blank verso, text vol. in buckram, plts. loose in ptd. wraps. & bd. folders, linen ties. (SG. May 3; 134) $175

DELATRE, Auguste
- **Eau-Forte, Pointe sèche et Vernis mou.** Ill.:– Delatre, Somm, Point, & Rops. Paris, 1887. 4to. 6 etched plts. in 2 states, hf.-title, cont. hf. mor. by Champs, spine gt., orig. wraps. preserved; Dr. Balp bkplt. (BBA. Jun.14; 200) *Sims, Reed & Fogg.* £150

DELAUNAY, Charles
- **Mémoire sur le Calcul des Variations.** [Paris], 1842. MS. dedication on inr. doubl., some slight browning, cont. bds. (HT. May 8; 492) DM 560

DELAUNAY, Sonia
- **Compositions Couleurs Idées.** Paris, ca. 1930. Fo. 40 cold. plts., slight discoloration, loose in portfo. as iss., stained. (SPB. May 17; 598) $900

DE LA VIGNE, A.
See— SAINT-GELAIS, O. de & DE LA VIGNE, A.

DEL BEN VIVER DE LE DONNE MARIDAD CHIAMATO GLORIA MULIERUM
See— DIOGENES LAERTIUS—PALMA VIRTUTUM—DEL BEN VIVER DE LE DONNE MARIDAD CHIAMATO GLORIA MULIERUM

DELBRUCK, H.
- **Geschichte der Kriegskunst in Rahmen der Politischen Geschichte.** Berlin, 1920-36. 7 vols. 1 vol. orig. hf. leath., rest orig. hf. cl., spines defect. (B. Oct.4; 386) Fls. 460

DELBRUECK, Max
See— MEITNER, Lise & Delbrueck, Max

DELCAMPE
[–] **La Connoissance Parfaite des Chevaux.** Paris, 1741. Engraved frontis., 7 plts., hf.-title, slightly offset, cont. cf., rebkd., spine gt., worn. (S. Mar.20; 766) *Symonds.* £120

DE LE RIME DI DIVERSI NOBILI POETI TOSCANI
Ed.:– Dionigi Atanagi. Venice, 1565. *1st. Edn.* 2 vols. in 1. Cont. vell., gt.-stpd. arms & ornaments, loose. (SG. Oct.27; 16) $140

DELFINI, D.
- **Sommario di Tutte le Scientie.** Venice., 1556. Sm. 4to. Heavy soiling at beginning & end, some cold. underlining., 18th. C. hf. coll. (D. Nov.23; 102) DM 400

DELFTLAND
- **'t Hooge Heemraed Schap van Delftland.** 1712-50. 510 x 595mm. 28 engraved maps including general map & 2 additional maps, dupls. of 2 maps & 2 title ll., margins, 5 maps soiled & frayed at edges with a few sm. tears, reprd., loose in portfo. (CH. May 24; 229) Fls. 1,800

DELICES DE LA FRANCE
Amst., 1699. 2 vols. 12mo. 2 engraved titles, 37 engraved plts., cl. (P. Jan.12; 218) *Reynold.* £160.

DELICES DE LA POESIE FRANCAISE
Ed.:– F. de Rosset. Paris, 1618. *2nd. Edn.* Lacks 5 prelim. ll. (1 blank) & table ll., cont. decor. mor., cypher (of Feydeau de Brou?); from H. de Backer liby. (HD. Mar.29; 25) Frs. 25,000

DE LIGNAC, Louis F.L.
[–] **De l'Homme et de la Femme, Considères Physiquement dans l'Etat du Mariage.** Lille, 1772. *1st. Edn.* 2 vols. Cont. cf., spines worn. (TA. Oct. 20; 235) £68

DE L'ISLE, Guillaume
- **Atlas Nouveau, contenant toutes les Parties du Monde.** Amst., ca. 1710. Fo. 50 etched double-p. maps, outl. cold., 1 folding map defect., lge. folding plt. defect., frontis. reprd., many inner margins reprd., mod. hf. cf., w.a.f. (SI. Dec.15; 70) Lire 4,200,000
- – **Anr. Edn.** Amst., J. Covens & C. Mortier, 1730. Fo. Additional engraved allegorical title, 47 (of 56?) double-p. engraved maps, hand-cold. in outl., engraved title fully cold., 1 or 2 short splits at centrefolds without loss of engraved surface, several map-sheets detchd., mod. vell. gt. (S. Dec.1; 201) *Burgess.* £1,400
- **[Collection of Maps of the World].** Paris, [maps dtd. 1700-32]. Ob. fo. 93 engraved maps, hand-cold. in outl., including 3 folding, 1 map torn, 3 maps with sm. tears in upr. outer corner, 1 map just shaved in foremargin, cont. cf., slightly worn. (C. Nov.16; 205) *Burgess.* £2,700
- **Mappemonde à l'Usage du Roi.** N.d. Fo. Bdg. not stated. (HD. Oct.14; 12) Frs. 7,000

DE L'ISLE, Guillaume & Buache, Ph.
- **Atlas Géographique des Quatre Parties du Monde.** Paris, 1800. Lge. fo. Wide margin, minimal spotting, cont. hf. leath., worn & bumped, jnts. partly split. (HK. May 15; 657) DM 2,100

DE L'ISLE, Guillaume & others
- **Atlas Géographique et Universel.** Paris, 1789. 2 vols. Fo. 2 allegorical titles, lists of maps, 143 (of 151) double-p. maps, all hand-cold. in outl., mntd. on guards, 1 title torn, both creased, tear in corner of Poitou, Brabant Meridional with piece torn from corner, l'Allemagne stained, tears in a few blank margins & corners, some minor dampstaining, last map in Vol. 1 with vertical crease, cont. cf., rubbed & worn. (C. Jun.27; 28) *Schuster.* £4,000

DELISLE, Léopold
- **Le Cabinet des Manuscrits de la Bibliothèque Impériale.** Paris, 1868-81. 4 vols., including plt. vol. Fo. Publisher's bds. (LM. Oct.22; 174) B. Frs. 8,000

DELLA LENGUEGLIA, Giovan Agostino
- **Guerra de Genovesi contro Alfonso Re di Aragona.** Ill.:– Cesare Bassani after H. de Ferrariis (frontis.). Genova, 1643. Old vell. (HD. Oct.21; 74) Frs. 2,100

DELLA ROCCA, Abbé
- **Traité Complet sur les Abeilles ...** Paris, 1790. *Orig. Edn.* 3 vols. Cont. marb. roan, spines decor., worn. (HD. Jun.26; 10) Frs. 3,000

DELLAVALE, Battista
- **Vallo Libro continente appertinente a Capitanii, retenere & fortificare una Cittá ...** Venice, 1539. Cont. limp vell. (GB. Nov.3; 986) DM 550

DELLOUX & DOURY
- **Historie Archéologique, Descriptive et Graphique de la Sainte-Chapelle du Palais.** Paris, 1865. Fo. Mor.-bkd. bds. gt., worn. (PNY. Oct.20; 206) $125

DELLOYE, H.L.
See— CHANTS ET CHANSONS POPULAIRES DE LA FRANCE

DELMET, P.
- **Chansons de Femmes.** Ill.:– Th. Steinlen. Paris, [1896]. Sm. 4to. Hf. leath. (V. Oct.1; 4160) DM 450

DE LONG, George W.
- **The Voyage of the Jeannette. The Ship & Ice Journals of ... Lieutenant Commander U.S.N. & Commander of the Polar Expedition of 1879-81.** Ed.:– Emma De Long. Boston, 1884. 2 vols. 1 map in rear pocket of Vol. 1, orig. gt.-decor. cl., rubbed. (TA. Mar.15; 1) £70

DELORD, Taxile
[–] **Un Autre Monde.** Ill.:– 'J.J. Grandville'. Paris, 1844. *1st. Edn.* Foxed, later hf. leath., bumped. (H. Nov.23; 659) DM 420
- – – **Anr. Copy.** 4to. Some foxing, 2 sm. tears in upr. jnt., orig. pict. & gt. linen. (BR. Apr.12; 1424) DM 400
- – – **Anr. Copy.** Lge. 8vo. Frontis., 35 (of 36) cold. plts., cont. hf. cf., decor. spine, many defects. (HD. Sep.21; 123) Frs. 1,100
- **Les Fleurs Animées.** Ill.:– 'J.J. Grandville'. Paris, 1847. *[1st. Edn.].* Col. frontis., 51 col. plts., qtr. mor. gt., w.a.f. (P. Nov.24; 165) *Finch.* £130
- – – **Anr. Copy.** 2 vols. Lge. 8vo. 2 cold. additional engraved titles, 2 plain & 50 cold. plts., some foxing, gt.-pict. cl., rebkd., Vol. 1 with orig. spine laid down. (SG. Nov.3; 89) $350
- – – **Anr. Copy.** 2 vols. in 1. 2 frontis., 2 uncold. plts., 49 (of 50) cold. plts., foxed, cont. hf. chagrin. (HD. Jan.24; 23) Frs. 1,900
- – – **Anr. Copy.** 3 pts. in 1 vol. Lacks Vol. 1 title & hf.-title, slightly foxed & soiled, some plts. partly soiled, 1 plt. pasted, new hf. linen. (GB. May 4; 1292) DM 550
- – – **Anr. Copy.** 2 vols. 2 frontis., 50 steel-engraved plts., cont. hand-cold. & gommées, some foxing, mainly in text, cont. elab. decor. cf. gt., slightly rubbed. (VG. Sep.14; 806) Fls. 900
- – – **Anr. Edn.** Intro.:– Alphonse Karr. Ill.:– J.-J. Grandville. Paris, [1847]. 2 vols. 2 frontis., 50 cold. engraved plts. & 2 plts. in black, some foxing, publisher's decor. bds. (HD. Jun.26; 13) Frs. 2,700
- – – **Anr. Copy.** 2 vols. Lacks 1 plt., foxing, publishers cl., special gt. & cold. tools. (HD. Mar.14; 43) Frs. 2,100
- – – **Anr. Copy.** 2 vols. 2 frontis., 49 cold. plts. (of 50) & 2 plts. in black, foxing, publisher's decor. bds. (HD. Jun.26; 14) Frs. 1,700
- – – **Anr. Edn.** Intro.:– A. Kerr. Ill.:– 'J.J. Grandville'. Brüssel, 1852. 2 vols. Some light foxing, cont. hf. leath., gt. (R. Oct.11; 230) DM 580
- – – **Anr. Edn.** Ill.:– 'J.J. Grandville'. Paris, 1867. 2 vols. 2 frontis., 2 black & white plts., 50 cold. & gommées plts., foxing, cont. hf. chagrin, decor. spines. (HD. Sep.21; 124) Frs. 1,050
- – – **Anr. Copy.** 2 vols. Engrs. hand-cold., hf. cf., 5 spine raised bands. (CR. Jun.6; 171) Lire 480,000
- – – **Anr. Edn.** Ill.:– 'J.J. Grandville'. Paris, [1867]. *New Edn.* 2 vols. Wide margin, last ll. Vol. 2 foxed, cont. lf. mor. gt. (R. Apr.3; 223) DM 900
See— SECOND, Albéric & Delord, Taxile

DE L'ORME, Philibert
- **L'Architecture** ... 1576. *3rd. Edn.* Fo. Cont. vell. (HD. Jun.29; 52) Frs. 1,850
- **Nouvelles Inventions pour bien Bastir et à Petits Fraiz** ... 1561. Fo. Dampstains, cont. vell. (HD. Jun.29; 51) Frs. 5,900
- **Le Premier Tome de l'Architecture.** Paris, 1568. *2nd. Edn.* Fo. Repair to title & some plts., dampstains, later roan, worn. (SM. Mar.7; 2013) Frs. 4,000

DELPHIKA GRAMMATA/The Sayings of the Seven Sages of Greece
Ed.:–Hans Mardersteig,. Trans.:– Betty Radice. Verona, Officina Bodoni, 1976. *(160) numbered on Magnani H.M.P.* In Greek & Engl., prospects laid in, qtr. vell., patterned bds., s.-c. (SG. May 17; 280) $300

DEL RIO, Capt. Don Antonio & Cabrera, Paul Felix
- **Description of the Ruins of an Ancient City.** 1822. Some light spotting, cont. cl., soiled. (CSK. Jul.6; 9) £380

DELRIO, Martin
- **Les Controverses et Recherches Magiques ausquels sont exactement et doctement confutées les Sciences Curieuses ... avecques la Manière de proceder en Justice contre les Magiciens et Sorciers ...** Trans.:– A. Duchesne. Paris, 1611. *1st. Fr. Edn.* Title-p. soiled, stained, cont. vell. (HD. Feb.22; 48) Frs. 3,700
- **Disquisitionum Magicarum Libri Sex.** Mainz, 1603. 3 pts. in 1 vol. Fo. Title with old name & monog. stp. in upr. margin, some sigs. slightly browned, some light stains in upr. margin, cont. blind-tooled pig. (R. Oct.12; 1544) DM 1,050
- – **Anr. Edn.** 1606. 3 vols. Slight soiling & dampstaining, sm. wormholes on a few ll., mostly marginal, Vol. 1 in later vell., slightly soiled, others in cont. blind-stpd. vell., worn, lacks clasps. (BBA. Nov.30; 35) *Walford.* £160
- – **Anr. Edn.** Lyon, 1608. 3 vols. in 1. Fo. 1 engraved title, margin stain's to some ll., corners reprd., cont. cf. gt. decor., centre motif, decor. spine; Claude Expilly ex-Libris. (HD. Jan.26; 94) Frs. 2,550
- – **Anr. Edn.** Mainz, 1624. 4to. Title with owner's mark, cont. limp vell., lacks ties. (HK. Nov.9; 1952) DM 520

DELTEIL, Joseph
- **Allo! Paris!.** Ill.:– Robert Delaunay. Paris, 1926. *(365) numbered.* 4to. Orig. wraps., unc. (S. Nov.21; 67) *Makiya.* £360
- – **Anr. Edn.** Ill.:– Robert Delaunay. Paris, 1926. *(365) numbered. (40) 'hors commerce'.* 4to. Orig. wraps., unc.; pres. copy, inscr. by author to Maurice Martin du Gard. (S. Nov.21; 12) *Rota.* £400
- – **Anr. Edn.** Trans.:– Robert Delaunay. Paris, [1926]. *(300) on Arches.* 4to. Hf.-title & 1 end-lf. browned, orig. wraps., lightly browned. (H. Nov.24; 2476) DM 1,600
- **Les Poilus. Epopée.** Paris, 1926. *Orig. Edn. (16) on china.* Sm. 4to. Jansenist maroon mor. by Alix, wrap. & spine, s.-c. (HD. Mar.27; 57) Frs. 1,550

DELTEIL, Loys
- **Catalogue Raisonné of the Etchings of Charles Meryon.** N.Y., 1924. 4to. Errata slips pasted in, slightly spotted, hf. mor., rubbed. (S. Apr.30; 136) *Brecht.* £180
- **The Graphic Works of Nineteenth & Twentieth Century Artists; Daumier.** N.Y., 1969. 10 vols. Lge. 4to. Orig. cl. (SI. Dec.15; 198) Lire 850,000
- **Manuel de l'Amateur d'Estampes des XIXe et XXe Siècles.** Paris, 1925. 2 vols. Cl., orig. wraps. bnd. in. (SI. Dec.15; 199) Lire 250,000
- **Manuel de l'Amateur d'Estampes du XVIIIe Siècle.—Manuel de l'Amateur d'Estampes des XIXe et XXe Siècles. Complément du Manuel ...** 1911-25-26. 5 vols. Hf. buckram. (HD. Jun.29; 53) Frs. 1,100
- **Le Peintre-Graveur Illustré.** [N.Y.], 1969. *Facs. Reprint of Paris 1926 Edn.* Vols. 20-29 & Index, together 11 vols. in 10. 4to. Orig. cl. (BBA. Sep.8; 45) *Leicester Art Books.* £140
- **Le Peintre Graveur Illustré: Charles-François Daubigny.** Paris, 1921. 4to. Hf. mor., spine faded,

rubbed, orig. wraps. bnd. in. (S. Apr.30; 23) *King.* £130
- **Le Peintre-Graveur Illustré: Corot.** Paris, 1910. *(50) numbered on japon.* 4to. Margin annots., cf., slightly rubbed & spotted. (S. Apr.30; 24) *Brecht.* £260
- **Le Peintre Graveur Illustré: Francisco Goya.** Paris, 1922. 2 vols. in 1. Fo. Orig. etched frontis., crimson hf. lev., orig. upr. wraps. bnd. in. (SG. Jan.26; 200) $325
- **Quarante Dessins de Claude Gelée dit Le Lorrain.** Intro.:– P. de Nolhac. Paris, 1920. *(150).* Sm. fo. Leaves, folder, sigd. by Nolhac. (HD. Jun.6; 43) Frs. 4,500

DELVAU, Alfred
- **Les Heures Parisiennes.** Ill.:– Emile Benassit. Paris, 1866. *1st. Edn. (200) on Dutch Bütten.* Etchings on vell., China & Bütten, some pp. lightly foxed, hand-bnd. hf. mor., orig. wraps. bnd. in, by Champs; Hauswedell coll. (H. May 24; 1263) DM 1,100

DEMACHY & Dübuisson
- **Der Liqueurfabrikant.** Trans.:– S. Hahnemann. Leipzig, 1785. 2 vols. New wraps. (B. Jun.21; 444) Fls. 460

DEMAISON, André
- **Le Livre des Bêtes qu'on appelle Sauvages.** Ill.:– Paul Jouve. Paris, 1934. *(50) with 2 added suites (1 heightened with gouache by Jean Berque & sigd.).* Fo. 44 orig. ills., hf. mor. by Semet et Plumelle, s.-c. (HD. Jun.13; 27) Frs. 6,500

DEMERSON, L.
- **La Botanique Enseignée en Vingt-Deux Leçons.** Paris, 1827. *3rd. Edn.* 12mo. Additional engraved title, frontis., 10 plts., all hand-cold., leath.-bkd. bds., edges worn. (SG. Dec.8; 71) $110

DEMIDOFF, Anatole de
- **Album de Voyage dans la Russie Méridionale et la Crimée.** Ca. 1850. Atlas vol. only. Fo. Litho. title, 100 plts., some light spotting, cont. mor.-bkd. bds. (CSK. Dec.16; 138) £150
- **Voyage dans la Russie Méridionale et la Crimée, par la Hongrie, la Valachie, et la Moldavie.** Ill.:– Raffet. Paris, 1840. *1st. Printing of ills.* 64 woodcuts, including 24 on chine appliqué, unnumbered mus. lf., cont. hf. cf., corners, blind-decor. spine. (HD. Sep.22; 230) Frs. 1,600
- – **Anr. Edn.** Ill.:– Raffet. Paris, 1854. *2nd. Edn.* Cont. havanna chagrin, blind-& gt.-decor. centre arms, decor. spine, inner roulette. (HD. Dec.9; 119) Frs. 4,800

DEMOCRITUS JUNIOR
See— BURTON, Robert 'Democritus Junior'

DE MOIVRE, Abraham
- **The Doctrine of Chances.** L., 1718. *1st. Edn.* 4to. Cont. cf., lettering piece replaced. (PNY. Jun.6; 478) $550

DEMOLDER, E.
- **Le Royaume Authentique du Grand Saint Nicolas.** Ill.:– F. Rops & E. Morannes. Paris, ca. 1890. *(10) De Luxe Edn. on Japan.* 4to. Cont. hf. mor. gt., orig. wraps. bnd. in, rubbed, upr. cover loose. (H. Nov.23; 749) DM 420

DEMOSTHENES
- **De Falsa Legatione contra Aeschinem Oratio.** Strassburg, 1550. Printer's mark on title cold., lr. margin slightly stained, some spotting, cont. vell. from 15th. C. Antiphonar MS., light wear, lacks ties; Conrad (Kunz) Lautenbach's copy, with his owner's mark on title & many old MS. annots., owner's mark of Philipp III. (HK. Nov.8; 160) DM 1,150
- **Logoi, kai Prooimia Demegorika, kai Epistolai [graece].** Paris, 1570. Fo. Some light spotting, 17th. C. Fr. mor., spine & covers with semé de fleurs-de-lys, rebkd. with orig. spine preserved, covers somewhat scuffed. (S. Oct.11; 394) *Maggs.* £120
- **Opera Graecolatina.** Ed.:– Hieronymus Wolf. Basel, 1572. Fo. Greek & Latin text, some foxing, old cf., disbnd. (SG. Apr.19; 70) $100
See— AESCHINES-DEMOSTHENES

DEMOTTE, G.J.
- **La Tapisserie Gothique.** Preface:– Salomon Reinach. Paris, 1924. Atlas fo. 100 mntd. cold. plts., each liby.-stpd. on blank verso. pict. cl. (SG. May 3; 135) $475

DE MOUSSY, V. Martin
- **Description Géographiquue et Statistique De La Confederation Argentine.** Paris, 1860-73. *Text: 1st. Edn.,Atlas: 2nd. Edn.* 3 vols. text & Atlas. Fo. & 8vo. Litho. title, 29 double-p. maps & diagrams, sm. liby. stp. on 3 title-pp., cont. cl., spines gt., not unif. (BBA. Feb.9; 282) *Remington.* £170

DENHAM, Maj. Dixon & Clapperton, Hugh
- **Narrative of Travels & Discoveries in Northern & Central Africa.** 1826. 2 vols. in 1. 4to. Steel-engraved frontis., 36 plts., 1 cold. aquatint, 1 folding map, cleanly torn, some light dampstaining, cont. diced cf., rebkd., lightly rubbed. (CSK. Jan.27; 103) £120
- – **Anr. Edn.** 1828. *3rd. Edn.* 2 vols. Folding map, 2 folding charts, 11 engraved plts., including 1 hand-cold., cont. cf., gt.-decor. spines. (TA. Nov.17; 2) £76

DENHAM, Hon. Sir John
- **Poems & Translations, with the Sophy.** 1684. *3rd.Imp.* Some ll. closely cropped on top margin, later hf. mor., gt.-decor. spine, rubbed. [Wing D1007] (TA. Jun.21; 346) £50

DENIS, Claudius
- **Etudes & Idées de Décoration Moderne.** Paris, ca. 1902. Fo. 32 pochoir-cold. plts., plts. with liby. stp. on verso, 1 stpd. in recto margin, plts. loose as iss., cl.-bkd. bd. folder. (SG. Jan.26; 172) $175

DENIS, Maurice
- **Carnets de Voyages en Italie ...** Ill.:– J.G. & G. Beltrand. 1925. *(175).* 4to. Leaves, portfo. (HD. Jun.29; 58) Frs. 1,700

DENNIS, Faith
- **Three Centuries of French Domestic Silver: Its Makers.** N.Y., 1960. 2 vols. Tall 4to. Silver-ornamented cl., box. (SG. Oct.13; 319) $375

DENNIS, John
- **The Grounds of Criticism in Poetry.** 1704. *1st. Edn.* Hf.-title, cont. cf. (BBA. Aug.18; 68) *Jarndyce.* £240

DENON, Dominique Vivant, Baron
- **Travels in Upper & Lower Egypt.** Trans.:– A. Aikin. 1803. *1st. Engl. Edn.* 3 vols. 60 engraved plts., some slight browning, cont. spr. cf., spines gt.; Sir Ivar Colquhoun, of Luss copy. (CE. Mar.22; 88) £240
- **Voyage dans Egypte.** L., ca. 1820. Fo. Frontis., folding map, folding plt., 3 double-p. plts., 54 single-p. plts., hf. cf., as a coll., w.a.f. (GM. Dec.7; 720) £130
- **Voyage Dans la Basse et la Haute Egypt.** L., n.d. Plt. vol. only. Fo. 61 plts., stained, hf. cf. defect. (P. May 17; 138) *Wood.* £85

DENSHIN, A.
- **Vyatskaya Clinyannaya Ingruschka [Viatka Terracotta Toys].** Moscow, 1917. *1st. Edn. (300).* 4to. decor. wraps., sigd. by author below 1st. ill., ills. hand-cold. & heightened with gold by author. (S. Nov.22; 375) *Glendale.* £220

DENTON, John Bailey
- **The Farm Homesteads of England.** 1865. *2nd. Edn.* Tinted litho. frontis., 68 plts., text & plts. loose, orig. cl. gt. (P. Jun.7; 308) £55

DENTON, Sherman Foote
- **As Nature Shows Them: Moths & Butterflies of the United States East of the Rocky Mountains.** Boston, [1898]-1900. *1st ltd. Edn. in book form. (500) numbered.* 2 vols. 4to. Black-&-white halftone photographic reproductions, & 56 full-p. plts. of butterflies & moths with their bodies engraved & hand-cold., their actual wing scales hand appliqued, almost all plts. include 2 examples, each on sm. sheets mntd. onto linen-hinged sheets, later crushed Turkey mor., raised bands, gt. panels with stpd. lepidoptera designs, duplicated at corners of cover panels, inner gt. dentelles. marb. end-papers. (HA. May 4; 248) £450

D'EON DE BEAUMONT, Chevalie
- Les Loisirs. Amst., 1775. *1st. Edn.* 13 vols. in 7. Vol. 4 with 1 lf. supplied in facs., cont. cf., slightly rubbed. (BBA. Jan.19; 22) *Aspin.* £60

DE ORATIONE ... /Sefer Hatarat Nedarim.
Verona, 1827. Owner's stps. in title & frontis. margins, cont. wraps. (SG. Feb.2; 171) $550

DE PAGES, M.
- Travels Round the World in the Years 1767, 1768, 1769, 1770, 1771 ... 1793. *2nd. Engl. Edn.* 3 vols. Hf. cf. (KH. May 1; 218) Aus. $550

DEPARCIEUX, Antoine
- Essai sur les Probabilitiés de la Durée de la Vie Humaine. Paris, 1746. *Orig. Edn.* Sm. 4to. Cont. diced roan, lr. cover rubbed, spine decor. (HD. Nov.9; 169) Frs. 3,600

DEPERTHES, Jean Louis Hubert Simon
- Histoire des Naufrages. Ill.:– Marillier. Paris, 1788-89. 3 vols. Hf.-titles, 6 engraved plts., cont. mott. cf., spines gt.; armorial bkplt. of Admiral Duff, 1858. (SG. Apr.26; 69) $325

DEPONS, Francois
- Travels in Parts of South America. L., 1806. (*Bound with:*) HELMS, Anthony Zachariah
- Travels from Buenos Ayres, by Potosi to Lima. L., 1807. Together 2 works in 1 vol. Some ll. rather soiled, mod. cf.-bkd. cl. (BBA. Dec.15; 52) *Waggett.* £60
- Travels in South America. L., 1807. 2 vols. Folding map foxed, hf. cf. [Sabin 19643] (S. Jun.25; 92) *Traylen.* £100

DEPORTE VELOCIPEDICO
Madrid, 1895. Nos. 1-44. Lge. fo. Publishers cl. (DS. Dec.16; 2016) Pts. 80,000

DEPPING, George Bernhard
- Les Jeunes Voyageurs en France. Paris, 1830. *3rd. Edn.* 6 vols. Sm. 12mo. 106 views & maps, cont. hf. cf., limp decor. spines, slightly soiled. (HD. Jan.30; 43) Frs. 1,150

DEPREAUX, Albert
- Costumes Militaires de France au XVIIIème Siecle. Paris, 1945. Hf. chagrin. (HD. Jan.27; 134) Frs. 1,500
- Exposition Coloniale, 1931. Armée Francaise d'Outre-Mer. Les Uniformes des Troupes de la Marine et des Troupes Coloniales et Ward Africaine. Paris, 1931. Hf. chagrin, wrap. preserved. (HD. Jan.27; 135) Frs. 1,300
- Soldats de la Grande Armée 1807-1808. Vu par un Artiste Allemand Contemporain. Paris, 1942-43. *(10) numbered.* Square 8vo. Nominative copy, 98 cold. plts. mntd. on guards, hf. chagrin, wrap.; Pierre Benigni copy. (HD. Jan.27; 133) Frs. 7,500

DE PRINGY
[–] Les Differents Caractères des Femmes du Siècle. Paris, 1694. *1st. Edn.* Inner margins slightly wormed, cont. cf. (TA. Nov.17; 415) £70

DE QUINCEY, Thomas
[–] Confessions of an English Opium-Eater. 1822. *1st. Edn.* 12mo. Hf.-title, lacks advt. lf. at end, slight spotting, cont. russ., gt.-decor. spine. (SKC. Jan.13; 2202) £210
- - **Anr. Copy.** 12mo. Hf.-title, lacks advt. lf. at end, cont. blind-stpd. cf., mor.-bkd. box. (S. Mar.20; 867) *Sawyer.* £180
- - **Anr. Copy.** 8vo. Hf.-title, lacks advt. lf., cont. cf.; George Augustus Legge bkplt. (BBA. Jan.19; 220) *Spencer.* £100
- - **Anr. Copy.** 12mo. Hf.-title, advt. lf., hf.-title partly glued to endpaper, offsetting from bkplt., orig. bds., unc., spine reprd. & worn, mor.-bkd. folding box; bkplt. of E.D.Lieberman, Fred A.Berne copy. (SPB. May 16; 211) $250
- Levana & Our Ladies of Sorrow. Ill.:– B. Shahn. N.Y., 1931. *(12) numbered with text sigd. by artist & publisher.* Fo. Plts. hinged & matted as iss., the 12 pp. of tall 8vo. text in self-wraps. inserted, 4 p. publisher's order form laid in, unbnd. in gt.-pict. four-way folder, worn & soiled, cl. ties; each plt. sigd. in pencil by artist. (SG. Nov.3; 190) $1,500

- The Works. Edinb., 1871. *3rd. Edn.* 16 vols. Panel. hf. cf. gt. (PD. Oct.19; 60) £90
- The Collected Writings. 1889-90. 14 vols. Hf. cf. gt., panel spines. (P. Feb.16; 220) £75

DERAND, Francois
- L'Architecture des Voutes, ou l'Art des Traits, et Coupe des Voutes. Paris, 1643. *1st. Edn.* Fo. 3A1 torn across & reprd. with some damage to diagram, sm. rusthole in Z4, a few slight margin defects not affecting text or diagrams, a few light stains, cont. Engl. cf., rebkd., corners worn; Earl of Bute & Luton Liby. bkplts. (S. Dec.20; 799) *Greenwood.* £120

DERHAM, William
- The Artificial Clock-Maker. A Treatise of Watch, & Clock-work. By W.D. L., 1696. *1st. Edn.* Folding engraved frontis. torn & reprd., last addenda lf. slightly torn, soiled thro.-out, mod. cf. [Wing D1099] (BBA. Nov.30; 100) *Walford.* £400
- - **Anr. Edn.** 1700. *2nd. Edn.* 2 pts. in 1 vol. 12mo. 1 folding plt. only, some light browning, cont. cf., rebkd., old spine preserved. [Wing D1100] (CSK. Dec.16; 100) £80

DERHAM, William
See— RAY, John

DE RICCI, Seymour
- Catalogue of a Collection of Mounted Porcelain belonging to E.M. Hodgkins. Paris, 1911. *(200) numbered.* Ob. fo. Slightly spotted, orig. cl., slightly soiled. (BBA. Nov.10; 273) *Leicester Art Books.* £65
- A Census of Caxtons. 1906. 4to. Orig. buckram-bkd. bds., spine a little worn; H.M. Nixon coll., with many MS. annots. (BBA. Oct.6; 199) *Quaritch.* £130
- English Collectors of Books & Manuscripts (1530-1930) & their Marks of Ownership. Camb., 1930. *[1st. Edn.].* Cl.; H.M. Nixon coll., with his MS. notes. (BBA. Oct.6; 40) *Quaritch.* £130
- - **Anr. Copy.** Orig. cl., d.-w. (S. May 1; 388) *Dawson.* £70

See— CLAWSON, John
See— SCHIFF, Mortimer L.

DE RICCI, Seymour & Wilson, W.J.
- Census of Medieval & Renaissance Manuscripts in the United States & Canada. N.Y., 1961, 1940, 1962. *Index & Supp.: 1st. Edns., rest: Kraus Reprints.* 3 vols., & Supp. 4to. Unif. buckram. (SG. Sep.15; 107) $175

DE RIENZI, G.L. Domeny
- Océanie, ou Cinquième Partie du Monde; Revue Géographique et Ethnographique ... Paris, 1836-37. 3 vols. Qtr. mor. (KH. May 1; 219) Aus. $170

DERING, Sir Edward
See— HENRY VIII, King of England—DERING, Sir Edward

DERLETH, August
- The Adventure of the Orient Express. Ill.:– Henry Lauritzen. N.Y., Candlelight Pr., 1965. *1st. Edn.* Lge. 12mo. Ills., pict. wraps., stapled, d.-w., publisher's ll-p. catalogue laid in; inscr. (SG. Apr.19; 262) $110
- Praed Street Papers. Ill.:– Frank Utpatel. N.Y., Candlelight Pr., 1965. *1st. Edn.* Lge. 12mo. Pict. wraps., stapled, d.-w. (SG. Apr.19; 266) $120

DE ROOS, Frederick Fitzgerald
- Personal Narrative of Travels in the United States & Canada in 1826. L., 1827. *1st. Edn.* Folding panorama, 2 maps, ll plts., lacks hf.-title, a few margin stains to panorama, cont. hf. cf., extremities worn; the Rt. Hon. Visc. Eccles copy. [Sabin 19677] (CNY. Nov.18; 83) $200
- - **Anr. Copy.** Light browning thro.-out. bkplt., early cf., rebkd. with orig. backstrip laid down, rubbed, some wear at corners. (HA. May 4; 365) $130

DE ROSSI, Azariah ben Moshe
- Meor Eynayim. Mantua, 18 Nov. 1573-75. 4to. Additional ll. at end, additional censorship lf. laid down on verso of title, slight trace of worming in margin & on a few prelim ll., slight staining & browning, margin glosses in several hands, bds.;

traces of Hochschule für die Wissenschaft des Judenthums stps. [Steinschneider 4448, 1] (SPB. Jun.26; 9) $3,250
- - **Anr. Edn.** Mantua, 1574. 4to. Repairs to title & a few final ll., traces of worming & staining with a few losses, 1 lf. torn with loss replaced in MS., bdg. not stated. (SPB. Feb.1; 38) $500

DE-ROSSI, Johannes Bernardus
- Annales Hebraeo-Typographici sec.XV. Parma, 1795. Fo. A few ll. slightly soiled, later hf. mor., rubbed. (BBA. Feb.9; 215) *Stewart.* £120

DERRIERE LE MIROIR
[Paris, 1957]. Nos. 94-103 in 5 vols. Fo. Unbnd. in col.-pict. wraps., orig. blind-pict. heavy linen folder, cl. ties. (SG. Mar.29; 128) $140
- - **Anr. Edn.** [Paris, 1960-64]. Nos. 118-122 in 5 vols. Fo. Unbnd. in col.-pict. wraps., orig. blind-pict. linen folder, cl. ties. (SG. Mar.29; 129) $110

DERRYDALE PRESS
See— BAKER, Charles H., Jr.
See— BUCKINGHAM, Nash
See— CLARK, Roland
See— CONNETT, Eugene V.
See— CURTIS, Paul A.
See— DE GOUY, L.P.
See— GEE, Ernest R.
See— GRAY, David
See— HERBERT, Henry William 'Frank Forester'
See— HERVEY, John
See— HUNT, Lynn Bogue
See— JENNINGS, Preston J.
See— KIRMSE, Marguerite
See— LANIER, Henry Wysham
See— MANCHESTER, Herbert
See— MARKLAND, Abraham
See— SHELDON, Col. Harold P.
See— SOMERVILLE, Edith Oenone & Martin, Violet Florence 'Martin Ross'
See— SPILLER, Burton L.
See— STONE, Herbert L. & Loomis, Alfred F.
See— VOSBURGH, Walter S.
See— WILLIAMS, Ben Ames

DESAGULIERS, John Theophilus
- A Course of Experimental Philosophy. L., 1734-44. *1st. Edn.* 2 vols. 4to. Subscribers list, errata, 1 lf. reprd., cont. cf., size not unif., some wear; E.N. de C. Andrade bkplts., John D. Stanitz copy. (SPB. Apr.25; 118) $600
- - **Anr. Edn.** L., 1763. *3rd. Edn.* 2 vols. 4to. Some light spotting & browning, cont. cf., spine gt., rebkd., orig. spine laid down, inner hinges strengthened, some chipping; John D. Stanitz coll. (SPB. Apr.25; 119) $175

DESARGES, Henri
- Grande Encyclopédie Pratique de Mécanique et d'Electricité. Paris, 1913. 5 vols. including Atlas. 4to. Bds. (HD. Mar.14; 183) Frs. 1,150

DESARGUES, Gaspard
- La Manière Vniverselle povr poser l'Essiev & placer les Heures & autres Choses aux Cadrans av Soleil. Ed.:– A. Bosse. Paris, 1643. *1st. Edn.* 4to. 2 pp. misbnd., minimal spotting & light browning, cont. cf., spine torn, slightly bumped, cover spotted & wormed. (H. May 22; 221) DM 550

DESAULT, Pierre Joseph
- Journal de Chirurgie. Paris, 1791. 4 vols. Cont. cf. (HD. Mar.21; 24) Frs. 4,000

DESBOEUF, Capt.
- Souvenirs—Les Etapes d'un Soldat de l'Empire (1800-1815). Paris, 1901. Hf. cf., wrap. preserved. (HD. Jan.27; 25) Frs. 1,100

DESCARTES, René
- Alle de Werken. Trans.:– J.H. Glasemaker. Amst., 1690-92. Pts. I-III (of 4). 4to. Cf. (B. Apr.27; 563) Fls. 800
- Discours de la Methode ... Paris, 1668. 4to. Cf. (DS. Feb.24; 2459) Pts. 95,000
- Epistolae. Amst., 1683. *1st. Latin Edn.* 3 pts. in 2 vols. 4to. Cont. vell.; Dr. Walter Pagel copy. (S. Feb.7; 92) *Morris.* £220
- Geometria Anno 1637. Ed.:– Florimondi de Beaune. Munich, 1651. Slightly browned, slightly spotted with minimal worming, cont. vell., spine

DESCARTES, René-*Contd.*

renewed, slightly spotted & defect. (D. Nov.23; 489a) DM 1,700
- L'Homme ... et la Formation de Foetus, avec les Remarques de Louis de La Forge.—Le Monde ou Traité de la Lumière. Ed.:– Clerselier. Paris, 1677. *[2nd. Edn.].* 4to. Cont. red mor., spine decor. (HD. Mar.29; 26) Frs. 28,000
- – Anr. Copy. 4to. Cont. cf., decor. spine. (HD. Sep.22; 233) Frs. 3,200
- Meditationes de Prima Philosophia. 1668. Sm. 4to. Sm. wormhole in outer margin, cf. (P. Sep.29; 166) £50
- Opera Philosophica. Amst., 1649/50. 4 works (6 pts.) in 1 vol. 4to. Some old spotting, especially in margin, vell., some wear. (V. Oct.1; 3731) DM 1,200
- Opuscula Posthuma, Physica et Mathematica. Amst., 1701. *1st. Edn.* 6 pts. in 1 vol. 4to. Faint stp. on title, cont. cf., worn. (SG. Oct.27; 83) $225
- Les Principes de la Philosophie. Paris, 1681. *4th. Edn.* 4to. Some light paper browning, cont. leath. gt., lr. corner slightly bumped. (R. Apr.3; 548) DM 530
- Principia Philosophiae: of Beginselen der Wysbegeerte ... Trans.:– J.H. Glazemaker. Amst., 1657. (*Bound with:*) LANDSBERGEN, P. - Bedenckingen op den Dagelijckschen, ende Iaerlijckschen Loop van den Aerdt-kloot ... Middleburgh, 1650. Together 2 works in 1 vol. Cont. vell., spine slightly darkened; from Dr. Hermann Rex liby. (VA. Apr.26; 111) R 170
- Principia Philosophiae; Specimina Philosophiae; Passiones Animae. Amst., 1656. 3 pts. in 1 vol. Sm. 4to. 1st. index lf. cropped 3rd. pt. lacks L3 & 2E4 (?blank), soiled thro.-out, some ll. trimmed or slightly worn, cont. cf. worn. (BBA. May 3; 24) *Rix.* £65
- – Anr. Copy. 3 pts. in 1 vol. Sm. 4to. Cont. hf. cf. (LM. Oct.22; 122) B. Frs. 10,000
- – Anr. Edn. Amst., 1692. 3 pts. in 1 vol. Mod. buckram. (SG. Oct.27; 84) $200

DESCHAMPS, P. & Brunet, G.
See— BRUNET, Jacques Charles

DESCOLE, Horacio R.
- Genera et Species Animalium Argentinorum. Buenos Aires, 1948-67. *Ltd. Edn., numbered & sigd. by Director.* 4 vols. Lge. 4to. Linen in antique herbal style, 1 vol. loose in bdg. (SKC. Oct.26; 354) £210

DESCOURTILZ, E.
- Code du Safranier, ou Traité Complet de la Culture et des Propriétés du Safran. 1809. Slight foxing, sewed, orig. wrap. (HD. Jul.6; 28) Frs. 2,200
- Flore [Pittoresque et] Medicale des Antilles. Paris, 1821-29. *1st. Edn.* (5) *in fo.* 8 vols. Fo. Vols. 3, 4 & 5 without title ll. (not publd.?), lacks 2 plts., 1 plt. double, cont. red hf. leath. gt., gold-tooled, crowned monog. of Marie Luise, corners slightly rubbed, vol. 1 upr. cover with scratch, vol. 3 spine faded & jnts. defect., some jnts. with slight worming. [Sabin 5,363] (D. Nov.23; 433) DM 25,000

DESCRIPTION DE L'EGYPTE, ou Recueil des Observations et des Recherches qui ont été faites en Egypte pendant l'Expédition de l'Armée Française.—Préface Historique.—Explication des Planches
Preface:– J.-B. Fourier. Paris, 1809-22. 13 vols. Lge. fo. & sheets. 892 plts. (of 894), proofs on vell., hf. cl., corners, unc.; from Maréchal Soult liby. (HD. May 16; 16) Frs. 35,200

DESCRIPTION DE TOUTES LES NATIONS DE L'EMPIRE DE RUSSIE ...
St. Petersb., 1776. 'Première Collection': 1 vol. 4to. 25 hand-cold. plts., hf. mor., w.a.f. (C. Nov.16; 77) *Al-Saud.* £240
- – Anr. Copy. 'Première Collection' & 'Seconde Collection': 2 pts. in 1 vol. 4to. 54 (of 55) hand-cold. engraved plts., titles in German, Fr. & Russian, no text, red hf. mor., w.a.f. (C. Nov.16; 76) *Hannas.* £190

DESCRIPTION DES CEREMONIES et des Fêtes qui ont eu Lieu pour le Baptême de S.A.R. Monseigneur le Duc de Bordeaux, Petit-fils de France
Ill.:– after Hittorff, Lecointe & Chasselat. Paris, 1827. Lge. fo. Cont. hf. russ. bds. gt., fleurs-de-lys on spine. (HD. May 21; 88) Frs. 3,000

DESCRIPTION OF ANIMALS, of Different Countries
Haverhill, [Mass.], 1809. 16mo. Lacks wraps., disbnd. (SG. Dec.8; 103) $110

DESCRIPTION OF ENGLAND & WALES, Containing a Particular Account of Each Country
L., 1769-70. *1st. Edn.* 10 vols. 12mo. 229 (of 240) engraved plts., cont. cf., spines gt. (S. Mar.6; 236) *Hayden.* £150
- – Anr. Copy. 10 vols. 12mo. Cont. spr. cf. gt. (LC. Jul.5; 190) £145

DESCRIPTION OF A SIEGE OF BASING CASTLE
Oxford, 1644. Unbnd. [Wing D 1170] (P. Jul.5; 132) £50

DESCRIZIONE ISTORICA DELL'ESTRA-ZIONE DELLA PUBBLICA NAVE, LA FENICE, Al Canal Spignon, in cui giacque tre Anni totalmente sommersa
Venezia, 1789. 4to. Cont. marb. bds., loose. (SI. Dec.15; 71) Lire 1,300,000

DESEINE, François
- Rome Moderne, Première Ville de l'Europe, avec Toutes ses Magnificences et ses Délices. Leyde, 1713. 6 vols. 12mo. Double-p. frontis., 105 plts., cont. cf., some sm. defects. (HD. Mar.19; 44) Frs. 2,200

DESFONTAINES, P.F.G.
[-] Der Neue Gulliver, oder die Reise J. Gulluivers, Sohnes des Capitain Lemuel Gulluivers. Trans.:– Abt. de Fontenelle & Selimontes (C.G. Weendt?). Hamburg, 1731. *1st. German Edn.* 2 pts. in 1 vol. Browned, cont. hf. vell., defect. (R. Oct.11; 432) DM 450

DESFONTAINES, René Louiche
- Les Bains de Diane, ou Le Trionphe de L'Amour. Paris, 1770. *1st. Edn.* Slightly soiled, later mor., spine gt., unc., rubbed. (BBA. Jul.27; 83) *Cavendish Rare Books.* £70

DESGODETZ, Antoine
- The Ancient Buildings of Rome. 1771. Vol. 1 only (of 2). Fo. 61 engraved plts., 1 spotted, cont. cf., brkn., covers detchd. (C. Dec.9; 184) *D'Arcy.* £65
- – Anr. Edn. 1771-95. 2 vols. Fo. 137 plts., text in Engl. & Fr., mod. cl.; Bg'ham. Liby. stp. on plts. (P. Feb.16; 170) £130
- Les Edifices Antiques de Rome. Ill.:– De Chastillon, Le Clerc, & others. Paris, 1682. *1st. Edn.* Fo. Engraved architectural title, 137 engraved plts., several double-p., a few margin tears reprd., 1 slightly affecting penultimate plt., cont. cf., rubbed. (C. Mar.14; 7) *Marlborough.* £380
- – Anr. Copy. Fo. Engraved architectural title, 137 plts., including 21 double-p., minor stains to 1 plt., a few margins slightly soiled, cont. mott. cf., worn; sigs. of Robert Williamson & Sir James Thornhill on title. (C. Dec.9; 183) *Weinreb.* £350
- – Anr. Copy. Tall fo. Engraved title, 137 full & double-p. engraved plts., few ll. stained, ex-liby., mod. qtr. mor. (SG. May 3; 136) $1,300

DESHAIRS, Leon
- Le Grand Trianon: Architecture, Decoration, Ameublement.—Le Petit Trianon. Paris, [1908]. Together 2 vols. Tall fo. 60 & 102 plts., ex-liby., crimson three-qtr. mor. (SG. May 3; 137) $275

DESIGNS FOR SHOP-FRONTS & DOOR CASES
Ca. 1785. Lge. 4to. Engraved title, 26 plts., slightly spotted & soiled thro.-out, cont. cf.-bkd bds., rebkd & recornered, slightly rubbed; owners stp. & sig. of Wm. Stephenson Feb. 1796 on front free end-paper. (BBA. Feb.9; 245) *Quevedo.* £380

DESMAREST, Anselme Gaëtan
- Histoire Naturelle des Tangaras, des Manakins et des Todiers. Ill.:– Gremilliet after Madame Knip (Pauline Decourcelles). Paris, 1805[-07]. Fo. 72 etched plts., ptd. in black & white & hand-cold.,

but for those showing the Todier Sylvain, where supporting tree-trunk is ptd. in green & brown, & that showing the Tangara Varie, where sm. part only of branch is ptd., in brown, generally including only name of artist, Pauline Decourcelles, & etcher, Gramilliet, few also include name of printer, Rousset (or Millevoy), some also show name of printer very faintly, slight spotting, cont. mor.-bkd. bds., rebkd., old spine laid down, rubbed. (S. Feb.1; 17) *Parker.* £5,500

DESMAREST, Jean
See— BONNE, Rigobert & Desmarest, Jean

DE SMET, Pierre Jean
- Letters & Sketches with a Narrative of a Year's Residence among the Indian Tribes of the Rocky Mountains. Phila., 1843. *1st. Edn. 1st. Iss.* with text ending on p.252. Folding explanatory plt., 12 litho. plts., folding plt. slightly frayed at edge, orig. cl., corners & spine ends worn; the Rt. Hon. Visc. Eccles copy. [Sabin 82262] (CNY. Nov.18; 84) $380

DESNARNOD, A.
See— SAYGER, C. & Desnarnod, A.

DESNOS, Louis Charles
- Atlases de la France. Paris, 1775. 12mo. Engraved dedication, title & frontis., 48 double-p. maps, table, cont. mor. gt. (P. Jun.7; 336) £55
- Nouvel Itinerarie Général ... Paris, 1766. Sections II-V in 1 vol. 4to. Double-p. engraved title, engraved list of maps, 24 double-p. hand-cold. maps, some folding, mntd. on guards, cont. wraps., upr. cover torn, lacks backstrip. (C. Nov.16; 206) *Burgess.* £150

DESNOS, Robert
- C'est les Bottes de 7 Lieues. Cette Phrase 'Je me vois'. Ill.:– André Masson. 1926. *Orig. Edn. (112).* 4to. On vergé d'Arches sigd. by author & artist, sewed. (HD. Dec.9; 122) Frs. 7,500
- Les Sans Cou. Ill.:– André Masson. Paris, 1934. *Orig. Edn., (113). (10)* on velin pur fil with 2 etchings. 4to. Sewed; sigd. in pencil by author & artist., autograph dedication to Adolphe Aymaud. (HD. Apr.13; 158) Frs. 7,800

DE SOTO, Hernando
- Histoire de la Conqueste de la Floride. Paris, 1685. *1st. Edn. in Fr.* 12mo. Liby. stps., cont. cf., rehinged; Astor Liby. copy. (SG. Oct.20; 131) $200
- – Anr. Edn. Leiden, 1731. *New Edn.* 2 vols. in 1. Cont. cf., spine worn. (TA. Oct.20; 63) £58

DESPARMET FITZ-GERALD, Xavière
- L'oeuvre Peint de Goya. Paris, 1928-50. *(764).* 2 text vols. 2 plt. vols. Lge. 4to. Orig. wraps. & orig. hf. linen portfo., s.-c., slight stains, unc., w.a.f. (HK. May 17; 3440) DM 400

D[ESPARS], N. & F.R.
- Chronyke van Vlaenderen ... Borgerlycke Oneenigheden Benginnende 621 tot 1725. Ill.:– J. Peeters (map) & N. Heylbrouck (engrs.). Brugge, [1725-]36. 3 vols. in 4. Fo. Lacks lge. folding prospect of Antw., foxing, cont. hf. cf., unc., spines slightly defect. (VS. Dec.9; 1194) Fls. 700

DESPAUTERIUS, Johannes
- [Works] Grammatica; Syntaxis; Rudimenta; Orthographia; De Figuris; Ars Versificatoria. [Lyon], 1530-31. 6 pts. in 1 vol. 4to. Some stains, wormed, cont. vell., shabby. (SG. Feb.9; 213) $200

DES PERIERS, Bonaventure
- Cymbalum Mundi ou Dialogues Satyriques sur Différents Sujets ... Notes:– Falconnet & Lancelot. Amst. [Paris], 1732. 12mo. Cont. spr. cf. gt., Pompadour arms, spine decor. (HD. Nov.9; 25) Frs. 6,200
- Recueil des Oeuvres. Lyon, 1544. Sm. 8vo. Lacks final lf. 'au lecteur', as usual, 18th. C. cf. gt., spine decor. (HD. Nov.9; 5) Frs. 15,500

D'ESPINELLE
[-] Les Muses Françoises ralliées Divers Pars. Paris, 1599. *Orig. Edn.* 2 pts. in 1 vol. 12mo. 'Les Ténèbres ... ', 1599, between the 2 pts., cont. mor., silver decor. (HD. Mar.29; 27) Frs. 32,000

DESPORTES, Philippe
- Les Oeuvres. Rouen, 1611. 12mo. Privilege lf. (dtd. 18 Feb. 1611), owner's stp., 19th. C. qtr. mor. by Pagnant. (SG. Oct.27; 85) $100

DESSINS SYMBOLISTES
Preface:– André Breton. Ill.:– Emile Bernard. Paris, 1958. *Orig. Edns. Vol. 1: (150) on Rives, sigd. by Breton.* 2 vols. Sm. sq. 8vo. Sewed; sigd. orig. pen ill. in 1st. vol. (HD. Dec.16; 110) Frs. 2,850

DESTAILLEUR, H.
- Receuil d'Estampes Relatives à l'Ornementation des Appartements au XVIe, XVIIe, et XVIIIe Siècles. Ill.:– Pfnor, Carresse & Reister, after Du Cerceau, Lepautre, Berain, Marot, Meissonier, La Londe & others. Paris, 1863-71. 2 vols. Fo. 144 plts. 'gravées en facsimile', some light foxing, cover & title-p. of Vol. I detchd., leath.-bkd. bds., spines chipped. (SG. Aug.25; 150) $130

DESTOMBES, M.
- Cartes Hollandaises. La Cartographie de la Compagnie des Indes Orientales 1593-1743. Saigon, 1941. *(250) numbered.* 4to. Catalogue loosely inserted, wraps.; pres. inscr. from author. (S. Jun.25; 289) *Tooley.* £220
- La Mappemonde de Petrus Plancius gravée par Josua van den Ende 1604. Saigon, 1944. *(260) numbered.* Fo. Orig. bds.; pres. inscr. from author. (S. Jun.25; 290) *Tooley.* £50

DESTOUCHES, Louis Ferdinand 'Louis Ferdinand Céline'
- Mort à Crédit, Roman. Paris, [1936]. *Orig. Edn.* Sewed; sigd. autograph dedication by author on hf.-title. (HD. May 3; 214) Frs. 1,700
– – Anr. Edn. Ill.:– Gen Paul. 1942. *1st. Ill. Edn. (12) on tinted vell.* 15 plts., hand-cold. by artist, chagrin by F. Thiébault, mosaic spine, wrap., s.-c.; added port., author's sig. & A.N. by artist. (HD. Apr.13; 155) Frs. 8,000

DESTOUCHES, Philippe Néricault
- Oeuvres de Théâtre. Paris, 1745. 5 vols. 12mo. Cont. marb. cf. gt., arms in centre; La Rochefoucauld ex-libris. (HD. Sep.22; 234) Frs. 3,500
- Oeuvres Dramatiques. Paris, 1757. 4 vols. 4to. Cont. cf. gt., decor. spines, inited roll-stp., 3 turn-ins restored. (HD. Sep.22; 304) Frs. 1,800
- Voyage au Bout de la Nuit. Ill.:– Gen-Paul. 1942. *1st. Ill. Edn. (285) on alfa.* Ills. heightened by artist, chagrin by F. Thiébault, mosaic spine, s.-c.; sigd. by author, long autograph dedication by artist. (HD. Apr.13; 157) Frs. 6,500

DESTREE, Joseph & others
- Les Musées Royaux du Parc du Cinquantenaire et de la Port-de-Hal à Bruxelles. Brussels, ca. 1930?. 2 vols. Tall fo. Plts., ach liby.-stpd. on blank verso, loose in bds., linen ties, 28 pt. covers preserved. (SG. May 3; 138) $200

DESTUTT DE TRACY
- Traité d'Economie Politique. Paris, 1823. 16mo. Cf. (HD. Feb.22; 50) Frs. 1,300

DETAILLE, Edouard
- L'Armée Francaise. Paris, 1885-89. 2 vols. Fo. Hf. chagrin, corners. (HD. Jan.27; 254) Frs. 2,800
- Types et Uniformes, L'Armée Francaise. Text:– Jules Richard. Paris, 1885-89. 2 vols. Hf. leath. & marb. bds., edges & spine nicked & rubbed. (RS. Jan.17; 464) $225

DETMOLD, Edward J.
- Twenty-Four Nature Pictures. N.Y. & L., n.d. *(500) numbered sets of 1st. proofs, sigd.* Fo. Cl.-bkd. ptd. bd. folder, bumped, lightly soiled flaps detchd., ex-liby. (SG. Jan.12; 84) $275

DETMOLD, Maurice & Edward
- [Illustrations of Subjects from Kipling's Jungle Book]. L., [1903]. Fo. 12 (of 16) mntd. cold. plts., orig. cl. gt. folder, stained & worn. (S. Nov.22; 318) *Demetzy.* £270

DE TRAFFORD, Sir Humphrey
- Horses of the British Empire. 1907. 2 vols. 4to. Orig. cl. gt., spines faded & rubbed. (TA. Dec.15; 158) £52

DETRI, Nic.
- Arithmetica Nova. Hamburg, 1654. 3 pts. in 1 vol. Slightly browned, MS. vell., slightly spotted. (R. Apr.4; 1513) DM 1,050

DEUCHAR, David
- A Collection of Etchings after the Most Eminent Masters of the Dutch & Flemish Schools. 1803. *1st. Edn.* Orig. cf. (LA. Mar.22; 150) £180
– – Anr. Edn. Edinb., 22 Dec., 1803. 3 vols. Fo. Etched titles & plts., some foxing, owner's stp. on title, cont. red str.-grd. mor., gt.-tooled, jnts. worn. (SG. Apr.26; 70) $1,000

DEUTSCH, Ernst
- Galante Frauen. Vienna, [1917]. *(50) numbered, sigd. & cold. by Deutsch.* Sm. fo. Plts. loose as iss. in lettered bd. folder. (SG. Mar.29; 104) $150

DEUTSCH, Nik. Manuel
- Todtentanz gemalt zu Bern um 1515-1520 lithographiert nach den Getreuen Copien d. Berühmten Kunstmalers. Wilh. Settler. [Bern & Den Haag], ca. 1838. Fo. Litho. title slightly foxed, orig. wraps., defect. (HK. Nov.9; 2214) DM 750

DEUTSCHE GEDENKHALLE
Ed.:– M. Herzig. [Berlin & Leipzig, 1905]. Lge. fo. Orig. pig over wood bds., decor. metal bosses, metal clasps, loose, enamel inlays, cold end-papers, slightly bumped & worn, 2 defects. (H. May 22; 486) DM 720

DEUTSCHE JUGENDKALENDER
Ill.:– L. Richter & others. Leipzig, 1847-58. 10 years (all publd.). Slightly foxed, late 19th. C. linen, orig. wraps. (GB. Nov.4; 1735) DM 1,000

DEUTSCHE KUNST UND DEKORATION
Ed.:– Alexander Koch. 1906, 1907, 1911, 1912. 4 vols. 4to. Approx. 25 ll. stained in 1st. vol., linen. (D. Nov.23; 1760) DM 520
– – Anr. Edn. Ed.:– Alexander Koch. Darmstadt, 1916-22. Vols. 39-50. 4to. Linen gt. (D. Nov.24, 3012) DM 520

DEUTSCHE ZEITUNG in der Niederlanden
Amst., 5 Jun. 1940-30 Apr. 1944. Years 1-4 in 10 vols. Lge. fo. Bnd. (B. Feb.8; 990) Fls. 1,500

DEUTSCHES BALLADENBUCH
Ill.:– A. Erhardt & others. Leipzig, 1852. *[1st. Edn.].* Slightly foxed, orig. linen gt. (R. Oct.11; 392) DM 460
– – Anr. Copy. Some foxing, cont. hf. leath. gt. (GB. Nov.4; 1736) DM 450

DE VANSSAY, 5ème Dragon
- Fragments des Mémoires Inédits Ecrits en 1817, sous le Titre de Souvenirs Militaires d'un officier de Dragons pendant les Campagnes de la Grand Armée des Années 1804 à 1811. Mortagne, 1864. 2 vols. in 1. Hf. chagrin, spine faded. (HD. Jan.27; 101) Frs. 2,300

DEVENTER, Hendrijk van
- Manuale Operationen. Ill.:– Ph. Bouttats. Leyden, 1746. *1st. Edn.* 4to. A little margin staining, cont. blind-stpd. cf., defect. (VS. Jun.7; 927) Fls. 725

DEVERIA, Achille
- Les Amours de Vénus et d'Adonis. Paris, N.Y. & L., n.d. Ob. 4to. Cont. hf. chagrin. *(With:)*
- Souvenirs du Théâtre Anglais à Paris. 1827. Light foxing, bradel hf. buckram. (HD. May 4; 248) Frs. 1,600
- Phèdre et les Personnages Historiques ... 1854. 4to. Orig. sketch & 51 orig. ink drawings, cont. hf. chagrin. (HD. May 4; 245) Frs. 8,200
- Rodope la Courtisane ... 1854. 4to. Orig. sketch of title frontis. & 10 orig. ink drawings, cont. hf. chagrin. (HD. May 4; 246) Frs. 2,700

DEVILLE, Achille
- Histoire de l'Art de la Verrerie dans l'Antiquité. Paris, 1871. Lge. 4to. 112 cold. litho. plts., each liby.-stpd. on blank verso. loose in cl.-bkd. ptd. bds., linen ties. (SG. May 3; 139) $275

DE VINNE, Theodore Low
- Title-Pages as Seen by a Printer. N.Y., Grol. Cl., 1901. *(325).* Lge. 8vo. Orig. hf. mor., unc., s.-c. (SG. Jan.5; 121) $225

DEVONSHIRE, Georgiana, Duchess of
- The Passage of Mount St. Gothard, a Poem. Priv. ptd., 1802. *(50).* 4to. Lacks title, some light spotting, cont. vell.-bkd. bds. (CSK. Oct.7; 46) £60

DE VRIESE, Hugo
- Puits et Fontaines. [Antw., 1573]. Ob. 4to. 24 engraved plts., mod. mor. (SSA. Jul.5; 103) R. 420

DEWALD, E.T.
- The Illustrations of the Utrecht Psalter. Princeton, [1932]. Tall fo. 144 plts., ex-liby., gt.-decor. buckram, sm. tear at 1 jnt. (SG. May 3; 140) $140

DEWEES, William P.
- A Treatise on the Physical & Medical Treatment of Children. Phila., 1825. *1st. Edn.* Very foxed, some stains, old cf., brkn. & loose. (SG. Oct.6; 125) $130

DE WINT, P.
- Sicilian Scenery. L., 1823. 4to. Engraved title, 60 steel-engraved plts., captions in Engl. & Fr., lightly foxed, some slight margin stains, cont. hf. leath. gt., slightly bumped. (R. Oct.13; 3139) DM 430

DE WITT, John
See— COURT, P. de la & Witt, John de

DEYRON, Jacques
- Des Anciens Bastimens de Nismes. Grenoble, 1656. *1st. Edn.* 4to. Cont. vell.; Liechenstein bkplt. (SG. Sep.22; 119) $125

DEYSSEL (Contrib.)
See— KRONIEK

DEZALLIER D'ARGENVILLE, Antoine Joseph
See— D'ARGENVILLE, Antoine Joseph Dezallier

DEZAUCHE, J.A.
See— DE L'ISLE, Guillaume & others

D'HAUTEFORT, Ch. V.
- Coup d'Oeil sur Lisbonne et Madrid en 1814 ... Paris, 1820. Bds. (DS. Apr.27; 2070) Pts. 26,000

D'HURCOURT, R.
- De l'eclairage au Gaz. Paris, 1845. Later hf. leath. (D. Nov.23; 673) DM 1,200

DIABLE AMOUREUX, Nouvelle Espagnol
Ill.:– J.E. Laboureur. Paris, 1921. *(475) numbered.* Red crushed lev. by Leonard Chatto, gt. designs on covers, gt. dentelles. (SG. Mar.29; 179) $175

DIABLE A PARIS (Le). Paris et les Parisiens.
Text:– G. Sand, P.J. Stahl, Gozlan, Balzac, G. Sue & others. Ill.:– Gavarni & Bertall. Paris, 1845-46. *1st. Printing of ills.* 2 vols. Lge. 8vo. Wide margins, some slight foxing, lacks plan of Paris (as often), cont. hf. cf., spines decor. (HD. May 4; 249) Frs. 2,100

DIAPER, William
[-] Nereides: or, Sea-Eclogues. L., 1712. *1st. Edn.* Old cf. gt., rebkd.; J.C. Lynn bkplt., Frederic Dannay copy. (CNY. Dec.16; 101) $300

DIARIO FESTIVO DE ... QUE CONTIENE TODAS LAS FIESTAS SOLEMNES ... desta Corte ...
Madrid, 1721. Vell. (DS. Apr.27; 2072) Pts. 30,000

DIAZ, Calvillo J.B.
- Sermon ... por la Victoria del Monte de las Cruces. Mexico City, 1811. 2 pts. in 1 vol. 4to. Qtr. sheep; inscr. of C.M. Bustamente. (SG. Oct.20; 132) $200

DIAZ DEL CASTILLO, Bernal
- The True History of the Conquest of Mexico. L., 1800. 4to. Frontis. map slightly offset onto title, cont. cf., slightly rubbed. (S. Jun.25; 93) *Traylen.* £200

DIAZ DE MONTALVO, Alonso
– **Repertorium Quaestionum super Nicolaum de Tudeschis.** [Nuremb., Anton Koberger], ca. 1485. Fo. Lge. copy, cont. MS. marginalia, slight worming at front & back, a few ll. browned, sm. liby. stp. in lr. margin of fo. 2, mod. bdg. from vell. antiphoner lf. [BMC II, 431; Goff D-174; HC 11565*] (SPB. Dec.14; 13) $1,000

DIAZ DE VALDERRAMA, Fr.-F. 'Don Fermin Arana de Var Dora'
– **Compendio Historico Descriptivo de la Muy Noble et Muy Leal Ciudad de Sevilla Metropoli de Andalucia.** Seville, 1789 [1790]. *2nd. Edn.* 2 pts. in 1 vol. Sm. 4to. Cont. vell. (HD. Dec.2; 85) Frs. 1,000

DIAZ MORANTE, Pedro
– **Arte de escribir.** Madrid, 1624. Fo. Vell. (DS. Apr.27; 2245) Pts. 30,000
– **Tercera Parte del Arte Nueva de Escrivir.** Madrid, 1629. Ob. fo. Linen. (DS. Mar.23; 2083) Pts. 110,000

DIBDIN, Charles
– **Observations of a Tour through Almost the Whole of England, & a Considerable Part of Scotland.** L., 1801; 1802. *1st. Edn.* 2 vols. Lge. 4to. 48 (of 60) aquatint plts, few retaining their tissue-guards, engraved folding plan, & folding table, cont. hf. leath., marb. bds., covers loose, lacks spines. (SG. Jun.7; 344) $100
– – **Anr. Edn.** [1801]. 2 vols. 4to. Cl. (LC. Oct.13; 262) £70

DIBDIN, Rev. Thomas Frognall
– **Aedes Althorpianae, or, An Account of The Mansion, Books, & Pictures at Althorp.** 1822. 2 vols., including Supp. 4to. 32 engraved plts., mor. gt., 1 cover detchd. (P. Sep.8; 54) *Jarndyce.* £90
– **A Bibliographical Antiquarian & Picturesque Four in France & Germany.** L., 1821. *1st. Edn.* 3 vols. 83 engraved plts., few imprints & captions cropped, 1 slightly creased, ills., many on india paper, cont. str.-grd. mor. gt. (S. Apr.9; 20) *Quaritch.* £340
– – **Anr. Copy.** Vols. 1 & 2 only (of 3). 4to. Russ., covers detchd., lacks hf. of 1 spine. (S. Nov.1; 77) *Schwedt.* £70
– – **Anr. Edn.** L., 1829. *2nd. Edn.* 3 vols. Hf.-titles, engraved plts. spotted, slightly browned, orig. cl. (BBA. Mar.7; 202) *C. Cox.* £60
– **The Bibliographical Decameron.** L., 1817. *[1st. Edn.].* 3 vols. 4to. L.P., cont. spr. cf. gt., panel. decor. spines. (P. Dec.8; 363) *Solomon.* £260
– – **Anr. Copy.** 3 vols. Hf.-titles, last imprint & errata ll., some ll. spotted, cont. hf. cf., hinges split. (BBA. Mar.7; 199) *W. Forster.* £150
– – **Anr. Copy.** 3 vols. Lge. 8vo. Hf.-title in each vol., Vol. II with the mntd. sample of gold printing with the binder's note, lacks errata lf. in Vol. I, orig. bds., spine chipped, unc. mod. s.-c.'s. (SG. Sep.15; 108) $300
– – **Anr. Copy.** 3 vols. Lge. 8vo. Some foxing & offsetting, three-qtr. mor. (SG. Sep.15; 109) $250
– – **Anr. Copy.** 3 vols. Lge. 8vo. Elab. gt. red mor. by Ramage, 3 corners bumped, few sm. scratches, unc. (VG. Sep.13; 509) Fls. 700
– **Bibliomania.** L., 1811. *2nd. Edn.* Hf.-title, slightly browned, mod. cl.-bkd. bds. (BBA. Mar.7; 198) *W. Forster.* £50
– – **Anr. Edn.** Ill.:– W.H. Bicknell after H. Pyle. Boston, 1903. *(483).* 4 vols. Sm. 4to. Frontis. etchings in 2 states (on Japan vell. & Holland paper), heavy bds., boxed; J.C. & E.S. Bernheim armorial bkplt. (SG. Sep.15; 111) $200
– – **Anr. Copy.** 4 vols. 4to. Etched frontis., bds., unc. (SG. May 17; 72) $120
– **An Introduction to the Knowledge of Rare & Valuable Editions of the Greek & Latin Classics.** L., 1827. *4th. Edn.* 2 vols. Lge. 8vo. Cf. gt. by Westerton, spines gt. with fleurons, gt. dentelles; armorial bkplt. of Christopher Turnor, Stoke Rochford Liby. (SG. Feb.16; 89) $250
– **Reminiscences of a Literary Life.** 1836. *[1st. Edn].* 2 vols. Cont. diced cf., rebkd. (BBA. Jul.27; 143) *Howes.* £70
– – **Anr. Copy.** 2 vols. Extra-ill. with plts., some cold., mor. gt. by Bayntun. (SPB. Dec.13; 657) $125

DICCIONARIO DE LE LENGUA CASTELLANA Madrid, 1780. Lge. fo. Cf. (DS. Mar.23; 2614) Pts. 28,000

DICK, Stewart
– **The Cottage Homes of England.** Ill.:– Helen Allingham. L., 1909. *(500) numbered & sigd. by artist.* 4to. Orig. cl., partly unc., soiled. (S. Jun.25; 313) *Sotheran.* £60

DICKENS, Charles
– **All the Year Round.** 1859-67. Vols. 1-17. A few ll. slightly spotted, later hf. cf., slightly rubbed. (BBA. Feb.9; 93) *Denison.* £55
– **American Notes for General Circulation.** L., 1842. *1st. Edn. 1st. Iss., with last contents p. in Vol. 1 numbered xvi.* 2 vols. 1 lf. advts. at beginning of Vol. 1, & 6 pp. at end of Vol. 2, gt.-panel cf. by Zaehnsdorf, with stp., entwined gt. reeded banding to bds., pale pink washed silk end-papers, slight fading to spines, orig. blind-blocked cl. bnd. in. (PD. Aug.17; 204) £110
– – **Anr. Copy.** 2 vols. Hf.-titles, 1st. lf. Vol. 1 & last 3 ll. Vol. 2 of advts., rather spotted thro.-out, orig. cl. by Leighton & Elles, with their ticket, faded & slightly rubbed. (BBA. Sep.29; 185) *Jarndyce.* £80
– – **Anr. Copy.** 2 vols. 6 pp. advts. in Vol. II, orig. cl., slight wear. (SG. Mar.15; 104) $300
– – **Anr. Copy.** 2 vols. Lacks advts., cont. three-qtr. pol. cf., lightly rubbed. (RO. Apr.23; 83) $135
– **Bleak House.** Ill.:– 'Phiz'. Mar.1852-Sep.1853. *1st. Edn.,* 20 orig. pts. in 19. Advts., including 'Village Pastor', orig. wraps., in buckram gt. box. (P. Dec.8; 365) *Joseph.* £420
– – **Anr. Copy.** 20 orig. pts. in 19. Lacks 8 advts., orig. wraps., cl. box; from Norman Tarbolton liby. (P. Apr.12; 2) *Jarndyce.* £360
– – **Anr. Copy.** 20 orig. pts. in 19, in 2 vols. Most advts. & slips as listed by Hatton & Cleaver, 2 p. unlisted advt. in Pt. XVI, advts. bnd. in Vol. 2, some items (mostly slips) lacking, gt.-panel. cf. by Zaehnsdorf, with stp., entwined gt. reeded banding to bds., silk liners, slight fading to spines, wraps. at end Vol. 1. (PD. Aug.17; 205) £200
– – **Anr. Copy.** 20 orig. pts. in 19. Advts., some wornholes, light foxing & browning on a few pts., orig. wraps., reprd. (SPB. May 16; 43) $550
– – **Anr. Copy.** 20 orig. pts. in 19. Most advts. as called for, plts., some plts. foxed or browned, orig. ptd. wraps., some repairs to spines, light soiling; Fred A.Berne copy. (SPB. May 16; 221) $400
– – **Anr. Edn.** Ill.:– 'Phiz'. L., 1853. *1st. Edn. in Book-Form.* Some offsetting of frontis. onto engraved title, orig. cl., some spotting; Fred A. Berne copy. (SPB. May 16; 222) $900
– – **Anr. Copy.** Some minor foxing & soiling, publisher's cl., worn, inner jnts. brkn. (RO. Apr.23; 86) $250
– – **Anr. Copy.** Minor foxing, soiling, &c., cont. diced cf., worn. (RO. Apr.23; 87) $140
– **A Child's History of England.** Ill.:– F.W. Topham. L., 1852-53-54. *1st. Edn.* 3 vols. Advt. lf. in each vol., gt.-panel. cf by Zaehndorf, with stp., entwined gt. reeded banding to bds., silk liners, slight fading to spines, orig. cl. bnd. in. (PD. Aug.17; 206) £225
– – **Anr. Copy.** 3 vols. Sm. sq. 8vo. Light spotting, orig. cl., some spotting; Fred A. Berne copy. (SPB. May 16; 223) $350
– – **Anr. Copy.** 3 vols. Hf.-titles, tissue guards, advts at end of each vol., some minor foxing & soiling, publisher's gt.-pict. cl. (RO. Apr.23; 89) $280
– – **Anr. Copy.** 3 vols. Tissue guard present in Vols. I & III, no advts., some light foxing, frontis. (probably inserted from anr. copy) loose & frayed in vol. II, three-qtr. mor., rubbed. (RO. Mar.21; 36) $160
– **The Chimes.** Ill.:– Arthur Backham. N.Y., Ltd. Edns. Cl., 1931. *(1500) numbered & sigd. by artist.* 4to. Orig. pict. cl. gt., spine soiled. (S. Dec.20; 574) *Russell.* £60
– – **Anr. Copy.** Tall 4to. Pict. buckram, spine darkened, s.-c. soiled & cracked. (SG. Jan.12; 228) $250
– – **Anr. Copy.** Tall 4to. Gt.- & black-stpd. pict. cl., pict. end-papers, spine discold., pict. s.-c., soiled. (SG. Jan.12; 300) $175
– **The Chimes.—The Cricket on the Hearth.—The Battle of Life.—The Haunted Man.** 1845-48. *1st. Edns. 1st., 2nd. & 4th. works: 1st. Iss., 3rd. work: 2nd. Iss.* Together 4 vols. 12mo. Some ll. slightly soiled, 1st. work stained, orig. cl. gt., 2nd. work rebkd. (BBA. Sep.29; 187) *Old Hall.* £85
– – **Anr. Edn.** 1845-48. *1st. Edns.* Together 4 vols. Tree cf. gt. (P. Oct.20; 46) £190
– **A Christmas Carol.** Ill.:– John Leech. 1843. *1st. Edn. 1st. Iss.* 12mo. Plts. hand-cold., hf.-title, last advt. lf., a few ll. slightly spotted, orig. cl. gt., slightly rubbed & soiled, small tear at spine head, s.-c. (BBA. Sep.29; 186) *Jarndyce.* £420
– – **Anr. Edn.** 1843. *1st. Edn. Iss. not stated.* 'Stave 1', plts. hand-cold., orig. cl. gt., cream end-papers. (P. Oct.20; 45) £260
– – **Anr. Copy.** 'Stave I', plts. hand-cold., hf.-title, advt. lf., orig. cl., green end-papers; autograph envelope sigd. to Mr. William Wilson, 14 Royal Exchange laid in, Fred A. Berne copy. (SPB. May 16; 225) $1,000
– – **Anr. Edn.** Phila., 1844. *1st. Amer. Edn.* Foxing, spotting, tears & repairs to inner margins, orig. cl., shaken. (SPB. Dec.13; 658) $225
– **A Christmas Carol in Prose.** N.Y., Wooly Whale Pr., 1930. *(200) numbered, for private distribution.* Fo. Vell.-bkd. cl. (SG. Jan.12; 367) $100
– **David Copperfield.** Ill.:– H.K. Browne. L., 1849-50. *1st. Edn* 20 orig. pts. in 19. With 'Life' on p.3 of Advertiser (pt.8), most advts. as called for, some spotting & foxing, light soiling, orig. wraps., lr. wraps. of pts. 4,5 & 10 supplied, spines chipped & worn, reprd., some stains, mor.-bkd. s.-c.; Fred A. Berne copy. (SPB. May 16; 239) $1,000
– – **Anr. Copy.** Some fraying, stains, &c., orig. wraps., cl. s.-c., backstrips chipped, lacks lr. wraps. to pts. I, VIII & XIX/XX, lacks both wraps. to pts. VII & XVIII, other wraps. frayed, chipped or loose, w.a.f. (RO. Apr.23; 91) $525
– – **Anr. Edn.** Ill.:– H.K. Browne. L., 1850. *1st. Edn. in Book Form. Early Iss.* Vig. title-p. dtd. 1850, lr. corner of most plts. lightly dampstained, publisher's cl., slightly worn & shaken. (RO. Apr.23; 119) $450
– – **Anr. Edn.** Ill.:– H.K. Browne. 1850. *1st. Edn. in Book Form. Iss. not stated.* Hf.-title, some ll. slightly soiled, spotted, cont. hf. cf., orig. upr. wrap. pt. 11 bnd. in. (BBA. Sep.29; 189) *Bauman.* £60
– – **Anr. Copy.** Most ills. with some margin browning, hf. cf., spine gt., scuffed; James F. Preston bkplt. (LC. Jul.5; 302) £50
– – **Anr. Copy.** Lacks hf.-title, date on engraved title cropped, three-qtr. cf. (SG. Nov.17; 41) $125
– **Dombey & Son.** Ill.:– H.K. Browne. L., 1846-48. *1st. Edn.* 20 orig. pts. in 19, in 2 vols. Lacks 'if' p. 426 line 9, p. 325 with misprint 'Capatain' on last line, with most advts. & slips as listed by Hatton & Cleaver, but lacks 10 items, advts. bnd. in Vol. 2, extra-ill. with 12 port. plts. by R. Young & H.K. Browne as publd. by Chapman & Hall in 1848, gt.-panel cf. by Zaehnsdorf, with stp., entwined gt. reeded banding to bds., silk liners, slight fading to spines, wraps. bnd. at end Vol. 1, orig. wraps. for the 2 iss. of plts. also bnd. in. (PD. Aug.17; 200) £190
– – **Anr. Copy.** 20 orig. pts. in 19. Early iss. points in pts. 9, 11 & 14, (except p. 431 is numbered), 2 line errata, advts. as called for in Hatton & Cleaver, some foxing, orig. wraps., some soiling, spines reprd., mor.-bkd. box. (SPB. Dec.13; 659) $400
– – **Anr. Copy.** 20 orig. pts. in 19. 8-line errata, with p. 431 numbered in pt. 15, & 'if' on p. 426 not present, in pt. 9 'Delight', some advts. as called for, some spotting & soiling, orig. ptd. wraps., some worn & reprd., some soiling, mor. solander case; Fred A. Berne copy. (SPB. May 16; 226) $250
– – **Anr. Edn.** Ill.:– H.K. Browne. L., 1848. *1st. Edn. in Book Form.* Lev. mor., double-ruled gt. borders., gt. ornaments, cover set with oval miniature ports. on ivory, framed in gt. borders, spine in 6 compartments, gt.-decor. panel., turn-ins gt., watered silk linings, by Riviere, stp.-sigd. by binders & artist on upr. & lr. turn-in respectively, inserted ptd. fly-lf. 'This is No.930 of Cosway Bindings invented by J.H. Stonehouse, with Miniatures on Ivory by Miss Currie', sigd. by both, fleece-lined cl. s.-c.; A.L.s. from author tipped in (but detchd.), as a bdg., w.a.f. (CNY. Dec.17; 590) $2,600
– **Dombey & Son.—David Copperfield.** Ill.:– H.K. Browne. L., 1848; 1850. *1st. Edns. in Book Form.*

Together 2 vols. Some foxing, 1st. vol. with last gathering of plts. loose, hf. leath., rubbed. (SG. Mar.15; 106) $120

– **Edwin Drood.** Ill.:– S.L. Fildes. L., 1870. *1st. Edn. Early Iss.* Pts. I-VI (all publd.). Thin cork advt. in pt. II, orig. pict. wraps., cl. s.-c., some fraying of wraps. (RO. Apr.23; 108) $275

– – **Anr. Edn.** Ill.:– S.L. Fildes. L., 1870. *1st. Edn. Iss not stated.* 6 orig. pts. Most advts. as called for, 'Cork Hat' slip in Pt.2, orig. ptd. wraps., some repairs to spines, chipped, soiled, mor. solander case. (SPB. May 16; 47) $250

– – **Anr. Copy.** 6 orig. pts. With 'Eighteenpence' slip pasted over price on pt. 6, 'Cork Hat' slip in pt. 2, most advts. & slips as called for, orig. ptd. wraps., some chipping & tears, some soiling, red mor. solander case; Fred A. Berne copy. (SPB. May 16; 236) $200

– – **Anr. Edn.** Ill.:– S.L. Fildes. L., 1870. *1st. Edn. in Book Form.* Last advt. lf., some ll. spotted, orig. cl., sawtooth border. (BBA. Sep.29; 193) *Jarndyce.* £65

– – **Anr. Copy.** Publisher's 32 p. catalogue dtd. 31 Aug. 1870, orig. gt.-lettered cl. (SG. Nov.17; 43) $150

– – **Anr. Copy.** W.H. Smith's catalogue, dtd. May 1872, some foxing, orig. black– & gt.-stpd. cl. [Carter's 1st. secondary bdg.], worn. (RO. Apr.23; 110) $105

– **Great Expectations.** L., 1861. *1st. Edn.* 3 vols. With advts. dtd. May 1861 in 3 places, with 'their' for 'her' on p. 162, Vol. 2 'raving' for 'staving' on p. 37, Vol. 3 'but' for 'was' on p. 145, 'led' for 'lead' on p. 150, orig. cl.; with 2 letters from Thomas Hatton to Mr. Charles S. Langstroth, pencilled annots., apparently in Hatton's hand, Fred A. Berne copy. (SPB. May 16; 227) $2,500

– **Hard Times.** 1854. *1st. Edn.* Gt.-panel. cf. by Zaehnsdorf, with stp., entwined gt. reeded banding to bds., silk liners, slight fading to spine, orig. blind-blocked cl. bnd. in. (PD. Aug.17; 207) £145

– – **Anr. Copy.** Hf.-title, orig. moire cl. (BBA. Sep.29; 190) *Jarndyce.* £130

– – **Anr. Copy.** Hf.-title, later hf. mor. by Riviere, orig. moire cl. preserved at end. (BBA. Dec.15; 205) *Jarndyce.* £60

– – **Anr. Copy.** Gt.-decor. maroon mor. by Rivière, gt. dentelles, light rubbing to covers, spine darkening, head chipped, orig. cl. covers bnd. in. (CBA. Mar.3; 161) $120

– **Hunted Down: A Story. With Some Account of Thomas Griffiths Wainewright, the Poisoner.** L., [1870]. *1st. Engl. Edn.* Hf.-titles & all advts., mor., orig. wraps. bnd. in, minor wear & soiling. (RO. Apr.23; 94) $150

– **The Lamplighter – a Farce (1838) now first printed from a Manuscript in the Forster Collection at the South Kensington Museum.** 1879. *1st. Edn. (250).* Gt.-panel cf., by Zaehnsdorf, with stp., entwined gt. reeded banding to bds., silk liners, slight fading to spine, orig. wrap. bnd. in. (PD. Aug.17; 212) £210

– **The Letters.** L., 1880-82. 3 vols. Lev. gt. extra, by Rivière, gt. dentelles, slightly stained. (SG. Nov.17; 44) $200

– **Little Dorrit.** Ill.:– H.K. Browne. L., Dec. 1855-Jun. 1857. *1st. Edn. 1st. Iss.* 20 orig. pts. in 19, in 2 vols. Name Rigand used instead of Blandois on pp. 469, 470, 472, & 473, with most advts. & slips as listed by Hatton & Cleaver, advts. bnd. in Vol. 2, gt.-panel cf. by Zaehnsdorf, with stp., entwined gt. reeded banding to bds., silk liners, slight fading to spines, orig. wraps. bnd. at end Vol. 1. (PD. Aug.17; 209) £350

– – **Anr. Copy.** 20 orig. pts. in 19. Correction slip on p. 481 of pt. XVI, some foxing, orig. pict. wraps. (some chipping or soiling), hf. mor. solander case. (RO. Apr.23; 101) $500

– – **Anr. Edn.** Ill.:– H.K. Browne. L., Dec. 1855-Jun. 1857. *1st. Edn. Iss. not stated.* 20 orig. pts. in 19. Advts., orig. wraps., hf. mor. box; from Norman Tarbolton liby. (P. Apr.12; 1) *Jarndyce.* £440

– – **Anr. Copy.** 20 orig. pts. in 19. Advts. as called for, some foxing of plts., orig. wraps., few spines reprd., some pts. lightly soiled, mor.-bkd. s.-c.; Thomas Hatton/Fred A. Berne copy. (SPB. May 16; 230) $650

– – **Anr. Copy.** 20 orig. pts. in 19. Many advts., some spotting & foxing, orig. wraps., tears & chipping, few covers loose. (SPB. May 16; 45) $225

– – **Anr. Edn.** Ill.:– H.K. Browne. L., 1857. *1st. Edn. in Book Form.* Some foxing, browning & soiling, &c., mor. gt., rubbed. (RO. Apr.23; 102) $110

– **Martin Chuzzlewit.** Ill.:– 'Phiz'. L., 1843-44. *1st. Edn. 1st. Iss.* 20 orig. pts. in 19, in 2 vols. Engraved vig. title with the transposed '£', with most advts. & slips as listed by Hatton & Cleaver, & 2 unlisted slips, advts. bnd. in Vol. 2, 4 p. publisher's list of George Young in Pt. X, 26 p. Mechi booklet in Pt. XVI, gt.-panel. cf. by Zaehnsdorf, with stp., slight fading to spines, orig. wraps. (marked with cont. writing) bnd. at end Vol. 1. (PD. Aug.17; 199) £390

– – **Anr. Edn.** Ill.:– 'Phiz'. L., 1843-44. *1st. Edn. Iss. not stated.* 20 orig. pts. in 19. With '£' on signpost transposed, slip 'Scones & Incidents of Foreign Travel', most slips & advts. as called for, some marginal spotting, orig. ptd. wraps., some spines reprd., some soiling, colour variation in wraps., red mor. solander cases; Fred A. Berne copy. (SPB. May 16; 231) $550

– – **Anr. Edn.** Ill.:– 'Phiz'. L., 1844. *1st. Edn. in Book Form.* Mor. gt. (LH. Sep.25; 521) $110

– **Master Humphrey's Clock.** Ill.:– G. Cattermole & H.K. Browne. L., 4 Apr. 1840-27 Nov. 1841. *1st. Edn.* 88 orig. weekly pts. in 85, in 3 vols. Ill. with additional plts. from Jacob Parallel's 'Hands to Humphries Clock', gt.-panel cf. by Zaehnsdorf, with stp., entwined gt. reeded banding to bds., silk liners, slight fading to spines, orig. wraps. bnd. at end each vol., orig. pict. wraps. to Pts. I & II of 'Hands to Humphries Clock bnd. at end Vol. 1. (PD. Aug.17; 198) £240

– – **Anr. Copy.** 20 orig. monthly pts. Fo. Most advts. as called for, orig. ptd. wraps., some repair to spines, lightly discold., cl. folding box; Fred A. Berne copy. (SPB. May 16; 233) $850

– – **Anr. Copy.** 88 orig. weekly pts. in 85. Lge. 8vo. Some soiling, spotting, orig. wraps., covers from iss. 45 detchd., soiling & stains on some pts., red mor.-bkd. case; Fred A. Berne copy. (SPB. May 16; 232) $550

– – **Anr. Copy.** 20 orig. monthly pts. Most advts., some browning, orig. wraps., slightly soiled & worn, some repairs. (SPB. May 16; 46) $475

– – **Anr. Edn.** Ill.:– G. Cattermole & H.K. Browne. L., 1840-41. *1st. Edn. in Book Form.* 3 vols. 4to. Frontispieces & titles foxed in Vols. I & II, gt.-decor. cl. (SG. Mar.15; 103) $110

– – **Anr. Copy.** 3 vols. Lge. 8vo. Minor soiling & foxing &c., cont. three-qtr. cf., worn. (RO. Apr.23; 106) $100

– – **Anr. Copy.** 3 vols. Foxing, cont. hf. cf., corners, decor. spine. (HD. Mar.14; 25) Frs. 1,800

– **Memoirs of Grimaldi, edited by Boz.** Ill.:– W. Greatbatch after S. Raven (engraved port.), George Cruikshank. L., 1838. *1st. Edn. 1st. Iss.* 'The Last Song' without border, 36 pp. advts at end Vol. 2, gt.-panel. cf. by Zaehnsdorf, with stp., entwined gt. reeded banding to bds., silk liners, slight fading to spine, orig. pink embossed covers bnd. in. (PD. Aug.17; 202) £230

– – **Anr. Edn.** Ill.:– George Cruikshank. L., 1838. *1st. Edn. Iss. not stated.* 4to. Inlaid red nor. by Guild of Women Binders, lightly rubbed; extra-ill. with ports. & plts. (many hand-cold.), 41 orig. playbills, 9 A.L.'s. from Charles Kemble & others, lge. clipped Cruikshank sig., &c. (RO. Apr.23; 107a) $850

– – **Anr. Copy.** 2 vols. Hf. titles, lacks 36 p. Bentley catalogue, gt.-ornamental crimson lev., by Bayntun, upr. covers with vari-col. mor. inlays, inner gt. dentelles, silk place markers, cl. s.-c.; extra-ill. with about 16 plts. & 2 facs plts. (SG. Nov.3; 58) $450

– **The Mudfog Papers.** 1880. *1st. Edn.* 6 pp. advts., orig. cl. (PD. Aug.17; 192) £92

– **Nicholas Nickleby.** Ill.:– 'Phiz'. L., 1838-39. *1st. Edn.* 20 orig. pts. in 19. With 'visiter' & 'latter', 1st. state of port., most of advts. & slips as called for, some foxing & spotting, few repairs, orig. pts. wraps., some spines reprd., some soiling & fraying; Fred A. Berne copy. (SPB. May 16; 229) $800

– – **Anr. Copy.** 20 orig. pts. in 19. Tall 8vo. 'Nickleby Advertiser' in 10 pts., many other advts., unc., pict. wraps., sewed, slight wear, a few sm. repairs to fore-edges of 4 upr. wraps. (SG. Nov.3; 57) $750

– – **Anr. Edn.** Ill.:– 'Phiz' & Finden. 1839. *1st. Edn. in Book Form. 1st. Iss.* With misprints 'visitor' on p. 123 line 17 & 'latter' on p. 160 line 6 from bottom, plts. 1-4 with publishers' imprint, caption on plt. facing p. 248 with 'in', that at p. 457 has long caption, some foxing, rebnd. panel. hf. cf. by Bayntun. (PD. Aug.17; 196a) £68

– – **Anr. Edn.** Ill.:– 'Phiz'. L., 1839. *1st. Edn. in Book Form. 2nd. Iss.* Plts. in 2nd. state excepting that facing p. 248 which is in 1st. state, publisher's pres. bdg. of red hard-grained mor. gt., elab. gt.-decor., stp. sigd. on inner turn-in, slight wear, spine slightly scarred; pres. copy from author to Lady Holland, with 2 A.L.s. from author to her laid in. (CNY. Dec.17; 411) *Holmes.* $20,000

– – **Anr. Edn.** Ill.:– 'Phiz'. L., 1839. *1st. Edn. in Book Form. Early Iss.* Imprint on frontis. & 1st. 4 plts., minor foxing & soiling, mor. by Bayntun, light wear. (RO. Apr.23; 99) $165

– – **Anr. Copy.** 2 vols. Frontis. & 1st. 4 plts. with publisher's imprint, long title for plt. after 457, hf.-title transposed to provide title of 2nd. vol., most plts. slightly browned (as usual), cont. (publisher's?) cl., some wear. (RO. Apr.23; 97) $160

– – **Anr. Edn.** Ill.:– 'Phiz'. L., 1839. *1st. Edn. in Book Form. Iss. not stated.* Minor soiling & foxing, orig. cl., some wear, brkn. (RO. Apr.23; 98) $400

– – **Anr. Copy.** Slightly foxed & soiled, some margin darkening, orig. cl., spine gt.-lettered, yellow end-papers, covers rubbed, corners bumped, backstrip faded, splitting & frayed at ends & jnts. (CBA. Mar.3; 162) $110

– **Novels.** Ca. 1890. 17 vols. Hf. cf. gt. (P. Sep.8; 279) £150

– **Oliver Twist.** Ill.:– G. Cruikshank. [L., 1837-39]. Text extracted from Bentley's 'Miscellany'. With hand-lettered title & ptd. title-pp. for 5 vols. of 'Miscellany', 25 etched plts., final plt. in 2 states (the 2nd. trimmed & mntd.) three-qtr. mor., gt.-panel. back. (SG. Feb.16; 90) $475

– – **Anr. Edn.** Ill.:– G. Cruikshank. 1838. *1st. Edn. 1st. Iss.* 3 vols. 12mo. Hf.-titles in Vols. 1 & 2, 1st. advt. ll. Vol. 3, list of ll. loosely inserted, some plts. & a few text ll. spotted, orig. cl., slightly rubbed & faded. (BBA. Sep.29; 183) *Jarndyce.* £640

– – **Anr. Copy.** 3 vols. With 'Fireside' plt., title-p. reading 'Oliver Twist, or the Parish Boy's Progress by 'Boz'', no list of ills. & no publisher's imprint at bottom of backs, 4 pp. advts. Vol. 1 & 2 pp. at beginning Vol. 3, orig. brown cl., blocked in blind, unc., slightly stained & shaken. (PD. Aug.17; 196b) £510

– – **Anr. Copy.** 3 vol. With 'Fireside' plt., hf.-titles in Vols. 1 & 2, advt. lf. at end of Vol. 3, list of plts. in facs., a few ll. slightly spotted, later hf. nor. by Riviere, spines gt. & faded, corners slightly bumped. (BBA. Dec.15; 200) *Jarndyce.* £210

– – **Anr. Copy.** 3 vols. With 'Fireside' plt., 4 pp. of publisher's advts. Vol. 1 & 2 pp. at beginning of Vol. 3 some spotting, orig. gt.-lettered cl., spines faded. (TA. Nov.17; 397) £160

– – **Anr. Edn.** Ill.:– G. Cruikshank. L., 1838. *1st. Edn. 2nd. Iss.* 3 vols. 24 etched plts., 1st. iss. 'Fireside' plt. bnd. in, hf.-titles to Vols. I & II (variant imprint on verso to that in Vol. I), list of ills., 4 pp. publisher's advts. at end Vol. I, without 2 pp. advt. at end Vol. III, 1 plt. slightly offset onto text, mod. crushed lev. mor. gt. by Zaehnsdorf, orig. cl. covers (without imprint at foot of spine) bnd. in; extra-ill. with hand-cold. vig. title & 20 hand-cold. etched plts. by Pailthorpe. (C. Nov.9; 60) *Jarndyce.* £400

– – **Anr. Edn.** Ill.:– G. Cruikshank. L., 1838. *1st. Edn. Iss. not stated.* 3 vols. With both states of title-p. & 'Fireside' plt., 2 advt. ll. in Vol. 1, 'Dickens' works listed in Vol. 2 dtd. Nov. 1838, advt. lf. in Vol. 3, orig. cl., without publisher's imprint on spine, lr. cover of Vol. 1 rehinged, recased with new end-papers; Hugh Walpole bkplt., Fred A. Berne copy. (SPB. May 16; 237) $500

– – **Anr. Edn.** 1846. *1st. 8vo. Edn. in Book Form.* Advts., mor. gt. by Zaehnsdorf; from Norman Tarbolton liby. (P. Apr.12; 5) *Jarndyce.* £320

– **Our Mutual Friend.** Ill.:– after Marcus Stone. L., 1864-65. *1st. Edn.* 20 orig. pts. in 19, in 2 vols.

DICKENS, Charles -Contd.

With most advts., slips as listed by Hatton & Cleaver, lacks mainly slips to advts. back but with white ribbed paper version of Scottish Union advt. Pt. IX, gt.-panel. cf. by Zachnsdorf, with stp., entwined gt. reeded banding to bds., silk liners, slight fading to spines. (PD. Aug.17; 211) £340
- - **Anr. Copy.** 20 orig. pts. in 19. Lacks some advts., orig. wraps., most rebkd., qtr. mor. box. (P. Jul.5; 229) £100
- - **Anr. Copy.** 20 orig. pts. in 19. Most advts. as called for, 'foreign bank notes' slip, slightly spotted, orig. ptd. wraps., some spines reprd., few short marginal tears, lightly soiled; Fred A. Berne copy. (SPB. May 16; 238) £500
- - **Anr. Copy.** 20 orig. pts. in 19. 'Foreign Bank Notes' slip in pts. 19/20, pict. wraps., lst. iss. front wrap. of pt. 1 without imprint at foot, some fraying, soiling, minor stains &c. (RO. Apr.23; 114) $325
- - **Anr. Copy.** 20 orig. pts. in 19. 40 wood engrs., most advts. including 'Foreign Banknotes', orig. wraps., some chipping & tears, repairs. (SPB. May 16; 48) $275
- - **Anr. Edn.** Ill.:- after Marcus Stone. L., 1865. *1st. Edn. in Book Form.* Some text browned, maroon lev. mor., covers triple gt.-ruled, gt. Gadshill device on upr. cover, spine in 6 compartments, decor. gt. panels, turn-ins gt., upr. doubl. set with watercolour painting on cf., watered silk linings, fleece-lined cl. s.-c., by Rivière & Son; A.L.s. from author tipped in (but detchd.), as a bdg., w.a.f. (CNY. Dec.17; 591) $700
- - **Anr. Copy.** 2 vols. in 1. Mor. by Zaehnsdorf, spine gt.-panel., wide gt. dentelles, marb. end-papers, covers lightly rubbed, spine lightly faded, sm. bookseller's label to rear pastedown, slight remnants of sm. label to front pastedown, orig. covers bnd. in, some slight edge tears; faint pencil name of Joe E. Brown. (CBA. Mar.3; 165) $300
- - **Anr. Edn.** Ill.:- after Marcus Stone. L., 1865. *1st. Edn. in Book Form. Later iss.* 2 vols. in 1. Publisher's remainder cl. bdg., unc., worn, spine ends slightly frayed. (RO. Apr.23; 117) $150
- **The Pic Nic Papers by Various Hands, edited by Charles Dickens Esquire.** Ill.:- Cruikshank, 'Phiz', & R.J. Hamerton. L., Palmer, 1841. *1st. Edn. Later Iss.* 10 pp. advts. (6 pp. Vol. 1 & 2 pp. to each of other vols.). gt.-panel cf. by Zaehnsdorf, with stp., entwined gt. reeded banding to bds., silk liners, slight fading to spines, orig. cl. bnd. in. (PD. Aug.17; 203) £190
- **Pickwick Papers.** Ill.:- Seymour, R.W. Buss, & 'Phiz'. L., 1836-37. *1st. Edn. Late Iss.* 20 orig. pts. in 19, in 2 vols. Vig. title has reading 'Weller', many typographical errors consistent with earlier iss., 2 plts. by Buss present in pt. 3, 1st. state of Seymour plts., lacks all advts. & slips prior to Pt. XIII, lacks Pickwick Advertiser to pt. 15, some foxing, gt.-panel. cf. by Zaehnsdorf, with stp., entwined gt. reeded banding to bds., silk liners, wraps. (all dtd. 1836/1837) bnd. in. (PD. Aug.17; 197) £500
- - **Anr. Edn.** N.Y., [1836-37?]. *Amer. iss.* Pts. I-XIII only (of the 20 orig. pts. in 19). Without advts., pict. wraps., unc., some fraying & soiling, worn. (RO. Apr.23; 124) $135
- - **Anr. Edn.** Ill.:- R. Seymour, Buss, & 'Phiz'. L., 1837. *1st. Edn. in Book Form. Early Iss.* 'Veller' title, 2 Chapters III, 2 sigd. & numbered Buss plts., &c., some foxing & browning of plts., slightly affecting text, some minor stains, soiling &c., three-qtr. cf., rubbed. (RO. Apr.23; 120) $100
- - **Anr. Edn.** Ill.:- R. Seymour, Buss, & 'Phiz'. L., 1837. *1st. Edn. in Book Form. Late iss., with errors in headings on pp. 26 & 375.* Lacks hf.-title, rebnd. panel. hf. cf. (PD. Aug.17; 195) £80
- - **Anr. Edn.** Ill.:- Seymour & 'Phiz'. L., 1837. *1st. Edn. in Book Form. No Iss. stated.* 30 plts. in 2 states, 7 in 3 states & 2 in 4 states, mor. gt. by Sangorski & Sutcliffe; Philip Dickens family copy, from Norman Tarbolton Liby. (P. Apr.12; 6)
Joseph. £470
- - **Anr. Copy.** A few plts. very slightly spotted, 1 reprd. in margin, mor., foliate design inlaid & gt., by Bayntun (Rivière), upr. cover inlaid with miniature hand-painted port. of Dickens, boxed. (S. Oct.4; 117) *Joseph.* £420
- - **Anr. Copy.** With 'Veller', slightly browned, elab.

red mor. gt., by Bayntun, Dickens' port. in gt. on upr. cover & his sig. in gt. on lr. cover; Fred A. Berne copy. (SPB. May 16; 240) $300
- - **Anr. Copy.** Plts. with some browning & foxing (as usual), lacks hf.-title, three-qtr. mor., rubbed. (RO. Apr.23; 121) $160
- - **Anr. Copy.** 'Veller' title & 2 Chapters III, without the 2 Buss plts., lacks directions to binder, minor soiling & browning, later three-qtr. mor. (RO. Apr.23; 122) $140
- - **Anr. Copy.** Lacks hf.-title, some plts. foxed or stained, cont. pol. cf. (SG. Nov.17; 35) $125
- - **Anr. Edn.** Launceston, Tasmania, 1838. *Pirated Edn.* Impft., bdg. not stated; Harry F. Chaplin copy. (JL. Jul.15; 282) Aus. $110
- - **Anr. Edn.** Ill.:- Cecil Aldin. 1910. *(250) numbered & sigd. by artist.* 2 vols. Fo. Orig. vell. gt., vol. 1 hinges brkn., unc.; extra-ill. with cold. plts. by Frank Reynolds. (SKC. Jan.13; 2122) £100
- - **Anr. Edn.** 1979. *Facs. of 1837 edn. Ltd. Edn.* Mor. gt. by Morrell, fore-e. pntg., fitted cl. box; from Norman Tarbolton liby. (P. Apr.12; 4a)
Hatchards. £75
- **Pictures from Italy.** Ill.:- Samuel Palmer. L., 1846. *1st. Edn.* Orig. cl., rubbed. (BBA. May 3; 236) *Jarndyce.* £55
- **The Plays & Poems.** L., 1882. *(150) numbered.* 2 vols. Lge. 8vo. Lev. gt. extra by Rivière, gt. dentelles, slightly stained. (SG. Nov.17; 45) $110
- **Sämmtliche Werke von Boz.** Trans.:- J. Seybt, H. Roberts & others. Leipzig, 1842-59. *1st. German Coll. Edn.* A few plts. slightly soiled or lightly browned, cont. marb. bds. gt. (GB. Nov.4; 1738)
DM 700
- **Sketches by 'Boz'.** L., 1836, 1837. *1st. Edn. in Book Form.* 1st. & 2nd. Series: 2 vols. 1st Series: plts. mottled, few pp. soiled, 2nd. Series: advts. dtd. Dec. 1836, 8 plts. lightly spotted, some marginal pencilled notes, orig. cl., some light soiling & fraying; Fred A. Berne copy. (SPB. May 16; 242) $2,800
[-] - **Anr. Edn.** Ill.:- George Cruikshank. L., 1839. *1st. Edn. in book form containing both series.* Lge. 8vo. With publisher's imprint on pl. 'The Greenwich Fair', & following plts., cf. gt., chipped. (SG. Mar.15; 102) $110
[-] **Sketches of Young Couples.** Ill.:- H.K. Browne. L., 1840. *1st. Edn.* 12mo. Hf.-title, 1 advt. lf. (of 2) at end, some ll. slightly spotted, cont. hf. cf., slightly rubbed. (BBA. Sep.29; 184)
Jarndyce. £56
- **Sketches of Young Gentlemen.** Ill.:- 'Phiz'. 1838. *1st. Edn.* 4 pp. advts., gt.-panel. cf. by Zaehnsdorf, with his stp., entwined gt. reeded banding to bds., silk liners, slight fading to spine, orig. pict. wraps. bnd. in. (PD. Aug.17; 201) £115
[-] - **Anr. Copy.** Mor. gt. by Ramage; from Norman Tarbolton liby. (P. Apr.12; 8) *Jarndyce.* £95
- **Speech of Charles Dickens Esquire, delivered at the Meeting of the Administrative Reform Association at the Theatre Royal, Drury Lane, Wednesday June 27 1855.** 1855. *1st. Edn.* Gt. panel cf., by Zaehnsdorf with his stp., entwined gt. reeded bands to bds., silk liners, spine slightly faded. (PD. Aug.17; 208) £150
- **The Speeches.** L., 1884. *L.P. Edn., (50) numbered.* Lge. 8vo. Lev. gt. extra, by Rivière, gt. dentelles,. (SG. Nov.17; 46) $130
- **A Tale of Two Cities.** Ill.:- H.K. Browne. 1859. *1st. Edn.* 8 orig. pts. in 7. With p.213 misnumbered, advts. as called for, orig. ptd. wraps., some repairs to spines, some soiling; Fred A. Berne copy. (SPB. May 16; 243) $2,600
- - **Anr. Edn.** Ill.:- H.K. Browne. L., 1859. *1st. Edn. in Book Form. Early Iss.* Some ll. spotted, cont. hf. cf., slightly rubbed. (BBA. Sep.29; 191) *Jarndyce.* £85
- - **Anr. Edn.** Ill.:- H.K. Browne. L., 1859. *1st. Edn. in Book Form. No Iss. stated.* P. 213 misnumbered 113, hf. cf. by Bumpus. (PD. Aug.17; 194) £105
- - **Anr. Copy.** Page 213 misnumbered 113, 2 extra plts. bnd. in, some captions cropped, some spotting, orig. upr. wrap. of 1st. pt. iss. & slip with publisher's announcement bnd. in, cont. red hf. mor. (S. Mar.20; 868) *Primrose.* £80
- **The Uncommercial Traveller.** 1861. *1st. Edn.* Lacks 22 pp. advts., gt. panel cf. by Zaehnsdorf

with his stp., entwined gt. reeded banding to bds.; silk liners, spine slightly faded. (PD. Aug.17; 210) £150
- **Works.** L., 1847-76. *Ill. Liby. Edn.* 29 vols. only (of 30, lacks Vol. 16). Cont. cf., rubbed, spines faded, a few worn. (BBA. May 3; 243)
Wieckenberg. £130
- - **Anr. Edn.** L., [1861-74],. *Liby. Edn.* 30 vols. Purple hf. mor., spines gt. (SPB. Dec.13; 520)
$650
- - **Anr. Edn.** Ill.:- after Darley, Gilbert, Cruikshank, Phiz & others. N.Y., 1867-69. *Riverside Edn.* 48 vols. Slightly foxed at beginning & end, lightly browned, later hf. leath. gt., spine lightly faded, worn. (H. May 22; 642)
DM 720
- - **Anr. Edn.** L., ca. 1870's. *Household Edn.* 17 vols. in 7, bnd. from monthly pts. 4to. Three-qtr. cf., spines gt. with fleurons, few wraps. bnd. in,1 cover detchd. (SG. Feb.16; 91) $130
- - **Anr. Edn.** L., 1881-82. *Ltd. Edn.* 30 vols. Imperial 8vo. A few plts. hand-cold., unc., cl., minor tears, a few vols. breaking. (C. Nov.9; 61)
Shapero. £100
- - **Anr. Edn.** L., 1882. 30 vols. in 60. Lge. 8vo. Hf. red mor., 1 spine wormed, 2 vols. cornerpieces badly wormed. (SPB. May 17; 726) $1,300
- - **Anr. Edn.** L., ca. 1890. 15 vols. Sm. 8vo. Three-qtr. cf. (SG. Feb.16; 92) $325
- - **Anr. Edn.** 1892. 48 vols. Cont. hf. cf., spines gt., by Maclehose, lightly rubbed. (CSK. Jan.13; 125) £380
- **The Writings.** Ill.:- after Cruikshank, Phiz, Leech & others. Boston, [1894]. *Standard Liby. Edn.* 32 vols. Gt.-stpd. cl., spines faded, spine ends slightly rubbed. (SG. Mar.15; 108) $140
- **Works.** Ed.:- A. Long. 1897-99. *Gadshill Edn.* 38 vols., including 'The Life ... '. Hf. mor. gt. (P. Jul.5; 259) £980
- - **Anr. Edn.** 1897-n.d. 36 vols. Orig. cl. (CSK. Jan.27; 83) £150
- - **Anr. Edn.** L., 1901. *Authentic Edn.* 21 vols. Cont. hf. cf., spines slightly faded. (S. Dec.13; 352)
Primrose. £130
- - **Anr. Edn.** 1906-08. *National Edn.* 40 vols. Some spotting. orig. cl., spines faded. (CSK. Jan.27; 172) £220
- **Werke.** Ed.:- M. Färber, P. Herrmann, K.M. Schiller, & Weizmann. Trans.:- C. Kolb. Ill.:- Phiz, Cattermole & Cruikshank. Leipzig & Meersburg, [1926-38]. Vols. 1-3 & 5-12 only (of 12). 4to. Lacks 'Die Pickwickier', orig. linen gt. (HK. Nov.10; 2379) DM 520
- - **Anr. Edn.** Ed.:- K.M. Schiller, M. Färber & P. Herrmann. Ill.:- after H.K. Browne, G. Cruikshank & others. Leipzig & Meersburg, [1927-33]. 12 vols. 4to. Orig. linen gt., w.a.f. (HK. May 16; 1972) DM 700
- **Works.** Nones. Pr., 1937-38. *(877) with orig. woodblock or metal plt.* 25 vols., including 'Dickensiana'. Woodblock of H.K. Browne's 'Kit enters the office' from the 'Old Curiosity Shop', orig. buckram, some slightly rubbed, woodblock in case. (S. Nov.22; 265) *Joseph.* £1,150
- - **Anr. Copy.** 25 vols., including 'Dickensiana'. Steel plt. of H.K. Browne's 'Mr. Pinch & the new pupil on a social occasion', prospectus, vari-col. buckram. (LH. Sep.25; 427) $2,800
- - **Anr. Edn.** Intro. & notes:-Andrew Lang. N.d. *Gadshill Edn.* 32 vols. Orig. cl. gt., partly unc., a few vols. a little faded or marked. (LC. Mar.1; 318) £70
- - **Anr. Edn.** N.d. *Liby. Edn.* 26 vols. Hf. cf. (SSA. Jul.5; 106) R 320

DICKENS, Charles (Contrib.)

See— ALBION, The: A Journal of the News, Politics, & Literature of Europe
See— IRVING OFFERING; A Token of Affection, for 1851

DICKENS, Charles & Collins, William Wilkie

- **The Wreck of the Golden Mary: A Saga of the California Gold Rush.** Ill.:- Blair Hughes-Stanton. Kentfield, 1956. *(200).* 4to. Prospectus laid in, slight margin darkening, title verse soiled, hf. bds. & marb. bds., bkplt. (CBA. Nov.19; 1a) $190

DICKENSIANA
- The Pickwick Songster. Edited by Sam Weller & the Honourable Members of 'The Pickwick Club'. L., ca. 1837-38. Nos. 3,5-9, 12-16, Pt.1 only of weekly pts.(all publd.). Ill., some soiling, self-wraps., with typed description sigd. by Thomas Hatton, dtd. Mar.4, 1935; Fred A. Berne copy. (SPB. May 16; 245) $200

DICKES, William Frederick
- The Norwich School of Painting. 1905. *(100)*. 4to. Mor. gt. (P. Oct.20; 35) £160

DICKESON, Montroville W.
- The American Numismatical Manual. Phila., 1859. *1st. Edn.* 4to. Gt.-decor. cl., spine worn; ex-liby., plts. unstpd. (SG. Jan.19; 165) $110

DICKEY, James
- Babel to Byzantium. N.Y., [1968]. Ptd. wraps.; uncorrected galley proof. (SG. Mar.1; 65) $120

DICKINSON, Emily
- Poems. Boston, 1890-91-96. *1st. Edns.* 1st., 2nd. & 3rd. Series; 3 vols. 12mo. 2 pp. in 1st. vol. stained, orig. cl. gt.; Frederic Dannay copies. (CNY. Dec.16; 102) $1,300
- - **Anr. Copy.** 1st., 2nd. & 3rd. Series, together 3 vols. Orig. cl. gt., not unif. (SPB. May 17; 601) $1,000
- - **Anr. Copy.** 1st., 2nd. & 3rd. Series: 3 vols. 12mo. 1st. vol. with ink inscrs. & title-p. & front fly-ll. wormed, orig. cl., 2 with ribbon marker, spines of 2nd. & 3rd. vols. worn; 2nd. vol. from liby. of Van Wyck Brooks, with sig of Eleanor Brooks, Frederic Dannay copies. (CNY. Dec.16; 103) $420
- - **Anr. Edn.** L., 1891. *1st. Engl. Edn.* 1st. Series only: 1 vol. 12mo. Orig. cl., partly unopened, slightly soiled: Frederic Dannay copy. (CNY. Dec.15; 106) $350
- - **Anr. Edn.** Boston, 1891-96. *1st. Edns.* 2nd. & 3rd. series only: 2 vols. 12mo. Orig. hf. cf. & decor bds., decor. end-papers, orig. maroon glazed limp cf., both worn; Frederic Dannay copies. (CNY. Dec.16; 105) $280
- - **Anr. Copy.** 2nd. & 3rd. Series only: 2 vols. 12mo. 2nd. vol. with long owner's inscr., orig. cl. gt., white ribbon marker, 2nd. vol. covers soiled; Frederic Dannay copies. (CNY. Dec.16; 104) $220
- The Single Hound, Poems of a Lifetime. Boston, 1914. *1st. Edn.* Orig. cl.-bkd. bds., sm. stain on upr. cover, orig. tissue d.-w. defect., cl. folding case; Frederic Dannay copy. (CNY. Dec.16; 107) $240

DICKINSON, J.
[-] Letters from a Farmer in Pennsylvania, to the Inhabitants of the British Colonies. 1768. *(Bound with:)* DUMMER, J.- A Defence of the New-England Charters. N.d. Together 2 works in 1 vol. Cont. cf. [Sabin 20044, 21197] (S. May 22; 316) *Traylen.* £220

DICKINSON, Page L.
See— SADLEIR, Thomas U. & Dickinson, Page L.

DICKS, John
- A New Gardeners' Dictionary or the Whole Art of Gardening. 1769. 4to. Cont. panel. cf., worn. (PD. Dec.14; 202) £100
- - **Anr. Copy.** Fo. Frontis., 13 engraved plts., frontis., title & 1st. lf. slightly torn, some staining thro.-out, qtr. cf. (P. Mar.15; 232) *Rota.* £60

DICKSON, R.W. 'Alexander McDonald'
- A Complete Dictionary of Practical Gardening, Comprehending all the Modern Improvements in the Art. Ill.:- F. Sansom after Sydenham Edwards. L., 1805-07. 2 vols. 4to. 73 engraved plts., 60 hand-cold., tiny holes in L2 Vol. I, & 3M2 Vol. II just touching text, light offsetting, light foxing to titles, cont. str.-grd. mor., gt. & blind borders on covers, gt. spines head of Vol. I slightly torn, lightly scuffed. (C. Jun.27; 117) *Campbell.* £1,000
- - **Anr. Edn.** [1805-]07. 2 vols. 4to. Slight spotting, mod. qtr. cf. (P. Sep.29; 59) *Shapiro.* £95
[-] - **Anr. Copy.** 13 plain & 61 col. engraved plts., some foxing, hf. mor. (SG. Nov.3; 60) $900
[-] - **Anr. Edn.** L., 1807. 2 vols. 4to. 74 engraved plts., 61 hand-cold., a few ll. browned, cont. cf.,

rebkd. & corners reprd. (BBA. May 3; 78) *Magee.* £740
- - **Anr. Copy.** 2 vols. 4to. Cont. mor. gt., 1 cover loose. (BR. Apr.12; 620) DM 3,000
- A Complete System of Improved Live Stock & Cattle Management. L., 1824. 2 vols. in 1. 4to. Port., 32 (of 33) plts., some spotting, hf. cf., worn. (P. May 17; 225) *Saunders.* £80
- The New Botanic Garden. Ill.:- Sansom after Sydenham Edwards. L., 1812. 2 vols. 4to. 61 hand-cold. engraved plts., some spotting, mod. hf. vell., unc. (C. Nov.16; 232) *Hart.* £480
- Practical Agriculture. 1805. 2 vols. 4to. Mod. cl.; from the Farmer's Club Liby. (P. Jul.5; 11) £130
- - **Anr. Edn.** L., 1807. *New Edn.* 2 vols. Lge. 4to. 87 plts. (27 hand-cold.), 1 frontis. preserved with glassine, 2 plts. torn at fore-edges, buckram, ex-liby. (SG. Mar.22; 99) £150

DICTIONARY OF AMERICAN BIOGRAPHY
Ed.:- Allen Johnson & Dumas Malone. N.Y., 1927-44. *Author's Edn. (500) numbered sigd. by Malone.* 22 vols. (including Index & Supp. One). 4to. Cl. (SG. May 17; 74) $550
- - **Anr. Edn.** Ed.:- Allen Johnson & Dumas Malone. N.Y., 1937. *(500) numbered.* 20 vols. & Index. No bdg. stated; sigd. by Malone. (LH. Sep.25; 216) $550
- - **Anr. Edn.** Ed.:- Allen Johnson. N.Y., 1943-44. 20 vols. & Index & Supp. vols. 4to. Cl., slight wear. (RO. May 22; 48) $460

DICTIONARY OF NATIONAL BIOGRAPHY
L., 1885-1927. 63 vols., & 1st. (-3rd.) Supp. in 7 vols., & 1 vol. Index. Some ll. loose, all but vol. 1 (rebnd.) in cont. hf. mor., some stained or worn. (S. May 1; 390) *Bobinet.* £420
- - **Anr. Edn.** Ed.:- Leslie Stephen, & others. L. & Oxford, 1908-59. 29 vols. 27 vols. in publisher's hf. mor., not. quite unif., some scratching, staining or mild fading, last 2 vols. in buckram. (KH. Nov.9; 464) Aus. $580
- - **Anr. Edn.** Ed.:- Leslie Stephen & Sidney Smith. L., 1921-22. 22 vols. including Supp. Orig. cl., slightly rubbed, 1st. vol. recased retaining orig. spine. (S. May 1; 389) *Schuster.* £220
- - **Anr. Edn.** Oxford, 1921-22. *India Paper Edn.* 22 vols., including Supp., with 3 further Supps., 1901-30. Orig. cl. (LC. Mar.1; 319) £200

DICTIONNAIRE ABREGE DU SURREALISME
Ed.:- [A. Breton & P. Eluard]. Ill.:- Yves Tanguy. Paris, 1938. *1st. Edn.* Orig. wraps. with cold. ill., wraps. loose & with fault. (H. Nov.24; 2566) DM 520

DICTIONNAIRE UNIVERSEL D'AGRICULTURE ET DE JARDINAGE, de Fauconnerie, Chasse, Pêche, Cuisine et Manège
Paris, 1751. 4to. Title lightly stpd., some ll. with light staining, cont. bds., gold-tooled mong., slightly bumped. (GB. May 3; 1081) DM 600

DICTIONNAIRE UNIVERSEL, Historique, Critique et Bibliographique
Paris, 1810-12. *9th. Edn.* 20 vols. Engraved plts. bnd. in at ends, slight browning & spotting, hf. cf., spines gt., soiled. (S. Mar.20; 767) *Booth.* £140

DICTYS CRETENSIS & Darius, Phrigius
- Warhafftige Histori von dem Troianischen Krieg. Trans.:- Marcus Tatius. Ill.:- Burgkmair, Schäufelein & others. Augsburg, 1536. *1st. Edn.* Fo. Lightly browned, mod. limp vell. (R. Oct.11; 31) DM 4,700

DIDEROT, Denis
- Les Bijoux Indiscrets. [Paris, 1748]. 2 vols. 12mo. Cont. cf., rebkd., orig. spine preserved. (C. May 30; 78) *Van Den Abbeel.* £100
- - **Anr. Edn.** Ill.:- S. Sauvage. 1923. 4to. Long-grd. mor., blind decor., unc., by R. Kieffer. (HD. Dec.9; 47) Frs. 1,800
- - **Anr. Edn.** Ill.:- Guirand de Scevola. Paris, 1928. *(50) on japan with 6 states of ills.* 2 vols. including album. 4to. Mor. gt. by Semet & Plumelle, watered silk end-ll., wrap., s.-c., mor. album, spine decor., wrap. preserved, spine slightly faded. (HD. Jun.13; 28) Frs. 7,500
- Comtes Moraux et Nouvelles Idylles de D[iderot] et S. Gessner. Ed.:- H. Meister. Trans.:- M. Huber.

Zürich, 1773. *1st. Fr. Edn.* 4to. Ex-libris, cont. marb. cf., gt. decor., inner & outer dentelle. (GB. Nov.4; 2018) DM 850
- Die Nonne. Trans.:- Carl Friedrich Cramer. Ill.:- W. Jury. Riga, 1797. *1st. German Edn.* Minimal foxing, end-paper pasted & written on, cont. bds. gt., rubbed, owners note. (GB. May 4; 1346) DM 800
- - **Anr. Copy.** Cont. bds. gt. (D. Nov.24; 2431) DM 480
- Oeuvres Complètes. Paris, 1875-77. 20 vols. Cont. hf. chagrin, slight defects. (HD. Nov.17; 21) Frs. 1,050
- Oeuvres Diverses. Paris, 1877-79. 6 vols. 12mo. Hf. mor., corners, decor. spines, by Pagnant. (HD. Apr.11; 19) Frs. 2,700
- Oeuvres Philosophiques. Amst., 1772. *1st. Coll. Edn.* 6 vols. Cont. cf. (HD. Apr.13; 14) Frs. 11,000
[-] Pensées Philosophiques. La Haye, 1746. Sm. 12mo. Cont. marb. cf., spine decor. (HD. Mar.19; 45) Frs. 1,700
See— GESSNER, Salomon & Diderot, Denis
See— GRIMM, Friedrich Melchior & Diderot, Denis

DIDEROT, Denis & Alembert, Jean le Rond d'
- Encyclopédie, ou Dictionnaire Raisonné des Sciences, des Arts et des Métiers. Paris, [Neuchâtel, Amst.], 1751-80. *Orig. Edn.* 17 text vols., 4 supp. vols. & 2 index vols., 10 plt. vols. only (of 12, Lacks plt. Vol. 9 & supp. plt. vol.). Lge. fo. Lacks 2 plts. in Vol. 2, 4 plts. in Vol. 5 & 6 plts. in Vol. 8, but extra plt. in Vol. 3 & Vol. 6, minimal marginalia, minimal browning, cont. leath. gt., some variation, 4 vols. in new bnd. cont.-style, some spine restorations, 2 spines very defect. (R. Oct.12; 1530) DM 19,500
- - **Anr. Edn.** 1773. Vol. 9 only. Fo. 210 engraved plts., some folding, some staining, hf. cf. worn, ex libris, as a collection of plts., w.a.f. (P. May 17; 251) *Levy.* £220
- - **Anr. Edn.** Geneve, 1777-79. 39 vols., including 3 plt. vols. (lacks vol. of tables). 4to. Cont. marb. cf. gt., decor. spines, slight defects. (HD. Sep.22; 235) Frs. 26,000
- - **Anr. Copy.** 39 vols. 4to. Lacks 5 plts., cont. porphyry roan, gt. decor., decor. spines, a little worn & stained. (HD. Mar.14; 27) Frs. 15,800
- - **Anr. Copy.** 39 vols. including 3 plt. vols., lacks 6 vols. Tables. 4to. Port. & 502 engraved plts., lacks plt. XIII of 'Armes et Machines de Guerre', spots & dampstains, cont. blind-decor. roan, decor. spines, slightly worn at edges. (HD. May 21; 26) Frs. 9,000
- - **Anr. Edn.** Genève, Lyon & Paris, 1778-87. 47 vols. including 3 plt. vols. & 2 atlas vols. 4to. Cont. marb. hf. roan.; from Château des Noës liby. (HD. May 25; 20) Frs. 9,200
- Encyclopédie ou Dictionnaire Universel des Connoissances Humaines. Yverdon, 1770-80. 58 vols., including 6 vols. supp. 4to. Approx. 20 text vols. stained or foxed in places, 4 plt. vols. stained, marb. cf., spines gt. (VG. May 3; 477) Fls. 12,000
- Encyclopédie ... Chasses. Paris, ca. 1765. Fo. 23 copper plts., hf. leath. (D. Nov.24; 4201) DM 1,400
- Encyclopédie ... Recueil de Planches. Paris, 1767. Vol. 4 only. Fo. Cont. cf., worn, stitching shaken, w.a.f. (CSK. Sep.30; 47) £140
[-] Planches pour l'Encyclopédie. 1770. *2nd. Edn.* Vol. 6 only: 'Natural History'. Fo. 236 engraved plts., light soiling, cont. vell.-bkd. bds., worn, stitching shaken, w.a.f. (CSK. Sep.30; 45) £180
- - **Anr. Edn.** Paris & Liége, 1774-75. Vols. 3 & 4 only. 4to. Some plts. removed, crude cl. & hf. leath., w.a.f. (SG. Oct.6; 127) $275
- - **Anr. Edn.** Livourne, 1778. *3rd. Edn.* Vol. 11 only: 'Textile Machinery'. Fo. Some soiling, cont. cf., worn, w.a.f. (CSK. Sep.30; 46) £120
- - **Anr. Edn.** Genf, 1779. 3 vols. 4to. Vol. 3 lacks 10 maps & other plts., 1 plt holed, cont. leath. gt., worn. (R. Oct.12; 2191) DM 2,300
- - **Anr. Edn.** Lausanne & Bern, 1780. Vol. 2. Sm. 4to. Cont. leath. gt. (R. Oct.12; 2192) DM 650
- Encyclopédie ... Planches sur les Sciences et les Arts. 1777. Fo. Cont. hf. roan. (HD. Jun.29; 61) Frs. 1,800
[-] Encyclopédie ... Recueil de Planches ... Sciences

DIDEROT, Denis & Alembert, Jean le Rond d' - *Contd.*
Mathématiques. [Paris, 1767]. Fo. Text & 102 plts. only, a few plts. browned, new hf. mor.; John D. Stanitz coll. (SPB. Apr.25; 121) $400
[–] **Encyclopédie ... Recueil de Planches par Ordre de Matières.** Paris, 1783-90. Vols. 1-4, 6-8, together 7 vols. Lge. 4to. Approx. 1600 plts., many double-p., some stained, cont. cf., disbnd., w.a.f. (SG. Apr.19; 73) $950
– **Encyclopédie ... Recueil de Planches, sur les Arts.** Paris, ca. 1770. Plt. vol. Fo. Together 17 copperplts., sewed. (D. Nov.24; 4177) DM 400
– **Recueil de Planches sur les Sciences, les Arts Libéraux, et les Arts Méchaniques.** Paris, 1768. *1st. Edn.* Fo. Lacks 6 plts., slightly browned, cont. leath. gt., spine with some sm. defects., reprd. (R. Apr.4; 2037) DM 2,000
– – **Anr. Copy.** Fo. Lacks 31 pp., cont. hf. leath. gt., rubbed & bumped. (HK. May 15; 377) DM 1,800
– **Encyclopedie ou Dictionnaire Raisonné des Sciences, des Arts et des Métiers.—Supplément. — Table Analytique et Raisonné des Sciences des Matières [par Mouchon].** Paris & Neufchatel; Amst. [Paris]; Paris, 1751-72; 1776-77; 1780. *Orig. Edns.* 28 vols., including ll plt. vols.; 5 vols. including plt. vol.; 2 vols. Fo. 3,129 plts., lacks frontis., cont. hf. cf., spines decor., some slight tears to turn-ins & corners. (LM. Mar.3; 1306) B. Frs. 650,000

DIEFFENBACH, Johann Friedrich
– **Der Aether Gegen den Schmerz.** Berlin, 1847. Hf.-title, liby. stp. on title, new bds., wraps. bnd. in; Dr. Walter Pagel copy. (S. Feb.7; 97) *Quaritch.* £480
– **Die Operative Chirurgie.** Leipzig, 1845-48. *1st. Edn.* 2 vols. Hf.-titles, errata lf., discold. in places, cl., mor. spines reprd.; Dr. Walter Pagel copy. (S. Feb.7; 96) *Quaritch.* £680

DIEHL, Edith
– **Bookbinding. Its Background & Technique.** N.Y., 1946. *[1st. Edn.].* 2 vols. Orig. cl. gt., s.-c.; H.M. Nixon coll. (BBA. Oct.6; 37) *Georges.* £50
– – **Anr. Copy.** 2 vols. Lge. 8vo. Ills., cl., s.-c., prospectus laid in. (SG. May 17; 76) $100

DIELMANN, J.
– **The Rhenish Portfolio.** Ill.:– after Dielmann. Frankfort, 1846. 3 pts. in 1 vol. Ob. 8vo. Chromolitho. titles, 80 engraved plts., some minor marginal spotting, orig. mor.-bkd. ptd. bds., rebkd. preserving orig. gt. spine, covers slightly stained, w.a.f.; from liby. of Luttrellstown Castle. (C. Sep.28; 1758) £850

DIEMERBROECK, Ysbrand van
– **Opera Omnia Anatomica et Medica.** Ed.:– T. de Diemersbrock. Utrecht, 1685. *1st. Coll. Edn.* Fo. 1st. p. & 1 plt. slightly crumpled in margin, cont. vell. (D. Nov.23; 545) DM 1,000

DIEMONT, Marius & Joy
– **The Brenthurst Baines ...** Johannesburg, 1975. *(850).* 4to. Cl., d.-w., s.-c. (VA. Oct.28; 420) R 1,200
– – **Anr. Copy.** Cl., d.-w. (SSA. Jul.5; 108) R 950
– – **Anr. Copy.** 4to. Cl., d.-w. (VA. Apr.27; 744) R 920
– – **Anr. Copy.** Cl., d.-w. (SSA. Sep.21; 123a) R 760

DIEPENBACH, W. & Stenz, C.
– **Die Mainzer Kurfürsten.** Mainz, [1935]. *(1725)* numbered. Fo. Lacks map, mod. hf. linen. (R. Oct.13; 2707) DM 520

DIEPENBROCK (Contrib).
See— KRONIEK

DIESEL, Mathias
– **Erlustierende Augenweide in Vorstellung Herrlicher Garten und Lustgebäude [–Erste Vortsetzung Erlustierender Augenweide].** [Augsburg, 1717-18]. 2 pts. in 1 vol. (bnd. in wrong sequence). Ob. fo. Engraved title, 100 plts., some margin staining, 19th. C. cf.-bkd. bds. (C. Dec.9; 36) *Goldschmidt.* £2,600
– **Erlustierender Augen-Weyde zweyte Fortsetzung, vorstellend die Weltberühmte Churfürstl. Residenz in München.** Ill.:– J.A. Corvinus & C. Remshart.

Augsburg, ca. 1720. Lge. ob. fo. Cont. hf. leath. (HK. Nov.9; 1399) DM 3,800

DIETRICH, A.
– **Flora Regni Borussici.** Berlin, 1833-44. 12 vols. 4to. 6 lithos. loose, margins frayed, 4 lithos. very spotted, text spotted or browned, some lithos. slightly foxed, cont. bds., some heavy wear. (H. May 22; 198) DM 4,000

DIETZ, U.
– **Calligraphia.** Nürnberg, ca. 1634. Ob. 4to. A little spotting, mod. bds., Hauswedel Coll. (H. May 23; 231) DM 4,200

DIEUSSART, Ch. Ph.
[–] **Theatrum Architecturae Civilis, in drey Bücher getheilet.** [Bayreuth, 1692?]. Fo. Lacks 1st. copper engraved title, ptd. title of 2 ll. prelims., text compl., copper engraved title very defect & mntd., 2 ll. MS. index bnd. at end, mod. hf. vell. (R. Apr.3; 696) DM 1,300

DIEZ, Fr.
– **La Poésie des Troubadours.** Trans.:– Baron Ferdinand de Roisin. Paris & Lille, 1845. *1st. Fr. Edn.* On vell., title verso stpd., cont. cf., gt. spine, covers, inner & outer dentelles, spine slightly faded; Hauswedell coll. (H. May 24; 1267) DM 620

DIEZEL, C.E.
– **Erfahrungen aus dem Gebiete der Niederjagd.** Offenbach, 1849. *1st. Edn.* Light wear, bds. (V. Sep.29; 1351) DM 650
– **Niederjagd.** Berlin, 1872. Cont. hf. leath. gt., rubbed. (R. Oct.12; 1970) DM 650

DIGBY, Sir Kenelm
– **Choice & Experimental Receipts in Physick & Chirurgery.** L., 1668. *1st. Edn.* With horizontal title-lf., cont. cf., roughly rebkd.; John Locke-Marsham family-Bernard Quaritch Ltd. copy, inscr. of William Elliot, bkplt. with initials CMHH surmounted with fleuron. [Wing D1423] (BBA. Nov.30; 103) *Pickering & Chatto.* £900
– **The Closet Opened ... Together with Excellent Directions for Cookery.** L., 1671. *2nd. Edn.* Sm. 8vo. Port., lacks K4-5, stained & browned, cont. sheep., worn. [Wing D1428] (S. Apr.10; 339) *Clarke.* £290

DIGGELMANN, A.W.
– **Die Jungfrau, Mein Berg.** N.d. Fo. 20 orig. lithos. & 2 panoramas, with accompanying text, bd. portfo., each lf. sigd. (G. Sep.15; 2096) Sw. Frs. 500

DIGGES, Sir Dudley
– **The Complete Ambassador.** 1655. *1st. Edn.* Fo. Some ll. browned, wormed in lr. edge, old spr. cf. (CE. Sep.1; 43) £65

DIGGLES, Silvester
– **Companion to Gould's Handbook; or, Synopsis of the Birds of Australia.** Ill.:– after Diggles. Brisbane, 1877. *Re-iss. of 'The Ornithology of Australia', 1866-70.* 2 vols. in 1. Fo. 82 (of 125) litho. plts., some foxing, cl.-bkd. bds., ex-liby. (SG. Oct.6; 175) $150

DIGHTON. R.
– **City Characters.** L., 1824. Fo. Ptd. title, 24 hand-cold. etched ports. dtd. individually between 1818 & 1824, further port. loosely inserted, many identified in pencil, later cf. (S. May 21; 2) *Quaritch.* £300

DIKDUKEI RASHI
[Riva di Trento], 1560. *1st. Edn.* 4to. Upr. margin of title reprd. without loss of text, slightly creased, staining mostly in lr. margins, mod. blind-tooled leath.; Moses Gaster Liby. stp. on p. 2. (S. Oct.24; 41) *Schwarzchild.* £350

DILHERR, Joh. Michael
– **Heilige Sonn– und Festags-Arbeit.** Ill.:– J.F. Fleischberger after G. Strauch. Nuremb., 1674. *2nd. Edn. 1st. Fo. Edn.* Fo. Cont. vell. (GB. May 3; 947) DM 1,600

DILLAYE, Frederic
– **La Practique en Photographies.** Paris, n.d. Qtr. mor., cl. bds., orig. paper covers bnd. in. (LH. Sep.25; 522) $140

D'ILLESCAS, Yakov
– **Imrei Noam.** Cremona, 1565. *2nd. Edn.* 4to. Mispaginated, faded, reprd., owner's sig, on title, staining mostly in margins, trimmed with loss of parts of some letters, mod. blind-tooled cf. (S. Oct.24; 141) *Stein.* £300

DILLEY, Arthur Urbane
– **Oriental Rugs & Carpets: a Comprehensive Study.** N.Y., 1931. *1st. Edn.* 4to. 80 plts., gt.-lettered cl. (SG. Jan.26; 258) $200

DILLON, Visc. Harold A. (Ed.)
See— ALMAIN ARMOURER'S Album, An

DILLON, Peter
– **Narrative & Successful Result of a Voyage in the South Seas.** 1829. *1st. Edn.* 2 vols. Hf.-titles, 2 folding frontis. (2nd. hand-cold.), engraved plt. & folding map, cont. cl.-bkd. bds.; pres. inscrs. 'from the author'. (S. May 22; 471) *Snow.* £530

DIMAND, Maurice S. (Ed.)
See— BALLARD COLLECTION

DINET, Etienne
[–] **Antar, Poème Héroïque Arabe des Temps Antéislamiques d'apres la Traduction de M. Davic.** Paris, 1898. *(300).* 4to. On vell. des Vosges, hf. mor., corners, mosaic spine, wrap. & spine preserved, by Klein. (HD. Dec.9; 123) Frs. 4,600

DINGE, M.
– **Discours sur l'Histoire de France.** Ill.:– Moreau Le Jeune. Paris, 1790. 4to. Cont. tree cf. gt., spine decor. (HD. May 3; 103) Frs. 1,000

DIODORUS SICULUS
– **Bibliothecae Historicae Libri VI.** Venice, Andreas de Paltasichis, 31 Jan. 1476/77. Fo. Considerable marginalia on 1st. few ll., MS. ex-libris on alr, 19th. C. maroon mor., elab. blind-tooled, brass clasps & bosses; the Walter Goldwater copy; A.L.s. by Margaret B. Stillwell relating to this edn. laid in. [BMC V, 251; Goff D-211] (SG. Dec.1; 121) $1,300
– – **Anr. Copy.** Fo. Rubricated, lacks 2 ll., sm. stain in lr. margin, last 2 ll. remargined at foot, old vell. [HC 6189; Goff D-211]. (HD. Jan.30; 7) Frs. 4,600
– – **Anr. Edn.** Venice, J. Tacuinus de Tridino, 20 Sep. 1496. Fo. Several ll. brownstained, later vell.; the Walter Goldwater copy. [BMC V, 530; Goff D-213; H. 6191] (SG. Dec.1; 122) $600
– **Bibliothecae Historicae Libri VI. Corneli Taciti Germania.** Trans.:– [Poggius]. Venice, Thomas de Blavis, de Alexandria, 25 Nov. 1481. Fo. A few MS. marginalia, some light spotting & staining, blind-stpd. cf., rebkd. with orig. spine laid down, foot of spine missing, corners & edges rubbed. [BMC V, 316; Goff D-212] (SPB. Dec.14; 14) $1,000
– **Bibliothecae Historicae Libri XVII.** Lyon, 1552. 32mo. Mod. red mor. (SG. Apr.19; 74) $120
– **Histoire.** Trans.:– Jacques Amyot. 1585. Fo. Cont. marb. cf., worn. (HD. Jun.29; 62) Frs. 1,000
– **Historiarum Libri Aliquot.** Ed.:– V. Obsopoeus. Basel, 1539. *1st. Edn.* 4to. Some light stains, later vell. (BBA. Jan.19; 4) *Quevedo.* £110

DIOGENES LAERTIUS
– **De Vitis Dogmatis et Apophthegmatis.** L., 1664. Fo. In Latin & Greek, slight browning, cont. red mor., gt. coats of arms on covers. (S. Mar.20; 822) *Blanko.* £220
– **Vitae et Sententiae Philosophorum.** Venice, [B. Locatellus] for Octavianus Scotus, 18 Dec. 1490. 4to. 1st. lf. remargined, some wrinkling & stains, old wood bds., cf. back, metal clasp; the Walter Goldwater copy. [BMC V, 438; Goff D-222] (SG. Dec.1; 123) $650

DIOMEDES
– **De Arte Grammatica Opus.** Venetiis, Christophorus de Pensis de Mandelo, 1491. Fo. 19th. C. Engl. jansenist mor. gt. [BMC V, 468; Goff D236] (HD. Nov.16; 72) Frs. 10,000

DION CASSIUS, Nicaeus
– **Delle Guerre & Fatti Romani.** Trans.:– Nicolo Leoniceno. Ill.:– Matheo da Treviso. [Venice,

1533]. 4to. Title in woodcut border, port., 32 woodcuts, some foxing, few marginalia, last 2 ll. reprd. with few letters in facs., old pol. cf. gt. (SG. Apr.26; 73) $225

DIONIGI, Maria Candidi
– Viaggi in Alcune Citta del Lazio. Rome, 1809. Ob. fo. Cont. hf. mor. (SKC. Nov.18; 2006) £120

DIONIS, Pierre
– The Anatomy of Humane Bodies Improv'd. 1703. 21 plts. (1 folding), some staining, folding plt. torn, panel. cf., rubbed. (P. Jun.7; 272) £65
– A Course of Chirurgical Operations, demonstrated in the Royal Garden at Paris. L., 1733. 2nd. Engl. Edn. Some dampstaining & soiling, minor margin tears, last lf. creased, cont. cf., spine defect., upr. cover detchd. (S. Dec.13; 263) Phillips. £120
– – Anr. Copy. Cf., brkn.; sig. of Dr. Benjamin Church. (LH. Sep.25; 523) $300
– A General Treatise of Midwifery. L., 1719. 1st. Engl. Edn. Advt. lf. at end, slight soiling, Q1-2 stained, cont. cf., worn. (S. Dec.13; 264) Phillips. £170

DIONYSIUS, Halicarnassus
– Antiquarium Romanarum. Lib. X. Paris, 1546-47. 2 pts. in 1 vol. Tall 8vo. Vell.; Michael Wodhull copy. (LH. Sep.25; 524) $300
– Antiquitates Romanae. Treviso, Bernardinus Celerius, 1480. Fo. Lge. copy, final lf. in revised state, with colophon in massed capitals, & translator's name given as 'LAPPUS', lacks 4 ll. (1 or more blank), old hf. vell.; the Walter Goldwater copy. [BMC VI, 895; Goff D-250] (SG. Dec.1; 124) $550
– – Anr. Copy. Fo. Wide margins, final lf. in revised state, 1st. & last 2 ll. reprd. in margins, considerably wormed at beginning, 18th. C. cf., rebkd.; the Walter Goldwater copy. (SG. Dec.1; 125) $375
– – Anr. Edn. Reggio Emilia, Franciscus de Mazalis, 12 Nov. 1498. 11 books in 1 vol. Fo. Initials painted in cols. & gold at beginning of each book, books I & IV specially decor. in margin, lacks blank 1st. lf., cont. blind-stpd. roan, end-papers renewed; from Fondation Furstenberg-Beaumesnil. [HC 6240; BMC VII, 1089; Goff D251] (HD. Nov.16; 41) Frs. 22,000
– Delle Cose Antiche della Citta di Roma. Trans.:– F. Venturi. Venezia, 1545. 4to. Hf. cf. (CR. Jul.6; 151) Lire 250,000

DIOSCORIDES, Anazarbei Pedanius
– De Medica Materia. Lyon, 1543. 16mo. Cf., by Simier, gt. decor., inner & outer roulette, decor. spines. (HD. Jan.26; 107) Frs. 1,600
– Historia de la Yerbas, y Plantas ... N.d. Sm. fo. Lacks ll. before A4 & after 203, soiled, browned, later roan-bkd. bds., w.a.f. (CSK. Nov.4; 133) £130

DIPPEL, J.C. 'Christiances Democritus'
– Analysis Cramatis Hyper-Metaphysico-Logico-Mathematica, Das ist Chymischer Versuch zu destilliren ... N.p., 1729 1st. Edn. 4to. Wide margins, bds. (R. Oct.12; 1545) DM 750

DIRKS, Jacob
– De Noord-Nederlandsche Gildenpenningen. Haarlem, 1878-79. 2 vols. text & 1 vol. plts. Later mor. gt., partly unopened. (S. May 1; 462) Drury. £170

DIROM, Alexander
– A Narrative of the Campaign in India, which terminated the War with Tippoo Sultan, in 1792. 1793. 4to. 1 neatline shaved, some slight offsetting & browning, cont. hf. cf., slightly worn. (S. Nov.1; 54) Edwards. £90

DIRSZTAY, V.
– Lob des Hohen Verstandes. Ill.:– O. Kokoschka. Leipzig, 1917. 1st. Edn. (200 Ltd. Iss. ?). Lge. 4to. Orig. bds. (H. May 23; 1333) DM 600

DISENOS OF CALIFORNIA RANCHOS. Maps of Thirty-Seven Land Grants 1822-1846
San Franc., 1964. (400). 4to. Linen-bkd. decor. paper bds. (LH. Sep.25; 328) $350

DISNEY, John
– Museum Disneianum, being a Collection of Ancient Marbles, Specimens of Ancient Bronze, & Various Ancient Fictile Vases. 1849. 4to. Litho. plts., some cold., cont. hf. mor., rebkd., slightly rubbed. (BBA. Jul.27; 260) Quaritch. £55

DISNEY, Walt
See— WALT DISNEY PRODUCTIONS

DISEPNSATORIUM REGIUM et Electorale Borusso-Brandenburgicum
Berlin, 1731. Fo. Browned thro.-out & some heavy spotting from pressing plants, 1 lf. defect., lacks 2 index ll., cont. hf. leath., defect., spine renewed. (HT. May 8; 534) DM 660

DISPUTATIO S. TRINITATIS
[Cologne, Arnold Ther Hoernen], ca. 1475. 4to. Lacks 1st. blank, blind-stpd. of.; from the Prince Arenberg liby., the Walter Goldwater copy. [BMC I, 208; Goff D-269] (SG. Dec.1; 126) $1,600
– – Anr. Edn. [Leipzig, Wolfgang Stoeckel], ca. 1500. 4to. Mod. hf. vell.; the Walter Goldwater copy. [BMC I, 157; Goff D-270] (SG. Dec.1; 127) $200

DISRAELI, Benjamin, Earl of Beconsfield
– Lord George Bentinck : A Political Biography. 1852. 2 pp. A.L.s. dtd. Feb. 26. 1849 from Disraeli to William Ansell Day, mntd. on front blank, 6 clipped sigs. from political figures, mntd. on dedication verso, cont. cf., rubbed, upr. cover neatly reprd. (CSK. May 18; 105) £120
– Novels & Tales by ... L., 1870-81. 11 vols. Unif. three-qtr. mor., gt.-decor. ribbed spines. (CBA. Dec.10; 191) $170
– – Anr. Edn. L., 1877. Coll. Edn. 10 vols. Sm. 8vo. Three-qtr. cf., spines gt. with fleurons. (SG. Feb.16; 94) $140
– – Anr. Edn. 1881. Hughenden Edn. 11 vols. Cont. hf. cf. (CSK. Dec.16; 111) £130
– – Anr. Edn. L., 1882. Hughenden Edn. 11 vols. Cont. hf. mor., spines gt. (S. Mar.20; 873) Wade. £70
– Voyage of Captain Popanilla. 1828. 1st. Edn. Cont. hf. cf. (CSK. Aug.19; 5) £140

D'ISRAELI, Isaac
– Curiosities of Literature. 1823. 2nd. Series: 1st. Edn. Orig. Series: 5 vols., 2nd. Series: 3 vols. Orig. bds. (BBA. Feb.9; 81) Bickersteth. £160

DISTELI, M.
– Schweizerischer Bilderkalender. Solothun, 1839-44. Years 1-6 only (of 9) in 1 vol. Browned, 4 folding plts. crumpled, some plts. torn & badly bkd., cont. bds., bumped. (R. Oct.11; 167) DM 750

DITHMAR, J. C.
– Geschichte des Ritterlichen Johanniter Orden und dessen Herren. Meisterthums ... Frankfurt/Oder, 1728. 4to. Some slight browning, 19th. C. linen, spine wormed. (R. Oct.11; 1133) DM 550

DITTERSDORF, Carl Ditters von
– Der Apotheker und Doktor im Clavierauszug ... Eine Deutsche Komische Opera ... Vienna, 1787. 2nd. Edn. 2 pts. in 1 vol. Fo. Some pp. misnumbered, a little spotted, a few cont. annots., cont. paper wraps., stiffened, stained, spine defect. (S. May 10; 46) Haas. £190

DIVINE, S.R.
– Photographic Manipulation or System of Practice for the Chemistry Department of the Portrait Gallery. N.Y., 1864. 1st. Edn. Orig. ribbed cl. (PNY. Dec.1; 98) $100

D'IVORI, Joan
– Vestidos Tipicos de España. Barcelona, 1936. Fo. 110 pochoir-cold. plts., each liby.-stpd. on blank verso, loose in bd. folder. (SG. May 3; 111) $100

DIX, O.
– Das Evangelium nach Matthäus. Berlin, 1960. (100) numbered De Luxe Edn. 4to. Orig. mor., bd. s.-c.; title sigd. by Dix in pencil. (HK. Nov.11; 3494) DM 550

DIXON, Charles
– The Game Birds & Wild Fowl of the British Islands. Ill.:– after Charles Whymper. Sheffield, 1900. 2nd. Edn. 4to. 41 cold. plts., orig. cl., soiled. (S. Apr.10; 495) Kouchak. £190
– – Anr. Copy. 4to. Orig. decor. cl., rubbed. (TA. Apr.19; 136) £65

DIXON, Capt. George
– Further Remarks on the Voyages of John Meares, Esq. L., 1791. 1st. Edn. 4to. Mod. bds.; the Rt. Hon. Visc. Eccles copy. [Sabin 20363] (CNY. Nov.18; 90) $4,000
– Remarks on the Voyages of John Meares, Esq. In a Letter to that Gentleman. L., priv. ptd., 1790. 1st. Edn. 4to. Hf.-title, cont. note to binder on title-p., mod. bds.; the Rt. Hon. Visc. Eccles copy. [Sabin 20361] (CNY. Nov.18; 88) $2,800
– A Voyage Round the World; But More Particularly to the North-West Coast of America: Performed in 1785, 1786, 1787 & 1788. L., 1789. 1st. Edn. 4to. Lge. & thick paper, lge. folding engraved map, 4 other folding maps, 17 full-p. engraved plts., including 7 hand-cold., 4 plts. foxed, old tree cf. gt., gt. spine, rebkd.; the Rt. Hon. Visc. Eccles copy. [Sabin 64590] (CNY. Nov.18; 87) $3,400
– – Anr. Edn. L., 1789. 2nd. Edn. 4to. Hf.-title, 5 folding engraved charts, 17 engraved plts., including 3 folding, short tears at folds of maps, 1 folding plt. with sm. tear in blank margin, cont. tree cf., rubbed, rebkd., corners reprd.; Stefansson Coll. liby. stp. [Sabin 20364] (C. Jun.27; 87) Traylen. £340
– – Anr. Copy. 4to. Lge. & thick paper, 22 maps, charts & plts., including 7 hand-cold., hf.-title, errata, directions to binder, some browning, some tears on folding plts., some pp. loose, disbnd., but with 2 covers, worn. (SPB. Dec.13; 441) $450
See— PORTLOCK, Capt. Nathaniel & Dixon, Capt. George

DOBAI, J.
See— NOVOTNY, F. & Dobai, J.

DOBBS, Arthur
– An Account of the Countries adjoining to Hudson's Bay, in the North-West part of America. L., 1744. 1st. Edn. 4to. Portion of blank margin torn from S4, cont. cf. [Sabin 20404] (S. Dec.1; 278) Brooke-Hitching. £1,250

DOBEL, Heinrich Wilhelm
– Eröffnete Jäger-Practica, Oder Der wohlgeübte u. Erfahrne Jäger. Leipzig, 1746. 1st. Edn. 3 pts. in 1 vol. Fo. Lacks hf.-title, some light foxing, jnts. strengthened with pasted strips inside, cont. leath., corners very bumped. (HK. May 16; 1574) DM 2,500
– Jäger-Practica. Leipzig, 1754. 2nd. Edn. 4 pts. in 1 vol. Fo. Some plts. slightly crumpled & with sm. repairs, slightly foxed or worn, cont. hf. leath., spine defect. (HK. Nov.9; 1772) DM 2,300
– Neueröffneter Jäger-Practica. Leipzig, 1783. 4 pts. in 1 vol. Fo. Title double stpd., plts. slightly crumpled, foxed & slightly stained thro.-out, cont. bds. (HK. Nov.9; 1773) DM 540

DOBIE, J. Frank
– Apache Gold & Yaqui Silver. Ill.:– Tom Lea. Boston, 1939. 1st. Edn. (265) numbered & sigd. by author & artist. Extra set of col. plts. in envelope laid in, cl.-bkd. bds., s.-c. (SG. Oct.20; 134) $350
– Tales of the Mustang. Ill.:– Jerry Bywaters. Dallas, 1936. (300). Paper bds. (LH. Sep.25; 218) $550

DOBLIN, A.
– Das Stiftsfräulein und der Tod. Ill.:– E.L. Kirchner. Berlin-Wilmersdorf, 1913. On vell., 5 orig. woodcuts, orig. sewed. (GB. May 5; 2773) DM 2,200

DOBRZENSKI, Jacobus Joannes Wenceslaus
– Nova et Amaenior de Admirando Fontium Genio ... Philosophia. Ferrara, 1659 [but 1657?]. 1st. Edn. Sm. fo. Short tear in engraved title, light stains towards end, lr. margins of last few ll. damaged by damp without affecting text, few sm. margin wormholes, cont. blind-stpd. vell., lr. cover defect.

DOBRZENSKI, Jacobus Joannes Wenceslaus - Contd.
near foot of spine; John D. Stanitz Coll. (SPB. Apr.25; 122) £1,200

DOBSON, Austin
- The Ballad of Beau Brocade. Ill.:– H. Thomson. L., 1892. (450) L.P. Mor. gt. decor. (P. May 17; 75) Marks. £100
– – Anr. Copy. Cont. red mor. gt. (CSK. Jan.27; 164) £85

DOBSON, Christopher
See— SPENCER, Earl & Dobson, Christopher

DOCUMENTS D'ART JUIF—Orfevrerie & Peinture
Preface:- Henri Guttmann. Paris, ca. 1925. 4to. 48 plts. (6 hand-cold.), plts. loose as iss., cl.-bkd. bd. folder, cl. ties, flaps detchd., spine frayed, ex-liby. (SG. Feb.2; 76) $250

DOCUMENTS OF BRITISH FOREIGN POLICY 1919-39
Ed.:- E.L. Woodward & Rohan Butler. L., 1946-72. 1st. Series, vols. 2-4, 6-13, 16-18, 2nd. series, vols. 1-8, 10-11, 3rd. series, vols. 1-10, together 34 vols. Some folding maps, orig. cl., few damp affected or slightly marked, d.-w.'s. (S. Apr.10; 353) Sayer. £190

DOCUMENTS pour servir à l'Etude de l'Art Egyptien
Paris, 1927-31. (612). 2 vols. Fo. Bds., unc. (B. Jun.21; 70) Fls. 1,000

DODDRIDGE, Joseph
- Notes on the Settlements & Indian Wars of the Western Parts of Virginia & Pennsylvania ... 1763-1783 ... Wellsburgh, Virginia, 1824. 1st. Edn. Foxing, heavy in places, later spr. cf. (LH. Apr.15; 301) $180

DODGE, Mary Mapes
- Hans Brinker, or, the Silver Skates. Ill.:– Darley & T. Nast. N.Y., 1866. 1st. Edn. 2 ll. of advts. [Blanck's state 'B'], some foxing, cl., worn. (SG. Dec.8; 138) $100

DODGE, Richard I.
- A Living Issue ... Wash., 1882. Orig. ptd. wraps. (LH. Apr.15; 302) $100

DODGSON, Campbell
- Catalogue of Early German & Flemish Woodcuts ... in the British Museum. L., 1911. 2 vols. 4to. Lightly browned, pencil entries, orig. linen, spine slightly bumped. (HT. May 8; 712) DM 750
- Catalogue of Etchings & Dry Points of Muirhead Bone. [L.], 1909. (275) numbered. Lge. 4to. Port.-frontis., ex-liby., orig. hf. leath. (SG. May 3; 52) $150
- A Catalogue of Etchings by Augustus John, 1901-14. 1920. (105) numbered, with frontis. self-port., sigd. by artist. 4to. Orig. buckram gt. (SKC. Nov.18; 1806) $200
– – Anr. Edn. L., 1920. (325) numbered. 4to. Orig. cl.-bkd. bds., rubbed. (S. Apr.30; 26) Sims. £80
– – Anr. Copy. Sm. fo. Port., 133 reproductions, ex-liby., hf. buckram. (SG. May 3; 221) $110
- Edmund Blampied: A Complete Catalogue of the Etchings & Dry-Points. L., 1926. (350) numbered, with sigd. etching. 4to. 100 plts., ex-liby., buckram. (SG. May 3; 50) $375
- Robert Austin: A Catalogue of Etchings & Engravings. L., 1930. (160) numbered. Sm. fo. Port., 89 reproductions, ex-liby., buckram. (SG. May 3; 26) $130
- Woodcuts of the XV Century in the ... British Museum. L., 1934-35. 2 vols. Fo. Cold. frontis., 262 reproductions on 117 plts., liby. buckram. (SG. May 3; 144) $120

DODGSON, Rev. Charles Lutwidge 'Lewis Carroll'
- Alice's Adventures in Wonderland. Ill.:– John Tenniel. N.Y., 1866. 1st. Edn. 2nd. [1st. Publd.] Iss. Sheets of suppressed first Engl. edn. of 1865 with cancel title, ills., cont. owner's inscr., orig. cl.; Perry Molstad copy. (SPB. May 16; 449) $3,500
– – Anr. Edn. L., 1866. 2nd. [1st. Publd.] Engl. Edn. Slight foxing to few ll., orig. publisher's cl.,

head & tail of spine slightly worn, bds. slightly soiled. (LA. Nov.29; 173) £460
– – Anr. Copy. 1st. lf. of prefatory poem detchd. & torn, dupl. lf. loosely inserted, lightly soiled thro.-out, orig. cl., spine worn, stitching brkn., light blue end-papers. (CSK. Oct.21; 25) £90
– – Anr. Copy. Lev. gt. by Bayntun, orig. cl. covers & spine bnd. in, s.-c. (SG. Dec.8; 91) $650
– – Anr. Copy. Pagination error on p.30, raised line on p.119, double rule above Poetical Intro., ills., writing on hf.-title & endpapers, some soiling or light browning, orig. cl., rebkd., soiled, red mor.-bkd. s.-c.; bkplt. of Alfred Hellman, Fred A. Berne copy, with An Easter Greeting ... N.p., ca. 1877, 16mo. (SPB. May 16; 246) $275
– – Anr. Edn. Ill.:– John Tenniel. Boston, 1869. 2nd. Amer. Edn. Ills., light browning, orig. cl. with gt. emblems on upr. & lr. cover in gt. rules; Fred A. Berne copy. (SPB. May 16; 247) $500
– – Anr. Copy. Darkening, orig. gt.-decor. cl., covers lightly rubbed & soiled, spine faded, extremities bumped, bookseller's stp. on front free end-paper verso; gift of Joe E. Brown to Marymount College, with bkplts. of both. (CBA. Mar.3; 74) $300
– – Anr. Edn. Ill.:– Arthur Rackham. L., [1907]. (1130) numbered. 4to. Orig. cl. gt., spine faded. (SKC. Sep.9; 1882) £160
– – Anr. Edn. Ill.:– Arthur Rackham. L., [1907]. 4to. Elab. red mor. gt. by Bayntun-Rivière. (SPB. Dec.13; 558) $900
– – Anr. Copy. 4to. Some browning & soiling, red hf. mor. (SPB. Dec.13; 557) $200
– – Anr. Edn. Ill.:– Arthur Rackham. L., 1919. 4to. Orig. cl.; pres. copy, inscr. by Rackham to Johan Briede, with pen & ink drawing on hf.-title, sigd. & dtd. 22.9.19. (S. Nov.22; 354) Joseph. £370
– – Anr. Edn. Ill.:– Marie Laurencin. Paris, Black Sun Pr., 1930. European Edn., (370) on Rives paper. Ob. 4to. Wraps. over light bds., glassine d.-w. slightly creased & torn, two-piece s.-c., worn; gift of Joe E. Brown to Marymount College, with their bkplts. (CBA. Mar.3; 81) $1,400
– – Anr. Edn. Ill.:– Marie Laurencin. Paris, Black Sun Pr., 1930. (790). (420) for sale in the U.S. Ob. 4to. Light foxing to a few pp., ptd. wraps., light foxing & staining to covers, glassine d.-w., darkened, chipped & torn. (CBA. Nov.19; 24) $325
– – Anr. Edn. Ill.:– after Sir John Tenniel. N.Y., Ltd. Edns. Cl., 1932. (1500) numbered. Mor. gt., owner's sig. on free end-paper; sigd. by Frederic Warde & Alice Hargreaves. (SG. Dec.8; 93) $275
– – Anr. Edn. Ill.:– Salvador Dali. N.Y., 1969. (2500) numbered & sigd. by artist. Fo. 2 copies of the prospectus in orig. pict. envelope, loose sheets as iss. in cl. folder, linen & mor. folder with ties. (SG. Dec.8; 94) $800
– – Anr. Copy. Fo. Leaves, wrap., box. (HD. Mar.27; 52) Frs. 1,800
- Alice's Adventures in Wonderland.—Through the Looking Glass & What Alice Found There. Ill.:– John Tenniel. 1867; 1872. 1st. work: 6th. thousand; 2nd. work: 1st. Edn. Together 2 vols. Orig. cl. gt. (SKC. Jan.13; 2136) £90
– – Anr. Edn. Ill.:– John Tenniel. N.Y., Ltd. Edns. Cl., 1932; 1935. (1500) numbered. Together 2 vols. Ills., mor. gt., s.-c.'s, spines slightly worn; each sigd. by Alice Hargreaves. (SG. Apr.26; 40) $500
- Alice's Adventures Under Ground. 1886. 1st. Edn. Orig. cl., a little faded. (LC. Mar.1; 114) £50
– – Anr. Copy. Slight stain to lr. corners, bookseller's entry tipped to hf.-title orig. gt.-lettered & ruled cl., slight wear to extremities, spine faded (gt. still bright), staining to foot of lr. cover. (CBA. Mar.3; 83) $120
- Aventures d'Alice au Pays des Merveilles. Ill.:– Arthur Rackham. Paris, [1907]. 1st. Fr. Edn. 4to. This copy with 'Exemplaire non destiné au Commerce' ptd. on verso of hf.-title, gt.-decor. white cl. (corresponds to Engl. Ltd. Edn. of 1130), rubbed & soiled, spine darkening, end-papers slightly foxed & darkened. (CBA. Aug.21; 507) $225
– – Anr. Edn. Ill.:– Arthur Rackham. N.d. (20) on Japan, sigd. by artist. 4to. No bdg. stated. (HD. Jun.26; 140) Frs. 11,000
- Doublets; a Word Puzzle. 1880. 3rd. Edn. 1 vol. Orig. cl. gt.; inscr. by author. (With:) - Through the Looking Glass, & What Alice Found There.

1872. 1st. Edn. 1 vol. Orig. cl. gt., badly soiled, spine worn. (LC. Mar.1; 113) £160
- The Hunting of the Snark. Ill.:– Henry Holiday. 1876. 1st. Edn. Orig. pict. cl. (LC. Jul.5; 23) £65
– – Anr. Copy. Ill., some browning, last few ll. & front endpaper loose, orig. pres. cl. gt.; pres. copy to Maria M.A. Synge, Fred A. Berne copy. (SPB. May 16; 248) $425
– – Anr. Copy. 2 pp. discold. by laid in newspaper clipping, orig. pict. cl., cl.-covered s.-c. (SG. Nov.17; 25) $140
- The Lewis Carroll Picture Book. Ed:– Stuart Dodgson Collingwood. L., 1899. 1st. Edn. Pict. gt. cl., covers lightly soiled, extremities mildly bumped, end-papers darkening. (CBA. Mar.3; 114) $100
- The Nursery 'Alice'. Ill.:– after John Tenniel, engraved by Edmund Evans. L., 1889. 1st. Edn. 4to. 2 pp. of advts. at end, 6 ills. in proof state on 3 fo. sheets laid in loose, contents darkening with some staining or soiling, proof sheets soiled & darkening, hf. cl. & pict. bds., designed by E. Gertrude Thomson, covers soiled & rubbed, extremities worn; William H. Woodin bkplt. (CBA. Mar.3; 87) $300
– – Anr. Edn. Ill.:– after Sir John Tenniel. N.Y., 1890. 1st. Amer. Edn. 4to. Orig. cl.-bkd. col.-pict. bds., designed by E.G. Thomson, covers spotted & scuffed at lr. edges. (SG. Dec.8; 92) $120
- Rhyme? & Reason? L., 1833. 1st. Edn. 1 vol. Orig. cl. gt. (With:) - The Game of Logic. L. & N.Y., 1887. 2nd. Edn. 1 vol. With envelope containing card/diagram, orig. cl. gt. (With:) - The Hunting of the Snark. L., 1876. 1st. Edn. 1 vol. Orig. ill. cl. (With:) - Sylvie & Bruno. L. & N.Y., 1889. 1st. Edn. 2 vols. Orig. cl. gt., spine faded, backstrip chipped. (LH. Sep.25; 507) $170
- Sylvie & Bruno. Ill.:– Harry Furniss. L., 1889. 1st. Edn. Few pp. lightly foxed, orig. gt.-decor. cl., light wear to covers, spine faded; pres. copy, inscr. to 'Mrs. Argles with sincere regards from the Author. Dec.12/89', Joe E. & Kathryn Brown bkplt., Marymount College bkplt. laid in loose. (CBA. Mar.3; 90) $250
- Sylvie & Bruno.—Sylvie & Bruno Concluded. Ill.:– Harry Furniss. L., 1889;1893. 1st. Edns. Together 2 vols. Orig. cl. gt., slightly worn; pres. copies, inscr. 'Mrs. Castle, from the Author. July 13, 1897'. (S. Dec.20; 642) Stacey. £155
– – Anr. Copy. Together 2 vols. Cont. mott. cf., spines gt. (CSK. Mar.9; 193) £65
– – Anr. Copy. Together 2 vols. Orig. cl., rubbed, 1st. with worn spine. (BBA. Jul.27; 153) Waggett. £50
– – Anr. Copy. Together 2 vols. An advt. dtd. C'mas. 1893 criticising the printing of the ills. of an edn. of 'Through the Looking-Glass ... ' laid in, gt.-decor. cl., 2nd. vol. with most of d.-w. (spine chipped), cl. folding box; pres. copies, inscr. to Grace Ellison, the 1st. dtd. 18 Sep. 1890, the 2nd. dtd. 28 Dec. 1893. (SG. Dec.8; 98) $550
- Sylvie & Bruno Concluded. Ill.:– Harry Furniss. L., 1893. 1st. Edn. Slight darkening, some foxing & dampstaining to end-papers & prelims., orig. gt.-decor. cl., some slight dampstaining to covers, spine slightly faded; pres. copy, inscr. to 'Mrs. Argles with sincere regards, from the Author. Dec.27, 1893', Joe E. & Kathryn Brown bkplt., Marymount College copy. (CBA. Mar.3; 91) $180
- Through the Looking-Glass, & What Alice Found There. Ill.:– Sir John Tenniel. L., 1872. 1st. Edn. 1st. Iss. Sm. 8vo. With 'wade on p. 21, lev. gt. by Bayntun, orig. cl. covers & spine bnd. in, s.-c. (SG. Dec.8; 95) $550
– – Anr. Edn. Ill.:– John Tenniel. L., 1872. 1st. Edn. With 'wade' on p.21, ill., light offsetting of frontis. onto tissue guard, orig. cl. gt.; pres. copy to Mary Brown, Frank J. Hogan bkplt., Fred A. Berne copy. (SPB. May 16; 249) $700
– – Anr. Edn. Ill.:– after Sir John Tenniel. N.Y., Ltd. Edns. Cl., 1935. (1500) numbered. Mor. gt., owner's sig. on end-paper; sigd. by Alice Hargreaves. (SG. Dec.8; 96) $225
- Wunderhorn. Ed.:– Max Ernst & Werner Spies. Ill.:– M. Ernst. Stuttgart, Manus Pr., 1970. De Luxe Edn., (69) numbered on papier d'Arches. Lge. 4to. Lacks double suite of lithos. on Japan, rough ll., in orig. linen portfo., orig. linen s.-c., printer's mark sigd. by artist. (HK. Nov.11; 3539) DM 1,300

- – Anr. Edn. Ill.:– Max Ernst. [Stuttgart], Manus Pr., 1970. *(1000)*. 4to. Orig. linen. (D. Nov.24; 3020) DM 400
- – Anr. Edn. Ed:– Max Ernst & Werner Spies. Ill.:– M. Ernst. Stuttgart, Manus Pr., 1970. *Ltd. Iss.* 4to. 36 orig. cold. lithos., orig. linen, spine faded. (GB. Nov.5; 2423) DM 450

DODGSON, D.S.
- General Views & Special Points of Interest of the City of Lucknow. L., 1860. Fo. Tinted litho. title, plan, 9 (of 11) plts., spotted, loose, orig. cl., spine worn. (S. Mar.6; 29) *Maggs.* £60

DODONAEUS or DODOENS, Rembertus
- Cruydt-Boeck. Antw., 1644. Fo. Some browning & margin staining, margin repairs to hf.-title, minor holes to a4-5 of index at beginning, cont. vell. bds., soiled, lacks ties. (S. Nov.28; 21) *Quaritch.* £1,100
- – Anr. Copy. Fo. Slightly stained at upr. margin of 1st. few ll., light browning, cont. blind-stpd. vell. over wood bds., lacks clasps, slightly stained, spine torn. (CH. May 24; 16) Fls. 3,500
- A New Herball, or Historie of Plants ... Trans.:– Henrie Lyte. 1586. 4to. Title cut-down & laid down, 1 lf. torn with loss, some margins reprd., some soiling, old cf., rubbed. (CSK. Jun.15; 49) £160
- Stirpium Historiae pemptades sex sive libri XXX. Antw., 1583. *1st. Latin Edn.* Fo. Wide margin, end lf. (containing privilege) with sm. bkd. excision & bnd. after title, prelims. mis-ordered, some corners stained, some other pp. browned, some margin repairs, hf. vell., spine renewed. (R. Oct.12; 1822) DM 6,000
- – Anr. Edn. Antw., 1616. *2nd. Latin Edn.* Fo. Copper engraved title bkd., sm. fault in side margin extended, some prelims. & end lf. partly restored in margins, many old Engl. MS. descriptions to woodcuts, some excised at side, stained nearly thro.-out, 19th. C. hf. vell. (R. Oct.12; 1822a) DM 2,200

DODSLEY, Robert
- A Collection of Poems. L., 1748-58. *1st. Edn.* 6 vols. 12mo. Engraved vig. on titles, S gathering browned in vol. 6, cont. cf. gt., tooled gt. spines slightly worn; bkplts. of Edward Lord Suffield. (SPB. May 16; 49) $450
- [-] Economie de la Vie Humaine. Edinb., 1752. 12mo. Cf. (HD. Feb.22; 51) Frs. 2,500

DODSWORTH, Roger
See— DUGDALE, Sir William & Dodsworth, Roger

DODWELL, Edward
- Views & Descriptions of Cyclopian of Pelasgic Remains in Greece & Italy ... L., 1834. 131 lithos., washed, many plts. reprd., stains, as a collection, w.a.f. (CR. Jul.6; 152) Lire 750,000
- Views in Greece. Ill.:– R. Havell, T. Fielding, F.C. Lewis, & others. L., 1821. *1st. Edn.* Lge. fo. Title with uncold. aquatint vig., 30 hand-cold. aquatint plts., mntd. on card, ptd. title slips pasted to mount versos (1 with different title to that in plt. list), 6 plts. with minor spotting, 3 title slips shaved, hf. mor. gt., s.-c. (C. Nov.16; 79) *Traylen.* £4,600
- – Anr. Copy. Lge. fo. Title with uncold. aquatint vig., 30 hand-cold. aquatint views, mntd. on card, plts. without the ptd. title slips on verso, cont. hf. mor., rebkd. (C. Mar.14; 45) *Tzakas.* £4,200
- – Anr. Copy. Fo. 29 engraved & cold. plts., Engl. & Fr. description, pasted on paper with caption on verso, lacks last plt. & description, hf. cf., corners. (HD. Dec.16; 44) Frs. 32,100
- – Anr. Edn. Ill.:– R. Havell, T. Fielding, F.C. Lewis, & others. [L., 1821]. *1st. Edn.* Lge. fo. Ptd. title with uncold. aquatint vig., 30 cold. aquatint plts., mntd. on card (without ptd. slips on verso of mounts), some faint offsetting, cont. red str.-grd. mor., gt.-decor. borders, blind-tooled & gt.-ruled frames, fan-shaped gothic window & arch cornerpieces, spine fully gt. in 5 compartments, rubbed, head of spine chipped. (S. Feb.1; 18) *Thomas.* £8,000

DOEFF, Hendrik
- Herinneringen uit Japan. Haarlem, 1833. Orig. bds. (VG. Mar.19; 238) Fls. 825

DOERING, H.
- Die Gelehrten Theologen Deutschlands um 18. und 19. Jahrhundert. Neustadt a.d. Orla, 1831-35. 4 vols. Slightly later hf. linen. (R. Oct.11; 1134) DM 550
See— WOLFF, Oscar Ludwig Bernhard & Doering, H.

DOES, J. van der
See— DOUSA or DOES, J. van der

DOEVEREN, Wouter van
- Musei Doevereniani Catalogus. [Leiden, 1785]. Auction catalogue, in Latin & Dutch, orig. unlettered wraps., chipped, untrimmed. (SG. Oct.6; 129) $100
- Specimen Observationum Academicarum, ad Monstrorum Historiam, Anatomen, Pathologiam & Artem Obstetricam praecipue Spectantium. Groningen & Leiden, 1765. 4to. Cont. marb. cf., spine gt. (VG. Nov.30; 752) Fls. 460

DOHME, R. (Ed.)
See— JAHRBUCH DER KONIGLICH PREUSSISCHEN KUNSTSAMMLUNGEN

DOHME, R. (Text)
See— RITTER, L.

D'OLLANDA, Francisco
- Os Desenhos das Antigualhas que vio ... Pintor Português (1539-40). Ed.:– Elias Tormo. Madrid, 1940. *Facs. of Codice Escurialense. (500).* Lge. fo. Mor., gt. & blind-tooled. (DS. Apr.27; 2211) Pts. 28,000

DOLLET, St.
- De Re Navali Liber ad Lazarum Bayfium. Lyon, 1537. *1st. Edn.* 4to. Some slight soiling, foxing & staining, mod. cont. style vell. (HT. May 8; 122) DM 1,400

DOLLFUS, Charles
See— HIRSCHAUR, L. & Dollfus, Ch.

DOLLFUS, Charles & Bouché, Henri
- Histoire de l'Aéronautique. Paris, 1932. Fo. Orig. decor. cl.; Hugh Oswald Short bkplt., John D. Stanitz copy. (SPB. Apr.25; 123) $150

DOLLINGER, C.
- Architektonische Reise-Skizzen. Stuttgart, ca. 1890. Lge. fo. Some plts. bumped in margin, loose in orig. hf. linen portfo., some sm. defects. & wear. (V. Sep.29; 46) DM 1,350

DOLLINGER, J.
- Die Reformation ... Regensburg, 1846-48. 3 vols. Cont. hf. leath. (D. Nov.25; 4865) DM 600

DOLLMAN, Lieut.-Col. W. & Skinner, Sgt. H.M.
- The Blue & Brown Diamond; A History of the 27th Battalion ... Adelaide, 1921. Bdg. not stated. (KH. May 1; 223) Aus. $100

DOLMETSCH, H.
- Der Ornamentschatz. Stuttgart, 1889. Lge. 4to. Orig. linen, spine defect. & pasted. (H. Nov.23; 179) DM 400

DOLPHIN, The: a Journal of the Making of Books N.Y., Ltd. Edns. Cl., 1933-41. Nos. 1-4 (the last in 3 pts.), together 6 vols. Lge. 4to. Cl., 1 vol. in ptd. wraps. (SG. Sep.15; 114) $475
- – Anr. Copy. Nos. 1-4 (lacks No. 4 pt. 1), together 5 (of 6) vols. Lge. 4to. Orig. cl., covers of 1 vol. soiled. (SG. Sep.15; 115) $250

DOMAT, Jean
- Les Loix Civiles. Paris, 1735. *New Edn.* 2 vols. in 1. Fo. Cont. cf. (HD. Feb.22; 52) Frs. 2,500

DOMBROWSKI, R. von
- Das Edelwild. Monograph. Beitrag zur Jagd Zoologie. Wien, 1878. Name excised from upr. title margin, orig. pict. hf. linen. (BR. Apr.12; 1200) DM 450

DOMENECH, Emmanuel E.H.D.
- Missionary Adventures in Texas & Mexico. L., 1858. *1st. Edn. in Engl.* 1 vol. Orig. cl., worn & shaken. [Sabin 20553] *(With:)* – Seven Years' Residence in the Great Deserts of North America. L., 1860. *1st. Edn.* 2 vols. Lge. folding map, 58

cold. & tinted wood-engraved plts. on yellow backgrounds (slightly oxidized), hf.-titles, hf. cf., jnts. & corners worn. [Sabin 20554] Together 3 vols. The Rt. Hon. Visc. Eccles copies. (CNY. Nov.18; 91) $300
- Seven Years' Residence in the Great Deserts of North America. L., 1860. *1st. Edn.* 2 vols. Hf.-titles, folding engraved map hand-cold., 58 'chromoxylograph' plts., orig. cl.; the Phillipps copy with the Middle Hill shelf-mark. [Sabin 20554] (S. May 22; 317) *Maggs.* £220
- – Anr. Copy. 2 vols. Folding map reprd., some ll. slightly spotted, orig. cl., reprd. (BBA. Oct.27; 296) *Sons of Liberty Books.* £75
- – Anr. Copy. 2 vols. Folding cold. map, 58 tinted wood-engraved plts., prelims. of Vol. 1 stained on inner margins, orig. cl., rubbed. (TA. Jun.21; 70) £58
- – Anr. Copy. 2 vols. Hf. cf., marb. paper bds. (LH. Sep.25; 220) $150
- Voyage Pittoresque dans les Grands Déserts du Nouveau Monde. Paris, 1862. *1st. Fr. Edn.* 4to. Foxed, cont. hf. leath. [Sabin 20555] (R. Oct.13; 2965) DM 610

DOMESDAY BOOK
- The Domesday Book of Kent. Ed.:– L.B. Larking. 1869. Fo. Red mor. (PWC. Jul.11; 575) £50
See— HENSHALL, Samuel—DOMESDAY BOOK

DOMINGUEZ ARGAIZ, Francisco Eugenio
- Platicas de los Principales Mysterios de Nuestra Sta. Fee ... Hechas en el idioma Yucateco. Mexico City, 1758. *1st. Edn.* Sm. 4to. A little worming, scarcely affecting text, very slight staining at head & foot of some ll., 19th C. cf.-bkd. marb. bds.; bkplts. of (E.C.) Brasseur de Bourbourg & A. Pinart. [Sabin 20568] (S. May 10; 262) *Walford.* £625

DOMINGUIN, Luis Miguel
- Toros y Toreros. Ill.:– Picasso. Paris, n.d. *1st. Edn. (150).* Lge. fo. Publishers stpd. cl. (DS. Nov.25; 2031) Pts. 90,000

DOMINICUS DE SANCTO GEMINIANO
- Lectura Super Secunda Parte Libri Decretalium. Ed.:– [Petrus Albinianus Trecius]. Venice, Johannes de Colonia & Johannes Manthen, 18 Nov. 1477. Fo. Tall copy, capitals & paragraph marks supplied in red or blue, lacks final blank, margin wormholes through 2nd. hf. affecting a few letters in last 3 quires, a few ll. browned, light margin dampstains at front, early liby. stp. on fo. 2 & at end, hf. vell. over marb. paper bds. [BMC V, 229; Goff D-310; HC 7541*] (SPB. Dec.14; 16) $1,500

DONALDSON, Thomas Leverton
- Pompeii. Ill.:– W.B. Cooke after Lieut.-Col. Cockburn. L., 1827. 2 vols. in 1. Atlas fo. 80 plts., text vigs., some foxing, ex-liby., cont. mor., each cover with lge. inlay of marb. paper, spine gt., worn. (SC. May 3; 145) $375

DONAT, Mrs.
See— HUDSON, Mrs. & Donat, Mrs.

DONATH, Ad.
- Ury Leser. Seine Stellung in der Modernen Deutschen Malerei. Berlin, 1921. *(110) numbered De Luxe Edn.* 4to. With sigd. orig. etching mntd. on Bütten, orig. chagrin, gt. decor. (GB. May 5; 3421) DM 3,300

DONATUS, Alexandro
- Constantinus Romae Liberator, Poema Heroicum. Rome, 1640. Cont. vell., decor., sm. loss from upr. cover border, Cardinal A.S. Piccolomini arms, silk ties; from Fondation Furstenberg-Beaumesnil. (HD. Nov.16; 116) Frs. 2,800
- Roma vetus ac recens utriusque aedificiis ad eruditam cognitionem expositis. Rome, 1665. *[3rd. Edn.].* 4to. Cont. spr. cf., spine gt. (C. Nov.16; 80) *Weinreb.* £100
- – Anr. Copy. Lge. 4to. Cont. vell. (SG. Feb.9; 320) $300

DONATUS, Ludovicus
- Oratio pro S. Augustini Solemnitae Habita. [Rome, Stephan Plannck], after 28 Aug. 1482?

DONATUS, Ludovicus -*Contd.*

4to. Mod. bds.; the Walter Goldwater copy. [BMC IV, 82; Goff D-357] (SG. Dec.1; 128) $125

DONDERS, Frans Cornelis
- Die Anomalien der Refraction und Accomodation des Auges. Ed.:– Otto Becker. Vienna, 1866. *1st. Edn. in German.* Chart separated at folds, old hf. mor., very worn, ex-liby. (SG. Oct.6; 130) $175

DONI, Antonio Francesco
- I Marmi ... diviso in Quattro Libri. Venice, 1609. Cont. leath. (D. Nov.24; 2255)   DM 700

DONKIN, Maj. Robert
- Military Collections & Remarks. N.Y., 1777. *1st. Edn.* Paragraph on p. 189 excised as usual, frontis. slightly stained in margin, cont. cf., slight wear to jnts. & corners; the Rt. Hon. Visc. Eccles copy. [Sabin 20598] (CNY. Nov.18; 92) $600

DONN, Benjamin
- Map of the County of Devon, with the City & County of Exeter. 1765. Fo. Key map of Devon, 11 sectional maps, 2 town plans on 1 sheet, mod. cl. (P. Jul.5; 381)   £140
-- Anr. Copy. Fo. 12 sectional maps, lacks general map, hf. cf., spine defect. (P. May 17; 429)   *Goodey.* £130

DONNE, John
- Biathanatos. A Declaration of that Paradoxe ... that Selfe-Homicide is not so Naturally Sinne. [1646-47]. *1st. Edn.* Sm. 4to. Cont. sheep, rubbed. [Wing D 1858] (P. Mar.15; 300)   *Quaritch.* £480
-- Anr. Edn. L., 1648. 4to. MS. notes in Fr. on front free end-paper, some ll. a little discold., cont. cf., rebkd.; John Towneley bkplt. [Wing D1859] (BBA. May 3; 120)   *Hannas.* £200
- Encaenia. The Feast of Dedication. Celebrated at Lincolnes Inne, in a Sermon there upon Ascension Day, 1623. At the Dedication of a New Chappell. L., 1623. *1st. Edn.* Sm. 4to. A4 blank cancelled, lacks final blank, corner torn from Cl, some staining, 19th. C. hf. cf. [STC 7039] (S. Dec.8; 17)   *Lawson.* £200
- Letters to Severall Persons of Honour. Ill.:– P. Lombert. L., 1651. *1st. Edn. 1st. Iss.* Engraved port., lacks A1 blank, N4 paper flaws, sm. wormholes in margin, early ll. rebkd.; bkplt. of Charles Hoare. [Wing D 1864] (SPB. May 16; 50) $225
- Poems ... with Elegies on the Authors Death. L., 1633. *1st. Edn.* Sm. 4to. 2 ll. restored with few letters in facs., few slight stains, slight reprd. tears & spotting in sig. K, sheets darkened, cf. gt. by Riviere, upr. cover detched.; Frederic Dannay copy. [STC 7045] (CNY. Dec.16; 110) $900
-- Anr. Edn. L., 1639. *3rd. Edn.* Lacks port., 1 side note & 1 or 2 headlines shaved, title-p. a little dust-stained, cont. cf., rebkd. [STC 7047] (BBA. May 3; 119)   *Bowers.* £95
-- Anr. Copy. Port., writing on recto, some spotting & browning, few sig. marks & catchwords cropped, sig. on title, mod. blindstpd. cf. (SPB. May 16; 51) $325
-- Anr. Edn. [L.], 1669. *7th. Edn.* Some browning thro.-out, sm. hole in D1, cont. mott. of., spine gt., new label, rebkd. with orig. backstrip laid down, corners reprd.; cont. bkplt. of Thomas Isted, later bkplt. of C.W.H. Sotheby, Frederic Dannay copy. [Wing D 1871] (CNY. Dec.16; 111) $200
- The Sermons ... Ed.:– George R. Potter & Evelyn M. Simpson. Calif., 1953-62. 10 vols. Orig. cl., d.-w.'s. (KH. Nov.8; 127)   Aus. $220

DONOVAN, Edward
- An Epitome of the Natural History of the Insects of China. L., priv. ptd., 1798. 4to. 50 hand-cold. engraved plts., some staining to plts. & text, cont. diced red mor. gt., rebkd. & worn. (CNY. May 18; 139) $600
-- Anr. Edn. L., 1798[-99]. 4to. 50 hand-cold. engraved plts., slight offsetting & discoloration, cont. russ. gt., rebkd., old spine laid down. (S. Nov.28; 22)   *Edinburgh.* £1,700
- An Epitome of the Natural History of the Insects of India, & the Island in the Indian Seas. L., 1800[-04]. 4to. 58 hand-cold. plts., lr. pt. of title-p. frayed, cf. gt. (P. May 17; 53)   *Rostron.* £1,100

- Instructions for Collecting & Preserving Various Subjects of Natural History. L., 1794. *1st. Edn.* Some spotting, cf.-bkd. bds., worn, upr. cover detchd. (S. Oct.4; 265)   *Quaritch.* £50
- The Natural History of British Birds. 1794-99. Vols. 1-5 only (of 10). 124 hand-cold. engrs. (1 loose), some slight spotting, cont. hf. cf., marb. bds., rubbed, 1 spine slightly defect. (SKC. Mar.9; 1932)   £600
-- Anr. Edn. 1802-08. 5 vols. in 3. 120 hand-cold. plts., cont. russ. gt., 1 hinge brkn. (SKC. Mar.9; 1933)   £750
-- Anr. Copy. 5 vols. in 3. Some slight text foxing, cont. hf. leath. gt., arms. (D. Nov.23; 702)   DM 4,200
- The Natural History of British Insects. L., priv. ptd., 1792-94. *1st. Edn.* Vols. I-III only (of 16). Tall 8vo. 108 hand-cold. copperplates, sm. liby. stp. at head of some text pp., cont. cf., defect. (SG. Oct.6; 131) $425
-- Anr. Edn. L., priv. ptd., 1792-1801. *1st. Edn. 1st. Iss.* Vols. I-X in 9. Plts. hand-cold., cont. red hf. mor., marb. bds., untrimmed. (SKC. Oct.26; 356)   £1,400
-- Anr. Edn. L., 1792-1801. *1st. Edn.* Vols. 1-10 only (of 16), in 5 vols. 360 engraved plts., most hand-cold., lacks title to Vol. 5, prelims. to Vol. 1 bnd. in Vol. 9, slight offsetting & spotting, cont. tree cf., rebkd., spines emblematically tooled, w.a.f. (S. Nov.23; 23)   *Robinson.* £600
-- Anr. Edn. L., 1792-1807. 10 (of 16) vols. in 9. 357 plts., most hand-cold., hf. red mor., unc., as a coll. of plts., w.a.f. (P. May 17; 298)   *Bailes.* £440
-- Anr. Edn. L., 1793-1811. 16 vols. in 8. 1 lf. with tear reprd. without loss, 1 plt. margin defect., cont. leath., renewed blind-tooled spine, 3 with slight wear, lacks 1 front-free end-paper. (D. Nov.23; 703)   DM 6,000
- The Naturalist's Repository of Exotic Natural History ... L., [1823]. [1st. Series:] 2 vols. 72 hand-cold. engraved plts., hf. mor. (C. Nov.16; 234)   *Junk.* £420
-- Anr. Edn. L., [1823-24]. 2 vols. Title with liby. stp., cont. linen, spine slightly brkn. (R. Apr.4; 1697)   DM 1,900
-- Anr. Edn. 1823-25. 2 vols. only (of 5). 74 hand-cold. plts., hf. cf. gt., as a coll. of plts., w.a.f. (P. Dec.8; 101)   *Schuster.* £420
-- Anr. Edn. L., 1834. 5 vols. 180 hand-cold. engraved plts., 2 plts. & text ll. detchd., cont. cl., orig. paper labels on spines. (C. Nov.16; 233)   *Neidhart.* £1,100

DON PIRLONE
Roma, 1848-49. Nos. 1-234 (all publd.). 4to. Hf. cf., defect. (CR. Jun.6; 186)   Lire 450,000

DON QUICHOTTE (Le)
Ed.:– Charles Gilbert-Martin. 26 Jun. 1874-25 Dec. 1875. Nos. 1-79 (2 different nos. 52) in 1 vol. Fo. Hf. roan. (HD. Jun.22; 33)   Frs. 1,400

DOOLITTLE, Hilda
[-] The Flowering of the Rod. By H.D. L., 1946. Ptd. stiff wraps.; inscr. to Richard Aldington. (SG. Mar.1; 73) $300
[-] Palimpset. [By] H.D. [Paris, 1926]. Sm. 4to. Ptd. wraps., spine worn; sigd. (SG. Mar.1; 77) $130
[-] Sea Garden. By H.D. L., 1916. *1st. Edn.* Orig. ptd. wraps., faded; Frederic Dannay copy. (CNY. Dec.16; 112) $150
[-] Selected Poems. [By] H.D. N.Y., [1957]. Ptd. wraps., lr. cover stained; inscr. to Richard Aldington. (SG. Mar.1; 80) $225
[-] Tribute to the Angels. By H.D. L., 1945. Ptd. wraps.; inscr. to Richard Aldington. (SG. Mar.1; 81) $450
- Two Poems. By H.D. Ill.:– Wesley Tanner. Berkeley, 1971. *(26) lettered & sigd. by artist.* Lge. 8vo. Qtr. cl., pict. bds. (SG. Mar.1; 82) $130
[-] What Do I Love? L., priv. publd., n.d. 12mo. Ptd. wraps.; inscr. to Richard Aldington. 1950. (SG. Mar.1; 84) $325

DOPPELMAYR, Johannes Gabriel
- Atlas Coelestis ... Secundum Nic. Copernaci et ex Parte Tychonis de Brahe ... Nuremb., 1742. *Orig. Edn.* Fo. Maps partly bkd., some with light staining in outer margin, some light spotting, defect., bds. (D. Nov.23; 395)   DM 7,000

DORAN, Dr. John
- 'Their Majesties' Servants'. Annals of the English Stage from Thomas Betterton to Edmund Kean. 1864. 2 vols. Orig. cl., rubbed & soiled; inscr. in Vol. 1 'To J. Hare Esq., Prince of Wales's Theatre ... with the best wishes of the author, John Doran', extra-ill. with many hand-cold. engraved ports. on India paper, wood engrs. of theatres, etc. (TA. Jul.19; 303)   £65
-- Anr. Edn. Ed.:– Robert W. Lowe. L., 1888. *(300) numbered on L.P., with ports. in dupl.* 3 vols. Lge. 8vo. Newspaper clippings laid or tipped in, two-tone cl., untrimmed. (SG. Nov.17; 208) $150

DORAT, Claude Joseph
- Les Baisers, précédés du Mois de Mai. Ill.:– Ponce after Eisen (port.), Eisen. La Haye, 1770. 4to. Orig. mor. (DS. Oct.28; 2325)   Pts. 30,000
-- Anr. Edn. Ill.:– Eisen & Marillier, engraved by Ponce, Aliamet De Longueil, Baquoy, Binet, Delaunay, Lignée, Masquelier & others. Den Haag, Paris, 1770. L.P. Hollande, some faulty pagination, bordeaux mor., sigd. by Rivière, gold-tooled, gt. outer dentelle., decor. inner dentelle, gt. decor. spine, double marb. paper end-papers. (D. Nov.24; 2257)   DM 3,000
-- Anr. Copy. L.P., Mois de Mai mispaginated, mor. gt. by Trautz-Bauzonnet, spine decor. (HD. May 3; 37)   Frs. 8,200
-- Anr. Edn. Ill.:– Eisen. Rouen, 1880. *Reprint of 1770 Edn. (50) on japan.* Lge. 8vo. Mor. by Quinet, spine decor., end-ll. lined with cf. (SM. Mar.7; 2015)   Frs. 2,500
- Les Baisers, précédés du Mois de Mai.— Imitations de plusieurs Poètes Latin. Ill.:– Eisen & Marillier. La Haye & Paris, 1770. Foxing, dampstains, str.-grd. mor., ca. 1830, spine decor., turn-ins & 1 corner defect., spine wormed. (SM. Mar.7; 2372)   Frs. 1,400
- Fables Nouvelles. Ill.:– Marillier. La Haye & Paris, 1773. *1st. Iss., with interlacing typographic ornament on p. III & p. 162 uncancelled.* 2 vols. in 1. On papier hollande, mor. gt. by Cuzin. (C. May 30; 79)   *Van den Abbeel.* £650
-- Anr. Edn. Ill.:– after Marillier. Paris, 1773. 2 vols. in 1. On large Dutch bütten, without repeated copperplt. pt. II, bnd. in MS. letter sigd. from author, 3 pp., 4to., with address, (margin tear reprd. without loss), & 1 port., mor., sigd. by Capé, gt. rococo style, gt. inner & outer dentelle; Léon Pather ex-libris. (D. Nov.24; 2256)   DM 3,900
-- Anr. Copy. 2 vols. On Bütten, minimal spotting, cont. marb. cf. gt., gold-tooled decor., gt. inner & outer dentelle. (HT. May 9; 1433)   DM 2,230
- Fables ou Allegories Philosophiques. Ill.:– Delaunay, Arrivet, Baquoy, Duflos, de Ghendt, Le Gouaz, Lebeau, & others, after Marillier. A La Haye, et se trouve à Paris, 1773. 2 vols. in 1. On Holland, Oo3-4, Ppl stained, title browned, light spotting, mor. gt. by Petit, lightly rubbed, soiling. (SPB. Dec.14; 49) $200

DORE, Gustave
- Des Agréments d'un Voyage d'Agrément. Paris, [1851]. Ob. 4to. Str.-grd. bordeaux hf. mor., corners, by Blanchetière, spine decor. (HD. May 4; 250)   Frs. 12,000

DORE, Gustave (Ill.)
See— ARIOSTO, Lodovico
See— BALZAC, Honoré de
See— BIBLES [French]
See— BIBLES [German]
See— CERVANTES SAAVEDRA, Miguel de
See— COLERIDGE, Samuel
See— DANTE ALIGHIERI
See— DAVILLIER, Baron Charles
See— DUPONT, Pierre
See— ENAULT, Louis
See— LA FONTAINE, Jean de
See— MICHAUD, Joseph
See— MILTON, John
See— PERRAULT, Charles
See— POE, Edgar Allan
See— RABELAIS, François
See— SAINTINE, X.B.
See— SONNETS ET EAUX-FORTES
See— TAINE, Hippolyte
See— TENNYSON, Alfred Lord

DORE, Gustave & Jerrold, Blanchard
- London. A Pilgrimage. 1872. Fo. Orig. cl. gt.,
worn. (LC. Mar.1; 59) £100
- - Anr. Copy. Fo. Hf. mor. gt., rubbed. (P. Jul.26;
182) £70

DORE, Henry
- Researches into Chinese Superstitions. Trans.:–
M. Kennelly. Shanghai, 1914/20. 6 vols. Orig. ptd.
bds., ties, some wear to spines. (TA. Jun.21; 613)
£120

DORGELES, Roland Lecavelé
- Les Croix de Bois. Paris, 1919. *Orig. Edn.* 12mo.
Jansenist mor. by Canape & Corriez, bordeaux
mor. doubls., faille end-ll., wrap. & spine preserved.
(HD. May 4; 251) Frs. 1,300
- - Anr. Edn. Ill.:– A. Dunoyer de Segonzac. Paris,
[1921]. *(600).* 4to. On tinted Lafuma, sewed. (HD.
May 4; 252) Frs. 1,800
- - Anr. Edn. *(With:)* – La Boule de Gui. Ill.:–
Dunoyer de Segonzac. *Orig. Edn. & 1st. Ill. Edn.*
(With:) – Le Cabaret de la Belle Femme. Together
3 vols. Paris, 1921-24. 4to. Cont. Lavallière mor.,
silk end-papers, wraps. preserved, s.-c.'s. (HD.
Nov.17; 111) Frs. 6,400
- Tombeau des Poètes. Ill.:– Beltrand after Dunoyer
de Segonzac. Paris, 1954. *Orig. Edn., (150).* 4to.
On Rives, leaves, publisher's box; artist's copy,
autograph dedications sigd. by author, artist &
engraver, with separate suite of 3 cold. double plts.,
special box. (HD. Jun.6; 48) Frs. 1,300

DORIGNY, Nicolas
- Psyches et Amoris Nuptiae ac Fabula a Raphaele.
Rome, 1695. *(Bound at end:)* Galeria Dipinta Del.
Palazzo dal Prencipe Panfilio da Pietro Berretini,
intaglialla da Carlo Cesio. Together 2 works in 1
vol. Fo. 18th. C. hf. roan, limp decor. spine. (HD.
Jan.26; 110) Frs. 1,800

DORLING, Adolph
- Royal Dresden Gallery. Dresden, Leipzig, & L.,
ca. 1850. 2 vols. 4to. Disbnd. (SG. Oct.13; 271)
$130
- - Anr. Copy. 2 vols. in 1. 4to. Not collated, orig.
gt.-decor. cf., worn & loose. (SG. Oct.13; 142)
$120

DORRA, Henri & Rewald, John
- Seurat ... l'Oeuvre Peint, Biographie et Catalogue
Critique. Paris, 1959. 4to. Orig. cl., d.-w. (S. Apr.30;
27) *Christies.* £60

DORTOMANN, Nicolas
- De Causis & Effectibus Thermarum
Belilucanarum Parvo Intervallo à Monspeliensi Urbe
Distantium. Lyon, 1579. *Orig. Edn.* Some sm.
wormholes, cont. mor., gt.-decor., centre arms,
decor. spine monogs. & arms, old reprd.; Jacques
Auguste de Thou copy, with his arms, from Baron
Jérôme Pichon liby. (HD. Jan.30; 8) Frs. 4,000

DORTOUS DE MAIRAN, J.J.
- Traité Physique et Historique de L'Aurore
Boréale. Paris, 1733. *1st. Edn.* 4to. Cont. cf.,
rubbed. (S. Dec.13; 265) *Quaritch.* £110

DORTU, Mme. G.
- Toulouse-Lautrec et son Oeuvre. N.Y., 1970. *Ltd.*
Edn. 6 vols. Orig. cl. (BBA. Nov.10; 165)
Howes. £140
- - Anr. Edn. N.Y., 1971. *(1450).* 6 vols. 4to. Orig.
cl. (S. Apr.30; 28) *Josefowitz.* £260
- - Anr. Copy. 6 vols. Lge. 4to. Cl., monog. end-
papers. (CBA. Jan.29; 461) $350
- - Anr. Copy. 6 vols. Lge. 4to. Orig. linen, wrap.
(HT. May 9; 1247) DM 1,200
- - Anr. Edn. N.Y., 1971. *Ltd. Edn.* 6 vols. 4to.
Orig. cl. (BBA. Apr.5; 35) *Zwemmer.* £150
- - Anr. Copy. 6 vols. Fo. Cl., unc. (VG. Sep.13;
713) Fls. 810

DOSIO, Giovanni Antonio
- Urbis Roma Aedificiorum Illustriumqua supersunt
Reliquiae. [Flor.], 1569. Ob. sm. fo. Engraved title,
50 engrs., few plts. with tears reprd., mod. vell.,
vell.-bkd. cl. folding case. (SG. Apr.26; 74) $900

DOS PASSOS, John
- The Head & Heart of Thomas Jefferson. Garden
City, 1953. 4to. Plain wraps., chipped, publisher's

typed label. dtd. 19 Nov. 1953, hand-corrected to
'Jan. 21'; uncorrected advance proof copy, text ptd.
on recto only. (SG. Jan.12; 86) $110
- One Man's Initiation—1917. L., [1920]. *1st. Edn.*
Sm. 8vo. Cl., d.-w. (SG. May 24; 280) $200

D'OSTERVALD, J.F.
- Voyage Pittoresque en Sicile. Paris, 1822/6. 2
vols. in 1. Lge. 4to. Single-p. engraved map, 87
uncold. or tinted aquatint plts. with tissue guards,
some minor spotting, mostly to margins, cont. hf.
mor. gt., partly untrimmed, rebkd. with orig. spine
relaid. (TA. Jun.21; 91) £1,350

DOSTOEVSKY, Fedor
- Besy [The Devils]. St. Petersb., 1873. *1st. Edn.* 3
vols. Hf.-titles, insert quotation lf. in Vol. I, some
spotting, sm. brown stain in upr. margins at end of
Vol. III, cont. hf. roan, a trifle rubbed. (S. May 10;
265) *Stockholm.* £850
- Brat'ya Karamazovy [Brothers Karamazov]. St.
Petersb., 1881. *1st. Edn.* 2 vols. Hf.-titles, some
very light browning, cont. hf. roan, slightly rubbed.
(S. May 10; 263) *Lyon.* £3,800
- Der Doppelgänger. Ill.:– A. Kubin. [1913]. *1st.*
Kubin. Edn. (800) numbered. 4to. Mor. (GB. May
5; 2842) DM 400
- - Anr. Edn. Ill.:– Kubin. München, [1913]. *1st.*
Kubin Edn. (50) numbered on Japan. Lge. 4to.
Printers mark sigd. by artist. orig. leath., gt. spine &
cover. (HK. May 17; 2926) DM 700
- Les Frères Karamazov. Trans.:– B. de Schloezer.
Ill.:– Alexandre Alexeieff. Paris, 1929. *(100) on*
Holland, with set of all ills. on thin Holland. 3
vols. Fo. Orange mor. gt., silk end-papers. (HD.
Nov.17, 112) Frs. 2,600
- Idiot. St. Petersb., 1874. *1st. Edn.* 2 vols. in 1.
Iss. with gathering 10 in Vol. I paginated correctly,
hf.-titles, some spotting, minor flaw in pp. 324 &
325 in Vol. II, cont. qtr. leath., slightly rubbed. (S.
May 10; 267) *Stockholm.* £1,800
- Podrostok [The Adolescent]. St. Petersb., 1876.
1st. Edn. 3 vols. in 1. A little margin spotting, mod.
hf. cl., upr. wraps. of each vol. preserved, unc.; liby.
stp. of Evgeniev-Maksimov. (S. May 10; 264)
Quaritch. £800
- Sämmtliche Werke. Ed.:– Moeller van den Bruck.
München, 1922. 22 vols. in 23, compl. Orig. hf.
linen. (V. Oct.1; 4012) DM 400
- Die Sanfte. Trans.:– A. Eliasberg. Ill.:– B.
Krauskopf. Berlin, [1920]. *(300). (70) De Luxe*
Edn. on Bütten. Orig. bds., gold-tooled upr. cover.
(HK. May 17; 3065) DM 520
- Vyechnyi Muzh [The Eternal Husband]. St.
Petersb., 1871. *1st. Edn.* Hf.-title, some light
spotting, cont. hf. mor., slightly rubbed. (S. May
10; 266) *Quaritch.* £700
- Zapeske ez Mertvago Doma [Memoirs from the
House of the Dead]. St. Petersb., 1862. *2nd. Edn.*
(1st. in book form). 2 vols. Hf.-titles, some
spotting & discolouration, cont. qtr. roan, rubbed.
(S. May 10; 268) *Quaritch.* £1,450

DOUCET, Jerome
- Trois Legendes d'Or, d'Argent et de Cuivre. Ill.:–
Georges Rochegrosse. Paris, 1901. *(220) numbered*
on velin d'Arches. Tall 8vo. 33 copperplts., gt. mor.-
bkd. bds., orig. wraps. bnd. in. (SG. Feb.16; 96)
$110

DOUGHTY, Charles Montrose
- Travels in Arabia Deserta. Camb., 1888. *1st. Edn.*
2 vols. Lge. cold. folding map in pocket of Vol. 1,
advt. ll. dtd. 1887 in Vol. 1, orig. cl. gt., spine of
1st. vol. frayed & reprd. (C. Nov.16; 81)
Irani. £750
- - Anr. Copy. 2 vols. Tall 8vo. Ills., folding cold.
map separated at folds & linen-bkd. in rear cover
pocket, 30-p. publisher's catalogue, orig. gt.-pict.
cl., corners worn, unc., mostly unopened. (SG.
Apr.26; 75) $500
- - Anr. Edn. Intro.:– T.E. Lawrence. 1936. 2 vols.
4to. Orig. cl., dampstains, d.-w.'s. (SKC. Sep.9;
2035) £50

DOUGLAS, David
- Journal Kept ... During his Travels in North
America 1823-1827. L., 1914. *1st. Edn.* Cl. (LH.
Sep.25; 221) $130

DOUGLAS, James
- Nenia Britannica: or a Sepulchral History of Great
Britain. L., 1793. *1st. Edn.* Fo. Extra title with vig.,
36 aquatint plts., inner margins of 1st. few ll.
stained, cont. diced russ., upr. hinge split, upr. cover
stained. (S. Apr.9; 210) *Marlborough.* £100

DOUGLAS, Mrs. M.
- [–] Notes of a Journey from Berne to England &
through France. Priv. ptd., [1796]. Cf. by
Kalthoeber, with his ticket, rebkd.; Beckford copy,
with inventory no. on fly-lf. & description from
1883 sale mntd. at end, Althorp liby. label. (BBA.
Sep.29; 99) *Thorp.* £90

DOUGLAS, Norman 'Normyx'
- Looking Back. L., 1933. *(535) numbered & sigd.*
2 vols. Orig. buckram-bkd. bds., d.-w.'s. (S. Dec.13;
354) *Forster.* £80
See— MAGNUS, Maurice—DOUGLAS, Norman
'Normyx'

DOUGLAS, Stephen A.
See— LINCOLN, Abraham & Douglas, Stephen
A.

DOURY
See— DELLOUX & Doury

DOUSA or DOES, J. van der
- Annales Rerum a Priscis Hollandiae Comitibus
per 346, Annos Gestarum. 's-Gravenhage, 1599.
Lge. 8vo. Some cont. annots. & underlinings, cont.
cf., back gt. (VG. Sep.14; 1151) Fls. 600

DOUWES, B.J.
See— GIETERMAKER, K.H.—DOUWES, B.J.

DOVES PRESS
See— BIBLES [English]
See— CREDO
See— FRANCIS OF ASSISI, Saint
See— GOETHE, Johann Wolfgang von
See— MACKAIL, John William
See— MILTON, John
See— RUSKIN, John
See— SHAKESPEARE, William
See— SHELLEY, Percy Bysshe
See— TACITUS, Publius Cornelius
See— WORDSWORTH, William

DOWER, John
- A New General Atlas of the World ... Henry
Teesdale, 1832. Engraved title, 45 hand-cold. maps
(1 double-p.), chart of rivers & mountains, map of
Persia & Arabia torn & frayed, title dampstained,
cont. hf. cf., worn, covers detchd. (TA. Mar.15; 58)
£110
- - Anr. Edn. 1841. Fo. Engraved title & 45 maps,
hand-cold. outl., cont. mor., rubbed. (CSK. Jul.6;
95) £220

DOWNING, Clement
- A Compendious History of the Indian Wars with
an Account of the Rise ... of Angria the Pyrate.
1737. 12mo. Some light spotting, cont. cf. (CSK.
Sep.30; 39) £95

DOWNMAN, Edward Andrews
- Blue Dash Chargers. 1919. 4to. Orig. parch.-bkd.
bds., slightly rubbed. (S. Nov.8; 513) *Thorp.* £50
- - Anr. Copy. Tall 8vo. Bds., spine stained. (SG.
Jan.26; 82) $150

DOWSON, Ernest
- Verses. L., 1896. *1st. Edn. (30) numbered on*
Japan vell. Orig. imitation vell. bds., upr. cover gt.-
stpd. in design after Aubrey Beardsley, with gt.-
stpd. 'AB' in corner, partly unc., slightly soiled;
pres. copy to Leonard Smithers, Frederic Dannay
copy. (CNY. Dec.16; 114) $10,000

DOYLE, Sir Arthur Conan
- The Adventures of Sherlock Holmes. Ill.:– Sidney
Paget. L., 1892. *1st. Edn.* Orig. cl. gt., vig. on upr.
cover without street-name on panel. (S. Dec.8; 101)
Sotheran. £180
- - Anr. Copy. Some spotting, orig. cl., spine ends
chipped. (CSK. Oct.7; 139) £95
- - Anr. Copy. Hf.-title & title loose, orig. cl., worn.
(P. Jun.7; 193) £65
- The Adventures of Sherlock Holmes.—The
Memoirs of Sherlock Holmes. Ill.:– Sidney Paget.

DOYLE, Sir Arthur Conan *-Contd.*

L., 1892; 1894. *1st. Edns.* Together 2 vols. Lge. 8vo. Orig. pict. cl. gt., 1st. imp. bdg. of 1st. title with street sign blank, red hf.-mor. s-c.; bkplt. of Barton Currie in 1st. vol., Frederic Dannay copies, inscr. 'Barnaby Ross'/'Ellery Queen'. (CNY. Dec.16; 115) $5,000
– – **Anr. Copy.** Together 2 vols. 4to. Unif. mor. gt. by Bayntun-Rivière. (SPB. Dec.13; 522) $850
– – **Anr. Copy.** Together 2 vols. 4to. Hf.-titles, ills., some foxing & light soiling, orig. cl. gt.; Fred A. Berne copy. (SPB. May 16; 253) $600
– **The Adventures of Sherlock Holmes.—The Later Adventures.—The Final Adventures.** Ed.:– Edgar W. Smith. Intro.:– Vincent Starrett. Ill.:– Frederick Dorr Steele, Sidney Paget & others. N.Y., Ltd. Edns. Cl., 1950-52. *(1500) numbered.* 3 vols.; 3 vols.; 2 vols. Tall 8vo. Hf. cl., patterned bds., medallion port. on covers, 3 s.-c,'s. (SG. May 17; 184) $275
– **Tha Captain of the Polestar & other Tales.** L., 1890. *1st. Edn.* Orig. cl., spine slightly faded. (BBA. May 23; 140) *Jarndyce.* £80
– **The Case Book of Sherlock Holmes.** L., 1927. *1st. Edn. in book form.* Light browning of few ll. & endpapers, orig. cl., lightly soiled; Fred A. Berne copy. (SPB. May 16; 250) $200
– **The Hound of the Baskervilles.** 1902. *1st. Edn. 1st. Iss.* Orig. decor. cl., spine faded. (BBA. Aug.18; 71) *Minerva.* £190
– – **Anr. Copy.** Sm. 8vo. 'You' for 'your' reading on p.13, plts., gt.-pict. cl. (SG. Apr.19; 225) $250
– – **Anr. Edn.** L., 1902. *1st. Edn.* Orig. cl. gt. (S. Mar.20; 875) *Steinfield.* £100
– – **Anr. Copy.** Plts., title & few ll. slightly spotted, orig. cl. gt. (S. Apr.9; 249) *Duschness.* £80
– – **Anr. Copy.** Frontis., hf.-title, ills., some spotting, orig. decor. cl. gt., few marks on upr. cover; Fred A. Berne copy. (SPB. May 16; 251) $275
– – **Anr. Edn.** Ill.:– Sidney Paget. [N.Y., 1901-02]. *1st. Amer. Edn. in pts.* Together 9 vols. Sm. 4to. Ills., orig. cold.-pict. wraps., spines worn with sm. tape repairs. (SG. Apr.19; 245) $150
– **The Lost World.** L., 1912. *1st. De Luxe Edn., (1000). (190) bnd. (rest transferred to 2nd. Iss.).* Orig. blind-stpd. cl., spine slightly soiled. (BBA. May 23; 155) *Minerva.* £450
– – **Anr. Edn.** L., [1912]. *Pre-publication Iss.* No foreword or chart at p. 128, 'Lord Roxton' (later revised to 'Lord John) p. 109 etc., red cl.; pres. inscr. on title from author to brother-in-law, dtd. 'Aug. 29/12'. (BBA. May 23; 156) *Ferret Fantasy.* £950
– – **Anr. Edn.** L., [1912]. *1st. Edn.* Orig. cl., slightly rubbed. (BBA. May 23; 158) *Col. O'Neill.* £50
– – **Anr. Copy.** Minor soiling or staining, gt.-pict. cl., covers lightly soiled & rubbed, spine slightly faded & stained. (CBA. Oct.29; 277a) $225
– – **Anr. Copy.** Plts., light spotting, orig. cl., with gt. port.; Fred A. Berne copy. (SPB. May 16; 252) $175
– **The Memoirs of Sherlock Holmes.** Ill.:– Sidney Paget. L., [1893]. *1st. Edn.* Orig. cl., spine rubbed. (BBA. May 23; 144) *Bledisloe.* £85
– – **Anr. Edn.** Ill.:– Sidney Paget. 1894. *1st. Edn.* Orig. cl., lightly soiled. (CSK. Oct.7; 140) £95
– – **Anr. Copy.** 4to. Orig. cl., worn. (PD. Apr.18; 125) £75
– – **Anr. Copy.** Orig. cl. gt., spine rubbed, upr. cover slightly damp spotted. (TA. Jul.19; 293) £66
– – **Anr. Copy.** Orig. cl. gt., slight wear. (P. Sep.29; 371) £55
– – **Anr. Copy.** Lge. 8vo. Some slight foxing, orig. cl., binder's cl. d.-w. (SG. Apr.19; 222) $130
– – **Anr. Copy.** Lge. 8vo. Scattered foxing, ills. clean, orig. gt.-lettered pict. cl., slightly worn & shaken. (SG. Mar.15; 111) $110
– – **Anr. Edn.** N.Y., 1894. *1st. Amer. Edn. 1st. Iss.* Orig. cl., slightly soiled. (BBA. May 23; 145) *Hunt.* £220
– – **Anr. Copy.** Sm. 8vo. Plts., 1 loose, orig. pict. cl., spine slightly frayed, hinges worn. (SG. Apr.19; 223) $100
– **Micah Clarke, his Statement.** L., 1889. *1st. Edn.* Embossed liby. stp. on title, orig. cl., upr. cover soiled. (BBA. May 23; 139) *Conan Doyle Bks.* £60
– **My Friend the Murderer, & other Mysteries & Adventures.** 1893. *1st. American Edn.* Orig. pict. cl. (BBA. May 23; 143) *Hunt.* £65
– **The Mystery of Clomber.** L., 1889. *1st. Edn.* Lacks advts., cont. cl., faded. (BBA. May 23; 166a) *Cockburn.* £80
– **The Poison Belt.** Ill.:– Harry Rowntree. L., 1913. *1st. Edn.* Orig. cl., spine faded. (BBA. May 23; 159) *Col. O'Neill.* £55
– **The Return of Sherlock Holmes.** Ill.:– Sidney Paget. L., 1905. *1st. Edn.* Orig. cl., rubbed. (BBA. May 23; 154) *Col. O'Neill.* £140
– – **Anr. Copy.** Ills., advts., orig. cl., front endpaper cut away; Fred A. Berne copy. (SPB. May 16; 255) $225
– – **Anr. Copy.** Sm. 8vo. Plts., some spotting, former owners' inscrs., orig. cl. (SG. Apr.19; 226) $110
– **Rodney Stone.** N.Y., 1897. *1st. Amer. Edn.* Silver & gold-stpd. cl., light wear, d.-w. (some fraying & chipping, split at hinge); Ken Leach coll. (RO. Jun.10; 391) $230
– **The Sign of Four.** 1890. *1st. Edn. in Book Form.* Fore-margins of pp. 13-14 & 15-16 cleanly torn, some light soiling, orig. cl., soiled. (CSK. Oct.7; 138) £200
– – **Anr. Copy.** Advts. dtd. Oct. 1890, few gatherings sprung, slight soiling, orig. cl., stain on upr. cover & spine; Fred A. Berne copy. (SPB. May 16; 256) $450
– – **Anr. Edn.** L. & Phila., 1890. *Special Engl. Edn. 1st. Serial Publication.* In Vol. 1 Lippincott's Monthly Magazine. Orig. cl., soiled. (BBA. May 23; 177) *Conan Doyle Bks.* £100
– – **Anr. Edn.** Phila., [1890]. *1st. Edn.* Lge. 8vo. Frontis., orig. wraps., qtr. mor., cl. s.-c.; Ellery Queen/Barnaby Ross copy, with his sig. (SG. Apr.19; 217) $650
– **Sir Nigel.** L., 1906. *1st. Edn. in Book Form.* Ill., spotting, orig. cl., red mor.-bkd. s.-c.; pres. copy, Fred A. Berne copy. (SPB. May 16; 257) $475
– **The Stark Munro Letters.** L., 1895. *1st. Edn. in Book Form.* Ill., 24-p. publisher's catalogue, orig. cl., spine worn, sm. tear at head; A.L.s. dtd. 21 June 1894. (SG. Apr.26; 76) $400
– **The Works.** Garden City & N.Y., 1930. *Crowborough Edn. (760) sigd.* 24 vols. Hf. mor. gt., partly unc., spines dull, some bd. edges & corners with slight wear. (CNY. May 18; 103) $1,000
See— **BARRIE, Sir James Matthew & Doyle, Sir Arthur Conan**

DOYLE, James William Edward
– **A Chronicle of England B.C. 55-A.D. 1485.** 1864. *[1st. Edn.].* 4to. Str.-grd. mor. gt., pres. inscr. on upr. cover; Kenneth Oldaker copy. (P. Jan.12; 13) *Cavendish.* £90
– – **Anr. Copy.** 4to. Str.-grd. mor. gt. (P. Feb.16; 51) £65
– – **Anr. Copy.** 4to. Str.-grd. mor. gt., gt. dentelles, by Riviere. (SG. Feb.16; 98) $130

DOYLE, John, Caricaturist
– **The Marmosite's Miscellany.** L., Hogarth Pr., 1925. Orig. wraps. (S. Mar.20; 877) *Mayou.* £85
[–] **Political Sketches, etc. by H.B.** 1829-35. Vols. 1-7. Ob. fo. 420 litho. plts. (1 folding), some light foxing, cont. hf. mor., gt.-lettered, slightly rubbed. (SKC. May 4; 1624) £220
– – **Anr. Edn.** 1829-48. 9 vols. Fo. Litho titles, 900 hand-cold. lithos., inlaid on card., contents lf. to each vol., cont. hf. mor. gt. (P. Dec.8; 33a) *Burdon.* £2,000
– – **Anr. Edn.** 1835-37. *(8) on India paper.* Vol. 5 only. 98 (of 100) litho. caricatures, many with characters identified in pencil, some foxing, cont. crimson mor. gt. by J. Mackenzie. (TA. Dec.15; 544) £56
– – **Anr. Edn.** N.d. *(8) on India paper.* Vol. 4 only. Fo. 99 litho. plts., mntd. on India paper, some margins spotted, cont. mor., worn. (CSK. Apr.6; 160) £50

DOYLE, Martin
– **The Illustrated Book of Domestic Poultry.** L., 1854. 20 cold. plts., hf. cf., bds. rubbed. (P. May 17; 151) *Comben.* £85

DOYLE, Richard
– **In Fairyland.** L., 1870. 4to. 16 col. plts., loose as usual, orig. cl. gt. (P. Nov.24; 304) *Joseph.* £240
– – **Anr. Copy.** 4to. Several ll. detchd., margins soiled, cont. cl., rubbed, w.a.f. (CSK. Jun.29; 167) £110
– – **Anr. Copy.** Fo. Pencil mark on title, spotting to some plts., 4 with tears, most reprd., orig. cl. gt., bd. edges worn. rebkd. preserving orig. spine. (LC. Mar.1; 115) £80
– – **Anr. Edn.** Ill.:– Edmund Evans. 1875. *2nd. Edn.* Plts. loose, some spotting, orig. cl. (CSK. Oct.21; 121) £190
– – **Anr. Copy.** Fo. Stain in 1 margin, 1 short tear, loose in orig. cl. gt., rubbed. (S. Nov.22; 377) *Subunso.* £140
– **Jack the Giant-Killer.** L., 1888. *Facs. Edn.* 4to. 'Publisher's Introduction' tipped in, orig. pict. cl. (S. Dec.20; 609) *Sawyer.* £60

D'OYLY, Sir Charles
– **Indian Sports.** Patna, Behar Amateur Litho. Pr., [plts. dtd. 1828-30]. 3 pts. in 1 vol. Ob. fo. 3 litho. titles, 31 (of 36?) plts., 1 a dupl., some margins little stained, cont. hf. vell., some stitching brkn. (BBA. Mar.21; 323) *Ad Orientem.* £1,000
[–] **Tom Raw, The Griffin.** L., 1828. *1st. Edn.* 25 hand-cold. aquatint plts., hf.-title, advt.-ll. at end, later red hf. mor. by Sangorski & Sutcliffe. (S. Oct.11; 518) *Hosain.* £220

D'OYLY, Charles (Ill.)
See— **WILLIAMSON, Capt. Thomas & Blagdon, Francis William**

DRAFT BOOK of Centennial Carriages
L., ca. 1876. Fo. Ills., first 3 ll., folding plan & last 2 ll. strengthened, mod. cl. (P. May 17; 252) *Allan.* £65

DRAKE, Edward Cavendish
– **A New Universal Collection of Authentic & Entertaining Voyages & Travels, from the Earliest Accounts to the Present Time.** L., 1769. Fo. 61 full-p. & folding maps, views, etc., some slight tears, etc., mod. crimson three-qtr. mor. (SG. Mar.29; 306) $325
– – **Anr. Edn.** 1770. Fo. Frontis. detchd., cont. bds., mor. backstrip, some wear. (TA. Nov.17; 60) £105
– – **Anr. Copy.** Lge. fo. Engraved frontis., 62 engraved plts., linen chagrin. (DS. Dec.16; 2532) Pts. 80,000

DRAKE, Sir Francis
[–] **Sir Francis Drake Revived.** L., 1653. *1st. Coll. Edn.* 3 pts. in 1 vol. Sm. 4to. Frontis. margins bkd. & reprd., title-p. mntd. with sm. repair to upr. corner, fore-margin of A3 bkd. & with sm. losses, lr. margin of D4 torn, rust holes to 2 ll., some spotting, 19th. C. blind-stpd. pol. cf., very worn, spine defect., upr. cover loosening; the Rt. Hon. Visc. Eccles copy. [Wing D 2122 (with incorrect date 1655)] (CNY. Nov.18; 93) $900

DRAKE, Francis, Surgeon
– **Eboracum: or the History & Antiquities of the City of York** ... 1736. Fo. Margins slightly soiled, few ll. dampstained, recent panel. cf., spine gt.-decor. (TA. Feb.16; 84) £150

DRAKE, James
– **Road Book of the London & Birmingham & Grand Junction Railways.** 1839. 2 folding col. maps, 9 plts., advts., text & plts. dampstained, col. worn, bdg. not stated. (P. Mar.15; 54) *Lomax.* £50

DRAMA: its History, Literature & Influence on Civilization
Ed.:– Alfred Bates. L., [1903]. *(250).* 20 vols. Three-qtr. mor. (CBA. Dec.10; 194) $140

DRAPARNAUD, J.P.R.
– **Histoire Naturelle des Mollusques Terrestres et Fluviatiles de la France.** Paris, 1805. 13 plts., some staining. (*Bound with:*) **MICHAUD, A.L.G.** – **Complément de l'Histoire Naturelle des Mollusques Terrestes et Fluviatiles de la France.** Verdun, 1831. 3 plts. stained. Together 2 works in 1 vol. 4to. Cf. (P. Jan.12; 220) *Way.* £90

DRAPER, J.W.
– **A Century of Broadside Elegies.** L., 1928. *(275) numbered.* 4to. Orig. qtr. buckram. (S. Oct.4; 219) *Walford.* £50

DRAPER, Sir William
– Colonel Draper's Answer to the Spanish Arguments, Claiming the Galeon, & refusing Payment of the Ransom Bills, for Preserving Manila from Pillage & Destruction. L., 1764. *1st. Edn.* Hf.-title, hf. roan; the Rt. Hon. Visc. Eccles copy. (CNY. Nov.18; 94) $170

DRAYTON, John
– Beschreibung von Sued-Carolina ... Mit Anmerkungen und Zusaetzen des Uebersetzers Begleitet. Weimar, 1808. *1st. German Edn.* 3 pts. in 1 vol. Some browning, cont. bds., slightly worn. (SG. Jan.19; 327) $100

DRAYTON, Michael
– Poems. L., 1613. Lf. A5 (Selden & Heyward) present, 2-p. index in neat 17th. C. hand at end, cont. limp vell., ties, loose. [STC 7221] (BBA. May 3; 101) *Maggs.* £320
– – **Anr. Edn.** [1630]. Mod. mor. [STC 7224] (BS. Nov.16; 47) £95
– Poly-Olbion. Ill.:– W. Hole. L., [1612]. *[1st. Iss.].* Fo. Lacks typographic title (as usual), 4 maps closely shaved on outer edge, sm. ink stains on 2 maps, light stains, cont. spr. cf., rebkd. (TA. Sep.15; 125) £660

DREAMLAND & GHOSTLAND
– Dream Warnings & Mysteries. L., [1888]. *Re-iss. of Vol. I of Dreamland & Ghostland.* Title-p. a cancel, some foxing, bkplt., orig. decor. cl., covers worn at spine ends, spine darkened. (CBA. Oct.29; 281) $180

DREISER, Theodore
– The 'Genius'. N.Y., L., Toronto, 1915. *1st. Edn.* Hf.-title, orig. cl., top edge unstained (indicating Amer. iss.), d.-w. (S. Oct.11; 326) *Sawyer.* £110
– Jennie Gerhardt. N.Y., & L., 1911. With misspelling 'is' in line 30, p. 22, orig. blue mott. cl., with author's full name on spine, slightly soiled. (S. Oct.11; 324) *Hamery.* £65
– – **Anr. Edn.** N.Y., 1911. 1st. state of text & bdg., some marginal soiling, orig. mott. cl., some light discoloration; pres. copy to W.E. Williams, Fred A. Berne copy. (SPB. May 16; 259) $275
– Sister Carrie. N.Y., 1900. *1st. Edn.* Hf.-title preceding text & title, marginal tear on 1st. text lf., slit in p.517, orig. cl., inr. hinges reprd.; Fred A. Berne copy. (SPB. May 16; 260) $450

DRESCHER, Karl
– Das Nuernbergische Schoenbartbuch. Ill.:– H. Gustav Brinckmann. Weimar, 1908. *(500) numbered hand-cold.* Sm. fo. 97 paintings on 78 handcold. plts., last 4-pp. text in photostat, ex-liby., orig. wraps., unc. (SG. May 3; 146) $325

DRESSER, Christopher
– Studies in Design. L., n.d. Fo. 60 cold. litho. plts., a few ll. lightly soiled, hf. cf., rubbed. (S. Apr.30; 180) *Henderson.* £620

DRESSER, Henry Eeles
– A History of the Birds of Europe. Ill.:– after Keulemans, Neale, Wolf, & Thorburn. L., priv. ptd., 1871-81, 1895-96 (Supp.). 9 vols., including Supp. 4to. Additional wood-engraved titles, 2 plain & 720 hand-cold. litho. plts., unif. hf. mor. gt., with additional vol. containing ptd. wraps. to 84 orig. pts. (C. Mar.14; 164) *Burden.* £3,500
– – **Anr. Edn.** Ill.:– after Keulemans, Neale, Wolf, & Thorburn. L., priv. ptd., 1871-81. 8 vols., without Supp. 4to. Additional wood-engraved titles, 2 plain & 631 hand-cold. litho. plts., cont. hf. mor. gt., spines slightly rubbed & faded. (C. Mar.14; 165) *Burden.* £3,000
– A Monograph of the Coraciidae, or Family of the Rollers. Ill.:– after J.G. Keulemans. Farnborough, 1893. Lge. 4to. 27 hand-cold. litho. plts., orig. cl., gt. vig., rubbed; pres. copy from author to his brother Arthur R. Dresser. (C. Mar.14; 166) *Franklin.* £1,400
– A Monograph on the Meropidae or Family of the Bee-eaters. Ill.:– J.G. Keulemans. Priv. ptd., 1884-86. Fo. Maroon hf. mor., spine gt., orig. wraps. bnd. in. (SKC. Nov.18; 1967) £2,100

DREUX, Alfred de
– Scènes Equestres. Paris, n.d. Ob. fo. Cont. hf. roan. (HD. Dec.9; 125) Frs. 6,700

DREUX DU RADIER, Jean François
– L'Europe Illustré. Ill.:– Eisen (frontis.), Odieuvre. 1777. 6 vols. 4to. Cont. marb. roan. (HD. Apr.13; 15) Frs. 3,500

DREVES, Friedrich & Hayne, F.G.
– Botanisches Bilderbuch für die Jugend und Freunde der Pflanzenkunde. Leipzig, 1794-98. 3 vols. in 1. 4to. German, Fr. & Engl. text, 87 cold. plts., some foxing to text, later hf. chagrin, spine raised bands. (HD. Jul.6; 29) Frs. 2,000
– – **Anr. Edn.** Ill.:– Capieux. Leipzig, 1794-95-98. Vols. 1-3 (of 5). 4to. German, Fr. & Engl. text, engraved vig. title-pp. & 102 plts. hand-cold., some text ll. discold., 1st. 2 title-pp. dampstained, cont. hf. cf., slightly rubbed; van Veen coll. (S. Feb.28; 143) £420

DREYFUS, Carle
See– NOCQ, Henri & Dreyfus, Carle

DRINKWATER, Capt. John
– A History of the Late Siege of Gibraltar. 1786. *1st. Edn.* 4to. 10 plts. & maps, 1 map preserved, 1 linen-bkd. & torn, hf. cf., lr. cover detch'd. (P. Sep.8; 261) *Elliott.* £60
– – **Anr. Edn.** 1786. *2nd. Edn.* 4to. 3 plts. slightly torn, some ll. rather spotted, cont. cf., gt. spine; loosely inserted A.L.s from Gen. Elliott, commander at Gibraltar, 30 Dec. 1784 1 p. 8vo. re power of attorney, D.s by John Watts of Victualling Office, 14 May 1781 1 p. 8vo. re chartering of the Ship Providence, with integral blank, woodcut of Gibraltar Bay, 1805. (BBA. Sep.29; 100) *Trocchi.* £140
– – **Anr. Edn.** 1786. *3rd. Edn.* 4to. 1 map, 10 engraved plts., all folding, 4 with tears, some soiling, cont. hf. cf., rubbed, rebkd. (CSK. Apr.6; 29) £85
– – **Anr. Edn.** 1790. *4th. Edn.* 4to. Cont. hf. cf. (TA. Jun.21; 94a) £80

DRINKWATER, John & Rutherston, Albert
– Claud Lovat Fraser. L., 1923. *(450) numbered & sigd.* 4to. Port. frontis., 39 plts., cl., partly untrimmed. (SG. Oct.13; 159) $140

DRONSFIELD, John
– Fifty African Improvisations. Cape Town, [1956]. *(80) numbered.* 4to. Wire bnd. cl.; letter from Janda Press loosely inserted. (VA. Apr.27; 773) R 240
– Non-Europeans Only. Cape Town, 1942. *(350) sigd.* 4to. Stiff wraps., wire bnd., covers slightly soiled; inscr. from 'Jack & Denis' to Lewis Hallett, Cape Town, May 1942. (VA. Apr.27; 774) R 170

DROSTE-HULSHOFF, Annette Elisabeth von
[–] Gedichte. Münster, 1838. *1st. Edn.* Foxing, orig. bds., slightly soiled & bumped; Hauswedell coll. (H. May 24; 1270) DM 5,000
– – **Anr. Edn.** Stuttgart & Tübingen, 1844. *1st. Coll. Edn.* Foxed, cont. linen gt., spine & corners bumped. (H. Nov.23; 635) DM 660
– Die Judenbuche. Ein Sittengemälde aus dem Gebirgigen Westfalen. Ill.:– Heinrich Nauen. Frankfurt, 1923. *(250) numbered.* Printers mark sigd. by Nauen, 10 orig. etchings, 9 monogrammed, orig. bds. (GB. May 5; 2011) DM 1,800
– – **Anr. Copy.** Printers mark sigd. by artist, 10 orig. etchings, including 9 monogrammed, orig. bds. (GB. Nov.5; 2838) DM 1,600
– Letzte Gaben. Nachgelassene Blätter. Ed.:– L. Schücking. Hannover, 1860. *1st. Edn.* Cont. linen. (H. May 22; 645) DM 520

DROUVILLE, G.
– Voyage en Perse, fait en 1812 et 1813. Paris, 1867. 2 vols. in 1. Map & 59 (of 60) cold. engraved lithos., cont. hf. cf., spine decor., 1 turn-in worn. (HD. Jun.26; 39) Frs. 2,500

DROZ, Gustave
– Monsieur, Madame et Bébé. Ill.:– Edmond Morin. Paris, 1878. 4to. Hf. mor., decor. & mosaic spine, corners, unc., wrap. & spine preserved, by Champs. (HD. Feb.17; 62) Frs. 1,300

DRUCE, Herbert & Gray, Thomas de, Lord Walsingham
See– BIOLOGIA CENTRALI-AMERICANA

DRUMMOND, Alexander
– Travels Through Different Cities of Germany, Italy, Greece & several Parts of Asia ... 1754. *1st. Edn.* Fo. Cont. cf., rubbed. (SKC. Mar.9; 2010) £300
– – **Anr. Copy.** Fo. Folding engraved frontis., 33 plts. & maps only, a few margins soiled, some clean tears, old cf., rubbed. (CSK. Jul.6; 70) £220
– – **Anr. Copy.** Fo. Folding allegorical frontis., 34 copperplts., many folding, rather foxed, old cf., shabby. (SG. Sep.22; 122) $450

DRUMMOND, Henry
[–] Histories of Noble British Families, with Biographical Notices; Illustrated by their Armorial Bearings, Portraits, Monuments, Seals, etc. L., 1846. 2 vols. Atlas fo. Hand-cold. ports. & arms, uncold. engraved views, etc., sm. liby. 'withdrawn' stp. on verso of titles, hf. cf., needs rebdg. (SG. Jun.7; 363) $200

DRUMMOND, James
– Sculptured Monuments of Iona & the West Highlands. Edinb., 1881. *Ltd. Edn., numbered.* Fo. Panel. qtr. mor. (PD. Oct.19; 76) £105
– – **Anr. Copy.** Fo. Orig. hf. mor., partly untrimmed, rubbed. (TA. Jul.19; 94) £66
See– ANDERSON, Joseph & Drummond, James

DRUMMOND, William, of Hawthornden
– The Works ... Ed.:– Thomas Ruddiman. Edinb., 1711. *1st. Coll. Edn.* Fo. Cont. panel. cf.; Sir Ivar Colquhoun, of Luss copy. (CE. Mar.22; 91) £230

DRUMPELMANN, Ernst Wilhelm
– Getreue Abbildungen und Naturhistorische Beschreibung des Thierreichs aus den Nördlichen Provinzen Russlands. Ill.:– Susemihl after Drümpelmann. Riga, 1807-11. 2 vols. 4to. (sizes not quite unif.). 7 fascicules only, lacks final fascicule, 7 engraved titles, folding table, 35 hand-cold. engraved plts., Vol. I includes 2 ll. of specially-ptd. dedication to Princess Catharina Pavlova, dtd. 25th. Feb. 1811, some very minor spotting, pres. badges. of cont. purple & olive silk-covered bds., Vol. II with gt. vig. on covers, spines rubbed. (C. Jun.27; 154) *Kaye.* £950

DRUON, M.
– La Fin des Hommes. Les Grandes Familles. Paris, 1948. *Orig. Edn.* Sm. 8vo. Hf. mor. by Devauchelle, unc., wrap. & spine, s.-c.; author's copy on chiffon d'Annonay, autograph dedication to Jean Louize, orig. pencil sketch by A. Jacquemin, letter by J. Loize, photo, visiting card, &c. (HD. Mar.27; 62) Frs. 3,200

DRURY, Dru.
– Illustrations of Exotic Entomology. Ed.:– J.O. Westwood. L., 1837. *New Edn.* 3 vols. 4to. 151 engraved plts., all but 1 hand-cold., mod. hf. leath. (SKC. Oct.26; 358) £700
– Illustrations of Natural History ... of Exotic Insects ... to which is added a translation into French. L., priv. ptd., 1770-82. *1st. Edn.* 3 vols. 4to. Uncold. key plt., 150 hand-cold. engraved plts., cont. red mor. gt., spines gt. (C. Mar.14; 167) *Bjorck & Borjesson.* £2,400
– – **Anr. Copy.** 3 vols. 4to. Uncold. engraved key plt., 150 hand-cold. engraved plts., on guards thro.-out, some plts. browned by tissues, late 19th. C. qtr. leath., spines worn & breaking. (CNY. May 18; 141) $550

DRYASDUST
See– HALIDON, M.Y. 'Dryasdust'

DRYDEN, John
– Absalom & Achitophel. L., 1681. *Pt. 1: 1st. Edn. 1st. Iss.* Fo. Mistakes on p.6 not corrected by hand, lacks 1st. blank lf., hf. mor.; William M. Fitzhugh, Jr. bkplt. [Wing D 2212] (SPB. May 16; 52) $950
– Annus Mirabilis. L., 1667. *1st. Edn. 3rd. Iss.* Lacks errata/licence lf. & final blank, slight browning & soiling, cont. sheep, worn. [Wing D2239] (S. Oct.11; 331) *Thorp.* £50
– Astraea Redux. A Poem on the Happy Restoration & Return of his Sacred Majesty Charles the Second. 1660. *1st. Edn.* Sm. fo. 2nd. state of p. 11 line 30, lacks 1st. lf. with Royal arms on verso, last p. slightly soiled, early 20th. C. cf. by Riviere &

DRYDEN, John -*Contd.*

Son, spine gt., slightly rubbed. [Wing D 2244] (BBA. Feb.23; 151) *Maggs.* £220
- **Cleomenes, the Spartan Heroe.** L., 1692. *1st. Edn.* Mod. spr. cf., gt. spine, inner gt. dentelles, new end-papers, by Sangorski & Sutcliffe. (CBA. Dec.10; 196) $160
- **An Evening's Love, or the Mock-Astrologer.** 1671. *1st. Edn.* 4to. Some staining, later hf. mor. [Wing D2273] (BBA. Jan.19; 129) *Maggs.* £100
- **The Fables** ... Ill.:– after Lady Diana Beauclerc. 1797. Fo. Cont. diced russ., covers decor., spine gt.; Sir Ivar Colquhoun, of Luss copy. (CE. Mar.22; 92) £460
- **Love Triumphant.** L., 1694. *1st. Edn.* 4to. Hf.-title, last lf. torn & reprd. with slight loss of text, margin wormholes, mod. mor. by Sangorski & Sutcliffe. [Wing D2302] (BBA. May 3; 176) *Finch.* £80
- **The Works.** L., 1691. *1st. Coll. Iss.* 33 pts. in 4 vols. 4to. Natural paper fault in G3, few headlines in 1 pt. wormed, other minor defects, cont. cf. gt. extra, slightly worn; bkplts. of the Fauconberg family & W. Marchbank. [Wing D 2207] (SG. Nov.3; 61) $3,200
- **The Dramatic Works.** Ed.:– Montague Summers. L., Nones. Pr., 1931-32. *(800) numbered. (50) on Van Gelder paper.* 6 vols. Tall 8vo. Orig. hf. vell. gt. & marb. bds., unc., end-papers browned. (CNY. May 18; 157) $110

DRYDEN, John & Lee, Nathaniel
- **Oedipus: a Tragedy.** L., 1679. *1st. Edn.* Some foxing, mod. lev. mor. & cl., new end-papers. (CBA. Dec.10; 197) $140

DRYDEN PRESS
- **Specimens of Type in use by J. Davy & Sons at the Dryden Press.** L., 1898. *(500).* 1 vol. 4to. Orig. cl. *(With:)* – **A Selection of Types, Ornaments, etc. of the Dryden Press.** L., 1907. *(200).* 1 vol. 4to. Dampstained, disbnd. (BBA. Apr.5; 321) *Questor.* £110

DUANE, William
- [–] **The System of Infantry Discipline ... with an Appendix ... containing the Elements of War.** N.P., 1814. Some foxing, orig. bds., upr. cover loose, spine partly chipped away, unc; with sig. of Joseph Bloomfield, Revolutionary General at top of p. 1 dtd. Dec. 22, 1814. (SG. Apr.5; 66) $175

DU BARTAS, Guillaume de Saluste, Seigneur
- **La Sepmaine, ou Création du Monde. — La Judith, l'Uranie, Le Triomphe de la Foy** ... Commentaries:– Simon Goulart. Paris, 1583. 2 works in 1 vol. 4to. Faint dampstain, cont. vell. gt., recovered, decor., name Guillaume Vernon & devices stpd. on covers; from Fondation Furstenberg-Beaumesnil. (HD. Nov.16; 117) *Frs. 12,000*

DUBE, Annemarie & W.-D.
- **E.L. Kirchner. Das Graphische Werk.** München, 1967. 2 vols. Lge. 4to. Orig. linen. (HK. Nov.11; 3689) DM 420
- **Erich Heckel. Das Graphische Werk.** Ill.:– Heckel. N.Y., 1964-74. 3 vols. 4to. 4 sigd. woodcuts, 1 sigd. etching & 1 sigd. litho., orig. linen. (HK. May 17; 2822) DM 2,200

DU-BEC-CRESPIN, Jean
- **The Historie of the Great Emperour Tamerlan.** Trans.:– H.M. L., 1597. *1st. Engl. Edn.* G8 misbnd., cf., rebkd. [STC 7263] (P. Mar.15; 303) *Thorp.* £270

DUBECH, Lucien
- **Histoire Générale Illustrée du Theatre.** Paris, 1931-34. 5 vols. 4to. Cont. hf. parch., spines slightly soiled, orig. wraps. bnd. in. (S. Mar.20; 677) *Duran.* £75

DU BELLAY, Joachim
- **Les Oeuvres Françoises.** Lyon, 1575. *2nd. Coll. Edn.* Orig. limp vell. gt., yapp edges, covers with gt.-stpd. leafy wreath, flat spine gt., sm. restoration to upr. yapp edge, sm. hole at foot of backstrip, qtr. parch. gt. box; Thomas B. Stevenson copy. (CNY. May 18; 104) $500
- **Recueil de Poésie Présenté à Tresillustre Princesse Madame Marguerite Soeur Unique du Roy, & Mis**

en **Lumière par le Commandement de Madicte Dame.** 1568. Inner margin wormed with loss of some letters, mod. vell. (HD. Mar.21; 25) *Frs. 2,000*

DU BELLAY, Martin
- **Les Mémoires.** Paris, 1569. *Orig. Edn.* Fo. Upr. margin of title cut, cont. vell. gt., François Grolier arms, spine decor., upr. turn-in reprd. (HD. May 21; 6) *Frs. 1,150*

DUBLIN HISTORICAL RECORD
Mar. 1938-Dec. 1981. Vol. 1 no. 1-Vol. 35 no. 1 (lacks Vol. 1 no. 2), & Indexes. Orig. wraps., w.a.f. (GM. Oct.5; 381) £130

DUBLIN PHILOSOPHICAL JOURNAL & SCIENTIFIC REVIEW
Dublin, 1825 & 26. Vols. I & II (all publd.?). Hf. mor., armorial motif on spine, as a periodical, w.a.f. (GM. Dec.7; 157) £100

DUBOIS, G.
- **Mémoires.** Ill.:– Jean Gradassi. Paris, 1950. *(3) on japan.* 4 vols. Sm. 4to. 6 orig. watercolours, 1 suite in black & 1 in sepia, lacks 2 double-p. plts. & orig. watercolour of 1 double-p. plt., leaves, wraps., box. (HD. Mar.27; 63) *Frs. 2,000*

DUBOIS, J.
- **Souvenirs de la Suisse. Dessiné d'après Nature.** Ill.:– A. Cuvillier, Himely & V. Pettit. Genf, ca. 1850. 45 cold. & tinted litho. views (10 double-p.), probably lacks 5 plts., cont. linen. (R. Apr.5; 3072) DM 1,700

DUBOIS, Abbé Jean Antoine
- **Description of the Character, Manners, & Customs of the people of India.** L., 1817. 4to. Diced cf. (GM. Dec.7; 638) £50

DU BOIS, John van Deusen
- **Campaigns in the West, 1856-1861: The Journals & Letters** ... Ed.:– George P. Hammond. Ill.:– after Joseph Heger. Tucson, [Grabhorn Pr.], 1949. *(300) numbered & sigd. by ed.* Sm. fo. Prospectus laid in, qtr. pig. & patterned bds., unc., spine nicked near head. (SG. Mar.29; 156) $130

DU BOIS, W.E. Burghardt
- **Black Reconstruction ... 1860-1880.** N.Y., [1935]. *1st. Edn.* Lge. 8vo. Cl.; from liby. of F.D. Roosevelt, inscr. 'For Mrs. Franklin D. Roosevelt with the admiration for her great courage & humanity, Walter White' (as Secretary of the NAACP). (SG. Mar.15; 16) $325

DUBOIS-FONTANELLE
- **Anecdotes Africains, depuis l'Origine ou la Découverte des Différents Royaumes qui composent l'Afrique, jusqu'à nos Jours.** Paris, 1755. Cont. marb. cf. gt., arms in centre, decor. spine; La Rochefoucauld ex-libris. (HD. Sep.22; 236) *Frs. 1,500*

DU BOSC, Claude
- **The Military History of the Late Prince Eugene of Savoy & of the Late John, Duke of Marlborough.** 1736. 2 vols. Fo. Some stains, cont. cf., spines gt. (BBA. Jun.28; 33) *Snelling.* £330

DUBOURDIEU, Rev. John
- **Statistical Survey of the County of Antrim.** Dublin, 1812. 1 vol. in 2. Linen-bkd. folding map & all the folding & single plts., etc., tree cf. (GM. Dec.7; 221) £150
- **Statistical Survey of the County of Down.** Dublin, 1802. *1st. Edn.* Engraved frontis. folding map, 12 plts., hf. mor. (GM. Dec.7; 427) £160

DUBOURG, Matthew
- **Views of the Remains of Ancient Buildings in Rome, & its Vicinity.** L., 1820 [but not before 1838]. Tall 4to. 26 cold. aquatint plts. (paper wtrmkd. 1838), no plt. list, orig. gt.-lettered cl., new red mor. back, matching s.-c. (SG. Mar.29; 307) $400
- – **Anr. Edn.** L., 1844. Fo. 26 engraved & col. ptd. plts., hf. cf. (CR. Jul.6; 153) *Lire 1,200,000*

DUBRAVIUS, Janus, Bp. of Olmutz
- **De Piscinis et Piscium qui in eis aluntur Naturis Libri Quinque.** [Zürich], 1559. 2 pts. in 1 vol. Lacks

last lf. (? blank), slightly stained, recent mor. (BBA. May 23; 320) *Von Knorring.* £120
- **Historia Boiemica.** Basel, 1575. *2nd. (1st. Basel) Edn.* Slightly browned, title soiled, several old owner's notes. *(Bound with:)* PIUS II, Aeneas Sylvius – **De Bohemorum et ex his Imperatorum** ... Basel, 1575. *Later Edn.* Margin's near end slightly soiled. Together 2 works in 1 vol. Fo. Cont. leath., lightly bumped, lr. cover wormed. (R. Oct.11; 34) DM 650

DU BREUIL, Jean
- [–] **Perspective Practica, oder Vollständige Anleitung zu der Perspectiv-Reiss-Kunst** ... Trans.:– J. Chr. Rembold. Augsburg, 1710. *1st. German Edn.* 4to. Lacks frontis., 3 ll. with bkd. tears & slight loss, a little light spotting, cont. cf., worn & slightly bumped. (H. May 22; 139) DM 800
- [– –] **Anr. Copy.** 4to. Lacks engraved frontis., 1 copper engr. extended in lr. corner, 1 copper engr. very browned, soiled, some foxing, mod. vell. (D. Nov.23; 1881) DM 500
- [–] **The Practise of Perspective** ... Trans.:– E. Chambers. L., 1749. *[3rd-Edn.].* 4to. 1 full-p. ill laid down (as called for), without final (?) blank, some browning, cont. cf., worn. (CSK. Nov.4; 138) £60
- [–] – **Anr. Copy.** 4to. Liby. stps. on title, erasure on title worn to sm. hole, slightly spotted, cont. cf., rebkd., worn. (S. Apr.30; 181) *Baker.* £50

DUBUAT-NANCAY, Comte Louis-Gabriel
- **Les Origines de l'Ancien Gouvernement de la France.** La Haye, 1757. *Orig. Edn.* 4 vols. 12mo. Cont. cf. (HD. Feb.22; 58) *Frs. 2,500*
- – **Anr. Edn.** La Haye, 1789. 3 vols. Hf. cl. (HD. Feb.22; 57) *Frs. 2,100*

DUBUFFET, Jean
- **La Botte d'Nique.** Geneva, 1973. *(210) sigd. with orig. serigraph.* 4to. & fo. Loose in folder & wraps. as iss., boxed. (SPB. Dec.13; 807) $175

DU BUISSON, Paul Ulric
- [–] **Tableau de la Volupté.** Ill.:– Eisen, engraved by Longueil. 1771. 12mo. Mor. gt. by Chambolle-Duru, spine decor. (HD. May 3; 39) *Frs. 1,600*

DUBUISSON
See— DEMACHY & Dübuisson

DU BUS (de Gisignies), Bernard L., Vicomte
- **Esquisses Ornithologiques, Descriptions et Figures d'Oiseaux Nouveaux ou peu Connus.** Ill.:– G. Severyns & J. Dekeghel. Brussels, 1845-48-50. Livraisons I-IV & supp. livraison (all publd.). No. 37 hand-cold. litho. plts., loose as iss. in orig. wraps., unc., s.-c. (C. Jun.27; 155) *Reid.* £350
- – **Anr. Edn.** Brüssel, 1845-48[-51]. 5 pts. (all publd.). Fo. Orig. wraps in linen box, box slightly rubbed. (D. Nov.23; 704) DM 3,100

DUCASSE, Isidore-Lucien 'Comte de Lautreamont'
- **Les Chants de Maldoror. Chants I, II, III, IV, V, VI.** Paris & Bruxelles, 1874. *Orig. Edn.* 12mo. Blind-decor. mor., inner gt. roll-stp., s.-c., by Semet & Plumelle. (HD. Sep.22; 271) *Frs. 7,000*
- – **Anr. Edn.** Paris & Bruxelles, 1874. *Orig. Edn. (except Chant I).* 12mo. Mor. gt. by Alix, wrap., box., edges untrimmed. (HD. Nov.29; 101) *Frs. 10,200*

DUCHAMP, Marcel & Halberstadt, V.
- **Opposition et Cases Conjugées sont Reconciliés par Duchamp et Halberstadt.** Paris & Brussels, 1932. *1st. Edn. Ltd. Iss.* 4to. In Fr., German & Engl., 1st. ll. slightly creased, orig. wraps.; MS. dedication by artist. (H. May 23; 1193) DM 1,000
- – **Anr. Edn.** Paris & Brüssel, 1932. *1st. Edn.* 4to. Orig. bds. (HK. Nov.11; 3510) DM 500

DUCHENNE DE BOULOGNE, G.B.A.
- **De l'Electrisation Localisée, et de Son Application à La Physiologie, à la Pathologue et à la Therapeutique.** Paris, 1855. *1st. Edn.* Lr. margins lightly dampstained, old hf. mor. (SG. Oct.6; 136) $200

DU CHESNE, Joseph 'Josephus Quercetanus'
- **Ad Veritatem Hermeticae Medicinae ex Hippocratis Veterumque Decretis ac Therapeusi.** Paris, 1604. *1st. Edn.* 2 pts. in 1 vol. 4 ll. with preface to

reader & errata at end, sm. hole in blank margin of title & following lf., few stains, some margin worming, new vell.; Dr. Walter Pagel copy. (S. Feb.7; 105) *Radziowsky.* £250
- Liber de Priscorum Philosophorum verae Medicinae Materia. Geneva, 1603. *1st. Edn.* 3 pp. errata, rubricated thro.-out, cont. Fr. limp vell., gt.-decor. sides, flat spine, outer margin of upr. cover defect., some stains; Dr. Walter Pagel copy. (S. Feb.7; 104) *Radziowsky.* £450
- - Anr. Edn. Geneva, 1609. *2nd. Edn.(?).* 1 word in imprint pasted over, qtr. cf.; Dr. Walter Pagel copy, w.a.f. (S. Feb.7; 103) *Heller.* £160
- Musée de Peinture et de Sculpture. Paris & L., 1820-30. Vols. 1-9 only (of 17). 12mo. Engl. & Fr. text, some spotting, cont. hf. cf., rubbed; Paul Wallraf bkplt. (S. Apr.30; 182) *Black.* £80
- Pestis Alexicacus sive Pestiferae Fuga. Paris, 1608. *1st. Edn.* Rubricated thro.-out, cont. limp vell.; Dr. Walter Pagel copy. (S. Feb.7; 102) *Quaritch.* £300
- Tetras Gravissimorum Totius Capitis Affectuum. Marburg, 1617. *Last Latin Edn.* (*Bound with:*) - Liber de Priscorum Philosophorum Verae Medicinae Materia, Praeparationis Modo, atque in Curandis Morbis, Praestantia. Geneva, 1603. *1st. Edn.* Together 2 works in 1 vol. Sm. 8vo. Early owner's sigs., early marginalia & underscoring, few liby. stps., early vell., slightly soiled. (SG. Mar.22; 104) $130

DU CHOUL, Guillaume
- Discorso sopra la Castrametatione et Disciplina Militare de Romani. Trans.:- Gabriel Symeoni. Lyon, 1556. Tall 4to. A woodcuts few crudely tinted, faint dampstain in lr. margin, vell. (SG. Feb.9; 215) $250
- Discours de la Religion des Anciens Romains. Lyons, 1556. (*Bound with:*) - Discours sur la Castrametation et Discipline Militaire des Romains. Lyons, 1557. Together 2 vols. in 1. Sm. 4to. Cont. blind-stpd. cf., rebkd. (BBA. Jun.28; 130) *Drury.* £260
- - Anr. Edn. Lyons, 1580. 2 pts. in 1 vol. 4to. Slightly browned & spotted, a few ll. marginally dampstained, cont. cf.-bkd. bds., worn. (BBA. Feb.23; 10) *Drury.* £85
- - Anr. Edn. Lyon, 1581. 4to. Sewed. (D. Nov.23; 103) DM 600

DUCKETT, W.A.
La Turquie Pittoresque. Paris, 1855. 20 engraved plts., slightly spotted, cont. hf. mor., spine gt., slightly rubbed. (BBA. Dec.15; 62) *Makiya.* £85

DUCLOS, Charles
[-] Acajou et Zirphile, conte A. Minutie. Ill.:- Chedel after Boucher. [Paris], 1744. 4to. Engraved frontis., 9 plts., later mor. (SPB. Dec.13; 808) $250

DUCOR, Henri
- Aventures d'un Marin de la Garde Impériale. Prisonnier de Guerre sur les Pontons Espagnols, dans l'île de Cabrera et en Russie. Paris, 1823. 2 vols. Mod. hf. chagrin. (HD. Jan.24; 26) Frs. 2,000

DUCREST, Charles Louis, Marquis
- Essai sur les Machines Hydrauliques. Paris, 1777. *1st. Edn.* Privilege lf., cont. sheep; John D. Stanitz coll. (SPB. Apr.25; 125) $300

DUCRET, Siegfried
- Fürstenberger Porzellan. Braunschweig, 1965. 3 vols. Lge. 4to. Orig. linen. (BR. Apr.13; 2054) DM 1,100
- Meissner Porzellan. Braunschweig, 1971-72. 2 vols. 4to. Orig. linen, orig. wraps. (GB. Nov.4; 1396) DM 420

DUDEVANT, Maurice 'Maurice Sand'
- History of the Harlequinade. L., 1915. 2 vols. 4to. Linen, corners. (DS. Dec.16; 2523) Pts. 20,000
- Masques et Bouffons. 1860. 2 vols. Cont. hf. chagrin. (HD. Jan.24; 84) Frs. 1,050
- - Anr. Edn. Paris, 1862. 2 vols. 50 hand-cold. plts., maroon mor. gt. extra, bkplt. (PNY. Jun.6; 554) $300
- Le Monde des Papillons. Paris, 1867. *1st. Edn.* 2 vols. in 1. 4to. Some slight browning & spotting,

mod. mor.; MS. dedication. (H. May 22; 181) DM 1,000

DUDIN, René Martin
- The Art of the Bookbinder & Gilder. Leeds, Elmete Pr., 1977. (*490*). Fo. Orig. mor.-bkd. gt. stpd. cl.; H.M. Nixon coll., with his typescript of a review loosely inserted. (BBA. Oct.6; 42) *Oak Knoll Books.* £80
- Arte del Legatore e Doratore di Libri. Milan, 1964. *Ltd. Edn.* Fo. Orig. wraps., s.-c.; H.M. Nixon coll., with his notes & corrected typescript of review for 'Book Collector' loosely inserted. (BBA. Oct.6; 38) *Book Press.* £70
- Art du Relieur. Ed.:- J.E. Bertrand. Ill.:- Bille. Paris, 1818. *New Edn.* 4to. Advt. lf., foxed & spotted, qtr. leath., shabby. (SG. Jan.5; 60) $275
- L'Art du Relieur Doreur de Livres. Ill.:- H. Ransonnette. [Paris], 1772. Fo. 16 copperplts., disbnd. (SG. Jan.5; 59) $350

DU FAY, M. L'Abbé
- Véritable Manière de bien Fortifier de Monsieur De Vauban ... Amst., 1702. 2 vols. in 1. Cont. cf., worn. (PD. Jun.13; 72) £50

DUFF, E. Gordon
- Catalogue of the Library. 1925. 2 pts. in 1 vol. 4to. Sale catalogue, cl.; H.M. Nixon coll., with his MS. notes. (BBA. Oct.6; 152) *Beres.* £60
- Fifteenth Century English Books. 1917. 4to. Orig. buckram-bkd. cl.; H.M. Nixon coll., with sigs. of L.H. & H.M. Nixon on front free endpaper, & some notes by H.M.N. (BBA. Oct.6; 205) *Cox.* £50

DUFLOS, P.
- Recueil d'Estampes. Paris, 1780. 158 hand-cold. plts. with borders & details heightened with gold. (*With:*) - Deuxième Recueil des Portraits. Paris, 1787. 100 plts. as above. Together 2 vols. Fo. Marb. bds. (S. May 21; 3) *Martinos.* £3,200

DUFLOT DE MOFRAS, Eugène
- Exploration du Territoire de l'Oregon, des Californies et de la Mer Vermeille ... Paris, 1844. 2 vols. only (lacks atlas). 1 lf. at end Vol. 1 supplied in facs., some staining, publisher's bds., rebkd. (S. Dec.13; 131) *Duviols.* £70

DU FOUILLOUX, Jacques
- La Vènerie. Paris, 1585. Sm. 4to. Without 'La Fauconnerie', at end 'De la Chasse du Loup, de la Chasse du Connin, Remèdes pour guarir les Chiens', late 17th. C. marb. roan, decor. spine. (HD. Feb.29; 12) Frs. 15,800

DUFOUR, L.
- Atlas des Champignons Comestibles & Vénéneux. 1891. Lge. 8vo. Some foxing to text, hf. chagrin, spine raised bands. (HD. Jul.6; 30) Frs. 1,100

DUFRESNE DE SAINT-LEON, A.
See— MARAIS, Paul & Dufresne de Saint-Leon, A.

DUFT, Johannes & Meyer, Peter
- The Irish Miniatures in the Abbey Library of St. Gall. Olten, Berne & Lausanne, 1954. (*600*). Fo. Niger, upr. cover stpd. in brown, spine lettered in brown, light wear to box; Estelle Doheny bkplt., Marymount College copy. (CBA. Mar.3; 256) $550

DUFY, Raoul
- Ten Colour Collotypes after Watercolours. 1961. (*200*). Fo. Orig. cl.-bkd. bds. (BBA. Feb.9; 186) *Price.* £75

DUGAST DE BOIS-SAINT-JUST, Jean Louis Marie, Marquis
[-] Paris, Versailles et les Provinces, au Dix-huitième Siècle. Paris, 1817. 3 vols., compl. Cont. hf. roan. (HD. Mar.27; 9) Frs. 1,300

DUGDALE, Florence E.
- The Book of Baby Birds. Ill.:- after Edward J. Detmold. L., ca. 1915. *1st. Edn.* Some light foxing, hf. cl. & pict. bds., slightly soiled. (CBA. Aug.21; 174) $150

DUGDALE, Thomas
- Curiosities of Great Britain. England & Wales Delineated. Tallis, 1835. Pts. 1-4, 6 & 7 only. 12 engraved views, 24 double-p. maps, some dampstains, orig. cl., spines worn. (TA. Sep.15; 123) £52
- - Anr. Edn. Ca. 1845. 8 vols. Double-p. county maps hand-cold. in outl., some minor stains & spotting, mostly to margins, orig. gt.-decor. cl., some wear. (TA. May 17; 94) £165
- - Anr. Copy. 10 vols. Steel-engraved frontis. & vig. title to each vol., 249 plts., 58 double-p. county maps, a few ll. detchd. & frayed at edges, orig. blind-stpd. cl., faded & rubbed on spines. (TA. Jun.21; 172) £155
- - Anr. Copy. 8 vols. only (of 11). 58 partly col. double-p. maps, 176 engraved plts., orig. cl. gt., worn & faded, as a collection of plts., w.a.f. (P. Nov.24; 119) *Willis.* £120
- - Anr. Copy. 8 vols. only. 185 engraved plts. & 54 maps, orig. cl. gt., as a collection of plts., w.a.f. (P. Sep.29; 218) *Eisler.* £100
- - Anr. Edn. L., ca. 1850. 8 vols. Engraved titles, frontis., 176 plts., 58 maps cold. in outl., some foxing to plts., orig. cl. gt. (P. Nov.24; 215) *Martin.* £130
- - Anr. Edn. Ed.:- E.L. Blanchard. Ca. 1860. 2 vols. Additional vig. titles, 58 double-p. hand-cold. county maps, 120 steel engrs., 1st. part of Vol. 1 dampstained, cont. hf. mor., worn, backstrips defect., covers detchd. (TA. Jul.19; 71) £165
- - Anr. Copy. 8 vols. in 4. Vig. title to each vol., 61 double-p. maps, 234 engraved plts., some spotting, cont. hf. cf. gt., some wear. (TA. Jan.19; 43) £150
- - Anr. Edn. N.d. Vols. 1-10 only (of 11). 58 double-p. maps, hand-cold. in outl., 227 plts., a few maps spotted, orig. cl., rubbed & faded. (BBA. Jan.19; 116) *Richards,.* £120
- - Anr. Copy. Vols. 1-10 only (of 11). 8vo. Engraved titles, 58 double-p. maps, 248 plts., some margins dampstained or torn, slightly soiled thro.-out, a few ll. loose, orig. cl., worn. (BBA. Dec.15; 91) *Jeffery.* £105
- - Anr. Copy. 4 vols. Engraved titles, 58 double-p. maps, 186 plts., some ll. slightly spotted, cont. hf. cf. (BBA. Oct.27; 275) *Jeffery.* £55

DUGDALE, Sir William
- The Antiquities of Warwickshire. Ill.:- W. Hollar, R. Vaughan, & others. L., 1656. *1st. Edn.* Fo. Engraved port. frontis., 16 double-p. maps, plans & plts., errata lf. at end, sm. holes touching engraved surface of 1 or 2 plts. with slight loss of engraved surface, some browning, cont. owner's inscr. on title, 18th. C. russ. gt., upr. cover detchd. [Wing D2479] (S. Dec.13; 203) *Wall.* £140
- - Anr. Copy. Fo. Extra port. (laid down), title & 1 plt. relaid, few margin tears thro.-out, cont. panel. cf. (TA. Sep.15; 126) £120
- The Baronage of England. L., 1675-76. *1st. Edn.* 3 vols. in 2. Fo. Some slight browning, short tear in title of Vol. 1, reprd., early 19th. C. russ. gt., rubbed. [Wing D 2480] (S. Dec.20; 831) *Samia.* £140
- - Anr. Edn. 1675[-76]. 2 vols. in 1. Fo. Vol 2 lacks prelims., some ll. slightly stained, or browned, sm. wormhole affecting some text, cont. cf., rebkd., rubbed; sig. of Lord Fauconberg 1677, Sir T. Frankland bkplt. [Wing D2480] (BBA. Feb.9; 12) *Wauchope.* £50
- The History of Imbanking & Drayning of Divers Fenns & Marshes. L., 1662. Fo. 11 folding maps, V2 margin torn, cont. cf., part of spine rebkd. [Wing D2481] (CSK. Feb.24; 1) £340
- The History of St. Pauls Cathedral in London. 1658. *1st. Edn.* Fo. Engraved frontis. port., 43 plts., cont. cf., rubbed; Sir Ivar Colquhoun, of Luss copy. [Wing D 2482] (CE. Mar.22; 93) £270
- - Anr. Copy. Fo. 1 plt. reprd., cf., rebkd.; R. & J.M. Paget bkplt. (P. Apr.12; 64) *Cavendish.* £160
- - Anr. Copy. Fo. Lacks 2 ll., later cf., rubbed. (CSK. Jan.13; 221) £50
- - Anr. Edn. L., 1716. Fo. Cf., defect. (DS. Dec.16; 2226) Pts. 20,000
- - Anr. Edn. Continuation:- Henry Ellis. 1818. Fo. Cont. diced cf., covers detchd., spine defect. (TA. Apr.19; 113) £60

DUGDALE, Sir William & Dodsworth, Roger
- Monastici Anglicani. L., 1673. 3 vols. Contents of Vols. 2 & 3 split in 2 sections, Vol. 1 lacks title-pp. & prelims. before preface & pp. 185-192, Vol. 3 lacks pp. 297-8, few ll. detchd., old cf., worn, covers detchd. (CBA. Dec.10; 82) $160
- Monasticon Anglicanum. L., 1693. 4to. 20 copper-engraved plts. (only?), some foxing & staining, ink markings on title-p. & front fly-lf., cont. cf., worn, rebkd. (CBA. Dec.10; 83) $190
-- Anr. Edn. Ill.:- after Hollar. L., 1718. Fo. Late 18th. C. russ. gt. (S. Oct.11; 519) *Clegg.* £130
-- Anr. Copy. Fo. Mod. hf. mor. (P. Jan.12; 65) *Clegg.* £100
-- Anr. Copy. 3 vols. in 1. Fo. Plt. 10 torn, cont. cf., rebkd. & worn. (CE. Sep.1; 36) £50
-- Anr. Edn. Continuation:- John Stevens. L., 1718-23. 3 vols. Fo. 1 plt. stained, 2 slightly torn in margins, some very light spotting, cont. russ., rebkd., spine gt. (S. Oct.11; 434) *Rhys-Jones.* £120
-- Anr. Edn. 1817-30. 6 vols. in 8. Fo. Cont. cf., very worn, all covers detchd., w.a.f. (BBA. Jul.27; 325) *Jeffrey.* £210

DUGUAY-TROUIN, René
- Mémoires de Monsieur Du Guay-Trouin, Lieutenant Général des Armées Navales de France. Ill.:- Larmessin (port.). [Amst], 1740. 4to. Cont. marb. cf., decor. spine. (HD. Sep.22; 237) Frs. 3,550
-- Anr. Copy. 12mo. Cont. spr. roan. (HD. Apr.13; 16) Frs. 2,500

DU HALDE, Jean Baptiste
- Description ... de l'Empire de la Chine. Paris, 1735. 4 vols. Fo. 15 engraved plts., 50 engraved maps, many folding or double-p., slight discoloration to 1 or 2 ll., cont. mott. cf., arms of Marquis Michel-Etienne Turgot on covers, dentelle in each vol. stpd. in gt. 'A. Monsieur Nervet'. (S. Dec.1; 377) *Arkway.* £1,800
- A Description of the Empire of China. L., 1738-41. 2 vols. Fo. 60 engraved maps & plts. only, some light spotting, 8 pp. of 2nd. index in MS., cont. cf., w.a.f. (CSK. Feb.24; 41) £360
-- Anr. Edn. 1741. Vol. II only. Fo. Minor stains, cont. hf. cf., worn. (TA. Oct.20; 51) £90

DUHAMEL DU MONCEAU, Henri Louis
- Abhandlung von dem Ackerbaue. Dresden, 1752. Some light soiling, cont. hf. vell., worn & slightly bumped. (HK. Nov.9; 1740) DM 440
- Art de la Draperie, Principalement pour ce qui Regarde les Draps Fins. [Paris], 1765. From the 'Description des Arts et Metiers' series. Tall fo. Disbnd. (SG. Oct.13; 122) $100
- Art du Serrurier. [Paris], 1767. From the 'Description des Arts et Metiers' series. Tall fo. 42 copperplates, disbnd. (SG. Oct.13; 226) $150
-- Anr. Copy. Tall fo. 42 copperplts., disbnd. (SG. Dec.15; 169) $130
- De l'Exploitation des Bois. Paris, 1764. 4to. Cont. leath. gt., rubbed., both spine extremities slightly defect. (R. Apr.4; 1699) DM 1,200
- Elemens de l'Architecture Navale. Paris, 1752. *1st. Edn.* 4to. Engraved frontis. & vigs., 23 engraved plts., including 22 folding, cont. MS. corrections & margin annots., cont. cf., corners & head of spine worn. (C. Nov.9; 61a) *Lawson.* £200
-- Anr. Copy. 4to. Cont. marb. cf., spine decor.; inscr. 'Cambry, procureur de la Commune de Lorient', dtd. 1792. (HD. Jun.18; 16) Frs. 5,200
-- Anr. Copy. 4to. Port. added, lacks 1 plt., cont. marb. cf., spine decor. (HD. Mar.9; 77) Frs. 3,500
-- Anr. Copy. 4to. Cont. marb. cf., decor. spine. (HD. Sep.22; 238) Frs. 3,000
- La Physique des Arbres. Paris, 1788. *2nd. Edn.* 2 vols. Vol. 1 slightly wormed, cont. leath. gt., slightly rubbed, Vol. 1 spine lightly wormed. (R. Apr.4; 1700) DM 1,200
- A Practical Treatise of Husbandry ... Trans.:- [John Mills]. 1759. *1st. Edn. in Engl.* 4to. Cf., head of spine worn; Dr. G.E. Fussell copy. (P. Jul.5; 57) £120
- Des Semis et Plantations des Arbres et de leur Culture ... Paris, 1760. *1st. Edn.* 4to. Cont. marb. cf., spine decor. (HD. Nov.9; 174) Frs. 1,900
-- Anr. Edn. Paris, 1780. *2nd. Edn.* 4to. Wide margin, cont. leath. gt., cover slightly worn. (R. Apr.4; 1701) DM 600

- Traité de la Fabrique des Manoeuvres pour les Vaisseaux, ou l'Art de la Corderie. Paris, 1747. *Orig. Edn.* 4to. Marb. hf. cf., spine decor. (HD. Mar.9; 76) Frs. 1,700
- Traité des Arbres et Arbustes qui se cultiven en France en Pleine Terre. Paris, 1755. *Orig. Edn.* 2 vols. 4to. Cont. restored cf. (HD. Dec.1; 67) Frs. 1,600
- Traité des Arbres Fruitiers ... Paris, 1768. 2 vols. 4to. 1 plt. torn, lacks corner of 1 plt., cf., spine decor., 2 corners crushed. (SM. Mar.7; 2435) Frs. 12,000
- Traité sur la Nature et sur la Culture de la Vigne ... Ed.:- Bidet. Paris, 1759. *2nd. Edn.* 2 vols. Sm. 8vo. 15 plts. (only?), cont. hf. roan. (HD. Nov.9; 185) Frs. 3,200

DUJARDIN
[-] Histoire Générale des Provinces-Unies. Paris, 1757-70. 8 vols. 4to. Some slight marks, cont. spr. vell., decor. spines ... (SI. Dec.15; 72) Lire 750,000

DU JON, François, the Younger
See— JUNIUS, Franciscus, or DU JON, François, the Younger

DULAC, Edmund (Ill.)
See— ANDERSEN, Hans Christian
See— ARABIAN NIGHTS
See— BRONTE, Emily, Charlotte & Anne 'Ellis, Currer & Acton Bell'
See— FAIRY GARLAND (A) Being Fairy Tales from the Old French
See— HAWTHORNE, Nathaniel
See— MILTON, John
See— OMAR KHAYYAM
See— PERRAULT, Charles
See— POE, Edgar Allan
See— PUSHKIN or POUCHKINE, Aleksandr Sergyeevich
See— QUILLER COUCH, Sir Arthur
See— ROSENTHAL, Leonard
See— SHAKESPEARE, William

DULAURE, Jacques Antoine
- Esquisses Historiques des Principaux Evénements de la Révolution Francaise ... Ill.:- Couché & Horace Vernet. Paris, 1823. 5 vols. Blind-decor. cf. by Dauphin. (HD. May 4; 253) Frs. 2,400
- Histoire Civile, Physique et Morale de Paris. Paris, 1825. *3rd. Edn. (Atlas 4th. Edn.).* 11 vols., including Atlas. 12mo. 85 engrs., cont. hf. cf., spines gt., Atlas hf. cf., spine decor., some worming to jnts. (HD. Mar.19; 93) Frs. 1,500
-- Anr. Edn. Paris, 1825-26. *3rd. Edn.* 10 vols. 12mo. Lavallière hf. cf. by Ponge, spines decor.; from Château des Noës liby. (HD. May 25; 22) Frs. 2,000

DU LAURENS, André
See— LAURENTIUS or DU LAURENS, Andreas

DULLAERT, Jean
See— BRADWARDINE, Thomas & others— DULLAERT, Jean

DULLER, Eduard
- Das Deutsche Volk ... Ill.:- after Doring, Schurig, & Muhlig. Leipzig, 1847. 50 hand-cold. litho. plts., no title or text, crayon scribbles at some inner margins, seriously affecting 5 plts., anr. plt. damaged by paper adhesion, a few plts. with minor dampstain in lr. outer corner, cont. mor. gt., w.a.f. (C. Nov.16; 82) *Gibbs.* £750
- Deutschland und das Deutsche Volk. Ill.:- after L. Richter & others, J. Döring & others. Leipzig, 1845. 2 vols. Some light text browning, cont. hf. leath., spine lightly bumped; Hauswedell coll. (H. May 24; 878) DM 16,000
-- Anr. Copy. 2 vols. Most plts. & text slightly foxed, lacks 1 plt., cont. linen gt., spine slightly defect. (R. Oct.12; 2359) DM 12,500
-- Anr. Copy. Vol. 1 only (of 2). 81 steel engraved plts., some slightly foxed, cont. hf. leath. gt., bumped & rubbed. (HK. Nov.8; 983) DM 4,000
- Die Geschichte des Deutschen Volkes. Ill.:- after L. Richter & J. Kirchhoff. Leipzig, 1840. Cont. hf. leath. gt. (R. Oct.11; 393) DM 480
- Die Malerischen und Romantischen Donauländer. Leipzig, ca. 1840. *1st. Edn.* 60 steel-engraved plts.,

browned & foxed, 2 sigs. loose, cont. hf. leath., bumped. (R. Oct.12; 2495) DM 1,300

DUMARCHAIS, Pierre 'Pierre Mac Orlan'
- Boutiques. Ill.:- L. Boucher. Paris, 1925. *1st. Edn. (496).* Linen, orig. upr. wrap. bnd. in. (H. Nov.24; 1793) DM 400
- Les Demons Gardiens. Ill.:- Chas Laborde. Paris, priv. ptd., 1937. 4to. Red mor. gt., silk end-papers, wrap. preserved, s.-c. (HD. Nov.17; 146) Frs. 2,100
- Eloge de Gus Bofa. Ill.:- G. Bofa. 1949. 4to. Leaves. (HD. Dec.9; 7x) Frs. 1,900
- Filles et Ports d'Europe. Ill.:- Gus Bofa. 1946. Sm. 4to. Sewed, s.-c.; Daragnès copy, notes sigd. by author & artist. (HD. Dec.9; 7t) Frs. 1,000
- Images Secrètes de Paris. Ill.:- G. Assire. Paris, ca. 1930. Ob. 4to. Mor., blind decor., decor. spine, unc., wrap., by R. Kièffer. (HD. Apr.11; 38) Frs. 1,200
- L'inflation Sentimentale. Ill.:- Chas. Laborde. 1923. 4to. Sewed (HD. Dec.9; 35d) Frs. 1,300
- Les Jeux du Demi-jour. Ill.:- Marcel Vertès. Paris, 1926. *Orig. Edn. 1st. Printing of lithos.* Fo. Lavallière hf. mor., corners, wraps. preserved. (HD. Nov.17; 147) Frs. 1,400
- Malice. Ill.:- Chas. Laborde. 1924. Sq. 8vo. Separate suite in ll. of 12 orig. preparatory ills., 11 proof etchings & 15 on vergé, hf. mor., corners. (HD. Dec.9; 35f) Frs. 1,750
- Maurice de Vlaminck. Paris, 1958. 4to. Orig. lithos., orig. pict. wraps. (GB. Nov.5; 3100) DM 500
- Père Barbançon. Ill.:- Gus Bofa. 1948. 4to. Leaves, wrap. & s.-c.; Daragnès copy, note from author, separate suite of 40 ills. & orig. ill. sigd. by Bofa. (HD. Dec.9; 7w) Frs. 2,600
- Port d'Eaux-Mortes. Ill.:- G. Grosz. Paris, 1926. *E. Edn. Ltd. Iss.* 8 orig. lithos., orig. wraps. (GB. May 5; 2631) DM 650
- Prochainement Ouverture ... de 62 Boutiques Litteraires. Ill.:- Henri Guilac. Paris, [1925]. *(1125) on Velin Lafuma.* Slight margin darkening, offset to end-papers, decor. bds., darkening to spine & edges. (CBA. Aug.21; 458) $150
- Rues et Visages de Londres. Ill.:- Ch. Laborde. Paris, 1928. *(100) numbered on velin de Rives.* Fo. Lge. etchings in col. & uncold. state, orig. hf. vell. portfo., slightly defect. (HK. Nov.11; 3473) DM 700
-- Anr. Edn. Ill.:- Charles Laborde. Paris, 1928. *(121) numbered with extra suite of uncold. plts.* Fo. 21 hand-cold. etched plts., all sigd. by artist, loose as iss. in orig. parch-bkd. bd. portfo., slightly rubbed; with orig. drawing for 'Green Park' plt. & 2 A.L.s. from artist to recipient of vol. (BBA. Jun.14; 221) *Makiya.* £1,300
- Tombeau de Pascin. Ill.:- Jules Pascin. N.p., [1944]. *(150) numbered.* 4to. Ptd. wraps., spine chipped; inscr. by author. (SG. Jan.12; 289) $450
-- Anr. Copy. 4to. 8 orig. ills. & sigd. orig. pen ill., Atelier stp. of Pascin, orig. hf. leath., partly unc., orig. wraps. bnd. in; this copy monogrammed by printer & designated 'Exemplaire imprimé pour Willy Michel', MS. dedication from author to Michel, with his ex-libris (engraved by P. Valéry), newspaper cuttings mntd. on end-paper. (GB. Nov.5; 2880) DM 4,400
- Vlaminck. Trans.:- J.B. Sidgwick. N.Y., [1958]. Lge. 4to. 4 orig. uncold. lithos. & an orig. double-p. col. litho. (sigd. on verso) laid in loose, frontis. & hf.-title detchd., title nearly so, col.-pict. wraps. over limp bds., light soiling & wear to covers. (CBA. Jan.29; 479) $160

DUMARESQ, Armand
- Uniformes de la Garde Impériale en 1857. Ill.:- Rousselot. Paris, 1858. *Not for sale.* Fo. 55 cold. lithos., including some heightened, leaves, hf. chagrin portfo., corners. (HD. Jan.27; 258) Frs. 9,000

DUMAS, Alexandre, Père
- Celebrated Crimes. Trans.:- I.G. Burnham. 1895. 8 vols. Some foxing, hf. mor. by Brentano's, spines faded. (BS. Nov.16; 69) £120
-- Anr. Copy. 8 vols. Crimson three-qtr. mor., spines gt. (SG. Feb.16; 101) $300
-- Anr. Copy. 8 vols. Three-qtr. mor., spines gt. (SG. Feb.16; 54) $200

- Le Comte de Monte-Cristo. Ill.:– Tony Johannot & Gavarni. Paris, 1846. 2 vols. Lge. 8vo. Lacks note to binder in Vol. II, minimal foxing, cont. hf. cf., spines decor. (HD. May 4; 254)
Frs. 1,600
- Grand Dictionnaire de Cuisine. Ill.:– Rajon (ports.). Paris, 1873. Some inner margins & ports. crudely reprd., some foxing, bnd. (B. Oct.4; 291)
Fls. 480
- La Maison de Savoie. Torino, 1852-57. 4 vols. 4to. Port. & many lithograph plts. in 3 cols., some stains, cont. hf. mor. (SI. Dec.15; 104)
Lire 440,000
- La Reine Margot. Ill.:– E. Lampsonius & Lancelot. Paris, 1853. 2 pts. in 1 vol. Lge. 8vo. Cont. hf. chagrin gt., spines decor. (HD. May 4; 255)
Frs. 1,900
- Les Trois Mousquetaires. Paris, 1894. 2 vols. 4to. Cont. hf. mor., spines slightly faded. (BBA. Jul.27; 87)   Cavendish Rare Books. £55
– – Anr. Copy. 2 vols. 1st. Printing. Cont. hf. red chagrin, corners, decor. spines, unc., wrap. (HD. Mar.14; 116)
Frs. 1,000
- Works. L., 1894-98. 60 vols. Plts., red hf. mor., slight variation in colour, spines gt. (S. Apr.9; 251)
Primrose. £300
- Writings. N.Y., ca. 1900. 10 vols. Lge. 8vo. Hf. cf., spines gt. (SG. Feb.16; 103) $150

DUMAS, Alexandre, Fils
- Camille. Trans.:– Edmund Gosse. Ill.:– Marie Laurencin. N.Y., Ltd. Edns. Cl., 1937. (1500) numbered & sigd. by artist. 4to. Gt.-decor. buckram, soiled. (SG. Jan.12; 191) $225
– – Anr. Copy. 4to. Cl., spine darkened, s.-c. slightly worn. (SG. Jan.12; 229) $150
– – Anr. Copy. 4to. 12 watercolour paintings, buckram gt., orig. s.-c. (SG. May 17; 187) $100
- La Dame aux Camélias. Preface:– Jules Janin. Ill.:– A. Lynch. Paris, [1886]. (100) numbered on japan. 4to. Etchings & heliogravures in 2 states, orig. etching on hf.-title, mor., lge. mosaic decor., inner dentelle, sigd. by Ch. Meunier, unc., wrap preserved. (HD. Feb.17, 65)   Frs. 5,000

DUMAS, F.G.
- Modern Artists, a Series of Illustrated Biographies. L., [1882-84]. Fo. Some engraved plts. on India-paper, hf. mor., worn, upr. cover detchd. (S. Oct.4; 147)   Vitale. £60

DU MAURIER, George
- Trilby. N.Y., 1895. (600) numbered. Lge. 8vo. Red crushed mor. gt., elab. gt.-decor., rounded spine in 6 compartments, gt.-decor., vell. linings, sigd. 'Doves Bindery 18 C-S 96'; A.L.s from author laid in, as a bdg., w.a.f. (CNY. Dec.17; 552)
$2,400

DUMEZ & Chanlaire, Pierre Gregoire
[–] Atlas National Portatif de la France. Paris, 1792. Ob. 4to. Cont. style leath., decor. (H. Nov.23; 305)
DM 2,200

DUMONT, Georges Marie
- Mémoires Historiques sur la Louisiane. Paris, 1753. 1st. Edn. 2 vols. 12mo. Hf.-titles, cont. spr. cf., spines gt., slightly rubbed. (BBA. Sep.29; 42)   Fletcher. £510

DUMONT, Henrietta
- The Language of Flowers. The Floral Offering: A Token of Affection & Esteem. Phila., 1856. Lge. 12mo. 6 hand-cold. litho. plts., tissue guards, orig. gt.-floral cl., cover corners frayed, long cont. inscr. dtd. 1856 on front free end-paper; from liby. of F.D. Roosevelt, inscr. by him (as Governor). (SG. Mar.15; 17) $150

DUMONT, Jean, Baron de Carlscroon
- A New Voyage to the Levant. L., 1696. 1st. Engl. Edn. Engraved frontis., 2 (of 8) engraved plts., some spotting, cont. cf., worn. [Wing D 2526] (S. Jun.25; 14)   O'Neill. £50

DUMONT, Jean & Huchtenburg, Jean
- Batailles Gagnées par le ... Prince Fr. Eugène de Savoye, sur les Ennemis de la Foi ... La Haye, 1725. Fo. 7 (of 15) plts. or maps, cont. cf., spine decor. (HD. Nov.29; 54)   Frs. 1,250

DUMONT D'URVILLE, Jules Sébastien César
- Malerische Reise um die Welt. Trans.:– A. Diezmann. Leipzig, 1835-37. 1st German Edn. 2 vols. in 1. 4to. 4 engraved maps (1 folding), 138 engraved plts., cont. hf. leath., worn. [Sabin 30942] (R. Oct.13; 3067)   DM 820
- Voyage de la Corvette l'Astrolabe Executé par Ordre du Roi Pendant les Années 1826-29. Paris, 1830-35. 13 vols. text in 26, & 5 atlases in 7. 8vo., 4to., & fo. Compl. set, Histoire du Voyage: without final (blank?) lf. in Vol. IV, pt. 1, Atlas with many lithos. hand-cold., plts. as numbered on list in Vol. I (including 4 bis plts.), plus 2 extra, being additional states of nos. 176 & 189, foremargins of 2 plts. shaved with loss of numeral, 2 sm. margin tears, some minor dampstaining, 1 vol. rebkd.; Botanique: liby. stps. on titles, Atlas with sm. stain in a few margins; Zoologie: Atlas with most plts. hand-cold., a few ll. slightly discold., text with 2 vols. rebkd.; Faune Entomologique de l'Océan Pacifique ... : the 12 fo. plts. to this pt. bnd. in Zoologie Atlas; Observations Nautiques, Meteréologiques, Hydrographiques, et de Physique: 1 text vol. rebkd. & lr. cover replaced; Philologie: lacks 1 blank? prelim., advt. lf. detchd; text in orig. ptd. bds. & wraps., unc., most vols. with orig. paper labels, atlases mntd. on guards, bnd. in cont. cf.-bkd. bds., Atlas Hydrographique rebkd. & recorrered, all but 1st. text vol. in mod. s.-c.'s. (C. Jun.27; 111)
Maggs. £12,000
- Voyage Pittoresque Autour du Monde ... Paris, 1834-35. 2 vols. 4to. Some foxing or soiling, early hf. roan, some defects, mainly to edges of papered bds. (KH. May 1; 229)   Aus. $400
- Voyage au Pole Sud et dans l'Océanie ... Histoire du Voyage ... Paris, 1841-46. 10 vols. Vol. 10 with lge. folding map of New Guinea & Torres Strait not called for, Vol. 5 misbnd. but compl., some foxing, orig. ptd. bds., a few minor defects., unc. & mostly unopened, Vol. 10 trimmed & in later bds. (KH. Nov.9; 587)   Aus. $480
– – Anr. Edn. Paris, 1852. Botanical atlas only. Fo. Title-p., hf.-title, contents lf., 66 plts., 1st. 5 supplied from a slightly smaller copy (3 torn across & reprd.), about hf. the plts. with some foxing, 1 with a pale stain, & about 7 with paper browned, old binder's cl. & qtr. roan, a little worn. (KH. Nov.9; 588)   Aus. $750
- Voyage au Pôle Sud et dans l'Océanie, sur les Corvettes, l'Astrolabe et la Zélée, Exécuté par Ordre du Roi pendant les Années 1837-1840: Atlas Pittoresque; Zoologie; Botanique. 1841 & later. Atlas: 207 plts., including 9 double-p. maps, most on 'chine appliqué'; Zoologie: 130 (of 140?) cold. engraved plts., including 36 illuminated bird plts.; some light dampstains, some ll. browned, cont. hf. mor., spines blind & gt. decor. (HD. Mar.9; 78)   Frs. 78,000

DU MOULIN, Cl.
- Tractatus Commerciorum. Köln, 1577. Cont. blind-tooled pig, blind-tooled centre-piece with oval port., arms on lr. cover, by Hans Wagner, Lauringen, lacks ties. (D. Nov.23; 132)   DM 2,400

DU MOULIN, G.
- Les Conquestes et les Trophées des Norman-François, aux Royaumes de Naples & de Sicile, aux Duchez de Calabre, d'Antioche de Galilée, & autres Principautez d'Italie & d'Orient. Roüen, 1658. Sm. fo. Old vell., worn.; from Châtean des Noës liby. (HD. May 25; 23)   Frs. 1,450

DUN, Maj. T.I.
- From Cairo to Siwa. Cairo, 1933. (175) bnd. thus. Fo. Orig. vell.-bkd. bds., cover designs impressed on gold tissue, scarab book mark, rubbed. (CSK. Mar.9; 124)   £65

DUNCAN, Archibald
- The British Trident, or Register of Naval Actions. 1804-06. 6 vols. 61 plts., cont. mott. cf. gt. (P. Dec.8; 320)   Burr. £150
– – Anr. Copy. 5 vols. 12mo. 1 folding plt. slightly torn, cont. cf., 1 vol. with head of spine damaged. (SKC. Jan.13; 2357)   £50

DUNCAN, James
- Entomology. 1840-41. From 'The Naturalist's Library': 7 vols. Sm. 8vo. Plts. hand-cold., lacks 1

plt., a few ll. detchd., later cl. gt., spines rubbed. (TA. May 17; 266)   £60
- The Natural History of British Butterflies. Edinb., 1840. From 'The Naturalist's Library'. Sm. 8vo. Port., 35 plts., including 33 hand-cold., hf. mor. (SKC. Oct.26; 360)   £50

DUNCAN, Raymond
- Poèmes de Parole Torrentielle. Paris, [1927]. 1st. Edn. (500). 2 line MS. dedication, black mor., red mor. inlays, art-deco., in Pierre le Grain style, silk doubls., gold marb. paper end-papers, orig. wraps. bnd. in, s.-c. (D. Nov.23; 160)   DM 1,200

DUNCAN, Robert
- Derivations. L., [1968]. (12) numbered out-of-series, sigd. Lge. 8vo. Cl., d.-w. (SG. Mar.1; 93)
$325
- Heavenly City, Earthly City. Berkeley, 1947. 1st. Trade Edn. Orig. pict. bds., d.-w.; sigd. handwritten limitation notice by publisher, Frederic Dannay copy. (CNY. Dec.16; 117) $350

DUNCKER, Alex
- Die Ländlichen Wohnsitze, Schlösser und Residenzen der Ritterschaftl Gutsbesitzer un der Preussischen Monarchie. Berlin, 1871-73. Ob. fo. Without index, lacks some text ll., some misbnd., 1 plt. & 1 text lf. very soiled, orig. linen, gold-tooled, spine renewed. (R. Oct.12; 2360)
DM 4,300

DUNDONALD, Archibald Cochrane, Earl of
- The Present State of the Manufacture of Salt Explained. 1785. Disbnd.; pres. copy. (P. Jun.7; 323)   £120
- A Treatise Shewing the Intimate Connection That Subsists between Agriculture & Chemistry. L., 1795. 1st. Edn. 4to. Hf.-title, foxed, mod. hf. cf. (SG. Oct.6; 138) $175

DUNLOP, John
- Mooltan, During & After the Siege. 1849. 4to. Some light spotting, litho. map trimmed & mntd. on verso of additional title, cont. cl., worn. (CSK. Jul.6; 47)   £130

DUNN, John
- History of the Oregon Territory & British North-American Fur Trade. L., 1844. 1st. Edn. Lge. folding map cut to border on hf. of inner margin, hf. mor. by Sangorski & Sutcliffe; the Rt. Hon. Visc. Eccles copy. [Sabin 21321] (CNY. Nov.18; 95) $130

DUNN, Samuel
- A New Atlas ... of Geography. 1788. Fo. 6 plts. & tables, 41 partly col. maps, 3 defect., hf. cf., cover detchd. (P. Jul.5; 387)   £220

DUNNHAUPT, G.
- Bibliographisches Handbuch der Barockliteratur. Stuttgart, 1980-81. 3 vols. 4to. Orig. linen; Hauswedell coll. (H. May 23; 376)   DM 820

DUNOYER, Ch. B.
- L'Industrie et la Morale Considerées dans leurs Rapports avec la Liberté. Paris, 1825. 1st. Edn. Sm. old stp. on title & end lf., cont. hf. leath gt., lightly rubbed. (R. Oct.11; 1311)   DM 600

DUNOYER DE SEGONZAC, André
- André Derain. Paris & Cologne, 1961. (360) on vell. d'Arches. Fo. Leaves, bds. (HD. Dec.16; 113)
Frs. 1,000

DUNRAVEN, Edwin Quin, Third Earl of
- Notes on Irish Architecture. Ed:– Margaret Stokes. L., 1875-77. 1st. Edn. 2 vols. Fo. 125 photos. on mounts, 161 text engrs., ex-liby., elab. gt.- decor. cl. (SG. May 3; 150) $1,200

DUNS SCOTUS, Johannes
- Quaestiones in Aristotelis Metaphysicam. Venice, B. Locatellus for O. Scotus, 20 Nov. 1497. Some margin dampstains. [BMC V, 448; Goff D-372] (Bound with:) - Commentaria ... in XII. Li. Metaphysice Aristo. Emendata ... Venice, B. Locatellus for heirs of O. Scoti, 1501. Together 2 works in 1 vol. Fo. Old vell.; the Walter Goldwater copy. (SG. Dec.1; 129) $850
- Quaestiones in Primum Librum Sententiarum. Venice, Vindelinus de Spira, 5 Nov. 1472. Fo. 1st.

DUNS SCOTUS, Johannes -Contd.

2 ll. bnd. at end, the work therefore opening at the 1st. text p. which is illuminated in cols. & silver, initials rubricated, & paragraph marks in red & blue, lacks final blank, dampstains thro.-out, causing erosion to outer & lr. margins, mostly confined to blank portions, later bds.; the Walter Goldwater copy. [BMC V, 159; Goff D-374] (SG. Dec.1; 130) $1,300

- **Quaestiones in Quattuor Libros Sententiarum.** Nuremb, Anton Koberger, 1481. (*Bound with:*) - **Quodlibeta.** Nuremb., Anton Koberger, 1481. Together 2 works in 1 vol. Lge. fo. Rubricated in red & blue, lacks last 3 ll. of 2nd. work, cont. stpd. roan over wood bds., defect., partly renewed, traces of clasps; from Fondation Furstenberg-Beaumesnil. [HC 6417 & 6435, BMC II, 419, Goff D380] (HD. Nov.16; 35) Frs. 13,500

- **Quaestiones Selecta.** [Venice], Vindelinus de Spira, ca. 1476/77. 4to. Lge. copy, last lf. in facs., some stains, etc., mod. red mor.; the Walter Goldwater copy. [BMC V, 248-9; Goff D-384] (SG. Dec.1; 131) $375

- **Quodlibeta.** Ed:- Tho. Penketh. Venice, J. de Colonia & J. Manthen, 7 Oct. 1477. Fo. Lge. margins, fully rubricated, some early margin notes, mod. three-qtr. lev.; the Walter Goldwater copy. [BMC V, 228; Goff D-393] (SG. Dec.1; 132) $3,200

- **Scriptum in Primum Librum Sententiarum.** Commentaries:- Pierre Lombard. Venice, Johannes de Colonia & Johannes Manthen, 26 Jul. 1477. (*Bound with:*) - **Quodlibeta.** Ed:- Tho. Penketh. Venice, Johannes de Colonia & Johannes Manthen, 7 Oct. 1477. Together 2 works in 1 vol. Fo. 1st. work has commentaries on 1st. pt. only (of 4), rubricated, cont. stpd. cf. over wood bds., richly decor.; from Fondation Furstenberg-Beaumesnil. [BMC V, 228; Goff D379 & D393] (HD. Nov.16; 63) Frs. 9,600

DUNSANY, Lord Edward J.M.D. Plunkett

- **The Chronicles of Rodriguez.** Ill.:- S.H. Hime (photogravure frontis.). N.Y., [1922]. *(500) numbered & sigd. by artist.* 4to. Vell.-bkd. bds. (LH. Sep.25; 528) $100

- **The King of Elfland's Daughter.** L., 1924. *(250) numbered & sigd. by author.* 4to. Vell.-bkd. bds., d.-w. (LH. Sep.25; 529) $160

- **Time & the Gods.** Ill.:- S.H. Hime. L., 1922. *(250) numbered & sigd. by author.* 4to. Vell.-bkd. bds., d.-w.; ills. sigd. by artist. (LH. Sep.25; 530) $150

DUNTHORNE, Gordon

Flower & Fruit Prints of the 18th & Early 19th Centuries. Wash., priv. ptd., 1938. *(2500). (1750).* 4to. Orig. buckram gt., s.-c. (P. Sep.8; 208) *Reid.* £170

- - **Anr. Copy.** 4to. Orig. cl., s.-c. (BBA. Sep.8; 50) *Mitchell.* £140

- - **Anr. Copy.** 4to. Buckram, spine dark, s.-c. (SG. Mar.22; 106) $225

- - **Anr. Copy.** Sm. fo. 72 plts., cl., spine darkened. (SG. Aug.25; 127) $190

- - **Anr. Edn.** Wash., priv. ptd., 1938. *(750) with added folding col. plt. listing subscribers.* Glazed buckram, s.-c. (SG. Mar.22; 105) $275

- - **Anr. Copy.** Fo. Plts., mostly cold., glazed buckram, buckram s.-c. (SG. May 17; 81) $225

- - **Anr. Copy.** Fo. Plts., mostly cold., liby. stp. on title, glazed buckram, buckram s.-c. (SG. May 17; 80) $175

DUNTON, John

[-] **The Phenix: or, a Revival of Scarce & Valuable Pieces.** L., 1707-08. 2 vols. Some margin pen markings, a little browned, cont. cf., rebkd., 1 cover loose. (BBA. Dec.15; 159) *Price.* £50

- **Religio Bibliopolae: In Imitation of Dr. Browns Religio Medici.** Ed:- Benjamin Bridgwater. L., 1691. *1st. Edn.* Sm. 8vo. Lev., triple gt. fillet borders, gt. dentelles, by Ramage: bkplt. of Luther Brewer, Cedar Rapids. (SG. May 17; 83) $350

DU PAN, J. Mallet

- **The British Mercury; or Historical & Critical Views of the Events of the Present Time.** 1798-1800. Vols. 1-5 (all publd.). Cont. cf.; Sir Ivar Colquhoun, of Luss copy. (CE. Mar.22; 95) £340

DUPATY, Ch.-M.J.B.

[-] **Briefe Über Italien vom jahr 1785.** Trans.:- G. Forster. Mainz, 1789-90. *1st. German Edn.* 2 vols. in 1. Erased stp. on Vol. 1 title, later bds. (R. Oct.13; 3141) DM 580

DU PERIER

[-] **A Complete Collection of Voyages made into North & South America ... by Monsr. l'Abbé Bellegarde ...** L., 1711. Old panel. cf., wormhole in upr. cover. [Sabin 4508] (C. Nov.16; 11) *Traylen.* £60

DUPIN, Amadine Aurore Lucie, Baronne Dudevant 'George Sand'

- **Histoire de ma Vie.** Paris, 1854-55. *Orig. Edn.* 2 vols. Some tears, lacks 3 hf.-titles & 1 title, hf. chagrin by Honnelaître, wrap. (HD. Mar.19; 141) Frs. 6,100

- **La Mare au Diable.** Ill.:- E. Rudeaux. 1889. Ills. in 2nd. state, decor. mor. by David. wrap. & spine preserved. s.-c. (HD. Jun.29; 184) Frs. 1,200

- **The Masterpieces of George Sand.** Trans.:- G. Burnham Ives. Phila., ca. 1900. *(1000) on japon vell.* 20 vols. Plts. in 2 states, elab. purple mor. gt.; A.N.s. tipped in Vol.1. (SPB. Dec.13; 561) $850

- **Mauprat.** Ill.:- Le Blant, engraved by H. Toussaint. Paris, 1886. *(100) on japan.* Lge. 8vo. Red bradel hf. mor., corners, by Carayon, wrap. & spine preserved; extra-ill. with watercol. by E. Van Muyden on frontis. (HD. May 4; 425) Frs. 1,400

- **Romans Choisis.** Ill.:- after Tony Johannot & Maurice Sand. 1852. 3 vols. Lge. 8vo. Port. of author added, cont. hf. chagrin, corners. (HD. Mar.21; 198) Frs. 1,900

DUPLESSI-BERTAUX, Jean

- **Album de la Jeunesse.** Paris, 1823. Ob. 4to. Port. & 25 plts. on chine collé, minimal foxing, cont. str.-grd. red mor., blind-decor., Comte d'Artois arms. (HD. May 4; 257) Frs. 3,600

- **Recueil de Cent Sujets de Divers Genres, Composés et Gravés à l'Eau-forte.** Paris, 1814. Port. & 96 plts., title reprd., 19th. C. Engl. red mor. gt., mor. doubls., spine decor. (HD. May 4; 256) Frs. 1,500

- **Recueil de Différentes Sujets.** Paris, [1807?]. Sm. 4to. 5 suites of 12 etched plts. each preceded by engraved folding view, slight foxing to some plts., hf. cf., limp decor. spine. (HD. Jan.30; 46) Frs. 1,000

- **Recueil des Principaux Costumes Militaires des Armées Alliées.** Paris, 1816. 3 pts. 4to. 36 engrs., heightened with cols., hf. chagrin. (HD. Jan.27; 259) Frs. 4,000

DUPLESSIS, George (Text)
See— SCHONGAUER, Martin

DUPONCHEL

- **Iconographie et Histoire Naturelle des Chenilles.** L. & Madrid, 1849. 2 vols. Foxing, mostly in text, cont. hf. chagrin. (HD. Feb.29; 18) Frs. 2,000
See— GODARD & Duponchel

DUPONT, Pierre

- **La Légende de Juif Errant ... Avec la Baliade de Béranger Mise en Musique par Ernest Doré.** Preface:- Paul Lacroix. Ill.:- Gustave Doré, engraved by Rouget, Jahyer & Gauchard. Paris, 1862. Fo. Publisher's bds., worn. (HD. Mar.27; 59) Frs. 2,300

DUPORT, James

- **Threnothriambos, sive Liber Job Graeco Carmine Redditus.** Camb., 1637. *1st. Edn.* Greek & Latin text, 17th. C. cf. gt. [STC 7365] (BBA. May 3; 115) *Traylen.* £70

DUPPA, Richard

- **Heads from the Fresco Pictures of Raffaello in the Vatican.** [1802]. Fo. 13 engraved ports., 5 tissue plts., cleanly torn, 1 with loss, cont. hf. mor. (CSK. Oct.7; 27) £55

DU PRAISSAC, Sieur

- **The Art of Warre.** Camb., 1639. *1st. Edn. in Engl.* 2 pts. Slight browning & soiling, title slightly defect. [STC 7366] (*Bound with:*) CAESAR, Caius Julius - **The Complete Captain.** Camb., 1640. 2 pts. Browned, a few tears & sm. holes, slightly affecting text. [STC 4338] Together 2 works in 1 vol. Cont. cf., worn. (S. Oct.11; 521) *Trotman.* £200

DUPRE, Louis

- **Voyage à Athenes et à Constantinople ...** Ill.:- after Dupre. Paris, 1825. Lge. fo. Double-p. passport plt., 38 (of 40) full-p. hand-cold. litho. plts., nos. on 2 plts. erased & incorrectly altered, plt. 18 detchd., plt. 22 with 6 inch tear, some text ll. spotted, text & plts. loose in bdg., old hf. mor., worn. (C. Nov.16; 83) *Athena.* £8,500

DUPUIS, Joseph

- **Journal of a Residence in Ashantee ...** 1824. 4to. Mod. mor. (HD. Jun.29; 63) Frs. 1,700

DURAND, Jean Nicolas Louise

- **Raccolta e Parallelo delle Fabbriche Classiche di tutti i Tempi d'ogni Popolo e di Ciascun Stile.** Venezia, 1833. 3 vols. Fo. Hf. cf. (CR. Jun.6; 154) Lire 420,000

- **Recueil et Parallèle des Edifices de Tout Genre.** Paris, 1801. Ob. fo. Engraved title & table, 90 plts., 1 torn, few little creased, cont. hf. cf. (C. Dec.9; 185) *Weinreb.* £300

- - **Anr. Edn.** Brussels, ca. 1850. Ob. atlas fo. 100 engraved plts., some foxing, marginal stains, ex-liby., cf.-bkd. marb. bds. (SG. May 3; 151) $475

DURAND-BRAGER, Henri

- **A Voyage in the Black Sea, the Bosphorus, the Sea of Marmara & the Dardanelles.** Ill.:- Sabatier, Eug. Ciceri & Pl. Benoist, after Braeger. L., n.d. Fo. Litho. title on mntd. china & 24 litho. views in black on tinted ground, prospectus bnd. at end, cont. hf. chagrin. (HD. Jun.18; 17) Frs. 11,000

DURANG, Mary

- **Love & Pride; being, the Histories of Julia Maydew, or, the Blind Girl, & Annette & Henriette, or Selfishness & Benevolence.** Phila., [1847]. *1st. Edn.* Lge. 16mo. 6 hand-cold. wood-engraved plts., orig. cl., soiled; from liby. of F.D. Roosevelt, inscr. by him. (SG. Mar.15; 18) $140

DURANTE, Castore

- **Herbario Novo ...** Ill.:- L. Norsino after I. Parasole. Venice, 1602. Fo. Some foxing, few stains, some corners reprd., some margin wormholes, cont. vell., upr. cover brkn. (VG. Nov.3; 753) Fls. 1,350

- - **Anr. Copy.** Fo. Stain on frontis., mod. vell. (SI. Dec.15; 154) Lire 1,600,000

DURANTI, Jean Stephane

- **De Ritibus Ecclesiae.** Cologne, 1592. Cont. stpd. cf. over wood bds., ports. & arms, clasps incompl.; from Fondation Furstenberg-Beaumesnil. (HD. Nov.16; 118) Frs. 1,700

- **Rationale Divinorum Officiorum.** Ed:- Johanne Aloiso Tuscano. Vicenza, Hermann Liechtenstein, 1478. Fo. Worming at end, cont. stpd. mor. over wood bds., decor., spine renewed; from Fondation Furstenberg-Beaumesnil. [H. 6480; BMC VII, 1037; Goff D417] (HD. Nov.16; 80) Frs. 9,000

- - **Anr. Edn.** [Strassburg, Georg Husner], ca. 1479. Fo. Wide margins, fully rubricated, initials in red & blue, several with added penwork decor., cont. cf. over wood bds., elab. blind-tooled, covers detchd., lacks 1 clasp; the Walter Goldwater copy. [Goff D-420] (SG. Dec.1; 133) $2,600

- - **Anr. Edn.** Strassburg, [Printer of the 1483 Jordanus de Quedlinburg], 1484. Fo. Illuminated floral border in cols. & gold on fo. 1, 7 initials illuminated in cols. & gold, many other initials in red & blue, lacks final blank, piece clipped from margin of lf. 2, a few ll. frayed, 2 sm. burnholes, disbnd.; the Walter Goldwater copy. [BMC I, 132; Goff D-428] (SG. Dec.1; 134) $1,600

- - **Anr. Edn.** Basle, Nicolas Kesler, 17 Jul. 1488. Fo. Cont. stpd. pig over wood bds.; from Fondation Furstenberg-Beaumesnil. [HC 6495; BMC III, 766; Goff D433] (HD. Nov.16; 11) Frs. 5,000

- - **Anr. Edn.** Strasbourg, [Printer of the 1483 Jordanus de Quedlinburg (Georg Husner)], 1 Sep. 1488. Fo. Lacks final blank, 1 or 2 margin wormholes in 1st. few & last few ll., light browning & spotting, cont. South German blind-stpd. cf. over wood bds., clasps, 5 bosses on each cover, rebkd., some of orig. spine preserved, head & foot of spine worn. [Goff D434] (S. Nov.17; 18) *Maggs.* £540

DURELLI, Gaetano & Francesco
- **La Certosa di Pavia.** Milan, [1823-53]. Fo. 70 engraved plts., including 8 folding, qtr. cl., ptd. bds., defect. (SG. Oct.13; 146) $175

DURENCEAU, André
- **Inspirations.** Woodstock, [1928]. Fo. 24 col. plts., loose as iss., cl.-bkd. decor. bd. folder, spine partially lacking. (SG. Aug.25; 128) $120

DURER, Albrecht
- **The Complete Woodcuts.** Ed.:– Willi Kurth. Intro.:– Campbell Dodgson. L., [1927]. *(500). (250) in buckram.* Tall fo. 346 reproductions, gt.-decor. buckram. (SG. May 3; 148) $140
- **De Symmetria Partium in Rectis Formis Humanorum Corporum.** Nuernberg, 1532. (*Bound with:*) – **De Varietate Figurarum et Flexuris Partium ac Gestib. Imaginum, Libri Duo.** Nuernberg, 1534. Lacks final blank, plts. reprd. at folds. 2 works in 1 vol. Fo. Lge. copy, very foxed, some tears, etc., loose in old vell. (SG. Nov.3; 64) $1,800
- **De Urbibus, Arcibus, Castellisque Condensis, ac Muniendis Rationes Aliquot, Praesenti Bellorum Necessitari Accommodatissime.** Trans.:– Camerarius. Paris, 1535. *1st. Edn.* Fo. 2 folding plts. tape-reprd., with some sm. holes, disbnd. (SG. Nov.3; 65) $1,100
- – **Anr. Copy.** Fo. Title lightly spotted, double ll. bds., unc. (HK. Nov.8; 168a) DM 2,300
- **Della Simmetria de i Corpi Humani Libri Quattro.** Trans.:– G.P. Galluci. Venice, 1591. Fo. A few ll. stained, sm. hole in 1 lf., sm. wormhole in final 21 ll. of text, minor incisions to a few ills., 17th. C. limp bds., rebkd. (C. May 30; 24) *Sims, Reed & Fogg.* £550
- **Hierinn sind begriffen vier Bücher von Menschlicher Proportion.** Arnhem, 1603. Fo. Monog. port., linen. (DS. Feb.24; 2431) Pts. 250,000
- **Die Kleine Passion.** Afterword:– H. Mardersteig. Trans.:– [Kosmos Ziegler]. Ill.:– L. Farina after Dürer. Verona, 1971. *(115) numbered.* 37 orig. woodcuts, hand-bnd. orig. hf. leath., orig. s.-c. (GB. May 5; 3040) DM 850
- **Kupferstiche: In Getreuen Nachbildungen.** Intro.:– Jaro Springer. Munich, 1914. Fo. 102 plts., loose in linen over bds. portfo., slightly soiled, inner lining chipping, ties. (CBA. Jan.29; 165) $110
- **La Passione di N.S. Giesu Christo.** Venice, 1612. *2nd. Edn. 5th. state of woodcuts.* 4to. 35 (of 37) woodcuts, lacks title & deposition, vig. from title cut away, soiled in places, cont. vell. (VS. Jun.7; 953) Fls. 5,100
- **Les Quatre Livres de la Proportion et des Parties & Pourtraicts des Corps Humains.** Trans.:– L. Meigret. Arnhem, 1613. *2nd Fr. Edn.* Fo. Lacks 4 double ll., 1 lf. misbnd., browned thro.-out, upr. margin soiled, 2 ll. with reprd. tears, cont. leath., defect. & loose. (R. Oct.11; 831) DM 600
- – **Anr. Edn.** Trans.:– Loys Meigret. Arnheim, 1614. *3rd. Fr. Edn.* Sm. fo. Outer margin of title lined, foxing, mod. vell. (HD. May 21; 27) Frs. 3,000
- **Quatuor his Suarum Institutionum Geometricarum Libris. Lineas, Superficies & Solida Corpora Tractavit.** Paris, 1535. *2nd. Edn. of this trans. 2nd. Iss.* Fo. Disbnd. (SG. Nov.3; 63) $850
- **Zeichnungen.** Ed.:– Friedrich Lippmann. Berlin, 1883-1929. *(300) numbered.* 7 vols. Atlas fo. 913 reproductions, most full-p., many cold., ex-liby., elab. pict. cl.; 20-p. 'Ubersicht ueber den Inhalt der Baende I-VII' laid in. (SG. May 3; 147) $1,700

DURET, Claude
- **Histoire Admirable des Plantes et Herbes Esmerueillabes et Miraculeuses en Nature ...** Paris, 1605. Wide margin, cont. vell. (HD. Dec.9; 33) Frs. 21,500

DURET, Théodor
- **Histoire des Peintres Impressionistes.** Ill.:– Pissaro (orig. woodcut) & Renoir, Monisot, & Guillaumin (orig. etchings). Paris, 1922. *3rd. Edn.* 4 orig. ills., margin slightly browned, hf. leath., orig. wraps. bnd. in. (GB. Nov.5; 2396) DM 400
- – **Anr. Edn.** Ill.:– L. Pissaro after C. Pissaro (orig. woodcut), Renoir, Berthe Morisot & Guillaumin (orig. etchings). Paris, 1922 [1923 on upr. wrap.].

4 orig. ills., orig. wraps., upr. wrap. loose. (GB. May 5; 2360) DM 450
- **Die Impressionisten.** Ill.:– Cézanne, Guillaumin, Morisot, Pissarro, Renoir & others. Berlin, [1909]. *(1000) numbered.* 4to. Frontis. holed, orig. linen, slightly holed. (HK. Nov.11; 3525) DM 1,500
- – **Anr. Copy.** 4to. Stain thro.-out in lr. margin, some light foxing, etchings foxed or mostly browned in margin, some in ill., title & end-paper with MS. owners mark, orig. leath., jnts. loose., partly pasted with leath. strips. (HK. May 17; 2699) DM 800
- **Renoir.** Paris, 1924. *1st. Edn.* 4to. Three-qtr. mor., ptd. wraps. bnd. in. (SG. Jan.12; 302) $150

D'URFEY, Thomas
- **The Comical History of Don Quixote ...** L., 1694-96. *1st. Edns.* 3 pts. in 1 vol. Sm. 4to. Advt. lf. at end of pt. 3, piece torn from B2 in pt. 3 affecting headline & text, a few other headlines shaved, MS. note on verso of last lf. of pt. 1, mor. by Sangorski. [Wing D 2712-14] (C. Nov.9; 58) *Temperley.* £220
- [-] **Wit & Mirth, or Pills to Purge Melancholy.** 1719-20. 6 vols. 12mo. Cont. cf., rubbed; Diouese of Southwark copy. (C. May 30; 132) *Macnutt.* £220

DURHAM, J.G. Lambton, First Earl of
- **Reports on the Affairs of British North America.** L., 1839. Sm. fo. Lacks Appendix B, hf. cf.; A.L.s. from the 2nd. Earl of Durham & 2 related ports. inserted. [Sabin 38747] (S. Dec.13; 132) *Quaritch.* £200

DURIEUX, Tilla
- **Spielen und Träumen.** Ill.:– Emil Orlik. [Berlin], 1922. *(25) sigd. by author & artist on printers mark.* 4to. Orig. silk. (H. Nov.24; 1916) DM 2,000

DU ROSOI, B.F.
- [-] **Les Sens. Poèmes en Six Chants.** Ill.:– after Eisen & Wille. L. [Paris], 1766. *1st. Edn.* Wide margin, minimal spotting, cont. red mor. gt., mod. hf. mor. cover & s.-c.; Hausswedell coll. (H. May 24; 1272) DM 1,500

DURRE, Dr. E.F.
- **Die Anlage und der Betrieb der Eisenhütten.** Leipzig, 1882-84. 3 text & 3 atlas vols. Hf. mor. gt. (P. Dec.8; 79) *Hildebrandt.* £50

DURRIE, Daniel S.
- **A History of Madison, the Capital of Wisconsin.** Ill.:– N.P. Jones (photos). Madison, 1874. 19 mntd. albumen photos (NYPL 285 calls for 10 only), cl., rubbed, bkplt. (SG. May 10; 42) $225

DURY, Andrew
- **A New, General & Universal Atlas.** L., 1761. *1st. Edn.* Sm. ob. 4to. Engraved title, dedication lf. & plt. list, 39 engraved maps (6 folding), hand-cold. in outl., cont. mott. cf., worn, spine & hinges crudely reprd. (SG. Dec.15; 5) $275
See– ANDREWS, John & Dury, Andrew

DUSSAULX, J.
- **De la Passion du Jeu ...** Paris, 1779. Cont. cf., spine decor. (HD. Feb.28; 32) Frs. 1,700

DUTCHESS COUNTY HISTORICAL SOCIETY
- **Records of the Town of Hyde Park, Dutchess County.** Ed.:– Franklin D. Roosevelt. Hyde Park, 1928. *Ltd. 1st. Edn.* Lge. 4to. Gt.-lettered cl.; from liby. of F.D. Roosevelt, inscr. 'For my son Franklin Delano Roosevelt Jr., This copy, No. 6, of an Edition of one hundred, Franklin Delano Roosevelt, Hyde Park, 1928'. (SG. Mar.15; 55) $1,500

DUTENS, Louis
- **Explication de quelques Médailles Grècques & Phéniciennes, avec une Paléographie Numismatique.** 1776. *2nd. Edn.* 4to. 9 folding engraved plts. (spotted), stp. on title, orig. bds., unc., worn. (S. May 1; 511) *Spink.* £90

DUTOT
- **Reflexions Politiques sur les Finances et le Commerce.** La Haye, 1738. *Orig. Edn.* 2 vols. 12mo. Cf., corners worn. (HD. Feb.22; 61) Frs. 3,300

DUTTON, Francis
- **South Australia & its Mines ...** 1846. *1st. Edn.* Map in end pocket, advt. slip (not called for by Ferguson), some foxing, bdg. not stated, unc.; inscr. to Capt. Fitzroy (of the Beagle?). (KH. May 1; 230) Aus. $450

DUTTON, Hely
- **A Statistical & Agricultural Survey of the County of Galway.** Dublin, 1824. *1st. Edn.* Orig. bds., unc. (GM. Dec.7; 420) £150
See– McPARLAN, James—FITZGERALD, George Robert—DUTTON, Hely

DUTUIT, Eugène & Auguste
- **La Collection Dutuit. Livres et Manuscrits.** Paris, 1899. *(350) numbered.* Fo. Orig. bds.; bkplt. & acquisition note of J.R. Abbey, H.M. Nixon coll., with front fly-lf. inscr. 'Howard M. Nixon dd. Henry Davis'. (BBA. Oct.6; 177) *Lyon.* £280

DUVAL, Amaury
- **Les Fontaines de Paris Anciennes et Nouvelles.** Ill.:– Moisy. Paris, [1812]. Fo. Engraved additional title, 60 plts., 2 plts. discold., faint dampstaines on anr., cont. russ., gt. key-pattern panel. & border in blind., rebkd. (C. Dec.9; 44) *Weinreb.* £160

DU VAL, Michael
- **Rosa Hispani-Anglica seu Malum Punicum Angl'Hispanicum.** [1623]. *1st. Edn.* 4to. Lr. margin shaved, later red mor. gt., slightly rubbed. [STC 7376] (BBA. Jun.14; 26) *Stuart Bennett.* £180

DU VAL, P.
- **La Carte Générale et les Cartes Pariculiéres des Costes de la Mer Mediterranée avec leurs Discours Necessaires.** Paris, 1665. Sm. ob. fo. Ptd. title, 12 full-p. engraved regional coastal charts, 1 chart torn & reprd. without loss of engraved surface, some faint browning, cont. cf., w.a.f. (S. May 21; 139) *Crete.* £360
- **La Géographie Universelle contenant les Descriptions, les Cartes, et le Blason des Principaux Pai Vis du Monde.** Paris, 1682. Double-p. engraved title (dtd. 1682), 51 (of 82?) double-p. engraved maps (without the maps of Europe), full-p. engraved dedication lf. (dtd. 1688) & 11 plts. of arms, mod. cf., w.a.f. (S. May 21; 112) *Franks.* £600

DUVERGER, J.
- **Nationaal Biografisch Woordenboek.** Brussel, 1964-81. 9 vols. Lge. 8vo. Cl. (VS. Dec.7; 256) Fls. 525

DUVEYRIER, M.
See– BOUET-VILLAUMEZ, Comte E.—FLEURIOT DE LANGLE, A.—DUVEYRIER, M.

DUVOTENAY, Ch.
- **Atlas Géographique, Historique, Statistique et Itinéraire de la Suisse.** Paris, 1837. *1st. Edn.* Lge. fo. 1 double-p. outl. cold. coll. map, 20 steel engraved maps (4 double-p.), 22 steel engrs., some foxing, last 2 text ll. slightly defect. & loose, cont. hf. leath., very bumped, spine defect. (R. Apr.5; 3074) DM 1,900

DWIGGINS, William Addison
- **Towards a Reform of the Paper Currency.** N.Y., Ltd. Edns. Cl., 1932. *(452) numbered, sigd.* Tall 8vo. Qtr. cf., patterned bds., orig. s.-c. (SG. May 17; 188) $100

DWIGHT, Timothy
- **Greenfield Hill.** N.Y., 1794. Sm. 4to. Some browning, margin repairs, mod. hf. leath., 3 bkplts. [Sabin 21554] (SPB. Dec.13; 442) $125
- **Travels in New England & New York.** L., 1823. *1st. Engl. Edn.* 4 vols. Offsetting from maps, cont. cf. gt., gt. spines; the Rt. Hon. Visc. Eccles copy. [Sabin 21556] (CNY. Nov.18; 97) $320
- – **Anr. Copy.** 4 vols. Port., 3 folding cold. maps, early marb. bds., cf. spines & tips, spines worn. (SG. Apr.5; 67) $110

DWINGLO, B.
See– UYTENBOGAERT, J. & Dwinglo, B.

DYKES, William Rickatson & E. Katherine
- **Notes on Tulip Species.** L., 1930. Fo. Unc., orig. cl., d.-w. (C. Nov.16; 239) *Marks.* £50

EACHARD, John
[–] **Some Opinions of Mr. Hobbs Considered in a Second Dialogue Between Philautus & Timothy.** 1673. *1st. Edn.* Cont. mott. cf., spine gt., little rubbed. [Wing E64] (BBA. Jun.28; 35)
Pickering & Chatto. £110

EACHARD, Laurence
See— ECHARD or EACHARD, Laurence

EAGLE
L., Apr. 1950-Jan. 1960. Vol. 1 no. 1-Vol. 11 no. 4 (lacks 5 nos.), & 3 dupls. 1 dupl. no. defect., 2 nos. torn, a few slightly frayed, orig. wraps. (S. Dec.20; 611)
Male. £350
– – **Anr. Edn.** L., May 1950-Dec. 1968. Vol. 1 no. 6-Vol. 19 no. 52 (625 iss. only, including 3 dupls.), & 2 Annuals 1968-70. 2 iss. defect., orig. wraps., frayed, some soiled, a few creased, 1 annual rather worn. (S. Nov.22; 379)
Avon. £140

EANDI, Giovanni
– **Statistica della Provincia de Saluzzo.** Saluzzo, 1833-35. 2 vols. 4to. Hf.-title, lightly stained, cont. hf. leath., loose. (SI. Dec.15; 105)   Lire 850,000

EAREE, Rev. R.B.
– **Album Weeds; Or, How to Detect Forged Stamps.** 1905. *3rd. Edn.* 2 vols. Publishers advts. to rear of each vol., orig. decor. cl., a little rubbed. (TA. Jun.21; 506)   £52

EARL, George Windsor
– **The Eastern Seas, or Voyages ... in the Indian Archipelago.** 1837. Title & folding map lightly spotted, cont. cl. (CSK. Oct.7; 81)   £200
– **Enterprise in Tropical Australia.** L., 1846. Cf. gt., spine rubbed, mor. labels torn; Lord Derby bkplt. (CA. Apr.3; 39)   Aus. $280

EARL, M. & Croxtonsmith, A.
– **The Power of the Dog.** L., n.d. 4to. 20 cold. plts., hf. vell. gt. (P. May 17; 41)   *Talbot.* £75

EARLE, Augustus
– **A Narrative of a Nine Months' Residence in New Zealand in 1827.** L., 1832. 4 ll. advts., some staining, orig. bds., defect. (P. Feb.16; 253)   £65

EARLE, Maj. Cyril
– **The Earle Collection of Early Staffordshire Pottery.** L., 1915. *1st. Edn.* Sm. fo. Gt.-embossed cl., spine chipped. (SG. Jan.26; 83) $130
– – **Anr. Edn.** N.d. *(250) numbered.* 4to. Orig. cl. gt., partly unc., a little worn on spine & corners, loosening. (LC. Mar.1; 7)   £90

EARLY ENGLISH DRAMATISTS
Ed.:– John S. Farmer. L., 1905-08. *(60).* 13 vols. Bdg. not stated. (CBA. Dec.10; 114) $100

EARLY ENGLISH TEXT SOCIETY
1867-1982. 39 vols. Some vols. in orig. ptd. wraps., spines worn, others cl. gt., 8 vols. with d.-w.'s. (TA. Dec.15; 237)   £110

EARLS OF KILDARE (The) & their Ancestors, from 1057-1773
Dublin, 1858. *2nd. Edn.* Royal 8vo. Mor., armorial motif on spine. (GM. Dec.7; 416)   £50

EARP, G. Butler
– **The Gold Colonies of Australia ... & Every Advice to Emigrants.** L., 1852. Hf. cf. (CA. Apr.3; 40)
Aus. $200

EASTAWAY, Edward (Pseud.)
See— THOMAS, Edward 'Edward Eastaway'

EASTMAN, Mary H.
– **The American Aboriginal Portfolio.** Phila., [1853]. 4to. Engraved title, 26 plts., spotted, a few wormholes, orig. cl., rubbed. (BBA. Jul.27; 286)
Remington. £300

EATON, Daniel Cady
– **Colored Figures & Descriptions with Synonymy & Geographical Distribution of the Ferns ...** Boston, 1878-1880. 2 vols. Lge. 4to. 91 cold. plts., cf. (CR. Jul.6; 155)   Lire 380,000
– **The Ferns of North America.** Ill.:– Emerton & Faxon. Salem, 1879, Boston, 1880. 2 vols. 4to. Some foxing, gt.-lettered cl., light wear. (RO. Dec.11; 96) $225

EATON, Elon Howard
– **Birds of New York.** Ill.:– L. Agassiz Fuertes. Albany, 1910-14. *1st. Edn.* 2 vols. Lge. 4to. 106 col. plts., few in Vol. 2 loose, orig. cl., Vol. 2 shaken, Vol. 1 ex-liby. (SG. Oct.6; 51) $110

EBBINGHAUS, Julius
– **Die Pilze und Schwämme Deutschlands.** Dresden, [1878]. 4to. Title lf. with old stp., cont. hf. leath., slightly rubbed. (GB. May 3; 1104)   DM 400

EBEL, Johann Gottfried
– **Anleitung, auf die Nützlichste und Genussvollste Art die Schweiz zu bereisen.** Zürich, 1809-10. *3rd. German Edn.* 4 vols. Cont. bds., some spines slightly defect. (R. Apr.5; 3075)   DM 920
– – **Anr. Edn.** Zürich, 1809-10. 4 vols. Some spotting, 1 map with tear, cont. hf. leath., rubbed. (D. Nov.23; 1122)   DM 420
– **Manuel du Voyageur en Suisse.** Zürich, 1805. Lightly browned, cont. hf. leath. gt., cover rubbed. (R. Apr.5; 3076)   DM 1,050

EBEQUE, J.C. de
– **Medicinae Helvetiorvm Prodromus, sive Pharmacopoeae Helvetiorvm Specimen.** Genf, 1677. (*Bound with:*) TACHENIUS, O. – **Tractatus de Morborum Principe.** Osnabrück, 1678. Together 2 works in 1 vol. 12mo. Slightly foxed & stained, cont. vell., defect., lacks ties. (HK. Nov.8; 702)   DM 800

EBERS, Georg
– **Aegypten in Wort und Bild.** Stuttgart & Leipzig, 1879-80. *1st. Edn.* 2 vols. Owners marks, vol. 1 slightly browned at beginning & end, orig. hf. leath., gt., gold-tooled upr. cover decor., lge. corner pieces, lge. gold-tooled cover centre-piece, slightly bumped wraps., box. (HT. May 10; 2731)   DM 440
– **Egypt: Descriptive, Historical, & Picturesque.** Intro. & Notes:– S. Birch. Trans.:– Clara Bell. L., ca. 1880. 2 vols. Fo. Three-qtr. mor., scuffed, ex-liby. (SG. Mar.29; 310) $200

EBERS, Georg & Guthe, Herm.
– **Palästina in Bild und Wort. Nebst der Sinaihalbinsel und dem Lande Gosen.** Stuttgart & Leipzig, n.d. 2 vols. Fo. Some foxing, gold & blind-tooled linen. (GF. Nov.12; 738)   Sw. Frs. 350

EBERSTADT, Edward & Sons, Booksellers
– **The Annotated Eberstadt Catalogs of Americana.** N.Y., 1965. *(750) sets.* 4 vols. Cl. (SG. Jan.5; 129) $100

ECCARD, Johannes
– **Geistlicher Lieder, auff den Choral oder gemeine Kirchen Melodey ... tenor part only.** Königsberg, 1597. *1st. Edn.* 2 pts. in 1 vol. Sm. 4to. Some staining, cont. vell. bds., dtd. 1621. (S. May 10; 49)   *Haas.* £320

ECHARD or EACHARD, Laurence
[–] **Flanders: or, the Spanish Netherlands most Accurately Described.** L., 1692. *2nd. Edn.* 12mo. Folding map, torn in fold, 2pp. advts., cont. cf., reprd. [Wing E144] (BBA. May 3; 267)   *Backus.* £50
– **The Gazetteer's, or Newsmen's Interpreter: being a Geographical Index of all the Considerable Cities ... in Europe.** L., 1692. *1st. Edn.* 12mo. Last 3 advt. pp., cont. sheep, rather worn. [Wing E144a] (BBA. May 3; 268)   *Coupe.* £60
– **Histoire Romaine, depuis la Fondation de Rome, jusqu'à la Translation de l'Empire par Constantin.** Ed.:– Abbé P. Fr. Guyot Desfontaines. Paris, 1744-66. 16 vols. 12mo. Cont. cf. gt., spines decor. (HD. May 21; 29)   Frs. 1,700

ECHEVERRIA, X.I. de
– **Geometria ... Necessaria a los Peritos Agrimensores.** San Sebastian, 1758. Leath. (DS. Dec.16; 2600)   Pts. 26,000

ECKARTSHAUSEN, K. von
– **Verschiedenes zum Unterricht und zur Unterhaltung für Liebhaber der Gaukeltasche, des Magnetismus und anderer Seltenheiten.** München, 1791. *1st. Edn.* Slightly foxed, cont. bds., unc. (R. Apr.4; 1432)   DM 700

ECKEL, John C.
– **The First Editions of the Writings of Charles Dickens & Their Values. A Bibliography.** L., 1913. *1st. Edn. (250) on L.P., sigd. by author & publishers.* 4to. Facs., orig. parch.-bkd. cl.; pres. copy to Col. H.J. Hughes, Fred A. Berne copy. (SPB. May 16; 172) $175
– – **Anr. Edn.** L., 1913. *1st. Edn. (750) numbered.* Orig. cl., d.-w. slightly worn. (KH. Nov.9; 590)   Aus. $160
– – **Anr. Copy.** Port., 36 plts., buckram; inscr. (SG. Jan.5; 125) $130
– – **Anr. Copy.** Port.-frontis., 36 plts., buckram, partly unc. (SG. May 17; 73) $110
– – **Anr. Edn.** N.Y. & L., 1932. *(750).* Orig. cl. (S. Oct.4; 149)   *Traylen.* £100
– – **Anr. Copy.** Some ll. spotted, orig. cl. (S. Oct.4; 148)   *Fletcher.* £70
– **Prime Pickwick in Parts. Census with Complete Collation, Comparison & Comment.** Foreword:– A. Edward Newton. N.Y. & L., 1928. *(440) numbered & sigd. by Eckel & Newton.* Cl., worn. (RO. Apr.23; 134) $110

ECKER, Paul, the Elder
– **Chinese Architecture.—Gothic Architecture.** 1759. 2 works (each in 2 pts.) in 1 vol. Ob. 4to. 36 & 24 engraved plts., cont. cf., gt. spine; Bute bkplt. (BBA. Sep.29; 79)   *Fletcher.* £720

ECKERMANN, J.P.
– **Gespräche mit Goethe.** Leipzig, 1837. 2 vols. in 1. Orig. marb. bds., roan bkd., worn; Robert Schumann's copy, with pres. inscr. by Walther von Goethe, 1 pencil annot. by Schumann; as an association copy. (S. May 10; 152)   *Benda.* £800

ECKHART, J. G. v.
– **Experimental-Oekonomie über das Animalische, Vegetabilische u. Mineralische Reich.** Ed.:– L.J.D. Suckow. Leipzig, 1782. Hf. leath. (V. Sep.29; 1354)   DM 435

ECKHEL, Abbé [J.H.]
– **Choix des Pierres gravées du Cabinet Imperial des Antiques.** Vienna, 1788. Fo. 40 engraved plts., some ll. spotted, cont. hf. cf., slightly rubbed. (BBA. Feb.23; 58)   *Thorp.* £100

EDDISON, E.R.
– **Styrbiorn the Strong.** Ill.:– Keith Henderson. 1926. *(12) numbered & sigd. on H.M.P.* Cl. gt., d.-w.; inscr. by author to Sir Henry Newbolt. (SKC. Jan.13; 2204)   £360
– **The Worm Ouroboros.** Ill.:– Keith Henderson. 1922. *1st. Edn.* 1 vol. Cl. decor. gt. (*With:*)
– **Mistress of Mistresses.** Ill.:– Keith Henderson. 1935. *1st. Edn.* Cl. gt., d.-w.; inscr. by author to Sir Henry Newbolt, A.L.s. from author loosely inserted. (SKC. Jan.13; 2205)   £300

EDEN, William
[–] **The History of New Holland from its First Discovering in 1616 to the Present Time.** L., 1787. *2nd. Edn.* Folding maps hand-cold., hf. cf., rebkd. (CA. Apr.3; 41)   Aus. $1,100

EDGEWORTH, Maria
– **Tales & Novels.** L., 1832. 16 vols. only (of 18). 12mo. Hf. mor. (GM. Dec.7; 194)   £50

EDGEWORTH, Richard Lovell
– **An Essay on the Construction of Roads & Carriages.** L., 1813. *1st. Edn.* 4 folding plts., some foxing, orig. bds., rebkd. (P. May 17; 253) *Georges.* £220
– **Essays on Professional Education.** 1809. *1st. Edn.* 4to. Tree cf., gt. (P. Feb.16; 254)   £110

EDGEWORTH, Richard Lovell & Maria
– **Memoirs ...** L., 1820. *1st. Edn.* 2 vols. Hf.-titles, bkplt., hf. mor., armorial motif on spine. (GM. Dec.7; 413)   £50

EDINBURGH CHRONICLE
Edinb., 22 Mar. 1759-15 Mar. 1760. Vol. 1 no. 1-Vol. 2 no. 130. 4to. Cont. hf. cf., unc.; Sir Ivar Colquhoun, of Luss copy. (CE. Mar.22; 96) £340

EDINBURGH MAGAZINE, The
1785-1800. Orig. Series: Vols. 1-16, New Series: Vols. 1-13, 15 & 16. Cont. panel. hf. cf. (PD. May 16; 183)   £460

EDKINS, J.
– **A Grammar of Colloquial Chinese as Exhibited in the Shanghai Dialect.** Shanghai, 1868.

Dampstained, cont. hf. cf. (BBA. Mar.7; 9)
Merrion Book Co. £55

EDMESTON, Lieut.-Gen.
- **A Short Narrative of his Conduct during the first four Years of the Rebellion in America.** Ca. 1783. 4to. Wraps. (P. Jun.7; 315) £400

EDMOND, Charles
- **Voyage dans les Mers du Nord à bord de la Corvette La Reinne Hortense.** Paris, 1863. Spotted, cont. sheep, slightly rubbed. (BBA. Jun.28; 210)
Hannas. £55

EDMONDES, Sir Clement
- **Observations upon Caesar's Commentaries.** 1604. Fo. Lacks ptd. title-p., cont. cf., rubbed. [STC 7489] (BBA. Feb.23; 140) *Fletcher.* £50

EDMONDS, Harfield H. & Lee, Norman N.
- **Brook & River Trouting. A Manual of Modern North Country Methods.** Bradford, priv. ptd., [1916]. *(50) numbered & sigd.* 4to. Frontis., 7 plts., plt. with 22 specimens of shades of silk, 39 flies with specimens of materials in sunken mounts, orig. cl., red hf. mor. box; Lee's copy, with note in his hand. (S. Oct.4; 19) *Head.* £1,800

EDMONDSON, J.L.
See— SUGDEN, Nan Victor & Edmondson, J.L.

EDMONDSON, Joseph
- **A Complete Body of Heraldry.** 1780. *1st. Edn.* 2 vols. Fo. Some offset from port. onto title, cont. cf. gt., rebkd. (P. Jun.7; 78) £65
See— SEGAR, Sir William & Edmondson, Joseph

EDOUARD-JOSEPH
- **Dictionnaire Biographique des Artistes Contemporains 1910-1930.** Paris, 1930. *(3000) numbered.* 3 vols. Cl. (SG. Aug.25; 132) $260

EDSCHMID, K.
- **Die Fürstin.** Ill.:– M. Beckmann. Weimar, 1918. *(95) on Zanders-Bütten De Luxe Edn.* 4to. All etchings sigd. by artist, margins slightly discold., last lf. with sm. tear, orig. hand-bnd. red-brown mor., tooled vig., by E.A. Enders, Leipzig, worn, spine lightly bumped & faded, ex-libris in cover. (H. May 23; 1143) DM 7,000
- – **Anr. Edn.** Ill.:– Max Beckmann. Weimar, 1918. *(370) numbered on Dutch Bütten.* 4to. 6 orig. etchings, orig. silk. (GB. Nov.5; 2272) DM 2,800

EDWARD, R. Dudley (Ed.)
See— IRISH HISTORICAL STUDIES

EDWARD OF NORWICH, 2nd. Duke of York
- **The Master of Game ... : The Oldest English Book on Hunting.** Ed.:– W.A. & F. Baillie-Grohman. Foreword: DEN Theodore Roosevelt. L., 1904. *(600) numbered.* Lge. 4to. Hf.-title, orig. suede gt., shabby, few smudges; sigd. by Theodore Roosevelt. (SG. Mar.15; 250) $400

EDWARDS, A. Cecil
- **The Persian Carpet.** L., 1960. 4to. Orig. cl., d.-w. torn. (BBA. Dec.15; 322)
Leicester Art Books. £60

EDWARDS, Bryan
- **An Historical Survey of the French Colony in the Island of St. Domingo.** L., 1797. *1st. Edn.* 4to. Lacks map, cont. cf., slightly worn. (S. Jun.25; 95)
Duval. £100
- **The History, Civil & Commercial, of the British Colonies in the West Indies.** L., 1794. *2nd. Edn.* 2 vols. 4to. Errata lf. at end of Vol. 2, 1 frontis. loose, cont. cf. gt. (S. Dec.13; 133) *Gabett.* £190
- – **Anr. Edn.** 1801. *3rd. Edn.* 3 vols. Some marginalia, cont. hf. cf., spines worn. (TA. Nov.17; 1) £105
- – **Anr. Copy.** 3 vols. Some browning & foxing, few sm. tears at folds of maps & plts., orig. tree cf., front. panel. Vol. 3 nearly detchd.; Castle Menzies Liby. bkplts. [Sabin 21901] (HA. Nov.18; 112) $160
- – **Anr. Edn.** L., 1807. 3 vols. Port., 11 folding maps, 10 plts., some slight foxing, hf. cf. (S. Jun.25; 94) *Faupel.* £120
- – **Anr. Edn.** 1818. Plt. vol. only. 4to. Engraved frontis., title vig., 10 plts. & 10 maps, 2 folding,

some light spotting, cont. bds., worn, w.a.f. (CSK. Apr.27; 130) £100

EDWARDS, Edward
- **Anecdotes of Painters.** L., 1808. 1 vol. extended to 2. 4to. A few plts. & text ll. spotted, later red hf. mor., slightly rubbed; extra-ill. with 280 engraved ports., landscapes, & other plts. (S. Apr.30; 31) *Alcaz.* £180
- **A Collection of Views & Studies after Nature.** 1790. Ob. 4to. Lightly soiled, lr. margins slightly wormed, cont. hf. cf., worn. (CSK. Jun.1; 29) £150

EDWARDS, Ernest
See— GEORGE, Hereford Brooks & Edwards, Ernest

EDWARDS, George
- **Gleanings of Natural History.** L., priv. ptd., 1758-64. 3 vols. 4to. Engraved port., 152 hand-cold. engraved plts., text in Engl. & Fr., 2 subscribers lists, cont. marb. cf., spines gt. (C. Nov.16; 241)
Neidhart. £1,600
- **A Natural History of Uncommon Birds.—Gleanings of Natural History.** L., priv. ptd., 1743-64. 4 vols.; 3 vols. 4to. Hand-cold. engraved frontis., port., 1 uncold. plt., 362 hand-cold. plts., text to 1st work in Engl., text to 2nd. work in Engl. & Fr., 3 plts. with tears affecting image, some minor tears in blank margins, some spotting, cont. diced russ. gt. (C. Nov.16; 240) *Walford.* £3,800
- – **Anr. Edn.** L., 1802-06. *(25) on L.P.* 4 vols.; 3 vols. Fo. Engraved port., frontis., 362 hand-cold. plts. (ptd. normally, most copies with plts. reverse ptd.), text to 1st. work in Engl., text to 2nd. work in Engl. & Fr., sm. hole in 1 plt., some short margin tears reprd., cont. purple hf. mor. (C. Nov.16; 242) *Smith.* £8,000
- – **Anr. Edn.** L., [1802-05?]. 7 vols. 4to. Port. of a Samojeed in Vol. 2, 359 (of 362) hand-cold. engraved plts., text in Engl. & Fr., without the cold. frontis. & 2 ports. of author, lacks Engl. title to Vol. 3, some offsetting, some spotting, slight soiling, piece torn from lr. margin of K1 in Vol. 5, 2K1 in Vol. 7 torn across, early 19th. C. bds., unc., corners worn, rebkd., w.a.f. (S. Nov.28; 26)
Schmidt. £3,100
- **Natural History of Uncommon Birds. / Histoire Naturelle des Oiseaux.** L., 1751. Vol. 3. 4to. Lacks Engl. title lf., foxed at end, most plts. lightly browned, cont. interim bds., unc. (R. Apr.4; 1702) DM 3,000

EDWARDS, Herbert Cecil Roth
See— MACQUOID, Percy & Edwards, Herbert Cecil Roth

EDWARDS, Jonathan
- **A Careful Strict Enquiry into the modern prevailing Notions of that Freedom of Will, which is supposed to be essential ...** Boston, 1754. *1st. Edn.* Errata slip pasted to recto of p. 2, 1st. 8 ll. washed, later hf. cf. gt. [Sabin 21930] (PNY. Jun.6; 481) $275

EDWARDS, Lionel
- **Famous Foxhunters.** 1932. *(100) sigd.* 4to. Hf. vell. gt. (P. Feb.16; 103) £120
- **My Hunting Sketch Book.** 1928. 4to. Orig. linen, stained. (LC. Mar.1; 481) £70
- – **Anr. Edn.** 1928-30. 2 vols. 4to. Orig. cl. (P. Oct.20; 161) £55
- **Huntsmen Past & Present.** 1929. *(150) sigd.* 4to. Qtr. vell. gt. (P. Feb.16; 102) £110
- **My Scottish Sketch Book.** L., 1929. *1st. Edn. (250) numbered & sigd.* 4to. 16 mntd. col. plts., light foxing, vell. & cl., gt. lettering. (HA. Nov.18; 256) $120
- **The Passing Seasons.** N.d. *(250).* Fo. 18 col. plts., slight spotting, cl., soiled; plts. sigd. in pencil by Edwards. (P. Jan.12; 174) *Way.* £190
- **Sketches in Stable & Kennel.** 1949. *De Luxe Edn., (50) numbered & sigd.* 4to. Orig. cf., slightly rubbed. (BBA. Feb.23; 132) *Smith.* £80

EDWARDS, Lionel & Wallace, H.F.
- **Hunting & Stalking the Deer.** 1927. *(156) sigd.* 4to. Orig. buckram gt. (SKC. Jan.13; 2312) £100

EDWARDS, Owen
- **Clych Atgot, Penodau yn Hanes fy Aggysg.** Gregy. Pr., 1933. Orig. sheep, lightly spotted, spine scuffed. (CSK. May 18; 191) £65

EDWARDS, Ralph
See— MACQUOID, Percy & Edwards, Ralph

EDWARDS, Sydenham Teak & Lindley, John
- **The Botanical Register.** 1815-17. Vols. 1-3. 263 hand-cold. plts., slight spotting, hf. cf., as a coll. of plts., w.a.f. (P. Mar.15; 148) £720
- – **Anr. Edn.** L., 1816. Vol. 2. Foxed & slightly browned, cont. hf. leath., bumped & defect. (R. Oct.12; 1825) DM 1,000
- – **Anr. Edn.** L., 1817. Vol. 3. Slightly browned & foxed, cont. hf. leath., defect. & loose. (R. Apr.4; 1704) DM 1,000
- – **Anr. Edn.** L., 1818. Vol. 4. Cont. hf. leath., unc., spine slightly brittle. (HK. Nov.8; 502) DM 1,100
- – **Anr. Edn.** L., 1824. Vol. 10. Lacks 4 cold. copperplts., some plts. slightly browned, cont. style leath. with cont. cover, worn. (HK. Nov.8; 504) DM 650
- – **Anr. Edn.** L., 1826. Vol. 12. Wide margin, cont. style leath., with cont. cover. (HK. Nov.8; 505) DM 750
- – **Anr. Edn.** L., 1827. Vol. 13. Cont. style leath., with cont. cover. (HK. Nov.8; 506) DM 800
- – **Anr. Edn.** L., 1828. Vol. 14. Minimal foxing, cont. style leath., with cont. cover. (HK. Nov.8; 507) DM 750
- – **Anr. Edn.** L., 1833-34. Vol. 19 & pt. of vol. 18 in 1 vol. Cont. hf. leath. (R. Oct.12; 1828) DM 1,300
- – **Anr. Edn.** L., 1835. Vol. 20. Cont. hf leath., defect. & loose. (R. Apr.4; 1706) DM 1,100
- – **Anr. Copy.** Vol. 20. Lacks some copper engrs., cont. hf. leath. (R. Oct.12; 1829) DM 1,050
- – **Anr. Edn.** L., 1843-44. 3 vols in 2. 187 hand-cold. plts., cf. gt., some orig. wraps. bnd. in. (P. Jan.12; 195c) *Reid.* £380

EEDEN, A.C. van
- **Album Van Eeden. Flora of Harlem.** Ill.:– Melle Arentine H. Arendsen. Haarlem, 1872-81. *1st. Edn.* Fo. 119 (of 120) chromolitho. plts., hand-stpd. on rectos, three-qtr. leath., worn, cover detchd., ex-liby. (RO. Dec.11; 97) $510

EFFIGIES DES SOVVERAINS PRINCES et Ducs de Brabant avec leur Chronologie, Armes et Devises [1610]. 4to. Extra port. of Isabella Austriaca, mor., stpd. 'EJG, 1908'. (TA. Oct.20; 379) £105

EGAN, Pierce
- **Boxiana.** L., 1823-29. 5 vols. Mixed set, orig. publisher's name in Vol. 1, George Virtue's decor. title-p. added to Vol. 2 & subsequently, extra-ill. thro-out with engrs., some folding, some laid onto blank ll. bnd. in, some foxing & soiling, mod. liby backram, new fly-ll. (CBA. Dec.10; 200) $200
- **The Finish of the Adventures of Tom, Jerry, & Logic.** L., 1889. Some plts. loose, orig. hf. leath. (R. Oct.12; 2145) DM 500
- **Life in London.** Ill.:– I.R. & G. Cruikshank. L., 1821. *1st. Edn. 1st. Iss., without footnote on p. 9.* 36 hand-cold. engraved plts., 3 engraved folding sheets of music (the 1st. unnumbered), hf.-title, no advt. ll. at end, red mor. gt., gt. pugilistic motif in compartments on spine, inner dentelles. (C. Mar.14; 46) *Quaritch.* £280
- – **Anr. Edn.** L., 1821. *1st. Edn.* Hand-cold. frontis., 35 plts., lacks hf.-title, some offset on text, cf. gt. (P. Sep.29; 261) *Haddon.* £120
- – **Anr. Edn.** 1821. *1st. Edn. 2nd. Iss.* Hand-cold. frontis., 35 hand-cold. plts., staining, few ll. reprd., cf., rebkd. (P. Apr.12; 65) *Solomon.* £75
- – **Anr. Edn.** Ill.:– I.R. & G. Cruikshank. L., 1822. Hand-cold. aquatint title, 35 plts., 3 folding plts. of music, 3 advt. ll., some soiling, spotting & offsetting, lacks hf.-title, cont. cf. (S. Mar.20; 678)
Haddon. £110
- [-] **Real Life in London.** Ill.:– Henry Alken & Thomas Rowlandson. 1821-22. 2 vols. Some foxing, hf. mor., spines brkn., unc. (BS. Nov.16; 62) £90
- – **Anr. Edn.** 1821-22 [some plts. dtd. 1823]. 2 hand-cold. frontis., 2 hand-cold. titles, 30 hand-cold. plts., some plts. cropped, crimson mor. gt. (P. Apr.12; 66) *Ayres.* £170

EGAN, Pierce -Contd.

[–] – **Anr. Edn.** Ill.:– Henry Alken & others. L., 1821-24. 2 vols. 2 hand-cold. engraved titles, 30 engraved plts., some browning & spotting, red hf. mor. by Zaehnsdorf. (SPB. Dec.13; 812) $200
– – **Anr. Edn.** Ill.:– Henry Alken & others. L., 1823. *1st. Edn.* 2 vols. 2 frontis., 2 titles, 28 plts. (dtd. 1821 or 1822), all hand-cold., offset from plts., some soiling & foxing, three-qtr. cf. & marb. bds., upr. bd. Vol. 1 detchd. (CBA. Aug.21; 7) $250
– – **Anr. Edn.** 1824. 2 vols. 2 hand-cold. titles, 2 frontis., 30 col. plts., few text ll. foxed, cont. cf., rebkd. (P. Sep.8; 270) £80

EGE, Otto F.

– **Original Leaves from Famous Bibles: Nine Centuries, 1121-1935 A.D.** Cleveland, n.d. Tall fo. 4 MS. ll. & 48 (of 56) ll., individually matted with attached caption, loose in orig. folding box. (SG. Jan.5; 131) $1,565

EGEDE, Hans Paulson

– **Description et Histoire Naturelle du Groenland.** Trans.:– D[es] R[oches] D[e] P[arthenay]. Coppenhague & Genève, 1763. Sm. 8vo. Stp. on title & anr. p., some foxing, cont. marb. cf., spine gt. [Sabin 22027] (VG. Nov.30; 816) Fls. 720

EGERTON, Francis

– **Journal of a tour in the Holy Land** ... L., 1841. 4 litho. plts., some light soiling, orig. cl., soiled, spine cracked. (CSK. Dec.2; 51) £95

EGERTON, Michael

– **Here & There over the Water. By M.E.** 1825. 4to. 4 plain & 23 hand-cold. plts., 1 plt. torn & reprd. with slight loss to surface, 2 text ll. torn, crudely reprd., some spotting, bdg. not stated. (P. Jul.25; 157) £240

EGERTON, William (Pseud.)

See– CURLL, Edmund 'William Egerton'

EGLI, Jean

– **Der Ausgestorbene Adel von Stadt und Landschaft Zürich.** Mühlebach, 1865. 4to. Gold-tooled leath. (GF. Nov.16; 1269) Sw. Frs. 750

EGLINTON TOURNAMENT

1843. Fo. Hand-cold. tinted litho. title & 13 plts. (of 21), cont. mor.-bkd. cl., lightly rubbed, w.a.f. (CSK. Jul.13; 169) £170

EGYPT

– **Sketches on the Nile [binder's title].** England(?), 19th. C. Sm. ob. fo. 1 double– & 25 single-p. litho. plts., orig. cl. (SG. Sep.22; 131) $100

EHRENBERG, Christian Gottfried

– **Organisation, Systematik und Geographisches Verhältnies der Infusionsthierchen** ... Berlin, 1830. Fo. Light stain & stp. on title, cont. bds., cont. notes inserted; Dr. Walter Pagel copy. (S. Feb.7; 109) *Quaritch.* £250
– **Symbolae Physicae** ... **Botanica.** Text:– C. Schumann. Berlin, 1900. Fo. 24 litho. or stipple engraved plts., all but 1 hand-cold., unstitched as iss. in orig. ptd. portfo. with ties, unc. (C. Jun.27; 156) *Quaritch.* £500

EHRENBERG, Herman

– **Der Freiheitskampf in Texas im Jahre 1836.** Leipzig, 1844. *2nd. Edn.* 16mo. Owner's stp. on heads of 3 ll., slightly foxed, qtr. leath. gt., dyed bds., cl. tips, worn & rubbed, cover detchd. (SG. Jan.19; 336) $400

EHRENBURG, Ilya

– **Ausgewählte Werke in Einzelausgaben.** Malik, 1927-32. *1st. German Edn.* Vols. 1-10 only (of 11). Orig. linen gt., Vol. 1 not unif., orig. wraps. (2 vols.) (GB. Nov.5; 2400) DM 400
– **Shest' Poviestei Olegkikh Kontsakh.** Ill.:– El Lissitzky. Moscow/Berlin, 1922. Orig. decor. ptd. paper wraps. by Lissitsky, slight abrasion on lr. cover. (C. Nov.9; 173) *Ungers.* £350
– – **Anr. Copy.** Some margin annots. in pencil, orig. wraps., rubbed, backstrip torn with some loss. (CSK. Jun.15; 145) £100

EHRENSTEIN, Albert

– **Die Gedichte.** Leipzig, 1920. *1st. Edn. (100)* numbered De Luxe Edn. 4to. Orig. mor. gt., gt. cover vig. (GB. May 5; 2365) DM 900

EHRET, Georg Dionysius

See– TREW, Christoph Jakob & Ehret, Georg Dionysius

EHRLICH, Paul

– **Das Sauerstoff-Bedürfnis des Organismus.** Berlin, 1885. *1st. Edn.* Hf. linen. (HK. Nov.8; 509) DM 420

EHRLICH, Paul & Hata, S.

– **Die Experimentelle Chemotherapie der Spirillosen.** Berlin, 1910. *1st. Edn.* Tall 8vo. Orig. cl., very worn, ex-liby. (SG. Oct.6; 148) $300

EHRMAN, Albert

See– POLLARD, Graham & Ehrman, Albert

EHRMANN, Th. F.

– **Neueste Kunde der Schweiz und Italiens.** Prag, 1809. Slightly browned & foxed, 1 folding plt. & map very crumpled, lacks main title lf., hf. linen, bumped. (R. Apr.5; 3077) DM 450

EICHENDORFF, Joseph, Baron von

– **Aus dem Leben eines Taugenichts.** Ill.:– E. Preetorius. München, 1914. *(500).* 4to. Orig. vell. by Fikentscher, Leipzig, cover vig.; sigd. by artist. (H. Nov.23; 1115) DM 1,800
– – **Anr. Copy.** 4to. Orig. vell., cover vig., bdg. not fixed, doubl. only pasted at margin inside cover. (H. May 22; 1046) DM 720
– – **Anr. Edn.** Ill.:– E. Preetorius. München, 1914. *(600) numbered.* 4to. Hf. vell. (HK. May 17; 2852) DM 600
– – **Anr. Copy.** 4to. Orig. vell. by Fikentscher, Leipzig, spine slightly spotted. (HK. Nov.11; 3863) DM 400
– – **Anr. Edn.** Ill.:– F. Staeger. München, [1919]. Fo. Remarks on thin japán, under guards, 7 sigd. etchings, bd. portfo. (HK. May 17; 3150) DM 610
– **Dichter u ihre Gesellen.** Ill.:– R.v. Haerschelmann. München, [1923]. *(75) DeLuxe Edn. with separate sigd. series of lithos.* 4to. Printers mark sigd. by artist., leaves in orig. bd. box. (HK. May 17; 2638) DM 440
– **Gedichte.** Berlin, 1837. *1st. Edn.* Errata lf. at end, title cut out & reinserted with tape, cont. hard-grd. mor. gt. (C. Dec.9; 211) *Post.* £350
– – **Anr. Edn.** Berlin, 1843. *2nd. Edn.* Cont. linen gt., cover blind-tooled, bumped, spine faded & with sm. defects. (HK. May 16; 1976) DM 1,300
– **Gesammelte Werke.** Ed.:– P. Ernst. München, 1909-13. Orig. hf. leath. gt. by P. Renner, minimal rubbing. (H. Nov.23; 1012) DM 470
– **Die Glücksritter.** [Leipzig, Ernst Ludwig Pr., 1911]. *(200)(50) De Luxe Edn. on Japan.* Orig. mor., gold-tooled centre-piece on upr. cover, by F.W. Kleukens, some sm. scratches. (HK. May 17; 2717) DM 850
– **Krieg den Philistern! Dramat. Märchen in fünf Abentheuern.** Berlin, 1824. *1st. Book Edn.* Minimal foxing, 2 ll. misbnd., marb. bds., orig. wraps. bnd. in, upr. wrap. with sm. margin fault & sm. owners stp., corners worn. (HK. Nov.10; 2384) DM 400
– **Lieder.** [Darmstadt, Ernst Ludwig Pr., 1921]. *(350).* Minimal browning, orig. mor., gt. spine cover & inner dentelle, spine slightly faded, ex-libris. (HK. May 17; 2718) DM 440
– **Ueber die Ethische und Religiöse Bedeutung der Neuren Romantischen Poesie in Deutschland.** Leipzig, 1847. *1st. Book Edn.* 3 ll. stained, slightly browned, some repairs, 1 sig. loose, sewed. (D. Nov.24; 2437) DM 500
– **Werke.** Ill.:– E. Eichens. Berlin, 1841. *1st. Coll. Edn. 1st. Printing.* 4 vols. Some foxing & light browning, some sm. brown spots, on prelim. lf. vol. 1 MS. entry & stp., cont. cf., supralibros, worn, slightly spotted & bumped. (H. May 22; 646) DM 2,400

EICHHOFF, F.G.

– **Parallèle des Langues de l'Europe et de l'Inde.** Paris, 1836. *1st. Edn.* Lge. 4to. Some light stains, with ptd. dedication lf. to Ferdinand Philippe, Duke of Orleans, cont. hf. cf., decor., crowned monog. on

upr. covers slightly loose. (SI. Dec.18; 107)
Lire 240,000

EICKSTEDT, C. v.

– **Reglements und Instructioneṅ für die Churfürstl. Brandenburgischen Truppen.** Berlin, 1837. 4to. Foxed, mod. vell. (R. Oct.12; 2278) DM 750

EIFFEL, Gustave

– **Nouvelles Recherches sur la Résistance de l'Air et l'Aviation faites au Laboratoire d'Auteil.** Paris, 1914. *1st. Edn.* 2 vols. (text & atlas). Lge. 4to. Orig. cl., d.-w.'s (spines faded & slightly frayed): John D. Stanitz coll. (SPB. Apr.25; 129) $300
– **La Résistance de l'Air et l'Aviation. Expériences effectués au Laboratoire du Champs-de-Mars.** Paris, 1910. *1st. Edn.* Fo. Cl., covers & spine of orig. wraps. laid down, some wear, shaken; John D. Stanitz coll. (SPB. Apr.25; 128) $175

EIKELENBERG, S.

– **Alkmaar en zyne Geschiedenissen.** Alkmaar, 1739. *(Bound with:)* – **Alkmaar en deszelfs Geschiedenissen.** Ed.:– G. Boomkamp. J. Punt & J.C. Philips after C. Pronk. Rotterdam, 1747. Together 2 works in 1 vol. 4to. Lacks 1 plt. in 2nd. work, folding maps reprd., some slight soiling, cont. hf. roan. (VS. Dec.9; 1278) Fls. 475
– **Gedaante & Gesteldheid v. Westvriesland voor 1300 en den Ondergang v. Vroone.** Alkmaar, 1714. Extra port., lacks map publd. again in 2nd. work. *(Bound with:)* – **Alkmaar e.z. Geschiedenissen.** Alkmaar, 1739. Together 2 works in 1 vol. 4to. Cont. marb. cf. gt., decor.; from Koch liby. (VG. Nov.30; 1023) Fls. 600

EINADO, J.M.

– **Instrucciones para la Constitución Fundamental de la Monarquia Española.** Guatemala, 1811. 4to. Leath. (DS. Nov.25; 2437) Pts. 32,000

EINSIEDEL, W. von (Ed.)

See– KINDLERS LITERATUR LEXIKON

EINSTEIN, Albert

– **Aether und Relativitätstheorie.** Berlin, 1920. Orig. ptd. wraps; Stanitz coll. (SPB. Apr.25; 136) $130
– **Ein Einfaches Experiment zum Nachweis der Ampereschen Molekularströme.** Brunswick, [1916]. Offprint from 'Verhandlungen der Deutschen Physikalischen Gesellschaft', pp. 173-77. Orig. ptd. wraps., holograph sig. 'Einstein' at head of upr. wrap.; John D. Stanitz copy. (SPB. Apr.25; 135) $425
– **Einheitliche Feldtheorie von Gravitation und Elektrizität.** [Berlin], 1925. 'Sitzungsberichte der Preussischen Akademie der Wissenschaften' XXII, pp. 414-19. Orig. ptd. wraps.; Stanitz coll. (SPB. Apr.25; 145) $175
– **Einheitliche Feldtheorie und Hamiltonsches Prinzip.** Berlin, 1929. Offprint from 'Sitzungsberichten des Preussischen Akademie der Wissenschaften', orig. ptd. wraps.; Stanitz coll. (SPB. Apr.25; 149) $125
– **Generalization of Gravitation Theory ..'. A Reprint of Appendix II fron the Fourth Edition of The Meaning of Relativity.** Princeton, 1953. Orig. ptd. wraps., stapled; review copy, publisher's slip & Princeton University press release, Stanitz coll. (SPB. Apr.25; 140) $275
– **Die Grundlage der Allgeméinen Relativitätstheorie.** Leipzig, 1916. *1st. Book Edn.* Title stpd., mod. bds. (HT. May 8; 370) DM 1,000
– – **Anr. Edn.** Leipzig, [1916]. Orig. wraps., unc. (R. Oct.12; 1664) DM 1,600
– **Die Kompatibilität der Feldgleichungen in der Einheitlichen Feldtheorie.** Berlin, 1929. Offprint from 'Sitzungsberichten der Preussischen Akademie der Wissenschaften', orig. ptd. wraps., creased; Stanitz coll. (SPB. Apr.25; 150) $175
– **Neue Möglichkeit für eine Einheitliche Feldtheorie von Gravitation und Elektrizität.** Berlin, 1928. Offprint from 'Sitzungsberichten der Preussischen Akademie der Wissenschaften', orig. ptd. wraps.; Stanitz coll. (SPB. Apr.25; 147) $325
– **Le Principe de Relativité et ses Consequences dans la Physique Moderne.** Trans.:– E. Guillaume. Genf, 1910. *1st. Separate Fr. Edn.* Orig. wraps., spine with paste marks; MS. dedication from author to E. Mach. (HK. Nov.8; 512) DM 500
– **Riemann-Geometrie mit Aufrechterhaltung des**

Begriffes des Fernparallelismus. Berlin, 1928. Offprint from 'Sitzungsberichten der Preussischen Akademie der Wissenschaften', orig. ptd. wraps.; Stanitz copy. (SPB. Apr.25; 146) $750
– **Theorie d'Opaleszenz v. Homogenen Flüssigkeiten u. Flüssigkeitsgemischen in d. Nähe des Krit. Zustandes.** Leipzig, 1910. *1st. Separate Edn.* Orig. wraps.; MS. dedication from author to E. Mach. (HK. Nov.8; 513) DM 580
– **Ueber das Relativitätsprinzip und die aus demselben gezogenen Folgerungen.** Leipzig, 1908. 'Jahrbuch der Radioaktivität und Elektronik', Vol. 4 (1907), pp. 411-62. Cl.-bkd. bds., slightly faded; John D. Stanitz coll. (SPB. Apr.25; 131) $550
– **Zur Affinen Feldtheorie.** [Berlin], 1923. 'Sitzungsberichte der Preussischen Akademie der Wissenschaften' XVII, pp. 137-40. Orig. ptd. wraps.; Stanitz coll. (SPB. Apr.25; 143) $125
– **Zur Einheitlichen Feldtheorie.** Berlin, 1929. *[1st. Edn.].* Offprint from 'Sitzungsberichten der Preussischen Akademie der Wissenschaften', orig. ptd. wraps., unopened; Stanitz coll. (SPB. Apr.25; 148) $350
– – **Anr. Copy.** Lge. 8vo. Thumbed, creased, ptd. wraps. (SG. Oct.6; 149) $110

EINSTEIN, Albert & Grommer, Jakob
– **Beweis der Nicht-existenz eines überall Regulären Zentrischen Symmetrischen Feldes nach der Feldtheorie von Th. Kaluza, in:** Scripta Universitatis atque Bibliothecae Hierosolymitanarum, Mathematica et Physica. Jerusalem, 1923. Vol. 1. 4to. Text in German & Hebrew, wraps. (S. Apr.10; 497)
Levy. £60

EINSTEIN, Albert & Grossmann, Marcel
– **Entwurf einer Verallgemeinerten Relativitätstheórie und einer Theorie der Gravitation. I Physikalischer Teil ... II Mathematischer Teil.** Leipzig & Berlin, 1913. *1st. Separate Edn.* Offprint from 'Zeitschrift für Mathematik und Physik', Vol. 62. Orig. ptd. wraps., faint foxing & rust stain at head, Stanitz coll. (SPB. Apr.25; 133) $650
– – **Anr. Edn.** Leipzig, 1914. Hf. linen. (R. Oct.12; 1666) DM 400

EISEN, Gustavus A. & Kouchakji, Fahim
– **Glass.** N.Y., 1927. 2 vols. 4to. Orig. cl.-bkd. bds., s.-c. (BBA. Nov.10; 324) *Demetzy.* £120

EISENBERG, Baron d'
– **L'Art de monter à Cheval ou Description die Manège Moderne dans sa Perfection.** Ill.:– B. Picart. La Haye, 1740. Ob. 4to. Title remntd., some stains, some plts. foxed, cont. marb. cf., decor. spine, sm. repairs. (HD. Feb.29; 13) Frs. 8,200
– – **Anr. Edn.** Ill.:– B. Picart. Amst. & Leipzig, 1747-59. Ob. fo. A few ll. lightly crumpled, cont. hf. leath., wear. (D. Nov.25; 4484) DM 6,800

EISENMENGER, Johann Andreas
– **Entdecktes Judenthum oder Gruendlicher und Wahrhaffter Bericht Welchergestalt die Verstockte Juden die Hochheilige Drey-Einigkeit ... laestern.** Koenigsberg, 1711. 2 vols. in 1. 4to. Errata lf. in each vol., some ll. in index pt. II misbnd., vell.; Dr. Walter Pagel copy. (S. Feb.7; 207) *Bondy.* £310
– – **Anr. Copy.** 2 vols. Sm. 4to. Each vol. with errata lf., 1st. with royal imprimatur on title verso, dtd. Coelln an der Spree, 6 Mar. 1711, some mild foxing or browning, old cf., worn, lacks spines. (SG. Feb.2; 44) $110

EISNER, H.
– **Umfassende Geschichte des Kaisers Napoleon mit Vollständiger Sammlung seiner Werke für Gebildete Leser.** Stuttgart, 1834-37. 10 vols. Lacks port., both folding plts. completely mntd. on linen, unif. red mor. gt., by Hatchards. (R. Apr.3; 1018) DM 1,200

EKELOF, Adolf
– **Ett Ar i Stilla Hafvet, reseminnen fran Patagonien ... Californien, British Colombia och Oceanien.** Stockholm, 1872. 4to. 17 litho. views & ports. on 12 sheets, orig. ptd. bds., mod. cl. backstrip. (S. May 22; 473) *Crete.* £280
– – **Anr. Copy.** 4to. Some ll. slightly browned, orig. blind-stpd. cl., gt. vig. on upr. cover. (C. Nov.16; 84) *Quaritch.* £100

ELAZER BEN YEHUDA ROKEACH of Worms
– **Sefer Ha'Rokeach.** Fano, 1505. *1st. Edn.* Fo. Censored with minor deletions & sigd. on final lf. by Camillo Yaghel, n.d., slight staining & soiling, sig. on title, bds. [Steinschneider 4924, 6] (SPB. Jun.26; 10) $6,000

ELDER, M.
See– ANDRE, A. & Elder, M.

ELDER SCIENTIFIC EXPLORING EXPEDITION, 1891-2
– **Journal.** Adelaide, 1893. 2 vols. with atlas. 2 folding maps in 4 pts., torn & reprd., slightly soiled thro.-out, text lacks wraps., maps in bds., worn. (BBA. May 3; 296) *Morrell.* £220

ELDRIDGE, G.W.
[–] **[Book of Harbour Charts New York to Boston].** Boston, [1902]. Fo. 49 litho. charts, hand-cold. in outl., some spotting, cont. cl. (CSK. Feb.10; 65) £70

ELEGANT EXTRACTS
N.d. 18 vols. 12mo. Lightly spotted, cont. mor. gt. (CSK. Jan.27; 2) £160

ELEONORA MARIA ROSALIA, Herzogin zu Troppau u. Jägerndorff
– **Freywillig-aufgesprungener Granat-Apffel, Des Christl. Samaritans ...** Wien, 1741. 2 pts. in 1 vol. 4to. Title side margin slightly defect., slightly soiled, lightly stained near end, cont. hf. leath., bumped & rubbed, lacks stpd. end-papers. (HK. Nov.8; 539) DM 1,100

ELGANBYURI, Eli (Pseud.)
See– ZDANEVICH, Ilya 'Eli Elganbyuri' or 'Ilyazd'

ELGAR, Francis
– **The Ships of the Royal Navy.** 1873. 4to. 47 col. litho. plts., lacks title, contents completely loose in orig. gt.-decor. cl., worn, w.a.f. (TA. Mar.15; 300) £190

ELGAR, Frank
– **Resurrection de l'Oiseau.** Ill.:– Georges Braque. Paris, 1959. *(225) numbered & sigd. by author & artist.* (25) on velin de Rives, with extra suite of the 4 lge. cold. lithos. Fo. Unsewn in orig. pict. wraps., unc., folder & s.-c. (S. Nov.21; 6) *Rota.* £980

ELGIN MARBLES (The) from the Temple of Minerva at Athens
1816. Fo. Engraved frontis., 61 plts. (from Stuart & Revett 'Antiquities of Athens'), including 58 double-p. or folding, frontis. offset, publisher's bds., unc., soiled & slightly worn. (S. Nov.1; 91) *Quaritch.* £240

ELIAHU BACHUR [ELIJAH LEVITA]
– **Sefer Ha'Tishbi.** Isny, 1541. 4to. Sigd. by Boniface del Asinary & Giovanni Dominico Carretto, 1608, slight soiling & staining, owners sigs., cl., rubbed; Hochschule für die Wissenschaft des Judenthums stps. [Steinschneider 4960, 46] (SPB. Jun.26; 16) $2,250

ELIAZAR BAR-ISAJAH P.
– **A Vindication of the Christians Messiah ... That Jesus Christ ... is the true Messiah ... foretold by all ... the Writers of the old Testament ... As also proved out of their own beloved Talmouth ...** L., 1653. Sm. 4to. Scattered minor stains, later wraps., trimmed, slightly worn & soiled. [Wing V500A] (SG. Feb.2; 121) $150

ELICAGARY, B. Renaud
[–] **La Théorie de la Manoeuvre des Vaisseaux.** Ed.:– J. Sauveur. Ill.:– Erlinger. 1689. *Orig. Edn.* Cont. cf., spine decor.; from Montesquieu liby. with MS. inscr. on title. (HD. Jul.2; 13) Frs. 3,800

ELIEZER HA-GADOL
– **Orhot Hayyim.** Venice, 1623. *(Bound with:)* HEILPRIN, Ya'akov – **Shoshanat Ya'akov.** Venice, 1623. Together 2 pts. in 1 vol. 12mo. Later stiff wraps. (SG. Feb.2; 172) $650

ELIEZER IBN SHANGI
– **Sefer Dat ve-Din.** Constantinople, 1726. *1st. Edn.* 2 pts. in 1 vol. 4to. Mild dampstaining, margin worming, later spr. cf., worn. (SG. Feb.2; 173) $250

ELIOT, George (Pseud.)
See– EVANS, Marian 'George Eliot'

ELIOT, Thomas Stearns
– **Ara Vus Prec.** Ovid Pr., 1919. *(264).* 4to. Bds., soiled. (P. Mar.15; 106) *Hosain.* £180
– – **Anr. Edn.** Ill.:– E.A. Wadsworth. [L.], Ovid Pr., [1920]. *1st. Edn., (264). (220) numbered.* 4to. Orig. cl.-bkd. bds., edges worn, covers dampd.; pres. copy(?), initialed, sigd. & dtd. by author, & with 2 corrections by him, Frederic Dannay copy. (CNY. Dec.16; 122) $1,800
– **Ash-Wednesday.** N.Y., 1930. *1st. Edn. (600) sigd. Out-of-series copy.* Bdg. not stated, covers lightly rubbed, free end-papers darkened, without orig. cellophane wrap. & box; Marymount College bkplt. (CBA. Mar.3; 188) $150
– – **Anr. Edn.** 1930. *(600) numbered & sigd. by author.* Orig. cl., lightly soiled. (CSK. Jan.27; 140) £80
– **Collected Poems 1909-1935.** L., 1937. *2nd. Impr.* Inscr. on title, orig. cl., slightly rubbed. (BBA. May 23; 84) *Maggs.* £100
– **Dante.** L., 1929. *(125) numbered on H.M.P. sigd. by author.* Orig. cl., slightly soiled. (BBA. May 23; 81) *Jolliffe.* £95
– **East Coker.** L., 1940. *1st. Edn.* Fo. Folded as iss., short tears at fold, reprd., slightly browned, inscr. by author. (S. Dec.8; 172) *Brenchley.* £180
– **Four Quartets.** L. [Verona, Bodoni Pr., 1960]. *(290) numbered & sigd.* Fo. Orig. parch.-bkd. bds., lacks publisher's box; Frederic Dannay copy. (CNY. Dec.16; 127) $550
– **Old Possum's Book of Practical Cats.** 1939. *1st. Edn.* Orig. cl., d.-w. (BBA. Aug.18; 15) *Minerva Books.* £60
– – **Anr. Copy.** Sm. 4to. Orig. cl., slightly discold., slightly soiled & frayed. (BBA. May 23; 85) *S.C. Smith.* £55
– **Poems 1909-1925.** L., 1925. *1st. Edn.* Orig. cl., d.-w., slightly soiled. (BBA. May 23; 79) *Words Etcetera.* £70
– – **Anr. Edn.** L., 1925. *1st. Iss.* Cl., discold.; I.A. Richard's copy, with MS. bkplt., annots. thro.-out, some presumably in his hand, 4 ll. of Eliot poems extracted from cont. periodicals mntd. on final blank verso & back end-paper. (SG. Mar.1; 101) $200
– **Prufrock & Other Observations.** L., The Egoist Ltd., 1917. *1st. Edn., (500).* 12mo. Orig. ptd. wraps., hf. mor. s.-c.; sigd. by author in 1933, Frederic Dannay copy. (CNY. Dec.16; 121) $2,200
– **A Song for Simeon.** Ill.:– E. McKnight Kauffer. L., n.d. *(500) L.P. numbered sigd. by artist.* Ariel Poem no. 16. Orig. bds., slightly soiled. (BBA. May 23; 80) *Bell, Book & Radmall.* £65
– **The Undergraduate Poems.** Camb., Mass., [1949]. Ptd. wraps. (SG. Mar.1; 102) $225
– **The Waste Land.** N.Y., 1922. *1st. Edn., (1000) numbered. 1st. Iss.* with 'mountain' correctly spelt in line 339, p. 41. Orig. flexible cl., glasine wrap. slightly frayed, mor. case. (BBA. Nov.30; 274) *Maggs.* £500
– – **Anr. Edn.** N.Y., 1922. Sm. 8vo. 2nd. state, cl. on stiff bds. (SG. Mar.1; 103) $350
– – **Anr. Edn.** Richmond, Hogarth Pr., 1923. *1st. Engl. Edn. (460).* Orig. marb. bds., slightly worn; Frederic Dannay copy. (CNY. Dec.16; 124) $400
– – **Anr. Edn.** L. [Verona, Bodoni Pr., 1962]. *(300) numbered & sigd.* Fo. Orig. parch.-bkd. bds., publisher's box worn; Frederic Danny copy. (CNY. Dec.16; 126) $750
– – **Anr. Copy.** Fo. Orig. parch.-bkd. bds., publisher's box worn; bkplt. of John Kobler, Frederic Dannay copy. (CNY. Dec.16; 125) $650

ELISABETH-CHARLOTTE DE BAVIERE, Princesse Palatine, Duchesse d'Orléans
– **Mémoires, Fragmens Historiques et Correspondance.** Paris, Nov. 1832. *1st. Compl. (partly Orig.) Edn.* On vell., 2nd. Empire blind-decor. mor. by Lortic père; added port. bnd. at beginning. (HD. May 16; 17) Frs. 1,750

ELISHA GALLICO
- **Beur Kohelet.** Venice, 1578. *1st. Edn.* 4to. Slightly soiled, creased, slight ink staining, cl., trimmed. (S. Oct.24; 143a) *Sol.* £200
- **Peirush Megillat Esther.** Venice, 1583. *1st. Edn.* 4to. Hf. leath., marb. paper cover. (S. Oct.24; 144) *Sol.* £220
- **Peirush Shir Ha'Shirim.** Venice, 1587. *1st. Edn.* 4to. Owner's stp. on title, slight worming in outer margin not affecting text, last 2 ll. reprd. affecting some letters, cl., trimmed. (S. Oct.24; 145) *Sol.* £210

ELIYAHU DI VIDAS
- **Reshit Chochma.** Venice, 1579. *1st. Edn.* 4to. A few repairs to margins, slight staining & soiling, a few margins frayed, mor.-bkd. bds., worn. (SPB. Feb.1; 39) $800

ELIYAHU MIZRAHI RE'EM
- **Peirush Rashi.** Venice, [1527]. *1st. Edn.* Sm. fo. Title & 2nd. lf. in facs., with text on title verso lacking, few ll. remargined or with sm. tears without loss, lacks 1 lf., 3 transposed, ostensibly anti-Christian words or passages blackened or inked over with MS. emendations, plastic-covered old hf. cl., slightly shaken. (SG. Feb.2; 174) $600

ELIZABETH I, Queen of England
- **Duo Edicta Elizabethae Reginae Angliae Contra Sacerdotes Societatis Jesu.** 1583. Cf. gt. (P. Jan.12; 222) *Georges.* £50
- **Queene Elizabeth's Speech to her Last Parliament.** N.p., 1601?. *1st. [& only] Edn.* 4to. Red hf. mor. gt.; the Lansdowne/Phillipps copy. [STC 7579] (SG. Oct.27; 89) $425

ELIZABETH, Princess
- [-] **Cupid Turned Volunteer** ... 1804. 4to. 12 hand-cold. aquatints, some stains, orig. bds., worn, backstrip defect. (TA. Apr.19; 263) £85

ELLEN, OR THE NAUGHTY GIRL RECLAIMED
1811. Sm. 8vo. 9 hand-cold. aquatint cut-out costumes, head, neck & 2 hats, lacks some hats, orig. ptd. wraps., w.a.f. (LC. Jul.5; 24) £140

ELLICOTT, Andrew
- **The Journal of ... for Determining the Boundary between the United States & the Possessions of His Catholic Majesty in America.** Phila., 1814. *1st. Edn.* Lge. 4to. With errata lf., lge. folding map partly detchd at folds & reprd., disbnd.; ex-liby. (SG. Apr.5; 69) $275

ELLIOT, Daniel Giraud
- **A Monograph of the Felidae or Family of the Cats.** Ill.:– after Joseph Smit & Joseph Wolf. [L.], priv. ptd., [1881-]83. Lge. fo. 43 hand-cold. litho. plts., slight crease in outer margin of plt. of Felis Temminckii, plt. of Felis Domestica foxed, some spotting (plts. mostly unaffected), hf. mor. by Zaehnsdorf, upr. wraps. to orig. ll pts. bnd. in. (S. Feb.1; 24) *Marlborough.* £10,500
- **A Monograph of the Paradiseidae, or Birds of Paradise.** Ill.:– Joseph Smit after Joseph Wolf. [L.], priv. ptd., 1873. Lge. fo. 36 litho. plts. hand-cold. by J.D. White, 1 uncold. plt., cont. dark red mor., gt.-decor., slightly rubbed & soiled, lacks front free end-paper, preserved in red qtr. mor. case. (S. Feb.1; 22) *Quaritch.* £10,500
- – **Anr. Copy.** Lge. fo. 36 litho. plts. hand-cold. by J.D. White, 1 uncold. plt., last plt. a little soiled, red hf. mor. gt. by Leighton, spine a little rubbed. (S. Feb.1; 23) *Taylor.* £10,000
- **A Monograph of the Phasianidae or Family of Pheasants.** Ill.:– Joseph Smit & J.G. Keulemans after Joseph Wolf. N.Y., priv. ptd., [1870-]72. 2 vols. Lge. fo. 79 litho. plts. cold. by J.D. White, 2 uncold. plts., plts. of Wild Turkey & Siamese Fireback slit by binder through captions at inner edge, some spotting (plts. mostly unaffected), cont. hf. mor. gt. (S. Feb.1; 21) *Klein.* £18,500
- **A Monograph of the Pittidae, or, Family of Ant Thrush.** N.Y., [1861-]63. *1st. Edn.* Fo. 31 hand-finished cold. litho. plts., frontis. loose, very slight soiling to margins of a few plts., three-qtr. mor., spine gt., end-papers foxed. (SG. Nov.3; 71) $5,600
- **A Monograph of the Tetraoninae, or Family of**

the Grouse. Ill.:– After Elliot, Joseph Wolf, & William S. Morgan. N.Y., priv. ptd., 1864-65. Orig. 4/5 pts. Lge. fo. 27 hand-cold. litho. plts., title & prelims. bnd. at end of pts. 4/5 (double no.), light offsetting from text onto plts., 1st. plt. in pts. 4/5 with margins chipped, a few other tears in margins, orig. ptd. bds., rebkd., preserved in qtr. mor. s.-c. (S. Feb.1; 19) *Taylor.* £7,000
- – **Anr. Edn.** Ill.:– Bowen, after Elliot & J. Wolf. N.Y., [1864-]65. Lge. fo. 27 hand-finished col. litho. plts., plt. 1 with short tear at foot, sm. stain to upr. margin of plt. 14 & facing p., plts. 8 & 9 cut close at lr. margin, plt. 16 cropped at lr. edge, some browning to edges of some plts., extreme lr. margins of text ll. stained, hf. mor. gt. by Stikeman. (CNY. Nov.18; 297) $3,000
- **The New & Heretofore Unfigured Species of Birds of North America.** N.Y., priv. ptd., [1866-]69. *1st. Edn.* 2 vols. Fo. 72 hand-cold. litho. plts., some foxing, mostly to text, a few margin tears, 1 reprd., several margin stains, hf. mor. (SG. Nov.3; 72) $6,200
- – **Anr. Copy.** 2 vols. Lge. fo. 72 hand-finished col. litho. plts., without the extra plt. 'Parus Occidentalis' (sometimes present), text lf. facing plt. 30 cut round & mntd., a few extreme outer margins stained, some finger– or dust DEN soiling to a few margins, 2 text ll. in Vol. 1 chipped at edges & browned, hf. mor. gt. by Stikeman. (CNY. Nov.18; 298) $4,500

ELLIOT, Robert & Roberts, Emma
- **Views in India, China & on the Shores of the Red Sea.** 1835. 2 vols. in 1. 4to. Col. frontis., 2 engraved titles, 61 engraved views, str.-grd. mor. gt. (P. Oct.20; 112) £95
- – **Anr. Copy.** 2 vols. 4to. Cold. frontis., 2 engraved titles, 61 views, orig. hf. mor., rebnd. (VG. Nov.30; 513) *Fls.* 500
- – **Anr. Edn.** N.d. 2 vols. in 1. 4to. Cold. frontis., steel-engraved additional titles, 61 plts., 1st. & last few ll. lightly spotted, cont. hf. mor., rubbed, lightly soiled. (CSK. Oct.21; 14) £95

ELLIOT, William
See– **BRANNEN, Noah & Elliot, William**

ELLIOTT, C.A.
- **Report on the History of the Mysore Famine of 1876-78.** Calcutta, 1878. 4to. Hf. cf., rubbed. (P. Jul.26; 143) £65

ELLIOTT, Grace Dalrymple
- **Journal of My Life During the French Revolution.** L., 1859. *1st. Edn.* 2 vols. Light foxing, some pencil notes in margins or on versos of some plts., providing identification & other pertinent information, later crimson mor. by Rivière, fleur-de-lis & other emblems gt.-stpd. at covers & backstrip, light scuffing at corners, covers with light wear, some wear & rubbing at jnts. light discolouration at base of 2 cover panels, extra-ill. with ca. lll full-& double-p. engraved scenes & ports., some hand-cold. (HA. May 4; 254) $110

ELLIS, G.V. & Ford, G.H.
- **Illustrations of Dissections ... Representing the Dissection of the Human Body.** L., 1867. Fo. 58 col. litho. plts., sm. tears in margins, slightly soiled, hf. cf., spine defect. (P. Nov.24; 129) *Evelyn.* £95

ELLIS, Henry
- **Voyage de la Baye de Hudson, fait en 1746 & 1747.** Paris, 1749. 2 vols. in 1. Engraved map, 10 plts., all folding, cont. cf., head of spine slightly worn. (S. Jun.25; 96) *Faupel.* £200
- **A Voyage to Hudson's Bay by the Dobbs Galley ... for Discovering a North West Passage.** L., 1748. *1st. Edn.* Cont. cf., a little worn. [Sabin 22312] (BBA. Sep.29; 43) *Morrell.* £340
- – **Anr. Copy.** 9 engraved plts., lacks map, cont. spr.-dc. cf. (TA. Dec.15; 57) £100
- – **Anr. Copy.** Folding map & plt. at p. 232 slightly torn, slight margin soiling, cont. cf. gt., rebkd., upr. jnt. brkn.; the Rt. Hon. Visc. Eccles copy. (CNY. Nov.18; 99) $500

ELLIS, John, Cartographer
- **English Atlas** ... L., 1768. Ob. 4to. 49 engraved maps only, including 1 folding, 2 reprd., 1 cleanly torn, later cl., soiled. (CSK. Nov.4; 10) £450

- – **Anr. Copy.** Ob. 4to. General map, 44 (of 50) uncold. county maps, lacks title, 1 map stained, disbnd. (P. Sep.8; 431) *Magna.* £340

ELLIS, John, Naturalist
- **An Essay Towards a Natural History of the Corallines.** L., 1755. *1st. Edn.* Lge. 4to. Frontis., 38 plts., most folding, cont. cf., spine gt., jnts. very worn. (SG. Apr.19; 80) $250

ELLIS, Tristram J.
- **On a Raft, & Through the Desert.** L., Leadenhall Pr., 1881. 2 vols. Lge. 4to. MS. limitation '25 Copies only. No. 20. Proofs. Tristram Ellis', map, 38 copper-etchings, some foxing, decor. vell., soiled. (SG. Sep.22; 137) $130

ELLIS, William, Farmer
- **Husbandry, Abridged & Methodized.** 1772. 2 vols. Cont. cf. gt. (PD. Dec.14; 217) £60
- **The Modern Husbandman or, the Practice of Farming.** 1744-47. 8 vols. Unif. cf., spines gt., rubbed; Sir Ivar Colquhoun, of Luss copy. (CE. Mar.22; 99) £360

ELLIS, Rev. William, Missionary
- **Polynesian Researches.** 1829. *1st. Edn.* 2 vols. 9 engraved plts., 2 maps, slight discolouration to a few plts., orig. bds., unc., spines with paper labels, worn & 1 detchd. (S. May 22; 474) *Quaritch.* £140
- – **Anr. Edn.** L., 1831-34. *2nd. Edn.* 4 vols. 16mo. Lacks map in 4th. vol., some foxing, &c., crude hf. mor., worn & torn, ex-liby. (SG. Sep.22; 138) $200

ELLIS, William, Surgeon
- **An Authentic Narrative of a Voyage performed by Captain Cook & Captain Clerke, in H.M.S. Resolution during the Years 1776, 1777, 1778, 1779, & 1780.** L., 1782. *1st. Edn.* 2 vols. Chart, 21 plts., cont. qtr. leath., worn. (JL. Jul.15; 379) *Aus.* $425

ELLMS, Charles
- **The Tragedy of the Seas; or, Sorrow on the Ocean, Lake, & River, from Shipwreck, Plague, Fire, & Famine.** N.Y., 1841. *1st. Edn.* Sm. 8vo. Some foxing, later cl.; from liby. of F.D. Roosevelt, inscr. by him. (SG. Mar.15; 19) $200

ELMES, James
- **Memoirs of the Life & Works of Sir Christopher Wren.** L., 1823. *1st. Edn.* 2 vols. Lge. 4to. Extra-ill. with over 150 engrs. of 18th. & early 19th. C. ports., views, etc., many hand-cold., all inlaid to size, ex-liby., three-qtr. lev., spines gt. (SG. May 3; 392) $850
- **A Scientific, Historical & Commercial Survey.** L., 1838. Fo. Additional engraved title with hemisphere projected on plane of horizon of L., 20 engraved maps & plans, hf. cf., defect., preserving portion of orig. prize bdg. on upr. cover, inner cover with mor. label recording award of Telford Premium to James Leslie, 1841. (S. May 21; 16) *Weinreb.* £250

ELMES, James
See– **SHEPHERD, Thomas Hosmer & Elmes, James**

ELMORE, H.M.
- **The British Mariner's Directory & Guide to the Trade & Navigation of the Indian & China Seas.** L., 1802. 4to. Cont. hf. cf., rebkd. & relined. (SG. Sep.22; 139) $200

ELOGES ET DISCOURS SUR LA TRIOMPHANTE RECEPTION DU ROY en sa Ville de Paris, après la Réduction de la Rochelle
Ill.:– after A. Bosse. 1629. Sm. fo. Pp. misnumbered, 2 plts. defect., stains, some ll. detchd., cont. havanna roan, decor., centre arms, decor. spine, defects., very worn. (HD. Feb.29; 14) *Frs.* 2,000

ELSASSER, Marie
- **Ausführliches Kochbuch für die Einfache und Feine Jüdische Küche.** Frankfurt, 1930. *4th. Edn.* Orig. pict. linen. (R. Oct.12; 2033) *DM* 520

ELSHOLTZ, J.S.
- **Neu angelegter Garten-Bau.** Frankfurt & Leipzig, 1727. Lacks 2nd. pt. Fo. Browned, some spotting, cont. rebnd. hf. leath. (H. Nov.23; 258) *DM* 420

ELSNER, H.
- Umfassende Geschichte des Kaisers Napoloen mit Vollständiger Sammlung seiner Werk für Gebildete Leser. Stuttgart, 1834-37. *1st. Edn. (vol. 1 2nd. Edn.).* 10 vols. 48 steel engrs. & 30 text woodcuts, some slight foxing, cont. decor. hf. leath., gt., gold-tooled, slightly rubbed & bumped. (HT. May 10; 2542b)   DM 480

ELSTOB, Eliza
- An English Saxon Homily on the Birthday of St. Gregory. 1709. *1st. Edn.* Cf., worn. (P. Jun.7; 271)
                                              £120

ELTON, John
See— BENNETT, Richard & Elton, John

ELUARD, Paul ie. Eugène Grindel
- Les Animaux et leurs Hommes. Les Hommes et leurs Animaux. Poèmes. Ill.:– Valentine Hugo. Paris, [1938]. *New Edn.* 12mo. Orig. sewed; Eluards MS. dedication on endpaper. (D. Nov.24; 3019)   DM 600
-- **Anr. Edn.** Ill.:– Valentine Hugo. Paris, n.d. *Re-edn.* Sm. 4to. Sewed; pres. inscr. by ill., 30 Dec. 1943, dedication by author, 15 Jun. 1944. (SM. Mar.7; 2121)   Frs. 1,300
- Au Rendez-vous Allemand. 1944. *Orig. Edn. (100).* Sm. 8vo. Sewed, turn-in defect.; pres. inscr., orig. drawing. (SM. Mar.7; 2122)   Frs. 1,200
- Collection Les Grandes Peintres par Leurs Amis: A Pablo Picasso. Ill.:– Pablo Picasso. Geneva & Paris, 1944. *(25) numbered & sigd. by author with 2 orig. etchings by Picasso, sigd. by artist.* 4to. Orig. wraps., parch.-bkd. bd. folder, s.-c. (BBA. Jun.14; 245)   *Sims, Reed & Fogg.* £1,400
-- **Anr. Edn.** Ill.:– Pablo Picasso. Geneva & Paris, 1944. *(90) numbered & sigd. by author with an orig. etching by Picasso, sigd. by artist.* 4to. Orig. wraps., loose, parch.-bkd. bds., s.-c. (BBA. Jun.14; 246)   *Barrie Marks.* £750
- Perspectives. Ill.:– A. Flocon. [Paris], 1948. 4to. Hf. vell., vell. corners, cover gold spr., sigd. by G. Gauché, unc. (D. Nov.24; 3019a)   DM 5,000

ELUARD, Paul [i.e. Eugène Grindel] (Ed.)
See— DICTIONNAIRE ABREGE DU SURRE-ALISME

ELUARD, Paul [i.e. Eugène Grindel] (Text)
See— RAY, Man

ELWE, Jan Barend
- Atlas. Amst., Priv. ptd., 1792. Fo. 33 (of 37) double-p. maps, including 2 astrological & genealogical charts & the distance table, & 1 additional man of Germany from anr. work, loosely inserted, hand-cold. in outl., & 22 pp. of letterpress, lacks title, some soiling & margin tears, reprd., hole in El, with loss of text, mod. mor. (CH. Sep.20; 63)
                                            Fls. 3,200

ELWE, Jan Barend & Langeveld, D.M.
- Vollkommen Reis-Atlas van Geheel Duitschland ... Amst., 1791. *1st. Edn.* Title with pasted over stp., cont. hf. leath. gt. (HK. Nov.8; 888)
                                            DM 4,200

ELWES, Henry James & Augustine Henry
- The Trees of Great Britain & Ireland. Edinb., priv. ptd., 1906-13. 8 vols., including Index. 4to. 7 floral titles, 5 cold. frontis., port., 414 plts., specially bnd. in cont. deer-bkd. wood bds. by Birdsall, of Northampton. (BBA. Oct.27; 219) *Fletcher.* £270

ELWES, Robert
- A Sketcher's Tour round the World. L., 1854. 21 tinted plts., some spotting, orig. embossed cl. gt., spine ends chipped; 3 A.L.s. from author to his sisters tipped in at beginning & end, each with pen & ink sketches & vigs. (C. Nov.16; 85)
                                            Castle. £400

ELYAKIM BEN NAFTALI
- Sefer Shem Tov. Venice, 1606. *1st. Edn.* Sm. 4to. Some dampstaining & soiling, title laid down, old hf. leath., spine & corners chafed; Van Biema copy. (SG. Feb.2; 175) $325

ELYOT, P.H.
- Ausführliche Geschichte aller Geistlichen und Weltlichen Kloster-und Ritterorden für beyderley

Geschlechte ... Leipzig, 1753-56. *1st. Edn.* 8 pts. in 4 vols. Some slight browning, cont. bds., 1 mod. vell. in cont. style. slightly spotted, light scratching. (HT. May 10; 2605)   DM 1,000

ELYOT, Sir Thomas
- The Dictionary. 1538. *1st. Edn.* Fo. Tear in 1 lf. without loss of text, paper fault in anr. lf. affecting a few letters, lacks 2 ll. of 'additamenta' Gg3 & 4, dupls. of Gg1 & 6 bnd. in their place, some minor margin dampstaining, cont. cf., very worn, stitching partly brkn.; cont. owners inscr. of Thomas Butterworth. [STC 7659] (C. May 30; 149)
                                        Pickering. £950
[-] Of the Knowledeg [sic] whiche maketh a wise man. L., 1533. *1st. Edn.* Sm. 8vo. Engraved port. after Bartolozzi inserted, sm. repair to blank inner margin of title, inner blank margin of A2 restored, headline on K4r distorted by printing flaw, mor. gt., spine gt., by Pratt. [STC 7668] (C. Nov.9; 62)
                                         Georges. £1,000

EMACLE, A.
- La Passante. Ill.:– Odilon Redon. Paris, 1892. *(400) numbered on Dutch Bütten.* Orig. etching as frontis., orig. sewed, unc. (GB. May 5; 3124)
                                            DM 1,000

EMBLEMATA: Handbuch der Sinnbildkunst des XVI & XVII Jahrhunderts
Ed.:– A. Henkel & A. Schoene. Stuttgart, [1967]. Lge. 4to. Art hf. mor., d.-w. slightly frayed. (SG. Jan.5; 133) $175

EMERSON, Peter Henry
- Wild Life on a Tidal Water. Ill.:– after Emerson & T.F. Goodall. L., 1890. *'Ordinary Edn., (500) numbered' [according to hf.-title].* 4to. 29 photogravures, lacks port. of Emerson, hf.-title & frontis. reinforced at hinge, 1st. few ll. & frontis. lightly foxed, some other light foxing, mostly to plt. margins, orig. gt.-lettered pict. cl, worn, leath. spine crudely reprd. (SG. Nov.10; 56) $325

EMERSON, Ralph Waldo
- Journals ... with Annotations. Boston, [1909-14]. *1st. Edn.* 10 vols. Slight margin darkening, bdg. not stated, 7 vols. with spine faded. (CBA. Mar.3; 190) $170
- Nature. Ill.:– A. Simons. München, Bremer Pr., 1929. *(130).* 4to. Hand-bnd. orig. vell., gold decor., by Fried Thiersch. (H. Nov.23; 948)   DM 500
- Writings. L., 1896-1902. 6 vols. Sm. 8vo. Three-qtr. lev., spines gt., partly unopened. (SG. Feb.16; 110) $130
- Complete Works. Boston & N.Y., [1903]. *Concord Edn.* 12 vols. 12mo. Few tiny pencil markings in few margins, crimson mor. & marb. bds., ornate gt. panels. (HA. May 4; 180) $250
- Works. Camb., Riverside Pr., 1903. *(600) numbered.* 12 vols. Tall 8vo. Mntd. photogravure port.-frontis., plts., lettered tissue-guards, A.MS. inlaid & tipped in as iss., few penciled marginalia, cl., minor stains on upr. cover of vol. 1, mostly unopened. (SG. Apr.26; 80) $750
-- **Anr. Edn.** Boston & N.Y., 1909. *Fireside Edn.* 12 vols. Maroon mor., gt.-panel. spines, 1 with sm. chip. (SG. Feb.16; 111) $275
- Complete Works. Boston & N.Y., Riverside Pr., n.d. *Centenary Edn.* 12 vols. Mor.-bkd. bds. (SPB. Dec.13; 525) $450

EMERSON, William
[-] The Elements of Optics. L., 1768. *1st. Edn.* Cont. cf. (S. Oct.4; 266)   *Marlborough.* £90
- Mechanics, or the Doctrine of Motion. L., 1769. *(Bound with:)* - The Projection of The Sphere. L., 1769. *(Bound with:)* - The Laws of Centripetal & Centrifugal Force. L., 1769. Together 3 works in 1 vol. Browning, cont. cf., rebkd. (PNY. Dec.1; 47)
                                              $100

EMERY, Henry
- La Vie Végétale. Histoire des Plantes. Paris, 1878. 4to. Publishers linen. (DS. Mar.23; 2090)
                                          Pts. 30,000

EMMONS, Arthur B.
See— BURDSALL, Richard L. & Emmons, Arthur B.

EMMRICH (Supp.)
See— SCHAUBACH, A.

EMORY, William H.
- Notes of a Military Reconnaisance, from Fort Leavenworth, in Missouri, to San Diego, in California. Wash., 1848. *Senate Edn., 1st. Iss., with the lge. folding map & with Emory's rank given also as Lieut.-Col.* Lge. folding map, 43 views, botanical drawings & plans, map with sm. tear, some light foxing, later cl. (LH. Jan.15; 284) $250
-- **Anr. Edn.** Wash., 1848. *1st. Edn. Senate Edn., 2nd. Iss., without the lge. folding map & with Emory's rank given as Brevet Major on title.* 3 full-p. maps, 14 botanical plts., 25 (of 26) litho. plts. & views, text ll. slightly browned, orig. cl., rubbed, spine label defect.; the Rt. Hon. Visc. Eccles copy, due to complexities of issues & variations of plts. & text, w.a.f. [Sabin 22536] (CNY. Nov.18; 101) $200
See— BAIRD, Spencer F.

EMPIRE PARLIAMENTARY ASSOCIATION
- An Account of the Arrangements & Procedure in Westminster Hall, Friday 7 May 1937 on the Occasion of the Luncheon of the Empire Parliamentary Association ... L., 1937. *(1000).* Sm. 4to. Mor. gt., cl. s.-c.; sigd. inscr. from R.G. Casey to Benson. (KH. Nov.8; 146)   Aus.$130

ENAULT, Louis
- Londres. Ill.:– Gustave Doré. 1876. *1st. Fr. Printing of ills.* 4to. Publisher's decor. hf. chagrin. (HD. May 4; 259)   Frs. 4,400
-- **Anr. Copy.** 4to. 52 plts., contents detchd. from bdg., publisher's decor. hf. chagrin. (HD. Mar.21; 144)   Frs. 1,650

ENCHUYSER LIED-BOECXKEN, behels, Bruylofts-Psalmen & seer Vermaeckelijcke Bruylofts Lidekens
Enkhuizen, [1686]. 75 x 50mm., miniature book. Orig. blind-stpd. vell., sm. silver clasp, loosening, some wear. (VG. Mar.19; 165)   Fls. 650

ENCICLOPEDIA JURIDICA ESPANOLA
Barcelona, [1943]. 67 vols. 4to. Publishers hf. cl. & leath. (DS. Nov.25; 2305)   Pts. 20,000

ENCOUNTER
L., 1953-83. Nos. 1-351. 4to. Orig. wraps., nos. 1-204 in easibinders. (BBA. May 23; 88)
                                        Sobun-So. £80

ENCYCLOPAEDIA BRITANNICA
Edinb., 1788-97. *3rd. Edn.?.* 18 vols. in 36 only. 4to. Lacks titles, orig. bds., most backstrips torn, some with loss, w.a.f. (CSK. Feb.10; 81)   £100
-- **Anr. Edn.** Edinb., [1788]-1797. *3rd. Edn.* 18 vols. Vol. 15 lacks 2 plts., 1 plt. & 1 map with sm. tear, cont. hf. leath. gt. (R. Oct.12; 2148)
                                            DM 7,800
-- **Anr. Edn.** Edinb., 1797. *3rd. Edn.* 20 vols., including 2 plt. vols. 4to. Cont. cf., some covers detchd. (CSK. Sep.30; 49)   £280
-- **Anr. Copy.** 18 vols. (lacks supps.). 4to. Cf., rubbed, as a coll. of plts., w.a.f. (P. Jan.12; 53)
                                         K.Books. £140
-- **Anr. Copy.** 16 vols. only (lacks vols. 1 & 11). 4to. Cont. cf., worn. (CSK. Dec.16; 220)   £120
-- **Anr. Edn.** Edinb., 1797, 1801. *3rd. Edn.* 22 vols., including 2 plt. vols. & Gleig's 2 vol. Supp. 4to. Plt. vols. with 542 engraved plts., Supp. with 50 engraved plts., unif. cont. tree cf., spines gt.; Sir Ivar Colquhoun of Luss copy. (CE. Mar.22; 100)
                                            £2,400
-- **Anr. Edn.** 1810. 20 vols. Hf. cf. (LA. Nov.29; 70)   £105
-- **Anr. Edn.** Edinb., 1823. *6th. Edn.* 20 vols. 4to. Cont. diced cf., spines gt., a few vols. neatly rebkd. preserving orig. spines; from liby. of Luttrellstown Castle, w.a.f. (C. Sep.28; 1815)   £350
-- **Anr. Edn.** Edinb., 1842. *7th. Edn.* 3 vols. of plts. only. 4to. 516 engraved plts. & maps, some folding, some spotted, cont. hf. cf., rubbed, 1 upr. cover detchd. (BBA. Feb.23; 206)   *Bailey.* £85
-- **Anr. Edn.** Edinb., 1875. *9th. Edn.* 25 vols. Red hf. mor. (PD. Feb.15; 59)   £165
-- **Anr. Edn.** 1875-79. *9th. Edn.* 25 vols., with Index. 4to. Hf. mor. gt. (P. Dec.8; 129)
                                        Finch. £160

ENCYCLOPAEDIA BRITANNICA -Contd.

– – **Anr. Edn.** 1875-1903. *9th./10th. Edn.* 35 vols. 4to. Cont. unif. hf. mor., spines gt.-decor., faded. (TA. Feb.16; 141) £65

– – **Anr. Copy.** 35 vols. 4to. Cont. unif. hf. mor., gt.-decor. spines, minor wear. (TA. Oct.20; 199) £50

– – **Anr. Edn.** Camb., 1910. *11th. Edn.* 29 vols. Cont. hf. mor., lightly rubbed. (CSK. Mar.9; 63) £160

– – **Anr. Copy.** 32 vols. bnd. in 16. Red hf. mor. (PD. Aug.17; 256) £85

– – **Anr. Edn.** 1910/11. 29 vols. 4to. Liby. stp. on titles & label pasted in each upr. cover, orig. mor. gt., faded & rubbed on spines. (TA. Jun.21; 629) £64

– – **Anr. Edn.** 1948. 24 vols. 4to. Orig. mock mor. gt., a little rubbed. (TA. Mar.15; 329) £58

– – **Anr. Edn.** 1961. 24 vols. 4to. Cl.; from liby. of Luttrellstown Castle, w.a.f. (C. Sep.28; 1816) £110

– – **Anr. Edn.** 1976. 30 vols. & yearbook for 1977. 4to. Orig. imitation mor. gt. (TA. Jul.19; 266) £170

– – **Anr. Edn.** N.d. *11th. Edn. Handy Edn.* 32 vols., including Supps. Dark red hf. mor. gt. (LC. Mar.1; 327) £90

ENCYCLOPAEDIA JUDAICA: Das Judentum in Geschichte und Gegenwart

Berlin, [1928-34]. 10 vols. Lge. 4to. Hf. leath., lacks 3 spines, others worn or chipped. (SG. Feb.2; 45) $550

– – **Anr. Copy.** 10 vols. 4to. Orig. hf. leath., some vols. slightly worn. w.a.f. (HK. Nov.11; 4348) DM 1,100

ENCYCLOPAEDIA METROPOLITANA

Ed.:– Smedley & Rose. L., 1845. *1st. Edn.* 29 vols. 4to. 547 engraved plts. & 30 maps, some spotting, cont. cf., rubbed, w.a.f. (S. May 21; 17) *Traylen.* £600

ENCYCLOPAEDIA, OR A DICTIONARY OF ARTS, SCIENCES & MISCELLANEOUS LITERATURE

Phila., 1798. 18 vols. Cf. (RS. Jan.17; 465) $475

ENCYCLOPAEDIA PERTHENSIS; or Universal Dictionary of Knowledge

Perth, [1796-1806]. 23 vols. Engraved frontis., approx. 350 plts., maps & plans (a few folding), cont. cf., spines gt., some worn or stained, w.a.f. (S. Nov.1; 4) *Jones.* £170

– – **Anr. Edn.** Perth, n.d. 23 vols. Imperial 8vo. Lacks title to Vol. I, 18th. C. tree cf., w.a.f.; from liby. of Luttrellstown Castle. (C. Sep.28; 1817) £300

ENCYCLOPAEDIE VAN NEDERLANDSCH-INDIE

Ed.:– J. Paulus, D.G. Stibbe & others. 's-Gravenhage, Leiden, 1917-39. 4 vols. & 4 vols. supp. Together 8 vols. Cl., some slight defects. (B. Apr.27; 682) Fls. 550

– – **Anr. Edn.** Ed.:– J. Paulus, D.G. Stibbe, & others. 's-Gravenhage/Leiden, 1917-40. *2nd. Printing.* 8 vols., including 4 supp. vols. in pts. as iss. lacks Vol. VI no. 18). Lge. 8vo. Cl. (VG. Nov.29; 138) Fls. 500

ENCYCLOPEDIA OF WORLD ART

1959-68. 15 vols. Buckram. (BS. May 2; 145) £100

– – **Anr. Copy.** 15 vols. Fo. No bdg. stated. (SPB. Nov.30; 246) $800

– – **Anr. Edn.** N.Y., [1959]. *Engl. Edn.* 15 vols. 4to. Bdg. not stated, minor soiling to 1 spine. (CBA. Jan.29; 171) $400

ENCYCLOPEDIE BOUASSE-LEBEL

Paris, ca. 1870. Atlas only. Fo. Cont. qtr. mor. gt. (TA. Sep.15; 518) £115

– – **Anr. Edn.** [Paris], late 19th. C. Atlas of plts. only. Lge. fo. 34 double-p. cold. plts., no title or text, a few plts. slightly cropped or spotted, mor.-bkd. cl., rubbed, w.a.f. (S. Dec.13; 307) *Erlini.* £100

ENCYCLOPEDIE CONCERNANT LA PECHE

– Recueil des Planches. Paris, 1793. 4to. 112 plts., dampstain on 1st. ll., later hf. sheep, decor. spine. (HD. Sep.22; 310) Frs. 2,000

ENCYCLOPEDIE DES METIER D'ARTS: DECORATION MODERNE

Paris, [1929]. 2 vols. 4to. Plts. loose as iss., Vol. I in 4 fascicules, each with ptd. wraps. (chipped), cl.-bkd. bd. folder. (SG. Aug.25; 18) $425

ENCYCLOPEDIE METHODIQUE

Paris, 1783. 4 vols., including plt. vol. 4to. 172 plts., most double-p., cont. hf. sheep, decor. spines. (HD. Sep.22; 283) Frs. 5,000

– **Marine.** Paris, Liège, 1783-87. 4 vols. including atlas. 4to. Hf. cf., ca. 1830, spine decor. (HD. Jun.18; 29) Frs. 5,800

– – **Anr. Copy.** 4 vols., including Atlas. 4to. & lge. 4to. 173 plts., cont. hf. roan & cont. bds. (HD. Mar.9; 101 & 132) Frs. 4,000

ENCYCLOPEDIE MODERNE. Dictionnaire Abrégé des Sciences, des Lettres des Arts ...

Paris, Firmin Didot. 1852. 27 vols. text & 3 vols. plts. 4to. Chagrin. (DS. Jan.27; 2211) Pts. 25,000

– – **Anr. Edn.** Paris, 1859. *New Edn.* Atlas Vols. 1-3 only. Vol. 1 hf. cf., rest ptd. wraps., frayed. (SG. Oct.6; 150) $100

ENCYCLOPEDIE PRATIQUE DE L'AGRICULTEUR

Ed.:– L. Moll. Paris, 1859-77. 13 vols. Cont. hf. cf., spine raised bands. (HD. Jun.22; 37) Frs. 1,000

ENDER, Thomas & others

– Malerische Ansichten der Donau von Engelhardszell bis Wien (von Theben bis Golumbacz). Pest, n.d. 2 vols. Ob. 8vo. 42 engraved plts., slightly spotted, orig. bd. portfos. (BBA. Sep.29; 101) *Branners.* £200

ENGEL, A. & Serrure, R.

– Répertoire des Sources Imprimées de la Numismatique Française. Paris, 1887-89. 2 vols. Some slight spotting, cont. cf.-bkd. bds., orig. frayed wraps. bnd. in. (S. May 1; 463) *Spink.* £100

ENGEL, Gabriel?

[–] American Oats: being a Rare Dish of Strange Kiplingana. N.p., priv. ptd., 1928. Ptd. tab on final p. notes 'only 90 copies printed ... ', on Japan vell., unbnd. (SG. Jan.12; 188) $150

ENGEL, Johann Jakob

– Schriften. Ill.:– Meil. Berlin, 1801-06. *1st. Coll. Edn.* 12 vols. Cont. hf. cf. (C. Dec.9; 212) *Braecklein.* £170

– – **Anr. Copy.** 12 vols. On fine ribbed Bütten, title lightly spotted, cont. marb. cf., decor. gt. spine, covers & outer dentelles, 3 covers with flat worm traces; engraved ex-libris, Hauswedell coll. (H. May 24; 1274a) DM 3,800

– – **Anr. Copy.** 12 pts. in 13 vols. Title slightly foxed, hf. leath. gt., ca. 1840, spine lightly faded, end-papers browned in corners. (HK. Nov.10; 2386) DM 1,250

ENGELBACH, Lewis

[–] Naples & the Campagna Felice. Ill.:– Rowlandson. L., 1815. Additional acquatinted title, 2 hand-cold. maps, & 15 hand-cold. aquatint plts., some sigd. by Rowlandson, hf. mor. (S. May 21; 226) *Traylen.* £170

ENGELBRECHT, Hans (van Brunswijk)

– De Werken. Trans.:– D. Jz. Kat. Amst., 1697. 2 vols. in 1. Sm. 8vo. Cont. vell. (VS. Dec.9; 1370) Fls. 500

ENGELBRECHT, M.

– Le Fabriche e Vedute di Venetia. Ill.:– L. Carlevaris. Augsburg, ca. 1730. Ob. fo. 1 plt. with sm. bkd. hole in plt. margin, 1 plt. slightly stained, lacks 12 plts., later hf. vell. (R. Oct.13; 3176) DM 4,200

ENGELMANN, J.B.

– Le Nouveau Merian ou Tems Anciens et Modernes du Rhin. Ill.:– Grape after Merian. Heidelberg, [1826]. 51 (of 50) engraved plts (1 double), title bkd., stp. partly painted over, minimal foxing & browning, marb. bds. (V. Sep.29; 94) DM 6,700

See– **ROCHETTE.**, Desiré, Raoul dit & Engelmann

ENGELS, H.

See– **NIBELUNGENLIED**

ENGLAND

– A New Display of the Beauties of England ... 1772-74. 2 vols. Cont. cf.-bkd. marb. bds., worn. (LC. Jul.5; 218) £85

– – **Anr. Edn.** 1776. 2 vols. 178 engraved plts., some loose, cont. cf. gt., as a coll. of plts., w.a.f. (P. Sep.29; 79) *Angle.* £150

– – **Anr. Edn.** L., 1776-77. *3rd. Edn.* 2 vols. Extra engraved titles, 180 engraved plts., few slightly soiled or plt.-marks shaved, ?lacks A1 of Vol.1, cont. hf. cf., worn, covers detchd. (S. Mar.6; 304) *W. Smith.* £140

– The Seaman's Opinion of a Standing Army in England, in Opposition to a Fleet at Sea, as the Best Security of this Kingdom. L., 1699. *1st. Edn.* Sm. 4to. Baldwin's list of 'Books written against a Standing Army' at end, mod. wraps. [Wing S2189] (SG. Oct.27; 221) $100

ENGLAND, Church of

– Aduertisements partly for due order in the Publique Administration of Common Prayers ... & partly for the Apparrell of all Persons Ecclesiasticall. L., [1565?]. 4to. With A2 catchword 'maiesties', A3 catchwood 'marche', A3. i. 'preaching', cont. margin notes, slightly cropped, later historical notes, bds., spine brkn. (SPB. Dec.13; 669) $150

ENGLAND DELINEATED

1804. 2 vols. Some spotting, orig. cl.-bkd. bds., unc., upr. cover marked. (LC. Jul.5; 194) £75

– – **Anr. Copy.** 2 vols. Engraved titles, 146 views, cf. gt. (P. May 17; 170) *Hollingsworth.* £70

ENGLAND ILLUSTRATED

Maps:– Kitchen. 1764. 2 vols. 4to. 28 engraved plts., 54 hand-cold. maps (2 folding), cont. cf., rubbed. (CSK. Jul.6; 98) £280

ENGLAND & WALES. Return of Owners of Land, 1873

L., 1875. 2 vols. Fo. Cont. hf. mor., slightly rubbed. (BBA. Dec.15; 93) *Heraldry Today.* £55

ENGLEFIELD, Sir Henry Charles

– A Description of the Principal Picturesque Beauties ... of the Isle of Wight. Ill.:– W. & G. Cooke & others. L., 1794. 4to. 50 engraved maps & plts., some maps folding, hf.-title, some minor spotting, sm. stains on 1 map, hf. mor. (S. Mar.6; 242) *Thackery.* £100

– – **Anr. Edn.** 1816. Fo. 3 folding maps, 47 plts., 1 map & 1 plt. hand-cold., cl., back damaged. (P. Oct.20; 68) £110

– – **Anr. Edn.** L., 1912. 4to. Tall copy, engraved port., 3 folding maps (1 hand-cold.), 47 plts. (1 hand-cold.), some folding, plts. spotted & stained, cont. maroon hf. mor., spine defect. (S. Jun.25; 316) *Shapiro.* £100

ENGLEHEART, Henry L.D.

See– **WILLIAMSON, George C. & Engleheart, Henry L.D.**

ENGLISH COACH BUILDERS', Illustrated Record of the International Exhibition, 1862

L., [1862]. 4to. 92 plts. (51 hand-cold.), 11 plts. of arms, 10 plts. monogs., some spotting, qtr. mor. (P. May 17; 254) *Henderson.* £580

ENGLISH DIALECT DICTIONARY

Ed.:– Joseph Wright. 1898. 6 vols. 4to. Hf. mor., worn. (PD. Apr.18; 120) £90

ENGLISH PILOT

– Part I ... the Southern Navigation Upon the Coasts of England, Scotland, Ireland, Holland, Flanders, Spain, Portugal, to the Streights Mouth. Charts:– John Seller, H. Moll & others. L., Thomas Page & William Mount, 1729. Fo. Ptd. title with woodcut royal arms, 24 engraved sea & coastal charts (22 double-p. or folding, 2 in text), 1 or 2 short tears without loss of engraved surface, some light browning mostly affecting text, a few annots. in cont. hand in text & on verso of 1st. chart, 19th. C. hf. cf., worn, w.a.f. (S. May 21;141) *Quaritch.* £1,000

ENGLISH SCENERY
1889. 120 chromolitho. views on 60 sheets, orig. cl. gt. (P. Feb.16; 146) £120
– – **Anr. Edn.** 1891. 120 chromolitho. views on 60 sheets, cl. gt., rubbed. (P. Apr.12; 163)
Hadden. £65
– – **Anr. Edn.** 1892. 120 chromolitho. views on 60 plts., lightly soiled, orig. cl., rubbed. (CSK. Mar.9; 116) £95

ENGLISH WATER-COLOUR
Ed.:– Charles Holme. Intro.:– Frederick Wedmore. L., 1902. Lge. fo. 66 mntd. cold. plts., lettered tissue-guards, ports., ex-liby., buckram. (SG. May 3; 155) $130

ENHINGER, John W.
– **Illustrations of Longfellow's Courtship of Miles Standish.** Ill.:– after Brady. N.Y., 1859. *1st. Edn.* Lge. ob. 4to. Plt. mounts foxed, orig. blind-decor. mor., covers scuffed & worn at extremities. (HA. Dec.16; 159) $120

ENSCHEDE, Charles
– **Fonderies de Caractères et leur Matériel dans les Pays-Bas du XVe au XIXe Siècle.** Haarlem, 1908. Fo. Orig. cl. gt., unopened. (BBA. Oct.27; 199)
Dailey. £120
– **Typefoundries in the Netherlands from the 15th to the 19th Cent.** Ed.:– L. Hellinga. Trans.:– H. Carter & N. Hoeflake. Haarlem, 1978. Fo. Imitation hf. cf. (VG. Sep.13; 392) Fls. 500

ENSKO, Stephen G.C.
– **American Silversmiths & Their Marks.** N.Y., 1937, 1948. Pts. II & III. Cl. (SG. Oct.13; 322) $120

ENSOR, James
– **La Gamme d'Amour.** Bruxelles, 1929. *Orig. Edn.* Ob. 4to. Leaves. (HD. Jun.6; 53) Frs. 8,000
– – **Anr. Edn.** Ill.:– after Ensor. Brussels, 1929. *(270) numbered. (250) on velin d'Arches.* Ob. fo. Unsewn in orig. wraps., worn; inscr. 'Pour Monsieur Scherzon et Vive la musique ce délicieux comple AACment de la peinture, James Ensor'. (S. Nov.21; 74) *Minou.* £450
– – **Anr. Copy.** Ob. fo. Unsewn in orig. wraps., slightly worn. (S. Nov.21; 20) *Marks.* £340
– – **Anr. Edn.** Brüssel, 1929. *(250) numbered on Bütten.* Ob. fo. Hf. leath. gt., orig. wraps. bnd. in. (GB. May 5; 2369) DM 2,800
– **Scènes de la Vie du Christ.** Bruxelles, 1921. *(285) sigd. 1st. Printing of ills.* Ob. 4to. Leaves. (HD. Jun.6; 54) Frs. 8,000

ENTFELDERS, Chr.
See– **SERARIUS or SERRURIER, P.**

ENTICK, Rev. John
– **The General History of the Late War ... in Europe, Asia, Africa, & America.** L., 1764-66. *Vol. I:3rd. Edn., Vols. II-IV: 2nd. Edn., Vol. V: 1st. Edn.* 5 vols. 8 folding maps, 41 port. plts., scattered foxing, few stains, cont. cf. (SG. Sep.22; 140) $175
– **A New & Accurate History & Survey of London, Westminster, Southwark & Places Adjacent.** 1766. *1st. Edn.* 4 vols. 4 engraved port. frontis., folding street map, 35 engraved plts., cont. spr. cf., spines gt. (LC. Oct.13; 266) £100

ENTREE TRIOMPHALE DE LEURS MAJESTEZ LOUIS XIV, Roy de France et de Navarre, et de Marie Thérèse d'Autriche, son Espouse, dans la Ville de Paris ...
Ill.:– F. Chauveau (frontis.), port engraved by P. van Schappen after Mignard, J. Lepautre. Paris, [1662]. Fo. Cont. grd. cf., corners a little worn. (HD. Dec.1; 68) Frs. 2,200

ENZENSBERGER, Chr.
– **Grösserer Versuch Über den Schmutz.** Ill.:– K. Fussmann. Berlin, 1980. *De Luxe Edn., (70) numbered.* Lge. 4to. Orig. monogrammed etchings, & separate series of etchings, orig. bds. & portfo. (GB. Nov.5; 2496) DM 600

ENZYKLOPADIE D. EISENBAHNWESENS
Ed.:– Frh. v. Röll. Berlin & Wien, 1912-23. 10 vols. 4to. Orig. linen & orig. hf. linen. (D. Nov.25; 4678) DM 670

EOBANUS HESSUS
– **Operum ... Farragines Duae.** Hall, [15]39. *1st. Edn.* 2 pts. in 1 vol. Title & some ll. with underlining & marginalia, sm. ink stains, cont. blind-tooled pig over wood bds., 2 clasps, lacks ties, ex-libris. (HK. Nov.8; 172) DM 950

EPHEMERA (Pseud.)
See– **FITZGIBBON, Edward 'Ephemera'**

EPICTETUS
– **Enchiridion, una cum Cebetis Thebani Tabula ...** Camb., 1655. 2 pts. in 1 vol. Cont. spr. cf.; from liby. of John Evelyn, with his press-mark P.2. & inscr. & motto. [Wing E3144] (S. Nov.17; 19)
A. Thomas. £160
– **[Works].** L., 1897. 2 vols. Red mor. gt. by Rivière. (LH. Sep.25; 465) $100

EPICURUS
– **Epicurus's Morals.** L., 1656. *1st. Engl. Edn.* 4to. Sm. hole in d4, frontis. & title-p. lightly dust-stained, cont. cf., reprd. & rebkd. [Wing E3155] (BBA. May 3; 135) *Howes Bookshop.* £75

EPISCOPIUS, J. (Pseud.)
See– **BISSCHOP, J. de 'J. Episcopius'**

EPISTOLAE DIVERSORUM Philosophorum; Epistolai Diaphoron Philosophon, Rhetoron, Sophiston
Venice, Aldine Pr., [29] Mar. 1499 [not before 17 Apr. 1499]. 2 vols. 4to. Greek type, washed, some margin worming, panel. mor., gt. anchor on covers, gt. dentelles. [Goff E64] (SG. Apr.26; 6) $1,800

EPISTOLAE ECCLESIASTICAE ET THEOLOGICAE, Praestantium et Erudit. Virorum
Text:– J. Arminius, J. Uytenbogardus, G.J. Vossius, Hug. Grotius & others. Amst., 1704. *3rd. Edn.* Fo. Cont. hf. roan, slightly rubbed, unc. (VG. Nov.30; 946) Fls. 460

ERAGNY PRESS
See– **FLAUBERT, Gustave**
See– **MOSELLY, Emile**
See– **RONSARD, Pierre de**
See– **RUST, Margaret**
See– **VILLON, François [i.e. François de Montcorbier]**

ERASMUS, Desiderius
– **Adagiorum.** Amst., 1650. 12mo. Chagrin. (DS. Mar.23; 2091) Pts. 40,000
– **Adagiorum Chiliades.** Ed.:– Froben. Ill.:– Urs Graf, Ambr. Holbein. Basel, 1523. Old MS. owners mark on title lf., stains in outer margins, especially last ll., cont. style hf leath, using old wood bds. (D. Nov.23; 160) DM 1,200
– – **Anr. Edn.** Basel, Mar. 1551. Fo. Slightly stained, browned & wormed, title with owners mark, 18th. C. hf. leath., rubbed & wormed. (HK. May 15; 123) DM 400
– **Adagiorvm Opvs.** Basel, 1530. Much cont. marginalia & underlining in red & black ink, lightly spotted & browned, cont. pig-bkd. wood bds., blind-tooled, clasps, rubbed, some worming. (H. Nov.23; 586) DM 500
– **Apophthegmatum Opus cum Primis Frugiferum ...** Lugduni, 1544. Cont. cf., crowned dolphin (mark of Francis II), 1 cover detchd., spine worn. (HD. Jun.29; 67) Frs. 1,000
– **Colloquiorum Familiarum Opus.** Lyons, 1542. Lacks last lf., blank (?), some light staining, cont. blind-stpd. pig. (BBA. Nov.30; 8) *Lapidus.* £60
– **Concio de Puero Jesu Olim Pronunciata a Puero in Schola Ioannis Coleti Londini Instituta, in qua Praesidebat Imago Pueri Jesu Docentis Specie.** Ed.:– S. Bentley. L., 1816. On vell., title in red & black, headings in red, facs. of Erasmus's handwriting at end & colophon lf. with device, mor. by Hering, his ticket, covers decor. in gt., broad inner gt. border decor., silk liners gt.; vell. lf. before title with calligraphic inscr. by Thomas Tomkins, preceded by anr. lf. confirming by anr. writer that Tomkins was writer of the inscr. (S. May 10; 274)
Marlborough. £550
– **De Octo Orationis Partium Constructione Libellus.** Trans.:– Iunius Rabirius. Paris, 1545. Many cont. marginalia, some slight spotting, cont. bds., slightly soiled. (HT. May 8; 128) DM 850

– **De Recta Latini Graeci'qve Sermonis Pronunciatione Dialogus. Eivsdem Dialogvs cvi Tivulus, Ciceronianus ...** [Venice], ca. 1530. Some initials, some foxing, title with owners mark, 18th. C. leath gt., wormed. (HK. May 15; 125) DM 800
– **Declamationes Quatuor.** Ill.:– Anton Woensam von Worms. Köln, 1525. Some slight text underlining, cont. style mod. vell. (HT. May 8; 126) DM 2,200
– **L'Eloge de la Folie.** Notes:– Gerard Listre. Trans.:– Gueudeville. Ill.:– after Holbein. Amst., 1728. *New Edn.* Sm. tear in corner of 1 lf., sm. stains on 3 others, late 18th. C. red mor. gt., decor., by Derôme. (HD. Nov.29; 55) Frs. 7,800
– – **Anr. Edn.** Trans.:– Gueudeville. Ill.:– Aliamet, De La Fosse, Flipart, Legrand & others. [Paris], 1751. *1st. Edn. ill. Eisen. De Luxe Edn. on L. Dutch P. with very wide margin.* 4to. Most copper engrs. sigd. in plt., Fr. hand-bnd. reddish brown mor., gt. spine, covers, inner & outer dentelles, by Chambolle-Duru, 2 sm. scratches; Hauswedell coll. (H. May 24; 1275) DM 1,700
– – **Anr. Edn.** Trans.:– Gueudeville. Ill.:– Eisen. [Paris], 1751. *New Edn. 1st. Printing of ills.* Sm. 4to. L.P., some light foxing, red mor. gt. decor. by David. (HD. May 3; 41) Frs. 3,100
– **Enchiridion Militis Christiani.** Basel, 1540. Woodcut device on title & final lf., cont. annots., cont. cf., slightly worn, spine reprd. (S. Apr.10; 315) *Kubicek.* £120
– – **Anr. Edn.** L., 1576. Cf., upr. cover detchd. [STC 10487] (P. Jan.12; 223) *Smallwood.* £140
– **Epistolarum libri XXXI et P. Melanc[h]thonis libri IV.** 1642. Fo. Sm. hole in 1 lf. affecting a few letters, cont. sheep, slightly worn; John, Marquis of Tweedale bkplt. (BBA. Feb.23; 146)
Lapidus. £120
– **Epitome Adagiorum.** Geneva, 1593. In latin & Greek, title-lf. cut away without loss of letters, cont. stpd. pig over wood bds., decor., arms of Johann Friedrich, Elector of Saxony, initials 'I.M.E.' & date 1597; from Fondation Furstenberg-Beaumesnil. (HD. Nov.16; 120) Frs. 1,300
– **Familiatrvm Colloqviorum Opus.** Strassb., 1529. Lacks 19 ll. of 'scholia' at end, slightly spotted title with lacks ties. (HK. May 15; 127) DM 400
– **Hern Erasmi vo Roterdam Vormanung das Heylige Euangeliü vnd der Heyligen Zwelf-Botè Schrifft flessig zu lesen.** Trans.:– Nic. Krumpach. Leipzig, 1522. 4to. Rubricated, title with old entries & browned, some spotting & margin tears, no bdg. stated. (HK. Nov.8; 173) DM 600
– – **Anr. Copy.** 4to. Rubricated, title & lr. (blank) cover lf. with old entries & browned, slightly spotted & margins torn or singed, 2 margin annots with slight loss, no bdg. stated. (HK. May 15; 129) DM 420
– **Hyperaspistes Diatribae adversus Servum Arbitrium Martini Lutheri.** Basel, 1526. *1st. Edn.* Title lf. slightly soiled, some light browning or staining, some margin underlining, later bds., slightly spotted. (HT. May 8; 127) DM 900
– **In Praise of Folly.** Ill.:– Fritz Eichenberg. N.Y. & Balt., Aquarius Pr., 1972. *1st. Edn. 'Principal Edn.', (10) hand-lettered, reserved for collaborators.* Elephant fo. Each print sigd. by artist in pencil at bottom margins, prints loose in orig. folder, all prints & texts laid into orig. cl. clam-shell box, box rubbed with some smudging. (HA. Feb.24; 245) $425
– **Liber Aureus de Civilitate Morum Puerilium.** Lübeck, 1646. Latin & German parallel text, browned. mod. bds.; Hauswedell coll. (H. May 24; 1660) DM 950
– **Lob der Narrheit.** Trans.:– Wilhelm G. Bekker. Ill.:– after Holbein. Basel, 1780. *1st. Bekker Edn.* Wide margin, L.P., 2 pp. with sm. hole & slight loss, cont. hf. leath. gt., tear at head of spine, cover, corners, etc. renewed. (HK. May 16; 1977)
DM 600
– **Moriae Encomium.** Oxford, [1663]. 12mo. A few sm. tears, with loss of a few letters to fo. N10, 19th. C. hf. cf., rubbed. [Wing E 3206] (BBA. Feb.23; 144) *Edwards.* £60
– **Opus de Conscribendis Epistolis.** Strassburg, 1522. *(Bound with:)–* **De Duplici Copia, Verborum et Rerum, Commentarii Duo.** Strassburg, 1522.

ERASMUS, Desiderius -*Contd.*

Together 2 works in 1 vol. Sm. wormholes at beginning & end, cont. blind-stpd. pig over bds., lacks clasps. (BBA. Nov.30; 7) *Maggs.* £160
- **Paraphrasis in Evangelium Secundum Ioannem ... in Acta Apostolorum ...** Paris, 1540. 2 pts. in 1 vol. (of 5). Title with owners mark, some slight spotting & staining, cont. leath., blind-tooled decor., gold-tooled corner fleurons, gold-tooled fleuron centre-piece, slightly defect., upr. cover loose. (HT. May 8; 129) DM 1,500
- **Pilgrimages to Saint Mary of Walsingham & Saint Thomas of Canterbury.** Trans.:- J.G. Nichols. Westminster, 1849. *1st. Edn.* Cont. cf., rebkd.; bkplt. & supralibros of William Stirling-Maxwell. (SG. Nov.17; 218) $100
- **Witt Against Wisdom or a Panegyrick upon Folly.** Trans.:- White Kennet. Oxford, 1683. *1st. Edn.* Cf. (CE. Sep.1; 59) £55

ERASTUS, Thomas [i.e. Thomas Liebler]
- **Disputationum de Medicina Nova Philippi Paracelsi.** Basle, 1572-73. 4 pts. in 1 vol.; & a dupl. vol. of pts. 1 & 2. but containing the 2 supp. pts. to pt. 2, without supp. to pt. 3. 4to. cont. blind-stpd. pig, 2 clasps; Dr. Walter Pagel copy. (S. Feb.7; 304) *Colombo.* £800

ERBADA, Ignacio de la
- **Las Fantasmas de Madrid y Estafermos de la Corte.** Salamanca, 1761-63. 3 vols. 4to. Vell. (DS. Apr.27; 2366) Pts. 75,000

ERCILLA Y ZUNIGA, Alonso de
- **Segunda parte de la Araucana.** Madrid, 1578. 4to. Body of text seems compl. [?], but title-p. reads only Segunda Parte, slip reading Primera pasted above it, final blank, lacks [?] 2 prelims. (replaced with 2 ll. from anr. edn.), some inner margin worming, cont. limp vell., due to uncertainty of completeness, w.a.f. (S. Nov.17; 20) *Quaritch.*

ERCKER, Lazarus
- **Aula Subterrancea ...** Frankfurt, 1736. Fo. Some browning, 1st. & last ll. wormed, cont. bds., rubbed. (GB. Nov.3; 1176) DM 1,300
- **Beschreibung allerfürnemisten Erzt und Bergwercksarten.** Frankfurt, 1598. 4to. Vell. (G. Sep.15; 2106) Sw. Frs. 950
- **Beschreibung Allerfürnemisten Mineralischen Ertz, und Berckwercks Arten ...** Prag, 1574. *1st. Edn.* Fo. Minimal browning, light soiling at beginning, old owner's note in lr. title margin, a little marginalia in old hand on a few pp., 6 ll. at end with old MS. chemical formulae, old vell., spine pasted with old paper. (R. Oct.11; 35) DM 19,000

ERCKMANN, Emile & Chatrian, Charles-Alexandre 'Erckmann-Chatrian'
- **Contes et Romans Populaires.** Ill.:- Théophile Schuler, Jundt, Riou, Benet, Bayard, Gluck. 1867. 2 vols. (*With:*) - **Romans Nationaux.** Riou & Fuchs. 1865. 2 vols. Together 4 vols. Lge. 8vo. Cont. hf. roan, corners. (HD. Mar.21; 149 & 150) Frs. 1,100

ERENBURG, Il'ya
- **Moi Parizh [My Paris].** Moscow, 1923. *1st. Edn., (5000).* Sm. ob. fo. Orig. decor. bds., slightly worn, d.-w., after design by El Lissitsky, sigd. El at corner of upr. cover, reprd. (S. Nov.21; 136) £300

ERGAS, Joseph
- **Divrei Yosef.** Livorno, 1742. (*With:*) **MORPURGO, Shimshon, of Ancona** - **Shemesh Tzedakah.** Venice, 1743. Pts. I & II in 1 vol. Together 2 vols. Fo. slight traces of spotting & soiling, vell.-bkd. bds., rubbed. (SPB. Feb.1; 42) $400
See— **CHAYUN, Nechemia—ERGAS, Joseph—SCHOLEM, Gershon**

ERHARD, J. Ch.
- **Neu Eröffnete Redschule.** Ill.:- Aegid. Touchemolin, etched by J. Ch. Erhard. Nuremb., Before 1822. 4to. Wide margin, hf. leath. gt., ca. 1860. (R. Oct.12; 1989) DM 3,300

ERLACH, Fr. K. Frh. von
- **Die Volkslieder der Deutschen.** Mannheim, 1834-36. *1st. Edn.* 5 vols. Lacks general register (1837),

hf. leath., decor. gt. spine; Hauswedell coll. (H. May 24; 1279) DM 660

ERMITAGE Revue Mensuelle de Litterature
Jun. 1906. 13th. Year no. 6. Orig. ptd. wraps. (LC. Oct.13; 392) £70

ERNST, Henri
- **Tapis de Pologne, de Lithuanie et de Yougoslavie.** - **Tapis de Finlande, Norvège, Suède.** Paris, ca. 1927. Together 2 portfos. Fo. 30 & 33 cold. plts., mntd. on art paper, each liby.-stpd. on blank verso, loose in pict. bds., cl.-bkd., linen ties. (SG. May 3; 156) $100

ERNST, Max
- **La Femme 100 Têtes.** Intro.:- André Breton. Paris, 1929. *Orig. Edn. 1st. Printing of ills.* 4to. Hf. roan, corners, by G. Gaucher, wrap. & spine, spine lightly faded. (HD. Nov.29; 133) Frs. 4,500
- - **Anr. Edn.** Paris, 1929. *(1000) numbered.* 4to. Orig. wraps., backstrip slightly worn. (S. Nov.21; 76) *Ars Libri.* £300
- - **Anr. Edn.** Ed.:- André Breton. Trans.:- Max Ernst. Paris, 1929. *Orig. Edn.* Sq. 4to. Numbered on tinted vell., Bradel bds., raw cl., pict. wrap. (HD. Dec.16; 115) Frs. 4,000
- - **Anr. Edn.** Ed.:- André Breton. Paris, 1929. *(1000) numbered on tinted vell.* 4to. Hf. mor. gt., orig. pict. wrap. bnd. in. (GB. May 5; 2450) DM 3,000
- **Histoire Naturelle.** Preface:- Hans Arp. Paris, 1926. *1st. Edn. (250).* Fo. Printers mark sigd. by artist, lightly foxed, 1 lf. with margin paper defect., loose in orig. hf. linen portfo., slightly rubbed, sm. hole in spine; Hauswedell coll. (H. May 24; 602) DM 3,800
- **Le Musée de l'Homme suivi de la Pêche au Soleil Levant.** [Paris, 1966]. *(333) numbered with monog. orig. etching.* 4to. Monogrammed orig. etching, orig. pict. wrap., orig. linen wrap. & s.-c. (GB. May 5; 2452) DM 800
- **Oeuvres de 1919 à 1936.** Contribs.:- Aragon, Breton, Eluard, Peret & others. Paris, 1937. *Orig. Edn.* Fo. Hf. mor., orig. pict. wraps. bnd. in; MS. dedication from author on hf.-title. (GB. Nov.5; 2418) DM 1,200
- **Rêve d'une Petite Fille qui Voulut entrer au Carmel.** Paris, 1930. *(1000) numbered.* 4to. Orig. wraps., unc., worn, upr. cover detchd. (S. Nov.21; 77) *Desk.* £330
- - **Anr. Edn.** Paris, 1930. *(40) numbered on Hollande Pannekoek.* 4to. Contents detchd. from bdg., pict. wraps., slightly discold. & chipped. (SG. Jan.12; 99) $550
- **Une Semaine de Bonté ou les sept Eléments Capitaux.** Paris, 1934. *1st. Edn. (800) numbered.* 4to. Orig. vari-cold. wraps., orig. s.-c.; MS. dedication & sig. of author on printer's mark. (GB. Nov.5; 2417) DM 3,600
- - **Anr. Copy.** 5 pts. 4to. Orig. cold. bds., orig. s.-c., slightly bumped, cover ill., spine & covers partly faded & spotted, 1 spine with sm. tear; Hauswedell coll. (H. May 24; 603) DM 3,200
- - **Anr. Copy.** Pts. 1-4 (of 5). 4to. Orig. cold. bds. (R. Oct.11; 195) DM 2,250

ERNST LUDWIG COLLECTION
- **Die Miniaturen-Sammlung. Seiner Königlichen Hoheit des Grossherzogs Ernst Ludwig von Hessen und Rhein.** Leipzig, 1917. *De Luxe Edn. (40).* Fo. Mor., rubbed. (SPB. Nov.30; 296) $275

ERNST LUDWIG PRESS
See— **BIBLIANA [German]**
See— **BINDING, R.G.**
See— **BOCK, A.**
See— **BUCH DER FABELN**
See— **GOETHE, Johann Wolfgang von**
See— **KLEUKENS, Chr. H.**
See— **LEON, G. von**
See— **NIEBERGALL, E.E.**
See— **PSALMS, PSALTERS & PSEUMES [German]**
See— **WAGNER, Richard**

ERXLEBEN, Johann Chr. P.
- **Anfangsgründe der Naturgeschichte.** Göttingen & Gotha, 1768. 2 vols. Cont. leath. gt. (R. Oct.12; 1531) DM 400

ES, N.J.A.P.H. van
- **De Twee Brigades Rijdende Artillerie onder de Republiek der Vreenigde Nederlanden, 1793-95.** [Arnhem, 1898]. 3 vols. (*With:*) - **Het Historisch Museum van het Korps Rijdende Artillerie, 1795-1898.** Arnhem, 1898. Vols. 2-5. Pres. copies to Prof. Dake, 2 sigd. 'van de schrijver'. (*With:*) - **Gedenkboek ter Herinnering aan de Teestviering van het Korps Rijdende Artillerie.** Arnhem, 1898. 1 vol. Sigd. 'present exemplaar van de Schrijver'. (*With:*) - **De Hippische Sport en het Korps Rijdende Artillerie, 1793-1908.** Arnhem, 1908. 2 vols. Together 10 vols. Fo. Plts. & ills. by H. van Papendracht, Krabbé, van Es, & others, many hand-cold., all in orig. decor. cl. gt. (CH. Sep.20; 51) Fls. 2,500

ES WAR EINMAL
Ill.:- Arthur Rackham. Zurich, 1920. *(1000) numbered.* 4to. Orig. cl. gt., slightly marked. (S. Dec.20; 570) *Crete.* £70

ESCHER, Maurits Cornelis
- **XXIV Emblemata, dat zijn Zinne-beelden.** Text:- A.E. Drijfhout. Bussum, 1932. *(300) numbered on Simili Japon van Gelder.* 4to. Orig. ill. wraps. (B. Oct.4; 570) Fls. 2,700

ESCOBAR Y MENDOZA, Antonius de
- **Liber Theologiae Moralis.** Lyon, 1659. Cont. roan, corners worn. (HD. Feb.22; 64) Frs. 1,300

ESMARCH, Fr.
- **Handbuch der Kriegschirurgischen Technik.** Hannover, 1877. *1st. Edn.* Cont. hf. leath. (BR. Apr.12; 654) DM 450

ESMERIAN, Raphael
- **Bibliothèque Raphaël Esmerian.** Paris, 1972-73. Pts. 1[-4] in 5 vols. (Lacks Pt. 5, but includes extra vol. for Pt.2). 4to. Sale catalogue, rubbings & photostats loosely inserted, orig. cl.; H.M. Nixon coll., with his sigs. & MS. notes. (BBA. Oct.6; 153) *Knuf.* £200
- - **Anr. Edn.** Paris, 1972-74. 5 vols. 4to. Sale catalogue, orig. cl. (BBA. Sep.8; 10) *Bennett & Kerr.* £70

ESNANS DE COURCHETET, Luc
- **Histoire des Negociations et du Traité de Paix des Pyrenees.** Amst. & Paris, 1750. 2 vols. 12mo. Cont. cf., spines faded. (HD. Feb.22; 65) Frs. 1,600

ESPAGNAC
- **Histoire de Maurice, Comte de Saxe, Duc de Courlande et de Semigalle ...** Utrecht, 1774. 2 vols. 12mo. Cont. roan, limp spines. (HD. Feb.22; 208) Frs. 1,600

ESPAGNET, Jean d'
[-] **Enchiridion Physicae Restitutae.** Paris, 1623. *2nd. Edn.(?).* 2 pts. in 1 vol. Errata lf., vell.; Dr. Walter Pagel copy. (S. Feb.7; 111) *Janssen.* £380
[-] - **Anr. Edn.** Paris, 1642. 2 pts. in 1 vol. !6mo. Some dampstains, cont. cf.; Dr. Walter Pagel copy. (S. Feb.7; 113) *Janssen.* £300

ESPINOLA, Nicolas
- **La Segunda Parte de Orlando. Con el Verdadero Sucesso de la Famosa Batalla de Roncesualles ...** Anvers, 1557. Mod. hf. cf. (LM. Mar.3; 173) B.Frs. 9,500

ESPOUY, Hector d'
- **Fragments d'Architecture Antique.** Paris, ca. 1897-1925. 4 vols. Atlas fo. 350 heliogravure plts., each liby.-stpd. on blank verso, loose in portfos., linen ties, Vol.4 in liby. cl. (SG. May 3; 157) $425

ESPRIT NOUVEAU. Revue Internationale d'Esthétique
[Paris, 1920 to 1922]. Nos. 1-17 (of 28) in 3 vols. Linen. (HT. May 9; 1786) DM 650

ESQUEMELING, Alexandre Olivier
See— **EXQUEMELIN or ESQUEMELING, Alexandre Olivier**

ESQUIROL, Jean Etienne Dominique
- **Die Geisteskrankheiten in Beziehung zur Medizin und Staatsarzneikunde.** Trans.:- Dr. W. Bernhard. Berlin, 1838. *1st. German Edn.* Advt. & errata ll.,

bds., cf. spine gt.; Dr. Walter Pagel copy. (S. Feb.7; 114) *Radziowsky.* £280
– **Des Maladies Mentales considerées sous les Rapports Medical Hygiénique et Médico-Légal.** Paris, 1838. *1st. Edn.* 3 vols. including Atlas. Tall 8vo. Owner's stps. on titles, plts. lightly foxed, atlas loose in bdg., qtr. mor., upr. cover of 1st. vol. stpd. 'Prix Esquirol/ Année 1880/ Mr Charles Vallon', worn. (SG. Mar.22; 112) $650

ESQUIROS, Alphonse
– **L'Angleterre et la Vie Anglaise.** Paris, ca. 1860's. Series 1-3: 3 vols. 12mo. Cont. elab. gt. mor., fore-e. pntg. in each vol. (SG. Nov.17; 227) $300

ESQUIVEL, Antonio Maria
– **Tratado de la Anatomia Pictórica.** Madrid, 1848. Lge. fo. Linen. (DS. Mar.23; 2097) Pts. 65,000

ESSAYS & OBSERVATIONS, Physical & Literary, read before a Society in Edinburgh
Edinb., 1754-56-71. Vols. I-III (all publd.). 22 engraved folding plts., similar cont. spr. cf.; Sir Ivar Colquhoun, of Luss copy. (CE. Mar.22; 101) £400

ESSEX HOUSE PRESS
See— ASHBEE, C.R.
See— ASHBEE, J.E.
See— COLERIDGE, Samuel Taylor
See— SHELLEY, Percy Bysshe
See— WHITMAN, Walt

ESSUILE, Comte d'
[–] **Traité Politique et Economique des Communes.** Paris, 1770. (*Bound with:*) SCOTT, Baron – Essai Patriotique ou Mémoire pour Servir à Prouver l'Inutilité des Communaux. Paris, 1775. Together 2 works in 1 vol. Cont. hf. roan, arms on spine, unc. (HD. Nov.9; 175) Frs. 1,700

ESTAMPE MODERNE
Paris, 1897-99. 2 vols. 4to. Orig. decor. cl. (SI. Dec.15; 201) Lire 4,000,000

ESTAMPES
Trans.:– R. Rey. Ill.:– after Braque, Brianchon, Chagall, Dufy & others. 1950. *(250) on holland.* Fo. Leaves, box ill. by Van Dongen. (HD. Jun.29; 68) Frs. 5,200

ESTIENNE, Charles
– **L'Agriculture et Maison Rustique ...** Paris, 1564. Wide margins, errata lf., occasional stains, red mor. by Huser, spine raised bands. (HD. Jul.6; 34) Frs. 38,000
– **La Dissection des Parties du Corps Humain diuisée en Trois Liures.** Paris, 1546. *1st. Fr. Edn.* Fo. Wide margin, some margin slits bkd. or strengthened, 1 text lf. torn across, 2 ll. ruled with red pen, some slight spotting, or margin soiling, lacks 2 pp., sm. hole in title, last lf. bkd. in lr. part, vell., ca. 1600, ties, lacks 1, soiled. (HK. May 15; 131) DM 3,800
– – **Anr. Edn.** Paris, 1965. *Facs. of the 1st. Fr. Edn. of 1546. (600).* Fo. 20 p. pamphlet 'L'Oeuvre de Charles Estienne et l'Ecole Anatomique Parisienne' by P. Huard & M.D. Grmek laid in, crushed mor. gt. extra. (SG. Oct.6; 153) $150
– **Paradoxes, ce sont Propos contre la Commune Opinion; debattuz en forme de Declamations Foreuses, pour exiter les Jeunes Esprits ...** Paris, 1554. Sm. 12mo. MS. annots., mor., spine decor.; Duc de La Vallière copy. (SM. Mar.7; 2018) Frs. 3,800

ESTIENNE, Charles & Liebault, John
– **XV Bücher von dem Feldbaw ...** Strassburg, 1588. Fo. Cont. blind-tooled pig over wood bds., rubbed, corners bumped, lr. cover brown spotted, 2 clasps, lacks ties. (HK. May 15; 132) DM 8,000
– **Maison Rustique; Or the Countrie Farme.** Trans.:– Richard Surflet. 1600. *1st. Engl. Edn.* 4to. Title relaid, lacks last lf. of index, prelims dampstained, later cf., rebkd. (TA. Feb.16; 355) £150
– – **Anr. Edn.** 1616. Sm. fo. D2 & D5 misbnd., Yy2 & Yy3 defect., title-p. & 1st. 284 pp. slightly wormed, old cf. [STC. 10549] (BS. May 2; 38) £120
– **Siben Bücher von dem Feldbau.** Strassburg, 1579. *1st. German Edn.* Fo. Lightly browned, some foxing or spotting in margins, soiling, some sm. margin slits, 3 ll. with longer margin tears, lacks 2 ll.

preface & 12 pp. with 6 woodcuts, cont-blind-tooled pig, very defect. (R. Apr.4; 1947) DM 1,200

ESTIENNE, Henri
– **Apologie pour Hérodote ou Traité de la Conformité des Merveilles Anciennes avec les Modernes.** La Haye, 1735. *New Edn.* 2 vols. in 3. Cont. red mor. gt., spines decor. (faded). (HD. May 3; 42) Frs. 1,400
– **Comicorum Graecorum Sententiae.** 1569. 24mo. Ruled, long-grd. red mor. by Rosa, gt.-decor., inner roulette, limp decor. spine, watered silk liners. (HD. Jan.26; 123) Frs. 1,200
– **L'Introduction au Traité de la Conformité des Mervilles Anciennes avec les Modernes.** [Genf.], 1566. *1st. Edn. 2nd. Printing.* Jansenist mor., gt. inner & outer dentelle, sigd. by Chambolle Duru. (D. Nov.23; 111) DM 4,000
– **A World of Wonders.** Edinb., 1608. 2 pts. in 1 vol. Fo. Foxing lf. at end, MS. ink sig. on title-p., sm. paper loss in lr. right corner B2, old cf., gt. embossed armoriäls on covers, worn. [STC 10554] (BS. May 2; 37) Fls. 110

ESTIENNE, Robert
– **Hebrea, Chaldaea. Graeca et Latina Nomina Virorum, Mulierum, Populorum, Idolorum, Urbium Flaviorum Caeterumque Locorum quae in Bibliis leguntur ...** Paris, 1537. Ruled copy, cont. cf., gt. decor., gt. centre motif, limp decor. spine, scratched. (HD. Dec.9; 34) Frs. 2,300

ESTOURMEL. Comte d'
– **Journal d'un Voyage en Orient.** 1844. *Orig. Edn. 1st. Printing.* 2 vols. 4to. Foxing, cont. hf. chagrin. (HD. Jun.29; 90) Frs. 3,200

ESTRADA, DIAZ Y LOPEZ
– **Caracteres del Establecimiento Tipográfico.** Madrid, 1865. Bdg. (DS. Mar.23; 2098) Pts. 20,000

ESTREES, Maréchal d'
[–] **Les Mémoires de la Regence de la Reine Marie de Medicis.** Paris, 1666. 12mo. Cont. cf. (HD. Feb.22; 66) Frs. 1,350

ETCHER, The
1879-82. Vols. 1-4. Fo. Hf. roan, Vol. 3 cover detchd. (SKC. Sep.9; 1803) £140

ETCHING CLUB
– **Etchings for the Art-Union of London.** Ill.:– Samuel Palmer & others. 1857. 4to. 30 engraved plts., plts. loose, orig. cl. gt., spine torn. (P. Sep.8; 5) *Heald.* £400

ETIQUETTE DU PALAIS IMPERIAL
Ed.:– Comte Louis-Philippe de Ségur & others. Paris, 1808. 18mo. Cont. spr. cf. gt., Napoleon I arms, spine decor., lightly rubbed; Napoleon's red liby stp. on title. (HD. May 4; 261) Frs. 10,000

ETRENNES DU PARNASSE pour l'Année Bissextile 1788
Paris, n.d. 18mo. Cont. gt. decor. mor., arms of Pierre Arnaud de la Briffe, watered silk end-ll. (HD. May 3; 44) Frs. 2,350

ETTENHARD, F.A. de
– **Compendio de los Fundamentos de la Verdadera Destreza y Filosofia de Las Armas.** Madrid, 1675. 4to. Cf. (DS. Nov.25; 2143) Pts. 32,000

ETTINGHAUSEN, Richard (Contrib.)
See— MEISS, Millard

EUCLID
– **Elementa Geometrica.** Venice, Erhard Ratdolt, 25 May 1482. *1st. Edn.* Fo. Lacks final blank, near-cont. annots., sm. repairs to lr. margins of 2 ll., sm. margin wormholes, few ll. spotted or soiled with early scribbles, some MS. marginalia cropped, later hf. cf. over marb. bds., early liby stp. of Count Hercules Silva (?), Stanitz coll. [BMC V, 285-86; Goff E113] (SPB. Apr.25; 153) $10,000
– – **Anr. Copy.** Fo. Black ptd. dedication letter, washed, wide lr. & side margin, some light browning in lr. margin, traces of old annots., slightly wormed in margin near end, lacks last lf. blank, leath. [H. 6693; BMC V, 285; Goff E113] (HK. Nov.8; 175) DM 15,000
– – **Anr. Edn.** Venice, 25 May 1482. *1st. Edn. 2nd.*

State of gathering a10. Fo. 137 ll. (of 138, lacks blank), woodcut border on a2r, woodcut capitals & diagrams thro.-out, some stains, sm. hole in a2, few marginal repairs, slight marginal worming, owners' inscrs., vell. antique. [Goff E113] (SG. Apr.26; 81) $4,800
– **Elementorum Libri XV. breviter Demonstrati.** Ed.:– I. Barrow. L., 1678. *4th. Barrow Edn.* (*Bound with:*) BARROW, Isaac – Lectio ... In qua Theoremata Archimedis de Sphaera et Cylindro, per Methodum Indivisibilium Investigata, ac breviter Demostrata exhibentur. L., 1678. *1st. Edn.* Together 2 pts. in 1 vol. Sm. 8vo. 2 headlines shaved, cont. spr. cf., minor wear; early owners inscr. of Henry Williams, bkplt. of Wilfrid Merton, 1945, with his (?) pencil notes on end-paper, Stanitz coll. (SPB. Apr.25; 154) $250
– **The First Six Books of the Elements of Euclid, ...** L., 1847. 4to. Spotted thro.-out, orig. vell., rubbed & soiled, w.a.f. (CSK. Dec.2; 18) £150
– **Op[er]a a Campano Interprete.** Venice, 22 May 1509. *4th. Edn.* Fo. Lacks final blank, some dampstaining, a little worming, slightly affecting text, title & last 4 ll. defect., 18th. C. vell. bds., slightly soiled. (S. Oct.11; 396) *Rix.* £180
– **La Perspectiva, y Especularia.** Madrid, 1585. *1st. Edn. in Spanish.* (*Bound with:*) GARCIA DE CESPEDES, Andres – Libro de Instrumentos Nuevos de Geometria. Madrid, 1606. *1st. Edn.* Together 2 works in 1 vol. 4to. Some soiling & stains, limp vell. (SPB. Dec.13; 671) $1,300
– **Ta Sozomena. Euclidis quae Supersunt Omnia.** Oxford, 1703. Fo. Last errata lf., browned thro.-out, cont. cf., worn. (BBA. May 3; 29) *Bickersteth.* £80

EUGEN, Prinz von Savoyen
– **Eugenius Nummis illustratus. Leben und Thaten des Grosen und Siegreichen Printzen Eugenii ...** Nuremb., 1726. Lightly browned or stained, later bds. (GB. May 3; 93) DM 400

EUGENIO DE S. FRANCISCO, Fr.
– **Relicario, Y Viaje, de Roma, Loreta, y Jerusalen ... ano de 1682.** Cadiz, [1693]. Sm. 4to. Title with portion of lr. margin cut away, some stains, cont. vell., soiled, some wear. (TA. May 17; 506) £60

EULER, Johann Albrecht
– **Enodatio Quaestionis quomodo Vis Aquae aliusve Fluidi cum Maximo Lucro ad Molas circum Agendas aliave Opera Perficienda impendi possit?.** Gottingen, 1754. Sm. 4to. Mor.-bkd. marb. bds.; Stanitz coll. (SPB. Apr.25; 155) $300

EULER, Leonhard
– **Dissertatio Physica de Sono.** Basel, [1727]. *1st. Edn.* Old wraps., upr. cover torn; Stanitz coll. (SPB. Apr.25; 156) $750
[–] **Geographischer Atlas.** Ill.:– N.F. Sauerbrey. Berlin, [1760]. Ob. fo. 44 copper-engraved maps, a few with tears & ink stains, title excised & pasted on, soiling, mostly in margin, MS. stp. on contents list, hf. vell., worn. (V. Sep.29; 10) DM 2,000
– **Institutiones Calculi Differentialis cum eius Usu in Analysi Finitorum ac Doctrina Serierum.** St. Petersb., 1755. *1st. Edn.* 2 vols. 4to. Foxing, mostly at beginning & end of each vol., 19th. C. mott. cf., gt. Signet arms, rebkd., orig. spines laid down, corners reprd.; Stanitz coll. (SPB. Apr.25; 157) $1,700
– **Institutionum Calculi Integralis.** St. Petersb., 1768-70. *1st. Edn.* 3 vols. 4to. Sm. liby. stp. on title versos, cont. cf.-bkd. bds. (C. Nov.9; 63) *Quaritch.* £300
– – **Anr. Edn.** St. Petersb., 1768-70-94. *1st. Edn.* 4 vols. including supp. 4to. Some minor discoloration, sm. liby stp. on verso of each title-p., cont. cf., spines gt., some slight wear; Stanitz coll. (SPB. Apr.25; 158) $1,800
– **Introductio in Analysin Infinitorum.** Lausanne, 1748. *1st. Edn.* 2 vols. 4to. Lacks dupl. frontis. in 2nd. vol., some light foxing & browning, cont. bds., unc., rebkd., corners renewed; Stanitz coll. (SPB. Apr.25; 159) $900
– – **Anr. Copy.** 2 vols. in 1. 4to. Both title ll. verso, port. & all plt. versos stpd. (1st. title lf. multi-stpd.), lacks engraved frontis., with Marians port., some light browning or foxing cont. leath. gt.,

EULER, Leonhard -*Contd.*

spine & lr. cover reprd. (R. Apr.4; 1516)
DM 1,300
- **Mechanica sive Motus Scientia analytice Exposita.** St. Petersb., 1736. *1st. Edn.* 2 vols. 4to. Light staining in Vol. I, some spotting, 19th. C. mott. cf., gt. Signet arms, rebkd., orig. spines laid down, corners reprd.; Stanitz coll. (SPB. Apr.25; 161)
$2,200
- - **Anr. Copy.** 2 vols. 4to. Old stp. on title, cont. hf. leath., Vol. 2 spine slightly brittle. (R. Oct.12; 1671)
DM 2,000
- **Methodus Inveniendi Lineas Curvas Maximi Minimive Proprietate Gaudentes.** Lausanne & Geneva, 1744. *1st. Edn.* (*Bound with:*) CLAIRAUT, Alexis-Claude – **Recherches sur les Courbes à Double Corbure.** Paris, 1731. *1st. Edn.* Together 2 works in 1 vol. 4to. Single wormhole thro.-out text & plts., cont. mott. cf., spine gt. (C. Nov.9; 66)
Pickering. £350
- - **Anr. Copy.** 4to. Title with 2 old names, some light browning, cont. leath. gt., slightly rubbed, head of spine defect. (R. Apr.4; 1518) DM 1,900
- **Scientia Navalis seu Tractatus de Construendis ac Dirigendis Navibus.** St. Petersb., 1749. *1st. Edn.* 2 vols. 4to. Light staining to lr. inner corner of Vol. I, some light browning & foxing, unc. edges slightly soiled & frayed, mod. cf.-bkd. bds., unc. & mostly unopened; Stanitz coll. (SPB. Apr.25; 164) $700
- **Theoria Motus Corporum Solidorum seu Rigidorum.** Rostock & Greifswald, 1765. *1st. Edn.* Sm. 4to. Slight browning, cont. cf. (C. Nov.9; 65)
Quaritch. £420
- - **Anr. Copy.** 4to. Light browning, cont. hf. sheep over marb. bds., spine gt., head of spine torn away; Stanitz coll. (SPB. Apr.25; 165) $950
- **Theoria Motuum Planetarum et Cometarum.** Berlin, [1744]. *1st. Edn.* 4to. Slight browning, cont. bds., unc. (C. Nov.9; 64) *Bozzolato.* £400
- **Théorie Complette de la Construction et de la Manoeuvre des Vaisseaux.** St. Petersb., 1773. Hf.-title, 10 folding plts., cont. cf., slightly rubbed. (S. May 21; 8) *Schumann.* £700
- **The True Principles of Gunnery** ... Trans.:– Hugh Brown. L., 1777. 4to. Cont. red mor. gt., spine decor. (C. Nov.9; 68) *Bickersteth.* £260

EURIPIDES
- **Opera Omnia.** Glasgow, 1821. 9 vols. Lge. 8vo. Crimson mor., gt.-tooled Greek-key borders, spines gt., inner dentelles gt., by Hodgson Singer, L'pool. (SG. Feb.16; 116) $375
- **Plays.** Trans.:– Gilbert Murray. Ill.:– R.A. Maynard & H.W. Bray. Gregy. Pr., 1931. (*500*) *numbered.* 2 vols. Fo. Orig. cl. gt., unc. (S. Nov.22; 276) *Makiya.* £160
- - **Anr. Copy.** 2 vols. Fo. Cl. (LH. Sep.25; 395)
$200
- **Supplices Mulieres, Iphigenia in Aulide et in Tauris.** Ed.:– Jer. Markland. Oxford, 1811. Lge. 4to. L.P., mod. antique-style cf. (SG. Feb.9; 222)
$225
- **Tragoedia Phoenissae.** Ed.:– H. Grotius, L. Casp. Valchenaer. Leiden, 1802. 4to. MS. note on endpaper, cont. vell. over wood bds., gt., gold-tooled decor., lacks ties. (D. Nov.24; 2443) DM 800

EUSEBIUS PAMPHILIUS, Bp. of Caesarea
- **Chronicon [with the continuations of Prosper Florentinus & M. Palmerius Pisanus. Edited by J.L. Santritter].** Venice, Erhard Ratdolt, 13 Sep. 1483. 4to. Lacks initial & final blank, 1st. 2 ll. slightly defect. & reprd. with some loss of text, some washing, vell. bdg. made out of a fragment of 16th. C. liturgical MS., some repairs. [Goff E117] (S. May 10; 275) *Duran.* £450
- **De Evangelica Praeparatione.** Treviso, Michael Manzolus, 12 Jan. 1480. Fo. Wide margins, lacks 1st. & last blanks, 1st. & last ll. reprd., mod. vell.; the Walter Goldwater copy. [BMC VI, 888; Goff E-121] (SG. Dec.1; 135) $550
- - **Anr. Copy.** Fo. Rubricated, lacks 2 blank ll., 19th. C. hf. chagrin; from Fondation Furstenberg-Beaumesnil. [HC 6702; BMC VI, 888; Goff E121] (HD. Nov.16; 55) Frs. 5,500
- - **Anr. Edn.** Venice, Bernardinus Benalius, 31 May 1497. Fo. Some margin dampstains, some

early marginalia, bds., cf. back; the Walter Goldwater copy. [BMC V, 376; Goff E-122] (SG. Dec.1; 136) $250
- - **Anr. Edn.** Venice, [Bartholomaeus de Zanis], 10 Nov. 1500. Fo. Bds., covered with incunable lf., vell. back; the Walter Goldwater copy. [BMC V, 435; Goff E-123] (SG. Dec.1; 137) $300
- **Ecclesiasticae Historiae Libri Decem.** Paris, 1659. 2 pts. in 1 vol. Fo. Title & text in Greek & Latin, hf.-title, cont. spr. cf., gt. spine; from John Evelyn's liby., pres. to him by Ralph Bohun, with inscr., Evelyn's press-mark A.21, & pencilled marks, notes & cross-references. (S. Nov.17; 21)
Quaritch. £520
- **Evangelicae Praeparationis** ... Paris, 1544. *1st. Edn.* Fo. Cont. stpd. cf., decor., jnts. reprd., clasps incompl., from Fondation Furstenberg-Beaumesnil. (HD. Nov.16; 121) Frs. 4,000
- **Historia Ecclesiastica.** Mantua, Johannes Schallus, not before 15 Jul. 1479. Fo. Fully rubricated, lacks final blank, some margin browning, 1 margin reprd., extensive marginalia, wood bds., blind-tooled cf. back; the Walter Goldwater copy. [BMC VII, 933; Goff E-127] (SG. Dec.1; 138)
$1,100
- **[Opera].** Ill.:– Holbein (title). Basilae, n.d. Fo. Sm. holes on title, cont. blind-stpd. pig. (HD. Jun29; 70) Frs. 2,000
See— JOANNES A CURRIBUS, Ferrariensis— EUSEBIUS PAMPHILIUS, Bp. of Caesarea— LACTANTIUS, Lucius Caecilius Firmianus

EUSEBIUS PAMPHILIUS, Bp. of Caesarea & others
- **The Auncient Ecclesiasticall Histories of the First Six Hundred Years after Christ, written [by] Eusebius, Socrates, & Evagrius.** Trans.:– Meredith Hanmer. 1585. Fo. Title-p. laid down & duststained, lacks last lf. (blank?), mod.mor. [STC 10573] (BBA. Feb.9; 1) *Vine.* £68

EUSTACHIUS, Bartolomaeus
- **De Ontleedkundige Plaaten.** Ed.:– A. Bonn. Ill.:– after Albinus. Amst., 1798. *New Edn.* Fo. Lacks 1 prelim lf. & 4 text ll., cont. hf. cf., spine gt., slightly rubbed. (VG. Mar.19; 266) Fls. 450
- **Opuscula Anatomica & de Dentibus.** Leiden, 1707. *2nd. Edn.* 3 pts. in 1 vol. 1 title lf. stpd., some light foxing, cont. vell. (R. Oct.12; 1391)
DM 2,150

EUSTOCHIUS, Laurentius
- **Dialogus, qui Inscribitur Studiosus** ... [Brescia, A. & J. Britannicus], after 1 Mar. 1488. 4to. Mod. wraps.; the Walter Goldwater copy. [GW 9482] (SG. Dec.1; 139) $1,600

EUTOCIOS, of Ascalon
- **In Archimedis Libros de Sphaera et Cylindro, atque alios Quosdam.** Basel, 1544. *1st. Edn.* 2 pts. in 1 vol. Fo. Lacks blank at end of each pt., mod. vell. (SPB. Dec.13; 622) $225

EUTROPIUS
See— CAESAR, Gaus Julius

EVAGRIUS
See— EUSEBIUS PAMPHILIUS, Bp. of Caesarea & others

EVANGILES, Les
- **Les Evangiles des Dimanches et Fêtes de l'Année.** Ed.:– Abbé Delaunay. Paris, 1864. 2 vols., including text vol. 4to. Inlaid mor., gt. dentelles, moire satin doubls. & end-ll., 2 elab. chased gt. clasps, text in qtr. mor.; copy no. 82, ptd. for Chevalier Louis de Brauz de Saldapenna. (SG. Nov.3; 124) $850

EVANS, A.H.
See— WILSON, S.B. & Evans, A.H.

EVANS, A.H. & Buckley, T.E.
- **A Vertebrate Fauna of the Shetland Isles.** Edinb., 1899. Orig. cl. gt. (PD. Dec.14; 110) £60

EVANS, Charles
- **American Bibliography: a Chronological Dictionary of all Books, Pamphlets & Periodical Publications printed in the United States of America.** Chic., priv. ptd., 1903-34. 12 vols. Lge. 4to. Buckram, spines gt., partly unc., some bdgs. soiled,

ex-liby.; each vol. numbered & sigd. by author. (SG. Sep.15; 129) $400
- - **Anr. Edn.** Chic., 1903-34. *Ltd. Edn., sigd.* 12 vols. 4to. Orig. cl., slightly soiled. (BBA. Apr.5; 284) *Hannas.* £330

EVANS, Charles Seddon
- **Cinderella.** Ill.:– Arthur Rackham. 1919. (*850*) *numbered & sigd. by artist.* 4to. Orig. bds., worn. (P. Mar.15; 361) *Marks.* £60
- - **Anr. Copy.** 4to. Cold. frontis., ills., orig. cl.-bkd. bds., slightly worn. (P. May 17; 378)
Primrose. £55
- - **Anr. Edn.** Ill.:– Arthur Rackham. L., [1919]. *1st. Trade Edn.* Slight margin darkening, decor. end-papers, decor. bds., cl. spine (darkened), bds. bumped at edges, corners just showing, orig. d.-w. rubbed & chipped. (CBA. Aug.21; 508) $120
- **The Sleeping Beauty.** Ill.:– Arthur Rackham. L., 1920. (*625*) *numbered, with additional ill., sigd. by artist.* 4to. Orig. parch.-bkd. bds. gt., slightly worn. (S. Dec.20; 583) *Rosenblatt.* £130

EVANS, George William
- **A Geographical, Historical & Topographical Description of Van Diemen's Land** ... L., 1822. Folding frontis. a little soiled & crushed, bds., qtr. cl. gt., unc. (KH. Nov.9; 595) Aus. $300

EVANS, Joan
- **English Jewellery from the Fifth Century A.D. to 1800.** L., [1921]. *1st. Edn.* Sm. fo. 34 plts., some foxing, gt.-lettered cl. (SG. Aug.25; 229) $280
- - **Anr. Copy.** Sm. fo. 34 plts. (2 cold.), ex-liby., cl. (SG. May 3; 160) $150
- **Pattern: A Study of Ornament in Western Europe from 1180 to 1900.** Oxford, 1931. *1st. Edn.* 2 vols. 4to. Gt.-decor. cl., spine ends worn. (SG. Aug.25; 138) · $160

EVANS, John
See— CORRY, John & Evans, John

EVANS, M.S.
See— WOOD, J. Medley & Evans, M.S.

EVANS, Marian 'George Eliot'
- **Adam Bede.** Edinb. & L., 1859. 3 vols. Gt.-panel. hf. cf., trimmed, orig. cl. bds. bnd. in. (PD. Aug.17; 168) £80
- **Complete Poems.** Intro.:– Matthew Browne. Boston, ca. 1900. (*200*) *numbered.* Lge. 8vo. Photogravure plts. on Japan vell., three-qtr. mor., elab. decor. gt. spine, by Bennett. (SG. Feb.16; 106)
$120
- **Daniel Deronda.** Edinb., 1876. *1st. Edn. 1st. Iss.* 4 vols. in orig. 8 pts. Sm. 8vo. Notice slip in pts. II-VII, & errata slip in books II & VI, orig. ptd. wraps., slight wear & some soiling, 2 spines frayed, other spines chipped at ends, 1 upr. wrap. loose. (SG. Nov.17; 53) $225
- - **Anr. Edn.** Edinb. & L., 1876. *1st. Edn. in orig. pts.* 8 pts. Notice slips inserted at end pts. 1-7 & erratum slips in pts. 3 & 6, orig. ptd. wraps., minor tears in 2 spines, cl. boxes; Fred A. Berne copy. (SPB. May 16; 261) $1,400
- - **Anr. Edn.** Edinb. & L., 1876. 4 vols. Errata slip for book II in Vol. 4, no advts., gt.-panel. hf. cf. (PD. Aug.17; 173) £60
- **Felix Holt the Radical.** Edinb. & L., 1866. *1st. Edn.* 3 vols. Hf.-titles, 4 pp. advt. at end of Vol. III, without 20 pp. catalogue, Carter 'A' bdg., orig. brown cl. (C. May 30; 146) *Maggs.* £220
- - **Anr. Copy.** 3 vols. 20-p. cat. in vol. 3, orig. cl., Carter's 'A' bdg. variant. (SPB. May 16; 262)
$650
- - **Anr. Copy.** 3 vols. Blackwood's 20-p. catalogue at end of Vol. III, publisher's cl., spines gt.-lettered, worn. (RO. Apr.23; 136) $175
- **The Mill on the Floss.** Edinb. & L., 1860. *1st. Edn.* 3 vols. Hf.-titles, 1 p. advt. in Vol. I, catalogue in Vol. III, titles & few ll. spotted, orig. cl. by Edmonds & Rennants with their ticket, slightly rubbed. (C. May 30; 147) *Pickering.* £200
- - **Anr. Copy.** 3 vols. Hf.-titles, 16 p. catalogue, cl. gt. by Hatchard, spines gt., gt. dentelles. (SG. Feb.16; 105) $175
- - **Anr. Edn.** Edinb. & L., 1860. 3 vols. Lacks advts., gt.-panel. hf. cf. (PD. Aug.17; 169) £65
- **Novels.** Edinb., 1880's. 8 vols. in 7. Sm. 8vo. Hf.

cf., spines gt. with fleurons. (SG. Feb.16; 107)
$170

- **Romola.** 1863. *1st. Edn.* 3 vols. 2 pp. advt., 2 ll. partly detchd., 1 with short tear in Vol. II, 6 ll. partly detchd. in Vol. III, sm. liby. stp. on titles, orig. cl., gt.-lettered spines (slightly rubbed), Buckram s.-c.; Michael Sadleir bkplt. (C. May 30; 148) *Jerndyce.* £280
- - **Anr. Copy.** 3 vols. Lacks advt. lf., gt.-panel. hf. cf., cl. spines bnd. in. (PD. Aug.17; 171) £98
- **Scenes of Clerical Life** ... Edinb. & L., 1858. *[1st. Edn.].* 2 vols. Gt.-panel. hf. cf., trimmed. (PD. Aug.17; 167) £85
- - **Anr. Copy.** 2 vols. Orig. cl.; Fred A. Berne copy. (SPB. May 16; 265) $375
- **The Works.** 1901. *Liby. Edn.* 10 vols. Panel. hf. cf. (PD. Oct.19; 59) £105
- - **Anr. Edn.** N.d. *Cabinet Edn.* 20 vols. Red hf. mor. (PD. Jun.13; 146) £150
- - **Anr. Edn.** Edinb. & L., n.d. 10 vols. Hf. cf. gt. (P. Sep.8; 52) *Woodruff.* £55
- - **Anr. Edn.** Ed.:- J.W. Cross. Edinb. & L., n.d. *Cabinet Edn.* 24 vols. Slight spotting & soiling, hf. mor. (SPB. May 17; 727) $450
- **Works, with Life.** Ed.:- J.W. Cross. Edinb., 1900's. *Warwick Edn.* 14 vols. 16mo. Three-qtr. cf., spines gt. (SG. Feb.16; 108) £110

EVANS, Maurice
- **The Aegis of England; or Triumphs of the Late War.** 1817. 1 vol. in 2. Lge. 8vo. Extra-ill. with 100 engraved ports., & letterpress titles, mor. gt. by Tout for Sotherans, with stps. on turndowns. (LC. Oct.13; 27) £80

EVANS, Oliver
- **The Young Mill-Wright's & Miller's Guide.** Octorara, PA., 1807. Browning & spotting, stitching loose in 1 place, cont. sheep, rubbed; Stanitz coll. (SPB. Apr.25; 167) $225

EVANS, Thomas
- **Old Ballads, Historical & Narrative, with Some of Modern Date.** 1784. *2nd. Edn.* 4 vols. 8vo. Engraved vig. on titles, offset, bkplts., hf.-titles, cont. marb. cf., spines gt.,. (BBA. Jul.27; 124) *Howes.* £80

EVANS, Walker
- **Message from the Interior.** N.Y., [1966]. *1st. Edn.* Sq. fo. Cl. (SG. Nov.10; 59) $120

EVANS CROW, Eyre
[-] **To-day in Ireland.** L., 1825. *1st. Edn.* 3 vols. 12mo. Hf.-titles, hf. mor., armorial motif on spine. (GM. Dec.7; 372) £85

EVELYN, John
- **Acetaria. A Discourse of Sallets.** L., 1699. *1st. Edn.* Lacks 1st. blank, browned, cont. panel. cf., spine worn. jnts. split. [Wing E3480] (S. Dec.8; 18) *Lewson.* £190
- **Memoirs for my Grand-son.** L., Nones. Pr., 1926. *Ltd. Edn. 1st. Iss.,* on Engl. H.M.P. Cont. cf.; bkplt. & inscr. of David Garnett. (BBA. Mar.21; 311) *Maggs.* £65
- **Numismata; a Discourse of Medals, Antient & Modern.** 1697. *1st. Edn.* Sm. fo. Cont. cf., rebkd. & reprd.; Sir George Shuckburgh bkplt. (BBA. Jun.28; 290) *Spring.* £70
- **Silva, or a Discourse of Forest Trees.** 1706. *4th. Edn.* Fo. Title-p. stained, cont. panel. cf., hinges brkn. (SKC. Mar.9; 1934) £70
- - **Anr. Edn.** Notes:- A. Hunter. 1776. 2 vols. 4to. Engraved frontis. port., 40 plts. (1 folding), folding table, cont. spr. cf., spines gt.; Sir Ivar Colquhoun, of Luss copy. (CE. Mar.22; 104) £320
- - **Anr. Copy.** 4to. Old cf., rebkd. (SKC. Nov.18; 1969) £100
- - **Anr. Copy.** 4to. Engraved port. (dampstained), & 40 plts., including 17 partly hand-cold., 1 folding, folding tables, some ll. slightly spotted or browned, cont. hf. cf., worn, covers detchd. (BBA. Nov.30; 104) *Demetzy.* £55
- - **Anr. Edn.** Ill.:- Bartolozzi (port), J. Miller & others. York, 1786. 2 vols. 4to. Cont. hf. cf., marb. bds., slightly rubbed. (SKC. Mar.9; 1935) £85
- - **Anr. Edn.** York, 1801. 2 vols. 4to. Hf. cf., spines defect. (CR. Jun.6; 156) Lire 320,000
- **Silva: or a Discourse of Forest Trees, to which is added Terra: a Philosophical Discourse of Earth.**

Ill.:- Bartolozzi (port.), Miller & others. York, 1786. 2 pts. in 1 vol. 4to. Slight spotting, cont. cf., covers detchd. (SKC. Nov.18; 1968) £75

EVERARD, Aegidius
- **Panacea; or the Universal Medicine ... Wonderfull Vertues of Tobacco.** 1659. *1st. Edn.* 8pp. booksellers' advts., title slightly defect. & soiled, 1 p. lacks corner, stpd. cf., slightly worn. (BS. Nov.16; 21) £240

EVERARD, Anne
- **Flowers from Nature.** L., 1835. Fo. 13 hand-cold. litho. plts., subscribers list with 4 names added in MS., cont. cl., spine ends rubbed. (C. Mar.14; 168) *Lindsay.* £270

EVERARD, H.S.C.
- **A History of the Royal & Ancient Golf Club St. Andrews 1754-1900.** Edinb., 1907. 4to. Orig. pict. cl., unc.; sigd. pres. copy from author. (PD. Oct.19; 97) £400

EVERHARDI, Nicolai
- **Consilia sive Responsa.** Frankfurt, 1577. Fo. Some dampstains, cont. blind-stpd. pig, soiled & worn. (TA. Sep.15; 427) £52

EVERITT, W.
- **Views in Bath & its Vicinity.** Bath, n.d. Ob. 8vo. Vig. title, 38 engraved views, 1 loose, orig. cl. gt. (P. Jun.7; 249) £170

EVERMANN, Barton Warren
See— JORDAN, David Starr & Everman, Barton Warren

EVERSON, William 'Brother Antoninus'
- **The Blowing of the Seed.** New Haven, 1966. *(200) numbered & sigd.* Lge. 8vo. Qtr. cf., bds.; inscr. to Kato & David Kherdian. (SG. Mar.1; 109) $150
- **The Dominican Brother.** [San Franc.], ca. 1965. 1 Vol. 4to. Self-wraps. *(With:)* - **John Chrysostom saint. Come, Then, Let us Observe the Feast [incipit title].** [Oakland, Calif.], n.d. 1 vol. Ob. 12mo. Fr.-fold unbnd.; sigd. by author. (SG. May 24; 53) $150
- **Eastward the Armies.** Ill.:- Tom Killion. [Torrance, Ca., 1980]. *(50) numbered on Hosho & Suzuki papers, sigd. by author & artist, with additional portfo. of 3 linocuts, 3 ptd. poems & an autograph MS. poem, each sigd. by author & artist.* Fo. Prospectus laid in, qtr. cl., decor. bds., s.-c. (SG. Mar.1; 112) $425
- - **Anr. Edn.** Ill.:- Tom Killion. [Torrence, Calif.], 1980]. *(200) numbered on Masa & Suzuki papers, sigd. by author & artist.* Fo. Prospectus laid in, qtr. cl., decor. bds., s.-c. (SG. May 24; 63) $175
- **The Illiterati.** Wyeth, Ore.; Waldport, Ore.; Pasadena, Calif., 1943; 1944-45; 1948. Nos. 1-5 (all publd.?). Sm. 4to. Pict. wraps., little chipped. (SG. May 24; 43) $250
[-] **The Last Crusade.** [Berkeley, 1969]. *Lettered out-of-series copy.* Sm. fo. Qtr. sheep., linen covers, acetate d.-w.; pres. copy, inscr. (SG. Mar.1; 115) $325
- - **Anr. Edn.** [Berkeley, 1969]. *(165) numbered & sigd.* Sm. fo. Qtr. sheep., linen covers, unlettered acetate d.-w.; inscr. (SG. May 24; 58) $100
- **The Masculine Dead: Poems, 1938-1940.** Prairie City. Ill. [1942]. *(Ca. 200).* Errata slip, cl.; inscr. to David Kherdian (SG. May 24; 41) $800
- **Poems Mcmxlii.** [Waldport, Ore.], 1945]. *(500).* Erratum slip tipped in, pict. wraps., trifle soiled; inscr. to David Kherdian. (SG. May 24; 46) $140
[-] **The Poet is Dead: A Memorial for Robinson Jeffers.** San Franc., Auerhahn Pr., 1964. *(200) sigd.* 4to. Qtr. lev., bds., d.-w.; inscr. to David Kherdian. (SG. Mar.1; 116) $200
- - **Anr. Copy.** 4to. Qtr. lev., bds., unc. (SG. Mar.1; 117) $150
- **A Privacy of Speech.** Ill.:- Mary Fabilli. Berkeley, Equinox Pr., 1949. *(100).* 4to. Qtr. vell., soiled, pict. bds., unc.; inscr. to Kato & David Kherdian. (SG. Mar.1; 118) $1,100
- **Psalmus I[-VII].** Oakland, Calif.?, the author?, 1952?. Fo. Unsewed & unbnd. (SG. May 24; 49) $650
- **Rattlesnake August.** Ill.:- Hans Burkhardt. [Northridge, Ca.], Santa Susana Pr., 1978. *(50) numbered & sigd. by author & artist.* Lge. 4to.

Sheets laid in cl. folding-case as iss. (SG. Mar.1; 120) $325
- **The Residual Years: Poems 1940-41.** [Waldport, Ore, The Untide Pr., 1944]. *(330) sigd.* Sm. 4to. Unlettered pict. wraps., owner's name on wraps. (SG. Mar.1; 121) $110
- **River-Root: A Syzygy for the Bicentennial of these States.** [Berkeley], 1976. *(50) Hors de Commerce, lettered 'Q', sigd.* 4to. Qtr. cf., pict. bds.; 4 lines of autograph verse. (SG. May 24; 61) $275
- **San Joaquin.** Los Angeles, Ward Ritchie Pr., 1939. *(100).* Sm. 4to. Qtr. cl., pict. bds.; inscr. to Kato & David Kherdian. (SG. Mar.1; 124) $1,100
- **Single Source: The Early Poems.** Intro.:- Robert Duncan. Berkeley, Oyez, [1966]. *(25) numbered & sigd.* Qtr. mor., pict. bds., d.-w. (SG. Mar.1; 125) $350
- **The Springing of the Blade.** Reno, Black Rock Pr., 1968. *(180) sigd.* 4to. Cl. (SG. Mar.1; 127) $110
- **There Will Be Harvest.** [Berkeley, Calif., 1960]. *(200).* 4to. Fr.-fold unbnd., as iss; sigd. (SG. May 24; 52) $110
- **These Are the Ravens.** San Leandro, Ca., 1935. Self-wraps.; inscr. to David Kherdian. (SG. Mar.1; 128) $800
- - **Anr. Copy.** Self-wraps., cover-title trifle chipped. (SG. May 24; 40) $275
- **Triptych for the Living.** Ill.:- Mary Fabilli. [Oakland, Calif.], [the author for] Seraphim Pr., 1951. *(Less than 100).* 4to. Unlettered limp goat suede, bnd. by author; inscr. to David Kherdian. (SG. May 24; 48) $800
- **Waldport Poems.** Waldport, Ore., 1944. *(975).* Lge. 8vo. Pict. wraps., slightly chipped, little stained, former owner's name on cover; inscr. to David Kherdian. (SG. May 24; 44) $110
- **X War Elegies.** Waldport, Ore, 1943. *(1000).* Wraps. serigraphed in black & yellow (1st. bdg.), trifle faded; inscr. to David Kherdian. (SG. May 24; 42) $425
- **War Elegies.** Waldport, Ore, Untide Pr., 1944. *(30) numbered & sigd.* Cf. (SG. Mar.1; 130) $350
- **The Year's Declension.** Berkeley, 1961. *(100) sigd. (50) publd.* Sm. fo. Emblematic bds. (SG. Mar.1; 131) $325

EVERSON, William 'Brother Antoninus' (Contrib.)
See— SELMA UNION HIGH SCHOOL

EVIDENCE BEFORE THE SELECT COMMITTEE ... on the State of the Coal Trade Newcastle, 1829. Orig. bds. (P. Jun.7; 324) £210

EVREINOV, Nikolai
- **Teatr dlya Sebya [Theatre for Oneself].** Ill.:- N. Kul'bin & Annenkov. Petrograd, 1911-16. 3 vols. 4to. Orig. wraps., unc. (S. Nov.21; 137)
Sutherland. £180

EWALD, Ernst
- **Farbige Decorationen.** Berlin, 1887. Fo. Chromolitho. plts., some double-p., detchd., orig. hf. cl., worn. (S. Apr.30; 183) *Gilbert.* £190
- - **Anr. Edn.** Berlin, 1889; 1896. 2 vols. Atlas fo. 160 chromolitho. plts., & 1 uncold. plt., each liby.-stpd. on blank verso, loose in ptd. bd. folders, linen ties. (SG. May 3; 161) $750

EXACT BOOK OF MOST APPROVED PRESIDENTS ... 1663. In Latin & Engl., some spotting, few minor margin defects., old sheep, some wear. [Wing E3628] (TA. Apr.19; 378) £90

EXCELLENCY (The) of the Pen & Pencil exemplifying the uses of them ... Drawing, Etching, Engraving ... L., 1688. *2nd. Edn.* Frontis. margins strengthened, fore-edge of 1 ill. & 1 headline shaved, dampstain & margin repairs on final ll. affecting a few letters, slight browning, mor. [Wing E 3779A] (C. Nov.9; 69) *Marlborough.* £320

EXEMPLEN DES GHELOOFS
See— ROESBRUGGE, V.M. van—EXEMPLEN DES GHELOOFS

EXERCICE SPIRITUEL
Ill.:- Moncornet. Paris, 1649. 12mo. Ills. cont. cold. & heightened with gold, 17th. C. red mor.,

EXERCICE SPIRITUEL -*Contd.*

probably by Rocelet factory, fanfare decor. (HD. Mar.21; 80) Frs. 1,600

EXHIBITION OF MODERN BOOKBINDINGS BY THE CHIEF EUROPEAN CRAFTSMEN, at the Caxton Head
L., 1891. (*With:*) INTERNATIONAL BOOK-BINDING EXHIBITION BY THE CHIEF CRAFTSMEN from all Parts of the World, at the Caxton Head L., 1894. Together 2 vols. 4to. Cold. plts., a few spots, orig. wraps. bnd. in, mor. gt. by Morreli; the exhibitors' (J. & M.L. Tregaskis) copies with bnd. in & mntd. reviews & notices & additional ills. of the bdgs., the 2nd with photographs of all but 2 of the exhibits. (S. May 1; 374) *Maggs*. £260

EXPILLY, Claude
- Poemes. Grenoble, 1624. *2nd. Edn.* 4to. Dedication lf. supplied in photostat, 17th. C. cf. gt. (SG. Oct.27; 99) $130

EXPOSITIO SEQUENTIARUM. Textus cum Optimo Commento
Cologne, H. Quentell, [1496]. (*Bound with:*) **EXPOSITIO HYMNORUM. Hymnarius cum Expositione et Commento** Cologne, H. Quentell, 1496. Together 2 works in 1 vol. 4to. Rubricated, cont. stpd. cf. over wood bds., richly decor., spine reprd., leath. & brass clasps; from Fondation Furstenberg-Beaumesnil. [HC 14686 & 6788; BMC I, 286] (HD. Nov.16; 23) Frs. 11,000

EXQUEMELIN or ESQUEMELING, Alexandre Olivier
- Bucaniers of America. L., 1684. *1st. Edn. in Engl.* 3 pts. in 1 vol. 4to. Lacks 2 prelims., cont. cf., scuffed. [Sabin 23479] (C. Nov.9; 136) *Faupel*. £110
- - Anr. Edn. L., 1684-85. 4 pts. in 2 vols., bnd. in 1. 4to. 11 plts., including 4 ports. & 3 folding maps (1 laid down), text engrs., mostly full-p. maps, woodcuts, red mor. gt., gt. dentelles, by Pratt; J.H. Bates bkplt. [Wing E3896-97] (SG. Apr.26; 82) $950
[-] Historie der Boecaniers, of Vreybuters van America. Amst., 1700. 4to. Added engraved title, folding map with sm. repair, red crushed lev., minor wear. [Sabin 23469] (SG. Apr.5; 71) $250
[-] Piratas de la America y Luz a la Defensa de las Costas de Indias Occidentales. Trans.:– Buena-Maison. Madrid, 1793. *3rd. Spanish Edn.* Margin slightly browned, cont. leath. [Sabin 23474] (D. Nov.23; 1319) DM 1,000

EXSTEENS, Maurice
- L'Oeuvre Gravé et Lithographié de Félicien Rops. Paris, 1928. (*500*) *numbered.* 4 vols. & portfo. of reproductions of plts. 694-807 & 942-959. Sm. fo. Ptd. wraps., spine ends chipped, unc. & unopened. (SG. Jan.26; 278) $275
- - Anr. Edn. Paris, 1928. 4 vols. in 1. Fo. Hf. leath. (SPB. Nov.30; 66) $400

EXTON, John
- The Maritime Dicaeologie or Sea Jurisdiction of England. L., 1664. *1st. Edn.* Fo. Cont. gt.-panel. cf.; owner's inscr. of Sir John Narbrough on front free end-paper. [Wing E 3902] (C. Nov.9; 10) *Quaritch*. £450

EYB, Albertus de
- Ob Einem Mann sei zu Nehmen ein Ehelich Weib oder Nicht. [Augsburg, Guenther Zainer], ca. 1473. Fo. Wide margins, rubricated initials, lacks? 1 lf. from last gathering, some age-stains, etc., disbnd.; the Walter Goldwater copy. [BMC II, 320; Goff E-181] (SG. Dec.1; 140) $1,300

EYBESCHUETZ, Yehonatan
- Sefer Kreiti u-Pleiti. Altona, 1743. *1st. Edn.* Sm. fo. Mild browning or dampstaining, title reprd., old pol. cf., chafed & worn, spine brittle & chipped. (SG. Feb.2; 176) $150

EYCK, P.N. von
See— ROYEN, J.F. von & Eyck, P.N. von

EYRE, Edward John
- Journals of Expeditions of Discovery into Central Australia. L., 1845. 2 vols. Lacks map, some slight stains in margin of some plts., rebnd. mor. (CA. Apr.3; 42) Aus. $650
- - Anr. Edn. Adelaide, 1964. *Facs. Edn.* 2 vols. Orig. cl. (KH. Nov.8; 148) Aus. $110
- Observations made at Paris during the Peace. Bath, 1803. Vol. 1 (all publd.). Cont. cf. gt. [by Kalthoeber?]; Beckford copy, with 2 pp. of notes in his hand, C.R. Spencer's bkplt. & his purchase note. (BBA. Sep.29; 164) *Finch*. £110

EYRE, Francis
[–] A Few Remarks on the History of the Decline & Fall of the Roman Empire. Relative Chiefly to the two last chapters. L., 1778. *1st. Edn.* (*With:*) GIBBON, Edward [–] A Vindication of Some Passages in the Fifteenth & Sixteenth Chapters of the History of the Decline & Fall of the Roman Empire. L., 1779. *1st. Edn.* Lf. M3 a cancel, a few stains, O1 torn. Together 2 vols. Orig. wraps., unc., mod. cl. sleeves & qtr. mor. folding box, 1st. work mis-attributed to Davis on sleeve & box; Thomas B. Stevenson copy. (CNY. Dec.17; 565) $750

EYRIES, J.
- Abrégé des Voyages Modernes depuis 1780 jusqu'à nos Jours ... Paris, 1822-24. 14 vols. in 7. Slight foxing, qtr. cf. (KH. May 1; 243) Aus. $300

EYRIES, Jean – Baptiste Benoît
See— ORBIGNY, Alcide de & Eyries, Jean Baptiste Benoît

EYTELWEIN, Johann Albert
- Handbuch der Hydrostatik. Berlin, 1826. *1st. Edn.* Stiff marb. wraps.; Stanitz coll. (SPB. Apr.25; 169) $175
- - Anr. Copy. Erased stp. on title, some foxing, cont. hf. leath. gt. (R. Oct.12; 1736) DM 420
- Handbuch der Mechanik Fester Körper und der Hydraulik. Berlin, 1801. *1st. Edn.* Slight foxing, 19th. C. cf.-bkd. bds., spine worn; J.A. Roebling's copy with his sig. on title-p., Stanitz coll. (SPB. Apr.25; 170) $475
See— GILLY, D. & Eytelwein, J.A.

F., J.J.
- Der Hermetische Nord-Stern oder Getreuer Unterricht ... wie zu der Hermetischen Meisterschaft zu Gelangen ... und sechs Tractaetlein Philippi Aureoli Th. Bombash ab Hochenhelm. Frankfurt & Leipzig, 1771. Inkstain on some blank corners, cf., worn; Dr. Walter Pagel copy. (S. Feb.7; 297) *Weiner*. £250

FABER, J.J.
- Specimen Zeli Justi Theologici contra Maleficos & Sagas. Stuttgart, 1667. Title with stp., cont. vell. (R. Oct.12; 1546) DM 1,200

FABER & Faur, G.
- Campagne de Russie, 1812, d'après le Journal Illustré d'un Témoin Oculaire. Intro.:– Armard Dayot. Paris, n.d. Cont. hf. roan. (HD. Jan.27; 32) Frs. 1,100

FABERT, Abraham
- Les Remarques sur les Coustumes Général du Duché de Lorraine ... Ill.:– S. Leclerc. Metz, 1657. Fo. Stains, cont. marb. cf., decor. spine, defects. (HD. Dec.9; 35) Frs. 2,900

FABIAN, Bentham
- Australia; Being a Brief Compendium ... The Whole forming a Complete Hand-Book or Guide to the Gold Regions, intended for intended for the Use of Merchants, Shipmasters, Intendent Emigrants, & Others ... N.Y., 1852. An amending pastedown dtd. 15 Nov. 1852 added at p. 113, mod. hf. mor., wraps. bnd. in. (KH. May 1; 245) Aus. $300

FABRE, Jean Antoine
- Essai sur la Manière la plus Avantageuse de Construire les Machines Hydrauliques, et en Particulier les Moulins à Bled ... Paris, 1783. *1st. Edn.* 4to. Hf.-title, cont. mott. sheep, some scraping, chipping to head of spine; Stanitz coll. (SPB. Apr.25; 171) $225
- Essai sur la Théorie des Torrens et des Rivières. Paris, 1797. *1st. Edn.* 4to. Cont. bds., slightly worn. (R. Oct.12, 1737) DM 400

FABRE, Jean-Henri
- Souvenirs Entomologiques. Paris, 1923-24. Lge. 8vo. 176 plts., hf. cf., unc., slightly faded, wraps. (HD. Mar.19; 47) Frs. 2,100

FABRI, A.
- Scherben. Ill.:– H.A.P. Grieshaber. Köln, 1964. *(140).* Fo. Printers mark sigd. by artist, woodcuts ptd. on black Orion bds. in gold & copper, loose ll., orig. wraps., orig. bd. box. (H. May 23; 1246) DM 1,200

FABRI, H.
- Tractatvs dvo:Qvorvm prior est de Plantis, et de Generatione Animalivm; posterior de Homine. Paris, 1666. 2 pts. in 1 vol. With 2 folding plts., lightly browned thro.-out, cont. pig, roll-tooled decor., brass clasps, lightly spotted, slightly rubbed, top of spine painted over. (HT. May 8; 536) DM 440

FABRI DE HILDEN, Guillaume
- Observations Chirurgiques. Geneva, 1669. 4to. 17 engraved plts., slight worming, stained, cont. cf., spine defect. (BBA. Mar.21; 42) *M.Phelps*. £65

FABRICII, Pr.
- Delle Allvsioni, Imprese et Embleni sopra la Vita, Opere, et Attioni di Gregorio, XIII. Pontefice Wassimo Libri VI ... Ill.:– Natal Bonifazio. Rome, [1588]. Sm. fo. Lacks 2 ll. & 3 etchings, title soiled & with 2 margin repairs, some browning or staining, cont. limp vell., slightly spotted & rubbed. (HK. Nov.8; 177) DM 1,700

FABRICIUS, Jo. Albertus
- Bibliotheca Graeca. Hamburg, 1708-28. 14 vols. 4to. (*With:*) - Bibliotheca Latina. Leipzig, 1773-74. 3 vols. 8vo. Together 17 vols. Rather browned, cont. vell., soiled. (BBA. Nov.30; 59) *Cressey*. £160

FABRICIUS AB AQUAPENDENTE, Hieronymus
- De Formatione ovi et Pulli Tractatus. Ed.:– Joannes Prevotius. Padua, 1621. *1st. Edn.* Fo. Errata lf., E2 & E3 & 1st. of 4 plts. at end in photo facs., 2 plts. shaved, sm. hole thro.-out most of book, unbnd.; Dr. Walter Pagel copy. (S. Feb.7; 117) *Maggs*. £320
- Opera Omnia Anatomica et Physiologica. Ed.:– B.S. Albini. Leiden, 1738. Fo. Port., 61 plts., some folding, hf.-title, lf. with directions to binder, hf. cf.; Dr. Walter Pagel copy. (S. Feb.7; 118) *Israel*. £680
- Operationes Chirurgicae. Venice, 1619. *1st. Edn.?.* 2 pts. in 1 vol. 1st. title dust-soiled, minor margin defects. (*Bound with:*) MERCADO, Luis - Institutiones Chirurgicae. Frankfurt, 1619. Together 2 works in 1 vol. Fo. Vell., dtd. 1621, soiled. (SG. Mar.22; 113) $500
- Wund DEN Art znei. Trans.:– J. Scultetus. Nürnberg, 1673. 2 vols. in 1. 4to. Lightly browned, cont. vell. (R. Oct.12; 1393) DM 2,700

FABRICZY, C. von
- Italian Medals ... Trans.:– Mrs. Gustavus W. Hamilton. L., 1904. Sm. 4to. Cont. red hf. mor. (S. May 1; 464) *Spring*. £50

FABRIS, Salvatore
- Scienza e Pratica d'Arme. Lipsia, 1677. Fo. In Italian & Dutch, browned, later vell. (SI. Dec.15; 49) Lire 650,000

FADEN, William
- Atlas Minimus Universalis ... L., 1798. Ob. 12mo. Engraved thro.-out, hand-cold. title, 54 (of 55) maps, hand-cold. in outl., piece cut from upr. margin of title, tears reprd. on title & 1st. list of maps, cont. cf. (C. Nov.16; 207) *Coss*. £160
- General Atlas. Ca. 1800. Lge. 4to. 50 double-p. & folding hand-cold. maps, most slightly affected by damp at lr. margins, some minor repairs, general chart of Cook's Voyages closely cropped top & bottom, recent hf. mor. (TA. Sep.15; 62) £660
[–] [A New General Atlas]. Ill.:– by or after H. Roberts, Laurie & Whittle, C.C. Lous, & others. L., [Maps dtd. 1790-99]. Lge. fo. 51 lge. double- or full-p. engraved mapsheets (only 50 called for in ptd. contents list), most hand-cold. in wash or outl., some dampstaining affecting engraved surfaces, a few margins strengthened, some dust soiling or slight offsetting, 1 or 2 mapsheets cut close affecting

neatlines, mod. hf. cf., orig. spine label preserved. (S. Dec.1; 206)   *Burgess.* £540
– – **Anr. Edn.** Ill.:– by or after H. Roberts, T. Kitchen, C.C. Lous, J. Cary, & others. L., [maps dtd. 1790-1806]. Lge. fo. 55 lge. double- or full-p. engraved mapsheets, most hand-cold. in wash & outl., lacks title, some slight offsetting, a few creases, 1 or 2 maps detchd., 1 or 2 cut close affecting some imprints, cont. hf. russ., worn 1 cover detchd. (S. Dec.1; 209)   *Burgess.* £760

FAGAN, Louis
– **Collectors' Marks.** Ed.:–M. Einstein & M.A. Goldstein. St. Louis, Laryngoscope Pr., 1918. *(300) numbered on Japan vell.* Sm. 4to. Cl., unopened. (SG. Sep.15; 96) $120

FAGNIEZ, Gustave
– **Le Père Joseph et Richelieu.** Paris, 1844. 2 vols. Sewed, spines brkn. (HD. Feb.22; 68)   Frs. 1,600

FAHEY, Herbert
– **Early Printing in California. From its Beginning in the Mexican Territory to Statehood.** San Franc., [Grabhorn Pr.], 1956. *(400).* Fo. Orig.? cl., unc., plain paper wraps. (RO. Dec.11; 102) $130

FAHEY, Jerome
– **The History & Antiquities of the Dioceses of Kilmacduagh.** Dublin, 1893. *1st. Edn.* Cl. (GM. Dec.7; 130)   £75

FAHNE, A.
– **Bilder aus Frankreich von Jahre 1831.** Berlin, 1835. Slightly foxed, spined, unc. (R. Apr.5, 2937)   DM 5,400

FAHY, K.
See— CRAIG, C. & others

FAIL, Noël du, Seigneur de la Herissaye
– **Les Contes et Discours d'Eutrapel.** Rennes, 1603. 12mo. Jansenist red mor. gt. by Capé, Masson-Debonnelle Sr. (HD. Mar.27; 11)   Frs. 1,900

FAIRBAIRN, James
– **Book of Crests.** Edinb., 1892. 2 vols. 4to. Qtr. mor. gt. (P. Dec.8; 85)   *Traylen.* £90
– – **Anr. Copy.** 2 vols. 4to. 229 plts., title slightly spotted, hf. mor., worn. (S. Apr.10; 354)
                                          Donald. £65
– – **Anr. Copy.** 2 vols. Sm. fo. 229 litho. plts., orig. mor.-bkd. cl. gt. (SG. Aug.4; 109) $220
– – **Anr. Copy.** 2 vols. 4to. Some foxing, purple hf. mor. (CBA. Dec.10; 258) $130
– – **Anr. Edn.** 1905. *4th. Edn.* 2 vols. 4to. Orig. cl. gt. (P. Sep.29; 317)   *Whittle.* £130

FAIRBAIRN, William
– **Treatise on Mills & Millwork.** L., 1861-63. *1st. Edn.* 2 pts. in 2 vols. hf.-title, slight spotting, orig. cl., Vol. 2 worn, inner hinge reprd., rubbed; Andrew Wyllie bkplt. in Vol. 1, Stanitz coll. (SPB. Apr.25; 172) $300

FAIRBRIDGE, Dorothea
– **Historic Houses of South Africa.** 1922. 4to. Orig. cl. gt. (LC. Oct.13; 28)   £70

FAIRFAX, Sir Thomas
– **Two letters from ... Sir Thomas Fairfax to the Right Honourable House of Peeres.** 1647. Title soiled, some stains in text, hf. mor., outer margin trimmed, rubbed. *(With:)* – **The Good & Prosperous Successe of the Parliaments Forces in Yorkeshire.** 1642. Title & 6 pp. text, browned, last lf. cropped, hf. mor. (P. Feb.16; 176)   £55

FAIRY GARLAND, A
Ill.:– Edmund Dulac. L., 1928. *(1000) numbered & sigd. by artist.* 4to. Qtr. vell., unc. (SKC. Nov.18; 1834)   £75
– – **Anr. Copy.** 4to. HP. vell. & cl., edges & endpapers lightly foxed. (CBA. Aug.21; 192) $300
– – **Anr. Edn.** Ill.:– Edmund Dulac. L. & N.Y., 1928. *(1000) numbered & sigd. by artist.* Vell.-bkd. bds., boxed. (LH. Sep.25; 527) $140

FALCON, Refael Moshe
– **Sefer Yashir Moshe.** Salonika, 1807. *1st. Edn.* Sm. fo. Includes 3-lf. index not noted by Friedberg, some dampstains, mod. str.-grd. mor. (SG. Feb.2; 177) $175

FALCONER, Capt. Richard (Pseud.)
See— CHETWOOD, William Rufus, attributed to

FALCONER, Thomas
– **The Oregon Question; or, a Statement of the British Claims to the Oregon Territory.** N.Y., 1845. *1st. Amer. Edn.* Marb. wraps., cl. s.-c.; the Rt. Hon. Visc. Eccles copy. [Sabin 23728] (CNY. Nov.18; 103) $150
[–] **The San Juan Boundary Question** [caption title]. [Usk, Monmouthshire, 1846?]. *1st. Edn.* MS. copy (probably in Falconer's hand) of a letter to Lord Ashburton & a 1 p. pencil sketch by Falconer bnd. in, mor. by Zaehnsdorf; the Rt. Hon. Visc. Eccles copy. (CNY. Nov.18; 104) $1,000

FALCONER, William
– **The Shipwreck.** Ill.:– Thomas Kitchin & J. Bayly. L., 1762. *1st. Edn.* 4to. Folding plts. offset, 1 with sm. repair at fold, old ink inscr. on title, 19th. C. hf. mor. gt.; bkplts. of George Grant Francis & H. Buxton Forman, Frederic Dannay copy. (CNY. Dec.16; 130) $180
– – **Anr. Edn.** Ill.:– Robert Dodd. 1811. 4to. Slight spotting, cont. hf. russ. (SKC. Jan.13; 2208) £80
– **An Universal History of the Marine.** L., 1776. 4to. Cont. cf.; W. Constable ex-libris. (HD. Mar.9; 80)   Frs. 1,400

FALDA, Giovanni Battista
– **Le Fontane di Roma.** Rome, 1691. *1st. Edn.* 4 pts. in 1 vol. Ob. 4to. Engraved titles, 103 plts., including 4 dedication ll., 2 laid down, red mor. by Sizier, gt. dentelle border, spine gt. (C. Dec.9; 45)
                                          Hammond. £1,800
– **Li Giardini di Roma.** Rome, ca. 1683?. *1st. Iss., with plts. unnumbered.* Ob. fo. Engraved title, 20 plts., some slight discoloration, 18th. C. stiff vell. (C. Dec.9; 46)   *Weinreb.* £600
– **Il Nuovo Teatro delle Fabriche et Edificii in Prospettiva di Roma Moderna.** Rome, 1665-99. 4 vols. in 1. Ob. fo. 142 engraved plts., including titles & dedication ll., plts. in Vol. 2 early iss., before numbering, 1 plt. in Vol. 1 misbnd. in Vol. 2, slight margin foxing, cont. vell. (C. Dec.9; 47)
                                          Weinreb. £900
See— FERRERIO, P. & FALDA, G.B.

FALKE, J.
– **Geschichte des Fürstlichen Hauses Liechtenstein.** Wien, 1868-82. 3 vols. Hf. chagrin, slightly rubbed. (VS. Dec.8; 722)   Fls. 1,000

FALKE, Otto Von
– **Decorative Silks.** N.Y., 1922. *New Edn.* Sm. fo. 10 plts. in colours & gold, 562 ills., ex-liby., decor. cl. (SG. May 3; 162) $175

FALLOPPIUS, Gabriel
– **Opera Genuina Omnia tam Practica quam Theoretica.** Venice, 1606. 3 vols. in 1. Fo. Cont. vell., blind-stpd. centrepiece on sides; Dr. Walter Pagel copy. (S. Feb.7; 115)   *Pickering & Chatto.* £420

FALLOU, L.
– **La Garde Impériale (1804-1815).** Paris, 1901. 4to. Hf. cf., corners, wrap. preserved. (HD. Jan.27; 142)   Frs. 1,900

FALLS, Capt. Cyril
See— MACMUNN, Sir George & Falls, Capt. Cyril

FAMILY CIRCLE & PARLOR ANNUAL
N.Y., 1849-52. Vols. X-XIII, for 1849-52, in 2 vols., as iss. Lge. 8vo. Each vol. with steel-engraved plts. & hand-cold. litho. plts., tissue gds., orig. gt.-floral red roan, both vols. somewhat worn; from liby. of F.D. Roosevelt, inscr. by him. (SG. Mar.15; 25) $250

FAMIN, Stanislas Marie César
See— GRANJEAN DE MONTIGNY & Famin, Stanislas Marie César

FANFROLICO PRESS
– **Fanfrolicana.** L., Jun. 1928. Qtr. mor.; inscr. by Jack Lindsay, Harry F. Chaplin copy. (JL. Jul.15; 254)   Aus. $120
See— ARISTOPHANES
See— HOMERIC HYMN to Aphrodite
See— LINDSAY, Jack

See— LOVING MAD TOM, Bedlamite Verses of the XVI & XVII Centuries
See— McCRAE, Hugh
See— MORRIS, William
See— NIETZSCHE, Friedrich
See— PETRONIUS ARBITER, Titus or Gaius
See— SLESSOR, Kenneth

FANG FUNG-MAO
– **Wupi Shih.** China, ca. 1900. Pts. 10-116 & 133-237 (of at least 237 pts.) in 71 (of at least 79) vols. Woodcut maps & diagrams, some pts. badly wormed, unlettered native wraps. (SG. Jun.7; 11)
                                          $150

FANIEL, S.
– **Collection Connaissances des Arts: Le XVIIe Siècle Français; Le XVIIIe Siècle Français; Le XIXe Siècle Français; Le Style Anglais.** 1750-1850. Together 4 vols. Fo. No bdgs. stated. (SPB. Nov.30; 248) $175

FANTE, John
– **Dago Red.** Ill.:– V. Angelo. N.Y., 1940. *1st. Edn.* Bdg. not stated, jacket worn & reprd. at folds, spine darkened; pres. inscr. from Fante to Angelo on front free end-paper, 4 T.L.s. from Fante to Angelo laid in loose. bdg. not stated, jacket worn & reprd. at folds, spine darkened. (CBA. Oct.1; 126) $350

FANTIN DES ODOARDS, Gen.
– **Journal, Etapes d'un Officier de la Grande Armée (1800-1830).** Paris, 1895. Hf. cf. (HD. Jan.27; 35)
                                          Frs. 1,500

FAR EAST: An Illustrated Fortnightly Newspaper
Yokohama, 30 May 1870-16 May 1872. Vol. I no. 1-Vol. II no. 14, together 48 nos. in 1 vol. 4to. Paper brittle, some edge fading, some foxing, hf. leath., worn, partly disbnd. (SG. Nov.10; 61) $2,800

FAR EASTERN CERAMIC BULLETIN
[1949]-60. 12 vols. (?) only in 7. 4to. Cont. cl. (CSK. Jun.29; 19)   £130

FARADAY, Michael
– **Chemical Manipulation.** 1827. *1st. Edn.* Cont. hf. vell., soiled. (BBA. Jul.27; 15)   *Laywood.* £130
– – **Anr. Copy.** Liby. stp. on title, orig. bds., rubbed. (BBA. Jul.27; 16)   *Laywood.* £110
– **Experimental Researches in Chemistry & Physics.** 1859. *1st. Coll. Edn.* Hf.-title, erratum slip, slight spotting, orig. cl., spine faded; pres. copy from author to Dr. Bence Jones. (S. Nov.1; 272)
                                          Pringle. £180
– – **Anr. Copy.** Orig. cl., slightly rubbed. (BBA. Jul.27; 17)   *Bickersteth.* £95
– – **Anr. Copy.** Hf.-title, erratum slip at p. 445, some light margin spotting, orig. cl., few splash marks on spine, rubbed mark on lr. cover; Stanitz coll. (SPB. Apr.25; 173) $425
– **Experimental Researches in Electricity.** L., 1839. Tear in 1 prelim lf. without loss of text, plts. spotted, orig. cl., unopened; Stanitz coll. (SPB. Apr.25; 174)
                                          $475

FARCY, Louis de
– **La Broderie du XIe Siècle.** Angers, 1890/1900. 4 vols. in 3. Atlas fo. 264 plts., text vol. with many intercalated plts., ex-liby., new buckram. (SG. May 3; 163) $200

FARGUE, Hon Paul
– **Banalité.** Ill.:– Loris & Parry. Paris, 1930. *(332) numbered.* 4to. On Hollande Pannekoek. Orig. wraps., printers mark sigd. by artist. (D. Nov.24; 3024)   DM 1,000
– – **Anr. Edn.** Ill.:– Loris & R. Parry. Paris, 1930. *(300) sigd. by artists.* Fo. Orig. wraps., slightly soiled; pres. copy inscr. to Vicomte Carlow. (BBA. Jun.14; 229)   *Quaritch.* £400
– **Contes Fantastiques.** Ill.:– André Villeboeuf. Paris, 1944. *Orig. Edn. 1st. Printing. (35) on Rives.* Suite of engrs. in black, hf. red mor., corners, wraps. preserved. (HD. Jan.26; 128)   Frs. 1,350

FARID AL-DIN ATTAR
– **Tezkereh-i-Evlia/Le Memorial des Saints.** Trans.:– A. Pavet de Courteille. Paris, 1889-90. 2 vols. Fo. Facs. & trans. of the 15th. C. Uighur MS., ptd. bds., extremities worn. (SG. Nov.17; 219)
                                          $325

FARINATOR, Matthias
See— LUMEN ANIMAE

FARINGTON, Joseph
– **The Farington Diary.** Ed.:– James Greig. 1922-28. 8 vols. Orig. cl., spines gt. (LC. Mar.1; 329)
£60
– – **Anr. Edn.** Ed.:– James Greig. 1923-28. 8 vols. Orig. cl. (BBA. Nov.10; 345) *Traylen.* £60
– **The Lakes of Lancashire, Westmoreland & Cumberland.** Descriptions:– Thomas H. Horne. L., 1816. *1st. Edn.* Fo. Mezzotint port., engraved double-p. hand-cold. map, 43 engraved plts. (proof imps. without captions), some on India paper, 1 plt. with minor staining, cont. str.-grd. red mor., covers & spine elab. gt., inner dentelles. (C. Nov.16; 87)
Steedman. £380
– **Views of the Lakes etc. in Cumberland & Westmoreland.** Ill.:– Byrne & others, after Farington. 1789. Ob. fo. 20 engraved plts., text in Engl. & Fr., slight marginal foxing & browning, gt. cf., upr. bd. detchd. (PD. Aug.17; 304) £130

FARMAN, Edgar
– **The Bulldog. A Monograph.** 1899. 4to. Orig. hf. vell. gt., soiled, new end-papers. (TA. Jul.19; 250)
£60

FARMER, John S. (Ed.)
See— EARLY ENGLISH DRAMATISTS

FARMER'S MAGAZINE, The
1800-73. Orig. Series: Vols. 1-18, 2nd. Series: Vols. 1-24, 3rd. Series: Vols. 1-44, & ll dupl. vols. (*With:*) **POLITICAL COMPANION to the Farmer's Magazine** 1834-38. Vols. 1-8. Together 105 vols. Various bdgs., most defect.; from the Farmer's Club Liby., as a periodical, w.a.f. (P. Jul.5; 32) £1,100
– – **Anr. Run.** Jan. 1843-Jun. 1847. 2nd. Series: Vols. 7-15. Some spotting, unif. hf. cf., lacks 1 label; Dr. G.E. Fussell copy, as a periodical, w.a.f. (P. Jul.5; 81) £130
– – **Anr. Run.** 1852-55. 3rd. Series: Vols. 1-7 only. 86 steel engrs., slight spotting, cont. unif. hf. cf., gt.-decor. spines, slightly rubbed. (TA. Dec.15; 182)
£115

FARNHAM, Thomas Jefferson
– **Travels in the Great Western Prairies, the Anahuac & Rocky Mountains & in the Oregon Territory.** N.Y. & L., 1843. orig. cl.-bkd. bds., paper label slightly chipped affecting a letter, unc.; the Rt. Hon. Visc. Eccles copy. [Sabin 23872] (CNY. Nov.18; 105) $250
– – **Anr. Edn.** Ploughkeepsie [sic], 1843. Tall 12mo. Later hf. cf., unc. (LH. Apr.15; 309) $130

FARREN, Robert
– **Cathedral Cities. Peterborough with the Abbeys of Crowland & Thorney.** Camb., 1888 [1889]. Fo. Etched title (sigd.), 22 plts., few ll. slightly spotted, orig. roan-bkd. cl., slightly worn. (BBA. Oct.27; 277) *Robertshaw.* £50

FARRERE, Claude (Pseud.)
See— BARGON, Frederic Charles Pierre Edouard 'Claude Ferrere'

FARSHVUNDENE VELT / The Vanished World
N.Y., 1947. Ob. sm. 4to. Text & captions in Yiddish & Engl., gt.-lettered cl. (SG. Feb.2; 78) $200

FASCH, Johann Rudolph
– **Brundmatzige Anweizung zu Aufreizung der Portale.** Nuremb., n.d. Sm. fo. Title, preface, 50 plts. (plt. 36 in dupl.), all mntd., slightly soiled & dampstained, cont. bds., rebkd. & recornered with cf., slightly rubbed. (BBA. Feb.23; 25)
Hildebrandt. £50

FASHIONABLE GUIDE & DIRECTORY to the Public Places of Resort
Ca. 1833. 4to. Some staining, hf. mor., as a coll. of plts., w.a.f. (P. Sep.29; 204) *Hadden.* £100

FASI, Joh. Conr.
– **Staats- und Erdbeschreibung der Ganzen Helvetischen Eidgenossschaft, derselben gemeinen Herrschaften und zugewandten Orten. Mit gemein-Eidgenössischen Allergnädigsten Priviligien.** Zürich, 1765-68. 4 vols. Cont. hf. leath. gt. (GF. Nov.16; 1187) *Sw. Frs.* 650

FASSAM, Thomas
– **An Herbarium for the Fair.** Ill.:– Betty Shaw-Lawrence. L., Hand & Flower Pr., 1949. *(250)* sigd. 4to. Engraved title, 20 botanical ills., each sigd. in pencil by artist, hf. mor. (SG. Mar.29; 163) $110

FASSBENDER, Adolf
– **Pictorial Artistry.** N.Y., [1937]. *(1000)* numbered & sigd. Fo. Metal spiral bdg. in gt.-lettered linen covers, scuffed & slightly soiled. (SG. Nov.10; 62) $110

FATIO, M.
See— BAYOT, A. & Fatio, M.

FAUJAS DE SAINT-FOND, Barthelemi
– **Description des Expériences de la Machine Aérostatique de MM. de Montgolfier.** Paris, 1783. *1st. Edn.* Short margin tear to 1 lf., 2 plt. margins shaved to engraved frame, cont. mott. cf., spine gt. (C. May 30; 113) *Thorp.* £240
– – **Anr. Copy.** Without separately publd. 'Première Suite' of plts. (as often), folding table browned, some light soiling, frontis. bkd., marb. bds., rebkd. with cf., rubbed; Stanitz coll. (SPB. Apr.25; 175) $500
– – **Anr. Copy.** 9 engraved plts., folding table, sm. stain on lr. text ll., sm. tear on frontis. margin, cont. mott. cf.; armorial bkplt. of E. De Payan Dumoulin. (SG. Apr.26; 83) $375
– – **Anr. Copy.** Title with old stp., cont. hf. leath. (R. Apr.4; 1492) DM 1,350
– **Natuurlijke Historie van den St. Pieters Berg bij Maastricht.** Trans.:– J.D. Pasteur. Amst., 1802-04. 2 vols. Some stains, some folding plts. weak or slightly stained in folds, cont. hf. cf., some restorations, unc. (VG. Sep.14; 1239) Fls. 750
– **Recherches sur les Volcans Eteints du Vivarais et du Velay.** Grenoble & Paris, 1778. *1st. Edn.* Fo. Engraved vig. on title, 20 plts., including 1 double-p., printing flaw on 5P1r, cont. Fr. mott. cf. gt., slightly worn. (S. Nov.28; 111) *Garman.* £500

FAULKNER, Henry
– **Elephant Haunts** ... L., 1868. Hf. cf. & marb. bds., slightly rubbed. (VA. Oct.28; 457) R 440

FAULKNER, Joseph P.
– **Eighteen Months on a Greenland Whaler.** N.Y., 1856. *1st. Edn.* 12mo. Cl., worn. (RO. May 29; 80) $125

FAULKNER, William
– **Mosquitoes: A Novel.** N.Y., [1927]. *1st. Edn.* Owner's stp. on end-papers, cl., d.-w. slightly chipped. (SG. Jan.12; 103) $325
– **Notes on a Horsethief.** Decors.:– Elizabeth Calvert. Greenville, Miss., 1950. *(975)* numbered & sigd. Pict. cl. (SG. May 24; 284) $350
– **Pylon.** N.Y., 1935. *1st. Trade Edn.* Cl., d.w. (spine ends slightly frayed), light wear. (RO. Apr.23; 141) $200
– **These 13.** N.Y., [1931]. *1st. Edn.* Two-tone cl., d.-w. (SG. Jan.12; 104) $250

FAUR, G.
See— FABER & FAUR, G.

FAUST
– **Histoire Prodigieuse et Lamentable du Docteur Fauste, avec sa Mort Espouentable** ... Rouen, 1627. *6th. Edn.* 12mo. Minor worming in top fore-corners slightly affects text, cont. limp vell., soiled. (S. Nov.17; 22) *Quaritch.* £140

FAUST, Camille Laurent Celestin
See— MAUCLAIR, Camille [i.e. Camille Laurent Célestin Faust]

FAUX, William
– **Memorable Days in America: being a Journal of a Tour to The United States** ... L., 1823. *1st. Edn.* Hf.-title, frontis. foxed & offset on title, some spotting, new end-papers, cont. pol. cf. gt., rebkd. with orig. backstrip laid down, corners reprd.; the Rt. Hon. Visc. Eccles copy. [Sabin 23933] (CNY. Nov.18; 106) $110

FAVANNE DE MONTCERVELLE, Guillième de
[–] **Catalogue Systématique et Raisonne AAC, ou Description du Magnifique Cabinet ... à M. le**

C[omte] de [la Tour d'Auvergne]. Paris, 1784. Cont. cf., upr. cover rubbed. (C. May 30; 193)
Weldon & Wesley. £170

FAVERET DE KERBRECH, Gen. de
– **L'Art de Conduire et d'Atteler autrefois-aujord'hui.** Paris, 1903. *Ltd. Edn.* Fo. Plts., ills., qtr. mor. gt. (P. May 17; 256) *Way.* £260
– – **Anr. Copy.** Fo. Plts., ills., orig. wraps. (P. May 17; 255) *Way.* £160

FAVIER, Alphonse
– **Péking. Histoire et Description.** Péking, 1897. *Orig. Edn.* Lge. 4to. Sewed, silk box. (HD. Jun.6; 57) *Frs.* 1,000

FAVRE, Jean Baptiste
– **Les Quatres Heures de la Toilette des Dames.** Ill.:– after Le Clerc. Paris, 1779. Ptd. overslip bnd. in, Paris & Geneva, J.E. Didier, 1781, later mor.-bkd. bds. (CSK. Jun.15; 200) £100

FAVRE-GUILLARMOD, L.
– **Les Champignons Comestibles du Canton de Neuchâtel et les Espèces Vénéneuses avec lesquelles ils pourraient être confondus.** Neuchâtel, 1861-69. 2 pts. in 1 vol. 4to. Some foxing in parts, cont. hf. vell. (GB. Nov.3; 1131) DM 900

FAWCETT, W.
– **Thoroughbred & Hunter.** Ill.:– Lionel Edwards. 1934. *(50)* numbered & sigd. by author & artist. 4to. Qtr. vell. gt. (P. Dec.8; 204) *Head.* £50

FAY, Theodore Sedgwick
– **Views in New York & Its Environs.** N.Y., 1831-[34]. *1st. Edn.* Lge. 4to. Engraved title, 15 engraved plts., (title & 5 plts. mntd. India-proofs), engraved folding map, partly hand-cold., most plts. slightly foxed & some offsetting from browned orig. tissue-guards, some light text foxing, cont. hf. roan, marb. bds., worn. (SG. Apr.26; 84) $3,600

FAYRER, Sir Joseph
– **The Thanatophidia of India being a Description of the Venomous Snakes of the Indian Peninsula.** L., 1874. *2nd. Edn.* Fo. 31 litho. plts., including 1 double-p., some spotting, orig. cl., worn & stained. (S. Dec.13; 270) *Phelps.* £200

FAZELLI, Fernando Tommaso
– **De Rebus Siculis Decades Duae** ... Palermo, 1558. Fo. Some pp. browned & stained, mod. vell. (CR. Jun.6; 28) Lire 200,000

FEA, Allan
– **After Worcester Flight.** L., 1904. Plts., slightly spotted, mor. gt., red onlays of stylised flowers, by Bayntun (Rivière), upr. cover inlaid with miniature hand-painted port. of Charles II, boxed. (S. Oct.4; 114) *Joseph.* £170
– **The Flight of the King.** L., 1897. Mor. gt. by Bayntun (Rivière), upr. cover inlaid with miniature hand-painted port. of Charles II, boxed. (S. Oct.4; 113) *Joseph.* £230

FEARNSIDE, William Gray
See— TOMBLESON, William & Fearnside, William Gray

FEATHERSTONHAUGH, George W.
– **A Canoe Voyage up the Minnay Sotor.** L., 1847. *1st. Edn.* 2 vol. 2 folding maps in pocket, slightly browned, orig. cl. (BBA. Dec.15; 42)
Remington. £140
– – **Anr. Copy.** 2 vols. 2 folding maps in pocket in upr. cover, orig. cl., slightly marked, heads of spines worn; the Rt. Hon. Visc. Eccles copy. [Sabin 351] (CNY. Nov.18; 107) $275
– **Excursions through the Slave States, from Washington to the Frontier of Mexico.** L., 1844. *1st. Edn.* 2 vols. Lge. 8vo. Murray's 8 p. book list (dtd. Apr. 1844) in Vol. 2, cl., crudely recased. (SG. Oct.20; 151) $100
See— JARVES, James Jackson—FEATHERSTONHAUGH, George W.

FECHTER, P.
– **Das Graphische Werk Max Pechsteins.** Berlin, [1920-21]. *(25)*, De Luxe Edn. on Zanders-Bütten with orig. ills. sigd. by artist. 4to. 10 sigd. orig. ills., hand bnd. orig. vell., cold. cover ill., slightly mis-cold. (H. May 23; 1448) DM 17,000

– – **Anr. Edn.** Berlin, [1921]. *Normal Edn., (400) numbered.* 4to. Slightly foxed, orig. pict. bds., slightly soiled. (HK. Nov.11; 3853) DM 1,000

FEDIX, P.A.
– L'Oregon et les cotes de l'Océan Pacifique du Nord ... Paris, 1846. *1st. Edn.* Folding map partially cold. in outl., orig. ptd. wraps., spine slightly chipped, hf. mor. s.-c. (LH. Apr.15; 311) $550

FEIGL, Friedrich
– Orient. Berlin, ca. 1914. Compl. set of 10 etchings & etchings with aquatint, on Japan paper, each individually matted, no title or text, Lacks orig. portfo. covers; each plt. sigd. & numbered 'X/XX' by artist. (SG. Dec.15; 144) $175

FELDIGL, Ferd. (Pseud.)
See— MEGGENDORFER, Lothar & Feldigl, Ferd.

FELDMANN, Friedr.
– Die Drey Aeltesten Geschichtlichen Denkmale der Teutschen Freymaurerbrüderschaft sammt Grundzügen zu e. allgem. Geschichte der Freymaurerey. Aarau, 1819. Cont. bds. (BR. Apr.12; 928)
DM 460

FELIBIEN DES AVAUX, André
[–] Description de la Grotte de Versailles. Ill.:– Le Pôtre, Picart, & others. Paris, 1676. *1st. Edn.* Fo. Lge. engraved armorial title vig., plan, 19 plts., margin worming thro.-out, partly affecting some plts., title slightly discold., cont. mott. cf. (C. Dec.9; 48) *Reilley.* £450
– Des Principes De L'Architecture. Paris, 1676. *[1st. Edn.].* 4to. Some ll. lightly browned, cont. cf. (P. Nov.24; 228) *Duran.* £180
– – **Anr. Copy.** 4to. Wide margin, cont. leath. gt., slightly rubbed & bumped, spine slightly defect. (D. Nov.23; 1886) DM 850
– Recueil Historique de la vie et des Ouvrages des plus Celèbres Architectes. 1705. (*Bound with:*)
– Les Plans et les Descriptions de deux des plus Belles Maisons de Campagne. 1707. Together 2 works in 1 vol. 12mo. cont. vell., spine slightly soiled. (S. May 1; 540) *Marlborough.* £120

FELIBIEN, Michel
– Histoire de l'Abbaye Royale de Saint-Denis en France ... Ill.:– Halle, Boulogne le jeune, Rubens, Oppenord & others. Paris, 1706. Fo. Cont. cf., spine decor., corners & turn-ins weak. (HD. May 3; 46)
Frs. 2,000
– Histoire de la Ville de Paris. Ed.:– Don Guy Alexis Lobineau. Paris, 1725. 5 vols. Fo. Cont. cf., decor. spines. (HD. Sep.22; 242) Frs. 3,500

FELIBIEN DES AVAUX, André
[–] Description de l'Eglise Royale des Invalides. Paris, 1706. Fo. Some foxing & slight margin stains at beginning & end, cont. red mor., Louis XIV arms, decor. spine with royal monog. (HD. Dec.1; 70) Frs. 3,800

FELICIANUS
– De Divina Praedestinatione. Memmingen, Albrecht Kunne, ca. 1486-89. 4to. Lge. copy, compl. with the 'Tractus de Decimis', some light stains, mod. marb. wraps.; the Walter Goldwater copy. [BMC II, 604; Goff F-55; H. 6952] (SG. Dec.1; 141) $600
– – **Anr. Edn.** [Speier, Conrad Hist], 1495. Lacks final blank, stiff vell., bdg. loose; the Walter Goldwater copy. [BMC II, 506-7; Goff F-57; HC 6954] (SG. Dec.1; 142) $550

FELIPE, Bartholomew
– Tratado del Consejo y de los Consejeros de los Príncipes. Turin, 1589. *2nd. Edn.* 4to. Leath. (DS. Apr.27; 2088) Pts. 35,000

FELIXMULLER, Conrad
– Das Maler-Leben. Dresden, 1927. *(160) numbered.* Lge. 4to. Sigd. on last lf., 16 orig. lithos., including wraps., orig. corduroy. (GB. Nov.5; 2462) DM 2,000

FELLIG, Arthur 'Weegee'
– Naked City. N.Y., [1945]. *1st. Edn.* 4to. Cl., d.-w. defect.; inscr. by Weegee to Frank Lewstik. (SG. Nov.10; 163) $150

FELLOWES, William Dorsett
– A Visit to the Monastery of La Trappe. L., 1815. *2nd. Edn.* 14 plts., including 12 hand-cold. aquatints, stitching slightly shaken, cont. mor. gt. (CSK. Nov.25; 29) £50
– – **Anr. Edn.** L., 1818. *2nd. Edn.* 12 cold. aquatint & 2 engraved plts., cont. str.-grd. red mor., 2 gt. borders, tools on covers, rebkd.; author's pres. copy. (C. Jun.27; 31) *Houle.* £100
– – **Anr. Copy.** aquatints hand-cold., 1 engr. on India paper laid on, cont. red grained & gt. mor., backstrip reprd.; Earl of Chichester bkplt. (CBA. Dec.10; 221) $100

FELLOWS, Charles
– Narrative of an Ascent to the Summit of Mont Blanc. L., priv. ptd., 1827. 4to. Litho. title-p., 9 plts., engraved table, spotted & soiled, cont. cf., worn, stained; inscr. to lady Kaye. (S. Mar.6; 83)
Lovett. £100

FELTHAM, Owen
[–] A Brief Character of the Low-Countries Under the States. L., 1660. 12mo. Lacks 1st. blank lf., cont. cf., spine slightly worn. [Wing F650] (BBA. May 3; 259) *Tooley.* £50

FELTON, S.
– Gleanings on Gardens, chiefly respecting those of the Ancient Style in England. L., 1829. Title & text ruled in green, extra-ill. with many engraved ports. & views, some folding, including cold. aquatint views, mor. gt. by Riviere, spine faded, w.a.f. (C. Mar.14; 48) *Chelsea Rare Books.* £350

FELTON, W.
– A Treatise on Carriages & Harness. L., 1805. *3rd. Edn.* 3 vols. 59 (of 60) plts., some spotting, few plts. worn, mod. hf. cf. (P. May 17; 257)
Blackwell. £460

FEMALE SOCIETY FOR THE RELIEF of British Negro Slavery
B'gham., 1828. 4to. L.P., cold. map, folding plan, 1 orig. photo, 11 plts., bdg. not stated, end-papers foxed. (LH. Apr.15; 373) $160

FENELON, François de Salignac de la Motte
– The Adventures of Telemachus. Ed.:– G. Gregory. Trans.:– John Hawkesworth. L., 1795. 2 vols. in 1. 4to. 12 col.-ptd. hand-finished engraved plts., in gt. & hand-cold. floral borders, front blank reprd., early mor. gt., mod. spine label. (SG. Dec.8; 150)
$250
– Les Aventures de Télémaque. Ill.:– after Coypel, Souville, Humblot, & others. Paris, 1730. *1st. Printing.* 2 vols. in 1. 4to. Cont. cf. gt., spine decor., upr. turn-in slightly soiled, 1 corner rounded. (HD. Nov.9; 35) Frs. 3,100
– – **Anr. Edn.** Ill.:– after Charles Monnet. Paris, 1773. 4to. Some slight foxing, cont. roan gt., spines decor., slightly rubbed. (HD. May 3; 48)
Frs. 1,250
– – **Anr. Edn.** Paris, 1784. *(350).* 2 vols. Stps. on title & last lf., 1st. ll. in both vols. defect. from chemical removal of stps., minimal spotting, cont. ox-blood red mor., gt. spine, cover, inner & outer dentelle, by Derome le jeune, with his ticket in Vol. 1; from Friedrich Wilhelm IV of Preussen coll. (HK. Nov.10; 3054) DM 1,200
– – **Anr. Edn.** Ill.:– Montulay, J.B. Tilliard after C. Monnet. [Paris], 1785. 2 vols. 4to. On vell., wide margin, some slight spotting, cont. red pol. mor. gt., decor., inner & outer dentelles, slightly spotted & rubbed. (H. Nov.23; 642) DM 2,400
– – **Anr. Edn.** Ill.:– Cochin & Moreau le jeune. Paris, 1790. 2 vols. Lge. 8vo. On vell., cont. red mor. gt., spines decor. (HD. May 3; 50) Frs. 2,800
– – **Anr. Edn.** Ill.:– Vivien, Lefevre & others. Paris, 1790. 2 vols. Lge. 8vo. L.P., marb. cf. gt. by Courteval, spines decor., some scratches, corner reprd. (HD. May 3; 49) Frs. 1,350
– – **Anr. Edn.** Ill.:– after Marillier. Paris, 1796. 2 vols. Hf.-titles, cont. red str.-grd. mor. gt. by Bozerian; bkplt. of Comte Louis Lanckoronski. (S. Nov.17; 23) *Fletcher.* £380
– – **Anr. Copy.** 4 vols. 16mo. Cont. red mor. gt. (HD. Mar.27; 12) Frs. 2,700
– – **Anr. Copy.** 4 vols. 18mo. Cont. tree cf. gt., spines decor., slight worming. (HD. May 3; 52)
Frs. 1,050

– – **Anr. Edn.** Ill.:– Manceau; after Lefebre; by Dambrun after Queverdo. Paris, 1796. *Ltd. Edn.* 4 vols. 12mo. 76 engraved plts., 26 in 1 state, 24 in 2 states, 26 in 3 states, later mor., slightly rubbed. (BBA. May 23; 349) *Greenwood.* £85
– – **Anr. Edn.** Ill.:– Vivien (port.) & Marillier. Paris, An IV [1796]. 2 vols. On vell., figures before the letter, dampstains, cont. red mor. gt., spines decor., light stains, end-papers renewed. (HD. May 3; 51)
Frs. 2,300
– – **Anr. Edn.** Ill.:– Delvaux & after le Febvre. Paris, 1802. 2 vols. On vell., copper engrs. in 3 states, bnd. in at beginning of vol. 1. A.L. from author dtd. 31.7.1704 to Countess de Monbron, 2 pp. with address, mor., sigd. by David Domont, gold. tooled decor., gt., red mor. doubls., decor., gt. outer dentelle. (D. Nov.24; 2266) DM 11,500
– – **Anr. Edn.** Ill.:– Manceau. 1821. 2 vols. Cont. blind-decor. cf. (HD. Jan.24; 12) Frs. 1,300
– – **Anr. Edn.** Ill.:– Foulquier. Tours, 1873. *(21) numbered on china.* Mod. jansenist mor., mor. doubl., silk end-ll., double end-papers, by Noulhac; Henri Beraldi ex-libris. (HD. Feb.17; 69)
Frs. 2,000
– Die Begebenheiten des Prinzen von Ithaca, oder: Derseinen Vater Ulysses suchende Telemach. Trans.:– B. Neukirch. Ill.:– Cochin after Le Clerc (engraved frontis), J.W. Winter & others, after Le Clerc & Sperling. Ansbach, 1727-39. *1st. Edn.* 3 vols. in 2. Fo. Wide margin, some margin soiling, especially at beginning Vol. 1, Vol. 1 1 1 lf. with tear reprd., 2 title ll. with sm. stp., lacks 2 ll. subscribers list at end, cont. vell. (R. Oct.11; 202) DM 1,500
– Directions pour la Conscience d'un Roi, composées pour l'Instruction de Louis de France, Duc de Bourgogne. La Haye, 1747. Engraved frontis., cont. red mor., spine decor. (HD. Mar.29; 30) Frs. 10,000
– Explication des Maximes de Saints sur la Vie Intérieure ... Paris, 1697. *Orig. Edn. 1st. Printing.* 12mo. Errata lf., fault on p. 48, red mor. gt. by David, spine decor. (HD. May 3; 47) Frs. 1,700
– – **Anr. Edn.** Brusselles, 1698. 12mo. Cont. mor.; Crémaux d'Entragues arms & armorial ex-libris, from La Baume Pluvinel Liby. (HD. Mar.29; 29)
Frs. 11,000
– Oeuvres. Paris, 1787-92. 9 vols. 4to. Device on title-pp., hf.-titles, sm. liby. stps. 'Bibliothèque de Picpen (?)', cont. Fr. mott. cf., spines gt. (S. Apr.10; 293) *Wade.* £120
– Traité du Ministère des Pasteurs. 1688. *Orig. Edn.* 12mo. Cont. red mor., spine decor. (HD. Mar.21; 28) Frs. 1,450
See— SPINOZA, Benoît de—FENELON, François de Salignac & others

FENESTELLA, Lucius
– De Romanorum Magistratibus. [Venice, Filippo de Pietro, ca. 1475]. 4to. Capital spaces with guide letters, a few early MS. notes & slip of paper pasted over inscr. on p. 1, old cf., worn. [BMC V, 218; Goff F61; H. 6958] (S. May 10; 277)
Fletcher. £520
– – **Anr. Edn.** Flor., Bartolommeo di Libri, ca. 1492. 4to. Later vell.; the Walter Goldwater copy. [BMC VI, 663, col. 2; Goff F-66; H. 6963] (SG. Dec.1; 143) $1,100

FENN, Sir John
– Original Letters, Written during the Reigns of Henry VI, Edward IV, & Richard III. 1787-1823. 5 vols. 4to. Hf, mor. gt. (P. Sep.29; 132)
Traylen. £110

FENNING, Daniel & Collier, J.
– A New System of Geography. 1769. 2 vols. Fo. Cont. cf. (CSK. Sep.16; 216) £140
– – **Anr. Edn.** 1773. 2 vols. Fo. Cf. gt., 1 cover detchd. (P. Dec.8; 27) *Map House.* £240

FENTON, Richard
– A Historical Tour through Pembrokeshire. 1811. 4to. Plts. slightly spotted & offset, hf. mor., rubbed. (S. Nov.1; 107) *Thorp.* £60

FER, Nicolas de
[–] Atlas Curieux. Paris, 1703. Ob. fo. Approx. 150 copper-engraved plts., approx. anr. 50 plts. added from other works, cf. over wood bds., metal reinforcements. (HD. Mar.19; 3) Frs. 10,500
– Les Forces de l'Europe ou Description des Principales villes avec leurs Fortifications. Paris, 1694-96.

FER, Nicolas de -*Contd.*

8 pts. in 1 vol. Ob. fo. Extra engraved title, 184 engraved plans & views, 3 additional folding engraved plts. from other books bnd. in, 1 title-p. defect., cont. panel. cf. (SKC. Sep.9; 2038) £1,000
– **Introduction à La Fortification.** Paris, [1705]. Ob. 4to. Cont. leath., arms supralibros on both covers, gt. spine. (D. Nov.23; 761) DM 8,200
– **Le Théâtre de la Guerre dans les Pais Bas.** Paris, 1703. 4to. Double-p. title frontis. decor., 19 outl. cold. maps (6 lge. format folding, rest double-P.), slight stains, later bds. (HD. Feb.29; 15) Frs. 1,500

FERBER, Johann Jacob
– **Physikalisch-Metallurgische Abhandlungen über die Gebirge und Bergwerke in Ungarn** ... Berlin & Stettin, 1780. *Orig. Edn.* Some slight foxing, cont. hf. leath. bumped or worn. (D. Nov.25; 4624) DM 520

FEREAL, M.
– **Ministerios de la Inquisición de España.** Buenos Aires, 1869. 2 vols. 4to. Linen. (DS. Dec.16; 2499) Pts. 20,000

FERET, Edouard
See— COCKS, Ch. & Feret, Edouard

FERGUSON, Charles D.
– **The Experiences of a Forty-Niner during Thirty-Four Years' Residence in California & Australia** ... Cleveland, 1888. Bdg. not stated, slight rubbing & marking. (KH. May 1; 253) Aus.$130

FERGUSON, James
– **Astronomy Explained upon Sir Isaac Newton's Principles.** 1673 [1773]. (*With:*) – **Lectures on Select Subjects in Mechanics, Hydrostatics, Pneumatics & Optics** ... 1773. 2 pts. in 1 vol. Together 2 vols. 4to. Cont. unif. spr. cf. (C. May 30; 114) Thorp. £240
– – **Anr. Edn.** L., priv. ptd., 1757. *2nd. Edn.* 4to. Fore-e. of 1 plt. frayed, mott. cf., slightly rubbed, lacks lr. compartment of backstrip. (B. Jun.21; 403) Fls. 700
– **Lectures on Select Subjects in Mechanics, Hydrostatics, Pneumatics, & Optics** ... L., 1760. *1st. Edn.* A few ll. spotted, cont. spr. cf.; from Westport House liby., Stanitz coll. (SPB. Apr.25; 176) $325

FERGUSON, James (Ed.)
See— BRITISH ESSAYISTS, The

FERGUSON, John
– **Bibliographica Paracelsica.** Glasgow, p.p., 1877-93. (*100*). Pts. 1-5 only (of 6). Hf. cl.; Dr. Walter Pagel copy. (S. Feb.7; 302) Janssen. £200
– **Bibliotheca Chemica: a Catalogue of ... Books in the Collection of the late James Young.** Glasgow, 1906. 2 vols. 4to. Original buckram, unopened. (S. Apr.10; 499) Symonds. £110
– – **Anr. Edn.** L., 1954. 2 vols. Orig. cl., Vol 1 with d.-w. (S. May 1; 393) Questor. £60
– – **Anr. Copy.** 2 vols. Orig. cl., slightly rubbed. (TA. Dec.15; 388) £52

FERGUSON, John Alexander
– **Bibliography of Australia.** Canberra, 1975-77. *Facs. Edn., (500).* 7 vols. Cl., d.-w. (BBA. Jan.19; 340) Clegg. £180
– – **Anr. Edn.** Canberra, 1975-77. *Facs. Reprint.* 7 vols. Orig. cl., d.-w.'s. (TA. Sep.15; 30) £120
– – **Anr. Edn.** 1976. *Facs. Edn.* 7 vols. Bdg. not stated, d.-w.'s. (JL. Mar.25; 771) Aus.$180

FERGUSON, Samuel
– **The Cromlech on Howth.** L., [1861]. Fo. Decor. cl. (GM. Dec.7; 308) £55

FERGUSSON, James
– **Illustrations of the Rock-Cut Temples of India.** Ill.:– T.C. Dibdin. L., 1845. *1st. Edn.* 2 vols. Atlas fo. & 8vo. 19 litho. plts., some cold. or tinted, & 10 plts. in text only, heavily spotted thro.-out, ex-liby., Weale's cat. dtd. 1844 & 1845 supp. bnd. in, mor.-bkd. cl., text vol. disbnd. (SG. May 3; 164) $400
– **Picturesque Illustrations of Ancient Architecture in Hindostan.** Ill.:– Dibdin. L., 1848. Lge. Fo. Hf. leath. gt. (V. Sep.29; 61) DM 600

– **The Rock-Cut Temples of India.** Ill.:– Maj. Robert Gill. L., 1864. 73 mntd. albumen photos, 1st. few ll. stained, some foxing thro.-out, hf. leath., heavily rubbed, 'Mrs. Gill' written on front fly-lf. in old hand, ex-liby. (SG. May 10; 57) $275

FERLINGHETTI, Lawrence
– **Pictures of the Gone World.** San Franc., [1955]. (*500*) sigd. Sq. 12mo. Owner's sig., ptd. wraps. (SG. Mar.1; 147) $200
– – **Anr. Edn.** [San Franc., 1955]. Sq. 12mo. Ptd. stiff wraps., ptd. yellow wraparound label; bkplt. of [Ruth Witt-Diamant?] partly removed from title. (SG. May 24; 66) $140

FERMIN, Philippe
– **Description Gén., Histor., Ge AACogr. et Physique de la Colonie de Surinam.** Amst., 1769. *1st. Edn.* 2 vols. Mod. cl. [Sabin 24114] (VG. Nov.30; 819) Fls. 550

FERNANDEZ DE CORDOVA, L.
– **Constituciones para el buen Govierno de el Colegio Seminario de S. Sebastián ... Ma AAClaga.** Granada, [1616]. Fo. Sewed. (DS. Nov.25; 2628) Pts. 22,000

FERNANDEZ DE MORATIN, Leandro
– **Obras Dramáticas y Li AACricas.** Barcelona, 1834. 6 vols. Leath. (DS. Nov.25; 2116) Pts. 50,000
– – **Anr. Edn.** Madrid, 1840-1. 6 vols. in 1. 4to. Linen. (DS. Apr.27; 2093) Pts. 35,000

FERNANDEZ NAVARRETE, Martin
– **Colección de los Viajes y Descubrimientos que hicieron por Mar los Españoles desde Fines del S. XV.** Madrid, 1858-59, 1829-37. 5 vols. 4to. Vell. (DS. Nov.25; 2060) Pts. 90,000

FERNEL, Jean
– **De Naturali Parte Medicinae Libri Septem.** Paris, 1532. *1st. Edn.* Old MS. underlining & marginalia, some slight browning & spotting, 1st ll. with slight slits in outer margin, some repairs, cont. limp vell., old MS. vell. ll. end-papers, some wear. (D. Nov.23; 552) DM 6,000
– – **Anr. Edn.** Venezia, 1547. Stain on frontis., cont. limp vell., lightly bumped. (SI. Dec.15; 155) Lire 400,000

FERRAR, J.
– **The History of Limerick.** Limerick, 1787. *1st. Edn.* Engraved frontis. & dedication, 11 (of 13) engraved views, folding plans & maps, subscribers list, cf. (GM. Dec.7; 211) £130

FERRARI, Filippo
– **Costumi di Roma.** Rome, 1835. 4to. Hand-cold. title, 30 hand-cold. plts., hf. mor. gt. (P. Oct.20; 54) £260
– **Costumi Ecclesiastici Civili et Militari Della Corte di Roma.** Roma, 1823. 4to. Engraved title, 26 (of 68) hand-cold. plts., some light foxing, near-cont. mor., spine tips chipped. (RO. Dec.11; 105) $130
– – **Anr. Edn.** Rome, 1842. 4to. Some plts. loose, cont. vell., gt. decor., slightly faded, red & dark green mor. inlays. (D. Nov.24; 4345) DM 1,700
– **Costumi n. 30 di Roma e di Aitri Paesi dello Stato Pontificio** ... Roma, 1835. 4to. Some plts. very discold., hf. cl., as a collection, w.a.f. (CR. Jun.6; 158) Lire 300,000

FERRARI, Giovanni Battista
– **De Florum Cultura Libri IV.** Rome, 1633. *1st. Edn.* 4to. Some text ll. slightly browned, frontis. & 1 prelim. lf. bnd. after p.96, 1st. sig. slightly loose, cont. leath., worn. (R. Apr.4; 1708) DM 2,000
– **Hesperides** ... Ill.:– Cornelis Bloemaerts, after Nicolas Poussin & others. Rome, 1646. *[1st. Edn.].* Fo. Engraved frontis., 100 engraved plts., old cf. gt., covers slightly rubbed & warped. (C. Nov.16; 244) Hart. £1,100
– – **Anr. Copy.** Fo. Some light browning, 1 sig. mis-ordered, cont. leath. bumped & slightly defect. (R. Oct.12; 1834) DM 3,550

FERRARIO, Giulio
– **Monumenti Sacri e Profani dell'Imperiale e Reale Basilica di Sant'Ambrogio.** Milan, 1824. Fo. Vig.

title, 31 copper-engraved plts., all cont. illuminated & gt., cont. hf. roan. (HD. Mar.9; 88) Frs. 2,600

FERRARIS, Lucius
– **Bibliotheca Canonica, Iuridica, Moralis, Theologica.** Rome, 1885-99. 8 vols. & supp. 4to. Cont. hf. cf., faded & soiled. (*With:*) – **Leggi e Memoire Venete sulla Prostituzione.** Venice, 1870-72. (*150*) numbered. 1 vol. 4to. Slightly spotted, mor., gt., by Rivière, very slightly marked. (S. Oct.11; 462) Erlini. £90

FERRARIUS, O.
– **De Re Vestiaria.** Padua, 1654. 2 pts. in 1 vol. 4to. Vell. (DS. Apr.27; 2246) Pts. 19,000

FERRE, J. & others
– **Watteau.** Madrid, 1972. 4 vols. Fo. No bdg. stated. (SPB. Nov.30; 71) $475

FERRERIO, P. & Falda, G.B.
– **Palazzi di Roma de piv Celebri Architetti.—Nvovi Disegni delle Architettvre, e Pianti de Palazzi di Roma.** Rome, ca. 1670. 2 vols. Ob. fo. Vol. 1 lacks 1 plt., some margins slightly foxed, cont. hf. vell., faded & slightly bumped, sm. worm-holes, loose, engraved ex-libris inside cover. (H. May 22;63) DM 2,200

FERRERIUS, Vincentius
– **Sermones de Sanctis.** Milan, Veldericus Scinzenzeler, 3 Mar. 1488. 4to. Rubricated in red & blue, mod. vell.; from Foundation Furstenberg-Beaumesnil. [HC 13422; BMC VI, 763; Goff F127] (HD. Nov.16; 31) Frs. 4,000
– **Sermones de Tempore [pars Aestivalis].** [Lyons, 1499?]. Later vell.; the Walter Goldwater copy. [C. 2473 (citing Pellechet 2371)] (SG. Dec.1; 147) $250
– **Sermones de Tempore et de Sanctis.** Lyons, [Mathias Huss], 23 Apr. 1497. 3 pts., bnd. in 1 vol. Some stains, later inscrs. on title-p. & at end, owner's inscr. in upr. cover, early vell., worn; the Walter Goldwater copy. [Goff F-138 (pts. 2 & 3 only)] (SG. Dec.1; 146) $1,400
– **Sermones Sancti Vicentii Fratris Ordinis Predicatoru[m] de Te[m]pore Pars Estivalis incipit feliciter.** [Lyon, Mathieu Huss], 1497]. 4to. Wide margins, inscr. on title & margin some lf.; sm. stain in lr. margin, lacks last lf. blank, 19th C. hf. roan. [C. 2472; Goff F-128] (HD. Jan.30; 9) Frs. 6,200

FERRETTUS, Julius
– **De Iure, & Re Navali et de Ipsius Rei Navalis, et Belli Aquatici Praeceptis legitimis Liber.** Venezia, 1579. 4to. Frontis. stained, cont. limp vell. (SI. Dec.15; 11) Lire 380,000

FERRIERE, Claude de
– **Corps et Compilation de Tous les Commentateurs Anciens et Modernes sur la Coutume de Paris.** Paris, 1714. *2nd. Edn.* 4 vols. Fo. Cont. cf., spines decor., minor defects. (HD. Mar.19; 90) Frs. 2,000

FERRIERES-SAUVEBOEUF, Cte. de
– **Mémoires Historiques, Politiques et Géographiques des Voyages** ... 1790. 2 vols. Errata ll., cont. gt.-decor. cf., dentelles, by Kalthoeber, with his ticket. (SKC. Sep.9; 2039) £180
See— LESSEPS, Jean Baptiste Barthelmy, Baron du

FERRIOL
– **Recueil de Cent Estampes représentant Différentes Nations du Levant** ... Ill.:– Cochin, Scottin, Hussard & others. Paris, 1714. Fo. 100 hand-cold. engrs., light foxing, marb. cf., spine decor., worn. (SM. Mar.7; 2437a) Frs. 26,000

FERRO, G.
– **Teatro d'Imprese.** Venice, 1623. 2 pts. in 1 vol. Fo. Vell., spine very defect., upr. cover loose, some ll. slightly foxed. (VG. May 3; 469) Fls. 750

FERRO, Saladino
– **Trattato della Peste et sua Preseruatione, & Cura.** Foligno, 1565. With last errata lf., stained, later limp vell. (SI. Dec.15; 156) Lire 600,000

FERRY, Gabriel
- **Der Waldläufer.** Ill.:– Max Slevogt. 1921. *(1,500).*
Ltd. Iss. 4to. Sigd. orig. litho. on japan, orig. pict.
hf. linen, spine foxed. (GB. May 5; 3335) DM 500
– – **Anr. Edn.** Ill.:– M. Slevogt. Berlin, [1921]. *De
Luxe Edn, (300) numbered.* 4to. 1 sigd. etching on
Japan, 2 ll. with some light browning, orig. hf.
leath., spine faded, slight scratches. (HK. Nov.11;
3980) DM 420
– – **Anr. Edn.** Ill.:– Max Slevogt. Berlin, [1921].
(500) De Luxe Edn. with sigd. etching on japan.
Orig. cf., gt. spine & cover, sm. spots & scratches,
spine discold., cold. paper end-papers. (HK. May
17, 3138) DM 800
– – **Anr. Edn.** Trans.:– J. Hoffmann. Ill.:– M. Slevogt. Berlin, [1921]. *Numbered on Bütten.* 4to. 1
hand-sigd. orig. litho. on japan, 9 orig. crayon
lithos., Engl. red mor., sigd. by O. Dorfner, minimal
spotting, gold-tooled star on covers, gt. spine &
inner dentelle, marb. paper end-papers. (D. Nov.24;
3191) DM 1,450
– – **Anr. Edn.** Trans.:– J. Hoffmann. Ill.:– after M.
Slevogt. Berlin, [1921]. *Ltd. Iss.* Lge. 4to. 1 sigd.
litho. on china, hand-bnd. red mor. by P.A.
Demeter, Hellerau, gt. spine, gt. decor. covers,
inner & outer dentelles, slightly rubbed. (H.
Nov.24; 2057) DM 900

FERTEL, Martin Dominique
- **La Science Pratique de l'Imprimerie.** Saint-Omer,
1723. Sm. 4to. Old marb. cf., spine decor. (LM.
Oct.22; 223) B.Frs. 21,000

**FETE PUBLIQUE donnée par la Ville de Paris à
l'Occasion du Mariage de Monseigneur le Dauphin**
Ill.:– Le Bas, Cochin, & others. Paris, 1745.
Engraved title, frontis., 19 plts., including 10 double-p., 1 discold. *(Bound with:)* PLANS ET DES-
SINS des Constructions et Décorations Ordonnées
par la Ville de Paris pour les Rejouissances
Publiques à l'Occasion de la Publication de la Paix,
le 12 Février 1749 Paris, 1749. Title, engraved
table & 6 plts., cut round & mntd. on 4 ll. Together
2 works in 1 vol. Fo. Cont. red mor. gt., fleur-de-
lys roll-tooled border & cornerpieces, arms of City
of Paris gt.-stpd. in centre, gt. spine with royal
cypher in comparments, few sm. repairs. (C. Dec.9;
93) *Meister.* £750
– – **Anr. Edn.** Ill.:– Eisen, Hutin & Cochin fils.
[Paris, 1745]. Fo. Sm. margin tear without loss to
2 plts., cont. cf. gt., spine decor., turn-ins & corners
worn. (HD. Jun.26; 12) Frs. 6,200
– – **Anr. Edn.** Ill.:– Marvye & others. [Paris, 1747].
Fo. Engraved title, frontis., 7 double-p. plts., 1 plt.
discold., 18th. C. inscr. erased from title, cont.
red mor. gt., palmette & fleur-de-lys roll-tooled
border & cornerpieces, arms of City of Paris gt.-
stpd. in centre, gt. spine with royal cypher in compartments, upr. cover stained, few sm. repairs. (C.
Dec.9; 92) *Meister.* £700

FEUCHT, Jak.
- **Kleinste oder Kinder Postill.** Köln, 1582. Title
with owner's mark & slit, lightly browned, some
staining or foxing, cont. leath. gt. & blind-tooled,
spine & end-papers renewed, gt. oxidised, lacks ties.
(HK. Nov.8; 178) DM 640

FEUERBACH, L.
- **Das Wesen des Christenthums.** Leipzig, 1841. *1st.
Edn.* Some slight foxing, mod. hf. leath. (H. May
22; 664) DM 600
– – **Anr. Copy.** 2 pp. misbnd., lacks last lf., some
annots., cont. hf. leath., rubbed & bumped. (HK.
Nov.10; 2392) DM 400

FEUILLE VILLAGEOISE
Paris, 1790. 1st. Year; nos. 1-49 in 2 vols., 2nd.
Year; nos. 1-52 in 2 vols. Prospectus in 1st. vol.,
cont. roan, 1 vol. disbnd. (HD. Feb.22; 185)
Frs. 2,400

FEULNER, Adolf
- **Frankfurter Fayencen.** Berlin, 1935. Fo. Orig.
linen. (R. Oct.11; 903) DM 1,100

FEVAL, Paul
- **Los Tribunales Secretos.** Ill.:– E. Planas. Barce-
lona, 1871. 2 vols. Fo. Linen. (DS. May 25; 2252)
Pts. 20,000

FEYERABEND, S.
- [–] **Reysbuch dess Heyligen Lands.** Ill.:– J. Amman.
Frankfurt, 1584. *1st. Edn.* Fo. MS. owner's mark
on title, lightly browned thro.-out, cont. blind-
tooled pig, slightly rubbed, a little worn. (GB.
Nov.3; 75) DM 2,700

FFOULKES, Charles John
- **Inventory & Survey of the Armouries of the Tower
of London.** N.d. 2 vols. 4to. Orig. cl., lightly soiled.
(CSK. Jun.15; 8) £70

FIAMMA, Gabriello
- **Le Vite de Sant' descritte.** Venice, 1581. Fo. Slight
defect. in blank margins at beginning, cont. Italian
black mor., covers with painted arms in gt. borders,
gt. spine, worn, arms partly rubbed away; H.M.
Nixon coll. (BBA. Oct.6; 228) *Quaritch.* £80

FICHTE, Johann Georg
- **Die Bestimmung des Menschen.** Berlin, 1800. *1st.
Edn.* Lightly foxed, name stp. on title, cont. bds.,
worn & bumped. (R. Apr.3; 550) DM 450
- **Der Geschlossne Handelsstaat.** Tübingen, 1800.
1st. Edn. Some slight foxing, cont. hf. leath., very
worn. (H. May 22; 665) DM 1,350
– – **Anr. Copy.** Title with weak monog. stp., foxing,
lacks 1st. & last ll. blank, cont. bds., bumped;
Hauswedell coll. (H. May 24; 1282) DM 800
- **Rede an die Deutsche Nation.** Berlin, 1808. *1st.
Edn.* Cont. bds., slightly rubbed & bumped. Biblio-
theca Türkheimiana ex-libris, name 'Türckheim'
on end-paper, Richard Boetsch Benziger monog.
stp.; Hauswedell coll. (H. May 24; 1283)
DM 1,400
– – **Anr. Copy.** Minimal spotting, cont. bds.,
spotted, spine torn. (H. May 22; 666) DM 400
– – **Anr. Edn.** Ed.:– C.G. von Massen. Ill.:– A.
Simons. München, Bremer Pr., 1922. *(270).* 4to.
Private mor. gt., gold-tooled decor., slight wear. (D.
Nov.24; 3026) DM 700
– – **Anr. Edn.** Ed.:– [C.G. v. Maassen]. Ill.:– Anne
Simons. München, Bremer Pr., 1922. *(270) num-
bered on Zandersbütten.* Lge. 4to. Orig. vell., gt.
decor., bd. s.-c. (HK. May 17; 2608) DM 420
- **Uber das Wesen des Gelehrten u. seine Erschei-
nungen im Gebiete d. Freiheit.** Berlin, 1806. *1st.
Edn.* New linen, unc. (BR. Apr.12; 1344) DM 500
- **Ueber den Begriff der Wissenschaftslehre oder der
Sogenannten Philosophie als Einladung zu seinen
Vorlesungen über diese Wissenschaft.** Weimar,
1794. *1st. Edn.* Cont. bd. s., spine bumped. (BR.
Apr.12; 1243) DM 600
- **Versuch einer Critik aller Offenbarung.** Königs-
berg, 1792. *1st. Edn.* Cont. bds., rubbed & bumped.
(HT. May 10; 2231) DM 780
– – **Anr. Edn.** Königsberg, 1792. *1st. Edn. Variant
Iss.* Title with MS. note, minimal browning, cont.
bds., very bumped. (HK. Nov.10; 2400) DM 650

FICINUS, Marsilius
- **De Triplici Vita.** Venice, 1498. 4to. Washed, 19th.
C. vell. (HD. Jan.26; 130b) Frs. 2,300

FICORONI, Francesco de'
- **La Vestigia e Rarita di Roma Antica.** Rome, 1744.
4to. 40 engraved plts., some ll. soiled, later cf.-bkd.
cl., rubbed. (BBA. Feb.23; 48) *Thorp.* £140

FIELD, Barron
- **Geographical Memoirs on New South Wales.**
1825. *1st. Edn.* Hf. cf. (BBA. Sep.29; 59)
Steedman. £290
– – **Anr. Copy.** Frontis. foxed, title offset, rebnd. hf.
cf. (CA. Apr.3; 44) Aus. $820
– – **Anr. Copy.** Bdg. not stated, slight discoloration,
rebkd. (JL. Mar.25; 582) Aus. $450

FIELD, Col. Cyril
- **Britain's Sea-Soldiers.** Foreword:– Admiral Earl
Beatty. L'pool., Lyceum Pr., 1924. 3 vols. 4to.
Lacks title-p. to Vol. 1, panel. hf. cf. (PD. Aug.17;
277) £50

FIELD, Eugene
- **Poems of Childhood.** Ill.:– Maxfield Parrish.
N.Y., [1922]. Orig. cl., corners lightly bumped, d.-
w. rubbed & chipped, reprd. on verso with paper
tape; sigd. by artist. (CBA. Aug.21; 442) $190
- **The Writings in Prose & Verse.** N.Y., 1920-14.
12 vols. Mor. gt., gt.-panel. sides, spines gt., red

mor. doubls. gt., watered silk free end-pp., partly
unc. (CNY. Dec.17; 558) $500

FIELD, George
- [–] **Chromatics, or, An Essay on the Analogy &
Harmony of Colours.** L., 1817. *1st. Edn.* 4to. Plts. &
ills. hand-cold., slight spotting, hf. roan, rubbed.
(S. Dec.13; 488) *Korn.* £110

FIELD, Nathaniel
See– MASSINGER, Phillip & Field, Nathaniel

FIELDE, John
- **A Caveat for Parsons Howlet ... & all the Rest
of that Darke Brood ... who ... seeke the Discredite
of the Trueth & the Disquiet of this Church of
England.** 1581. Sm. 8vo. A few margin repairs to
last ll., recent cf. (TA. Jun.21; 523) £210

FIELDING, Anna Marie
See– HALL, Anna Marie, née Fielding

FIELDING, Henry
- **Amelia.** L., 1752. *1st. Edn.* 4 vols. Advt. lf. in
Vol. 2, cont. cf., spines gt. (C. Nov.9; 138)
Ximenes. £620
– – **Anr. Copy.** 4 vols. 12mo. Lacks advt. lf. in Vol.
2, a few margins cropped with loss of running-title
in Vol. 1, cont. hf. cf., rubbed. (SKC. May 4; 1668)
£80
– – **Anr. Copy.** 4 vols. 12mo. 'At the Universal-
Register-Office' lf. at end of Vol. II, p. 39 in Vol.
III not paginated, 'her lovely nose was beat all to
pieces' on p. 95 Vol. I, no blanks or hf.-titles, edges
yellowed, 19th. C. cf., spines gt., lightly rubbed.
(RO. Apr.23; 144) $220
– – **Anr. Copy.** 4 vols. 12mo. Advt. lf., vol.1 lacks
final blank, slight soiling, some sm. margin tears,
spr. cf. gt., spines gt., by Riviere; Fred A. Berne
copy. (SPB. May 16; 271) $200
– – **Anr. Copy.** 12mo. Some slight browning, cont.
Fr. mott. cf., gt. spines, not unif., armorial bkplt.
in each vol. (SPB. May 16; 54) $150
- [–] **The Author's Farce & The Pleasures of the
Town, by Scriblerus Secundus.** L., 1730. *1st. Edn.*
Some foxing, hf. cf., cover detchd. (SG. Feb.9; 226)
$325
- **Geschichte des Thomas Jones.** Trans.:– [J.J.
Bode]. Wien, 1788. 6 vols. in 3. Cont. hf. leath. gt.,
corners slightly bumped. (R. Oct.11; 203a)
DM 520
- **Histoire de Tom Jones.** Trans.:– M. de La Place.
Ill.:– Gravelot, engraved by Punt. Amst., 1750. 4
vols. in 2. 12mo. Some light foxing, cont. cf. gt.,
spines decor., some scratches. (HD. May 3; 53)
Frs. 1,150
- **Joseph Andrews.** 1742. 2 vols. Cf., defect. (LA.
Nov.29; 168) £97
– – **Anr. Edn.** L., [1742]. *1st. Edn.* 2 vols. 12mo.
Advt. ll., some spotting, few gatherings sprung,
cont. cf.; bk-label of Scotney Castle, Lamberhurst.
(SPB. May 16; 55) $650
– – **Anr. Edn.** 1742. *2nd. Edn.* 2 vols. 12mo. Cf.,
worn. (P. Mar.15; 309) *Maggs.* £50
- **Journal of a Voyage to Lisbon.** L., 1755. *1st. Edn.*
12mo. Some spots & stains, cont. cf.; bkplt. of
Baron [John] Rolle, from liby. of Bicton House.
(S. Dec.8; 44) *Pickering & Chatto.* £190
– – **Anr. Copy.** 12mo. Hf.-title, misnumbering of
pp.241-6, sig. on title, cont. cf. (SPB. May 16; 57)
$250
- **Miscellanies.** 1743. *1st Edn. 1st. Iss.* 3 vols. Sub-
scribers list in Vol. 1, cf. (P. Jan.12; 150)
Bickersteth. £190
- **Novels.** Oxford, Shakes. Hd. Pr., 1926. *(1000) for
sale.* 10 vols. Orig. cl. (KH. Nov.8; 150)
Aus. $180
- **Tom Jones.** L., 1749. *1st. Edn.* 6 vols. 12mo. With
all cancels as listed in Rothschild, cont. cf., spines
gt. (C. Nov.9; 139) *Ximenes.* £2,600
– – **Anr. Copy.** 6 vols. 12mo. Final blanks in vols.
1 & 3, in vol. 3 the cancels H8, H9 & H10 correctly
inserted, some browning, cont. cf., lr. endpaper on
vols. 1 & 3 loose; Herbert L. Carlebach-Hannah
D. Habinowitz-Stockhausen copy. (SPB. May 17;
606) $1,800
– – **Anr. Copy.** 6 vols. 12mo. B10 in Vol. I a cancel,
in Vol. III H8-10, M3 & Q11 are cancels, lacks
final blank in Vol. I, minimal foxing to 3 title-pp.,
later gt.-ruled mott. cf., spines gt.-panel., by W.
Pratt; J.G.F. Lund bkplts. (SG. Nov.3; 76) $700

FIELDING, Henry -Contd.

– – **Anr. Copy.** 6 vols. 12mo. Some light foxing, cont. cf., worn, early rebacking, 2 covers detchd. (SG. Apr.19; 86) $200

– – **Anr. Edn.** L., 1749. *1st. Edn. Vol. 1: 2nd. Iss.* 6 vols. Slight foxing or soiling, a few sigs. slightly sprung, cont. cf., Vols. 2-6 with .gt.-stpd. crown on spine, sm. remnant of mor. label on 1 spine, covers slightly rubbed & darkening, extremities bumped, Vol. 1 recased & with new end-papers, extensive collation on 1st. rear pastedown, several vols. lack 1 or more end-papers or fly-ll., scrawls on some end-papers, bkplts. (CBA. Dec.10; 212) $425

– – **Anr. Edn.** 1749. *2nd. Edn.* 6 vols. 12mo. Without errata, cont. cf., spines gt., Diocese of Southwark. copy. (C. May 30; 133) *Maggs.* $200

– – **Anr. Copy.** 6 vols. 12mo. Final blank ll. in vols. 1,3 & 5, some stains, cont. cf., spines gt.-ruled, s.-c.; Fred A. Berne copy. (SPB. May 16; 272) $200

– – **Anr. Edn.** L., 1749. 6 vols. 12mo. Final blank in vol. 1, few marginal tears & repairs, panel. cf. gt., spines gt., by Pratt, mor. solander cases; Perry Molstad copy. (SPB. May 16; 453) $650

– **Tom Jones ou l'Enfant trouvé.** Trans.:– De La Place. Londres/Paris, 1777. 4 vols. in 2. Linen. (DS. Dec.16; 2114) Pts. 30,000

– – **Anr. Edn.** 1833. 4 vols. Lge. 8vo. On vell., engr. before the letter by Moreau le jeune, in 2 proofs (1 foxed), cont. cf. gt. by Petit, spines decor.; Henri Thuile ex-libris. (HD. Jul.6; 103) Frs. 1,800

– **Works.** 1784. 10 vols. End-paper Vol. 1 torn, cont. cf. gt. (P. Sep.29; 137) *Kassow.* £220

– – **Anr. Edn.** Ed.:– Arthur Murphy. L., 1821. 10 vols. Cf. gt., spines gt. with fleurons. (SG. Feb.16; 119) $225

– – **Anr. Edn.** Ill.:– H. Railton & E.J. Wheeler. 1893. *(150) numbered.* 12 vols. L.P., red mor. gt., dentelles, spines decor. gt., by Morrell. (SKC. Jan.13; 2210) £260

– **The Works ... with The Life of the Author ... to which is now first added, The Fathers.** L., 1783. 12 vols. 12mo. Some offsetting from frontispieces, early tree cf., neatly rebkd., extremities worn. (SG. Mar.15; 113) $175

FIELDING, Sarah

[–] **The Adventures of David Simple.** L., 1744. *1st. Edn.* 2 vols. 12mo. Cont. cf., some wear. (SPB. May 16; 58) $425

FIELDING, Theodore Henry

– **British Castles or a Compendious History of the Ancient Military Structures of Great Britain.** L., 1825. Ob. 4to. 25 hand-cold. aquatint plts., mod. hf. cf., orig. gt. mor. label on upr. cover. (C. Jun.27; 32) *Zanzotto.* £280

– **Cumberland, Westmoreland & Lancashire Illustrated.** L., 1822. Fo. 44 hand-cold. engraved plts., cont. hf. mor., slightly rubbed. (BBA. Dec.15; 79) *Quevedo.* £500

FIELDING, Theodore Henry & Walton, J.

– **A Picturesque Tour of the English Lakes.** L., 1821. 4to. Title with cold. aquatint vig., 48 hand-cold. aquatint plts., mod. maroon str.-grd. mor. gt. (C. Jun.27; 33) *Zanzotto.* £500

– – **Anr. Copy.** 4to. Cold. aquatint vig. on title & 48 hand-cold. aquatint views, 1st. plt. & prelims. slightly spotted, cont. hf. mor. (S. May 21; 68) *Myerscough.* £480

FIERENS, Paul

– **Survage.** Paris, [1931]. *(5) numbered on imperial japan with sigd. orig. gouache & orig. etching in 3 states, 1 numbered & sigd.* Lge. 4to. Linen box. (D. Nov.24; 3204) DM 1,400

FIERENS-GEVAERT, Hippolyte

– **Histoire de la Peinture Flamande des Origines à la Fin du Xve Siècle.** Paris & Brussels, 1927-29. 3 vols. Tall 4to. Ptd. wraps. (SG. Aug.25; 143) $180

FIEVEE, Joseph

– **Correspondance Politique et Administrative commencée au Mois de mai 1814.** Paris, 1816-Feb. 1818. 13 pts. in 3 vols. (compl. series). Cont. bds. (HD. Feb.22; 70) Frs. 3,000

FIGARO-SALON

Paris, 1885-1901. In 9 vols. Fo. & 4to. Cont. hf. mor., rubbed. (BBA. Feb.23; 66) *Erlini.* £110

FIGDOR, Dr. Albert

– **Die Sammlung Dr. Albert Figdor Wien.** Berlin, 1930. 5 vols. 4to. Priced sale catalogue, orig. wraps., some chipping. (SG. Aug.25; 141) $240

FIGULUS, Benedictus

– **Pandora Magnalium Naturalium Aurea et Benedicta ...** Strassburg, 1608. In Latin & German, symbol on title hand-cold., dyed vell.; Dr. Walter Pagel copy. (S. Feb.7; 120) *Ritman.* £700

FILHOL, Antoine Michel

– **Galerie du Musée de France.** Paris, 1814. 10 vols. Lge. 8vo. L.P., port., 720 engrs., some foxing, early str.-grd. mor., gt. design on all covers in border & crowned 'N'S' spines gt.; armorial bkplt. of Mackenzie of Portmore. (SG. Apr.26; 87) $500

– – **Anr. Copy.** 10 vols. Lacks 7 copperplts., lightly browned, slightly foxed, cont. gold-tooled leath. (R. Apr.4; 2089) DM 500

FILIPPI, Filippo de

– **Karakoram & Western Himalaya 1909. An Account of the Expedition of H.R.H. Prince Luigi Amedeo of Savoy.** N.Y., 1912. 1 vol. only (lacks Atlas vol.). 4to. Cl., worn, unc. (RO. Sep.13; 51) $290

FILIPPINI, Antonio Pietro

– **La Historia di Corsica.** Tournon, 1594. Sm. 4to. Some light foxing & dampstains, 18th. C. cf., spine decor. (HD. Oct.21; 82) Frs. 26,000

– **Istoria di Corsica.** Ed.:– G.C. Gregori. Pisa, 1827-31. *2nd. Edn.* 5 vols. Publisher's bds. (HD. Oct.21; 83) Frs. 3,000

FILMLIGA

Ed.:– M. Ter Braak, J. Ivens. H. Scholte. Amst. & Rotterdam, 1927-35. Yrs. I-VIII (= VII) (all publd.). 7 vols. bnd. in 3. 4to. Hf. cl., not unif. (B. Apr.27; 620) Fls. 3,400

FINALY, Mme. of Florence

See— LANDAU, Baron Horace de & Finaly, Mme. of Florence

FINDEN, Edward Francis

– **Illustrations of the life and Works of Lord Byron.** Ill.:– W. Brockedon. 1833-34. 4to. Engraved titles, 123 plts., some browned, cont mor., slightly rubbed. (BBA. Feb.9; 71) *Dimakarakos.* £120

– – **Anr. Copy.** 3 vols. 3 engraved titles, 123 engraved views, ports., etc., hf. mor. (GM. Dec.7; 601) £90

– – **Anr. Copy.** 3 vols. Lge. 8vo. 146 engraved plts., cont. hf. mor., backs gt. decor. (SG. Jun.7; 347) $150

– – **Anr. Copy.** 3 vols. Some foxing & offsetting, orig. three-qtr. str.-grd. mor., elab. gt.-decor. spines. (CBA. Dec.10; 214) $140

– – **Anr. Copy.** 3 vols. 3 engraved titles, 123 steel engraved plts., later leath. (R. Oct.13; 3140) DM 620

– – **Anr. Edn.** 1835-33-34. 3 vols. 4to. Cont. mor. gt. (SKC. May 4; 1626) £80

FINDEN, Edward Francis & William

– **Malerische Ansichten von den Hafen- und Küstenlandschaften Grossbritanniens und Irlands.** Ill.:– W.H. Bartlett. L., [Leipzig, 1839]. *1st. German Edn.* 4to. Engraved title with vig., 79 steel engraved plts., foxed & stained, cont. hf. linen, bumped. (BR. Apr.12; 79) DM 450

– **Ports, Harbours, Watering Places, & Coast Scenery of Great Britain.** 1839. Vol. 1 only (of 2). 4to. Engraved vig. title, 64 plts., stained, hf. cf., defect., as a coll. of plts., w.a.f. (P. Jan.12; 109) *Macdonald.* £130

– – **Anr. Copy.** Vol. 2 only (of 2). 4to. 58 plts., some spotting, cf. gt. (P. Sep.29; 206) £110

– – **Anr. Edn.** Ill.:– N.H. Bartlett. 1842. 2 vols. 4to. 123 (of 124) engraved plts., some foxing, cont. hf. mor. gt. (SKC. Jan.13; 2150) £240

– – **Anr. Copy.** 2 vols. 4to. Vig. & ptd. title to each vol., 124 steel engrs., some spotting, mainly to margins, cont. hf. mor., gt.-decor. spines, rubbed. (TA. Jun.21; 210) £210

– – **Anr. Copy.** 2 vols. 4to. 123 engraved views, some foxed, cont. mor. gt. (P. Sep.29; 308) *Shapiro.* £180

– – **Anr. Edn.** Ill.:– Bartlett, Harding, Creswick, & others. L., [1842]. 2 vols. 4to. Additional engraved pict. titles, 142 plts., some foxing, marginally affecting plts., early hf. cf. gt., worn, spines brittle, cover detchd. (SG. Mar.29; 313) $200

– – **Anr. Edn.** [1874]. 2 vols. 4to. Engraved additional titles, 142 plts., some light spotting, cont. cf. spines rubbed. (CSK. Nov.4; 30) £220

[–] **The Royal Gallery of British Art.** L., ca. 1880. Fo. 48 engraved plts., 7 litho. ll. of subscribers' sig., a few ll. spotted, cont. hf. mar., spine gt., rubbed. (BBA. Dec.15; 309) *Erlini.* £260

– **Tableaux of National Character, Beauty, & Costume.** L., 1837-41. 5 vols. Fo. Some spotting, orig. mor., gt. & blind-stpd., rubbed. (BBA. Dec.15; 80) *Erlini.* £70

– – **Anr. Edn.** 1843. 2 vols. in 1. Fo. Vig. title, 60 steel engrs., some spotting, cont. hf. mor., spine gt.-decor. (TA. Feb.16; 296) £60

– – **Anr. Copy.** 2 vols. 1 additional engraved title, 62 steel-engraved plts., later hand-cold., some foxing, later three-qtr. red gt.-ruled mor., gt.-stpd. spines, some staining to covers, corners worn, Vol.1 lr. edges gouged. (CBA. Dec.10; 215) $130

– **Views of Ports & Harbours, Watering Places, Fishing Villages, & Other Picturesque Objects on the English Coast.** L., 1838. 4to. 50 steel-engraved plts., some foxing & soiling, publisher's gt.-stpd. mor., worn. (RO. Dec.11; 108) $100

– – **Anr. Edn.** 1839. 4to. Engraved title, 49 engraved views, orig. cl. gt., spine slightly torn. (P. Oct.20; 230a) £100

– – **Anr. Edn.** N.d. 2 vols. 4to. 2 engraved titles, 142 plts., hf. cf., rubbed. (P. Mar.15; 188) £250

– – **Anr. Copy.** 2 vols. in 1. 4to. 2 steel-engraved extra titles, 137 plts. only, some spotting, cont. hf. mor., 1 cover loose, lightly soiled. (CSK. Feb.24; 130) £220

FINDEN, Edward Francis & William & Horne, Rev. Thomas Hartwell

– **Landscape Illustrations of the Bible.** 1836. 2 vols. Some slight spotting, cont. leath. 'cathedral' bdg., spines gt. (LC. Oct.13; 46) £70

– – **Anr. Copy.** 2 vols. 2 engraved titles, 94 plts., some spotting & staining, diced cf. gt., rubbed. (P. Mar.15; 234) £65

– – **Anr. Copy.** 2 vols. Lge. 8vo. Orig. maroon mor., spines gt., rubbed, spines chipped at head. (LC. Jul.5; 202) £50

FINDLAY, F.R.N.

– **Big Game Shooting & Travel in South-East Africa.** L., 1903. *1st. Edn.* Three-qtr. leath., rubbed. (RO. Jun.26; 67) $150

FINDLAY, G.G. & Holdsworth, W.W.

– **The History of the Wesleyan Methodist Missionary Society.** L., 1921-24. *1st. Edn.* 5 vols. Orig. cl. (KH. Nov.8; 152) Aus. $140

FINE, Oronce

[–] **Giuoco d'Arme dei Sovrani e degli Stati d'Europa.** Trans.:– B. Giustiniani. Naples, 1681. 16mo. 52 engraved plts., vell., soiled. (P. Jan.12; 224) *Duran.* £70

FINIGUERRA, Maso

– **A Florentine Picture-Chronicle.** Ed.:– Sir Sidney Colvin. L., 1898. *(300).* Tall fo. 99 plts. in sepia, 99 text ills., tipped-in errata slip, ex-libry., Decor. cl. (SG. May 3; 165) $120

FINLEY, Anthony

– **A New American Atlas, Designed Principally to Illustrate the Geography of the United States of North America.** Phila., Finley, 1826. *1st. Edn.* Atlas fo. Title, plt.-list, 15 cold. maps, slight foxing, some wear at centre folds, qtr. mor., worn. (SG. Jun.7; 13) $1,000

– **A New General Atlas.** Phila., 1824. *1st. Edn.* Lge. 4to. Engraved title, index & 59(of 60) cont. hand-cold. engraved maps, lacks plt. 60: table, margin stains, cont. hf. cf., foot of spine defect. (VS. Jun.7; 787) Fls. 725

FINN, Edmund 'Garryowen'

[–] **The Chronicles of Early Melbourne, 1835 to 1852 ... by 'Garryowen' ...** Melbourne, 1888. *Centennial*

Edn. 2 vols. 4to. Sewing weak, publisher's mor.
(KH. Nov.8; 153)   Aus. $350
– – **Anr. Edn.** Melbourne, n.d. *Facs. Edn. (500)*
numbered. 3 vols. 4to. Bdg. not stated. (KH. May
1; 256)   Aus. $160

FIORENTINI, J. v. & Löhneysen, Georg Engelherd
von
– **Zwey Gute und sehr Nutzlich Bücher von Stangen**
und Mund-stücken, sambt einer Beschreibung der
Complexion und Nature der Pferde ... Frankfurt,
1609. Fo. 1 folding plt. with light crumpling, cont.
vell., slightly spotted, lacks lr. tie. (HK. Nov.9;
2018)   DM 2,850

FIRMIN-DIDOT, Frères
– **Nouvelle Biographie Générale depuis les**
Temps les plus reculés jusqu'à nos Jours ... Ed.:–
M. Hoefer. Paris, 1858-73. 46 pts. in 23 vols. Cont.
red hf. leath., some spines lightly bumped. (HK.
Nov.11; 4396)   DM 650

FIRST EDITION CLUB
– **A Bibliographical Catalogue of the First Loan**
Exhibition of Books & Manuscripts held by the
First Edition Club 1922. Priv. ptd., 1922. *(500) sigd.*
by 10 members of the First Edition Club. Orig. cl.-
bkd. bds., unc.; 2 letters from A.J. Symons (1
to Laver), & receipt sigd. by G.B. Shaw loosely
inserted. (S. May 1; 371)   *Libris.* £80

FIRST [SECOND] REPORT OF THE COMMIS-
SIONERS for Inquiring into the State of Large
Towns & Populous Districts
L., 1844-45. *1st. Edns.* 2 reports in 4 vols. 47 plts. &
maps, some cold. & folding, 1 vol. orig. ptd. wraps.,
slightly worn, 3 vols. cont. cl. (S. Mar.20; 715)
                                                    Drury. £70

FIRTH, Sir Charles Harding
See— GARDINER, Samuel Rawson & Firth, Sir
Charles Harding

FISCHART, Joh.
– **Geschichtklitterung.** Ill.:– Br. Goldschmitt.
[München, 1914-15]. 2 pts. & 1 vol. 4to. Leath.,
blind-tooled, s.-c. (HK. May 17; 2845)   DM 700

FISCHBACH, Gustave
– **Album du Siège et du Bombardement de Stras-**
bourg ... Ca. 1870. 4to. 19 litho. plts., some foxing,
qtr. mor. gt. (P. Dec.8; 324)   *Mann.* £170

FISCHBACH, Johann
– **Malerische Ansichten von Salzburg und Ober-**
Oesterreich. Ill.:– Robock, Huber, Lang & others
after Johann Fischbach. Salzburg, ca. 1850. Ob.
fo. Wide margin, 1 litho. title, 41 steel engraved
plts., some plts. foxed, cont. linen. (D. Nov.23; 847)
                                                    DM 2,800

FISCHER, F. O. J.
– **Uber die Probenächte der Teutschen Bauer-**
mädchen. Berlin & Leipzig, 1780. *1st. Edn.* Stp. on
title pasted over on verso, some slight foxing, hf.
leath. (HK. Nov.9; 2105)   DM 850

FISCHER, Isidor
– **Biographisches Lexikon der Hervorragenden**
Aerzte der Letzten Fuenfzig Jahre. Berlin &
Vienna, 1932-33. *1st. Edn.* 2 vols. in 4. Lge. 8vo.
Liby. buckram. (SG. Mar.22; 207) $350

FISCHER, Max
– **Das Heidelberger Schloss.** Karlsruhe, ca. 1845.
Ob. fo. Title & 15 litho. views, lge. folding panorama, torn without loss, some spotting to text &
tissues, orig. cl., loose. (S. Apr.9; 22) *Nolan.* £210

FISCHER, S. (Ed.)
See— NEUE RUNDSCHAU

FISCHER, V.F. (Ed.)
See— SYLVAN

FISCHER VON ERLACH, Johann Emmanuel
– **Anfang Einiger Vorstellungen der Vornehmsten**
Gebäude ... **Vorstädten von Wien.** Ill.:– Delsenbach.
Augsburg, [1719]. Ob. fo. Engraved title, 27 plts.
(numbered 4-10, 10a, 11-29/30), privilege lf., cont.
cf. gt., rebkd. in red mor. gt. with Devonshire
cypher. (C. Dec.9; 50)   *Hedworth.* $6,000
– **Entwurff Einer Historischen Architectur** ...

Leipzig, 1725. *2nd. Edn.* 5 pts. in 1 vol. Ob. fo.
Engraved title, dedication lf., frontis., map, 84 plts.,
5 hf.-titles, plts. discold., 2 minor margin tears
reprd., sm. stain on 1 plt., cont. cf., spine gt., head
of spine reprd. (C. Dec.9; 49)   *Waldersee.* £1,200

FISHER, J.
See— SITWELL, Sacheverell & others

FISHER, John, Bp. of Rochester
– **Assertationis Lutheranae Confutatio iuxta Verum**
ac Originalen Archetypum. Venice, Aug. 1526. Fo.
e2 & 5 misbnd. in sig. c, upr. & outer margin of
L1 reprd., owner's inscr. erased from title-p. with
repair on verso & soiled, 19th. C. mor. gt. by
Wright, slightly rubbed; Harmsworth bkplt. (S.
Nov.17; 24)   *A. Thomas.* £280

FISHER, John Dix
– **Description of the Distinct, Confluent, and Inocu-**
lated Small Pox, Varioloid Disease, Cow Pox and
Chicken Pox. Boston, 1829. *Only Edn.* 4to. 13
hand-cold. plts., stpd. on verso, captioned in pencil,
liby. stp., mod. hf. cf., unc.; sig. of William Holme
Van Buren on title & orig. pastedown, mntd. &
bnd. in. (SG. Mar.22; 120) $275

FISHER, Jonathan
– **A Picturesque Tour of Killarney.** Dublin, 1790.
2nd. Edn. Ob. fo. Tinted map, 20 hand-cold. plts.,
liby. stp. obliterated on title & intro., crimson hf.
mor. (GM. Dec.7; 175)   £1,200

FISHER, R.S.
See— COLTON, G.W. & Fisher, R.S.

FISHER, Thomas
– **A Series of Antient Allegorical, Historical &**
Legendary Paintings ... **at Stratford-upon-Avon.** L.,
1836. Fo. Some plts. hand-cold., some spotting,
mostly marginal, later hf. mor., slightly rubbed. (S.
Dec.13; 447)   *Price.* £80

FISHER, Son & Co., Publishers
– **Fisher's Illustrations of Devon & Cornwall.** 1810.
1st. Edn. Mor., orig. bds. (LA. Jul.20; 137) £130

FISSCHER, J.F. van Overmeer
– **Bijdrage tot de Kennis van het Japansche Rijk.**
Amst., 1833. 4to. Hf.-title, 15 hand-cold. engraved
plts., several with added gold, light margin stains
affecting a few ll. of text, hf. mor. (S. May 22; 439)
                                            Orientum. £550

FITCH, John A.
– **The Steel Workers.** Ill.:– after Lewis W. Hine &
others. N.Y., 1910. *1st. Edn.* From 'Pittsburgh
Survey'. 4to. Cl., rubbed & stained. (SG. Nov.10;
83) $475

FITCH, Samuel Sheldon
– **A System of Dental Surgery.** N.Y., 1829. *1st.*
Edn. Some offsetting, 19th. C. suede, extremities
worn; Asbell bkplt. (SG. Mar.22; 90) $110

FITE, Emerson D. & Freeman, Archibald
– **A Book of Old Maps, Delineating American His-**
tory from the Earliest Days Down to the Close of
the Revolutionary War. Camb. [Mass], 1926. *1st.*
Edn. Fo. Buckram, rubbed. (SG. Jun.7; 148) $175

FITTLER, James & Love, John
– **[Views of Waymouth].** Ill.:– Nixon, Beaumont, Le
Cave, & others. 1791. Ob. fo. Etched dedication,
12 sepia etched & aquatint plts., cont. red hf. mor.,
spine gt.; the Hinton House copy. (LC. Oct.13;
437)   £520

FITZ-ADAM, ADAM (Pseud.)
See— MOORE, Edward

FITZGERALD, E.A.
– **Climbs in the New Zealand Alps.** L., 1896. *1st.*
Edn. (60) numbered. Folding map mntd. on linen
in pocket at end, cont. hf. mor., slightly rubbed.
(BBA. May 3; 345)   *Bob Finch Books.* £210
– **The Highest Andes** ... **with Chapters by Stuart**
Vines. L., 1899. *(60) numbered.* 4to. 1 folding map
torn, some ll. slightly, orig. cl.-bkd. bds., rubbed;
pres. inscr. to Arthur Lightbody by Stuart Vines.
(BBA. May 3; 346)   *Bob Finch Books.* £220
– – **Anr. Edn.** 1899. Cl. gt. (P. Feb.16; 149)   £60

FITZGERALD, Edward
[–] **Euphranor: A Dialogue for Youth.** L., 1851. *1st.*
Edn. 12mo. Errata-p., orig. cl., spine faded, owner's
sig. on end-paper. (SG. Mar.15; 114) $110

FITZGERALD, Francis Scott
– **The Beautiful & Damned.** N.Y., 1922. *1st. Edn.*
1st. Printing. Inscr. 'Sincerely F. Scott Fitzgerald',
cl., tear on spine reprd. (SG. Nov.3; 77) $400
– – **Anr. Edn.** N.Y., 1922. *1st. Edn.* Cl. (SG. May
24; 287) $200
– – **Anr. Edn.** N.Y., 1922. *1st. Edn. 3rd. Printing.*
Orig. cl., slight foxing to end-papers; inscr. by
author to Dorothy Bissell. (CNY. Dec.17; 414).
                                                $650
– **Flappers & Philosophers.** N.Y., 1920. *1st. Edn.*
1st. Printing. Cl., slightly worn, spine ends nicked.
(SG. May 24; 286) $150
– **The Great Gatsby.** N.Y., 1925. *1st. Edn. 2nd.*
Printing. Few pp. lightly foxed, orig. cl., few sm.
stains on spine, inscr. by author to Dorothy Bissell.
(CNY. Dec.17; 415) $2,200
– **Tales of the Jazz Age.** N.Y., 1922. *1st. Edn.* With
'and' at p. 232, perfect type on pp. 22, 27, etc.,
without list of works on p. [B], with cancellans title-
lf. identical with integral title described by Bruccoli
A9.1.a., cl., spine ends rubbed. (SG. May 24; 290)
                                                $150
– **The Vegetable.** N.Y., 1923. Lightly browned, orig.
cl.; pres. copy to Martha Wolcott. (SPB. May 17;
607) $600

FITZGERALD, George Robert
See— McPARLAN, James—Fitzgerald, George
Robert—DUTTON, Hely

FITZGERALD, Robert D.
– **Australian Orchids.** Sydney, 1882. Fo. Vol. 1 in
book form, Vol. 2 in 5 orig. pts., 26 plain & 92 col.
litho. plts., mostly hand-cold., 1 plt. & 4 ll. of text
torn in lr. outer margin, liby. stps. on title &
wraps., hf. mor. gt. & orig. wraps. (P.
Nov.24; 248)   *Walford.* £1,350

FITZGIBBON, Edward 'Ephemera'
[–] **A Handbook of Angling: teaching Fly-Fishing,**
Trolling, Bottom-Fishing, & Salmon-Fishing; ... **by**
Ephemera. L., 1847. *1st. Edn.* 1 vol. Orig. cl., spine
faded. *(With:)* – **The Book of the Salmon.** ... **By**
Ephemera, assisted by A. Young. L., 1850. *1st. Edn.*
1 vol. 9 plts., including 8 hand-cold., slight spotting,
stitching loose, orig. cl., spine faded, stained. (S.
Oct.4; 20)   *Marlborough.* £130

FITZROY, Capt. Robert, King, Adam P.P. &
Darwin, Charles
– **Narrative of the Surveying Voyages of His**
Majesty's Ships Adventure & Beagle, 1826-1836.
L., 1839. *1st. Edn. Vol. 3: 2nd. Iss.* Vols. 1 & 3
only, & Appendix to Vol. 2. 2 folding maps each
in front pockets of Vol. 1 & Appendix, 16 engraved
plts. in Vol. 1, 6 engraved plts. in Appendix, folding
map in Vol. 3, some light stains & foxing in Vol.
1 & Appendix, some underlining in Vol. 3, blind-
stpd. cl., Vol. 1 & Appendix unc., Vol. 1 loose, 2
spines torn, covers stained, ex-liby. (CA. Apr.3; 14)
                                               Aus. $1,100
– – **Anr. Edn.** L., 1839. *1st. Edn.* 3 vols. Engraved
plts. & charts, 4 folding charts only (of 8) in pockets
at beginning or end, lacks Appendix to vol.2, orig.
cl., slightly worn; inscr. to Maj. Chipchase from
FitzRoy, as an assoc., w.a.f. (S. Apr.9; 18)
                                            Maggs. £950

FIXIMILLNER, P.
– **Meridianus Speculae Astronomicae Cremifanensis**
seu Longitudo eius Geographica per Magnum Illud
Solis Deliquium ... Steyr, 1765. *1st. Edn.* 4to. Cont.
leath., rubbed. (R. Apr.4; 1519)   DM 480

FLACCUS, Siculus & others
– **De Agrorum.** Paris, 1554. 4to. Title laid down
with section supplied in MS., Y1 cleanly torn
affecting text, blank margins of X3 & 201 torn
with loss, old limp vell. (CSK. Nov.4; 126)   £140

FLACH
– **Les Origines de l'Ancienne France.** Paris, 1886-
1917. 4 vols. Hf. cl. (HD. Feb.22; 71) Frs. 1,700

FLACHAT, Stéphane
- Atlas de l'Histoire des Travaux et de l'Amenagement des Eaux du Canal Caledonian. Paris, [1828]. Fo. Some soiling, title reprd., cont. hf. cf. (CSK. Aug.5; 55) £100

FLACOURT, Sieur Etienne de
- Histoire de la Grande Isle Madagascar. Paris, 1661. *2nd. Edn.* 4to. Cont. spr. cf., decor. spine, very worn. (HD. Dec.9; 36) Frs. 3,300
- – Anr. Copy. 4to. Cont. cf., worn. (HD. Jun.29; 73) Frs. 2,700

FLAGG, Ernest
- Small Houses: Their Economic Designs & Construction. N.Y., 1922. Tall fo. 50 plts., many text ills., ex-liby., cl., worn. (SG. May 3; 167) $140

FLAMAND, Claude
- Les Mathématiques et Géométrie de Parties en Cinq Livres. - La Guide des Fortifications et Conduitte Militaire, pour bien Fortifier & Deffendre. - La Practique et Usage d'Arpenter et Mesurer Toutes Superficies de Terre. Montbeliart, [1611]. *1st. Edn. of 3rd. work.* 3 works in 1 vol. Foxing & dampstains, old vell., mod. bdg. (HD. Apr.13; 70) Frs. 6,000

FLAMEL, Nicolaus
- Zwey Ausserlesene Chymische Buechlein I. das Buch der Hieroglyphischen Figuren ... Kirchhof der un-schuldigen Kinder zu Paris ... II. Das Warhaffte Buch des Gelahrten Griechischen Abts Synesii vom Stein der Weisen ... das Original der Begierde. 1673. Together 2 works in 1 vol. Folding plt. in 1st. work, few stains, D1 torn in upr. & lr. corners, old bds., spine worn; Dr. Walter Pagel copy, due to possible lack of a plt., w.a.f. (S. Feb.7; 122) *Ritman.* £600

FLAMEN, Albert
- Devises et Emblesmes d'Amour Moralisez. Paris, 1672. Sm. 8vo. Additional engraved title & 50 emblematical engrs., a few minor tears, all rather crudely reprd., a few stains, cont. cf., gt. spine, worn. (S. May 10; 278) *Watson.* £220

FLAMSTEED, John
- Atlas Celeste de Flamsteed, Approuvé par L'Académie Royale des Sciences. Ed.:– M.J. Fortin. Paris, 1776. *2nd. Edn.* 4to. Cont. qtr. cf. gt. (SG. Mar.22; 122) $325
- – Anr. Copy. Sm. 4to. 30 double-p. & 3 supp. copper-engraved maps, cont. leath. gt., bumped, spine slightly defect. (R. Oct.13; 2844) DM 1,100
- – Anr. Edn. Paris, 1795. 4to. Linen. (DS. Mar.23; 2106) Pts. 30,000

FLANAGAN, Mrs.
[–] Antigua & the Antiguans. L., 1844. *1st. Edn.* 2 vols. Orig. cl. gt., unc. (F. May 17; 4) *Kossow.* £190

FLANAGAN, Roderick
- The History of New South Wales ... 1862. 2 vols. Old hf. mor., partly unc., slightly spotted & marked. (KH. May 1; 260) Aus. $110

FLANDIN
See— BOTTA & FLANDIN

FLASSAN, DE
- Histoire Générale et Raisonné de la Diplomatie Française. Paris, 1809. 6 vols. Hf. cf. (HD. Feb.22; 72) Frs. 2,100

FLAUBERT, Gustave
- Bouvard et Pécuchet. Paris, 1881. *Orig. Edn.* 12mo. Mor. by Semet et Plumelle, spine decor., wrap. preserved. (HD. Jun.13; 31) Frs. 3,900
- – Anr. Edn. Paris, 1881. *Orig. Edn. (10) on china.* 12mo. Jansenist mor. by Marius Michel, spine raised bands (slightly faded), mor. gt. doubls., sewed silk end-ll., wrap. & spine. HD. May 16; 20) Frs. 25,000
- Un Coeur Simple. Preface:– A. de Claye. Ill.:– Emile Adam, engraved by Champollion. Paris, 1894. *(200) with suite of ills. before the letter.* Jansenist mor. gt., Grollie decor, wrap. preserved. (HD. Jun.13; 30) Frs. 3,200
- L'Education Sentimentale. Paris, 1870. *Orig. Edn.* 2 vols. Hf. mor. by Semet et Plumelle, spines decor. (slightly faded), wrap. preserved; author's brother's copy. (HD. Jun.13; 35) Frs. 25,100

– – Anr. Copy. 2 vols. Bradel hf. mor., corners. by V. Champs, unc., wraps. & spines; with 32 pp. catalogue. (HD. May 16; 19) Frs. 8,800
- Herodias. Ill.:– Champollion after Georges Rochegrosse. Paris, Sociéte AAC des Beaux Arts, ca. 1900. *Edn. des Deux Mondes. (20) lettered on Japan vell.* 4to. Plts. & text engrs. in 3 states (plain, India-proof & cold.), all (excepting 1 state of the text engrs.) with vig. remarque, orig. lev. gt., cold. mor. inlays, dentelles elab. gt.-decor., lev. doubls., upr. doubl. with inlaid oval hand-cold. engraved vig. on vell., moire grosgrain cl. liners, partly unc. (SG. Feb.16; 283) $1,300
- – Anr. Edn. Berlin, 1919. *(200) numbered on Zanders bütten.* Fo. Slightly foxed, orig. hf. vell. (HK. May 17; 3142) DM 540
- – Anr. Edn. Trans.:– W. Unus. Ill.:– M. Slevogt. Berlin, [1919]. *De Luxe Edn., (50).* Lge. 4to. Hand-bnd. orig. vell., by O. Dorfner, Weimar, slightly rubbed; sigd. litho. (H. Nov.24; 2058) DM 1,050
- – Anr. Edn. Ill.:– Gustave-Adolphe Mossa, pochoir-cold. by Berthelot. Paris, 1927. *(1200) numbered on velin teinte du Marais, initialed by publisher.* Sm. 8vo. Red three-qtr. mor., cold. pict. wraps. bnd. in. (SG. Feb.16; 121) $130
- La Légende de Saint Julien L'Hospitalier. Ill.:– Lucien Pissaro. [L., Eragny Pr., 1900]. *(226).* 16mo. Linen-bkd. paper bds. (LH. Sep.25; 362) $160
- Madame Bovary. 1 & 15 Oct., 1 & 15 Nov., 1 & 15 Dec. 1856. *1st. Edn. in orig. pts. from 'Revue de Paris'.* 6 pts. in 1 vol. Hf. mor., corners, by Canape, spine decor. (HD. May 4; 263) Frs. 2,900
- – Anr. Edn. Paris, 1857. *Orig. Edn.* 2 vols. 12mo. Hf. mor., corners, by Forbin, wraps. (lightly soiled), spine unif. faded. (HD. May 4; 264) Frs. 1,300
- – Anr. Copy. 2 vols. Light margin browning or soiling, orig. wraps., bd. cover & s.-c.; Hauswedell coll. (H. May 24; 1285) DM 2,600
- – Anr. Copy. 2 pts. in 1 vol. Square 12mo. On thick vell., jansenist mor. by Canapé, 1904, spine raised bands, mor. gt. doubls., sewed silk end-ll., s.-c. (HD. May 16; 18) Frs. 16,100
- – Anr. Copy. 2 vols. in 1. Without catalogue, jansenist mor. by Marius Michel, mor. liners, watered silk end-ll., wrap. preserved., spine faded. (HD. Jun.13; 34) Frs. 5,500
- – Anr. Edn. Preface:– Leon Hermique. Ill.:– C. Chessa after A. de Richemond. Paris, 1905. *(200) numbered.* 4to. On japan, mor. gt. by Zaehnsdorf, 1911, wrap. & spine, s.-c.; with suite with remark of all ills. on japan. (HD. May 21; 116) Frs. 4,100
- – Anr. Edn. Ill.:– Grau-Sala. 1945. *(35).* Separate suite in black & orig. aquatint, sewed, s.-c.; Daragnès copy. (HD. Dec.9; 30) Frs. 1,000
- Novembre. Ill.:– Edgar Chahine. Paris, 1928. *(237). (150) on vélin d'Arches.* 4to. Leaves, folder & s.-c. (HD. May 4; 269) Frs. 2,200
- Oeuvres Complètes. Paris, 1910. *Coll. Edn.* 18 vols. Hf. chagrin, corners, decor. spines, wrap. & spine preserved. unc. (B. Apr.27; 626) Fls. 925
- Oeuvres Diverses. Paris, n.d. 9 vols. 12mo. Cont. hf. red mor., corners. (HD. Apr.11; 21) Frs. 1,400
- Die Sage von Sankt Julian dem Gastfreien. Trans.:– Else v. Hollander. Ill.:– Max Kaus. 1918. *(100) De Luxe Edn. on Bütten.* 12 monogrammed & dtd. orig. lithos., orig. hf. suede, silk covered, gold-tooled cover vig., end-papers slightly spotted. (GB. May 5; 2762) DM 1,200
- Salammbo. Paris, 1863. *Orig. Edn.* With fault 'effraya', jansenist mor. gt. by Noulhac, silk liners & end-ll., wrap. preserved, s.-c.; with A.L.s. to Eugène Crepet, ca. 1862. (HD. Jun.13; 32) Frs. 11,000
- – Anr. Copy. Foxing, hf. mor., corners, by Vauthrin, unc., wrap. & spine; 8 etchings by P. Vidal for 1879 lemerre edn. bnd. in. (HD. May 21; 115) Frs. 1,500
- – Anr. Edn. Preface:– Léon Hennique. Ill.:– G. Rochegrosse. Paris, 1900. *Hors Commerce, on vell. decuve des Vosges.* 2 vols. Engrs. in 3 states including pure etching & with remarks, decor. & mosaic spines, blind centre cover motif, gt. & mosaic decor., decor. wtrd. silk doubls & end-papers, pict wrap. preserved, s.-c.'s, by Gruel, sigd. (HD. Feb.17; 71) Frs. 7,800
- – Anr. Edn. Preface:– Léon Hennique. Ill.:– G. Rochegrosse, engraved by Champollion. Paris, 1900. *(600).* 2 vols. 4to. On Arches, red hf. mor.,

corners, by Yseux, wraps. & spines preserved. (HD. May 4; 267) Frs. 5,800
- – Anr. Edn. Ill.:– Fritz Heubner. München, 1924. *(220) numbered. (35) De Luxe Edn. with orig. etching plt.* Lge. 4to. Printers mark sigd. by artist, orig. etchings, each etching with MS. monog., orig. vell. gt., inner dentelle borders, orig. vell. s.-c., orig. etching plt. inlaid. (GB. May 5; 2684) DM 1,000
- – Anr. Edn. Ill.:– F. Heubner. München, 1924. *(145) on Bütten.* 4to. Orig. hand-bnd. vell. gt., 4 slight scratches; printer's mark sigd. by artist. (H. Nov.24; 1851) DM 640
- – Anr. Edn. Ill.:– William Walcot. Paris, 1926. *(50) on japon impérial with 2 states of etchings.* 4to. Sewed. (HD. Jun.13; 120) Frs. 1,200
- – Anr. Edn. Ill.:– F. Hertenberger. Paris, 1947. *De Luxe Edn., (300) numbered.* Fo. Double series of etchings in 1st. state, orig. wraps. (HK. Nov.11; 3614) DM 520
- A Simple Heart. Ill.:– Champollion after Emile Adan. Paris, Sociéte AAC des Beaux Arts, ca. 1900. *Edn. des Deux Mondes. (20) lettered on Japan vell.* 4to. Plts. & text engrs. in 3 states (plain, India-proof & cold.), all (excepting 1 state of the text engrs.) with vig. remarque, orig. lev. gt., cold. mor. inlays, dentelles elab. gt.-decor., lev. doubls., upr. doubl. with inlaid oval hand-cold. engraved vig. on vell., moire grosgrain cl. liners, partly unc. (SG. Feb.16; 284) $1,100
- The Temptation of Saint Anthony. Ed.:– Francis Carmody. Trans.:– Lafcadio Hearn. Kentfield, 1974. *(140).* Fo. Hand-blocked cl., orig. acetate wrap., orig. shipping box. (CBA. Nov.19; 2) $300
- La Tentation de Saint-Antoine. Paris, 1874. *Orig. Edn.* Cont. hf. red mor., corners, grotesque spine decor. (HD. Mar.14; 120) Frs. 2,600
- – Anr. Edn. Ill.:– Georges Rochegrosse, engraved & cold. by E. Decisy. Paris, 1907. Hf. mor., spine decor. (slight defect), wrap. preserved. (HD. Jun.13; 33) Frs. 2,900
- – Anr. Edn. Ill.:– after Odilon Redon. Paris, 1933 [publd. 1938]. *(220). (185) numbered on velin d'Arches.* Fo. Jansenist lev. mor. by Henri Creuzevault, sigd. on upr. turn-in, smooth spine gt. in thin sans serif lettering with author's name & title, suede doubls. & free end-pp., partly unc., orig. ptd. wraps. & backstrip preserved, matching hf. mor. chemise with matching gt. lettering on backstrip, matching mor.-edged s.-c. (CNY. May 18; 198) $8,500
- – Anr. Edn. Intro:– Paul Valéry. Ill.:– J.G. Daragnes. Paris, 1942. *On vell. de Rives.* 4to. With orig. full-p. aqua sigd., sewed, box. (HD. Mar.14; 121) Frs. 1,000
- Complete Works. Intro:– Ferdinand Brunetiere. Preface:– Robert Arnot. N.Y. & L., 1904. *Ltd. 'Edition Premiere' Edn. (26) Lettered on Japan vell.* 10 vols. Plts. in 2 forms, cold. & uncold., crushed lev. mor., gt.-panel. borders, gt. onlays, gt. spines in 3 compartments, mor. doubls. gt., silk brocade free end-pp., silk-covered fly-ll., partly unc.; inscr. by M. Walter Dunne 'This is to certify that this ... is my personal copy.'. (CNY. Dec.17; 559) $2,800

FLAVEL, J.
- The Balm of the Covenant. 1826. Mor. gt., double fore-e. pntg. (P. Jun.7; 322) £140

FLAVIUS JOSEPHUS
See— JOSEPHUS, Flavius

FLAXMAN, John
- Compositions from the Works, Days & Theogony of Hesiod. Ill.:– William Blake after Flaxman. 1817. *[1st. Edn.].* Ob. fo. Engraved title, 37 engraved plts., light spotting, margins browned, cont. mor., rubbed. (CSK. Mar.9; 172) £130
- – Anr. Copy. Ob. fo. Lightly browned, mod. hand-bnd. hf. vell., orig. wrap. title mntd. on upr. cover. (HT. May 9; 1448) DM 560

FLAYDERMAN, E. Norman
- Scrimshaw & Scrimshanders: Whales & Whalemen. Ed.:– R.L. Wilson. New Milford, [1973]. 4to. Cl., d.-w. (SG. Aug.4; 277) $110

FLECKER, James Elroy
- The Golden Journey to Samarkand. L., 1913. *1st. Edn. (50) numbered & sigd.* Orig. bds., partly

unopened; Frederic Dannay copy. (CNY. Dec.16; 141) $280

- **Letters to Frank Savery.** [L., Beaumont Pr., 1926]. *(310) numbered.* Qtr. vell., decor. bds., unc., mostly unopened, glassine d.-w. (SG. Mar.1; 158) $110

FLEETWOOD, Bp. William
- **Chronicon Preciosum.** 1745. *2nd. Edn.* Mod. hf. cf. (P. Dec.8; 264) *Tzakas.* £90
- – **Anr. Copy.** Cont. cf., worn. (S. Oct.11; 527) *Drury.* £50
- – **Anr. Edn.** 1845. Advt. lf., later cf. by Clarke & Bedford, defect.; the Thomas Gray copy, with his notes to back of plt. I. (PD. Aug.17; 125) £150

FLEISCHER, V.
- **Till Eulenspiegel, Dem Volksbuch nacherzählt.** Ill.:– O. Laske. Wien, [1920]. *De Luxe Edn., (100) on Hadern paper.* Orig. leath., orig. cold. pict. wraps. bnd. in, some light wear; printer's mark sigd. by artist. (HK. Nov.11; 3719) DM 500

FLEMING, Hans Friedrich von
- **Der Vollkommene Teutsche Soldat.** Leipzig, 1726. Fo. Lacks hf.-title, Index & approx. last 50 pp. stained, 2 copper engrs. torn, some worming, lightly browned thro.-out, old hf. leath. (R. Oct.12; 2281) DM 2,400

FLEMING, Ian
- **Casino Royale.** L., 1953. *1st. Edn. 1st. Iss.* Orig. cl., d.-w. in 1st. state, review copy. (BBA. Nov.30; 303a) *Howell.* £520
- – **Anr. Edn.** 1953. *1st. Edn.* Orig. cl., slight wear. (P. Oct.20; 228) £160
- – **Anr. Copy.** Orig. bds. (S. Mar.20; 883) *Udall.* £70
- **Diamonds are Forever.** 1956. *1st. Edn. (With:)*
- **Dr No.** 1958. *1st. Edn. (With:)* – **From Russia with Love.** 1957. *1st. Edn.* Together 3 vols. Cl., d.-w.'s. (PD. Oct.19; 185) £65
- **The Diamond Smugglers.** L., 1957. *1st. Edn.* Hf.-title, orig. cl., d.-w.; bkplt. inscr. 'To Eileen Cond ... from Ian Fleming 1957', T.L.S. from Fleming to Miss. Cond loosely inserted. (S. Dec. 8; 174) *Rudy.* £720
- – **Anr. Copy.** Orig. bds., d.-w., slightly frayed & soiled; pres. inscr. 'To Dorothy Cooper ... from Ian Fleming 1957' on front free end-paper. (BBA. Feb.23; 279a) *Gegosci.* £650
- – **Anr. Copy.** Orig. cl. & d.-w. (torn); pres. copy from author to 'John Blaize', with A.N. from Fleming to Blaize. (LC. Mar.1; 332) £550
- **Dr. No.** L., 1958. *1st. Edn.* Hf.-title, orig. decor. cl., d.-w.; bkplt. inscr. 'To Eileen Cond ... from Ian Fleming'. (S. Dec.8; 175) *Rudy.* £470
- **From Russia, With Love.** 1957. *1st. Edn.* Orig. cl., with gun & rose on upr. cover, orig. d.-w. (LC. Mar.1; 335) £80
- **Live & Let Die.** L., 1954. *1st. Edn.* Orig. cl., d.-w. (S. Mar.20; 886) *De F.* £130
- **Moonraker.** L., 1955. *1st. Edn.* Orig. cl., d.-w. slightly soiled. (S. Dec.13; 360) *Heywood.* £105
- – **Anr. Copy.** Orig. cl. & d.-w. (a little soiled). (LC. Mar.1; 334) £80
- **On Her Majesty's Secret Service.** L., 1963. *1st. Edn. (250) on mould-made paper, sigd., specially bnd.* Hf.-title, orig. vell.-vkd. decor. cl., upr. cover slightly marked. (S. Dec.8; 180) *Joseph.* £520
- – **Anr. Edn.** L., 1963. *1st. Edn.* Hf.-title, errata slip at end, Orig. decor. cl., d.-w.; bkplt. inscr. 'To Eileen ... from Ian Fleming'. (S. Dec.8; 177) *Rudy.* £440
- – **Anr. Edn.** [N.Y.], 1963. *1st. Amer. Edn.* Orig. cl.-bkd. bds., bds. discold., d.-w.; sigd. (S. Mar.20; 888) *Reuter.* £130
- – **Anr. Edn.** [1963]. Orig. wraps.; uncorrected proof copy. (CSK. Feb.10; 69) £160
- **The Spy Who Loved Me.** L., 1962. *1st. Edn.* Hf.-title, 'orig. decor. cl., d.-w.; bkplt. inscr. 'To ... Eileen from Ian Fleming'. (S. Dec.8; 176) *Joseph.* £380
- **Thrilling Cities.** L., [1963]. *1st. Edn.* Lge. 8vo. Hf.-title, errata slip at end, orig. buckram-bkd. bds., d.-w.; bkplt. inscr. 'To ... Eileen from Ian Fleming',. (S. Dec.8; 178) *Rudy.* £270
- **Thunderball.** L., 1961. *1st. Edn.* Orig. bds., worn.; pres. copy to Mike Calvert. (S. Mar.20; 889) *Gekoski.* £260

FLERIEU, Charles Pierre Claret, Comte de
- [–] **Discoveries of the French in 1768 & 1769, to the South-East of New Guinea.** L., 1791. *1st. Edn. in Engl.* 4to. 12 folding engraved maps & plts., hf.-title dust-soiled, title & A3 transposed, some foxing & offsetting, few margin repairs, buckram. (SG. Sep.22; 141) $600

FLERS, Robert de
- **Ilsea. Princezna Tripolisska.** Trans.:– J.J. Benesovsky-Vesely. Ill.:– A. Mucha. Prag, 1901. *(200) on vell.* 4to. Minimal soiling, orig. pt. wrap., orig. bd. portfo., spine slightly defect., portfo. bumped. (HK. Nov.11; 3828) DM 1,900
- **Ilsée, Princesse de Tripoli.** Ill.:– Alphonse Mucha. Paris, 1897. Fo. Lithos. on China, orig. cold. pict. wraps., bds. with linen white on japan, woodcut self port. on japan with MS. 5-line dedication, orig. ill. with MS. annots. (D. Nov.24; 3151) DM 9,000

FLETCHER, John
- **The Elder Brother, a Comedie.** L., 1637. *1st. Edn.* Sm. 4to. Slight browning, sm. hole in B3, with loss of a few letters of text, disbnd. [STC 11066] (S. Oct.11; 336) *Blackwells.* £160
See— BEAUMONT, Francis & Fletcher, John

FLETCHER, John Gould
- **Fire & Wine.** L., [1913]. Sm. 8vo. Cl.; inscr. to Charles May in 1935, & again in 1945. (SG. Mar.1; 159) $500

FLETCHER, Phineas
- [–] **The Purple Island, or the Isle of Man.** Camb., 1633. *1st. Edn.* 2 pts. in 1 vol. Sm. 4to. Lacks blank preceding title, slight staining, cont. sheep., rebkd., corners reprd. [STC 11082] (SPB. May 16; 60) $250

FLETCHER, William Younger
- **Bookbinding in France.** L., 1894. 4to. Later hf. cf. (BBA. Mar.7; 308) *D.Ralph.* £70
- **English Bookbindings in the British Museum.** 1895. *(500) numbered.* Fo. Few plts. just affected by tissue guard adherence, orig. cl., spine worn; H.M. Nixon coll., with his sig. & some MS. annots., MS. index & a rubbing loosely inserted. (BBA. Oct.6; 46) *Zeitlin & Verbrugge.* £320
- – **Anr. Copy.** Lge. fo. 66 chromolitho. plts., moire cl. (SG. Jan.5; 61) $250
- **Foreign Bookbindings in the British Museum.** 1896. *(500) numbered.* Fo. Traces of tissue guard on few plts., orig. cl.; H.M. Nixon coll., with his sig. & some MS. annots. (BBA. Oct.6; 47) *Zeitlin & Verbrugge.* £260
- – **Anr. Copy.** Fo. Mod. hf. mor. (BBA. Nov.10; 14) *Forster.* £180

FLEURET, Fernand
- **Friperies.** Ill.:– Raoul Dufy. Paris, 1923. *Orig. Edn. 1st. Printing. (320) numbered on Raphia Naturel.* MS. dedication from author on end-paper & artist's sig., orig. sewed. (GB. May 5; 2353) DM 400

FLEURIEU, Charles-Pierre Claret de
- **Découvertes des Francois, en 1768 & 1769, dans le Sud-Est de la Nouvelle Guinée.** Paris, 1790. *1st. Edn.* 4to. 12 folding engraved maps & plts., sm. liby. stp. on title, cont. mott. cf., spine gt. [Sabin 24748] (C. Jun.27; 88) *Lindh.* £380

FLEURIOT DE LANGLE, A.
See— BOUET-VILLAUMEZ, Comte E.—FLEURIOT DE LANGLE, A.—DUVEYRIER, M.

FLEURON (THE), a Journal of Typography.
Ed.:– S. Morison. Camb. & N.Y., 1920-26. Vols. V & VII. 4to. Vol. V slightly spotted. orig. cl., slightly rubbed. (S. May 1; 416) *Landry.* £80
- – **Anr. Edn.** Ed.:– O. Simon & St. Morison. L., & (from year V) Cambridge & N.Y., 1923-30. Years I-VII (all publd.). 4to. Years II-VII with MS. owners note, orig. linen (3), linen (2) & hf. linen (2), some slight wear. (HK. Nov.11; 4400) DM 1,600

FLEURY, Arthus
See— NERVAL, Gerard de & Fleury, Arthus

FLIGHT ACROSS THE ATLANTIC
N.Y., 1919. No bdg. stated; sigd. on end-flap by people mentioned in text, including Glenn Curtiss,

E.K. Gordon & J. Allan Smith. (RS. Jan.17; 481) $250

FLINDERS, Matthew
- **Narrative of his Voyage in the Schooner Francis, 1798** ... Gold. Cock. Pr., 1946. *1st. Edn. (750) numbered.* Sm. fo. Bdg. not stated. (KH. May 1; 261) Aus. $170
- – **Anr. Copy.** Sm. fo. Bdg. not stated, covers slightly marked. (KH. May 1; 262) Aus. $150
- – **Anr. Edn.** Intro.:– Geoffrey Rawson. Ill.:– John Buckland-Wright. Gold. Cock. Pr., 1946. *(750) numbered. (100) specially bnd.* Sm. fo. Orig. mor. gt., s.-c.; from D. Bolton liby. (BBA. Oct.27; 135) *Howell.* £300
- – **Anr. Edn.** Intro.:– Geoffrey Rawson. Ill.:– John Buckland-Wright. Gold. Cock. Pr., 1946. *(750) numbered.* Sm. fo. Orig. cl. (S. Nov.21; 230) *Duschness.* £130
- – **Anr. Copy.** Sm. fo. Orig. cl., a little flecked, a couple of bruises. (KH. Nov.9; 598) Aus. $230
- – **Anr. Edn.** Ill.:– J.B. Wright. Gold. Cock. Pr., 1946. Fo. Mor. by Sangorski & Sutcliffe. (JL. Jun.24; 93) Aus. $550
- **A Voyage to Terra Australis.** L., 1814. *1st. Edn.* 2 vols. (without Atlas). 4to. Hf.-titles, plts. browned & offset onto text, cont. cl., slightly worn. (S. Jun.25; 19) *Fossitt.* £480
- – **Anr. Copy.** Atlas vol. only. Fo. 16 double—& single-p. engraved maps, 13 engraved views & plts., offsetting, margin tears, creases, some foxing, orig. bds., worn, brkn. (SPB. Dec.13; 496a) $4,000
- – **Anr. Copy.** 2 vols. text only. 4to. Plts. slightly discold., hf. cf., rebkd., covers worn. (CA. Apr.3; 45) Aus. $1,300
- – **Anr. Edn.** Adelaide, 1966. *Facs. Edn.* 2 vols., with box of maps. 4to. Orig. cl.; ptd. pres. slip to Benson on his retirement as Chairman of the Building Trustees & Deputy President of the Liby. Council of Victoria. (KH. Nov.8; 158) Aus. $480
- – **Anr. Copy.** 2 vols. 4to. Orig. cl., maps boxed. (KH. Nov.9; 599) Aus. $450
- – **Anr. Copy.** 2 vols. & Atlas. No bdg. stated. (JL. Jun.24; 66) Aus. $420
- – **Anr. Copy.** 2 vols., with folder of charts. 4to. Bdg. not stated. (KH. May 1; 265) Aus. $380

FLINT, James
- **Letters from America, containing Observations on the Climate & Agriculture of the Western States, the Manners of the People** ... Edinb., 1822. *1st. Edn.* Bnd. without advt. ll., cont. cf. gt., spine & corners slightly rubbed; the Rt. Hon. Visc. Eccles copy. [Sabin 24780] (CNY. Nov.18; 110) $110

FLINT, Timothy
- **Recollections of the Last Ten Years ... in the Valley of the Mississippi.** Boston, 1826. *1st. Edn.* Mod. cl.-bkd. bds., unc. *(With:)* – **Indian Wars of the West.** Cinc., 1833. *1st. Edn.* 12mo. Some slight staining, maroon hf. mor. by Sangorski & Sutcliffe. Together 2 vols. The Rt. Hon. Visc. Eccles copies. (CNY. Nov.18; 111) $200

FLINT, Sir William Russell
- **Drawings.** 1950. 4to. Cl., d.-w., carton, s.-c. (P. Sep.8; 46) *Snell.* £55
- – **Anr. Edn.** L., 1950. *(125) numbered & sigd., with orig. sigd. drawing in separate envelope.* Fo. Qtr. mor. & linen, orig. box. (SKC. Jan.13; 2105) £280
- **Etchings & Drypoints, Catalogue Raisonné.** L., 1957. *1st. Edn. (135) numbered & sigd.* 4to. Frontis. sigd., 12 reproductions showing 2 states, orig. hf. mor., s.-c. (S. Nov.22; 326) *Houle.* £170
- **Minxes Admonished, or Beauty Reproved.** Gold. Cock. Pr., 1955. *(550) numbered. (150) sigd., with 8 extra plts. not in the book, specially bnd.* 4to. Orig. red mor. gt., s.-c. (S. Nov.21; 236) *Joseph.* £140
- – **Anr. Copy.** Fo. Orig. red mor. gt., spine slightly faded, s.-c. (S. Nov.21; 235) *Joseph.* £130
- – **Anr. Copy.** Sm. fo. Scarlet crushed mor. by Sangorski & Sutcliffe, marb. bd. s.-c. (SG. Jan.12; 127) $225

FLINT, Sir William Russell (Ill.)
See— AURELIUS, Marcus Antoninus, Emp.
See— BRADSHAW, Percy V.
See— CHAUCER, Geoffrey
See— HERRICK, Robert

FLINT, Sir William Russell (Ill.) -*Contd.*

See— **KINGSLEY, Charles**
See— **MALORY, Sir Thomas**
See— **SOLOMON, King of Israel**

FLISCO, Maurice, Comte de
– Decas de Fato Annisque Fatalibus. Francofurti, 1665. *1st. Edn.* 4to. Some foxing & browning, later three-qtr. leath., jnt. brkn. (RO. Dec.11; 110)
$110

FLISCUS, Hector
– Oratio ad Innocentium VIII. [Rome, Stephan Plannck], after 27 Apr. 1485. 4to. Some dampstains, disbnd., laid into lf. from a vell antiphomal; the Walter Goldwater copy. [BMC IV,85; Goff F-196; H. 7133] (SG. Dec.1; 148) $175

FLITNER, Joannes
– Nebulo Nebulonum, hoc est Jocoseria nequititiae Censura ... Carmine Jambico Dimetri adornata a Joanne Flitnero. Frankfurt, 1620. *1st. Edn.* 1 text lf. with old MS., sm. trace of worm in 1st. sigd., later vell. (GB. May 4; 1387) DM 700

FLOGEL, Karl Friedrich
– Geschichte der Komischen Literatur. 1784-87. *1st. Edn.* 4 vols in 2. (*With:*) – Geschichte des Groteske-komischen. Geschichte der Hofnarren. 1788-89. *1st. Edn.* 2 vols. (*With:*) – Geschichte des Burlesken. 1794. *1st. Edn.* 1 vol. Together 3 works in 5 vols. Cont. unif. hf. leath. (B. Oct.4; 625) Fls. 500

FLOOD, James
– The James Flood Book of Early Motoring. Ed.:– H.H. Paynting. Melbourne, 1968. *1st. Edn.* 4to. Slight yellowing of fore-edges, bdg. not stated. (KH. May 1; 266) Aus. $220

FLORA BATAVA
Text:– J. Kops. Ill.:– G.J. van Os. Amst., [1800]-14. Vols. I-III in 2. 4to. Dutch & Fr. text, 1 engraved title & 240 hand-cold. plts., lacks Vol. 2 title, cont. hf. cf., worn, 1 spine-end slightly defect.; 26 hand-cold. plts. with descriptive text-ll. from Vol. 4 inserted. (VG. Mar.19; 267) Fls. 4,000

FLORA & SYLVA, a Monthly Review
1903-05. 3 vols. 4to. Orig. hf. vell., lightly soiled. (CSK. Sep.16; 45) £85
– – **Anr. Copy.** 3 vols. 4to. Cont. hf. mor., slightly soiled. (CSK. Jun.15; 192) £55

FLORA ROSSICA, edita jussu et auspiciis Augustissimae Rossorum Imperatricis Catharinae II
Petropoli, 1784. Fo. 99 (of 100) hand-cold. botanical plts., some margin repairs, 2 plts. stained, recent hf. mor. (TA. Sep.15; 519) £185

FLORA VON DEUTSCHLAND
Ed.:– D.F.L. v. Schlechtendal, L.E. Langenthal & E. Schenk. Revised:– E. Hallier. Gera-Untermhaus, 1880-88. 30 vols. Orig. hf. leath., slightly rubbed, w.a.f. (HK. May 15; 397)
DM 2,800

FLORE DES SERRES ET DES JARDINS DE L'EUROPE
Gand, 1845-54. 9 vols. (not quite compl.). 838 cold. lithos., hf. cf., some slight defects., as a period, w.a.f. (VG. May 3; 377) Fls. 2,500
– – **Anr. Edn.** Gent, 1850-56. Vols. 6 & 8-11. Plts. not completely collated, cont. hf. leath., bumped, w.a.f. (R. Oct.12; 1839) DM 2,000

FLORENCE
– Reminiscenze Pittoriche di Firenze ... con Descrizioni e Illustrazioni de Valenti e conosciute Penne. Ill.:– after Nocchi engraved by Campantico. Flor., 1845. 4to. 47 cont. cold. plts., cont. hf. roan. (HD. Dec.2; 91) Frs. 1,000

FLORES, Jose
– Del Meraviglioso Specifico delle Lucertole, or Ramarri, per la Radical Cura del Cancro, della Lebbra, e Lue Venera. Trans.:– C.M. Toscanelli. Venice, 1785. Liby. stps. on title & at end, cont. bds., untrimmed, spine defect. (SG. Oct.6; 157)
$150

FLOREZ, Henrique
– Memorias de las Reynes Catholicas ... de Castilla, y de Leon. Madrid, 1761. 2 vols. in 1. A few margin tears, cont. cf., rebkd. with orig. spine, rubbed, lr. cover detchd. (BBA. Nov.30; 68) *Duran.* £60
– – **Anr. Edn.** Madrid, 1770. 2 vols. 4to. Cf. (DS. Feb.24; 2242) Pts. 60,000

FLOREZ, Jose Segundo
– Espartero Historia de Su Vida Militar y Politica y de los Sucesos Contemporáneos. Madrid, 1844-45. 4 vols. Linen. (DS. Oct.28; 2058) Pts. 20,000

FLORIAN, Jean Pierre Claris de
– Fables. Paris, 1792. *1st. Edn.* Gold-tooled cf. (CR. Jun.6; 161) Lire 220,000
– Galatée, Roman Pastorale imité de Cervantes. Paris, 1793. 4to. 4 col.-ptd. engraved plts. before numbers, some light spotting, cont. cf. gt., slightly worn. (S. Dec.20; 776) *Mediolanum.* £200
– – **Anr. Copy.** 4to. L.P., plts. in proofs before letters, some spotting, tear on 1 plt. reprd., cont. mott. cf. gt., rubbed & scuffed, some wear to spine; Henri Bonasse bkplt. (SPB. Dec.14; 52) $425
– – **Anr. Copy.** Lge. 4to. L.P., figures before the letter, cont. marb. cf. gt., spine decor. (HD. May 3; 54) Frs. 7,300
– Oeuvres. Ill.:– Queverdo. Paris, 1786-99. 13 vols. 18mo. Cont. grd. cf., gt. decor., limp decor. spine. (HD. Jan.26; 132) Frs. 1,500
– – **Anr. Edn.** Ill.:– after Vignaud, Choquet, Monet & others. Paris, 1802-07. 24 vols. 12mo. Cont. red str.-grd. mor. gt. by Thouvenin, sigd. at foot of 2 spines. (C. May 30; 80)
Quaritch. £1,400
– – **Anr. Edn.** Paris, 1803. *New Edn.* 8 vols. 1 plt. detchd., cont. cf. (CSK. Jun.1; 189) £60
– Oeuvres Complettes. Ill.:– Queverdo, Le Barbier, & others. Paris, 1803. 8 vols. 19th. C. diced cf. (GM. Dec.7; 682) £90
– Les Six Nouvelles. Ill.:– Quéverdo. Paris, 1784. *1st. Printing.* 16mo. Lacks frontis., str.-grd. red mor. gt., spine decor., watered silk liners & end-ll. (HD. May 21; 31) Frs. 1,000

FLORIANI, Pietro Paolo
– Difesa et Offesa delle Piazze. Venice, 1654. *2nd. Edn.* Fo. Title & 1st. lf. stpd., slightly stained, vell., ca. 1800, bumped. (HK. Nov.9; 1887) DM 540

FLORICULTURAL CABINET & Florists' Magazine
Ed.:– J. Harrison. 1833-39. Vols. 1-7. Engraved title to each vol., 92 hand-cold. plts., some minor spotting, orig. cl., spine ends slightly worn. (TA. Aug.18; 2) £95
– – **Anr. Run.** L., [1833-38]. *2nd. Edn.* (Vol. 1), Vols. 1-6 (of 27). Extra engraved title in Vols. 2-4 only, 79 hand-cold. plts. only, cl., stained, w.a.f. (S. Apr.10; 508) *Haddon.* £140
– – **Anr. Run.** Ed.:– J. Harrison. 1833-42. 10 vols. Engraved titles, 133 hand-cold. plts., slight spotting, hf. cf. gt., some orig. wraps. bnd. in. (P. Jan.12; 195d) *Duran.* £190
– – **Anr. Copy.** Vols. 1-10 in 5 vols. Engraved titles, 134 hand-cold. plts., cont. hf. cf., some spines worn. (SKC. Jan.13; 2319) £180
– – **Anr. Run.** Ed.:– Joseph Harrison. 1838; 1839-40. Vols. 6, 7 & 8. (Vols. 7 & 8 in 1 vol.). 41 hand-cold. plts., many pp. advts., slight browning & offsetting, Vol. 6 hf. cf., Vols. 7 & 8 cont. hf. cf. (SKC. Jan.13; 2320) £60
– – **Anr. Run.** 1848. 1851-52-56. 4 vols. 50 hand-cold. plts., cont. non-unif. hf. cf. or mor., some wear. (TA. Aug.18; 5) £50

FLORIDA
– Relation of the Invasion & Conquest of Florida by the Spaniards under the Command of Fernando de Soto ... by a Gentleman of Elvas. L., 1686. Tears to lr. portions of C4 & P7, disbnd., end-papers soiled. [Sabin 24865] (SPB. Dec.13; 436) $1,100

FLORIDI, Francisci
See— **POLITIANUS, Angelus—FLORIDI, Francisci**

FLORINUS, Franciscus Phillipus [i.e. Franz Philipp von Subzbach]
– Allgemeiner Klug- und verständiger Hauss-Vatter,
wie auch Adeliches Land-Leben ... Basel, 1748/49. 2 pts. in 2 vols. Fo. Minimal foxing, leath. gt., worn & bumped. (V. Sep.29; 1376) DM 1,800
– Oeconomus Prudens et Legalis. Nuremb., ca. 1750?. 9 pts. in 1 vol. Fo. Many double-p., full-p. & text engraved plts., lacks title & prelims., & index beyond T, mod. cf., w.a.f. (SG. Apr.19; 87)
$600
– Oeconomus Prudens. Oder Hausz-Vatter. Nuremb., Frankfurt, Leipzig, 1750-51. 4 vols. Fo. Marb. cf., a little rubbed. (VG. May 3; 488)
Fls. 4,400

FLORIO, John
– Queen Anna's New World of Words. Or Dictionarie of the Italian & English Tongues ... 1611. Sm. fo. Port. frontis. & woodcut title with cont. annots., lacks last lf./ll., later cl. bds., mor. backstrip, rubbed. (TA. Jun.21; 379) £50

FLORIST (THE), FRUITIST & GARDEN MISCELLANY
1856-60. 5 vols. 63 hand-cold. litho. plts., some light spotting. orig. cl., slightly soiled. (CSK. Apr.27; 16) £180

FLORIST & POMOLOGIST
Ed.:– R. Hogg & others. [1862-64]. 2 vols. 23 & 12 chromolitho. plts., hf. leath., 1 spine damaged. (SKC. Jan.13; 2315) £55
– – **Anr. Edn.** Ed.:– Robert Hogg. 1864. Tall 8vo. 23 hand-cold. plts., a few slightly frayed at outer edge, recent cl. (TA. May 17; 302) £55
– – **Anr. Edn.** 1868-84. 17 vols. 357 col. plts., 2 folding plts. torn, hf. cf. gt., as a coll. of plts., w.a.f. (P. Jan.12; 168) *Noble.* £620
– – **Anr. Edn.** Ed.:– Th. Moore. L., 1882-84. 3 vols. Cont. hf. leath. (R. Oct.12; 1840) DM 700

FLORIST'S JOURNAL & GARDENER'S RECORD to which is appended the Dictionary of Flowers & Hardy Trees & Shrubs.
Ca. 1850. 3 vols. Cold. titles, 37 hand-cold. plts., orig. cl. gt., slightly worn. (SKC. Jan.13; 2314)
£85

FLORUS, Lucius Annaevs
See— **LIVIUS, Titus & Florus, Lucius Annaeus**
See— **SALLUSTIUS CRISPUS, Gaius & Florus, Lucius Annaeus**

FLORUS, Publius Annaeus
– Rerum Romanorum ... Ed.:– Cl. Salmasius. Lugduni Batavorum, 1638. *1st. Iss.* 18mo. Pages 200 & 336 misnumbered, moderate browning, some foxing, light old stain at rear portion, later str.-grd. mor., gt. rules, ornate gt. panels, lacks spine label, spine ends & edges moderately scuffed. (HA. May 4; 441) $150

FLOWER, Desmond (Ed.)
See— **BOOK COLLECTOR'S QUARTERLY**

FLOWER, John
– Views of the Ancient Buildings in the Town & County of Leicester. Leicester, ca. 1830. Fo. 26 lithos., qtr. cf. (HBC. May 17; 335) £170
– – **Anr. Copy.** Fo. Some slight browning, cont. hf. roan, worn. (S. Nov.1; 108) *Laywood.* £120

FLOYER, Sir John
– The Physician's Pulse-watch. L., 1707. *1st. Edn.* Advt. lf., cont. spr. cf. (S. Apr.10; 501)
Phelps. £520

FLUDD, Robert
– De Morborum Signis. Frankfurt, 1631. 4to. Rebnd. paper bds. (LH. Sep.25; 533) $170

FLY-FISHING in Salt & Fresh Water
L., 1851. *1st. Edn.* 6 plts., including 5 hand-cold., hf.-title & advt. lf. browned, orig. cl.; bkplt. & liby. stps. of Flyfishers' Club liby. (S. Oct.4; 21)
Marlborough. £80

FOILLET, Jacques
– New Modelbuch, darinnen Allerley Aussgeschnittens Arbeit, in Kleiner, Mittelmaessiger und Grosser Form Erst Newlich Erfunden. Muempelgarten, 1598. 4to. Title in woodcut border, 83 woodcut plts., very foxed & stained, old vell. covers from rubric acid MS., worn. (SG. Apr.26; 113) $4,200

– Nouveaux Pourtraicts de Point Coupe et Dantelles en Petite Moyenne & Grande Forme. Montbeliard, 1598. 4to. Title in woodcut border, 83 woodcut plts., lacka A4 (blank), early vell., leath. ties defect. (SG. Apr.26; 112) $4,200

FOKKER, T.H.
– Roman Baroque Art. The History of a Style. L., 1938. 2 vols. 4to. No bdg. stated. (SPB. Nov.30; 99) $125

FOLENGO, Teofilo 'Merlinus Cocaius'
– Merlini Cocaii Opus Macaronicum. Amst., 1768. 2 vols. 4to. Port., engraved initials, head & tall pieces, cont. qtr. cf., 1 spine slightly torn. (P. May 17; 188) *Marinoni.* £70
– – **Anr. Edn.** Amst., 1768-71. 2 vols. 4to. 19th. C. hf. leath., slightly loose. (SI. Dec.15; 74) Lire 300,000

FOLIO SOCIETY
– Original Leaves from Famous English Books. L., n.d. *(200).* In solander case. (SSA. Jul.5; 141) R. 250

FOLLOT, Charles
See— CLOUZOT, Henri & Follot, Charles

FOLLOT, Paul
– Documents de Bijouterie et Orfevrerie Modernes. Paris, ca. 1895. Fo. 24 plts., including 12 pochoir-cold., loose as iss., 1 plt. stpd. on recto, cl.-bkd. pict. bds. (SG. Aug.25; 34) $425

FOLNESICS, J. (Ed.)
See— MAYER, Karl

FOLON, Jean-Michel
– Manifesti di Folon. [Milan, 1978]. *1st. Edn. (200) with numbered & sigd. orig. litho.* Fo. Unbnd., loose in decor. folder, cl. ties. (CBA. Jan.29; 192) $130

FOLTZ, F.
– Halenza's Rheinisches Album. Mainz, ca. 1850. Ob. 4to. 22 steel engrs., orig. gold & blind-tooled linen. (R. Oct.13; 2693) DM 1,200
– – **Anr. Edn.** Mainz, ca. 1860. Lge ob. 4to. 16 (of 22) steel engraved views, lightly foxed thro.-out, orig. linen, spine defect. (HT. May 10; 2963b) DM 480
– – **Anr. Edn.** Mainz, ca. 1880. 4to. 66 steel-engraved views, cl. gt., worn, top hinge separated. (PNY. Oct.20; 280) $400
– – **Anr. Edn.** Mainz, n.d. Ob. 8vo. Bdg. not stated. (HD. Oct.14; 3) Frs. 2,400
– Rhein-Album. Frankfurt, ca. 1880. Sm. ob. fo. 1 woodcut plt. & 21 steel engrs. plts. slightly foxed, orig. linen, gold-tooled, rubbed. (R. Oct.13; 2683) DM 850
– – **Anr. Edn.** Frankfurt, ca. 1890. Ob. 4to. Orig. pict. linen. (GB. Nov.3; 213) DM 425

FONTAINE, Nicolas
[–] Histoire du Vieux et de Nouveau Testament (Histoire de la Bible). Amst., 1700. 2 vols. Fo. Several plts. partly cut away, cont. vell., worn, w.a.f. (BBA. Feb.23; 31) *Weston.* £140

FONTAINE, Pierre François Léonard
See— PERCIER, Charles & Fontaine, Pierre François Léonard

FONTANA, Carlo
– Il Tempio Vaticano ... Ill.:– A. Specchi after Fontana. Rome, 1694. *1st. Edn.* Fo. Parallel Latin & Italian text, pagination partly irregular, minimal browning, early 19th. C. mor., gt. decor. spine covers & outer dentelles, slightly rubbed, Alexander I armorial ex-libris on both covers. (H. May 22; 65) DM 10,500
– – **Anr. Edn.** Rome, 1694. Fo. Cont. bdg. (HD. Dec.15; 12) Frs. 5,000
– Templum Vaticanum et Ipsius Origo. Ill.:– Alessandro Specchi. Rome, 1694. *1st. Edn.* Fo. 79 engraved plts., some double-p. folding, titles & text in Latin & Italian, 1 plt. slightly shaved, cont. panel. cf., rubbed. (C. Mar.14; 8) *Lamartia.* £1,000
– Ultissimo Trattato dell'Acque Correnti. Rome, 1696. Fo. Vell., worn. (P. Jul.26; 194) £380

FONTANA, Felice
– De Irritabilitatis Legibus. Siena, 1767. 4to. Vell.; Dr. Walter Pagel copy. (S. Feb.7; 123) *Quaritch.* £150
– I Pregi della Toscana, nell'imprese più segnalate de' Cavalieri di Santo Stefano. Flor., 1701. Fo. Hf.-title, engraved frontis., port., & 37 plts., sm. wormhole affecting last few ll., vell. bds., unc., soiled, worn. (S. May 21; 9) *Schrire.* £640
– Ricerche Filosofiche sopra la Fisica Animale. Flor., 1775. *1st. Italian Edn.* 4to. Thick & L.P., stp. on title, cont. marb. bds., unc.; Dr. Walter Pagel copy. (S. Feb.7; 124) *Nat.Lib. of Medicine.* £120
– Richerche Fisiche sopra il Veneno della Vipera. Lucca, 1767. *1st. Edn.* Some stains, cont. limp bds., unc. (SI. Dec.15; 157) Lire 240,000

FONTANA, Jean
– Essai sur l'Histoire du Droit Privé en Corse (Etude Critique des Statuts Corses du XVIe Siècle). Paris, 1905. Hf. chagrin, wrap.; A.L.s. to J.D. Guelfi. (HD. Oct.21; 85) Frs. 1,500

FONTANE, M.
– Voyage Pittoresque à travers l'Isthme de Suez. Ill.:– E. Ciceri. Paris, 1870. Fo. Some staining at end of vol., publisher's bds., some staining. (HD. Dec.16; 47) Frs. 2,400
– – **Anr. Edn.** Ill.:– Riou, lithographed by Eug. Ciceri & J. Didier. Ca. 1870. Fo. Publisher's bds., spine slightly unstuck. (HD. Mar.21; 153) Frs. 4,800

FONTANE, Theodor
– Aus England. Studien u. Briefe über Londoner Theater, Kunst u. Presse. Stuttgart, 1860. *1st. Edn.* Title with owner's note, cont. hf. leath. gt. (HK. Nov.10; 2406) DM 650
– Balladen. Berlin, 1861. *1st. Edn.* Orig. linen, gt. spine & upr. cover, slightly bumped, spine slightly faded. (HK. Nov.10; 2407) DM 600
– Effi Briest. Ed.:– J. Rodenberg. Berlin, [Oct.]1894-[Mar.]1895. Vols. 81 & 82 in 2 vols. Deutsche Rundschau Yr.21, pts. 1-6. Orig. gold-tooled linen. (D. Nov.24; 2447) DM 880
– – **Anr. Edn.** Ill.:– M. Liebermann. Berlin, 1927. *(325) numbered for members of Maximilian Gesellschaft.* 4to. 21 orig. lithos., 3 full-p., 1 sigd., orig. vell. gt., decor. Marcus Behmer. (GB. May 5; 2885) DM 5,500
– – **Anr. Edn.** Ill.:– M. Liebermann. [Berlin, 1927]. *(325).* Sm. 4to. 1st. full-p. litho. sigd. by artist, orig. vell. gt. by Hübel & Denck. (H. May 23; 1356) DM 6,000
– – **Anr. Copy.** Sm. 4to. Hand-bnd. orig. vell. gt., by Hübel & Denck (design by M. Behmer); 1 sigd. litho. (H. Nov.24; 1778) DM 5,200
– – **Anr. Copy.** 4to. Orig. vell., gt. spine & cover, orig. bd. s.-c. (HK. May 17; 3036) DM 4,800
– Frau Jenny Treibel. Berlin, 1893. *1st. Book Edn.* Orig. linen, minimal rubbing. (R. Apr.3; 192) DM 720
– Grete Minde. Berlin, 1880. *1st. Edn.* Orig. linen. (GB. May 4; 1255) DM 550
– – **Anr. Edn.** Berlin, 1880. Name above title, orig. linen. (V. Oct.1; 3814) DM 420
– Ost-Havelland. Die Landschaft um Spandau, Potsdam, Brandenburg. Berlin, 1873. *1st. Edn.* Cont. linen gt. (GB. Nov.4; 2034) DM 460
– Die Poggenpuhls. Berlin, 1896. *1st. Edn.* Orig. linen. (GB. Nov.4; 2036) DM 480
– Der Stechlin. Stuttgart & Leipzig, 1897-98. 2 vols. Fo. Hf. linen gt. (GB. Nov.4; 2037) DM 1,400
– – **Anr. Edn.** Berlin, 1899. *1st. Book Edn.* Orig. linen, rubbed. (R. Apr.3; 193) DM 900
– Unterm Birnbaum. Berlin, 1885. *1st. Edn.* Margins slightly discold., orig. linen. (H. Nov.23; 643) DM 600
– Unwiederbringlich. Ed.:– J. Rodenberg. Berlin, [Jan.-Jun.] 1891. Vols. 66 & 67 in 2 vols. Deutsche Rundschau. Orig. gold-tooled linen. (D. Nov.24; 2449) DM 470
– – **Anr. Edn.** Ed.:– J. Rodenberg. Berlin, [1891]. Vol. 66 & 67. Cont. hf. leath. (GB. May 4; 1258) DM 400

– Von der Schönen Rosamunde. Dessau, 1850. *1st. Edn.* Sm. 4to. Old owners note on end-paper & title, 1 sig. loose, slightly stained, cont. romantic linen gt. (GB. May 4; 1253) DM 700

FONTANINI, Giusto
– Biblioteca dell'Eloquenza Italiana. Annots.:– Apostolo Zeno. Venice, 1753. 2 vols. 4to. Qtr. leath. & patterned bds., end-ll. mildly foxed or dampstained. (SG. Oct.27; 106) $110

FONTENELLE, Bernard le Bovier de
– Oeuvres Diverses. Ill.:– Bernard Picart. La Haye, 1728-29. *Partly Orig. Edn.* 3 vols. Fo. Cont. mor. gt., spines decor., Samuel Bernard (1651-1739) arms, ungilded & retinted. (HD. Mar.27; 13) Frs. 16,000
– – **Anr. Copy.** 3 vols. 4to. Cont. cf. gt., spines decor., sm. repairs to turn-ins. (HD. May 3; 55) Frs. 2,600
– – **Anr. Copy.** 3 vols. 4to. Cont. cf.; A.N.s. by Fontenelle, 'Extrait des Registres de l'Académie Royale des Sciences du 17 déc. 1740'. (HD. Jun.6; 60) Frs. 2,000
[–] A Plurality of Worlds. Trans.:– Mr. Glanvill. L., 1688. *1st. Engl. Edn.* E4 & F1 cancels, cont. cf., spine gt. [Wing F1416] (BBA. May3; 169) *Ximenes.* £90

FOOT, M.M.
– The Henry Davis Gift, A Collection of Bookbindings. 1978. Vol. 1 only (of 2). 4to. Plts., orig. ptd. wraps.; proof copy, H.M. Nixon coll., with typescript copy of his review loosely inserted. (BBA. Oct.6; 48) *Oak Knoll Books.* £85

FOPPENS, F.
See— CHRYSTIN, Jean Baptisti & Foppens, F. & Pierre

FORAIN, Jean-Louis
– Album. N.d. *(50) on japan, sigd. by artist.* 4to. Lavallière hf. mor., corners, by Allo, unc., wraps. (HD. May 4; 272) Frs. 1,250
– Rires & Grimaces. Paris, [1890-1900?]. *(50) on papier de Chine.* Sm. fo. 20 wood-engrs. in 2 states (1 before letters), bds., cl. spine, (?) upr. cover showing a clown, sigd. Jan van Beers bnd. in; from Esmerian coll. (S. May 10; 279) *Koch.* £280

FORBERG, Frederick Karl
– Manuel d'Erotologie Classique. Paris, 1906. *(500).* Ob. 8vo. Engraved title & 19 plts., each plt. in 2 states, 1 cold., some soiling, hf. mor., combination lock. (SPB. May 17; 605) $425

FORBES, Alexander
– California: a History of Upper & Lower California. L., 1839. *1st. Edn.* Folding engraved map, port. & 9 litho. plts. (some foxing), orig. cl. [Sabin 25035] (S. May 22; 318) *Michael.* £750
– – **Anr. Copy.** Lge. folding engraved map, 10 full-p. litho. plts. & views, ptd. slip inserted at p. 339, several plts. foxed, cont. mor. gt., covers with motto of the Earls of Minto; the Rt. Hon. Visc. Eccles copy. [Sabin 25035] (CNY. Nov.18; 112) $320

FORBES, Alexander Kinloch
– Ras Mala; Or, Hindu Annals of the Province of Goozerat, in Western India. 1856. 2 vols. Minor spotting, orig. cl. (TA. Sep.15; 78) £50

FORBES, Edwin
– Life Studies of the Great Army ... N.Y., [1876]. Ob. fo. Compl. portfo. of 40 etchings, orig. plt.-list & descriptions mntd. inside upr. cover, 1st. plt. soiled & chipped, some foxing, chipping, soiling, & creasing on other plts., some remains of orig. cl. covers. (SG. Sep.22; 96) $325

FORBES, Elizabeth Stanhope
– King Arthur's Wood: A Fairy Story. L., ca. 1910. Fo. Hessian-like cl. over bds., lightly worn. (CBA. Aug.21; 226) $200

FORBES, Lieut. Frederick E.
– Dahomey & the Dahomans; Being, a Journal of Two Missions to the King of Dahomey, & Residence at his Capital, in the Years 1849 & 1850. L., 1851. *1st. Edn.* 2 vols. Sm. 8vo. Errata slip, recent three-qtr. mor. gt. extra. (SG. Sep.22; 142) $150
– Five Years in China; from 1842 to 1847. 1846.

FORBES, Lieut. Frederick E. -*Contd.*

Frontis. spotted & sm. part of top corner torn away, cont. hf. roan gt. (TA. Sep.15; 80) £72

FORBES, James
- Oriental Memoirs. L., 1813. *1st. Edn.* 4 vols. 4to. Port. with sm. stain at foot, 93 plts., some cold. & including a series of lithos. on thin paper, errata lf. at end, largely free from expected discolouration in uncold. plts., 1 or 2 plt. imprints shaved, cont. russ. gt., spines rubbed. (S. May 22; 438) *Trivedi.* £700
- - **Anr. Copy.** 4 vols. 4to. Port., 65 engraved views & plts., 2 cold. engraved plts., 26 hand-cold. natural history plts., hf.-titles, minor dampstain to a few uncold. plts., cont. diced cf., Vols. 1-3 rebkd. preserving orig. spines; Leigh bkplt. (C. Mar.14; 49) *Deacon.* £550
- - **Anr. Copy.** 4 vols. 4to. Engraved port., 92 (of 93) plts., including 29 hand-cold., some stains in Vol. 2, mod. cl. gt. (P. Sep.8; 227) *Sweet.* £250
- - **Anr. Copy.** 4 vols. 4to. Engraved port., 64 plain & 28 cold. plts., including 7 lithos., spotted thro.-out. cont. hf. cf., worn, covers detchd. (BBA. Dec.15; 6) *Scott.* £170
- Oriental Memoirs; Illustrations to Oriental Memoris. L., 1834-35. 3 vols. 8vo. & 4to. 83 engraved or litho. plts. (23 cold.), liby, stp. on title, cont. hf. cf. & cf., rubbed, covers detchd., spine defect. (BBA. Dec.15; 7) *Makiya.* £160

FORBES, James David
- Norway & its Glaciers visited in 1851. 1853. Liby. stp. on title, cf. (P. Apr.12; 168) *Scott.* £80
- Travels through the Alps of Savoy & other Parts of the Pennine Chain. Edinb., 1843. *1st. Edn.* 4to. 1 folding map slightly torn, a few ll. slightly spotted, orig. cl. (BBA. Sep.29; 102) *Lovatt.* £140

FORBES, Dr. P.
- A Full View of Public Transactions in the Reign of Q. Elizabeth ... 1740-41. 2 vols. Fo. Hf.-titles, spr. cf., spines gt.; Sir Ivar Colquhoun, of Luss copy. (CE. Mar.22; 106) £150

FORBES, Patrick
- Funerals of a Right Reverend Father in God ... Aberdeen, 1635. Sm. 4to. Cont. vell. gt., upr. cover with central floral tool surround by initials ADR, soiled; Sir Ivar Colquhoun, of Luss copy. [STC 11151] (CE. Mar.22; 105) £550

FORBIN, Louis Nicholas Philippe Auguste, Comte de
- Voyage dans le Levant en 1817 et 1818. Ill.:- after Forbin, Lecomte, Bourgeois, Fragonard, & others. Paris, 1819. Lge. fo. 2 plans, 77 (of 78) plts., comprising 8 sepia aquatint views & 69 litho. views, title, hf.-title & 2 plts. with edges torn & frayed, cont. bds., unc. & unstitched, worn, backstrip defect., w.a.f. (C. Mar.14; 50) *Hantzis.* £1,500
- - **Anr. Copy.** Fo. Lacks 7 plts., some foxing, cont. hf. roan, corners, decor. spine. (HD. Mar.14; 29) Frs. 7,500

FORBONNAIS
- Elemens du Commerce. Leiden & Paris, 1754. 2 vols. 12mo. Cont. roan. Vol. 1 lacks spine. (HD. Feb.22; 74) Frs. 1,300
- Recherches et Considerations sur les Finances de la France. Liège, 1758. 6 vols. 12mo. Old roan. (HD. Feb.22; 75) Frs. 5,000

FORCE, Peter (Ed.)
See— UNITED STATES OF AMERICA

FORD, Ford Madox
See— HUEFFER or FORD, Ford Madox

FORD, G.H.
See— ELLIS, G.V. & Ford, G.H.

FORD, Gerald R.
- A Vision for America. Northridge, Ca., 1980. *1st. Edn. (500)* numbered & sigd. Cl. (PNY. Jun.6; 380) $100

FORD, John
[-] The Chronicle Historie of Perkin Warbeck. 1634. *1st. Edn.* Sm. 4to. Sig. F in corrected form, Ll with 2 rows of ornaments, dampstain to title & a few ll., sm. hole at title affecting 1 letter of

imprint, A3 shaved at head & foot, piece torn from margin of Ll, 19th. C. mor.-bkd. bds., rubbed; Discase of Southwork copy. [STC 11157] (C. May 30; 134) *Bennett.* £250

FORD, Paul Leicester (Contrib.)
See— BOWEN, Clarence W.

FORD, Richard
[-] A Hand-book for Travellers in Spain. 1845. *1st. Edn.* 2 vols. Orig. cl., spines faded; 2 p. A.L.s from author to Dawson Turner tipped in. (BBA. Sep.29; 104) *Bean.* £160

FORD, Sally Rochester
- Raids & Romance of Morgan & his Men. Mobile, 1864. *2nd. Edn.* Advt. lf., some foxing thro.-out, old hf. mor., orig. wallpaper wraps. bnd. in. (SG. Oct.20; 110) $375

FORDRIN, Louis
- Nouveau Livre de Serrurerie. Paris, [1723]. 30 engraved plts., including title & dedication lf., some folding, 1 sm. fold tear, slight wormhole in last 3 plts., 2 plts. browned, 3 shaved. (*Bound with:*)
- Livre de Serrurerie de Composition Angloise. Paris, [1723]. 20 engraved plts., including title, artists' & engraver's names masked, a few plts. shaved. Together 2 works in 1 vol. Fo. Cont. cf. gt., gt. spine, rebkd. preserving orig. spine; inscr. of Françoois Soufflot. (C. Dec.9; 51) *Marlborough.* £1,600

FORDYCE, George
- Elements of the Practice of Physic. L., 1771. *3rd. Edn.* 2 pts. in 1 vol. Cont. owners' sigs., cont. cf., annots. on rear end-papers. (SG. Mar.22; 124) $100
- - **Anr. Edn.** L., 1784. *5th. Edn.* Interleaved thro.-out, with many early owner's annots., derived in part from Fordyce's own lectures, disbnd., ex-liby. (SG. Oct.6; 158) $120

FOREIGN FIELD SPORTS, Fisheries, Sporting Anecdotes ... With a Supplement of New South Wales.
Ill.:– Samuel Howitt & others. L., 1814-13. *1st. Edn.* 4to. 110 hand-cold. engraved plts., some soiling, text lf. reprd., red mor. gt., spine worn. (SPB. Dec.13; 584) $1,300
- - **Anr. Edn.** 1819. Fo. 108 (of 109) hand-cold. aquatints, lacks title, 1st. plt. badly soiled, some margin discoloration, cont. mor. gt., covers detchd. (TA. Nov.17; 314) £500

FORES, Samuel William 'John Blunt'
- Man-Midwifery Dissected; or, The Obstetric Family-Instructor. Ill.:– I. Cruikshank (frontis.). L., [1795?]. *1st. Edn. Later Iss., with frontis. cold. & imprint date erased.* 12mo. Lacks hf.-title, hf. cf. (SG. Oct.6; 159) $800

FORES'S SPORTING NOTES & SKETCHES
L., 1884-91. Vols. 1-7. Hf. mor., spines gt., by J. Larkins, orig. wraps. & advts. bnd. in. (S. Mar.20; 769) *Spake.* £70
- - **Anr. Edn.** 1884-1907. 24 vols. Crimson hf. mor. gt., panel. spines. (P. Dec.8; 226) *Joseph.* £280

FOREST, Louis
See— MONTORGUEIL, Georges & Forest, Louis

FORESTER, Frank (Pseud.)
See— HERBERT, Henry William 'Frank Forester'

FORESTER, Thomas
- Rambles in the Islands of Corsica & Sardinia. 1858. *1st. Edn.* Cold. engraved map, 8 litho. plts., text ills., top blank area of frontis. replaced, orig. cl., faded, 1st. sig. loose. (BS. May 2; 11) £100
- - **Anr. Edn.** L., 1861. *2nd. Edn.* 8 cold. & tinted litho. plts., 1 folding (torn), engraved map hand-cold. in outl., hf.-title, cont. cf., spine gt., rubbed. (BBA. Dec.15; 69) *Erlini.* £50
- - **Anr. Copy.** Cont. cf., spine decor. (worn). (HD. Oct.21; 86) Frs. 2,200

FORESTIERO illuminato intorno le Cose piu Rare e Curiose, Antiche e Moderne della Citta di Venezia
Venezia, 1740. 70 engrs., cont. bds. (CR. Jun.6; 162) Lire 500,000
- - **Anr. Edn.** Venezia, 1784. 70 engrs. (of 72), cont. bds., defect., w.a.f. (CR. Jun.6; 163) Lire 350,000

FORFAIT, Pierre Alexandre Laurent
- Traité Elémentaire de la Mâture des Vaisseaux. Ill.:– Benard. Paris, 1788. *Orig. Edn.* 4to. Cont. marb. cf., spine decor. (slightly worn). (HD. Jun.18; 18) Frs. 2,800
- - **Anr. Copy.** 4to. Cont. marb. cf., 1 turn-in reprd. (HD. Mar.9; 82) Frs. 2,000

FORGUES, Paul Emile Daurand 'Old Nick' & Gérard, Jean Ignace Isidor 'Jean Jacques Grandville'
- Petites Misères de la Vie Humaine. 1843. *Orig. Edn. 1st. Printing.* 50 plts., hf. chagrin. (HD. Jan.24; 20) Frs. 1,400

FORKEL, Joh. Nic.
- Allg. Gesch. der Musik. Leipzig, 1788-1801. *1st. Edn.* 2 vols. 4to. Both titles with ex-libris pasted on, Vol. 2 title with bkd. tear, some soiling, Vol. 2 browned near end, cont. hf. leath. gt., rubbed & bumped, vol. 2 spine slightly defect. (HK. Nov.9; 2243) DM 750

FORMAN, Harry Buxton
- The Books of William Morris. L., 1897. *1st. Edn. (75)* Japan vell., for private circulation. Sm. 4to. Orig. buckram, slightly soiled, spine darkened; Cortlandt F. Bishop bkplt. (SG. Sep.15; 234) $180

FORMULARIUM INSTRUMENTORUM ad Usum Romanae Curiae
Rome, Stephanus Plannck, 22 Oct. 1482. (*Bound with:*) FORMULARIUM PROCURATORUM et Advocatorum Romanae Curiae Rome, Stephanus Plannck, 15 Jan. 1483. [BMC IV, 82; Goff F265] Together 2 works in 1 vol. 4to. Initials painted in red or blue, 1st. initials gt., title inscr. in ink on lr. edge, cont. stpd. roan over wood bds., richly decor., clasps, lacks ties; from Fondation Furstenberg-Beaumesnil. (HD. Nov.16; 42) Frs. 8,500

FORREST, Charles Ramus Lieut.-Col.
- A Picturesque Tour along the Rivers Ganges & Jumna in India. L., 1824. 4to. L.P., engraved folding map, title with hand-cold. aquatint vig., 24 hand-cold. aquatint plts., later red hf. mor., spine gt., partly unc. (C. Nov.16; 89) *Foyle.* £900
- - **Anr. Copy.** Bdg. not stated, cover worn. (JL. Jul.15; 324) Aus. $1,250

FORREST, John
- Explorations in Australia. L., 1875. Cf. gt. (CA. Apr.3; 46) Aus. $700
- - **Anr. Copy.** 40 pp. of book advts. at end, some slight foxing to folding maps, margins of plts. & some ll. foxed, inscr. on title & end-paper, orig. blind-stpd. cl. gt., unc., covers worn. (CA. Apr.3; 47) Aus. $360

FORREST, Capt. Thomas
- A Picturesque Tour along the Rivers Ganges & Jumna in India. 1824. Lge.4to. Engraved aquatint pict. title, 1 vig., 24 plts., all hand cold., 1 engraved folding map, a few ll. slightly spotted, cont. cf., rebkd., slightly rubbed; Signet Liby.copy. (BBA. Feb.9; 316) *Ayres.* £640
- Voyage aux Moluques et à la Nouvelle Guinée fait sur la Galère La Tartare en 1774-1776, par Ordre de la Compagnie Angloise. Trans.:– J. Nicolas Demeunier. Paris, 1780. *Orig. Edn. of 1st. Fr. Trans.* 4to. Sm. paper loss from corner of 1 plt., 1 lf. with loss of text, some stains, cont. marb. cf., defects. (HD. Mar.19; 48) Frs. 1,300
- - **Anr. Copy.** 4to. Cont. cf., spine defect. (VG. Sep.14; 1096) Fls. 600
- A Voyage to New Guinea, & the Moluccas ... during the Years 1774, 1775 & 1776. L., 1779. *1st. Edn.* 4to. Engraved port., 27 (only, of 31), engraved maps & plts., mod. cf.-bkd. bds. (C. Jun.27; 90) *Piks.* £140
- - **Anr. Edn.** 1780. *2nd. Edn.* 4to. Orig. bds., old cl. reback, worn, unc.; MS. order to Lt. Mitchell of Gun Vassel Acute. (BBA. Sep.29; 75) *Morrell.* £240
- - **Anr. Copy.** 4to. Lacks 6 plts., plts. mostly crumpled, some with long tears, 1 plt. with lge. excision, slightly browned or foxed, 1st. ll. stained, MS. annots. on inner doubl., cont. leath., defect., cover loose. (HT. May 10; 2843) DM 480
- - **Anr. Copy.** 4to. Some foxing, some maps frayed, cont. marb. cf., rebkd., covers slightly rubbed. (VS. Dec.9; 1280) Fls. 625

FORRESTER, Alfred Henry 'Alfred Crowquill'
- Absurdities, in Prose & Verse. L., 1827. Etched frontis., vig. title, 13 hand-cold. plts., cont. hf. mor. (S. Dec.20; 602) *Drummond.* £130
- The Tutor's Assistant, or Comic Figures of Arithmetic. Ill.:– Percy Cruikshank after Forrester. L., 1843. Orig. cl. gt., s.-c. (S. Dec.20; 644) *Drummond.* £120

FORSHAW, Joseph M. & Cooper, William T.
- Australian Parrots. Ill.:– W.T. Cooper. Melbourne &c., 1980. *2nd. Edn. (1000) sigd. by author & artist.* 2 vols. Fo. Mor., cold. onlays of parrots on upr. covers, cl. box. (C. Mar.14; 169) *Hill.* £900
- – Anr. Copy. Vol. 1 only. Fo. Publisher's inlaid leath., boxed. (KH. May 1; 268) Aus. $140
- Parrots of the World. Ill.:– W.T. Cooper. Melbourne, 1973. *1st. Edn.* Fo. Bdg. not stated, d.-w. (KH. May 1; 270) Aus. $140

FORSTER, Johann Georg Adam
- A Chart of the Southern Hemisphere. 1770. 660 x 630mm, folding to 4to. Engraved map, slightly soiled, cont. hf. cf., worn, lr. cover detchd. (BBA. Jan.19; 65) *Brooke-Hitching.* £140
- Erinnerungen aus dem Jahr 1790 in Historischen Gemälden und Bildnissen ... Ill.:– D. Chodowiecki & others. Berlin, 1793. *1st. Edn.* 18 plts., cont. bds. (S. Apr.10; 317) *Koch.* £110
- Kleine Schriften. Ein Beytrag zur Völker- und Länderkunde, Naturgeschichte und Philosophie des Lebens. Ill.:– Berger, Bolt & Kohl; Berger & Ringk after Chodowiecki. Berlin, 1794-1803. *1st. Edn.* Lacks title with medallion copper engr., cont. style later hf. leath. gt. (GB. Nov.4; 2041) DM 1,300
- Voyage Philosophique et Pittoresque sur les Rives du Rhin ... Trans.:– Ch. Pougens. Paris, [1795]. 2 vols. Cont. bds. (D. Nov.24; 2450) DM 480
- – Anr. Edn. Paris, 1796. Cont. marb. sheep, decor. spine, 1 cover scratched. (HD. Sep.22; 247) Frs. 1,100
- A Voyage Round the World. 1777. 2 vols. 4to. Owners inscrs. clipped out of upr. margins of titles with loss, margins of title & 1st. few ll. of Vol. 1 lightly wormed, mod. hf. cf. (CSK. Jul.6; 23) £280
- – Anr. Copy. 2 vols. 4to. Chart offset, some ll. foxed, blind-stpd. cf. gt., rebkd. (CA. Apr.3; 48) Aus. $1,800

FORSTER, John
- The Life of Charles Dickens. 1872-74. 3 vols. Cont. cf. gt.; Anthony Trollope bkplt. in each vol., his sig. in Vol. II. (C. May 30; 151) *Quaritch.* £260
- – Anr. Copy. 3 vols. in 6 Lge. 8vo. Extra-ill. with over 450 engraved port. & view. plts., mostly inlaid, few hand-cold., & 33 A.L.s., plus 2 other autograph items, together 48 pp., 4to. & smaller, few inlaid, vol. 1 lacks title-p., crushed mor. gt., gt. dentelles, partly unc., by Riviere, jnts. very worn, with D.s & Accomplished by Dickens, bank cheque to pay Miss Dickens, sheet of engraved Tavistock Square letter head sigd. by Dickens & Forster. (SG. Apr.26; 72) $950

FORSTER, Johann Reinhold
- Observations Made During a Voyage Round the World, on Physical Geography, Natural History, & Ethic Philosophy. 1778. *1st. Edn.* 4to. Lacks map, text misbnd., cont. cf., rebkd. (TA. Feb.16; 24) £120
- – Anr. Copy. 4to. Title slightly foxed, old tree cf., spine reinforced. (CA. Apr.3; 49) Aus. $780

FORSYTH, Robert
- The Principles of Moral Science. Edinb., 1805. Vol. 1 (all publd.). Orig. bds., unc., defect.; Sir Ivar Colquhoun, of Luss copy. (CE. Mar.22; 109) £180

FORSYTH, William
- Life of Marcus Tullius Cicero. L., 1867. School prize bdg. of cont. blind-tooled mor., fore-e. pntg. (SG. Nov.17; 228) $120

FORT ST GEORGE GAZETTE
Madras, 1834. Nos. 276-321 only in 1 vol. 4to. Some ll. detchd., cont. cf., covers detchd., w.a.f. (CSK. May 4; 138) £150

FORTALITIUM SCIENTIAE das ist die Unfehlbare Volkommeliche Unerschatzliche Kunst aller Kuensten und Magnalien ... hocherleuchte Bruederschafft des Rosencreutzes zu Eröffnen Gesandt
[Nuremb.?], 1617. *1st. Edn.* 23 ll., lacks last lf. (blank?), some underlinings & few notes in red, bds., old. wraps. bnd. in; Dr. Walter Pagel copy. (S. Feb.7; 125) *Janssen.* £280

FORTE, Giovanni Bernardo
- Incomincia sul al Nel Nome de Xpo Yesu. Incomincia el Vocabulista Ecclesia/stico. Ricolto & ordinato dal Pouero Sacerdote de Christo./ Frate Johane Bernardo Sauonese. Milan, Alexander Pelizonus, 21 [or 23] Mar. 1500. Some staining, later hf. vell., slightly bumped. (SI. Dec.15; 12) Lire 650,000

FORTESCUE, Sir John
- De Laudibus Legum Angliae ... the Two Summes of Sir Ralph de Hagham. L., 1616. *1st. Edn.* 2 pts. in 1 vol. Lacks 1st. lf. (? blank), cont. sheep, a little worn. [STC 11197] (BBA. May 3; 103) *Frognall.* £110

FORTESCUE, Sir John William
- A History of the British Army. 1910-30. 13 vols. in 14, & 6 map vols. Orig. cl. gt. (P. Dec.8; 195) *Remington.* £260

FORTH BRIDGE, (The) in its Various Stages of Construction, & Compared with the Most Notable Bridges of the World
Edinb., n.d. Ob. 4to. Orig. cl. (P. Sep.29; 242) *Bickersteth.* £60

FORTHOFFER, R.
- Le Manuscrit de Marckolsheim, 1800-1814. N.d. 2 vols. 4to. 306 cold. plts., leaves, publisher's bdgs. (HD. Jan.27; 144) Frs. 2,550

FORTUNATIANUS, Chirius Consultus
- Rhetorica. [Venice, C. de Pensis de Mandello, 1498-1500]. 4to. Some margin dampstains, loose in later bds., the Walter Goldwater copy. [BMC V, 1475; Goff F-273; HC 7305] (SG. Dec.1; 149) $950
- – Anr. Copy. 4to. Lacks the 12 separately sigd. ll. of the 'Dialecta', loose in early vell.; the Walter Goldwater copy. [BMC V, 1475; Goff F-273; HC 7305] (SG. Dec.1; 150) $125
- Rhetorica, et De Officio Oratoris. [Venice, C. de Pensis de Mandello, 1494-1500]. 4to. Lacks blank ll. a1 & h6, heavily stained, with some erosion, loose in later marb. bds., leath. back; the Walter Goldwater copy. [Goff F-275] (SG. Dec.1; 151) $200

FORTUNATUS, Patavinus Monachus
- Decas Elementorum Mysticae Geometriae Quibus Praecipua Divinitatis arcana Explicantur. Padua, 1617. Outer margin of title shaved, short tear in E1. (*Bound with:*) MEURSIUS, Joannes – Denarius Pythagoricus sivo de Numerorum usque ad Denarium Qualitate. Leiden, 1631. Some ll. misbnd., pinholes in inner blank margins. Together 2 works in 1 vol. 4to. Cont. cf.; Trotter & Dr. Walter Pagel copy. (S. Feb.7; 126) *Weiner.* £240

FORTUNE, Robert
- A Residence Among the Chinese Inland, On the Coast, & at Sea. 1857. Hf. cf. gt. (P. Feb.16; 211) £55
- Wanderungen in China. Trans.:– J. T. Zenker. Leipzig, 1854. *2nd. German Edn.* Slightly browned, liby. hf. linen. (R. Oct.13; 3002) DM 550
- – Anr. Copy. Cont. bds. (HK. Nov.8; 870) DM 520

FORTUNE, T.
See— PHIPPS, Joseph—FORTUNE, T.

FOSBROOKE, Dudley
- Abstracts of Records & Manuscripts respecting the County of Gloucester. Gloucester, 1807. 2 vols. 4to. Engraved title, 29 plts., some spotting, cont. hf. mor., rubbed; Joseph Nield Bkplt. (BBA. Feb.9; 334) *Parsloe.* £190

FOSBROOKE, Thomas
- Original History of the City of Gloucester. 1819. 4to. Engraved title, 36 plts., some spotted, cont. cf., rubbed. (BBA. Feb.9; 335) *Paraloe.* £75

FOSKETT, Daphne
- Dictionary of British Miniature Painters. N.Y. & Wash., 1972. 2 vols. 4to. Orig. cl., d.-w.'s. (BBA. Sep.8; 136) *Bearnes.* £130
- – Anr. Edn. [1972]. 2 vols. 4to. Orig. cl., d.-w. (CSK. Apr.6; 125) £120

FOSS, Henry
See— PAYNE, Thomas & Foss, Henry

FOSTER, Birket
- Pictures of English Landscape. Ed.:– Tom Taylor. 1881. *(1000) numbered.* Fo. Orig. decor. vell. bds. (TA. Dec.15; 349) £60

FOSTER, Joshua J.
- French Art from Watteau to Prud'hon. Together with ... some Studies in the Social History of the Period. L., 1905. *Edn. Royale. (35).* 3 vols. Fo. Parch. (SPB. Nov.30; 37) $425
- Miniature Painters British & Foreign. 1903. *(175) numbered & sigd.* 2 vols. Fo. Liby. stp. on titles, orig. vell.; Hornby bkplt. (BBA. Nov.10; 167) *Bennett.* £70
- – Anr. Edn. N.Y. & L., 1903. *(210) numbered & sigd. by author.* 2 vols. Some ll. loose. orig. cl.-bkd. bds., slightly rubbed. (S. Apr.30; 121) *Spink.* £60
- Samuel Cooper & the English Miniature Painters of the XVII Century. L., 1914-16. *De Luxe Edn. (125).* 3 vols., including Supp. Fo. Purple mor. gt. (SPB. Nov.30; 293) $475

FOSTER, T.T.
- The Stuarts. L. & N.Y., 1902. *(550) numbered & sigd.* 2 vols. Fo. Cl. gt. (GM. Dec.7; 653) £50

FOSTER, Thomas
- Review of the Labours of Several Explorers of Australia ... Melbourne, &c., 1863. Continuosly paginated to p. 16, excluding wraps. (Ferguson calls for only 12 + [2] pp.), sm. section torn from fore-edge of title-p. without loss of text, sewn in wraps., folding cf. case. (KH. May 1; 271) Aus. $300

FOSTER, Thomas Campbell
- Letters on the Conditions of the People of Ireland. L., 1846. *1st. Book Edn.* Hf. mor., armorial motif on spine. (GM. Dec.7; 154) £85

FOSTER, William Harnden
- New England Grouse Shooting. N.Y., 1942. *1st. Edn.* Lge. 4to. Hf.-title, pict. linen, spine a bit darkened, covers slightly soiled; sig. of Franklin D. Roosevelt Jr. (SG. Mar.15; 256) $110

FOUCHE, Joseph, Duc d'Otrante
- Mémoires. 1824. *Orig. Edn.* 2 vols. Hf. cf. by Monier. (HD. Jan.24; 14) Frs. 1,300

FOUCHER, A. & Bazin-Foucher, Mme. E.
- La Vielle Route de l'Inde de Bactres à Taxila. Paris, 1942-47. 2 vols. Fo. Orig. wraps. (BBA. Nov.10; 319) *Sims, Reed & Fogg.* £180

FOUCHET, Max-Pol
- Femme de Nuit et d'Aube. Ill.:– C.G. Beverloo 'Corneille'. Paris, 1966. *Orig. Edn., (110) sigd. by author & artist.* Lge. ob. fo. 7 orig. cold. lithos., leaves, portfo., cl. (B. Feb.8; 365) Fls. 1,100

FOUCQUET, Jean
- Oeuvre. Paris, 1866. 2 vols. Lge. 8vo. Elab. red mor., black intertwined strapwork on covers, some scuffing. (SPB. Nov.30; 38) $450

FOUJITA, Tsuguharo Léonard
- Légendes Japonaises. Preface:– Claude Farrère. Paris, 1922. *Orig. Edn. 1st. Printing.* On vell. alfa., red hf. chagrin, corners, limp spine, wrap. & spine preserved. (HD. Dec.9; 128) Frs. 2,900
- – Anr. Edn. Preface:– A. Farrère. Paris, 1923. *Orig. Edn.* On vell. d'alfa, sewed. (HD. Apr.11; 22) Frs. 1,900
- – Anr. Copy. Sewed. (HD. Jun.13; 121) Frs. 1,450

FOUQUERAY, Charles
- Les Fusiliers-Marins au Front des Flandres. Preface:– Le Goffic. Paris, [1916]. *(25) on vell., with orig. sigd. water-colour.* Fo. 32 drawings, sketches & watercolours, loose in folder. (HD. Sep.21; 120) Frs. 1,100

FOUR ADDRESSES OF THE KEELMEN of the River Tyne
Newcastle, 1823. Bds. (P. Jul.5; 321) £50

FOURIER, Jean Baptiste Joseph, Baron de
- The Analytical Theory of Heat. Trans.:– Alexander Freeman. Camb., 1878. *1st. Edn. in Engl.* Errata, some pencil marginalia, some light spotting, orig. cl., shaken; Stanitz coll. (SPB. Apr.25; 179) $200

FOURNIER, Edouard
See— MICHEL, Francisque & Fournier, Edouard

FOURNIER, Georges, S.J.
- Hydrographie contenant la Théorie et la Pratique de toutes les Parties de la Navigation. Paris, 1667. *2nd. Edn.* Fo. Title reprd., some foxing, cont. cf., spine decor., end-papers renewed. (HD. Jul.2; 14) Frs. 2,000
- Traité des Fortifications ou Architecture Militaire. Mainz, 1668. 12mo. Lacks engraved frontis., margins cut close affecting a few sigs., or catch-words, recent cf.; sig. of Hester Maria Thrale (eldest daughter of Mrs. Piozzi) on front free end-paper. (BBA. May 23; 336) *Snelling.* £70

FOURNIER, le Jeune
- Dissertation sur l'Origine et les Progrès de l'Art de graver en Bois ... Paris, 1758. *(Bound with:)–* De l'Origine et des Productions de l'Imprimerie Primitive en Taille de Bois. Paris, 1759. *(Bound with:)–* Observations sur un Ouvrage intitulé Vindiciae hypographicae, pour servir de Suite au Traité. Together 3 works in 1 vol., old marb. cf., sm. worm hole, decor. spine. (HD. Mar.30; 6) Frs. 5,000

FOURNIER, Pierre Simon
- Manuel Typographique. Paris, 1764; 1766. *1st. Edn.* 2 vols. Sm. 8vo. Hf.-title, engraved frontis., 5 folding ll. mus. notat., lacks 16 folding engraved plts., frontis. & hf.-title stained, red crushed levant, triple gt. fillet borders, spines gt. (SG. May 17; 88) $500
- – **Anr. Edn.** Ill.:– Fessard after Gravelot & de Sèvre. Paris, 1764-66[68]. 2 vols. Some foxing & browning, 1 text lf. & mus notat. lf. with sm. margin repair, cont. red mor., gt. decor., gt. inner & outer dentelle, slightly worn, some spotting & scratches. (H. May 22; 15) DM 7,200

FOWLER, Thomas
- Medical Reports of the Effects of Arsenic in the Cure of Agues, Remitting Fevers, & Periodic Headachs. L., 1786. *(Bound with:)* – Medical Reports of the Effects of Tobacco in the Cure of Dropsies & Dysuries, or Cases of Pain & Difficulty of Passing Urine. L., 1788. *2nd. Edn.* *(Bound with:)* – Medical Reports of the Effects of Blood-Letting, Sudorifics, & Blistering in the Cure of the Acute & Chronic Rheumatism. L., 1795. Together 3 works in 1 vol. Cont. tree cf., extremities worn, covers starting, liby. bkplts., stps. (SG. Mar.22; 127) $120

FOWLES, Joseph
- Sydney in 1848: Illustrated by Copper-plate Engravings of its Principal Streets, Public Buildings, Churches ... Sydney, [1848]. 4to. 40 hand-cold. plts., 1 plt. with edges torn & laid down, 'Opinions of the Press' lf. with slight tear, reprd., 2 plts. shaved just affecting headings, orig. ptd. bds., worn, some staining, rebkd. (LC. Jul.5; 197) £480

FOX, George
- Gospel Truth Demonstrated, in a collection of Doctrinal Books. 1706. *1st. Edn.* Fo. 18th C. owner's inscr. on title-p., later brown mor., spine gt. (BBA. Feb.9; 28) *Waterfield.* £70

FOX, John, Jr.
- The Little Shepherd of Kingdom Come. Ill.:– N.C. Wyeth. N.Y., 1931. *1st. Edn.* Orig. cl. & box; mor. & sigd. by artist. (CBA. Aug.21; 674) $350

– – **Anr. Edn.** Ill.:– N.C. Wyeth. N.Y., 1931. *(512) sigd. by artist.* 4to. Orig. vell.-bkd. cl., glassine d.-w., publisher's box stained, 1 corner worn. (SPB. May 17; 719) $325

FOX, Lady Mary (Ed.)
See— WHATELY, Rev. Richard, attributed to

FOX-DAVIES, A.C.
- The Art of Heraldry, An Encyclopaedia of Armory. 1904. Fo. 153 plts., orig. gt.-pict. cl., bkplts. (SKC. May 4; 1725) £70
- The Book of Public Arms. L., 1915. Orig. cl., foxed; author's copy, many autograph annots. & pasted-in material. orig. cl., boxed. (S. Oct.11; 533) *Thorp.* £270

FOXE, Luke
- North-West Fox, or, Fox from the North-West Passage. L., 1635. *1st. Edn.* 4to. Woodcut frontis., folding map, woodcut map in text, port. of Charles I inserted, a little, mainly marginal, worming, printing flaw on K2, blank margin of K4 reprd., some light stains, cont. cf., edges just worn. [Sabin 25410; STC 11221] (BBA. May 3; 258) *Brooke-Hitching.* £11,000

FOXON, D.F.
- English Verse, 1701-1750. 1975. 2 vols. 4to. Orig. cl., d.-w.'s, s.-c. (TA. Dec.15; 304) £70

FRACASTORIUS, Hieronymus
- Opera Omnia. Ed.:– Andreae Naugerii. Venice, 1555. *1st. Coll. Edn.* 2 pts. in 1 vol. 4to. 2 ll. sig. Kk misbnd., sm. tear in inner margin of 1st. ll. reprd., some worming, closely cut at top, pol. cf. gt., rebkd.; Dr. Walter Pagel copy. (S. Feb.7; 127) *Phelps.* £200

FRACCUS, Ambrosius Novidius
- Sacrorum Fastorum Libri XII. Rome, 1547. 4to. Title-p, dust-stained, later bds. (BBA. Nov.30; 9) *George's.* £90

FRANÇAIS PEINTS PAR EUX-MEMES
Paris, 1840-41. *1st. Edn.* Vols. 1-4, 6, 7 & 9 only (of 9). 4to. Vol. 1 woodcut title with sm. fault pasted, minimal foxing, cont. hf. leath. gt., slightly rubbed & bumped. (HK. Nov.10; 3057) DM 1,100
– – **Anr. Edn.** Texts:– Balzac, Gautier, Janin & others. Ill.:– after Daumier, Gavarni, Gerard, Meissomier, Lami, & others. Paris, 1840-42. *Orig. Edn.* 9 vols. Lge. 8vo. Approx. 1,500 vigs. & 400 cont. cold. figures, lacks Vol. 1 frontis., some plts browned, cont. hf. mor., blind decor. (HD. Jan.30; 54) Frs 7,000
– – **Anr. Edn.** Ill.:– Gavarni. Paris, n.d. 1 vol. only. 4to. 69 lumés of wood engraved ills., all but 1 on hire., hf. mor. corners, spine detchd. (HD. Jan.26; 138) Frs. 1,900

FRANCE, Anatole [ie. Anatole François Thibault]
- L'Affaire Crainquebille. Ill.:– Steinlen, engraved by Deloche, E. & F. Florian, the Fromonts, Gusman, Mathieu, & Perrichon. Paris, 1901. *Orig. Edn.* 4to. On old japan, unnumbered, 2 ll. inverted, hf. mor., corners, by Alix, unc., s.-c. (HD. Mar.27; 68) Frs. 5,800
– – **Anr. Edn.** Ill.:– Steinlen. Paris, 1901. *(400).* Lge. 8vo. This copy numbered & nominative on velin du Marais, maroon mor. gt. by Ch. Meunier, 1902, spine decor., wtrd. silk liners & end-ll., wrap. & spine, s.-c.; orig. cold. drawing, sigd., bnd. at beginning. (HD. Jun.26; 1a) Frs. 36,000
- Balthasar. Paris, 1889. *Orig. Edn.* 12mo. Hf. mor., corners, spine decor., unc., wrap. & spine, s.-c.; author's autograph dedication to Francis Magnard, A.N. by author at head of 'Temps'. (HD. Mar.27; 66) Frs. 1,200
– – **Anr. Edn.** Ill.:– after Henri Caruchet. Paris, 1900. Jansenist mor., inner fillet, wrap. preserved, by Manùs Michel, slightly faded. (HD. Feb.17; 72) Frs. 2,000
- Clio. Ill.:– Alphonse Mucha. Paris, 1900. *[1st. Edn.].* Red hf. mor., orig. pict. wraps. (soiled) bnd. in. (S. Nov.21; 112) *Desk.* £100
– – **Anr. Copy.** Margins lightly browned, 2 tears, cont. vell., soiled. (CSK. Oct.21; 154) £75
– – **Anr. Copy.** Three-qtr. lev., spine elab. gt. with floral design, orig. pict. wraps. bnd. in. (SG. Nov.3; 148) $325

– – **Anr. Copy.** Sm. 8vo. Lev., slightly worn, cold. pict. wraps. bnd. in. (SG. Feb.16; 216) $130
- Les Contes de Jacques Tournebroche. Paris, [1908]. *(60) numbered on china, with 2 separate suites of all ills.* Sm. 8vo. Cont. hf. mor. gt., corners, by H. Blanchetière, spine decor., wrap. & spine. (HD. May 16; 25) Frs. 2,100
- Les Dieux ont Soif. Paris, 1912. *Orig. Edn.* 12mo. On japan, jansenist red mor., mor. liners, wrap. & spine preserved; from Louis Barthou liby., author's dedication, A.L.s. to Barthou. (HD. Jun.13; 42) Frs. 10,000
– – **Anr. Edn.** Paris, 1912. *(200) on hólland.* 12mo. Recovered vell. by Vauthrin, decor. with paintings by Joseph Hémard, sigd., unc., wrap. & spine, s.-c.; 176 orig. watercolours by J. Hémard, sigd. by author, author's autograph dedication to Albert Henraux. (HD. Mar.27; 71) Frs. 7,500
– – **Anr. Copy.** 12mo. Jansenist red mor. by Ch. Septier, spine raised bands, pink mor. doubls., silk end-ll., wrap. & spine, s.-c. (HD. May 16; 26) Frs. 3,000
- Histoire Comique. Paris, [1903]. *Orig. Edn.* 12mo. Sewed, lacks upr. cover of wrap.; Georges Courteline copy with autograph dedication. (HD. May 16; 24) Frs. 1,000
– – **Anr. Edn.** Ill.:– Edgar Chahine. Paris, 1905. Jansenist mor., red mor. liners, watered silk end-ll., wrap. & spine preserved, s.-c. (HD. Jun.13; 37) Frs. 3,800
- Histoire Contemporaine. Le Mannequin d'Osier. Paris, 1897. *(50) on holland.* 12mo. Mor. gt. by Lortic, watered silk liners & end-ll., wrap. & spine preserved. (HD. Jun.13; 40) Frs. 3,200
– – **Anr. Edn.** Paris, 1899. *(40) on japan.* 12mo. Red mor. gt. by Lortic, spine decor., watered silk liners & end-ll. (HD. Jun.13; 41) Frs. 3,500
- Histoire de Dona Maria d'Avalos et de Don Fabricio, Duc d'Andria. Ill.:– Illumination:– Léon Lebègue. Paris, 1902. *(240). (25) on japan with suite in black on china.* Sm 4to. Hf. mor., corners, by Yseux, spine decor., unc., wrap. & spine preserved; autograph dedication on end-paper from Lebègue to Jules Claretie. (HD. May 4; 274) Frs. 1,800
- L'Ile des Pingouins. [1908]. *Orig. Edn. (75) on japan.* 12mo. Bordeaux hf. mor., corners, spine decor. (HD. Apr.13; 161) Frs. 1,800
– – **Anr. Edn.** Ill.:– Louis Jou. Paris, 1926. *(535). (20) on japon impérial.* 2 vols. in 1. Red hf. mor. by Cretté, wrap. & spine preserved, s.-c. (HD. May 4; 275) Frs. 2,600
- Le Lys Rouge. Paris, 1894. *Orig. Edn.* 12mo. Cont. blind-decor. old red mor. by Joly for Henri Vever, 1917, after sketch by Jules Claudel, silk doubls. & end-ll., wrap. & spine, s.-c. (HD. May 16; 23) Frs. 6,700
– – **Anr. Edn.** Paris, 1894. *Orig. Edn. (30) on japan.* Mor. by Iseux, spine decor. (faded), watered silk liners & end-ll., wrap. & spine preserved. (HD. Jun.13; 39) Frs. 2,900
- Les Noces Corinthiennes. Paris, 1876. *Orig. Edn.* 12mo. Hf. mor., corners, spine decor., wrap. & spine. *(With:)* - Thaïs. Paris, 1891. *Orig. Edn.* 12mo. Hf. mor., corners, by P.L. Martin, wrap. (HD. May 16; 21) Frs. 1,000
- Oeuvres Complètes Illustrées. Ill.:– G. Belot, Carlegle, Brissaud, Chahine & others. 1925-35. 25 vols. Sm. 4to. Hf. chargrin, corners. (SM. Mar.7; 2130) Frs. 1,500
– – **Anr. Edn.** Ill.:– Ed. Chahine (port.), Dufour, Leroux, Naudin, Marty, Mirande, Belot, etc. (wood engrs.). Paris, 1925-36. *1st. Coll. Edn. Ltd. Edn. on Van Gelder numbered.* 28 vols. including 3 for separate suites of engrs. Port. in 2 states, hf. chagrin, corners, gt. & mosaic decor. spines, unc., wrap. preserved, s.-c., separate printing of suites on chine in 3 states in leaves in wrap. in 3 unif. decor. s.-c.'s. (HD. Mar.30; 29) Frs. 9,000
- Les Opinions de M. Jérôme Coignard, recueillies par Jacques Tournebroche et publiées par Anatole France. Paris, 1893. 12mo. Jansenist mor. by Champs, spine raised bands (slightly faded), wrap. & spine, s.-c. (HD. May 16; 22) Frs. 1,500
- Le Petit Soldat de Plomb. Ill.:– Gustave-Adolphe Mossa. Paris, 1919. *(1200) numbered & initialled by publishers. (With:)* - La Legende des Saintes Oliverie et Liberette. Gustave-Adolphe Mossa, pochoir-cold. by Berthelot. Paris, 1924. *(1200)*

numbered & initialled by publishers. Together 2
vols. 12mo. Crushed three-qtr. lev., spines gt., &
with inlaid mor. designs, cold. pict. wraps. bnd. in.
(SG. Feb.16; 127) $275
- **La Rôtisserie de la Reine Pédauque.** Ill.:– Auguste
Leroux. Paris, 1911. *1st. Ill. Edn.* Red mor. gt. by
Semet et Plumelle, spine decor., wrap. & spine
preserved, s.-c. (HD. Jun.13; 38) Frs. 8,100
- - **Anr. Copy.** 4to. On vell., numbered, 18th. C.
style roan, spine decor., unc., wrap. & spine. (HD.
May 21; 117) Frs. 3,100
- - **Anr. Edn.** Ill.:– Guy de Montable & Jacomet.
Paris, [1925]. *(83) numbered on Japon imperial.*
4to. 75 aquarelles, hand-cold., with compl. extra
suite ptd. on China paper, lev., with inlaid strapwork
pattern on covers & spine, wide gt. dentelles, satin
doubls. & end-ll., by Subirana. (SG. Feb.16; 126)
$300
- **Les Sept Femmes de Barbe-bleue** ... Ill.:– G.A.
Mossa. Paris, 1921. *De Luxe Edn. (70) numbered
on japan, with 3 suites of dry-points & separate
suite.* Lge. 8vo. States in black ptd. on china, orig.
bdg. (HD. Apr.26; 108) Frs. 1,300
- **Sur la Pierre Blanche.** Paris, [1905]. *Orig. Edn.*
12mo. Hf. mor., corners, by Semet & Plumelle,
spine blind-decor., unc., wrap. & spine; author's
autograph dedication to Robert Dreyfus. (HD.
Mar.27; 70) Frs. 1,500
- **Thaïs.** Ill.:– Georges Rochegrosse, engraved by
E. Decisy. Paris, 1909. Numbered copy on vélin
d'Arches, hf. mor., corners, by Durvand, mosaic
spine, unc. & spine, ill. wrap. & spine. (HD. Jul.2; 66)
Frs. 1,100
- - **Anr. Edn.** Ill.:– R. Freida. Paris, 1924. *(50)
numbered on vell. de Hollande.* 4to. With double
suite of ills. in black & sanguine, bordeaux mor.,
gt. decor., gt. inner decor., pict. wrap. & spine, s.-
c., by Mabilde. (HD. Mar.14; 122) Frs. 3,500
- **Vie de Jeanne d'Arc.** Paris, 1904-08. *Orig. Edn.*
2 vols. Slight foxing to 1st. ll. of Vol. II, hf. cf.,
corners, unc., wraps.; author's autograph dedication
to Georges Clémenceau. (HD. Mar.27; 68)
Frs. 2,600
- **Works.** N.Y., 1924. *Autograph Edn. (1075) sigd.*
30 vols. Elab. tooled mor. gt. (SPB. Dec.13; 530)
$950

FRANCE AU XIXe SIECLE
Text:– Ch. J. Delile. Ill.:– after Thomas Allom.
Paris, L., ca. 1830. 2 vols. 4to. Approx. 60 engraved
plts., publisher's decor. buckram. (HD. Jun.22; 42)
Frs. 1,700

FRANCE ILLUSTRATED
L., Paris, ca. 1830. 3 vols. 4to. 96 steel-engraved
plts., some light foxing, cont. hf. cf., spines gt. (HD.
Mar.19; 49) Frs. 1,850

FRANCHIERES, J. de
- **La Fauconnerie.** Paris, 1618. Sm. 4to. At end 'La
Fauconnerce de Messire Arthelouche de
Alagona' & 'Recueal de tous les Oiseaux de Proye
qui servent à la Vollerie et Fauconnerie' by G.-B.,
mor., gt. decor., s.-c., by Zaehnsdorf. (HD. Mar.14;
30) Frs. 2,950

FRANCIA, L.
- **Progressive Lessons tending to Elucidate the Character of Trees.** 1813. 4to. 14 plts., including 13
hand-cold., 1 trimmed & loose, qtr. mor., defect.
(P. Dec.8; 161) *Marlborough.* £110

FRANCIS, George Grant
- **Charters Granted to Swansea.** 1867. *(100).* Fo.
Slightly spotted, orig. mor. gt. (BBA. Aug.18; 255)
Korn. £80

FRANCIS, Grant R.
- **Old English Drinking Glasses.** 1926. *[1st. Edn.].*
4to. Orig. cl., d.-w. (BBA. Sep.8; 243)
Belanske. £85
- - **Anr. Copy.** 4to. Orig. cl. gt., partly unc., spine
faded. (LC. Jul.5; 44) £65
- - **Anr. Copy.** 4to. 72 plts., orig. buckram, covers
lightly worn, some light foxing, d.-w. worn & reprd.
(CBA. Jan.29; 215) $180
- - **Anr. Edn.** 1926. *(100).* 4to. Orig. parch.-bkd. cl.
(BBA. Nov.10; 325) *Traylen.* £85

FRANCIS, James B.
- **Lowell Hydraulic Experiments being a Selection
from Experiments on Hydraulic Motors.** Boston,
1855. 4to. Some spotting of plts., cf. prize bdg.,
slight rubbing: presented to James Amos, 10 Jan.
1859, by Society of Engineers, pres. plt. sigd. by
Henry P. Stephenson & Alf. Williams, Stanitz coll.
(SPB. Apr.25; 181) $650

FRANCIS OF ASSISI, Saint
- **I Fioretti** ... [Chelsea], Ash. Pr., 1922. *(252).
(240) on paper.* Vell. (LH. Sep.25; 317) $325
[-] **Laudes Creaturarum.** Trans.:– M. Arnold.
[Hammersmith, Doves Pr., 1910]. *(250).* On
Bütten, hand-bnd. orig. cf. (H. Nov.23; 991)
DM 700
- **Les Petites Fleurs.** Ill.:– Emile Bernard. Paris,
1928. 4to. Chagrin gt., wraps. preserved, s.-c.'s.
(HD. Nov.17; 169) Frs. 1,850
- - **Anr. Copy.** On vergé d'Arches, leaves, wrap.,
some tears. (HD. Jan.24; 63) Frs. 1,000
- **Den Wijngaert va[n] Sinte Franciscus vol Schoonre
Historien Legenden, end Duechdelijcke Leeringhen
Allen Menschem seer Profijtlijck.** Antw., 1518. Sm.
fo. Title, 1st. 2 ll. & 1 index lf. reprd. with transparent paper, with loss of a few letters, colophon
lf. defect. & mntd., affecting address, few sm.
repairs, mainly in margins, cont. panel. & blind-
stpd. decor. cf. over wood, lge. brass corner-pieces,
central pieces & brass strip, catches, lacks clasps,
spine reprd. (VG. Sep.14; 1322) Fls. 3,200

FRANCISCO DE ACOLTIS, de Aretio
See— **ANDREAE, Johannes—FRANCISCO DE
ACOLTIS, de Aretio**

FRANCISCUS DE MAIRONIS
- **Conflatus sive Scriptum super Primum Sententiarum.** Basle, Nicolas Kesler, 1489. Fo. Initials
painted in red, cont. blind-stpd. roan, richly decor.,
brass boss in centre, spine rebkd. with old pig, clasps
incompl.; from Fondation Furstenberg-Beaumesnil. [H. 10535; BMC III, 768] (HD. Nov.16;
13) Frs. 6,500

FRANCK, P. & others
[-] **Kunstrichtige Schreibart allerhand Versalie[n]
oder Anfangs Buchstabe[n] der Teütschen Lateinischen und Italienischen Schrifften, aus unterschiedlichen Meistern der Edlen Schreibkunst.** Nürnberg,
after 1655. 4to. Title loose, lacks 3 ll., minimal
spotting, cont. bds., bumped; Hauswedell coll. (H.
May 23; 235) DM 1,700

FRANCK, Sebastian
- **Chronica, Zeitbuch vnnd Geschichtbibel von
Anbegyn biss in diss Gegenwertig M.D.L. Jahr ver-
lengt.** [Bern], 1550-51. Fo. Cont. owners note on
title, some ll. stained, engraved ex-libris inside
cover, cont. blind-tooled pig-bkd. wood bds.,
rubbed, bumped, lacks clasps. (H. Nov.23; 588)
DM 2,400
- - **Anr. Edn.** Bern, 1550-51. *4th. Edn. 2nd.
printing.* 2 pts. in 1 vol. Fo. Some heavy soiling in
margins, most margins spotted, especially at end,
some worm-holes, mostly in margins, in pt.1 3 ll.
with side margin partly cut off, ptd. marginelia on
2 ll. cut off in part, 1 ll. with corner tear at top, 1
lacking lf. replaced by 2 ll. old MS., pt. II 3 ll. with
margin or corner tears, lacks 1 lf., cont. wood bds.,
very wormed & defect., upr. cover loose, lacks
clasps. (R. Apr.3; 42) DM 900
- **Germaniae Chronicon.** Augsburg, 1538. Title facs.
on old paper, slightly browned & foxed, some
underlining, old entries on end-papers, 2 end-ll.
with margin repairs, cont. wood bds., lacks cover
material & clasps. (HK. May 15; 135) DM 1,200
- **Paradoxa Ducenta Octaginta, das ist CCLXXX
Wunderred vnd Gleichsam Räterschafft, auss der H.
Schrifft.** Ulm, ca. 1535. *[2nd. Edn. ?].* 4to. 2 short
reprd. tears in title-p., some staining, several cont.
marginalia, mod. vell., slightly soiled & warped.
(S. May 10; 281) *Bruno.* £380
[-] **Sprichworter.** Frankfurt, 1615. Browned,
stained, wormed, title with owners mark, margin
defect., cont. vell., slightly wormed, lacks ties. (HK.
May 16; 1447) DM 400
- **Weltbüch: Spiegel und Bildtniss des Gantzen Erd-
bodens** ... Tübingen, 1534. *1st. Edn.* 4 vols. in 1.
Fo. R4 blank, cont. inscr. on title & in text, (?)

lacks colophon lf., new cf. antique. [Sabin 25468]
(S. May 21; 164) *Quaritch.* £350

FRANCO, Ceres
- **H.** Ill.:– C.G. Beverloo 'Corneille'. Epinay, 1974.
(99) sigd. by author & artist. 4to. 5 cold. plts., each
numbered & sigd. by artist, leaves, wood box. (B.
Feb.8; 366) Fls. 600

FRANÇOIS DE PAULE, Saint
- **Les Figures et l'Abrégé de la Vie, de la Mort et
des Miracles.** Paris, 1671. Sm. fo. 'Portraits de
quelques personnes ... de l'Ordre des Minimes' at
end, cont. red mor., Du Seuil decor on covers, spine
decor. (HD. Jun.6; 61) Frs. 3,000

FRANCOIS DE SALES, Saint
- **Les Oeuvres.** Tolose, 1637. Sm. fo. Cont. red mor.,
Du Seuil decor. on covers, spine decor. (HD. Jun.6;
62) Frs. 2,100
- **Les Sentiments du Bien-heureux François de Sales,
Evesque de Genève, touchant la Grace.** Ed.:– R.P.
Dom Pierre de Saint Joseph. Paris, 1647. 12mo.
Cont. decor. red mor., crowned cypher of Anne of
Austria; 18th. C. ex-libris 'Demonge' on end-lf.,
pres. inscr. dtd. 1698 on anr. lf., stp. on title. (HD.
Mar.29; 31) Frs. 36,000

FRANCOLIN, H. von
- **Thurnier Buch Wahrhafftiger Thate, som in dem
Monat Junii des Vergangenen LX. Jars in vnd aus-
serhalb des Statt Wienn zu Ross vnd zu Fuess, auff
Wasser vnd Lannd gehalten worden** ... Wien, [1561].
1st. German Edn. Fo. Title & last lf. with sm.
margin defects., stained thro.-out, 2 other works
removed from bdg., cont. vell. (HK. Nov.8; 184)
DM 620

FRANCQUART, Jacobus
- **Pompa Fvnebris Optimi Potentissimiq. Principis
Alberti Pii, Archidvcis Avstriae.** Ill.:– C. Galle.
Brüssel, 1623. *1st. Edn.* Ob. fo. Lacks 1 copperplt.,
2 plts. slightly defect. & mntd. on linen, lightly
browned thro.-out, hf. vell. (HK. Nov.8; 930)
DM 850
- - **Anr. Edn.** Ill.:– C. Galle after Francquart. Brus-
sels, 1623. *2nd. Edn.* Fo. Latin, Fr., Flemish &
Spanish text, 2 plts. folded, title & some copper
engrs. slightly browned, some sm tears, later cf. gt.,
lightly rubbed, spine torn. (H. May 22; 361)
DM 1,100

FRANCUS, Jacobus [i.e. Conrad Memmius or Lau-
tenbach]
- **Historicae Relationis Continuatio.** (Frankfurt,
after 1607/1639). 8 vols. 4to. Lacks copperplts.,
bds., 3 vols. without bdg. (HK. Nov.8; 987)
DM 860

FRANK, J.P.
- **System einer Vollständigen Medicinischen
Polizey.** Mannheim, 1780-84. Cont. hf. leath. (D.
Nov.23; 554) DM 460
- - **Anr. Edn.** Mannheim, 1783. *1st. Edn.* Some
light foxing, cont. hf. leath., spine slightly defect.
(R. Apr.4; 1299) DM 480

FRANK FEIGNWELL'S Attempts to Amuse his
Friends on Twelfth-Night
L., 1811. *1st. Edn.* 16mo. 8 loose hand-cold. cut-
out figures, with 1 moveable head, 1 (of 3?) hats &
1 wig, 1 figure lacks arm, ptd. wraps., orig. ptd. s.-
c. (SG. Dec.8; 256) $200

FRANKAU, Julia
- **Eighteenth Century Colour Prints.** 1900. *(60).* 1
vol., lacks plt. portfo. Fo. Some light spotting, cont.
mor. gt. decor. by Bickers & Son, watered silk end-
ll., upr. cover & spine slightly faded. (CSK. Jul.13;
187) £220
- - **Anr. Copy.** 4to. Slight spotting, orig. cl.,
discold., spine rubbed at head & tail. (S. Apr.30;
137) *Erlini.* £50
- **John Raphael Smith: His Life & Works.** L., 1902.
1st. Edn. Portfo. of plts. only. Lge. fo. 50 full-p.
mntd. plts., plt. list, hf.-title loose, linen over bds.
envelope-style case, rubbed & soiled, 1 flap detchd.
(HA. Nov.18; 81) $125
- **The Story of Emma, Lady Hamilton.** 1911. *(250)
numbered & sigd.* 2 vols. Fo. Some light spotting,
orig. parch. gt., slightly soiled. (CSK. Jun.1; 22)
£65

FRANKEL, L.
– Handbuch für die Erkenntnis und Heilung der Kinderkrankheiten. Berlin, 1838. Foxed, cont. bds., bumped. (R. Apr.4; 1298) DM 420

FRANKEL, Paul T.
– Form & Re-Form. N.Y., [1930]. Orig. cl., rubbed & lightly soiled. (CSK. Mar.1; 201) £100

FRANKLAND RUSSELL, Sir Robert
– Sketches of Deer Stalking. N.d. Ob. fo. No title (?called for), 10 mntd. litho. plts., most stained, cont. red hf. mor. gt., title label on upr. cover, as a coll. of plts., w.a.f. (LC. Mar.1; 487) £120

FRANKLIN, Benjamin 'Richard Saunders'
– Oeuvres. Trans.:– Barbeu Dubourg. Paris, 1773. 2 vols. in 1. 4to. Cont. vell., blind motif. (HD. Jan.26; 141) Frs. 2,400
– Poor Richard, 1736: An Almanack for the Year of Christ 1736. Phila., [1735]. 12mo. Lacks 2 ll. (1 supplied in facs.), several ll. stained, mor. by Rivière. (SG. Jan.19; 171) $1100
– Works. Ed.:– William Duane. Phila, 1808-18. 6 vols. Engraved general title in all but 1st. vol., some foxing, hf. leath. gt., spines scuffed. (SG. Apr.5; 72) $175

FRANKLIN, Dr.
– Chess Made Easy: New & Comprehensive Rules for Playing the Game of Chess ... & the Morals of Chess, Written by the Ingenious & Learned Dr. Franklin. Phila., 1802. 12mo. 4 pp. advts., 1st. line excised from title, disbnd. (SG. Mar.15; 191) $110

FRANKLIN, John
– Narrative of a Journey to the Shores of the Polar Sea, in the Years 1819, 20, 21, & 22. Ill.:– E. Finden & others. L., 1823. 1st. Edn. 4 folding maps, 30 engraved plts., all uncold. plts. on India paper, mntd., the cold. plts. in 2 states (cold. & uncold.), 4 additional engraved ports. not called for, together 4 maps & 44 plts. [Sabin 25622] (With:) – Narrative of a Second Expedition to the Shores of the Polar Sea, in the Years 1825, 1826 & 1827. E. Finden. L., 1828. 1st. Edn. 6 engraved folding maps, 31 engraved plts., many on India paper, mntd., 2 additional ports. on India paper, both with Murray's 1828 imprint. [Sabin 26228] Together 2 vols. 4to. Some light foxing to several plts. & a few text pp., unif. old lev. mor., rebkd.; the Rt. Hon. Visc. Eccles copies. (CNY. Nov.18; 114) $2,400
– – Anr. Copy. 4to. 36 maps & plts., some folding, including plt. 'Dufourea Arctica & Cetraria Richardsonii' not called for in list of plts., early hf. mor. (SG. Mar.29; 314) $350
– – Anr. Copy. 4to. 31 plts. (12 cold.), some foxing & browning, lacks hf.-title, hf.-mor., worn, endpaper crudely reprd. (SPB. May 17; 609) $325
– – Anr. Edn. 1824. 2nd. Edn. 2 vols. Hf. cf. gt. (P. Jun.7; 24) £120
– Narrative of a Second Expedition to the Shores of the Polar Sea. L., 1828. 1st. Edn. 4to. Some foxing, str.-grd. mor., gt. extra. (PNY. Dec.1; 49) $375
– – Anr. Copy. 4to. Some foxing, linen, loose, slightly rubbed. [Sabin VII, 30] (D. Nov.23; 1344) DM 490

FRANZETTI, Agapito
– Riccolta ... Della Citta di Roma e di Alcuni Luoghi Suburbani. Ill.:– Barbazza, Pronti, Cipriani, Morelli, Porretta, & others, after Franzetti. Rome, [18th. C.]. Ob. 4to. 80 plts., each with 4 sm. engrs., some plts. foxed or stained, title worn, mntd. to anr. lf., bds., shabby, lacks spine. (SG. Jun.7; 348) $225

FRASER, Ed.
See— JOURDAIN, Lt.-Col. H.F.N. & Fraser, Ed.

FRASER, James
– The History of Nadir Shah ... The Present Emperor of Persia. 1742. Cont. spr. cf. (CSK. Feb.10; 192) £75

FRASER, James H.
– The Paste Papers of the Golden Hind Press. 1983. (70) numbered & sigd. by Delight Lewis. Tall 8vo. 15 mntd. paper samples, cl.-bkd. bds., unc., slight wear. (RO. May 22; 63) $110

FRASER, Robert
– General View of the Agriculture & Mineraology, Present State & Circumstances of the County of Wicklow. Dublin, 1801. 1st. Edn. Hf. mor.; inscr. by author to Marquis of Sligo. (GM. Dec.7; 428) £170
– – Anr. Copy. Orig. bds. (GM. Dec. 7; 429) £110
– – Anr. Copy. Title-p. soiled, plain wraps., unc. (GM. Dec.7; 421) £90

FRASER, Sir William
– The Red Book of Menteith. Edinb., 1880. (150). 2 vols. 4to. Plts., some spotting, orig. cl. (S. Apr.10; 359) Young. £90

FRAUENZIMMERTASCHENBUCH für das Jahr 1819.
Nuremb., n.d. Slightly browned, orig. bds., by C. Heideloff; ex-libris. (GB. May 4; 1264) DM 700

FRAZER, Sir James George
– The Golden Bough. 1930-36-35. 3rd. Edn. 12 vols. Orig. gt.-decor. cl. (SKC. May 4; 1672) £75
– – Anr. Edn. L., v.d. 3rd. Edn. 12 vols. Cl., moderate wear. (RO. May 22; 64) $100

FREAR, William H.
– Five Weeks in Europe. A Photographic Memorandum. N.p., 1891. (500). Fo. Cl., some wear & soiling, spine ends worn; sigd. 'Mark Twain' on limitation lf. (RO. Apr.23; 359) $230

FRECULPHUS, Bp. of Lisieux
See— LEO I, the Great, Pope—FRECULPHUS, Bp. of Lisieux

FREDERICK (Pseud.)
See— NEWHOFF, Friedrich von 'Frederick'

FREDERICK II, the Great, King of Prussia
– L'Antimachiavel ou Prince de Machiavel. München, Ruprecht Pr., 1922. (130) numbered on wide margin Zanders-Bütten with colophon wtrmrk. Fo. Orig. bds., wrap. (GB. May 5; 3190) DM 600
– Briefe Friedrichs des Grossen. Ed.:– M. Hein. Trans.:– Fr. v. Oppelen-Bronikowski & E. König. Ill.:– after Adolph von Menzel. Berlin, 1914. 4to. Orig. vell. gt. (D. Nov.24; 3629) DM 400
– Bücher v. der Natur der Vögel u. der Falknerei. Berlin, 1896. Fo. Orig. pict. hf. linen gt. (HK. May 16; 1576) DM 750
– De Arte Venandi cum Avibus. Graz, 1969. Facs. of MS. Pal. Lat. 1071 from Vatican. Ltd. Iss. Fo. Suede & hf. suede, s.-c.; Hauswedell coll. (H. May 23; 443) DM 1,400
[–] Examen du Prince de Machiavel, avec des Notes Historiques et Politiques. Ed.:– Voltaire. La Hay, 1741. Cont. marb. fr., spine decor., Madame de Pompadour arms; Pompadour's MS. note 'Par le Roy de Prusse' on hf.-title, from Madame Daulnoy liby. (HD. Mar.29; 102) Frs. 22,000
– Grundsätze der Lager-Kunst und Tactic. N.p., 1771. 4to. Wide margin, cold. paper end-papers, cont. leath. gt., corners lightly bumped. (HK. Nov.9; 1889) DM 3,600
– Hinterlassene Werke. Berlin, 1788. 1st. German Edn. 15 vols. Lacks 1789 supp., title versos stpd., slight foxing to some vols., cont. hf. leath., gt. decor., vol. 2 jnts. slightly brittle, slightly worn, w.a.f. (HK. May 16; 1998) DM 2,900
– – Anr. Copy. 15 vols. in 7. Browned, slightly foxed, some ll. with light stain, cont. hf. leath., bumped, spine with sm. tears, engraved ex-libris inside cover. (H. May 22; 675) DM 1,500
– Instruction Militaire du Roi de Prusse pour ses Généraux. N.p., 1761. Cont. marb. leath. gt. (HK. Nov.9; 1888) DM 1,400
[–] Mémoires pour Servir à l'Histoire de la Maison de Brandebourg. Ill.:– Schley & Fokke. Berlin & La Haye, 1751. 2 vols. 4to. Cont. red mor.; 73 MS. ll. bnd. at end of 2nd. vol. (HD. Apr.13; 18) Frs. 2,200
– Recueil de plans de Batailles, Sièges et Combats, arrivés dans les Expéditions Memorables de la Guerre de Sept Ans, pour Servir à l'Intelligence des Oeuvres Posthumes de Frederic II. Amst., 1789. Fo. Engraved title-vig., 18 engraved plans &c., hand-cold. outl., 1 folding engraved map, cont. hf. cf.,

spine gt., slightly rubbed. (CH. May 24; 51) Fls. 1,300
– Ueber die Deutsche Litteratur, die Mängel, die man ihr vorwerfen kann ... Trans.:– [C.W. von Dohm]. Berlin, 1780. 1st. Edn. 1st. ll. spotted, browned, cont. bds., faded, Hauswedell coll. (H. May 24; 1288) DM 1,100
– Die Werke. Ill.:– Ad. v. Menzel. Berlin, 1913-14. 10 vols. Lge. 4to. Orig. hf. cf. gt., some sm. spots. (HK. May 15; 825) DM 500
– Die Werke.—Briefe. Ed.:– G.B. Volz & M. Hein. Trans.:– Fr. von Oppelln-Bronikowski & others. Ill.:– A. von Menzel. Berlin, 1913-14. 12 vols. 4to. Margins lightly browned thro.-out, orig. hf. leath. gt., some heavy wear & bumping, stains, Brief vols. partly slightly cockled & stained. (H. May 22; 1023) DM 500

FREDERICK HENRY, Prince of Orange
– Mémoires. Qui Contiennent ses Expeditions Militaires depuis 1621 jusqu'à l'Année 1646. Ill.:– Bernard Picart. Amst., 1733. 4to. Few ll. spotted, cont. cf., spine gt. (BBA. Jun.28; 135) Dilua. £90

FREDERICKS, J.W.
– Dutch Silver. The Hague, 1950-58. 3 vols. only (of 4). Fo. No bdg. stated. (SPB. Nov.30; 339) $425
– – Anr. Edn. The Hague, 1952-61. 1st. Edn. 4 vols. Sm. fo. Gt.—& blind-pict. cl., d.-w.'s. (SG. Oct.13; 323) $475
– – Anr. Edn. The Hague, 1952-61. De Luxe Edn. 4 vols. Fo. Orig. mor., embossed decor. on upr. covers, spines gt. (VS. Jun.6; 35) Fls. 1,900
– – Anr. Edn. The Hague, 1952-61. 4 vols. 4to. Orig. cl., d.-w.'s torn. (S. May 1; 685) Dreesman. £300
– – Anr. Copy. 4 vols. Fo. Many plts., cl. (VG. May 3; 281) Fls. 950

FREEDMAN, Barnett
– Proof Lithographs, Title-pages Cloth Covers & End-papers for Anna Karenina by Tolstoy. Camb., Ltd. Edns. Cl., 1951. Orig. cl., s.-c., pres. inscr. & A.L.s. by author. (BBA. May 23; 188) Maggs. £220

FREELING, Arthur
– The Grand Junction Railway Companion to Liverpool, Manchester & Birmingham. L'pool., 1837. Sm. 8vo. Advts. bnd. in at end, orig. cl. gt., spine faded & rubbed. (TA. May 17; 155) £58
– The Railway Companion, from London to Birmingham, Liverpool & Manchester. [1838]. (Bound with:) – The Grand Junction Railway Companion to Liverpool, Manchester & Birmingham. 1838. Together 2 works in 1 vol. Sm. 8vo. Advts. at end of each pt., orig. cl. gt., rubbed. (TA. May 17; 154) £78

FREEMAN, Archibald
See— FITE, Emerson D. & Freeman, Archibald

FREEMAN, Douglas Southall
– R.E. Lee. A Biography. N.Y., 1934. 4 vols. Cl., spines faded; pres. copy from author to Winston Churchill, with his & R.S. Churchill's bkplts. (LH. Jan.15; 261) $2,200
– – Anr. Copy. 4 vols. Cl. gt., orig. box. (LH. Sep.25; 227) $110

FREEMAN, R. Austin
– The Red Thumb Mark. [L.], 1907]. 1st. Edn. 12mo. Orig. cl., author's thumb-print reproduced on upr. cover; Frederic Dannay copy. (CNY. Dec.16; 142) $700
– – Anr. Copy. 12mo. Some foxing, last lf. stained, orig. wraps., author's thumb-print reproduced on upr. cover, spine slightly frayed; Frederic Dannay copy. (CNY. Dec.16; 143) $600

FREEMASONS
– The Constitutions of the Free-Masons, Containing the History ... For the Use of the Lodges. L., 1723. 1st. Edn. of Anderson's Version. 4to. Slight browning & soiling, sm. stp. on title & hf.-title, some worming at end, cont. mott. cf., spine gt., worn. (S. Dec.8; 317) Marquis of Northampton. £800

FREGNAC, C.
- Collection Connaissance des Arts, 'Grands Artisans d'Autrefois': Les Ebenistes du XVIIIe Siècle Français; Les Grands Orfèvres de Louis XIII à Charles X; XVIIIe siècle Francais. 1963-66. Together 4 vols. Fo. No bdgs. stated. (SPB. Nov.30; 41) $250

FREHER, Paul
- Theatrum Virorum Eruditione Clarorum. Nuremb., 1688. *1st. Edn.* Fo. Lacks final plt. (?), 19th. C. diced cf., lacks spine. (C. May 30; 26) *Parikian.* £100
- – Anr. Copy. Fo. Lightly browned, cont. leath., slightly rubbed & bumped. (R. Oct.12, 2261) DM 1,250

FREIHERR, D.
- Deutschlands Armée in Feldgrauer Kreige und Friedens Uniformen. Ill.:– Paul Casberg. Berlin, n.d. Ob. 4to. Leaves, publisher's ill. buckram portfo. (HD. Jan.27; 145) Frs. 1,300

FREILIGRATH, F.
See— SCHUCKING, Christoph B. Levin & Freiligrath, F.

FREITAGIO, A.
- Mythologia Ethica. Antw., 1579. Some margins reprd., stained lr. part of margin trimmed, hf. vell., w.a.f. (P. Jan.12; 157) *Edmunds.* £190

FREKE, William
- Select Essays Tending to the Universal Reformation of Learning. 1693. Licence lf., upr. inner hinge worn, cont. cf., rubbed. (BBA. Jul.27; 105) *Lawson.* £90

FREMANTLE, Adm. Sir C.H.
- Diary & Letters ... Relating to the Founding of the Colony of Western Australia, 1829. Ed.:– Lord Cottesloe. Priv. ptd., 1928. Buckram; 2 p. sigd. letter from ed. tipped in. (KH. May 1; 275) Aus. $130

FREMONT, John Charles
- Report of the Exploring Expedition to the Rocky Mountains in the Year 1842 & to Oregon & California in the Years 1843-44. Wash., 1845. *1st. Edn.* 2 vols. (the lge. map separately bnd.). Lge. folding map, 3 (of 4) other maps, 22 litho. plts., the folding map bkd. with linen, later pol. cf.; the Rt. Hon. Visc. Eccles copy. [Sabin 25845] (CNY. Nov.18; 115) $380
- – Anr. Edn. Wash., 1845. *House Iss.* Lge. 8vo. 4 maps, 9 plts., 13 litho. views, lge. folding map in cover pocket, some foxing, orig. gt.-tooled roan, gt.-lettered spine. (SG. Oct.20; 160) $300

FREMPERGER, Thomas
- Historia Translationis Tunicae Jesu Christi. Cologne, Ludwig von Renchen, after 1500? 4to. Lacks 1st. lf., mod. antique-style cf.; the Walter Goldwater copy. [BMC I, 269; Goff F-309 (this copy only); HC 3759] (SG. Dec.1; 152) $125

FRENAUD, André
- Vieux Pays, suivi de Campagne. Ill.:– Raoul Ubac. Paris, 1967. *(185) numbered & sigd. by author & artist.* Fo. 13 etchei plts., ptd. in high relief, unsewn in orig. wraps., unc., cl. case. (S. Nov.21; 123) *Makiya.* £100

FRENCH, James Weir
- Modern Power Generators. 1908. 2 vols. Fo. Orig. decor. cl. gt. (SKC. Mar.9; 1909) £55

FRENE, Roger
- Les Nymphes. Ill.:– Modigliani. 1921. *Orig. Edn. 1st. Printing of ills. (120) on old japan.* Sm. 4to. Sewed; autograph dedication (scratched). (HD. Apr.13; 163) Frs. 1,600

FRENEVA, G.F.
- Verídica Narración ... Célebres Aplausos ... que en ... Sevilla han tenido los ... Reyes ... desde su Feliz Entrade ... Sevilla, 1729. 4to. Sewed. (DS. Apr.27; 2099) Pts. 25,000

FRESHFIELD, Douglas W.
- Across Country from Thonon to Trent. L., priv. ptd., 1865. Orig. cl., slightly rubbed; inscr. 'John L.

Anderdon from the author' lightly crossed through. (BBA. May 3; 347) *Ximenes.* £300
- Round Kangchenjunga. L., 1903. Orig. cl., slightly rubbed. (BBA. May 3; 348) *Quaritch.* £200

FREUD, Sigmund
- Collected Papers. Ed.:– Ernest Jones. Trans.:– Joan Riviere. L., 1924-25. *1st. Coll. Edn. in Engl.* Nos. 7-10 of the 'International Physcho-Analytical Library': 4 vols. 4to. Unif. cl. gt., worn; T.N.s from Jones to Dr. Meyer presenting him with a copy of Vol. 1 of the papers. (SG. Oct.6; 164) $100
- Drei Abhandlungen zur Sexualtheorie. Leipzig & Wien, 1905. *1st. Edn.* Sigs. loose, some staining & light foxing, orig. wraps., upr. wrap. with pasted strips, spine pasted, unc. (HK. Nov.8; 561) DM 440
- The Ego & the Id. Trans.:– Joan Rivière. Hogarth Pr., Institute of Psycho-Analysis, 1927. *1st. Edn. in Engl.* Hf.-title, advt. lf. at end, cl., unc.; pres. copy, insur. by author 'Dem judischen Museum in Nikolsburg der Verf. 1935' on fly-lf. (S. Nov.28; 114) *Crete.* £290
- Gesammelte Schriften. Vienna, [1925-28]. 11 vols. Lge. 8vo. Liby. buckram, ex-liby. (SG. Mar.22; 130) $130
- Der Witz und Seine Beziehung zum Unbewussten. Leipzig & Vienna, 1905. *1st. Edn.* Cont. hf. cl. (S. Dec.13; 271) *Crete.* £100

FREUDEN DER KINDER
Wien, ca. 1830. Marb. bds., bumped, sm. defect. (V. Oct.1; 3926) DM 1,300

FREYCINET, Louis
See— PERON, Francois Auguste & Freycinet, Louis

FREYER, Johan
- Negenjaarige Reyse door Oostindien en Persien, 1672-82. 's-Gravenhage, 1700. *1st. Dutch Trans.* 4to. Cont. vell. (VG. Nov.30; 822) Fls. 1,250

FREZIER, Amedée François
- Reis-beschryving door de Zuid-Zee, langs de Kusten v. Chili, Peru en Brazil ... in 1712-14. Amst., 1718. 4to. Cont. cf., spine gt., corners slightly rubbed. [Sabin 25927] (VG. Nov.30; 823) Fls. 770
- A Voyage to the South-Sea, & Along the Coasts of Chili & Peru, in the Years 1712, 1713 & 1714 ... Postscript:– Dr. Edmund Halley. L., 1717. *1st. Edn. in Engl.* 4to. 37 engraved maps & plts., many folding, frontis. map frayed at margin & laid down, with slight offset, repair to blank margin of title, sm. rust-hole in blank margin of O03, minor worming to upr. blank margins of some ll. & plts., cont. cf. [Sabin 25926] (C. Jun.27; 91) *Lindh.* £220
- – Anr. Copy. 4to. 37 maps & plts., many folding, some spotting & offsetting, mott. cf., spine worn. [Sabin 25926] (SPB. Dec.13; 445) $650

FRICKER, Dr. Karl
- The Antarctic Regions. 1900. Cl. gt. (P. Jun.7; 25) £75

FRICX, Eugène Henry
- Cartes des Provinces des Pays Bas ... Paris, 1744. Fo. 15 double-p. engraved maps, some discoloration, cont. wraps., torn & frayed. (C. Nov.16; 12) *Traylen.* £280

FRIEDERICH, Capt. J.C.
- Mémoire d'un Mort (1805-1828). Faits de Guerre et Exploits d'Alcoves. Paris, n.d. 3 vols. Hf. chagrin, wrap. (HD. Jan.27; 37) Frs. 1,600

FRIEDLANDER, Lee
- The American Monument. N.Y., [1976]. *1st. Edn. (2000).* Ob. 4to. Ptd. cl.; sigd. by author on fly-lf. (SG. Nov.10; 66) $400
- – Anr. Copy. Ob. fo. Ptd. cl. (SG. May 10; 49) $200

FRIEDLANDER, Max J.
- Die Altniederländische Malerei. Berlin, 1924-37. 14 vols. 4to. Orig. cl.-bkd. bds., soiled. (S. Apr.30; 38) *Sims.* £190
- – Anr. Copy. 14 vols., compl. 4to. Over 1,300 plts., orig. hf. linen, slightly bumped. (H. May 22; 109) DM 1,200

- – Anr. Edn. Leiden, 1934-36. 14 vols. 4to. Two-tone cl. (SG. Oct.13; 161) $110
- Early Netherlandish Painting. Leyden & Brussels, 1967-76. 14 vols. in 16, including Supp. Lge. 4to. Orig. cl. gt. (VS. Dec.7; 63) Fls. 2,500
- Max Liebermann. Berlin, [1923?]. *(100) numbered.* 2 sigd. etchings on Japan, spine faded, lightly bumped, orig. leath. gt., cold. paper end-papers. (HK. May 17; 2958) DM 1,800

FRIEDMANN, H.
See— RIDGWAY, Robert & Friedmann, H.

FRIEDRICH, C.G.
- Naturgeschichte aller Deutschen Zimmer—, Haus—und Jagdvögel, nebst einem Anhange über die ausländischen Vögel ... Stuttgart, 1849. *1st. Edn.* Some slight foxing, orig. pict. bds., rubbed, inner jnt. reprd. (GB. May 3; 1107) DM 420

FRIEDRICH, G.
See— KITTEL, G. & Friedrich, G.

FRIENDSHIP'S OFFERING, & Winter's Wreath; A Christmas & New Year's Present for 1844.— ... , for 1845.— ... , for 1846
Boston, [1843]; 1845; 1846. 3 vols. 12mo. & lge. 12mo. 2 ll. loose in 2nd. vol., orig. gt.-floral & blind-floral red leath., each vol. very rubbed on extremities, 3rd. vol. with tear on head of spine & portion of rear free end-paper torn away; from liby. of F.D. Roosevelt, each vol. sigd. & inscr. by him. (SG. Mar.15; 26) $325

FRIES, Laur
- Ein Hochnutzlicher Tractat. Strassburg, 1538. 4to. Title with old MS. ex-libris, upr. margin cut close, mod. mor., blind-tooled, s.-c. (D. Nov.23; 511) DM 3,600

FRISCH, Johann Leonhard
- Beschreibung von allerley Insecten in Teutschland. Berlin, 1721-66. 13 pts. in 1 vol. 4to. Some light browning, cont. bds., soiled & bumped. (GB. Nov.3; 1134) DM 540
- Vorstellung der Vögel Deutschlands (in Teutschland) und beyläufig auch einiger Fremden. Berlin, ca. 1745-63. Klassen 9-12 & Supp. in 1 vol. Fo. Lacks 2 copperplts., few plts. slightly spotted, cont. hf. leath., bumped, lacks spine. (BR. Apr.12; 842) DM 11,000

FRITH, Francis
- Egypt & Palestine. L., [1857]. 1st. & 2nd. Divisions: 2 vols. Fo. 31 orig. mntd. photos., including port., no titles, few sm. margin stains, orig. cl., slightly worn. (S. Mar.6; 16) *Samiramis.* £320
- – Anr. Edn. L., [1858-59]. 2 vols. in 1. Fo. 76 mntd. albumen photographs, 2 p. list of British subscribers bnd. in at end, front fly-lf. with inscr., stained & partly detchd., hf. leath., scuffed, pict. wraps. for 'Egypt & Palestine' pt. 5 for sale from Virtue, Emmins & Co., N.Y. bnd. in. (SG. Nov.10; 66a) $1,300
- Sinai & Palestine. Ca. 1862? Fo. Additional titles with mntd. photograph, 36 plts. of mntd. albumen photographs, orig. red mor. gt. (LC. Mar.1; 213) £340

FRITZ, J.H. & Schultze, B.
[-] Orientalisch—und Occidentalischer Sprachmeister. Leipzig, 1748. 2 pts. in 1 vol. Some foxing, later hf. mor., slightly rubbed. (VG. Mar.19; 239) Fls. 1,200

FRITZE, H.E.
- Arthroplastik. Lemgo, 1842. 4to. Some light foxing, wraps., unc. (R. Oct.12; 1396) DM 1,600

FROBEL, Frédéric
- Manuel Pratique des Jardins d'Enfants, à l'Usage des Institutrices et des Mères de Famille, composé par J.F. Jacobs. Brussels, 1859. 4to. Cont. roan-bkd. bds., slightly rubbed, van Veen coll. (S. Feb.28; 116) £50

FROBEL, J.
[-] Die Wahrhaftige Geschichte vom Deutschen Michel und seinen Schwestern. Ill.:– M. Disteli. Zürich & Winterthur, 1843. *1st. Edn.* Some foxing, title verso stpd., no bdg. stated. (GB. Nov.4; 1741) DM 800

FROEHLICH, W.
– **Orientalische Teppiche: Ein Vorlagenwerk zum Studium von Farbe und Ornament.** Berlin, n.d. Fo. Plts. loose as iss., cl.-bkd. bds. (SG. Aug.25; 281) $110

FROEHLICH-BUME, L.
– **Ingres: His Life & Art.** Trans.:– M.V. White. L., 1926. Lge. 4to. 80 plts., buckram. (SG. Oct.13; 205) $110

FROELICH, J.
– **Annales Compendiarii Regum, & Rerum Syriae, Numis Veteribus Illustrati.** Vienna, 1754. Fo. Hf. title, cont. spr. cf., slightly rubbed. (S. May 1; 467)
Azezian. £100

FROGER, François
– **Relation d'un Voyage fait en 1695, 1696 et 1697 aux Côtes d'Afrique, Détroit de Magellan ... par une Escadre des Vaisseaux du Roy commandée par M. de Gennes.** Paris, 1698. *Orig. Edn.* 12mo. Lacks 1 plt., lacks frontis., several plts. torn with loss, cont. cf., spine decor., worn. (HD. Jun.26; 41)
Frs. 2,000
– – **Anr. Edn.** Amst., 1699. 12mo. Cont. cf., spine decor. (HD. Nov.17; 26) Frs. 2,320
– **A Relation of a Voyage ... on the Coasts of Africa** ... L., 1698. *1st. Edn. in Engl.* Engraved frontis., 15 plts. & maps, (2 double-p.), frontis. reprd., cf. gt. [Sabin 26004] (SG. Apr.26; 86) $600

FROHAWK, Frederick William
– **The Complete Book of British Butterflies.** L., 1934. Orig. cl. (SKC. Oct.26; 366) $110
– **Natural History of British Butterflies.** L., 1914. 2 vols. Fo. 60 cold plts. & 4 other plts., orig. cl., d.-w.'s. (SKC. Oct.26; 365) £300
– – **Anr. Copy.** 2 vols. Fo. 60 cold. plts., 4 other plts., orig. cl., d.-w.'s. (SKC. Jan.13; 2316) £150
– – **Anr. Edn.** L., [1914]. 2 vols. Fo. 5 plain & 60 cold. plts., hf. cf. (C. Mar.14; 138)
Wheldon & Wesley. £90
– – **Anr. Copy.** 2 vols. Fo. 64 plts. (60 cold.), cl. gt., d.-w.'s. defect. (P. May 17; 299) *Bookroom.* £80
– – **Anr. Edn.** [1926]. 2 vols. Fo. Orig. cl., lightly soiled. (CSK. Aug.19; 81) £80
– **Varieties of British Butterflies.** L., 1938. 4to. Orig. cl. (SKC. Oct.26; 367) £90

FROHLICH, A.E.
– **Fabeln.** Ill.:– M. Distelli. Aarau, 1829. *1st. Edn.* Slightly foxed thro.-out, cont. bds., gold-tooled, slightly rubbed & bumped. (HT. May 9; 1432)
DM 440

FROISSART, Sir John
– **Chronicles of England, France & the Adjoining Countries ...** Trans.:– Thomas Johnes. Cardiganshire, 1803-05. *1st. Edn. thus.* 4 vols. 4to. Old cf., arms of Earl of Lonsdale, rubbed, unlettered rebacking. (KH. Nov.8; 164) Aus. $260
– – **Anr. Edn.** Trans.:– Thomas Johnes. L., 1808. *3rd. Edn.* 12 vols. Aquatint folding plts. bnd. in at rear of each vol., later three-qtr. cf., new endpapers. (CBA. Dec.10; 230) $160
– **Chronicles of England, France, Spain.** 1855. 2 vols. Hf. mor. gt. (P. Sep.29; 168) Traylen. £140
– – **Anr. Edn.** Trans.:– Johnes. L., 1868. 2 vols. Plts. hand-cold., hf. mor., spines gt. (S. Oct.4; 84)
Traylen. £150
– – **Anr. Copy.** 2 vols. Lge. 8vo. Cont. crimson hf. mor., spines gt.-decor. (TA. Feb.16; 267) £84
– **Chroniques.** Paris, 1824. 15 vols. Some foxing, cont. hf. cf., corners, spines decor. (HD. Nov.17; 28) Frs. 1,900
– – **Anr. Edn.** Paris, 1881. 4to. Publishers cl.; Antoine d'Orléans ex-libris. (DS. Oct.28; 2164)
Pts. 22,000
– **Cronycles.** Stratford-upon-Avon, Shakes. Hd. Pr., 1927. *(350).* 8 vols. Lge. 8vo. Heraldic decors. handcold., prospectus laid in 1st. vol., cl.-bkd. bds., spines spotted, spine labels worn, unc. (SG. Jan.12; 313) $225
– – **Anr. Edn.** Stratford-upon-Avon, Shakes. Hd. Pr., 1927-28. *(350) numbered.* 8 vols. Orig. linenbkd. bds., unopened. (P. Sep.8; 308) *Ralph.* £160
– – **Anr. Copy.** 8 vols. Armorial ills. hand-cold., prospectus loosely inserted, orig. cl.-bkd. bds., spines lightly soiled. (CSK. Jan.27; 51) £130
– – **Anr. Copy.** 2 vols. in 8 (as publd.). 4to. Bds.,

qtr. linen, cold. & illuminated armorials, unc. (KH. Nov.8; 165) Aus. $270
– **Histoire et Chronique.** Ed.:– Denis Sauvage. Lyon, 1559-60. 4 pts. in 2 vols. Fo. Some ll. dampstained, 18th. C. marb. roan, some wear, spines decor. (HD. Nov.17; 27) Frs. 4,800
– **Histoire et Chronique Memorable.** Ed.:– Denis Sauvage. Paris, 1574. 4 vols. in 1. Fo. 18th. C. cf. (SG. Feb.9; 233) $225
– **Le Premier [—Quart] Volume de Froissart des Croniques de France, Dangleterre, Descoce, Despaigne [& c.].** Paris, 14 Jul. 1513. 4 vols. in 2. Sm. fo. Last lf. of Vol.IV supplied in facs., lge. hole in title-p. of Vol. I with partial loss of device & some text on verso, a few ll. stained, title-p. of Vol. III mntd., early 19th. C. diced cf. gt., rebkd.; 16th. C. sig. of [Sir] Hewett Osborne & other members of Osborne family in both vols., Duke of Leeds bkplts. (S. Nov.17; 26) *Tzakas.* £440
– **Le Premier Volume de l'Histoire et Cronique ...** — **Le Second Volume ...** Lyon, 1559. 2 vols. in 1. Fo. Lr. margins stained thro.-out, last 4 ll. with margin repairs, mod. marb. bds., vell.-bkd., with medievalstyle painted title. (SG. Apr.19; 88) $250
– **Le Second Volume des Croniques de France, d'Angleterre ...** Pairs, [1518]. Fo. Lacks 2 ll., some worming, cont. Engl. blind-stpd. sheep over wood bds., centre blind fillet pattern with tool & floral roll round, lacks clasps, hinged on upr. cover, worn & defect., w.a.f.; from liby. at Lacock Abbey, H.M. Nixon coll. (BBA. Oct.6; 229)
Bloomsbury Rare Bks. £130

FROME, Capt. Edward Charles
– **Outline of the Method of Conducting a Trigonometrical Survey ...** 1850. *2nd. Edn.* Slight wear, bdg. not stated, unc. & largely unopened; inscr. (KH. May 1; 278) Aus. $200

FROMENTIN, Eugène
– **Sahara et Sahel.** Ill.:– Le Rat, Coutry & Bajon. Paris, 1887. 4to. Hf. mor., corners, decor. spine, s.-c. (HD. Jan.30; 55) Frs. 1,200

FROMMEL, Carl
– **Pittoreskes Italien.** Ed.:– W. v. Lüdemann & C. Witte. Leipzig, 1840. 3 steel engraved titles with vig. & 100 steel engraved plts., some slight browning, cont. hf. leath. gt., decor. (HK. May 15; 888) DM 750
– – **Anr. Copy.** 3 engraved titles, 100 steel engraved plts., lightly foxed, cont. hf. leath., spine rubbed. (HT. May 10; 2810) DM 490

FRONTINUS, Sextus Julius
– **De Aquaeductibus Urbis Romae Commentarius.** Ed.:– Joannis Poleni. Padua, 1722. 4to. Cont. cf., worn. (TA. Apr.19; 419) £75
– – **Anr. Edn.** Padua, 1722. *1st. Printing.* 4to. Sm. bookseller's stp. on title-p., cont. blind-stpd. vell.; Stanitz coll. (SPB. Apr.25; 180) $325

FROST, Donald McKay
– **Notes on General Ashley, the Overland Trail & South Pass.** Worcester, 1945. *1st. Edn. (50).* L.P., map in lr. cover, cl.-bkd. paper bds. (LH. Sep.25; 228) $100

FROST, Robert
– **A Boy's Will.** L., 1913. *1st. Edn. 1st. Iss.* Orig. cl., bdg. A, mor.-bkd. s.-c.; inscr. with 10-line verse. to George Matthew Adams, Prescott copy. (SPB. May 17; 610) $1,500
– – **Anr. Copy.** Orig. cl. [bdg. 'A'], cl. s.-c.; Frederic Dannay copy. (CNY. Dec.16; 145) $950
– **Collected Poems.** N.Y., 1930. *(1000) numbered & sigd.* Lge. 8vo. Cl., partly unc. (SG. Mar.1; 164) $100
– **The Complete Poems.** Intro.:– Louis Untermeyer. Ill.:– Thomas W. Nason. N.Y., Ltd. Edns. Cl., 1950. *(1500). sigd. by author, artist & printer.* 2 vols. Sm. 4to. Bdg. not stated, box slightly darkened at extremities. (CBA. Nov.19; 365) $300
– – **Anr. Copy.** 2 vols. Tall 8vo. Col., s.-c., worn. (SG. May 17; 192) $225
– **A Further Range.** N.Y., [1936]. *1st. Edn.* Cl., d.-w.; 4 lines of verse in Frost's hand, sigd. & dtd. Jun. 1936. (SG. Jan.12; 117) $175
– **North of Boston.** L., 1914. *1st. Edn. 1st. Iss. (350).* Sq. 8vo. Orig. buckram, mor.-bkd. s.-c.; inscr. by author, & with 2 sm. corrections by him, Paul

Lemperly copy, with note by him laid in, Frederic Dannay copy. (CNY. Dec.16; 146) $2,000
– **West-Running Brook.** N.Y., [1928]. *(1000) numbered & sigd.* Lge. 8vo. Qtr. cl., decor. bds., s.-c. worn. (SG. Mar.1; 165) $110
– **A Witness Tree.** N.Y., 1942. *1st. Edn. (735) sigd.* *(With:)* **Complete Poems.** N.Y., 1949. *1st. Edn. (500) sigd.* Title torn. Together 2 vols., various bdgs., s.-c.'s, 1 cracked. (SG. May 24; 296) $110

FROUDE, James Anthony
– **The English in Ireland in the Eighteenth Century.** L., 1872-74. 3 vols. Mor., tooled lined borders, armorial motif on spine. (GM. Dec.7; 248) £100
– **History of England.** L., 1870. 12 vols. Leath., some minor wear to covers. (JL. Jul.15; 656)
Aus. $160

FRY, Joseph Storrs
– **An Essay on the Construction of Wheel-Carriages.** L., 1820. *1st. Edn.* Diagrams, hf. cf., hinges reprd. (P. May 17; 259) *Georges.* £300
– – **Anr. Edn.** Bristol, 1820. 4to. Woodcut dedication, some light spotting, orig. bds., inscr. 'The author to William Dickenson'. (TA. Dec.15; 88)
£165

FRYKE or FRICK, Christopher & Schweitzer, Christopher
– **A Relation of two several Voyages made into the East-Indies.** 1700. *1st. Engl. Edn.* Last advt. lf., cont. cf., gt. spine; Lord Hardwicke bkplt. [Wing F2211] (BBA. Sep.29; 74) *Maggs.* £400

FUCHS, Eduard
– **Illustrierte Sittengeschichte.** Müchen, 1909-12. 3 vols. & 3 supp. vols. Orig. linen. (GB. May 4; 2014)
DM 400
– – **Anr. Edn.** Müchen, [1909-12]. 3 vols. & 3 supp. vols. 4to. Orig. linen & orig. mole. (D. Nov.24; 3967) DM 480
– – **Anr. Copy.** 3 main vols. & 3 supp. vols. 4to. Orig. linen, cover of supp. vols. slightly worn, w.a.f. (HK. Nov.9; 2108) DM 400

FUCHS, G.B.
– **Abenteuerliche Geschichten ohne Abenteuer.** Berlin, 1968. *(99) numbered.* 4to. 9 orig. woodcuts, printers mark sigd., orig. pict. hf. linen. (GB. May 5; 3270) DM 560

FUCHS, G.F. Ch. & others
[–] **Systematische Beschreibung aller Gesund. brunnen und Bäder der Bekannten Länder.** Jena & Leipzig, 1801. *2nd. Edn.* Vol. 1 (all publd.?). Cont. hf. leath. (R. Oct.12; 1350) DM 800

FUCHS, Leonhard
– **De Curandi Ratione Libri Octo.** Lyon, 1548. Some old marginalia & notes on title & inside covers, some staining, cont. leath., gold-stpd. centre-piece, blind-tooled borders, 4 corner fleurons, slightly defect., upr. cover loose. (D. Nov.23; 117)
DM 1,300
– **New Kreüterbuch.** Basel, 1543. *1st. German Edn.* Fo. Some ll., with stains & some foxing, 6 ll. with sm. repairs in inner margin, sm. part of title with slight loss reprd., later vell., slightly spotted; Hauswedell coll. (H. May 24; 859) DM 22,000
– – **Anr. Copy.** Fo. Lacks title lf. (with port. verso), replaced by excised printers mark from last lf., lf. with 3 port. woodcuts misplaced with ports. on verso & plant woodcut on recto, index & 1st. 2 sigs. with some margin strenthening & other pasting, stained or foxed, especially margins, early 17th. C. wood bds. with leath. cover, spine old painted over & torn at top, worn, lacks clasps. (HK. Nov.8; 186) DM 5,000

FUCHS, Samuel
– **Metoposcopia & Ophthalmoscopia.** Strassburg, 1615. *1st. Edn.* Lightly browned thr.-out, some slight spotting & staining, later limp MS. vell. (HT. May 8; 566) DM 900

FUCHSPERGER, D.
– **Ain Grundlicher Klarer Anfang der Naturlichen und Rechten Kunst der Waren Dialectica ... auss dem Latein ins Teutsch Transferiert.** Augsberg, 1533. 4to. 19th. C. cf. (BBA. Nov.30; 22)
Maggs. £260

FUENTES, Marmel A.
- Lima or Sketches of the Capital of Peru ... Paris, 1866. 4to. Slightly foxed, orig. bds., spine with late linen, corners bumped. [Sabin 26118] (HK. Nov.8; 830)　　　　　　　　　　　　　　　DM 480

FUERST, M. (Ed.)
See— GRIESHABER, Hap

FUERST, Walter René & Hume, Samuel J.
- XXth Century Stage Decoration. 1928. 2 vols. 4to. Orig. cl.-bkd. bds. (BBA. Nov.10; 348)
　　　　　　　　　　　　　　　Zwemmer. £50

FUERSTINN, Rosina Helena
- Das Neue Modelbuch von Schoenen Naedereyen, Ladengewuerck und Paterleinsarbeit. Nuremb., [1666]. 1st. Edn. Pt. 2. Ob. sm. 4to. Engraved title-p., 44 (of 50) engraved plts., some foxing on plt. margins, old marb. bds., disbnd., unc. (SG. Apr.26; 114)　　　　　　　　　　　　　　$425

FUESSLY, Johann Caspar
- Archiv der Insectengeschichte. Zurich & Winter-thur, 1781-86. 8 pts. in 1 vol. Sm. 4to. 51 engraved plts. (47 hand-cold.), text misbnd., some dampstaining to lr. portion of text, cont. str.-grd. mor., gt. borders on covers, spine gt. with insect stp., slightly scuffed; Ely bkplt., w.a.f. (C. Jun.27; 119)　　　　　　　　　　　　　Maggs. £380
- Archives de L'Histoire des Insectes. Winterthous, 1794. 4to. 50 plts. (numbered 1-54, plts. Nos. 37-42 are omitted as called for by the author, plts. Nos. 19 & 28 have 'a' & 'b' versions, plts. Nos. 6, 7 & 13 are uncold. & plt. 7 has minimum colouring), cont. cf., covers detchd. (SKC. Oct.26; 368)　　　　　　　　　　　　　　£420

FUGGER, Wolffgang
- Ein Nutzlich vnd wolgegrundt Formular, Mancherley schöner Schriefften, als Teutscher, Lateinischer, Griechischer, vnnd Hebrayscher Buchstaben ... Nurmberg, 1553 [Colophon: 1597-1605]. 2nd. Edn. Sm. ob. 4to. Title verso with mntd. copper engr. with monog. & dtd. 1535, hand-bnd. cf. ca. 1870, wear; William Stirling-Maxwell supra-libros & paper ex-libris, Hauswedell coll. (H. May 23; 219)　　　　　　　　　　　　DM 5,000

FULGENTIO DE RINALDI, Père F.
- Monimenti Historiali dell'Antico, e Nobile Castello d'Iseo ... Brecia, 1685. 3 pts. in 1 vol. Sm. 4to. Bds. (HD. Dec.2; 92)　　　　　　Frs. 1,750

FULKERSON, H.S.
- Random Recollections of Early Days in Mississippi. Vicksburg, 1885. 1st. Edn. Orig. cl. gt., cover worn. (LH. Jan.15; 292)　　　　　　　　　$140

FULLARTON, A.
- The Companion Atlas. Ca. 1850. Fo. Partly cold. maps, hf. mor., covers loose. (P. Sep.29; 432)
　　　　　　　　　　　　　　　　£140
- The Royal Illustrated Atlas of Modern Geography. Ca. 1860. Fo. 74 maps, plans & ills., a few closely cropped on outer edge, some minor spotting & margins a little browned, cont. hf. mor., worn. (TA. Mar.15; 56)　　　　　　　　　　　£370
- - Anr. Edn. N.d. Fo. Engraved title & 76 maps, hand-cold. in outll., some double-p., cont. hf. cf., lacks spine. (CSK. May 4; 29)　　　　　　£350
- - Anr. Copy. Engraved title & 76 maps (some double-p.), hand-cold. outll., lightly soiled, cont. hf. mor., slightly rubbed. (CSK. Jul.6; 94)　　£190

FULLER, Ronald
See— WHISTLER, Laurence & Fuller, Ronald

FULLER, Samuel
- Practical Astronomy. Dublin, 1732. Title loose, cont. cf. (SKC. Jan.13; 2283)　　　　　　£75

FULLER, Dr. Thomas, 1608-61, DD. Prebendary of Salisbury
- The Church-History of Britain. 1655. [1st. Edn.]. Sm. fo. A few ll. reprd., cont. mott. cf., rubbed. (BBA. Jul.27; 100)　　　　　　　Howes. £55
- - Anr. Copy. Fo. 18th. C. bds., leath. back & tips, rubbed, cover detchd. (RO. May 29; 89)　　$110
- The Historie of the Holy Warre. L., 1647. 3rd. Edn. [Wing F 2438] (Bound with:) - The Holy State. L., 1652. 3rd. Edn. Engraved title supplied from 2nd. edn. [Wing F 2445] Together 2 works

in 1 vol. Fo. Dampstained, sm. tear to map, old cf., worn. (SG. Oct.27; 118)　　　　　　　$120
- The History of the Worthies of England. L., 1662. 1st. Edn. Fo. Spotted, cf., slightly rubbed, corners reprd., recased. (S. Dec.13; 362) Smallwood. £80
- A Pisgah-Sight of Palestine. L., 1650. Fo. Engraved allegorical additional title, engraved armorial plt., lge. folding general map, 27 double-p. plts. (including 20 regional maps), a few tears reprd., some browning, mostly affecting text, mod. cf., gt., extra-ill. by insertion of 16 dupl. maps & plts., w.a.f. [Wing F2445] (S. May 22; 279)
　　　　　　　　　　　　　Hague. £1,000

FULLER, Thomas, M.D. 1654-1734
- Exanthematologia; or, An Attempt to give a Rational Account of Eruptive Fevers, Especially of the Measles and Small Pox. L., 1730. 1st. Edn. 2 pts. in 1 vol. 4to. Few ll. dampstained at corners, cont. panel. cf. (SG. Mar.22; 133)　　　　$110

FULMAN, William
- [-] Notitia Oxoniensis Academiae. L., 1675. 2nd. Edn. Sm. 4to. Interleaved copy, numerous additions & extensions in Latin in unknown cont. hand (note on p. 81 records death of Edward Pococke, Prof. of Hebrew & Arabic), cont. cf., rebkd. [Wing F2524] (S. Oct.11; 532)　　　　Waterfield. £90

FULTON, John F.
- A Bibliography of ... Robert Boyle. L., 1961. 2nd. Edn. 4to. Orig. cl.; long T.L.s. to Robert Birley loosely inserted. (S. Oct.4; 221)　　Thomas. £60

FULTON, Robert of Brockley
- The Illustrated Book of Pigeons. Ca. 1886. 4to. Some ll. soiled, orig. cl. gt. (F. Dec.8; 78)
　　　　　　　　　　　　　Walford. £50
- - Anr. Edn. Ca. 1890. 4to. 50 col. plts., inner hinges reprd. with tape, orig. cl. gt., partially split on spine, rubbed. (TA. Jun.21; 246)　　　　£50
- - Anr. Edn. N.d. 4to. Soiled, cont. hf. cf., worn. (CSK. Aug.5; 71)　　　　　　　　　　£55

FULTON, Robert, Civil Engineer
- Recherches sur les Moyens de Perfectionner les Canaux de Navigation ... Paris, An VII [1798/99]. Cont. cf. gt. [Sabin 26202] (PNY. Jun.6; 488)
　　　　　　　　　　　　　　　$225

FUNF JAHRE SOWJET HERRSCHAFT IN RUSSLAND
Berlin, 1923. Fo. Orig. sewed. (GB. May 4; 2042)
　　　　　　　　　　　　　　　DM 420

FUNFSTUCK, M.
- Naturgeschichte des Pflanzenreichs. Stuttgart, [1885-88]. [1st. Edn.]. Fo. Mod. linen. (R. Apr.4; 1722)　　　　　　　　　　　　　DM 430
- - Anr. Copy. Sm. fo. 1 plt. with margin tear, last plts. slightly browned & foxed. orig. hf. leath. gt. (BR. Apr.12; 668)　　　　　　　　　DM 400

FUNKE, C. Ph.
See— LIPPOLD, G. H. C. & Funke, C. Ph.

FUNNELL, William
- A Voyage Round the World. 1707. Cont. cf. (CSK. Jul.6; 20)　　　　　　　　　　　£400
- - Anr. Copy. 5 maps, 10 plts., staining, 1 map loose, 1 torn, panel. cf., rubbed. (P. Feb.16; 255)
　　　　　　　　　　　　　　　£300

FUR, FEATHER & FIN SERIES
Ed.:- A.E.J. Watson. 1895-1903. Various Edns. 10 vols. Orig. hf. mor. (CSK. Oct.7; 94)　　£150

FURBER, Robert & Bradley, Richard
[-] The Flower-Garden Displayed. L., 1734. 2nd. Edn. 4to. 12 col. engraved plts., cont. panel. cf., rebkd., later qtr. cf. s.-c. (SG. Nov.3; 80) $1,300

FURETIERE, Antoine
- Fables Morales et Nouvelles. 1671. Orig. Edn. 12mo. Cf. by Petit (successor of Simier), spine decor. (HD. Mar.21; 28)　　　　Frs. 1,200
- Les Paraboles de l'Evangile Traduites en Vers. Paris, 1672-73. Orig. Edn. 2 vols. in 1. 12mo. Cont. red mor. gt., spine decor.; from Colbert liby., MS. note on title & arms of J.-B. Colbert on cover. (HD. Nov.9; 36)　　　　　　　　Frs. 6,000

FURLEY, Robert
- A History of the Weald of Kent, with an Outline of the Early History of the County. Ashford, 1871-74. 2 vols. in 3. Orig. cl. gt., rubbed. (TA. Feb.16; 81)　　　　　　　　　　　　　　£50

FURLONG, Capt. Lawrence
- The American Coast Pilot. N.Y., 1850. 16th. Edn. 17 charts, cont. sheep, some dampstaining; owner's inscr. of Charles Skolfield. (PNY. Mar.27; 109)
　　　　　　　　　　　　　　　$100

FURST, Herbert
- The Decorative Art of Frank Brangwyn. 1924. (120) with orig. sigd. woodcut. 4to. Cl. gt. (P. Jun.7; 293)　　　　　　　　　　　　　£80
- - Anr. Edn. L., 1924. (120) numbered on Dutch Rag paper. 4to. Buckram, sigd. woodcut self. port. by Brangryn. (KH. Nov.8; 228)　　Aus. $140

FURSTENBERG, H. & Tammaro de Marinis
- Die Italienischen Renaissance-Einbände der Bibliothek Fürstenberg. Hamburg, 1966. Fo. Orig. cl.; H.M. Nixon coll., with his sig. & acquisition note. (BBA. Oct.6; 49)　　Mariboro' Rare Books. £80

FURSTNERIUS, Caesarinius (Pseud.)
See— LEIBNITZ, Gottfried Wilhelm 'Caesarinius Fürstnerius'

FURTTENBACH, Joseph
- Architectura Universalis. D.i.: Von Kriegs: Statt-u. Wasser Gebäwen. Ulm, 1635. Fo. Lightly stained at foot, cont. vell. (HK. May 16; 1453) DM 1,900
- - Anr. Copy. Fo. 1 plt. margin torn, last plt. loose, cont. vell., loose. (D. Nov.23; 1889)　　DM 700
- Büchsenmeisterey-Schul. Augsburg, 1643. (Bound with:) - Architectura Martialis. Ulm, 1630. Lacks title lf., 1 supp. vol. removed. Together 2 works in 1 vol. Fo. Cont. blind-tooled vell., slightly rubbed, spine restored, clasps. (GB. Nov.3; 988)
　　　　　　　　　　　　　DM 2,000
- Mannhafter Kunst- Spiegel oder Continuatio und Fortsetsung allerhand Mathematisch- und Mechanisc- hochnutzlich Künsten. Augsburg, 1663. 1st. Edn. Fo. Many plts. torn, some with pasted or bkd. tears, & 5 mntd., margins foxed, lacks last lf. (errata or plt. index?), cont. blind-tooled pig over wood bds., lacks clasps. (R. Oct.12; 1742)
　　　　　　　　　　　　　　　DM 600

FURTWAENGLER, Adolf
- Die Antiken Gemmen: Geschichte der Steinschnei-idekunst im Klassischen Altertum. Leipzig & Berlin, 1900. 3 vols. Lge. 4to. 70 plts., 237 text ills., ex-liby., hf. mor. (SG. May 3; 171)　　　　$1,100

FURUKAKI, Tetsuro
- Paris de mon Coeur. Ill.:- Bernard Buffet. Paris, 1961. (197). (122) numbered on offset Sirène. 4to. Leaves, double wrap., box; B. Buffet autograph dedication. (HD. Mar.27; 73)　　　Frs. 1,600

FUSELIER & de Blamont
- Les Fêtes Grecques et Romaines. Paris, 1762. 4to. Cont. red mor., fleur-de-lis dentelle, gt. tooled centre arms, decor. fleur-de-lis spine, wtrd. silk doubl. & guards. (HD. Mar.14; 32)　　Frs. 8,100

FUTURISTY. DOKHLAYA LUNA [Futurists. The Croaked Moon]
Ed.:- V. Shershenevich. Ill.:- D. & V. Burliuk. Moscow, 1914. 2nd. Edn. 4to. 2 etched plts., 17 plts. ptd. in blue, orig. pict. wraps., backstrip reprd. (S. Nov.21; 139)　　　　　　　Quaritch. £280

FUTURISTY GILEYA. DOKHLAYA LUNA [Futurists Hylaea. The Croaked Moon]
Contribs.:- D. & N. Burliuk, V. Khlebnikov, A. Kruchenykh, B. Livshits, & V. Mayakovsky. Ill.:- D. & V. Burliuk. Moscow, 1913. 1st. Edn., [300]. Sm. 4to. 2 cold. etched plts., 16 litho. plts., orig. wraps., rebkd. (S. Nov.21; 138)　　　Makiya. £750

FUX, Joh. Jos.
- Gradus ad Parnassum od. Anführung zur Regelmässigen Musicalischen Composition. ... Ill.:- L. Mitzler. Leipzig, 1742. 4to. Title in photocopy, mntd. on old paper, 2 pp. stpd., sm. margin tears,

1 lf. with tear in side margin with minimal loss, some slight soiling, some plts. with partly reprd. margin defects., cont. leath., worn, sm. defects. (HK. Nov.9; 2245) DM 550
- Gradus ad Parnassum, sive Manuductio ad Compositionem Musicae Regularem, Methodo Nova. Ill.:– G.A. Müller after J. van Schuppen. Wien, 1725. *1st. Edn.* Wide margin, frontis. slightly defect. & sm. tears, cont. leath. gt., slightly rubbed & bumped, spine partly defect., with sm. repair. (HK. Nov.9; 2244) DM 1,600

FYFE, Andrew
- A System of the Anatomy of the Human Body. Edinb., 1814. *3rd. Edn.* 3 vols. 4to. Many plts. hand-cold., stained thro.-out. Vols. 1 & 3 cont. hf. cf., Vol. 2 mod. hf. mor., mor. rebkd. (BBA. Mar.21; 43) *R.V. Elliott.* £60

G., A.P.D.
- Sketches of Portuguese Life, Manners, Costume, & Characters. 1826. Engraved mus. plt., 20 hand-cold. aquatint plts., lacks hf.-title, some ll. spotted., cont. cf. by E. Nettleton, Plymouth, spine gt., rubbed. (BBA. Jan.19; 329) *Remington.* £130

G.H.
[-] Scanderbeg Revivivus. An Historical Account of the Life & Actions of ... John III, K. of Poland. 1684. Engraved port., little trimmed, folding engraved plt. with explanation lf., cont. cf., rubbed, upr. cover wormed; owner's inscr. of Tho. Ottley, 1684. [Wing G26] (BBA. Jun.28; 317) *Maggs.* £60

G., U.
- Sketches of Newfoundland & Labrador. Ipswich, ca. 1857. Ob. fo. Litho. title with vig., 24 full-p. litho. line views on heavy stock, 2 lf. list of plts., the 2 ll. of text loose in bdg., orig. cl.-bkd. paper wraps., worn, edges & corners frayed; the Rt. Hon. Visc. Eccles copy. (CNY. Nov.18; 118) $750

GABELENTZ, Hans von der
- Zeichnungen Alter Meister in Kupferstich-Kabinett des Grossherzoglichen Museums zu Weimar. Frankfurt, Prestel-Gesellschaft, 1912-33. *Ltd. Edn., numbered.* 2 vols. Atlas fo. 60 plts., each liby.-stpd. on mount verse, text laid in, loose in bd. folders, linen ties. (SG. May 3; 289) $175

GABELSBERGER, F.X.
- Anleitung zur Deutschen Redezeichenkunst oder Stenographie. München, 1834. *Orig. Edn.* 4to. 1st. 2 ll. slightly discold. at upr. margin, light foxing, cont. hf. leath., spine slightly torn. (R. Apr.3; 677) DM 600

GABIROL, Schlomo Ibn
- Mivchar Ha'Peninim. Cremona, 1558. *3rd. Edn.* Upr. margin of title reprd. without loss of text, last 12 ll. with wormholes affecting some letters, some staining, hf. leath., marb. paper bds. (S. Oct.24; 155) *Toporwitch.* £230

GABIROL, Schlomo Ibn & Pseudo-Aristotle
- Goren Nachon-Tikun Midot Ha'Musrei Ha'Philosophim-Ha'Tapu'ach. Riva di Trento, 1562. 4to. Owners' stp. & sig. on title, some staining mostly in margins, mod. mor. (S. Oct.24; 154) *Dzialowski.* £420

GABISHON, Avraham
- Sefer Omer ha-Shikheha. Livorno, 1748. *1st. Edn.* Sm. 4to. Dampstained, sm. repairs to title & final 2 ll., later mor., trimmed, extremities rubbed,. (SG. Feb.2; 179) $110

GABLER, A.
- Ausrufende Personen in Nürnberg mit Prospecten der Stadt, nebst einer Kurzen Beschreibung. Nürnberg, 1805. *2nd. Edn.* 8 cold. copperplts., 4 pp. text, some spotting, orig. ptd. wraps., slightly creased; Hauswedell coll. (H. May 23; 37) DM 9,800

GACON DE LOUANCY
[-] Lettres de Deux Curés des Cévennes sur la Validité des Mariages des Protestans et sur leur Existence Légal en France. L., 1779. 2 vols. Cf., spines decor., Le Roux d'Esneval arms, corners worn. (SM. Mar.7; 2021a) Frs. 1,800

GADBURY, J.
- London's Deliverance predicted : in a Short Discourse shewing the Cause of Plagues in General. 1665. Sm. 4to. Last few pp. slightly shaved at bottom, some browning & spotting thro.-out, cf. gt., by Ramage, some wear. (BS. May 2; 42) £65

GADFLY, The
Ed.:– J.W. Gillingham. L., 14 Feb. 1906-11 Dec. 1907. 96 iss., in 2 vols. Some wear, carbon typescript list of names used is the publication by C.J. Dennis loosely enclosed, old hf. roan, very worn. (KH. Nov.8; 171) Aus. $780

GADOW, G.
- Zehn Jahre im alten Südafrika. Königsberg, 1903. Wraps. (SSA. Sep.21; 161) R 210

GAEDECHENS, O.C.
- Hamburgische Münzen und Medaillen. Hamburg, 1852-76. Vols. 2 & 3 (of 3) in 4 pts. 4to. Sewed. (D. Nov.24; 4424) DM 600

GAETANI, Pietro Antonio
- Museum Mazzuchellianum, seu Numiamata Virorum Doctrima Praestantium. Venice, 1761-63. *1st. Edn.* 2 vols. Lge. fo. Frontis., vig. titles, port., 208 copperplates, text in Italian & Latin, early vell. (SG. Nov.3; 81) $375

GAFFAREL, Jacques
- Abdita Divinae Cabalae Mysteria. Paris, 1625. *1st. Edn.* Sm. 4to. Errata lf., new cl.; Dr. Walter Pagel copy. (S. Feb.7; 129) *Weiner.* £170
- Curiositez Inouyés sur la Soulpture Talismanique des Perses, Horoscopes des Patriarches et Lecture des Etoiles. Paris, 1629. *1st. Edn.* 1 plt. mntd. & creased, with hole, the other plt. torn in one fold, cont. vell.; Dr. Walter Pagel copy. (S. Feb.7; 130) *Colombo.* £160
- Unheard-of Curiosities. L., 1650. *1st. Engl. Edn.* 2 folding woodcut plts. torn & mntd., 1st. Testimony lf., 19th. C. cf. by J. Larkins, rubbed, upr. cover loose. [Wing G105] (BBA. May 3; 129) *Finch.* £60

GAGARINE, Prince P.G.
[-] Les Treize Journées ou la Finlande. St. Petersb., 1809. *[100].* Cont. hf. cf. (CSK. Oct.21; 1) £150

GAGE, Thomas
- The English-American his Travail by Sea & Land. L., 1648. Fo. Browning & foxing, mott. cf. gt., worn, upr. cover detchd. (SPB. Dec.13; 446) $500
- Nouvelle Relation contenant ses Voyages dans la Nouvelle Espagne. Trans.:– De Beaulieu-Hues O'Neil. Amst., 1699, *3rd. Edn.* 4 pts. in 2 vols. 12mo. Cont. cf., spines decor.; Maynon de Fargeville copy. (HD. Mar.21; 30) Frs. 2,600

GAGNON, Phileas
- Essai de Bibliographie Canadienne. Quebec, 1895. Lge. 8vo. New cl. (SG. Jan.5; 142) $150

GAGUINUS, Robertus
- Compendium de Origine et Gestis Francorum. Lyons, Johannes Trechsel, 24 Jun. 1497. Fo. Very stained, 2 old liby. stps. on 1st. lf., bds.; the Walter Goldwater copy. [BMC VIII, 301; Goff G-14; H. 7412] (SG. Dec.1; 153) $375
- Co[m]pe[n]diu[m] Roberti Gagiuni Sup[er] Fra[n]Cor[um] Gestis. [Paris, Thielman Kerver for Jean Petit, Jan. 1507]. Wide margin, red rubric, annots. thro.-out in 2 16th. C. MSs., 18th. C. cf., soiled. (HD. Jan.30; 10) Frs. 1,800

GAIETANUS DE THIENIS
- Recollectae super Octo Libros Physicorum Aristotelis. Venice, Johannes Hamman, 28 Jul. 1500. Fo. Some capitals left blank with guide letters, some browning, a few sm. filled wormholes affecting text, 1st. gathering guarded at inner margins, mod. parch.-bkd. bds., Stanitz coll. [Goff G36] (SPB. Apr.25; 182) $800

GAILER, J.E. (Ed.)
See– COMENIUS or KOMENSKY, John Amos

GAILER, J.G.
- Neues Fabelbuch: eine Auswahl des Schoensten aus der Fabelnwalt. Tuebingen, [1836]. Tall 8vo. 36 hand-cold. engraved ills. on 18 plts., text in German, Fr., Engl. & Latin, some foxing or mild staining, not affecting plts., 1st. gathering loose, pict. bds., rubbed, spine worn. (SG. Dec.8; 6) $140

GAILHABAUD, Jules
- L' Architecture du V au XVII Siècle en Temoignage de Reconaissance. Paris, for Subscribers, 1858. 4 vols. 4to. Some spotting, later hf. mor. (BBA. Dec.15; 315) *Bennett & Kerr.* £50
- Monuments Anciens et Modernes. 1850. 4to. Hf. chagrin, corners, 2 hf. chagrin portfos. (HD. Jun.29; 74) Frs. 1,050
- - **Anr. Copy.** 4 vols. 4to. Hf.-title, some stains, cont. hf. mor., decor. spine, slightly loose. (SI. Dec.15; 110) Lire 300,000
- - **Anr. Edn.** Paris, 1853. 4 vols. each in 2 pts., together 8 vols. Sm. fo. Engraved plts., ex-liby., some foxing, cont. hf. mor. (SG. May 3; 172) $175

GAINSBOROUGH, Thomas
- Collection of Prints, illustrative of English Scenery. Ill.:– W.F. Wells & J. Laporte. L., [1802-05]. Ob. fo. 72 etched plts., some etchings white heightened on blue ground, washed or cold., 8 plts. foxed, cont. leath. gt., slightly rubbed. (GB. Nov.3; 880) DM 1,600
- - **Anr. Edn.** Ill.:– W.F. Wells & J. Laporte, after Gainsborough. L., 1821 or later. Fo. 60 engrs., including 37 hand-cold., text & plts. wtrmkd. J. Whatman 1821, cont. str.-grd. red mor. gt. (S. Dec.8; 385) *Marlborough.* £300

GALANTE, Abraham & Joel Ibn Sho'ib
- Kol Bochim. Ed.:– Menachem Azaria di Fano. Venice, 1589. *1st. Edn.* 4to. Title washed, slight worming not affecting text, index ll. shorter, margin glosses, hf. leath., marb. paper bds. (S. Oct.24; 157) *Sol.* £260

GALANTE, Moshe, of Safed
- Sh'eilot U'Teshuvot. Venice, 1608. Fo. A few ll. stained & browned, 19th. C. hf. cf., rubbed. (SPB. Feb.1; 45) $450

GALANTE, Moshe
See– CHAGIZ, Yakov—GALANTE, Moshe

GALATINO, Pietro di
- De Arcanis Catholicae Veritatis Libri XII. Frankfurt, 1612. Fo. Register lf., marb. bds., vell. spine; bkplt. of J.B. Craven, Dr. Walter Pagel copy. (S. Feb.7; 131) *Ritman.* £480

GALENUS, Claudius
- De l'Usage des Parties du Corps Humain. Trans.:– [J. Dalechamps]. Lyons, 1566. Closely cut, discold., some stains, some worming, 18th. C. Fr. mott. cf., spine gt., corners worn; Dr. Walter Pagel copy. (S. Feb.7; 135) *Gurney.* £90
- De Usu Partium Corporis Humani. Trans.:– Nicolao Regio Calabro. Paris, 1528. *1st. Separate Edn.* 4to. Many underlinings & margin annots., some stains, short tear H4, title soiled, stp. erased, new bds., cf. spine; Dr. Walter Pagel copy. (S. Feb.7; 132) *Gurney.* £280
- - **Anr. Edn.** Trans.:– Nicolao Regio Calabrio; Sylvium & Martinum Gregorium. Paris, 1543. 2 works in 1 vol. Fo. 1st. work in Latin, 2nd. work in Greek, hf. cf.; from colls. of John Haviland, William Selwyn & Dr. Walter Pagel. (S. Feb.7; 134) *Rosenfeld.* £450
- Galeno ascriptus Graecus Liber. de Urinis ... Wittenberg, 1586. *1st. Edn.* Parallel Grt. & Latin Edn., hf. vell. (R. Oct.12; 1400) DM 450
- Omnia quae extant. Opera. Venice, 1565. 11 pts. in 6 vols. Fo. Lacks Index vol., some old MS. marginalia, some underlining, some light browning, 17th. C. leath., spine restored or renewed, 1 vol. loose. (R. Oct.12; 1399) DM 1,400
- Opera Omnia. Basel, 1549. 4 vols. Fo. Some light margin dampstains, cont. histor. pig, metal clasps (most defect.), 1 vol. with scattered worming affecting bdgs. & some ll. (SG. Mar.22; 134) $850
- - **Anr. Edn.** Ed.:– C.G. Kuhn. Leipzig, 1821-33. 20 vols. in 22, including Index. In Greek & Latin, hf. cf. (*With:*) SCHUBRING, Konrad
- Bemerkungen zu der Galenausgabe ... Hildesheim, 1965. 1 vol. Wraps. Together 23 vols. Dr. Walter Pagel copies. (S. Feb.7; 136) *Poole.* £1,200

– Recettario ... a Tutte le Infirmità. Trans.:– Z. Saracino. [Venice, Jan. 1535]. Browned, loose in old qtr. cf. (previously bound with anr. work). (SG. Oct.27; 121) $150

GALERIE CONTEMPORAINE des Illustrations Françaises
Paris, after 1885?. 8 vols. Fo. Approx. 140 mntd. Woodburytype ports. of artists, many mntd. Woodburytype reproductions of their work, some minor foxing, a few plts. detchd., hf. mor., extremities rubbed. (SG. May 10; 51) $2,600

GALERIE DES ARTISTES DRAMATIQUES
Ill.:– Alexandre Lacauchie. [Paris], ca. 1840. 4to. 28 tipped in litho. ports. on India paper, MB. title-p. & index, a few margins worn, a few tears, several plts. loose, cont. hf. roan, rbkd., worn. (S. Dec.20; 724) *Dennistoun.* £55

GALERIE DES FEMMES DE SHAKESPEARE
Paris, 1838. 45 metal engraved ports., romantic red mor., gt. decor., sigd. by Boutigny. (HD. Jan.30; 56) Frs. 1,500

GALERIE DRAMATIQUE. Costumes des Théâtres de Paris
[Paris, 1844-70]. 2 vols. 4to. 1 plt. soiled, some slight margin browning, red hf. mor. gt., slightly bumped. (D. Nov.24; 4395) DM 2,300

GALERIE du Muséé de France
See— FILHOL, Antoine Michel

GALERIES HISTORIQUES DE VERSAILLES
Paris, ca. 1840. *De Luxe Edn.* Series III-V & VII in 3 vols. Imp. fo. Plts. on China, wide margin, 13 ills. loose in vol. VI (Series V), cont. hf. leath. gt., slightly bumped. (R. Oct.12; 2362) DM 8,000

GALET
– Le Corps de l'Homme. Paris, 1835-36. Pts. 1 & 2 (of ?) in 1 vol. 4to. Some heavy staining, some spotting, multi-folding plts. partially torn, cont. hf. leath., gt., bumped & worn, spine with sm. defect. (HT. May 8; 539) DM 720

GALIBERT, L.
– Histoire de la République de Venise. Ill.:– after Rouargue. Paris, ca. 1850. 24 steel engrs., double-p.,. Slightly foxed, cont. leath. (R. Apr.5; 2986) DM 400

GALILEI, Galileo
– Dialogo ... sopra i Due Massimi Sistemi del Mondo Tolemaico, e Copernicano. Flor., 1632. *1st. Edn.* 4to. Slip pasted in margin of p.92, erratum lf., lacks engraved frontis. & final blank, sm. hole affecting colophon, some browning, early 19th. C. hf. vell. over marb. bds., slightly scuffed; Stanitz coll. (SPB. Apr.25; 183) $3,100
– – Anr. Copy. 4to. Engraved frontis., woodcut diagrams, slip pasted in margin of p.02, errata lf., some browning, few ll. marginally stained, later parch. bds., spine soiled. (SPB. May 17; 613) $2,500
– – Anr. Edn. Fiorenza [= Napoli], 1710. *2nd. Edn.* 2 pts. in 1 vol. 4to. Some light foxing, cont. leath. gt., slightly rubbed. (R. Oct.12; 1672) DM 460
– Discorsi e Dimonstrazioni Matematiche, intorno a Due Nuove Scienze attenenti alla Mecanica & i Movementi Locali. Leyden, 1638. *1st. Edn.* Sm. 4to. Errata lf., faint dampstain on title, cont. limp vell., sm. flaw in lr. corner; inscr. on title 'Ex. Lib. Dni J.B. de Secondat', from Montesquieu's liby. (C. May 30; 115) *Turner.* £3,000
– – Anr. Copy. Sm. 4to. Errata lf., some light browning & spotting, cont. MS. mathematical notes at foot of last p. & following lf., later vell., Stanitz coll. (SPB. Apr.25; 184) $5,500
– Galileo a Madame Cristina di Lorena. Padua, Salmin, 1896 [1897]. 17 x 11mm. Miniature Book. Some ll. worn at outer margin with some loss of text, mor., decor. gt. end-papers. (S. Nov.22; 424) *Fletcher.* £120
– Istoria e Dimonstrazioni intorno alle Macchie Solari e Loro Accidenti. Rome, 1613. *1st. Edn. Iss. without Scheiner's letters to Welser & double-p. plt.* Sm. 4to. 2 repairs to title-p. where owners inscrs. deleted, some foxing, cont. vell., mor. solander case; Stanitz coll. (SPB. Apr.25; 185) $3,000

– Nov-Antiqua Sanctissimorum Patrum, & Probatorum Theologorum, de Sacrae Scripturae Testimoniis, in Conclusionibus vere Naturalibus. Strassburg, 1636. *1st. Edn.* Sm. 4to. Last 2 ll. in facs., title restored in margins, few sm. tears reprd., mod. limp vell. (S. Apr.10; 502) *Faurre.* £50
– Opera. Flor., 1718. 3 vols. 4to. Old name on all 3 title ll., cont. hf. leath. gt., rubbed. (R. Apr.4; 1520) DM 600
– – Anr. Edn. Padua, 1744. 4 vols. 4to. Wide margin, cont. vell. (D. Nov.23; 399) DM 950
– Opere. Bologna, 1655-56. *1st. Coll. Edn.* 2 vols. 4to. Engraved frontis., port. & folding plt., woodcut ills. & diagrams, separate title to each work but lacks 1, cont. limp vell. (SPB. May 17; 615) $600
– Systema Cosmicum. In quo Dialogis IV de Duobus Maximis Mundi Systematibus. Ptolemaico & Copernicano.—Discursus & Demonstrationes Mathematicae Pert. ad Mechanicam & Motum Localem. Leyden, 1699. 2 works in 1 vol. 4to. Cont. vell., slightly soiled, lacks sm. strip from spine. (VG. Sep.14; 1241) Fls. 1,000

GALILEI, Galileo & Castelli, Benedetto
– Riposta alle Oppositioni del Sign. Lodovico delle Colombe e del Sig. Vincenzo di Gratia, contro al Trattato del Sig. Galileo Galilei delle Cose che stanno su l'Acque, o che on quella si muovono. Bologna, 1655. 4to. Lev. mor. by Sangorski & Sutcliffe; Stanitz coll. (SPB. Apr.25; 186) $475

GALITZIN, Fürst N.S.
– Allgemeine Kriegsgeschichte aller Völker und Zeiten. Trans.:– Streccius & Eichwald. Kassel, 1874-89. 4 pts. in 13 vols. Liby. stp. on title lf., hf. linen, rubber & bumped. (D. Nov.24; 3644) DM 600

GALL, E. (Ed.)
See— REALLEXIKON ZUR DEUTSCHEN KUNSTGESCHICHTE

GALLAEUS, Servatius
– Dissertationes de Sibyllis, earymque Oraculis. Amst., 1688. *1st. Edn.* 4to. Lacks last blank, cont. mott. cf., spine gt. (BBA. Jan.19; 17) *Maggs.* £100

GALLARDO, Bartolomé José
– Bibliotheca Nacional de Cortes ... Madrid, 1838. Fo. No bdg. stated. (DS. Apr.27; 2101) Pts. 30,000
– Diccionario Crítico Burlesco ... Cadiz, 1811. 2 pp. with variants, leath. (DS. Apr.27; 2102) Pts. 20,000

GALLARDO DE BONILLA. L.
– Descripcioń de la Proclama que se executó en ... Badajoz ... [Coronación] Fernando VI. Madrid, 1747. 4to. Cl. (DS. Mar.23; 2109) Pts. 34,000

GALLE, Theodor
– Illvstrivm Imagines, ex Antiquis Marmoribus. Nomismatibus, et Gemmis expressae : Quae exstant Romae. Antw., 1606. 4to. Leath., gt. spine & upr. cover. (HK. Nov.9; 1493) DM 580
– Sammelband mit 3 Heiligenviten in Bilderfolgen. Amst., ca. 1600. Some margin defects., reprd., some old soiling, cont.-style leath., gt. & blind-tooled decor., gt. inner & outer dentelle, slightly bumped. (V. Oct.1; 3738) DM 480

GALLEGARIS, B.
– Lo Strvcciero. Venice, 1646. *1st. Edn.* 19th. C. vell. (HK. May 16; 1577) DM 400

GALLERIA UNIVERSALE DI TUTTI I POPOLI DEL MONDO
Venezia, 1838-42. 4 vols. in 5. 4to. Many stains, cont. hf. leath., slightly loose. (SI. Dec.15; 111) Lire 300,000

GALLERY OF MODERN BRITISH ARTISTS
Ill.:– J.M.W. Turner, D. Roberts, & others. 1834. 4to. Steel-engraved frontis., additional title, 76 plts., spotted, cont. russ. (CSK. Nov.4; 155) £150

GALLESIO, Giorgio
– Pomona Italiana. Pisa, 1817-39. 2 vols. in 4. Fo. Tall copy, engraved table, 3 double-p. ptd. tables, 160 hand-finished col.-ptd. plts. (Nissen incorrectly calling for 170), 3 plts. with faint staining of

background surround, 2 plts. browned, 1 with slight offsetting, cont. hf. roan gt., spines tooled. (C. Nov.16; 246) *Makrocki.* £12,000

GALLETTI, G. Abbé J.A.
– Allgemeine Weltkunde. Pest & Wien, 1822. 4to. Cont. hf. leath., worn & partly loose spine torn. (D. Nov.23; 872) DM 500

GALLI DA BIBIENA, Ferdinando
– L'Architettura Civile. Parma, [1711]. *1st. Edn.* Fo. 72 unnumbered engraved plts., name erased from title, 1 lf. reprd., rust mark on 1 plt., cont. vell., rebkd., orig. spine preserved. (C. Dec.9; 53) *Thomas-Scheler.* £2,600
[–] Basilica Carolina Opus Grande ... Ill.:– Jos. & Joh. Klauber. Mannheim, 1760. Fo. Double-p. engraved allegorical title, 19 plts., including 7 double-p., cont. mott. cf. (C. Dec.9; 54) *Weinreb.* £600

GALLI DA BIBIENA, Giuseppe
[–] Architetture, e Prospettive. Ill.:– A. & J. Schmuzer, Pfeffel, & others, after Bibiena. Augsburg, 1740[-44]. *1st. Edn.* Lge. fo. Engraved title with vig., engraved port., engraved dedication, 50 engraved plts., lacks frontis., additional plt. & ptd. preface lf., title reprd., minor dampstain to a few blank margins, sm. wormhole in 1st. 23 ll., mod. hf. mor. (C. Dec.9; 55) *Lyon.* £2,600

GALLICIUS, J.
– Geometria Militaris ... in Operibus Militaribus existentes considerantur ... München, 1676. Fo. 1 plt. with tear, some with creases, title with owners mark, cont. vell. (HK. May 16; 1677) DM 420

GALLICO, Paul
– The Snow Goose. Ill.:– after Peter Scott. [1946]. *(750) numbered & sigd.* 4to. Orig. cl., d-w. (CSK. Sep.30; 85) £55

GALLICO, Shmuel
See— MENACHEM AZARIA DI FANO & Gallico, Shmuel

GALLIEUR, E.H.
See— SCHAUB & Gallieur, E.H.

GALLING, K. & others
– Die Religion in Geschichte und Gegenwart. H Handwörterbuch für Theologie und Religionswissenschaft. Tübingen, 1957-65. *3rd. Edn.* 6 vols. & index. Hf. leath. (1 vol. cl.). (B. Jun.21; 281) Fls. 480

GALLINI, Giovanni-Andrea Battista
– Critical Observations on the Art of Dancing ... to which is added a Collection of Cotillans on French Dancies. Ca. 1770. 50 engraved musical scores, cont. hf. cf. gt. (PD. Oct.19; 276) £115
– A Treatise on the Art of Dancing. 1772. Cont. hf. cf., worn. (PD. Oct.19; 277) £125

GALLO, Agostino
– Le Vinti Giornate dell' Agricoltura, et de' Piaceri della Villa. Venice, 1572. 4to. 19 full-p. woodcut ills., title with sm. hole slightly affecting 1 character, some old dampstaining, a few blank margins lightly wormed, later hf. vell., lightly soiled. (CSK. Apr.27; 114) £200

GALLON, Colon
– Machines et Inventions Approuvées par l'Académie Royale des Sciences, depuis son Etablissement jusqu'à Présent. Paris, 1735-77. *1st. Edn.* Vol. 1-7. 4to. Hf.-titles, browning & staining to some pp., old cf., reprd., painted; liby. stps. of K.u.K. Technische Bibliothek, Militar-Akademie, on backs of plts., Stanitz coll. (SPB. Apr.25; 187) $3,800

GALLONIUS, Antonius
– De SS. Martyrum Cruciatibus Liber. Ill.:– after Tempesta. Paris, 1660. 4to. Washed & replaced in bdg., cont. marb. cf. gt., Cardinal Mazarin arms, spine decor. (HD. Nov.9; 67) Frs. 5,100

GALLOWAY, Elijah & Herbert, Luke
– History & Progress of the Steam Engine. 1829. Cf. gt. (P. Jan.12; 226) *Edwards.* £70
– – Anr. Edn. 1831. Hf. cf., rubbed. (P. Jan.12; 225) *Edwards.* £50

GALLUCCI, Giovanni Paolo
- De Fabrica, et Usu Hemisphaerii Uranici, Nova Fabricandi Horaria Mobilia, et Permanentia. Venezia, 1596. 2 pts. in 1 vol. Sm. fo. Black & red stain on frontis. 1st. pt., 1st. pt. with large worm hole in margins with slight loss, 2nd. pt. with stain on frontis., some worming in margins, later vell. (SI. Dec.18; 158)   Lire 250,000

GALLUP, Joseph A.
- Sketches of Epidemic Diseases in the State of Vermont; from its first Settlement to the year 1815; with a Consideration of their Causes, Phenomena, & Treatment; to which is added Remarks on Pulmonary Consumtion. Boston, 1815. 1st. Edn. Light dampstaining, cont. crude hf. leath., unc., chipped & soiled, cover detchd. (SG. Mar.22; 135)
                                                    $100

GALLUZZI, R.
- Storia del Granducato di Toscana. Firenze, 1822. 11 vols. bnd. in 5. Hf. vell. (CR. Jun.6; 166)
                                            Lire 250,000

GALLWEY, Sir Ralph Payne
- The Book of Duck Decoys. 1886. 4to. Orig. cl. gt. (SKC. Mar.9; 1938)   £120

GALLWITZ, Dr. Klaus
- Max Beckmann. Die Druckgraphik. Karlsruhe, 1962. Orig. pict. bds. (H. Nov.24; 2453) DM 440

GALSWORTHY, John 'John Sinjohn'
- The Works. L., 1923-36. Manaton Edn. (530) numbered. 30 vols. Some vols. dampstained, orig. parch.-bkd. bds., soiled; bkplt. of David Garnett. (BBA. Mar.21; 292)   Bowers. £60
-- Anr. Edn. N.Y., 1926-29. 22 vols. Some margin staining to prelims., three-qtr. mor., gt.-decor. spine, some covers stained, one badly. (CBA. Dec.10; 231) $170
-- Anr. Edn. N.Y., 1929. 1st. Compact Edn. (500) sigd. 6 vols. Hf. red mor. gt., publisher's boxes. (SPB. May 17; 744) $300

GALT, John 'Micah Balwhidder'
- The Lives of the Players. 1831. 1st. Edn. 2 vols. Extra-ill., hf. mor., rubbed; inscr. by author, with 12 line annot. on p. 231, as an extra-ill. copy, w.a.f. (P. Mar.15; 138)   Hannas. £220
- Poems. L., 1833. Title spotted, orig. cl., partly unopened, faded; inscr. by author to [Isaac] Disraeli. (P. Feb.16; 256)   £70
- Voyages & Travels, in the Years 1809, 1810, & 1811; Containing ... Observations on Gibraltar, Sardinia, Sicily, Malca, Serigo, & Turkey. L., 1812. 1st. Edn. 4to. Some light foxing, offsetting, qtr. cl., unc. (SG. Sep.22; 146) $100

GALTON, Francis
- Finger Prints. L., 1892. [1st. Edn.]. Pres. inscr., 16 plts., review pasted on hf.-title verso, a few ll. slightly marked, orig. cl., faded, unc. (S. Dec.20; 840)   Rota. £120
-- Anr. Copy. Orig. cl., unc. & mostly unopened, rubbed & faded. (TA. May 17; 148)   £64
-- Anr. Copy. Orig. cl., spine ends slightly worn, untrimmed; Harvey Cushing & Yale Medical Liby. bkplts. (SG. Oct.6; 166) $500
- Inquiries into Human Faculty & its Development. L., 1883. 1st. Edn. Cl., light wear & spotting. (RO. Dec.11; 114) $160
- Vacation Tourists & Notes of Travel in 1860. Camb., 1861. 8vo. Orig. cl., slightly worn. (BBA. Jan.19; 105)   Quaritch. £50

GALTON, S.J.
[-]The Natural History of Birds ... Intended for the Amusement & Instruction of Children. 1791. 3 vols. 12mo. 115 (of 116) hand-cold. plts., slightly soiled, cont. cf., 1 vol. covers detchd. (SKC. Mar.9; 1939)
                                                    £80

GALWAY ARCHAEOLOGICAL & HISTORICAL SOCIETY
- Journal. Galway & Dublin, 1900-49; 1913. Vols. I-XXIII, & Index for Vols. I-VII. Royal 8vo. Buckram-bkd. cl., as a periodical, w.a.f. (GM. Dec.7; 191)   £700

GAMBADO, Geoffrey
See— BUNBURY, Henry W. 'Geoffrey Gambade'

GAMBLE, John
- Views of Society & Manners in the North of Ireland. L., 1819. 1st. Edn. Bkplt., crimson hf. mor., gh-tooled spine. (GM. Dec.7; 390)   £130

GAMBOA Y ERASO, Luis de
- Verdad de lo Sucedido con Ocasión de la Venida de la Armada Inglesa del Enemigo sobre Cádiz. 1626. Fo. Linen. (DS. Mar.23; 2110) Pts. 110,000

GAMELIN, Jacques
- Nouveau Recueil d'Ostéologie et de Myologie, dessiné d'après Nature, pour l'Utilité des Sciences et des Arts. Ill.:– Gamelin & Lavallée. Toulouse, 1779. 2 pts. in 1 vol. Fo. 2 frontis., 80 plts., dampstains, 2 plts. torn without loss, mod. chagrin gt., spine decor., unc. (HD. Mar.21; 32)
                                              Frs. 32,000

GAMOND, A.T. De
- Account of the Plans for a New Project of a Submarine Tunnel Between England & France. L., 1870. 2nd. Edn. 2 vols. 4to. 3 cold. folding plans, orig. wraps. & bds. (P. Dec.8; 138) Walford. £100

GANDINI, F.
- Itineraire de l'Europe. Ill.:– Fumagalli. Milan, 1821. 3 engraved folding maps & 10 aquatinted views, text spotted, orig. wraps., slightly worn, unc. (S. Apr.9; 24)   Elliott. £90

GANDY, John P.
See— GELL, Sir William & Gandy, John P.

GANGHOFER, L.
See— ALLERS, C.W. & Ganghofer, L.

GANIER, Henry
- Costumes des Régiments et des Milices Recrutés dans les Anciennes Provinces d'Alsace ... pendant les XVIIe et XVIIIe Siècles. 1882. (500). Fo. Leaves, lacks cartouche. (HD. Mar.21; 154)   Frs. 1,300

GANILH, Charles
- Essai Politique sur le Revenu Public. Paris, 1806. 1st. Edn. 2 vols. Some slight spotting & soiling, cont. mott. cf., 1 jnt. split; each cover with gt. stp. of Signet Liby. (S. Apr.10; 361)   Drury. £80
-- Anr. Edn. Paris, 1823. 2 vols. Sewed. (HD. Feb.22; 76)   Frs. 2,000
- La Théorie de l'Economie Politique. Paris, 1815. 1st. Edn. 2 vols. Hf.-titles, folding tables, cont. cf., spines slightly worn, each cover with gt. stp. of Signet Liby. (S. Apr.10; 360)   Drury. £80

GANNET, William C.
- The House Beautiful. In a setting designed by Frank Lloyd Wright. River Forest, Illinois, Ptd. ... at the Auvergne Pr. ... by William Herman Winslow & Frank Lloyd Wright, Winter 1896/97 [publd. 1897]. (90) numbered & sigd. by Winslow & Wright. Lge. 4to. Suite of 12 oriental-style photogravure ills. on 14 tall 8vo. ll. of thin Japon vergé stitched with flap to upr. free end-paper, 8 blank margins of text dampstained, orig. qtr. cf. gt. & paper bds., partly unc., covers worn & nearly detchd., backstrip brkn. (CNY. May 18; 171)
                                                  £1,700

GANSLER, R.
- Lugenschmid.—Anderer Theil. Augsburg & Dillingen, [1698]. 1st. Edn. Pt. 2. 2 pts. in 1 vol. Frontis. & title bkd. in margin with sm. fault & cut short, 1st. ll. wormed, with slight loss, some slight browning, cont. pig, partly defect. (HT. May 9; 1300)   DM 750

GANYMED, Jahrbuch für die Kunst
Ed.:– J. Meier-Graefe. Ill.:– Beckmann, Grossmann, Schinnerer, Bech, Hofer & Kubin. München, 1921. (200) numbered for members of Marees Gesellschaft. Vol. 3. 4to. 6 orig. ills., orig. hf. linen, slightly spotted. (BR. Apr.13; 1705)
                                                  DM 500
-- Anr. Copy. Vol. 3. 4to. Without Ganymed portfo., orig. hf. vell. (HK. May 17; 2763)
                                                  DM 450
-- Anr. Edn. Ed.:– J. Meier-Graefe. W. Hausenstein. Trans.:– Texts:– A. Döblin, A. Kolb, H. Mann, H. von Hofmannsthal, A. Kubin & A.

Einstein. Ill.:– M. Beckmann, E. Heckel, A. Kubin, R. Grossmann, R. Seewald M. Unold. München, 1921-25. Vols. III-V. 4to. Vol. IV slightly stained in some outer margins, orig. hf. linen, wear. (HT. May 9; 1804)   DM 880

GANZ, Paul
- Malerei der Frührenaissance in der Schweiz. Zurich, 1924. Fo. 1st. few ll. with sm. tear, orig. wraps., slightly torn. (BBA. Nov.10; 169)
                                              Schwarz. £50

GANZO, Robert
- Lespugue. Ill.:– O. Zadkine. [Paris, 1966]. (175) on Papier d'Auvergene à la main. Lge. 8vo. Printers mark sigd. by author & artist, loose ll. in orig. wraps. & bd. covers. (H. May 23; 1570) DM 500
- Oeuvre Poétique. Ill.:– Jacques Villon. Paris, 1957. (185) sigd. by author & artist. (25) numbered on Arches, with extra suite of the plts. in sanguine & an additional plt. of frontis. in 1st. state. 4to. Crushed mor. by Roger Devauchelle, sigd. on upr. turn-in, covers with onlaid glossy cold. papers forming an abstract multi-pointed design, smooth spine gt.-lettered, partly unc., orig. wraps. & backstrip preserved, matching mor.-edged s.-c. (CNY. May 18; 179) $1,800

GAPE, Tim
- The Comical Fellow; or, Wit & Humour, for Town & Country. L., ca. 1780. 3rd. Edn. 12mo. Engraved frontis., mod. three-qtr. mor. (SG. Apr.19; 89) $175

GARCIA, Gregorio
- Origen de los Indios en el Nuevo Mundo e Indias Occidentales. Madrid, 1729. 2nd. Imp. Fo. Partly dampstained, cont. vell. [Sabin 26567] (SG. Jan.19; 173) $450

GARCIA CONDE, Pedro
- Verdadera Albeyteria. Madrid, 1658. Fo. Linen. (DS. Mar.23; 2113)   Pts. 150,000
-- Anr. Edn. Madrid, 1707. Fo. Some ll. remargined, mod. cf. (DS. Nov.25; 2003)
                                              Pts. 24,000

GARCIA DE CESPEDES, Andres
See— EUCLID—GARCIA DE CESPEDES, Andres

GARCIA DE LA CONCEPCION, José
- Historia Bethlehemitica: Vida ... del ... Pedro de San Joseph Betancúr, Fundadór de el Regulafr Instituto de Bethlehen en las Indias Occidentales. Seville, 1723. 1st. Edn. Fo. Slightly dampstained, margin defects in title-p., cont. vell., relined; Bibliotheca Lindesiana bkplt. [Sabin 26571] (SG. Jan.19; 174) $300

GARCIA LORCA, Federico
- Llanto por Ignacio Sánchez Meiias. Ill.:– José Caballero. Madrid, 1935. 1st. Edn. Fo. Wraps. (DS. Jan.27; 2496)   Pts. 30,000
- Noces de Sang. Trans.:– Marcelle Auclair. Ill.:– Jansen. Paris, 1977. (200). Fo. On Arches, leaves, wrap, publishers velours box. (HD. Dec.16; 125)
                                              Frs. 2,200
- Poema del Cante Jondo. Madrid, 1931. 1st. Edn. Mor., s.-c. (DS. Jan.27; 2303)   Pts. 28,000

GARCILASO DE LA VEGA, called El Inca
- La Florida del Inca. Madrid, 1723. 2nd. Edn. Fo. Linen, corners. (DS. Feb.24; 2473) Pts. 25,000
-- Anr. Edn. Madrid, 1723. 3rd. Edn. Fo. Without Ensaio Cronologica as usual, 1 lf. reprd. at outer margin, with very slight loss of text, old mott. cf., jnts. worn. [Sabin 98745] (SG. Apr.5; 76) $200
- Primera parte de los Commentarios Reales ... del Origen des los Incas. Lisbon, 1609. 1st. Edn. 4to. Hole on title-p. affecting 1 letter, some dampstains, vell., soiled, vell. ties (1 defect.). (P. Jan.12; 241)
                                              Duran. £600
-- Anr. Edn. Madrid, 1723. (With:) – Historia Generál del Peru. Madrid, 1722. Together 2 vols. Sm. fo. Unif. cont. cf. gt., rubbed. (BBA. Jun.28; 227)   Baldwin. £190
- The Royal Commentaries of Peru. 1688. 2 pts. in 1 vol. Fo. Mod. cf. [Wing G215] (CSK. Jul.6; 88a)
                                                  £220

GARDEN, Alexander
– Anecdotes of the Revolutionary War in America. With Sketches of Persons ... in the Southern States. Charleston, S.C., 1822. *1st. Edn.* Lacks last 2 ll. of subscribers list & fly-ll., slightly foxed, orig. bds., soiled, slightly shaken, spine chipped, partly unopened, qtr. mor. s.-c.; inscr. on front free endpaper by Sir William Middleton. (SG. Jan.19; 175) $110

GARDENER'S MAGAZINE
Ed.:– J.C. Loudon. 1836-41. Vols. 12-17. Cont. hf. cf. (TA. Aug.18; 8) £60
– – **Anr. Edn.** Ed.:– Thomas Moore & William P. Ayres. Jan. 1850-Jan. 1852. Vols. I-XXII & New Series pt. I, together 23 vols. 102 cold. & uncold. plts., no bdg. stated. (WW. Nov.23; 150) £350

GARDILANNE, Gratiane de & Moffatt, Elizabeth Whitney
– Les Costumes Regionaux de la France. Ed.:– Henry Royer. Preface:– Princesse Bibesco. N.Y., Pegasus Pr., 1929. *(500) numbered.* 4 vols. Atlas fo. 200 cold. plts., each matted, ex-liby., buckram. (SG. May 3; 112) $150

GARDINER, A.B. (Contrib.)
See— BOWEN, Clarence W.

GARDINER, Alan H.
See— DAVIES, Nina M. & Gardiner, Alan H.

GARDINER, Samuel Rawson & Firth, Sir Charles Harding
– History of England 1603-1656. L., 1863-1901. *1st. Edns.* Hf. mor., by Bayntun (Rivière), spines gt. (S. Oct.4; 85) *Foyles.* £240

GARDNER, Alexander
– Photographic Sketch Book of the War. Ill.:– Gardner, O'Sullivan, Barnard & Gibson, & others. Wash., [1866]. Vol. 1. Ob. fo. Litho. title, 50 mntd. albumen photos, all plts. with some edge fading, publisher's mor., loose, upr. spine tape reprd. (SG. May 10; 52) $2,000

GARDNER, J. Starkie
– Old Silver-Work Chiefly English. 1903. Fo. Orig. cl., spine soiled. (CSK. Sep.30; 2) £55

GARGIARIA, G.B.
– Tractatus Varii. [Bologna, 1643]. Lge. 4to. L.P., cont. red mor. gt. super extra, arms of Frederick II de Medici on covers (the dedication copy?), rebkd. & relined, old spine laid down. (SG. Nov.17; 168) $110

GARIOT, J.B.
– Tradé des Maladies de la Bouche. Paris, 1805. *1st. Edn.* Some light spotting in margins, cont. style bds., cont. wraps. bnd. in, unc. (R. Oct.12; 1506) DM 1,100

GARMANN, Chr. Fr.
– De Miraculis Mortuorum Libri tres. Ed.:– Imm. H. Garman. Ill.:– Bodenehr. Dresden & Leipzig, 1709. *2nd. Edn.* 4to. Browned, some heavy spotting, cont. vell., 4 ties. (HK. Nov.8; 569) DM 550

GARNER, Thomas & Stratton, Arthur
– The Domestic Architecture of England during the Tudor Period. 1911. *[1st. Edn.].* 3 vols. Fo. Orig. hf. mor., slightly rubbed. (BBA. Jul.27; 258) *Crisford.* £55
– – **Anr. Copy.** 2 vols. Lge. fo. Plts., text ills., ex-liby., loose in pict. buckram folders. (SG. May 3; 173) $225
– – **Anr. Copy.** 3 vols. Lge. fo. Liby. buckram. (SG. Jan.26; 198) $130
– – **Anr. Edn.** L., 1929. *2nd. Edn.* 2 vols. Fo. Orig. cl., d.-w.'s. (S. Oct.4; 153) *Scrimgeour.* £90

GARNERAY, Jean François
[–] Collection des Nouveaux Costumes des Autorités Constituées Civils et Militaires. Ill.:– P.M. Alix after Garneray. ca. 1796. 26 hand-cold. engraved plts., lacks title & 2 ll. [bound with:] – Collection Générale des Portraits de M.M. les Deputés à l'Assemblée Nationale. Ill.:– Allais, P.M. Alix & others. ca. 1790. 63 ports. only, stipple or line-engraved with mezzotint, some light staining or spotting in margins. 2 works in 1 vol, 4to. Cont. hf. roan. (S. Apr.9; 25) *Russell.* £90

GARNERAY, Louis
– 9 Années de Captivité en Angleterre. Mes Pontons. Suite au Mémoires d'un Vrai Matelot. Limoges, n.d. Bradel buckram. (HD. Jan.27; 39) Frs. 1,000

GARNET, J.R. & Conabere, Betty
– Wildflowers of South-Eastern Australia. Melbourne, 1974. *(775) numbered & sigd.* 2 vols. Fo. Bdg. not stated, cl. s.-c. (KH. May 1; 282) Aus. $140

GARNETT, Thomas
– Observations on a Tour through the Highlands & part of The Western Isles of Scotland. 1800. *1st. Edn.* 2 vols. 4to. 2 engraved maps (1 folding), 51 aquatint plts., cont. spr. cf.; Sir Ivar Colquhoun, of Luss copy. (CE. Mar.22; 130) £340
– – **Anr. Copy.** 2 vols. in 1. 4to. Cont. cf. gt., w.a.f.; from liby. of Luttrellstown Castle. (C. Sep.28; 1737) £160

GARNIER, Charles George Thomas (Ed.)
See— VOYAGES IMAGINAIRES ...

GARNIER, Marie-Joseph Francis
– Voyage d'Exploration en Indo-Chine. Ill.:– after Delaporte & others. Paris, 1873. 4 pts. in 3 vols. Fo. & 4to. Few plts. & col. maps in text, Atlas with 9 engraved plans, 12 partly cold. engraved maps, including 2 double-p., 2 engraved plts., 39 col. or tinted litho. views, including 6 double-p., disbnd. (SG. Nov.3; 82) $375
– – **Anr. Copy.** 2 vols., & Atlas vol. (2 pts. in 1 vol.). Fo. & lge. fo. Glazed hf. cf., 1 cover loose, atlas vol. lacks part of spine. (V. Sep.29; 66) DM 1,600

GARRAN, Hon. Andrew
– Australasia Illustrated. 1892. 3 vols. Leath. (JL. Mar.25; 583) Aus. $220
– Picturesque Atlas of Australasia. Sydney, 1886. 3 vols. 4to. Titles slightly spotted, orig. hf. mor., rubbed. (S. Nov.1; 25) *Eisler.* £130
– – **Anr. Copy.** 3 vols. Fo. 1 vol. with margin staining thro.-out, 3 or 4 ll. with some soiling or margin tears, publisher's hard-grain cl., rebkd. with buckram, a few marks. (KH. May 1; 283) Aus. $280
– – **Anr. Edn.** L., ca. 1886. 2 vols. in 4. Fo. Not collated, bdg. not stated, rebkd. & recornered. (KH. Nov.9; 604) Aus. $240

GARRARD, George
– A Description of the Different Varieties of Oxon Common in the British Isles. L., priv. ptd., 1800 [i.e. 1799-1815]. Ob. fo. 52 etched plts., without the 'order for binding' slip or author's advt. lf., a few plts. spotted, a few with fore-margins cropped, last plt. cut across & reprd., 2 plts. creased, hf. mor., soiled. (C. Mar.14; 123) *Schuster.* £950

GARRARD, William
– The Arte of Warre. L., 1591. *1st. Edn.* Sm. 4to. 6 (of 7) folding woodcut diagrams, errata lf., quire Z misbnd., L4 (sigd. K2) slashed for cancelling, sm. hole in Kk1, cont. limp vell., soiled, loose. [STC 11625] (S. Dec.8; 3) *Smallwood.* £170

GARRETT, John
– The Kingdome of England & Principality of Wales Exactly Described [Quarter Master's Map]. Ill.:– W. Hollar. L., by John Garrett, ca. 1752. Engraved title, sm. map of the Isle of Man, 6 lge. folding maps, hand-cold. in outl., a few sm. tears at folds, some reprd., mod. hf. cf. (C. Nov.16; 92) *Burgess.* £280

GARRICK, David
– The Dramatic Works. L., 1768. 3 vols. Sm. 8vo. A few margins slightly browned, cont. spr. cf., gt. Signet Liby. arms on covers. (C. Nov.9; 73) *Scott.* £100

GARRIDO, Fernando
– Historia del Reinado del Ultimo Borbón de España. Barcelona, 1868-69. 3 vols. 4to. Cf. (DS. Nov.25; 2057) Pts. 40,000

GARRYOWEN (Pseud.)
See— FINN, Edmund 'Garryowen'

GARSAULT, Fr. de
– Le Nouveau Parfait Maréchal, ou la Connoissance Générale et Universelle du Cheval. Paris, 1771. *4th.*

Edn. 4to. Cont. marb. roan, spine decor.; from Château des Noës liby. (HD. May 25; 28) Frs. 2,000
– – **Anr. Copy.** 4to. Old cf., spine decor., worn, reprd. (LM. Mar.3; 122) B.Frs. 10,000
– – **Anr. Edn.** Paris, 1843. *5th. Edn.* 4to. Cont. hf. leath. (D. Nov.25; 4487) DM 400

GARTENLAUBE, Die. Illustrirtes Familienblatt
Contribs.:– Gerstäcker, Eichendorff, Groth, Rückert & others. Leipzig, 1855-57. 3 vols. Lge. 4to. 1857 lacks 8 pp., 2 hf. linen, 1 spine reprd., 1 hf. leath. (BR. Apr.12; 96) DM 500
– – **Anr. Edn.** Contribs.:– Gerstäcker, Storm, Rückert. Leipzig, 1862-64. 3 vols. Hf. linen. (BR. Apr.12; 97) DM 500

GARTLER, I. & Hikmann, Barbara
– Wienerisches Bewährtes Kochbuch. Wien, 1795. Title with traces of stp., plts. slightly crumpled. some light browning, cont. bds., slightly bumped. (HK. Nov.9; 1669) DM 460

GARTNER, Fr. von
– Ansichten der am meisten erhaltenen Griechischen Monumente Siciliens. Ill.:– J.E. Mettenleiter (2 litho. titles), F. v. Gärtner & A. Falger. München, 1819. Ob. fo. German & Fr. text & captions, title, text & last 6 plts. slightly soiled, 1 plt. misbnd., cont. hf. leath., bumped, some soiling, spine defect. (HK. Nov.8; 1075) DM 2,000

GARZONI, Thomas
– Piazza Universale. Ill.:– M. Merian. Frankfurt, 1626. *2nd. German Edn.* Fo. Browned, some staining, cont. vell., soiled, end-papers soiled. (HK. Nov.9; 1547) DM 700

GASKELL, Mrs. Elizabeth Cleghorn
– Cranford. Ill.:– Hugh Thomson. L., 1891. Mor. gt. by Kelliegram Bindery, with inlaid port. on upr. cover & inlay on lr. cover; inscr. on blanks, Perry Molstad copy. (SPB. May 16; 411) $175
– Works. 1906. 8 vols. Qtr. vell. gt. (P. Feb.16; 2) £85

GASON, Samuel
– The Dieyerie Tribe of Australian Aboriginals ... Ed.:– George Isaacs. Adelaide, 1874. Some staining & foxing, stiff wraps., crude repair to backstrip. (KH. May 1; 284) Aus. $220

GASPA Y ESPINOSA, G.J.
– Manual de Avisos para el Perfecto Cortesano. Madrid, 1681. 4to. Linen. (DS. Mar.23; 2653) Pts. 25,000

GASPEY, William
– Tallis's Illustrated London. L., [1851]. Ob. 8vo. Advt. ll., approx. 80 engrs., some browning, bdg. not stated, w.a.f. (S. Apr.9; 167) *Burlington.* £300
– – **Anr. Edn.** [1851-52]. 2 vols. 2 vig. titles, 222 views on 150 sheets, hf. mor. gt. (P. Dec.8; 6) *P. Martin.* £90
– – **Anr. Copy.** 2 vols. Engraved titles, 150 engraved plts., 1 loose, hf. cf. gt. (P. Sep.8; 183) *Evellyn.* £70
– – **Anr. Edn.** L., 1852. 16mo. Approx. steel engrs. (full-p. & hf.-p.), cl., as a collection, w.a.f. (CR. Jun.6; 167) Lire 280,000

GASS, Patrick
– A Journal of the Voyages & Travels of a Corps of Discovery, under the Command of Capt. Lewis & Capt. Clarke ... from the Mouth of the River Missouri through the Interior Parts of North America to the Pacific Ocean ... Pittsb., 1807. *1st. Edn.* 12mo. Sm. tape repair to fore-edge of hf.-title, moderate foxing, fore-edge of text trimmed with text on a few pp. slightly affected, cont. ink inscr. at front blank, cont. marb. bds., recased with later cf. backstrip. (HA. Feb.24; 339) $650
– – **Anr. Edn.** L., 1808. *1st. Engl. Edn.* 4 cont. grey wash drawings of 5 animal subjects bnd. in, all by the same hand, 1 sigd. 'Ireton', 3 with pen & ink captions, a few margin sketches of animals & some notes, MS. contents & game list on 1 lf. bnd. at end, without advt. lf., near-cont. hf. mor. gt. by J. Robinson of Whitehaven, with his ticket; Frederick Straker bkplt., the Rt. Hon. Visc. Eccles copy. [Sabin 26741] (CNY. Nov.18; 119) $2,800
– – **Anr. Copy.** 2 pp. advts. at end, slightly browned,

GASS, Patrick -*Contd.*

mod. qtr. cf.; the Rt. Hon. Visc. Eccles copy, unc. [Sabin 26741] (CNY. Nov.18; 120) $400

GASSENDI, Pierre
- **Institutio Astronomica.** L., 1675. *5th. Edn.* Sm. 8vo. Woodcuts, some full-p., old cf., spine worn. [Wing G292] (SG. Apr.26; 88) $320
- **Tychonis Brahei ... Vita ... Accessit Nicolai Copernici ... The Hague, 1655. *2nd. Edn.* 3 pts. in 1 vol. General title, separate title to each pt., engraved ports., 2 woodcut diagrams, some foxing, owner's inscr. on general title, old vell. bds., gt. arms of the Signet, warped & soiled. (SPB. May 17; 616) $450
- **The Vanity of Judiciary Astrology.** 1659. Edge of title-p. strengthened, old cf., rebkd. & worn. (BS. Nov.16; 27) £70

GASSER, A.P.
[-] **Historiarum et Chronicorum Mundi Epitomes Libellus.** Venice, 1533. Sm. 8vo. Slightly cropped, old vell. (SG. Jan.19; 176) $300

GASTALDI, Girolamo
See— CURLO, Girolamo—GASTALDI, Girolamo

GASTINEAU, Henry
- **Wales Illustrated.** Ca. 1832. 2 pts. in 1. vd. 4to. 2 engraved titles, 208 engrs. on 104 sheets, lacks 1 title, blind-stpd. cf., rubbed, as a coll. of plts., w.a.f. (P. Jul.5; 272) £120
- **Wales Illustrated; South Wales Illustrated.** L., 1830. 2 pts. in 1 vol. 4to. L.P., engraved titles with vigs., 112 plts., lightly spotted, some plts. stained, cont. hf. roan, slightly worn. (S. Mar.6; 247)
Chesters. £150

GASTINEAU, Henri
See— WRIGHT, Thomas—GASTINEAU, Henri

GASTRELL, Francis
- **The Certainty of the Christian Revalation, & the Necessity of Believing it, Established.** 1699. *1st. Edn.* Cont. cf., Harley arms gt. on covers, spine gt., rebkd., orig. spine preserved; pres. inscr. on title-p., bkplt. & gt. sig. of Robert Harley stpd. on verso of title. [Wing G301] (BBA. Jun.14; 67)
Quaritch. £85

GAUDIOL, Jose
- **Goya Biography, Analytical Study & Catalogue of his Paintings.** N.Y., n.d. 4 vols. 4to. Orig. cl. (BBA. Sep.8; 141) *Leicester Art Books.* £60

GAUGER, Nicolas
- **La Mechanique du Feu.** Amst., 1714. *2nd. Edn.* Cont. leath. gt., spine slightly bumped. (R. Apr.4; 1602) DM 550

GAUGUIN, Paul
- **Letters to Ambroise Vollard & André Fontaines.** Ed.:– John Rewald. San Franc., Grabhorn Pr., 1943. *(250).* Fo. Linen-bkd. paper bds. (LH. Sep.25; 369) $240
- – **Anr. Copy.** Fo. Ills. on Chinese H.M.P., hf. linen & decor. bds., 1 corner slightly bumped. (CBA. Nov.19; 221) $125
- **Noa Noa (Voyage de Tahiti).** [München. 1926]. Fo. Orig. linen, orig. pict. wraps. (GB. Nov.5; 2501) DM 3,000
- – **Anr. Copy.** 4to. Without title & printer's mark, orig. linen. (H. Nov.24; 1516) DM 2,700

GAULE, John
- **Pys-mantia. The Mag-astro-mancer, or the magicall-astrological-diviner posed, & puzzled.** 1652. *1st. Edn.* 4to. Unpaginated sigs. i., k. & l. present, mod. hf. cf. [Wing G377] (BBA. Jan.19; 147) *Quaritch.* £110

GAULTIER, L'Abbé Aloysius Edouard Camille
- **A Complete Course of Geography.** 1800. Fo. 13 partly cold. maps, hf. cf., worn. (P. Dec.8; 406)
McNutty. £50

GAULTIER, Bon
- **The Book of Ballads.** Ill.:– Crowquill & others. L., n.d. 4to. engraved frontis., chromo-litho. title, text ills., red mor., jnts. reprd., double fore-e.pntg., as a fore-e.pntg., w.a.f. (SPB. May 17; 733) $750

GAURINI, Gaurino
- **Architettura Civile ... Opera Postuma.** Ed.:– Vittone. Ill.:– G. Abbati, & Ioan Fayneau, Gaurini & others. Turin, 1737. *1st. Compl. Edn.* Fo. Engraved frontis., 79 plts., a few discold., cont. mott. cf., spine gt., covers slightly scuffed; bkplt. of A.A. Palisot. (C. Dec.9; 60) *Weinreb.* £1,500

GAUSS, Carl Friedrich
- **Disquisitiones Generales circa Superficies Curvas.** Göttingen, 1828. *1st. Edn.* 4to. Slight spotting on a few pp., remains of wraps. along inner hinges of title & last lf., mod. cl.; Dr. G. Holzmüller libry stp., his (?) MS. notes laid in, Ludwig Illo Peters bkplt., Stanitz coll. (SPB. Apr.25; 189) $650
- **Intensitas Vis Magneticae Terrestris ad Mensuram Absolutam Revocata.** Göttingen, 1833. *1st. Separate Edn.* Title stpd. ir; lr. outer corner, slightly foxed, mod. leath., unc. (R. Oct.12; 1673) DM 750

GAUTIER, Léon
- **La Chevalerie.** Paris, 1884. 4to. Mor., decor., by Pagnant. (HD. Apr.11; 26) Frs. 2,100

GAUTIER, Théophile
- **L'Eldorado ou Fortunio ...** Ill.:– Millius & M. Avril. Paris, 1880. *Nominative Edn., (115) with ills. in 2 states.* Hf. mor., corners, by Yseux, unc., wrap. & spine preserved. (HD. May 4; 281)
Frs. 1,050
- **Emaux et Camées.** Preface:– M. du Camp. Ill.:– G. Fraipont. Paris, 1887. *De Luxe Edn. (200) numbered & monogrammed.* Ills. in 2 states, orig. aqua. on hf-title, red mor., gt. decor., gold-tooled outer dentelle, gt. decor. spine, decor. inner dentelle, sigd. by Chambolle-Duru. (D. Nov.24; 2272) DM 1,600
- **Fortunio.** Ill.:– A. Lunois. Paris, 1898. *(600).* 4to. On vélin du Marais, bradel hf. mor., corners, by Carayon, mosaic spine, unc., wraps. & spines preserved. (HD. May 4; 283) Frs. 2,400
- – **Anr. Edn.** Ill.:– P.E. Becat. 1956. *(19) with orig. copper engr., 2 orig. drawings, 2 suites, 2 proofs on silk, 1 refused engr. in 2 states.* 4to. Leaves, box. (HD. Jul.6; 108) Frs. 1,350
- **Jean et Jeannette.** Preface:– Léo Claretie. Ill.:– Ad. Lalauze. Paris, 1894. *On Japan.* Engrs. in 3 state, including pure etching & state with remarks, cont. lavallière mor., gt. & mosaic decor. on upr. cover, inner dentelle, wtrd. silk end-papers, wrap. & spine preserved, by Ch. Meunier. (HD. Feb.17; 74) Frs. 5,000
- – **Anr. Edn.** Ill.:– A. Lalauze. Paris, Société des Beaux Arts, ca. 1900. *Edn. des Deux Mondes. (20) lettered on Japan vell.* 4to. Plts. & text engrs. in 3 states (plain, India-proof & cold.), all xcepting 1 state of the text engrs.) with vig. remarque, orig. lev. gt., cold. mor. inlays, dentelles elab. gt.-decor., lev. doubls., upr. doubl. with inlaid oval hand-cold. engraved vig. on vell., moire grosgrain cl. liners, partly unc. (SG. Feb.16; 285) $1,000
- **King Candaules.** Ill.:– Paul Avril. Paris, Société des Beaux Arts, ca. 1900. *Edn. des Deux Mondes. (20) lettered on Japan vell.* 4to. Plts. & text engrs. in 3 states (plain, India-proof & cold.), all (excepting 1 state of the text engrs.) with vig. remarque, orig. lev. gt., cold. mor. inlays, dentelles elab. gt.-decor., lev. doubls., upr. doubl. with inlaid oval hand-cold. engraved vig. on vell., moire grosgrain cl. liners, partly unc. (SG. Feb.16; 286) $900
- **A Night of Cleopatra.** Ill.:– Paul Avril. Paris, Société des Beaux Arts, ca. 1900. *Edn. des Deux Mondes. (20) lettered on Japan vell.* 4to. Plts. & text engrs. in 3 states (plain, India-proof & cold.), all (excepting 1 state of the text engrs.) with vig. remarque, orig. lev. gt., cold. mor. inlays, dentelles elab. gt.-decor., lev. doubls., upr. doubl. with inlaid oval hand-cold. engraved vig. on vell., moire grosgrain cl. liners, partly unc. (SG. Feb.16; 287) $1,000
- **Oeuvres Diverses.** Paris, n.d. 30 vols. 12mo. Cont. hf. red mor., corners. (HD. Apr.11; 27) Frs. 5,000
- **Poésies.** Paris, 1830. *Orig. Edn.* 12mo. Some stains & foxing, sewed, decor. red hf. mor. folder, s.-c.; Victor Hugo's copy, dedication on wrap. (HD. Jun.13; 43) Frs. 1,300
- **Le Roman de la Momie.** Ill.:– Alex Lunois, engraved by Leon Boisson. Paris, 1901. *(30) on Japon, with ills. in 3 states.* 4to. Mor. gt. by

Carayon, mosaic decor., silk end-ll., wraps. preserved, s.-c. (HD. Nov.17; 126) Frs. 3,300

GAUTIER, Théophile de (Text)
See— FRANÇAIS PEINTS PAR EUX-MEMES

GAUTROT, Jean-Edouard
See— BLAIZOT, Claude & Gautrot, Jean-Edouard

GAVARD, Charles
- **Collection des Principales Vues de Paris.** Paris, ca. 1840. Ob. fo. 24 (of 31) aquatints, minimal soiling, cont. hf. linen, gold-tooled, worn. (HK. Nov.8; 1004) DM 420

GAVARNI, Paul (i.e. Guillaume-Sulpice Chevalier)
- **La Correctionnelle.** Paris, 1840. 100 pts. in 1 vol. 4to. Mod. bradel hf. vell., corners, unc., wrap. preserved. (HD. May 4; 284) Frs. 2,300
- – **Anr. Copy.** 4to. 100 orig. lithos. in 1st. printing, hf. roan, unc. (HD. Jan.30; 57) Frs. 1,900
- **Le Diable à Paris.** Paris, 1845. (*With:*) – **Paris et les Parisiens.** Paris, 1846. Together 2 vols. Lge. 8vo. Qtr. mor., worn. (SG. Dec.15; 147) $125
- **Les Etudians de Paris.** Paris, [1840]. 4to. Cont. buckram. (HD. Dec.1; 71) Frs. 2,900
- **Impression de Menage.** Paris, [1870?]. 4to. 30 lithos., sewed. (CR. Jun.6; 168) Lire 320,000
[-] **Perles et Parures; Les Joyaux; Les Parures.** Text:– J. Mary. Ill.:– Gavarni, engraved by Geoffroy. Paris, Leipzig, [1850]. *Orig. Edn. 1st. Printing.* 2 vols. Lge. 8vo. Repeated frontis., 31 plts., all on mntd. china, plts. in 2 states including cold. with margins cut in dentelles, late 19th. C. Bradel hf. mor., corners, unc., wraps. & spines. (HD. Mar.27; 15) Frs. 5,000
- **Les Parures. Fantaisies.—Les Perles. Fantaisie.** Text:– Méry. Ill.:– Ch. Geoffroy for Gavarni. Paris, Leipzig, [1850]. *Orig. Edn. 1st. Printing.* 2 vols. Lge. 8vo. Hf. red chagrin. (HD. Jan.30; 58) Frs. 1,100
- **Paris.** [Paris], ca. 1839. Lge. 4to. 6 orig. lithos. in 1st. printing, hf. buckram, corners; Henri Beraldi ex-libris. (HD. Jun.22; 26) Frs. 2,000

GAVIN, Charles Murray
- **Royal Yachts.** 1932. *(1000) numbered.* 4to. Orig. mor. gt., unc. (SKC. Nov.18; 1929) £75
- – **Anr. Copy.** 4to. Mor. gt., unc. (SKC. Sep.9; 2021) £65
- – **Anr. Copy.** Lge. 4to. Hf.-title, gt.-pict. mor., partly unc.; inscr. to 'F.D.R. from H.B.R., Jul. '33'. (SG. Mar.15; 313) $175

GAY, John
- **Achilles. An Opera.** L., 1733. *1st. Edn.* Page of advts., 19th. C. pol. cf., spine gt. (BBA. May 3; 192) *Traylen.* £85
- **The Beggar's Opera.** L., 1728. *1st. Edn. 2nd. Iss., with the 3 lines of music on p. 53.* 16 pp. of engraved music at end, disbnd. (S. Dec.13; 364)
Hannas. £180
- – **Anr. Edn.** L., 1728. *2nd. Edn.* Lacks? hf.-title, mod. three-qtr. leath., some wear. (RO. Dec.11; 115) $140
- – **Anr. Edn.** 1728. 8 ll. engraved music, some lr. margins shaved, title slightly soiled, mod. cf., spine gt.; Henry Yates Thompson bookplt. (CSK. May 18; 157) £200
- **The Distress'd Wife. A Comedy.** L., 1743. *1st. Edn.* Variant advt. slip tipped-in on verso of hf.-title, hf.-title & verso of last lf. a little discold., recent mor.-bkd. bds. (BBA. May 3; 193)
Ximenes. £65
- **Fables.** 1727-38. *1st. Edn.* 2 pts. in 1 vol. 4to. Some light spotting, cont. cf. (CSK. Aug.19; 39) £180
- – **Anr. Copy.** 2 vols. 4to. L.P., 51 engraved headpieces in vol.1, engraved frontis. & 16 engraved plts. in vol.2, browning & spotting, worming of lr. margins of vol.2, cont. cf., not quite unif., rebkd., spines gt. (SPB. May 16; 61) $250
- – **Anr. Edn.** Ill.:– William Blake & others. L., 1793. *[1st. Edn.].* 2 vols. in 1. Title slightly cropped affecting engraved surface, hf. cf. (S. Oct.11; 450)
Vine. £80
- – **Anr. Copy.** 2 vols. in 1. Titles trimmed, bdg. not stated, but defect. (BS. May 2; 52) £50
- – **Anr. Copy.** 2 vols. in 1. 69 (of 70) engrs., plts. offset onto facing p., contents darkening & lightly

foxed, armorial tree cf., rebkd. with portion of spine leath. laid on, scuffed. (CBA. Aug.21; 54) $425
– – **Anr. Edn.** Ill.:– William Blake & others. L., '1793' [i.e. 1811]. 2 vols. Plts., some spotting of 1st. few pp. & endpapers, engraved title margins trimmed, cont. tree cf., inscr. on endpaper. (SPB. May 16; 62) $175
– **The Fan. A Poem. In Three Books.** L., 1714. [1713]. *1st. Edn.* Fo. Upr. margin of a few ll. slightly discold., disbnd. (BBA. May 3; 187)   *Hannas.* £380
– **The Rehearsal at Goatham.** L., 1754. Disbnd. (BBA. May 3; 194)   *Ximenes.* £60
– **The Shepherd's Week. In Six Pastorals.** Ill.:– L. du Guernier. L., 1714. *1st. Edn. L.P. Iss.* Cont. cf. gt., upr. jnt. a little worn; pres. copy, inscr., 'from the author'; bkplt. of Arthur a. Haughton. (BBA. May 3; 188)   *Maggs.* £700
– **Trivia; or, The Art of Walking the Streets of London.** L., [1716]. *1st. Edn. Iss. on fine paper.* Mott. cf. gt. extra, by Riviere, gt. dentelles. (SG. Nov.3; 83) $550
– – **Anr. Edn.** L., [1716]. *1st. Edn. Thick Paper Iss.* Some spotting, cont. cf., double-ruled gt. spine, worn; Frederic Dannay copy. (CNY. Dec.16; 150) $350
– **Two Epistles.** L., [1715 or 1720?]. *1st. Edn.* 4pp. advts., later wraps. (BBA. May 3; 190)   *Ximenes.* £270
– **The Wife of Bath. A Comedy.** L., 1730. Some light foxing, cont. cf., upr. hinge slightly rubbed. (BBA. May 3; 191)   *Ximenes.* £65

GAY, Jules
[–] **Bibliographie des Ouvrages Relatifs à l'Amour ...** Turin [etc.], 1871-73. *3rd. Edn.* 6 vols. Hf.-titles, cont. mor.-bkd. bds.; bkplt. of David Garnett. (BBA. Mar.21; 32)   *Bondy.* £90
– **Les Chats ...** Paris & Bruxelles, 1866. 12mo. Unique(?) copy on yellow vell. paper, orig. drawing & 2 orig. watercolours sigd. by H. Thirioz on title & hf.-title of 1st. pt., mor. gt. by R. Kieffer, richly decor., laquer by Madame Jerebtsoff, doubls., silk end-papers, box. (HD. Nov.29; 92) Frs. 6,500

GAY, Walter
– **Paintings of French Interiors.** Ed.:– Albert Gallatin. Ill.:– Bruce Rogers (design & decor.). N.Y., 1920. *(950).* Fo. 50 plts., cl-bkd. bds., spine ends & tips worn. (SG. Aug.25; 159) $120

GAY DE VERNON, Joseph
[–] **A Treatise on the Science of War & Fortification,.** Trans.:– J.M. O'Connor. N.Y., 1817. *1st Edn. in Engl.* 2 vols. in 1, plus atlas. 8vo & 4to. 31 folding maps & plans, old hf. cf., spine reprd. (SG. Sep.22; 149) $150

GAZETTE DU BON TON
Ed.:– Lucien Vogel. Ill.:– Lepape, Brissaud, Barbier & others. Paris, 1913. Vol. 2 nos. 7-12 only. 56 cold. plts. only, some hand-finished, lacks 4 plts. in iss. ll, cold. ills., cont. hf. mor., lightly rubbed. (CSK. Mar.23; 126)   £550
– **Le Bon Ton d'Après-Guerre ... Collection de 200 Planches en Couleurs de George Barbier, Benito ... Extraites des Années 1920 à 1922 de la Gazette du Bon-Ton.** Ill.:– Barbier, Benito, Drian & others. Paris, [1920-22]. 2 vols. 195 cold. plts. only, some hand-finished, orig. bds., spines & jnts. rubbed. (CSK. Mar.23; 127)   £1,500

GAZETTE NATIONALE ou le Moniteur Universal [1789-1790]. Nos. 1-38 & 1-181b. Lge. fo. No bdg. stated. (DS. Apr.27; 2109)   Pts. 110,000

GAZOLA, Giovambattista
– **Ittiolitologia Veronese del Museo Bozziano ... e di Altri Gabinetti di Fossili Veronesi.** Verona, 1796. 2 vols., including plt. vol. 4to. 76 engraved plts., Vol. 1 title soiled, cont. wraps., vol. 1 disbnd., unc. (TA. Nov.17; 340)   £100

GEBAUER, Dr. August (Pseud.)
See– BAUER, A. 'Dr. August Gebauer'

GEBER [Jabir ibn Hayyan]
– **De Alchimia Libri Tres.** Strassburg, 10 Mar. 1529. *1st. Edn.* Sm. fo. Title lf. with bkd. margin slit, slight stains, some soiling, especially title lf., cont leath., blind-tooled, rubbed, spine defect. (D. Nov.23; 471)   DM 4,800

GEBHARDT, V.
– **Los Dioses de Grecia y Roma.** Barcelona, 1880. 2 vols. Lge. Fo. Publishers stpd. cl. (DS. Mar.23; 2320)   Pts. 26,000

GEBHART, Emile
– **Cloches de Noël et de Pâques.** Ill.:– A. Mucha. Paris, 1900. *(252) numbered.* 4to. Floral borders hand-cold., slightly spotted, orig. pict. wraps., unc. (S. Nov.21; 111)   *Desk.* £780
– **Sandro Botticelli et son Epoque.** Paris, 1907. *(50) on papier Japon, with additional suite of plts.* Fo. Red mor., hinges reprd. (SPB. Nov.30; 88) $125

GEDIK, Simon
[–] **Disputatio Perjucunda, qua Anonymus Probare Nititur, Mulieres Homines Non Esse; cui opposita est, Simonis Gedicci Defensio Sexus Muliebris.** Paris, 1693. *Late Edn.* Sm. 12mo. Later bds. (SG. Mar.22; 136) $110

GEDIKE, F.
See– BERLINISCHE MONATSCHRIFT

GEE, Ernest R.
– **Early American Sporting Books, 1734 to 1844.** Derrydale Pr., 1928. *(500).* Lge. 8vo. Qtr. cl., unopened. (SG. Mar.15; 218) $150

GEFFROY, Gustave
– **Les Bateaux de Paris.** Ill.:– E. Béjot & Ch. Huard, J. Beltrand (wood engrs.). Paris, 1903. *(25) on japan, with separate printing.* 4to. Cont. red mot., decor., inner fillet, wrap. preserved, s.-c., by Carayon. (HD. Feb.17; 75)   Frs. 4,000

GEIB, Karl
– **Malerische Wanderungen am Rhein von Constanz bis Cöln, nebst Ausflügen ...** Karlsruhe, 1838. *1st. Edn.* 3 pts. in 1 vol. 96 steel engraved plts., 1 sub-title with defect. & light stp., some slight browning, cont. hf. leath. gt., rubbed. (HT. May 10; 2963)   DM 3,000
– – **Anr. Copy.** 3 vols. in 1. Vol. II lacks 1 plt., some slight foxing or light browning, cont. hf. leath., slightly worn. (H. Nov.23; 411)   DM 2,400
– **Schilderachtige Wandelingen aan de Boorden van het Meer van Constanz ...** Amst., 1839. 2 vols. Sm. 8vo. 96 steel engrs., some foxing, mainly on text ll., hf. mor. (B. Oct.4; 670)   Fls. 2,200

GEIGER, Benno
– **I Disegni del Magnasco.** Padova, 1945. *Ltd. Iss.* Lge. 4to. Bds., loose. (SI. Dec.15; 203)   Lire 320,000

GEIGER, W.
– **Corrida de Toros.** München, 1923. *(125) on Van Gelder.* 4to. All etchings sigd. by artist, 21 etchings, 2 ll. with sm. brown mark, loose in orig. linen portfo., spine faded. (H. May 23; 1228) DM 1,700
– **Die Kreuzigung.** Berlin, 1911. *(50) numbered & sigd. by artist. (10) ptd. on Japon before the plts. were steel-faced.* 4to. 40 etched plts., orig. hf. pig, spine torn, unc. (S. Nov.21; 79)   *Erasmus.* £100
– **Stierkampf. 20 Radiering** (binder's title). Ca. 1925. *Ltd. Edn.* Lge. fo. All etchings sigd. by artist, lightly browned, some foxing in margins, orig. linen portfo., slightly spotted. (H. May 23; 1229)   DM 2,000

GEIKIE, Walter
– **Etchings Illustrative of Scottish Character & Scenery ...** Edinb., 1885. *(366) numbered.* 4to. Engraved proof plts., orig. cl. gt., unc. (PD. Apr.18; 201)   £72

GEILER V. KAISERSBERG, J.
– **Das Buch d[er] Sünden des Munds ...** Ill.:– D. Hopfer, H. Baldung Grien, & others. Strassburg, 27. I - 6. III. 1518. *1st. Edn.* 2 pts. in 1 vol. Fo. Minimal worming & soiling, vell. (HK. Nov.8; 193)   DM 8,000
– **Peregrinus—Navicula Penitentiae.** Ed.:– J. Ottherus. Strassburg, 1513 & May 1512. 2 works in 1 vol. 4to. Dedication letters to Johannes Brisgoicus & G. Ruysch, cont. owners mark on 1st. title, 2nd title with long old MS. entry, 1st. sig. re-hinged, 1 lf. in each work with margin or corner tear, cont. blind-tooled pig over wood bds., 2 brass clasps. (R. Apr.3; 44)   DM 520

GEISBERG, Max
– **Der Buchholzschnitt im 16. Jahrhundert.** Berlin, 1937. *(50) numbered.* Fo. Some guards spotted & defect., some ptd. trials with slight loss. 1 lf. text & 19 (of 100) orig. ll. under guards, without box. (GB. May 3; 889)   DM 600

GEISENDORF DES GOUTTES
– **Les Prisonniers de Guerre sous le Premier Empire.** Genève & Paris, 1932-37. 2 vols. Hf. chagrin, wraps. (HD. Jan.27; 40)   Frs. 1,500

GEISER, Bernhard
– **Picasso. Peintre-graveur. Cat. illustré de l'oeuvre gravé et lithographié 1899-1931. Cat. Raisonné de l'oeuvre Gravé et des Monotypes.** Bern, 1955-68. *Vol. 1: (900). (100) not for sale; Vol. 2: (2000). (50) not for sale.* 2 vols. Fo. Orig. wraps. (HK. Nov.11; 3856)   DM 800

GEISLER, Maria
[–] **Collection de Vues des Principaux Palais, Eglises, Batimens Publics ... Wien.** Wien, [1812]. 66 (of 100) numbered cold. copper engrs. on 64 plts., German & Fr. captions, lacks 8 plts., some light soiling, cont. hf. leath. gt., rubbed. (HK. Nov.9; 1173)   DM 2,000

GEISSLER, G.H.
See– GRUBER, J.C. & Geissler, G.H.

GEISSLER, J.G.
– **Der Uhrmacher oder Lehrbegriff der Uhrmacherkunst.** Leipzig, 1796-99. Pts. 7-10 (of 10) in 1 vol. Cont. hf. leath. gt. (HK May 15, 546)   DM 750

GELDNER, Ferdinand
– **Bucheinbände aus Elf Jahrhunderten.** Munich, 1958. Fo. Orig. buckram-bkd. bds.; H.M. Nixon coll., with his sig. & acquisition note on fly-lf., & some MS. notes. (BBA. Oct.6; 50)   *Quaritch.* £90

GELEE, Claude
See– CLAUDE LE LORRAIN [i.e. Claude Gelée]

GELENIUS, Aegidius
– **Vindex Libertatis Ecclesiasticae et Martyr S. Engelbertus Archiepiscopus Coloniensis ...** Köln, 1633. *1st. Edn.* 1 sig. unptd., some heavy browning & spotting. (*Bound with:*) – **Preciosa Hierotheca Duodecim Unionibus Coloniensis Historiae exornata** Köln, 1634. *1st. Edn.* Light browning & spotting. Together 2 works in 1 vol. Sm. 4to. Vell., restored, end-papers renewed. (V. Sep.30; 2937)   DM 1,100

GELIOT, L.
– **La Vraye et Parfaite Science des Armoires ... augmenté de Nombre de Termes ... par Pierre Palliot.** Dijon, Paris, 1664. Fo. MS. name on title, several ll. reprd., foxing, cont. vell. gt., spine decor. (HD. Jun.26; 15)   Frs. 9,500

GELIS-DIDOT, P.
– **Le Peinture Décorative en France du XVIe au XVIIIe Siècle.** Paris, ca. 1895. Tall fo. 60 chromolitho, plts., text engrs., each plt. liby.-stpd. on blank verso, loose in cl. folder, linen ties. (SG. May 3; 175) $350

GELL, Sir William & Gandy, John P.
– **Pompeiana: the Topography, Edifices, & Ornaments of Pompeii.** 1817-19. *1st. Edn.* 4to. Cont. russ., gt. decor., w.a.f.; from liby. of Luttrellstown Castle. (C. Sep.28; 1738)   £130

GELLERT, Christian Furchtegott
– **Fabeln.** Ill.:– R. Seewald. Berlin, 1920. *(125) numbered, with 1 woodcut sigd. by artist.* Fo. Orig. hf. linen, cold. woodcut on upr. cover, lightly soiled. (HK. Nov.11; 3967)   DM 900
– – **Anr. Copy.** Lge. 4to. Some foxing, owner's note on end-paper, orig. hf. leath., sm. cover vig., soiled, corners bumped & spine defect. (H. Nov.24; 2041)   DM 580

GELLERT, Leon
– **The Isle of San: A Phantasy ...** Ill.:– Norman Lindsay. Sydney, 1919. *(100) numbered & sigd. for sale.* Fo. Qtr. imitation vell., a little marked. (KH. Nov.8; 173a)   Aus. $2,500

GELLIUS, Aulus
- Noctes Atticae. Venice, B. Locatellus for Octavianus Scotus, 13 Nov. 1494. Fo. Vell.; the Walter Goldwater copy. [BMC V, 444; Goff G-125; H. 7525] (SG. Dec.1; 154) $750

GEM (THE): A Christmas & New Year's Present for 1840.— ... for 1842
Phila., [1839; 1841]. *1st. Iss.'s.* 2 vols. (all publd. under this title). Sm. 12mo. Orig. blind-stpd. roan & gt.-ornamental cf., edges rubbed on both vols., head of jnt. torn on 2nd. vol.; from liby. of F.D. Roosevelt, 1st. inscr. & 2nd. sigd. by him, 2nd. also inscr. 'For F.D. from M.A.L., Dec. 25, 1929'. (SG. Mar.15; 28) $175

GEMINIANI, Francesco
- The Art of Playing on the Violin ... Opera IX ... L., 1751. *1st. Edn.* Fo. Overall browning, some foxing, cont. marb. bds., worn, spine brkn., upr. cover detchd. (S. Nov.17; 105)   *Baron.* £540

GEMINUS, Thomas
- Compediosa Totius Anatomie Delineato. Trans.:– Nicholas Udall. 1559. *3rd. Iss. of Engl. version.* Fo. Engraved title & 21 engraved plts. only (of 40), a few stained, lacks lf. before title & F, later cf., rebkd. & reprd. (BBA. Jul.27; 20)   *Rix.* £310

GEMMA, Cornelius
- De Arte Cyclognomica. Antw., 1569. *1st. Edn.* 3 pts. in 1 vol. 4to. Privilege/errata lf. at end, dedication to Frederick of Toledo called for by Ruelens lacking (never bnd. in?), cont. blind-stpd. pig, with histor. rolls & other tools, spine stained at bottom, hinge brkn. (SG. Oct.27; 123) $140
- De Naturae Divinis Characterismis. Ill.:– Ant. Van Leest & G. Janssen van Kempen. Antw., 1575. 2 vols. in 1. 12mo. Lacks Index & errata at end of vol., cont. vell. (HD. Mar.14; 33)   Frs. 7,000

GEMS OF ANCIENT ART, or Select Specimens from the Old Masters
1827. 4to. Engraved aquatint plts., all on India paper, mntd., margins lightly spotted, cont. hf. mor., soiled. (CSK. Apr.27; 12)   £60

GEMS OF SCENERY FROM PICTURESQUE EUROPE
L., 1884. *(300) numbered on India paper.* Fo. 50 engraved plts. on India paper, 1 lf. of text loose, orig. hf. roan, worn. (BBA. Dec.15; 70)   *Erlini.* £160

GENAUER, Emily
- Rufino Tamayo. N.Y., ca. 1974. Lge. ob. 4to. Sigd. by artist, 146 plts., bdg. not stated, light wear to d.-w. (CBA. Jan.29; 446) $130

GENEALOGISCHE EN HERALDISCHE BLADEN
Ed.:– E.B.F.F. Wittert v. Hoogland. ['s-Gravenhage], 1906-15. 10 vols. Orig. cl., 1 spine reprd. (VS. Dec.8; 718)   Fls. 500

GENEALOGISCHES HANDBUCH der Fürstlichen Häuser
Ed.:– H.F. v. Ehrenkrook. Glücksburg, 1951-75. Ed. 1-42, 44, 45 & 50. Sm. 8vo. Orig. cl. (VS. Dec.8; 727)   Fls. 825

GENERAL STUD BOOK, The
1858-1957. Vols. 1-16 & 18-38, in 41 vols. Mott. cf. gt., w.a.f. (P. Dec.8; 203)   *Way.* £550

GENET, Edmond Charles
- Memorial on the Upward Forces of Fluids & their Applicability to Several Arts, Sciences & Public Improvements ... Albany, 1825. *1st. Edn.* Spotting, margin staining, orig. ptd. bds., some chipping of lr. spine; John P. Bausman Jr. bkplt., Stanitz coll. (SPB. Apr.25; 190) $1,500
- – Anr. Copy. Tall 8vo. Orig. ptd. bds., lightly soiled, cl. s.-c.; pres. copy, inscr. by author's wife on front free end-paper. (SG. Mar.22; 137) $700

GENET, Jean
- Querelle de Brest. Ill.:– Jean Cocteau. N.p., [1947]. *Orig. Edn., (525) on vell.* Leaves, box. (HD. May 11; 152)   Frs. 2,600

GENEVOIX, Maurice
- Raboliot. Ill.:– Jean Commère. Paris, 1974. *(275). (4) on japan super nacré, sigd. by author & artist.* Fo. Compl. suites on japan super nacré & on Arches sigd. by artist, lge. orig. aqua sigd., orig. full-p. wash ill. sigd. opposite title, 2 sketches sigd., 1 orig., other engraved, leaves wrap., publishers velours box. (HD. Dec.16; 126)   Frs. 4,500

GENIUS. Zeitschrift für Alte und Werdende Kunst.
Trans.:– Hans Mardersteig. Ill.:– Heckel, M. Kaus, Masereel, Rouveyre & others. München, 1912-21. 1st. book, years II & III. 4to. 10 orig. ills., orig. wraps. & orig. hf. vell., year II spotted. (GB. May 5; 2558)   DM 1,600
- – Anr. Edn. Ed.:– G. Heise, H. Mardersteig & K. Pinthus. Ill.:– K. Caspar, I. Epper, H. Nauen, F. Marc, K. Schmidt-Rottlof &. R. Seewald. München, 1919. Yr. 1 in 2 pts. Lge. 4to. Orig. sewed. (D. Nov.24; 3031)   DM 680
- – Anr. Edn. Munich, 1919-21. 6 vols. (all publd.). 4to. Orig. wraps. (S. Oct.4; 154)   *Hamery.* £440
- – Anr. Copy. 3 yrs (all publd.) in 6 vols. Lge. 4to. 8 woodcuts., 7 lithos., 1 etching, many partly cold. plts. & ills., orig. wraps., 1 wrap loose, slightly bumped, spine browned. (HK. May 17; 2769)   DM 2,400
- – Anr. Copy. 3 vols. (All publd.). Fo. 16 orig. ills., lacks 2 mntd. plts., minimal wear. orig. hf. vell., some light rubbing, unc. (HT. May 9; 1809)   DM 1,605
- – Anr. Edn. Ed.:– C.G. Heise & H. Madersteig. Ill.:– E. Heckel, M. Kaus, F. Masereel. A. Rouveyre & others. [München, 1920-21]. Fo. 10 orig. ills, orig. linen, loose, some wear. (HK. Nov.11; 3562)   DM 850

GENLIS, Stephanie Felicite Ducrest, Comtesse de
- Memoirs. L., 1825-26. 8 vols. 12mo. Extra-ill. with 86 engraved ports. & views (30 cold.), mor., gt.-decor., gt. spines in 6 compartments, by Bayntun, w.a.f. (CNY. Dec.17; 561) $550
- Théâtre à l'Usage des Jeunes Personnes. Paris, 1779-80. *1st. Edn.* 4 vols. 12mo. Cont. cf.-bkd. bds. unc., slightly rubbed; van Veen coll. (S. Feb.28; 64)   £80
- – Anr. Edn. Paris & Maestecht, 1780. 4 vols. 12mo. Hf.-titles, last 3 approbation pp. in Vol.1, few ll. slightly soiled, cont. cf., rebkd. with gt. spines. (BBA. Mar.21; 28)   *Bondy.* £60
- – Anr. Edn. Paris, 1781. *1st. III. Edn.?.* 4 vols. 12mo. Cont. cf.-bkd. bds., unc., slightly rubbed; van Veen coll. (S. Feb.28; 65)   £100

GENOA
- Della Storia di Genova dall Trattato di Worms fino alla Pace d'Aquisgrana. Leida, 1750. 4to. Cont. vell. (HD. Oct.21; 90)   Frs. 2,300

GENOUILLAC, H. Gourdon de
- Paris à Travers Les Siècles. Paris, 1879-82. 5 vols. 4to. Over 300 full-p. & text black-&-white engrs., & 112 full-p. hand-cold. engrs., lge. folded hand-cold. engraved street map of New Paris, some foxing or few spots, some pp. & plts. lightly chipped at edges, orig. mor. & marb. bds., raised bands, edges moderately worn with some scuffing to bds., slight remnants of spine stickers, lge. bkplts. at front pastedowns. (HA. May 4; 257) $170

GENT, K. van
[-] Het Beginsel en Voortganck der Geschillen onder de Gene die Doops-Gesinden genoemt worden. Amst., 1658. 4to. Loose, mod. vell. (VG. Sep.14; 1324)   Fls. 480

GENTHE, Arnold
- Old Chinatown, A Book of Pictures. Intro. & Commentary:– Will Irwin. N.Y., 1913. Cl. gt., laid in 3 Christmas greetings from Genthe, each with photo from book, & 2 sm. silverprint photos, each sigd. by Genthe. (PNY. Jun.6; 492) $270

GENTIL, M. le
- Nouveau Voyage autour du Monde. Amst., 1728. 3 vols. in 2. Lacks title to Vol. 3, cont. spr. cf., gt.-decor. spines. (TA. Sep.15; 109)   £95
- – Anr. Copy. 3 vols. in 2. Lacks title to Vol. 3, cont. spr. cf., gt.-decor. spines. (TA. Oct.20; 44)   £90

GENTILLET, Innocent
[-] Discours sur les Moyens de bien gouverner et maintenir en Bonne Paix un Royaume, contre Nicolas Machiavel, Florentin. N.p., 1579. *3rd. Edn.* 12mo. Early 18th. C. roan, spine decor. (HD. Mar.21; 33)   Frs. 1,000
- Examen: das ist, Ergründunge und Widerlegunge des Tridentinischen Conciliums. Trans.:– Nic. Höniger. Basel, 1587. *1st. German Edn.* 1st. & last ll. lightly wormed cont. limp vell., lightly soiled. (R. Oct.11; 41)   DM 480

GENTLEMAN OR TRAVELLER'S POCKET-FARRIER, The
Northampton, 1732. Title & some text soiled, cont. sheep, rubbed. (P. Mar.15; 311)   £130

GENTLEMAN'S MAGAZINE, The
1731-1802. Vols. 1-72 & index for Vols. 1-56, in 96 vols. Cont. spr. cf., spines gt.; Sir Ivar Colquhoun, of Luss copy. (CE. Mar.22; 131)   £4,400
- – Anr. Edn. L., 1731-1838. Orig. Series: Vols. 1-103 pt. 2, New Series: Vols. 1-10, & 5 vols. of Indexes. together 169 vols. Vols. to 1823 bnd. in unif. hf. cf., others cf., some spines gt., 1 cover detchd., some vols. rebkd., as a periodical, w.a.f. (C. Nov.9; 74)   *Kinross.* £2,200
- A Selection of Curious Articles from the Gentleman's Magazine. 1811. 4 vols. Minor spotting, hf. cf., spines gt. (BBA. Jan.19; 216)   *Quaritch.* £60

GENTLEMAN'S MAGAZINE OF FASHIONS, Fancy Costumes, & the Regimentals of the Army
L., 1829. Vol. 2 nos. 9-20 only, in 1 vol. Frontis., 37 hand-cold. etched or aquatint plts., frontis. slightly spotted, a few slight offsets, some plts. cropped, diced cf. gt., rebkd., as a periodical, w.a.f. (S. Mar.20; 719)   *Maggs.* £220

GENTY
- Costumes Militaires—Infanterie Russe (1815) Première Suite. Paris, n.d. 4to. 5 plts. repeated in different cols., guards, Bradel hf. chagrin. (HD. Jan.27; 263)   Frs. 3,000
- Deuxième Suite de Costumes Militaires. Infanterie Prussienne (1815). N.d. 4to. Frontis., 31 (of 36) plts., 2 extra plts., together 34 plts., 3 disbnd., str.-grd. mor. (HD. Jan.27; 265)   Frs. 3,300

GEOFFROY, Etienne Louis
- Histoire Abrégée des Insectes. Paris, 1764. 2 vols. 4to. 22 folding plts., folding table, hf.-titles, few ll. spotted, cont. cf., spines gt., recased. (S. Mar.20; 772)   *Shapero.* £55

GEOFFROY SAINT-HILAIRE, Etienne & Cuvier, Baron Georges Leopold Chretien
- Histoire Naturelle des Mammifères. Ill.:– after J.C. Werner, N. Huet, & others. Paris, [1819-]24-42. 7 vols. in 5. Fo. 431 hand-cold. litho. plts. (compl.), some browning & spotting, 1 plt. in Vol. I & 2 plts. in Vol. IV mntd. to size (possibly inserted from a smaller copy), title-pp. in Vols. I-III & V only (latter is for Vol. VII with blank slip pasted over no.), hf.-titles in Vols. I-IV, cont. red mor.-bkd. bds., partly unc., w.a.f. (S. Feb.1; 25)   *Taylor.* £12,000

GEOGRAFISCHES LEXIKON DER SCHWEIZ
Neuenburg, 1902/10. 6 vols. 4to. Hf. leath. (G. Sep.15; 2247)   Sw.Frs. 500

GEOGRAPHISCH-TONEEL, of Uitgezochte Kaarten, tot Gemak der Officieren, Registers en Liefhebbers
Amst., 1735. 41 folding engraved maps in cont. hand-col., lacks 3 maps of Netherlands, but 5 extra maps, some folds slightly torn, cont. hf. roan, lacks part of chintz on upr. cover. (VS. Jun.7; 991)   Fls. 1,600

GEOPONICA
- De Re Rvstica Selectorvm Libri XX. Ed.:– Io. A. Brassicani. Basel, 1539. *1st. Edn.* Title stpd., browned, vell., gold-tooled ex-libris on covers, hf. linen s.-c. (HK. Nov.8; 195)   DM 560

GEORG, J.M.
- Vollständiges Handbuch der Jagdwissenschaft. Ed.:– Leonhardi. Leipzig, 1797-98. 2 pts. in 1 vol.

Foxed, 19th. C. hf. leath. gt. (R. Apr.4; 1874)
DM 1,150

GEORGE IV, King of England
- Brief Account of the Coronation of His Majesty. George IV. L., 1821. 8 plts., 6 cold., interleaved, mor.-bkd. bds., rubbed. (BBA. May 23; 203)
Quaritch. £55

GEORGE, Ernest
- Etchings in Belgium. 1883. *2nd. Edn.* Fo. 30 etched plts., orig. cl., loose. (BBA. Oct.27; 251)
Bookroom. £55
- Etchings of Old London. L., 1884. Fo. 20 etched plts., orig. cl., loose. (BBA. Mar.21; 119)
Levy. £50
- Etchings of Venice. 1888. *(300).* Fo. 12 etched plts. sigd., orig. cl., slightly soiled. (CSK. Feb.10; 145)
£150
- Sketches, German & Swiss. 1870. Fo. Frontis. & 44 plts. on India paper, orig. cl., dampstained. (P. Feb.16; 188)
£260

GEORGE, Hereford Brooks & Edwards, Ernest
- The Oberland & its Glaciers. 1866. *[1st. Edn.].* 4to. Some light spotting, orig. cl., rebkd., old spine preserved. (CSK. Sep.30; 76)
£70
- - Anr. Copy. 4to. Double-p. map, 28 mntd. albumen photos, some minor foxing, tissue guards discold., gt.-pict. cl., heavily rubbed & faded. (SG. May 10; 44)
$110

GEORGE, Stefan
- Algabal. Paris, 1892. *2nd. Edn.* Orig. vell. wrap., slightly spotted, some sm. faults. (H. Nov.24; 1524)
DM 1,600
- Die Bücher der Hirten- und Preisgedichte, der Sagen und Sänge, und der Hängenden Gärten. Berlin, 1895. *1st. Edn. (200) on yellowish Bütten.* Suede, orig. ptd. wrap. bnd. in, slightly spotted. (H. Nov.24; 1525)
DM 720
- Gesamt-Ausgabe der Werke. Berlin, 1927-34. *1st. Coll. Edn.* 18 vols. in 15. Orig. linen gt. (GB. May 5; 2560)
DM 1,200
- Maximin. Ill.:- M. Lechter. Berlin, 1907. *1st. Edn. (200).* Fo. Red title on Japan, orig. vell., gold-tooled ill. (H. Nov.24; 1528)
DM 5,200
- - Anr. Copy. Lge. 4to. Orig. linen gt., corners rubbed, stained. (GB. May 5; 2564)
DM 650
- Der Teppich des Lebens und die Lieder von Traum und Tod, mit einem Vorspiel. Ill.:- M. Lechter. [Berlin], 1900. *1st. Edn. (300).* Lge. 4to. On heavy grey Bütten, orig. wood bds. with linen over. (H. Nov.24; 1531)
DM 3,400
- Werke. Berlin, [1928-34]. *1st. Compl. Edn. (Vol. I: 2nd. Edn.). De Luxe Edn. on japan.* 18 vols. in 15. Orig. vell., 6 spines lightly browned & with sm. spots. (H. May 23; 1231)
DM 4,400

GEORGI, Joh. G.
- Bemerkungen einer Reise im Russischen Reich. Petersburg, 1775. *1st. Edn.* 2 pts. in 1 vol. Lge. 4to. Wide margin, 2 folding engraved maps, 4 folding copperplts., lightly foxed, hf. leath. (HK. Nov.9; 1219)
DM 950

GEORGIAN SOCIETY
- Records of Eighteenth-Century Domestic Architecture & Decoration in Dublin. Dublin, 1910-13. *Ltd. Edns.* Vols. 2, 4 & 5 only. 4to. Orig. cl., slightly soiled. (S. Nov.8; 520)
Clegg D. £110
- - Anr. Edn. Dublin, 1911, 1969. *Vol. III: Orig. Edn. Vols. I, II & IV: Reprints.* Vols. I-IV only (of 5). 4to. Cl. & mor.-bkd. bds. (GM. Dec.7; 88)
£70

GEORGYEVSKY, G.
- Old Russian Miniatures. Preface & Notes:- Wladimirov & Georgyevsky. Moscow, 1934. 4to. 100 loose col. plts., cl. folder. (SG. Aug.25; 262) $100

GERALDINUS, Antonius
- Oratio in Obsequio Nomine Ferdinandi et Elisabeth Innocentio VIII Exhibito. [Rome, Stephan Plannck, 1488-91]. 4to. Disbnd.; the Walter Goldwater copy. [BMC IV, 93; Goff G-161; H. 7613] (SG. Dec.1; 155)
$125

GERARD, Jean Ignace Isidor 'Jean Jacques Grandville'
- Un Autre Monde. Paris, 1844. *[1st. Edn.].* Hf. mor. gt. (P. Mar.15; 112)
£140

- - Anr. Copy. Lge. 8vo. Cont. hf. chagrin, spine blind-decor. (HD. May 4; 290) Frs. 3,600
- - Anr. Copy. Browning & foxing, cont. hf. red chagrin, corners. (HD. Mar.14; 40) Frs. 1,050
- - Anr. Copy. Title stpd., some slight foxing, cont. hf. leath. gt., slightly bumped & rubbed, spine faded. (HT. May 9; 1481) DM 650
- - Anr. Copy. 4to. Light spotting, cont. hf. leath., slightly rubbed & bumped, lr. jnt. defect. (HK. May 17; 2442) DM 520
- Cent Proverbs. Paris, 1845. *Orig. Edn. 1st. Printing.* Some foxing, cont. hf. long-grd. mor., gt. decor. spine. (HD. Mar.14; 41) Frs. 1,600
- - Anr. Edn. Paris, 1845. *1st. Edn.* Lge. 8vo. Cl., rebkd., orig. spine laid down, end-papers soiled. (SG. Jun.7; 355) $120
- Les Etoiles, Dernière Féérie ... Astronomie des Dames. Text:- Mery. Paris, Lepizig, [1849]. *1st. Printing of plts.* 2 pts. in 1 vol. Lge. 8vo. Light foxing, decor. buckram, lacks front end-paper. (HD. May 4; 292) Frs. 2,700
See— FORGUES, Paul Emile Daurand 'Old Nick' & Gérard, Jean Ignace Isidor 'Jean Jacques Grandville'

GERARD, Jean Ignace Isidor 'Jean Jacques Grandville' (Ill.)
See— DELORD, Taxile
See— HETZEL, Pierre Julius 'P.J. Stahl'
See— SECOND, Albéric & Delord, Taxile

GERARD, P. & Vandermaelen, Ph.
- Atlas Topographique de la Belgique. Ill.:- J.E. Dekeyser. Bruxelles, 1846. Lge. fo. Title & 24 double-p. maps on guards, 1 map torn, hf. cf., worn. (LM. Oct.22; 60) B.Frs. 40,000

GERARD OF CREMONA
See— SACROBOSCO, Johannes de – GERARD OF CREMONA

GERARDE, John
- The Herball, or Generall Historie of Plantes. L., 1597. *1st. Edn.* Fo. Lacks title, sm. rusthole at Ff5, short tear at 4Q4 & 3F1, margin worming to prelims. slightly affecting side-note, upr. hf. only of colophon lf. & laid down, 19th. C. tree cf., rubbed. [STC 11750] (C. Mar.14; 107) *Sotheran.* £500
- - Anr. Copy. Fo. Title-p. reprd., qtr. cf., rebkd. (PWC. Jul.11; 546) £350
- - Anr. Copy. Fo. Lacks engraved title, 6 prelims. & final lf. of table, port. torn without loss, commendation & preface ll. incompl., some ll. of table soiled & frayed at edges with slight loss, some light stains, cont. panel. reversed cf., spine worn. (TA. May 17; 321) £210
- - Anr. Copy. Fo. Lacks title, port. & some prelim. & final ll. supplied in facs., some repairs, soiling & staining, old blind-stpd. cf., rebkd., worn, w.a.f. (SPB. Dec.13; 834) $225
- - Anr. Edn. [1597]. Fo. Lacks title & some ll., some ll. torn with loss, cont. cf., worn, lacks upr. cover, largely disbnd., w.a.f. (CSK. Apr.27; 180) £250
- - Anr. Edn. Ed.:- Thomas Johnson. L., 1633. *2nd (1st. Johnson) Edn.* Fo. Lacks 1st. & last blanks, some dampstaining at end, mostly marginal, a few headline-rules cropped, sm. hole in 5D3 & 1 or 2 rust holes, 18th. C. diced russ. gt., jnts. reprd., some wear. [STC 11751] (S. Nov.28; 24) *Quaritch.* £900
- - Anr. Copy. Fo. Lacks 1st. & last blanks, engraved title cut round & mntd., & margins frayed, a few ll. at beginning & end stained, B4-5 remargined, a few other repairs, 18th. C. reversed cf., worn. [STC 11751] (S. Nov.28; 25) *Allegretti.* £550
- - Anr. Copy. Fo. Title, dedication lf. & last 5 ll. of 'The Table of Vertues' at end supplied in MS., some ll. stained, old cf., rubbed, rebkd. (LC. Mar.1; 147) £400
- - Anr. Copy. Fo. Woodcuts thro.-out, title torn & laid down with loss of plt., A.5, F2-F5, 2B6, 2C1, 215, torn & defect., cf. gt., rebkd., w.a.f. (P. May 17; 46) *Donovan.* £300
- - Anr. Copy. Fo. Lacks engraved title, dedication lf. detchd., dampstained, cont. cf., worn & brkn. (TA. May 17; 322) £210
- - Anr. Copy. In 2 vols. Fo. Lacks engraved title, pp. 1,483/4 & last lf. of table, margins of prelims. &

last few ll. strengthened with some loss of text, later hf. cf., some wear. (TA. May 17; 323) £160
- - Anr. Copy. Fo. Title cut round & mntd., 7B5 laid down, 7A1 inserted from shorter copy, tears to 11 leaves, some worming, some dampstains, 18th. C. cf., rebkd., corners reprd., w.a.f. [STC 11751] (CNY. Dec.17; 562) $750
- - Anr. Edn. 1636. *2nd. Edn. (Revised).* Fo. Engraved title laid down, lacks bottom right hand corner, lacks 24 ll. at end & a further 14 ll. from main text, most ll. stained, some torn or defect., cf., worn, w.a.f. (LC. Mar.1; 146) £260
- - Anr. Edn. L., 1636. *3rd. Edn.* Fo. Engraved title, upwards of 2,600 woodcuts in text, some minor dampstaining, 1 or 2 wormholes running through inner margins & affecting border of title & 1 or 2 letters of text, cont. cf., rebkd., sm. tear at head of spine. [STC 11752] (C. Jun.27; 120)
Dunsheath. £700
- - Anr. Copy. Fo. Engraved title-p. reprd., some sm. stains at end, new fly-ll., cont. cf., rebkd., with Leyden label. (SKC. Sep.9; 1992) £460

GERARDINI, M.
- Capricci di Varie Figure di ... N.p., n.d. 1 vol. 4to. Linen. (DS. Mar.23; 2115) Pts. 100,000

GERARDUS DE ZUTPHANIA
- De Spiritualibus Ascensionibus. [Basel, Amerbach & Petri], not after 1489. Richly ornamented floral 'B' on 1st. p. of text, other initials & paragraph marks in red & blue. [BMC III, 752; Goff G-177; HC 16296] *(Bound with:)* CHRYSOSTOMUS, Saint Johannes, Archbp. of Constantinople - De Compunctione Cordis. Basel, Michael Furter, ca. 1500. Rubricated, lacks f5 (?). [BMC III, 786; Goff J-279; HC 5046] Together 2 works in 1 vol. Cont. blind-stpd. pig over wood bds., metal clasps; the Walter Goldwater copy. (SG. Dec.1; 156) $1,100

GERASCH, Franz
- Das Oesterreichische Heer von Ferdinand II Römisch Deutschen Kaiser bis Ferdinand I Kaiser von Osterreich. Vienna, ca. 1854. 4to. 66 (of 153) lithos., leaves, wraps. (HD. Jan.27; 272)
Frs. 1,400

GERBERON, Dom Gabriel
- [-] Histoire Générale du Jansénisme. Amst., 1700. 3 vols. Sm. 8vo. Cont. cf., spines decor. (HD. May 3; 57) Frs. 1,200

GERBETT, G.F.
- Ost-Indische Natur-Geschichte, Sitten und Alterthümer. Halle, 1752. Lacks last index lf., hf. leath., rubbed. (GB. Nov.3; 76) DM 480

GERICAULT
- Etudes de Chevaux. Paris, n.d. Fo. Stains & foxing, publisher's bdg., chagrin spine. (HD. Feb.29; 16) Frs. 14,500

GERMAIN, Pierre
- Elements d'Orfevrerie. Ill.:- J.F. Pasquier. Paris, 1748. 2 pts. in 1 vol. 4to. Engraved titles, 100 plts., 1 plt. stained in margin, anr. foxed, sm. ink alterations to few plts., cont. mott. cf., spine gt.; author's sig. at foot of title. (C. Dec.9; 56)
Quaritch. £800

GERMAN THEATRE, The
Trans.:- Benjamin Thompson. 1801. 6 vols. Cont. spr. cf.; Sir Ivar Colquhoun, of Luss copy. (CE. Mar.22; 308) £170

GERMANES, Abbé de
- Histoire des Révolutions de Corse depuis ses Premiers Habitants jusqu'à nos Jours. Paris, 1771-76. 3 vols. in 2. 12mo. Cont. marb. cf., spines decor., bdgs. not unif. (HD. Oct.21; 91) Frs. 4,500

GERMERSHAUSEN, Chr. Fr.
- [-] Die Hausmutter in allen ihren Geschäften. Leipzig, 1780-81. *Vols. 4 & 5: 1st. Edn.* 5 vols. Vol. 1 title lightly torn, some margins with sm. repairs, cont. hf. leath. gt., lightly rubbed. (HK. Nov.9; 1743) DM 950

GERNING, Johann Isaac von
- Beschreibung der Vierundzwanzig Rheinansichten. L., 1820. 4to. Wide margins, folding engraved map

GERNING, Johann Isaac von -Contd.

cold. in outl., 24 hand-cold. aquatint views, orig. ptd. wraps., slightly rubbed, with advts. in Engl. on inside covers. (S. May 21; 228)   *Bailey.* £1,400
- A Picturesque Tour along the Rhine from Mentz to Cologne. 1820. *1st. Engl. Edn. 1st. Iss.* 4to. Folding map, 24 hand-cold. plts., some offset, crimson mor. gt. by Bayntun. (P. Mar.15; 121)
Tzakas. £1,550
- - Anr. Edn. L., 1820. *[1st. Engl. Edn.].* 4to. Folding map & 24 hand-cold. aquatint views, some slight discolouration to a few ll. of text & some faint offsetting onto plts., cont. qtr. mor., rubbed. (S. May 21; 227)   *Bailey.* £1,400
- - Anr. Copy. Lge. 4to. Engraved folding map, 24 hand-cold. aquatint plts., some staining, affecting map & 1 plt., disbnd. (SG. Nov.3; 84) $1,900
- - Anr. Copy. Fo. Wide margin, on vell., 20 (of 24) cold. aquatint etchings, 1 folding map, title verso stpd., later hf. leath. gt., supralibros Ernst August von Hannover, spine faded & slightly worn; Hauswedell coll. (H. May 24; 879)   DM 7,200
- - Anr. Copy. Lge. 4to. 3 plts. cut to subject separated & present loose, (very browned), 4 text ll. at beginning loose, cont. linen, gold-tooled, bumped & spotted. (R. Apr.4; 2492)   DM 4,000

GERNSHEIM, Helmut & Alison
- The History of Photography. L., [1969]. 4to. Gt.-stpd. cl., d.-w. (SG. May 10; 56) $225

GERSAINT, Edme François
- A Catalog & Description of the Etchings of Rembrandt van-Rhyn, with some Account of his Life. L., 1752. Margin darkening to prelims. & a few later ll., cont. cf., covers rubbed & worn, sm. bkplt. (CBA. Jan.29; 382) $170

GERSDORFF, Hans von
- Feldtbuch der Wundartzney. Strassburg, 1526. Sm. 4to. 23 cont. cold. text-engrs., lacks ll. 26 & 27 with trepanation figure, cont. stpd. pig. (HD. Mar.21; 34)   Frs. 25,000

GERSHON, Yitzhak & David Ibn Hin
- Likutei Shoshanim. Venice, 1602. *1st. Edn.* 4to. Owner's sig. on title, slight staining, trimmed, mod. mor. (S. Oct.24; 161)   *Jts.* £260

GERSHON BEN SHLOMO, of Catalonia
- Sha'ar Ha'Shamaim. Venice, 1547. *1st. Edn.* 4to. Owners' sigs. on title, slight staining mostly in margins, slightly creased, hf. leath. with marb. paper bds.; Berlin Jewish Community stp. (S. Oct.24; 160)   *Jansen.* £480

GERSHWIN, George
- Song-book. Ill.:– Alajalov. N.Y., 1932. *1st. Edn. (300) numbered.* Sm. fo. The sheet music for 'Mischa, Yascha, Toscha, Sascha' (Tall 4to. Self-wraps., tied) inserted in lr. sleeve as iss., some light finger-soiling to text, mor. gt., worn; sigd. by Gershwin & Alajalov. (SG. Nov.3; 85) $650
- - Anr. Copy. Sm. fo. Sheet music for 'Mischa, Yascha, Toscha, Sascha' (Tall 4to. Self-wraps., tied) inserted in rear sleeve, as iss., mor. gt., minor staining to covers, jnts. & corners worn. (SG. Jan.12; 121) $425
- - Anr. Edn. Ill.:– Constantin Alajalov. N.Y., 1932. 4to. Cl., d.-w. worn & frayed; pres. inscr. from Gershwin to Alice de Lamar on front free end-paper, with additional inscr. from Alajalov. (PNY. Jun.6; 494) $375

GERSON, Johannes
- Bibliotheca. Ed.:– I. Simler. Zürich, Mar. 1573. Fo. Title with 2 owner's marks, 1 excised, last lf. with MS. note, some soiling in upr. margin, several sigs. slightly wormed, stain in 1 corner near end, end-papers with MS. entry, cont. cf. gt., defect. (HK. Nov.8; 199)   DM 850
- Copia Bullae, sive Sententiae Concilii Basiliensis de Conceptione Mariae. [Cologne, Johann Guldenschaff], ca. 1480. 4to. Rubricated, 2 corners reprd., slightly affecting text, later bds.; the Walter Goldwater copy. [BMC I, 254; C. 1763; Goff G-217] (SG. Dec.1; 158) $275
- De Custodia Linguae et Corde Bene Ruminanda. [Cologne, Ulrich Zel], ca. 1470. 4to. With blank

sheet around text (not called for in BMC), rubricated, disbnd., hf. lev. folding case; the Walter Goldwater copy. [BMC I, 184; Goff G-219; H. 7683] (SG. Dec.1; 159) $1,000
- De Passionibus Animae. [Paris, Pierre Poulhac], ca. 1495. Sm. 8vo. Fully rubricated, mod. wraps.; the Walter Goldwater copy. [Goff 249a (this copy only)] (SG. Dec.1; 160) $650
- Opera. [Nuremb., Georg Stuchs], 22 Nov. 1489. Pt. 1 only (of 3). 4to. Bds., cover detchd.; the Walter Goldwater copy. [Goff G-188; HC 7623] (SG. Dec.1; 157) $325
- - Anr. Edn. [Strasburg, Johannes Pruss, 1488 (pts. I-III)]; Strasburg, Martin Flach & Mathias Shürer, 1502 (pt. IV). 4 vols. Fo. 1st. 3 vols. rubricated, initials painted in red & blue, index bnd. at beginning of 1st. vol., cont. unif. stpd. pig over wood bds., decor., brass clasps; from Fondation Furstenberg-Beaumesnil. [BMC I, 170; Goff G186] (HD. Nov.16; 48)   Frs. 48,000
- Sermo de Passione. Basle, 1515. Light dampstains in corners of some ll., spr. bds.; from Fondation Furstenberg-Beaumesnil. (HD. Nov.16; 124)
Frs. 3,000
- - Anr. Edn. Basel, 1518. 6 pts. in 2 vols. Fo. 2 pasted in ex-libris, cont. blind-tooled leath. over wood bds., lacks clasps & bosses. (HK. Nov.8; 196)   DM 2,900
- Tractatus de Simonia, De Probatione Spiritum, De Eruditione Confessorum. [Cologne, Ulrich Zell, ca. 1470]. 4to. Rubricated, initials painted in red, lge. 1st. initials painted on gold with continuations in margins, lacks last 5 ll. ('De Remediis contra Recidivum Peccandi'), 19th. C. str.-grd. hf. mor.; from Fondation Furstenberg-Beaumesnil. [BMC I, 184; Goff G267] (HD. Nov.16; 19)   Frs. 8,500
- Tractatus per Modum Dialogi de Perfectione Cordis. [Cologne, Joh. Koelhoff], n.d. Fo. Compl. fragment, 15 ll. (II-XVI, A. 2-B 8), 37 (of 40) lines, 2 columns, rubric in red & blue, 2 lge. decor. initials fleuronné, some old MS. marginalia, 1 lf. with slight stain, hf. vell., marb. paper. (D. Nov.23; 118)   DM 800

GERSONIDES-RALBAG
See— LEVI BEN GERSHON [Gersonides-Ralbag]

GERSTACKER, Friedrich
- Herrn Malhubers Reiseabenteuer. Ill.:– E. Preetorius. München, 1917. *De Luxe Edn., (40) on Japan.* Without portfo., orig. hand-bnd. vell., cover slightly discold. (H. Nov.23; 997)   DM 500
- Nach Amerika! Ill.:– Th. Hosemann (Vol. 1). & C. Reinhardt. Leipzig, 1855. 6 vols. Lightly browned, some slight foxing, cont. hf. leath. gt. (GB. May 4; 1272)   DM 480
- Narrative of a Journey Round the World ... L., 1853. *1st. Edn. in Engl.* 3 vols. Orig. cl., a few corners slightly worn; the Rt. Hon. Visc. Eccles copy. (Sabin 27183) (CNY. Nov.18; 121) $220

GERSTENBERG, K. von
See— STREICH, T.F. & Gerstenberg, K. von

GERSTINGER, Hans
- Die Wiener Genesis: Farbenlichtdruckfaksimile der Griechischen Bilderbibel. Vienna, [1931]. 2 vols. Fo. Vol. 1, 152 ills. on 26 plts., vol. 2, cold. facs. on 48 pp., vell.-bkd. bds., facs. vol. loose. (SG. May 3; 39) $300

GERSZI, Teréz
- Netherlandish Drawings in the Budapest Museum, Sixteenth-Century Drawings. Amst. & N.Y., 1971. 2 vols. Fo. Orig. cl. (S. Apr.30; 40)
Dreesman. £70

GERUSEZ, Victor 'Crafty'
See— CRAFTY [ie Victor Gerusez]

GERVAIS, M.
See— RAMEAU, Jean Philippe – GERVAIS, M.

GERVAIS, Paul
- Histoire Naturelle des Mammifères. Paris, 1854-55. 2 vols. 4to. Many engrs. hand-cold., pebbled cl. gt., end-papers soiled, ex-liby. (SG. Oct.6; 171) $100

GERVINUS, G.G.
- Insurrection et Régénération de la Grèce. 1863. 2 vols. Sm. defects & foxing, cont. hf. roan, corners, by Loisellier. (HD. Jun.29; 94)   Frs. 1,800

GESELLSCHAFT, Internat. Revue f. Sozialismus u. Politik
Ed.:– Rud. Hilferding. Berlin, 1924-33. Years 1-10, pt. 2 (lacks 11 pts.). Some sm. faults, 1½ yrs. bnd., rest orig. pts. (V. Sep.30; 2355)   DM 500

GESNER, Abraham
- The Industrial Resources of Nova Scotia. Halifax, Nova Scotia, 1849. Orig. cl., rebkd., part of spine laid down. (CSK. Jul.6; 122)   £130

GESNER, Conrad
- Gesnerus redivivus auctus & emendatus. Oder: Allgemeines Thier-Buch [und] Vogel- und Fisch-Buch. Frankfurt, 1669. [-1672]. *1st. Coll. Edn.* 5 vols. & supp. vol. (Schlangen-Buch) in 1 vol. Fo. 1 (of 3?) engraved titles, over 1000 woodcuts (some full-p.), cont. leath., worn. (R. Apr.4; 1725)
DM 3,800
- Historiae Animalium. Frankfurt, 1617-20. 5 pts. in 3 vols. Fo. Browning & dampstains, colophon laid down on last lf. of index, cont. cf., gt. shield on cover with arms of England, T. Barrington, Montagu, Nevill & Pole. (P. Mar.15; 155)   £950
- Historiae Animalium Liber II De Quadrupedibus Oviparis. Appendix Historiae Quadrupedum Viviparorum & Oviparorum. Zürich, 1554. *1st. Edn. Bk. 2.* 2 pts. in 1 vol. Fo. Lr. margin stained, some ll. strengthened with paper strips, erased title stp., 2 old erased entries, crudely pasted, spotted, cont. blind-tooled leath., bumped, spine renewed. (R. Apr.4; 1726)   DM 800
- Historiae Animalium Liber III qui est de Avium Natura. [Zürich, 1555]. *1st. Edn.* Fo. Lacks 1st. sig. & prelims., title lf. reptd. in 18th. C., misdtd. 1554, lightly browned & slightly foxed, 18th. C. vell. (R. Oct.12; 1848)   DM 2,400
- Historiae Animalium Liber IIII ... Zürich, 1558. *1st. Edn.* Fo. Title with deleted owner's mark, 1st. & last ll. with slightly frayed margins & side margin stained, 1 lf. defect. & reprd., lr. margin slightly stained thro.-out, minimal browning, late 19th. C. hf. vell. (HK. Nov.8; 198)   DM 2,000
- The Practice of the New & Old Phisicke ... Newly Corrected & Published in English, by George Baker. 1599. Lacks some ll., others loosely inserted but supplied from anr. copy, dampstained, 18th. C. cf., spine worn, w.a.f. [STC 11799] (CSK. Mar.23; 52)   £130
- Schlangenbuch. Zürich, 1589. *1st. German Edn.* 2mo. Later hf. vell., lacks spine. (D. Nov.23; 708)   DM 1,850
[-] Thesaurus de Remediis Secretis. Venice, 1556. 12mo. Lr. quarter of 1st. 240 pp. wormed, 1 lf. with sm. tear, 1 lf. with sm. tear in upr. corner, last ll. soiled, some light spotting, cont. vell., slightly soiled, wormed & bumped. (HK. Nov.8; 575)   DM 420
- Vogelbuch. Zürich, 1557. *1st. German Edn.* Wide margin, 1 lf. torn, some later pencil notes, lightly browned, cont. blind-tooled pig-bkd. wood bds., metal clasps, very worn & bumped, 2 pasted tears; Hauswedell coll. (H. May 24; 867)
DM 6,800

GESS, F.W.
- Das Alte u. das Neue Griechenland. Reutlingen, 1835. 73 litho. plts. Slightly foxed, lacks 1 litho. plt.(?), hf. linen. (HK. May 15; 841)   DM 600

GESSNER, C.F.
- Die so Nöthig als Nützliche Buchdruckerkunst und Schrift Giesserey, mit ihren Schriften, Formaten und allen dazu Gehörigen Instrumenten abgebildet auch Klärlich Beschrieben ... mit einer Vorrede Herrn Johann Erhard Kappens. Leipzig, priv. ptd., 1740-45. *1st. Edn.* Vols. I, II & IV only (of 4). Double-p. engraved frontis., 92 ports. & plts. (1 torn), 4 folding ptd. specimen plts., some browning. (*Bound with:*) PEUCER, Daniel – D. Martin Luthers Merckwürdiger Sendbrief vom Dollmetschen ... nebst eben Desselben Erläuterten Ausprüchen von der Buchdruckerey und den Buchdruckern. Leipzig, 1740. *1st. Edn.* 11 folding engraved plts. (*Bound with:*) LESSER, F.C. - Typographia Iubilans, das ist: Kurtzgefasste Historie der Buckdruckerey. Leipzig, 1740. *1st.*

Edn. Together 3 works in 1 vol. Cont. vell. (S. Nov.17; 27) *Marlboro' Bks.* £620

GESSNER, Salomon.
- Contes Moreaux et Nouvelles Idylles. Zürich, 1773. *1st. Fr. Edn.* 4to. Slightly spotted, cont. bds., bumped, spotted. (HK. May 17; 2441) DM 700
- Idyllen. Zürich, 1756. *1st. Edn.* Wide margin, cont. hf. gt. gt. (GB. Nov.4; 2046) DM 1,300
- - Anr. Edn. Berlin, n.d. *(60)* numbered. *De Luxe Edn. on Zanders Bütten.* Lithos. sigd. by artist, orig. leath. gt., slightly worn. (HK. May 17; 3159) DM 420
- Mort d'Abel ... Trans.:– Hubert. Ill.:– after Monsiau. Paris, 1793. 4to. 5 col.-ptd. plts. before numbers, some light spotting, cont. cf. gt., slightly worn. (S. Dec.20; 777) *Mediolanum.* £180
- - Anr. Copy. 4to. Cont. cf., rebkd. & reprd. (S. Oct.11; 535) *Thulins.* £150
- - Anr. Copy. Lge. 4to. Plts. before pagination, cont. red mor. gt., leath. creased & discold., sm. repairs to corners & head of spine. (SPB. Dec.14; 53) $500
- - Anr. Copy. Lge. 4to. Wide margin, cont. marb. leath. gt., slightly rubbed. (R. Apr.3; 202) DM 1,500
- Oeuvres. Ill.:– Le Barbier. Paris, [1786-93]. *1st. Printing.* 3 vols. 4to. Cont. tree cf. gt., spines decor., slightly rubbed. (HD. May 3; 58) Frs. 2,600
- - Anr. Edn. Paris, n.d. 3 vols. 4to. Bdg. not stated. (HD. Oct.14; 69) Frs. 1,100
- Oeuvres Complètes. Trans.:– M. Huber. Ill.:– Blanchard after Binet. Paris, 1796. 3 vols. Wide margin, hf. mor. gt., ca. 1880. (HK. Nov.10; 3058) DM 400
- Schriften. Zürich, 1770-72. *4th. pict. coll. Edn.* 5 vols. Wide margin, cont. hand-bnd. cf., gt. decor.; Hauswedell coll. (H. May 24; 1291) DM 3,000
- - Anr. Edn. Zürich, 1777-78. *1st. German 4to. Edn.* 2 vols. On vell., wide margin, cont. marb. leath., gt. spine, cover & outer dentelle, gold-tooled arms supralibros on upr. covers, slightly rubbed. (HK. May 16; 2011) DM 7,000
- - Anr. Copy. 2 vols. 4to. Wide margin, on Bütten, lacks 3 etchings, but 4 new etchings, slightly browned, mostly in margins, 1 lf. lightly creased, cont. red mor., gold-tooled decor. cover, spines, inner & outer dentelles, slightly rubbed; Hauswedell coll. (H. May 24; 1292) DM 6,600
- - Anr. Copy. 4to. Title & a few pp. slightly foxed, cont. leath. gt., end-paper stpd. (GB. Nov.4; 2045) DM 1,500
See– CHATEAUBRIAND, François August René, Vicomte de & Gessner, Salomon

GESSNER, Salomon & Diderot, Denis
- Moralische Erzählungen und Idyllen. Zürich, 1772. *1st. Edn.* Cont. hf. leath., rubbed. (GB. May 4; 1274) DM 480

GEUFFROY, A.
- Hoffhaltung des Türckischen Keisers ... Basel, 1573. *1st. German Edn.* Some slight browning, light stain at beginning & end in upr. corner, 1 lf. with lr. margin tear, cont. blind-tooled pig over wood bds., 18th. C. leath. spine gt., spine slightly rubbed, lacks clasps. (R. Oct.11; 42) DM 3,500

GHERARDI, Evarista
- Le Théâtre Italien. Paris, 1741. 6 vols. 12mo. Old cf., decor. spines. (HD. Mar.14; 36) Frs. 2,600
- - Anr. Copy. 6 vols. 12mo. Cont. spr. cf., decor. spines; Montmorency ex-libris. (HD. Sep.21; 122) Frs. 1,500

GHEYN, Jacques de
- Maniement d'Armes d'Arquebuses, Mousquetz, et Piques. Ill.:– J. de Gheyn. La Haye, 1607. *1st. Edn. in Fr.* Fo. Some light spotting in margins, cont. leath., gold decor. & centre-pieces, scratched. (R. Oct.12; 2285) DM 9,700

GHIRARDELLI, Cornelio
- Cefalogia Fisonomica ... dive ... si esaminano le Fisonomie di cento Teste Humane. Bologna, 1674. Cont. vell. (SI. Dec.15; 160) Lire 320,000

GIACOMETTI, Georges
- La Vie et l'Oeuvre de Houdon. Preface:– Camille Mauclair. Paris, [1929]. *1st. Edn. (50)* numbered on imperial Japan paper. 2 vols. Sm. fo. Mntd.

India-proof copperplate port., 105 photogravure plts., 1 plt. loose, pict. wraps., slightly worn, unc. & partly unopened. (SG. Oct.13; 200) $200
- - Anr. Edn. Paris, [1929]. *Ltd. Edn.* 2 vols. Fo. Hf. leath. (SPB. Nov.30; 45) $225

GIAFEY, A.F.
- Historia Germaniae Polemica. Frankfurt & Leipzig, 1722. *1st. Edn.* 4to. Cont. leath., rubbed. (R. Apr.3; 991) Frs. 440.

GIAFFERI, Paul-Louise de
- L'Histoire du Costume Feminin de l'an 1037 à l'an 1870. Paris, 1922. 10 pts. Cl. folder, ties. (RS. Jan.17; 466) $150
- - Anr. Edn. Paris, [1922-23]. 10 pts. 4to. 120 hand-cold. plts., some margins defect., orig. pict. wraps., orig. linen portfo., 2 wraps. defect., spine of portfo torn. (D. Nov.24; 4346) DM 700
- L'Histoire du Costume Feminin Français. Paris, ca. 1925. 10 sections. Fo. 120 cold. plts., loose as iss., cold. pict. wraps., pict. cl. folder, spine worn. (SG. Aug.25; 102) $200
- - Anr. Edn. Paris, ca. 1929. 10 fascicules in 1 vol. Sm. fo. 120 cold. plts., ex-liby., buckram, orig. pict. wraps. for 10 pts. bnd. in. (SG. May 3; 116) $150
- The History of the Feminine Costume of the World. N.Y., ca. 1925. 20 fascicules in 2 vols. Fo. 200 cold. plts., ex-liby., cl., very worn, 20 orig. cold. pict. wraps. bnd. in. (SG. May 3; 114) $200
- - Anr. Edn. N.Y., late 1920's. 20 sections. Fo. 200 cold. plts., loose in cold. pict. wraps., 2 pict. cl. folders, spines worn. (SG. Aug.25; 103) $110
- The History of French Masculine Costume. N.Y., ca. 1927. Orig. 10 fascicules in 1 vol. Fo. 100 cold. plts., ex-liby., cl., cold. pict. upr.-cover, 10 orig. cold. pict. wraps. bnd. in. (SG. May 3; 115) $175

GIARRE, Gaetano
- Raccolta di Caratteri. 1814. Ob. 4to. Engraved title, 17 engraved plts., last plt. reprd., vell.-bkd. bds. (P. Oct.20; 215) £50

GIBB, William
See– HIPKINS, Alfred James & Gibb, William

GIBBINGS, Robert
- Fourteen Wood Engravings from Drawings made on Orient Line Cruises. Gold. Cock. Pr., [1932]. Fo. Orig. cl.-bkd. bds., worn. (BBA. Feb.23; 240) *Elliott.* £75
- The Wood Engravings ... Ed.:– Patience Empson. 1959. 4to. Orig. cl., d.-w. (LC. Oct.13; 24) £55

GIBBON, Edward
[–] Critical Observations on the Sixth Book of the Aeneid. L., 1770. *1st. Edn.* Hf.-title, new wraps., cl. s.-c., slightly browned; Thomas B. Stevenson copy. (CNY. May 18; 106) $400
- Essai sur l'Etude de Littérature. L., 1761. *1st. Edn.* Errata, slight spotting, cont. tree cf. (SPB. May 16; 64) $700
- Geschichte des Verfalls u. Untergangs d. Römischen Reichs. Leipzig, 1805-20. 19 pts. in 10 vols. Title stpd. & with MS. owners mark, some slight browning, cont. hf. leath., gt. decor. (HK. May 15; 889) DM 540
- The History of the Decline & Fall of the Roman Empire. Ill.:– after Reynolds. 1776-88. *[1st. Edn.].* 6 vols. 4to. 3 maps, 2 folding, lightly spotted, hf.-titles lack, 2 blank margins cleanly torn, cont. cf., rubbed, vol. 1 rebkd. with old spine preserved, some jnts. cracked, spines gt., slightly chipped; Henry Yates Thompson bookplt. (CSK. May 18; 158) £450
- - Anr. Copy. 6 vols. 4to. 1st. state of Vol. 1, with cancels & errata uncorrected, engraved port. bnd. in Vol. 2, sm. tear to errata lf. in Vol. 1, 1st. map in Vol.2 torn, few ll. slightly spotted in Vol.2, cont. cf., spines gt., upr. cover of Vol.1 detchd.; Thomas B. Stevenson copy. (CNY. Dec.17; 564) $1,600
- - Anr. Copy. 6 vols. 4to. Cancels in vol.1, frontis.-port., 3 folding maps, errata in each vol., spotting & browning, lacks 5 hf.-titles, some marks from ribbons, cont. cf., rebkd., orig. spines laid down, bkplt. of Richard Cox, Quarley, Hants. (SPB. May 16; 66) $1,200
- - Anr. Edn. Ill.:– Maps:– Thomas Kitchen. 1777-88. *3rd. Edn.* 6 vols. 4to. Cont. hf. cf., scuffed. (TA. Dec.15; 538) £90
- - Anr. Edn. 1781-88. *Vol. 1: 4th. Edn., Vols. 2 &*

3: 2nd. Edn., Vols. 4-6: 1st. Edn. 6 vols. 4to. Nearunif. cont. spr. cf., spines gt.; Sir Ivar Colquhoun, of Luss copy. (CE. Mar.22; 132) £680
- - Anr. Edn. L., 1788. *1st. Edn.* 6 vols. 4to. Vol. I with X4 & a4 sigd. & with errata-lf. at end (lacking in Vols. II & III), 2 (of 3) folding engraved maps, lacks port., each vol. lacks hf.-titles, Vol. I lacks title (supplied in ptd. quasi-facs.) & A3-4 (replaced by the full Table of Contents iss. in Vol. II), cont. spr. cf., rebkd. (S. Oct.11; 339) *Womersley.* £130
- - Anr. Edn. 1788-90. *New Edn.* 12 vols. Cont. cf., spines gt., rubbed, some jnts. reprd. (CSK. Jan.27; 79) £120
- - Anr. Edn. 1820. 12 vols. Port. loose, hf. cf. gt., slightly rubbed. (P. Feb.16; 1) £100
- - Anr. Edn. 1828. 8 vols. Panel. cf. gt. (PD. May 16; 73) £78
- - Anr. Copy. 8 vols. Later hf. cf. gt. (PNY. Jun.6; 450) $750
- - Anr. Edn. 1848. 8 vols. Pol. cf., by Maclehose, gt.-decor. spines. (SKC. Sep.9; 1911) £110
- - Anr. Edn. 1855. 8 vols. Cf. gt. (P. Sep.8; 280) £130
- - Anr. Edn. Ed.:– Bury. L., 1909-14. 7 vols. Hf. mor., by Bayntun (Rivière), spines gt. (S. Oct.4; 86) *Foyles.* £280
- Miscellaneous Works. Ed.:– John, Lord Sheffield. L., 1796. *1st. Edn.* 2 vols. 4to. Frontis.-silhouette, errata, lacks advt. lf. at end vol.2, some spotting & soiling, cont. cf. gt., bkplt. of Richard Cox. (SPB. May 16; 67) $100
- - Anr. Edn. 1796-1815. 3 vols. 4to. Cont. cf., rebkd. in mor. (BBA. Jul.27; 128) *Womersley.* £75
- - Anr. Copy. 3 vols. Lge. 4to. Silhouette port., engraved port., early mott. cf., spines gt., defect. (SG. Apr.19; 93) $300
See– EYRE, Francis – GIBBON, Edward

GIBBON, Lardner
See– HERNDON, William Lewis & Gibbon, Lardner

GIBBS, J.
- Twenty Four Country Dances for the Year 1754. [1754]. Ob. Engraved title, 12 sheets of engraved music, title browned & stained with candle wax, some staining thro.-out, unbnd. (BS. Nov.16; 8) £240

GIBBS, James
- Bibliotheca Radcliviana. L., 1747. Fo. 2 engraved ports., 21 plts., light dampstain in lr. margin of some plts., orig. wraps. (C. Dec.9; 57) *Lyon.* £220
- A Book of Architecture. L., 1728. *1st. Edn.* Lge. fo. 149 (of 150) engraved plts., including 4 doublep., cont. panel. cf. (C. Dec.9; 58) *Weinreb.* £500
- - Anr. Copy. Fo. 150 engraved plts., dampstained at foot, 1 plt. reprd. in margin, hf. cf., somewhat worn. (S. May 1; 543) *Berschoyle.* £420
- - Anr. Copy. Fo. 150 engraved plts., some folding or double-p., subscribers list, title lightly browned, margins of title & dedication ll. restored, later hf. sheep, very worn, lacks spine, covers detchd. (SG. Oct.13; 173) $650

GIBBS, Josiah Willard
- Elementary Principles in Statistical Mechanics Developed with Especial Reference to the Rational Foundation of Thermodynamics. N.Y., L., 1902. *1st. Edn.* Orig. cl., rubbed; William Howell Williams bkplt., Stanitz coll. (SPB. Apr.25; 191) $125
- On the Equilibrium of Heterogeneous Substances [Concluded]. New Haven, 1878. *1st. Printing.* Pt. 2 only, 'Transactions of the Connecticut Academy of Arts & Sciences', Vol. III. Orig. wraps., upr. outer corner torn, slight chipping; Stanitz coll. (SPB. Apr.25; 192) $250
- The Scientific Papers. L., N.Y. & Bombay, 1906. *1st. Edn.* Orig. linen, unc. (HT. May 8; 407) DM 620

GIBLIN, R.W.
- The Early History of Tasmania ... L. & Melbourne, 1928-39. 2 vols. Bdg. not stated, 1 vol. with chipped d.-w. (KH. May 1; 289) Aus. $170

GIBRALTER COMMERCIAL LIBRARY
- A Catalogue of Books in the Gibralter Commercial Library Established in the Year 1806. 1823. Cont. cf. gt. (PD. Dec.14; 250) £125

GIBRAN, Kahlil
- **Twenty Drawings.** Intro.:– Alice Raphael. N.Y., 1919. *1st. Edn. (100) sigd.* 4to. Hf. vell. & decor. bds. (CBA. Aug.21; 245) $300

GIBSON, Charles Dana
- **The Gibson Book.** N.Y., 1906. 2 vols. Ob. fo. Slight darkening & other wear to contents, gt.-decor. cl., covers spotted & faded at spines & edges. (CBA. Jan.29; 209a) $110
- **London.** N.Y., 1897. *(250) numbered with orig. proof sigd. by author.* Lge. ob. 4to. Cl., light wear. (RO. Mar.21; 162) $120

GIBSON, Frank
- **Charles Conder, His Life & Work.** L., 1914. 4to. Invitation to a private view of an exhibition of Conder's work 1913 loosely inserted, orig. decor. cl., with d.-w. lettered by Pickford Waller; Waller bkplt., designed by J. Guthrie. (S. Nov.22; 317) *Arnold.* £200
- – **Anr. Copy.** 4to. Spotted, orig. cl., soiled, spine slightly rubbed. (S. Apr.30; 41) *Arnold.* £90
- – **Anr. Copy.** 4to. Decor. cl., slight wear & soiling, lacks front free end-paper. (KH. May 1; 290) *Aus.* $320

GIBSON, John
- **Atlas Minimus Illustratus.** 1779. 32mo. Engraved frontis., 52 maps, cont. vell.-bkd. bds., worn. (BBA. Jan.19; 66) *Angle Books.* £280.

GIBSON, Strickland
- **Early Oxford Bindings.** 1903. 4to. Additional rubbings inserted, orig. buckram-bkd. bds.; H.M. Nixon coll., with his sig. & MS. notes. (BBA. Oct.6; 193) *Quaritch.* £130

GIBSON, W.H.
See— ANDERTON, Basil & Gibson, W.H.

GIBSON, William Sydney
- **The History of the Monastery Founded at Tynemouth.** 1846-47. 2 vols. 4to. Cont. qtr. mor. (S. Nov.1; 109) *Turton.* £50

GIBSON CRAIG, James T.
- **Catalogue of the Valuable & Very Extensive Library.** 1887-88. *(100) L.P.* 3 pts. in 1 vol. Lge. 4to. Prices ptd. at end of each pt., cont. hf. mor.; H.M. Nixon coll., with inscr. on fly-lf. 'Howard M. Nixon. dd. Henry Davis. 1.1.68'. (BBA. Oct.6; 154) *Traylen.* £180

GIDE, André
- [–] **Les Cahiers d'André Walter. Oeuvre Posthume.** Paris, 1891. *Orig. Edn.* 12mo. 1 of approx. 70 copies not destroyed (mostly dedication copies), without dedication, jansenist mor., decor., doubls., by Yseux, wrap. preserved, spine of wrap. defect., s.-c. (HD. Nov.9; 105) *Frs.* 6,400
- **Les Caves du Vatican.** Paris, 1914. *(500) numbered.* 2 vols. Mor. by Margaret Levy, 1973, palladium tooling, suede liners, s.-c.'s, sigd. on turn-ins, orig. wraps. preserved. (BBA. Jun.14; 214) *Greenwood.* £85
- **Les Nourritures Terrestres. Gravures de Galanis.** Paris, 1930. *(8) on old tinted Japon, with 2 orig. sigd. drawings & 4 states of etchings.* Lge. 4to. Mntd. on guards, edges untrimmed, mor., by Paul Bonet, gt.- & silver-decor., mosaics, silk doubls. & end-papers, wrap. & spine, hf. mor. box & folder matching spine decor. with typed certificate stating that bdg. was done between Oct. 1930 & Mar. 1931. (HD. Nov.29; 135) *Frs.* 39,000
- – **Anr. Edn.** Ill.:– Galanis. Paris, 1930. *(339). (16) on Montval vergé blanc with suite.* 4to. Sewed, folder, s.-c. (HD. May 4; 286) *Frs.* 2,500
- **Oeuvres Complètes.** Paris, 1932-39. *1st. Coll. (partly Orig.) Edn., (3232).* 15 vols. Felt by Muriel Morin Pons. (SM. Mar.7; 2133) *Frs.* 1,600
- **Paludes** ... Ill.:– Roger de La Fresnaye. Paris, 1921. *(312), on papier velin Lafuma-Navarre. (300) numbered.* 4to. Art Deco bdg. of Cubist design in red hf. mor. & red marb. paper sides in vertical bands by Paul Bonet, sigd. at upr. turn-in, upr. cover elab. decor. gt. & ruled, rules obscured by paper sides, lr. cover plain, smooth spine gt.-lettered, red marb. paper linings, partly unc., orig. ptd. wraps. & spine preserved. (CNY. May 18; 173) $2,000
- **Philoktet od. der Traktat von den drei Arten der**

Tugend. Trans.:– Rud. Kassner. Leipzig, 1904. *(500) numbered.* Mor., gt. & gold-tooled decor., inner & outer dentelle, by Bruno Scheer, Berlin. (HK. Nov.11; 3504) DM 900
- **Les Poésies d'André Walter.** 1892. *Orig. Edn.* Pink hf. mor., corners. (HD. May 11; 24) *Frs.* 1,200
- **Le Voyage d'Urien.** Ill.:– Maurice Denis. Paris, 1893. *(300) on lightly tinted papier vergé.* Sm. 4to. 30 orig. lithos., mor. gt. by René Kieffer, unc., wrap. & spine. (HD. May 16; 30) *Frs.* 29,100

GIETERMAKER, K.H.
- **'t Vergulde Licht er Zeevaard, ofte Konst der Stuurlieden.** Amst., [1774]. *9th. Printing.* Port. frontis. slightly defect. *(Bound with:)* DOUWES, B.J. – **Tafelen, bev. de Sinussen, Tangenten en Secanten** ... Amst., 1779. *New Edn.* Together 2 works in 1 vol. 4to. Slight margin staining, old vell., spine defect. (VS. Dec.9; 1281) Fls. 450
- – **Anr. Edn.** Amst., ca. 1775. 4to. Some slight spotting, 19th. C. vell., slightly bumped & spotted. (HK. Nov.9; 1870) DM 800

GIFFORD, John
- **The History of France.** 1791-94. 5 vols. 4to. Cont. tree cf., spines gt.; Sir Ivar Colquhoun, of Luss copy. (CE. Mar.22; 134) £290

GIFT (The); A Christmas & New Year's Present ...
Ed.:– Miss Leslie. Trans.:– Contrib.:– Edgar Allen Poe. Phila., [1835; 1839]; [1842]. 3 vols. Lge. 16mo. & 12mo. Orig. gt.-pict. vari-cold. roan, 1st. vol. nicked on spine ends & foxed, 2nd. shaken, 3rd. with torn front jnt.; from liby. of F.D. Roosevelt, each vol. with his inscr., 3rd. vol. also dtd. by him (as President). (SG. Mar.15; 29) $275
- – **Anr. Edn.** Contribs.:– Edgar Allan Poe & others. Phila., [1841]. *1st. Printing of 'Eleonora'.* Some foxing, publisher's gt.-stpd. cf., rubbed. (RO. Apr.23; 249) $135
- – **Anr. Edn.** Phila., [1841; 1842]. 2 vols. Lge. 12mo. Elab. gt.-ornamental cf., by S. Moore, 1842 iss. sigd. by Moore on both covers, both vols. very rubbed & a little discold. on extremities; from liby. of F.D. Roosevelt, both vols. inscr. by him, 1st. also inscr. by him 'Poe's Eleonor', & 2nd. inscr. by him as 'rare, Poe's The Pit & The Pendulum'. (SG. Mar.15; 30) $475
- – **Anr. Edn.** Contribs.:– Edgar Allan Poe & others. Phila., [1842]. *1st. Printing of 'The Pit & the Pendulum'.* Sm. 8vo. Some foxing, minor stains & soiling &c., publisher's gt.-stpd. cf., rubbed. (RO. Apr.23; 250) $135

GIGLIOLI, Prof. Dott. E.H.
- **Appunti Intorno ad una Collezione Etnografica fatta durante il Terzo Viaggio di Cook** ... Flor., 1893-95. In Vol. 23 pt. II & Vol. 25 pt. I of the 'Archivo per l'Antropologia e la Etnologia'. Wraps. (KH. May 1; 291) *Aus.* $190

GIGNOUX, Régis
- **L'Appel du Clown.** Ill.:– André Dunoyer de Segonzac. Paris, 1930. *(20) numbered on Japon Impérial with an extra suite of plts.* 4to. Loose as iss. in orig. wraps., s.-c. (BBA. Jun.14; 205) *Lyon.* £850

GIKATILA, Joseph
- **Sha'arei Orah.** Mantua, 1561. *1st. Edn.* 4to. 1836 Russian censorship stp. on 1st. lf., owners' sigs. & stp. on title, soiled, staining, some worming affecting some words, cl. (S. Oct.24; 163) *Stein.* £300
- **Sha'arei Zedek.** Riva di Trento, 1561. *1st. Edn.* 4to. Slight staining in margins, slightly creased, cl. (S. Oct.24; 164) *Schwarzchild.* £400

GIL BLAS ILLUSTRE
Contribs.:– Verlaine, Maupassant, Zola, Baudelaire & others. Ill.:– Steinlen & others. Paris, 1891-97. Fo. Some slight staining, some sm. slits in early ll., hf. linen. (GB. May 5; 2567) DM 2,000
- – **Anr. Edn.** Texts:– Barbey d'Aurevilly, Baudelaire, S. Bernhardt, Colette Daudet, Gautier, Maupassant, Mendes, Verlaine, Zola & others. Ill.:– Steinlen & others. Paris, 1894-96. Years 4-6. 154 (of 156) in 1 vol. Fo. Lacks pts. 4 & 43 of 4th. year, margins browned & brittle, hf. leath., spine decor., rubbed. (HK. Nov.11; 3571a) DM 1,100

- – **Anr. Edn.** Ill.:– Steinlen, Bac, Guillaume, Louis Legrand & others. Paris, 1896-98. 3 vols. Fo. Cont. hf. buckram. (HD. Jun.22; 47) *Frs.* 1,680

GILBERT, Charles Sandoe
- **Historical Survey of the County of Cornwall.** 1817. 3 vols. Hf. mor. (LA. Nov.29; 121) £170

GILBERT, Davies
- **The Parochial History of Cornwall.** 1858. *1st. Edn.* 4 vols. Orig. bds. (LA. Nov.29; 100) £85

GILBERT, J.T.
- **An Account of the Parliament House, Dublin.** Dublin, 1896. 4to. News cutting pasted in covers, cl. (GM. Dec.7; 296) £50
- **Calendar of Ancient Records of Dublin.** 1889-1922. Vols. I-XVIII only (of 19). Lge. 8vo. Mor.-bkd. bds., w.a.f. (GM. Oct.5; 297) £160

GILBERT, Paul & Bryson, C.L.
- **Chicago & its Makers.** Chic., 1929. *(2000) numbered.* 4to. Orig. buckram. (SG. Jan.19; 148) $200

GILBERT, Rose
- **A Treatise on the Aeropleustic Art ... by means of Kites, or Buoyant Sails.** Ill.:– David Cox. L., 1851. 6 litho. plts., some foxing, orig. bds. (P. May 17; 261) *Hopkinson.* £170

GILBERT, Thomas
See— WHITE, John – GILBERT, Thomas

GILBERT, William
- **De Magnete.** L., 1600. *1st. Edn.* Fo. 18th. C. hf. vell., decor. paper bds. [STC 11883] (C. Nov.9; 75) *Franklin.* £3,800
- – **Anr. Copy.** Fo. Inner margin of title strengthened, sm. wormholes in inner margins of next few ll., some dampstains in upr. portions, & also in some outer margins mainly towards end & on the plt., a few spots, 19th. C. qtr. vell. [STC 11883] (S. Nov.28; 115) *Franklin.* £1,500
- **On the Magnet.** Chiswick Pr., 1900. *(250).* Fo. Orig. holland-bkd. bds., rubbed, s.-c. (BBA. Feb.23; 88) *Thorp.* £55

GILBEY, W.
- **George Morland.** 1907. *(250) sigd. by author.* 4to. Pict. cl., slightly worn. (BS. May 2; 141) £55

GILCHRIST, Alexander
- **The Life of William Blake.** L., 1863. 2 vols. Orig. cl. (BBA. Apr.5; 43) *Graser.* £50
- – **Anr. Edn.** L., 1880. 2 vols. Cl. gt., slightly worn; inscr. to D.G. Rossetti from Anne Gilchrist. (P. Oct.20; 37) £95
- – **Anr. Edn.** 1888. 2 vols. Orig. cl. gt., rebkd. with orig. spine. (BBA. Sep.8; 55) *Price.* £55

GILDER, R.W. (Contrib.)
See— BOWEN, Clarence W.

GILDON, Charles
See— LANGBAINE, Gerard & Gildon, Charles

GILES
- **Sunday Express & Daily Express Cartoons.** 1947-82. Series 1-36 (lacks nos. 1 & 31). Ob. 4to. Cold. pict. covers. (SKC. Nov.18; 1836) £60

GILES, Ernest
- **Australia Twice Traversed** ... 1889. *1st. Edn.* 2 vols. Some soiling & minor defects or repairs, liby. stps., orig. cl., rebkd. with mor., orig. backstrip preserved. (KH. May 1; 292) *Aus.* $480
- – **Anr. Edn.** Adelaide, 1964. *Facs. Edn.* 2 vols. Orig. cl., slight soiling. (KH. Nov.8; 174) *Aus.* $140

GILES, Herbert A.
- **A Chinese Biographical Dictionary.** L. & Shanghai, 1898. *1st. Edn.* Lge. 8vo. Three-qtr. mor. (SG. Nov.17; 189) $100

GILIBERTI, V.
- **La Polizia Ecclesiastica de Regno di Napoli.** [Neapel, 1797]. Hf. leath. gt. (D. Nov.25; 4904) DM 500

GILIO, Giovanni Andrea
- **Trattato ... de la Emulatione, che il Demonico ha fatta a Dio, ne l'Adoratione, ne Sacrificii, & ne le Altre Cose appartenenti alla Divinità.** Venezia,

1563. Frontis. stained, cont. limp vell., spine slightly bumped. (SI. Dec.15; 13)　　　　　Lire 360,000

GILKIN, I.
– Ténèbres. Ill.:– O. Redon. Brüssel, 1892. *1st. Edn. (150) numbered on Van Gelder-Bütten.* 4to. Hf. vell. (HK. Nov.11; 3892)　　　　　DM 1,800

GILL, Eric
– And Who Wants Peace? San Franc., Greenwood Pr., 1948. *(100).* Fo. Cl.-bkd. bds., in wrap. (PNY. Dec.1; 51)　　　　　$200
– Clothing without Cloth. Gold. Cock. Pr., 1931. *(500) numbered.* With separate imps. of all ills. on 2 sheets, & 9 imps. of 6 ills. for the Cranach Pr.'s 1931 'Canticum Canticorum Salomonis', 1 partly cold. with blue crayon, orig. cl. gt. (S. Nov.21; 222)　　　　　*Desk.* £520
– Engravings. Bristol, 1929. *(490).* Fo. Orig. cl. (SPB. Dec.13; 826)　　　　　$325
– Sculpture, an Essay. Ditchling, 1918. *1st. Separate Edn.* Orig. wraps., unc. (P. Mar.15; 312)　　　　　*Bookroom.* £70

GILL, Eric (Ill.)
See— BREBEUF, Jean de
See— CHAUCER, Geoffrey
See— GOETHE, Johann Wolfgang von
See— HOMER
See— NEW TESTAMENTIANA [English]
See— PASSIO DOMINI NOSTRI JESU CHRISTI
See— PLATO
See— RILKE, Rainer Maria
See— SHAKESPEARE, William
See— SIMON, H. E. & others
See— SOLOMON, King of Israel
See— VALERY, Paul
See— VERGILIUS MARO, Publius

GILL, Samuel Thomas
[–] Victoria Illustrated. Melbourne & Sydney, 1857. Ob. 4to. Orig. cl. gt. (P. Dec.8; 277)　　　　　*Nicholson.* £340
– – Anr. Edn. Melbourne & Sydney, 1857 [but ca. 1880]. *Facs. of 1st. Edn.* Ob. 4to. Pict. title, 45 plts., orig. cl., upr. cover & spine soiled. (S. Apr.9; 26)　　　　　*Nolan.* £230

GILL, Thomas of Glen Osmond, South Australia
– Colonel William Light: Founder of Adelaide, Sailor, Soldier, Artist ... Adelaide, 1911. *(200) numbered on H.M.P., sigd.* Additional inscr. to J.H. Maiden, publisher's crimson vell. gt.; the Hobill Cole copy. (KH. Nov.9; 607)　　　　　Aus. $200

GILLEN, F.J.
See— SPENCER, Sir Baldwin & Gillen, F.J.

GILLESPIE, Alexander
– Gleanings & Remarks Collected during Many Months of Residence at Buenos Ayres, & within the Upper Country. Leeds, 1818. *1st. Edn.* Orig. bds., ptd. label eroded, untrimmed. (SG. Oct.20; 164)　　　　　$200

GILLET, Henri
– Nouvelles Fantaisies Décoratives. Paris, ca. 1925. Tall fo. 36 designs on 20 plts. in colours & gold, ex-liby., each plt. stpd. on blank verso, loose in cl.-bkd. pict. bd. folder, linen ties. (SG. May 3; 23)　　　　　$275

GILLIS, Lieut. James Melville
– The U.S. Naval Astronomical Expedition to the Southern Hemisphere during the Years 1849-50-51-52. Wash., 1855. 2 vols. 4to. Lge. folding view, 9 maps & plans (4 folding), 41 plts. (19 cold., 5 tinted), 1 loose, some foxing, sm. liby. stp. on title-pp., orig. decor. cl. gt., Vol. 2 rebkd. [Sabin 27419] (BBA. Feb.9; 273)　　　　　*Sons of Liberty Books.* £100
– – Anr. Copy. Vol. II only. Lge. 4to. 2 maps, 35 litho. plts. (1 dupl. in place of anr. plt.), offsetting & some foxing, gt.-pict. cl., jnts. crudely reinforced with tape, ex-liby. (SG. Sep.22; 149a)　　　　　$100

GILLMAN, Federico
– Enciclopedia Popular ilustrada de Ciencias y Artes. Madrid, 1881-85. 4 vols. text & 4 vols. plts. Fo. Cf. (DS. Feb.24; 2340)　　　　　Pts. 25,000

GILLRAY, James
– The Suppressed Plates from The Works. L., 1851. Fo. 43 (of 45) engraved plts. on 22 sheets, lacks title-p., dampstained thro.-out, orig. red hf. mor., rubbed. (S. Dec.20; 540)　　　　　*Collman.* £70
– The Works ... , from the Original Plates, with the Addition of Many Subjects Not Before Collected. L., ca. 1849. Fo. Lacks vol. of suppressed plts., frontis. port., 586 plts., some minor foxing, cont. hf. leath., spine gt., rubbed. (SG. Jun.7; 353) $600

GILLY, D. & Eytelwein, J.A.
– Praktische Anweisung zur Wasserbaukunst. Berlin, 1803-09. *1st. Edn.* 4 pts. in 2 vols. 4to. Some light plt. foxing, cont. hf. leath., slightly bumped. (R. Oct.12; 1743)　　　　　DM 900
– – Anr. Edn. Berlin, 1805-36. 4 pts. in 2 vols. Cont. hf. leath., slightly rubbed. (GB. Nov.3; 1180)　　　　　DM 1,000

GILPIN, William
– Observations on the Coasts of Hampshire, Sussex, & Kent. L., 1804. *1st. Edn.* 6 aquatint plts., lacks hf.-title. *(Bound with:)* – Observations on ... Cambridge, Norfolk, Suffolk, & Essex; also on Several Parts of North Wales. L., 1809. *1st. Edn.* 20 aquatint plts. Together 2 works in 1 vol. Offsetting, cont. str.-grd. mor. (SG. Nov.17; 247)　　　　　$110
– Observations relative chiefly to Picturesque Beauty ... particularly the High-Lands of Scotland. 1787. *1st. Edn.* 2 vols. 40 aquatint plts. & maps, some minor offset foxing, cont. tree cf., spines gt.; Sir Ivar Colquhoun, of Luss copy. (CE. Mar.22; 136)　　　　　£120
– Observations Relative chiefly to Picturesque Beauty ... particularly the Mountains & Lakes of Cumberland & Westmoreland. L., 1788. *2nd. Edn.* 2 vols. 30 plts., lacks hf.-title?, offsetting, cont. str.-grd. mor. (SG. Nov.17; 249)　　　　　$100
– – Anr. Edn. 1792. *3rd. Edn.* 2 vols. 40 aquatint plts. & maps, cont. mott. cf., covers & spines decor.; Sir Ivar Colquhoun, of Luss copy. (CE. Mar.22; 135)　　　　　£230
– Observations, Relative Chiefly to Picturesque Beauty ... of Cumberland & Westmoreland. –Observations on the Western Parts of England. L., 1788; 1798. *2nd. Edn.; 1st. Edn.* 2 vols. & 1 vol. 1st. work, 29 aquatint plts., 3 maps, slightly offset, unc., 2nd. work, 18 aquatint plts., spotted, cont. hf. roan. (S. Apr.9; 168)　　　　　*Scott.* £90
– Remarks on Forest Scenery & other Woodland Views ... L., 1791. *1st. Edn.* 2 vols. 32 plts., lacks hf.-titles?, offsetting, cont. str.-grd. mor. (SG. Nov.17; 251)　　　　　$100

GIMAT DE BONNEVAL
[–] Voyage de Mantes ou les Vacances de 17 ... Ill.:– Moreau l'ainé (engraved title), & Moreau le Jeune? Amst. [Paris], 1753. 12mo. Sm. rust-stain on 1 plt., cont. cf., spine decor. (HD. Nov.9; 37) Frs. 2,600

GIN
– Les Vrais Principes du Gouvernement Français demontrés par la Raison et par les Faits. Genève, 1777. Cont. cf., corners worn, up. cover vol. 1 with loss. (HD. Feb.22; 77)　　　　　Frs. 1,500

GINOUVIER
– Tableau de l'Interieur des Prisons de France. Paris, 1824. Cont. hf. roan, worn. (HD. Feb.22; 78)　　　　　Frs. 1,200

GINSBERG, Allen
– Howl & Other Poems. Intro.:– William Carlos Williams. San Franc., 1956. *1st. Edn.* 12mo. Orig. ptd. wraps.; Frederic Dannay copy. (CNY. Dec.16; 151)　　　　　$200
– – Anr. Edn. San Franc., [1956]. Sq. 12mo. Ptd. wraps., wire-stitched; sigd., Witt-Diamant sig. & ticket on title. (SG. Mar.1; 168)　　　　　$475
– The Moments Return: A Poem. Ill.:– Robert LaVigne. San Franc., 1970. *(200) sigd. by author & artist.* Ob. fo. Qtr. cl. (SG. Mar.1; 169)　　　　　$100

GINTRAC, E.
– Observations et Recherches sur la Cyanose, ou Maladie Bleue. Paris, 1824. Orig. hf. leath. gt., slightly rubbed & bumped. (D. Nov.23; 560)　　　　　DM 450

GINZBURG, M.Y.
– Stil i Epocha. Problemy Sovremennoj Architectury. Moskau, 1924. 4to. Pencil transcript of Russian text on title, paper lightly browned & brittle, especially at beginning, sm. margin defects., linen, upr. orig. wrap. bnd. in, very defect. & mntd. (HK. Nov.11; 3572)　　　　　DM 1,100

GIONO, Jean
– Angelo. Roman. Paris, 1958. *(35) on holland.* *(With:)* – Les Terrasses de l'Ile d'Elbe. Paris, 1976. *(45) on holland.* Together 2 vols. Sewed. (HD. Jun.26; 81)　　　　　Frs. 1,480

GIONO, Paul
– Regain. Ill.:– Andre Minaux. Paris, 1965. *(54) on Auvergne with added suites on japon nacré & Rives.* 4to. Decor. cf., folder, s.-c., suite on Rives in leaves, box. (HD. Jun.13; 44)　　　　　Frs. 2,200

GIORGI, A.A.
– Alphabetum Tibetanum. Rome, 1762. 4to. Hf.-title, title ptd. in red & black with device ptd. in blue, 6 engraved plts. (all but 1 folding), faint liby. stp. on title, cont. qtr. vell., slightly worn. (S. May 22; 441)　　　　　*Randall.* £820

GIORGI, Federigo
– Libro di ... Giorgi, del Modo di Conoscere i Buoni Falconi, Astori, e Sparavieri, di Farli, di Governali, & di Medicarli. Venice, 1558. Sm. 8vo. Without final lf. G8, headlines of some ll. shaved, some inner margins reinforced, old vell. (CSK. Nov.4; 125)　　　　　£120

GIORGIO, Francesco
– De Harmonia Mundi Totius Cantica Tria. [Venice, Sep. 1525]. *1st. Edn.* Fo. 1 of the 2 blanks at end present, some worming, sm. stain on folios Y6-8, many underlinings by early student, few margin markings & notes, vell.; stp. 'Bliot. Bonderici' on title, bkplt. of G. Girolamo Bolognetti, Dr. Walter Pagel copy. (S. Feb.7; 144)　　　　　*Janssen.* £2,600

GIOVIO, Paolo, Bp. of Nocera, the Elder
– Elogia Virorum Bellica Virtute Illustrium. Ill.:– T. Stimmer. Basel, 1596. Fo. Some foxing, some old underlining & notes, mod. hf. leath. (D. Nov.23; 125)　　　　　DM 1,800
– Elogia Virorum Bellica Virtute Illustrium.–Elogia Virorum Literis Illustrium. Ill.:– Tob. Stimmer. Basel, 1575; 1575. Together 2 works in 1 vol. Fo. Vol. 1 title with owner's note, some old annots., cont. vell., lr. spine defect., & lr. cover lightly worn. (HK. Nov.8; 241)　　　　　DM 2,000
– Elogia Virorum Literis Illustrium. Basel, 1577. *1st. Edn.* Fo. Sm. liby. stps., cont. limp vell.; bkplt. of Dukes of Brunswick-Luneberg. (SPB. Dec.13; 680)　　　　　$150
– Historiarum sui Temporis Tomus Primus [Secundus]. Flor., 1550. *1st. Edn.* 2 vols. Fo. Some spotting, late 17th./early 18th. C. Fr. red mor. gt., royal arms on covers & royal cypher in compartments of spines; late 17th. C. sig. of N. Bentzon, the Woodhull copy with his sig., provenance & price £4.4s. (S. Nov.17; 28)　　　　　*Maggs.* £600
– Libellus de Legatione Basilii Magni Principis Moschoviae ad Clementem VII Pont. Max. Rome, 1525. Sm. 4to. Woodcut border round title trimmed, last imprim. lf., browned thro.-out, mod. cf.-bkd. cl. (BBA. May 23; 311)　　　　　*Hannas.* £240
– La Vita di Gonzalvo Ferrando di Cordova. Flor., 1550. Vell. (DS. Apr.27; 2114)　　　　　Pts. 36,000
– Vitae Illustrium Virorum. –Elogia Virorum Bellica Virtute Illustrium. – Elogia Virorum Literis Illustrium. Basel, 1578/77; 1596; 1577. 3 works in 1 vol. (1st. work 2 pts.). Fo. Cont. leath. gt., slightly worn. (R. Oct.11; 53)　　　　　DM 2,300

GIOVONI, Carulu
– I Profumi di l'Isula; Vers Corses et Traduction Littérale Française. Marseille, 1930. *(With:)* – Mon Ile; Poèmes Corses (lère Série). Bordeaux, Paris, 1934. Together 2 vols. Sewed. (HD. Oct.21; 95)　　　　　Frs. 1,900

GIRALDI, J.B.
– Commentario delle Cose di Ferrara. Venice, [1556]. Cont. vell., gt. decor., centre arms, repeated spine cypher. (HD. Dec.9, 37)　　　　　Frs. 6,500

GIRALDI CINTHIO, Giovanni Battista
See— HOBBES, Thomas–GIRALDI CINTHIO, Giovanni Battista

GIRARD, A.
– Les Mémorables Journées des Français où sont décrites leurs Grandes Batailles ... 1647. *Orig. Edn.* 4to. Mod. hf. roan. (HD. Jan.24; 16) Frs. 1,400

GIRARD, Bernard de
– De l'estat et succez des affaires de France. Paris, 1619. 2 pts. in 1 vol. Lr. fore-corners lightly stained thro.-out cont. cf. gt.; from John Evelyn's liby. with press-marks P.8, 28 Minerva & I.52 (all deleted), & inscr. & motto (2 words deleted). (S. Nov.17; 30)
Quaritch. £140

GIRARD, Pierre Simon
– Description Générale des Différens Ouvrages à Executer pour la Distribution des Eaux du Canal de l'Ourcq dans l'Intérieur de Paris. Paris, 1812. 4to. Mod. bds., unc. & unopened; Stanitz coll. (SPB. Apr.25; 193) $225
– Traité Analytique de la Résistance des Solides et des Solides d'Egale Résistance. Paris, 1798. *1st. Edn.* 4to. Hf.-title, errata, slight spotting, hf. cl., marb. bds., light rubbing, faded mark at foot of spine; Stanitz coll. (SPB. Apr.25; 194) $275

GIRAUD, Jane Elizabeth
– The Flowers of Milton. [L., 1850]. Lge. 4to. Litho. dedication dtd. 1846, cont. hf. leath. gt., upr. jnt. rubbed. (BR. Apr.12; 697) DM 650
– – **Anr. Edn.** L., n.d. 4to. Hand-cold. title, dedication, 28 col. plts., mor. gt., slightly rubbed. (P. Nov.24; 57) *Ayres.* £130
[–] The Flowers of Shakespeare. Faversham, 1845. 4to. Orig. cl., lacks most of backstrip. (SKC. Mar.9; 1777) £145

GIRAUDOUX, Jean
– Rues & Visages de Berlin. Ill.:– Ch. Laborde. Paris, 1930. *(90) numbered on vélin d'Arches.* Fo. Lge. etchings in col. & uncold. state, orig. hf. linen portfo. (HK. Nov.11; 3472) DM 1,350

GIROLAMI CORTONA, Abbé F.
– Georgraphie Générale de la Corse. Ajaccio, 1893. Lacks map, mod. hf. roan, wrap. (HD. Oct.21; 96)
Frs. 1,200

GIRTIN, Thomas
– A Selection of Twenty of the most Picturesque Views in Paris & its Environs, drawn & etched in the Year 1802 ... L., 1803. Fo. 17 (of 20) aquatints cont. cold. proofs, light foxing, red str.-grd. hf. mor. by Champs-Stroobants, corners, spine decor., unc. (HD. May 21; 33) Frs. 4,600
See— TURNER, Joseph Mallord William & Girtin, Thomas

GISSING, George
– Born in Exile. 1892. *1st. Edn.* 3 vols. Hf.-titles, orig. cl., worn. (P. Feb.16; 257) £60

GIULINI, J.
– Tägliche Erbauung eines Wahren Christen ... Ill.:– after I.W. Baumgartner. Wien & Augsburg, 1753-54. Vols. 1 & 2 only (of 4). Sm. 4o. Lacks 1 plt. & some pp. at end, cont. leath. gt., very rubbed & bumped. (HK. Nov.9; 1514) DM 1,400

GIUSTINIANO, Agostino
– Castigatissimi Annali con la loro Copiosa Tavola della Eccelsa & Illustrissima Republ. di Genoa. Genova, 18 Mar. 1537. *1st. Edn.* Fo. Outside frontis. margin strengthened, 2 worm holes at end with slight loss of text, many sm. margin defects., most reprd., some stains, 19th. C. hf. leath. (SI. Dec.15; 14) Lire 600,000
– – **Anr. Edn.** Genova, 1537. Fo. Title restored & remntd., cont. cf., spine decor., worn; Auria ex-libris. (HD. Oct.21; 97) Frs. 4,500

GIUSTINIANI, F.
– El Atlas abreviado. Lyon, 1739. Vol. 1 (of 4?). 2 maps cut close at side margin, cont. leath. gt. (R. Oct.13; 2841) DM 950

GIUSTINIANI, P.M.
[–] Riflessioni intorno ad un Libro Intitolato Giustificazione della Rivoluzione di Corsica. N.p., [1760].

Old vell.; D. de Auria ex-libris. (HD. Oct.21; 99)
Frs. 4,200
[–] Riposta ad un Libello Famoso Intitolato Disinganno intorno alla Guerra di Corsica. Friburgo, 1737. Sm. 8vo. Old Bradel vell.; Auria ex-libris. (HD. Oct.21; 98) Frs. 3,600

See— BOSWELL, James–GIUSTINIANI, P.M.

GIUSTINIANUS, P.
– Delle Guerre di Fiandra. Antw., 1609. 4to. Some holes & repairs, browned, 19th. C. hf. cf. (VG. May 3; 553) Fls. 2,000

GLADDEN, Washington
– From the Hub to the Hudson; with Sketches of Nature, History & Industry in North-Western Massachusetts. Boston, 1869. *1st. Edn.* 12mo. Orig. cl., institutional bkplt.; from liby. of F.D. Roosevelt, inscr. by him. (SG. Mar.15; 48) $150

GLADKY, Serge
– Nouvelles Compositions Décoratives. Paris, 1920's. 1st. Series. 4to. 48 pochoir-cold. plts., loose as iss., cl.-bkd. decor. bds. (SG. Aug.25; 163)
$250
– – **Anr. Edn.** Paris, ca. 1930. 1st. & 2nd. Series: in 2 portfos. 4to. Some spotting, margins slightly browned, cold. pict. orig. hf. linen portfos., slightly faded & worn. (H. Nov.24; 2445) DM 660

GLADWIN, Francis
– The Persian Moonshee. 'Calcutta ptd., re-ptd. in L. at the Oriental Pr.', 1801. 2 vols. in 1. 4to. In Persian & Engl., orig. bds., spine defect., unopened. (C. Nov.9; 140) *Franklin.* £220

GLANVIL, Joseph
– Saducismus Triumphans: Or, Full & Plain Evidence concerning Witches & Apparitions. 1681. *1st. Edn.* Errata lf. at end, some slight staining to corners of some early ll., name cut from title, old cf., worn, spine torn at foot. (LC. Jul.5; 319) £120
– – **Anr. Edn.** 1682. *2nd. Edn.* Ppl holed with loss of 1 letter, old cf. [Wing G823] (CSK. Sep.30; 118) £95
– – **Anr. Edn.** L., 1682-81. *2nd. Edn.* 2 pts. in 1 vol. Sig. obliterated on title, lacks? hf.-title or privilege lf., newer three-qtr. leath., brkn. (RO. Dec.11; 121)
$200

GLAPTHORNE, Henry
– The Ladies Priviledge. 1640. *1st. Edn.* 4to. Title-p. dust-stained, later mor.-bkd. bds.; bkplts. of Thomas Holley, F.S.A. [STC 11910] (BBA. Jan.19; 128) *Maggs.* £160

GLASER, Curt
– Die Graphik der Neuzeit vom Anfang des XIX. Jahrhunderts bis zur Gegenwart. Ill.:– E. Munch, L. Corinth, Liebermann, Pechstein, Slevogt & Purmann. 1922. *(150) numbered De Luxe Edn.* 4to. 6 orig. ills., orig. burgundy pold. mor. gt. (GB. May 5; 2573) DM 1,500
– – **Anr. Edn.** Berlin, 1922. 4to. Orig. cl., soiled. (S. Oct.4; 155) *Hamery.* £50

GLASER, C. & others
– Max Beckmann. [1924]. *(180) numbered De Luxe Edn.* 4to. 4 sigd. orig. ills., orig. hf. leath. gt. (GB. May 5; 2180) DM 6,800

GLASGOW, Ellen
– Works. N.Y., 1938. *Virginia Edn. (810) numbered & sigd. by author.* 12 vols. Lge. 8vo. Vell.-bkd. buckram, orig. cl. s.-c.'s, partly unc. & unopened. (SG. Nov.3; 86) $375
– – **Anr. Copy.** 12 vols. Orig. parch.-bkd. cl. (SPB. Dec.13; 532) $225

GLASSE, Hannah
– The Complete Confectioner: or, the Whole Art of Confectionary Made Plain & Easy, ... N.d. 8vo. (in 4's). Cancellans title, otherwise conforms to 1762 edns. cited in Bitting, some browning & dampstaining. cont. cf., worn, lacks end-papers. (CSK. Mar.9; 97) £130

GLASSER, E.
– Costumes Militaires. Paris, 1900. Hf. chagrin, wrap. preserved. (HD. Jan.27; 333) Frs. 1,300

GLATZ, Jacob
– Die Frohen Kinder, oder Erzählungen und Bilder aus der Kinderwelt. Ill.:– Weiss. Vienna, Trieste & Baden, [1806]. *1st. Edn.* Ob. 4to. German & Fr. text, 6 hand-cold. engraved plts., slightly spotted, cont. marb. bds.; van Veen coll. (S. Feb.28; 145)
£320

GLAUBER, J.R.
– Des Teutschlands Wohlfahrt. Amst., 1656-61. *1st. German Edn.* 6pts. & Appendix to pt. 5 in 1 vol. Pt. 6. cut slightly close in upr. margin, pt. 3 with wear, some slight browning, cont. vell., blind-tooled monog. 'FK' on both covers. (R. Apr.4; 1434)
DM 5,800

GLEASON'S PICTORIAL DRAWING ROOM COMPANION
Boston, 7 Jan.-30 Dec. 1854. Vol. 6 no. 1-Vol. 7 no. 21, in 2 vols. Fo. Slightly darkening, some creasing or chipping, orig. stpd. gt.-decor. cl., Vol. 7 incorrectly labeled Vol. 5 on cover, covers moderately worn. (CBA. Mar.3; 222) $100

GLEESON, Rev. J.
– History of the Ely O'Carroll Territory or Ancient Ormond. Dublin, 1915. *1st. Edn.* Frontis. map in zerox, cl. (GM. Dec.7; 238) £70

GLEICHEN-RUSSWORM, A. von
– Im Ring der Zeit. Ill.:– Ferdinand Staeger. Dresden & Leipzig, 1924. *(200) numbered.* 4to. 5 sigd. orig. etchings, hf. mor., gt. decor. (GB. May 5; 3354) DM 400

GLEICHMANN, Otto
– Judas Makkabäus. 1919. *(50) numbered sigd. by artist.* Fo. On Japan, 10 sigd. orig. lithos., loose ll. under guards, bd. portfo., slightly defect. (GB. May 5; 2574) DM 1,900

GLEIG, George Robert
[–] A Narrative of the Campaigns of the British Army at Washington & New Orleans ... in the Years 1814 & 1815. L., 1821. *1st. Edn.* Lacks errata lf., orig. bds., rebkd., corners bumped, the Rt. Hon. Visc. Eccles copy, unc. [Sabin 27568] (CNY. Nov.18; 122) $110

GLEIM, Betty
[–] Bremisches Kochbuch. Bremen, [1808]. *1st. Edn.* Pt. 1 (of 2). Title with sm. tear bkd., slightly browned & foxed, cont. bds, spine defect. (D. Nov.24; 4142) DM 650
– – **Anr. Edn.** Bremen, 1830. *5th. Edn.* Cont. bds., bumped. (BR. Apr.12; 1162) DM 450

GLEIM, Johann Wilhelm Ludwig
[–] Gedichte nach den Minnesingern. Berlin, 1773. *1st. Edn.* Dedication copy, 2 pp. torn, slightly browned & foxed, mod. mor., cont. bds. bnd. in, unc; Hauswedell coll. (H. May 24; 1294)
DM 1,400
– Preussische Kriegslieder. Ill.:– Meil. Berlin, 1758. *1st. Edn.* Sm. 8vo. Orig. bds., unc. (C. Dec.9; 220) *Wenner.* £100

GLEIZES, Albert
– Kubismus. (Bauhausbücher Bd. XIII.). München, [1928]. *1st. German Edn.* Orig. linen, bdg. & typography by L. Moholy-Nagy. (H. Nov.24; 1344) DM 680

GLEIZES, A. & Metzinger, J.
– Du Cubisme. Ill.:– M. Duchamp & others. Paris, 1947. *(400) on pur fil Lana.* Lge. 8vo. 7 orig. ills., loose ll. in orig. wraps. (H. May 23; 1239)
DM 1,750

GLENDINING & CO.
– Coin Catalogues. 1963-79. 33 vols. A run. 4to. Priced thro.-out, cont. cl., orig. wraps. bnd. in. (S. May 1; 469) *Dreesman.* £360

GLEN INNES DISTRICT
– The Land of 'The Beardies', being the History of the Glen Innes District ... Glen Innes, 1922. Ob. 8vo. Tear in hf.-title, several rubber stps., wraps. (KH. May 1; 302) Aus. $100

GLEZ. DE MEDINA BARBA, D.
– Examen de Fortificación. Madrid, 1599. 4to. Cf. (DS. Apr.27; 2675) Pts. 125,000

GLIDDEN, Charles J. (Ed.)
See— AERONAUTICAL DIGEST

GLISSON, Francis
- Anatomia Hepatis. Amst., 1665. 12mo. Cf., worn; Dr. Walter Pagel copy. (S. Feb.7; 141) *Pratt.* £90

GLONER, Samuel
- Novae Sacrorum Bibliorum, Figurae Versibus Latinis & Germanicis ... ; Epigrammatum Bibliorum Latino-Germanicorum. Strassburg, 1625. Together 2 works in 1 vol. Sm. 8vo. Very browned thro.-out, old vell. (SG. Feb.9; 116) $325

GLORIEUX, G.
See— COCKX-INDESTEGE, E. & Glorieux, G.

GLUCK, Chr. W.
- Orfeo ed Euridice. Azione Theatrale. Ill.:– N. Le Mire after C. Monnet. Paris, 1764. *1st. Edn.* Fo. Frontis., title & next ll. slightly foxed, 1 p. with pasted tear, minimal browning, 19th. C. hf. leath., bumped, slightly loose. (HK. Nov.9; 2246)
DM 2,500

GLUTZ VON BLOTZHEIM, U.N.
See— BAUER, K.M. & Glutz von Blotzheim, U.N.

GLYPTOTHEQUE NY-CARLSBERG (LA)
Munich, 1896. 3 vols. Fo. 220 mntd. photographs, loose in folding buckram cases, some soiling. (S. May 1; 695) *Heneage.* £210

GOBEL, Heinrich
- Die Wandteppiche. Leipzig & Berlin, 1923-34. 3 pts. in 6 vols. Fo. Orig. linen, 2 vols. slightly faded, 1 spine with sm. defect at foot. (HK. May 17; 3483)
DM 3,600
- Wandteppiche – Die Niederlande. Leipzig, 1923. 2 vols. 4to. Orig. cl. (SKC. Sep.9; 1804) £70

GOBERT, Théodore
- Liége à travers les Ages. Les Rues de Liége. Liége, 1924-29. 6 vols. 4to. Hf. mor., corners, spine decor., wrap. preserved. (LM. Oct.22; 245) B.Frs. 16,000

GOBET, Nicholas
See— PICHON, Thomas Jean & Gobet, Nicolas

GOBINEAU, Arthur Graf von
- Die Liebenden von Kandahar. Trans.:– Franz Werner Schmidt. Ill.:– H. Steiner-Prag. Berlin, ca. 1925. *(200).* Printers mark sigd., 3 vigs. in orig. etching, 6 full-p. sigd. orig. etchings, vell. gt., monog. orig. aquarelle. (GB. May 5; 3359)
DM 1,700

GOBINEAU, Joseph-Arthur, comte de
- Les Pléiades. Stockholm, 1874. *Orig. Edn.* 12mo. Sewed. (HD. Dec.16; 130) Frs. 1,650

GOCHHAUSEN, H.F. v.
[–] Notabilia Venatoris. Nuremb., 1731. *9th. Edn.* Last & index ll. wormed in lr. margin, cont. hf. leath. gt., 3 sm. wormholes in spine. (R. Oct.12; 2001)
DM 1,500
– – Anr. Edn. Ill.:– Brühl. Weimar, 1751. Some wear, 3 sm. wormholes, leath. gt. (V. Sep.29; 1387)
DM 2,300

GOCLENIUS, Rodolph
- Tractatvs de Magnetica Curatione. Marburg, 1609. *1st. Edn.* (Bound with:) – Tractatvs de Portentosis Luxuriosis ac Monstrosis. Marburg, 1609. Together 2 works in 1 vol. Foxed, cont. limp vell., slightly loose, lacks ties. (HK. Nov.9; 1959)
DM 420

GODART & Duponchel
- Histoire Naturelle des Lepidoptères ou Papillons de France. 1821-44. 14 vols., with Supp. 'Papillons d'Europe' & 1 vol. 'Catalogue Méthodique' & 4 vols. Atlas. 1 plt. in black, 545 engraved & cold. plts., some foxing, cont. unif. hf. cf. (HD. Feb.29; 17) Frs. 13,000

GODDARD, T. & Booth, John
- Costume of the Armies of Europe in 81 Plates. 1812-15. 96 hand-cold. engraved plts., a few slightly stained or soiled, many ll. loose, later cl., covers detchd., as a coll. of plts., w.a.f. (LC. Mar.1; 66)
£480

GODDEN, Geoffrey A.
- Encyclopaedia of British Pottery & Porcelain Marks. L., 1964. *1st. Edn.* No bdg. stated. (JL. Jun.24; 221) Aus. $140

GODEFROID, A.
- Armées des Souverains Alliés, Années 1814 et 1815. Paris, n.d. Ob. fo. 3 extra plts., hf. chagrin. (HD. Jan.27; 273) Frs. 6,600

GODEFROY, Louis
- L'Oeuvre Gravé de Jean-Emile Laboureur, Première Partie: Gravures en Taille Douce. Paris, 1929. 4to. Orig. engraved frontis., sewed. (HD. Dec.16; 135) Frs. 3,100

GODEFROY or GOTHOFREDUS, Denis or Dionysius
- Opuscula Juridica, Politica, Historica. Geneva, 1654-68. 7 pts. in 1 vol. Inserted port., few blank margins slightly stained, cont. vell. (VG. Sep.14; 951) Fls. 850

GODEY'S LADY'S BOOK
Phila., 1850, 1853-55, 1857-58, 1860, 1862, 1865. 9 vols. Many ills. hand-cold., orig. leath., all bdgs. etched, very shabby, w.a.f. (SG. Dec.15; 150)
$225
– – Anr. Edn. Phila., [1853-61]. 9 vols. Lge. 8vo. Nearly every no. contains a hand-cold. plt., few double-p. plts. reprd., plts. not collated but apparently all present, unif. mod. gt. hf. mor., cl., w.a.f. (SG. Jun.7; 354) $250

GODFREY, Col. M.J.
- Monograph & Iconograph of Native British Orchidaceae. Ill.:– Hilda M. Godefery. Camb., 1933. *1st. Edn.* Lge. 4to. Perforated liby. stp. on title, buckram, shelf mark on spine. (SG. Mar.22; 139)
$110

GODLEY, Alexander
- Life of an Irish Soldier. L., [1939]. Cl., pres. copy from author to Winston Churchill, 28 Jan. 1940, with his & R.S. Churchill's bkplts. (LH. Jan.15; 260) $190

GODMAN, Eva M.
See— ARCHER, Sir Geoffrey & Godman, Eva M.

GODMAN, Frederick du Cane & Salvin, Osbert
See— BIOLOGIA CENTRALI-AMERICANA

GODMAN COLLECTION
- Persian Ceramic Art – The Thirteenth Century Lustred Vases. Ed.:– Henry Wallis. L., for private circulation, 1891. *(200) numbered.* Fo. 46 litho. plts., gt.-lettered cl., rubbed, spine ends frayed. (SG. Jan.26; 93) $225

GODWIN, William 'Edward Baldwin'
- Thoughts on Man. 1831. 19th. C. hf. cf. (BBA. Sep.29; 181) *Price.* £150

GOEBEL, H.
- Wandteppiche. 1. Teil: Die Niederlande. Leipzig, 1923. 2 vols. (text & plts.). Sm. fo. 509 plts., some cold., orig. cl. gt., partly discold. (VS. Jun.6; 38)
Fls. 625

GOEBEL, Theodor
- Die Graphische Kuenste der Gegenwart. Ed.:– Felix Krais. Stuttgart, 1902. Sm. fo. Cold.-pict. cl. gt.; from Grol.Cl. Liby., given in 1903 by T.L.De Vinne, with his T.L.s. tipped in. (SG. Jan.5; 145)
$175

GOEDAERDT, Jan
- Metamorphosis Naturalis ofte Historische Beschryvinghe. Middelburgh, [1662-69]. *1st. Edn.* 3 vols. Sm. 8vo. Additional hand-cold. engraved titles, port., 126 hand-cold. plts., those in Vol. III lettered A-Y, 1 plt. shaved, mor. gt. [Nissen 1603 (erroneously calling for an additional plt. in Vol. I)] (C. Nov.16; 247) *Quaritch.* £580
– – Anr. Edn. Middelburgh, ca. 1669. *1st. Edn.* Vols. 1 & 2 only (of 3). Sm. 8vo. Additional hand-cold. engraved titles, port., 105 (of 106) hand-cold. plts., some captioned in ink in early hand, some slightly wormed, port. shaved, lacks frontis.'s(?), cont. spr. cf. gt., spines partly loose. (SG. Mar.22; 140) $220

GOEDEKE, K.
- Grundriss zur Geschichte der Deutschen Dichtung aus den Quellen. Ed.:– [H. Rambaldo]. Leipzig, Dresden & Berlin, 1884-1964. Pts. 1-15 & New Series vol. 1 & Index vol. Orig. linen. (R. Apr.3; 635) DM 2,500

GOELDI, Dr. Emilio A. (Ed.)
See— ALBUM DE AVES AMAZONICA

GOES, Damiano de
- Fides, Religio, Moresque Aethiopium sub Imperio Preciosi Ioannis (quem vulgò Presbyterum Ioannem vocant) degentium ... Paris, 1541. Sm. 8vo. Lacks last lf. with printer's mark, slightly browned & stained, some old annots., including some lines in Coptic, later vell. (VG. Nov.30; 827) Fls. 450

GOESIUS, Wilhelm
- Rei Agrariae Auctores Legesque Variae. Amst., 1674. 2 pts. in 1 vol. 4to. LP., sm. section of blank margin of 2XI torn & reprd., late 19th. C. mor., gt. (CSK. Nov.4; 121) £220

GOETGHEBUER, P.J.
- Choix des Monuments, Edifices et Maisons les Plus Remarquables du Royaume des Pays-Bas. Gand, 1827. Fo. 120 plts., heightened with col., hf. cf., worn. (LM. Oct.22; 290) B.Frs. 40,000

GOETHE, Johann Wolfgang von
- Auserlesene Lieder und Balladen. Ein Strauss. Hammersmith, Doves Pr., 1916. *(175) on Bütten.* Orig. vell. (D. Nov.24; 3037) DM 1,500
– – Anr. Copy. Hand-bnd. orig. vell. (H. Nov.23; 996) DM 1,100
- Aus Meinem Leben, Dichtung und Wahrheit. Tübingen, 1811-17. *1st. Edn.* 5 vols. (Band I-III, 2. Abt. I-II). Sm. 8vo. Cont. paper bds., marb. sides, spines gt. (slightly rubbed). (C. May 30; 26a) *Hannas.* £200
- Balladen. Ill.:– S. Frank. Berlin, 1919. *(85) on Japan Imperial.* Lge. 4to. Orig. vell., gold-tooled cover ill. & inner gt. dentelle, slightly spotted; printers mark sigd. by artist. (H. Nov.24; 1509)
DM 680
– – Anr. Edn. [Darmstadt, Ernst Ludwig Pr., 1924]. *(30) numbered Deluxe Edn. on Japan.* Leath., gt. spine, cover & inner & outer dentelle, sigd. Ernst Rehbein, spine slightly faded, sm. scratches on corner. (HK. May 16; 2720) DM 1,100.
- Briefwechsel zwischen Goethe und Zelter. Berlin, 1833-34. *1st. Edn.* 6 vols. Slightly browned, some foxing, 1 title lf. loose, cont. bds., corners restored with linen. (GB. May 4; 1282) DM 580
- Clavigo. Leipzig, 1774. *1st. Edn. 1st. Printing.* Some slight foxing, bds., col. paper covered, spine faded, unc.; from Richard Doetz-Benziger liby.; Hauswedell coll. (H. May 24; 1309) DM 1,200
– – Anr. Edn. Ill.:– H. Steiner-Prag. Weimar, 1917. *De Luxe Edn., (25) on Bütten.* Sm. 4to. Hand-bnd. orig. vell., slightly discold., all lithos. sigd. (H. Nov.24; 2103) DM 420
- Drei Märchen. Ill.:– Karl-Georg Hirsch, Rolf Münzer, Rainer Herold. Leipzig, 1981. *(300). (100) numbered for trade.* Fo. 9 sigd. orig. ills., orig. hf. vell. gt. (GB. May 5; 2584) DM 400
- Egmont, ein Trauerspiel. Leipzig, 1788. *1st. Edn.* Slight browning thro.-out, orig. paper bds., spine defect., unc. (C. Dec.9; 221) *Fischer.* £240
– – Anr. Copy. Light browning, cont. style bds.; Hauswedell coll. (H. May 24; 1315) DM 1,000
- Erklärung der zu Goethe's Farbenlehre Gehörigen Tafeln; Anzeige und Uebersicht des Goethischen Werkes zur Farbenlehre. [Tübingen, 1810]. Sm. 4to. 15 plts. only (of 17) including 11 cold., without 2 text vols., cont. qtr. cf. (S. Apr.10; 319)
Kubicek. £60
– – Anr. Copy. 4to. 17 plts. (numbered 16), including 12 hand-cold., cont. hf. chagrin, spine & corners slightly defect. (VG. Nov.30; 756)
Fls. 1,300
- Erwin und Elmire. Leipzig, 1788. Special printing from vol. 5 of 8 vol. coll. Edn. 1787-90, slightly browned thro.-out, early 19th. C. red mor., blind-tooled & gt. spine, covers, inner & outer dentelles; from R. Doetsch-Benziger liby; Hauswedell coll. (H. May 24; 1316) DM 1,500
- Faust. Ein Fragment. Leipzig, 1790. *8th. Edn. 1st. Book Edn.* Slightly foxed thro.-out, no bdg. stated. (HK. Nov.10; 2437) DM 4,500

GOETHE, Johann Wolfgang von *-Contd.*

– – **Anr. Copy.** Lightly soiled & browned thro.-out, title with old owners mark, bds.; Hauswedell coll. (H. May 24; 1318) DM 2,800

– **Faust. Erster Theil.** Tübingen, 1808. *1st. Edn. of Compl. 1st. Pt.* Sm. sq. 8vo. Slightly browned or spotted, cont. bds., spine reprd.; Frederic Dannay copy. (CNY. Dec.16; 152) $380

– – **Anr. Copy.** MS. dedication & poem by Schiller on end-paper dtd. Feb. 1903, old bds. (BR. Apr.12; 1413) DM 1,000

– – **Anr. Edn.** Ill.:– Sepp Frank. München, 1921. *(190). (25) De Luxe Edn.* Fo. 25 full-p. sigd. orig. etchings, Orig. copperplt. worked in s.-c. cover, orig. vell., gt., sigd. Knorr & Hirth, inner dentelle, doubl. & end-paper with orig. etching, orig. vell. s.-c. (GB. May 5; 2539) DM 1,500.

– – **Anr. Copy.** Fo. Orig. vell., gt. spine, covers, inner dentelles & etched doubls., by Knorr & Hirth, München, orig. vell. s.-c., copperplt. laid in cover, printer's mark & all etchings sigd. by artist. (H. Nov.24; 1508) DM 800

– – **Anr. Edn.** Ill.:– J. Holtz. [Zürich], ca. 1925. *(400) B. Edn.* Pt. 1. Fo. Hand-bnd. hf. linen. (H. May 23; 1296) DM 420

– **Faust. Zweiter Theil.** Ill.:– Max Slevogt. Berlin, [1926-] 1927. *(250) numbered.* Lge. fo. Red mor., gold-tooled. (HK. May 17; 3143) DM 9,200

– – **Anr. Edn.** Ill.:– M. Slevogt. Berlin, 1927. *(250).* Fo. Incorrect no. of lithos. mentioned, hand-bnd. red mor., printer's mark sigd. by artist. (H. Nov.24; 2059) DM 7,000

– **Faust. Erster & ZweiterTheil.** Ill.:– E.R. Gill. [(Hammersmith, Doves Pr., 1906 & 1910)]. *(25) or (22) on vell. De Luxe Edn.* Pts. I & II. Lge. 8vo. Hand-bnd. orig. red mor., gt. decor. spine, covers, inner & outer dentelles, slight printing fault on lr. cover Pt. II; William Davignon ex-libris inside cover. (H. May 22; 1005) DM 14,000

– – **Anr. Edn.** Ill.:– E.R. Gill (initials). [Hammersmith, Doves Pr., 1906 & 1910]. *(300) & (250) on Bütten.* 2 vols. Hand-bnd. orig. vell. (H. Nov.23; 989) DM 2,400

– – **Anr. Edn.** Ill.:– F.H. Ehmcke. Jena, 1908-09. *Jubilee Edn. Ltd. Iss. numbered.* 2 pts. in 1 vol. Orig. blind-tooled leath. gt, 1 (of 2) clasps (2nd. clasp present but detchd.). (GB. May 5; 2363) DM 550

– – **Anr. Edn.** [L., Doves Pr., 1910]. *(275). (250) on paper.* 2 vols. 4to. Vell., s.-c.'s.; Joseph Manuel Andreini bkplt. (LH. Sep.25; 360) $375

– – **Anr. Edn.** Darmstadt, Ernst Ludwig Pr., 1922-23. Pts. 1 & 2 (of 3) in 1 vol. 4to. Red mor., decor. spine, cover & inner dentelle, bd. s.-c., by Rudolf Lang, München. (HK. May 17; 2721) DM 1,050

– – **Anr. Edn.** München, Bremer Pr., 1925. Red-brown mor., decor., ex-libris. (HK. Nov.11; 3441) DM 420

– – **Anr. Edn.** Ed.:– Max Hecker. Ill.:– Anna Simons. [Munich, Bremer Pr., 1925]. On Zanders Alfa papier, mor., cont. owner's gift inscr. on blank fly-lf. (SG. Mar.29; 25) $100

– **Faust. Erster, Zweiter Teil & Urfaust.** [Frankfurt, Ernst Ludwig Pr., 1922-24]. *Ltd. Iss. on Bütten.* 3 vols. Sm. 4to. Orig. hf. vell., faded. (H. Nov.23; 1040) DM 800

– **Faust [English].** Trans.:– John Auster. Ill.:– Harry Clarke. N.Y., ca. 1925. *1st. Edn. Amer. Iss., (1000) sigd. by artist.* 4to. Ink inscr. to fly, hf. vell. & bds., some spotting to tail of spine. (CBA. Aug.21; 103) $120

– **Faust. Tragédie. [French].** Trans.:– Albert Stapfer. Ill.:– E. Delacroix. Paris, 1828. *1st. Edn.* Fo. Lithos. on white vell., port. on China, 1 sm. tear, on verso of 1st. litho. coll. stp. EB (Eugène Bouvy), hf. title with thin place, 3 ll. with sm. corners torn off, hand-bnd. hf. leath. by P. Martin, orig. litho. wraps. bnd. in, slightly spotted, sm. repairs; Hauswedell coll. (H. May 24; 1335) DM 27,000

– – **Anr. Edn.** Trans.:– Gérard de Nerval. 1835. *2nd. Edn.* 16mo. Washed & mntd., hf. cf., corners, by Yseux, spine decor., wrap. (HD. May 4; 373) Frs. 1,400

– – **Anr. Edn.** Ill.:– Tony Johannot. Paris, 1847. *1st. Johannot Edn.* Some foxing in places, cont. black mor., gt. decor. & inner & outer dentelles, sigd. Kaufmann. (GB. Nov.4; 1807) DM 440

– – **Anr. Edn.** Ill.:– after F.L. Schmied. Paris, 1938. *(100). (20) De Luxe Edn. with 2 series of woodcuts.* Lge. 4to. Loose ll. in orig. linen wrap., orig. linen s.-c., printers mark not sigd. (D. Nov.24; 3184) DM 2,600

– **Gedichte.** Ill.:– E. Barlach. Berlin, 1924. *(100).* Fo. On Bütten, 31 orig. lithos., some full-p., 2 ll. creased, loose in orig. hf. vell. box, defect. (BR. Apr.13; 1633) DM 1,800

– – **Anr. Edn.** Ed.:– H.G. Gräf. Berlin, Maximilian-Gesellschaft, 1924-25. *(300) on Bütten.* 4 vols. 4to. Hand-bnd. hf. leath., by Heyne-Ballmüller, Berlin, spine darkened. (H. Nov.23; 1167) DM 460

– **Geschichte Gottfrieds von Berlichingen mit der Eisernen Hand.** Ill.:– L. Corinth. Berlin, 1921-22. *(192) numbered.* 4to. Printers mark sigd. by artist, 26 orig. etchings (2 full-p.), some margin browning, orig. bds. (GB. May 5; 2291) DM 2,800

– – **Anr. Edn.** Ill.:– L. Corinth. Berlin, [1921-22]. *De Luxe Edn., (46).* Lge. 4to. Hand-bnd. mor., gold decor. spine, covers, inner & outer dentelles, printer's mark sigd. by artist. (H. Nov.24; 1455) DM 7,200

– – **Anr. Edn.** Ill.:– Werner Schmidt. Leipzig, [1925]. *(220) numbered.* 4to. 29 orig. lithos., hand-bnd. orig. mor., gt. outer dentelle, orig. bd. s.-c., sigd. by Enders. (BR. Apr.13; 1711) DM 400

– **Gott und Welt.** [Leipzig, Ernst Ludwig Pr., 1913]. *De Luxe Edn., (30) on Japan.* Orig. hand-bnd. cf. (H. Nov.23; 1034) DM 620

– **Götz von Berlichingen mit der Eisernen Hand.** [Darmstadt], 1773. *1st. Edn.* Wide margin, title with sm. MS. owners mark, spotting, mostly light, some heavier, 2 ll. with sm. margin erosions, cont. marb. hf. leath. gt., worn, corners slightly bumped, lr. jnt. lacks sm. piece of leath. (HK. May 16; 2031) DM 10,000

– **Hermann und Dorothea.** Ill.:– Chodowiecki; Grepius after Gilly. Berlin, [1797]. *De Luxe 1st. Edn. 1st. Printing.* Lightly foxed thro.-out, orig. red mor. s.-c., slightly rubbed; Hauswedell coll. (H. May 24; 1323) DM 1,900

– – **Anr. Edn.** Ill.:– F. Oberkogler [after Lips], after Chodowiecki & Dunker. [Bern], 1804. Orig. bds., engraved ills., slightly spotted & bumped; Hauswedell coll. (H. May 24; 1326) DM 400

– – **Anr. Edn.** Ill.:– Esslinger after H. Chr. Kolbe. Braunschweig, 1829. *De Luxe Edn. in lge. Bodoni type on vell.* Some browning, cont. chagrin, gt. decor. spine, blind-tooled, gt. outer dentelle, corner fleurons inside cover, wtrd. silk doubls., lacquered end-papers, Hauswedell coll. (H. May 24; 1336) DM 2,600

– – **Anr. Edn.** Ill.:– F.W. Kleukens. Leipzig, Ernst Ludwig Pr., 1908. *(180) on Bütten.* Orig. suede, gold-tooled title vig., some fading. (HK. May 17; 2724) DM 1,300

– – **Anr. Edn.** Ed.:– E. Schulte-Strathaus. Ill.:– A. Simons. München, Bremer Pr., 1922. *(500).* 4to. Hand-bnd. orig. vell., by Frieda Thiersch. (H. Nov.23; 955) DM 480

– **Iphigenie auf Tauris.** Leipzig, 1787. *1st. separate Edn.* Special printing from Vol. III of 8 vol. coll. Edn., lightly spotted thro.-out, red mor. 1804, gt. spine, gold borders, gt. inscr. on upr. cover: 'presenté à Mademoiselle Marie Meroni' & on lr. cover dtd. 4 Aug. 1804, from Richard Doetsch-Benziger liby; Hauswedell coll. (H. May 24; 1312) DM 4,000

– – **Anr. Edn.** Leipzig, 1787. *1st. Edn. 2nd. Printing.* Without vigs., slightly browned & foxed, slightly stained in margin at beginning, cont. red hf. leath. gt., worn & slightly bumped, MS. dedication on end-paper. (HK. May 16; 2033) DM 1,200

– – **Anr. Edn.** [Hammersmith, Doves Pr., 1912]. *(200).* Orig. hand-bnd. mor., gold decor. (H. Nov.23; 994) DM 2,200

– – **Anr. Edn.** Ed.:– M. Hecker. Ill.:– A. Simons. München, Bremer Pr., 1922. *(300) on Bütten.* 4to. Orig. hand-bnd. vell., by Frieda Thiersch, gt. decor. (H. Nov.23; 934) DM 620

– **Italian Journey.** Trans.:– W.H. Auden & Elizabeth Mayer. [Verona], Giovanni Mardersteig, Pantheon Books, [1962]. *(2500).* 4to. Decor. cl., jacket, box lightly faded. (CBA. Aug.21; 249a) $100

– **Italienische Reise.** Ed.:– Georg von Gravenitz. 1912. *1st. Edn.* Fo. Orig. hf. leath. gt., by E.R. Weiss. (GB. May 5; 2578) DM 700

– – **Anr. Copy.** Fo. MS. dedication on early blank lf., some foxing, orig. hf. leath., corners lightly worn. (HK. May 16; 2034) DM 420

– – **Anr. Edn.** 1925. Fo. Red mor. gt., d.-w., s.-c. (P. Oct.20; 78) £95

– – **Anr. Copy.** Fo. Orig. red mor. gt. (R. Oct.11; 275a) DM 700

– – **Anr. Edn.** N.p., n.d. Lge. 4to. Orig. hf. leath. gt. (D. Nov.24; 2279) DM 460

– **Leben des Benvenuto Cellini.** Tübingen, 1803. *1st. definitive separate Edn.* 2 vols. in 1. 2 ll. reprd., minimal spotting, hf. leath., old spine, slightly worn; Hauswedell coll. (H. May 24; 1325) DM 720

– **Die Leiden des Jungen Werthers.** Ill.:– A.F. Oeser. Leipzig, 1774. *1st. Edn.* 2 pts. in 1 vol. 1st Printing. with list of printing errors on last p., no. 36 on p. 39, 2 press corrections, 3 Kartonblätter, slightly browned, minimal spotting, title with old name in lr. margin, cont. cf. gt., slightly worn; Hauswedell coll. (H. May 24; 1310) DM 14,000

– – **Anr. Copy.** 2 pts. in 1 vol. Weak stp. on 2 pp., 8 pp. slightly spotted, hf. leath., ca. 1850, gt., spine & corners worn, gt. partly defect., inner jnts. strengthened with linen. (HK. May 16; 2035) DM 7,000

– – **Anr. Edn.** Leipzig, 1775. *2nd. Edn.* 2 pts. in 1 vol. Foxed, cont. hf. leath. gt., corners slightly bumped. (R. Apr.3; 211) DM 850

– – **Anr. Edn.** Ill.:– Graily Hewitt. [Hammersmith, Doves Pr., 1911]. *De Luxe Edn., (5) on vell., with initials in gold.* Orig. hand-bnd. vell. (H. Nov.23; 992) DM 4,800

– – **Anr. Edn.** [L., Doves Pr., 1911]. *(225). (200) on paper.* Vell. (LH. Sep.25; 359) $170

– **Liebesgedichte.** Ed.:– H.G. Graf. Ill.:– E.R. Weiss (binding design). Leipzig, 1912. *De Luxe Edn., (200) on China.* 1st. & last ll. & end-papers foxed, ex-libris, hand-bnd. red mor., by Enders, Leipzig, slightly rubbed. (H. Nov.23; 1064) DM 470

– **Das Maerchen.** Ill.:– M. Slevogt. Dresden, [1922]. *(260) numbered.* Orig. sigd. litho., orig. gt.-decor. vell. (GB. Nov.5; 3019) DM 450

– **Der Mann von Fünfzig Jahren.** Ill.:– Bangemann & Hönemann after M. Liebermann. Berlin, 1922. *(100) numbered.* On Bütten, orig. hf. vell. (HK. May 17; 2959) DM 480

– – **Anr. Edn.** Ill.:– M. Liebermann. Berlin, 1922. *Ltd. Edn.* 4to. Printers mark sigd. by artist, some foxing, orig. hf. vell., browned, slightly spotted & bumped. (H. May 23; 1357) DM 500

– **Marienbader Elegie.** [München, Bodoni Pr., 1923]. *(151) on Van Gelder Bütten.* 4to. Orig. bds., end-papers lightly browned. (H. Nov.24; 1209) DM 1,400

– **Neue Schriften.** Berlin, 1792-1800. *1st. Edn.* 7 vols. Sm. 8vo. 8 inserted folding ll. of music, directions to binder in Vol. 4, advt. lf. at end of Vol. 7, lacks? separate title lf. to 'Wilhelm Meister' in Vol. 6, 1 engraved plt. slightly stained, early 19th. C. cf.-bkd. bds. (C. Dec.9; 227) *Bender.* £380

– – **Anr. Edn.** Berlin, 1794-1800. *2nd. definitive coll. Edn.* Vol. 1 with year 1800 (for 1792), vol. IV states Frankfurt & Leipzig, with last mus. supp. in MS., cont. cf., decor. spine gt., cover slightly rubbed, 1 corner bumped, Hauswedell coll. (H. May 24; 1303) DM 5,200

– **Die Novelle.** Ill.:– O. Bangemann after M. Liebermann. Berlin, 1921. *Ltd. Iss.* 4to. Orig. pict. bds.; printer's mark sigd. by artist. (H. Nov.24; 1780) DM 420

– **Pandora, Ein Festspiel.** Ill.:– Ludwig v. Hofmann. Zürich & Hellerau, 1923. *(300). (270) numbered.* 4to. Printers mark MS. sigd. by artist, 8 full-p. orig. woodcuts, orig. hf. vell. gt. (GB. May 5; 2700) DM 450

– – **Anr. Edn.** Ill.:– L. von Hoffmann. Zürich, [1923]. *(300).* Lge. 4to. Orig. hf. vell.; printer's mark sigd. by artist. (H. Nov.24; 1610) DM 420

– **Les Passions du Jeune Werther.** Trans.:– Aubry. Manheim & Paris, 1777. *Orig. Edn.* Cont. marb. cf., decor. spine. (HD. Sep.22; 252) Frs. 1,150

– **Promethée.** Trans.:– André Gide. Ill.:– Henry Moore. Paris, 1950. *(183) numbered.* Fo. This copy unnumbered, with extra suite of all lithos. except lettering for title-p. in early state, mor., by Leroux, covers decor., lightened by paring leath. linked by irregular raised strips of cold. cf., title tooled on spine in cols., Japanese end-papers, hf. mor. folder, s.-c. (S. Nov.21; 199) *Minou.* £3,200

– – **Anr. Edn.** Trans.:– André Gide. Ill.:– Mourlot

Frères after Henry Moore. [Paris], 1950 [i.e. 1951]. *(183) numbered on Marais wove paper. 1 of a few extra copies for collaborators, unnumbered.* Fo. 'Sculptured' bdg. of lev. mor. by P.L. Martin, sigd. on upr. turn-in, dtd. '1962' on lr. turn-in, covers with lge. inset suede panels, upr. cover panel filled with design of variously cut abstract shapes in pol. iridescent cf. onlaid to the suede & forming the letters of title, lr. cover plain, smooth spine gt.-lettered horizontally at top & foot & title set vertically in between, partly unc., orig. ptd. wraps. & backstrip preserved, matching hf. mor. chemise, unif. gt.-lettered on spine, matching mor.-edged s.-c.; publisher's copy, sigd. by artist on hf.-title. (CNY. May 18; 189) $11,000

– Prometheus. Darmstadt, Kleukens Pr., 1922. *(250) numbered.* Orig. gt.-decor. vell., sigd. Kleukens-Binderei. (GB. Nov.5; 2685) DM 430

– Propyläen. Ill.:– J. Chr. E. Müller & Horny after Müller & J.H. Meyer. Tübingen, 1798-1800. Vol. 1 pt. 1-Vol. 3 pt. 2. Together 6 pts. (all publd.). 2 advt. ll. in vol. 3, pt. 1, minimal spotting, margins slightly crumpled & dog-eared, orig. decor. wraps., 1 faded, 1 spine torn, partly unc.; Hauswedell coll. (H. May 24; 1324) DM 3,600

– Reineke Fuchs. Ill.:– after W. von Kaulbach. 1846. *1st. Edn.* Fo. Some light foxing, cont. leath., elab. gt., spine very defect., corners bumped, jnts. partly brkn. (GB. May 4; 1280) DM 520.

– – Anr. Edn. Ill.:– Wilhelm von Kaulbach. Stuttgart & Tübingen, 1846. 4to. Publisher's decor. cf., sm. scratch. (HD. Jun.13; 122) Frs. 1,000

– – Anr. Edn. Ill.:– after W. v. Kaulbach engraved by R. Rahn & A. Schleich. Stuttgart, [1846?]. Lge. 4to. Slightly foxed, mainly in margins, 2 pp. with 2 sm. margin tears, orig. leath., very rubbed. (R. Apr.3; 212) DM 460

– – Anr. Edn. Ill.:– W. von Kaulbach. Stuttgart, 1867. 4to. Orig. mor. gt., lightly rubbed. (CSK. Jun.15; 79) £55

– – Anr. Copy. Fo. Foxed thro.-out, affecting some plts., gt.-embossed & blind-stpd. mor. (CBA. Dec.10; 243) $200

– – Anr. Edn. Ill.:– Walther Klemm. 1916. *(650). (150) numbered De Luxe Edn. on van Gelder Bütten.* Fo. 47 orig. woodcuts, including 22 full-p. & monogrammed, Hf.-title & end-papers lightly margin browned, orig. leath. (GB. May 5; 2802) DM 800

– – Anr. Edn. Ill.:– Otto Schubert. 1921. *(250). (185) numbered on Bütten.* 4to. Printers mark sigd. by artist, orig. bds. (GB. May 5; 2580) DM 500

– Das Römische Carneval. Ill.:– H. Lips (title vig.), Georg Schütz engraved by Georg Melchior Kraus. Berlin, 1789. *(250).* 4to. On Dutch paper, plts. with some sm. tears outside plt. margin, text pp. slightly spotted, red hf. mor., decor. gt. spine, s.-c., early 19th. C. paper lined causing traces of lime on upr. cover, sm. ink number in lr. margin, unc.; Hauswedell coll. (H. May 24; 1317) DM 34,000

– – Anr. Edn. 1905. *Orig. Edn. (250) numbered.* 4to. Orig. gt.-decor. mor., orig. pict. wraps. bnd. in. (GB. Nov.5; 2520) DM 600

– – Anr. Edn. [Montagnola, 1924]. *(224) on Bütten.* Lge. 4to. Orig. vell., spine slightly faded. (HK. May 17; 3034) DM 1,300

– Sämmtliche Werke. Hersau, 1835-38. *1st. Swiss Edn.* 12 vols. Vol. VI mispaginated, Vol. III completed by photocopy, some slight foxing, cont. hf. leath., gold-tooled, bumped. (HT. May 9; 1471) DM 440

– – Anr. Edn. Stuttgart, 1857-58. *Compl. Edn.* 30 vols. Some light spotting, cont. hf. leath. gt., spine partly reprd. in 7 vols., some scratches, w.a.f. (HK. May 16; 2022) DM 950

– – Anr. Edn. Stuttgart & Berlin, [1902-07]. *[Jubiläums Edn.].* Vols. 1-36 (of 45) & 2 (of 4) Supp. vols. 4to. Orig. mor., gt., partly unc., w.a.f. (HK. May 16; 2025) DM 1,000

– – Anr. Copy. 40 vols. Lacks index vol., orig. hf. leath. gt., w.a.f. (HK. May 16; 2024) DM 540

– – Anr. Copy. 40 vols. Orig. pict. linen, spine slightly faded, some spines bumped, vol. 1 loose. (H. Nov.23; 1057) DM 420

– – Anr. Edn. München, & (from vol. 29) Berlin, 1909-25. 43 (of 45) vols. & 4 supp. vols. (Lacks vols. 42 & 43). Slightly browned in outer margin, vols. 1-3 slightly foxed, orig. bds. (vol. 41), rest orig. hf. leath. (R. Apr.3; 207a) DM 420

– Schriften. Leipzig, 1718-90. *1st. Authorised Edn.* 8 vols. Sm. 8vo. Vols. 1 & 2 with Austrian copyright imprint 'Wien & Leipzig, Stahel und Goschen', Vol. 3 dtd. 1790, cancel lf. 01 in Vol. 5, subscribers list in Vol. 1, without the additional 5 engraved plts. by Chodowiecki & Vol. 5 without the 4 unnumbered ll. containing the privilege, title of Vol. 5 slightly stained, early 19th. C. cf.-bkd. bds. (C. Dec.9; 226) *Bender.* £380

– – Anr. Edn. Karlsruhe, 1778-80. *1st. Edn.* 4 pts. in 2 vols. Some foxing & soiling, cont. hf. leath. gt., slightly bumped & rubbed, 1 jnt. torn. (HK. May 16; 2014) DM 620

– – Anr. Edn. Leipzig, 1787-89. *1st. authorised coll. Edn.* 7 vols?. 3 supp. copper engrs. by Chodowiecki (in vols. 1, 2 & 4) withdrawn by Goethe, vol. 1 with Goethe's notice, vol. 3 with later bd. ll. with title vig. by Lipps, vol. 5 with Imperial privilege, vols. 3-5 & 7 in orig. printing, cont. bds., rubbed, foxed. (BR. Apr.12; 1409) DM 3,300

– – Anr. Edn. Ill.:– H. Lips, F. Grögory & Geyser, partly after Oeser, Mechau, Chodowiecki & A. von Kauffmann. Wien & Leipzig, 1787-90. Pts. 3-8 (of 8) in 3 vols. 3 frontis. versos with owners marks, lightly browned, cont. hf. leath. gt., rubbed & bumped, slightly wormed, cold. paper end-ll. (HK. May 16; 2015) DM 580

– – Anr. Edn. Ill.:– J.W. Meil, F. Grögory after Oeser & H. Lips. Leipzig, 1787-91. 4 vols. Browned, ex-libris, cont. style hf. leath. gt., slightly rubbed. (H. Nov.23; 651) DM 400

– – Anr. Edn. Ill.:– after Chodowiecki, Kauffmann, Meil, engraved by Lips, etc. Leipzig, 1790 [1789 vol. VIII]. Lacks subscriber list vol. IV, some underlining & slight spotting, cont. hf. leath., some sm. faults, some jnts. slightly brittle, spine partly spotted. (HT. May 9; 1469) DM 600

– Schriften.–Neue Schriften. Ill.:– J. Mansfeld & D. Weis., Chodowiecki, Lips, Meil & others. Mannheim, 1801-23. Vols. I-VII (of 8) & Vols. VIII-X (of 10) in 10 vols. Title lf. vol. VI with pasted tears, 1st. sigs. vol. VIII stained, some slight spotting, cont. hf. leath., decor. gt. spine, some spines slightly defect.; Hauswedell coll. (H. May 24; 1304) DM 520

– Les Souffrances du Jeune Werther. Ill.:– Moreau le jeune. Paris, 1909. Wide margin, cont. red hf. mor.; Hauswedell coll. (H. May 24; 1327) DM 800

– Taschenbuch für 1798. Hermann u. Dorothea. Ill.:– Meil. Berlin, [Oct. 1797]. *1st. Edn. Variant.* 12mo. Minimal spotting, orig. red mor. Brieftasche, worn, spine extremities slightly bumped; MS. dedication on end-paper. (HK. May 15; 2032) DM 1,500

– Torquato Tasso. Leipzig, 1790. *1st. separate Edn.* Browned & spotted, last ll. with light stain, bds., spine slightly faded; Hauswedell coll. (H. May 24; 1321) DM 420

– – Anr. Edn. Leipzig, 1816. Some foxing, cont. leath. gt., blind-tooled, bd. s.-c., sm. slit on upr. cover. (R. Apr.3; 214) DM 500

– – Anr. Edn. [Hammersmith, Doves Pr., 1913]. *(15) on vell. De Luxe Edn.* Lge. 8vo. Orig. hand-bnd. red mor., gt. decor., covers, inner & outer dentelles, slight print mark on upr. cover; engraved ex-libris inside cover. (H. May 22; 1008) DM 5,200

– – Anr. Edn. [Hammersmith, Doves Pr., 1913]. *(200) on Bütten.* Orig. hand-bnd. mor., gold decor. spine, covers, inner & outer dentelles. (H. Nov.23; 995) DM 1,900

– – Anr. Copy. Limp orig. vell., sigd. by Doves Binderey. (D. Nov.24; 3036) DM 1,500

– Trilogie der Leidenschaft. [Leipzig, Ernst Ludwig Pr., 1912]. *De Luxe Edn., (50) on Japan.* Hand-bnd. orig. cf., slightly scratched. (H. Nov.23; 1036) DM 720

– Triumph der Empfindsamkeit. Leipzig, 1787. *1st. separate Edn.* Wide margin, title with crease, 1st. & last ll. slightly browned & spotted, cont. hf. leath., slightly worn & bumped, owners mark & ex-libris E. Redslob; Hauswedell coll. (H. May 24; 1313) DM 400

– Ueber Kunst und Alterthum. Stuttgart, 1816-32. 6 vols. & 3 pts. = 18 pts. (all publd.). Some foxing, cont. hf. leath., lightly rubbed, lacks ptd. orig. wraps.; Hauswedell coll. (H. May 24; 1331) DM 1,600

– Unbekannte Erotische Epigramme. Ill.:– C.H. Roon. Venedig, priv. ptd. 1924. *(30).* All etchings with monog., 1 etching browned, hand-bnd. hf. vell., red mor. cover & gt. vig., spine slightly scratched. (H. Nov.23; 1069) DM 1,100

– Unterhaltungen Deutscher Ausgewanderten. Frankfurt, Kleukens Pr., 1919. *(250) numbered.* Orig. red mor. gt., orig. box. (R. Oct.11; 294) DM 760

– Versuch die Metamorphose der Pflanzen zu Erklären. Gotha, 1790. *[1st. Edn.].* Liby. stp. on title, cont. red str.-grd. bds. (C. Dec.9; 222) *Quaritch.* £450

– – Anr. Copy. Wide margin, title with 2 lge. margin defects., some slight foxing, no bdg. stated. (HK. Nov.10; 2451) DM 700

– Die Wahlverwandschaften. Tübingen, 1809. *1st. Edn.* 2 pts. Slightly spotted & browned thro.-out, hf. leath., ca 1900, spine rubbed; Hauswedell coll. (H. May 24; 1328) DM 1,600

– – Anr. Copy. 2 pts. in 1 vol. Leath., slightly rubbed. (HK. May 16; 2041) DM 1,300

– Walpurgisnacht. Ill.:– Ernst Barlach. 1923. 4to. 20 orig. woodcuts., some full-p., orig. bds., margin lightly faded. (GB. May 5; 2155) DM 600

– – Anr. Copy. Orig. bds., slightly browned. (HK. May 17; 2558) DM 420

– Werke. Stuttgart & Tübingen, 1806-19. *1st. compl. Edn.* 20 vols. in 19. Minimal spotting, cont. cf., gt. spine, decor. covers, last 6 vols. slightly different; Hauswedell coll. (H. May 24; 1305) DM 4,200

– – Anr. Edn. Stuttgart & Tübingen, 1815-18. Vols. 1-8 (of 20). Lightly browned, some foxing, cont. hf. leath., slightly bumped. (R. Apr.3; 206) DM 600

– – Anr. Edn. Stuttgart & Tübingen, 1815-19. *2nd. Edn.* 20 vols. Cont. hf. leath. gt., minimal wear, spine rubbed & partly faded, w.a.f. (HK. Nov.10; 2432) DM 1,500

– – Anr. Edn. Wien, Stuttgart, 1816-22. *Orig. Edn.* 26 vols. Sm. 8vo. Engraved & ptd. titles, vol. 21 lacks engraved title, vol. 2 browned, heavily in parts, 2 vols. with col. or pencil marking, 1 vol. with sm. nail marks, cont. hf. leath., worn, corners bumped, vols. 21-26 not unif. (H. May 22; 690) DM 500

– – Anr. Edn. 1827-30. *'Taschenausgabe'.* Vols. 1-40 (of 60). Some slight foxing, cont. bds., bumped; ex-libris. (GB. May 4; 1276) DM 800

– – Anr. Edn. Stuttgart & Tübingen, 1827-30. *Compl. Edn.* Vols. 1-40. Cont. hf. cf., spines gt. (VG. Nov.29; 236) Fls. 500

– – Anr. Edn. Stuttgart & Tübingen, 1827-33. *Compl. Edn.* Vols. 1-55. Cont. hf. leath, gt. lightly rubbed & some slight slits. (GB. Nov.4; 2050) DM 3,500

– – Anr. Copy. Pts. 1-55 in 27 vols. Without 'Nachgelassene Werke', minimal spotting, cont. hf. leath. gt., lightly rubbed & bumped, w.a.f. (HK. May 16; 2019) DM 1,300

– – Anr. Edn. Stuttgart & Tübingen, 1827-33, 1835. *Compl. Edn.* 55 vols., & Musculus' Index vol. (bnd. in as Vol. 56). Some old spotting, heavier in places, hf. leath., sigd. 'Bound by Faser Regent St.', some vols. lightly bumped. (V. Oct.1; 3822) DM 2,600

– – Anr. Copy. 55 vols, & Musculus' Index vol. Vol. 17 lacks pp. 177-192, bds., vol. 17 slightly differs, Vols. 7-29 very bumped. (V. Oct.1; 3823) DM 1,400

– – Anr. Edn. Stuttgart & Tübingen, 1827-42. *Definitive Edn.* 60 pts. & index in 34 vols. Lge. 8vo. With Musculus index, pts. 35-36 replaced by 1 vol. from sm. 8vo. Edn., 2 pp. pt. 16 torn, pt. 33 lacks 12 pp. (?), pt. 52 lacks 2 pp., 4 vols. slightly stained, 34 title ll. stpd. & numbered in upr. right corner, cont. marb. hf. leath., pts. 35/36 in 1 cont. hf. leath. vol., 3 vols. with slight creases, some slightly worn, pts. 55-60 not quite unif., w.a.f. (HK. May 16; 2018) DM 5,200

– – Anr. Edn. Stuttgart & Tübingen, 1828-33. *Compl. Definitive Edn.* 40 vols. in 20 & Nachgelassene Werke Vol. 1-15 (of 20) in 8 vols. Cont. unif. hf. leath. gt. (HT. May 9; 1470) DM 1,600

– – Anr. Edn. Stuttgart & Tubingen, 1828-35. 56 vols. in 51, including Index. Sm. 8vo. Cont. hf. cf. (C. Dec.9; 229) *Wenner.* £750

– – Anr. Copy. 29 vols. Title & 2 ll. with hole, some vols. blind-stpd., some browning, cont. hf. leath.,

GOETHE, Johann Wolfgang von -*Contd.*

blind-tooled, loose, slightly rubbed. (H. Nov.23;
652) DM 2,600
- - **Anr. Edn.** Stuttgart, 1867. 36 pts. in 18 vols.
Minimal spotting, orig. red hf. leath. gt., spines
gold-tooled decor., slightly rubbed, w.a.f. (HK.
May 16; 2023) DM 560
- - **Anr. Edn.** Weimar, 1887-1919. Pt. 1: 55 pts. in
63 vols., Pt. II: 13 pts. in 14 vols., Pt. III: 15 pts.
in 16 vols., Pt. IV: 50 vols., together 143 vols. 4to.
L.P., orig. hf. leath. linen (142) & orig. hf. leath., w.a.f.
(HK. Nov.10; 2434) DM 7,800
- **West-oestlicher Divan.** Stuttgart, 1819. *1st. Edn.*
Old spr. bds. (C. Dec.9; 224) *Fischer.* £230
- - **Anr. Copy.** Light browning, cont. bds. (C. Dec.9;
223) *Post.* £220
- - **Anr. Copy.** Faulty pagination, upr. margin
lightly browned, cont. bds., gt. spine, corners
bumped, jnts. split; Hauswedell coll. (H. May 24;
1333) DM 1,400
- - **Anr. Copy.** With 2 bd. ll. for 4 pp., 'hier' &
'Talismane', pagination jumps, 2 pp. numbered in
duplicate, very browned in margins thro.-out, last
sigs. stained, cont. bds., defect. (H. May 22; 694)
DM 780
- - **Anr. Copy.** With corrected quarter sheet (pp.
7-10), pp. 399/400 paginated double, pp. 495/96
missed, some slight foxing, cont. bds., rubbed &
bumped. (GB. May 4; 1278) DM 500
- - **Anr. Edn.** Ed.:- Max Hecker. Ill.:- Marcus
Behmer. Leipzig, 1910. Mor., gt. decor., wide gt.
inner dentelle, by Bruno Scheer. (HK. May 17;
2577) DM 9,000
- - **Anr. Edn.** [München, 1910]. *(100) unnumbered
on Bütten.* Brownish red mor., sigd. by K. Ebert,
München, gold-tooled decor., gt. inner dentelle,
spine & corners with slight wear, cover slightly
scratched. (D. Nov.24; 3033) DM 850
- **Wilhelm Meisters Lehrjahre.** Berlin, 1795. *1st.
separate Edn.* 4 vols. With all mus. supps., some
heavy spotting & browning, hf. leath., ca. 1900,
slightly worn, Hauswedell coll. (H. May 24; 1322)
DM 460
- - **Anr. Edn.** Mus. Supps.:- J.F. Reichardt. Berlin,
1795-96. *1st. Edn.* 4 vols. With 7 (of 8) folding mus.
supps., title with owner's mark, some slight
browning & foxing, cont.-style hf. leath. gt. (HK.
Nov.10; 2452) DM 650
- **Wilhelm Meisters Wanderjahre.** Tübingen, 1821.
1st. Book Edn. Vol. 1 (all publd.). Lacks last
lf. blank, foxed, cont. long-grd. mor. blind-tooled,
decor., gt. spine, cover, inner & outer dentelle,
jnts. & end-papers renewed. (HK. May 16; 2042)
DM 1,900
- - **Anr. Copy.** Lacks hf.-title with poem, minimal
spotting, cont. hf. leath. gt., slightly rubbed. (R.
Oct.11; 222) DM 1,000
- **Zur Farbenlehre.** Tübingen, 1810. *1st. Edn.* 2
text & 1 plt. vol. 8vo. & 4to. Copperplts. with MS.
changes, plt. sizes vary slightly, 4 pp. vol. II slightly
soiled, some foxing, last pp. with sm. ink stain, hf.
linen & orig. wraps., rubbed, plt. nos. on spine
changed, sm. margin tears, Hauswedell coll. (H.
May 24; 1329) DM 7,400
- - **Anr. Edn.** Tübingen, ca. 1820. 4to. 17 copperplts. (12 cold.), text minimal browned, orig.
linen, orig. wraps. bnd. in. (HK. May 16; 2029)
DM 900
- **Zur Morphologie.** Stuttgart & Tübingen, 1817-
23. *1st. Book Edn.* 2 vols. Vol. II lacks 1 copper
engr., some slight spotting, 1 lf. pasted, later bds.,
spine slightly bumped, Hauswedell coll. (H. May
24; 1332) DM 600
- **Zur Naturwissenschaft Uberhaupt, Besonders zur
Morphologie.** Stuttgart & Tübingen, 1817-24. *1st.
Edn.* 2 vols. in 1. Originally iss. in 6 pts., with orig.
ptd. title to each pt. bnd. in, & final paper wrap. to
Vol. 1 with errata, 3 engraved plts. only in Vol. 2,
lacks the 3 plts. in Vol. 1, cont. marb. bds. (C.
Dec.9; 225) *Bjorck.* £200
- - **Anr. Edn.** Stuttgart/Tübingen, 1820-22. Pts.
3 & 4 in 1 vol. Cont. mor. gt., gold & blind-tooled
decor., gt. inner & outer dentelles. (BR. Apr.12;
700) DM 650

GOETZ, Hermann
See— KUHNEL, Ernst & Goetz, Hermann

GOEVERNEUR, J.J.A.
- **Fabelboek.** Ill.:- O. Eerelman. Leeuwaerden,
1882. 4to. 9 hand-cold. lithos., foxed in places, 2 ll.
reprd., mod. cl. pasted over with pts. of orig. bdg.
(VG. Sep.13; 743) Fls. 450

GOFF, Frederick R.
- **Incunabula in American Libraries.** N.Y., 1964.
Orig. cl. (BBA. Apr.5; 286) *Aspin.* £55
- - **Anr. Edn.** N.Y., 1964; 1972. 2 vols. with Supp.
4to. Cl. (SG. May 17; 94) $100

GOGOL, Nikolai Vassilievitch
- **Les Ames Mortes.** Trans.:- Henri Mongault. Ill.:-
M. Chagall. Paris, 1948. *(285) on vell. d'Arches.*
Printers mark sigd. by artist in ink, full-p. aqua
(37.8 × 28 cm.), sigd. & dtd. 1952, full-p. etchings
with light browning, loose ll. in orig. wraps., bd.
covers & s.-c., soiled, Hauswedell coll. (H. May 24;
594) DM 38,000
- **Der Mantel.** Ed.:- F. Gaber. Ill.:- W. Gramatte.
Potsdam, ca. 1924. *Ltd. Iss.* Sm. 4to. Margins
lightly browned, orig. hf. linen, slightly faded. (H.
Nov.24; 1554) DM 460
- **The Overcoat; from the Tales of Petersburg.** Ill.:-
Pietro Annigoni. Verona, Officina Bodoni, 1975.
(160) numbered, sigd. by artist. 4to. Russian &
Engl. text, 6 etchings, vell.-bkd. gt.-decor. bds.,
partly unc., buckram s.-c., text lf. by printer laid
in. (SG. May 17; 281) $550
- **Der Unhold.** Ill.:- Walter Becker. Heidelberg,
1920. *(250) numbered.* Lge. fo. Printers mark sigd.
by artist, on Zanders Bütten, orig. pict. bds., slightly
spotted, spine defect., unc. (GB. May 5; 2177)
DM 440

GOLBERY, Ph. de
- **Histoire et Description de la Suisse et du Tyrol.**
Paris, 1838. 1 folding map, 92 steel engraved plts.,
slightly foxed, cont. hf. linen gt. (R. Oct.13; 3256)
DM 920
[-] **Schweiz und Tyrol.** Stuttgart, 1840. 87 (of 92)
engraved plts., 1 multi-folding litho. map, some
staining & browning, 1 plt. with margin tear, cont.
hf. leath., rubbed. (HT. May 10; 2857) DM 620
- - **Anr. Copy.** Lacks 1 steel engraved plt., foxed,
or browned, cont. hf. leath. gt. (GB. Nov.3; 110)
DM 600

GOLD, Capt. Charles
- **Oriental Drawings.** 1806. 4to. 46 (of 49) cold.
aquatint plts., very slight staining to 2 plts., & to
margins of 6 others, cont. hf. cf. gt. (LC. Oct.13;
269) £320

GOLD, H.
- **Die Juden und Judengemeinden Böhmens [Mäh-
rens u. Bratislavas] in Vergangenheit und Gegenwart.**
Brünn, 1729-34. 3 works in 3 vols. 4to. Orig. pict.
linen. (R. Oct.11; 1085) DM 800

GOLDAST V. HAIMISFELD, M.
- **Collectio Constitutionum Imperialium ...** Frank-
furt, 1673. *3rd. Edn.* 3 pts. in 1 vol. Fo. Cont. leath.
(R. Oct.11; 1257) DM 900

GOLDEN COCKEREL PRESS
- **Chanticleer, a Bibliography of the Golden Cock-
erel Press, April 1921-August 1936.** Gold. Cock.
Pr., 1936. *(300) numbered & sigd. by the partners.*
(*With:*) - **Pertelote, A Sequel to Chanticleer, being
a Bibliography of the Golden Cockerel Press.** Gold.
Cock. Pr., 1943. *(200) numbered & sigd. by the
partners.* Together 2 vols. Orig. mor.-bkd. cl., 2nd.
vol. slightly stained, 1st. vol. with d.-w. torn; from
D. Bolton liby. (BBA. Oct.27; 130) *Webb.* £85
- **The Illustrators of the Golden Cockerell Press.**
Hereford, Five Seasons Pr., 1980. *(75) numbered &
sigd. by C. & L. Sandford.* Sm. fo. Decor. wraps.
(SG. Aug.4; 136) $100
See— AESOP
See— BEAUMONT, Francis
See— BELL, Gertrude
See— BIBLIANA [English]
See— BLIGH, William
See— BREBEUF, Jean de
See— CABELL, James Branch
See— CAESAR, Gaius Julius
See— CAREY, Henry

See— CHAIR, Somerset de
See— CHASE, Thomas & other
See— CHAUCER, Geoffrey
See— CHESTER PLAY OF THE DELUGE, The
See— FLINDERS, Mathew
See— FLINT, Sir William Russell
See— GIBBINGS, Robert
See— GILL, Eric
See— GRAY, Thomas
See— GREEK ANTHOLOGY, The
See— HERIZ, Patrick de
See— HERRICK, Robert
See— HOMERIC HYMN TO APHRODITE
See— HUDSON, William Henry
See— KEATS, John
See— LACOMBE, Sieur Jean de
See— LAWRENCE, Thomas Edward 'T.E. Shaw'
See— LUCIAN, of Samosata
See— MALLARME, Stephane
See— MILLER, Patrick
See— MILTON, John
See— MORE, Sir Thomas
See— MORRISON, James
See— MUSAEUS
See— NEW TESTAMENTIANA [English]
See— OMAR KHAYYAM
See— PASSIO DOMINI NOSTRI JESU
CHRISTI
See— PLATO
See— POWYS, Llewelyn
See— RUTTER, Owen
See— SOLOMON, King of Israel
See— SPARRMAN, Anders
See— STERNE, Laurence
See— SWIFT, Jonathan
See— SWINBURNE, Algernon Charles
See— SWIRE, Herbert
See— TOUSSAINT, Franz

GOLDMANN, C.S.
- **South African Mines ... : Rand Mining Companies;
Miscellaneous Companies; Maps & Plans.** 1895-
96. Together 3 vols. 4to. Some ills. in book which
fits into bdg., orig. bdgs.; from Signet Liby. (VA.
Oct.28; 467) R 720

GOLDMANN, Nic.
- **Vollst. Anweisung zu der Civil-Bau-Kunst ...** Ed.:-
L. Chr. Sturm. Leipzig, 1708. 2 pts. in 1 vol. Lge.
fo. Wide margin, lacks both engraved titles, pt. 2
lacks 4 plts. & 2 pp., title with sm. margin tear, some
browning & foxing, cont. vell., slightly rubbed &
bumped. (HK. May 16; 513) DM 800

GOLDONI, Carlo
- **Commedie.** Venezia, 1829-31. 74 vols. bnd. in 19.
12mo. Hf. cf., some spines lightly defect. (CR.
Jun.6; 33) Lire 300,000

GOLDSCHMIDT, Ad.
- **Die Deutsche Buchmalerei.** Leipzig, 1928. Lge.
4to. Orig. linen. (HK. Nov.11; 4413) DM 560

GOLDSCHMIDT, Ernest Philip
- **Gothic & Renaissance Bookbindings.** 1928. 2 vols.
4to. Orig. cl., faded, spines worn; H.M. Nixon coll.,
with many MS. notes, A.L. from author loosely
inserted. (BBA. Oct.6; 52) *Beres.* £220.
- - **Anr. Copy.** 2 vols. 4to. 113 plts., cl., d.-w.'s.
(SG. Sep.15; 51) $300
- - **Anr. Copy.** Text & plt. vol. 4to. 110 plts., orig.
linen. (D. Nov.23; 198) DM 700
- **The Printed Book of the Renaissance.** Camb.,
1950. *(750).* 4to. Cl., d.-w. (SG. Jan.5; 146) $150

GOLDSCHMIDT, Ernest Philip (Contrib.)
See— MINER, Dorothy

GOLDSMITH, Oliver
- **The Deserted Village.** L., 1770. *1st. Edn. 1st. Iss.*
4to. Mor. by Rivière & Son, sigd.; George Jameson
copy. (GM. Dec.7; 347) £725
- - **Anr. Copy.** 4to. Title vig., hf.-title, with 'Careless' catchword on p.9, p.no. '23' is punched
through & sm. repair in margin, later cf., triple gt.
fillet borders, spines & dentelles. (SG. Apr.26;
89) $600
- - **Anr. Edn.** L., 1770. *1st. Edn.* 4to. Lacks hf.-title,
few inner margins reprd., some faint dampstaining,
mod. hf. cf. gt.; Frederic Dannay copy. (CNY.
Dec.16; 154) $110

[-] **An Enquiry into the Present State of Polite Learning in Europe.** L., 1785. *1st. Edn.* Hf.-title, cont. cf. (SPB. May 16; 69) $400
- **The Grecian History, from the Earliest State to the Death of Alexander the Great.** L., 1774. *1st. Edn.* 2 vols. With the blank after Vol. 2 title (often lacking), owner's sig. on titles, cont. tree cf. (SG. Oct.27; 132) $250
- **The Haunch of Venison.** L., 1776. *1st. Edn.* 4to. Hf.-title with 'Price One Shilling & Six-Pence' & imprint 'Entered at Stationers Hall', etched port., red mor. by Riviere, rebkd.; Roderick Terry-Hogan copy. (SPB. May 16; 70) $550
- - **Anr. Copy.** 4to. Lacks hf.-title, few margins lightly soiled & 3 with sm. repair, lf. C1 torn & reprd., mor. by W. Pratt, gt. & gt.-panel., Christie-Miller arms on sides, party unc.; Frederic Dannay copy. (CNY. Dec.16; 155) $400
- **An History of the Earth & Animated Nature.** 1774. *1st. Edn.* 8 vols. 101 engraved plts., minor wormhole affecting index margin, cont. cfs., spines gt., 2 spines slightly defect.; Sir Ivar Colquhoun, of Luss copy. (CE. Mar.22; 137) £250
- - **Anr. Copy.** 8 vols. Some light soiling, cont. cf. (CSK. Aug.19; 23) £110
- - **Anr. Copy.** 8 vols. Margin stains, cont. cfs., rubbed, jnts. slightly worn. (BBA. May 23; 278) *S. Finch.* £50
- - **Anr. Edn.** Ed.:– W. Turton. L., 1805. *New Edn.* 6 vols. in 3. 105 plts., qtr. cl., marb. bds., cover detchd., ex-liby. (SG. Mar.22; 141) $100
- - **Anr. Edn.** L., ca. 1825. 4 vols. 4 hand-cold. frontis., 34 hand-cold. plts., lacks some text, hf. mor. (GM. Dec.7; 691) £90
- - **Anr. Edn.** L., 1850. 2 vols. Engrs. hand-cold., hf. cf. (CR. Jun.6; 175) Lire 200,000
- - **Anr. Edn.** Intro:– Cuvier. Edinb., ca. 1865. 2 vols. Some slight spotting or soiling, 1 plt. pasted, torn in margin, some plts. with sm. tears, later hf. leath., gt. spine, slightly worn & bumped, 1 sm. stain. (H. May 22; 220a) DM 900
- - **Anr. Edn.** L., 1873. 2 vols. Royal 8vo. 36 hand-cold. plts., many black & white plts., hf. mor. (GM. Dec.7; 695) £60
- - **Anr. Edn.** N.d. 2 vols. Port., 2 hand-cold. vig. titles, 71 hand-cold. plts., hf. cf., worn. (P. Jun.7; 133) £65
[-] **The Life of Richard Nash.** L., 1762. *1st. Edn.* Fo. C6 a cancel, 1st. 2 ll. a little stained, cont., rubbed. (BBA. Nov.30; 228) *Scott.* £60
- **Poems.** Ill.:– Thomas & John Bewick. 1795. 4to. Hf. cf. gt.; Sir Ivar Colquhoun, of Luss copy. (CE. Mar.22; 140) £270
- **The Poetical Works.** Remarks:– R.H. Newell. Ill.:– S. Alken after designs by Newell. L., 1820. *[2nd. Edn.].* 4to. Additional pict. title & 6 aquatint plts., last few ll. torn, orig. bds., worn. (SG. Mar.15; 118) $100
- - **Anr. Edn.** L., 1846. Mor. gt., reprd., as a fore-e. pntg., w.a.f. (SPB. May 17; 734) $275
- **She Stoops to Conquer.** L., 1773. *1st. Edn. 1st. Iss.* Mod. qtr. cf. (SPB. May 16; 71) $400
- - **Anr. Edn.** Ill.:– Hugh Thomson. [1912]. *(350) numbered & sigd. by artist.* 4to. Orig. decor. vell. gt.; Sir Ivar Colquhoun, of Luss copy. (CE. Mar.22; 139) £160
- - **Anr. Copy.** Sm. fo. Broadside advertising Thomson's watercolours laid in, heavy vell., upr. cover & spine elab. gt.-stpd., soiled, mostly on spine, lacks cl. ties. (SG. Jan.12; 340) $140
- **The Traveller, or Prospect of Society.** L., 1765. *1st. Publd. Edn.* 4to. Advts., lacks hf.-title, 4 sm. wormholes thro.-out, mor. gt., gt. panel., Christie-Miller gt. arms on sides, by W. Pratt, partly unc.; Frederic Dannay copy. (CNY. Dec.16; 153) $500
[-] **The Vicar of Wakefield.** Dublin, 1766. *1st. Dublin Edn.* 2 vols. in 1. 12mo. Early cf. (SG. Feb.9; 236) $110
- - **Anr. Edn.** Phila., 1772. *1st. Amer. Edn.* 2 vols. in 1. 12mo. Lacks P6 (?final blank), some soiling, mor. (SPB. May 16; 73) $400
- - **Anr. Edn.** Ill.:– Th. Rowlandson. L., 1817. *1st. Rowlandson Edn.* MS. dedication on 1st. plt. verso, L., 3 Oct. 1818, ink stain, cont. hf. leath., corners lightly bumped, spine worn. (HK. Nov.10; 3104) DM 1,000
- - **Anr. Edn.** Ill.:– William Mulready. L., 1843. 14 p. catalogue bnd. in, lev., elab. gt. borders, gt. centrepiece, spines & dentelles gt., moire silk

doubls. & end-ll., by Sangorski & Sutcliffe, orig. cl. covers & spine bnd. in. (SG. Feb.16; 142) $250
- - **Anr. Edn.** Ill.:– E.J. Sullivan. L., 1914. *(500) sigd. by artist.* 4to. Light offset to pp. 12-13 from laid in material, bdg. not stated, covers rubbed, spine fading, end-papers darkening. (CBA. Aug.21; 613) $110
- - **Anr. Edn.** Ill.:– Arthur Rackham. L., [1919]. 4to. Mor. gt., inlaid frontis. ill. on upr. cover, light discoloration, edges scuffed, s.-c. (SPB. Dec.13; 559) $325
- - **Anr. Edn.** Ill.:– Arthur Rackham. L., 1929. *(575) numbered & sigd. by artist for England.* 4to. Orig. parch. gt., slightly spotted, yawning spine darkening. end-papers slightly darkening. (CBA. Aug.21; 514) $225
- - **Anr. Edn.** Ill.:– Arthur Rackham. Phila., 1929. *(200) numbered for the U.S., sigd. by artist.* 4to. Gt.-ruled vell., pict. end-papers, bd. s.-c. (SG. Mar.29; 253) $250
- - **Anr. Edn.** Ill.:– Arthur Rackham. L., [1929]. *(775) sigd. by artist.* 4to. Orig. vell. gt. (SPB. Dec.13; 887) $275
- **The Works.** N.Y. & L., 1900. *Wakefield Edn. (500).* 12 vols. Lge. 8vo. Hf. mor. gt. (SPB. May 17; 745) $850
- - **Anr. Copy.** 12 vols. Sm. 4to. Each double frontis. includs black-&-white engraved or gravure frontis. preceded by dupl. hand-cold. inserted plt., 4 examples are unsigd. ports., remaining 8 represent scenes from Goldsmith's works, each of latter also sigd. by orig. artist in bottom margin of black-&-white plt., each frontis. & text plt. ptd. on Japan vell., elab. mor., gt. roses stpd. on spines & at corners & centre of each cover panel, inner gt. dentelles, marb. end-papers, text untrimmed & partly unopened, publisher's watermarked laid paper. (HA. May 4; 187) $575
- - **Anr. Copy.** 12 vols. Sm. fo. Hf. mor. (SPB. Dec.13; 534) $300
- - **Anr. Edn.** Ed.:– Peter Cunningham. Ill.:– Frederick Simpson Coburn. N.Y. & L., ca. 1908. *Primrose Hundred/Turks Head Edn. (100).* 10 vols. Lge. 8vo. Photogravures, mor. (SPB. May 17; 746) $1,400

GOLDWURM, C.
- **Kirchen Calender.** Ill.:– H. Weiditz. Frankfurt, 1559. *1st. Edn.* 4to. Browned, bds. (HK. Nov.8; 203) DM 650

GOLFER'S MANUAL, The
Intro:– Bernard Darwin. 1947. *(740) numbered.* Buckram, d.-w. (HBC. May 17; 214) £65

GOLF ILLUSTRATED
5 Jan.-30 Mar. 1900. Vol. III. Bdg. not stated. (PD. Jul.13; 54) £140
- - **Anr. Run.** 4 Apr.-27 Jun. 1902. Vol. XII. Bdg. not stated. (PD. Jul.13; 52) £140
- - **Anr. Run.** 3 Oct.-26 Dec. 1902. Vol. XIV. Cl. (PD. Jul.13; 50) £170
- - **Anr. Run.** 25 Jun.-17 Sep. 1909. Vol. XLI. Bdg. not stated. (PD. Jul.13; 53) £130
- - **Anr. Run.** 24 Dec. 1909-18 Mar. 1910. Vol. XLIV. Bdg. not stated. (PD. Jul.13; 51) £130

GOLL, Claire
- **Journal d'un Cheval.** Ill.:– Marc Chagall. Paris, 1952. *(200) numbered.* 4to. 2 orig. etchings & 4 orig. lithos., loose ll. in orig. wraps. with cold. litho. in orig. bd. portfo. (GB. May 5; 2272) DM 2,000

GOLL, Claire & Ivan
- **Poèmes d'Amour.** Ill.:– Marc Chagall. Paris, 1925. *1st. Edn. (600) numbered.* MS. dedication from I. Goll, sigd. by both authors on end-paper, orig. wraps. (GB. May 5; 2588) DM 650
- **Poèmes de Jalousie.** Ill.:– T. Foujita. Paris, 1926. *1st. Edn. (300) numbered.* 1 orig. etching, MS. dedication from I. Goll, sigd. by both authors on end-paper, orig. wraps., loose., sm. margin tear, lacks lr. wrap. (GB. May 5; 2589) DM 440
- **Sodom et Berlin.** Paris, 1929. *1st. Edn.* MS. dedication on end-paper, lightly browned, orig. sewed, lacks upr. cover & spine covering. (GB. May 5; 2591) DM 850

GOLL, Ivan
- **Bouquet de Rêves pour Neila.** Ill.:– Joan Miro. Paris, 1967. *(200) numbered & sigd. by artist.* 4to. Unsewn in orig. wraps., decor. covers, folder & s.-c., unc. (S. Nov.21; 105) *Simons.* £300
- **Elegie Iphetonga, suivi de Masques de Cendre.** Ill.:– Pablo Picasso. Paris, 1949. *(220) numbered.* 4to. Unsewn in orig. wraps., unc. (S. Nov.21; 35) *Rota.* £280
- **Jean sans Terre: Landless John.** Preface:– Allen Tate. Trans.:– [Lionel Abel, Wm. Carlos Williams & others]. Ill.:– Eugène Berman. San Franc., Grabhorn Pr., 1942. *(175).* Fo. Hf. cl. & marb. bds., covers lightly soiled & slightly warped, corners bumped; leath. monog. of the Rosenwald Coll., plt. & stp. of the Liby. of Congress. (CBA. Nov.19; 188a) $150
- **Poèmes de la Vie et de la Mort.** Paris, 1927. *1st. Edn. (350) numbered.* MS. dedication from I. Goll, sigd. by both authors on hf.-title, orig. wraps., sm. spine tear. (GB. May 5; 2590) DM 650

GOLL, Ivan (Text)
See– MUNCHNER BLATTER FUR DICHTUNG UND GRAPHIK

GOLOVNIN, Vasily Mikhailovich
- **Voyage contenant le Récit de sa Captivité chez les Japonais, pendant les Années 1811, 1812 et 1813 ... suivi de la Relation du Voyage de M. Ricord ...** Trans.:– J.-B.-B. Eyriès. Paris, 1818. *1st. compl. Fr. Edn.* 2 vols. Cont. tree roan, spines decor., worn. (HD. May 21; 34) Frs. 1,200
- - **Anr. Copy.** 2 vols. Multi-stpd., map with lengthy reprd. tear, minimal browning & light foxing, cont. hf. leath. gt., cover slightly rubbed. (H. Nov.23; 341) DM 400

GOLTZIUS, Hubert
- **Graeciae eiusque Insularum et Asiae Minoris Nomismata.** Antw., 1644. Fo. Additional engraved title, engraved plts., cont. mott. cf. gt., rebkd. preserving orig. spine, rubbed. (S. May 1; 588) *Azezian.* £150
- **Icones Imperatorum Romanorum ex Priscis Numismatibus ad Vivum Delineatae.** Ill.:– Christoph Jeger, Gevartius & others. Antw., 1645. Fo. Hf.-title, engraved title after Rubens, 153 medallion ports. in chiaroscuro, 7 shields left blank, last lf. with printer's device, vell. (S. May 10; 290) *Fletcher.* £350

GOMEZ DE AVELLANEDA, Gertrudis
- **Obras ...** Madrid, 1869. 6 vols. 4to. Publishers cl., oxidised. (DS. Jan.27; 2212) Pts. 20,000

GOMEZ DE NAVIA, José
- **Suite of 12 Views of the Escorial.** Ill.:– Thomas Lopez Enguidanos & Manuel Alegre. Madrid, [1800]. Ob. fo. Cont. bds., new cf. spine & corners; bkplts. of J. Miguel de Carvajal & Holland House. (C. Dec.9; 59) *Weinreb.* £5,500

GOMEZ DE SOMORROSTRO, A.
- **El Aqueducto y otras Antigüedades de Segovia.** Madrid, 1820. Lge. fo. Linen. (DS. Mar.23; 2119) Pts. 30,000

GOMEZ ORTEGA, C.
- **Historia Natural de la Malagueta o Pimienta de Tabasco.** Madrid, 1780. 4to. Sewed. (DS. Oct.28; 2519) Pts. 40,000

GONCOURT, Edmond
- **La Fille Elisa.** Paris, 1895. On china, jansenist mor. gt. by Franz, silk liners & end-ll., wrap. preserved, s.-c., spine faded; pres. copy without suite of etchings, publisher's prospectus added. (HD. Jun.13; 46) Frs. 2,200
- - **Anr. Edn.** Ill.:– Georges Jeanniot. 1895. *1st. Edn., (300). (38) on china with 4 states of etchings & 2 states of other ills.* Str.-grd. hf. mor., corners, spine decor., cover wrap. preserved, with specimen. (HD. Jul.6; 110) Frs. 1,000

GONCOURT, Edmond de (Text)
See– TYPES DE PARIS

GONCOURT, Edmond & Jules
- **La Femme au Dix-huitième Siècle.** Ill.:– Dujardin. Paris, 1887. *1st. Ill. Edn. (75) on Japon.* 4to. Mor.,

GONCOURT, Edmond & Jules -Contd.

gt. decor., centre cypher, decor. spine, by Allo. (HD. Dec.9; 133) Frs. 2,000
- **Idées et Sensations.** Paris, 1866. *Orig. Edn.* Hf. bradel buckram, wrap. preserved; Champfleury copy with pencil commentary. (HD. Jun.13; 45) Frs. 1,100
- **Journal.** 1956. *(350) numbered on Vergé.* 25 vols. Square 12mo. Folder. (SM. Mar.7; 2137) Frs. 1,400
- **Les Maîtresses de Louis XV.** Ill.:– St. Aubin, Cochin, Madame de Pompadour, etc. Paris, 1860. *Orig. Edn. (8) on Hollande.* 2 vols. With promisary note sigd. by Comtesse du Barry, dedication sigd. by Edmond de Goncourt, 154 ports. before the letter, red mor., gt. decor., decor. spines, Lavallière mor. doubls., inner dentelle, unc.; from Robert Hoe & F. Kettaneh libys. (HD. Dec.8; 132) Frs. 18,500

GONSE, Louis

- **L'Art Japonais.** Paris, 1883. *(1400) numbered.* 2 vols. Fo. Orig. cl., d.-w.'s. (BBA. Nov.10; 293) *Ralph.* £90
- – **Anr. Copy.** 2 vols. 4to. Some plts. heightened in gold, three-qtr. lev., rubbed & faded. (SG. Jan.26; 212) $275
- – **Anr. Copy.** 2 vols. Tall fo. 64 chromolitho. plts., text ills., ex-liby., pict. linen, very frayed, hinges loose. (SG. May 3; 179) $175
- **Eugène Fromentin Peintre et Ecrivain.** Paris, 1881. *(100) on Hollande.* 4to. Etchings in 2 states, hf. mor., gt. & mosqic spine, unc., wrap. preserved. (HD. Feb.17; 32) Frs. 1,250

GONTSCHAROW, Iwan

- **Gesammelte Werke.** 1920. 4 vols. Orig. linen, by E.R. Weiss. (GB. May 5; 2593) DM 400

GONZALES CARRANZA, Domingo

- **A Geographical Description of the Coasts, Harbours, & Sea Ports of the Spanish West Indies, Particularly of Porto Bello, Cartagena, & the Island of Cuba.** L., 1740. *1st. Edn.* 3 folding maps (of 4 or 5), lr. margins browned, disbnd. [Sabin 27799] (SG. Jan.19; 178) $275

GONZALEZ, A.

- **Hierusalemsche Reyse.** Antw., 1673. 2 pts. in 1 vol. 4to. Some foxing & staining, sm. margin wormholes, cont. hf. roan, slightly rubbed. (VG. Nov.30; 829) Fls. 900

GONZALEZ DE MEDINA BARBA, Diego

- **Examen de Fortificación.** Madrid, 1599. 4to. Linen, superlibris & ex-libris. (DS. Mar.23; 2121) Pts. 75,000

GONZALEZ DE MENDOZA, Juan

- **Dell'Historia della China.** Genoa, 1586. 2 pts. in 1 vol. Sm. 4to. Some browning & foxing, limp vell., soiled. (SG. Mar.29; 316) $375
- – **Anr. Edn.** Trans.:– Francesco Avanzo. Venice, 1590. Title soiled, cont. vell.-bkd. bds., rubbed. (BBA. Jun.28; 214) *Erasmus.* £90
- **Historia del gran Regno della China.** Trans.:– F. Avanzi. 'Vinegia, per Andrea Musch' [L., John Wolfe], 1587. 12mo. Corner torn from title with loss of date & 2 letters of text, reprd., early 19th. C. red str.-grd. mor., slightly rubbed; the William Beckford copy. [STC 12004] (S. Dec.1; 376) *Baker.* £300

GONZALEZ HOLGUIN, P.D.

- **Vocabulario de la Lengua General de Todo el Peru Llamada Lengua Qqichua o del Inca.** Lima, 1608. 4to. Lacks last 2 ll. after the colophon, pre-lims., pp. 321/2 pt. 1 & 3-14, 85-94, 147-158, 207/8 in pen facs. on new paper, new cf., w.a.f. (S. Dec.13; 135) *Quaritch.* £140

GOOD, John Mason

See— POLEHAMPTON, Edw. & Good, John M.

GOOD, John Mason & others

- **Pantologia: a New Cyclopaedia, comprehending Essays, Treatises, & Systems.** L., 1813. *1st. Edn.* 12 vols. Many plts. hand-cold., some foxing, cont. cf., brkn. (SG. Oct.6; 284) $275

GOOD SHUNAMMITE, The

1847. 11 ll. reproducing illuminations in gold & cols., by Lewis Gruner, orig. papier-mâché bdg.; H.M. Nixon coll. (BBA. Oct.6; 244)
Oak Knoll Books. £110

GOODALE, George L.

- **Wild Flowers of America.** Ill.:– after Isaac Sprague. Boston, 1882. Lge. 4to. 50 chromolitho. plts., perforated liby. stp. on title, some plts. loose in bdg., red three-qtr. mor., very worn, shelf mark on spine. (SG. Mar.22; 142) $110

GOODALL, Walter

See— RUDDIMAN, Thomas & others

GOODE, George Brown

- **Game Fishes of the United States.** Ill.:– S.A. Kilbourne. [N.Y., 1879]. Lge. ob. fo. 19 (of 20) cold. litho. plts., & some accompanying wraps. & text ll., some margin chipping, some plts. with adhesion, wrinkling, etc., loose in bd. portfo., worn, w.a.f. (RO. Dec.11; 123) $650

GOODRICH, Lloyd

- **Raphael Soyer.** N.Y., ca. 1972. *1st. Edn.* Fo. 77 tipped-in col. plts., linen, d.-w. (CBA. Jan.29; 419) $170

GOODRICH, Samuel Griswold 'Peter Parley'

[–] **Tales about Europe, Asia, Africa, & America.** By Peter Parley. L., 1839. *4th. Edn.* Sq. 16mo. 4 pp. publishers advts., orig. gt. pict. cl., spine defect.; from liby. of F.D. Roosevelt, inscr. by him (as President). (SG. Mar.15; 49) $140
[–] **Tales About Great Britain & Ireland.** By Peter Parley. L., 1839. *3rd. Edn.* Lge. 16mo. Orig. gt.-pict. cl., spine badly worn; from liby. of F.D. Roosevelt, inscr. by him (as President). (SG. Mar.15; 50) $200

GOODSIR, Robert Anstruther

- **An Arctic Voyage to Baffin's Bay & Lancaster Sound, in Search of Friends with Sir John Franklin.** L., 1850. *1st. Edn.* Orig. cl., spine faded; sig. on front end-paper of Edward Whymper, the Rt. Hon. Visc. Eccles copy. [Sabin 27931] (CNY. Nov.18; 123) $550

GOODWIN, Francis

- **Domestic Architecture.** L., 1833-34. *1st. Edn.* 2 vols. in 1. 4to. 40 cold. aquatint views (wtrmkd. 1827 or 1833), 43 uncold. aquatint or line-engraved plans, hf.-title in Vol. 2, some light foxing & offsetting, cont. mor. gt. extra, gt. dentelles. (SG. Nov.3; 87) $1,800.
- – **Anr. Edn.** L., 1843. *2nd. Edn.* 2 vols. 4to. 99 aquatint & engraved plts., liby. stps. on versos of titles, cont. hf. mor., rubbed. (S. May 1; 544) *Dennistoun.* £100

GOOS, Abraham

See— BLAEU, Willem or Guilielmus Janszoon

GOOS, Pieter

- **De Zee-Atlas, ofte Water-Wereld, waer in Vertoont Werden alle de Zee-Kusten van het Bekende des Aerd-Bodems.** Amst., 1669. Fo. A tall copy, Dutch text, ptd. title in elab. engraved allegorical border incorporating vig., dedication to Johann de Witt, ptd. text Kort Verhael ... der Scheep-Vaart on 16 pp., list of contents, & 41 double-p. or folding engraved sea- & coastal-charts including world map in twin hemispheres & 12 charts relating to the Americas, title & all charts richly cold. by cont. hand & heightened with gold thro.-out, on thick paper, faint unif. browning, lr. blank margins of 1 or 2 charts holed without affecting engraved surface, cont. gt.-panel. vell. central & corner arabesques on upr. & lr. corners, slightly soiled, lacks ties. (S. Feb.1; 26) *Dew.* £26,000

GORDON, Alexander

- **Itinerium Septentrionale: or a Journey Thro' Most of the Counties of Scotland, & Those in the North of England.** 1726. Fo. Engraved map, 65 plts., some folding, cont. panel. cf., spine gt., rubbed; Sir Ivar Colquhoun, of Luss copy. (CE. Mar.22; 141) £140

GORDON, G.B. & Mason, J. Alden

- **University of Pennsylvania: Examples of Maya Pottery in the Museum & Other Collections.** Phila.,

1925-28-43. 3 pts. in 3 vols. Fo. 66 plts., ptd. wraps., cl.-bkd. portfo., jnts. torn. (SG. Jan.26; 126) $300

GORDON, George H.

- **History of the Campaign of the Army of Virginia, under. John Pope ... from Cedar Mountain to Alexandria, 1862.** Boston, 1880. *1st. Edn.* (*With:*) – **A War Diary of Events in the War of the Great Rebellion, 1863-1865.** Boston, 1882. *1st. Edn.* (*With:*) – **Brook Farm to Cedar Mountain in the War of the Great Rebellion, 1861-1862.** Boston, 1883. *1st. Edn.* Together 3 vols. Tall & sm. 8vo. Orig. cl., lettering, 1st. & 3rd. vols. with light wear & rubbing, 2nd. with covers spotted; 3rd. with armorial bkplt. of George Meade. (HA. Sep.16; 340) $120

GORDON, Patrick

- **Geography Anatomized.** 1744. Cont. cf. gt. (P. Oct.20; 89) £80
- – **Anr. Edn.** Maps:– Emanuel Bowen. L., 1754. *20th. Edn.* Sm. 8vo. 22 folding maps, crude hf. linen, ex-liby. (SG. Dec.15; 7) $150

GORE, Mrs. Catherine

- **The Lover & the Husband; the Woman of a Certain Age.** 1841. *1st. Edn.* 3 vols. Cont. figured cl., paper labels slightly worn; H.M. Nixon coll. (BBA. Oct.6; 227) *Murray Hill.* £90

GOREY, Edward

- **The Unstrung Harp.** N.Y. & Boston, [1953]. *1st. Edn.* 12mo. Pict. bds., d.-w. (price clipped). (SG. May 24; 299) $200

GORI, Antonio Francesco

- **Antique Numismata Aurea et Argentea Praestantiora et Aerea Maximi Moduli quae ...** Firenze, 1740-42 & 1764. 3 vols. Fo. Cont. russ. cf. (CR. Jun.6; 35) Lire 900,000
- **Monumentum sive Columbarium Libertorum et Servorum Liviae Augustae et Caesarum Romae detectum in Via Appia ...** Ed.:– A.M. Salvinius. Flor. & Frankfurt, 1727. *1st. Book Edn.* Fo. Title stpd., some light browning, some plts. slightly crumpled & foxed, cont. bds., lightly browned, spotted & bumped. (HT. May 9; 996) DM 450

GORLING, Adolph

- **Belvedere oder die Galerien von Wien.** Leipzig, & Dresden, ca. 1850. 2 vols. 4to. Cont. hf. leath. (R. Oct.12; 2245) DM 220
- **Die Dresdener Galerie.** Leipzig, ca. 1850. 2 vols. in 1. 4to. Lightly browned, cont. gold-tooled leath. (R. Apr.4; 2090) DM 750
- – **Anr. Copy.** 2 vols. in 1. 4to. 1 plt. with lengthy tear, some foxing. cont. hf. leath. gt., rubbed & loose. (R. Oct.12; 2246) DM 700
- **Royal Dresden Gallery.** A.H. Payne, ca. 1850. 2 vols. in 1. 4to. Hf. cf. gt. (P. Oct.20; 97) £120
- – **Anr. Copy.** 4to. Some slight foxing & light browning, cont. hf. leath. gt. (R. Apr.4; 2100) DM 610
- – **Anr. Edn.** Dresden & Leipzig, A.H. Payne, ca. 1880. Vol. 2 (of 2) & Coll. Vol. with plts. from vols. 1 & 2 in 2 vols. 4to. Lightly foxed, mod. liby. linen. (R. Oct.12; 2257) DM 600
- – **Anr. Edn.** Dresden, Leipzig & L., A.H. Payne, n.d. 2 vols. 4to. Some browning, cont. hf. cf., rubbed, w.a.f. (CSK. Jun.15; 58) £150
- – **Anr. Copy.** Vols. I & II in 1 vol. 4to. Cont. red hf. mor. gt., rubbed. (LC. Oct.13; 71) £120
- **Stahlstich-Sammlung nach den Vorzueglichsten Gemaelden der Dresdener Galerie.** Leipzig & Dresden, A.H. Payne, ca. 1850. 2 vols. 4to. Foxed, hf. mor., spines elab. gt., worn. (SG. Oct.13; 178) $150
- – **Anr. Copy.** 4to. Lacks 1 engraved title, text slightly foxed, lightly browned. (R. Oct.12; 2247) DM 850
- – **Anr. Copy.** 2 steel engraved titles, 134 steel engraved plts., a few pp. a little stained, foxing, cont. cl., a little worn, spine gt. (VS. Jun.6; 188) Fls. 600

GORLING, Adolph, Meyer, B. & Woltmann, A.

- **Art Treasures of Germany.** Boston, ca. 1860. Hf. leath. gt., foxed, bumped & rubbed. (HK. Nov.9; 1734) DM 480

GORRES, J.
- **Reden gegen Napoleon. Aufsätze und Berichte des Rheinischen Merkur 1814/15.** Ed.:– B. Ihringer. 1914. *(100) Privilege Edn.* Orig. mor. gt., cover slightly soiled & scratched. (R. Oct.11; 349a)
DM 480
- **Die Teutschen Volksbücher.** Heidelberg, 1807. *1st. Edn.* Many (mid 19th. C.?) margin annots., commentaries & contents list inside cover, in text & on 34 ll. bnd. in at end, some slight browning, most in margins, cont. hf. leath., spine bumped; Hauswedell coll. (H. May 24; 1297) DM 580

GORTER, Johannes de
- **Medicinae Compendium in Usum Exercitationis Domesticae.** Leiden, 1731. Latin MS. additions in many hands to margins thro.-out, leath. (DM. May 21; 79) $100

GOSSAERT, G.
- **Gedichte.** Trans.:– R. Schröder. Ill.:– Anna Simons. [München, Bremer Pr., 1929]. *1st. Edn. (180) on Bütten for Friends of Bremer Pr.* Sm. 4to. Orig. hand-bnd. burgundy mor., gt. decor. spine, covers, inner & outer dentelle, by Frieda Thiersch, lr. cover with 2 light spots & 1 scratch. (H. May 22; 983) DM 1,200
- – **Anr. Copy.** Sm. 4to. Hand-bnd. orig. vell., gold decor., by Frieda Thiersch. (H. Nov.23; 949)
DM 600
- – **Anr. Copy.** 4to. Orig. vell., decor., s.-c. (HK. May 17; 2613) DM 500

GOTCH, J. Alfred
- **Architecture of the Renaissance in England.** 1894. 2 vols. Fo. Orig. hf. mor. gt. (BBA. Jul.27; 259)
Cavendish. £70
- – **Anr. Copy.** 2 vols. Tall fo. 145 plts., 180 text engrs., plts. liby.-stpd. on blank verso, loose in mor.-bkd. gt.-decor. cl., linen ties. (SG. May 3; 181)
$150

GOTENDORF, A.N
See— HAYN, H. & Gotendorf, A.N.

GOTHEIN, Marie Luise
- **A History of Garden Art.** Ed.:– W.P. Wright. 1928. *[1st. Edn.].* 2 vols. 4to. Cl., d.-w.'s. (P. Sep.8; 212) £100
- – **Anr. Copy.** 2 vols. 4to. Orig. cl. gt., slightly rubbed. (TA. Jun.21; 243) £70

GOTTFRIED, Johann Ludwig
- **Archontologia Cosmica.** Ill.:– after Blaeu, Braun, Hogenberg, Jansson, & others. Frankfurt am Main, Matthaeus Merian, 1649. *2nd. Edn.* 3 vols. Sm. fo. Engraved allegorical additional title, hf.-title, ptd. title with lge. woodcut device in red & black, 197 engraved plts., many sigd. by M. Merian, including 43 maps (40 double-p.), 142 plans, views & panoramas (136 double-p.), many showing 2 or more subjects, & 8 lge. folding plans & panoramas, a few outer margins strengthened without loss of engraved surface, 1 or 2 minor tears, some margin wormholes, browning mostly affecting text, cont. vell., spines lettered in ink, w.a.f. (S. May 21; 106)
Lawrence. £11,000
- **Historische Chronica.** Frankfurt, 1642. Fo. Probably lacks 3 copperplts., 1 plt. very defect., some ll. with tear, cont. blind-tooled pig over wood bds., slightly worn, spine leath. reprd. later, 2 clasps, lacks ties. (HK. Nov.8; 1021) DM 1,100
- **Historische Chronick.** Ill.:– M. Merian. Frankfurt, 1743. 8 pts. in 1 vol. 1 lf. with sm. text incision, some sm. tears, some soiling or browning, blind-tooled pig, 2 brass clasps. (V. Sep.29; 58)
DM 3,200.
- **Historische Kronyck ... tot 1698.** Ed.:– S. de Vries. Ill.:– after M. Merian I & II, partly by J. Luiken. Leyden, 1698-1700. 3 vols. Fo. Frontis. & some engrs. hand-cold., lacks world map & some plts. with ports., some ll. defect. with loss of text, partly roughly reprd., some tears & stains, volume-indication on 2nd. & 3rd. titles erroneous, cont. cf. (2 vols.) & hf. vell., defect. & crudely reprd., w.a.f. (VG. Mar.19; 248) Fls. 550
- **Inventarium Sueciae.** Frankfurt, 1632. *[1st. Edn.].* Fo. 5 ports., 87 sm. views, 15 plts. trimmed or torn, 2 maps with tears, vell., w.a.f. (P. Dec.8; 188) *Heald.* £1,750
- – **Anr. Copy.** Fo. Lacks copper engraved title, 2 folding ills. cut to subject at side, lightly browned, cont. vell. (R. Oct.12; 2365) DM 9,000
- **Neuwe Archontologia Cosmica ...** Frankfurt, 1638. Fo. Engraved frontis., 86 engraved plts. & maps, fore-margin of frontis. shaved, & with sm. owner's stp., many of the folding views & some other plts. with tears, repairs & some loss, some discoloration & stains, hf. vell., w.a.f. (S. Dec.1; 189) *Schuster.* £3,200
- – **Anr. Edn.** Ill.:– Matthew Merian. Frankfurt, 1646. Fo. 100 engrs., lacks a few text prelims., text browned, a few minor tears & slight spotting towards end, mor. gt. (SPB. Dec.13; 488) $1,800

GOTTHELF, Jeremias
- **Uli der Pächter.** Ill.:– T. Hosemann. Berlin, 1850. *1st. Hosemann Edn.* A few ll. slightly browned, cont. gt.-decor. linen. (GB. Nov.4; 1800) DM 500

GOTTLIEB, Theodor
- **K.K. Hofbibliothek. Bucheinbände.** Vienna, 1910. Fo. Loose as iss. in orig. cl. portfo., spine a little worn, s.-c.; J.R. Abbey bkplt. & acquisition note, H.M. Nixon coll., with sig., note re acquisition & MS. annots. (BBA. Oct.6; 53) *Quaritch.* £450

GOTTSCHALCK, Fr.
- **Die Ritterburgen und Bergschlösser Deutschlands.** Halle, 1810-25. 6 vols. (of 9) bnd. in 3. Later bds. (D. Nov.23; 1411) DM 400

GOTTSCHED, Joh. Christ.
- **Gedichte.** Ed.:– J.J. Schwabe. Leipzig, 1736. *1st. Edn.* Cont. vell., ex-libris. (HK. Nov.10; 2460)
DM 460

GOTZ, T.
- **Monographie des Hundes.** Gotha, 1834. Text slightly stained thro.-out, 2 plts. slightly cut, cont. bds., loose, spine defect. (R. Apr.4; 1891)
DM 1,400

GOTZ, W.
- **Geograph.-historisches Handbuch von Bayern.** München, 1895. Orig. linen, blind-tooled, vol. 2 spine torn. (R. Oct.12; 2499) DM 3,100
- – **Anr. Edn.** München, 1895-98. 2 vols. 4to. Orig. linen. (HK. Nov.9; 1358) DM 2,300

GOTZKOFSKY, J.C.
- **Geschichte eines Patriotischen Kaufmanns aus Berlin, Namens J.C. Gotzkofsky, von ihm selbst geschrieben.** Augsburg, 1789. Later sewed. (GB. Nov.3; 270) DM 560

GOUDAR, Ange
- [-] **Histoire des Fripons, Ouvrage Néccessaire aux Honnestes Gens pour se préserver des Grecs, qui scavent corriger la Fortune au Jeu.** Amst., 1773. 12mo. Sewed, old wrap. (HD. Feb.28; 36)
Frs. 1,200

GOUDY, Frederic W.
- **The Story of the Village Type, by Its Designer.** N.Y., Pr. of the Wolly Whale, 1933. *1st. Edn. (450) on Arnold paper.* Qtr. linen, bds., publisher's broadside advt. laid in. (SG. May 17; 98) $110

GOUFFE, Jules
- **Le Livre des Conserves.** Paris, 1869. Some light foxing, cont. hf. roan, limp, blind-tool decor. spine, spine faded. (HD. Dec.9; 134) Frs. 1,700
- **Le Livre de Cuisine.** Paris, 1870. *2nd. Edn.* 4to. Cont. hf. leath. gt., loose. (R. Apr.4; 1912)
DM 450
- – **Anr. Edn.** Ill.:– E. Roujat. Paris, 1884. *6th. Edn.* Some foxing, publishers bds. (HD. Dec.9; 135)
Frs. 1,400
- **Le Livre de Patisserie.** Paris, 1873. *1st. Edn.* Cont. hf. leath. gt. (R. Apr.4; 1820) DM 620
- **The Royal Cookery Book.** Trans.:– A. Gouffé. L., 1868. 4to. Margins at beginning & end frayed, some tears reprd., orig. linen gt., corners bumped, spine & end-papers renewed. (HK. Nov.9; 1670)
DM 420

GOUGER, Robert (Pseud.)
See— WAKEFIELD, Edward Gibbon 'Robert Gouger'

GOUGH, Richard
- [-] **British Topography.** L., 1780. 2 vols. 4to. Engraved vig. titles, 9 engraved folding maps, some offset, some slight browning or spotting, Vol. 1 lacks last blank, cont. cf., rebkd. (S. Mar.6; 250)
Kidd. £110
- [-] **Sepulchral Monuments in Great Britain.** L., 1786-96. 2 vols. in 5. Fo. Hf.-titles, engraved plts., folding tables, sm. liby. stps., some slight spotting, mor. gt., jnts. rubbed. (S. May 21; 60)
Chaddock. £350

GOULART, S.
See— CRESPIN, J. & Goulart, S.

GOULD, John
- **The Birds of Asia.** Ill.:– Gould, H.C. Richter, Joseph Wolf, & W. Hart. L., priv. ptd., 1850-83. 7 vols. in orig. 35 pts. Fo. 530 hand-cold. litho. plts., title-pp. & prelims. bnd. at end of pt. 35, some slight margin soiling, a few spots, orig. cl.-bkd. bds., unc., slightly worn & soiled, stp. on covers of Ernest Augustus, King of Hanover, preserved in 7 qtr. mor. cases, gt. spines. (S. Feb.1; 28)
Didier. £46,000
- **Birds of Asia. — Birds of South America. — Birds of Europe. — Birds of Australia. — Birds of New Guinea.** Texts:–A. Rutgers. 1966-72. 5 vols. Orig. cl., d.-w.'s. (LC. Mar.1; 149) £80
- **The Birds of Australia.** Melbourne, 1972-75. *Facs. Edn.* 8 vols., with accompanying 8vo. Handbook. Fo. Orig. cl. (KH. Nov.9; 610)
Aus. $750
- – **Anr. Copy.** Vols. II-IV & VI only. Fo. Bdg. not stated. (KH. May 1; 308) Aus. $350
- **The Birds of Australia & the Adjacent Islands.** Melbourne, 1979. *Facs. Edn. (500).* Bdg. not stated. (KH. May 1; 310) Aus. $240
- **The Birds of Europe.** Ill.:– after J. & E. Gould & Edward Lear. L., [1832-]37. 5 vols. Fo. 448 hand-cold. litho. plts., subscribers list, some plts. slightly soiled in margins & some slight offsetting, mainly onto text, margin tear reprd. in plt. 183 in Vol. 3, plt. 347 in Vol. 5 slightly frayed, 3 or 4 other plts. with very sm. margin tears, some prelims. in Vol. 1 slightly torn in upr. margin, short margin tear to title in Vol. 4, margin stain to plt. 327 & facing text lf. in Vol. 4, Vol. 2 lacks front free end-paper, cont. gt.-panel. red mor., red mor. doubls., worn & soiled, 1 cover detchd. (S. Nov.28; 28)
Robinson. £15,500
- **The Birds of Great Britain.** L., 1862-73. 5 vols. in 25 pts. Fo. 367 hand-finished col. plts., titles, dedication, lists of plts. & subscribers bnd. in pt. 25, orig. cl.-bkd. bds. (P. Nov.24; 240)
Taylor. £13,000
- – **Anr. Copy.** 25 orig. pts. Lge. fo. 367 hand-finished cold. litho. plts., some very minor spotting, orig. cl.-bkd. ptd. bds. (C. Nov.16; 248)
Craddock & Barnard. £12,000
- – **Anr. Edn.** Ill.:– after Gould, Joseph Wolf, H.C. Richter, & W. Hart. L., priv. ptd., [1862-]73. 5 vols. Fo. 367 hand-cold. plts., cont. hf. mor. gt., spines gt. in compartments, slightly rubbed. (S. Feb.1; 30) *Borgessons.* £15,000
- – **Anr. Copy.** 5 vols. in 10. Fo. 367 hand-cold. litho. plts., subscribers list, plts. guarded at inner edge thro.-out, in a few cases obscuring artists' & printers' names, 19th. C. maroon hf. mor., rubbed & slightly stained. (S. Nov.28; 29)
Marshall. £12,000
- – **Anr. Edn.** Ill.:– after Gould, J. Wolf, & H.C. Richter. L., priv. ptd., [1862-]75. 5 vols. Lge. fo. 367 hand-finished cold. litho. plts., cont. mor. gt., spines gt. in compartments, by Zaehnsdorf; C. Kennard bkplt. (C. Mar.14; 171)
Old Hall. £16,000
- **A Monograph of the Odontophorinae, or Partridges of America.** Ill.:– Gould & H.C. Richter. L., priv. ptd., [1844-]50. Fo. 32 hand-cold. litho. plts., slight offsetting on plts. of Plumed Partridge & Californian Partridge, title dampstained, mod. mor. gt., dark green watered silk linings. (S. Feb.1; 27)
Lester. £8,000
- **A Monograph of the Pittidae.** Ill.:– Gould, W. Hart, & H.C. Richter. L., priv. ptd., 1880-81. Pts. 1 & 2 (all publd.). Lge. fo. 10 hand-cold. litho. plts., orig. cl.-bkd. ptd. bds., slightly soiled, orig. wrap. to pt. 2 bnd. in, mod. buckram portfo., buckram s.-c. (C. Nov.16; 250) *Craven.* £1,200
- **A Monograph of the Ramphastidae, or Family of Toucans.** Ill.:– Hullmandel, after J. & E. Gould & E. Lear. L., priv. ptd., 1834. *1st. Edn.* Fo. 34 litho.

GOULD, John -*Contd.*

plts. (33 cold.), cont. cl., upr. cover gt.-lettered, slightly worn & stained. (C. Mar.14; 170)
Quaritch. £7,500
– – **Anr. Edn.** Ill.:– Gould & H.C. Richter, & G. Scharf. L., priv. ptd., [1852-]54. *2nd. Edn.* Fo. 51 hand-cold. litho. plts., 1 uncold. plt., some slight spotting, cont. mor. gt.; Lord Braybrooke bkplt. (S. Feb.1; 29)
Didier. £15,500
– **A Monograph of the Trochilidae, or Family of Humming-Birds.** Ill.:– Hullmandel & Walton, & Walter & Cohn, after Gould & H.C. Richter. L., [1849-]61. 5 vols. Lge. fo. 360 hand-finished col. litho. plts., sm. abrasion to 1 plt. in Vol. 3, slight margin tear to 1 plt. & anr. plt. slightly soiled in Vol. 4, sm. mark to 1 plt. in Vol. 5, last text lf. in Vol. 2 creased, margin tear to 1 text lf. in Vol. 3, extremities of text & plts. slightly darkened, hf. mor. gt., sm. portions of covers to Vol. 2 slightly scored, slight wear to a few corners. (CNY. Nov.18; 299)
$27,000
– – **Anr. Edn.** Ed.:– Richard Bowdler Sharpe. Ill.:– after Gould, H.C. Richter, & W. Hart. L., priv. ptd., [1849-]61, [1880-]87. 6 vols., including Supp. Lge. fo. 418 hand-finished cold. litho. plts., plt. 1 foxed, some browning to fore-margins of some text thro.-out lst. 5 vols., affecting about 15 plts., extremities of text & plts. slightly darkened, sm. spot on plt. 36 in Vol. 3, mor. gt. by Zaehnsdorf, extremities of spines & some outer jnts. & corners with slight wear. (CNY. May 18; 142) $44,000
– **A Monograph of the Trogonidae, or Family of Trogons.** Ill.:– C. Hullmandel, after J. & E. Gould. L., priv. ptd., 1838. Lge. fo. 36 hand-cold. litho. plts., including double-p. folding 'Trogon Resplendens', subscribers list, 1 plt. & facing text lf. stained at inner blank margin, a few plts. with slight dampstain at lr. blank margin, cont. mor. gt., spine gt. (C. Nov.16; 251)   *Papp.* £3,500

GOULD, John W.
– **Private Journal of a Voyage from New-York to Rio de Janeiro** ... N.Y., priv. ptd., 1839. *1st. Edn.* Tall 8vo. Foxed, 1 final blank lf. loose, orig. gt.-armorial cl.; sigd. inscr. of John Fairchild on free end-paper, inscr. by author to Mrs. Childs. 14[Sabin 28116]. (SG. Oct.20; 167) $200

GOULD, Robert Freke
– **The History of Freemasonry.** Edinb., n.d. 6 vols. 4to. Orig. gt.-decor. cl. (SKC. May 4; 1591)   £55

GOURDAULT, Jules
– **La Suisse, Etudes et Voyages, Premier Partie: Genève, Vaud, Valais** ... 1879. 4to. Foxing, publisher's chagrin, arms of Switzerland. (SM. Mar.7; 2489)   Frs. 2,200
– – **Anr. Edn.** Paris, 1879-80. 2 vols. Fo. 750 text woodcuts, including 141 full-p. cont. hf. leath., worn. (R. Oct.13; 3257)   DM 2,500
– – **Anr. Copy.** 2 vols. Fo. Cont. hf. leath., slightly bumped. (HK. Nov.9; 1256)   DM 2,300
– **La Suisse Pittoresque.** Paris, 1892. 4to. 134 woodcut text ills., (64 full-p.), some slight foxing, MS. owners mark, orig. linen, gold & black-tooled. (HT. May 10; 2858)   DM 401

GOURDON DE GENOUILLIAC, H.
– **Paris à travers les Siècles.** Paris, 1881-82. 5 vols. Lge. 8vo. Cont. hf. roan, spines faded. (HD. Mar.19; 95)   Frs. 1,500

GOURMONT, Remy de
– **Couleurs.** Ill.:– J.E. Laboureur. Paris, 1929. Jansenist mor. gt. by Semet & Plumelle, red mor. liners, watered silk end-ll., wrap. preserved, s.-c., spine slightly faded. (HD. Jun.13; 47) Frs. 4,800
– **Histoires Magiques.** 1894. *Orig. Edn.* (7) *on japon impérial.* No bdg. stated. (HD. May 11; 27)
Frs. 3,300
– **Le Latin Mystique. Les Poètes de l'Antiphonaire et la Symbolique au Moyen-âge.** Preface:– J.K. Huysmans. Paris, 1892. *Orig. Edn.* (7) on 'Pourpre Cardinalice' japan. Lge. 8vo. Red bradel hf. mor., corners, by Louise Leveque, unc., wrap. & spine, cold. ill. by Charles Filiger on wrap.; sigd. autograh dedication to Francois Coulon, MS. article by Marcel Schwob bnd. at beginning. (HD. May 16; 34)   Frs. 5,000
– **Les Saintes du Paradis.** Ill.:– Georges d'Espagnat.

Paris, 1898. 19 orig. woodcuts, sewed, unc. (GB. May 5; 2471)   DM 500
– **Le Songe d'Une Gemme.** Ill.:– J.E. Laboureur. Paris, 1925. *(385).* Hand-bnd. red hf. mor., orig. wraps. bnd. in, end-papers foxed. (H. Nov.24; 2518)   DM 800

GOURSAT, E.
– **Cours d'Analyse Mathématique.** Paris, 1910-15. *1st. Edn.* 3 vols. Sm. 4to. Private hf. linen, unc. (HT. May 8; 409)   DM 580

GOURY, Jules
See— JONES, Owen & Goury, Jules

GOURY DE CHAMPGRAND, Charles Jean
– **Traité de Vènerie et de Chasses.** 1769. *Orig. Edn.* 2 pts. in 1 vol. 4to. Some pp. stained, cont. marb. cf., decor. (HD. Feb.29; 19)   Frs. 4,500

GOUTHOEVEN, Valerius van
– **D'Oude Chronijcke ende Historien van Holland (met West-Vriesland) van Zeeland ende van Utrecht. (Met Vervolg tot 1620.).** Dordrecht, 1620. 2 pts. in 1 vol. Fo. Few sm. wormholes, vell. (B. Feb.8; 602)   Fls. 1,100

GOWER, John
– **De Confessione Amantis.** L., 1554. *3rd. Edn.* Fo. Lacks final blank lf., some minor staining, mainly marginal, clean tear without text loss in O2, outer blank margin of Bb6 frayed, 19th. C. hard-grained red mor.; owners' inscrs. of William Howard & Edward, Lord Morpeth. [STC 12144] (C. Nov.9; 77)   *Gregory.* £650

GOWER, Lord Ronald Sutherland
– **Sir Thomas Lawrence. With a Catalogue of the Artist's Exhibited & Engraved Works.** L., 1900. *Ltd. Edn.* Fo. Mor. gt. by Zaehnsdorf. (SPB. Nov.30; 5) $275

GOWINIUS, S.
– **Enfaldiga tankar om Nyttans om England kan hafva of Sina Nybyggen i Norra America.** Ed.:– Peter Kalm. Abo (Turku), [1763]. Sm. 4to. Later bds. [Sabin 36990] (S. Dec.1; 282)   *Israel.* £200

GOYA, Francisco
– **Los Desastres de la Guerra.** Madrid, 1903. *(100).* Ob. fo. 80 aquaforte engrs., port. & 2 typographical pp., linen. (DS. May 25; 2191)   Pts. 725,000
– **Les Dessins.** Rome, 1908. 3 vols. Fo. Unbnd. as iss. in orig. cl. portfo., lightly soiled. (CSK. Jun.29; 82)   £100
– **Los Dibujos** ... Intro. & Notes:– F.J. Sanchez Canton. Madrid, 1954. 2 vols. Tall 4to. Cl.-bkd. pict. bds., slightly shaken. (SG. Oct.13; 186) $130
– **Los Proverbios Coleccion de Diez y Ocho Laminas Inventadas y Grabadas al Agua Fuerte** ... Madrid, 1864. *1st. Edn.* Ob. fo. Bradel hf. cl. (HD. Jun.13; 48)   Frs. 140,000
– **Tauromachia.** Ed.:– Hugo Kehrer. 1923. *(500)* numbered. 4to. Orig. vell. gt., s.-c. (TA. Oct.20; 329)   £100

GOYDER, G.W.
– **Official Atlas of South Australia** ... Adelaide, 1885. Lge. fo. Lacks 2 sheets (as usual), lge. tipped in slip states they 'will be forwarded when published', some fraying, mainly marginal, bdg. not stated, worn & brkn. (KH. May 1; 312)
Aus. $400

GOZ, Fr. A.
– **Neues Theoretisch-praktisches Zeichnungsbuch zum Selbetunterricht für Angehende Künstler und Handwerker** ... 1803-07. 3 pts. in 1 vol., compl. Fo. Pt. 2 lacks 4 supp. copperplts., some plts. lightly soiled, some foxing, mod. hf. vell. (H. May 22; 141)   DM 620

GRAAF, Regner de
– **De Virorum Organis Generationi Inservientibus, de Clysteribus et de Usu Siphonis in Anatomia.** Leiden, 1668. *1st. Edn.* (*With:*) – **Tractatus Anatomico-Medicus de Succi Pancreatici Natura & Usu.** Leiden, 1671. *1st. Edn.* 1 folding plt. cropped, margin of A1 clipped away. (*With:*) – **Partium Genitalium Defensio.** Leiden, 1673. *1st. Edn.* Together 3 works in 2 vols. Few stains, etc., unif. blind-tooled cf. antique. (SG. Nov.3; 88) $500

– **De Mulierum Organis Generationi Inservientibus.** Leiden, 1672. Several plts. shaved or cleanly torn, lacks additional engraved title & frontis., old cf., rubbed, rebkd. (CSK. Jun.1; 25)   £90
– **Tractatus Anatomico-Medicus de Succi Pancreatici Natura & Usu.** Leiden, 1671. Lacks port., blank corner of title torn off, vell.; Dr. Walger Pagel copy. (S. Feb.7; 143)   *Israel.* £90

GRAAH, Wilhelm August
– **Undersøgelses-Reise till Østkystens af Grønland.** Copen., 1832. 4to. Lge. folding engraved map, 8 hand-cold. plts., some offsetting (as usual), qtr. cf. (S. Dec.1; 307)   *Israel.* £320

GRAAUWHART, H.
– **Leerzame Zinnebeelden; Bestaande in Christelyke Bedenkingen.** Ill.:– C. Huyberts. Amst., 1704. *1st. Edn.* Sm. 8vo. Cont. blind-stpd. vell. (VS. Dec.9; 1137)   Fls. 500

GRABBE, Chr.
– **Dramatische Dichtungen.** Frankfurt, 1827. *1st. Edn.* Foxed, cont. hf. leath., worn & slightly bumped., 1 spine with sm. defect., liby. & bookseller stp. inside cover. (H. May 22; 704)   DM 440

GRABHORN, Edwin & Marjorie
– **Figure Prints of Old Japan.** Intro.:– Harold P. Stern. San Franc., [Grabhorn Pr.], 1959. *(400).* Fo. Hf. cl. & decor. bds., covers lightly rubbed. (CBA. Nov.19; 184) $325
– **Landscape Prints of Old Japan** ... **Illustrated from Original Prints in the Collection of Edwin & Marjorie Grabhorn.** Ed.:– Jack Hillier. San Franc., Grabhorn Pr., 1960. *(450).* Fo. Hf. cl. & decor. bds. (CBA. Aug.21; 780) $250

GRABHORN PRESS
See— AESOP
See— BIBLIANA [English]
See— CABECA DE VACA, Alvar Nunez
See— CALVERT, George Chambers
See— DU BOIS, John van Deusen
See— GAUGUIN, Paul
See— GOLL, Yvan
See— GRABHORN, Edwin & Marjorie
See— HARLOW, Neal
See— HARTE, Bret
See— HELLER, Elinor Raas & Magee, David
See— HITTELL, Theodore H.
See— JEFFERS, Robinson
See— KAISER, Henry J.
See— KNOX, Capt. Dudley W.
See— KURTZ, Benjamin P.
See— LEWIS, Oscar
See— LITTLEJOHN, David
See— LYTELL GESTE OF ROBYN HODE & HIS MEINY
See— MANDEVILLE or MAUNDEVILLE, Sir John
See— METZGAR, Judson D.
See— MINASIAN, Khatchik
See— MUMFORD, Lewis
See— PATTISON, Mark
See— ROBERTSON, John
See— SCHULZ, H.C.
See— SHAKESPEARE, William
See— SKELTON, R.A.
See— SWINBURNE, Algernon Charles
See— VESPUCCI, Amerigo
See— VIZCAINO, Sebastian
See— WHEAT, Carl I.
See— WHITMAN, Walt
See— WILDE, Oscar
See— WOOLF, Virginia

GRACE, Sheffield
– **Memoirs of the Family of Grace.** L., 1823. Royal 8vo. Sigd. pres. copy from author, unopened, mor.-bkd. (GM. Dec.7; 301)   £90

GRACQ, Julien
– **Le Rivage des Syrtes.** Ill.:– Camille Josso. Paris, 1956-57. *(18)* on vélin de Rives, with plt. in 3 states. 2 vols. 4to. Leaves, box. (HD. Nov.17; 131)
Frs. 2,500

GRADUALE CARTUSIENSE
– **Incipit Liber Graduale Cartusiense** ... Seville, 1630. Lge. fo. Ptd. in 2 cols., leath. (DS. Dec.16; 2166)   Pts. 20,000

GRADUALE ROMANUM juxta Missale ex Decreto Sacrosancti Concilii Tridentini Restitutum Antverpiae, 1774. Fo. Privilege lf., mus. notat., blind-decor. cf., copper clasps, 1 corner defect. (LM. Mar.3; 226b)   B. Frs. 13,000

GRAEF, Abraham de
– De Seven Boeken v.d. Groote Zeevaert, ofte de Konste der Stuer-luyden. Amst., 1657 [1658]. 7 pts. in 1 vol. Sm. fo. Lacks engraved general title, 1st. section-title & prelims. slightly damaged & stained, stains at end, later hf. vell. (VG. Sep.14; 997)   Fls. 2,000

GRAESSE, Jean George Th.
– Trésor de Livres Rares et Precieux. 1950. 8 vols., including Supp. 4to. Orig. cl. (BBA. Apr.5; 288)   Oak Knoll Books. £250
– – Anr. Edn. Milan, [1950]. 8 vols., including Supp. 4to. In various languages, cl., light dusting to covers. (CBA. Nov.19; 726) $250
– – Anr. Copy. 8 vols., including Index. Lge. 8vo. Cl. (VS. Dec.7; 270)   Fls. 925

GRAEVIUS, Johann Georg
– Thesaurus Antiquitatum et Historiarum Italiae ... Ill.:– Stoopendaal, Mulder, & others. Leiden, 1704-25. 22 vols. Fo. Engraved dedicatory title, frontis., folding port., 15 additional engraved titles to pts., titles with engraved vigs., about 800 engraved maps, town plans, views & plts., many double-p. or folding, hf.-titles, Vol. 9 pt, 1 sig. Mm inverted, pt. 10 portion 02 torn away, some margin dampstains, a few blank margins reprd., a few ll. loose, bdg. not stated, w.a.f. (C. Mar.14; 140)   Crossley. £4,500
– Thesaurus Antiquitatum Romanarum. Traject. ad Rhen & Lugd. Batavor, 1694. 1st. Edn. 12 vols. Fo. Perforation stps. in titles, old cf., worn, few covers detchd., ex-liby. (RO. Dec.11; 124) $350
– – Anr. Edn. 1694-99. 12 vols. Fo. 219 engrs., including 2 double-p., cont. panel. cf. gt. (P. Dec.8; 130)   Weinreb. £520

GRAF, O.M.
– Amen und Anfang. Ill.:– G. Schrimpf. München, 1919. 1st. Edn. (300) numbered. 4to. Orig. hf. linen; printers mark sigd. by author, orig. woodcut sigd. (GB. Nov.5; 2528)   DM 500

GRAFFIGNY, Françoise d'Issembourg d'Happoncourt de
[–] Lettre d'une Péruvienne. [1747]. Orig. Edn. 12mo. Cont. mor., gt. decor. (HD. Dec.9; 38)   Frs. 2,000

GRAFSTROM, Anders Abraham
– Ett ar i Sverige. Ed.:– C. Forssell. Ill.:– J.G. Sandberg. Stockholm, 1827[-36]. 1st. Edn. Sm. 4to. Vig. title, 2 engraved mus. plts., 45 chromolitho. plts., (all supplied from the 1864 edn.?), slight foxing & offsetting, 20th. C. hf. mor. gt., marb. bds. (SG. Sep.22; 151) $200

GRAHAM, Ernest R.
[–] The Architectural Work of Graham Anderson Probst & White, Chicago ... L., 1933. (300) numbered, for private circulation. 2 vols. Fo. 386 photogravure plts., ex-liby., lev., triple gt. fillet borders, raised hands, gt. dentelles, by Sangorski & Sutcliffe, boxed; pres. copy to Richard C. Lilly, sigd. (SG. May 3; 182) $850

GRAHAM, J.
See— MONTGOMERY, James & others

GRAHAM, Maria
– Journal of a Residence in India. Edinb. & L., 1812. 4to. Hand-cold. engraved frontis., 15 plts., some folding, cont. hf. cf., rebkd. (C. Nov.16; 93)   Shapero. £80
– – Anr. Edn. Edinb., 1813. 2nd. Edn. 4to. No hf.-title, cont. hf. cf., a little worn. (BBA. Sep.29; 63)   Primrose Hill Books. £65
[–] Voyage of H.M.S. Blonde to the Sandwich Islands in the Years 1824-1825; Captain the Right Hon. Lord Byron, Commander. 1826. 4to. Some 15 ll. foxed or stained, a few sm. defects, later hf. cf. (KH. May 1; 313)   Aus. $380

GRAHAM, William
– The Art of Making Wines, from Fruits, Flowers, & Herbs, ... To Which is now Added,

The Complete Method of Distilling Pickling, & Preserving. L., 1776. Title browned, disbnd. (P. Jan.12; 228)   £140

GRAHAME, Kenneth
– Dream Days. Ill.:– E.H. Shepard. 1930. Ltd. Edn., sigd. by author & artist. Qtr. vell. gt., s.-c., unopened. (P. Sep.8; 307)   £80
– – Anr. Edn. Ill.:– Ernest H. Shepard. [1930]. (275) numbered & sigd. by author & artist. Orig. hf. vell., orig. s.-c. (CSK. Jan.27; 133)   £90
– The Golden Age. Ill.:– E.H. Shepard. 1928. Ltd. Edn., sigd. by author & artist. Qtr. vell. gt., s.-c., unopened. (P. Sep.8; 306)   £80
– – Anr. Edn. Ill.:– Ernest H. Shepard. [1928]. (275) numbered & sigd. by author & artist. Orig. hf. vell., spine lightly soiled, orig. s.-c. (CSK. Jan.27; 134)   £65
– The Wind in the Willows. 1908. 1st. Edn. Orig. cl., gt.-decor., unc., slightly rubbed, ink inscrs. on front end-papers & fly-lf. (SKC. Mar.9; 1780)   £120
– – Anr. Edn. Ill.:– Ernest H. Shepard. 1931. (200) numbered & sigd. by author & artist. 4to. Cont. cl.-bkd. bds., bumped. (CSK. Jan.27; 162)   £240
– – Anr. Edn. Intro.:– A.A. Milne. Ill.:– Arthur Rackham. N.Y., Ltd. Edns. Cl., 1940. (2020) numbered, designed & sigd. by Bruce Rogers. Lge. 4to. 16 mntd. cold. plts., buckram, batik bds., s.-c. cracked. (SG. May 17; 194) $500
– – Anr. Copy. Tall 4to. Cl.-bkd. bds., rubbed & soiled, lacks s.-c. (SG. Dec.8; 297) $375
– – Anr. Edn. Ill.:– Arthur Rackham. L., [1951]. (500). 4to. Sheep, gt.-lettered spine, covers slightly soiled, spine slightly darkened & dried, box lightly rubbed; gift of Mrs. Joe E. Brown to Marymount College, with their bkplt. (CBA. Mar.3; 459) $225

GRAHAM'S MAGAZINE
Ed.:– Edgar Allan Poe. Phila., Jan.-Jun. 1842. Vol. XX. Contains Poe's 'Masque of the Red Death', 'Life in Death', 'To One Departed', & 'A Few Words About Brainard', foxed thro.-out, some stains & tears, three-qtr. diced mor. & bds., covers rubbed, chipped, corners showing, pencil scrawls to end-papers. (CBA. Oct.29; 671a) $110
– – Anr. Edn. Contribs.:– Edgar Allan Poe & others. Phila., Jan.-Jun. 1943. Tall 8vo. Some foxing, publisher's red mor. gt., owner's name embossed on cover, rubbed. (RO. Apr.23; 251) $125

GRANADA
– Ordenanzas que los Muy Ilustres y Muy Magníficos Señores de Granada mandaron guardar par la Buena Governación de su República. Granada, 1672. Fo. Vell. (DS. Oct.28; 2054)   Pts. 65,000
– Razón del Juicio seguido en Granada contra Varios Falsificadores de Escrituras Públicas. Tradiciones. Reliquias y Libros ... Madrid, 1781. Fo. L.P., orig. leath. (DS. Oct.28; 2664)   Pts. 75,000

GRANADOS DE LOS RIOS, C.
– Discurso de las Grandezas de Toledo. Toledo, 1635. 4to. Leath. (DS. Dec.16; 2610) DM 80,000

GRAND-CARTERET, Jean
– L'Histoire, la Vie, les Moeurs et la Curiosité. Paris, 1927-28. 5 vols. 4to. Orig. mor.-bkd. cl. gt., slightly rubbed. (BBA. Feb.23; 75)   Duran. £140
– – Anr. Copy. 5 vols. 4to. Hf. chagrin, corners, spines decor. (SM. Mar.7; 2490)   Frs. 1,000
– – Anr. Edn. Paris, 1927-28. (1000) numbered on alfa paper. 5 vols. Very tall 4to. Some plts. hand-cold., orig. gt.-decor. mor.-bkd. cl., spine ends worn. (SG. Oct.13; 187) $150
– – Anr. Copy. 4to. Publisher's hf. chagrin. (SM. Mar.7; 2138)   Frs. 1,400
– Raphaël et Gambrinus ou l'Art dans la Brasserie. Ill.:– Desboutin (frontis.), Pille, Jeanniot, etc. Paris, 1886. Orig. Edn. (30) numbered on japan paper. Frontis. in 2 states, some ills. hand-cold, hf. mor., unc. (HD. Apr.11; 25)   Frs. 1,500
– Vieux Papiers, Vieilles Images; Cartons d'un Collectionneur. Paris, 1896. 1st. Edn. 4to. 6 plts. (3 cold.), 461 text reproductions, liby. buckram, pict. upr. wrap. bnd. in. (SG. May 17; 104) $100

GRANDES COUSTUMES DU ROYAUME DE FRANCE ...
1522. 4to. Some dampstains, cont. cf., reprd. (HD. Jun.29; 48)   Frs. 2,500

GRANDI, Guido
– Instituzioni Meccaniche. Flor., 1739. 1st. Edn. Plts. slightly frayed at fore-edges, old vell. bds., slightly wormed; Stanitz coll. (SPB. Apr.25; 195) $200

GRANDIN, F.
– Souvenirs Historiques du Capitaine Krettly, Ancien Trompette Major ... Paris, 1839. 2 vols. Mod. hf. chagrin, wraps. preserved. (HD. Jan.27; 46)   Frs. 2,200

GRANDJEAN, Serge (Text)
See— ROTHSCHILD, Edouard de

GRANDVILLE, Jean Jacques (Pseud.)
See— GERARD, Jean Ignacio Isidor 'Jean Jacques Grandville'

GRANJEAN DE MONTIGNY & Famin, Stanislas Marie César
– Architecture Toscane ... – Tombeaux et Monuments de la Renaissance dans les XVe et XVIe Siècles. 1846. New Edn. Fo. Foxing, later cl. (HD. Feb.29; 20)   Frs. 1,300

GRANNISS, Robert
See— COWAN, Robert E. & Granniss, Robert

GRANT, C.H.B
See— MACKWORTH-PRAED, C.W. & Grant, C.H.B.

GRANT, Charles, Viscount de Vaux
– The History of Mauritius, or the Isle of France, & the Neighbouring Islands ... 1801. 4to. Some foxing & offsetting, cont. hf. cf., worn. (TA. Nov.17; 22)   £52

GRANT, James
– Narrative of a Voyage of Discovery ... to New South Wales. L., 1803. 1st. Edn. 4to. Hand-cold. frontis., folding map, 6 plts., including 1 folding, spotting, mod. mor. gt. (P. Dec.8; 356)   Burgess. £800
– – Anr. Copy. 4to. With additional 'List of Encouragers' lf., Folding frontis. set down in linen, folding map bnd. inverted, later hf. cf. by Morrell. (KH. Nov.9; 611)   Aus. $3,800
– – Anr. Copy. 4to. Folding plan offset, sig. at head of title, old cf. (CA. Apr.3; 51)   Aus. $3,200

GRANT, Col. Maurice Harold
– Jan Van Huysum 1682-1749. 1954. (500) numbered. Fo. Orig. buckram, d.-w. (CE. Sep.1; 82)   £50
– The Makers of Black Basaltes. Edinb., 1910. 1st. Edn. 4to. Frontis., 96 plts., sm. repair to frontis., gt.-pict. cl., spine end chipped. (SG. Jan.26; 95) $110
– Old English Landscape Painters. Leigh-on-Sea, [1957-61]. (500) numbered. 8 vols. Orig. cl. (CSK. Dec.16; 121)   £65

GRANT, Ulysses S.
– Personal Memoirs. N.Y., 1885-6. 1st. Edn. 2 vols. Unopened, unbnd., cl. s.-c.'s., unc. (LH. Sep.25; 230) $355

GRANVILLE, A.B.
– The Spas of Germany. L., 1843. 2nd. Edn. Minimal spotting, cont. hf. leath., spine defect. (HK. May 15; 837)   DM 400

GRAPALDI, Francesco Mario
– De Partibus Aedium. [Turin], 14 Dec. 1516, 1517. 2 pts. in 1 vol. 4to. Lr. edge of title trimmed, removing early owner's name, some bad stains & minute worming thro.-out, cont. tooled leath. on bds., worn & loose, lacks clasps. (SG. Feb.9; 238) $350

GRAPHEUS, C.
– Spectaclorvm in Susceptione Philippi Hisp. Prin. Divi. Caroli. V ... Antwerpiae Aeditorvm, Mirificvs Apparatvs. Antw., 1550. 1st. Latin Edn. Sm. fo. 1st. & last lf. slightly torn, 2 ll. pasted over in fold, some light spotting, mod. cf., worn. (H. May 22; 362)   DM 1,700

GRAPHIC ILLUSTRATIONS OF THE MOST PROMINENT FEATURES OF THE FRENCH CAPITAL; with Characteristic Figures in the Foregrounds
Ill.:– Angus, Sparrow, Dadley, Porter, & others. L., [early 19th. C.],. Fo. Title detchd., 12 double-p. engrs., foxed thro.-out, later cl., worn. (SG. Jun.7; 383) $110

GRAPHISCHEN KUNSTE
Ed.:– O. Berggruen. Ill.:– Ludwig Richter & H. Bürkner & others. Wien, 1882-87. Yrs., IV-IX in 6 vols. Fo. 148 etchings & heliogravures, many text woodcuts & ills., 2 orig. etchings, orig. blind-gold– & silver-tooled linen, some light bumping. (HK. May 16; 1518) DM 480

GRAPPE, Georges
– **H. Fragonard, Peintre de l'Amour au XVIIIe Siècle.** Paris, 1913. 2 vols. 4to. Cont. hf. mor. by Ch. De. Samblanx., spines gt. decor., partly untrimmed, orig. wraps. bnd. slightly rubbed. (TA. Feb.16; 265) £64
– **Un Soir à Cordue.** Ill.:– Jose Pedro Gil. Paris, 1933. *(152) numbered.* 4to. Wraps., s.-c. (DS. Oct.28; 2141) Pts. 34,000

GRASSET, Eugène
– **La Plante et ses Applications Ornementales.** Paris, n.d. [1st. vol. intro. dtd. 1896]. 1st. & 2nd. Series: 2 vols. Fo. 144 pochoir-cold. plts., few plts. with minor margin tape repairs, plts. liby.-stpd. on verso, 4 stpd. in margin, qtr. mor., lacks spine, covers & end-papers detchd. (SG. Dec.15; 152) $700
– **Voyage Historique, Littéraire et Pittoresque dans les Isles et Possessions ci-devant Vénetiennes du Levant ...** An VIII [1800]. 3 vols. in 2, including atlas. 8vo. & 4to. Cont. hf. roan, worn. (HD. Jun.29; 93) Frs. 5,600
– – **Anr. Copy.** 3 vols. 1 map & 1 text lf. with sm. hole, cont. hf. leath. gt. (R. Oct.13; 3144) DM 2,250

GRASSET DE SAINT-SAUVEUR, Jacques
– **Encyclopédie des Voyages ...** Paris, 1796. 4 pts. (of 5) in 4 vols. 4to. 349 (of 432) cold. copperplts., text foxed, plts. foxed mostly in margin, title ll. with excisions & partly loose, cont. hf. leath., worn & bumped. (GB. May 3; 8) DM 2,700
[–] **Les Fastes du Peuple Français.** Ill.:– after Labrousse. [1796]. Sm. 4to. 19th. C. hf. red chagrin. (HD. Feb.29; 21) Frs. 6,000
– **Voyages Pittoresques dans les Quatre Parties du Monde. Tome Premier; contenant, les Peuples de l'Europe.** Paris, 1806. *[1st. Edn].* Additional engraved title, frontis., 2 double-p. maps, 79 hand-cold. plts., cont. mott. cf. gt. (SG. Sep.22; 152) $275
– – **Anr. Copy.** 4to. Wide margin, 1 plt. with side margin tear, cont. hf. vell. (R. Apr.4; 2042) DM 3,400

GRASSHOFF, Johann
[–] **Aperta Arca Arcani Artificiosissimi oder des Grossen und Kleinen Bauers Eroeffneter ... durch eine Visionem Chymicam Cabalisticam ...** Hamburg & Stockholm, 1687. Slight tear in title margin, browned, many blank ll. bnd. in, vell.; Dr. Walter Pagel copy. (S. Feb.7; 146) *Quaritch.* £320
– **Geheimniss der Natur des Grossen und Kleinen Bauers.** [Strassburg?], 1731. Title stpd., 5 pp. with MS. marginalia, lightly browned, cont. hf. vell., spine partly burst, old pasted over. (R. Oct.12; 1548) DM 2,300

GRASSMANN, H.
– **Gesammelte Mathematische und Physikalische Werke.** Ed.:– Fr. Engel. Leipzig, 1894-1904. *1st. Coll. Edn.* Pts. 1-4 (of 6), 2 vols. (of 3) in 4 vols. Margins slightly browned, private hf. leath. (HT. May 8; 410) DM 950

GRASTORF, Dennis J.
– **Wood Type of the Angelica Press.** Brooklyn, Angelica Pr., 1975. *(220).* Lge. fo. Posters & 50 font specimens ptd. directly from wood type, ll. loose in wraps. in specially-designed wood case, as iss., 2 prospectuses laid in. (SG. May 17; 342) $150
– – **Anr. Copy.** Fo. Posters & 46 (of 50) font specimens, ll. loose in wraps., specially designed wood case, as iss. (SG. Jan.5; 320) $130

GRATIANUS, Benedictine Monk
– **Decretum.** Basle, Michael Wenssler, 1482. Lge. fo. 1st. initial painted in blue on gt. ground, lge. initials painted in blue, cont. stpd. roan over wood bds., richly decor., brass boss, lacks brass corner, clasps incompl.; from Fondation Furstenberg-Beaumesnil. [BMC III, 728; Goff G371] (HD. Nov.16; 9) Frs. 55,000
– – **Anr. Edn.** Nuremb., Anton Koberger, 30 Nov. 1493. Fo. Capital H on a2r illuminated in cols. & gold, lge. capitals supplied in blue thro.-out, lacks b7 & the final blank, a2 supplied from anr. copy & dampstained, some slight worming, mostly marginal, 18th. C. vell., worn, soiled; MS. ex-libris & ptd. bkplt. of the cloister at Leubus. [BMC II, 437; Goff G-386; Hain 7913*] (SG. Oct.27; 161) $400

GRATIUS, O.
– **Gemma Prenosticationum.** [Köln], 1517. Title with old note, slightly browned & soiled, bds. (HK. Nov.8; 204) DM 1,150

GRATTAN, Henry
– **Memoirs of the Life & Times of the Rt. Hon. Henry Grattan.** L., 1839. *1st. Edn.* 2 vols. Crimson hf. mor., armorial motif on spine. (GM. Dec.7; 249) £85
– **The Speeches** ... 1822. 4 vols. Cont. tree cf. gt., w.a.f.; from liby. of Luttrellstown Castle. (C. Sep.28; 1704) £120

GRAU SALA
– **Doce Puntes Seques i un Autorretrat de Grau Sala.** Ed.:– Jaume Pla & Josep Janés. Barcelona, 1958. *(90).* Fo. 12 full-p. dry-points, s.-c.; artists copy sigd. (DS. Jan.27; 2584) Pts. 75,000

GRAVELOT, Hubert François Bourguignon & Cochin, Charles Nicolas
– **Iconologie par Figures ou Traité Complet des Allégories, Emblèmes & c.** Paris, [1789]. 4 vols. L.P., some light browning or spotting, 19th. C. hf. cf., slightly rubbed. (SPB. Dec.14; 55) $475
– – **Anr. Edn.** Ill.:– Choffard, De Launay, Le Mire & others after Gravelot & Cochin. Paris, [1791]. 4 vols. Wide margin, some plts. loose, some soiling, some sm. margin defects., cont. bds., lightly bumped, spine defect. (HK. Nov.9; 1626) DM 2,500
– – **Anr. Copy.** 4 vols. L.P., cont. leath., gt. covers, inner & outer dentelles. (R. Oct.11; 185) DM 1,700

GRAVES, Algernon
– **Century of Loan Exhibitions 1813-1912.** 1913-15. *(250) numbered.* 5 vols. Hf. mor., spines gt. (BBA. Sep.8; 140) *Wood Gallery.* £110
– **The Royal Academy of Arts, A Complete Dictionary of Contributors & their Work from its Foundation in 1769 to 1904.** 1970. 4 vols. Orig. cl., recovered. (S. Nov.8; 524) *Chung.* £75

GRAVES, Algernon & Cronin, W.V.
– **A History of the Works of Sir Joshua Reynolds.** 1899-1901. *(125).* Hf. mor. gt. by Kelly. (P. Jun.7; 1) £240
– – **Anr. Edn.** L., 1899-1901. 4 vols. 4to. Gt. mor., spines unif. faded, 1 spine slightly chipped. (SPB. Nov.30; 7) $1,200

GRAVES, George
– **British Ornithology.** L., 1821. *2nd. Edn.* 3 vols. 144 hand-cold. plts., pp. numbered in ink in upr. margins, mod. hf. cf. gt., unc. (P. Dec.8; 33) *Maggs.* £700
– **Hortus Medicus.** Edinb., 1834. 4to. Plts. hand-cold., cont. cf., spine rubbed & worn; pres. copy. (SSA. Jul.5; 161) R 660

GRAVES, Robert
– **Adam's Rib.** Ill.:– James Metcalf. L., Trianon Pr., 1955. *1st. Edn. (2026) numbered & sigd. by author & artist.* Sm. fo. Orig. cl., d.-w., s.-c. (S. Mar.20; 894) *Hawthorn.* £65
– **Contemporary Techniques of Poetry: A Political Analogy.** L., Hogarth Pr., 1925. Pict. wraps., worn, a little soiled; dedication copy, inscr. by author beneath ptd. dedication. (SG. May 24; 74) $600

– **Goliath & David.** [1916]. *1st. Edn. (200).* Sm. 4to. Orig. wraps., unc., slightly soiled; 2 A.L.s. from author to Ralph Edwards, undtd. with envelope postmarked 1921, loosely inserted. (SKC. Jan.13; 2214) £500
– **Good-bye to all That.** L., 1929. *1st. Edn. 1st. Iss.* Orig. cl., d.-w. (S. Mar.20; 900) *Hawthorn.* £170
– – **Anr. Copy.** With Sassoon poem, mark from bkplt., orig. cl., d.-w., sm. stain on spine, red mor.-bkd. s.-c.; Perry Molstad copy. (SPB. May 16; 455) $425
– **John Kemp's Wager, a Ballad Opera.** Oxford, 1925. *1st. Edn. (100) numbered & sigd.* Orig. bds. (S. Mar.20; 902) *Sawyer.* £110
– **Over the Brazier.** L., 1916. *1st. Edn. 1st. Iss.* A few ll. slightly spotted, orig. wraps. (BBA. Nov.30; 276) *Johnson & O'Donnell.* £280
– – **Anr. Edn.** L., 1916. *1st. Edn.* Some foxing, orig. pict. wraps.; Frederic Dannay copy. (CNY. Dec.16; 156) $380
– **Poems (1914-27).** L., 1927. *1st. Edn. (115) numbered & sigd.* Orig. vell.-bkd. bds., partly unc., d.-w., s.-c. worn. (S. Mar.20; 907) *Sawyer.* £180
– **Poems, 1929.** L., Seizin Pr., 1929. *1st. Edn. (225) numbered & sigd.* Orig. buckram. (S. Mar.20; 909) *Joliffe.* £80
– **Poems, 1953.** L., [1953]. *(250) sigd.* Qtr. linen, unlettered tissue d.-w. *(With:)* – **The More Deserving Cases.** [Marlborough], 1962. *(400) sigd.* Mor., bkplt. *(With:)* – **Love Respelt Again.** N.Y., [1969]. *(1000) sigd.* Cl., ptd. d.-w. (SG. May 24; 76) $200
– **The Shout.** L., 1929. *[1st. Edn.]. (530) numbered & sigd.* Sm. 4to. Orig. bds., unc. & unopened, spine faded. (SG. May 24; 75) $200
– – **Anr. Copy.** Pict. bds., d.-w., unopened. (SG. Jan.12; 138) $150
– **Whipperginny.** L., 1923. *1st. Edn.* Orig. bds., d.-w. (S. Mar.20; 916) *Hawthorn.* £70

GRAVESANDE, Guillaume Jacob
– **Elements de Physique démontrés Mathématiquement et confirmés par des Expériences; ou Introduction à la Philosophie Newtonienne.** Leiden, 1746. 2 vols. 4to. Cont. marb. cf. (HD. Jan.26; 156) Frs. 1,800
– **Mathematical Elements of Natural Philosophy ...** Trans.:– J.T. Desaguilère. 1747. *6th. Edn.* 2 vols. 4to. 127 folding plts., plt. 10 defect., with portion lacking?, bdg. not stated. (P. Jul.26; 28) £50
– – **Anr. Copy.** 2 vols. 4to. 127 folding copperplates, some spotting, etc., cont. cf., worn. (SG. Oct.6; 176) $150

GRAY, Andrew
– **The Experienced Millwright or, a Treatise on the Construction of some of the most useful Machines.** Edinb., 1804. Sq. fo. 44 engraved plts., offset foxing from plts., cont. spr. hf. cf. gt.; Sir Ivar Colquhoun, of Luss copy. (CE. Mar.22; 143) £800

GRAY, B.
See– BINYON, J.V.S. Wilkinson & Gray, B.

GRAY, David
– **The Sporting Works.** Ill.:– Paul Brown. Derrydale Pr., 1929. *Hitchcock Edn. (750) numbered.* 3 vols. Sm. 4to. Gt.-pict. cl.; inscr. & sigd. in each vol. by author 'For Sue & F.D.R. Jr. by their aff. Uncle David G', inscr. again by author to Alice & Roger, & sigd. on hf.-title by Gray, in Vol. I; inscr. by F.D. Roosevelt Jr. in Vol. I, & sigd. by him in 2 other vols. (SG. Mar.15; 223) $200

GRAY, George
– **The Earlier Cambridge Stationers & Bookbinders & the First Cambridge Printer.** 1904. 4to. Orig. buckram-bkd. bds.; H.M. Nixon coll., with some MS. notes, draft letter to J.B. Oldham loosely inserted. (BBA. Oct.6; 195) *Quaritch.* £80

GRAY, George Robert
– **The Entomology of Australia in a Series of Monographs ...** 1833. Pt. 1 (all publd.). 4to. Plts. hand-cold., plain watered cl., sewing loose. (KH. May 1; 315) Aus. $3,300

GRAY, Harold St. George
See– BULLEID, Arthur & Gray, Harold St. George

GRAY, Henry
- Anatomy, Descriptive & Surgical. Ill.:– after H.V. Carter. Phila., 1859. *1st. Amer. Edn.* 4to. Cont. cf., gt.-decor. spine. (CBA. Dec.10; 309) $150

GRAY, John
- Spiritual Poems. Ill.:– Charles Ricketts. L., Ballantyne Pr., 1896. Mor., blind-tooled decor., gt. inner & outer dentelle. (GB. Nov.5; 2255)
DM 2,900

GRAY, John Edward
[-] Gleanings from the Menagerie & Aviary at Knowsley Hall. — Gleanings from the Menagerie & Aviary at Knowsley Hall. Hoofed Quadrupeds. Ill.:– after Edward Lear; by B.W. Hawkins. Knowsley, 1846; 1850. 2 vols. Fo. 17 hand-cold. lithos. in 1st. work, 62 lithos. in 2nd. work, 1 plt. in 2nd. work detchd. & slightly chipped, & some 12 plts. foxed, gt.-lettered cl., lacks spine, ex-liby.; the Zoological Soc. of Phila. copies; pres. inscr. 'with J.E. Gray's kindest regards' in 2nd. work. (SG. Nov.3; 91)
$4,800
- Illustrations of Indian Zoology. Ca. 1835. Fo. 16 (of 20) hand-cold. lithos. & engrs., 1 plt. soiled on outer margin, bds., worn, as a collection of plts. w.a.f. (P. Oct.20; 83) £110

GRAY, Maxwell (Pseud.)
See— TUTTIETT, Miss Mary Gleed 'Maxwell Gray'

GRAY, Thomas
- Designs by Mr. Bentley for Six Poems. L., 1753. *1st. Edn.* 4to. Hf.-title reading 'Drawings, &c.', 6 full-p. engrs., 12 sm. text engrs., light soiling, cont. cf.-bkd. marb. bds., some wear. (SPB. May 16; 76)
$275
- - Anr. Edn. L., 1775. 4to. Thick paper, engraved vig. on title, frontis., 5 plts., 13 vigs., offset, rather spotted, cont. cf. (S. Apr.9; 257) *Barker.* £50
- Elegy Written in a Country Church-yard. Ill.:– Gwenda Morgan. Gold. Cock. Pr., 1946. *(80) numbered, specially bnd.* Orig. mor., s.-c. (BBA. Dec.15; 259) *Marks.* £120
- - Anr. Copy. Orig. mor. gt. by Sangorski & Sutcliffe, spine slightly faded. (CSK. Mar.9; 207)
£50
- Odes by Mr. Gray. L., Straw. Hill Pr., 1757. *1st. Edn.* 4to. Thin paper, with 'Ilissus' on p.8 & comma after 'Swarm' on p.16, hf.-title, engraved vig. on title, light offsetting, red mor. gt. by Riviere. (SPB. May 16; 77) $600
- Poems. L., 1768. *1st. Coll. Edn.* Old cf., early rebkd., worn. (RO. Apr.23; 152) $100
- - Anr. Edn. Ill.:– E. Radclyffe after C.W. Radclyffe. Eton, Eton College Pr., 1902. 4to. Prize bdg. of cf., gt. arms in borders, spines gt., by Spottiswoode & Co.; with lf. presenting the vol. to Archibald Fox Lambert, 1903. (SG. Feb.16; 148)
$125

GRAY, Thomas de, Lord Walsingham
See— DRUCE, Herbert & Gray, Thomas de, Lord Walsingham

GRAZIANI, Antonio Maria
- De Bello Cyprio. Rome, 1624. *1st. Edn.* Sm. fo. Papal imprimatur lf. & final lf. containing errata & register, considerably foxed & spotted, old spr. cf. gt. (SG. Sep.22; 153) $600

GRAZZINI, Anton Francesco
- The Story of Doctor Manente ... Trans.:– D.H. Lawrence. Flor., 1929. *[1st. Edn.]. (200) numbered & sigd. by trans.* Orig. bds., unopened, s.-c. slightly worn. (BBA. Feb.23; 325)
Forster. £75
- - Anr. Copy. Unlettered bkplt. comprising the Lawrence phoenix on front pastedown, ptd. bds., unc. (SG. Jan.12; 200) $175
- - Anr. Copy. Orig. ptd. bds., unopened, spine darkened, publisher's box (slightly worn); punctuation correction by author in limitation notice. (CNY. May 18; 118) $100

GREAT & ANCIENT CHARTER (THE) of the Cinque-Ports
- L., 1682. L., 1682. *1st. Edn.* 12mo. Recent hf. cf. [Wing G1632] (BBA. May 3; 162)
Howes Bookshop. £95

GREAT BRITAIN
- Abstract of the Answers & Returns Made pursuant to an Act, passed in the Forty-first Year of His Majesty King George III intituled 'An Act for taking an Account of the Population of Great Britain, & the Increase or Diminuation thereof'. Parish Registers; Enumeration. 1801-02. 2 vols. Fo. Diced hf. russ. gt.; Sir Ivar Colquhoun, of Luss copy. (CE. Mar.22; 3) £400
- Serious Reflections on the Present Condition of Great Britain ... L., 1733. Cont. gt. flowered wraps., paper by Stoy of Augsberg, sigd. along back wrap. (BBA. Nov.30; 213) *George's.* £50

GREAT EXHIBITION
- Dickinson's Comprehensive Pictures of the Great Exhibition ... Ill.:– after Nash, Haghe, & Roberts. L., 1854. 2 vols. Lge. fo. 55 hand-finished chromolitho. plts., 1 plt. slightly defect., 4 loose, orig. red hf. mor., gt. vig. on upr. covers, rubbed, lr. cover of Vol. 1 dampstained. (C. Mar.14; 51)
Walford. £1,300
- - Anr. Copy. 2 vols. Fo. 55 cold. plts., few plts. with slight foxing to margins, red hf. mor. gt., slightly rubbed. (P. Apr.12; 273) *Shapiro.* £1,200
- Exhibition of the Works of Industry of All Nations. Reports by the Juries ... L., 1852. *1st. Edn. 2nd. Iss.* 4to. Orig. cl. gt., some rubbing & soiling; Stanitz coll. (SPB. Apr.25; 168) $300
- Official Descriptive & Illustrated Catalogue. 1851. Vols. 1-3. *(With:)* - Reports by the Juries. 1852. 1 vol. *Together 4 vols.* Cl., soiled. (P. Feb.16; 133) £60

GREAT WESTERN RAILWAY MAGAZINE
Jan. 1924-Dec. 1954. Vols. 36-57. 4to. Hf. leath. gt.; the Eighth Earl Poulett copy. (LC. Oct.13; 457)
£180

GREAVES, John
- Pyramidographia: or a Description of the Pyramids of Aegypt. L., 1646. 2 folding plts., text ills., 1 folding plt. reprd., later wraps. [Wing G 1804] (S. Apr.9; 27) *Azezian.* £120

GRECO, Gioachino
- Le Jeu des Eschets. Paris, 1689. Sm. 12mo. Cont. spr. cf., spine decor., worn. (HD. Jun.6; 68)
Frs. 1,000
- The Royall Game of Chesse-Play. L., 1656. *1st. Edn.* Sm. 8vo. With final lf. K1, outer typographic border of title & 1 headline shaved, stain, a few later MS. notes, 18th. C. spr. cf [Wing G 1810] (C. Nov.9; 80) *Phelps.* £400

GREEK ANTHOLOGY
Ed.:– F.L. Lucas. Ill.:– Lettice Sandford. Gold. Cock. Pr., 1937. *(80) numbered, with 20 ills.* Fo. Orig. hf. pig over cl. gt., s.-c.; from D. Bolton liby. (BBA. Oct.27; 140) *Duschnes.* £120
- - Anr. Edn. Ed.:– F.L. Lucas. Ill.:– L. Sandford. Gold. Cock. Pr., 1937. *(206) numbered.* Qtr. pig. (P. Sep.29; 108) *Blackwells.* £65
- - Anr. Edn. Ed.:– F.L. Lucas. Gold. Cock. Pr., [1937]. *(206). (74) numbered on H.M.P., with 6 extra plts.* Fo. Orig. hf. mor. gt., lightly soiled, lightly rubbed. (CSK. Dec.2; 103) £70

GREELY, Adolphus W.
- Report of the Proceedings of the United States Expedition to Lady Franklin Bay, Grinnell Land. Wash., 1888. 2 vols. 4to. Margin dampstains, cl., slightly discold., bumped. *(With:)* - Cruise of the Revenue-Steamer Corwin in Alaska & the N.W. Arctic Ocean in 1881. Wash., 1883. 1 vol. 4to. Cl. (SG. Sep.22; 28) $125
- Three Years of Arctic Service. An Account of the Lady Franklin Bay Expedition of 1881-84 & the Attainment of the Farthest North. N.Y., 1886. 2 vols. Some spotting, orig. decor. cl., slightly frayed at top & bottom of spines. (TA. Mar.15; 2) £80

GREEN, Charles R.
See— CLYMER, W.B.S. & Green, Charles R.

GREEN, Emanuel
- Bibliotheca Somersetensis: A Catalogue of Books, Pamphlets, Single Sheets, & Broadsides ... connected with the County of Somerset. Taunton, 1902. 3 vols. Lge. 8vo. Orig. cl., unc., soiled. (LC. Jul.5; 49) £150

GREEN, George
- Mathematical Papers. Ed.:– N.M. Ferrers. L., 1871. *1st. Edn.* Hf.-title, errata, front end-paper marked with inked liby. stps., orig. cl., some rubbing, sm. paper tags on spine; William Walton sig. & bkplt., released from Magdalene College with stps., Stanitz coll. (SPB. Apr.25; 196) $225

GREEN, Jacob, M.D.
[-] Astronomical Recreations; or Sketches of the Relative Position & Mythological History of the Constellations. Phila., 1824. *1st. Edn.* 4to. Extra-engraved title, 19 engraved plts., most hand-cold., some foxing, old bds., cf. back, later paper spine label, some wear, front end-paper removed, inner jnts. tape-reprd. (RO. Dec.11; 127) $260
- - Anr. Copy. 4to. 19 plts., including 17 hand-cold., foxing to text, cont. hf. sheep, unc.; inscr. pres. copy. (PNY. Oct.20; 221) $140

GREEN, John
- Remarks, In Support of the New Chart of North & South America ... L., 1753. 4to. Cont. qtr. cf. & paper bds.; the Rt. Hon. Visc. Eccles copy. [Sabin 28538] (CNY. Nov.18; 124) $480

GREEN, John (Ed.)
See— ASTLEY, Thomas

GREEN, Prof. John Richard
- History of the English People. 1878-80. 4 vols. *(With:)* - The Making of England. 1882. 1 vol. *(With:)* - The Conquest of England. 1883. 1 vol. *Together 6 vols.* Unif. panel. cf. gt., by Hopkins of Glasgow, gt.-decor. spines & dentelles. (SKC. Sep.9; 1915) £65
- A Short History of the English People. L., 1907. Mor. gt., fore-e.pntg. of Lord Nelson, as a fore-e.pntg., w.a.f. (SPB. May 17; 735) $375

GREEN, Jul.
- Mont-Cinère. Ill.:– Vlamminck. Paris, [1930]. *(325). (280) on velin d'Arches.* Sm. 4to. Linen. (HK. Nov.11; 4041) DM 1,400

GREEN, Russell (Ed.)
See— COTERIE

GREEN, S.G.
- Pictures from the German Fatherland. L., 1893. 4to. Frontis., 37 woodcut plts., many text woodcuts, orig. pict. linen, spine faded. (HT. May 10; 2914)
DM 420

GREEN, Thomas
- The Universal Herbal. 1816. 2 vols. 4to. 2 engraved hand-cold. frontis. & title, 101 hand-cold. plts., sheep. (P. Mar.15; 68) *Walford.* £320
- - Anr. Edn. L'pool., [1816-20]. 2 vols. 4to. Additional cold. engraved title in Vol. 1, 2 frontis., 106 hand-cold. plts., some offsetting on text, Vol. 2 slightly soiled at beginning, sm. stain on p. 539 in Vol. 2 affecting text, cont. cf. gt., rebkd. (S. Nov.28; 30) *Ward.* £400

GREEN, Gen. Thomas J.
- Journal of the Texian Expedition Against Mier; Subsequent Imprisonment of the Author; His Sufferings & Final Escape from the Castle of Perote. N.Y., 1845. Orig. cl., faded, boxed. (LH. Sep.25; 231) $325

GREEN, William
- A Description of a Series of Sixty Small Prints. Ambleside, 1814. 60 etched plts., slightly spotted, cont. hf. cf., spine defect. (S. Apr.9; 169)
Hollett. £70

GREENAWAY, Kate
- Almanachs. Paris, [1882-94]. 13 vols. 24mo. & 32mo. 1st. vol. slightly spotted, 1884 in orig. wraps., rest in orig. cl.-bkd. bds., slightly soiled, in mor.-bkd. box by Riviere. (BBA. Dec.15; 280)
Snelling. £400
- - Anr. Run. L., for 1883-85 & 1888-95. 11 vols. 12mo. & 24mo. 8 in orig. cl.-bkd. bds., rest in orig. imitation mor., wraps. or cl., some slightly worn. (S. Nov.22; 380) *Steedman.* £240
- - Anr. Run. L., for 1885-88, 1890 & 1892-95. *1st. Edns.* Together 10 vols., including variant dupl. for 1890 (with different end-papers & bdg.). 4 x 3 inches. Various states, vol. for 1887 a variant not

GREENAWAY, Kate -Contd.

listed by Thomson, some slight soiling or offset, 1st. bdg. not stated, 2 vols. imitation mor., 4 vols. pict. bds., 1 vol. gt.-decor. cl., 1 vol. col. & gt.-decor. cl.-bkd. bds., 1 vol. gt.-decor. silk, 1 bdg. slightly frayed. [Thomson 49a, 50c, 52a, 54a, 54c, 57b, 58c, 59a & 60a] (CBA. Aug.21; 253) $550
- A Day in a Child's Life. Music by Myles B. Foster. L., [1881]. *1st. Edn.* 4to. Cl.-bkd. pict. bds., pict. d.-w. chipped. (SG. Mar.29; 69) $200
- - Anr. Edn. Trans.:– Music:– Myles B. Foster. L., n.d. *1st. Edn.* 4to. Decor. bds., cl. spine, worn. (RO. Mar.21; 33) $110
- Pictures from Originals Presented by her to John Ruskin ... Appreciation:– H.M. Cundall. L., 1921. *1st. Edn.* 4to. Gt.-lettered cl., d.-w., edges darkened. (CBA. Aug.21; 278) $150

GREENAWAY, Kate & Crane, Walter
- The Quiver of Love. Text:– B.M. Ranking & T.K. Tully. 1880. Orig. cl., slight wear. (P. Sep.8; 102) *Marks.* £60

GREENBANK, Thomas K., Publisher
- Views of American Scenery. Ill.:– J. Yeager, T. Birch, & others. Phila., 1828. 12 engraved plts., 2 just shaved at fore-margin, 1 also tightly bnd. with partial loss of caption, a few slight reprd. tears, cleaned, cf., orig. ptd. upr. wrap. bnd. in, upr. portions of wrap. defect. & restored, w.a.f.; the Rt. Hon. Visc. Eccles copy. (CNY. Nov.18; 125) $1,600

GREENE, Bella Da Costa
See— MINER, Dorothy

GREENE, Graham
- The Basement Room, & Other Stories. 1935. Bdg. not stated, d.-w. slightly frayed, slightly dust soiled along top edge. (TA. May 17; 521) £200
- The Labyrinthine Ways. N.Y., [1940]. *1st. Amer. Edn.* Cl., d.-w. chipped. (HA. Nov.18; 191) $160
- The Name of Action. L., 1930. *1st. Edn.* Hf.-title, price inscr. on front free end-paper, orig. cl., slightly marked. (S. Dec.13; 368) *Mayon.* £80
- The Quiet American. 1955. *1st. Edn.* Orig. cl., d.-w. (BBA. Feb.23; 265) *Heuer.* £70

GREENE, Maurice [?]
- The Chaplet, being a Collection of Twelve English Songs, for Voice & Continuo with Flute. L., 1738. *1st. Edn.* Advt. for J. Walsh, orig. ? blue paper wraps., with tears, a little dust-stained. (S. May 10; 155) *Macnutt.* £260

GREENE, William Thomas
- Parrots in Captivity. L., 1884-87. 3 vols. 81 cold. plts., without 9 supp. plts., slight spotting, orig. cl. gt. (P. May 17; 346) £380
- - Anr. Copy. 3 vols. 81 cold. plts. (without 9 supp. plts.), vol.1 with plt. at p.7 & pp.111-112 torn, some ll. & plts. detchd. & frayed, orig. cl., worn, stained, inside hinges weak or brkn.; pres, copy; w.a.f. (S. Apr.10; 505) *Reid.* £340
- - Anr. Copy. 3 vols. Tall 8vo. 80 (of 81) col. hand-finished plts., orig. cl., spines worn. (TA. Dec.15; 140) £280
- - Anr. Copy. 3 vols. (without the supplementary Vol. 4). 81 hand-cold. engraved plts., hf. mor. & gt.-pict. cl., worn, Vol. 3 loose, ex-liby. (SG. Oct.6; 177) $500

GREENER, William
- Die Geheinnisse d. Engl. Gewehrfabrikation u. Büchsenmacherkunst so wie d. Enzeugung d. Versch. Eisensorten zu d. Feinsten Jagdwehren. Ill.:– C.H. Schmidt. Weimar, 1836. *1st. Edn.* Cont. bds., upr. jnt. with sm. defects., slightly bumped. (HK. May 16; 1578) DM 1,100
- The Science of Gunnery, as Applied to the Use & Construction of Fire Arms. 1841. Orig. cl., spine faded. (TA. May 17; 145) £72

GREENHOW, Robert
- The History of Oregon & California, & the Other Territories on the North-West Coast of North America. L., 1844. *1st. Engl. Edn.* Errata slip, lge. folding map with 3 inch tear, orig. cl.; the Rt. Hon. Visc. Eccles copy. [Sabin 28632] (CNY. Nov.18; 126) $220

GREENWALT, Crawford H.
- Hummingbirds. Garden City, N.Y., [1960]. *(500) numbered. & sigd. by author.* Lge. 4to. Orig. leatherette, s.-c. (CSK. Apr.27; 83) £160

GREENWAY, John
- Bibliography of the Australian Aborigines ... Sydney, 1963. Bdg. not stated, d.-w. (KH. May 1; 318) Aus. $140

GREENWOOD, Charles
- An Epitome of County History. 1838. Vol. 1: 'County of Kent'. 4to. Partly cold. map, 82 lithos., cl. by R. Hynes, Dover. (PWC. Jul.11; 571) £230
- - Anr. Copy. Vol. 1: 'Kent'. 4to. Hand-cold. double-p. map, 82 litho. views, slight spotting, cl. gt. (P. Nov.24; 62) £210
- - Anr. Copy. Vol. 1: 'Kent'. 4to. 83 litho. plts., few torn & reprd., many with stains in margins, lacks some text, hf. mor. gt., as a collection of plts., w.a.f. (P. Sep.8; 370) *Cranbrook.* £130

GREENWOOD, Charles & John
- [-] Atlas of the Counties of England. L., [1834]. Lge. fo. 12 double-p. engraved maps only (of 46), hand-cold., some offsetting & faint dust-soiling, cont. hf. cf., worn. (S. Apr.9; 137) *Windsor.* £170
- - Anr. Copy. Lge. fo. 12 double-p. engraved maps only (of 46), hand-cold., some faint dust-soiling, cont. hf. cf., worn. (S. Apr.9; 138) *Charles.* £150
- Map of the County of Devon, From an Actual Survey made in the Years 1825 & 1826. 20 Feb. 1827. Lge. fo. (650 x 400mm). 9 engraved sheets, inset of Lundy Island & lge. vig. view of Exeter Cathedral, sm. hole affecting vig. sheet, few minor stains, some faint creases, cont. hf. russ., worn, unc. (S. Nov.1; 162) *Ambra.* £80
- Map of the County of Gloucester, From an Actual Survey Made in the Year 1823. 22 Nov. 1824 (atlas map 1831). Lge. fo. (650 x 455mm.). 6 engraved sheets & fully cold. atlas map, lge. inset vig. view of Gloucester Cathedral, some faint offsetting, mod. hf. cf., unc. (S. Nov.1; 163) *Burgess.* £170

GREENWOOD, William
- Bouleuterion, or a Practical Demonstration of County Judicatures. 1659. *1st. Edn.* Hf.-title, slightly stained in upr. margin, cont. sheep, rebkd. & reprd., rubbed. [Wing G1870] (BBA. Jul.27; 101) *Blackwell's.* £640

GREG, Sir Walter Wilson
- A Bibliography of the English Printed Drama to the Restoration. 1939-59. 4 vols. 4to. Orig. cl.-bkd. bds., faded. (CSK. Apr.6; 21) £70
- - Anr. Copy. 4 vols. 4to. Some ll. spotted, orig. holland-bkd. bds., spine of Vol. 1 torn. (BBA. Aug.18; 20) *Sutherland.* £60
- - Anr. Edn. L., 1970. 4 vols. 4to. Cl., light wear. (RO. Dec.11; 128) $110

GREGO, Joseph
- Pictorial Pickwickiana. Ill.:– after 'Phiz', Crowquill, Pailthorpe, Seymor, & others. L., 1899. *1st Edn.* 2 vols. Darkening & rippling, some margin dampstaining, gt.-decor. cl., covers mildly soiled & stained, extremities lightly bumped & rubbed, free end-papers irregularly darkened. (CBA. Mar.3; 173) $130
- Rowlandson the Caricaturist. L., 1880. 2 vols. 4to. Orig. mor.-bkd. cl., worn, 1 hinge brkn. (S. Dec.13; 449) *Solomons.* £100
- - Anr. Copy. 2 vols. 4to. Some ll. spotted, orig. mor.-bkd. cl., rubbed. (BBA. Feb.9; 188) *Brailey.* £60

GREGOIRE, Gaspard
- Explication des Cérémonies de la Fête-Dieu d'Aix en Provence. Aix-en-Provence, 1777. Orig. Edn. 12mo. Engraved port.-frontis., 13 folding plts., early hf. leather, slightly worn. (SG. Apr.19; 98) $130
- - Anr. Copy. Cont. gt.-decor. pol. cf. (GB. Nov.3; 962) DM 650

GREGOIRE, Pierre
- Syntaxes Artis Mirabilis, in Libros Septem Digestae. Venetiis, 1588. Some staining & soiling, title lf. torn affecting device. *(Bound with:)*
- Syntaxeon Artis Mirabilis, Alter Tomus. Venetiis, 1588. Some staining & soiling. Together 2 works in 1 vol. Old limp vell., loose in casing. (RO. Dec.11; 129) $110

GREGORAS, N.
- Romanae, hoc est Byzantinae Historiae Libri XI. Basel, Aug. 1562. *1st. Edn.* Fo. Some ll. at beginning & end stained & lightly wormed, cont. blind-tooled pig, centrepiece & corner fleurons, lacks ties. (HK. Nov.8; 205) DM 800

GREGORIUS IX, Pope
- Decretales. Venice, Baptista de Tortis & Franciscus de Madiis, 7 Sep. 1484. Lge. fo. Rubricated, initials in red & blue, cont. MS. table on verso of blank 1st. lf., repeated on last lf., cont. pig, decor., studs & corners, clasps; from Fondation Furstenberg-Beaumesnil. [HC 8017; BMC V, 323; Goff G458] (HD. Nov.16; 70) Frs. 11,100
- - Anr. Edn. Nuremb., Anton Koberger, 1493. Fo. Initials painted in blue, cont. cf. over wood bds., blind-decor., spine reprd., lacks 1 clasp; from Fondation Furstenberg-Beaumesnil. [HC 8030; BMC II, 436; Goff G470] (HD. Nov.16; 36) Frs. 8,500
- Decretales, cum Glossa. Basel, Michael Wenssler, 15 Mar. 1482. Fo. Capitals & paragraph marks supplied in red or blue, headlines in quire f supplied in MS. (as usual), cont. MS. index on initial blank, some slight worming, few other margin defects, few early marginalia, early blind-stpd. pig over wood bds., brass bosses & clasps, lacks corner-pieces; release stp. of the Stadtbibliothek, Frankfurt. [BMC III, 728; Goff G-454; Hain 8012*] (SG. Oct.27; 162) $1,900
- - Anr. Edn. Venice, Thomas de Blavis, de Alexandria, 22 Dec. 1486. 4to. Light stains, margin foxing, MS. list of rubrics bnd. in at end, near-cont. limp vell., torn, upr. hinge brkn. [BMC V, 318; Goff G-463; HC 8021*] (SPB. Dec.14; 18) $500

GREGORIUS MAGNUS I, Pope
- Commentum super Cantica Canticorum. [Cologne, Ulrich Zel], not after 1473. Fo. Rubricated, lacks final blank, old cf., worn; the Walter Goldwater copy. [BMC I, 192; Goff G-394; H. 7937] (SG. Dec.1; 161) $1,100
- Dialogorum Libri Quattuor. Venice, Hieronymus de Paganinis, 13 Nov. 1492. 4to. Lacks last blank, later vell.; the Walter Goldwater copy. [BMC V, 457 (IA 23310); Goff G-405; H. 7963] (SG. Dec.1; 163) $375
- - Anr. Edn. Basel, Michael Furter, 1496. [Goff G-407] *(Bound with:)* - Homiliae super Ezechielem. [Basel, Michael Furter], 1496. [Goff G-425] *(Bound with:)* - Pastorale. Basel, [Michael Furter], 15 Feb. 1496. [Goff G-441] Together 3 works in 1 vol. 4to. Rubricated, later vell.; the Walter Goldwater copy. (SG. Dec.1; 167) $1,200
- Homeliae super Evangelis. [Augsburg, Gunther Zainer], 28 Aug. 1473. *1st. Edn.* Fo. Rubricated, initials painted in red, some continued in margins, mod. vell.; from Fondation Furstenberg-Beaunesnil. [BMC II, 319; Goff G417] (HD. Nov.16; 2) Frs. 8,500
- Moralia, sive Expositio in Job. Paris, Ulrich Gering & Berthold Rembolt, 31 Oct. 1495. Fo. Lacks blank TT10, slight worming, mostly to index ll., old cf., worn, covers detchd. the Walter Goldwater copy. [BMC VIII, 29-30; Goff G-431; H. 7932] (SG. Dec.1; 162) $425
- - Anr. Edn. Venice, Andreas Torresanus de Asula, 11 Apr. 1496. Fo. Some margins strengthened, some heavy staining, considerable early marginalia, bds., covered with lf. from an old vell. antiphonary; the Walter Goldwater copy. [BMC V, 312; Goff G-433; H. 7933] (SG. Dec.1; 164) $375
- Pastorale, sive Regula Pastoralis. Venice, Hieronymus de Paganinis, 13 Dec. 1492. 4to. Old liby. stp. on A1, qtr. cf.; the Walter Goldwater copy. [BMC V, 457 (IA 23311); Goff G-440; H. 7986] (SG. Dec.1; 166) $300
- Sopra la Vita di Job. Flor., N. Laurentii, Alamanus, 15 Jun. 1486. *1st. Edn. in Italian.* In 2 vols. Fo. Bds., vell. backs; R.W. Martin armorial bkplt., the Walter Goldwater copy. [BMC VI, 631; Goff G-435; H. 7935] (SG. Dec.1; 165) $1,100
- Vita et Miracula Santissimi Patri Benedicti. Ill.:– Bernardinus Passerus & others. Rome, 1579. Fo. Engraved title in border of 14 sm. engrs., 46 (of 48?) engraved plts., each with 6 lines of engraved text, 2 plts. trimmed & mntd., some fraying &

spotting, old mott. cf., worn. (SG. Apr.19; 165)
$500

GREGORIUS NYSSANUS
See— BERTHORIUS, Petrus — NAUSEA,
Fredericus — GREGORIUS NYSSANUS

GREGOROVIUS, Ferdinand
- Corsica. Stuttgart & Tübingen, 1854. *1st. Edn.*
2 vols. Cont. hf. chagrin. (HD. Oct.21; 100)
Frs. 1,500
- Die Insel Capri. Leipzig, 1868. *1st. Edn.* Fo. Title
stpd., ex-libris, hf. linen. (GB. Nov.3; 111)
DM 560

GREGORY, Lady Augusta
- Kincora. N.Y., 1905. *1st. Amer. Edn.* (50)
numbered, for securing copyright in the U.S. Orig.
wraps.; sigd. by author. (S. Dec.8; 187)
Sutherland. £120
- Spreading the News. N.Y., 1905. *1st. Amer. Edn.*
(50) *numbered, for securing copyright in the U.S.*
Orig. wraps., a few spots on lr. cover; sigd. by
author. (S. Dec.8; 188) *Sutherland.* £120
- The White Cockade. N.Y., 1905. *1st. Amer. Edn.*
(30) *numbered, for securing copyright in the U.S.*
Sigd. by author, initialled by publisher, hf.-title,
orig. wraps. (S. Dec.8; 189) *Sutherland.* £150

GREGORY, Augustus Charles & F.T.
- Journals of Australian Explorations. Brisbane,
1884. Orig. cl., recased, new backstrip. (KH. Nov.9;
613) Aus. $260

GREGORY, David
- Astronomiae Physicae & Geometricae Elementa.
Geneva, 1726. *2nd. End.* 2 vols. 4to. Engraved port.,
48 folding plts. only, some light dampstaining, cont.
cf., lightly rubbed. (CSK. Jan.27; 108) £75

GREGORY, John
- The Works. L., 1671. 4to. Little light browning,
cont. cf., slightly worn. [Wing G 1914] (BBA.
Mar.21; 192) *R.V. Elliott.* £55

GREGORY, John Walter
- The Great Rift Valley. 1896. *1st. Edn.* Cont. cf.
gt. (BBA. Aug.18; 190) *Morrell.* £65

GREGORY, Olinthus
See— GOOD, John Mason & others

GREGORY, W.
- Zigtbaare Tusschenkoomst der Goddelijke
Voorzienigheid. Trans.:— G. Outhuis. Dordrecht,
1803. Later hf. cl. (VG. Nov.30; 830) Fls. 450

GREGSON, Matthew
- Portfolio of Fragments Relative to the History &
Antiquities ... of the County of ... Lancaster.
1869. *3rd. Edn.* Fo. L.P., panel. mor. gt. by Rivière.
(P. Mar.15; 21) *Thorp.* £100

GREGYNOG PRESS
See— AESOP
See— BIBLIANA [English]
See— BROOKE, Lord Fulke Greville
See— DAVIES, W.H.
See— EURIPIDES
See— JOHN, Saint, the Divine
See— JOINVILLE, Jean de
See— LAMB, Charles
See— MADARIAGA, Salvador de
See— MILTON, John
See— PARRY, Robert William
See— PEACOCK, Thomas Love
See— ROSSETTI, Christina
See— SHAW, George Bernard

GREHAN, Amédée
- La France Maritime. Paris, 1837-38. *1st. Edns.*
vols. II & III. 3 vols. (of 4). 4to. MS. owners mark
on hf.-title, some slight browning, cont. hf. leath.,
rubbed, lightly spotted. (HT. May 8; 646)
DM 850
- - **Anr. Edn.** Paris, 1837-42. 4 vols. 4 frontis., 178
plts., lacks 2 title-ll., some foxing, cont. hf. sheep,
not quite unif., decor. spines. (HD. Sep.21; 145)
Frs. 2,100
- - **Anr. Edn.** Ill.:— Pardinel after Fatio. [Paris],
1848. *2nd. Edn.* Plt. vol. only, 3 pts. in 1 vol.
Lge. ob. 8vo. 2 steel-engraved titles, 108 steel-
engraved & etched views & plts., some foxing (as

usual), some margin stains, cont. chagrin, richly gt.
(VS. Dec.8; 787) Fls. 500
- - **Anr. Edn.** Ill.:- after Isabey, Morel-Fatio,
Garneray, Decamp & others. Paris, 1852-53. 4 vols.
4to. 4 frontis., 195 steel-engraved plts., minimal
foxing, cont. hf. chagrin, decor. spines. (HD.
Sep.21; 149) Frs. 3,300

GREIG
[-] A Narrative of the Cruise of the Yacht Maria
among the Feroe Islands in the Summer of 1854.
1856. *2nd. Edn.* 4to. Some staining, mod. cl. (P.
Mar.15; 151) £70

GREIG, John
See— STORER, James Sargent & Greig, John

GREK, T.V
See— IVANOVA, A.A. & others

GRELLMANN, Heinrich Moritz Gottlieb
- Dissertation on the Gipseys. Trans.:— [Raper]. L.,
1807. Light spotting, mod. bds. (S. Dec.20; 843)
£55
- Histoire des Bohémiens, ou Tableau des Moeurs,
Usages et Coutumes de ce Peuple Nomade; suivie
de Recherches Historiques sur leur Origine, leur
Langage et leur Première Apparition en Europe.
Paris, 1810. Cont. tree cf. gt., decor. spine. (HD.
Sep.22; 254) Frs. 1,500

GRENET, Abbé
- Atlas Portatif à l'Usage des Collèges. N.d. 4to.
Double-p. engraved title, 86 outl.-cold. double-p.
maps (dtd. 1779-90), str.-grd. hf. mor., spine gt.,
as an atlas, w.a.f. (LC. Oct.13; 270) £130

GRENIER DE SAINT MARTIN, François
- Victoires et Conquêtes. Recueil des Principaux
Evénements de l'Histoire de nos Combats. Paris,
[1819-22]. Fo. The 11 orig. title-pp. bnd. in at end,
plts. hand-stpd. on face, mostly in blank section, 1
with perforation stp. in margin, some foxing &
soiling, bds., disbnd., lacks lr. cover, upr. wrap. for
1st. pt. bnd. in, ex-liby. (RO. Dec.11; 130) $225

GRENOBLE
- Décorations faites dans la Ville de Grenoble ...
pour la Réception de Mgr le Duc de Bourgogne et
de Mgr le Duc de Berry. Ill.:— after Sevin. Grenoble,
1701. Lge. 4to. Title vig., 6 plts. (1 folding), with
'Remarques, et Réflexions sur la Pratique des
Decorations, later parch., s.-c. (HD. Feb.29; 9)
Frs. 4,800

GREVE, F.P.
See— ARABIAN NIGHTS

GREVILLE, Charles C.F.
- Memoirs. L., 1874-87. [Pt. 1], 2 & 3, 8 vols.
Extra-ill. with many plts., some hand-cold., mor.,
gt., by Bayntun (Rivière). (S. Oct.4; 87)
Traylen. £380

GREVILLE, Robert Kaye
- Scottish Cryptogamic Flora. Edinb., 1823-28. 6
vols. in 4, bnd. from the orig. pts. 358 (of 360) cold.
engraved plts., titles & indexes at end, cont. hf. cf.,
bdgs. brkn. (C. Nov.16; 253) *Walford.* £280

GREW, Nehemiah
- The Anatomy of Vegetables begun; with a General
Account of Vegetation founded thereon. L., 1672.
1st. Edn. Sm. 8vo. Lacks Royal Soc. licence lf., 1st.
few ll. spotted, some light corner dampstains, early
cf., upr. cover detchd.; early sig. of G. Colvill on
verso of title, with MS. note 'Ex dono Charissimi
Fratris Alexandri Colvill.'. [Wing G1946] (SG.
Mar.22; 143) $250
- Musaeum Regalis Societatis. 1681. *[1st. Edn.].*
Fo. Cont. panel. cf., rebkd. (TA. May 17; 382)
£190
- - **Anr. Copy.** Fo. 5 extra engrs. pasted in, engraved
port. frontis. slightly frayed, cont. cf., old reback.
[Wing G1952]. (TA. Sep.15; 497) £80
- - **Anr. Copy.** 2 pts. in 1 vol. Fo. Engraved port.
of Colwal, 31 plts., 1 torn on plt. mark, cont. cf.,
upr. cover detchd.; Sir Ivar Colquhoun, of Luss
copy. [Wing G 1952] (CE. Mar.22; 145) £50

GREY, Sir George
- Journals of Two Expeditions of Discovery in
North-West & Western Australia. 1841. *1st. Edn.*

2 vols. 2 folding maps in pocket at beginning of
Vol. 1, 22 litho. plts. (several cold.), some slight
foxing, advt. ll. at end of Vol. 1, 4pp. advts. for
Gould's Birds of Australia & the Kangaroos at
beginning of Vol. 2, orig. cl. (S. May 22; 475)
Maggs. £600
- - **Anr. Copy.** 2 vols. 2 folding maps, 22 plts., lacks
advts., Vol. 1 frontis. stained, tears in folds of maps,
stps. on titles, pol. cf. gt., Vol. 1 covers detchd.
(CA. Apr.3; 52) Aus. $800
- - **Anr. Copy.** 2 vols. Lacks folding map from 1
end pocket, some foxing to plts., cl., unc., worn.
(KH. May 1; 320) Aus. $300
- - **Anr. Edn.** Adelaide, 1964. *Facs. Edn.* 2 vols.
Orig. cl. (KH. Nov.8; 191) Aus. $130

GREY, Thomas de
- The Compleat Horse-Man & Expert Ferrier.
1670. *4th. Edn.* Sm. 4to. Cont. cf., rebkd. [Wing
D859] (TA. Feb.16; 119) £62

GRIBBLE, Ernest R.
See— CESCINSKY, Herbert & Gribble, Ernest R.

GRIEBEN, T.
- Le Vrai Guide et Conducteur de Berlin et de
Potsdam et de leurs Environs. Berlin, 1857. Some
foxing, cont. hf. leath. gt. (GB. Nov.3; 271)
DM 460

GRIEG, Edvard
- Lyrische Stucke. Leipzig, 1904. *1st. Edn.* Cont.
(unstated) bdg.; autograph inscr. sigd. (S. Nov.17;
112) *Simeone.* £200

GRIERSON, J.
- Twelve Select Views of the Seat of War including
Views Taken in Rangoon, Cachar & Andaman
Islands. Calcutta, 1825. Ob. fo. 7 (of 12) ll. of
litho. text in MS., lacks title, bds. defect., staining,
margins frayed, w.a.f. (P. Sep.29; 195)
Shapiro. £130

GRIESHABER, Hap
- Affen und Alphabete. Stuttgart, 1962. *(300)*
numbered. Lge. fo. 34 orig. woodcuts, Printers mark
sigd. by artist, orig. pict. wraps., orig. pict. s.-c.
(GB. May 5; 2602) DM 1,800
- Erster Dürerpreisträger der Stadt Nürnberg.
Stuttgart, 1971. *1st. Edn.* Fo. 10 orig. woodcuts,
orig. pict- bds. (GB. May 5; 2607) DM 450
- Der Holzschneider. Hap Grieshaber. Stuttgart,
1964. Fo. With supp. pt. : by M. Fuerst & series
'The Lord's Black Nightingale gewidmet' with 6
cold. orig. woodcuts, orig. pict. bds. (GB. May 5;
2603) DM 500
- - **Anr. Copy.** with supp. Fo. 6 orig. cold. woodcuts,
2 woodcuts with nail traces, orig. pict. bds. (GB.
Nov.5; 2536) DM 440
- Malbriefe. Ed.:— M. Fuerst. Stuttgart, 1967. *De
Luxe Edn., (50) numbered, with sigd. orig. woodcut
on separate MS. Malerbrief.* 4to. Orig. pict. linen,
orig. wraps. (GB. Nov.5; 2537) DM 700
- Stop dem Walfang. Düsseldorf, [1973]. Fo. 7 sigd.
orig. woodcuts, 1 double-p., 5 cold., including wrap.,
orig. bds., sigd. woodcut on silver. (GB. May 5;
2610) DM 900
- Totentanz von Basel. Ill.:— Albert Kapr. Leipzig,
1966. Fo. 40 orig. cold. woodcuts with 2 ll. text
each in German, Engl., Fr., text partly in woodcut,
orig. linen, blind-tooled emblem & red end-papers.
(GB. May 5; 2604) DM 1,400
- - **Anr. Edn.** Dresden, [1966]. Fo. German,
Engl. & French text, orig. pict. linen, orig. wraps.
(D. Nov.24; 3044) DM 2,600
- - **Anr. Copy.** Fo. Tri-lingual text, orig. linen; coll.
stp. inside cover. (H. May 22; 451) DM 1,800

GRIEVE, Christopher Murray 'Hugh MacDiarmid'
- First Hymn to Lenin & Other Poems. Unicorn
Pr., 1931. *(500). (50) numbered & sigd.* Orig. hf.
mor., s.-c.; pres. inscr. to J.F. Moors. (CSK. Jun.15;
78) £120
- Sangschaw. 1925. *1st. Edn.* Orig. cl., d.-w. (BBA.
Oct.27; 97) *Joseph.* £60
- Selected Lyrics. Verona, Bodoni Pr., for Kulgin D.
Duval & Coln H. Hamilton, 1977. *(135) numbered.*
4to. Orig. vell.-bkd. decor. bds., s.-c. (S. Nov.22;
273) *Duschness.* £140

GRIEVE, Symington
- The Great Auk, or Garefowl. 1885. 4to. Folding maps partially split on folds, recent crimson hf. mor.; author's pres. copy. (TA. Dec.15; 138) £105

GRIFFITH, Charles
- The Present State & Prospects of the Port Phillip District of New South Wales ... Dublin, 1845. Lge. 12mo. Some soiling or mild discoloration, mod. qtr. mor., unc. (KH. May 1; 322) Aus. $380
- - Anr. Copy. Some foxing, cl. (JL. Nov.13; B21) Aus. $200

GRIFFITH, J.E.
- Pedigrees of Anglesey & Carnarvonshire Families. Horncastle, 1914. Fo. Cont. hf. mor., soiled & scuffed; inscr. by Gen. Hugh Gough. (CSK. Feb.24; 136) £280

GRIFFITH, Samuel Y.
- History of Cheltenham & its Vicinity. Oxford, 1838. 3rd. Edn. 4to. Engraved title, port, dedication, map, 33 engraved plts. on India paper, cont.hf.cf., rubbed. (BBA. Feb.9; 336) Parsloe. £75
- New Historical Description of Cheltenham & its Vicinity. Cheltenham, 1826. 1st. Edn. 4to. L.P., engraved title, 2 plans, folding map, 71 plts., a few spots, cont. cf., slightly rubbed. (S. Jun.25; 324) Traylen. £160

GRIFFITHS, Acton Frederick
- [-] Bibliotheca Anglo-Poetica. L., 1815. Hf.-title, cont. cf., rebkd. (BBA. Mar.7; 219) M. Whitby. £55

GRIFFITHS, Anselm John
- Observations on Some Points of Seamanship; with Practical Hints on Naval Oeconomy. Cheltenham, 1824. Mod. hf. cf., unc. & Partly unopened. (SG. Sep.22; 154) $100

GRIFFITHS, T.E.
- Colour Printing: A Practical Demonstration ... L., [1948]. 2 vols., including portfo. of charts. Sm. 4to. Cl., s.-c., ex-liby. (SG. Jan.5; 149) $125

GRIGORIEW, Boris
- Russische Erotik. [München, 1919]. Fo. Loose ll. in orig. hf. linen portfo., corners bumped. (GB. Nov.5; 2548) DM 450

GRILLION'S CLUB
- Portraits of Members of Grillion's Club. Priv. ptd., 1864. 2 vols. Fo. Some light spotting, cont. hf. mor. (CSK. Sep.30; 184) £90

GRILLPARZER, Franz
- Die Ahnfrau, ein Trauerspiel. Vienna, 1817. 1st. Edn. Mod. mor. gt., orig. ptd. wraps. bnd. in. (C. Dec.9; 231) Quaritch. £200
- Der Arme Spielmann. Ill.:– J. Hoffmann. Wien, 1915. De Luxe Edn., (50) on Bütten. 4to. Orig. mor. gt. decor., corners slightly worn. (HK. Nov.11; 4062) DM 5,200
- - Anr. Edn. Ill.:– Josef Hoffmann. Wien, 1915. (500) numbered. Sm. 4to. Orig. linen gt. (GB. May 5; 2698) DM 600

GRIMALDI, Giacinto
- Dell'alchimia. Palermo, 1645. 4to. Vell. (DS. Nov.25; 2162) Pts. 45,000

GRIMALDI, Stacy
- [-] The Toilet. 1821. 2nd. Edn. Sm. 4to. Plts. hand-cold., 8 with overslip, cont. pencil & watercol. drawing pasted on fly-lf., cont. cf. (TA. Aug.18; 353) £64

GRIMAUD DE CAUX, G. & Martin Saint-Ange, G.-J.
- Physiologie de l'Espèce, Histoire de la Gèneration de l'Homme. Paris, 1837. 2 vols. 4to. 12 plts. in double state, cont. leath. (HD. Mar.27; 175) Frs. 1,000

GRIMBLE, Angustus
- The Salmon Rivers of England & Wales. 1904. (350). 2 vols. 4to. Red hf. mor. gt. by Morrell. (P. Jul.5; 105) £140
- The Salmon Rivers of Ireland. 1903. (250). 2 vols. 4to. Red hf. mor. gt. by Morrell. (P. Jul.5; 103) £120
- The Salmon Rivers of Scotland. 1899-1900. 4 vols. 4to. Hf. mor. gt. (LC. Mar.1; 153) £200
- - Anr. Edn. 1899-1900. Ltd. Edn. 4 vols. 4to. Red hf. mor. gt. by Morrell. (P. Jul.5; 104) £190
- The Salmon & Sea Trout Rivers of England & Wales. 1904. (350). 2 vols. 4to. Hf. mor. gt. (LC. Mar.1; 151) £120
- Shooting & Salmon Fishing. 1892. (With:)
- Deer-Stalking. 1888. (With:) - Highland Sport. 1894. Together 3 vols. 4to. Red mor. gt. (P. Jul.5; 106) £220

GRIMM, Friedrich Melchior & Diderot, Denis
- Correspondance ... — Correspondance inédité. Recueil de Lettres Retranchées par la Censure Impériale. Paris, 1829. 15 vols. & 1 vol. Bds., several spines with loss. (HD. Feb.22; 81) Frs. 3,800

GRIMM, Jacob Ludwig Karl
- Ueber den Altdeutschen Meistergesang. Göttingen, 1811. 1st. Edn. Title verso with liby. stp., cont. marb. bds. (GB. Nov.4; 2061) DM 650

GRIMM, Jakob Ludwig Karl & Wilhelm Karl
- Das Blaue Licht. Mappenwerk. Ill.:– M. Slevogt. 1923. (100) numbered. Fo. 15 sigd. pen ills. on Japan under guards, lacks typographical title as often & contents lf., orig. hf. vell. portfo. (GB. May 5; 3340) DM 650
- - Anr. Edn. Ill.:– M. Slevogt. Berlin, [1924]. (400). Lge. 4to. Printers mrk. sigd. by artist, orig. pict. hf. vell. (H. May 23; 1510) DM 500
- - Anr. Edn. Ill.:– M Slevogt. [1924]. Portfo. Edn., (100). Fo. 15 sigd. pen lithos. on Japan under passepartouts, lacks typographical title & contents list as usual, orig. hf. vell. portfo. (GB. Nov.5; 3025) DM 1,100
- Die Deutsche Heldensage. Göttingen, 1829. 1st. Edn. Title stpd., cont. bds., bumped, spine worn. (R. Oct.11; 247) DM 700
- Deutsche Märchen. Ill.:– M. Slevogt. (1918). De Luxe Edn., (100) numbered on Zanders Bütten. 4to. Orig. suede [by E.R. Weiss]. (GB. Nov.5; 3020) DM 450
- Deutsche Sagen. Berlin, 1816-18. 1st. Edn. Cont. hf. leath., slightly bumped. (R. Oct.11; 246) DM 1,050
- - Anr. Copy. Some browning, especially 1st. & last ll., owners mark on end-paper & inside cover, cont. style hand-bnd. hf. leath.; Hauswedell coll. (H. May 24; 1342) DM 850
- The Fairy Tales. Trans.:– E. Lucas. Ill.:– A. Rackham. L., 1909. Sm. 4to. 2 plts. loose, 1 slit, orig. pict. linen gt., spine faded & torn, loose. (H. May 23; 1469) DM 580
- - Anr. Edn. Trans.:– Mrs. Edgar Lucas. Ill.:– A. Rackham. L., 1909. (750) numbered & sigd. by artist. Lge. 4to. Perforated liby. stp. on title, pict. vell., partly unc., very discold., shelf mark on spine, lacks ties. (SG. Mar.29; 252) $250
- Der Gelernte Jäger. Ill.:– M. Slevogt. [1924]. (100) numbered De Luxe Edn. 4to. 13 sigd. pen ills. on China, lacks typographical title & imprint, title foxed, orig. hf. vell. portfo., clasp. (GB. May 5; 3338) DM 700
- - Anr. Copy. 4to. 13 ll. sigd. pen lithos. on China, lacks typographic title & imprint, lacks portfo. (GB. Nov.5; 3024) DM 580
- - Anr. Copy. Sm. fo. All ll. sigd. by artist & under guards, lacks double title lf., 1st. litho. foxed, loose ll in orig. pict hf. vell. box, 2 sm. spine tears. (H. May 23; 1507) DM 520
- German Popular Stories. L., 1823. 1st. Engl. Edn. 3rd. Iss. Plts. darkened with some text offset, some foxing or soiling, darkened at edges, period cf., bkplt., end-papers. (CBA. Aug.21; 145) $225
- - Anr. Edn. Ill.:– G. Cruikshank. L., 1823. 2nd. Edn. Vol. 1. Lacks. hf-title & ptd. title & advt. ll. at end., 1 sm. margin excision reprd., hand-bnd. mor. gt., gold decor., wide inner dentelle, by Wood, London, spine slightly discold.; Hauswedell coll. (H. May 24; 1665) DM 700
- Hansel & Gretel & Other Stories. Ill.:– K. Nielsen. L., [1925]. (600) numbered & sigd. by artist. 4to. Bkplt., gt.-pict. cl. (SG. Dec.8; 251) $900
- - Anr. Copy. 4to. Gt.-pict. cl., lightly soiled. (SG. Nov.3; 154) $475
- - Anr. Copy. 4to. Lacks 3 tissue guards, front end-paper slightly defect., hf. cl. & patterned bds.,

extremities badly worn, partly unc. (SG. Jan.12; 274) $325
- Kinder– und Haus-Märchen. Berlin, 1819. 2nd. Edn. 2 vols. 16mo. Pagination of 1 foreword lf. cropped, short tear in 1 lf., sm. hole in Vol. 2 engraved title, a few ll. slightly spotted, 19th. C. hf. cf.; van Veen coll. (S. Feb.28; 146) £1,350
- - Anr. Edn. Göttingen, 1843. 3rd. Edn. 2 vols. Lacks 2 copper engrs. (by L.E. Grimm), 6 line dedication to Bettina v. Ariam, hf. leath., rubbed, jnts. brittle. (D. Nov.24; 2474) DM 850
- - Anr. Edn. Ill.:– H. Vogel. München, ca. 1900. Mor., ca. 1920, gt. spine, cover, inner & outer dentelle, both covers with cold leath insets. (HK. May 17; 2349) DM 850
- [-]Der Königssohn der sich vor nichts fürchtet. Ill.:– M. Slevogt. Berlin, 1923. (400). Lge. 4to. Printers mark sigd. by artist, orig. pict. hf. vell., lightly foxed, end-papers, doubls. foxed. (H. May 23; 1509) DM 400
- Little Brother & Little Sister. Ill.:– Arthur Rackham. [1917]. (525) numbered & sigd. by artist. 4to. 13 mntd. cold. plts., orig. cl., lightly soiled. (CSK. Jun.29; 162) £300
- Sechs Behmer. Ed.:– J. Bolte. Ill.:– M. Behmer. [Berlin, 1918]. (260). Sm. 8vo. Orig. hand-bnd. cf., gt. decor., by H. Fikentscher, slightly rubbed, spine lightly faded. (H. May 23; 1147) DM 1,550
- Der Treue Johannes und Andere Märchen. Ill.:– M. Slevogt. Berlin, (1923). (100) De Luxe Edn. Sm. 4to. Orig. red mor. gt., spine lightly faded, sm. scratches & wear. (H. May 23; 1508) DM 1,150
- Die Zwei Brüder. Ill.:– M. Slevogt. [1924]. (400) numbered on Handbüttenpapier. Lge. 4to. 29 orig. lithos., pol. mor., cold. insets, gold-tooled decor., centre-piece, gt. inner dentelles, orig. pict. vell. wraps. bnd. in, cold. paper s.-c.; printer's mark sigd. by artist. (GB. Nov.5; 3022) DM 2,900
- - Anr. Copy. Lge. 4to. Unnumbered copy, hf.-title with dtd. MS. dedication by artist, orig. pict. vell. (H. May 23; 1506) DM 800
- - Anr. Copy. Printers mark sigd. by artist, orig. vell., litho. on upr. cover. (HK. May 17; 3144) DM 420
- Die Zwölf Brüder. Ein Märchen. Ill.:– Martha Müller. Hamburg, ca. 1910. Ob. 4to. Orig. pict. cold. hf. linen, corners bumped. (GB. May 5; 2990) DM 450
- Die Zwölf Jäger. Ill.:– M. Slevogt. [Berlin, 1925]. Lge.4to. Lithos. on china & sigd. by artist in orig. passepartouts, loose in mod. hf. leath. (HT. May 9; 2045) DM 3,200

GRIMM, Wilhelm Karl
- Die Deutsche Heldensage. Göttingen, 1829. 1st. Edn. Cont. bds., slightly rubbed; 2 ll. with 4 pp. altered text bnd. in, Hauswedell coll. (H. May 24; 1345) DM 460
- Vridankes Bescheidenheit. Göttingen, 1834. 1st. Edn. Title verso stpd., cont. bds., unc. (HK. Nov.10; 2467) DM 400

GRIMMELSHAUSEN, J. Chr. von
- Der Erste Beernhäuter. Ill.:– M. Behmer. [Berlin, 1919]. (200). Hand-bnd. orig. hf. leath., spine worn. (H. May 23; 1148) DM 900
- - Anr. Edn. Ill.:– M. Behmer. Berlin, 1919. (300) numbered. 5 full-p. orig. etchings, gt.-decor. red mor., sigd. G. Dietz Freiburg. (GB. Nov.5; 2278) DM 1,800
- - Anr. Copy. This copy with number replaced in printers mark by initials 'mb', 5 orig. full-p. etchings, orig. hf. linen, slightly soiled. (GB. May 5; 2187) DM 1,200
- [-] Navigare necesse est. Eine Festgabe für A. Klippenberg zum 22 Mai 1924. Contribs.:– Carossa, Th. Däuber, Hofmannsthal, Rilke, Schröder, Zweig, & others. Ill.:– M. Behmer & G.A. Mathey (orig. etching), L.V. Hofmann, Masereel, & W. Tiemann (orig. woodcut), E.R. Weiss (orig. litho.). 1924. (500) numbered. 4to. 5 orig. ills., graphic supps. on special paper, orig. hf. vell. (GB. Nov.5; 2280). DM 900

GRIMOD DE LA REYNIERE, Alex. Bathasar
- [-] Almanach des Gourmands. Paris, 1803-12. [1st.-]8th. Years: 8 vols. 12mo. Old pol. cf. gt., 1 vol. rebnd. to style, anr. rehinged, some wear. (SG. Aug.4; 142) $220

GRINDLAY, Capt. Robert Melville
- Scenery, Costumes and Architecture, chiefly on the Western side of India. L., 1826. Pts. 1-4 only (of 6) in 1 vol. Fo. Engraved vig. title, 27 (of 36) hand-cold. plts., some offsetting, cont. hf. mor., spine worn, rubbed. (BBA. Dec.15; 8)
Remington. £440
- - Anr. Copy. Pt. 1 only (of 6). Fo. Col. vig. title, 6 hand-cold. plts., text dampstained, some stains to plt. margins, orig. bds., worn. (P. Jul.5; 208) £140
- - Anr. Edn. L., [1826]. Vol. 1 only (of 2). 4to. Hand-cold. vig. title, 18 hand-cold. plts., 3 with inner margin slightly torn, lacks contents lf., hf. mor. gt., rubbed. (P. Apr.12; 219) *Evelyn.* £380
- - Anr. Edn. L., 1826-30. 2 vols. in 1. Fo. Engraved hand-cold. title to Vol. I, 36 hand-cold. aquatint views, lacks title to Vol. II, cont. red hf. mor., spine gt.; Reuben D. Sassoon & T.A. Oldham bkplts. (C. Nov.16; 94) *Map House.* £900
- - Anr. Copy. 2 vols. in 1. Fo. Engraved title to Vol. I, 24 (of 36) hand-cold. aquatint views, lacks title to Vol. II, hf. cf., defect., as a coll. of plts., w.a.f. (P. Oct.20; 118) £360
- - Anr. Edn. 1830. 6 pts. in 2 vols. bnd. in 1. 4to. Col. vig. title to Vol. 1, uncold. vig. title on India paper to Vol. 2, 36 hand-cold. plts., cl., spine worn. (P. Jul.5; 209) £720
- - Anr. Copy. Foxing thro.-out, not affecting etchings, pp. loose, bdg. not stated, spine detchd. (JL. Jul.15; 326) Aus. $475

GRINGO, Harry (Pseud.)
See— WISE, Lieut. Henry A.

GRINNELL, George Bird
- The Cheyenne Indians. New Haven, 1923. *1st. Edn.* 2 vols. Orig. cl. (SG. Apr.5; 80) $150

GRINNELL, George Bird (Text)
See— HARRIMAN ALASKA EXPEDITION

GRIOIS, Gen.
- Mémoires. Ed.:– A. Chaquet. Paris, 1901. *2nd. Edn.* 2 vols. Hf. chagrin. (HD. Jan.27; 48)
Frs. 1,100

GRITSCH, Johannes
- Quadragesimale. [Cologne], Heinrich Quentell. 1481. Fo. Cont. stpd. cf. over wood bds., clasps; from Fondation Furstenberg-Beaumesnil. [HC 8068; BMC I, 263; Goff G498] (HD. Nov.16; 22) Frs. 9,000
- - Anr. Edn. [Strasbourg, Printer of the 1483 Vitas Patrum], 5 Feb. 1484. Fo. Initial C on clr in blue & red on gold ground & in green & red frame, foliate decor. in outer & lr. margins with stork perched on topmost branch, some initials supplied in red, mostly rubricated, 2 sm. wormholes at end slightly affecting text, later end-papers, cont. German blind-stpd. pig over wood bds., clasps, metal cornerpieces & centrepieces with bosses, a few tears in upr. part of spine & repairs to lr. part, author's name in ink at head of upr. cover; 17th. C. inscr. of Carmelites at Bamberg. [Goff G500] (S. Nov.17; 31) *Fletcher.* £1,300

GROBER, Karl
- Children's Toys of Bygone Days. 1928. 4to. Liby. stp. on some ll. & plts., orig. cl. (LC. Jul.5; 51) £55

GROENWEGEN, Gerrit
- Verscheide Soorten van Hollandse Vaartuigen. Rotterdam, 1786-91. 6 pts. (of 7) in 1 vol. Sm. 4to. 72 plts. (of 84), last 2 pts. misbnd., 1 plt. laid down (from anr. copy?), 1 or 2 ll. foxed, later roan-bkd. bds. (CH. May 24; 48) Fls. 12,000

GROHMANN, Joh. Gottfried
- Ländliche Vergnügungen. Leipzig, [1801]. Lr. title margin detchd. & extended, text browned, wraps. (R. Oct.12; 2335) DM 420
- Recueil d'Idées Nouvelles pour la Décoration der Jardins et des Parcs dans le Gout Anglois, Gothique, Chinois etc. Leipzig, 1797-99. Pts. 1-12 in 1 vol. Sm. fo. Each pt. with 2 ll. explanation of text in German & Fr., foxing at end, cont. hf. leath., slightly rubbed. (GB. Nov.3; 885) DM 1,100

GROHMANN, Will
- Kandinsky. Ill.:– W. Kandinsky. Paris, 1930. *(500)* numbered on *Vélin de Torpes.* Orig. cold.

woodcut, orig. sewed, spine restored. (GB. Nov.5; 2648) DM 500
- Kirchner-Zeichnungen. Ill.:– E.L. Kirchner. Dresden, 1925. 2nd. Series 6. 18 orig. woodcuts, including title & bdg., orig. pict. linen. (GB. Nov.5; 2664) DM 2,800

GROLIER CLUB
- Catalogue of Original & Early Editions ... from Langland to Wither. N.Y., Grol. Cl., 1893. *(400).* Lge. 8vo. Qtr. roan, worn, cover detchd., mostly unopened. (SG. May 17; 108) $100
- Catalogue of Original & Early Editions ... Wither to Prior. N.Y., Grol. Cl., 1905. *(400).* 3 vols. Lge. 8vo. Qtr. roan, worn, covers detchd., mostly unopened. (SG. May 17; 109) $100
- One Hundred Books Famous in English Literature. N.Y., Grol. Cl., 1902. *(305).* (With:)
- Bibliographical Notes on One Hundred Books Famous in English Literature. By Henry W. Kent. N.Y., Grol. Cl., 1903. *(305).* Together 2 vols. Paperback & bds. (LH. Sep.25; 399) $190

GROLIER DE SERVIERE, Nicolas
- Recueil d'Ouvrages Curieux de Mathématique et de Mécanique ... Ill.:– Daudet & others. Lyon, 1733. *2nd. Edn.* 4to. Cont. mott. sheep, spine gt. (rubbed); sig. of Erasmus Philipps, inscr. 'Bought at Lyons of Mr. Rivoli, who has the care of this Cabinet, Nov. 1737'. (C. May 30; 116)
Sims, Reed & Fogg. £320
- - Anr. Copy. 4to. No plts. 48 & 76, cont. cf., spine decor. (HD. Nov.9; 177) Frs. 4,000

GROMMER, Jakob
See— EINSTEIN, Albert & Grommer, Jakob

GROMORT, Georges
- L'Architecture Romane. Paris, 1928-31. 3 vols. Tall 4to. 234 photo. plts., text ills., each plt. liby.-stpd. on blank verso, loose in cl.-bkd. ptd. bds., linen ties. (SG. May 3; 185) $300

GRONOVIUS, Jacobus
- Thesaurus Graecarum Antiquitatum. Lugduni Batavorum, 1697-1702. 13 vols. Fo. Perforation stps. in titles, old cf., worn, few covers detchd., ex-liby. (RO. Dec.11; 131) $200

GRONOW, Capt. Rees Howell
- The Reminiscences & Recollections of ... L., 1892. 2 vols. Extra-ill. with over 90 ports., views, sigs., etc., red mor., gt. panel., spines gt., cl. case (soiled), by Bayntun, w.a.f. (CNY. Dec.17; 566) $200

GROOT, Constantin de
- Voor-Bereidselen Wysheid, en Gebruik der Heilige en Kerklijke Historien. Amst., 1690. 2 vols. Fo. Cont. mott. cf. (SG. Feb.9; 117) $275

GROOT, J.J.M. de
- The Religious System of China. Leyden, 1892-1901. Vols. I-IV (of 6). Lge. 8vo. Hf. cl. (VG. Mar.21; 522) Fls. 600

GROOTE or GROTIUS, Hugo de
- Annales et Histoires des Troubles du Pays-Bas. Amst., 1662. *1st. Edn. in Fr.* Fo. Cont. cf. (HD. Feb.22; 82) Frs. 2,300
- Annales et Historiae de Rebus Belgicis. Amst., 1657. *1st. Edn.* Fo. Lge. device on title, engraved port., cont. blindstpd. vell. (SG. Apr.19; 99) $150
- Annotata ad Vetus Testamentum. Lutetiae & Amst., 1644. *1st. Edn.* 3 pts. in 1 vol. Fo. Blind-tooled vell., lacks ties. (B. Jun.21; 511) Fls. 500
- De Jure Belli ac Pacis Libri III. Notes:– G. v.d. Muelen & J.F. Gronovius. Utrecht, 1696-1703. 3 vols. Fo. Some foxing, cont. blind-stpd. vell., not quite unif., covers slightly dampstained & defect., lacks ties. (VS. Dec.9; 1162) Fls. 550
- Le Droit de la Guerre et de la Paix. Trans.:– Courtin. Ill.:– Vermeulen. Paris, 1687. 2 vols. 4to. Cont. cf., decor. spine. (HD. Jan.26; 159)
Frs. 1,200
- - Anr. Edn. Trans.:– J. Barbeyrac. Amst., 1729. 2 vols. 4to. Cont. cf. (HD. Feb.22; 83) Frs. 4,000
- Hugo Grotius, his Most Choice Discourses. L., 1658. 4 pts. in 1 vol. 12mo. Cont. cf., reprd. [Wing G2112] (BBA. May 3; 140)
Howes Bookshop. £55

- Nederlandtsche Jaerboeken en Historien (1555-1609). Trans.:– J. Goris. Ill.:– Luyken &c. Amst., 1681. Fo. Vell. (B. Jun.21; 483) Fls. 1,600

GROOTE TAFEREEL DER DWASHEID, Vertoonende de Opkomst Voortgang en Ondergang der Actie, Bubbel en Wind Negotie, in Vrankryk, Engeland en de Nederlanden, in den Jaare MDCCXX 1720. Fo. Cont. hf. roan, corners, spine decor., lacks upr. turn-in. (HD. May 3; 64) Frs. 11,000
- - Anr. Copy. Fo. 5 pts. text, including section of 4 unnumbered ll., engraved frontis., title, 2 double-p. maps, 69 engraved plts., including 51 double-p., cont. hf. cf., corners torn. (CH. Sep.20; 42)
Fls. 2,200
- - Anr. Copy. Fo. 5 copper engrs. with sm. tears in fold, 2 copper engrs. excised & pasted on, browning, some text heavier, some sm. spots, cont. cf. gt., worn & bumped, upr. cover loose, jnt. torn, lr. cover with 4 sm. holes. [Sabin 28932] (H. May 22; 380)
DM 3,600

GROPIUS, Walter
- Internationale Architektur. (Bauhausbücher Bd. I.). München, [1925]. Orig. linen, bdg. & typography by H. Moholy-Nagy. (H. Nov.24; 1341) DM 600

GROSE, Francis
- The Antiquities of England & Wales. 1772-87. 6 vols. 4to. Cf. gt., 1 cover detchd. (P. Sep.29; 199)
Campbell. £150
- - Anr. Edn. 1773-87. 6 vols., including 2 vol. Supp. 4to. 6 engraved titles, 42 county maps, hand-cold. in outl., 626 plts., 1 folding map cleanly torn, some light staining, cont. cf., worn, w.a.f. (CSK. Dec.16; 172) £340
- - Anr. Edn. [1783-]97. 8 vols. Some ll. browned or spotted, cont. str.-grd. mor., rubbed. (BBA. Feb.9; 345) *Hulme.* £300
- - Anr. Edn. [1783-]99. 8 vols. Hf. cf. gt. (P. Sep.8; 389) *Martin.* £320
- - Anr. Edn. L., [1784-87]. 8 vols. including Supp. Engraved titles with vigs., folding engraved map hand-cold. in outl., engraved plts. (including folding plans), engraved maps in text (outl. col.), some discolouration, liby. stps. at beginning of each vol., cf., rebkd. in mor. (S. May 21; 61) *Walford.* £380
- - Anr. Edn. N.d. & 1785-87. 8 vols. 4to. Cont. hf. cf., marb. bds., slightly worn. (SKC. Mar.9; 1980) £260
- - Anr. Copy. 8 vols., including Supp. 4to. Engraved titles, many engraved plts., sm. hand-cold. text maps, some foxing, ex-liby., cont. cf., wood-grained cf. inlays, rebkd., orig. gt-decor. spines laid down. (SG. May 3; 186) $325
- - Anr. Edn. L., n.d. 8 vols., including Supp. 4to. Some spotting & offsetting, cont. hf. cl. preserving orig. bds., unc., rubbed & soiled. (S. Dec.13; 204) *Kidd.* £220
- The Antiquities of England & Wales. — The Antiquities of Scotland. — The Antiquities of Ireland. 1773-76, 1777-87, [1787]; 1789-91; 1791-95. 7 vols., including 2 vol. Supp. & Addenda; 2 vols.; 2 vols. Lge. 4to. Unif. cont. spr. cf.; Sir Ivar Colquhoun, of Luss copies. (CE. Mar.22; 146)
£1,650
- - Anr. Edn. N.d. & 1797; 1797; 1791-97. 8 vols.; 2 vols.; 2 vols. (With:) - Military Antiquities repsecting a History of the English Army. 1801. 2 vols. Together 14 vols. 4to. Cont. decor. russ. gt. (SKC. Mar.9; 1979) £620
- The Antiquities of Ireland. L., 1791. *1st. Edn.* 2 vols. Lge. 4to. 2 engraved frontis., 2 engraved titles, 264 engraved plts., bkplt., hf. cf., Vol. 1 lacks 1 cover, other detchd. (GM. Dec.7; 327) £240
- - Anr. Copy. 2 vols. Lge. 4to. About 250 plts., most hand-cold., ex-liby., disbnd. (SG. May 3; 188)
$225
- - Anr. Copy. 2 vols. Fo. L.P., old cl.-bkd. bds., worn, 1 cover detchd., some spine tears. (RO. Dec.11; 132) $150
- - Anr. Copy. 2 vols. 4to. Contents loose in bdgs., orig. bds. (SSA. Jul.5; 171) R 410
- - Anr. Edn. 1797. 2 vols. 4to. L.P., minor spotting, cont. crimson str.-grd. mor. gt. (TA. Sep.15; 158) £280
- - Anr. Copy. 2 vols. 4to. L.P., minor spotting, cont. crimson str.-grd. mor. gt. (TA. Oct.20; 64) £220

GROSE, Francis -*Contd.*

- **The Antiquities of Scotland.** 1789-91. *1st. Edn.* 2 vols. Engraved titles, folding hand-cold map, 192 plts., cont. str.-grd. mor., rubbed. (BBA. Feb.9; 346) *Edwards.* £80
- – **Anr. Copy.** 2 vols. Lge. 4to. Engraved titles, many engraved plts., ex-liby., early cf., inlaid marb. cf. panels on all covers, very worn. (SG. May 3; 187) $275
- **Military Antiquities, Respecting a History of the English Army.** L., 1786. *1st. Edn.* 2 vols. 4to. Cf., 2 covers loose. (GM. Dec.7; 619) £75
- – **Anr. Edn.** 1786-88. 2 vols. 4to. Some foxing, cont. tree cf. gt., spines decor., rubbed; Sir Ivar Colquhoun, of Luss copy. (CE. Mar.22; 147)£210
- – **Anr. Copy.** 2 vols. 4to. 2 engraved vig. titles, 2 frontis., 78 engrs., cf. gt. (P. Jul.26; 55) £70
- – **Anr. Edn.** [L.,], 1812. *New Edn.* 2 vols. 4to. Scattered light foxing, hf. cf. gt. (SG. Sep.22; 156) $175

GROSE, Francis & others

- **The Antiquarian Repository: a Miscellany intended to preserve & Illustrate several valuable Remains of Old Times.** 1780-84. *Vol. 1: 2nd. Edn., Vols. 2-4: 1st. Edn.* 4to. A few plts. in Vol. 2 stained, cont. tree cf. gt.; Sir Ivar Colquhoun, of Luss copy. (CE. Mar.22; 13) £700
- – **Anr. Edn.** 1807-09. *New Edn.* 4 vols. 4to. L.P., 1 ill. hand-cold., subscribers list, cont. pol. cf. gt. (SKC. Mar.9; 1978) £220
- – **Anr. Copy.** 4 vols. Fo. Hf. mor. gt. (P. Sep.8; 175) *Robertshaw.* £85

GROSE, S.W.

- **Catalogue of the McLean Collection of Greek Coins ... Fitzwilliam Museum.** Camb., 1923-29. 3 vols. Lge. 8vo. Cl. (B. Feb.8; 866) Fls. 550

GROSIER, Abbé J.B.G.

- **Atlas Général de la China.** 1785. Lge. fo. 65 maps, plans & plts. (most folding), publisher's bds. (HD. Jun.29; 110) Frs. 7,500

GROSIUS, Henningus, Comp.

[-] **De Spectris et Apparitionibus Spirituum; item De Magicis & Diabolicis Incantionibus: De Miraculis, Oraculis, Veticiniis ... & Imposturis Malorum Damonum ...** Islebiae, 1591. *1st. Edn.* Washed, browned thro.-out, later hf. cf. (PNY. Dec.1; 53) $200

GROSLIER, George

- **Danseuses Cambodgiensis Anciennes et Modernes.** Paris, [1913]. Lge. 4to. Cont. hf. mor., lightly rubbed. (CSK. Jul.27; 29) £50

GROSSE, K.

- **Geschichte der Stadt Leipzig.** Leipzig, 1839-42. 2 vols. 1 coll. view & plan completely mntd., 1 folding plt. defect., 5 copper engrs. cut close, lightly crumpled, 2 bkd., mod. hf. leath. (R. Oct.13; 2773) DM 1,000

GROSSMANN, Marcel

See— EINSTEIN, Albert & Grossman, Marcel

GROSSMANN, Rudolf

- **Illustrationen zu E.T.A. Hoffmann. Ritter Gluck.** Ill.:– J. Tempel & A. Fallscheer after Grossmann. [Tölz, Bremer Pr., 1920]. *De Luxe Edn., (65).* Fo. Separate series on Japon, all sigd., all ll. dry-stpd. by Marees-Gesellschaft, under guards, no text, loose in orig. hf. linen portfo., slightly spotted. (H. Nov.24; 1567) DM 800
- **Unold von Kaltenquell.** Berlin, 1922. *(180) numbered.* Fo. Printers mark sigd. by artist, orig. silk with cold. litho. on upr. cover. (HK. Nov.11; 3586) DM 400

GROSZ, GEORG

- **Ecce Homo.** Berlin, 1923. *C Edn.* Fo. Minimal foxing to inside cover, orig. bds. (GB. Nov.5; 2555) DM 2,000
- – **Anr. Copy.** Fo. Orig. wraps. (HK. May 17; 2792) DM 1,700
- – **Anr. Copy.** Fo. Slightly foxed, orig. pict. bds., slightly foxed. (GB. May 5; 2621) DM 1,300
- – **Anr. Edn.** Berlin, [1923]. *D Edn.* Sm. fo. Last plts. with 2 sm. holes, orig. pict. wraps., spotted, sm. margin tears. (H. Nov.24; 2486) DM 1,000

- **Im Schatten.** Berlin, 1921. *(30) numbered C Edn.* Fo. All ll. except title-lf. pencil sigd. by artist, 9 sigd. orig. lithos. on H.M. Bütten, slight stain in upr. right corner, loose ll. in orig. hf. silk portfo. (GB. May 5; 2619) DM 16,000
- **Mit Pinsel und Schere. 7 Materialisationen.** 1922. 4to. Orig. typographic pict. wraps., spine slightly rubbed. (GB. May 5; 2620) DM 650

GROTE, George

- **A History of Greece.** L., 1888. *New Edn.* 10 vols. Sm. 8vo. Cf., gt. arms of Chelton College on upr. covers, spines gt.; label presenting the set as prize to a Chelton student, 1889. (SG. Feb.16; 150) $400

GROTE-HASENBALG, Werner

- **Masterpieces of Oriental Rugs.** N.Y., [1921]. With 2 portfos. containing 120 cold. plts., cl.-bkd. bds. (PNY. Oct.20; 222) $150
- **Der Orientteppich. Seine Geschiechte u. Seine Kuttur.** Berlin, 1922. Text vol. & 2 plt. vols. 4to. 1 folding map, 26 partly cold. plts., plt. vol. with 120 mntd. cold. ills., orig. linen, engraved ex-libris. (V. Sep.30; 1659) DM 1,350

GROTIUS, Hugo de

See— GROOTE or GROTIUS, Hugo de

GROUSSET, R.

- **Histoire des Croisades et du Royaume Franc de Jerusalem.** Paris, 1934-36. 3 Vvols. Cl., vol. 1 with slight loss. (HD. Feb.22; 84) Frs. 3,000

GROVE, Sir George

- **Dictionary of Music & Musicians.** Ed.:– Eric Blom. 1954. *5th. Edn.* 10 vols. Cl., d.-w.'s. (PD. Aug.17; 216) £170
- – **Anr. Edn.** Ed.:– E. Blom. N.Y., 1960, 1961. *5th. Edn.* 9 vols., & Supp. Lge. 8vo. Buckram, d.-w.'s. (SG. Nov.17; 258) $225

GROVE, William Robert

- **On the Correlation of Physical Forces: Being the Substance of a Course of Lectures Delivered in the London Institution in the Year 1843.** L., 1846. *1st. Edn. Iss. with title in unif. type & Highley imprint.* Mod. claret mor.; Stanitz coll. (SPB. Apr.25; 200) $250

GRUBER, J.C. & Geissler, Ch. G.H.

- **Sitten, Gebräuche und Kleidung der Russen in St. Petersburg, dargestellt in Gemälden mit Beschreibungen.** Ill.:– Geissler & J. G. Scheffner. Leipzig, [1801-03] & [1805]. 2 vols. 4to. Some slight browning, some repairs. (*Bound with:*) RICHTER, J. & Geissler, Ch. G.H. - **Sitten, Gebräuche und Kleidung der Russen aus den Niedern Ständen.** 2 vols. bnd. in 1. 4to. Some slight browning, some repairs, hf. leath., ca. 1900, rubbed; Hauswedell coll. (H. May 23; 163) DM 4,400

GRUBER, Jacques

- **Le Vitrail à l'Exposition Internationale des Arts Decoratifs Paris 1925.** Paris, [1926]. 4to. 42 plts., including 11 pochoir-cold., loose as iss., cl.-bkd. pict. bds. (SG. Aug.25; 26) $160

GRUEL, Leon

- **Manuel Historique et Bibliographique de l'Amateur de Reliures.** Paris, 1887. *(1000) numbered.* 4to. Cont. hf. mor., a little rubbed, orig. wraps. preserved; H.M. Nixon coll., with his sig. & acquisition note. (BBA. Oct.6; 56) *Quaritch.* £110

GRUENPECK, Jos.

- **Pronosticvm ab Anno Trigesimo secundo usque ad Annum Quadragesimum Imperatoris Caroli, quinti plerasque Futuras Historias continens.** Regensburg, 1532. 4to. Minimal soiling, sewed. (HK. Nov.8; 206) DM 400
- **Tractatus de Pestilentiali Scorra sive Mala de Franzos. Originem Remediaqz eivsdem continens ...** [Augsburg], 1496. Sm. 4to. Mod. bds. [Hain 8091] (HD. Dec.2; 95) Frs. 23,500

GRUN, A.

See— MONTAIGNE, Michel Eyquem de — GRUN, A.

GRUNDLICHER BERICHT VOM HEILIGEN ABENDMAL unsers Herren Jesu Christi ...

Heidelberg, 1574. *3rd. Edn.* 4to. Some old

underlining on last pp., hf. vell. (R. Oct.11; 48) DM 680

GRUNDSATZE DER HOHERN KRIEGSKUNST und Beyspiele Ihrer Zweckmässigen Anwendung für die Generale der Osterreichischen Armee.

Wien, 1808. Fo. Bds. (HD. Feb.22; 85) Frs. 2,600

GRUNENBERG, Arthur

- **Phoenix.** Ca. 1920. *(100) numbered.* Fo. 10 sigd. & numbered orig. etchings under guards, some ll. cold. in, partly with gold, orig. linen portfo. (GB. May 5; 2636) DM 500

GRUNER, Elioth

- **24 Reproductions in Colour from Original Oil Paintings.** *(2000) numbered.* No bdg. stated. (JL. Jun.24; 181) Aus. $250

GRUNER, Lewis

- **Fresco Decorations & Stuccoes of Churches & Palaces in Italy.** Contrib.:– J.J. Hittorff. L., 1844. *1st. Edn.* Lge. fo. Engraved title, 46 plts., including 26 hand-cold., few ll. spotted at beginning, cont. red mor., richly gt., slightly rubbed. (S. Nov.8; 522) *Thorp.* £320
- – **Anr. Copy.** Lge. fo. Engraved title, 46 plts., 26 hand-cold., a few ll. spotted at beginning, lacks text, cont. red mor., richly gt. (S. May 1; 548) *A. Henderson.* £190
- – **Anr. Edn.** Contrib.:– J. J. Hittorff. L., 1854. *New Edn.* Lge. fo. Engraved title, 56 plts., some foxing, cont. red hf. mor. gt. (S. Nov.8; 523) *Thorp.* £125
- – **Anr. Copy.** 3 pts. in 1 vol. Lge. fo. 56 engraved plts., cont. hf. mor. (SKC. Sep.9; 1807) £50
- **Specimens of Ornamental Art.** Text vol.:– Emil Braun. L., 1850. *1st. Edn.* 2 vols., including text vol. Fo. & 4to. 80 plts., most cold., 3 plts. & 2 ll. of text crudely remargined, tears, slightly soiled, detchd. from bdg., cont. red hf. mor., worn, w.a.f. (S. Apr.30; 185) *Sims.* £210

GRUNER, Vincentius

See— AUGUSTINUS, Saint Aurelius, Bp. of Hippo — GRUNER, Vincentius

GRUTERUS, Janus

[-] **Delitiae C. Poetarum Gallorum, huius Superiorisque Aevi illustrium ... collectore Ranutio Ghero (pseud.).** [Frankfurt], 1609. 3 vols. (*With:*) - **Delitiae Poetarum Germanorum ... collectore A.F.G.G. (J. Gruterus).** Frankfurt, 1612. 6 vols. in 9. (*With:*) - **Delitiae C. Poetarum Belgicorum ... collectore Ranutio Ghero.** Frankfurt, 1614. Vols. I & II only (of 4). Together 14 vols. 16mo. All rather browned, later 17th. C. Fr. red mor. gt., arms of Jean-Baptiste Colbert in triple gt. fillet à la Du Seuil, & his cypher in gt. compartments of spines. (S. Nov.17; 32) *Chapponiere.* £1,200

GRYPHIUS, Andreas

- **Ausgewählte Sonette, Gedichte und Epigramme.** Ill.:– Otto Rohse. Hamburg, 1970 & 1977. *(195).* 2 vols. 4to. Vol. II with sigd. printers mark, orig. blind-tooled hf. leath., by Chr. Zwang; Hauswedell coll. (H. May 24; 766) DM 660

GRYPHIUS, Chr.

[-] **Ars Apophthegmatica.** Nürnberg, 1655-56. *1st. Edn. (Vol. 1), 2nd. Edn. (Vol. 2).* 2 vols. in 1. Without engraved main title & probably lacks 1 lf. errata, 1st. title lf. verso with stp., end-paper & inner cover with old owners mark, lightly browned, cont. vell., jnts. brittle, slightly spotted; Hauswedell coll. (H. May 24; 1154) DM 3,800

GSELL-FELS, Theodor

- **Die Bäder und Klimatischen Kurorte der Schweiz.** Zürich, 1880. Orig. linen. (R. Oct.13; 3258) DM 600
- **Die Schweiz.** München & Berlin, [1876-77]. 2 vols. Fo. 60 woodcut plts., end-papers renewed, linen, using cont. linen bds., soiled. (HK. Nov.9; 1258) DM 1,400
- – **Anr. Edn.** München & Berlin, ca. 1880. 2 vols. Fo. 60 plts. & approx. 300 wood engraved ills., cont. hf. leath. gt. (R. Oct.13; 3259) DM 1,400
- – **Anr. Copy.** Vol. 1 (of 2). Fo. 30 plts., approx. 150 wood engraved ills., mod. linen. (R. Apr.5; 3081) DM 400
- **Switzerland: its Scenery & People.** Trans.:– G.G.

Chisholm. L., 1881. Fo. Orig. pict. linen, bumped & loose. (R. Oct.13; 3261)　　　DM 1,400

GUALTHERUS, Phillipus
- **Alexandreidos Libri Decem.** Ingolstadt, 1541. Head of title-p. shaved, some stains, lacks last lf. blank, cont. limp vell. (BBA. May 23; 313)
　　　Quaritch. £70

GUARINI, Giambattista
- **Il Pastor Fido.** Paris, 1656. Sm. 4to. Hf.-title, 18th. C. Fr. red mor., flat spine gt., gt. border à la Du Seuil, arms of Anne-Marguerite-Gabrielle de Beauvau-Craon, duchesse de Lévis-Mirepoix. (S. Nov.17; 29)　　　*Tzakas.* £320

GUASCO
- **De l'Usage des Statues chez les Anciens.** Brussels, 1768. 4to. Last errata lf., browned thro.-out, cont. vell., slightly rubbed. (BBA. Feb.23; 55)
　　　Thorp. £60

GUAZZO, Fr. M.
- **Compendium Maleficarum.** Mailand, 1608. *1st. Edn.* 4to. Slightly stained near end, some slight foxing, later vell. (D. Nov.23; 120)　　　DM 4,000

GUAZZO, Stefano
- **La Civil Conversatione.** Brescia, 1574. *1st. Edn.* 4to. 17th. C. leath. gt., very bumped. (HK. Nov.8; 210)　　　DM 480
- **Van den Heuschen Burgerlycken Ommegangh ...** Trans.:– Gomes van Triers. Alckmaer, 1603. 4to. Slightly browned, few light stains, cont. vell. (VG. Nov.30; 580)　　　Fls. 600

GUEDEVILLE, N.
- [–] **Le Grand Théâtre Historique, ou Nouvelle Histoire Universelle, tant Sacrée que Profane.** Leiden, 1703. *1st. Edn.* 5 vols. Fo. Some slight browning, cont. leath. gt., slightly rubbed & worn. (GB. Nov.3; 8)　　　DM 950

GUEGAN, Bertrand
- **Le Cuisinier Français, ou les Meilleures Recettes d'Autrefois et d'Aujourd'hui.** Paris, 1934. 4to. Sewed, wrap. unglued. (HD. May 16; 88)
　　　Frs. 2,000

GUENTHER, Chr. W.
- [–] **Kindermährchen aus Mündlichen Erzählungen gesammelt.** Erfurt, 1787. Browned, cont. bds. gt., bumped; ex-libris; Hauswedell coll. (H. May 24; 1672)　　　DM 740

GUER, Jean Antoine
- **Moeurs et Usages des Turcs.** Ill.:– Duflos after François Boucher & Halle. Paris, 1746-47. *Vol. I: 1st. Edn., Vol. II: 2nd. Edn.* 2 vols. 4to. 30 copperplts., some folding, 2 plts. crudely reprd., few sm. margin stains or light foxing, 1 lf. with sm. repair, early cf. gt. (SG. Sep.22; 157)　　　$700
- – **Anr. Edn.** Ill.:– Boucher & Hallé. Paris, 1746-47. 2 vols. 4to. Cont. marb. roan, spines decor. (HD. May 3; 61)　　　Frs. 6,200

GUERICKE, Otto von
- **Experimenta Nova (ut vocant) Magdeburgica de Vacuo Spatio ...** Amst., 1672. *1st. Edn.* Fo. Additional engraved title, port., 23 engrs., including the 2 folding plts. at pp. 27 & 105, the unnumbered plt. on p. 24, the 2 dupls. of plt. 18 on pp. 142 & 148 (the latter ptd. inverted), plts. 19/20 on 1 sheet, in this copy a 4th. copy of plt. 18 (without text on verso) inserted at p. 149, errata lf., port. slightly discold., stain on pp. 149-153, vell. (S. Nov.28; 116)
　　　Pickering & Chatto. £1,700
- – **Anr. Copy.** Fo. Some light browning or foxing, port. with excision, pasted on front-free end-paper, full-p. copper engr. with old part col., 1 plt. with 3 sm. red spots in upr. inner corner, some old text underlining, 1 lf. errata, cont. vell., 1 upr jnt. slightly broken. (R. Apr.4; 1523)　　　DM 7,500
- – **Anr. Copy.** Fo. Approx. 1st. 25 pp. slightly wormed, 1 plt. cut to subject & 1 other plt. cut, some slight foxing, cont. vell. (R. Oct.12; 1675)
　　　DM 6,000

GUERIN, Charles
- **Le Coeur Solitaire.** Paris, 1898. *Orig. Edn., (413).* Sm. 8vo. Old red hf. mor., corners, by Stikeman & Co., spine gt., unc.; sigd. autograph dedication to

---

Swinburne on hf.-title, Swinburne's ex-libris. (HD. May 16; 35)　　　Frs. 2,600

GUERIN, Jules
See– PARRISH, Maxfield & Guerin, Jules

GUERIN, Léon
- **Histoire Maritime de France.** Paris, 1851. 6 vols. 40 plts., including 36 ptd. on chine appliqué, preface ll. bnd. at beginning of vol. II, cont. hf. damson chagrin, corners, limp decor. spines. (HD. Jan.26; 162)　　　Frs. 2,050

GUERIN, Marcel
- **Gaugin: L'Oeuvre Gravé.** Paris, 1927. *(600) numbered.* 2 vols. 4to. Port., 96 plts., ptd. wraps. (SG. Aug.25; 158)　　　$650

GUERIN, Vict.
- **La Terre Sainte.** Paris, 1882-84. 2 vols. Fo. Orig. hf. leath., slightly rubbed, MS dedication on Vol 1 end-paper. (HK. Nov.8; 871)　　　DM 450
- – **Anr. Edn.** Paris, [1882-84]. 2 pts. in 2 vols. Fo. Elab. gt.-decor. cl., rubbed, extremities worn. (SG. Feb.2; 103)　　　$200

GUERIN DE BOUSCAL, Guyon
- **Don Quichotte de la Manche. Comédie.** 1639. *1st. Edn.* 4to. Cont. cf. (HD. Jan.24; 25)　　　Frs. 1,700

GUERIN MENEVILLE, Felix Edourd
- **Dictionnaire Pittoresque d'Histoire Naturelle et des Phénomènes de la Nature.** Paris, 1833-39. Vols. 1 & 2, 4-9. 4to. Cont. hf. leath., defect., 2 vols. lack spine, 1 vol. lacks half of spine. (D. Nov.23; 710)
　　　DM 3,200
- – **Anr. Edn.** Paris, 1834-39. 9 vols. Lge. 8vo. 720 engraved plts., heightened with col., hf. roan, spines decor., worn. (LM. Oct.22; 161)　　　B.Frs. 18,000

GUERINET, Armand
- **L'Architecture Française.** Paris, ca. 1900?. 14 vols. Tall fo. Approx. 840 photoplts., each liby.-stpd. on blank verso, loose in ptd. bds., linen ties. (SG. May 3; 189)　　　$130

GUERMONT, Remy de
- **Des Pensées Inédites.** Ill.:– Raoul Dufy. Paris, 1920. *(100) numbered.* Fo. 10 ll. preface & 1 lf. printers mark in MS. facs. by G. Apollinaire, 4 ll. in MS. facs. by de Gourmont, hf. mor. gt. (GB. May 5; 2354)　　　DM 850

GUERNIERI, Giovanni Francesco
- **Disegno del Monte Situato Presso la Citta Metropolitana di Cassel.** Kassel, 1706. *Re-iss. of the Rome, 1705 edn.* Fo. Titles with engraved armorial vig., 16 engraved plts. (7 double-p. & 3 folding), titles in Italian & Latin, text in Latin, Italian, German & Fr., minor tears in fold of 1 plt., creases in 3 plts., a few plts. slightly foxed, some browning thro.-out, cont. sheep, rubbed; sig. of Erasmus Philipps. (C. Mar.14; 9)　　*Weinreb.* £800
- **Plans et Desseins des Batimens.** Rome, 1749. Fo. Titles with engraved armorial vig., lge. engraved folding plan on 2 sheets, 4 lge. folding views, including 1 on 3 sheets, 13 plts., including 6 double-p., titles in Latin & Fr., text in Latin, Fr., German & Italian, sm. tear in fold of 1 view, old marb. paper bds., later mor. spine. (C. Dec.9; 61)
　　　Weinreb. £1,700

GUEROULT DU PAS, J.
- [–] **Les Différens Bâtimens de la Mer Océanne, présentez à Monsieur de Vanolles, Grand Audiencier de France et Trésorier Général de la Marine.** Paris, ca. 1710. Ob. 12mo. Cont. roan gt., spine decor. (HD. Jul.2; 16)　　　Frs. 3,000

GUERRA, Francisco
- **American Medical Bibliography, 1639-1783: a Chronological Catalogue.** Ed.:– Lawrence C. Wroth. N.Y., 1962. Cl. (SG. May 17; 112)　$100

GUERRAZI, F.D.
- **Pasquale Paoli ossia la Rotto di Pontenuovo.** Ill.:– Masutti, Vagani & others. Milano, 1864. *2nd. Edn.* 2 vols. Lge. 8vo. Cont. hf. roan, spines decor. (HD. Oct.21; 103)　　　Frs. 1,500

GUEVARA, Antonio de
- **Las Obras.** Valladolid, 1545. *2nd. Edn.* Fo. Some soiling & worming, old cf., worn. (SPB. Dec.13; 682)　　　$125
- **Speculum Religiosorum & Exercitum Virtuosorum.** Trans.:– [Aegidius Albertinus]. München, 1599. *1st. German Edn.* 1st. & last ll. slightly foxed & stained, cont. wood bds. & leath., 2 clasps, 1 with light worming. (HK. May 15; 60)
　　　DM 600

GUEVARA, Giovalli de
- **In Aristotelis Mechanicas Commentarii.** Rome, 1627. *1st. Edn.* 4to. Title with engraved vig. (lightly cold. red), some browning & foxing, cont. vell. gt., slightly soiled; Stanitz coll. (SPB. Apr.25; 201)
　　　$400

GUGLIELMINI, Domenico
- **Della Natura de'Fiumi Trattato Fisico-matematico.** Bologna, 1697. *1st. Edn.* 4to. 1 lf. torn, cont. vell.-bkd. bds.; Stanitz coll. (SPB. Apr.25; 202)　　　$200

GUIA DE BILBAO y Conductor del Viagero en Vizcaya
Bilbao, 1846. Cl. (DS. Apr.27; 2111)　Pts. 26,000

GUIA DE FORASTEROS en la Ciudad y Virreynato de Buenos Ayres para el Año de 1793
Buenos Aires, 1792. Leath. (DS. Oct.28; 2564)
　　　Pts. 55,000

GUIA DE FORESTEROS EN FILIPINAS
1857. Linen. (DS. Mar.23; 2127)　　Pts. 25,000

GUICCIARDINI, Francesco
- **La Historia de ...** Baeza, 1581. Fo. Port. reprd., 18th. C. bdg. (DS. Mar.23; 2128)　Pts. 150,000
- **Historie ... Containing the Warres of Italie & other Partes.** Trans.:– Geffray Fenton. L., 1579. *1st. Edn. in Engl.* Fo. Title device, woodcut initials & ornaments, device & 1st. ornament hand-cold., 1st. blank lf. before title mntd. with details of a Medici family tree in 17th. C. hand, few corners wormed, tiny rust-hole in 3T.4 & 4N.1, new cf. (S. Apr.10; 341)　　　*Maggs.* £210
- **The History of Italy from the Year 1490 to 1532.** Trans.:– A.P. Goddard. Chelmsford, 1753-56. 10 vols. Cont. cf., spines gt., by Johnson, some spine ends chipped, cont. bookseller's ticket. (C. Nov.9; 80a)　　　*Howes.* £90
- – **Anr. Copy.** 20 books in 10 vols. Cont. cf. gt. (LH. Sep.25; 538)　　　$140

GUICCIARDINI, Ludovico
- **Belgicae sive Inferioris Germaniae descriptio.** Amst., 1635. Vol. 2 only (of 2). 12mo. 28 folding maps & town plans, title reprd., cont. vell. bds. (S. Jun.25; 162)　　　*Loose.* £85
- **Belgium dat is Nederlandt ofte Beschrijvinge derselviger Provincien ende Steden.** Amst., 1648. *1st. Edn.* Fo. 98 plts., including some double-p., marb. cf., spine decor. (LM. Oct.22; 291)
　　　B.Frs. 175,000
- **Beschryving der Nederlanden.** Amst., 1660-62. 2 vols. 12mo. Lacks 6 double-p. plans, vell. (B. Jun.21; 484)　　　Fls. 950
- **Description de tout le Pais-Bas autrement dict la Germanie Inférieure, ou Basse-Allemagne.** Antw., 1568. Sm. fo. Plt. torn & reprd., cont. decor. cf., re-cased, spine & corners bumped. (SI. Dec.15; 16)
　　　Lire 1,100,000
- – **Anr. Edn.** Amst., 1625. Fo. Cont. vell. (D. Nov.23; 829)　　　DM 5,500
- **Descrittione di Tutti i Paesi Bassi.** Antw., 1567. Fo. Hand-cold. engraved title, arms & port. (partly bkd.), 16 hand-cold. double-p. maps, plans & plts. (all restored & lacking parts of plt.), wormhole in margin affecting few letters of text, mod. cf., w.a.f. (P. Sep.29; 233)　　　*Edmunds.* £150
- – **Anr. Edn.** Antw., 1588. Fo. Hf.-title, plts. browned, mainly at margins, some browning or spotting to text, sm. repair to 1 plan, cont. gt.-panel. vell., spine soiled. (C. May 30; 28)
　　　Burgess. £750
- – **Anr. Copy.** Fo. Engraved title, 61 engraved maps, some browning & staining, a little worming, vell., as a coll. of plts., w.a.f. (SPB. Dec.13; 496)　　$750
- **Omnium Relgii, sive Inferioris Germaniae,**

GUICCIARDINI, Ludovico -Contd.

Regionum Descriptio. Arnhem, J. Jansson, 1616. Ob. sm. fo. 9 full-p. maps, 99 town plans & 1 full-p. ill. of coats-of-arms, etc., 2 plans cut down & loose, 1 damaged, minor worming, mostly to margins, 1 or 2 weak impressions of plans, corner of 2M2 torn away & supplied (loose) from anr. copy, 1 or 2 other minor defects, cont. vell., as an atlas, w.a.f. (C. Jun.27; 34) *Dreesmann.* £900

GUIDE PITTORESQUE DU VOYAGEUR EN FRANCE

1838. Vols. 1-4 & 6. Cont. hf. cf., spine decor., worn. (HD. Jul.6; 40) Frs. 1,600
– – Anr. Edn. [1838]. 6 vols. Cont. hf. bdg., some staining. (HD. Feb.17; 13) Frs. 1,500

GUIDOL, J.

– **Goya, 1746-1828. Biografia, Estudio Analitico y Catalogo de sus Pinturas.** Barcelona, 1970. 4 vols. 4to. No bdg. stated. (SPB. Nov.30; 185) $175

GUIDOTT, Thomas

– **A Discourse of Bathe, and the Hot Waters There; also, Some Enquiries into the Nature of the Water of St. Vincent's Rock ... with an Account of the Lives & Character of the Physicians of Bathe.** L., 1676. *1st. Edn.* Few ll. lightly soiled, few holed in margins, slight text loss to 1, mod. cf., spine ends & extremities rubbed. [Wing G2192] (SG. Mar.22; 145) $200

GUIFFREY, Jules

– **Comptes des Batiments du Roi sous le Regne de Louis XIV.** Paris, 1881-1901. 5 vols. 4to. Cl., spines gt., orig. wraps. preserved. (BBA. Apr.5; 182) *Weinreb.* £150

GUIGARD, Joannes

– **Nouvel Armorial du Bibliophile.** Paris, 1890. 2 vols. Lge. 8vo. Cont. hf. chagrin, spines decor. (HD. Jun.6; 70) Frs. 2,100

GUIGO, I.

– **Statuta Ordinis Cartusiensis.** Ill.:– Urs Graf. Basel, 18.11.1510. 6 pts. in 1 vol. Fo. Wide margin, rubricated thro.-out & with many red pen initials, old MS. note at end, some slight foxing, spotting or staining, 18th. C. leath. gt., arms supralibros on both covers of Society of Writers to the Signet, worn & bumped. (HK. Nov.8; 211) DM 2,100

GUIJARRO, Miguel

– **Las Mujeres Españolas Portuguesas y Americanas.** Madrid, 1872-76. 3 vols. Fo. All plts. mntd., some slight spotting, cont. elab. gt. mor. by Zaehnsdorf. (BBA. Sep.29; 105) *Duran.* £320

GUILLAUME, A.

See— BAC, F. & Guillaume, A.

GUILLAUMET, G.

– **Tableaux Algériens ...** Paris, 1888. *Orig. Edn., (900). (100) Nominiative Iss. with 2 states of etchings & port (1 before the letter).* 4to. Lavallière mor. gt. by Magnin, watered silk doubl. & end-paper, unc. (HD. May 4; 293) Frs. 4,200

GUILLEMARD, Francis Henry Hill

– **The Cruise of the Marchesa to Kamschatka & New Guinea.** Ill.:– Keulemans. 1886. *[1st. Edn.].* 2 vols. Sm. 4to. Some plts. hand-cold., hf. mor. gt. (BBA. Sep.29; 76) *Thorp.* £110
– – Anr. Copy. 2 vols. Frontis.'s hand-cold., minor spotting to first & last few ll., orig. cl. gt. (TA. Sep.15; 10) £85

GUILLEMEAU, Jacques

– **Les Oeuvres de Chirurgie.** Paris, 1598. 2 pts. in 1 vol. Fo. Engraved titles, 33 plts. (1 folding), lacks engraved general title, also possibly 4 prelims., stained, several ll. with rough margin repairs, corners of 4 ll. cut away, 1 plt. defect., 1 torn, tear & sm. hole in x4 pt. 2, 18th. C. medical MS. bnd. in at end, 18th. C. cf., worn; Dr. Walter Pagel copy, w.a.f. (S. Feb.7; 151) *Phelps.* £380

GUILLEN, Jorge

– **7 Estudis per Máscares sobre Faunes de Picasso.** Intros.:– Vazquez Montalban & Terenci Moix. Ill.:– Guillen after models by Picasso. [Barcelona, 1981]. *(60) numbered, with each plt. & upr. cover*

numbered & sigd. Fo. 7 cold. etchings with relief printing, cut-out portions & onlays of string & hair, bds., upr. cover with papier mâché & collage relief decor. in acrylic, lr. cover with abstract brush design, linen ties. (PNY. Jun.6; 485a) $1,300

GUILLERMUS AVERNUS, Bp. of Paris

– **De Fide et Legibus.** [Augsburg, Gunther Zainer, 1475-76]. Fo. Rubricated, cont. hf. mor. over wood bds., traces of clasps; from Fondation Furstenberg-Beaumesnil. [H. 8317; BMC II, 319; Goff G417] (HD. Nov.16; 3) Frs. 7,500
– **Postilla super Epistolas et Evangelia.** [Reutlingen, Michael Greyff], ca. 1478. *[BMC's 2nd. Iss. (but see below)].* Fo. Colophon with 1st. iss. reading 'evage', also 1st. lf. with several variations from the 2nd. iss.: on line 2 'Gwillermus', line 6 ends with 'exper', on line 7 'ac', & on verso last line has lr. case 'i' in incipit, fully rubricated thro.-out, with rubricator's date at end of 1479, cont. MS. of Matthew on 27 blank ll. bnd. in at end, cont. stpd. pig over wood bds., lacks 1 metal clasp; the Walter Goldwater copy. [BMC II, 575; Goff G-653] (SG. Dec.1; 170) $3,600
– – Anr. Edn. Lyons, Jean de Vingle for S. Gueynard, 11 Feb. 1500/01. 4to. 256 ll. (of 260?, with note (in Dr. Scholderer's? hand) laid in stating that this copy lacks 4 prelims.), all histor. woodcuts & pict. woodcut initials hand-cold., initial on lf. 211 recto inscr. in red 'Conradus Z ... 1501', sm. hole & repair on fo. 1, some dampstaining, final blank with early writing on both sides, mod. vell.-bkd. bds.; the Walter Goldwater copy. [Goff G-707] (SG. Dec.1; 171) $1,700

GUILLERMUS BAUFET

– **Episcopus Parisiensis. Dialogus de Septem Sacramentis.** [Mainz, Jacob Meydenbach], ca. 1492. 4to. Rubricated, mod. cl.; the Walter Goldwater copy. [BMC I, 45; Goff G-720; H. 8310] (SG. Dec.1; 172) $500

GUILLIM, John

– **A Display of Heraldry.** 1679. *[5th. Edn.].* 2 pts. in 1 vol. Fo. Cont. cf. gt., rebkd. (P. Jun.7; 79) £75
– – Anr. Copy. Fo. Over 100 full-p. ports. & arms, many text woodcuts, mod. crimson three-qtr. mor. (SG. Apr.19; 100) $400
– – Anr. Edn. 1724. *6th. Edn.* Fo. 16 ports., 48 plts., cf., rebkd., new end-papers. (P. Mar.15; 189) *Ayres.* £120
– – Anr. Copy. Fo. 47 engraved plts., 17 ports., 1 extra plt. cropped & loosely inserted, woodcut coats-of-arms, few ll. spotted or browned, cont. cf., worn. (S. Apr.9; 214) *Russell.* £90
– – Anr. Copy. Fo. Fo. Most engraved plts. hand-cold., some ll. spotted or discold.,. Most engraved plts. hand-cold., some ll. spotted or discold., head of title cut away, cf., slightly worn. (S. Nov.8; 527) *McNulty.* £60

GUINOT, Eugène

– **L'été à Bade.** Ill.:– T. Johannot & others. Paris, [1847]. *1st. Edn.* Engraved port., 1 outl. cold. map, 11 (of 12) steel engraved views, 5 (of 6) cold. litho. costume plts. & many text woodcuts, orig. linen, gold & cold. decor. (R. Apr.4; 2290) DM 500
– – Anr. Edn. Paris, ca. 1855. *3rd. Edn.* Lacks 3 plts. & both ports., cont. leath. gt. (R. Oct.12; 2455) DM 850
– – Anr. Edn. Paris, [1857]. *2nd. Edn.* Port., cold. map, 6 cold. costume plts. & 12 views, publishers red mor., decor., centre arms, decor. spine, inner dentelle; Robert de Billy copy. (HD. Jan.30; 62) Frs. 1,900
– **A Summer at Baden-Baden.** L., [1853]. Engraved port., map, 18 engraved plts., including 6 hand-cold. costume plts., slight spotting, mostly marginal, orig. pict. cl. gt., rubbed. (S. Jun.25; 163) *Dupont.* £155
– – Anr. Copy. 4to. Port. frontis., map, 6 cold. costume plts., 12 view plts., some light foxing, three-qtr. mor. gt., spine nicked. (SG. Mar.29; 317) $300

GUINTERIUS, J.

– **Institvtionvm Anatomicarvm Secvndvm Galeni Sententiam ad Candidatos Medicinae Libri Quatuor.** Basel, 1536. *2nd. Edn.* Title with 2 owner's marks, some ll. with slight browning & worming in margin,

incunable paper covered bds. (HK. Nov.8; 212) DM 1,400

GUIOL

– [–] **Essai sur la Composition et l'Ornement des Jardins.** Paris, 1818. *1st. Edn.* Orig. pict. wraps., sm. slits, unc. (GB. Nov.3; 886) DM 600

GUISCHARDT, Charles

– **Mémoires Militaires sur les Grecs et les Romains où l'on a fidelement rétabli, sur le Texte de Polybe et des Tacticiens Grecs et Latins, la plupart de Bataille & des Grands Opérations de Guerre.** La Haye, 1758. 2 vols. in 1. 4to. Cont. diced cf. (HD. Feb.22; 86) Frs. 2,500

GUITRY, Sacha

– **De Jeanne d'Arc à Philippe Pétain.** Texts:– P. Benoît, G. Duhamel, Cocteau, Giraudoux, P. Morand, P. Vallery etc. Ill.:– P. Bonnard, Dignimont, A. Maillot, Utrillo etc. Paris, 1944. *(675) on chiffon.* Lge. 4to. Leaves, s.-c. (HD. Dec.9; 136) Frs. 1,500

GULIELMUS DE GOUDA

– **Expositio Mysteriorum Missae.** [Cologne, Peter Ther Hoernen], ca. 1486. 4to. Rubricated, lacks 1st. blank, stained, hf. vell.; G.W. Davis bkplt. [Goff G619] (SG. Feb.9; 253) $800

GULL, Fr.

– **Kinderheimath in Bildern und Liedern.** Foreword:– Gustav Schwab. Ill.:– F. Pocci. Stuttgart, 1846. Some slight foxing, bds., orig. upr. & lr. cover ills. mntd. (GB. Nov.4; 1875) DM 900

GULLY, John

– **New Zealand Scenery.** Ed.:– Dr. Julius Von Haast. L., 1877. Fo. Some adhesion to few plts., corner of 1 chipped, minor margin chipping, cl., brkn., ex-liby. (RO. Dec.11; 133) $350

GUMPERT, Thekla von

– **Hymnen für Kinder.** Ill.:– L. Richter. Berlin, 1846. *1st. Edn.* Cont. hf. linen. (GB. Nov.4; 1918) DM 450

GUMUCHIAN & Cie

– **Catalogue de Reliures du XVe au XIXe Siècle.** Paris, [1930]. *(1000).* Fo. Small hole thro' 1st. 4 ll., affecting a few words, later mor.-bkd. marb. bds.; H.M. Nixon coll., with some notes in his hand. (BBA. Oct.6; 167) *Quaritch.* £180
– – Anr. Edn. Paris, n.d. 4to. Cl. gt., upr. cover slightly marked. (LC. Oct.13; 40) £110
– **Les Livres de l'Enfance du XVe au XIXe Siècle.** [1930]. *(100).* 2 vols. 4to. 4 plts. replaced with photocopies, sewed. (HD. Mar.21; 159) Frs. 1,800

GUNN, Thom

– **Mandrakes.** Ill.:– Leonard Baskin. [L., Rampant Lions Pr., Camb., for] Rainbow Pr., [1973]. *(150) numbered & sigd.* Sm. fo. Qtr. vell., s.-c. (SG. May 24; 77) $250

GUNSAULUS, Helen C.

– **The Clarence Buckingham Collection of Japanese Prints: The Primitives.** Chic., [1955]. *(500) numbered.* Tall fo. 8 cold. plts., many reproductions, ex-liby., buckram. (SG. May 3; 190) $550

GUNTHER, J. Chr.

– **Gedichte.** Breslau & Leipzig, 1764. Lightly foxed, port. bkd., early 19th. C. hf. leath; MS. dedication on end-paper. (GB. May 4; 1304) DM 600
– **Sammlung bis anhero edirten Deutschen und Lateinischen Gedichten.** Ed.:– G. Fessel. Ill.:– Barth. Strahowsky. Breslau & Leipzig, 1735. *1st. Coll. Edn.* Minimal spotting, cont. vell., spines with 3 sm. nail holes; Hauswedell coll. (H. May 24; 1348) DM 800

GURK, E.

– **Abbildung der Neuesten Adjustirung der Tuerkischen Armee in Constantinopel.** Vienna, ca. 1830. 4to. Col. engraved title, 19 hand-cold. aquatints, each linen-bkd., with Engl. caption in lr. blank margin, MS. list of Turkish words tipped onto fly-lf., crude hf. leath.; sig. of H.W. Benham, U.S. Army. (SG. Sep.22; 158) $250

GURLITT, C.

- **Beschreibende Darstellung der Alteren Bau– und Kunstdenkmäler des Königreichs Sachsens.** Dresden, 1896-1923. Vols. 18, 20 (last pt.), 21-36 & 38-41. Sm. 4to. Not collated, orig. linen, 3 spines lightly discold. (H. May 22; 80) DM 840
- **Das Französische Sittenbild des Achtzehnten Jahrhunderts im Kupferstich.** Ill.:– A. Lambert. Berlin, 1913. *(100) on Van Gelder.* 4to. Publishers bordeaux mor., gt. decor., decor. spines, s.-c.; from F. Kettaneh liby. (HD. Dec.9; 138) Frs. 1,800

GURLITT, Fritz

- **Das Graphische Jahr.** Ill.:– L. Corinth, F. Meseck, M. Pechstein, & G. Grosz. Berlin, 1921. *(100)* *numbered & sigd. (50) with 4 sigd. orig. ills.* Orig. hf. leath., cold. cover litho., lightly soiled. (V. Oct.1; 4209) DM 1,600

GURLT, Dr. E.

- **Geschichte der Chirurgie.** Berlin, 1898. 3 vols. Cl.; Dr. Walter Pagel copy. (S. Feb.7; 152)
Phelps. £160

GURNEY, Joseph John

- **A Journey in North America, described in Familiar Letters to Amelia Opie.** Norwich, priv. ptd., 1841. Some foxing, cl., recased; inscr. by author. (SG. Oct.20; 169) $110
- **Notes on a Visit Made to Some of the Prisons in Scotland & the North of England in Company with Elizabeth Fry** ... 1819. *2nd. Edn.* later cl. gt. (KH. May 1; 329) Aus. $100

GURNEY, Thomas

- **Easy & Compendious System of Short Hand.** Ed.:– T. Sergeant. Ill.:– Birch after Sergeant. Phila., 17 Jun. 1799. *2nd. Amer. Edn.* 12mo. Cont. tree cf., slightly worn. (SG. Aug.4; 288) $110

GUSMAN, Pierre

- **L'Art Décoratif De Roma de la Fin de la Republique au IVe Siècle.** Paris, [1914]. 3 vols. Sm. fo. 180 plts., each liby.-stpd. on blank verso, loose in ptd. bd. folders, linen ties. (SG. May 3; 193) $120
- **La Villa Imperiale de Tibus.** Paris, 1904. Lge. 4to. Over 600 ills., liby. buckram, orig. gt.-pict. upr. wrap. bnd. in. (SG. May 3; 192) $140

GUTERMANN, Georg Friederich

- **Erklaerte Anatomie fuer Hebammen, samt derselben Nutzanwenung zur Praxi, nach Oberherrlichen Auftrage und Genehmhaltung Geschrieben.** Augsburg, 1752. *1st. Edn.* Sm. 8vo. Errata lf., index, disbnd. (SG. Oct.6; 180) $225

GUTH, P.

- **Memoires d'un Naïf.** Ill.:– Yves Brayer. Pujls, 1967. *(15) on vell.* 4to. Orig. full-p. aqua., sigd., added suite of all ills., each sigd., on japan nacré, leaves, wrap., box. (HD. Dec.16; 132) Frs. 1,100

GUTHE, Herm.

See— EBERS, Georg & Guthe, Herm.

GUTHERIUS, Jacobus

- **De Veteri jure Pontifico Urbis Romae Libri Quatuor.** Paris, 1612. *1st. Edn.* 4to. Ptd. slip pasted on lr. corner of V3, light margin dampstain towards end, pol. cf., spine gt., spine & hinges rubbed & worn; the Chatsworth copy. (S. Dec.20; 778)
Maggs. £70

GUTHMANN, Joh.

- **Eurydikes Wiederkehr in drei Gesängen.** Ill.:– Max Beckmann. 1909. *(35) numbered with lithos. on Strathmore Japan.* 4to. 9 orig. lithos., including 8 sigd., black mor., red mor. inlays, decor., cold. paper s.-c., by Paul Cassirer, 1909. (GB. Nov.5; 2274) DM 11,500

GUTHRIE, James

- **A Child's Good Day.** 1908. 16mo. Text tipped in as iss., orig. wraps.; pres. copy to George Buchanan. (P. Mar.15; 274) *Quaritch.* £110

GUTHRIE, William

- **Atlas to Guthrie's System of Geography.** 1811. Fo. 26 hand-cold. double maps, hf. russ., worn, w.a.f. (BBA. Jun.14; 256) *Faupel.* £160
- **A New Geographical, Historical, & Commercial Grammar; & Present State of the Several Kingdoms of the World.** Ill.:– Thomas Kitchen (maps). 1788.

11th. Edn. 20 folding engraved maps, & extra map of Capt. Cook's Voyages & engraved plt. of Artificial Sphere, cont. hf. roan. (TA. Sep.15; 115) £50

GUTIERREZ DE LA VEGA, J.

- **Los Perros de Caza Españoles.** Sevilla, 1890. *(200).* 4to. Rag paper, cl., wraps. (DS. Apr.27; 2676) Pts. 20,000

GUTIERREZ DE VEGAS, Fernando

- **Los Enredos de un Lugar o Historia de los Prodigios y Hazañas del Célebre Abogado de Conchuela el Licenciado Tarugo, del Famoso Escribano Corrales y Otros** ... Madrid, 1778-81. 3 vols. Orig. cf., flat spines. (DS. Dec.16; 2072) Pts. 22,000

GUTIERREZ SOLANA, José

- **Aguafuertes.** Ed.:– Ramon Gomez de la Serna. Madrid, 1963. *(230) numbered.* Lge. fo. 5 etchings, publisher cl. portfo. (DS. Jan.27; 2457) Pts. 250,000

GUTENBERG-GESELLSCHAFT

- **Veröffentlichungen.** Mainz, 1902-32. Vols. I-XXII, in 12 vols. 4to. Orig. wraps., bumped & browned, unc. (H. Nov.23; 83) DM 480

GUTTMANN, Heinrich

See— BOSSERT, Helmuth Theodor & Guttmann, Heinrich

GUYOT, Charles

- **Le Printemps sur la Neige.** Ill.:– Arthur Rackham. Paris, [1922]. *1st. Edn. (1300) numbered.* 4to. 16 mntd.cold. plts., three-qtr. mor., orig. wraps. bnd. in. (SG. Feb.16; 247) $225

GUYOT, Edme Gilles

- **Nieuwe Natuur– en Wiskonstige Vermaaklykheden** ... Rotterdam, 1771-75. 4 vols. Sm. 8vo. 77 folding engraved plts., most cont. hand-cold., cont. marb. cf., spines gt. (VS. Dec.9; 1316) Fls. 800
- **Nouvelles Récréations Physiques et Mathématiques.** Paris, 1798-1800-1798. *New Edn.* 3 vols. Minimal soiling, cont. leath. gt., lightly bumped & worn. (HK. Nov.8; 578) DM 700

GUYS, P.A.

- **Voyage Littéraire de la Grèce** ... 1783. 2 vols. Cont. red mor. (HD. Jun.29; 96) Frs. 3,000

GUZMAN, José Maria

- **Breve Noticia que da al Supreme Gobierno del Actual Estado del Territorio de la Alta California** ... Mexico, 1833. *1st. Edn.* Orig. plain paper wraps., tied as iss., hf. mor. s.-c. (LH. Apr.15; 317) $450

H., Madame

- **Galerie Industrielle, ou Application des Produits de la Nature aux Arts et Métiers** ... **à l'Usage de. l'Enfance et de la Jeunesse.** Paris, 1822. *1st. Edn.* Ob. 4to. Slightly spotted, cont. hf. roan, slightly rubbed; van Veen coll. (S. Feb.28; 73) £400

HAAN, F. de

- **Oud Batavia.** Bandoeng, 1935. *2nd. Printing.* Text vol. & atlas. 4to. Orig. cl. (VG. Mar.21; 698) Fls. 500

HAARLEM

- **Een Korte Beschrijvinge van de Stadt Haerlem, behels. de Voorn. Geschiedenissen.** Contrib.:– J.A. Leegh-water. Haerlem, 1669. 12mo. Upr. margins slightly short, mod. hf. vell.; Erven Ch. Enschedé bkplt. (VG. Sep.14; 1135) Fls. 850

HAAS, Aad de

- **De Dood en het Meisje.** Intro.:– Ko Sarneel. Dan Haag, 1973. *(90).* Lge. fo. 20 lino-cuts ptd. on japan by Nel de Haas, leaves, orig. box, cl. (B. Feb.8; 377) Fls. 700

HABERSHON, W.G.

- **Records of Old London.** Ca. 1880. Fo. Col. title, 36 mntd. col. plts., hf. mor., rubbed. (P. Mar.15; 190) *Marsden.* £55

HABERT, Abbé de Cerisy

- **La Vie du Cardinal de Berulle.** Paris, 1746. *Orig. Edn.* 4to. Ruled, cont. red mor. gt., arms of Charron Marquis de Mesnars, spines gt., sm. repair to upr. cover. (HD. May 3; 62) Frs. 3,000

HABICHT, T.

- **Die Rheingegend von Mainz bis Düsseldorf.** Ill.:– F. Foltz & others. Bonn, ca. 1845. Cold. litho. title & 60 steel engraved views, plts. stained in upr. & side margin thro-out, orig. hf. leath. gt., slightly rubbed & soiled. (R. Oct.12; 2692)
DM 3,000

HABINGTON, William

- **Castara.** L., 1640. *3rd. Edn. [1st. Compl. Edn.].* 3 pts. in 1 vol. 12mo. Lacks A3, printing fault with loss of text on 1 lf., cont. cf., spine gt. [STC 12585] (BBA. May 3; 123) *Hannas.* £65

HACHETTE, Jean Nicolas Pierre

- **Traité Elémentaire des Machines.** Paris [St. Petersb.], [1809]. *1st. Edn.* 4to. Hf.-title, browning & foxing, blank corner of 1 lf. reprd., mod. mor., unc., cl. s.-c.; Stanitz coll. (SPB. Apr.25; 203) $175
- – **Anr. Edn.** Paris & St. Petersb., 1811. *2nd. Edn.?.* 4to. Hf.-title, slight brown stain affecting a few margins, some paper flaws (no loss of text), orig. bds., rubbed; Stanitz coll. (SPB. Apr.25; 204) $175

HACHISUKA, Masauji

- **The Birds of the Philippine Islands.** L., 1931-35. 2 vols. Lge. 8vo. 101 plts., many cold., 2 folding maps, cl.-bkd. bds. (S. Apr.10; 421) *Evans.* £440
- – **Anr. Copy.** 2 vols. in 4 pts. Orig. wraps. (CSK. May 18; 176) £240

HACKENBROCH, Yvonne (Ed.)

See— UNTERMEYER, Irwin

HACKET, Bp. John

- [–] **Loiola [Stoicus Vapulans; Cancer; Paria].** L., 1648. *1st. Edn.* 4 pts. in 1 vol. 12mo. MS. cast-list (for the performances in 1622-23?) & extensive MS. emendations, dtd. at end 'Junii 27. 1665', a few line borders & headlines shaved, early 19th. C. pol. cf.; Duke of Devonshire bkplt., Chatsworth Liby. label. [Wing H 170] (S. Dec.8; 22)
Quaritch. £200

HACKETT, James

- **Narrative of the Expedition ... to join the South American Patriots.** L., 1818. Hf. cf. (P. Dec.8; 336)
Burton Garbett. £180

HACKLANDER, F.W.

See— STIELER, Karl, Wachenhusen, K.S.H. & Hacklander, F.W.

HACKNEY, Louise Wallace & Chang-Foo, Yau

- **A Study of Chinese Paintings in the Collection of Ada Small Moore.** 1940[-41]. Fo. Supp. loosely inserted, orig. cl. (BBA. Nov.10; 294) *Howes.* £60

HADELN, Detlev F. von

- **Venezianische Zeichnungen der Hochrenaissance.** Berlin, 1925. 4to. Orig. cl., spine faded. (BBA. Sep.8; 60) *Quaritch.* £50
- **Venezianische Zeichnungen des Quattrocento.** Berlin, 1925. 4to. Orig. cl., spine faded. (BBA. Sep.8; 61) *Quaritch.* £50

HADEN, Sir Francis Seymour

- **About Etching.** [L.], 1879. 2 pts. in 1 vol. Sm. fo. Etching as frontis., 15 facs., ex-liby., orig. qtr. mor., worn. (SG. May 3; 194) $200

HADFIELD, William

- **Brazil & the River Plate.** L., 1877. With supp. Leath. (D. Nov.23; 1306) DM 730

HAEBLER, Konrad

- **Bibliografia Iberica de Siglo XV.** The Hague & Leipzig, 1903; 1917. 2 vols. 4to. Vell. gt., orig. wraps. bnd. in. (SG. May 17; 117) $225
- **Deutsche Bibliophilen des 16. Jahrhunderts.** Leipzig, 1923. *(20) De Luxe Edn.* Fo. Orig. leath. gt. (R. Apr.3; 637) DM 700
- **The Early Printers of Spain & Portugal.** 1897. 4to. Orig. buckram-bkd. bds., spine stained; H.M. Nixon coll. (BBA. Oct.6; 184) *Quaritch.* £80
- – **Anr. Copy.** 4to. Liby. stp. on some pp., cont. mor.-bkd. cl. (BBA. Nov.10; 68) *Duran.* £60
- – **Anr. Copy.** 4to. Frontis., 33 plts., hf. linen, partly unc.; armorial bkplt. of Sir D'Arcy Power. (SG. Jan.5; 179) $200
- **The Study of Incunabula.** N.Y., Grol. Cl., 1933.

HAEBLER, Konrad -*Contd.*

1st. Edn. in Engl. (350) numbered. Orig. cl., d.-w. stained. (SG. Jan.5; 180) $275
- - **Anr. Copy.** Gt.-decor. cl. (SG. May 17; 118) $150
- **Der Westeuropäische Wiegendruck in Original-Typenbeispielen.** München, 1928. *(103). (13) hand-numbered.* 2 vols: text vol. & plt. vol. 60 specimen ll. from incunables, orig. cl. (LM. Oct.22; 229b) B.Frs. 130,000

HAECKEL, Ernst
- **Anthropogenie oder Entwickelungsgeschichte des Menschen.** Leipzig, 1874. *1st. Edn.* Margins lightly browned & some soiling, cont. leath., worn. (HK. Nov.8; 579) DM 400
- **Kunstformen der Natur.** Leipzig & Wien, [1899-]1904. With Supp. vol. Lge. fo. Orig. linen, lr. cover worn. (V. Sep.29; 1664) DM 550
- **Natürliche Schöpfungsgeschichte.** Berlin, 1868. *1st. Edn.* Title & end-paper stpd., cont. hf. leath. gt. (GB. May 3; 1058) DM 600

HAEFTEN, Benedictus van
[-] **The School of the Heart.** Trans.:- [Christopher Harvey]. L., 1676. 12mo. Engraved frontis., orig. ills. pasted over with 47 emblematic engrs. from an earlier edn., 1 engr. defect., 1 blank margin torn, cf. gt., rebkd. [Wing H185a] (BBA. Mar.21; 196) *Baldwin.* £95

HAEMMERLE, Albert
- **Buntpapier.** Munich, 1961. 4to. 18 specimens of cold. paper, orig. cl.-bkd. bds., d.-w., s.-c.; H.M. Nixon coll., with his sig., & MS. notes on front free end-paper & loosely inserted. (BBA. Oct.6; 57) *Temperley.* £120

HAEMSTEDE, A.C. van & others
[-] **De Historie der Martelaren ... tot 1655 ... Met Vervolg –1686.** Ed.:- J. G[ysius] O[stendanus]. Ill.:- C. Bruin. Leiden, 1747. Fo. Cont. red mor. gt., decor., mor. inlay; from Koch liby. (VG. Nov.30; 953) Fls. 1,800

HAER, Fl. van der
- **De Initiis Tumultuum Belgicorum ... Libri II.** Douai, 1587. *1st. Edn.* Sm. 8vo. Cont. mott. cf., spine richly gt. (VG. Sep.14; 1159) Fls. 480

HAESAERTS, Luc & Paul
- **Flandre. Essai sur l'Art Flamand depuis 1880. L'Impressionisme.** Paris, 1931. *(1000) numbered on Papier Couché, Strathesk.* 4to. Publisher's bds. (LM. Mar.3; 72) B.Frs. 13,000

HAFIZ, S.M., of Shiraz
- **Eine Sammlung Persischer Gedichte.** Trans.:- G. Fr. Daumer. Ill.:- F.H.E. Schneidler. Jena, 1912. Orig. red mor. gt. (GB. Nov.5; 2990) DM 640
- - **Anr. Copy.** Orig. red leath., bd. s.-c. (HK. Nov.10; 2478) DM 410
- - **Anr. Edn.** Trans.:- G. Fr. Daumier. Ill.:- F.H.E. Schneidler. Jena, 1912. *(50) numbered on Bütten.* Orig. linen gt. (V. Oct.1; 4039) DM 420

HAGELSTANGE, R.
- **Balthasar.** Ill.:- F. Masereel. 1951. *1st. Edn. (600) numbered.* 4to. 8 full-p. orig. woodcuts, dedication on end-paper, orig. pict. bds.; printer's mark sigd. by author & artist. (GB. Nov.5; 2781) DM 450
- **Der Grosse Filous.** Ill.:- K.H. Hansen-Bahia. Hamburg, 1975. Lge. 4to. 27 orig. cold. woodcuts, orig. pict. bds; printer's mark sigd. by author & artist. (GB. May 5; 2647) DM 400

HAGEN, Fr. H. von der
- **Minnesinger.** Leipzig, 1838 & Berlin, 1856-61. *1st. Complete Edn.* Atlas & supp. atlas in 5 vols. 4to. & lge. 4to. Plts. of supp. atlas bnd. in main vol., vols. I-III with monog. GB on titles, atlas loose, cont. hf. leath., gt. spine, bumped & worn, 3 spots, newer linen & hf. linen; Hauswedell coll. (H. May 24; 1349) DM 950
- **Der Nibelungen Lied.** Berlin, 1807. *1st. Edn.* Hf. linen, ca. 1870. (HK. Nov.10; 2625) DM 580

HAGEN, V.W. von
- **La Fabricacion del Papel entre los Aztecas y los Mayas.** Ed.:- Dard Hunter. Trans.:- J. Romero. Mexico City, [1945]. *(750) numbered.* 4to. 2 paper

specimens tipped in, orig. cl., d.-w. (SG. Jan.5; 246) $125

HAGER, H.
- **Handbuch der Pharmaceutischen Praxis.** Berlin, 1880. 2 vols. Orig. hf. leath., slightly rubbed. (GB. May 3; 995) DM 420

HAGGADAH
(arranged chronologically)
- **Haggadah Shel Pessach.** Commentary:- Don Yitzhak Abarbanel. Riva di Trento, 1561. Fo. Unpaginated, owners' stp. & sigs. on title, mod. blind-tooled mor., s.-c. (S. Oct.24; 166) *Davis.* £2,200
- **Haggadah Shel Pessah-Chiluka De'rababbanan.** Amst., 1695. 4to. With commentaries Mate Aron, Ktonet Passim, Shnei Luchot Habrit, instructions in Yiddish, part of last lf. in facs., lightly stained, mod. hf. leath., w.a.f. (S. Oct.25; 31) £260
- **Haggadah Shel Pessah.** Commentary:- Don Yitzhak Abarbanel. Yiddish trans.:- Chad Gadya. Amst., 1712. Fo. Also with commentary Mate Aron, title worn, not affecting engr., artist's name Abran Bar Yakov faded, lr. margins torn not affecting text, map of Palestine split in centre without loss of text, orig. leath., central gold medallions, w.a.f. (S. Oct.25; 32) £800
- **[Haggada].** Commentary:- Abarbanel & others. Amst., 1712. Sm. fo. Stains, some worming with negligible loss, map stained, remargined & reinforced at folds, sm. tear with loss, old hf. leath., worn, covers loose. (SG. Feb.2; 180) $2,200
- **Nasu'Kol Magid David Haggadah Shel Pessach.** Commentary:- Joseph David Aiash. Livorno, 1720. 4to. Slightly creased, hf. leath., patterned bds., slightly worn. (S. Oct.24; 167) *Bragadin.* £150
- **[Haggadah].** Commentary:- Eliezer Ashkenazi. Fuerth, 1754. Sm. fo. Stained, a few ll. slightly frayed at edges, sm. tear & wormholes in title minimally affecting text, cl.-bkd. bds. (SG. Feb.2; 182) $425
- **Passover Haggadah.** Amst., 1765. 4to. In Hebrew & Yiddish with commentaries Eli Esh & Zevach Pessach, lightly stained, bds., w.a.f. (S. Jul.3; 104) £220
- **Haggadah Shel Pessah [Bet Chorin].** Amst., 1781. 4to. Lacks map of Palestine, lightly stained, orig. leath., new spine, w.a.f. (S. Oct.25; 33) £350
- **Passover Haggadah.** Amst., 1783. 4to. In Hebrew & Old Yiddish, stained, browned, cl., w.a.f. (S. Jul.3; 105) £200
- - **Anr. Copy.** 4to. In Hebrew & Old Yiddish, stained & soiled, hf. leath., marb. bds. (S. Oct.24; 168) *Durschlag.* £130
- **Pessach Me'ubin Haggadah Shel Pessach.** Ed.:- Chaim Benveniste. Livorno, 1788. 4to. Owners' sigs. on title, some staining, discold., lr. corner of last lf. torn without loss of text, bds., slightly worn. (S. Oct.24; 169) *Durschlag.* £200
- **Shevach Pessach. Haggadah Shel Pessach.** Commentary:- Ishmael Cohen, of Modena. Livorno, 1790. Fo. Stained & browned, bds., worn. (S. Oct.24; 170) *Schimmel.* £140
- **[Haggadah Shel Pessah].** Commentary:- Elisha Chabilio. Livorno, 1794. Instructions in Ladino, lightly browned, hf. cl., w.a.f. (S. Oct.25; 35) £180
- **[Haggadah].** Offenbach, 1795. 12mo. Few ll. with minimal browning, dyed vell. (SG. Feb.2; 184) $275
- **Passover Haggadah. Maale Bet Chorin.** Vienna, 1804. 4to. Very stained, bds., w.a.f. (S. Jul.3; 106) £190
- **Haggadah Shel Pessach Minhag Sefaradim.** L., 1813. 4to. In Hebrew & Spanish, lacks Slaves of Egypt plt., maps reprd. with some loss, some ll. torn & crudely reprd., some foxing, mod. blind-tooled mor. (S. Oct.24; 172) *Davis.* £1,500
- **Passover Haggadah. Maale Bet Chorin.** 1813. 4to. Stained, bds., w.a.f. (S. Jul.3; 107) £180
- **Seder Haggadah Le'Pessach Im Otiot Gedolot Ve'Gam Im Ziurim.** Amst., 1815. In Hebrew & Yiddish, soiled & stained, trimmed, bds. (S. Oct.24; 173) *Davis.* £150
- **Haggadah Zikhron Yetsi'at Mitsrayim.** Vienna, 1815. Sm. 8vo. Scattered stains, later qtr. leath., extremities worn. (SG. Feb.2; 187) $200
- **Passover Haggadah. Maale Bet Chorin.** Vienna,

1823. 4to. Stained, bds., detchd., w.a.f. (S. Jul.3; 109) £190
- **[Haggadah].** Livorno, 1827. Sm. 4to. With Spanish trans., stained, edges frayed or chipped with some loss, disbnd. (SG. Feb.2; 188) $110
- ... **Meforash be-Ma'amar Afikoman.** Sulzbach, 1830. 12mo. Some staining, hf. leath., worn, crudely rebkd. (SG. Feb.2; 189) $130
- **Haggadah Shel Pessach Im Ha'Pitaron Bilshon Sefaradi.** Livorno, 1839. 4to. Some worming not affecting text, some staining, hf. cl. (S. Oct.24; 174) *Davis.* £150
- **Seder Haggada le-Leil Shemarim ... / Service for the First Nights of Passover according to the Custom of the German & Polish Jews.** Trans.:- A.P. Mendes. L., 1862. *2nd. Edn.* In Hebrew & Engl., some staining, orig. cl., rubbed, extremities slightly worn. (SG. Feb.2; 190) $325
- ... **Service for the Two First Nights of Passover, with an English Translation.** N.Y., 1863. *7th. (Stereotype) Edn.* Scattered browning. cont. qtr. cl., extremities worn. (SG. Feb.2; 191) $375
- **Haggadah Shel Pessach.** Music:- M. Naumbourg. Trans.:- A. Ben Baruch Crehange. Paris, 1864. 12mo. In Hebrew & Fr., few stains, cl., w.a.f. (S. Oct.25; 43) £280
- - **Anr. Edn.** Livorno, 1864. 4to. In Hebrew & Italian, some staining, bds. (S. Oct.24; 176) *Davis.* £160
- - **Anr. Edn.** L., 1879. In Hebrew & Engl., lightly stained, cl., w.a.f. (S. Oct.25; 50) £140
- - **Anr. Edn.** L., 1885. In Hebrew & Engl., lightly stained, cl., w.a.f. (S. Oct.25; 55) £190
- **Haggadah Shel Pessach Im Serach Aravi.** Bombay, 1887. In Hebrew & Judaeo-Arabic, stained & browned, edges frayed, bds. (S. Oct.24; 179) *J.T.S.* £130
- **Baghdad rite, in Hebrew & Arabic.** Livorno, 1887. Sm. 4to. Leatherette. (SG. Feb.2; 193) $100
- **Die Darmstader Pessach-Haggadah.** Leipzig, 1927. *Facs. Edn.* 2 vols., including plt. vol. Lge. 4to & fo. Limitation lf. removed, slight traces of browning, orig. mor.-bkd. bds., plt. vol. with publisher's s.-c., slight rubbing. (SPB. Feb.1; 3) $1,800
- - **Anr. Edn.** Leipzig, 1927[-28]. *(15)? in facs. bdg.* Facs. vol. only. Fo. Elab. blind-tooled leath., brass corner & centrepieces & clasps, in facs. of orig. bdg., defect. folding bd. case. (SG. Feb.2; 197) $4,800
- **Haggadah Shel Passah.** Trans.:- Cecil Roth. Ill.:- Albert Rutherston. Soncino Pr., 1930. *(110) numbered. (100) on H.M.P.* 4to. In Hebrew & Engl., orig. mor. gt., spine & edges worn, s.-c. worn; inscr. 'for Eric Lipson with affection, Cecil Roth'. (S. Nov.22; 361) *Pappenheim.* £270
- **Haggadah.** Trans.:- Cecil Roth. Ill.:- Arthur Szyk. L., Sun Engr. Co., for the Beaconsfield Pr., 1939. *British Empire Iss., (125) numbered on vell., sigd. by trans. & artist.* Lge. 4to. In Hebrew & Engl., lev. mor. gt. by Sangorski & Sutcliffe, spine gt., mor. inner dentelles gt., ptd. silk liners, velvet-lined hf. mor. gt. folding box. (C. Nov.9; 175) *Gregory.* £6,800
- - **Anr. Copy.** Lge. 4to. In Hebrew & Engl., lev. mor. gt. by Sangorski & Sutcliffe, lined in silk, velvet-lined box, w.a.f. (S. Jul.3; 114) £4,200
- - **Anr. Copy.** Lge. 4to. Lev. mor. gt. by Sangorski & Sutcliffe, lined in silk, velvet-lined box, w.a.f. (S. Jul.3; 113) £4,000
- - **Anr. Copy.** Lge. 4to. Mor. gt. extra by Sangorski & Sutcliffe, hf. mor. gt. folding box, spine slightly chipped. (SPB. Feb.1; 48) $6,500
- **La Haggadah de Pesaj.** Trans.:- Prof. Zelik Shifmanovich. Ill.:- Yosef Durno. Mexico, 1946. Sm. 4to. In Hebrew & Spanish, pict. cl. (SG. Feb.2; 201) $110
- **Die Darmstädter Pessach-Haggadah.** Ed.:- J. Gutmann & others. Ill.:- G. de Beauclair. Berlin, [1972]. Facs. & text vol. Lge. 4to. German & Engl. text, orig. hf. leath. (H. Nov.23; 64) DM 650
- **Passover Haggadah [Reproduction of Amsterdam Haggadah of 1712].** Milano, 1980. *(79) numbered.* Fo. On vell., leath., velvet case, w.a.f. (R. Oct.25; 121) £700

See— **ME'AH BRACHOT [with Passover Haggadah, Hebrew & Ladino]**

HAGGARD, Sir Henry Rider
- **A Farmer's Year.** 1899. *(100) numbered on L.P.* 4to. Margins browned, orig. bds., spine soiled. (CSK. Apr.27; 163)   £55
- **The Missionary & the Witch-Doctor.** N.Y., 1920. Darkening, wraps., irregularly darkened, spine chipping. (CBA. Oct.29; 369) $1,100
- **Montezuma's Daughter.** L., 1893. *1st. Edn.* Cl., worn, spine ends slightly chipped; pres. copy sigd. & inscr. by author, photo of author loosely inserted. (RO. Apr.23; 156) $190
- - **Anr. Edn.** Ill.:– Maurice Greiffenhagen. L., 1898. Some foxing, no bdg. stated, 1 corner bumped & rubbed; sigd. by author & dtd. 1900. (CBA. Oct.29; 370) $160
- **Works.** 1884-87. 11 vols. Hf. mor. gt., spines faded. (P. Sep.29; 138)   *Spake.* £440

HAGGER, Conrad
- **Neues Saltzburgisches Koch-Buch. Für Hochfürstl. u. andere Vornehme Höfe, Clöster, Herren-Häuser** ... Ausgb., 1719. 4to. Lacks frontis. & title, replaced in photocopy, lacks 2 prelim. ll., 2 copper engrs. & 1 text lf. pt. 3 with lr. tear, a few ll. in 1st. bk. slightly browned or spotted, cont. blind-tooled pig over wood bds., decor., spine slightly wormed, 2 clasps. (HK. May 16; 1467) DM 5,300

HAGUE, Arnold
See— **UNITED STATES GEOLOGICAL SURVEY**

HAHN, L.
- **Friedrich der Grosse.** Berlin, 1855. 4to. Hf. linen. (D. Nov.24; 3632)   DM 540

HAHN, Otto & Strassman, F.
- **Ueber die Entstehung von Radiumisotopen aus Uran durch Bestrahlen mit Schnellen und Verlangsamten Neutronen.** Berlin, 18 Nov. 1938. *1st. Edn.* 'Die Naturwissenschaften', Vol. 26, no. 46, pp. 755-56. 4to. Sm. margin stain with chipping, orig. wraps., some browning, article name underlined in red; Stanitz coll. (SPB. Apr.25; 206) $850

HAHNEMANN, S.
- **Organon der Heilkunst.** Dresden, 1824. Cont. marb. bds. (HK. May 15, 408)   DM 420

HAHNLOSER, Hans R.
- **Villard de Honnecourt. Kritische Gesamtausgabe des Bauhuttenbuches ms. fr 19093 der Pariser Nationalbibliothek.** Vienna, 1935. *1st. Edn.* Lge. 4to. Orig. cl., d.-w., 1 corner slightly bumped, slight darkening of d.-w. spine; Stanitz coll. (SPB. Apr.25; 207) $125

HAIDER, M.
- **Die Jagd in Bildern.** München, [1862]. 4to. Title vig., 1 text woodcut & 50 woodcut plts., wear, cont. hf. linen. (BR. Apr.12; 1204)   DM 450

HAI GAON
- **Ha'Mikach Ve'Hamimkar.** Venice, 1602. *1st. Edn.* 1st. & last ll. defect. & reprd. affecting some letters, staining thro.-out, slightly creased, cl. (S. Oct.24; 193)   *Sol.* £180
- **Pitron Halomot.** Venice, 1623. *1st. Edn.* 16mo. Dampstained & soiled, trimmed slightly, affecting title border, mod. cl. (SG. Feb.2; 206) $800

HAI GAON, attributed to
- **Mishpetei Shavuot Ve'Dinei Mamonot.** Venice, 1602. *1st. Edn.* 4to. Slight staining, short tears in margins of last lf. reprd. without loss of text, cl. (S. Oct.24; 194)   *Sol.* £180

HAILE, Martin
- **James Francis Edward the Old Cavalier.** L., 1907. Extra-ill. with 12 plts., a few hand-cold., a few ll. slightly spotted, mor., elab. gt., by Bayntun (Rivière), upr. cover inlaid with miniature hand-painted port. of Clementina Walkinshaw, boxed. (S. Oct.4; 115)   *Joseph.* £360

HAILEY, C.
- **Thoroughbred Sires.** Newmarket, 1908. Ob. 4to. 63 plts., orig. cl. gt. (P. Dec.8; 209)   *Allen.* £55

HAILS, W.A.
- **An Enquiry Concerning the Invention of the Life Boat** ... Gateshead, 1806. Title slightly spotted, hf.

cf. gt.; pres. copy to R. Murray. (P. Jan.12; 229)   *Quaritch.* £80

HAINES, Elijah M.
- **Historical & Statistical Sketches of Lake County, State of Illinois** ... Waukegan, Illinois, 1852. *1st. Edn.* 16mo. Orig. ptd. wraps., imprint on upr. wrap. partly obliterated. (LH. Apr.15; 318) $325

HAIR, T.H.
See— **ROSS, Metcalf & Hair, T.H.**

HAJEK-HALKE, Heinz
- **Experimentelle Fotografie.** Contrib.:– Robert d'Hooghe. Bonn, 1955. *1st. Edn.* 4to. Cl., d.-w. rubbed. (SG. May 10; 60) $100

HAJOS, E.M. & Zahn, L.
- **Architektur der Nachkriegszeit.** Intro.:– E. Redslob. Berlin, [1928]. 4to. Orig. linen. (GB. Nov.3; 273)   DM 400

HAKE, Henry M.
See— **O'DONOGHUE, Freeman Marius & Hake, Henry M.**

HAKEWILL, James
- **The History of Windsor & its Neighbourhood.** 1813. 4to. Subscribers list, hf. cf., spine gt.-decor.; Henry Carrington Bowles bkplt. (SKC. Mar.9; 1981)   £85
- **A Picturesque Tour of Italy.** L., 1820. 4to. Extra engraved title, engraved views & plans, some spotting, hf. mor. (S. Apr.9; 30)   *Perham.* £140
- - **Anr. Copy.** 4to. 63 steel engrs., browning, hf. cf., spine defect. (CR. Jun.6; 179)   Lire 380,000

HAKLUYT, Richard
- **The Principall Navigations, Voiages & Discoveries of the English Nation.** L., 1589. *1st. Edn.* Fo. With the 12 unnumbered pp. relating to Drake's voyages inserted between pp. 643 & 644, & 2nd. iss. of Bowes ll., owners inscrs. & pen-trials on title & at end, wormholes affecting lr. margin of 1st. ll., portion of fore-margin in B2 to B5, weak with slight loss of letters, sm. rustholes affecting individual letters in A4 & 2X3, corner torn from 205 with loss of p. no., a few ll. slightly soiled or with light stains at beginning & end, without a map as sometimes found, russ., covers detchd. [STC 12625; Sabin 29594] (S. May 21; 165)
                                    Quaritch. £1,200
- - **Anr. Edn.** L., 1599. *3rd. Edn.* Vols. I & II only (of 3) in 1. Fo. Title a little creased, short tear in a1 & a2, sm. hole in Rrr4 with slight loss of text, slight dampstain towards end, cont. cf., lacks ties. [Sabin 29596/7; STC 12626a] (C. Jun.27; 35)
                                    Scott. £350
- - **Anr. Edn.** L., 1599-1600. 3 vols. in 2. Fo. Church's 1st. Iss. of 'The Voyage to Cadiz' in Vol. 1, with p. 608 misnumbered 605, sm. rust hole to Cc4 in Vol. 2, a few slight spots, vol. 2 ll. of Vol. 1 rehinged. [Sabin 29596-8; STC 12626] *(With:)*
- **A Selection of** ... **Voyages** ... **intended as a Supplement.** L., 1812. 1 vol. 4to. [Sabin 29600] Together 3 vols. Unif. 19th. C. russ. gt., 1st. vol. rebkd. with orig. backstrip laid down, upr. jnt. of 2nd. vol. & jnts. of last vol. worn; the Minto & Rt. Hon. Visc. Eccles copies. (CNY. Nov.18; 128)
                                    $3,500
- - **Anr. Edn.** L., 1809-12. *(250) on royal paper.* 5 vols. 4to. Hf. cf., rebkd. in mor., worn. (SPB. Dec.13; 447) $350
- - **Anr. Edn.** Glasgow, 1903-05. *(100) numbered.* 12 vols. Plts. & maps on japan paper, orig. vell.-bkd. cl., lightly soiled. (CSK. Jan.13; 5)   £240
- - **Anr. Edn.** Glasgow, 1903-05. 12 vols. Orig. cl. gt., untrimmed. (SKC. Mar.9; 2014)   £100
- - **Anr. Edn.** Intro.:–John Masefield. L., 1927-28. 10 vols., including 2 supp. vols. Orig. cl., d.-w.'s chipped. (KH. Nov.8; 194)   Aus. $100

HAKLUYT SOCIETY
- **[Publications].** 1946-74. Series II: Vols. 93-142, 144-145. Orig. cl. gt., 36 vols. with d.-w. (P. Dec.8; 355)   *Quaritch.* £360

HALBERSTADT, V.
See— **DUCHAMP, Marcel & Halberstadt, V.**

HALCYON. Driemaandelijks Tijdschrift voor Boek-, Druk– en Prentkunst
Rijswijk, 1940-41. Pts. 1-4 & 6-12 only (of 12), in

9 vols. Fo. With article on Escher (often missing), including 2 woodcut plts. & 2 woodcut ills., loose as iss. in orig. portfos., uncollated, w.a.f. (VS. Dec.7; 52)   Fls. 1,100

HALDORSON, Biörn
- **Lexicon Islandico-Latino-Danicum.** Copen., 1814. 2 vols. in 1. Sm. 4to. Later cf., spine gt. (BBA. Mar.7; 76)   *D. Loman.* £65

HALE, Edward Everett
- **The Man Without a Country.** Boston, 1865. *1st. Edn.* 12mo. Without publisher's announcement, a few ll. soiled, ptd. wraps., detchd., spine chipped, qtr. mor. folding case, rubbed; clipped inscr. 'I am glad to do what you wish. Edward E. Hale.' mntd. on rear blank. (SG. Dec.8; 188) $175

HALE, Sir Matthew
- **A Discourse Touching a Provision for the Poor.** 1683. Red str.-grd. mor. (BS. Nov.16; 22)   £130

HALE, Sarah Josepha
- **Flora's Interpreter; or, the American Book of Flowers & Sentiments.** Boston, ca. 1840. *14th. Edn.* Sm. 8vo. 2 hand-cold. plts., orig. gt.-floral cl., spine ends nicked; from liby. of F.D. Roosevelt, inscr. by him (as Governor). (SG. Mar.15; 51) $225

HALE, Thomas
- **A Compleat Body of Husbandry.** 1756. Fo. Engraved frontispiece & 13 plts., 1 folding, 1 with letterpress explanation ptd. on recto & verso, some light offsetting, cont. cf., spine label chipped. (CSK. Apr.27; 52)   £150
- - **Anr. Copy.** Fo. Cont. cf. gt. (P. Dec.8; 133)
                                    Traylen. £75
- - **Anr. Copy.** Fo. Frontis. & double-p. plt. torn without loss, cont. cf., covers detchd. (TA. Nov.17; 315)   £50

HALENZA'S RHEINISCHES ALBUM
See— **FOLTZ, F.**

HALES, Stephen
- **A Description of Ventilators.** 1743. *1st. Edn.* Cf.-bkd. marb. bds., unc., 18th. C. armorial bkplt. (SKC. May 4; 1729)   £270
- **Instructions pour les Mariniers, contenant la Manière de rendre l'eau de Mer Potable** ... Den Haag, 1740. Cont. leath. gt., rubbed. (R. Apr.4; 2139)
                                    DM 620
- **Vegetable Staticks: or, an Account of some Statical Experiments on the Sap in Vegetables** ... 1727. *1st. Edn.* *(With:)* - **Statical Essays: containing Haemastaticks: or, an Account of some Hydraulick & Hydrostatical Experiments made on the Blood & Blood-Vessels of Animals.** 1733. *1st. Edn.* Together 2 vols. Cont. panel. cf. (SKC. May 4; 1728)   £320

HALEVY, Ludovic
- **L'Abbé Constantin.** Ill.:– Madeleine Lemaire. Paris, 1888. Jansenist mor. gt. by Canapé, satin doubls., watered silk end-ll., wrap. & spine, s.-c.; 9 added orig. watercolours by F. Coindre (2 on doubles., 1 as hf.-title & 6 in vol. on japan). (HD. Mar.27; 75)   Frs. 3,200
- **La Famille Cardinal.** Intro:– Marcel Guérin. Ill.:– Edgar Degas, engraved by Maurice Potin. Paris, 1939. *(350) on Rives.* 4to. Leaves, box. (HD. May 4; 295)   Frs. 3,500
- - **Anr. Copy.** Fo. Hf. mor., orig. wraps. bnd. in. (GB. May 5; 2317)   DM 1,800

See— **MEILHAC, H. & Halevy, Ludovic**

HALEY, J. Evetts
- **The Xit Ranch of Texas. And the Early Days of the Llano Estacado.** Chic., 1929. *1st. Edn.* Cl. (LH. Sep.25; 232) $200

HALFORD, Frederick M.
- **An Angler's Autobiography.** L., 1903. *(100) numbered & sigd.* Mor. gt., spine emblematically tooled, faded, partly unc. (S. Oct.4; 26)   *Angle.* £300
- **Dry Fly Entomology.** L., 1897. *(100) numbered & sigd.* 2 vols. 28 plts., 100 artificial flies in 12 sunken mounts, slightly spotted, red hf. mor. gt., spines emblematically tooled, by Bayntun; bkplt. of Bibliotheca Piscatoria Lynniana. (S. Oct.4; 30)
                                    Nolan. £800

HALFORD, Frederick M. -Contd.

- Dry-Fly Fishing in Theory & Practice. L., 1889. *(100)* numbered & sigd. 26 mntd. plts., including frontis., text ills. on India paper, mor. gt., partly unc. (S. Oct.4; 24) *Head.* £190
- The Dry-Fly Man's Handbook. A Complete Manual ... 1913. *1st. Edn. (100) De Luxe Edn.,* sigd. 4to. Red hf. cf., spine gt. (LC. Mar.1; 154) £340
- Floating Flies & How to Dress Them. L., 1886. *1st. Edn.* Advts., orig. cl., slightly marked; author's P.S. slip tipped in. (S. Oct.4; 23) *Selby.* £100
- Modern Development of the Dry Fly. 1910. *(75) De Luxe Edn.* 2 vols. 4to. Some slight spotting to mounts, red hf. cf., spine gt., partly unc. (LC. Mar.1; 155) £750

HALFPENNY, William & John

- Rural Architecture in the Chinese Taste. 1752. *2nd. Edn.* 4 pts. in 1 vol. Engraved title & sub-title, 60 plts., including 11 folding & 1 dupl., faint offset on a few plts., several trimmed to plt.-mark, cont. cf. gt. (C. Dec.9; 62) *Lyon.* £350
- Rural Architecture in the Gothick Taste. 1752. 16 engraved plts., some slight discoloration, hf. cf. (C. Dec.9; 63) *Weinreb.* £300

HALIDOM, M.Y. 'Dryasdust'

- Tales of the Wonder Club. L., [1899-1900]. *1st. Edn.* 3 vols. Orig. maroon cl. (CBA. Oct.29; 282) $130

HALIFAX, Charles Montagu, Earl of
See— PRIOR, Matthew & Montagu, Charles, Earl of Halifax

HALKETT, John

[-] Statement Respecting The Earl of Selkirk's Settlement upon the Red River, in North America. L., 1817. *1st. Publd. Edn.* Hf.-title, offsetting to folding map, hf. mor., jnts. worn; the Rt. Hon. Visc. Eccles copy. [Sabin 20704] (CNY. Nov.18; 129) $300

HALKETT, Samuel & Laing, Rev. John

- A Dictionary of the Anonymous & Pseudonymous Literature of Great Britain. 1882-88. 4 vols. 4to. Orig. cl., spines defect., some covers detchd. (TA. Dec.15; 346) £75
- - Anr. Copy. 4 vols. 4to. Prelims. spotted, orig. cl., faded & little worn on spines. (TA. Aug.18; 308) £70
- - Anr. Edn. 1926-62. *New & Enlarged Edn.* Vols. 1-9. Sm. fo. Liby. stp. on each title, label pasted in each upr. cover, orig. cl. gt., a little rubbed. (TA. Jun.21; 406) £360
- - Anr. Copy. Vols. 1-9. 4to. Sm. liby. stp. on titles, orig. cl. gt., untrimmed, some vols. faded & rubbed, classification no. on spine. (TA. Jul.19; 415) £300

HALL

- Le Gentilhomme Cultivateur ou Cours Complet d'Agriculture. Trans.:- Dupuy Demportes. Paris & Bordeaux, 1761-64. 8 vols. 4to. Cont. hf. cf., spine decor. (HD. Nov.9; 178) Frs. 2,300

HALL, Anne Marie, née Fielding

- Pilgrimages to English Shrines. L., 1853. Mod. red mor., elab. gt. with design in panels, mor. inlaid border, fore-e. pntg., as a fore-e. pntg., w.a.f. (SPB. May 17; 736) $950

See— HALL, Samuel Carter & Anne Marie

HALL, Capt. Basil

- Account of a Voyage of Discovery to the West Coast of Corea, & the Great Loo-Choo Island. 1818. *[1st. Edn.].* 4to. 10 plts., including 8 hand-cold. aquatints, 5 charts, hf.-title lightly spotted, cont. red mor., lightly rubbed, later end-papers. (CSK. May 4; 116) £280
- - Anr. Copy. 4to. 15 maps & plts., including 8 hand-cold., hf.-title & advt. ll., recent hf. mor., partly unopened. (BBA. Sep.29; 80) *Howell.* £200
- Forty Etchings, from Sketches made with the Camera Lucida, in North America ... 1829. 4to. Folding hand-cold. map, 40 engrs. on 20 sheets, stained, hf. cf., defect. (P. Jun.7; 213) £110
- Travels in North America in the Years 1827 & 1828. Edinb., 1829. 3 vols. Hf.-titles, col. folding map torn at bottom, linen-bkd. bds., binder's ticket

of R. Jackson & Co. in each vol., covers worn; A.L.s. from author presenting this set tipped onto front end-paper, dtd. 15 Feb. 1832. (LH. Jan.15; 301) $170

HALL, Basil, M.A.

- The Great Polyglot Bibles: Including a Leaf from the Complutensian of Acala ... San Franc., [Allen Pr.], 1966. *(400).* Fo. Unsewn sheets, paper cover, as iss., box. (LH. Sep.25; 310) $350
- - Anr. Copy. Fo. Unsewn folded sheets in H.M.P. folder, cl. box, upr. edge of box lightly soiled. (CBA. Nov.19; 3) $300
- - Anr. Copy. Fo. Unsewn folded sheets in H.M.P. folder, cl. box, orig. carton. (CBA. Nov.19; 46) $250

HALL, Chapman (Ed.)
See— COTERIE

HALL, Fairfax

- Paintings & Drawings by Harold Gilman & Charles Ginner in the Collection of Edward Le Bas. Fairfax Hall, [Stourton Pr.], 1965. *(105) numbered.* Fo. 36 lge. cold. reproductions, separate text in mor.-bkd. cl., in orig. hf. mor. fitted case. (S. Nov.22; 298) *Makiya.* £220

HALL, Lieut. Francis

- Travels in Canada, & the United States, in 1816 & 1817. L., 1818. *1st. Edn.* Cont. hf. cf., rebkd. preserving orig. spine; the Rt. Hon. Visc. Eccles copy. [Sabin 29769] (CNY. Nov.18; 131) $150

HALL, James
See— M'KENNEY, Thomas L. & Hall, James

HALL, John

- A Series of Select & Original Modern Designs for Dwelling Houses, for the Use of Carpenters & Builders, adapted to the Style of Building in the United States. Balt., 1848. *2nd. Edn.* 4to. 24 full-p. litho. plts., some liby. pencil markings, recent buckram. (HA. Feb.24; 257) $300

HALL, Manly P.

- An Encyclopedic Outline of Masonic, Hermetic, Quabbalistic & Rosicrucian Symbolical Philosophy. Ill.:- J.A. Knapp. San Franc., 1928. *King Solomon Edn. (550) numbered.* Tall fo. Batik bds., vell. back & corners, spine stained & worn at extremities, box very worn. (SG. Nov.17; 261) $350

HALL, Rev. Peter

- A Brief History of Old & New Sarum. Salisbury, Roxb. Cl., 1834. *(32).* 4to. 4 engraved plts on India paper, spotted, orig. mor.-bkd. bds., rubbed; pres. inscr. to William Pickering & A.L.s. loosely inserted from author. (BBA. Sep.29; 113) *Congleton.* £120

HALL, Samuel Carter

- The Baronial Halls & Ancient Picturesque Edifices of England. 1858. 2 vols. Fo. 71 tinted litho. plts., some light spotting, cont. hf. mor. (CSK. Jun.15; 83) £150
- - Anr. Edn. Ill.:- Harding, Prout & Holland. L., 1881. 2 vols. Some pp. loose, no bdg. stated, but spine & edges rubbed. (RS. Jan.17; 468) $120
- - Anr. Edn. L., n.d. *2nd. Edn.* Fo. 71 (of 72) litho. plts., 1 cut round & mntd., spotted, cont. hf. roan. (S. Mar.6; 252) *Harris.* £50
- Gems of European Art. 1846. 1st. & 2nd. Series: in 1 vol. 4to. 90 engraved plts., a few with margin foxing, crimson mor. gt. (P. Mar.15; 268) *Erlini.* £80
- - Anr. Edn. N.d. Vol. 2 only. Fo. Some margins lightly soiled, no bdg. stated. (CSK. Jun.29; 143) £50
- The Royal Gallery of Art. Ca. 1850. Vols. 1, 3 & 5-8 only (of 8). 4to. Many plts. loose, orig. cl. gt., spines faded (P. Mar.15; 31) *Erlini.* £90
- The Vernon Gallery of British Art. 1850-54. 4 vols. 152 engraved plts., cont. hf. mor., marb. bds., slightly rubbed. (HD. Nov.18; 1812) £160

See— JEWITT, Llewellynn & Hall, Samuel Carter

HALL, Samuel Carter (Ed.)
See— BOOK OF GEMS

HALL, Samuel Carter & Anne Marie

- The Book of the Thames, From its Rise to its Fall. L., 1867. 4to. Sm. blind-stp. on 2 text ll., gt.-stpd. leath., without mntd. photographs on covers. (SG. Nov.10; 67) $200
- - Anr. Edn. 1869. Mor. gt. (P. Apr.12; 170) *Primrose.* £55
- Ireland; Its Scenery, Character, etc. L., 1841. 3 vols. Royal 8vo. 2 engraved frontis., 3 woodcut titles, map of Ireland, 18 other maps, 46 engraved plts., mor. gt., armorial motif on spine. (GM. Dec.7; 438) £280
- - Anr. Copy. 3 vols. Royal 8vo. 19 engraved maps, 49 engraved plts., hf. mor. (GM. Dec.7; 460) £160
- - Anr. Edn. L., 1841-43. 3 vols. Hf. cf., defect. (P. Nov.24; 131) *Goddard.* £85
- - Anr. Copy. 3 vols. Tall 8vo. 17 single-p. maps, 50 steel engrs., some minor margin dampstains, cont. diced cf. gt., rubbed. (TA. Mar.15; 216) £64
- - Anr. Copy. 3 vols. Lge. 8vo. Cont. hf. cf., spines gt., jnts. worn. (SG. Feb.16; 163) $150

HALL, Sidney

- Pocket County Maps. Chapman & Hall, n.d. 45 folding maps, 42 county maps, 3 general maps, lacks Scotland, hand-cold. in outl., bkd. on linen, each in cl. folder, mor., case defect. (P. Sep.29; 450) *Hadden.* £95
- Travelling Atlas of the English Counties. Chapman & Hall, n.d. 45 maps, col. in outl., title loose, a few maps stuck together, orig. limp leath., torn. (P. Mar.15; 386) *Martin.* £75
- A Travelling County Atlas: With all the Railroads Accurately Laid Down. Ca. 1840. 46 double-p. folding maps, hand-cold. in outl., orig. wallet-style mor., rebkd. (TA. Mar.15; 244) £100

HALL, T.

- The Queen's Royal Cookery. L., n.d. *5th Edn.* 12mo. Title & 1 lf. slightly torn, lightly browned thro.-out, cont. cf., spine torn. (P. Jan.12; 230) *Jarndyce.* £130

HALL, William Henry

- The New Royal Encyclopaedia; Or, Complete Modern Dictionary of Arts & Sciences. Ca. 1770. 3 vols. Fo. Some spotting, cont. cf., some wear to spines. (TA. Apr.19; 256) £50
- - Anr. Edn. L., [?1788]. 3 vols. Fo. 1 plt. affected by offsetting, dampstain at end Vol. 3, cont. cf., worn. (S. Mar.20; 721) *Haddon.* £180

HALLE, Johann Samuel

- Magie oder die Zauberkräfte der Natur. Berlin, 1784. *1st. Edn. vol. II, 2nd. Edn. vol. I.* 2 vols. Vol. 2 with holes thro.-out & loss, 19th. C. hf. leath., spine restored. (GB. Nov.3; 1184) DM 400

HALLER, Albrecht von

- De Partium Corporis Humani Praecipuarum Fabrica et Functionibus. Bern & Lausanne, 1778. 8 vols. Cont. leath., gt. decor. spine, some bumping. (D. Nov.23; 564) DM 600
- Deux Mémoires sur le Mouvement du Sang et sur les Effets de la Saignée. Lausanne, 1756. *1st. Separate Edn.* Errata lf., cont. cf., spine worn; Dr. Walter Pagel copy. (S. Feb.7; 155) *Phelps.* £190
- - Anr. Copy. Cont. cf. gt. (SG. Oct.6; 181) $250
- - Anr. Copy. Lightly foxed, cont. leath. gt., bumped. (R. Oct.12; 1409) DM 520
- Epistolarum ab eruditis viris ad. Alb. Halierum Scriptarum. Bern, 1773-75. *1st. Edn.* Pt. 1 (all publd.) in 6 vols. Some light staining vol.4, cont. wraps. (R. Apr.4; 1306) DM 850
- Opera Minora emendata, aucta et renovata. Lausanne, 1762-68. *1st. Edn.* 3 vols. 4to. Vol. 1 with light stain in lr. corner in centre portion, cont. interim hf. leath., rubbed, 1 spine slightly defect., unc. (R. Apr.4; 1305) DM 850
- - Anr. Edn. Lausanne, 1763-68. 3 vols. 4to. Vol. 3 stained in lr. margin, cont. hf. leath., spine defect., bumped. (HK. Nov.8; 580) DM 560

HALLEY, Edmund

[-] Miscellanea Curiosa. 1705-08. *1st. Edn.* 3 vols. 21 plts., most folding, no advt. lf. before title, lacks blanks, 1 plt. reprd., anr. torn, mod. hf. cf. (P. Jun.7; 227) £140

– – **Anr. Edn.** 1726-23-27. 3 vols. Cont. cf., rubbed. (CSK. Jun.29; 147) £85

HALLIWELL or HALLIWELL-PHILLIPS, James Orchard
– **Some Account of a Collection of Several Thousand Bills, Accounts, & Inventories, Illustrating the History of Prices between 1650 & 1750.** Brixton Hill, 1852. *(80), for priv. circulation.* 4to. Spotted, orig. cl., worn. (S. Oct.11; 539) *Kraus.* £100

HALMA, François & Brouer van Niedek, Mathias
– **Tooneel der Vereenighde Nederlanden en Onderhorige Landschappen.** Leeuwaarden, 1725. 2 pts. in 1 vol. Fo. Vell., some stains & defects. (B. Oct.4; 724) Fls. 1,700
– – **Anr. Copy.** 2 pts. in 1 vol. Fo. 8 folding maps only, hf. cf., w.a.f. (VG. Sep.14; 1161) Fls. 450

HALOANDER, Gregorius [i.e. Meltzer]
– **Quinquaginta Librorum Digestorum sive Pandectorum Juris Caesarei ...** Paris, 1540. *Early Edn.* Sm. 8vo. Some slight browning, 18th. C. cf., spines gt., slightly defect. (VS. Dec.9; 1164) Fls. 600

HALSBURY, Earl of
– **The Laws of England. – General Index. – Consolidated Table of Cases.** Ed.:– Visc. Simonds. 1952-66; 1941-42; 1940. 52 vols., including indexes & cumulative supps.; 2 vols.; 1 vol. 52 vols. orig. cl. gt., 3 vols. cl. gt. (P. Dec.8; 367a) *Tooley.* £190

HAMANN, R
See— **MARBURGER JAHRBUCH FUR KUNSTWISSENSCHAFT**

HAMBURG
– **Hamburg mit 16 Stahlstichen und Geschichtlich beschreibenden Text.** München, ca. 1850. Mod. bds. (R. Oct.12; 2599) DM 1,350

HAMBURGER AUSRUF in Bildern und Verses
Ed.:– H. Ney (verses). Ill.:– C. Niedorf. Hamburg, ca. 1860. 12 ll. with cold. lithos. on linen, 7 ills. with monog. CN, 1 sig. with 4 ll. loose, orig. linen, cold. & litho. cover ill., soiled; Hauswedell coll. (H. May 23; 32) DM 400

HAMECONS EN USAGE AU JAPON
N.d. Orig. drawings on rice paper, text in Fr. & Japanese, hf. tree sheep. (HD. Sep.22; 309) Frs. 3,800

HAMERTON, Philip Gilbert
– **The Art of the American Wood-Engraver.** N.Y., 1894. Fo. Compl. series of 40 wood engrs., each an India-proof, matted & sigd. by engraver, red three-qtr. mor., scuffed. (SG. Jun.7; 358) $225
– **Etching & Etchers.** Ill.:– Rembrandt, Callot & others. L., 1868. *1st. Edn.* Lge. 8vo. 35 plts., including etchings, ex-liby., some light foxing, orig. mor.-bkd., gt.-decor. cl., very worn. (SG. May 3; 197) $1,000
– **The Graphic Arts.** L., 1882. Fo. Orig. cl., soiled. (BBA. Apr.5; 136) *Subun-So.* £60
– **Landscape.** 1885. *(500) numbered on L.P.* Lge. 4to. Gt. vell. bds., unc. (PD. Feb.15; 176) £52
– – **Anr. Copy.** Fo. 50 plts., orig. parch. gt., soiled. (S. Dec.20; 564) *Davidson.* £50
– – **Anr. Copy.** Lge. fo. Plts., etchings, ex-liby., gt.-decor. vell., soiled, unc. (SG. May 3; 199) $250

HAMILTON, Alexander, Statesman
– **Report of the Secretary of the Treasury ... Containing a Plan for the Further Support of Public Credit.** [Phila.], 1795. Lacks the 10 lge. folding charts. *(With:)* – **Report ... for the Improvement & Better Management of the Revenues of the United States ...** Phila., 1795. Together 2 vols. lightly browned, saddle-stitched with few extra stab holes, removed from bdgs. (HA. Nov.18; 116) $100

HAMILTON, Alexander & others
– **The Federalist.** N.Y., 1788. *1st. Coll. Edn.* 2 vols. Some spotting, liby. blind-stps. & owners' sigs., cont. cf., worn. bds. detchd. on Vol. 1 & upr. bd. detchd. on Vol. 2. (SPB. Dec.13; 448) $1,300

HAMILTON, Count Anthony
– **Mémoires de la Vie du Comte de Grammont.** Cologne, 1713. *Orig. Edn.* 12mo. Mor., gt. decor., decor. spine, sm. inner dentelle, by Chambolle-Duru. (HD. Mar.14; 48) Frs. 1,800

– – **Anr. Edn.** L., [1792]. 4to. 72 engraved ports., mor. gt. (SG. Feb.9; 242) $150
– – **Anr. Edn.** Ill.:– after S. Harding & Vaet. L., [1793]. 4to. With 'Notes et éclaircissements' (often lacking), imprint slightly erased from title, cont. Engl. str.-grd. red mor. gt., spine decor. (HD. Jun.26; 17) Frs. 2,200
– – **Anr. Copy.** With 'Notes et éclaircissements' (often lacking), foxing, cont. Engl. str.-grd. red mor. gt., spine decor., rubbed; George IV copy, with his mark on spine. (HD. Jul.2; 17) Frs. 1,500
– **Memoirs of Count Grammont.** [1794]. 4to. Engraved vig. title, frontis. port., 77 port. plts., cont. diced russ. gt., spine faded; Sir Ivar Colquhoun, of Luss copy. (CE. Mar.22; 148) £70
– – **Anr. Edn.** Ed.:– Henry Vizetelly. L., 1889. 2 vols. in 4. Extra-ill. with many plts., mostly engraved, & a few MS. notes in pencil, spotted, mor., spines slightly discold. (S. Oct.4; 88) £100

HAMILTON, J.C.
[–] **Experiences of a Colonist Forty Years Ago ... by An Old Hand.** Adelaide, 1880. Without (as always) plt. at p.34, sm. corner cut from front free end-paper, orig. cl. (KH. Nov.9; 616) Aus. $350

HAMILTON, Sinclair
– **Early American Book Illustrators & Wood Engravers 1670-1870.** Princeton, 1968. 2 vols., including Supp. 4to. Cl., light wear. (RO. May 22; 83) $175

HAMILTON, Sir William
– **Campi Phlegraei, observations on the volcanos of the two Sicilies.** Ill.:– after Pietro Fabris. Naples, 1776-79. 2 vols. in 1. Fo. Double-p. hand-cold. engraved map, 59 hand-cold. engraved plts., edged in black with grey wash borders, titles & text in Engl. & Fr., early 19th. C. vell. gt. (C. Mar.14; 52) *Franklin.* £9,000
– – **Anr. Edn.** Intro.:– Gino Doria. Milano, 1962. Fo. Publishers bos., box. (CR. Jul.16; 180) Lire 230,000
– **Collection of Engravings from the Anicent Vases of Greek Workmanship discovered ... of the two Sicilies.** Napoli, 1791-95. 2 vols. (of 3). Fo. Approx. 120 engrs., cf., defect., as a collection. w.a.f. (CR. Jun.6; 40) Lire 550,000
– **Observations on Mount Vesuvius, Mount Etna & other Volcanoes.** 1773. *2nd. Edn.* Folding map slightly torn, some ll. slightly soiled, cont. cf., worn. (BBA. Feb.9; 323) *Bickersteth.* £120
– – **Anr. Copy.** Cont. cf., spine ends chipped, rubbed. (TA. Feb.16; 40) £85
– – **Anr. Copy.** Map torn, cf. (P. Apr.12; 93) £50

HAMILTON, William, of Gilbertfield
– **A New Edition of the Life & Heroick Actions of the Renoun'd Sir William Wallace.** Glasgow, 1722. *1st. Edn.* Title slightly soiled, bdg. not stated; Sir Ivar Colquhoun, of Luss copy. (CE. Mar.22; 149) £65

HAMM, Margherita Arlina.
– **Famous Families of New York.** N.Y., [1902]. 2 vols. 4to. Bds., gt. decor. vell. backs. (SG. Apr.5; 153) $140

HAMMA, W.
– **Meister Italienischer Geigenbaukunst.** Stuttgart [1964]. *Ltd. numbered Iss.* 4to. German, Engl. & Fr. parallel text, lr. inner doubl. stpd., orig. hf. leath. (HT. May 10; 2644a) DM 500

HAMMACHER, A.M.
– **De Wereld van Henry van de Velde.** s'Gravenhage, 1967. 4to. Orig. parch.-bkd. cl., s.-c. (BBA. Apr.5; 183) *Thorp.* £65

HAMMER or HAMMER-PURGSTALL, J. von
– **Der Diwan von Mohammed Schemsed-din-Hafis.** Stuttgart & Tübingen, 1812-13. *1st. Book Edn.* 2 vols. Title lf. mntd., cont. style hand-bnd. mor. gt., spine slightly faded. (H. Nov.23; 670) DM 420
– **Geschichte der Schönen Redekünste Persiens.** Wien, 1818. *1st. Edn.* 4to. 1 engraved mus. supp., minimal foxing, hf. linen. ca. 1840. (HK. Nov.10; 2480) DM 1,000

HAMMETT, Dashiel
– **The Maltese Falcon.** Knopf, N.Y., 1930. *1st. Edn.* Orig. decor. cl., spine faded. (PNY. Dec.1; 54) $400

– – **Anr. Copy.** Some spotting, orig. cl., some soiling; Fred A. Berne copy. (SPB. May 16; 215) $150
– **Red Harvest.** Knopf, N.Y., 1929. *1st. Edn.* Orig. decor. cl. (PNY. Dec.1; 55) $300
– **The Thin Man.** N.Y., 1934. *1st. Edn. 1st. Iss.* With 'seep' for 'sleep' on p.209, slight marginal stain, light spotting, orig. cl., d.-w. as ill. in Layman but with tag laid on upr. cover, some creasing & soiling; sigd., Fred A. Berne copy. (SPB. May 16; 216) $1,200

HAMMOND, John
– **The Practical Surveyor.** 1725. *1st. Edn.* Text browned, cont. cf., rebkd. (BBA. Jul.27; 21) *Laywood.* £95

HANAPIS, Nicolaus de [i.e. Pseudo-Bonaventura]
– **Auctoritates utrisque Testamenti ...** [Strassb., H. Eggestein.], ca. 1475. Fo. Wide margin, rubricated, many red & blue initials, 1 lf. 'Tabula' in neat cont. MS., some cont. MS. marginalia, 1 lf. with tear in lr. corner, 1 lf. bkd. in upr. corner & slightly spotted, some slight browning, hf. vell. [H. 3534; BMC I, 72] (HK. Nov.8; 294) DM 2,600

HANCARVILLE, Pierre François Hughes de
– **Antiquités Etrusques, Grecques et Romaines, Tirées du Cabinet de M. Hamilton.** Naples, 1766-67. 4 vols. Fo. 8 cold. titles, 183 cold. plts., 246 (of 254?) other plts. including dedication ll., engraved initials & vigs. in text (those in Vol. 4 ptd. in cols.), 1 or 2 ll. in Vol. 1 stained, 1 plt. reprd., several laid down, light brng. stps. on verso of plts. & elsewhere, a few margins dust-soiled, cont. Engl. red mor. gt., slightly rubbed, 2 vols. rebkd. (S. May 21; 231) *Hitching.* £6,500
[–] **Monumens de la Vie Privée des Douze Césars.** Caprée, 1780. *1st. Edn. 2nd. Iss., with mod. 's' & 10-line title.* 4to. Extra engraved title, 50 copperplts., purple lev., gt. dentelles, by Pagnant. (SG. Feb.16; 74) $375
– – **Anr. Edn.** 1780. *(With:)* – **Monuments du Culte Secret des Dames Romaines ...** 1780. Together 2 vols. 4to. Cont. roan. (HD. Jan.24; 26) Frs. 1,500
– – **Anr. Edn.** [Nancy], 1782. 4to. Worming, foxing, later red hf. mor., spine decor. *(With:)* – **Monumens du Culte Secret des Dames Romaines.** [Nancy], 1784. 4to. Ex-libris, foxing, cont. decor. roan. (SM. Mar.7; 2376) Frs. 2,500
– – **Anr. Edn.** Rome, 1785. 1 vol. *(With:)* – **Monumens du Culte Secret des Dames Romains.** Rome, 1787. 2 vols. Together 3 vols. Lge. 8vo. Cont. marb. cf. gt., spines decor., slightly rubbed. (HD. Nov.9; 39) Frs. 4,600
– – **Anr. Edn.** Rome, 1786. *New Edn. (With:)* – **Monumens du Culte Secret des Dames Romaines.** Rome, 1790. *New Edn.* Together 2 vols. Cont. tree cf. gt., spine decor., turn-ins slightly worn. (HD. Nov.9; 40) Frs. 1,600
[–] **Monumens du Culte Secrèt des Dames Romaines.** Caprée, 1780 [after 1784]. *Re-iss., with mod. 's'.* 4to. Extra engraved title, 50 copperplts., purple lev., raised bands, gt. dentelles, by Pagnant. (SG. Feb.16; 75) $375

HANCKE, Erich
– **Max Liebermann. Sein Leben und Seine Werke.** Berlin, 1923. Lge. 4to. Frontis. stained, vell.-bkd. bds., soiled. (SG. Aug.25; 250) $110

HANDBUCH DER KUNSTWISSENSCHAFT
Ed.:– F. Burger & A.E. Brinckmann. Berlin & Potsdam, [1913-39]. 31 vols. 4to. 1 vol. rippled, 1 vol. with light margin staining, some light spotting, title stpd., orig. hf. linen, partly lightly bumped, 1 rippled, 1 with sm. defect. (HT. May 9; 1002) DM 502

HANDBUCH DER MUSIKWISSENSCHAFT
Ed.:– E. Bücken. Potsdam, [1927-31]. 4to. Some end-papers with owners mark, orig. pict. linen. (HT. May 10; 2645) DM 450

HANDEL, Georg Friedrich
– **Coronation Anthems. — The Funeral Anthem for Queen Caroline. — Te Deum & Jubilate.** L., [1743-45]. *Early Edns.* 3 works in 1 vol. Orig. cf. bds. (S. Nov.17; 114) *MacNutt.* £150
– **Messiah.** N.d. No bdg. stated; sigd. (twice) & inscr. in pencil by Sir Edward Elgar, Worcester, 1923. (S. Nov.8; 467) *Reuter.* £60

HANDEL, Georg Friedrich -Contd.

- Sosarme. L., John Walsh, ca. 1733. *1st. Edn.* Fo. Music ptd. on recto of lf. only, elsewhere both sides of lf. used, corrections & annots., probably in hand of John Walsh or one of his assistants, offsetting onto blank pp., lr. corners stained with printer's ink, cont. marb. bds., worn; proof copy, without title-p. or table of contents. (S. Nov.17; 117) *Otto Haas.* £2,200
- Vocal Works, mostly Sacred. Ca. 1800. 13 vols. Fo. Cont. hf. cf., gt.-decor. spines, some spine ends slightly worn. (TA. May 17; 547) £50

HANDTKE, F.
See— SOHR, K. & Handtke, F.

HANFLAND, C.
- Das Motorrad und seine Konstruktion. Berlin, 1925. Orig. linen. (R. Apr.4; 1573) DM 420

HANFSTAENGL, F.
- Die Vorzüglichsten Gemälde der Kgl. Galerie in Dresden. Dresden, 1836. Vol. 1 (of 3). Imp. Fo. Some plts., slightly creased, 1 plt. with pasted tear, some margin foxing, cont. hf. leath. gt. (R. Oct.12; 2248) DM 8,500
-- Anr. Edn. Dresden, 1836-41. Imp. fo. Lacks some plts.(?), some cut close, slightly foxed, loose in 5 orig. wraps. (HK. Nov.9; 1598) DM 3,600

HANNOVER, Emil
- Kunstfaerdige Gamle Bogbind indtil 1850 det Danske Kunstindustrimuseums Udstilling 1906. Copen., 1907. *(500).* Tall 4to. Cont. hf. cl., a little stained, H.M. Nixon coll., with some MS. notes. (BBA. Oct.6; 58) *Goldschmidt.* £130
- Pottery & Porcelain: A Handbook for Collectors. Ed.:– Bernard Rackham. N.Y., 1925. 3 vols. Orig. cl. (BBA. Nov.10; 274) *Bowers.* £50
-- Anr. Copy. 3 vols. Tall 8vo. Cl., spine ends frayed. (SG. Jan.26; 97) $110

HANSARD, George Agar
- The Book of Archery. 1841. Steel-engraved additional title, 38 plts., spotted, orig. cl., lightly soiled. (CSK. Sep.30; 22) £55

HANSBROW, Rev. G.
- An Improved Topographical & Historical Hibernian Gazetteer. Dublin, 1835. Cl. (GM. Dec.7; 388) £50

HANSEN, P.
- Schweoz i Skildringer og Billeder. Lge. 4to. Orig. hf. leath., bumped & rubbed. (D. Nov.23; 1129) DM 400

HANSI [i.e. Jean Jacques Waltz]
- L'Histoire d'Alsace racontée aux Petits Enfants. Paris, 1912. 1st. Printing. 4to. Publisher's decor. cl. bds.; from Château des Noës liby. (HD. May 25; 30) Frs. 1,200

HANWAY, Jonas
- An Historical Account of the British Trade Over the Caspian Sea ... 1753. *1st. Edn.* 4 vols. in 3. 4to. Cont. cf., rubbed. (SKC. Mar.9; 2015) £160
-- Anr. Edn. 1754. *2nd. Edn.* 4 vols. 4to. Engraved frontis., 17 plts. & 9 folding maps, 5 torn, cont. cf., rebkd.; Ely Cathedral Liby. bkplts. & cancellation stps. (CSK. Feb.10; 199) £110

HAPPEL, Everhard Guerner
- Gröste Denckwürdigkeiten der Welt. Hamburg, 1683-91. 5 vols. 4to. 10 plts. partly torn, slightly spotted, 1 sig. loose, hf. leath., slightly loose & worn. [Sabin 30277]. (D. Nov.24; 2286) DM 3,000
-- Anr. Copy. Vols. 1, 3, 4 & 5 (of 5). 4to. 147 (of 169) plts. & woodcuts, bds., defect., w.a.f. (VG. Mar.19; 241) Fls. 500
- Historischer Kern. Hamburg, 1706-10. 5 pts. in 1 vol. 23 (of 30) most folding copperplts., lacks 1 lf., cont. vell. (R. Oct.11; 1012) DM 600

HARANGUES (The) or Speeches of Several Celebrated Quack-Doctors in Town & Country
L., 1762. Wraps. (P. Jan.12; 231) *Laywood.* £140

HARBAVILLE
- Mémorial Historique et Archéologique du Département du Pas-de-Calais. Arras, 1842. 2 vols. in 1. Hf. roan. (HD. Mar.19; 57) Frs. 1,100

HARCOURT, R. & M. d'
- La Céramique Ancienne du Perou. [Paris, 1924]. 2 vols., including plt. vol. Fo. Plt. vol. with 65 loose plts., ptd. wraps., cl.-bkd. bd. portfo., soiled, spine torn. (SG. Jan.26; 98) $175

HARDENBERG, Friedrich von 'Novalis'
- Heinrich von Ofterdingen. Ed.:– [L. Tiéck]. Berlin, 1802. *1st. Separate Edn.* 2 pts. in 1 vol. Title & a few ll. lightly foxed, lacks last lf. blank, cont. hf. leath. gt., lightly rubbed, corners bumped. (R. Oct.11; 364) DM 7,300
- Hymnen an die Nacht. [München, 1910]. *4th printing.* On Strathmore Japan. Lge. 4to. Some light margin browning, hand-bnd. orig. mor. gt., by Carl Sonntag jun., Leipzig. (H. Nov.23; 1106) DM 1,050
-- Anr. Edn. [München, Hundertdrucke, 1920]. On Strathmore Japan. Lge. 4to. Some light browning in margins, hand-bnd. orig. mor. gt., by Carl Sonntag jun., Leipzig, slight foxing to doubls. (H. May 22; 1044) DM 900
- Das Märchen aus Heinrich von Ofterdingen. Ill.:– F. Meseck. München, 1920. *(65) numbered De Luxe Edn. on japan.* Lge. 4to. 13 orig. etchings, orig. vell., cover slightly defect. (GB. May 5; 2966) DM 400
- Schriften. Ed.:– Fr. Schlegel & L. Tieck. Berlin, 1802. *1st. Coll. Edn.* 2 vols. Some spotting & browning, 2 pp. unptd. in vol. 1, cont. hf. leath., rubbed & bumped. (H. Nov.23; 728) DM 820
-- Anr. Edn. Ed.:– Fr. Schlegel & L. Tieck. Tieck & E. von Bülow (vol. III). Berlin, 1802 & 1846. *1st. coll. Edn.* 3 vols. Lightly browned, I & II slightly browned, title I with erased owners mark, II with old MS. dedication, format III slightly larger, later hf. linen, lightly rubbed; Hauswedell coll. (H. May 24; 1494) DM 3,400
-- Anr. Edn. Ed.:– L. Tieck & Fr. Schlegel. Berlin, 1805. *2nd. Edn.* With hf.-titles, title ll. with old owners marks, cont. bds., lacquered end-papers with ex-libris, lightly rubbed. (H. May 22; 815) DM 1,400
-- Anr. Edn. Ed.:– L. Tieck & Fr. Schlegel. Berlin, 1815. 2 vols. Title lightly browned, cont. hf. leath., lightly rubbed; Hauswedell coll. (H. May 24; 1495a) DM 680

HARDIE, David
- Notes on some of the More Common Diseases in Queensland, in Relation to Atmospheric Conditions, 1887-91. Brisbane, 1893. 2 vols. with atlas. Folding table, 8 tables & booklet in s.-c., orig. cl., slightly rubbed. (BBA. May 3; 39) *Levy.* £100

HARDIE, Martin
- The Etched Work of W. Lee-Hankey. L., [1921]. *(350) numbered.* 4to. 187 reproductions, ex-liby., bds., soiled. (SG. May 3; 236) $150
- Etchings & Dry Points of James McBey. L., 1925. *(500) numbered, with orig. sigd. etching.* Tall 4to. Frontis., 223 reproductions, ex-liby., orig. hf. cf. (SG. May 3; 246) $300
- Water-colour Painting in Britain. 1967-68. 3 vols. Orig. cl. gt., d.-w. (P. Apr.12; 259) *Henderson.* £60
-- Anr. Edn. 1968. 3 vols. Fo. Cl., d.-w.'s, slightly worn. (BS. May 2; 129) £95
-- Anr. Edn. 1969-71. 3 vols. 4to. Orig. cl., d.-w.'s. (S. Nov.8; 528) *Jenkins.* £80

HARDIMAN, James
- The History of the Town & County of the Town of Galway. Dublin, 1820. *1st. Edn.* 4to. Folding frontis., folding map, 8 (of 9) engraved plts., including 2 folding, bkplt., hf. mor., armorial motif on spine. (GM. Dec.7; 434) £210
-- Anr. Copy. 4to. Folding engraved frontis., 6 plts., 4 maps & plans, some folding, some light spotting, cont. cf., rebkd., old spine laid down, corners rubbed. (CSK. May 4; 65) £180
-- Anr. Edn. Dublin, 1975. *Facs. of 1820 Edn.* 4to. Qtr. mor. (GM. Dec.7; 489) £50

HARDING, Edward
- Costume of the Russian Empire. L., 1803. 4to. Engl. & Fr. text, 70 hand-cold. lithos., hf. red mor., corners, gold-tooled. (CR. Jun.6; 181) Lire 650,000

HARDING, James Duffield
- Drawing Book for the Year 1838. L., [1838]. Ob. fo. Some slight foxing, mostly in wide margin, orig. hf. leath., slightly rubbed & soiled. (R. Oct.12; 2694a) DM 2,500
- Harding's Portfolio. Ill.:– Hullmandel. L., [1837]. Fo. Tinted litho. title, 23 tinted litho. views, cont. hf. mor. gt., edges & corners a little rubbed. (C. Jun.27; 36) *Marlborough.* £220
- Seventy-Five Views of Italy & France. L., 1834. 77 engraved plts., some spotting in margins, mor. gt., rubbed, upr. portion of spine defect. (P. Mar.15; 12) *Ayres.* £190
- Sketches at Home & Abroad. L., [1836]. Lge. fo. 50 litho. 2-tone plts., heavy foxing, title nearly disbnd., cont. hf. chagrin, corners, rubbed. (HD. Feb.29; 22) Frs. 7,200
-- Anr. Edn. N.d. 50 plts., title-p. loose, some foxing, orig. hf. mor. & bds., slightly defect. (LA. Jul.20; 140) £660

HARDINGE, Charles Stewart
- Sketches in the Camp before Sebastopol. L., 1855. Fo. Tinted litho. title, 19 tinted litho. views, list of plts., short margin tears to a few plts., some light spotting, plts. loose in bdg., cont. red mor.-bkd. bds. gt. (C. Nov.16; 95) *Shapero.* £50

HARDWICK, C.
- History of the Borough of Preston ... 1857. Folding map, 30 engraved plts., orig. cl. gt., worn. (P. Feb.16; 44) £60

HARDY, Thomas
- The Dynasts. 1927. *(525) sigd.* 3 vols. 4to. Qtr. vell. gt., unopened, d.-w.'s, 1 torn. (P. Jul.26; 68) £180
-- Anr. Copy. 3 vols. 4to. L.P., Orig. qtr. vell., unc. (SG. Jan.12; 151) $300
-- Anr. Copy. Vell.-bkd. bds., s.-c. (LH. Sep.25; 539) $180
-- Anr. Copy. 3 vols. 2 or 3 spots of foxing, bds., qtr. vell. (KH. Nov.8; 198) Aus. $200
- Far from the Madding Crowd. L., 1874. *1st. Edn. in book form.* 2 vols. With '1' lacking in pagination of p.91, no exclamation point on p.261 vol.2, & 'Sacrament' on p.2 vol.1, ill., advts., some spotting, orig. decor. cl., some fraying; Fred A. Berne copy. (SPB. May 16; 282) $1,900
- The Hand of Ethelberta. L., 1876. *1st. Edn. in book form.* 2 vols. B4 a cancel, F1 not, ill., advts., orig. decor. cl., mor.-bkd. s.-c.; Fred A. Berne copy. (SPB. May 16; 283) $550
- Jude the Obscure. Dec. 1894-Nov. 1895. *1st. Serial Publication (In Harper's New Monthly Magazine).* 12 iss. Lge. 8vo. Light browning or marginal soiling, orig. ptd. wraps. lightly soiled, Fred A. Berne copy. (SPB. May 16; 284) $350
-- Anr. Edn. Ill.:– H. Macbeth-Raeburn. [L., 1896]. *1st. Edn.* Sm. 8vo. 1st. state, with all pp. through sig. H numbered, hf.-titles, lev. gt., gt. dentelles, by Bayntun (Rivière). (SG. Feb.16; 154) $200
-- Anr. Edn. Ill.:– A.M. Parker. Ltd. Edns. Cl., 1969. 1 vol. Orig. bdg. *(With:)* - The Mayor of Casterbridge. A.M. Parker. Ltd. Edns. Cl., 1964. 1 vol. Orig. bdg. (P. Sep.8; 228) *Georges.* £75
- A Laodicean. L., 1881. *1st. Engl. Edn.* 3 vols. With 'or' in hf.-title of vol.1, without advts., spotting & foxing, orig. cl., slight variation in cl., hole in vol.1 lr. endpaper; Fred A. Berne copy. (SPB. May 16; 285) $175
- The Mayor of Casterbridge: the Life & Death of a Man of Character. L., 1886. *1st. Edn.* 2 vols. Hf.-titles, Vol. I lacks advt. lf. at end & Vol. II the 2 advt. ll. at end, a little spotting, mod. hf. cf. by Bayntun, Bath, spines gt., slightly faded. (S. Oct.11; 343) *Scott.* £170
-- Anr. Copy. 2 vols. Hf.-titles, advts., hf. mor. gt., orig. cl. spines bnd. in; sigd., Fred A. Berne copy. (SPB. May 16; 286) $600
- A Pair of Blue Eyes. L., 1873. *1st. Edn.* 3 vols. 16-pp. advts. dtd. Mar. 1873, vols. 2 & 3 hf.-titles

reprd., some spotting & soiling, orig. cl., jnts. reprd.;
Fred A. Berne copy. (SPB. May 16; 287) $700
- **The Return of the Native.** L., 1878. *1st. Edn. in book form.* 3 vols. Photo. laid down on frontis.-map verso, light marginal browning, orig. cl., 3rd. vol. not quite unif., some fraying, mor.-bkd. s.-c.'s.; Fred A. Berne copy. (SPB. May 16; 288) $750
- - **Anr. Copy.** 3 vols. Some soiling, marginal tears, 1st. bdg., orig. cl., recased, mor.-bkd. s.-c.; Perry Molstad copy. (SPB. May 16; 456) $200
- - **Anr. Edn.** Ill.:– after Clare Leighton. L., 1929. *(1500) sigd. by artist.* Lge. 8vo. Some mild offsetting, vell.-bkd. batik bds., spine slightly soiled. (SG. Jan.12; 218) $100
- **Satires of Circumstance.** L., 1914. *1st. Edn.* Orig. cl., unopened, d.-w. chipped with some tears, lightly soiled, mor.-bkd. s.-c.; Fred A. Berne copy. (SPB. May 16; 289) $175
- - **Anr. Copy.** Orig. cl., unopened, d.-w. slightly frayed; Frederic Dannay copy. (CNY. Dec.16; 160) $160
- **Tess of the D'Urbervilles.** L., 1891. *1st. Edn. 1st. Imp.* 3 vols. Vols. 2 & 3 lack final blank, mod. hf. mor. gt. by Bayntun. (S. Dec.8; 103)
Sotheran. £300
- - **Anr. Edn.** [L., 1891]. *1st. Edn. 1st. Iss., with chapter 35 misnumbered 25, the reading 'horse-tracks' on p. 206 in Vol. II, 'road' for 'load' on p. 198 in Vol. III, & 'without' on p. 257 in Vol. III misspelled.* 3 vols. Sm. 8vo. Without blank lf. before hf.-title in Vol. III, blank top corner of 1 lf. torn off, owner's stp. on prelims. of 2 vols., gt.-floral cl., worn & very soiled, label removed from upr. covers, slightly shaken, cl. folding case; A.E. Newton bkplts.; A.L.s. from Hardy to Mr. Secombe mrtd. on hf.-title in Vol. I. (SG. Nov.3; 94) $475
- - **Anr. Edn.** L., [1891]. *1st. Edn.* 3 vols. Some spotting, orig. cl. with gt. design after Charles Ricketts, cl. folding box; Prescott copy. (SPB. May 17; 621) $3,500
- - **Anr. Copy.** 3 vols. Some spotting of fore-edges, orig. cl. gt., mark where labels removed, vol.3 lr. cover buckled; Fred A. Berne copy. (SPB. May 16; 290) $600
- **The Trumpet-Major.** L., 1880. *1st. Edn.* 3 vols. Orig. cl., some browning of endpapers, inr. hinges reprd., some fraying, faint mark where labels removed; Fred A. Berne copy. (SPB. May 16; 291) $475
- **Two on a Tower.** L., 1882. *1st. Edns.* 3 vols. Orig. cl., mor.-bkd. s.-c.; Fred A. Berne copy. (SPB. May 16; 292) $1,000
- **Under the Greenwood Tree.** L., 1872. *1st. Edn.* 2 vols. 2 gatherings loose, stitching loose, some spotting, orig. cl., some soiling & fraying, mor.-bkd. s.-c.; inscr. to B.C. Johns from W. Tinsley (publisher), Fred A. Berne copy. (SPB. May 16; 293) $650
- **The Well-Beloved.** L., 1897. *1st. Edn.* Orig. cl., d.-w. worn, s.-c.; sigd., Fred A. Berne copy. (SPB. May 16; 294) $350
- **Wessex Poems & Other Verses.** [L. & N.Y., 1898]. *1st. Edn. (500).* Orig. cl., mostly unopened, faint marks on upr. cover; pres. copy from author to Sir James Crichton-Browne, Frederic Dannay copy. (CNY. Dec.16; 159) $3,400
- **Wessex Tales.** L., 1888. *1st. Edn.* 2 vols. Advts., orig. cl., some spotting; with A.N.s, Fred A. Berne copy. (SPB. May 16; 296) $650
- **The Woodlanders.** L., 1887. *1st. Edn. in book form.* 3 vols. Ownership sig. & liby. label in vol.3, light margin discoloration, orig. cl., some fraying, mor.-bkd. s.-c.; Fred A. Berne copy. (SPB. May 16; 298) $325
- **Works.** L., 1906-02-27. *Macmillan's Coll. Edn.* 19 vols. Mod. hf. cf., spines gt. (BBA. May 3; 244)
Traylen. £520
- **The Works in Prose & Verse.** L., 1912-13. 21 vols. Tall 8vo. Maroon str.-grd. mor. gt., gt.-decor. spines, gt. dentelles, by Zaehnsdorf. (SG. Feb.16; 155) $1,700
- **Works.** L., 1919-20. *Mellstock Edn. (500) numbered & sigd. by author.* 37 vols. Three-qtr. mor. by Bennett, spines gt., unc., lightly rubbed. (RO. Apr.23; 161) $1,800
- **The Writings.** N.Y. & L., n.d. *Autograph Edn., (153) sigd.* 20 vols. Plts. on Japon vell., light margin browning, orig. cl., soiled. (SPB. Dec.13; 536) $650

HARGRAVE, Catherine Perry
- **A History of Playing Cards & a Bibliography of Cards & Gaming.** Boston & N.Y., at the Riverside Pr., Camb., 1930. *[1st. Edn.].* 4to. Orig. cl. gt. (LC. Jul.5; 54)   £190
- - **Anr. Copy.** Fo. Orig. cl. gt., a little dampstained & rubbed. (TA. Jun.21; 471)   £85
- - **Anr. Copy.** 4to. Cl., probably rebnd., covers lightly soiled, spine rubbed & worn, bkplt. (CBA. Jan.29; 356) $150

HARGRAVES, Edward Hammond
- **Australia & its Gold Fields** ... 1855. *1st. Edn.* Early hf. roan, worn; Will Sowden copy. (KH. May 1; 334)   Aus. $150

HARISSE, H.
- **Découverte et Evolution cartographique de Terre-Neuve et des pays Circonvoisins 1497-1501-1769.** L. & Paris, 1900. *(380).* 4to. Orig. wraps., backstrip defect. (S. Jun.25; 288)   *Lowendahl.* £100

HARLAN, Robert D.
- **Bibliography of the Grabhorn Press 1957-1966.** San Franc., 1977. *(225).* Fo. Qtr. cf., cl. bds. (LH. Sep.25; 370) $250

HARLEY, Robert & Edward, Earls of Oxford
- **Harleian Miscellany.** 1808-11. Vols. 1-12. Most vols. spotted to some extent, hf. cf., spines faded, slight tear in 1 spine. (S. Oct.11; 540)*Davids.* £85
- - **Anr. Edn.** 1808-12. 9 vols. only (of 10). 4to. Mod. hf. cf. (BBA. Jul.27; 131)
The Bookroom. £50

HARLOW, Neal
- **The Maps of San Francisco Bay from the Spanish Discovery in 1769 to the American Occupation.** San Franc., [Grabhorn Pr.], 1950. *(375).* 4to. Red mor.-bkd. decor. paper covers. (LH. Sep.25; 330) $350
- - **Anr. Copy.** 4to. With prospectus, red mor.-bkd. decor. paper covers, spine defect. (LH. Apr.15; 270) $250

HARNISCH, Wilhelm
- **Die Wichtigsten Neuern Land- und Seereisen.** Leipzig, 1829-32. 16 vols. Cont. bds. (C. Dec.9; 232)   *Edwards.* £270

HARPER, Charles G.
- **The Old Inns of Old England.** 1906. 2 vols. Orig. cl. gt., spines faded, partly untrimmed. (TA. May 17; 107)   £75
- **Stage-Coach & Mail in Days of Yore. A Picturesque History of the Coaching Age.** 1903. 2 vols. Orig. decor. cl., spines faded, partly untrimmed. (TA. May 17; 106)   £50

HARPER, Henry Andrew
- **Walks in Palestine.** 1888. *(100) numbered.* 24 photogravured plts. (on India paper mntd.), some light spotting, orig. vell. (CSK. Sep.16; 116)   £60

HARPER, Ida Husted
- **The Life & Work of Susan B. Anthony.** Indianapolis, 1899. 2 vols. Orig. cl.; inscr. by Anthony, 26 Aug. 1905. (LH. Jan.15; 303) $160

HARPER, Robert Goodloe
- **Dispute Between the United States & France.** Phila., 1797. *1st. Edn.* Dampstained, foxed, 4 ll. chipped, later crude bds., sigd. by John Marshall on hf.-title. (SG. Jan.19; 45) $200

HARPER'S BAZAAR
N.Y., 1868. Vol. 1. Fo. Cont. three-qtr. mor., moderate wear. (RO. Jul.24; 108) $155

HARPER'S WEEKLY
N.Y., Apr. 9, 1859-Dec. 29, 1860. Vol. II, no. 119-Vol. IV, no. 209. In 2 vols. Fo. Not collated, but likely compl., hf. leath., worn, w.a.f. (SG. Jun.7; 359) $275
- - **Anr. Edn.** N.Y., 1861-64. Vols. 5-8. Fo. Vol. 8 bnd. with title-p. from Vol. 12, some foxing, staining & chipping, old hf. leath., shabby, not collated, w.a.f. (SG. Dec.15; 156) $850
- - **Anr. Edn.** N.Y., 1864. Vol. 8. Fo. Old hf. leath. (SG. Dec.15; 154) $300
- - **Anr. Edn.** Ill.:– Thomas Nast. N.Y., 1880. Vol. 24. Sm. fo. Hf. leath., lacks spine. (SG. Dec.15; 155) $200

HARRADEN, Richard
- **Picturesque Views of Cambridge.** Camb., 1800. Ob. fo. Plan, 21 (of 31) aquatint views, 2 views supplied from anr. copy, cut down & mntd., spotted in margins, mod. hf. cf. (S. Jun.25; 327)
Webb. £260

HARRIMAN ALASKA EXPEDITION
Text:– John Burroughs, John Muir, G.B. Grinnell, & others. N.Y., 1901. *1st. Edn.* Vols. I & II only. Lge. 8vo. Orig. cl. (SG. Sep.22; 14) $250
- - **Anr. Copy.** Vols. I & II only. 4to. Gt.-pict. cl., orig. cl. d.-w.'s. (SG. Nov.10; 49) $225
- - **Anr. Edn.** L., 1901. Vols. I & II only (of 14). Orig. cl. gt. (P. Nov.24; 8)   *Cavendish.* £70
- - **Anr. Edn.** N.Y., 1902, Wash., 1914. Vols. 1-5 & 8-14, in 13 vols. Orig. cl., 2 sm. holes in 1 spine. (SPB. Dec.13; 449) $900

HARRINGTON, Charles
[–] **Summering in Colorado.** Ill.:– J. Collier. Denver, 1874. A few plts. somewhat faded, orig. gt.-lettered cl., extremities worn. (SG. Nov.10; 48) $150

HARRINGTON, H. Nazeby
- **Engraved Work of Sir Francis Seymour Haden.** Liverpool, 1910. *(75) numbered, sigd.* Lge. 4to. 109 plts., ex-liby., orig. hf. mor. (SG. May 3; 195) $400

HARRINGTON, James
- **The Commonwealth of Oceana.** L., 1656. *Orig. Edn.* Sm. fo. Cf., corners & spine reprd. (HD. Feb.22; 88)   Frs. 7,500
- **The Oceana, & other Works.** Ed.:– John Toland. L., 1700. *1st. Coll. Edn.* Fo. Lacks port., disbnd. (SG. Oct.27; 138) $100

HARRIS COLLECTION
- **Dictionary Catalog of the Harris Collection of American Poetry & Plays. Brown University Library, Providence, Rhode Island.** Boston, 1972. 16 vols. including 3 supps. Fo. Buckram, minimal wear. (RO. Apr.23; 163) $250

HARRIS, Joel Chandler
- **The Tar-Baby, & Other Rhymes of Uncle Remus.** Ill.:– A.B. Frost & E.W. Kemble. N.Y., 1904. *1st. Edn.* Gt.-pict. cl. (SG. Dec.8; 190) $100
- **Uncle Remus.** Ill.:– Freerick S. Church & James H. Moser. N.Y., 1881. *1st. Edn. 1st. Iss.* With 'presumptive' on p.9, 1st. iss. of advts., margin repair & creasing on p.25, sm. tears, light margin stain, few ll. cracked, orig. cl., sm. repair to spine, some soiling; Fred A. Berne copy. (SPB. May 16; 300) $250
- - **Anr. Copy.** Reading 'presumptive' for 'presumptuous' in last line of p. 9, orig. gt.-decor. cl., butterfly end-papers, covers lightly soiled, spine ends slightly nicked; Joe E. Brown bkplt., Marymount College copy. (CBA. Mar.3; 239) $225
- - **Anr. Copy.** With 'presumptive' on p.9, 1st. iss. of advts., some light marginal discoloration, orig. cl., some soiling; Perry Molstad copy. (SPB. May 16; 457) $200

HARRIS, Dr. John, F.R.S.
- **The History of Kent.** L., 1719. *[1st. Edn.].* Vol. 1 (all publd.). Fo. Index, diced cf., embossed with armorials; Sir S.R.B. Taylor bkplt. (HBC. May 17; 367)   £720
- - **Anr. Copy.** Vol. 1 (all publd.). Fo. Engraved port., 5 folding maps, 36 (of 38) plts. (33 folding), blank margins of few ll. lightly wormed, cont. cf., rebkd. & cornered, later end-papers, w.a.f. (CSK. Feb.24; 61)   £700
- - **Anr. Copy.** Vol. 1 (all publd.). Fo. Engraved port., folding map, 3 plts., 4 maps, 34 double-p. views (1 folding), 19th. C. qtr. mor. gt., marb. bds. (PWC. Jul.11; 585)   £560
- - **Anr. Copy.** Vol. 1 (all publd.). Fo. Engraved port., 3 maps, 40 plts., several lightly browned, cont. cf., rebkd., upr. cover detchd. (CSK. Dec.2; 36)   £480
- - **Anr. Copy.** Vol. 1 (all publd.). Fo. Engraved port. cropped & mntd., 43 plts. & maps, a few mntd., a few torn affecting ill., some ll. soiled & browned, a few tears reprd., cont. cf., rebkd., rubbed. (BBA. May 3; 316)   *Russell.* £400
- - **Anr. Copy.** Vol. 1 (all publd.). Fo. 35 (of 49)

HARRIS, Dr. John, F.R.S. -*Contd.*

plts., some text ll. loose, cf., rebkd., as a collection of plts., w.a.f. (P. Sep.8; 252) *Frankland.* £280
– – **Anr. Copy.** Vol. 1 (all publd.). Fo. 41 (of 49) maps & plts., county map defect., 2 plts. with lr. margin trimmed, many with tears in fold, cf., spine defect., as a collection of plts., w.a.f. (P. Sep.8; 365) *Frankland.* £240
– **Navigantium Atque Itinerantium Bibliotheca: or a Complete Collection of Voyages & Travels.** 1705. 2 vols. Fo. 2 engraved ports., 18 engraved plts. only, 9 folding maps, 2 slightly soiled, cont. cf., rubbed. (CSK. Jul.6; 24) £320
– – **Anr. Edn.** L., 1744-48. 2 vols. Fo. 39 engraved plts., 22 engraved maps, including 15 folding, lf. T2 in Vol. I reprd. without loss, cont. cf., shabby, brkn. (SG. Sep.22; 162) $850
– – **Anr. Copy.** 2 vols. Fo. 62 engraved maps & plts., some lr. margins in Vol.2 defect. & reprd., some dampstaining, 2 ll. detchd., 2 maps & few plts. cropped, 1 map torn, cont. cf., worn, covers detchd., w.a.f. (CNY. May 18; 107) . $450
– – **Anr. Edn.** Maps:– E. Bowen. 1748. *2nd. Edn.* Vol. 2 only. Fo. 11 engraved maps, 22 plts., cont. cf., worn, w.a.f. (CSK. Feb.10; 15) £500
– – **Anr. Edn.** Ill.:– Maps:– Emmanuel Bowen & Thomas Kitchen. 1764. 2 vols. Fo. Cont. russ. gt. (SKC. Mar.9; 2016) £950

HARRIS, Moses
– **The Aurelian.** 1766. *1st. Edn. 1st. Iss.* Fo. Engraved frontis., vig. title, 41 hand-cold. plts., plt. 35 in 1st state, plt. 17 corrected in MS. to 2nd. state, errors in pagination to pp. 71-81 corrected in MS., frontis. reprd., 2 plts. torn affecting engraved area, a few margins torn, cont. cf., covers scuffed, 1 detchd., lacks part of spine. (CSK. Dec.16; 49) £1,700
– – **Anr. Edn.** L., 1778. *2nd. Edn.* Fo. L.P., hand-cold. frontis., engraved vig. on title-p., 45 hand-cold. plts., text in Engl. & Fr., later hf. cf., marb. bds. (SKC. Oct.26; 375) £1,900
– – **Anr. Edn.** L., 1778 [= 1814]. *2nd. Edn. 3rd. Printing.* Lge. fo. Wide margin, lacks Fr. title & index at end, most plts. with 'WZ' dtd. 1794, text slightly foxed, some light soiling in plt. margins, cont. leath., bumped, spine renewed. (R. Oct.12; 1852) DM 5,000
– – **Anr. Edn.** Ed.:– J.O. Westwood. L., 1840. *New [4th.] Edn.* 4to. Hand-cold. frontis., engraved vig. on title-p., 45 hand-cold. plts., orig. cl., worn & shaken. (SKC. Oct.26; 374) £700
– – **Anr. Copy.** Fo. Lacks frontis., minimal spotting, cont. hf. leath., very worn, upr. cover loose. (H. May 22; 179) DM 3,800
– **The Exposition of English Insects.** 1782. *2nd. Edn. 1st. Iss.* 4to. Hand-cold. frontis., engraved title, 51 plts., including 50 hand-cold., 1 watercolour diagram inserted, many plts. slightly soiled, MS. notes in ink, hf. mor. gt. (P. Dec.8; 103) *Negro.* £190
– – **Anr. Edn.** L., 1782. *2nd. Edn.* 4to. Hand-cold. frontis., engraved title, 51 copperplates, all but 1 hand-cold., text in Engl. & Fr., mod. hf. cf., marb. bds. (SKC. Oct.26; 376) £320

HARRIS, R.
– **South Africa Illustrated by a Series of One Hundred & Four Permanent Photographs.** Port Elizabeth, priv. ptd., 1888. 4to. 104 mntd. woodbury-type photographs including town & mining scenes, a few margins slightly dust-soiled, publisher's mor., rubbed, covers detchd. (S. May 22; 415) *Bonham.* £140

HARRIS, S.
– **The Coaching Age.** Ill.:– J. Sturgess. 1885. 1 vol. Hf. mor. gt. (*With:*) – **Old Coaching Days.** J. Sturgess. 1882. 1 vol. Hf. mor. gt. (P. Sep.8; 98) *Solomon.* £52

HARRIS, Tomas
– **Goya Engravings & Lithographs.** Oxford, 1964. 2 vols. Fo. Orig. cl., d.-w.'s. (S. Apr.30; 46) *Rota.* £200
– – **Anr. Copy.** 2 vols. Fo. Orig. cl., d.-w.'s. (S. Apr.30; 44) *Dreesman.* £190
– – **Anr. Copy.** 2 vols. Fo. No bdg. stated. (SPB. Nov.30; 186) $425

– – **Anr. Copy.** 2 vols. Fo. Many plts. mntd., orig. cl., wraps. (SI. Dec.18; 205) Lire 300,000
– – **Anr. Edn.** San Franc., 1983. 2 vols. 4to. Bdg. not stated, d.-w.'s, orig. shipping box. (CBA. Jan.29; 219) $150

HARRIS, Walter B.
– **The Land of an African Sultan.** 1889. *(200)* numbered. 4to. Orig. cl., rubbed; 2 Letters from author pasted down on front end-papers, mntd. newspaper cuttings. (CSK. Jan.27; 158) £120

HARRIS, William
– **A Catalogue of the Library of the Royal Institution of Great Britain.** L., 1809. *1st. Edn.* Hf.-title, few ll. slightly spotted, cont. cf., splits in hinges. (BBA. Mar.7; 335) *Quaritch.* £60

HARRIS, Sir William Cornwallis
– **The Highlands of Aethiopia.** 1844. *2nd. Edn.* 3 vols. Orig. cl. (SKC. Mar.9; 2017) £110
– – **Anr. Copy.** 3 vols. 3 litho. plts., 1 cold., folding map torn, some slight spotting, orig. cl., 1 spine torn. (S. Apr.9; 31) *Trophy.* £80
– **Portraits of the Game & Wild Animals of Southern Africa.** 1840. Fo. 30 hand-cold. plts., hf.-title (loose), list of subscribers, text foxed, cont. hf. cf., end-paper loose. (SSA. Jul.5; 188) R 6,100
– – **Anr. Copy.** 30 hand-cold. litho. plts., slight foxing on pict. title, slight foxing & browning on edges of text ll., hf. mor. by Sangorski & Sutcliffe, spine gt. (VA. Apr.27; 672) R 6,000
– – **Anr. Edn.** Ill.:– Frank Howard after Harris. L., 1840[-42]. *1st. Edn. Iss. on L.P.* 5 orig. pts. in 1 vol. Fo. Cold. additional litho. vig. title, 30 cold. litho. plts., subscribers list, short margin tears to 1 plt. reprd., some light foxing, hf. mor., extremities slightly chafed. (SG. Nov.3; 95) $6,400
– **The Wild Sports of Southern Africa.** L., 1839. *1st. Edn.* 12mo. Folding map, 7 plts., title trimmed, orig. cl. (P. Dec.8; 337) *Robertshaw.* £50
– – **Anr. Edn.** L., 1841. *3rd. Edn.* Additional engraved title with hand-cold. vig., folding map, 25 hand-cold. plts., a few margins slightly soiled, orig. cl. (S. May 22; 416) *Reford.* £280
– – **Anr. Copy.** Frontis. & title-p. stained, hf. cf. (SSA. Jul.5; 189) R 340
– – **Anr. Edn.** L., 1844. *4th. Edn.* Some foxing on plts., marks in margin, hf. cf. (VA. Apr.27; 674) R 480
– – **Anr. Edn.** L., 1852. *5th. Edn.* Sm. 4to. Hand-cold. litho. title, folding map, 25 plts., some ll. slightly spotted or soiled, mod. cf. (BBA. Mar.21; 325) *Clarkes Bookshop.* £300

HARRIS, William Tell
– **Remarks Made During a Tour Through the United States of America, in the Years 1817, 1818 & 1819.** L'pool., [1819]. *1st. Edn.* Tall 8vo. Hf.-title, cont. gt.-tooled hf. russ. by C. Smith, spine gt. with alternating cinquefoil & cross patte of William Beckford, partly unc., Earl of Rosebery bkplt., the Rt. Hon. Visc. Eccles copy. (CNY. Nov.18; 132) $700

HARRISON, John, Publisher
– **D'Anville's Atlas, Containing a Map of the World, the World in Twelve Maps; & Twelve Maps of the Most Interesting Parts of the World upon a Large Scale. Also Eleven Maps of Ancient Geography for the Study of Ancient History.** 1792. Fo. Engraved title, 36 maps (13 double-p.), based on D'Anville's originals, engraved by Neele, Sudlow, Bowen & others, some hand-cold. in outl., on guards thro.-out, some maps a little soiled, a few leaving guards, some very sm. margin wormholes, cont. hf. cf., marb. bds., worn, lacks some leath., w.a.f. (LC. Mar.1; 261) £220

HARRISON, Walter
– **New & Universal History, Description & Survey of the Cities of London & Westminster.** 1776. Fo. 99 maps, town plans & engraved plts., title torn & reprd. affecting text, some text ll. torn, cf. gt., upr. cover detchd., as a collection of plts., w.a.f. (P. Sep.29; 253) *Reid.* £200
– – **Anr. Copy.** Fo. Lacks 5 plts., some offsetting, cont. hf. cf., worn. (S. Nov.1; 113) *Haddon.* £120
– – **Anr. Edn.** L., ca. 1780. Title, frontis., plts., some defect., browning, cf. worn, w.a.f. (P. May 17; 354) *Haden.* £170

HARRISSE, Henri
– **Bibliotheca Americana Vetustissima.** N.Y., 1866. *1st. Edn. (590).* Dark purple mor. gt. (*With:*) – **Bibliotheca Americana Vetustissima – Additions.** Paris, 1872. *1st. Edn.* Dark purple qtr. mor., gt. spine. Together 2 vols. Sm. fo. The Rt. Hon. Visc. Eccles copies. (CNY. Nov.18; 133) $350
– **Excerpta Colombiniana: Bibliographie de Quatre Cents Pièces Gothique** ... Paris, 1887. Lge. 8vo. Three-qtr. mor., unc., orig. wraps. bnd. in. (SG. Jan.5; 159) $110

HARRSEN, Meta
– **Nekcsei-Lipocz Bible: a Fourteenth Century Manuscript from Hungary in the Library of Congress.** Wash., 1949. *(600)* numbered. Fo. Mor.-bkd. gt.-decor. cl. (SG. Sep.15; 242) $100

HARSDORFFER, G. Ph.
– **Vollst. Trincir Büchlin.** Nuremb., [1640?]. Ob. 4to. Typographic title with sm. tear in upr. margin, lacks 1 sig. & ll pp. with 5 full-p. copper engrs., 1st. copperplt. very defect., minimal staining, cont. MS. vell., 4 ties (lacks 1), slightly soiled. (HK. Nov.9; 167 2) DM 1,300

HART, Capt. Liddell & Storrs, Sir Ronald
– **Lawrence of Arabia.** Corvinus Pr., 1936. *(128)* numbered & sigd. *(25)* on Barcham Green 'Boswell' paper. 4to. Orig. hf. cl. by Sargorski & Sutcliffe; pres. copy, inscr. 'To Nanny from [Viscount] Carlow who printed this book'. (CSK. Sep.16; 71) £170

HART, Capt. Lockyer Willis
– **Character & Costumes of Afghaunistan.** 1843. Fo. Litho. pict. title, dedication, map. 26 plts., orig. cl., rebkd. in mor. (BBA. Sep.29; 64) *Traylen.* £180

HARTE, Bret
– **The Luck of Roaring Camp.** Boston, 1870. *1st. Edn.* 12mo. Orig. blindstp. cl., mor.-bkd. folding box; inscr. on end-paper, Fred A.Berne copy. (SPB. May 16; 301) $550
– – **Anr. Edn.** Intro.:– Oscar Lewis. Ill.:– Mallette Dean. San Franc., [Grabhorn Pr.], 1948. *(300).* Sm. fo. Bkplt., hf. cl. & bds., corners slightly bumped. (CBA. Nov.19; 194) $110
– **A Millionaire of Rough-end-Ready.** Kentfield, 1955. *(220).* Lge. 8vo. Gt.-decor. two-tone bds. (CBA. Nov.19; 4) $130
– **The Queen of the Pirate Isle.** Ill.:– Kate Greenaway. L., [1886]. *1st. Edn.* Some darkening & soiling, unnamed bkplt. on front free end-paper, blue end-papers, pict. cl., Blanck's bdg. 'A'; bkplt. of Walter Crane, & pres. inscr. to his son Lionel. (CBA. Aug.21; 276) $120
– **Stories & Poems & Other Uncollected Writings.** Boston/N.Y., 1914. 20 vols. Hf. leath., marb. end-pp. (JL. Jul.15; 654) Aus. $170

HARTENFELS, E.
– **12 Lieder v. Goethe, Herder, Uhland, Chamisso, Heine, Brentano Komponiert m. Begleitung d. Pinoforte oder d. Guitarre.** Ill.:– Levy-Elkan & Fay, Preyer, Clasen, Heine & others. Düsseldorf, n.d. Ob. fo. Light old soiling or browning, hf. leath. (V. Oct.1; 3828) DM 750

HARTIG, G.L.
– **Einleitung zur Forst-und Weidmanns-Sprache oder Erklärung der älteren und Neueren Kunstwörter beym Forst- und Jagdwesen.** Tübingen, 1809. *1st. Edn.* Cont. bds., spine rubbed. (BR. Apr.12; 1206) DM 1,400
– **Lehrbuch für Jäger.** Tübingen, 1811. *1st. Edn.* 2 vols. Cont. bds., corners lightly bumped. (R. Apr.4; 1879) DM 1,600

HARTINGER, A.
– **Atlas der Alpenflora.** Text:– K.W. Dalls Torre. Wien, 1882-84. *1st. Edn.* 5 vols. (1 text & 4 plt. vols.). Cont. hf. leath. (R. Apr.4; 1731) DM 2,100

HARTKNOCH, Ch.
– **Preussische Kirchen-Historia.** Frankfurt & Leipzig, 1686. *1st. Edn.* 4to. Title with sm. corner tear, lacks port., some old MS. annets., cont. vell. (R. Oct.13; 2639) DM 1,100

HARTLAND, Frederick D.
- Tapographia: Or, A Collection of Tombs ... [L.], 1856. *(12)* lithod. & ptd. by author & pres. to Sir Thomas Phillipps. Sm. fo. Ills., plans, hf. mor. (SG. Apr.26; 92) $225

HARTLEY, J. & others
[–] History of Westminster Election. 1784. 4to. 15 engraved plts., mod. cl.-bkd. bds. (CSK. May 4; 97) £60

HARTLIEB, Jacob
- De Fide Meretricum in suos Amatores ... [Ulm, 1501?]. Old bds. (GB. May 3; 950) DM 1,000

HARTMANN, J.F.
- Abhandlung von der Verwandschaft und Ahnlichkeit der Elektrischen Kraft mit den Erschrecklichen Lluft- Erscheinungen. Hannover, 1759. *1st. Edn.* Cont. leath. gt., very rubbed. (R. Apr.4; 1524) DM 750

HARTMANN VON AUE
- Der Arme Heinrich. Trans.:– W. Grimm. Ill.:– R. Seewald. Dachau, [1920]. *(80) De Luxe Edn. on Bütten.* Not sigd. & numbered by artist, orig. cf., cover ill., slightly worn, spine faded. (H. Nov.24; 2042) DM 480

HARTT, Frederick
- Donatello: Prophet of Modern Vision. L., 1974. Fo. No bdg. stated. (SPB. Nov.30; 96) $200

HARVEY, T.
See— STURGE, J. & Harvey, T.

HARVEY, W. 'Aleph'
[–] Geographical Fun: Being Humorous Outlines of Various Countries ... by 'Aleph'L., ca. 1863. 4to. 12 chromolitho. caricature maps, publisher's catalogue at end, publisher's pict. bds., defect., w.a.f. (S. May 21; 175) *Map House.* £540

HARVEY, William
- The Anatomical Exercises. Ed.:– Geoffrey Keynes. Nones Pr., [1928.]. *(1450) numbered.* Orig. mor. (BBA. May 23; 189) *Maggs.* £75
– – **Anr. Copy.** Some edges browned, niger mor., partly unc. & unopened. (SG. Oct.6; 183) $125
- Exercitationes Anatomicae de Motu Cordis et Sanguinis Circulatione. Glasgow, 1751. Discold. in places, cont. cf. spine reprd.; Dr. Walter Pagel copy. (S. Feb.7; 156) *Studd.* £140
- Exercitationes de Generatione Animaluim. Amst., 1651. Title verso with owners mark, stained, some sm. margin defects., bds. (HK. May 15; 412) DM 400
– – **Anr. Edn.** Amst., 1662. 12mo. Cont. cf., worn; bkplt. of Henri Petit, Dr. Walter Pagel copy. (S. Feb.7; 157) *Studd.* £140
- Observationes et Historiae Omnes & Singulae e ... Libello De Generatione Animalium Excerptae. Amst., 1674. *1st. Ill. Edn.* 12mo. Engraved allegorical title, 8 engraved plts., partly dampstained, cont. vell.; bkplts. & stp. of the Osler Liby. at McGill University. (SG. Oct.6; 184) $275
- Opera. Ed.:– B.S. Albinus. Leiden, 1737. *1st. Coll. Edn.* 2 pts. in 1 vol. 4to. Hf.-title & 1st. lf. of preface misbnd., lacks 3 blank ll. & advt. lf., some stains, new hf. cf.; Dr. Walter Pagel copy. (S. Feb.7; 162) *Phillips.* £440
- Opera Omnia. Ed.:– Mark Akenside. Ill.:– I. Hall after Cornelius Jonson. L., 1766. 4to. Offset from port. onto title, margin of port. stained, hf. cf., unc.; Dr. Walter Pagel copy. (S. Feb.7; 158) *Studd.* £250
- The Works. L., 1847. Ex-liby. (*With:*) – An Anatomical Dissertation upon the Movement of the Heart & Blood. Canterbury, priv. ptd., 1894. (*With:*) - The Anatomical Exercises: De Motu Cordis, 1628; De Circulatione Sanguinis, 1649. Ed.:– Keynes. L., Nones. Pr., [1928]. *(1450) numbered.* Together 3 vols. 4to. & 8vo. Cl. & niger, 1st. vol. lacks spine. (SG. Mar.22; 147) $175

HARVEY PIRIE, J.H.
See— RUDMORE BROWN, R.N. & others

HARVIE-BROWN, J.A.
- Travels of a Naturalist in Northern Europe. 1905. 2 vols. Orig. cl., partly untrimmed. (TA. Jun.21; 50) £50

HARVIE-BROWN, J.A. & Buckley, T.E.
- A Fauna of the Moray Basin. Ill.:– after Annan. Edinb., 1895. 2 vols. Orig. cl. gt. (PD. Dec.14; 107) £65
- A Vertebrate Fauna of the Orkney Isles. Edinb., 1891. Orig. cl. (PD. Dec.14; 109) £55
- A Vertebrate Fauna of the Outer Hebrides. Ill.:– after Millais. Edinb., 1888. (*With:*) – A Vertebrate Fauna of Argyll & the Inner Hebrides. Edinb., 1892. Together 2 vols. Cl. gt. (PD. Dec.14; 108) £90

HARVIE-BROWN, J.A. & MacPierson, Rev. H.A.
- A Fauna of the North-West Highlands & Skye. Edinb., 1904. Orig. cl. gt. (PD. Dec.14; 113) £50

HASENTODTER, J.
- Chronica. Königsberg, 1569. *1st. Edn.* 1st. ll. slightly soiled, title lf. defect. with loss, 181 19th. C. bds. (R. Oct.11; 46) DM 800

HASIUS, J.M.
- Regni Davidici et Salomonaei Descriptio Geographica et Historica, una cum Delineatione Syriae et Aegypte ... Nuremb., 1739. Fo. 19th. C. hf. leath. (R. Oct.13, 3029) DM 1,075

HASKELL, Daniel C.
See— STOKES, I.N.Phelps & Haskell, Daniel C.

HASSALL, Mary
[–] Secret History; or, the Horrors of St. Domingo. Phila., 1808. 12mo. Spotted, cont. cf., worn, upr. cover nearly detchd. [Sabin 30807] (S. Jun.25; 99) *Maggs.* £280

HASSELL, John
- Memoirs of the Life of The Late George Morland. 1806. 4to. Hf. mor., rebnd. (WW. Nov.23; 118) £60
- Tour of the Grand Junction. L., 1819. *[1st. Edn.].* 4 hand-cold. aquatint plts, dedication lf. present, some light offsetting, sm. strip torn from blank margin of 1 plt., cont. mor. gt., jnts. slightly worn. (BBA. May 23; 217) *Quaritch.* £400
– – **Anr. Copy.** Some plt. margins trimmed affecting publication line, str.-grd. mor. gt., slightly defect. (BS. Nov.16; 36) £240
– – **Anr. Copy.** 24 hand-cold. plts., str.-grd. mor. gt., wc. (P. Oct.20; 212) £220
- Tour of the Isle of Wight. L., 1790. 2 vols. Titles slightly spotted, cont. cf., slightly worn. (S. Mar.6; 254) *Morrell.* £80
– – **Anr. Copy.** 2 vols. Place in ink on outer margins of plts., cf. gt. (P. Oct.20; 230d) £55

HASTED, Edward
- The History & Topographical Survey of the County of Kent. Canterbury, 1778-99. *[1st. Edn.].* 4 vols. Fo. 60 engraved plts., 39 folding maps & plans, extra-ill. with 2 additional ports., some light soiling, later tree cf. gt. by J. Mackenzie, rebkd., old spine laid down. (CSK. Dec.2; 37) £800
– – **Anr. Copy.** 4 vols. Fo. 99 maps & plts., diced cf. gt., 1 spine damaged. (P. Oct.20; 62) £720
– – **Anr. Copy.** 4 vols. Fo. 100 engraved plts, some ll. spotted or soiled, last 6 ll. in Vol. 2 stained, cont. cf., worn, most covers detchd. (BBA. Feb.9; 348) *Cumming.* £640
– – **Anr. Edn.** 1778-82-90. 3 vols. only (of 4). Fo. Rebkd. in cf. (PWC. Jul.11; 586) £500
– – **Anr. Edn.** 1779-99. *1st. Edn.* 4 vols. Fo. Handcold. folding county map, 98 engraved maps & plts., 2 slightly torn, 1 reprd., few ll. slightly spotted, hf. cf. gt., hinges reprd. (P. Sep.8; 366) £820
– – **Anr. Edn.** 4 vols. Fo. Hand-cold. folding county map (loose), 96 (of 98) maps & plts., slight trim to some plts. on outer margin, cf. g., Vol. 3 reprd., part of upr. corner of back in Vol. 1 lacking. (P. Sep.29; 97) *Fancycrest.* £500
– – **Anr. Edn.** Canterbury, 1797-1801. *2nd. Edn.* 12 vols. 69 views & maps, some spotting, a few sm. tears & repairs, hf. cf. gt.; A.L.s. from author. (P. Nov.24; 61) *Fancycrest.* £380
– – **Anr. Copy.** 12 vols. 35 (of 36) engraved folding maps & plans, 33 plts., many maps with tears reprd. & offset, few plt.-marks & captions cropped, few ll. reprd., some spotting, cont. cf., slightly worn, rebkd. (S. Mar.6; 426) *Frankland.* £340
– – **Anr. Edn.** 1972. *Facs. of 1797-1801 2nd. Edn.* 12 vols. Orig. cl., d.-w.'s. (TA. Nov.17; 193) £100

HASTINGS, James
- Encyclopedia of Religion & Ethics. 1908-26. 13 vols. 4to. Orig. cl. (BBA. Jul.27; 155) *Quaritch.* £90

HASTREL, A. d'
- Album de la Plata o' Colleccion de las Vistas y Costumbres Remarcables de esta Parte de la America del Sur. Paris, ca. 1850. *New Edn.* Lge. fo. Some slight foxing, orig. hf. leath. (HK. Nov.8; 832) DM 460

HATA, S.
See— EHRLICH, Paul & Hata, S.

HATCH, Benton J.
- A Check List of the Publications of Thomas B. Mosher ... 1891-1923. Biographical Essay:– R. Nash. Northampton, Gehenna Pr., 1966. *(500) sigd. by L. Baskin.* 4to. Cl.-bkd. bds., spine lightly soiled, unc., s.-c. cracked. (SG. Sep.15; 236) $140

HATCH, William Henry Paine
- The Principal Uncial Manuscripts of the New Testament. Chic., [1939]. *1st. Edn.* Tall 4to. 76 plts., cl. (SG. Sep.15; 25) $100

HATCHER, Henry
See— BENSON, Robert & Hatcher, Henry

HATCHET-SOUPLET, Pierre
- Le Dressage des Animaux et les Combats des Bêtes. Paris, [1895?]. Orig. pict. cl. gt., slightly worn. (S. Dec.20; 672) *Hackhofer.* £80

HATTIN, L.E.
- Histoire Pittoresque des Voyages dans les Cinq Parties du Monde. Paris, 1843. 5 vols. 48 cold. engraved plts., cont. hf. chagrin, spines decor. (HD. May 16; 36) Frs. 3,400

HATTON, Thomas
- An Introduction to the Mechanical Part of Clock & Watch Work. L., 1773. Hf.-title torn & mntd., slightly soiled thro.-out., mod. mor.-bkd. cl. (BBA. Nov.30; 101) *Walford.* £280

HATTON, Thomas & Cleaver, Arthur H.
- A Bibliography of the Periodical Works of Charles Dickens. 1933. *(250) sigd. by authors.* Orig. cl. gt.; from Norman Tarbolton liby. (P. Apr.12; 13) *Joseph.* £130
– – **Anr. Edn.** 1933. *(750).* Orig. cl.; H.M. Nixon coll. (BBA. Oct.6; 60) *Sawyer.* £100
– – **Anr. Edn.** L., 1933. *Ltd. Edn.* 4to. Buckram. (GM. Dec.7; 639) £50
– – **Anr. Edn.** L., 1953. *(50) L.P.* 4to. Last few ll. spotted, orig. cl., unc. (S. May 1; 400) *Branners.* £120

HAUDICQUER DE BLANCOURT, François
- L'Art de la Verrerie. Paris, 1718. *2nd. Edn.* 2 vols. MS. entry, cont. leath. gt., slightly bumped. (R. Oct.12; 1745) DM 800
– – **Anr. Copy.** 3 pts. in 2 vols. Plt. margins slightly browned or spotted, 1 plt. with sm tear, end-papers stpd., cont. hf. leath., slightly defect. (HT. May 8; 631) DM 520
– – **Anr. Copy.** 2 vols. 12mo. Cont. cf., decor. spines. (HD. Jan.26; 167) Frs. 1,300

HAUER, D.A.
- Kurtze und Gründliche Anweisung nach der Neuesten Art zierlich zu Schreiben. Nürnberg, ca. 1765. Ob. 4to. Title stpd., mod. bds.; Hauswedell coll. (H. May 23; 291) DM 560

HAUFF, W.
- Mittheilungen aus den Memoiren des Satan. Stuttgart, 1827-29. *1st. Edn.* 3 vols. Title with 2 stps., cont. hf. leath. gt., blind-tooled, crowned initials on covers, spine vol. 1 slightly stained. (HK. Nov.10; 2484) DM 1,400
- Sämmtliche Schriften. Ed.:– G. Schwab. Stuttgart, 1830. *1st. Coll. Edn.* 36 vols. in 12. 12mo. 2 ll. loose, minimal spotting, with litho. port., cont. lacquered bds., decor., spines darkened; Eduard Erdmann ex-libris; Hauswedell coll. (H. May 24; 1357) DM 1,500
– – **Anr. Copy.** 36 vols. in 5. Slightly browned, cont. bds., gold-tooled, slightly defect., some tears, slightly defect., some tears, slightly bumped & worn. (HT. May 9; 1497) DM 750

HAUGUM, J. & Low, A.M.
- A Monograph of the Birdwing Butterflies. Klampenberg, 1978-80. Vol. I: Pts. I-III, Vol. II: Pts. I & II. 4to. Orig. wraps. (SKC. Oct.26; 377) £50

HAUKSBEE, Francis
- Physico-Mechanical Experiments ... L., 1709. 2nd. Edn. Cont. panel. cf., rebkd., new end-papers. (P. Jan.12; 233) *Bickersteth.* £180

HAUPT, Albrecht
- Renaissance Palaces of Northern Italy & Tuscany, With Some Examples of Earlier Styles from the 13th to the 17th Century. L., 1931. *Revised Edn.* 3 vols. Fo. Orig. bdgs. (VA. Apr.26; 231) R. 180

HAUPT, Albrecht & others
- Palast-Architektur von Ober-Italien und Toscana. Berlin, 1886-1922. 6 vols. Atlas fo. Approx. 600 plts., & text ills., each plt. liby-stpd. on blank versos, not collated, loose in ptd. bds., linen ties. (SG. May 3; 201) $550

HAUPT, M.T. von
- [–] Blüten aus Italien. Darmstadt, 1808. *1st. Edn.* 2 pts. in 1 vol. Lightly foxed, cont. bds. (R. Apr.5; 2967) DM 550

HAUPTMANN, Aug.
- Neues Chym. Kunst Project u. sehr wichtigen Bergk Bedencken, über die allergrösten Hauptmängel des Bergckwercks ... Leipzig, 1658. Sm. stp. on title verso, lightly browned, cont. bds., worn & slightly wormed. (HK. Nov.8; 453) DM 900

HAUPTMANN, Gerhard
- Der Biberpelz. Berlin, 1893. *1st. Edn.* MS. owners list, ex-libris, orig. wraps. (R. Oct.11; 259) DM 420
- Das Bunte Buch. Beerfelden, 1888. *1st. Edn.* 1st. corners lightly creased, margins lightly browned, orig. wraps., slightly faded, spine slightly bumped, 1 sm. corner torn off. (H. Nov.24; 2490) DM 600
- Fasching. Ill.:– A. Kubin. 1925. *1st. Edn.* (450) numbered. 4to. Printers mark sigd. by author, 12 orig. lithos., 1 sigd., 10 full-p., orig. pict. hf. leath. (GB. May 5; 2845) DM 750
- Der Ketzer von Soana. Ill.:– Hans Meid. 1926. (130) numbered De Luxe Edn. on H.M.P., (120) for sale. 4to. Printers mark sigd. by author, 14 sigd. orig. etchings, orig. vell., gold-tooled cover vig. (GB. May 5; 2953) DM 1,300
- – Anr. Copy. 4to. Orig. vell.; printer's mark sigd. by author. (HK. Nov.11; 3809) DM 1,100

HAUPTNER, H.
- Katalog der Instrumenten-Fabrik für Tiermedizin und Tierzucht. Berlin, 1907. 4to. Orig. linen. (GB. Nov.3; 1016) DM 430

HAUSCHNER, A.
- Der Tod des Löwen. Ill.:– H. Steiner-Prag. Leipzig, [1922]. (400). (145) numbered De Luxe Edn. A with sigd. orig. etchings with remarks. 4to. 11 orig. etchings (including 10 full-p. sigd.), orig. mor., sm. defect. on upr. cover, inset centrepiece, gold-tooled vig., gt. spine. (GB. May 5; 3362) DM 800

HAUSDORFF, F.
- Grundzüge der Mengenlehre. Leipzig, 1914. *1st. Edn.* Cont. hf. leath., spine slightly faded. (HT. May 8; 413) DM 750

HAUS, STADT UND LAND, in 12 Col. Bildlichen Darstellungen aus dem Leben
Nürnberg, [inscr. dtd. 1857]. Lge. ob. 4to. 12 lge. hand-cold. litho. scenes, Fr. German & Engl. captions, short tear in upr. margin of last plt. reprd., orig. bds., pict. label on upr. cover hand-cold., rebkd., slightly worn; van Veen coll. (S. Feb.28; 147) £880

HAUSENSTEIN, W.
See— CORINTH, L. & Hausenstein, W.

HAUSWEDEL, E.L. (Ed.)
See— IMRIMATUR
See— PHILOBIBLON

HAUTECOEUR, L. & Wiet, G.
- Les Mosquées du Caire. Paris, 1932. 2 vols. 4to. Private hf. leath., worn. (D. Nov.23; 1238) DM 1,100

HAUTHAL, F.
- Geschichte der Sächsischen Armee in Wort und Bild. Leipzig, 1859. *2nd. Edn.* Fo. Plts. with minimal spotting, cont. linen. (R. Oct.12; 2289) DM 4,100

HAUTORTHON, Josaphat Friedrich
- [–] Der Verlängerte dritte Anfang der Mineralischen Dinge oder vom Philosophischen Saltz nebenst der waren Preparation Lapidis et Tincture Philosophorum ... Amst., 1656. *1st. Edn.* Colophon lf., hf. cf., marb. wraps. bnd. in; Dr. Walter Pagel copy. (S. Feb.7; 169) *Ritman.* £500

HAVARD, Abbé
See— ROGISSART, Le Sieur de & Havard, Abbé

HAVARD, Henry
- Dictionnaire de l'Ameublement et de la Décoration. Paris, ca. 1890. 4 vols. Lge. 4to. 250 plts., including many chromolithos., 2500 text engrs., liby. buckram. (SG. May 3; 202) $325
- – Anr. Copy. 4 vols. 4to. Prelims. to 1st. vol. detchd., some darkening & brittling, bdg. not stated, but worn, lacks backstrips, end-papers partly detchd. (CBA. Jan.29; 233) $140
- Histoire des Faiences de Delft. Amst., 1909. *2nd. Edn.* 2 vols. 4to. Three-qtr. leath., rubbed, spines crudely taped. (SG. Jan.26; 100) $110
- Histoire de l'Orfevrerie Française. Paris, 1896. Lge. 4to. 40 plts., many chromolithos., liby. buckram, orig. pict. cover wrap. detchd. (SG. Aug.25; 170) $190

HAVELL, Robert
- The Tour, or Select Views of the Southern Coast. L., 1827. Engraved title & 57 hand-cold. aquatint views on 25 plts., 1 folding, cont. mor.-bkd. bds., rubbed. (BBA. May 23; 218) *Quaritch.* £480

HAVEN, Charles T. & Belden, Frank A.
- A History of the Colt Revolver & Other Arms Made by Colt's Patent Fire Arms Manufacturing Company from 1836 to 1940. N.Y., 1940. *1st. Edn.* 4to. Orig. gift bdg. of gt.-pict. mor., boxed; Sigd. & dtd. by authors on front free end-paper. (SG. Aug.4; 111) $160

HAVERS, Clopton
- Novae Quaedem Observationes de Ossibus. Ed.:– J.C. Heyne. Leiden, 1734. 3 pp. errata, cont. marb. bds., cf. spine, unc.; Dr. Walter Pagel copy. (S. Feb.7; 165) *Heller.* £180

HAWEIS, Thomas (Ed.)
See— BIBLIANA [English]

HAWKER, James C.
- Early Experiences in South Australia. Adelaide, 1899. Orig. cl.; the Hobill Cole copy. (KH. Nov.9; 618) Aus. $140

HAWKER, Col. Peter
- The Diary, 1802-1853. Intro.:– Sir Ralph Payne-Gallwey. 1893. *1st. Edn.* 2 vols. Publisher's 24 p. catalogue dtd. Aug. 1893, orig. cl. gt. (SKC. May 4; 1758) £110
- Instructions to Young Sportsmen in All that Relates to Guns & Shooting. L., 1824. *3rd. Edn.* 10 plts., including 4 hand-cold., lacks title (supplied in ptd. facs.), & hf.-title, mod. red hf. mor. gt., spine tooled in compartments with ornaments, by Bayntun slightly soiled. (S. Oct.4; 269) *Old Hall.* £60
- – Anr. Edn. 1833. *7th. Edn.* Hf.-title, mod. hf. cf. gt.; extra-ill. with 1 plain & 5 cold. plts. (SKC. May 4; 1757) £70

HAWKESWORTH, John
- An Account of the Voyages ... in the Southern Hemisphere. 1773. *1st. Edn.* 3 vols. 4to. 51 engraved charts, maps & plts. (of 52), some slight soiling or offsetting, sm. inscr. on titles, cont. hf. cf., worn. (S. May 22; 470) *Marshall.* £480
- – Anr. Edn. 1773. *2nd. Edn.* 3 vols. 4to. Hf. cf., spines gt., spines faded, slight scuffing to jnts. & corners; Lord Mexborough copy, J.A. Bushfield bkplt. (LC. Jul.5; 200a) £460

- – Anr. Copy. 3 vols. A few pp. spotted, cf., rebkd. (JL. Nov.13; B84) Aus. $1,200
- – Anr. Edn. L., 1773. 3 vols. 4to. Some staining & foxing, liby. stps., hf. cf., covers detchd., 1 lacking, worn, as a coll. of plts., w.a.f. (SPB. Dec.13; 502) $275
- – Anr. Edn. Dublin, 1775. *1st. Authorized Irish Edn.* 2 vols. Cont. tree cf., covers detchd. (SG. Sep.22; 103) $150
- [–] Almoran & Hamet: An Oriental Tale. L., 1761. *1st. Edn.* 2 vols. Hf.-titles, errata lf., cont. tree cf.; bkplt. of Rev. T. Streatfeild. (SPB. May 16; 78) $200
- Geschichte der See-Reisen und Entdeckungen im Süd-Meer. Berlin, 1774. *1st. German Edn.* 3 vols. 4to. Cont. leath., slightly worn. [Sabin 30942] (R. Oct.13; 3068) DM 3,000
- Relation des Voyages ... pour faire des Découvertes dans l'Hemisphère Méridional. Trans.:– Suard. Paris, 1774. *1st. Fr. Edn.* 4to. Bds., unc. [Sabin 30940] (D. Nov.23; 1320) DM 1,800

HAWKESWORTH, John
See— COOK, Capt. James & Hawkesworth, John

HAWKESWORTH, John (Ed.)
See— ADVENTURER, The

HAWKINS, Sir Anthony Hope 'Anthony Hope'
- Works. N.Y., 1902. *Ltd. 'Authors' Edn.* (50) numbered, 'made for Andrew J. McDuffee'. 15 vols. Maroon mor., gt.-tooled, gt.-panel. spines in 6 compartments, turn-ins gt. with suede doubls., satin free end-pp., partly unc.; A.L.s. from author to Robert Russell, with envelope, tipped in. (CNY. Dec.17; 569) $550

HAWKINS, Ernest
- [–] The Colonial Church Atlas. 1842. 4to. 18 partly cold. maps. orig. cl., dampstained. (P. Feb.16; 297) £65

HAWKINS, G.
- The Holy Land. Day & Haghe, ca. 1840. Ob. fo. 13 tinted lithos., no text, some foxing, no bdg. stated. (P. Sep.8; 340) *Shapiro.* £75

HAWKINS, Sir John
- A General History of the Sciences & Practice of Music. L., 1776. *1st. Edn.* 5 vols. 4to. Hf.-titles, slight offsetting onto text, 19th. C. pol. cf., gt., rubbed, a few minor defects in spines; bkplt. recording in Latin gift of books to (Sir) Walter Morley Fletcher from M.R. James in 1904. (S. May 10; 68) *Baron.* £380
- – Anr. Copy. 5 vols. 4to. Hf.-titles, a few spots & stains, tear in last lf. of Vol. I & wormholes in last few ll. of Vol. V, reprd., early 20th. C. hf. mor., spines gt., partly unc., slightly rubbed. (S. May 10; 69) *Baron.* £250

HAWKINS, Rush C.
- Titles of the First Books from the Earliest Presses ... before the End of the Fifteenth Century. N.Y. & L., 1884. (300) numbered. 4to. Cl.,-ex-liby., unc. (SG. Aug.4; 162) $150

HAWKS, Francis Lister
- Narrative of the Expedition ... under ... M.C. Perry. Wash., 1856. *1st. Edn.* 3 vols. 4to. With suppressed nude bathers plt. & plt. showing photographer at work, lacks 1 plt. & 2 folding charts, many fold separations, liby. buckram; sigd. pres. set from grandson of G.B. Perry, w.a.f. (SG. Sep.22; 171) $300
- – Anr. Copy. 3 vols. 4to. With the photographer plt., but without the nude bathers plt., orig. cl. or cont. cf., worn. (SG. Mar.29; 332) $225
- – Anr. Edn. N.Y., 1857. 11 folding maps, 77 plts., orig. cl., rebkd., orig. spine preserved. (S. Apr.9; 32) *McCall.* £180
- – Anr. Copy. 4to. Nude bathers & photographer plts., scattered light foxing & dampstaining, mor., worn. (SG. Sep.22; 173) $100
- [–] Uncle Philip's Conversations with the Young People about the Whale Fishery, & Polar Regions. L., 1837. 16mo. Orig. gt. & blind-stpd. cl.; from liby. of F.D. Roosevelt, inscr. by him (as President). (SG. Mar.15; 52) $400

HAWLEY, Walter A.
- Oriental Rugs, Antique & Modern. 1925. 4to. Orig. cl., lightly soiled. (CSK. Oct.7; 97) £55

HAWLEY COLLECTION
- The Hawley Collection of Violins. Chic., 1904. *(2000) numbered.* 4to. Port. & cold. plts. spotted, orig. cl.-bkd. bds., spine soiled & rubbed (affecting label), s.-c. worn & defect. (S. May 1; 663)
Baron. £110

HAWTHORNE, Nathaniel
- The House of Seven Gables. Boston, 1851. *1st. Edn.* Advts. dtd. Mar. 1851, bdg. B, orig. blindstpd. cl.; Fred A. Berne copy. (SPB. May 16; 303) $550
- The Scarlet Letter. Boston, 1850. *1st. Edn.* Advts. dtd. Mar.1, 1850, with 'reduplicate' instead of 'repudiate' on p.21, slight browning on advts. from newspaper clipping on endpaper, orig. cl., upr. cover stained, Spoor/Fred A.Berne copy. (SPB. May 16; 304) $425
- - **Anr. Copy.** 4-pp. advts. dtd. Mar. 1, 1850, orig. cl., spine & corners worn, mor. s.-c.; Perry Molstad copy. (SPB. May 16; 458) $400
- - **Anr. Copy.** Inserted publisher's advts. dtd. Mar.1, 1850, orig. cl., spine ends chipped. (SPB. Dec.13; 686) $275
- - **Anr. Copy.** Sm. 8vo. Cf. gt., by Bayntun. (SG. Mar.15; 121) $200
- Tanglewood Tales. Ill.:– Edmund Dulac. L., [1918]. *(500) numbered & sigd. by artist.* 4to. Orig. hf. vell., s.-c. (S. Nov.22; 321) *Desk.* £280
- - **Anr. Copy.** 4to. Fore-e.'s foxed, three-qtr. gt.-decor. vell. & bds., end-papers darkening. (CBA. Aug.21; 193) $200
- A Wonder Book. Ill.:– after Arthur Rackham. L., [1922]. *1st. Rackham Edn. (600) numbered.* 4to. Some minor foxing, mainly at end-papers, gt.-decor. linen, lightly soiled. (CBA. Aug.21; 517) $275
- [Works]. Ill.:– Childe Hassam, Howard Pyle, Eric Pape, Alice Barber Stephens, F.C. Yohn, & others. Boston, 1900. *(500) numbered.* 22 vols. Tall 8vo. Engraved vig. titles, frontispieces, & plts. each present in mntd. India-proof & cold. states, India proof frontispieces sigd. in pencil by artists, cl., unopened, spines faded, few labels lightly soiled. (SG. Mar.15; 122) $500
- - **Anr. Copy.** 22 vols. Cl., mostly unopened, some staining to spines. (CBA. Dec, 10; 256) $140

HAXTHAUSEN, A. Freiherr von
- Studien über die Inneren Zustände, das Volksleben und insbesondere die Ländlichen Einrichtunges Russlands. Hannover & Berlin, 1847-52. *1st. Edn.* 3 pts. in 3 vols. Some sigs. lightly browned, some slight foxing, cont. linen, spine slightly faded. (HT. May 10; 2849) DM 580

HAY, Peter, of Naughton
- An Advertisement To the Subjects of Scotland, Of the fearfull Dangers threatned to Christian States ... by the Ambition of Spaine ... Aberdeen, 1627. 4to. Some stains, old vell., worn & defect.; Sir Ivar Colquhoun, of Luss copy. [STC 1271] (CE. Mar.22; 151) £460

HAY, Robert
- Illustrations of Cairo. Ill.:– J.C. Bourne after Hay, O.B. Carter & C. Laver. L., 1840. Fo. Frontis., dedication lf. & 30 litho. views on 29 sheets, a few minor spots, publisher's qtr. mor., spine defect. (S. May 22; 281) *Hague.* £1,750

HAY, Roy & Synge, Patrick M.
- The Dictionary of Garden Plants. Arcadia Pr., 1969. *Ltd. Edn., sigd. by authors.* 4to. Mor. by Zaehnsdorf, upr. cover gt. & with col. mor. onlays, cl. box. (C. Nov.16; 256) *Hill.* £100

HAYASHI, Shunko
- Shippo no Moyo. Tokyo, Showa 52 [1977]. Lge. 4to. 91 col. plts., cl., cl. folding case, publisher's corrugated-bd. box. (SG. Jan.26; 214) $110

HAYDEN, Ferdinand Vandeveer
- Geological & Geographical Atlas of Colorado. 1877. Lge. fo. 20 double-p. litho. maps & views, orig. hf. mor., worn. (CSK. Feb.24; 26) £150
- - **Anr. Copy.** Fo. 18 double-p. litho. maps, most in col., 2 double-p. plts. of panoramic views in the Rockies, liby. stp. on title, lr. margins lightly dampstained, cl., scuffed. (SG. Jun.7; 16) $225

HAYDN, Joseph
- Laurette. Paris, [1791]. *1st. Edn.* Fo. Title with MS. publisher's name, title double stpd. & with MS. owner's mark, erased stps. in lr. margins, slightly browned thro.-out & some light foxing, 2 ll. with sm. tear in lr. corner, 1 p. with blue stain, cont. hf. vell., MS. title on upr. cover. (HK. Nov.9; 2249) DM 400
- Die Schoepfung. Ein Oratorium. [Partitur]. Wien, 1800. *1st. Edn. Ltd. Iss.* Fo. Lacks port. (as often), oval stp. on title with monog., some slight foxing, lr. corner lightly soiled thro.-out, some recent blue pencil entries, hf. linen, ca. 1870; Haydn's monog. round stp. on title & his MS. sig. (HK. Nov.9; 2251) DM 4,600

HAYDON, G.H.
- Five Years' Experience in Australia Felix ... 1846. Some foxing, some pencil marginalia, bdg. not stated, unc., recased. (KH. May 1; 339) Aus. $190
- - **Anr. Copy.** Title slightly foxed, margins of some plts. foxed, blind-stpd. cl. gt., unc., rebkd., covers chipped. (CA. Apr.3; 53) Aus. $160

HAYES, Charles
- A Treatise of Fluxions. L., 1704. *1st. Edn.* Fo. Overlay inserted on verso of 1 lf., cont. panel. cf., rebkd., orig. label laid down, some rubbing; John Wilkes sig., Stanitz coll. (SPB. Apr.25; 209) $900

HAYES, Sir Henry Browne
- The Only Genuine Edition: The Trial of Sir Henry Browne Hayes, Knt., for forcibly & feloniously taking away Miss Mary Pike, on the Twenty-Second Day of July, 1797 ... Cork, ca. 1801. Sm. 4to. Stained & discold., paper fault on B3 affecting a few words of text, old hf. cf., worn, no free end-papers. (KH. May 1; 340) Aus. $120

HAYES, Isaac Israel
- The Open Polar Sea. L., 1867. Cl. gt.; pres. copy from Donald B. Macmillan, with his bkplt. (P. Nov.24; 10) *Cavendish.* £60

HAYES, J.G.
- Antarctica; A Treatise on the Southern Continent. 1928. *1st. Edn.* Copy of Royal Warrant for Polar Medal inserted, buckram, d.-w. slightly torn. (P. Jun.7; 26) £85

HAYES, Samuel
- A Practical Treatise on Planting ... By S.H. Dublin, 1794. *1st. Edn.* Bds., unc. (GM. Dec.7; 12) £130

HAYES, William
- [A Collection of 39 Hand-Coloured Etched Plates of Birds]. 1777. Fo. Many proofs before letters sigd. by artist & dtd. 1777, 1 plt. detchd. from bdg., mod. hf. cf., as a coll. of plts., w.a.f. (C. Jun.27; 160) *Parkway.* £3,000
- A Natural History of British Birds, &c. With their Portraits. Ill.:– after Hayes. L., [?1771-]75. Fo. 25 (of 40) hand-col. plts., lacks engraved dedication & pp. 5-6, last plt. creased & frayed, a few margin tears, stitching brkn., cont. hf. cf., very worn, covers detchd. (S. Nov.28; 33) *Reid.* £980

HAYES, William & Family
- Portraits of Rare & Curious Birds with their Descriptions from the Menagery of Osterly Park in the County of Middlesex. L., priv. ptd., 1794. 4to. 91 hand-col. etched plts. (of 100), a few sigd. by Hayes or members of his family, some captions cropped or shaved, cont. hf. cf., worn, spine torn, w.a.f. (C. Jun.27; 161) *Burden.* £1,100
- - **Anr. Copy.** 4to. 39 (of 100) hand-col. ills., of which at least 12 are either orig. wtrcol. drawings or very light impressions of plts. hand-col., many sigd. by Hayes, mor. gt., w.a.f. (C. Jun.27; 162) *Kaye.* £700
- - **Anr. Copy.** Vol. 1 only. 4to. 50 hand-col. etched plts., lacks frontis. & several tissue guards, many ptd. captions cropped & replaced in MS., few plts. with light margin soiling, cont. cf., worn, covers & 1st. sig. detchd., ex-liby. (SG. Oct.6; 188) $1,000
- - **Anr. Edn.** L., 1794 [-99]. *1st. Edn.* 2 vols. in 1. 4to. 100 hand-col. etched plts., lacks frontis. to Vol. I, & title & prelims., 1 lf., to Vol. II, 1st. plt. a little stained, some minor foxing, 19th. C. red hf. mor. gt. (C. Jun.27; 162) *Maggs.* £1,700

- - **Anr. Edn.** Ill.:– after Hayes & others. L., 1794-99. 2 vols. in 1. 4to. 100 hand-cold. engraved plts., lacks frontis. (a view of Osterly menagerie inserted) & title & prelims. to Vol. 2, some plts. trimmed, slight spotting & soiling, cont. red mor., gt. borders & spine, covers lettered 'Mrs. Davison 1805', spine rubbed. (S. Nov.28; 32)
Schuster. £860

HAYGARTH, W.
- Greece, a Poem. 1814. 4to. Diced cf. gt. (P. Mar.15; 225) *Tzakas.* £520

HAYLEY, William
- Ballads ... Founded on Anecdotes Relating to Animals. Ill.:– William Blake. 1805. Cf. gt., rebkd. (P. Apr.12; 269) *Marks.* £260
- The Life of George Romney. Chichester, 1809. 4to. 1 plt. cleanly torn & reprd., orig. bds., rebkd. (CSK. Aug.5; 51) £70
- The Triumphs of Temper. Ill.:– William Blake after Maria Flaxman. Chichester, 1803. *12th. Edn.* Sm. 8vo. Hf.-title, cont. tree cf., rebkd., spine gt. (BBA. Jan.19; 206) *Thomas, A.* £160.

HAYM, N.F.
[-] Thesauri Britannici pars Prima [& altera] seu Museum. Vienna, 1762-[64]. 2 vols. 4to. Spotted & browned, 2nd. vol. with additional work bnd. in, cf.-bkd. bds spines & jnts. worn. (S. May 1; 512)
Spink. £90

HAYMO, Bp. of Halberstadt
See– SULPICIUS SEVERUS — HAYMO, Bp. of Halberstadt

HAYN, H. & Gotendorf, A.N.
- Bibliotheca Germanorum Erotica et Curiosa. München, 1912-14. 8 vols. Orig. hf. leath., rubbed. (HK. May 17; 3340) DM 500

HAYNE, Freidrich G.
- Termini Botanici Iconibus Illustrati. Berlin, 1799–1807. *1st. Edn.* 2 pts. in 1 vol. 4to. 1 copper engraved title browned & stpd. in margin, cont. leath., rubbed. (GB. Nov. 3; 1137) DM 900

See– DREVES, Friedrich & Hayne, F.G.
See– WILLDENOW, C.L. & Hayne, Fr. G.

HAYNE, Fr. G. & Otto, Fr.
- Abbildung der Fremden, in Deutschland ausdauernden Holzarten. Ed.:– Fr. Guimpel. Berlin, 1825. Vol. 1 (of 2). 4to. 108 old cold. copperplts., some plts. slightly spotted, some slightly browned, text slightly foxed, cont. mor. gt., slightly rubbed & bumped. (HT. May 8; 295) DM 1,700

HAYTER, Rev. John
- A Report upon the Herculaneum Manuscripts. 1811. 4to. 6 engraved plts. (5 hand-cold.), some ll. browned, cont. pres. bdg. to Edward Cook (Under Secretary of State), rebkd., worn, upr. cover detchd. (BBA. Jan.19; 341) *Maggs.* £140

HAYWARD, John
- English Poetry. [1950]. *(550) numbered.* Orig. cl., d.-w. (CSK. Nov.25; 205) £80
- - **Anr. Copy.** Sm. 4to. Orig. buckram, d.-w. slightly reprd.; Frederic Dannay copy. (CNY. Dec.16; 162) $140

HAYWARD, Sir John 1564–1627
- The Life & Raigne of Kind Edward the Sixt. L., 1630. *1st. Edn.* 4to. Engraved title-p., cut close & stained, port. of author, lacks 1st. lf. (? blank), cont. limp vell., arms blind-stpd. on covers. [STC 12998] (BBA. May 3; 110) *Robertshaw.* £70

HAZAN, Yisrael Moshe
- Sefer Nahala le-Yisrael. Na Amon [Alexandria], 1862. *2nd. Edn. (Bound with:) -* Sefer She'eirit ha-Nahala. Na Amon [Alexandria], 1862. *1st. Edn.* Together 2 works in 1 vol. 4to. Mild browning, scattered margin worming, Italian title-p. soiled, cont. qtr. leath., spine ends badly chafed, covers spotted. (SG. Feb.2; 207) $130

HAZEN, E.
- The Panorama of Professions & Trades. Phila., 1836. Sm. 4to. Foxed & partly browned, cont. hf. leath., bumped, spine defect. (R. Apr.4; 2044) DM 550

HAZLITT, William
- **Characters of Shakespear's Plays.** L., 1817. *1st. Edn.* Slightly foxed, cf. gt. by Sangorski & Sutcliffe. (LH. Sep.25; 540) $110
- **Lectures on the English Comic Writers.** L., 1819. *1st. Edn.* Pict. prize certificate of Ancheas Mitchell on front pastedown, gt. armorial cf. by Carss, spine gt. (SG. Nov.17; 170) $110
- **Liber Amoris.** L., 1823. *1st. Edn.* 12mo. Hf.-title, slightly browned, dampstains on a few ll., cont. cf., spine gt., rubbed. (BBA. May 3; 235) *Korn.* £90
- [-] **The Plain Speaker: Opinions on Books, Men & Things.** 1826. *1st. Edn.* 2 vols. 8vo. Cont. hf. cf., rebkd. in mor.; author's name inscr. on titles. (BBA. Jan.19; 230) *Wauchope.* £120
- [-] **A Reply to the Essay on Population, by the Rev. T.R. Malthus.** 1807. *1st. Edn.* Some foxing, later hf. mor. gt., partly untrimmed. (TA. Nov.17; 373) £160
- [-] **The Spirit of the Age.** 1825. *1st. Edn.* 1st. & last lf. spotted, cont. cf. slightly rubbed. (BBA. Feb.9; 84) *Scott.* £55
- **A View of the English Stage.** L., 1818. *1st. Edn.* Lacks hf.-title & last (? blank) lf., some ll. slightly browned, cont. hf. cf., rebkd., slightly rubbed. (BBA. May 3; 234) *Murray Hill.* £65

HEAD, C.F.
- **Eastern & Egyptian Scenery, Ruins & c.** L., 1833. Ob. fo. Vig. on title, 3 maps (1 hand-cold. in outl.), 22 litho. views, errata slip, margin stains affecting title & some plts., orig. ptd. bds., worn. (S. May 22; 282) *Shapiro.* £650

HEAD, Sir Francis Bond
- **A Narrative.** L., 1839. *1st. Edn.* Orig. cl. gt. (P. May 17; 1) *Blackwells.* £70
- **Reports Relating to the Failure of the Rio Plata Mining Association.** L., 1827. Hf.-title, mod. bds., unc.; pres. inscr. by author to Woodbine Parrish on title. [Sabin 31136] (BBA. Dec.15; 53) *Quevedo.* £80
- - **Anr. Copy.** Orig. bds. [Sabin 31136] (SG. Oct.20; 179) $100

HEAD, Richard
- [-] **The Life & Death of Mother Shipton.** L., 1687 [but later?]. Sm. 4to. Woodcut frontis. guarded & offset onto title, some spotting, mod. panel. cf., gt. spine. [cf. Wing H1259] (S. Oct.11; 542) *Thorp.* £50
- [-] **Proteus Redivivus: or the Art of Wheedling, or Insinuation.** L., 1675. *1st. Edn.* Corner of K8 defect., 2 natural flaws affecting a few letters, X1 torn, some headlines cropped, a little browned, later cf. [Wing H1272] (BBA. May 3; 155) *Howes Bookshop.* £80
- - **Anr. Copy.** Old cf., rebkd. & relined, much of old spine laid down. (SG. Oct.27; 140) $200

HEAL, Ambrose
- **The English Writing-Masters & their Copy-Books.** L., 1st. Edns. Club, 1931. *(100) De Luxe Edn. for members.* Lge. 4to. Orig. hand-bnd. hf. leath., spine faded, Hauswedell coll. (H. May 23; 342) DM 1,700
- - **Anr. Edn.** Intro.:- Stanley Morison. Hildesheim, 1962. 4to. Cl., light wear. (RO. Dec.11; 141) $100
- **The London Furniture Makers.** 1953. 4to. Orig. cl.-bkd. bds., d.-w. (BBA. Sep.8; 193) *Quantin.* £80
- - **Anr. Copy.** 4to. Orig. cl.-bkd. bds., d.-w. (BBA. Apr.5; 220) *Bowers.* £50
- **The London Goldsmiths, 1200-1800.** Camb., 1935. *1st. Edn.* Sm. fo. Frontis., 80 plts. of trade cards, gt.-pict. cl. (SG. Oct.13; 180) $325
- **The Signboards of old London Shops.** 1947. *(1000).* 4to. Orig. cl., d.-w. (BBA. Nov.10; 351) *Litherland.* £50

HEALY, Rev. William
- **History & Antiquities of Kilkenny [County & City].** [Kilkenny, 1893]. Vol. 1 (all publd.). Mod. mor. (GM. Dec.7; 422) £70

HEANEY, Seamus
- **Bog Poems.** Ill.:- Barrie Cooke. [L.], Rainbow Pr., 1975. *(150) numbered & sigd.* 4to. Hf. lev., papyrus covers, cl. s.-c., by Sangorski & Sutcliffe. (SG. Mar.1; 172) $300

HEAP, Gwinn H.
- **Central Route to the Pacific, from the Valley of the Mississippi to California: Journal of the Expedition of E.F. Beale** ... Phila., 1854. 13 tinted lithos., advts. at end, lacks map, orig. cl., covers faded. (LH. Jan.15; 306) $110

HEARN, Geoge A.
- **Collection of Watches loaned to the Metropolitan Museum of Art of the City of New York.** [N.Y.], 1907. 4to. Hf. leath. (R. Oct.12; 1778) DM 400

HEARN, Lafcadio
- **Shadowings.** Boston, 1900. *1st. Edn.* Decor. cl., d.-w., light wear, d.-w. with minor fraying & taped on verso; Ken Leach coll. (RO. Jun.10; 584) $100

HEARNE, Samuel
- **A Journey from Prince of Wales's Fort in Hudson's Bay, to the Northern Ocean.** L., 1795. *1st. Edn.* 4to. 4 folding plts., 5 folding engraved maps, the 1st. with journeys hand-cold., some light foxing to plts., cont. diced russ. gt., rebkd. with orig. backstrip laid down, corners just worn; the Rt. Hon. Visc. Eccles copy. [Sabin 31181 (noting 4 maps & 8 plts.)] (CNY. Nov.18; 135) $1,900
- - **Anr. Copy.** 4to. 5 folding maps, 4 engraved ills., cf. [Sabin 31181] (LH. Sep.25; 234) $1,600

HEARNE, Thomas & Bryne, W.
- **Antiquities of Great Britain, Illustrated in Views of Monasteries, Castles, & Churches, now existing.** 1786. *[1st. Edn.].* Vol. 1 only (of 2). Ob. fo. Engraved additional title, 51 plts., including tail-piece, text in Engl. & Fr., cont. tree cf., spine gt.; Sir Ivar Colquhoun, of Luss copy. (CE. Mar.22; 153) £150
- - **Anr. Copy.** Fo. Additional engraved title, 51 engraved plts., subscribers list, lacks index lf., some browning in margins, cont. cf., rubbed, spine ends frayed. (SKC. May 4; 1782) £150
- - **Anr. Edn.** L., 1786-1806. 2 vols. in 1. 4to. 79 views (1 laid down), crimson mor. gt., panel spine. (P. Apr.12; 222) *Thorp.* £230
- - **Anr. Edn.** 1807. 2 vols. Ob. 4to. 2 engraved titles, 83 engraved views, some margin foxing, hf. cf., rubbed. (P. Mar.15; 265) *Fraser.* £220

HEARTMAN, Charles F.
- **John Peter Zenger.** Highland Park, N.J., 1934. *(99) numbered.* Fo. Marb. paper bds., s.-c. (LH. Sep.25; 235) $650

HEARTMAN, Charles F. (Ed.)
See— AMERICAN BOOK COLLECTOR, The

HEATH, Charles
- **Gallery of British Engravings.** 1836-37. Vols. I-III only. Cont. mor. gt. by R. Spencer. (LC. Mar.1; 74) £50
- - **Anr. Edn.** Ill.:- Heath after Turner, Landseer, Maclise, Stanfield, Westall, & others. L., 1836-38. 4 vols. Lge. 8vo. Engraved titles & 216 engraved plts., each with lf. of text & tissue-guard, some light foxing, orig. gt.-decor. mor. (SG. Jun.7; 361) $175
- **The Shakespeare Gallery.** L., n.d. 4to. 45 hand-cold. engraved plts., title spotted, mor. gt. (S. Oct.11; 455) *Erlini.* £110

HEATH, Charles
See— PUGIN, Augustus Welby & Heath, Charles

HEATH, Christopher
- **A Course of Operative Surgery.** Ill.:- Hanhart after Leveille. Phila., 1878. *1st. Amer. Edn.* Tall 4to. 20 hand-cold. litho. plts., hf. mor., covers detchd. (SG. Oct.6; 189) $100

HEATH, Henry
- **The Caricaturist's Scrap Book.** Ca. 1850?. Ob. fo. General title, Omnium Gatherum, title & 7 plts., 2nd. Series, 6 plts., Demonology & Witchcraft, 6 plts., Old Way's & New Way's, title & 6 plts. Nautical Dictionary, title & 6 plts., The Art of Tormenting, title & 6 plts., Sayings & Doings, 6 plts., Scenes in London, 12 plts., orig. gt.-lettered cl., chipped, partly loose in bdg. (SG. Jun.7; 362) $120

HEATH, William, Artist, 1795-1840
- **The Life of a Soldier.** L., 1823. 4to. 18 hand-cold. aquatint plts., inserted hand-cold. folding engraved

frontis. caricature, hf.-title, advt. lf. at end, plt. 13 smudged, some minor finger soiling, some text darkened, red hf. mor. gt., partly unc. (CNY. May 18; 108) $220
- **Theatrical Characters.** L., Thomas M'Lean, n.d.?. Fo. 10 hand-cold. engrs., pencil identification to each plt., slight soiling, plts. loose, orig. wraps., worn, covers loose, as a coll. of plts., w.a.f. (SPB. Dec.13; 832) $225
- [-] **A Trip to Margate.** [1828]. Ob. 4to. 12 hand-cold. plts., hf. cf. gt. (P. Mar.15; 256) *Reid.* £190

HEATH, William & others
- **Political Caricatures during the Reign of George 4th.** [Plts. dtd. 1824-31]. 3 vols. Fo. Mntd. litho. titles, 300 hand-cold. engraved or litho. plts., including 1 mntd. & 1 folding with a few margins shaved or sm. tears, some spotting, cont. hf. mor., worn. (CSK. Oct.21; 148) £2,400

HEATHCOTE, Evelyn D.
- **Flowers of the Engadine.** Winchester, 1891. Lge. 8vo. 224 col. plts., orig. cl. gt. (LC. Mar.1; 157) £80
- - **Anr. Copy.** 224 cold. plts., orig. cl. gt., worn. (P. May 17; 155) *Way.* £65

HEATON, John Aldam
- **Furniture & Decoration in England During the Eighteenth Century.** 1890-92. 2 vols. in 4. Fo. Orig. cl. gt. (P. Sep.29; 366) *Reynard.* £90
- - **Anr. Copy.** 2 vols. in 4. Lge. fo. Orig. cl. gt., spines slightly worn. (TA. Apr.19; 299) £60
- - **Anr. Edn.** L., 1890-93. 2 vols. in 4. Fo. Slightly soiled, end-papers torn, hinges brkn., orig. cl., soiled & rubbed. (S. May 1; 706) *Kapusi.* £80

HEAVISIDE, Oliver
- **Electrical Papers.** L. & N.Y., 1892. *1st. Edn.* 2 vols. Orig. cl., sm. paper liby. tags on spines, light rubbing, slight browning of end-papers; released from Taylor Liby., Sidney College, with stps., Stanitz coll. (SPB. Apr.25; 211) $200

HEBBEL, Friedrich
- **Aus den Tagebüchern.** Ill.:- Emil Schumacher. Berlin, 1970. *(100) on tinted paper.* 6 full-p. sigd. orig. etchings, relief decor., orig. linen. (GB. May 5; 3299) DM 400
- **Judith. Eine Tragödie in 5 Akten.** Ill.:- Th. Th. Heine. München, 1908. *(100).* Orig. vell., gt. decor., end-papers slightly foxed. (GB. May 5; 2668) DM 460
- - **Anr. Edn.** Ill.:- Th. Th. Heine. München, 1908. *(1000).* Orig. vell. gt. (GB. Nov.5; 3172) DM 600
- - **Anr. Copy.** 4to. Light foxing, orig. vell., slightly holed. (HK. Nov.11; 3613) DM 420
- **Die Nibelungen.** Ill.:- Alois Kolb. Leipzig, 1924. *De Luxe Edn. [?]. (450) numbered.* Supp. 2nd. series of 15 full-p. ills., leath., lightly rubbed. (R. Apr.3; 291) DM 400

HEBEL, Johann Peter
- **Allemannische Gedichte.** Karlsruhe, 1804. Some ll. at beginning slightly crumpled, cont. hf. leath., corners bumped, cover slightly rubbed. (HK. Nov.10; 2491) DM 460
- - **Anr. Edn.** Ill.:- Zix. Carlsruhe, 1806. *1st. Ill. Edn.* 4 mus. supps., copper engrs. lightly foxed, cont. leath. gt. (GB. Nov.4; 2078) DM 460
- **Sämmtliche Werke.** Karlsruhe, 1832-34. *1st. Coll. Edn.* 1 litho. port., 4 folding litho. mus. supps., cont. hf. leath. gt. (HK. Nov.10; 2488) DM 6,200

HEBER, Richard
- **Bibliotheca Heberiana. Catalogue of the Library of the Late Richard Heber.** L., 1834-36. 12 (of 13) pts. in 5 vols. All but 1 pt. with prices written in, mod. cl., unc., with related material. (S. Oct.11; 463) *Quaritch.* £350
- **An Historical List of Horse-Matches Run.** 1752-69. 18 vols. Cont. cf. gt., rebkd. (P. Dec.8; 215) *Way.* £140

HECK, Johann Caspar
- **Iconographic Encyclopaedia of Science, Literature, & Art.** Trans.:- Spencer F. Baird. N.Y., 1851. *1st. Amer. Edn.* 6 vols., including 2 atlas vols. Tall 8vo. & ob. 4to. 2 plts. defect., text & atlas

vols. foxed, cont. hf. mor. gt. & marb. bds., worn. (SG. Oct.13; 190) $225

HECKETHORN, C.W.
- **The Printers of Basle in the XV & XVI Centuries.** L., 1887. Fo. Plts., facs., little stained, orig. cl. gt., unc. (SG. May 17; 120) $130

HECKEWELDER, John
- **Nachricht von der Geschichte der Sitten und Gebräuchen der Indianischen Völkerschaften, welche ehemals Pennsylvanien und die Benachbarten Staaten bewohnten.** Trans.:– F. Hesse. Ill.:– Contrib.:– G.E. Schutze. Göttingen, 1821. *1st. German Edn.* Liby. hf. leath. [Sabin 31208] (R. Oct.13; 2972) DM 850

HECKFORD, N.
- **Sailing Directions & Coasting Guide from the Sand Heads to Rangoon & Moulmein** ... Calcutta, 1857. Bds., detchd. (PNY. Mar.27; 155) $100

HECQUET, Philippe
[-] **Le Naturalisme des Convulsions dans les Maladies de l'Epidemie Convulsionnaire.** Solothurn [i.e. Paris?], 1733. 2 pts. in 1 vol. 12mo. Cont. cf., rebkd. (SG. Oct.6; 190) $140

HEDBERG, Arvid
- **Stockholm Bok Bindare 1460-1880.** Stockholm, 1949-60. 2 vols. Tall 4to. Orig. ptd. wraps; H.M. Nixon coll. (BBA. Oct.6; 61) *Quaritch.* £180

HEDELIN, François de, Abbé d'Aubignac
See— D'ASSOUCY, Charles Coypeau de — HEDELIN, François de, Abbé d'Aubignac

HEDENBORG, J.
- **Turkiska Nationens Seder och Kläderdrägter.** Stockholm, 1839. 4to. Some plts. with outlines in pencil, few sm. faults, orig. linen, gt. & blind-tooled, orig. litho. wraps. bnd. in. (HK. Nov.9; 1834) DM 540

HEDENDAAGSCHE HISTORIE
- **Switzerland en Italië.** Amst., 1760-61. 2 vols. (*With:*) - **Groot Brittannie.** Amst., 1755. 2 pts. in 1 vol. Together 3 vols. Some stains in text, unif. cont. hf. cf. slight rubbed. (VG. Mar.19; 244) Fls. 950

HEDGE, Frederic H.
- **Prose Writers of Germany.** Phila., 1848. 4to. Red mor., gt. decor. emblems, fore-e.pntg., as a fore-e.pntg., w.a.f. (SPB. May 17; 737) $275

HEDIN, Sven
- **Through Asia.** 1898. 2 vols. Orig. cl. gt. (P. Sep.8; 275) £75

HEDWIG, Joannes
- **Species Muscorum Frondosorum Descriptae.** Lipsiae & Parisiis, 1801. 4to. Vig. title & 77 cold. plts., some foxing to text, cont. bds., worn. (HD. Jul.6; 43) Frs. 1,700

HEER, J.C.
- **Le Lac des Quatre-Cantons et la Suisse Primitive.** Zürich & Leipzig, 1900. Lge. 4to. 800 photogravure & wood engraved ills., linen. (GF. Nov.16; 1144) Sw. Frs. 650

HEERINGEN, G. von
- **Wanderungen durch Franken.** Ill.:– Ludwig Richter. Leipzig, [1840]. 31 steel engrs., cont. hf. leath. gt. (GB. May 3; 169) DM 2,400
- - **Anr. Copy.** 28(of 31) steel engraved plts., foxed, cont. hf. leath. (D. Nov.23; 815) DM 1,700

HEFNER-ALTENECK, J. H. von.
- **Deutsche Goldschmiede-Werke des Sechzehnten Jahrhunderts.** Frankfurt, 1890. Tall fo. 30 chromolitho. plts., loose as iss., cl.-bkd. bd. folder, stiff flaps detchd. (SG. Aug.25; 168) $100
- **Trachten, Kunstwerke und Geräthschaften vom Frühen Mittelalter bis Ende des Achtzehnten Jahrhunderts.** Frankfurt, 1879-89. *2nd. Edn.* 10 vols. Lge. 4to. Minimal spotting, cont. hf. leath., slightly worn & bumped. (H. Nov.23; 166) DM 1,400

HEGEL, G. W.
- **Hebräische Melodien.** Berlin, [1918]. *(40) numbered De Luxe Edn. on Jap.Imp.* 4to. Orig. vell.,

gt. spine & upr. cover, by O. Dorfner, Weimer. (HK. May 16; 2083a) DM 600

HEGEL, Georg Wilhelm Frederick
- **Encyclopädie der Philosophischen Wissenschaften im Grundrisse.** Heidelberg, 1830. *3rd. Edn.* MS. dedication from author on upr. end-paper, some light foxing, MS. pencil annots. on a few pp., cont. bds., bds. from orig. bdg. bnd. in, worn & slightly bumped. (R. Apr.3; 558) DM 2,700
- **Vorlesungen über die Geschichte der.Philosophie.**Ed.:– K.L. Michelet. Berlin, 1833-36. *1st. Edn.* 3 vols. Some slight foxing, cont. linen, spine browned. (R. Apr.; 559) DM 400
- **Werke.** Berlin, 1832-40. 18 pts. in 21 vols. Title & last p. in each vol. stpd., minimal spotting, cont. hf. leath., gt. decor., partly rubbed, w.a.f. (HK. May 16; 2080) DM 1,800

HEGEL, Joh. P.
- **Wissenschaft der Logik.** Nürnberg, 1812-16. *1st. Edn.* 2 vols. Vol. II with main title & individual title lf., some heavy foxing, cont. bds., slightly worn & bumped. (H. May 22; 727) DM 3,800

HEGEMANN, W.
- **City Planning Housing.** Ed.:– W.W. Forster & R.C. Weinberg. N.Y., 1938. Vol. 3. 4to. Orig. linen. (D. Nov.23; 1894) DM 450

HEGEMANN, Werner & Peets, Elbert
- **The American Vitruvius.** N.Y., 1922. Lge. fo. Over 1200 ills., ex-liby., cl. (SG. May 3; 203) $200

HEGESIPPUS
See— JOSEPHUS, Flavius – HEGESIPPUS

HEGI, Gustav
- **Illustrierte Flora von Mitteleuropa.** München, [1906-31]. 7 vols. in 13. Sm. 4to. Orig. linen, 7 spines browned, slightly bumped & rubbed, 1 vol. reprd. (H. May 22; 199) DM 1,200

HEIDELOFF, Nicolas
[-] **Gallery of Fashion.** L., 1798-1802. Vols. 5-8 in 1 vol. 4to. Hand-cold. engraved titles, 96 hand-cold. plts., titles & many plts. heightened with silver & gold, cont. str.-grd. citron mor., blue & red onlays forming borders on covers & compartments of spine, gt., lettered 'Vol. 2', slightly rubbed. (S. Dec.1; 387) *Walford.* £2,500

HEIDEN, Jan van der
- **Beschryving der Nieuwlyks uitgevonden en geoctrojeerde Slang-Brand-Spuiten, en haare wyze ven Brand-blussen** ... Amst., 1735. *2nd. Edn.* Fo. Hf. roan, back rubbed. (B. Apr.27; 564) Fls. 3,400

HEIDENREICH, F.W.
- **Orthopaedie oder Werth der Mechanik zur Heilung** ... Berlin, 1827-31. *1st. Edn.* 2 vols. Mod. bds. (R. Oct.12; 1415) DM 600

HEIDMANN, J.A.
- **Vollständige auf Versuche und Vernunftschlüsse Gegründete Theorie der Electricität** ... Wien, 1799. *1st. Edn.* 2 vols. in 1. 1st. title stpd., cont. bds., slightly worn. (R. Apr.4; 1525) DM 500

HEILPRIN, Yakov
- **Nachlat Yakov.** Padua, 1623. *1st. Edn.* 4to. Margins of title & 1st. p. reprd. without loss of text, stained & soiled, hf. leath. (S. Oct.24; 198) *Heitner.* £320

HEILPRIN, Ya'akov
See— ELIEZER HA-GADOL — HEILPRIN, Ya'akov

HEIM, Albert
- **Geologie der Schweiz.** Leipzig, 1919-22. 3 vols. 4to. Hf. vell., gold-tooled. (GF. Nov.16; 1179) Sw. Frs. 420

HEIM, Roger & Wasson, R. Gordon
- **Les Champignons Hallucinogènes.** Paris, 1958. 4to. Orig. wraps. (BBA. Dec.15; 133) *Browning.* £75

HEINE, Heinrich
- **Aus den Memoiren des Herrn. von Schnabelewopsky.** Ill.:– Julius Pascin. Berlin, 1910. *(60) De Luxe Edn. on Japan.* 4to. Printers mark & 9 lithos. (6 cold.) sigd. by artist, hand-bnd. orig. vell., cold. cover ill.; Hauswedell coll. (H. May 24; 674) DM 13,500
- - **Anr. Edn.** Ill.:– Jules Pascin. Berlin, 1910. *(250) numbered on Old Stratfort paper.* 4to. 6 ills. hand-cold., silk, with litho. cover design by Pascin, plain wraps., s.-c., worn. (SG. Jan.12; 290) $850
- - **Anr. Copy.** 4to. Orig. silk, cover ill., soiled. (H. Nov.24; 1219) DM 2,200
- - **Anr. Edn.** Ill.:– J. Pascin,. Berlin, Pan Pr., 1910. *(60) De Luxe Edn. on Japan.* 4to. Hand-bnd. orig. vell., cold. cover ill.; printer's mark & 9 lithos. (including 6 cold.) sigd. (H. Nov.24; 1920) DM 6,200
- - **Anr. Edn.** Ill.:– Julius Pascin. Berlin, 1910. *(310) numbered.* 4to. Some ills. hand-cold., orig. bds., slightly soiled. (BBA. Jun.14; 240) *Sims, Reed & Fogg.* £450
- **Briefe aus Berlin.** Ill.:– Hans Baluschek. Berlin, 1924. *De Luxe Edn. A. (100) numbered.* 4to. 10 orig. lithos. cont.-style hand-bnd. orig. pol. cf., gt.-decor., by Spamerschen Buchbinderei, Leipzig, slightly rubbed & bumped. (GB. Nov.5; 2259) DM 800
- - **Anr. Copy.** Orig. leath., gt. (HK. May 17; 2554) DM 750
- **Das Buch Le Grand ... 1826. Kapitel 1 bis X.** Ill.:– M. Oppenheimer. Berlin, Pan Pr., 1914. *(10) on van Geldern-Bütten.* 4to. Without portfo. with 2nd. series of ills., name on end-paper, hand-bnd. orig. mor. gt.; all etchings sigd. by artist. (H. Nov.24; 1906) DM 1,300
- **Buch der Lieder.** Hamburg, 1827. *1st. Edn.* Some spotting, orig. roan-bkd., blind-stpd. cl. bds., green end-papers; Robert Schumann's copy, with his sig., inscr., & annots. (S. Nov.17; 168) *Otto Haas.* £5,000
- - **Anr. Copy.** With the 4 dedicatory ll., advt. lf. at end, cont. paper bds. (C. Dec.9; 233) *Fischer.* £650
- - **Anr. Copy.** With dedications, dedication lf. to Merkel in 2 versions: after title to 'Merckel' & with other spelling later, lacks hf.-title, cont. hf. leath., gt. spine, rubbed; Hauswedell coll. (H. May 24; 1360) DM 5,600
- - **Anr. Copy.** Cont. hf. leath., slightly rubbed. (R. Apr.3; 245) DM 1,900
- - **Anr. Copy.** With hf.-title & dedication lf., lacks advt. lf. at end, brown spotted, margins browned, cont. bds., notes inside cover, very bumped & rubbed. (H. May 22; 729) DM 1,000
- - **Anr. Copy.** Foxed, slightly stained, cont. bds., gt. decor., spine & corners rubbed. (HK. Nov.10; 2499) DM 580
- **Der Doktor Faust. Ein Tanzpoem.** Hamburg, 1851. *1st. Edn.* Orig. pict. wraps., slightly soiled, mostly unopened, case damaged. (LH. Sep.25; 541) $325
- - **Anr. Edn.** Ill.:– Josef von Diveky. Berlin, 1912. *(400) numbered.* Orig. hf. vell., cold. paper doubl. & end-papers. (GB. May 5; 2335) DM 420
- **Dreiunddreissig Gedichte.** Ed.:– F.W. Gubitz. Berlin, 1824. 4to. Minimal foxing, cont. bds., lacks spine, corners bumped. (GB. May 4; 1319) DM 2,100
- **Gespenstische Balladen.** Ill.:– H. Steiner-Prag. 1924. *(200). (100) numbered De Luxe Edn. with special etching on Japan.* 4to. Printers mark & all ll full-p. etchings sigd. by artist, title vig. etching, red mor., gt. decor., gt. inner & outer dentelle & spine. (GB. May 5; 3363) DM 1,800
- - **Anr. Copy.** 4to. On Bütten, hand-bnd. red orig. mor., gt. spine, inner & outer dentelle, gt. cover vig., by A.G. Fritzsche; printer's mark & all full-p. etchings sigd. (H. Nov.24; 2107) DM 1,300
- **Neue Gedichte.** Hamburg, 1844. *1st. Edn.* Slight spotting at end, cont. hf. cl., worn. (C. Dec.9; 234) *Pollak.* £140
- **Die Nordsee.** Ill.:– F.W. Kleukens. Leipzig, Ernst Ludwig Pr., 1909. *(50) De Luxe Edn. on Japan.* Cf., gold-tooled cover vig., by Carl Sonntag Jun., Leipzig, sm. scratches, some light wear. (HK. May 17; 2729) DM 750
- **Oeuvres. La France.** Paris, 1833-35. *1st. Fr. Edn.* Together 6 vols. Hf. mor., gt. & cold mor. mosaic,

HEINE, Heinrich -*Contd.*

sigd. by Noulhac, orig. Wraps. bnd. in. (D. Nov.24; 2481) DM 8,200
- Der Rabbi von Bacherach. Ill.:- M. Liebermann. Berlin, 1923. *(100) De Luxe Edn.* Lge. 4to. 1 supp. litho. & 16 other proofs on Japan sigd. by artist, orig. hand-bnd. mor., gt. leath. medallion-shaped inset on upr. cover. (H. Nov.24; 1781) DM 6,200
- - **Anr. Copy.** 4to. 17 orig. lithos., extra series of lithos. on Japan, each lf. sigd. by artist, orig. mor., gt. inset on upr. cover. (GB. Nov.5; 2748) DM 6,000
- - **Anr. Copy.** 4to. 17 orig. lithos., without extra series of lithos., orig. mor., gt. inlay on upr. cover. (GB. May 5; 2887) DM 1,700
- Romanzero. Hamburg, 1851. *1st. Edn. 1st. Printing.* Lacks hf.-title (as usual), bd. ll for 2 pp. included with spelling Atriden. *(Bound with:)* - Der Doktor Faust. Hamburg, 1851. 1st. Edn. 1st. Printing, probably lacks 1 lf. hf.-title & lf. adverts at end. Together 2 works in 1 vol., slightly foxed, cont. hf. leath. gt., slightly rubbed. (R. Apr.3; 247) DM 420
- Sämmtliche Werke. Hamburg, 1861-66. *1st. Coll. Edn.* Ex-libris, cont. hf. leath. gt., slightly rubbed, w.a.f. (HK. Nov.10; 2495) DM 550
- Shakespeares Maedchen und Frauen, mit Erlaeuterungen. Paris, 1839. *1st. Edn.* Lge. 8vo. 45 engraved plts., some foxing thro.-out, orig. hf. roan, spine gt. (C. Dec.9; 237) *Fischer.* £180
- - **Anr. Copy.** 4to. 2 steel engrs. lightly browned, a few light margin spots, 4 engrs. & 5 ll. loose, mor. gt., lightly rubbed & faded, 2 sm. margin tears. (H. May 22; 731) DM 1,000
- Tragödien. Berlin, 1823. *1st. Edn.* Cont. bds. (R. Apr.3; 248) DM 750
- Vermischte Schriften. 1854. *1st. Edn.* Lightly browned, some slight foxing, cont. blind-tooled linen. (GB. May 4; 1321) DM 450
- Werke. Ed.:- H. Laube. Wien, 1884-88. *De Luxe Edn.* 6 vols. Orig. linen. (GB. Nov.4; 1788) DM 450

HEINECKEN, K.H. von

[-] Idée Générale d'une Collection Complette d'Estampes avec une Dissortation sur l'Origine de la Gravure. Leipzig & Vienna, 1771. Slightly browned, cont. hf. leath. gt. (R. Apr.3; 642) DM 680
- - **Anr. Copy.** Foxed, cont. leath., gold-tooled border decor., rubbed, upr. cover loose, ex-libris. (HT. May 8; 750) DM 480

HEINEKEN, Paul

- Lucidum Prospectivae Speculum. Augsburg, 1717. Fo. Engraved frontis., 95 plts., some folding, cont. vell.-bkd. bds. (C. Dec.9; 64) *Goldschmidt.* £400

HEINLEIN, Robert A.

- The Discovery of the Future. [Los Angeles], 1941. *2nd. Edn. (100).* Spirit duplicated, stapled wraps., chip from upr. left corner of upr. wrap., slight darkening; inscr. by publisher. (CBA. Oct.29; 400) $700
- Space Cadet. Ill.:- Clifford N. Geary. N.Y., 1948. *1st. Edn.* 1 corner lightly bumped, d.-w. with very slight wear at extremities, spine slightly darkened. (CBA. Oct.29; 402) $250

HEINS, Henry Hardy

- A Golden Anniversary Bibliography of Edgar Rice Burroughs. West Kingston, 1964. *Revised Edn.* 4to. Slight darkening to extreme edges, bdg. not stated, jacket darkened. (CBA. Oct.29; 174b) $130

HEINSE, G.H.

- Fiormona oder Briefe aus Italien. Berlin, 1794. *1st. Edn.* Some slight foxing, last p. mis-paginated, later cf. gt. (H. May 22; 732) DM 620

HEINSE, Joh. J.W.

- Sämmtliche Schriften. Ed.:- H. Laube. Leipzig, 1838. *1st. Coll. Edn.* 10 vols. in 6. Lacks port., later marb. bds., gt. spine, slightly rubbed, spine faded; Hauswedell coll. (H. May 24; 1366) DM 1,100
- - **Anr. Copy.** 10 vols. Some slight foxing, & some light browning, cont. linen, foxed. (GB. May 4; 1323) DM 450

HEINSIUS, Daniel

- Poematum Editio Nova. Accedunt Prater Alia Libri, De Contemptu Mortis. Leiden, 1621. 2 pts. in 1 vol. 18th. C. Fr. mor. gt., decor., flat spine tooled in compartments; sig. of De Saint Jullien & anr. inscr. (cropped) on title-p., Schiff-Abbey copy. (S. Nov.17; 33) *Tzakas.* £160

HEINSIUS, Nicolas

- Catalogi Bibliothecae Heinsianae. Leiden, 1682. 2 pts. in 1 vol. 12mo. Priced in MS. thro-out, lacks port.?, cont. vell., spine soiled. (CSK. Feb.24; 200) £120

HEINZMANN, J.G.

- Appell an meine Nation. Uber die Peste der dt. Literatur. Ill.:- B.A. Dunker. Bern, 1795. *1st. Edn.* 2 pp. paginated double, cont. bds., bumped & rubbed. (D. Nov.24; 2482) DM 520

HEISE, G. (Ed.)
See— GENIUS. Zeitschrift für Alte und Werdende Kunst

HEISENBERG, Werner

- Die Physikalischen Prinzipien der Quantentheorie. Leipzig, 1930. *1st. German Edn.* Margin browning, erased stps. on title, orig. ptd. wraps., browning; Stanitz coll. (SPB. Apr.25; 212) $325

HEISTER, Lorenz

- Chirurgie. Nuremb., 1731. *3rd. Edn.* Some light soiling, some margin worming, plt. 1 with light defect. in upr.-corner, lacks large part of plt. 23, cont. vell., slightly spotted. (R. Apr.4; 1309) DM 2,100
- - **Anr. Edn.** Nuremb., 1770. 3 pts. in 1 vol. 4to. Some plts. with slight bkd. tear, lacks port. at beginning, 19th. C. hf. leath., rubbed & worn. (D. Nov.23; 567) DM 1,900
- - **Anr. Copy.** Leath. (G. Sep.15; 2158) Sw. Frs. 1,800
- Institutiones Chirurgicae. Amst., 1739. *1st. Latin Edn.* 2 vols. 4to. Vol. 1 with light spotting in some margins, folding plts. with margin defects., cont. style hf. leath. (R. Oct.12; 1416) DM 2,400
- - **Anr. Edn.** [Venice, 1740]. 4to. Lacks title & part of preface & 10 ll., minimal soiling, cont. restored vell. (HK. Nov.8; 584) DM 440
- - **Anr. Edn.** Amst., 1750. *2nd. Latin Edn.* 2 vols. 4to. Old owners note on title, all plt. versos stpd., cont. hf. leath., bumped, spine defect., vol. 2 ptly. loose. (R. Oct.12; 1417) DM 1,100
- Kleine Chirurgie od. Handbuch der Wundarzney. Wien, 1787. Plts. loose, lacks plt. 8, cont. bds., rubbed & bumped. (HK. Nov.8; 585) DM 450

HELD, Julius (Contrib.)
See— MEISS, Millard

HELDENBUCH darinn Viel Seltsamer Geschichten und Kurzweilige Historien ven den Grossen Helden ...
Frankfurt, 1590. 4to. Cont. stpd. cf. over wood bds., blind-decor., clasps, chain reprd.; from Fondation Furstenberg-Beaumesnil. (HD. Nov.16; 126) Frs. 17,500

HELFT, Jacques

- Les Grands Orfèvres de Louis XIII à Charles X. Paris, 1965. 4to. Publisher's bds. (HD. Jun.26; 86) Frs. 1,500
- Le Poinçon des Provinces Françaises. Paris, 1968. Tall 4to. Cl., d.-w. (SG. Oct.13; 324) $120

HELIODORUS

- Aethiopicorum Libri X ... Notes:- Commelino. Lugduni, 1611. 12mo. Red mor., Louis XIII arms & cypher, turn-in & corners defect., lacks 1 end-lf. (SM. Mar.7; 2022) Frs. 3,400
- - **Anr. Edn.** Paris, 1619. In Greek & Latin, 18th. C. pol. cf. gt. (SG. Oct.27; 141) $110
- Amours de Théagene et Chariclée. Trans.:- Jean de Montlyard. Ill.:- Rabel, Briot, Matheus, Crispin de Passe, & Michel Lasne. Paris, 1626. *2nd. Edn.* 2 vols. 18th. C. mor. gt., spine decor., 1 corner defect. (HD. Nov.9; 41) Frs. 4,200

HELIODORUS
See— HORTENSIUS, L. - HELIODORUS

HELLER, D.

- A History of Cape Silver; Further Researches in Cape Silver. Cape Town, 1949-53. 2 vols. 4to. Orig. bdgs., d.-w.'s; Vol. 1 sigd. by author. (VA. Apr.27; 804) R 270

HELLER, Elinor Raas & Magee, David

- The Bibliography of the Grabhorn Press, 1915-40. San Franc., [Grabhorn Pr.], 1940. Fo. Cf.-bkd. linen bds. (LH. Sep.25; 371) $550

HELLOT, Jean

- L'Art de la Teinture des Laines, et des Etoffes de Laine, en Grand et Petit Teint. Paris, 1750. *1st. Edn.* 12mo. Hf.-title, cont. cf., rebkd. (S. Apr.10; 512) *Perceval.* £60
- - **Anr. Copy.** Hf.-title, cont. cf., worn, rebkd. & recornered. (SG. Oct.6; 142) $110

HELLWIG, Chr. von

[-] Curiöser und Vernünftiger Urin-Arzt ... von Val. Kräutermann. Frankfurt & Leipzig, 1724. *(Bound with:)* RIEDLIN, V. - Methodus Curandi Febres. Ulm, 1705, 1st. Edn. Together 2 works in 1 vol. Mod. leath. gt. (GB. May 3; 1000) DM 500

HELMAN, Isidore Stanislas Henri

- Abrégé Historique des Principaux Traits de la Vie de Confucius. Paris, [1782]. Lge. 4to. Engraved text, title & 24 plts., title soiled, some stains sm. tear on 8 ll., mod. crude qtr. cl., heavy bds. (SG. Apr.19; 102) $175
- - **Anr. Edn.** Paris, [1788]. 4to. 1 plt. with sm. margin worm-holes, cont. bds. (HD. Jan.26; 169) Frs. 2,000
- Faits Memorables des Empereurs de la Chine. Paris, 1788. 4to. 24 plts., early tree cf. gt. (SG. Mar.29; 319) $175

HELMHOLTZ, Herman Ludwig Ferdinand von

- Beschreibung eines Augen-Spiegels zur Untersuchung der Netzhaut im Lebenden Auge. Berlin, 1851. *1st. Edn.* Cont. marb. bds., rubbed or slightly worn. (GB. May 3; 1001) DM 6,500
- Die Lehre von den Tonempfindungen als Physiologische Grundlage filr die Theorie der Musik. Braunschweig, 1863. *1st. Edn.* Light wear, some lead or cold. pencil underlining, some pencil marginalia, cont. hf. leath., slightly rubbed. (R. Apr.4; 1310) DM 1,600
- Handbuch der Physiologischen Optik. Leipzig, 1867. *1st. Edn.* Cont. hf. leath., slightly rubbed. (R. Oct.12; 1677) DM 2,200
- On the Conservation of Force. [L., 1853]. *1st. Edn. in Engl.* 'Scientific Memoirs (Natural Philosophy)', Vol. I, pt. II, pp. 114-62. Some soiling of 1st. text lf., mod. hf. cf.; Lord Kelvin's copy with his stps. on title & free end-paper, Stanitz coll. (SPB. Apr.25; 214) $425
- Uber die Erhaltung der Kraft. Berlin, 1847. *1st. Edn.* Old liby. stp. on title verso, end lf. & end-papers, slightly foxed, hf. linen, orig. wraps. bnd. in. (R. Oct.12; 1679) DM 5,000
- Ueber die Wechselwirkung der Naturkräfte und die darauf Bezüglichen Neuesten Ermittlungen der Physik. Königsberg, 1854. *1st. Edn.* Some spotting, cl.; Hermann Stobbe sig. & many notes on end-papers, Stanitz coll. (SPB. Apr.25; 215) $200
- Vorlesungen über Theorestische Physik. Ed.:- A. König & others. Leipzig, 1898-1922. Vols. 1 - 6. 4to. Orig. hf. linen, some sm. defects. (HT. May 8; 418) DM 420

HELMHOLTZ, R. & Staby, W.

- Die Entwicklung der Lokomotive im Gebiete des Vereins Deutscher [Später Mitteleuropäischer] Eisenbahnverwaltungen. München & Berlin, 1930-37. 4to. Orig. linen. (R. Oct.12; 1597) DM 450

HELMOLDUS

- Chronica Slavorum. Ed.:- H. Bangertus. Luebeck, 1659. *1st. Compl. Edn.* 4to. Cont. vell., soiled. (SG. Feb.9; 245) $140

HELMONT, Johannes Baptista van

- Aufgang der Artzney-Kunst. Trans.:- C. Knorr von Rosenroth. Ill.:- J.J. de Sandrart (frontis.). Sulzbach, 1683. *1st. Edn. in German.* Fo. Hf.-title,

cont. cf.; Dr. Walter Pagel copy. (S. Feb.7; 176) *Klingsor.* £700
- **Les Oeuvres Traittant des Principes de Médecine et Physique.** Trans.:– Jean Le Conté. Lyons, 1671. *1st. Edn. in Fr.* 4to. Title vig. written on, old bds., soiled, unc.; Dr. Walter Pagel copy. (S. Feb.7; 172) *Heller.* £180
- **Opera Omnia.** Ill.:– J.J. Vogel. Frankfurt, 1682. *6th. Edn.* 2 pts. in 1 vol. 4to. Discold. & browned in places, vell.; Dr. Walter Pagel copy. (S. Feb.7; 173) *Wilkinson.* £170
- **Opuscula Medica Inaudita.** Cologne, 1644. *1st. Edn.* 4 pts. in 1 vol. Errata lf., blind-stpd. cf., spine worn; Dr. Walter Pagel copy. (S. Feb.7; 166) *Sneider.* £400
- **Ortus Medicinae.** Amst., 1648. *1st. Edn.* 4 pts. in 1 vol. Sm. 4to. Approx. 20 ll. soiled, reprd. & bkd., some with loss, title lf. completed with MS. letters, cont. vell., ties. (GB. Nov.3; 1018) DM 560
- – **Anr. Edn.** Ed.:– Francisco Mercurio van Helmont. Venice, 1651. *2nd. Edn.* Fo. Hf.-title, vell.; Dr. Walter Pagel copy. (S. Feb.7; 167) *Mayo Clinic.* £200
- – **Anr. Edn.** Ed.:– Fr. M. van Helmont. Amst., 1652. *3rd. Edn.* 2 pts. in 1 vol. 4to. Name erased from title, few sm. wormholes, some stains, vell., wormed; Dr. Walter Pagel copy. (S. Feb.7; 170) *Gurney.* £110
- – **Anr. Edn.** Lyons, 1667. *5th. Edn.* 2 pts. in 1 vol. Fo. Hf.-title, engraved title with ports., last lf. blank, new bds. cf. spine gt. (S. Apr.10; 513) *Kurzer.* £120
- **Tumulus Pestis.** Trans.:– Johannes Henricus Seyfrid. Sulzbach, 1681. Old bds.; Dr. Walter Pagel copy. (S. Feb.7; 175) *Thoemmes.* £250

HELMS, Anthony Zachariah
See— DEPOMS, F. — HELMS, Anthony Zachariah

HELVETIUS, Claude Adrien
[–] **De l'Esprit.** Paris, 1758. *1st. Edn.* 4to. Hf.-title, cont. mott. cf. gt. (SG. Nov.3; 96) $500
- – **Anr. Copy.** 4to. Without cancels & with privilege, cont. marb. cf., spine decor. (HD. Mar.21; 38) Frs. 1,000
- **Oeuvres Complètes.** Liège, 1774. 4 vols. Some sm. restorations, cont. cf. gt., grotesque decor. spines. (HD. Sep.22; 257) Frs. 3,500
- – **Anr. Edn.** L., 1781. *New Edn.* 5 vols. Hf. roan. (HD. Feb.22; 90) Frs. 3,200
- – **Anr. Edn.** Paris, 1794. 5 vols. Cont. marb. cf. gt., decor. spines. (HD. Sep.21; 129) Frs. 1,100

HELWIG, Helmuth
- **Handbuch der Einbandkunde.** Hamburg, 1953. 3 vols. 4to. Orig. linen. (D. Nov.23; 203) DM 500

HELY-HUTCHINSON, J.W.
- **Catalogue of the Celebrated Library of Valuable Printed Books, Fine Bindings & Manuscripts.** 1956. Prices & buyers' names, cont. mor.-bkd. bds., orig. wraps. preserved; H.M. Nixon coll., with some MS. annots., some rubbings loosely inserted. (BBA. Oct.6; 155) *Beres.* £160

HELY HUTCHINSON, John
[–] **The Commercial Restraints of Ireland** ... Dublin, 1779. *1st. Edn.* Hf.-title, bkplt., mott. cf. (GM. Dec.7; 452) £180

HELYOT, Pierre
[–] **Histoire des Ordres Monastiques, Religieux et Militaires.** Paris, 1714-19. 8 vols. 4to. Cont. cf., spines & jnts. worn. (CSK. Apr.6; 65) £160

HEMARD, Joseph
- **Code Civil: Livre Premier des Personnes.** Paris, [1925]. *(50) numbered on Japan vell., with extra suite of drawings in black & white, & a sigd. cold. unpubld. drawing by Hemard.* Sm. 4to. Red lev., cold. mor. inlays, wide dentelles, orig. wraps. bnd. in, s.-c. (SG. Feb.16; 156) $350
- **Forumulaire Magistral.** Paris, [1927]. *(800) numbered on vergé de cuve.* Lev. by Rene Kieffer, lge. design stpd. on covers, decor. spine, orig. wraps. bnd. in. (SG. Feb.16; 171) $130

HEMINGWAY, Ernest
- **A Farewell to Arms.** N.Y., 1929. *1st. Edn. 1st. Iss.* Without legal disclaimer, cl. gt., d.-w. (lightly

frayed & soiled), light wear. (RO. Apr.23; 166) $240
- – **Anr. Edn.** N.Y., 1929. *1st. Edn.* Without disclaimer on p. [x], stain in lr. margin on 1st. 6 ll., endpapers & d.-w., slight spotting & soiling, orig. cl., orig. d.-w. by Cleon; Fred A. Berne copy. (SPB. May 16; 305) $150
- – **Anr. Edn.** N.Y., 1929. *(510) numbered & sigd.* Lge. 8vo. Bds., vell. back & tips, faded, spine slightly discold. (SG. Nov.3; 98) $650
- – **Anr. Edn.** May-Oct., 1929. 6 iss. (contained in 'Scribner's Magazine'). Fo. Orig. pict. wraps. decor. by Rockwell Kent; Fred A. Berne copy. (SPB. May 16; 306) $375
- **In Our Time.** Paris, Three Mountains Pr., 1924. *1st. Edn. (170).* Fo. Orig. ptd. bds., endpapers browned; pres. copy to Alma Estelle Lloyd. (SPB. May 17; 626) $6,750
- – **Anr. Edn.** N.Y., 1925. *1st. Edn.* Sm. 8vo. Cl. gt., hinge brkn., cover detchd.; inscr. by author to Jeannette Menell, extensive autograph revisions by author in chapter 9. (SG. Jan.12; 155) $3,800
- **Men Without Women.** N.Y., 1927. *1st. Edn.* 1st. hf.-title loose, cl. gt., 2nd. iss. d.-w. with added reviews, unc., at edges; press. copy to B.F. Hart, sigd. & inscr. by author on front free end-paper. (RO. Apr.23; 167) $975
- – **Anr. Copy.** With perfect '3' on p.3, light marginal browning, orig. cl., orig. 1st. iss. d.-w. with errors in blurb; Fred A.Berne copy. (SPB. May 16; 308) $225
- **Oeuvres Complètes.** Ill.:– Masson, Carzou, Commère, Fontanarosa & others. Paris, 1963-65. *(52000) numbered.* 8 vols. 4to. Leaves, orig. wraps., unc. & untrimmed, box; unique copy, with suite of all lithos. except. that by Masson on japon nacré, each litho. sigd. & numbered, gouache by each artist except Masson & Carzou. (SM. Mar.21; 2337) Frs. 14,000
- **Le Vieil Homme et la Mer.** Trans.:– J. Dutourd. Ill.:– A. Totero. Grenoble, n.d. 1 vol. Separate suite of ills. on japan, box. (HD. Apr.11; 29b) Frs. 1,000

HEMMERLIN, Felix
- **De Nobilitate et Rusticitate Dialogus et Alia Opuscula. - Opuscula et Tractatus.** [Strassburg, Johann Pruess], ca. 1493-1500. 2 vols. in 1. Fo. Some worming, considerable marginalia in early hands, early wood bds. & blind-stpd. vell. back, lacks clasps; the Walter Goldwater copy. [BMC I, 129; Goff H-15 & 16; H. 1426 & 1425] (SG. Dec.1; 173) $1,000

HEMMERSAM, M.
- **West-Indiamisk Reese-Beskriffning, fran ahr 1639. till 1645** ... Visingsborg, 1674. Sm. 4to. Sm. liby. stp. at foot of title, later bds. [Sabin 31290] (S. Dec.1; 283) *Israel.* £400

HEMPEL, Charles W.
[–] **The Commercial Tourist; or Gentleman Traveller.** Ill.:– I.R. Cruikshank. L., 1822. Proem lf. present, sigs. on title-pp., a few stains, sm. piece torn from margin of title, cont. cl-bkd. bds., by John W. Dixon of Falmouth. (BBA. May 23; 219) *Bledisloe.* £55

HEMPEL, Michael
- **Psalmodiarum** ... Preface:– Martin Luther. Wittenberg, 1578. Ports., cont cf., silver-decor.; owner's name 'D. Eliae Vogelio Secretario' on upr. cover, initials 'M.H.F.' & date 1578 on lr. cover, from Fondation Furstenberg-Beaumesnil. (HD. Nov.16; 127) Frs. 1,000

HEMSLEY, W.B.
See— CHEESEMAN, Thomas Frederick & Hemsley, W.B.

HENCKEL, J.F.
- **Anweisung zum Verbesserten Chirurgischen Verbande.** Berlin & Stralsund, 1779. Browned, approx. 25 pp. with sm., worm-holes in margin, 6 ll. preface misbnd. between pp. 226/227, cont. hf. leath., rubbed & bumped. (R. Apr.4; 1311) DM 450
- **Pyritologia** ... Leipzig, 1725. *1st. Edn.* Minimal soiling, cont. hf. vell., worn. (HK. Nov.8; 654) DM 1,500

HENDERSON, C.C.
[–] **Road Scrapings.** L., 1840. Ob. 4to. 12 plts. on India paper, some foxing, 1 soiled, limp leath., orig. wraps. bnd. in. (P. May 17; 266) *Johnson.* £85
- – **Anr. Copy.** Ob. 4to. 12 engraved plts., on India paper, some spotting, mor. gt., orig. upr. wrap. bnd. in. (P. Sep.8; 13) *Clatworthy.* £55

HENDERSON, Ebenezer
- **Iceland; or the Journal of a Residence in that Island.** Edinb., 1818. 2 vols. Stained towards beginning of Vol. 2, orig. cl.-bkd. bds., unc. & worn. (S. Jun.25; 164) *Hannas.* £50

HENDERSON, Harold G. & Ledoux, Louis V.
- **Sharaku: The Surviving Works.** N.Y., 1939. Sm. fo. Buckram. (SG. Oct.13; 101) $150

HENDERSON, John
- **Excursions & Adventures in New South Wales** ... 1851. 2 vols. 12mo. Bdg. not stated, unc., 1 vol. with slight chipping, the other with defect. backstrip. (KH. May 1; 343) Aus. $100
- **Observations on the Colonies of New South Wales & Van Diemen's Land.** Calcutta, 1832. A few slight imperfections, pig, lightly rubbed. (KH. May 1; 342) Aus. $500

HENDERSON, Robert W.
- **Early American Sport: A Chronological Check-List of Books Published Prior to 1860.** Intro.:–Harry T. Peters. N.Y., Grol. Cl., 1937. *(400).* Lge. 8vo. Cl. (SG. Mar.15; 262) $100

HENDERSON, Thomas
- **Picturesque 'Bits' from Old Edinburgh.** Ill.:– Archibald Burns. Edinb., 1868. Sm. 4to. 15 mntd. albumen photos, edge fading to plts., orig. gt.-pict. cl., worn, spine faded, partially detchd. (SG. May 10; 21) $120

HENDERSON, William
- **My Life as an Angler.** L., 1879. *1st. Edn.* L.P., hf. mor., gt.; inscr. by author, bkplt. of A.H. Thompson. (S. Oct.4; 29) *Marlborough.* £70

HENDERSON, William Augustus
- **The Housekeeper's Instructor; or, Universal Family-cook; ... To which is Added the Complete Art of Carving.** Ed.:– Jacob Christopher Schnebbelie. ca. 1811. *17th. Edn.* 8vo. A few ll. stained, mod. cl.-bkd. bds. (BBA. Jan.19; 217) *Bloomsbury Rare Books.* £70
- – **Anr. Edn.** N.d. *5th. Edn.* Frontis., 11 plts., frontis. worn, last 4 plts. stained, qtr. cf., worn. (P. Mar.15; 71) *Marshall.* £55
- – **Anr. Edn.** L., n.d. *6th. Edn.* 2 plts. torn, some ll. slightly soiled, cont. sheep, worn. (BBA. May 3; 212) *Quaritch.* £70

HENDLEY, Thomas Holbein
- **Damascening on Steel or Iron, as Practised in India.** Ill.:– W. Griggs. L., 1892. Fo. 104 designs on 32 plts., ex-liby., leath.-bkd. gt.-pict. bds., slightly worn & soiled. (SG. May 3; 204) $225

HENDLEY, T.H.
See— JACOB, S. S. & Hendley, T. H.

HENFREY, H.W.
- **Numismata Cromwelliana.** L., 1877. 4to. Orig. cl., slightly rubbed & soiled. (S. May 1; 471) *Drury.* £60

HENISCH, G.
See— RAMUS, P. - THEODOSIUS TRIPOLITA - HENISCH, G.

HENKEL, A. (Ed.)
See— EMBLEMATA ...

HENKELS, F.R.A.
[–] **Bij Gesprek.** [Groningen, Priv. Ptd.], Mar. 1942. *(199) (120).* Lge. 4to. Text lf. with sm. tear, cold. pictor. wraps., loose, slightly crumpled. (H. Nov.24; 2206) DM 2,500

HENLEY, William Ernest
- **A Book of Verses.** L., 1888. *1st. Edn.* Light spotting, mostly of endpapers, orig. wraps.; 1½ p. A.L.s. with initials laid in, Fred A. Berne copy. (SPB. May 16; 309) $125
- **London Types.** Ill.:– William Nicholson. L., 1898.

HENLEY, William Ernest *-Contd.*

4to. 12 cold. litho. plts., orig. bds. (CSK. Feb.24; 113) £95
– – **Anr. Copy.** 4to. 12 col. litho. plts., orig. cold. pict. cl.-bkd. bds., slightly spotted. (LC. Mar.1; 499) £60

HENNEBUTTE, Bl.
– **France et Espagne, Album des deux Frontières vues des Environs Bayonne et de St. Sébastien.** Ca. 1840. 4to. Title, 27 tinted litho. plts., 14 foxed, cl., spine defect. (P. Nov.24; 45) *Dupont.* £260

HENNEPIN, Louis
– **A New Discovery of a Vast Country in America, Extending above Four Thousand Miles, Between New France & New Mexico ... ; with a Continuation.** L., 1698. *1st. Edn. in Engl. 'Tonson' Iss. (2nd. Iss.?).* 2 pts. in 1 vol. Lacks maps, some plts. torn, old cf., worn & stained. (SG. Jan.19; 184) $275
– **Nouveau Voyage d'un Pais plus Grande que l'Europe** ... Utrecht, 1698. *1st. Edn. Variant Iss., with the name Voskuyl on title-p. instead of Schouten.* 12mo. Title-p. bkd. & with sm. restorations at gutter– & fore-margin, plts. & map lightly foxed, orig. vell.; the Rt. Hon. Visc. Eccles copy. [Sabin 31351 (the Schouten iss.)] (CNY. Nov.18; 137) $1,200
– **Nouvelle Découverte d'un très Grand Pays Situé dans l'Amérique, entre le Nouveau Mexique et la Mer Glaciale.** Utrecht, 1697. *1st. Edn.* 12mo. 1 map with a few minor tears, light dampstains to fore-margins of many ll., orig. vell.; the Rt. Hon. Visc. Eccles copy. [Sabin 31349] (CNY. Nov.18; 136) $2,200
– – **Anr. Copy.** Last ll. slightly stained, cont. leath., bumped. [Sabin 31349] (BR. Apr.12; 15) DM 900

HENNEQUIN-REVEUR
– **Motifs Inedits pour toutes Industries d'Art dans le Gout du Jour.** Paris, ca. 1910. Fo. Title & plts. stpd. in lr. margin, orig. pict. hf. linen portfo., lightly rubbed & bumped. (HT. May 9; 1030) DM 800

HENNEZEL, Henri d'
– **Le Décor des Soieries d'Art Anciennes et Modernes.** Paris, ca. 1926. Fo. 56 cold. plts. mntd. on art paper, each liby.-stpd. on blank verso, loose in ptd. bd. folder, linen ties. (SG. May 3; 205) $200

HENNINGER
– **Der Rhein u. d. Rheinlande.** Ill.:– Rohbock & Cooke engraved by Kolb & others. Darmstadt, 1856. Engraved title with vig., 38 steel-engraved plts., some old spotting, mostly in margin, bds., lightly bumped. (V. Sep.29; 95) DM 3,000

HENNINGUS, Marcus
– **Tirolensium Principum Comitum ... Genuinae Eicones.** Augsburg, 1599. Fo. Lacks last blank, stains, vell., stained. (BBA. Jan.19; 8) *Maggs.* £150

HENREY, Blanche
– **British Botanical & Horticultural Literature before 1800.** L., 1975. 3 vols. 4to. Cl., boxed. (SG. Oct.6; 192) $140

HENRICUS de Vrimaria
– **Opus Sermonŭ Exactissimorŭ de Sanctis.** Hagenau, Nov. 1513. 4to. Cont. blind-stpd. pig over wood bds., clasps, bevelled edges, a trifle soiled. (S. Oct.11; 398) *Fletcher.* £210

HENRIOT, Gabriel
– **Encyclopédie du Luminaire.** Paris, [1933]. 6 pts. Fo. 240 plts., each liby.-stpd. on blank verso, loose in ptd. wraps., enclosed in 2 folders with cl.-bkd. ptd. bds., linen ties. (SG. May 3; 206) $325

HENRY VIII, King of England
– **Assertio Septem Sacramentorum adversus Martin Lutherŭ** ... 1521. *1st. Edn.* Title cut close on tail edge, minor wormhole affecting text & stains, mostly at hinges. [STC 13078] *(Bound with:)* DERING, Sir Edward **- A Collection of Speeches.** 1642. Last lf. defect. [Wing D 1104] Together 2 works in 1 vol. 4to. Old cf., rubbed; Sir Ivar Colquhoun, of Luss copy. (CE. Mar.22; 154) £580

– – **Anr. Edn.** N.p., ca. 1522. *Early Edn.* Last lf. with sm. margin repair, cont. MS. annots., bds. (HK. Nov.8; 216) DM 2,000

HENRY, Frederick, Prince of Orange
[–] **Het Leven van Frederik Henrik.** Ill.:– after B. Picart. The Hague, 1737. 2 vols. Cont. cf. gt. extra, slightly stained. (SG. Oct.27; 112) $110

HENRY, George Morrison Reid
– **Coloured Plates of the Birds of Ceylon.** Ed.:– W.E. Wait. 1927-35. 4 pts. (all publd.) in 1 vol. 4to. 64 cold. plts., cont. cl. (TA. Oct.20; 148) £100
– – **Anr. Copy.** 4 pts. in 1 vol. (all publd.). 4to. 64 cold. plts., cont. cl. (TA. Aug.18; 23) £65

HENRY, John Joseph
– **An Accurate & Interesting Account of the Hardships & Sufferings of that Band of Heroes, who Traversed the Wilderness in the Campaign Against Quebec in 1775.** Lancaster, Pa., 1812. *1st. Edn.* 12mo. Copyright notice pasted on verso of title-p., text quite browned, cont. sheep, worn at head of spine; the Rt. Hon. Visc. Eccles copy. (CNY. Nov.18; 138) $160

HENRY, O.
See– PORTER, William Sydney 'O. Henry'

HENRY, Robert
– **The History of Great Britain, from the first invasion of it by the Romans under Julius Caesar** ... Edinb., 1771-93. *1st. Edn.* 6 vols. 4to. Cont. tree cf., spines gt., spines faded; Sir Ivar Colquhoun, of Luss copy. (CE. Mar.22; 155) £260

HENSHALL, Samuel
– **Specimens & Parts; containing an History of the County of Kent.** L., 1789. *(Bound with:)* DOMESDAY BOOK – **Domesday; or, an Actual Survey of South-Britain** ... Samuel Henshall & J. Wilkinson. L., 1799. Together 2 works in 1 vol. 4to. Some browning & spotting, some margin annots. (partly trimmed), later hf. cf., slightly rubbed. (S. Mar.6; 427) *Sanders.* £50

HENSLOW, John Stephen
See– Maund, Benjamin & Henslow, John Stephen

HENTY, W.
– **On Improvements in Cottage Husbandry.** Launceston, [1860?]. Title wraps., outer ll. slightly worn. (KH. Nov.8; 208) Aus. $550

HENTZE, Carl
– **Chinese Tomb Figures.** 1928. 4to. Hf.-title loose, orig. cl. (BBA. Sep.8; 213) *Han Shan Tang.* £80
– – **Anr. Copy.** Lge. 4to. 114 plts., ex-liby., buckram. (SG. May 3; 207) $200

HENTZNER, Paul
– **A Journey into England.** Straw. Hill Pr., 1757. Lacks final blank, cont. mott. cf. (S. Nov.1; 114) *Thorp.* £100
– **Travels in England, During the Reign of Queen Elizabeth.** Trans.:– Horace Walpole. 1797. 11 engraved plts. (6 tinted), minor foxing, cont. hf. cf., unc.; Sir Ivar Colquhoun, of Luss copy. (CE. Mar.22; 156) £150

HEPPLEWHITE, Alice
– **Cabinet Maker & Upholsterer's Guide.** 1963. *Thames Facs.* No bdg. stated. (JL. Jun.24; 195) Aus. $200

HERAEUS, C.G.
– **Bildnisse der Regierenden Fürsten und Berühmter Männer vom 14. bis zum 18. Jahrhundert in einer Folgereihe von Schaumünzen.** Wien, 1828. Lge. fo. Some slight foxing, cont. hf. leath. gt., slightly rubbed. (R. Oct.11; 1055) DM 1,800
– **Gedichte und Lateinische Inschriften.** Nürnberg, 1721. *1st. Edn.* Lightly browned, 19th. C. paper covered bds., new red leath. spine gt. (GB. Nov.4; 2085) DM 400

HERBELOT DE MOULAINVILLE, Barthelemy de
– **Bibliothèque Orientale; ou, Dictionnaire Universel, Contenant Généralement Tout ce qui Regarde la Connoissance des Peuples de l'Orient.** Maastricht, 1776. Fo. Hf.-title, cont. hf. sheep, worn; from J.W.

Rimington Wilson chess liby. (SG. Sep.22; 166) $110
– – **Anr. Edn.** Maastricht, 1776-80. Fo. Cont. leath. gt., slightly worn. (R. Oct.13; 3014) DM 800

HERBERSTAIN, Siegmund von, Baron
– **Moscouiter Wunderbare Historien.** Basel, 1567 [i.e. St. Petersb., 1795]. *Facs. Edn.* Fo. Cont. Russian str.-grd. red mor. gt., covers gt.-decor., spine gt. in 6 compartments, bd. edges & turn-ins gt., marb. end-papers, slight wear to extremities; ink stp. on title of the Bibliothèque de Tsarskoe Solo. (CNY. May 18; 110) $750

HERBERT, Lord Edward, of Cherbury
– **The Life of Edward, Lord Herbert of Cherbury.** Strawberry Hill, 1764. *[1st. Edn.].* 4to. Cont. mott. cf., spine gt.-decor.; Sir Ivar Colquhoun, of Luss copy. (CE. Mar.22; 157) £210
– – **Anr. Copy.** 4to. Folding engraved frontis., folding pedigree, slightly browned, cont. red mor. gt., spine gt. in compartments. (SPB. May 16; 148) $450

HERBERT, Frank
– **Dune.** Phila., [1965]. *1st. Edn.* Edges & a few pp. lightly spotted, ink scrawl to rear pastedown, lightly shaken, d.-w. rubbed & creased, covers rubbed, spine leaning, tiny tear to outer joint. (CBA. Oct.29; 405) $180

HERBERT, George
– **A Priest to the Temple.** L., 1671. *2nd. Edn.* 1st. 'Imprimatur' lf. present, lacks last blank, some lr. margins cut close, later panel. cf. gt.; pres. inscr. by Charles Whibley. [Wing H1513] (BBA. May 3; 151) *Robertshaw.* £55
– **The Temple. Sacred Poems & Private Ejaculations.** Camb., 1641. *6th. Edn.* 12mo. Cont. cf., sig. & bkplt. of Maurice Baring. [Wing H1516] (BBA. May 3; 125) *Quaritch.* £150

HERBERT, Henry William 'Frank Forester'
[–] **The Warwick Woodlands, by Frank Forester.** Ill.:– Robert Ball & Forester. Derrydale Pr., 1934. *(250) numbered.* Tall 8vo. Hand-cold. frontis. & title, 6 plts., gt.-pict. leatherette, back gt. (SG. Mar.15; 227) $150

HERBERT, Luke
See– GALLOWAY, Elijah & Herbert, Luke

HERBERT, Thomas
[–] **A Relation of some yeares travaile** ... **into Afrique & the greater Asia, especially the Territories of the Persian Monarchie. By T.H.** L., 1634. *1st. Edn.* Fo. A few minor stains, cont. cf. [STC 13190] (S. Dec.1; 358) *Lyon.* £260

HERBERT, William, Librarian to the Corporation of the City of London
– **Antiquities of the Inns of Court & Chancery** ... L., 1804. 24 engraved plts., orig. bds., unc. & unopened. (C. Nov.16; 14) *Steedman.* £140

HERBERT, Hon. William, Dean of Manchester, 1778-1847
– **Amaryllidaceae.** 1837. 48 engraved plts., including 43 hand-cold., stitching shaken, orig. cl., lightly soiled. (CSK. Sep.16; 127) £200
[–] **Musae Etonenses: seu Carminum Delectus.** L., 1795. *1st. Edn.* 2 vols. Final errata lf. in both vols., cont. str.-grd. mor., gt., slightly marked; inscr. 'From W. Herbert Janr. 1796', Dr. J. Goodall's & Robert Birley's copy. (S. Oct.11; 399) *Georges.* £180

HERBILLON, A
See– BALASCHOFF, P. de & Herbillon, A.

HERBOLARIO VOLGARE Nequal e le Virtu de le Herbe & Moltri altri Simpoici se Dechiarano Venice, 15 Nov. 1534. Title woodcut, 146 (of 151) woodcuts, closely cut affecting some headlines, title margin reprd., some staine, few wormholes, new cf.; Hunger & Dr. Walter Pagel copy, w.a.f. (S. Feb.7; 181) *Rix.* £230

HERBORT, J.A. de
– **Nouvelles Méthodes pour fortifier les Places et pour remedier à la Foiblesse des Anciens.** Augsburg, 1735. Cont. leath. gt. (R. Apr.4; 2109) DM 550

HERBST, Joh. Fr. Wilh.
- Versuch e. Naturgesch. d. Krabben u. Krebse. Zürich, 1782. Pts. 1-3 only (of 4). 4to. Lacks end of 3rd. pt., text partly foxed & stained, especially in 1st. part, mostly loose, hf. linen, ca. 1870. (HK. Nov.8; 590) DM 1,200
See— JABLONSKY, Carl Gustav & Herbst, Johan Friedrich Wilhelm

HERD, Sandy
- My Golfing Life. 1923. *1st. Edn.* Bdg. not stated. (PD. Jul.13; 39) £90

HERDER, Johana Georg
- Abhandlung über den Ursprung der Sprache. Berlin, 1772. *1st. Edn.* Cont. bds. (BR. Apr.12; 1073) DM 750
- Ideen zur Philosophie der Geschichte der Menschheit. Riga & Leipzig, 1784-87. *1st. Edn.* 3 (of 4) pts. in 3 vols. Some browning, cont. hf. leath. gt., slightly rubbed & spotted. (HT. May 10; 2251) DM 450
[-] Kritische Wälder. Riga, 1769. *1st. Edn.* 3 vols. in 1. Vol. I title stpd., later hf. leath., elab. gt. spine, slightly rubbed, reprd.; Hauswedell coll. (H. May 24; 1371) DM 400
- Leider der Liebe. Leipzig, 1778. *1st. Edn.* Slightly browned, cont. bds., slightly bumped & worn. (HK. May 16; 2090) DM 440
- Sämmtliche Werke. 1827-30. *2nd. Coll. Edn.* 60 vols. in 30. Hf. leath., romantic gt., corners bumped. (GB. May 4; 1326) DM 1,400
- - Anr. Copy. 60 vols. & 1 supp. vol. in 34 vols. Slightly browned, cont. bds., some vols. slightly bumped. (R. Apr.3; 251) DM 1,100
- Terpsichore. Lübeck, 1795-96. *1st. Edn.* 3 vols. Engraved ex-libris inside cover, cont. hf. leath., gt. spine, slightly discold.; Hauswedell coll. (H. May 24; 1377) DM 500
[-] Von Deutscher Art und Kunst. Hamburg, 1773. *1st. Edn.* Some light browning, sm. coll. stp. on title, tooled arms & ex-libris, mod. bds., faded; Hauswedell coll. (H. May 24; 1372) DM 2,400

HERDMAN, William Gawin
- Pictorial Relics of Ancient Liverpool. L. & L'pool., 1843. 4to. Additional litho. title, 48 plts., lightly dampstained thro.-out, cont. hf. mor., rubbed, w.a.f. (CSK. Jan.13; 23) £290
- - Anr. Copy. Fo. Tinted litho. title (loose), 48 litho plts., 3 slightly soiled, hf. mor. gt. (P. Dec.8; 63) *Nicholson.* £220
- - Anr. Edn. 1858. Fo. Hf. mor. gt. (P. Dec.8; 64) *Nicholson.* £220

HERE, Emmanuel
- Recueil des Plans, Elevations et Coupes, tant Géometrales qu'en Perspective des Chateaux ... que le Roi de Pologne Occupe en Lorraine. Ill.:– Lotharing, Lattre, Girardet, & others. Paris, ca. 1750. 2 vols. Engraved titles, port. frontis., engraved dedication, 60 engraved plts., including 34 double-p., some folding, 1 margin slightly frayed. (*With:*) - Plans et Elevations de la Place Royale de Nancy ... F. Lotharing. Paris, 1753. 1 vol. Engraved title, 13 engraved double-p. plts., including 2 folding. Together 3 vols. Lge. fo. Unif. cont. mott. cf. gt., covers with gt. arms of Stanislaus Leszczynski, King of Poland, spines gt., slightly rubbed, corners strengthened. (C. Dec.9; 65) *Lyon.* £4,200

HERE & THERE a book of Transformation Pictures
L. & N.Y., n.d. 2 plts. cleanly torn, orig. cl.-bkd. pict. bds., d.-w. (CSK. Jun.1; 178) £120

HEREDIA, Jose Maria
- Les Trophées. Paris, 1907. *(175) numbered.* Fo. Vell., red mor., gt. tools, s.-c. (DS. Nov.25; 2196) Pts. 50,000
- - Anr. Edn. Ill.:– G. Rochegrosse & others. Paris, 1914. *(512).* 4to. On vélin d'Arches, bordeaux hf. mor., corners, by Yseux, unc., wrap. & spine preserved. (HD. May 4; 296) Frs. 2,200

HERIOT, George
- Travels through the Canadas. 1807. *[1st. Edn.].* 4to. Folding frontis., folding hand-cold, map, 26 plts., some folding, mod. cl. (P. Mar.15; 244) *Tzakas.* £820
- - Anr. Copy. 4to. Hand-cold. engraved folding

chart, 27 sepia-ptd. plts. on thin paper, many folding, some offsetting, cont. tree cf. [Sabin 31489] (C. Nov.16; 96) *Blackwells.* £600
- - Anr. Copy. 4to. Scattered light foxing, few margin repairs, antique hf. cf. (SG. Jan.19; 134) $650

HERIZ, Patrick de
- La Belle O'Morphi. Ill.:– after François Boucher. Gold. Cock. Pr., [1947]. *(100) numbered, specially bnd.* Orig. mor.-bkd. cl. gt., slightly dampstained, s.-c.; from D. Bolton liby. (BBA. Oct.27; 136) *Duschnes.* £55

HERLICIUS, David (Ed.)
See— HERMETISCHE ROSENKRANTZ ...

HERLITZ, G. (Ed.)
See— JUDISCHES LEXIKON

HERMAN, Morton
- The Early Australian Architects & Their Work. Sydney, 1954. *Ltd. 1st. Edn. (100) numbered & sigd.* No bdg. stated. (JL. Jun.24; 163) Aus. $100

HERMANN, Johann
- Tabula Affinitatum Animalium. Strassburg, 1783. *1st. Edn.* Lge. 4to. Some liby. stps., buckram. (SG. Mar.22; 152) $130

HERMANN, Paul
- Horti Academici Lugduno-Batavi Catalogus. Lugduni Batavorum, 1687. Some spots & dampstains, cont. parch. (HD. Jul.6; 46) Frs. 1,300
- Sechs Kaltnadelarbeiten zu Liedern von Coethe. Munich, ca. 1922. *(150) numbered.* This copy unnumbered, 5 (of 6) dry-point etchings, orig. ptd. wraps., with verses for each etching in covers; each dry-point sigd. by artist. (SG. Dec.15; 158) $150

HERMANT, Godefroy
- La Vie de S. Athanase Patriarche d'Alexandrie. Paris, 1671. 2 vols. 4to. Cont. red mor., Du Seuil gt. decor., spines decor., from Lamoignon liby. (HD. May 3; 63) Frs. 1,550

HERMES, Trismegistus
- Mercurius Trismegistusi Peomander, seu de Potestate ac Sapientia Divina. Parisiis, 1554. Text in Greek & Latin, some ll. stained, title brown, notes on blank lf. at end, later hf. cf., rubbed. (BBA. Jun.28; 158) *Whitby.* £140

HERMETISCHE ROSENKRANTZ das ist Vier Schoene Ausserlesene Tractaetlein nemlich Artephii ...
Ed.:– David Herlicius. Hamburg, 1659. *1st. Edn.* Lacks last blank lf., sm. repair to title margin, bds.; Prof. M. Nierenstein & Dr. Walter Pagel copy. (S. Feb.7; 182) *Ritman.* £420

HERNANDEZ, Estevan
- Diario de Un Viage desde el Puerto de San Rafael del Diamante hasta el de San Lorenzo en las Puntas del Río Quinto ... Buenos Aires, 1837. *1st. Edn.* Lge. fo. Sewed. (DS. Oct.28; 2539) Pts. 35,000

HERNANDEZ, Miguel
- El Labrador de más Aire. Madrid/Valencia, 1937. *1st. Edn.* Orig. wraps. (DS. Jan.27; 2304) Pts. 25,000

HERNDON, William Lewis & Gibbon, Lardner
- Exploration of the Valley of the Amazon. Wash., 1853-54. 2 vols. & 2 folders of maps. 5 folding litho. maps, 52 tinted litho. plts., some browning & spotting, sm. tears at folds of maps, 1 map loose, orig. cl., foot of 1 spine worn. [Sabin 31524] (C. Nov.16; 97) *Bonham.* £200

HERNSHEIM, Franz
- Südsee-Erinnerungen (1875-1880) ... Foreword:– Dr. Otto Finsch. Berlin, ca. 1883. 4to. Old qtr. roan, rubbed. (KH. May 1; 346) Aus. $130

HERO of Alexandria
- De Gli Automati overo Machine se moventi, Libri Due. Trans.:– Bernaldus Baldus. Venice, 1589. *1st. Italian Edn.* 4to. 18th. C. wraps. (R. Apr.4; 1605) DM 1,400
- The Pneumatics. Ed.:– Bennet Woodcroft. L., 1851. *1st. Edn. in Engl.* 4to. Prelims. slightly foxed, mod. hf. cf. over marb. bds.; Stanitz coll. (SPB. Apr.25; 219) $200

- Spirituali [Italian]. Trans.:– A. Giorgio. Urbino, 1592. Sm. 4to. 1 lf. defect. & reprd. at upr. margin affecting a few words, some light foxing, mostly towards end, later parch., soiled; Liechtenstein bkplt., Stanitz coll. (SPB. Apr.25; 218) $275
- Spiritualium Liber. Trans.:– F. Commandino. Urbino, 1575. *1st. Edn.* Sm. 4to. A few ll. browned, 1st. 2 ll. guarded, slight worming to inner margins of last 2 ll., later vell.; Stanitz coll. (SPB. Apr.25; 217) $750

HERO OF CONSTANTINOPLE, the younger
- Liber de Machinis Bellicis necnon de Geodaesia. Trans.:– F. Barozzi. Venice, 1572. *1st. Edn.* Sm. 4to. Sm. hole in blank part of title-p., 1 prelim. lf. very browned, a few other ll. less browned, new hf. mor.; armorial bkplt. & label of Comte/Marquis de Fortia, Kenney copy with label, 2 military drawings & some Greek notes on tracing paper tipped in, Stanitz coll. (SPB. Apr.25; 220) $650

HERODIANUS OF ALEXANDRIA, Historian
- History of Twenty Roman Caesars & Emperors of his Time. Trans.:– I. M[axwell]. 1629. 1 lf. trimmed with loss of few words of margin note, last lf. trimmed, some spotting, diced cf. [STC 13222] (P. Jan.12; 236) *Smallwood.* £70

HERODOTUS
- Historiarum libri IX. Amst., 1763. Fo. Title & text in Greek & Latin, late 18th. C. Engl. russ. gt. (S. Oct.11; 400) *Maggs.* £70
- History ... Trans.:– George Rawlinson. L., 1862. 4 vols. Early pol. cf., slight rubbing, with Scotch College prize stp. (KH. Nov.8; 209) Aus. $170
- - Anr. Edn.:– A.W. Lawrence. Trans.:– G. Rawlinson. Ill.:– V. Le Campion (wood engrs.) & T. Poulton (maps). Bloomsbury, Nones. Pr., 1935. *(675) numbered.* Sm. fo. Vell.-bkd. buckram, spine gt., & slightly spotted, partly unc. (SG. Aug.4; 234) $260
- - Anr. Copy. 4to. Qtr. vell. gt., partly unc. (SG. Jan.12; 276) $200
- Les Neuf Livres des Histoires de Herodote ... intitulés du Nom des Muses ... plus un Recueil de Georges Gemiste dict Plethon, des Choses avenues depuis la Journée de Mantinée ... Trans.:– P. Saliat. Paris, 1556. Fo. Mod. vell. (HD. Feb.22; 91) Frs. 2,500

HERON DE VILLEFOSSE, René
- L'Ile de France. Ill.:– A. Dunoyer de Segonzac. 1966. Fo. On japon nacré, red mor., wrap. & spine preserved, s.-c.; with suite on Arches. (HD. Jun.29; 115) Frs. 4,500
- La Rivière Enchantée. Ill.:– Foujita. Paris, 1951. *(300). Unnumbered on vélin d'Arches.* 4to. 26 orig. etchings (14 cold.), leaves, ill. wraps., box. (HD. Mar.27; 76) Frs. 69,000

HEROUVILLE DE CLAYE
[-] Mémoires sur l'Infanterie ou Traité des Légions. La Haye, 1753. Sm. 8vo. Cont. marb. cf., spine decor.; 18th. C. ex-libris 'Lallemant de Betz'. (HD. Nov.9; 127) Frs. 1,000

HERRAUDS OCH BOSA SAGA ...
Ed.:– Olaus Verelius. Uppsala, 1666. Mod. bds. (S. Jun.25; 165) *Hannas.* £90

HERRENSCHWAND, J.F. von
- Abhandlung von den Vornehmsten und Gemeinsten Innerlichen und Ausserlichen Krankheiten. Bern, 1788. *1st. German Edn.* 4to. Light stain in early upper corners, a few ll. slightly spotted, cont. leath., slight spotted, rubbed, spine defect. (R. Oct.12; 1418) DM 540

HERRERA, Antonio de
- The General History of the Vast Continent & Islands of America ... Trans.:– Capt. John Stevens. L., 1725-6. *1st. Engl. Edn.* 6 vols. 2 maps, 15 engraved plts., lacks hf.-titles, cf. (LH. Sep.25; 236) $775

HERRGOTT, M.
- Genealogia Diplomatica Augustae Gentis Habsburgicae. Wien, 1737. Fo. Some light foxing, cont. vell. (R. Apr.5; 3085) DM 20,000

HERRICK, Robert
- **One Hundred & Eleven Poems.** Ill.:– Sir William R. Flint. Gold. Cock. Pr., 1955. *(550) numbered & sigd. by artist. (105) specially bnd., with an extra set of ills. not in the book.* 4to. Prospectus loosely inserted, orig. sheep gt., s.-c. (S. Nov.21; 234)
Blackwells. £210

HERRIGEL, Eugen
See— SUZUKI, D.T. & Herrigel, Eugen

HERRIOT, Edouard
- **Madame Recamier.** Trans.:– Alys Hallard. L. & N.Y., 1906. 2 vols. Extra-ill. with 68 plts. (20 cold.), crushed lev. mor., gt.-panel., spines in 6 compartments, gt., mor. gt. doubls. in cf. gt. strip border, upr. doubls. with oval miniature ports. of Madame Recamier & Benjamin Constant, watered silk linings, silk markers, fleece-lined cl. s.-c., by Bayntun, as a bdg., w.a.f. (CNY. Dec.17; 534)
$800

HERRLIBERGER, D.
- **Basslerische Ausruff-Bilder.** N.p., n.d. *Litho. reprint of 1749 Edn.* 52 numbered, cold. & litho. ills., plts. loose & slightly spotted, hf. linen, slightly bumped, Hauswedell coll. (H. May 23; 167)
DM 1,900
- **Zürcherische Ausruff-Bilder.** Zürich, 1748-51. 3 pts. in 1 vol. Fo. 18 etchings with 156 numbered ills., each plt. in 9 numbered pts., Swiss German captions & high German rhyme, 1 sm. tear, 1 bkd. corner, mod. bds.; Hauswedell coll. (H. May 23; 158)
DM 8,400

HERRMANN[-NEISSE], Max
- **Das Buch Franziskus. Gedichte.** Berlin-Wilmersdorf, 1911. *1st. Edn. (400) numbered.* End-paper with MS. dedication from author, wide margin, orig. pict. wraps. (GB. May 5; 2670)
DM 400
- **Einsame Stimme. Ein Buch Gedichte.** Ill.:– G. Grosz. Berlin, 1927. *1st. Edn. (900).(200) numbered De Luxe Edn.* Orig. lithos., orig. hf. leath. (GB. May 5; 2672)
DM 500

HERROLD-HEMPSALL, W.
- **Bee-Keeping, New & Old.** 1930-37. Cl. (P. Jul.5; 215)
£95

HERSCHEL, J.F.W.
See— PEACOCK, George — HERSCHEL, J.F.W. — BABBAGE, Charles

HERTEL, C.G.
- **Vollständige Anweisung zum Glass-Schleiffen, wie auch zu Verfertigung der Optischen Maschinen ...** Preface:– C. Wolffes. Halle, 1716. *1st. Edn. (Bound with:)* LEUTMANN, J.G. - **Neue Anmerckungen vom Glasschleiffen.** Halle, 1738. Together 2 works in 1 vol. Browned, erased liby. stp., cont. leath., some slight wear & minimal worming. (HT. May 8; 632)
DM 900

HERTTWIG, Chr.
- **Neues und Volkommenes Berg-Buch.** Dresden & Leipzig, 1710. *1st. Edn.* Fo. Slightly browned, cont. cf., spine with short tears. (H. May 22; 171)
DM 900
- - **Anr. Edn.** Dresden & Leipzig, 1734. *2nd. Edn.* Fo. Some light browning, cont. hf. vell. (R. Oct.12; 1574)
DM 1,000

HERTZ, Heinrich
- **Electric Waves being Researches on the Propagation of Electric Action with Finite Velocity through Space.** Preface:– Lord Kelvin. Trans.:– D.E. Jones. L., 1893. *1st. Edn. in Engl.* Orig. cl.; Stanitz coll. (SPB. Apr.25; 222)
$275
- **Ueber die Einwirkung einer Geradlinigen Schwingung auf eine Benachbarte Strombahn. — — Ueber Inductionserscheinungen, Hervorgerufen durch die Electrischen Vorgänge in Isolatoren. — — Ueber die Ausbreitungsgeschwindigkeit der Electrodynamischen Wirkungen. — — Ueber Electrodynamischen Wellen im Luftraume und deren Reflexion.** Leipzig, 1888. *1st. Edn.* 4 papers in 'Annalen der Physik und Chemie', Vol. XXXIV, New Series. Light browning, orig. cl.; Stanitz coll. (SPB. Apr.25; 223)
$200
- **Untersuchungen ueber die Ausbreitung der Elektrischen Kraft ...** Leipzig, 1892. *1st. Edn.* Title

hinged at inner margin to free end-paper, cont. hf. mor., rubbed; sig. of Dr. G.J.M. Coolhans, Dec. 1892, on title, Stanitz coll. (SPB. Apr.25; 221)
$1,300

HERTZ, Henry
- **Le Guignol Horizontal.** 1923. *(112) with 4 lithos. by José de Togorès.* Sewed. (HD. Jun.29; 116)
Frs. 1,100
- **Vers un Monde Volage. Illustré de Dix Eaux-Fortes Originales Hors Texte par Marcel Gromaire.** Paris, 1926. *(250) numbered.* 4to. Orig. ptd. wraps., untrimmed. (TA. Jun.21; 598)
£75

HERTZ, Wilhelm
- **Schlüssel zur Praktischen Gartenkunst.** Stuttgart, 1840. Some foxing, orig. bds. (GB. Nov.3; 1103)
DM 1,200

HERTZBERG
- **Histoire de la Grèce sous la Domination des Romains.** Trans.:– A. Bouche Leclercq. Paris, 1887-90. 3 vols. Hf. chagrin. (HD. Feb.22; 92)
Frs. 1,600

HERVEY, J.
- **Godsvruchtige Bespeigelingen & Overdenkingen.** Ill.:– S. Fokke. Amst., 1754-56. 2 vols. 18th. C. panel. marb. cf. gt., richly decor. (VG. Nov.30; 546)
Fls. 460

HERVEY, James
- **Meditations & Contemplations.** 1796. 2 vols. Cont. russ., spines gt.-decor., spines slightly faded; Sir Ivar Colquhoun, of Luss copy. (CE. Mar.22; 159)
£80

HERVEY, John
- **Messenger: The Great Progenitor.** Derrydale Pr., [1935]. *(500).* Tall 8vo. Two-toned bds., unopened. (SG. Mar.15; 228)
$150
- **Lady Suffolk: The Old Grey Mare of Long Island.** Foreword:–Harry T. Peters. Derrydale Pr., [1936]. *(500).* Lge. 8vo. Two-toned bds., unopened. (SG. Mar.15; 229)
$150

HERVEY, John & Vosburgh, Walter S.
- **Racing in America, 1665-1936.** [1922-37-44]. *(800) numbered.* 4 vols. 4to. Orig. cl.-bkd. bds. (P. Dec.8; 216)
Head. £180

HERZIG, M. (Ed.)
See— ARS NOVA

HERZL, Theodor
- **Der Baseler Congress.** Vienna, 1897. *1st. Edn.* Sm. 4to. Ptd. wraps., loose, owner's sig. on upr. wrap. (SG. Feb.2; 132)
$700
- - **Anr. Copy.** Soiled, mod. leath. (R. Oct.11; 1089)
DM 500
- **Der Judenstaat. Versuch einer Modernen Loesung der Judenfrage.** Vienna, 1896. *1st. Edn.* Hand-drawn owner's mark on title & 2 other pp., binder's cl., slightly worn. (SG. Feb.2; 133)
$1,500
- - **Anr. Copy.** Orig. wraps., upr. wrap with margin slit & mntd., lacks lr. wrap. (D. Nov.24; 4233)
DM 3,500
- - **Anr. Copy.** Wide margin, hf. linen, orig. upr. wrap. bnd. in, soiled, crumpled, bkd. corner tear. (HK. Nov.9; 1793)
DM 2,800
- - **Anr. Copy.** Title lf. lightly soiled, later bds. (GB. Nov.4; 1453)
DM 2,600

HESIOD
- **Opera Omnia.** Parma, 1787. 4to. Cont. mor., blind-tooled decor., gt. inner & outer dentelle, silk doubl. & end-papers; from Mirabeau liby. (D. Nov.24; 2395)
DM 1,600
- **[Opera] quae extant cum Graecis Scholiis Procli, Moschupoli, Tzetzae ... Item Notae ...** Ed.:– Daniel Heinsius. Antw., 1603. 2 pts. in 1 vol. 4to. Text in Greek, some commentaries in Latin, vell.; pres. copy inscr. by Ed. to Nicolaus Seyslius, with 10 line inscr. in Latin; later owner's entry of Otho Zeyst. (S. May 10; 299)
Goldschmidt. £220
- **Opuscula Inscripta Ega kai Emerai.** Basel, 1539. Sm. 8vo. In Greek & Latin, mod. bds. (SG. Feb.9; 247)
$110
- **Theogonie** [Greek]. Ill.:– G. Braque. Paris, 1955. *(150).* Fo. On auvergne H.M.P., Printers mark sigd. by artist, loose ll. in cold etched orig. wraps., orig.

s.-c., wear & slightly bumped; Hauswedell coll. (H. May 24; 529)
DM 16,000

HESS, C.A.
- **Abbildungen der Chur. Sächsischen Truppen in ihren Uniformen unter der Regierung Fried. Aug.** Dresden, 1805-07. Fo. 8 cold. engraved plts., hf. chagrin. (HD. Jan.27; 275)
Frs. 6,000

HESS, David
- **Die Badenfahrt.** Ill.:– Fr. Hegi & others. Zürich, 1818. Engraved title vig., 26 copper engrs. & vig., 1 multi folding plan, slightly foxed, cont. style hf. leath., orig. wraps. bnd. in. (GF. Nov.16; 1153)
Sw. Frs. 3,400

HESS, J.L. von
- **Topographisch-politisch-historische Beschreibung der Stadt Hamburg.** Hamburg, 1796. *1st. Edn.* 3 vols. 1 copper engr. with sm. tear, some maps cold., some with sm. pasted tear, plan partly bkd., browned & slightly foxed thro.-out, later hf. leath. (H. Nov.23; 378)
DM 500

HESS, L.
- **Folge von 54 num. Kupferstichen mit Ansichten von Jena und seiner Umgebung.** Jena, 1829-31. Loose ll., versos blank, cont. leath. cover, cont. vell. s.-c., both rubbed. (R. Oct.13; 2769)
DM 4,000

HESS, Moses
- **Rom und Jerusalem, die letzte Nationalitaetsfrage.** Leipzig, 1862. *1st. Edn.* Mildly browned, few minor stains, owner's stp. on title, mod. leath. (SG. Feb.2; 135)
$1,600

HESS, P.
- **Album of Greek Heroism being Scenes from the War of Independence in Greece (1820-1829).** N.d. 31 plts., loose, some spotting, orig. portfo., soiled, as a coll. of plts., w.a.f. (P. Oct.20; 120) £1,450

HESS, Thomas B.
- **Willem de Kooning Drawings.** Greenwich, [1972]. *1st. Amer. Edn.* 4to. 128 plts., bdg. not stated, owner's sig. on front end-paper, d.-w. clipped. (CBA. Jan.29; 288)
$160

HESSE (Contrib.)
See— NEUE RUNDSCHAU

HESSE, Hermann
- **Gedichte des Malers.** Bern, 1920. *1st. Edn. (100) De Luxe Edn. numbered on japan.* 4to. Printers mark sigd., hand-bnd. orig. hf. vell., partly faded. (HT. May 9; 1860)
DM 650
- **Italien: Verse.** Ill.:– Hermann Struck. Berlin, 1923. *(100) numbered with each plt. sigd.* Fo. Last plt. & limitation lf. discold. by laid in clippings, dampstain at upr. margins of end-papers, orig. stiff vell., very soiled; inscr. by author on, fly-lf. ' ... To our dear Joe. Berlin 18 X 26. Hermann and Mally'. (SG. Jan.12; 326)
$300
- - **Anr. Edn.** Ill.:– H. Struck. Berlin, 1923. *1st. Edn. (200) with sigd. title etching.* Sm. fo. Orig. pict. hf. vell. (H. Nov.24; 1604)
DM 620
- **Jahreszeiten. Zehn Gedichte mit Bildern.** Zürich, 1931. *1st. Edn. (500) numbered.* Orig. hf. vell. (GB. May 5; 2677)
DM 700
- **Neue Garten-Lust.** [Leipzig], 1696. 4to. Browned, lightly stained near end, cont. vell., spine defect. (R. Apr.4; 1871)
DM 800

HESSEL, A.
- **Kort Berettelse om then Swenska Kyrkios Narwarande tilstand i America.** Norrkoping, 1725. Sm. 4to. Stain affecting title & some other ll., 18th. C. decor. bds., cf. spine. [Sabin 31616] (S. Dec.1; 284)
Sawyer. £320

HESSEL, P.
- **Hertzfliessende Betrachtungen von dem Elbe-Strom.** Hamburg, 1675. Pt. 1. Sm. 4to. Frontis., port., 23 plts. only, lacks pp. 155-158, vell., soiled, w.a.f. (P. Jul.5; 267)
£160

HESSE-WARTEGG, E. von
- **China und Japan. Erlebnisse, Studien, Betrachtungen auf einer Reise um die Welt.** Leipzig, 1897. Sm. 4to. Several sm. tears pasted, orig. leath., 1 (of 2) pasted metal ornams., very bumped, spine defect. (R. Oct.13; 3004)
DM 420

HESYCHIUS
See— STEPHANUS Byzantius — POLLUX, Julius — HESYCHIUS

HETHERINGTON, Arthur Lonsdale
- The Art of the Chinese Potter. Ed.:– R.L. Hobson. 1923. 4to. Orig. buckram, spine slightly faded. (S. Nov.8; 535)   *Perkins.* £100

HETZEL, Pierre Jules 'P.J. Stahl'
- Nouvelles et Seules Veritables Aventures de Tom Pouce. Ill.:– Bertall. Paris, 1844. *Orig. Edn.* Hf. mor., corners, decor. spine, wrap. preserved, by Champs-Stroobants, sm. repair to cover. (HD. Dec.9; 187)   Frs. 1,500
- Scènes de la Vie Privée et Publique des Animaux. Ill.:– 'Grandville'. Paris, 1842. 2 vols. Lge. 8vo. Hf. chagrin by Peiffer & Vernier, spines gt., unc. (HD. May 21; 90)   Frs. 2,800
- – Anr. Copy. 2 vols. Chagrin, unc., by Cuzin. (HD. Mar.14; 39)   Frs. 1,800
- – Anr. Copy. 2 vols. Lge. 8vo. Minimal foxing, 2 ll. disbnd., lacks 1 plt., cont. hf. chagrin, corners, spines decor., slightly rubbed. (HD. May 4; 428)   Frs. 1,400
- – Anr. Copy. 2 vols. 4to. Wide margin, lightly foxed, cont. romantic hf. leath. gt., slightly rubbed & bumped, upr. part of orig. wraps. bnd. in. (HK. May 17; 2443)   DM 460
- – Anr. Copy. 2 vols. Slightly foxed, cont. hf. leath. gt., slightly worn. (R. Oct.11; 235)   DM 440
See— MUSSET, Alfred de & Hetzel, Pierre Jules 'Pierre Jules Stahl'

HEUBACH, J.P.
- Histoire Militaire de la Suisse et celles des Suisses dans les Differents Services de l'Europe. Lausanne, 1788. 8 vols. Old hf. roan, spine decor., lacks some vol. labels; May Schostland copy. (HD. Jan.27; 332)   Frs. 4,500

HEUCHLER, E.
- Die Bergknappen in ihren Berufs- und Familien-leben. Dresden, 1857. Ob. fo. Slightly foxed, cont. hf. linen, defect. (R. Apr.4; 1464)   DM 680

HEUGLIN, Martin Theodor von
- Reisen in Nord-Ost-Afrika. Gotha, 1857. Cont. linen gt. (GB. May 3; 34)   DM 550

HEULLAND, d'
[-] Théâtre de la guerre Présente en Allemagne. Paris, 1758. Text & atlas vol., 2 vols. 1 map defect, 2 maps slightly crumpled, 2 others loose, lightly soiled thro.-out, cont. paper wraps., rubbed, spine defect. (R. Oct.12; 2369)   DM 1,300

HEUNISCH, A. J.
- Beschreibung des Grossherzogthums Baden. Stuttgart, 1836. Map. multi torn, defect., cont. bds., bumped & worn. (R. Oct.12; 2463)   DM 1,750

HEURES DE PAPHOS, Contes Moraux par un Sacrificateur de Venus
[Paris], 1787. Mor. by Pagnant, box. (SM. Mar.7; 2439)   Frs. 11,000

HEUSS, A.
See— MANN, Golo & Heuss, A.
See— MANN, G. & others

HEVELIUS, Johannes
- Annus Climatericus. Danzig, 1685. Fo. Wide margin, sm. hole in hf.-title, some light browning or foxing, cont. hf. vell. (R. Oct.12; 1680)   DM 1,050
- Selenographia, sive Lunae Descriptio ... Danzig, 1647. *1st. Edn.* Lge. fo. Engraved title with ports., hf.-title, port., 111 engrs., some double-p. many text engrs., unlisted plt. 'RRR', light marginal dampstains on few ll., cont. cf., rebkd., orig. spine laid down, with 3-p. ptd. letter with engr. to Eich-stadt, dtd. 5 Jan. 1650. (SG. Apr.26; 93) $6,000
- – Anr. Copy. Fo. Some slight foxing, cont. leath., gt. à la grotesque, decor. & arms supralibros J.A. de Thou on both covers, slightly rubbed. (D. Nov.23; 402)   DM 10,500

HEWATT, Alexander
[-] An Historical Account of the Rise & Progress of the Colonies of South Carolina & Georgia. L., 1779. *1st. Edn.* 2 vols. Cont. cf.; the Rt. Hon. Visc.

Eccles copy. [Sabin 31630] (CNY. Nov.18; 139) $1,700

HEWITSON, William C.
- British Oology; Being Illustrations of the Eggs of British Birds. Newcastle, priv. ptd., [1831-42]. 2 vols. 169 hand-cold. litho. plts., cont. mor., spines gt. (CSK. Dec.2; 138)   £130
- Coloured Illustrations of the Eggs of British Birds. 1856. '3rd. Edn.'. 2 vols. 149 plts., including the 4 starred plts., cont. hf. mor., 1 spine defect. (SKC. Mar.9; 1943)   £85

HEWITT, Graily
- Lettering for Students & Craftsmen. L., 1930. *(380) numbered & sigd.* 4to. Orig. buckram, partly unc., slightly soiled. (S. May 1; 401) *Forster.* £50

HEWLETT, Maurice
- Quattrocentisteria: How Sandro Botticelli Saw Simonetta in the Spring. Ill.:– V. Angelo. N.Y., Golden Cross Pr., 1937. *(175) sigd. by artist.* Tall 4to. Hand-illuminated, announcement & xerox review laid in loose, end-papers slightly discold., three-qtr. parch. & bds., very slightly soiled, s.-c. worn & reprd.; the V. Angelo copy. (CBA. Oct.1; 137) $120

HEY, Mrs. Rebecca
[-] The Moral of Flowers. 1836. 23 hand-cold. plts., hf. mor. gt. (P. Sep.8; 37)   *Hollingsworth.* £130
[-] The Spirit of the Woods. 1837. 26 hand-cold. plts., hf. mor. gt. (P. Sep.8; 38)   *Trevor.* £65

HEYDENREICH, L.H. (Ed.)
See— REALLEXIKON ZUR DEUTSCHEN KUNSTGESCHICHTE

HEYLYN, Peter
- Cosmographie. Maps:– after Hondius by P. Chetwynd. For P. Chetwynd & A. Seile, 1677. *5th. Edn.* Fo. Engraved allegorical additional title, ptd. title in red & black, 4 folding engraved maps of continents, all with wide margins, browning affecting text, 1 or 2 margin tears, sm. liby. stps. on title & versos of maps, mod. cl. [Wing H1694] (S. May 21; 166)   *Burgess.* £250
- Cosmography in Four Books. 1703. Fo. Some light offsetting, cont. cf. (CSK. Sep.16; 218) £160

HEYM, Georg
- Umbra Vitae. Ill.:– Ernst Ludwig Kirchner. München, 1924. *(500).* 47 orig. woodcuts, orig. pict. linen; Hauswedell coll. (H. May 24; 649)   DM 8,500
- – Anr. Copy. Orig. pict. linen, 2 sm. scratches, spine & upr. margin slightly faded. (H. Nov.24; 2508)   DM 7,500
- – Anr. Copy. Lge. 8vo. Brown spotting, especially at beginning & end, orig. pictor. linen, owners mark on lr. end-paper. (H. May 23; 1325)   DM 6,600
- – Anr. Edn. Ill.:– E.L. Kirchner. München, 1924. *(510).* Orig. pict. linen. (H. Nov.24; 1696)   DM 8,800
- – Anr. Copy. 47 orig. lithos., some foxing, orig. pict. linen. (V. Oct.1; 4227)   DM 6,500

HEYNS, Zacharias
- Emblemata. Emblèmes Chrestiennes et Morales. Sinne-Beelden. Ill.:– Swelinck (engraved title), Goltzius (port.), & others. Rotterdam, 1625. 4 pts. in 1 vol. 4to. Some light wear & browning, cont. vell., ties, recased. (VG. Sep.14; 912)   Fls. 1,500

HEYRENBACH, J.C.
- Medicus. Steyr, 1753. Some slight foxing, 6 pp. with sm. cleanly reprd. tear, cont. leath. gt. (R. Apr.4; 1884)   DM 600

HEYTESBURY, William
- De Sensu Composito et Diviso. Venice, 17 Jul. 1501. Sm. 4to. 24 ll. (including final blank), lev. mor. by Sangorski & Sutcliffe; Stanitz coll. (SPB. Apr.25; 224) $350

HIBBERD, Shirley
- New & Rare Beautiful-Leaved Plants. 1870. 4to. Orig. gt.-decor. cl. (SKC. Sep.9; 1994)   £55

HIBBERD, S.
See— HULME, F.E. & Hibberd, S.

HIBERNIA VINDICATA
Hamburg, 1691. Sm. 4to. In German, later hf. leath. (SKC. Jan.13; 2218)   £100

HIEROCLES
- In Aureos Versus Pythagorae Opusculum. Trans.:– Joannes Aurispa. Patavii, Bartholomaeus de Val de Zoccho, 1474. *1st. Edn.* 4to. Lacks last blank lf., cont. MS. annots. at beginning, 17th. C. Italian stpd. roan; from Fondation Furstenberg-Beaumesnil. [HC 8545; BMC VII, 906] (HD. Nov.16; 38)   Frs. 16,600

HIERONYMUS, Saint Eusebius
- Epistolae. Mainz, Peter Schoeffer, 7 Sep. 1470. *Iss. with colophon beginning '[I] am decet ut nostris [con]corde[n]t'.* 2 vols. in 1. Fo. Most rubrics ptd., a few supplied in red, capitals & paragraph marks supplied in red or blue in intro. & index, folios 114 & 123 supplied from a vell. copy, 1st. & last 2 ll. heavily restored, some minor tears & repairs, mostly marginal, some spotting & slight staining, a few cont. MS. marginalia, cont. blind-stpd. pig over wood bds., slightly wormed, covers reprd., brass bosses, cornerpieces & clasps, lacks ties., vell antiphoner ll. supplied as free end-papers, new pastedowns; the Frederick Spiegelberg copy. (SPB. Dec.14; 19) $5,000
- – Anr. Edn. Parma, 1480. *Reprint of 1476 Edn.* 2 vols. Lge. fo. Initial on 1st. table lf. of each vol. decor. in cols. & gold, 1st. initial on 1st. text lf. richly painted in cols. & gold, cont. Venetian stpd. black mor. over wood bds., each vol. differently decor., spines renewed, traces of clasps; from Fondation Furstenberg-Beaumesnil. [H. 8457; BMC VII, 942; Goff H169] (HD. Nov.16; 39)   Frs. 24,000
- – Anr. Edn. Basle, Nicolaus Kesler, 8 Aug. 1489. Fo. Initials & rubrics painted in red or blue, lacks last blank lf., 1st, lf. mntd., some repairs to next 2 ll., much worming towards end, most margins dampstained, 18th. C. spr. cf., blind-decor., faded. [H. 8559; BMC III, 768; Goff H171] (SM. Mar.7; 2440)   Frs. 4,500
- – Anr. Edn. Venice, Bernardinus Benalius, 14 Jul. 1490. 2 vols. Tall fo. Lacks the 6 prelims. (1 blank) in Vol. I & 4 in Vol. II, limp linen; the Walter Goldwater copy. [BMC V, 372; Goff H-172; H. 8560] (SG. Dec.1; 175) $350
- – Anr. Edn. Venice, J. Rubeus Vercellensis, 7 Jan & 12 Jul. 1496. Fo. Title-lf. mntd., with some repairs, cf., brkn.; the Walter Goldwater copy. [BMC V, 419; Goff H-175; H. 8563] (SG. Dec.1; 176) $375
- – Anr. Edn. [Venice, Dominus Pincius], after 1500?. Fo. Lacks title-lf., register lf. & final lf. possibly inserted from anr. edn., prelims. & final lf. defect., some stains, etc. thro.-out, later vell.; the Walter Goldwater copy. [Goff H-177; H. 8564] (SG. Dec.1; 177) $325
- Expositio in Psalterium. Venice, J. G. de Grego-riis, 1498. Pt. 3 only (of 4) of 'Commentaria in Vetus & Novum Testamentum'. Fo. 19th. C. vell. [H. 8581; BMC V, 350] (HD. Nov.16; 77)   Frs. 5,000
- Opera. Ed.:– J. Martianay & A. Pouget. Parisiis, 1693-1706. *St. Maur Edn.* 5 vols. Lge. fo. L.P., stp. on title, corner of approx 60 ll. stained, blind-tooled vell. (B. Oct.4; 804)   Fls. 750
- Opera Omnia ... accessit his in Epistolarvm Tomos Nova Scholiorum. Ed.:– Erasmus. Paris, 1533/34. 9 pts., Supp. & Index, in 4 vols. Fo. 2 ll. in pt. 7 double, some old annots. & entries, some staining or browning, 18th. C. leath., spine & end-papers renewed, cover rubbed, corners very bumped. (HK. Nov.8; 221)   DM 1,600
- Ordo, seu Regula Vivendi Deo ad Eustochium. Bologna, Caligula de Bazaleriis, 28 Mar. 1498. 4to. Some light stains, 1 sm. wormhole thro.-out, mod. vell.-bkd. bds.; the Walter Goldwater copy. [Goff H-186] (SG. Dec.1; 178) $475
- Vita et Transitus. Flor., Francesco Bonaccorsi, 13 Feb. 1490. 4to. In Italian, lacks title-lf., sigs. a & b supplied from di Dino's 1492 edn., very foxed & stained, old vell.; the Walter Goldwater copy. [BMC VI, 72; Goff H-259] (SG. Dec.1; 179) $200
- – Anr. Edn. Flor., [Francesco di Dino], 13 Feb.

HIERONYMUS, Saint Eusebius -*Contd.*

1492. 4to. In Italian, lacks title-lf., some foxing, mod. vell.; the Walter Goldwater copy. [Goff H-261] (SG. Dec.1; 180) $125
- - **Anr. Edn.** Paris, [Ledru?], ca. 1498?. Title headed 'Transitus beati hieronymi quem presertim tres sancti ... ', blank corner of title restored, 18th. C. cf., supralibros eradicated from cover; the Walter Goldwater copy. (SG. Dec.1; 181) $450
- **Vitas Patrum.** Lyon, Apr. 1502. 4to. Worming at beginning & end slightly affects text, mod. vell. (S. Oct.11; 401) *K. Books.* £130

HIGDEN, Ranolphus
- **Polychronicon.** William Caxton, 1482. 1 lf. only, margin notes in red, cl. folder. (P. Apr.12; 34) *Questor.* £80
- - **Anr. Copy.** Fo. 1 lf. only, comprising fo. 104 from Book 2, sm. margin hole, early marginalia, tipped into mor.-bkd. binder. (SPB. Dec.13; 648) $175
- - **Anr. Edn.** Westminster, Wynkyn de Worde, 13 Apr. 1495. Sm. fo. Title, colophon & x2 & 7 supplied in facs., 17th. C. cf., upr. cover gt.-stpd. 'Mr. John Berridge to Christ's Hospital', with gt. arms of the school, rebkd.; the Walter Goldwater copy. [Goff H-268; H. 8660] (SG. Dec.1; 182) $9,750
[-]- **Anr. Edn.** Trans.:- [John de Trevisa]. L., 16 May 1527. *3rd. Edn.* Fo. Lacks X1, MS. notes in several 16th. C. hands, title 'Pope' frequently deleted, some staining, few short tears & sm. holes, colophon lf. torn & reprd., title mntd., old cf., rebkd., upr. cover detchd. [STC 13440] (S. Dec.8; 4) *Rix.* £360

HIGHWAYS & BYWAYS
L., 1914-48. 24 vols. Ills., orig. cl. gt. (P. May 17; 356) *Grange.* £100

HIKMANN, Barbara
See— GARTLER, I. & Hikmann, Barbara

HILARY, Saint, Bp. of Poitiers
- **Opera Complura.** Paris, [1510]. 1 vol. Fo. 17th. C. panel. cf., rebkd., brkn. (*With:*) - **Lucubrationes.** Basel, 1535. 1 vol. Fo. Cont. blind-tooled cf., rebkd., brkn. (SG. Oct.27; 143) $110

HILDEBRAND, W.
[-] **Das Grosse Planeten-Buch.** Leipzig, 1695. Slightly browned thro.-out, some soiling, cont. leath., spine slightly defect., loose. (R. Oct.12; 1550) DM 600
- **New augirte ... Magia Naturalis.** Erfurt, 1863-64. 4 pts. in 1 vol. 4to. Vol. 1 title with deleted owners mark, slightly wormed near end, browned, 19th C. bds. gt., lightly bumped. (HK. Nov.9; 1764) DM 420

HILL, Daniel Harvey
- **Bethel to Sharpsburg: a History of North Carolina in the War Between the States.** Raleigh, 1926. *1st. Edn.* 2 vols. Light dusting & foxing to text edges, gt.-lettered buckram. (HA. Sep.16; 451) $100

HILL, David Octavius
- **Sketches of Scenery in Perthshire.** Ill.:- C. Hullmandel, & J. Robertson, after Hill. N.d. Fo. 30 litho. plts., 1 with no imprint, but lettered in pencil & sigd. D.O. Hill, apparently in artist's hand, orig. bds., mor. spine & corners, neatly rebkd. (BBA. Sep.29; 134) *Marlboro' Rare Books.* £390

HILL, John
- **The British Herbal.** [L.,], 1756. Fo. Hand-cold. frontis., cold. vig. on title, 75 hand-cold. plts., cont. diced cf., rebkd. (P. Jan.12; 195a) *Shapiro.* £480
- - **Anr. Copy.** Fo. Engraved frontis., vig. title, 75 engraved plts., a few partly hand-cold., lacks portion of plt. 4, diced cf. gt., rubbed. (P. Mar.15; 32) *Walford.* £100
- - **Anr. Copy.** Fo. A little foxing, cf.-bkd. linen bds. (LH. Sep.25; 544) $275
- **The Construction of Timber, from its Early Growth** ... L., 1770. 46 engraved plts., including 2 hand-cold., cont. spr. cf., spine ends slightly frayed. (C. Nov.9; 82) *Thorp.* £400
- **Decade di Alberti Curiosi ed Eleganti Piante delle Indie Orientali, e dell'America.** Ill.:- after Majoli. Rome, 1786. 4to. 10 cold. engraved plts.,

dampstains, mainly to margins, cont. bds., worn, untrimmed. (SG. Oct.6; 194) $350
- **The Family Herbal.** Bungay, ca. 1810. Sm. 8vo. 54 hand-cold. plts., mod. leatherette. (SG. Oct.6; 195) $250
- **A General Natural History.** L., 1751. [Vol. II: 'A History of Plants']. Fo. Some spotting & discoloration, cont. cf. (C. Nov.16; 15) *Schuster.* £70
- - **Anr. Copy.** Vol. II only: 'Plants' (of 3). Fo. 16 hand-cold. engraved plts., slight offsetting from text, cont. mott. cf., spine gt., worn, reprd. (*With:*)
- **The British Herbal.** L., 1756. 1 vol. Fo. Engraved frontis., 75 plts., plt. 1 torn, plt. 2 frayed, slight browning, title & last p. dustsoiled, a few p. numerals on the latter erased, 19th. C. hf. mor., some wear. (S. Nov.28; 34) *Schuster.* £250
- **An History of Animals.** L., 1752. Fo. 28 engraved plts., cont. cf. gt., scuffed. (P. Jun.7; 175) £150
- - **Anr. Edn.** 1752. Fo. 28 hand-cold. engraved plts., some detchd. & slightly frayed at edges, cont. cf., worn. (TA. May 17; 380) £50
- **The Vegetable System.** 1769-70. Vols. 15 & 16 only: 'Five Petal'd Plants'. Fo. 119 uncold. plts., title reprd. (P. Jul.5; 281) £380

HILL, P. & Co.
- **Travelling Atlas of Scotland.** Maps:- Lizars, Edinburgh. Edinb., [1820]. Sm. 8vo. 30 engraved partly cold. maps, index, advt. lf., &c., orig. hf. cf. (PD. Apr.18; 162) £65

HILLIER, Jack
- **Japanese Prints & Drawings from the Vever Collection.** L., 1976. *(2000)* numbered. 3 vols. Fo. Orig. cl., d.-w.'s. (S. May 1; 590) *Stodart.* £50

HILLIER, Jack (Ed.)
See— GRABHORN, Edwin & Marjorie

HILLS, John Waller
- **A Summer on the Test.** Ill.:- Norman Wilkinson. L., 1924. *(325)*. *(300)* numbered & sigd. 4to. Orig. cl., slightly rubbed & faded, unc. (S. Oct.4; 31) *Inge.* £180
- - **Anr. Edn.** Ill.:- Norman Wilkinson. L., [1924]. *(300)*. 4to. 12 dry-points, orig. cl. (S. Apr.10; 514) *Head.* £130

HILSCHER, P.C.
- **Beschreibung des so Genannten Todten Tantzes.** Dresden & Leipzig, 1705. *1st. Edn.* Sm. 8vo. Title partly bkd., ex-libris on verso, slightly browned, old bds. (H. May 22; 453) DM 520

HILTON, Harold H.
- **My Golfing Reminiscences.** L., 1907. Bdg. not stated. (PD. Jul.13; 49) £80

HILTON, Harold H. & Smith, Gordon G.
- **The Royal & Ancient Game of Golf.** L., 1912. *(900)* numbered. Red leath.; subscriber's copy of F. Ormesby Cooke. (PD. Jul.13; 77) £850
- - **Anr. Edn.** 1912. *De Luxe Edn.*, *(100)* numbered. 4to. Orig. vell. gt., silk doubls. (SKC. May 4; 1759) £620

HIMLY
- **Histoire de la Formation Territoriale des Etats de l'Europe Centrale.** Paris, 1894. *2nd. Edn.* Mor. (HD. Feb.22; 93) Frs. 1,300

HIND, Arthur M.
- **An Introduction to the History of Woodcut.** L., 1935. *1st. Edn.* 2 vols. 4to. Buckram, d.-w.'s. (SG. Oct.13; 193) $100

HIND, Arthur M. & others
- **Engraving in England in the Sixteenth & Seventeenth Centuries.** Camb., 1952-64. 3 vols. 4to. Orig. cl., slightly soiled. (BBA. Nov.10; 211) *Blackwell.* £200

HIND, Henry Youle
- **Explorations in the Interior of the Labrador Peninsula in the Country of the Montagnais & Nasquapee Indians.** L., 1863. *1st. Edn.* 2 vols. 2 maps, 12 cold. plts., orig. cl. [Sabin 31933] (S. May 22; 319) *Sawyer.* £480
- **Narrative of the Canadian Red River Exploring Expedition of 1857 & of the Assinnibone & Saskatchewan Exploring Expedition of 1858.** L., 1830. *1st. Edn.* 2 vols. Hf.-titles, 3 engraved maps (2 folding),

folding profile, 4 hand-cold. plans, 20 chromoxylograph plts., advts. at end of both vols., orig. cl. [Sabin 31934] (S. May 22; 320) *Crete.* £320
- - **Anr. Edn.** L., 1860. 2 vols. 1 folding plan, 7 maps, including 2 folding, 20 cold. plts. on yellow backgrounds (slightly oxidized), hf.-titles, cont. pol. cf., gt. spines, some scuffing; the Rt. Hon. Visc. Eccles copy. [Sabin 31934] (CNY. Nov.18; 140) $600

HINDERWELL, Thomas
- **The History & Antiquities of Scarborough & the Vicinity.** York, 1798. 4to. Margin pencil notes, cont. tree cf. gt. (TA. Nov.17; 158) £65

HINTON, J.W.
- **Organ Construction.** L., 1900. *1st. Edn.* 4to. Cl. (PNY. Dec.1; 68) $100

HINTON, John Howard
- **The History & Topography of the United States.** 1830-32. 2 vols. 4to. Port., 2 engraved titles, 98 maps & plts., hf. mor. gt., rubbed. (P. Jun.7; 208) £200
- - **Anr. Copy.** 2 vols. 4to. Port., 95 engraved maps & plts., diced cf. gt. (P. Mar.15; 7) *Martin.* £180
- - **Anr. Edn.** Ed.:- S.L. Knapp, J.O. Choules. Boston, 1852-53. *3rd. Edn.* 2 vols. 4to. Some plts. foxed, hf. mor., extremities slightly worn. [Sabin 31966] (SG. Jan.19; 185) $100

HINTON, Richard J.
- **The Hand-Book to Arizona.** San Franc., 1878. *1st. Edn.* Thick lge. 12mo. 4 maps (lge. folding map), 20 litho. plts., orig. gt. pict. cl., jnts. frayed, upr. hinge split. (SG. Apr.5; 10) $175

HIPKINS, Alfred James & Gibb, William
- **Musical Instrument: Historic, Rare & Unique.** Edinb., 1888. *1st. Edn.* *(1040)*. Fo. 50 chromolitho. plts., red hf. mor. & vell. gt., spine gt., worn & soiled. (SG. Nov.17; 297) $150

HIPKISS, E.J. (Ed.)
See— KAROLIK, M. & M.

HIPPEL, Th. G. von
[-] **Kreuz– und Querzüge des Ritters A bis Z.** Ill.:- J. Penzel. Berlin, 1793-94. *1st. Edn.* 2 vols. Erased sig. on title-lf., later hf. linen. (GB. Nov.4; 2094) DM 420

HIPPOCRATES
- **Les Aphorismes d'Hippocrates, Prince des Medecins** ... Commentaries:- Gabien & Jean Brèche. Trans.:- Jean Brèche. Paris, 1558. (*Bound with:*) DAMAS, Jan de - **Aphorismes** ... J. Brèche. Paris, 1557. Together 2 works in 1 vol. 16mo. Cold. printer's mark at end of each work, old vell. (HD. Mar.19; 59) Frs. 1,100
- **The Aphorismes ... with a Short Comment on each one, taken out of those larger Notes of Galen, Heurnius, Fuchsius, & c.** L., 1655. 24mo. Lacks A1 (blank?), disbnd. [Wing H 2071] (SG. Oct.6; 196) $150
- **Oeuvres.** Paris, 1839-61. 10 vols. Some spotting, later hf. mor., spines gt., a few lightly rubbed. (CSK. Mar.9; 200) £350
- **Oeuvres Complètes.** Intro.:- George Duhamel. Ill.:- Jean Chièze. Paris, 1955. 5 vols. 4to. On vell., blind-decor. roan. (HD. Jul.2; 73) Frs. 1,300
- **Upon Air, Water, & Situation; upon Epidemical Diseases; & upon Prognostics.** Trans.:- Francis Clifton. Ill.:- G. Vander Gucht after Rubens (port.). L., 1734. *1st. Edn.* of this trans. Cont. Camb. cf., upr. cover detchd. (RO. Dec.11; 144) $100

HIPPOLYTUS DE MARSILIIS
- **Tractat. de Questionib: in quo Materie Maleficioru y Tractant.** [Lyon, 1532-31]. 4 pts. in 1 vol. Dampstained, old vell., worn. (CSK. Nov.4; 173) £55

HIRSCH, August & others
- **Biographisches Lexikon der Hervorragenden Aertze Aller Zeiten und Voelker.** Vienna & Leipzig, 1884-88. *1st. Edn.* 6 vols. Lge. 8vo. Lacks 1st. prefatory lf., 1st. title-p. reprd., mod. buckram, ex-liby. (SG. Oct.6; 197) $550

-- Anr. Edn. München & Berlin, 1962. 6 vols. 4to. Orig. linen. (HK. Nov.11; 4429)   DM 1,300

HIRSCH, J. Chr.
- Der Fränkische Bienen-Meister. Ansbach, 1767. *1st. Edn.* Title soiled, some slight foxing. (*Bound with:*) – Abhandlungen und Erfahrungen der Fränkisch-Physicalisch-ökonomischen Bienengesellschaft auf das Jahr 1770. Nuremb., 1770. Together in 1 vol., cont. bds. (GB. May 3; 1108)
                                                      DM 420

HIRSCHAUER, L. & Dollfus, Ch.
- L'Annee Aeronautique. 1920-39. Vols. 1-20 (all publd.). Sm. fo. Advts., orig. ptd. wraps. or cont. hf./full mor. gt., some vols. slightly rubbed or worn. (TA. Dec.15; 486)   £90

HIRSCHFELD, Al
- Harlem as Seen by Hirschfeld. Text:–William Saroyan. N.Y., [1941]. *(1000) numbered.* Fo. Pict. cl., heavily soiled, spine partially torn. (SG. Jun.7; 364) $350

HIRSCHFELD, C.C.L.
- Das Landleben. Ill.:– C.L. Crusius. Leipzig, 1776. *3rd. Ill. Edn.* Brown spotting, cont. leath. slightly rubbed; Hauswedell coll. (H. May 24; 1383)
                                                      DM 400
- Theorie der Gartenkunst. Leipzig, 1779-85. 5 vols. 4to. Some browning & foxing, a few ll. with sm. stain, 2 pp. with marginalia, cont. hf. leath., slightly rubbed. (GB. May 3; 1085)   DM 3,700

HIRSHBERG, Leonard Keen
See— MENCKEN, Henry Louis & Hirshberg, Leonard Keen

HIRT, F.
- Geographische Bildertafeln. Ed.:– A. Oppel & Ludwig. Pts. 2 & 3 in 4 vols. 4to. Orig. linen. (D. Nov.23; 804)   DM 850

HISTOIRE ABREGEE DES PROV.-UNIES DES PAIS-BAS, leurs Progrès, Conquêtes, Gouvernement, Compagnies en Orient & en Occident ...
Amst., 1701. Fo. Maps & folding plts. slightly browned, cont. cf., back gt. (VG. Sep.14; 1165)
                                                      Fls. 500

HISTOIRE DE LA TRIOMPHANTE ENTREE du Roy et de la Reyne dans Paris le 26 Août 1660.
Ill.:– Pautre, Marot & others. Paris, 1665. Fo. Mod. chagrin gt., spine decor., w.a.f. (HD. May 3; 40)
                                                      Frs. 1,900

HISTOIRE DES INQUISITIONS où l'on rapporte l'Origine et le Progrès de ces Tribunaux, leurs Variations et la Forme de leur Jurisdiction
Cologne [Paris], 1759. *1st. Edn.* 2 vols. 12mo. Cont. marb. cf., spine decor. (HD. Mar.21; 40)
                                                      Frs. 1,000

HISTOIRE LITTERAIRE DE LA FRANCE, Ouvrage Commencé par des Religieux Bénédictins de la Congrégation de Saint-Maur et Continué par des Membres de l'Institut
1733-1962. 39 vols. 4to. Cf. & marb. sheep, decor. spines, arms at foot. (HD. Sep.22; 258) Frs. 8,300

HISTOIRE DU LIVRE et de l'Imprimerie en Belgique. Des Origines à nos Jours
Bruxelles, 1923-24. 5 pts. in 1 vol., & Index vol. 4to. Cl., orig. upr. wraps. bnd. in, some wear, Index in orig. wraps. (RO. Dec.11; 145) $100

HISTOIRE NATURELLE Eclaircie dans Deux de ses Parties Principales: La Lithologie et la Conchyliologie ...
Paris, 1742. 2 pts. in 1 vol. 4to. Copper-engraved frontis., 32 copper-engraved plts., title-p. & frontis. soiled, some other minor soiling, some spotting & darkening, cont. cf., gt.-tooled spine, marb. endpapers, covers rubbed & worn. (CBA. Jan.29; 132a)
                                                      $130

HISTOIRE NATURELLE ET POLITIQUE DE LA PENSYLVANIE ET DE L'ETABLISSEMENT DES QUAKERS ...
Paris, 1768. Leath. (DS. Mar.23; 2149)
                                                      Pts. 100,000

HISTOIRE UNIVERSELLE depuis le Commencement du Monde
Paris, 1779-91. 125 vols. No bdg. stated. (HD. Oct.14; 80)   Frs. 3,100

HISTORIA SECRETA DE LA CORTE Y GABINETE DE ST. CLOUD
Cadiz, 1808. 4to. Cf. (DS. Mar.23; 2134)
                                                      Pts. 40,000

HISTORICAL COLLECTION OF THE MOST MEMORABLE ACCIDENTS & TRAGICALL MASSACRES OF FRANCE
L., 1598. *1st. Edn.* 2 pts. in 1 vol. 4to. Lacks Ai (blank?), title strengthened, a few outer margins reprd., cont. cf., rebkd. (P. Nov.24; 222)
                                                      Peck. £75

HISTORICAL RECORDS OF AUSTRALIA
1914. Series 1 (vols. 1-26) Governors Despatches to & from England. No bdg. stated. (JL. Jun.24; 124)   Aus. $550

HISTORISCH-BIOGRAPHISCHES LEXIKON DER SCHWEIZ
Neuenburg, 1921-34. 7 vols. & 1 supp. vol. 4to. Linen, gold-tooled, Vol. 3 spine loose. (GF. Nov.16; 1185)   Sw. Frs. 800

HISTORISCHE GENEALOGISCHER CALENDER, oder Jahrbuch der Merkwuerdigsten Neuen Welt-Begebenheiten fuer 1784
Ill.:– Chodowiecki & others. Leipzig, [1783]. 32mo. Engraved title, 13 plts. (1 double-p.), folding (single-p.) map, 3 hand-cold. plts. (1 with matching pennon), orig. vell. bds., soiled, partly loose. (SG. Apr.26; 94) $950

HISTORISCHER WARHAFFTIGER BERICHT unnd Lehre Göttliches Worts, v.d. Gantzen Streit u. Handel d. Hl. Abendmals
Ed.:– Chr. Pezelius. Amberg, 1592. Sm. 8vo. Some stains, cont. limp vell. (VG. Nov.30; 911) Fls. 500

HISTORY & Adventures of Little Henry
L., 1810. 7 hand-cold. figures, 1 head & 3 hats, orig. wraps., s.-c. (P. May 17; 396)
                                                      Bickersteth. £100

HISTORY OF INK including its Etymology, Chemistry & Bibliography
N.Y., n.d. Orig. cl. gt. (LC. Mar.1; 9)   £70

HISTORY OF JACK & his Seven Brothers
L., n.d. Orig. wraps., worn. (P. Jul.5; 362)   £140

HISTORY OF LITTLE FANNY, The
L., 1810. *1st. Edn.* 16mo. 7 loose hand-cold. figures, with 1 moveable head & 3 (of 4) hats, 1 hat slightly defect., ptd. wraps., badly worn ptd. s.-c. (2nd. edn.). (SG. Dec.8; 257) $110
-- Anr. Edn. L., 1810. *6th. Edn.* 7 figures, 1 head & 4 hats, loose as iss., orig. wraps. (P. May 17; 395)
                                                      Cavendish. £55

HISTORY OF NEW HOLLAND ... & a Description of Botany Bay
1787. *1st. Edn.* 2 folding engraved maps (handcold. in outl.), advt. lf. at end, orig. bds., unc., backstrip renewed, s.-c. (S. May 22; 476)
                                                      Maggs. £750
-- Anr. Copy. Maps discold. & tears reprd. at folds, mod. hf. cf. (S. Nov.1; 27)   *Maggs.* £340

HISTORY OF THE SEVEN WISE MASTERS OF ROME, The
L., 1697. Sm. 8vo. Paperfault causing margin defect to title, a few catchwords shaved, cont. sheep. [Wing H 2187] (C. Nov.9; 14)   *Hirsch.* £210

HISTORY OF TECHNOLOGY
Ed.:– Singer, Holmyard & Hall. N.Y. & L., 1954-58. *1st. Edn.* 5 vols. 4to. Unif. cl., some spines lightly faded, ptd. d.-w.'s (some with sm. tears). (HA. Nov.18; 371) $120

HISTORY OF VAN DIEMENS LAND
1832-33. Hand-cold. plts., list of contents provided in MS., later hf. cf. (CSK. Nov.25; 41)   £80

HITCHCOCK, Enos
- Memoirs of the Bloomsgrove Family. Boston, 1790. *1st. Edn.* 2 vols. 12mo. Some browning, cont.

marb. sheep, spines worn; pres. copy, inscr. to Mrs. Windsor. (CSK. Oct.21; 2)   £90

HITLER, Adolf
- Mein Kampf. München, 1925-27. *1st. Edn.* Orig. linen. (R. Oct.11; 1192)   DM 3,100

HITTELL, Theodore H.
- El Triumfo de la Cruz. Ill.:– V. Angelo. San Franc., Grabhorn Pr., 1930. *(50) sigd. by artist.* A few pp. mott., bds., yawning; the V. Angelo copy. (CBA. Oct.1; 160) $100

HITTORFF, J.J. (Contrib.)
See— GRUNER, Lewis

HOAK, Edward W. & Church, Willis H.
- Masterpieces of Architecture in the United States. Intro.:– Paul P. Cret. N.Y., 1930. Tall fo. Plts., exliby., buckram. (SG. May 3; 210) $130

HOARE, Sir Richard Colt
- Collection of Forty-Eight Views of Nobleman's & Gentlemen's Seats ... in North & South Wales. L., ca. 1800. Ob. 4to. 48 engraved plts., some spotting, cont. red mor. gt. (S. Mar.6; 257) *Old Hall.* £150
-- Anr. Edn. N.d Ob. 4to. 48 engraved plts. (dtd. 1792-1806), 1 detchd., some lightly stained, cont. mor. (CSK. Dec.16; 227)   £55
- A Tour through the Island of Elba. 1814. 4to. L.P., bds., defect. (P. Sep.29; 295)   *Erlini.* £95
See— BENSON, Robert & Hatcher, Henry

HOBBES, Thomas
- Behemoth; or, an Epitome of the Civil Wars of England. L., 1679. *1st. Edn.* 12mo. Margins trimmed close, lightly damp-wrinkled, early spr. cf., worn. (SG. Apr.19; 104) $190
- Historia Ecclesiastica Carmine Elegiaco Concinnata. Augustae Trinobantum [= L.], 1688. *1st. Edn.* Stain. [Wing H2237]. (*Bound with:*) GIRALDI CINTHIO, Giovanni Battista – Poemata. Basle, 1540. Early notes, title defect. at foot, stained. Together 2 works in 1 vol., cont. mott. cf., little rubbed. (BBA. Jun.28; 52)
                                                      Pickering & Chatto. £140
- Hobb's Tripos, in Three Discourses. L., 1684. *3rd. Edn.* Title-p. rubricated, later mor. [Wing H2266] (BBA. May 3; 163)   *Hannas.* £130
- Leviathan. L., 1651. *1st. Edn. 1st. Iss.*, with the 'head' ornament on title. Fo. Titles & final 3 ll. reprd. at blank outer margin, sm. hole in K3 affecting 2 words, cont. cf., rebkd. [Wing H 2246] (C. Nov.9; 83)   *Harry.* £900
-- Anr. Edn. 1651. *1st. Edn. 3rd. Iss.* Sm. fo. Cont. cf.; early bkplt. of I. Hungerford, owners stp. of A.L. Smith, E.C. Hodgkin copy. (C. May 30; 127)   *Weinkle.* £120
-- Anr. Edn. L., 1651. *1st. Edn.* Fo. Winged head ornament on ptd. title, folding ptd. table, cont. MS. marginalia, engraved title (from anr. copy?), tear in F1, light marginal stain, few ll. soiled, cont. cf., rebkd., sm. wormholes. [Wing H2246] (SPB. May 16; 79) $1,300
-- Anr. Edn. L., 1651 [but Amst., ca.1651]. *2nd. Edn.* Fo. 'Bear' ornament on title, some foxing & minor soiling, later cf., rubbed. (RO. Apr.23; 168) $450
-- Anr. Edn. [Amst.], 1651 [but ca. 1680]. Fo. Spotted, browned, cont. cf., worn, rebkd., upr. hinge brkn. (S. Mar.20; 922)   *Malcolm.* £80
-- Anr. Edn. Amst., 1670. *1st. Edn. in Latin.* Sm. 4to. Last erratum lf., armorial bkplt. pasted on verso of title-p., cont. panel. cf. (SKC. Sep.9; 1917)   £150
-- Anr. Copy. Cont. cf., rebkd., shabby. (SG. Apr.19; 103) $375
- Philosophicall Rudiments concerning Government & Society. 1651. *1st. Edn. in Engl.* 12mo. Engraved title-p. reinforced in lr. margin on 1st. engraved plt., slight browning & spotting thro-out, panel cf., worn. (BS. May 2; 31)   £150
- The Moral & Poetical Works of ... 1750. 4to. Cont. cf., rebkd. (PD. Aug.17; 228)   £100

HOBERG, R.
- Die Graph. Techniken u. Ihre Druckverfahren. Ill.:– Corinth, Geiger, Grossmann, Kubin, Pechstein & others. Berlin, 1923. *De Luxe Edn., (1000).* 4to. 15 sigd. orig. ills., orig. vell. (HK. Nov.11; 3621) DM 1,150

HOBHOUSE, John Cam
- A Journey through Albania & other Provinces of Turkey in Europe & Asia to Constantinople during the years 1809 & 1810. 1813. *1st. Edn.* 4to. Cont. cf. gt., w.a.f.; from liby. of Luttrellstown Castle. (C. Sep.28; 1740) £540

HOBSON, A.R.A.
- French & Italian Collectors & their Bindings illustrated from Examples in the Library of J.R. Abbey. Oxford, Roxb. Cl., 1953. 4to. Orig. mor.-bkd. cl., H.M. Nixon coll., with some MS. annots. & corrections. (BBA. Oct.6; 115) *Maggs.* £1,600

HOBSON, Geoffrey D.
- Bindings in Cambridge Libraries. Camb., 1929. *(250).* Fo. Orig. cl. gt., worn; H.M. Nixon coll., with his acquisition note, many MS. annots. & additions thro-out, a few cuttings loosely inserted. (BBA. Oct.6; 64) *Beres.* £700
- English Binding before 1500. 1929. *(500).* Fo. Some ll. detchd., orig. cl., rubbed. (TA. May 17; 440) £70
- English Bindings 1490-1940 in the Library of J.R. Abbey. Chiswick Pr., 1940. *(180) numbered & sigd. by Hobson & Abbey.* 4to. Orig. buckram, a little rubbed; H.M. Nixon coll., with his sig., note & many MS. annots. (BBA. Oct.6; 66) *Maggs.* £1,900
-- **Anr. Copy.** Fo. Orig. buckram, slightly faded; pres. copy inscr. by Abbey. (S. May 1; 403) *Quaritch.* £780
- Maioli, Canevari & others. L., 1926. *[1st. Edn.].* 4to. Orig. cl., top of spine defect.; H.M. Nixon coll., with his sig., acquisition note & many MS. annots. (BBA. Oct.6; 62) *Beres.* £650
-- **Anr. Copy.** 4to. 64 plts. (6 cold.), orig. cl. (BBA. Mar.7; 311) *Zeitlin & Verbrugge.* £300
-- **Anr. Copy.** 4to. Orig. cl., d-w. (BBA. Nov.10; 15) *Blackwell.* £110
-- **Anr. Copy.** 4to. On Antique de Luxe wtrmkd. laid paper, owner's name at 1 p. margin, light foxing, gt.-lettered cl., sm. tears at spine tips with sm. chips at intersections with upr. jnt., covers slightly worn. (HA. Nov.18; 410) $150
-- **Anr. Copy.** 4to. Orig. linen. (HK. Nov.11; 4432) DM 650
- Les Reliures à la Fanfare. Le Problème de l'S fermmé. Chiswick Pr., 1935. *(215) numbered & sigd.* Fo. Photostat copy of A.R.A. Hobson's 'Additions et Corrections', Amst., 1970, loosely inserted; H.M. Nixon coll., with his acquisition note & some MS. notes. (BBA. Oct.6; 65) *Beres.* £350
- Thirty Bindings. 1926. *(600).* 4to. Orig. buckram gt., spine a little faded; H.M. Nixon coll., with his sig. & many MS. notes. (BBA. Oct.6; 63) *Temperley.* £140

HOBSON, Robert Lockhart
- A Catalogue of Chinese Pottery & Porcelain in the Collection of Sir Percival David. 1934. *(680) numbered.* Fo. Orig. cl. by Morrell, lightly rubbed, publisher's box. (CSK. Jun.29; 1) £480
-- **Anr. Copy.** Fo. Orig. silk by Morrell, spine slightly rubbed, cl. box, dampstained. (S. Oct.4; 163) *Libris Ant.* £360
-- **Anr. Copy.** Sm. fo. 180 plts., many cold., ex-liby., cl., folding s.-c. (SG. May 3; 81) $750
-- **Anr. Copy.** Fo. Orig. silk, orig. box, slightly soiled. (VS. Jun.6; 21) Fls. 1,200
- Catalogue of the Collection of English Pottery in the ... British Museum. L., 1903. *1st. Edn.* 4to. 42 plts., some foxing, cl., spine ends rubbed. (SG. Jan.26; 102) $110
- Catalogue of the Leonard Gow Collection of Chinese Porcelain. 1931. *(300) numbered & sigd. by Gow.* 4to. Orig. cl., slightly soiled. (BBA. Sep.8; 214) *Han Shan Tang.* £230
-- **Anr. Copy.** 4to. This copy unnumbered, orig. mor. by Sangorski & Sutcliffe, cl. box. (CSK. Jun.1; 4) £160
- Chinese Pottery & Porcelain. N.Y. & L., 1915.

1st. Edn., (1500). 2 vols. Gt.-decor. cl. (PNY. Oct.20; 223) $225
-- **Anr. Copy.** 2 vols. Buckram gt.; Baron Leverhulme bkplt. (PNY. Dec.1; 85) $175
-- **Anr. Copy.** 2 vols. 136 plts., orig. gt.-decor. cl., covers lightly rubbed, bkplts. (CBA. Jan.29; 365) $160
-- **Anr. Edn.** L., 1915. *Ltd. Edn.* 2 vols. No bdg. stated. (SPB. Nov.30; 156) $250
- The George Eumorfopoulos Collection: Catalogue of the Chinese, Korean & Persian Pottery & Porcelain. L., Chiswick Pr., [1925]. *1st. Edn. (725).* 6 vols. Fo. Orig. hf. cl., Vols. 3-5 in s.-c.'s. (PNY. Dec.1; 86) $1,600
-- **Anr. Edn.** [1928]. *(725) numbered.* Vol. 6 only. Fo. Orig. cl., s.-c. (CSK. Jun.1; 6) £100
- The Later Ceramic Wares of China. 1925. 4to. Orig. buckram, spine slightly faded. (S. Nov.8; 534) *Perkins.* £100
-- **Anr. Edn.** L., 1925. *(250) numbered & sigd.* 4to. Orig. pig. (S. May 1; 591) *Tang.* £50
-- **Anr. Copy.** 4to. 81 plts. (31 cold.), ex-liby., gt.-decor. pig. (SG. May 3; 79) $325
-- **Anr. Copy.** 4to. Pig, worn. (PNY. Dec.1; 87) $150
- The Wares of the Ming Dynasty. L., 1923. *1st. Edn. (256) on H.M.P.,* sigd. 4to. Pig, worn. (PNY. Dec.1; 89) $250
-- **Anr. Edn.** L., 1923. *2nd. Imp.* 4to. Orig. cl., very slightly soiled. (S. Oct.4; 164) *Leicester.* £50
-- **Anr. Edn.** L., 1923. 4to. Orig. buckram, spine slightly faded. (S. Nov.8; 533) *Sweet.* £80
-- **Anr. Copy.** 4to. Text lightly spotted, orig. cl., spine slightly faded, slightly soiled. (S. May 1; 592) *Renard.* £50
- Worcester Porcelain, a Description of the Ware from the Wall Period to the Present Day. 1910. *[1st. Edn.].* Fo. Orig. cl. gt. (LC. Jul.5; 56) £100
-- **Anr. Copy.** Fo. Orig. cl., faded. (BBA. Sep.8; 215) *Renard.* £60
-- **Anr. Copy.** Fo. No bdg. stated. (SPB. Nov.30; 267) $150
-- **Anr. Copy.** Fo. Gt.-decor. cl., spine ends rubbed, faded, partly unc. (SG. Jan.26; 104) $130

HOBSON, Robert Lockhart & others
- Chinese Ceramics in Private Collections. 1931. *(625). Out-of-series copy.* 4to. Orig. buckram gt., slightly soiled. (SKC. Mar.9; 1718) £120
-- **Anr. Edn.** 1931. *(625).* 4to. Cl., slightly bumped. (SG. Jan.26; 71) $130

HOBURG, Chr.
- Christ-Fürstl. Jugend-Spiegel. Frankfurt, 1645. Cont. black mor., gt.-decor., monog. on upr. cover. (HK. Nov.9; 1765) DM 400

HOCKER, Jost
- Der Teufel selbs. Oberursel, 1568. *1st. Edn.* 3 pts. in 1 vol. Some old annots., lightly browned, cont. limp vell. (HK. Nov.8; 222) DM 2,000

HOCKIN, Rev. John Pearce
See– KEATE, George – HOCKIN, Rev. John Pearce

HOCKNEY, David
- Paper Pools. L., 1980. *(1000) numbered & sigd. by artist & with orig. sigd. litho. in folder.* 4to. Orig. cl., s.-c. (S Apr.30; 50) *Lennert.* £100

HODDESDON, John
[–] The History of the Life & Death of Sr. Thomas More. L., 1662. *1st. Edn.* Some margins cut close. [Wing H2292] *(Bound with:)* BROOKE, Lord Fulke Greville – The Life of the Renowned Sr. Philip Sidney. L., 1652. *1st. Edn.* Fore-e. of title & some other margins shaved. [Wing B4899] Together 2 works in 1 vol. 12mo. Cf., a little rubbed; 18th. C. Earl of Egmont bkplt. (BBA. May 3; 146) *Howes Bookshop.* £65

HODGES, Sir Benjamin
[–] An Impartial History of Michael Servetus. L., 1724. Without separate lf. at end (sometimes present), new cl.; Dr. Walter Pagel copy. (S. Feb.7; 342) *Quaritch.* £160

HODGES, Nathaniel
- Loimologia or an Historical Account of the Plague in London ... Ed.:– John Quincy. L., 1720. *1st. Edn. in Engl.* Text stained, cf.; Dr. Walter Pagel copy. (S. Feb.7; 190) *Heller.* £60

-- **Anr. Copy.** Cont. panel. cf., rebkd., cont. armorial bkplt. (SG. Mar.22; 158) $175

HODGES, William
- Travels in India. L., 1793. *1st. Edn.* 4to. Engraved folding map, 14 plts., some spotting, cont. spr. cf., rebkd. (S. Mar.6; 31) *Samiramis.* £140
-- **Anr. Copy.** 4to. Some foxing, cont. mor. gt. by H. Walther, with his label. (SPB. Dec.13; 451) $150

HODGKIN, John Eliot
- Rariora. L., 1900-02. 3 vols. 4to. Cl. (SG. Jan.5; 164) $140
-- **Anr. Edn.** L., [1900-02]. 3 vols. 4to. Orig. cl., slightly soiled. (BBA. Mar.7; 223) *Bowers.* £130

HODGKIN, John Eliot & Edith
- Examples of Early English Pottery Named, Dated, & Inscribed. 1881. *L.P. Edn. (50) numbered & sigd. by authors.* Fo. Orig. cl., a little worn. (LC. Mar.1; 10) £50

HODGKIN, Thomas
- Italy & Her Invaders. Oxford, 1892. *2nd. Edn.* 8 vols. in 9. Maps, ills., slight browning, cf. gt., by Zaehnsdorf. (SPB. May 17; 747) $350

HODGKINSON, Clement
- Australia, from Port MacQuarie to Moreton Bay. L., 1845. Book advts. bnd. in at front & back, map foxed, orig. blind-stpd. cl., unc. & partly unopened. (CA. Apr.3; 55) Aus. $1,300
-- **Anr. Copy.** Advt. ll. bnd. in, tree cf. by Rivière, partly unc., orig. cl. covers bnd. in at end. (KH. May 1; 352) Aus. $580
-- **Anr. Copy.** Lacks book advts., some staining in margins of some plts., stp. on title & p. 1, blind-stpd. cl., unc., covers torn & faded. (CA. Apr.3; 54) Aus. $300

HODGSON, Adam
- Letters from North America, Written During a Tour in the United States & Canada. L., 1824. *1st. Engl. Edn.* 2 vols. Hf.-titles & errata slip, offset from plt. on title-p. of Vol. 1, title-p. of Vol. 2 bkd. & with inscr. cut from upr. margin, cont. hf. cf.; the Rt. Hon. Visc. Eccles copy. [Sabin 32357] (CNY. Nov.18; 141) $150
- Remarks during a Journey through North America in 1819-21 ... with an Appendix, containing an Account of Several of the Indian Tribes ... also a Letter to J.B. Say on the Comparative Expense of Free & Slave Labour. Ed.:– Samuel Whiting. N.Y., 1823. *1st. Edn.* Small tear at head of title, penultimate lf. with tear, some foxing, disbnd. (SG. Apr.5; 89) $120

HODGSON, James
- The Doctrine of Fluxions Founded on Sir Isaac Newton's Method. L., priv. ptd., 1736. *1st. Edn.* Slight soiling, tear on 1 lf. affecting 2 letters, cont. cf., sm. chips from head of spine, rubbed; John Earl of Bute bkplt., Stanitz coll. (SPB. Apr.25; 225) $550

HODGSON, Ralph
- The Last Blackbird & Other Lines. L., 1907. *1st. Edn. 1st. Iss.* 12mo. Orig. cl., partly unc.; pres. copy, inscr. from author to Galloway [Fraser?], followed by 17 line poem, Frederic Dannay copy. (CNY. Dec.16; 170) $230

HOE, Robert
- A Catalogue of Books in English later than 1700. N.Y., priv. ptd., 1905. *(100).* 3 vols. Ptd. wraps., unc. (SG. Jan.5; 165) $225
- [Catalogue of the Library]. N.Y., priv. ptd., 1903-09. *De Luxe Edn., (100).* 12 vols. only. Tall 8vo. 2 titles on Japan vell., gt.-panel. hf. mor. by Stikeman, orig. wraps. bnd. in. (SG. Sep.15; 172) $550
-- **Anr. Edn.** N.Y., 1903-09. 16 vols. Orig. wraps., worn. (SG. Sep.15; 173) $425
-- **Anr. Edn.** N.Y., 1911-12. 4 pts. in 8 vols. Price lists for pts. 3 & 4 laid in, ptd. wraps., cl. folding-case. (SG. Jan.5; 166) $200
- A Lecture on Bookbinding as a Fine Art, delivered before the Grolier Club, February 26, 1885. Ill.:– E. Bierstadt. N.Y., Grol. Cl., 1886. *(200).* 4to. On Holland, cl. & bds., gt.-lettered, untrimmed, covers moderately worn with rubbing & some soiling; Francis Bullard bkplt. (HA. Feb.24; 152) $100

- One Hundred & Seventy-six Historic & Artistic Book-Bindings dating from the Fifteenth Century to the Present Time ... from the Library of Robert Hoe. N.Y., 1895. *(200) on Japan Imperial paper.* 2 vols. Fo. Cont. hf. mor., slightly rubbed; H.M. Nixon coll., with his sig. & MS notes. (BBA. Oct.6; 69) *Kokoro.* £650

HOEFER, E.
- Küstenfahrten an der Nord– und Ostsee. Stuttgart, [1881]. Fo. 66 plts. & approx. 200 woodcuts, some foxing, some ll. with margins stained, orig. linen, corners bumped. (GB. May 3; 173) DM 900
– – Anr. Edn. Ill.:– G. Schönleber. Stuttgart, ca. 1890. Fo. Orig. pict. linen. (R. Oct.12; 2615)
DM 1,400

HOEFER, Jean Chrétian Ferdinand
- Nouvelle Biographie Universelle. Paris, 1852-66. 46 vols. Cont. hf. chagrin, decor. spines. (HD. Jan.26; 175) Frs. 3,900

HOEFNAGEL, J.
- Diversae Insectarum Volatilium Icones ad Vivum Accuratissime Depictae. [Amst.], 1630. Slightly foxed & soiled, mostly in margins, 1 plt. brown spotted, cont. hf. leath., spine defect. (R. Apr.4; 1735) DM 3,800

HOEKSTRA, Cdr. Klaas
- Dagverhaal van het Verongelukken van het Galijootschip Harlingen, in Straat-Davids. Harlingen, 1828. Hf. cf., hinges worn. (P. Jun.7; 28) £150

HOEPLI, [U.]
- Collezione Artistica Hoepli: Il Bronzo e il Rame; Il Ferro Battuto; Il Legno e la Mobilia. Milan, 1926-29 & n.d. Together 3 vols. 4to. A few cold. plts., somewhat damp affected, orig. cl. (S. Apr.30; 189) *Erlini.* £65

HOERNERUS VON DINCKELSPUEHL, Johannes
- Problemata Summum Mathematicum & Cabalisticum. Nuremb., 1619. 2 pts. in 1 vol. 4to. 2 advt. ll., many MS. notes in cont. German hand, new hf. vell.; Dr. Walter Pagel copy. (S. Feb.7; 191) *Ritman.* £880

HOFFBAUER, Fédor
- Paris à Travers les Ages. Text:– Fournier, Lacroix, & others. Paris, 1875-82. 2 vols. Fo. 90 chromolitho. plts., three-qtr. mor., nicked. (SG. Jan.26; 205) $250
– – Anr. Edn. Paris, 1885. *2nd. Edn.* 2 vols. Fo. Litho. plts., some double-p., some cold., woodengraved text ills., maps, plans, some with diagrammatic tissue overlays, owner's stp., cont. hf. leath., lightly worn, 1st. vol. hinges reinforced. (SG. Apr.19; 306) $300

HOFFMAN, T.
- Jacob Abraham und Abraham Abrahamson 55 Jahre Berliner Medaillenkunst. Frankfurt, 1927. *(350).* 4to. Later purple mor. gt. (S. May 1; 472) *Spink.* £240

HOFFMANN, C.G.
- Scriptores Rerum Lusaticarum Antiqui & Recentiores. Inter quos Chr. Manlii Rerum Lusaticarum Commentarii deprehenduntur; in Corpus conjecti, et ex Bibliotheca Senatus Zitaviensis editi. Leipzig & Bautzen, 1719. 4 pts. in 1 vol. Fo. Some light browning or foxing, cont. vell. (R. Oct.13; 2641)
DM 1,200

HOFFMANN, Ernst Theodor Amadeus
- Ausgewählte Schriften. Ill.:– C.F. Thiele after Hoffmann & Callot. Berlin, 1827-28. *1st. Coll. Edn.* 10 vols. Browned, some staining, cont. linen, gt. spine, spotted, spine faded; Hauswedell coll. (H. May 24; 1388) DM 1,000
– – Anr. Edn. Berlin & Stuttgart, 1827-28, 1839. *1st. Coll. Edn.* 15 vols., 2 copper engrs. defect., (hole in centre), lacks separate title Vol. 11, foxed, cont. bds., rubbed & bumped, Vols. 1-10 spines defect., lacks orig. wraps (usually bnd. in). (R. Apr.3; 255) DM 420
- Contes Fantastiques. Trans.:– Loeve-Veimar. Ill.:– André Lambert. Paris, 1924. *(421) numbered on velin d'Arches.* 4to. Pict. engraved title, 21

etched cold. plts., three-qtr. cf., spine gt., orig. wraps. bnd. in. (SG. Feb.16; 158) $150
- Dichtungen und Schriften. Ed.:– W. Harich. Weimar, 1924. 15 vols. Hand-bnd. hf. leath., by W. Hacker, Leipzig, spine slightly faded. (H. Nov.23; 1100) DM 950
[–] Die Elixiere des Teufels. Berlin, 1815-16. *1st. Edn.* 2 vols. Wide margin, minimal foxing, cont. hf. leath. gt., bumped. (HK. Nov.10; 2515)
DM 2,100
- Erzählungen aus seinen Letzten Lebensjahren, seine Leben u. Nachlass. Ed.:– Micheline Hoffmann. Stuttgart, 1839. *1st. Edn.* 5 vols. in 3. Lacka 1 hf.-title, cont. hf. linen. (BR. Apr.12; 1450)
DM 460
- Fantasiestücke in Callot's Manier. Blätter aus dem Tagebuche eines reisenden Enthusiasten. Preface:– Jean Paul Richter. Bamberg, 1814-15. *1st. Edn.* 4 vols. in 2. Lge. copy, hf. mor., unc. (S. May 10; 306) *Braecklin.* £600
– – Anr. Copy. 4 vols. Foxed thro.-out & lightly browned, cont. hf. leath., slightly rubbed, jnts. partly split, old owners mark on end-lf. & MS. contents list. (H. May 22; 742) DM 1,200
- Das Fräulein von Scuderi. Ill.:– K.M. Schultheiss. Dresden-Hellerau, 1923. *(200) numbered De Luxe Edn.* Orig. leath. gt., s.-c. (D. Nov.24; 3189)
DM 400
- Gesammelte Schriften. Ill.:– Theodor Hosemann & Jaene, after Callot. Berlin, 1844-45. 12 vols. Sm. 8vo. Cont. hf. roan gt., some spines scuffed, orig. ptd. wraps. bnd. in each vol. (C. Dec.9; 245) *Kaldewey.* £440
– – Anr. Copy. Some light browning, plts. slightly darkened as usual, cont. hf. leath., romantic gt. spine, slightly rubbed & faded; Hauswedell coll. (H. May 24; 1389) DM 3,200
- Der Guldne Topf. Ill.:– K. Thylmann. Leipzig, 1913. *(25) De Luxe Edn. on Japan.* Sm. 4to. All lithos. sigd. by artist, hand-bnd. reddish-brown orig. mor., gold-tooled, by A. Köllner, Leipzig, light scratching. (H. Nov.24; 2140) DM 520
- Das Majorat. Ill.:– H. Steiner-Prag. Berlin, n.d. *De Luxe Edn., (100) numbered.* 12 sigd. etchings,, remarks on all plts., orig. leath., spine slightly worn. (HK. Nov.11; 3992) DM 600
- Meister Floh. Ill.:– Otto Nückel. München, [1922]. *(100) numbered De Luxe Edn. on Bütten.* 40 orig. woodcuts, orig. hf. mor. gt. (GB. May 5; 3036) DM 500
– – Anr. Copy. Hf. leath. (HK. May 17; 3033)
DM 440
- Musikalische Novellen. Berlin, 1923. *(100) numbered on Bütten.* All etchings sigd, slightly foxed, orig. leath., slightly rubbed. (HK. May 17; 3038)
DM 420
[–] Nachtstücke. Berlin, 1817. *1st. Edn.* 2 vols. Text slightly foxed thro.-out, cont. hf. russ. *(With:)* **- Meister Floh.** Frankfurt, 1822. *1st. Edn.* 1 vol. Foxed thro.-out, orig. decor. paper bds., spine defect. & reprd., covers rubbed. (C. Dec.9; 242) *Kaldewey.* £350
– – Anr. Copy. 2 vols. Some slight spotting, later red mor., elab. gt. spines & covers; Prinz Wilhelm von Braunschweig stp. on title-lf.; Hauswedell coll. (H. May 24; 1390) DM 13,000
- Prinzessin Brambilla. Ill.:– Callot. Breslau, 1821. *1st. Edn.* Sm. 8vo. Errata lf. & 4 pp. advts. at end, cont. hf. cf. (C. Dec.9; 243) *Quaritch.* £550
– – Anr. Copy. Lightly foxed thro.-out, last p. with sm. excision in lr. margin, orig. bds., 2 spots, slightly bumped, unc.; Hauswedell coll. (H. May 24; 1392)
DM 1,900
- Ritter Gluck. Ill.:– Rud. Grossmann. Tölz, Bremer Pr., 1920. *(200). (135) numbered on Zanders-Bütten.* Orig. hf. vell. (GB. May 5; 2245)
DM 480
- Die Serapions-Brüder, gesammelte Erzöhlungen und Mährchen. Berlin, 1819-21. *1st. Edn.* 4 vols. Sm. 8vo. Some light foxing, cont. hf. cf. (C. Dec.9; 307) *Quaritch.* £420
- Signor Formica. Ill.:– R. Hadl. [Leipzig], 1920. *(120) on Bütten.* Fo. Supp. orig. pencil ill., handbnd. orig. mor., gold decor. spine, covers & inner dentelle, gold-tooled cover vig, by A. Köllner, Leipzig; printer's mark sigd. by artist. (H. Nov.23; 1103) DM 620

HOFFMANN, Fr.
- Gründl. Anweisung, wie ein Mensch vor d. Frühzeitigen Tod u. allerh. Arten Kranckheiten ... sich verwahren könne. Halle, Frankfurt & Leipzig, 1715-17. 2 pts. in 1 vol. 1st. title stpd. on verso & end-lf. with old owners note. 1st. sig. cut in lr. margin, cont. leath. gt. (HK. Nov.8; 595) DM 500

HOFFMANN, H.
- Les Monnaies Royales de France depuis Hughues Capet jusqu à Louis XVI. Ill.:– Dardel. Paris, 1878. Lge. 4to. Cont. hf. red mor., corners. (HD. Dec.9; 141) Frs. 2,500

HOFFMANN, Heinrich
- Der Struwwelpeter ... fuer Kinder von 3 bis 6 Jahren. Leipzig, ca. 1900. 12mo. Accordion-folded in orig. col.-pict. bds. (SG. Dec.8; 197) $100

HOFFMANN, J.G.
- Die Hauszimmerkunst. Königsberg, 1802. *1st. Edn.* Title stpd., cont. bds., worn & scratched. (R. Oct.12; 1751) DM 460

HOFFMANN, Karl
- Lehrbuch der Praktischen Pflanzenkunde. Stuttgart, 1880's? Plt. vol. only. Ob. fo. 60 col. litho. plts., no title, plt.-list or text, liby. stp. on few plts., bds., w.a.f. (SG. Oct.6; 199) $250

HOFFMANN, Leonh. Wilib.
- Alter und Neuer Münz-Schlüssel. Nuremb., 1683. Leath. (G. Sep.15; 2165) Sw.Frs. 1,000
- Gründlicher und Ausführlicher Bericht ... mancherley Arten der Güld- und Silbernen Müntz-Sorten geschlagen worden ... [Nuremb.], 1680. *1st. Edn.* 4to. Browned, cont. style blind-tooled cf. (R. Apr.3; 1062) DM 800

HOFFMANN VON FALLERSLEBEN, A.H.
- Mein Leben. Hannover, 1868. *1st. Edn.* 6 vols. Cont. bds. (BR. Apr.12; 1452) DM 650

HOFFY, Alfred
- North American Pomologist. Ed.:– William D. Brinckle. Phila., 1860. *1st. Edn.* Vol. I (all publd.). 4to. 36 litho. plts., several with orig. tissue-guard, 4 plts. loose (3 crudely reprd.), some plts. brittle at fore-edges, port. & text ll. soiled at edges, liby stp. on title, binder's buckram. (SG. Mar.22; 159)
$475

HOFMANN, E.
- Die Gross-Schmetterlinge Europas. Stuttgart, 1887. *1st. Book. Edn.* 4to. Orig. linen. (HK. May 15; 520) DM 500

HOFMANN, Friedrich H.
- Frankenthaler Porzellan. Munich, 1911. *(400) numbered.* 2 vols. Lge. 4to. 208 plts., mntd. on art paper, parch.-bkd. bds., 1 spine defect., rubbed. (SG. Jan.26; 108) $750
- Geschichte der Bayerischen Porzellan-Manufaktur Nymphenburg. Leipzig, 1923. 3 vols. Fo. Orig. hf. vell. (HT. May 9; 1173) DM 1,600

HOFMANN, Johann Baptiste & Weigel, Joh. Chr.
- Lucidissimum Artis Scriptoriae Speculum. Nürnberg, after 1700. Minimal spotting, 18th. C. leath., rubbed, sm. wormholes; Hauswedell coll. (H. May 23; 251) DM 1,050

HOFMANN, U.
- Gründlicher Vorbericht eines vollstänoligen Werckes der Zierlichsten Schreib-Kunst. Nürnberg, 1659. Ob. 4to. Slightly spotted, mod. bds., Hauswedell coll. (H. May 23; 242) DM 820

HOFMANNSTHAL, Hugo von
- Ariadne auf Naxos. Ill.:– Willi Nowack. München, 1922. Fo. On Bütten, orig. bds., unc. (GB. May 5; 2709) DM 400
- Jedermann. Ill.:– E. Lang. Wien & Leipzig, [1922]. *(25) De Luxe Edn. with 2nd suite of sigd. etchings in orig. bd. portfo.* Lge. fo. Printers mark sigd. by author & artist, orig. hand-bnd. pig, light spotting & wear. (H. May 23; 1288) DM 700
- Der Kaiser und die Hexe. Ill.:– H. Vogeler-Worpswede. Berlin, 1900. *1st. Edn. (200) numbered on Bütten.* Orig. vell., gt. inner dentelle. (R. Oct.11; 266) DM 13,500
– – Anr. Copy. With cold. double title, decor. cold. endpapers & initials, hand-bnd. orig. vell., gt. decor.

HOFMANNSTHAL, Hugo von -*Contd.*

inner dentelle, spine slightly faded; MS. dedication from artist on 2nd. end-paper, engraved ex-libris on verso of pict. end-paper. (H. Nov.24; 1624)
DM 10,500

– **Lucidor.** Ill.:– K. Walser. Berlin, Prospero Pr., [1919]. *1st. Edn. (18) De Luxe Edn. on Bütten.* 4to. All etchings sigd. by artist, hand-bnd. orig. cf., by H. Fikentscher, Leipzig, spine slightly discold. (H. May 23; 1553)
DM 1,100

– – **Anr. Edn.** Ill.:– Karl Walser. Berlin, Prospero Pr., [1919]. *1st. Edn. (52) De Luxe Edn.* 4to. 6 sigd. etchings, with extra suite of sigd. etchings in 1st. state, orig. silk, silk doubls., bumped, spine silk brkn.; author's name on end-paper dtd. 1923. (H. Nov.24; 2184)
DM 1,400

– – **Anr. Edn.** Ill.:– F. Hoffmann. [Frankfurt, 1959]. *(500).* Sm. 4to. Printers mark sigd. by artist, orig. hf. vell. (H. Nov.24; 1625)
DM 460

– **Prinz Eugen.** Ill.:– F. Wacik. Wien, [1915]. *(50) numbered De Luxe Edn., sigd by author & artist.* Ob. 4to. Orig. vell.(H. Nov.24; 1627)   DM 740

– **Anr. Copy.** Ob. 4to. Orig. vell. (V. Oct.1; 4228)
DM 500

– **Rodauner Nachträge.** [Wien], 1918. *1st. Edn. (170) numbered on Hadern paper.* 3 vols. 4to. Orig. hf. vell. (HK. Nov.11; 3633)   DM 700

– **Der Thor und der Tod.** Ill.:– H. Vogeler. Berlin, 1900. *1st. Book Edn. (500) on Bütten.* Orig. pict. bds., margins lightly browned, engraved ex-libris inside cover. (H. May 23; 1290a)   DM 400

– **Der Turm.** München, Bremer Pr., 1925. *1st. Edn. (260) numbered.* Printers mark sigd. by author, orig. vell. (HK. Nov.11; 3634)   DM 650

– **Die Wege und die Begegnungen.** Bremer Pr., [Mar. 1913]. *1st. Edn. (10).* Orig. vell. (H. Nov.23; 919)
DM 5,000

– – **Anr. Edn.** [Bremer Pr., 1913]. *1st. Edn. (200) on Van Gelder-Bütten.* Orig. red hand-bnd. mor., blind-tooled, gt. inner & outer dentelle; MS. dtd. dedication on end-paper, engraved ex-libris inside cover. (H. Nov.23; 923)   DM 4,400

– – **Anr. Copy.** Orig. hand-bnd. red mor., gt. inner & outer dentelle, end-paper with slight margin browning, torn in inner fold. (H. May 22; 984)
DM 2,600

– – **Anr. Copy.** Minimal browning, ex-libris, orig. red mor., gt. inner & outer dentelle, blind-tooled. (HK. Nov.11; 3444)   DM 1,900

– **Der Weisse Fächer.** Ill.:– E. Gordon Craig. Leipzig, 1907. *(850). (800).* Fo. Foxing, vell.-bkd. bds. (PNY. Oct.20; 205) $100

– – **Anr. Copy.** Fo. Ptd. in yellow & black, some plts. with sm. spots, orig. hf. vell., s.-c. (HK. Nov.11; 3636)
DM 500

HOFMANNSTHAL, Hugo von (Texts)
See— GANYMED
See— NEUE RUNDSCHAU

HOFMILLER, J. (Ed.)
See— BALLADS & SONGS OF LOVE
See— CHANSONS D'AMOUR

HOFSTEDE DE GROOT, Dr. Cornelis
– **Beschreibendes u. krit. Verzeichnis d. Werke d. Holländ, Maler d. XVII Jhs.** Esslingen, 1907-23. *Orig. Edn.* Vols. 1-8 only (of 10). 39 plts., Vol. 8 stained in first third, hf. linen gt., upr. cover Vol. 8 defect. (V. Sep.30; 1681)   DM 850

– – **Anr. Edn.** Paris, 1907-28. 10 vols. Plts., some browning, cont. pig, gt., soiled, lacks 1 spine label. (CSK. Mar.23; 91)   £350
See— BODE, Dr. Wilhelm & Hofsted de Groot, Cornelis

HOGARTH, William
– **L'Analisi della Bellezza.** Ill.:– F. Violanti after Hogarth. Livorno, 1761. *1st. Italian Edn.* 2 engraved vigs., 2 lge. folding engraved plts., few ll. lightly stained, cont. vell., spine slightly wormed. (SG. Apr.19; 105) $130

– **The Analysis of Beauty.** 1753. 4to. Folding plts. slightly torn & reprd., cont. cf. (P. Jun.7; 92) £70

– **Colección de Ochenta y Ocho Grabados.** 18th. C. Lge. ob. fo. Cf. (DS. Oct.28; 2151)   Pts. 40,000

– **The Genuine Graphic Works.** Ill.:– T. Cook. L., 1812. Fo. 2 frontis., 157 engrs., linen. (DS. Feb.24; 2264)
Pts. 65,000

– – **Anr. Edn.** L., 1813. Fo. 158 engrs., including 1

folding & defect., leath., covers detchd. (DS. Feb.24; 2344)   Pts. 50,000

– **Graphic Illustrations of ... in the Possession of Samuel Ireland.** N.p., n.d. 2 vols. 4to. 104 engrs., some folding, leath. (DS. Jan.27; 2489)
Pts. 26,000

– **Hogarth Moralized** ... 1768. Sm. 4to. Engraved additional title, frontis., 75 ills., cont. red mor. gt., spine lightly rubbed. (CSK. Jan.27; 31)   £70

– **Hogarth Restored.** Ill.:– T. Cook. L., 1801. Fo. 111 copper engrs. on 90 plts., some plts. slightly foxed & soiled some margin tears, 1 plt. torn in plt. margin, MS. plt. numbering at beginning, later hf. leath., bumped. (GB. May 4; 1336)   DM 3,300

– – **Anr. Copy.** Lge. fo. Lacks text, some plts. foxed & soiled, some margin tears, 1 plt. torn in plt. margin, cold. pen plt. numbering at beginning, later hf. leath., bumped, upr. cover loose. (H. Nov.23; 679a)   DM 1,050

– – **Anr. Edn.** L., 1802. Lge. fo. 111 engraved plts., 1 engr. by anr. hand loosely inserted, cont. hf. roan. (SKC. Jan.13; 2111)   £560

– – **Anr. Copy.** Imp. fo. Lacks ptd. title, plts. lightly browned & some soiling & staining, a few plts. with light margin tears, cont. mor. gt., defect., very rubbed & bumped. (HT. May 9; 1015) DM 1,400

– – **Anr. Edn.** 1806. Fo. Port., 67 full-p. plts., 38 plts. on 19 sheets, 6 plts. on 2 sheets, 11 extra plts. from different edns. inserted, hf. cf., covers detchd., as a coll. of plts., w.a.f. (P. Dec.8; 189)
Macdonald. £420

– – **Anr. Copy.** Atlas fo. 111 plts., some foxing & staining, old qtr. cf., needs rebdg. (SG. Jun.7; 365)
$450

– **Zergliedrung der Schönheit, die Schwankenden Begriffe von dem Geschmack festzugesetzen.** Preface:– G.E. Lossing. Trans.:– C. Mylius. Berlin & Potsdam, 1754. *Revised Edn.* 4to. Minimal browning, cont. vell., slightly soiled. (H. May 22; 145)   DM 620

– – **Anr. Copy.** Some slight browning or spotting, plts. browned, slightly stained, sm. margin slits, 19th. C. hf. linen, very rubbed. (GB. May 4; 1335)
DM 500

– **The Complete Works.** L., [1840?]. 4to. 150 steel engrs., hf. cf., corners. (CR. Jun.6; 184)
Lire 280,000

– – **Anr. Edn.** Ed.:– J. Hannay. L., ca. 1870. *New & revised Edn.* Fo. 144 (of 151) steel engraved plts., some light foxing, cont. decor. linen, gold & blind-tooled. (HT. May 9; 1017)   DM 400

– **Original Works.** 1790. Lge. fo. 76 sheets of engrs. only, cf., defect., as a coll. of plts., w.a.f. (P. Sep.29; 31)   *Collmann.* £820

– **Works.** Ed.:– J. Nichols. Ca. 1830. Lge. fo. 81 full-p. sheets, 61 engrs. on 32 sheets, no suppressed plts., hf. mor. gt., as a coll. of plts., w.a.f. (P. Dec.8; 250)   *Woodruff.* £480

– – **Anr. Copy.** Elephant Fo. 143 engrs. on 113 ll., lacks suppressed plts., title torn, 2 plts. trimmed, some stains, lacks covers, as a coll. of plts., w.a.f. (P. Jan.12; 113)   *Collmann.* £300

– – **Anr. Edn.** Ed.:– Rev. Dr. John Trusler. 1833. 2 vols. in 1. 4to. Cf. gt., upr. cover detchd. (P. Apr.12; 114)   *Fontanella.* £60

– – **Anr. Copy.** 2 vols. 4to. Minimal light brown spotting, cont. crushed mor., gt. decor. spine, covers & inner dentelles, corners lightly worn; Hauswedell coll. (H. May 24; 1398)   DM 520

– – **Anr. Edn.** Ed.:– John Trusler. 1833-n.d. 2 vols. 4to. Spotted, cont. hf. cf., rubbed, lightly dampstained. (CSK. Jan.13; 148)   £55

– – **Anr. Edn.** Ed.:– John Nichols. L., 1835-37. Fo. 116 engraved plts., without the 3 suppressed plts. at end, some foxing, cont. red hf. mor., spine gt., rebkd. preserving orig. spine, scuffed. (CN.9; 84)   *Collmann.* £480

– – **Anr. Copy.** Fo. 80 plts., disbnd., w.a.f. (SSA. Sep.21; 210)   R 230

– – **Anr. Edn.** Ed.:– John Nichols. L., [1835-37]. Lge. fo. 2 engraved ports., 114 engraved plts., & 2 suppressed plts. in pocket at end, title & some text ll. spotted, cont. hf. mor., slightly worn. (S. Nov.22; 330)   *Coulman.* £550

– – **Anr. Copy.** Lge. fo. 116 engrs., some staining, frontis. torn, cont. hf. mor., worn. (S. Dec.8; 386)
Finch. £350

– – **Anr. Copy.** Lge. fo. Some spotting, hf. cf.,

defect., as a collection of plts., w.a.f. (P. Sep.29; 30)   *Collmann.* £300

– – **Anr. Edn.** L., [1840?]. 4to. 150 steel engrs., hf. red mor., corners. (CR. Jun.6; 185) Lire 220,000

– – **Anr. Edn.** Ed:– Rev. John Trusler. L., ca. 1870. 2 vols. 4to. 150 steel engrs., 1st. engraved title chipped & detchd., moderate foxing & soiling, embossed cl., covers rubbed & scuffed, 2nd. vol. lacks portion of spine head. (CBA. Jan.29; 236)
$130

– – **Anr. Edn.** L., n.d. Lge. fo. 154 plts. on 114 sheets, 3 suppressed plts. in end pockets, title & 2 text ll. creased, hf. mor. gt. (P. Apr.12; 237)
Collmann. £500

– – **Anr. Copy.** 2 vols. 4to. 150 engraved plts., hf. mor. gt. (P. Mar.15; 10)   *Duran.* £50

– – **Anr. Copy.** 2 vols. Fo. Linen. (DS. May 25; 2419)   Pts. 26,000

– – **Anr. Copy.** Lge. fo. Hf. leath. & marb. bds., brkn., edges & spine rubbed & torn. (RS. Jan.17; 491) $350

HOGARTH PRESS
See— KEYNES, John Maynard

HOGENBERG, Franz
[–] [**Afbeeldinghe ende Beschrijvinghe van alle de Veldslagen Belegeringen ...**]. Ill.:– M. Quad, G. Ens, W. Salsman, & others. [Cologne, &/or The Netherlands, 1583?-1629]. Ob. fo. A series of approx. 400 engraved plts., mostly views, town & battle plans, relating to the period 1535-1622, most with engraved German captions of approx. 12 lines in rhyming couplets, a few with additional Fr. descriptions, with a further 10 unnumbered plts., (8 with separate letterpress description with the Antw. imprint of A. Verhouen, plan of the siege of Breda by N. Goelkerken dtd. 1624, & route map from Milan to Antw. by M. Coignet), 2 of these additional plts. possibly listed by Muller, but without reference to the letterpress, wormholes affecting 1st. 2 plts., several early plts. loose or slightly defect., light stains at end, a few fore-margins shaved, faint liby. stp. on margin of 1st. plt., cont. (Dutch?) blind-stpd. cf. over wood bds., worn, as a collection, w.a.f. (S. Dec.1; 188)
Ochs. £6,500
See— BRAUN or BRUIN, Georg & Hogenberg, Franz

HOGENBERG, Nicolaus
– **Gratae et Laboribus aequae Posteritati Caesareas Sanctique Patris Longo Ordine Turmas Aspice.** [Antw.?, 1532]. Fo. Iss. with space above plts. unengraved but with arms of emperor's ancestors & their names & titles in Fr. drawn & written in Flemish hand & sigd. & dtd. by scribe, Jehan Ruchie Gantois Prestre en lan MDXXXII, 2 plts. & inscrs. (at beginning & end) cold. & the 38 plts. of procession cold. (all presumably by Ruchie), all plts. trimmed close to engraved area & inlaid, 6 plts. slightly rubbed, a few other plts. with white colouring showing oxidisation, some light staining, 2 plts. misbnd., 19th. C. light red mor., gt. extra, covers ornately gt. to an 18th. C. Scottish pattern, slightly faded. (S. Nov.17; 35)   *Harper.* £25,000

HOGG, A., Publisher
– **Ruins & Antient Buildings in England & Wales.** Maps:– T. Kitchin. Ca. 1790. Fo. No title or pre-lims., approx. 330 views on 317 sheets, 44 maps, no bdg. stated, as a collection of plts., w.a.f. (P. Oct.20; 197)   £360

HOGHELANDE, Theobald de
– **De Alchemiae Difficultatibus.** Cologne, 1594. *1st. Edn.* Errata lf., new bds.; Dr. Walter Pagel copy. (S. Feb.7; 195)   *Ritman.* £500

HOGREWE, J.L.
– **Beschreibung der in England seit 1759 angelegten, und jetzt grösstentheils vollendeten Schiffbaren Kanäle, zur inneren Gemeinschaft der Vornehmsten Handelstädte.** Hannover, 1780. 4to. Title lf. with erased stp., cont. marb. leath., rubbed. (GB. Nov.3; 1207)   DM 680

HOHBERG, Wolff Helmhard von
[–] **Georgica Curiosa.** Nuremb. 1687. Pt. 2 only (of 2). Fo. Lacks title, 4pp. & several end ll., 4 ll. defect. with loss, several ll. defect. & reprd., some

browning & staining, 19th. C. hf. leath., slightly rubbed. (HK. Nov.9; 1745) DM 520
- - **Anr. Edn.** Nuremb., 1701. *4th. Edn. (Vol. 1), 5th. Edn. (Vvol. 2); 2nd. Edn. (Vol. 3)*. 3 vols. Title & frontis. Vol. 2 & some other ll. with margin slits or tears, Vol. 1 lacks frontis., lightly browned, cont. bds., slightly spotted. (R. Oct.12; 2013)
DM 1,500
- - **Anr. Edn.** Nuremb., 1716. Vol. 1 only (of 2). Fo. Old owner's note on title, copper engraved title slightly torn, bdg. not stated, rubbed, spine defect. (HK. Nov.9; 1746) DM 400

HOJAH EFFENDI, Sa'd Al-Din
- The Reign of Sultan Orchan Second King of the Turks ... Trans.:– William Seaman. L., 1652. *1st. Edn.* Sm. 8vo. Cont. cf. gt., slightly worn. [Wing S 225] (C. Nov.9; 86) *Wood.* £200

HOJEDA, F. Diego de
- La Christiada. Ill.:– Murillo, Rubens, Rafael, Pellicer, Llimona etc. Barcelona, n.d. Leath. over wood bds., gt. engraved, bronze clasps. (DS. Dec.16; 2433) Pts. 22,000

HOKUSAI MANGA
1819 [but later]. Vol. 10. Some foxing or light brown stains, wraps., bnd. in Japanese manner, stitching partly brkn., wraps. rubbed. (HA. May 4; 90) $150
- - **Anr. Edn.** [Tokyo?], 1936-39. Vols. 3-5, 7, 9, 12-14. Orig. wraps. (SG. Jan.26; 215) $175

HOLANDRE, Fr.
- Planches pour l'abrégé d'Histoire Naturelle. Zweibrücken, 1790. Some slight foxing, cont. bds., rubbed & bumped. (HK. Nov.8; 480) DM 460

HOLBACH, Paul Henri Thyri, Baron d'
[–] Système de la Nature ... Par M. Mirabaud. L. [= Amst.], 1770. *1st. Edn. 1st. Printing.* 2 pts. in 1 vol. Pt. 1 lacks hf.-title, 2 errata ll. at end pt. 2, 1 lf. with pasted tear, 1st. & last ll. foxed, 19th. C. hf. leath. (R. Oct.11; 1261) DM 1,000
- Système Social ou Principes Naturels de la Morale et de la Politique avec un Examen de l'Influence du Gouvernement sur les Moeurs. L., 1774. *Orig. Edn.* 3 vols. in 1. Cf., worn. (HD. Feb.22; 97)
Frs. 2,600

HOLBEIN, Hans, the Younger
- The Dance of Death. Ill.:– David Deuchar. 1803. Sm. 4to. Frontis., port., engraved title, 48 etched plts., cont. cf. gt. (P. Dec.8; 122) *Symonds.* £70
- - **Anr. Edn.** 1898. 16mo. Cont. mor. gt. by D[ouglas] C[ockerel], lightly rubbed; inscr. 'To my friend Grant Richards with best wishes J.H. Isaacs'. (CSK. Mar.23; 190) £50
- Icones Mortis. Trans.:– G. Aemilius. Ill.:– H. Lützelbürger. Bâle, 1554. Sm. 8vo. Washed, corner of 1 lf. reprd., late 19th. C. vell. (HD. Nov.9; 6)
Frs. 7,500
- The Images of the Old Testament, lately Expressed, set forthe in Ynglishe & Frenche. [Buenos Aires, 1947]. *Facs. of Frellon's 1549 Edn. (15) numbered on imperial Japan vell., with orig. copper laid into folding case.* 4to. Loose as iss. in vell. wraps., bd. folding case worn. (SG. Oct.13; 196) $110
- Imagines de Morte, et Epigrammata. Trans.:– Georgio Aemylio. Lyon, 1542. *1st. Edn. in Latin.* Last lf. blank, some stains, sm. wormhole in some lr. blank margins, cont. cf. gt., title lge. on upr. cover. (S. May 10; 300) *Lacquaforte.* £1,000
- Imitations of Original Drawings. Ill.:– Bartolozzi. L., 1792[-1800]. Atlas fo. 3 ports. (2 cold.), & 80 tinted engraved plts., many on cold. paper & including 32 trimmed & mntd., slight foxing, cont. crimson str.-grd. mor., gt.-tooled, inner dentelles gt., slightly worn. (SG. Apr.26; 95) $2,600
- Oeuvre ou Recueil de Gravures. Basel, 1780. Lacks 1st. plt. (*Bound with:*) — La Passion de Notre Seigneur. Basel, 1784. Together 2 works in 1 vol. Slightly foxed or browned, cont. hf. leath. gt. (HK. Nov.9; 2215) DM 600
- Les Simulacres & Historiées Faces de la Mort. Lyon, 1538. *1st. Edn.* Sm. 4to. Apparently lacks 1 or more ll. at end (including colophon), old cf. (LM. Oct.22; 251) B.Frs. 16,000

HOLBERG, Ludwig 'Nicholas Klimius'
[–] Onderaardsche Reis van Claas Klim. The Hague, 1761. 1 vol. Top of frontis. shaved, later cl.-bkd. bds. (*With:*) – Nicolai Klims unterirdische Reise. Copen. & Leipzig, 1780. 1 vol. Some light staining, later hf. mor., partly unopened. (BBA. Feb.23; 52)
Bennett. £60
- Des Weltberühmten Niclas Klim Höchst Merkwürdige Reisen. Nürnberg, 1824. Sm. 8vo. 4 handcold. plts., a few stains, some foxing, cont. bds. (VG. Mar.21; 451) Fls. 500

HOLCROFT, Thomas
- Memoirs. Ed.:– [William Hazlitt]. L., 1816. *1st. Edn.* 3 vols. 12mo. Hf.-titles, 1st. 2 advt. ll. in Vol. 1, spotted, later hf. mor., partly unc., rubbed. (BBA. May 3; 233) *Murray Hill.* £120
- Travels from Hamburg through Westphalia, Holland & the Netherlands. 1804. 2 vols. 4to. Plts. spotted, diced russ. (BS. Nov.16; 61) £110

HOLDERLIN, Friedrich
- Gedichte. Stuttgart & Tübingen, 1826. *1st. Edn.* Title with 2 names, newspaper cutting on verso, lr. endpaper with MS. entries, cont. new bnd. red mor. with old spine, slightly rubbed. (H. Nov.23; 676)
DM 9,500
- - **Anr. Copy.** 1 lf. with pasted tear, some foxing, especially in margins, stp. on end-paper, later bds., MS. spine title; Hauswedell coll. (H. May 24; 1386) DM 7,200
- - **Anr. Copy.** 13 ll. with pencil entries, some slight foxing, some stains in upr. margin, cont. bds., very spotted & bumped & ex-libris & liby. label inside cover. (H. May 22; 740) DM 6,200
- - **Anr. Copy.** Title lacks ptd. centrepiece fragment, some sm. MS. text corrections, some light foxing, cont. hf. leath. (HK. May 16; 2096)
DM 4,200
- Hymnen. München, Rupprecht Pr., 1919. *(200) numbered.* 4to. Hand-bnd. mor., sigd. by W. Voigt, Weimar, gt. cover vig. (GB. Nov.5; 2955)
DM 400
- Hyperion oder der Eremit in Griechenland. Stuttgart & Tübingen, 1822. *2nd. Edn.* 2 vols. in 1. Minimal spotting, cont. bds., lightly bumped; Hauswedell coll. (H. May 24; 1385) DM 3,200
- - **Anr. Edn.** Ed.:– Fr. Zinkermgel. Leipzig, Ernst Ludwig Pr., 1912. *(200).* 4to. Orig. vell., cover slightly warped. (HK. May 17; 2730) DM 450
- Poèmes. Trans.:– A. Bouchet. Ill.:– M. Ernst. [Paris, 1961]. *(90) De Luxe Edn. on Velin de Rives.* 4to. Printers mark sigd. by artist, translator & publishers, loose ll. in orig. wraps. & linen cover, s.-c. (H. May 23; 1213) DM 2,250
- Sämmtliche Werke. Ed.:– Chr. Th. Schwab. Stuttgart & Tübingen, 1846. *1st. Coll. Edn.* 2 pts. in 1 vol. Some foxing, mor., ca. 1870, decor., slightly worn, stain on upr. cover; pres. inscr. dtd. 1878 on end-paper. (HK. Nov.10; 2513) DM 1,500
- - **Anr. Copy.** 2 vols. Some foxing, cont. bds. (GB. Nov.4; 2097) DM 900

HOLDITCH, Robert
- Observations on Emigration to British America, & the United States. Plymouth-Dock, priv. ptd., [1818]. *1st. Edn.?* Errata slip at end, margin tear in last 2 ll. reprd., maroon hf. mor., unc.; the Rt. Hon. Visc. Eccles copy. (CNY. Nov.18; 142) $600

HOLDSWORTH, W.W.
See— FINDLAY, G.G. & Holdsworth, W.W.

HOLE, William
See— NORDEN, John & Hole, William

HOLFORD, G.
- The Convict's Complaint in 1815, & the Thanks of the Convict in 1825; or, Sketches in Verso of a Hulk in the Former Year, & of Millbank Penitentiary in the Latter ... 1825. Mod. hf. mor. (KH. May 1; 355) Aus. $160
- Letter to the Rt. Hon. the Secretary of State for the Home Department ... on the Propriety of taking Other Measures for the Supply of Women to the Settlements in New South Wales ... 1827. Mod. hf. mor. (KH. May 1; 357) Aus. $170
- Substance of the Speech ... on the Bill 'To Amend the Laws relative to the Transportation of Offenders' ... 1815. Later hf. mor. (KH. May 1; 360)
Aus. $100

- Third Vindication of the General Penitentiary shewing that there is no Ground whatever for supposing that the Situation of that Prison had any Share in producing the Late Disease ... 1825. Mod. hf. mor. (KH. May 1; 361) Aus. $100

HOLINSHED, Raphael
- The Firste Volume of the Chronicles of England, Scotlande & Irelande. L., 1577. *1st. Edn.* 3 pts. in 1 vol. Fo. Cont. panel. cf., gt. arabesque decor., w.a.f. [STC 13568b] (C. Nov.9; 15)
Snelling. £160
- - **Anr. Edn.** L., [1577]. 4to. Lacks title & last few index ll., dedication lf. (impft.) is followed by 'Description of Britaine', 127 pp. plus errata, in all 1,872 pp. plus index, not otherwise collated, mod. gt. brocaded covers, w.a.f. (SG. Feb.9; 248) $475

HOLITSCHER, A.
- Gesang an Palästina. Ill.:– H. Struck. Berlin, 1922. *[1st. Edn.]. (320).(100) numbered on H.M.P.* Fo. 12 full-p. orig. etchings sigd., orig. red mor. gt., slightly spotted or worn. (GB. Nov.5; 3056)
DM 1,200
- - **Anr. Copy.** 1 sigd. etching, slightly browned & foxed, orig. mor., corners slightly bumped. (HK. May 17; 3168) DM 850

HOLLAND, Henry, Bookseller
[–] Herwologia Anglica. By H.H. Ill.:– Willem & Magdalena van de Passe. [Arnhem, 1620]. *1st. Edn.* 2 vols. in 1. Fo. Index-lf. at end, prelims. lack 5 & 6 & Gruterus lf., some dampstaining, a few tears, slightly affecting text & a few plts., reprd., title & plt. of tomb of Queen Elizabeth cut down & mntd., early 19th. C. russ. gt., rebkd., old spine preserved. [STC 13582] (S. Oct.11; 544) *Rix.* £70

HOLLAND, Sir Henry, Bart
- Travels in the Ionian Isles, Albania, Thessaly, Macedonia, etc. during the years 1812 & 1813. 1815. *1st. Edn.* 4to. Engraved map, 12 engraved plts., cont. gt.-decor. russ., spine gt., lacks piece at head of spine. (SKC. May 4; 1808) £150

HOLLANDER, O.
- Nos Drapeaux et Etendards de 1812 á 1815 ... Paris, 1902. Hf. chagrin. (HD. Jan.27; 240)
Frs. 1,000

HOLLEY, Mary Austin
- Texas. Observations, Historical, Geographical & Descriptive, in a Series of Letters, Written during a Visit to Austin's Colony ... in the Autumn of 1831. Balt., 1833. 12mo. Hooker's 'Map of the State of Coahuila & Texas' laid in, foxed thro.-out, last 40 pp. dampstained, orig. cl., lr. cover blistered, lacks spine labels, shabby. (SG. Jan.19; 186) $750

HOLLIS, Thomas & George
- The Monumental Effigies of Great Britain. L., 1840-42. *1st. Edn.* 6 pts. (all publd.). Fo. 61 engraved plts., announcements present, hf. mor., unc., wraps, present. (PNY. Oct.20; 224) $250

HOLM, P.
- Stuurmans Zee-meeter, inh. het Geene dat een Stuurman Nodig is. [Amst.], priv. ptd., 5844 [1748]. 3 pts. in 1 vol. Sm. 8vo. Cont. marb. cf., slightly warped, spine reprd. (VS. Dec.9; 1286) Fls. 600

HOLME, Charles
- Modern Pen Drawings: European & American. Ill.:– after J. King, L. Housman, Seton-Thompson, & others. L., 1901. *(300) numbered.* Tall 4to. Title & end-papers lightly foxed, blind-stpd. vell. (SG. Dec.8; 67) $130

HOLME, Charles (Ed.)
See— ART IN PHOTOGRAPHY
See— ENGLISH WATER COLOUR

HOLME, Randal
- The Academy of Armory. Chester, priv. ptd., 1688. 1 vol. Fo. Extra engraved title with margins reprd. & laid down, some discoloration, anagram lf. reprd. with loss, cont. cf., rebkd. [Wing H 2513] (*With:*) – An Index of the Names of Persons contained in the Academy of Armory. L., 1821. 1 vol. Fo. Cl.-bkd. bds. (S. Mar.6; 484) *Page.* £120

HOLMES, Oliver Wendell

- The Autocrat of the Breakfast-Table. Boston, 1858. *1st. Edn. 1st. Printing.* Orig. cl. [bdg. 'A'], 3 corners a little worn, gt. spine frayed; Frederic Dannay copy. (CNY. Dec.16; 172) $160.
- Currents & Counter-Currents in Medical Science, with Other Addresses & Essays. Boston, 1861. *1st. Edn., with 16 pp. of advts. at end & 'Ticknor & Co' on spine.* 12mo. Cl. (SG. Oct.6; 200) $110
- Songs of Many Seasons. 1862-1874. Boston, 1875. *1st. Edn.* 12mo. Cl.; pres. copy, inscr. by author to J.P. Coolee, & dtd. 23 Nov. 1874, bkplt. (SG. Nov.17; 67) $100
- The Writings. Boston & N.Y., ca. 1891. *Riverside Edn.* 14 vols. Purple hf. mor. (SPB. Dec.13; 538) $275
- - Anr. Edn. Camb., Riverside Pr., 1891-96. *(175)* numbered on L.P. 16 vols. Cl.-bkd. bds., unc. & unopened, light wear, d.-w.'s with extra flaps turning over top & bottom of books, light wear; Ken Leach coll. (RO. Jun.10; 176) $130

HOLMES, R.R.

- Specimens of Royal Fine & Historical Book-binding, selected from the Royal Library, Windsor Castle. 1893. Fo. Dedication lf. loose, cont. buckram, a little rubbed; H.M. Nixon coll., with his sig. & some MS. notes. (BBA. Oct.6; 71) *Traylen.* £600

HOLMES, Thomas

- Great Metropolis. Ill.:- W.G. Fearnside & T. Harrel. [1851]. Engraved title, 48 plts., orig. cl. gt., slightly soiled. (P. Oct.20; 30) £70
- - Anr. Edn. Ill.:- W.G. Fearnside & T. Harrel. L., n.d. Some spotting, cf. gt. (P. Sep.29; 264) *Leycester.* £60

HOLMES, Thomas James

- Increase Mather: A Bibliography. Cleveland, 1931. *(500).* 2 vols. (*With:*) - Cotton Mather: A Bibliography. Camb., Mass., 1940. *(500).* 3 vols. (*With:*) - The Minor Mathers: A List of their Works. Camb., Mass., 1940. *(200).* 1 vol. Together 6 vols. Three-qtr. lev., partly unc., s.-c.'s. (SG. Jan.5; 219) $375

HOLROYD, James E. (Ed.)
See— SHERLOCK HOLMES JOURNAL

HOLSTEIN, Lucas

- Collectio Romana Bipartita Veterum Aliquot Historiae Ecclesiasticae Monumentorum. Rome, 1662. 2 pts. in 1 vol. With final errata lf., cont. Fr. red mor. gt., 2 borders à la Du Seuil round covers, arms of Pierra Séguier, spine gt. with his cypher & arms in alternate compartments. (S. Nov.17; 36) *Maggs.* £350

HOLT, James

- Virgin Gold & How to Win It. Moonee Ponds, n.d. New hf. mor., wraps. bnd. in. (KH. May 1; 363) Aus. $160

HOLTY, L.H. Ch.

- Gedichte. Hamburg, 1783. *1st. Edn.* Cont. hf. leath. (D. Nov.24; 2491) DM 4,400

HOLUB, Emil

- Sieben Jahre in Sud-Afrika. Vienna, 1881. 2 vols. Some light browning, cont. hf. cl., rubbed, inner hinges reprd. (CSK. May 4; 85) £55

HOLUB, E & Pelseln, A. von

- Beiträge zur Ornithologie Südafrikas. Wien, 1882. Slightly browned, orig. linen; dedication from author. (R. Oct.13; 2902) DM 480

HOLWELL, J.Z.

- India Tracts. 1764. *2nd. Edn.* 4to. Lightly soiled, cont. cf. (CSK. Sep.30; 40) £95

HOLZSCHUHER, Johann Friedrich Siegmund von 'Jtzig Feitel Stern'

- Das Schabbes Gaertle vun unnere Leut ... Zweite Ouflag. Meissen, 1835. (*Bound with:*) - Die Schabbes Lamp vun Pollische Messing. Meissen, 1835. Together 2 works in 1 vol. Later hf. leath., orig. pict. wraps. bnd. in. (SG. Feb.2; 80) $350

HOMANN, Johan Baptiste

- Atlas. [Nuremb.], ca. 1730? Fo. 25 hand-cold. engraved maps, without title, some dampstaining,

edges frayed, 1st. map torn at fold, last map defect., cont. cf., publisher's device(?) on covers, worn, edges torn. (CH. Sep.20; 65) Fls. 2,600
- Atlas Minor. Nuremb., [1729]. Lge. fo. Stained thro.-out, 5 maps bkd. in side margin or corner, some foxing, hf. linen with cont. limp leath. cover, rubbed. (HK. Nov.8; 889) DM 2,500
- - Anr. Edn. Nuremb, ca. 1745. Lge. fo. 27 old cold. double-p. copper engraved maps (of 36 in plt. index), 10 others bnd. in, 1 cold. plt., many maps torn, some crumpled, cont. hf. leath., defect. (R. Oct.13; 2846) DM 3,200
- Atlas Novus. Amst., ca. 1755 or later. Fo. Engraved title, 1 key map & table, 85 double-p. engraved maps, all but 4 hand-cold., mntd. on guards, some light marginal staining, last map slightly creased & with marginal tear, cont. cf., worn, jnts. brkn. (CH. Sep.20; 64) Fls. 9,000
- Atlas Novus Terrarum Orbis Imperia, Regna et Status. Nuremb., ca. 1724. *Early Edn.* 2 vols. Fo. Engraved allegorical title, engraved full-length port. of Charles VI, 2 ptd. dedication ll., 21 ll. intro. text, 198 double-p. engraved mapsheets, including 145 maps, 31 town plans & views on 28 plts., 19 astronomical & cosmographical diagrams, 3 battle plans & 3 naval & military plts., index lf. at end, all but port. cont. hand-cold., 1 or 2 short tears without loss of engraved surface, cont. cf.-bkd. bds., unc., worn, w.a.f. (S. May 21; 124) *Burgess.* £20,000
- Schul-Atlas. Nuremb., 1745[-46]. Fo. Partly bkd., spotted & browned, especially in margins, corners crumpled, cont. limp leath., spotted, worn, torn. (H. Nov.23; 307) DM 1,600

HOMANN, Johann Baptiste & Heirs

- Atlas Geographicus Maior. Nuremb., 1759. Lge. fo. 173 cold. copper engraved maps, maps dated variously, 4 maps loose & with creases & sm. margin slits, some maps stained & slightly spotted, some with margin annots., cont. hf. leath., defect. (D. Nov.23; 765) DM 24,000

HOMANN, Johann Baptiste, Heirs of

- Atlas Germaniae Specialis. Nuremb., 1753. Fo. Engraved cold. frontis., engraved title with vig., 4 dedication ll. with engraved vig., engraved index, 144 (of 147?) double-p. outl. & surface cold. copper engraved maps, very browned, newly bnd. & restored cont. cf. using old material, gold-tooled decor., corner pieces, gold-tooled Roman-German imperial arms, supralibros, gold-stpd. decor. (D. Nov.23; 764) DM 27,200
- Atlas Silesiae. Nuremb., 1750. Imp. fo. Title & plt. index engraved, 20 double-p. old cold. copper engraved maps with figure cartouche, most maps dtd. 1736 (some to 1751), slight wormholes thro.-out, cont. bds. (R. Oct.13; 2642a) DM 4,000

HOME, Henry, Lord Kames

- Elements of Criticism. Edinb., 1762. *1st. Edn.* 3 vols. Cont. cf., spines gt.-decor.; Sir Ivar Colquhoun, of Luss copy. (CE. Mar.22; 162) £580
- The Gentleman Farmer. Edinb., 1779. *2nd. Edn.* 2 pp. advts., plts. foxed, cont. cf., spine gt., rubbed. (LC. Jul.5; 137) £55
- Memoirs. Ed.:- A.F. Tytler. Edinb., 1807. 2 vols. 4to. Orig. bds., unc.; pres. copy to A. Boswell, of Blackadder. (PD. Dec.14; 209) £130
- [-] Sketches of the History of Man. Edinb., 1774. *1st. Edn.* 2 vols. 4to. Hf.-titles, cont. cf., spines gt.; Sir Ivar Colquhoun, of Luss copy. (CE. Mar.22; 163) £420
- - Anr. Copy. 4to. Hf.-titles, cont. tree cf. gt., later gt. spines, corners & minor abrasions reprd. (C. May 30; 156) *Drury.* £350

HOME, John

- [-] Douglas: A Tragedy. Edinb., 1757. *1st. Edinb. Edn.* (*Bound with:*) - Agis: A Tragedy. Edinb., 1758. (*Bound with:*) - The Siege of Aquileia. A Tragedy. Edinb., 1760. Together 3 works in 1 vol. Cont. cf., spine gt.; Sir Ivar Colquhoun, of Luss copy. (CE. Mar.22; 164) £85
- The History of the Rebellion in the year 1745. 1802. *1st. Edn.* 4to. Errata lf., cont. spr. cf., spine gt.; Sir Ivar Colquhoun, of Luss copy. (CE. Mar.22; 166) £80

HOME, Robert

- Select Views in Mysore. L., 1794. *1st. Edn.* 4to. Lge. copy, 4 folding engraved maps, 29 engraved plts., cont. str.-grd. red mor. gt. by Hering, with his ticket, head of spine slightly rubbed. (S. Dec.1; 372) *Kossow.* £280
- - Anr. Copy. 4to. 4 engraved folding maps (torn at folds), 29 plts., some ll. foxed, some worming, cont. mor., worn. (S. Mar.6; 32) *Samiramis.* £120
- - Anr. Copy. Lge. 4to. Lacks 2 engraved plts., some faint spotting, cont. hf. russ. gt., worn. (S. Nov.1; 57) *Shapiro.* £70

HOMER

- The Iliad [English]. Trans.:- Alexander Pope. L., 1715-20. 6 vols. Fo. Lacks map, some browning, cont. mott. cf., spines worn. (SPB. Dec.13; 724) $125
- Iliad [Greek & Latin]. Glasgow, 1747. 6 vols. Lf. of advts. at end of Vol. 6 with 'Ciceronis Opera omnia 20 vols' listed (a late iss.?, possibly 1749), cont. mott. cf., spines gt.-decor.; Sir Ivar Colquhoun, of Luss copy. (CE. Mar.22; 115) £170
- Ilias [German]. Trans.:- Th. v. Scheffer. München & Leipzig, 1913. *De Luxe Edn., (150)* numbered on Bütten. Orig. leath. (HK. Nov.11; 4235) DM 480
- The Iliad. — The Odyssey. [English]. Trans.:- Alexander Pope. L., 1715-26. Together 11 vols. 4to. Cont. cf., spines gt., 2 covers detchd.; bkplt. of Earl of Holderness & Leeds. (BBA. Mar.21; 204) *S. Bennett.* £280
- - Anr. Copy. Together 6 vols. in 11, as iss. 4to. Hf.-title to Iliad, privilege & errata ll., subscribers lists, early mott. cf. gt. (SG. Feb.9; 310) $650
- - Anr. Edn. Trans.:- Alexander Pope. Ill.:- Miller after Vanloo (port. of Pope). L., 1760. 11 vols. Cont. cf. gt., decor. spines. (HD. Sep.22; 261) Frs. 1,800
- - Anr. Edn. Trans.:- Alexander Pope. L., 1771. Together 9 vols. 12mo. cont. cf., spines gt. (SG. Feb. 16; 159) $140
- - Anr. Edn. Trans.:- A. Pope. L., 1813-06. 12 vols. in 6. Cont red mor. gt. by J. White, of Pall Mall & F.J. du Roveray, ties; Kenneth Oldaker copy. (P. Jan.12; 11) *Cavendish.* £420
- - Anr. Edn. Boston & N.Y., 1905. *(600)* numbered. 4 vols.; 4 vols. Hf. mor. gt. over bds. (LH. Sep.25; 466) $170
- - Anr. Edn. Trans.:- Alexander Pope. Ltd. Edns. Cl., 1931. *(1500)* numbered & sigd. by the designer J. van Crimpen. 2 vols. 4to. Mor.-bkd. bds., unopened. (S. Nov.22; 278) *Houle.* £60
- Iliad. — Odyssey. [Greek]. Glasgow, Foulis Pr., 1756-58. 4 vols. Fo. Interleaved copy, hf. title in each vol., few pp. slightly spotted, 1st. quire in Vol.1 of Odyssey loosening, cont. Engl. red mor. gt.-decor., spines gt.; bkplts. of Sophia Streatfield, Myles Standish Slocum & Thomas B. Stevenson. (CNY. Dec.17; 560) $1,100
- - Anr. Edn. Ed.:- E. Schwartz. Ill.:- A. Simons. München, Bremer Pr., 1923-24. *(615)* on Bütten. 2 vols. Sm. fo. Hand-bnd. red mor. by P.A. Demeter, Hellerau, blind-tooled & gt. on spine, covers, inner & outer dentelles. (H. Nov.23; 938) DM 2,000
- The Iliad. — The Odyssey. [Greek & English]. Nones. Pr., 1931. *(1450)* numbered; *(1300)* numbered. Together 2 vols. Orig. mor., slightly mottled, s.-c.'s. (BBA. Oct.27; 170) *Joseph.* £140
- - Anr. Copy. Together 2 vols. Orig. mor., foot of spines dampstained, s.-c.'s. (BBA. Sep.29; 221) *Old Hall Books.* £80
- L'Iliade et l'Odyssée [French]. Trans.:- Madame Dacier. Paris, 1741. *New Edn.* 8 vols. 12mo. Cont. marb. cf., spine decor. (HD. Nov.9; 42) Frs. 2,000
- Iliadis Fragmenta Antiquissima cum Picturis idem Scholia Vetera ad Odysseam. Ed.:- Angelus Maius. Milan, 1829. Ro. Hf.-title, mod. hf. leath., unc. (SI. Dec.18; 115) Lire 240,000
- The Iliads. — The Odysseys. — Batrachomyomachia, Hymns & Epigrams. [English]. Ed.:- Richard Hooper. Trans.:- George Chapman. L., 1857-58. *Liby. of Old Authors Edn.* Together 5 vols. Sq. 16mo. Cl. gt., spines gt. with fleurons. (SG. Feb.16; 160) $140
- Ilias ... Ulyssea. Batrachomyomachia. Hymni. XXXII. Venice, Apr. 1524. 2 vols. Title-pp. lightly soiled with faded liby. stps., str.-grd. mor. by Roger

Payne, covers gt.-decor., gt.-panel. spines, extremities a little rubbed; John Scott, of Halkshill bkplt. (SPB. Dec.14; 20) $650
- **Nausikaa-Episoden. Fyra Sänger ur Odysseen.** Intro.:– Knut Hagberg. Ill.:– Johnny Friedlaender. Lund, 1953. *(365). (125).* 8 orig. sigd. etchings, sepia ptd. on Marais-Bütten, orig. mor. gt. (GB. May 5; 2542) DM 2,000
- **Odyssea [Latin].** Ed.:– Henrico Stephano. Paris, 1624. Fr. mor., sides gt. with arms of Marius Philomardy or Filomardi, Archbp. of Avignon 1624-44, flat spine gt. decor., slightly worn, as a bdg., w.a.f. (S. Apr.10; 294) *Maggs.* £220
- **L'Odyssée [French].** Trans.:– Hughes de Picou. Ill.:– François Chauveau. Paris, 1650. *Orig. Edn.* 4to. Mor. by Cuzin, blind- & gt.-decor. (HD. Mar.19; 132) Frs. 2,400
- **– Anr. Edn.** Trans.:– Victor Bérard. Ill.:– F.L. Schmied. Paris, 1929-33. *(145) numbered on vell.* 4 vols. 4to. Engrs. cold. & heightened with gold & silver by Saudé, minor foxing, wraps., vell. folder & box, Vol. III wrap. foxed; 2 orig. gouaches sigd. by Schmied. (HD. Jul.2; 74) Frs. 48,000
- **– Anr. Edn.** Trans.:– Victor Bérard. Ill.:– F.-L. Schmied. Paris, 1930-33. *De Luxe Edn. (140) numbered on parch.* 4 vols. 4to. Boxes, recovered with parch. (HD. Apr.26; 256) Frs. 20,000
- **Die Odyssee [German].** Trans.:– R.A. Schröder. Ill.:– A. Maillol, E. Gill (initials). [Leipzig], Cranach Pr., [1907-10]. *(350) for sale.* 2 vols. 4to. On Bütten, orig. hf. vell. gt. (H. Nov.23; 982) DM 3,200
- **– Anr. Copy.** Vol. I (of II). On Bütten, some margins lightly browned orig. hf. vell., gt. spine, lr. inner cover torn, slightly rubbed & corners bumped; Hauswedell coll. (H. May 24; 732) DM 660
- **– Anr. Edn.** Trans.:– R.A. Schröder. Ill.:– Maillol, E. Gill. Leipzig, 1910. *(425) numbered.* 2 vols. 4to. Orig. hf. vell., gt., corners slightly bumped. (HK. May 17; 2970) DM 2,000
- **– Anr. Edn.** Ill.:– L. v. Hofmann. Berlin, 1924. *Ltd. Iss., numbered.* 4to. Orig. hf. vell. gt., gt. cover vig. (GB. Nov.5; 2609) DM 750
- **– Anr. Edn.** Ed.:– C.G. v. Maassen. Trans.:– J.H. Voss. Ill.:– Anna Simons. München, Bremer Pr., 1926. *(200) on Zanders Bütten.* 4to. Orig. red orange mor., gt. spine, cover, inner & outer dentelle, s.-c. (HK. May 17; 2618) DM 1,000
- **– Anr. Edn.** Trans.:– Johann Heinrich Voss, C.G. von Massen. Ill.:– A. Simons. München, Bremer Pr., 1926. *(280) on Bütten.* 4to. Hand-bnd. orig. vell., gold decor., by Frieda Thierach. (H. Nov.23; 943) DM 1,200
- **Odyssee ... Die Heimkehr, Gesänge XIII-XXIV.** Ill.:– G. Marcks. [Starnberg, 1976]. Fo. Orig. linen. (H. Nov.24; 1814) DM 620
- **The Odyssey [English].** Trans.:– T.E. Lawrence. L., 1932. *1st. Edn. of this Trans. (530).* Fo. Orig. mor., s.-c. (C. Nov.9; 177) *Howes.* £320
- **– Anr. Copy.** Fo. Orig. mor., s.-c. (C. Nov.9; 177a) *Blackwells.* £300
- **– Anr. Copy.** 4to. Pol. cf., s.-c. (LH. Sep.25; 556) $525
- **– Anr. Copy.** Sm. fo. Gt. medallions on title & at head of each book, niger mor., partly unc. (SG. May 17; 304) $425
- **The Odyssey [Greek & English].** Trans.:– Alexander Pope. Ill.:– Rudolf Koch & Fritz Kredei. [L.], Nones, Pr., 1931. *(1300).* Gt.-stpd. mor., spine darkened, marb. end-papers, some wear to box, partly unc. (CBA. Nov.19; 472) $160
- **Oeuvres.** Trans.:– Dugas Montbel. Paris, 1833. 9 vols. Fr. & Greek, old hf. cf., decor. spines. (HD. Dec.9; 142) Frs 2,000
- **Oeuvres Complètes.** Paris, 1786. 4 vols. 4to. Bdg. not stated. (HD. Oct.14; 82) Frs. 1,600
- **Opera Omnia. Graece.** Ed.:– A.P. Manutius. Venetiis, 1524. 2 vols. Some light stains, 18th. C. cf., gt. decor. covers & spine, inner & outer dentelles, 1 jnt. partly split, light worming; Hauswedell coll. (H. May 24; 1126) DM 920
- **Speculum Heroicum.** Ill.:– C. de Passe. Arnhemiae, 1613. Sm. 4to. Title slightly soiled, Fr. red mor. gt., 'Newby Hall' stpd. on upr. cover; bkplts. of Earl de Grey & Nevile Gwynne. (BS. Nov.16; 39) £160
- **Werke.** Trans.:– J.H. Voss. Altona, 1793. *1st. Coll. Edn.* 4 vols. Title stpd., foxed, cont. hf. leath.

gt., rubbed, spine lightly defect. (HK. Nov.10; 2760) DM 600

HOMERIC HYMN TO APHRODITE
L., Fanfrolico Pr., 1928. *(500) numbered.* Leath.; long inscr. by Jack Lindsay, Harry F. Chaplin copy. (JL. Jul.15; 258) Aus. $100
- **– Anr. Edn.** Trans.:– F.L. Lucas. Ill.:– Mark Severin. Gold. Cock. Pr., 1948. *(100) numbered, specially bnd.* Sm. fo. Orig. mor. gt., s.-c.; from D. Bolton liby. (BBA. Oct.27; 142) *Duschnes.* £150

HOMES OF AMERICAN STATESMEN
Ill.:– John A. Whipple (frontis.). N.Y., 1854. Frontis. captioned in pencil 'Hancock House Boston / an original sun picture', additional engraved title age-darkened, orig. gt.-pict. cl., corners worn, lacks front free end-paper. (SG. May 10; 151) $175

HONDORFF, A.
- **Promptuarium Exemplorum.** Frankfurt, 1595. Fo. 1st. ll. slightly wormed, cont. pig over wood bds., blind-tooled roll-stp., decor., sm. ports., lge., centre-piece with floral border on upr. cover, same border on lr. cover & centre-piece, 2 brass clasps, owners monog. & date 1612, lr. cover partly rubbed. (D. Nov.23; 121) DM 1,800

HONDT, Pieter de
- **Figures de la Bible.** The Hague, 1728. 2 vols. in 1. Fo. 2 engraved titles, 207 (of 212?) plts., many double-p., a few splits or tears at folds, some light staining, mainly marginal, 19th. C. red hf. roan, worn, w.a.f. (S. Nov.17; 34) *Snelling.* £280

HONEY, W.B.
- **European Ceramic Art.** 1949-52. *[1st. Edn.].* 2 vols. 4to. Orig. cl. (LC. Jul.5; 61) £50
- **– Anr. Copy.** 2 vols. 4to. Cl., faded, 2nd. vol. with spine ends torn. (SG. Jan.26; 110) $150

HONEYMAN COLLECTION of Scientific Books & Manuscripts ... sold by Auction ...
L., 1978-81. 7 vols. 4to. Estimate leaflet in each vol., wraps. (SG. Aug.4; 153) $150
- **– Anr. Copy.** 7 vols. Sm. 4to. Ills., unif. wraps., estimate sheets inserted in each vol. (SG. May 17; 126) $120
- **– Anr. Copy.** 7 vols. 4to. Orig. sewed. (HT. May 8; 755) DM 550

HONTER, J.
[–] **Reformatio Ecclesiae Coronensis ac Totius Barcensis Provinciae.** Preface:– Ph. Melanchthon. Wittenburg, 1543. Old underlining, stained, browned near end, bds. (HK. Nov.8; 279) DM 1,100

HOOD, John
- **Australia & the East.** L., 1843. Lacks errata slip & advts. as called for by Ferguson, blind-stpd. cf. gt. (CA. Apr.3; 56) Aus. $130

HOOD, Thomas
- **The Comic Annual.** L., 1830-39, 1842. *1st. Edns.* Together 11 vols. Sm. 12mo. Hand-cold. woodcut plts. & text woodcuts, advts., unif. dyed cf., gt.-panel. backs., by Root, each vol. with orig. pict. wraps. bnd. in (last vol. orig. gt.-pict. cl.); armorial bkplts. of Herbert Rivington Pyne. (SG. Apr.19; 292) $130
- **– Anr. Edn.** L., [1872-91]. 7 vols. Sq. 8vo. Qtr. cf., rubbed. (SG. Mar.15; 123) $200
- **The Headlong Career & Woful Ending of Precocious Piggy.** L., 1864. 4to. Pict. bds., cl. spine, worn; added verses, extra-ill. with pen-&-ink drawings on blank versos. (RO. Mar.21; 55) $100

HOOFT, Peter Cornelis
- **Nederlandsche Historien, Seedert de Oover-dragt der Heerschappye van Karel V op Philips zynen Zoon.** Ill.:– Th. Matham after J. Sandrart (title). Amst., 1642. *1st. Edn.* Fo. Some minor margin stains, cont. blind-stpd. vell. over wood bds., spine reprd., clasps. (VS. Dec.9; 1205) Fls. 600
- **Nederlandsche Historien. Met het Vervolgh (1555-1587).** Ill.:– C. Decker. Amst., 1677. *3rd. Printing.* Fo. Lacks 1 port., foxing, cont. blind-stpd. vell. (VS. Dec.9; 1206) Fls. 525
- **– Anr. Copy.** Fo. 1 or 2 minor repairs, upr. fly-lf. a little wormed, cont. vell., rebkd., six ties. (CH. May 24; 17) Fls. 500

HOOGEWERFF, Godefridus Joannes
- **De Noord-Nederlandsche Schilderkunst.** The Hague, 1936. 5 vols. Orig. cl. (BBA. Sep.8; 145) *Zwemmer.* £140
- **– Anr. Edn.** s'Gravenhage, 1936-47. 5 vols. Orig. cl., Vol. 3 stained. (BBA. Apr.5; 49) *Zwemmer.* £150
See— **BYVANCK, Alexandre William & Hoogewerff, Godefridus Joannes**

HOOGHE, Romein de
- **Aesopus in Europe.** Den Haag, 1737-38. *2nd. Printing.* 40 pts. in 1 vol. 4to. Some slight spotting or staining, cont. wraps., very worn, unc. (H. May 22; 751) DM 440
- **Hieroglyphica of Merkbeelden** ... Ed.:– A.H. Westerhovius. Amst., 1735. 4to. Engraved port., dedication, title vig., etched port., additional engraved title, emblematic frontis., 62 emblematic plts., 19th. C. hf. cf. (C. Nov.9; 87) *Snelling.* £360
- **Première Partie-Troisième Partie des Guerres des Flandres.** N.p., ca. 1680? 3 pts. in 1 vol. Fo. 3 engraved titles, 5 full-p. ports., 22 double-p. cop-perplts., old vell.-bkd. marb. bds. (SG. Feb.9; 370) $550

HOOGSTRAETEN, Samuel van
- **Inleyding tot de Hooge Schoole der Schilderkonst anders de Zichtbaere Werelt.** Rotterdam, 1678. 4to. Additional engraved title, engraved port., 16 engraved plts., including 2 folding, old MS. plt.-list at end of preface, cont. velli., soiled, loose. (SG. Oct.13; 198) $275

HOOKE, Robert
- **Lectures De Potentia Restitutiva, or of Spring Explaining the Power of Springing Bodies** ... L., 1678. *1st. Edn.* Sm. 4to. Lacks 1st. blank, title-p. soiled, some light browning & staining, outer margins of 2 plts. cropped with loss of engraved fig. 1, mod. cf.; Stanitz coll. [Wing H2619] (SPB. Apr.25; 226) $1,300
- **Micrographia: or some Physiological Descriptions of Minute Bodies made by Magnifying Glasses** ... L., 1665. *1st. Edn.* Fo. Unpressed copy, title with engraved arms, 38 plts., including 17 folding & 4 double-p., imprimatur lf., several plts. slightly trimmed or with sm. tears or repairs, cont. cf., rebkd., worn. [Wing H 2620] (S. Nov.28; 119) *Danckers.* £3,300

HOOKER, Sir Joseph Dalton
- **The Flora of British India.** L., 1875-97. 7 vols. Orig. cl. gt., slightly worn; Royal Commonwealth Soc. copy. (P. Nov.24; 284) *Wheldon & Wesley.* £60
- **The Rhododendrons of Sikkim-Himalaya.** Ed.:– Sir W.J. Hooker. Ill.:– W.H. Fitch after Hooker. L., 1849-51. *1st. Edn.* 3 pts. in 1 vol. Fo. Vig. title, 30 hand-cold. litho. plts., slight soiling, mor.-bkd. cl.; Plesch bkplt. (S. Nov.28; 40) *Heuer.* £1,800

HOOKER, Richard
- **Works.** Ed.:– J. Keble. Oxford, 1845. *3rd. Edn.* 3 vols. Cont. mor., gt. floral borders enclosing lge. circular devices, spines gt., fore-e. pntg. in each vol.; school pres. inscr. dtd. 1847. (SG. Nov.17; 229) $600

HOOKER, Sir William Jackson
- **A Century of Ferns** ... Ill.:– W.H. Fitch. L., 1854. 98 hand-cold. litho. plts., numbered to 100 (2 double-p. plts. with double numeration), cont. hf. mor., spine & corners rubbed. (C. Mar.14; 175) *Wheldon & Wesley.* £110
- **Exotic Flora.** Edinb., 1823-27. 3 vols. 233 hand-cold. plts., some spotting, liby. stp. on title, cl., rubbed, split, loose. (P. Nov.24; 249) *Walford.* £780
- **Journal of a Tour in Iceland.** Yarmouth, 'not publd.', 1811. *1st. Edn.* Frontis. hand-cold., cont. hf. cf., rubbed, spine worn. (S. Jun.25; 166) *Hannas.* £140
- **Musci Exotici; containing, Figures & Descriptions of New or Little Known Foreign Mosses & other Cryptogamic Subjects.** L., 1818-20. *1st. Edn.* 2 vols. Lge. 8vo. 176 engraved plts., some foxing on fore-edges of a few plts., liby. stps., buckram. (SG. Mar.22; 160) $200
- **Pomona Londinensis.** L., priv. ptd., 1818. Vol. 1

HOOKER, Sir William Jackson -Contd.

(all publd.). 4to. 49 aquatint & stipple-engraved hand-cold. plts., hf. cf. by W. Francis, Jnr. of Ludlow, spine gt. in compartments. (C. Mar.14; 173)   Jones. £4,800
– – Anr. Copy. Vol. 1 (all publd.). 4to. 49 hand-cold. plts., a few lightly soiled, title soiled, hf. mor. gt. (P. Nov.24; 250)   £1,950
– – Anr. Copy. Vol. 1 (all publd.). 4to. 28 (of 49) aquatint & stipple-engraved hand-cold. plts., orig. ptd. wrap. to pt. 2 bnd. in as title, cl., w.a.f. (C. Mar.14; 174)   Jones. £1,700

HOOPER, John, Bp.

– A Declaratyon of the Ten Holy Commaunde-mentes. 1540. Sm. 8vo. Cont. owners inscr. on title-p., some light staining at end, later red mor. gt., slightly rubbed. [STC 13747] (BBA. Jun.14; 19)
Duffield. £250

HOOPER, William, M.D.

– Rational Recreations ... L., 1774 [frontis. dtd. 1815]. 1st. Edn. 4 vols. 12mo. 65 folding engraved plts., Vol. 1 with a few MS. ink corrections & slight margin worming in 1st. few ll., Vol. 2 with tear in fold of plt. 3 & sm. portion lacking from margin of plt. 18, slightly spotted or browned in parts, cont. mott. cf., rubbed; J.R. Culson bkplt. (S. Dec.20; 674)   Lotman. £250
– – Anr. Edn. 1783-82. 2nd. Edn. 4 vols. 65 folding engraved plts., slight spotting & offsetting, cont. cf., spines rubbed; Kenney copy. (S. Nov.1; 276)
Hackhofer. £150

HOOYER, G.B.

– De Krijgsgeschedenis v. Nederl.-Indie. 1811-94. 's-Gravenhage/Batavia, 1895-87. 4 vols., including atlas. Lge. 8vo. 64 maps, most folding, loose in portfo. as iss., orig. bds., loose. . (VG. Nov.29; 143)
Fls. 550

HOPE, Anthony (Pseud.)

See— HAWKINS, Sir Anthony Hope 'Anthony Hope'

HOPE, G.W.

– Copies or Extracts of any Correspondence relative to the Establishment of a Settlement at Port Essington. Map:– J. Arrowsmith. 1843. Fo. Folding litho. map partly hand-cold., disbnd. (BBA. Jan.19; 76)   McCormick. £240

HOPE, W.H. St. John

– Windsor Castle, An Architectural History. 1913. (1050) numbered. 3 vols., including vol. of plans. Fo. Orig. vell. gt., slightly soiled. (P. Jun.7; 90)
£95

HOPE, Sir William, of Balcomie

– A New, Short & Easy Method of Fencing. Edinb., 1707. 1st. Edn. 4to. Cont. cf., stain on upr. cover. (C. Nov.9; 143)   Brooke-Hitching. £380

HOPF, K.

– Historisch-genealogischer Atlas. Abtheilung l. Deutschland. Gotha, 1858[-66]. Vols. 1 & 2 pts. 1-4 in 2 vols. (all publd.). Fo. Orig. leath. gt., bumped, Vol. 2 cont. linen. (R. Oct.11; 1056)   DM 630

HOPKINS, Albert A.

– Magic: Stage Illusions & Scientific Diversions. L., 1897. 1st. Edn. Orig. buckram, soiled & slightly worn. (S. Dec.20; 675)   Dawson. £60

HOPKINS, Charles

– Pyrrhus King of Epirus. A Tragedy. 1695. 1st. Edn. 4to. Hf.-title & Epilogue ll., mod. hf. cf. [Wing H2726] (BBA. Jan.19; 143)   O'Neil. £80

HOPKINS, Edward I. & Rimbault, E.F.

– The Organ, its History & Construction ... by Hopkins ... Preceded by ... New History of the Organ ... by ... Rimbault. 1855. Cleanly torn, some light spotting, cont. hf. cf., rubbed. (CSK. Mar.9; 145)   £55

HOPKINS, Gerard Manley

– Poems. Ed.:– Robert Bridges. L., [1918]. 1st. Edn. Orig. cl.-bkd. bds.; Frederic Dannay copy. (CNY. Dec.16; 173) $260

HOPPE, E.O.

– Studies from the Russian Ballet. L., [1911]. Fo. Gt.-lettered cl., rubbed. (SG. May 10; 67) $275
– – Anr. Copy. Fo. Plt. mounts slightly soiled, loose as iss. in gt.-lettered bd. portfo., lacks spine, heavily chipped; inscr. on 1 photo 'To my dear pupil Eleanor Block ... from Adolph Bolm'. (SG. May 10; 66)
$175

HOPPEL, E.G.

– Tomi IV. Erster Theil der Grössten Denkwürdig-keiten der Welt. Hamburg, 1688. Sm. 4to. Cont. leath., rubbed. (GB. Nov.3; 976)   DM 600

HOPTON, Arthur

– A Concordancy of Yeares. Containing a New, Easie, & Most Exact Computation of Time. According to the English Account. 1616. Later cf.; bkplt. of John Hopton of Can-frome. [STC 13780] (BBA. Jun.14; 25)   Sokol. £95

HORAE

[Arranged chronologically irrespective of use]
– Heures à Luisage de Rome. Philippe Pigouchet for Simon Vostre, 22 Aug. 1498. Sm. 4to. On vell., lacks ll. c7 & c8 & last 2 quires, early 16th. C. blind-stpd. vell., shabby, lacks spine. (HD. Mar.21; 39)   Frs. 9,500
– Ces Present Heures à lusaige de Romne sont Toutes au Long sans riens requerir avecques les Quinze Oraisons Saincte Brigide et Plusieurs Autres Oraisons. Paris, 20 Sep. 1517. On vell., privilege, 14 lge. ills., 14 sm. ills. & 9 decor. borders, all illuminated in cols., heightened with gold, initials illuminated thro.-out, title slightly rubbed, slight margin staining & sm. ill. rubbed on 1 lf., slight paper fault or tear reprd. in 1 lf., red mor. gt. by Belz-Niedrée, silver initials 'LH' crowned on upr. cover, silver fleur-de-lys cornerpieces, silk liners, lacks clasps. (C. May 30; 31)   Soloman. £1,200
– Heures à l'Usaige de Romme, Tout au Long, sans rien requerir. Paris, ca. 1520? [Calendar dtd. 1509-24]. 4to. On vell., lacks 15 ll., illuminated floral border at outer edge of each p., 7 full-p. & 26 sm. miniatures richly illuminated with gold & cols., initials & line-endings in gold on red or blue grounds, lge. illuminated cut of anatomical man on verso of A1, wormhole in 4 ll. not affecting text, C2 creased & worn affecting lge. miniature on verso & text on recto, sm. flaw in border of 1 lf., 1st. & last pp. discold. & worn, recased in 17th. C. sheep gt., traces of worm, spine defect. (C. May 30; 32)
King. £850
– Oraria ad Vsum Diocesis Monasteriensis Vltimo iam ad Vnguè castigata ... Ill.:– A. Waensam v. Worms. Köln, 1538. 12mo. 12 month & star ills. at beginning, minimal browning, linen, ca. 1850. (HK. May 15; 209)   DM 700
– Heures à lusage de Sens: au long sans rien requerir. Sens, 1569. 12mo. Short reprd. tear in B7 & 8, early 17th. C. Fr. cf., double gt. fillet border round flat spine & covers, olive wreath at centre of both covers enclosing inscr. 'Claude de la Mare 1622'; from Firmin-Didot & Duc de Parme colls. (S. May 10; 303)   Lyon. £740
– Heures de Senault. Ed.:– L. Senautt. Paris, ca. 1682. Engraved thro.-out, old mor., decor. spine, dentelle, clasps, sm. inner dentelle, watered silk end-papers. (HD. Mar.30; 7)   Frs. 6,500
– Heure[s] de Cour, contenant les Sept Offices de la Semaine, les Sept Pseaumes, Vespres Hymn et les Litan ... Paris, 1684. Miniature Book. 47 x 30mm. Title-p. & anr. lf. reinserted, outer margin of title-p. & a few other ll. worn with slight loss of text, orig. mor., slightly rubbed, limp mor. wrap. with fastening. (S. Nov.22; 428)   Bimmey. £350
– Heures Royales et Prières Chrétiennes contenant les offices, Vespres, Hymnes et Proses de l'Eglise. Ed.:– R.P. Simon Le Bossu. Paris, 1693. 12mo. Ruled, text heightened with gold & silver, cont. galuchat, silver nail border, lge. centre monog. of sm. silver nails, silk doubls., soiled. (HD. Jan.30; 85)   Frs. 1,700
– Heures imprimées par l'Ordre de Mgr. le Cardinal de Noailles, Archevesque de Paris. Paris, 1703[?]. Ruled, 1 lf. torn with slight loss, cont. red mor. gt. dentelle, gt. centre arms, gt. motif decor. spines, inner dentelle. (HD. Jan.30; 87)   Frs. 1,100

– Heures Royales. Paris, [1818]. 16mo. Cont. str.-grd. mor. gt., Talleyrand arms, spine decor.; from A. de Caillavet liby. (HD. May 4; 297) Frs. 9,000
– Livre d'Heures de la Reine Anne de Bretagne. [Paris, 1861]. Chromolitho. reproduction of orig. MS., publisher's red mor., decor. spine, Bictagne crowned cypher & arms, gt. clasps, inner dentelle, watered silk end-papers, box. (HD. Feb.17; 15)
Frs. 3,250
– Nouvelles Heures et Prières Composées dans le Style des Manuscripts du XIV au XVI Siècle. Paris, ca. 1870. Mor. by Blanchard of Orléan, sigd. with his ticket, silver monog. on upr. cover, silk end-sheets. (PNY. Jun.6; 466) $200
– Heures du Moyen Age. 1887. 12mo. 17th. C. style mor. gt. by Gruel, sewed silk doubls., clasps. (HD. Jun.29; 171)   Frs. 5,600

HORAE B.V.M.

[Arranged chronologically irrespective of use]
– Hore Beate Marie Virginis secundum Usum Romane Curie. Paris, Anthoine Verard, 20 Aug. 1490. On vell., 13 lge. & 36 sm. miniatures, all richly illuminated with gold & cols., initials & line-endings in gold on red or blue grounds, lge. illuminated printer's device on verso of last lf., romantic cf., blind-decor., crowned cypher of Marie Amélie, Queen of France (1830-48) on upr. cover, arms of France on lr. cover, vell. paste-downs & end-ll., chemise & s.-c.; Lucien-Graux bkplt. (C. May 30; 29)   Stein. £8,000
– Hore Intemerate Virginis Marie secundum Usum Romanum. Paris, 18 Sept. 1506. On paper, initials supplied in red & blue, upr. borders of a few ll. shaved, 19th. C. blind-stpd. cf. by Dauphin; inscr. at head of 1st. lf. 'A l'usage du Convent de St. André de Lisn' (C. May 30; 30)   Lyon. £2,800
– Diurnale Monasticum Secundum Rubricam Romanam & secundum Ratum & Consuetudinem Monasterii B.M.V., alias Scotorum Vien[en]se Ordinis S. Benedicti. Venice, 13. VII. 1515. 3 ll. with prayers in cont. MS. at end, some old annots., minimal soiling, vell. with old MS. ca. 1500. (HK. Nov.8; 162)   DM 650
– Cursus B.M.V. ad Usum Romanum. Paris, 3. XII. 1516. Lightly browned, slightly soiled, sm. margin defects, old MS. annots. & deletions, early 19th. C. leath., spine wormed. (HK. Nov.8; 157)
DM 1,350
– Hore Dive Virginis Marie secu[n]dum Usu[m] Romanum. Paris, [1526]. On vell., calendar for 1526-41, incompl., lacks 17 ll. Most sm. woodcuts old cold., or cold in, title lf. very spotted, col. rubbed from printers mark, end-lf. spotted, 2 ll. slightly cut in side margin, some ll. slightly cut in upr. margin (gold border only), other slight spotting, old vell., ties. (R. Apr.3; 49)   DM 1,450
– Rosario della Gloriosa Vergine Maria. [Venice, 1575]. Some sm. wormholes in 1st. ll., 19th. C. red chagrin, blind decor., inner dentelle. (HD. Jan.30; 12)   Frs. 1,600

HORAPOLLO

– De Sacris Aegyptiorum Notis. Paris, 1574. 1st. Edn. 2 woodcuts inverted, lacks 4 ll., slightly stained at beginning, title border slightly cut at outer right side, 18th. C. cf. gt., corners bumped, spine slightly wormed. (D. Nov.23; 107)   DM 1,500

HORATIUS FLACCUS, Quintus

– Art of Poetry. Trans.:– Ben Jonson. L., 1640. 1st. Edn. 2nd. Iss. 12mo. Engraved frontis., imprimatur lf., lacks blanks at front & back & following p.40, collation A11, B12 ,C11, D5, E4, e12, F12, G11, some soiling & fraying of edges, mor. by Riviere, bkplts. of Charles L. Dana, William Stone. [STC 13798] (SPB. May 16; 90) $125
– Commentariis & Enarrationibus Commentatoris Veteris, et Jacobi Cruquii Messenii ... Accedunt, Jani Dousae Nordovicis. 1611. 4to. Slightly browned, old vell., gt. armorial on both covers, spine worn; ex-libris George Augustus Sala, with bkplt. & MS. notes on fly-lf. (TA. Oct.20; 470)   £50
– Odes & Epodes. Boston, Bibliophile Soc., 1901[-03]. (467). 7 vols. in 9. Engraved frontis. in 2 states, before & after sigs., red mor., elab. gt. onlaid decor., gt. spines in 5 compartments, mor. doubls. with onlaid Art Nouveau border of mor. gt., watered silk free end-pp., silk markers, partly unc. (CNY. Dec.17; 571) $800

- **Opera.** Ed.:– Jacob Locher. Strassburg. Johannes [Reinhard] Gruninger, 12 Mar. 1498. Fo. Lacks fo. 214 blank, spaces left for capitals, some early interlinear & other MS. notes in margins, worming in a few extreme inner blank corners, very short tear in margin of FF 4-5, sm. hole in upr. margin of FF6-GG2 just affecting head-lines, some sm. wormholes, cont. (?) Nuremb. bdg. of blind-stpd. pig over oak bds., decor. panels stpd. orig. spine, 1 clasp defect., 1 clasp torn; from Abbey at Ottobeuren. [BMC I, 112; Goff H461; H. 8898] (S. May 10; 305) *Rosenthal.* £4,800

– **– Anr. Copy.** Fo. 213 ll. (of 220, lacks blanks & 6 minor ll.), capital spaces with guide letters, some wormholes thro.-out filled in, title margin reprd., blind-stpd. vell., some worming & wear. (SPB. May 17; 628) $950

– **[–] Anr. Edn.** Venice, Aldus, 1501. *1st. Aldine Edn.* With final blank, title-p. soiled, lr. margins cropped affecting sigs. & catchwords & a few bottom lines of text, 19th. C. red mor. gt., spine worn, jnts. brkn.; Lord Hill & John Scott, of Halkshill bkplts. (SPB. Dec.14; 21) $500

– **– Anr. Edn.** Ed.:– Richard Bentley. Camb., 1711. *1st. Edn.* Lge. 4to. Hf.-titles, cont. name on title-p., mod. niger three-qtr. lev. by Cambridge Binding Guild. (SG. Feb.9; 249) $250

– **– Anr. Edn.** L., 1733-37. *Pine's 1st. Edn. 1st. Iss., with 'Post Est' on p.108 in Vol.2.* 2 vols. Some spotting, cont. red str.-grd. mor., decor. in gt. & blind. (BBA. Jul.27; 116) *Quaritch.* £200

– **– Anr. Copy.** 2 vols. Cf. gt., rebkd. (P. May 17; 176) *Serefino.* £80

– **– Anr. Copy.** 2 vols. Lge. 8vo. Early 19th. C. vell. gt. extra, cf. lettering-pieces. (SG. Nov.3; 102) $375

– **– Anr. Iss.** L. 1733-37. Pine's 1st. Edn. 2nd. Iss., with 'potest' on p. 108 in Vol.2. 2 vols. Cont sheep, elab. gt.-tooled, rubbed, fore-e. pntg. in each vol. (BBA. Feb.9; 34) *Quevedo.* £320

– **– Anr. Copy.** 2 vols. 2nd. State, with reading 'potest' on p.108 in Vol.2, 6 ll. sprung in Vol.2, 18th. C. Irish red mor. gt., smooth spines, a Trinity College, Dublin prize bdg. with gt. stps. on covers, the blind-stps. of the recipient, Thos. Burgh. on upr. covers & prize bkplts.; Apley Library bkplts. Thomas B. Stevenson copy. (CNY. Dec.17; 570) $280

– **– Anr. Edn.** Ed.:– John Prior. L., 1733-37. Wide margin, Dutch paper, 18th. C. dentelle style mor., gt. spine with monog. & crown, gt. borders & centrepieces, arms & crown on covers, gt. inner & outer dentelle; Hauswedell coll. (H. May 24; 1500) DM 2,000

– **– Anr. Edn.** Parma, Bodoni Pr., 1793. Later mott. cf., spine gt.; Harvard College Liby. plt. & stps. (CBA. Dec.10; 71) $140

– **– Anr. Edn.** Trans.:– F.W. Cornish. Ill.:– Alma Tadema. L., 1888. 16mo. Crushed lev. gt. by Zaehnsdorf, spine & inner dentelles gt., satin endll., partly unc., unopened. (SG. Feb.16; 161) $175

– **Opera cum Novo Commentario ad Modum Joannis Bond.** Preface:– Ambr. Firmin Didot. Ill.:– after Barrais, Benouville, & Rosa. Paris, 1855. *De Luxe Edn.* Cont. Renaissance style mor. gt. (GB. Nov.4; 1796) DM 700

– **Poemata.** Amst., 1676. 12mo. Red str.-grd. mor. gt. extra by Bozérian le Jeune, rubbed. (SG. Oct.27; 90) $250

– **Poems of Horace, Consisting of Odes, Satyrs & Epistles.** Trans.:– Alexander Brome & others. L., 1666. *1st. Edn.* Ports., imprimatur lf., lacks a8 (?blank), sig. on title. cont. mott. cf., gt. lozenge on covers, rebkd; pres. copy from trans., bkplts. of Charles B. Foote, Edwin Holden & William S. Stone. [Wing H 2781] (SPB. May 16; 17) $550

– **Quinti Horatii Flacci Carmina. — Odes d'Horace.** Trans.:– Delort. Ill.:– A. Maillol. Paris, 1939 [-58]. *(300) numbered on Chanvre et Lin H.M.P.* Together 2 vols. Printer's mark numbered & monogrammed, 121 orig. woodcuts, loose ll. in orig. pict. wraps. (GB. Nov.5; 2758) DM 1,600

– **[Works].** Trans.:– P. Francis. 1827. 12mo. Cont. mor. gt., fore-e. pntg. (P. Sep.8; 142) £110

HORBLIT, Harrison D.
- **One Hundred Books Famous in Science.** N.Y., Grol. Cl., 1964. *(1000).* Tall 4to. Two-tone cl. gt., boxed. (SG. Sep.15; 174) $350

– **Anr. Copy.** 4to. Prospectus laid in, cl., s.-c. (SG. Jan.5; 151) $250

– **– Anr. Copy.** 4to. Facs. ills., cl., s.-c. (SG. May 17; 127) $225

– **– Anr. Copy.** 4to. Facs. ills., cl., s.-c. (SG. May 17; 110) $200

– **– Anr. Copy.** Orig. linen; Hauswedell coll. (H. May 23; 472) DM 820

HOREN
Ed.:– Schiller. Mus. supp.:– J.F. Reichardt. 1795-97. *1st. Edn.* 36 pts. in 6 vols. (all publd.). Some light browning & foxing, vol. 1 cockled thro.-out, 8 pp. cut in margin, later hf. leath., spine faded. (GB. May 4; 1447) DM 2,700

HORGAN, Paul
- **Great River. The Rio Grande in American History.** N.Y., 1954. *(1000) sigd.* 2 vols. Buckram, s.-c. (LH. Jan.15; 312) $140

- **The Return of the Weed.** Ill.:– Peter Hurd. N.Y., 1936. *(350) numbered & sigd. by author & artist.* 4to. Cl., spine faded, s.-c. defect. (LH. Jan.15; 313) $160

HORIZON; A Review of Literature & Art
Ed.:– Cyril Connolly. [L.], 1940-43. Nos. 1-23, 25, 27-37. Ptd. wraps., sewed. (SG. May 24; 307) $110

– **– Anr. Run.** Ed.:– Cyril Connolly. L., 1940-50. Nos. 1-121 & Index, in 119 vols. Orig. wraps., lacks 1 spine. (BBA. May 23; 108) *Bloomsbury Rare Bks.* £120

HORN. W. & Schenkling, S.
- **Index Litteraturae Entomologicae.** Berlin, 1928-29. *Ltd. Iss.* Series 1: 4 vols. Orig. wraps., unc. (GB. May 4; 1825) DM 500

– **– Anr. Copy.** 4 vols. Orig. wraps., unc. (GB. Nov.4; 1295) DM 440

HORN, W.O. v. [i.e. W. Oertel]
- **Der Rhein. Geschichte und Sagen Seiner Bürgen, Abteien, Klöster und Städte.** Wiesbaden, 1881. *3rd. Edn.* Some margin foxing, ink MS. owners entry on frontis., orig. hf. leath., gt., spine brkn. (R. Oct. 13; 2695) DM 800

HORNBY, Charles Harry St. John
See— ASHENDENE PRESS

HORNE, Rev. Thomas Hartwell
See— FINDEN, William & Edward Francis & Horne, Rev. Thomas Hartwell

HORNEMAN, Frederick
- **The Journal of Frederick Horneman's Travels from Cairo to Mourzouk, the Capital of the Kingdom of Fezzan, in Africa, in the Years 1797-98.** 1802. 4to. Cont. cf., some wear. (TA. Nov. 17; 19) £60

HORNOR, William Macpherson
- **Blue Book Philadelphia Furniture.** Phila., 1935. *(400) numbered & sigd. by author.* 4to. Cl., unc., s.-c. (scuffed), worn. (RO. Mar.28; 94) $265

HORNUNG, E.W.
- **The Boss of Taroomba.** L., 1894. *1st. Edn.* Orig. cl., spine soiled; pres. inscr. from author's brother-in-law. (BBA. May 23; 181) *Preston.* £190

HORODISCH, A.
- **Alfred Kubin als Buchillustrator.** Amst., 1949. *(100) De Luxe Edn. with 3 unpublished etchings sigd. by Kubin.* 4to. Printers mark sigd. by author, hf. leath. (H. May 23; 1345) DM 560

- **Alfred Kubin Book Illustrator.** Ill.:– A. Kubin. N.Y., 1950. *(50) De Luxe Edn. with 3 supp. plts. sigd. by artist.* 4to. Orig. hf. vell., s.-c. (HK. May 17; 2931) DM 550

HORREBOW, Niels
- **The Natural History of Iceland** ... L., 1758. Fo. Cont. cf. (C. Nov.16; 16) *Foyle.* £280

– **– Anr. Copy.** Fo. Some discolouration to text, cont. russ., rebkd. (S. May 22; 454) *Tonge.* £150

HORSBRUGH, Maj. Boyd
- **The Game-Birds & Water-Fowl of South Africa.** Ill.:– C.G. Davies. 1912. 67 col. plts., some spotting, hf. mor., rubbed. (P. Jul.5; 159) £280

HORSEY, J.G.
- **A Voyage from Australia to England** ... L., 1867. Soiled & foxed, old hf. roan. (KH. Nov.8; 215) *Aus.* $100

HORSFIELD, Thomas Walker
- **The History, Antiquities & Topography of the County of Sussex.** Lewes, 1835. 2 vols. 4to. Plt. list in Vol. 2 loose, some light stains or discoloration, cont. hf. cf.; ticket on upr. pastedown 'Subscriber's copy'. (S. Mar.6; 259) *Sanders.* £100

– **– Anr. Copy.** 2 vols. 4to. Port., 2 hand-cold. maps, 54 engraved plts., 1 torn & reprd. in margins, 1 map torn & reprd., cf. gt., 1 cover detchd. (P. Oct.20; 230g) £65

HORSLEY, John
- **Britannia Romana: or the Roman Antiquities of Britain.** 1732. Fo. Cont. cf., lightly rubbed. (CSK. Jul.6; 51) £170

HORSMANDEN, Daniel
- **The New York Conspiracy** ... N.Y., 1810. *2nd. Edn.* Cont. owners sig. on title lf., 1 lf. defect., some foxing, 5 p. list of committals at end, cont. qtr. sheep, chafed, worn. lacks front free end-papers. (SG. Apr.5; 134) $110

HORST, G.A.
- **Der Starnberger See.** Ill.:– H. Wolf. München, 1876. Lge. 4to. Orig. linen, gold & black tooled. (HK. Nov.9; 1468) DM 520

HORST, Jakob
- **De Aureo dente Maxillari pueri Silesii** ... Leipzig, 1595. *1st. Edn.* Browned, cont. vell., lacks ties. (S. Nov.28; 122) *Quaritch.* £480

HORST, Tieleman van der
- **Neue Bau-Kunst** ... Nürnberg, 1763. *1st. German Edn.* Fo. Wide margin, copperplts. loose, margins & 8 middle folds slightly browned, text browned, newer hf. linen & hf. linen portfo. (H. May 22; 66) DM 900

- **Theatrum Machinarum Universale; of Keurige Verzameling** ... **Waterwerken, Schutsluizen, Waterkeringen, Ophaal en Draaibrugen.** Amst., 1736. *1st. Edn.* Margins dust-soiled, stitched in wraps., unc. & unopened, margins worn, cl. folder & s.-c.; Stanitz coll. (SPB. Apr.25; 228) $425

– **– Anr. Copy.** 2 pts. in 1 vol. Lge. fo. Cont. gt.-panell cf., rebnd. (VG. Sep.14; 1274) Fls. 900

– **– Anr. Edn.** Amst., [1757-74]. *2nd. Edn.* 2 vols. in 1. Lge. fo. Text ll. guarded, cont. bds., later cf. back & corners, scuffed; Stanitz coll. (SPB. Apr.25; 229) $1,100

- **Theatrum Machinarum Universale; of Nieuwe Algemeene Bouwkunde** ... Ill.:– J. Schenk after Horst. Amst., 1739. Fo. Bnd. (B. Oct.4; 693) Fls. 550

HORT, W. Jillard
- **The New Pantheon; or. An Introduction to the Mythology of the Ancients.** L., 1839. *New Edn.* Lge. 16mo. Orig. gt. mor., worn; from liby. of F.D. Roosevelt, inscr. by him (as President). (SG. Mar.15; 53) $175

HORTENSIA, Queen Consort of Louis, King of Holland
- **Mémoires sur Mme la Duchesse de St.-Leu, ex-Reine de Hollande.** L., 1832. Sm. ob. fo. Orig. glazed bds., slightly worn. (VG. Sep.14; 791) Fls. 550

HORTENSIUS, Lambertus
- **Secessionum Ciuilium ultra Jectinarum, et Bellorum.** Basel, 1546. *1st. Edn.* Wide margin, MS. owners mark on title, lr. margin title & end-paper soiled, erased stp. on title-lf. & verso of preceding lf. *(Bound with:)* HELIODORUS – Aethiopicae Historiae Libri Decem. Basel, 1552. *1st. Latin Edn.* Together 2 works in 1 vol. Fo. Cont. limp vell., soiled, lacks clasps. (D. Nov.23; 122) DM 720

- **Tumultum Anabaptistarum Liber Unus.** Basel, 1548. 4to. Wide margin, MS. entry on title, some sm. wormholes, cont. limp vell., slightly spotted & cockled. (HT. May 8; 146) DM 960

HORTICULTURAL SOCIETY OF LONDON
- **Transactions.** Ill.:– after William Hooker & others. L., 1820-26. 1st. Series: Vols. 1-6 only of 7). 4to. Engraved titles, approx. 116 plts., including 60 cold. plts. of fruit & flowers, some col.-ptd., all

HORTICULTURAL SOCIETY OF LONDON - Contd.
hand-finished, some folding, a few plts. just shaved, cont. hf. mor., spines faded, as a periodical, w.a.f. (C. Mar.14; 124) *Campbell.* £2,400
-- **Anr. Run.** Ill.:– William Hooker & others. 1822-30. 1st. Series: Vols. 4-7. 4to. Engraved titles, 36 col. plts., some folding, 32 uncold. engraved plts., spotting to titles & some plts., cont. hf. leath., spines gt., rubbed. (LC. Jul.5; 430) £540
-- **Anr. Run.** 1835-42. 2nd. Series: Vols. 1-3 in 2. 4to. Part of Vol. 7 from 1st. Series bnd. at end, panel. hf. cf., rubbed. (PD. May 16; 258) £310

HORTULUS ANIMAE
Antw., 1564. Lacks 8 unnumbered ll. at beginning & 1 numbered lf., title & last 2 ll. with bkd. margin defects., some light browning. 18th. C. leath., lr. cover wormed. (HK. Nov.8; 226) DM 440
-- **Anr. Edn.** Trans.:– H.D. van den Houte. Antw., 1590. Slightly browned, cont. blind-stpd. & panel. cf. over wood, few repairs, clasps & catches preserved. (VG. Nov.30; 957) Fls. 1,300

HORTUS SANITATIS DE HERBIS ET PLANTIS
[Strassburg, Johannes Pruess], not after 21 Oct. 1497. 3 pts. Fo. Lacks Iil in pt. 1 & A1 & I7-8 in pt. 2, title, prologue & next 2 ll. torn & reprd. with some loss of text, B1, C6 & O2 torn & defect., 3 other ll. with sm. tears, a few sm. margin dampstains, recent Spanish cf., blind-stpd. panels on covers, gt., s.-c., w.a.f. [Goff H-487] (C. Mar.14; 176) *Harcourt-Williams.* £2,200

HORWOOD, Richard
- **Plan of the Cities of London & Westminster, the Borough of Southwark, & parts adjoining.** L., 1792-99. Fo. Town plan in 32 engraved mapsheets, joined as 16, parish boundaries hand-cold. in outl., some slight soiling or margin fraying touching engraved surface of 1 or 2 plts., cont. bds., defect. (S. Dec.13; 192) *Johns.* £340
-- **Anr. Edn.** 1799. Fo. 16 double-p. partly cold. town plans, including title, also Bowle's 1 sheet plan of London bnd. in, hf. cf., defect. (P. Sep.29; 437) *Burgess.* £250

HOSIUS, Stanislaus
- **Confession.** Trans.:– Johann zu Wege. Ingolstadt, 1560. Fo. Title lf. with sm. excision, old MS. owners mark on verso, some slight foxing, lr. cover slightly rubbed, cont. blind-tooled pig over wood bds., decor., 2 brass clasps. (D. Nov.23; 123) DM 800

HOSKINS, George Alexander
- **Travels in Ethiopia.** 1835. 4to. 53 litho. plts. (2 hand-cold.), 1 folding map, some light soiling, orig. cl., spine reprd. (CSK. Jul.6; 35) £350

HOSTE, Paul
- **L'Art des Armées Navales ... Théorie de la Construction des Vaisseaux.** Lyons, 1697. 1st. Edn. 2 pts. in 1 vol. Fo. 145 engraved plts., including 11 folding, hf.-title, slight discoloration, cont. cf., worn, portion of spine loose. (S. Dec.1; 381) *Brooke-Hitching.* £500
-- **Anr. Copy.** 2 pts. in 1 vol. Fo. 145 plts., vell. (HD. Mar.9; 86) Frs. 9,000
-- **Anr. Copy.** 2 pts. in 1 vol. Fo. Dampstains, cont. cf. gt., spine decor., some repairs. (HD. Jul.2; 18) Frs. 5,600
-- **Anr. Copy.** Fo. Slightly browned, some staining, 2 plts. with sm. margin tear, title with corner tear, cont. leath. gt., wear. (HT. May 10; 2628a) DM 2,050
- **Naval Evolutions; or a System of Sea-Discipline.** Trans.:– Christopher O'Bryen. 1762. 4to. 18 folding engraved plts., folding tables at end, a few sm. tears at folds, later hf. leath. (SKC. Jan.13; 2362) £210
- **A Treatise on Naval Tactics.** Trans.:– Capt. J.D. Boswall. Edinb., 1834. 4to. Engraved title-p., 52 engraved plts., hf.-title, mod. cl. (SKC. Jan.13; 2359) £65

HOTMAN, Jean, Seigner de Villiers
- **L'Ambassadeur.** 1603. Sm. 4to. 9 ll. errata on verso of last lf., vell. (P. Jan.12; 238) *Georges.* £130

HOTTENROTH, F.
- **Deutsche Volkstrachten.** Frankfurt, 1898-1902. 3 vols. Orig. pict. linen. (R. Apr.4; 2202) DM 2,500

HOTTENROTH, Johann Edmund
- **Geschichte der Sächsischen Fahnen und Standarten.** Dresden, 1910. Hf. bdg., corners. (HD. Jan.27; 241) Frs. 1,300

HOUBRAKEN, Arnold
- **De Groote Schouburgh der Nederl. Konstschilders.** 's-Gravenhaage, 1753. 3 vols. Frontis. & 47 ports., cont. cf., slightly defect., covers loose, stains. (VG. May 3; 481) Fls. 480

[HOUCKGEEST], Andre Everard van Braam
- **An Authentic Account of the Embassy of the Dutch East-India Company to the Emperor of China.** L., 1798. 2 vols. Last advt. lf. in Vol. 2, a few ll. spotted, cont. hf. cf., slightly rubbed; bkplt. of John Selwyn. (BBA. Dec.15; 18) *Edwards.* £140

HOUDIN, Robert
- **Les Tricheries des Grecs Dévoilées; l'Art de Gagner à tous les Jeux.** Paris, 1861. Orig. Edn. Light foxing, sewed. (HD. Feb.28; 45) Frs. 2,200

HOUDINI, Harry (Pseud.)
See– WEISS, Erich 'Harry Houdini'

HOUEL, Jean Pierre Louis Laurent
- **Histoire Naturelle des Deux Eléphants Mâle et Femelle, du Musée de Paris venus de Hollande en France en l'An VI.** Paris, An XII [1803]. *1st. Printing of ills.* Sm. fo. Minimal foxing, old hf. russ., spine decor. (HD. May 4; 298) Frs. 4,000

HOUGH, Romeyn B.
- **American Woods.** Lowville, 1888. Pts. I & II. Accompanying text pamphlet in Pt. I, ex-liby., loose in cl. portfos., as iss., s.-c. (RO. Nov.30; 95) $105
-- **Anr. Edn.** Lowville, N.Y., 1888-1928. Vol. of text & 13 (of 14) portfos. Each portfo. with approx. 75 specimens of the orig. wood, in orig. cl. cases with metal clasp, text bnd. in 1 cl. vol., orig. covers bnd. in, w.a.f. (C. Nov.16; 257) *Quaritch.* £500

HOUGHTON, Rev. William
- **British Fresh-Water Fishes.** Ill.:– A.F. Lydon. L., 1879. 1st. Edn. Fo. Frontis., 40 chromolithos., cont. hf. mor., slightly rubbed. (SKC. Jan.13; 2322) £280
-- **Anr. Copy.** Fo. 41 full-p. cold. litho. plts., 1 loose, roan-bkd. cl. (SKC. Jan.13; 2321) £240
-- **Anr. Edn.** L., [1879]. *[1st. Edn.].* Fo. 41 cold. plts., ills., text spotted, few ll. loose & frayed, mor.-bkd. cl., worn, covers detchd., lacks spine. (S. Apr.10; 518) *Perham.* £400
-- **Anr. Copy.** Fo. 40 (of 41) cold. plts., some dampstained in margin, hf. cf., worn, reprd. (S. Dec.13; 277) *Schuster.* £180
-- **Anr. Copy.** 2 vols. Fo. Some text foxing, orig. linen, slightly bumped. (R. Oct.12; 1837) DM 1,300
-- **Anr. Copy.** 2 vols. Fo. Slightly foxed, orig. linen, slightly bumped. (R. Apr.4; 1710) DM 1,100
-- **Anr. Edn.** Ill.:– A.F. Lydon. N.d. 2 vols. Fo. 41 plts. ptd. in cols. from woodblocks, 2 with blank margins dampstained, orig. cl., soiled. (CSK. Feb.10; 197) £320
-- **Anr. Copy.** Fo. 41 col. plts., a few ll. slightly spotted, hf. mor. gt. by Bayntun-Rivière. (LC. Mar.1; 161) £280
-- **Anr. Copy.** Fo. 31 plts. only, margins of few plts. tattered, some ll. detchd., orig. mor.-bkd. cl., spine worn, ex-liby., w.a.f. (CSK. Jan.13; 102) £150
-- **Anr. Copy.** Vol. 2 only. Fo. 21 cold. litho. plts., gt.-decor. cl. (SKC. May 4; 1853) £130

HOUSE, Homer D.
- **Wild Flowers of New York.** Albany, 1923. 2nd. Printing. 2 vols. Lge. tall 4to. 264 col. photographic plts., some light foxing, orig. cl. (SG. Oct.6; 378) $150

HOUSE OF COMMONS
- **[Blue Papers:] Irish Education Reports.** 1825. 9 vols. Fo. Wraps., w.a.f. (GM. Oct.5; 337) £130
- **... Copies of all Correspondence ... on the Subject of the Military Operations lately Carried on Against the Aboriginal Inhabitants of Van Diemen's Land.** L., 1831. Sm. fo. Folding Arrowsmith litho. map with some col., bnd. with endorsement lf., later hf. roan. (KH. Nov.9; 729) Aus. $620
- **Report from the Select Committee on the Conduct**
of General Darling while Governor of New South Wales. 1835. Sm. fo. A few rubbed paper defects on title-p., a few ll. at end stained, early hf. roan, rubbed. (KH. May 1; 197) Aus. $350

HOUSMAN, Alfred Edward
- **Introductory Lecture delivered ... in University College, October 3.** Camb., 1892. Outer ll. soiled, stitched as iss. (BBA. Feb.23; 286) *Quaritch.* £380
- **Last Poems.** L., 1928. *Reprint.* Orig. cl., d.-w. torn; pres. copy from author. (S. Mar.20; 925) *Wise.* £50
- **Manili Astronomicon.** L., 1930. *1st. Edn.* Proof copy. Orig. wraps., cl. case; author's own copy, sigd. on upr. wrap. & with pencilled notes & MS. corrections, Perry Molstad copy. (SPB. May 16; 470) $600
- **A Shropshire Lad.** L., 1896. *1st. Edn. (500). (350)* Engl. Iss. 1 vol. Orig. hf. vell., slightly worn & soiled; inscr. from Laurence Houseman to Percy Wallace. (With:) - **The Name & Nature of Poetry.** L., 1933. *1st. Edn.* 1 vol. Bds.; James Stephen's copy, with his pencil notes. (BBA. Dec.15; 227) *Blackwell.* £350
-- **Anr. Copy.** 12mo. Orig. bds., Carter & Sparrow's 'A' label, spine slightly soiled, cl. s.-c.; pres. copy to Mrs. Wise, Perry Molstad copy, 2 T.L.s. from John Carter to Molstad. (SPB. May 16; 462) $8,000
-- **Anr. Copy.** 12mo. Orig. bds., corners bit worn, hf. mor. folding box; laid in is publisher's ptd. pres. slip, Frederic Dannay copy. (CNY. Dec.16; 175) $800
-- **Anr. Copy.** 12mo. Orig. bds., Carter & Sparrow's 'B' label, soiled, mor. solander case; A.L.s. to Edward Hall, Perry Molstad copy. (SPB. May 16; 463) $425
-- **Anr. Copy.** Some browning & soiling, orig. parch.-bkd. bds., cl. folding box; Fred A. Berne copy. (SPB. May 16; 317) $400
-- **Anr. Edn.** N.Y., 1897. *1st. Edn. (500). (150)* Amer. Iss. 12mo. Orig. bds., Carter & Sparrow's 'B' label; sigd. & with A.L.s. to I.R. Brussell, also sigd. carte-de-visite photo of author, Perry Molstad copy. (SPB. May 16; 464) $1,200
-- **Anr. Edn.** L., Riccardi Pr., 1914. *(12) numbered on vell.* 4to. Orig. vell., silk ties, cl. s.-c.; Perry Molstad copy. (SPB. May 16; 466) $750

HOUSMAN, Clemence
- **The Were-Wolf.** Ill.:– Laurence Housman. L., 1896. 1st. Edn. Second bdg., end-papers darkened. (CBA. Oct.29; 420) $120

HOUSSAYE, J.G.
- **Monographie du Thé.** Paris, 1843. Some light staining, orig. cl., lightly scuffed. (CSK. Dec.16; 147) £65

HOUTEN, H. van
- **Vertandelinge van de Grontregeln der Doorzigtkunde, of Tekenkonst [Perspectef].** Amst., 1705. Sm. 4to. Title brown spotted, cont. vell., upr. cover with long defect. (R. Apr.3; 800) DM 720

HOUTTUYN, Martinus
See– NOZEMAN, Cornelius & Houttuyn, Martinus

HOUVET, Etienne
- **Cathédrale de Chartres.** N.p., ca. 1930. 5 vols. in 7. Sm. fo. Photo. plts., each liby.-stpd. on blank verso, loose in ptd. bds., linen ties, not collated, w.a.f. (SG. May 3; 212) $250

HOUVILLE, Gérard d'
- **Le Diadème de Flore.** Ill.:– A. E. Marty, wood engraved by G. Beltrand. Paris, 1928. Orig. Edn. Special ptd. for publisher on japon nacré. (25) numbered. 12mo. Autograph dedication sigd. by publisher, 3 suites of ills. on japan, in cols. on Hollande & on japan, 3 suites of decompositions of cols., 1 unique on Chine, leaves, wrap., pink hf. chagrin s.-c., box. (HD. Mar.14; 127) Frs. 3,850

HOVORKA, O. von & Kronfeld, A.
— **Vergleichende Volksmedizin.** Stuttgart, 1908-09. 4to. Orig. hf. leath., lightly rubbed. (R.Apr.4; 1317) DM 450

HOW THE BOERS MADE WAR, Comprising Battle Scenes, Generals, Transvaal Executive Council, Field Artillery, Commandos, etc.
Cape Town, n.d. Ob. 8vo. In Engl. & Afrikaans, pict. wraps. (VA. Jan.27; 199)   R 240

HOWARD, George Selby
- The New Royal Cyclopaedia, & Encyclopaedia. L., [1788]. 3 vols. Lge. fo. Not collated, cont. mott. cf. (SG. Oct.6; 204) $275

HOWARD, H. Eliot
- The British Warblers. A History with Problems of their Lives. Ill.:– after Henrik Gronvold. Feb. 1907-Jun. 1915. Pts. 1-9 & separately iss. plates for pts. 6 & 9, in 2 vols. Tall 8vo. Slight damage to text in pt. 3, some spotting, orig. ptd. bds., linen backstrips, untrimmed, rubbed, mod. qtr. mor. & marb. bds. boxes. (TA. Feb.16; 97)   £320

HOWARD, John
- An Account of the Principal Lazarettos in Europe. Warrington, 1789. 1st. Edn. 4to. Folding table, 22 plts. & plans, mostly folding, lf. with directions to binder, some plts. stained, lacks hf.-title & 1st. blank lf., cont. cf., rebkd. (S. Mar.6; 88)
                Damakarkos. £200

HOWARD, Leland O. & others
- The Mosquitoes of North and Central America and The West Indies. Wash., 1912-17. 1st. Edn. 4 vols. Sm. 4to. Cl., Vol. I loose, ex-liby. (SG. Mar.22; 166) $130

HOWARD, Robert E.
- Skull-Face & others. Appreciations:– Love-craft & E. Hoffman Price. Sauk City, 1946. 1st. Edn. (3000). Bdg. not stated, faint erasure marks to front fly, d.-w., slightly worn at margins, some light rubbing to cover lr. edge, a corner & spine head lightly bumped. (CBA. Oct.29; 424) $425
- - **Anr. Copy.** Lge. 8vo. Cl., spine ends rubbed, d.-w., with design by Hannes Bok, minor tears. (SG. Jan.12; 161) $225

HOWARD, W.
See— LOWE, Edward Joseph & Howard, W.

HOWARD-BURY, Lieut.-Col. C.K.
- Mount Everest. The Reconnaissance, 1921. L., 1922. (200) numbered on L.P. with extra plts. Fo. Errata slip, orig. parch.-bkd. cl., slightly rubbed. (BBA. May 3; 349) *Cavendish Rare Books.* £290

HOWE, Ellic
- List of London Bookbinders 1648-1815. 1950. Sm. 4to. Notes, letters & typescripts loosely inserted, orig. buckram-bkd. bds.; H.M. Nixon coll., with his MS. notes. (BBA. Oct.6; 219)
                Oak Knoll Books. £95
- The London Bookbinders, 1780-1806. Ill.:– Gwen-dolen Raverat. 1950. (250) numbered. Buckram, d.-w. (HBC. May 17; 157)   £75
- - **Anr. Copy.** Buckram, d.-w. (HBC. May 17; 156)   £65

HOWE, Henry
See— BARBER, John W. & Howe, Henry

HOWE, Visc. William
- The Narrative ... Relative to his Conduct during his Late Command of the King's Troops in North America. 1780. L.P. 4to. Cont. hf. mor., gt.-decor. spine. (TA. Oct.20; 248)   £80
See— BURGOYNE, Lieut.-Gen. John — HOWE, Visc. William — SAYER, Robert & Bennett, John, Publishers

HOWELL, James
- Dendrologia. Dodona's Grove, or the Vocall For-rest. Camb., 1645. 3rd. Edn. 4 pts. in 1 vol. 12mo. Printing flaws on lr. part of frontis. & anr. lf., cont. cf. gt., slightly worn; bkplt. of Richard Hopton of Can-frome. [Wing H3060] (BBA. Jun.14; 47)
                Waterfield. £60
[-] Instructions for Forreine Travell. L., 1642. 12mo. Last lf. stained, old cf. [Wing H3082] (P. Dec.8; 338)   *P. King.* £180
- Londinopolis; an Historicall Discourse or Per-lustration of the City of London. L., 1657. Fo. Acquisition note dtd. 1657 on front free end-paper, printing imperfections on title, a little stained, sm.

wormholes, later cf. [Wing H3091] (BBA. May 3; 137)   *Howes Bookshop.* £200
- - **Anr. Copy.** Sm. fo. Engraved frontis. & double-p. panorama of L., mntd. & cut down, slightly dampstained, Nn1-Qq3 dampstained, later cf. (CSK. Feb.10; 155)   £95

HOWELL, T.B. & T.J.
- A Complete Collection of State Trials. L., 1811-28. Vols. 1-33 & Index vol. Some titles & a few ll. spotted, hf. cf., spine heads of 4 vols. worn or reprd. (S. Dec.20; 847)   *Professional Books.* £260

HOWELLS, William Dean
- A Foregone Conclusion. Boston, 1875. 1st. Edn. Gt.-decor. cl., light wear; pres. copy from author to Edmund C. Stedman, inscr. on front end-paper, Camb., Nov. 28, 1874, Stedman bkplt., A. Edward Newton 'hobby-horse' bkplt. (RO. Apr.23; 172)
                $160

HOWES, Wright
- U.S.-Iana. N.Y., 1954. 1st. Edn. Cl.; inscr. by author to De Witt O'Kieffe. (LH. Sep.25; 239)
                $110
- - **Anr. Copy.** Sm. 4to. Buckram. (SG. Aug.4; 155)
                $100
- - **Anr. Edn.** N.Y., 1962. 2nd. Edn. 4to. Buckram. (SG. May 17; 130) $140
- - **Anr. Copy.** 4to. Cl. (SG. Jan.5; 169) $110

HOWITT, Richard
- Australia; Historical, Descriptive, & Statistic ... 1845. Bdg. not stated, unc., slight wear. (KH. May 1; 369)   Aus. $180

HOWITT, Samuel
- The Angler's Manual, or Concise Lessons of Experience. L'pool., 1808. 1st. Edn. Ob. 8vo. Hf.-title, three-qtr. mor. (SG. Mar.15; 270) $150
- British Preserve. L., 1824. 4to. Engraved vig. title, 36 engrs., some spotting, hf. cf. (P. May 17; 217)
                Perham. £150
- The British Sportsman. L., 1812. New Edn. 4to. 71 engraved plts., all loose, slight soiling, cont. hf. cf., covers detchd. (SKC. May 4; 1760)   £450
- - **Anr. Copy.** Ob. 4to. Some slight foxing, mostly in margin, light stain in upr. left corner, more near end, frontis. crumpled, sm. margin tear bkd., cont. hf. leath., slightly bumped & worn, spine restored. (R. Apr.4; 1888)   DM 3,000
- Groups of Animals. L., 1811. 4to. 44 etched plts., some stains, cl., stained. (S. Apr.10; 521)
                Elliott. £70
- - **Anr. Copy.** 4to. 44 engraved plts., some staining, hf. cf., defect. (P. Mar.15; 145)   *Roberts.* £60
- Miscellaneous Etchings, Old & New. 1812. New Edn. 4to. Engraved vig. title, 50 plts., some spotted, orig. cl., worn. (BBA. Jun.28; 220)   *Erlini.* £55
- - **Anr. Copy.** Bdg. not stated; sigd. by Conrad Martens on title-p. (JL. Mar.25; 358)   Aus. $550
- New Work of Animals. L., [1809]. 4to. 101 plts., slight staining, lacks title-p., cf., upr. cover detchd., as a coll. of plts., w.a.f. (P. May 17; 218)
                Bailey. £130
- - **Anr. Edn.** 1811. 4to. 100 engraved plts., cont. panel. cf. gt. (P. Dec.8; 361)   *Beetles.* £120
- - **Anr. Edn.** 1818. 4to. 100 engraved plts., some ll. slightly soiled & spotted, owner's stp. on title, cont. cf. gt., rubbed. (BBA. Jan.19; 33)
                Printers Devil. £110
See— WILLIAMSON, Capt. Thomas & Howitt, Samuel

HOWITT, William
- Land, Labour & Gold, or Two Years in Victoria. 1855. Cl., slight foxing. (JL. Mar.25; 590)
                Aus. $200
- Life in Germany. L., 1849. Slightly foxed, cont. linen gt., bumped. (R. Oct.12; 2179)   DM 400

HOWITT, William & Mary
- Ruined Abbeys & Castles of Great Britain. Ill.:– Bedford, Sedgfield, G.W. Wilson, Fenton, & others. L., 1862. 4to. Title detchd., some foxing thro.-out, not affecting plts., orig. gt.-decor. cl., mntd. albumen photograph on covers, spine defect. (SG. Nov.10; 88) $130

HOWLETT, Bartholomew
- A Selection of Views in the County of Lincoln. L., 1797-1805. 4to. Cold. engraved map, engraved

dedication, 53 plts., slight spotting, cont. hf. russ., binder's label of J. Townley, of Boston. slightly worn. (S. Mar.6; 260)   *Clarke.* £280
- - **Anr. Edn.** 1805. 4to. L.P., engraved title, dedi-cation & 53 plts., 1 hand-cold. map, some margins dampstained, cont. hf. cf., rubbed. (CSK. Jul.13; 143)   £120
- - **Anr. Copy.** 4to. Hand-cold. map, engraved dedi-cation, 53 engraved plts., hf.-title, subscribers list, hf. cf. gt., unc., rubbed. (LC. Jul.5; 422)   £100
- - **Anr. Copy.** 4to. L.P., engraved title, dedica-tion & 53 plts., 1 hand-cold. map, some margins dampstained, cont. hf. cf., rubbed. (CSK. May 4; 60)   £50

HOWLETT, Robert
- The Angler's Sure Guide ... L., 1706. 1st. Edn. Text browned & stained, rust-hole in H2, 19th. C. cf. gt., spine emblematically tooled. (S. Oct.4; 34)
                Petty. £240
- - **Anr. Copy.** Plt. of fish with sm. tear (reprd.), slight browning, stain on A2, rust-hole in B5, tiny hole in M1-2, a few margin repairs, mod. panel. cf.; bkplt. of the Bibliotheca Piscatoria Lynniana. (S. Oct.4; 33)   *Quaritch.* £150
- The School of Recreation: or, a Gu'de to the Most Ingenious Exercises ... by R.H. L., 1732. Late Edn. 12mo. Old cf., neatly rebkd. (SG. Mar.15; 271) $110

HOWLEY, James P.
- The Beathucks or Red Indians. Camb., 1915. 4to. Orig. cl., lightly dampstained. (CSK. Aug.19; 65)
                £55

HOYM, Ch. d'
- Catalogus Librorum Bibliothecae ... Paris, 1738. Cont. spr. cf., spine decor.; prices marked. (HD. Jun.6; 75)   Frs. 2,200

HOYTEMA (Ill.)
See— KRONIEK

HOZIER, Capt. Henry Montague
- The France-Prussian War. L., 1870-72. 2 vols. 4to. Vol. 2 lacks engraved title & 1 map, slightly spotted, hf. mor., worn, w.a.f. (S. Mar.6; 89)
                Beisler. £160
- - **Anr. Edn.** L., [1870-72]. 6 vols. (without the Supp. 'Paris during the Siege'). 4to. A few plts. & maps slightly spotted, orig. cl. gt., worn. (S. Dec.20; 848)   *Russell.* £80
- - **Anr. Edn.** Ca. 1875. 2 vols. 4to. Cont. hf. cf. (TA. Aug.18; 58)   £140
- - **Anr. Copy.** 6 orig. divisions. 4to. Minor spotting, orig. cl. gt. (TA. Sep.15; 104)   £125
- - **Anr. Edn.** L., n.d. 7 orig. pts. 4to. 1 engraved title only, 79 plts. & maps, orig. cl., lightly soiled. (CSK. Dec.2; 16)   £160
- - **Anr. Copy.** 2 vols. Hf. cf., rubbed, as a coll. of plts., w.a.f. (P. Jan.12; 110)   *Mann.* £130
- - **Anr. Copy.** Pts. 1-5 only. Lge. 4to. 4 wood-engraved plts., 17 ports., 18 steel-engraved views, 19 maps, margin of 1 view cleanly torn, orig. cl., soiled, w.a.f. (CSK. Sep.16; 201)   £110
- - **Anr. Copy.** 3 pts. in 2 vols. Lacks engraved title to Vol. II, some slight foxing, cont. gt.-panel. hf. cf. (PD. Aug.17; 58)   £80

HOZIER, Louis-Pierre d'
- Armorial Général de la France. 1865-1908. 12 vols. Lge. 4to. Cont. hf. chagrin, corners. (HD. Mar.21; 112)   Frs. 3,900

HU, Hsen-Hsu & Chun, Woon-Young
- Icones Planatarum Sinicarum. Shanghai, 1927-35. Fascicles 1-4, in 2 vols. Fo. 200 plts., text in Engl. & Chinese, liby. cl. (SG. Mar.22; 167) $300

HUART, Louis
- Muséum Parisien. Ill.:– Grandville, Gavarni, Daumier, Traviés, Lécurieur, & Henri Monnier. Paris, 1841. 1st. Printing. Some slight foxing, sm. tear in 1 margin, cont. hf. chagrin, corners. (HD. Nov.29; 97)   Frs. 2,100
- - **Anr. Copy.** No bdg. stated. (HD. Oct.14; 83)
                Frs. 1,700
See— ALHOY, Maurice, & others

HUARTE, J.
- Prüfung der Köpfe zu den Wissenschaften. Trans.:– G.E. Lessing. Zerbst, 1752. 1st. Edn. of

HUA

HUARTE, J. -*Contd.*

this trans. Slightly wormed, lightly browned, a few cold. pencil crossings, cont. bds., worn & bumped. (GB. May 4; 1374).   DM 700

HUARTE Y NAVARRO, Juan
- **Examen de Ingenios, the Examination of Mens Wits.** Trans.:– R. C[arew]. 1616. Sm. 4to. Mod. mor. by Riviere, gt. (BBA. Jul.27; 93)
                                            Frognal. £230
- **Examen de Ingenios: or, the Tryal of Wits.** Trans.:– Mr. Bellamy. L., 1698. Browned, tear in margin of F7 not affecting text, panel. cf., worn. [Wing H 3205] (P. Mar.15; 316)   *Jarndyce.* £90

HUBBACK, Theodore R.
- **To Far Western Alaska for Big Game.** 1929. *1st. Edn.* Lge. folding map in rear pocket, publisher's advts. bnd. in at end, orig. cl. gt., rubbed, spine faded. (TA. Jul.19; 11)   £54
- – **Anr. Copy.** Black & white ills., folding map contained in rear pocket, orig. gt.-decor. cl., a little faded & rubbed on spine. (TA. Jun.21; 42)   £50

HUBER, F. & Senebier, J
See— SENEBIER, J. — HUBER, F. & Senebier, J.

HUBER, J.W.
- **Vues Pittoresques des Ruines les plus Remarquables de l'Ancienne Ville de Pompei.** Zurich, 1824. Fo. Spotted, cont. cl., soiled. (CSK. Dec.16; 137)
                                                    £100

HUBER, M.
- **Handbuch für Kunstliebhaber und Saunmler über die Vornehmsten Kupferstecher und Ihre Werke.** Ed.:– C.C.H. Rost (Vols. 1-5) & C.G. Martini (Vols. 6-9). Zürich, 1796-1808. 9 vols. Browned, mod. bds. (R. Apr.3; 801)   DM 950

HUBERS, Francis S.
- **Hubers Uniform Plates. The British Army 1800-1850.** Ill.:– R.P. North. L., 1956-62. *Ltd. Edn., not for sale.* 3 vols. 4to. 44 plts., leaves, box. (HD. Jan.27; 157)   Frs. 1,200

HUBERT, Sir Francis
- [–] **The Deplorable Life & Death of Edward II, King of England** ... L., 1628. *1st. Edn.* Engraved port., lacks A1 & K4 blanks, few sm. marginal repairs, port. & title cropped, light browning, new mor. [STC 13900] (SPB. May 16; 80) $250

HUBNER, Johann, the Elder
- **Curieuses und Reales Natur-, Kunst-, Berg-., Gewerck- und Handlungs-Lexicon** ... [Leipzig], 1746. Cont. vell., slightly spotted. (R. Oct.12; 1533)
                                                    DM 520
- **Neu-Vermehrtes und Verbessertes Reales Staats-, Zeitungs- und Conversations-Lexicon.** Regensburg & Vienna, 1761. Browned & foxed, cont. leath. gt., sm. spine defect. (R. Apr.3; 656)
                                                    DM 500
- **Reales Staats-, Zeitungs- und Conversations-Lexicon.** Leipzig, 1744. Slightly wormed, browned thro.-out, cont. hf. cf., worn. (BBA. Jun.28; 142)
                                Bloomsbury Rare Books. £55
- **Zeitungs- und Conversations-Lexikon.** Ed.:– F.A. Rüder. Leipzig, 1824-28. 4 vols. Slightly rubbed, cont. hf. leath. gt. (BR. Apr.12; 986)   DM 1,000

HUBOTTER
See— HIRSCH, A. & Hübotter

HUBRECHT, Alphonse
- **Grandeur et Suprematie de Peking.** Peking, 1928. *(100) numbered, with initials 'enluminêes par les meilleurs artistes'.* Lge. 4to. Red mor., col.-pict. wraps. bnd. in. (SG. Mar.29; 300) $250

HUBSCH, H.
- **Monuments de l'Architecture Chretienne.** Paris, 1866. Fo. Some spotting, mostly to next, cont. red hf. mor., worn, foot of spine torn; inscr. 'A M Poynter from E Burne-Jones'. (S. May 1; 551)
                                                Thomas. £385

HUCHTENBURG, Jean
See— DUMONT, Jean & Huchtenburg, Jean

HUCKELL, John
- [–] **Avon, a Poem.** 1758. 4to. 1st. blank lf., a few ll. slightly soiled, cont. hf. cf., rubbed. (BBA. Nov.30; 223)   *Hannas.* £90

HUDSON, Rev. Charles
- **Where There's a Will there's a Way; an Ascent of Mont Blanc.** L., 1856. *1st. Edn.* Folding cold. map torn, some ll. slightly soiled, orig. cl., rubbed. (BBA. May 3; 352)   *Ximenes.* £140

HUDSON, Mrs. & Donat, Mrs.
- **The New Practice of Cookery,** ... Edinb., 1804. Index, errata, advt. lf., cont. cf. (PD. Aug.17; 32)
                                                    £80

HUDSON, William Henry
- **Birds of La Plata.** Ill.:– H. Gronvold. L., 1920. *1st. Edn.* 2 vols. 4to. Owner's sigs., gt.-lettered cl., d.-w.'s chipped. (SG. Mar.22; 169) $100
- **Green Mansions: a Romance of the Tropical Forest.** L., 1904. *1st. Edn.* Hf.-title, mod. hf. mor. by Bayntun, Bath. (S. Oct.11; 344)   *Hamery.* £150
- **Letters to R.B. Cunninghame Graham.** Ill.:– Sir William Rothenstein. Gold. Cock. Pr., 1941. *(250) numbered.* Orig. mor.-bkd. bds., s.-c.; from D. Bolton liby. (BBA. Oct.27; 137)   *Swales.* £55
- **The Collected Works.** L. & Toronto, 1922-23. *(750).* 24 vols. Orig. cl. gt., partly unopened. (VS. Dec.8; 541)   Fls. 550

HUEFFER or FORD, Ford Madox
- **The Cinque Ports.** Ill.:– W. Hyde. 1900. 4to. Orig. cl. gt. (P. Oct.20; 230e)   £70
- **Ford Madox Brown: A Record of his Life & Work.** L., 1896. *1st. Edn.* Decor. cl., spine worn. (SG. Aug.25; 71) $130
- **Mister Bosphorus & the Muses.** Ill.:– Paul Nash. 1923. 4to. Orig. pict. linen-bkd. bds., d.-w. (P. Oct.20; 39)   £95
- **Women & Men.** Paris, Three Mountains Pr., 1923. *(300) on H.M.P.* 4to. Ptd. wraps., unc., slightly soiled. (SG. May 24; 294) $200
See— CONRAD, Joseph & Hueffer or Ford, Ford Madox

HUELSENBECK, R.
- **En Avant Dada. Die Geschichte des Dadaismus.** Hannover, 1920. *1st. Edn.* Title with owners mark & verso ex-libris, orig. sewed, slightly browned. (GB. May 5; 2719)   DM 400

HUERTE, Roque de
- **Recopilación de Notas de Escrituras Públicas.** Salamanca, 1551. Fo. Vell. (DS. Mar.23; 2138)
                                                Pts. 100,000

HUFELAND, Chr. W.
- **Die Kunst des Menschliche Leben zu verlängern.** Jena, 1797. *1st. Edn.* Lacks copper engraved title, cont. hf. leath., rubbed & bumped. (HT. May 8; 549)   DM 400
- – **Anr. Edn.** Jena, 1798. *2nd. Edn.* 2 vols. in 1. Some pencil marginalia & underlining, cont. bds., slight rubbing. (R. Apr.4; 1319)   DM 420

HUFELAND, Chr. W. (Ed.)
See— JOURNAL DER PRACTISCHEN HEILKUNDE

HUGEL, C. von
- **Kaschmir und das Reich der Siek.** Stuttgart, 1840-48. 4 vols. in 5. Lightly browned, orig. bds. (R. Oct.13; 3043)   DM 680
- – **Anr. Copy.** 4 vols. in 5 pts. Slightly browned, some ll. & plts. slightly foxed, new linen. (GB. Nov.3; 79)   DM 400

HUGHES, George R.
See— CARRINGTON, John B. & Hughes, George R.

HUGHES, Griffith
- **The Natural History of Barbados.** 1750. Fo. Title & 1 plt. holed, several plts. shaved with loss of blank margin, mod. hf. cf. (CSK. Jun.1; 39)
                                                    £300

HUG

HUGHES, H.
- **The Beauties of Cambria.** L., 1823. Ob. 4to. 60 wood-engraved plts., some spotting, cont. cf., worn. (CSK. Nov.4; 166)   £85

HUGHES, John
- **Views in the South of France, chiefly on the Rhone.** Ill.:– after P. Dewint. L., 1825. 4to. 24 engraved views, a few slightly spotted, cont. hf. roan, rubbed. (S. Jun.25; 167)   *Dupont.* £100

HUGHES, John T.
- **Doniphan's Expedition, Containing an Account of the Conquest of New Mexico.** Cinc., [1847]. *1st. Edn.* Orig. paper wraps., boxed; Littell bkplt. (LH. Sep.25; 243) $550

HUGHES, Josiah
- **Australia Revisited in 1890.** L. & Bangor, 1891. Orig. cl., slightly rubbed; pres. inscr. to W. Williams from author. (BBA. May 3; 297)
                                        Palace Books. £55

HUGHES, Talbot
See— SELIGMAN, G. Saville & Hughes, Talbot

HUGHES, Ted
- **Animal Poems.** [1967]. *(100) numbered & sigd. (20) with orig. MS. poem 'Hawk Roosting'.* 4to. Orig. wraps. (CSK. Jun.15; 162)   £75
- **Crow – from the Life & Songs of the Crow** ... Ill.:– Leonard Baskin. 1973. *Ltd. Edn., numbered.* 4to. Buckram, cl. spine, s.-c. (PD. Aug.17; 105)
                                                    £52
- **Eat Crow.** L., Rainbow Pr., 1971. *(150) numbered & sigd.* Sm. 4to. Cf., partly untrimmed, s.-c., by Zaehnsdorf. (SG. May 24; 83) $200
- **Moortown Elegies.** Ill.:– Leonard Baskin. [L., Rampant Lions Pr., for Rainbow Pr., 1978]. *(26) lettered & sigd.* 4to. Mor. gt., cf. gt. emblem on upr. cover, gt. dentelles, partly untrimmed, cl. s.-c., by Sangorski & Sutcliffe. (SG. Mar.1; 176)
                                                    $300
- **Orts.** L., Rainbow Pr., 1978. *(200) numbered & sigd.* Sm. 4to. Cf., partly untrimmed, s.-c., by Zaehnsdorf. (SG. May 24; 88) $100
- **Remains of Elmet.** Ill.:– Fay Godwin. [L., Rampant Lions Pr., for] Rainbow Pr., 1979. *(70) numbered & sigd. by author & artist.* 4to. Tree cf., partly untrimmed. cl. s.-c. (SG. Mar.1; 177) $100

HUGHES, Thomas
- [–] **Tom Brown at Oxford.** Camb., 1861. *1st. Edn.* 3 vols. 24 p. publisher's catalogue at end of Vol. III, lacks final blank in last vol., orig. cl., worn, spines darkened. (SG. Nov.17; 75) $200
- [–] **Tom Brown's School Days.** Camb., 1857. *1st. Edn.* Hf. title, mor. gt. by Rivière, s.-c.; from Norman Tarbolton liby. (P. Apr.12; 19)
                                                Georges. £220
- – **Anr. Copy.** Lacks advt. lf. & 24 p. publisher's catalogue at end, orig. cl., worn, spine darkened; A.L.s. by Hughes laid in. (SG. Nov.17; 74) $350

HUGHES, Thomas of Chester
- **Ancient Chester; a Series of Illustrations of the Streets of this Old City.** L., 1880. *(300). (100) on India paper.* Fo. 29 plts., slightly stained in inner margin, slightly spotted, mor.-bkd. bds. (S. Mar.6; 486)   *Hepner.* £130

HUGHES, Thomas Smart
- **Travels in Greece & Albania.** 1830. *2nd. Edn.* 2 vols. Sm. stain just affecting margin of last plt. in Vol. 1, orig. cl., unopened. (S. Nov.1; 92)
                                                Clegg. £220

HUGHSON, David [i.e. David Pugh]
- **London; being an Accurate History & Description ... to Thirty Miles extent from an actual Perambulation.** L., 1807-05-06-09. 6 vols. Some plts. & maps folding & hand-cold., lacks 1 map, some browning, cont. hf. russ., lightly rubbed, w.a.f. (CSK. Dec.2; 178)   £200
- – **Anr. Edn.** L., 1805-09. 6 vols. 5 engraved folding maps, 154 plts., spotted, few sm. tears, cont. cf., worn, some covers detchd. (S. Mar.6; 385)
                                                Eisler. £130

HUGNET, Georges
- **L'Apocalypse.** Ill.:– S.W. Hayter. 1937. *Orig. Edn. (70) on Montval, sigd.* 12mo. Sewed. (HD. Apr.13; 165) Frs. 1,200
- **40 Poésies de Stanislas Boutemer.** Ill.:– Max Jacob. Paris, 1928. *(170) numbered, with 2 orig. lithos by Jacob.* Orig. wraps., s.-c.; pres. copy inscr. to Vicomte Carlow on hf.-title, loose sketch by artist. (BBA. Jun.14; 220)
Sims, Reed & Fogg. £150

HUGO, Hermannus
- **Pia Desideria.** Ill.:– Carolus Blancus. Milan, 1634 [colophon 1633]. 16mo. Few light stains, later cf.-bkd. bds., spine defect. (BBA. Mar.21; 16)
Snelling. £80

HUGO, Jean
- **Le Miroir Magique.** Ill.:– Saude. Paris, 1927. *(50) numbered on Arches paper, sigd.* Tall fo. 20 pochoir-cold. plts., no title-p., loose in bd. folder with title label mntd., linen ties. (SG. Dec.15; 160)
$125

HUGO, Count Jean Abel
- **France Militaire.** Paris, 1838. 4to. Foxed., cont. hf. leath gt., worn. (R. Oct.12; 2370) DM 2,000
- **France Pittoresque ou Description Pittoresque, Topographique et Statistique des Départements et des Colonies ...** Paris, 1835. 3 vols. Lge. 8vo. Cont. hf. roan. (HD. Jun.22; 52) Frs. 1,100
- **Histoire Générale de France ...** Paris, 1836-43. 5 vols. 4to. Cont. hf. chagrin, spines decor.; from Château des Noës liby. (HD. May 25; 31)
Frs. 1,550

HUGO, Thomas
- **The Bewick Collector.** L., 1866-68. 2 vols., including supp. 4to. Port. stained, slightly soiled, Vol. 1 mod. cl., Supp. orig. cl., rebkd. with orig. spine. (BBA. Mar.7; 225) *Bondy. £75*
- – **Anr. Copy.** 2 vols., with Supp. Orig. cl., worn. (BBA. Nov.10; 213) *Traylen. £60*

HUGO, Valentine
- **Les Aventures de Fido Caniche.** Paris, 1947. Sm. ob. 4to. Publisher's ill. bds.; with dedication. (SM. Mar.7; 2145) Frs. 1,200

HUGO, Victor
- **L'Année Terrible.** Ill.:– L. Flameng & D. Vierge. Paris, 1874. *1st. printing of Vierge ills. (20) on china.* Some worming, bradel red mor. by Carayon, wrap. preserved. (HD. Jun.13; 49) Frs. 1,250
- **L'Art d'être Grand-père.** Paris, 1877. *Orig. Edn. (20) on china.* Sm. 4to. Sewed, glazed wrap. (HD. May 16; 37) Frs. 3,500
- **Les Châtiments.** Genève & N.Y., 1853. *Orig. Edn. 1st. Printing.* 32mo. On thin tinted paper, cont. chagrin. (HD. Apr.13; 88) Frs. 1,800
- **Correspondance 1815-1882.** Paris, 1896-98. *Orig. Edn. (10) on japan (1st. vol.), (5) on japan (2nd. vol.).* 2 vols. Lge. 8vo. Hf. cf., corners, by Semet & Plumelle, spines decor., wrap., unc. (HD. Apr.13; 89) Frs. 2,800
- **Cromwell. Drame.** Paris, 1828. *Orig. Edn.* In leaves, washed, unsewn, wrap., folder, spine decor., s.-c. (HD. Nov.9; 96) Frs. 1,350
- **Dessins.** Text:– Théophile Gautier. Ill.:– Paul Chenay. Paris, 1863. *Orig. Edn.* Lge. 4to. Some foxing, cont. publishers red decor. buckram, some defects. (HD. Dec.9; 145) Frs. 1,300
- **Extraits de l'Oeuvre Complète de Victor Hugo.** Paris, May 1885. 12mo. Unique copy on well., red hf. mor., corners, by Semet & Plumelle, bnd. ca. 1935, unc.; from Georges Hugo liby. (HD. Apr.26; 146) Frs. 2,000
- **Les Misérables.** Ill.:– after E. Morin, D. Vierge, Valnay & others. Paris, ca. 1890. 5 vols. Lge. 8vo. Hf. chagrin. (HD. Mar.27; 77) Frs. 1,300
- **Notre-Dame de Paris.** Ill.:– Tony Johannot. Paris, 1831. *Orig. Edn. '4th. Edn.'.* 2 vols. Cont. hf. red mor. roan, corners, decor. spines. (HD. Dec.9; 144) Frs. 4,600
- – **Anr. Copy.** 2 vols. Russ. by Pagnant, spines decor.; added port. by Devéria. (HD. Apr.13; 90) Frs. 4,000
- – **Anr. Edn.** Ill.:– L. Boulanger, A. & T. Johannot, Raffet, Rouargue & others. Paris, 1836. 3 vols. Cont. hf. cf., spines decor. (HD. Jun.6; 76) Frs. 1,500

- – **Anr. Edn.** Ill.:– after M. & E. de Beaumont, L. Boulanger, d'Aubigny, Johannot & others. Paris, 1844. *1st. Printing.* Lge. 8vo. Bordeaux mor. gt. by Chambolle-Duru, spine decor. (HD. May 4; 301) Frs. 2,400
- – **Anr. Edn.** Ill.:– after Luc-Olivier Merson. Paris, 1889. *Edition Nationale, on vergé.* 2 vols. 4to. Ills. in 2 states, cont. mor., decor. spines, decor. 'à la cathédrale', inner dentelle, wrap. & spine preserved, by Champs. (HD. Feb.17; 79) Frs. 2,800
- **Nouvelles Odes.** Paris, 1824. 12mo. Hf. chagrin; Vigny copy, with dedication. (HD. Jun.13; 51)
Frs. 32,000
- **The Novels ...** L., 1895. *(100) on japan imperial paper.* 28 vols. 8vo. Engrs. in 2 states, bkplts. (*With:*) – **Romances: The Gallery of Illustrations.** L., 1895. *(100) on japan imperial paper.* 1 vol. 4to. Engrs. in 3 states. Together 29 vols. Unif. gt.-ruled lev. mor. by H.S. Nichols, elab. gt.-decor. spines, inner gt. dentelles. (CBA. Dec.10; 262) $550
- **Odes.** Ill.:– after Devéria. [1827]. *3rd. Edn.* 2 vols. 18mo. Jansenist mor., mor. doubl., wrap & spine preserved, s.-c.'s, by Huser. (HD. Feb.17; 12t) Frs. 1,300
- **Odes et Ballades.** Paris, 1827. 12mo. Hf. chagrin; Vigny copy, with dedication. (HD. Jun.13; 50) Frs. 25,800
- – **Anr. Edn.** Paris, 1828. *4th. Edn. (1) on pink chine.* 2 vols. Cont. hf. mor., spines decor.; letter from author to Laure Jourdain, from Jules Janin liby. (HD. Nov.9; 97) Frs. 17,500
- **Oeuvres.** Paris, 1840-57. 18 vols. Lge. 8vo. No bdg. stated. (HD. Oct.14; 84) Frs. 1,350
- – **Anr. Edn.** 1857-60. 18 vols. On holland, hf. mor., corners, by David, unc.; from J. de Rothschild liby. (HD. Jul.6; 111) Frs. 2,500
- – **Anr. Edn.** Paris, 1875 & later. 30 vols. Sm. 12mo. On china, cont. old red mor. by Marius Michel, spine raised bands, mor. gt. doubls.; binder's copy, justified & paraphed by Alphonse Lemerre. (HD. May 16; 39) Frs. 10,200
- **Oeuvres Complètes.** Ill.:– Merson, Rodin, Flameng, Giacomelli & others. Paris, 1885-95. 43 vols. 4to. Cont. bordeaux hf. mor., corners, spines decor. (slightly faded), unc. (HD. Jul.2; 75) Frs. 4,000
- **Les Orientales.** Paris, 1829. *Orig. Edn.* Hf.-title 'Oeuvres de Victor Hugo', frontis. by C. Cousin on mntd. china, 16 pp. subscription at end sigd. E.T. (Sainte-Beuve), hf. mor., corners, spine decor., wrap. preserved, unc., slight tear to turn-in, 1 corner worn. (SM. Mar.7; 2495) Frs. 1,200
- – **Anr. Edn.** Ill.:– Gérome & Benjamin Constant, engraved by Los Rios. 1882. *(135) on japan with plts. in 2 states.* Lge. 4to. Mor. gt. by Gruel, spine decor., s.-c.; nominative copy, with list of Society members. (HD. Jul.6; 112) Frs. 1,200
- **William Shakespeare.** Paris, 1864. *Orig. Edn.* On holland, red hf. mor., corners, by Bernasconi, spine decor., unc., wrap. & spine preserved; with extract from Nouvelle Revue de Paris, Mar. 1864, sigd. by Amédée Roland. (HD. May 4; 302) Frs. 3,500

HUGO DE SANCTO CARO
- **Expositio Missae, seu Speculum Ecclesiae.** [Rome, Stephan Plannck], ca. 1485. 4to. Mod. vell.; the Walter Goldwater copy. [Goff H-518] (SG. Dec.1; 184) $175

HUGUENIN DU MITAND, Louis
- **A New System of Reading; or, the Art of Reading English.** L., 1787. *1st. Edn.* 12mo. Early cf. gt. (SG. Dec.8; 245) $200

HUHN, E.
- **Heidelberg und seine Umgebungen.** Darmstadt, 1854. Stained from p. 13 to end, including 7 engrs., orig. bds., bumped & spotted, spine defect. (R. Oct.12; 2459) DM 850

HUISH, Marcus B.
- **Japan & its Art.** L., [1912]. *3rd. Edn.* Decor. cl. (PNY. Dec.1; 91) $140
See– TURNER, Joseph Mallord William & Huish, M.B.

HUISH, Robert
- **The Last Voyage of Captain Sir John Ross ...** 1835. Some minor spotting, liby. stp. on engraved & ptd. titles, recent qtr. cf. gt. (TA. Jul.19; 15) £52

HULBERT, Archer Butler
- **Historic Highways of America.** Cleveland, 1902-05. 15 vols. & Index. Cl. (LH. Sep.25; 241) $150

HULLS, Jonathan
- **Description & Draught of a Newly Invented Machine for carrying Vessels or Ships out of or into any Harbour, Port or River.** 1737 [but ca. 1860]. *Facs. Edn.* Front free-endpaper inscr. '12 copies reprinted on old paper, sm. 4to. No. 5 large paper copy', cont. hf. mor., lightly rubbed; pres. copy to Robert Napier dtd. Oct. 27 1860, with his bkplt. (CSK. May 18; 183) £120

HULME, F.E.
- **Familiar Wild Flowers.** L., [1877-1900]. Series I-V (of IX) in 5 vols. Aquarelles monogrammed & dtd. some slight spotting, private hf. leath. gt. (HT. May 8; 297) DM 1,700
- – **Anr. Edn.** L., n.d. 5 vols. Orig. decor. cl., orig. boxes. (BBA. Mar.21; 46) *J. Brailey. £70*

HULME, F.E. & Hibberd, S.
- **Familiar Garden Flowers.** L., ca. 1880. 5 vols. in 2. Many cold. plts., cont. hf. linen. (SI. Dec.15; 161) Lire 380,000

HULSENBECK, Rich. (Ed.)
See– DADA ALMANACH

HULSIUS, Levinus
- **Die Siebenzehende Schiffart.** Frankfurt, 1620. *1st. Edn.* 4to. 1 plt. reprd., hf. vell. [Sabin 33670] (D. Nov.23; 1321) DM 750

HULSMANNS, Dieter
- **Paroxysmus. Les Lois d'un Paroxysme Interne.** Preface:– E. Roditi. Ill.:– Peter Brüning. Flensburg, Petersen Pr., 1963. *(570). (60) Roman numbered De Luxe Edn. with 4 sigd. orig. etchings.* Orig. linen, initials DHP in gold. (GB. May 5; 3281) DM 700

HULTON, Paul & Quinn, David Beers
- **The American Drawings of John White.** L., 1964. *(600).* 2 vols. Fo. Orig. cl., s.-c. (BBA. Sep.8; 68) *Belanske. £250*
- – **Anr. Copy.** 2 vols. Fo. Orig. buckram, publisher's box; the Rt. Hon. Visc. Eccles copy. (CNY. Nov.18; 284) $350

HUMBER, William
- **A Practical Treatise on Cast & Wrought Iron Bridges & Girders.** L., 1857. Fo. Litho. view & 57 plts., cont. hf. mor. (S. Apr.9; 171) *Traylen. £170*

HUMBOLDT, Baron Friedrich Heinrich Alexander von
- **Ansichten der Natur mit Wissenschaftlichen Erlaeuterungen.** Tubingen, 1808. *1st. Edn.* Vol. 1 (all publd.). Hf. roan, wraps. bnd. in; Dr. Walter Pagel copy. [Sabin 33702] (S. Feb.7; 198)
Quaritch. £100
- – **Anr. Edn.** 1826. *1st. Compl. Edn.* 2 pts. in 1 vol. Title verso stpd., late 19th. C. marb. bds. (GB. Nov.3; 11) DM 480
- **Gesammelte Werke.** Stuttgart, [1889]. 12 vols. in 7. Orig. hf. leath. (D. Nov.23; 377) DM 400
- **Kosmos.** Stuttgart & Tübingen, 1845-58. *1st. Edn.* Vols. 1-4 in 5 vols. (lacks vol. 5 & Atlas as often). Cont. hf. leath. gt. (R. Apr.4; 1414) DM 450
- – **Anr. Edn.** Stuttgart & Tubingen, 1845-62. *1st. Edn.* 5 vols. (without atlas vol.). Some light foxing, cont. roan-bkd. bds., slightly rubbed. (C. Jun.27; 38) *Weiner. £70*
- – **Anr. Copy.** 5 vols. in 6 & Atlas. 8vo. & ob. 4to. Some foxing, hf. linen, atlas orig. hf. leath., rubbed & bumped. (D. Nov.23; 875) DM 1,300
- – **Anr. Copy.** 5 vols. & atlas. 8vo. & ob. fo. Cont. hf. leath. gt., atlas not unif. (HK. Nov.8; 599) DM 950
- – **Anr. Copy.** 6 vols., including atlas. Ob. fo. Cont. hf. leath. (B. Oct.4; 355) Fls. 1,100
- **Mineralog. Beobachtungen über einige Basalte am Rhein.** Braunschweig, 1790. *1st. Edn.* Title with MS. owner's mark, verso stpd., annots. at beginning, cont. bds., slightly soiled & lightly bumped. (HK. Nov.8; 655) DM 850
- **Political Essay on the Kingdom of New Spain.** L., 1822. *3rd. Edn.* 4 vols. Qtr. cf. (LH. Sep.25; 242) $120

HUMBOLDT, Baron Friedrich Heinrich Alexander von -*Contd.*
- **Reisen in die Aequinoctial-Gegenden des Neuen Continents.** Trans.:– H. Hauff. 1861-62. 6 vols. in 3. 1 lf. torn, cont. hf. linen. (GB. May 3; 44) DM 600
- – **Anr. Edn.** Ed.:– Hermann Hauff. Stuttgart, n.d. 4 vols. in 2. Title stpd., orig. linen. (GB. Nov.3; 12) DM 450
- **Researches Concerning the Institutions & Monuments of the Ancient Inhabitants of America.** L., 1814. 2 vols. 16pp. advts., some light soiling, orig. bds., worn. (CSK. Nov.4; 201) £70
- – **Anr. Edn.** L., n.d. 2 vols. 5 plts. hand-cold., slight spotting, hf. cf. gt. (P. Apr.12; 217) *Burton Garbett.* £110
- **Versuche über die Gereizte Muskel– und Nerven-faser nebst Vermuthungen über den Chemischen Process des Lebens in der Thier- und Pflanzenwelt.** Posen & Berlin, 1797. *1st. Edn.* 2 vols. Hf.-titles, some spotting & discoloration, hf. cf., worn; Dr. Walter Pagel copy. (S. Feb.7; 196) *Bickersteth.* £220

HUMBOLDT, Baron Friedrich Heinrich Alexander von & Bonpland, Aimé
- **Monographie des Melastomacées ... Rhexies.** L., 1833. 2 pts. in 1 vol. Fo. 64 col. plts., some light foxing or offsetting, old moiré cl., worn, rebkd., orig. spine laid down. (SG. Mar.22; 170) $600

HUMBOLDT, Wilhelm von
- **Briefe an eine Freundin.** Leipzig, 1848. 2 pts. in 1 vol. Wide margin, some slight foxing, cont. hf. leath. gt., lightly worn & bumped. (HK. May 16; 2106) DM 400
- **Memoiren.** Leipzig, 1861. *1st. Edn.* 2 vols. Title with owners mark, cont. linen gt., spine faded. (HK. May 16; 2108) DM 1,050

HUMBOLDT, Wihelm von & Caroline von
- **Wilhelm und Caroline von Humboldt in Ihren Briefen.** Ed.:– Anna v. Sydow. Berlin, 1910-16. 7 vols. On Bütten, orig. gold-tooled linen, unc. (GB. May 4; 1340) DM 800

HUME, David, Baron of the Exchequer in Scotland
- **Commentaries on the Law of Scotland, respecting the Description & Punishment of Crimes.** Edinb., 1797. *1st. Edn.* 2 vols. (*With:*) - **Commentaries on the Law of Scotlad, respecting Trial for Crimes.** Edinb., 1800. *1st. Edn.* 2 vols. Together 4 vols. 4to. Hf.-title to each vol., unif. cont. cf., spines gt.; Sir Ivar Colquhoun, of Luss copies. (CE. Mar.22; 169) £420
- – **Anr. Copy.** 2 vols. 4to. Orig. bds., unc. (PD. Dec.14; 208) £65
- – **Anr. Edn.** Edinb., 1819. *2nd. Edn.* 2 vols. in 1. 4to. Bdg. defect. (PD. Dec.14; 32) £60

HUME, David, Historian
- **An Enquiry Concerning the Principles of Morals.** L., 1751. *1st. Edn.* L3 a cancellans, cont. cf., gt. spine, a trifle worn. (BBA. Nov.30; 218) *Quaritch.* £480
- – **Anr. Copy.** L3 in orig. state, before cancellation, no hf.-title, errata corrected in early hand, some soiling & slight staining, inscr. erased from title, cont. cf., rebkd., worn. (BBA. Nov.30; 217) *Quaritch.* £320
- **Essays, Moral & Political.** Edinb., 1742. *2nd Edn.* Vol. 1 only (of 2). 8vo. Cont. cf. (BBA. Jan.19; 190) *Boyle.* £90
- **Essays & Treatises, on Several Subjects.** L., 1767. *New Edn.* 2 vols. Vol. 1 title with loss, cf., corners worn. (HD. Feb.22; 98) Frs. 2,100
- **Four Dissertations.** L., 1757. *1st. Edn.* 12mo. Hf.-title with advts. on verso placed preceding title, fly title to Dissertation 1 between gathering a & B, errata on M8v, cancel lf. C12, sig. on title, cont. cf. (SPB. May 16; 81) $400
- **The History of England.** Edinb. & L., 1754-62. *1st. Edn.* 6 vols. 4to. Lacks. hf.-titles in Vols. 1-3, some foxing & browning, cont. tree cf., greek-key border, rebkd., spines gt. (SPB. May 16; 82) $400
- – **Anr. Edn.** 1782. 8 vols. Unif. cf. (*With:*) SMOLLETT, Tobias - **The History of England Continued.** 1759-65. 8 vols. Unif. cf. (PD. Aug.17; 89) £52
- – **Anr. Edn.** 1789. *New Edn.* Vols. 1-8. (*With:*) SMOLLETT, Tobias - **The History of England**

Continued. 1812. *New Edn.* Vols. 9-13. Together 13 vols. Unif. cf. (PD. May 16; 71) £60
- – **Anr. Edn.** Maps:- [Thomas Moule]. Ca. 1850. 8 divisions. Sm. fo. 68 engraved ports. & plts., 30 folding county maps, orig. cl. gt., spines ends chipped. (TA. Nov.17; 154) £240
- **Philosophical Essays Concerning Human Understanding.** L., 1748. *1st. Edn.* 12mo. 2-pp. advts., cont. mott. cf., new label, spine reprd.; bkplt. of Joseph Townsend. (SPB. May 16; 83) $750
- **A Treatise of Human Nature.** 1739. Vols. 1 and 2 only. Cont. cf., spine rubbed & slightly split. (CSK. Jul.27; 43) £550

HUME, Martin
- **The Love Affairs of Mary Queen of Scots.** L., 1903. Extra-ill. with 13 engraved plts., a few hand-cold. or offset, mor., elab. gt., by Bayntun (Rivière), upr. cover inlaid with miniature hand-painted port. of Mary Queen of Scots, boxed. (S. Oct.4; 116) *Joseph.* £320

HUME, Samuel J.
See— FUERST, Walter Rene & Hume, Samuel J.

HUMPHREY, Maud
- **Children of the Revolution.** Ill.:– Maud & Mabel Humphrey. N.Y., [1900]. 4to. Col.-pict. bds., moderate shelf-wear. (RO. Jul.24; 138) $360

HUMPHREYS, Arthur L.
- **Old Decorative Maps & Charts.** L., 1926. *1st. Edn. (1500) numbered.* 4to. 79 plts. (19 cold.), buckram gt. (SG. Jan.5; 170) $125

HUMPHREYS, Henry Noel
- **A Genera & Species of British Butterflies.** Ca. 1859. Col. title, 33 col. plts., orig. cl. gt. (P. Jul.5; 203) £60
- – **Anr. Edn.** [1860]. Tall 8vo. 33 hand-cold. plts., including title, slight spotting, orig. cl., decor. gt., recased. (SKC. Oct.26; 381) £130
- **The Genera of British Moths.** L., ca. 1860. 62 hand-cold. plts., orig. cl., decor. gt., spine reprd. (SKC. Oct.26; 382) £210
- – **Anr. Copy.** 2 vols. Tall 8vo. 62 hand-cold. plts., slight spotting, orig. gt.-decor. cl. (SKC. Sep.9; 1996) £100
- – **Anr. Copy.** 2 vols. in 1. Orig. cl. gt., slightly worn. (P. Sep.29; 49) *Shapero.* £55
- – **Anr. Edn.** Ca. 1870. Tall 8vo. 62 hand-cold. plts., orig. cl. gt., recent mor. backstrip. (TA. May 17; 285) £65
- – **Anr. Copy.** Tall 8vo. 62 hand-cold. plts., orig. cl. gt., recent mor. backstrip. (TA. Jun.21; 258) £56
- – **Anr. Edn.** N.d. 62 col. plts., orig. cl. gt., slightly worn. (P. Feb.16; 79) £85
- **A History of the Art of Printing.** 1867. *1st. Iss. (300).* Limitation notice bnd. in, orig. cl. gt., rebkd., orig. spine preserved; Wellington College copy. (C. May 30; 4) *Breker.* £220
- – **Anr. Edn.** 1868. *[2nd. Iss.].* Fo. Cont. hf. mor. (CSK. Feb.10; 164) £70
- – **Anr. Copy.** Fo. 100 photolitho. plts., elab. gt.-decor. cl., worn, rebkd., ex-liby. (SG. Sep.15; 178) $150
- **Masterpieces of the Early Printers & Engravers.** 1870. Fo. Later hf. mor., gt. spine. (BBA. Nov.10; 79) *Hartley.* £150
- – **Anr. Copy.** Sm. fo. 72 plts., some foxing, decor. cl. (SG. Aug.4; 159) $100
[-] **The Miracles of Our Lord.** L., 1848. Thick paper, title-p. slightly soiled, orig. decor. embossed mor. by Hayday, vell. medallion onlays to both covers lettered in black & 2 cols., bevelled edges. (CBA. Aug.21; 315) $170
- **The Night Flyers.** L., ca. 1866. Hand-cold. litho. title, 14 hand-cold. plts., slightly soiled, orig. lac-quered bds., worn. (P. Nov.24; 46) *Ayres.* £90
- **The Origin & Progress of the Art of Writing.** L., 1855. *2nd. Edn.* 4to. 29 litho. plts., including 11 cold., some light spotting, orig. mor.-bkd. papier-maché bds., covers slightly chipped, spine rubbed & chipped at ends, recased. (CSK. Dec.2; 101) £90
- – **Anr. Copy.** Orig. bdg. (P. Apr.12; 84) *Maggs.* £80
- **Sentiments & Similies of W. Shakespeare.** 1851. Sm. 4to. Slight spotting, orig. papier-mâché, inset port. medallion, spine slightly worn. (SKC. May 4; 1632) £75

HUMPHREYS, Henry Noel & Jones, Owen
- **The Illuminated Books of the Middle Ages.** L., 1849. Sm. fo. Ptd. & illuminated titles, 2 uncold. plts., 39 chromolitho. plts., some double-p., most with extra text ll., mntd., with lge. & sm. initials & elab. decor. borders in colours & gold, few plts. bnd. out of order, ex-liby., orig. mor., blind-tooled with medieval-style ornaments; Michael Tomkinson bkplt. (SG. May 3; 213) $275
- – **Anr. Copy.** Atlas fo. L.P., ptd. & illuminated titles, 1 uncold. plt., 39 mntd. litho. plts., ptd. in colours, most with lf. of explanation with sm. illuminated initial, marginal stains thro.-out with no serious effect on plts., old liby. bkplt., cont. hf. mor., shabby. (SG. May 17; 133) $110

HUMPHREYS, Henry Noel & Westwood, John Obadiah
- **British Butterflies & their Transformations.** L., 1841. *[1st. Edn.].* 4to. Litho. pict. title, 42 plts., all hand-cold., 1 frayed & soiled, orig. cl., recased. (BBA. Mar.21; 47) *P. Roberts.* £340
- – **Anr. Copy.** 4to. Hand cold. title, 42 plts., crimson mor. gt. (P. Dec.8; 102) *Graham.* £250
- – **Anr. Edn.** 1849. 4to. Hand-cold. additional litho. title, 42 plts., cont. hf. mor., spine gt., rubbed. (CSK. Apr.6; 137) £240
- – **Anr. Edn.** L., 1857. 4to. Hand-cold. title, 47 (of 48) hand-cold. plts., mor. gt. (P. May 17; 304) £120
- – **Anr. Edn.** L., 1860. *New Edn.* 4to. Hand-cold. additional title, 42 hand-cold. engraved plts., orig. cl., decor. gt. (SKC. Oct.26; 451) £320
- – **Anr. Copy.** 4to. Hand-cold. title, 42 hand-cold. plts., orig. cl. gt. (P. Oct.20; 219) £120
- – **Anr. Copy.** 4to. Hand-cold. frontis., 21 plts., including 19 hand-cold., hf. mor. (SKC. Oct.26; 453) £95
- **British Moths & Their Transformations.** L., 1841-43. *1st. Edn.* 2 vols. Lge. 4to. 124 hand-cold. plts., some foxing, liby. stp. on titles, gt.-pict. cl., rehinged. (SG. Mar.22; 171) $325
- – **Anr. Edn.** L., 1843-45. *1st. Edn.* 2 vols. 4to. Hf. mor. (SKC. Oct.26; 452) £240
- – **Anr. Copy.** 2 vols. 4to. 124 col. plts., 19th. C. qtr. mor. (SG. Oct.6; 207) $275
- – **Anr. Edn.** 1849. 2 vols. 4to. 124 hand-cold. litho. plts., some light browning, cont. hf. mor., spines gt., rubbed. (CSK. Apr.6; 136) £200
- – **Anr. Edn.** L., 1854. 2 vols. 4to. 124 hand-cold. plts., cl., defect., Vol. 1 brkn. (P. Jul.5; 153) £200
- – **Anr. Edn.** 1857. *New Edn.* 2 vols. 4to. 124 hand-cold. engraved plts., some light staining to top margins in Vol. 1, some spotting to text, cont. hf. cf., rubbed. (TA. Feb.16; 105) £160

HUMPHREYS, James
[-] **The Oriental Navigator ...** Phila., 1801. *1st. Amer. Edn.* Browning thro.-out, cont. cf., upr. cover loose. (PNY. Mar.27; 156) $300

HUNDORPH, J.
- **Encomuim Ecfurtinum. Encomii Erfurtini Continuatio ...** Erfurt, 1651. Cont. bds. (R. Oct.13; 2755) DM 480

HUNNIUS, Nicholas
- **Christliche Betrachtung der newen Paracelsischen und Weigelianischen Theologie.** Wittemberg, 1622. Apparently lacks prelim. lf. before p.1 of text (subtitle?), discold., cont. vell.; Dr. Walter Pagel copy. (S. Feb.7; 202) *Ritman.* £650

HUNOLD, C.F. 'Menantes'
- **Die Manier Höflich und wohl mit Hohen, Vornehmen Personen, seines Gleichen und Frauenzimmer.** Hamburg, 1710. *1st. Edn.* Lightly browned, cont. hf. vell. (R. Oct.11; 270) DM 500

HUNT, James Henry Leigh
- **Critical Essays on the Performers of the London Theatres.** 1807 [1808]. 2 pts. in 1. Hf.-titles, prospectus of 'The Examiner' bnd. at end, later mott. hf. cf., spine gt.; A.L.s. from author tipped in. (BBA. Jan.19; 213) *Jarndyce.* £110
[-] **The Liberal.** 1822-23. *1st. Edn.* 2 vols. Hf. cf. gt., rubbed. (P. Feb.16; 120) £55
- **Table-talk, to which are added Imaginary Conversations of Pope & Swift.** L., 1851. *1st. Edn.* 8 ll. of advts., sm. piece cut from top corner of title-p.,

orig. cl., gt., rebkd., cl.-lined box; pres. inscr. from author to his daughter, Julia Trelawney Leigh Hunt. (BBA. Dec.15; 212) *Swales.* £80
See— KEATS, John — HUNT, James Henry Leigh — PROCTOR

HUNT, John
- Historical Surgery. Loughborough, 1801. 4to. Hf. cf. (S. Apr.10; 523) *Phillips.* £160

HUNT, Lynn Bogue
- An Artist's Game Bag. N.Y., Derrydale Pr., 1936. *(1225).* 4to. Slight margin browning, orig. bdg., slight scuffing. (SPB. Dec.13; 588) $175
- - Anr. Copy. 4to. Ink inscr., gt.-decor. leatherette, light wear to covers. (CBA. Nov.19; 130) $110

HUNT, P. Francis
- Orchidacae. Ill.:– M. Grierson. L., 1973. *(600) sigd. by author & artist.* Fo. 40 cold. plts., orig. vell. by Zaehnsdorf, cl. s.-c.; subscriber's copy. (C. Nov.16; 260) *Young.* £130

HUNT, Rachel McMasters Miller
- Catalogue of Botanical Books in the Collection of ... 1477-1800. Ed.:– J. Quinby & A. Stevenson. Pittsb., Anthoensen Pr., 1958-61. *1st. Edn. (750).* 2 vols. in 3, as iss. 4to. Gt.-pict. cl. *(With:)* – The Hunt Botanical Library ... Its Collections, Program, & Staff. Pittsb., 1961. 1 vol. 4to. Unif. gt.-pict. cl. (SG. Sep.15; 179) $700
- - Anr. Edn. Pittsb., 1958-61. 2 pts. in 3 vols. 4to. Orig. linen. (R. Apr.3; 645) DM 950

HUNT, T.F.
- Exemplars of Tudor Architecture. L., 1830. 4to. Some spotting, later hf. cf., slightly rubbed. *(With:)* – Archittetura Campestre. L., 1827. 4to. Spotted, orig. roan-bkd. bds., slightly rubbed. (S. May 1; 552) *Roe.* £70

HUNT, William, Gauger
- Gauger's Magazine. 1687. Title & 1st. few ll. soiled, some margin defects, cont sheep, worn. [Wing H373] (TA. Dec.15; 89) £52

HUNT, William Southworth
- Frank Forester: a Tragedy in Exile. Newark, Carteret Book Cl., 1933. *(200).* Errata slip tipped in, cl., spotted, s.-c. (SG. Mar.15; 263) $100

HUNTER, Dard
- Old Papermaking. Ill.:– Ralph Pearson. [Chilicothe], 1923. *(200) sigd.* Fo. Etched frontis. tipped-in, sigd. by artist, mntd. plts., text engrs., 9 mntd. specimens, orig. marb. bds., orig. box. (SG. Apr.26; 96) $1,100
- Papermaking by Hand in India. N.Y., 1939. *(370) numbered & sigd. by author & publisher Out-of-series copy.* 4to. 27 paper specimens bnd. in at end, prospectus laid in, qtr. cf. & patterned cl.-covered bds., spine very chipped, s.-c. (SG. Nov.3; 104) $800
- A Papermaking Pilgrimage to Japan, Korea & China. N.Y., 1936. *(370) numbered & sigd. by author & Elmer Adler.* Lge. 4to. Plts. & specimens of papers, liby. stps., pamphlet laid in, elab. patterned bds., lev. spine, by Gerhard Gerlach, boxed. (SG. Apr.26; 97) $1,000
- Papermaking: The History & Technique of an Ancient Craft. N.Y., 1947. *2nd. Edn.* 1 vol. Orig. cl., d.-w. *(With:)* – Papermaking in Pioneer America. Phila., 1952. 1 vol. Orig. qtr. cl. (SG. Jan.5; 173) $150

HUNTER, G.L.
- Decorative Textiles. Phila. & L., 1918. *Ltd. Edn.* 4to. Orig. cl. gt., unc., slightly marked. (S. May 1; 652) *Potterton.* £90

HUNTER, Capt. John
- An Historical Journal of the Transactions at Port Jackson & Norfolk Island. L., 1793. *1st. Edn.* 4to. Engraved frontis. port., engraved vig. title, 15 engraved plts. & charts, some folding, list of subscribers & list of plts., cont. cf. gt.; subscriber's copy. (LC. Oct.13; 277) £3,800
- - Anr. Copy. 4to. Engraved title with vig. (imprint slightly shaved, inner margin soiled), port., 15 engraved plts., (including 2 folding maps), neatline of the Norfolk Island map just shaved, subscribers list, cont. cf., ship device in compartments of spine;

Edward Earl of Powis bkplt. (S. May 22; 480) *Hammond.* £1,500
- - Anr. Copy. 4to. Title-p. & a few ll. with a little pale foxing, corner of 1 lf. restored, mod. hf. mor. (KH. Nov.9; 624) Aus. $2,900
- - Anr. Copy. 4to. Date shaved from foot of engraved title (as usual), folding map laid down, a few sm. defects, later (19th. C.?) hf. mor. (KH. May 1; 370) Aus. $2,100
- - Anr. Copy. 4to. Engraved title, port., 5 engraved maps, 10 engraved plts., title & frontis. foxed, most maps & some plts. slightly foxed, hf. cf., spine reinforced. (CA. Apr.3; 59) Aus. $2,000
- - Anr. Edn. Adelaide, 1968. *Facs. Edn.* 4to. Orig. cl. (KH. Nov.8; 224) Aus. $140
- - Anr. Copy. 4to. Orig. cl. (KH. Nov.9; 625) Aus. $100

HUNTER, Dr. John
- The Natural History of the Human Teeth. L., 1778. *2nd. Edn.* 2 pts. in 1 vol., including Supp. 4to. Lacks hf.-title, 1 text lf. & 1 plt. slightly torn & reprd., cont. cf. gt., rebkd. (P. Dec.8; 359) *Phillips.* £750
- - Anr. Edn. Ed.:– E. Parmly. N.Y., 1839. 2 pts. in 1 vol. Title verso stpd., liby. linen. (R. Oct.12; 1507) DM 470
- Traité des Maladies Venériennes. Trans.:– M. Audiberti. Paris, 1787. 7 folding plts., cont. cf. gt. (P. Dec.8; 90) *Clements.* £65
- Treatise on the Natural History & Diseases of the Human Teeth. Notes:– Thomas Bell. Phila., 1839. Some light foxing, later marb. wraps. (SG. Oct.6; 208) $100

HUNTER, W.S.
- Eastern Townships Scenery, Canada East. Ill.:– J.H. Bufford after Hunter. Montreal, 1860. *1st. Edn.* Sm. fo. Additional litho. title-p., 10 litho. plts., tissue guards, map, some plt. foxing, minor staining at top of few plts., orig. cl., soiled, nearly disbnd. [Sabin 33936] (SG. Apr.5; 41) $650

HUNTER, W.W.
- Orissa. 1872. 2 vols. Cont. hf. cf., gt.-decor. spines. (TA. Sep.15; 83) £78

HUNTINGTON, A.T. & Brownne, J.S.
- Medical Library & Historical Journal. Contribs.:– Osler, Pilcher, Packard, Billings, Chadwick, & others. Brooklyn, 1903-06. Vols. I-IV in 2 vols. Lge. 8vo. Later buckram. (SG. Oct.6; 252) $125

HUNTLEY, Lydia Howard
See— SIGOURNEY, Lydia Howard, née Huntley

HURD, W.
- A New Universal History of the Religions, Rites, Ceremonies, & Customs of the Whole World. [1788]. Fo. Engraved frontis., 60 plts., 2 ll. of advts. cropped, cf. (P. Mar.15; 191) *Azezian.* £140

HURLBUTT, Frank
- Bristol Porcelain. L., 1928. 4to. Orig. cl., d.-w. worn. (KH. Nov.9; 626) Aus.$130

HURSTHOUSE, Charles Flinders
- An Account of the Settlement of New Plymouth, in New Zealand. L., 1849. *1st. Edn.* Hand-cold. litho. folding plan (reprd.), 5 plts., 32 pp. advts., errata slip, some soiling, orig. cl., spine reprd. (S. Mar.6; 33) *Maggs.* £130

HURTADO DE MENDOZA, Diego
- Guerra de Granada. Lisboa, 1627. *1st. Edn.* 4to. Vell. (DS. Dec.16; 2633) Pts. 25,000

HURTAUD, Pierre & Magny, P.
- Dictionnaire Historique de la Ville de Paris et de ses Environs. Paris, 1779. 4 vols. Cont. hf. roan, spines decor. (HD. Mar.19; 99) Frs. 1,800

HURVITZ, Yesha'ya
- Sefer Beit ha-Levi. Venice, 1676. *1st. Edn.* Sm. 4to. Mild dampstaining, title soiled with minor worming, cont. blind-tooled cf., trimmed, shabby. (SG. Feb.2; 208) $175

HUSAIN IBN 'ABD ALLAH, Abû Alî, called Ibn Sînâ, or Avicenna
- Compendium de Anima. Venice, 1546. *1st. Latin Edn.* 4to. Some worming, especially last ll., lightly

stained in upr. part, loose, cont. vell. wraps. (R. Nov.8; 96) DM 520

HUSBAND, Edward
- A Collection of all the publicke Orders Ordinances & Declarations. 1646. Fo. Old cf. gt. [Wing H3808] (P. Feb.16; 259) £140

HUSKE, John
[-] The Present State of North America, etc. L., 1755. *1st. Edn.* Pt. 1 (all publd.). 4to. A few minor stains, stitched, as iss., unc. & partly unopened, cl. folding case; the Rt. Hon. Visc. Eccles copy. [Sabin 34027] (CNY. Nov.18; 144) $800

HUSSEY, Christopher
- English Country Houses. 1955-58. 3 vols. 4to. Orig. cl. (CSK. Jul.27; 99) £240
- - Anr. Copy. 3 vols. Orig. buckram, d.-w.'s. (S. Nov.8; 539) *Renard.* £220
See— JEKYLL, Gertrude & Hussey, Christopher

HUSSEY, Cyrus M.
See— LAY, William & Hussey, Cyrus M.

HUSSEY, Mrs. Thomas John
- Illustrations of British Mycology. L., 1847. 1st. Series only. 4to. 87 (of 90) hand-cold. litho. plts., cont. cf.-bkd. cl., w.a.f. (C. Mar.14; 125) *Shapiro.* £450

HUSUNG, M. J.
- Buch und Bucheinband, Aufsätze und Geographische Blätter zum 60. Geburtstage von H. Loubier. Contribs.:– G.A.E. Bogeng, H. Degering, M.J. Husung & others. Ill.:– M. Behmer & H. Wolff (orig. etchings), R. Koch & E.R. Weiss (orig. woodcuts). Leipzig, 1923. 4to. 2 orig. etchings, 2 orig. woodcuts, orig. vell. (R. Apr.3; 662) DM 420
- Bucheinbände aus der Preussischen Staatsbibliothek zu Berlin. Leipzig, 1925. Fo. Orig. cl. gt.; J.R. Abbey bkplt. & acquisition note, H.M. Nixon coll., with sig. & note. (BBA. Oct.6; 73) *Maggs.* £850

HUTCHESON, Francis
[-] An Essay on the Nature & Conduct of the Passions & Affections with Illustrations on the Moral Sense. 1728. *1st. Edn.* Cont. panel. cf., rubbed; Sir Ivar Colquhoun, of Luss copy. (CE. Mar.22; 170) £320
- An Inquiry into the Origin of our Ideas of Beauty & Virtue. 1738. *4th. Edn.* Cont. cf. (PD. Feb.15; 115) £78
- A System of Moral Philosophy in three books ... To which is prefixed some account of the life, writings, & character of the author, by the Reverend William Leechman. Glasgow, 1755. *1st. Edn.* 2 vols. 4to. Cont. spr. cf., spines gt.; Sir Ivar Colquhoun, of Luss copy. (CE. Mar.22; 116) £680

HUTCHINS, John
- History & Antiquities of the County of Dorset. 1861. *3rd. Edn.* Vols. 1 & 2 only (of 4). Fo. Lacks some text ll., disbnd., w.a.f. (LC. Jul.5; 204) £150
- - Anr. Edn. 1861-70. *3rd. Edn.* 4 vols. Fo. 120 (of 127) plts., plans, etc., lacks intros. & part of Domesday appendix, 3 plts. laid down, hf. vell. gt., w.a.f. (LC. Jul.5; 205) £320
- - Anr. Copy. 4 vols. 128 (of 133) plts., slightly spotted, some autograph material inserted, cont. hf. cf., slightly worn. (S. Mar.6; 261) *Gilbert.* £240
- - Anr. Edn. Ed.:– W. Shipp & J.W. Hodson. 1973. *Facs. of 1861-74 3rd. Edn.* 4 vols. Fo. Orig. cl., d.-w.'s. (TA. Nov.17; 180) £80

HUTCHINSON, Francis
- Historical Essay concerning Witchcraft. 1718. *1st. Edn.* Hf.-title, slight worming thro.-out affecting text, reprd. tear on hf. title-p., MS. sigs. in ink on title-p., panel cf., worn, rebkd. (BS. May 2; 40) £75
- - Anr. Edn. 1720. *2nd. Edn.* Cont. cf., worn. (BBA. Oct.27; 23) *Robertshaw.* £55

HUTCHINSON, Frank & Myers, Francis
- The Australian Contingent ... Sydney, 1885. Some foxing, mostly of fore & lr. ll., crimson mor. gt. (KH. Nov.9; 627) Aus. $180

HUTCHINSON, H.
- The Golfing Pilgrim. 1898. *1st. Edn.* Bdg. not stated. (PD. Jul.13; 36) £220

HUTCHINSON, Lucy
- Memoirs of the Life of Col. Hutchinson. L., 1806. *1st. Edn.* 4to. Extra-ill. with approx. 130 engraved plts., some folding, some spotting, few trimmed or offset, cont. maroon mor., rebkd.; 2 MS. ll. on author inserted. (S. Apr.10; 363)   *Haddon.* £80

HUTCHINSON, Thomas
- The History of the Colony of Massachusetts-Bay. L., 1760 [i.e. 1765-]68, L., 1828. *Vols. 1 & 2: 2nd. [1st. Engl.] Edn., with 1st. iss. of the Vol. 1 title before cancellation; Vol. 3: 1st. Edn., Engl. Iss., with the 16 pp. Dedication & Preface & a different title-p.* 3 vols. Title of Vol. 1 rehinged & with slight restoration to blank margin. [Sabin 34076, 34079, & 34082] (*With:*) - A Collection of Original Papers Relative to the History of the Colony of Massachusetts-Bay. Boston, 1769. *1st. Edn.* 1 vol. [Sabin 34069] Together 4 vols. Mor. gt. by Pratt; the Rt. Hon. Visc. Eccles copies. (CNY. Nov.18; 145) $480
- The History of the Province of Massachusetts Bay from 1749-1774. 1828. Orig. cl.-bkd. bds., unopened. (P. Jun.7; 310)   £110

HUTCHINSON, William
- A Treatise on Naval Architecture. L'pool., 1794. 13 engraved plts., 1 in facs., some spotting, pencilled marginalia, cont. hf. cf., slightly rubbed. (CSK. Dec.2; 66)   £80

HUTCHINSON, William, Topographer
- The History of the County of Cumberland. Carlisle, 1794. *1st. Edn.* 2 vols. 4to. Extra engraved titles, folding map, 54 views, plans & maps (1 cold.), some spotting, cont. cf., worn; letter from author to C.J. Harford tipped in. (S. Mar.6; 262)   *Chesters.* £100

HUTH, Alfred H.
- Catalogue of the Fifty Manuscripts & Printed Books Bequeathed to the British Museum. 1912. Fo. Orig. cl., faded. (BBA. Nov.10; 29)   *Marlborough Rare Books.* £75

HUTH, Henry
- Catalogue of the Famous Library ... collected by Henry Huth. L., 1911-20. 9 pts. in 3 vols. 8 pts. with lists of prices & buyers names, vell.-bkd. cl., orig. wraps. bnd. in, lists separate in orig. wraps. (S. Oct.11; 466)   *Lawson.* £220

HUTTEN, Ulrich von
- De Unitate Ecclesiae Conservanda, et Schismate ... Mainz, 1520. *1st. Edn.* 4to. Blank part of title lf. with close old MS., mod. bds. (R. Oct.11; 49)   DM 1,900

HUTTEN-CZAPSKI, M. Graf von
- Die Geschichte des Pferdes. Ed:– B. Graf von Hutten-Czapski. Trans:– L. Koenigk. Berlin, 1876. Cont. red mor., gt. inner & outer dentelle, goldtooled Franz-Joseph arms on both covers, sigd. by Belz-Niedrée, corners slightly bumped, lr. cover with slight wear. (D. Nov.25; 4498)   DM 800

HUTTON, Edward
- The Pageant of Venice. Ill.:– Frank Brangwyn. 1922. *(75) numbered & containing orig. litho. sigd. by Brangwyn.* 4to. Some light soiling, later hf. mor. (CSK. Mar.23; 187)   £75

HUTTON, William
- A Voyage to Africa ... in the Year 1820. 1821. 4 hand-cold. plts., slight browning, spr. cf. gt., rebkd., new end-papers. (SKC. Mar.9; 2018)   £140

HUTTON, William Rich
- California, 1847-1852. Intro.:– W.O. Waters. San Marino, Grabhorn Pr., 1942. *(700).* Ob. 4to. Liby. stp. on title, marb. bds., cl. back, shelf mark on spine. (SG. Apr.5; 94) $150

HUXLEY, Aldous
- Brave New World. L., 1932. *1st. Edn. (324) sigd., specially bnd.* Lge. 8vo. Orig. buckram, slightly soiled, partly unc. (S. Dec.8; 213)   *Hosian.* £250
- – Anr. Copy. Lge. 8vo. Buckram, partly untrimmed. (SG. Jan.12; 164) $550
- – Anr. Edn. L., 1932. *1st. Edn.* Slightly browned, orig. cl., d.-w. slightly discold.; Perry Molstad copy. (SPB. May 16; 473) $300

- The Burning Wheel. Oxford, 1916. *1st. Edn.* Few pencil notes, orig. wraps., dust-soiled, spine chipped; review copy, 'For Review' stpd. on hf.-title, Frederic Dannay copy. (CNY. Dec.16; 179) $200
- Eyeless in Gaza. L., 1936. *1st. Edn. (200) numbered & sigd.* Qtr. buckram, buckram folding case. (SG. Jan.12; 165) $250
- Texts & Pretexts: an Anthology with Commentaries. L., 1932. *1st. Edn. (214) specially ptd. & bnd., sigd.* Orig. cl.-bkd. decor. bds., slightly marked, partly unc. (S. Oct.11; 345)   *Byrne.* £80
- They Still Draw Pictures. N.Y., 1938. *1st. Edn. (100) numbered & sigd.* Spiral bnd. wraps., worn; orig. drawing by Spanish child for plt. 25. (RO. Apr.23; 175) $300

HUXLEY, T.H.
- [Lectures] On ... the Causes of the Phenomena of Organic Nature. 1862. *1st. Edn.* Orig. cl. (BBA. Jun.28; 271)   *Jarndyce.* £140

HUYGENS, Christiaan
- Horologium Oscillatorium, sive de Motu Pendulorum ad Horologia Aptato Demonstrationes Geometricae. Paris, 1673. *1st. Edn.* Fo. Lacks e4 (as usual), spotting, mostly affecting 1st. few & last few ll., front free end-paper loose, cont. cf., rebkd. with orig. spine laid down, corners renewed, light rubbing; Stanitz coll. (SPB. Apr.25; 230) $3,400
- Kosmotheoros, sive de Terris Coelestibus, earumque Ornatu, Conjecturae. The Hague, 1699. *2nd. Edn.* 4to. 1 plt. repeated, cont. Engl. panel. cf., slightly defect., jnt. brkn. (VG. Nov.30; 763)   Fls. 800
- Oeuvres Complètes. 's-Gravenhage, 1888-1950. *Ltd. Edn.* 21 vols. (of 22) in 22. 4to. On laid paper, sewed, unc., sm. defects. (B. Jun.21; 385)   Fls. 1,900
- Opera Reliqua. Amst., 1728. 3 pts. in 2 vols. 4to. Wide margin, browned & foxed, cont. vell. (HK. May 15; 434)   DM 550
- Opera Varia. Leiden, 1724. *1st. Edn.* 2 vols. 4to. 2 ll. advts., advice to binder lf., hf.-titles, lacks front free end-paper in 1st. vol., some browning, cont. cf., spines gt., some rubbing & chipping, lacks title labels; bkplts. of Earl of Bute, Luton Liby. & E.N. da C. Andrade, Stanitz coll. (SPB. Apr.25; 231) $250
- – Anr. Copy. 2 vols. Port. frontis., 56 folding plts., hf.-titles, lf. of binder's directions, advts. at end. (*With:*) - Opera Reliqua. Leiden, 1728. 2 vols. 58 folding plts., 1st. vol. dampstained. Together 4 vols. 4to. Unif. cont. pol. cf. gt. extra. (SG. Nov.3; 105) $700
- De Wereld-beschouwer, of Gissingen over de Hemelsche Aardklooten. Trans.:– P. Rabus. Rotterdam, 1699. Sm. 8vo. Slightly foxed, cont. vell. (VG. Nov.30; 764)   Fls. 450

HUYSHE, G.L.
See– BRACKENBURY, H. & Huyshe, G.L.

HUYSMANS, Joris-Karl
- A Rebours. 1884. *Orig. Edn.* Hf. chagrin. (HD. May 11; 31)   Frs. 1,250
- A Vau-l'Eau. Ill.:– Edgar Chahine. Paris, 1933. *(200) numbered.* 4to. Leaves, wrap., s.-c. (HD. Mar.30; 31)   Frs. 2,700
- La Bièvre, les Gobelins, Saint-Severin. Ill.:– A. Lepère. Paris, 1901. *(75) on china for libraire Conquet.* 2 vols. Red mor. by Carayon, blind- & gt.-decor., wrap., mor. album, s.-c.'s. (HD. Jun.13; 54)   Frs. 14,500
- Le Drageoir aux Epices. Ill.:– A. Brouet. Paris, 1929. *(215). (40) on japon impérial with ills. in 2 states.* 4to. 54 orig. etchings, leaves, folder, s.-c. (HD. May 4; 305)   Frs. 2,700
- Gilles de Rais. Trans.:– A. Döppner. Ill.:– W. Geiger. Berlin, 1919. *(40) De Luxe Edn. on thick Bütten.* 'Der Venuswagen', 1st. Series, Vol. IX. 4to. Printers mark & all litho. plts. sigd. by artist, orig. burgundy mor. (H. May 23; 1230)   DM 920
- Le Quartier de Notre-Dame. Ill.:– Ch. Jouas. Paris, [1905]. *(30) with 3 states of etchings & 2 states of wood engrs.* Blind-decor. mor. by Kieffer, wrap. & spine preserved, s.-c., spine faded; pen

drawing by Jouas as title. (HD. Jun.13; 52)   Frs. 3,500
- – Anr. Edn. Ill.:– Ch. Jouas. Paris, [1905]. *(130) on Arches with 3 states of engrs.* Mor. by M. Lortic, Renaissance decor., wraps. (HD. May 4; 304)   Frs. 4,500
- Les Soeurs Vatard. Preface:– Lucien Descaves. Ill.:– J.F. Raffaelli. Paris, 1909. *(60) on japan with 2 states of etchings.* Hf. mor., corners, mosaic spine (slightly faded), wrap. & spine preserved. (HD. Jun.13; 53)   Frs. 3,600

HYDE, Donald
- [-] Four Oaks Library. Ed.:– Gabriel Austen. Somerville, 1967. *(1250).* Tall 8vo. Cl.-bkd. bds.; Xmas greeting sigd. by Mary Hyde laid in. (SG. Sep.15; 181) $100

HYDE, Edward, Earl of Clarendon
See– CLARENDON, Edward Hyde, Earl of

HYDE, R.
- The Regent's Park Colosseum. 1982. *(200) numbered & sigd. by author.* 4to. 6 hand-cold. plts., mor. gt., lined box. (P. Apr.12; 68)   *Woodruff.* £130

HYDE, Thomas
- Veterum Persarum et Parthorum et Medorum Religionis Historia. Ed.:– George Costard. Oxford, 1760. *2nd. Edn.* 4to. 20 plts., including 4 folding, age-browned, cont. vell., blind-stpd. ornaments. (SG. Nov.3; 106) $400

HYETT, Francis A. & Bazeley, Rev. William
- The Bibliographers Manual of Gloucestershire Literature. *(250).* 3 vols. (*With:*) - Biographical Supplement. *(110).* 2 vols. Together 5 vols. Gloucester, 1895-1906. Orig. cl., paper labels on spines torn. (BBA. Feb.9; 337)   *Parsloe.* £170

HYGINUS, Caius Julius
- Poeticon Astronomicon. Venice, Erhard Ratdolt, 14 Oct. 1482. 4to. Lacks 1st. blank, c1, c8, g2 & g9 in facs., considerable dampstaining, loose in old bds.; the Walter Goldwater copy. [BMC V, 286; Goff H-560; HC 9062] (SG. Dec.1; 185) $550

HYMNALS [English & Ojibwa]
- A Collection of Chippeway & English Hymns. Toronto, 1840. 16mo. Thumbed, few stains, old cl. over cont. sheep. (SG. Oct.20; 191) $170

HYPERION
Ed.:– F. Blei & C. Sternheim. Ill.:– E. Gordon-Craig, J. Laboureur, A. Thomann, J.J. Vrieslander, E. Bloos & others. München, 1908-10. *Ltd. Iss.* 2 series in 6 pts. each, bnd. together in 6 vols. (all publd.). 4to. Orig. hf. linen, decor. by W. Tiemann, spine spotted. (H. Nov.24; 1651)   DM 1,100
- – Anr. Copy. Years I & II in 6 vols. (all publd.). Orig. hf. linen, spine soiled, sm. scratches, ex-libris, w.a.f. (HK. Nov.11; 3643)   DM 900

I*, M. le C. d'**
- Bibliographie des Ouvrages Relatifs à l'Amour, aux Femmes, au Mariage ... 1871. *3rd. Edn.* 6 vols. in 3. Sm. 8vo. Orig. hf. mor., partly untrimmed, some wear to spine ends. (TA. May 17; 348)   £70

IACOVLEFF, Alexander
- Dessins et Peintures d'Afrique. Paris, 1927. *Ltd. Edn.* Fo. 50 cold. plts., loose as iss., with text, in orig. mor.-bkd. limp cl., all preserved in orig. mor. portfo., ties. (BBA. Apr.5; 104)   *Greenwood.* £120
- – Anr. Edn. [Paris, 1927]. *(1000) on Lafuma paper.* 1 vol. only (lacks text vol.). Fo. 50 col. plts. (1 double-p.), 1 torn, loose as iss. in leath. folder, worn. (SG. Jan.26; 207) $140
- Les Dessins & Peintures d'Extrême-Orient. Text:– V. Goloubew. Paris, 1922. *(150) numbered.* Fo. On China, plts. on Dutch Bütten, 50 plts. (38 in 2-col. gravure, 12 col.-ptd.), text pt. 23 pp., with 5 mostly full-p. ills., including port., in orig. vell. box. (R. Oct.11; 870)   DM 700
- Le Théâtre Chinois. Text:– Tchou-Kia-Kien. Paris, 1922. 4to. Publisher's bds. (HD. Jun.6; 79)   Frs. 1,000

IAMBLICHUS

- **De Mysteriis [with other tracts].** Trans.:– Marsilius Ficinus. Venice, Aldus, 1497. *1st. Edn.* Fo. Lr. margin of title mntd. to mask stp., 18th. C. vell., spine reprd.; from Fondation Furstenberg-Beaumesnil. [BMC V, 557; Goff J216] (HD. Nov.16; 76) Frs. 18,300
- **De Mysteriis Aegyptiorum.** Ed.:– M. Ficinus. Venice, Nov. 1516. Fo. Some margin stains, hf. cf.; Dr. Walter Pagel copy. (S. Feb.7; 203) *Colombo.* £400
- **De Mysteriis Liber.** Ed.:– Thomas Gale. Oxford, 1678. Fo. In Greek & Latin, errata lf., cont. cf.; Andrew Fletcher & Dr. Walter Pagel copy. [Wing I 26] (S. Feb.7; 204) *Heller.* £320
- **De Vita Pythagorica & Protrepticae Orationes ad Philosophiam.** [Franecker], 1598. 4to. Cont. vell., corner repair to bdg. & end-paper; Eusèbe Salverte's copy (according to MS. note), with his autograph slip pasted to end-paper, from Fondation Furstenberg-Beaumesnil. (HD. Nov.16; 129) Frs. 1,800

IBANEZ DE ECHEVARRI, B.

- **Histoire du Paraguay sous les Jésuites.** Map:– Guillaume de l'Isle. Amst., 1780. *1st. Edn.* 3 vols. Hf.-titles, old bds. [Sabin 21763] (SG. Jan.19; 190) $175

IBARRA, G.

- [-] **[Trages y Costumbres de la Provincia de Buenos Aires].** [Buenos Aires, 1839]. Sm. fo. 12 (of 24) litho. plts., unbnd. (S. Dec.13; 145) *Henig.* £90

IBIS, The: a Quarterly Journal of Ornithology

L., British Ornithologists' Union. 1920-83. Plts., cold. maps, last 12 years in orig. wraps., rest hf. cl., w.a.f. (S. Apr.10; 424) *Evans.* £360

IBN SINA

See– HUSAIN IBN 'ABD ALLAH, Abû Alî, called Ibn Sînâ or Avicenna

IBN YECHIAH, Don Yosef

- **Torah Or.** Bologna, 1538. *1st. Edn. (Bound with:)*
- **Seder Olam.** [Venice], 1545? Together 2 works in 1 vol. 4to. Poem on verso of 1st. work title, uncensored, title stained with repairs & sigs., a few other margin repairs, some staining, 2nd. work lacks title, some worming, staining & repairs, bds.; Hochschule für die Wissenschaft des Judenthums stps. [Steinschneider 5934] (SPB. Jun.26; 12) $1,600

IBSEN Heinrik

- **Die Kronprätendenten.** Ill.:– A. Kolb. Leipzig, 1911. *(250).* Fo. Hand-bnd. blind-tooled pig, silk liners & doubls., gt. inner dentelle, by Hans Dannhorn, Leipzig. (H. Nov.24; 1716) DM 520
- **Peer Gynt.** Ill.:– Arthur Rackham. L., 1936. *(460) numbered & sigd. by artist.* 4to. Orig. parch. gt., spine darkened. (S. Dec.20; 577) *Rosenblatt.* £190

ICONES ARBORUM, FRUTICUM ET HERBARUM EXOTICARUM quarundam a Rajo, Mentzelio ... ut et Animalium Peregrinorum Rarissimorum

Leiden, ca. 1720. Ob. 4to. Engraved title, 80 engraved plts., cont. hf. vell., slightly rubbed. (C. Jun.27; 166) *Quaritch.* £400

IDE, Simeon

- **A Biographical Sketch of ... William B. Ide.** [Claremont, N.H., 1880]. *1st. Edn.* 16mo. Orig. cl., slightly faded. (LH. Apr.15; 323) $110

IDEAL TRIFLES, published by a Lady

L., 1774. 12mo. Errata lf., advt. lf., few spots & light stains, orig. bds., worn, unc. (S. Apr.9; 260) *Bennett.* £90

IDEN PARK ESTATE

L., 1879. 4to. 3 col. folding maps (1 torn & loose), 2 litho. plts., orig. wraps., upr. cover loose, torn & soiled. (P. Nov.24; 64) *Fancycrest.* £60

IDES, Ekert Ysbrants

- **Dreijaarige Reize naar China, te Land gedaan over Groot Ustiga, Siriania ... tot in China.** Map:– Nic. Witsen. Amst., 1704. *1st. Edn.* 4to. Slight margin staining, cont. hf. cf., covers rubbed, spine slightly defect. (VS. Dec.9; 1287) Fls. 625

- **Three Years Travel from Moscow Over-Land to China.** 1706. 4to. Lf. of directions to binder at end, minor foxing, cont. cf., rebkd. (BBA. Sep.29; 81) *Hossain.* £370
- – **Anr. Copy.** 4to. Additional engraved title, lge. folding map (reprd. in folds), 30 engraved plts. (a few double-p. or folding), cont. panel. cf. (S. May 22; 442) *Bonham.* £240

IDYLLE PRINTANIERE

N.p., n.d. 4to. Vergé d'Arches, leaves, publishers portfo. (HD. Dec.9; 18) Frs. 3,000

IGNATIUS, of Loyola

See– AUGUSTINUS, Saint Aurelius, Bp of Hippo & Ignatius, of Loyola

IHLE, Johann Eberhard

See– PREISLER, Johann Martin & Ihle, Johann Eberhard

ILES MAURICE ET DE LA REUNION

N.p., n.d. Sm. 4to. Album of 84 photos., cont. damson chagrin, blind decor., decor. spine, box. (HD. Dec.9; 146) Frs. 4,900

ILLINOIS

[-] **Debates & Proceedings of the Constitutional Convention of the State of Illinois.** Springfield, 1870. 2 vols. 4to. Maroon mor.-bkd. bds., corners bumped, a few slight stains. (LH. Sep.25; 244) $120
- **The History of Adams County.** Chicago, 1879. *1st. Edn.* Hand-cold. double-p. map, many view & port. plts., some foxing, hf. mor., gt. decor. cl., spine extremities frayed. (SG. Apr.5; 95) $120

ILLUSTRATED BOTANY, The

N.Y., 1846. Vol. I. 2 plain & 47 col. litho. plts., few browned, some foxing, cont. hf. leath., spine chipped. (SG. Oct.6; 210) $140

ILLUSTRATED JOURNAL OF AUSTRALASIA, The

See– JOURNAL OF AUSTRALASIA, The [later The Illustrated Journal of Australasia]

ILLUSTRATED LONDON NEWS

May 1842-Jun. 1843. Vols. 1 & 2 in 1. Fo. Folding panorama of London (2 pts. on single sheet), some damage, cont. hf. mor. (TA. Oct.20; 191) £52
- – **Anr. Run.** Jan. 1843-Jun. 1846. Vols. 2-8. Fo. Orig. cl. gt., dampstained, not affecting contents. (TA. Aug.18; 287) £88
- – **Anr. Run.** Jul. 1849-Jun. 1850. Vols. 15 & 16 in 1. Fo. Cont. hf. roan, base of spine torn. (TA. Oct.20; 194) £54
- – **Anr. Run.** Jul. 1849-Dec. 1863. In 27 vols. (lacks Jul.-Dec. 1852). Lge. fo. 11 vols. in cont. cl. gt., others in hf. roan; from liby. of Luttrellstown Castle, w.a.f. (C. Sep.28; 1827) £700
- – **Anr. Run.** 1850-51. 3 vols. Fo. Orig. cl. gt. (P. Apr.12; 271) *Robertshaw.* £60
- – **Anr. Run.** Jan. 1852-Dec. 1854, Jan. 1864-Dec. 1865, Jan. 1868-Dec. 1896. 64 vols. Variously bnd. (LC. Mar.1; 504) £1,200
- – **Anr. Run.** L., 1852-71. 6 vols. Fo. Cont. cl. or hf. sheep, mostly shabby. (SG. Dec.15; 161) $250
- – **Anr. Run.** Jan.-Jun. 1860. Vol.XXXVI. Fo. Lacks 3 or 4 ll., 6 double-p. cold. supps. (with foxing & slight adhesion) bnd. at end, old hf. mor., slightly worn & rubbed. (KH. May 1; 374) *Aus.* $130
- – **Anr. Run.** Jul.-Dec. 1860. Vol.XXXVII. Fo. 4 cold. supps., old hf. mor. (KH. May 1; 375) *Aus.* $150
- – **Anr. Run.** L., 1861-63. Vols. XXXVIII-XLII in 6 vols. Fo. Some slight browning, sm. margin tears, orig. linen & 2 cont. linen, not collated, w.a.f. (HT. May 10; 2827) DM 600
- – **Anr. Run.** L., 1867-69. Vols. L-LV in 6 vols. Fo. Some slight browning, some sm. margin tears, various cont. bdgs., some with slight defects. or light wear, not collated, w.a.f. (HT. May 10; 2828) DM 650
- – **Anr. Run.** 1941-45. 9 vols. Fo. Recent cl. (TA. Aug.18; 288) £50

ILLUSTRATED SYDNEY NEWS

1882-87. Fo. Hf. cf. gt., rubbed. (P. Jun.7; 236) £400

ILLUSTRATION

Paris, 1843-49. Vols. I-VIII & X-XIV only, in 10 vols. Fo. Vols. I-VIII hf. roan, rest publisher's hf. chagrin. (B. Feb.8; 611) Fls. 1,100
- – **Anr. Edn.** Paris, 1847-52. 11 vols. Fo. Some foxing, cont. hf. mor. gt., a little rubbed, 3 spines defect. (VS. Jun.6; 189) Fls. 500
- – **Anr. Edn.** Paris, 1908-19. 24 vols. Fo. Hf. chagrin; from Château des Noës liby. (HD. May 25; 32) Frs. 2,000

ILLUSTRATION THEATRALE

Paris, 1901-14. In 22 vols. only. 4to. Cont. hf. roan, some spines worn, few covers detchd. (BBA. Oct.27; 336) *Kohler.* £70

ILLUSTRES FEES (Les). Contes Galans, Dédiez aux Dames

Paris, 1709. 12mo. Red mor. by Duru, 1853, blind- & gt.-decor. (HD. Mar.27; 18) Frs. 1,800

ILLUSTRIRTES KONVERSATIONS- LEXIKON

Berlin, 1870-82. 8 vols. & 2 supp. vols. in 10 vols. 4to. 1st. half of vol. 3 stained in upr. margin, cont. hf. linen, vols. 7 & 10 slightly loose. (R. Apr.4; 1190) DM 1,500
- – **Anr. Edn.** Leipzig & Berlin, 1885-92. 8 vols. Orig. hf. leath. gt., slightly rubbed. (GB. Nov.3; 979) DM 1,500

ILYAZD (Pseud.)

See– ZIANEWICH, Ilya 'Eli Elganbyuri' or 'Ilyazd'

IMAGE. A Quarterly of the Visual Arts

See– ALPHABET & IMAGE - IMAGE. A Quarterly of the Visual Arts

IMAGE, Revue Littéraire et Artistique Ornée de Figures sur Bois

Ill.:– Jeanniot, Maurice Denis, Renouard, Chéret, Doudelet & others. Paris, Dec. 1896-Dec. 1897. Nos. 1-12 (all publd.). 4to. Publisher's bdg., special tools, unc. (LM. Oct.22; 57) B.Frs. 15,000

IMAGO MUNDI

L., 1939-82. Vols. 3-34. 4to. Vols. 3-26 in wraps., 1 or 2 worn, rest in cl.; several vols. with MS. notes by G.R. Crone loosely inserted. (S. Jun.25; 296) *Tooley.* £460

IMLAY, Gilbert

- **A Topographical Description of the Western Territory of North America.** L., 1797. *3rd. Edn.* 1 folding plan, 3 engraved folding maps, hf.-title, lacks advt., some faint browning, cont. cf., spine gt., worn. [cf. Sabin 34358 (calling for 2 maps & 1 plan only)] (S. Dec.13; 136) *Edwards.* £170

IMMERMANN, K.

- **Münchhausen. Eine Geschichte in Arabesken.** Düsseldorf, 1838-30. *1st. Edn.* 4 vols. Cont. bds. gt., slightly bumped. (HK. Nov.10; 2533) DM 420
- **Tulifäntchen.** Ill.:– M. Slevogt. Berlin, 1923. *(300) numbered.* 20 orig. etchings, title etching sigd. by artist, orig. hf. leath. gt., unc. (GB. May 5; 3343) DM 650

IMPERIAL GALLERY OF BRITISH ART, The

Ca. 1870. Fo. 46 (of 48) engraved plts., title torn, some margin foxing, hf. mor., defect. (P. Mar.15; 261) *Erlini.* £260

IMPERIALE REGIO GOVERNO DI VENEZIA. ...

See– ISTRUZIONE SULLA PROCEDURA DA OSSERVARSI nella Prestazione di Giuramento degli Israeliti ... –IMPERIALE REGIO GOVERNO DI VENEZIA. ...

IMPRIMATUR. Ein Jahrbuch für Bücherfreunde

Hamburg & Weimar, 1930-51. *Ltd. Iss.* Orig. Series: Vols. I-X. 4to. Orig. hf. linen & linen. (H. Nov.23; 96) DM 720
- – **Anr. Edn.** Hamburg, 1930-55. Orig. Series: Vols. I-XII. 4to. Orig. hf. linen & linen. (HK. Nov.11; 4439) DM 1,000
- – **Anr. Copy.** Orig. Series: Vols. I-XII. Sm. 4to. 1 lf. prelims. stained & discold., orig. linen & hf. linen, Vol. I upr. cover discold. & cockled. (H. Nov.23; 95) DM 900
- – **Anr. Edn.** Ed.:– S. Buchenau, G.K. Schauer, &

IMPRIMATUR. Ein Jahrbuch für Bücherfreunde - *Contd.*
others. Frankfurt, 1957-76. Vols. I-VIII & index Vols. I-XII, New Series: Vols. I-IV. together 9 vols. Orig. linen. (H. Nov.23; 97) DM 620

IMPRINT (THE)
L., 1913. Vol. 1 nos. 1-6 & Vol. II nos. 1, 8 & 9, in 3 vols. 4to. A few stains, orig. wraps., some spines defect., in 3 cl.-bkd. bd. folders. (S. May 1; 405)
Sawyer. £100

INCHBALD, Mrs. Elizabeth
– A Collection of Farces. L., 1809. 7 vols. 12mo. Early cf. gt., jnts. worn. (SG. Feb.16; 162) $120

INCWADI YABANTWANA
Durban, 1869. *1st. Edn.* Sm. 8vo. Orig. woodcut-pict. wraps., sewed, spine slightly chipped. (SG. Mar.29; 83) $100

INDAGINE, Ioannes ab
– Introductiones Apotelesmatice Elegantes, in Chyromantiam, Physionomiam, Astrologiam Naturalem ... Lugduni, 1556. Cont. decor. vell. gt. (LM. Mar.3; 203) B. Frs. 14,500

INFANT'S LIBRARY, The
L., ca. 1800. Books 1-15, & 'A Short History of England'. Miniature Book. 57 x 45mm. Several ll. in Book 1 torn with some paper loss, affecting 1 ill., orig. bds., 2 vols. detchd. from bdg., all but 3 rebkd., orig. wood box, additional engraved label on rear, lid chipped. (SG. Dec.8; 207) $1,100

INGERSOLL, Robert G.
– The Works. N.Y., [1901-]11. *(50) numbered.* 13 vols. 1st. title & engraved plts. in 2 states, purple mor., covers with gt.-panel borders, spines in 6 compartments, gt.-panel., mor. gt. doubls., watered silk end-pp., partly unc.; A.L.s from author tipped in. (CNY. Dec.17; 572) $550

INGERSOLL-SMOUSE, Florence
– Joseph Vernet: Peintre de Marine, 1714-1789. Paris, 1926. *1st. Edn. (500) numbered.* 2 vols. Sm. fo. 357 reproductions on 152 plts., cl. (SG. Oct.13; 354) $300

INGLEBY, Thomas
– Whole Art of Legerdemain, containing all the Tricks & Deceptions ... as performed by the Emperor of Conjurors. L., [frontis. dtd. 1815]. *1st. Edn.* 12mo. Frontis. hand-cold., offset on title-p., a few ll. slightly spotted, orig. bds., unc., worn, lacks backstrip. (S. Dec.20; 676) *Huber.* £260

INGLETON, G.C.
– Charting a Continent ... Sydney, 1944. Bdg. not stated, d.-w. slightly frayed. (KH. May 1; 376) Aus. $170
– True Patriots All or News From Early Australia. Sydney, 1952. *(150) numbered & sigd. & with 3 sigd. etchings by Ingleton.* No bdg. stated. (JL. Jun.24; 119) Aus. $475

INGOLDSBY, Thomas (Pseud.)
See– BARHAM, Rev. Richard H. 'Thomas Ingoldsby'

INGRAM, Dale
– Practical Cases & Observations in Surgery, with Remarks ... not only for the Improvement of all Young Surgeons, but also for the Direction of Such as are Farther Advanced. L., 1751. *1st. Edn.* Cont. cf., rather worn. (SG. Mar.22; 173) $175

INGRAM, James
– Memorials of Oxford. Ill.:– J. Le Keux. Oxford, 1837. *[1st. Edn.].* 2 vols. only (of 3). 2 vig. titles, 68 engraved views, hf. cf. gt. (P. Sep.8; 234)
Jarndyce. £150
– – Anr. Copy. 3 vols. 4to. Cont. hf. mor., spines gt. (SG. Mar.29; 321) $200

IN HET CIRCUS - Tijl Uilenspiegel en Zijn Streken
Ill.:– Jan Franse. Amst., ca. 1910. 2 vols. 4to. Moving picture book, 1 ill. in 2nd. vol. lacks sm. part, text browned, orig. limp pict. bds., slightly worn; van Veen coll. (S. Feb.28; 273) £110

IN MEMORIAM N.Z.A.S.M.
Amst., [1909?]. Lge. 4to. Orig. bdg. (VA. Jan.27; 200) R 180

INNES, Cosmo
– The Black Book of Taymonth ... with other Papers from the Breadalbane Charter Room. Edinb., priv. ptd., 1855. 4to. Later red panel. hf. mor. by Rivière. (PD. Jun.13; 57) £230

INNES-LILLINGTON, Lieut. F.G.
– The Land of the White Bear. Portsmouth & L., 1876. 8 plts., folding map detchd. with sm. tears, some spotting, orig. cl., slightly worn; pres. copy to Mr. Ball from Allen Young. (S. Mar.6; 65)
Hitching. £480

INNOCENTIUS VIII, Pope
– Bulla Canonizationis Sancti Leopoldi Machionis. [Vienna, Stephen Koblinger?], after 6 Jan. 1485. 4to. Initial 'I' at opening, sig. 'a' on 1st. p., & 'nostri' in the last line, untrimmed & unbnd. sheets, in cl. folding case; the Walter Goldwater copy. [BMC III, 809; Goff I-102; C. 3267] (SG. Dec.1; 187) $800

INSTITORIS, H.
See– SPRENGER, J. & Institoris, H.

INSTRUCCION FORMADA EN VIRTUD DE REAL ORDEN DE S.M., que se dirige al Senor Comandante General de Provincias Internas ... [Mexico, 1786]. Fo. Disbnd. (S. May 22; 340)
Cortes. £6,000

INSTRUCTION DUR LES MESURES Deduites de la Grandeur de la Terre
Auxerre, An 2 [1793/94]. Cont. wraps., untrimmed. (SG. Oct.6; 212) $150

INTELLECTUAL OBSERVER: Review of Natural History, Microscopic Research, & Recreative Science
1862-65. Vols. 1-7. Cont. hf. cf., gt.-decor. spines, slightly rubbed. (TA. May 17; 354) £50

INTERESTING & AFFECTING HISTORY OF PRINCE LEE BOO, a Native of the Pelew Islands
L., 1789. 12mo. Bds. (P. Feb.16; 260) £55

INTERNATIONAL AUCTION RECORDS
Ed.:– E. Mayer. [Paris], for 1970, 1971, 1973-78, 1980 & 1981. 10 vols. Unif. cl. (SG. Jan.26; 208) $350

INTERNATIONAL BOOKBINDING EXHIBITION BY THE CHIEF CRAFTSMEN from all Parts of the World, at the Caxton Head
See– EXHIBITION OF MODERN BOOKBINDINGS BY THE CHIEF EUROPEAN CRAFTSMEN, at the Caxton Head – INTERNATIONAL BOOKBINDING EXHIBITION BY THE CHIEF CRAFTSMEN from all Parts of the World, at the Caxton Head

INWOOD, Henry William
– The Erechtheion at Athens. Ill.:– M.A. Nicholson. L., 1827. *1st. Edn.* Atlas fo. 35 plts., some double-p., ex-liby., some foxing, later red three-qtr. mor. (SG. May 3; 215) $700

IOHARA, Shizuka
– Man-shi Zuan Seika Taisei. Tokyo, Showa 11 [1936]. 4to. Possibly impft., text in wraps., laid in with loose plts. in cl. folding case, as iss., slightly soiled, extremities rubbed. (SG. Jan.26; 185) $150

IRBY, Charles Leonard & Mangles, James
– Travels in Egypt & Nubia, Syria, & Asia Minor during the years 1817 & 1818. L., 1823. Orig. bds., unc. & unopened, foot of spine chipped. (C. Nov.16; 98) *Wood.* £200

IREDALE, Tom
– Birds of New Guinea. Melbourne, 1956. 2 vols. *(With:)* – Birds of Paradise & Bower Birds. Together 3 vols. No bdgs. stated, together in s.-c. (JL. Jun.24; 139) Aus. $400
– – Anr. Copy. 2 vols. 4to. Qtr. mor., s.-c., covers & s.-c. soiled. (CA. Apr.3; 62) Aus. $260
– – Anr. Copy. 2 vols. Publisher's qtr. mor., d.-w.'s. (KH. May 1; 378) Aus. $190
– Birds of Paradise & Bower Birds. Ill.:– Lilian Medland. Melbourne, 1950. 4to. Qtr. mor., covers soiled, spine rubbed, sig. on front end-paper. (CA. Apr.3; 61) Aus. $140

– – Anr. Copy. Publisher's qtr. mor., d.-w. (KH. May 1; 379) Aus. $100
– – Anr. Edn. N.d. 4to. Qtr. mor. (WW. Nov.23; 144) £75

IRELAND
– Address & Resolutions of the Two Houses of Parliament in Ireland, & Account of the Commerce & Revenue of Great Britain & Ireland. Dublin, 1800. Fo. Bkplt., hf. cf. (GM. Dec.7; 474) £220
– Return of Owners of Land of One Acre & Upwards ... in Ireland. Dublin, 1876. Fo. Hf. mor., rubbed. (GM. Dec.7; 178) £170
– A Tour through Ireland, Wherein the Present State of that Kingdom is Considered. Dublin, 1780. 12mo. No folding map, lacks front blank, cf., spine cracked. (GM. Dec.7; 201) £65

IRELAND, John
– Hogarth Illustrated. L., 1791-94. 3 vols. Engraved frontis. & vig. titles to Vols. 1 & 2, 112 engraved plts., fore-edge of 1 plt. shaved, Vol. 2 browned towards end, cont. russ., spines faded. (C. Nov.9; 142) *Traylen.* £70
– – Anr. Edn. Ill.:– N. Cook. 1801. Fo. 93 engraved plts., cont. cf. gt., worn, upr. cover detchd. (PD. May 16; 234) £310

IRELAND, Samuel
– A Picturesque Tour Through Holland, Brabant & Part of France. L., 1790. 2 vols. 4to. L.P., 2 engraved titles with sepia aquatint oval vigs., 25 plts., mostly sepia aquatint views, some spotting & offsetting, cont. hf. cf., slightly rubbed. (C. Jun.27; 39) *Zanzotto.* £250
– – Anr. Copy. 2 vols. 2 vig. titles, 45 plts., cf., rebkd. & corners reprd. (P. Feb.16; 156) £120
– – Anr. Edn. L., 1796. *2nd. Edn.* 2 vols. Additional engraved titles, 46 plts., cont. spr. cf. gt. (C. Nov.16; 18) *Bradley.* £450
– – Anr. Copy. 2 vols. Extra engraved titles, 48 plts., mostly aquatint views, 7 with pencil sketches on reverse, spotted & offset, cont. mor. (S. Apr.9; 34)
Ayres. £140
– – Anr. Copy. 2 vols. Fo. L.P., engraved title, 48 aquatints & plts., cont. cf., rebkd., orig. spines laid down, worn; pres. copy from author to his daughter. (SPB. Dec.13; 845) $275
– Picturesque Views on the River Medway. 1793. Hf.-title, hf. mor., partly unc., rubbed. (S. Nov.1; 115) *Scott.* £90
– – Anr. Copy. Hf. cf. gt. (P. Sep.29; 91)
Hodden. £65
– – Anr. Copy. Additional aquatint title, engraved map, 28 aquatint views, hf.-title, plts. slightly dampstained in lr. corner, cont. hf. cf., rubbed. (S. Jun.25; 329) *Elliott.* £50
– Picturesque Views on the River Thames. 1792. *[1st. Edn.].* 2 vols. 4to. 2 engraved additional titles, 2 engraved maps, 52 aquatint plts., some margins spotted, cont. diced cf., rebkd. (CSK. Dec.16; 70) £180

– – Anr. Copy. 2 vols. Aquatint titles, 2 maps, 52 plts., hf.-title & last errata lf. in Vol. 1, last advt. & errata ll. in Vol. 2, some ll. spotted, cont. hf. cf. (BBA. Sep.29; 115) *Clack.* £150
– – Anr. Edn. 1801-02. 2 vols. Tall 8vo. Additional aquatint titles, 2 uncold. maps, 52 aquatint plts., some offset to text, some margin stains, recent qtr. mor. (TA. May 17; 91) £190
– – Anr. Copy. 2 vols. 4to. Additional aquatint titles, 2 maps, 53 plts., a few imprints shaved, a few ll. spotted, cont. hf. cf., rubbed. (S. Jun.25; 328)
Young. £170
– Picturesque Views of the Severn. L., 1824. 2 vols. Lge. 8vo. 102 plts., cl. (HBC. May 17; 366) £75
– Picturesque Views on the Upper, or Warwickshire Avon. 1795. *[1st. Edn.].* Tall 8vo. Aquatint title, map, 31 plts., orig. marb. bds., parch. backstrip, untrimmed, spine worn. (TA. Dec.15; 94) £85
– – Anr. Copy. Aquatint frontis. & 31 plts., ills to text, some margin dampstains, recent qtr. cf. (TA. Jun.21; 173) £75
– Picturesque Views with an Historical Account of the Inns of Court. 1800. 4to. L.P., cf. gt. (P. Sep.29; 270) *Solomons.* £85

IRELAND, William Henry
– The Confessions ... Containing the Particulars of his Fabrication of the Shakespeare Manuscripts. L., 1805. *1st. Edn.* 12mo. 2 plts. torn along a fold, later vell.-bkd. cl. (BBA. Dec.15; 183) *Bowers.* £60
– England's Topographer, or A New & Complete History of The County of Kent. L., 1828-29. 4 vols. Engraved title, folding map, 124 engraved views, many stained, mod. cl. gt. (P. Nov.24; 66) *Fancycrest.* £150
– – Anr. Copy. 4 vols. 1 engraved title, folding map, 113 (of 124?) plts., some foxing, hf. mor. gt. (P. Oct.20; 63) £100
– – Anr. Edn. 1828-30. 4 vols. Vig. title, folding map, 123 engraved plts., hf. cf. gt. (P. Sep.8; 367) *Frankland.* £130
– – Anr. Copy. 4 vols. Engraved title, 124 engraved plts., cf. gt., some covers loose. (PWC. Jul.11; 581) £100
– – Anr. Copy. 4 vols. Engraved title, folding map, 92 (of 124) plts., some imprints cropped, spotted, some browning, later hf. cf. (S. Mar.6; 428) *Swift.* £60
– The Life of Napoleon Bonaparte. Ill.:– George Cruikshank. 1823. 4 vols. Some plts. hand-cold., some spotting, recent hf. mor., gt.-decor. spines. (TA. May 17; 83) £76
– – Anr. Edn. Ill.:– George Cruikshank. 1828. 4 vols. 27 folding engraved plts. (24 hand-cold.), hf. cf., spines gt.-decor., slightly rubbed. (SKC. Mar.9; 1752) £400
– – Anr. Copy. 4 vols. 3 plain plts., 24 hand-cold. plts., folding, each bkd., some browning, cf. gt. (SPB. Dec.13; 846) £150
– Miscellaneous Papers & Legal Instruments under the hand & Seal of William Shakespeare. 1796. Fo. Some plts. hand-cold., 1 p. with 2 tears, orig. bds., rebkd. (P. Apr.12; 53) *Vine.* £140

IRENAEUS, Saint
– Opus Eruditissimum Divi Irenaei Episcopi Lugdunensis in Quinque Libros ... Basilea, 1526. Fo. 16th. C. blind-stpd. cf., turn-ins worn. (HD. Jun.29; 121) Frs. 2,300

IRIBE, Paul
– Blanc et Rouge. – Rose et Noir. – Bleu, Blanc, Rouge. Paris, 1930-32. Fo. Orig. wraps. (GB. May 5; 2725) DM 800
– Choix. Bagneux, 1930. 4to. Sewed, spiral bound. (HD. Dec.1; 48) Frs. 4,200
– Le Temoin. Paris, 1933-35. Nos. 1-60, lacks no. 46. In parts. (HD. Dec.1; 49) Frs. 3,000

IRIBE, P. & others
– L'Eventail et la Fourrure chez Paquin. N.p., ca. 1925. *(300).* Fo. Publisher's decor. bds. (HD. Jun.29; 122) Frs. 5,300

IRISH HISTORICAL STUDIES
Ed.:– R. Dudley Edward & T.W. Moody. Dublin, 1938-80. Vol. I no. 1-Vol. XVIII no. 70, & nos. 74, 75, 77, 79, 80-82, 85, & 86. Orig. painted wraps., as a periodical, w.a.f. (GM. Dec.7; 181) £220

IRISH RAILWAY COMMISSION
– Atlas to Accompany 2nd Report of the Railway Commissioners, Ireland 1838. Dublin, 1838. Lge. atlas fo. 6 double-p. maps, including 1 hand-cold., some stains, cl., as an atlas, w.a.f. (GM. Dec.7; 496) £130

IRVING, Washington
– Astoria; or Enterprise beyond the Rocky Mountains. – Adventures of Captain Bonneville, or Scenes beyond the Rocky Mountains of the Far West. Paris, 1836, 1837. Cont. hf. leath. (D. Nov.23; 1275) DM 450
– Bracebridge Hall. Ill.:– R. Caldecott. 1877. Publisher's catalogue bnd. in at end, mor. gt. by Rivière, orig. cl. gt. upr. cover & backstrip bnd. in. (TA. May 17; 502) £50
[–] The Crayon Miscellany. Phila., 1835. *1st. Amer. Edns. v. 1st. 2 vols. Blanck's 1st. State, 3rd. vol. Blanck's state 'A'.* 3 vols. 12mo. Some foxing, orig. cl., spine labels darkened & slightly chipped, some wear, upr. cover of 3rd. vol. slightly chewed. (RO. Apr.23; 181) $135
– The Legend of Sleepy Hollow. Ill.:– Arthur Rackham. [1928]. *(250) numbered & sigd. by*

artist. Bdg. not stated. (JL. Mar.25; 447) Aus. $180
– – Anr. Edn. Ill.:– Arthur Rackham. Phila., [1928]. *(375) sigd. by artist.* 4to. Orig. vell. gt. (SPB. Dec.13; 888) $350
– The Life of George Washington. N.Y., 1889. *'Ltd. Centennial Edn.' (300) numbered.* 5 vols. 4to. Cl., spines gt., light wear, d.-w.'s (light wear, a few minor tears &c.), each vol. in separate gt.-lettered publisher's box, worn; Ken Leach coll. (RO. Jun.10; 120) $100
– Rip Van Winkle. Ill.:– Arthur Rackham. 1906. 4to. On Whatman, no bdg. stated. (HD. Jun.26; 127) Frs. 1,900
– – Anr. Edn. Ill.:– Arthur Rackham 1908. 4to. Orig. cl. gt. (P. Feb.16; 287) £55
– The Rocky Mountains: Or, Scenes, Incidents, & Adventures in the Far West. Phila., 1837. *1st. Edn.* 2 vols. 12mo. Without publisher's catalogue, a few sigs. sprung, maps with minor tears &c., orig. cl. (Blanck's variant 'A'), some wear, 1 label slightly chipped. (RO. Apr.23; 185) $120
– Salmagudi: or the Whim-Whams & Opinions of Launcelot Langstaff & Others. N.Y., 1807-08. *Mixed Edns.? [see below].* 2 vols. Marked 3rd. Edn. in Vol. 1 pt. 1 & 2nd. Edn. in pts. 2 & 3, Vol. 1 apparently bnd. mainly from 2nd. state pts. & Vol. 2 from 1st. state, cf., covers lightly rubbed, slight age darkening. (CBA. Mar.3; 259) $110
– Works. N.Y., 1850-69. 27 vols. 4to. Orig. cl. (DS. Feb.24; 2178) Pts. 38,000
– – Anr. Edn. N.Y., 1889. *Hudson Edn.* 27 vols. Hf. mor. (SPB. Dec.13; 539) $375
– – Anr. Edn. Ill.:– Rackham, Coburn, Darley, & others. N.Y., [1901]. *Joseph Jefferson Edn. (250) numbered & sigd.* 40 vols. Illuminated additional titles, col., frontispieces, many photogravure & other plts. on Japan vell., lettered tissue guards, gt.-lettered hf. vell., partly unc., spines lightly soiled & scuffed. (SG. Mar.15; 126) $400

IRVING OFFERING; A Token of Affection, for 1851
Ill.:– John Sartain. N.Y., 1851. Lge. 12mo. Extra engraved title & 5 mezzotint plts., mod. gt. red mor., covers spotted; from liby. of F.D. Roosevelt, inscr. by him, 'First app. of Lizzie Leigh by Chas. Dickens & Descent into Maelstrom by E.A. Poe, etc., etc ... '. (SG. Mar.15; 31) $600

ISACHAR BAER BEN PETACHIA MOSHE
– Pitchei Yah. Prague, 1609. *1st. Edn.* 4to. 16th. C. German MS. inserted at beginning, edges slightly frayed, staining, mod. blind-tooled mor. (S. Oct.24; 199) *Toporwitch.* £380

ISACHI, A.
– Relatione Intorno l'Origine Solennita Traslatione, et Miracoli della Madonna di Reggio. N.p., 1619. 4to. Cont. vell., worn. (HD. Dec.2; 100) Frs. 2,200

ISELIN, J. Ch.
– Neu-vermehrtes Historisch – und Geographisches Allgemeines Lexicon. Basel, 1726-29. 4 vols. 1st. & last lf. with some sm. faults in margin, leath., old spotting & wear. (V. Sep.30; 2137) DM 700

ISENDAHL, W.
– Automobil u. Automobilsport. Berlin, 1908. 2 vols. 4to. Orig. pict. linen, Vol. 2 bumped. (HK. Nov.8; 433) DM 440

ISHERWOOD, Christopher
See– AUDEN, Wystan Hugh & Isherwood, Christopher

ISIDORUS HISPALENSIS
– De Fide Catholica contra Judaeos ... Rome, ca. 1485. 4to. Mod. stiff vell.; the Walter Goldwater copy. [BMC VII, 1132; Goff I-189; H. 9306] (SG. Dec.1; 188) $950
– De Summo Bono. [Cologne, Ulrich Zel, not after 1472]. Sm. 4to. Initials & paragraph marks supplied in red & blue, sm. slit affecting 4 letters, 1 lf. misbnd., 18th. C. mor., spine rubbed; Heber Liby. stp., Earl of Carlisle bkplt. [H. 9281; BMC I, 187; Goff 1193] (C. May 30; 34) *Rik.* £380
– Etymologiarum Libri XX. [Augsburg], Gunther Zainer, 1472. Fo. Rubricated, capitals painted in blue & red, 2 ll. (with 3 lge. tables & trees) in facs., cont. pig over wood bds., clasps incompl.;

from Fondation Furstenberg-Beaumesnil. [H. 9273; BMC II, 317; Goff I181] (HD. Nov.16; 1) Frs. 5,500
– Etymologiae. De Summo Bono. Venice, Peter Löslein, 1483. Fo. Capital spaces with guide letters, full-p. woodcut slightly cropped, a few ink stains, 1 margin tear, some light browning, mostly at inner margins, cont. limp vell. MS. lf., mor. box; London Liby. stp. & release, Stanitz coll. (SPB. Apr.25; 236) $1,200

ISLE OF WIGHT FLOWERS, by Botanica
Portsea, 1866. 104 engraved plts., some partly hand-cold., completely loose in orig. cl. gt., spine faded. (TA. Nov.17; 326) £52

ISCHYRIUS, Christianus
– In Psalmos Poenitentiales, in Psalmos Horarii sive Cursus de Beata Maria Virgine. Cologne, ca. 1535. 16mo. Errata list, 8 lf. supp., some margin fraying & stains, soiled, last lf. defect. with woodcut device damaged, cont. blind-panel. cf., lacks ties. (SG. Feb.9; 256) $300

ISNARD
[–] Traité des Richesses. L. & Lausanne, 1787. 2 vols. Cf., spine decor., Le Roux d'Esneval arms. (SM. Mar.7; 2024) Frs. 11,000

ISOGRAPHIE DES HOMMES CELEBRES, ou Collection de Fac-similé de Lettres Autographes et de Signatures
Paris, 1828-30. 3 vols. (lacks supp.). 4to. Cont. hf. cf., worn. (HD. Jun.6; 78) Frs. 2,300

ISRAELS (Contrib.)
See– KRONIEK

ITALY
– Beknopte Beschrÿving van Italien. Amst., 1703. Engraved frontis, 25 folding engraved maps & plans, cont. hf. cf., gt. spine, slightly rubbed. (CH. May 24; 3) Fls. 450
– Italie illustrée en CXXXV figures ... Leyden, 1757. 2 pts. in 1 vol. Fo. Engraved title, 2 sub-titles, frontis., 135 double-p. plts., cont. Fr. red mor. gt., in style of Derome, spine gt.; Richard Heber stp. & A.N. (C. Dec.9; 66) *Turner.* £3,500
– – Anr. Copy. 2 pts. in 1 vol. Ob. fo. Captions in Italian, Latin & Fr., lacks 1 plts., 1 plt. misbnd., 7 plts. torn without loss, inner margin wormed, some margin stains, last plt. slightly crumpled, trace of centrefold in plts., disbnd., spine sewed. (B. Feb.8; 639) Fls. 7,500

IVANOVA, A.A. & others
– Album of Indian & Persian Miniatures, XVIth-XVIIIth Century. Moscow, 1962. 4to. Russian text, plts., some cold., loose in orig. cl. folder, slightly soiled. (S. Apr.30; 122) *Sims.* £180

IVENS, J. (Ed.)
See– FILMLIGA

IVES, Brayton (Contrib.)
See– BOWEN, Clarence W.

IVES, Joseph C.
– Report upon the Colorado River of the West. Wash., 1861. *Senate Iss.* 4to. Folding maps reprd., browned & spotted, orig. cl., worn. (S. Dec.13; 137) *Faupel.* £70
– – Anr. Copy. 4to. 3 folding maps, 31 plts., later buckram. (LH. Jan.15; 320) $120

IVSIC, Radovan
– Mavena. Ill.:– Joan Miro. Paris, 1960. *(95) on H.M.P., sigd. by author & artist, with numbered sigd. litho. by Miro.* 4to. Loose in orig. wraps., folder, box, slight darkening & rubbing. (SPB. Dec.14; 69) $850

IZOBRAZITEL 'NOE ISKUSSTVO [Visual Art]
Contribs.:– Malevich, Kandinsky, & others. Ill.:– after Tatlin, Malevich, Shterenberg, & others. Petersburg, 1919. No. 1 (all publd.). Fo. Orig. wraps., cover design by Shterenberg, backstrip split. (S. Nov.21; 142) *Makiya.* £100

JABLONSKY, Carl Gustav & Herbst, Johan Friedrich Wilhelm
– Natursystem aller bekannten in-und auslandischen Insecten ... Der Schmetterlinge. Ill.:– Bodenehr &

JABLONSKY, Carl Gustav & Herbst, Johan Friedrich Wilhelm -*Contd.*
L. Schmidt, after Jablonsky & Kruger. Berlin, 1783-1804. 14 vols., including 3 plt. vols. 8vo. & ob. 4to. Engraved frontis. in Vol. 1, 11 engraved title vigs., all hand-cold., 327 hand-cold. engraved plts. of butterflies, 1 cold. plt. of instruments, single sm. brown stains to blank areas of plts. 13 & 52, some text browned, cont. marb. paper wraps., spines gt., extremities of text vols. with slight wear, spines & corners of plt. vols. worn; wax stp. of G. Loos, Frederick Du Cane Godman bkplts. (CNY. May 18; 143) $5,400
- - **Anr. Edn.** Ill.:– Ludw. Schmidt. Berlin, ca. 1800. Pt II: Schmetterlinge. Plt. vol. Ob. fo. Some light foxing at beginning, with guard ll., cont. hf. leath., worn & bumped. (HK. May 15; 521) DM 3,400

JACK, J.H.
- **Taschenbibliothek der Wichtigsten und Interessantesten See– und Landreisen, von der Erfindung der Buchdruckerkunst bis auf unsere Zeit.** Graz & Nuremb., 1831-33. 85 vols. in 28. Cont. bds. gt. (HT. May 10; 2820) DM 2,300

JACK, Robert Logan
- **Northmost Australia.** L., [1921]. 2 vols. Lacks maps A-H, but with dupls. of maps K-R, cl. gt. (CA. Apr.3; 63) Aus. $240

JACK, Thomas
- **Onomasticon Poeticum.** Edinb., 1592. Sm. 4to. Cont. cf., spine gt. [STC 14293] (BBA. Mar.21; 162) *Maggs.* £200

JACKSON, Andrew
- **Robert O'Hara Burke & the Australian Exploring Expedition of 1860.** L., 1862. Map foxed with sm. tears in folds, orig. blind-stpd. cl., unc., covers slightly faded, spine chipped. (CA. Apr.3; 64) Aus. $160

JACKSON, A.V. Williams
- **History of India.** L., Grol. Soc., [1906-07]. *Connoisseur Edn., (200). (200).* 9 vols., & an additional vol. containing dupl. set of photographic plts. Lge. 8vo. Crushed three-qtr. mor., spines elab. gt. with inlaid ornaments, partly untrimmed. (SG. Nov.17; 266) $325
- - **Anr. Edn.** L., Grol. Soc., [1906-07]. *Baroda Edn.* 9 vols. Lge. 8vo. Most vols. dampstained in part, three-qtr. lev., spines gt. with floral onlays, slight wear, last vol. heavily worn. (SG. Nov.17; 264) $150

JACKSON, Lady Catherine Charlotte
- **Works.** 1899. 14 vols. Hf. mor. gt. (P. Dec.8; 185) *Cavendish.* £70

JACKSON, Sir Charles J.
- **English Goldsmiths & their Marks ...** 1921. *2nd. Edn.* 4to. Orig. buckram cl., d.-w. (PD. Feb.15; 231) £50
- - **Anr. Copy.** Lge. 4to. Buckram gt., slightly shaken. (SG. Oct.13; 181) $100
- **An Illustrated History of English Plate.** 1911. 2 vols. 4to. Hf. mor. (S. May 1; 687) *Heneage.* £70
- - **Anr. Copy.** 2 vols. 4to. Some stains, mostly affecting photogravures in Vol. 1, hf. mor. by B.T. Batsford, partly untrimmed. (TA. Jul.19; 442) £50

JACKSON, E. Nevill
- **Silhouette Notes & Dictionary.** 1938. (*With:*)
- **Ancestors in Silhouette cut by August Edouart.** 1921. (*With:*) - **The History of Silhouettes.** 1911. Some slight spotting. Together 3 vols. 4to. Orig. cl., spine of 1st. faded. (S. Apr.30; 123) *Burwood.* £60

JACKSON, Sir Frederick John & Sclater, William Lutley
- **The Birds of Kenya Colony & the Uganda Protectorate.** L., 1938. 3 vols. Lge. 8vo. Port., cold. folding map, 24 cold. plts., map with short tear in inner margin, owner's stp. in margin of a few ll., orig. cl., some wear. (S. Nov.28; 39) *Miller.* £280

JACKSON, Helen Hunt
- **The Procession of Flowers in Colorado.** Ill.:– Alice A. Stewart. Boston, 1886. *1st. Edn. (100) numbered & sigd. by artist.* 4to. 12 orig. watercolour

floral borders, cl., worn, upr. jnt. brkn. (RO. Dec.11; 153) $160

JACKSON, Holbrook
- **The Anatomy of Bibliomania.** L., 1930-31. *1st. Edn. (1000) numbered.* 2 vols. Orig. cl., d.-w.'s; inscr. (*With:*) - **The Fear of Books.** L., 1932. *1st. Edn. (2000) numbered.* 1 vol. Orig. cl. (SG. Jan.5; 187) $200
- - **Anr. Copy.** 2 vols. Cl., light wear, d.-w.'s lightly soiled & frayed. (RO. Dec.11; 154) $110
- - **Anr. Copy.** 2 vols. Prospectus loosely inserted, buckram, this set for review & unnumbered. (KH. Nov.9; 628) Aus. $160
- - **Anr. Edn.** 1930. 2 vols. Orig. cl., 1 vol. with d.-w. (P. Jun.7; 191) £50

JACKSON, James Grey
- **The Empire of Morocco.** L., 1809. 4to. 9 engraved plts., 2 hand-cold., 2 folding maps, 1 torn, some spotting, cont. hf. cf., worn, upr. cover detchd. (BBA. May 3; 302) *Adab.* £60

JACKSON, John
- **The Practical Fly-Fisher, more Particularly for Grayling or Umber.** 1899. *4th. Edn.* 10 hand-cold. plts., panel. mor. gt. by Sangorski & Sutcliffe, spine & top edge of upr. cover slightly faded. (TA. May 17; 290) £55

JACKSON, Mr. [John Baptist]
- **An Essay on the Invention of Engraving & Printing in Chiaro Oscuro ...** L., [1754]. 4to. Advt. & list of 8 'studied historical compositions of Mr. Wills' bnd. in at end, some foxing thro.-out, several pp. stained from plt. colouring, p. 19 defect., mod. cl., recased, trimmed. (SG. Jan.26; 210) $3,400

JACKSON, William
- **The New & Complete Newgate Calendar.** [1795-1802]. 7 vols. Cont. cf., worn, most covers detchd. (TA. Feb.16; 234) £50

JACKSON, William A.
[-] **An Annotated List of the Publications of T.F. Dibdin, based mainly on those in the Harvard College Library.** Camb., Mass., Stinehour Pr., for the Houghton Liby., 1965. *1st. Edn. (500).* Tall 4to. Cl. (SG. Sep.15; 112) $100
- **General Note of the Prices of Binding of all Sorts of Books, 1669.** Camb., Mass., 1951. *(350).* Fo. Photocopies of other 17th. C. ptd. 'Prices for Binding' bnd. in, cl., H.M. Nixon coll., with many annots. & many loosely inserted notes. (BBA. Oct.6; 74) *Quaritch.* £400

JACKSON, William A. (Ed.)
See— PFORZHEIMER, Carl

JACKSON, William Henry
- **Descriptive Catalogue of Photographs of North American Indians.** Wash., 1877. Orig. ptd. wraps., spine chipped. (LH. Jan.15; 321) $160

JACOB, Giles
- **The Compleat Sportsman.** 1718. *1st. Edn.* 12mo. Cont. cf., rebkd. & reprd. (BBA. Feb.23; 135) *Rota.* £240
[-] **The Poetical Register.** L., 1719-20. *1st. Edn.* 2 vols. Errata lf. in Vol.2, 8 ll. advts., some browning, cont. cf., rebkd. (BBA. Mar.21; 205) *John Andrew.* £140

JACOB, J.
- **Observations on the Structure & Draught of Wheel-Carriages.** L., 1773. *1st. Edn.* 4to. 14 folding plts., some offset, mod. blind-stpd. cf. (P. May 17; 271) *Joseph.* £220

JACOB, Max
- **Le Cornet à Des.** N.P., [1917]. *Orig. Edn.* Hf. marb. roan, unc., wrap.; autograph dedication to Jacques Dyssord & autograph poem dedicated to Dyssord, sigd. & dtd. 7 Jul. 1916, bnd. in front of vol. (HD. Dec.16; 133) Frs. 2,900
- - **Anr. Edn.** 1923. 12mo. Sewed; autograph dedication to Cingria. (HD. Apr.13; 167) Frs. 1,200
- **Ne Coupez pas Mademoiselle, ou les Erreurs des P.T.T.** Ill.:– Juan Gris. 1921. *Orig. Edn. (110) on Holland van Gelder. (10) with suite in black on old china.* 4to. Sewed. (HD. Apr.13; 168) Frs. 34,000

- **Picasso. Chronique des Temps Héroïques.** 1956. *Orig. Edn. (175) numbered on vergé, sigd. by Picasso.* Sm. 4to. 3 orig. lithos. (2 cold.), 3 orig. dry-points & 24 engraved woodcuts, leaves, s.-c. (slightly torn); with prospectus with printing of s.-c. litho. in cols. (SM. Mar.7; 2148) Frs. 12,000

JACOB, N.H. & Rados, L.
- **Storia Naturale delle Scimie e dei Maki.** Torino, 1816. Fo. Some staining at end, cont. decor. hf. leath. (SI. Dec.15; 116) Lire 950,000

JACOB, S. S. & Hendley, T. H.
- **Jeypore Enamels.** L., 1886. Sm. fo. 28 chromolitho plts., pict. bds., disbnd. (SG. Aug.25; 192) $110

JACOB, William
- **Travels in the South of Spain. 1809 & 1810.** L., 1811. Fo. Cf. (DS. Mar.23; 2143) Pts. 75,000

JACOB LE BIBLIOPHILE (Pseud.)
See— LACROIX, Paul 'Jacob le Bibliophile'

JACOBI, Carl Gustav Jacob
- **Vorlesungen über Dynamik nebst Fünf Hinterlassenen Abhandlungen desselben.** Ed.:– A. Clebsch. Berlin, 1866. *1st. Edn.* 4to. Some spotting, mostly to lr. margin of pp. 111-16, orig. cl.-bkd. bds., rubbed, chipping, fading, corners bumped, some fraying of cl. spine; Stanitz coll. (SPB. Apr.25; 238) $200

JACOBI, Friedrich Heinrich
- **Auserlesener Briefwechsel.** Ed.:– Fr. Roth. Leipzig, 1825-27. *1st. Edn.* 2 vols. Vol. 1 1st. ll. spotted in margin, cont. hf. leath. gt., jnts. slightly torn. (BR. Apr.12; 1454) DM 500
- **Werke.** Ed.:– [Köppen & Roth]. Leipzig, 1812-25. *1st. Coll. Edn.* 6 vols. Cont. hf. cf. (C. Dec.9; 309) *Bender.* £90
- - **Anr. Copy.** 6 vols. in 7. Owners mark on endpaper, hf. leath. gt., corners slightly bumped, jnts. slightly rubbed. (GB. May 4; 1587) DM 800
- **Wider Mendelssohns Beschuldigungen Betreffend die Briefe über die Lehre des Spinoza.** Leipzig, 1786. *1st. Edn.* Hf. cf., spine torn (anr. book removed). (*With:*) - **Ueber die Lehre des Spinoza in Briefen an den Herrn Moses Mendelssohn.** Breslau, 1789. *New Enlarged Edn.* Title stained, bds. Together 2 vols. Dr. Walter Pagel copies. (S. Feb.7; 208) *Janssen.* £140

JACOBI, Johann Georg
- **Saemtliche Werke.** Halberstadt, 1770-74. *1st. Edn.* 3 vols. in 1. Cont. hf. cf. (C. Dec.9; 310) *Bender.* £70

JACOBSON, Oscar B.
- **Kiowa Indian Art.** Nice, C. Szwedzicki, [1929]. *(750) numbered, sigd. by publisher.* Tall fo. Portfo. of 30 cold. plts. on vari-cold. paper, ex-liby., each plt. stpd. on blank verso, loose in orig. bd. folder, lge. cold. plt. on cover, linen ties. (SG. May 3; 9) $900

JACOBUS DE CLUSA
- **Sermones de Sanctis.** [Speier, Printer of the Gesta Christi], ca. 1472. Fo. Fully rubricated, some margin dampstains, bds., leath. back; the Walter Goldwater copy. [BMC II, 483; Goff J-38; H. 9329] (SG. Dec.1; 191) $750

JACOBUS DE VORAGINE
See— VORAGINE, Jacobus de

JACOBUS PHILIPPUS DE BERGOMENSIS FORESTUS
See— BERGOMENSIS FORESTUS, Jacobus Philippus de

JACOBY, H.
- **Eine Sammlung Orientalischer Teppiche.** Berlin, 1923. 4to. Orig. cl., lightly soiled. (CSK. Sep.16; 131) £95

JACQUE, Fr.
- **Le Livre d'or de J.-F. Millet par un Ancien Ami.** Paris, 1891. *(50) on Japan.* 4to. 17 orig. etchings in text & on plts. & supp. series of plts. all sigd., burgundy mor., mosaic inlay gold decor., inner & outer dentelles, doubl. & end-paper covered with silk, orig. s.-c., slightly spotted. (HT. May 9; 1574) DM 1,000

JACQUEMART, Albert & Le Blant, E.
- Histoire Artistique Industrielle et Commerciale de la Porcelaine. 1861. 3 pts. in 1 vol. Fo. Mod. cl., orig. wraps. bnd. in. (P. Dec.8; 292) *Tzakas.* £50

JACQUEMIN, Raphael
- Iconographie Générale et Méthodique Costume du IVe au XIXe Siècle. Paris, 1869. Fo. 200 hand-cold. plts., slightly soiled, some tears, mostly marginal, loose in cont. portfo., worn. (BBA. May 23; 221) *Nolan.* £180
- - Anr. Edn. Paris, [1869]. Lge. fo. 200 cold. plts., ex-liby., later hf. leath. (SG. May 3; 118) $225
- Supplement à l'Iconographie Générale et Méthodique du Costume du IVe au XIXe Siècle. Paris, ca. 1872. Tall fo. 80 hand-cold. plts., ex-liby., later hf. mor. (SG. May 3; 119) $150

JACQUES, Henri
- Sous le Signe du Rossignol. Ill.:- K. Nielsen. Paris, [1923]. *(150) De Luxe Edn.* Lge. 4to. With second series of ills., hand-bnd. mor. by Jeanne Ruinit, leath. onlays, gold-tooled decor. on cover, striped silk end-papers & doubls., spine darkened, doubls. cockled. (H. Nov.24; 1680) DM 820

JACQUET, E.
See— BURNOUF, Eugene & Jacquet, E.

JACQUIN, Abbé
- Abhandlung von der Gesundheit. Trans.:- G. Neuhofer. Augsburg, 1764. Bds. (D. Nov.23; 577) DM 650

JACQUIN, Nicholas Joseph von
- Icones Plantarum Rariorum. Wien, 1781-86. Vol. 1 (of 3). Lge. fo. 19th. C. hf. leath., rubbed. (R. Oct.12, 1858) DM 5,200
- Observationum Botanicarum, Iconibus ab Auctore Delineatis Illustratum. Ill.:- Wangner. [Wien, 1764-71). 4 pts. in 1 vol. Fo. Pt. II lacks title, plts. 94-100 misbnd., partly browned & stained, lacks bdg. (GB. Nov.3; 1144) DM 2,000

JACQUINOT DE PRESLE
- Cours d'Art et d'Histoire Militaires à l'usage de MM. les Officiers de l'Ecole Royale de Cavalerie. Saumur, 1829. Cont. red mor., blind-stpd. & gt. decor., decor. spine. (HD. Dec.9; 44) Frs. 1,700

JAECKEL, Willy
- Mathäus-Passion. Berlin, [1920]. *(40) numbered.* Lge. fo. Bdg., title & printers mark sigd. by artist, title slightly crumpled, 14 orig. lithos., orig. vell. portfo. (HT. May 9; 1892) DM 640

JAEGER, B.
- The Life of North American Insects. Providence, priv. ptd., 1854. *1st. Edn.* Tall 8vo. Plts. hand-cold., orig. gt.-pict. cl. (SG. Oct.6; 215) $100

JAEGER, Doris U.
- The Faculty of the College of Physicians & Surgeons, Columbia University in the City of New York: Twenty-Four Portraits. N.Y., 1919. *1st. Edn.* Fo. Liby. stp. on plt. versos, cl.-bkd. bds., slightly scuffed. (SG. Nov.10; 160) $120

JAHNS, Max
- Geschichte der Kriegswissenschaften. Munich & Leipzig, 1889-91. 3 vols. Cont. cf.-bkd. bds., rubbed. (BBA. Feb.23; 67) *Tumarkin.* £100

JAHR, G.H.G.
- Ausführlicher Symptomen-Kodex der Homöpath. Arzneimittellehre. Düsseldorf, 1843. *1st. Edn.* 2 pts. in 4 vols. slightly foxed, cont. hf. leath. (R. Oct.12; 1421) DM 900

JAHRBUCH DER AUKTIONSPREISE Für Bücher, Handschriften und Autographen
Hamburg, 1972-79. Vols. XXIII-XXX. Lge. 8vo. 1 quire misprinted, cl. (VS. Dec.7; 290) Fls. 900

JAHRBUCH DER EINBANDKUNST
Leipzig, 1927-37. 4 vols. Fo. Cl.; H.M. Nixon coll., with his sig. (Vol. 1) & some MS. notes. (BBA. Oct.6; 75) *Quaritch.* £1,000

JAHRBUCH DER ERFINDUNGEN u. Fortschritte auf den Gebieten der Physik u. Chemie, der Technologie u. Mechanik, der Astronomie u. Meteorologie

Leipzig, 1865-92. Yrs. 1-28. Slightly spotted, cont. hf. linen gt., some wear, spine faded, w.a.f. (HK. May 15; 435) DM 420

JAHRBUCH DER JUNGEN KUNST
Ed.:- G. Biermann. Ill.:- Pechstein, Eberz, & others (lithos.). Leipzig, 1920. Vol. 1. 4to. 8 orig. ills., 4 ills. slightly spotted, last part of vol. with lge. stain, owner's name inside cover, orig. pict. hf. linen, spotted, sm. reprd. tears, spine renewed. (H. Nov.24; 2498) DM 400
- - Anr. Edn. Ed.:- G. Biermann. Ill.:- M. Beckmann, B. Kretzschmer, F.M. Jansen, W. Kohlhoff & others. Leipzig, 1922. Vol. 3. 4to. 6 orig. ills., orig. linen, orig. bd. s.-c. (HK. Nov.11; 3649) DM 600

JAHRBUCH DER KONIGLICH PREUSSISCHEN KUNSTSAMMLUNGEN
Ed.:- W. Bode, R. Döhme, H. Grimm, M. Jordan & others. Berlin, 1880-89. Vols. 1-10. Lge. 4to. Slightly browned, some staining, cont. hf. leath., partly defect.; ex-libris. (HT. May 9; 1027) DM 1,000

JAHRBUCH FUR BRANDENBURGISCHE LANDESGESCHICHTE
Berlin, 1950. Vols. 1-32. 4to. Orig. sewed. (GB. Nov.3; 285) DM 400

JAHRBÜCHER DER BERG UND HUTTENKUNDE
Ed.:- K.E. v. Moll. Salzburg, 1797-1801. Vols. 1-5 (all publd.) in 6 vols. Cont. bds., lightly rubbed. (R. Oct.12; 1575) DM 1,250

JAILLOT, Hubert
See— SANSON, Nicholas & Jaillot, Hubert

JAILLOT, Hubert & Mortier, Pieter
- Le Neptune François, ou Recueil des Cartes Marines. Paris, 1693. Pt. 1 (of 2). Lge. fo. Engraved title, 6pp. text, engraved table, 29 double-p. engraved charts, hand-cold. in outl., some with inset maps, mntd. on guards, 1 chart with vertical crease, orig. bds., slightly rubbed; loosely inserted at end chart of the Straits Mouth of Gibralter, by Richard Bolland, engraved chart on 2 sheets, mntd., title cartouches & some outl. hand-colouring, slightly wormed at centre, sm. margin tear; Earl of Lonsdale bkplt. (C. Jun.27; 40) *Lindh.* £1,900
- - Anr. Edn. Paris & Amst., 1693-1700. 3 pts. in 1 vol. Lge. fo. 3 ptd. titles, additional engraved titles to pts. 1 & 2 (the 1st. hand-cold.), 31 plts. of ships & flags (the flags with cont. colouring), chart of the winds, 72 engraved charts, all with cont. outl. hand-colouring, most double-p., 1st. title, a few text ll. & some charts slightly discold., some minor repairs, cont. panel. cf., rebkd. & reprd., slightly rubbed. (C. Mar.14; 53) *Burgess.* £18,000
- - Anr. Edn. Amst., 1710-1700. 3 pts. in 2 vols. Lge. fo. Vol. I pt. 1: elab. engraved allegorical title by Jan van Vianen, ptd. title in red & black with fully cold. vig., dtd. 1700, full-p. engraved table of comparative nautical scales, 6 pp. of ptd. text in Fr., index to both vols., 12 full-p. engraved plts. of naval ensigns, & 31 double-p. or folding sea- & coastal-charts (several dtd. 1692 or 1693) covering Northern & Western Europe including a world chart on Mercator's projection; pt. 2, 'Cartes Marines à l'usage des armées du Roy de la Grande Bretagne', ptd. title in red & black, with fully cold. vig., dtd. 1710, & 9 elab. engraved & etched charts (mostly double-p.) of Fr. & Engl. Channel coasts & including lge. folding chart of Mediterranean all by Romein de Hooghe incorporating insets showing ports. & harbours; Vol. II: elab. engraved allegorical title by Romein de Hooghe, ptd. title 'Suite du Neptune François' dtd. 1700, 5 pp. ptd. text in Fr., full-p. engraved table of wind directions, & 23 full-p. naval plts. including the engraved title 'Plan de plusieurs bâtimens', & 37 mostly double-p. sea-& coastal-charts, including Edmond Halley's isogonal world chart on Mercator projection with accompanying lf. of ptd. text, 10 charts devoted to North America & 2 charts covering the Canary & Cape Verde Islands from the Blaeu Atlas Major & from Olfert Dapper's 'Description de l'Afrique' in place of charts with same titles with Covens & Mortier imprint, together 76 charts & 36 plts., engraved titles (heightened with gold), charts & plts. cold.

thro.-out in cont. hand. several charts in Vol. I bkd. with archive tissue, some damage by green paint reprd., 1 or 2 minor tears without significant loss of engraved surface, slight staining at end of Vol. II, cont. Dutch mott. cf., gt.-panel., lge. atlas devices on covers, rebkd. preserving spines; sm. liby. stp. of R.H. Laurie on front pastedowns. (S. Feb.1; 32) *Hatch.* £36,000

JAILLOT, Jean-Baptiste Renou de Chauvigné
- Recherches Critiques, Historiques et Topographiques sur la Ville de Paris. Paris, priv. ptd., 1772-82. Pts. 1, 2, 3, 8, 11, 13, 18 & 20 only, in 6 vols. or pamphlets. Various bdgs. (HD. Mar.19; 101) Frs. 1,400

JAIME, Ernest
- Musée de la Caricature. Text:- Brazier, Ch. Nodier, J. Janin & others. Paris, 1838. 2 vols. 4to. Cont. hf. roan, spines decor. (HD. May 4; 307) Frs. 3,300

JAL, Auguste
- Archéologie Navale. Paris, 1840. *Orig. Edn.* 2 vols. 19th. C. hf. russ., spines decor. (HD. Mar.9; 91) Frs. 2,000

JALLABERT, L.
- Experiences sur l'électricité. Paris, 1749. *2nd. Edn.* Cont. hf. leath. gt. (D. Nov.25; 4632) DM 400
- Versuche über die Electricität. Basel, 1771. *2nd. German Edn.* 2 pts. in 1 vol. Cont. bds., slightly spotted, spine defect. (R. Apr.4; 1530) DM 520

JAMES I, King of England
[-] Basilikon Doron. Or His Majesties Instructions to his Dearest Sonne, Henry the Prince. 1603. Title & last lf. soiled, lacks 1st. & last (?) blanks, some blank margins with corners torn away without loss of text, 19th. C. mor., spine worn. [STC 14350] (CSK. Jun.1; 86) £65
- Two Broad-sides against Tobacco. L., 1672. 4to. Full-p. woodcut, few early marginalia, few stains, old qtr. cf., shabby, unc. [Wing J147] (SG. Apr.19; 108) $250
- The Workes ... L., 1616. *1st. Edn.* Fo. Head of engraved title shaved, port. slightly stained, cont. cf. gt., scuffed, extremities of spine chipped. [STC 14344] (C. Nov.9; 144) *Maggs.* £260
- - Anr. Copy. Fo. Slight worming, slightly affecting text, additional title shaved at head, portion torn from fore-margin of 2X5, just touching line border, cont. cf., rebkd., covers detchd. [STC 14344] (S. Dec.13; 373) *Coulter.* £85

JAMES IV, James V, Kings of Scotland & Mary, Queen of Scotland
- Epistolae Jacobi Quarti, Jacobi Quinti, et Mariae Regum Scotorum ... Ad Imperatores, Reges Pontifices, Principes Civitates et Alios ab anno 1505 ab Annum 1545. Edinb., 1722-24. 2 vols. Cont. spr. cf., spines gt.-decor.; pres. inscr. in Latin from Thomas Ruddiman (the publisher, & ed.?) to John Drummond in each vol., Sir Ivar Colquhoun, of Luss copy. (CE. Mar.22; 174) £140

JAMES, E.
- Account of an Expedition from Pittsburgh to the Rocky Mountains. L., 1823. 3 vols. Hf.-titles in vols. 2 & 3 (as usual), 8 aquatint plts. (3 cold.), folding map with tear in folds & 1 sm. hole, engraved folding section (detchd. at fold), advts. at end of Vol. 1, cont. qtr. cf., edges unc. [Sabin 35683] (S. May 22; 321) *Hammond.* £640
- - Anr. Copy. 3 vols. 3 plts. hand-cold., lacks hf.-titles in Vols. 2 & 3, light foxing to folding map, several uncold. plts. spotted, cont. diced cf. gt., rebkd.; the Rt. Hon. Visc. Eccles copy. [Sabin 35683] (CNY. Nov.18; 148) $600

JAMES, Edwin
- The Lives & Battles of the Champions of England from the Year 1700 to the Present Time. N.Y., [1879]. 12mo. Pict. wraps., soiled, lacks pts. of spine. (SG. Mar.15; 183) $150

JAMES, Grace
- Green Willow & Other Japanese Fairy Tales. Ill.:- Warwick Goble. L., 1910. *1st. Goble Edn.* Some foxing & darkening thro.-out, orig. gt.-decor. cl., spine ends frayed. (CBA. Aug.21; 248) $100

JAMES, Grace -*Contd.*

– – **Anr. Edn.** Ill.:– Warwick Goble. 1910. *De Luxe Edn., (500).* 4to. 1 plt. slightly creased, orig. vell., gt.-decor., untrimmed, slightly rubbed, lacks ties. (SKC. Mar.9; 1778) £55

JAMES, Henry
– **The Ambassadors.** N.Y., 1903. *1st. Amer. Edn.* Orig. bds., orig. fabric-paper d.-w. slightly worn. (SG. Mar.29; 169) $110
– **The Complete Tales.** Ed.:– Leon Edel. Phila., [1962-64]. 12 vols. Cl., all but 1 vol. with d.-w. (SG. Mar.29; 171) $175
– **The Novels & Tales** ... Ill.:– A.L. Coburn. N.Y., 1922. 26 vols. Cl. gt., spines faded with light wear. (PNY. Jun.6; 451) $450
– **The Portrait of a Lady.** 1881. *1st. Edn.* 3 vols. Orig. cl., rebkd. (BBA. Feb.23; 288) *Quaritch.* £180
– – **Anr. Edn.** Boston, 1882. *1st. Amer. Edn. 1st. Iss.* Orig. decor. cl. gt., buckram portfo., mor.-bkd. buckram s.-c. (C. May 30; 154) *Maggs.* £100

JAMES, John Thomas
– **Journal of a Tour in Germany, Sweden, Russia, Poland.** L., 1819. *3rd. Edn.* 2 vols. 12 aquatint plts., cont. gt. & blind-stpd. cf., slightly rubbed. (BBA. Dec.15; 71) *Hannas.* £65

JAMES, Dr. Montague Rhodes
– **The Canterbury Psalter.** 1935. *(450).* 4to. Orig. cl. gt., slight wear. (P. Oct.20; 91) £90
– – **Anr. Copy.** 4to. Prospectus loosely inserted, orig. cl. (BBA. Sep.8; 12) *Maggs.* £55
– – **Anr. Edn.** L., 1935. *(450).* Fo. Orig. cl., slightly rubbed. (S. May 1; 407) *Dawson.* £120

JAMES, Lieut.-Col. Thomas
– **The History of the Herculean Straits, now called the Straits of Gibraltar.** 1771. 2 vols. 4to. Cont. cf. gt. (P. Sep.8; 343) *Maggs.* £220
– – **Anr. Copy.** 2 vols. 4to. 16 engraved plts. & maps, 1 torn & reprd., some ll. spotted, cont. cf., rebkd. & reprd. (BBA. Oct.27; 33) *Bookroom.* £95

JAMES, W.S.
– **Cow-Boy Life in Texas, or 27 Years a Mavrick.** Chic., [1893]. *1st. Edn.* Decor. cl., boxed. (LH. Sep.25; 248) $120

JAMES, William
– **A Full & Correct Account of the Military Occurrences of the Late War Between Great Britain & the United States.** 1818. 2 vols. Some ll. spotted, cont. hf. cl., rubbed, upr. cover Vol. 1 detchd. (BBA. Feb.9; 300) *Armstrong.* £110
– – **Anr. Copy.** 2 vols. 1 folding map slightly torn, cont. cf., spines gt. with arms of Frederick Augustus, Duke of York & Albany, upr. corners bumped; Thomas Watkin Forster bkplt., the Rt. Hon. Visc. Eccles copy. [Sabin 35718] (CNY. Nov.18; 149) $280

JAMESON, Robert
– **Mineralogy of the Scottish Isles.** Edinb., 1800. 2 vols. 4to. Lge. folding map (laid down), 12 maps & plts., errata lf., foxed, short tear in 1 margin, cf., lacks labels. (S. Mar.6; 366) *Korn.* £100

JAMIESON, Alexander
– **A Celestial Atlas.** 1822. *[1st. Edn.].* Ob. 4to. Engraved title & dedication pp., 30 engraved plts., errata slip, cont. hf. cf. (SKC. Jan.13; 2380) £140
– – **Anr. Copy.** Ob. 4to. Engraved title, dedication, 30 engraved plts., mostly hand-cold., errata slip at end, some faint stains, cont. hf. roan gt. (S. Jun.25; 268) *Shapiro.* £130
– – **Anr. Copy.** Ob. fo. Engraved title, 31 plts., slightly spotted & soiled, cont. hf. roan, worn, upr. cover loose. (BBA. Jan.19; 45) *Franks.* £70

JAMIESON, John
– **An Etymological Dictionary of the Scottish Language.** Edinb., 1808. *1st. Edn.* 2 vols. 4to. Orig. bds., unc. & unopened, spines chipped at foot, 1 cover loose; Sir Ivar Colquhoun, of Luss copy. (CE. Mar.22; 175) £130

JAMIESON, John & Brown, William
– **Select Views of the Royal Palaces of Scotland.** Edinb., 1830. 4to. Minor foxing, cont. mor., by Carss, decor. borders, spine gt. (CE. Sep.1; 94) £55

JAMOT, Paul & Wildenstein, Georges
– **Manet.** Paris, 1932. 2 vols. 4to. Cl. (BBA. Apr.5; 52) *Sims, Reed & Fogg.* £190

JANER, Florencio
– **Condición Social de los Moriscos de España.** Madrid, 1857. 4to. Linen; with coll. of documents. (DS. Feb.24; 2238) Pts. 24,000

JANIN, Jean
– **Mémoires et Observations Anatomiques, Physiologiques et Physiques sur l'oeil, et sur les Maladies qui affectent cet Organe.** Lyon, Paris, 1772. Cont. roan, spine decor., 1 turn-in worn. (HD. Mar.19; 83) Frs. 1,500

JANIN, Jules
– **La Bretagne.** Ill.:– H. Bellange, Gigoux, Isabey, Morel-Fatio, Daubigny & others. Paris, [1844]. *1st. Printing.* Lge. 8vo. Lacks instructions to binder, decor. bds. by Le Nègre. (HD. May 4; 310) Frs. 2,600
– **Un Hiver à Paris.** Ill.:– Eugène Lami. Paris, 1843. Cont. hf. mor., spine decor. (HD. Jun.22; 55) Frs. 1,200
– **Un Hiver à Paris. – Un Eté à Paris.** Ill.:– after E. Lami. Paris, 1843. *1st. Printing of ills.* 2 vols. Lge. 8vo. Foxing, decor. blue & red mor. (SM. Mar.7; 2150) Frs. 1,800
– – **Anr. Edn.** Ill.:– E. Lami. Paris, [1843]. *1st. Work Orig. Edn. 1st. Printing.* 2 vols. Some slight foxing, hf. chagrin (1st. work by Andrieux), spines decor., 2nd. work rubbed. (HD. May 4; 309) Frs. 1,150
– **Voyage en Italie.** Paris, 1839. *Orig. Edn. 1st. Printing.* Hf. gladed cf., by Champs, decor. spine, corners, wrap, & spine preserved, ca. 1880. (HD. Feb.17; 14) Frs. 3,900

JANIN (Text)
See— **FRANÇAIS PEINTS PAR EUX-MEMES**

JANINET, Jean-François
– **Vues Pittoresques des Principaux Edifices de Paris.** Paris, 1792. Sm. 4to. Many prints before the numbers, added proofs, chagrin by A. Knecht, spine decor.; from Eugène von Wasserman liby. (HD. Jun.18; 19) Frs. 43,000

JANNEAU, Guillaume
– **L'Art Cubiste. Théories et Réalisations. Etude Critique.** Paris, [1929]. 4to. 48 plts. including 12 stencil gouaches, sewed. (HD. Jun.22; 30) Frs. 1,300
– **Le Luminaire et les Moyens d'Eclairages Nouveaux.** Paris, ca. 1925. 1st. & 2nd. Series: 2 vols. 4to. 48 & 50 loose plts., cl.-bkd. bd. folders, 2nd. vol. worn. (SG. Aug.25; 21) $240

JANSCHA, Lorenz & Ziegler, Johann
– **Collection de Cinquante Vues du Rhin** ... **Fünfzig Malerische Ansichten des Rhein-Stromes von Speyer bis Düsseldorf** ... Ill.:– Ziegler after Janscha. Vienna, 1798. Fo. Engraved title, 50 hand-cold. plts. of views, in ink & wash borders, interleaved with decriptive text in German & Fr., slight tear in lr. margin of plt. 9 touching wash border, reprd., some smudging of outer inkline border on about 8 plts., early 19th. C. hard-grained mor., spine ends reprd.; Horatio Noble Pym bkplt. (C. Mar.14; 54) *Moglihi & Nesa.* £35,000

JANSON, Charles William
– **The Stranger in America.** L., 1807. *1st. Edn.* 4to. Lacks 1 plt. & 6 pp. advts. at end, some browning, some offsetting from plts., cont. hf. hf. gt., marb. bds. (SG. Jan.19; 199) $175

JANSON, Horst Waldemar
– **The Sculpture of Donatello.** Princeton, 1957. 2 vols. 4to. No bdg. stated. (SPB. Nov.30; 97) $225

JANSSON, Johannes
– **Atlantis Majoris Quinta Pars, Orbem Maritimum.** Amst., priv. ptd., 1650. *1st. Latin text Edn.* [Novus Atlas vol. V]. Fo. Engraved title with ptd. paste-on slip, 33 double-p. engraved mapsheets, cont. hand-cold. thro.-out, title (heightened with gold) & all embellishments fully so, some browning thro.-out (as usual), cont. gt.-panel. vell., slightly soiled, w.a.f. (S. May 21; 143) *Hillman.* £4,500
– **Novus Atlas, sive Theatrum Orbis Terrarum** ... **Tomus Quartus, Novus Atlas.** Amst., 1646. *1st. Edn. with Latin text.* Vol 4. [British Isles]. Fo. Engraved allegorical title, & 56 double-p. engraved regional & country maps, title fully cold. & heightened with gold, maps hand-cold. in outl., all embellishments fully so, engraved & woodcut ills. in text, browning, cont. vell., gt.-panel, slightly soiled, w.a.f. (S. May 21; 24) *Mizon.* £2,800
– – **Anr. Edn.** Amst., 1649. Fo. Engraved allegorical title, 56 double-p. engraved maps, on guards, title fully cold., maps cold. in outl., with cold. cartouches & embellishments, engraved & woodcut ills. in text, some hand-cold., maps seem identical to 1st. 1646 edn., without additional dedication to reader, tear in fold of map of England, orig. map 44 Lancashire lacking but inserted from Fr. Edn., cont. vell. gt. (C. Jun.27; 40a) *Burgess.* £3,600
– **Le Théâtre du Monde ou Nouvel Atlas.** Amst., 1658-62. 10 vols. Fo. 10 frontis. & 633 double-p. maps, cont. cold. & heightened with gold, publisher's recovered vell. gt., spines decor. (HD. Jun.18; 20) Frs. 720,000

JANUS PRESS
– **Silver Anniversary Miscellany, 1955-80.** Ill.:– Jerome Kaplan & others. [Newark, Vermont, Janus Pr., 1980]. *(75).* 4to. 19 examples of printing, type design & book ill., few sigd. in pencil by artists, wraps. & self-wraps., unbnd., cl. folding case. (SG. May 17; 143) $150

JAPANESE TEMPLES & their Treasures
Tokyo, 1910. 3 vols. Fo. 529 plts., all liby.-stpd. on blank verso, unbnd. in brocaded folding cases, linen ties. (SG. May 3; 219) $225

JARDIN DE MONCEAU près de Paris, appartenant à S.A.S. Mgr. le Duc de Chartres
Ill.:– L. de Carmentelle. Paris, 1779. *1st. Printing of ills.* Fo. Some ll. slightly yellowed, paper bds., arms. stpd. in gold. (HD. May 21; 40) Frs. 40,000
– – **Anr. Copy.** Fo. Old. hf. roan, corners. (HD. Jul.2; 19) Frs. 25,000

JARDINE, Sir William
– **British Salmonidae.** [Edinb., 1639-41]. Pts. 1 & 2 (all publd.). Fo. A coll. of 58 preparatory ills. for the 12 plts. to the work, comprising orig. pencil studies, watercolours, proof etchings (some with backgrounds added), etchings on Chine appliqué & cold. etchings by W.H. Lizars, some inscr. with pencil notes, some wtrmkd. 'J Whatman Turkey Mills', '1838', '1839' or '1840', some stains & tears at edges, preserved under passe-partout mounts in 3 lge. portfor. (S. Nov.28; 41) *Marks.* £4,000
– – **Anr. Edn.** L., 1979. *Facs. Edn. (500) numbered.* Lge. fo. 12 cold. plts., orig. mor.-bkd. cl., s.-c. (CSK. Feb.24; 202) £120
– – **Anr. Copy.** Lge. fo. Orig. mor.-bkd. cl., s.-c. (CSK. Jun.1; 154) £75
– **Foreign Butterflies.** Text:– James Duncan. Edinb., 1837. From 'The Naturalist's Library'. Port. frontis., additional vig. title, 30 hand-cold. plts., orig. cl., untrimmed. (TA. Aug.18; 20) £66
– **Leaves from the Book of Nature.** Edinb., n.d. Lge. Atlas Fo. Hand-cold. ills. on 34 lge. plts., including cover, as a coll., w.a.f. (GM. Dec.7; 725) £275
– **The Natural History of Humming Birds.** 1833. From 'The Naturalist's Library': 2 vols. 2 frontis., 2 col. vig. titles, 64 hand-cold. plts., cl., worn. (P. Jul.5; 136) £100
– – **Anr. Copy.** 2 vols. 2 hand-cold. vig. titles, port., 62 (of 64) hand-cold. plts., hf. mor. stained. (P. May 17; 91) *Sambos.* £80
– – **Anr. Edn.** Edinb., 1833. From 'The Naturalist's Library', 2 vols. Sm. 8vo. 2 engraved ports., additional hand-cold. engraved titles, 64 hand-cold. plts., cont. cl. (C. Nov.16; 261) *Traylen.* £110
– – **Anr. Copy.** From 'The Naturalist's Library, 2 vols. in 1. 2 port. frontis., 2 titles with cold. vigs., 63 (of 64) hand-cold. plts., slightly soiled, red hf. mor., gt. spine. (SKC. Sep.9; 1999) £60
– – **Anr. Copy.** 2 vols. Sm. 8vo. Port. frontis.'s,

additional pict. titles, 64 hand-cold. plts., hf. cf., rubbed. (SG. Mar.22; 180) $225
– – **Anr. Edn.** Edinb., 1834. From 'The Naturalist's Liby.' series: 2 vols. in 1. Sm. 8vo. Port. frontis.'s, hand-cold. vig. titles, 64 hand-cold. plts., cont. hf. cf., worn. (TA. Jul.19; 246) £70
– – **Anr. Edn.** Edinb., 1840. 2 vols. 62 (of 64) hand-cold. plts., lacks 2 plts. in 1st. vol., crushed three-qtr. mor. gt. by Root & Son, extremities slightly scuffed. (SG. Mar.22; 181) $325
– – **Anr. Edn.** L., ca. 1845 & 50. 2 vols. Cont. hf. leath. & orig. linen, bumped & defect. (R. Oct.12; 1860) DM 450
– – **Anr. Edn.** Edinb., n.d. 2 vols. in 1. Sm. 8vo. 64 hand-cold. plts., few trimmed, lacks hf.-title, port. & vig. title to vol. 1, cl. (S. Apr.10; 426)
Wesley. £65
– **The Natural History of the Birds of Great Britain & Ireland.** L., 1838-42. Pts. 1-3 in 3 vols. 3 engraved vig. titles, 2 hand-cold., 3 ports., 97 hand-cold. plts., cl. not unif. (P. May 17; 342)
Steinhager. £80
– **The Naturalist's Library.** Edinb., 1833-43. 40 vols. Sm. 8vo. Many hand-cold. plts., some browning, mainly text, hf. cf., gouge on upr. cover of 1 vol. (SPB. May 17; 634) $1,200
– – **Anr. Edn.** Edinb., 1833-52. *Various Edns.* 10 vols. only, including 'Hummingbirds', 'Butterflies' & 'Game Birds'. Hand-cold. engraved plts., cont. cl., worn, w.a.f. (CSK. Nov.4; 80) £170
– – **Anr. Edn.** 1835-37. Vols. 2-5 only of 'Entomology'. Plts. hand-cold., orig. cl., worn & defect. (BBA. Aug.18; 215) *London Library.* £50
– – **Anr. Edn.** Ill.:– W.H. Lizars. Edinb., L., 1838-66 & n.d. 25 vols. various. 12mo. Plts. hand-cold., orig. cl., some chipping & fading, ex-liby. (SG. Oct.6; 216) £650
– – **Anr. Edn.** Edinb., 1843. *[2nd. Edn.].* 40 vols. Many title vigs. hand-cold., most plts. hand-cold., some tears at head of 1st. few ll., hf. cf. gt., rebkd., some corners worn. (LC. Jul.5; 140) £700
– – **Anr. Copy.** Vols. 34-40: 'Entomology'. Hand-cold. plts., pol. cf., gt. spines, lacks 3 labels. (SKC. Sep.9; 2000) £100
– – **Anr. Copy.** 40 vols. Hand-cold. engrs., hf. leath. & marb. bds., spines lightly nicked, edges rubbed. (RS. Jan.17; 489) $1,000
– – **Anr. Copy.** 40 vols. Slightly foxed, cont. hf. leath. gt. (R. Oct.12; 1859) DM 4,050
– – **Anr. Edn.** Edinb., [1845-46]. 40 vols. Vol. 2 lacks ptd. title, lacks 1 plt. each in Vols. 11 & 22, most vols. without hf.-titles, some plts. trimmed, some offsetting, mostly affecting text, hf. cf., Vols. 28-40 not unif., spines worn, lacks most labels, w.a.f. (S. Nov.28; 42) *Schuster.* £700
– – **Anr. Edn.** L., [1852-64]. 42 vols. Sm. 8vo. Plts. hand-cold., liby. blind-stps. to text only, orig. two-tone cl., some spines defect. & chipped. (SG. Nov.3; 107) $1,200
– – **Anr. Edn.** N.d. 17 vols., various. Engraved plts., most hand-cold., some vols. slightly shaken, orig. cl., rubbed, 2 spines split, w.a.f. (CSK. Mar.23; 177) £250
– **The Naturalist's Library: Mammalia.** Vol. 6 on the ordinary Cetacea or Whales. 1837. Cont. linen. (R. Oct.12; 1929) DM 450
– **The Naturalist's Library: Mammalia: Ornithology.** Edinb., 1834-40. Vols. 2-5, 7, 9 & 10; Vols. 4, 9 & 10, together 10 vols. Extra engraved titles with vigs., ports., hand-cold. plts., cont. hf. cf., worn, w.a.f. (S. Apr.10; 526) *Hildebrandt.* £190
– **The Naturalist's Library: Ornithology.** Edinb., 1833. Vols. 1 & 2. Extra engraved titles with hand-cold. vigs., 2 engraved ports., 64 hand-cold. plts., ills., advts., some slight spotting or offsetting, orig. cl., worn. (S. Apr.10; 527) *Demetzy.* £70

JARDINE, Sir William & Selby, Prideaux John
– **Illustrations of Ornithology.** Edinb., n.d. New Series: pts. 1 & 2 only. 4to. 32 (of 53) engraved plts. only, all hand-cold., part of orig. engraved wrap. preserved as title, cont. hf. cf., worn. (BBA. Oct.27; 224) *Madrid.* £200

JARS, Gabriel
– **Voyages Métallurgiques.** Lyon, 1774. 4to. Some margin stains, cont. cf., defect. (VG. Mar.19; 112)
Fls. 500

JARVES, James Jackson
– **History of the Hawaiian Islands.** Honolulu, 1847. *(Bound with:)* FEATHERSTONHAUGH, George W. – **Excursion through the Slave States.** N.Y., 1844. Together 2 works in 1 vol. Some foxing, bdg. not stated, cover torn, edges & spine rubbed. (RS. Jan.17; 472) $225
– – **Anr. Edn.** Honolulu, 1872. *4th. Edn.* 9 ll. with advts. for Honolulu business establishments, minor soiling, cl., roan back & tips, some wear, spine chipped. (RO. Dec.11; 158) $180

JAUGEON, N.
– **Le Jeu du Monde** ... Ill.:– Guerard. Paris, 1684. Sm. 12mo. Cont. cf., spine decor.; Comte de Noé stp. (HD. Feb.8; 48) Frs. 1,600

JAUME SAINT HILAIRE, Jean Henri
– **Plantes de la France.** Paris, 1808-09 [i.e. 1805-09]. *1st. Edn., (400). 8vo. Iss. on laid paper.* 4 vols. 400 col.-ptd. stipple-engraved plts., subscribers list, errata lf., 1 plt. nicked, some foxing, old bds., unc., defect. (SG. Nov.3; 108) $1,600

JAUSSIN
[–] **Mémoires Historiques Militaires et Politiques sur les Principaux Evènements arrivés dans l'Isle et Royaume de Corse depuis ... 1738 jusqu'à 1741.** Lausanne, 1769. *2nd. Edn.* 2 vols. 12mo. Lacks map, cont. marb. roan, spines decor. (HD. Oct.21; 108) Frs. 4,000

JAY, John
See– HAMILTON, Alexander & others

JEAKE, Samuel
– **Charters of the Cinque Ports.** L., 1728. *1st. Edn.* Fo. Advt. lf., reprd., slight worming in lr. margin, reprd. at end, some faint spotting, margin annots. in cont. hand, cont. cf., slightly worn, rebkd., corners reprd. (S. Mar.6; 430) *Frankland.* £70

JEANNERET, Charles Edouard 'Le Corbusier' & Jeanneret, P.
– **L'Architecture Vivant.** Paris, 1927-[36]. 1st.-7th. series in 7 vols. 4to. Orig. paper bds. & ties. (VA. Apr.26; 57) R 350
– **Poème de l'Angle Droit.** [Paris, 1955]. *(250) sigd.* Fo. (18 of 19) orig. cold. lithos., loose in orig. wraps. as iss., folder & box worn, as a coll. of plts., w.a.f. (SPB. Dec.13; 856) $450

JEFFERIES, Richard
– **After London.** 1885. *1st. Edn.* Hf.-title, 10 pp. of advts. at end, orig. cl., spine gt. (LC. Oct.13; 347) £110
– **Bevis, The Story of a Boy.** 1882. *1st. Edn.* 3 vols. Hf.-titles in each vol., orig. cl. gt. (LC. Oct.13; 344) £200
– **Greene Ferne Farm.** 1880. *1st. Edn.* Hf.-title, 6 pp. of advts. at end, slight foxing to some ll., orig. cl., upr. cover slightly marked. (LC. Oct.13; 340) £50
– **Hodge & His Masters.** 1880. *1st. Edn.* 2 vols. Hf.-titles, 4 pp. of advts. at end Vol. 2, orig. cl. gt.; William Crampton bkplt. (LC. Oct.13; 341) £90
– **Jefferies' Land, A History of Swindon & its Environs.** Ed.:– Grace Toplis. 1896. *1st. Edn. (350).* Folding map, 12 plts., hf.-title, advts., some slight spotting, orig. cl. (LC. Oct.13; 349) £50
– **The Scarlet Shawl.** 1874. *1st. Edn.* Hf.-title, 4 pp. of advts. at end, slight spotting to title & some other ll., some corners turned down, orig. cl., soiled, liby. label removed from upr. cover. (LC. Oct.13; 336) £180

JEFFERS, Robinson
– **Brides of the South Wind: Poems 1917-22.** Ed.:– William Everson. N.p, 1974. *(185) numbered & sigd. by ed.* Lge. 8vo. Qtr. sheep. & cl. (SG. Mar.1; 186) $140
– **Californians.** N.Y., 1916. Cl. (SG. Mar.1; 187) $150
– **Cawdor, & Other Poems.** N.Y., 1928. *(375) numbered & sigd.* Qtr. cl., s.-c. worn. (SG. Mar.1; 189) $250
– – **Anr. Edn.** N.Y., 1928. *Trade Iss.* Qtr. cl., d.-w.; inscr. to Byrd & Ralph Whitehead. (SG. Mar.1; 190) $350
– **Dear Judas.** N.Y., 1929. *1st. Edn.* 1 vol. 8vo. Orig. qtr. cl., d.-w. chipped. *(With:)* – **Give your Heart to the Hawks.** N.Y., 1933. *1st. Edn. (200)*

sigd. 1 vol. Sm. 4to. Orig. qtr. cf., rubbed. (SG. Jan.12; 170) $130
– **Descent to the Dead.** N.Y., [1931]. *(500) numbered & sigd.* Lge. 8vo. Qtr. vell., s.-c.; Rockwell Kent copy. (SG. May 24; 92) $150
– – **Anr. Copy.** Lge. 8vo. Qtr. vell., s.-c. (SG. May 24; 91) $140
– **The Double Axe, & Other Poems.** N.Y., [1948]. Lge. 8vo. Cl., d.-w.; sigd. on tipped in lf. (SG. Mar. 1; 191) $750
– **Flagons & Apples.** Los Angeles, 1912. *1st. Edn., (500).* 12mo. Orig. cl.-bkd. bds., cl. s.-c.; Frederic Dannay copy. (CNY. Dec.16; 186) $500
– – **Anr. Edn.** Los Angeles, 1912. Some light foxing, qtr. cl. (SG. Mar.1; 192) $650
– **Granite & Cypress.** Santa Cruz [Calif.], 1975. *(100) numbered.* Ob. lge. 4to. Unlettered coarse linen; sigd. by William Everson. (SG. May 24; 60) $140
– **Poems.** Intro.:– B.H. Lehman. Ill.:– A. Adams & V. Angelo. San Franc., [Grabhorn Pr.]. 1928. *(310) sigd. by author & artists.* Slight margin darkening, buckram, spine faded, s.-c. worn & tape reprd.; the V. Angelo copy. (CBA. Oct.1; 162) $350
– **Return, An Unpublished Poem.** San Franc., [Grabhorn Pr.], 1934. *(250) numbered.* Sm. fo. Ptd. bds.; Herbert McLean Evans bkplt. (SG. Mar.1; 193) $250
– **Roan Stallion, Tamar & Other Poems.** N.Y., 1925. Qtr. cl., gt.-stpd.; inscr. (SG. Mar.1; 194) $225
– **Such Counsels You Gave to Me, & Other Poems.** N.Y., [1937]. *(300) numbered & sigd.* Qtr. mor., patterned bds. & s.-c.; Clifton Waller Barrett bkplt. (SG. Mar.1; 195) $250
– – **Anr. Copy.** Sm. 8vo. On Gelre H.M.P., mor. & bds., untrimmed, orig. bd. s.-c. with matching design to covers, faded & rubbed. (HA. Feb.24; 202) $140
– **Tamar, & Other Poems.** N.Y., [1924]. *(500).* Cl.; Clifton Waller Barrett bkplt. (SG. Mar.1; 196) $275
– – **Anr. Copy.** Gt.-stpd. cl. (SG. May 24; 89) $175
– **Themes in my Poems.** Ill.:– Mallette Dean. San Franc., 1956. *(350).* 4to. Qtr. cl., decor. bds., unc. (SG. Mar.1; 197) $100
– **Tragedy Has Obligations.** Ill.:– Alison Clough. [Santa Cruz, 1973]. *(200) sigd. by artist & printer.* Fo. Announcement laid in, hf. mor. & linen. (CBA. Nov.19; 140) $160
– – **Anr. Copy.** Fo. Facs. plt. tipped in, qtr. art leath., cl. covers. (SG. Mar.1; 145) $110
– **Two Consolations.** [San Mateo, Calif., Quercus Pr.], 1940. *(250).* 4to. Ptd. bds. (SG. Mar.1; 198) $200

JEFFERS, Robinson (Text)
See– WESTON, Edward

JEFFERS, Una
– **Visits to Ireland: Travel-Diaries.** Foreword:– Robinson Jeffers. Los Angeles, Ward Ritchie Pr., 1954. *(300).* Sm. 4to. Qtr. cl., marb. bds., s.-c.; photo. of Robinson Jeffers & his sons laid in, inscr. on verso by Una Jeffers. (SG. Mar.1; 206) $400

JEFFERSON, Thomas
– **Notes on the State of Virginia.** L., 1787. Orig. bds., unc., worn. (P. Jun.7; 309) £500
– – **Anr. Edn.** Phila., 1788. *1st. Amer. Edn.* Title soiled, lr. edges of text ll. stained, table partly torn, slightly foxed, cont. mott. cf., upr. jnt. defect.; sigd. on title by William Woodbridge, Governor of Michigan & U.S. Senator. (SG. Apr.5; 103) $225

JEFFERYS, Thomas
– **The American Atlas: or, A Geographical Description of the Whole Continent of America.** L., Ptd. & Sold by R. Sayer & J. Bennett, 1775. *1st. Edn.* Atlas fo. 22 engraved maps on 29 sheets with guards, all hand-cold. in outl., most folding, index lf., 4 maps with faint spotting, 1 with sm. tear at fold, very minor dust soiling, mainly at edges, edges of title darkened & brittle, cont. tree cf., brkn. [Sabin 35953 (note)] (CNY. Nov.18; 300) $7,500
– – **Anr. Edn.** L., 1776. Fo. Title, 29 folding engraved maps as called for in index, partially hand-cold. in outl., some wrinkling & tears at folds, slight soiling & offsetting, liby. stps. on versos, orig.

JEFFERYS, Thomas -Contd.

bds., disbnd., worn, mod. folding box. (SPB. Oct.26; 3) $5,000
- **A Collection of the Dresses of Different Nations, particularly Old English Dresses.** L., 1757. Vol. 1 only. 4to. 117 hand-cold. plts., qtr. cf. & marb. bds. (HBC. May 17; 107) £105
- **The Great Probability of a North West Passage: Deducted from Observations on the Letter of Admiral de Fonte ... With an Appendix, Containing the Account of a Discovery of Part of ... Labrador, the Whole Intended for the Advancement of Trade & Commerce.** L., 1768. 4to. 3 folding engraved maps, 1 hand-cold. in outl., 1st. with left border cropped & torn at fold, 3rd. cut across with minimal loss of text, disbnd. [Sabin 28460] (C. Jun.27; 41)
Quaritch. £420
- **The Natural & Civil History of the French Dominions in North & South America.** L., 1760. 2 pts. in 1 vol. Fo. 18 folding engraved maps & plans, with the 7 ll. LL*-Nr* & the pastedown slip on p. 80 in Pt. 2, tape repairs to sm. tear in 1 map & to preceding text lf., slight tear to 1 plan, old pastedown over lr. margin of verso of final lf. covering paper flaws, cont. diced russ. gt., gt.-stpd. Lowther Castle arms on covers, upr. jnt. with old repair but brkn., repairs to spine & corners; the Rt. Hon. Visc. Eccles copy. [Sabin 35964] (CNY. Nov.18; 150)
$5,500

JEFFREYS, Lieut. Ch.

- **Van Diemen's Land** ... L., 1820. A little foxing or spotting, bds., qtr. roan; the Sticht copy. (KH. Nov.9; 630) Aus. $350

JEFFRIES, D.

- **Traité des Diamants et des Perles.** Ill.:- Baquoy after Cochin. Paris, 1753. Slightly foxed, hf.-title verso with 2 old liby. plts., spr. leath. ca. 1860, gt. (HK. May 16; 1594) DM 480

JEFFS, William

- **Recollection of Italy in Fifteen Select Views.** [1829]. Fo. 15 mntd. litho. plts., slight spotting, orig. cl. (LC. Jul.5; 423) £105

JEKYLL, Gertrude

- **Some English Gardens.** Ill.:- G. S. Elgood. 1910. 4to. Cl. gt. (P. Mar.15; 74) £35

JEKYLL, Gertrude & Hussey, Christopher

- **Garden Ornament.** 1918. *1st. Edn.* Fo. Orig. cl. gt., worn. (LC. Mar.1; 162) £70
- - **Anr. Edn.** 1927. Fo. Orig. cl. gt. (P. Sep.29; 302) *Henderson.* £80
- - **Anr. Copy.** Fo. Orig. cl. (P. Dec.8; 154) *Weinreb.* £60
- - **Anr. Copy.** Fo. Orig. cl., stained. (P. Dec.8; 76) *Walford.* £50
- - **Anr. Edn.** [1927]. *2nd. Edn.* Orig. cl., lightly soiled. (CSK. Mar.23; 25) £70

JENKINS, James

- **The Martial Achievements of Great Britain & her allies from 1799 to 1815.** Ill.:- after W. Heath. L., priv. ptd., [1814-15]. 4to. Engraved title, hand-cold. dedication with arms, 52 hand-cold. aquatint plts., including frontis. entitled 'Martial Achievements vol. 1', bnd. without list of subscribers & port. of Wellington, maroon mor. by Bayntun, covers with diamond-shaped gt. ornament & gt.-tooled borders, rebkd. preserving orig. gt. backstrip. (C. Mar.14; 54a) *Heald.* £3,000
- - **Anr. Edn.** Ill.:- Havell & others, after W. Heath. L., 1814-15 [text & plts. wtrmkd. 1812]. 4to. Engraved title with uncold. vig., hand-cold. coat of arms, 52 hand-cold. aquatint views in wash borders, list of subscribers, without port. of Wellington, cont. mor. by Hering, with his ticket, covers with elab. blind- & gt.- stpd. panels, gt. vigs. in spine compartments, inner gt. dentelles, blind- & gt.-stpd. pink paper doubls., rubbed; Luffness Liby. copy. (C. Mar.14; 55) *Marshall.* £700
- - **Anr. Edn.** L., [1815]. 4to. Engraved title with vig., hand-cold. aquatint frontis., dedication, 51 hand-cold. aquatint views, without any of the ports. which are not called for but occasionally included, plt.-margins unusually filled in with light grey wash, some margins slightly soiled, hf. cf. (S. May 21; 11) *Ross.* £800

- **The Naval Achievements of Great Britain.** Ill.:- after T. Whitcombe & others. L., priv. ptd., [1816-17]. 4to. Engraved title, uncold. plt., 55 hand-cold. aquatint plts. (wtrmkd. 1812-16), without the ports. of Lord St. Vincent & Nelson, but with different cold. port. of Nelson inserted, crimson str.-grd. mor. by Bayntun, covers with diamond-shaped gt. ornament & gt.- & blind-tooled borders, spine gt. (C. Mar.14; 55a) *Davidson.* £3,000
- - **Anr. Edn.** L., [1817]. Engraved title with vig. (uncold., & therefore according to Abbey an early iss.), without ptd. list of subscribers & ports. of Nelson & St. Vincent, short tear in margin of 1st. plt. reprd. *(With:)* - **The Martial Achievements of Great Britain & Her Allies.** L., [1815]. Engraved title with vig., hand-cold. port. & dedication lf., 52 hand-cold. aquatint plts., a few minor repairs or tears in margins, a few ll. with slight spotting. *(With:)* ORME, Edward - **Historic, Military & Naval Anecdotes.** L., ca. 1819. 40 hand-cold. aquatints, slight discolouration to a few ll. of text. Together 3 works. 4to. Unif. bnd. in hf. mor., partly unc., tall copies. (S. May 21; 10) *Traylen.* £5,500
- - **Anr. Copy.** 4to. Engraved title with uncold. vig., 2 hand-cold. aquatint ports., 55 hand-cold. aquatint plts. (wtrmkd. 1816), lacks plan of Algiers & Battle of Trafalgar, cont. red mor. gt., lightly rubbed, rebkd., old spine laid down. (CSK. Dec.2; 40) £3,000
- - **Anr. Copy.** 4to. Hand-cold. vig. title, 56 plts., including 55 hand-cold., 2 p. dedication, 6 p. intro., 2 p. list of dates, lacks subscribers list, orig. red hf. roan, unc. (P. Dec.8; 32) *Heald.* £2,800

JENKINS, John

- **The Art of Writing, Reduced to a Plain & Easy System, on a Plan Entirely New. Book I. Containing & Plan Easily & Familiar Introduction.** Camb., priv. ptd., [1813]. Some foxing, old bds., roan back, some wear. (RO. Dec.11; 159) $200

JENKS, Silvester

- [-] **The Blind Obedience of an Humble Penitent.** [L.], 1698. *1st. Edn.* 12mo. Little slight browning, cont. mott. cf., spine gt. [Wing J629] (S. Mar.20; 829) *Thorp.* £110

JENNER, Edward

- **An Inquiry into the Causes & Effects of the Variolae Vaccinae.** Springfield, Mass., 1802. *1st. Amer. Edn.* Sm. 8vo. Dampstained, 2 ll. torn without loss, early sheep, brkn. (SG. Mar.22; 182) $450

JENNER, Thomas

- **A Book of the Names of all Parishes, Market Towns, Villages, Hamlets, & Smallest Places in England & Wales.** L., 1657. *Reprint of Mathew Simons' 'A Direction for the English Traviller', 1643.* Additional engraved title dtd. 1643, engraved map of England with general table, 39 sm. county maps with tables, lists of the hundreds ptd. below & on versos, table of roads, 3 maps & table of roads laid down & folding, interleaved thro.-out, old cf. (C. Nov.16; 100) *Burden.* £380

JENNINGS, Preston J.

- **A Book of Trout Flies, containing a List of the Most Important American Stream Insects & Their Imitations.** Ill.:- Alma W. Froderstrom. Derrydale Pr., [1935]. *(850) numbered.* Gt.-decor. cl., partly unc., unopened. (SG. Mar.15; 230) $375

JEPPE, F.

- **Jeppe's Transvaal Almanac & Directory for 1889.** Cape Town, 1889. Limp cl., upr. cover loose. (VA. Jan.27; 206) R. 210

JEROME, Saint
See— HIERONYMUS, Saint Eusebius

JERRARD, Paul

- **Floral Groups.** Ca. 1860. 4to. Title, 10 hand-finished plts., loose, orig. cl. gt., lr. part of spine defect. (P. Mar.15; 231) *Heald.* £210
- **Flowers from Stratford on Avon.** - **The Floral Offering.** L., 1852. Together 2 vols. Lge. 8vo. 1st. work, pict. title & text ptd. in gold, with decor. borders & initials, 13 hand-cold. plts., some spotting, few ll. stained, loose, orig. enamelled bds. gt., leath. spine, worn, 2nd. work, 14 hand-cold. plts. including title & lf. for pres. inscr., text ptd. in gold

with decor. borders & initials, slight soiling & spotting, cf., gt. (S. Apr.10; 529) *Korn.* £160
- **The Humming Bird Keepsake ... poems by F.W.N. Bailey.** L., ca. 1850. Fo. 12 hand-cold. litho. plts., gt. litho. title & text, publisher's advt., orig. cl., upr. cover with card, panel of litho. title with hand-cold. vig., lr. cover with blind- & gt.-stpd. vig. panel, slightly soiled. (C. Mar.14; 177)
Traylen. £300
- **The Humming Bird Offering.** L., ca. 1850. Imperial 8vo. Hand-cold. title, 10 hand-cold. litho. plts., gt. litho. text, publisher's advt., orig. decor. cl. gt., rubbed. (C. Mar.14; 178) *D'Arcy.* £120

JERRARD, Paul & Bayley, F.W.N.

- **Gems for the Drawing Room.** L., ca. 1855. Fo. Text, title, dedication & advt. lf. ptd. in gold, 12 hand-cold. litho. plts., slight offsetting from text, loose, orig. cl., defect. (S. Apr.10; 530)
Elliott. £170

JERROLD, William Blanchard

- **Life of George Cruikshank.** L., 1882. 2 vols. in 4. Lge. fo. Text inlaid thro.-out, specially ptd. title-p. dtd. 1880 for each vol., extra-ill. with about 1100 ills., many cold., some later imps., red crushed lev. mor. in gt. & blind, by Bayntun; 3 A.L.s by R.W. Elliston, T. Grenville & W.E. Gladstone, 8 sigs. of Cruikshank, W.H. Ainsworth, C. Kean, & others, Eldridge R. Johnson copy, James William Ellsworth bkplts., w.a.f. (CNY. Dec.17; 547)
$1,600
- **London; a Pilgrimage.** Ill.:- Gustave Doré. L., 1872. Fo. Some light spotting, cont. hf. mor., rubbed. (CSK. Dec.2; 60) £60
See— DORE, Gustave & Jerrold, Blanchard

JESSE, John Heneage

- **Memoirs of the Pretenders & their Adherents.** L., 1845. 2 vols. Extra-ill. with many plts., some hand-cold., mor. gt. by Bayntun (Rivière). *(With:)* - **Memoirs of the Life & Reign of King George the Third.** L., 1867. 3 vols. Extra-ill. with many plts., some hand-cold., hf. mor., by Bayntun (Rivière). spines gt. (S. Oct.4; 89) *Chelsea.* £120

JESSEN, H.

- [-] **Album Hamburgischer Costume.** Ca. 1850. Litho. title, 50 hand-cold. litho. plts., some light soiling, mod. cl. (CSK. Aug.19; 77) £650
- - **Anr. Copy.** Minimal spotting, orig. hf. leath., ptd. covers, slightly rubbed. (R. Oct.12; 2604)
DM 5,700

JESUIT TRAVELS

- **The Travels of Several Learned Missioners of the Society of Jesus, into Divers Parts of the Archipelago, India, China, & America.** L., 1714. *1st. Edn. in Engl.* 2 ll. advts. at end, some soiling & minor stains, old cf., jnts. worn. (RO. Dec.11; 161)
$130

JESUITS

- **Lettres Edifiantes et Curieuses, écrites des Missions Etrangères, par quelques Missionaires de la Compagnie de Jesus.** Paris, 1707-43. *Some later vols. 1st. Edns.* Recueils 1-26 only (of 34), in 24 vols. 12mo. 33 engraved plts., plans & maps, including 1 map hand-cold. in outl., single plts. in Recueils 16 & 24 torn, Recueil 23 dampstained, cont. cf., spines & corners worn; Thomas Eyre 1792 bequest bkplts., the Rt. Hon. Visc. Eccles copy, w.a.f. [Sabin 40697] (CNY. Nov.18; 151) $1,600

JESUS, Thomas de

- **Stimulus Missionum: Sive de Propaganda a Religiosis per Universum Orbem Fide.** Rome, 1610. Liby. stp., owner's cypher branded onto edges, 17th- & 18th. C. inscrs., cont. limp vell. (SPB. Dec.13; 693) $125

JESUS MARIA, Joseph de

- **Hechos Heroycos de la Portentosa Vida y Virtudes de N. Seraphico y Glorioso Padre S. Juan de la Cruz** ... Malaga, 1717. Fo. Errors in pagination, upr. margin cut close, cf. (DS. Dec.16; 2409)
Pts. 50,000
- - **Anr. Copy.** Fo. Upr. margin short, cf. (DS. Apr.27; 2401) Pts. 40,000

JEURAT, E.S.
- Traité de Perspective à l'usage des Artistes. Paris, 1750. 4to. 105 (of 110) full-p. & 7 (of 8) hf.-p. copper engrs. (numbered 1-100), 19 double, 10 copperplts. (numbered 101-110), 69 (of 73) engraved vigs., 1 plt. soiled, 2 plts. torn, 1 reprd. in margin, cont. hf. leath. (D. Nov.23; 2041)
DM 600

JEUX DE LA POUPÉE, OU LES ETRENNES DES DEMOISELLES
Paris, 1806. Ob. 8vo. Slightly spotted, lacks hf. of lr. end-lf., orig. bds., backstrip worn; van Veen coll. (S. Feb.28; 76)
£140

JEWEL (THE); or, Token of Friendship. A Christmas or New-Year's Present
Hartford, n.d. Lge. 16mo. Orig. gt.-floral cl.; from liby. of F.D. Roosevelt, inscr. by him (as governor). (SG. Mar.15; 32)
$275

JEWEL, John
- A Replie unto M. Hardinges Answeare. L., 1565. 1st. Edn. Fo. Cont. & later inscrs., some soiling, including title, old blind-stpd. cf., spine defect. [STC 14606] (SG. Feb.9; 258)
$200

JEWELL, J. Grey
- Among Our Sailors. N.Y., 1874. 1st. Edn. Sm. 8vo. Orig. gt.-pict. cl., cont. sig. of David Achenbach, from liby. of F.D. Roosevelt, inscr. by him. (SG. Mar.15; 56)
$175

JEWETT, Sarah Orne
- Betty Leicester's English Xmas. Balt., priv. ptd., 1894. 1st. Edn. Gt.-decor. cl., worn, lacks front free end-paper, linen d.-w., gt. school seal, some chipping, spine frayed; Ken Leach coll. (RO. Jun.10; 263)
$110

JEWISH MANUEL (The); or Practical Information in Jewish & Modern Cookery ...
L., 1846. Cl., new spine; dedication by J. Franklin to Mrs. J.M. Isaac, 2 Oct. 1851, w.a.f. (S. Jul.3; 127)
£620

JEWISH MUSEUM of London
- Catalogue of ... Ed.:– R.D. Barnett. L., [1974]. Lge. 4to. Orig. cl., d.-w. (SPB. Feb.1; 2)
$350

JEWISH NATION: Containing an Account of their Manners & Customs, Rites & Worship, Laws & Polity
Ed.:– D.P. Kidder. N.Y., 1850. 12mo. Scattered foxing, orig. cl., worn, some fraying of extremities. (SG. Feb.2; 8)
$150

JEWITT, John R.
- Narrative of the Adventures & Sufferings of ... Only Survivor of the Crew of the Ship Boston, during a Captivity among the Savages of Nootka Sound. Ed.:– R. Alsop. N.Y., 1815. 1st. Edn. Tall 12mo. Text dampstained at lr. inner portion, orig. cl.-bkd. woodcut-pict. bds., worn. (SG. Aug.4; 168)
$160

JEWITT, Llewellynn & Hall, Samuel Carter
- The Stately Homes of England. 1881. 2 vols. 4to. Extra-ill. with engraved ports. & views, cont. panel. cf. gt., lacks 2 spine labels. (TA. Sep.15; 147)
£50

JIMENEZ, Juan Ramon
- Españoles de Tres Mundos. Buenos Aires, 1942. 1st. Edn. 4to. Wraps. (DS. Dec.16; 2116)
Pts. 70,000

JOANNES A CURRIBUS, Ferrariensis
- De Coelesti Vita. [Venice,], Matteo Capcasa (di Codeca), 19 Dec. 1494. [HC 6982; BMC V, 485] (Bound with:) EUSEBIUS PAMPHILIUS, Bp. of Caesarea - Evangelica Preparatio. Trans.:– Gorgio Trapezuntio. Venice, Bernard Benalius, 31 May 1497. [HC 6706; BMC V, 376; Goff E122] (Bound with:) LACTANTIUS, Lucius Caecilius Firmianus - De Divinis Institutionibus. De Ira Dei. De Opticio Dei. De Phoenice. Nephytoman. Venice, Simon Bevilacqua, 4 Apr. 1497. [HC 9818; BMC V, 522; Goff L13] Together 3 works in 1 vol. Fo. 3rd. work lacks blank last lf., cont. stpd. pig, decor.; from Fondation Furstenberg-Beaumesnil. (HD. Nov.16; 74)
Frs. 11,000
-- Anr. Copy. [HC 6982, BMC V, 485]. (Bound with:) EUSEBIUS CAESARIENSIS - De Evangelica Praeparatione a Georgio Trapezuntio e Graeco

in Latinam Tractatus. [Ed.:– Hieronymus Bononius]. Venice, Bernardinus Benalius, 31 May 1497. [HC. 6706; BMC V, 376; Goff E-122]. (Bound with:) LACTANTIUS FIRMIANUS - Opera. [Ed.:– Joh. Andreae]. Venice, Simon Bevilaqua, 14 Apr. 1497. [HC. 9818; BMC V, 522; Goff L-13]. Together 3 works in 1 vol. Fo. Some light browning, upr. margin lightly stained, lacks last lf. blank, cont. blind-tooled pig over wood bds., 2 brass clasps, slightly worn, some worm-holes in jnts. (R. Apr.3; 4)
DM 7,000

JOB [i.e. Jacques Marie Gaston Orfroy de Bréville]
See— MONTORGUEIL, Georges & Job

JODELLE, Etienne
- Les Oeuvres et Meslanges Poétiques. Paris, 1583. Vol. I (all publd.). 12mo. A few ll. lightly browned, sig. erased at title slightly affecting a few letters, cont. mor. gt., head of spine rubbed. (C. May 30; 82)
Henner. £110

JOEL IBN SHO'IB
See— GALANTE, Abraham & Joel Ibn Sho'ib

JOHANN ALBRECHT I, Hzg. v. Mecklenburg
- Epistola ad Illyricum, de Osiandrica Haeresi, Pie, Dei Beneficio Sopita. 1556. Short appendix by M. Flacius Illyricus at end, title with MS. dedication Flacius to Nic. Gallus, later note on title mostly erased, lightly browned, vell. (HK. Nov.8; 232)
DM 700

JOHANN FRIEDRICH I of Saxony
- Das Gantze Leben vnd Historia, dess ... Hertzogen Johann Friderichen, Geborenen Churfürsten zu Sachsen ... Ca. 1561. Fo. Some slight spots, hand-bnd. red mor. by F. Bedford, gt. decor., arms & ex-libris. (H. May 22; 556)
DM 9,000

JOHANNESBURG
- Grocott & Sherry's Album of Johannesburg. Johannesburg, 1898. Cl. (SSA. Jul.5; 170)
R 250

JOHANNES CHRYSOSTOMUS, Saint, Archbp. of Constantinople
See— CHRYSOSTOMUS, Saint Johannes, Archbp. of Constantinople

JOHANNES DE AQUILA
- Sermones Quadragesimales. Venice, P. de Quarengiis for A. Calcedomius, 21 Oct. 1499. Very stained, etc. thro.-out, old vell., worn, with tears; the Walter Goldwater copy. [BMC V, 514; Goff J-252; H. 1327] (SG. Dec.1; 199)
$350

JOHANNES DE BROMYARD
- Summa Praedicantium. [Basel, Johann Amerbach. not after 1484]. 1st. Edn. Pt. 1 only (of 2). Fo. Lge. & sm. capitals supplied in red or blue, paragraph marks in red or blue, underscores in red, lacks final blank, k6 & P4 holed, with slight loss, o2 stained, few ll. thumbed, slight worming, mostly marginal, few margin defects & repairs, owners' inscrs., early blind-stpd. pig, worn, lacks clasps; stp. & release stp. of the Stuttgart Liby. [BMC III, 747; Goff J-260; Hain 3993] (SG. Oct.27; 163)
$800

JOHANNES DE CAPISTRANO
- Tractatus de Cupidatate. [Cologne, J. Koelhoff, the Elder], ca. 1482. Fo. Partly rubricated, lacks the 2 blanks, margin repairs on 1st. & last few ll., old cf.-bkd.; the Walter Goldwater copy. [BMC I, 225; Goff J-267; HC 4376] (SG. Dec.1; 200)
$500

JOHANNES DE JANDUNO
- De Physico Auditu Noviter Emendate. [Venice], 14 Oct. 1501. Fo. 155 ll. (lacks last lf. blank?), some ll. stained, margins of 4 ll. roughly reprd., few sm. wormholes, new cf.; Dr. Walter Pagel copy. (S. Feb.7; 209)
Colombo. £280
- Super Libros Aristotelis de Anima Subtilissimae Quaestiones. Venice, 1552. Fo. 115 ll. (lacks last lf. blank?), title cut round & mntd., some sm. wormholes, new bds.; Dr. Walter Pagel copy. (S. Feb.7; 206)
Colombo. £180

JOHANNES DE LAPIDE
- Resolutorium Dubiorum. [Strassburg, J.R. Grueninger], n.d. 4to. Lightly soiled, mod. wraps.; the Walter Goldwater copy. [BMC III, 860; Goff J-375; HC 9900] (SG. Dec.1; 204)
$250

JOHANNES DE SEGOVIA
See— CONRAD DE ALEMANNIA - JOHANNES DE SEGOVIA

JOHANNES STOBNICENSIS
[–] Parvvlvs Philosophiae Natvralis; Inventibvs Ingeniis Phisicen Desiderantibvs Oppido qvam Necessariva. Wien, 1510. 1st. Edn. 4o. 2 sm. wormholes at beginning, some soiling, bds. (HK. Nov.8; 237)
DM 800

JOHN, Saint, the Divine
- The Revelation of Saint John the Divine. Ill.:– Blair Hughes-Stanton. Newtown, Gregy. Pr., 1932. Fo. Orig. mor., a little worn. (BBA. Sep.29; 223)
Thorp. £140

JOHN OF THE CROSS, Saint
- Obras del Beato. Madrid, 1693. 2 vols. 4to. Vell. (DS. Oct.28; 2165)
Pts. 46,000

JOHN, of Fordun
- Scotichronicon, cum Supplementis et Continuatione Walteri Boweri ... Praefixa est ad Historiam Scotorum Introductio brevis cura Walteri Goodall. Edinb., 1759. 1st. Edn. 2 vols. Fo. Old cf., spines gt.; Sir Ivar Colquhoun, of Luss copy. (CE. Mar.22; 108)
£150

JOHN, Augustus
- Fifty-Two Drawings with an Introduction by Lord David Cecil. 1957. (150) numbered & sigd. by John & Cecil. Fo. Orig. hf. vell. by Zaehnsdorf, s.-c. (SKC. Mar.9; 1720)
£110

JOHN, W.
- Erzherzog Karl der Feldherr und Seine Armee. Vienna, 1913. Ltd. Edn. 4to. Orig. cl. gt. (S. Dec.20; 548)
Crete. £50

JOHN, William David
- Nantgarw Porcelain. Newport, 1948. 1st. Edn. No bdg. stated. (JL. Jun.24; 203)
Aus. $200
- The Nantgarw Porcelain Album. 1974. 4to. Red mor. gt. (PD. Oct.19; 263)
£70
- Swansea Porcelain. Newport, 1958. 4to. Orig. cl. gt., partly untrimmed, spine slightly faded. (TA. Dec.15; 370)
£56
- William Billingsley. Newport, 1968. 1st. Edn. No bdg. stated. (JL. Jun.24; 205)
Aus. $180

JOHNSON, Alfred Forbes
- Decorative Initial Letters. 1931. (500). 4to. Orig. cl., partly untrimmed, rubbed & soiled. (TA. Dec.15; 324)
£50
- German Renaissance Title-borders. 1929. 4to. Orig. buckram-bkd. bds.; H.M. Nixon coll. (BBA. Oct.6; 208)
Bennett & Kerr. £50

JOHNSON, Arthur Henry
- The History of the Worshipful Company of the Drapers of London. Oxford, 1914-22. 5 vols. including Index. 4to. Orig. cl. gt. (S. Dec.20; 849)
Subunso. £100

JOHNSON, A.W.
- The Birds of Chile & Adjacent Regions of Argentina, Bolivia & Peru. Buenos Aires, 1965. 2 vols. Orig. cl., d.-w.'s. (LC. Mar.1; 163)
£50

JOHNSON, Allen (Ed.)
See— DICTIONARY OF AMERICAN BIOGRAPHY

JOHNSON, Alvin Jewett & Colton, Joseph H.
- Johnson's New Illustrated (Steel Plate) Family Atlas, with Physical Geography, & with Descriptions Geographical, Statistical, & Historical. N.Y., Johnson & Ward, 1863. Fo. Approx. 100 engraved plts., almost all hand-cold., dampstain through lr. right corner, gt.-pict. cl., leath. back, partially disbnd. (SG. Jun.7; 20)
$200

JOHNSON, Charles, Botanist
- British Poisonous Plants. 1856. 28 hand-cold. plts., orig. cl. (LC. Jul.5; 141)
£50

JOHNSON, Capt. Charles
- A General History of the Lives & Adventures of the Most Famous Highwaymen, Murderers, Street-Robbers, etc. ... 1734. Fo. Engraved frontis., 25 plts., margin of index lf. reprd., later cf., worn. (CSK. Jan.27; 30)
£300

JOHNSON, Capt. Charles -*Contd.*

- – **Anr. Copy.** Fo. Title & final lf. reprd., frontis. & preceding page loose, some browning & spotting, old cf., rebkd. (SPB. Dec.13; 695) $275
- **A General History of the Pirates.** L., 1724. *2nd. Edn.* 3 engraved plts. (folding), early spr. cf. gt., worn. (SG. Apr.19; 149) $175
- **The History of the Lives & Actions of the most Famous Highwaymen, Street-Robbers, & c. & c.** Edinb., 1813. Hf. mor. retaining orig. bds., spine gt., unc. (LC. Oct.13; 350) £55

JOHNSON, Charles Pierpoint
See— SOWERBY, John Edward & Johnson, Charles Pierpoint

JOHNSON, G.W.
See— WINGFIELD, W. & Johnson, G.W.

JOHNSON, J.
- **A Copy Book, containing both Experimental Precepts & usual Practices of Fair & Speedy Writing.** 1669. Sm. ob. 4to. Engraved additional title, frontis. & 19 plts. (?) only, last plt. cleanly torn, some text ll. shaved with loss, some browning & spotting, no bdg. stated, w.a.f. (CSK. Jun.1; 95) £100

JOHNSON, John
- **A Journey from India to England through Persia, Georgia, Russia, Poland & Prussia.** 1818. 4to. 1 engraved plan, 12 aquatint plts. (5 hand-cold.), 3 plts. offset, later roan, rebkd. (CSK. Feb.10; 52) £130

JOHNSON, John, Printer
- **Typographia, or the Printer's Instructor.** 1824. 2 vols. 12mo. Later cl., loose. (BBA. Nov.10; 83) *Hogg.* £75
- – **Anr. Copy.** 2 vols. Sm. 8vo. Cont. hf. cf. (VG. Sep.13; 394) Fls. 600

JOHNSON, Lionel
- **Poems.** L. & Boston, 1895. *1st. Edn., 1st. Iss.* (25) numbered & sigd. Orig. cl., cl. case; Frederic Dannay copy. (CNY. Dec.16; 187) $800
- – **Anr. Edn.** L. & Boston, 1895. *1st. Edn. 2nd. Iss., (750).* Orig. buckram (an advance, trial or special bdg.), unopened; note initialed 'P.D.' & dtd. 4/11/30 regarding bdg. laid in. Frederic Dannay copy. (CNY. Dec.16; 188) $1,300
- – **Anr. Copy.** Orig. ptd. bds., unopened, Frederic Dannay copy. (CNY. Dec.16; 189) $800

JOHNSON, Richard
[-] **The Drawing School for Little Masters & Misses.** 1774. Orig. bds., worn. (P. Jun.7; 334) £200

JOHNSON, Robert U. & Buel, Clarence C.
- **Battles & Leaders of the Civil War.** N.Y., [1887-88]. *'Grant-Lee Edn.'.* 4 vols. in 8. 4to. Unif. cl., covers lightly worn & spotted, some rubbing to backstrips. (HA. Sep.16; 346) $130

JOHNSON, Dr. Samuel
- **An Account of the Life of Mr. Richard Savage.** L., 1744. *1st. Edn.* Hf.-title, errata line & misnumbering of pp.185-6, lacks advt. lf., mott. cf.; armorial bkplt. (PSB. May 16; 84) $550
- **A Dictionary of the English Language.** L., 1755. *1st. Edn.* 2 vols. Fo. Some browning & soiling, few short tears, cont. cf., rebkd., old spines preserved; book label of I.C. Searle, with her inscr. on endpaper. (S. Dec.8; 54) *Quaritch.* £2,000
- – **Anr. Copy.** 2 vols. Fo. Title-pp. soiled, 1st. with sm. liby. stp., some creasing, one p. reprd., approx. 30 pp. spotted, late 18th. C. hf. cf., new chemises, three-qtr. gt.-decor. cf. boxes with owner's name in gt. (CBA. Dec.10; 270) $3,250
- – **Anr. Copy.** 2 vols. Fo. Minor spotting, cont. cf., rebkd., corners reprd., new endpapers. (SPB. May 17; 634a) $2,200
- – **Anr. Copy.** 2 vols. Fo. Titles bkd., some inkspots, slight soiling, marginal stains in vol.1, sig. on title, later hf. cf., marb. bds. (SPB. May 16; 85) $1,400
- – **Anr. Edn.** L., 1755. *2nd. Edn.* Vol. 1 only (of 2). Fo. Title-p. reprd., title & 1st. few pp. of preface detchd., cf., covers detchd., spine split in several places, bands split & lifted, nearly disbnd.; Marymount College copy. (CBA. Mar.3; 264) $120

- – **Anr. Edn.** 1756. [1st. Abridged Edn.]. 2 vols. Some ink annots. in margin, cont. cf., covers detchd. (SKC. Nov.18; 1892) £70
- – **Anr. Edn.** L., 1765. *3rd. Edn.* 2 vols. Fo. Tear in 18U2 margin, some spotting & browning, new hf. cf. (SPB. Dec.13; 696) $375
- – **Anr. Edn.** L., 1770. 2 vols. in 1. 4to. Some light soiling, later hf. mor., lightly rubbed. (CSK. Nov.25; 45) £60
- – **Anr. Edn.** L., 1773. *4th. Edn.* 2 vols. Fo. Some spots & stains, holes in Vol.1 title, cont. russ.; bkplt. of Thomas Boswall of Blackadder. (S. Dec.8; 53) *Quaritch.* £560
- – **Anr. Copy.** 2 vols. Fo. Cont. russ. gt.; cont. booklabel & sig. of Chas. Thos. Coryndon Luxmoore. (S. Dec.8; 52) *Maggs.* £550
- – **Anr. Copy.** 2 vols. Fo. Some spotting & browning, foxing, some worming, cont. tree cf., rebkd. (SPB. May 17; 634b) $800
- – **Anr. Edn.** L., 1775. 2 vols. Fo. Cont. mott. cf., spines gt., slightly scuffed, scratch on lr. cover of Vol. I. (C. Nov.9; 146) *Maggs.* £5,200
- – **Anr. Edn.** 1784. *5th. Edn.* 2 vols. Fo. Vol.1 title torn & reprd., mod. cl. gt. (P. Dec.8; 266) *Traylen.* £110
- – **Anr. Edn.** 1785. *6th. Edn.* 2 vols. 4to. 1st. few ll. of Vol. 1 slightly wormed in margins, cont. cf. (TA. Apr.19; 259) £80
- – **Anr. Edn.** 1785. *7th. Edn.* Fo. Minor worming in blank margin, cont. rough cf., slightly worn. (BBA. Jun.14; 75) *Cavendish Rare Books.* £180
- – **Anr. Edn.** L., 1786. 2 vols. 4to. Wormhole in Vol. 2 affecting a few letters & words of text, cf., defect., upr. cover of Vol. 2 detchd. (P. Jan.12; 177) *Jarndyce.* £100
- – **Anr. Copy.** Lge. fo. Old cf., brkn. (SG. Aug.4; 170) $300
- – **Anr. Edn.** Dublin, 1798. *8th. Edn.* 2 vols. 4to. Mod. cl. gt. (P. Jul.5; 144) £90
- – **Anr. Edn.** Phila., 1818. *1st. Amer. Edn.* 2 vols. in 4. Tall 4to. Publisher's broadsheet announcement at beginning of Vol. I, some minor foxing & stains, orig. bds., ptd. paper spines (darkened & partly chipped away), unc., worn, covers detchd. (RO. Apr.23; 191) $310
- – **Anr. Edn.** L., 1818. 5 vols. 4to. Hf. cf., Dublin bdg.? (GM. Dec.7; 613) £100
- – **Anr. Edn.** Phila., 1818-19. *1st. Amer. Edn.* 4 vols. 4to. Minor margin dampstains in Vol. 2, cont. cf., upr. cover Vol. 2 slightly singed. (RO. Dec.11; 164) $275
- **Irene.** L., 1749. *1st. Edn.* Lacks hf.-title, spotted, soiled, stained, mod. hf. cf. (S. Apr.9; 262) *Salloways.* £50
- **A Journey to the Western Islands of Scotland** ... 1775. *1st. Edn. 1st. Iss.,* with the cancellantia D8 & *U4.* 12 Line errata slip,. Slight foxing & browning to title & end-pp., cont. panel. mott. cf. gt., worn. (PD. Aug.17; 159) £115
- – **Anr. Copy.** Tall 8vo. Sm. tear to errata lf., front free end-paper loose, cont. tree cf., spine brittle. (SG. Nov.17; 269) $200
- – **Anr. Edn.** L., 1775. *1st. Edn.* 12 line errata lf. sm. portion torn from blank margin of 1 lf. without loss of text, cont. tree cf., spine gt. (C. Nov.9; 147) *Maggs.* £380
- – **Anr. Copy.** 1 vol. 12 line errata lf., cont. cf., rebkd. (With:) - **A Diary of a Journey into North Wales.** L., 1816. *1st. Edn.* 1 vol. Hf.-title, lacks errata slip, cont. hf. cf., rubbed. (With:) - **Prayers & Meditations.** L., 1796. *3rd. Edn.* 1 vol. Cont. cf., rubbed. (BBA. Nov.30; 234) *Buxton.* £160
- – **Anr. Copy.** 12-line errata, cont. cf., spine gt., edges rubbed. (C. May 30; 155) *Traylen.* £70
- **Lives of the Most Eminent British Poets.** Ed.:– Peter Cunningham. L., 1854. 3 vols. Prize bdg, of cf., with school arms on covers. (SG. Feb.16; 168) $100
- **The Lives of the Most Eminent English Poets.** 1781. 4 vols. Spotted, cont. cf., covers detchd. (SKC. May 4; 1678) £60
- – **Anr. Copy.** 4 vols. Cont. tree cf. (CBA. Dec.10; 271) $160
- – **Anr. Edn.** 1783. *New Edn.* 4 vols. Cont. cf., lightly rubbed. (CSK. Jan.13; 202) £110
- – **Anr. Copy.** 4 vols. Engraved frontis.-port., cont. cf., upr. cover of one vol. separated.; armorial bkplt.

of W[alter Savage?] Landor in each vol. (SG. Apr.19; 110) $130
- – **Anr. Edn.** L., 1885. *1st. Authorised Edn.* 4 vols. Lge. 8vo. Vol.4 lacks advt. lf., some foxing, cont. cf., spines gt., jnts. & spines worn. (SG. Feb.16; 167) $200
- **London: a Poem & the Vanity of Human Wishes.** Introductory Essay:– T.S. Eliot. L., 1930. *(150)* numbered sigd. by Eliot. Fo. Orig. bds., slightly soiled, unopened. (BBA. May 23; 87) *Words Etcetera.* £140
- **Poetical Works.** 1785. 2 pp. advts., mod. hf. cf. (CSK. Jun.1; 61) £90
- **Prayers & Meditations.** L., 1785. *1st. Edn.* Spotted, cont. cf. (S. Apr.9; 263) *Salloways.* £85
- **The Prince of Abissinia. A Tale.** L., 1759. *1st. Edn.* 2 vols. Sm. hole in 1 lf. affecting a numeral, a little light staining, cont. cf., 1 cover detchd., slightly rubbed, not unif. (BBA. May 3; 207) *Maggs.* £280
- – **Anr. Copy.** 2 vols. Sm. 8vo. Sm. hole affecting page no., cont. spr. cf., slight scuffing & worming on lr. covers & spines. (SPB. May 16; 87) $950
- – **Anr. Edn.** L., 1759. *2nd. Edn.* 2 vols. A few stains, cont. cf., 1 cover detchd. (BBA. May 3; 208) *Jarndyce.* £75
[-] **Thoughts on the Late Transactions Respecting Falkland's Islands.** 1771. *2nd. Edn.* Later sheep, slightly rubbed. (BBA. Jun.28; 222) *Rudge.* £130
- **The Vanity of Human Wishes.** L., 1749. *1st. Edn.* 4to. Some spots, mod. lev. hf. mor. gt.; bkplt. of William Marchbank. (S. Dec.8; 51) *Quaritch.* £1,600
[-] **A Voyage to Abyssinia.** L., 1735. *1st. Edn.* Some soiling, cont. spr. sheep., rebkd. with pt. of orig. spine, corners reprd.; bkplt. of Earl Cornwallis. (SPB. May 16; 88) $350
- **Works.** 1792. 12 vols. Some light soiling, cont. tree cf., lightly rubbed, a few jnts. worn. (CSK. Jan.27; 10) £170
- – **Anr. Edn.** Essay:– Arthur Murphy. L., 1823. *New Edn.* 12 vols. Early diced cf. (KH. Nov.8; 254) Aus. $480
- – **Anr. Edn.** 1825. 6 vols. Cf. gt. (P. Sep.29; 135) *Allen.* £75
- – **Anr. Copy.** 6 vols. Cont. cf., gt. spines, lightly worn. (PNY. Jun.6; 453) $130
- – **Anr. Edn.** Troy, [1903]. *Connoisseurs' Edn., (150).* 16 vols. Slight offsetting, hf. mor. (SPB. Dec.13; 540) $600
See— POETS – JOHNSON, Dr. Samuel

JOHNSON, T.
- **Johnson's Atlas of England with All the Railways.** Manchester, 1847. 4to. 41 hand-cold. litho. county maps on 42 full-p. sheets, Publisher's cl. gt., slightly soiled, w.a.f. (S. May 21; 37) *Quaritch.* £240

JOHNSON, Theodore
[-] **Illustrations of British Hawk Moths & their Larvae.** 1874. *1st. Edn.* 4to. 36 orig. watercolour drawings on card., cont. cl. (SKC. May 4; 1856) £680

JOHNSTON, Alexander Keith
- **The National Atlas of Historical, Commercial, & Political Geography.** L., [1844]. *1st. Edn.* Fo. Engraved title, 45 (of 46) double-p. engraved maps, hand-cold. in wash or outl., some faint offsetting, publisher's hf. mor. gt., very worn, defect. (S. Dec.1; 211) *Liberty.* £350
- – **Anr. Edn.** Edinb., 1850. Fo. Engraved title & 46 double-p. engraved maps, hand-cold. in outl., some margins slightly soiled, cont. hf. mor., rubbed. (CSK. May 4; 28) £120
- **The Physical Atlas.** L., 1849. Fo. Cont. hf. mor., worn. (BBA. Mar.21; 132) *G. Jeffery.* £110
- – **Anr. Edn.** Edinb. & L., 1856. Lge. fo. Cont. hf. roan gt.; from liby. of Luttrellstown Castle, w.a.f. (C. Sep.28; 1742) £120
- **The Royal Atlas of Modern Geography.** L., 1861. Fo. 48 col. maps, hf. mor. gt., rubbed. (P. Nov.24; 316) *Graham.* £75
- – **Anr. Copy.** Fo. Partly cold. maps, hf. cf. (P. May 17; 431) *Jeffreys.* £55
- – **Anr. Copy.** Fo. 48 double-p. engraved maps, hand-cold. in outl., cont. hf. mor. (BBA. Sep.29; 131) *Spivey.* £50
- – **Anr. Edn.** Edinb., 1867. Fo. 48 double-p. maps,

hand-cold. in outl., cont. hf. mor., worn. (CSK. Mar.9; 67) £50

JOHNSTON, Sir Harry
- Liberia. L., 1906. 2 vols. 4to. A few spots, hf. mor. (S. Jun.25; 66) *Haile.* £90
- – **Anr. Copy.** 2 vols. Orig. cl. gt. (BBA. Sep.29; 8) *Morrell.* £50
- The Uganda Protectorate. 1902. 4to. Orig. cl. gt. (*With:*) – **British Central Africa.** 1897. 4to. Cl. (SKC. Mar.9; 2020) £75

JOHNSTON, Joseph E. & others
- Reports of the Secretary of War, Reconnaissances of Routes from San Antonio to El Paso. Wash., 1850. *1st. Edn.* 2 lge. folding maps, 72 litho. plts., including 3 folding, maps with some slight darkening, text foxed, red hf. mor.; the Rt. Hon. Visc. Eccles copy. [Sabin 36377] (CNY. Nov.18; 153) $120

JOHNSTON, Theodore T.
- Sights in the Gold Region, & Scenes by the Way. N.Y., 1849. *1st. Edn.* 12mo. Lacks hf.-title, title hinged, orig. cl. (SG. Jan.19; 126) $225

JOHNSTON, W. & A.K.
- Johnston's Royal Atlas of Modern Geography. Special Index to Each Map. Edinb., 1914. Fo. 60 double-p. chromolitho. map plts., gt.-pict. hf. mor., shaken; Henry Sanderson bkplt. (SG. Jun.7; 21) $110

JOHNSTONE, G.H.
- Asiatic Magnolias in Cultivation. 1955. 4to. Orig. cl. (CSK. Apr.27; 93) £90
- – **Anr. Copy.** Cl.; W. Norman bkplt. by Rex Whistler. (P. Jun.7; 104b) £75
- – **Anr. Copy.** 4to. Cl. gt. (P. Sep.8; 211) *Dartmoor.* £60

JOHNSTONE or JONSTON, Dr. John
- Description of Four-footed Beasts. 1678. Fo. 79 engraved plts. only, several torn with a little loss, stained, old cf., re-bkd., worn, w.a.f. [Wing J1015B] (CSK. May 18; 104) £140
- Historia Naturalis [De Quadrupedibus, De Ovibus, etc. ...]. Amst., 1657. 6 pts. in 1 vol. Fo. Light staining to upr. margins, hf. vell., recently reprd. (CR. Jun.6; 189) Lire 1,500,000
- Historiae Naturalis de Avibus. Heilbronn, 1756. Extra engraved title (dtd. 1650), 62 engraved plts. (*Bound with:*) – **Historiae Naturalis de Insectis.** Heilbronn, 1757. Extra engraved title (dtd. 1653), 28 engraved plts. Together 2 pts. in 1 vol. Fo. Some minor tears & foxing, old cf., gt. spine. (RO. Dec.11; 166) $270
- Theatrum Universale de Avibus. Ill.:– M. Merian. Heilbronn, 1756. Fo. Title with engraved vig., 62 engraved plts., some staining, cont. vell. (S. Apr.10; 427) *Wesley.* £260

JOINVILLE, Jean, Sire de
- Histoire de Saint Louis. 1761. *1st. Edn.* Fo. Cont. marb. cf., spine decor. (HD. Mar.21; 43) Frs. 2,200
- The History of Saint Louis. Trans.:– Joan Evans. Ill.:– Alfred J. Fairbank, Reynolds Stone, B. Wolpe. Gregy. Pr., 1937. (*200*) *numbered on Arnold & Foster H.M.P.* Fo. Armorials hand-cold., orig, prospectus, slight stain at foot of hf.-title, orig. mor., arms of France gt. on upr. cover, partly unc., orig. s.-c. (LC. Mar.1; 79) £380
- – **Anr. Copy.** Sm. fo. Wood-engraved ornaments hand-cold., liby. accession no. at foot of p. 1, crushed plum lev., by the Gregy. Pr. Bindery, gt. coat of arms, minor scratch on upr. cover, partly untrimmed. (SG. Nov.3; 92) $750

JOLI JEU DE LA MAISON QUE PIERRE A BATIE
Paris, [Inscr. dtd. 1821]. 16mo. 10 hand-cold. ills., loose in orig. ptd. wraps.; van Veen coll. (S. Feb.28; 77) £130

JOLL, Evelyn
See— BUTLER, Martin & Joll, Evelyn

JOLLY OLD MAN Who sings Down Derry Down
[Lr. cover dtd. 1863]. 4to. 8 ills. hand-cold., 3-dimensional face with holes in ills. & upr. cover, orig. cl.-bkd. pict. bds. (S. Feb.28; 274) £260

JOMBERT, Charles-Antoine
- Architecture Moderne ou l'Art de bien bâtir pour toutes Sortes de Personnes. Paris, 1728. 2 vols. 4to. Lacks 1 plt., cont. spr. cf., spines decor.; from Château des Noës liby. (HD. May 25; 33) Frs. 1,600
- – **Anr. Edn.** Paris, 1764. 2 vols. 4to. Cont. marb. cf. (HD. Dec.1; 73) Frs. 2,100
- Méthode pour apprendre le Dessin. Paris, priv. ptd., 1755. 4to. Title with old owners mark, minimal light spotting, text slightly browned, cont. cf., gt., worn & slightly bumped, 1 hole in spine. (H. May 22; 146) DM 700

JOMMELLI, Nicolò
- La Passione. L., ca. 1765. *1st. Edn.* Fo. Ptd. subscribers' list, some 19th. C. MS. corrections, cont. marb. bds. (S. Nov.17; 119) *MacNutt.* £150

JONAH GERONDI, attributed to
- Issur Ve'Heter. Ferrara, 1555. *1st. Edn.* 4to. Mispaginated, last 2 ll. (index) in facs., margins of 1st. 10 ll. crudely reprd., soiled & stained, edges frayed, hf. leath. (S. Oct.24; 200) *Herzfeld.* £700

JONAS, Arngrimus
- Specimen Islandiae Historicum et magna ex Parte Chorographicum. Amst., 1643. *1st. Edn.* 4to. Cont. vell., upr. hinge brkn.; Patrick Hume, 1st. Earl of Marchmont bkplt. (S. Jun.25; 171) *Hannas.* £200

JONES, David
- An Introduction to the Rime of the Ancient Mariner. Clover Hill Edns. 1972. (*330*) *roman-numbered.* (*115*) *sigd. & dtd. by author.* 4to. Orig. parch.-bkd. cl., s.-c.; Prospectus & 9 letters or cards from Douglas Cleverdon loosely inserted. (S. Nov.21; 185) *Appleton.* £200

JONES, E. Alfred
- The Gold & Silver of Windsor Castle. 1911. (*285*) *numbered.* Fo. Orig. cl. (BBA. Sep.8; 248) *Greenhalgh.* £120

JONES, Henry
See— LOWTHORP, John & others

JONES, Herschel V.
- Adventures in Americana, 1492-1897 ... Being a Selection of Books from the Library of herschel V. Jones ... N.Y., 1928. (*200*) *numbered.* 2 vols. Tall 4to. Cl., boxed. (SG. May 17; 4) $130

JONES, Inigo
- The Designs of Inigo Jones ... Ed.:– William Kent. L., 1727. *1st. Edn.* 2 vols. in 1. Fo. Vol. 1: engraved frontis., 51 plts. (numbered 1-73), including 7 double-p. & 5 folding, Vol. 2: 46 plts. (numbered 1-63), including 17 double-p., slight foxing on 1 plt., late 18th. C. russ. gt., spine gt. (C. Dec.9; 70) *Quaritch.* £1,200
- – **Anr. Copy.** 2 vols. Fo. Engraved frontis., 136 plts. on 97 sheets, list of subscribers, cont. cf., rebkd. (P. Nov.24; 161) *Evelyn.* £320
- The Most Notable Antiquity of Great Britain, Vulgarly called Stone-Heng ... Restored ... Chorea Gigantum ... by Dr. Charleton & Mr. Webb's Vindication of Stone-Heng Restored. L., 1725. *2nd. Edn.* 3 vols. in 1. Fo. Lacks both ports., minimal spotting, some stains, cont. cf., bumped, spine reprd. (H. May 22; 67) DM 750

JONES, John B.
- A Rebel War Clerk's Diary at the Confederate States Capital. Phila., 1866. *1st. Edn.* 2 vols. Sm. 8vo. Some pencil underlines & margin markings in Vol. II, orig. cl., gt.-lettered, minimal wear, bkplts. (HA. Feb.24; 327) $110

JONES, Owen
- Details & Ornaments from the Alhambra. L., 1845. Fo. Additional decor. title, 50 plts., most chromolithos., titles with margin chipping, some foxing, disbnd. (SG. Aug.25; 232) $225
- Examples of Chinese Ornament Selected from Objects in the South Kensington Museum. L., 1867. Tall 4to. Chromolitho. additional title, 99 chromolitho. plts., disbnd. (SG. Aug.25; 233) $400
- Grammar of Ornament. L., 1856. Fo. Extra chromolitho. title, 100 plts., lightly soiled, few ll. torn, disbnd., worn, lacks lr. cover, w.a.f. (CSK. Feb.24; 125) £220

- – **Anr. Copy.** Fo. 112 cold. plts., some foxing & stains, cont. hf. cf., top of spine torn. (BBA. Jan.19; 330) *Quaritch.* £110
- – **Anr. Copy.** Fo. Chromo-illuminated title & 111 plts., some spotting, a few margin repairs, recent hf. mor. (TA. Jun.21; 449) £65
- – **Anr. Copy.** Lge. fo. Extra chromolitho. title, 100 chromolitho. plts., sm. liby. stp. on title-p., three-qtr. mor. (SG. Nov.3; 111) $1,200
- – **Anr. Copy.** Lge. fo. 100 chromolitho. plts., ex-liby., rebnd. in leath.–bkd. buckram. (SG. May 3; 222) $900
- – **Anr. Edn.** L., [1865]. Fo. Chromolitho. title & 111 plts., text slightly foxed at beginning & end, cont. mor. gt., rubbed & stained. (S. Apr.30; 195) *Gilbert.* £70
- – **Anr. Edn.** L., 1868. Fo. Slightly spotted, orig. cl. gt., very slightly worn. (*With:*) – **A Theoretical & Practical Treatise on the Five Orders of Architecture.** L., 1839. 4to. Spotted, cont. cf., rubbed, upr. cover detchd. (S. May 1; 554) *Jones.* £90
- – **Anr. Copy.** Fo. Some spotting, some ll. loose & frayed, cont. red mor., very worn, loose. (S. Apr.30; 191) *Gilbert.* £65
- – **Anr. Copy.** Fo. 112 chromolitho. plts., three-qtr. mor., rubbed, ex-liby. (SG. Jan.26; 237) $150
- – **Anr. Edn.** 1910. Fo. Col. title, 104 col. plts., orig. cl. gt. (P. Feb.16; 10) £100
- – **Anr. Copy.** 4to. Orig. cl. gt. (P. Sep.29; 314) *Thorp.* £70
- – **Anr. Edn.** L., 1928. Fo. Orig. cl. gt., lr. cover slightly stained. (S. Apr.30; 193) *Scott.* £80
- A Welcome to Alexandria. 1863. 4to. Orig. cl. gt. (P. Apr.12; 38) *Henderson.* £50
See— HUMPHREYS, Henry Noel & Jones, Owen

JONES, Owen & Goury, Jules
- Plans, Elevations, Sections & Details of the Alhambra. L., 1841-45. 2 vols. Lge. fo. L.P., additional chromolitho. titles, 102 plts., the uncold. engrs. on India paper, some spotting in margins, cont. hf. mor. gt. (C. Nov.16; 101) *Irani.* £2,600
- Views on the Nile: from Cairo to the Second Cataract. Ill.:– George Moore. 1843. Fo. Some minor spotting, loose in orig. qtr. mor. (TA. Nov.17; 26) £620
- – **Anr. Copy.** Fo. Minor spotting, somewhat loose in orig. qtr. mor. (TA. Sep.15; 38) £580

JONES, William
- The Gentlemens or Builders Companion. L., priv. ptd., 1739. 4to. Engraved decor. title, 56 engraved plts., (numbered 1-60), including 4 folding, 6 lf. engraved list of plts., cont. cf., rebkd. (C. Dec.9; 68) *Wood.* £550
- – **Anr. Edn.** L., n.d. Pt. 1 only. Pict. title-p. & 30 plts. (*Bound with:*) – **A Specimen of Antient Carpentry ... Collected by James Smith Carpenter.** L., 1736. Together 2 vols. in 1. 4to. Cont. hf. roan, rubbed; Blair Adam Liby. bkplt. (S. May 1; 555) *Weinreb.* £100

JONES, Sir William
- The Works. 1799. 6 vols. 4to. Cont. tree cf. gt. (SKC. Mar.9; 1844) £170

JONES, William & others
- Clavis Campanalogia, or a Key to the Art of Ringing. L., 1788. 12mo. Engraved title & 1st. lf. loose, soiled thro.-out, cont. cf., slightly worn, upr. cover detchd.; inscr. of John Corder, Polstead, Suffolk, 1827. (BBA. Nov.30; 236) *Maggs.* £240

JONES & CO., Publishers
- Views of the Seats ... of Noblemen & Gentlemen in England. L., 1829. 4 vols. (lacks 1 vol., but 1 dupl.). 4to. 2 engraved titles only, engraved plts., spotted, various bdgs., worn, w.a.f. (S. Apr.9; 173) *Erlini.* £170
- – **Anr. Copy.** 3 vols. only (of 4). 4to. 3 engraved titles with vigs., 194 plts. on India paper, some spotting, lacks? 2 ptd. titles, cont. hf. roan, slightly rubbed. (S. Jun.25; 330) *Shapiro.* £120
- – **Anr. Copy.** 2 vols. 4to. Additional engraved title with vig., 122 plts. on India paper, some spotting, cont. cf. gt., rubbed, spines defect. (S. Nov.1; 116) *Vitale.* £80
- – **Anr. Copy.** 4to. Engraved title, 192 views on 96 ll., some minor margin spotting, cont. hf. cf., wear. (TA. Apr.19; 92) £72
- – **Anr. Copy.** 4to. Engraved title, 198 views on 99

JONES & CO., Publishers -*Contd.*

sheets, some foxing, hf. cf. (P. Sep.8; 17)
Primrose. £65
– – **Anr. Edn.** Ill.:– after J. P. Neale. L., [1829-31]. Vols. 1-3 only (of 6), in 4 vols. Lge. 4to. 384 mntd. India-proof views on 192 plts., without engraved titles, some foxing to about 25 plts., hf. mor. gt., cl. covers gt.-lettered, leath. nicked & rubbed. (SG. Mar.29; 323) $200
– – **Anr. Edn.** [1831]. 2 vols. 4to. Cont. hf. mor. gt., worn, 1 upr. cover detchd. (TA. Sep.15; 132) £82

JONSON, Ben
– **Sejanus his Fall.** L., 1605. *1st. Edn.* 4to. Title & last 2 ll. supplied in facs., cropped, mostly in side-notes & direction-lines, but also with loss of 4 text lines, few repairs, cf. antique by Middleton. [STC 14782] (SG. Oct.27; 176) $150
– **Volpone or The Fox.** L., 1607. 4to. Title washed, light margin dampstaining thro.-out, cont. cf. [STC 14783] (PNY. Dec.1; 58) $425
– – **Anr. Edn.** Ill.:– Aubrey Beardsley. L., 1898. *(100) numbered on Japan vell., with extra suite of initials.* 4to. Orig. vell. gt. extra, partly unc. (SG. Nov.3; 9) $450
– – **Anr. Edn.** Ed.:– V. O'Sullivan. R. Ross. Ill.:– A. Beardsley. L., 1898. *(100) De Luxe Edn.* Sm. 4to. Imperial Japan vell. with extra set of plts. ptd. in photogravure, orig. vell., gold-tooled. (H. Nov.24; 1353) DM 550
– **The Workes.** L., 1616; 1640. *1st. Edns.* 3 vols. in 2. Fo. Vol.1; engraved title, initial blank not in border & imprint reads London/Printed by William Stansby, MDCXVI, gathering 2P sprung, tear in D6, stain on Oo1, 4Q4 torn, 3Q5 slit, p.73 reprd. in margin, light spotting & browning thro.-out, vol.2 with some pts. bnd. haphazardly, cont. cf., wormed, vol.2 rebkd., corners renewed. (SPB. May 16; 91) $1,400
– – **Anr. Edn.** L., 1692. *1st. Compl. Coll. Edn.* Fo. Few margin defects, few rustholes, cont. cf., worn, relined. (SG. Oct.27; 177) $350
– – **Anr. Edn.** L., 1816. 9 vols. Mor. gt., covers scuffed. (LH. Sep.25; 547) $140
– – **Anr. Edn.** L., 1875. 9 vols. Cont. cf. by Bickers & Son, spines gt., lacks sm. part of 1 spine. (S. Mar.20; 777) *Booth.* £110

JONSSON, Jon, of Stadhar-hool
– **Meditationes Triumphales edur Sigurhroofs Hugvekiur.** Holar in Hjaltadulur, Iceland, 1749. Tear in title, dust-soiled, cont. sheep. (S. Jun.25; 172) *Hannas.* £100

JONSTON, Dr. John, Naturalist
See— **JOHNSTONE or JONSTON, Dr. John, Naturalist**

JORDAN, David Starr & Evermann, Barton Warren
– **The Aquatic Resources of the Hawaiian Islands.** Ill.:– after A.H. Baldwin, C.H. Hudson, & others. Wash., 1905. Vol. XXIII pt. 1 of the 'Bulletin of the United States Fish Commission'. 4to. Folding map, 138 litho. plts., contents slightly darkened, three-qtr. mor. & cl., marb. end-papers, spine detchd., covers & end-papers partly detchd. (CBA. Jan.29; 188) $140

JORDAN, Karl
See— **ROTHSCHILD, Hon. Walter & Jordan, Karl**

JORDAN, S.R.
– **Escuela de a Cavallo.** Ill.:– Donato, Julian & Galcera. Madrid, [1751]. Light staining at beginning, old wear, limp vell. (V. Sep.29; 1416) DM 900

JORDANA Y MORERA, Don Ramon
– **Bosquejo Geografico e Historico-natural del Archipielago Filipino.** Madrid, 1885. Lge. 4to. Orig. cl.; inscr. to Baron Selys-Longchamps. (CSK. Oct.21; 18) £170

JORDANES, Bp. of Ravenna
– **De Rebus Gothorum. Paulus Diaconus Foroiuliensis de Gestis Langobardorum.** Ill.:– H. Burgkmair. Augsburg, 1515. *1st. Edn.* 2 pts. in 1 vol. Fo. 1 tear restored, hf. leath. (HK. Nov.8; 238) DM 2,000

JORDANSZKY, A.
– **Kurze Beschreibung der Gnadenbilder der Seligsten Jungfrau Mutter Gottes Maria ... nach dem Vortittre der Zwei, von Wailand Fürsten Paul Eszterás.** Ill.:– Derneck & Kern. Presbourg, 1836. 4to. 1 added figure pasted on guard-lf., hf. roan. (HD. Dec.2; 103) Frs. 1,100

JORDANUS NEMORARIUS
– **Liber ... de Ponderibus Propositiones XIII.** Nuremb., 1533. *1st. Edn.* Sm. 4to. Oxidized ink-stain on last p. causing sm. hole in colophon, some slight discoloration, new vell.; E.N. da C. Andrade bkplt., Stanitz coll. (SPB. Apr.25; 239) $1,100

JORG, J. Chr. G.
– **Handbuch zum Erkennen und Heilen der Kinderkrankheiten nebst der Physiologie, Psychologie und Diätetischen Behandlung des Kindes.** Leipzig, 1826. Cont. hf. leath. gt., slightly rubbed. (HT. May 8; 550) DM 400

JORGE, Juan
– **Compendio de Navegación para el Uso de los Caballeros Guarda-Marinas.** Cádiz, 1757. *1st. Edn.* 4to. Cf. (DS. Jan.27; 2485) Pts. 36,000

JOSEF BEN MOSHE, of Kremnitz
See— **YACOV HEILPERUN** – **JOSEF BEN MOSHE, of Kremnitz**

JOSEF IBN EZRA
– **Atzmot Yosef.** Saloniki, 1601. Title mntd. (*Bound with:*) – **Masa Melech.** Saloniki, 1600. together 2 works in 1 vol. Fo. Slight staining & soiling, a few minor repairs, roan-bkd. bds., rubbed. (SG. Feb.1; 51) $1,800

JOSEPH CHAYUN
– **Milei De'avot.** Venice, 1600. *1st. Edn.* 4to. Stained & reprd., owner's sig. on title, inner margins towards beginning & end strengthened not affecting text, creased & browned, hf. leath. (S. Oct.24; 201) *Toporwitch.* £230

JOSEPH COLON, Maharik
– **She'eilot U'Teshuvot.** Venice, 1519. *1st. Edn.* Sm. fo. 1st. 4 ll. xerox replacements, 5th. lf. reprd. with loss of some letters, staining mostly in margins, slight worming not affecting text, slightly creased, hf. leath. (S. Oct.24; 202) *Ludmir.* £260

JOSELAND, Howard
– **Angling in Australia & Elsewhere.** Sydney, 1921. Qtr. cl., bds. (KH. May 1; 386) Aus. $160

JOSENHANS, J.
– **Scènes Missionaires, offertes à la la Jeunesse ... d'après l'original Anglais.** Mainz, Ca. 1885. 2 vols. Ob. 4to. 40 hand-finished cold. litho. plts., short tear in Vol. 1 title-p. reprd., some outer margins in Vol. 1 dampstained, text slightly browned, orig. decor. bds., backstrips worn, 1 lr. cover stained, the other slightly dampstained, van Veen coll. (S. Feb.28; 78) £460

JOSEPH IBN REI
[–] **Sepher Ha'Masorot.** Venice, 1607. *1st. Edn.* 4to. Foxed & creased, slight staining, blind-tooled leath. (S. Oct.24; 204) *Toporwitch.* £250

JOSEPH ZARFATI
– **Yad Joseph.** Ill.:– Yakov Ben Abram (title). Amst., 1700. *2nd. Edn.* Fo. Slight soiling, mod. cf. (S. Oct.24; 206) *Dzialowski.* £120

JOSEPHUS, Flavius
– **Alle Bücher.** Strassburg, 1556. Fo. Lightly browned thro.-out, cont. vell., lacks clasps. (GB. Nov.3; 942) DM 1,100
– **Alle de Werken ... in't Nederduytsch overgebragt door W. Sewel.** Ill.:– Jan & Kaspar Luiken. Amst., 1732. Fo. Mod. blind-tooled leath., metal bosses, unc. (SG. Feb.2; 87) $350
– **De Antiquitate Judaica.** Venice, J. Rubeus Vercellensis for O. Scotus, 23 Oct. 1486. 2 pts. in 1 vol. Fo. Lacks final blank, slight worming & stains, 18th. C. leath.; the Walter Goldwater copy. [BMC V, 415; Goff J-486; HC 9454] (SG. Dec.1; 206) $1,400
– **De Bello Judaico.** Trans.:– Rufinus Aquileiensis. Verona, Petrus Maufer, 25 Dec. 1480. Fo. Lacks 1st. 2 ll. including dedication & last 30 ll. ('De

antiquitate Judaeorum'), MS. annots. in margins, some inner margins stained, 18th. C. red mor. gt., spine decor.; from Fondation Furstenberg-Beaumesnil. [BMC VII, 951; Goff J484] (HD. Nov.16; 79) Frs. 7,000
– **Della Guerra Iudaica ...** Venice, 1531. Light margin worming at beginning, a few sm. wormholes at end slightly affect text, some light stains, cont. Northern Italian mor. gt., title 'IOSE.D.B.I.' & 'D PIERO' stpd. in gt. on upr. cover, rebkd. with most of orig. spine preserved. (S. Nov.17; 40) *Maggs.* £170
– **Des Hochberuempten Histori Beschreibers alle Buecher.** Strassburg, 1556. Fo. General title, many woodcut initials, lightly browned, some marginal stains, cont. inscr. on title, last lf. remargined, cont. pig. on wooden bds., worn, spine slightly wormed, lacks clasp. (SG. Apr.19; 112) $325
– **Histoire de Fl. Josephe.** Trans.:– François Bourgoing. Lyon, 1569. 2 vols. in 1. Fo. 1st. title & last lf. restored, lightly wormed, trace of old dampstain, some sm. stains, old cf., spine decor., worn. (LM. Oct.22; 250) B.Frs. 9,000
– **Histoire des Juifs ecrite [...] sous le Titre des Antiquités Judaiques.** Trans.:– Arnauld d'Andilly. Amst., 1700. Sm. fo. Cont. roan. (HD. May.22; 73) Frs. 3,000
– **Historico delle Antichita, e Guerre Giudaiche.** Trans.:– Pietro Lauro. Venice, 1616-14-04. 3 pts. in 1 vol. 4to. Foxed & spotted, cont. vell., brkn. (SG. Feb.9; 261) $140
– **Historien und Bücher.** Trans.:– J. Spreng. Ill.:– Amman. Frankfurt, 1569. *1st. German Edn.* 3 pts. in 1 vol. Fo. Some slight browning or soiling, 3 ll. with tears pasted, 1 lf. pt. 1 with corner tear with loss at foot, later leath. (R. Oct.11; 51) DM 2,100
– – **Anr. Edn.** Trans.:– [K. Lautenbach]. Ill.:– T. Stimmer. Strassburg, 1578. (*Bound with:*) HEGESIPPUS –Fünff Bücher: Vom Jüdischen Krieg. [Trans.:– K. Lautenbach]. Strassburg, 1578. Together 2 works in 1 vol. Fo. Light paper browning thro.-out, light soiling in margins, especially title lf., some light stains in upr. margin, cont. blind-tooled pig over wood bds., clasps, some repairs. (R. Apr.3; 51) DM 1,600
– – **Anr. Edn.** Trans.:– [K. Lautenbach]. Ill.:– T. Stimmer. Strassburg, 1590. Some light soiling, some staining in upr. margins, few sm. wormholes, lacks 2 ll., replaced in MS. (*Bound with:*) HEGESIPPUS –Fünff Bücher: Vom Jüdischen Krieg ... Trans.:– [K. Lautenbach. Ill.:– T. Stimmer. Strassburg, 1590]. Some ll. reprd. 2 works in 1 vol., fo. later black leath. over wood bds., very rubbed, spine defect. (R. Oct.11; 52) DM 950
– – **Anr. Edn.** Trans.:– Conrad Lautenbach. Ill.:– Tobias Stimmer. Strassburg, 1603. Title with sm. bkd. defect., (*Bound with:*) HEGESIPPUS – Fünff Bücher vom Jüdischen Krieg. Strassburg, 1603. Trans.:– Conrad Lautenbach. 21 text woodcuts reprd. from Flavius. Together 2 works in 1 vol. Fo. Some sm. wormholes, most in margin, cont. leath. (BR. Apr.12; 868) DM 1,200
– – **Anr. Edn.** Ill.:– T. Stimmer. Strassburg, 1617. (*Bound with:*) (HEGESIPPUS) – Fünff Bücher: Vom Jüd. Krieg ... Strassburg, 1617. 2 works in 1 vol. Fo. Some ink spotting, foxed thro.-out & very browned, vell., 4 ties. (HK. May 15; 881)DM 420
– **Josephus Teütsch.** Ed.:– Caspar Hedion. Strassburg, 1531. *1st. German Edn.* 3 pts. in 1 vol. Fo. Many short old marginalia & some old MS. underlining, pt. 1 prelims. cut close at side, pt. 2 lacks 9 ll. prelims. & intro., pt. 3 lacks 2 ll. prelims., titles present, cont. blind-tooled pig over wood bds., clasps renewed, slightly worn. (R. Oct.11; 50) DM 750
– [Opera:] **Antiquitates Judaicae. De Belle Judaico [& De Antiqutate Judaeorum contra Appionem].** Ed.:– [Hieronymus Squarzaficus]. Trans.:– Rufinus Aquileiensis. Venice, Joannes Rubeus Vercellensis, 23 Oct. 1486. 2 vols. Fo. short marginalia & some old MS. underlining, some soiling in margins, some ll. at beginning wormed, 14 ll. reprd., stained, including 10 ll. with slight loss or reprd., lacks 2 blank ll. at beginning & end, mod. cf. [HC. 9454; BMC V, 415; G. J-486] (R. Oct.11; 4) DM 2,000
– **Opera Omnia.** Ill.:– Jost Amman & others. Frankfurt, 1580. Lge. fo. A few ll. with frayed margins, 2 ll. torn, 18th. C. cf., spine gt. (SG. Feb.9; 260) $700

- Preclara Opera. Ed.:– R. Goullet. Paris, 1514. 3 pts. in 1 vol. Fo. Slight staining & browning to some ll., trace of worming, a few minor tears, old blind-stpd. vell. over bds., vell. rubbed, upr. cover reprd., traces of clasps. (SPB. Feb.1; 6a) $600
- Sämtliche Werke. Zürich, 1736. 5 pts. in 1 vol. Fo. Some browning in parts, old liby. note erased on end-paper, cont. vell. (GB. Nov.3; 943) DM 950
- Los veynte Libros de las Antiguedades Iudaycas. Antw., 1554. Fo. Some ll. slightly wormed, soiled thro.-out, upr. corner marginally chewed, mod. cf., slightly rubbed. (BBA. Feb.23; 8)
Bloomsbury Rare Books. £190
- Works. Trans.:– Ebenezer Thompson & William Charles Price. Ill.:– after Luyken. L., 1777-78. *1st. Edn.* 2 vols. 4to. 70 copperplts. & maps, 8 p. list of subscribers, cont. mott. cf., 1 cover detchd. (SG. Feb.9; 262) $250
- The Whole Works. Ed.:– Mr. Yorke. Trans.:– Charles Clarke. L., 1785. Fo. 60 copperplts., old cf., brkn. (SG. Feb.9; 263) $110
- The Whole Genuine & Complete Works. Ed.:– Edward Kimpton. Trans.:– George Henry Maynard. Ill.:– Grignion & others. L., ca. 1785. Lge. fo. 60 copperplts., subscribers lf., some margin stains cont. mott. cf., cover detchd. (SG. Feb.9; 264) $175

JOSSELYN, John
- An Account of Two Voyages to New-England. L., 1674. *1st. Edn.* 1st. lf. present with Widdows's device, sm. hole in K2 affecting a few words, sm. margin wormhole, cont. sheep, spine a little worn. [Sabin 36672; Wing J1091] (BBA. May 3; 263)
Brooke-Hitching. £2,100

JOU, Louis
- Le Chemin de Croix. Paris, 1916. *(40).* In sheets. On japan, 15 orig. woodcuts, legends heightened with watercol., all plts. mntd. under paper-masks & sigd. by artist, leaves, publisher's portfo. (HD. May 16; 89b) Frs. 2,000

JOUFFROY, A.
- Aube à l'Antipode. Ill.:– René Magritte. Paris, 1966. *(77) numbered with state in wide margins of 2 ills. numbered & sigd. by ill.* Square 8vo. Sewed, box, justified & sigd. by ill. on bdg. (HD. Jun.26; 90) Frs. 6,300

JOUHANDEAU, Marcel
- Ximenès Malinjoude. Ill.:– André Masson. 1927. *Orig. Edn. (10) on japan.* Sm. 8vo. Sewed. (HD. Apr.13; 169) Frs. 6,000

JOUIN, Henry
- Ancien Hôtel de Rohan. Ill.:– after Simonneau (1700). Paris, 1889. Fo. On vell., hf.-title, hf. red mor., corners, decor. spine. (HD. Feb.29; 24) Frs. 1,500

JOULE, James Prescott
- On the Calorific Effects of Magneto-Electricity, & on the Mechanical Value of Heat. L., 1843. *1st. Edn.* 3 pts., 'London, Edinburgh & Dublin Philosophical Magazine & Journal of Science', 3rd. Series, nos. 152-54. Orig. wraps., unc. & unopened; Stanitz coll. (SPB. Apr.25; 240) $1,100

JOURDAIN, Lt.-Col. H.F.N. & Fraser, Ed.
- The Connaught Rangers. L., 1924-28. *1st. Edn.* 3 vols. (compl.). Royal 8vo. Bkplt., cl. gt. (GM. Dec.7; 304) £180

JOURDAIN, Margaret
- Regency Furniture 1795-1830. Country Life, 1965. *(With:)* – English Interior Decoration 1500-1830. 1950. Together 2 vols. No bdgs. stated. (JL. Jun.24; 193) Aus. $800

JOURDIN, J.
[–] Le Grand Mareschal, où il est traité de la Parfaite Connaissance des Chevaux ... Paris, 1667. *3rd. Edn. (1st. Edn. with this title).* Fo. Cont. roan, spine decor. (HD. Oct.4; 58) Fls. 3,500

JOURNAL DER PRACTISCHEN HEILKUNDE
Ed.:– Chr. W. Hufeland & E. Osann. Berlin, 1826-27. Vols. 62-65. Cont. hf. leath. gt. (BR. Apr.12; 728) DM 480

JOURNAL DES DAMES ET DES MODES
[Paris, Nov. 1797-Aug. 1801]. 4 vols. Approx. 317 hand-cold. plts., cont. Swedish red mor. gt., as a periodical, w.a.f. (S. Dec.1; 388) *Walford.* £1,000
– – Anr. Run. Frankfurt, 1818. Yrs. 10, Pts. 1-25, 27-30, 32-52 in 50 pts.,. 47 (of 52) cold. copperplts., slightly torn in places, 1st. lf. stpd., orig. wraps. (HK. May 16; 1643) DM 1,100
– – Anr. Run. Paris, 1819-33. 15 vols. 1,965 hand-cold. engraved costume plts., some minor foxing, mainly affecting text, liby. stps. on most titles, orig. bds., as a periodical, w.a.f. (C. Mar.14; 56)
Horst Koch. £5,200
– – Anr. Run. Frankfurt, 1821. 52 nos. in 2 vols. 50 (of 52) copper engrs., a few plts. slightly foxed, cont. bds. (R. Apr.4; 2054) DM 1,200

JOURNAL DES DEMOISELLES
Bruxelles, 1847-49-51. 3 vols. Lge. 4to. 4 plts. hand-cold., cont. cf.-bkd. bds., van Veen coll. (S. Feb.28; 117) £120
– – Anr. Run. 1863-65. 3 vols. 115 hand-cold. plts., few loose, hf. cf., spines defect., as a coll. of plts., w.a.f. (P. May 17; 154) *Walford.* £240
– – Anr. Run. Paris, 1869-80. 13 vols. Imperial 8vo. Approx. 700 plts. & inserts, many cold., some ptd. in silver & gold, including costume plts., lace patterns, sheet music, etc., cont. red hf. mor., as a periodical, w.a.f. (C. Mar.14; 57) *Fletcher.* £2,200
– – Anr. Run. Paris, 1870-71-72. 3 vols. 4to. Linen. (DS. Mar.23; 2588) Pts. 20,000
– – Anr. Run. Ca. 1880. Lge. 4to. 83 cont. cold. proof plts., 5 slightly stained, no bdg. stated. (HD. Feb.28; 162) Frs. 2,100

JOURNAL DES VOYAGES
Paris, 1818-28. 40 vols. Cont. hf. roan, limp decor. spines. (HD. Jan.27; 191) Frs. 2,400

JOURNAL FUR ORNITHOLOGIE
Cassel & Berlin, 1853-91; 1903; 1911-12, 1922, 1925-Apr. 1983, Index to 1853-67. Plts., some cold., last 12 years orig. wraps., rest hf. or qtr. cl., w.a.f. (S. Apr.10; 428) *Quaritch.* £850

JOURNAL OF AUSTRALASIA, The [later The Illustrated Journal of Australasia]
Melbourne, Jul.-Dec. 1856. Vol. 1. New hf. mor., most wraps. bnd. in, 1 wrap. & 2 advt. ll. torn; sigs. of John Shillinglaw. (KH. May 1; 387) Aus. $120
– – Anr. Run. Melbourne, Jul. 1856-Jun. 1858. 4 vols. Some slight foxing, mod. hf. cf., many wraps. bnd. in. (KH. May 1; 388) Aus. $550

JOURNAL OF INDIAN ART
Ill.:– W. Griggs. L., 1886-92. Vols. I-IV, nos. 1-37. Fo. Several plts. torn, some reprd., qtr. mor., 1 vol. disbnd., uncollated, w.a.f. (SG. Aug.25; 234) $400

JOURS DE GLOIRE
Contribs.:– Paul Eluard, Paul Valery, Colette, & others. Ill.:– Picasso, Daragnès, Touchagues, & Dignimont. Paris, n.d. *(1070) numbered.* 4to. 10 etched plts., unsewn in orig. wraps., unc. (S. Nov.21; 38) *Duran.* £100

JOUTEL, Henri
- Journal Historique du Dernier Voyage que feu M. de la Sale fit dans le Golfe de Mexique ... Paris, 1713. *1st. Edn.* 12mo. Tear to map along central fold, old. cf., rebkd. preserving gt. spine; the Rt. Hon. Visc. Eccles copy. [Sabin 36760] (CNY. Nov.18; 154) $1,900
- A Journal of the last Voyage performed by Monsr. De La Sale to the Gulph of Mexico. L., 1714. *1st. Edn. in Engl.* Cont. cf., gt. spine slightly rubbed; bkplt. of Richard Banner. (BBA. Dec.15; 54)
Remington. £1,500
– – Anr. Copy. Cont. cf.; the Rt. Hon. Visc. Eccles copy. [Sabin 36762] (CNY. Nov.18; 155) $1,600

JOVELLANOS, M.G.
- Memoria en que se rebaten las Calumnias divulgadas contra los Individuos de la Junta Central. Coruna, 1811. 4to. Linen. (DS. Mar.23; 2146) Pts. 26,000

JOVIUS, Bp. Paulus
See– GIOVIO or JOVIUS, Paolo, Bp. of Nocera, the Elder

JOYANT, Maurice
- Henri de Toulouse-Lautrec. Paris, 1926. *1st. Trade Edn.* 4to. 8 cold. plts., reproductions, 1 drypoint etching, ex-liby., buckram, orig. pict. upr. wrap. bnd. in. (SG. May 3; 356) $130

JOYCE, James
- Anna Livia Plurabelle. Preface:– Padraic Colum. N.Y., 1928. *(800) sigd.* 12mo. Cl. (SG. Jan.12; 175) $450
- Chamber Music. L., 1907. *Ltd. 1st. Edn. 1st. Iss.* 12mo. Orig. cl., few faint stains on sides; Frederic Dannay copy. (CNY. Dec.16; 190) $1,400
- Dubliners. L., [1914]. *1st. Edn.* Orig. cl., discold. (LH. Sep.25; 548) $275
– – Anr. Edn. N.Y., 1916. *1st. Amer. Edn., (504).* Cl., spine darkened & ends frayed. (SG. Jan.12; 171) $110
- Finnegan's Wake. 1939. *1st. Edn.* Orig. cl. gt. (P. Mar.15; 88) *Marshall.* £120
– – Anr. Copy. Orig. linen. (GB. May 5; 2743) DM 800
– – Anr. Edn. N.Y., 1939. *1st. Amer. Edn. Trade Iss.* Lge. 8vo. (in 16s). Cl., d.-w. (SG. Mar.1; 210) $110
- The Mime of Mick, Nick & the Maggies. Ill.:– Lucia Joyce. L., & The Hague, 1923. *(1000).* Initial letter, tailpiece, orig. wraps., s.-c. (BBA. May 23; 110) *Blackwell.* £90
- A Portrait of the Artist as a Young Man. N.Y., 1916. *1st. Edn.* Owner's embossed stps. & sig., cl., minimum wear. (SG. May 24; 312) $300
– – Anr. Copy. 12mo. Owner's sig. on end-paper, cl., spine ends rubbed. (SG. Jan.12; 172) $200
- Sämmtliche Werke. Frankfurt, 1969-74. 9 vols. Orig. leath., orig. wraps. (D. Nov.24; 2188) DM 950
- Tales Told of Shem & Shaun. Paris, Black Sun Pr., 1929. *1st. Edn. (650).* Sm. 4to. Orig. wraps., s.-c., unc. (S. Dec.13; 374) *Ghani.* £190
– – Anr. Edn. Ill.:– Constantin Brancusi. Paris, Black Sun Pr., 1929. *(500) numbered.* Sm. 4to. Wraps., gt. s.-c. (SG. Mar.1; 211) $375
– – Anr. Copy. Ptd. wraps. (SG. Jan.12; 176) $350
- Ulysse. Paris, 1929. *(1000). (875) numbered on alpha vergé.* 4to. Later hf. mor., lightly rubbed, orig. wraps. bnd. in. (CSK. Jan.27; 136) £60
- Ulysses. Paris, Shakespeare & Co., 1922. *1st. Edn. (750) numbered on H.M.P.* 4to. Wraps., sm. tear on upr. wrap., unc. & unopened. (SG. Jan.12; 173) $3,600
– – Anr. Edn. Paris, for the Egoist Pr., L., 1922. *1st. Edn. for England. (2000) numbered.* 4to. Hf. mor., orig. wraps. bnd. in. (PNY. Jun.6; 506) $400
– – Anr. Edn. Paris, 1922. *1st. Edn., (1000). (150) on verge d'Arches.* 4to. Some pp. soiled, some spotting, cf. (CNY. Dec.17; 574) $1,000
– – Anr. Edn. L., Egoist Pr., 1922. *Ltd. Iss.* Margins & 1st. ll. slightly browned, hf. linen, orig. wrap. covers pasted on, lightly spotted & discold. (H. Nov.24; 1673) DM 1,500
– – Anr. Edn. Paris, 1924. *4th. Printing.* 4to. Hf.-title, 2 errata ll., slight browning, buckram, orig. wraps. preserved; few MS. notes & sig. by Oliver Edwards. (S. Mar.20; 930) *Hatterway.* £80
– – Anr. Edn. Ed.:– G. Goyert. [Basel], Priv. ptd., 1927. *1st. German Edn. (1000) numbered on Bütten.* 3 vols. Cont. hf. leath., unc. (BR. Apr.13; 1773) DM 2,000
– – Anr. Copy. 3 vols. Orig. hf. leath., lightly browned & rubbed. (H. May 23; 1309b) DM 920
– – Anr. Edn. Trans.:– Georg Goyert. [Basel], Priv. Ptd., 1927]. *1st. Edn. Ltd. Iss.* 3 vols. Hf. leath. gt. (GB. May 5; 2742) DM 620
– – Anr. Edn. Ill.:– Henri Matisse. N.Y., The Print Cl., 1935. *(150).* Fo. Ptd. title & 6 softground etchings, sigd. proofs, each numbered in pencil by artist, loose as iss. in folding buckram portfo. (SG. Apr.26; 137) $3,200
– – Anr. Edn. Ill.:– Henri Matisse. N.Y., Ltd. Edns. Cl., 1935. *(250) sigd. by author & artist.* 4to. 6 orig. etchings, each with reproductions of preliminary studies, orig. cl., box worn. (SPB. Dec.13; 866) $1,600
– – Anr. Edn. Intro.:– Stuart Gilbert. Ill.:– Henri Matisse. N.Y., Ltd. Edns. Cl., 1935. *(200) sigd. by author & artist.* 4to. 6 soft-ground etchings, many

JOYCE, James -*Contd.*

facs. on cold. paper, gt.-pict. buckram, s.-c. slightly worn. (SG. Apr.26; 102) $2,000
– – **Anr. Edn.** Intro:– Stuart Gilbert. Ill.:– after Henri Matisse. N.Y., Ltd. Edns. Cl., 1935. *(1500) sigd. by artist.* 4to. Gt.-decor. cl., spine slightly darkening, box lightly soiled, extremities rubbed. (CBA. Nov.19; 375) $800
– – **Anr. Copy.** 4to. 6 orig. etchings, each with reproductions of the preliminary studies, light spotting of fore-edges, orig. cl., publisher's box (some wear). (SPB. Dec.14; 66) $550
– – **Anr. Edn.** L., 1936. *(900) numbered.* 4to. Orig. cl. gt., spine faded. (P. Jun.7; 255) £85
See— TWO WORLDS MONTHLY

JOYCE, P.W., etc
- Atlas & Cyclopedia of Ireland. N.Y., 1903. 4to. Cl. (GM. Dec.7; 99) £60

JOYNER, William
- The Roman Empress: A Tragedy. 1671. *1st. Edn.* 4to. Little staining, mor. by Sangorski & Sutcliffe. [Wing J1159] (BBA. Jan.19; 131) *Maggs.* £140

JTZINGER, Karl
- Das Blutgericht am Haushamerfeld. Ill.:– K.U. Wilke. Leipzig, n.d. Minor spotting, gt.-pict. cl., spine ends frayed; sigd. pres. copy from Heinrich Himmler. (SG. Sep.29; 124) $110.

JUAN, Georges
- Examen Maritime, Théorique ou Traité Mechanique, Appliqué à la Manoeuvre des Vaisseaux et Autres Bâtiments. Trans.:– P. Levêque. Nantes, priv. ptd., 1783. *Orig. Edn. of trans.* 2 vols. 4to. Cont. tree cf., spines gt. (HD. Mar.9; 92) Frs. 2,100

JUAN Y SANTACILLA, Jorge
See— ULLOA, Antonio de & Juan y Santacilla, Jorge

JUBE, Auguste
- Le Temple de la Gloire ou les Fastes Militaires de la France depuis le Règne de Louis XIV jusqu'à nos Jours. Paris, 1819. 2 vols. Foxing, hf. parch. (SM. Mar.7; 2500) Frs. 2,000
– – **Anr. Edn.** Paris, 1819-20. 2 vols. Fo. Mod. hf. bdg. (LM. Oct.22; 145) B. Frs. 24,000
– – **Anr. Copy.** 14 pts. in 2 vols. Lge. fo. 19th. C. hf. chagrin, spines decor. (LM. Mar.3; 140) B. Frs. 12,000
– – **Anr. Edn.** Ill.:– after Martinet. Paris, 1819-21. 2 vols. Fo. Hf. cl. (HD. Nov.17; 40) Frs. 1,400

JUBINAL, Achille
- La Armeria Reál. Paris, 1839. 2 vols. & supp. Lge. fo. Linen & supp. in portfo. (DS. Apr.27; 2136) Pts. 250,000

JUCH, K.W.
- Abbildung v. Beschreibung v. 48 Giftpflanzen. Augsburg, 1819. Fo. Title slightly foxed, marb. bds., lightly bumped. (V. Sep.29; 1417) DM 1,350

JUDISCHES LEXIKON. Enzyklopäd. Handbuch des Jüdischen Wissens
Ed.:– G. Herlitz & B. Kirschner. Berlin, 1927-30. Minimal foxing, orig. hf. leath., rubbed & partly bumped. (R. Oct.11; 1094) DM 900

JUGEL, C., Publisher
- Rheinisches Album. N.d. Ob. 4to. 4 col. titles, 71 engraved views, some staining, orig. pict. bds. (P. Sep.8; 66) *Traylen.* £800
[–] Vues Pittoresques de Francfort sur le Mein et de ses Environs. Ill.:– Ehemant engraved by Martens. Frankfurt, 1836. Sm. 4to. 1st. ll. & plt. slightly stained, orig. hf. leath, blind-tooled cover, orig. s.-c. (R. Oct.12; 2560) DM 4,000

JUGEL, F.
See— WOLF, L. & Jugel, F.

JUGEL, F. & Lieder, Fr.
- Darstellung der Königl. Preussischen Infanterie in 36 Figuren ... Potsdam, n.d. Fo. 14 engraved aquatint plts., some foxing, hf. chagrin. (HD. Jan.27; 290) Frs. 1,200

JUGER, J.G.
- Sehr geheim Gehaltene und nunmehre frey Entdeckte Experimentirte Kunst-Stücke. Zittau & Leipzig, 1789. *Revised Edn.* 2 pts. in 1 vol. Title & preface bnd. after p. 288, lacks last lf. blank, some slight spotting & light browning, cont. cf., bumped, spine defect. (H. May 22; 147) DM 640

JUILLARD-HARTMANN, G.
- Iconographie des Champignons supérieurs. N.d. 5 vols. Leaves, publisher's folders. (HD. Jul.6; 49) Frs. 1,750

JUKES, Joseph Beete
- Narrative of the Surveying Voyage of H.M.S. Fly ... in Torres Strait, New Guinea ... together with an Excursion into the Interior of the Eastern Part of Java. 1847. 2 vols. Frontispieces (1st. slightly spotted), 34 ills. on 17 plts., 2 folding maps, 9 advt. ll., hf. cf. (S. May 22; 477) *Cavendish.* £420

JULIAN, Emp.
- Opera. Paris, 1630. 4to. In Latin & Greek, some browning, cf. gt. with semé of fleur-de-lys & crowned L's, surrounding Royal arms in chain of Order of St. Esprit, 1 hinge reprd., top of spine defect. (P. Sep.8; 72) *Azezian.* £110
- Opera quae supersunt Omnia et Cyrilli Alexandr. contra Julianum Lib. X. Ill.:– S. & C.F. Blesendorff. Leipzig, 1696. Fo. In Greek & Latin, very foxed, cont. vell., decor., arms; from Fondation Furstenberg-Beaumesnil. (HD. Nov.16; 130) Frs. 1,100

JULIAN OF NORWICH
- XVI Revelations of Divine Love. N.p., 1670. Sm. 8vo. Late 17th. C. decor. red mor.; Richard O'Brien MS. ex-libris on title, statement on end-paper 'Given by her Majesty the queen Dowager of England Ano-1695'. (HD. Mar.21; 81) Frs. 1,600

JULIEN, Adolphe
- Richard Wagner. Sa Vie et ses Oeuvres. Ill.:– H. Fantin-Latour. Paris & L., 1886. 4to. 14 orig. lithos., 3 orig. etchings, slightly foxed, orig. hf. leath. gt., corners bumped. (GB. Nov.5; 2458) DM 850
– – **Anr. Edn.** Ill.:– Fantin-Latour. Paris & L., 1888. 2 vols. 4to. Unif. mor.; pres. copies from author to Albert Dayrolles. (SPB. Dec.13; 697) $200

JUNCKER, Johann Chr. Wilhelm
- Archiv der Aerzte und Seelsorger wide die Pockennoth. Leipzig, 1796-99. Pts. 1-7 in 7 vols. (all publd.). Cont. bds., rubbed & slightly spotted. (GB. May 3; 1010) DM 450

JUNCO, Pedro
- Fundación, Nombres y Armas de la Ciudad de Astorga. Pamplona, 1639. 4to. Leath. (DS. Mar.23; 2148) Pts. 120,000

JUNG, Franz Wilhelm
See— KLEIST, Heinrich von – JUNG, Franz Wilhelm

JUNGE DEUTSCHLAND, Monatschrift für Literatur und Theater
Ed.:– A. Kahane & others. Berlin, 1918-19. Yrs. I & II (of III). Lacks 1 litho., browned, hf. linen, soiled. (GB. May 5; 2748) DM 400

JUNGK, H.
- Die Bremischen Münzen. Bremen, 1875. Some slight spotting, later cl.; owner's inscr. of Dr. Werner Koch. (S. May 1; 473) *Spink.* £100

JUNGER, J.F.
[–] Der Kleine Cäser. Ill.:– D. Chodowiecki. Leipzig, 1782. *1st. Edn. of this trans.* 2 vols. 1 copper engr. with sm. paste mark, cont. hf. leath., worn. (GB. May 4; 1225) DM 420

JUNGHUHN, F.
- Java, seine Bestatt, Pflanzendecke und Innere Bauart. Trans.:– J.K. Hasskarl. Leipzig, 1857. *2nd.*

Edn. 3 vols. Cont. hf. leath., rubbed. (R. Oct.13; 3026) DM 750
- Topographischer und Naturwissenschaftlicher Atlas zur Reise durch Java. Ed.:– C.G. Nees v. Esenbeck. Magdeburg, 1845. Ob. fo. Some light foxing, cont. hf. leath, loose, spine defect. (R. Apr.5; 2834) DM 440

JUNG STILLING, H.
- Jugend, eine Wahrhafte Geschichte. Ed.:– Goethe. Ill.:– Chodowiecki. Berlin & Leipzig, 1777. *1st. Edn.* Sm. 8vo. 2 ll. reprd., later cl.-bkd. bds. (C. Dec.9; 251) *Braecklein.* £120
- Sämmtliche Werke. Stuttgart, 1841-42. *2nd. Coll. Edn.* 12 vols. Some foxing, vol.10 stained, cont. bds., bumped. (R. Apr.3; 271) DM 850
[–] Die Siegesgeschichte der Christlichen Religion in einer Gemeinnützigen Erklärung der Offenbarung Johannis. Nuremb., 1799. *1st. Edn. 1st. Printing.* Minimal spotting at end, cont. hf. leath., spine slightly bumped. (R. Apr.3; 272) DM 620
- Theorie der Geister-Kunde. Nuremb., 1808. *1st. Edn.* Lightly foxed, cont. hf. leath. gt. (R. Oct.12, 1551) DM 500

JUNIUS, Adrian
- The Nomenclator ... Trans.:– Iohn Higins. L., 1585. *1st. Edn.* Title with A. Fleming's name as compiler of the index but without Latin verses to him on verso, slight browning, lacks 1st. blank, sm. portion torn from head of last lf., with loss of a few letters, 17th. C. cf. [STC 14860] (S. Oct.11; 550) *Georges.* £85

JUNIUS, Franciscus, or DU JON, François, the Younger
- De Schilder-konst der Oude. Middelburg, 1641. *1st. Edn. in Dutch.* 4to. Sm. margin stairs, cont. hf. cf., spine gt. (defect.). (VG. Mar.19; 144) Fls. 450

JUNKER, Wilhelm
- Reisen in Afrika. Ed.:– Richard Buchta. Wien, 1889-91. *1st. Edn.* 3 vols. Some foxing & soiling, orig. pict. linen. (R. Oct.13; 2905) DM 580

JURIN, J. (Essay)
See— SMITH, Robert

JURINE, L.
- Histoire des Monocles qui se trouvent aux Environs de Genève. Genf-Paris, 1820. 4to. Some foxing or light staining, hf. leath. (D. Nov.23, 713) DM 650

JUSTICE, James
- The British Gardener's Director Chiefly Adapted to the Climate of Northern Countries. Edinb., 1764. Advt. lf., cont. cf. (PD. Dec.14; 255) £65

JUSTIN MARTYR, Saint
- [Opera]. Paris, 1551. Fo. In Greek, cont. vell., spine ends worn, soiled. (TA. Apr.19; 370) £60

JUSTINIANUS I, Flavius Anicius, Emp.
- Codex Imperatoris semper maximi Diui Iustiniani ... Lugduni, 1584. Lge. 4to. Title reprd. & soiled, vell. (VA. Apr.26; 295) R 250
- Codices Justiniani. Lyon, 1548-50. 3 vols. Fo. Printers marks in MS., stained nearly thro.-out, some corners & margins bumped, newer hf. leath. over wood bds. end-papers renewed. (V. Oct.1; 3743) DM 400
- Instituta. Venice, 1516. *New Edn.* Some stains, mod. vell. (HD. Apr.13; 19) Frs. 1,300
- Institutiones. Basel, Michael Wenssler, 31.V.1476. Fo. With Gloss, old MS. column titles, pagination, underlining & marginalia, some in red ink & slightly faded, some light soiling, sm. tear in 1 upr. margin, slightly wormed thro.-out, especially 1st. & last ll., lacks 1 lf., mod. cf. [H.9499; G. J. 513] (R. Oct.11; 5) DM 3,300
[–] Institutiones Imperiales. Ed.:– J. Chappuis. Lyon, 15.XII.1509. 2 pts. in 1 vol. Fo. Slightly wormed at beginning, lightly browned & stained, last lf. with corner tear, no bdg. stated, but loose, spine with remains of bdg. (HK. Nov.8; 244) DM 540
- Institutionum Libri Quattuor. Gaesbeeck, 1678. 16mo. in 8's. L.P., engraved title-p., cont. red mor. gt.; inscr. 'D. of Grafton. 1781'. (BBA. May 23; 338) *King.* £60

JUSTINUS, Marcus Junianus
- Epitomae in Trogi Pompeii Historiae. [Venice, J. Rubeus Vercellensis], after 1489-90. Fo. Later vell.; the Walter Goldwater copy. [BMC V, 421; Goff J-619; H. 9633] (SG. Dec.1; 208) $450
- Justino Vulgarizato. [Venice, J. de Colonia & J. Manthen], not before 12 Sep. 1477. Fo. Lacks 1st. blank, some worming, considerable early marginalia, 17th. C. vell.; the Walter Goldwater copy. [BMC V, 233; Goff J-625; H. 9659] (SG. Dec.1; 209) $1,000
- Trogi Pompeii Historiarum Philippicarum Epitoma. In Justini Historias Notae. Paris, 1581. 2 pts. in 1 vol. Cont. vell. gt., spine decor.; from Fondation Furstenberg-Beaumesnil. (HD. Nov.16; 131)   Frs. 2,000

JUVENALIS, Decimus Junius
- Satyrae. Venice, Andreas de Paltascichis, 24 Mar. 1488. A few stains, some sm. wormholes affecting letters. [Goff J653; H. 970] (Bound with:) PERSIUS FLACCUS, Aulus – Satyrae. Venice, Reynaldus de Novimagio, 24 Dec. 1482. A few tiny round wormholes in margins. [Goff P345; HC 12722]. Together 2 works in 1 vol Fo. Cont. Venetian mor. over wood bds., elab. tooled decor., incorporating tools of grotesque head, sm. strip with title removed from upr. cover, 4 metal studs, 2 clasps, spine reprd. (S. May 10; 311)   Robinson. £1,700
- - Anr. Edn. Nuremb., Anton Koberger, 6 Dec. 1497. Fo. Rubricated, initials painted in red, cont. MS. annots. in margins, cont. stpd. cf. over wood bds., richly decor., clasps lack 1 tie; from Fondation Furstenberg-Beaumesnil. [HC 9711; BMC II, 443; Goff J664] (HD. Nov.16; 37)   Frs. 15,100

JUVENALIS, Decimus Junius & Persius Flaccus, Aulus
- Satyrae. Venice, 1501 [i.e. ca. 1517]. 2nd. Edn. Few stains, early marginalia, old pol. cf. gt., extremities chaffed. (SG. Oct.27; 4) $250
- - Anr. Edn. Bg'ham., 1761. 4to. Cont. marb. cf., tooled in gt. & worked in black, gt. inner dentelles in star & lozenge pattern; bkplt. of Sir Henry Campbell-Bannerman. (CSK. Aug.19; 41)   £50
- Satirae Decem et Sex. L., 1845. Fo. (in 4's). L.P., few margins stained, mor. gt. by White, decor. borders, panels & spine, gt. arms of Earl of Derby on upr. cover; E.C. Hawtrey's long ink inscr.; Thomas B. Stevenson copy. (CNY. Dec.17; 575) $240

KA HOPE NO KA HELUNAAU ...
Oahu, 1835. Sm. 8vo. Marb. bds., spine taped. (LH. Jan.15; 305) $375

KABBALA DENUDATA seu Doctrina Hebraerum Transcendentalis et Metaphysica ...
Trans.:– [C. Knorr von Rosenroth]. Sulzbach & Frankfurt, 1677-78-84. 2 vols. (compl. set of all pts., including the 2 rare tracts 'Adumbratio kaballae christianae' & 'Liber seu coelorum'). 4to. Folding frontis. slightly torn & shaved, 2nd. section of Vol. 1 misbnd. in Vol. 2, Yy3 in Vol. 1 torn, plt. 15 shaved, Kk 2 from sig. 3E-4L & following section (a)-(i) with lr. corners stained & paper brittle, a few tears or sm. holes reprd., cf., rebkd., not quite unif.; Atwood-South bkplt. & inscr., Dr. Walter Pagel copy. (S. Feb.7; 224)   Ritman. £1,800

KABINET VAN CHRISTELYKE GEBEDEN VOR DE NEDERLANDSCHE JEUGD
s'Gravenhage, 1754. 51 x 37 mm., miniature book. Cont. cf. gt.; van Veen coll. (S. Feb.28; 183) £380

KADEN, Woldemar
- Durchs Schweizerland. Gera, 1895. Some light browning, orig. linen. (GB. Nov.3; 116)   DM 750
- - Anr. Edn. Gera, 1898. 1st. Edn. 6 cold. lithos., 19 wood engraved plts. (13 double-p.), 103 text woodcuts, orig. pict. linen. (BR. Apr.12; 196)   DM 550
- Das Schweizerland. Stuttgart, ca. 1880. Fo. 1st. 12 ll. loose, cl., defect. (P. Jul.5; 173)   £300
- - Anr. Copy. Fo. 500 woodcut ills. in text & 90 tinted plts., orig. linen gt. (R. Oct.13; 3264)   DM 1,800
- - Anr. Edn. Stuttgart, ca. 1890. Fo. 90 tinted woodcut plts. & many text woodcuts, title slightly foxed, orig. linen. (HK. Nov.9; 1260) DM 1,300
- - Anr. Copy. Fo. 90 tinted woodcut plts., many

text woodcuts, some slight foxing & soiling, orig. linen, corners bumped. (HK. May 15; 1098)   DM 1,000
- Switzerland its Mountains & Valleys. 1878. 4to. 90 wood-engraved plts., orig. cl., lightly soiled. (CSK. May 4; 99)   £350
- - Anr. Copy. 4to. Orig. cl. (S. Jun.25; 175)   Burgess. £340
- - Anr. Copy. 4to. 90 full-p. plts., orig. cl. gt. (P. Oct.20; 95)   £280
- - Anr. Copy. Hf. leath. & marb. bds., spines nicked, edges rubbed. (RS. Jan.17; 494) $210

KAEMPFER, Engelbert
- De Beschryving van Japan. Amst., 1733. Fo. Additional engraved title, 48 engraved maps & plts., most double-p. or folding, hf.-title, slight margin worming at end, sm. stain to gutter of sig. N, cont. cf., spine gt., upr. jnt. & inner bdg. cracked, extremities slightly worn. (CNY. May 18; 111) $750

KAFKA, Franz
- Amerika. Munich, 1927. 1st. Edn. A few ll. slightly spotted, orig. cl., soiled, sm. tears in spine. (BBA. Jan.19; 30)   Francis Edwards. £50
- Betrachtung. Leipzig, 1913. 1st. Edn. (800) numbered. Some slight wear, orig. hf. leath. (HK. Nov.11; 3678)   DM 2,200
- Ein Hungerkünstler. Berlin, 1924. 1st. Edn. Orig. bds. (GB. Nov.5; 2642)   DM 450
- - Anr. Copy. Orig. linen, slightly defect., spine faded. (HK. Nov.11; 3679)   DM 420
- In der Strafkolonie. Leipzig, 1919. 1st. Edn. (1000). Orig. hf. roan, rubbed, lacks spine. (BBA. Jan.19; 28)   Francis Edwards. £60
- - Anr. Copy. Hf. leath. (HK. Nov.11; 3681)   DM 700
- Ein Landarzt. [Leipzig & München, 1919]. 1st. Edn. Orig. hf. leath., worn & slightly discold. (H. Nov.24; 1684)   DM 460
- Der Prozess. Berlin, 1925. 1st. Edn. Orig. bds., rubbed, sm. tears in spine. (BBA. Jan.19; 29)   Francis Edwards. £60

KAFKA, Franz (Contribs.)
See— GENIUS

KAHANE, A. (Ed.)
See— JUNGE DEUTSCHLAND

KAIN, Saul (Pseud.)
See— SASSOON, Siegfried 'Saul Kain'

KAISER, Henry J.
- Twenty-Six Addresses Delivered during the War Years. Ill.:– Mallette Dean. San Franc., [Grabhorn Pr.]. 1945. (30). Fo. Hf. mor. & decor. bds., d.-w. (CBA. Nov.19; 205) $200

KAKIEMON, IMARI, JUTANI, NABESHIMA
Ca. 1900. 2 vols. Fo. Loose as iss. in portfos. (SPB. Nov.30; 159) $300

KALKEISEN, J.J. & Cherbuin, L.
- Recueil des Vues Principales de Milan et de ses Environs. Ill.:– Mazzola, Falkeisen, & Cherbuin. Milan, n.d. Ob. fo. 2 litho. views, 55 aquatint views, cont. roan, covers with blind-tooled rustic decor., enclosing monog. on upr. cover, corners rubbed, upr. jnt. reprd. (C. Mar.14; 47)   Walford. £1,700

KALLIMORGEN, F.
- In's Land der Mitternachtssonne. Tagebuch eines Malers. Ca. 1900. Ob. fo. Title stpd., some slight spotting, orig. linen, slightly spotted. (HT. May 10; 2823)   DM 521

KALM, Pehr
- Reis door Noord Amerika. Ill.:– C.J. de Huyser. Utrecht, 1772. 1st. Dutch Edn. 2 vols. 4to. Some foxing & margin stains, cont. hf. cf. [Sabin 36988] (VS. Dec.9; 1288)   Fls. 600
- Travels into North America; containing its Natural History ... Trans.:– J. R. Forster. Warrington, 1770-71. 1st. Edn. in Engl. 3 vols. Lge. folding engraved map, 6 engraved plts., folding map slightly torn near inner margin, lf. U1 in Vol. 1 torn & reprd., Q1 & 2 in Vol. 2 stained, some ll. browned, cont. cf. gt., heads of spines chipped, corners worn; the Rt. Hon. Visc. Eccles copy. [Sabin 36989] (CNY. Nov.18; 156) $2,600

KAMES, Henry Home, Lord
See— HOME, Henry, Lord Kames

KAMPEN, Nicolaas Godfried van
- The History & Topography of Holland & Belgium. [1837]. Engraved title, folding map, 61 engraved view, some spotting, mor. gt., rebkd. (P. Sep.8; 243)   Sperling. £85
- - Anr. Edn. Ill.:– W.H. Bartlett, [1837]. Some slight spotting & offsetting, orig. cl., rubbed. (S. Jun.25; 173)   Traylen. £80
- Vues de la Hollande et de la Belgique. Ill.:– after W.H. Bartlett. Londres, ca. 1840. Title-frontis., folding map, 61 steel-engraved plts., some light foxing, str.-grd. mor., blind-decor. covers, spine gt. (HD. Mar.19; 60)   Frs. 1,200

KANDINSKY, Wassily
- Punkt und Linie zu Fläche. Ed.:– Gropius & Moholy-Nag. Ill.:– Typography:– H. Bayer. München, 1926. 1st. Edn. Sm. 4to. Orig. linen, orig. wraps. (partly bkd.). (V. Oct.1; 4246)   DM 700
- - Anr. Copy. Orig. linen, spotted. (GB. May 5; 2757)   DM 650
- - Anr. Edn. München, [1928]. 2nd. Edn. Orig. linen, spine faded. (H. May 23; 1137)   DM 520

KANDINSKY, Wassily & Marc, Franz
- Der Blaue Reiter. Munich, 1912. 1st. Edn. 4to. 4 hand-cold. plts., 137 ills., 3 music. inserts, liby. stp. on title, pict. buckram, shelf mark on spine. (SG. Apr.26; 104) $1,600

KANE, Paul
- Paul Kane's Frontier ... Ed.:– J. Russell Harper. Austin, [1971]. (300). 4to. Suede, s.-c. (SG. Oct.13; 216) $120
- Wanderings of an Artist among the Indian Tribes of North America. L., 1859. 1st. Edn. Hf.-title, folding map (tear reprd.), port. & 7 chromolitho. plts., advts. at end, orig. cl. [Sabin 37007] (S. May 22; 322)   Watt. £480
- - Anr. Copy. Engraved folding map, 8 chromolitho. plts., text ills., soiled, map & few margins slightly frayed, orig. cl., worn, jnts. brkn. (S. Apr.9; 36)   McCall. £300
- - Anr. Copy. Engraved outl. cold. folding map, 8 cold. litho. plts., cont. pol. cf. gt.; the Rt. Hon. Visc. Eccles copy. [Sabin 37007] (CNY. Nov.18; 157) $1,600

KANE, Saul (Pseud.)
See— SASSOON, Siegfried 'Saul Kain'

KANITZ, Charlotte
[-] Erste Nahrung für den Keimenden Verstand guter Kinder. Ill.:– J.J. Wagner. Leipzig, 1824. 5th. Edn. Sm. 4to. German & Fr. text, 25 hand-cold. plts., 1 plt. reprd., few slight stains, 19th. C. bds., slightly worn; J.H. Krelage bkplt.; von Veen coll. (S. Feb.28; 150)   £220

KANT, Immanuel
- Critik der Practischen Vernunft. Puga, 1788. 1st. Edn. Title verso stpd., end-papers renewed, cont. bds. (R. Apr.3; 563)   DM 2,800
- Critik der Urtheilskraft. Ill.:– after Lowe. Berlin & Libau, 1790. 1st. Edn. Cont. hf. leath., gt. spine, slightly rubbed; Hauswedell coll. (H. May 24; 1406)   DM 5,600
- - Anr. Copy. Some margin notes, underlining & ink spots, cont. bds., rubber & bumped. (HT. May 10; 2259)   DM 1,450
- - Anr. Copy. Stp. on title verso pasted over with ex-libris, some foxing, hf. leath. (HK. May 16; 2117)   DM 1,200
- Grundlegung zur Metaphysik der Sitten. Ill.:– A. Simons. München, Bremer Pr., 1925. (285) on Bütten. 4to. Hand-bnd. orig. vell., gold decor. (H. Nov.23; 941)   DM 420
- - Anr. Copy. 4to. Orig. vell., s.-c. (HK. May 17; 2620)   DM 400
- Kritik der Reinen Vernunft. Riga, 1781. 1st. Edn. Light browning & some spotting, title with erased stp. & owners mark, cont. bds., slightly rubbed; Hauswedell coll. (H. May 24; 1405)   DM 6,000
- - Anr. Edn. Riga, 1794. Some light browning, er lf. with sm. hole & slight loss, cont. hf. leath. Apr.3; 564)   DM
- Die Metaphysik der Sitten in zwey T'

KANT, Immanuel *-Contd.*

Königsberg, 1797. *1st. Edn.* 19th. C. bds., rubbed. (R. Apr.3; 565) DM 600
– **Prolegomena zu einer jeden Künftigen Metaphysik** ... Riga, 1783. *1st. Edn. 2nd. Iss.?* Cont. marb. bds., buckram s.-c. (C. Dec.9; 312) *Bender.* £150
– **Von der Macht des Gemüths durch den Blossen Vorsatz seiner Krankhaften Gefühle Meister zu seyn.** Jena, 1798. *1st. Separate Edn. 1st. Printing.* Lightly foxed, some pencil underlining on 2 pp., cont. bds., unc. (R. Oct.11; 505) DM 750
– **Werke.** Ed.:– H. Cohen, A. Buchenau & Ernst Cassirer. Berlin, 1912-18. 11 vols. Orig. hf. leath., some spines slightly rubbed. (D. Nov.25; 4800) DM 1,000
– – **Anr. Edn.** Ed.:– E. Cassirer & others. Berlin, 1912-22. 11 vols. Vol. 3 with light stain in upr. margin at beginning, orig. hf. leath., lightly rubbed. (R. Apr.3; 562) DM 680
– **Zum Ewigen Frieden.** Königsberg, 1795. *1st. Edn. 1st. Printing.* Minimal foxing, cont. bds., slightly rubbed. (HK. Nov.10; 2538) DM 950
– – **Anr. Copy.** Wide margin, new bds. (V. Oct.1; 3839) DM 520

KARL, Johann Friedrich
– **Vue et Prospect des Différentes Parties du Parc Près du Chateau de Freundenhaim Appartenant à le Cardinal et Prince Regnant de Passau.** Passau, ca. 1770. Ob. 4to. Engraved title, 30 plts., (9 unnumbered) including folding plan (laid down & reprd.), mod. bds. (C. Dec.9; 69) *Weinreb.* £1,300

KARO, Joseph
– **Bedek Ha'Bait.** Venice, 1606. *2nd. Edn.* 4to. 2 special pp. (usually missing), margins of 2nd. & last ll. reprd. affecting some letters, some foxing, hf. leath. (S. Oct.24; 209) *Dzialowski.* £320
– **She'eilot U'Teshuvot.** Saloniki, 1597. *1st. Edn.* Fo. Staining, worming affecting some letters, creased, cl. (S. Oct.24; 210) *Klein.* £300
– **Shulchan Aruch.** Ed.:– Moshe Isserles [Rama] & Gur Arye Ha'Levi. Mantua, 1722-23. *20th. Edn.* 4 vols. 4to. Owners' sigs. on titles, staining, creased, some worming not affecting text, browned, leath., rebkd., slightly worn. (S. Oct.24; 212) *Alex.* £400

KARO, Yitshak
– **Sefer Toledot Yitshak.** Amst., 1708. 4to. Early dyed vell. over bds., worn, loose, rebkd. & rehinged; sig. of David Milhaud. (SG. Feb.2; 214) $150

KARO, Yosef
– **Shulkhan Arukh Beit Yosef.** Venice, 1567. *2nd. Edn.* Sm. fo. Title & numerous ll. remargined with some loss, some text supplied in MS., Hebrew marginalia in early hand, last lf. loose & defect., some dampstaining, later qtr. leath., worn. (SG. Feb.2; 216) $650

KAROLIK, M. & M.
– **Collection of American Water Colors & Drawings 1800-1875.** Boston, 1962. 2 vols. 4to. Cl.-bkd. bds., s.-c., light wear. (RO. Oct.18; 93) $105
– **Eighteenth Century American Arts. The M. & M. Karolik Collection of Paintings, Drawings, Engravings, Furniture, Silver ... of the Period from 1720 to 1820.** Ed.:– E.J. Hipkiss. Camb., 1941. 4to. No bdg. stated. (SPB. Nov.30; 197) $125

KARR, Alphonse
– **Voyage autour de mon Jardin.** Ill.:– Steinhell, Miessonier, Gavarni, Daubigny & others. Paris, 1851. *1st. Printing.* Lge. 8vo. Some foxing, decor. buckram. (HD. May 4; 311) Frs. 1,100

KASCHNITZ-WEINBERG
– **Sculture del Magazzino del Museo Vaticano.** The Vatican, 1936-37. 2 vols. Fo. No bdg. stated. (SPB. Nov.30; 317) $275

KAUFFER, Edward McKnight
– **The Art of the Poster.** L., 1924. 4to. Orig. cl.-bkd. bds.; inscr. by author. (CSK. Aug.5; 37) £90
– – **Anr. Copy.** 4to. Cl.-bkd. bds., spine worn, shaken. (SG. Aug.25; 292) $120

KAUFMANN, E.F.
– **Orbis Pictus.** Intro.:– G.H. v. Schubert. Stuttgart, 1841. Slightly foxed, cont. hf. leath., rubbed & bumped. (R. Apr.4; 2036) DM 800

KAUKOL, M.J.C.
[–] **Christlicher Seelen-Schatz Ausserlesner Gebetter.** [Bonn, 1729]. On Bütten, slightly foxed & soiled, leath., ca. 1780, blind & gold-tooled decor., slightly rubbed & bumped, 1 jnt. brkn., partly disbnd. (GB. May 4; 1348) DM 1,600
– – **Anr. Copy.** On H.M.P. slightly browned & soiled, later leath., blind-tooled, decor., slightly rubbed. (H. Nov.23; 692) DM 720
– – **Anr. Copy.** Last ll. slightly soiled, minimal foxing, leath., ca. 1840, cathedral style, gold inner & outer dentelles, lightly rubbed. (HK. Nov.9; 1519) DM 500

KAVANAGH, Arthur
– **The Cruise of the R.Y.S. Eva.** Dublin, 1865. *1st. Edn.* Cl., defect. (GM. Dec.7; 604) £55

KAWAKAMI, K.
See— **TAKENOBU, Y. & Kawakami, K.**

KAWAKITA, Michiaki
See— **AKIYAMA, Terukazu & others**

KAY, John
– **A Series of Original Portraits & Caricature Etchings.** Edinb., 1837. 2 vols. 4to. Hf. cf., worn. (PD. Jun.13; 60) £80
– – **Anr. Edn.** Edinb., 1837-38. *Orig. Edn.* 2 vols. 4to. 14-p. list of subscribers, over 350 etched plts., disbnd. (SG. Jun.7; 374) $200
– – **Anr. Edn.** Edinb., 1837, n.d. 2 vols. & Appendix. 4to. & 8vo. 237 engraved plts., Appendix with 30 (of 31) plts., lacks title-p. to Appendix, hf. mor. gt., Appendix in cl. (PD. May 16; 170) £230
– – **Anr. Edn.** Edinb., 1842. 2 vols. in 4, with Appendix. 360 engraved plts., a few folding, orig. cl., 2 vols. with hinges brkn. (SKC. May 4; 1634) £75
– – **Anr. Copy.** 2 vols. in 4. Orig. cl., worn on spines. (TA. Mar.15; 373) £70
– – **Anr. Edn.** Edinb., 1877. 4 vols. 4to. Cont. hf. mor. (CE. Sep.1; 34) £100
– – **Anr. Copy.** 2 vols. 4to. 361 engraved plts., orig. qtr. mor. gt., partly untrimmed. (TA. May 17; 605) £50
– – **Anr. Edn.** Edinb., 1878. *(20) numbered, with India proof imps.* 2 vols. in 4. 4to. 361 hand-cold. mntd. etchings, hf. mor., brkn., ex-liby. (SG. Nov.17; 273) $325

KAYE, J.W.
See— **FORBES WATSON, G. & Kaye, J.W.**

KAYSER, J.C.
– **Deutschlands Schmetterlinge mit Berücksichtigung Sämmtlicher Europäischer Arten.** Leipzig, 1859. Plts. lightly foxed, mostly in margin, cont. linen spine renewed with old material. (R. Oct.12; 1911) DM 1,700

KAZNELBOGEN, Shmuel Juda
– **Shneim Asar Drashot.** Venice, 1594. *1st. Edn.* 4to. Some outer margins reprd. not affecting text, slightly soiled & stained, hf. leath., marb. bds., slightly worn. (S. Oct.24; 216) *Sol.* £180

KEANE, Marcus
– **The Towers & Temples of Ancient Ireland.** Dublin, 1867. *1st. Edn.* 4to. Mor. (GM. Dec.7; 61) £110

KEATE, George
– **An Account of the Pelew Islands.** 1788. *1st. Edn.* 4to. Mott. cf. (P. Dec.8; 340) *Lawson.* £70
– – **Anr. Copy.** 4to. Few plts. with light margin foxing, diced cf., spines reprd. (SG. Sep.22; 180) $200
– – **Anr. Copy.** (*With:*) **HOCKIN, Rev. John Pearce – Supplement.** L., 1803. Together 2 vols. 4to. Some ll. spotted or soiled, orig. bds., unc., worn, loose. (BBA. Mar.21; 74) *Morell.* £60
– – **Anr. Edn.** 1788. *2nd. Edn.* 4to. Cont. cf., worn. (CSK. Jul.6; 22) £80
– – **Anr. Copy.** 4to. Folding map & plt. laid down, a few ll. foxed, later hf. mor. (KH. May 1; 389) Aus. $120

KEATING, George T.
– **A Joseph Conrad Memorial Library.** Garden City, 1929. *(501) numbered.* Cl., s.-c., spine faded. (LH. Sep.25; 552) $150

KEATING, William H.
– **Narrative of an Expedition to the Source of St. Peter's River, Lake Winnepeek ... in the year 1823** ... L., 1825. *1st. Engl. Edn.* 2 vols. Sm. repair to folding map, some spotting & offsetting, orig. bds., covers worn, rebkd., using orig. spine labels, unc.; the Rt. Hon. Visc. Eccles copy. [Sabin 37137] (CNY. Nov.18; 158) $280

KEATS, John
– **Endymion: A Poetic Romance.** L., 1818. *1st. Edn. 1st. Iss., with 1 line erratum.* Without inserted advts., crushed lev. mor., covers richly gt. with central medallions, spine in 6 compartments, matching mor. doubls. with lge. gt. pointille lozenge & corner ornaments, watered silk liners gt., sprig of leaves from poet's grave mntd. before fly-lf., by Zaehnsdorf, sigd. & dtd. 1905, & with his oval gt. stp., marb. bds. s.-c.; Thomas Wentworth Higginson's copy, with sig. & carte de visite on fly-lf., Frederic Dannay copy. (CNY. Dec.16; 192) $1,600
– – **Anr. Edn.** L., 1818. *1st. Edn. 2nd. Iss., with 5 line errata.* 2 leaves advts. inserted, some foxing, faint staining to some ll., orig. bds., unc., upr. cover detchd., backstrip brkn., covers soiled, red mor. gt. box brkn.; Frederic Dannay copy. (CNY. Dec.16; 193) $850
– – **Anr. Edn.** Ill.:– John Buckland-Wright. Gold. Cock. Pr., 1947. *(100) numbered & sigd., specially bnd.* Fo. Orig. vell. gt., s.-c.; from D. Bolton liby. (BBA. Oct.27; 139) *Maggs.* £340
– – **Anr. Copy.** Sm. fo. Orig. vell. gt., s.-c. (S. Nov.21; 231) *Maggs.* £240
– – **Anr. Copy.** Fo. A few ll. slightly browned, orig. vell. gt., s.-c. (S. Nov.21; 232) *Hawkins.* £170
– **Hyperion.** Corvinus Pr., Jun. 1945. *(55) numbered.* Lge. 8vo. Qtr. vell. & buckram, case. (HBC. May 17; 203) £52
– **Lamia, Isabella, The Eve of St. Agnes & Other Poems.** L., 1820. *1st. Edn.* 12mo. 4 ll. advts. inserted, some slight spotting, orig. bds., unc., spine slightly defect., covers worn, qtr. mor. gt. s.-c.; Charles B. Foote & John Gribbel bkplts., Frederic Dannay copy. (CNY. Dec.16; 194) $1,600
– – **Anr. Copy.** 12mo. Lacks hf.-title, mor. by Rivière. (RO. Dec.11; 168) $375
– – **Anr. Edn.** Ill.:– Robert Gibbings. Gold. Cock. Pr., 1928. *(500) numbered.* Cont. snakeskin-bkd. bds., lightly soiled. (CSK. Jun.1; 59) £100
– – **Anr. Copy.** Sm. fo. A.L.s. from Gibbings & a sigd. print of a wood engr. laid in, partly unc., qtr. shark, buckram bds., by Sangorski & Sutcliffe, spine ends badly chipped. (SG. Jan.12; 129) $200
– **Life, Letters, & Literary Remains.** Ed.:– R.M. Milnes. 1848. 2 vols. Publisher's advts., orig. cl. (P. Feb.16; 261) £75
– **Poems.** L., 1817. *1st. Edn.* Sm. 8vo. Hf.-title, title washed & vig. soiled, 2 ll. detchd., orig. bds. unc., rebkd. with parts of orig. backstrip laid down; Frederic Dannay copy. (CNY. Dec.16; 191) $2,200
– – **Anr. Edn.** Kelms. Pr., 1894. *(300).* 8vo. Orig. limp vell., ties, slightly soiled. (BBA. Dec.15; 252) *Fletcher.* £160
– **The Poetical Works.** L., 1884. Lev. mor. gt. with rococo gt. borders, upr. cover set with oval miniature port. of Keats, spine in 6 compartments, watered silk linings, silk markers, fleece lined folding cl. box, by Bayntun, as a bdg., w.a.f. (CNY. Dec.17; 530) $850
– **The Poetical Works & Other Writings.** Ed.:– H. Buxton Forman. & Maurice Buxton Forman. Trans.:– Intro.:– John Masefield. N.Y., 1938-39. *Hampstead Edn. (1050) numbered, sigd. by Masefield & M.B. Forman.* 8 vols. Plts., three-qtr. mor. (SG. Apr.26; 105) $650
– – **Anr. Copy.** 8 vols. Cl., s.-c.'s. (SG. Mar.15; 128) $175

KEBLE, John
[–] **The Christian Year.** Oxford, & L., 1827. *1st. Edn.* 2 vols. Hf.-titles, errata lf., some ll. spotted, owners inscrs., orig. bds., unc., backs reprd.; A.L.s. from author laid in, bkplts. of William Warren Carman, Frederic Dannay copy. (CNY. Dec.16; 195) $160

KEENE, Foxhall (Contrib.)
See— BOOK OF SPORT

KEENE, J. Harrington
- Fly-Fishing & Fly-Making for Trout, Bass, Salmon, etc. M.Y., 1891. *3rd. Edn.* Orig. cl., worn. (RO. May 29; 120) $150

KEEPSAKE, The
Ed.:– Frederic Mansel Reynolds. L., 1828-57. 29 vols. only (of 30). 28 vols. bnd. in three-qtr. vell., elab. gt.-decor. spines, 1 vol. in watered silk. (CBA. Dec.10; 275) $350

KEEPSAKE D'HISTOIRE NATURELLE. Description des Mammifères. Classification de Cuvier.
Ed.:– Charles d'Orbigny. Text:– Buffon. Ill.:– Victor Adam. Paris, [1840]. Hf. red chagrin, corners, decor. spine, corners weak. (HD. Dec.9; 150) Frs. 1,500

KEIM, Albert
- Le Beau Meuble de France. Preface:– Paul Léon. Paris, ca. 1925. Fo. 80 photographic plts., loose as iss., bd. folder, spine detchd. (SG. Aug.25; 151) $120

KEIM, F. (Ed.)
See— NIBELUNGEN

KELLER, Gottfried
- Der Grüne Heinrich. Stuttgart, 1874. *New Edn.* 4 vols. in 2. Margins slightly browned, old owners mark on prelim lf., orig. linen. (H. May 22; 766) DM 560
- Züricher Novellen. Stuttgart, 1878. *1st. Edn.* 2 vols. Title & 1st. ll. slightly foxed, cont. linen gt. (GB. May 4; 1351) DM 400

KELLER, W.B.
- Catalogue of the Cary Collection of Playing Cards in the Yale University Library. New Haven, 1981. 4 vols. (2 text & 2 plt.). Orig. linen. (R. Oct.11; 768) DM 1,000

KELLEY, Hall J.
- A Narrative of Events & Difficulties in the Colonization of Oregon & the Settlement of California. Boston, 1852. *1st. Edn.* Orig. ptd. wraps., punched but not sewn, wraps. chipped with some paper loss, not affecting text, spine partly perished, red mor. box; Donald McKay Frost bkplt. (LH. Apr.15; 328) $750

KELLNER, D.
- Officina Chymico-metallica Curiosa. Nordhausen, 1723. *1st. Edn.* A few old MS. notes & underlining, narrow margin, 19th. C. bds. (R. Apr.4; 1438) DM 1,200
- – Anr. Copy. Some cont. marginalia & underlining, slightly browned, cut close, marb. bds., ca. 1850. (HK. Nov.8; 613) DM 620

KELLY, C.
- History of the French Revolution. 1819-19. 2 vols. 4to. Engraved frontis., 54 plts., including 8 handcold. maps & plans, some staining, cf. gt., rubbed. (P. Mar.15; 115) *Hadden.* £80

KELLY, Michael, Actor
- Reminiscences of Michael Kelly of the King's Theatre. L., 1826. *1st. Edn.* 2 vols. Hf. mor., gt.-tooled spine with armorial motif. (GM. Dec.7; 156) £110

KELLY, Michael
See— STORACE, Stephen – KELLY, Michael

KELLY, Rob Roy
- American Wood Types ... 1828-1900. [Kansas City, 1964]. *(45) numbered, sigd.* Vol. 1 (all publd.). Tall fo. Spiral-bnd. ptd. wraps. together with 97 same-size specimen sheets ptd. directly from wood type & ornaments, loose as iss., cl. folding case slightly worn. (SG. Apr.26; 209) $800

KELMSCOTT, DOVES & ASHENDENE: the Private Press Credos
Intro.:– Will Ransom. Los Angeles, 1952. *(300).* 12mo. Cl.-bkd. bds. (SG. Jan.12; 179) $120

KELMSCOTT PRESS
See— AMIS & AMILE
See— BEOWULF
See— CHAUCER, Geoffrey
See— COLERIDGE, Samuel Taylor
See— DEGREVAUNT
See— KEATS, John
See— MACKAIL, John William
See— MORRIS, William
See— PERECYVELLE
See— PSALMS, PSALTERS & PSEUMES [Latin]
See— ROSSETTI, Dante Gabriel
See— RUSKIN, John
See— SWINBURNE, Algernon Charles
See— VORAGINE, Jacobus de

KELSON, George M.
- The Salmon Fly ... L., 1895. *1st. Edn.* 4to. 45 pp. advts. of tackle, orig. cl., slightly worn. (S. Oct.4; 36) *Joseph.* £160
- – Anr. Copy. 4to. 46 pp. advts., orig. cl. (CSK. Sep.30; 65) £110
- – Anr. Copy. 4to. Orig. pict. cl., spine defect. (CE. Sep.1; 9) £60

KEMBLE, Edward Windsor
- A Coon Alphabet. N.Y., 1898. *1st. Edn.* Square 8vo. Cl.-bkd. pict. bds., worn, shaken, d.-w., very chipped; Ker Leach coll. (RO. Jun.10; 458) $120

KEMBLE, John Philip
- Macbeth & King Richard the Third: an Essay. L., 1817. Hf.-title, advts., slightly spotted, orig. bds., unc., spine worn. (S. Mar.20; 931) *Sutherland.* £50

KEMSLEY, Lord
- Anglo American Concord. Dec. 1945. *(25) numbered.* 4to. Mor. by Sangorski & Sutcliffe, d.-w., case. (HBC. May 17; 222) £75
- – Anr. Copy. 4to. Mor. by Sangorski & Sutcliffe, d.-w., case. (HBC. May 17; 223) £65

KENDALL, Edward A.
- Travels through the Northern Parts of the United States in the Years 1807 & 1808. N.Y., 1809. *1st. Edn.* 3 vols. Some fore-margins lightly dampstained, some foxing, paper bds., spines gt., minor wear to spine ends, unc.; the William Beckford & Rt. Hon. Visc. Eccles copy. [Sabin 37358] (CNY. Nov.18; 159) $320

KENDALL, George Wilkins
- Narrative of the Texan Santa Fe Expedition ... & the Final Capture of the Texans, & their March as Prisoners, to the City of Mexico. N.Y., 1844. *1st. Edn.* 2 vols. Sm. 8vo. Folding map, 5 engraved plts., orig. cl. [Sabin 37360] (S. May 22; 323) *C. Christensen.* £380
- – Anr. Copy. 2 vols. Orig. cl., boxed. (LH. Sep.25; 250) $475
- – Anr. Edn. N.Y., 1856. *7th. Edn.* 2 vols. Embossed cl., boxed. (LH. Sep.25; 251) $1,600
- The War Between the United States & Mexico. Ill.:– Carl Nebel. N.Y./Phila., 1851. Hand-cold. lithos., hf. leath., edges & spine nicked & rubbed. (RS. Jan.17; 473) $5,000

KENDRICK, A.F. & Tattersall, C.E.C.
- Hand-woven Carpets Oriental & European. 1922. *Ltd. Edn.* 2 vols. 4to. Orig. cl. gt. (BBA. Nov.10; 328) *Trivedi.* £200
- – Anr. Copy. 2 vols. 4to. Orig. cl., slightly soiled. (BBA. Sep.8; 195) *Traylen.* £150

KENMUIR, D.
See— BRADLOW, R.F. & Kenmuir, D.

KENNEDY, Edward G.
- The Etched Work of James A. McNeill Whistler. Ed.:– Royal Cortissoz. N.Y., Grol. Cl., 1910. *(402).* 1 text vol. & 9 plt. vols. 4to. & fo. Many mntd. collotype reproductions, ex-libry., text vol. cl.-bkd. bds., worn, 9 portfos. mor., raised bands. (SG. May 3; 381) $3,400

KENNEDY, John
- A Treatise upon Planting, Gardening, & the Management of the Hot-House. 1777. *2nd. Edn.* 2 vols. Cont. cf., spines gt., rubbed. (LC. Jul.5; 143) £55

KENNEDY, John Fitzgerald
- As We Remember Joe. Camb., Mass., priv. ptd., 1945. *1st. Edn.* Orig. cl.; pres. copy, inscr. by recipient 'Arthur S. Mann presented by John F. Kennedy'. (S. Dec.13; 375) *Oneill.* £170
- The Burden & the Glory. Ed.:– Allan Nevins. Foreword:– L.B. Johnson. N.Y., [1964]. *1st. Edn.* Orig. gift bdg. of cf., gt.-stpd. with Seal of United States in gt. rules on upr. cover, boxed; sigd. by Jacqueline Kennedy, inscr. by Ler to Lynn Forster, 1964. (SG. Sep.29; 195) $225
- Profiles in Courage. Foreword:– Allan Nevins. N.Y., [1961]. *Inaugural Edn.* Cl.-bkd. bds., d.-w. worn; sigd. by author, & inscr. 'For John Trefry, Jr. ... ', also sigd. & inscr. by Trefry on same lf. (SG. Sep.29; 136) $475

KENNEDY, R.F.
- Catalogue of Prints in the Africana Museum. Johannesburg, 1975. 2 vols. *(With:)* - Catalogue of Pictures in the Africana Museum. Johannesburg, 1966-72. 7 vols. including supp. Together 9 vols. 4to. Orig. cl. (BBA. Jun.14; 155) *Heald.* £150

KENNET, Basil
- De Aaloudheden van Rome. Amst., 1704. Fo. Cont. vell. (SI. Dec.15; 77) Lire 600,000

KENNY, Thomas
See— SANDS, John & Kenny, Thomas

KENT, Henry W
See— GROLIER CLUB

KENT, Rockwell
- The Bookplates & Marks. - Later Bookplates & Marks. N.Y., 1929; 1937. *(1250) numbered & sigd.* Together 2 vols. 12mo. Gt.-pict. cl., spines faded. (SG. Jan.12; 183) $175
- – Anr. Copy. 2 vols. Ills., orig. cl., d.-w.'s, prospectus for 2nd. work inserted; Perry Molstad copy. (SPB. May 16; 408) $150
- Greenland Journal. N.Y., [1962]. *1st. Edn.* *(1000) numbered & sigd.,* with suite of 6 litho. plts., the 1st. sigd. Orig. cl., s.-c. (SG. Jan.12; 184) $175
- N. by E. N.Y., 1930. *(900) numbered & sigd.* 4to. Decor. cl., s.-c. (PNY. Dec.1; 61) $100
- Wilderness: a Journal of Quiet Adventure in Alaska. N.Y., 1920. *1st. Edn.* 4to. Gt.-lettered gray buckram (1st. iss. bdg.), covers slightly warped. (SG. Jan.12; 182) $125

KENTISH, N.L.
- Proposals for Establishing in Melbourne, the Capital of Victoria ... a Company on the Mutual Principle ... To Be Designated, the Victoria Sheep & Cattle Assurance Company. Melbourne, 1850. With the extra advt. lf., mod. hf. mor., wraps. bnd. in; inscr. (KH. May 1; 393) Aus. $320

KEPHALIDES, A.W.
- Reise durch Italien und Sicilien. Leipzig, 1818. *1st. Edn.* 2 vols. Cont. bds. (R. Apr.5; 2970) DM 600

KEPLER, Johannes
- Ad vitellionem Paralipomena, quibus Astronomiae Pars Optica traditur. Frankfurt, 1604. *1st. Edn.* 4to. Copperplt. & 1 table with sm. bkd. tear, 2 tables with sm. worm-hole in upr. margin, old name dtd. 1664 on title lf., cont. vell. (R. Apr.4; 1532) DM 5,800
- Dioptice. Augsburg, 1611. *1st. Edn.* Cont. style leath. (R. Apr.4; 1533) DM 7,500
- Epitome Astronomiae Copernicae. Linz, 1618. *1st. Edn.* 3 pts. in 1 vol. A few ll. slightly browned, paper break on 1 lf., liby stp. erased from title-p. & verso of last lf. with some weakening of paper, cont. vell.; Stanitz coll. (SPB. Apr.25; 242) $2,600
- – Anr. Edn. Linz & Frankfurt (Pt. V-VII), 1618-21. *1st. Edn.* 7 pts. in 1 vol. Title lf. with MS. owners mark & sm. upr. margin defect., some cont. marginalia, slightly browned, cont. vell., minimal soiling, lightly cockled. (HT. May 8; 269) DM 8,500
- Harmonices Mundi Libri V. Linz, 1619. *1st. Edn. Early Iss., without dedication to James I.* Fo. 1st. state of title-p., a few ll. browned, cont. vell., some losses to spine, mor. folding box; Stanitz coll. (SPB. Apr.25; 243) $6,000
- – Anr. Edn. Linz, 1619; Frankfurt, 1622. *1st. Edn. 1st. Printing.* Fo. Bnd. in reverse order, darkened

KEPLER, Johannes -*Contd.*

stp. on title verso, cont. bds., rubbed. (R. Oct.12;
1685) DM 19,000

KEPLER, Johannes & Bartsch, Jacobus
- **Tabulae Manuales Logarithmicae ad Calculum Astronomicum in specie Tabb. Rudolphinarum ... Utiles.** Strassburg, 1700. Errata lf., vell. (S. Apr.10;
535) *Perceval.* £50

KEPPEL, Maj. George Thomas
- **Narrative of a Journey across the Balcan.** 1831.
2 vols. Hand-cold. frontis., 3 maps, including 2 folding, orig. bds. (S. Nov.1; 93) *Clegg.* £150
- **Personal Narrative of a Journey from India to England.** 1834. *New Edn.* 2 vols. 4 hand-cold. aquatint plts., 1 folding map, browned, cont. mor. gt.; inscr. to Princess Frederick of the Netherlands.
(CSK. Jul.6; 57) £160

KEPPEL, Henry
- **The Expedition to Borneo of H.M.S. Dido for the Suppression of Piracy.** 1846. 2 vols. 1st. & last few ll. spotted, orig. cl., spines slightly faded. (CSK.
Oct.21; 19) £110
- **The Expedition to Borneo of H.M.S. Dido for the Suppression of Piracy; With Extracts from the Journal of James Brooke Esq. of Sarawak.** 1847.
3rd. Edn. 2 vols. Uncold. litho. port., 10 tinted lithos., 6 folding maps, folding chart, cont. hf. cf., rubbed. (TA. Mar.15; 25) £120

KERCHOVE DE DETERGHEM, O. de
- **Les Palmiers Histoire Iconographique.** Paris,
1878. 40 col. plts., cf. gt., unopened. (P. Mar.15;
150) *Hill.* £220

KERCKRING, Th.
- **Spicelegium Anatomicum.** Amst., 1670. *1st. Edn.*
2 pts. in 1 vol. 4to. Frontis. with sm. tear, 2 ll.
prelims, loose, light stain thro.-out, slightly foxed, bds., defect. (D. Nov.23; 580) DM 1,000

KERGER, Martin
- **De Fermentatione Liber Physico-Medicus.** Wittemberg, 1663. 4to. L.P.(?), sig. on title, vell. gt., arms of Schaffgotsch on sides; bkplt. of Reichsgraf von Nostitz, Dr. Walter Pagel copy. (S. Feb.7; 215) *Klingsor.* £380

KERGUELEN TREMAREC, Yues Jos de
- **Beschreibung seiner Reise nach der Nordsee ...** Leipzig, 1772. *1st. German Edn.* 2 folding copper engraved maps, slightly crumpled, 1 copper engraved plt., cont. bds., rubbed & bumped. (R.
Apr.5; 3112) DM 410
- **Relation d'un Voyage dans la Mer du Nord, aux Cotes d'Islande, du Groenland, des Orcades & de Noruege ...** Paris, 1771. Fo. Cf. (DS. Mar.23; 2150) Pts. 60,000
- - **Anr. Edn.** Amst., 1772. 4to. Cont. hf. cf., spine gt., slightly rubbed. (VG. Nov.30; 839) Fls. 825

KERITOT
Commentaries:– Rashi & Tosafot. Venice, 1528.
2nd. Edn. Fo. Slight staining mostly in margin, discold., mod. vell. (S. Oct.25; 388) *Klein.* £900

KERN, Jerome
- **The Library of Jerome Kern.** N.Y., 1929. 2 vols.
4to. Sale catalogue, prices & buyer written in pencil, list of corrections tipped in, limp roan; the William Roberts copy, A.L. by T.J. Wise & 3 Y.L.s by Mitchell Kemerby loosely inserted. (S.
Oct.11; 468) *Quaritch.* £200

KERN DER KERKELYKE HISTORIE
Dordrecht, 1755. *1st. Edn.* 2 vols. 46 x 31mm., miniature book. Cont. cf. gt., 1 cover slightly rubbed, lacks ties; van Veen coll. (S. Feb.28; 186) £350

KERN DER NEDERLANDSCHE HISTORIE
Amst., 1753. *1st. Edn.* 2 vols. 43 x 26 mm., miniature book. 1st. folding plt. frayed at folds slightly affecting caption & upr. edge of ill., cont. cf., spines gt.; van Veen coll. (S. Feb.28; 188) £350

KERNDORFER, Heinrich August
[–] **Wirthschaftliches ABC und Bilderbuch für Mädchen, nebst einer Anweisung Kindern leicht lesen zu lehren.** Pirna, [1812]. *2nd. Edn.* 2 pts. in

1 vol. Square 12mo. Upr. edges slightly cropped, short tear in 1st. text lf., slight pencil marks & scribbling, lacks sub-title to 2nd. pt. (?), 4 p. catalogue at end, 19th. C. bds.; J.H. Krelage bkplt., van Veen coll. (S. Feb.28; 151) £220

KERNER, J.S.
[–] **Darstellung vorzüglicher Ausländischer Bäume und Gesträuche.** Tübingen, 1796. Vol. 1 (all publd.).
4to. Title & a few plts. slightly foxed at side, newer linen, orig. wraps. bnd. in. (R. Apr.4; 1746) DM 3,600

KERNER, Justinus
- **Die Dichtungen.** Stuttgart & Tübingen, 1834.
[1st. Edn.]. Orig. red mor. gt., marb. end-papers, ribbon; Robert Schumann's copy, sigd. & with autograph annots.; as an association copy. (S. May 10; 151) *Benda.* £1,000
- - **Anr. Copy.** Lightly foxed at beginning, hf.
leath., ca. 1870, slightly worn. (HK. Nov.10; 2544) DM 450
- **Die Lyrischen Gedichte.** 1854. *Definitive Edn.*
MS. dedication sigd. from author, orig. linen gt., jnt. rubbed. (GB. May 4; 1352) DM 530
- **Die Scherin von Prevorst.** Stuttgart & Tübingen,
1829. *1st. Edn.* 2 pts. in 1 vol. Hf. leath., slightly rubbed & old spotting. (V. Oct.1; 3842) DM 420

KERR, Alfred
- **Krämerspiegel. Zwölf Gesänge für eine Singstimme mit Klavierbegleitung komponiert von Richard Strauss, opus 66.** Ill.:– Michel Fingesten.
1921. *1st. Edn. (120). (90) numbered on Zanders-Bütten.* Fo. Printers mark sigd. by Fingesten & Strauss, 12 orig. lithos., orig. hf. vell. gt., slightly spotted, by Paul Cassirer 1921. (GB. May 5; 2528) DM 1,150

KERSHAW, Capt. James
See– MOORE, Lieut. Joseph – KERSHAW, Capt.
James & Daniell, William

KERTESZ, André
- **Of New York.** Ed.:– Nicolas Ducrot. N.Y., 1976.
1st. Edn. 4to. Leath.; a Knopf card, sigd. by Kertesz, mntd. to front free end-paper, front & pastedown end-papers sigd. by 22 others (including E.L.
Doctorow, Rona Jaffe, Robert Bernstein & Sam Levenson). (SG. Nov.10; 95) $150

KESSLER, Joh. W.
- **Lehrbuch der Kunst schön und geschwind zu schreiben.** Heilbronn & Rotenburg, 1793. Sm. 4to.
Slightly spotted, cont. hf. vell.; slightly rubbed & bumped, owners mark on end-paper, Hauswedell coll. (H. May 23; 312) DM 700

KESSLER VON WETZLER, Franz
- **Kurtzer Einfaeltiger und doch Aussfuehrlicher Verstaendlicher Bericht ... oder Geometrische und Ringkoestige Proportional Instruments ...** Oppenheim, 1612. *1st. Edn. (Bound with:)*
- **Eygendtlicher Bericht vom Nutzem und Gebrauch des Proportional-Instruments.** Oppenheim, 1613.
1st. Edn. Together 2 works in 1 vol. 4to. Mod. qtr.
cf. (SG. Feb.9; 265) $500

KEULEN, Joannes van
- **De Groote Nieuwe Vermeerderde Zee-Atlas.** 1681-
86? *Various Edns.* Lge. fo. 32 double-p. maps (ptd.
index lists 37), hand-cold. in outl., cartouches, etc.
fully hand-cold. & partly heightened in gold, an extra 4 double-p. maps by N. Visscher bnd. at beginning, lacks title, margins partly short or slightly frayed, some slight stains or dust-soiling, some sm. repairs, cont. gt.-stpd. decor. vell., rebnd., dust-soiled, new fly-ll. (VG. Sep.14; 1072) Fls. 12,000

KEY, Eugene George
- **Mars Mountain.** Ill.:– Irving E.G. Bjorkman.
Everett, Pa., Fantasy Pr., ca. 1935. *1st. Edn. (200 or less?).* Darkened, pict. wraps. after Bjorkman, light wear & soiling. (CBA. Oct.29; 456) $450

KEYNES, Geoffrey
- **A Bibliography of Robert Hooke.** 1960. 4to.
(With:) - **John Evelyn, a Study in Bibliophily.** 1968.
2nd. Edn. Together 2 vols. 4to. Orig. cl., d.-w.'s.
(BBA. Jul.27; 225) *Batho.* £60

- **Bibliotheca Bibliographica.** Trianon Pr., 1964.
(500). Orig. cl. (BBA. Nov.10; 86) *Maggs.* £65
- **Engravings by William Blake, the Separate Plates.**
Dublin, 1956. *(500).* 4to. Orig. cl. (S. Apr.30; 52) *Christies L.* £90
- **A Study of the Illuminated Books of William Blake.** L. & Paris, Trianon Pr., [1964]. *1st. Edn.
(525) numbered & sigd.* 4to. Hf. mor., some light wear & discolouration at spine tips, s.-c. (RO.
Dec.11; 172) $110

KEYNES, Geoffrey (Ed.)
See– BLAKE, William

KEYNES, Geoffrey L. (Contrib.)
See– MINER, Dorothy

KEYNES, Geoffrey & Wolf, Edwin
- **William Blake's Illuminated Books: A Census.**
N.Y., Grol. Cl., 1963. *(400).* Tall 4to. Cl. (SG.
Sep.15; 157) $100

KEYNES, John Maynard
- **The End of Laissez-faire.** Hogarth Pr., 1926. *1st.
Edn.* Orig. cl.-bkd. bds., slightly rubbed. (BBA.
Nov.30; 308) *Quaritch.* £50
- **The General Theory of Employment Interest & Money.** L., 1936. *1st. Edn.* Orig. cl. (BBA. Nov.30;
309) *Quaritch.* £130
- - **Anr. Copy.** Orig. cl. (BBA. Jan.19; 277) *Zeitlin & Ver Brugge.* £100
- - **Anr. Copy.** Orig. cl. (BBA. Dec.15; 243) *Blackwell.* £65
- **A Revision of the Treaty.** L., 1922. *1st. Edn.* Orig.
cl., d.-w. (BBA. Nov.30; 283) *Quaritch.* £65
- **Treatise on Money.** L., 1930. *1st. Edn.* 2 vols.
Orig. cl., d.-w.'s. (BBA. May 23; 112) *Thorpe.* £150
- **A Treatise on Probablity.** 1921. *1st. Edn.* Orig.
cl. (BBA. Jan.19; 276) *Pickering & Chatto.* £80
- - **Anr. Copy.** Slightly browned, orig. cl., slightly rubbed. (BBA. May 23; 111) *Drury.* £70

KEYSER, H. de
- **Architectura Moderna ofte Bouwinge van ossen Tyt ...** Ed.:– C. Danckerts. Amst., 1631. *1st. Edn.*
Fo. Engraved title, 44 plt., including 4 double-p., title slightly defect. & lined, outer margin weakened by damp, margin of 6 defect. & lined, outer margin weakened by damp, margin of 6 ll. strengthened, sm. wormhole, vell. (B. Oct.4; 688a) Fls. 1,100

KEYSSLER, Johann Georg
- **Neueste Reisen.** [Hannover, 1751]. Pt. 2 only (of
2). 4to. Hf.-title with MS. name & verso stpd., cont. vell. (HK. Nov.8; 1095) DM 420

KHAIRALLAH, K.T.
- **Caïs.** Ill.:– Gio. Colucci. [Paris, 1921]. *(500) with etching frontis.* Square 12mo. Cont. blind-decor.
roan by Levitsky, unc., wrap.; artist's copy, 5 proofs (4 sigd.) bnd. at beginning. (HD. Jun.22; 23) Frs. 1,000

KHEVENHULLER, Ludwig Andrea v.
- **Observations-Puncten ... bey deme Ihme anvertrauten Dragoner– Regiment vorgeschrieben.** Wien,
1738-39. *2nd. Edn.* 3 pts. in 1 vol. *(Bound with:)*
KOSTKA, J. - **Observationes Militares,Theoretico-practicae über den Kayserlichen Articuls Brief Leopoldi primi ...** Wien, 1738. *2nd. Edn.* Together 2 works in 1 vol. 4to. cont. vell. (R. Oct.12; 2297) DM 850

KHMUROGO, V.
- **Anatol Petrits'ki: Teatral'ni Stoy [Anatole Petritski: Theatrical Designs].** Kiev, 1929. Fo.
Reproductions captioned in Ukrainian & German,
1 lf. slightly frayed, & reinserted, orig. bds., rebkd. & recornered. (S. Nov.21; 147) *Quaritch.* £230

KIDSON, Joseph R. & Frank
- **Historical Notices of the Old Leeds Pottery.**
Leeds, 1892. 4to. Orig. cl., unc. (S. May 1; 627) *Heneage.* £80

KIECHEL, Johann Fr.
- **Die Teutsche Kurrent = Kanzlei = und Fraktur = Schrift ...** Strassburg, 1788. Ob. 4to. Wide margin, later marb. bds., slightly rubbed; crowned eagle stp.
on end-paper, Hauswedell coll. (H. May 23; 310) DM 600

KIEFFER, Fritz
- Les Garnisons d'Alsace au 19ème Siecle. Strasbourg, 1911. 100 cold. plts., hf. chagrin, corners, mntd. on guards. (HD. Jan.27; 159)   Frs. 2,000
- - **Anr. Copy.** Leaves, publisher's portfo. (HD. Jan.27; 160)   Frs. 1,500

KIEPERT, H. & Weiland, C.F.
- Grosser Hand-Atlas des Himmels und der Erde. Weimar, 1874. Fo. (590 x 375mm.). Double-p. litho. title, 67 double-p. engraved or litho. map-sheets, maps mostly hand-cold. in outl., some light spotting, few maps detchd., publisher's bds., worn. (S. Nov.1; 185)   Marlboro Rare Bks. £155

KIES, Helmut
- Im Garten der Venus. Hildesheim, 1965. (100) numbered. Fo. 10 sigd. & numbered orig. etchings, orig. hf. linen portfo. (GB. May 5; 2771) DM 500

KIKI
- Souvenirs. Preface:- Foujita. Ill.:- after Man Ray & others. Paris, [1929]. Sm. 4to. Orig. wraps. (SG. Nov.10; 107) $225

KILBURNE, Richard
- A Topographie or Survey of the County of Kent. 1659. 1st. Edn. County map by John Speede inserted, later cf. (PWC. Jul.11; 583)   £250
- - **Anr. Copy.** 4to. Bkplt. pasted on title verso, tear in A4 reprd., cont. cf., rebkd. [Wing K434] (S. Mar.6; 433)   Smallwood. £190
- - **Anr. Copy.** Sm 4to. Cf., rebkd. (P. Sep.29; 99)   Fancycrest. £90
- - **Anr. Copy.** Sm. 4to. Port., title & 1st. 3 ll. outer margins reprd., cont. cf., rebkd. (P. Nov.24; 74)   Fancycrest. £70
- - **Anr. Edn.** 1659. 4to. Engraved port. trimmed & mntd. on verso of title, R4 reprd., some light staining, later hf. cf., worn, w.a.f. [Wing K434] (CSK. May 4; 90)   £55

KILIAN, G.C.
- Li Contorni delle Pitture Antiche d'Ercolano. 1779-95. 7 vols. in 3. Text & plts. extended to fo. size, hf. mor. gt. (P. Mar.15; 157)   £110

KILIAN, Wolfgang
See— FUGGER, Family of — KILIAN, Wolfgang

KILLEEN, W.D.
- The Ecclesiastical History of Ireland. L., 1875. 1st. Edn. 2 vols. Mor. by Seighton, Brewer St., armorial motif on spine. (GM. Dec.7; 414)   £50

KILLIGREW, Henry
- The Conspiracy a Tragedy, as it was Intended, for the Nuptialls, of the Lord Charles Herbert, & the Lady Villiers. L., 1638. 1st. Edn. Sm. 4to. Final blank, sig. E3 correctly ptd., foot of E1 & E4 irregularly trimmed, with catchword shaved at foot of verso, sm. hole in D2, with loss of 1 letter of text, slight browning, some MS. underlinings in 1st. few ll., disbnd. [STC 14958] (S. Oct.11; 347)   Hannas. £140

KILLIGREW, Thomas
- Comedies & Tragedies. L., 1664. 1st. Coll. Edn. Fo. All titles of plays dtd. 1663, extra title for 'The Prisoners' dtd. 1664 inserted after Cccc4, engraved port. with 2nd. state of escutcheon, some foxing & browning, rustholes, 19th. C. cf. [Wing K450] (SPB. May 16; 92) $800

KILMER, Joyce
- Trees & Other Poems. N.Y., 1914. 1st. Edn. 1st. State. Orig. bds.; Perry Molstad copy. (SPB. May 16; 475) $200
- - **Anr. Copy.** Without 'Printed in U.S.A.', some spotting, orig. bds.; Fred A.Berne copy. (SPB. May 16; 318) $150

KIMBALL, Horace
[-] The Naval Temple: a Complete History of the Battles Fought by the Navy of the United States. Boston, 1816. 1st. Edn. Additional engraved title, 19 engraved plts., some stains & foxing in text, 2 ll. loose, cont. cf., spine very worn; sigd. by M. v. Buren & dtd. 26 Feb. 1816, inscr. & sigd. by his father Abr. v. Buren. (SG. Oct.20; 360) $400

KIMBER, Edward
[-] The Life & Adventures of Joe Thompson. 1751. 2nd. Edn. 2 vols. 1 engraved frontis. torn, 2 ll. in Vol. 2 holed with loss, blank margins of 2 ll. torn with loss, cont. cf., rubbed. (CSK. Oct.21; 68)£50

KIMBERLEY, W.B.
- Bendigo & Vicinity ... Melbourne, 1895. 4to. Bdg. not stated, weakening, covers stained. (KH. May 1; 395)   Aus. $120

KIMCHI, David [Radak]
- Shoroshim. Ed.:- Isaiah Parnas & Elijah Levita. Venice, 1529. 5th. Edn. Fo. Worming affecting some letters, margins crudely reprd. affecting some words, slight staining & foxing, hf. leath., marb. paper bds. (S. Oct.24; 219)   Toporwitch. £400
- - **Anr. Edn.** Venice, 1546. Title reprd. at inner margin. (Bound with:) - Michlol. Venice, 1545. Together 2 works in 1 vol. Fo. Staining to lr. portion, 18th. C. tinted vell. gt., worn. (SPB. Feb.1; 52) $1,300

KIND, Johann Friedrich
- Der Freischütz. Leipzig, 1822. 1st. Edn. Sm. 8vo. Cont. bds. (C. Dec.9; 254)   Hoffman. £200

KINDER, Stephen
- The Sabretooth: a Romance of Put-in-Ray. Chic., [1902]. No bdg. stated, spine slightly darkening. (CBA. Oct.29; 457) $250

KINDERSLEY, Mrs. Jemima
- Letters from the island of Teneriffe, Brazil, the Cape of Good Hope & the East Indies. L., 1777. 1st. Edn. Hf.-title, cont. cf., gt. spine; bkplt. of Marquess of Donegal. (BBA. Dec.15; 55)   Lawson. £110

KINDERVREUGD
Amst., ca. 1860. Lge. 4to. Moving picture book, 4 ills. hand-cold., 2 limbs & lever in last ill. detchd., dampstained thro.-out, orig. cl.-bkd. pict. bds., slightly worn; van Veen coll. (S. Feb.28; 276) $210

KINDLEBN, Chr. W.
- Vermischte Aufsätze für das Denkende Publikum. Eine Berlinische Wochenschrift. Berlin & Leipzig, 1780. 2 vols. in 1. Title stpd., cont. sewed., unc. (GB. Nov.3; 290)   DM 460

KINDLERS LITERATUR LEXIKON
Ed.:- W. von Einsiedel. Zürich, 1965-74. 7 vols. & supp. vol. Orig. linen. (GB. May 4; 1777)DM 410
- - **Anr. Edn.** Ed.:- W. von Einsiedel. Zürich, [1965-74]. 7 vols. & supp. vol. With loose index pts., orig. linen. (H. Nov.23; 102)   DM 560
- - **Anr. Edn.** Zürich, 1970-74. 12 vols. Orig. bdg., wraps. (D. Nov.24; 4329)   DM 520

KING, Daniel
- The Cathedrall & Coventuall Churches of England & Wales. 1672. 2nd. Imp. Ob. fo. Engraved title, 90 plts., lacks frontis. & 1 plt., some plts. remntd., a few slightly defect., cont. panel. cf., upr. cover detchd. [Wing K 486] (TA. Dec.15; 457)   £160
- The Vale-Royall of England. L., 1656. 1st. Edn. Fo. Extra engraved title (laid down), 2 folding maps, 17 engraved plts., few sm. reprs., slight browning & margin staining, cont. cf., rebkd. [Wing K488] (S. Mar.6; 487)R. Budenberg. £220
- - **Anr. Copy.** 4to. Engraved title (margins trimmed & preserved), 2 maps, 1 town plan, 16 plts., crimson mor. gt. (P. Sep.8; 9)   Chesters. £190
- - **Anr. Copy.** Fo. Engraved additional title, 17 plts., 1 double-p., 2 double-p. maps, ills., later mor., rubbed. (CSK. May 4; 68)   £150

KING, Edward, F.R.S., Antiquary
- Munimenta Antiqua; or Observations on Ancient Castles. 1799-1805. 4 vols. Fo. 167 plts., some folding, hf. cf. gt., rubbed. (P. Mar.15; 192) £190
- - **Anr. Copy.** 4 vols. Fo. 158 aquatint & engraved plts., some spotting & browning, cont. russ. (S. Mar.6; 282)   M. Scott. £80
- Vestiges of Oxford Castle. Or a Small Fragment of a Work, Intended to be Published Speedily; on the History of Antient Castles; & on the Progress of Architecture. 1796. Fo. 5 uncold. aquatint plts. &

plans, & extra double-p. plan bnd. in at rear, some margin dampstains, later hf. vell. (TA. Jun.21; 206)   £58

KING, Edward D., of Springfield
- The Southern States of North America: a Record of Journeys. Ill.:- after J. Wells Champney. L., 1875. 1st. Engl. Edn. 3 vols. 4to. Orig. cl., liby. labels removed from upr. covers; the Rt. Hon. Visc. Eccles copy. (CNY. Nov.18; 161) $320

KING, Capt. James (Ed.)
See— COOK, Capt. James

KING, Jeff & Oakes, Maud
- Where the Two Came to Their Father: A Navajo War Ceremonial. Commentary:- Joseph Campbell. N.Y., 1943. Compl. set of 18 silkscreen prints, with text, linen portfo. (LH. Sep.25; 252) $300
- **Anr. Edn.** Commentary:- Joseph Campbell. N.Y., [1943]. Lge. fo. 18 cold. plts., text laid in, ex-liby., each plt. stpd. on verso, loose as iss. in 2-toned cl. folder, linen ties. (SG. May 3; 8) $700

KING, Capt. Phillip Parker
- Narrative of a Survey of the Intertropical & Western Coasts of Australia. L., 1826. 1st. Edn. Titles & folding map offset, some minor discolouration to some plt. margins, hf. cf. (CA. Apr.3; 65)   Aus. $2,500
See— FITZROY, Capt. Robert, King, Capt. Philip Parker & Darwin, Charles

KING, Ronald
- Stampart I-III. [Guildford], Circle Pr., ca. 1979. 1st. Edn. (100). Square 4to. 3 mono-ptd. plts. with 4 stps., each loose, numbered & sigd. by King at bottom margin, white-lettered folder. (HA. Feb.24; 229) $110

KING, Stephen
- Carrie. Garden City, 1974. 1st. Edn. Bdg. not stated, d.-w.; sigd. & dtd. 1/15/82 by King. (CBA. Oct.29; 458) $250
- Christine. N.Y., [1983]. 1st. Trade Edn. Bdg. not stated, d.-w.; inscr., sigd. & dtd. 5/19/83 by King. (CBA. Oct.29; 459) $110
- The Dead Zone. N.Y., [1979]. 1st. Edn. Bdg. not stated, d.-w.; lengthy inscr. by King, sigd. & dtd. 10/1/82. (CBA. Oct.29; 461) $100
- The Stand. Garden City, 1978. 1st. Edn. Bdg. not stated, d.-w. lightly rubbed; inscr., sigd. & dtd. 9/8/79 by King. (CBA. Oct.29; 463) $250

KING, William
[-] The Art of Cookery, in Imitation of Horace's Art of Poetry. L., [1708]. 1st. Edn. Hf.-title, browned & stained, cont. sheep, worn, covers detchd. (S. Oct.4; 298)   Temperley. £50

KING, William, of the British Museum
See— HOBSON, Robert Lockhart & others

KINGSBOROUGH, Lord Edward
- Antiquities of Mexico. Ill.:- Augustine Aglio. L., 1831, Bonn, 1848. 1st. Edn. 9 vols. Atlas fo. Many hand-cold. ills., over 150 uncold. litho. plts. in mntd. India-proof state, sm. liby. stp. at foot of each title-p., three-qtr. mor., spines gt. (SG. Apr.26; 106) $60,000

KINGSLEY, Charles
- The Heroes, or Greek Fairy Tales. for my Children. Ill.:- Sir William Russell Flint. L., 1912. (500) numbered. 4to. Prospectus loosely inserted, orig. limp vell., ties, s.-c. (S. Nov.22; 325)   Desk. £260
- The Life & Works. L. & N.Y., 1901-03. (525). 19 vols. Mor. gt. (SPB. Dec.13; 542) $400
- The Water-Babies. Ill.:- J. Noel Paton. L., 1863. 1st. Edn. Later Printing. Without dedication lf., some slight foxing & margin darkening, gt.-ruled pol. cf. by Bayntun, gt.-decor. spine, gt. dentelles, marb. end-papers, orig. cl. covers bnd. in at end; Joe E. & Kathryn Brown bkplt., Marymount College copy. (CBA. Mar.3; 316) $120
- - **Anr. Edn.** Ill.:- Warwick Goble. 1909. De Luxe Edn., (260). 4to. Orig. vell. gt., partly untrimmed, soiled, lacks ties. (TA. Nov.17; 466)   £52
- - **Anr. Edn.** Ill.:- W. Heath Robinson. L., [1915]. Slight margin darkening, orig. gt.-decor. cl., spine darkening. (CBA. Aug.21; 559) $100
- - **Anr. Edn.** Ill.:- Jessie Willcox Smith. N.Y.,

KINGSLEY, Charles -*Contd.*

[1916]. 4to. Some minor foxing, pict, cl., decor. end-papers. (CBA. Aug.21; 600) $130

KINGSMILL, Andrew
- **A Most Excellent & Comfortable Treatise ... for all such are Troubled in Minde. & also A Conference Containing a Conflict had with Satan. (A Forme of Thankesgiving & Praier ...).** 1577. 3 pts. in 1 vol. Cont. vell. [STC 15000] (P. Dec.8; 89) *Quaritch.* £520

KINNELL, Galway
- **First Poems, 1946-1954.** Mt. Horeb, Wis., Perishable Pr., 1970. *(87) numbered.* Qtr. lev., marb. bds., unc. (SG. Mar.1; 217) $110

KINNEY, Troy
- **The Etchings.** Garden City, 1929. *(990) numbered & sigd.* Sm. fo. 25 aquatone plts., ex-liby., cl.-bkd. bds. (SG. May 3; 224) $150

KINSEY, Rev. William Morgan
- **Portugal Illustrated.** N.p., 1828. *1st. Edn.* Lge. 8vo. Most plts. are mntd. India proofs, costume plts. hand-cold., no ptd. title, foxed, later mor. gt. (SG. Sep.22; 251) $100

KINZIE, Mrs. John H.
- **Wau-Bun, The 'Early Day' in the Northwest.** Chic., 1857. *2nd. Edn.* Hf. cf. & cl. (LH. Jan.15; 330) $160

KIP, Joannes
- **Britannia Illustrata** ... L., [1707?]. Vol. I (all publd.). Fo. Engraved title, 79 double-p. engraved views, lacks 2nd. title, tables & text, 4 plts. with sm. tears at fold in lr. margin, old reversed cf., blind-panel., rebkd., as a coll. of plts., w.a.f. (C. Nov.16; 102) *Burgess.* £950
- **Nouveau Théâtre de la Grande Bretagne.** D. Mortier, 1708. Vol. 1 only. Fo. 80 engraved plts., a few wormholes in 40 plts., old cf., worn, as a coll. of plts., w.a.f. (P. Jun.7; 7) £1,100
- - **Anr. Edn.** L., 1724. Vol. 3 only. Fo. Engraved additional title in Fr. & Engl. dtd. 1719, Fr. title, 47 engraved plts. only (42 double-p., 8 folding), a few clean tears along folds, 1 plt. slightly trimmed at lr. margin, later russ., extremities rubbed, rebkd. (CSK. May 4; 33) £1,700
- - **Anr. Copy.** Vol. 3 only. Fo. Additional engraved title with vig., 42 (of 49) engraved plts., most double-p., some folding, 2 additional plts. bnd. in, lacks 'Table Généalogique & Chronologique de la Ligne Royale d'Angleterre', short tears to a few plts., mod. cf. (C. Nov.16; 104) *Burgess.* £1,300
- **Anr. Edn.** L., 1724-28. 6 vols. in 3, including Supp. & 'Atlas Angloise'. Lge. fo. Title to Vol. I with engraved Royal arms, 391 engraved maps, plans & views, many double-p., mntd. on guards thro.-out, list of plts. in each vol., lacks 1 plt. each in Vol. 4 & Supp. (but the former including 1 plt. not called for), without the genealogical table of the Kings & Queens in Vol. 3, & with the entry on the plt. list. pasted over, 1 plt. with margin tear reprd., 2 plts. remargined, 1 plt. detchd., old cf., gt. arms on covers of James Beech of Warwick, rebkd. & recornered. (C. Nov.16; 103) *Burgess.* £11,500

KIP, William
See— **NORDEN, John & Kip, William**

KIPLING, Rudyard
- **Captains Courageous, a Story of the Grand Banks.** L., 1897. *1st. Edn.* Cl. gt., hf. mor. s.-c. (PNY. Oct.20; 240) $160
- - **Anr. Copy.** Some light foxing, gt.-decor. cl., covers lightly rubbed, fly-lf. creased; Joe E. Brown bkplt., Marymount College copy. (CBA. Mar.3; 317) $140
- **Departmental Ditties & Other Verses.** Lahore, 1886. *1st. Edn. (350).* Tall 8vo. Orig. ptd. wraps., with flap designed to resemble official envelope, pink ribbon, slightly chipped at edges. (SKC. Jan.13; 2224) £540
- - **Anr. Edn.** Lahore, [1886]. *1st. Edn. Approx. (350).* Tall 8vo. Owner's sig. & date, orig. wraps. with flap, slightly foxed, lacks red tape; Frederic Dannay copy. (CNY. Dec.16; 197) $1,700
- **A Fleet in Being.** L., 1898. *1st. Edn.* Sm. 8vo. Three-qtr. mor., upr. corners of covers badly chipped, orig. pict. wraps. bnd. in; author's sig. on title, & inscr. 'To Josephine's bachelor, Nelson Spencer, from The Author of Josephine'. (SG. Nov.17; 85) $120
- **The Jungle Book. — The Second Jungle Book.** Ill.:– John Lockwood Kipling & others. L., 1894; 1895. *1st. Edns.* Together 2 vols. Some light foxing, orig. cl. gt.; Frederic Dannay copy, inscr. 'Barnaby Ross'/'Ellery Queen'. (CNY. Dec.16; 198) $380
- - **Anr. Copy.** Together 2 vols. Some light foxing, orig. gt.-decor. cl., covers slightly rubbed, lightly soiled; Joe E. Brown bkplts., Marymount College copies. (CBA. Mar.3; 318) $160
- - **Anr. Edn.** N.Y., 1894; 1895. *1st. Amer. Edns.* Together 2 vols. Sm. 8vo. Decor. cl.; author's name on 2nd. title-p. scratched through, & beneath is inscr. 'To Nelson Spencer from The Author ... ', Spencer's bkplt. in 1st. vol. (SG. Nov.17; 84) $750
- **Just So Stories.** L., 1902. *1st. Edn.* Orig. decor. cl., d.-w., boxed. (LH. Sep.25; 554) $400
- - **Anr. Copy.** Gt.-ruled pol. cf. by Bayntun, gt.-decor. spine, gt. inner dentelles, marb. end-papers, orig. cl. covers bnd. in; Joe E. & Kathryn Brown bkplt., Marymount College bkplt. laid in loose. (CBA. Mar.3; 319) $150
- **Kim.** 1901. *1st. Edn.* Orig. cl., faded; inscr. pres. copy from author to W.E. Henley, sigd. again on title. (SKC. Mar.9; 1846) £220
- - **Anr. Edn.** L., 1901. *1st. Engl. Edn.* Gt.-ruled pol. cf. by Bayntun, gt.-decor. spine, inner gt. dentelles, marb. end-papers, orig. covers bnd. in at end; Marymount College copy. (CBA. Mar.3; 320) $160
- **Kim [French].** Trans.:– Louis Fabulet & Ch. Fountaine-Walker. Lausanne, 1930. 2 vols. 4to. On japan with suite, lacks 3 plts.(?), jansenist red mor. by Semet & Plumelle, wrap. preserved, s.-c. (HD. Jun.13; 56) Frs. 31,100
- **Letters of Marque.** Allahabad, 1891. *Ltd. 1st. Edn.* Pol. cf. by Zaehnsdorf. (KH. Nov.9; 283) Aus. $240
- **Le Livre de la Jungle.** Trans.:– Louis Fabulet & Robert D'Humières. Ill.:– Paul Jouve, engraved by F.L. Schmied. Paris, 1919 [1918]. *(125) on velin d'Arches.* 4to. Some foxing, leath. by Trinckvel, incised & painted, dtd. 1922 & sigd. by Malo Renault, spine blind-decor., painted silk liners & end-ll., unc., ill. wrap. & spine, s.-c.; orig. china ink drawing by artist heightened with watercol. on japan, A.L.s. by Jouve & A.L. by Michel-Dansac. (HD. Jul.2; 78) Frs. 24,000
- **Le Livre (le Second Livre) de la Jungle.** Trans.:– Louis Fabulet & Robert d'Humières. Ill.:– Deluermoz. 1930. On Rives, suite on china in 1st. vol., suite on japan in 2nd. vol., red hf. mor., corners, by Richard, unc., wraps. & spines preserved. (HD. May 4; 312) Frs. 3,500
- - **Anr. Edn.** Ill.:– Henri Deluermoz, engraved by Théo Schmied. Paris, 1941. *(250).* 2 vols. Lge. 4to. On vell., leaves, wrap., box. (HD. Mar.27; 78) Frs. 1,350
- **Poems, 1886-1929.** Ill.:– F. Dodd (port.). L., 1929. *(525) numbered on L.P., sigd. by Kipling & Dodd.* 3 vols. Lge. 4to. Red mor. gt. (SG. Nov.3; 114) $300
- **Schoolboy Lyrics.** Lahore, priv. ptd., 1881. *1st. Edn. (50?).* 12mo. Orig. white wraps., sm. stain & some foxing on upr. cover, red mor. solander case; sigd. by author on title-p., A.L.s. from author's wife tipped in, Charles C. Auchinloss bkplts., Frederic Dannay copy. (CNY. Dec.16; 196) $7,500
- - **Anr. Copy.** 12mo. Elab. gt. mor., spine detchd.; inscr. 'To Nelson Spencer ... ' on title, & sigd. at end 'Rudyard Kipling Sep. 1901. The Elms'. (SG. Nov.3; 113) $2,400
- **A Song of the English.** Ill.:– W. Heath Robinson. [1909]. *(500) numbered & sigd. by artist.* 4to. 30 mntd. cold. plts., orig. vell., lightly soiled, lacks 1 tie. (CSK. Jun.29; 158) £180
- - **Anr. Copy.** 4to. Light foxing thro.-out, vell., decor. in cols. & gt., rubbed & soiled, slightly yawning, ribbon ties, bkplt. (CBA. Aug.21; 560) $180
- - **Anr. Edn.** Ill.:– W. Heath Robinson. N.d. Cl. gt. (P. Jul.5; 366) £65
- **Songs of the Sea.** 1927. *(500) sigd.* L.P., qtr. vell., d.-w., s.-c. (SSA. Jul.5; 224) R 180
- **Under the Deodars.** Allahabad, 1890?. 'Bandra' hand-stpd. above imprint on title-p., ptd. pict. wraps. (chipped), some wear & soiling. (RO. Apr.23; 199) $110
- **The Works** ... 1897-98. *Edn. de Luxe. (1050).* 34 vols. Silk cl., gt. spines., unc. (PD. Aug.17; 165) £92
- - **Anr. Edn.** N.Y., 1897-1937. 36 vols. Red hf. mor., slightly worn. (BS. Nov.16; 75) £320
- - **Anr. Edn.** 1913-38. *Bombay Edn.* 31 vols. Imperial 8vo. Orig. cl.-bkd. bds., unc., short split to 1 spine, a few labels frayed; sigd., A.L.s. by author to 'My dear Swettenham' 15 Oct. [1923] tipped in at front free end-paper. (C. May 30; 157) *Traylen.* £350
- - **Anr. Edn.** L., 1913-38. *Bombay Edn. Vols. 1-26: (1050) sigd., Vols. 27-31: (500).* 31 vols. Cl.-bkd. bds. (PNY. Jun.6; 454) $225
- - **Anr. Edn.** Garden City, 1914-20. *Seven Seas Edn. (1050) numbered & sigd.* 26 vols. Lge. 8vo. Qtr. linen, boards, some wear, most vols. unopened. (SG. Apr.19; 296) $200
- - **Anr. Edn.** Garden City, 1914-26. *Seven Seas Edn. (1050) numbered & sigd.* 27 vols. Lge. 8vo. Linen-bkd. bds., unc., paper labels chipped. (SG. Mar.15; 129) $350
- **The Writings in Prose & Verse.** N.Y., 1897-1932. *(204) sets on Japan paper.* 34 vols. only. Lev. mor. gt., spines in 6 compartments, by Stikeman, some spines browned, w.a.f. (CNY. Dec.17; 578) $1,900
- **[Collected Works].** V.p., v.d. *1st. Edns.* 9 vols. 'Letters of Marque' lacks front end-paper & advts., all orig. cl. (PD. Aug.17; 164) £350
- - **Anr. Copy.** 16 vols. Unif. cl. gt. (PD. Aug.17; 162) £52

KIPLING, Rudyard (Text)
See— **NICHOLSON, William**

KIPPING, Heinrich
- **Antiquitatum Romanarum.** Ed.:– Justus Lipsius. Leiden, 1713. *New Edn.* Folding map, 13 folding plts., old bds., untrimmed; sig. of Jean Senebier. (SG. Oct.13; 218) $120

KIPPIS, Andrew
- **Biographia Brittanica or, the Lives of the Most Eminent Persons ... in Great Britain & Ireland.** 1778-93. *2nd. Edn.* Vols. 1-5 (all publd.). Fo. Cont. tree cf., spines gt.; Sir Ivar Colquhoun, of Luss copy. (CE. Mar.22; 183) £320
- **The Life & Voyages of Captain James Cook.** Edinb., 1840. 16mo. 6 steel-engraved plts., including additional engraved title-p., orig. gt.-floral cl., soiled, front hinge brkn., tear in 1 plt.; from liby. of F.D. Roosevelt, inscr. by him (as President). (SG. Mar.15; 57) $175
- **Vie du Capitaine Cook.** Trans.:– Castera. Paris, 1789. *1st. Edn. in Fr.* 2 vols. Hf.-titles, cont. cf. gt., spine ends & corners worn. (S. Nov.1; 29) *Thorp.* £90

KIRBY, Thomas
See— **BOWDITCH, Nathaniel & Kirby, Thomas**

KIRBY, William Forsell
- **The Butterflies & Moths of Europe.** L., 1907. 4to. Orig. pict. cl. gt. (SKC. Oct.26; 390) £65
- **European Butterflies & Moths.** L., 1882. 4to. 61 cold. plts. & anr. plt., orig. pict. cl. gt. (SKC. Oct.26; 389) £120
- - **Anr. Copy.** 4to. 61 (of 62) plts., orig. cl., worn, w.a.f. (S. Oct.4; 271) *Erlini.* £100
- - **Anr. Copy.** 4to. 1 plain & 61 col. plts., hf. cf. (P. Sep.8; 268) *Leadley.* £85
- - **Anr. Copy.** 4to. Hf. cf., spine gt. (SKC. Nov.18; 1973) £70
- - **Anr. Copy.** 4to. Publishers cl. (CR. Jun.6; 192) Lire 420,000
- - **Anr. Edn.** L., 1889. 4to. 62 plts., title spotted & with sm. piece cut out where inscr. inlaid, hf. cf., worn. (S. Nov.1; 280) *Quaritch.* £90
- - **Anr. Copy.** 4to. Publishers cl., defect. (CR. Jun.6; 193) Lire 450,000
- - **Anr. Edn.** 1898. 4to. Recent qtr. mor., gt.-decor. spine. (TA. May 17; 313) £95

KIRCHEN ORDNUNG im Churfurstenthum der Marcken zu Brandemberg
See— **CATECHISMUS oder Kinder Predig — VON DER GEBRAUCH der Heiligen Hochwirdigen Sacramenten — KIRCHEN ORDNUNG**

im Churfurstenthum der Marcken zu Brandemberg

KIRCHER, Athanasius
- Arithmologie. Rome, 1665. *1st. Edn.* 4to. Old owners note on frontis., cont. leath., rubbed. (HK. Nov.9; 1964) DM 1,400
- Ars Magna Lucis et Umbrae. Amst., 1671. *2nd. Edn.* Fo. Partly dampstained, foxed, folding plt. torn, cont. inscrs., sm. stp. on title, old blind-stpd. pig, metal clasps, spine very worn. (SG. Oct.27; 178) $450
- China Monumentis. Amst., 1667. *[1st. Edn.].* Fo. Engraved title, port., 2 maps, 13 full-p. plts. only, 52 hf.-p. plts., cont. vell., w.a.f. (P. Feb.16; 189) £420
- - Anr. Copy. Fo. Engraved frontis., port., 23 plts., lacks 2 maps, 1 plt. detchd., 3 plts. torn, cont. vell. (C. Nov.16; 105) *Hart.* £60
- La Chine Illustrée de Plusieurs Monuments ... Amst., 1670. Fo. Double-p. frontis. (from 1667 edn.), 1 (of 2) maps, 19 (of 23) plts., lacks port., cont. roan, worn. (HD. Jan.24; 28) Frs. 2,200
- Lingva Aegyptica Restituta Opus Restitutum. Rome, 1643. *1st. Edn.* 4to. Engraved title with year 1644, verso stpd., lacks 1 lf. (hf.-title), title browned & slightly spotted, 19th. C. hf. vell., worn & bumped, upr. cover & spine loose. (H. May 22; 261) DM 900
- Magneticum Naturae Regnum ... Amst., 1667. 12mo. Frontis. with sm. stp., bds. (HK. Nov.8; 615) DM 540
- Mundus Subterraneus. Amst., 1665. *1st. Edn.* 2 vols. in 1. Fo. 2 engraved titles (dtd. 1664), 1 (of 2) ports., 19 maps & plts. (12 double-p. or folding), 7 double-p. or folding tables, volvelles on pp. 132, 154 & 156, sm. woodcut inserted at p. 30 in pt. 1, sm. engr. inserted at p. 384 in pt. 2, short tears in 3 plts., a few sm. wormholes, some margin stains, margins of 4 index ll. defect., with last lf. tissued & parts of text lacking, vell. bds.; Dr. Walter Pagel copy. [Sabin 37967] (S. Feb.7; 219) *Browning.* £400
- - Anr. Edn. Amst., 1678. *3rd. Edn.* 2 vols. Fo. Some browning, several ll. shaved, old cf., lightly rubbed. (CSK. Jul.6; 25) £420
- - Anr. Copy. 2 vols. Fo. Lacks 2nd. title & port., very browned thro.-out, old liby. stp. on title, cont. cf., spines hand-lettered. (SG. Mar.22; 187) $225
- - Anr. Copy. 2 pts. in 1 vol. Fo. Title with erased owners mark, various plts. with bkd. tears, pt. 1 several ll. & plts. with mntd. lr. corner, with some slight loss, pt. II 4 text ll. with tears, some browning & foxing, cont. vell., slightly soiled, spine with 2 tears. (HK. Nov.8; 616) DM 2,800
- Musurgia Universalis. Rome, 1650. *1st. Edn.* 2 vols. Fo. 2 engraved frontis., port., 20 (of 23) copperplts., Index & errata/register ll., table of contents, liby. stp. on titles, mod. vell. (SG. Feb.9; 266) $550
- - Anr. Copy. 2 vols. Fo. Title lf. with MS. owners. mark, with plt. of copper engrs. XI & XII bnd. as frontis. in Vol II, engrs. IV & V on 1 plt., 2 pp. paginated double, lightly browned, some spotting, cont. vell., slightly browned & spotted; ex-libris in cover, from Fürstl. Averspergschen Fideicommiss Liby. (H. May 22; 404a) DM 4,400
- D'Onder-aardse Weereld. Amst., 1682. 2 vols. Fo. Stps. on titles, lacks 2 tables(?), light staining, cont. cf., spines gt., loosening, minor defects. (VG. Mar.19; 269) Fls. 1,300
- Physiologie Kircheriana Experimentalis. Amst., 1680. Fo. Some spotting & browning, cont. vell., slightly spotted, 1 corner defect. (H. Nov.23; 277) DM 1,600
- Scrutinium Physico-Medicum Contagiosae Luis quae Dicitur Pestis. Leipzig, 1659. *2nd. Edn.(?).* 12mo. Vell.; Dr. Walter Pagel copy. (S. Feb.7; 217) *Phelps.* £160
- Sphinx Mystagoga, sive Diatribe Hieroglyphica. Amst., 1676. *1st. Edn.* Fo. 2 plts. with sm. tears, browned, cont. hf. leath., very worn & bumped. (H. May 22; 262) DM 850
- Tariffa Kircheriana. — Principis Christiani Archetypon Politicum Sive Sapientia Regnatrix. Rome, 1679; Amst., 1672. *1st. Edns.* 2 vols. in l; 1 vol. 8vo.; 4to. 1st. work: 23 (of 24?) sm. folding woodcut diagrams, foxed, cont. vell.; 2nd. work: browned, cont. blind-stpd. cf., rebkd. (SPB. Dec.13; 698) $400

KIRCHHOFF, Gustav Robert
- Vorlesungen über Mathematische Physik, Mechanik; Mathematische Optik; Electricität und Magnetismus; Theorie der Wärme. Leipzig, 1883-94. *1st. vol. 3rd. Edn., 2nd. & 3rd. vols. reprints, 4th. vol. 1st. Edn.* 4 vols. Some browning, various bdgs., some fading, 1st. vol. in roan-bkd. marb. bds., rubbed; Georg Quincke bkplt., sig. of D. Minkhoff on end-paper, Stanitz coll. (SPB. Apr.25; 247) $100

KIRCHNER, A.
- Ansichten von Frankfurt am Main, der Umliegenden Gegend und den Benachbarten Heilquellen. Frankfurt, 1818. 2 vols. Wide margin, lacks hf.-titles, slightly foxed, cont. red mor., gt. spine, inner & outer dentelle, gold decor. cover. (R. Oct.12; 2561) DM 9,200

KIRCHNER, Raphael
- De la Brune à la Blonde. Paris, n.d. Fo. 16 prints in 2 cols., in portfo., with ties. (SKC. Sep.9; 1872) £55

KIRCHWEGER, Anton Joseph
- Microscopium Basilii Valentini. Berlin, 1790. Later vell., slightly soiled, unc. (D. Nov.23; 582) DM 1,400

KIRK, T.
- The Forest Flora of New Zealand. Wellington, 1889. Fo. 1 lf. (blank?) before title removed, title-p. with slight foxing & slight chipping of fore-edge, orig. pres.(?) mor. gt., slightly rubbed. (KH. May 1; 397) *Aus.* $170

KIRKPATRICK, William
- An Account of the Kingdom of Nepaul. L., 1811. *1st. Edn.* 4to. Engraved folding map, 14 plts. (1 cold.), some ll. stained & spotted, lacks hf.-title, cf., slightly rubbed. (S. Jun.25; 39) *Shaw.* £260

KIRMSE, Marguerite
- Dogs in the Field. Foreword:- John Taintor Foote. Derrydale Pr., [1935]. *(685) numbered, with frontis. drypoint sigd. by artist.* Ob. 4to. Extra portfo. of 6 plts. laid in, qtr. cl., orig. box. (SG. Mar.15; 231) $600

KIRNBERGER, Joh. Ph.
- Grundsätze des Generalbasses als erste Linien zur Composition. Wien, ca. 1810. 4to. Title 'Inkunabel der Lithographie', title with cont. MS. dedication & slightly soiled, a few engraved mus. notats. lightly soiled, wraps. (HK. Nov.9; 2253) DM 550

KIRSCHNER, B. (Ed.)
See— JUDISCHES LEXIKON

KIRSCHNER, Fr.
- Sammlung von Blumen zum Zeichnen und Stiken. Augsburg, ca. 1785. Pt. II. 4to. Engraved title & 12 copperplts., some slight brown spotting, some slight offsetting, loose in mod. bd. portfo. (H. May 22; 148) DM 420

KIRSCHNER, Zdenek
- Josef Sudek: Vyben Fotografii z Celozivotniho Dila. [Prague, 1982]. *1st. Edn.* 4to. Cl., outer corners slightly bumped, d.-w. (SG. May 10; 143) $100

KIT-CAT CLUB
- Memoirs of the Celebrated Persons Composing the Kit-Cat Club. Ill.:- after Sir Geoffrey Kneller. 1821. Fo. 48 engraved ports., cont. str.-grd. mor., gt. fillets & corners enclosing blind-stpd. border, gt.-decor. spine. (SKC. Jan.13; 2285) £110

KITCHEN OR KITCHIN, Thomas
- General Atlas. L., Sayer & Bennett, 1777. Fo. 26 engraved maps on 37 sheets, all hand-cold. in outl., 1 detchd., lacks title, some margins soiled, old hf. cf., worn, w.a.f. (CSK. Dec.2; 13) £1,200
- - Anr. Edn. Laurie & Whittle, 1800. Fo. 40 partly cold. maps, hf. cf., covers detchd. (P. Sep.8; 425) *Burgess.* £480
- A New Universal Atlas. L., J. Laurie & J. Whittle, 1798. *2nd. Edn.* Lge. fo. 47 engraved maps on 56 (of 70) double-p. folding sheets, all hand-cold., mntd. on guards thro.-out, world chart torn at fold, 1 map with sm. tear in 1 sheet, cont. paper wrap.,

lacks lr. wrap. & backstrip. (C. Mar.14; 59) *Burgess.* £750
- Post-Chaise Companion through England & Wales. 1767. General map, 103 roadmaps on 52 sheets, 6 p. Index, limp leath. folder, with tie. (P. Jun.7; 337) £250
- - Anr. Copy. Ob. 4to. Title browned, limp leath. (P. Dec.8; 405) *P. Martin.* £230
See— BOWEN, Emmanuel & Kitchen or Kitchin, Thomas

KITCHENER, H.H.
- A Trigonometrical Survey of the Island of Cyprus. L., 1885. Lge. ob. fo. Litho. title, 1 outl. cold. litho. map (index map) & 15 outl. cold. litho. map ll., loose in orig. hf. leath. portfo., spine & corners rubbed. (R. Oct.13; 3138) DM 710

KITCHIN, Thomas
See— KITCHEN or KITCHIN, Thomas

KITTEL, G. & Friedrich, G.
- Theologisches Wörterbuch zum Neuen Testament. Stuttgart, 1933. 10 vols. in 11. 4to. Orig. cl., 3 vols. with orig. wraps. (B. Jun.21; 279) Fls. 650

KITTENBERGER, Kalman
- Big Game Hunting & Collecting in East Africa 1903-1926. N.Y., 1929. Cl., light wear. (RO. Jun.26; 99) $100

KJOPING, N.M. & others.
- Een kort Beskriffning vppa trenne resor och peregrinationer, sampt konungarijket Japan. Visingsborg, 1667. Sm. 4to. Light stain affecting title, browned thro.-out, bdg. not stated. (S. Dec.1; 374) *Israel.* £900

KLABUND, A. Henschke
- Kleines Bilderbuch vom Krieg. München, 1914. *(30) De Luxe Edn. on China.* Fo. MS. sig., loose ll. in orig. bd. portfo., cold. cover woodcut, spine torn. (H. Nov.24; 2044) DM 1,200

KLAJ, Johann
- Engel- und Drachen-Streit. Nürnberg, [1649]. *1st. Edn.* Sm. 4to. Minimal foxing, 19th. C. hf. leath. gt. (R. Oct.11; 293) DM 1,900
- - Anr. Copy. Title with cont. MS. note at foot, printers mark excised from lr. part of last lf. & cont. bkd., slightly browned & foxed, hf. linen. (HK. Nov.10; 2546) DM 750

KLASEN, K.H.
- Die Mittelalterliche Bildhauerkunst im Deutschordensland. Die Bildwerke bis zur Mitte des 15. Jahrhunderts. Berlin, 1939. 4to. Orig. linen. (R. Apr.3; 741) DM 420

KLAUBER, Joseph & Johann
- Biblische Geschichten, des Alten und Neuen Testaments. Augsburg, ca. 1750. Ob. fo. 100 copperplts., cont. cf., worn, rebkd. (SG. Feb.9; 127) $320

KLEEMAN, Ch. F.
See— ROSEL V. ROSENHOF, A. J.

KLEIN, F.
- Die Entwicklung der Mathematik im. 19. Jahrhundert. Ed.:- E. Staiger. Göttingen, 1914-18. 5 pts. in 5 vols. 4to. Many MS. entries, various bdgs. (HT. May 8; 429) DM 820
- Vorlesungen über die Theorie der Elliptischen Modulfunctionen. Ed.:- R. Fricke. Leipzig, 1890-92. *1st. Edn.* Cont. hf. leath. (HT. May 8; 428) DM 420

KLEIN, Jacob Theodor
- Ordre Naturel des Oursins de Mer et Fossiles ... Paris, 1754. *1st. Fr. Edn.* Some plts. cut short in lr. margin, cont. leath. gt., very defect. (R. Apr.4; 1747) DM 440

KLEIN, William
- Moscow. Preface:- Harrison E. Salisbury. N.Y., [1964]. *1st. Edn.* Fo. Cl., lightly soiled, d.-w. worn. (SG. Nov.10; 97) $175
- New York. [L., 1956]. *1st. Edn.* 4to. Gt.-lettered cl., d.-w. reprd. (SG. May 10; 76) $200
- Tokyo. Preface:- Maurice Pinguet. N.Y., [1964]. *1st. Edn.* Fo. Cl., d.-w. chipped. (SG. Nov.10; 98) $130

KLEINE UNIVERSUM
Stuttgart, 1840. 117 (of 144) views, 1 lf. torn, title & 3 ll. stpd. in margin or on verso, partly washed, loose ll. in cont. hf. linen. (GB. Nov.3; 13)
DM 450

KLEINER, G. (Ed.)
See— SYLLOGE NUMMORUM GRAECORUM DEUTSCHLAND

KLEINER, Salomon
- Dilucida Repraesentatio ... Eigentliche Vorstellung der Vortreflichen und Kostbaren Kaiserlich Bibliothec. Vienna, 1737. Pt. 1 (all publd.), Lge. ob. fo. 12 (of 13) engraved plts., including 2 folding, title & text in Latin & German, cont. hf. vell.; Liechtenstein Liby. bkplt. (C. Dec.9; 71)
Weinreb. £300
- Représentation exacte du Château de Chasse de S.A. Sme Monseigneur l'Evêque de Bamberg ... Ill.:– M. Steidlin, G. Weber & A. Friderich. Augsburg, 1731. Ob. fo. Engraved title, 6 plts., patterned paper bds. (C. Dec.9; 73)
Weinreb. £2,200
- Représentations au Naturel des Châteaux de Weissenstein au Dessus de Pommersfeld et de Celui de Geubach ... Augsburg, 1728. 2 pts. in 1 vol. Ob. fo. Engraved title, 27 plts., including 6 folding, cont. spr. cf., gt. spine (defect). (C. Dec.9; 72)
Weinreb. £3,200
- Residences Mémorables de l'Incomparable Héros de Notre Siècle ou Représentation Exacte des Edifices et Jardins de ... Monseigneur le Prince Eugène François. Augsburg, 1731-38. 9 pts. in 1 vol. Fo. 9 engraved titles, engraved dedication, frontis., 80 plts., some folding, captions in Fr. & German, sm. repair on title verso, few plts. with sm. tear at fold, cat's-paw cf. gt. (C. Dec.9; 74)
Weinreb. £3,000
- Vera et Accuratio Delineatio Omnium Templorum et Coenobiorum ... Ed.:– J.A. Pfeffel. Augsburg, 1724-37. 4 pts. in 1 vol. 4 engraved titles, 4 pict. dedications, dedication lf., 132 plts., including 2 folding, lf. from ed. (*Bound with:*) – Viererley Vorstellungen Angenehm– und Zierlicher Grundrisse Folgender Lustgarten und Prospecten ... Augsburg, n.d. Pt. 1 (but publd. as 5th. pt. of preceding work). Engraved title, dedication, 33 plts., including 2 folding, some minor margin tears reprd., some with tape. Together 2 works in 1 vol. Ob. fo. Cont. cf., spine gt. (C. Dec.9; 75)
Lyon. £3,000

KLEINSCHMIDT, A.
- Die Eltern und Geschwister Napoleons I. Berlin & Potsdam, 1886. *2nd. Edn.* Red mor. gt., by Hatchards. (R. Apr.3; 1021)
DM 450

KLEIST, E. Chr. von
- Sämmtliche Werke. Ed.:– W. Körte. Berlin, 1803. *De Luxe Edn.* on vell. 2 vols. Vol. 1 with double hf.-title, cont. decor. cf. gt., some wear, spines slightly faded; Paul Hirsch ex-libris inside cover, MS. notice on end-paper; Hauswedell coll. (H. May 24; 1408)
DM 1,650

KLEIST, Heinrich von
- Das Erdbeben in Chili. Ill.:– A. Kolb. Berlin, [1921]. *(25) De Luxe Edn. on Japan.* Lge. 4to. Orig. vell. by E.A. Enders, Leipzig. (HK. May 17; 2907)
DM 500
-- Anr. Edn. Ill.:– Otto Rohse. Hamburg, 1981. *(45) De Luxe Edn.* Sm. 4to. 2 numbered & sigd. special pulls of woodcuts, printers mark sigd., orig. blind-tooled mor. by Chr. Zwang; Hauswedell coll. (H. May 24; 767)
DM 700
- Erzählungen. Berlin, 1810-11. *1st. Edn.* 2 vols. Vol. II. with some heavier spotting, title cut, cont. marb. bds. gt., slightly rubbed & bumped, ex-libris & stp. on end-papers; Hauswedell coll. (H. May 24; 1415)
DM 6,400
-- Anr. Edn. Berlin, 1910. 3 vols. Orig. leath. gt., minimal rubbed. (HK. May 16; 2126) DM 800
- Friedrich von Homburg. Ill.:– K. Walser. Berlin, 1916. *(250).* 4to. Printers mark sigd. by artist, orig. pictor. vell., cover slightly spotted & warped. (HK. May 17; 3215)
DM 500
- Gesammelte Schriften. Ed.:– L. Tieck. Berlin, 1826. 3 vols. Lightly browned, later marb. bds., slightly bumped; Hauswedell coll. (H. May 24; 1412)
DM 3,200
-- Anr. Edn. Ed.:– L. Tieck. J. Schmidt. Berlin,

1859. 3 vols. Cont. hf. leath., gt., lightly rubbed. (GB. May 4; 1353) DM 450
- Hinterlassene Schriften. Ed.:– L. Tieck. Berlin, 1821. *1st. Edn.* Cont. hf. cf. gt. (C. Dec.9; 255)
Quaritch. £480
-- Anr. Copy. Title bkd., minimal spotting, cont. marb. bds., slightly bumped; Hauswedell coll. (H. May 24; 1411) DM 1,200
- Das Käthchen von Heilbronn. Berlin, 1810. *1st. Edn.* Some light spotting, marb. bds., unc.; Hauswedell coll. (H. May 24; 1416) DM 1,600
- Kleine Schriften. Ill.:– Max Liebermann. Berlin, [1917]. *(250) numbered on Bütten.* 4to. Sigd. by artist, some slight spotting, orig. vell. (D. Nov.24; 3123) DM 1,500
- Les Marionnettes. Trans.:– R. Valancay. Ill.:– Hans Bellmer. Paris, [1969]. *(150).* Lge. 4to. On brownish Fabrario Bütten, 2nd. series of etchings on Japan, all ll. sigd. by artist, loose ll. in orig. silk cover & s.-c., slightly spotted & bumped; Hauswedell coll. (H. May 24; 584) DM 5,600
- Die Marquise von O ... Ill.:– K.M. Schultheiss. Dresden, 1924. *(50).* Printers mark sigd. by artist, orig. bdg., silk covered, s.-c. (D. Nov.24; 3105)
DM 800
- Michael Kohlhaas. Ill.:– Alois Kolb. Berlin, 1912. *(300) numbered.* 4to. 8 full-p. sigd. orig. etchings, orig. leath., corners bumped. (GB. Nov.5; 2698)
DM 420
- Penthesilea. Tübingen, [1808]. *1st. Edn.* Title with thin place, minimal spotting, cont. bds., spine reprd.; Hauswedell coll. (H. May 24; 1414)
DM 3,800
-- Anr. Copy. (*Bound with:*) JUNG, Franz Wilhelm – Odmar, dramatisches Gedicht, zweite Auflage. Mainz, 1821. Together 2 works in 1 vol. Old bds., mod. hf. mor. (C. Dec.9; 256)
Quaritch. £1,450
-- Anr. Edn. München, 1914. 4to. Hand-bnd. bds. by Eva Aschoff; Hauswedell coll. (H. May 24; 747)
DM 520
- Prinz Friedrich von Hamburg. Ill.:– E. Böhm, Renee Sintenis & W. Wagner after E.R. Weiss. Berlin, Maximilian-Gesellschaft. 1913. *(300) for members of Maximilian-Gesellschaft.* 4to. Hand-bnd. red mor., decor., gt. inner & outer dentelle, by Hans Glökler, Berlin. (H. Nov.23; 1171)
DM 1,700
-- Anr. Copy. 4to. Orig. red mor., by E.A. Enders, gt. decor., blind-tooled supralibros, slight tear in lr. outer jnt. (GB. May 5; 2790) DM 480
-- Anr. Edn. Ill.:– Karl Walser. Berlin, 1916. *(250) numbered.* Lge. 4to. Printers mark sigd. by artist, orig. pict. vell., slightly spotted, unc. (BR. Apr.13; 1905) DM 1,100
- Der Rabbi von Bacharach. Ill.:– M. Liebermann. 1917. *(250) numbered.* Lge. 4to. Printers mark sigd. by artist, 56 (of 54) orig. lithos., slightly foxed, orig. pict. vell. (GB. May 5; 2888) DM 1,200
- Robert Guiskard Herzog der Normänner. Fragment aus der Trauerspiel. Tölz, Bremer Pr., 1919. *(270) numbered.* 4to. Margins lightly browned, orig. leath., gt. spine, cover, inner & outer dentelle, ex-libris. (HK. Nov.11; 3448) DM 2,400
-- Anr. Copy. Sm. 4to. Hand-bnd. orig. mor., gt. decor., inner & outer dentelles, by Frieda Thiersch, spine lightly discold. (H. Nov.23; 926) DM 1,100
- Der Zerbrochene Krug. Berlin, 1811. *1st. Edn.* Slightly foxed or soiled, lacks last lf. blank, pold. cf. gt., gold decor., centre fleuron, gt. outer dentelle, by W. Collin, Berlin; Jean Fürstenberg ex-libris. (R. Apr.3; 280) DM 3,500
-- Anr. Copy. Some spotting, cont. style hf. leath. gt., corners slightly bumped, traces of erased owners mark on end-papers; Hauswedell coll. (H. May 24; 1417) DM 2,200
See— LIEBERMANN, Max

KLEIST, Heinrich von (Ed.)
See— PHOBUS

KLEMM, Walther
- 100 Monogrammierte Orig.-Holzschnitte zu Till Eulenspiegel. N.p., ca. 1920. 4to. Loose ll. in hf. linen portfo. (GB. May 5; 2793)
- Das Paradies. [Weimar, 1920]. Lge. fo. 6 handcold. & sigd. orig. lithos., loose ll. with passepartouts in hf. leath. portfo. (GB. Nov.5; 2670)
DM 1,800
-- Anr. Copy. Lge. fo. On Bütten, 6 hand-cold. &

sigd. orig. lithos., lacks title lf., loose ll. in hf. linen portfo. (GB. May 5; 2792) DM 900
- Radierungen zu Balzacs Succubus. [Weimar, 1924]. 4to. Hf. linen portfo. (HK. Nov.11; 3695)
DM 400
- 10 Signierte und Handkolierte Orig.-Radierungen zu Voltaires Prinzessin von Babylon. [Weimar], ca. 1925. 4to. Loose ll. under guards in hf. linen portfo. (GB. May 5; 2797) DM 550

KLEMMING, G.E.
- Sveriges Aldre Liturgiska Literatur. Bibliografi. Stockholm, 1879. Fo. 13 mntd. ll. inserted (only, of 20?), including 4 on vell. & 2 facs., 1 with 2 holes, wraps. & cl. portfo. (S. Nov.17; 43)
Hannas. £2,300

KLETTE, A.
- Neu-erfundenes Trenchir-Buch. [Leipzig], 1665. Ob. 4to. Some light browning, cont. vell., slightly soiled. (HK. Nov.9; 1675a) DM 3,800
- Neuverbesserte u. Wohlinformirter Tafel-Decker u. Trenchant ... Nürnberg, ca. 1680. Sm. ob. 8vo. Some spotting, bds., slight wear. (V. Sep.29; 1424)
DM 2,500

KLEUKENS, Chr. H.
- Die Fabel vom Wind u. andere Fabeln. [Darmstadt, Ernst Ludwig Pr., 1923]. *(50) on Japan.* Orig. leath., gt. spine, inner & outer dentelle, by Kleukens, corners slightly worn. (HK. May 17; 2734) DM 800
- Reinke Voss. Ill.:– F.W. Kleukens. Darmstadt, Ernst Ludwig Pr., 1913. *(350).* Sm. 4to. Orig. pict. hf. vell. (H. Nov.23; 1033) DM 480
- Ein Trostbüchlein für Vormänner. Darmstadt, Ernst Ludwig Pr., 1940. *Ltd. iss., not for sale.* Presentation note mntd. inside cover, orig. hf. vell., gt. cover ill. (H. May 3; 2461) DM 800

KLEUKENS, Chr. H. (Ed.)
See— BUCH DER FABELN

KLEUKENS, F.W.
[-] Zwölf Monatsbilder. Darmstadt, Ernst Ludwig Pr., 1911. Vell. (HK. May 17; 2737) DM 420

KLEVENHULLER, L. von
- Observations–Puncten ... Dragoner-Regiment. Wien, 1734. *2nd. Edn.* 2 pts. in 1 vol. (*Bound with:*) - Exercitium zu Pferd und zu Fuss. Wien, 1734. Together 2 works in 1 vol. 4to. Cont. leath. (GB. Nov.3; 989) DM 450

KLIMIUS, Nicholas (Pseud.)
See— HOLBERG, Ludwig von 'Nicholas Klimius'

KLIMT, Gustav
- Fünfundzwanzig Handzeichnungen. Wien, 1919. *(500) numbered.* Lge. fo. 2 ll. title & contents & 25 partly cold. plts. mntd. under passepartouts, loose in orig. hf. linen portfo. (R. Oct.11; 876)
DM 1,700

KLIMT, Gustav & others
[-] Allegorien Neue Folge. Vienna, ca. 1890. Lge. fo. Title-p., introduction, plt. list & 120 tinted & cold. plts., some marginal wear, liby. stps., loose in portfo. as iss. (SPB. May 17; 635) $2,700

KLINCKOWSTROM, Alex L.
- Bref om de Förenta Staterna Författade under en Resa Till Amerika, Aren 1818, 1819, 1820. Stockholm, 1824. 2 vols. & Atlas. 8vo. & ob. fo. Text with additional engraved titles (without errata lf. in Vol. I) & Atlas with litho. title with vig., list of plts. & 16 litho. or aquatint maps, plans & views, including 2 maps hand-cold. in outl., all disbnd. & mntd. in mod. album, upr. margin of title stained & with tears reprd., a few plts. with margin tears reprd., foremargin of 1 plt. torn & reprd., slightly defect., text in cont. hf. roan, atlas in mod. hf. mor. [Sabin 38053] (C. Jun.27; 42) *Faupel.* £1,100

KLING, C.
- Geschichte der Bekleidung, Bewaffnung und Ausrüstung des Königlich. Preussischen Heeres. Weimar, 1902-12. 3 vols. 4to. Hf. chagrin. (HD. Jan.27; 161) Frs. 3,200

KLINGEMANN, Aug. 'Bonaventura'
- **Kunst und Natur; Blätter aus meinem Reisetagebuche.** Braunschweig, 1823-28. Slightly foxed, hf. linen. (GB. May 4; 1356) DM 530
- **Nachtwachen.** Penig, 1805. *1st. Edn.* Title torn, some spotting, cont. marb. bds., decor., bumped; Bibliotheca Muddendorfiana ex-libris, Hauswedell coll. (H. May 24; 1421) DM 5,200

KLINGER, Friedrich Maximilian
- **Die Geschichte vom Goldenen Hahn. Ein Beytrag zur Kirchen-Histoire.** [Gotha], 1785. *1st. Edn.* Lightly foxed, stained at beginning, some ll. with sm. margin or corner tears, cont. paper wraps., unc. (HT. May 9; 1535) DM 600
- **Werke.** Königsberg, 1809-16. *1st. Coll. Edn.* 12 vols. Vol. I lacks port. as often, some foxing, Vols. VIII, XI & XII lack main title-ll., sewed in 4 bd. boxes, faded & spotted; Hauswedell coll. (H. May 24; 1418) DM 600

KLINGER, Max
- **Intermezzi. Rad. Op. IV.** München, [1881]. Lge. fo. Lacks title lf. as often, orig. hf. linen portfo., some light spotting, some faults, ex-liby. (HK. Nov.11; 3704) DM 1,300
- - **Anr. Copy.** Nürnberg, [1881]. Lge. fo. Orig. aquatint etchings on China, some ll. soiled & stained, loose in orig. hf. linen portfo., slightly soiled or rubbed, ties. (GB. Nov.5; 2688) DM 1,600
- - **Anr. Edn.** N.d. 12 mntd. engraved plts., last plt. dtd. Nuremb., [1881], portfo. vol. in orig. bds. (PD. Feb.15; 241) £220
- **Radierungen zu Apulejus' Märchen Amor u. Psyche.** Trans.:– R. Jachmann. München, [1880]. *1st. Edn.* Fo. Lightly stained thro.-out, at beginning at foot, at end at head, new linen, with orig. upr. cover & spine, lightly bumped, sm. defects., ex-libris. (HK. Nov.11; 3703) DM 850
- - **Anr. Edn.** Nuremb., [1880]. Portfo. 1 (of 2),. Fo. Plts. on China, some slight spotting & staining, orig. pict. hf. linen, slightly spotted; ex-libris. (HT. May 9; 1536) DM 700
- **Zelt.** Berlin, 1915. Pts. I & II. Lge. fo. Wide margin, 1 sm. corner tear to title lf., minimal browning to verso some ll., loose in orig. pict. linen portfos. (H. Nov.24; 1703) DM 15,500

KLIPSTEIN, Dr. August
- **Käthe Kollwitz. Verzeichnis des Graphischen Werkes.** Bern, 1955. *(600).* 4to. Orig. linen. (H. Nov.24; 2510) DM 1,300

KLOPSTOCK, Fr. G.
- **Die Deutsche Gelehrtenrepublik.** Hamburg, 1774. *1st. Edn.* Pt. 1 (all publd.). Wide margin, with bd. ll. with corrections of printing errors, subscribers list, title lf. with owners entry, cont. hf. leath., slightly bumped & worn, spine torn; Hauswedell coll. (H. May 24; 1425) DM 600
- **De Messias.** Trans.:– Joh. Meerman. Ill.:– F. John after H. Füger. Den Haag, 1803-05 & 1815. *On Bütten.* 4 pts. & 'Narede' in 2 vols. & Atlas vol. with text. 4to. & fo. Wide margin, minimal browning, copper engrs. slightly foxed, cont. red mor. gt., spine faded, some spotting & scratches, copper engrs. loose in hf. leath. portfo., slightly spotted; Hauswedell coll. (H. May 24; 1427) DM 680
- - **Anr. Edn.** Ill.:– H. Schmidt. Leipzig, 1813. 4 vols. Cont. crushed red mor., gt. decor. spine, gt. cover & outer dentelles, lacquered end-papers & doubls., name on 1st. end-paper verso; Hauswedell coll. (H. May 24; 1427) DM 1,800
- **Oden.** Hamburg, 1771. 4to. Wide margin, on Roman vell., arms of dedicatee, some ll. slightly foxed, especially at beginning & end, 2 ll. bnd. at end with 4 in orig. printing, engraved ex-libris in cover, cont. cf. gt., by C. Kalthoeber, London, with label, upr. cover loose, spine torn, worn; Hauswedell coll. (H. May 24; 1424) DM 600
- **Werke.** Troppau & Brünn, 1785/86. 8 vols. in 4. Some slight spotting, lightly browned, cont. cf., gt. spine, cold. paper end-ll., slightly worn, some sm. wormholes, 1 lr. cover defect.; Hauswedell coll. (H. May 24; 1422) DM 520
- [-] - **Anr. Edn.** Ill.:– F. John after Schnorr von Carolsfeld & Füger (title copper engrs.) A.W. Böhm after Juel (port.). Leipzig, 1798-99 & 1809. *1st. Definitive Coll. Edn. De Luxe Edn. on vell.*

'Fürstenausgabe'. 7 vols. in 5. Lge. 4to. Wide margin, title ll. with liby. stp., some slight foxing or browning, later mor., gt. decor. spines, covers, inner & outer dentelles, some slight discol., 2 vols. with scratches, 1 vol. with lengthy tear; Hauswedell coll. (H. May 24; 1423) DM 6,400

KLOSS, Dr. George Franz Burkhard
- **Catalogue of the Library of Dr. Kloss.** L., 1835. Mod. hf. cf., unc. (S. Oct.11; 469) *Quaritch.* £200

KLUGE, Kurt & Lehmann-Hartleben, K.
- **Die Antiken Grossbronzen.** Berlin & Leipzig, 1927. 3 vols. 4to. Orig. cl., lightly soiled. (CSK. Sep.16; 135) £280
- - **Anr. Copy.** Fo. Orig. linen. (R. Oct.11; 784) DM 900
- - **Anr. Copy.** 3 vols. Lge. 4to. Margins slightly browned, orig. linen, slightly spotted, spine faded. (H. May 22; 355) DM 520

KNAPP, Andrew & Baldwin, William
- **The Newgate Calendar; Comprising interesting Memoirs of the Most Notorious Characters ...** 1824-28. 4 vols. Hf. mor. gt. by Birdsall. (TA. May 17; 340) £145

KNEELAND, Samuel
- **The Wonders of the Yosemite Valley, & of California.** Ill.:– John P. Soule. Boston, 1871. *1st. Edn.* 4to. 10 mntd. albumen photos, orig. gt.-lettered cl., rubbed & faded, spine ends chipped, later clippings & a map tipped to rear end-papers. (SG. May 10; 133) $200
- - **Anr. Edn.** Ill.:– John P. Soule. Boston, 1872. *2nd. Edn.?.* 4to. 2 maps, 10 mntd. albumen photos, some minor foxing, affecting 1st. plt., orig. gt.-lettered cl., lightly rubbed. (SG. May 10; 134) $130

KNICKERBOCKER, Dietrich (Pseud.)
See— IRVING, Washington

KNIGGE, A. von
- **Brife auf einer Reise aus Lothringen nach Niedersachsen geschrieben.** Hannover, 1793. Title verso stpd., cont. bds. (R. Oct.11; 297) DM 560
- **Die Reise nach Braunschweig.** Ill.:– G. Osterwald. Hannover, 1839. *1st. Ill. Edn.* 1st. & last ll. light brown spotted, cont. hf. leath. gt., old owners mark inside cover. (H. May 22; 771) DM 460
- **Uber den Umgang mit Menschen.** Hannover, 1788. *1st. Edn.* 2 vols. Vol.1 title & a few text ll. slightly foxed, cont. hf. leath. gt. (R. Oct.11; 299) DM 2,000
- **Uber Eigennutz und Undank.** Leipzig, 1796. *1st. Edn.* Lacks errata lf. & title copper engr., foxed, hf. leath., ca. 1850, bumped. (R. Apr.3; 288) DM 480

KNIGHT, Charles Raleigh
- **Scenery on the Rhine.** L., priv. ptd., [1846?]. Lge. fo. Tinted pict. litho. title (detchd.), 16 plts., list of subscribers at end, interleaved text, orig.? hf. mor., slightly rubbed. (C. Mar.14; 59a) *Schuster.* £1,800

KNIGHT, Henry Gally
- **The Ecclesiastical Architecture of Italy.** L., 1842. Vol.1 only (of 2). Fo. Litho. title, 40 plts. (3 cold.), a few loose, 1 slightly frayed, few spotted, cont. maroon hf. mor. (S. Mar.6; 90) *Rabbecchi.* £120
- - **Anr. Edn.** L., 1842-44. 2 vols. Atlas fo. Illuminated title-pp., 81 tinted litho. plts., mod. liby. buckram. (SG. May 3; 226) $600

KNIGHT, Laura
- **A Book of Drawings.** Foreword:– Charles Marriott. L., 1923. *(500) numbered.* 4to. Holland-bkd. bds. (SKC. Jan.13; 2114) £50
- **Twenty-one Drawings of the Russian Ballet.** Intro.:– P.G. Konody. 1920. *(350). Out of series copy.* Fo. A few plts. lightly soiled, title spotted, unbnd. as iss. in orig. holland-bkd. portfo., soiled. (CSK. Oct.21; 145) £75

KNIGHT, Richard Payne
- **An Account of the Remains of the Worship of Priapus.** L., 1786. *1st. Edn.* 4to. Frontis. offset onto title, 18 engraved plts., some slight spotting, orig. bds., unc., slightly rubbed; sigd. by Lawrence Dundas on pastedown & with receipt to him from

---

Drummonds Bank loosely inserted. (S. Apr.30; 197) *Sims.* £210
- **A Discourse on the Worship of Priapus, & its Connection with the Mystic Theology of the Ancients. ... To which is added an Essay on the Worship of the Generative Powers during the Middle Ages of Western Europe.** Priv. ptd., 1865. *New Edn.* 4to. Orig. qtr. mor., partly untrimmed, rubbed. (TA. Mar.15; 403) £62

KNIGHT, Thomas Andrew
- **Pomona Herefordiensis: Containing Coloured Engravings of the Old Cider & Perry Fruits of Herefordshire, with such New Fruits as have been Found to Possess Superior Excellence.** Ill.:– William Hooker. L., 1811. 4to. 30 hand-cold. plts., index supplied in MS., lacks map, plts. 9 & 15 a little short, cont. str.-grd. hf. mor., slightly rubbed. (C. Jun.27; 167) *Harcourt Williams.* £1,200
- - **Anr. Copy.** 4to. 30 hand-cold. plts., no frontis. or map, cf. gt., upr. cover detchd. (P. Nov.24; 253) *Heald.* £620

KNIP, Madame Antoinette Jacqueline, née Pauline des Courcelles
- **Les Pigeons.** Text:– C.J. Themminck. Ill.:– C. Macret. Paris, [1808-]11. Imp. fo. Wide margin. 85 (of 87) cold. engrs., some tears & margin excisions, some tape bkd., some slight foxing, cont. red hf. mor. gt. (D. Nov.23; 715) DM 23,000
- - **Anr. Edn.** Ill.:– after Mme. Knip. Paris, [1808-]11 & [1838-43]. *1st. Edn.* 2 vols. Fo. 147 cold. plts., partly ptd. in col. & hand-finished, many proof imps.: plt. XLVIII has caption supplied in pencil, & directions to colourist, & has been stained, possibly from oil on lithographic stone, & bears slight indentation surrounding figure of bird, other plts. carry similar stains, lack captions, or have captions supplied in MS., 2 ptd. on paper of smaller format than rest of vol., some MS. additions possibly in hand of Mme. Knip (none of these corresponds with ptd. errata list), plts. in Vol. I generally clean but several in Vol. II lightly stained or spotted, some spotting of text, 19th. C. red hf. mor. gt. (not quite unif.), jnts. Vol. I rubbed; Frederic Ducane Godman bkplt., owner's entries of A.J. Dearden, 1925. (S. Feb.1; 33) *Taylor.* £20,000

KNOLLES, Richard
- **The General Historie of the Turkes ..., together with the Lives & Conquests of the Othoman Kings & Emperors, unto the Yeare 1621.** 1621. *3rd. Edn.* Fo. Engraved title slightly shaved, some worming in margin, old panel. cf., worn. [NSTC 15053] (CE. Sep.1; 41) £140

KNOOP, Johann Hormann
- **Beschrijving en Afbeeldingen van de Beste Soorten van Appelen en Pearen.** Ill.:– J.C. Philips & J. Folkema after Knoop. Amst. & Dordrecht, 1790. *2nd. Edn.* 20 cold. folding plts., the 1st. creased. *(Bound with:)* - **Beschrijving van Vruchtboomen en Vruchten.** Amst. & Dordrecht, 1790. *2nd. Edn.* 19 cold. folding plts. *(Bound with:)* - **Beschrijving van Plantagie-Gewassen.** Amst. & Dordrecht, 1790. *2nd. Edn.* Together 3 works in 1 vol. Fo. Some browning to text, cont. cf.-bkd. bds., unc., spine worn, upr. cover loose. (S. Nov.28; 46) *Goldschmidt.* £700
- - **Anr. Copy.** 20 cont. hand-cold. engraved plts. *(Bound with:)* - **Beschryving van Vruchtboomen en Vruchten.** Amst. & Dordrecht, 1790. *2nd. Edn.* 19 cont. hand-cold. engraved plts. *(Bound with:)* - **Beschrijving van Plantagie-Gewassen.** Amst. & Dordrecht, 1790. *2nd. Edn.* Together 3 works in 1 vol. Sm. fo. Some minor defects., cont. hf. cf., unc. (VS. Dec.9; 1319) Fls. 1,300
- **Pomologia. — Fructologia. — Dendrologia.** Leeuwarden, 1758, 1763, 1763. *1st. Edns.* 3 pts. in 1 vol. Fo. 39 hand-cold. plts., some staining, most in margins, mod. hf. roan. (VG. Sep.14; 1254) Fls. 1,200
- - **Anr. Edn.** Leeuwarden, ca. 1770. *2nd. Edn.* 3 pts. in 1 vol. Fo. Cont. hf. leath. gt., rubbed. (BR. Apr.12; 732) DM 1,900
- - **Anr. Edn.** Leeuwarden, n.d. 3 pts. in 1 vol. 39 hand-cold. engraved plts., some light browning, cont. hf. cf. (CSK. Sep.16; 25) £350

KNORR, Georg Wolfgang
- Auserlesenes Blumen-Zeichenbuch für Frauenzimmer. Ill.:– Knorr & Barbara Regina Dietzsch. Nürnberg, ca. 1790. *3rd. Iss.* 2 pts. in 1 vol. Fo. Lacks 1st. plt. pt. II, some sm. spots, sm. brown spot in upr. margin thro.-out, cont. cf., worn & slightly spotted; with 4 ll. pencil ills. (H. May 22; 149) DM 2,600
- Délices Physiques Choisies. Nuremb., 1766-67. Fo. Additional hand-cold. engraved title, dtd. 1754, 91 cont. hand-cold. engraved plts. (1 double-p.), ptd. titles & text in German & Fr., lacks port., russ.-bkd. bds., slightly rubbed. (C. Mar.14; 180) *Campbell.* £2,800
- Die Edle Jagd Lust. Nuremb., ca. 1750. 12mo. in ob. 4to. 19th. C. bdg. mntd. in hf. leath. (R. Oct.12; 2032) DM 1,400
[–] Thesavrvs Rei Herbariae Hortensisqve Vniversalis. Nürnberg, 1770-72. 2 text & 2 plt. vols. in 2 vols. Fo. Minimal browning, cont. cf. gt., plt. vol. slightly worn & spotted, sm. defects., 1 sm. spine tear; Hauswedell coll. (H. May 24; 860) DM 36,000
- Verlustiging der Oogen en van den Geest ... Amst., 1770-75. 6 pts. in 2 vols. 4to. Thick paper, 190 cont. hand-cold. plts., cont. panel cf. gt., decor. (VG. Nov.30; 765) Fls. 7,500
- - **Anr. Edn.** [Amst., ca. 1775]. 4to. 190 hand-cold. plts., lacks text, Dutch names of shells in cont. MS., 19th. C. hf. cf., spine gt. (VG. Sep.14; 1255) Fls. 2,800

KNORR VON ROSENROTH, Christian (Trans.)
See— KABBALA-UDATA ...

KNOTEL, Rich.
- Uniformenkunde. Rathenow, 1890-1914. 2 vols. 4to. 174 cold. loose plts., orig. linen portfo. (HK. Nov.9; 1898) DM 3,400

KNOTTS, Benjamin (Ed.)
See— METROPOLITAN MUSEUM OF ART

KNOWLER, William
- The Earl of Stafforde's Letters & Dispatches. Dublin, 1740. *1st. Dublin Edn.* 2 vols. Fo. Cont. cf., rubbed. (GM. Dec.7; 86) £90

KNOX, Alexander
- The Irish Watering Places. Dublin, 1845. *1st. Edn.* Bkplt., hf. mor., armorial motif on spine. (GM. Dec.7; 228) £65

KNOX, Capt. Dudley W.
- Naval Sketches of the War in California. Intro.:– Franklin D. Roosevelt. Ill.:– William H. Meyers. N.Y., [Grabhorn Pr.], 1939. Fo. Vell.-bkd. bds. (LH. Sep.25; 372) $150

KNOX, Hubert T.
- The History of the County of Mayo. Dublin, 1908. *1st. Edn.* Royal 8vo. Orig. buckram; pres. copy. (GM. Dec.7; 292) £95

KNOX, John
- A Tour through the Highlands of Scotland & the Hebride Isles in 1786. 1787. Orig. bds., worn. (PD. May 16; 97) £70

KNOX, Capt. John
- An Historical Journal of the Campaigns in North-America, for the Years 1757, 1758, 1759, & 1760. L., priv. ptd., 1769. *1st. Edn.* 2 vols. 4to. Cont. cf., extremities worn; the Rt. Hon. Visc. Eccles copy. [Sabin 38164] (CNY. Nov.18; 162) $1,200
- A New Collection of Voyages, Discoveries & Travels. 1767. 7 vols. 48 engraved maps & plts. only, some folding, a few loose, some ll. slightly soiled, cont. cf., rather worn. (BBA. Sep.29; 29) *Bauman.* £100

KNOX, Robert
- An Historical Relation of the Island Ceylon in the East-Indies. L., 1681. *1st. Edn.* Fo. Engraved folding map, 15 plts., lacks port., cont. panel. cf., rebkd. [Wing K 742] (C. Nov.16; 106) *Obeyesekera.* £400
- - **Anr. Copy.** Fo. Map (laid down), 15 plts., some partly cold., lacks port., margin repairs, some browning & soiling, old cf., worn, rebkd., covers detchd. (SPB. Dec.13; 452) $150

KOBAYASHI, Yukio
See— TAMURA, Jitsuzo & Kobayashi, Yukio

KOBBE, Th. & Cornelius, W.
- Wanderungen an der Nord– und Ostsee. Leipzig, ca. 1840. 2 vols. in 1. Plts. slightly foxed & soiled, some text ll. with sm. margin tears, cont. hf. leath. gt., rubbed. (BR. Apr.12; 297) DM 1,800
- - **Anr. Copy.** 2 vols. in 1. Lge. 8vo. Some heavy browning, especially in margins, cont. bds., slightly bumped. (H. May 22; 338) DM 1,400
- - **Anr. Edn.** Leipzig, [1841]. 2 pts. in 1 vol. Some foxing, 1 lf. loose, cont. hf. leath. gt., corners rubbed. (GB. May 3; 175b) DM 1,700

KOBELL, Ferdinand
- Radierungen. Ed.:– Franz Kugler. Nuremb., [1841]. *1st. Edn. Later iss., with Carl Mayer imprint overslip.* Fo. 178 etched plts. on 79 ll., some foxing, few stains, orig. bds., worn. (SG. Apr.26; 107) $550

KOCH, A.
- Encyklopädie der Gesammten Thierheilkunde und Thierzucht. Wien & Leipzig, 1885-94. Orig. hf. leath. gt., liby. label. (D. Nov.23; 716) DM 500

KOCH, Alexander (Ed.)
See— DEUTSCHE KUNST UND DEKORATION

KOCH, P. de
- La Grande Ville, Nouveau Tableau de Paris ... Ill.:– Gavarni, V. Adam, Daumier, Daubigny, H. Emy & others. Paris, 1842. *Orig. Edn.* 2 vols. Cont. hf. chagrin, spines decor. (HD. May 4; 313) Frs. 2,200

KOCH, Rudolf & Kredel, Fritz
- Das Blumenbuch. Ill.:– Fritz Kredel after Koch, hand-cold. by Emil Wallner. Mainz, 1929-30. *(1000).* 3 vols. in 1. 4to. 250 hand-cold. engraved plts., crushed russet mor. gt., blind-stpd. 'TH'; pencil note 'Sir Meynell's copy 1963'. (C. May 30; 190) *Quaritch.* £580
- - **Anr. Copy.** 3 vols. Lge. 4to. 250 hand-cold. woodcut plts., orig. bds. (R. Oct.11; 276) DM 2,000
- - **Anr. Copy.** Lge. 4to. Orig. bds., s.-c. (HK. May 17; 2895) DM 1,200
- - **Anr. Edn.** Ill.:– Fritz Kredel after Koch, hand-cold. by Emil Wallner. [Mainz, 1929-30]. *(1000).* 3 vols. 4to. Bds., spines darkening, box extremities darkening. (CBA. Nov.19; 425) $650

KOCH, W. & Opitz, C.
- Eisenbahn und Verkehrs Atlas von Europe. Leipzig, 1912. Sm. fo. 83 double-p. cold. maps, orig. pict. linen, spine loose. (BR. Apr.12; 631) DM 400

KOCH UND KELLERMEYSTEREY
Magdeburg, 1684. 1st. ll. wormed, slightly browned & soiled in parts, bds. (HK. Nov.9; 1678) DM 1,700

KOCHNO, Boris & Luz, Maria
- Le Ballet. [Paris, 1954]. *1st. Edn.* 4to. Orig. litho. frontis. by Picasso, decor. cl., acetate wrap. slightly chipped. (CBA. Jan.29; 346) $200

KOCK, Charles Paul de
- Novels, Tales, Vaudevilles, Reminiscences & Life. Intro.:– Jules Claretie. Trans.:– Mary H. Ford & others. Illumination:– Helen Sinclair Patterson & Ella G. Brown. Ill.:– John Sloan, W. Glackens, E. Boyd Smith, & others. Boston, L., Paris, Frederick J. Quinby Co., [1902-04]. *Bibliomaniac Edn. (10) on vell.* 31 vols. (of 49, all publd.?). 3 notarized statements sigd. by publisher, printer, trans. & illuminators, without the ptd. note on a prelim. stating the work was to comprise 100 vols. (present in the Kistler copy), lev. mor., covers with lge. mor. gt. onlays, spines gt. in 4 compartments, turn-ins gt., gt.-decor. mor. doubls., mor. free end-pp. with 'SLE' gt. monog., corded silk markers, in watered silk-lined folding mor. gt. boxes, spines gt., metal folding clasps, by the Harcourt Bindery, a few clasps defect. (CNY. Dec.17; 579) $26,000
- Works. Intro.:– Jules Claretie. Ill.:– John Sloan, W. Glackens, Everett Shinn, & others. Boston, [1902-04]. *Gregory Edn., (1000) numbered.* 23 vols.

only (of 25, lacks Vols. 13 & 14). Cl. (SG. Jan.12; 189) $275
- - **Anr. Edn.** Intro.:– Jules Claretie. Ill.:– William Glackens, John Sloan, Louis Meynell, Charles White, George B. Luks. Boston, [1902-08]. *Artists' Edn. (1000).* 22 vols., plus separate vol. of Kock's Memoirs. On Exeter wove paper, unif. cl., untrimmed, light shelf wear, some rubbing, sm. bkplts. (HA. Feb.24; 237) $340
- - **Anr. Edn.** Intro.:– Jules Claretie. Trans.:– Edith Mary Norris. Ill.:– John Sloan & others. N.Y., etc., [1905-09]. *Memorial Edn. (250) numbered.* 42 vols. only (of 50, all publd.). 53 orig. etchings by Sloan, three-qtr. red mor. by Harcourt Bindery, inlaid mor. floral decor. on spines, unc., slight wear. (RO. Dec.11; 175) $1,400

KODALY, Zoltán
- Magyar Népzene. Budapest, 1925. *1st. Edn.* Fo. Some browning & dust-staining, no bdg. stated; sigd. & inscr. (S. Nov.17; 120) *Simeone.* £100

KOECKER, Leonard
- A New Treatise on the Theory & Practice of Dental Surgery, Exhibiting a New Method for treating the Diseases of the Teeth & Gums. Balt., 1842. 2 pts. in 1 vol. Scattered foxing, slight margin dampstains, mod. bds. (SG. Mar.22; 91) $100

KOEHLER, Johann David
- Bequemer Schul-und Reisen-Atlas ... Nuremb., 1718. Fo. Double-p. title, double-p. engraved frontis., 2 pp. privilege, 3 engraved double-p. text ll., 3 double-p. ptd. text ll., 120 double-p. engraved maps, views, plts. & tables, all maps & most plts. hand-cold., mntd. on guards thro.-out, without dedication & descriptive text plt. 26-31 called for by contents list, map of Hungary torn & defect. replaced by a different folding map of Hungary loosely inserted, 2 maps with sm. tears, cont. Spanish tree cf., labelled 'Zeitungs Atlas', vell. index tabs. (C. Nov.16; 106a) *Neidhart.* £4,000
- Descriptio Orbis Antiqui. Nuremb., ca. 1720. Sm. fo. Engraved title, contents list, 44 double-p. engraved mapsheets, hand-cold., dampstains & some browning, a few margin wormholes, some maps detchd., cont. hf. cf., worn, w.a.f. (S. May 21; 118) *Trotter.* £230
- - **Anr. Copy.** Ob. fo. Engraved title, 43 hand-cold. plts., index, orig. cl.-bkd. bds. (P. Dec.8; 409) *Tooley.* £220
[–] Der Durlauchtigen Welt ... Geschichts-Geschlechts-und Wappen-Calender auf ... 1737. Nürnberg, [1736]. Year XV. Title lf. with sm. stp., 1st. sigs. with light stain, 1 copper engr. torn, cont. cf. gt., slightly worn. (H. May 22; 373) DM 420
- Gründl. Erzehlung d. Merckwürdigen Welt-Geschichten aller Zeiten ... Ill.:– Chr. Weigel. Nürnberg, 1726. 4to. 1 copper engr. with old ink scribble in lr. margin, copper engr. with sm. tear in upr. corner, minimal foxing, cont. leath., lightly rubbed. (HK. Nov.10; 2893) DM 1,300
- Historischer Münz-Belustigung Erster (-Vierter) Theil. Intro.:– J. Luckius. Nürnberg, 1729-32. 4 vols. in 2. 4to. 1 frontis. loose, minimal browning, cont. cf. gt., very rubbed & spotted, vol. 1 brkn. in jnt., II torn. (H. May 22; 402) DM 1,750
- Orbis Terrarum in Nuce. Nürnberg, 1722. 4to. Some heavy browning & foxing, hf. leath. (V. Oct.1; 3746) DM 500

KOEHLER, S. R.
- A Chronological Catalogue of the Engravings, Dry-Points, & Etchings of Albert Duerer. N.Y., Grol. Cl., 1897. *(400) on Holland.* 4to. 1 plt. taped, cl. (SG. Aug.25; 125) $120
- Etching: an Outline of the Technical Processes & its History. N.Y., [1885]. Fo. 30 plts., many text ills., ex-liby., some marginal fraying, cl., worn, partly loose. (SG. May 3; 227) $700

KOEMAN, C.
- Atlantes Neerlandici. Bibliography of Terrestial, Maritime & Celestial Atlases & Pilot Books, publ. in the Netherlands up to 1880. Amst., 1967-71. 5 vols. Sm. fo. Cl. (VS. Dec.7; 298) Fls. 925
- - **Anr. Copy.** 5 vols. Fo. Cl. (VG. May 3; 162) Fls. 700

KOETSCHAU, Karl
- **Rheinisches Steinzeug.** Munich, [1924]. *1st. Edn.*
Sm. fo. 73 plts., last plt. taped along gutter, not
affecting image, cl., spine crudely taped. (SG.
Jan.26; 119) $120
- - **Anr. Edn.** München, 1924. Fo. 1st. lf. lightly
spotted, orig. linen, lightly spotted. (V. Sep.30;
1775) DM 400

KOHL, J.G.
- **Ireland, Dublin, The Shannon, Limerick, ... & the
Giant's Causeway.** L., 1843. Bkplt., hf. cf., armorial
motif on spine. (GM. Dec.7; 396) £120

KOHLER, W.
- **Die Karolingischen Miniaturen.** Berlin, 1958-63.
3 pts. in 4 vols. Sm. 4to & lge. fo. Orig. linen &
plts. loose in 3 orig. linen portfos. (HT. May 8;
699) DM 2,300

KOKOSCHKA, Oskar
- **Ann Eliza Reed.** Hamburg, 1952. *(660).* 4to. Sigd.
by artist, all lithos. sigd., bds. (DS. Nov.25; 2134)
Pts. 190,000
- - **Anr. Edn.** [Hamburg, 1952]. *(600) for Maximil-
iam-Gesellschaft.* Printers mark sigd. by artist,
orig. bds., litho. upr. cover. (HK. Nov.11; 3706)
DM 420
- **Handzeichnungen 1906-65.** Ed.:– E. Rathenau.
N.Y., [1966]. *(600).* 4to. Orig. linen. (HK. May
17; 2904) DM 420
- **Die Träumenden Knaben.** Berger & Chwala, 1908.
(500). Ob. 4to. 1st. ll. lightly soiled, orig. linen, cover
ill., gold-painted, some light oxidisation; Philipp
Häusler stp. on title; Hauswedell coll. (H. May 24;
651) DM 18,000
- - **Anr. Edn.** Wien, 1908. Ob. 4to. Orig. linen,
mntd. litho. cover ill., upr. paste-down with ex-libris
removed, lr. paste-down & endpaper renewed. (HK.
Nov.11; 3709) DM 14,000

KOLB, C.F.A.
- **Naturgeschichte des Thierreichs.** Stuttgart, 1868.
Fo. Some margin soiling, 2 plts. with margin tears,
cont. hf. leath., defect. (HT. May 8; 605)
DM 1,300

KOLBEN, Peter
- **Naaukeurige en Uitvoerige Beschryving van de
Kaap de Goede Hoop.** Trans.:– A. Zeeman. Amst.,
1727. 2 vols. in 1. Engraved frontis. port., 4 (of 6)
folding maps, 39 (of 46) fine engraved plts., a little
soiled & stained in places, 19th. C. hf. cf., a little
rubbed. (VS. Jun.7; 1014) Fls. 800
- **The Present State of the Cape of Good Hope.**
1738. *2nd. Edn.* 3 vols. Cont. cf., spines rubbed; Sir
George Farrar bkplt. (SSA. Jul.5; 228) R 670
- - **Anr. Edn.** L., 1738-31. 2 vols. Port., frontis., 43
ills. on 27 plts. (3 folding), folding map & a plan,
later panel. cf. (S. May 22; 418) Sawyer. £240

KOLBENHEYER, Erich
- **Designs of the Homes-Industry Embroideries in
Bukovina ...** [Vienna, 1912]. Fo. Map, 75 col. plts.,
loose as iss., title & text in German, Fr., & Engl.
cl.-bkd. decor. bd. portfo. (SG. Aug.25; 375) $250

KOLBENSCHLAG, Sixtus
- **Ein Troestliche Fruchtbare Ordnung und Unterricht wider die Schroecklichen Schnellen Kranckhait
der Vergifften Lufft und Pestilentz.** [Nuremb.],
1540. Sm. 4to. Paper discold., light dampstain in
lr. corner, cl.-bkd. bds.; Dr. Walter Pagel copy. (S.
Feb.7; 223) Quaritch. £280

KOL BO
[Italy], ca. 1485?. *1st. Edn.* Fo. Uncensored, lacks
6 ll., no bdg. stated. [Steinschneider 3589; Goff
Heb-67] (SPB. Jun.26; 14) $20,000
- - **Anr. Edn.** Venice, 1567. *5th. Edn.* Fo. Washed,
top corner of title torn & reprd. with loss of part
of 7 lines, owners' sigs. on fly-lf. & title, staining
mostly in margins, mod. blind-tooled mor. (S.
Oct.24; 45) Stern. £400

KOLLWITZ, Ottilie
- **Das Buch vom Kleinen Peter.** Berlin, 1923. *(300)*
numbered. 4to. Title sigd. by artist, orig. pict. bds.
(HK. Nov.10; 2894) DM 560

KOLYN, Klass
- **Geschicht-Historical Rym of Rymchronyk.**
Hague, 1745. Fo. Some light browning, cont. vell.;
Augustus Pugin bkplt. (CSK. Jun.1; 149) £60

KOMENSKY, John Amos
See— **COMENIUS or KOMENSKY, John Amos**

KONIG, A.B.
[–] **Annalen der Juden in den Preussischen Staaten
besonders in der Mark Brandenburg.** Berlin, 1790.
Stained thro.-out, especially 1st. ll., later linen. (R.
Oct.11; 1096) DM 480

KONIG, F.N.
- **Nouvelle Collection de Costumes Suisses.** Berne,
priv. ptd., n.d. 12 hand-cold. engraved plts., offsetting to some plts., orig. paper-covered bds. gt., spine
chipped, corners worn; Spencer-Churchill family
bkplt. (LC. Jul.5; 66) £390

KONIGSHOVEN, Jakob von
- **Die älteste Teutsche so wol Allgemeine als Inson-
derheit Elsassische und Strassburgische Chronicke.**
Ed.:– D. Johann Schilter. Strassburg, 1698. 4to. As
Supp.: **'Origines Civitatis Friburgi in Brisgovia ...'**,
vell. (V. Oct.1; 3748) DM 800

KONODY, Paul George
- **The Art of Walter Crane.** 1902. *(100)* numbered.
Cl. gt., rubbed. (P. Apr.12; 240) DeMetzy. £190
- - **Anr. Edn.** 1902. Fo. Ancoats Brotherhood
card & 2 Scottish Widows Fund bookmarks
inserted, orig. cl. gt. (P. Jun.7; 295) £80

**KONST OCH NYHETS MAGASIN for Medorgare
of alla Klasser [continued as Magasin fur Konst]**
Stockholm, 1818-23. Vols. 1-5 (all publd. with
this title). 4to. Titles lithographed or in woodblock
borders, 172 numbered plts. on 166 sheets, some
hand-cold., apparently lacks 11 plts. in Vol. 1 & 9
in Vol. 4, short tears to a few folding plts., later
qtr. roan, as a periodical, w.a.f. (S. Dec.1; 392)
Marlborough. £450

**KOOKER EN TAS ALMANACH VOOR HET
JAAR 1778**
Amst., [1777]. miniature book, 67 x 27 mm. Letters
at margins of a few pp. cropped or shaved, orig.
Dutch floral wraps., similar decor. s.-c.; van Veen
coll. (S. Feb.28; 190) £140

KOOP, Albert J.
- **Frühe Chinesische Bronzen.** Berlin, 1924. Fo.
Orig. cl. (S. Oct.4; 169) Leicester. £52

KOOPS, Matthias
[–] **Historical Account of the Substances which have
been used to Describe Events, & to Convey Ideas,
from the Earliest Date, to the Invention of Paper.**
L., 1800. Sm. fo. Last 4 ll. (Appendix) brittle &
loose, old cl., worn. (SG. Apr.26; 108) $425

KOPERA, F.
- **Pomniki Krakowa.** Ill.:– Maximilian & Stanislaus
Cercha. 3 vols. Lge. 4to. Text Polish, plt. captions
Polish-Fr., linen. (D. Nov.23; 1096a) DM 450

KOPPEN, F. von
- **Die Hohenzollern und das Reich bis zur Wie-
derherstellung des Deutschen Kaiserthums.** Glogau,
[1884-87]. 4 vols. Orig. pict. linen, elab. gold-
tooied. (GB. May 3; 294) DM 520

KOPPMANN, K.
- **Alt-Hamburg in Wort u. Bild. Von seiner Grün-
dung bis z. grossen Brande v. 1842.** Hamburg, ca.
1870. Ob. 4to. 30 tinted lithos., orig. linen, gt. &
blind-tooled. (BR. Apr.12; 278) DM 550

KOPS, Jan
- **Flora Batava.** Amst., [1800-]14. Vols. 1-3 only
(of 28). 4to. Engraved titles, the 1st. with cold. vig.,
260 hand-cold. engraved plts., subscribers list &
errata slip in Vol. 1, cont. hf. cf., spines gt., w.a.f.
(S. Nov.28; 47) Edinburgh. £800
- - **Anr. Copy.** Vols. 1-3 only (of 28). 4to. Engraved
titles, the 1st. with cold. vig., 260 hand-cold.
engraved plts., subscribers list in Vol. 1, plts. erratically numbered in MS., 1 plt. reprd. at foot, some
slight discoloration, hf. cf. gt., worn, w.a.f. (S.
Nov.28; 48) Marks £520
- - **Anr. Copy.** Vols. 1-3 only (of 28). Engraved

titles, the 1st. with cold. vig., 256 hand-cold.
engraved plts., cont. hf. cf., worn, w.a.f.; from the
Signet Liby. (S. Nov.28; 49) Varekamp. £380
- - **Anr. Edn.** Amst., 1807-32[-44]. Vols. 2-6 only
(of 28), & index to Vols. 1-8. Engraved titles to
Vols. 2-6, 409 (of 410) hand-cold. engraved plts.,
hf. cf., unc., rubbed, w.a.f. (S. Nov.28; 50)
Varekamp. £620

KORAN, The
- **Alcoranus Mahometicus.** Nuremb., 1616. 4to.
Title with owner's mark, some MS. text annots.,
slightly browned, vell., with 16th. C. MS. anti-
phonar, spine defect., upr. cover loose. (HK. Nov.9;
1823) DM 1,000
- **Al- Coranus. s. Lex Islamitica Muhammedis, Filii
Abdallae Pseudoprophetae ...** Hamburg, 1694. 4to.
Latin title stpd., foxed, cont. vell., cover lightly
wormed. (R. Oct.11; 1143) DM 4,200
- **Le Coran.** Trans.:– Savary. Paris, 1783. 2 vols.
Cont. marb. cf., spine decor., sm. hole below 1 turn-
in. (HD. Nov.9; 49) Frs. 2,600
- - **Anr. Edn.** Late 18th.-early 19th. C. Fo. Oriental
gt.-decor. red mor., slightly worn. (LM. Oct.22;
115) B. Frs. 8,500
- **Le Coran. Précédé d'une Etude de Jacques Berque
... accompagné du Manuscrit d'Ibn-al-Bawwab,
commenté par D.S. Rice.** Trans.:– Jean Grosjean
(1st. work) & J. Bernard (2nd. work). Ill.:– Zender-
oudi. Paris, 1972. 4 vols. 4to. & 8vo. On vell.,
publisher's decor. roan. (HD. Jul.2; 49) Frs. 1,450
- **The Koran; Commonly Called the Alcoran of
Mohammed.** Trans.:– George Sale. 1734. Lge. 4to.
Cont. cf., worn. (CSK. Jan.13; 188) £80
- - **Anr. Edn.** Trans.:– Arthur Jeffery. Ill.:– V.
Angelo. N.Y., Ltd. Edns. Cl., 1958. *(1500).* This
copy specially illuminated, Newsletter announcing
this vol. laid in, wallet-style bdg. in folding box; the
V. Angelo copy, with publisher's pres. blind-stp.,
later note in his hand, & T.L.s. from George Macy.
(CBA. Oct.1; 268) $130
- - **Anr. Edn.** Trans.:– George Sale. L., n.d. Sm.
margin tears, mor. gt., by Zahn, cold. inlaid designs
on upr. cover, lightly rubbed. (SPB. Dec.13; 544)
$500
- **Mahomets Alkoran.** Trans.:– J.H. Glazemaker.
Amst., 1658. *1st. Dutch Trans.* Light staining, no
bdg. stated. (VG. Mar.19; 196) Fls. 500

KORIN GAFU
Kyoto, 1895. 2 vols. Lge. 8vo. 24 double-p. col.
woodblock ills., native wraps., brkn. (SG. Jan.26;
219) $130

KORN, Chr. H.
[–] **Geschichte der Kriege in und ausser Europa vom
Anfange des Aufstandes der Brittischen Kolonien in
Nordamerika an.** Nuremb., 1776-79. 18 pts. (of 30)
in 3 vols. Pts. 1 & 13 lack title, lacks 1 engraved &
partly cold. folding map, cont. hf. leath., bumped &
rubbed. [Sabin VII, 27213] (D. Nov.23; 1278)
DM 450

KORNFELD, Eberhard W.
- **Verzeichnis des Graphischen Werkes von Paul
Klee.** Bern, 1963. *(1400) in German.* Fo. Orig. linen,
orig. wraps. (GB. May 5; 2787) DM 450

KOSCIUSKO, General
- **Manoeuvres of Horse Artillery.** Trans.:– Jonathan
Williams. N.Y., 1808. Foxed & stained, owners'
inscrs. on blank ll., early cf. gt., defect. (SG. Jan.19;
200) $450

KOSTER, E.
- **Schetsbaek. Nederlandsche Stads- en Havenge-
zigten.** Ill.:– Steuerwalt, Hilverdink, C. Springer
after Koster. Amst., 1858. Light foxing, excpially
in margin, staining in margin, hf. leath., sm. fault
in spine. (V. Sep.29; 86)

KOSTER, Henry
- **Travels in Brazil.** L., 1817. *2nd. Edn.* 2 pts. in 1
vol. Sm. hole in 1 lf., later hf. mor., rebkd. [Sabin
38272] Fls. 500

KOSTIGOVA, G.I.
- **Abrazcj Kalligrafii Irana y Sredneyi Azii. [Samples
of the Calligraphy of Iran & Central Asia, Fif-
teenth-Nineteenth Centuries].** Moscow, 1963. Sm.
fo. Cl., slightly soiled. (S. Apr.16; 234) £130

KOSTKA, J.
See— KHEVEN HULLER, L.A.v. – KOSTKA, J.

KOTTENKAMP, Dr. F.
- History of Chivalry & Ancient Armour. Trans.:–
Rev. A. Löwy. L., 1857. Ob. 4to. 62 hand-cold.
plts., some slightly soiled, orig. cl., worn. (P. May
17; 317)   *Bickersteth.* £320

KOTZEBUE, Augustus. v.
- Ausgewählte Prosaische Schriften. Wien, 1842-
43. 45 pts. in 23 vols. Slightly foxed, cont. hf. leath.
gt., w.a.f. (HK. May 16; 2136)   DM 600
- Theater. Wien & Leipzig, 1840-41. 40 pts. in 20
vols. Lightly foxed, cont. hf. leath. gt., slightly
bumped & rubbed, w.a.f. (HK. May 16; 2137)
                                             DM 550

KOTZEBUE, Otto von
- A New Voyage round the World. L., 1830. *1st.
Edn. in Engl.* 2 vols. 12mo. Foxed, buckram, ex-
liby. (SG. Sep.22; 183) $750

KOUCHAKJI, Fahim
See— EISEN, Gustavus A. & Kouchakji, Fahim

KOYTHAR, Joh.
- Thesaurus, Pauperum, Haussapotek ... Wittemberg, 1600. Old MS. annots. at end, last lf. reprd.
in lr. margin, browned thro.-out, mod. linen. (D.
Nov.23; 655)   DM 600

KRACKHART, C.
- Illustriertes Conditoreibuch. München, 1819. Hf.
linen. (G. Sep.15; 2212)   Sw. Frs. 1,200

KRAEMER, H.
- Der Mensch und die Erde. Berlin, [1906-13]. 10
vols. 4to. Orig. leath., richly decor., inlaid metal
relief on upr. covers. (B. Feb.8; 813)   Fls. 460

KRAFFT, Johann Carl
- Recueil d'Architecture Civile. Paris, 1812. Fo.
Engraved frontis., 120 plts., a few discold., cont.
russ., wide roll-tool borders in gt. & blind, inner gt.
panel, spine gt. (C. Dec.9; 76)   *Weinreb.* £700

KRAME, J.H.
- Afbildningar af Nordiska Drägter. Stockholm,
1891. Ob. 4to. 14 col. litho. plts., orig. cl. gt. (P.
Oct.20; 137)   £160

KRANTZ, Albertus
- Saxonia. Cologne, May 1520. *1st. Edn.* With the
8 ll. (hf.-title & index) preceding title-p. & final
blank. (*Bound with:*) – **Wandalia.** Cologne, Apr.
1519. *1st. Edn.* With the 7 unsigd. ll. preceding
title-p. (hf.-title, index & woodcut armorial
frontis.), with final register/ colophon lf., lacks
initial blank, some lr. margins stained. (*Bound
with:*) – **Chronica Regnorum Aquilonarium Daniae,
Suetiae, Norvagiae ... Descripta.** Strasbourg, Feb.
1548. Brown stain in fore-margins at end, lr. fore-
corners lightly gnawed; owner's inscr., dtd. 1568,
of Nicolaus Everardus. 3 works in 1 vol. Sm. fo.
Cont. German blind-stpd. cf. over wood bds. (S.
Nov.17; 44)   *Maggs.* £750
- **Anr. Edn.** Trans.:– Basilius Fabrus Soranus.
Leipzig, 1563. Fo. Lightly stained, title with old
owner's mark. cont. vell., soiled. (GB. Nov.3; 182)
                                             DM 680

KRASHENINNIKOV, Stefan P.
- Beschreib. des Landes Kamtschatka. Trans.:– J.T.
Köhler. Lemgo, 1789. *2nd. Iss.* 4to. Cont. cf., gt.
stp. 'Bibl. Commercii.' on upr. cover, slightly
rubbed. (VG. Nov.30; 841)   Fls. 620
- [-] The History of Kamtschatka, & the Kurilski
Islands. Gloucester, 1764. *1st. Engl. Edn.* 4to. 2
folding engraved maps, 5 engraved plts., cont. cf.;
Caher bkplt. [Sabin 38301] (S. May 22; 478)
                                            Kossow. £460

KRAUSS, Ferdinand
- Das Thierreich in Bildern nach Familien und Gattungen. Stuttgart & Esslingen, 1851. Fo. 50 litho.
plts., including 43 hand-cold., text spotted, liby. stp.
on title, orig. cl. gt., slightly rubbed. (S. Nov.22;
385)   *Baer.* £150

KRAUSS, Friedrich S.
- Anthropophyteia. Jahrbuch für Ethnologische,
Folkloristische und Kulturgeschichtliche Sexualfor-
schungen. Leipzig, priv. ptd., 1904-13. *Ltd. Iss.,
numbered.* Vols. I-VI & VIII-X only (of 10). Lge.
8vo. Orig. cl., not unif., traces of wear, 1 spine
defect. (B. Feb.8; 913)   Fls. 500

KRAUSS, Johann Carl
- Afbeeldingen der Fraaiste, meest Uitheemsche
Boomen en Heesters ... Amst., 1802. 4to. 114 (of
126) cont. hand-cold. plts., cont. hf. cf. (VG.
Nov.30; 766)   Fls. 4,000

KRAUSS, Johann Ulrich
- Ausserlesene Fabeln. Trans.:– Veneroni & Nick-
isch. Augsburg, 1713. Slightly browned & soiled,
1 lf. badly tape reprd., cont. style leath. (R. Oct.11;
306)   DM 520
- Historische Bilder Bibel. Augsburg, 1702. *1st.
Edn.* 5 pts. in 1 vol. Sm. 4to. Slightly foxed &
soiled, 3 plts wormed in lr. margin, cont. leath.,
worn, spine defect. (R. Oct.12; 2232)   DM 480
- Historische Bilder Bibel.-Heilige Augen und
Gemüths – Lust. — Biblisches Engel– u. Kunst.-
Werk. Ill.:– Krauss. Augsburg, 1705; 1706; 1705.
3 works in 1 vol. Fo. Lacks 3 plts., 2 plts. with torn
corners, some plts. with sm. defects in margin, some
old spotting & soiling, especially in margin, hf.
leath. gt., cover loose, rubbed & bumped.
(V. Oct.1; 3749)   DM 1,400
- Tapisseries du Roy ... Königl. Französischen
Tapezereyen, oder überaus shöne Sinn-Bilder, in
welchen die vier Elemente samt den Vier Jahr-Zeiten
... Augsburg, 1687. *1st. German Edn.* Fo. Cont.
bds. (BR. Apr.12; 908)   DM 2,000

KRAUTERMANN, Valentin (Pseud.)
See— HELLWIG, L. Christoph von

KREA, Henri
- Thermes. Ill.:– after René Laubies. Paris, 1958.
*(75) numbered on straw cold. 'Chiffon' paper, sigd.
by author & artist.* 4to. Hf. mor. & paper sides
over wood bds. in vertical bands by Alain Lobstein,
sigd. on verso of 1st. free end-paper, bands at outer
edges ending near foot of upr. cover & near head
of lr. cover, upr. cover with onlaid mor. abstract
design reaching upwards from lr. edge, smoth spine
brown-lettered, inner bds. inner bds. painted black
with facing & matching black free end-pp., partly
unc., orig. ptd. wraps. & backstrip preserved.
(CNY. May 18; 186) $450

KREBS, B.
[-] Handbuch der Buchdruckerkunst. Frankfurt,
1827. Bds., sm. old defects. (V. Sep.30; 2151)
                                            DM 420

KREDEL, Fritz
- Wer will unter die Soldaten?. Frankfurt, 1933.
(100) De Luxe Edn. 4to. Printers mark sigd. by
artist, orig. bds., slightly rubbed & faded, some
parts reprd. with col. (H. Nov.24; 2512)   DM 400
See— KOCH, Rudolf & Kredel, Fritz

KREFFT, Gerard
- The Mammals of Australia. Ill.:– Harriet Scott &
Helena Forde. Sydney, 1871. Fo. Some foxing, sm.
defect. to advt. lf. & final text lf., title-p. reprd. &
laid down, mod. mor. gt. (KH. May 1; 399)
                                            Aus. $980
- The Snakes of Australia. Sydney, 1869. Leath.
(JL. Nov.13; B535)   Aus. $1,050

KREITTMAYR, W.X.A. v.
- Anmerkungen üb. d. Codicem Maximilaneum
Bavaricum Civilem. München, 1758-68. 5 pts.,
Supp. & General Index in 3 vols. Fo. Some foxing,
Vol. 2 stained in lr. margin, cont. vell., some corners
bumped. (HK. Nov.9; 1376)   DM 1,000
[-] Codex Maximilianeus Bavaricus, Civilis.
München, 1756. *1st. Edn.* Fo. Title lf. with old
faded stp., cont. hf. linen, rubbed. (GB. Nov.3;
1000)   DM 1,000
[-]Anr. Copy. Fo. Slightly foxed, cont. vell. (HK.
Nov.9; 1375)   DM 850

KRETSCHMER, Albert
- Deutsche Volkstrachten. Leipzig, 1870. *1st. Edn.*
4to. Cont. leath., red & gold-tooled, spotted, spine
defect. (D. Nov.24; 4349)   DM 2,900

- - Anr. Copy. 4to. Chromolitho. titles, 88 (of 89)
chromolitho. plts., text in German, Fr. & Engl.,
cont. hf. cf., foot of spine a little torn. (CH. Sep.20;
7)   Fls. 3,000
- - Anr. Edn. Leipzig, [1887-90]. *2nd. Edn.* Sm.
fo. Some plts. loose, gold & blind-tooled, defect. &
loose. (R. Oct.12; 2374)   DM 4,000
- - Anr. Copy. 4to. Chromolitho. title, 2 repairs, &
90 chromolitho. plts., 1 text lf. inverted, 1 lf. creased, mod. linen. (H. May 22; 388)   DM 3,200
- - Anr. Copy. Lge. 4to. Lacks 9 chromolitho. plts.,
loose, with separate orig. pt. wraps, (fayed). (HK.
May 16; 1645)   DM 2,000

KRETSCHMER, Konrad
- Die Entdeckung Amerikas. Berlin, 1892. 2 vols.
Fo. & lge. fo. Mod. hf. leath. (R. Oct.13; 2978)
                                          DM 1,200
- - Anr. Copy. 1 text & 1 atlas vol. Fo. & lge. fo.
Orig. hf. leath., worn. (HK. Nov.8; 837) DM 950

KRISTELLER, Paul
- Andrea Mantegna. Trans.:– S. Arthur Strong.
1901. Fo. Some spotting, orig. cl. gt., slightly
rubbed & soiled. (TA. May 17; 434)   £50
- Early Florentine Woodcuts. L., 1897. *(300) numbered.* 4to. Orig. hf. leath., unc. (SI. Dec.15; 206)
                                         Lire 550,000

**KRISTNI-SAGA, sive Historia Relioginia Christi-
anae in Islandiam Introductae**
Copen., 1773. Hf.-title with vig., 6 folding genealogical tables, 19th. C. cf., spine gt., slightly rubbed.
(BBA. Feb.23; 56)   *Quevedo.* £180

KRONENBERG, M.E.
See— NIJHOFF, Wouter & Kronenberg, M.E.

KRONFELD, A.
See— HOVORKA, O. von & Kronfeld, A.

KRONIEK
Ed.:– P.L. Tak. Trans.:– Contribs.:– Diepenbrock,
Berlage, Israëls, Deyssel, & others. Ill.:– Bauer,
Berlage, Hoytema & others. Amst., 1895-1907. 12
vols. (of 13). Years I-XIII. Lacks Vol. IV. Fo. &
4to. Cl. & hf. cl. (B. Apr.27; 954)   Fls. 1,800

KROON, John
- Akvareller och Techningar av Elias Martin.
Malmo, 1943. *(400).* Fo. Orig. cl. portfo., slightly
worn. (BBA. Nov.10; 215)   *Zwemmer.* £50

KROSINSKY, B. & Lindner, Fr.
- Geogrpahisch-statistisch-topographisches
Lexikon von Würtemberg. Stuttgart, 1833. Cont.
hf. leath., slightly rubbed. (HT. May 10; 2998)
                                            DM 520

KRUCHENYKH, A.
- Stikhi Mayakovskago [The Poetry of
Mayakovsky]. Petersburg, 1914. *1st. Edn.* Sm. 4to.
Litho. by Malevich, titled 'Universal Landscape',
tipped in as frontis. (usually replaced by anr. litho.
by Rozanova), orig. ptd. wraps., port. of
Mayakovsky on upr. cover, unc. (S. Nov.21; 150)
                                          Weston. £750
- Vozropshchem [Let's Grumble]. Ill.:– Malevich &
Rozanova. Petersburg, 1913. *1st. Edn., [1000].* Sm.
4to. Lithos. tipped in before title, orig. wraps, unc.
(S. Nov.21; 148)   *Weston.* £500
- Vzorval' [Explodity]. Ill.:– Malevich, Roanova,
Goncharova, Kul'bin, & others. Petersburg, [1913].
2nd. Edn., [450]. Orig. litho. pict. wraps. by
Rozanova, partly hand-cold., probably by artist,
rebkd., a few short tears reprd. (S. Nov.21; 149)
                                          Carus. £600

KRUG, W.T.
- Allgemeines Handwörterbuch der Philosophischen
Wissenschaften. Leipzig, 1827-29. 5 vols. Cont. hf.
leath., bumped. (R. Oct.11; 508)   DM 500

KRUGER, E.
- Die Jagd. Hamburg, ca. 1860. Ob. fo. Corner of
dedication lf. restored, loose in orig. hf. linen
portfo., spine renewed. (R. Oct.12; 2043)
                                          DM 1,350

KRUGER, F.
See— BRANDES, R. & Krüger, F.

KRUGER, J.G.
- **Naturlehre.** Halle, 1748-50. 4 pts. in 3 vols. Lacks 1 folding plt., cf., spines gt., some rubbing. (B. Jun.21; 389) Fls. 850

KRUNITZ, Johann. Georg.
- **Auszug aus des Herrn D.J.G. Krünitz ökonomisch -technologischen Encyklopädie.** Ed.:– M.C. von Schütz. Berlin, 1786-1812. 32 vols. (all publd.?). Cont. hf. leath. gt., light wear, 4 sm. tears or spine defects. (D. Nov.24; 4330) DM 3,200
- **Oeconomisches Encyclopädie.** Berlin, 1775. Pt. 5. 15 (of 16) folding copperplts., cont. bds., bumped. (R. Apr.4; 1842) DM 450
- **– Anr. Copy.** Pt. 6. 1 folding plt. defect., cont. hf. leath., slightly bumped. (R. Apr.4; 1848) DM 400
- **– – Anr. Edn.** Berlin, 1783. Pt. 29. Cont. bds., bumped. (R. Apr.4; 1589) DM 400
- **– – Anr. Edn.** Brünn, 1788. Pt. 18. Cont. hf. leath. gt. (R. Oct.12; 1746) DM 520

KRUSENSTERN, Capt. A.J. von
- **Voyage round the World in the Years 1803, 1805, 1805 & 1806.** Trans.:– Richard B. Hoppner. L., 1813. *1st. Engl. Edn.* 2 vols. in 1. Vol. 1 lacks title-p., frontis. restored, a few prelims. with margins reinforced, 1 p. with sm. repair, title to Vol. 2 foxed, bdg. not stated. (JL. Mar.25; 412) Aus. $120

KUBIN, Alfred
- **Am Rande des Lebens.** München, 1921. *(150) numbered De Luxe Edn.* Fo. 4 ll. & 21 plts. in passepartouts, loose in orig. bd. portfo.; imprint sigd. by artist. (R. Oct.11; 308) DM 440
- **– Anr. Copy.** Lge. fo. Printers mark sigd. by artist, 4 text ll. at beginning slightly foxed, orig. hf. vell. portfo., lightly bumped. (HK. May 17; 2915) DM 400
- **Heimliche Welt.** Heidelberg, [1927]. *(550) numbered.* Ob. fo. Minimal foxing, orig. hf. linen. (HK. May 17; 2913) DM 560
- **Rauhnacht.** Preface:– O. Stroessl. Berlin, 1925. *[1st. Edn.].* Ob. 4to. Orig. linen portfo., slightly faded, printers mark sigd. by artist. (D. Nov.24; 3112) DM 900
- **– Anr. Copy.** Ob. fo. Printer's mark sigd. by artist, orig. pict. hf. linen portfo. (HK. Nov.11; 4105) DM 750
- **– – Anr. Edn.** [Berlin, 1925]. *1st. Edn.* Lacks pp. 1/2 (ptd. title), slight wear, orig. hf. linen portfo. (HK. May 17; 2916) DM 500
- **Die 7 Todsünden.** Berlin, [1914]. Lge. fo. Orig. pict. hf. linen. (HK. Nov.11; 4109) DM 1,600
- **Von Verschiedenen Ebenen.** Berlin, [1922]. *(400) numbered.* Sm. fo. Lightly foxed, orig. hf. linen, slightly browned. (HK. Nov.11; 4117) DM 1,200
- **Zwanzig Bilder zur Bibel.** München, 1924. *De Luxe Edn., (80).* 4to. Printer's mark sigd., plts. cold. by artist, orig. hf. leath., s.-c. (HK. Nov.11; 4096) DM 2,600
- **Zwanzig Lichtdrucke nach A. Kubin.** N.p., n.d. Orig. hf. leath. (HK. Nov.11; 4097) DM 750

KUBIN, A. (Texts)
See— GANYMED

KÜCHELBECKER, J.B.
- **Allerneueste Nachricht von Römisch- Kayserl. Hofe. Nebst Beschreibung der Residentz-Stadt Wien.** Ill.:– J.G. Schmidt. Hannover, 1730. 2 pts. in 1 vol. Lacks 1 blank lf., leath. gt., slightly worn. (V. Sep.29; 144) DM 550

KUEHNEL, Ernst
See— VOLBACH, W.F. & Kuehnel, Ernst

KUGLER, Franz Theodor
- **Geschichte Friedrich des Grossen.** Leipzig, 1840. *1st. Edn.* 2 vols. Lge. 4to. Cont. linen, elab. romantic decor. gt., slightly bumped. (HK. May 15; 826) DM 720
- **– Anr. Copy.** Lightly foxed, blind-tooled linen, slightly bumped. (V. Sep.30; 2387) DM 430
- **– – Anr. Edn.** Ill.:– A. V. Menzel. Leipzig, 1910. Orig. linen. (D. Nov.24; 3633) DM 540

KUHLMANN, Quirinus
- **Recht dunkelt mich das Dunkel.** Ill.:– Uwe Bremer, G.B. Fuchs & others. [Berlin], 1964. Fo.

Author's copy, 20 sigd. orig. woodcuts, orig. hf. linen, slight scratch, slightly rubbed. (GB. May 5; 3161) DM 1,000

KUHN, A. (Ed.)
See— AUSSTELLUNG DEUTSCHER ZEIT-GENOSSISCHER ARCHITEKTUR

KUHNEL, Ernst & Goetz, Hermann
- **Indian Book Painting.** L., 1926. Fo. Orig. buckram, d.-w.; inscr. to Sir Leslie & Lady Wilson from the Chief & Rani of Sangli on hf.-title. (BBA. Apr.5; 239a) *Sims, Reed & Fogg.* £60

KULMUS, Johann. Adam.
- **Anatomische Tabellen.** Ed.:– K.G. Kühn. Leipzig, 1814. 4to. Lacks part of 1 plt., cont. hf. leath., rubbed. (D. Nov.23; 588) DM 500

KUMMEL, Otto
- **Chinesische Kunst.** Berlin, 1930. *(300) numbered.* Fo. Orig. cl., slightly rubbed. (S. May 1; 597) *Zwemmer.* £70

KUNCKEL v. LOWENSTERN, J.
- **Ars Vitraria Experimentalis.** Frankfurt & Leipzig, 1679. 2 pts. in 1 vol. Sm. 4to. Cut slightly close, pt. 1 title date defect., 1 lf. pt. 1 with reprd. tear, 2 pp. omitted in numbering, 4 pp. mis-bnd., browning, some marginalia, MS. entry in pt. 2 dtd. Würzburg, 1730, hf. leath., ca. 1820, rubbed & slightly bumped. (R. Oct.12; 1748) DM 4,400
- **– – Anr. Edn.** Nuremb., 1743. 2 pts. in 1 vol. 4to. Wormed with some slight loss, some browning, cont. leath., wormed, spine partly restored, MS. note on upr. end-paper. (HK. May 15; 403) DM 850

KUNST GEWERBLICHE SCHMUCKFORMEN FUER DIE FLAECHE: Vierteljahrshefte fuer die Verzierende Kunst
Plauen i. V., ca. 1925. Vols. XIII-XVI (lacks XIV pt. 1), together 4 vols. 4to. 82 (of 84) mntd. plts. 'reproduced machinally by stencils', loose as iss., ptd. wraps., 2 with covers detchd. (SG. Aug.25; 22) $130

KUNST TOOVERBOEK OF VERANDERING VAN VOORSTELLINGEN
Rotterdam, 1839. Flick book, orig. ptd. bds., slightly worn, rebkd.; van Veen coll. (S. Feb.28; 244) £420

KUNST UND KUNSTLER
1924-33. Vols. XXII-XXXIII, 11 vols. in 10. 4to. & 8vo. Some spotting, some orig. upr. covers bnd. in, cl. or bds., 1 vol. slightly soiled. (S. Apr.30; 310) *Landry.* £50

KUNST UND VERLEGER
Contribs.:– Eulenberg, Friedländer, Glaser, Preetorius & others. Ill.:– L. Corinth, R. Grossmann & E. Orlik, M. Liebermann. Berlin, 1922. *(100) numbered.* Year 1, Pt. 1. Lge. 4to. 3 sigd. lithos. & 1 sigd. etching, orig. pict. wraps., slightly soiled, margins lightly frayed, spine slightly defect. (HK. Nov.11; 3718) DM 1,800

KUNZ, C.
- **Vedute Principali di Venezia.** Venice, ca. 1860. Sm. ob. 4to. Cold. litho. title & 12 cold. litho. views, minimal browning, orig. hf. linen, bumped, slightly spotted. (R. Oct.13; 3177) DM 450

KUNZ, George Frederick
- **Ivory & the Elephant in Art, in Archaeology & in Science.** Garden City, 1916. *1st. Edn.* Lge. 8vo. Ills., ex-liby., buckram, lge. pict. labels on cover & spine. (SG. May 3; 229) $225

KUNZE, R.
- **Die Bringer Beethovens.** Ill.:– H.A.P. Grieshaber. [Düsseldorf, Eremiten-Pr., 1976]. *(225) De Luxe Edn. with woodcut sigd. by artist.* 4to. Printers mark sigd. by artist, orig. pict. wraps. (H. May 23; 1207) DM 420

KUON, R. (Ed.)
See— MUNCHNER BLATTER FUR DICH-TUNG UND GRAPHIK

KURODA, Magamichi
- **The Birds of the Island of Java.** Tokyo, 1933-36. 2 vols. Fo. Some browning, cl., orig. spines laid down. (SPB. Dec.13; 590) $275

KURSCHNER, Joseph
- **Deutsche National Litteratur.** Berlin & Stuttgart, n.d. 206 vols., various. Mor.-bkd. bds., worn, w.a.f. (CSK. Jan.27; 114) £170

KURTZ, Benjamin P.
- **The Life & Works of William Caxton.** Ed.:– Edwin Grabhorn. San Franc., Grab. Pr., 1938. *(297) for Book Cl. of California.* 4to. Lf. from Caxton's 1482 edn. of Polycronicon, fo.336, tipped in, cl., decor. bds. (SG. May 17; 102) $600

KURZ, M.
See— POPPEL, J. & Kurz, M.

KUSMIN, M.
- **Die Abenteuer des Aimé Lebeuf.** Trans.:– P. Barchan. Ill.:– Hans Meid. 1922. *(100) numbered.* 4to. 24 sigd. etchings, margin lightly browned, orig. cf., corners lightly rubbed, spine lightly worn. (GB. Nov.5; 2802) DM 1,400

KUTHAN, Georges
- **Aphrodite's Cup.** [North Vancouver], Honeysuckle Pr., [1964]. *(275) numbered, 'published privately by the artist ... '.* Sq. 4to. This copy unnumbered, pict. cl., slightly rubbed. (SG. Mar.29; 113) $275

KUYPER, J.
- **Gemeente-Atlas v. Nederland. IV: Noord-Holland.** Leeuwarden, ca. 1870. Ob. 8vo. 138 maps, hand-cold. outl., orig. cl. gt., spine worn. (VG. Mar.19; 8) Fls. 2,200

KWANGETSU, Shitomi
- **Ise Sangu Meisho Zuye** ... Kyoto & Osaka, 1797. 8 vols. Collation not certified, Japanese bdg. style (material not stated). (KH. Nov.9; 700)Aus. $350

KYPSELER, G. 'Abraham Ruchat'
See— RUCHAT, Abraham [i.e. G. Kypseler]

KYRIOLES ou Cantiques qui sont chantez à l'Eglise de Mesdames de Remiremont, par des Jeunes Filles de Différentes Parroisses des Villages Voisins de Cette Ville ...
Remiremont, 1773. Added 1 ptd. lf., 19th. C. mor. (HD. Dec.2; 104) Frs. 2,750

KYRISS, Ernst
- **Festschrift Ernst Kyriss.** Stuttgart, 1961. Orig. cl.; H.M. Nixon coll., with some MS. notes & rubbings, corrected proof of his Review for The Library & cards loosely inserted. (BBA. Oct.6; 78) *Oak Knoll Books.* £120
- **Verzierte Gotische Einbände im Alten Deutschen Sprachgebiet.** Stuttgart, 1951-58. 4 vols. in 1. Buckram, H.M. Nixon coll., with a few MS. notes loosely inserted. (BBA. Oct.6; 77) *Maggs.* £350

KYSER, H.
- **Tango Argentino.** Ill.:– E. Oppler. Berlin, ca. 1925. *(100) De Luxe Edn.* Sm. 4to. All etchings sigd. by artist, printers mark sigd. by author & artist, owners note on end-paper, hand-bnd. mor. gt. (H. Nov.24; 1908) DM 840
- **– – Anr. Edn.** Ill.:– E. Oppler. Berlin, n.d. *(550) numbered.* 4to. Printers mark sigd. by author & artist, all etchings sigd. by artist, name on endpaper, orig. leath., by E. Nicolas, corners slightly bumped. (HK. Nov.11; 3843) DM 650

KYSTER, Anker
- **Bookbindings in the Public Collections of Denmark.** Copen., 1938. *(250).* Vol. 1. 4to. Orig. cf.-bkd. bds.; H.M. Nixon coll., with his sig., acquisition note & some MS. notes. (BBA. Oct.6; 79) *Beres.* £600

LAAR, G. van
- **Magazijn v. Tuin-sieraden of Verzam. v. Modellen Lust-hoven.** Amst., 1802. *1st. Edn.* 4to. Engraved title & 190 plts., all hand-cold., title soiled, cont. hf. cf., covers & corners detchd. (VG. Mar.19; 41) Fls. 3,900
- **– – Anr. Copy.** 4to. Title-vig., 190 plts., sm. tears

LAAR, G. van -*Contd.*

in 1 plt., 2 text ll. reprd., later hf. cl. (B. Oct.4; 243) Fls. 700
– – **Anr. Edn.** Zalt-Bommel, [1819]. *New Edn.* 4to. Engraved title, 190 hand-cold. engraved plts., cont. marb. cf., spine gt. (VG. Sep.14; 933) Fls. 3,600
– – **Anr. Copy.** 4to. Title-vig., 190 plts., all hand-cold., hf. roan, rubbed, slightly defect. (B. Oct.4; 243a) Fls. 1,500

LABACCO, Antonio
– **Libro ... Appartenente a l'Architettura.** [Rome, 1557]. Engraved title, 26 engraved plts., including 4 double-p., 2 additional engraved plts., including 1 double-p., bnd. at beginning (both ascribed to Labacco by former owner), plt. '29-30' bnd. as a folding plt. & slightly worn. (*Bound with:*) **BAROZZI, Giacomo, called Vigiola** – **Cinque Ordini d'Architettura.** [Rome, 1563?]. 32 engraved plts. Together 2 works in 1 vol. Fo. Few marginalia, old cf. gt., worn. (SG. Nov.3; 117) $1,500

LABADIE, Jean de
– **Kort-begryp van 't Rechte en Ware Christendom.** Amst., 1685. *2nd. Printing.* Sm. 8vo. New endpapers, cont. vell., slightly soiled. (VS. Dec.9; 1378) Fls. 525
– **La Reformation de l'Eglise par le Pastorat.** Middelburg, 1667. *1st. Edn.* 2 vols. in 1. (*Bound with:*) – **L'Idée d'un Bon Pasteur et d'une Bonne Eglise.** Amst., 1667. *1st. Edn.* (*Bound with:*) – **Le Triomphe de l'Eucharistie.** Amst., 1667. *1st. Edn.* Together 3 works in 1 vol. Some foxing, cont. vell.; J.W. Six bkplt. (VS. Dec.9; 1379) Fls. 1,200

LA BARRE, Michel de
– **Le Triomphe Des Arts ... Livre Troisième.** Paris, [1700]. *1st. Edn.* Ob. 4to. A few sm. tears, some affecting text, cont. mott. cf., gt. ornamental spine, lacks part of head & foot, some sm. holes in upr. cover, corners reprd.; from liby. of St. Michael's College, Tenbury, & [?] from Toulouse-Philidor Collection. (S. May 10; 76) *Macnutt.* £1,200

LA BARRE DE BEAUMARCHAIS, Antoine de
[–] **Le Temple des Muses.** Ill.:– B. Picart le Romain. Amst., 1733. Fo. Cont. vell. (HD. May 3; 67) Frs. 1,900

LABARTE, Jules
– **Histoire des Arts Industriels au Moyen Age et à l'Epoque de la Renaissance.** Paris, 1872-75. *2nd. Edn.* 3 vols. Sm. fo. 79 plts., most chromolithos., text engrs., ex-liby., hf. mor. (SG. May 3; 230) $100

LABASTIDE
– **Recueil de Dessins au Crayon ... représentant des Vues, Scènes et personnages Populaires de la Russie d'avant 1914.** N.d. Fo. 28 pieces, 19th. C. russia havanna cf album, blind & gt. fillet decor., restored. (HD. Feb.29; 39) Frs. 5,500

LABAT, Jean Baptiste
– **Nouvelle Relation de l'Afrique Occidentale.** Paris, 1728-29. *1st. Edn.* 5 vols. Titles with excised owners mark, slightly spotted, cont. leath., lightly bumped, gt. oxidised. (HK. May 15; 585) DM 850
– – **Anr. Edn.** Paris, 1728. 5 vols. 12mo. 75 plts., many folding, cf. (P. Dec.8; 341) *Shapero.* £75

LABAT, P.
– **Voyages en Espagne et en Italie.** Paris, 1730. *1st. Edn.* 8 vols. 12mo. Cont. marb. cf., spines decor. (HD. Jun.26; 42) Frs. 2,900

LABBE, Ph.
– **Bibliotheca Bibliothecarum Curis Secundis auctior. Acc. Bibliotheca Nummaria in duas Partes tributa ...** Paris, 1664. Cont. vell. (HK. Nov.11; 4468) DM 480

LABE, Louise
– **Oeuvres.** Lion, 1555. *Orig. Edn.* Sm. 8vo. Privilege lf., ink inscrs. on title, apparently 18th. C., some ink underlinings in text without damage to paper, faint dampstain affecting upr. corners of last 30 ll., some corners rounded, orig. vell. from MS. p., upr. corner wormed. (HD. Nov.9; 7) Frs. 251,000

LA BEAUMELLE, Angliviel de
– **Mémoires pour Servir à l'Histoire de Mme de Maintenon et à celle du Siècle Passé ...** Amst., priv. ptd., 1755-56. *Orig. Edn.* 6 vols. in 3. 12mo. Cont. cf. gt., spines decor., turn-ins & corners lightly worn. (HD. May 3; 68) Frs. 1,100
– – **Anr. Edn.** Hambourg, 1756. *New Edn.* 5 vols. (*With:*) – **Lettres de Madame de Maintenon ...** Glascow, 1756. 7 vols. Together 12 vols. 12mo. Cont. marb. cf., spines decor., lacks 2 title labels; from Château des Noës liby. (HD. May 25; 34) Frs. 1,900

LA BEDOLLIERE, Emile de
– **Le Bois de Vincennes.** Ill.:– I. Rousset. Paris, 1866. 4to. 25 mntd. albumen photographs, some light foxing, mostly affecting text & plt. margins, orig. gt.-pict. cl. (SG. Nov.10; 141) $475
– **Histoire de la Garde Nationale.** Ill.:– Pauquet. Paris, 1848. 12mo. Frontis. & 10 plts., cont. cold., red hf. mor., corners, by V. Champs, spine gt., unc.; Paul Gavault ex-libris. (HD. Jun.22; 28) Frs. 1,500
– **Les Industriels, Métiers et Professions en France.** Ill.:– H. Monnier. Paris, 1842. *1st. Edn.* Minimal spotting, later hf. mor. gt., by Weidle, orig. pict. wraps. bnd. in, corners bumped; name, title stp. & ex-libris of Graf Grigorij Alexandrowitch Stroganoff, Hauswedell coll. (H. May 23; 114) DM 420

LA BEDOYERE, H. Huchet de
[–] **Voyage en Savoie et dans le Midi de la France en 1804 et 1805.** Paris, 1807. *Orig. Edn.* On vell., str.-grd. red mor. gt. by P. Rosa, Napoleon I arms, spine decor. (HD. May 4; 314) Frs. 26,000

LABEYLE, Charles, Engineer
– **The Result of a View of the Great Level of the Fens.** 1745. Sm. 4to. Interleaved, recent hf. mor.; 'pres. copy'. (BBA. Sep.29; 117) *Traylen.* £110

LABILLARDIERE, Jacques-Julien Houton de
– **An Account of a Voyage in Search of La Perouse.** L., 1802. *2nd. Edn.* 2 vols. & Atlas. 8vo. & 4to. Atlas with 44 engraved plts., text vols. orig. cf., rebkd., atlas hf. cf., covers rubbed. (CA. Apr.3; 66) Aus. $1,000

LA BOETIE, Etienne de
– **De la Servitude Volontaire ou le Contre'un.** Ill.:– Louis Jou. Paris, 1922. *(335). (10)* on japon impérial. Square 8vo. Jansenist bordeaux mor. by Lavaux, wrap. & spine preserved, s.-c. (HD. May 4; 315) Frs. 1,800

LABORDE, Alexandre de
– **Itinerario Descriptivo de las Provincias de Espàna.** Valencia, 1826. 4to. Linen. (DS. Mar.23; 2151) Pts. 40,000
– **Voyage Pittoresque et Historique de l'Espagne.** Paris, 1806-1820. 4 vols. Lge. fo. On thick vell., 272 engraved plts., cont. str.-grd. hf. mor., spines gt., slight tears. (HD. Mar.9; 93) Frs. 29,000
– – **Anr. Edn.** Paris, 1807-20. 4 vols. Lge. Fo. Frontis., port., 2 maps, 272 engrs., cont. chagrin, corners. (DS. May 25; 2292b) Pts. 800,000
– – **Anr. Edn.** Paris, 1812. Vol. 2 (2 pts. in 1) only (of 2). Fo. 174 plts., plans & maps on 137 sheets, lacks 1 sheet, some plts. partly hand-cold., mor., rubbed, as a coll. of plts., w.a.f. (P. Apr.12; 295) *Shapiro.* £580

LABORDE, Jean Benjamin de
– **Choix de Chansons Mises en Musique.** Ill.:– Moreau, Masquelier, & Nee, after Moreau, & others. Paris, 1773. *Early Iss., without ports. of Laborde or Mme. Laborde.* 4 vols. in 2. Titles, dedication with arms, 3 frontis., 100 plts., cont. cf., spines gt. (C. Dec.9; 196a) *D'Arcy.* £1,500
– – **Anr. Edn.** Ill.:– Moreau le jeune, Masquelier, & Née, after Moreau, Le Barbier, Le Bouteux, & Saint-Quentin. Paris, 1773. 4 vols. in 2. Lge. 8vo. With 1774 port., title, 4 frontis., 100 ills., some light spotting & discoloration, cont. mott. cf., spines gt., 1st. vol. carefully reprd. at head of spine. (SPB. Dec.14; 57) $1,500
See— **ZURLAUBEN, B.F.A., Baron de & Laborde, Jean Benjamin de**

LABOUREUR, Jean Emile
– **Graphismes.** 1931. *(99).* 4to. Lightly foxed, leaves, wrap. & box. (HD. Jan.24; 67) Frs. 3,250

LABOUR MONTHLY
1921-41. Vols. 1-5, 7 & 9-23 only. Cont. cf., rubbed. (BBA. Feb.9; 127) *Koffler.* £60

LA BROUE, S. de
– **Le Cavalerice François ...** Paris, 1620. *3rd. Edn.* 3 pts. in 1 vol. Fo. Lacks several ll. at beginning of each pt., old vell.; from Château des Noës liby. (HD. May 25; 35) Frs. 4,000

LA BRUYERE, Jean de
– **Les Caractères de Théophraste. Traduits du Grec. Avec Les Caractères, ou Les Moeurs de ce Siècle.** Paris, 1688. *1st. Edn.* 12mo. With 1st. privilege & 'Fautes d'impression', cont. red mor. gt., spine decor., Chancelier Boucherat arms. (HD. Mar.29; 32) Frs. 260,000
– – **Anr. Edn.** Paris, 1689. *4th. Edn.* 12mo. Errors corrected in pen, cont. red mor., spine decor., Jean-Baptiste Henrion arms. (HD. Mar.29; 33) Frs. 48,000
– – **Anr. Edn.** Paris, 1690. *5th. Edn.* 12mo. MS. key in margins, cont. red mor., fleurs-de-lys, spine decor.; from Comte de Lignerolles liby. (HD. Mar.29; 34) Frs. 25,000
– – **Anr. Edn.** 1692. *Orig. 7th. Edn.* 12mo. Cont. roan, spine decor., turn-ins worn. (HD. Mar.21; 45) Frs. 1,100
[–] – **Anr. Edn.** Paris, 1716. 12mo. Mor. gt., spine decor., by Yseux. (HD. Nov.17; 41) Frs. 1,900
– – **Anr. Edn.** Notes:– M. Coste. Paris, 1765. *1st. Printing of ills.* 4to. Cont. marb. cf., University of Paris arms, spine decor.; from Château des Noës liby. (HD. May 25; 36) Frs. 2,100
– – **Anr. Edn.** Paris, 1824. 2 vols. Minimal foxing, cf. by Dauphin, blind- & gt.-decor. (HD. May 4; 317) Frs. 4,100

LA CALPRENEDE, Gaultier de Coste
[–] **Cassandra; the Fam'd Romance ...** Trans.:– Sir Charles Cotterel. 1661. Fo. Engraved frontis., creased & torn with slight loss, cont. cf., rubbed, base of spine worm-holed. [Wing L107] (CSK. Apr.27; 143) £60

LACASSAGNE
– **Traité Général des Eléments du Chant.** Versailles, priv. ptd., 1766. *Orig. Edn.* Mor., spine decor. (SM. Mar.7; 2025) Frs. 2,200

LACEPEDE, Comte Bernard Germaine Etienne de
– **Histoire Naturelle comprenant les Cétacés, les Quadrupèdes, Ovipares, les Serpents et les Poissons.** Paris, 1839. 2 vols. Lge. 8vo. Cont. cold. engraved plts., cont. hf. chagrin, spines decor. (HD. Jun.22; 59) Frs. 1,300
– **Oeuvres.** Bruxelles, 1833-34. Part of plt. pt. Lacks 75 plts., 5 plts. defect., some light browning, loose in 27 orig. pts. (R. Oct.12; 1838) DM 500
– – **Anr. Edn.** Paris, 1836. 3 vols. 150 steel-engraved plts., cont. cold & gommées, some foxing, cont. hf. sheep, decor. spines. (HD. Sep.22; 263) Frs. 2,500
– **Oeuvres, comprenant l'histoire Naturelle des Quadrupèdes Ovipares, des Serpents, des Poisson, et des Cetacés.** Paris, ca. 1840. Cont. hf. leath. gt. (BR. Apr.12; 736) DM 550

LACEPEDE, Comte Bernard Germaine Etienne de & Cuvier, Baron Georges Leopold Chretien
– **La Ménagerie du Museum National d'Histoire Naturelle.** Ill.:– Miger after Maréchal. Paris, 1801. Fo. Foxing in lr. margin thro.-out, cont. hf. leath. (D. Nov.23; 718) DM 4,000

LA CHAU, Abbé Geraud de
– **Dissertation sur les Attribus de Vénus ...** Ill.:– Saint Aubin after Titien. Paris, 1776. 4to. 'Vénus Anadyomène' plt. in 3 states, jansenist mor. by Gruel; from Le Barbier de Tinan liby. (HD. May 3; 69) Frs. 2,800

LA CHAU, Abbé Geraud de & Le Blond, Abbé
– **Description des Principales Pierres Gravées du Cabinet de S.A.S. Monseigneur le Duc d'Orléans.** Paris, 1780-84. 2 vols. Fo. 178 engraved plts., hf.-titles, cont. cf. gt., rebkd. (SKC. Nov.18; 1814) £150
– – **Anr. Copy.** 2 vols. Fo. 1 plt. yellowed in Vol. II,

lacks 7 medal plts. sometimes added, red hf. mor. by Champs. (HD. May 3; 70) Frs. 1,150

LACKNER, Stefan
- **Der Mensch ist kein Haustier.** Ill.:– M. Beckmann. Paris, 1937. *1st. Edn.* 7 orig. lithos., orig. pict. sewed. (GB. May 5; 2181) DM 450
- – **Anr. Copy.** 7 orig. lithos., orig. pict. wraps. (GB. Nov.5; 2275) DM 400
- – **Anr. Edn.** Paris, [1937]. *Ltd. Iss.* Orig. bds. (HK. Nov.11; 3412) DM 460

LACLOS, Pierre Ambroise François Choderlos de
- **Les Liaisons Dangereuses.** Amst. [France?], 1782. 4 vols. in 2. 12mo. Vol. IV hf.-title omitted by binder, cont. red mor., spine decor. (HD. Mar.29; 35) Frs. 56,000
- – **Anr. Edn.** Ill.:– Baquoy, Langlois, & others, after Monnet, Fragonard fils, & Mlle Gérard. L., 1796 [1812]. *Counterfeit Edn.* 2 vols. Hf. mor., corners, decor. spines, by Arnaud. (HD. Sep.22; 217) Frs. 1,850
- – **Anr. Edn.** Ill.:– Lubin de Beauvais. Paris, 1908. *De Luxe Edn., (40) on Japan.* 4to. Separate series of cold. lithos., hand-bnd. mor., gt. inner & outer dentelle, pink mor. doubls. gt., silk end-papers, orig. wraps. bnd. in, by René Assourd; publisher's no. 1 copy. (H. Nov.24; 1356) DM 3,200
- – **Anr. Edn.** Trans.:– [Ernest Dowson]. Ill.:– 'Alastair'. Paris, Black Sun Pr., 1929. *(1000) numbered.* 2 vols. Tall 4to. Ptd. wraps., unc. (SG. Jan.12; 3) $275
- – **Anr. Copy.** 2 vols. 4to. Some margins lightly browned, linen, unc., orig. wraps. bnd. in; Franz Goldstein ex-libris inside cover. (H. Nov.24; 1310) DM 460
- – **Anr. Edn.** Ill.:– S. Sauvage. Paris, 1930. *(40) with suite & orig. drawing.* 2 vols. 4to. Mor. by Semet & Plumelle, blind– & silver-decor, watered silk end-ll., wrap. preserved, s.-c.; 2 engrs. on silk & 2 orig. copper engrs. mntd. in s.-c.'s. (HD. Jun.13; 57) Frs. 15,000
- – **Anr. Edn.** Ill.:– S. Sauvage. Paris, 1930. *(175) on Montval.* 2 vols. Lge. 4to. Leaves, wrap., autograph dedication from artist. (HD. Dec.16; 97) Frs. 2,550

LACOMBE, Sieur Jean de
- **A Compendium of the East being an Account of Voyages to the Grand Indies.** Gold. Cock. Pr., 1937. *(300) numbered.* Fo. Orig. cl., head of spine reprd. (BBA. Oct.27; 163) *Primrose Hill.* £85

LA CONDAMINE, Charles Marie de
- **Journal du Voyage fait par Ordre du Roi à l'Equateur ... – Mesure des Trois Premiers Degrés du Meridien ...** Paris, 1751. *Orig. Edns.* 2 pts. in 1 vol. 4to. Lacks 2 figures, maps or plts., cont. marb. cf., spine decor.; from Château des Noës liby. (HD. May 25; 37) Frs. 2,400
- **Journal du Voyage fait par Ordre du Roi, à l'Equateur ... –Mesure des Trois Premiers Degrés du Mendies dans l'Hemisphère Austral. –Supplement au Journal Historique du Voyage à l'Equateur.** 1751; 1751; 1752. *1st. Edn.* Together 3 works in 1 vol., Supp. pt. 1 only (of 2). 4to. 1 folding plt. slightly torn in 1st. work, slight browning & spotting, cont. cf., very worn. [Sabin 38479; 38483; 38490] (S. Nov.28; 123) *Pickering & Chatto.* £250
- **Relation abrégée fait dans l'Intérieur de l'Amerique Meridionale.** Paris, 1745. *1st. Edn.* A few margins dampstained. (Bound with:) **Lettre à Madame ***sur l'Emeute Popul** Paris, 1746. Together 2 works in 1 vol. 19th. C. cf.-bkd. bds., slightly rubbed. (S. Jun.25; 102) *Quaritch.* £180

LACOSTE, C.
See— VUILLEMIN, Thullier & Lacoste, C.

LACRETELLE, Jacques, i.e. Amauny Jacques de
- **Silbermann.** Ill.:– J.E. Laboureur. Paris, 1925. *1st. pict. Edn. (15) on imperial japan.* Autograph dedication sigd. & dtd. from author, sewed, pict. wrag. (HD. Mar.14; 130) Frs. 2,400

LA CROIX, A. Pherotée de
- **Relation Universelle de l'Afrique Ancienne et Moderne.** Lyons, 1688. 4 vols. 12mo. Cont. Fr. citron mor., spines gt., sm. abrasion on 1 upr. cover, traces of worming at foot of 2 spines, corners scuffed. . (C. Nov.16; 107) *Braunschweig.* £250

LACROIX, J.
- **Nouveau Guide Générale du Voyageur en Suisse.** Paris, ca. 1860. Orig. linen. (R. Oct.13; 3269) DM 410

LA CROIX, J.F. de
- [–] **Dictionnaire Historique Portatif des Femmes Célèbres.** Paris, 1769. *1st. Edn.* 2 vols. Some slight foxing, 1 leaf with slight loss, cont. leath., blind-tooled decor., gt. spine, rubbed. (D. Nov.24, 4351) DM 800

LACROIX, Paul
- **Les Arts au Moyen Age et à l'Epoque de la Renaissance.** Paris, 1874. *5th. Edn.* 4to. Some foxing, three-qtr. red mor., spine gt. in 6 compartments. (RO. Dec.11; 179) $125
- **Costumes Historiques de la France, d'après les Monuments les Plus Authentiques ... avec un Texte Descriptif. Par le bibliophile Jacob.** Paris, [1852]. 8 vols. (without the 2 additional vols.). Lge. 8vo. 640 hand-cold. engraved plts., many heightened with gold & silver, 2 plts. slightly chipped, some light foxing, rarely affecting plts., some titles & hinges crudely reprd., liby. stp. to plt. versos, disbnd. (SG. Sep.22; 113) $475
- **Moeurs, Usages et Costumes au Moyen Age et à l'Epoque de la Renaissance.** Paris, 1874. *4th. Edn.* 4to. Some foxing, three-qtr. red mor., spine gt. in 6 compartments. (RO. Dec.11; 180) $135
- **Moyen Age et Epoque de la Renaissance: Les Arts.**
- **Moeurs et Usages et Costumes, Sciences et Arts.**
- **XVIIe Siècle, Institutions, Usages et Costumes, Lettres, Sciences et Arts. – XVIIIe Siècle, Institutions, Usages et Costumes, Lettres, Sciences et Arts.**
- **Directoire, Consulat et Empire.** Paris, 1877-84. 9 vols. Lge. 8vo. 142 chromolitho. plts., unc., publisher's hf. chagrin, corners, richly decor. (LM. Mar.3; 166) B.Frs. 20,000

LACROIX, Silvestre Francois
- **An Elementary Treatise on the Differential & Integral Calculus.** Trans.:– C. Babbage, G. Peacock & J.F. Herschel. Camb., 1816. *1st. Edn. in Engl.* Errata ll., some browning & soiling, hf. cf., rubbed; Stanitz coll. (SPB. Apr.25; 249) $375
- **Traité du Calcul Différential et du Calcul Intégral.** Paris, 1797-98. *1st. Edn.* 2 vols. (With:) **Traité des Différences et des Séries.** Paris, 1800. 1 vol. Together 3 vols. 4to. A few gatherings browned, cont. tree cf., spines gt., 2nd. work not unif., upr. jnt. reprd.; 2nd. work with (Baron Gaspard?) De Prony bkplt., Stanitz coll. (SPB. Apr.25; 248) $325
- – **Anr. Edn.** Paris, 1810-19. Minimal browning, cont. hf. leath. (HT. May 8; 356) DM 500

LACTANTIUS, Lucius Caecilius Firmianus
- **Divinarum Institutionum Libri Septem.** Venice, Aldine Pr., Apr. 1515. 2 words in 1 vol. Aldine device on title. [*bound with:*] **TERTULLIANUS, Quintus Septimus Florens** – **Apologeticus Adversus Gentes.** Device on title & final lf. verso. 2 works in 1 vol. 17th. C. vell. (SG. Apr.19; 7) $175
See— JOANNES A CURRIBUS, Ferrariensis – EUSEBIUS PAMPHILIUS, Bp. of Caesarea – LACTANTIUS, Lucius Caecilius Firmianus

LA CURNE DE SAINTE-PALAYE, Jean Baptiste de
- **Mémoires sur l'Ancienne Chevalerie.** Ed.:– Ch. Nodier. Paris, 1829. *New Edn.* 2 vols. Bds. (HD. Feb.22; 204) Frs. 2,100

LACY, Thomas Hailes
- **Female Costumes Historical, National & Dramatic.** 1865. Lge. 8vo. 96 hand-cold. plts., hf. mor. gt., rebkd. (P. Oct.20; 247) £65
- **Male Costumes, Historical, National & Dramatic.** 1868. 200 plts., marb. bds. (JL. Jun.24; 214) Aus. $320

LADBACH, E.
- **Charakterische Holzbauten der Schweiz.** Berlin, 1896. Lge. fo. Loose ll. in limp portfo., wear. (GF. Nov.16; 1241) Sw. Frs. 950

LADIES MONTHLY MAGAZINE, The World of Fashion
1860, 1862, & 1863. Vols. 37, 39, & 40. 36 uncold. plts. of hats, 144 hand-cold. costume plts. (2 with

edges torn), hf. roan, worn, spines defect., lacks 1 cover. (LC. Mar.1; 80) £280

LADIES' WREATH; An Illustrated Annual for MDCCCXLVIII-IX
Ed.:– Mrs. S.T. Martyn. N.Y., 1848-49. Lge. 8vo. 11 hand-cold, flower plts. & ll. steel-engraved plts., orig. gt.-ornamental mor., very rubbed on edges, corners nicked; from liby. of F.D. Roosevelt, inscr. by him. (SG. Mar.15; 33) $150

L'ADMIRAL, Jacob
- **Naauwkeurige Waarneemingen omtrent de Veranderingen van veele Insekten of Gekorvene diertjes.** Amst., 1774. Fo. Title with cold. vig., 33 hand-cold. engraved plts., in reversed imps., plts. 26 & 27 stained & smudged, plt. 15 smudged at foot, margin repairs to plt. 28, G1 stained, mod. cf.-bkd. cl. (S. Nov.28; 51) *Schmidt.* £270

LADY'S ANNUAL: A Christmas & New Year Gift
N.Y., n.d. Sm. 8vo. Gt. & blind-ornamental maroon mor., rubbed & somewhat foxed; from liby of F.D. Rooosevelt, inscr. by him. (SG. Mar.15; 34) $130

LADY'S BOOK OF FLOWERS & POETRY
Ed.:– Lucy Hooper. N.Y., 1842. Sm. 8vo. 10 hand-cold. flower plts., tissue guards, including additional pict. title-p., orig. gt.-pict. mor., covers rubbed, with nicks; from liby. of F.D. Roosevelt, inscr. by him. (SG. Mar.15; 58) $130

LAENNEC, René Théophile Hyacinth
- **Abhandlung von den Krankheiten der Lungen des Herzens und der Mittelbaren Auscultation als ein Mittel zu ihrer Erkenntniss.** Trans.:– Fr. L. Meissner. Leipzig, 1832. *1st. Edn. in German.* 2 vols. 8 litho. plts. on 4 folding sheets, cont. hf. cf.; Dr. Baumgarten, Dr. O[scar] Minkowski & Dr. Walter Pagel copy. (S. Feb.7; 221) *Phelps.* £260
- **De l'Auscultation Médiate ou Traité du Diagnostic de Maladies des Poumons et du Coeur.** Paris, 1819. *1st. Edn.* 2 vols. Vol. I pagination begins (after title-lf.) with VIII, Vol. II with VI, lacks hf.-title & dedication(?), some heavy foxing, cont. hf. leath., spine restored. (GB. Nov.3; 1029) DM 1,100
- – **Anr. Edn.** 1826. *2nd. Edn.* 2 vols. Cont. hf. cf., spines decor. (HD. Mar.21; 164) Frs. 3,100

LA FAILLE, Jacob Baart de
- **Les Faux Van Gogh.** Paris & Brussels, 1930. *Ltd. Edn.* 4to. Cont. cl. (BBA. Apr.5; 34) *Zwemmer.* £75
- **L'Oeuvre de Vincent Van Gogh, Catalogue Raisonné.** Paris & Bruxelles, 1928. *(650) numbered.* 4 vols. 4to. Vol. 2 loose & lacks plt. 204, a few others creased, cont. hf. cf., rubbed. (BBA. Jul.27; 239) *Hetherington.* £100
- – **Anr. Copy.** 4 vols. Lge. 4to. 446 plts., liby. buckram. (SG. May 3; 363) $950

LA FARE, Marquis de
- **Mémoires et Réflexions sur les Principaux Evènements du Règne de Louis XIV et sur le Caractère de ceux qui ont eu la Principale Part.** Amst., 1734. 12mo. Cont. cf. (by Boyet?), spine decor.; from libys. of J.-J. de Bure & James Hartmann. (HD. Mar.29; 36) Frs. 5,200

LA FAYETTE, Comtesse de
- **Histoire de Madame Henriette Dangleterre, Première Femme de Philippe de France Duc d'Orléans.** Amst., 1742. 12mo. Cont. cf., spine decor.; Mareˊchal de Rohan-Soubise copy. (HD. Mar.29; 38) Frs. 9,000
- **Histoire de Madame Henriette d'Angleterre ... Prèmiere Femme de Philippe de France, Duc d'Orleans. — Mémoires de la Cour de France, pour les Années 1688 et 1689.** Amst., 1742. 2 works in 1 vol. Cont. marb. cf., spine decor., Madame d'Epinay arms. (HD. Mar.29; 39) Frs. 9,000
- **Mémoires de la Cour de France, pour les Années 1688 et 1689.** Amst., 1731. *Orig. Edn.* 12mo. Cont. blind-decor. cf. (HD. Mar.29; 40) Frs. 7,000
- **La Princesse de Clèves.** Paris, 1678. *Orig. Edn.* 4 vols. in 2. 12mo. Cont. cf., spine decor. (HD. Mar.29; 37) Frs. 300,000

LA FAYETTE, Comtesse de -*Contd.*

– – **Anr. Edn.** Ill.:– F. Masson. Paris, 1878. Jansenist mor. by Kaufmann-Petit. (HD. May 4; 320) Frs. 1,700
– – **Anr. Edn.** Ill.:– M. Leloir. Paris, 1926. Hf. mor., decor. & painted vell. centre band, by Max Fonsèque, wrap., s.-c. (HD. Jan.30; 67) Frs. 1,050
– – **Anr. Edn.** Ill.:– Maurie Laurencin. Paris, 1947. *(280). (230) on Vell.* 4to. 10 orig. cold. etchings, loose double ll. in orig. wraps. in orig. hf. linen box. (GB. May 5; 2869) DM 2,200
– **La Princesse de Montpensier.** Paris, 1804. 12mo. Str.-grd. mor. by Bozérian, spine decor. (HD. May 4; 319) Frs. 1,200

LA FEUILLE, D. De
[–] **Lettres sur l'etat Present de l'Europe.** Amst., 1696. *2nd. Edn.* 4to. 46 plts., cont. bds., defect. & loosening, some stains. (VG. May 3; 660) Fls. 570

LAFITAU, Joseph-François
– **Histoire des Découvertes et Conquestes des Portugais dans le Nouveau Monde** ... Paris, 1734. 4 vols. Sm. 8vo. A few tears & minor defects, several liby. stps., early cf., some slight rubbing. (KH. May 1; 402) Aus. $420
– – **Anr. Edn.** Ill.:– Scotin. Paris, 1753. *Orig. Edn.* 2 vols. 4to. Some ll. stained, cont. marb. of., decor. spines, some reprs. (HD. Dec.9; 45) Frs 4,000
– **Moeurs des Sauvages Amériquains.** Paris, 1724. *1st. Edn.* 2 vols. 4to. Frontis. map & 41 engraved plts., without privilege lf. in Vol. 2, short tear in 3K2 (Vol. 1), cont. cf., rebkd. [Sabin 28596] (S. May 22; 324) *Quaritch.* £480
– – **Anr. Copy.** 2 vols. 4to. Errata lf. in each vol., cont. mott. cf., gt. spines. (SKC. Sep.9; 2049) £460
– – **Anr. Copy.** 2 vols. 4to. Engraved frontis, map, 41 full-p. plts., repair to 1 lf, in Vol. 1, minor wormholes at front of Vol. 2, early paper bds., mod. cf., gt. spines, unc.; purchase inscrs. dtd. 1725 of Randolph Greenway, Jnr., the Rt. Hon. Visc. Eccles copy. [Sabin 38596] (CNY. Nov.18; 169) $1,000

LAFOND, Capt. G.
– **Voyages autour du Monde et Naufrages Célèbres.** 1844. 8 vols. 76 engraved plts., including 31 handcold., spotted thro.-out, cont. cf.-bkd. bds., gt. spines. (BBA. Sep.29; 30) *Bauman.* £120

LA FONTAINE, Jean de
– **Adonis.** Intro.:– Paul Valéry. Ill.:– Pierre-Yves Trémois. Paris, 1955. *(165) numbered on vélin du Marais.* Fo. Leaves, wrap., folder, box. (HD. May 21; 126) Frs. 4,500
– **Les Amours de Psiché et de Cupidon.** La Haye, 1700. *3rd. Edn.* 12mo. Cont. red mor. gt., spine decor., sm. stain to 1 cover; from libys. of C.S. d'Esmazières (with 18th. C. ex-libris), Jean-Jacques de Bure (with autograph inscr., sigd. & dtd. 22 Jul. 1825), & Marquis de Coislin. (HD. May 16; 42) Frs. 5,800
– – **Anr. Edn.** Ill.:– after Schall. Paris, 1791. *1st. Printing.* Lge. 4to. Advt. for Milton's Paradise Lost at end, marb. cf., spine decor., corners worn. (SM. Mar.7; 2026) Frs. 3,200
– – **Anr. Edn.** Ill.:– Bonnefoy, Colibert, & De Monchy, after Schall. Paris, 1791. 4to. Lacks portion of title, & with some surface damage, laid down, slight staining to early ll., stain to inner margin of last few ll. & 1 plt., mod. mor.-bkd. cl. gt. (LC. Oct.13; 54) £80
– – **Anr. Copy.** Fo. Advt. for 1792 'Le Paradis perdu' at back, some browning & spotting, light staining on a few pp., sm. stp. on title, cont. tree cf. gt., rubbed, sm. wormholes on spine. (SPB. Dec.14; 58) $450
– – **Anr. Edn.** Paris, 1793. Cont. decor. red mor. gt. (P. Jan.12; 240) *Cavendish.* £75
– – **Anr. Edn.** Paris, 1795 [An III]. 4to. Engraved port., 8 plts., slightly offset, some spotting, cont. red blind-ruled mor. (S. Apr.10; 321) *Tile.* £180
– – **Anr. Edn.** Ill.:– Moreau le Jeune. Paris, [1795]. Lge. 4to. Port., 8 engraved plts., each in 2 states, crimson crushed lev., double gt. fillet borders, gt.-panel. back, gt. dentelles, by Zaehnsdorf; Royal copy, hf.-title inscr. 'de la Bibliothèque de S.M. Louis Philippe, à Mme. Marie Saxe ... '. (SG. Apr.26; 110) $800
– – **Anr. Copy.** 4to. Some light spotting & browning, cont. tree cf. gt., l-inch tear in leath. at upr. lr. jnt., rubbing along jnts. & on spine, sm. wormholes, wormhole in end-paper; Jean Pierre Platzmann, Robert Walsingham Martin & Edward S. Marsh bkplts. (SPB. Dec.14; 59) $200
– – **Anr. Copy.** 4to. On vell., cont. tree cf. gt., spine decor., sm. loss from upr. turn-in. (HD. May 3; 79) Frs. 1,950
– – **Anr. Edn.** Ill.:– L. Jou. 1930. 4to. Jansenist mor. by Septier, wrap. (HD. Jan.24; 70) Frs. 1,250
– – **Anr. Edn.** Ill.:– Becat. Paris, 1950. *Ltd. Edn.* 4to. Loose ll. in publishers bds., box. (CR. Jun.6; 197) Lire 300,000
– – **Anr. Edn.** Ill.:– P.E. Becat. 1955. *(13) with orig. copper engr., orig. drawing, 2 suites with remarks, 1 extra plt.* 4to. Leaves, box. (HD. Jul.6; 114) Frs. 1,100
– **Contes et Nouvelles. — Fables.** Ill.:– Grandville. Paris, 1839; 1838. 1 vol., 2 vols. Foxed, unif. hf. mor. cf., decor. spines. (HD. Feb.22; 110) Frs. 1,600
– **Contes et Nouvelles en Vers** ... Ill.:– Romain de Hooghe. Amst., 1685. *1st. Coll. & 1st. Ill. Edn. 1st. Printing.* 2 vols. in 1. 12mo. Str.-grd. red mor. gt. by R. Payne, spine decor. (slightly faded). (HD. May 3; 74) Frs. 5,000
– – **Anr. Edn.** Ill.:– Romain de Hooghe. Amst., 1685. *1st. Coll. & 1st. Ill. Edn. 2nd. Iss.* 2 vols. in 1. 12mo. Cont. vell. (HD. Sep.22; 265) Frs. 2,450
– – **Anr. Edn.** Ill.:– R. de Hooghe. Amst., 1699. 2 vols. in 1. Sm. 8vo. Extra pict. title, 62 copperplts., mor. by René Kieffer, jnts. & edges worn. (SG. Feb.9; 268) $100
– – **Anr. Edn.** Amst., 1732. *New Edn.* 2 vols. Cont. cf., Vol. 1 rebkd., old spine preserved. (CSK. Sep.16; 42) £75
– – **Anr. Copy.** 2 vols. Sm. 8vo. Cont. marb. cf., spines decor. (HD. May 3; 75) Frs. 1,650
– – **Anr. Edn.** Ill.:– Eisen & Choffard. Amst. [Paris], 1762. *Fermiers Généraux Edn. 1st. Printing.* 2 vols. Sm. 8vo. 11 refused plts., some light foxing, str.-grd. red mor. gt. by Bozérian jeune, spines decor., watered silk liners & end-ll. (HD. May 21; 42) Frs. 20,500
– – **Anr. Copy.** 2 vols. Late 19th. C. red mor., inner & outer dentelle, wtrd. silk doubl. & end-papers, by Puvière. (HD. Mar.30; 10) Frs. 12,000
– – **Anr. Edn.** Ill.:– Aliamet, Choffard & others after Eisen. Amst. [Paris], 1762. *Fermiers Généraux Edn.* 2 vols. Cont. mor. gt. decor. by Derome le Jeune, watered silk liners. (C. May 30; 83) *Beres.* £11,500
– – **Anr. Copy.** 2 vols. 2 frontis. ports., 82 plts., text engrs., cont. Fr. red mor. gt., gt. dentelles; J.H. Bates bkplts. (SG. Apr.26; 109) $1,600
– – **Anr. Copy.** 2 vols. Cont. mor., limp decor. spines, gt. decor., centre arms, inner dentelle; from Lindeboom liby. (HD. Dec.9; 48) Frs. 75,000
– – **Anr. Copy.** 2 vols. Some light foxing, some ll. yellowed, cont. red mor. gt., spines decor. (HD. May 3; 76). Frs. 28,500
– – **Anr. Edn.** Ill.:– after Eisen & others. Amst., 1764. 2 vols. Hf.-titles, engraved port. & 80 plts., 60 culs-de-lampe, some light browning & foxing, red crushed mor. gt. by Sangorski & Sutcliffe, partly unc., s.-c., sm. ex-libris of G.M.O. Barclay. (S. May 10; 313) *Simonds.* £250
– – **Anr. Edn.** Ill.:– port. after Rigault, plts. based on orig. Eisen plts, culs-de-lampe after Choffard. [Paris], 1777. 2 vols. Mod. red mor. gt. (S. Oct.11; 402) *Traylen.* £240
– – **Anr. Edn.** Ill.:– Desrais. L., 1780. 2 vols. 18mo. Cont. cf. gt., spines decor. (HD. May 3; 77) Frs. 2,100
– – **Anr. Edn.** Paris, 1792. 2 vols. Engraved frontis. ports., 83 engraved plts., including 3 additional plts. in different versions from the originals, cont. elab. gt. mor., flat spines gt.-tooled, jnts. & spine extremities slightly worn, s.-c. (C. Nov.9; 89) *Mascardi.* £500
– – **Anr. Copy.** 2 vols. Hf. cf., ca. 1840, initials 'A.R.' on spines (faded). (HD. Mar.21; 46) Frs. 1,150
– – **Anr. Edn.** Ill.:– Fragonard, Le Barbier, Monnet, Touzé, Mallet & others. Paris, 1795. 2 vols. 4to. 20 cont. publd. plts. & 3 plts. not publd. at this time (in mod. printing), mod. bordeaux hf. mor., corners, spines decor., unc.; extra-ill. with 80 figures by Eisen from Fermiers Généraux edn., other ills. by Deveria, Marillier & Johannot, 8vo engrs. remntd. to 4to. (HD. May 3; 78) Frs. 10,500
– – **Anr. Edn.** Ill.:– after Fragonard. Paris, An III [1795]. 2 vols. 4to. 20 plts., including 3 before the letter, some light foxing, 19th. C. mor.-bkd. bds., rubbed. (SPB. Dec.14; 61) $450
– – **Anr. Edn.** Ill.:– Picquet after Rigaud (engraved port.). Paris, 1874. *(100) numbered on Whatman.* 2 vols. Wide margin, Several ll. double in 1st. vol., slightly foxed, mor., gt. spine, cover & inner dentelle, decor., watered silk liners, by A. Chatell, slightly bumped, spine slightly darkened. (HK. Nov.10; 3073) DM 600
– – **Anr. Edn.** Ill.:– A. Derain. Paris, 1950. *(160) numbered on velin de Montval.* 2 vols. 4to. Rough ll. in orig. wraps., orig. bd. covers & s.-c., wraps. browned, covers with some wear. (HK. Nov.11; 3488a) DM 570
– – **Anr. Edn.** Ill.:– André Derain. Paris, priv. ptd., 1950. *(200).* 2 vols. 4to. On vélin de Montval, set of lithos. on Chine, set of 15 unused plts. on Japon, 1 orig. drawing, leaves, box. (HD. Nov.17; 142) Frs. 10,100
– **Dix Contes Choisis.** Paris, 1931. 10 orig. etchings in cols., Jansenist red mor., red mor. doubls., orig. copper engr. inset in upr. cover, by Septier, s.-c. (HD. Dec.9; 37) Frs. 1,450
– **L'Eunuque, Comédie.** Paris, 1654. *Orig. Edn.* 4to. Red mor. by Duru, spine decor.; from Baron Walkenaer & Armand Bertin libys. (HD. Mar.29; 47) Frs. 36,000
– **Fables.** Ill.:– Simon & Coing after Vivier. Paris, 1796. 4 vols. Some ll. remargined, cont. marb. cf., decor. spines, inner roll-stp. (HD. Sep.22; 267) Frs. 11,000
– – **Anr. Edn.** Ill.:– Vivier, engraved by Simon & Coiny. Paris, An IV [1796]. 4 vols. Some slight foxing, spr. cf. gt. by Gaudreau, spines decor. (slightly faded). (HD. May 3; 73) Frs. 3,200
– – **Anr. Edn.** Ill.:– 'J.J. Grandville'. Paris, 1838. *New Edn. 2nd. Printing.* 2 vols. Frontis. on chine, 120 engrs., hf.-titles, some slight foxing, hf. chagrin, corners, by Arnaude, spine decor. with gt. animals by Grandville. (HD. Nov.29; 100) Frs. 2,100
– – **Anr. Edn.** Ill.:– 'Grandville'. Paris, 1859. 19th. C. red mor., gt.-inner dentelle. (HD. Mar.14; 46) Frs. 2,000
– – **Anr. Edn.** Ill.:– Gustave Doré. Paris, 1867. 2 vols. Fo. Plts. & text vigs., elab. gt. cl., worn, shaken, spines reinforced. (SG. Apr.19; 214) $200
– – **Anr. Edn.** Ill.:– G. Doré. Paris, 1868. Fo. Slightly foxed, cont. hf. leath. (HK. May 17; 2454) DM 400
– – **Anr. Edn.** Ill.:– A. Delierre, A. Delâtre. Paris, 1883. *(50) numbered on Whatman.* 2 vols. 4to. Engrs. in 2 states, hf. titles covered by orig. aqua. sigd., mor., decor. & mosaic spines, gt. cover decor., inner dentelle, wrap. & spine preserved, by Champs-Stroobants. (HD. Feb.17; 80) Frs. 3,100
– – **Anr. Edn.** Ill.:– A. Delierre. Paris, 1883. 2 vols. 4to. Red hf. mor. by Champs, spines decor., unc. (HD. Jun.26; 96) Frs. 2,000
– – **Anr. Edn.** Eloge:– Chamfort. Ill.:– Emile Adan etchd. by Le Rat. Paris, 1885. *De Luxe Edn., (10) on Japan.* 2 vols. in 1. Triple series of ills., proof pull with lightly browned plt. margin, hand-bnd. burgundy mor. gt., decor. covers, inner & outer dentelle, mor. doubls. decor., cold. leath. inlays, by Marius Michel. (H. Nov.23; 698a) DM 1,100
– – **Anr. Edn.** Ill.:– Paul Jouve. N.p., 1929. *(30) with suite on japan.* 4to. Leaves, vell. box. (HD. Jun.13; 59) Frs. 4,800
– **Fables. — Contes.** Preface:– Paul Lacroix (2nd. work). Ill.:– Emile Adan (1st. work); Edouard de Beaumont (2nd. work). Paris, 1885. 4 vols. 12mo. On papier vergé, cont. hf. mor., corners, sigd. by Canapé, spines decor., wraps. & spines. (HD. May 16; 43) Frs. 1,900
– – **Anr. Edn.** Ill.:– J. Touchet. Paris, 1941. 4 vols. Hf. mor., corners, mosaic spines, wraps. & spines. (HD. Jun.6; 85) Frs. 2,000
– – **Anr. Edn.** Ill.:– H. Lemarié. Paris, 1966; 1970. 3 vols.; 3 vols. 2nd. work sm. 4to. On vélin de Rives, leaves, ill. wrap., box. (HD. Jun.26; 97) Frs. 4,200
– **Fables Choisies.** Ill.:– J. Cause. La Haye, 1688-94. 5 pts. in 2 vols. 12mo. Cont. cf., decor. spines, some wear. (HD. Dec.9; 46) Frs. 3,200

– – **Anr. Edn.** Ill.:– Jan Van Vianen. Amst., 1693-94. 5 pts. in 1 vol. 12mo. Cont. cf. gt., decor. spine. (HD. Sep.22; 266) Frs. 2,000
– **Fables Choisies mises en Vers.** Ill.:– François Chauveau. Paris, 1668. *1st. Edn.* 4to. Privilege lf. dtd. 31 Mar. 1668, orig. blank at end, 2 tears in Fl affecting text, lge. tear across K3 with loss of 1 letter, tear in O2 affecting text, tear in X3 affecting text, all crudely reprd., several margin tears reprd., title discold. & tear in margin, a few spots & stains, cont. panel mor. gt., head & foot of spine reprd., end-papers renewed. (C. May 30; 86)
Spinoit. £2,000
– – **Anr. Edn.** Paris, 1678-79. 4 pts. in 2 vols. 12mo. Cont. red mor., spines decor.; autograph correction to p. 99, Book II, from Vaux-le-Vicomte liby. (HD. Mar.29; 41) Frs. 68,000
– – **Anr. Edn.** Ill.:– François Chauveau, N. Guérard, & others. Paris, 1709. 5 vols. 12mo. Some minor defects, cont. cf., spines gt. (HD. Mar.19; 64) Frs. 1,800
– – **Anr. Edn.** Ill.:– Aubert, Cochin, Dupuis, & others, after J.B. Oudry. Paris, 1755-59. *(100)* L.P. 4 vols. Lge. fo. Frontis., 275 engraved plts. (2nd. state of 'Le Singe et le Léopard' plt., with legend on banner), hf.-titles, without port. (not always present), margins of 3 plts. in Vol. 1 darkened, margins of 2 text ll. stained & 1 margin of a text lf. slightly torn in Vol. 3, cont. cf. gt., covers gt.-decor., spines gt.-decor. in 7 compartments, foot of spine of Vol. 3 & head of spine of Vol. 4 just chipped, corners slightly worn, slight worming to covers of Vols. 1 & 3. (CNY. May 18; 113)
$6,000
– – **Anr. Edn.** Ill.:– Oudry. Paris, 1755-59. *1st. Edn. 1st. Printing.* 4 vols. Lge. fo. Leath. [by Joseph Cooper?], Vol. 1 covers loose; George IV arms superlibris. (DS. Jan.27; 2178) Pts. 450,000
– – **Anr. Copy.** 4 vols. Fo. Orig. cf. (DS. Oct.28; 2075) Pts. 375,000
– – **Anr. Copy.** 4 vols. Fo. Lacks 5 plts., washed, plts. re-gilded, cont. red mor., greek key decor., roulette & lge. gt. dentelle, sm. tools, angle arms, decor. spines, some scratches & defects. (HD. Dec.9; 47) Frs. 28,000
– – **Anr. Copy.** 4 vols. Fo. Wide margins, some slight foxing, cont. cf. gt., spines decor. (HD. May 3; 72) Frs. 26,000
– – **Anr. Edn.** Ill.:– after Oudry. Paris, 1755-59. *Iss. with plt. for 'La Singe et le Léopard' without lettering on banner.* 4 vols. Fo. 19th. C. hf. mor., slight wear to corners & jnts. (SPB. Dec.14; 62)
$2,500
– – **Anr. Edn.** Ill.:– after Jean Baptiste Oudry. 1755-59. 4 vols. Fo. Wood-engraved vig. titles, port., frontis., 275 plts., hf.-titles, cont. mott. mor. gt. (P. Jun.7; 6) £1,900
– – **Anr. Copy.** 4 vols. Fo. With Oudry port. engraved by Tardieu after Largillière, some light foxing or stains, 1 lf. with sm. paper loss at foot, others with light tears, old red mor., gt. decor., sm. inner dentelle. (HD. Mar.30; 9) Frs. 52,000
– – **Anr. Copy.** 4 vols. Lge. fo. Cont. cf. & mod. hf. cf., 1st. 2 vols. rebnd. in unif. style. (HD. Apr.13; 20) Frs. 6,900
– – **Anr. Copy.** 4 vol. in 2. Lge. fo. Without Oudry port., 1st. ll. slightly soiled, cont. leath. gt., bumped. (BR. Apr.12; 1469) DM 4,600
– – **Anr. Copy.** 4 vols. Fo. Lacks frontis., some browning or staining, cont. marb. leath., gt. spine, & inner dentelle, decor., slightly bumped, corners slightly defect. (HK. Nov.10; 3074) DM 3,000
– – **Anr. Edn.** Ill.:– Fessard. Paris, 1765-75. 6 vols. Cont. Fr. red mor. gt., spines slightly faded, head of spine of Vol. I chipped. (C. May 30; 87)
Lyon. £1,600
– – **Anr. Copy.** 6 vols. Engraved titles, 23 engraved plts., cont. cf. (SPB. Dec.13; 853) $500
– – **Anr. Copy.** 6 vols. Frontis. & 1st. 3 ll. of Vol. I from anr. copy, cont. marb. cf. (HD. Apr.13; 21)
Frs. 4,500
– **Fables Choisies pour les Enfants.** Ill.:– De Monvel. Paris, ca. 1900. Ob. 4to. Slight darkening, orig. decor. cl. (CBA. Aug.21; 413) $110
– **Fables Nouvelles et Autres Poèmes.** Ill.:– François Chauveau. Paris, 1671. *Partly Orig. Edn.* 12mo. Cont. cf., spine decor. (HD. May 3; 71) Frs. 2,300
– **Le Florentin, Comédie.** La Haye [France], 1702. *1st. Imp.* 12mo. Jansenist mor. by Lortic frères,

mor. liners, watered silk end-ll.; from Rattier liby. (HD. Mar.29; 480) Frs. 5,500
– **La Fontaine en Estampes ou Nouvelle Edition des Fables.** Paris, 1821. 4to. Hand-cold. plt. on title, 110 cont. hand-cold. engraved plts., cont. richly blind-stpd. Romantic-style cf., spine gt.; Andres Rours (Barcelona) mor. bkplt. (VS. Dec.7; 404) Fls. 950
– **Ode pour la Paix.** Paris, 1679. *Orig. Edn.* 4to. Jansenist red mor. by A. Cuzin; from Guyot de Villeneuve & E. Daguin libys. (HD. Mar.29; 50)
Frs. 30,000
– **Oeuvres Complettes.** Ill.:– Ribault after Rigault (port.), after J.M. Moreau (copperplts.). Paris, 1814. *1st. Coll. Edn.* Cont. marb. leath. gt., monog. stpd. on title verso, sm. liby. label on spine. (R. Apr.3; 299) DM 2,800
– – **Anr. Edn.** Ill.:– Devéria. 1826. Foxing, chequered cf. by Labreveux, blind- & gt.-decor. (HD. Jan.24; 29) Frs. 2,000
– **Poème de la Captivité de Saint Malc.** Paris, 1673. *Orig. Edn.* 12mo. Jansenist mor. by Trautz-Bauzonnet; dedication corrected in ink (by author?), from libys. of Bertin, Solar, Firmin-Didot, Guyot de Villeneuve & E. Daguin. (HD. Mar.29; 49)
Frs. 16,000
– **Recueil de Poësies Chrétiennes et Diverses.** Ed.:– Louis-Henri Loménie de Brienne. Paris, 1679. *Reprint of 1671 Edn.* 3 vols. 12mo. Cont. red mor., Du Seuil decor, spine decor., red mor. liners. (HD. Mar.29; 51) Frs. 47,000
– **Schwänke und Mährchen von Hans La Fontaine.** Boston [i.e. Berlin], 1811. On vell., cont. hf. leath. gt., marb. paper covered, leath. corners, sm. defects. on lr. cover vol. 1. (GB. May 4; 1365) DM 800
– **Tales & Novels, in Verse.** Paris & N.Y., 1883. *(400)* numbered. 2 vols. Cont. red mor. gt. by Rivière, gt. inner dentelles. (CSK. May 18; 190)
£150
– **Vingt Fables.** Ill.:– Jean Lurcat. Lausanne, 1950. *(250) numbered & sigd. by artist & publisher.* 4to. Loose as iss. in orig. wraps., vell.-bkd. bd. folder, s.-c. (BBA. Jun.14; 230) *Makiya.* £250

LAFOREST
– **L'Art de Soigner les 'Pieds.** Paris, 1782. 12mo. Mod. hf. marb. roan, decor. spine. (HD. Dec.9; 48b) Frs. 1,400

LAFORGUE, Jules
– **Some Poems of** ... Ill.:– Patrick Caulfield. [L.], Petersburg Pr., 1973. *1st. Engl. Edn. (200).* Sq. fo. Identified & sigd. by artist in pencil at limitation p., with the requisite sleeve containing 6 loose col. screenprints, each numbered & sigd. by artist on blank versos, cf., sleeve in matching cf., both inserted in orig. s.-c., bnd. in similar cf., all bdgs. by Rudolph Rieser in Cologne, 1972. (HA. Feb.24; 268) $450

LAFORGUE, L.
– **Die Zahnarzneikunst.** Trans.:– C.F. Angermann. Leipzig, 1803-06. *1st. German Edn.* 3 pts. in 2 vols. Some text ll. lightly foxed, 18 plts. more foxed, cont. style hf. leath. (R. Oct.12; 1508) DM 2,000

LA FOSSE, Jean Charles de
– **Premier [–Septième] Livre de Trophées.** Paris, ca. 1760. Fo. 59 engraved plts., sm. tear reprd., sm. piece torn from 1 corner, cont. mott. cf., spine gt. (C. Dec.9; 78) *Goldschmidt.* £500

LAFRENTZ, Ferdinand W.
– **Cowboy Stuff.** Ill.:– Henry Ziegler. N.Y., 1927. *'Author's Autograph Edn.'. (500) numbered & sigd. by author, artist & publishers.* 4to. Bds., gt.-lettered paper parch. back, unc., light wear, s.-c., some wear. (RO. Dec.11; 183) $170

LAFRERI, Antoine
– **Speculum Romanae Magnificencae.** Rome, 1575. Fo. Title sigd. by Lafreri, 120 plts. (34 sigd. by Lafreri alone), 8 added plts. sigd. by Duchat or his heirs, dtd. 1582-87, anr. plt. dtd. 1565, all cold., outer margins of many engrs. old renewed, cont. vell., Du Seuil decor. (HD. Jun.18; 23)
Frs. 250,000

LAFUENTE, Modesto
– **Historia General de España.** Ed.:– Juan Valera. Barcelona, 1877. 6 vols. Lge. fo. Linen, corners, 1

vol. lacks corners, not unif. (DS. Mar.23; 2335)
Pts. 60,000

LAGARDETTE, DE
– **Les Ruines de Paestum ou Posidonia, mesurées et dessinées sur les Lieux.** Paris, 1799. Lge. fo. Cont. bdg. (HD. Dec.15; 16) Frs. 2,600

LAGRANGE, Ch.
– **Etude sur le Système des Forces du Monde Physique.** Brüssel, 1892. *1st. Edn.* 4to. Author's dedication to Caratheodory, margins slightly browned, cont. hf. leath. (HT. May 8; 434) DM 440

LAGRANGE, Joseph Louis
– **Méchanique Analytique.** Paris, 1788. *1st. Edn.* 4to. Hf.-title, some spotting & light browning, early 19th. C. mott. bds., top of spine slightly worn; Stanitz coll. (SPB. Apr.25; 252) $2,300
– **Théorie des Fonctions Analytiques Contenant les Principes du Calcul Différentiel.** Paris, [1797] An V. *1st. Edn.* 4to. Lacks hf.-title & last blank, liby. stp. on title, new bds., cf. spine. (S. Apr.10; 538)
Perceval. £60
– – **Anr. Copy.** 4to. Errata, mod. cont. style hf. cf., unc. (HD. Apr.13; 71) Frs. 2,000
– – **Anr. Copy.** 4to. Hf.-title, without final blank, sm. ink spots on a few pp., some light spotting, later marb. bds., some wear; Stanitz coll. (SPB. Apr.25; 250) $275
– – **Anr. Edn.** Ed.:– J.A. Serret. Paris, 1847. *3rd. Edn.* 4to. Slightly browned, later hf. leath., slightly bumped & worn; ex-libris. (HT. May 8; 357)
DM 420

LA GRANGE-CHANCEL, François Joseph de
– **Oeuvres Meslées.** Den Haag, 1724. *1st. Edn.* Cont. style cf., gold-tooled decor., gt. spine, inner & outer dentelle. (D. Nov.24; 2507) DM 400

LA GUERINIERE, François-Robichon de
– **Ecole de Cavalerie Contenant la Connoissance, l'Instruction et la Conservation du Cheval.** Ill.:– after Parrocel & Coquart. Paris, 1733. 3 pts. in 1 vol. Sm. fo. Engraved title, 23 plts., including 4 double-p., ½p. engraved plts. to each pt., cont. panel. cf., slightly worn. (PD. Oct.19; 73) £550
– – **Anr. Copy.** Fo. 1 plt. torn & partly reprd., a few tears in text margins, cont. cf. gt., rebkd. (P. Jan.12; 9a) *Greenwood.* £420
– – **Anr. Copy.** Fo. Lacks frontis. & prelims., cont. cf., covers detchd. (P. Dec.8; 297) £300
– – **Anr. Edn.** Ill.:– Audran, Avenline, Beauvais, & others, after Parrocel. Paris, 1751. Fo. Engraved frontis., 24 engraved plts., some folding, 4 prelims. (1 authority calling for 6, but appears compl.), cont. cf., rebkd. (C. Mar.14; 181) *Walford.* £700
– – **Anr. Copy.** Fo. Cont. marb. cf., spine decor., worn; from Château des Noës liby. (HD. May 25; 39) Frs. 11,000

LA GUILLETIERE, Seigneur de
– **Lacédémone, Ancienne et Nouvelle.** 1676. 2 pts. in 1 vol. 12mo. Spr. cf., some defects. (HD. Jun.29; 95) Frs. 1,100

LA HARPE, Jean François de
– **Abrégé de l'Histoire Générale des Voyages.** Ill.:– Bernard. Paris, 1780. 22 vols. including atlas. 8vo. & 4to. 82 plts. (lacks plt. 57, dupl. of plt. 56), 77 maps, mostly folding, 3 loosely inserted, text vols. cont. Fr. mott. cf., spines gt., some scraped or very sm. wormholes, atlas cont. bds., cf. spine gt. (S. Apr.10; 295) *Marshall.* £640
– – **Anr. Edn.** Paris, 1780-1801. *1st. Edn.* 32 vols. Lacks all maps, cont. mott. cf. gt., worn. (SG. Sep.22; 184) $175
– – **Anr. Edn.** Paris, 1825. 24 vols. & atlas. 8vo. & sm. fo. Foxing, decor. red mor. (Vol. 3 defect.), atlas hf. roan. (SM. Mar.7; 2156) Frs. 2,000
– **Correspondance Littéraire adressée à son Altesse Impériale Monseigneur le Grand-Duc, aujourd'hui Empereur de la Russie.** Paris, 1801. 6 vols. Cont. spr. cf., decor. spines. (HD. Sep.22; 269)
Frs. 1,400
– **Lycée ou Cours de Littérature Ancienne et Moderne.** Paris, 1816. 15 vols. Some foxing, bradel decor. tree cf., Louis XVIII arms. (SM. Mar.7; 2157) Frs. 4,800
– – **Anr. Edn.** Paris, 1827. 16 vols. Cont. decor. cf. (HD. Mar.19; 63) Frs. 1,000

LA HARPE, Jean François de -*Contd.*

– **Tangu et Féline.** Ill.:– Marillier. Paris, 1780. Lge. 8vo. On holland, jansenist red mor. by Gruel, arms. (HD. May 3; 80) Frs. 1,100

LA HIRE, Philippe de
– **La Gnomonique ou Méthodes Universelles pour Tracer des Horloges Solaires ou Cadrans sur Toutes Sortes de Surfaces.** Paris, 1698. 12mo. Cont. cf., spine decor. (HD. Nov.9; 179) Frs. 1,200
– **Traité de Mécanique.** Paris, 1695. *1st. Edn.* 12mo. Cont. spr. cf., spine gt., spine slightly worn; E.N. da C. Andrade bkplt., Stanitz coll. (SPB. Apr.25; 254) $400

LAHONTAN, Louis Armand, Baron de
– **New Voyages to North America** ... L., 1703. *1st. Engl. Edn.* 2 vols. 4 engraved maps, including 3 folding, 20 engraved plts., including allegorical frontis. in Vol. 2 (not present in all copies), advt. lf. at end Vol. 1, cont. mott. panel. cf., spine ends chipped; the Rt. Hon. Visc. Eccles copy. [Sabin 38644] (CNY. Nov.18; 165) $1,100
– – **Anr. Edn.** L., 1735. 2 vols. Frontis., 43 ills. on 13 plts. (3 folding), 5 maps on 4 sheets (2 folding), 2 plans (1 folding), cont. cf. [Sabin 38645] (S. May 22; 325) *McCall.* £500
– **Nouveaux Voyages ... dans l'Amérique Septentrionale. — Memoires de l'Amérique Septentrionale.** The Hague, 1703. *1st. Edn. 1st. Iss., with angel vig. on title & larger folding maps.* Together 2 vols. 4 engraved frontis., 3 engraved maps, including 2 folding, 22 folding engraved plts., 2 plts. just shaved, 1 very slightly defect. at corner, some slight browning. [Sabin 38635-6] (*With:*) – **Suite du Voyage, de l'Amérique** ... Amst., 1704. *1st. Edn. Re-iss., with a new title-p.* 2 pts. in 1 vol. 2 folding engraved maps, 4 folding engraved plts., some slight browning. [Sabin 38643] Together 3 vols. 16mo. Cont. spr. cf., rebkd. & gt. with corners restored; Philip, Earl of Hardwicke bkplts., the Rt. Hon. Visc. Eccles copies. (CNY. Nov.18; 164) $1,400
– **Voyages ... dans l'Amérique Septentrionale. — Mémoires de l'Amérique Septentrionale.** Amst., 1705. Together 2 works in 1 vol. 1 engraved folding map detchd., sm. holes at fold, 1st. 2 ll. of 2nd. vol. wormed. [Sabin 38641-2] (*Bound with:*) – **Suite du Voyage, de l'Amérique.** Amst., 1704. *1st. Edn.* [Sabin 38643] Together 3 works in 1 vol. 12mo. Cont. bds. (C. Nov.16; 109) *Faupel.* £650

LAIGNEL-LAVASTINE, Prof. M.
– **Histoire Générale de la Médecine, de la Pharmacie, de l'Art Dentaire et de l'Art Vétérinaire.** Paris, 1936/49. 3 vols. 4to. Orig. ptd. wraps., worn on spines. (TA. Jun.21; 466) £85

LAING, David
– **Hints for Dwellings, consisting of Original Designs for Cottages, Farm-Houses, Villas &c. &c.** L., 1841. 4to. 34 engraved plts., margins dampstained, orig. bds. worn, covers detchd., loose. (*With:*) – **Catalogue du Cabinet de Tableaux de l'Abbé Du Jardin.** Bruges, ca. 1860. Fo. 47 litho. ills. on 46 plts., some top margins dampstained, some ll. spotted, cont. roan-bkd. bds., covers detchd., worn. (S. Apr.30; 311) *Elliott.* £90

LAING, John
– **Voyage to Spitzbergen.** Edinb., 1818. *2nd. Edn.* 12mo. Head of title-p. cropped, lacks last lf. (blank?) cont. hf. cf., slightly rubbed. (BBA. Feb.9; 329) *Hannas.* £65

LAING, Rev. John
See— **HALKETT, Samuel & Laing, Rev. John**

LAIRE, F.-X.
– **Index Librorum ab Inventa Typographia ad Annum 1500.** Senonges, 1791. 2 vols. Prices & buyers in red ink, cont. Fr. mor., gt. decor., inner & outer dentelle, slightly spotted. (HK. Nov.11; 4452) DM 500

LAIRESSE, Gerard de
– **Anleitung zur Zeichen-Kunst. Wie man dieselbe durch Hülff der Geometrie, gründlich und vollkommen erlernen Könne** ... Trans.:– S.T. Geriken. Berlin, [1705]. *1st. German Edn.* (*Bound with:*) **BOSSE, A. – Regel — mässige Zeichnungen und Vortheilhafte Hand-Griffe wonach man die Steine richtig hauen** ... Nürnberg, 1721. Together 2 works in 1 vol. Sm. 4to. Cut slightly short in upr. margin, some light discol., cont. vell. (H. May 22; 152) DM 1,300
– **Groot Schildersboek, waar in de Schilderkonst Grondig werd onderweezen** ... Amst., 1714. *3rd. Edn.* 2 pts. in 1 vol. 4to. Engraved titles, port., 66 plts., some stains in text, cont. vell., soiled. (VG. Sep.14; 926) Fls. 500
– – **Anr. Edn.** Ill.:– Pool, G. v. Gouwen, Lairesse & others. Haarlem, 1740. *2nd. Edn.* 2 vols. in 1. 4to. Engraved frontis. port. & 60 engrs. & etched plts., some folding, some foxing, cont. vell., a little soiled. (VS. Jun.7; 868) Fls. 550
– **The Principles of Drawing.** L., 1730. 2 vols. 4to. 53 engraved plts., 1 soiled, orig. wraps., spines torn. (P. May 17; 186) *Jarndyce.* £130

LAIRITZ, Johann Georg
– **Neu-angelegter Histor.-Genealog. Palm-Wald** ... Nuremb., 1686. Fo. Cont. vell. (HK. Nov.8; 1102) DM 620

LA JONCHERE, L. de
– **Nouvelle Méthode de Fortifier les plus Grandes Villes** ... Paris, 1718. *Orig. Edn.* 12mo. Cont. red mor. gt., polychrome double. & end-papers on gold ground. (HD. Mar.19; 106) Frs. 1,300

LAKE, William
– **The Parochial History of Cornwall.** 1867. *1st. Edn.* 4 vols. Orig. cl. (LA. Nov.29; 109) £68

LAKING, Sir Guy Francis
– **A Record of European Armour & Arms through Seven Centuries.** 1920-22. 5 vols. 4to. Orig. buckram, unc. (PD. Oct.19; 257) £230
– **Sevres Porcelain of Buckingham Palace & Windsor Castle.** L., 1907. *[1st. Edn.].* 4to. Later mor. gt. (S. Dec.13; 457) *Jameson.* £120
– – **Anr. Copy.** Lge. 4to. 63 cold. plts., lettered tissue-guards, ex-liby., hf. mor., loose, with dupls. of 16 cold. plts., each stpd. on verso. (SG. May 3; 83) $200
– – **Anr. Copy.** 4to. A few edges with minor chips, disbnd. (SG. Jan.26; 157) $150

LALAISSE, Hippolyte
– **Empire Français.** Paris, 1853-55. 4to. Lacks 8 plts., Hf. cl. bds.; from Château des Noës liby. (HD. May 25; 40) Frs. 1,000
– **Galérie Armoricaine. Costumes et Vues Pittoresques de la Bretagne** ... Text:– J.C. Le Meder. Nantes, 1858. 5 pts. in 2 vols. 4to. 5 litho. title-frontis., 5 maps, 100 costume lithos., cold. & gommées, 25 camaîeu lithos., publisher's gt. cl. bds., covers soiled. (HD. Jul.2; 21) Frs. 12,500
– **Uniformes de l'Armée et de la Marine (1848-1852).** N.d. *1st. Printing.* 4to. 32 (of 40) chromolitho. plts., hf. mor., corners, spine faded. (HD. Jan.27; 278) Frs. 2,200

LALANDE, Jerome le Français
– **Astronomie.** Paris, 1792. *3rd. Edn.* 3 vols. Lge. 4to. Hf.-titles, port., 33 folding engraved plts., cont. mott. cf., jnts. brkn., armor. bkplt. in each vol. of Sir George Shuckburgh. (SG. Apr.26; 122) $500

LALANDE, Michel-Richard de
[–] **Ballet De La Jeunesse, Divertissement Meslé de Comédie & de Musique ... libretto.** Paris, 1686. 4to. Engraved frontis. trimmed at lr. margin, mod. 18th. C. style bds. (S. May 10; 80) *Macnutt.* £700
– **Motets ... Avec un Discours sur la Vie et les Oeuvres de L'Autheur** ... Paris, 1729. *1st. Edn.* Books I-XIX in 10 vols. Fo. Blank corners of a few ll. torn away, some staining, cont. pol. cf., some gt. ornamental spines & corners reprd., others a little rubbed & worn; stp. of Bibliothèque Du Roi Palais Royal on 4 title-pp., gt. arms of Comte & Comtesse de Toulouse in triple gt. fillets on covers, a little rubbed & stained; from Toulouse-Philidor collection. (S. May 10; 78) *Macnutt.* £5,000
– – **Anr. Copy.** Books I-IV, V-VII & XVII-XX, in 3 vols. Fo. Margins of several ll. wormed & stained in 1st. vol., a few minor tears, 1 corner reprd., cont. spr. vell. bds., rebkd. with spr. cf., corners reprd., mod. labels on spines; from collection of St. Michael's College, Tenbury. (S. May 10; 79) *DPL.* £2,500

LALLEMENT DE METZ, Guillaume
[–] **Choix de Rapports, Opinions et Discours à la Tribune Nationale depuis 1789 jusqu'à ce Jour.** Paris, 1818-21. Vol. 1, year 1789 – vol. XVI, year 1795-99 in 16 vols. Hf. roan. (HD. Feb.22; 186) Frs. 8,000
– – **Anr. Edn.** 1818-22. 21 vols. (lacks table vol.). Foxing, cont. roan. (HD. Jan.24; 31) Frs. 2,500

LA LAURENCIE, L.
See— **LAVIGNAC, A. & La Laurencie, L.**

LA LOUBERE, Simon de
– **Du Royaume de Siam.** Paris, 1691. 2 vols. 12mo. 40 maps & plts., cf. (P. Dec.8; 342) *Shapero.* £90
– **A New Historical Relation of the Kingdom of Siam.** L., 1693. 2 pts. in 1 vol. Sm. fo. 11 engraved plts. & maps, some spotting, cont. hf. cf., crudely reprd. [Wing L201] (BBA. Jul.27; 110) *Ad Orientem.* £500
– **Anr. Copy.** 2 vols. in 1. Fo. 11 engraved plts. & maps, slight browning, bkplt. pasted to title verso, cont. mott. cf., slightly rubbed, rebkd. (S. Dec.13; 153) *Edwards.* £300

LALSZ, Gyula
See— **BRASSAI**

LA MARCHE, Olivier de
– **Le Chevalier Delibère.** Ed.:– F. Lippmann. 1898. 4to. Orig. buckram-bkd. bds.; H.M. Nixon coll. (BBA. Oct.6; 187) *Blackwell.* £55

LAMARCK, Jean Baptiste, Chevalier de
– **Flore Française, ou Description Succincte de Toutes les Plantes qui croissent naturellement en France.** Paris, 1795. *2nd. Edn.* 3 vols. Cont. tree cf. gt., decor. spines, upr. turn-ins restored. (HD. Sep.21; 138) Frs. 1,000
– **Histoire Naturelle des Animaux sans Vertèbres.** Paris, 1815-22. *1st. Edn.* 7 pts. in 8 vols. Slightly browned thro.-out, 2 sigs. loose vol. IV, 2 margin defects. vol. VI, end-paper with defect. in vol. VII, cont. hf. leath., slightly rubbed & bumped. (HT. May 8; 606) DM 1,900
– **Tableau Encyclopédique et Méthodique des Trois Règnes de la Nature: Botanique.** 1793. 7 vols. 4to. Over 650 engraved plts. (incompl.), text incompl., practically unbnd. (HD. Jul.6; 51) Frs. 3,300

LAMARTINE, Alphonse Marie Louis Prat de
– **Histoire de la Restauration.** Bruxelles, 1851-53. *Belgian Edn.* 8 vols. Sm. 8vo. Cont. marb. cf. gt., spines decor. (HD. Jun.26; 18) Frs. 1,000
– **Méditations Poétiques.** Paris, 1837. 2 vols. Cont. glazed cf. gt. (HD. Mar.27; 19) Frs. 4,600
– **Raphaël.** Ill.:– Sandoz, engraved by Champollion. Paris, n.d. Red mor. gt. by Rivière & Son. (HD. May 4; 327) Frs. 1,800

LA MARTINIERE, Pierre Martin de
– **Voyage des Pays Septentrionavx.** Paris, 1676. *2nd. Fr. Edn.* Lightly browned & stained, cont. leath., spine renewed. (HK. Nov.8; 1110) DM 460

LA MARTINIERE, Pierre Martin de & Martens, Friedrich
– **De Noordsche Weereld; Vertoond in Twee Nieuwe ... Reysen.** Trans.:– S. de Vries. Amst., 1685. 4to. Frontis., map (incompl.), 18 (of 20) plts., stained & soiled, cont. vell., soiled. (VG. Sep.14; 1104) Fls. 500

LAMB, Lady Caroline
[–] **Ada Reis, A Tale.** 1823. *1st. Edn.* 3 vols. in 1. 4pp. engraved mus., cont. cf. gt., lightly faded. (CSK. May 18; 97) £300

LAMB, Charles
– **Elia. — Last Essays of Elia.** L., 1823; 1833. *1st. Edn.; 1st. Engl. Edn.,. 1st. work 1st. Iss.* Together 2 vols. 1st. work without final 3 advt. ll., 2nd. work, hf.-title, single lf. only of advts., hf. mor. gt., by Tout, s.-c.; Fred A. Berne copy. (SPB. May 16; 320) $300
– – **Anr. Edn.** Ill.:– H.W. Bray. Gregy. Pr., 1931. *(285) numbered. (25) specially bnd.* 2 vols. Orig. blind-tooled mor., spines & top of upr. cover of 2nd. vol. faded. (S. Nov.22; 275) *Maggs.* £350
– **The Works** ... L., 1894-1907. 7 vols. Hf. mor. gt. (PNY. Jun.6; 455) $110

See— **COLERIDGE, Samuel Taylor, Lamb, Charles & Lloyd, Charles**

LAMB, Charles & Mary
- Tales from Shakespeare. Ill.:– A. Rackham. 1909. *(750) numbered & sigd. by artist.* 4to. Cl. gt., slightly soiled, ties. (P. Sep.29; 382) *Dee.* £220
- – Anr. Copy. 4to. Cl. gt., spine discold. (LH. Sep.25; 442) $225

LAMB, Edward Buckton
- Studies of Ancient Domestic Architecture. L., 1846. Fo. 20 litho. plts., slightly spotted, some plts. & ll. loose & slightly frayed, orig. roan-bkd. cl., worn. (S. Mar.6; 283) *Weinreb.* £50

LAMB, H.
- Sketches of Malvern & its Vicinity. Ca. 1830. Ob. 4to. 12 cold. litho. plts., orig. cl. (P. Apr.12; 40) *Tempetley.* £130

LAMB, Horace
- Hydrodynamics. Camb., 1895. *2nd. Edn.* Orig. cl., slight spotting of fore-e. & end-papers; Ernst Mach's stp. on title, Stanitz coll. (SPB. Apr.25; 255) $275

LAMB, Roger
- An Original & Authentic Journal of Occurrences during the late American War. Dublin, 1809. 24 p. list of subscribers, cont. tree cf., spine gt.; the Rt. Hon. Visc. Eccles copy. [Sabin 38724] (CNY. Nov.18; 166) $380

LAMBARDE, William
- Archaionomia. L., 1568. *1st. Edn.* 4to. In Anglo-Saxon & Latin, margin annots. in cont. & near-cont. hands, cont. cf., corners reprd., spine rebkd. [STC 15142] (S. Mar.6; 434) *Seibu.* £320
- Eirenarcha: Or of the Office of the Justices of Peace in Foure Bookes. 1592. *2nd. Edn.* Sm. 4to. Title slightly soiled & frayed at edges, lacks last lf./ll.?, cont. vell., soiled. (TA. Nov.17; 539) £58
- – Anr. Edn. L., 1594. Corner torn from A4 & Oo3, 1 side-note cropped. [STC 15168] *(Bound with:)* - The Duties of Constables, Borsholders, Tythingmen ... L., 1594. Slight worming in a few lr. margins, occasionally affecting text. [STC 15150] Together 2 works in 1 vol. Sm. 8vo. Cont. cf.; inscr. 'John Vincent 1678' on end-lf. (S. Mar.6; 437) *Page.* £280
- A Perambulation of Kent. L., 1576. *1st. Edn.* 4to. Lacks Lyne's map, lr. margins of prelims. & headlines cropped, margin repairs to title, Oo3 & Iii1, some staining & spotting, cont. cf., spine slightly wormed. [STC 15175] (S. Mar.6; 436) *Sanders.* £150
- – Anr. Edn. 1596. *2nd. Edn.* Lacks folding map, names on title, little staining, old cf., worn, partly loose. [STC 15176] (BBA. Jul.27; 333) *Bennett & Kerr Books.* £120

LAMBECK, P. & Nessel, Daniel de
- Catalogus, sive Recensio Specialis Omnium Codicum Manuscriptorum Graecorum ... Augustissimae Bibliothecae Caesareae Vindobonensis. Vienna & Nuremb., 1690. 6 pts. in 2 vols. Fo. 112 copper engrs. (28 folding), 18th. C. marb. cf., spines decor. (HD. Mar.9; 62) *Frs.* 2,900

LAMBERT, Abbé
- Histoire Litteraire du Regne de Louis XIV. Paris, 1751. *1st. Edn.* 3 vols. 4to. Hf.-titles, cont. cf. (GM. Dec.7; 612) £75

LAMBERT, Jean Clarence
- Jardin Errant. Ill.:– C.G. Beverloo 'Corneille'. Milan, 1963. *(121) sigd. by author & artist.* 4to. 8 orig. cold. lithos., orig. wrap., box, cl. (B. Feb.8; 367) *Fls.* 700

LAMBERT, John
- Travels through Lower Canada & the United States of North America, in the years 1806, 1807, & 1808. L., 1810. *1st. Edn.* 3 vols. Folding engraved map, hand-cold. engraved chart, 16 aquatint plts., map torn at fold, some ll. browned, particularly quire 2H in Vol. 1, some staining & offsetting, cont. hf. cf., rebkd., new end-papers, corners worn; the Rt. Hon. Visc. Eccles copy. [Sabin 38734] (CNY. Nov.18; 167) $950

– – Anr. Edn. L., 1813. 2 vols. Cold. folding map, cold. plan, 16 aquatints (6 cold.), cf., rebkd. [Sabin 38734] (S. Jun.25; 104) *Faupel.* £280
– – Anr. Edn. 1814. *2nd. Edn.* 2 vols. Engraved folding map hand-cold., cont. cf., spines gt.; from liby. of Luttrellstown Castle, w.a.f. (C. Sep.28; 1746) £320
– – Anr. Edn. L., 1816. 2 vols. Cold. folding map, cold. plan, 16 aquatints (6 cold.), map with tear reprd., orig. roan-bkd. bds., unc. [Sabin 38734] (S. Jun.25; 103) *Remmington.* £300

LAMBERT, P. (Ed.)
See— **ROSEN-ZEITUNG**

LAMBETH, William A. & Manning, Warren H.
- Thomas Jefferson: As an Architect & a Designer of Landscapes. Boston, 1913. *1st. Edn. (535) numbered on L.P.* 4to. 54 plts., sm. owner's stp. on title & 3 other ll., cl. (SG. Oct.13; 209) $110

LAMBRICHS, G.
- Chaystre ou les Plaisirs Incommodes. Ill.:– Wols. Paris, 1948. *(50) De Luxe Edn. with 2 etchings sigd. & numbered by Wols.* Sm. 8vo. On alfa paper, orig. wraps. (H. May 23; 1565) DM 3,100

LAMBTON, J.G., First Earl of Durham
See— **DURHAM, J.G. Lambton, First Earl of**

LA MENARDAYE, M. de
- Examen et Discussion Critique de l'Histoire des Diables de Loudon de la Possession des Religieuses Ursulines et de la Condamnation d'Urbain Grandier. Liège, 1749. 12mo. Cont. marb. cf., decor. spine. (HD. Dec.9; 49) *Frs.* 1,200

LA MESANGERE, Pierre Antoine Leboux de
- Collection de Meubles et Objets de Goût. Ca. 1805. Fo. 123 cont. cold. plts., wraps. (HD. Mar.14; 54) *Frs.* 10,000
- Costumes des Femmes Françaises du XII au XVIIIe Siècle. Ill.:– after Lante, ptd. by Wittman. Paris, 1900. *New Edn. of 1827 'Galerie Française de Femmes Celèbres'.* Sm. 4to. 70 hand-cold. copperplts., three-qtr. mor. (SG. Aug.25; 107) $110
- Journal des Dames et des Modes. Paris, 1806-12. 3 vols. 485 cold. plts., incompl., hf. chagrin, ca. 1860, spines decor.; from Château des Noës liby. (HD. May 25; 41) *Frs.* 7,500
- Les Petits Mémoires de Paris. Ill.:– Henri Boutet. Paris, 1908-09. *(50) De Luxe Edn. on japan with supp. series of etchings.* 6 vols. Hand-bnd. cf. gt., cover vig., wear; Hauswedell coll. (H. May 24; 1231) DM 460

LA METTRIE, Julien Offray de
- Système de Monsieur Herman Boerhaave, sur les Maladies Vénériennes. Paris, 1735. *Orig. Edn.* 12mo. Sm. ink stains in corners of 3 ll., cont. cf., spine decor.; Author's copy, with his MS. corrections. (HD. Nov.29; 59) *Fls.* 13,000

LAMI, Eugene
- Collection des Armes de la Cavalerie Française en 1831 (1834). Paris, n.d. Fo. 8 (of 10) lithos., 1 loose with trace of fold, bds. (HD. Jan.27; 282) *Frs.* 2,500
- Souvenirs de Londres. Paris, 1826. Ob. 4to. 12 hand-cold. lithos., later hf. mor., orig. wraps. bnd. in. (CSK. Dec.2; 32) £400

LA MODE. Revues des Modes. Galérie de Moeurs. Album des Salons
Oct. 1829– Sep. 1830. 4 vols. Plts. partly browned or foxed, no bdg. (D. Nov.24; 4353) DM 600

LA MORLIERE, Chevalier Rochette de
- [-] Angola Histoire Indienne. Ill.:– Eisen. 1751. *New Edn.* 2 vols. in 1. 16mo. With vig. 'au carosse', red mor. gt. by Lortic, spine decor.; from libys. of Danyau, Delbergue, Cormont & Jules Lemaître. (HD. May 3; 81) *Frs.* 3,100

LAMOTHE LE VAYER, François de
- Oeuvres. Paris, 1671-70. 15 vols. 12mo. Cont. cf., spines decor. (HD. Mar.19; 66) *Frs.* 1,050

LA MOTTE, Antoine Houdart de
- Fables Nouvelles. Ill.:– after Coypel (frontis.), after Gillot, Picart & others (copper engrs.). Paris, 1719. 4to. Some pp. slightly browned, cont. leath. gt. (R. Apr.3; 300) DM 1,300

– – Anr. Edn. [Paris], ca. 1730. MS. title on 2nd. leaf, 65 (of 100) copperplts., lightly browned, some staining, cont. leath., defect., upr. cover loose. (HT. May 9; 1467) DM 500
- Neue Fabeln. Trans.:– C.G. Glafey. Ill.:– G. Böhmer (frontis.). Frankfurt & Leipzig, 1736. Title lf. & last lf. with upr. corner excised, slight loss, 1 vig. mntd., cont. vell., slightly spotted & bumped, cont. owners mark on end-paper. (HT. May 9; 1468) DM 500

LA MOTTE, Guillaume Mauquest de
- A General Treatise of Midwifery. Trans.:– Thomas Tomkyns. L., 1746. *1st. Engl. Edn.* Cont. cf., slightly rubbed. (S. Dec.13; 281) *Phillips.* £180

LAMOTTE, T.
- Voyage dans le Nord de l'Europe. 1813. 4to. Extra engraved title, folding map, engraved plts., slight spotting & offsetting, short tear in map, later hf. mor. (S. Apr.9; 37) *Hannas.* £105

LA MOTTE FOUQUE, Friedrich Heinrich Karl, Baron de
- Dramatische Spiele von Pellegrin. Berlin, 1804. *1st. Edn.* 1 vol. *(With:)* - Der Held des Nordens. Berlin, 1810. *1st. Edn.* 3 vols. in 1. Together 2 vols. Sm. 8vo. Cont. hf. cf. (C. Dec.9; 214) *Quaritch.* £240
- Undine. Ill.:– Julius Höppner. L., ca. 1880's. Fo. 9 cold. plts., orig. pict. cl. gt. (P. Dec.8; 390) *Ferret Fantasy.* £58
– – Anr. Edn. Ill.:– Julius Höppner. Wandsbeck, [1884]. Lge. fo. Some light foxing, orig. cl. gt., decor., by J.E. Bösenberg of Leipzig. (B. Oct.4; 642) *Fls.* 480
– – Anr. Edn. Ill.:– Arthur Rackham. L., 1909. *1st. Trade Edn.* Gt.-decor. cl., ill. end-papers. (CBA. Aug.21; 511a) $140
– – Anr. Edn. Ill.:– A. Rackham. L., 1909. *(1000) numbered & sigd. by artist.* 4to. Vell. gt., soiled, lacks ties. (P. Sep.29; 383) £130
– – Anr. Copy. 4to. Orig. parch. gt., spine soiled, worn, lacks ties. (S. Dec.20; 575) *Roberts.* £100
– – Anr. Edn. Ill.:– Arthur Rackham. 1912. *(40) numbered on japon impérial, sigd. by artist.* 4to. No bdg. stated. (HD. Jun.26; 131) *Frs.* 3,300

LA MOTTRAYE, Aubrey de
- Travels. Ill.:– Hogarth, Vertue & others. L., 1723. *1st. Edn.* Vols. I & II only, lacks Vol. III. Fo. 4 folding maps, 44 plts., most folding, subscribers list, privilege lf., plt. 6 defect., some foxing, few tears, prelims. remargined, hf. mor. gt. (SG. Sep.22; 185) $550

LAMOUR, Jean
- Recueil des Ouvrages en Serrurerie que Stanislas le Bienfaisant Roy de Pologne ... a fait poser sur la Place Royale de Nancy. Ill.:– Collin & Nicole. Nancy, priv. ptd., 1767. Lge. fo. Engraved title, dedication with ill., lge. folding plt. in 3 sheets, 18 single-sheet plts., an additional plt. (cut & laid down) at end, & 2 orig. ll. of ink & wash drawings, lge. plt. with tears at folds & some wear, mod. hf. cf., w.a.f. (C. Dec.9; 79) *Lyon.* £300

LAMPADIUS, Wilhelm August
- Handbuch der Allgemeinen Hüttenkunde. Göttingen, 1804-05. 2 vols. Cont. hf. leath. gt. (R. Oct.12; 1578) DM 540

LAMPE, M.A. & Davenport, H.
- Das Pferd. Leipzig, 1902-04. *1st. Edn.* 2 vols. Orig. pict. linen. (GB. May 3; 1111) DM 450

LAMPORT, Felicia
- Light Metres. Ill.:– Edward Gorey. N.Y., [1982]. *1st. Edn. (26) lettered, sigd. by author & artist.* Sm. 8vo. Gt.-pict. cl., tissue d.-w., s.-c. (SG. May 24; 300) $120

LAMPRONTI, Yitshak
- Pahad Yitshak. Venice; Livorno, 1750, 1796; 1840. *1st. Edns.* Vols. 1, 2 pt. 2, & 5 only (of 5). Fo. Some browning or dampstaining, owners' stps., qtr. leath. shabby. (SG. Feb.2; 220) $325

LAMY, Bernard
- De Tabernaculo Foederis, De Sancta Civitate Jerusalem, et De Templo Ejus Libri Septem. Paris,

LAMY, Bernard -*Contd.*

1720. Fo. Owner's stp. on title, cont. vell., soiled, vell. sprung, end-paper defect. near upr. cover fore-e. (SG. Feb.2; 92) $200

LANA [TERZI], Francesco
- **Prodromo overo Saggio di Alcune Inventione Nuove.** Brescia, 1670. *1st. Edn.* Fo. Some margins lightly foxed, cont. vell. (R. Oct.12; 1622)
DM 2,200

LANCASTER, Albert
- **Quatre Mois au Texas: Notes de Voyage.** Mons, 1887. *2nd. Edn.* Ptd. bds., worn. (SG. Aug.4; 304)
$175

LANCHESTER, F.W.
- **Aerodynamics.** L., 1907. *1st. Edn.* (*With:*)
- **Aerodonetics.** L., 1908. *1st. Edn.* Together 2 vols. Orig. cl.; sig. of A.E. Bush, R.A.F., Stanitz coll. (SPB. Apr.25; 258) $300
- **The Flying Machine: Two Papers, The Aerofoil & the Screw Propeller.** L., 1915. *1st. Edn.* 'With author's compliments' stp. on end-papers. (*With:*)
- **Aerodynamics.** L., 1907. *1st. Edn.* J.P. Den Hartog sig. on title. (*With:*) - **Aerodonetics.** N.Y., 1909. *1st. Amer. Edn.* James S. Stephens sig. on end-papers, Together 3 vols. Orig. cl., 1st. vol. soiled; John D. Stanitz coll. (SPB. Apr.25; 6)
$125

LANCISI, Joannes Maria
- **De Subitaneis Mortibus Libri II.** Rome, 1707. *1st. Edn.* 4to. Cont. bds., spine slightly defect., unc. (BR. Apr.12; 738) DM 550
- - **Anr. Edn.** Lucca, 1707. *2nd. Edn.* 4to. Sm. tear in M1 & 2, cf., rebkd.; Dr. Walter Pagel copy. (S. Feb.7; 226) *Phelps.* £280
- **Dissertatio de Nativis, deque Adventitiis Romani Coeli Qualitatibus, cui accedit Historia Epidemiae Rheumaticae.** Rome, 1711. 4to. Some browning, cont. Italian red mor. gt., Pope Clement XI arms, some light staining, traces of worn in spine. (C. May 30; 117) *Quaritch.* £500

LANCKISCH, Friedrich
- **Concordantiae Bibliorum Germanico-Hebraico-Graecae ...** Leipzig & Frankfurt, 1688. Lge. fo. Cont. pig. over wooden bds., bdg. wormed, lacks clasps. (SG. Feb.9; 128) $225

LANCKORONSKA, Maria & Oehler, R.
- **Die Buchillustration des XVIII Jahrhunderts in Deutschland, Osterreich und der Schweiz.** Leipzig, 1932-34. *(300).* 3 vols. 4to. On Bütten, orig. bds., spotted. (H. Nov.23; 12) DM 600
- - **Anr. Edn.** Frankfurt, 1932-34. *(200) numbered for Frankfurt Bibliophilen Ges.* 3 vols. 4to. Orig. bds., spines faded. (HK. Nov.11; 4471) DM 850
- - **Anr. Copy.** 3 vols. 4to. On Bütten, orig. bds., lightly browned. (H. Nov.23; 45) DM 720

LANCKORONSKA, Maria & Rümann, A.
- **Geschichte der Deutschen Taschenbücher und Almanache aus der Klassisch-romantischen Zeit.** München, 1954. *Ltd. Iss.* Orig. hf. leath., s.-c. (GB. Nov.4; 1248) DM 500
- - **Anr. Copy.** Orig. hf. leath., s.-c. (GB. May 4; 1781) DM 480

LANCOSME-BREVES, Le comte Savary de
- **De l'équitation et des Haras.** Paris, 1843. 4to. L.P., later hf. cl., wraps. preserved. (HD. Jan.27; 200) Frs. 1,500

LAND WE LIVE IN (The)
N.d. 3 vols. 48 pp. of plts., spotting, hf. mor., rubbed. (P. Feb.16; 130) £65

LANDAU, E.
- **Vorlesungen Uber Zahlentheorie.** Leipzig, 1927. *1st. Edn.* 3 vols. Orig. linen, vol. 1 with MS. dedication to Caratheodory. (HT. May 8; 437)
DM 950

LANDAU, G.
- **Beiträge zur Geschichte der Jagd und der Falknerei in Deutschland.** Kassel, 1849. Foxed, cont. hf. leath. gt., bumped, spine worn. (R. Apr.4; 1925)
DM 650

LANDAU, Baron Horace de & Finaly, Mme., of Florence
- **Catalogue of Very Important Illuminated Manuscripts & Printed Books selected from the Renowned Library.** 1948-49. 3 pts. in 1 vol. 4to. Sale catalogue, cl.; H.M. Nixon coll., with Pt. 1 heavily annotated by him. (BBA. Oct.6; 156)
Beres. £120

LANDE, Lawrence
- **The Lawrence Lande Collection of Canadiana in the Redpath Library of McGill University. A Bibliography.** Montreal, 1965. *(950) numbered & sigd.* Fo. Orig. mor.-bkd. cl., s.-c., unc. (BBA. Nov.10; 30) *Howes.* £110
- - **Anr. Copy.** Lge. fo. Qtr. pig & holland bds., partly unc., boxed; the Rt. Hon. Visc. Eccles copy. (CNY. Nov.18; 168) $300
- - **Anr. Copy.** Sm. fo. Pig-bkd. buckram, boxed. (SG. Sep.15; 203) $200
- **Rare & Unusual Canadiana: First Supplement to the Lande Bibliography.** Montreal, 1971. *(500) numbered & sigd.* 4to. Two-tone buckram. (SG. Sep.15; 204) $150

LANDI, B.
- **De Origine et Cavsa Pestis Patauinae, Anni MDLV.** Venice, 1555. Some old notes & underlining, last ll. lightly stained in side margin, bds. (HK. Nov.8; 249) DM 400

LANDO, Ortensio
[-] **Commentario della piu Notabili & Mostruose Cose d'Italia, & Altri Luoghi.** [Venezie, 1554]. Frontis. marked, stained, later bds. (SI. Dec.15; 19) Lire 600,000

LANDOLT, H.
- **100 Master Drawings of the 15th & 16th Centuries from the Basle Print Room.** 1972. 4to. Orig. bds., s.-c. (P. Apr.12; 286) *Dreesman.* £50

LANDON, Charles Paul
- **Annales du Musée et de l'Ecole Moderne des Beaux-Arts.** Paris & L., 1815. 21 vols. Cont. str.-grd. mor., gt., slight surface wear, spines faded (S. Oct.4; 170) *Erlini.* £130
- - **Anr. Copy.** 19 vols., including the 2 vol. 'Paysage et Tableaux de Genre du Musée Napoléon' (dtd. 1805 & 1815). Cont. str.-grd. mor., covers & spines elab. gt., slight wear. (SG. Oct.13; 221) $375
See— **LEGRAND, J.G. & Landon, Charles Paul**

LANDON, Perceval
- **A Lhassa. La Ville Interdite. Description de Tibet Central et des Coutumes de ses Habitants. Relation de la Marche de la Mission envoyée par le Gouvernement Anglais (1903-04).** Paris, 1906. Lge. 8vo. Hf. chagrin, unc., ill. wrap. (HD. May 21; 127)
Frs. 1,550

LANDOR, Arnold Henry Savage
- **China & the Allies.** 1901. 2 vols. Orig. decor. cl., soiled. (BBA. Jun.14; 296) *T. Scott.* £55

LANDOR, Walter Savage
- **The Longer Prose Works, Poems etc.** L., 1891-93. 10 vols., compl. Orig. cl. (GM. Dec.7; 664)
£50
- **Pericles & Aspasia.** L., 1836. *1st. Edn.* 2 vols. Hf.-titles, 2 advt. ll., orig. drab bds., repairs, cl. folder & cf. s.-c.; Hogan copy. (SPB. May 16; 93)
$100
- - **Anr. Edn.** N.Y., Chiswick Pr., 1903. *(210) numbered for America, priv. ptd. for the Scott-Thaw Co.* Fo. Two-tone cl., unc. & unopened, the 2 extra spine labels tipped in. (SG. Jan.12; 62) $100

LANDRIANI, Marsilio
- **Opuscoli Fisico-Chimici.** Milan, 1781. Hf.-title, cont. mott. cf., spine defect. (SG. Oct.6; 224)
$100

LANDSBERG [Landsperger], J.
- **Ein Edels Schatzbüchlein der Göttlichen Liebe.** Trans.:- Ph. Dobreinner. Dillingen, 1564. *2nd. Edn.* Cont. blind-tooled cf. over wood bds., clasps, 2 lge. stps. & gt. monog. AP & date 1565, spine slightly defect. (R. Apr.3; 53) DM 1,900

LANDSBOROUGH, [William]
- **Journal of Landsborough's Expedition from Carpentaria, in Search of Burke & Wills.** Melbourne, 1862. Folding map laid down & torn at folds, rebnd. qtr. mor., orig. upr. wrap. preserved (laid down,

reprd. & soiled); Thomas Gill bkplt. (CA. Apr.3; 68) Aus. $450
- - **Anr. Copy.** Minor wear, frontis. with pale stain, 2 ll. roughly opened, stiff wraps. (KH. May 1; 403)
Aus. $300

LANDSCAPE ANNUAL, The
Ill.:- after S. Prout & J.D. Harding. L., 1830-34. Vols. 1-5 only (of 10). L.P., extra engraved titles & vigs., 127 engraved plts., on India paper, some spotting, cont. roan gt. (S. Mar.6; 91) *Ayres.* £290
- - **Anr. Edn.** Ill.:- after S. Prout & J.D. Harding. L., 1830-35. 4 vols. only (of 10). Some slight spotting, cont. mor. (S. Mar.6; 92) *Clarke.* £130
- - **Anr. Edn.** Ed.:- Thomas Roscoe & W.H. Harrison. L., 1830-39. Vols. 1-10 (all publd.). Some foxing, mor. (RO. Dec.11; 184) $300

LANDSCAPE GALLERY: A Series of Fine Line Engravings, Views of Scenery, Edifices, Cities, &c., &c., in Various Parts of the World, Copied from Nature, & Executed by the First Artists.
L., 1856. Ob. 8vo. Considerably foxed, gt.-decor. cl., rubbed, spine torn. (SG. Jun.7; 391) $130

LANDSEER, Thomas
- **Monkey-Ana or Men in Miniature.** L., 1927. Fo. 27 engrs., including 1 in dupl., on India paper & mntd. mor. gt., lr. cover detchd., Orig. sigd. watercolor drawing & note sigd. by artist tipped in. (SPB. Dec.13; 855) $450

LANDSEER SERIES OF PICTURE BOOKS
Descriptions:- Mrs. Surr. L., ca. 1880. Nos. 1-4, in 1 vol. 4to. Text ll. with heavy offsets from plts. (despite the tissue guards), mod. gt.-lettered buckram, orig. col.-pict. wraps. bnd. in. (SG. Dec.8; 213) $100

LANE, F.C.V.
- **The Bookplates of Norman Lindsay.** Adelaide, 1944. *(375) numbered.* Stiffened wraps. (KH. Nov.9; 306) Aus. $170

LANE-POOLE, Stanley
- **Social life in Egypt.** L., ca. 1840. 4to. Leath. over wood bds., gt. decor., sm. fault in spine. (D. Nov.23; 1241) DM 700

LANFRANCUS de Oriano
- **Tractatus de Arbitris.** Pescia, Laurentius & Francus Cennis for Bastianus & Raphael de Orlandis, 5 Dec. 1486. Fo. Some worming at beginning diminishing to single wormhole as far as b6 affects text, a few cont. marginalia, early bdg. of medical MS. fragment; early 17th. C. sig. of Luce Sanguineti on front free end-paper. [HC 9888] (S. May 10; 314) *Quaritch.* £950

LANG, Andrew
- **The Blue Fairy Book.** Ill.:- H.J. Ford & G.P. Jacomb Hood. L., 1889. *1st. Edn. (113) L.P.* Some slight margin soiling, hf. parch. & bds., paper on upr. bd. splitting where attached to parch., light soiling, light wear to extremities. (CBA. Aug.21; 361) $225
- **The Blue Poetry Book.** Ill.:- H.J. Ford & Lancelot Speed. 1891. *(150) numbered on L.P.* Lge. 8vo. Orig. bds., unc. (BBA. Jun.14; 11)
Blackwell's. £60
- **The Brown Fairy Book.** Ill.:- H.J. Ford. L., 1904. *1st. Edn.* Some slight margin darkening, gt.-ruled pol. cf. by Bayntun, spine gt.-decor., gt. dentelles, marb. end-papers, orig. cl. covers bnd. in at end; Marymount College copy. (CBA. Mar.3; 325)
$110
- **The Fairy Books [Violet, Green, Orange, Crimson, Brown, Yellow, Grey, Olive, Pink, Rcd, Lilac & Blue].** Ill.:- H.J. Ford. 1889-1910. *1st. Edn.* 12 vols. Mod. cold. cf. by Bayntun, spines gt. (BBA. Jun.14; 10) *Cavendish Rare Books.* £450
- **The Green Fairy Book.** Ill.:- H.J. Ford & Lancelot Speed. 1892. *(150) numbered on L.P.* Lge. 8vo. Orig. bds., unc. (BBA. Jun.14; 12)
Blackwell's. £60
- - **Anr. Copy.** Hf. parch. & bds., unopened, darkening & soiling to covers, spine darkened, ends bumped, corners defect., offset to end-papers, bkplt. (CBA. Aug.21; 363) $200
- - **Anr. Edn.** Ill.:- H.J. Ford. L., 1892. *1st. Edn.* Few pp. lightly foxed, gt.-ruled pol. cf. by Bayntun, gt.-decor. spine, gt. dentelles, marb. end-papers,

orig. covers bnd. in at end; Marymount College copy. (CBA. Mar.3; 326) $120
- **The Library.** L., 1881. 2 vols. Fo. Inlaid & extra-ill. with 250 ports., views & ills., most engraved, some hand-cold., some folding, mod. cl.; A.L.s. from J. Northcote. (BBA. Mar.7; 235)
A. Lenton. £150
- **The Orange Fairy Book.** Ill.:– H.J. Ford. L., 1906. *1st. Edn.* Few pp. lightly soiled, gt.-ruled pol. cf. by Bayntun, gt.-decor. spine, gt. dentelles, marb. end-papers, orig. covers bnd. in at end; Marymount College copy. (CBA. Mar.3; 327) $110
- **The Princess Nobody.** Ill.:– E. Evans after Richard Doyle. L., [1884]. *1st. Edn.* Sm. 4to. Cl.-bkd. pict. bds., tips worn. (SG. Dec.8; 139) $275
- **The True Story Book.** Ill.:– H.J. Ford & others. 1893. *(150) numbered on L.P.* Lge. 8vo. Orig. bds., unc. (BBA. Jun.14; 13) *Blackwell's.* £60
- **The Violet Fairy Book.** Ill.:– H.J. Ford. L., 1901. *1st. Edn.* Gt.-ruled pol. cf. by Bayntun, gt.-decor. spine, gt. dentelles, marb. end-papers, covers lightly rubbed & scratched, spine slightly faded, some offset from dentelles to end-papers, orig. cl. covers bnd. in at end; Marymount College copy. (CBA. Mar.3; 328) $120
- **The Yellow Fairy Book.** Ill.:– H.J. Ford. 1894. *(140) numbered on L.P.* Lge. 8vo. Orig. bds., unc. (BBA. Jun.14; 14) *Blackwell's.* £60
- - **Anr. Edn.** Ill.:– H.J. Ford. L., 1894. *1st. Edn.* Some light foxing & soiling to a few pp., gt.-ruled pol. cf. by Bayntun, gt.-decor. spine, gt. dentelles, marb. end-papers, orig. cl. covers bnd. in at end; Marymount College copy. (CBA. Mar.3; 329) $120
- **[Collected Works].** N.d. *Mostly 1st. Edns.* 21 vols. Orig. pict. gt. cl. (PD. Oct.19; 91) £175

LANG, Carl
- **Geschichtliche Denkwürdigkeiten und Seltenheiten der Natur.** Nuremb., 1813. 1 vol. (of 3). Slightly browned or foxed, cont. bds., rubbed & bumped. (GB. May 4; 1538) DM 400
- - **Anr. Edn.** Nuremb., 1814. 2 vols. 89 engraved cold. ills. on 47 plts., subscribers list, cont. bds. (C. Dec.9; 259) *Schwing.* £220

LANG, Henry C.
- **Phopalocera Europae, The Butterflies of Europe.** L., N.d. 2 vols. 4to. 82 col. plts., hf. mor., spine decor. gt., orig. wraps. bnd. in. (SKC. Oct.26; 395) £110

LANG, John Dunmore
- **An Historical & Statistical Account of New South Wales.** L., 1834. *1st. Edn.* 2 vols. Folding map hand-cold. in outl., diced cf., covers slightly rubbed. (CA. Apr.3; 69) Aus. $190
- - **Anr. Copy.** 2 vols. 12mo. Liby. blind-stps. on titles, mod. hf. cf. (KH. May 1; 405) Aus. $190
- - **Anr. Edn.** 1840. *3rd. Edn.* 2 vols. Advt. lf. at end Vol.1, folding map reprd., slightly browned., orig. cl., rebkd. (TA. Dec.15; 49) £70
- - **Anr. Copy.** 2 vols. Advt. lf. bnd. in at end of Vol. 1, folding map reprd., slight browning, orig. cl., rebkd. (TA. Nov.17; 38) £60

LANGALLERY, Marquis de
- **Mémoires.** La Haye, 1743. *1st. Edn.* 12mo. Cont. marb. cf., spine decor. with Rohan-Soubise arms. (HD. Mar.21; 47) Frs. 1,100

LANGBAINE, Gerard
- **An Account of the English Dramatick Poets.** Oxford, 1691. *1st. Edn.* Some MS. corrections, lacks last lf., some margin worming, cont. cf. [Wing L373] (BBA. Jun.14; 64) *J. Price.* £190
- - **Anr. Copy.** Errata lf. & longitudinal title lf. at end, cf., defect.; E. Peddler, Jnr. bkplt. (P. Mar.15; 318) *Lawson.* £95

LANGBAINE, Gerard & Gildon, Charles
- **The Lives & Characters of the English Dramatick Poets.** [1699]. *1st. Edn.* Extra lf. *L4 present, advt. ll. at end, lacks last blank, some staining, cont. cf. [Wing L375] (BBA. Jun.14; 65) *J. Price.* £280

LANGDON, John E.
- **American Silversmiths in British North America 1776-1800.** Toronto, 1970. *(350) numbered.* Tall 8vo. Cl.-bkd. bds., s.-c. (SG. Jan.26; 285) $125

- - **Anr. Copy.** Tall 8vo. Cl.-bkd. bds., s.-c. slightly soiled. (SG. Oct.13; 326) $120

LANGE, Ludwig
- **Original Ansichten der Historisch Merkwürdigsten Staedte in Deutschland.** Darmstadt, 1832. Vol. 1. 4to. Engraved title dtd. 1837, 65 ills. on 41 plts., cont. hf. mor. (C. Nov.16; 110) *Kistner.* £1,150
- - **Anr. Edn.** Darmstadt, 1837. Vol. 1. 4to. Soiling, especially text, cont. hf. leath., rubbed & bumped. (HK. Nov.8; 1103) DM 4,800
- - **Anr. Edn.** Ill.:– E.&.C. Rauch, Joh. Poppel, G.A. Müller. Darmstadt, 1837[-46?]. Vols. I-V. 4to. All vols. with text, I-IV with plt. index, lacks engraved title V & 1 view in III & IV, & 4 (of 6) views in V, some foxing & browning, cont. hf. leath., spotted, slightly bumped, 2 spines defect. (H. Nov.23; 366) DM 16,000
- - **Anr. Edn.** Darmstadt, 1840. Vol. 2. 4to. Engraved title, 54 plts., some minor spotting in margins, cont. hf. mor. (C. Nov.16; 111) *Weissert.* £1,000
- - **Anr. Edn.** Darmstadt, 1843. Vol. 4. 4to. Engraved title, 52 (of 54) plts., some spotted, cont. hf. mor. (C. Nov.16; 112) *Weissert.* £1,100
- - **Anr. Edn.** Darmstadt, 1850. Vol. 8. 4to. Engraved title, 53 plts., some spotting, cont. hf. mor. (C. Nov.16; 115) *Weissert.* £1,200
- **Original - Ansichten der Vornehmsten Städte in Deutschland.** Ill.:– Ernst Rauch, L. Hoffmeister, J. Poppel & others. Darmstadt, 1832-52. Vols. 1-10 (lacks Vols. 3 & 8), & 'Sammelband'. 4to. Vols. 5 & 6 lack 1 plt., lacks title to Sammelband, 5 vols. with some foxing, especially text & early ll. Vol. 1 & some plts. Vol. 9, Vol. 5 with stain, hf. leath. gt., marb. cover, wraps., Vol. 2 lacks bdg., 2 vols. lack spine. (V. Sep.29; 77) DM 33,500
- - **Anr. Edn.** Darmstadt, 1852. vol. 9. 4to. 53 steel engrs., including engraved title with vig., some foxing, slight. hf. linen, defect., lacks spine. (R. Oct.13; 3200) DM 2,150
- **Original Ansichten von Deutschland.** Darmstadt, 1846. Vol. 6. 4to. Engraved title, 52 plts., some spotting & staining in margins, cont. hf. mor. (C. Nov.16; 113) *Burden.* £750
- - **Anr. Copy.** Vol. 5. 4to. 67 steel engrs. incld. 8 supp., supp. plts. intered in index in old ink MS., foxed, liby. hf. lines, defect. (R. Oct.12; 2376) DM 2,800
- - **Anr. Edn.** Darmstadt, 1848. Vol. 7. 4to. Engraved title, 60 plts., title & some margins spotted, cont. hf. mor. (C. Nov.16; 114) *Kistner.* £1,050
- - **Anr. Copy.** Vol.7. 4to. Engraved title, 61 steel engrs., including 1 supp., foxed, cont. hf. leath. (R. Oct.12; 2377) DM 2,500
- - **Anr. Edn.** Darmstadt, 1851. Vol. 9. 4to. Engraved title, 52 engraved plts., some spotting, cont. hf. mor. (C. Nov.16; 116) *Kistner.* £600
- - **Anr. Edn.** Darmstadt, 1852. Vol. 10. 4to. Engraved title, 53 plts., staining in some margins, some spotting, cont. hf. mor. (C. Nov.16; 117) *Weissert.* £1,150
- - **Anr. Copy.** vol. 10. 4to. 58 steel engrs., including 5 supp., lacks 1, foxed & slightly stained, hf. linen, rubbed. (R. Oct.12; 2378) DM 4,200
- - **Anr. Edn.** Darmstadt, 1859. Vol. 12. 4to. Engraved title, 53 plts., some minor spotting & staining, cont. hf. mor. (C. Nov.16; 118) *Weissert.* £1,200
- **Der Rhein und die Rheinlande ...** Ill.:– J. Poppel. Darmstadt & Wiesbaden, 1842. Steel engraved title with vig., 101 steel engraved plts., Slightly browned, cont. hf. leath., bumped & rubbed, spine defect. & loose. (HK. May 15; 1014) DM 3,600
- - **Anr. Edn.** Darmstadt, 1847. Qtr. mor., worn. (P. Oct.20; 195) £750
- - **Anr. Edn.** Ill.:– J. Poppel after Lange. Darmstadt, 1849. 104 (of 105) steel-engraved plts., foxed, cont. hf. leath. gt. (HK. Nov.9; 1197) DM 2,800
- - **Anr. Edn.** Ill.:– J. Poppel. Darmstadt, 1852. Lge. 8vo. Engraved title with vig., 102 steel engrs., (lacks 11 : c.f. plt. index), 11 others bnd. in, browned & brown spotted, hf. leath., spotted, very rubbed. (H. May 22; 342) DM 2,800

LANGENBECK, C.J.M. von
- **Icones Anatomicae: Neurologiae.** Göttingen, [1826-30]. Pts. I-III in 1 vol. Lge. fo. Cont. hf.

---

leath., bumped, spine defect. (R. Apr.4; 1327) DM 1,700

LANGENES, Barent
- **Caert-Thresoor, Inhoudende de Tafelen des gantsche Werelts Landen.** Amst., Cornelis Claesz, 1599. *2nd. Edn.* 2 pts. in 1 vol. Sm. ob. 8vo. Ptd. title with engraved vig., engraved 'Victoria' plt., 115 + 56 full-p. engraved maps & plts. (of 172), with the additional maps of America & Asia, 'Gotland' torn without loss of engraved surface, some staining or slight surface dirt, cont. cf., spine gt. (S. Dec.1; 180) *Franks.* £1,150

LANGENTHAL, L.E. (Ed.)
See— FLORA VON DEUTSCHLAND

LANGEREN, Jacob van
- [-] **A Book of the Names of all Parishes, Market Towns, Hamlets, & Smallest Places in England & Wales.** L., 1657. 4 folding maps,? inserted from anr. work, folding table, 37 ll. incorporating maps, some ll. a little stained, cont. cf., as an atlas, w.a.f. [Wing B3717] (BBA. May 3; 246) *Ingol Maps.* £600
- [-] **A Direction for the English Traviller.** L., 1636. *2nd. Edn.* 40 ll. only (of 45, lacks Suffolk [supplied in photostat] & the 4 folding tables) ptd. on 1 side, 36 incorporating maps, last lf. stained & reprd., title-p. frayed, light stains, ptd. lf. 'To the gentle reader' supplied in photostat (? called for). (*Bound with:*) SACRED GEOGRAPHIE. Or Scriptural Mapps Trans.:– Joseph Moxon. L., 1671. Folding table, no maps, some margins shaved. Together 2 works in 1 vol. Ob. 4to. Cont. cf., rebkd., as an atlas, w.a.f. (BBA. May 3; 245) *Burton.* £400
- - **Anr. Edn.** L., [1677?]. 4to. and as. sm. 8vo. 43 ll. only (of 44), ptd. on 1 side, 4 folding, 39 incorporating maps, lacks Buckinghamshire & Westmorland, 2 copies of Herefordshire, 1 folding lf. torn, cont. cf., 2 clasps, as an atlas, w.a.f. [Wing D1528] (BBA. May 3; 247) *Ingol Maps.* £540

LANGEVELD, D.M.
See— ELWE, Jan Barend & Largeveld, D.M.

LANGFORD, Nathaniel Pitt
- **Diary of the Washburn Expedition to the Yellowstone & Firehole Rivers in the Year 1870.** N.p., priv. ptd., [1905]. Pict. cl.; pres. copy from author. (LH. Jan.15; 333) $110

LANGHANS, C. [F.]
- **Uber Theater oder Bemerkungen über Katakustik in Beziehung auf Theater.** Berlin, 1810. 4to. 5 folding copperplts. (for 4), some ll. slightly crumpled, hf. linen. (GB. May 3; 897) DM 460

LANGIUS, Rodolphus
- **Urbis Hierosolyme Templique in ea origo, & Horum rursus excidium.** [Cologne, Jan. 1517]. Sm. 4to. Bds., spine defect. (S. May 10; 315) *McKiddrick.* £180

LANGLAND, William
- [-] **The Vision of Pierce Plowman.** L., 1550. *1st. Edn.* Sm. 4to. Woodcut title border, date '1505' corrected by pen, cont. sigs. on title-p., MS. diagram on verso & note at end, lacks last lf. (blank), 2 sm. holes in margin of title, a few side notes shaved, 1 margin torn, some stains, later mor., cf. spine a little worn. [STC 19906] (BBA. May 3; 92) *Thomas.* £5,200
- - **Anr. Edn.** L., 1550. *2nd. Edn.?.* Sm. 4to. 'Tyme' on title, 'Imprynted' on colophon, 2 ll. reprd. & defect., affecting text, slight staining, 18th. C. cf., spine gt., 2 compartments of spine restored; Frederic Dannay copy. [STC 19907] (CNY. Dec.16; 200) $3,000

LANGLEY, Batty
- **The Builder's Director, or Bench-Mate.** N.d. 184 engrs. on 92 ll., some ll. slightly soiled, cont. sheep, rebkd. with cf., rubbed. (BBA. Feb.12; 171) *Thorp.* £80
- **New Principles of Gardening.** 1728. 4to. 27 engraved plts. only, several cleanly torn, 3 with loss, cont. cf., spine chipped. (CSK. Nov.4; 94) £100
- **Pomoná; or, The Fruit-Garden Illustrated.** 1729. Fo. 67 engraved plts. only, a few tears, title & 9 ll. defect., cont. cf. (P. Oct.20; 208) £220
- - **Anr. Copy.** Fo. 79 engraved plts., some folding,

LANGLEY, Batty -Contd.

slight wormholes thro.-out, cont. hf. cf. (SKC. May 4; 1858)   £140

LANGLEY, E. & Belch, W.
- **New County Atlas of England & Wales.** L., J. Phelps, 1820. Ob. 4to. 49 (of 53) full-p. engraved regional & county maps, hand-cold. in wash & outl., lacks title, some maps loose, a few with liby. stps., not touching engraved surface, cont. hf. roan, defect. (S. Dec.1; 162)   *Cartographia.* £520

LANGLEY, Samuel Pierpoint
- **Experiments in Aerodynamics.** Wash., 1891. *1st. Edn.* Lge. 4to. Orig. cl., remains of paper label on lr. cover, some spotting; Langley's card as Secretary of Smithsonian Institute laid in, Stanitz coll. (SPB. Apr.25; 260) $175

LANGLY, Wilhelm
- **Observationes et Historiae Omnes et Singulae Guilelmi Harvei.** Ill.:– Romeyn de Hooghe. Amst., 1674. 12mo. Engraved frontis., 8 plts., vell.; Dr. Walter Pagel copy. (S. Feb.7; 161)
Goldschmidt. £420

LANGSDORF, Karl Christian
- **Lehrbuch der Hydraulik.** Altenburg, 1794-96. *1st. Edn.* 2 vols. in 1. 4to. Cont. vell. bds., Prussian eagle stpd. in gt. on covers; Stanitz coll. (SPB. Apr.25; 262) $475
- – **Anr. Copy.** 2 pts. in 1 vol. Cont. hf. cf., spine rubbed & slightly defect. (VG. Mar.19; 113)
Fls. 900

LANGUET, Hubert
[–] **Vindiciae contra Tyrannos.** 'Edimburgii' [Basle], 1579. *1st. Edn.* Sm. 8vo. Mor. by the Camb. Bdg. Guild, slightly discold. [STC 15211] (C. Nov.9; 90)   *Quaritch.* £500

LANIADO, Avraham Ben Yitshak
- **Magen Avraham.** Venice, 1603. *1st. & only Edn.* Sm. 4to. Some soiling & dampstaining, lacks last 5 ll. (part of index), early vell., soiled, spine darkened, covers bowed. (SG. Feb.2; 221) $350

LANIADO, Shmuel
- **Sefer Kli Yakar.** Venice, 1603. Fo. (in 6's). Hole in centre of title reprd. with some text loss on recto & verso, 1 lf. out of sequence, lacks ll. 12, 182-184, mod. binder's buckram, end-ll. marginally wormed. (SG. Feb.2; 222) $400

LANIER, Henry Wysham
- **A.B. Frost: the American Sportsman's Artist.** Derrydale Pr., [1933]. *(950).* 4to. Gt.-lettered cl., spine rubbed, bumped at head & foot. (SG. Mar.15; 232)
$175

LANIER, Sidney
- **Poems.** Phila. & L., 1877. *1st. Edn.* 12mo. Orig. cl., spine slightly worn; pres. copy from author to Epes Sargent, & with author's corrections & revisions, Frederic Dannay copy. (CNY. Dec.16; 201) $750

LANIGAN, Rev. John
- **An Ecclesiastical History of Ireland.** Dublin, 1822. 4 vols. List of subscribers, hf. cf. (GM. Dec.7; 133)   £50

LANOUE, Pierre de
- **La Cavalerie Françoise et Italienne.** Lyon, 1620. *1st. Edn.* Fo. Title & pp. 1-70 bkd. in upr. margin, with some slight loss, last 11 ll. reprd. in lr. right corner, some slight staining, later bds. (D. Nov.25; 4503)   DM 950

LANSBERGEN, Ph.
- **Bedenckinghen, op den Daghelijckschen, ende Iaerlijckschen Loop vanden Aerdt-cloot.** Middelburg, 1629. *1st. Edn.* 4to. 19th. C. hf. vell. (VG. Nov.30; 767)   Fls. 950

LANTE, Louis Marie & others
- **Galerie Française des Femmes Célèbres.** Paris, 1827. *1st. Printing of plts.* Lge. 4to. Mod. bradel hf. buckram, corners, unc. (HD. May 4; 328)
Frs. 7,000
- – **Anr. Edn.** Paris, 1827. Fo. 70 hand-cold. engraved plts., hf.-title, some slight foxing, cont.

hf. chagrin, spine decor., worn. (SM. Mar.7; 2508)
Frs. 1,500
- – **Anr. Edn.** [1832]. 4to. 70 cold. engraved plts. (1 repeated, 4 slightly short), hf. mor., corners, by Stroobants. (HD. Jul.6; 106)   Frs. 1,750

LANTIER, Etienne François de
- **Voyages d'Anténor en Grèce et en Asie.** Ill.:– Bornet, engraved by Adam. Paris, 1809. 3 vols. Orig. cf. gt. by P. Lalande, spines decor. (HD. May 4; 329)   3,600

LANZ, Philippe Louis & Betancourt y Molina, Augustin de
- **Analytical Essay on the Construction of Machines.** L., ca. 1820 [wtrmkd. 1817]. *1st. Edn. in Engl.* 4to. Slight spotting & soiling, bds., unc., rebkd., splash mark on cover, newspaper clippings on end-papers; G.E. Kenney label, earlier sig. of J. Perry on title-p., Stanitz coll. (SPB. Apr.25; 264) $325
- **Essai sur la Composition des Machines.** Preface:– Hachette. Paris, 1808. *1st. Edn.* 4to. Hf.-title, light spotting, marb. bds., unc., lightly rubbed; Stanitz coll. (SPB. Apr.25; 263) $325

LAPAUZE, Henry
- **Ingrès. Sa Vie et Son Oeuvre.** Paris, 1911. Fo. Hf. mor. (SPB. Nov. 30; 49) $225

LA PEROUSE, Jean François Galaup de
- **Atlas du Voyage de la Perouse.** Ill.:– after Prevost & others. [Paris, 1797]. *[1st. Edn.].* Fo. Engraved title, port., 69 charts & plts., some double-p. & folding, some spotting & minor dampstaining, some tears, 2 plts. with some loss of ptd. caption, cont. bds., rubbed & worn, w.a.f. [Sabin 38960] (C. Mar.14; 60)   *Faupel.* £600
- – **Anr. Copy.** Lge. fo. Engraved title & 69 copper engraved plts., (1 folding & 20 double-p), foxed thro.-out, some plts. loose, cont. hf. leath., rubbed, spine slightly defect. [Sabin 38960] (R. Apr.5; 2897)   DM 3,200
- **Voyage de La Perouse autour du Monde.** Ed.:– L.A. Milet-Mureau. Paris, 1796-97. *1st. Edn.* 4 vols. only (lacks Atlas). Lge. 4to. 1st. few ll. of Vol. I dampstained, some foxing, &c. elsewhere, old cf., needs rebdg. (SG. Sep.22; 186) $400
- – **Anr. Edn.** Ed.:– L. Millet-Mureau. Paris, An V [1797]. *Orig. Edn. 1st. Printing.* 4 vols. text & 1 atlas vol. 4to. & fo. Some stains, cont. grd. cf., gt. dentelle, decor. spines. (HD. Dec.16; 51)
Frs. 20,000
- – **Anr. Edn.** Ed.:– L.A. Millet-Mureau. Ill.:– Moreau le Jeune (port.). Paris, 1797. *Orig. Edn.* 5 vols., including Atlas. 4to. & fo. 69 plts., most double-p., cont. cf., spines decor, atlas in old bdg., worn. (HD. Mar.9; 93b)   Frs. 14,000
- – **Anr. Edn.** 1799. 3 vols., including Atlas. 4to. & fo. Engraved title, 68 maps & plts., some double-p., lacks ports., cf. & hf. cf. (P. Dec.8; 357)
Walford. £720
- **Voyage Round the World.** L., 1798. Atlas vol. only. Sm. fo. Engraved title, port., 68 engraved plts., some double-p., some soiling or staining, some plts. creased, few detchd., cont. bds., defect. (S. Apr.9; 76)   *Burgess.* £480
- – **Anr. Copy.** 3 vols. 42 engraved maps & plts., titles foxed, some plts. or maps offset or foxed, old cf., rebkd. (CA. Apr.3; 71)   Aus. $620
- – **Anr. Edn.** 1798-99. Atlas vol. only. Sm. fo. Early hf. cf., brkn., covers detchd. (KH. May 1; 211)
Aus. $1,250
- – **Anr. Edn.** 1799. 2 Vols. 4to. Port., 69 plts. & maps, including 1 map hand-cold. in outl., mott. cf., rebkd. (P. Oct.22; 77)   £750
- – **Anr. Copy.** Atlas vol. only. Fo. Engraved title, 69 engraved charts & plts., dtd. 1798, some double-p. & folding, orig. bds., unc., lacks spine, loose in covers, w.a.f. [Sabin 38962] (C. Nov.16; 119)
Quaritch. £600

LA PERRIERE, Guillaume de, Tolosan
- **Les Considérations des Quatre Mondes.** Ill.:– Guiraud Agret? Lyon, 1552. Sm. 8vo. Mor. gt., decor., by Chambolle-Duru. (HD. Nov.9; 8) Frs. 17,500
- **La Morosophie.** Lyon, 1553. Blank upr. margin renewed & short tear renewed in title, sm. area rubbed in title & 3 woodcuts, 19th. C. str.-grd. mor. gt. (C. May 30; 88)   *Parikian.* £1,400

LAPIE, Pierre & Alexandre Emile
- **Atlas Universel de Géographie Ancienne et Moderne.** Paris, 1838. Fo. 50 double-p. litho. mapsheets, mostly hand-cold. in outl., some spotting, few minor splits at centrefolds, cont. roan-bkd. bds., worn. (S. Mar.6; 108)   *Cassidy.* £120

LA PLACE, Adml. Cyrille Pierre Théodore
- **Reis rondom de Wereld door de Zeeën van Indië en China.** Zaltbommel, 1834-36. 7 vols. 2 vols. slightly stained, orig. bds., unc., slightly impft. (VG. Mar.19; 247)   Fls. 600

LAPLACE, Pietre Simon, Marquis de
- **Exposition du Système du Monde.** Paris, [1796]. *1st. Edn.* 2 vols. Some heavy browning, cont. sewed, defect. (R. Oct.12; 1690)   DM 450
- **Mécanique Céleste ... Translated.** Trans.:– Nathaniel Bowditch. Boston, 1829-39. *1st. Edn., (250).* 4 vols. 4to. Hf.-titles, light spotting, some soiling, orig. cl., unc., faded, labels chipped; Stanitz coll. (SPB. Apr.25; 265) $1,900

LA POPELINIERE, Henri Lancelot Voisin de
- **Les Trois Mondes.** Paris, 1582. 3 pts. in 1 vol. Privilege lf. & blank g8, lacks map & final blank gg4, 19th. C. mor. gt. (C. May 30; 89)
Quaritch. £450

LAPORTE, John
- **Progressive Lessons Sketched from Nature.** L., [1798-99, wtrmkd. 1794]. Pts. I-IV. Ob. fo. 16 plts., a few margins slightly soiled, orig. paper wraps., 1 spine torn. (C. Mar.14; 11)   *Henderson.* £55

LA QUINTINYE, Jean de
- **The Compleat Gard'ner.** Trans.:– J. Evelyn. L., 1693. Fo. Port., 10 (of 11) plts., old cf. (P. Nov.24; 254)   *Weldon & Wesley.* £120
- **Instruction pour les Jardins Fruitiers et Potagers, avec un Traité des Oranges, suivi de Quelques Réflexions sur l'Agriculture ... augmentée d'un Traité de la Culture des Melons & de nouv. Instructions pour cultiver les Fleurs.** Amst., 1697. 3 pts. in 1 vol. 4to. Minimal spotting, cont. leath., corners partly bumped. (HK. May 16; 1536)   DM 420

LARA (Pseud.)
See— ARMOUR, Robert, Jr. 'Lara'

LARBAUD, Valery
- **Allen.** Ill.:– O. Coubine. Paris, 1927. *(120)* numbered. 4to. Orig. wraps. (BBA. Jun.14; 198)
Makiya. £170
- **Enfantines.** Ill.:– Jeanne Rosoy, Germaine Labaye, Halicka, Hermine David. Paris, 1926. *(20)* numbered on japon impérial, with separate suite on old japan. 4 vols. Square 12mo. 24 orig. etchings, publisher's bds., unc., s.-c. (HD. May 16; 91)
Frs. 2,200
- **Fermina Marquez.** Ill.:– Chas. Laborde. 1925. 4to. Cont. vell., orig. acqua on upr. cover with gt. calligraphed title, orig. inner decor. (HD. Dec.9; 35k)   Frs. 1,200

LARCHER, P.H.
- **Mémoire sur Vénus ...** Paris, 1775. 12mo. With 'Huitième Index' by Le Blond, red mor. gt. by Hardy-Mennil, spine decor.; orig. drawing bnd. in, replacing engr. by A. de Saint-Aubin usually added. (HD. Jul.2; 22)   Frs. 1,800

LARDNER, Nathaniel
- **The Works, with a Life by Dr. Kippis.** 1838. 10 vols. Some spotting of prelims., cont. cf., gt.-decor. spines, a little rubbed. (TA. Jun.21; 358)   £50

LA RISA
N.O., 1849. 3 vols. in 1 (compl.). 4to. Linen. (DS. Apr.27; 2579)   Pts. 190,000

LARKIN, Philip
- **The North Ship.** L., Fortune Pr., [1945]. *1st. Edn.* 12mo. Orig. cl., unopened, d.-w.; Frederic Dannay copy. (CNY. Dec.16; 202) $320
- **XX Poems.** [Belfast, priv. ptd.], 1951. *1st. Edn. (100).* Orig. wraps., stapled as iss., covers soiled; Frederick Dannay copy. (CNY. Dec.16; 203)
$1,100

LARKING, L.B. (Ed.)
See— DOMESDAY BOOK

LA ROCCA, Jean de
- Abbatucci, Garde des Sceaux, Ministre de la Justice ... Paris, 1855. Some foxing, mod. hf. chagrin. (HD. Oct.21; 111) Frs. 1,000

LAROCHE, H.J.
- Cuisine. Ill.:– Edouard Vuillard, A. Dunoyer de Segonzac & André Villebouef. Paris, 1935. *(170) numbered.* Fo. Hf. mor., orig. wraps. bnd. in., leath. corners, sigd. by Lobstein-Laurenchet. (D. Nov.24; 3117) DM 3,200

LA ROCHE, Sophie von
- Melusinens Sommer-Abende. Ed.:– C.M. Wieland. Halle, 1806. *1st. Edn.* Some light browning, title & end-paper stpd., cont. hf. leath. gt., lightly rubbed. (H. Nov.23; 700) DM 600

LA ROCHEFOUCAULD, François VI, Duc de, Prince de Marcillac
- Maximes et Reflexions Morales. Parma, 1812. *(220).* Lge. 8vo. Wide margin, some light foxing, hand-bnd. cf., by Zaehnsdorf, lightly worn & scratched, 1 spot. (H. May 22; 617) DM 1,000
- Mémoires. Cologne, 1662. *2nd. Edn.* Sm. 12mo. Cont. cf., spine decor., Lambert de Thorigny arms; old ex-libris of Le Fors de Chessimot. (HD. Mar.29; 53) Frs. 7,000
- – Anr. Edn. Cologne, [Bruxelles], 1662. *2nd. Orig. Edn.* 16mo. Lacks errata lf., cont. cf., worn, lr. cover detchd. (HD. Feb.22; 112) Frs. 1,500
- – Anr. Edn. Cologne, 1664. *4th. Edn.* Sm. 12mo. Cf. gt. by Closs, spine decor. (HD. May 3; 82) Frs. 1,000
- Réflexions ou Sentences Morales. Paris, 1693. *6th. Edn.* 12mo. Cont. cf., J.-B. Poulett crowned cypher. (HD. Mar.29; 52) Frs. 10,000

LA ROCHE-GUIHEM, Mlle. de
[–] Histoire des Favorites. Constantinople [Amst.], [1699]. 2 vols. Cont. leath. (D. Nov.24; 2296) DM 400

LA ROCQUE, Gilles André de
- Traité de la Noblesse et de Toutes ses Différentes Espèces. Rouen, 1735. *New Edn.* 4to. Cont. marb. cf., spine decor. (HD. Nov.9; 129) Frs. 1,050

LAROON, Marcellus
- The Cryes of the City of London. L., [1711 ?]. Fo. Wide margin, dte. on title very indistinct, 74 numbered copperplts., all but 4 with captions in Engl., Fr. & Italian, some margin repairs, 1 lf. with crayon scribble on blank verso, 1 copper engr. slightly cold. in, later leath., blind-tooled, gt. outer dentelle, wear, jnts. partly torn; Hauswedell coll. (H. May 23; 43) DM 7,200

LAROUSSE, Pierre
- Grand Dictionnaire Universel du 19e Siècle. Paris, 1866 & following. 16 vols. 4to. Cont. hf. mor., lacks 2nd. supplement. (HD. Apr.11; 33) Frs. 4,500
- – Anr. Edn. N.d. 17 vols. 4to. Publishers hf. havanna chagrin. (HD. Dec.9; 151) Frs. 6,000
- – Anr. Copy. 17 vols., including 2 supps. 4to. Publisher's hf. chagrin. (HD. Jan.27; 201) Frs. 5,200
- Grande Larousse Encyclopédique. Paris, [1960-64]. 10 vols. Sm. 4to. Orig. bdgs. gt. (H. Nov.23; 101) DM 440

LARRAMENDI, Manuel de
- Diccionario Trilingue de Castellane, Bascuence, y Latin. San Sebastien, 1745. 2 vols. Sm. fo. 1 title soiled, a few ll. reprd., later spr. cf., spines gt., rubbed; bkplt. of Milton, Peterborough. (BBA. Jul.27; 79) *Loman.* £95

LARRETA, Enrique
- La Gloire de Don Ramire. Trans.:– R. de Gourmont. Ill.:– Jean Gabriel Daragnes. Paris, 1934. *(130) numbered on vélin de Rives.* 3 vols. 4to. Leaves, wraps., folders & s.-c. (HD. May 16; 77) Frs. 1,300

LARREY, Dominique Jean, Baron
- Mémoires de Chirurgie Militaire et Campagnes. 1812 & 1817. *1st. Edn.* 4 vols. Cont. decor. spr. cf.; autograph dedication 'à Monsieur l'Intendant Général Daure'. (HD. Mar.21; 165) Frs. 14,300

- Relations Médicales de Campagnes et Voyages, de 1815 à 1840. Paris, 1841. *1st. Edn.* Some foxing, disbnd. (SG. Mar.22; 191) $100

LARREY, I. de
- Gesch. v. Engelandt, Schotlandt en Ierlandt. Trans.:– J.L. Schuer. Ill.:– Rom. de Hooghe. Amst., 1728-41. 4 vols. Fo. Vol. 4 stained in upr. margins, cont. hf. cf., unc., slightly worn. (VG. Sep.14; 1105) Fls. 580

LARSEN, H.
- Skisser fra Zululand. Decorah, Iowa, 1905. Orig. bdg. (VA. Oct.28; 496) R 300

LARTIGUE, J.-H.
- Boyhood Photos of J.-H. Lartigue: The Family Album of a Gilded Age. [Lausanne, 1966]. *1st. Edn. in Engl.* Ob. 4to. Gt.-lettered cl., with mntd. photographic reproduction, orig. shipping box. (SG. May 10; 81) $200
- – Anr. Copy. Ob. 4to. Gt.-lettered cl., with mntd. photographic reproduction. (SG. Nov.10; 101) $175
- Les Photographies de ... Un Album de Famille de la Belle Epoque. [Lausanne, 1966]. *1st. Edn.* Ob. 4to. Gt.-lettered cl., with mntd. photographic reproduction. (SG. Nov.10; 100) $120

LA RUE, Charles de
- Carminum Libri Quatuor. Paris, 1680. 4to. Cont. mott. cf., worn. (BBA. Jun.28; 147) *Dilua.* £80
- Idyllia. Paris, 1672. 12mo. Roan, richly gt., sm. wormhole to 1 jnt. (HD. Mar.19; 138) Frs. 1,000

LA RUE, J. de
- Traité de la Coupe des Pierres. Paris, 1764. 3 plts. with overslips (as called for), cont. mott. cf., spine gt., jnts. slightly split. (CSK. May 18; 77) £220

LASALLE, M. de
See— POUQUEVILLE, Francois Charles Hughes Laurent - ARTAUD, Chevalier - LASALLE, M. de

LAS CASAS, Bartolome de
- An Account of the First Voyages & Discoveries made by the Spanish in America. L., 1699. Some browning, cont. bkplt., spr. cf. [Sabin 12289; Wing C797] (S. May 22; 391) *Frers.* £400
- Conquista dell'Indie Occidentali. Trans.:– Marco Ginammi. Venice, 1645. *1st. Italian Edn.* Sm. 4to. Spanish & Italian text, mod. mor., gt. back, leath.-edged cl. s.-c. [Sabin 11248] (SG. Apr.5; 45) $200
- La Decouverte des Indes Occidentales par les Espagnols et les Moyens dont ils se sont servis pour s'en rendre Maîtres. Trans.:– Abbé de Bellegarde. Ill.:– P. Giffart (frontis.). Paris, 1701. 12mo. Cont. spr. roan, spine decor. (HD. Nov.9; 130) Frs. 1,400
- Entre los Remedios. Seville, 1552. 4to. Browned & foxed, mod. parch. covered bds. [Sabin 11229] (SPB. Dec.13; 699) $750
- Istoria o Brevissima Relatione della Distruttione dell' Indie Occidental. Trans.:– Gicaomo Castellani. Venice, 1643. Sm. 4to. Spanish & Italian text, mod. mor., gt. back, leath.-edged cl. s.-c. [Sabin 11244] (SG. Apr.5; 46) $200
- – Anr. Edn. Venecia, n.d. 4to. Vell. (DS. Mar.23; 2044) Pts. 90,000
- Narratio Regionvm Indicarvm per Hispanos quosdam Deuastatarum Verissima. Ill.:– De Bry. Frankfurt, 1598. *1st. Latin Edn.* 4to. Title lf. with worming, lr. margin bkd., MS. owners mark cut from lr. margin, some slight soiling or browning, 2 ll. reprd. in fold, lacks last lf. blank, 6 copper engrs. slightly cold. in some places, old bds., slightly bumped, spine pasted. [Sabin 11283] (H. May 22; 272) DM 1,900
- Relations des Voyages et des Découvertes que les Espagnols ont fait dans le Indes Occidentales; L'Art de Voyager Utilement. Amst., 1698. 12mo. Bkplt. on title verso, cont. cf., slightly worn. (S. Jun.25; 90) *Duval.* £180
- Il Supplice Schia Indiano. Trans.:– Marco Ginammi. Venice, 1657. Sm. 4to. Spanish & Italian text, mod. mor., gt. back, leath.-edged cl. s.-c. [Sabin 11247] (SG. Apr.5; 47) $175
- Warhafftiger und gründlicher Bericht der Hispanier Grewlich und Abschewlichen Tyranney von Ihnen in den West Indien ... Ill.:– after J. van Winghe.

Oppenh., 1613. *3rd. German Edn.* 4to. Wide margin, some ll. slightly stained, new bds. [Sabin 11280] (D. Nov.23; 1324) DM 4,200

LAS CASES, Emmanuel Auguste Dieu-Donné Marius Joseph, Marquis de, Comte de 'A. Le Sage'
- Atlas Historico, Genealogico, Cronologico, Geografico, etc. Paris, 1826. Fo. Ptd. title in woodcut device, 37 double-p. tables, mostly hand-cold., some browning, publisher's bds. (S. Mar.6; 109) *Browning.* £70
- Mémorial de Sainte Hélène; Journal of the Private Life & Conversations of the Emperor Napoleon at Saint Helena. 1823. *1st. Edn. in Engl.* 8 vols. Cont. hf. cf., spines gt. (LC. Oct.13; 358) £80
- – Anr. Edn. Ill.:– Charlet. 1842. *1st. Printing.* 2 vols. Lge. 8vo. Cont. hf. cf. (HD. Mar.21; 166) Frs. 1,200

LA SERRE, Jean Puget de
See— PUGET DE LA SERRE, Jean

LASINIO, Carlo
- Ornati Presi da Graffiti e Pitture Antiche esistenti in Firenzi. Firenzi, 1789. Fo. Frontis. & 40 engraved plts., hf. cf. (CR. Jul.6; 200) Lire 200,000

LASINIO, G.P.
- Pitture a Fresco del Camposanto di Pisa. Ill.:– G.P. Lasinio after G. Rossi. Flor., 1832. Fo. Slightly foxed, hf. vell. (HK. Nov.8; 1078) DM 620

LASINSKY, J.A.
- Croquis Pittoresques. Cinquante-Cinq Vues de Rhin. Frankfurt, 1829. Ob. 4to. Engraved title, folding map, 55 plts., orig. bds., worn. (P. Mar.15; 229a) *Burgess.* £1,450

LASKER-SCHULER, Else
- Gesamtausgabe. 1919-20. *1st. Edn. (3 vols.).* 10 vols. Orig. hf. vell., s.-c., some slight slits, end-papers mostly slightly foxed. (GB. May 5; 2864) DM 800

LASSAGA, J.L. de & others
[–] Representaciones del Real Tribunal de Mineria a Favor de su Importante Cuerpo. Mexico, 1781. Fo. Disbnd. (S. May 22; 401) *Cortes.* £380

LASSAIGNE, Jacques
- Chagall. Paris, 1957. Orig. litho. wraps. (R. Oct.11; 822) DM 1,200
- – Anr. Copy. 14 (of 15) orig. cold. lithos., orig. bds. with cold. orig. graphic wrap. ill. (GB. May 5; 2273) DM 950
- – Anr. Copy. 12 (of 15) orig. cold. lithos., orig. pict. bds., orig. cold. pict. wrap. (GB. Nov.5; 2342) DM 800
- – Anr. Edn. [Paris, 1957]. *1st. Edn.* Sm. 4to. Col. litho. stiff wraps., glassine d.-w. (SG. Mar.29; 44) $400
- – Anr. Copy. 4to. Lacks 3 cold. lithos., 1 plt. loose, margins slightly browned, orig. bds., cold. lithos. pict. orig. bds., slightly browned. (HK. Nov.11; 3467a) DM 750
- Le Plafond de l'Opéra de Paris. Ill.:– Chagall. Monte-Carlo, 1965. 4to. Orig. litho. loose, orig. linen, orig. wraps. (D. Nov.24; 2977) DM 400

LASSAIGNE, Jacques (Text)
See— CHAGALL, Marc

LASSALLE, L.
- Costumes Suisses des 22 Cantons. Genf, ca. 1850. Cont. bds., orig. ptd. wraps. mntd. over, slightly bumped. (R. Oct.13; 3272) DM 3,100

LASSELS, Richard
- The Voyage of Italy. 1686. 2 pts. in 1 vol. Sig. on title-p., some browning, cont. cf. [Wing L466b] (BBA. Jun.14; 60) *Marlborough Rare Books.* £90

LASSERE, Loys
- La Vie de Monseigneur Sainct Hierosme. Paris, 1541. *Latest Edn.* 4to. Early 19th. C. hf. cf., spine decor.; cont. MS. note, sigd. by Picart, to 'sa très chère niepce et amye'. (HD. Nov.9; 9) Frs. 3,600

LATHAM, Charles
- In English Homes. L., 1904-09. 3 vols. Orig. cl. gt., very slight wear. (S. May 1; 557) *Potterton.* £90

LATHAM, Charles -*Contd.*

– – **Anr. Copy.** 3 vols. Fo. Cl. gt., rubbed. (P. Mar.15; 78)   *Clegg.* £70
– – **Anr. Copy.** 3 vols. Fo. Photo. ills., ex-liby., elab. gt.-pict. buckram. (SG. May 3; 232) $400
– – **Anr. Edn.** L., 1909. Vols. [I] & III only. Fo. Gt.-pict. cl., rubbed & shaken. (SG. Jan.26; 240) $120

LATHAM, John
– **A General Synopsis of Birds. — Supplement to the Synopsis of Birds. — Index Ornithologicus.** L., 1781[-1802]. 6 vols.; 2 vols.; 2 vols. Together 10 vols. 4to. 8 hand-cold. engraved titles, 142 hand-cold. engraved plts., cont. spr. cf. gt., gt. spines; John Plumtre bkplts. (C. Jun.27; 121)   *Maggs.* £2,000
– **Index Ornithologicus, sive Systema Ornithologiae.** Priv. ptd., 1790. *1st. Edn.* 2 vols. 4to. Mott. cf. gt. (BBA. Jan.19; 35)   *Evans.* £110

LATHAM, Simon
– **Falconry, or, the Faulcons Lure & Cure.** L., 1633. *2nd. Edn.* 2 vols. in 1. 4to. With lf. of Acrostic of author's name before sig. B & integral blank lf. between 2 pts., mod. crushed mor., by French Bindery, Garden City. [NSTC 15267.7] (SG. Apr.26; 124) $850

LATIUM
– **Description of Latium or La Campagna di Roma.** L., 1805. 4to. 20 engrs., cf., defect. (CR. Jun.6; 87)   Lire 280,000

LA TORRECILLA, Marques de
– **Indice de Bibliografia Hipica Espagnola y Portuguesa.** Madrid, 1916-21. Fo. Leath. (R. Apr.3; 652)   DM 700

LATOUR, Charlotte de
– **Le Language des Fleurs.** Paris, n.d. *2nd. Edn.* Hand-cold. vig., 14 hand-cold. plts., some spotting, cf., rubbed. (P. Jan.12; 156)   *Edmunds.* £50

LATOUR, J.L.F.D.
– **Essai sur le Rhumatisme.** Paris, 1803. *1st. Publd. Edn.* Some light foxing, cont. leath. gt., corners lightly bumped. (R. Apr.4; 1328)   DM 400

LATROBE, Charles Joseph
– **The Rambler in North America** ... 1835. *1st. Edn.* 2 vols. Orig. cl., unc.; Sir Ivar Colquhoun, of Luss copy. (CE. Mar.22; 185)   £220

LATROBE, Rev. Christian Ignatius
– **Journal of a Visit to South Africa in 1815, & 1816.** L., 1818. *1st. Edn.* 4to. Lge. engraved folding map, 16 full-p. plts., including 12 hand-cold., title & 1 or 2 ll. spotted, fore-margins of 1 or 2 plts. slightly frayed, cont. cf. gt. (S. Dec.1; 361)   *Botts.* £440
– – **Anr. Copy.** 4to. Lge. engraved folding map & 16 plts., including 12 hand-cold. aquatints, title & a few ll. spotted, cont. cf., slightly rubbed. (S. May 22; 419)   *Sawyer.* £380
– – **Anr. Copy.** 4to. Lacks folding map, some light foxing, newer bds. (GB. Nov.3; 37)   DM 1,000
– – **Anr. Copy.** 4to. Cont. hf. cf., upr. cover loose, lr. section of spine lacking. (SSA. Jul.5; 234)   R 470
– – **Anr. Copy.** 4to. Foxing, hf. cf. & marb. bds., rubbed, edges worn. (VA. Apr.27; 679)   R 450
– – **Anr. Copy.** Hf. cf., covers loose, spine worn. (SSA. Jul.5; 233)   R 380

LATUADA, S.
– **Descrizione di Milano** ... Milan, 1737. 5 vols. 12mo. Old Bradel bds., gt. dentelle. (HD. Dec.2; 107)   Frs. 3,800
– – **Anr. Edn.** Milan, 1737-38. 5 vols. Frontis., lge. plan & 45 plts., 1 plt. reprd., vell. (VG. May 3; 661)   Fls. 450

LAUCHE, Wilhelm
– **Deutsche Pomologie.** Berlin, [1879-]1882. 1st. Series: 4 vols. Some foxing, loose in linen box, defect. (R. Oct.12; 1841)   DM 1,100

LAUCKHARD, C.F.
– **Orbis Pictus.** Leipzig, [1857 &] ca. 1862. *1st. Edn. Vol. I, 3rd. Edn. Vol. III.* Vols. I & III (of 3) in 2 vols. 4to. 60 cold. steel engraved plts., some

plts. slightly browned, vol. II slightly spotted & cut close at upr. margin, text with slight browning, hand-bnd. hf. leath., 1 orig. wrap. cover bnd. in. (H. Nov.23; 848)   DM 640
– – **Anr. Edn.** Ill.:– W. Müller, G. Brinckmann & others after Neu, Jaede & Lucas. Leipzig, Ca. 1860. *1st. Edn.?* Vols. 2 & 3 (of 3). 4to. 60 hand-cold. engraved plts., slightly spotted, orig. cl.-bkd. ptd. bds.; van Veen coll. (S. Feb.28; 153)   £240
– **Die Welt in Bildern.** Leipzig, [1860]. 4to. Minimal spotting, red leath. with old gt. (R. Nov.10; 2912)   DM 1,500

LAUER, Ph.
See— BLUM, A. & Lauer, Ph.
See— MARTIN, H. & Lauer, Ph.

LAUGHTON, L.G. Carr
– **Old Ship Figure Heads & Sterns.** 1925. 4to. Orig. cl., d.-w. (CSK. May 4; 127)   £95
– – **Anr. Edn.** 1925. *(1500)* numbered. 4to. Some ll. spotted, orig. cl. gt., d.-w. (BBA. Nov.10; 333)   *Blackwell.* £130
– – **Anr. Edn.** L., 1925. *(100)* numbered. 4to. Plts., some cold., ills., hf. mor., partly unc. (S. Apr.9; 216)   *Edwards.* £70

LAUGIER, Marc Antoine
[–] **Histoire de la République de Venise.** Paris, 1759-68. 12 vols. 12mo. Bdg. not stated. (HD. Oct.14; 98)   Frs. 1,300

LAUGIER DE TASSY
– **Histoire du Royaume d'Alger.** Amst., 1725. 12mo. Engraved vig. title & 2 folding maps, 1 torn, browned, cont. cf., rubbed. (BBA. Jul.27; 77)   *Adab Books.* £60

LAUJON, Pierre de
– **Les A Propos de Sociéte.** Ill.:– Moreau, [Paris], 1773. 2 vols. *(With:)* – **Les A Propos de la Folie.** Ill.:– Moreau, [Paris], 1773. 1 vol. Together 3 vols. Cont. marb. cf., spines decor. (HD. May 3; 83)   Frs. 2,100

LAUNAY, Marie de
See— BEY, Hamdy & Launay, Marie de

LAURENCE, E.
– **The Duty of a Steward to his Lord.** 1727. 4to. Cf., upr. cover detchd.; from the Farmers' Club Liby. (P. Jul.5; 15)   £80

LAURENCE, John
– **A New System of Agriculture, Being a Complete Body of Husbandry & Gardening.** 1726. *1st. Edn.* Fo. Cont. panel. cf. (TA. Oct.20; 144)   £100

LAURENCIN, Marie
– **Deuxième Album.** Ill.:– after Paul Rosenberg & others. Paris, n.d. *(250).* Fo. Leaves, folder. (HD. Jun.6; 88)   Frs. 1,600
– **Eventail.** Poems:– Louis Codet, Jean Pellerin, R. Allard, A. Breton, F. Carco & others. 1922. *Orig. Edn. (300) on vergé de Hollande.* Sewed. (HD. Apr.13; 170)   Frs. 10,500

LAURENT DE L'ARDECHE, Paul Mathieu
– **Histoire de l'Empereur Napoléon** ... Ill.:– Clerget (frontis.) & H. Bellangé. 1840. *New Edn.* Lge. 8vo. Str.-grd. red mor. gt. by F. Michon, spine decor. (unif. faded), unc., wraps. (lightly soiled) (HD. May 4; 331)   Frs. 3,300
– – **Anr. Copy.** Lge. 8vo. 2 frontis. & 44 cold. plts., cont. hf. roan, spine decor., worn. (HD. Jun.26; 19)   Frs. 1,850

LAURENTIUS or DU LAURENS, Andréas
– **Historia Anatomica Humani Corporis.** Frankfurt, [1600]. *2nd. Edn. Ill. Edn.* Fo. Sm. worm-hole at head, mostly in margin, minimal loss, blind-tooled leath. (HK. May 15; 450)   DM 1,600

LAURIE, Robert & Whittle, James
– **[Atlas].** L., [maps dtd. 1794]. Fo. 64 engraved maps, hand-cold. in outl., many frayed, torn or brittle at edges, loose, disbnd. (BBA. Dec.15; 123)   *Jeffery.* £260
– **Laurie & Whittle's Welsh Atlas; Comprehending New & Accurate Maps of the Respective Counties of North & South Wales, Divided into Hundreds, with the Turnpike Roads.** 1805. Ob. 4to. Additional engraved title, engraved frontis., 13 hand-cold. engraved maps, engraved explanation plt., offsetting onto text ll., orig. hf. roan, spine gt., marb.

bds., a little rubbed, w.a.f. (LC. Mar.1; 257) £150
– **New Traveller's Companion: Exhibiting a Complete & Correct Survey of all the Direct & Principle Cross Roads, in England, Wales & Scotland ... by Nathaniel Coltman.** 1814. *7th. Edn.* Tall 8vo. 25 hand-cold. double-p. maps, some spotting, orig. wallet-type mor., worn. (TA. Jun.21; 181)   £58
– – **Anr. Edn.** L., 1834. Sm. 4to. Engraved title, folding general map, 25 double-p. engraved road maps, mostly hand-cold. in outl., some light offsetting, cont. limp roan. (S. Mar.6; 286)   *Burgess.* £130

LAUROP, C.P. (Ed.)
See— SYLVAN

LAUTENBACH, Conrad
See— FRANCUS, Jacobus [i.e. Conrad Memmius or Lautenbach]

LAUTREAMONT, Comte de (Pseud.)
See— DUCASSE, Isidore-Lucien, 'Comte de Lautreamont'

LAUTTE, J.
[–] **Le Iardin d'Armoires cont. les Armes de Plusieurs Nobles Royaumes & Maisons de Germanie Inferieure, De Boomgaert der Wapenen.** Gendt, 1567. Sm. 8vo. Title reprd., some cont. annots., lacks last lf. with arms & errata, 19th. C. hf. cf., defect. (VS. Dec.9; 1213)   Fls. 725

LAVAL
– **Sentences, Prières et Instructions Chrestiennes.** 1676. 17th. C. decor. red mor., François de Harlay-Chamvallon arms. (HD. Mar.21; 82)   Frs. 1,600

LAVAL, Antoine Jean de
– **Voyage de la Louisiane fait par ordre du Roy.** Paris, 1728. *1st. Edn.* 4to. 20 engraved maps, diagrams & charts, some folding, 11 folding tables, cont. cf., gt. spine, upr. cover loosening; the Rt. Hon. Visc. Eccles copy. [Sabin 39276] (CNY. Nov.18; 169) $1,200

LAVALLEE, Joseph
– **Travels in Istria & Dalmatia, drawn up from the Itinerary of L.F. Cassas.** L., 1805. *1st. Engl. Edn.* Cont. hf. leath., slightly defect. (BR. Apr.12; 58)   DM 550
– **Voyage Dans les Departements de la France.** 1792-1803. 12 vols. 343 maps & plts., maps hand-cold., hf. cf. gt., as a coll. of plts., w.a.f. (P. Dec.8; 116)   *Shapero.* £700
– **Voyage Pittoresque et Historique de l'Istrie et de la Dalmatie.** Ill.:– Née, after Cassas. Paris, 1802. Fo. Hf.-title, subscribers list, additional engraved title with lge. vig., head-pieces, 2 engraved double-p. maps, frontis., 70 engraved architectural & other views & plts. on 65 ll., some double-p. or folding, cont. red str.-grd. mor., covers with gt. ornamental border & decor., spine gt. in compartments, corners & jnts. rubbed. (C. Jun.27; 43)   *Campbell.* £2,000
– – **Anr. Edn.** An X [1802]. Fo. Lge. vig. on title, frontis., map & 66 engrd. plts., subscribers list, mod. spr. hf. cf., corners. (HD. Jun.18; 8)   Frs. 13,000

LA VALLIERE, Duchesse de
– **Réflexions sur la Misericorde de Dieu.** Paris, 1697. *7th. Edn.* 12mo. Cont. Jansenist red mor., blind-decor. (HD. Mar.29; 54)   Frs. 7,000

LA VALLIERE, Louis-César de La Baume Le Blanc, Duc de
– **Bibliothèque du Théâtre Français.** Dresde, 1768. *Orig. Edn.* 3 vols. Sm. 8vo. Cont. marb. cf., spine decor. (HD. Nov.9; 44)   Frs. 1,000

LA VARENDE, Jean de
– **L'Homme aux Gants de Toile.** Ill.:– Louis Soulas (frontis.). Paris, 1943. *Orig. Edn. (30) numbered on vélin pur chiffon.* 12mo. Hf. mor. by Houdart, unc., wrap. & spine. (HD. Mar.27; 81) Frs. 1,300

LA VARENNE, François Pierre
– **Le Cuisinier François.** Rouen, ca. 1735. 12mo. Some upr. corners torn at beginning, re-used limp vell. (HD. Mar.19; 54)   Frs. 2,100
– **Le Vray Cuisinier François.** Paris, 1682. 2 pts. in 1 vol. 12mo. 1st. advt. lf., some ll. slightly soiled, cont. cf., spine gt., slightly rubbed. (BBA. Nov.30; 54)   *Segal.* £150

-- **Anr. Edn.** Amst., ca. 1690. Cont. leath. gt., lightly rubbed. (R. Apr.4; 1915)   DM 950

LAVATER, Johann Kaspar
- L'Art de Connâitre les Hommes par la Physionomie. Paris, 1806-07. 10 vols. 4to. Lacks 2 engrs., hf. chagrin, corners, ca. 1840. (HD. Mar.21; 167)   Frs. 4,800
- Essai sur la Physiognomonie destinée à faire connaître l'Homme et à le faire aimer. La Haye, 1781-86. *1st. Fr. Edn.* 3 vols. Fo. Lacks 2 title pieces, & 1 plt. Vol. II, cont. cf. (HD. Feb.22; 113)   Frs. 2,400
-- **Anr. Edn.** Ill.:– Chodowiecki, Berger, Lips, Schellenberg & others. Den Haag, [1781-]1803. *1st. Fr. Edn.* 4 vols. Fo. Wide margin, minimal browning, cont. cf. gt., spine cold. red, worn. (H. Nov.23; 701)   DM 2,300
- Essays on Physiognomy. Trans.:– T. Holcroft. L., 1789. 3 vols. Orig. marb. bds. (PD. Dec.14; 241)   £75
-- **Anr. Copy.** 3 vols. Hf. cf., gt. spines. (CR. Jul.6; 46)   Lire 350,000
-- **Anr. Edn.** Trans.:– Henry Hunter. Ill.:– Thomas Holloway. L., 1789-98. 3 vols. in 5. 4to. Cont. russ. gt., spines gt.-decor., slightly faded; Sir Ivar Colquhoun, of Luss copy. (CE. Mar.22; 186) £360
-- **Anr. Copy.** 3 vols. in 5. Lge. 4to. Lacks hf.-titles, scattered foxing, mainly marginal, cont. cf., lacks 1 spine label, jnts. defect.; cont. sigs. of Robert Milligan, Henry Davidson armorial bkplts. (SG. Mar.22; 192) $500
-- **Anr. Copy.** 3 vols. in 5 pts. 4to. Some foxing, later owner's stps., cont. diced cf. gt. extra, defect., rebkd.; subscriber's copy, armorial bkplts. of James Caulfield, 1st. Earl of Charlemont. (SG. Nov.3; 118) $400
-- **Anr. Copy.** 5 vols. 4to. Cf., spines slightly worn. (CR. Jul.6; 201)   Lire 750,000
-- **Anr. Edn.** L., 1792. 3 vols. in 5. 4to. Cont. cf. gt., 2 covers slightly rubbed. (S. Dec.13; 283)   *Traylen.* £250
-- **Anr. Copy.** 3 vols. in 4. Fo. Minor foxing or soiling, 19th. C. gt.-decor. & blind-stpd. cf., Vol. 1 lacks orig. fly-ll., new end-papers, few minor defects, rebkd. with gt.-decor. ribbed spines, light scuffing to extremities, several corners defect. (CBA. Aug.21; 374) $275
-- **Anr. Edn.** Ed.:– Gessner. L., 1804. 3 vols. in 4. Port., 424 plts. (irregularly numbered?), 1 plt. with short tear Vol. 3, cont. hf. cf., rubbed, some covers loose; w.a.f. due to possible lack of plts. (S. Apr.10; 540)   *Diaz.* £75
-- **Anr. Edn.** Trans.:– Henry Hunter. Ill.:– William Blake & others. L., 1810. 3 vols. in 5. 4to. 174 plts., text engrs., many offsets onto text, cont. hf. mor. (S. Apr.10; 541)   *Jones.* £150
- Hand-Bibliotheck für Freunde ... 1793. [Zürich, 1793]. 6 vols. 12mo. Cont. hf. cf., spines gt.; each vol. inscr. by author to 'Freund Steiner'. (C. Dec.9; 260)   *Braecklein.* £420
- Physiognomische Fragmente, zur Beförderung der Menschenkenntniss und Menschenliebe. Ill.:– Chodowiecki, Lips & others. Leipzig & Winterthur, 1775-78. *1st. Edn. (750).* 4 vols. 4to. Vols. I & II stained, some slight browning, cont. mor., gt., slightly discold. & spotted, rubbed; Hauswedell coll. (H. May 24; 1440)   DM 6,800
-- **Anr. Edn.** Ed.:– J.M. Armbruster. Winterthur, 1783-87. 3 vols. Title lf. vols. 2 & 3 with top corner torn, vol. 1 title lf. & dedication ll. vols. 2 & 3 with name stp., vol. 2 lacks 1 plt., cont. bds. (R. Apr.3; 301)   DM 580
-- **Anr. Copy.** 3 vols. Later name on title, cont. hf. leath. gt. (R. Oct.11; 323)   DM 540
-- **Anr. Edn.** Ed.:– J.M. Armbruster. Winterthur, 1783-87, 1830 (Vol. 4). *2nd. Edn.* 4 vols. Wide margin, some slight foxing, cont. bds. gt., bumped. (HK. Nov.10; 2568)   DM 1,500
-- **Anr. Edn.** Zürich, 1968. *Facs. Reprint of Leipzig & Winterthur 1st. Edn.* 4 vols. Lge. 4to. Orig. linen, orig. wraps. (GB. Nov.4; 1231)   DM 500

LAVATER, Ludwig
- De Spectris, Lemuribus et Magnis atque Insolitis Fragoribus, Variisque Praesagitionibus ... Ill.:– R. de Hooghe. Gorinchem, 1683. *3rd. Edn.* 12mo. Some ll. & 2 copper engrs. stained, lightly browning, cont. vell., monog stp. pasted on. (H. May 22; 354)   DM 480
- Of Ghostes & Spirites, walking by Night ... Trans.:– R. H[arrison]. L., 1596. *2nd. Edn. in Engl.* Sm. 4to. Most headlines cropped or shaved, margin wormholes sometimes affecting text, 2 corners torn away without text loss, stained, early 17th. C. spr. sheep, rebkd. [STC 15321] (S. Dec.20; 677)   *Maggs.* £240

LAVAUX
- Manuel du Tribunal de Cassation, ou Règles de la Justice Civile, Criminelle, Correctionnelle et de Police ... Paris, An VI [1797]. 12mo. Cont. str-grd. red mor. gt., dedication to Citoyen Reubel on upr. cover, spine decor. (HD. May 3; 84)   Frs. 2,300

LAVER, James
- Arthur Briscoe: A Complete Catalogue of the Etchings & Dry-Points. L., 1930. *(250) numbered, with etched frontis. sigd. by artist.* 4to. Frontis., 151 reproductions, ex-liby., cl. (SG. May 3; 60) $225

LAVERRENZ, C.
- Die Medaillen und Gedächtniszeichen der Deutschen Hochschulen ... Berlin, 1887. *2nd. Edn. (Vol. 1).* 2 vols. Hf.linen, orig. wraps. mntd. on upr. cover. (R. Apr.3; 1065)   DM 620

LAVIGNAC, A. & La Laurencie, L.
- Encyclopedie de la Musique et Dictionnaire du Conservatoire. Paris, 1921-31. 2 pts. in 11 vols. 4to. Hf. chagrin, spines decor. (slightly faded). (HD. Jul.2; 79)   Frs. 1,300

LA VIGNE, André de
See— SAINT-GELAIS, Octavien de & La Vigne, André de

LA VIGNE, D. de
- La Manière de se bien preparer à la Mort par des Considérations sur la Cène, la Passion et la Mort de Jésus-Christ. Ed.:– M. de Chertablon. Ill.:– R. de Hooghe. Antw., 1700. *1st. Fr. Edn.* 4to. Stain thro.-out, some slight browning & spotting, 1 plt. with sm. hole, cont. cf., very worn, spine tear, inside cover sm. wormhole & coll. stp. (H. May 22; 456)   DM 1,600
- Spiegel om wel te Sterven, Aanwyzende met Beeltenissen v.h. Lyden onses Zaligmaakers Jesu Christi. Amst., 1694. 42 engraved plts. (*Bound with:*) DE CHERTABLON – La Manière de se bien Préparer à la Mort. Anvers, 1700. Together 2 works in 1 vol. 4to. Fr. text apparently from anr. edn., some foxing, mod. black mor. gt. by Hardy, silk end-ll. (VS. Dec.9; 1144)   Fls. 650

LAVISSE, Ernest & Rambaud, A.
- Histoire Générale du IVe Siècle à nos Jours. 1922-25. 12 vols. Hf. chagrin, some spines faded. (HD. Dec.9; 152)   Frs. 1,200

LAVOISIER, Antoine Laurent
- Elements of Chemistry. Trans.:– Robert Kerr. Edinb., 1790. *1st. Edn. in Engl.* 13 double-p. or folding plts., 2 folding tables, lacks hf.-title, slight browning, mod. hf. cf. (S. Apr.10; 542)   *Bickersteth.* £120
-- **Anr. Edn.** Edinb., 1799. *4th. Edn. in Engl.* Hf.-title, some ll. dampstained. (*Bound with:*) SCHERER, Dr. A.N. – A Short Introduction to the Knowledge of Gaseous Bodies. 1800. Together 2 works in 1 vol. Cont. hf. cf., worn. (BBA. Jan.19; 47)   *Gurney.* £110
-- **Anr. Copy.** 13 folding engraved plts. (& dupl. of plt. 9), hf.-title, tables, cont. marb. cf. gt., rebkd. (LC. Mar.1; 167)   £70
- Recueil de Mémoires et d'Observations sur la Formation & sur la Fabrication du Salpetre. Paris, 1776. *1st. Edn.* Cont. marb. leath. gt., lightly rubbed & bumped. (HK. Nov.8; 633) DM 1,200
- Traité Elémentaire de Chimie. Ill.:– Mme Lavoisier. Paris, 1789. *1st. Edn. 2nd. Iss.* 2 vols. Sm. repairs to 2 plts., some discoloration, cont. Spanish mott. cf., labels possibly later, traces of worm in spines, sm. repair to 1 spine & 1 corner. (C. May 30; 118)   *Gurney.* £600
-- **Anr. Edn.** 1793. *2nd. Edn.* 2 vols. Cont. cf. (HD. Jan.24; 33)   Frs. 1,400
-- **Anr. Edn.** Paris, An IX/1801. *3rd. Edn.* 2 vols. Cont. hf. leath. (R. Oct.12; 1691)   DM 1,300

LAVOISNE, C.V.
- Complete Genealogical, Historical, Chronological & Geographical Atlas. 1814. Fo. 64 handcold. double-p. maps & charts, cont. hf. cf., upr. cover detchd. (SKC. Jan.13; 2383)   £50
-- **Anr. Edn.** Ed.:– J. Satchell. 1840. 26 hand-cold. maps, cold. tables, mor. gt. (P. Oct.20; 269)   £60

LAW, John of Lauriston
- Considerations sur le Commerce & l'Argent. La Haye, 1720. *1st. Fr. Edn.* With port., cf., gt. back, top of spine & corners slightly defect. (VG. May 3; 453)   Fls. 900

LAWATZ, H.W.
- Ueber die Tugenden und Laster ... Flensburg, Schleswig, Leipzig, 1789-92. 3 vols. Cont. hf. leath. (D. Nov.23; 3986)   DM 400

LAWRENCE, David Herbert
- Amores. L., [1916]. 16 pp. advts., cl. mostly unopened, partly unc.; Albert Parsons Sachs bkplt. (SG. Mar.1; 220) $175
- Apocalypse. Flor., 1931. *(750) numbered.* Emblematic bds., partly unopened, d.-w. (SG. Mar.1; 222) $130
- Bay: a Book of Poems. Ill.:– Anne Estelle Rice. [L., Beaumont Pr., 1919]. *1st. Edn. (30) numbered on Japan vell., sigd. by author & artist.* 12mo. Orig. vell.-bkd. bds. (CNY. May 18; 114) $850
- Birds, Beasts & Flowers. N.Y., 1923. Sm. 4to. Cl., qtr. mor. s.-c. (SG. Mar.1; 224) $110
-- **Anr. Edn.** Ill.:– Blair Hughes-Stanton. L., Cresset Pr., 1930. *1st. Ill. Edn. (500) numbered on H.M.P.* Fo. Extra suite of proofs of ills. in lr. cover pocket, orig. pig, partly unc., slightly scuffed. (CNY. May 18; 122) $400
- The Escaped Cock. Paris, Black Sun Pr., 1929. *(450) numbered.* Sm. 4to. Ptd. wraps., glassine d.-w. (SG. Mar.1; 229) $275
- Glad Ghosts. L., 1926. *(500).* 12mo. Ptd. wraps., later qtr. mor. s.-c. (SG. Mar.1; 230) $100
- Lady Chatterley's Lover. Flor., priv. ptd., 1928. *1st. Edn. (1000) numbered & sigd.* Lge. 8vo. Red hf. mor., partly unc., slightly marked. (S. Dec.8; 232)   *Beecham.* £300
-- **Anr. Copy.** Some light soiling, orig. bds., rebkd., old spine laid down, lightly soiled. (CSK. Jan.13; 119)   £200
-- **Anr. Copy.** Orig. bds., covers loose, spine defect. (P. Apr.12; 255)   £100
-- **Anr. Copy.** Lge. 8vo. Orig. bds., unc., extremities slightly worn, d.-w. badly worn, buckram folding case. (SG. Jan.12; 198) $650
-- **Anr. Copy.** Title torn & tissue-bkd., few stains, emblematic bds., unc., rebkd. & recornered, orig. backstrip laid down. (SG. Mar.1; 231) $275
-- **Anr. Edn.** Priv. ptd., 1929. *Unabridged Popular Edn.* Crimson mor. gt. by Maltby, upr. cover decor. with leafy sprays, 'John Thomas A New Gospel' on spine, orig. wraps. bnd. in. (P. Jul.5; 119)   £140
- Last Poems. Flor., 1932. *1st. Edn. (750) numbered.* Lge. 8vo. Bds., buckram folding case. (SG. Jan.12; 206) $100
- The Lost Girl. L., [1920]. *1st. Edn. 1st. Iss.* Sm. 8vo. Cl., buckram folding case. (SG. Jan.12; 196) $175
- Love Poems & Others. L., 1913. *[1st. Edn.].* Lge. 8vo. With reading 's' for 'is' on p. xlv, cl. (SG. Mar.1; 235) $140
-- **Anr. Copy.** Lge. 8vo. Cl. (SG. Jan.12; 193) $110
- The Paintings. L., Mandrake Pr., [1929]. *1st. Edn. (500) numbered.* Fo. 26 cold. plts., hf.-title, colophon/limitation-lf. at end, orig. hf. mor., partly unc., stained. (S. Oct.11; 349)   *Subunso.* £150
-- **Anr. Copy.** Fo. Orig. maroon hf. mor., partly unc., slight scuffing at corners. (CNY. May 18; 119) $260
- Pansies. L., [1929]. *1st. Edn. (250) numbered & sigd.* Orig. bds., d.-w. worn; Frederick Dannay copy. (CNY. Dec.16; 204) $200
-- **Anr. Edn.** L., priv. ptd., 1929. *Definitive Edn. (500) numbered & sigd.* Frontis., orig. wraps., unc., s.-c. (S. Apr.9; 266)   *Gerrard.* £150
-- **Anr. Copy.** Orig. ptd. wraps., tissue overlay d.-w., publisher's box slightly worn; Frederick Dannay copy. (CNY. Dec.16; 205) $210

LAWRENCE, David Herbert *-Contd.*

- - **Anr. Copy.** Orig. ptd. wraps., tissue overlay d.-w., publisher's box worn. (CNY. May 18; 120) $200
- - **Anr. Edn..** [L.], priv. ptd., 1929. *Definitive Edn. (50) numbered & sigd., specially bnd.* Orig. flexible pig., publisher's box slightly worn; bkplt. of John Kobler, Frederick Dannay copy. (CNY. Dec.16; 206) $800
- - **Anr. Copy.** Orig. pig, spine faded, some foxing on covers. (CNY. May 18; 121) $300
- **The Prussian Officer & other Stories.** L., 1914. *1st. Edn.* 20 pp. catalogue, orig. cl.; bkplt. of David Garnett. (BBA. Mar.21; 297)
     W. Forster. £100
- - **Anr. Edn.** N.Y., 1916. *1st. Amer. Edn.* Cl., d.-w. slightly worn. (SG. May 24; 318) $110
- **Rawdon's Roof.** L., 1928. *(530) numbered & sigd.* Sm. 4to. Decor. bds. (SG. May 24; 93) $250
- - **Anr. Copy.** Sm. 4to. Decor. bds., d.-w. (SG. Mar.1; 242) $175
- **Sun.** L., 1926. *1st. Edn. (100) numbered.* 4to. Orig. ptd. mott. wraps., unopened, discold. (CNY. May 18; 116) $450
- - **Anr. Edn.** Paris, Black Sun Pr., 1928. *1st: Unexpurgated Edn. (165). (150).* 1 vol. Orig. ptd. wraps., slight stains at lr. edges of tissue overlay, publisher's portfo. case (worn). (With:) - **Rawdon's Roof.** L., 1928. *1st. Edn. (530) numbered & sigd.* 1 vol. Orig. bds., d.-w. slightly frayed. (CNY. May 18; 117) $400
- **The Virgin & the Gypsy.** Flor., 1930. *1st. Edn. (810) numbered on H.M.P.* 4to. Orig. bds., d.-w. slightly torn. (BBA. Nov.30; 284) *Belanske.* £120
- - **Anr. Copy.** Orig. cl., untrimmed, d.-w. (SKC. Jan.13; 2227)   £90
- **The White Peacock.** N.Y., 1911. *1st. Edn., 1st. Imp. 2nd. Iss.* Sm. 8vo. Cancellans title-lf. reading 'Copyright, 1911', pict. cl., rubbed, slightly discold., buckram folding case. (SG. Jan.12; 192) $600
- - **Anr. Edn.** L., 1911. *1st. Edn. 1st. Engl. Imp.* Cancel title, 1911 copyright notice, & cancel pp. 227-230 with modified text, hf.-title with advts. on verso, a little slight spotting, mod. hf. mor. gt. by Bayntun. (S. Oct.11; 348)   *Primrose Hill.* £110
- **Women in Love.** N.Y., 1920. *1st. Edn. (1250) numbered.* Cl., slight wear. (P. Mar.15; 63)   £90
- - **Anr. Copy.** Tall 8vo. Cl. (SG. May 24; 319) $300
- - **Anr. Copy.** Lge. 8vo. Cl. (SG. Mar.1; 245) $130
- - **Anr. Edn.** N.Y., 1920 [L., 1922]. *1st. Edn. Engl. Iss., (50) numbered & sigd.* Tall 8vo. Sm. stain to lr. edge of 1st. 12 ll., orig. cl. (SG. Nov.3; 119) $1,300
- - **Anr. Copy.** Dampstain towards bottom of ll. on 2nd. hf. of book, orig. cl., dampstain on spine & lr. cover. (CNY. May 18; 115) $450

LAWRENCE, George N.
See— BAIRD, Spencer F. & others

LAWRENCE, Sir Henry
[–] **Some Passages in the Life of an Adventurer in the Punjaub.** Delhi, 1842. Browned, cont. cl., lightly damp-affected. (CSK. Sep.30; 26)   £240

LAWRENCE, John 'William Henry Scott'
- **British Field Sports.** 1818. *[1st. Edn.].* Additional ill. title, 33 (of 34) engraved plts., spotting to some plts. & text ll., cf. gt., rebkd., rubbed. (LC. Mar.1; 184)   £70
- - **Anr. Copy.** Some light browning, later hf. mor. gt. (R. Oct.12; 2047)   DM 680
- - **Anr. Copy.** Lacks (supp.?) 4 ll. with 'The sportsman's progress' as usual, cont. hf. leath. gt., jnts. torn. (BR. Apr.12; 1215)   DM 650
- - **Anr. Edn.** 1820. *2nd. Edn.* Additional title, 34 engraved plts., 2 slightly wormholed, mod. hf. cf. gt., spine gt. in compartments. (SKC. May 4; 1761)   £130
- **The History & Delineation of the Horse.** 1809. 4to. Some plts. lightly spotted or dampstained, some browning, later mor., rubbed. (CSK. Jun.1; 133)   £95
- - **Anr. Copy.** 4to. Frontis., engraved title, 12 plts., some spotting, hf. cf. gt., covers detchd. (P. Mar.15; 36)   *Ackermann.* £85

- - **Anr. Copy.** 4to. Engraved frontis., title, dedication, 12 engrs., some spotting, bds., unc. & worn. (P. Mar.15; 105)   *Hilde.* £70
- **The Sportsman's Repository.** Ill.:– J. Scott after Stubbs, Cooper & others. L., 1826. 4to. Engraved title with date 1820 (1st. Edn.), foxed thro.-out, cont. hf. leath., worn. (HK. Nov.9; 2188) DM 400

LAWRENCE, Richard
- **The Complete Farrier & British Sportsman.** L., 1831. 4to. Minimal spotting, leath., gold-tooled decor., flannel lined s.-c. (GF. Nov.12; 741)
     Sw.Frs. 600

LAWRENCE, Thomas Edward 'T.E. Shaw'
- **Crusader Castles.** Gold. Cock. Pr., 1936. *(1000) numbered.* 4to. Maps in loosely inserted envelope, orig. hf. mor., spines faded, slightly soiled. (S. Nov.21; 224)   *Makiya.* £320
- - **Anr. Copy.** 2 vols. 4to. Lacks inserted folder containing maps, orig. hf. mor. (TA. Dec.15; 479)   £80
- **The Diary ... MCMXI.** Corvinus Pr., 1937. *(203) numbered.* 4to. Orig. qtr. mor., vell. tips, partly untrimmed, s.-c. defect. (TA. Jul.19; 497)   £360
- **From a Letter of T.E. Lawrence.** Priv. ptd. [at the Bodoni Pr.], 1959. *[60] for pres. to members of the Double Crown Cl.* Orig. wraps., unc. (S. Nov.22; 268)   *Quaritch.* £260
- **The Mint.** 1955. *(2000).* 4to. Orig. mor.-bkd. cl., s.-c. (BBA. Feb.23; 293)   *Birnie.* £50
- - **Anr. Copy.** 4to. Qtr. lev., partly unc., s.-c. (SG. May 24; 322) $200
- **Revolt in the Desert.** L., 1927. *1st. Edn. (315) numbered.* Lge. 8vo. With 40 pp. prospectus for 'Seven Pillars of Wisdom', 1925, 4to., orig. cf.-bkd. bds., rebkd. preserving orig. spine, prospectus in orig. wraps.; 2 A.L.s from 'T.E. Shaw' to Col. M.V.B. Hill, & related correspondence from various persons to Hill, 13 pp. in all. (C. Nov.9; 176)   *Harry.* £800
- - **Anr. Copy.** 4to. Mor.-bkd. buckram., d.-w. torn. (SKC. Nov.18; 2012)   £80
- **Secret Despatches from Arabia.** Gold. Cock. Pr., [1939]. *1st. Edn. (1000) numbered.* 4to. Orig. mor.-bkd. cl., partly unc., slightly marked, bd. s.-c. (S. Oct.11; 351)   *Smith.* £130
- **Seven Pillars of Wisdom.** Ill.:– E. Kennington, W. Roberts, P. Nash, B. Hughes-Stanton, & others. L., [priv. ptd.], 1926. *1st. Edn. [170 compl. copies].* 4to. 2 folding cold. maps (each in dupl.), 66 plts., including 4 double-p., leaflet 'Some Notes on the Writing of The Seven Pillars of Wisdom by T.E. Shaw' loosely inserted, blind-stpd. & gt. mor. by Roger de Coverly & Sons; page XIX with MS. correction by author & note at foot 'Complete copy. 1.XII.26 TES'. (S. Dec.8; 234)   *Spiro.* £8,200
- - **Anr. Edn.** N.Y., 1926. *1st. Amer. Edn. (22) numbered & sigd. by publisher, for securing copyright in the U.S.* 4to. Orig. hf. vell. bds., label slightly chipped, partly unc.; inscr., 'G.C. R[amsey] ... from T.E.S. ... 29.VII.290. (S. Dec.8; 235)
     Maggs. £6,200
- - **Anr. Edn.** L., 1935. *1st. Trade Edn. (750) specially bnd.* 4to. Orig. pig-bkd. buckram, partly unc. (S. Mar.20; 935)   *Maggs.* £140
- - **Anr. Copy.** 4to. Orig. pig-bkd. buckram gt., unc. (S. Oct.4; 90)   *Joseph.* £110
- - **Anr. Copy.** 4to. Gutter margin of hf.-title slightly torn, orig. qtr. pig. & buckram, sides gt., partly unc.; 2 A.L.s from author to Meinertzhagen tipped in, R. Meinertzhagen bkplt. & note, Thomas B. Stevenson copy. (CNY. Dec.17; 580) $2,400
- - **Anr. Copy.** Sm. 4to. Qtr. pig., cl. covers, mostly unopened, spine slightly soiled. (SG. Mar.1; 264) $250
- **To his Biographer Liddell Hart; To his Biographer Robert Graves.** N.Y., 1938. *(1000) numbered & sigd. by biographer.* Together 2 vols. Orig. cl., spines soiled, s.-c. defect. (S. Mar.20; 936)
     Kassis. £65
- - **Anr. Copy.** Together 2 vols. Cl., d.-w.'s. (SG. Mar.1; 265) $265
- - **Anr. Copy.** Together 2 vols. Buckram, s.-c. (PNY. Dec.1; 63) $125
See— WOOLLEY, C. Leonard & Lawrence, Thomas Edward

LAWS OF CRICKET
Ill.:– Charles Crombie. L., n.d. Ob. fo. 12 chromo-litho. plts., 1 chromolitho. advt. lf., orig. cl.-bkd. bds., soiled, spine worn, stitching brkn. (CSK. Dec.2; 187)   £120

LAWSON, Henry
- **Kiss in the Ring.** Ill.:– G.D. Nicol. 1924. Bdg. not stated. (JL. Mar.25; 444)   Aus.$110

LAWSON, John
- **A New Voyage to Carolina.** 1709. *1st. Edn.* 4to. Last advt. lf., lacks plt., upr. margin wormed, cont. spr. cf. (BBA. Sep.29; 46)   *Brook-Hitching.* £210

LAWSON, John Parker
- **Scotland Delineated in a Series of Views ...** Ill.:– J.D. Harding after C. Stanfield, D. Roberts, & others. L., 1847. *1st. Edn.* 2 vols. Lge. fo. 60 plts., a few foxed or stained, hf. leath., spines defect. (SKC. Sep.9; 2052)   £240
- - **Anr. Edn.** Ill.:– J.D. Harding, Carrick, Cauci, Needham, & others. L., 1854. 4 vols. in 2. Lge. fo. Additional litho. title dtd. 1847, 89 uncold. views, lacks titles to Vols. 3 & 4, a few plts. spotted, last plt. in each vol. severely, cont. red hf. mor., spines gt. (C. Nov.16; 120)   *Hart.* £580
- - **Anr. Copy.** Vol. 2 only. Lge. fo. 52 engraved plts., hf. mor. gt., rubbed. (PD. May 16; 194)
     £230
- - **Anr. Edn.** L., ca. 1854. Sm. fo. Litho. title, 71 views, some spotting & staining, few sm. tears, loose, cont. hf. mor. (S. Mar.6; 368)   *Eisler.* £70
- - **Anr. Edn.** L., n.d. 4to. Orig. cl. gt., shaken & loose. (PD. Dec.14; 162)   £50

LAY, William & Hussey, Cyrus M.
- **A Narrative of the Mutiny on Board the Ship Globe, of Nantucket, in the Pacific Ocean, Jan. 1824; & the Journal of a Residence of Two Years on the Mulgrave Islands.** New London, priv. ptd., 1828. *1st. Edn.* 12mo. Foxed, some pp. at beginning & end dampstained at extremities, cont. tree cf. (SG. Oct.20; 202) $400

LAYARD, Austen Henry
- **Discoveries in the Ruins of Nineveh & Babylon.** 1853. *1st. Edn.* Orig. embossed cl. (SKC. May 4; 1810)   £50

LAYARD, Edgar Leopold
- **The Birds of South Africa.** Ed.:– R. Bowdler Sharpe. L., 1875-84. *New Edn.* Tall 8vo. 12 hand-cold. litho. plts., three-qtr. mor., lr. cover loose & sellotape reinforced, ex-liby. (SG. Oct.6; 231)
     $425

LAYARD, George Somes
- **The Life & Letters of Charles S. Keene.** 1892. *(250) numbered & sigd.* 4to. Cont. red hf. mor. gt.; added sig. & 4 line inscr. by author., Dyson Perrins bkplt. (BBA. Sep.8; 75)   *Heneage.* £55
See— SPIELMANN, Marion Harry & Layard, George Somes

LAYE, Elizabeth
[–] **Social Life & Manners in Australia ... by a Resident.** 1861. No book advts. (as iss.), bdg. not stated, slight wear. (KH. May 1; 408)   Aus.$150

LAYMOUR, Jean
- **Recueil des Ouvrages en Serrurerie, que Stanislas le Bienfaisant, Roy de Pologne ... a fait poser sur la Place Royale de Nancy.** Berlin, 19th. C. Fo. Pict. title & dedication lf., 28 facs. plts., several double-p., dedication lf. with minor margin repairs, loose as iss. in bd. folder, spine worn. (SG. Aug.25; 199)
     $150

LAZIO, P.A. de
- **Selections from the Work.** Ed.:– Oakley Williams, Essay:– R. de Montesquiou. L., [1921]. *(300) numbered.* Fo. This copy unnumbered, 64 photogravure plts., text in Fr. & Engl., 2-tone cl., spine ends worn. (SG. Aug.25; 245) $160

LAZIUS, Wolfgang
- **De Gentium Aliqvot Migrationibvs, Sedibvs Fixis, Reliqviis, Linguarumque ...** Frankfurt, 1600. Fo. Old MS. entry on title, some tears in margin, browned, cont. blind-tooled pig, roll-stpd., slightly rubbed & browned. (HT. May 8; 157)   DM 400

- Titvli ac Catalogi cvm Opervm qvorvnndam Magnorvm, tum Vetervm Avtorvm, qvi in Theologicis, Historiis, Caeterisq. Scientiis ... Vienna, ca. 1553. Fo. Slightly stained & wormed, bds. (HK. Nov.8; 251) DM 750

LAZZARI, Antonio
- Nuova Raccolta delle Principali Vedute della R. Citta di Venezia. Venice, 1831. Ob. 4to. Cont. marb. paper bds. (HD. Jun.18; 24) Frs. 3,200

LEA, Isaac
See— CAREY, Henry Charles & Lea, Isaac

LEA, Philip
See— SAXTON, Christopher & Lea, Philip

LEA, Tom
- George Catlin, Westward Bound a Hundred Years Ago. Sketches by Tom Lea. El Paso, n.d. *(350)*. Paper covers; advance copy. (LH. Sep.25; 402) $475

LEABHAR BREAC, The Speckled Book, Otherwise Styled Leabhar Mor Dúna Deighre
Dublin, 1872. *(200)*. 2 vols. Fo. No bdg. stated. (GM. Dec.7; 173) £100

LEACH, Bernard
- A Potter's Portfolio. L., 1951. 4to. Orig. cl., slightly soiled. (S. May 1; 630) *Zwemmer.* £50

LEACH, Henry
- Great Golfers in the Making. 1910. *1st. Edn.* *(With:)* - Letters of a Modern Golfer to his Grandfather. 1910. Together 2 vols. Bdgs. not stated. (PD. Jul.13; 31) £220

LEACOCK, John, attributed to
- The School for Scandal. A Comedy. 1779. *1st. Edn.* Some slight spotting to a few ll., final blank lf., disbnd. (LC. Mar.1; 389) £420

LEAKE, William Martin
- Travels in the Morea. L., 1830. 3 vols. Hf.-titles. *(With:)* - On Some Disputed Questions of Ancient Geography. L., 1857. 1 vol. Together 4 vols. Qtr. leath. or orig. cl. (SG. Sep.22; 187) $375

LEAR, Edward
- The Birds of Edward Lear. Ed.:– A. Thorpe. 1975. *Ltd. Edn.* Fo. Cl., d.-w. (P. Mar.15; 258) £70
[-] A Book of Nonsense by Derry Down Derry. [L.], 10 Feb. 1846. *1st. Edn.* [Pt. 2 only]. Ob. 8vo. 29 (of 37) litho. designs, including pict. title, without a complement set of sheets (as often), a single yellow end-paper bnd. in the middle of the book, orig. cl.-bkd. pict. wraps., lightly soiled. (SG. Dec.8; 219) $2,800
- Illustrated Excursions in Italy. L., 1846. 2 vols. Fo. 2 maps, 55 litho. views, engraved music, hf.-titles, contents slightly loose, orig. cl. (S. Dec.1; 341) *Wise.* £720
– – **Anr. Copy.** 2 vols. 4to. Map, 55 tinted litho. views, 2 ll. of engraved music, Vol. 2 spotted, cont. roan-bkd. cl. & orig. ribbed cl. gt., spines faded & slightly rubbed. (C. Mar.14; 61) *Bifolco.* £480
- Illustrations of the Family of Psittacidae, or Parrots. L., priv. ptd., 1832. Fo. 42 hand-cold. plts., 2 p. list of subscribers, some spotting affecting some plts., slight tear to lr. margin of 1 plt., lacks very sm. portion of lr. corner of title-p., hf. mor. gt. (P. Oct.20; 122) £12,000
- Journals of a Landscape Painter in Albania, etc. L., 1851. *1st. Edn.* Some foxing, orig. cl. (PNY. Dec.1; 64) $270
– – **Anr. Copy.** 4to. Frontis. map, 20 col. litho. plts., slight darkening to contents, orig. blind-stpd. cl., gt.-lettered spine, spine & cover edges darkening, slight wear to extremities. (CBA. Mar.3; 332) $170
– – **Anr. Edn.** 1852. *2nd. Edn.* Maps, 20 litho. plts., slight spotting, orig. cl. gt., slight tear in spine, soiled. (P. Feb.16; 108) £200
– – **Anr. Copy.** Sm. stain at foot of map, orig. cl., slightly worn. (S. Nov.1; 94) *Crete.* £190
- Journal of a Landscape Painter in Corsica. 1870. Cont. tree cf., rebkd. (BBA. Feb.9; 235) *Parsons.* £75
– – **Anr. Copy.** Lge. 8vo. Map, 40 plts., orig. cl., slightly worn. (S. Dec.13; 182) *King.* £70

– – **Anr. Copy.** Lge. 8vo. Bradel bds. (HD. Oct.21; 112) Frs. 1,400
- Journals of a Landscape Painter in Southern Calabria. 1852. Tall 8vo. 2 maps, 20 tinted litho. plts., publisher's advts. bnd. in at end, minor spotting, orig. cl., spine gt.-decor., untrimmed, slightly worn; pres. copy from author to Rev. Charles M. Church, inscr. on title & dtd. 4 Nov. 1857. (TA. Feb.16; 50) £150
– – **Anr. Copy.** 2 maps, 20 litho. plts., maps & 6 plts. foxed, orig. cl., worn. (P. Sep.8; 43) £100
Craddock & Barnard. £100
- Nonsense Songs, Stories, Botany & Alphabets. L., 1871. *1st. Edn.* Hf. cf. gt. (P. Jan.12; 298) *Dee.* £65
– – **Anr. Copy.** Some soiling, pp. darkening, cl., paper edges at spine lifting with minor chipping to edges, corners bumped, adhesion damage to rear end-papers. (CBA. Aug.21; 385) $180
- On My Shelves. Ill.:– Annettee von Eckardt (colouring). [München], Bremer Pr., 1933. *(155)* on Bütten. Lge. 4to. With catalogue of books ill. by Lear, orig. hf. linen. (H. Nov.23; 953) DM 1,400
- Views in Rome & its Environs. L., 1841. Fo. Litho. title with vig., 25 litho. views, a few plts. slightly spotted, publisher's qtr. mor., hinges brkn. (S. May 21; 232) *Sotheran.* £450
- Views in the Seven Ionian Islands. 1863. Fo. Tinted litho. title, 20 tinted litho. views, list of plts., intro. lf., subscribers list at end, 10 plts. with some foxing, text & plts. loose, orig. cl. gt. (P. Jul.5; 274) £650
See— SOWERBY, James de Carle & Lear, Edward

LEARMONTH, N.F.
- The Portland Bay Settlement ... Melbourne, 1934. *1st. Edn.* Orig. cl., some wear.; inscr. & sigd. (KH. Nov.9; 298) Aus. $170

LEAUTAUD, Paul
- Journal Littéraire 1893-1956. 1954-66. *Orig. Edn. (300) on Vélin de Rives or Johannot.* 19 vols. Sewed. (HD. Mar.21; 168) Frs. 2,600
– – **Anr. Copy.** 19 vols. including index. On vélin de Rives, sewed, s.-c.'s for 1st. 9 vols. (HD. Jun.26; 100) Frs. 2,200
– – **Anr. Edn.** Paris, 1966. 19 vols. Sewed. (SM. Mar.7; 2510) Frs. 1,100
- Le Petit Ami. Roman. Paris, 1903. *Orig. Edn. 1st.* Printing with 1st. wrap. 12mo. Hf. chagrin, corners, by Flammarion-Vaillant, spine blind-decor., unc., wrap. & spine; author's autograph dedication. (HD. Mar.27; 83) Frs. 1,300

LEAVITT, Thadeus W.H.
- The Jubilee History of Tasmania ... Melbourne, n.d. 2 vols. 4to. Orig. cl., slight fading & marking, due to erratic collation, w.a.f. (KH. Nov.9; 299) Aus. $210

LE BAS, Philippe
- Allemagne. Paris, 1838. 2 vols. 1 engraved frontis., 2 multi-folding steel-engraved maps, 200 steel engraved plts., slightly stained, especially margins, cont. hf. leath. gt. (HK. May 15; 916) DM 900
– – **Anr. Copy.** Vol. II. 100 steel engrs., 2 folding maps, 1st. text plts. very spotted & browned, some plts. slightly spotted, later hf. leath., spotted & bumped. (H. May 22; 309) DM 440
- Estados de la Confederacion Jermanica. Barcelona, 1843. Foxing, cont. leath., wear. (D. Nov.23; 817) DM 550
- Recueil de Divers Morceaux gravés d'après plusieurs Tableaux de David Teniers, de Boott, de Berghem, de Vouvremans, Lancret, Oudry ... Paris, 1746. Lge. fo. Cont. red mor. gt., spine decor. (HD. Jul.2; 23) Frs. 15,000

LE BEAU, C.
- Avantures ... ou Voyage Curieux et Nouveau, parmi les Sauvages de l'Amérique Septentrionale, dans le quel on trouvera une Description du Canada. Amst., 1738. *1st. Edn.* 2 vols. Sm. 8vo. Engraved map & 6 plts. (folding), early owners stp. on dedication lf. & 2nd. title, cont. cf., slightly worn, preserved in s.-c. [Sabin 39582] (S. May 22; 326) *Remmington.* £320

LEBEL, Robert
- Marcel Duchamp. Trans.:– G.H. Hamilton. N.Y., [1959]. *1st. Edn. in Engl.* 4to. Orig. linen; MS.

dedication Duchamp on hf.-title. (H. May 23; 1191a) DM 500

LEBERT, Herman
- Traité d'Anatomie, Pathologie Générale et Spéciale ... Paris, 1857-61. 4 vols. Fo. With atlas of 200 steel engraved plts., cont. hf. red chagrin, decor. spines. (HD. Dec.1; 58) Frs. 3,000

LEBESGUE, Octave
See— MONTORGUEIL, Georges [i.e. Octave Lebesgue]

LE BLANC, Charles
- Manuel de L'Amateur d'Estampes. Paris, 1854-n.d. 3 vols. only (of 4). Cont. hf. mor., 1 jnt. split. (BBA. Apr.5; 144) *Heald.* £80

LE BLANC, Fr.
- Traité Historique des Monnoyes de France, avec leur Figures, depuis le Commencement de la Monarchie jusqu'à Présent. Ill.:– Ertinger. 1690. 4to. 59 plts., cont. cf., spine decor., corners worn. (HD. Mar.21; 48) Frs. 2,600
– – **Anr. Copy.** 4to. 1 lf. disbnd., cont. marb. cf., decor. spine. (HD. Dec.9; 50) Frs. 1,400

LE BLANC, Hubert
- Defense de la Basse de Viole contre les Entreprises du Violon et les Pretentions du Violoncel. Amst., 1740. *1st. Edn.* 12mo. Hf.-title, repairs in inner margins in quires D-F affecting a few letters of text, lightly browned thro.-out, some quires sprung, cont. vell.; stp. of Bibliotheca Landsbergiana on title-p. (S. May 10; 168) *Macnutt.* £320

LE BLANT, E
See— JACQUEMART, Albert & Le Blant, E.

LE BLOND, Abbé
See— LA CHAU, Abbé de & Le Blond, Abbé

LE BLOND, Alex
- La Théorie et la Pratique du Jardinage. Paris, 1722. 4 pts. in 1 vol. 4to. Mott. cf. (P. Jan.12; 242) £200
– – **Anr. Copy.** 4to. Cont. marb. cf., spine decor.; from Château des Noës liby. (HD. May 25; 43) Frs. 2,000
[-] The Theory & Practise of Gardening. Trans.:– John James. 1712. 4to. Errata lf., cont. cf. gt. (P. Sep.8; 203) *Evelyn.* £230

LE BRETON
- La Marine du XIXe Siècle. Paris, n.d. Ob. 4to. Some foxing on title, publisher's bds., decor. with litho. on tinted ground. (HD. Jun.18; 25) Frs. 4,500

LEBRIXA, Antonio de
See— NEBRISSENSIS or LEBRIXA, Aelius Antonius or Antonio de

LE BRUIN
- Galerie des Peintres Flamands, Hollandais et Allemands. 1792-96. 3 vols. Lge. 4to. 201 engrs., on holland, 19th. C. hf. long-grd. red mor., corners, decor. spine. (HD. Feb.29; 25) Frs. 14,800

LEBRUN, Charles
- Dissertation sur un Traité ... concernant le Rapport de la Physionomie Humaine avec celle des Animaux. Paris, 1806. Lge. fo. Lightly browned, cont. bds. (CR. Jun.6; 47) Lire 380,000
- Expressions des Passions de l'Ame. N.p., ca. 1800? Fo. Engraved title, 20 stipple-engraved plts., several repairs, mainly marginal, some soiling or foxing, mod. blind-tooled leath. (SG. Jan.26; 241) $130

LE BRUN, Cornelius
- Travels in Muscovy, Persia, & part of the East-Indies. L., 1737. 2 vols. Fo. Frontis., port., 113 engraved plts., many folding, some worming, 1 plt. in Vol. 2 damaged by adhesion, cont. cf., worn, w.a.f. (S. Jun.25; 40) *Shapiro.* £200
- Voyage au Levant. Paris & Rouen, 1725. 5 vols. 4to. Cont. spr. cf., spines decor.; from Château des Noës liby. (HD. May 25; 44) Frs. 4,900

LEBRUN, Pierre & Thiers, J.B.
- Superstitions Anciennes et Modernes: Prejugés Vulgaires. Amst., 1733-36. *1st. Edn.* 2 vols. Fo.

LEBRUN, Pierre & Thiers, J.B. *-Contd.*

Some foxing & soiling, cont. cf., marb. end-papers, covers rubbed & chipped, corners showing, upr. cover of Vol. 1 detchd., lacks lge. portions of back-strips. (CBA. Mar.3; 423) $110

LECALDANO, Paolo
– Les Sommets de l'Art: Rubens. La Galérie Medicis au Palais du Luxembourg. 1969. (*With:*) – Michel-Ange et la Chapelle Sistine. 1965. (*With:*) – El Greco. Les Dernières Années de Tolède. 1969. (*With:*) – Goya y sus Pinturas Negras en la Quinta del Sordo. 1963. Together 4 vols. Fo. No bdgs. stated. (SPB. Nov.30; 233) $350

LE CARRE, John
– The Spy Who Came in from the Cold. L., 1963. *1st. Edn.* Orig. cl., d.-w. (BBA. Nov.30; 339a)
Johnson & O'Donnell. £120

LE CAT, Claude Nicolas
– Traité de la Couleur de la Peau Humaine en Générale, de Celle des Nègres cen Particulier, et de la Métamorphose d'une de ces Couleurs en l'autre ... Ill.:– Gravelot. Amst., 1765. Cont. marb. roan, decor. spine, slight defects. (HD. Jan.27; 204)
Frs. 1,700

LECCHI, Antonio
– Memorie Idrostatico-storiche delle Operazioni eseguite nell'inalveazione del Reno di Bologna, e degli altri Minori Torrenti per la Linea di Primaro al Mare. Modena, 1773. 2 vols. in 1. 4to. Cont. hf. leath., slightly loose. (SI. Dec.15; 162)
Lire 250,000

LECHTER, Melchior
– Tagebuch der Indischen Reise. Berlin, Einhorn Pr., 1912. *MS. Facs. 1st. Edn. (15) on Japan imperial.* Lge. 4to. Printers mark sigd. by artist, orig. vell., leath. inlays, gold-tooled, 2 metal clasps. (H. Nov.24; 1768) DM 3,400
– – **Anr. Edn.** Berlin, Einhorn Pr., 1912. *(333). (315) numbered on Bütten.* Fo. Printer's mark monogrammed & numbered, orig. hf. vell. (R. Oct.11; 325) DM 780
– – **Anr. Copy.** 4to. Printers mark monog. & numbered by artist, hand-bnd. orig. cf. gt., leath. inlay, spine faded, slightly rubbed, doubl. with glue marks. (H. May 23; 1354) DM 640
– – **Anr. Copy.** Fo. Printers mark monog. & numbered by artist, orig. leath., gt. inner dentelle, leath. onlay on upr. cover, gold-tooled, spine faded, very worn, slightly brittle at top. (HK. May 17; 2949) DM 420

LECKY, Hatton Stirling
– The King's Ships. 1913-14. Vols. 1-3 (all publd.). 4to. Orig. cl., lightly soiled. (CSK. May 4; 129)
£120

LECKY, William Edward Hartpole
– A History of England in the Eighteenth Century. L., 1892. *Cabinet Edn.* 7 vols. Sm. 8vo. Three-qtr. mor., spines gt. with fleurons. (SG. Feb.16; 178)
$275

LECLAIR, J.-M.
– Troisième Livre de Sonates à Violon Seul avec la Basse Continue. Oeuvre V. Paris, priv. ptd., n.d. Fo. Old roan. (HD. Nov.9; 45) Frs. 1,700

LE CLERC, Jean
– Atlas de la Géographie Ancienne, Sacrée, Ecclesiastique et Profane. Maps:– after Sanson, P. de la Rue, C. van Adrichom, G. de l'Isle & others. Amst., J. Covens & C. Mortier. [1725]. Fo. Additional engraved title, 2 ptd. titles (1 in red & black), 93 double-p. or folding engraved mapsheets covering all parts of ancient world (including maps of world & 4 continents), hand-cold. in outl., MS. contents list at end, some faint dust-soiling, cont. vell.-bkd. bds., unc., worn, w.a.f. (S. May 21; 122)
Harris. £1,500
– Théâtre Géographique du Royaume de France. Contenant les Cartes & Descriptions particulières des Provinces d'iceluy. Paris, 1631. Fo. 49 (of 50) uncold. double-p. engraved maps, lacks 'Carte Universelle', several maps closely cropped, particularly on outer edges, some browning, all dampstained, later qtr. cf., rubbed. (TA. Mar.15; 59) £875

LE CLERC, Nicholas Gabriel
– Histoire Physique, Morale, Civile et Politique de la Russie ... Paris, 1783-An II [1794]. 6 vols., lacks atlas. 4to. Cont. marb. cf., spines decor., last vol. not quite unif.; from Château des Noës liby. (HD. May 25; 46) Frs. 3,500
– – **Anr. Edn.** [Paris, 1794]. Atlas vol. only. Fo. 38 plts., some folding, 16 military, revenue & census tables, most folding, sm. margin tear to a few folding plts., cont. mott. cf., very worn. (SG. Mar.29; 340) $450

LE CLERC, Sebastien
– Traité d'Architecture. Paris, 1714. 2 vols., including plt. vol. 4to. 1 plt. remntd. & shorter, cont. spr. roan, spines decor.; from Château des Noës liby. (HD. May 25; 45) Frs.1,900
– – **Anr. Copy.** 2 vols., including plt. vol. 4to. Some light spotting, cont. cf., rubbed. (CSK. Jul.13; 161)
£170
– Traité de Géometrie. Paris, 1690. *1st. Edn.* Lge. 8vo. Engraved frontis./dedication, 16 full-p. engrs., cont. cf. gt., worn. (SG. Oct.6; 233) $120
See– CORNEILLE, Jean-Baptiste & Le Clerc, Sebastien

LECLERE, Paul
– Amante Des Fontaines. Ill.:– Houplain. Paris, n.d. *Ltd. Edn. on Japon nacré.* Sm. 4to. 9 orig. text engrs., additional suite of 23 loose engrs., 1 MS. poem & 1 orig. sigd. engr., all accompanied by an engraved copper plt. representing one of the text. ills., orig. wraps., folder & box. (SPB. Dec.13; 836) $175
– Venise Seuil des Eaux. Ill.:– Van Dongen. Paris, 1926. *De Luxe Edn., (10) on Japan Imperial.* Lge. 4to. Double series of 11 ills. on vell. (cold.) & China (monotone), orig. pict. wraps., loose. (H. Nov.24; 1470) DM 1,100

LECLERE, Tristan
– Les Femmes de Théâtre du XVIIIe Siècle. Ill.:– after La Tour, Fragonard & others. Paris, [1911]. *(275) numbered on specially produced Holland H.M.P.* Lge. 4to. 40 plts., crimson lev. by Mad. Pinard, gt. borders & spine, wide gt. dentelles, orig. wraps. bnd. in. (SG. Feb.16; 179) $120

LE CLERT, Louis
– Le Papier ... 1926. *(675).* 2 vols. Fo. Sewed. (HD. Jun.29; 129) Frs. 1,650

LECOINTE DE LAVEAU, G.
– Guide du Voyageur à Moscou. Moscow, 1824. Cont. diced russ. (S. Mar.6; 93) *Quaritch.* £130

LE COMTE, P.
– Praktikale Zeevaartkunde en Theoretische Kennis voor Handel en Scheepvaart. Ill.:– D. Veelwaard. Amst., 1842. 4to. 121 steel-engraved plts., some foxing, slight margin staining, mod. bds. (VS. Dec.8; 801) Fls. 500

LECONTE DE LISLE, Charles Marie Rene
– Poèmes Barbares. Ill.:– Jouve. Lausanne, 1929. *(25) with suite in black on japon impérial, 1 suite of several states & 1 suite of trial etchings.* 4to. Leaves, box. (HD. Jun.13; 60) Frs. 15,000

LE COQ, Albert von
– Die Buddhistische Spaetantike in Mittelasien. Berlin, 1922-33. Vols. 1-7. Tall fo. Plts., some cold., ills., ex-liby., leath.-bkd. pict. bds. (SG. May 3; 235) $2,200

LE CORBUSIER (Pseud.)
See– JEANNERET, Charles Edouard 'Le Corbusier'.

LE COULTEUX DE CANTELEU, Bon.
– La Venerie Française. 1858. *Orig. Edn.* 4to. Cont. hf. mor., corners. (HD. Jun.29; 130) Frs. 2,200

LECUYER, Raymond
– Histoire de la Photographie. Paris, 1945. *1st. Edn.* Fo. Lacks the 3-dimensional glasses from pocket in upr. cover, cl.-bkd. bds., spine defect. & partly reprd. (SG. Nov.10; 103) $325

LEDERMULLER, Martin Frobenius
– Amusement Microscopique. Nuremb., 1764-66. *1st. Fr. Edn.* Vols. 1-2 (of 3). 4to. Mod. hf. leath. (R. Apr.4; 1619) DM 2,500

– Versuch, bey angehender Frühlings Zeit die Vergrösserungs Werckzeuge zum nüzlich u. angenehmen Zeitvertreib ansuwenden ... Nuremb., 1764. German-Fr. parallel text, cont. bds., spine defect., unc. (HK. May 15; 451) DM 3,400

LEDOUX, Cl. N.
– L'Architecture considerée sous le Rapport de l'Art, des Moeurs et de la Legislation. Paris, 1962. 2 vols. Fo. Phototype reproduction, publishers bdg. (HD. Dec.15; 20) Frs. 10,000

LEDOUX, Louis Vernon
– A Descriptive Catalogue of an Exhibition of Japanese Figure Prints from Moronobu to Toyokuni. N.Y., Grol. Cl., 1924. *(300) on Van Gelder Zonen paper.* 28 plts., bds., worn. (SG. Jan.26; 235) $100
See– HENDERSON, Harold G. & Ledoux, Louis V.

LEDWICH, Edward
– Antiquities of Ireland. Dublin, 1790. *1st. Edn.* 4to. List of Subscribers, errata at end, tree cf., rubbed. (GM. Dec.7; 280) £140
– – **Anr. Edn.** Dublin, 1803. *2nd. Edn.* 4to. Engraved frontis. & title, 40 engraved plts., list of Subscribers, advts. at end, cf., defect. (GM. Dec.7; 319) £60

LEE, Nathaniel
– Gloriana, or the Court of Augustus Caesar. L., 1676. Mod. lev. mor., new end-papers. (CBA. Dec.20; 284) $110
See– DRYDEN, John & Lee, Nathaniel

LEE, Norman N.
See– EDMONDS, Harfield H. & Lee, Norman N.

LEE, Sidney
– Shakespeare's Comedies, Histories, & Tragedies ... containing a Census of Extant Copies, with some Account of their History & Condition. Oxford, 1902. *1st. Edn.* (*Bound with:*) – Notes & Additions to the Census of Copies of the Shakespeare First Folio. L., 1906. Together 2 works in 1 vol. Fo. Cont. red hf. mor. gt., orig. wraps. to 2nd. work bnd. in. (SG. Sep.15; 298) $100

LEECH, John
– Follies of the Year. L., n.d. Ob. 4to. Hand-cold. title, 21 plts., a few lightly spotted or stained, some text ll. spotted & margins tattered, orig. hf. mor., soiled, recased, later end-papers. (CSK. Feb.24; 79) £55
– – **Anr. Copy.** Ob. 4to. 21 cold. plts., orig. hf. mor. (KH. May 1; 411) Aus. $350
[–] [Mr. Briggs & his doings. Fishing.] Ill.:– after Leech. N.d. Ob. fo. 12 hand-cold. litho. plts., lightly soiled, cont. hf. mor., worn, disbnd., orig. upr. wrap. bnd. in. (CSK. Sep.16; 168) £90

LEECH, John (Ill.)
See– A'BECKETT, Gilbert Abbott
See– DICKENS, Charles
See– PUNCH
See– SURTEES, Robert Smith

LEECH, John Henry
– Butterflies from China, Japan & Corea. 1892-94. 3 vols. 4to. Hf. mor. gt. by Arthur B. Colley, orig. wraps. bnd. in. (SKC. Nov.18; 1974) £780

LEEDS, H.A.
See– BRIGHT, P.M. & Leeds, H.A.

LEES, Lady
– Illustrations to Alfred Tennyson's Poem, the Princess. N.d. Lge. chromolitho. title & 9 plts., some hand-finished, some mounts slightly spotted affecting plt. area, orig. velvet, covers with blind-stpd. borders, upr. cover with title blocked in gt., elab. gt. metal clasp, extremities rubbed, watered silk end-papers, cont. book mark loosely inserted. (CSK. Mar.23; 50) £320

LEESER, Isaac
– The Claims of the Jews to an Equality of Rights. Phila., 5601 [1841]. Orig. wraps., spine chipped, cellotape repair at head. (SG. Feb.2; 7) $350
– Discourses on the Jewish Religion ... Phila., 1867-68. 3rd. Series: Vols. IV-X. Orig. cl., sunned, worn, 1 spine defect. (SG. Feb.2; 9) $425

LEEUWENHOEK, Anthony van
- **Anatomia** ... Leiden, 1687. *1st. Edn.* 2 pts. in 1 vol. Sm. 4to. Slightly browned or foxed, some pencil underlinings, some ll. with sm. reprd. faults in corners, cont. vell., spotted; title lf. with MS. owners mark A. Forel. (HT. May 8; 559a)   DM 1,500
- **The Collected Letters.** Amst., 1939-41. 2 vols. Lge. 4to. In Dutch & Engl., cl., soiled, ex-liby. (SG. Mar.22; 193) $110
- **[Letters].** Delft, Leiden, 1695-97. *Various Edns.* 4 vols. in 2. 4to. Cont. cf. gt., rubbed; the Sir Thomas Molyneux set. (SG. Nov.3; 120) $600

LEEWARD ISLANDS
- **Acts of Assembly, passed in the Charibbee Leeward Islands from 1690 to 1730.** 1734. Fo. Some browning, hf. cf., worn. (P. Mar.15; 67)   £120

LE FANU, Joseph Sheridan
- **All in the Dark.** 1866. 2 vols. Orig. cl., soiled. (P. Sep.29; 116)   *Stevens.* £280

LE FERON, J.
- **Catalogue des Très Illustres Ducz et Connestables de France** ... Paris, 1555. 6 pts. in 1 vol. 4to. Blazons in 1st. printing, lr. margin gnawed in almost hf. of vol.; from Château des Noës liby. (HD. May 25; 47)   Frs. 1,000
- **[-] Catalogue des Très-Illustres Grand Maistres de France.** Paris, 1628. 4 pts. (only) in 1 vol. Fo. Margins extra-illuminated with 9 MS. arms, later cf.-bkd. bds. (CSK. Mar.23; 137)   £65

LEFEVRE, Georges
- **La Croisière Jaune. Troisième Mission.** Paris, 1933. *Ltd. Edn.* 4to. Decor. mor., unc., box; autograph dedication by Andre Citroën. (LM. Oct.22; 59)   B.Frs. 9,000

LE FORT DE LAMORINIERE, A. Cl.
- **[-] Bibliothèque Poétique.** Ill.:– after Titon du Tillet (frontis.). Paris, 1745. 4 vols. 4to. Cont. marb. cf., decor. spines. (HD. Dec.16; 23)   Frs. 1,800

LEFOULON, P.J.
- **A New Treatise on the Theory and Practice of Dental Surgery.** Balt., 1844. *Only Edn. in Engl.* (*Bound with:*) BLANDIN, P.F. - **Anatomy of the Dental System, Human & Comparative.** Balt., 1845. *Only Edn. in Engl.* Together 2 works in 1 vol. Scattered browning, cont. sheep, extremities rubbed; inscr. by Elisha Townsend to J.R. McCurdy, Asbell bkplt. (SG. Mar.22; 92) $200

LEFRANC DE POMPIGNAN, Jean-Jacques, Marquis de
- **[-] Eloge Historique de Monseigneur le Duc de Bourgogne.** Ill.:– Frédou (port.) & Cochin. Paris, 1761. Cont. red mor. gt., spine decor. (HD. May 3; 85)   Fls. 1,500

LE FRANCQ VAN BERKHEY, J.
- **Natuurl. Historie v. Holland.** Amst., 1769-79. Pts. I-IV in 7 vols. (of 9). Map hand-cold., lacks 1 plt., some staining, cont. hf. roan, slightly worn. (VG. Mar.19; 271)   Fls. 680

LE GALLIENNE, Richard
- **The Romance of Perfume.** Ill.:– George Barbier. 1928. 8 cold. plts., additional advertising pamphlet in pocket at back (as called for), orig. pict. bds., s.-c. (CSK. Dec.16; 186)   £50

LE GENTIL, Guillaume Joseph
- **Voyage dans les Mers de l'Inde** ... Paris, 1781. 2 vols. Fo. Leath. (DS. Mar.23; 2155) Pts. 125,000

LEGER, Fernand
- **Mes Voyages, avec un Poème d'Aragon.** Paris, 1960. *(291) numbered.* Fo. Unsewn in orig. wraps., unc., folder & s.-c. (S. Nov.21; 86)   *Rota.* £500
- – **Anr. Copy.** Fo. Unsewn in orig. wraps., unc., folder & s.-c. (S. Nov.21; 87)   *Makiya.* £300
- – **Anr. Copy.** Sm. fo. Loose in ptd. wraps. as iss., s.-c. slightly worn. (SG. Nov.3; 121) $400

LEGGE, William Vincent
- **A History of the Birds of Ceylon.** Ill.:– after J.G. Keulemans. L., priv. ptd. [1878-]80. 3 pts. in 2 vols. 4to. Map, cold. plt. of eggs, key plt., 33 hand-cold. litho. plts., minor stains to 1 plt., hf. mor., spines gt.-tooled, by Bayntun. (C. Nov.16; 266)
                            Traylen. £800

- – **Anr. Copy.** 3 vols. 4to. Cold. map, key plt., cold. plt. of eggs & 33 hand-cold. plts., cont. hf. mor., ptd. wraps. to orig. 3 pts. bnd. in. liby. stps. on wraps. (C. Jun.27; 169)   *Traylen.* £700
- – **Anr. Edn.** Ill.:– J.G. Keulemans. L., priv. publd., 1880. 3 pts. in 1 vol. 4to. Cold. map, 1 plain plt., 34 hand-cold. litho. plts., cont. hf. mor. gt. (SKC. May 4; 1859)   £750
- – **Anr. Copy.** 4to. Map, title & dedication reprd. at edges, 8 text pp. marginally reprd., some other edge repairs, cont. hf. mor. (SSA. Sep.21; 249)
                            R 360

LEGRAIN, Pierre
- **Repertoire Descriptif et Bibliographique de 1236 Reliures.** Intro.:– Prof. J. Millot. Etudes:– J. Ant. Legrain, G. Blaizot, R. Bonfils, M. Dormoy, J. Guignard. Paris, 1965. *(600) on vell. de Rives. This 1 of (100) for members of Société de la Reliure Originale.* 4to. Sewed, box. (HD. Dec.16; 143)
                            Frs. 3,000

LE GRAND, Anthony
See— GEULINCX, A. — SCHOTANUS, J. — LE GRAND, Anthony

LEGRAND, Augustin
- **Album de la Jeunesse, Mélange d'Histoire Naturelle, Minéraux, Plantes, Animaux.** Ca. 1830. Ob. 4to. Some ll. dampstained at head, cont. hf. roan, slightly rubbed; van Veen coll. (S. Feb.28; 82)
                            £450

LE GRAND, Abbé J.
- **Histoire du Divorce de Henry VIII, Roy d'Angleterre et de Catherine d'Aragon.** Paris, 1688. *Orig. Edn.* 3 vols. Cont. red mor., gt. decor., gt. tooled centre arms, decor. spines, gt. inner dentelle. (HD. Mar.14; 55)   Frs. 5,300

LEGRAND, Jacques Guillaume & Landon, Charles Paul
- **Description de Paris et de ses Edifices.** Paris, 1806, 1809. 2 vols. Folding map, approx. 130 engraved plts., cont. red hf. mor. (SG. Apr.26; 126)
                            $550

LEGRAND, Louis
- **Cours de Danse Fin de Siècle.** Paris, 1892. *(350).* Lge. 8vo. On vell., hf. mor., corners, by Bretault, spine decor. (unif. faded), wrap.; with invitation card ill. by Legrand, greeting card ill. by Lobel-Riche & postcard. (HD. May 4; 332)   Frs. 4,700
- – **Anr. Edn.** Paris, 1892. *De Luxe Edn. on japan.* 4to. Quadruple series of etchings, private vell with title & vig., orig. wraps. with etched vig. bnd. in, inner doubl. & free end-papers with green silk, linen s.-c. (HT. May 9; 1552)   DM 3,300
- **La Petite Classe.** Paris, ca. 1908. *(100) with each etching individually numbered & stpd. by publisher.* Fo. Loose as iss. in pict. wraps., with etching on upr. wrap., bd. portfo., lacks 2 ties; each etching sigd. by artist in pencil in lr. margin. (SG. Nov.3; 123) $4,500

LE GRAND D'AUSSY, Pierre Jean Baptiste
- **Fabliaux or Tales, Abridged from French Manuscripts of the XIIth & XIIIth Centuries.** Ill.:– Thomas Bewick. L., 1815. *1st. 3 vol. Edn.* 3 vols. Some foxing, orig. bds., corners bumped & showing, spines darkened, with some chipping. (CBA. Aug.21; 50) $150
- **Histoire de la vie Privée des Français, depuis l'Origine de la Nation jusqu'à nos Jours.** Paris, 1782. *Orig. Edn.* 3 vols. Cont. marb. roan, spines gt. (HD. Mar.19; 55)   Frs. 2,700

LEGUAT, François
- **Voyage et Avantures ... en Deux Isles Desertes des Indes Orientales.** L., 1708. 2 vols. in 1. 12mo. 34 plts. & maps (16 folding), cont. cf., spine gt., some wear. (S. Apr.10; 430)   *Smitskamp.* £220

LE HAY
- **Explication des Cent Estampes qui représentent Differentes Nations du Levant** ... Ill.:– Scotin, Simonneau, &c. Paris, 1715. *2nd. Iss.* Lge. fo. Cont. mor., worn. (HD. Nov.9; 45b)   Frs. 6,100
- **Recueil de Cent Estampes representant Differentes Nations du Levant.** Paris, 1714. *1st. Edn.* Fo. Engraved title & preface, 102 engraved plts., including 3 folding, creased at folds, 1 reprd., cont.

vell., rebkd., worn, ties. (C. Dec.9; 82)
                            Cratsos. £750
- – **Anr. Copy.** Fo. 102 engraved plts., including 3 double-p., plt.-list, plts. stpd. on verso, 2 plts. stpd. in margins, early cf., worn. (SG. Sep.22; 188)
                            $1,900
- – **Anr. Copy.** Fo. Cont. cf., decor. spine, worn. (HD. Mar.14; 56)   Frs. 14,000
- – **Anr. Edn.** Paris, 1714, 1715. *1st. Compl. Edn.* Fo. Wide margin, cont. red mor., gold-tooled decor., arms supralibros, mor. inlay, silver tooling, gt. inner & outer dentelle, marb. end-papers, linen box. (D. Nov.23; 172)   DM 52,000
- – **Anr. Copy.** 2 pts. in 1 vol. Fo. With mus. plt. (often lacking), cont. spr. cf., spine decor., worn; from Château des Noës liby. (HD. May 25; 48)
                            Frs. 7,000

LEHMANN
See— NETTO & Lehmann

LEHMANN, K.
- **Samothrace Excavations Conducted by the Institute of Fine Arts, New York University.** 1960-64. Vols. 2-4 in 7 pts. 4to. Orig. cl., d.-w. (P. Mar.15; 26)   *Martinos.* £80

LEHMANN, P.A.
- **[-] Die Vornehmsten Europäischen Reisen.** Hamburg, 1703. 2 pts. in 1 vol. Title slightly browned, 2 maps with tears, cont. vell., spine sprung. (GB. May 3; 111)   DM 840

LEHMANN, Walter
- **Kunstgeschichte des Alten Peru.** Paris, 1924. Lge. 4to. Orig. cl., slightly rubbed, spine faded. (S. Apr.30; 200)   *Brecht.* £80

LEHMANN-HARTLEBEN, K
See— KLUGE, K. & Lehmann-Hartleben, K.

LEHR, F.H. (Ed.)
See— MARBURGER JAHRBUCH FUR KUNSTWISSENSCHAFT

LEHRS, Max
- **Geschichte und Kritischer Katalog des Deutschen, Niederländischen und Franzosischen Kupferstichs im XV Jahrhundert.** [N.Y.], n.d. *Facs. Reprint of the Vienna, 1908-34 Edn.* 10 vols., including plt. vol. 8vo. & fo. Orig. cl. (BBA. Nov.10; 178)
                            London Library. £75
- – **Anr. Copy.** 10 vols. 8vo. & 4to. Orig. cl. (BBA. Apr.5; 56)   *Ernsting.* £65
- – **Anr. Copy.** 10 vols. Orig. hf. leath. (HT. May 9; 1069)   DM 620
- – **Anr. Copy.** 9 text vols. & 1 plt. vol. Lge. 8vo. & fo. Orig. linen, lightly bumped. (H. Nov.23; 152)
                            DM 420

LEIBNITZ, Gottfried Wilhelm von 'Caesarinus Fürstnerius'
- **De Jure Suprematus ac Legationis Principum Germaniae.** N.p., 1677. Minimal browning, cont. hf., vell., cover lightly rubbed. (R. Oct.11; 1266)
                            DM 800
- **Lehr-Saetze ueber die Monadologie ... Discurs des Uebersetzers ueber das Licht der Natur.** Frankfurt & Leipzig, 1720. *1st. Edn.* (*Bound with:*)
- **Merck-Würdige Schriften** ... Frankfurt & Leipzig, 1720. Together 2 works in 1 vol. Old bds.; Dr. Walter Pagel copy. (S. Feb.7; 230)
                            Ritman. £2,600
- **Oeuvres Philosophiques Latines et François** ... Ed.:– R.E. Raspe. Amst. & Leipzig, 1765 (colophon: Hanover, 1764). *1st. Edn.* 4to. Hf.-title, errata lf., new bds., cf. spine; Dr. Walter Pagel copy. (S. Feb.7; 231)   *Duran.* £180
- **Protogaea sive de Prima Facie Telluris et Antiquissimae Historiae Vestigiis in ipsis Naturae Monumentis Dissertatio.** Ed.:– Chr. L. Scheidius. Goettingen, 1749. *1st. Edn.* 4to. Title with engraved royal arms, 12 folding plts., contents lf., title badly soiled, new bds., cf. spine, Dr. Walter Pagel copy. (S. Feb.7; 233)   *Morris.* £350
- **Theodice, das ist, Versuch v. der Güte Gottes, Freyheit des Menschen u. vom Ursprunge des Bösen** ... Ed.:– J.C. Gottsched. Hannover & Leipzig, 1744. *4th. German Edn. 1st. Gottsched Edn.* Cont. hf. vell., spine lightly defect., lacks lr. free end-paper. (HK. Nov.10; 2572)   DM 750
- – **Anr. Edn.** Ed.:– J.C. Gottsched. Hannover &

LEIBNITZ, Gottfried Wilhelm von 'Caesarinus Fürsternius' *-Contd.*
Leipzig, 1783. *5th. German Edn.* Some pencil lining, cont. hf. leath., rubbed. & bumped. (R. Oct.11; 509) DM 480

LEIBNITZ, Gottfried Wilhelm von & Bernouilli, Johann
- Commercium Philosophicum et Mathematicum. Lausanne & Geneva, 1745. *1st. Edn.* 2 vols. in 1. 4to. Some spotting & soiling, title soiled, later marb. bds., some wear; J.C.H. Gebauer's sig. with date on verso of titles, Stanitz coll. (SPB. Apr.25; 267) $600
-- **Anr. Copy.** 2 vols. 4to. Wide margin, some light browning, cont. leath., wear, liby. stp. (HT. May 8; 439) DM 620

LEIBNITZ, Gottfried Wilhelm von & Clarke, Samuel
- A Collection of Papers, which passed between the Late Learned Mr. Leibnitz, & Dr. Clarke ... relating to the Principles of Natural Philosophy & Religion ... L., 1717. *1st. Edn.* 2 pts. in 1 vol. Cont. blind-stpd. vell., corners rubbed; Stanitz coll. (SPB. Apr.25; 266) $425

LEIBNITZ, Gottfried Wilhelm von & others
- Recueil de Diverses Pièces sur la Philosophie, la Religion Naturelle, l'Histoire, les Mathématiques ... Amst., 1720. 2 vols. 12mo. Cont. cf.; from Montesquieu liby., MS. inscr. on title. (HD. May 21; 43) Frs. 1,800

LEICESTER, R. Dudley, Earl of
See— ROHAN, Henri, Duc de — BUCKINGHAM, G. Williams, Duke of — LEICESTER, R. Dudley, Earl of

LEICHHARDT, Dr. Ludwig
- Journal of an Overland Expedition in Australia, from Moreton Bay to Port Essington, a Distance of Upwards of 3,000 Miles, during the Years 1844-5. 1847. *1st. Edn.* 14 steel engrs., publisher's advts. bnd. in both front & rear, orig. blind-stpd. cl. gt., unc., a little rubbed, sm. tear at head of spine. (TA. Mar.15; 11) £640
-- **Anr. Copy.** 2 vols. 7 engraved plts., without accompanying set of 3 maps, cont. cf., rebkd. (S. May 22; 479) *Maggs.* £420
-- **Anr. Copy.** 2 stps. erased, late 19th. C. hf. mor. (KH. May 1; 413) Aus. $900
-- **Anr. Copy.** No early book advts. (as usual), bdg. not stated, unc., a few marks & sm. defects. (KH. May 1; 412) Aus. $550

LEIDEN
- De Vermakelyke Leidsche Buiten-cingels, Aangenaame Dorpen en Landstreken, rondom die Stad Gelegen. Leiden, 1734. Sm. 8vo. Cont. vell. (VG. Sep.14; 1141) Fls. 600

LEIDINGER, George
- Meisterwerke der Buchmalerei. München, 1920. *(100) numbered.* Lge. fo. Lightly browned & spotted, orig. linen. (HT. May 8; 700) DM 500
-- **Anr. Edn.** Munich, [1920]. *(1000).* Fo. 50 cold. plts., envelope with description tipped to upr. free endpaper, qtr. vell., bds. (SG. May 17; 139) $120

LEIGH, Charles
- The Natural History of Lancashire, Cheshire & the Peak in Derbyshire. Oxford, 1700. *1st. Edn.* Fo. Port., col. map, 24 plts., cont. cf., reprd. (P. Jul.26; 66) £85
-- **Anr. Copy.** 3 pts. in 1 vol. Fo. Engraved folding map, hand-cold. in outl., 24 (of 25) plts., lacks explication lf. & errata to 3rd. pt., spotted & stained, a few tears reprd., cont. cf., rebkd. (S. Mar.6; 488) *Page.* £65

LEIGH, G.
- The Accedence of Armorie. L., 1591. Sm. 4to. A few woodcut coats of arms in text cold., corner torn from D7, later hf. cf. [STC 15391] (S. Mar.6; 489) *Maggs.* £120

LEIGH, M.A.
- New Pocket Atlas of England & Wales ... Corrected since the passing of the Reform Bill. L., 1834. Sm. 8vo. Additional engraved title with lge. vig., folding general map, 52 (of 55) engraved county maps, publisher's catalogue at end, publisher's hf. roan. (S. Jun.25; 432) £80

LEIGH, W.H.
- Reconnoitering Voyages & Travels, with Adventures in the New Colonies of South Australia. L., 1839. *1st. Edn.* Hf.-title, additional litho. title with vig., 7 litho. plts., 24 pp. publisher's advts., title, frontis. & few plts. spotted, orig. cl., spine faded; Rosebery blind-stpd. at head of ptd. title. (C. Jun.27; 95) *Dunsheath.* £110
-- **Anr. Copy.** 24 pp. of advts. at end, some foxing on plts. & text pp., orig. blind-stpd. cl., unc., covers faded. (CA. Apr.3; 76) Aus. $180

LEIGHLY, John
- California as an Island. San Franc., 1972. Fo. Decor. paper bds., mor. spine. (LH. Sep.25; 327) $625
-- **Anr. Edn.** San Franc., 1972. *(450).* Sm. fo. Prospectus & extra copy of plt. VII laid in, qtr. leath. (SG. Mar.29; 157) $450

LEISCHING, E.
- Die Bildnis-Miniatur in Osterreich von 1750 bis 1850. Wien, 1907. *(400).* Lge. 4to. Lacks 1 plt., some soiling, orig. leath, wear, spine reprd. (D. Nov.23; 2090) DM 1,300

LEISCHING, Julius
- Ferdinand Staeger. Vienna, 1913. *(550) numbered.* 4to. 3 hand-cold. ills., title & few mounts spotted, unbnd. as iss. in orig. hf. cl. portfo. (CSK. Feb.10; 31) £85
- Schabkunst. Wien, 1913. *(350) numbered.* 4to. Hf. leath. (R. Oct.11; 886) DM 520

LEITE, Solidonio
- Catalogo Annotado da Bibliotheca. Rio de Janeiro, ca. 1910. *(50) numbered & sigd. by author.* Pt. 1 (all publd.). Thick sm. 4to. A little foxed, cont. qtr. cf. & marb. bds., orig. ptd. wraps. bnd. in, a little shaken. (SG. Apr.5; 212) $100

LEITER, Levi Ziegler
- Leiter Library: A Catalogue of Books, Manuscripts & Maps relating principally to America collected by the late ... Ed.:– Hugh A. Morrison. Wash., priv. ptd., 1907. *(100) numbered.* 4to. Cont. gt.-panel. hf. mor.; pres. copy to Charles Pike, sigd. by J. Leiter, T.L.s. from J.F. Bell to A.S.W. Rosenbach,. (SG. Sep.15; 207) $200

LEITSCHUB, Franz Friedrich
- Albrecht Dürer's Sämtliche Kupferstiche. Leipzig. 1912. Lge. fo. 104 plts., cont. hf. mor., lightly rubbed. (CSK. Jan.13; 230) £50

LE KEUX, John
- Memorials of Cambridge. 1841-42. 2 vols. Steel-engraved titles, 1 map, 73 plts., some light spotting, cont. hf. mor., lightly rubbed. (CSK. Jan.13; 8) £170

LE KEUX, John (Ill.)
See— INGRAM, James

LE LABOUREUR, Claude
- Discours de l'Origine des Armes et des Termes Receus & Usités pour l'Explication de la Science Héraldique. Lyon, 1658. *1st. Edn.* Sm. 4to. Cont. vell.; author's ex-dono 'pour le R. Père Ainé au Petit Collège à Lyon,' 'Claudia Br. F.' on title. (HD. Mar.21; 118) Frs. 2,000

LELAND, John
- De Rebus Britannicis Collectunea. Oxford, 1715. *[150].* 6 vols. Some later pencil margin annots., cont. cf., rubbed. (CSK. Jul.27; 140) £110

LELAND, Thomas
- The History of Ireland from the Invasion by Henry II. 1773. *1st. Edn.* 3 vols. 4to. Hf.-titles, cont. spr. cf., spines gt.; Sir Ivar Colquhoun, of Luss copy. (CE. Mar.22; 188) £220
-- **Anr. Copy.** 3 vols. Lge. 4to. Hf. mor., armorial motif on spine. (GM. Dec.7; 465) £120
-- **Anr. Copy.** 3 vols. 4to. Cf., rubbed. (GM. Dec.7; 464) £65

LELOIR, Maurice
- Vie de Lazarille de Tormes. Paris, 1866. *(105) numbered. (5) sigd. by artist.* Fo. Orig. aquatint port., with suite of vigs. on Japan, 3 states of ills. on vell., mor.; aquatint port. sigd. by artist. (DS. Feb.24; 2024) Pts. 34,000

LE LONG, Jacques
- Bibliothèque Historique de la France. Paris, 1719. *[1st. Edn.].* Fo. Cont. cf. gt., worn. (BBA. Jun.28; 148) *Quaritch.* £75
-- **Anr. Copy.** Lge. fo. Cont. cf., spine decor. (HD. Nov.9; 131) Frs. 1,050

LE LOYER, Pierre
- A Treatise of Spectres or Straunge Sights, Visions & Apparitions. L., 1605. *1st. Edn. in Engl.* 4to. Variant without trans. name on A3r, errata lf., few headlines shaved, 19th. C. cf., shabby. [STC 15448] (SG. Apr.19; 115) $175

LELY, Gilbert
- Ma Civilisation. Ill.:– Lucien Coutaud. Paris, 1947 [1948]. 4to. On velin du Marais, leaves, wrap., folder & s.-c.; orig. pen drawing dtd.1 Dec. 1948 facing hf.-title, sigd. by artist with dedication to Mme Gompel. (HD. May 16; 76) Frs. 1,700

LEMAIRE, Charles & others
- Flore des Serres et des Jardins de l'Europe, ou Descriptions des Plantes les Plus Rares et le Plus Méritantes. Gand, 1845-80. Vols. 1-13 & 15-23. Some soiling, plts. hand-stpd. on rectos, mostly in blank space, hf. leath., worn, few vols. brkn., ex-liby. (RO. Dec.11; 186) $1,100

LEMAITRE, Jules
- A.B.C. Ill.:– Job. Paris, 1919. *(10) numbered on japan, with suite in black.* 4to. Str.-grd. hf. mor., corners, spine decor., ill. wrap. (HD. Apr.26; 153) Frs. 4,000

LE MAITRE DE SACY
- L'Histoire du Vieux et du Nouveau Testament, Représentée avec des Figures. Paris, 1770. 4to. Cont. cf., decor. spine, slight defects. (HD. Sep.22; 273) Frs. 1,700

LE MARIE DE BELGES, J.
- Les Illustrations de Gaulle et Singularitez de Troye ... Paris, 1548 (last pt. dtd. 1549). 5 pts. in 1 vol. 4to. Old inscr. cancelled on title, 3 ll. defect. in margin with sm. loss of text, lacks last lf., 2 ll. out of order, cont. vell., worn. (HD. May 21; 45) Frs. 1,500

LE MASCRIER, Abbé
See— BANIER, Abbé & Le Mascrier, Abbé

LEMBERGER, E.
- Die Bildnis-Miniatur in Deutschland von 1550-1850. München, [1909]. *(400).* Lge. 4to. Orig. mor. gt., gt. inner dentelle, some wear, spine faded, watered silk end-papers. (D. Nov.23; 2091) DM 1,300
- Die Bildnis-Miniatur in Skandinavien. Berlin, 1912. *(500).* 2 vols. Fo. Roan, rubbed, some wear. (SPB. Nov.30; 297) $200
-- **Anr. Copy.** 2 vols. Sm. fo. 100 col. plts., 1st. ll. lightly browned, orig. cf. gt., very worn & bumped, spine loose. (H. May 22; 105) DM 650
-- **Anr. Edn.** Berlin, 1912. *(510).* 2 vols. Fo. Orig. linen. (D. Nov.23; 2092) DM 1,400
- Meisterminiaturen aus fünf Jahrhunderten. Stuttgart, 1911. 4to. Lightly foxed, orig. linen. (D. Nov.23; 2093) DM 950
-- **Anr. Copy.** 4to. 76 mntd. cold. ills. on 75 plts., some foxing, orig. mor., gold-tooled borders; E. Lemberger ex-libris. (HT. May 9; 1103) DM 480

LEMERY, Louis
- A Treatise of Foods. L., 1704. Some stains, cropped, cont. cf., worn. (BBA. May 3; 48) *Jarndyce.* £110
-- **Anr. Edn.** Trans.:– D. Hay. L., 1745. 12mo. Cf. gt., rebkd. (P. Jan.12; 244) *Maggs.* £140

LEMERY, Nicholas
- Cours de Chymie, oder Der Vollkommene Chymist. Dresden, 1705. *New Edn.* 2 vols. in 1. Title & 2 ll. stpd., pagination jumps in vol. II, light browning, cont. vell. (H. May 22; 175) DM 1,250
-- **Anr. Edn.** Dresden & Leipzig, 1734. 2 pts. in 1 vol. Title verso stpd., some light browning, cont. vell., re-cased. (R. Oct.12; 1692) DM 1,350

- A Course of Chymistry. 1686. *2nd. Edn.* Licence
lf. used as front pastedown, last advt. lf., title soiled,
cont. cf., crudely rebkd. (BBA. Jul.27; 36)
Demetzy. £50
- Dictionnaire Universel des Drogues Simples. 1760.
New Edn. 4to. Cont. marb. roan, spine raised bands
(some losses). (HD. Jul.6; 57) Frs. 2,400

LEMNIUS, Levinus
- De gli Occulti Miracoli. Venice, 1567. Old wraps.
(SG. Oct.6; 235) $200
- Occulta Naturae Miracula. Leipzig, 1592. *3rd.
German Edn.* Browned & foxed thro.-out, cont.
vell., lacks 4 ties. (HK. May 15; 454) DM 950
- - **Anr. Edn.** [Heidelberg], 1600-01. 2 pts. (with
10 bks.) in 1 vol. Title with old name, minimal
browning, cont. blind-tooled vell., with date 1603.
(R. Apr.4; 1331) DM 1,800

LEMOISNE, Paul André
- Degas et Son Oeuvre. 1946. *(980).* 4 vols. Fo.
Orig. wraps. & s.-c.'s. (SPB. Nov.30; 28) $1,900
- la Vie et l'Art Romantiques: Gavarni, Peintre et
Lithographe. Paris, 1924-28. 2 vols. 4to. Orig.
wraps. (BBA. Apr.5; 145) *Lenton.* £85
- Les Xylographies du XIVe et du XVe Siècle au
Cabinet des Estampes de la Bibliothèque Nationale.
Paris & Brussels, 1927-30. *[650 numbered.].* 2 vols.
Fo. Liby. stps. on title, orig. hf. cl., embossed paper
bds. (BBA. Sep.8; 78) *Arts et Metiers.* £200
- - **Anr. Copy.** 2 vols. Fo. 130 mntd. reproductions,
ptd. wraps., minor chipping. (SG. Aug.25; 247)
$250

LEMONNIER, Camille
- Felicien Rops: L'Homme et l'Artiste. Paris, 1908.
4to. Hf. leath. by Bernard, orig. pict. wraps. bnd.
in; Pierre Bellanger bkplt. (SG. Jan.26; 277) $475
- - **Anr. Copy.** 4to. Hf. mor., corners, by Saulnier.
(HD. Jun.29; 132) Frs. 1,500

LE MONNIER, Pierre Charles
[-] Description et Usage des Principaux Instruments
d'Astronomie. Ill.:- Barnard after Goussier. [Paris],
1774. From the 'Description des Arts et Metiers'
series. Tall fo. 14 folding copperplates, mod. three-
qtr. cl. (SG. Oct.6; 19) $175
- Histoire Celeste. Paris, 1741. *1st. Edn.* 4to. Hf.-
title, Privilege lf., 7 folding engraved plts., full-p.
view, cont. mott. cf., back gt., jnts. very worn. (SG.
Apr.26; 127) $225

LE MOYNE, Pierre
- La Gallerie des Femmes Fortes. Paris, 1647. Fo.
Engraved frontis., 20 full-p. text engrs., lacks il &
most of Bb2, several ll. & ills. torn & reprd., early
19th. C. cf. gt., gt. cypher of Duke of Devonshire
on spine. (S. Apr.10; 322) *S. Levy.* £170
- Les Oeuvres Poétiques. Ill.:- G. Scotin after P.
Mignard. Paris, 1671. *1st. Coll. Edn.* Fo. Slightly
browned, cont. leath. gt., gold-tooled arms supralibros. (HK. Nov.10; 3078) DM 420

LE MUET, Pierre
- Maniere de Bastir pour toutes Sortes de Personnes
... Paris, chez François Jollain, [1647?]. *1st. Edn.*
Pt. 2. 2 pts. in 1 vol. Fo. 1st. title reprd., slight tear
in 1 plt., sm. hole in anr., antique-style panel of
cf. (C. Dec.9; 83) *Gimcrack.* £550
- - **Anr. Edn.** 1681. 2 pts. in 1 vol. Fo. Cont. marb.
cf., worn. (HD. Jun.29; 133) Frs. 1,550

LE NAIL, Ernest
- Le Château de Bois. Paris, 1875. Tall fo. 8 chromolitho. plts., plan & 43 mntd. photos., liby.
buckram. (SG. May 3; 238) $130

LENAU, Nicolaus
- Sämmtliche Werke. Ed.:- Anastasius Grün.
Stuttgart & Augsburg, 1855. *1st. Coll. Edn.* 4 vols.
19th. C. hf. mor., spines gt., partly unc. (C. Dec.9;
316) *Wenner.* £80

LENFANT, Jacques
- Histoire de la Guerre des Hussites et du Corricle
de Basle. Udrecht, 1731. 2 pts. in 1 vol. Stp. on hf.-
title & title, cont. vell. (R. Oct.11; 1022) DM 400

LENGLET DUFRESNOY, Pierre Nicolas
- Geographia Antiqua et Nova ... L., 1742. 4to. 33
double-p. engraved maps, mntd. on guards, cont.
cf. (C. Nov.16; 211) *Coss.* £140

LENIHAN, M.
- Limerick; its History & Antiquities. Dublin, 1866.
1st. Edn. Royal 8vo. Errata slips, bkplt., cl., loose.
(GM. Dec.7; 443) £70

LENIN, Vladimir Ilych [i.e. Vladimir Ilych Ulyanov]
- Doklad ob obedinitel'nom sëzde Rossiiskoi sotsial-
democraticheskoi rabochei partii [Report on the
Unification Conference of the Russian Social-Demo-
cratic Workers' Party. Letter to Petersburg Wor-
kers]. Moscow, 1906. *1st. Edn.* Loose as iss. in orig.
ptd. wraps., slightly soiled & discold. (BBA. Feb.9;
151) *Dury.* £100
- Ekonomicheskie Etyudy i Stat'i [Economic
Studies & Articles]. St. Petersb., 1899. Cont. cf.-
bkd. bds., rubbed. (S. May 10; 316)
Quaritch. £1,500
- K deevenskoi bednote [To the Village Poor].
Moscow, 1905. Appendix loosely inserted, orig.
wraps., spine slightly torn. (BBA. Feb.9; 152)
Drury. £130
- Razvitie Kapitalizma v Rossii [The Development
of Capitalism in Russia]. St.Petersb., 1899. *1st. Edn.*
Last errata lf., folding ptd. table, folding plt. with
margin tear, last text lf torn affecting 3 lines of
text, title slightly soiled, cont. cf. bkd. bds., slightly
rubbed. (BBA. Feb.9; 150) *Drury.* £400

LENOIR, Albert
- Statistique Monumentale de Paris. Paris, 1867. 3
vols. in 5. Atlas fo. & lge. sq. 4to. Frontis., approx.
300 engraved plts., ex-liby., text. vol. hf. mor., 4
atlas vols. qtr. mor. (SG. May 3; 239) $1,400

LENOIR, Marie Alexandre
- Musée des Monumens Français: Histoire de la
Peinture sur Verre, et Description des Vitraux
Anciens et Modernes; Description Historique et
Chronologique des Statues en Marbre et en Bronze,
Bas-Beliefs et Tombeaux des Hommes et Femmes
Célèbres. Ill.:- Guyot, after Lenoir & Percier. Paris,
1802-06. 5 vols. 5 additional pict. titles, 223 engrs.
(of 224?, lacks? port.), 1 plt. clipped, some foxing,
bds., chipped. (SG. Aug.25; 248) $150

LENOTRE, G.
- The Flight of Marie Antoinette. Trans.:- Mrs.
Rodolph Stewell. L., 1908. Extra-ill. with 15 plts.,
including 5 hand-cold., spotted, mor., elab. gt., by
Bayntun (Rivière), upr. cover inlaid with miniature
port. of Marie Antoinette, boxed. (S. Oct.4; 121)
Joseph. £320

LENTULO, Scipio
- An Italian Grammer [sic] written in Latin ... &
turned into Englyshe ... Trans.:- H. Grantham.
1575. *1st. Edn.* Sm. 8vo. Many MS. annots. (those
on title & last lf. mostly owners marks), a few ink
marks, title slightly soiled, corners folded over with
use & sometimes frayed, cont. vell., stitched, upr.
cover defect., lr. cover slightly torn at edges &
corner creased. [STC 15469] (C. May 30; 158)
Quaritch. £200

LENZ, Jakob Michael Reinold
- Gesammelte Schriften. Ed.:- L. Tieck. Berlin,
1828. *1st. Coll. Edn.* 3 vols. Later hf. linen,
romantic gt.; 2 ex-libris; Hauswedell coll. (H. May
24; 1441) DM 1,600
- - **Anr. Copy.** 3 vols. Lightly browned, cont bds.,
bumped & slightly rubbed. (HK. May 16; 2144)
DM 540
- - **Anr. Edn.** Ed.:- Franz Blei. München &
Leipzig, 1909-13. 5 vols. 1st. pp. vols. II & III
slightly crumpled, orig. hf. leath., gold-tooled spine
lightly worn. (HT. May 9; 1931) DM 750
- - **Anr. Edn.** Ed.:- E. Lewy. 1909. 4 vols. Cont.
patterned bds., orig. pict. wraps. bnd. in; ex-libris.
(GB. May 4; 1372) DM 650

LEO I, the Great, Pope
- Omnium Sermonum, Homiliarum & Epistolarum
... Cologne, 1546. *(Bound with:)* FRECULPHUS,
Bp. of Lisieux - Chronicorum ... Cologne, 1539. *1st.
Edn.* Together 2 works in 1 vol. Fo. Cont. stpd. cf.
over wood bds., decor.; from Fondation Fursten-
berg-Beaumesnil. (HD. Nov.16; 132) Frs. 1,500

LEO, Marsicanus
- Chronica Sacri Casinensis Coenobii. Ed.:- L.
Vicentius. Venice, 1513. *1st. Edn.* 4to. Without

final blank, mod. bds., spine darkened. (C. May 30;
37) *Parikian.* £150

LEO AFRICANUS, Joannis
- Joannis Leonis Africanus Africae descriptio IX
lib. absoluta. Lugduni Batavorum, 1632. 2 pts. in 1
vol. 16mo. Orig. bdg. (VA. Apr.27; 835) R 190

LEON, G. von
- Rabbinische Legenden. [Leipzig, Ernst Ludwig
Pr., 1913]. *DeLuxe Edn., (30) on Japan.* Orig.
hand-bnd. mor., some light scratches. (H. Nov.23;
1035) DM 920
- - **Anr. Edn.** Darmstadt, Ernst Ludwig Pr., 1913.
(100). Orig. vell., gold-tooled title. (HK. May 17;
2738) DM 400

**LEON SANCHEZ, Manuel & Cascales Muñoz,
José**
- Antologia de la Cuerda Granadina. Mexico, 1928.
(500) numbered. 4to. Orig. wraps.; autograph dedication. (DS. Feb.24; 2127) Pts. 22,000

LEON Y GAMA, Antonio de
- Descripcion Historica y Cronologica de las dos
Piedras que con Ocasion del Nuevo Empedrado que
se esta formando en la Plaza Principal de Mexico,
se hallaron en ella el ino de 1790. Mexico City,
1792. *1st. Edn.* Sm. 4to. Lf. of subscribers' names
at end, a few spots & stains, a little worming, not
affecting text, cont. mott. Spanish cf., spine gt.,
rubbed. [Sabin 40059] (S. May 10; 318)
Quaritch. £1,600

LEONARD
- Histoire de Jeanne lère, Reine de Naples, Comtesse
de Provence. Monaco, 1932-37. 3 vols. Hf. vell.,
vol. 1 with loss. (HD. Feb.22; 117) Frs. 1,000

LEONARD, R.L. (Ed.)
See— STYLE, Blätter für Mode ...

LEONARD, William Ellery
- Two Lives. [Binghampton, N.Y., priv. ptd., 1922].
1st. Edn. Tall 8vo. Orig. bds., spine worn; sigd. pres.
copy from author to Prof. & Mrs. M.I. Rostovtzeff,
Frederic Dannay copy. (CNY. Dec.16; 208) $750

LEONARDI, Domenico Felice
- Le Delizie della Villa di Castellazzo. Ill.:- Marc-
Antonio Dal Re. Milan, 1743. Fo. Engraved double-
p. port., 23 double-p. plts., orig. wraps. (C. Dec.9;
84) *Hedworth.* £2,800

LEONARDO DA VINCI
- Codex Madrid I & II. 1974. *Facs. Edn. (1000)
numbered.* 2 vols. 4to., with Commentary, Transcription & Translation, by Ladislac Reti. 8vo. & 4to.
Compl. with sigd. certificate contained in matching
book-box, orig. crimson mor., gt.-decor. spines.
(TA. Mar.15; 485) £55
- De Codices Madrid. Utrecht/Antw., 1974. *Facs.
of 1493 Edn.* 5 vols. Engl. transcription & commen-
tary, no bdgs. stated, s.-c. (VG. Mar.21; 548)
Fls. 480
- Del Moto e Misura dell'Acqua. Bologna, 1923. 2
plts. stuck together, some browning & spotting,
orig. ptd. wraps., some spotting, some wear to spine;
Stanitz coll. (SPB. Apr.25; 269) $150
- The Literary Works ... Ed.:- Jean Paul Richter.
L., 1939. *2nd. Enlarged Edn.* 2 vols. 4to. Buckram,
d.-w.'s chipped, card. case. (KH. Nov.9; 302)
Aus. $150
- The Madrid Codices. Trans.:- Ladislao Reti.
N.Y., 1974. *MS. Facs. Edn., with Engl. trans.
(1000).* 6 vols. Gt.-decor. red mor., clear acrylic
box, orig. shipping carton. (CBA. Jan.29; 291)
$400
- I Manoscritti e i Disegni di Leonardo da Vinci.
Rome, 1936-41. *(300).* Vols. II, III & V in 3 vols.
Fo. Orig. sewed, slightly spotted, some margin
tears. (HT. May 9; 1075) DM 520
- Trattato della Pittura ... con la Vita dell'Istesso
Autore Scritta da Rafaelle du Fresne ... Paris, 1651.
1st. Edn. 2 pts. in 1 vol. Fo. Lacks 8 unnumbered
introductory ll., short tear to title, cont. cf., spine
gt., w.a.f. (C. Nov.9; 18) *Vianini.* £160
- - **Anr. Edn.** Ed.:- R. du Fresne. Bologna, 1786.
New Edn. Fo. Engraved title vig., 7 text vigs. & 19
copperplts., title & some ll. lightly brown spotted,
cont. bds., very bumped, stain. (H. May 22; 155)
DM 860

LEONARDO DA VINCI -*Contd.*

- - **Anr.** Copy. Fo. Cont. hf. roan, corners, decor. spine, worn. (HD. Dec.9; 89)   Frs. 2,300
- **A Treatise of Painting.** L., 1721. Port., 35 engraved plts., cont. panel. cf. gt., rebkd. (P. Feb.16; 18)   £50

LEONARDO OF PISA
- **Scritti de Leonardo Pisano Matematico del Secolo Decimoterzo: Il Liber Abbaci; Practica Geometriae, Opusculi.** Ed.:– B. Boncompagni. Rome, 1857-62. *1st. Edn.* 2 vols. Fo. Some light spotting, mod. mor., unc.; Stanitz coll. (SPB. Apr.25; 268) $1,300

LEONHARD, H. (Ed.)
See— WELTBUHNE

LEONHARD, K.
- **Ida Kerkovius. Leben und Werk.** Koln, 1967. *(100). (20) roman numbered for the artist.* 4to. Orig. linen, orig. wraps.; MS. dedication on endpaper. (GB. Nov.5; 2661)   DM 600

LEONHARDI, F.G.
- **Der Förster u. Jäger in s. Monatl. Amtsverrichtungen u. Beschäftigungen.** Supp.:– E.M. Schilling. Leipzig, 1828. Cont. hf. leath. gt., spine slightly defect. & worn, jnts. brittle. (HK. May 16; 1580)   DM 850

LEONHARDT, Richard
- **Dekorative Farbige Ornamente.** Leipzig, 1907. Fo. 16 chromolitho. plts. loose as iss., cl.-bkd. bd. folder. (SG. Aug.25; 35) $130

LEONICENUM, Nicolaus
- **Opuscula** ... Ed.:– D. Andreas Leenius. Basle, 1532. Fo. Some sm. wormholes, mainly marginal, vell., spine worn; Dr. Walter Pagel copy. (S. Feb.7; 232)   *Quaritch.* £420

LEOPOLD, Duke of Austria
- **Compilatio ... de Astrorum Scientia.** Venice, 1520. *2nd. Edn.* Sm. 4to. Deleted inscr. on title-p. oxidized with slight paper loss, wormholes at head of title covered on verso, 2 sm. wormholes in margins through about hf. of book, slight foxing at beginning & end, cont. limp vell; Stanitz coll. (SPB. Apr.25; 271) $750

LEOPOLD, Rudolf
- **Egon Schiele. Gemälde, Aquarelle, Zeichnungen.** Ill.:– E. Schiele. Salzburg, 1972. *(200) De Luxe Edn.* Lge. 4to. 2 orig. engrs., orig. leath., slightly worn, orig. bd. s.-c. (HK May 17; 3106)   DM 1,100
- **Egon Schiele, Paintings, Watercolours, Drawings.** L., 1972. Lge. 4to. No bdg. stated. (SPB. Nov.30; 336) $550

LE PAGE DU PRATZ, Antoine Simon
- **Histoire de la Louisiane ... Deux Voyages dans le Nord du Nouveau Mexique.** Paris, 1758. *1st. Edn.* 3 vols. 12mo. Lge. folding engraved map, folding plan, 40 full-p. engraved plts., hf.-titles, cont. mott. cf., spines gt., rubbed; Edward Gibbon bkplt. in Vol. 1, the Rt. Hon. Visc. Eccles copy. [Sabin 40122] (CNY. Nov.18; 170) $650
- **The History of Louisiana** ... L., 1763. *1st. Edn. in Engl.* 2 vols. 12mo. Cont. cf., spines gt. [Sabin 40123] (C. Nov.16; 19)   *Kossow.* £460
- - **Anr.** Copy. 2 vols. 12mo. Hf.-titles, 1 folding map wrinkled with a minor inch tear, cont. cf.; the Rt. Hon. Visc. Eccles copy. [Sabin 40123] (CNY. Nov.18; 171) $420

LE PAUTRE, Antoine
- **Les Oeuvres d'Architecture.** Paris, [1652?]. Fo. 2 engraved double-p. titles, frontis., double-p. port. plt., 58 plts., including 35 double-p. views & plans, no text (as in the 1st. edn., this possibly a reiss. of the plts. only), vell.-bkd. bds. (C. Dec.9; 85)   *Waldersee.* £550
- - **Anr.** Copy. 2 pts. in 1 vol. Fo. 59 (of 62?) copperplates, 1 text lf. clipped at head & foot of inner margin, old cf., nicked. (SG. Oct.13; 224) $425
- [–] **Les Plans, Profils et Elevations de Ville et Chateau de Versailles.** Paris, ca. 1725. Fo. 2 engraved titles, 54 plts. & plans on 53 ll., including

22 double-p., cont. marb. bds., slightly worn & reprd. (C. Dec.9; 86)   *Waldersee.* £500

L'EPEE, Abbé Charles Michel de
- [–] **Institution des Sourds et Muets, par la Voie des Signes Methodiques** ... Paris, 1776. 2 pts. in 1 vol. Cont. cf. gt., lr. jnt. defect., lacks label. (SG. Oct.6; 151) $150
- [–] **La Veritable Manière d'Instruire les Sourds et Muets.** Paris, 1784. *1st. Edn.* Lge. 12mo. Few stains, cont. sheep gt. (SG. Oct.6; 152) $200

LEPERE, Auguste
- **La Forêt de Fontainebleau.** [1910]. *(35).* Fo. 34 woodcuts, leaves. (HD. Jun.6; 93)   Frs. 12,500
- **Le Long de la Seine et et des Boulevards.** [Paris, 1910]. Fo. Title-frontis. & 19 orig. woodcuts ptd. on japon pelure, under thick vell. masks, leaves, folder; without justification. (HD. Jun.6; 94)   Frs. 12,500
- **Nantes en 1900.** Preface:– Roger Marx. Nantes, 1900. Pink bradel hf. mor. by Franz, wrap. & spine preserved; prospectus bnd. at end. (HD. Jun.13; 85)   Frs. 2,800
- **Rouen Illustrée.** Paris, 1913. *(50).* Fo. 14 woodcuts on japon pelure, leaves. (HD. Jun.6; 95)   Frs. 12,500
- **Voyage autour des Fortifications.** Ca. 1910. *(35).* Fo. 27 plts. on japon pelure (including 3 supp. plts.), leaves. (HD. Jun.6; 96)   Frs. 11,500

LE PETIT, Jean François
- **Le Grande Chronique Ancienne et Moderne de Hollande.** Dordrecht, 1601. 2 vols. Fo. Lightly stained, titles misbnd., old cf., rebkd. (CSK. Sep.30; 166)   £85

LE PRIEUR, J.C.
- **Description d'une Partie de la Vallée de Montmorenci et de ses plus Agréable Jardins.** Paris, 1784. *2nd. Ill. Edn.* 23 added 18th. & 19th. C. plts. bnd. in, mod. grd. roan, decor. spine, unc. (HD. Dec.16; 24)   Frs. 1,450
- [–] **Vue de Monumens Construits dans les Jardins de Franconville-la-Garenne Appartenans à Madame la Comtesse d'Alban.** Paris, 1784. *1st. Edn.* 19 engraved plts., including 2 folding, extra plt. loosely inserted, cont. cold. Dutch gt. wraps. (C. Dec.9; 87)   *Weinreb.* £1,000

LE PRINCE DE BEAUMONT, Jean Baptiste
- **Divers Ajustements et Usages de Russie.** [Paris, plts. dtd. 1764-74]. 8 pts. in 1 vol. 4to. 71 engraved plts., including frontis. & 8 title-pp., little light margin staining, hf. cf., rebkd.; bkplt. of David Garnett. (BBA. Mar.21; 327)   *Erlini.* £220
- - **Anr. Edn.** Ca. 1775. 4to. Engraved title, 85 plts., some minor spotting, mod. qtr. cf. & decor. bds. by Sangorski & Sutcliffe. (TA. Oct.20; 380)   £155
- - **Anr. Edn.** N.d. 8 pts. in 1 vol. 4to. 64 etched & 7 aquatint plts. (dtd. 1764-74), including 8 titles, stained, later hf. cf., rebkd., old spine preserved, w.a.f. (CSK. Dec.16; 44)   £180

LE RIRE
Ill.:– Brunelleschi, Fabiano, Godefroy, Gris, Guillaume, Jeanniot, Leandre, Steinlen, Vallotton, Villon, & others. Paris, 10.XI.1894-24.XII.1909. Years I-XIV (=Orig. Series: pts. 1-430, New Series: pts. 1-360), in 15 vols. Fo. Some margins slightly brittle, some slight defects, cont. red hf. mor., decor. spine, some slight defects., lacks 1 spine, orig. cold. pict. wraps. bnd. in, w.a.f. (HK. Nov.11; 3914)   DM 2,200

LERMONTOV, Mikhail Yurievitch
- **A Song about Tsar Ivan Vasilyevitch.** Ill.:– Paul Nash. Aquila Pr., 1929. *(750) numbered.* Orig. rust mor., geometric black & white mor. onlays after design by Nash, unc., fitted case with yellow mor. centrepiece with arms of Maj. Abbey. (S. Nov.21; 202)   *Marks.* £130

LE ROUGE, George Louis
- **Atlas Nouveau Portatif à l'Usage des Militaires, Collèges et du Voyageur. Introduction à la Géographie.** Paris, priv. ptd., 1756. 2 vols. 4to. 2 double-p. frontis. & 193 maps heightened with cols., cont. marb. cf., spines decor.; from Château des Noës liby. (HD. May 25; 49)   Frs. 7,500
- - **Anr. Edn.** Paris, 1756-59. 2 vols. 4to. Maps. sm.

ob. fo., cont. hf. leath., bumped, spine slightly worn. (R. Oct.13; 2859)   DM 7,400
- [–] **Detail des Nouveaux Jardins à la Mode. Jardins Anglo-chinois à la Mode.** [Paris, 1776]. 4 pts. in 1 vol. Ob. fo. Without general title, 103 metal engraved plts. old bds., soiled. (HD. Dec.1; 85)   Frs. 3,000
- [–] **Jardins Anglois-Chinois et Jardins de la Mode.** Paris, 1776-88. 21 pts. in 11 vols. 4to. 492 double-p. or folding engraved plts., including numbered engraved ll. of 'Table', some plts. trimmed, few folding plts. splitting at centrefold, few slightly discold., with margin dampstains or rust marks, few short tears reprd., 19th. C. cf.-bkd. bds., w.a.f. (C. Dec.9; 88)   *Weinreb.* £9,000
- - **Anr. Edn.** [1776-87]. 8 pts. only (of 21), in 1 vol. Ob. fo. 207 plts., titles to pts. 4 & 7 bnd. at end, lacks 2 ll. & 1 plt., 30 plts. oil-stained, 19th. C. hf. chagrin. (HD. Nov.9; 180)   Frs. 4,100
- **Le Parfait Aide de Camp.** Paris, 1760. Ob. 4to. Slight worming in right margin, sm. hole with loss in 1st. 6 text ll., cont. bds. (R. Oct.12; 2382)   DM 3,300
- **Recueil des Côtes Maritimes de France.** Paris, 1757. 4to. Double-p. engraved title, folding general map & 50 double-p. engraved charts, mntd. on guards thro.-out, cont. mott. cf. gt., slightly rubbed. (C. Jun.27; 44)   *Shapero.* £190
- - **Anr.** Copy. Ob. 4to. 50 engraved maps & plans, cont. bds. (HD. Mar.19; 67)   Frs. 3,500

LE ROUX, Philibert Joseph
- **Dictionnaire Comique, Satyrique, Critique, Burlesque, Libre et Proverbal.** Lion, 1735. *New Edn.* Marb. cf., spine decor., slightly worn. (LM. Oct.22; 244)   B. Frs. 8,000
- - **Anr. Edn.** Lyon, 1752. *New Edn.* 2 vols. Some light staining, cont. hf. vell., soiled. (CSK. Jan.27; 64)   £50

LE ROUX DE LINCY, A.J. V.
- **Recherches sur Jean Grolier sur la Vie et sa Bibliothèque.** Paris, 1866. 2 vols. 4to. & 8vo. 6 plts. bnd. separately, cont. hf. mor. gt.; H.M. Nixon coll., with his sig., acquisition note & a few MS. notes. (BBA. Oct.6; 82)   *Traylen.* £220
- - **Anr.** Copy. Lge. 8vo. Cont. hf. cf., corners. (HD. Jun.6; 97)   Frs. 1,700
- **Researches concerning Jean Grolier, His Life & His Library.** N.Y., Grol. Cl., 1907. *(300).* 1 vol. in 2. 4to. Hf. mor.; H.M. Nixon coll., with many annots. on interleaves in Vol. 2. (BBA. Oct.6; 83)   *Beres.* £4,500

LEROY, Alphonse
- **Recherches sur les Habillements des Femmes et des Enfans.** Paris, 1772. *Orig. Edn.* 12mo. Chagrin, unc. (HD. Feb.28; 170)   Frs. 2,500

LEROY, C.F.M.
- **Souvenirs de ... Major d'Infanterie Vétéran des Armées de la République et de l'Empire (1767-1851).** Ed.:– G. Dumay. N.p., n.d. Hf. cf. (HD. Jan.27; 61)   Frs. 1,700

LE ROY, Julien David
- **Les Ruines des plus Beaux Monuments de la Grèce.** Ill.:– Le Bas & others, after Le Roy. Paris, 1758. *1st. Edn.* 2 pts. in 1 vol. Fo. 60 plts., cont. cf., spine gt. in 7 compartments, corners rubbed. (C. Mar.14; 62)   *Tzakas.* £2,200
- - **Anr.** Copy. 2 pts. in 1 vol. Lge. fo. On holland, cont. red mor., spine decor. (HD. Jun.18; 26)   Frs. 35,000
- - **Anr. Edn.** Paris, 1770. *[2nd. Edn.].* 2 vols. in 1. Fo. Sm. brown stains on table lf., cont. marb. roan, decor. spine; E. de Laplane ex-libris. (HD. Dec.16; 52)   Frs. 11,500
- - **Anr.** Copy. 2 vols. in 1. Fo. Stain in lr. margin, cont. hf. roan, worn. (HD. Mar.14; 58)   Frs. 9,100
- - **Anr.** Copy. 2 vols. in 1. Lge. fo. Lacks hf.-title of Vol. II & 1 plt., new hf. cf., corners. (B. Oct.4; 698)   Fls. 2,000

LERSNER, A.A. von
- **Der Weit-berühmten Freyen Reichs-Wahl-und Handels-Stadt Franckfurt am Mayn Chronica.** [Frankfurt], 1706. Vol. 1; 2 pts. in vol. 4to. Cont. vell., slightly spotted; 2 engraved Braunschweig-Luneburg ex-libris. (H. Nov.23; 538)   DM 1,200

LE SAGE, Alain René
- **The Adventures of Gil Blas de Santillane.** L., 1800. 4 vols. Hf. mor. by Morell, L., tooled gt. spine. (GM. Dec.7; 681) £65
- **– – Anr. Edn.** Trans.:– Smollett. L., 1819. 3 vols. 15 hand-cold. aquatint plts., cont. red mor. gt. (BBA. Oct.27; 50) *Fletcher.* £120
- **– – Anr. Copy.** Cf. bkd. bds. (S. Oct.11; 352) *Soloman.* £55
- **Le Bachelier de Salamanque.** Paris; The Hague, 1736-1738. *1st. Edn.* 2 vols. Sm. 8vo. 6 engraved plts., cont. spr. cf., jnts. worn, upr. cover of 1 vol. detchd. (SG. Apr.19; 116) $110
- **– – Anr. Copy.** 2 vols. 12mo. Cont. spr. cf., spines decor., corners rounded. (HD. Nov.9; 47) Frs. 1,650
- **Le Diable Boiteux.** Ill.:– Mageleine Horthemels (frontis.). 1707. *Orig. Edn.* 12mo. Cont. cf., Duc de Luynes arms. (HD. Apr.13; 22) Frs. 2,000
- **– – Anr. Edn.** Ill.:– Tony Johannot. Paris, 1840. 4to. Crimson three-qtr. mor., spine gt., by Durvand, spine & corners slightly worn. (SG. Feb.16; 177) $110
- **Histoire de Gil Blas de Santillane.** Paris, 1747. *1st. Compl. Edn. 1st. Printing of ills.* 4 vols. 12mo. 1 lf. torn, cont. spr. cf., spines decor., some turn-ins. reprd. (HD. May 3; 86) Frs. 1,300
- **– – Anr. Edn.** Ill.:– Bornet, Charpentier & Duplessi-Bertaux. Paris, An 3 [1795]. 4 vols. Some light foxing, cont. marb. cf. gt., spines decor. (HD. May 3; 87) Frs. 2,800
- **– – Anr. Edn.** Ill.:– Guétard (port.) & Marillier. Paris, 1805. 4 vols. *(With:)* – **Le Diable Boîteux.** Paris, 1805. 2 vols. *(With:)* – **Histoire de Guzman d'Alfarache.** Paris, 1806. 2 vols. *(With:)* – **Le Bachelier de Salamanque.** Paris, 1807. 2 vols. Together 10 vols. 12mo. Cont. str.-grd. red mor. gt., spines decor. (HD. May 4; 333) Frs. 4,800
- **– – Anr. Edn.** Ill.:– after R. Smirke. L., 1809. 4 vols. 4to. Lacks 2 copper engrs., cont. Engl., burgundy long-grd. mor., gt. & blind-tooled in Bozérian style. (D. Nov.24; 2297) DM 1,200
- **– – Anr. Edn.** Ill.:– Godard (port.), J. Gigoux (vigs.). Paris, 1835. *1st. Printing.* Cont. long-grd. mor., gt. decor., buckram doubls. & endpapers, s.-c., sigd. by Valentin. (HD. Dec.16; 25) Frs. 2,500
- **– – Anr. Edn.** Ill.:– after Jean Gigoux. Paris, 1835. Lge. 8vo. Port. ptd. on china, cont. hf. mor., corners, sigd. by Lanne, spine gt., unc. (HD. Mar.19; 68) Frs. 1,200
- **Gil Blas de Santillane ...** Ill.:– Maucie Leloir. [1899]. *(50) on japan.* Lge. 8vo. Bordeaux mor. gt. by Chambolle-Duru, spine decor., wraps. (HD. May 4; 335) Frs. 2,700
- **Oeuvres Choisies.** Amst., 1783. 15 vols. Cont. marb. cf. (HD. Jun.29; 134) Frs. 1,400
- **Recueil des Pièces mises au Théâtre François.** Paris, 1739. *1st. Edn.* 2 vols. 12mo. Cont. red mor., Marie-Thérèse de Savoie arms; from libys. of Baron de Franchetti & Baron de La Roche-Lacarelle. (HD. Mar.29; 56) Frs. 33,000
- **Le Théâtre de la Foire.** Amst., 1723. 5 vols. 12mo. Cont. cf., arms, decor. spine. (HD. Jan.27; 210) Frs. 1,950
- **– – Anr. Edn.** Ill.:– Bonnart (frontis.) & Marillier. Paris, 1810. Vols. 13-16 of 'Oeuvres choises'. Some foxing, unc., cont. red hf. mor., Duchesse de Berry arms on upr. cover, decor. spines, unc., Château de Rosny ex-libris. (HD. Sep.22; 274) Frs. 3,100

LESCALLIER, Daniel
- **Traité Pratique du Gréement des Vaisseaux et Autres Bâtiments de Mer.** Paris, L., Amst., 1791. *Orig. Edn.* 2 vols. in 1. 4to. Some slight stains, vell. (HD. Mar.9; 96) Frs. 4,100
- **– – Anr. Copy.** 2 vols. 4to. Cont. marb. roan, spine decor., worn, turn-ins reprd. (HD. Jun.18; 27) Frs. 4,000
- **[-] Vocabulaire des Termes de Marine Anglois et François.** Paris, 1777. 4to. Cont. cf.; Quimper liby. stp. (1885), Marquis de Granges de Surgères ex-libris. (HD. Mar.9; 95) Frs. 1,900

LESCURE, Jean
- **La Saint-Jean d'Eté.** Ill.:– Leon Gischia. Paris, 1963. *(123) numbered & sigd. by author & artist. (20) with extra suite of the woodcuts on Auverre,*

each print sigd. by artist. 4to. Unsewn in orig. wraps., unc., folder & s.-c. (S. Nov.21; 80) *Landau.* £150

LESLIE, Col.
- **Historical Records of the Family of Leslie from 1067-1869.** Edinb., 1869. 3 vols. Cl. gt. (PD. Dec.14; 103) £65

LESLIE, Frank
- **Pictorial History of the American Civil War.** Ed.:– E.G. Squier. N.Y., 1862. Compl. in 25 nos. Tall fo. Lr. margins slightly stained, hf. leath.; ex-liby. (SG. Apr.5; 55) $175

LESLIE, John
- **An Experimental Inquiry into the Nature & Propagation of Heat.** L., 1804. *1st. Edn.* Lacks last (blank?) lf., a few ll. misbnd., later hf. cf. (BBA. Nov.30; 110) *Phillips.* £75
- **De Origine, Moribus et Rebus Gestis Scotorum.** Rome, 1578. 4to. Some slight staining or spotting, hf. roan by Bretherton, with ticket; Phillipps copy, with press-marks. (S. Mar.20; 831) *Erasmus.* £90

LESPINASSE, Pierre
- **La Miniature en France au XVIIIe Siècle.** Paris & Brussels, 1929. 4to. Mor.-bkd. bds., partly unc. spine & jnts. slightly rubbed, orig. wraps. bnd. in. (S. Apr.30; 124) *Gerino.* £110

LESSEPS, Jean Baptiste Barthelmy, Baron du
- **Reise durch Kamtschatka und Siberien nach Frankreich.** Trans.:– J.R. Forster. Berlin, 1791. *1st. German Edn. (Bound with:)* FERRIERES-SALVEBOEUF, L.F. de – **Reisen in der Turkei, Persien und Arabien,** pp. 303-544, cont. hf. leath. gt. (R. Oct.13; 3053) DM 550

LESSER, F.C.
See– GESSNER, C.F. — PEUCER, Daniel — LESSER, F.C.

LESSING, Gotthold Ephraim
- **Emilia Galotti.** Ill.:– F. Bolt after Schnorr. Leipzig, 1803. *De Luxe Edn. on vell.* Lge. 4to. Slightly foxed thro.-out, 1 lf. with sm. tear. hf. leath., ca. 1900, gold-tooled monog.; Ernst Magnus ex-libris. (GB. May 4; 1373) DM 400
- **Fabeln Drey Bücher.** Ill.:– K. Nebel. [Darmstadt, Kleukens Pr., 1920]. *(250) numbered.* Orig. vell. gt. (HK. May 17; 2889) DM 600
- **Laokoon.** Berlin, 1766. *1st. Edn.* Pt. 1 (all publd.). Cont. hf. cf. (C. Dec.9; 262) *Bjorck.* £500
- **– – Anr. Copy.** Pt. 1 (all publd.). Cont. hf. leath.; Borries v. Münchhausen engraved ex-libris. (BR. Apr.12; 1478) DM 1,600
- **Lustspiele.** Berlin, 1767. *1st. Edn.* 2 vols. Some light browning & spotting, upr. inner cover with traces of pasting, cont. hf. leath., slightly worn. (H. Nov.23; 704) DM 2,400
- **Minna von Barnhelm.** Berlin, 1767. *1st. Separate Edn. 1st. Printing.* Slightly browned & soiled, cont. hf. leath., rubbed. (HK. Nov.10; 2577) DM 2,000
- **Nathan der Weise.** N.p., 1779. *1st. Edn. 1st. Iss.,* with 'Introite' on title & misprint on p. 95. Sm. 8vo. Stp. cut from title & reprd., some foxing thro.-out, cont. cf. (C. Dec.9; 263) *Pollak.* £190
- **– – Anr. Copy.** Title with MS. owner's mark, 2 sm. worm traces, some light browning & foxing, bds. with old col. & end-paper, unc. (HK. Nov.10; 2578) DM 1,500
- **– – Anr. Copy.** Sm. 8vo. 'Introite' on title, 'reichre' on p. 95., title verso & last lf. with liby. stp., browned & foxed, cont. bds., new spine, spotted & defect. (H. May 22; 788) DM 680
- **– – Anr. Edn.** [Berlin], 1779. *1st. Edn. 2nd. Iss.* Browned thro.-out, cont. hf. sheep, rubbed. (BBA. Jan.19; 23) *Bickersteth.* £75
- **– – Anr. Edn.** Leipzig, [1910]. *Facs. of 1779 1st. Edn. (200) numbered De Luxe Edn.* Lacks facs. of subscribers invitation & MS. sketch of 'Nathan', orig. leath., gt. spine, inner & outer dentelle, corners slightly bumped. (D. Nov.24; 3121) DM 500
- **Sämmtliche Schriften.** Ill.:– Frisch. Berlin, 1784-94. 30 vols. Port. slightly stained in upr. margin, cont. hf. russ. gt. (C. Dec.9; 266) *Wohler.* £390
- **– – Anr. Edn.** Ed.:– J.F. Schink. Berlin, 1825-27. 32 vols. Pts. 1-28. Lacks 2 copperplts.(?), all titles stpd. in upr. right corner, MS. numbered, cont. bds., some slight foxing, w.a.f. (HK. May 16; 2146) DM 400

– – Anr. Edn. Trans.:– K. Lackmann. Berlin, 1838-40. *1st. critical coll. Edn.* 13 vols. Foxed, cont. hf. leath. gt.; Hauswedell coll. (H. May 24; 1447) DM 2,600
- **Schrifften.** Ill.:– J.W. Meil. Berlin, 1753-55. *1st. Coll. Edn.* 6 vols. Slightly spotted & browned, vol. IV some ll. with sm. wormhole, cōnt. cf., gt. decor., 2 spines lightly defect., slightly bumped; Hauswedell coll. (H. May 24; 1446) DM 3,600
- **Theologischer Nachlass.** Ed.:– [K.G. Lessing.]. Ill.:– Endner (title vig.), Berlin, 1784. *1st. Edn.* 19th. C. bds. (R. Apr.3, 307) DM 450

LESSING, Julius
- **Alt Orientalische Teppichmuster, nach Bildern und Originalen des XV-XVI. Jahrhunderts.** Berlin, 1877. Fo. 30 col. litho. plts., 2-tone cl., spine crudely taped. (SG. Aug.25; 282) $600
- **Das Tafelsilber ihrer Koniglichen Hoheiten des Prinzen und der Prinzessin Wilhelm von Preussen.** Berlin, 1883. Fo. Some dampstaining, mostly marginal, loose as iss. in orig. hf. cl. portfo., rubbed & soiled. (S. Dec.13; 458) *Green.* £70

LESSING, Julius
- **Die Gewebe-Sammlung des Koeniglichen Kurstgewerbe-Museum.** Berlin, 1900-[13]. 11 vols. Atlas fo. 330 plts., most in colours & gold., text on tissue-guards, each plt. liby.-stpd. on blank verso, loose in cl.-bkd. ptd. bds., linen ties. (SG. May 3; 240) $3,200

LESSON, René Primevère
- **Historie Naturelle des Oiseaux-Mouches.** Paris, [1829-30]. 86 hand-finished col.-ptd. plts. *(With:)* – **Histoire Naturelle des Colibris, suivie d'un Supplement à l'Histoire Naturelle des Oiseaux-Mouches.** Paris, [1830-32]. 65 (of 66) hand-finished col.-ptd. plts. *(With:)* – **Les Trochilidées.** Paris, [1832-33]. 66 hand-finished col.-ptd. plts. Together 3 vols. No hf.-titles, pp. IX-XLVI of Vol. 1 bnd. at end of Vol. 3, some foxing, mostly affecting text, 19th. C. red mor. gt. by D. Batten, with his ticket, slightly rubbed. (S. Nov.28; 43) *Schuster.* £820
- **– – Anr. Copy.** 86 cold. plts., some spotting, mainly to text, cont. red hf. mor. gt., partly unc. (S. Nov.28; 44) *Reid.* £380
- **– – Anr. Copy.** 86 cold. plts., foxed, hf. mor. (SPB. Dec.13; 591) $350
- **Voyage autour du Monde ... sur la Corvette la Coquille.** Paris, 1839. *1st. Edn.* 2 vols. 42 engraved plts. (19 hand-cold.), titles & many plts. & ll. foxed, Vol. 2 loose with many ll. partly detchd., cont. decor. bds., unc., covers very rubbed. (CA. Apr.3; 77) Aus. $190
- **– – Anr. Copy.** 4 vols. in 2. Some slight foxing, hf. leath., gt. spine, spine defect. (D. Nov.23; 900) DM 450

LESSORE, E.
See– WYLD, W. & Lessore, E.

LESTER, W.W. & Bromwell, W.J.
- **A Digest of the Military & Naval Laws of the Confederate States ...** Columbia, 1864. *1st. Edn.* Sm. 8vo. Cl.-bkd. marb. bds.; pencil note on flylf. stating the book was taken when 'Genl. Lee's Baggage train was captured ... '. (SG. Oct.20; 111) $200
- **– – Anr. Copy.** Incidental ageing & foxing, a few pp. roughly opened, orig. cl., & marb. bds., lack backstrip, covers worn; Huston Lee (Major & Chief Quartermaster, C.S.A.) copy, sigd. with rank in pencil at front pasted own & title, 1864. (HA. Sep.16; 324) $150

L'ESTOILE, Pierre de
- **[-] Journal ... de Henri III. — Description de l'Isle des Hermaphrodites ... — Journal du Règne de Henri IV. — Supplément au Journal du Règne de Henri IV.** Cologne, 1720-36. 7 pts. in 5 vols. 12mo. Slight foxing, some ll. slightly short at head, 19th. C. blind-decor. russ. (HD. May 3; 88) Frs. 3,700

LETAROUILLY, Paul
- **Edifices de Rome Moderne.** Paris, 1860; 1850; 1857. Text vol. & 3 plt. vols. Lge. 4to. & Atlas fo. Port., frontis., 354 plts., ex-liby., some foxing, text vol. red hf. mor., plt. vols. red-mor.-bkd. marb. bds. (SG. May 3; 241) $400
- **Le Vatican et la Basilique de Saint-Pierre de**

LETAROUILLY, Paul -*Contd.*

Rome. Paris, 1882. 2 vols. Elephant fo. Cl. (SKC. Sep.9; 1811) £70
- - **Anr. Copy.** 4 pts. in 2 vols. Atlas fo. Approx. 250 engraved & heliotype plts., some cold., ex-liby., hf. mor. (SG. May 3; 242) $650

LETCHFORD, Albert
- **A Series of Seventy ... Illustrations to ... Burton's 'Arabian Nights'.** 1897. *(280). (250) 'choice Edition de Luxe'.* Lge. fo. This copy unnumbered, port., 71 plts., some spotting, cont. hf. mor., rubbed & soiled. (CSK. Oct.21; 133) £60

LE TELLIER, H.
- **Defense des Nouveaux Chrestiens et des Missionaires de la Chine, du Japon & des Indes.** Paris, 1688. Cf., detchd. (DS. Feb.24; 2031) Pts. 20,000

LETH, Hendrik de
- **Het Oud Adelyk Huys en Ridderhofstad te Meer Toebehoorende ... Vincent Maximilian, Baron von Lockhorst ... Chateau de Ter Meer.** N.p., ca. 1730. Fo. Lge. folding engraved view, 26 plts. on 13 ll., cont. blind-decor. stiff vell. (C. Dec.9; 90) *Quaritch.* £1,000
[-] **Nieuwe Geographische en Historische Atlas van de Zeven Vereengde Nederlandsche Provintien.** Amst., [1766]. Ob. 8vo. Engraved title (stained), 1 plt., 36 outl.-cold. maps, bnd. (B. Oct.4; 730a) Fls. 2,800
- - **Anr. Copy.** Narrow 8vo. Engraved folding title, 1 folding plt., 50 cont. outl. cold. folding maps, 2 hand-cold. folding tables, outer margins slightly frayed, some slightly torn, cont. hf. cf., covers rubbed, corners defect. (VG. Nov.30; 798) Fls. 1,800

LETI, Gregorio
- **Critique Historique, Politique ... Comique sur les Loteries Anciennes et Modernes, Spirituelles et Temporelles, des Etats et des Eglises.** Amst., 1697. *1st. Edn.* 2 vols. Browned, cont. recovered vell. (HD. Feb.28; 58) Frs. 2,300

LE TONNELIER DE BRETEUIL, A.F.V.
- **Missale Montalbanense** ... Tolosae, 1784. 4to. Red mor. gt. by Stradel, cathedral blind-decor. (HD. May 3; 89) Frs. 1,100

LETRASME, Jacques
- **Hardes et Uniformes de Matelots (de Louis XIV à nos Jours).** Ill.:– A. Goichon. Paris, 1937. Fo. Leaves, bds. (HD. Jan.27; 169) Frs. 1,000

LETTER ADDRESSED TO TWO GREAT MEN on the Prospect of Peace; & on the Terms Necessary to be insisted upon in the Negociation
L., 1760. *1st. Printing.* Attrib. to John Douglas, William Pulteney & Junius ... mod. crushed qtr. mor., marb. bds. (SG. Apr.5; 73) $120

LETTERE DI PRINCIPI
Venice, 1564-81. 3 vols. Sm. 4to. Piece of paper pasted over 'Libro Primo' on title-p. of Vol. I, a few stains, late 17th. C. Italian vell. (S. Oct.11; 403) *Maggs.* £240

LETTERS FROM FRANCE
See— S., M.

LETTRE D'UN BENEDICTIN A MONSIEUR L'EVFSQUE DE BLOIS, touchant le Discernement des Anciennes Reliques, au Sujet d'un Dissertation de Mr Thiers, contre la Saint Larme de Vendome.
Paris, 1700. 12mo. Text attrib. to Mabillon, 19th. C. hf. cf. (HD. Dec.2; 109) Frs. 1,100

LETTRE D'UN CANDIDAT ou l'Entrée à Bibliopolis
Ill.:– Paul Avril, engraved by Gaujean. Paris, 1896. *(115) on Whatman.* 4to. Ills. in 3 states, mor. gt. by Petitot, wraps. preserved; from Paul Lacombe liby. (B. Oct.4; 657) Fls. 700

LETTS, Son & Company
- **Popular Atlas.** L., 1881-83. 4 vols. Fo. Cont. hf. mor., lightly rubbed. (CSK. Dec.2; 15) £75

LETTS, John M.
[-] **California Illustrated.** Ill.:– J. Cameron after G.V. Cooper. N.Y., 1852. *1st. Edn.* 48 full-p. handcold. litho. plts., moderate foxing to some text ll. & most plts., 1 plt. partly loose, later hf. cf., partly unc., rubbed, corners; the Rt. Hon. Visc. Eccles copy. (CNY. Nov.18; 172) $600

LETTSOM, John Coakley
- **Hints Designed to promote Beneficence, Temperance, & Medical Science.** 1816. *Revised Edn.* 3 vols. Browned & spotted, orig. bds., rebkd., rubbed. (BBA. Jul.27; 37) *Gurney.* £160

LEU, Thomas de
- **Septem Praecipuae Effusiones Preciosissimi Sanguinis D.N. Jesu Christi.** N.p., [late 16th. C.]. Ob. 4to. Bds. (HD. May 21; 47) Frs. 1,100

LEUCHS, Johann Carl
- **Allgemeines Waaren-Lexicon.** Nuremb., [1825]-26. 2 vols. in 4. Cont. hf. leath., slightly rubbed. (R. Oct.12; 1757) DM 410

LEUPOLD, J. Chr.
- **Geistliche Herzens-Einbildungen Inn (je) 250 Biblischen Figur-Sprüchen.** Augsburg, ca. 1740. 2 pts. in 1 vol. Ob. 4to. Lacks pt. 1 16 ll. preface & 4 plts., 1st. copper engr. pt. 2 cold. in 1 plt. pt. 2 with lge. tear, slightly soiled, 1st. 10 ll. pt. 1 worn, pt. 2 browned in upr. margin, bds. (HK. Nov.9; 1629) DM 950
- **Theatrum Machinarum Generale. Schaü-Platz des Grundes Mechanischer Wissenschaften.** Leipzig, 1724. Fo. Hf.-title, text slightly browned, light stain affecting a few plts., cont. vell.; C.E. Kenney copy, Stanitz coll. (SPB. Apr.25; 272) $650
- **Theatrum Machinarum Hydrotechnarum. Schau-Platz der Wasser-Bau-Kunst.** Leipzig, 1724. *(With:)* - **Theatri Machinarum Hydraulicarum** ... Leipzig, 1725. *(With:)* - **Theatri Machinarum Supplementum das ist; Zusatz zum Schau-Platz der Machinen und Instrumenten.** Leipzig, 1739. Together 3 works in 1 vol. Fo. Lacks hf.-titles, paper losses to 2 title-pp., text very brown, some stains & foxing to plts., sm. margin wormholes at beginning & end, cont. cf., spine gt., jnts. reprd., slightly rubbed; Stanitz coll. (SPB. Apr.25; 273) $1,600
- - **Anr. Copy.** Fo. Slightly browned or spotted, hf. leath. using old cover paper. (D. Nov.25; 4640) DM 2,700
- - **Anr. Copy.** Vol. II. Fo. Slight browning, some plts. slightly crumpled, cont. hf. vell., slightly defect. (HT. May 8; 641) DM 700
- **Theatrum Machinarum Moliarum.** Ed.:– J.M. Beyer, J.K. Weinhold (pt. 3). Dresden, 1767-88. 3 pts. in 1 vol. Fo. Lacks 1 copperplt. in pt. 3, title pts. 1 & 2 stpd., cont. hf. leath., rubbed & bumped. (HK. May 15; 456) DM 1,050
- **Theatri Machinarum Supplementum.** Leipzig, 1739. Fo. Some light browning, some plts. slightly spotted, cont. hf. vell., rubbed & bumped. (HT. May 8; 642) DM 600
- **Theatri Statici Universalis, sive Theatrum Staticum, das ist: Schau-Platz der Gewicht-Kunst und Waagen.** Leipzig, 1726. 4 pts. in 1 vol. Fo. Text lightly discold., plts. unc. & slightly frayed at foreedges, cont. vell.; C.E. Kenney copy, Stanitz coll. (SPB. Apr.25; 274) $1,000
- **Theatrum Pontificiale.** Leipzig, 1726. Fo. Some light browning, title lf. with erased stp., cont. hf. leath. gt. (D. Nov.25; 4639) DM 2,700

LEUSDEN, Johannes
- **Philologus Hebraeo-Mixtus.** Utrecht, 1682. *2nd. Edn.* 4to. Engraved frontis. & plts., printer's devices out from title & final lf., some ll. frayed & reprd., some stains, cont. cf., crudely rebkd. (S. Apr.10; 323) *Hirschler.* £120

LEVAILLANT, François
- **Erste Reise in das Innere von Afrika.** Ed.:– J.R. Forster. Berlin, 1790. *1st. German Edn.* Cont. hf. leath. gt. (R. Oct.13; 2913) DM 550
- **Histoire Naturelle des Oiseaux d'Afrique.** Ill.:– C.M. Fessard & J.L. Peree, after J. Lebrecht Reinold. Paris, 1805-02-08. *Re-iss. of Vols. 1 & 2.* 6 vols. Lge. fo. 300 engraved plts. in 2 states, 1 ptd. in cols. & hand-finished, the other uncold., no hf.-titles, some foxing & offsetting, particularly at beginning & end of vols., minor flaw slightly affecting text on I2r in Vol. 5, cont. gt.-panel. mott. cf., spines decor., several covers becoming loose or detchd. (S. Nov.28; 52) *Maggs.* £8,000
- **Histoire Naturelle des Oiseaux de Paradis et des Rolliers, Suivie de Celle des Toucans et des Barbus.** Ili.:– Bouquet, Grémilliet, & Pérée, after Barraband. Paris, [1801-]06. 2 vols. Lge. fo. Without subsequently iss. 'Histoire naturelle des promerops, et des guêpiers', 114 plts. in 2 states, ptd. in cols. & hand-finished & uncold., col. plt. 18 in Vol. II loosely inserted (ptd. on a smaller sheet of paper), a few sm. margin repairs, some light spotting, cont. russ. gt., rebkd. (S. Feb.1; 35) *Thorolds.* £19,000
- - **Anr. Edn.** Ill.:– Jacques Barraband. Paris, [1801-]1806 & [1806-18]. Lge. fo. Wide margin, on vell.; some foxing, mostly in margins, some sm. tears, mod. hf. mor.; Hauswedell coll. (H. May 24; 868) DM 50,000
- **Histoire Naturelle des Perroquets.** Ill.:– Langlois, under direction of Bouquet, after Barraband. Paris, 1801-05. 2 vols. A lge. copy, 145 plts., ptd. in cols., retouched by hand, some slight spotting or discolouration, plt. 102 with margin tear reprd., mod. red hf. mor. gt., unc.; sm. embossed stp. of Pavlovsk Muzei in lr. corners of plts. (S. Feb.1; 36) *Parker.* £18,000
- **Histoire Naturelle d'une Partie d'Oiseaux Noureaux et Rares de l'Amérique et des Indes.** Paris, 1801[-02]. *1st. Edn.* Vol. 1 (all publd.). Lge. 4to. A few plts. with minimal spotting, later hf. leath., unc. (R. Oct.12; 1865) DM 6,000
- **New Travels into the Interior Parts of Africa by the way of the Cape of Good Hope.** L., 1796. 3 vols. Frontis. map, 22 plts., some folding, hf. cf., w.a.f. (GM. Oct.5; 510) £170
- **Nouvelle Bibliothèque des Voyages, ou Choix des Voyages.** Paris, 1830. 9 vols. Cont. hf. cf. (SSA. Jul.5; 242) R 180
- **Travels into the interior parts of Africa.** L., 1796. *[2nd. Edn.].* 2 vols. Frontis., 11 plts. (2 folding), a few light margin stains, hf. cf. (S. Jun.25; 67) *Barrows.* £100
- - **Anr. Copy.** 2 vols. 12 copperplt. engrs. (compl., including Hottentot Woman, often suppressed), cont. mott. cf., rubbed, spine ends worn. (TA. Feb.16; 8) £56
- **Travels in South Africa & His Collection of 165 Watercolour Paintings ... Cape Town, 1973. *(250) in Engl.* 2 vols. 4to. Cf. (VA. Apr.26; 160) R 280
- - **Anr. Copy.** Covers slightly spotted. (VA. Apr.27; 681) R 170

LE VAILLANT DE ST. DENIS
- **Recueil d'Opuscules sur les Differentes Parties de l'Equitation.** Versailles, Paris, 1789. Pagination faulty, some staining, dark red fine-grd. & pol. mor. gt., decor., gt. arms, gt. inner & outer dentelle, lightly bumped & soiled. (V. Sep.29; 1448) DM 480

LEVANTO, Francesco Maria
- **Prima Parte dello Specchio del Mare.** Genoa, Gerolamo Marino & Benedetto Celle, 1664. (All publd.). Fo. Ptd. title in engraved border, 25 engraved mapsheets (all but 1 double-p.), numerous woodcut coastal profiles & other diagrams in text, 1 or 2 plts. trimmed in plt.-mark, last lf. of text reprd., cont. cf. gt., reprd., w.a.f. (S. May 21; 146) *Martinos.* £3,500

LEVASSEUR, Victor
- **Atlas.** [Before 1860]. Ob. fo. Lacks title-p., some stains, some margins torn, hf. cl., corners. (HD. Jul.6; 57b) Frs. 2,100
- **Atlas Illustré des 86 Départements et des Possessions de la France.** Paris, 1852. Fo. 100 maps (1 double-p.), cont. hf. roan. (HD. Mar.19; 5) Frs. 3,200
[-] **Atlas national de la France.** [Paris], 1856 or later. 1 vol. in 2. Ob. fo. 91 (of 100) engraved maps, hand-cold. in outl., mntd. on card. thro-out, hf. mor., worn. (S. Jun.25; 262) *Jefferies.* £180

LEVEL, André
- **Souvenirs d'un Collectioneur.** Ill.:– Picasso. Paris, 1959. *(2,200). This copy one of (100) numbered in*

Roman. 4to. Orig. litho. sigd. in plt., sewed. (CR. Jun.6; 203) Lire 250,000

LEVEQUE, Jean-Jacques
- **December Song** ... Ill.:- Jean Berthier. Paris, 1965. *(100), on papier vélin de Rives, sigd. by author & artist. (10) numbered with orig. sigd. & dtd. drawing in cols. tipped in after title.* Sm. 4to. Dark red mor. by Roger Devachelle, sigd. at foot of upr. doubl., covers with onlaid cold. papers forming concentric circles, the design cut in & quarters, smooth spine with title vertically gt.-lettered, lr. cover with paper sleeve attached containing the 45 r.p.m. recording of 'Visage d'Ombre' & '3+2=1', orig. wraps. & backstrip preserved. (CNY. May 18; 180) $1,200

LEVER, Charles
- **Confessions of Con Cregan: The Irish Gil Blas.** Ill.:- H.K. Browne. L., [1849]. *1st. Edn.* Orig. 14 pts. in 13. Sm. 8vo. Pict. wraps., 1st. pt. unopened, other pts. unc., some soiling, 4 upr. wraps. reprd. at top, 2 cl. s.-c.'s; A.L.s. from Lever to J.R. Flanagan laid in. (SG. Nov.3; 125) $200
- **Luttrell of Arran.** Ill.:- H.K. Browne. L., 1865. *1st. Edn. in Orig. Pts.* 16 pts. in 15. Advts., 'Luttrell of Arran Advertiser' in each pt., 32 plts., pict. wraps., some spines frayed, cl. folding-case. (SG. Apr.19; 299) $165
- **The Novels.** L., 1897. *Copyright Edn., (1000).* 37 vols. Hf. cf., gt. spines, some rubbing & soiling. (SPB. Dec.13; 545) $350
- **Works.** 1872-73. 17 vols. Hf. cf. gt. (P. Oct.20; 86) £55
- **[Collected Works].** Ill.:- 'Phiz', Browne, & others. V.p., 1841-65 & n.d. *Mostly 1st. or 2nd. Edns.* 27 vols. 18 vols. in unif. gt.-panel. hf. cf. by Brown of Edinb., remainder in hf. mor., slightly faded. (PD. Aug.17; 77) £135

LEVER, Christopher
- **The Historie of the Defendors of the Catholique Faith.** L., 1627. 4to. Ptd. & engraved titles, mor. gt., gt. dentelles, by Pratt; Huth copy. [STC 15537.] (SG. Apr.26; 128) $150

LEVER, Darcy
- **The Young Sea Officer's Sheet Anchor** ... 1808. *1st. Edn.* 4to. 110 engraved plts. on 55 thick ll., cont. hf. cf., rebkd., orig. spine preserved, new endpapers. (SKC. Jan.13; 2361) £260
- **- Anr. Edn.** Ed.:- George W. Blunt. N.Y., 1858. 4to. Engraved title, 113 plts. (2 folding), later cf. (PNY. Mar.27; 159) $600

LE VERRIER DE LA CONTERIE, Jean Baptiste Jacques
- **Vénerie Normande, ou Ecole de la Chasse aux Chiens Courants, pour le Lièvre, le Chevreuil, le Cerf** ... Rouen, 1778. *2nd. (partly Orig.) Edn.* Lacks blank lf. (as often), mod. old-style marb. roan, spine decor.; from Château des Noës liby. (HD. May 25; 51) Frs. 2,100

LEVERTON, Denise
- **The Cold Spring, & Other Poems.** [N.Y.?], 1968 [i.e. 1969]. *(100) numbered & sigd.* Bds., d.-w. (SG. Mar.1; 266) $250
- **Conversation in Moscow.** [Camb., Mass.], 1973. *(200) numbered & sigd.* 1 vol. Sm. 4to. Ptd. wraps. *(With:)* **Chekhov on the West Heath.** Andes, N.Y., 1977. *(200) numbered & sigd.* 1 vols. 8vo. Marb. wraps. (SG. Mar.1; 272) $100
- **The Double Image.** L., 1946. Sm. 8vo. Cl., d.-w.; inscr. (SG. Mar.1; 267) $225
- **Here & Now.** San Franc., [1956]. Sq. 12mo. Ptd. wraps., wire-stitched; sigd. (SG. Mar.1; 268) $175
- **- Anr. Edn.** San Franc., [1956]. *(1000).* Sq. 12mo. Ptd. wraps., ptd. wraparound label; Michael Rumaker copy, with his sig., laid in is ptd. lf. including Levertov's appreciation of Rumaker's The Butterfly. (SG. May 24; 96) $110
- **A New Year's Garland for My Students.** Mt. Horeb, Wis., 1970. *(125) numbered for sale.* Ptd. on Wilson's 'pale rasberry' paper, wraps., d.-w. (state Wilson ascribes only to hors-de-commerce copies). (SG. May 24; 102) $130
- **- Anr. Copy.** Wraps., d.-w. (SG. Mar.1; 270) $110
- **Overland to the Island.** Highlands [N.C.], 1958.

1st. Iss., (450) sigd. Lge. 8vo. Unlettered wraps., d.-w. (SG. Mar.1; 271) $175

LEVESQUE, Pierre Charles
- **Histoire des Différents Peuples soumis à la Domination des Russes, ou Suite de l'Histoire de Russie.** Paris, 1783. 2 vols. 12mo. Cont. cf. (HD. Feb.22; 118) Frs. 1,000

LEVETUS, A.S.
- **Frank Brangwyn der Radierer.** Wien, 1924. *(60) with 2 etchings sigd. by artist. De Luxe Edn.* 4to. 1 margin browned (recto lighter), orig. vell. (H. May 23; 1165) DM 520

LEVI BEN GERSHOM, Gersonides-Ralbag
- **Milchamot Ha'Shem.** Riva di Trento, 1560. *1st. Edn.* Fo. Title mntd., creased, owner's stp. on last lf., staining, slightly discold., short tear in 1 margin, hf. leath., marb. paper bds., trimmed, stained. (S. Oct.24; 223) *Klein.* £600
- **- Anr. Copy.** Fo. Lacks title-p., slight browning & staining, mod. vell.-bkd. bds.; stp. of Rabbi Yaakov Zvi Mecklenburg, of Koenigsberg. (SPB. Feb.1; 53) $300
- **Peirush Al Ha'Torah.** [Mantua], Avraham be Shlomo Conat & Avraham Yedidiah Ha'ezrachi of Cologne, [1474-77]. Fo. Lacks 6 ll., sigd. by censors, Andrea di Mante (?) & Dominico Irosolomitano (Yerushalmi), 1597, a few words deleted, slight staining, mostly in margins, a few minor margin repairs, slight soiling & browning to final & prelim. ll., bds., worn; traces of Hochschule für die Wissenschaft des Judenthums stp. on final lf. [Steinschneider 6138, 3; Goff Heb-69] (SPB. Jun.26; 15) $77,500
- **Toaliot Ha'Ralbag.** Riva di Trento, 1560. *1st. Edn.* 2 pts. in 1 vol. 4to. Stained & browned, slightly creased, mod. mor. gt. (S. Oct.24; 225) *Toporwitch.* £300

LEVINSON, André
- **Bakst.** [Berlin], 1922. *(300) numbered, for Great Britain & the Colonies.* Fo. 68 plts., mostly col. & mntd., vell., soiled & buckled, nicked at 1 edge. (SG. Nov.17; 158) $350
- **- Anr. Edn.** Berlin, [1925]. *'A' Edn. (250) numbered.* Fo. Orig. hf. vell., gold-tooled cover vig., unc., corners worn. (GB. Nov.5; 2254) DM 1,400

LEVIS, Howard C.
- **A Descriptive Bibliography of the Most Important Books in the English Language relating to ... Engraving.** L., 1912. Fo. Cl.-bkd. bds. (P. May 17; 118) *Blackwell.* £110

LEVITA, Elijah Bachur
- **Dikduk.** Isny, 1542. *5th. Edn.* 4to. Some ll. crudely reprd. affecting some letters, slightly discold., mod. blind-tooled leath., trimmed. (S. Oct.24; 227) *Rosenfeld.* £420
- **Meturgeman [Hebrew, Aramaic & Old Yiddish dictionary].** Isny, 1541. *1st. Edn.* Fo. Lacks Latin title-p., title mntd. without loss of text, owners' sigs. & stp. on 1st. 2 ll., some ll. reprd. without loss of text, some staining, slightly soiled, slight worming, mod. mor.; sig. of Kalman Lieben, of Prague. (S. Oct.24; 229) *Jansen.* £600
- **Tishbi.** Basel, 1601. 4to. Slight staining & foxing, some markings to text, mor., spine faded. (SPB. Feb.1; 54) $700
See— **MUNSTER, Sebastian & Levita, Elia Bachur**

LEVRAULT, L. & others
- **Musée Pittoresque et Historique de l'Alsace.** Ill.:- J. Rothmuller. 1863. 4to. 72 plts. (1 double-p.), cont. hf. chagrin, corners, spine decor. (HD. Mar.21; 170) Frs. 7,500

LEVY
See— **BRAUNE & LEVY**

LEVY, Saul
- **Laques Venitiennes du Dix-huitième Siècle.** Paris, 1968. 2 vols. Fo. No bdg. stated. (SPB. Nov.30; 278) $125

LEWENKLAU [Leundavius], H.
- **Neuwer Musulmanischer Histori, Türckischer Nation.** Frankfurt, 1595. *2nd. German Edn.* Fo. Prelims. old bkd. in partly defect. margins, last

index ll. with light stains in lr. corner defect., cont. blind-tooled pig, slightly soiled, spine leath. 18th. C. renewed. (R. Apr.3; 54) DM 1,100
- **- Anr. Edn.** Frankfurt, 1596. *2nd. German Edn.* Fo. 1st. & last ll. stained & defect., slightly spotted, cont. blind-tooled pig, defect., leath. bnd. in 18th. C. (H. Nov.23; 589) DM 570

LEWES, Louis
- **The Women of Shakespeare.** N.Y. & L., 1895. 1 vol. in 2. Extra ill. with 45 steel-engraved plts., red mor. gt. (SKC. Mar.9; 1798) £80

LEWIN, J.W.
- **A Natural History of the Birds of New South Wales** ... Melbourne, 1978. *Facs. Edn. (500).* Sm. fo. Bdg. not stated, boxed. (KH. May 1; 414) Aus. $100

LEWIN, Lieut.-Col. Thomas H.
- **A Fly on the Wheel, Or How I Helped to Govern India.** 1885. Later pol. cf., gt.-decor. spine, by Zaehnsdorf, author's pres. copy. (TA. May 17; 11) £72

LEWIN, William
- **The Birds of Great Britain.** L., priv. ptd., 1789-94. *1st. Edn. (60).* 7 vols. Fo. 323 orig. watercolour drawings, 5 p. index at end of Vol. 7, cont. red str.-grd. mor. gt. by Staggemeier(?), spines gt. (C. Mar.14; 182) *Toscani.* £10,000
- **- Anr. Copy.** 7 vols. in 3. 4to. 272 orig. watercolour drawings of birds, & 52 of eggs, in addition to the usual bis plts. (18, 19, 244, 250 & 260) this copy with extra plt. numbered 255 in Vol. 7, slight offsetting & a little margin soiling or spotting, margin tear reprd. in plt. 50 in Vol. 2, margin tear in D2 in Vol. 5, cont. diced russ. gt., rebkd. preserving most of old spines. (S. Nov.28; 57) *Libris.* £7,800
- **- Anr. Edn.** L., 1789-94. *1st. Edn. Early Iss.* 7 vols. in 3. 4to. 393 orig. watercolour drawings, sm. liby. stp. on titles & borders of plts., old ink stain on some lr. blank corners in vols. 1 & 2, cont. diced russ. gt., rebkd. (SPB. May 17; 636) $9,000
- **- Anr. Edn.** L., 1795-1801. *2nd. Edn.* 8 vols. in 4. 4to. 336 hand-cold. engraved plts., text in Engl. & Fr., some slight browning or offsetting, cont. russ. gt., rebkd., some wear. (S. Nov.28; 58) *Antik Koch.* £900
- **The Papillions of Great Britain.** L., 1795. 4to. 46 hand-cold. engraved plts., title & text in Engl. & Fr., hf.-title, mod. hf. cf., marb. bds. (SKC. Oct.26; 396) £580

LEWIS, Cecil Day
- **Beechen Vigil & Other Poems.** L., Fortune Pr., [1925]. *1st. Edn.* Orig. wraps.; Frederic Dannay copy. (CNY. Dec.16; 97) $140

LEWIS, Charles Thomas Courtney
- **George Baxter the Picture Printer.** N.d. *(1000) numbered.* Light spotting, orig. cl. (CSK. Feb.10; 88) £65
- **The Picture Printer of the Nineteenth Century, George Baxter 1804-1867.** L., 1911. Lge. 8vo. A few ll. spotted, orig. cl., unc. (S. Apr.30; 143) *Aus. Nat. Gall.* £60
- **The Story of Picture Printing in England during the Nineteenth Century.** [1928]. 4to. Spotted, orig. cl., spine faded, inner hinges worn. (BBA. Jul.27; 244) *Maggs.* £60
- **- Anr. Copy.** 4to. Orig. cl. (SG. Jan.5; 195) $150

LEWIS, Frederick Christian
- **The Scenery of the River Exe.** 1827. Fo. Engraved title, 29 views on 27 plts., all on india paper, mntd., spotted, mod. cl.-bkd. bds. (CSK. Jul.6; 31) £130

LEWIS, George
- **A Series of Groups ... of the People of France & Germany.** 1823. 4to. Engraved dedication, 52 plts. on India paper, some ll. spotted or slightly soiled, orig. bds., unc., rebkd. with cl. (BBA. Oct.27; 253) *Erlini.* £120

LEWIS, George Cornewall
- **On Local Disturbances in Ireland, on the Irish Church Question.** L., 1836. Hf. mor., armorial motif on spine. (GM. Dec.7; 225) £120

LEWIS, H.C.
- A Descriptive Bibliography of books relating to the Art & History of Engraving & Collecting Prints. L., 1912. *(350) numbered.* Lge. 4to. Some light soiling, orig. cl.-bkd. bds., soiled, spine torn. (CSK. Feb.24; 207) £70

LEWIS, James O.
- The Aboriginal Port-Folio. Phila., 1835. 50 cold. engraved plts., with 3 ll. of 'Advertisement' from nos. 1, 2 & 3 & wraps. for nos. 3 & 9, 10 plts. tipped in mats, anr. 8 sewn together with title-p., 6 more sewn together with mor. wrap. for no. 3, 26 plts. loose, together with a single plt. from the M'Kenney & Hall series, some plts. badly worn, with serious paper looses, some others torn & soiled, as a coll. of plts., w.a.f. [Sabin 40812] (SPB. Dec.13; 453) $2,250

LEWIS, John Frederick
- Illustrations of Constantinople ... L., [1838]. Fo. Tinted litho. title, dedication, 25 tinted litho. plts., a few plts. foxed, orig. gt.-lettered mor.-bkd. bds., spine torn & defect. (C. Nov.16; 122)
Shapero. £450
- Sketches & Drawings of the Alhambra. L., [1835]. Fo. Litho. title, dedication & plt. list, 25 tinted litho. plts., some lightly spotted, cont. mor.-bkd. cl., spine torn. (CSK. Feb.24; 24) £550
– – **Anr. Copy.** Fo. Litho. title, dedication, 25 tinted litho. views, some spotting, orig. mor.-bkd. cl., spotted. (C. Nov.16; 123) *Duran.* £350
- Sketches of Spain & Spanish Character. L., [1835]. Fo. Litho. title, dedication & plt. list, 25 tinted litho. plts., some lightly spotted, cont. mor.-bkd. cl. (CSK. Feb.24; 23) £550

LEWIS, Rev. John
- The History & Antiquities of the Abbey Church of Faversham in Kent. L., 1727. Extra-ill. with 3 plts. from Grose's 'Antiquities'. *(Bound with:)* - A Dissertation on the Antiquity & Use of Seals in England ... L., 1736. Together 2 works in 1 vol. 4to. Additional addenda at end relating to the 1st. work, 18th. C. hf. cf. (S. Mar.6; 438) *Frankland.* £110
- The History & Antiquities ... of the Isle of Tenet, in Kent. L., 1736. *2nd. Edn.* 2 pts. in 1 vol. 4to. Mezzotint port., 25 engraved plts., some folding, some stains along inner margins, sm. hole in B1, cont. cf., slightly worn, spine reprd. (S. Mar.6; 439) *Sanders.* £120

LEWIS, Matthew Gregory, 'Monk'
- Journal of a West India Proprietor, Kept During a Residence in the Island of Jamaica. 1834. *1st. Edn.* Hf.-title & advt. lf., some staining, later hf. mor. [Sabin 40821] (BBA. Jan.19; 89) *Scott.* £60
- The Monk, a Romance. 1796. *1st. Edn. 1st. Iss.* 3 vols. 12mo. Cf. gt., rubbed. (P. Jan.12; 245) *Jarndyce.* £580
- Poems. 1812. *1st. Edn.* Mod. red hf. mor. by W. Pratt, gt. spine; bkplt. of John Byram. (BBA. Oct.27; 44) *Snelling.* £100

LEWIS, Meriwether & Clark, William
[-] Message from the President ... Communicating Discoveries Made in Exploring the Missouri, Red River, & Washita. N.Y., 1806. *1st. N.Y. Edn.* Browned, orig. bds., unc., worn, spine defect. (SG. Jan.19; 206) $475
- Original Journals of the Lewis & Clark Expedition. Ed.:– Reuben G. Thwaites. N.Y., 1904. 8 vols. Gt. decor. buckram. (SG. Apr.5; 109) $450
- The Travels of ... from St. Louis, by Way of the Missouri & Columbia Rivers, to the Pacific Ocean ... L., 1809. *[1st. Engl. Edn.].* Faint dampstain to folding map, a few ll. spotted & browned, cont. paper-bkd. bds., unc., foot of spine worn. [Sabin 40827] (C. Mar.14; 13) *Morrell.* £320
– – **Anr. Copy.** Map offset to title-p., some spotting, orig. bds., unc., spine worn, folding buckram case; Holland House bkplts., the Rt. Hon. Visc. Eccles copy. [Sabin 40827] (CNY. Nov.18; 174) $650
- Travels to the Source of the Missouri River & across the American Continent to the Pacific Ocean ... in the Years 1804, 1805, & 1806. L., 1814. *1st. Engl. Edn.* 4to. Sm. tear & some creasing at inner fold of 1st. map, cont. pol. cf. gt., rebkd. with orig. backstrip laid down, corners reprd., upr. jnt. brkn.; Sir William Young bkplt., the Rt. Hon. Visc. Eccles copy. [Sabin 40829] (CNY. Nov.18; 173) $2,000

– – **Anr. Copy.** 4to. Hf.-title, scattered minor stains, map slightly frayed, qtr. leath., unc. (SG. Jan.19; 205) $800

LEWIS, Oscar
- The Origin of the Celebrated Jumping Frog of Calaveras County. Ill.:– V. Angelo. San Franc., [Grabhorn Pr.,], 1931. *(250).* Hf. buckram & marb. bds.; pres. copy from Lewis to Angelo, sigd. by Angelo below inscr., C'mas. card dtd. 1978 from Lewis to 'Val' laid in loose. (CBA. Oct.1; 163) $225

LEWIS, Samuel
- Atlas to the Topographical Dictionary of England & Wales. 1844. Folding general map, plan of London, 55 county maps, outl. hand-cold., some folding. *(With:)* – Atlas. Counties of Ireland. 1846. Engraved vig. title, general map, 32 county maps, outl. hand-cold. *(With:)* – Map of Scotland. 1846. 6 folding maps, hand-cold. in outl. Together 3 vols. 4to. Cl. gt. (P. Jan.12; 327) *Hadden.* £200
– – **Anr. Edn.** 1848. 4to. General map, folding London plan, 55 county maps, most single-p., outl. hand-cold., orig. blind-stpd. cl., soiled, some wear. (TA. May 17; 99) £80
- A Topographical Dictionary of England. L., 1831. 4 vols. 4to. Engraved maps, cont. diced cf. gt., worn. (P. May 17; 430) *Martin.* £75
– – **Anr. Copy.** 4 vols. 4to. 45 maps, slight staining, hf. cf. gt. (P. Jun.7; 342) £60
– – **Anr. Edn.** 1833. *2nd. Edn.* 5 vols., including Atlas Vol. Lge. 4to. Some spotting, orig. cl., spines faded, lacks spine of atlas vol. (CSK. Oct.7; 151) £75
– – **Anr. Edn.** 1835. 4 vols. 4to. Orig. cl., lacks 2 spines. (P. Sep.29; 428) *Whittle.* £85
– – **Anr. Edn.** L., 1837. *1st. Edn.* 2 vols. & Atlas. Lge. 4to. Engraved title, lge. folding map, 31 single-p. maps, cl., as an atlas, w.a.f. (GM. Dec.7; 472) £130
– – **Anr. Copy.** 2 vols. 4to. List of Subscribers, cl. (GM. Dec.7; 324) £50
- View of the Representative History of England. L., 1835. 4to. 116 maps, cold. in outl., cl., upr. cover detchd. (P. Nov.24; 313) *Haddon.* £160

LEWIS, Sinclair
- Main Street. Ill.:– Grant Wood. N.Y., Ltd. Edns. Cl., 1937. *(1500) numbered & sigd. by artist.* 4to. Cl.-covered limp bds., s.-c. worn. (SG. Jan.12; 365) $300

LEWIS, William, 1714-81
[-] Neues verb. Dispensatorium od. Arzneybuch. Hamburg, 1768-72. *1st. German Edn.* 2 vols. Title with MS. owner's mark, verso stpd., some light browning, foxing & staining, cont. bds. (HK. Nov.8; 636) DM 1,100

LEWIS, William, Bookseller
- New Traveller's Guide. L., [1819]. Sm. 4to. Engraved title, 43 hand-cold. engraved maps, including 1 folding, cont. hf. roan, slightly rubbed & stained. (S. Dec.13; 207) *Burgess.* £150

LEWIS, Wyndham
- Thirty Personalities & a Self-Portrait. L., 1932. *(200) numbered & sigd.* Fo. Loose in portfo. (C. Nov.9; 178) *Howes.* £280
– – **Anr. Copy.** Fo. Title soiled, liby. stp. on title & in upr. cover, loose as iss. in orig. cl.-bkd. portfo., ties. (S. Nov.22; 334) *Brook.* £160
- Wyndham Lewis the Artist. L., 1939. Cold. frontis., plts., orig. cl. gt., d.-w., lightly stained. (P. May 17; 161) *O'Neill.* £50

LEWISOHN, Lewis
- The Last Days of Shylock. Ill.:– after Arthur Szyk. N.Y., 1931. *1st. Edn. (125) numbered on special paper & sigd. by author.* Hf. cl., unopened. (SG. Feb.2; 116) $200

LEWKENOR, Samuel
- A Discourse not Altogether Unprofitable, nor Unpleasant for such as are Desirous to Know the Situation & Customes of Forraine Cities ... L., 1600. *1st. Edn.* Sm. 4to. 2 short tears in A4, reprd., mod. limp vell., spine gt.; the Heber-Britwell-W.A. White copy, Penrose bkplts. [STC 15566] (S. Dec.8; 21) *Quaritch.* £500

LEYBOURN, William
- Dialling ... Shewing, How to Make all such Dials, & to Adorn them with all Useful Furniture. L., 1682. *1st. Edn.* Fo. Lacks last (blank?) lf., 1 plt. slightly torn, some ll. slightly soiled, outer margin of 1 lf. cropped affecting & few letters, type faded on Q2r, mod. cf. [Wing L1912] (BBA. Nov.30; 102) *Walford.* £300
– – **Anr. Copy.** Fo. Engraved port. loose, few margin tears, some ll. rather soiled, cont. reversed cf., worn, upr. cover detchd. [Wing L1912] (BBA. Aug.18; 217) *Page.* £100
- Pleasure with Profit. ... Also, A Treatise on Algebra by R. Sault. L., 1694. *1st. Edn.* 2 pts. in 1 vol. Fo. Some stains & foxing, old panel. suede, crudely rebkd., worn. (SG. Feb.9; 271) $300
- The Seamans New Kalender, of the Sun, Moon & Fixed Stars. L., 1706. Sm. 4to. L2-3 torn with some loss of text, soiled thro.-out, cont. cf., worn. (BBA. May 3; 49) *Phillips.* £200

LEYCESTER, Sir Peter
- Historical Antiquities ... containing Particular Remarks concerning Cheshire. L., 1773-72. *1st. Edn.* Fo. 2 extra engraved mntd. plts., Speede map closely cropped, some light staining, later cf. (S. Mar.6; 490) *Hepner.* £160

LEYDEN, John
[-] A Comparative Vocabulary of the Barae. Malayu & Thai Languages. Serampore, Mission Pr., 1810. Cont. hf. cf., slightly rubbed; liby. stp. on title. (BBA. May 23; 351) *Kossow.* £320

LEYEN, Friedrich von der
See– WOLFSKEHL, K. & Leyen, Friedrich von der

LEYES CON QUE SE GOVIERNA LA MUY NOBLE Y MUY LEAL PROVINCIA DE ALAVA
Vitoria, 1671. Fo. Vell. (DS. Jan.27; 2244) Pts. 25,000

LEYMARIE, Jean (Text)
See– CHAGALL, Marc

LEZARDIERE, Mlle. de
- Théorie du Droit Politique de la Monarchie Française. Paris, 1844. *New Edn.* 4 vols. Hf. roan, stain on vol. 4 spine. (HD. Feb.22; 119) Frs. 1,600

LEZIUS, Martin
- Das Ehrenkleid des Soldaten. Berlin, [1936]. 4to. Cold. plts., ills., cont. hf. mor. (CSK. May 18; 82) £60

L'HOPITAL, Guillaume François Antoine, Marquis de
- Analyse des Infiniment Petits, Pour l'Intelligence des Lignes Courbes. Paris, 1696. *1st. Edn.* 4to. Colophon lf., some gatherings lightly browned, some soiling, cont. cf., chipping & cracking along head & tail of spine, rubbed; sig. of J. Fanshawe on end-paper, Stanitz coll. (SPB. Apr.25; 275) $500
– – **Anr. Edn.** Paris, 1768. *3rd. Edn.* Some slight spotting, lacks upr. front free end-paper, cont. leath., slightly defect. (HT. May 8; 393) DM 680
- Traité Analytique des Sections Coniques et de leur Usage pour la Résolution des Equations ... Paris, 1720. 4to. Cont. diced cf., spine decor. (HD. Nov.9; 181) Frs. 1,600

LHOTE, André & Cocteau, Jean
- Escales. Paris, 1920. 4to. Litho. plts., many hand-cold., orig. pict. wraps., slightly soiled, lacks back-strip. (BBA. Jun.14; 228) *Makiya.* £75

LIBER SCRIPTORUM
N.Y., Authors Cl., 1893. Lge. 4to. Elab. mor., embossed in black, gt., corners a little rubbed. (LH. Sep.25; 319) $700

LIBRI, Guillaume
- Monuments Inedits ou Peu Connus, faisant Partie du Cabinet.de Guillaume Libri. 1864. *2nd. Edn.* Fo. Some margin annots. sigd. 'C', cont. hf. mor. gt., rubbed; Bibliotheca Lindesiana bkplt., H.M. Nixon coll., with his acquisition note & MS. annots. (BBA. Oct.9; 84) *Knuf.* £450

LICETO, Fortunio
- De Lucernis Antiquorum reconditis ... Udine, 1653. Fo. Frontis. stained & torn, 1st. ll. stained, 17th. C. cf., spine defect., w.a.f. (CR. Jun.6; 49)
Lire 200,000

LICHT, H.
- Sittengeschichte Griechenlands. Dresden & Zürich, [1925-28]. 2 vols. & Supp. vol. 4to. Orig. linen, gold-tooled cover ill. (GB. Nov.4; 1485)
DM 400

LICHTENBERG, G. Chr.
- Ausführliche Erklärung der Hogarthischen Kupferstiche. Göttingen, 1794-1835. *1st. Edn.* 14 pts. in 4 vols. 8vo. & ob. fo. Cont. hf. leath., slightly rubbed, 1 spine torn; Hauswedell coll. (H. May 24; 1455)
DM 1,200
- Vermischte Schriften nach dessen Tode aus den Hinterlassenen Papieren gesammlet. Ed.:– L. Chr. Lichtenberg & F. Kries. Göttingen, 1800-06. *1st. Edn.* 9 vols. Traces of wear, some slight foxing & browning, 1 vol. stained, cont. hf. leath. gt., rubbed, vol. 9 slightly different. (GB. May 4; 1376)
DM 850
- - **Anr. Edn.** Ill.:– Chodowiecki. Göttingen, 1844-53. *Orig. Edn.* 14 pts. in 12 vols. Title stpd., some foxing, cont. marb. bds., decor., last 3 vols. slightly different, w.a.f. (HK. May 16; 2148)
DM 400
- - **Anr. Edn.** Göttingen, 1844-54. *2nd. Coll. Edn.* 14 pts. in 5 vols. Some foxing, title verso & end-papers stpd., cont. linen gt., pts. 9-14 (in 1) not unif. (GB. Nov.4; 2122)
DM 600

LICHTENSTEIN, Heinrich
- Travels in Southern Africa. 1812. 2 vols. in 1. Foxed, cont. hf. mor., rubbed. (SSA. Jul.5; 251)
R 500
- - **Anr. Edn.** 1815. 2 vols. 5 pp. in Vol. 1 heavily foxed, orig. bds. (SSA. Jul.5; 250)
R 520

LICHTENSTEIN, H. & Winckler, E.
- Die Veredelte Hühnerzucht. Berlin, 1857-58. 2 pts. in 1 vol. Fo. Wide margin, cont. hf. leath., orig. litho. wraps. bnd. in, spine partly reprd. (R. Oct.12; 1859)
DM 2,600

LIDDELL, Col. Robert Spencer
- The Memoirs of The Tenth Royal Hussars. 1891. Orig. cl. gt. (P. Jan.12; 88) *Trotman.* £75

LIE, [M.] S.
- Theorie der Transformationsgruppen. Ed.:– Fr. Engel. Leipzig, 1888-93. *1st. Edn.* Some light browning, cont. hf. leath. (HT. May 8; 440)
DM 720
- Vorlesungen über Continuirliche Gruppen mit Geometrischen und Anderen Anwendungen. Ed.:– G. Scheffer. Leipzig, 1893. *1st. Edn.* Some slight browning, cont. hf. leath. (HT. May 8; 441)
DM 400

LIEB, Christophus J.
- Practica et Arte di Cavalleria. Ubung und Kunst des Reitens. Dresden, 1616. *1st. German Edn.* 2 pts. & 'Gebissbuch' in 1 vol. Fo. 1st. pt. lacks copper engraved title, some sm. wormholes, some slight spotting, cont. limp vell from old Antiphonar, spine worn, dedication prefaces in both parts MS. sigd. by author. (GB. May 4; 2091)
DM 600

LIEBAULT, Jean
- Trois Livres de l'Embellissement et Ornement dv Corps Humain. Paris, 1582. *1st. Fr. Edn.* Some staining near end, cont. limp bds., stained, sm. faults, lacks ties, end-papers defect. (HK. Nov.8; 252)
DM 420
See— ESTIENNE, Charles & Liebault, Jean

LIEBE, Christian Sigismund
- Gotha Numeria, sistens Thesauri Fridericiani Numismata Antiqua. Amst., 1730. Fo. Title frayed, margin stains, cont. vell. bds., slightly rubbed & soiled, head & foot of spine defect. (S. May 1; 477)
Spink. £120

LIEBERKUHN, Joannes Nathaniel
- Anatomici, dum Viveret, Summi, et Medici Experientissimi ... Ed.:– J. Sheldon. L., 1782. 4to. Advt. lf. for Sheldon's 'History of the Absorbent System', browned & soiled, cont. hf. roan, worn. (CSK. Nov.4; 135)
£250

LIEBERMANN, Max
- Die Handzeichnungen. 1922. *(480) numbered with sigd. orig. etchings.* Fo. 2 sigd. orig. etchings, etchings slightly foxed, doubl. with stain, orig. leath. (GB. May 5; 2884)
DM 1,800
- Dreissig Holzschnitt-Zeichnungen von Max Liebermann. Geschnitten von Reinhold Hoberg. Intro.:– Willy Kurth. Berlin, 1922. *(400) numbered.* 4to. Orig. hf. leath. (D. Nov.24; 3124)
DM 2,400
- Holländisches Skizzenbuch. Text:– Oscar Bie. Berlin, 1911. *A Edn. (100) numbered with orig. litho.* Ob. 4to. 1 orig. litho., orig. pict. linen, slightly soiled. (GB. May 5; 2881)
DM 600
- 54 Steindrucke zu Kleinen Schriften von H. von Kleist. Berlin, [1917]. *(250) on Bütten, sigd. by artist.* 4to. Hand-bnd. orig. vell., cover vig., orig. hf. linen box, spotted & slightly bumped. (H. Nov.24; 1783)
DM 1,400
- - **Anr. Edn.** Berlin, n.d. *(270) numbered & sigd. by artist.* Lge. 4to. Orig. vell. (S. Nov.21; 29)
Desk. £280

LIEBLER, Thomas
See— ERASTUS, Thomas [i.e. Thomas Liebler]

LIECHTENSTEIN, Eleonora Maria Rosalia von, Herzogin zu Troppau u. Jögerndorf
- Freywillig–auffgesprungener Granat-Apfel des Christlichen Samaritans. Wien, 1701. 2 pts. in 1 vol. 4to. Cont. blind-tooled pig-bkd. wood bds., 2 brass clasps, end-papers renewed. (R. Oct.12; 1987)
DM 1,700

LIEDER, Fr.
See— JUGEL, F. & Lieder, Fr.

LIEDER DER DEUTSCHEN MYSTIK
Ed.:– J. Bernhart. Ill.:– A. Simons. München, Bremer Pr., 1922. *(270) on Bütten.* 4to. Hand-bnd. orig. vell., gold decor., by Frieda Thiersch. (H. Nov.23; 935)
DM 800
- - **Anr. Copy.** 4to. Mor., gt. & blind-tooled spine, gt. outer dentelles, hf. mor. s.-c. (HK. May 17; 2622)
DM 750

LIEDERBUCH MIT STEINZEICHNUNGEN
Ill.:– M. Slevogt. Berlin, [1919]. *(85).* Ob. 4to. On Japan, 2nd. last lf. with sm. margin hole, orig. hf. leath.; 1st. litho. sigd. (H. Nov.24; 2067) DM 740

LIEURE, Jules
- Jacques Callot. N.Y., 1969. 8 vols. Lge. 4to. Orig. cl. (SI. Dec.18; 207)
Lire 900,000

LIEUTAUD, Joseph
- Historia Anatomico-Medica; sistens, Numerosissima Cadaverum Humanorum Extispicia. Ed.:– Antonius Portal. Paris, 1767. *1st. Edn.* 2 pts. in 1 vol. 4to. Hf.-titles, 4 pp. advts. at end of 1st. pt., errata lf., owner's embossed stp. on title & few other ll., few minor defects reprd., mod. hf. cf. gt. (SG. Mar.22; 194)
$140

LIEVEN, Doroteya K., Princess
- Letters of Princess Lieven to Lady Holland, 1847-1857. Ed.:– E.A. Smith. Roxb. Cl., 1956. 4to. Orig. qtr. mor. (S. Oct.4; 237) *Traylen.* £60

LIFE MAGAZINE
Sep. 1939-Jul. 1945. In 31 vols. (lacks Jan.-Mar 1942). Lge. 4to. No bdg. stated; from liby. of Luttrellstown Castle, w.a.f. (C. Sep.28; 1828)
£400

LIFE & PUBLIC SERVICES of Hon. Abraham Lincoln of Illinois & Hon. Hannibal Hamlin of Maine
Boston, 1860. *1st. Edn.* Slightly soiled, orig. pict. wraps., box. (LH. Apr.15; 335)
$275
- - **Anr. Copy.** Bdg. not stated, lge. portion of upr. wrap. reprd. & incorporated into new bdg., w.a.f. (LH. Apr.15; 336)
$225

LIGER, Louis
- La Nouvelle Maison Rustique, ou Economic Générale de tous les biens de Campagne ... Paris, 1721. 2 vols. 4to. Engraved frontis., 27 plts., Vol. 1 title & 1 plt. in Vol. 2 reprd., cf., worn; Dr. G.E. Fussell copy. (P. Jul.5; 59)
£50
- - **Anr. Edn.** Paris, 1749. *6th. Edn.* 2 vols. 4to. Old

marb. cf., decor., slight wear. (LM. Mar.3; 169)
B. Frs. 8,000
- - **Anr. Edn.** 1768. *9th. Edn.* 2 vols. 4to. Engraved frontis. & 36 plts., 2 folding, some blank margins wormed, cont. cf., worn, w.a.f. (CSK. Apr.27; 50)
£85
- - **Anr. Edn.** Ill.:– H. Besnier. Paris, 1775 & 1768. 2 vols. 4to. Cont. marb. leath., gt. spine & outer dentell. (HK. May 16; 1537)
DM 1,300
- - **Anr. Edn.** Paris, 1775. *10th. Edn.* 2 vols. 4to. Cont. mott. cf. (S. Oct.11; 552) *Boin.* £110

LIGHT, Henry
- Travels in Egypt, Nubia, Holy Land, Mount Libanon, & Cyprus, in the Year 1814. L., 1818. *1st. Edn.* 4to. 20 plts. & maps, stained, old cl., worn. (SG. Sep.22; 189)
$200

LIGHT, William
- Sicilian Scenery. Ill.:– P. de Wint. 1823. Fo. L.P., Fr. & Engl. text, steel-engraved title & 61 plts., all but 1 with dupl. plt. in proof state, together 121 plts. only, all on india paper, mntd., some light spotting, cont. hf. mor., rubbed. (CSK. Jul.6; 7)
£220
- - **Anr. Copy.** Lge. 8vo. Engraved title & 60 plts., slightly dampstained, hf.-title, cont. cf., rebkd., slightly rubbed. (BBA. May 3; 324) *Soave.* £80
- - **Anr. Copy.** Cont. str.-grd. mor. gt., minor rubbing. (KH. May 1; 416)
Aus. $170

LIGHTFOOT, Rev. John
- Flora Scotia ... Edinb., 1792. *2nd. Edn.* 2 vols. Slight foxing, cont. cf., worn. (PD. May 16; 254)
£75

LIGNE, Charles Joseph, Prince de
- Lettres et Pensées. Paris, 1809. *2nd. Edn.* Minimal foxing, cont. tree cf. gt., Napoleon I arms, spine decor. (HD. May 4; 337) Frs. 6,000

LIGNIERES, Marie Henry de
- Souvenirs de la Grande Armée et de la Garde Impériale. 1785-1866. Paris, n.d. Hf. chagrin. (HD. Jan.27; 62) Frs. 1,550

LIGNY, François de
- Histoire de la Vie de Jésus-Christ. Paris, 1804. 4to. Red mor. by Simier, spine decor. (SM. Mar.7; 2165) Frs. 1,400

LIHARZIK, F.
- Das Quadrat die Grundlage aller Proportionalität in der Natur und das Quadrat aus der Zahl Sieben die Uridee des Menschiichen Körperbaues. Wien, 1865. *1st. Edn.* 4to. 10 line dedication from author, cont. hf. leath. (HT. May 8; 442)
DM 860

LILFORD, Thomas Littleton Powys, Fourth Baron
- Coloured Figures of the Birds of the British Islands. Ill.:– after Thorburn, Keulemans, & others. L., 1885-97. 7 vols. Port., 421 chromolitho. plts., some hand-cold., some spotting, mostly marginal, cont. hf. mor. gt., spines faded. (S. Nov.28; 53)
Schuster. £1,200
- - **Anr. Edn.** Ill.:– after A. Thorburn, J.G. Keulemans, & others. L., 1891-97. *2nd. Edn.* 7 vols. Port., 421 chromolitho. plts., on guards thro-out, cont. hf. mor., spines slightly faded. (C. Nov.16; 267) *Grahame.* £1,350
- Notes on the Birds of Northamptonshire & Neighbourhood. Ill.:– after A. Thorburn & G.E. Lodge. 1895. 2 vols. 4to. L.P., cont. hf. mor. by R.H. Porter, partly untrimmed, rubbed, obituary notice from I.L.N. & port. of author pasted on fly-lf. of Vol. 1. (TA. Feb.16; 96)
£120
- - **Anr. Copy.** 2 vols. Tall 8vo. Orig. cl., partly untrimmed, rubbed. (TA. Apr.19; 141)
£60

LILI, Cam.
- Dell'Historia di Camerino. Ill.:– J. Ant. Antoniucci. Macerata, 1652. 2 pts. in 1 vol. 4to. Without ptd. titles & lacks pp. 219 - 224 & from p. 257 to end pt. 1 as usual, cont. vell ... (HD. Dec.2; 112)
Frs. 1,000

LILIENTHAL., Otto
- Birdflight as the Basis of Aviation. A Contribution towards a System of Aviation. L., 1911. *1st. Edn. in Engl.* Light margin browning, orig. blue cl.; Stanitz coll. (SPB. Apr.25; 277)
$200
- Der Vogelflug als Grundlage der Fliegekunst. Ein

LILIENTHAL., Otto -*Contd.*

Beitrag zur Systematik der Flugtechnik. Berlin, 1889. *1st. Edn.* Margin browning, orig. decor. cl., light rubbing; bkplt. of Dr. Ing-Arthur Wormser, stp. of W. Luther of Frankfurt, Stanitz coll. (SPB. Apr.25; 276) $750

LILLY, John
See— LYLY or LILLY, John

LILLY, William
- **The Starry Messenger.** L., 1645. *1st. Edn.* 4to. No blanks, mod. qtr. mor. gt. (P. Dec.8; 50)
Finch. £70

LILY, William, Grammarian
- **A Short Introduction of Grammar; Brevissima Institutio, seu, Ratio Grammatices Cognoscendae.** Oxford, 1714. 2 pts. in 1 vol. Cont. panel. cf., sm. piece of cover lacking. (SG. Oct.27; 195) $130

LIMBORCH, Philip Van
- **De Veritate Religionis Christianae Amica Cellatio cum Erudito Judaeo.** Gouda, 1687. 4to. Little foxed, few dampstains, cont. cf., worn. (SG. Feb.2; 1) $275
- **Historia Inquisitionis.** Amst., 1692. *1st. Edn.* fo. A few minor repairs, cont. spr. cf., rebkd. in mor. (BBA. Jun.28; 149) *Dilua.* £65

LIMITED EDITIONS CLUB
- **Quarto-Millenary: the First 250 Publications & the First 25 Years of the Limited Editions Club.** N.Y., Ltd. Edn. Cl., 1959. *(1500) numbered.* Sm. fo. Ills., many cold., cl. with medallion, mor. spine, orig. s.-c. (SG. May 17; 217) $130

LINCE GONZALEZ, J.A.
- **Reglamento u Ordenanzas de Ensayadores.** Mexico, 1789. Fo. Disbnd. (S. May 22; 389)
Cortes. £500

LINCOLN, Abraham
- **Complete Works.** Ed.:– J.G. Nicolay & J. Hay. N.Y., [1905]. *Gettysburg De Luxe Edn., (700) numbered.* 12 vols. Cl., some bdgs. spotted. (SG. Aug.4; 176) $220
- **The Proclamation of Emancipation, by the President of the United States** ... [Boston, Dec. 1862]. 32mo. Brown paper cover, with title on upr. cover & quotation from the speech of A.H. Stephens on lr. cover. (SPB. May 23; 43) $600

LINCOLN, Abraham & Douglas, Stephen A.
- **Political Debates ... in the Celebrated Campaign of 1858, in Illinois.** Columbus, 1860. *1st. Edn. 1st. Iss., with no rule above imprint on copywright p., no advts., & '2' at foot of p. 17.* Lge. 8vo. Foxed, lacks free end-paper, orig. blind-stpd. cl., slightly spotted. (SG. Jan.19; 207) $130
- – **Anr. Copy.** No rule over printer's name, no advts., '2' at foot of p. 17, orig. stpd. cl. (SG. Apr.5; 110) $120

LINCOLNSHIRE PARISH REGISTERS
1905-14, 1916. *(150).* Vols. 1-10, & Index to Vols. I-VI. All orig. cl. gt., rubbed on spines; sigd. by compiler. (TA. Mar.15; 242) £80

LINDANUS, W.D.
- **Apologeticum ad Germanos, pro Religionis Catholicae Pace** ... Antw., 1568-70. 3 pts. in 1 vol. 4to. Sm. wormhole in 1st. 50 ll., blind-tooled pig over wood bds., slightly rubbed, brass clasps. (B. Apr.27; 582) Fls. 700

LINDBERGH, Charles A.
- **'We.'** N.Y., 1927. *(100) [sic] numbered pres. copies sigd.* Hf. art vell., spine faded, s.-c. (SG. May 24; 325) $800
- – **Anr. Copy.** Qtr. art vell., unc., box. (SG. May 24; 326) $500
- – **Anr. Copy.** Lge. 8vo. Bds., parch. back & tips, lightly spotted, spine darkened. (SG. Jan.12; 241) $265

LINDEBERG, H.T.
- **Domestic Architecture of H.T. Lindeberg.** Intro.:– Royal Cortissoz. N.Y., 1940. *1st. Edn. (1000).* Tall fo. 6 p. subscribers list, gt.-ptd. two-tone cl., spine ends soiled. (SG. Oct.13; 225) $450

LINDEN, Jean Jules & Lucien
- **Lindenia: Iconography of Orchids.** Ed.:– J. Linden & others. Gent, 1881-94. Vols. 1, 2, 5 & 7 in 22 pts. Fo. Orig. pt. wraps., loose in hf. linen portfo. (R. Oct.12; 1884) DM 2,300
- – **Anr. Edn.** Ghent, 1891-93. 5 vols. 4to. 120 chromolitho. plts., some foxing, cont. hf. mor. (SPB. May 17; 637) $1,600
- – **Anr. Edn.** Ghent, 1891-97. *1st. Engl. Edn.* 13 vols. in 7. 4to. 312 plts. (304 cold.), numbered 265-576, some spotting, cont. hf. mor., slightly rubbed. (BBA. Nov.30; 110a) *Howell.* £1,800

LINDHOUT, Henricus a
- **Introductio in Physicam Judiciariam, in qua** ... **Astrologiae Fundamenta** ... Hamburg, 1597. Sm. 4to. 4 folding tables, woodcut diagrams, few text woodcuts, blank margin of title defect., some worming in margins, 1 table reprd., 12 torn without loss, cont. vell., decor. in blind, initials MCC, central piece on lr. cover slightly torn, 2 ties, discold. (S. Apr.10; 324) *Tile.* £280

LINDLEY, John
- **Rosarum Monographia.** L., 1830. *New Edn.* Cont. cl. (BBA. May 23; 280) *Quaritch.* £260
See— EDWARDS, Sydenham Teak & Lindley, John
See— MOORE, Thomas & Lindley, John
See— PAXTON, Sir Joseph & Lindley, John

LINDLEY, John (Ed.)
See— POMOLOGICAL MAGAZINE, The

LINDNER, Fr.
See— KROSINSKY, B. & Lindner, Fr.

LINDNER, Ilse
- **Literarische Visionen.** Essays. Ill.:– Ch. Berend. Berlin, 1920. *(100) sigd.* 4to. 9 orig. port. lithos. of Lichtenberg, Lenz, Schlegel, Bettina, Schleiermacher, Hoffmann, Andersen, & others, orig. hf. leath.; orig. lithos. sigd. (GB. Nov.5; 2287) DM 500

LINDNER, O.
- **Arthur Schopenhauer.** Ed.:– J. Frauenstädt. Berlin, 1863. *1st. Edn.* Some pencil underlining, 1 errata lf., cont. linen. (R. Apr.3; 583) DM 650

LINDSAY, David, Bp. of Edinb.
- **A True Narration of all the passages of the proceedings in the general Assembly of the Church of Scotland holden at Perth 25. of August, Anno Dom, 1618** ... **Against a seditious Pamphlet.** 1621. 4to. (in 8's). Old vell., worn; Sir Ivar Colquhoun, of Luss copy. [NSTC 15657] (CE. Mar.22; 190) £90

LINDSAY, Jack
- **Fauns & Ladies.** Ill.:– Norman Lindsay. Kirribilli, 1923. *(210).* Unsigd. copy, woodcuts initialled & variously numbered, bds., qtr. cf., backstrip rubbed. (KH. May 1; 417) Aus. $420
- **The Passionate Neatherd.** Ill.:– Norman Lindsay. Sydney, Fanfrolico Pr., 1926. *(75) numbered.* Fo. Mor. by Riviere; long inscr. by Jack Kirtley (the printer), anr. inscr. by artist, Harry F. Chaplin copy. (JL. Jul.15; 247) Aus. $475

LINDSAY, Jack (Ed.)
See— LOVING MAD TOM, Bedlamite Verses of the XVI & XVII Centuries

LINDSAY, Sir Lionel
- **The Art of Sir Lionel Lindsay.** Ed.:– Peter Lindsay & Joanna Mendelssohn. Sydney, 1982. *(300) numbered.* Bdg. not stated. (JL. Mar.25; 729) Aus. $270
- **Conrad Martens, the Man & his Art.** Sydney, 1920. No bdg. stated, case. (JL. Jun.24; 179) Aus. $300

LINDSAY, Norman
- **Creative Effort.** Sydney, 1920. *(120) with orig. sigd. etching.* Bds., qtr. cl. (KH. Nov.9; 308) Aus. $450
- **The Etchings** .... L., 1927. *(31) numbered & sigd.* Spotting & foxing to edges, bdg. not stated, some discoloration to cover. (JL. Jul.15; 574) Aus. $1,050
- **Exhibition of Norman Lindsay's Watercolours & Etchings** – **Catalogue.** Adelaide, 1926. *(250) numbered.* Leath. (JL. Mar.25; 728) Aus. $200
- **Micomicana.** Melbourne, 1979. *(527) numbered & sigd.* Hf. leath. & cl., boxed. (JL. Mar.25; 852) Aus. $600
- **Paintings in Oil.** N.d. *(1000) numbered.* Fo. No bdg. stated. (JL. Jun.24; 184) Aus. $320
- **The Pen Drawings.** Ed.:– Sydney Ure Smith & Bertram Stevens. Sydney, 1918. *(150) for sale.* Bds., qtr. cl., d.-w. worn; sigd. inscr. from both eds. (KH. May 1; 427) Aus. $270
- – **Anr. Edn.** Sydney, 1924. *(500) numbered & sigd.* 4to. Some pale foxing, bds., slight soiling. (KH. May 1; 428) Aus. $300
- – **Anr. Copy.** Title-p. & text foxed, bdg. not stated. (JL. Mar.25; 851) Aus. $120
- **Water Colour Book.** Sydney, 1939. *Ltd. Edn.* Cl., slightly discold. (JL. Mar.25; 727) Aus. $230
- **Watercolours.** Sydney, 1969. Bdg. not stated, d.-w.; Harry F. Chaplin copy. (JL. Jul.15; 278) Aus. $100

LINDSAY, Vachel
- **Adventures While Preaching the Gospel of Beauty.** N.Y., 1914. Cl., lr. cover slightly stained, d.-w. stained; inscr., with 12 line autograph poem & autograph correction. (SG. Mar.1; 280) $275
- **The Art of the Moving Picture.** N.Y., 1916. MS. ex-libris on title, pict. cl.; inscr. with 2 autograph poems sigd. – 'Epitaph for John Bunny, Motion Picture Comedian', 20 lines, initialled, & 'To Mae Marsh– Motion Picture Actress', 20 lines, sigd. & dtd. 17 Nov. 1917. (SG. May 24; 327) $275
- **Rhymes to Be Traded for Bread.** [Springfield, Ill., 1912]. Self-wraps. (SG. Mar.1; 288) $150
- **The Tramp's Excuse & Other Poems.** [Springfield, Illinois, 1909]. *1st. Edn.* Orig. ptd. wraps., tied with cord at top; inscr. by author, Frederic Dannay copy. (CNY. Dec.16; 213) $1,700

LINDSTROEM, C.
- **Costumi Romani.** Rome, 1830. Sm. fo. Engraved title, 20 engraved plts., all hand-cold., several titled in ink, title & few margins soiled or slightly frayed, disbnd. (S. Nov.1; 79) *Erlini.* £180

LINGARD, John A.
- **A History of England.** Paris, 1826-31. *4th. Edn.* 14 vols. Some spotting, hf. cf. gt. (P. Jan.12; 4)
Way. £100

LINHARTA, Lubomira
- **Josef Sudek: Fotografie.** Prague, 1956. *1st. Edn.* Lge. 8vo. Buckram, d.-w. rubbed & chipped. (SG. Nov.10; 154) $325

LINNE or LINNAEUS, Sir Charles or Carolus
- **Critica Botanica ... Accedit J. Browallii De Necessitate Historiae Naturalis Discursus.** Leiden, 1737. *1st. Edn.* 2 pts. in 1 vol. Borwalis 'Discursus' with own title-lf., *(Bound with:)* - **Fundamenta Botanica.** [Paris, 1744]. *4th. Edn.* Bnd. between pts. 1 & 2 of 1st. work. Together 2 works in 1 vol., cont. leath. gt., head of spine lightly defect. (R. Oct.12; 1866) DM 1,100
- **Fauna Svecica.** Stockholm, 1761. Cont. cf., worn, lacks upr. cover. (LC. Mar.1; 168) £60
- **A General System of Nature** .... Ill.:– William Jurton. L., 1802. 4 vols. Liby. stp. on title-pp., hf. cf., gt. spines. (SKC. Oct.26; 397) £70
- **Hortus Upsaliensis.** Stockholm, 1748. 1 gathering misbnd.? at end, browning, title stained, old sheep, worn. (SPB. Dec.13; 703) $175
- **Vollstaendiges Pflanzensystem nach der Dreyzehnten Lateinischen Ausgabe.** Nuernberg, 1778-86. Pts. 3, 5 & 8-13 only (of 14). 69 folding plts., cont. cf., spines gt. (RO. Dec.11; 188) $150

LINPERGH, Pieter
- **Architectura Mechanica. Moole Boek....** Amst., 1725? *1st. Edn.* Fo. Browned, cont. vell., parts of covers blackened; Stanitz coll. (SPB. Apr.25; 279) $850
- – **Anr. Edn.** Amst., 1727. *2nd. Edn.* Fo. 18th. C. bds., later roan back & corners, scuffed; Stanitz coll. (SPB. Apr.25; 280) $850

LINSCHOTEN, Jan Huygen van
- **Le Grand Routier de Mer...** — **Description de l'Amérique & des Parties d'Icelle,....** Amst., 1619. 2 works in 1 vol. Fo. Scattered browning, map reprd., mod. hf. leath. [Sabin 41371-72] (SG. Jan.19; 211) $450

- Histoire de la Navigation ... aux Indes Orientales .... Amst., 1638. *2nd. Fr. Coll. Edn. (pts. I & II: 3rd. Edn., pt. III: 2nd. Edn.).* 3 vols. in 1. Fo. Pts. I & III lack folding engraved maps, pt. II lacks 15 copperplts. & 8 pp., 10 pp. missed, 4 sm. views cut close, some plts. with scribble on verso & partly bkd., 1 lf. with sm. holes, some heavy spotting & browning, wear, cont. cf., spine slightly defect., worn & bumped. [Sabin 41373] (H. Nov.23; 343)
DM 2,000

LINSCHOTEN-VEREENIGING
- Werken. 's-Grav., 1909-16. Pts. 1-11 in 13 vols. Lge. 8vo. Orig. cl. gt., stained. (VG. Mar.21; 625)
Fls. 650
-- **Anr. Edn.** 's-Gravenhage, 1915-34. Pts. 9-13 & 16-39, in 29 vols. Orig. cl. gt., unc. (VG. Mar.21; 626)
Fls. 1,350

LINTON, Anthony
- Newes of the Complement of the Art of Navigation, & the Mightie Empire of Cataia, together with the Straits of Anian [by A.L.]. 1609. Sm. 4to. Headlines shaved, lacks last lf. (blank?), 19th. C. pol. cf; Scott Liby. bkplt. [STC 15692] (C. May 30; 159)
Arkway. **£600**

LINTON, William
- The Scenery of Greece & its Islands. 1856. 4to. Map, 50 engraved plts. on India paper, some spotting thro.-out, orig. cl. bds., soiled, plts. & text disbnd., w.a.f., as a coll. of prints. (BS. May 2; 10)
£220
-- **Anr. Copy.** 4to. 1 lf. reprd., some spotting, loose in orig. cl., spine defect. (TA. Aug.18; 62) **£125**
-- **Anr. Edn.** 1857. 4to. Map, 50 plts., cl., disbnd. (WW. Nov.23; 12) **£85**

LINTON, William James
- The History of Wood-Engraving in America. L., 1882. *Ltd. Edn., sigd.* 4to. Orig. bds., slightly worn. (P. Nov.24; 225) *Robertshaw.* **£55**
- The Masters of Wood-Engraving. New Haven & L., 1889. *(600) numbered, sigd.* Lge. fo. Cold frontis., full-p. & text ills., many of latter mntd. India proofs, ex-liby., buckram. (SG. May 3; 243)
$150
-- **Anr. Copy.** Fo. Many text ills. mntd. India-proofs, cl., spine ends worn. (SG. Aug.25; 251)
$120

LIONI, Ottavio
- Ritratti di Alcuni Celebri Pittori del Secolo XVII. Rome, 1731. 4to. Hole in fo. G3 affecting ill., a few ll. slightly browned, later hf. cf., rubbed. (BBA. Feb.23; 42) *Maggs.* **£170**

LIORE, A. & Cailler, P.
- Catalogue de l'Oeuvre Gravé de Dunoyer de Segonzac. Genf, 1958-59. *(100). (50) De Luxe Edn. numbered.* Vols. I & II (of 8). Sm. fo. 4 orig. etchings & 464 text ills., some full-p., orig. bds., orig. wraps. (HT. May 9; 958) **DM 600**

LIPPERHEIDE, Franz Joseph von
- Katalog der Kostumbibliothek. Ed.:– N.G. Wagner-Neumann. Berlin, 1965. 2 vols. Orig. cl. (BBA. Nov.10; 89) *Goldschmidt.* **£100**

LIPPMANN, Edmund O. von
- Entstehung und Ausbreitung der Alchemie. Berlin, 1919-31-54. 3 vols. Qtr. cl., not unif., & wraps.; Dr. Walter Pagel copy. (S. Feb.7; 227)
Weiner. **£260**

LIPPMANN, Friedrich
- Drawings by Sandro Botticelli for Dante's Divina Commedia. L., 1896. *(500).* 4to. Orig. cl., slightly soiled. (BBA. Apr.5; 107)
Sims, Reed & Fogg. **£60**
- Engravings & Woodcuts by Old Masters. L., [1899-1900]. 5 vols. Fo. Hf. mor., defect., w.a.f. (SPB. Dec.13; 859) **$450**

LIPPMANN, Fr. & A.
- [-] Zeichnungen von Albrecht Dürer in Nachbildungen. [Berlin, 1883ff]. Pts. 1-4 only (of 7), in 5 vols. Lge. fo. Approx. 490 partly cold. plts., lacks title & text for plts. 78, 219 & 220, orig. linen portfo., w.a.f. (HK. Nov.12; 4655) **DM 1,200**

LIPPOLD, G.H.C. & Funke, C. Ph.
- Neues Natur- u. Kunstlexicon. Weimer, 1801-05. *1st. Edn.* 3 pts. & Supp. in 3 vols. All titles stpd., vol. 1 title with old MS. owners mark, vols. 1 & 3 very, stained, cont. hf. leath., lr. cover stained, rubbed & bumped. (HK. May 15; 458) **DM 400**

LIPSIUS, Justus
- De Militia Romana Libri Quinque. Antw., 1596. 2 pts. in 1 vol. Sm. 4to. Last 2 approbation ll. to pt. 2, cont. vell., soiled, lacks ties. (BBA. Mar.21; 11) *Snelling.* **£80**
- Epistolarum Selectarum Centuriae. Antw., 1611-14. 11 pts. in 1 vol. 4to. Browned, slight stain at beginning, cont. vell., slightly soiled. (R. Oct.11; 57) **DM 560**
- Epistolarum Selectarum Centuria Prima [Tertia] ad Belgas. – Epistolarum...ad Germanos & Gallos. — Epistolarum...ad Italos & Hispanos. Epistolica Institutio. Antw., 1604-05. *Reprints of 1601-02 Edns.* Together 3 works in 1 vol. 4to. Ex-dono on free end-paper & foot of title, dtd. 1613 & 1636, cont. vell., decor.; from Fondation Furstenberg-Beaumesnil. (HD. Nov.16; 133) **Frs. 2,000**
- Saturnalium Sermonum, qui de Gladiatoribus. Antw., 1582. *(Bound with:)* – De Amphitheatro Liber. Antw., 1585. Together 2 works in 1 vol. 4to. Cont. vell., worn & soiled. (SG. Oct.27; 196) **$250**
See— **BUXTORFF, John – LIPSIUS, Justus**

LIRER, Thomas
[-] Chronica von Allen Künig und Keiseren; von Anfang Rom. Auch von Vil Geschüchten bisezu unsem Zeiten .... Strassburg, [B. Kistler uff Grüneck, 1499 or 1500]. Sm. 4to. Title with sm. bkd. margin defects & sm. wormhole in woodcut, 1st. lf. slightly defect. in margin, stained, some worming, some old MS. marginalia, newer leath., spine pasted with leath. strips: Bibliotheca Lindesiana ex-libris. [H. 4493; BMC 504] (V. Oct.1; 3755) **DM 2,800**
- Schwäbische Chronik. Ulm, Dinckmut, 1486. *1st. Dtd. Edn.* Fo. Wide margin, lacks 32 ll. (including woodcuts, 1st. & last ll.), very stained & soiled, old annots. & underlining, vell., defect. [H. 10117; BMC II,535; Goff L 226] (HK. Nov.8; 254)
DM 500

LISKENNE, Ch. & Sauvan
- Bibliothèque Historique et Militaire dédiée à l'Armeé et la Garde Nationale de France. Paris, 1838-44. 6 (of 7) text vols. & Atl. Lge. 8vo. & fo. 96 (of 114) plts. in Atl. vol., cont. hf. leath. & hf linen portfo., portfo. very worn. (D. Nov.24; 3697)
DM 425

LISLE, Edward
- Observations in Husbandry. 1757. *1st. Edn.* 4to. Port. offset onto title, cf., rebkd. & reprd.; Dr. G.E. Fussell copy. (P. Jul.5; 60) **£140**
-- **Anr. Copy.** 4to. Slightly spotted, cont. cf., spine gt., rubbed. (BBA. Jul.27; 29) *Honeyfield.* **£90**
-- **Anr. Edn.** 1757. 4to. Engraved port. frontis., offset to title, cont. cf., gt.-decor. spine. (TA. Jun.21; 270) **£70**

LIST, Frans
- Gesammelte Schriften. Ed.:– L. Häusser. Stuttgart & Tübingen, 1850-51. *1st. Coll. Edn.* 3 vols. Minimal spotting, cont. hf. linen, slightly rubbed & bumped; name on end-paper; Hauswedell coll. (H. May 24; 1457) **DM 680**

LIST OF ALL THE OFFICERS OF THE ARMY & ROYAL MARINES
L., 1807. *55th. Edn.* Fo. L.P., cont. red str.-grd. mor., spine gt. with gt. borders round covers. (BBA. May 3; 230) *Traylen.* **£80**

LISTE DES LEGITIMISTES FIDELES QUI se rendirent en Pélerinage à Belgrave-Square d'Octobre 1843 à Janvier
N.d. 4to. Cont. embroidered velvet, richly decor., royal arms, gt. bronze corners, silk doubls. & end-papers, 1 serving as portfo.; Comte Chambord copy. (HD. Nov.29; 95) **Frs. 5,200**

LISTER, Joseph, Baron
- Contributions to Physiology & Pathology. L., 1859. From 'Philosophical Transactions', pt. 2 for 1858: 3 pts. in 1 vol. Under special title-p., cl.; inscr.

by author, Dr. Walter Pagel copy. (S. Feb.7; 239)
Goodrich. **£120**

LISZT, Franz
- Lohengrin et Tannhauser der Richard Wagner. Leipzig, 1851. Cont. marb. bds., orig. upr. wrap. bnd. in. (CSK. Oct.21; 45) **£70**

LITHGOW, William
- The Totall Discourse of the Hare Adventures .... L., 1632. Sm. 4to. Frontis. trimmed & laid down, some light browning, cont. cf. gt., rebkd. [STC 15713] (P. Dec.8; 263) *Tzakas.* **£130**

LITORAL. Revista de la Poesía y el Pensamiento
May 1968-May 1980, Nov. 1980-May 1982. 8 vols. *2nd. Epoque,* & 2 vols. 4to. Linen, wraps., last 2 vols. unbnd. (DS. Nov.25; 2117) **Pts. 55,000**

LITTLE, Thomas, of the Opera Colonnade
[-] Confessions of an Oxonian. Ill.:– after J. Findlay. L., 1826. *1st. Edn.* 3 vols. 36 engraved cold. plts., text slightly browned, imprint of a few plts. shaved, cf. gt. by Rivière, partly unc. (C. Nov.9; 91)
Scott. **£250**

LITTLE, Thomas (Pseud.)
See— **MOORE, Thomas, Poet 'Thomas Little'**

LITTLEJOHN, David
- Dr. Johnson & Noah Webster: Two Men & their Dictionaries. San Franc., 1971. *[1st. Edn.]. (500).* Sm. fo. With ll. from each dictionary (1755 & 1828) bnd. in, hf. buckram. (SG. Jan.5; 203) **$225**
-- **Anr. Copy.** Sm. fo. With 2 ll. from orig. edns. of the dictionaries bnd. in, qtr. cl. & gt.-ornamented bds., covers slightly warped. (SG. Sep.15; 145)
$160
-- **Anr. Copy.** Lge. 4to. With matched pair of orig. ll. from Johnson's (1775) & Webster's (1828) dictionaries tipped in, some ageing of ll., hf. cl. & bds. (CBA. Nov.19; 59) **$120**

LITTLETON, Sir Thomas
- Tenures in English. 1612. Cont. vell., soiled. [STC 15780] (CSK. Sep.16; 52) **£80**

LITTMANN, E.
- Vom Morgenländischen Floh. Ill.:– M. Behmer. Leipzig, 1925. *De Luxe Edn., (12) sigd. by artist.* On Bütten, hand-bnd. orig. vell. gt., by B. Scheer, Berlin. (H. Nov.24; 1367) **DM 4,200**
-- **Anr. Edn.** Ill.:– M. Behmer. Leipzig, 1925. *(300).* On Bütten, some ll. with light brown spots, hand-bnd. hf. vell. (H. May 23; 1149) **DM 1,800**
-- **Anr. Edn.** Ill.:– M. Behmer. 1925. *(330) numbered.* On printers mark 'unverstählt Probedruck I', also on 1st. etching next to sig., etchings on printers mark 'U.-V.-E.D.-P.D.-Eigendruck. Marcus Behmer 25', 13 orig. etchings brown ptd., orig. hf. vell. gt. (GB. May 5; 2188) **DM 4,400**

LITTRE, Emile
- Dictionnaire de la Langue Française. Paris, 1875-77. 5 vols. including supp. 4to. Cont. hf. chagrin, corners, spines decor. (HD. Jun.6; 99) **Frs. 1,000**

LIVES OF THE CANDIDATES, No. 1 Abe Lincoln, No. 2 S.A. Douglas
N.p., 1860. 2 vols. Miniature book 1¾ x 1¼ inches. Ptd. wraps. (LH. Apr.15; 333) **$1,800**

LIVES OF THE SAINTS, The
Ill.:– V. Angelo. Chic., Catholic Pr., [1958]. 3 vols. Gt.-decor. mor., decor. end-papers, box defect.; the V. Angelo copy. (CBA. Oct.1; 306) **$140**

LIVINGSTON, William
[-] A Review of the Military Operations in North America, from the Commencement of the French Hostilities on the Frontiers of Virginia in 1753, to the Surrender of Oswego, 1756. Dublin, 1757. *1st. Irish Edn.* 12mo. Later hf. leath., worn, new leath. spine labels. (SG. Nov.3; 129) **$1,200**

LIVINGSTONE, David
- Cambridge Lectures. Ed.:– W. Monk. Camb., 1858. *1st. Edn.* Orig. cl.; pres. copy. (S. Jun.25; 69)
Haile. **£180**
- Letzte Reise in Centralafrika. Ed.:– H. Waller. Trans.:– J.M. Boyes. Hamburg, 1875. *1st. German Edn.* 2 vols. Cont. hf. leath. (R. Oct.13; 2914)
DM 580

LIVINGSTONE, David -Contd.

- **Missionary Travels & Researches in South Africa.**
1857. *1st. Edn. 1st. Iss.* Cont. hf. cf., gt.-decor.
spine. (TA. Oct.20; 10)   £62
- - **Anr. Copy.** Orig. cl. (P. Dec.8; 343)
Walford. £60
- - **Anr. Copy.** Tinted litho. folding frontis., folding
map, wood engrs., publishers advts. bnd. in at rear,
some minor spotting, recent qtr. cf. (TA. Jun.21;
41)   £52
- - **Anr. Edn.** L., 1857. *1st. Edn.* 1 folding map in
pocket, orig. cl., spine slightly faded. (S. Jun.25;
68)   *Haile.* £90
- - **Anr. Copy.** Orig. cl. gt. (P. Dec.8; 95)   £55
- - **Anr. Copy.** Orig. cl., unc.; John King copy. (KH.
Nov.9; 311)   *Aus.* $280
- - **Anr. Copy.** 1 vol. 8 pp. advts. dtd. Nov. 1, orig.
cl. (*With:*) - **The Last Journals of David Livingston
in Central Africa.** 1874. 2 vols. Orig. cl. gt., soiled,
hinges brkn. (SKC. Mar.9; 2026)   £100
- - **Anr. Copy.** Orig. cl., hinges reprd. (P. Apr.12;
44)   *Simper.* £55

LIVINGSTONE, David & Charles

- **Narrative of an Expedition to the Zambesi & its
Tributaries.** L., 1865. *1st. Edn.* Folding map, 13
plts., ills., orig. cl., rebkd.; ex-liby. (S. Apr.9; 38)
£77
- - **Anr. Copy.** A few ll. slightly spotted, orig. cl.,
slightly soiled. (BBA. Sep.29; 25)   *Thorp.* £60

LIVIUS, Titus

- **Decades.** Venice, 1520. Fo. Title with woodcut
port. & device, woodcuts at head of each chapter,
cont. MS. marginalia, few ll. browned or lightly
stained, later parch.-bkd. bds., spine damaged.
(SPB. May 17; 640) $650
- **Histoire Romaine.** Trans.:– Antoine de la Faye.
1582. Fo. Worming at foot of vol., cont. stpd. pig,
gt. initials 'N.V.M.' on upr. cover. (HD. Mar.21;
98)   Frs. 1,700
- - **Anr. Edn.** Trans.:– Dureau de Lamalle. Paris,
1810-12. 15 vols. Latin & Fr. parallel text, cont.
tree cf. gt., decor. spines. (HD. Sep.22; 361)
Frs. 2,200
- **Historiae Romanae Decades.** Ed.:– Lucas Porrus.
Treviso, Johannes Rubeus Vercellensis, 1485.
Reprint of 1482 Edn. Fo. Initials painted in red or
blue, 1st. initials decor. in gt. & cols., arms &
initials 'TH. O.' in 1 lr. margin, lacks 3 blank ll.,
cont. margin MS. notes at beginning, 17th. C.
vell.; from Fondation Furstenberg-Beaumesnil. [H.
10136; BMC. VI, 897; Goff L244] (HD. Nov.16;
57)   Frs. 10,000
- **Historiarum.** Ed.:– Thomas Ruddiman. Edinb.,
1751. 4 vols. Cont. spr. cf., spines gt.; Sir Ivar
Colquhoun, of Luss copy. (CE. Mar.22; 118) £75
- **Historicus Duobus Libris.** [Venice, 1520]. Fo.
Heavily reprd. title, few other repairs, some wear,
some sections heavily annotated by early owner,
mod. vell. (SG. Feb.9; 272) $250
- **Latinae Historiae Principis Decas Quarta....** Lug-
duni, 1537. 16th. C. mor., blind- & gt.-decor.
Fantuzzi arms, slightly disbnd., turn-ins worn. (HD.
Jun.29; 197)   Frs. 2,700
- **Libri Omnes.** Ill.:– J. Amman. Frankfurt, 1568.
1st. Amman Edn. 5 pts. (of 6) in 1 vol. Fo. Some
light soiling in 1st. third, last ll. lightly stained,
some sm. wormholes at beginning, & some old
MS. marginalia, cont. leath., some restoration. (R.
Oct.11; 59)   DM 2,000
- **Rhömische Historien.** Mainz, 1557. 4 pts. in 1
vol. Sm. fo. Some light browning or old spotting,
some woodcuts pale, pig over wood bds., roll stpd.,
defects., pasted on leath. strips, lacks 1 brass clasp.
(V. Oct.1; 3756)   DM 1,200
- **Roemsche Historie of Gesten, nu eerst mael in
Nederlandscher Spraken ghedrucht.** Antw., Gra-
pheus for J. Gymnious, 1542. *1st. Dutch Edn.* 4
pts. in 1 vol. Fo. Lacks title, some old spotting,
leath., wear. (V. Oct.1; 3758)   DM 1,300
- **Römische Geschichte.** Ed.:– G.C. Adler. Trans.:–
G.C. Maternus v. Alano. Altona, 1777-79. *1st. Edn.*
Title stpd., slightly browned & brown spotted, cont.
leath. gt., spine & jnts. worn. (R. Apr.3; 955)
DM 400
- **Römische Historien.** Trans.:– N. Carbach & J.
Micyllus. Mainz, 1538. Sm. fo. Lr. margin cut in
1st. title lf., lacks part of 2nd. leaf, approx. 100 ll.

torn in lr. margin, 2 ll. with lengthy tear, 1 lf. with
corner torn off, some browning, 2 ll. blue spotted
in lr. margin, blind-tooled pig over wood bds.,
spotted, lacks clasps. (GB. May 3; 114) DM 5,400
- **Titi Livi Patavini Romanae Historiae Principis,
Libri Omnes.** Frankfurt, 1568. Cont. stpd. pig over
wood bds., decor., clasps; from Fondation Furstenberg-Beaumesnil. (HD. Nov.16; 176)   Frs. 1,400

LIVIUS, Titus & Florus, Lucius

- **Von Ankunfft und Ursprung dess Römischen
Reichs.** Trans.:– S. Müntzer. Ill.:– Ammann.
Frankfurt, 1571. Fo. Lacks last lf. blank, some
spotting & staining, some ll. with pasted or extended
margin tears, later vell. gt., slightly spotted. (H.
Nov.23; 590)   DM 980
- - **Anr. Edn.** Trans.:– Z. Muentzer. Ill.:– T.
Stimmer & Bocksberger. Strassburg, Riehl. [1574].
Fo. Woodcuts partly bkd., margins lightly defect.,
browned thro.-out, & light stain in parts, 6 index
ll. with loss, last lf. only present in part, blind-
tooled leath., upr. cover defect & re-bnd., lacks 1
brass clasp. (V. Oct.1; 3757)   DM 900
- - **Anr. Edn.** Ill.:– T. Stimmer. [Strassburg, 1581].
Fo. Slightly browned & foxed, cont. blind-tooled
pig over wood bds., lightly soiled, 2 clasps. (HK.
Nov.8; 255)   DM 2,700

LIVRE DE CHASSE

Paris, [1886]. Ob. fo. 24 engraved plts., sigd.
J.A.M.S., liby. perforation stp. in title, some hand-
soiling, cl., leath. back, worn & brkn. (RO. Dec.11;
192) $185

LIVRE D'OR DU BIBLIOPHILE

Paris, [1927, 1929]. *Ltd. Edn., numbered.* Nos.
1 & 3 only (of 3). Lge. 4to. Lacks hf.-title(?) &
limitation lf. in Vol. 1, paper wraps. (SG. Aug.4;
185) $100

LIVRE DE QUATRE COULEURS, Le

Paris, 1757. Cont. cf., rebkd. (P. Mar.15; 9)
Marks. £100

LIVRE MAGIQUE (Le) Tombé de la Lune 1500
Ans avant la Creátion du Monde et Retrouvé en
1870

Metz, 1870. Flick book, hand-cold. ills., title-p.
stained, 1 lf. loose; anr. reinserted incorrectly,
wraps.; van Veen coll. (S. Feb.28; 246)   £120

LIVRE POUR UNE PETITE FILLE BIEN SAGE

Paris, 1817. 12mo. 14 hand-cold. litho. plts., minor
tear to title, cont. bds., spine chipped. (SG. Dec.8;
222) $375

LIZARS, Daniel

- **The Edinburgh Geographical & Historical Atlas.**
Ca. 1840. Fo. 58 hand-cold. double-p. maps, a few
folding, 1 map torn along fold, hf. cf., covers detchd.
(P. Mar.15; 385)   *Burr.* £300

LIZARS, William Home

- **Edinburgh Geographical General Atlas.** Ca. 1840.
Fo. 69 partly cold. maps, hf. cf., defect. (P. Sep.29;
430)   £180
- - **Anr. Edn.** Edinb., n.d. Fo. 62 engraved plts.
only, cont. hf. mor., rubbed. (BBA. Dec.15; 129)
Jeffery. £180
- **General Atlas.** Edinb., [1831]. 61 engraved maps
only, hand-cold. in outl., some light soiling, cont.
cf., worn, covers detchd., w.a.f. (CSK. Oct.7; 21)
£200
- **New Edinburgh School Atlas.** Edinb., n.d. Fo.
Litho. title, 32 (of 33) hand-cold. maps, some torn,
1 defect., soiled thro.-out, cont. roan-bkd. cl., worn.
(BBA. Feb.9; 256)   *Argosy Bookstore.* £70

LLEWELLYN, Martin

[-] **Men-Miracles with other Poems.** [Oxford],
1646. *1st. Edn.* Lacks A1 (?blank), title margin
reprd., final text lf. soiled, mark from bkplt., tree
cf.; bkplts. of Fairfax of Cameron & Robert S.
Pirie. (SPB. May 16; 94) $850

LLONVILLE & others

- **Memoires tirés des Papiers d'un Homme d'Etat
....** Paris, 1828-38. 13 vols. Hf. cf. (HD. Feb.22;
137)   Frs. 2,500

LLOYD, Charles

See— COLERIDGE, Samuel Taylor, Lamb,
Charles & Lloyd, Charles

LLOYD, Edward

- **Natural History.** 1896. 16 vols. Orig. cl., spines
faded, liby. labels pasted in covers, ink numbers on
spines. (TA. Apr.19; 162)   £75
- - **Anr. Copy.** 16 vols. Orig. cl., spines faded, ink
liby. nos. at head of spines, labels pasted in covers.
(TA. May 17; 275)   £65
- - **Anr. Copy.** 16 vols. 16mo. Publishers cf., some
spine defects. (CR. Jun.6; 109)   Lire 420,000
- - **Anr. Edn.** L., 1896-97. 16 vols. Some ll. slightly
spotted, orig. mor.-bkd. cl., slightly rubbed. (BBA.
May 23; 281)   *Bailey.* £100

LLOYD, Lewis

- **The Game Birds & Wild Fowl of Sweden &
Norway.** 1867. *1st. Edn.* 48 chromolitho. plts., slight
spotting, slightly loose, orig. gt.-decor. cl. (SKC.
May 4; 1861)   £80
- **Scandinavian Adventures.** 1854. *2nd. Edn.* 2 vols.
Map, 12 tinted litho. plts., cont. patterned pol. cf.
gt. (SKC. May 4; 1811)   £60

LLOYD, Lodowick

- **The Pilgrimage of Princes.** [1573?]. *1st. Edn.* 4to.
1st. 4 & last 6 ll. inlaid, other margin repairs, recent
cf. [STC 16624] (BBA. Jun.14; 21)   *Maggs.* £190
- **The Stratagems of Ierusalem: with the Martiall
Laws & Militarie Discipline, as well of the Iewes
as of the Gentiles.** 1602. Sm. 4to. Some headlines
shaved & a few cropped, lacks last lf. (blank?),
minor foxing to prelims., sm. repair to 1 lf., mod.
red mor. gt. [STC 16630] (C. May 30; 160)
Rik. £100

LLOYD, T.H.

- **The Diary of Capt. Eyre Lloyd.** L., ptd. for Private
Circulation, 1905. Some light foxing, decor. vell.
gt., mark on upr. cover. (VA. Oct.28; 501) R 270

LLYWD, Humphrey

See— TWYNE, Joannis — LLYWD, Humphrey

LOBELIUS [L'OBEL], Mathias de

- **Icones Stirpium.** Antw., 1591. *2nd. Edn.* Some
marginalia, lacks last lf. of Engl. name index &
last lf. (blank), last lf. of Engl. index defect with
loss, 1-2 sm. wormholes in lr. margin of last ll.,
some slight spotting, cont. hf. leath., rubbed. (R.
Oct.12; 1867)   DM 4,900
- **Plantarum seu Stirpium Historia.** Antw., 1576.
1st. Edn. 4to. Replacement woodcuts pasted to
R3 & R4, 24 p. index to the companion vol. 'Nova
Stirpium Adversaria' bnd. at end, natural paper
flaw at lr. outer corner of DD3, slight discolouration
thro.-out, old blind-stpd. vell. over wood bds. (C.
Mar.14; 184)   *Thorp.* £400

LOBEL-RICHE, Almery

- **Arabesques Intimes....** Paris, 1937. *(50) on vell.*
Lge. 4to. Orig. ill., sigd. & annotated by Lobel-
Riche, cont. hf. mor., limp spine, mosaic vertical
title, decor. wrap. & s.-c., by Hauttecoeur, unc.
(HD. Dec.9; 41)   Frs. 3,200

LOBINEAU, Gui Alexis

- **Histoire de Bretagne.** Paris, 1707. 2 vols. Fo.
Cont. cf., rebkd. (BBA. Aug.18; 195)
Nat. Library of Wales. £80

LOBO, R.P.J.

- **Voyage Historique d'Abissinie.** Ed.:– M. Le
Grand, Prieur de Neuville-les-Dames. Ill.:– Cochin.
Paris & La Haye, 1728. 4to. Cont. marb.cf., decor.
spine. (HD. Dec.9; 51)   Frs. 2,800

LOCARD & COTTEAU

- **Description de la Faune des Terrains Tertiaires
Moyens de la Corse.** Paris, 1877. (*Bound with:*)
PERON, A. - **Description du Terrain Tertiaire du
Sud de l'Ile de Corse.** N.d. Together 2 works in 1
vol. Later hf. chagrin. (HD. Oct.21; 114)
Frs. 1,000

LOCH, James

- **An Account of the Improvements on the Estates
of the Marquess of Stafford in the Counties of
Stafford & Salop & the Estate of Sutherland.** 1820.
Folding frontis. map, 38 (of 39) plts., cont. tree cf.
(PD. May 16; 182)   £170

LOCHMAIR, Mich.

- **Sermones de Sanctis Perutiles cum Vigintibus
Sermonibus ... Pauli wann Annexis ...** [Passau, Petri,

LOC column 1

1490-91]. *1st. Edn.* Fo. Title soiled & with owner's note, some old text annots., some browning or staining & worming, 1st. sigs. loose, cont. blind-tooled pig over wood bds., upr. cover brkn. & nearly loose, very rubbed & bumped, defect. [H. 10172; BMC II, 617; Goff L 270] (HK. Nov.8; 256)
DM 800

LOCKE, Harold
– A Bibliographical Catalogue of the Writings of Sir Arthur Conan Doyle. Tunbridge Wells, 1928. Cl.-bkd. bds., unc., moderate wear. (RO. May 22; 112) $130

LOCKE, John
– A Collection of Several Pieces of Mr. John Locke, Never Before Printed. L., 1720. *1st. Edn.* Advts. at end, sm. tear to inside margin of title, b2 & 3 with corners torn away, recent cl.; the Rt. Hon. Visc. Eccles copy. (CNY. Nov.18; 175) $550
– – **Anr. Copy.** Some margin stains &c., lacks hf.-title (?), old cf., rubbed, cover detchd. (RO. Apr.23; 206) $160
[–] A Common-place Book to the Holy Bible. 1697. *1st. Edn.* Sm. 4to. Browned, cont. panel. cf., rebkd. & reprd., rubbed. (BBA. Jul.27; 106)
Peter Murray Hill. £50
[–] An Essay Concerning Humane Understanding. L., 1690. *1st. Edn. 1st. Iss.* Fo. 18th. C. ink margin notes, 2 early owners' sigs., later cf. [Wing L 2738] (C. Nov.9; 92) *Thomas.* £2,600
– [–] **Anr. Copy.** Fo. Lacks E1, 2E1 & 2Y1, lf. 2Q4 torn, some stains, marginal wear, disbnd., w.a.f. (SG. Apr.19; 121) $550
– – **Anr. Edn.** L., 1694. *2nd. Edn.* Fo. Slight stain at beginning & end, cont. cf., lr. cover detchd. [Wing L 2740] (C. Nov.9; 93) *Maggs.* £380
– – **Anr. Copy.** Fo. Worming to some blank margins, frontis. rehinged & with 2 short tears reprd., cont. blind-panel. cf., rebkd., rubbed, stained. [Wing L2740] (C. May 30; 161) *Thorp.* £180
– – **Anr. Edn.** L., 1706. *5th. Edn.* Fo. Cont. panel. cf., old reback, some wear. (TA. Mar.15; 404) £54
– Posthumous Works. L., 1706. *1st. Edn.* Cont. panel. cf. (SPB. May 16; 95) $325
– – **Anr. Copy.** Old cf. (SG. Oct.27; 197) $200
– Reply to the Right Reverend the Lord Bishop of Worcester. 1699. *1st. Edn.* Errata lf., cont. cf. [Wing L2754] (P. Feb.16; 264) £70
– Some Familiar Letters Between Mr. Locke & Several of his Friends. L., 1708. *1st. Edn.* Cont. panel. cf., spine slightly worn. (SPB. May 16; 96) $375
– Some Thoughts Concerning Education. L., 1699. *4th. Edn.* Cont. cf., head of spine cracked; Thomas Stonor & Austin Dobson bkplts. [Wing L2764] (BBA. May 3; 172) *Quaritch.* £110
– The Works. 1714. *[1st. Coll. Edn.].* 3 vols. Fo. Some slight staining, cont. panel. cf. gt. (P. Apr.12; 232) *Cavendish.* £95
– – **Anr. Copy.** 3 vols. Fo. Some minor stains &c., cont. cf., early rebkd., rubbed, 1 cover detchd., lacks spine labels. (RO. Apr.23; 207) $150
– – **Anr. Edn.** L., 1751. *5th. Edn.* 3 vols. Fo. Cont. spr. cf., rubbed; Sir Ivar Colquhoun, of Luss copy. (CE. Mar.22; 193) £320
– – **Anr. Edn.** L., 1794. *9th. Edn.* 9 vols. Spr. cf., spines gt. (SG. Feb.16; 183) $400
– – **Anr. Edn.** L., 1823. 10 vols. Bds., brkn. (HD. Feb.22; 121) Frs. 2,100

LOCKER, Edward Hawke
– Memoirs of Celebrated Naval Commanders. 1832. 4to. 20 engraved plts. on India paper, mntd., margins lightly stained, cont. hf. mor., lightly rubbed. (CSK. May 4; 80) £60
– Views in Spain. L., 1824. 4to. Some light spotting, cont. hf. cf. (CSK. Sep.30; 71) £400
– – **Anr. Copy.** 55 (of 60) plts., 8 extra plts. (5 trimmed at 1 edge), some foxing, mod. hf. cf. gt. (P. Dec.8; 310) *Shapero.* £280
– – **Anr. Copy.** 4to. Port. with litho. vig., 60 lithos., orig. mor., corners. (DS. Oct.28; 2268) Pts. 80,000

LOCKHART, Sir Robert B.
– My Rod, My Comfort. Ill.:– J. Gaastra. Dropmore Pr., 1949. *(550) numbered & sigd. by author & artist.* 4to. Cf., d.-w. (HBC. May 17; 164) £55

LOC column 2

LOCKWOOD, Luke Vincent
– Colonial Furniture in America. N.Y., 1913. 2 vols. 4to. Orig. cl., spines faded. (BBA. Jul.27; 255)
Demetzy. £90

LOCOMOTIVE RAILWAY CARRIAGE & Wagon Review, The
Jan. 1923-Nov. 1959. Vols. 29-65. 4to. Cl., spines gt.; Earl Poulett the Eighth copy. (LC. Oct.13; 458) £200

LODDIGES, Conrad & Sons
– The Botanical Cabinet. 1817-33. 20 vols. 2,000 hand-cold. & partly col. plts., a few folding, some slight staining, hf. mor., unc., some vols. rebkd., Vol. 10 hinges worn, Vol. 20 loose. (P. Jun.7; 291) £850
– – **Anr. Edn.** Ill.:– George Cooke, after G. Loddiges & others. L., 1818-21. Vols. 1-6. Sm. 4to. Wide margins, engraved titles, 600 hand-cold. engraved plts., Vols. 1-3 cont. green hf. mor., spines gt., Vols. 4-6 cont. purple hf. mor., a few spines rubbed; sig. of Lady James Murray. (C. Nov.16; 269) *Sotheran.* £850
– – **Anr. Edn.** Ill.:– G. Cooke, after G. Loddiges & family, Miss. Rebello, & Thomas S. Boys. L., 1818-33. 20 vols. 4to. L.P., 20 engraved titles, 1 uncold. plt., 2,000 hand-cold. engraved plts., 'Catalogue of Plants'. 1820. 12th. Edn. (containing 2 engraved plts. of hothouses) bnd. at end of Vol. 1, a few plts. slightly cropped, cont. Engl. purple str.-grd. mor., broad gt. borders & gt.-panel, covers, spines gt.-decor. & gt.-lettered, watered silk linings, ticket of Henry Gough, bookbinder to the Duke of Sussex, in Vols. 7-10, spines & jnts. slightly rubbed, corners slightly worn; Lord Dinorben bkplt., as a periodical, w.a.f. (CNY. May 18; 144) $3,500
– – **Anr. Edn.** L., n.d.-1824. Vols. 9 & 10 only (of 20). Sm. 4to. Engraved title to Vol. 10 (lacking in Vol. 9), 190 hand-cold. plts., slight offsetting, maroon mor. gt., slightly rubbed, w.a.f. (S. Nov.28; 54) *Wedekind.* £250
– – **Anr. Edn.** N.d. Vols. 18 & 19 in 1 vol. Nos. 18 to 126 (of 129) hand-cold. plts., 1 torn, lacks title-pp. & 1 index, cont. hf. mor., slightly worn, w.a.f. (SKC. Jan.13; 2328) £110
– – **Anr. Copy.** Nos. 1524-1640 (lacks 1 no.). 73 hand-cold. engraved plts., lacks title & 1 cover, bdg. not stated, w.a.f. (SKC. Nov.18; 1975) £100

LODGE, Edmund
– Portraits of Illustrious Personages of the Court of Henry VIII. L., 1812. 4to. 84 hand-cold. plts., hf. mor. gt. (P. May 17; 43) *Joseph.* £300
– – **Anr. Edn.** 1828. 4to. 84 cold. engraved plts., some on pink paper, cont. red mor. gt. by J. Wright, slightly rubbed. (C. May 30; 188)
Cavendish. £250
– – **Anr. Copy** Sm. fo. 84 engrs., red three-qtr. mor., worn. (SG. Nov.3; 99) $400
– Portraits of Illustrious Personages of Great Britain. L., 1814-34. 4 vols. Fo. Cont. Engl. decor. cf. (SI. Dec.15; 117) Lire 500,000
– – **Anr. Edn.** 1821. Vols. I & II only. Fo. Cf. gt., inner dentelles; subscriber's copy. (LC. Oct.13; 57) £70
– – **Anr. Edn.** L., 1821-34. 4 vols. in 5. Fo. Slight browning, 1 title torn, cont. russ., worn, 1 vol. rebkd., others with covers loose or detchd. (S. Mar. 20; 728) *Rebecchi.* £50
– – **Anr. Copy.** 4 vols. Fo. L.P., 240 mntd. India-proof plts., some foxing to plts., chiefly in margins, not collated, but likely compl., 19th. C. mor., gt.- & blind-stpd., spines & extremities rubbed. (SG. Jun.7; 375) $150
– – **Anr. Edn.** L., 1823-34. 12 vols. in 6. Some ports. spotted, later hf. mor., spines faded. (S. Oct.4; 92)
Dempster. £50

LODGE, George E.
See— BANNERMAN, David Armitage & Lodge, George E.

LOEFFLER, Berthold
– Die Flaeche: Dekorative Entwuerfe Neue Folge. Vienna, ca. 1910. Vol. II pts. 1 & 2, together 2 vols. 4to. 32 accordion-folding col. plts., ptd. wraps. on bd., lacks spines. (SG. Aug.25; 322) $220

LOH column 3

LOEILLET, Jean-Baptiste
– Six Suits of Lessons for the Harpsichord or Spinnet .... L., ca. 1730. *1st. Edn. 2nd. Iss.* Fo. Some dust-staining, orig. marb. bds., worn, spine brkn. (S. Nov.17; 134) *Jeffrey.* £210

LOF EN NUTTIGHEID DER DRUKKONST
Middelberg, 1770. Miniature book, 55 x 39 mm. Cont. cf. gt. decor.; van Veen coll. (S. Feb.28; 192) £1,900

LOFFLER, Konrad
– Schwäbische Buchmalerei in Romanischer Zeit. Augsburg, [1928]. Lge. 4to. Orig. linen. (HK. Nov.11; 4478) DM 400

LOGAN, James, Antiquary
– The Clans of the Scottish Highlands. Ill.:– after R.R. McIan. L., 1845. 2 vols. Fo. 2 cold. frontis., 49 hand-cold. plts. only, the whole loose, decor. mor. gt., w.a.f. (GM. Dec.7; 654) £400
– – **Anr. Edn.** L., 1845-47. 2 vols. Fo. 2 illuminated frontis. with arms, 72 hand-finished col. litho. plts., some plts. & text, particularly Vol. 2, detchd. from gutta-percha bdg., cont. mor.-bkd. embossed cl. gt. (C. Mar.14; 63) *Foyle.* £1,200
– – **Anr. Copy.** 2 vols. Fo. 2 illuminated armorial frontis., 72 hand-finished col. litho. plts., titles spotted, cont. mor.-bkd. embossed cl., gt. arms on upr. covers, spines gt. (C. Nov.16; 125)
Traylen. £900
– – **Anr. Copy.** 2 vols. Fo. Chromolitho. additional titles, 72 hand-cold. litho. plts., orig. mor.-bkd. cl. (CSK. Aug.19; 47) £480
– – **Anr. Edn.** L., 1847. 2 vols. Fo. Cold. armorial frontispieces, 72 hand-cold. litho. costume plts., all. plts. on new guards & few with sm. owners stps. on verso, orig. mor.-bkd. cl., jnts. & edges renewed, fold-over cl. boxes. (S. May 21; 5) *Pringle.* £1,100

LOHENSTEIN, D.C. von
– **Grossmüthiger Feld-Herr Arminius oder Herrmann, Nebst seiner Durchlauchtigsten Thusnelda ....** Ill.:– J. Tscherning (port.), Sandrart (frontis.). Leipzig, 1731. *2nd. Edn.* 4 pts. in 2 vols. 4to. Coll. title with owner's note, frontis. & title pt. 3 & 2 pp. defect. with loss, cont. blind-tooled pig over wood bds., spine later leath., rubbed, spine wormed, lacks clasps. (HK. Nov.10; 2586)
DM 800

LOHLEIN, George Simon
– Clavier-Schule. Leipzig, 1791 & 1788. 4 pts. in 2 vols. Ob. 4to. Vol. 1 title & last lf. with MS. name, Vol. 1 title with sm. tear in upr. corner, cont. hf. leath., rubbed & bumped. (HK. Nov.9; 2260)
DM 440

LOHMEYER, J.
– Was willst Du werden?. Ill.:– H. Bürkner after Pletsch. Leipzig, ca. 1875. 4to. Minimal soiling, orig. hf. linen. (GB. Nov.4; 1868) DM 2,000

LOHMEYER, K.
Heidelberger Maler d. Romantik. Heidelberg, 1935. 4to. Orig. linen, lacks upr. endpaper. (HK. Nov.12; 4729) DM 440

LOHNEYSS or LOHNEISEN, Georg Engelhard von
– Bericht vom Bergwerck. N.p., ca. 1660. *2nd. Edn.* Fo. Stp. on title, cont. vell., spotted, slightly loose. (H. Nov.23; 215) DM 3,000
– Neu eröffnete Hof Kriegs - und Re-it-Schul. Trans.:– Val. Trichter. Nürnberg, 1729. 6 pts. in 1 vol. Fo. Lacks hf.-title, frontis. (with slight loss), title & 2 prelim. ll. (1 with slight text loss) bkd. in margins, 5 plts with partly bkd. tears, 4 slightly spotted, a few text ll. with bkd margin tears (most small), cont. hf. leath., rubbed, end-papers renewed. (R. Apr.4; 1926) DM 2,700
See— FIORENTINI, J.V. & Löhneysen, Georg Engelhard von

LOHR, Johann Andreas Christian
– Erste Lehren u. Bilder. Ill.:– Gapieux. Leipzig, ca. 1823. Lacks 2 pp. & 1 copperplt., some offsetting, plt. ll. very cut with slight loss, wear, hf. linen with orig. cold. pict. cover, rubbed. (HK. Nov.10; 2914) DM 540
– Das Fabelbuch für Kindheit und Jugend. Ill.:– H. Rosmäsler. Leipzig, [1824]. *3rd. Edn.* Engraved

LOHR, Johann Andreas Christian -*Contd.*

frontis., pict. title & 14 plts., hand-cold., orig. pict. bds., soiled, backstrip discold. & slightly chipped; van Veen coll. (S. Feb.28; 154)   £230
- - **Anr. Copy.** Engraved frontis., pict. title & 14 plts., hand-cold., a few ll. slightly stained, cont. hf. cf.; New Year present from Earl Stanhope to his daughter Caroline, inscr. by her, van Veen coll. (S. Feb.28; 155)   £220

LOHSE, Ernest (Ill.)
See— ALBUM DE AVES AMAZONICA

LOMBARDO, Josef Vincent
- **Chaim Gross: Sculptor.** N.Y., 1949. *1st. Edn.* 4to. Cl.; pen-&-ink drawing by Gross on front free end-paper, inscr. to a student, Jan. 1956. (SG. Feb.2; 75) $120

LOMBARDUS, Marcus
- **Gründtlicher Bericht und Erklärung von der Juden Handlungen und Ceremonien, Schelten und Fluchen wider Jesum Christum und seine Kirchen.** Basel, 1573. 4to. Sm. stains at end, many old MS.marginalia, mod. wraps. (R. Oct.11; 60)   DM 1,450

LOMENI, I.
- **Notizie Storico-istruttive intorno la Introduzione, la Moltiplicazione, la Coltura del Gelso delle Isole Filippine ....** Mailand, 1837. Lge. 4to. L.P., wide margin, cont. mor. gt., blind-tooled. (R. Oct.12; 1773)   DM 620

LOMIER
- **Le Bataillon des Marins de la Garde 1803-1815.** Ill.:– G. Amoretti. Paris, 1911. Hf. chagrin. (HD. Jan.27; 174)   Frs. 1,300

LONCLE, M.
- **Eloge de Dunoyer de Segonzac.** 1963. *(250)* numbered on vélin de Rives with suite of 4 double-p. ills. 4to. 10 orig. etchings, leaves, wrap., box. (HD. Jul.2; 64)   Frs. 3,000

LONDON
- **Britannia Illustrata or Views of all the Kings Palaces, Several Seats ... Publick Buildings & Squares in London & Westminster.** Ill.:– B. Cole, J. Harris, & others. Hen. Overton & J. Hoole at the White Horse without Newgate, [1727]. Ob. fo. Engraved title, 100 engraved views (contents lf. calls for 107), 1 additional plt. intended for the work by J. Clark & dtd. 1724, 2 plts. inserted from anr. copy, & cut down & mntd., title margins shaved affecting neatline at head, also headline on contents lf., later hf. cf. (S. Dec.1; 174)   *Shapero.* £600
- **London County Council Survey of London.** 1900-80. Vols. 1-40. 4to. Vols. 1-3 cont. cl., slightly soiled, Vol. 1 with orig. ptd. wraps. preserved, Vols. 3-12 orig. ptd. wraps., untrimmed, Vols. 13-40 orig. cl. gt., all but Vol. 17 with d.-w.'s. (TA. Dec.15; 76)   £500
- **London & its Environs Described.** L., 1761. 6 vols. Lge. folding map & the 2 plans with sm. tears, slight offsetting, cont. cf. (S. Mar.6; 389)   *Hayden.* £70
- **Public Edifices of the British Metropolis.** 1820. 4to. Mod. qtr. cf. (P. Sep.29; 263) *Burgess.* £65
- **Select Views of London & its Environs.** 1804-05. 2 vols. 4to. 2 vig. titles, 60 plts., some foxing, cont. diced cf., spines defect. (P. Jun.7; 14)   £75
- **Several Plans & Drawings referred to in the Third Report ... upon the Improvement of the Port of London.** L., 1800. Lge. fo. 21 engraved & aquatint folding or double-p. plans (5 hand-cold.), some margins soiled, orig. wraps., soiled, w.a.f. (CSK. Feb.24; 20)   £260
See— PORT OF LONDON

LONDON BIBLIOGRAPHY OF THE SOCIAL SCIENCES
Ed.:– B.M. Headicar & C. Fuller. Vols. 1-5 & 7-10 only. 4to. A few ll. torn, orig. wraps., torn & soiled. (BBA. Feb.9; 124)   *Koffler.* £55

LONDON & COUNTRY BREWER
1744. *5th. Edn.* 4 pts. in 1 vol. General title, 16pp. publishers advts., some light spotting, cont. cf., rubbed. (CSK. May 18; 179)   £80

LONDON ENCYCLOPAEDIA, Or Universal Dictionary of Science, Art, Literature, & Practical Mechanics
1829. 22 vols. Tall 8vo. Cont. hf. cf., rubbed, some a little worn. (TA. Jan.19; 384)   £80

LONDON GAZETTE
3 Oct. 1695-8 Aug. 1698. Nos. 3119-3416 (lacks nos. 3142, 3370 & 3376). 4to. Some nos. lightly browned, cf., spine reprd., as a periodical, w.a.f. (P. Sep.29; 272)   *Paper Heritage.* £300

LONDON INTERIORS: a Grand National Exhibition
Ill.:– after T.H. Shepherd & others. 1841. 2 vols. 4to. Some minor spotting, cont. pol. cf., covers panel. in gt. & blind, spines gt.; from liby. of Luttrellstown Castle, w.a.f. (C. Sep.28; 1829)   £130

LONDON MAGAZINE
L., 1747-78. Over 300 copperplts., many folding, cont. mott. cf., rehinged. (SG. Dec.15; 170) $1,700

LONDON MISSIONARY SOCIETY
- **A Missionary Voyage to the Southern Pacific Ocean... compiled from the Journals of the Officers & the Missionaries.** L., 1799. *1st. Edn.* 4to. 7 engraved maps (5 folding), 6 engraved plts., some offsetting from plts. & slight discolouration, 19th. C. hf. cf., rubbed. (S. May 22; 481)   *Cavendish.* £200

LONDON, Jack
- **The Call of the Wild.** Ill.:– P.R. Goodwin & C. Bull. N.Y., 1903. *1st. Edn.* Publisher's 4-p. advt. flyer laid in, orig. decor. cl., mor.-bkd. s.-c.; Charles Platt-Prescott copy. (SPB. May 17; 641) $550
- - **Anr. Copy.** Owner's sig. on frontis. recto, pict. vertically ribbed cl., upr. cover darkened at edges, spine ends bumped. (SG. Jan.12; 243) $200
- - **Anr. Copy.** Col.-pict. cl., tips & spine ends rubbed. (SG. Dec.8; 224) $110
- **The House of Pride & Other Tales of Hawaii.** N.Y., 1912. *1st. Edn.* Pict. cl., worn. (RO. Aug.23; 104) $110
- **Jerry of the Islands.** N.Y., 1917. *1st. Edn.* Cl., worn, d.-w. frayed. (RO. Aug.23; 106) $300
- **Les Mutinés de l'Elseneur.** Trans.:– Paul Gruyer & Louis Postif. Ill.:– Charles Fouqueray. Paris, 1934. *(300)* on vell. 4to. Hf. roan by Randeyne et fils, unc., upr. cover ill. wrap., s.-c. (HD. Mar.27; 84)   Frs. 1,050
- **Scorn of Women.** N.Y., 1906. *1st. Edn.* (*With:*)
- **Theft.** N.Y., 1910. *1st. Edn.* Together 2 vols. Cl., worn. (RO. Aug.23; 114) $1,050

LONG, Sydney
- **The Etched Work ...** Attic Pr., 1942. *(300)* numbered & sigd. Bdg. not stated; inscr. 'To My Friend C.Q. Williamson'. (JL. Mar.25; 844)   Aus. $120

LONGA, G. della
See— MOSCHETTI, Allessandro & others

LONGCHAMPS, M.
See— RENGGER, J.R. & Longchamps, M.

LONGFELLOW, Henry Wadsworth
- **Ballads & Other Poems.** Camb., 1842. *3rd. Edn.* *(70)* on L.P. Tall 8vo. Few ll. reprd., orig. bds., rebkd., sides soiled, cl. jacket; pres. copy from author, & A.N.s. laid in, Frederic Dannay copy. (CNY. Dec.16; 215) $220
- **Evangeline, a Tale of Acadie.** Boston, 1848. *(50)* L.P. Some spotting, orig. cl., elab. gt.-blocked, spine frayed; Frederic Dannay copy. (CNY. Dec.16; 216) $250
- - **Anr. Edn.** Ill.:– Violet Oakley & Jessie Wilcox Smith. Boston, 1897. Gold-decor. cl., d.-w. (some chipping & fraying); Ken Leach coll. (RO. Jun.10; 405) $155
- **Hyperion: a Romance.** L., 1865. Sm. 4to. 24 mntd. photos., orig. decor. cl. (BBA. Mar.21; 274)   *Fenning.* £50
- - **Anr. Edn.** Ill.:– Francis Frith. L., 1868. 4to. Some foxing, cl. gt., some wear, rear jnt. brkn. (RO. Dec.11; 111) $100
- [-] **Outre-Mère; A Pilgrimage Beyond the Sea.** Boston, 1833; [1834]. *1st. Edn.* 2 pts. in 1 vol. With publisher's name on title & copyright page of 1st.

pt., 2nd. pt. with title-p. only in 1st. gathering, some spotting, mod. marb. wraps., red mor.-bkd. folding box; Fred A. Berne copy. (SPB. May 16; 326) $125
- **The Song of Hiawatha.** Boston, 1855. *1st. Amer. Edn. 1st. Iss.,* with all the points cited in BAL. Sm. 8vo. The 'n' on p. 279 lacking, 12 p. catalogue dtd. Oct. 1855, blind-stpd. cl. (SG. Nov.17; 90) $150
- **Writings, with Bibliographical & Critical Notes.** Camb., Riverside Pr., 1886. *(500)* numbered on L.P. 11 vols. Lge. 8vo. Hf. cl., unc. & unopened. (SG. Nov.17; 94) $120

LONGMAN, W. & Trower, H.F.
- **Journal of Six Weeks' Adventures in Switzerland, Piedmont, & on the Italian Lakes. [By W.L. & H.F.T.].** L., 1856. Orig. cl., rubbed; hf.-title inscr. 'Herman Merivale Esq. ...' from Longman. (BBA. May 3; 353)   *Cavendish Rare Books.* £95

LONGMORE, Capt. C.
- **The Old Sixteenth; Being a Record of the 16th Battalion, A.I.F. ...** Perth, 1929. Frontis. & front. free end-paper removed, buckram gt. (KH. May 1; 432)   Aus. $100

LONGOLIUS, Christopher
- **Opera.** 1533. Old vell. (P. Mar.15; 320)   *Poole.* £80

LONGUS
[-] **Les Amours Pastorales de Daphnis et Chloé.** Ill.:– Scotin &c. [Paris], 1731. 12mo. Cont. mor. gt., spine decor. (slightly faded). (HD. May 3; 90)   Frs. 1,100
- - **Anr. Edn.** Ill.:– after Cochin, Scotin. [Paris], 1745. *Reprint of 1731 Edn.* Cont. cf. gt., rubbed, margin tear; Hauswedell coll. (H. May 24; 1458)   DM 420
- - **Anr. Edn.** Trans.:– M. Amiot. Ill.:– Fokke, Eisen & Cochin. Paris, 1757. 4to. Cont. spr. cf., gt. decor., decor. spine, sm. scratches. (HD. Dec.9; 52)   Frs. 1,600
- - **Anr. Edn.** Trans.:– Jacques Amyot. L. [Paris], 1779. 4to. Engraved frontis. (misbnd.), 29 plts., fore-edge of 1st. few ll. stained & corners reprd., vell. wraps., unc., s.-c. (BBA. Mar.21; 26)   *Snelling.* £100
- - **Anr. Edn.** Ill.:– Martinet. Paris, 1787. Lge. 4to. Wide margin, L.P., some light browning, & foxing, cont. mott. cf. gt., wear, 1 spine torn, end-lf. slightly crumpled, engraved ex-libris inside cover; Hauswedell coll. (H. May 24; 1461)   DM 1,500
- - **Anr. Edn.** Ill.:– Binet. 1795. *New Edn.* 18mo. Red mor. gt. by Simier, spine decor. (HD. May 3; 91)   Frs. 1,000
- - **Anr. Edn.** Trans.:– J. Amyot. Ill.:– A. de Saint-Aubin (port.), Eisen & Wille. Paris, 1863. *New Edn.* Cont. red mor. gt., spine decor. (HD. May 4; 339)   Frs. 1,300
- - **Anr. Edn.** Ed.:– A. Pons. Trans.:– Courier. Ill.:– Scott. Paris, 1878. Hand-bnd. mor. by Ammand, gt. inner & outer dentelle, leath. inlays multi-cold., orig. wraps. bnd. in, sm. tear, Hauswedell Coll. (H. May 24; 1466)   DM 520
- - **Anr. Edn.** Ed.:– P.-L. Courier. Preface: – Anatole France. Ill.:– J. Amyot. Paris, 1878. *(50)* De Luxe Edn. on China. Wide margin, etched port & 6 etchings, hand-bnd. mor., gt. spine, cover, inner & outer dentelles, by J. Kauffmann; Hauswedell coll. (H. May 24; 1464)   DM 400
- - **Anr. Edn.** Ill.:– Raphael Collin. Paris, Société des Beaux Arts, ca. 1900. *Edn. des Deux Mondes.* *(20)* lettered on Japan vell. 4to. Plts. & text engrs. in 3 states (plain, India-proof & cold.), all (excepting 1 state of the text engrs.) with vig. remarque, orig. lev. gt., cold. mor. inlays, elab. gt.-decor. dentelles, lev. doubls., upr. doubl. with inlaid oval hand-cold. engraved vig. on vell., moire grosgrain cl. liners, partly unc. (SG. Feb.16; 288) $1,000
- - **Anr. Edn.** Ed.:– P.L. Courier. Trans.:– J. Amyot. Paris, 1902. *(40)* De Luke Edn. on China. Lge. 4to. Title slightly crumpled due to thin paper, some pp. slightly darkened, hand-bnd. crushed mor., decor., by Collin, spine discold., corners bumped, Hauswedell coll. (H. May 24; 589)   DM 10,000
- - **Anr. Edn.** Trans.:– J. Amyot. Ill.:– Pierre Bonnard. Paris, 1902. *(200)* numbered on Holland van Gelder wtrmkd. 'Daphnis et Chloe'. 4to. Crushed

mor. gt. by Altermat, partly unc., orig. wraps. bnd. in, spine faded, mor.-edged bd. s.-c. (C. May 30; 184) *Lyon*. £1,800

– – **Anr. Edn.** Trans.:– J.A. Amyot. Ill.:– Pierre Bonnard. Paris, 1902. *(250) numbered.* 4to. Mor., cf. end-ll., orig. wraps. bnd. in, mor.-bkd. folder & s.-c., by P.L. Martin. (S. Nov.21; 54) *V. & A.* £4,300

– – **Anr. Edn.** Trans.:– J. Amyot. Ill.:– Carlegle. Paris, 1919. *(100) on imperial Japon.* Mor. gt., inlaid, by Ch. de Samblank, 1924, s.-c. (SPB. Dec.13; 547) $650

– – **Anr. Edn.** Trans.:– Amyot, revised by paul Louis Courier. Paris, 1920. *(10) not for sale on japon nacré with suite on japon nacré.* 4to. Some foxing, mor. gt. by Semet & Plumelle, spine decor. (faded), cf. liners, watered silk end-ll., wrap. preserved, s.-c. (HD. Jun.13; 61) Frs. 4,800

– – **Anr. Edn.** Ed.:– Jules Claretie. Ill.:– Champollion after Raphael Collin. Paris, [1922]. 4to. L.P., 12 etched plts., crimson three-qtr. lev., spines gt., mor. inlays, orig. wraps. bnd. in, s.-c. (SG. Feb.16; 184) $175

– – **Anr. Edn.** Trans.:– J. Amyot. Ill.:– Sylvain Sauvage. Paris, 1925. *(115) on velin d'Arches special, sigd. by artist.* Some offsetting from woodcuts, orange mor., with black design, by G. Huser, some rubbing, s.-c. (SPB. Dec.13; 563) $125

– – **Anr. Edn.** Trans.:– J. Amyot. Ill.:– G. Raverat. L., Ash. Pr., 1933. *(20) on vell.* Woodcuts, 4 initials in gold, others hand-painted in blue, mor. gt., s.-c. (P. May 17; 55) *H.M. Fletcher.* £4,000

– – **Anr. Edn.** Ed.:– Paul-Louis Courier. Trans.:– Jacques Amyot. Ill.:– Leonnec. Paris, [1934]. *Ltd. Edn., numbered.* 4to. 16 cold. plts., maroon lev., covers & spine decor. with inlaid pattern, gt. dentelles, moire satin end-ll., cold. pict. wraps. bnd. in, matching mor. s.-c. (SG. Feb.16; 185) $275

– – **Anr. Edn.** Ed.:– P.L. Courier. Trans.:– J.A. Amyot. Ill.:– Aristide Maillol. Paris, 1937. *(500) on Maillol-Butten, sigd. by artist & publisher.* 48 woodcuts, including wraps., orig. wraps. in handbnd. mor., vell. inlays, gold decor., patterned endpapers, writing in cover. (H. Nov.24; 1796) DM 3,200

– – **Anr. Edn.** Ill.:– Aristide Maillol. Paris, 1937. *(500) numbered & sigd. by artist.* Loose as iss. in orig. wraps., bd. folder, s.-c. (BBA. Jun.14; 233) *Landau.* £400

– – **Anr. Edn.** Ed.:– P.L. Courier. Trans.:– J.A. Amyot. Ill.:– Aristide Maillol. Paris, 1937. *(525) numbered & sigd. by artist.* Unsewn in orig. wraps., unc., folder & s.-c., slightly soiled. (S. Nov.21; 99) *Sims.* £310

– **Daphnis & Chloe. [English].** Trans.:– George Thornley. Ill.:– Aristide Maillol. L., 1937. *(250) numbered & sigd. by artist.* With additional suite of the woodcuts, orig. vell., unc., additional suite in vell.-bkd. portfo., s.-c. (S. Nov.21; 30) *Haas.* £660

– – **Anr. Copy.** On H.M.P., edges slightly browned, orig. vell., unc., slightly soiled. (BBA. Feb.23; 257) *Maggs.* £220

– – **Anr. Copy.** On Maillol-Bütten, printers mark sigd. by artist, margins lightly browned, hand-bnd. vell., browned. (H. May 23; 1366) DM 1,400

– **Die Liebesgeschichte v. Daphnis u. Chloe.** Trans.:– L. Wolde. Leipzig, Ernst Ludwig Pr., 1910. *(300).* 4to. Orig. leath., gt. inner dentelle, by P.A. Demeter, Leipzig, partly faded, rubbed, scratched. (HK. May 17; 2739) DM 400

– – **Anr. Edn.** Ill.:– O. Hettner. München, Phantasus Pr., [1923]. *(270) on Bütten, sigd. by artist.* Sm. 4to. Hand-bnd. mor. gt. by H. Glökler, Berlin. (H. Nov.24; 1223) DM 840

– – **Anr. Edn.** Ill.:– O. Hettner. München, [1923]. *(300) on Bütten.* 4to. Orig. vell., slightly spotted, printers mark sigd. by artist. (D. Nov.24; 3126) DM 450

– – **Anr. Edn.** Ill.:– Renée Sintenis. Hamburg, [1935]. *(200) numbered sigd. in printers mark by artist.* 31 orig. woodcuts, orig. hf. vell. (R. Apr.3; 441) DM 950

– **Pastoralium de Daphnide et Chloe [Graece].** Ill.:– Cagnoni after Lucatelli. Parmae, 1786. *(150) on 'Carta real f. azzurra'.* 4to. Wide margin, last p. slightly spotted, cont. red mor., decor. spine, inner & outer dentelles, spine rubbed & discold.; ex-libris; Hauswedell coll. (H. May 24; 1226) DM 1,400

– **Pastoralium de Daphnide & Chloë. Libri Quatuor. [Graece et Latine].** Ed.:– R. Columbianus. Flor., 1598. *1st. Edn.* Sm. 4to. Old owners mark on title, dtd. 1699, slightly spotted & browned; Hauswedell coll. (H. May 24; 1159) DM 1,200

– – **Anr. Edn.** Paris, 1778. 2 vols. in 1. Cont. cf. gt., supralibros, slightly spotted & rubbed. Hauswedell coll. (H. May 24; 1460) DM 420

LONITZER, LONICER or LONICERUS, Adam
– **Botanicon. Plantarum Historiae, cum earundem ad vivum artificiose expressis iconibus, tomi duo.** Frankfurt, 1565 [colophon dtd. 1551]. *2nd. Edn.* 2 vols. in 1. Fo. All but 7 ills. hand-cold. (those in Vol. 1 with cont. col., those in Vol. 2 cold. slightly later?), some worming to fore-margins of 1st. 190 ll., sm. hole in 13, a few ll. & some lr. margins & corners dampstained thro.-out, some brown offsetting from col. in Vol. 2, cont. cf. gt., backstrip defect., covers worn, tissue repairs to fly-ll.; sig. of Thomas Knyvett, 'C. & P.' mark of Thomas Rawlinson on upr. pastedown. (CNY. May 18; 145) $2,000

– **Kreuterbuch, Künstl. Conterfeytunge de Bäume, Stauden, Hecken, Kreuter, Getreyde... Gechteren der Erden. Dessgleichen von Metallen...** Frankfurt, 1587. Fo. Cut slightly close, some marginalia, title mntd., lacks 15 ll., 1 lf. misbnd., 3 ll. with tear, partly reprd., frayed margins reprd., tears partly bkd., index ll. with loss, lacks 1 index lf., last index lf. mntd. on MS. lf., spotted, mainly near end, no bdg. stated. (HK. May 15; 460) DM 2,200

LONITZER, LONICER or LONICERUS, Joh. Adam
See— BEISSARD, Jean Jacques – LONICER, Joh. Adam

LONNBERG, Einar (Text)
See— WRIGHT, Magnus, W. & F. von

LOOFFT, M.
– **Nieder-Sächisches Koch-Buch.** Altona & Lübeck, 1761. *4th. Edn.* Cont. bds., defect, some spotting. (D. Nov.24; 4151) DM 650

LOOMIS, Alfred F.
See— STONE, Herbert L. & Loomis, Alfred F.

LOON, Gerard van
– **Aloude Hollandsche Histori der Keyzeren, Koningen, Hertogen en Graaven.** 's-Gravenhage, 1734. 2 vols. Fo. Cont. cf. gt. (VG. Sep.18; 1175) Fls. 460
– **Beschr. der Nederl. Historipenningen...** 's-Gravenhage, 1723-31. 4 vols. Fo. L.P., some browning, 19th. C. hf. cf., slightly rubbed, corners & some spine-ends slightly defect. (VG. Mar.19; 173) Fls. 900

LOOSJES, A.Pz.
– **Hollands Arkadia of Wandelingen in de Omstreeken van Haarlem.** Haarlem, 1804. Title vig., 3 folding plts., hand-cold., 9 ll. mus., hf. roan, slight defects. (B. Apr.27; 538) Fls. 650
– **Nederland in Beeld.** Amst., ca. 1925-36. 17 vols. only (of 18, lacks 'De Zuiderzee'). 4to. Decor. cl. (B. Feb.8; 657) Fls. 1,500

LOPES, Jose Joaquim Rodrigues
– **Plani-Historia ou. Resume Synopti co-Historico-Genealogico do Imperio do Brazil e Do Reino de Portugal e das Familias Reinantes Nestes Paizes.** Rio de Janeiro, 1877. Tall fo. Giant fo. litho. folding genealogical tree, outlined in various cols. by hand, 12 text pp., top edges slightly nicked, mod. wraps., uncropped. (SG. Apr.5; 258) $150

LOPEZ, Joan Luys
– **Discurso Legal, Theologico-Practico en Defense de la Provision y Ordenanza de Govierno de XX de Febrero MDCLXXXIV.** Lima, 1685. *1st. Edn.* Fo. Mod. three-qtr. mor. (SG. Oct.20; 279) $150

LOPEZ, L.
– **Instructorii Conscientiae ...** Lyon, 1587-88. *1st. Edn.* 2 pts. in 2 vols. Cont. owners mark on titles, some light browning, cont. leath., blind-tooled decor., lge. gold-tooled decor. centre-pieces on upr. covers, lr. cover with blind-tooled decor. & roll stps., some defects., vol. 1 with lge. fault & jnt. torn, lacks clasps. (HT. May 8; 158) DM 550

LOPEZ CANCELADA, J.
– **Cartilla o sean Reglas Utiles para la Tropas Españolas que pasan a Mexico...** Cadiz, 1811. 12mo. Vell. (DS. Nov.25; 2414) Pts. 32,000

LOPEZ DE AYALA, I.
– **Historia de Gibraltar.** Madrid, 1782. Sm. 4to. Cont. vell. (HD. Mar.14; 37) Frs. 1,500

LOPEZ FERREIRO, Antonio
– **Galicia en el Ultimo Tercio del Siglo XV.** La Coruña, 1896-97. *2nd. Edn.* 2 vols. in 1. Cont. linen. (DS. Oct.28; 2248) Pts. 34,000

LORAIN, Paul
– **La Flore Decorative: Receuil de Plantes Dessinées d'après Nature.** Paris, ca. 1895. Fo. 48 hand-cold. plts., loose as iss., cl.-bkd. bds. (SG. Aug.25; 36) $130

LORD, Henry
– **Historie de la Religion des Banians; Histoire de la Religion des Anciens Persans.** Paris, 1667. 2 pts. in 1 vol. 12mo. Spotted, cont. russ. (S. Apr.10; 325) *Marshall.* £60

LORENZ, H.F.
– **Ornament.** St. Petersb., 1898. 4to. Cont. hf. mor. (CSK. Sep.30; 159) £60

LORENZ, K. (Ed.)
See— ROTE ERDE

LORENZ, OTTO
– **Catalogue Général de la Librairie Française.** Paris, 1867-1906. 17 vols. Cont. hf. red mor. (HD. Jan.27; 214) Frs. 1,600

LORING, Rosamond B.
– **Decorated Book Papers: Being an Account of their Designs & Fashions.** Camb., 1942. *(250) numbered.* Lge. tall 8vo. 8 sepia plts., 25 mntd. col. plt. samples, cl.-bkd. patterned bds. (SG. Sep.15; 210) $400

L'ORME, Philippe de
– **Architecture.** Paris, 1626. *4th. (1st. Compl.) Edn.* Fo. Numbering faulty, 2 sm. holes & margin tears, several ll. & double-p. plts., with sm. margin stains & tears, margins lightly browned, title with old owners mark, cut slightly close, mod. red cf. (H. May 22; 62) DM 2,800

– – **Anr. Edn.** Rouen, 1648. Fo. Hf.-title, thumbed, some stains & tears, mostly marginal, old pol. cf. gt., spine defect. (SG. Nov.3; 131) $325

– **L'Oeuvre.** Paris, 1894. Lge. fo. Facs., 1st. 2 pp. inverted, wraps. (DS. Dec.16; 2516) Pts. 30,000

LORRAIN, Jean
– **L'Aryenne.** 1907. *Orig. Edn. (25) on holland.* Ill. wrap. by Van Welie, unc. (HD. May 11; 42) Frs. 1,300

LORRIS, Guillaume de & Meung, Jean de
– **Le Romant de la Rose.** Ed.:– Jean Molinet. [Lyon, G. Balsarin, 1503]. Sm. fo. Lacks blank a4, red mor. gt., decor., mor. doubls., by Trautz-Bauzonnet. (HD. Nov.9; 10) Frs. 91,000

– – **Anr. Edn.** Notes:– Lantin de Damerey. Paris, 1735, Vol.IV: Dijon, 1737. 4 vols. 12mo. Cont. cf. gt., spines decor. (HD. Nov.9; 48) Frs. 1,100

– **The Romaunt of the Rose.** Trans.:– Geoffrey Chaucer. Ill.:– K. Henderson & N. Wilkinson. L., 1908. *(500) numbered.* 4to. Plt. guard slightly adhered to title-p., orig. cl.-bkd. bds., s.-c., unc. (S. Dec.20; 546) *Salinas.* £50

LORY, Gabriel
– [–] **Picturesque Tour through the Oberland.** L., 1823. Lge. 8vo. Engraved map, 17 hand-cold. aquatint views, slight offsetting from map onto title, cont. hf. mor. (S. May 21; 234) *Schumann.* £2,000

– – **Anr. Copy.** 1 cont. copper engraved map & 17 cold. aquatint plts., cont. hf. leath., unc. (R. Oct.13; 3273) DM 11,500

LOSACK, William
See— STEEL, David — LOSACK, William

LOSADA Y PRADA, J.A.
– **Nuevo Mapa ... Real Máscara ... que ofreció la Lealtad Amante de los Dependientes de las Reales Fabricas de Tabaco para celebrar la Real Jura ... [de] Fernando Vi.** Sevilla, 1748. 4to. Vell. (DS. Mar.23; 2164) Pts. 30,000

LOS ANGELES COUNTY
- **An Illustrated History of Los Angeles County** ...
Chic., 1889. *1st. Edn.* 4to. 8 photographic plts., 54
engraved port. plts., lacks plt. at p. 712 (never
present?), orig. mor., blind-stpd. & gt. (LH.
Apr.15; 339) $150

LOSKIEL, George Henry
- **Geschichte der Mission der Evangelischen Brüder
under den Indianern** ... Barby, 1789. *1st. Edn. 2nd.
Iss.* Mod. three-qtr. mor. (LH. Apr.15; 340) £110
- - **Anr. Edn.** Barby, 1789. *1st. Edn.* Foxed, old hf.
mor., defect. (SG. Jan.19; 192) $150
- - **Anr. Copy.** Cont. hf. leath., lightly bumped.
[Sabin 42109] (HK. Nov.8; 838) DM 650
- **History of the Mission of the United Brethren
among the Indians in North America.** L., 1794. *1st.
Edn. in Engl.* Cont. cf. gt., spine & corners slightly
worn; the Rt. Hon. Visc. Eccles copy. [Sabin 42110]
(CNY. Nov.18; 176) $130

LOSSING, Benson J.
- **The Life & Times of Philip Schuyler.** N.Y.,
[1872]-73. 2 vols. Orig. cl.; ex-liby., 2 A.L.s. by
Schuyler tipped into Vol. 1. (SG. Jan.19; 42) $275

LOSTALOT-BACHOUE, M.E. de
- **Le Monde, Histoire de tous les Peuples.** Paris,
1859. 10 vols. 4to. Linen. (G. Sep.15; 2252)
Sw. Frs. 850
- - **Anr. Copy.** Some slight foxing, orig. linen. (R.
Oct.13; 2817) DM 650

LOTHIAN, J.
- **New Edinburgh General Atlas.** Glasgow, n.d. Fo.
46 maps, hand-cold. in outl., hf. mor., soiled. (P.
Nov.24; 311) *Map House.* £90

LOTHROP, S.K. (Ed.)
See— BLISS, Robert Woods

LOTI, Pierre [i.e. Louis Marie Julien Viaud]
- **Au Maroc.** 1890. *Orig. Edn.* (25) on japan. Hf.
mor., corners, by Semet & Plumelle. (HD. May
11; 57) Frs. 1,200
- **Aziyadé...** Paris, 1879. *Orig. Edn.* 12mo. Jansenist
mor. by Huser, gt. doubls., silk end-ll., wraps. &
spine preserved, folder, s.-c. (HD. May 4; 340)
Frs. 7,200
- **Le Château de la Belle-au-bois-dormant.** Paris,
1910. *Orig. Edn.* (15) numbered on japan. 12mo.
Hf. mor., corners, unc., wrap. & spine, s.-c., spine
slightly faded; Claude Farrère copy, with author's
autograph dedication, 1910 (in name of Ch. Bar-
gone), Farrère's pencil margin annots. & A.L. (HD.
Mar.27; 87) Frs. 3,200
- **Les Desenchantées. Roman des Harems Turcs
Contemporains.** Paris, 1906. *Orig. Edn.* (25) num-
bered on japon impérial. 12mo. Lacks port., jan-
senist mor. by Affolter, unc., wrap. & spine; A.L.
by author. (HD. Mar.27; 86) Frs. 1,600
- - **Anr. Edn.** [1906]. *Orig. Edn.* (75) on holland.
No bdg. stated. (HD. May 11; 55) Frs. 1,100
- **La Mort de Philae.** Paris, 1908. *Orig. Edn.* (60)
numbered on holland. 12mo. Cont. mor., decor.,
gt. inner fillet, unc., wrap. & spine preserved, by
Stroobants. (HD. Feb.17; 95b) Frs. 2,200
- **Oeuvres Complètes.** Ill.:– Bourgoin & Leveille.
Paris, [1908-09]. 10 vols. Hf. mor., spines faded.
(HD. Jul.2; 80) Frs. 1,250
- **Pêcheur d'Islande.** Ill.:– E. Rudaux. Paris, 1893.
(650). (25) on japan, with triple suite of etchings,
separate suite of woodcuts & orig. watercol. Jansenist mor. by J. Bettenfeld, wtrd. silk doubls. &
end-ll., wrap. & spine. (HD. Jun.6; 100)
Frs. 2,100
- - **Anr. Edn.** Ill.:– E. Rudeaux, J. Huyot (wood
engrs.). Paris, 1893. (50) numbered on china. Separate printing of wood engrs., 3 states of etchings
including pure etching & state with remark, cont.
mor., decor., inner dentelle, wtrd. silk end-papers,
wrap. & spine preserved, by Champs. (HD. Feb.17;
95) Frs. 4,700
- **Un Pèlerin d'Angkor.** 1912. *Orig. Edn.* (100) on
holland. Hf. mor., corners, by Semet & Plumelle.
(HD. May 11; 59) Frs. 1,200
- - **Anr. Edn.** Ill.:– Paul Jouve. 1930. 4to. Red mor.
by Semet & Plumelle, lacquer-work by Dunand,
mor. liners, watered silk end-ll., wrap. preserved,
s.-c. (HD. Jun.13; 62) Frs. 190,000
- **La Troisième Jeunesse de Madame Prune.** Ill.:–

T. Foujita. Paris, 1926. (457) numbered. (325) on
velin d'Arches. 4to. 11 col.-ptd. plts., orig. wraps.,
unc., s.-c. worn. (S. Nov.21; 78) *Marks.* £400
- - **Anr. Edn.** Ill.:– Foujita. 1926. (458). 4to. 17
orig. cold. etchings, sewed, s.-c. (HD. Jun.29; 137)
Frs. 3,600

LOTICHIUS, Joannes Petrus
- **Rerum Germanicarum.** Frankfurt am Main, 1650.
Pt. 2 only (of 2). Fo. Engraved & ptd. titles, 55
engraved plts. (including folding views, double-p.
map & full-p. plts. showing port. subjects), a few
short tears, some repairs affecting engraved surface,
some browning or slight soiling, sm. liby. stp. on
both titles, cont. vell., soiled & worn, w.a.f. (S. May
21; 233) *Lawrence.* £1,000

LOTTER, Tobias Conrad
- **Atlas Geographicus Portatilis.** Ill.:– Tobias
Lobeck. N.p., 17th. C. 12mo. Engraved frontis., 29
maps, all double-p., cont. cold., leath. (DS. Dec.16;
2427) Pts. 22,000
- - **Anr. Edn.** Augsburg, ca. 1740. Copper-engraved
title cold., lacks 1st. map, soiled thro.-out, slightly
foxed, some pencil scribbling, 1 map with ink
scribble on verso, map with sm. tear, cont. leath.,
rubbed. (HK. Nov.8; 890) DM 1,100
- - **Anr. Edn.** [Augsburg, ca. 1760?]. 32mo. Double-p. pict. title, frontis., engraved table, 28 (of 29)
double-p. maps, fully cold., cont. cf., elab. gt.-stpd.
cover. (SG. Dec.15; 8) $325
- **Atlas Minor Praecipua Orbis Terrarum Imperia.**
Ill.:– M.G. Grophius after J.C. Weyerman, Augsburg, ca. 1750. Ob. 4to. 1st. 6 maps with sm.
wormholes, sm. bkd. margin tears, title partly
slightly spotted, cont. limp leath., light wear, 1 tie.
(HK. May 15; 662) DM 6,500

LOUANDRE, Charles
- **Les Arts Somptuaires: Histoire du Costume et
de l'Ameublement des Arts et Industries qui s'y
rattachent.** Ill.:– Ciappori, ptd. by Hangard-Mauge.
Paris, 1857-58. 2 text vols. bnd. in 1, 2 plt. vols.,
together 3 vols. Lge. 4to. 2 cold. frontis in text vols.,
322 chromolitho. plts., cl., some wear, 1 vol. disbnd.
(SG. Aug.25; 253) $120
- - **Anr. Edn.** 1858. 2 vols. 4to. 324 chromolithos.,
hf. chagrin, corners, ca. 1870. (HD. Apr.13; 95)
Frs. 1,400

LOUBAT, Joseph F.
- **The Medallic History of the United States of
America 1776-1876.** Ill.:– Jules Jacquemart. N.Y.,
1878. 2 vols. Bdg. not stated, edges nicked &
rubbed; sigd. by author, 1879. (RS. Jan.17; 474)
$200

LOUBIER, Hans
- [**Festschrift**] **Buch und Bucheinband.** Leipzig,
1923. (50) numbered & sigd. by artists. 4to. 3 orig.
engrs., 25 plts., orig. vell.-bkd. bds., a little rubbed;
H.M. Nixon coll., with his sig. & a few MS. notes.
(BBA. Oct.6; 85) *Maggs.* £130

LOUDON, Mrs. Jane Webb
- **British Wild Flowers.** L., 1846. *1st. Edn.* 4to.
60 hand-cold. litho. plts., cont. hf. mor., slightly
rubbed. (C. Mar.14; 185) *Parker.* £420
- - **Anr. Copy.** 4to. 60 hand-cold. litho. plts., no hf.-
title, some spotting, hf. mor. gt. (S. Nov.28; 55)
Quaritch. £320
- - **Anr. Copy.** 4to. 60 cold. litho. plts., some
staining, mostly slight, to 14 plts., cont. str.-grd. hf.
mor., spine gt. (LC. Oct.13; 199) £200
- - **Anr. Copy.** 4to. Lacks 1 hf. title(?), approx. 20
lithos. very spotted or browned, cont. hf. leath. gt.,
slightly spotted. (H. May 22; 201) DM 1,600
- - **Anr. Edn.** 1847. 4to. 60 cold. litho. plts., advt.
lf., hf.-title, orig. gt.-decor. cl., partly unopened.
(SKC. Jan.13; 2329) £420
- - **Anr. Edn.** L., 1849. 4to. 60 cold. litho. plts., 1
creased, slight margin soiling, 1 text lf. loose &
frayed, orig. cl., lacks spine, covers loose or detchd.
(S. Nov.28; 59) *Walford.* £250
- - **Anr. Edn.** Ca. 1849. *2nd. Edn.* 4to. 60 col. plts.,
cl., defect. (P. Jan.12; 195b) £260
- - **Anr. Edn.** 1859. *3rd. Edn.* 4to. 60 col. plts., orig.
cl., rebkd. (P. Oct.20; 82) £180
- **The Ladies' Flower-Garden of Ornamental
Annuals.** 1840. *1st. Edn.* 4to. Mor. gt. (P. Dec.8;
100) *Wilton.* £550

- - **Anr. Copy.** 4to. 48 hand-cold. litho. plts., hf.-
title, slight staining to 8 plts., cont. hf. str.-grd.
mor. gt. (LC. Oct.13; 198) £380
- - **Anr. Copy.** 4to. 48 hand-cold. litho. plts., few
plts. marginally foxed, old hf. leath., spine gt., worn,
endpapers loose. (SG. Apr.26; 131) $1,300
- - **Anr. Edn.** 1842. 4to. Orig. cl. gt., spine reprd.
(P. Dec.8; 106) *Heald.* £380
- **The Ladies' Flower Garden of Ornamental Bulbous
Plants.** 1841. *1st. Edn.* 4to. Mor. gt. (P. Dec.8; 99)
Map House. £620
- - **Anr. Edn.** L., 1841. 4to. 51 (of 58) plts. & 9
supp. plts., cont. hf. leath., lacks spine. (R. Apr.4;
1754) DM 2,800
- **The Ladies' Flower Garden of Ornamental Peren-
nials.** 1843. *1st. Edn.* 2 vols. 4to. 96 hand-cold.
plts., cont. hf. mor. gt. (PD. Oct.19; 105) £520
- - **Anr. Edn.** 1843-44. *1st. Edn.* 2 vols. 4to. 85 (of
96) hand-cold. plts., 1 with outer margin trimmed,
some loose, orig. cl., worn, as a coll. of plts., w.a.f.
(P. Oct.20; 17) £620
- - **Anr. Copy.** 2 vols. 4to. 95 (of 96) hand-cold.
litho. plts., few plts. minimally foxed, orig. hf.
leath., richly gt., rubbed, extremities worn. (SG.
Mar.22; 195) $1,600
- - **Anr. Copy.** 2 vols. 4to. Vol. 1 lacks plt. 24,
1st. & last ll. & some plts. in both vols. misbnd.,
Vol. 1 last text lf. & lr. cover loose, cont. hf. leath.,
Vol. 2 spine & upr. cover loose, lr. cover nearly
loose, bumped & worn. (HK. Nov.8; 641)
DM 4,800
[–] **The Mummy, a Tale.** 1827. *1st. Edn.* 3 vols. Hf.
cf., jnts. reprd. (P. Jan.12; 142) *Jarndyce.* £310

LOUDON, John Claudius
- **Arboretum et Fruticetum Britannicum.** 1835-38.
1st. Edn. 8 vols., including 4 plts. vols. Orig.
embossed cl., unc. & unopened; from liby. of Lut-
trellstown Castle, w.a.f. (C. Sep.28; 1777) £240
- **An Encyclopaedia of Cottage, Farm & Villa
Architecture & Furniture.** 1833. Some light soiling,
cont. bds., rebkd. (CSK. Apr.27; 165) £80
- **Observations on the Formation & Management
of Useful & Ornamental Plantations.** Edinb., 1804.
Advt. lf., 10 plts., slight offsetting, cont., spine worn.
(S. Apr.10; 546) *Primrose.* £90
- **A Treatise on Forming, Improving, & Managing
Country Residences.** L., 1806. 2 vols. 4to. 32
engraved plts., 1 with overslip, some spotting, cont.
cf., lacks head of spines. (S. Oct.4; 273)
Scrimgour. £190

LOUIS XV, King of France
- **Le Sacre de Louis XV, Roy de France et de
Navarre.** Ill.:– d'Ulin, Audran, Beauvais Cochin
père, & others. [Paris, 1723]. Fo. Engraved title,
engraved double-p. table, 8 lge. vigs., 9 double-p.
plts., 30 costume plts., light margin dampstain
towards end, 1 plt. & 1 lf. slightly browned, traces
of foxing, cont. mott. cf., gt. spine, spine extremities
chipped. (C. Dec.9; 95) *Meister.* £700

LOUTHERBOURG, Philippe Jacques de
- **The Romantic & Picturesque Scenery of England & Wales.** L., 1805. *1st. Iss.* Fo. 18 hand-cold.
aquatint views, titles & text in Engl. & Fr., cont.
hf. roan. (C. Nov.16; 126) *Wolff.* £800

LOUVET DE COUVRAY, Jean-Baptiste
- **Les Amours du Chevalier de Faublas.** Ill.:– Colin.
1825. 4 vols. Engrs. lightly foxed, Engl. cf. by
Hatchard & Son, spine decor. (HD. Jul.6; 115)
Frs. 1,800

LOUYS, Pierre
- **Aphrodite.** Ill.:– Clara Tice. N.P., priv. ptd., 1926.
(650). (110) numbered, hand-cold. Lge. 8vo. 10
etchings, three-qtr. lev., cover gt. with female nude
by Tice, spine gt. with emblematic devices. (SG.
Feb.16; 187) $200
- - **Anr. Edn.** Ill.:– Pierre Rousseau. Paris, 1929.
(970) numbered on papier de Rives. Hf. lev., decor.
inlaid spine, orig. cold. wraps. bnd. in. (SG. Feb.16;
77) $150
- - **Anr. Edn.** Ill.:– Andre Morty. Paris, 1936. Sm.
4to. Leaves, wrap. & s.-c. (HD. Dec.9; 43)
Frs. 1,200
- **Aphrodite. Moeurs Antiques.** Ill.:– after Antoine
Calbet. Paris, [1923]. (500) numbered on vell. Lge.
4to. L.P., burgundy hf. mor., leath. corners, gt. &
3 col. inlay decor., orig. wraps. bnd. in, s.-c., sigd.

by G. Mercier, 1923. (D. Nov.24; 2967)
DM 1,500
– – **Anr. Edn.** Ill.:– Edouard Chimot. Paris, 1929. *(16) on Japon blanc supernacré, with orig. copperplt.* Lge. 4to. 1 plt. in 14 states, including orig. drawings, separate vol. of 5 plts. in 5 states, 15 plts. in main vol. in 5 states & 1 in 4 states, red mor. by Durvand, 1929, elab. inlaid doubls., inlaid decor., watered silk liners, red hf. mor. wrap-around, s.-c., folder with copperplate & separate plt. vol. bnd. in unif. red hf. mor.; pres. copy from artist to Daniel Sickles. (SPB. Dec.14; 48) $3,500
– **Archipel.** Paris, 1906. *(50) on holland.* Hf. chagrin, corners, spine decor., wrap. & spine preserved. (HD. Jun.13; 63)   Frs. 1,000
– **Les Aventures du Roi Pausole.** Ill.:– J. Touchet. Paris, [1939]. *(160) on holland with suite.* Hf. mor., corners, by Aussourd, mosaic spine, wrap. & spine. (HD. Jun.6; 101)   Frs. 1,500
– **Les Chansons de Bilitis.** Ill.:– Sylvain Sauvage. Paris, [1927]. *(12) reserved for 'collaborators'.* 4to. Mor. by Jean Lambert, elab. mor. doubls., decor. inlay in gt. border; this copy for Sauvage, with orig. sigd. drawing for ill. on p.95. (SPB. Dec.14; 80)
$1,800
– – **Anr. Edn.** Ill.:– P.E. Becat. Paris, [1938]. 4to. Artists copy with artists dedication, loose ll. in orig. pict. wraps., foxed, cont. hf. vell. portfo., hf. vell. s.-c. (HT. May 10; 2418)   DM 440
– – **Anr. Edn.** Ill.:– M. Lydis. Paris, [1948]. *(365) numbered.* Lge. 4to. Loose ll. in orig. wraps., orig. bd. portfo. & s.-c. (HK. Nov.11; 3758)   DM 600
– **Contes Antiques.** Ill.:– Sylvain Sauvage. Paris, 1929. *(237).* 4to. Light offsetting of a few plts., elab. mor. gt. by Jean Lambert, wrap-around design at head & tail of gt. & blind slanted lines in double fillet border gt.-decor. & inlaid strip on either side of slanted design, cf. doubls., light rubbing on a few spots. (SPB. Dec.14; 81) $1,200
– **La Femme et le Pantin. Roman Espagnol.** Paris, 1898. *(10) on Whatman.* Sewed, recovered hf. mor. folder by Mercier, s.-c.; Georges Louys copy, cold. pencil dedication, A.L.s. dtd. 10 Feb. 1895. (HD. Jun.13; 65)   Frs. 16,000
– – **Anr. Edn.** Ill.:– E. Chimot. Paris, 1928. *(211). (125) on vélin d'Arches with definitive col. state of etchings.* 4to. Leaves, folder & s.-c. (*With:*) – **Les Poésies de Méléagre.** Paris, [1926]. 4to. This copy not for sale, on vell., 2 states of engrs., leaves, box, sigd. by artist. (HD. May 4; 343)   Frs. 2,800
– **Oeuvres Complétes.** Ill.:– Calbet. Paris, 1929-30. 13 vols. Hf. chagrin, corners, wraps. preserved. (HD. Nov.17; 145)   Frs. 1,600
– **Les Poésies de Méléagre.** Ill.:– Edouard Chimot. Editions d'Art Devamblez, 1926. *(230) numbered. (50) on japon imperial, with plts. in 3 states.* 4to. Black mor., tan mor. onlays between gt. & blind tooling, extending foot of spine & covers in chevron form, tan mor. doubls., s.-c., by V. Ollivier, s.-c. brkn.; with extra state of frontis. & crayon drawing sigd. by artist. (S. Nov.21; 62)
Marks. £380
– **Pybrac; Quatrains.** Ill.:– Marcel Vertès. Narbonne, ca. 1928. 4to. On vell. du Marais, leaves, wrap., s.-c. (HD. Dec.9; 56)   Frs. 1,300
– **Sanguines.** Ill.:– Lobel-Riche. [1945]. *(300).* 4to. Suite with remarks & orig. sketch, leaves, box. (HD. Mar.21; 224)   Frs. 1,050

LOVAT, Simon, Lord
– **The Whole Proceedings in the House of Peers upon the Impeachment...against Simon Lord Lovat, for High Treason.** 1747. Fo. 1st. licence lf., few ll. slightly soiled, cont. hf. cf., unc., worn; bkplt. of Earl of Portland. (BBA. Oct.27; 26)
Melbourne. £55

LOVE, G.T.
[–] **A Five Years' Residence Buenos Ayres.** L., 1825 [i.e. 1826?]. *1st. Edn.* Title cropped, old qtr. sheep, shabby & brkn. (SG. Oct.20; 205) $150

LOVE, John
See— FITTLER, James & Love, John

LOVECRAFT, Howard Phillips
– **Beyond the Wall of Sleep.** Ed.:– August Derleth & Donald Wandrei. Sauk City, 1943. *1st. Edn. (1200).* Bdg. not stated, ink inscr. on front free end-paper,

---

d.-w. chipped, rubbed, darkened at edges, vol. spine & edges faded. (CBA. Oct.29; 521) $225
– **The Shadow over Innsmouth.** Everett [Pa.], 1936. *1st. Edn. Ca. (400).* Publisher's announcement laid in loose, bdg. not stated, covers lightly rubbed, extremities mildly bumped. (CBA. Oct.29; 523)
$700
– **The Shunned House.** Athol [Mass.], 1928. *1st. Edn.* Unbnd. sigs., 59 pp., darkening; 1941 letter from Everett F. Bleiler to R.H. Barlow, apparently never received, typewritten publishing history laid on over copyright statement with some mild staining from glue. (CBA. Oct.29; 524) $1,700

LOVELESS, George
– **The Victims of Whiggery; A Statement of the Persecutions experienced by the Dorchester Labourers...Also, a Description of Van Diemen's Land...** Ca. 1838. *8th. Edn.* Mod. hf. roan. (KH. May 1; 436)   Aus. $220

LOVELL, Robert
– **Panbotanologia, sive Enchiridon Botanicum, or a Compleat Herball.** Oxford, 1659. *1st. Edn.* Sm. 8vo. Cont. cf., rebkd. [Wing L 3243] (C. Nov.9; 94)
Quaritch. £170

LOVER, S.
– **Legends & Stories of Ireland.** L., 1834. 2nd. Series: 3 vols. 12 mo. Hf. mor., rubbed, spine with armorial motif. (GM. Dec.7; 367)   £60

LOVETT, Richard
– **The English Bible in the John Rylands Library.** L., priv. ptd., 1899. Fo. Cont. mor., little worn. (BBA. Apr.5; 297)   *Hartley.* £140

LOVING MAD TOM, Bedlamite Verses of the XVI & XVII Centuries
Ed.:– Jack Lindsay. Ill.:– Norman Lindsay. Fanfrolico Pr., 1927. *(375) numbered.* 4to. Orig. parch.-bkd. bds., slightly soiled. (S. Dec.20; 552)
Blackwells. £60
– – **Anr. Copy.** 4to. Bds., qtr. imitation vell., a little mild soiling. (KH. Nov.9; 636)   Aus. $210
– – **Anr. Copy.** Bdg. not stated; long inscr. by ed., Harry F. Chaplin copy. (JL. Jul.15; 251)
Aus. $180

LOW, A.M.
See— HAUGUM, J. & Low, A.M.

LOW, Charles Rathbone
– **Her Majesty's Navy.** L., [1890-93]. 3 vols. in 6. 4to. 3 cold. titles, 43 cold. plts., cl. (P. May 17; 92)
Erlini. £160
– – **Anr. Edn.** Ill.:– W. Christian Symons & W. Fred. Mitchell. L., 1890's. 3 vols. 4to. 46 col. lithos., lacks many tissue-guards, hf. mor. gt., worn. (SG. Sep.22; 193) $250
– **History of the Indian Navy.** 1877. 2 vols. Orig. cl. (SKC. Nov.18; 1936)   £90

LOW, David
– **The Breeds of the Domestic Animals of the British Islands.** Ill.:– W. Nicholson after W. Shiels. L., 1842. 2 vols. Fo. 56 hand-finished cold. litho. plts., cont. str.-grd. mor., covers with gt. & blind-tooled borders enclosing gt.-stpd. arms with cold. onlays, rebkd. preserving orig. gt. spines. (C. Jun.27; 171)
Parkway. £4,000
– – **Anr. Copy.** 2 vols. in 1. Fo. Hf. mor., marb. bds.; with bookplt. of John Waldie & his inscr. on front blank fly-lf. (BS. May 2; 6)   £3,800

LOW, Hugh
– **Sarawak; Its Inhabitants & Productions: Being Notes during a Residence in that Country with H.H. the Rajah Brooke.** 1848. Orig. cl., spine faded. (TA. Nov.17; 17)   £90

LOWE, Edward Joseph
– **Ferns, British & Exotic.** L., 1856-60. 8 vols. Cold. plts., hf. cf. gt. (P. May 17; 36)   *Georges.* £120
– – **Anr. Edn.** 1861-64. 8 vols. Tall 8vo. Orig. blind-stpd. cl., faded on spines, some a little worn at top & bottom. (TA. Mar.15; 254)   £80
[–] **Les Plantes à Feuillage Coloré.** Intro.:– Charles Naudin. Paris, 1867-70. *2nd. Edn.* 2 vols. Sm. 4to. 120 chromolitho. plts., unif. cont. mor.-bkd. cl., soiled. (SG. Oct.6; 238) $450

LOWE, Edward Joseph & Howard, W.
– **Beautiful Leaved Plants.** 1872. 60 col. plts., orig. cl. gt. (P. Jul.5; 114)   £60
– – **Anr. Copy.** 60 cold. plts. (*With:*) – **Coloured Foliage Plants** [spine title]. L., 1872. 55 cold. plts., no. title-p. Together 2 vols. Three-qtr. mor. (CBA. Dec.10; 347) $160

LOWELL, James Russell
[–] **Class Poem.** Camb., Mass., 1838. *1st. Edn.* Cont. inscr., orig. ptd. wraps, piece chipped from upr. cover, hf. mor. s.-c.; Frederic Dannay copy. (CNY. Dec.16; 219) $200
– **The Courtin'.** Ill.:– Winslow Homer. Boston, 1874. 4to. 8 plts., gt.-pict. cl., soiled. (SG. Apr.19; 301) $110

LOWELL, Robert
– **The Voyage & other Versions of Poems by Baudelaire.** Ill.:– Sidney Nolan. 1968. *(200) numbered & sigd. by author & artist.* 4to. Orig. cl., s.-c. (BBA. Jan.19; 304)   *Primrose Hill Books.* £55

LOWER CANADA
– **Reports of the Commissioners Appointed to Inquire into the Grievances Complained of in Lower Canada.** L., 1837. Fo. Folding hand-cold. map, cont. hf. cf., slightly rubbed. [Sabin 10582] (S. May 22; 328)   *Quaritch.* £280

LOWNDES, William Thomas
– **The Bibliographer's Manual of English Literature.** L., 1857-64. *New Edn.* 11 vols. 12mo. Orig. cl., numbers hand-lettered on spine, worn,. (RO. Mar.28; 118)   £110
– – **Anr. Edn.** L., 1858-65. *Revised Edn.* 11 vols. Light soiling & darkening, orig. ptd. cl., covers slightly rubbed, some bumping & soiling. (CBA. Nov.19; 625)   £110
– – **Anr. Edn.** Ed.:– H.G. Bohn. L., [1864]. *New Edn.* 4 vols. Sm. 8vo. Orig. hf. mor. (SG. Aug.4; 187) $100
– – **Anr. Edn.** Appendix:– H.G. Bohn. L., 1883-85. *New Edn.* 6 vols. in 4. Tall 12mo. Mod. hf. mor. gt. (SG. Sep.15; 212) $160
– – **Anr. Edn.** Ed.:– H.G. Bohn. 1900. 6 vols., including Appendix. Cl. gt. (P. Jul.5; 293)   £110

LOWTH, George T.
– **The Wanderer in Arabia.** L., 1855. *1st. Edn.* 2 vols. 22 ll. of advts., title & plts. spotted, orig. cl., slightly soiled & rubbed; inscr. 'to Mr Wyld'. (S. Jun.25; 16)   *Maggs.* £100

LOWTHORP, John & others
– **The Philosophical Transactions.** 1749-56. 10 vols. in ll. 4to. 315 engraved plts. & maps (?) only, some browning, cont. cf., rubbed, spine labels detchd. or lacking, w.a.f. (CSK. Apr.27; 138)   £180

LOYSEAU
– **Ses Oeuvres.** Paris, 1640. *New Edn.* Fo. Cf., spine renewed. (HD. Feb.22; 123)   Frs. 1,800

LOYSEL, J.B.
– **Versuch einer Ausführlichea Anleitung zur Glasmacherkunst.** Frankfurt, 1802. 1 text lf. with sm. hole & slight loss, minimal spotting, cont. bds., worn. corners bumped. (HK. May 15; 404)
DM 1,000
– – **Anr. Edn.** Frankfurt, 1802-18. 2 vols. 4to. Some slight foxing, cont. bds., slightly bumped. (R. Oct.12; 1749)   DM 2,500

LOZANO, Pedro
[–] **A True & Particular Relation of the Dreadful Earthquake...at Lima.** L., 1748. *1st. Edn. in Engl.* Title-p. browned, antique cf. (SG. Jan.19; 301)
$175

LUARD, John
[–] **Views in India, Saint Helena & Car Nicobar.** L., [1833]. Fo. 26 (of 60) litho. plts. on india paper, lacks title & prelims., some marginal spotting or staining, few plts. loose, cont. cl., defect. (S. Apr.9; 40)   *Hosains.* £55
– – **Anr. Edn.** [1835]. Fo. Litho. title, 60 mntd. litho. plts. on India paper, foxing to surrounds of some plts., hf. mor. gt., slightly rubbed. (LC. Jul.5; 208)   £230
– – **Anr. Edn.** L., [1838]. 4to. Litho. title, 60 litho. plts., all on India paper, some spotting in margins,

LUARD, John -*Contd.*

cont. hf. mor., spine defect. (C. Nov.16; 127)
Shapero. £140

LUBBOCK, Basil
- **Adventures by Sea from Art of Old Time.** 1926.
(1750) numbered. Lge. 4to. Plts., some mntd. &
cold., orig. cl., d.-w. (CSK. Jul.13; 174) £50
- **Barlow's Journal of his Life at Sea in King's Ships,
East & West Indiamen & Other Merchant Men
from 1659 to 1703.** 1934. *(100) numbered & sigd.*
2 vols. Tall 8vo. Orig. qtr. cf. gt., partly untrimmed,
pict. end-papers. (TA. May 17; 61) £105
- **The Colonial Clippers.** L., 1955. *(With:)* - **The
Last of the Windjammers.** L., 1963. 2 vols. Together
3 vols., no bdgs. stated. (JL. Jun.24; 232)
Aus. $150
- **The Nitrate Clippers. — The Opium Clippers.**
1932; 1933. *1st. Edns.* Together 2 vols. 4to. Orig.
cl. gt., both rubbed on spinec. (TA. Mar.15; 303)
£50

LUBBOCK, B.
See— SPURLING, J. & Lubbock, B.

LUBKE, W.
- **Die Mittelalterliche Kunst in Westfalen.** Ill.:-
Laeillot. Leipzig, [1853]. Plt. vol. only. Ob. fo. 30
litho. plts. on 29 sheets, some plts. slightly bumped,
some old spotting loose in paper portfo. (V. Sep.29;
143) DM 600

LUCAE, Friedrick
- **Des. Heel Römischen Reichs uhr alter Fürsten-
Saal.** Frankfurt, 1705. 4to. Cont. hf. vell. (R. Apr.3;
1066) DM 480

LUCANAS, Marcus Annaeus
- **Pharsalia.** Venice, Aldine Pr., Apr. 1502. *1st.
Aldine Edn.* Slight marginal browning, some
worming, 19th. C. cf. gt., worn. (SG. Apr.19; 8)
$150
- - **Anr. Edn.** [Venice, Apr. 1502]. Marginalia, qtr.
cf., vell. tips. (SG. Oct.27; 5) $250
- - **Anr. Edn.** Venezia, 1515. Last p. stained, some
cont. margin notes, cont. pig, slightly bumped. (SI.
Dec.15; 21) Lire 500,000
- - **Anr. Edn.** Trans.:- Nicholas Rowe. L., 1718.
1st. Edn. of this trans. Fo. Folding map & frontis.,
errata, lf. 5X browned, some browning, cont. panel.
cf., rebkd.; Richard Brinsley Sheridan's bkplt. &
sig. (SPB. May 16; 135) $400
- - **Anr. Edn.** Ed.:- Hugo Grotius & Richard
Bentley. Strawberry Hill, Strawberry Hill Pr.,
1760. *(500).* 4to. Some foxing, lacks lst. & last
blanks, mor. gt. by Lewis; Herbert Norman Evans-
Sir William Vernon Guise-Thomas B. Stevenson
copy. (CNY. Dec.17; 606) $350
- - **Anr. Edn.** Ed.:- Richard Bentley & Hugo Grotius. L., Straw. Hill Pr., 1760. 4to. 1st. Iss. of
prelims., cont. cf.-bkd. marb. bds.; pres. copy from
Bentley to Bendall Martyn, bkplt. of P. Littlehales.
(SPB. May 16; 149) $300
- - **Anr. Copy.** 4to. Red mor. gt. (LH. Sep.25; 446)
$275

LUCAS
- **Deleyte de Cavalleros y placer de los Cavallos.**
Madrid, ca. 1736. Fo. Title remntd. & doubld.,
some foxing, mod. vell. (HD. Mar.14; 61)
Frs. 1,300

LUCAS, Edward Verrall
- **Playtime & Company: a Book for Children.** Ill.:-
E.H. Shepard. L., [1925]. *(100) numbered on
H.M.P., sigd. by author & artist.* 4to. Buckram-
bkd. bds., d.-w., unc. (SG. Dec.8; 225) $110

LUCAS, Edward Verrall
See— BENSON, Arthur Christopher & others

LUCAS, Frank Laurence
- **Gilgamesh, King of Erech.** Ill.:- Dorothea Braby.
Gold. Cock. Pr., 1948. *(60) numbered & sigd.,
specially bnd.* Orig. hf. mor.; from D. Bolton liby.
(BBA. Oct.27; 141) *Duschnes.* £110

LUCAS, Frederic W.
- **The Annals of the Voyages of the Brothers
Nicolo & Antonio Zeno in the North Atlantic... &
the Claim ... to a Venetian Discovery of America:
A Criticism & an Indictment.** L., 1898. *1st. Edn.*

Sm. Fo. Approx. 10 ll. misbnd., cl., orig. lr. wrap.
bnd. in, upr. wrap. laid down on cover, slightly
shaken. (SG. Jan.19; 212) $130

LUCAS, Paul
- **Voyage fait en 1714...par Ordre de Louis XIV
dans la Turquie, l'Asie, Sourie, Palestine, Haute et
Basse Egypte....** Rouen, 1724. 3 vols. 12mo. Lge.
folding map, 30 plts., cont. cf., spines decor. (HD.
Mar.19; 69) Frs. 2,000

LUCAS, Pierre Hippolyte
- **Histoire Naturelle des Lepidoptères Exotiques.**
Ill.:- Pauquet. Paris, 1835-[36]. *1st. Edn.* Lge. 8vo.
Ptd. & hand-cold. engraved title-pp., hf.-title, 80
hand-cold. litho. plts., tissue guards, text foxed,
cont. gt.-decor. qtr. cf., marb. bds., unc. (SG.
Apr.26; 132) $900

LUCAS, Richard
- **Practical Christianity.** 1693. *4th. Edn.* Cont. gt.-
decor. red crushed mor., rubbed. (TA. Dec.15; 445)
£50

LUCAS, S.E.
- **Catalogue of Sassoon Chinese Ivories.** 1950. *(250)
numbered sigd. by Sir Victor Sassoon & S.E.
Lucas.* 3 vols. Fo. Hf. vell., s.-c.'s. (BS. May 2; 112)
£360

LUCAS, W.J.
- **British Dragon-Flies.** L., 1900. 27 col. plts., orig.
pict. cl. (SKC. Oct.26; 402) £50

LUCCIANA
See— DE CARAFFA & LUCCIANA

LUCIAN, of Samosata
- **I Dialoghi Piacevoli.** Venice, 1551. Some margin
worming & repairs, few dampstains, mostly marginal, old vell., loose. (SG. Oct.27; 203) $140
- **Dialogues.** Ill.:- Henri Laurens. Paris, 1951. *(275)
numbered & sigd. by artist.* Fo. Unsewn as iss. in
orig. pict. wraps., folder & s.-c. (S. Nov.21; 84)
Rota. £550
- **Die Hetaerengespräche.** Ill.:- Fr. Blei. Leipzig,
1907. *(50) De Luxe Edn. on Japan.* Sm. fo. Hand-
bnd. orig. linen, marb. end-papers & doubls.; Hauswedell coll. (H. May 24; 650) DM 5,600
- - **Anr. Edn.** Ill.:- Franz Blei. Leipzig, 1907. *(450)
numbered.* Fo. Orig. linen. (HT. May 10; 2411)
DM 1,600
- - **Anr. Edn.** Ill.:- Hansen-Bahia. Hamburg, 1971.
(50) De Luxe Edn. Lge. fo. All ll. sigd. by artist,
loose ll. in orig. linen portfo.; Hausewedell coll. (H.
May 24; 622) DM 1,050
- **Mimes des Courtisanes.** Trans.:- Pierre Louys.
Ill.:- Maurice Potin after Edgar Degas. Paris, 1935.
4to. 4 key plts., 22 engraved plts., unc., unsewn,
orig. wraps. (S. Nov.21; 17) *Rota.* £330
- - **Anr. Copy.** Fo. Chagrin. (DS. Feb.24; 2187)
Pts. 120,000
- **[Oeuvres].** Trans.:- N. Perrot. Amst., 1709. 2 vols.
Sm. 8vo. Str.-grd. mor. by Thouvenin, blind- &
gt.-decor. (HD. May 3; 93) Frs. 2,600
- **Sämtliche Werke.** Ed.:- H. Floerke. Trans.:-
C.M. Wieland. 1911. *(150) Privilege Edn. on Dutch
Bütten.* 5 vols. Orig. red mor. gt., unc. (R. Oct.11;
350) DM 1,200
- **Scènes des Courtisanes.** Ill.:- R. Ranft. 1901. On
vell., hf. mor., corners, by Maylander, wrap. (HD.
Jan.24; 73) Frs. 1,200
- **Scènes de la Vie des Courtisanes.** Ill.:- Pierre
Louys. Paris, 1894. *Orig. Edn. (10) numbered on
japan.* Square 16mo. Mor. gt. by Creuzevault,
wrap. & spine preserved. (HD. Apr.26; 178)
Frs. 1,400
- **True History.** Trans.:- Francis Hickes. Ill.:- Wil-
liam Strang, J.B. Clark, & Aubrey Beardsley. L.,
Priv. Ptd., 1894. *(54) numbered.* Linen. (LH.
Sep.25; 323) $180
- - **Anr. Edn.** Ill.:- Robert Gibbings. Waltham St.
Lawrence, [Gold. Cock. Pr.], 1927. *(275).* Fo. Mor.-
bkd. cl., publisher's box. (SPB. Dec.13; 829) $250
- **The Works** .... Ed.:- Thomas Francklin. L., 1781.
4 vols. Royal 8vo. Hf.-titles, cont. tree cf., gt.-tooled
borders. (GM. Dec.7; 698) £65

LUCIDAIRE (Le)
Lyon, 22 May 1501. 4to. Lacks title, mor. by
Missol. (HD. Jun.29; 138) Frs. 3,500

LUCRETIUS CARUS, Titus
- **De la Nature des Choses.** Trans.:- Lagrange. Ill.:-
Gravelot. Paris, 1768. *1st. Printing of ills.* 2 vols.
Lge. 8vo. On holland, parallel Latin text, cont. tree
cf. gt., spines decor. (HD. May 3; 94) Frs. 1,100
- - **Anr. Edn.** Trans.:- La Grange. Ill.:- Monnet.
Paris, An III [1795]. 2 vols. L.P., figures before the
letter, cont. tree cf. gt., spines decor., some slight
defects. (HD. May 3; 95) Frs. 1,800
- **Della Natura delle Cose Libri Sei.** Trans.:- Ales-
sandro Marchetti. Amst., Priv. ptd., 1754. 2 vols.
Some slight stains, cont. Fr. red mor., recent decor.,
slightly loose. (SI. Dec.15; 79) Lire 550,000
- **De Rerum Natura.** 1832. Lge. 4to. Cont. gt.-
tooled red mor., lightly rubbed, double fore-e. pntg.
(CSK. Jul.27; 32) £280
- **De Rerum Natura Libri Sex.** Bg'ham., 1772. 4to.
Bkplt., later fly-ll., cont. gt.-decor. tree cf., inner
gt. dentelles. (CBA. Dec.10; 31) $100
- - **Anr. Edn.** Ed.:- H.A.J. Munro. L., 1900-03. 3
vols. Maroon mor., college arms in gt. on upr.
covers; each vol. with label in upr. cover presenting
set to I.J. Cash as 1st. prize in Senior Class of Latin
at University College, L., each label sigd. by A.E.
Housman, Prof. (SG. Mar.15; 124) $250

LUDECUS, M.
- **Historia von der Erfindung, Wunderwercken vnd
Zerstörung des Vermeinten Heiligen Bluts zur
Wilssnagk...** Wittenburg, 1586. 4to. Slightly
browned & some light staining, incunable paper-
covered bds. (HK. Nov.8; 257) DM 700

LUDEMANN, W. von (Text)
See— FROMMEL, C.

LUDERT, T.
- **Fünf Jahre in Transvaal, 1895-1900.** Hamburg,
1901. Map in pocket at end, decor. cl., part of upr.
cover faded. (V. Oct.28; 503) R 200

LUDEWIG, J.H.
- **Francfort sur le Mein et ses Environs.** Trans.:-
J.L. Trenel. Frankfurt, ca. 1845. Orig. bds, spine
reprd. in hf. linen. (R. Oct.12, 2563) DM 950
- **Frankfurt am Main und Seine Umgebung.** Frankfurt, 1843. *2nd. Edn.* Lacks 1 steel engraved plt.,
slightly browned, stain in upr. margin near end,
orig. bds., spine renewed. (R. Oct.12; 2562)
DM 720

LUDEWIG, Johann Peter
- **Scriptores Rerum Episcopatus Bambergensis [et
Germanicarum].** Frankfurt & Leipzig, 1718. 2 pts.
in 1 vol. Fo. Badly paginated, some browning, hf.
leath., ca. 1880, rubbed & bumped. (HK. Nov.9;
1384) DM 800

LUDLOW, William
- **Report of a Reconnaissance of the Black Hills of
Dakota, made in the Summer of 1874.** Wash., 1875.
1st. Printing. Lge. 4to. 1 folding map partly hand-
cold., pencil nos. at front blank, maps with some
foxing, orig. cl., covers lightly spotted, sm. chips at
spine tips, ex-liby.; 1 text sentence crossed out by
author & his ptd. note pasted at bottom of p. (HA.
Nov.18; 124) $105

LUDOLFF, Hiob
[-] **Allgemaine Schau-Buhne der Welt; oder Beschre-
ibung der Vornhemsten Welt-Geschichte.** Ill.:-
Romeyn De Hooghe. Frankfurt, 1699. Fo. 1
engraved frontis. & 3 ll. of plts. only, 1 holed with
very slight loss. 1 cleanly torn, hf.-title & title
reprd., prelims. wormed, vell., soiled, w.a.f. (CSK.
Dec.16; 74) £120
- - **Anr. Copy.** 2 pts. in 1 vol.: Vol. I (of 5). Fo.
Lacks hf.-title, title slightly short, last ll. & lr. cover
dampstained, cont. vell. (VG. Mar.19; 183)
Fls. 950
- - **Anr. Edn.** Frankfurt, 1701-18. *1st. Edn. (pts.
II-IV), 2nd. Edn. (pt. 1).* Pts. I-IV (of V) in 2 vols.
Fo. 3 (of 4) engraved titles, browned thro.-out,
slightly stronger in parts, cont. bds., spotted & with
light defects. (HT. May 10; 2532) DM 1,700
- **Historia Aethiopica.** Frankfurt, 1681. *(Bound
with:)* - **Iobi Ludolfi ... Ad suam Historiam Aethiop-
icam ... Commentarius.** Frankfurt, 1691. Together
2 works in 1 vol. Fo. Some ll. browned or soiled,
some tears in 1st. title-p. with minor loss, early vell.,
soiled, torn at head of spines. (SG. Feb.2; 46) $250

- A New History of Ethiopia. L., 1682. *1st. Engl. Edn.* Sm. fo. Some spotting in margins of text, cont. cf. (P. Oct.20; 244) £200

LUDOLPHUS DE SAXONIA
- Compendium Orationum, nuper Reformatum & Auctum. Venetiis, 1559. Early inscr. on title, few ll. browned, later velvet, gold end-papers decor. in pink, becoming loose, 1 hinge crudely reprd. (BBA. Jun.28; 150) *P.J. King.* £60
- Dit es d'Leve ons Liefs heren Jhesu Christi .... Antw., 27 Apr. 1521. 4to. (in 6's). Woodcuts fully cold. by early owner, lacks 2 ll. in sig. z, 1st. & last few ll. soiled, 1 index lf. reprd. at blank margin, old blind-tooled cf. over wood bds., metal clasps defect. (SG. Nov.3; 132) $3,200
- Vita Christi. Cologne, Nicolaus Götz, 30 Apr. 1474. Lacks pt. 1. Fo. Rubricated in red & blue, initials painted in red & blue, 4 cont. MS. table ll. at end, cont. stpd. cf. over wood bds., richly decor., scratched & reprd., spine renewed, traces of clasps; from Fondation Furstenberg-Beaumesnil. [HC 10291; BMC I, 238; Goff L338] (HD. Nov.16; 21) Frs. 6,500
- - **Anr. Edn.** Venice, Simon Bevilaqua (for Paganino de Paganinis?), 7 Dec. 1498. Sm. 4to. Red ink rubric, some painted initials, lacks last lf., 1 lf. with margin tear, 1 lf. partly remargined, 16th. C. pig over wood bds., blind decor., clasps. [Goff L-349] (HD. Jan.30; 16) Frs. 7,800

LUDWIG, Christianus Gottlieb
- Terrae Musei Regii Dresdensis ... accedunt Terrarum Sigillatarum Figurae. Lipsia, 1749. Fo. Lightly browned, cont. hf. cf., decor. spine. (SI. Dec.15; 80) Lire 250,000

LUDWIG, Karl, Elector Palatine of the Rhine 'Philotheus'
[–] Symbola Christiana. Frankfurt, 1677. Fo. Some dampstaining & soiling, margin tear in L3, some ll. loose & slightly frayed, mott. cf., rebkd., worn, inside hinges reprd. (S. Oct.11; 404) *Snelling.* £120

LUGAR, Robert
- Architectural Sketches for Cottages, Rural Dwellings, & Villas ... Suitable to Persons of Genteel Life & Moderate Fortune. L., 1840. 4to. 38 engraved plts., including 22 hand-cold., dampstained, loose, orig. cl.-bkd. bds., worn, lacks spine. (S. Oct.11; 553) *Bookroom.* £50
- Plans & View of Ornamental Domestic Buildings, Executed in the Castellated & Other Styles. L., 1836. *2nd. Edn.* Fo. 16 plans, 16 cold. aquatint views, lacks hf.-title(?), text ll. with margin dampstain, gt.-lettered cl., spine chipped, ex-liby. (SG. Jan.26; 243) $275
- Villa Architecture ... in England, Scotland, &c. Ill.:– Matthew Dubourg & others. L., 1828. *1st. Edn.* Fo. 16 uncold. plans, 26 cold. aquatint plts. (wtrmkd. 1828, text wtrmkd. 1820-22), hf.-title, few minor margin stains, some light foxing & offsetting, hf. mor., old marb. bds., unc. (SG. Nov.3; 133) $1,600
- - **Anr. Copy.** Tall fo. 15 uncold. plans, 15 full-p. col. aquatint views, 12 other plts., publisher's 8 p. catalogue tipped in at end, orig. cl., lacks end of spine, liby. bkplt. (SG. Jan.26; 244) $750

LUGARD, Capt. F.D.
- The Rise of Our East African Empire. Early Efforts in Nyasaland & Uganda. 1893. 2 vols. 2 maps in front & rear pockets of Vol. 1, orig. decor. cl., rubbed, corners bumped. (TA. May 17; 40) £74

LUGT, Frits
- Les Marques de Collections de Dessins & d'Estampes. Amst., 1921. 2 vols. 4to. Orig. linen. (R. Apr.3; 840) DM 720
- - **Anr. Edn.** Amst., 1921; Den Haag, 1956. 2 vols. Orig. linen. (R. Oct.11; 890) DM 620
- - **Anr. Edn.** Amst., 1921 [San Franc., 1975]. 2 vols., including facs. reprint Supp. Orig. cl. (BBA. Apr.5; 108) *Zwemmer.* £110
- - **Anr. Edn.** The Hague, 1956. *1st. Edn. of Supp.* 2 vols., including Supp. 4to. Unif. cl., covers crudely reinforced with cl. tape, ex-liby. (SG. Jan.26; 245) $325

- - **Anr. Edn.** La Haye, 1956. *Reprint of 1921 Edn.* 2 vols. 4to. Orig. linen. (V. Sep.30; 2170) DM 800
- - **Anr. Edn.** 1975, Den Haag, 1956 (Supp.). *Vol. I: Reprint.* 2 vols. 4to. Orig. linen. (GB. Nov.4; 1372) DM 600
- - **Anr. Copy.** 2 vols. 4to. Orig. linen. (HK. Nov.11; 4484) DM 500
- - **Anr. Edn.** N.Y., 1975, & Den Haag, 1956. 2 vols. 4to. Orig. linen. (GB. May 4; 1882) DM 480

LUIKEN or LUYKEN, Jan
- Afbeeldingen der Merkwaardigste Gesch. v.h. Oude en Nieuwe Testament. Amst., 1729. Fo. Some slight browning in text, cont. cf. gt., slightly rubbed. (VG. Mar.19; 209) Fls. 2,000
- Beschouwing der Wereld, bestaande in Hondert Konstige Figuren. Amst., 1708. *1st. Edn.* Lacks frontis., title spotted, with old MS. annots., 2 slits, 3 text ll. with excisions, without loss, 1 copper engr. with defect., some spotting, later hf. leath., slightly spotted, upr. end-paper renewed; ex-libris. (HT. May 9; 1320) DM 400

LUIKEN, Jan & Kaspar
- Spiegel v.h. Menselyk Bedryf... Amst., 1718. 1 quire loosening, cont. vell., sm. 8vo. (VG. Mar.19; 194) Fls. 3,500

LUITPOLD, Herzog in Bayern
- Die Fränkische Bildwirkerei. München, [1925]. *Ltd. Iss.* Text & plt. vol. Fo. Stp. on title & endpapers, orig. nf. leath., slightly worn; text vol. endpapers with author's MS. dedication. (H. Nov.23; 207a) DM 720

LUKOMSKI, George K.
- Les Demeures des Tsars: Les Palais des Eupereurs de Toutes les russies. Paris, 1929. *(370) numbered & initialed by publisher.* Fo. 24 hand-cold. hf.-tone plts., loose as iss., decor. wraps. over bd. folder, spine & edges worn. (SG. Aug.25; 317) $120

LULLIUS, or LULLY Raymundus
- Opera ea quae ad adinventam ab ipso Artem Universam ... Strassb., 1598. *1st. Coll. Edn.* A few old underlinings at beginning, some light soiling, mostly in upr. margin, cont. vell., slightly spotted. (R. Oct.12; 1552) DM 1,000
- Testamentum Duobus Libris Universam Artem Chymican Complectens item Ejusdem Compendium Animae Transmutationis Artis Metallorum. Cologne, 1573. *2nd. Edn.* 1 folding table slit in fold, old cf.; Rolle bkplt., Dr. Walter Pagel copy. (S. Feb.7; 241) *Van Aorst.* £240

LUMEN ANIMAE
Ed.:– Matthias Farinator. [Strasburg, printer of 1481 Legenda Aurea], 22 Mar. 1482. Fo. Rubricated in red & blue, cont. stpd. cf. over wood bds., richly decor., spine renewed; from Fondation Furstenberg-Beaumesnil. [HC 10333; BMC I, 97; Goff L393] (HD. Nov.16; 45) Frs. 28,000

LUMHOLTZ, Carl
- Among Cannibals. L., 1889. Decor. cl., unc., covers soiled, spine faded, sig. on front end-paper. (CA. Apr.3; 78) Aus. $150
- Au Pays des Cannibales...L'Australie orientale. Paris, 1890. Lge. 8vo. Hf.-title, later hf. mor., gt. ornaments on spine. (BBA. Dec.15; 26) *Quevedo.* £50
- Through Central Borneo. An Account of Two Years' Travel in the Land of the Head-Hunters, 1913-1917. N.Y., 1920. 2 vols. Orig. cl. gt., spines slightly faded. (TA. Oct.20; 22) £155

LUMISDEN, Andrew
- Remarks of the Antiquities of Rome & its Environs. L., 1797. Lge. 4to. Cont. watercold. aquatints, cont. str.-grd. mor. gt., spine decor.; from libys. of Hibbert, Chalfont House & Sir Abdy. (HD. Jun.18; 28) Frs. 32,000

LUNARDI, Vincent
- An Account of Five Aerial Voyages in Scotland. -- Account of his Ascension & Aerial Voyage, from the New Fort, Liverpool. L.; n.p., 1786; 1785. *1st. Edns.* 2 vols. in 1. Lge. 8vo. 1st. work, engraved frontis.-port., 2 engraved plts., 4 (of 6) 114, [1] pp., lacks hf.-title, 2nd. work, port. & final lf. tipped in on free endpapers, title soiled, later qtr. leath. bds., worn, 1st. work unc., 2nd. unopened; Vailima

---

bkplt. of Robert louis Stevenson & bkplt. of Herschel V. Jones. (SG. Apr.26; 133) $1,200

LUND or LUNDIUS, Johannes
- Die Alten Jüdischen Heiligthümer, Gottesdienste u. Gewohnheiten. Hamburg, 1704. Fo. Some foxing & browning, cont. leath., very worn & defect. (HK. Nov.9; 1802) DM 600
- - **Anr. Edn.** Hamburg, 1738. Sm. fo. Some mild browning, old cf., worn, lacks spine & free end-papers. (SG. Feb.2; 94) $110

LUNDBORG, H.
- Medizinisch-biologische Familienforschungen ... 2 vols. Fo. Orig. hf. leath. (D. Nov.23; 626) DM 500

LURCAT, Jean
- Géographie Animale. Lausanne, 1948. *(315) numbered & sigd. by artist & publisher.* Unsewn in orig. wraps., unc., parch.-bkd. folder & s.-c. (S. Nov.21; 90) *Makiya.* £160

LURIA, Shlomo [Maharshal]
- Beurei Sefer Semag. — Amudei Shlomo. Ed.:– Elijah Loanz. Basle, 1600. 2 pts. in 1 vol. 4to. Worming thro.-out crudely reprd. affecting some words, staining, browned, buckram, trimmed. (S. Oct.24; 234) *Sol.* £140

LURIA, Shlomo [Maharshal] & Yitzhak, of Duren
- Sha'arei Dura. Ed.:– Elijah Loanz. Basle, 1599. *7th. Edn. [2nd. Edn. of Commentary].* 4to. Owners' stps. on title & last p., stained, browned, mod. cf., trimmed. (S. Oct.24; 236) *Dr K.* £380

LUSUS WESTMONASTERIENSES
L., 1740. Mor. gt. by Bozerian, the Elder. (BBA. Mar.21; 225) *Thorp.* £50

LUTHER, Clair Franklin
- The Hadley Chest. Hartford, 1935. *1st. Edn. (525) numbered.* 4to. Supp. loosely inserted, cl., worn, covers soiled. (RO. Sep.13; 110) $180

LUTHER, Martin
- An den Durchleüchtigiste[n] Hochgebornen Fürsten un[d] Herrn Albrechte[n]/Erzbischoffen zu Meintz und Magdeburg/Churfürsten und Marggraffen zu Brandenburg... N.p., 1527. Staining, last lf. with defect, reprd. with minimal loss, mod. sewed. (HT. May 8; 161a) DM 750
- Ad Librum Eximii Magistri Nostri Ambrosii Catharini Defensoris Silvestris Prieratis Acerrimi Responsio. Cum Exposita Visione Danielis viii. De Antichristo. Wittenberg, 1521. *1st. Edn.* 4to. Wide margin, minimal worming & paper browning, hf. vell. (R. Apr.3; 61) DM 1,400
- Das Ander Tayl wider die Hymlischen Prophete[n] vom Sacrament. [Augsburg], 1525. 4to. Many cont. MS. annots., 19th. C. jansenist mor., sigd. by Hans Asper, gt. outer dentelle & wide gt. inner cover borders, marb. paper end-papers. (D. Nov.23; 126) DM 3,200
- Appellation odder Beruffung an ein Christlich Frey Conciliu[m] von dem Bapst Leo .... Wittenberg, [1520]. *2nd. Edn.* 4to. Hf. leath. (R. Oct.11; 66) DM 560
- Assertio Omnuim Articulorum M. Lutheri, per Bullam Leonis X Novissima[m] Damnatoru[m]. Ill.:– L. Cranach. Wittenberg, 1520. *1st. Edn.* 4to. Slightly spotted & browned, especially title, end-lf. partly bkd., hf. vell. (R. Apr.3; 60) DM 1,600
- Ein Brieff an die zu Franckfort am Meyn. Wittenberg, 1533. *1st. Edn.* 4to. Lacks end lf. with printèrs mark, title slightly soiled, wraps. (R. Oct.11; 76) DM 1,300
- Ein Brieff D. Mart. Luth. Von seinem Buch der Winckel messen, an einen guten Freund. Wittenberg, 1534. *1st. Edn. 1st. Printing.* 4to. Some light spotting, some cont. marginalia, bds. (R. Apr.3; 65) DM 1,300
- Colloquia Mensalia: or ... Divine Discourses at His Table, &c. L., 1652. *1st. Edn. in Engl.* Fo. Port. frayed, cont. cf., worn. (SG. Oct.27; 205) $275
- A Commentarie of M. Doctor Martin Luther upon the Epistle of S. Paul to the Galatians.... 1575. Old cf., covers detchd. (SKC. Nov.18; 1897) £80
- De Votis Monasticis Iudicum. Basel, 1522. *2nd. Edn.* Sm. 4to. Wormed thro.-out, some ll. soiled, new hf. vell. (BR. Apr.12; 878) DM 1,000

LUTHER, Martin -*Contd.*

- **Deuttung der Zwo Grewlichen Figuren Bapstesels zu Rum und Munchkabos zu Freyberg in Meyssen funden.** Wittenberg, 1523. *1st. Edn. 1st Printing.* 4to. Wide margin, mod. vell. (R. Oct.11; 65)   DM 3,700
- **Epistel S. Petri.** [Tübingen], 1524. Sn. lr. part of title & 1st. few ll. reprd. (*Bound with:*) – **Die Ander Epistel S. Petri u. eine S. Judas.** [Tübingen], 1524. Together 2 works in 1 vol. 4to. Bds., covered with German incunable lf., F. Heitz bkplt. (VG. Sep.14; 1339)   Fls. 500
- **Erklerung etlicher Artickel: in seinem Sermon: von dem Heyligen Sacrament.** [Nuremb., 1520]. 4to. Slightly stained, some old MS. marginalia, hf. vell. (R. Apr.3; 58)   DM 450
- **Der Erste [bis Achte ... und Letzte] Teil aller Bücher und Schrifften.** Ed.:– [N. von Amsdorff, J. Aurifaber & others]. Jena, 1555-62. *1st. Edn. (vols. I-IV & VI, rest 2nd. Edn.).* 8 vols. Some cont. marginalia, some old MS. entries on end-papers, stain with sm. paper flaw in VII,1, some soiling, lightly browned thro.-out, cont. pig over wood bds., blind-tooled, metal clasps, defects. at head of Vol. II & VII, some spotting, wear or tears. (HT. May 8; 161)   DM 5,000
- **Der Erste Theil d. Bücher, Schrifften, Predigten...vom 1516. bis 1529.** Ill.:– Lucas Cranach the Elder & Hans Seb. Beham. Eisleben, 1564. Vol. 1 only (of 2). Fo. Some light foxing & browning, cont. blind-stpd. decor. pig over wood, binder's monog. L.W., rather worn, recased, new end-papers & clasps, catches. (VG. Sep.14; 901)   Fls. 2,200
- [–] **Eyn Deutsch Theologia.** Wittenb., 1518. *1st. Compl. Edn.* 4to. Wide margin, title with old note, title & 10 other ll. with sm. reprd. margin defects., last 6 ll. slightly wormed in 1 corner, slightly browned thro.-out & lightly stained near end. bds. (HK. Nov.8; 258)   DM 5,000
- **Formula Missae et Commvnionis pro Ecclesia Vuittembergensi.** Wittenb., 1523. *1st. Edn.* 4to. Wide margin, title lightly spotted & creased, sm. lr. corner repair, 1 sm. wormhole, hf. vell. (HK. May 15; 181)   DM 1,000
- **Der Fünffte Teil der Bücher.** Wittenberg, 1552. Vol. 5 of 1st. German Coll. Edn. Fo. Blind-tooled pig over wood bds., dtd. 1552, clasps brkn. (R. Oct.11; 62)   DM 600
- **Hauspostilla vber die Sontags vnd der Fürnemesten Feste Euangelien, Durch das Gantze Jar.** Ill.:– H. Brosamer. Wittenburg, 1547-58. 3 pts. in 1 vol. Fo. Title lf. probably from anr. copy, title with pasted tear, lightly browned, some slight spotting, cont. blind-tooled pig, centrepiece, lightly rubbed & soiled, lr. cover slightly wormed, corners & end-papers renewed, ex-libris. (HK. Nov.8; 265)   DM 2,700
- **Eine Heerpredigt widder den Türcken.** Ill.:– L. Cranach. Wittenberg, 1529. *1st. Edn.* Sm. 4to. Woodcut title border cut at foot, title with sm. margin tears bkd., spotted, some underlining & marginalia in old MS., new vell. (BR. Apr.12; 879)   DM 800
- **In Cantica Canticorum.** Wittenberg, 1539. Title verso with stp., hf. leath. ca. 1900, Hauswedell coll. (H. May 24; 1161)   DM 1,600
- **In Epistolam S. Pauli ad Galatas Commentarius** ... Wittemberg, 1535. *1st. Edn.* Some staining, lacks p. 337, front free end-paper & fly-lf., cont. cf. over wood bds., very worn, some worming, remmants of brass & leath. clasps. (CBA. Dec.10; 457) $325
- **Kirchenpostilla.** Nuremb., [15]60. 4 pts. in 1 vol. Fo. Slightly browned & stained thro.-out, some slight worming, some ll. with sm. tears, last ll. with margins worn, cont. blind-tooled pig, blind-tooled arms supralibros, spine gt., 2 clasps, lacks ties & corner bosses, end-papers 19th. C. renewed. (HK. Nov.8; 266)   DM 480
- **Das Magnificat verteutschet und aussgelegt.** Wittenb., [1521]. *2nd. Edn.* 4to. Rubricated, title side margin frayed, corner torn off with slight loss, old MS. annots., lightly browned, especially 1st. 2 ll., no bdg. stated. (HK. May 15; 175)   DM 650
- **Resolutio[n]es Disputationum, de Indulgentia[rum] Virtute.** Leipzig, 1519. 4to. Many old MS. marginalia, & some MS. on last lf. blank, title margin defect., wraps. (R. Oct.11; 63) DM 1,200

- **Römscher Key. Maiestat Verhorung Rede vnd Widerrede Doctor Martini Luters.** [Basle, 1521]. Sm. 4to. Inner margins reinforced, mod. bds. (S. Dec.20; 758)   *Crete.* £230
- **Eyn Schrecklich Geschicht und Gericht Gotes über Thomas Müntzer** ... [Wittenberg, 1525]. *1st. Printing.* 4to. Light stain in upr. margin, some tiny worm-holes thro.-out, incunable paper wraps. (R. Apr.3; 69)   DM 2,600
- **Der Sechs un Dreyssigst Psalm David eynen Christlichen Menschen tzu Leren un Trosten widder die Mutterey der Botzenn unnd Freueln Gleytzner.** [Wittembergt], 1521. *1st. Edn.* Sm. 4to. Rubricated hand-lettered title, 15 unnumbered ll. & facs. title, few faint old margin stains, light foxing, few early ink margin annots., later vell. over bds., s.-c. (HA. Nov.18; 357) $100
- **Eyn Sendebrieff von dem Harten Büchlin wider die Bawrn.** [Nürnberg], 1525. 4to. Foxed, title with old note & notes in upr. margins, mod. leath. (R. Oct.11; 71)   DM 2,600
- **Sermo de Meditatione Dominice Passionis.** Wittenberg, 1521. 4to. 2 sm. worm-holes, hf. vell. (R. Apr.3; 56)   DM 1,000
- **Ain Sermon v. der Beraytung zum Sterben.** Ill.:– Hans Schäufelein. [Augsburg, 1519]. 4to. Wide margin, lightly browned, underlining & marking in old MS., margins lightly frayed, last. lf. with bkd. margin hole, no bdg. stated. (HK. May 15; 177)   DM 700
- **Ein Sermon von dem Sacrament der Buss.** [Nuremb., 1520]. 4to. Bds. (R. Apr.3; 57)   DM 480
- **Eyn Sermon von dem Vnrechten Mammon.** Ill.:– L. Cranach. Wittenburg, 1522. 4to. A few cont. MS. marginalia, upr. margin cut close, bds. (HK. Nov.8; 260)   DM 500
- **Die Sieben Buszpsalm** ... Leyptzick, 1520. 4to. Title spotted in inner margin, name on title, lightly browned. bds. (B. Apr.27; 583)   Fls. 525
- **Das Siebe [n]d Capital S. Pauli zu den Chorinthern Ausgelegt.** Ill.:– L. Cranach. Wittenberg, 1523. *1st. Edn.* 4to. Lightly spotted or browned, hf. vell. (R. Apr.3; 62)   DM 1,250
- **Operationes in Duas Psalmorum Decades.** Basle, 1521. Fo. Cont. stpd. pig over wood bds., emblem (ex-libris?) dtd. 1542 on upr. cover, claspa; from Fondation Furstenberg-Beaumesnil. (HD. Nov.16; 134)   Frs. 14,500
- **Sendbrief an die Christen im Niederland.** Groningen, May 1941. *(90).* Orig. pict. wraps., one corner slightly defect. (H. Nov.24; 2205)   DM 1,400
- **Tessaradecas Consolatoria pro Labora[n]tibus et Oneratis.** Wittenberg, 1520. *1st. Edn.* 4to. Wide margin, many old MS. marginalia, title slightly spotted, hf. vell. (R. Apr.3; 59)   DM 1,000
- **Eyn Trost Brief an die Christen zu Augspurg.** Wittenberg, [1523]. *1st. Edn.* 4to. Bds. (R. Oct.11; 70)   DM 1,100
- **Ein trostliche Predigt von der Zukunfft Christi, und den Vorgehenden Zeichen des Jüngsten Tags.** Wittenberg, 1536. *3rd. Edn.* 4to. Corners slightly soiled, hf. vell. (R. Oct.11; 75)   DM 700
- **Vom Eelichen Leben.** [Augsburg, 1522]. Sm. 4to. Lacks last lf. blank, title brown spotted in places, old MS. page nos., stains in margin, last p. with sm. owners stp., hf. vell., Hauswedell coll. (H. May 24; 1160)   DM 420
- **Vom Schem Ham-phoras: Vnd von Geslecht Christi.** Wittenberg, 1543. *2nd. or 3rd. Printing.* 4to. Many MS. annots. & underlining, last lf. verso with MS. annots. & underlining, last lf. verso with MS. data, 2 ll. loose, some spotting, later pencil pagination, wraps. from old printing, spine renewed. (H. Nov.23; 591)   DM 900
- **Von Beyder Gestalt des Sacraments tzu Nemen.** [Wittenberg, 1522]. *2nd. Edn.* 4to. Old coll. stp. on title, slightly soiled, bds. (R. Oct.11; 67) DM 850
- **Von Heim/lichen und Gestolen/Brieffen, sampt einem/Psalm, ausgelegt,/widder Hertzog/Georgen zu Sachsen.** Wittenberg, 1529. *1st. Edn.* Sm. 4to. Title verso with engraved owners entry, sewed, without bdg. (GB. May 3; 923)   DM 1,100
- **Von Jhesu Christo eine Predigt ... zu Hofe zu Torgaw Gepredigt.** Wittenberg, 1533. *1st. Edn.* 4to. Title verso stpd., MS. correction of publication date on title from 1532, slightly browned or soiled, 2 traces of worm, with light loss, cf., by Riviere. (HK. May 15; 187)   DM 800

- **Von der Sunde widder den Heiligen Geist. Ein Sermon.** Wittenberg, 1529. *1st. Edn.* 4to. Partly rubricated, some cont. marginalia & underlining, hf. vell. with incunable paper. (R. Oct.11; 73)   DM 1,200
- **Warnunge An seine Lieben Deudschen.** Ill.:– G. Lemberger. Wittenberg, 1531. *1st. Edn. 2nd. Printing.* 4to. Minimal worming, wraps. (R. Apr.3; 64)   DM 1,500
- **Was auff dem Reichstag zu Nuremberg, von wegen Bepstlicher Heiligkeit ... Lutherischer Sachen halben belangt, vnd darauff geantwortet worden ist** ... Ill.:– Lukas Cranach. Wittenberg, 1538. *1st. German Edn.* Part wraps., vell. box. (GB. May 3; 924)   DM 1,000

LUTSCH, H.
- **Verzeichnis der Kunstdenkmäler der Provinz Schlesien.** Breslau, 1886-1903. Vols. 1, 2, 4 & 5 (of 6) in 4 vols. All titles multi-stpd., cont. hf. linen, very rubbed. (R. Apr.3; 841)   DM 1,000

LUTYENS, Sir Edwin Landseer
- **Houses & Gardens.** 1914. Fo. Buckram-bkd. bds., worn. (BS. Nov.16; 103)   £55

LUTYENS, Robert
- **The Old Burgundians.** Priv. ptd., 1962. *(50)* numbered & sigd. 4to. Mntd. & loose in orig. folder with ties. (TA. Oct.20; 362)   £62

LUYKEN, Jan
See— LUIKEN or LUYKEN, Jan

LUZ, Maria
See— KOCHNO, Boris & Luz, Maria

LUZZATTO, A.
See— BIBLIOTECA AMBROSIANA, MILAN

LUZZATO, Moshe Chaim
- **Leshon Limudim.** Mantua, 1727. *1st. Edn.* Slightly foxed & creased, leath.; sig. & margin glosses of Ben Zion Ettlinger. (S. Oct.24; 238)   *Abramsky.* £190
- **Mesilat Yesharim.** Amst., 1740. *1st. Edn.* 12mo. Browned, some staining, leath., sliightly worn. (S. Oct.24; 240)   *Ludmir.* £220
- **Sefer Hoker u-Mekubbal.** Shklov, 1785. *1st. Edn.* Sm. 8vo. Repairs to title with minimal loss, remaining tear in centre of lf., owners' stps., soiled & dampstained, cl.-bkd. bds., worn. (SG. Feb.2; 225) $175

LYALL, Robert
- **The Character of the Russians & a Detailed History of Moscow ... with a Dissertation on the Russian Language.** 1823. 4to. Mod. hf. mor.; from liby. of Luttrellstown Castle, w.a.f. (C. Sep.28; 1748)   £350

LYCETT, Joseph
- **Views in Australia, or New South Wales & Van Diemen's Land Delineated.** L., 1824. Ob. fo. Cold. litho. title with oval 'View in Bathurst Plains near Queen Charlotte's Valley', ptd. dedication to Earl Bathurst, advt. lf., 16pp. intro. account & list of plts., 2 engraved maps, 48 cold. aquatint plts., folding map reprd. & slightly defect., sky colouring of 2 plts. oxidised, some minor spotting & soiling in margins, 2 plts. with sm. rust spot, mod. mor.-bkd. marb. bds.; pres. inscr. from Charles Bean dtd. 1827 on title. (C. Jun.27; 96)   *Gordon.* £10,075
- – Anr. Edn. Melbourne, n.d. *Facs.* S.-c. (JL. Jun.24; 67)   Aus. $340

LYCOSTHENES, Conrad [ie. Conrad Wolffhart]
- **Apophthegmatum ex Optimis Utriusque Linguae Scriptoribus.** Lyon, 1573. Sm. 8vo. Mod. red lev., gt. dentelles. (SG. Dec.9; 275) $175
- **Apophthegmatum sive Responsorum Memorabilium ... Loci Communes** ... Basel, 1555. *1st. Edn.* Fo. Title with fault in upr. margin reprd. without loss, 1st. & last ll. wormed, slightly soiled, minimal browning, 2 ll. with ink spots, some underlining, cont. bdg., spine blind-tooled pig, covers 15th. C. vell., slightly defect., wear; ex-libris. (HT. May 8; 167)   DM 820

LYDEKKER, Richard
- **Animal Portraiture.** Ill.:– after W. Kuhnert. [1912]. 2 vols., including plt. vol. Orig. cl., affected

by damp, plts. unbnd. as iss. in orig. portfo. (CSK. Oct.21; 127) £65
– – **Anr. Copy.** Lge. 4to. 50 mntd. cold. plts., slight spotting, maroon hf. mor., worn, unc. (S. Apr.10; 547) *Head.* £50
– – **Anr. Edn.** N.d. Fo. 50 mntd. cold. plts., orig. gt.-pict. cl., fore-edge slightly damp-marked. (SKC. May 4; 1862) £50

LYELL, Charles
– **Elements of Geology.** Phila., 1839. *1st. Amer. Edn.* Frontis. hand-cold., orig. cl., spine faded, slightly spotted. (SG. Mar.22; 199) $110
– **The Geological Evidences of the Antiquity of Man.** L., 1863. *1st. Edn.* Frontis. plt., text ills., advts., oirg. cl. gt.; bkplts. of H. Gueneau de Mussy, M.D., & Henry Dunand. (S. Apr.10; 548) *Primrose.* £55
– **Geologie.** Berlin, 1857-58. *1st. Edn.* 2 vols. Title with old stp., some light foxing, cont. hf. leath., very rubbed. (R. Oct.12; 1583) DM 480
– **Travels in North America in the Years 1841-2.** N.Y., 1845. *1st. Amer. Edn.* 2 vols. 12mo. 3 plts. foxed, orig. cl., corners nicked. (SG. Jan.19; 213) $100
– **Travels in North America: with Geological Observations on the United States, Canada & Nova Scotia.** L., 1845. *1st. Edn.* 2 vols. Plts. somewhat spotted, orig. cl., spine slightly faded; the Rt. Hon. Visc. Eccles copy. [Sabin 42763] (CNY. Nov.18; 179) $190

LYELL, Denis D.
– **Hunting Trips in Northern Rhodesia.** L., 1910. 4to. 55 plts., pict. cl., top of spine defect. (VA. Oct.28; 504) R 220

LYELL, J.P.R.
– **Early Book Illustration in Spain.** 1926. 4to. Cl. (P. Sep.29; 300) *Forster.* £70

LYLE, Robert Charles
– **The Aga Khan's Horses.** Ill.:– Lionel Edwards. [1938]. *(140) numbered & sigd. by author, artist & H.H. Aga Khan.* 4to. Qtr. vell. gt. (P. Feb.16; 100a) £130
– **Brown Jack.** Ill.:– Lionel Edwards. [1934]. *(250) numbered sigd. by author, artist & owner.* 4to. Qtr. vell. gt. (P. Dec.8; 205) *Mar.* £70

LYLY or LILLY, John
– **Euphues: The Anatomie of Wit. — Euphues & His England ....** L., 1630; 1631. 2 pts. in 1 vol. 1st. title-p. laid on new lf., both title-pp. underlined red, some foxing, margin notes & underlining, new fly-ll., later three-qtr. mor. (CBA. Dec.10; 290) $100
– **Sixe Court Comedies.** L., 1632. *1st. Coll. Edn.* 12mo. 3rd. state of prelims., lacks 1st. blank, few margin repairs, title little soiled, cf. antique, by Riviere. [STC 17089] (SG. Apr.26; 134) $400

LYNDEWODE, Bp. William
– **Provinciale seu Constitutiones Anglie cum Summariis.** Ed.:– Badius Ascensius. 1501. Fo. Title, 1st. 2 & last ll. defect. with text loss, many repairs in lr. margin, some stain, old blind-stpd. cf., rebkd. [STC 17107] (P. Sep.8; 356) *Rix.* £140
– – **Anr. Edn.** [Antw, 20 Dec. 1525]. 2 pts. in 1 vol. Fo. Last 3 ll. of Tabula defect., some worming, some tears & sm. holes in title & other ll., 17th. C. cf., worn, war. cover detchd.; Edward Taylor bkplt., apparently from Liby. of Robert Dudley, Earl of Leicester. [STC 17111] (S. Dec.8; 5) *Coulter.* £500

LYNDSAY, Sir David
– **Facsimile of an Ancient Heraldic Manuscript.** Edinb., 1822. *[100].* Fo. Hand-col. engraved title, 136 plts. on 134 ll. (2 ptd. recto & verso), cont. mor., elab. gt.-tooled (CSK. Dec.16; 197) £110

LYON, Capt. George Francis
– **A Brief Narrative of an unsuccessful Attempt to reach Repulse Bay.** 1825. Lacks hf.-title, hf. cf. gt.; inscr. 'from Lieut.-Gen. Coghlan' on title. (BBA. Sep.29; 47) *Acadia.* £65
– **A Narrative of Travels in Northern Africa, in the Years 1818, 19 & 20.** 1821. *1st. Edn.* 4to. Prelims. misbnd., folding map slightly torn, some light offsetting, 1 lf. loose, anr. torn & reprd., some light staining, mott. hf. cf. (BBA. Sep.29; 9) *Thorp.* £180

– **The Private Journal ... during the Recent Voyage of Discovery under Captain Parry.** L., 1824. *1st. Edn.* Map with sm. tear at inner margin, plts. offset, orig. bds., unc., spine & corners worn; the Rt. Hon. Visc. Eccles copy. [Sabin 42853] (CNY. Nov.18; 180) $180
– **The Private Journal. – Brief Narrative of an Unsuccessful Attempt to reach Repulse Bay.** L., 1824; 1825. *1st. Edns.* Together 2 vols. 1st. work, folding map, 7 engraved plts., slightly foxed, cont. hf. cf., 2nd. work, folding map, 7 engraved plts., some slightly spotted, qtr. cf., unc. (S. Apr.9; 41) *Traylen.* £140

LYSONS, Rev. Daniel
– **The Environs of London.** 1782-1811. 5 vols., with Supp. 4to. 4 vig. titles, 77 plts. & maps, a few hand-cold., hf. cf. gt. (P. Dec.8; 4) *Drewett.* £80
– – **Anr. Edn.** 1810-11. 2 vols. in 4. 4to. Orig. bds., unc. (P. Jul.5; 146) £50
– – **Anr. Edn.** 1811. *2nd. Edn.* 2 vols. 4to. 48 engraved plts. (1 cold.), including maps, 1 folding map loose, offsetting, hf. roan, rubbed, head of 1 spine defect. (SKC. Mar.9; 1982) £65
– – **Anr. Edn.** 1811-1800. *2nd. Edn.* 5 vols. (including 1 vol. Parishes of Middlesex). 4to. Cont. hf. cf. (CSK. Mar.23; 6) £95
– – **Anr. Copy.** 2 vols. in 4, & Supp. 'An Historical Account of Those Parishes in the County of Middlesex'. 4to. Some spotting, cf. gt. (P. Sep.29; 260) *Hasley.* £50

LYSONS, Daniel & Samuel
– **Magna Britannia.** L., 1806. Vol. 1 only. 4to. Slight margin spotting & offsetting, cont. diced cf. gt., rebkd., orig. spine preserved. (S. Mar.6; 291) *Gaunt.* £80
– – **Anr. Edn.** 1806-17. 5 vols. 4to. Some spotting & minor dampstains, Vols. 1 & 2 cont. cl., untrimmed, some wear, Vol. 3 orig. cl., rubbed, untrimmed. Vols. 4 & 5 cont. cf., gt.-decor. spines, rubbed. (TA. May 17; 112) £220
– – **Anr. Copy.** 5 vols., matched set. 4to. Maps, folding copperplt. engrs. & other ills., some spotting & minor dampstains, Vols. 1 & 2 cont. cl., untrimmed. some wear, vol. 3 untrimmed, orig. cl., rubbed, Vols. 4 & 5 cont. cf., gt.-decor., rubbed. (TA. Jun.21; 199) £190
– – **Anr. Edn.** 1806-22. Vols. 1-6. 4to. Engraved maps & plts., several hand-cold., cont. hf. mor. (CSK. Jul.6; 61) £320
– – **Anr. Copy.** Vols. I-VI only. Lge. 4to. A few plts. & maps hand-cold., some browning, cont. hf. mor., w.a.f. (CSK. Oct.7; 150) £300
– – **Anr. Edn.** 1814. *1st. Edn.* Vol. III: 'Cornwall'. Pol. cf., front hinge defect. (LA. Nov.29; 122) £170
– – **Anr. Copy.** Vol. III only: 'Cornwall'. 4to. Hf.-titles, publisher's catalogue inserted, publisher's bds., unc. & partly unopened, lacks spine. (S. Nov.1; 117) *Wise.* £60
– – **Anr. Edn.** 1822. Vol. VI pts. 1 & 2 only: 'Devonshire'. 4to. Some spotting, cont. hf. cf. (TA. Oct.20; 86) £70

LYSONS, Samuel
– **A Collection of Gloucestershire Antiquities.** L., 1803. Fo. Engraved title, 110 plts. (11 cold.), few imprints shaved, slightly spotted, cont. cf., 1 cover detchd. (S. Mar.6; 290) *Sanders.* £50

LYTELL GESTE OF ROBYN HODE & HIS MEINY
Ill.:– Valenti Angelo. [San Franc., priv. ptd. for Herbert L. Rothschild at the Grabhorn Pr.], 1931. *(25).* Niger, spine gt.-lettered, covers slightly spotted & slightly bowed, spine slightly faded. (CBA. Mar.3; 228) $300
– – **Anr. Edn.** Intro.:– Oscar Lewis. Ill.:– V. Angelo. San Franc., Westgate Pr., at the Grabhorn Pr., 1932. *(280) sigd. by artist.* Hf. niger & decor. bds.; the V. Angelo copy. (CBA. Oct.1; 164) $200

LYTTON, Lord Edward George Bulwer 'Pisistratus Caxton'
[–] **Eugene Aram.** 1832. *1st. Edn.* 3 vols. Pol. cf., gt. fillets, dentelles, gt. decor. spine, by Zaehnsdorf. (SKC. Jan.13; 2230) £75.
– **Night & Morning.** Phila., 1862. 2 vols. Pol. hf. cf. over marb. bds.; each vol. inscr. 'Mary Lincoln 1864'. (LH. Jan.15; 150) $750

– **What Will He Do With It?** L., 1859. *1st. Edn.* 4 vols. Orig. blind-stpd. cl., covers stained; inscr. by Lytton 'With kind regards from the author. Jan. 1, 1859' in Vol. 1. (SG. Nov.17; 19) $110
– **Works.** 1860-69. *Liby. Edn.* 40 vols. Hf. cf., spines gt.; the Hinton House copy. (LC. Oct.13; 444) £180
– – **Anr. Edn.** L., [1892-93]. *Edn. de Luxe,. (500).* Plts., ex-liby., orig. cl., soiled, few labels torn, unc. (S. Apr.9; 267) *Wormsley.* £70

M., A.
[–] **The Bairds of Gartsherrie – some Notices of their Origin & History.** Glasgow, priv. ptd., 1875. Red mor. gt. by Maclehose. (PD. Dec.14; 387) £75

M., W.
– **The Queens Closet Opened.** L., 1674-5. 3 pts. in 1 vol. Frontis., 'A Queens delight' & 'The compleat Cook' both with separate titles, few minor flaws, mod. leath. [Wing M102] (BBA. Nov.30; 199) *Walford.* £400

M., W. & Wright, F. von
– **Svenska Faglar efter Naturen och på sten Ritade.** Text:– E. Lönnberg. Stockholm, [1927-29]. *New Edn. 2nd. Iss. (Vols. I & III), 1st. Iss. (Vol. II).* 3 vols. Sm. fo. 2 cf. & 1 hf. leath., spine faded, lightly scratched, slightly bumped. (H. May 22; 223) DM 1,800

MA'ASE YEHUDIT. [With] Ma'ase Daniel
Venice, ca. 1650?. Sm. 8vo. Lightly soiled, mod. cl. (SG. Feb.2; 227) $425

MABILLON, Jean
– **De Re Diplomatica Libri VI.** Paris, 1681. *1st. Edn.* Fo. Some light staining, cont. spr. cf. (S. Nov.17; 45) *A. Thomas.* £250

McADAM, John Loudon
– **Remarks on the Present System of Road Making with Observations ...** 1820. *3rd. Edn.* Orig. bds. (PD. May 16; 225) £80

MACADAM, M.F. Laming
– **The Temples of Kawa.** Oxford & L., 1949; 1955. 4 vols. Lge. 4to. 200 plts., ex-liby., cl. (SG. May 3; 245) $250

McALLISTER, Ward
– **Society as I Have Found It.** N.Y., [1890]. *(400) numbered & sigd.* Lge. 8vo. Silver & gt. cl. (SG. Aug.4; 188) $100

MacARTHUR, James
– **New South Wales, Its Present State & Future Prospects.** L., 1837. Map torn, title & some ll. stained, hf. cf. (CA. Apr.3; 79) Aus. $140

McARTHUR, John
See— CLARKE, James Stanier & McArthur, John

MACARTHY, M.E.
See— BELCHER, J. & Macarthy, M.E.

MACAULAY, Lord Thomas Babington
– **The History of England.** L., 1885. 8 vols. Sm. 8vo. Tree cf., spines gt., by Riviere. (SG. Feb.16; 188) $325
– **The Works.** Ed.:– Lady Trevelyan. L., 1871. 8 vols. Lge. 8vo. Tree cf. gt. (SG. Feb.16; 189) $350
– – **Anr. Edn.** N.Y., 1874-75. 16 vols. Hf. cf. gt., lightly worn. (PNY. Oct.20; 186) $150

McBANE, Donald
– **The Expert Sword-Man's Companion.** Glasgow, 1728. Sm. 8vo. Lacks port. & gathering H, plts. supplied in facs. & separately bnd. in wraps, foxed, hf. cf.; cont. MS. ex-libris of James Buchanan. (SG. Sep.22; 196) $200

McCALL, H.B.
– **Story of the Family of Wandesforde of Kirklington & Castlecomer.** L., 1904. *1st. Edn.* Lge. 4to. Orig. buckram, gt. (GM. Dec.7; 289) £85

Mac CARTHY, J.
– **Choix de Voyages dans les Quatre Parties du Monde ... Entrepris depuis l'Année 1806 jusqu'à ce Jour.** 1821-22. 8 vols. only (of 10). Cont. roan. (HD. Jan.24; 34) Frs. 1,000

McCLAUSLAND, Elizabeth
- **Changing New York.** Ill.:– after Bernice Abbott. N.Y., 1939. *1st. Edn.* 4to. Lr. outer corners worn, cl. (SG. Nov.10; 1) $175

M'CLINTOCK, Sir Francis Leopold
- **The Voyage of the 'Fox'.** L., 1859. *1st. Edn.* Later hf. cf., spine gt.; A.l.s. from author tipped in. (BBA. Dec.15; 13) *Sons of Liberty books.* £70

McCLURE, Michael
- **Passage.** Big Sur, Ca., 1956. *1st. Edn.* (200). Tall 8vo. Orig. wraps., sewn. as iss.; sigd. by author & Marshall Clements, Frederic Danney copy. (CNY. Dec.16; 221) $180

McCOOK, Henry C.
- **American Spiders & Their Spinningwork: A Natural History of the Orbweaving Spiders of the United States.** Phila., priv. ptd., 1889-93. *1st. Edn.* (250) numbered. 3 vols. Lge. 4to. 35 litho. plts., orig. cl.; sigd. (SG. Mar.22; 200) $450

McCORMACK, Joseph, of Prestonpans
- **State-Papers & Letters addressed to William Carstares, confidential secretary to King William** ... Edinb., 1774. 4to. Cont. panel. cf. (PD. May 16; 147) £52

McCORMICK, Richard C.
- **Arizona: Its Resources & Prospects. A Letter to the Editor of the New York Tribune.** N.Y., 1865. *1st. Edn.* Folding map tipped in, paper wraps., s.-c. (LH. Sep.25; 263) $140

McCRACKEN, Harold
- **The Frank Tenney Johnson Book. A Master Painter of the Old West.** N.Y., 1974. *(350)* numbered. 4to. Naugahyde, cast relief bronze port. set in upr. cover; sigd. by author. (LH. Sep.25; 264) $130
- **George Catlin & the Old Frontier.** N.Y., 1959. *[1st. Edn.]. (250) numbered & sigd.* 4to. Leath. gt., cl. s.-c. (SG. Jan.19; 146) $250
- **– Anr. Copy.** Cf. gt., s.-c. (LH. Jan.15; 353) $200
- **– Anr. Copy.** Gt. pict. mor., corners scuffed. (SG. Apr.5; 50) $130

McCRAE, Hugh
- **Forests of Pan.** Sydney, 1944. Qtr. leath.; drawing & MSS. by McCrae inserted, Harry F. Chaplin copy. (JL. Jul.15; 275) Aus. $160
- **Satyrs & Sunlight.** Intro.:– Thomas Earp. Ill.:– after Norman Lindsay. L., Fanfrolico Pr., 1928. *(550).* 4to. 1 plt. creased, leath., rubbed, partly unc. (SG. Jan.12; 101) $120
- **– Anr. Copy.** Bdg. not stated; long inscr. by Jack Lindsay, Harry F. Chaplin copy. (JL. Jul.15; 252) Aus. $230

MCCULLOCH, John Ramsey
- **Catalogue of Books, The Property of a Political Economist.** 1862. A few margins lightly spotted, mor.-bkd. bds. (CSK. May 18; 95) £320
- **A Dictionary, Geographical, Statistical, & Historical.** 1841-42. 2 vols. 1 folding map hand-cold., slight tears, spotting, hf. cf. gt. (P. Jul.5; 270) £75
- **A Treatise on the Principles** ... **of Taxation.** 1845. *1st. Edn.* Hf.-title, publisher's advts., orig. cl. gt., unc. (P. Feb.16; 265) £120
- **Treatises & Essays** ... **on Economical Policy.** Edinb., 1853. *1st. Edn.* Orig. cl. gt., spine bleached. (P. Feb.16; 265a) £95

MacCURTIN, H.
- **A Brief Discourse in Vindication of the Antiquity of Ireland.** Dublin, 1717. *1st. Edn.* 2 pts. in 1 vol. Sm. 4to. Hf.-title, subscribers list, cont. cf. (SKC. Jan.13; 2232) £90

MacDIARMID, Hugh (Pseud.)
See— GRIEVE, Christopher Murray 'Hugh MacDiarmid'

McDONALD, Alexander (Pseud.)
See— DICKSON, R.W. 'Alexander McDonald'

MACDONALD, James D.
See— CAVE, Col. Francis O. & Macdonald, James D.

M'DONNELL, Alexander Greenfield
- **A Narrative of Transactions in the Red River Country; from the Commencement of the Operations of the Earl of Selkirk, till the Summer of the Year 1816.** L., 1819. *1st. Edn.* D1 in facs., old hf. mor.; the Rt. Hon. Visc. Eccles copy. [Sabin 43170] (CNY. Nov.18; 182) $400

MAC DONNELL, Eneas
- **The Hermit of Glenconella.** L., 1820. *1st. Edn.* 16mo. Mor., gt.-tooled. borders & panel. centre. (GM. Dec.7; 352) £110

M'DOUGALL, Capt. George F.
- **The Eventful Voyage of H.M. Discovery Ship 'Resolute'.** 1857. Some foxing to text, orig. cl., worn. (P. Oct.20; 148) £75

MACEDA, M.J. de
- **Actas de los Santos Saturino, Honesto y Fermín.** Madrid, 1798. 4to. Leath. (DS. Apr.27; 2154) Pts. 25,000

MACER FLORIDUS, Aem.
- **De Herbarum Virtvtibus.** Basel, 1527. Lacks last lf. blank, slightly browned, margins lightly stained, incunable paper-covered bds. (HK. Nov.8; 268) DM 560

M'EWEN, George
- **The Culture of the Peach & Nectarine.** Ed:– J. Cox. L., 1859. Frontis. hand-cold., orig. cl. gt. (P. Nov.24; 255) *Henderson.* £50

MACFALL, Haldane
- **The French Pastellists of the Eighteenth Century.** 1909. 4to. Cont. buckram, soiled; extra-ill with MS. annots. by author. (S. Nov.8; 549) *Thorp.* £110

M'FARLAN, John
- **Inquiries Concerning the Poor.** Edinb., 1782. Cont. cf., spine gt. (S. Oct.11; 561) *Laywood.* £140

MACFARLANE, Charles
- **Constantinople in 1828.** 1829. *2nd. Edn.* 2 vols. Hf.-titles, orig. bds. (S. Nov.1; 95) *Scott.* £150

MACFARLANE, John
- **Antoine Verard.** 1900. 4to. Orig. buckram-bkd. bds.; H.M. Nixon coll. (BBA. Oct.6; 189) *Traylen.* £60

MAC-GEOGHEGAN, Abbé
- **Histoire de l'Irlande, Ancienne et Moderne.** Paris, 1758. 3 vols. 4to. Mott. cf. (GM. Dec.7; 294) £85

MACGIBBON, David & Ross, Thomas
- **The Castellated & Domestic Architecture of Scotland** ... Edinb., 1887-92. 5 vols. 4to. Orig. buckram cl. gt. (PD. Feb.15; 223) £210
- **– Anr. Copy.** 5 vols. Orig. cl. (S. Mar.6; 371) *Hatchwell.* £180
- **The Ecclesiastical Architecture of Scotland.** 1896-97. 3 vols. Orig. decor. buckram gt. (CE. Sep.1; 85) £95
- **– Anr. Copy.** 3 vols. Orig. cl. (PD. Jun.13; 69) £65

MacGILLIVRAY, John
- **Narrative of the Voyage of H.M.S. Rattlesnake.** L., 1852. 2 vols. Folding maps, 13 plts., map torn, many plts. stained, liby. stps. on titles, plt. versos & many ll., orig. blind-stpd. cl., unc., covers stained, spines reinforced & reprd., end-paper in Vol. 2 detchd. (CA. Apr.3; 80) Aus. $700

MacGILLIVRAY, William
- **The Edinburgh Journal of Natural History & Physical Sciences.** Edinb., [1835-]40. Pts. A-G (all publd.): 7 vols. 4to. 130 hand-cold. engraved plts. (Nissen calls for 206 engrs., but compl. according to binder's plt.-lists mntd. on front pastedowns), some foxing, cl.-bkd. ptd. bds., soiled & stained, last 2 pts. brkn. (SG. Oct.6; 241) $475
- **– Anr. Edn.** 1839. 2 vols. Fo. Hf. cf., gt. spines, some staining. (WW. Nov.23; 134) £85

McGOVERN, Melvin
- **Specimen Pages of Korean Movable Types.** Los Angeles, 1966. *(300). Primary Edn., (95).* Fo. 22 specimen pp. tipped in, orig. cl.-bkd. bds., publisher's box; Stanitz coll. (SPB. Apr.25; 286) $350

MCGRATH, Daniel F.
- **Bookman's Price Index: A Guide to the Values of Rare & Other Out-of-Print Books.** Detroit, 1973-78-79. Vols. VII, XIII, XV-XVII. in 5 vols. 4to. Cl., some wear, few corners lightly bumped; exliby., some markings. (HA. May 4; 156) $150

MCGREGOR, John
- **Historical & Descriptive Sketches of the Maritime Colonies of British America.** 1828. Slightly soiled thro.-out, cont. cl.-bkd. bds., worn. (BBA. Jan.19; 86) *Quaritch.* £65
- **Observations on the River Tyne with a View to the Improvement of its Navigation** ... Newcastle, 1832. Orig. bds., spine reprd., mostly unopened. (P. Jan.12; 247) *Quaritch.* £100

McGUIRE, Joseph D.
- **Pipes & Smoking Customs of the American Aborigines.** [Wash., 1898]. Offprint from the 'U.S. National Museum Report', pp. 353-645. New buckram. (SG. Nov.17; 328) $130

MACH, Ernst & Salcher, P.
- **Photographische Fixirung der durch Projectile in der Luft Eingeleiteten Vorgange.** Vienna, 1887. *1st. Separate Edn.* Offprint from 'Sitzungsberichte der Akademie der Wissenschaften', Vol. 95. 1st. p. slightly browned, orig. wraps., slight wear; presented to Société de Physique, inscr. on wrap., stp. of Societé Française de Physique, Stanitz coll. (SPB. Apr.25; 282) $200

MACHADO, Rafael
- **Memoria sobre los Trabajos en que se ha occupado el Consulado de Comercio de la Republica de Guatemala. — Inform y Estados con que Dui Cuenta a la Junta de Gobierno del Consulado de Comercio de la Republica de Guatemala.** Guatemala, 1862; 1865. *1st. Edns.* Together 2 vols. Orig. decor. wraps., sewed, 2nd. vol. nearly disbnd.; 1st. vol. with cont. sig. of Col. P. Brun on upr. wrap. (SG. Apr.5; 81) $110

MACHIAVELLI, Niccolo
- **Gesammelte Schriften.** Ed.:– H. Floerke. Trans.:– Ziegler & Nicolaus. München, 1925. 5 vols. Orig. linen. (V. Oct.1; 4063) DM 550
- **Historie.** 'Piacenza' [L.], 1587. 12mo. Slight dampstaining, a few short tears, old vell. bds., soiled. [STC 17161] (S. Oct.11; 405) *Lurie.* £90
- **– Anr. Copy.** Lge. 12mo. Title & last lf. little soiled, cont. vell. [STC 17161] (TA. Nov.17; 537) £70
- **Oeuvres.** Trans.:– Giraudet. Paris, 1803. *2nd. Edn.* 9 vols. Bds. (HD. Feb.22; 125) Frs. 1,300
- **Opere.** 'Italia' [Flor.?], 1826. 10 vols. Hf. cf. gt., worn. (BBA. Jun.28; 154) *Georges.* £60
- **Opere Inedite.** Londra, 1760. Slightly browned, cont. vell., slightly soiled. (BBA. Feb.23; 51) *Thorp.* £50
- **Tutte le Opere.** N.p., 1550 [but 1645]. *4th. 'Testina' Edn.* 5 pts. in 1 vol. 4to. Slightly browned & spotted, cont. cf., worn. (S. Mar.20; 805) *Quaritch.* £85
- **– Anr. Edn.** L., 1747. 2 vols. 4to. Engraved plt. browned, few ll. slightly spotted, later cf., spines gt. (BBA. Aug.18; 83) *Page.* £70
- **The Works.** L., 1695. Sm. fo. Lightly dampwrinkled, ex-liby., early spr. cf., worn. (SG. Apr.19; 122) $150

MACHIR, Moshe Ibn
- **Seder Ha'Yom.** Venice, 1599. *1st. Edn.* 4to. Some staining, trimmed, cl. (S. Oct.25; 244a) *Ludmir.* £300

MACHSOR LIPSIAE: ... 68 Facsimile Plates of the Mediaeval, Illuminated, Hebrew Manuscript in the possession of the Leipzig University Library Flor., [1964]. 2 vols. 4to. & fo. Plts. loose as iss., qtr. cl., both in specially designed worn bd. foldingcase. (SG. Feb.2; 228) $500

MACHZOR ASHKENAZ SHA'AR BAT RABBIM Venice, 1711-15. 4 vols. Fo. Short tear in 1st. title, some staining, creased, discold., hf. leath. (S. Oct.25; 247) *Halprin.* £650

MACHZOR SEFARADIM YAMIM NORAIM Commentary:– Moshe Cordovero. Venice, 1576, 1583-84. *1st. Edn. of Commentary.* Lacks 24 ll. &

Luach Ha'Moadim booklet, title in facs., some ll. torn with loss of text, stained thro.-out, soiled, trimmed, mod. blind-tooled mor. (S. Oct.25; 245) *Moriah.* £700

McIAN, Robert Ronald
See— LOGAN, James & McIan, Robert Ronald

McILVANNEY, William
See— ACKROYD, Norman & McIlvanney, William

MACKAIL, John William
- Biblia Innocentium being the Story of God's Chosen People. Kelms. Pr., 1892. *(200).* 4to. Vell., rebkd.; May Morris's card tipped in. (BBA. Dec.15; 254) *The Bookroom.* £68
- William Morris: an Address at Kelmscott House. Hammersmith, Doves. Pr., 1901. *(300).* 4to. Orig. vell. by the Doves Bindery, unc. (SG. Aug.4; 95) $110
– – **Anr. Copy.** Hand-bnd. orig. vell. (GB. May 5; 2344) DM 500

MACKANESS, George
- Admiral Arthur Phillip. Sydney, 1937. Orig. cl., d.-w. fraying. (KH. Nov.9; 394) Aus. $120
- The Art of Book-Collecting in Australia. Sydney, 1956. *(500) numbered & sigd.* Bdg. not stated. (KH. May 1; 451) Aus. $200
- Historical Monographs. Sydney, 1935-62. *Orig. Edns. Numbered & sigd.* 41 titles in 47 pts., as iss. Stiff wraps., some minor defects, in 6 cl. boxes. (KH. May 1; 456) Aus. $1,600

MACKAY, Andrew
- The Complete Navigator ... Phila., 1807. *1st. Amer. Edn.* Light foxing, plt. 4 torn, cont. cf. (PNY. Mar.27; 160) $100

MACKAY, Charles
- The History of the United States of America ... Ca.1870. 2 vols. Lge. 8vo. 6 col. double-p. maps, 65 steel engrs., some spotting, cont. hf. cf., spines gt.-decor., rubbed. (TA. Feb.16; 30) £70

MACKAY, George
- The History of Bendigo. Melbourne, 1891. *1st. Edn.* Orig. cl. (KH. Nov.9; 319) Aus. $130

MacKAYE, Percy
- The Mystery of Hamlet, King of Denmark. N.Y., [Lakeside Pr.], 1950. *Memorial Edn., (357) numbered & sigd. by author & designer.* Fo. Gt.-lettered buckram, buckram s.-c. (SG. Jan.12; 246) $150

M'KEEVOR, Thomas
- A Voyage to Hudson's Bay, during the Summer of 1812. L., 1819. *1st. Edn. Iss. with the Preface.* 19th. C. hf. roan, edges worn, unc.; the Rt. Hon. Visc. Eccles copy. [Sabin 43396 (different iss.)] (CNY. Nov.18; 184) $180

MacKENNA, F. Severne
- Chelsea Porcelain: The Red Anchor Wares. Leigh-on-Sea, [1951]. *(With:)* - Chelsea Porcelain: The Gold Anchor Wares. Leigh-on-Sea, [1952]. *(500) sigd.* Together 2 vols. 4to. Gt.-lettered cl., d.-w.'s. (SG. Jan.26; 124) $200
- Worcester Porcelain. Leigh-on-Sea, 1950. *(500) sigd.* 4to. Orig. cl. (BBA. Sep.8; 221) *Renard.* £65

M'KENNEY, Thomas L. & Hall, James
- History of the Indian Tribes of North America. Phila., 1837-44. 3 vols. Fo. 120 hand-cold. litho. plts. & ports., 1 uncold. map & 17 pp. of subscribers' sigs. in facs., faint offsetting on some plts., some spotting, mainly to text, cont. mor. gt., rubbed. (S. Dec.1; 279) *Burgess.* £6,200
– – **Anr. Edn.** Phila., 1838, 1842-44. 3 vols. Fo. 1 p. of litho. maps, 120 hand-finished cold. litho. plts., 17 pp. litho. sigs. of subscribers, errata slip, some offsetting and some foxing & stains to text, cont. hf. red mor. gt., badly worn, jnts. brkn.; Butler Place bkplts. [Sabin 43410a] (CNY. Dec.17; 581) $8,000
– – **Anr. Edn.** Phila., 1848-55. 3 vols. 118 (of 120) hand-cold. lithos., blind-stpd. cf., Vol. 2 not unif., as a coll. of plts., w.a.f. (SPB. Dec.13; 454) $1,500
– – **Anr. Edn.** Phila., 1855. 3 vols. Lge. 8vo. 120 hand-finished col. litho. plts., some foxing & smudges, mostly marginal, cont. red mor. gt. extra, defect. (SG. Nov.3; 135) $2,600

– – **Anr. Edn.** Boston, ca.1880?. 3 vols. 4to. 120 col. litho. plts., three-qtr. mor., rubbed, few end-papers detchd.; ex-liby., plts. unstpd., preface sigd. by publisher. (SG. Jan.19; 214) $1,200
– – **Anr. Edn.** Phila., n.d.-1842-44. 3 vols. Fo. 120 hand-finished cold. lithos., 1 sheet of maps, without subscribers lists, 1st. port. in Vol. I browned, some foxing & light offsetting, mostly of text, p. 185 Vol. III has black spots, a few plts. foxed, title of Vol. I creased, later hf. mor. (SPB. Dec.14; 64) $10,000
- The Indian Tribes of North America, with Biographical Sketches & Anecdotes of the Principal Chiefs. Ed.:- Frederick Webb Hodge. [Edinb.], 1933-34. *New Edn.* 3 vols. 4to. Orig. cl. gt., partly untrimmed. (TA. May 17; 62) £125
– – **Anr. Copy.** 3 vols. Thick sm. 4to. Cl., d.-w.'s. (SG. Apr.5; 113) $175
– – **Anr. Edn.** Ed.:- F.W. Hodge. Edinb., 1933-34. 3 vols. Mor. gt., by Bayntun (Rivière), s.-c.'s. (S. Oct.4; 93) *Traylen.* £280
– – **Anr. Copy.** 3 vols. 4to. Orig. cl. (CSK. Jul.6; 14) £130
– – **Anr. Copy.** 3 vols. 2 folding maps, 124 plts., all but 2 cold., orig. cl., lightly rubbed. (S. Jun.25; 107) *Traylen.* £90

MACKENZIE, Alexander
- Voyages d'Alexandre. Mackenzie, dans l'Intérieur de l'Amérique Septentrionale, faits en 1789, 1792 et 1793. Trans.:- J. Castera. Paris, 1802. *1st. Edn. in Fr.* 3 vols. 12mo. Hf.-title, title & port. in Vol. 1 slightly stained, cont. cf., gt. spines, some wear. (RO. Dec.11; 196) $325
- Voyages from Montreal, on the River St. Lawrence, through the Continent of North America ... L., 1801. *1st. Edn.* 4to. Hf.-title, 2 p. errata, each of the 3 maps with clean tear from careless opening, cont. mott. cf. gt., gt. spine; the Rt. Hon. Visc. Eccles copy. [Sabin 43414] (CNY. Nov.18; 185) $1,400
– – **Anr. Edn.** N.Y., 1802. *1st. Amer. Edn.* Tall 8vo. Slight browning, sm. tears in map, cont. tree sheep, worn, covers detchd. (SG. Jan.19; 135) $200

McKENZIE, D.F.
- The Cambridge University Press 1696-1712. Camb., 1966. 2 vols. 4to. Orig. cl., d.-w.'s; H.M. Nixon coll., with his sig. & notes on front free endpaper of Vol. 1. (BBA. Oct.6; 87) *Devas.* £80

MACKENZIE, Sir E.M. Compton
- My Life & Times. 1963-71. *1st. Edn.* 10 vols. Some vols. with owner's sig. on front free endpaper, all in orig. cl., d.-w.'s, some slightly soiled & torn. (BBA. Jul.27; 208) *Parsons.* £60

MACKENZIE, George, M.D.
- The Lives & Characters of the Most Eminent Writers of the Scots Nation; with an Abstract & Catalogue of their Works. Edinb., 1708-11-22. 3 vols. Fo. Cont. cf., spines gt., worn; Sir Ivar Colquhoun, of Luss copy. (CE. Mar.22; 202) £110

MACKENZIE, Sir George, of Rosehaugh
- Observations on the Acts of Parliament made by King James I-VI, Queen Mary, King Charles I & II. Edinb., 1687. 4to. Cont. cf. (PD. May 16; 164) £65
- The Works ... Edinb., 1716-22. *1st. Coll. Edn.* 2 vols. Fo. Engraved frontis. port. in Vol. 2, 31 plts., cont. panel. cf., worn; Sir Ivar Colquhoun, of Luss copy. (CE. Mar.22; 200) £220

MACKENZIE Sir George Stuart
- Travels in the Island of Iceland. Edinb., 1812. *2nd. Edn.* 4to. Some foxing, 2pp. replaced by photo facs., cont. style hf. leath. (D. Nov.23; 1009) DM 1,500

MACKENZIE, Henry
[-] The Man of the World. L., 1773. 2 vols. 12mo. Some staining, mostly light, 1 margin defect. just shaving text, cont. cf.; Sir Velters Cornewall Bt. bkplts. (BBA. Dec.15; 176) *Finch.* £95

McKENZIE, Kenneth
- Our Earth. Ill.:- Norman Lindsay. Sydney, 1937. *(225) numbered.* Orig. sigd. etching, qtr. cl., some minor wear to cover. (JL. Jul.15; 563) Aus. $750

MACKENZIE, Roderick
- Strictures on Lt. Col. Tarleton's History of the Campaigns of 1780-81 ... 1787. Orig. bds., unc., worn. (P. Jun.7; 311) £160

M'KERRELL, T.
- Kilmarnock to Johannesburg. Kilmarnock, 1899. Orig. bdg., covers slightly faded. (VA. Apr.27; 859) R 190

McKERROW, R.B. & others
- A Dictionary of Printers & Booksellers in England, Scotland & Ireland. 1910-32. 4 vols. Sm. 4to. Orig. buckram-bkd. bds., 1 spine a little worn; H.M. Nixon coll., with his MS. notes. (BBA. Oct.6; 200) *Knuf.* £85

MACKINNON, Capt. Lauchlan Bellingham
- Atlantic & Transatlantic Sketches, Afloat & Ashore. L., 1852. *1st. Edn.* 2 vols. Orig. cl., spines faded; the Rt. Hon. Visc. Eccles copy. [Sabin 43461] (CNY. Nov.18; 186) $180
- Steam Warfare in the Parana. 1848. 2 vols. Folding map, 3 plts., stained, liby. stps. on titles, orig. cl., spines defect., worn. (BBA. Jun.28; 230) *Wise.* £58

MACKWORTH-PRAED, C.W. & Grant, C.H.B.
- African Handbook of Birds. L., 1952-63. *1st. Edns.* Series 1 & 2, 4 vols. Plts., most. cold., text ills., orig. cl. (S. Apr. 10; 432) *Temperley.* £80
- Birds of Eastern & North Eastern Africa. 1952-55. *1st. Edns.* 2 vols. Orig. cl. gt., little faded. (TA. Sep.15; 515) £50
- Birds of West Central & Western Africa. 1970-73. *1st. Edn.* 2 vols. Orig. cl., d.-w. (LC. Mar.1; 171) £60

MACLAURIN, Colin
- An Account of Sir Isaac Newton's Philosophical Discoveries. 1748. *1st. Edn.* 4to. Hf.-title, cont. spr. cf.; Sir Ivar Colquhoun, of Luss copy. (CE. Mar.22; 203) £320
- A Treatise of Fluxions. Edinb., 1742. *1st. Edn.* 2 vols. 4to. Hf.-title in Vol. I, lacks hf.-title in Vol. II (?), 1 plt. very defect. & largely replaced in early pen facs., some margin tears (no loss of text), some soiling & staining, cont. cf., rebkd. worn; Stanitz coll. (SPB. Apr.25; 284) $300

M'LEAN, Thomas, Publisher
- Historical Portraiture of Leading Events in the Life of Ali Pacha. Ill.:- G. Hunt after W. Davenport. L., 1823. Fo. 6 hand-cold. plts., hf. cf., defect. & loose. (GM. Dec.7; 658) £150

MACLEHOSE, J.
- Maclehose's Picture of Sydney, & Strangers' Guide in New South Wales for 1839 ... Sydney, 1839. MS. key added to map, a few minor defects, 19th. C. mor., slight rubbing. (KH. May 1; 448) Aus. $2,500

MACLEISH, Archibald
- New Found Land, Fourteen Poems. Paris, Black Sun Pr., 1930. *1st. Edn., (135). (25) numbered on Japan vell., sigd.* Orig. ptd. wraps., tissue overlay d.-w., publisher's box slightly worn; Frederick Dannay copy. (CNY. Dec.16; 222) $320

M'LEOD, John
- Voyage of His Majesty's Ship Alceste. 1818. Plts. hand-cold., hf. cf. gt. (P. Mar.15; 92) £55
– – **Anr. Edn.** L., 1819. *3rd. Edn.* Engraved folding chart, port., 5 hand-cold. aquatints, cont. mor. gt., slightly worn. (S. Mar.6; 36) *Falk.* £60
– – **Anr. Copy.** Cont. leath. gt., spine a little worn. (BBA. Sep.29; 31) *Scott.* £50

MACLER, Frederic
- Documents d'Art Armeniens. Paris, 1924. 2 vols. Sm. fo. Vol.1, 36 ills., some cold., vol.2, 260 ills. on 103 plts., ex-liby., each plt. stpd. on blank verso, ptd. wraps. & loose in bd. folder with ties. (SG. May 3; 16) $175
- Miniatures Arméniennes. Paris, 1913. 1 vol. Fo. Orig. cl.-bkd. bd. portfo. *(With:)* - Documents d'Art Arméniens. Paris, 1924. 2 vols. Fo. Orig. wraps. & portfo. (BBA. Sep.8; 15) *Saidi.* £95

MACLURE, A.
- Obsequies of the Late Illustrious Field Marshall the Duke of Wellington. N.d. Fo. Cont. hf. mor., worn. (CSK. Dec.16; 127) £110

McCLURE, Michael
- -!The Feast! [caption title]. [San Franc., 1960]. *(Bound with:)* - The Blossom; or, Billy the Kid [caption title]. [N.Y.], 1964 [i.e. 1966?]. Together 2 works in 1 vol. 4to. Stationers' wraps., unlettered; each work with author's autograph title-lf. & several autograph corrections & emendations. (SG. Mar.1; 295) $140
- Passage. Big Sur [Ca.], 1956. *(200)*. Lge. 8vo. Pict. wraps., unc. (SG. Mar.1; 305) $275
- Solstice Blossom. Ill.:– Wesley Tanner. [Berkeley], Arif Pr., 1973. *(30) numbered & sigd. by author & artist.* 4to. Watercolour frontis., pict. wraps. (SG. Mar.1; 311) $110

McMICHAEL, William
- The Gold-headed Cane. L., 1827. *1st. Edn.* Vig. on title, wood-engrs., title discold., few stains, orig. bds., soiled, rebkd., unc. (S. Apr.10; 554)
Bickersteth. £50

McMINN, G.R. & Rendle, J.J.
- Abridged Report on the Northern Territory of South Australia; its Natural Features, Pastures, Mineral, Present Resources, & Future Possibilities ... Melbourne, 1902. Sm. fo. Ptd. wraps., detchd. & slightly chipped. (KH. May 1; 449) Aus. $100

MACMUNN, G.F.
- The Armies of India. 1911. 4to. Limitation lf. inscr. 'Presented to me by the authors R.G. Alexander. Delhi 1911', mntd. cold. plts., orig. cl., slightly soiled. (CSK. May 18; 86) £100

MACMUNN, Sir George & Falls, Capt. Cyril
- Military Operations. Egypt & Palestine. 1928-30. 2 vols. in 5, including 2 portfos. of maps. Orig. cl. (BBA. Aug.18; 283) *F. Edwards.* £60

McNAUGHTON, Arnold
- The Book of Kings, a Royal Genealogy. Arcadia Pr., 1973. *(55) numbered.* 3 vols. Fo. Mor. gt. by Zaehnsdorf, s.-c., stained. (BBA. Dec.15; 334)
Heraldry Today. £60

MACNEICE, Louis
- Blind Fireworks. L., 1929. *1st. Edn.* 12mo. Orig. cl., d.-w. soiled; Frederic Dannay copy. (CNY. Dec.16; 223) $240

MACNICOL, Donald
- Remarks on Dr. Samuel Johnson's Journey to the Hebrides. 1779. Cont. spr. cf., spine gt.-decor., pres. inscr. on end-paper; Sir Ivar Colquhoun, of Luss copy. (CE. Mar.22; 204) £280

MACOMB, Capt. John N. & Newberry, J.S.
- Report of the Exploring Expedition. From Santa Fe, New Mexico, to the Junction of the Grand & Green Rivers of the Great Colorado of the West, in 1859, ... Wash., 1876. 4to. Cl.; Navarre Macomb copy. (LH. Sep.25; 259) $200
- -Anr. Copy. 4to. Cl.; the Navarre Macomb copy. (LH. Jan.15; 348) $150

MACONOCHIE, Capt. Alexander
- Thoughts on Convict Management ... Hobart, 1838. Cl., worn & stained. (KH. May 1; 457)
Aus. $350

MAC ORLAN, Pierre (Pseud.)
See— DUMARCHAIS, Pierre 'Pierre Mac Orlan'

McPARLAND, James
- Statistical Survey of the County of Mayo. Dublin, 1802. *1st. Edn. (Bound with:)* FITZGERALD, George Robert - Authentic Memoirs of George Robert Fitzgerald Esq. [of Castlebar] with a Full Account of his Trial & Execution. L., 1786. *(Bound with:)* DUTTON, Hely - A Statistical & Agricultural Survey of the County of Galway. Dublin, 1824. *1st. Edn.* Together 3 works in 1 vol. Hf. cf. (GM. Dec.7; 215) £200
- -Anr. Copy. Folding map loose, crimson hf. mor.; inscr. by author. (GM. Dec.7; 417) £150

MacPHAIL, Ian (Ed.)
See— MELLON, Paul & Mary

MACPHERSON, James
- The History of Great Britain, from the Restoration, to the accession of the House of Hannover. 1775. *1st. Edn.* 2 vols. 4to. Errata lf. in 1st. vol., cont. spr. cf., spines gt.; Sir Ivar Colquhoun, of Luss copy. (CE. Mar.22; 206) £90

MACPHERSON, James (Ed.)
See— OSSIAN

MacPIERSON, Rev. H.A
See— HARVIE-BROWN, J.A. & MacPierson, Rev. H.A.

McQUEEN, James
- A Geographical & Commercial View of Northern Central Africa. Edinb., 1821. Cont. cf., spine rubbed; Sir George Farrar bkplt. (SSA. Jul.5; 292)
R 360
- The West India Colonies; the Calumnies & Misrepresentations Circulated Against Them by the Edinburgh Review, Mr. Clarkson, Mr. Cropper, etc.1824. *1st. Edn.* Cont. spr. cf., rebkd.; ex-Signet liby. (TA. Jun. 21; 66) £74

MACQUER, Pierre-Joseph
- Dictionaire de Chymie Contenant la Théorie et la Pratique de cette Science. Paris, 1777. *2nd. Edn.* 3 vols. Sm. 8vo. Cont. marb. roan, spines decor. (HD. Nov.9; 182) Frs. 1,650
- -Anr. Edn. Paris, 1786. 2 vols. 12mo. Roan. (HD. Feb.22; 127) Frs. 2,000

MACQUOID, Percy
- A History of English Furniture. L., 1904-06. 3 vols. only (lacks Age of Stinwood). Fo. Some ll. loose & frayed, orig. cl., slightly rubbed, spines faded. (S. May 1; 709) *Potterton.* £100
- -Anr. Copy. 3 vols. only. Fo. Some light soiling, orig. cl. (CSK. Sep.30; 92) £65
- -Anr. Edn. L., 1904-08. 4 vols. in 2. Fo. Hf. cf. (S. May 1; 712) *Kapusi.* £350
- -Anr. Copy. 4 vols. Fo. Cont. hf. mor.; front blank of 1st. vol. inscr. by author to Anthony Prinsep & sigd. (CSK. Feb.10; 174) £220
- -Anr. Copy. 4 vols. Fo. Orig. cl., slightly rubbed & faded. (S. Nov.8; 553) *Thorp.* £140
- -Anr. Copy. 4 vols. Fo. 60 col. plts., gt.-lettered cl., spine ends frayed. (SG. Aug.25; 154) $350
- -Anr. Edn. L., 1904 (Vol.1), 1923. 4 vols. Fo. Orig. buckram, rubbed. (S. Nov.8; 550)
Sims. £100
- -Anr. Edn. [1904-38-38]. 3 vols. only. Fo. Orig. cl., dampstained, 1 vol. rebkd. (CSK. Jan.27; 107)
£85
- -Anr. Edn. L., 1919. 4 vols. Fo. 1st. few ll. of The Age of Mahogany defect. or stained due to damp, orig. buckram, stained. (S. May 1; 713)
Heneage. £70
- -Anr. Copy. 4 vols. Fo. Loose in orig. cl. (TA. Nov.17; 502) £56
- -Anr. Edn. L., 1919-23. 4 vols. Fo. Orig. buckram, spines very slightly faded; 2 vols, pres. copies to Princess Mary, with her bkplt. (S. Oct.4; 172) *Allegretti.* £150
- -Anr. Edn. 1923-28. 4 vols. Fo. Orig. cl. gt., spines & covers faded. (LC. Jul.5; 70) £180
- -Anr. Edn. 1938. 4 vols. Fo. Orig. cl. gt. (LC. Jul.5; 70a) £190
- -Anr. Copy. 4to. Cl., d.-w.'s, faded. (BS. May 2; 114) £130
- -Anr. Edn. [1938]. 4 vols. Fo. 1 plt. detchd., orig. cl., lightly soiled. (CSK. Jul.27; 25) £220
- -Anr. Edn. N.d. 4 vols. 4to. Cl., spines damaged. (P. Oct.20; 104) £75

MACQUOID, Percy & Edwards, Herbert Cecil Ralph
- The Dictionary of English Furniture. L., 1924-27. 3 vols. Fo. Orig. cl. (S. May 1; 714) *Kapusi.* £320
- -Anr. Copy. 3 vols. Fo. Orig. cl.; J.R. Abbey bkplt. (S. Oct.4; 173) *Wais.* £300
- -Anr. Copy. 3 vols. Fo. Some text with margin tears, not affecting text, hf. mor. gt. (P. Nov.24; 164) £260
- -Anr. Copy. 3 vols. Fo. Orig. cl., 2 vols. in orig. d.-w. (LC. Oct.13; 58) £190

- -Anr. Copy. 3 vols. Fo. Orig. linen, corners bumped. (GB. May 4; 1912) DM 600
- -Anr. Edn. L., 1954. *2nd. Edn.* 3 vols. Fo. Orig. cl. & d.-w.'s,w.a.f.; from liby. of Luttrellstown Castle. (C. Sep.28; 1789) £450
- -Anr. Copy. 3 vols. Fo. Orig. cl. gt., d.-w.'s slightly torn. (C. Nov.9; 95) *Sancroft-Baker.* £350

MACQUOID, T.R.
See— WARING, John Burley & Macquoid, T.R.

MACREDIE, A.
- Atlas Minima. Edinb., ca. 1814. 12mo. Engraved title, index lf. & 30 miniature hand-cold. maps, cont. hf. cf. (S. Apr.9; 78) *Traylen.* £120

MACROBIUS, Aurelius Theodosius
- In Somnium Scipionis ex Ciceronis VI Libro de rep. eruditissima Explanatio. Venezia, 1528. Stained at beginning & end, lacks 2 blank ll. at beginning, 18th. C. cf., decor. spine, Duke of Marlborough ex-libris. (SI. Dec.15; 22)
Lire 480,000
- Opera J.I. Pontanus recensuit: & Saturnaliorum Libros ... Leyden, 1597. Cont margin annots. & text underlining, slightly browned, some sigs. with light stain, cont. vell., slightly spotted, upr. cover lightly cockled. (HT. May 8; 168) DM 480
- [Somnium Scipionis et Saturnalia]. Ed.:– Joannes Rivius. Venice, 15 Jun. 1513. Fo. Many inner margins stained, light worming in last 3 ll., 17th. C. qtr. vell., edges worn. (S. Nov.17; 46)
Maggs. £680

MACULLOCH, John
- Remarks on the Art of Making Wine. 1821. *3rd. Edn.* Some spotting, orig. bds. (CSK. Oct.7; 113)
£60

McVICKAR, H.W.
- Our Amateur Circus; or a New York Season. N.Y., 1892. Ob. 8vo. Gt.-decor. watered silk, box worn. (SG. Aug.4; 190) $140

MADAN, F.F.
- A New Bibliography of the Eikon Basilike. Oxford, 1950. Cf., cf.-bkd. box. (S. May 1; 411)
Georges. £50

MADARIAGA, Fr. Juan de
- Vida del Seráfico Padre San bruno Patriarca de la Cartuxa. Valencia, 1596. 4to. Vell. (DS. Nov.25; 2523) Pts. 38,000

MADARIAGA, Salvador de
- Don Quixote. L., Gregy. Pr., 1934. *(250) numbered.* Orig. holland-bkd. bds., slightly discold.; bkplt. of David Garnett. (BBA. Mar.21; 309)
Palace Books. £50

MADDEN, Sir Frederick
See— SHAW, Henry & Madden, Sir Frederick

MADDEN, R.R.
- The United Irishmen, their Lives & Times. L., 1842. 2 vols. Sm. 8vo. Hf. mor., armorial motif on spine. (GM. Dec.7; 384) £100

MADDOCK, James
- The Florist's Directory, a Treatise on the Cultivation of Flowers. L., 1822. Some offsetting, sig. on title, cont. hf. cf., spine gt. (BBA. May 23; 282)
Thorpe. £85

MADERNUS, Carolus
- [-] Recueil de Plans et Elevations du Vatican et des Eglises Romaines. N.d. Fo. Lacks title, coll. of 30 plts., 1 sigd. 'Carolus Madernus inventor'. bdg. brkn. (HD. Dec.15; 24) Frs. 1,200

MADISON, James
See— HAMILTON, Alexander & others

MADOL, Roger
See— SITWELL, Sacheverell & Madol, Roger

MADOU, Jean Baptiste
- Evénements de la Belgique. Bruxelles, n.d. Ob. 4to. Red mor., blind- & gt.-decor., wrap. (doubled) preserved. (LM. Mar.3; 34) B.Frs. 32,000
- Vie de Napoléon. Bruxelles, 1827. 2 vols. Ob. 4to. 141 (of 145) litho. plts., hf. roan. (LM. Oct.22; 278) B.Frs. 16,000

MADOX, Thomas
– Baronia Anglica; an History of Land-Honors & Baronies ... L., 1741. Fo. Cont. cf., gt. dentelles, rebkd. gt.-decor. mor., worn. (CBA. Dec.10; 90)
$160

MADRID
– Guía de Litigantes y Pretendientes para le Año 1808. Madrid, 1807. 16mo. Mor. (DS. Nov.25; 2425)
Pts. 30,000

MAELEN, Philippe Vander
– [Atlas Universel de Géographie, Physique, Statistique et Mineralogique]. [Brussels], 1827 or later. Fo. 180 numbered double-p. litho. maps from the above, or similar series, hand-cold. in outl., a few with sm. tears at centre, loose in portfo. (C. Mar.14; 64)
Crossby. £1,100

MAESTRE DE SAN JOAN
– Deleyte de Cavalleros, y placer de los Cavallos. Madrid, [1736]. Sm. fo. Browning & staining, heavier in parts, vell. (V. Sep.29; 1456) DM 550

MAESTRE Y CANAMARES, A.
– Derrotero de la Navegación a las Islas Filipinas. Sevilla, 1862. 4to. L.P., bdg. (DS. Dec.16; 2292)
Pts. 35,000

MAETERLINCK, Maurice
– Hours of Gladness. Ill.:– E.J. Detmold. L./N.Y., 1912. 4to. 20 cold. plts., margin edges little stained, orig. decor. cl. gt., d.-w., spine defect. (BBA. Mar.21; 342)
M.Ayres. £50
– – Anr. Edn. Ill.:– E.J. Detmold. [1912]. 4to. Orig. pict. cl. gt., slightly soiled. (P. Apr.12; 318)
Dennis. £80
– – Anr. Copy. 4to. Some pp. & end-papers lightly foxed, decor. cl., covers spotted, corners slightly bumped, spine darkened, bkplt. (CBA. Aug.21; 176)
$110
– Poésies Choisies dans 'Serres Chaudes'. Ill.:– Charles Doudelet. Vienne, 1921. *(15) on holland cold. by Doudelet, sigd. by author & artist.* 4to. Some slight foxing, bradel vell. gt. (HD. Jun.26; 102)
Frs. 2,100
– Serres Chaudes. Ill.:– Georges Minne. 1899. *Orig. Edn., (155) on holland.* Hf. mor., corners. (HD. May 11; 64)
Frs. 3,500
– La Vie des Abeilles. Ill.:– Adolphe Giraldon. 1914-18. Square 8vo. On vélin d'Arches, hf. mor., corners, by Affolter, mosaic spine, wrap. & spine preserved. (HD. May 4; 345)
Frs. 2,400
– La Vie des Abeilles. — La Vie des Fourmis. — La Vie des Termites. Ill.:– J.E. Laboureur. Paris, 1930. *On vell. de Rives.* 3 vols. Sewed, box. (HD. Dec.16; 148)
Frs. 2,300
– La Vie des Fourmis, la Vie des Termites, la Vie des Abeilles. Ill.:– J.E. Laboureur. Paris, 1930. *(680) on Rives.* 3 vols. Mor. gt. by Bernasconi, spine raised bands, wrap. preserved, s.-c. (SM. Mar.7; 2173)
Frs. 6,000

MAFEKING MAIL
– Special Siege Slips. Ed.:– G.N.H. Whales. 1 Nov. 1899-[31 May 1900]. Nos. 1-152, lacks no. 56 (not iss.), compl. Fo., 4to. & 8vo. Cancelled no. 45 present, explanation lf. in place of no. 56, 'seige' on no. 1, some foxing, gt.-lettered cl. (VA. Apr.27; 850)
R 720

MAFFEI, Alessandro
– Raccolta di Statue Antiche e Moderne. Ed.:– Domenico De Rossi. Roma, 1704. Fo. 163 engraved plts., browning & staining, hf. vell. (CR. Jun.6; 51)
Lire 400,000

MAFFEI, Giovanni Pietro
– Le Historie delle Indie Orientali. Venice, 1589. 4to. 1st. 2 ll. impft. & reprd., some foxing, light dampstains, old vell. (SG. Sep.22; 197)
$150

MAFFEI, Scipione
– Verona Illustrata. Verona, 1731-32. 4 vols. bnd. in 1. Fo. Some slight staining, hf. vell., defect. (CR. Jun.6; 52)
Lire 400,000

MAGASIN FUR KONST
See— KONST OCH NYHETS MAGASIN for Medorgare af alla Klasser [continued as Magasin fur Konst]

MAGASIN PITTORESQUE ...
Ed:– E. Cazeaux & E. Charton. Paris, 1833-63. Pts. I-XXXI (lacks IX, XII, XX & XXVI), in 27 vols. Sm. fo. Some foxing, cont. cf.-bkd. bds., worn, spines defect. (CH. Sep.20; 8)
Fls. 1,100
– – Anr. Run. Ill.:– T. Johanot, C. Nanteuil, Grandville. Paris, 1833-89. Years 1-57 & 1st. series table vol. 4to. Cont. hf. roan, some light scratches. (HD. Jun.22; 60)
Frs. 3,000

MAGATUS SCANDIANENSIS, Caesar
– De Rara Medicatione Vulnerum seu de Vulneribus Raro Tractandis. Venice, 1616. *1st. Edn.* Fo. Errata lf. for pt. 1 in dupl., index ll. at beginning short (from anr. copy?), few stains, new qtr. cf., marb. sides; Dr Walter Pagel copy. (S. Feb.7; 242)
Maggs. £240

MAGAZINE OF ART
[1878-]94. Vols. 1-17. 4to. & 8vo. Some ll. slightly soiled, cont. hf. mor. & orig. cl., slightly worn. (BBA. Nov.10; 219)
Sanders. £60

MAGAZINE OF THE BEAU MONDE
Vol. 4 only. 4to. Hand-cold. frontis. (cleanly torn) & 49 plts., cont. hf. cf., worn. (CSK. Jul.13; 166)
£70

MAGAZIN VOR AERZTE – NEUES MAZAZIN FUR AERZTE
Ed:– Ernst Gottfried Baldinger. Leipzig, 1778-96. Pts. 1-12 in 2 vols.; Vols. 1-8 & 11-13 & Vol. 18 in 12 vols. Together 14 vols. Cont. bds. (GB. May 3; 1016)
DM 900

MAGDEBURG, Joachim
– Dialogvs Oder. Ein Gespreche eines Esels vnd Bergknechts, Jhesu Christo vnserm einigen Erlöser, vnd seiner Göttlichen Wahrheit zun Ehren ... N.p., 1557. Title & 10 further ll. with reprd. margin defects., title soiled, with underlining & sm. stp., some slight browning, early 19th. C. bds. (HK. Nov.8; 270)
DM 480

MAGEE, David
– Victoria R.I.: A Collection of Books, Manuscripts ... by the Lady Herself & her Loyal Subjects. San Franc., [1969-70]. *(625).* 3 vols. 4to. Slip laid in announcing sale to Brigham Young University, decor. wraps. (SG. Jan.5; 212)
$100
See— HELLER, Elinor Raas & Magee, David

MAGEN BUCHLEIN
Strassburg, [1540]. 4to. Slightly browned & soiled thro.-out, old MS. marginalia, lacks 1 lf., mod. hf. mor. (D. Nov.23; 590)
DM 1,700

MAGGI, G.A.
– Principii della Teoria Matematica del Movimento dei Corpi. Milan, 1896. *1st. Edn.* Slightly browned, cont. hf. linen, slightly worn. (HT. May 8; 446)
DM 1,200

MAGGI, Giovanni
– Nuova Raccolta di Fontane. Rome, ca. 1645. 4to. Engraved title, 58 plts., including 7 folding, many sigd. & dtd. 1618, slight offset on 1 plt., cancelled liby. stp. on title & plt. versos, early 18th. C. vell. (C. Dec.9; 96)
Niystad. £500

MAGGS BROS.
– Biblotheca Americana et Philippina. 1922-28. 7 pts. in 6 vols. 4to. Cl.-bkd. bds. (BBA. Jan.19; 344)
Remington. £160
– – Anr. Edn. L., 1926-28. Pts. 5-7 only. Sm. 4to. Buckram. (SG. Jan.5; 213)
$110
– Catalogue No. 491, Australia & the South Seas. L., 1927. 4to. Qtr. mor., sig. on front end-paper. (CA. Apr.3; 81)
Aus. $130
– – Anr. Copy. Title from wrap., orig. wraps. (KH. Nov.9; 639)
Aus. $110

MAGIC WAND, The
Ed:– George Johnson & others. L., 1920-52. Vols. 9-41 (lacks nos. 206 & 207). 4to. & 8vo. Vols. 9-12 in cl., rest in orig. wraps. (S. Dec.20; 678)
Hackhofer. £120

MAGIUS, Hieronymus
– De Tintinnabulis Liber Postumus ... Amst., 1644. 1 text lf. detchd. & frayed at edges. (*Bound with:*)
– De Equuleo Liber Postumus ... 1664. 1 plt. torn

with slight loss. Together 2 works in 1 vol. 12mo. Cont. vell., soiled. (TA. Feb.16; 359)
£125

MAGNA CARTA
– Magna Carta. 1816. Fo. 15 ll., ptd. in gold on vell., all elab. illuminated in gold & cols., 2 ports., dedication lf., title & 11 text ll., cont. mor., by J. Whittaker, elab. gt. in gothic style tracery, gt. spine, broad inner gt. borders, pink watered silk doubls., spine & corners reprd., cl. s.-c. (BBA. Sep.29; 168)
Heywood Hill. £2,400
– Magna Carta et cetera Antiqua Statuta. 1556. 2 pts. in 1 vol. Sm. 8vo. Lacks A1 (blank?), a few margin notes & underlinings, some staining, later cf., spine gt. [STC 9277] (BBA. Jun.14; 20)
White. £150
– Magna Charta cum Statutis. 1587. Slight staining to last few ll., lacks corner from last 3 ll., affecting text on 2 ll., old vell., with ties. [STC 9282] (LC. Jul.5; 398)
£85
– – Anr. Edn. L., 1608. Dampstained, old cf., worn, rebkd. [STC 9284] (SG. Oct.27; 186)
$130

MAGNAN, Domenico
[-] La Ville de Rome. Rome, 1787. 4 vols. Lge. fo. Light old soiling, plt. versos & margin multi-stpd., 19th C. hf. leath., unc. (V. Sep.29; 121)
DM 1,200

MAGNAN, J.M.
– Taureaux pour ... El Cordobes. Ill.:– J. Cocteau. [Paris, 1963?]. Fo. Separate series of 17 cold. lithos. on vell. d'Arches, orig. wraps. (HK. Nov.11; 3478)
DM 550

MAGNE, Emile
– Nicolas Poussin Premier Peintre du Roi 1594-1665 (Documents Inédits), suivi d'un Catalogue Raisonné ... Brussels & Paris, 1914. *(500) numbered.* Fo. Cl., unc., soiled, orig. wraps. bnd. in; pres. copy, inscr. by author to Henri Roujon. (S. Apr.30; 59)
Leicester. £100

MAGNI PHILOSOPHORUM ARCANI REVELATOR. Quo Hermetis Discipuli Magnique Scrutatores Operis Omnia ... Invenient
Geneva, 1688. 12mo. Stp. on title, some worming, cont. red mor. gt., spine gt.; Dr. Walter Pagel copy. (S. Feb.7; 243)
Janssen. £240

MAGNI PIACENTINO, Pietro-Paolo
– Discorsi sopra il Modo di Sanguinare. Roma, 1586. 4to. 1st. proofs of plts., cont. limp vell. (LM. Mar.3; 186)
B.Frs. 52,000

MAGNUS, Maurice
[-] Memoirs of the Foreign Legion. By M.M. Intro.:– D.H. Lawrence. L., 1924. *1st. Edn.* 1 vol. Sm. 8vo. Orig. cl., d.-w. slightly worn; inscr. 'To Pino Orioli from D.H. Lawrence even in Florence'. (*With:*) DOUGLAS, Norman 'Normyx' – D.H. Lawrence & Maurice Magnus. L., 1924. 1 vol. Sm. 8vo. Wraps. (SG. Jan.12; 207)
$550

MAGNUS, Olaus
– Historia delle Genti et della Natura delle Cose Settentrionali. Venice, 1565. *1st. Edn. in Italian.* Fo. Ptd. title with lge. woodcut device, full-p. engraved map of Scandinavia, & upwards of 450 woodcut ills. in text, a few ll. lightly stained in margins, vell. bds., slightly soiled. (S. May 21; 238)
Martyon. £1,100
– – Anr. Copy. Fo. Title-p. spotted, some spotting & browning thro.-out, light staining to upr. edges at end, 18th. C. tree cf., spine gt.; Stanitz coll. (SPB. Apr.25; 285)
$1,800
– Historien de Mittnachtigen Lander. Basle, 1567. Fo. Folding map cut close at head, just touching headline, margin stains at beginning & end, headline of title shaved, 18th. C. spr. cf. (S. Dec.1; 308)
Hannas. £1,150

MAGNUSSON, Eirikr
See— MORRIS, William & Magnusson, Eirikr

MAGNY, P.
See— HURTAUT, Pierre & Magny, P.

MAHARAM, of Rottenburg
See— MEIR BEN BARUCH [Maharam, of Rottenburg]

MAHLER, Gustav
- **Zehnte Symphonie.** Foreword:– Alma Mahler. [Vienna, 1924]. *Ltd. 1st. Edn., numbered.* Fo. Unbnd. as iss. in bd. & cl. folder, folder slightly frayed & dampstained at inner portion, slightly affecting top edges of text & facs. sheets, cl. ties; this copy for 'Herrn Direktor Felix Stransky', inscr. on 1st. text lf. 'Zur Erinnerung an das Musik und Theaterfest der Stadt Wien 1924' in an unknown hand, & sigd. 'Fritz M[ahler?]'. (SG. Nov.17; 279) $275

MAHLMANN, S. Aug.
- **Sämmtliche Schriften. Nebst Mahlmanns Biographie.** Leipzig, 1839-40. *1st. Coll. Edn.* 8 pts. in 2 vols. Cont. marb. bds., lightly bumped. (HK. Nov.10; 2591)   DM 500

MAHON, Philip Henry Stanhope, Lord
See— STANHOPE, Philip Henry, Lord Mahon

MAHR, Adolf
- **Christian Art in Ancient Ireland.** Dublin, 1932. Vol. 1 only (of 2). Fo. Cl. (GM. Dec.7; 484) £55

MAIDEN, Joseph Henry
- **Critical Revision of the Genus Eucalyptus.** L., 1909-33. 75 pts. in 8 vols. 4to. 296 plain & 12 col. plts., qtr. cf., rubbed, cover of Vol. 1 detchd; Royal Commonwealth Soc. copy. (P. Nov.24; 278)
Wheldon & Wesley. £400
- **The Forest Flora of New South Wales.** L., 1904-25. 77 pts. in 8 vols. 4to. 295 plts. (stained), a few ll. torn, qtr. mor., rubbed; Royal Commonwealth Soc. copy. (P. Nov.24; 279)
Wheldon & Wesley. £280

MAIER, Mich.
- **Arcana Arcanissima hoc est Hieroglyphica Aegyptio-Graeca** ... [Oppenheim], 1612. *1st. Edn.* 4to. Title with owner's note, some text annots., slightly browned & stained, cont. vell., using 15th. C. note book, slightly spotted & wormed. (HK. Nov.9; 1968)   DM 2,100

MAILLARD, Leon
- **Auguste Rodin.** 1899. *(60) on japan with suite.* 4to. Sewed; sigd. autograph dedication by Rodin. (HD. Jun.29; 139)   Frs. 1,400
See— BOUTET, Henri - MAILLARD, Leon

MAIMBOURG, Louis
- **Histoire de l'Arianisme depuis sa Naissance jusqu'à sa Fin.** Paris, 1686. 2 vols. 4to. Cont. cf., arms, decor. spines. (HD. Dec.9; 54) Frs. 3,000
See— NALSON, John — MAIMBOURG, Louis

MAIMONIDES
See— MOSHE BEN MAIMON [Maimonides]

MAINDRON, Ernest
- **Les Programmes Illustrés des Théâtres et des Cafés** ... Paris, ca. 1897. 4to. Orig. decor. paper covers bnd. in, anr. set pasted onto bds. (LH. Jan.15; 349) $160

MAINWARING, Sir Thomas
- **A Defence of Amicia, Daughter of Hugh Cyveliok, Earl of Chester.** L., 1673. *1st. Edn.* 3pp. advts., lacks last blank lf., cont. mor. gt. [Wing M300] (*With:*) - **A Reply to Sir Peter Leicester's Answer to Sir Thomas Mainwaring's Admonition.** Manchester, 1854. *1st. Edn. (100).* Cont. hf. mor. (BBA. May 3; 154)   *Robertshaw.* £75

MAIRAN, J. de
- **Traité Physique et Historique de l'Aurore Boréale.** Ill.:– after Ph. Simmoneau. Paris, 1754. 4to. Cont. marb. cf., spine decor.; from Château des Noës liby. (HD. May 25; 52) Frs. 1,300

MAIRE, N.M.
- **Atlas Administratif de la Ville de Paris.** Paris, 1821. Fo. 14 cold. engraved double-p. plans, old bds. (HD. Mar.19; 110) Frs. 2,300

MAISON, Karl Erik
- **Honoré Daumier; Catalogue Raisonné.** L., 1967. *(1500) numbered.* 2 vols. 4to. Orig. cl., orig. s.-c. (CSK. Feb.24; 152)   £260
- - **Anr. Edn.** L., 1968. *(1500) numbered.* 2 vols. 4to. Orig. cl., s.-c. (S. Apr.30; 60)
Rainsford. £350

MAISON RUSTIQUE (La) du XIXe Siècle
Paris, 1836. 5 vols. Lge. 8vo. Hf. roan, spine decor. (HD. Nov.9; 183)   Frs. 1,100
- - **Anr. Edn.** Ed.:– Bailly, Bixio & Malpeyre. Paris, ca. 1850. 4 vols. Lge. 8vo. Cont. hf. roan. (HD. May 16; 45)   Frs. 1,600

MAISTRE, Xavier [i.e. François-Xavier, comte de]
- **Oeuvres. — Oeuvres Posthumes.** Lyon, 1830. 4 vols.; 4 vols. Sewed, 4 s.-c.'s. (HD. Feb.22; 126)
Frs. 2,800

MAITLAND, William
- **The History of Edinburgh.** Edinb., 1753. Fo. Few ll. foxed, cont. hf. cf., covers detchd., unc. (CE. Sep.1; 4)   £65
- **The History of London.** L., 1756. 2 vols. Fo. 130 engraved plts. & maps, several folding, 1 hand-cold., cont. cf., rebkd., old spine laid down. (CSK. Nov.4; 45)   £350
- - **Anr. Copy.** Fo. 110 plts., including folding maps & plans, few short tears, slight margin worming in Vol.1, some browning or spotting, cont. cf., rebkd. gt., worn. (S. Mar.6; 392) *Pack.* £240
- - **Anr. Copy.** 2 vols. Fo. Some plts. & maps detchd., cont. hf. cf., worn, covers detchd., w.a.f. (CSK. Sep.16; 20)   £140
- - **Anr. Copy.** 2 vols. Fo. Some foxing, old bds., cf. back, some wear. (RO. Dec.11; 199) $220
- - **Anr. Edn.** L., 1756-60. 2 vols. Fo. 121 engraved maps, plans & plts., some folding, a few plts. cut close or shaved, cont. cf., rebkd. (S. Dec.1; 170)
Walford. £300
- - **Anr. Edn.** Ill.:– B. Cole & others. L., 1772. 2 vols. Fo. Few plts. shaved, some margin staining, minor margin worming at end of Vol. 2, cont. cf. gt., slightly worn. (S. Nov.1; 118) *Woodruff.* £280
- - **Anr. Edn.** Ill.:– B. Cole & others. L., 1775. 2 vols. Fo. 133 plts., some folding, 1 or 2 additional folds worn affecting engraved surface, some slight staining or browning, cont. hf. russ. gt. (S. Dec.13; 210)   *Levy.* £260

MAITRE-JAN, Ant.
- **Tractat von den Kranckheiten des Auges.** Nuremb, 1725. *1st. German Edn.* 4to. Frontis verso stpd. & with MS. owners mark, some light browning & foxing, cont. leath. gt., slightly rubbed & worn, head of spine slightly split, cont. MS. entry on lr. end-paper. (H. May 15; 317)   DM 3,000

MAITRES DE L'AFFICHE
Preface:– Roger Marx. Ill.:– after Bonnard, Chéret, Mucha, Steinlen, Toulouse-Lautrec etc. Paris, 1895-1900. 5 vols. Complete coll. Fo. Hf. red chagrin, unc. (HD. Feb.17; 44) Frs. 48,000

MAITRES ILLUSTRATEURS, Les
Paris, 1901-03. *(50) numbered on chine.* Special edn. from the monthly review 'L'Oeuvre et l'Image': 12 orig. pts. in 1 vol. 4to. 1 lf. creased, qtr. cl. & marb. bds., unc., corners slightly rubbed, orig. upr. & lr. wraps. for each of the issues & wraps. for the coll. preserved; blind-stp. of Comte Tony de Vibraye on hf.-title, Raphael Esmerian bkplt. (CNY. May 18; 188) $850

MAIUS, Iunianus Parthenopeus
- **Liber de Priscorum Proprietate Verborum.** Venetiis, Octavianus Scotus, 1483. Fo. Lacks 4 pp., initial letter & genealogical tree in col. & gold at beginning, blue & red initials, recent bds. (CR. Jun.6; 208)   Lire 1,500,000

MAIUS, Th.
See— BRIAN, T. — MAIUS, Th.

MAIZEROY, Reńe
- **La Mer.** Ill.:– Bracquemond, & after Courbet, Daubigny, Isabey & others. Paris, 1895. Fo. 2 orig. etchings, including 1 on cover, red hf. mor., corners, decor. spine, wraps. preserved. (HD. Sep.22; 277)
Frs. 2,000

MAJOLINO, L.
- **Peintures Murales Pompei.** Naples, ca. 1840. Ob. fo. 24 mntd. col. litho. plts., some heightened with gouache, orig. cl. gt., rubbed. (TA. Apr.19; 264)   £135
- - **Anr. Edn.** Naples, n.d. [late 19th. C.]. Ob. 4to. Litho. title (no text) & 24 litho. plts. hand-cold. with black backgrounds, trimmed & mntd. on thick

paper, cont. cl. gt. (C. Jun.27; 45)
Campbell. £300

MAJOR, John
- **Historia Majoris Britannia, tam Angliae quam Scotiae.** [Paris], 1521. *1st. Edn.* Printers mark on title, woodcut arms, initials, inner margin of title-p. strengthened, some light water-staining, later cf., rebkd. (BBA. May 23; 309) *Sokol.* £130

MAJOR, Thomas
- **The Ruins of Paestum, otherwise Posidonia in Magna Graecia.** 1768. Fo. Some stains, cont. cf.-bkd. bds., worn. (BBA. Jun.28; 232) *Dilua.* £280
- - **Anr. Copy.** Lge. fo. 31 plts. & cuts, some spotting, affecting margins, old cf.-bkd . marb. bds.; Sir Ivar Colquhoun, of Luss copy. (CE. Mar.22; 211)
£260

MALAGA
- **Noticia sobre el Establecimiento y Progresos de la Compania Marítima de Málaga.** Madrid, 1792. 4to. Linen. (DS. Nov.25; 2505) Pts. 22,000

MALAVOLTI, Orlando
- **Historia de'Fatti e Guerre de'Sanesi** ... Venezia, 1599. 3 vols. bnd. in 1. Light browning, vell. (CR. Jun.6; 53)   Lire 320,000

MALCOLM, James Peller
- **Anecdotes of the Manners & Customs of London.** L., 1808-11. 2 vols. 4to. 68 engraved plts. (24 hand-cold.), slightly spotted & browned, cont. cf., rebkd. (S. Mar.6; 393) *Rix.* £75
- **An Historical Sketch of the Art of Caricaturing, with Graphic Illustrations.** L., 1813. *1st. Edn.* 4to. 31 engraved plts., plts. lightly foxed, mod. mor. gt. (SG. Jan.26; 182) $140

MALCOLM, Sir John
- **The History of Persia.** Ill.:– Heath after Smidt. L., 1815. *1st. Edn.* 2 vols. 4to. L.P., hf.-titles, lge. folding engraved map (short tear reprd.), 21 engraved plts., some slightly foxed, cont. russ. gt., rebkd. preserving orig. spines, arms of Earl of Cawdor on covers. (S. May 22; 284)
Gibson. £1,100
- **The Life of Robert Lord Clive.** 1836. 3 vols. Cont. mor. gt. by Hering, Derome-style dentelle decors., elab. gt. inner dentelles, extremities lightly rubbed. (CSK. Mar.23; 199)   £110

MALCOLME, David
- [-] **A Collection of Letters, in which the Imperfection of learning ... The Usefulness of the Celtic** ... Edinb., 1739. Cont. mott. cf.; Sir Ivar Colquhoun, of Luss copy. (CE. Mar.22; 212)   £260

MALEBRANCHE, Nicolas
- **De la Recherche de la Vérité.** Paris, 1712. *6th. Edn.* 2 vols. in 1. 4to. (*With:*) - **Treatise Concerning the Search after Truth** ... Trans.:– T. Taylor. Oxford, 1694. Fo. Last lf. a little frayed at edges. [Wing M317] Together 2 vols. Cont. cf., worn. (TA. Jan.19; 370)   £60

MALEFACTOR'S REGISTER; or, the Newgate & Tyburn Calender ...
N.p., ca. 1780. 5 vols. 57 engraved plts., including frontis.'s, cont. cf.; Sir Ivar Colquhoun, of Luss copy. (CE. Mar.22; 213)   £600

MALET, Capt. Harold Esdaile
- **Annals of the Road.** L., 1876. *1st. Edn.* 10 cold. plts., orig. cl. gt., spine slightly soiled. (P. May 17; 272)   *Allan.* £60
- - **Anr. Copy.** Orig. cl. gt. (P. May 17; 14)
Allen. £55

MALEUS MALEFICARUM
Trans.:– Montague Summers. N.p., 1928. *1st. Edn. in Engl. (1275) numbered.* Fo. Orig. cl., partly unopened. (SG. Oct.6; 242) $120
- - **Anr. Copy.** On H.M.P., bdg. not stated, d.-w. (JL. Mar.25; 414)   Aus. $150

MALEVICH, Kasimir
- **O Novykh Sistemakh v Iskusstve [On New Systems in Art].** Vitebsk, 1920. *1st. Edn.* 4to. Orig. ptd. wraps., double imp. of woodcut cover design, frayed, top edge of upr. cover reprd., covers reattached. (S. Nov.21; 153)   *Weston.* £850

MALEZIEUX, Emile
- Travaux Publics des Etats-Unis d'Amérique en 1870. Paris, 1875. Atlas vol. only. 4to. 61 double-p. & folding plts. & maps, some soiling, minor stains, margin fraying, etc., hf. mor., worn. (RO. Nov. 30; 123) $175

MALHERBE, François de
- Les Oeuvres. Ed.:– Antoine Godeau. Ill.:– Vostermann. Paris, 1631. 2nd. Edn. 18th. C. hf. marb. cf., corners, decor. spine; ex-libris of André Felibien & his sons. (HD. Jan.27; 221) Frs. 1,500
- Les Poésies de Malherbe. Notes:– Ménage. Paris, 1689. 2nd. Edn. 12mo. Red mor. by Du Seuil, Marie-Anne d'O. arms; from Guyot de Villeneuve liby. (HD. Mar.29; 57) Frs. 24,500
- Vers du Sieur de Malherbe à la Reine. Paris, 1611. Orig. Edn. Red mor. by Capé, spine decor.; from Guyot de Villeneuve liby. (HD. Mar.29; 58) Frs. 18,000

MALIBRAN, H.
- Guide à l'Usage des Artistes et des Costumiers, contenant la Description des Uniformes de l'Armée Française de 1780 à 1848. Paris, 1904-07. 2 vols., including plt. vol. Hf. cf., corners. (HD. Jan.27; 335) Frs. 1,300

MALLARME, Stéphane
- L'Après-midi d'un Faune. Paris, 1876. Recovered marb. paper bds. by M. Brisson, unc., wrap. (HD. May 16; 46) Frs. 51,600
- – Anr. Edn. Trans.:– Aldous Huxley. Ill.:– John Buckland-Wright. Gold. Cock. Pr., 1956. (200) numbered. (100) specially bnd., with 4 extra plts. not in the book. Lge. 8vo. Prospectus loosely inserted, orig. mor. gt., s.-c. (S. Nov.21; 237) Hamer. £200
- Herodiade. 1957. Pict. vell., hand-painted end-papers. (D. Nov.24; 3173) DM 1,200
- Madrigaux. Ill.:– Raoul Dufy. Paris, 1920. (20) numbered with extra suite of plts. in black. 4to. Hand-cold. plts., loose, orig. wraps., spine slightly torn. (BBA. Jun.14; 208) Makiya. £380
- Les Poésies ... Paris, 1887. Orig. Edn., (47) on japan. 9 pts. in 1 vol. 4to. Cont. mor. gt. decor. by Marius Michel, sewed silk doubls. & end-ll., unc., upr. covers of wraps., s.-c.; with 10 orig. watercols. by Carloz Schwabe, 1893, verse dedication sigd. by Mallarmé. (HD. May 16; 47) Frs. 280,100
- – Anr. Edn. Bruxelles, 1899. 2nd. Edn. Jansenist mor. by Weckesser et fils. (HD. May 11; 65) Frs. 2,500
- – Anr. Copy. Lge. 8vo. Bradel bordeaux hf. mor. by Lemardeley, wrap. (HD. May 4; 348) Frs. 2,000
- – Anr. Edn. Ill.:– Henri Matisse. Lausanne, 1932. (25) numbered on Japon, sigd. by artist, with extra suite of plts. in black. 4to. Loose as iss in orig. wraps., orig. roan-bkd. bds., jnts. weak, s.-c., slightly soiled. (BBA. Jun.14; 236) Sims,. Reed & Fogg. £14,000

MALLERY, Garrick
- Picture-Writing of the American Indians. Wash., 1893. 4to. 54 plts., cl. (SG. Oct.20; 209) $120

MALLET, Allain Manesson
- Beschreibung des Ganzen Welt-Kreises. Frankfurt, 1719. Vols. 4 & 5 only (of 5) in 1. Thick sm. 4to. Additional engraved titles, 228 copperplts., old vell., w.a.f. (SG. Dec.15; 9) $600
- – Anr. Copy. Pts. 1-3 only (of 5) in 1 vol. 4to. 332 (of 333?) copperplts., cont. vell., spotted, end-papers renewed. (R. Oct.13; 2819) DM 1,500
- – Anr. Copy. Pt. 4 only (of 5),. 4to. Lacks 3 unnumbered plts., foxed, cont. leath. (HK. Nov.8; 1109) DM 420
- Description de l'Univers. Paris, 1683. [1st. Edn.]. 5 vols. Cont. cf., spines wormed. [Sabin 44130] (C. Nov.16; 128) Franks. £1,500
- – Anr. Copy. 5 vols. Approx. 10 ll. & 1 text lf. with bkd. tears (2 to subject), vol. 1 lacks 1 lf. with copper engr., vol. 3 lacks 1 lf. with copper engr. & 1 index lf., slightly browned, stained & spotted thro.-out, heavier in places, late 18th. C. leath., gold-tooled cover borders, gt. spine. (HT. May 10; 2831) DM 6,800
- La Géométrie Pratique. Paris, 1702. Orig. Edn. 4 vols. Cont. spr. cf., Arenberg arms, spines decor. (HD. May 21; 52) Frs. 5,100

- Le Travaux de Mars ou la Fortification Nouvelle tant Regulière, qu'Irregulière. Paris, 1671-72. 1st. Edn. 3 vols. Cont. cf., gt. decor. spine. (D. Nov.24; 3490) DM 2,400

MALLET, David
[-] Edwin & Emma. Bg'ham., 1760. 1st. Edn. 1st. Iss. 4to. Pol. cf.; Ralph Straus bkplt. (SG. Feb.9; 167) $150

MALLETT, D.
See— THOMSON, J. & Mallett, D.

MALO, Charles
- Les Capitales de l'Europe. Promenades Pittoresque. Berlin. Paris, ca. 1825. Cont. blind-tooled bds. (GB. Nov.3; 301) DM 500
- Histoire des Roses. Ill.:– after P. Bessa. Paris, [1818]. 12mo. Slightly foxed, cont. hf. linen gt., spine & end-papers renewed. (HK. Nov.8; 645) DM 580
- Les Papillons. Paris, [1817]. 12mo. Plts. hand-painted, pink silk, decor. in gold, orig. card. case. (SKC. Oct.26; 404) £160
[-] Parterre de Flore. Paris, [1820.]. Plts. lightly browned, cont. bds., lightly faded. (With:) - Guirlande de Flore. Paris, [1815]. Sm. 8vo. Slightly browned & spotted thro.-out especially in margins, cont. bds. (H. May 22; 585) DM 700
[-] Voyage Pittoresque de Paris au Havre sur les Rives de La Seine. Paris, [1828]. Engraved title with cold. vig., 10 cold. aquatint views, hf.-title, some slight discoloration to a few ll. of text, cont. cf., blind cathedral-style design on covers. (S. Dec.1; 339) Cavendish. £160

MALO, Felix Vanancio
See— VALCARCEL, Domingo & Malo, Felix Vanancio

MALONE, Dumas (Ed.)
See DICTIONARY OF AMERICAN BIOGRAPHY

MALONE, Edmund
- An Inquiry into the Authenticity of Certain Papers attributed to Shakespeare. 1796. 4 pp. publishers prospectus, cont. hf. cf., rubbed. (CSK. Jun.1; 11) £60

MALORY, Sir Thomas
- Le Morte D'Arthur. Ed.:– H. Oskar Sommer. Trans.:– William Caxton. L., 1889-91. 3 vols. in 4. 4to. Parch. bds., wallet edges, unc., worn & soiled. (SG. Mar.29; 232) $110
- – Anr. Edn. Ill.:– A. Beardsley. L., 1893-94. (300) on Dutch H.M.P. 3 vols. 4to. Most plts. & ills. discold., orig. vell., gt., slightly soiled. (BBA. May 23; 191) Thorpe. £380
- – Anr. Copy. 1 vol. in 12 pts., bnd. in 3 vols. Lge. 8vo. 1 wood-engraved frontis., 2 etched frontis., 17 wood-engraved plts. (5 double-p.), some foxing, three-qtr. mor., partly unc., mostly unopened. (SG. Jan.12; 28) $800
- – Anr. Edn. Ill.:– Aubrey Beardsley. L., 1893-94. (1500). 4to. Orig. pict. cl. gt., spotted. (S. Nov.22; 307) Joseph. £250
- – Anr. Copy. 2 vols. 4to. Orig. cl. gt., partly untrimmed, rubbed. (TA. Mar.15; 413) £120
- – Anr. Copy. 2 vols. 4to. Some light offsetting, orig. gt.-decor. cl., spines darkened, slightly shaken, partly untrimmed, unopened. (SG. Nov.17; 8) $225
- – Anr. Edn. Ill.:– Aubrey Beardsley. N.Y., 1909. 2nd. Edn. (500) for America. 4to. Faint offset from some plts., many pp. unopened, gt.-decor. cl., bkplt. (CBA. Aug.21; 37) $225
- – Anr. Edn. Ill.:– William Russell Flint. Medici Soc., 1910-11. (500) numbered on Riccardi H.M.P. 4 vols. 4to. Holland-bkd. bds., unc. (SKC. May 4; 1628) £120
- – Anr. Edn. Ill.:– William Russell Flint. Medici Soc., 1921. Ltd. Edn. 4 vols. 4to. Orig. vell. gt., ties, unc., soiled. (P. Jul.5; 121) £120
- – Anr. Edn. Intro.:– J. Rhys. Ill.:– Aubrey Beardsley. [L.], 1927. [3rd. Edn.]. (1600). 4to. Dutton reading on title verso, elab. gt.-stpd. cl., shaken. (SG. Aug.4; 29) $180
- – Anr. Copy. 4to. Decor. cl. gt., spine frayed. (PNY. Dec.1; 12) $100

- – Anr. Edn. Intro.:– John Rhys. Notes.:– A. Vallance & R.A. Walker. Ill.:– Aubrey Beardsley. [N.Y.], 1927. (1600). 4to. Elab. gt.-decor. cl., beveled edges, covers lightly rubbed, slight darkening to pastedowns. (CBA. Mar.3; 22) $300
- The Romance of King Arthur ... Ed.:– Alfred W. Pollard. Ill.:– Arthur Rackham. 1917. (500) numbered & sigd. by artist. 4to. Orig. parch. gt., soiled. (CSK. Mar.9; 132) £190
- – Anr. Copy. 4to. Orig. vell. gt., spine defect., worn & soiled. (P. Sep.8; 407) Elliott. £95

MALPIGHI, Marcello
- Dissertationes Epistolicae Duae, una de Formationis pulli in Ovo, altera de Bombyce. L., 1673[-1669]. 2 pts. in 1 vol. 4to. 16 folding plts., a few slightly trimmed, some browning, cont. cf., worn. [Wing M 351] (S. Nov.28; 125) Quaritch. £980
- Opera Omnia. L., 1685. 1st. Coll. Edn. 2 vols. in 1. Engraved frontis. in Vol. 1, 123 plts., including the 7 sm. ones, without the repeated frontis. in Vol. 2 (sometimes present), cont. cf., hinges reprd.; Dr. Walter Pagel copy. [Wing M 342a] (S. Feb.7; 246) Sheider. £600
- – Anr. Edn. L., 1686. 2 vols. in 1. Fo. Some stains thro.-out, cont. panel. cf., slightly worn. [Wing M 342b] (TA. Jul.19; 380) £160
- Opera Posthuma. Ed.:– Petrus Regis. Amst., 1698. Frontis., 19 folding plts., pp. 247-325 wormed, hf. cf.; Dr. Walter Pagel copy. (S. Feb.7; 247) Phelps. £160
- Tetras Anatomicarum Epistolarum de Lingua ... Anonymi Accessist Exercitatio de Omente, Pinguedine & Adiposis Ductibus. Bologna, 1665. 12mo. Pages 97/8 & 119/20 are cancels, 2 (of 3) plts., limp vell., loose; Dr. Walter Pagel copy. (S. Feb.7; 245) Shaftel. £80

MALRAUX, André
- La Condition Humaine. Paris, 1933. Orig. Edn. 12mo. On vélin Lafuma, jansenist red mor. by Semet & Plumelle, mor. doubls., watered silk end-ll., wrap. & spine preserved, folder & s.-c. (HD. May 4; 350) Frs. 8,600
- Les Conquerants. 1928. Orig. Edn. (20) specially ptd. on vélin d'Arches la cuve, sigd. by author, with double wrap. Jansenist red mor. by Devauchelle, spine decor., watered silk doubls. & end-ll., wraps. & spines preserved, folder, s.-c. (HD. May 4; 349) Frs. 5,500
- – Anr. Edn. Ill.:– André Masson. Paris, [1949]. Lge. 4to. On pur fil du Marais, lacks justification lf., leaves, wrap., folder, box. (HD. May 21; 131) Frs. 2,750
- Psychologie de l'Art. Le Musée Imaginaire, La Création Artistique. La Monnaie de l'Absolu. Genève, 1947-50. Orig. Edn. 3 vols. 4to. Sewed (HD. May 4; 351) Frs. 1,600

MALRAUX, André & Dali, Salvador
- 'Roi, je t'attends à Babylone'. Genève, 1973. Orig. Edn., (150) on vélin de Rives. (138) numbered & sigd. by author, artist & publisher. Fo. 12 dry-points on thick paper, leaves, ill. wrap., mor. folder, parch. covers, upr. cover ill., mor. s.-c.; each plt. sigd. by artist. (HD. Jun.26; 105) Frs. 22,200

MALTBY, Albert E.
- Old Glory ... The Flag of Our Country. Slippery Rock, Pa., 1897. Lge. 8vo. Gt. & col.-pict. cl., spine darkened, covers spotted; from liby. of F.D. Roosevelt, inscr. 'Given me by James T. Maltby at Fayetteville, N.Y., July 17, 1930 ... the Brother of the Author of this book ... '. (SG. Mar.15; 59) $325

MALTE-BRUN, Victor-Adolphe
- L'Allemagne Illustrée. Paris, 1885-88. 5 text vols. & Atlas vol. in 6 vols. 4to. Lightly foxed, cont. lf. leath. (R. Apr.4; 2217) DM 6,900
- – Anr. Copy. 6 vols., including Atlas. 93 wood engraved plts., 100 engraved cold. double-p. maps, many text woodcuts, some light browning, cont. decor hf. leath. gt., spine slightly faded. (HT. May 10; 2942) DM 5,000
- La France Illustrée. Paris, 1881-84. New Edn. 5 vols. & 1 Atlas vol. 4to. Cont. lf. leath. (D. Nov.23; 979) DM 2,200

MALTHUS, Rev. Thomas Robert
- An Essay on the Principle of Population. L., 1817. *5th. Edn.* 3 vols. Some spotting, cont. cf., jnts. split, labels defect. or missing. (S. Apr.10; 368)
Drury. £120
- Principles of Political Economy. 1820. *1st. Edn.* Lacks hf.-title, dampstained, hf. cf., worn. (P. Jul.5; 154)
£220

MALTON, James
- A Picturesque & Descriptive View of the City of Dublin ... L., 1794. Ob. fo. Engraved title & dedication, folding plan, 2 engraved surveys & key panorama, 25 hand-cold. aquatint plts., lacks frontis. & prelims., title torn, map stained & taped on verso, engraved key very stained, 1 plt. lightly stained, 2 plts. creased (1 with some offsetting), tear to right margin of 1 plt., slightly affecting image, view of Dublin torn & dampstained, some dampstaining to text & margins of some plts. thro.-out, disbnd., as a coll. of plts., w.a.f. (PNY. Jun.6; 521)
$3,400
- - **Anr. Edn.** [Dublin], n.d. Lge. ob. fo. Engraved title, dedication & key panorama plt., aquatint frontis., 2 maps only, 24 plts. only (wtrmkd. 1811, text wtrmkd. 1802), title, dedication & frontis. torn in half & reprd., blank margins wormed, dampstained, cont. hf. mor., worn, w.a.f. (CSK. Dec.16; 34)
£460
- The Young Painter's Maulstick: Being a Practical Treatise on Perspective. L., 1800. *1st. Edn.* Tall 4to. 23 aquatint plts., including 2 with overlay, cont. marb. bds., cf. gt. spine & corners, worn & foxed. (SG. Jan.26; 247)
$225

MALTON, Thomas, the Elder
- A Compleat Treatise on Perspective in Theory & Practice. 1779. 2 pts. in 1 vol., & vol. of plts. Fo. 58 plts., some with moveable parts, qtr. mor., rubbed. (P. Jul.5; 206)
£160

MALTON, Thomas, the Younger
- A Picturesque Tour through the Cities of London & Westminster. L., 1792. 2 vols. in 1. Fo. Engraved titles, dedication with aquatint arms, 99 (of 100) aquatint views, some ptd. in sepia, 2 pp. list of subscribers, cont. red hf. mor., edges & corners rubbed, w.a.f. (C. Mar.14; 65)
Burgess. £4,000

MAME ET FILS
- Notice et Specimens. Tours, 1867. Fo. Cl. (SG. Jan.5; 215)
$275

MANCHESTER, Herbert
- Four Centuries of Sport in America, 1490-1890. N.Y., Derrydale Pr., 1931. *1st. Edn. (850).* Lge. 4to. Orig. cl.; Van Santvoord Merle-Smith bkplt. (LH. Apr.15; 299)
$130

MANDAT-GRANCEY, Baron Edmond de
- Dans les Montagnes Rocheuses. Paris, 1884. *1st. Edn.* Hf.-title, hf. mor.; the Rt. Hon. Visc. Eccles copy. (CNY. Nov.18; 187)
$110

MANDELSLOH, Johann Albert von
- Morgenländische Reyse-Beschreibung ... Ed:– Adam Olearius. Schleswig, 1658. Fo. Cont. vell. (C. Mar.14; 66)
Braecklein. £320
- Voyages Célèbres & Remarquables, faits de Perse aux Indes Orientales. Ill.:– P. v.d. Aa. Amst., 1727. 2 vols. Additional engraved title, port., 43 engraved maps, views, etc., many folding, hf.-titles, later bds. (S. Dec.1; 365)
Quaritch. £580
- - **Anr. Copy.** 2 vols. in 1. Sm. fo. Frontis. dtd. 1718, 21 maps & plans, 23 plts., old hf. roan. (HD. May 21; 51)
Frs. 6,800
- - **Anr. Copy.** 2 pts. in 1 vol. Fo. 37 double-p. maps, unc., mod. hf. cf., corners, blind-decor. (LM. Mar.3; 235)
B. Frs. 24,000

MANDER, Carel van
- Het Leven der Doorluchtige Nederlandsche en Eenige Hoogduitsche Schilders. Amst., 1764. 2 vols. Engraved frontis., 52 port. plts., cont. pol. tree cf. gt. extra. (SG. Oct.13; 230)
$120

MANDEVILLE, Bernard de
- [-] La Fable des Abeilles, ou les Fripons deverus Honnêtes Gens. L. [Amst], 1740. 4 vols. Cont. marb. cf., decor. spines. (HD. Jan.27; 224)
Frs. 1,150

- The Virgin Unmask'd: or, Female Dialogues Betwixt an Elderley Maiden Lady & her Niece. L., 1724. *2nd. Edn.* Cont. cf., rebkd. & cornered, spine laid down. (CSK. Nov.25; 157)
£140

MANDEVILLE or MAUNDEVILLE, Sir John
- The Voiage & Travaile of ... which Treateth of the Way to Hierusalem, & of Marvayles of Inde, with other Ilands & Countryes. Ill.:– V. Angelo. N.Y., [Grabhorn Pr.], 1928. *(150) sigd. by artist.* Fo. Initials hand-illuminated, specially bnd. in red niger, margins of end papers darkened, buckram s.-c.; the V. Angelo copy. (CBA. Oct.1; 182)
$1,500
- Voyages & Travels. 1684. 4to. Title-p. reprd., restored paper loss in margin on K2, just affecting text, restored margin area on p. 119, some browning & spotting thro-out, cf. gt., by W. Pratt, spine slightly faded. (BS. May 2; 43)
£170

MANDEY, Venterus & Moxon, Joseph
- Mechanick-Powers: or, the Mistery of Nature & Art Unvail'd. L., [1696?]. *1st. Edn. Iss. with shorter imprint & without date on title.* 4to. Final 2 ll. of errata & Moxon's advts., margin worming in 1st. few ll., touching rule border of title & 2 letters on verso, a few plts. torn or partly detchd. (in 2 cases slightly affecting engraved area without loss), paper flaw in 1 lf. affecting a few letters, some soiling, cont. cf., worn, top of spine & corners reprd., inner hinges strengthened; old owners inscr. on end-paper, later inscr. to Banner Mill Liby. with their ptd. labels, Stanitz coll. [Wing M419]. (SPB. Apr.25; 287)
$1,100

MANDRIL
Ed.:– C. Boost, E. Elias, H. Knap, F. v.d. Molen & c. Amst., 1948-52. Years I-IV (lacks year III, nos. 6-8) in 3 vols. Sm. fo. Part of 1 lf. cut out, cl., orig. wraps. preserved, 3 wraps. defect. (VG. Mar.21; 751)
Fls. 770

MAN-FONG, Lee
- Paintings & Statues from the Collection of President Sukarno. Tokyo, 1964. 5 vols. Lge. 4to. Orig. cl., d.-w.'s. (CSK. Jun.1; 141)
£80

MANGAN, Terry W. & others
- William Henry Jackson's Rocky Mountain Railroad Album. Silverton, 1976. *(3000) numbered.* Lge. fo. Gt.-lettered two-tone cl. (SG. Nov.10; 93)
$275

MANGET, Jean Jacques
- Bibliotheca Chemica Curiosa, seu Rerum ad Alchemiam Pertinentium Thesaurus Instructissimus. Genf., [1702]. 2 pts. in 1 vol. Fo. Lacks port., 1st. ll. & 1st. 74 pp. pt. 1 completed in photocopy, also lacking plt. 7 pt. 2., slightly browned, minimal soiling, last plts. slightly stained, margin fraying, hf. vell. (HK. Nov.8; 646)
DM 550

MANGIN, Nicole S.
- Catalogue de l'Oeuvre de Georges Braque. Paris, 1959-68. 5 vols. 4to. Spiral-bnd., orig. linen, cold. cover ill., spine browned. (H. Nov.24; 2458)
DM 700

MANGLES, James
See– IRBY, Charles Leonard & Mangles, James

MANIFESTO della Serenissima Republica di Genova con le Riposte de Corsi
Campoloro, 1760. Sewed. (HD. Oct.21; 118)
Frs. 1,500

MANILIUS, Marcus
- Astronomicon. Ed:– Joseph Scaliger. Leiden, 1599-1600. 2 pts. in 1 vol. 4to. Title & prelims. to pt.2 misbnd., few ll. browned, limp vell., ties. (S. Apr.10; 549)
Poole. £90
- - **Anr. Edn.** Ed:– Joseph Scaliger. Strassburg, 1655. 4to. Some ll. loose, few marginal stains, sm. repair on dedication lf., cont. vell., blistered. (SG. Apr.26; 135)
$300
- - **Anr. Edn.** Commentaries:– Michel Faye, P.-D. Huet & J. Scaliger. Ill.:– Edelinck (frontis.). Paris, 1679. 4to. Cont. vell., decor., Utrecht city arms; from Fondation Furstenberg-Beaumesnil. (HD. Nov.16; 135)
Frs. 3,800
- - **Anr. Edn.** Ed.:– Richard Bentley. Ill.:– Vertue (port.). L., 1739. *1st. Bentley Edn.* 4to. Port.,

folding engraved plt., mod. cl. (SG. Apr.19; 123)
$175
- - **Anr. Edn.** Trans.:– G. Pingré. Paris, 1786. 2 vols. Parallel texts, cont. tree cf., spines decor. (HD. Nov.17; 47)
Frs. 1,000
- - **Anr. Edn.** Ed.:– A.E. Housman. L., [priv. ptd.], 1903-30. *1st. Housman Edn.* 5 vols. Qtr. cl., ptd. bds., 1 label frayed, buckram folding-case. (SG. May 24; 308)
$400

MANIPULUS
- Officia Sacerdotum Ordinem Septem Sacramentorum perbreviter complectens. Cologne, H. Quentel, 1492. 4to. With accipies woodcut, upr. margins short, old margin annots., old hf. cf., worn, some stains, 18th. C. ex-libris. [HC 8203] (VG. May 3; 494)
Fls. 1,500

MANKELL, J.
- Anteckingar Rörande Svenska Regementers Historia. Ill.:– Nordmann. Stockholm, 1864. Fo. Later hf. leath. (D. Nov.24; 3510)
DM 3,600

MANKOWITZ, Wolf
- Wedgwood. L., 1953. *(1500).* No bdg. stated. (JL. Jun.24; 202)
Aus. $100

MANLEY, Mary de la Riviere
- The Power of Love: in Seven Novels. L., 1741. A little browning, cont. cf., edges slightly rubbed. (BBA. May 3; 201)
Jarndyce. £160
[-] Secret Memoirs & Manners of Several Persons of Quality. — Memoirs of Europe. L., 1709; 1710. *2nd Edn.; 1st. Edn.* 2vols.; 2 vols. Engraved frontis. in 1st. work, cont. red mor. gt., spines gt., 1 jnt. reprd.; leather labels of Edward George Hibbert & the Earl of Rosebery. (SPB. May 16; 98)
$900

MANN, Golo & Heuss, A.
- Universele Wereldgeschiedenis. Trans.:– J. Huizinga, L.F. Janssen, & others. Den Haag, 1975-79. 12 vols. Royal 8vo. Cl. (B. Oct.4; 338)
Fls. 500

MANN, Golo & others
- Propyläen-weltgeschichte. Eine Universalgeschichte. Berlin, Frankfurt &c., 1960-65. 12 vols., including 2 supps. Lge. 8vo. Cl. (B. Feb.8; 885)
Fls. 460

MANN, Heinrich
- Das Wunderbare und andere Novellen. Ill.:– Bruno Paul (pict. title), Th. Th. Heine (vigs.). 1897. *1st. Edn.* Owners entry on end-paper, cont. linen gt. (GB. May 5; 2909)
DM 550

MANN, Heinrich (Texts)
See– GANYMED

MANN, Thomas
- Bekenntnisse d. Hochstaplers Felix Krull Der Memoiren erster Theil. [Frankfurt, 1954]. *1st. Edn. publd. in Europe. (500) numbered De Luxe Edn.* Printers mark sigd., orig. cf. gt., slight scratches. (HK. May 17; 2973)
DM 680
- Bemühungen. 1925. *1st. Edn.* Orig. linen; MS. 8 line dedication from author on end-paper. (GB. May 5; 2917)
DM 480
- Buddenbrooks. Berlin, 1901. *1st. Edn.* 2 vols. Cont. vell.-bkd. buckram; autograph dedication 'Meinem lieben Kurt Martens in herzlicher Freundschaft! Munchen 9.ix.1904 Thomas Mann' on title of Vol. 1, with Martens bkplt. on hf.-titles. (C. Dec.9; 317)
Quaritch. £7,200
- - **Anr. Copy.** 2 vols. Prelim. ll. stpd., orig. linen, lightly rubbed, 2 sm. spots. (H. May 23; 1375)
DM 6,800
- Doktor Faustus. Stockholm [& N.Y.], 1947. *1st. Edn. (50) Special Edn. with printer's mark sigd. by author.* 4to. Orig. linen. (H. May 23; 1377)
DM 2,800
- Gesammelte Werke [in Einzelausgaben]. 1922-36. *1st. Edn.* 15 vols. (all publd.). Orig. linen gt. (GB. Nov.5; 2761)
DM 600
- - **Anr. Edn.** Ill.:– after M. Liebermann. 1925. *2nd. Coll. Edn.* Orig. linen by H.E. Mende, spine lightly rubbed, end-papers foxed. (GB. May 5; 2913)
DM 500
- Des Gesetz. Ed.:– E. Gottlieb & F. Guggenhelm. Los Angeles, priv. ptd., [1944]. *(250) De Luxe Edn.* Printers mark sigd., orig. hf. leath., margins slightly browned, spine rubbed. (H. May 23; 1379)
DM 450

- **Joseph & his Brothers.** N.Y., 1934. *1st. Amer. Edn.* Cl., minor spotting to covers, upr. corners & spine end worn; inscr. & sigd. (partly in German & partly in Engl.) to Grace Spranz(?), 8 Jun. 1934. (SG. Jan.12; 252) $150
- **Kino.** Gera, 1926. *1st. Edn.* 4to. Orig. wraps. (HK. Nov.11; 3781) DM 460
- **The Magic Mountain.** N.Y., 1927. *1st. Amer. Edn. (200) numbered.* 2 vols. Vell.-bkd. bds., s.-c. torn; sigd. by author. (LH. Sep.25; 562). $200
- **Thamar.** Ill.:– G. Böhmer. [Frankfurt], 1956. *(250) De Luxe Edn.* Sm. 4to. On Bütten, printers mark sigd. by artist, hand-bnd. orig. mor., by W. Pingel. (H. May 23; 1383) DM 440
- **Der Tod in Venedig.** Berlin, 1913. Orig. wraps., light wear; MS. dedication on prelim. lf. (H. May 23; 1384) DM 920
- **Tonio Kröger.** Ill.:– E. Simon. [1913]. *1st. Edn.* Orig. bds. (GB. Nov.5; 2762) DM 400
- **The Transposed Heads: a Legend of India.** Kentfield, Calif., Allen Pr., 1977. *(140) on St. Cuthberts Mill all-rag paper.* Fo. Text ills., hand-blocked patterned cl. from India. (SG. May 17; 7) $300
- **Tristan.** Ill.:– E. Scharff. München, [1922]. *(250).* On Bütten, printers mark sigd. by artist, orig. hf. leath.; (H. Nov.24; 1810) DM 820
- **Wälsungenblut.** Ill.:– Th. Heine. München, [1921]. *1st. Book Edn. (200).* Sm. 4to. printers mark sigd by author & artist, some light browning, orig. pict. bds., very defect., spine pasted. (H. Nov.24; 1811) DM 820
- **Werke.** Stockholm, Berlin & Frankfurt, 1947-58. 14 vols. Orig. linen. (HK. Nov.11; 3768) DM 700

MANN, William
- **A Description of a New Method of Propelling Locomotive Machines.** L., 1830. Folding plt., some light foxing, orig. bds. stained. (P. May 17; 273) *Fletcher.* £130
- **Six Years' Residence in the Australian Provinces.** L., 1839. Some foxing, bdg. not stated, worn. (JL. Mar.25; 594) Aus. $200
- – **Anr. Copy.** 12mo. Some foxing & discoloration, map reprd., bdg. not stated, recased. (KH. May 1; 465) Aus. $180
- – **Anr. Copy.** Map & some pp. offset, map with tear reprd., title foxed, orig. blind-stpd. ribbed cl., unc., rebkd. preserving orig. spine. (CA. Apr.3; 83) Aus. $130
- – **Anr. Copy.** Map & some ll. offset, title foxed, p. 359 to end-paper detchd., orig. blind-stpd. ribbed cl., unc., covers stained, spine torn. (CA. Apr.3; 82) Aus. $110

MANNERS, Lord J.
See– SCHETKY, J. & Manners, Lord J.

MANNERS, John Henry, Duke of Rutland
See– RUTLAND, John Henry Manners, Duke of

MANNERS, Lady Victoria & Williamson, G.C.
- **Angelica Kauffmann, RA, Her Life & Works.** L., 1924. *(1000).* 4to. Orig. cl.-bkd. bds., slightly soiled; pres. copy inscr. by Williamson to his son, letter to author loosely inserted. (S. Apr.30; 107) *Dreesman.* £100
- **John Zoffany, R.A., his Life & Works.** L., 1920. *(500).* 4to. Orig. cl.-bkd. bds., d.-w.; 2 letters to Williamson & pres. slip from him loosely inserted. (S. Apr.30; 108) *Dreesman.* £180

MANNERS & CUSTOMS OF THE FRENCH
See– S., M.

MANNFELD, B.
See– RITTERHAUS, E. & Mannfeld, B.

MANNING, Rev. Owen & Bray, William
- **The History & Antiquities of Surrey.** 1804-14. 3 vols. Fo. 85 engraved plts. & maps, 2 folding slightly torn, 13 folding ptd. tables. Vol. 1 lacks last blank lf., rather spotted thro.-out, cont. cf. (BBA. Sep.29; 118) *Thorp.* £340
- – **Anr. Copy.** 3 vols. Fo. Slight offsetting, cont. hf. cf., worn, some covers detchd. (SKC. Mar.9; 1985) £260
- – **Anr. Copy.** 3 vols. Fo. Cont. cf. gt. (P. Oct.20; 202) £180
- – **Anr. Edn.** 1974. *Facs. of 1804-14 Edn.* 3 vols. Fo. Orig. cl., d.-w.'s. (TA. Nov.17; 181) £60

MANNING, Warren H.
See– LAMBETH, William A. & Manning, Warren H.

MANNINGHAM, Sir Richard
- **An Exact Diary of what was Observ'd during a Close Attendance upon Mary Toft** ... L., 1726. *1st. Edn.* Hf.-title, mod. three-qtr. leath. (SG. Oct.6; 243) $110

MANOACH HENDEL BEN SHEMARYA
- **Chochmat Manoach.** Prague, 1612. *1st. Edn.* 4to. Lacks pp. 129-132, slight browning, old cf., rubbed. (SPB. Feb.1; 62) $700

MANSFIELD, Katherine
- **The Garden Party & Other Stories.** Ill.:– Marie Laurencin. Bodoni Pr., 1939. *(1200) designed by Mardersteig.* Slight foxing, bds. (KH. Nov.9; 324) Aus. $400

MANSON, J.B. & Meynell, Mrs.
- **The Work of John S. Sargent.** L. & N.Y., 1927. *(360) numbered.* Lge. fo. Approx. 90 gravure reproductions, lettered tissue-guards, ex-liby., buckram. (SG. May 3; 323) $225

MANUAL OF POLICE REGULATIONS for the Guidance of the Constabulary of Victoria
Melbourne, 1856. Broadside list of police districts & stations in end pocket, vell. 'saddle-bag' bdg.; sig. of John Shillinglaw. (KH. May 1; 726) Aus. $550

MANUALE PAROCHIALIUM SACERDOTUM
[Cologne, H. Quentell], ca. 1492. Sm. 4to. Lacks final blank, sm. repair in upr. margin of last 2 ll., stained, mod. bds. [Goff M221] (S. Nov.17; 47) *Maggs.* £280

MANUEL II, King of Portugal
- **Early Portuguese Books, 1489-1600, in the Library of His Majesty the King of Portugal.** L., 1929. 3 vols. Lge. 4to. In Engl. & Portuguese, publisher's bradel cl. bds. (HD. Jun.6; 105) Frs. 4,000
- **Livros Antigos Portuguezes, 1489-1600.** 1932-35. *(45) inscr. by the King.* Vols. II & III only (of 3). Text in Portuguese & Engl., facs. thro.-out, buckram gt., d.-w.'s torn. (P. Jan.12; 158) *K Books.* £180

MANUTIUS, Aldus
- **Institutionum Grammaticarum.** [Venice, 1508]. *2nd. Edn.* 4to. Lacks 2a7-8 of Appendix, wormed, few stains, mostly marginal, old pol. blind-panel. sheep, restored. (SG. Oct.27; 6) $475
- **Orthographiae Ratio.** Venice, 1591. Owners mark on title, lightly spotted thro.-out, later decor. vell. (HT. May 8; 172) DM 480
- **Vita di Cosimo de' Medici.** Bologna, 1586. Engraved title, title & hf.-title reprd., some margins lightly browned, & with some soiling or staining, cont. vell., soiled, sm. hole in upr. corner. (CSK. Mar.23; 180) £75

MANUTIUS, Paulus
- **In Epistolas Ciceronis ad Atticvm Commentarivs.** Venice, 1547. *1st. Edn.* Title with owners mark, lacks lf. with 2 printers marks at end, some sm. reprd. defects., 1st. & last ll. soiled, cont. limp vell., some sm. tears, lacks ties. (HK. May 15; 191) DM 440

MANUFACTURES DE HAUT RHIN
Ill.:– G. Engelmann after J. Mieg. Ca. 1825. Ob. fo. Lacks 2 plts., cont. hf. roan, corners. (HD. Mar.21; 175) Frs. 4,000

MAP COLLECTORS' CIRCLE, The
- **Map Collector's Series.** Ed.:– R.V. Tooley. 1963-73. Nos. 1-92. Orig. ptd. wraps. (TA. Jul.19; 56) £200
- – **Anr. Run.** Ed.:– R.V. Tooley. L., 1963-74. Nos. 1-110. Sm. 4to. Orig. wraps. (BBA. Apr.5; 298) *Tooley.* £140
- – **Anr. Run.** Ed.:– R.V. Tooley. 1964-69. Nos. 1-60 in 6 vols. 4to. Cont. cl. (BBA. Nov.10; 91) *Shapero.* £180

MAPEI, Camillo
- **Italy, Classical, Historical & Picturesque.** Glasgow, 1847. 4to. Engraved title, 60 plts., spotting, hf. cf., rubbed. (P. Mar.15; 193) *Acquaforte.* £300
- – **Anr. Edn.** Glasgow, [1847?]. Fo. Engraved title, 60 engraved views, slight spotting, hf. cf. gt. (P. Sep.8; 242) *Edistar.* £270
- – **Anr. Copy.** 4to. Engraved title, 60 engraved plts., cont. purple mor. gt. (SPB. Dec.13; 865) $300
- – **Anr. Copy.** 4to. Plts. stpd. on versos, disbnd., ex-liby. (RO. Dec.11; 201) $110
- – **Anr. Edn.** N.d. Fo. Some spotting, mor. gt., spine ends worn slightly. (LC. Oct.13; 279) £250

MAPEI, Camillo & Carlyle, G.
- **Italy, illustrated & described.** L., 1864. Lge. 4to. Some foxing, red hf. mor., ca. 1880, orig. spine. (HK. Nov.8; 1076) DM 1,050

MAPPUS, Marcus
- **Historia Plantarum Alsaticarum.** Strasburg, 1742. 4to. Many old margin annots., cont. bds. (HD. Mar.21; 52) Frs. 1,800

MAQUARIE, Lachlan
- **Journal of his Tours in New South Wales & Van Diemen's Land 1810-22.** Public Liby. N.S.W., 1956. *1st. Edn.* No bdg. stated. (JL. Jun.24; 89) Aus. $100

MARAIS, Paul & Dufresne de Saint-Leon, A.
- **Catalogue des Incunables de la Bibliothèque Mazarine.** Paris, 1893. 2 vols, including Supp. Lge. 8vo. Vell., spines gt., orig. wraps. bnd. in. (SG. May 17; 245) $150

MARAN, René
- **Batouala.** Ill.:– Alexandre Iacovleff. Paris, 1928. *(48) hors commerce, with orig. full-p. pencil sketch. (35) on rives.* 4to. Mor. gt., upr. cover with wood inset & mor. onlays., by Lobstein, s.-c. (SPB. Dec.13; 847) $275

MARBACH, G.O. (Trans.)
See– NIEBELUNGENLIED

MARBOT, Gal. Bon. de
- **Mémoires.** Paris, 1891. *2nd. Edn.* 3 vols. Hf. mor., decor. spines, wrap., by Girard. (HD. Mar.14; 191) Frs. 1,000

MARBURGER JAHRBUCH FUR KUNSTWISSENSCHAFT
Ed.:– R. Hamann & F.H. Lehr. Ill.:– Paul Baum (etching), Alexander Kanoldt, K. Doerbecker, P. Baum (lithos.), Ewald Matare (woodcut). Marburg, 1924. *(500).* 4to. 4 orig. ills., orig. hf. vell., corners bumped, end-papers foxed. (GB. Nov.5; 2774) DM 450

MARC, Franz
- **Sechszehn Farbige Handzeichnungen aus dem Skizzenbuch von Franz Marc.** Potsdam, [1922]. *B Edn. (500). (450) numbered.* 4to. Loose ll. in orig. hf. linen portfo. (GB. May 5; 2927) DM 500
- **Stella Peregrina.** Ill.:– Annette von Eckardt after Marc (col.). München, 1917. *(110).* Fo. Hand-bnd. orig. bds., bumped, spine defect. (H. Nov.24; 2526) DM 500
See– KANDINSKY, Wassily & Marc, Franz

MARCAGGI, J.B.
- **Les Chants de la Mort et de la Vendetta de la Corse.** Paris, 1898. 12mo. Sewed. (HD. Oct.21; 122) Frs. 1,000

MARCAIS, Georges & Poinssot
- **Objets Kairouanais IXe au XIIIe Siècle. Reliures, Verreries, Cuivres et Bronzes, Bijoux.** Tunis, 1948. Orig. wraps.; H.M. Nixon coll., with his sig. (BBA. Oct.6; 88) *Quaritch.* £300

MARCASSUS, Pierre de
- **Le Timandre.** Ill.:– Crispin de Passe (frontis.). Ca. 1630. 12mo. Red mor. by Chambolle & Duru, 1862, some stains. (HD. Mar.21; 53) Frs. 3,200

MARCEL, Gabriel
- **Réproductions de Cartes & de Globes Relatifs à la Découverte de l'Amérique du XVI au XVIII Siècle.** Paris, 1893-94. 2 vols, including Atlas. 4to. & fo.

MARCEL, Gabriel -Contd.

Some perforation stps., plts. hand-stpd. on versos, three-qtr. leath., worn, ex-liby. (RO. Dec.11; 204) $130

MARCELLINUS, Ammianus
- Rerum Gestarum ... Libri XVIII ... Omnia nunc Recognita ab Jacobo Gronovio. Leiden, 1693. Fo. Cont. limp vell. (S. Oct.11; 407)   *Fletcher.* £80

MARCGRAF DE LIEBSTAD, George
See— PISO, Gulielmus & Marcgraf de Liebstad, George

MARCHAND, Prosper
- Dictionaire Historique ou Mémoires concernant la Vie et les Ouvrages de Divers Personnages dans la République des Lettres. 's-Gravenhage, 1758-59. 2 pts. in 1 vol. Fo. Some foxing, cont. vell. (VG. Mar.19; 100)   Fls. 480
[–] Histoire de l'Origine et des Premiers Progrès de l'Imprimerie. The Hague, 1740. 4to. Some browning & soiling, old parch., soiled. (CSK. Feb.24; 215)   £75

MARCHEN VON DEM FISCHER UN SYNER FRU
Ill.:– E. Würtenberger,. Bern, Seldwyla Pr., 1921. *(300).* Lge. 4to. Hand-bnd. vell. by W. Hacker, Leipzig. (H. Nov.24; 1268)   DM 700

MARCHI, F.M.
- Motti Risposte e Burle del Celebre Minuti Grosso. Bone, 1923. Marb. hf. roan, corners, wrap. (HD. Oct.21; 123)   Frs. 1,000

MARCO (Pseud.)
See— MOUNTBATTEN, Louis, Earl, of Burma

MARCUS, Jacob Ernst
- Het Studie-prentwerk. (Etudes Gravées). Amst., ca. 1830. Fo. Dutch & Fr. text, engraved title & 105 plts., few light stains, cont. hf. cf., rubbed, some repairs. (VG. Mar.19; 48)   Fls. 1,000

MARCY, Randolph B.
- Exploration of the Red River of Louisiana, in the Year 1852. Wash., 1854. With the 2 lge. folding maps, both linen mntd., lacks 1 plt., replaced with dupl. of anr., 1 folding map worn at folds with some tears reprd., orig. cl., maps in separate cl. covers, rebkd. (SG. Oct.20; 212) $130

MARDERSTEIG, Giovanni or Hans
- The Making of a Book at the Officina Bodoni. Ill.:– Frans Masareel. Verona, Bodoni Pr., 1973. *(300).* Orig. bds., s.-c. (BBA. Oct.27; 197)
Monk Bretton. £210
- The Officina Bodoni, an Account of the Work of a Hand Press 1923-1977. Trans.:– Hans Schmoller. Verona, Edizioni Valdonega, 1980. *(99) numbered, with 2nd. vol. containing orig. ll. from books of the Pr.* 2 vols. 4to. The keepsake 'Giovanni Mardersteig 8.1.1892-27.12.1977' in orig. wraps. loosely inserted, orig. mor.-bkd. cl., s.-c. (S. Nov.22; 274)
Houle. £270
- Pastonchi, a Specimen of the New Letter for Use on the 'Monotype'. Verona, Bodoni Pr., 1928. *(200).* 4to. Slight foxing, orig. cl. (BBA. Oct.27; 195)
Erlini. £50

MARDERSTEIG, Giovanni or Hans (Ed.)
See— GENIUS Zeitschrift für Alte und Werdende Kunst.

MARDON, E.R.
- Billiards. Brighton, [1844]. 4to. 41 plts., orig. cl. gt., lacks spine. (P. Dec.8; 82)   *Haddon.* £65

MARDRUS, Dr. Joseph Charles
- Histoire Charmante de l'Adolescente Sucre d'Amour. Ill.:– F.L. Schmied. Paris, 1927. *1st. Edn. (150) numbered on papier d'Arches, sigd. by artist.* 4to. 14 cold. wood-engraved ills., many vigs. & decors., patterned bds., some foxing on end-ll., unc., clear plastic d.-w.; inscr. to artist. (SG. Apr.26; 178) $550
- - Anr. Edn. Ill.:– F.L. Schmied. Paris, 1927. *(170) on Arches, sigd. by Schmied.* 4to. Faint offsetting of some ills., elab. mor., inlaid border of mor., by René Assourd. (SPB. Dec.14; 82) $2,300
- - Anr. Edn. Ill.:– Schmied. Paris, 1927. 4to. Red

mor. gt. by Gonin, mosaic decor, red mor. liners & end-ll., wrap. preserved, s.-c. (HD. Jun.13; 67)
Frs. 33,000
- Le Livre des Rois. l'Avenement de Salomon. Ill.:– F.L. Schmied, wood engraved in col. by Ph. Gonin. Lausanne, 1930. *(175) sigd. by Gonin. 1st. (25) with double series of col. woodcuts on Japon.* This number 152 but with separate series, some slight foxing, loose ll. in orig. wraps., lightly spotted, hf. linen cover & s.-c., slightly spotted & bumped. (H. Nov.24; 2558)   DM 1,800
- Ruth et Booz. Ill.:– F.L. Schmied. Paris, 1930. *(162).* 4to. Some foxing, leaves, box. (HD. Jun.13; 66)   Frs. 3,800
- - Anr. Edn. Ill.:– F.L. Schmied, engraved by Th. Schmied. Paris, 1930. *(172).* Lge. 4to. On madagascar paper, mor. in red mor. border, by F.L. Schmied, decor. gt. & silver, upr. cover recovered, red mor. doubl. in black mor. border, wrap., hf. mor. s.-c. & box, watered silk end-ll. & double endpapers; sigd. by artist, with double suite of ills. on japan, in black & cols, from Jacques Andre liby. (HD. Dec.16; 185)   Frs. 106,000

MARDRUS, Dr. Joseph Charles (Trans.)
See— ARABIAN NIGHTS

MARECHAL, Pedro
- Arte de conservar y arreglar los Reloxes ... Madrid, 1767. Leath. (DS. Apr.27; 2168)
Pts. 25,000

MARECHAL, Pierre Sylvain
- Costumes Civils Actuels de Tous les Peuples Connus ... Ill.:– after Grasset de St Sauveur; Daisrais (titles). Paris, 1788. 4 vols. Sm. 4to. 4 engraved titles & 278 cold. engraved plts., cont. mor. finish hf. roan, corners, spines decor. (HD. May 3; 96)
Frs. 16,500
[–] Projet d'une Loi portant Défense d'Apprendre à Lire aux Femmes. An IX. 1801. *1st. Edn.* Hf. cl., corners, ca. 1880. (HD. Mar.21; 176)   Frs. 1,400

MAREES-GESELLSCHAFT
See— ARNIM, Ludwig Achim von

MARESTIER, Jean Baptiste
- Mémoire sur les Bateaux à Vapeur des Etats-Unis d'Amérique. Paris, 1824. Atlas vol. only. Lge. fo. 17 litho. plts., light spotting, damp-damaged, cont. hf. cf. (CSK. Aug.5; 54)   £180

MARGERAND, J.
- Armement et Equipement de l'Infanterie Française du XVIème au XXème Siècle. Ill.:– J.E. Hilpert. Paris, 1945. Hf. chagrin. (HD. Jan.27; 179)
Frs. 1,550
- Les Coiffures de l'Armée Française. N.d. 2 vols. 4to. Hf. chagrin, corners, pt. wraps. preserved. (HD. Jan.27; 177)   Frs. 7,500

MARGERIT, R.
- Lobel-Riche. Paris, 1946. 4to. Hf. chagrin, corners, by Yseux, wrap. & spine; dedication & orig. drawing sigd. by artist. (HD. Jun.6; 106)
Frs. 1,500

MARGUERITE D'ANGOULEME, Queen of Navarre
- [Heptaméron François] Les Nouvelles. Ill.:– Eichlet after Dunkler,. Bern, 1780-81. *1st. Edn.* 3 vols. Vols. I & II on Bütten, Vol. I lacks hf.-title, title verso stpd., 1 lf. reprd. Vol. I & text completed in MS., some slight foxing & browning, later red mor., gt. decor. spine, covers, inner & outer dentelles, some wear; Hausewedell coll. (H. May 24; 1471)   DM 3,600
- - Anr. Copy. 3 vols. Vols. 2 & 3 lack hf.-title & title, red mor. gt. (R. Oct.11; 331)   DM 2,700
- - Anr. Copy. 3 vols. Slight foxing to first 2 vols., old long-grd. red mor., gt. decor., decor. spines, sm. scratches. (HD. Dec.9; 57)   Frs. 5,100
- - Anr. Copy. 3 vols. On papier vergé fort, cont. red mor. gt., Racine-Demonville's name gt. on upr. covers., decor. spines, inner roll-stp., spines renewed. (HD. Sep.22; 282)   Frs. 3,700
- The Heptameron of the Tales of Margaret, Queen of of Navarre. Ill.:– Freudenberg. 1894. *(312) numbered on H.M.P.* Ills. on japan, mntd., mor. gt. by Zaehnsdorf, untrimmed & unopened. (SKC. Mar.9; 1880)   £160
- Neuigkeiten. Trans.:– [J.R. von Sinner]. Bern,

1791. *(400) on dutch paper.* 2 vols. in 1. 2 ll. with hole or margin tear, a little spotting, cont. hf. leath., gt. spines, slightly bumped, spine with short tears; Hauswedell coll. (H. May 24, 1472)   DM 2,000

MARGUERITE DE VALOIS, Queen of Navarre
- Les Mémoires de la Roine Marguerite. Paris, 1628. *1st. Edn.* Vell., worn. (P. Mar.15; 322)
Duran. £50
- - Anr. Copy. Some ll. dampstained, cont. elab. decor. red mor., end-ll. renewed. (HD. Mar.29; 59)
Frs. 50,000

MARGUERITTE, Victor
- La Garçonne. Ill.:– after K. van Dongen. Paris, 1926. *Ltd. Edn. on H.M.P.* 4to. Hf. mor., orig. wraps. preserved. (VG. Nov.29; 204)   Fls. 480

MARIANA, Jean de, S.J.
- Histoire Générale d'Espagne. Trans.:– Joseph-Nicolas Charenton. Ill.:– after J.B. Nolin. Paris, 1725. 5 vols. 4to. Supp. to Vol. 5: Dissertation by Mahuda, 2 vols. stained with sm. wormholes, blind-tooled vell., some wear. (V. Sep.29; 137)   DM 420
- Historiae de Rebus Hispaniae Libri XXX. Mainz, 1605. 1 vol. bnd. in 2. 4to. 'Summarium' bnd. at end vol. II, Maguncia, 1619, leath. (DS. Feb.24; 2523)   Pts. 20,000

MARICHAL, Robert (Ed.)
See— CHARTERS

MARIE, A.
- Le Peintre Poète Louis Boulanger. — Henry Monnier (1799-1877). — Alfred et Tony Johannot. Peintres, Gravures et Vignettistes. — Celestin Nanteuil. Peintre Aquafortiste et Lithographe, 1813-1873. Paris, 1924-31. Together 4 vols. 4to. Orig. wraps., 1 in leath. (SPB. Nov.30; 53) $125

MARIESCHI, Michael
- Magnificentiores Selectioresque Urbis Venetiarum Prospectus. Venice, 1741. Fo. Engraved double-p. title, & 21 etched double-p. views, all on guards, reprd. sm. tear & minor margin stain in 1st. dedication plt., old patterned bds.; bkplts. of Wm. M. Sale, Sir John Wolfe Barry, G. Fummach & Leo Olschki. (C. Dec.9; 98)   *Thomas-Scheler.* £11,000

MARIETTE, Pierre Jean
- Traité des Pierres Gravées. Ill.:– Edme Bouchardon, engraved by le Comte de Caylus. Paris, 1750. *Orig. Edn. 1st. Printing.* 2 vols. Sm. fo. Cont. marb. cf. gt., 1 cover rubbed, spines decor. (HD. Nov.9; 184)   Frs. 2,050
- - Anr. Edn. Paris, 1750. 2 vols. Sm. fo. Engraved titles & dedication, 130 plts. on 67 sheets & 129 hf.-p. plts., cont. cf., rubbed. (P. Feb.16; 132)   £150
- - Anr. Copy. 2 vols. Lge. fo. Leath. (DS. Mar.23; 2174)   Pts. 200,000

MARILLIER, Henry Carrie
- Dante Gabriel Rossetti. 1899. *[1st. Edn.].* Fo. Orig. cl. gt. (P. Jun.7; 294)   £65
- - Anr. Copy. Lge. fo. Plts. & text ills., ex-liby., gt.-pict. cl. (SG. May 3; 319) $200

MARINE AU XIXEME SIECLE (La)
Ill.:– Becquet after Lebreton. N.p., n.d. Lge. ob. 8vo. Publisher's decor. cl. bds.; from Château des Noës liby. (HD. May 25; 53)   Frs. 5,200

MARINER, William
- Nachrichten über die Freundschaftlichen, ober die Tonga Inseln. Weimar, 1819. *1st German Edn.* Slightly browned thro.-out, orig. bds., worn, mod. hf. cf. box, spine gt. (BBA. Dec.15; 28)
Quevedo. £80

MARINES DEDIEES A S.A.R. MGR LE PRINCE DE JOINVILLE
Ill.:– after Hue, Gudin, Van Bree, Isabey, & Morel-Fatio. Paris, 1842. Lge. fo. 49 steel-engraved plts. on 'chine appliqué', cont. hf. mor. by Andrieux, spine decor.; Duc de Chartres copy. (HD. Mar.9; 105)   Frs. 4,500

MARINIS
- Opera Juridica. Venise, 1758. 6 vols. in 5. Fo. Cont. vell. (HD. Feb.22; 131)   Frs. 2,000

MARINIS, Tammaro de
- Appunti e Ricerche Bibliografiche. Milan, 1940. Hf. mor., orig. wraps. preserved; H.M. Nixon coll., with his sig., acquisition note & many MS. notes. (BBA. Oct.6; 89) *Maggs*. £300
- Catalogue d'un Collection Anciens Livres à Figures Italiens. Preface:– Seymour de Ricci. Milan, [1925]. Sm. fo. Cold. frontis., 277 plts., ptd. wraps., unc., unopened. (SG. May 17; 247) $275
- [Festschrift] Studi di Bibliografia e di Storia. Verona, 1964. 4 vols. Tall 4to. Orig. cl., s.-c.'s; H.M. Nixon coll., with his sig. in Vol. 1 & a few MS. notes, autograph card from Marinis to Nixon loosely inserted. (BBA. Oct.6; 90) *Parikian*. £420
- La Legatura Artistica in Italia nei Secoli XV e XVI. Flor., 1960. 4 vols. Fo. Orig. hf. leath. (D. Nov.23; 1024) DM 2,100

MARIN-MARIE
- Grands Coureurs et Plaisanciers. Livre d'Or du Yachting. Paris, 1957. *Unnumbered on vélin de hollande*. Fo. Leaves, wrap., box. (HD. Mar.27; 89) Frs. 5,600
- - Anr. Copy. Leaves, ill. wrap., box. (HD. Jun.26; 108) Frs. 4,600

MARINO, Giambattista
- La Sampogna. Ill.:– I. Isaac (title-frontis.). 1620. *Orig. Edn*. 12mo. Cont. Italian red mor., richly decor. (HD. Mar.21; 55) Frs. 1,300

MARIOTTE, Edme
- Oeuvres. The Hague, 1740. *2nd. Edn*. 2 vols. 4to. 'Nouvelle edition' slip of Paris bookseller Jombert pasted over orig. imprint, prelim. blank present in Vol. 1, browning, severe in places, cont. mott. cf., spines gt., slight wear, corners bumped; Stanitz coll. (SPB. Apr.25; 290) $175
- Traité du Mouvement des Eaux et des Autres Corps ... Paris, 1686. *1st. Edn*. Hf.-title, some spotting & browning, cont. sheep, rubbed, slight chipping of head of spine; Stanitz coll. (SPB. Apr.25; 288) $750
- A Treatise of the Motion of Water & other Fluids. Trans.:– J.T. Desaguliers. L., 1718. *1st. Engl. Edn*. Cont. cf. (P. Dec.8; 265) *Tzakas*. £240
- - Anr. Copy. Advt. lf., some spotting & browning, mostly at back, writing on end-papers, liby bkplt., panel. cf., rebkd., corners renewed; Stanitz coll. (SPB. Apr.25; 289) $550

MARIVAUX, Pierre Carlet de Chamblain de
- Les Fausses Confidences. Ill.:– Brianchon. Paris, 1959. *(147) numbered*. Fo. Loose as iss. in orig. wraps., cl. folder & s.-c. (BBA. Jun.14; 192) *Makiya*. £200
- Le Théâtre. Amst., Leipzig, 1756. *New Edn*. 4 vols. 12mo. Cont. porphyry cf., decor. spines, sm. slits. (HD. Dec.9; 58) Frs. 2,300

MARKHAM, C.A.
See– CHAFFERS, M. & Markham, C.A.

MARKHAM, Edwin
- The Man with the Hoe. [San Franc.], 1899. *1st. Edn*. Fo. Some corners & margins chipped; inscr. by author in 3 places, Frederic Dannay copy. (CNY. Dec.16; 224) $130
- - Anr. Edn. San Franc., 1899. *1st. Edn. in Book Form*. 12mo. Orig. ptd. wraps., sewn as iss., slight tear on upr. cover, reprd. on verso, orig. ptd. mailing envelope, hf. mor. s.-c.; inscr. by author, Frederic Dannay copy. (CNY. Dec.16; 225) $120

MARKHAM, Francis
- Five Decades of Epistles of Warre. L., 1622. *1st. Edn*. Fo. Cont. cf., lacks end-papers. (SG. Sep.22; 201) $225

MARKHAM, Gervase
- Country Contentments; or the Husbandmans Recreations ... Hunting, Hawking, Coursing with Greyhounds ... Angling. L., 1683. Sm. 4to. Slight staining & soiling, hf. mor. gt. (S. Oct.4; 276) *Old Hall*. £75
- [–] The English Housewife. 1649. Lacks 1st. blank, text browned, some stains, 19th. C. hf. cf. gt. [Wing M629] (P. Jan.12; 249) *Cavendish*. £180
- Farewell to Husbandry. 1638. *4th. Edn*. (*With:*)
- Country Contentments. 1654. *7th. Edn*. Together 2 vols. Sm. 4to. Both works browned & spotted,

later cf.-bkd. cl., slightly rubbed. (BBA. Jul.27; 30) *Rix*. £120
- Masterpiece: containing all Knowledge belonging to the Smith, Farrier, or Horse-Leech. L., 1668. 2 vols. in 1. Leath. (G. Sep.15; 2263) Sw.Frs. 1,400
- The Pleasures of Princes ... Contayning a Discourse of the Generall Art of Fishing ... Together with the Choyce, Breeding, & Dyeting of the Fighting Cock. L., 1635. Sm. 4to. Browned, 19th. C. mor. (S. Oct.4; 39) *Old Hall*. £110

MARKLAND, Abraham
- Pteryplegia: The Art of Shooting-Flying. Foreword:–Col. H.P. Sheldon. Ill.:– Robert Ball. Derrydale Pr., 1931. *(200) numbered with ills. hand-cold., sigd. by artist*. Lge. 8vo. Hf. art vell., extremities lightly soiled or faded. (SG. Mar.15; 234) $275

MARKWELL, Marmaduke [Pseud.]
- Advice to Sportsmen, Rural or Metropolitan, Noviciates or Grown Persons. Ill.:– Thomas Rowlandson. L., 1809. *1st. Edn*. 12mo. 16 etched plts., pol. cf. gt. by Rivière. (S. Dec.13; 316) *Fletcher*. £80

MARLBOROUGH, G. Spencer, Third Duke of
- Catalogue of the Marlborough Gems. 1899. Sale catalogue, prices & some buyers' names supplied in MS., bds. (P. Jul.5; 149) £65

MARLE, Raimond van
- Iconographie de l'art Profane au Moyen-Age et à la Renaissance et la Décoration des Demeures. La Haye, 1931-32. 2 vols. Lge. 4to. 10 heliogravure & 1,047 plts. & ills., orig. decor. cl. gt. (VS. Jun.6; 81) Fls. 1,050

MARLES, Michel de
- Histoire de la Domination des Arabes et des Maures en Espagne et en Portugal. Paris, 1825. 3 vols. 4to. Mor.; Maria Luisa superlibris. (DS. Jan.27; 2122) Pts. 24,000

MARLIANUS, Joannes Bartholomaeus
- Urbis Romae Topographia. Rome, 1540. Fo. Some wormholes in margins, several sm. margin stains, sm. liby. stp. at foot of title, later hf. vell. (S. Dec.1; 343) *Callea*. £350
- - Anr. Edn. [Rome, Sep.] 1544. Fo. Slightly wormed, mainly to margins, old hf. vell. (TA. Sep.15; 70) £130
- - Anr. Copy. Fo. Some margin dampstaining & spotting, last lf. stained, mod. cf., spine gt.-lettered, bd. edges rubbed, s.-c.; Thomas B. Stevenson copy. (CNY. May 18; 125) $600
- - Anr. Edn. Basel, 1550. Fo. Upr. right corner excised thro.-out (without loss), dedication pasted with Japan paper strips in right margin, stained at foot thro.-out, mod. bds. (D. Nov.23; 1033) DM 450

MARLOWE, Christopher
- Lusts Dominion; or, The Lascivious Queen. L., 1657. *1st. Edn. 1st. Iss*. 8vo. & 12mo. Inlaid thro.-out, lacks final blank, B2 in facs., stained, many ll. cracked, without loss, pol. cf. gt. by Sangorski & Sutcliffe; Quaritch collation note. (SG. Oct.27; 212) $325

MARLOWE, Christopher & Chapman, George
- Hero & Leander. Ill.:– Charles Ricketts or Charles Shannon. L., Ballantyne Pr., 1893-94. *(220). (6) bnd. by Ricketts*. 7 orig. woodcuts, orig. vell., gold-tooled decor., gold-tooled corner-pieces, unc., with orig. prospectus. (GB. May 5; 3136) DM 4,000

MARMIER, Xavier
- Reis in Zwitserland. Trans.:– S.J. van den Bergh. Ill.:– after brothers Rouargue. Utrecht, 1864. 2 pts. in 1 vol. Lge. 8vo. A few plts. slightly foxed, mainly in margin, hf. cl. (B. Jun.21; 532) Fls. 700
- Voyage en Suisse. Paris, 1862. 4to. 26 partly cold. steel engraved plts., foxed, mainly text, linen, lacks back. (GF. Nov.16; 1147) Sw.Frs. 750
- - Anr. Edn. Ill.:– Rouargues. Paris, [1862]. 4to. Cont. hf. leath. gt. (R. Oct.13; 3277) DM 1,050

MARMION, Anthony
- The Ancient & Modern History of the Maritime Ports of Ireland. L., 1855. *1st. Edn*. Decor. cl. (GM. Dec.7; 250) £55

MARMOCCHI, F.C.
- Raccolta di Viaggi dalla Scoptera del Nuovo Continente fino a' di Nostri. Prato, 1840-45. 18 vols. Lge. 8vo. Cont. hf. cf. (SG. Mar.29; 325) $200

MARMOL CARVAJAL, Luis del
- Historia del [sic] Rebelion y Castigo de los Moriscos del Reyno de Granada. Malaga, 1600. Fo. Cf. (DS. Mar.23; 2175) Pts. 200,000

MARMONTEL, Jean François
- Belisaire. Paris, 1767. *Orig. Edn*. Cf., worn. (HD. Feb.22; 132) Frs. 1,400
- Les Incas, ou la Destruction de l'Empire de Pérou. Ill.:– de Launay, Duclos, de Ghendt & others, after Moreau. Paris, 1777. 2 vols. 5 figures with proof added before the letter, cont. tree cf. gt., decor. spine, inner roll-stp. (HD. Sep.22; 284) Frs. 2,350
- Oeuvres Complettes. Ill.:– after Gravelot. Liege, 1777-80. 9 vols. 3 frontis., 26 plts., cont. bds., vell. corners, cf. spines gt. (S. Apr.10; 296) *Marshall*. £240

MARMORA, Andréa
- Della Historia di Corfu. Venice, 1672. 4to. Old vell. (HD. Mar.9; 124) Frs. 2,600

MARMOTTAN, P.
- Le Peintre Louis Boilly (1761-1845). Paris, 1913. Fo. Red mor. (SPB. Nov.30; 14) $225

MARNO, Ernst
- Reisen im Gebiete des Blauen und Wissen Nil. Wien, 1874. *1st. Edn*. Mod. linen. (R. Oct.13; 2917) DM 650

MARNOCK, Robert
- The Floricultural Magazine & Miscellany of Gardening. L., 1836-42. Vols. I-VI & Vol. VI duplicate, 7 vols. Many hand-cold. plts., hf. cf., as a collection of plts., w.a.f. (CR. Jun.6; 219) Lire 330,000

MAROLLES, Michel de
- Tableaux du Temple des Muses. Ill.:– Bloemaert. Paris, 1655. *[1st. Edn.]*. Fo. Engraved title, 2 ports., 58 engraved plts., some foxing & light stains, old bds., shabby. (SG. Apr.19; 126) $325
- - Anr. Copy. Fo. Lacks engraved title, some light browning, stained thro.-out in lr. & upr. right corners, cont. marb. cf. gt., rubbed & bumped. (H. Nov.23; 713) DM 420
- - Anr. Edn. Ill.:– after Bloemaert. Amst., 1676. 4to. Some plts. slightly stained in margins, cont. cf., rubbed & slightly loosening. (VG. Sep.14; 918) Fls. 500

MAROLOIS, Sam.
[–] Sintagma in quo Varia Eximiaque Corporum Diagrammata ex Praescriptio Opticae, Artis Perspectivae etc. Amst., 1624[?]. Cont. leath. (GB. Nov.3; 893) DM 450

MAROT, Clement
- Les Oeuvres de Clément Marot de Cahors, Vallet de Chambre du Roy. Lyon, 1544. 2 pts. in 1 vol. 17th. C. red mor., spine decor.; sig. of Etienne Baluze on title, from L. de Montgermont liby. (HD. Mar.29; 60) Frs. 95,000
- - Anr. Edn. La Haye, 1700. *New Edn. 1st. Printing*. 2 vols. 16mo. Red mor. gt. by Reymann, spines decor. (HD. Mar.27; 22) Frs. 3,000
- - Anr. Copy. 2 vols. 12mo. Cont. mor., gt. decor., limp decor. spines, sm. faults. (HD. Dec.9; 59) Frs. 1,900
- - Anr. Copy. 2 vols. 12mo. Cont. cf., spine decor. (HD. Mar.21; 57) Frs. 1,050
- Oeuvres de Clément Marot, Valet de Chambre de François 1er ... Avec les Ouvrages de Jean Marot son Père et ceux de Michel Marot son Fils. La Haye, 1731. 6 vols. 12mo. On papier fort, cont. cf., inscr. 'Mr. Croismare' on upr. covers, decor. spines, slightly defect.; Emmanuel Martin ex-libris. (HD. Sep.22; 285) Frs. 1,900
- - Anr. Edn. La Haye, 1731. 4 vols. 4to. Cont. cf., spines decor. (HD. Nov.17; 49) Frs. 1,200
- Oeuvres Complètes. Paris, 1824. *Paul Lacroix Edn*. 3 vols. On 'vélin satiné', cont. hf. russ., spines gt., unc. (HD. Mar.19; 72) Frs. 1,400

MAROZZO, Achille
- Arte dell'Armi. Venezia, 1569. 4to. Lge. wormhole in outer margin with slight loss of text, some other

MAROZZO, Achille *-Contd.*

defects., some stains, cont. vell., slightly discold.
(SI. Dec.15; 25)   Lire 750,000

MARPERGER, Paul Jacob
- **Beschreibung der Messen u. Jahr-Märckte.**
Leipzig, 1710. *1st. Edn.* Cut slightly close in places,
cont. leath. gt. decor., slightly worn. (HK. May 16;
1621)   DM 1,900
[-] **Die Neu-Eröffnete Kauffmans-Börse.** Hamburg,
1704. 1 plt. loose, wraps. (HK. Nov.9; 1819)
                    DM 600
- - **Anr. Copy.** 12mo. Mod. hf. leath. (VG. May 3;
455)   Fls. 700
- **Trifolium Mercantile Aureum, oder Dreyfaches
Güldenes Klee-Blatt der Werthen Kauffmannschaft.**
Dresden & Leipzig, 1723. Cont. leath., spine
rubbed, wormed. (GB. May 3; 954)   DM 760

MARPURG, Fr. W.
- **Anfangsgründe der Theoretischen Musik.** Leipzig,
1757. *1st. Edn.* 4to. Slightly stained thro.-out in lr.
margin, cont. vell. (HK. Nov.9; 2265) DM 2,400
- **Anleitung zur Singcomposition.** Berlin, 1758. *1st.
Edn.* 4to. Title & 1 lf. torn, title partly bkd. in
lr. margin, some slight soiling, cont. bds., slightly
bumped, sm. defect. & spotting. (HK. Nov.9; 2266)
                    DM 2,700
- **Handbuch bey dem Generalbasse u. der Composition mit zwo-acht u. mehr. Stimmen für Anfänger
u. Geübte.** Berlin, 1757-62 (Pts. 2 & 3 & Supp.).
1st. Edn. 3 pts. & Supp., in 1 vol. 4to. Some light
spotting or browning, cont. hf. leath. gt., rubbed,
slightly bumped. (HK. Nov.9; 2267)   DM 2,300

MARQUART, Joseph
- **Die Benin-Sammlung des Reichsmuseums.** Leiden,
1913. Fo. Orig. cl. (CSK. Sep.16; 139)   £200
- - **Anr. Copy.** Orig. linen. (D. Nov.23; 1245)
                    DM 450

MARRYAT, Frank S.
- **Borneo & the Indian Archipelago.** L., 1848. *1st.
Edn.* 4to. 22 tinted litho. plts., orig. blind-decor. cl.,
spine gt. (SKC. Mar.9; 2027)   £160
- - **Anr. Copy.** Col. frontis., litho. title, 20 litho.
plts., a few foxed, hf. cf. gt. (P. Oct.20; 225) £140
- - **Anr. Copy.** Sm. fo. Cold. litho. frontis. & title
frayed at edges, some spotting, orig. cl., crudely
reprd. on spine, untrimmed. (TA. Oct.20; 17) £70
- - **Anr. Copy.** Orig. cl., some tears. (SPB. Dec.13;
456) $150

MARRYAT, Capt. Frederic
- **Novels.** Ed.:- R. Brimley Johnson. L., 1895. *(750)*
on H.M.P., for America. 24 vols. Hf. mor. gt. (SPB.
Dec.13; 548) $500

MARSDEN, Samuel
- **The Letters & Journals** ... Ed.:- John Rawson
Elder. Dunedin, 1932. Orig. cl., d.-w. worn. (KH.
Nov.9; 330)   Aus.$100

MARSDEN, William
- **The History of Sumatra.** L., 1811. 4to. Folding
engraved map, 28 plts., errata slip, most plts.
offset & slightly spotted, 1 imprint shaved, cont.
cf., covers detchd. (S. Jun.25; 41)
                    Remmington. £300

MARSH, Othniel Charles
- **Dinocerata: a Monograph of an Extinct Order of
Gigantic Mammals.** Ill.:- F. Berger, lithographed
by E. Crisand, New Haven. Wash., 1884. *1st. Edn.*
Fo. 56 plts., minor soiling & darkening, marb. end-
papers, period three-qtr. red mor. & mott. bds.,
worn, some glue stains from attempted repair; inscr.
to Gen. W[illiam] T. Sharmon. (CBA. Aug.21;
405) $100

MARSH, Lieut. Col. W. Lockwood
- **Aeronautical Prints & Drawings.** L., 1924. *(100)*
numbered. 4to. Some ll. spotted, orig. pig, slightly
rubbed. (BBA. Nov.10; 220)   *Blackwell.* £160
- - **Anr. Edn.** L., 1924. *(1000) numbered.* 4to. Gt.-
lettered cl., soiled, lr. hinge strengthened. (SG.
Oct.6; 2) $150

MARSHALL, H. Rissik
- **Coloured Worcester Porcelain of the First Period
(1751-1783).** Newport, 1954. *1st. Edn.* 4to. Orig.
cl. gt. (LC. Jul.5; 72)   £70
- - **Anr. Copy.** 4to. Orig. cl. (BBA. Nov.10; 281)
                    Zwemmer. £55
- - **Anr. Edn.** Newport, 1954. *(1200).* No bdg.
stated. (JL. Jun.24; 210)   Aus. $550

MARSHALL, John
- **The Life of George Washington.** Phila., 1804-07.
5 vols. & atlas, together 6 vols. 8vo. & 4to. Port.,
10 maps (8 double-p.), subscribers' list, foxing,
spotting, tears mostly marginal, cont. tree cf. & cf.-
bkd. marb. bds (atlas); Fred A. Berne copy. (SPB.
May 16; 328) $350

MARSHALL, William
- **The Rural Economy of the West of England.** 1796.
1st. Edn. 2 vols. Mott. cf. gt. (P. Jun.7; 118) £130

MARSHMAN, Joshua
- **Dissertation on the Characters & Sounds of the
Chinese Language.** [Serampore, 1809]. 4to. Errata
lf., folding tables, few fore-margins slightly stained,
cont. bds., unc., rebkd. (S. Mar.6; 38)
                    Orientum. £200
- **Elements of Chinese Grammar.** Serampore, 1814.
*1st. Edn. 2nd. Iss., with the Sino-Engl. title, errata
lf., expanded preface, cancelled blank N4, & the
completed 'Ta-Hyoh'.* 4to. Cont. diced cf. gt. extra,
rehinged; Joseph Dart armorial bkplt. (SG. Nov.3;
136) $225

MARSIGLI, Luigi Ferdinando
- **Danubius Pannonico-Mysicus** ... The Hague &
Amst., 1726. 6 vols. Fo. 6 engraved frontis., 284
numbered plts. & maps, some double-p. or folding,
some browning, a few stains, margin repair to
frontis. in Vol. 5, cont. Fr. mott. cf. gt., rebkd. &
reprd.; titles inscr. 'Le Duc de Valentinois, 1728',
James Franck Bright bkplt. (S. Nov.28; 126)
                    Obodda. £1,300
- **L'Etat Militaire de l'Empire Ottoman.** Den Haag,
1732. 2 vols. Fo. Parallel Italian & Fr. text, Vol. 1
probably lacks 2 ll., some slight text browning, hf.
leath., very rubbed & bumped. (D. Nov.24; 3437)
                    DM 600
- **Histoire Physique de la Mer.** Amst., 1725. Fo. 2
plts. cleanly torn, 1 affecting plt. area, cont. cf.,
spine gt. (CSK. Dec.16; 5)   £420

MARSOLLIER, Abbe Jacques
[-] **The Life of St. Francis of Sales.** Trans.:- William
Henry Coombes. L., 1737. *1st. Edn.* 3 vols. Mor.
gt. (BBA. Mar.21; 224)   *H.M. Fletcher.* £80

MARSTON, G.
See— **MURRAY, J. & Marston, G.**

MARSYAS: Eine Zweimonatsschrift
Ill.:- Pechstein, Grossman, & others. Berlin, 1917-
19. *(200).* Vol.1 nos. 1-6 (all publd.). Fo. Approx.
120 lithos. & etchings, some dupls., loose, but
including orig. pict. upr. wraps.; sigs. of collector
Heinrich Stinnes on wraps., not collated, w.a.f.
(SG. Dec.15; 173) $475

MARTEL, André
- **Le Mirivis des Naturigies.** Ill.:- Jean Dubuffet.
[Paris, 1963]. *(110) sigd. by author & artist.* 4to.
Loose in orig. wraps. as iss., folder & box, slight
rubbing. (SPB. Dec.14; 50) $950

MARTENS, Friedrich
See— **LA MARTINIERE, Pierre Martin de &
Martens, Friedrich**

MARTIAL, A.R.
- **Paris pendant le Siège. Paris sous la Commune.
Paris Incendié.** N.d. Fo. Hf. roan, corners, wrap.
preserved, bdg. defect.; many MS. notes (by Sully-
Prudhomme?). (HD. Jun.29; 190)   Frs. 2,500

MARTIALIS, Marcus Valerius
- **Epigrammata.** Venice, [1480]. Fo. Lacks last
blank lf., late 18th. C. hf. roan, rubbed; from
Fondation Furstenberg-Beaumesnil. [HC 10814;
BMC V, 296; Goff M304] (HD. Nov.16; 66)
                    Frs. 8,100
- - **Anr. Edn.** Ed.:- Domitius Calderinus. Milan,
Leonardus Pachel & Uldericus Scinzenzeler, 15

Aug. 1483. Lacks a (blank), y3 & 8 & last 1f.
[Goff M-307] (*Bound with:*) **PERSIUS FLACCUS,
Aulus – Satirarum Opus.** Milan, Antonius Zarottus,
1484. Lacks a1 (blank). Together 2 works in 1 vol.
Some light staining, vell. (BBA. Mar.21; 1)
                    Fletcher. £450
- - **Anr. Edn.** Commentaries:– [Domitius Calder-
inus]. Milan, Ulderich Scinzenzeler, 20 Sep. 1490.
Fo. 1st. & last ll. mntd., 6 ll. at beginning with
margins reprd., upr. margins dampstained, a few
sm. tears & wormholes in text, some ll. browned
with slight stains, 18th. C. marginalia, cont. vell.,
worn. [BMC VI 764] (BBA. Nov.30; 23)
                    Fazzi. £380
- **Ex Otio Negotium. Or, Martiall his Epigrams
Translated with Sundry Poems & Fancies,** ...
Trans.:– R. Fletcher. L., 1656. *1st. Edn.* 4 supp. ll.
present, cont. inscr. on recto of 1st. lf., 17th. C.
MS. poem at end, a few headlines shaved, 19th. C.
cf., spine gt.; sig. of Charles Taylor, 1672, John
Drinkwater, 1921, bkplt. & sig. [Wing M381]
(BBA. May 3; 136)   *Ximenes.* £250

MARTIN, Alexander
- **La Suisse Pittoresque.** Paris, 1834. 4to. Engraved
frontis. & 85 steel engraved plts., some plts. with
liby. stp. on verso, orig. linen. (GF. Nov.16; 1148)
                    Sw. Frs. 1,200
- **La Suisse Pittoresque & ses Environs.** Paris, 1835.
Frontis., folding map & 82 steel engraved plts. &
views, lacks map & 2 plts., stained, 1st. ll. loose &
defect., bds. (VG. May 3; 392)   Fls. 900

MARTIN, Arthur
See— **CAHIER, Charles & Martin, Arthur**

MARTIN, Benjamin
- **Philosophia Britannica; or, a New & Comprehensive System of the Newtonian Philosophy.** L., 1759.
2nd. Edn. 3 vols. Some foxing &c., old cf., rubbed,
worn at tips & edges. (RO. Jun.26; 116) $180
- **The Philosophical Grammar; Being a View of
the Present State of Experimented Physiology, or
Natural Philosophy** ... 1755. *5th. Edn.* Little
browned, cont. cf. (TA. Sep.15; 472)   £54

MARTIN, Charles & Leopold
- **The Civil Costume of England to the Present
Period.** 1842. 4to. Hand-cold. title, 59 (of 60) plts.,
hf. mor. gt. (P. Sep.29; 249)   *Shapiro.* £80

MARTIN, Clara Barnes
- **Mount Desert, on the Coast of Maine.** Portsmouth, 1885. *6th. Edn.* 5 mntd. hf. stereo albumen
photos., 2 extra photos. inserted in rear sleeve
with folding map, orig. cl., front free end-paper &
frontis. brkn. on inner margin. (SG. Apr.5; 116)
                    $140

MARTIN, David, of Utrecht, 1639-1721
- **Histoire du Vieux et du Nouveau Testament.** Ill.:-
after Picart & others. Amst., 1700. 2 vols. in 1.
Lge. fo. 2 lge. vigs. on title-p., 2 extra engraved
titles, 3 double-p. maps, 426 (of 428) copperplts.,
blank margins stained, 1 plt. reprd., old liby. stp.
on title-p., cont. mott. cf., lge. gt.-stpd. design on
covers, that on upr. cover partly worn away, lacks
most of spine; armorial bkplt. of Thomas Winford,
Glashampton, Worcs. (SG. Feb.9; 130) $275
[-] **Historie des Nieuwen Testaments. Tweede Deel.**
Ill.:- Luyken, Van der Gouwen, Picart & others.
Amst., 1700. *1st. Edn.* Fo. Cont. vell., decor., gold-
tooled centre-piece, gt. spine. (D. Nov.24; 2304)
                    DM 1,200

MARTIN, Fredrik R.
- **Miniatures from the Period of Timur in a MS. of
the Poems of Sultan Ahmad Jalair.** Vienna, 1926.
Fo. Authors MS. dedication on endpaper, slightly
soiled, orig. hf. vell. (D. Nov.23; 1965)   DM 600
- **The Miniature Painting & Painters of Persia
India & Turkey.** L., 1968. *(500).* Fo. Orig. cl., d.-
w. (S. Apr.30; 126)   *Randall.* £60

MARTIN, H. & Lauer, Ph.
- **Les Principaux Manuscrits à Peinture de la Bibliothèque de l'Arsenal à Paris.** Paris, 1929. Fo. 92
plts., loose as iss. in orig. bds., worn; H.M. Nixon
coll. (BBA. Oct.6; 91)   *Maggs.* £50

MARTIN, Henri
- Historie de France ... Paris, 1878. 17 vols. Hf. mor., gt. spines, bkplt. (PNY. Jun.6; 456) $160

MARTIN, Dom Jacques
[–] Le Réligion des Gaulois Tirée des plus Pures Sources de l'Antiquité. Paris, 1727. 2 vols. 4to. Cont. diced roan, covers lightly rubbed, spines decor. (HD. Nov.9; 137) Frs. 1,250

MARTIN, Jean Baptiste
- Collection de Figures Théatrales. Ill.:– Gaillard & Martin. Paris, 1760. Fo. Wide margins, engraved title, 20 plts., mod. bds. (C. Dec.9; 99) *Goldschmidt.* £1,800

MARTIN, John
- Illustrations of the Bible. 1939. 4to. 20 engraved plts., orig. cl. gt. (P. Mar.15; 110) *Joseph.* £280
- – Anr. Copy. Fo. Spotted, orig. cl. gt. (P. Sep.29; 12) *Frankel.* £160

MARTIN, Martin
- A Description of the Western Islands of Scotland. 1703. *1st. Edn.* Folding engraved map & engraved plt. torn, cont. panel. cf., upr. cover detchd. (CE. Sep.1; 1) £145

MARTIN, P., von Cochem
- Der Verbesserte Grosse Baum-Garten. Wurzburg, 1763. Cont. velvet, worn, white metal corner-pieces & clasp. (CSK. Dec.2; 174) £60

MARTIN, Robert Montgomery
- Australia Comprising New South Wales ... [1853]. 4to. 8 ports., 3 engraved views, 8 double-p. partly cold. maps, orig. cl. gt., slightly worn. (P. Oct.20; 230b) £200
- The British Colonies. Ill.:– Maps:– Tallis. Ca. 1850. Vol. 1 only. 18 partly col. maps, hf. cf., rubbed. (P. Jul.5; 237) £300
- – Anr. Copy. 6 vols. in 12 pts. 4to. Some maps & plts. misbnd., some light foxing, gt.-decor. cl., spines gt., a few spines chipped & loose. (SG. Mar.29; 326) $500
- – Anr. Edn. Ill.:– Maps:– Rapkin. N.d. 6 vols. in 3. 4to. 42 hand-cold. double-p. maps, cont. hf. mor., lightly rubbed. (CSK. Jul.6; 18) £480
- History of Austral-Asia ... 1839. *2nd.-Edn.* Mod. hf. cf. (KH. May 1; 471) Aus. $120
- The Illustrated Atlas. Ill.:– Tallis (maps). Ca. 1850. 4to. Frontis., vig. title, 2 plts., 81 maps, orig. cl. gt. (P. Oct.20; 264) £700
- – Anr. Copy. 96 maps (including 31 dupls.), hand-cold. in outl., several lightly stained, disbnd., w.a.f. (CSK. Dec.2; 23) £650
- – Anr. Edn. Ill.:– Tallis. 1851. 4to. Frontis., engraved title, 81 hand-cold. maps with vigs., hf. cf., upr. cover detchd. (P. Oct.20; 256d) £740
- – Anr. Copy. Fo. Additional engraved title with vig., engraved frontis., 81 full-p. steel-engraved maps, hand-cold. in outl., 2 engraved thematic plts., frontis., title & last map soiled, some dust-soiling, 1 or 2 outer margins chipped, 1 crudely reprd. affecting engraved surface, later bds., worn, w.a.f. (S. May 21; 135) *Ross.* £720
- – Anr. Copy. Fo. Engraved frontis., additional title, 81 maps, hand-cold. in outl., some light soiling, some text ll. cleanly torn, cont. hf. mor., worn. (CSK. Dec.16; 167) £550
- – Anr. Edn. Ill.:– J. Rapkin. L. & N.Y., J. & F. Tallis, [1851]. Fo. Engraved title with vig., 2 engraved plts., 77 (of 81?) full-p. steel-engraved maps, hand-cold. in outl., sm. tear in title, some browning affecting text, cont. hf. cf. gt., worn. (S. Dec.1; 212) *Delmre.* £820
- – Anr. Edn. Ill.:– after Rapkin. N.d. Fo. Engraved frontis., title, 80 maps, hand-cold. in outl., title & frontis. lightly stained, cont. hf. cf., rubbed. (CSK. Jan.13; 27) £800
- – Anr. Copy. Fo. Engraved title, 2 tables & 80 maps only, hand-cold. in outl., 1 folding plan, some light soiling, cont. cf., worn, upr. cover detchd. (CSK. May 4; 47) £650
- – Anr. Copy. Fo. Folding plan of L. badly torn, old hf. mor., rubbed, w.a.f. due to uncertainty of completeness. (KH. May 1; 472) Aus. $1,400

MARTIN, Violet Florence 'Martin Ross'
See— SOMERVILLE, Edith Osbone & Martin, Violet Florence 'Martin Ross'

MARTIN, William, Naturalist
- Petrificata Derbiensia. Wigan, 1809. Vol.1 (all publd.). 4to. 52 hand-cold. engraved plts., some light spotting & offsetting, cont. hf. vell., worn. (S. Mar.6; 293) *Marlborough.* £180

MARTIN, Sir William
[–] The Laws of England Compiled & Translated into the Maori Language by Direction of His Excellency Colonel Thomas Gore Browne ... Auckland, 1858. Sm. fo. In Engl. & Maori, cont. or early semi-limp binder's cl. gt., with colonial ticket. (KH. May 1; 473) Aus. $140

MARTIN CANO, F.
- Glorias de Alaurin ... Exaltación de ... Carlos III. Madrid, 1760. 4to. Sewed. (DS. Nov.25; 2631) Pts. 20,000

MARTINDALE, Lieut.-Col
See— CARLILE, Lieut. & Martindale, Lieut.-Col.

MARTIN DU GARD, Roger
- L'Eté 1914. Paris, 1936. *Orig. Edn. (300) on pur fil Lafuma.* 3 vols. 12mo. Orig. bdg. (HD. Apr.26; 191) Frs. 1,520
- Les Thibault. Paris, 1922-40. *Orig. Edn.* 11 vols., compl. 12mo. Some vols. foxed, sewed; autograph dedications to Béatrice Appia, Eugéne Dabit, Jean Paulhan, Schiffrin, Louis Jouvet. (HD. Jun.26; 109) Frs. 2,800

MARTIN SAINT-ANGE, G.-J.
See— GRIMAUD DE CAUX, G. & Martin Saint-Ange, G.-J.

MARTINEZ, Martin
- Anatomia Completa del Hombre. Madrid, 1738. 4to. Vell. (DS. Feb.24; 2079) Pts. 20,000

MARTINEZ DE LA ROSA, Francisco
- Hernán Peréz del Pulgar et de las Hazanas. Madrid, 1834. *1st. Edn.* Sewed. (DS. Feb.24; 2126) Pts. 30,000

MARTINEZ DE TOLEDO, Alfonso
- Oratio in Vitam et Merita S. Bonaventurae. [Rome], Joannes Philippus de Lignamine, not before 14 Apr. 1482. 4to. Lacks ll. 1 (woodcut) & 7, ll. 2-3 bnd. at end & stained, bds., brkn.; G.W. Davis bkplt. [H. 10830 (SG. Feb.9; 254) $175

MARTINI, Friedrich Heinrich Wilhelm
- Neues Systematisches Conchylien-Cabinet. Ill.:– C.B. Glassbach after A. Fr. Happe. Nuremb., 1768. Vol. 1 only (of 12). Lge. 4to. Slightly browned or stained, 2 plts. with slight margin defects., cont. vell. (HK. Nov.8; 623) DM 550

MARTINI, Martin
- Historia om thet tartariiske krijget uthi konunga-rijket Sina, sampt theras seder. Preface:– A. Nidelberg. Visingsborg, 1674. Sm. 4to. Later bds. (S. Dec.1; 375) *Israel.* £150
- Sinicae Historiae Decas Prima Res a Gentis Origine ad Christum Natum in Extrema Asia, sive Magno Sinarum Imperio Gestas complexa. München, 1658. *1st. Edn.* Title with cont. owners mark, engraved ex-libris, cont. vell., lightly spotted, lacks ties. (HT. May 10; 2535a) DM 650

MARTINS, Wilson
- A Palavra Escrita: Historia do Livro, da Imprensa e da Biblioteca. Sao Paulo, 1957. *1st. Edn.* Orig. cl. (SG. Apr.5; 213) $100

MARTIUS, Karl Friedrich Philipp von
- Icones Plantarum Cryptogamicarum. München, 1828-34. Fo. Some plt. margins slightly faded, cont. hf. leath., worn & bumped, cover loose. (H. Nov.23; 260) DM 2,000
See— SPIX, Johann B. von & Martius, Karl F.P. von

MARTY, Andre
- L'Imprimerie et les Procédés de Gravures au Ving-tième Siècle. Paris, priv. ptd., 1906. *(100) numbered.* 4to. Hf. lev. mor. by Salvator David, spine gt.-lettered, partly unc., orig. ptd. wraps. & spine preserved; Raphael Esmerian bkplt. (CNY. May 18; 190) $1,300

MARTY, Marcel
- Images d'une Petite Ville Arabe. Ill.:– Albert Marquet. Paris, [1947]. *(225) numbered.* 4to. Unsewn in orig. pict. wraps., folder & s.-c. (S. Nov.21; 32) *Makiya.* £190

MARTYN, Benjamin
[–] An Impartial Enquiry into the State & Unity of the Province of Georgia. L., 1741. *1st. Edn.* Hf.-title, maroon hf. mor.; the Rt. Hon. Visc. Eccles copy. [Sabin 45001] (CNY. Nov.18; 189) $380

MARTYN, John
See— LOWTHORP, John & others

MARTYN, Thomas 1760-1816, Entomologist
- Aranei; or, A Natural History of Spiders. L., 1793. Lge. 4to. 2 engraved titles, 2 engraved plts. of medals, 28 col. engraved plts., lacks frontis., cont. red str.-grd. mor. gt. extra, rebkd. (SG. Nov.3; 137) $375
- English Spiders. N.d. Lge. 4to. 17 hand-cold. plts., hf.-title, no title, unc., orig. bds. (GM. Dec.7; 657) £80

MARTYN, Thomas, Botanist, 1735-1825
- Flora Rustica. Ill.:– Frederick P. Nodder. 1792. 2 vols. in 1. 144 hand-cold. engraved plts. (including dupl. plt. 88), cont. cf., worn, w.a.f. (CSK. Jul.13; 150) £180
- – Anr. Edn. Ill.:– F.P. Nodder. L., 1792-94. 4 vols. 144 hand-cold. engraved plts., some browning & spotting, cont. tree cf., worn. (S. Nov.28; 60) *Payne.* £250
- – Anr. Copy. 4 vols. in 2. 144 hand-cold. plts., no title-p. to Vol. 2, some spotting, hf. cf., worn, upr. cover to Vols. 3 & 4 detchd. (P. Sep.29; 331) *Maggs.* £110
[–] Sketch of a Tour through Swisserland. 1787. 12mo. Tree cf. gt. (P. Mar.15; 323) *Cavendish.* £70
- Thirty-Eight Plates ... to Illustrate Linnaeus's System of Vegetables. 1788. 38 hand-cold. engraved plts., orig. paper-bkd. bds. (CSK. Oct.7; 47) £75
- – Anr. Edn. 1794. 38 hand-cold. plts., cont. mott. cf. gt. (P. Feb.16; 88) £65
- – Anr. Copy. 38 hand-cold. plts., cf. (P. Sep.29; 330a) *Omniphil.* £60
See— MILLER, Philip & Martyn, Thomas

MARTYN, William Frederic
- A New Dictionary of Natural History. L., 1785. Vol. 2 only. Fo. 99 (of 100) hand-cold. engraved plts., few faintly spotted, 3 marginal tears, cont. cf.-bkd. bds., worn, unc. (S. Apr.10; 551) *Cumming.* £280
- – Anr. Copy. 2 vols. in 1. Fo. Not collated, over 90 hand-cold. plts., disbnd., w.a.f. (SG. Mar.22; 201) $275

MARTYR, Peter, of Anghiera
- De Rebus Oceanicis & Orbe Novo Decades tres ... Eiusdem Praeterea Legationis Babylonicae. Basle, 1533. Fo. Cont. inscr. on title giving the approval of the Inquisitor at Modena, same hand has also erased the printer's name, light stains at beginning & end, red mor. [Sabin 1557] (S. Dec.1; 286) *Baker.* £520
- The Historie of the West Indies, Contaynig the Actes & Adventures of the Spanyardes, which have Conquered & Peopled Those Countries ... L., 1612. Sm. 4to. Cf., boxed; Barlow copy, Littell bkplt. (LH. Sep.25; 261) $900

MARVELL, Andrew
- Miscellaneous Poems. 1681. *1st. Edn.* Sm. fo. Lacks pp. 117-30 (as usual), cont. MS. insertion at p. 110, frontis. with repair to sm. tear just into engraved area & slightly offset onto title, sm. rust-hole at D3 & 4 affecting a few letters, some minor spotting, mod. blind-panel cf. by Hodgson; Lord Derby bkplt. [Wing M872] (C. May 30; 162) *Bennett.* £400
- – Anr. Copy. Fo. Engraved frontis.-port., minor marginal stains, port. margin very slightly frayed, sm. blank piece torn from margin of last lf., some ll. after R1 cancelled, early marb. wraps., unc., cl. folder, qtr. mor. s.-c.; Arthur A. Houghton copy. [Wing M872] (SPB. May 16; 100) $6,000

MARX, Karl
- **Capital: A Critical Analysis of Capitalist Prod-uction.** Ed.:– Frederick Engels. L., 1887. *1st. Edn.* 2 vols. Orig. cl., covers worn, hinges reprd. (LH. Sep.25; 563) $750
- **Das Kapital.** Ed.:– F. Engels (Vols. 2 & 3). Hamburg, 1867-94. *1st. Edn.* 3 vols. (Vol. 3 in 2 pts.). All 3 title ll. with traces of removed stp., some pencil annots. & underlining vol. 2, mod. red mor. gt., decor., orig. pt. wraps. bnd. in, unif. s.-c. (R. Oct.11; 1203) DM 20,500
- - **Anr. Edn.** Ed.:– Fr. Engels. Hamburg, 1883-94. *Partly 1st. Edn.* 3 vols. Cont. hf. leath. or hf. linen, slightly rubbed. (GB. May 4; 1590) DM 700
- - **Anr. Edn.** Ed.:– F. Engels. Hamburg, 1903 & 1885. *Vol. 1: 5th. Edn., Vol. 2: 1st. Edn.* Vols. 1 & 2 only. Cont. hf. mor., not unif., rubbed. (BBA. Feb.9; 172) *Hall.* £75
- **Zur Kritik d. Polit. Oekonomie.** Berlin, 1859. *1st. Edn.* Pt. 1 (all publd.). Text slightly browned & foxed, orig. wraps., spine defect., loose. (VG. May 3; 81) Fls. 8,500

MARX, Roger
- **La Lole Fuller.** Ill.:– P. Roche. [Paris, 1904]. *Nominative Edn., (130) for the 'Cent Bibliophiles' with 17 orig. compositions.* Sm. 4to. Leaves, portfo. (HD. May 4; 353) Frs. 14,500

MARY, André
- **Tristan.** Ill.:– Jean Berque. Paris, 1937. *(150) numbered & sigd. by author & artist with extra suite of plts.* 4to. Loose as iss. in orig. wraps., vell.-bkd. bds., s.-c. (BBA. Jun.14; 187) *Makiya.* £200

MARYLAND
- **A Relation of the Successful Beginnings of the Lord Baltemore's Plantation in Mary-Land.** ... [L.], 1634. 4to. 14 pp., A-B4, some staining thro.-out, sm. wormhole, margin fraying & tears, hardly touching text, mod. wraps., buckram s.-c. [Sabin 69291; STC 4371] (C. Nov.9; 99) *Sawyer.* £13,000

MASCLEF, A.
- **Atlas des Plantes de France, Utiles, Nuisables et Ornamentales.** 1891. 3 vols. including 2 plt. vols. Light foxing to text, leaves, publisher's cl. folders. (HD. Jul.6; 61) Frs. 2,000

MASEFIELD, John
- **The Country Scene.** Ill.:– Edward Seago. L., 1937. *(50) sigd. by author & artist.* 4to. Orig. mor.-bkd. cl., soiled. (S. Mar.20; 682) *Words.* £125
- **Reynard the Fox.** L., 1919. *1st. Edn., (275). (250) numbered & sigd.* Orig. imitation vell.-bkd. bds., partly unc.; pres. copy from author to Lillah McCarthy, with her inscr., & with 54 pen & ink & watercolour drawings on 58 pp. by author, Frederic Dannay copy. (CNY. Dec.16; 229) $2,800
- **Salt-Water Ballads.** L., 1902. *1st. Edn. (500).* Orig. buckram [1st. bdg.], partly unc., cl. s.-c.; A.L.s. from William Collinge to Charles J. Sawyer laid in. Frederic Dannay copy. (CNY. Dec.16; 227) $1,100
- - **Anr. Copy.** Orig. buckram [2nd. bdg.], partly unc., hf. mor. s.-c.: bkplt. of William Marchbank, Frederic Dannay copy. (CNY. Dec.16; 228) $250
- - **Anr. Edn.** L., 1902. *1st. Edn.* Slightly spotted, orig. buckram, cl. case; Perry Molstad copy. (SPB. May 16; 478) $175

MASEKHET DEREKH ERETS RABBA VE-ZUTA
Luneville, 1804. 16mo. Some worming to last few ll. with minimal loss, last lf. remargined, mod. cl. (SG. Feb.2; 224) $150

MASEREEL, Franz
- **Du Noir au Blanc – Vom Schwarz zu Weiss.** Paris & N.Y., 1939. *1st. Edn. (100) De Luxe Edn.* 4to. Printers mark sigd. by artist, 57 orig. woodcuts, orig. pict. silk. (GB. May 5; 2932) DM 1,800
- **Expiations. Douze Bois Gravés.** Paris, 1933. *(88) on vell. d'Ardes.* Italian–Fr. parallel text slightly foxed nearby thro.-out, 12 orig. monograved wood-cuts, loose in orig. hf. linen portfo. (R. Oct.11; 333) DM 1,000

MASERES, Francis
- [-] **An Account of the Proceedings of the British, & other Protestant Inhabitants, of the Province of Quebec, in North-America, in order to obtain an** House of Assembly in that Province. L., 1775. *1st. Edn. (With:)* [-] **Additional Papers Concerning the Province of Quebeck: being an Appendix to the Book entitled, 'An Account of the Proceedings'.** L., 1776. *1st. Edn.* Together 2 vols. Cont. hf. cf., worn; the Rt. Hon. Visc. Eccles copies. [Sabin 45411] (CNY. Nov.18; 190) $1,100
- **Proposal for Establishing Life–Annuities in Parishes for the Benifit of the Industrious Poor.** L., 1772. Mod. mor. (D. Nov.24; 3701) DM 1,800

MASJUTIN, W.
- **Der Goldene Hahn.** Berlin, ca. 1925. Fo. Sigd. & cold. orig. woodcuts, orig. hf. vell. portfo., gold-litho. paper covered, corners bumped. (GB. Nov.5; 2787) DM 1,300

MASK, The: A Monthly Journal of the Art of the Theatre
1908-29. Vols. 1-7 & 9-15. 4to. & 8vo. Cl. (P. Sep.29; 126) *Marks.* £330

MASLEN, T.J.
- [-] **The Friend of Australia, or, A Plan for Exploring the Interior & for Carrying on a Survey of the Whole Continent ... By A Retired Officer** ... 1830. Tear in folding map taped, early hf. cf., sm. defects. (KH. May 1; 475) Aus. $880

MASON, George Henry
- **The Costume of China.** L., 1800. 4to. 60 hand-cold. engraved plts., titles & text in Engl. & Fr., lacks text for plt. 52, a dupl. description of plt. 51 included in error, 1 plt. with sm. margin tear, mor.-bkd. bds., unc. (C. Nov.16; 132) *Collmann.* £220
- - **Anr. Copy.** 4to. 60 hand-cold. engraved plts., text in Engl. & Fr., soiled & spotted, cont. hf. roan, worn, upr. cover detchd. (S. Mar.6; 39) *Shapero.* £120
- - **Anr. Copy.** Sm. fo. 60 hand-cold. aquatint plts., each with text lf. in Engl. & Fr., advt. dtd. 1818, ex-liby., some foxing, orig. bds., crudely rebkd., unc. (SG. May 3; 109) $475
- - **Anr. Edn.** 1804. [Wtrmkd. 1819]. Fo. Titles & text in Fr. & Engl., 60 hand-cold. engraved plts., cont. red mor., worn, upr. cover detchd., w.a.f. (CSK. May 4; 70) £280
- [-] **The Punishments of China.** L., 1830. Lge. 4to. Date 'MDCCCXXX' stpd. after letters on Engl. title, Fr. title undtd., 22 cold stipple-engraved plts. (wtrmkd. 1830, text wtrmkd. 1829), fly-lf. loose, cont. red str.-grd. mor. gt. extra, rubbed, end-papers loose. (SG. Sep.22; 254) $150

MASON, J. Alden
See— GORDON, G.B. & Mason, J. Alden

MASON, M. (Pseud.)
See— MONCK, Thomas

MASON, William Monck
- **Hibernia Antiqua et Hodierna, Being a Topo-graphical Account of Ireland.** Dublin, 1819. *1st. Edn.* Lge. 4to. Bkplt., cf., gt.-tooled spine. (GM. Dec.7; 326) £310

MASSA, Nicolaus
- **Liber de Febre Pestilentiali ac de Pestichiis, Mor-billis, Variolis & Apostematibus Pestilentialibus.** Venice, 1566. *2nd. Edn.* 4to. Some margin worming, old wraps.; from Prof. Lucas Schönlein liby., with stp. on title, Dr. Walter Pagel copy. (S. Feb.7; 249) *Gurney.* £110

MASSAIA, G.
- **I Miei Trentacinque Anni di Missione nell'Alta Etiopia.** Roma-Milano, 1885-93. 12 vols. bnd. in 6. 4to. Hf. vell. (CR. Jun.6; 220) Lire 300,000

MASSENET, Jules
- **Esclarmonde [vocal score].** Paris, 1890. *1st. Edn.* Lge. 8vo. Limp cf.; autograph mus. quotation & inscr. sigd. by author. (S. Nov.8; 473) *Lionheart.* £80

MASSILON, Jean-Baptiste
- **Sermons.** Petit Carème. Paris, 1745. *Orig. Edn.* 12mo. Cont. red mor., spine decor., Marquise de Pompadour arms. (HD. Mar.29; 61) Frs. 17,500

MASSINGER, Philip
- **The Dramatick Works.** Ed.:– John Monck Mason. L., 1779. 4 vols. Some foxing, cont. tree cf., rubbed. (RO. Apr.23; 231) $100
- **The Picture.** L., 1630. *1st. Edn.* 4to. 2nd. state of gathering A, 1st. state of gathering I, lacks initial blank, last lf. impft., B1 reprd., other defects, mod. qtr. cf. [NSTC 17640.5] (SG. Oct.27; 213) $200

MASSINGER, Phillip & Field, Nathaniel
- [-] **The Fatall Dowry: a Tragedy. By P.M. & F.N.** L., 1632. *1st. Edn.* Sm. 4to. Slight browning, tears in last lf., with crude repair to margin, disbnd. [STC 17646] (S. Oct.11; 353) *Maggs.* £100

MASSON
- **Histoire des Etablissements et du Commerce Fran-çais dans l'Afrique Barbaresque.** Paris, 1903. Hf. roan. (HD. Feb.22; 133) Frs. 1,200

MASSON, André
- **Anatomy of my Universe.** N.Y., Golden Eagle Pr., Mount Vernon. 1943. *1st. Amer. Edn. De Luxe Iss., (10) on Sevir.* 4to. Orig. pict. wraps.; 1 sigd. pen ill. & 1 sigd. etching, printers mark sigd. by artist. (H. Nov.24; 2529) DM 1,800

MASSON, Frédéric
- **Cavaliers de Napoléon, Illustrations d'après les Tableaux et Aquarelles d'Edouard Detaille.** Paris, n.d. 4to. Red hf. mor., corners, wraps. preserved. (HD. Jan.27; 182) Frs. 2,000
- **Joséphine, Impératrice et Reine.** Paris, 1899. 4to. On vell., str.-grd. mor. by Durvand, imperial arms, spine decor. (HD. May 4; 354) Frs. 2,600

MASTERS, Edgar Lee
- **Spoon River Anthology.** N.Y., 1915. *1st. Edn.* 1st. state,. Orig. cl., d.-w., hf. mor. s.-c.; inscr. by author, sigd. autograph MS. (fair copy) laid in; Frederic Dannay copy. (CNY. Dec.16; 230) $1,200
- - **Anr. Copy.** Orig. cl., mor. solander case, inscr. to H. Kanti with 13-line autog. quotation, sigd., Perry Melstad copy. (SPB. May 16; 479) $600

MATE, P.
- **Kleines Deutsch-Kaffrisches-Wörterbuch.** Mari-annhill, 1891. Sm. 8vo. Slightly browned, paper bds. & leath spine. (VA. Oct.28; 514) R 310

MATEU, F.
- **Antipronostico a la Victoria que se pronostica ... Richelieu contra. El Rey de Espâna ... 1635.** Valencia, 1636. 4to. Bds. (DS. Nov.25; 2411) Pts. 34,000

MATHER, Cotton
- **Magnalia Christi Americana.** L., 1702. *1st. Edn.* 7 pts. in 1 vol. Fo. Folding engraved map, advt. ll., lacks errata ll., mor. gt. by A. de Coverly, early MS. bkplt. of William Irvine, bkplt. of J.H. Bates. (SG. Apr.26; 136) $1,400
- - **Anr. Copy.** Fo. L.P., folding map mntd. & reprd. & bnd. following table of contents, liby. stp. on title-p., trimmed & reprd., ll. (A2-A3) reprd. at outer margins, some pp. lightly browned, with scattered foxing, stains at inner margins of 1st. 16 ll. & pp. 80-120, panel.cf., worn & scuffed, lr. cover separating from spine, spine with liby. catalogue nos. (Brown University Liby.) & reprd. with tape. (SPB. Oct.26; 22) $1,300

MATHEWS, Gregory M.
- **Birds of Australia.** Ill.:– Groenvold, Keule-mans, & others. L., 1910-27. *(225) numbered.* 12 vols., & Supps. 1-5 (Checklist & Bibliography), in 23 vols. Fo. 597 (of 600) hand-cold. litho. plts., lacks prelims. & 65 text pp. in Vol. XI, 1 plt. with sm. hole not affecting ptd. image, buckram, many orig. wraps. bnd. in, ex-liby.; the Zoological Soc. of Phila. copy. (SG. Nov.3; 17) $4,500
- **Birds & Books, The Story of the Mathews Orni-thological Library.** Ed.:– L.F. Fitzhardinge. Can-berra, 1942. *(200) numbered & sigd.* Wraps. (CA. Apr.3; 84) Aus. $130

MATHEY, J.
See— PARKER, J.T. & Mathey, J.

MATHISON, Gilbert Farquhar
- **Narrative of a Visit to Brazil, Chile, Peru & the Sandwich Islands.** L., 1825. Some browning, cf.,

blind-tooled decor., gt. outer dentelle & spine, slightly spotted & rubbed, 1 sm. defect. [Sabin XI, 46856] (D. Nov.23; 1310) DM 780

MATISSE, Henri
- Dernières Oeuvres de Matisse 1950-1954. Paris, 1958. Verve no. 35/36. Fo. Orig. bds. (BBA. Sep.8; 181) *Kinnaird.* £75
- Dessins. Thémes et Variations. Précédés de 'Matisse-en-France' par Aragon. Paris, 1943. *On vell.* 4to. Leaves, bds. (HD. Mar.14; 137) Frs. 1,800
- Portraits. Monte Carlo, 1955. *(500).* 4to. Pict. wraps., s.-c. (SG. Jan.12; 257) $450

MATON, William George
- Observations relative chiefly to the Natural History ... of the Western Counties of England. 1797. 2 vols. in 1. Lacks hf.-titles, mod. hf. cf. (P. Apr.12; 177) *Bennett.* £80

MATSCHOSS, C.
- Die Entwicklung der Dampfmaschine. Berlin, 1908. 2 vols. 4to. Orig. hf. leath. (R. Oct.12; 1760) DM 400

MATSUBARA, Subara
See— AKIYAMA, Terukazu & others

MATTHAEUS DE CRACOVIA
See— AUGUSTINUS, Saint Aurelius, Bp. of Hippo — ANTONINUS FLORENTINUS — MATTHAEUS DE CRACOVIA

MATTHESON, Joh.
- Kleine General-Bass-Schule. Worin ... aus den ... Anfangs-Gründen des Clavier-Spieles ... durch versch. Classen u. Ordnungen der Accorde ... zu mehrer Vollkommenhelt in dieser Wissenschaft ... angeführet werden. Hamburg, 1735. *1st. Edn.* 4to. Lacks engraved port., with title copper engr. (dtd. 1934), some slight spotting, cont.-style hf. leath. (HK. Nov.9; 2269) DM 700

MATTHEWS, Brander
- Bookbindings Old & New ... with an Account of the Grolier Club of New York. N.Y., 1895. *(150) on Japan vell.* Crushed mor., by Stikeman, gt. dentelles, spine slightly faded. (SG. Sep.15; 53) $100
- - Anr. Edn. 1896. *(75) numbered on Japan vell.* Orig. wraps.; H.M. Nixon coll., with his sig. (BBA. Oct.6; 92) *Oak Knoll Books.* £90

MATTHEWS, Lieut. John
- Twenty-One Plans, with Explanations, of Different Actions in the West-Indies, during the Late War. Chester, 1784. 4to. 12 (of 21) folding hand-cold. engraved maps, lacks 2 text ll., slight offsetting, disbnd. [Sabin 46887] (SG. Jan.19; 217) $200
- Voyage to the River Sierra-Leone. 1788. Hf. cf. (P. Dec.8; 344) *Rota.* £160

MATTHIEU, Pierre
[-] Unhappy Prosperity Expressed in the History of Aelius Scianus, & Philippa the Catanian, ... Trans.:– Sir Thomas Hawkins. L., 1639. 4 pts. in 1 vol. 12mo. 2 margins reprd., cont. cf. [STC 17667] (BBA. May 3; 121) *Howes Bookshop.* £100

MATTIOLI, Petrus Andreas
- Commentaires sur les Six Livres de Ped. Dioscoride ... mis en François sur la Dernière Edition Latine ... Trans.:– Jean des Moulins. Lyon, 1572. *3rd. Fr. Edn. (1st. Moulins Edn.).* Fo. Lacks 2 table ll., old cf., worn. (HD. Jun.6; 108) Frs. 1,700
- - Anr. Edn. Trans.:– Antoine du Pinet. Lyon, 1680. *Latest Edn.* Fo. Cont. hf. leath. gt. (D. Nov.23; 448) DM 850
- Commentarii Denue aucti in Libros Sex Pedacii Dioscoridis Anazarbei de Medica Materia ... Lyon, 1653. 4to. Lacks last lf., title discold. & defect., laid down, 1 text lf. with tear in lr. margin, somewhat discold. thro.-out, some underlining & margin annots. in ink in early hand, cont. limp vell., lacks ties, w.a.f. (C. Mar.14; 187) *Barker.* £150
- Commentarii Secundo aucti in Libros Sex Pedacii Dioscoridis Anazarbei de Medica Materia ... Venice, 1559. 2 pts. in 1 vol. Fo. Lacks 1 index lf., final lf. & 6 prelims.?, title torn & defect. with old repairs & sigs., 1 text lf. torn, stain in some upr.

margins, cont. limp vell., worn, lacks lr. cover, w.a.f. (C. Mar.14; 186) *La Fenice.* £450
- Commentariorum ... Pedacii Dioscoridis Anazarbei, de Medica Materia ... Venice, 1583. Pt. 2 only. Fo. Title torn at inner margin, cont. limp vell., with ties, w.a.f. (C. Mar.14; 188) *Bifolco.* £400
- I Discorsi ne i Sei Libri della Materia Medicinale di Pedacio. Vinegia, 1557. Fo. Map & various ll. reprd., stains & browning, 18thc C. hf. cf., w.a.f. (CR. Jun.6; 221) Lire 1,100,000
- Discorsi ne' sei Libri di Pedacio Discoride Anazarbeo della Materia Medicinale. Venice, 1744. Fo. Cont. leath. gt., very rubbed & slightly bumped. (R. Apr.4; 1756) DM 2,700
- Herbarz ginak bylinarz. Wytisstieno w Starém Miestie per Th. Hagek ... Prag, 1562. *1st. Czech. Edn.* Fo. Lacks title, 19th. C. MS. completion, lightly browned & some soiling & staining thro.-out, 1st. & last sigs. with reprd. margin defects., also some text ll., some old annots., cont. blind-tooled pig over wood bds., 19th. C. bdg., slightly rubbed, spine with sm. tear, 2 clasps. (HK. Nov.8; 649) DM 2,200
- Neu Vollkommenes Kräuter-Buch. Basel, 167[8]. Fo. Lacks pp. 5-8 & large part of index, frontis., copper engrs. & ptd. title with faults & mntd., 1 lf. with lge. defect. completed in MS., margin tears partly bkd., some worming, cont. marginalia, slightly browned or soiled thro.-out, margin staining, some ll. loose, cont. hf. leath., defect. (HT. May 8; 301) DM 1,850

MATTSBERGER, Melchior
[-] Geistliche Herzens-Einbildungen inn [je] 250 Biblischen Figur-Sprüchen. Augsburg, [1717]. 2 pts. in 1 vol. Ob. 4to. Lacks 7 copper engrs., 2 ll. with sm. corner tear, last lf. torn with loss, cont. hf. leath., spine defect., very worn. (GB. Nov.3; 920) DM 2,000

MATURIN, Charles Robert
[-] The Wild Irish Boy. L., 1808. *1st Edn.* 3 vols. 12mo. Hf. mor., rubbed. (P. Jan.12; 252) *Jarndyce.* £240

MATUTE I LUQUIN, Gaspar
- Collección de los Autos Generales i Particulares de Fe celebrados por ... la Inquisicion de Córdoba. Cordoba, n.d. Leath. (DS. Nov.25; 2016) Pts. 20,000

MATY, Paul (Ed.)
See— PHILOSOPHICAL TRANSACTIONS

MATEIL NEFASHOT
Venice, 1664. 12mo. Inner margins crudely reprd., lightly stained, cl., w.a.f. (S. Oct.25; 144) £100

MAUCLAIR, Camille
- Jean-Baptiste Greuze. Paris, n.d. *(500) on velin vergé.* Fo. Mor. (SPB. Nov.30; 44) $400
- Jules Cheret. Paris, 1930. *(730) numbered.* Sm. fo. Prospectus loosely inserted, orig. wraps., unc. (S. Apr.30; 62) *Maino.* £70
- Les Miniatures du Dix-huitieme Siècle. Portraits de Femmes. Paris, 1912. *(50) on panier Japon.* *(With:)* - Portraits de Femmes. Paris, 1913. *Ltd. Edn.* Together 2 vols. Fo. Mor. gt. by Durvand, spines lightly faded. (SPB. Nov.30; 298) $200
- Trois Femmes de Flandre. Ill.:– H. Cassiers. Paris, 1905. *Numbered on vell à la cuve.* Sm 4to. Hf. mor., decor. & mosaic spine, corners, unc., wrap. & spine preserved. (HD. Feb.17; 98) Frs. 2,300

MAUDE, John
- Visit to the Falls of Niagara, in 1800. L., 1828. *(308). (50).* Royal 8vo. L.P., engraved title, 7 engraved plts., each marked 'Proof', some foxing to plts., some early ll. detchd., orig. cl. over bds., rebkd. preserving fragment of label (Lande notes that the spine label states 'Only 250 copies printed', the above limitation is taken from Sabin), covers worn, new end-papers, w.a.f.; the Rt. Hon. Visc. Eccles copy. [Sabin 46913] (CNY. Nov.18; 191) $380

MAUDSLEY, Anne Cary & Alfred Percival
- A Glimpse of Guatemala & Some Notes on the Ancient Monuments of Central America. L., 1899. *1st. Edn.* 4to. Prelims. with few faint liby. stps., newer cl., unc., orig. cover label & end-papers, light wear. (RO. Dec.11; 206) $310

MAUGHAM, William Somerset
- The Bishop's Apron. 1906. *1st. Edn.* Orig. cl., sigd. on front free end-paper. (BDA. Aug.18; 94) *Bell, Book & Radmall.* £65
- Cakes & Ale. Ill.:– Graham Sutherland. [1954]. *(1000) numbered & sigd. by author & artist.* Orig. cf., s.-c. (BBA. Aug.18; 96) *Brook.* £70
- - Anr. Copy. Mod. cl. leath. (BBA. Feb.23; 329) *Duschnes.* £60
- The Casuarina Tree. 1926. *1st. Edn. (With:)*
- Ashenden. 1928. *1st. Edn. (With:)* - The Gentleman in the Parlour. 1930. *1st. Edn. (With:)*
- Cakes & Ale. 1930. *1st. Edn. (With:)* – First Person Singular. 1931. *1st. Engl. Edn.* Together 5 vols. Orig. cl. (BBA. Aug.18; 97) *Maggs.* £70
- The Explorer. 1908. *1st. Edn.* Last 2 advt. ll., orig. cl.; sigd. by author on front free end-paper. (BBA. Aug.18; 100) *'Freddie'.* £55
- The Land of the Blessed Virgin. 1905. *1st. Edn. 2nd. Iss.* Frontis., 7 ills. inserted, orig. parch.-bkd. bds., soiled; sigd. by author & inscr. 'Written in Seville 1898-1899' on front free end-paper. (BBA. Aug.18; 102) *Glendevon.* £120
- Liza of Lambeth. L., 1897. *1st. Edn.* Orig. cl.; Perry Molstad copy. (SPB. May 16; 480) $300
- A Man of Honour. L., 1903. *1st. Edn. (150).* Orig. ptd. wraps., soiled, cl. s.-c.; inscr., Perry Molstad copy. (SPB. May 16; 481) $750
- Of Human Bondage. 1915. *1st. Engl. Edn.* Last 8 advt. ll., orig. cl.; sigd. by author; inscr. of Gerald Kostoris, bkplt. of Herbert Parsons. (BBA. Aug.18; 109) *Glendevon.* £130
- - Anr. Copy. Orig. cl., recased, cl. s.-c.; inscr. to E.A.Jones, Perry Molstad copy. (SPB. May 16; 483) $225
- - Anr. Edn. Ill.:– Randolph Schwabe. Garden City, 1936. *(751) numbered & sigd. by author & artist.* Linen, d.-w., s.-c. (LH. Sep.25; 564) $350
- - Anr. Edn. Ill.:– John Sloan. N.Y., Ltd. Edns. Cl., 1938. *(1500) numbered & sigd. by artist.* 2 vols. Cl. (SG. Jan.12; 317) $375
- - Anr. Copy. 2 vols. Lge. 8vo. Cl., s.-c. cracked. (SG. May 17; 206) $325
- - Anr. Copy. 2 vols. Cl., spines lightly faded, s.-c. cracked. (SG. Jan.12; 234) $275
- Orientations. L., 1899. *1st. Edn.* Remainder Iss. 1 vol. Orig. cl., worn, sigd. by author. *(With:)*
- Mrs. Craddock. L., 1903. *1st. Edn. 2nd.* *'Times Book Cl.' iss., with cancel title-p.* 1 vol. Orig. cl., worn; sigd. by author. *(With:)* - The Magician. L., 1908. *1st. Edn.* 1 vol. Cancel title-p. slightly torn, orig. cl., worn; sigd. by author. (BBA. Nov.30; 315) *'Freddie'.* £70
- The Painted Vell. 1925. *1st. Engl. Edn. 3rd. Iss.* Orig. cl., sm. tear at head of spine; sigd. by author & inscr. 'The scene was in Hong Kong. It changed to Tching-Yen on the threat of an action by the Colonial Secretary of Hong Kong'. (BBA. Aug.18; 111) *Bell, Book & Radmall.* £85
- A Writer's Notebook. L., 1949. *1st. Edn. (1000) numbered & sigd., specially bnd.* Lge. 8vo. Hf.-title, final blank, orig. vell.-bkd. buckram, partly unc., slightly marked. (S. Mar.20; 938) *Maggs.* £55

MAULEON, Auger de
[-] Memoirs de la Reyne Marguerite. Brussels, 1653. *Nouvelle Edn.* 12mo. Sheep., spine reprd., mor.-bkd. s.-c.; John Locke's copy with sig., as an association copy, w.a.f. (SPB. May 16; 97) $950

MAUND, Benjamin
- Botanic Garden. 1825. *[1st. Edn.].* Vols. I-VI & Appendix. Engraved titles, 146 hand-cold. plts., a few cropped, spotting, Vols. IV-VI badly stained on outer margin, no bdg. stated, as a coll. of plts., w.a.f. (P. Apr.12; 116) *Thomas.* £520
- - Anr. Copy. Vol. 1. Engraved title, 96 cold. ills. on 24 copperplts., copper engraved title browned, 1st. copperplt, lightly browned, cont. hf. leath., gold-tooled. (HT. May 8; 302) DM 950
- - Anr. Copy. Vol. 1 only (of 13). Cont. bds., defect., upr. cover loose. (HK. Nov.8; 650) DM 930
- - Anr. Copy. Engrs. hand-cold., browned & stained, cl. (CR. Jun.6; 222) Lire 400,000
- - Anr. Edn. L., 1825-26. Vol. 1. 4to. Cont. hf. leath. (R. Apr.4; 1757) DM 1,000
- - Anr. Edn. L., 1825-28. Vols. 1 & 2 in 1 vol. 1 (of 2) engraved titles, lacks ptd. title, 48 cold.

MAUND, Benjamin -Contd.

copper engrs., cont. hf. leath gt. (R. Oct.12; 1871) DM 1,300
- - **Anr. Edn.** L., 1825-39. Vols. 1-8 only (of 13), bnd. from the pts.?. Sm. 4to. 8 additional engraved titles, dedication, 192 hand-cold. engraved plts., without plt. 137, text for nos. 545-548 & 1 text lf. of 'Auctarium', but with dupl. plt. 145, 2 titles spotted, cont. hf. cf., bookseller's note on the bdg. from pts. & the upr. wrap. of gt. 97 bnd. in Vol. 5, 2 spines slightly faded, w.a.f. (C. Nov.16; 273) *Schuster.* £950
- - **Anr. Edn.** L., 1825 [-ca.1842]. Vol. 1. 4to. Cont. leath., worn, spine defect. (R. Oct.12; 1870) DM 750
- - **Anr. Edn.** 1827. Vols. 1 & 2 only. 2 engraved titles, 48 hand-cold. plts., 2 spotted, panel. cf., stained, rebkd. (P. Oct.20; 76) £210
- - **Anr. Edn.** L., 1827-8. Vol. 2 only. 24 hand-cold. plts., 1 loose, a few with light stain in outer margins, orig. bds., defect., as a collection of plts., w.a.f. (P. Nov.24; 49) *Ayres.* £120
- - **Anr. Copy.** Vol. 2 only. Wide margin, some light foxing, cont. hf. leath., bumped, upr. cover loose. (HK. Nov.8; 651) DM 800
- - **Anr. Edn.** 1830. Vol. 3. Sm. 4to. L.P., 24 hand-cold. plts., slight offsetting, lacks end-papers, orig. cl. decor. gt. (SKC. Jan.13; 2332) £90
- - **Anr. Edn.** L., 1830-35. Vols. 3-5 only (of 13). 4to. Additional engraved titles, 72 hand-cold. plts., engraved titles foxed, bds., lacks spines, covers loose, w.a.f. (S. Nov.28; 61) *Burden.* £360
- - **Anr. Edn.** L., 1833-34. Vol. 5 in 2 pts. Cont. bds., defect. & loose. (R. Oct.12; 1874) DM 650
- - **Anr. Edn.** L., 1834-35. Vol. 5 & vol. 6 pt. 1. Cont. hf. leath., gt. (R. Oct.12; 1874a) DM 900
- - **Anr. Copy.** Vol. 5. 4to. Cont. hf. leath. gt. (R. Apr.4; 1758) DM 800
- - **Anr. Edn.** 1835-36. Vol. 6. Sm. 4to. L.P., 24 hand-cold. plts., qtr. mor., gt. spine; inscr. by Maund. (SKC. Jan.13; 2333) £160
- - **Anr. Copy.** Vol. 6 only. Sm. 4to. 22 (of 24) hand-cold. engraved plts., hf. mor. (SKC. Nov.18; 1978) £100
- - **Anr. Copy.** Vol. 6. Cont. bds., defect. & loose. (R. Oct.12; 1875) DM 700
- - **Anr. Edn.** L., 1835-37. Vol. 6/II & 7/1 in 1 vol. Cont. hf. leath. gt. (R. Oct.12; 1875a) DM 650
- - **Anr. Edn.** L., [1842]. Cont. hf. leath. (BR. Apr.12; 755) DM 950
- - **Anr. Edn.** L., 1848-50. 32 orig. pts. (nos. 277-294, 296, 298-310). 4to. 64 hand-cold. engraved plts., 32 of flowers, each with 4 figures & 32 of fruit with text beneath, as iss. in orig. ptd. paper wraps., w.a.f. (C. Jun.27; 173) *Reid.* £450
- - **Anr. Edn.** L., n.d. Vols. 3 & 4 in 1 vol. 1 (of 2) engraved titles, lacks ptd. title, engraved dedication, 49 cold. copper engrs., cont. hf. leath. gt. (R. Oct.12; 1873) DM 1,300
- **Orchard & Garden Fruits: Their Description, History, & Management.** Ca. 1875. 4to. 24 hand-cold. engrs. with descriptive text below, orig. cl. gt., rubbed. (TA. Jun.21; 548) £50

MAUND, Benjamin & Henslow, John Stephen
- **The Botanist.** 1825. 50 hand-cold. plts., qtr. mor. gt. (P. Sep.8; 35) *Trevor.* £120
- - **Anr. Edn.** Ca. 1825. Vols. 1 & 2 only. 100 hand-cold. plts., hf. mor. gt. (P. Sep.8; 207) *Edistar.* £240
- - **Anr. Edn.** [1837-46]. Vols. 1, 2 & 4 only. 3 engraved titles, 150 hand-cold. plts., titles spotted, hf. mor. & cl. gt., as a coll. of plts., w.a.f. (P. Jul.5; 253) £340

MAUNDEVILLE, Sir John
See— **MANDEVILLE or MAUNDEVILLE, Sir John**

MAUPASSANT, Guy de
- **Bel-Ami.** Paris, 1885. *Orig. Edn. (200) on papier vergé de Hollande.* 12mo. Sewed. (HD. May 16; 48) Frs. 4,400
- - **Anr. Edn.** Ill.:– Grau Sala. Paris, 1945. *(275).* 2 vols. Sm. 4to. On white paper, 118 orig. cold. lithos., leaves, ill. wrap., box. (HD. Mar.27; 91) Frs. 2,800
- - **Anr. Edn.** Ill.:– Grau Sala. Paris, 1945. 2 vols.

4to. Numbered, with specimen of work, leaves, pict. wraps., wrap. boxes. (HD. Dec.16; 153) Frs. 1,400
- **Clair de Lune.** Ill.:– Maurice Boutet de Monvel, Eugène Gradset, & others. Paris, 1884. *Ltd. Edn., numbered, on Japan paper, sigd. by publisher.* 4to. 21 orig. drawings, 12 of the textual lithos. in 2 states, 5 two colour proofs of selected images on various papers, orig. pict. wraps., with orig. watercolour & pen & ink drawing for wraps. & title, mor. by Canapé-Belz. (SPB. Dec.13; 867) $2,000
- **Contes de la Bécasse.** Ill.:– Pierre Falké. Paris, 1931. *(310).* 4to. On Arches, leaves, pict. wrap., box. (HD. Dec.16; 152) Frs. 2,500
- **Le Horla.** Paris, 1887. *(40) on holland.* Red bradel hf. mor., wrap. preserved; extra-ill. with 136 watercold. pen drawings by Henriet, dtd. 1888. (HD. Jun.13; 69) Frs. 13,500
- **La Maison Tellier.** Ill.:– Lobel Riche. Paris, 1926. On Japan, not for sale, triple state of etchings, decor. mor. by Gilbert, embroidered silk liners & end-ll., wrap. preserved, s.-c.; with refused plt. in 4 states. (HD. Jun.13; 71) Frs. 15,000
- - **Anr. Edn.** Ill.:– after Edgar Degas. Paris, 1934. *(305) on vélin de Rives.* 4to. Orange mor., s.-c. (HD. Nov.17; 150) Frs. 2,700
- - **Anr. Edn.** Ill.:– after Edgar Degas. Paris, 1934. *(325) on Rives.* 4to. Sewed. (HD. May 4; 355) Frs. 4,100
- **Oeuvres Complètes.** Paris, 1908-10. *Definitive Edn. On vergé, Gelder van Zoneo with Maupassant wtrmkd.* 29 vols. Hf. linen, 2 vols. very stained on upr. cover. (V. Oct.1; 4311) DM 480
- - **Anr. Edn.** Paris, 1908-10. 22 vols. Three-qtr. red mor., by Canape, gt.-ruled spine,. (CBA. Dec.10; 301) $160
- - **Anr. Edn.** Paris, 1910. *(20) numbered on Japon Imperial, initialed by publisher.* 23 vols. Three-qtr. leath., unopened. (SG. Feb.16; 197) $150
- **Oeuvres Complètes Illustrées.** Ill.:– Falke, Dunoyer de Segonzac, Laboureur & others. 1934-38. *(2015).* 15 vols. Sm. 4to. Publisher's hf. bds.,. (SM. Mar.7; 2179) Frs. 1,700
- **Pierre et Jean.** Ill.:– E. Duez & A. Lynch. Paris, 1888. 4to. Hf. mor., decor. spine, corners, unc., wrap. preserved, by Champs. (HD. Feb.17; 99) Frs. 1,100
- - **Anr. Copy.** 4to. Silk end-papers, cont. mor., gt. & blind decor., decor. spine, inner dentelle, s.-c., sigd. by Th. Veloppé. (HD. Jan.30; 70) Frs. 1,000
- **Le Rosier de Madame Husson.** Ill.:– Dys & Despres. 1888. *Orig. Edn. 1st. Printing.* Sm. 4to. On vélin du Marais, hf. chagrin, spine raised bands. (HD. Jul.6; 116) Frs. 1,200
- **Le Vagabond.** Ill.:– T.-A. Steinlen. Paris, 1902. *(115) numbered on velin de Rives.* 4to. Extra suite of the cold. lithos. before text (not usually found), 'cuir inciselé' bdg. of crushed lev. mor. by Marius Michel, sigd. on upr. turn-in, upr. cover with lge. inset rectangular cf. panel showing the vagabond walking along a tree-lined road, carved, cold. & stp.-sigd. by artist, lr. cover plain, spine in 6 compartments, gt.-lettered in 2, turn-ins with double gt. rule, canvas linings, partly unc., orig. ptd. wraps. & backstrip preserved, mor.-edged s.-c.; Steinlen's copy, with his name ptd. below limitation, René Descamps Scrive bkplt., Georges Rivieres copy. (CNY. May 18; 192) $5,500
- **Une Vie.** Paris, 1883. On holland, mor. gt. by Semet & Plumelle, spine decor. (lightly faded), red mor. liners, wrap. preserved, s.-c. (HD. Jun.13; 68) Frs. 10,000

MAUPASSANT, Guy de (Contrib.)
See— **GIL BLAS ILLUSTRE**

MAUPASSANT, Guy de (Text)
See— **TYPES DE PARIS**

MAUPERTUIS, Pierre Louis, Moreau de
- **La Figure de la Terre determinée par les Observations de Maupertuis, Clairaut, Camus, Le Monnier, Outhier** ... Amst., 1738. *1st. Edn.* Cont. leath. gt., rubbed, 1 jnt. defect. (GB. May 3; 1063) DM 400
[-] **Oeuvres Diverses de Mr. M.P.T.** Provins, 1810. *(3).* Bradel bds. (HD. Jan.27; 228) Frs. 1,050

MAURER, F.
- **Observationes Curioso–Physicae.** Frankfurt & Leipzig, 1713. Last index ll. with 1 or 2 sm. wormholes, cont. vell., head of spine defect. (R. Apr.4; 1439) DM 750

MAURICE, R.T.
- **Extracts from Journals of Explorations ... Fowler's Bay to Rawlinson's Ranges, & Fowler's Bay to Cambridge Gulf** ... Adelaide, 1904. Recent hf. mor., some wear. (KH. May 1; 477) Aus. $120

MAURICE, Thomas
- **Grove Hill - a Descriptive Poem with Ode to Mithra.** Ill.:– Anderson after Samuel. 1799. 4to. Orig. bds., unc. (PD. Dec.14; 358) £70

MAURICEAU, François
- **Traité des Maladies des Femmes Grosses et de celles qui Sont Accouchées.** Paris, priv. ptd., 1681. *3rd. Edn.* 4to. Some foxing & stains, sm. wormholes, mostly marginal, cont. cf. gt. (SG. Mar.22; 247) $225

MAUROIS, André
- **Rouen** ... Ill.:– Othon Friez. 1929. *1st. Ill. Edn.* 4to. On japon impérial, 3 proofs of each litho., hf. mor. by Vermuyse, spine decor., unc., wrap. & spine preserved; from L. van Malderen liby. (HD. May 4; 356) Frs. 1,700

MAURY, Matthew Fountaine
- **Explanations & Sailing Directions to accompany the Wind Current Charts** ... Wash., 1858. *8th. Edn.* Vol. 1 only. 4to. 12 wind current maps, 39 plts., cont. cf., covers detchd. (PNY. Mar.27; 161) $150

MAUVILLON, Eleazor de
[-] **Histoire du Prince François Eugène de Savoie.** Amst., 1740. 5 vols. 12mo. Cont. spr. cf., arms, spines decor. (HD. May 21; 54) Frs. 1,600

MAVELOT, Charles
- **Nouveau Livre de Differens Cartouches, Couronnes, Casques, Supports et Tenans** ... [Paris], Privilege dtd. 1685 at end. Sm. ob. 4to. Red mor., gt. inner & outer dentelle, marb. paper end-papers, sigd. by Ouzin. (D. Nov.24; 2305) DM 4,000

MAW, George
- **A Monograph of the Genus Crocus.** 1886. 4to. Hand-cold. litho. plts., some spotting, cont. mor. gt., slightly rubbed; autograph pres. slip to author's cousin pasted in at front. (BBA. Jul.27; 43) *Kehl.* £750

MAWE, John
- **Travels in the Interior of Brazil Particularly in the Gold & Diamond Districts.** 1812. 4to. 9 engraved plts., 1 hand-cold., title offset, cont. cf., rebkd. (BBA. Jun.28; 234) *Waggett.* £180

MAWSON, Sir Douglas
- **The Home of the Blizzard.** 1915. *1st. Edn.* 2 vols. Orig. cl.; pres. copy from author to Sir Philip Brocklehurst. (P. Jun.7; 30) £460
- - **Anr. Copy.** 2 vols. Orig. cl. (P. Jun.7; 31) £180

MAWSON, Thomas H.
- **Civic Art: Studies in Town Planning** ... L., 1911. *1st. Edn.* Fo. Cold. frontis., 272 full-p. & text ills., ex-liby., orig. cl. (SG. May 3; 249) $140

MAXIMILIAN, Prinz zu Wied(-Neuwied)
- **Reise in das Innere Nord-America in den Jahren 1832 bis 1834.** Ill.:– Carl Bodmer. Koblenz, 1839-41. *1st. Edn.* 2 text vols. & 1 plt. portfo. Lge. 4to. & lge. ob. fo. L.P., Wide margin, all plts. with Bodmers blind stp., some plts. & text very foxed, some slight browning, 2 plt. corners renewed, some margins crumpled or with sm. tears, some bkd., 2 text ll. torn w/out sm. holes, plts. loose in cont. bd. portfo., spine renewed, slightly worn, cont. hf. leath., very defect., partly loose. [Sabin 47014]. (H. Nov.23; 333) DM 16,000
- **Reise nach Brasilien.** Frankfurt, 1820. 3 vols., including Atlas. 4to. & fo. Atlas with 3 engraved maps, including 2 folding, 22 engraved plts., 19 engraved plts. in text, some spotting to plts. in text, text cont. hf. cf., slightly worn, atlas mod. portfo., orig. wrap. preserved on upr. cover. [Sabin 47018]. (S. Dec.1; 287) *Ewart.* £4,000

MAXIMILIAN-GESELLSCHAFT
See— GOETHE, Johann Wolfgang von
See— KLEIST, Heinrich von
See— SALLUSTIUS CRISPUS, Gaius

MAXIMUS, Pacificus
- Elegie nun nulle Iocose & Festive. Camerino, 15 May 1523.. Sm. 4to. Lacks lf. g4, a few stains, sm. ink stain in upr. margin of A7, new bds.; the Broxbourne copy. (S. Dec.20; 759)   £80
- Pacifici Magnifici, Poete Asculani, De Componendis Hexametris & Penthametris, Opusculum Rarissimum. Wittemberg, 1516. 4to. 7 (of 8) ll., many MS. notes in very early hand, later bds. (SG. Feb.9; 282) $175

MAXWELL, Sir Herbert
- Trees – a Woodland Notebook ... Glasgow, 1915. *(275) numbered.* Mor.-bkd., bds., unc., d.-w. (PD. Jun.13; 125)   £52

MAXWELL, James Clerk
- A Dynamical Theory of the Electromagnetic Field. L., 1865. *1st. Edn.* 'Philosophical Transactions', Vol. 155, pp. 459-512. 4to. Light margin browning, loose in gatherings; Stanitz coll. (SPB. Apr.25; 293) $425
- A Treatise on Electricity & Magnetism ... Oxford, 1873. *1st. Edn.* 2 vols. Hf.-titles, 15 pp. advts. Vol. II, orig. cl. (PD. Aug.17; 135)   £285
-- Anr. Copy. 2 vols. Advts., slight spotting, lacks errata slip, orig. cl., rubbed, some spotting on spine; bkplt. of William Durham F.R.S.E., Stanitz coll. (SPB. Apr.25; 294) $1,400

MAXWELL, W.
- Iona & the Ionians ... Glasgow, 1857. Sm. 8vo. Orig. cl. (PD. Apr.18; 85)   £75

MAXWELL, William Hamilton
[-] Wild Sports of the West. 1832. *1st. Edn.* 2 vols. Orig. bds. (P. Jan.12; 253)   *Cavendish.* £75
- Rambling Recollections of a Soldier of Fortune. Dublin, 1842. *1st. Edn. (With:)* – Wild Sports of the West. L., 1838. Together 2 vols. 12mo. Hf. mor., armorial motif on spine. (GM. Dec.7; 193)   £70

MAY, A.E. & W.
- Choice Flowers ... from the Garden & Conservatory. L., 1849. Fo. Additional cold. litho. title, 28 (of 31) hand-cold. litho. plts., a few with minor spotting, 1 shaved in lr. margin, cont. red mor., covers blind-tooled, upr. cover with central gt. ornament, w.a.f. (C. Nov.16; 274)   *Marks.* £520

MAY, Caroline
- The American Female Poets. N.Y., [1869]. Mor., inlaid wood panels on covers. (SG. Feb.16; 4) $150

MAY, J.C.
- Versuch einer Allgemarien Einleitung in die Handlungs– Wissenschaft. Altona & Lübeck, 1770. *2nd. Edn.* 2 vols. Cont. hf. leath. gt. (R. Apr.3; 1228)   DM 510

MAY, Robert
- The Accomplisht Cook. L., 1685. Lacks 4 plts., slightly spotted, cont. cf. [Wing M 1394] (S. Mar.20; 732)   *Hoppen.* £95

MAY, Sophie (Pseud.)
See— CLARKE, Rebecca Sophie 'Sophie May'

MAY, W.
See— BANNERMAN, David Armitage & May, W.

MAYAKOVSKY, V.
- Dlia Golosa [For the Voice]. Ill.:– El Lissitzky. Berlin, 1923. *1st. Edn.* Orig. wraps. (S. Nov.21; 157)   *Phillips.* £500

MAYENVILLE
- Chronique du Temps qui fut la Jacquerie. Ill.:– L.O. Merson. 1903. *(500).* Lge. 8vo. On velin de cuve d'Arches, 3 states of all compositions, hf. mor., corners, by Yseux, unc., wrap. & spine preserved. (HD. May 4; 357)   Frs. 1,800

MAYER, Anton
- Wiens Buchdrucker-Geschichte. Wien, 1883-87. 2 vols. Lge. 4to. Cont. hf. vell. (HK. May 17; 3416)   DM 440

MAYER, Henry Leonard
- Coloured Illustrations of British Birds & their Eggs. 1842-50. *1st. 8vo. Edn.* 7 vols. 8 plain plts. of anatomical details, etc., 322 hand-cold. plts. of birds, 102 hand-cold. plts. of eggs, slight spotting at beginning of some vols., cont. hf. mor. gt., corners & spines slightly rubbed. (LC. Jul.5; 146)   £410

MAYER, Johann Christoph Andreas
- Anatomische Kupfertafeln. Berlin, & Leipzig, 1783-84 (pts. 1-4), Berlin, 1794. *1st. Edn.* 6 pts., compl. Some browning, plts. stained thro.-out, crumpled, especially margins, cont. leath. gt., slightly rubbed & stained. (GB. Nov.3; 1034)   DM 600

MAYER, Julius Robert von
- Die Mechanik der Wärme in Gesammelten Schriften. Stuttgart, 1867. *1st. Edn.* Spotted, cl.-bkd. bds., rubbed; Stanitz coll. (SPB. Apr.25; 295) $250

MAYER, Karl
- Die Wiener-Porzellan-Sammlung Karl Mayer: Katalog und Historische Einleitung. Ed.:– J. Folnesics. Vienna, 1914. *1st. Edn., (350) numbered. (50) roman-numbered not for sale.* 4to. Orig. cf., rubbed. (SG. Jan.26; 90) $150

MAYER, Luigi
See— Ainslie, Sir Robert & Mayer, Luigi

MAYHEW, Henry
- 1851, or the Adventures of Mr. & Mrs. Sandboys. Ill.:– G. Cruikshank. N.d. Some staining, hf. cf., rubbed. (P. Apr.12; 72)   *Ayres.* £60
- Great Exhibition of 1851. Ill.:– G. Cruikshank. 1851. Fo. 11 plts. in orig. cl. folder. (P. Apr.12; 270)   *Robertshaw.* £55
- London Labour & the London Poor. L., n.d. 3 vols. Some plts. loose, orig. cl., rubbed & stained, ex-liby. (BBA. Dec.15; 229)   *Primrose Hill Books.* £70
- The Lower Rhine & its Picturesque Scenery. — The Upper Rhine: the Scenery of its Banks. Ill.:– after Birket Foster. L., 1860. Together 2 vols. Additional engraved titles, 38 plts., some spotting, orig. cl. (S. Dec.13; 177)   *Chancery.* £260
- The Rhine & its Picturesque Scenery. Ill.:– after Birket Foster. l., 1856. Extra engraved title, 19 plts., spotted, orig. cl. gt., spine slightly worn. (S. Mar.6; 94)   *Clarke.* £150
- The Upper Rhine. Ill.:– after B. Foster. L., 1858. Steel-engraved title, 18 (of 19) steel engraved plts., some foxing, some margin defects., orig. linen, gt., very bumped, jnts. split, upr. jnt. detchd. (HK. May 15; 1016a)   DM 800
-- Anr. Edn. after Birkett Foster, 1860. A few ll. slightly spotted, orig. gt.- & blind-stpd. cl. (BBA. Sep.29; 107)   *Thorp.* £130

MAYHEW, Jonathan
- Two Discourses ... for the Success of His Majesty's Arms, more Especially in the Intire Production of Canada. Boston, 1760. *1st. Edn.* Lacks hf.-title, mod. cl. (SG. Jan.19; 136) $350

MAYO, Herbert
- Anatomical & Physiological Commentaries. L., Aug. 1822 & Jul. 1823. Nos. 1 & 2. 15 plts., liby. stp. on title, mod. bds., unc., rebkd.; A.L.S. from Prof. Wood Jones to Sir Geoffrey Jefferson, 10 May 1944, inserted, Dr. Walter Pagel copy. (S. Feb.7; 251)   *Quaritch.* £1,100

MAYO, John Horsley
- Medals & Decorations of the British Army & Navy. L., 1897. *1st. Edn.* 2 vols. 55 plts., may cold., orig. cl. gt.,. (P. May 17; 159)   *Hill.* £85

MAYOR, J.
- Kiosques & Pavillons Urbains Destinés à l'Exposition Internationale des Arts Decoratifs Modernes Paris 1925. Paris, ca. 1925. Sm. fo. 32 partially pochoir-cold. plts., loose as iss., cl.-bkd. lettered bds. (SG. Aug.25; 23) $190

MAZAL, Otto
- Europäische Einbandkunst aus Mittelalter und Neuzeit. 270 Einbände der Osterreichischen Nationalbibliothek. Graz, 1970. Fo. Orig. decor. cl.; H.M. Nixon coll. (BBA. Oct.6; 93)   *Quaritch.* £150

MAZARD, J.
- Corpus Nummorum Numidiae Mauretaniaeque. Paris, 1955. *Ltd. Edn.* 4to. Mod. hf. mor. (S. May 1; 479)   *Baker.* £60

MAZINUS, Paulus
- De Elementorum Natura et Eorum Situ Paradoxa. Paris, 1549. Cl., leath. spine; Dr. Walter Pagel copy. (S. Feb.7; 253)   *Heller.* £70

MAZUCHELLI, Mrs. Nia E.
[-] The Indian Alps & how we crossed them,. L., 1876. 4to. Folding map, 10 chromolitho. plts., some spotting & offsetting, inscr. on hf.-title & author's name written on title, mor. gt. by Bayntun. (S. Dec.13; 152)   *King.* £80
-- Anr. Copy. 4to. Orig. pict. cl. gt., worn. (BS. Nov.16; 17)   £75

MAZZEI, Filippo
- Recherches Historiques et Politiques sur les Etat-Unis de l'Amérique Septentrionale ... Paris, 1788. *1st. Edn.* 4 vols. Hf.-titles, cont. cf. [Sabin 47206] (LH. Sep.25; 262) $250

MAZZUCHELLI, Gian-Maria
- Notizie Istoriche e Critiche Intorno alla Vita, alle Invezioni ed agli Soritti di Archimede. Brescia, 1737. 4to. Light staining, cont. vell., soiled & warped; Marchese Salsa & Earl of Dudley bkplts. (S. Dec.20; 782)   *Brown.* £50

MEAD, Richard
- A Mechanical Account of Poisons in Several Essays. L., 1702. *1st. Edn.* Minor margin worming, cont. cf., very worn. (SG. Mar.22; 205) $140
-- Anr. Edn. 1747. *4th. Edn.* Cont. cf. (PD. Dec.14; 242)   £60

MEADE, H.
- A Ride through the Disturbed Districts of New Zealand. 1870. *1st. Edn.* Chromolitho. frontis., 3 plts., 2 maps, including 1 folding, mod. hf. mor. gt. (S. Nov.1; 34)   *Scott.* £70

ME'AH BRACHOT [with Passover Haggadah, Hebrew & Ladino]
Ed.:– Moshe Sacut. Venice, 1780. Lightly stained, trimmed, leath., w.a.f. (S. Jul.3; 134)   £140

MEANS, James
- Manflight. Boston, priv. ptd., 1891. *1st. Edn. (With:)* – The Problem of Manflight. Boston, 1894. *1st. Edn. (With:)* - Epitome of Aeronautical Annual. Boston, 1910. *2nd. Edn.* Together 3 vols. Orig. wraps., 2nd. vol. reprd., 3rd. vol. slightly worn; John D. Stanitz coll. (SPB. Apr.25; 126) $175

MEARES, John
- An Answer to Mr. George Dixon ... in which the Remarks of Mr. Dixon ... are Fully Considered & Refuted. L., 1791. *1st. Edn.* 4to. Cont. note regarding the mis-bdg. of the pamphlet on hf.-title, mod. bds.; the Rt. Hon. Visc. Eccles copy. [Sabin 47257] (CNY. Nov.18; 89) $3,200
- Collection des Cartes, Vues, Marines ... Relatives au Voyage ... Paris, 1795. 4to. No bdg. stated. (HD. Oct.14; 11)   Frs. 1,600
- Voyages Made in the Years 1788 & 1789, From China to the North West Coast of America ... Ill.:– T. Stothard, T. Foot, R. Pollard, & others. L., 1790. *1st. Edn.* 4to. Stipple-engraved port., 3 folding engraved maps, 24 full-p. engraved plts., including the optional plt. of the Philippines at p. 17, 1 map lightly spotted, 1 plt. with abrasion, cont. tree cf., rebkd. preserving orig. gt. spine; Duke of Leeds bkplt., the Rt. Hon. Visc. Eccles copy. [Sabin 47260] (CNY. Nov.18; 192) $1,800

MECHAM, Clifford Henry
- Sketches & Incidents of the Siege of Lucknow ... with Descriptive Notices by George Couper. L., 1858. Fo. Tinted litho. title & 26 tinted litho. plts. on 17 sheets, title & some margins spotted, cont. purple cl. gt., rebkd. (C. Jun.27; 47)   *Enzler.* £120
-- Anr. Copy. Fo. Tinted litho. title (spotted), 25

MECHAM, Clifford Henry -*Contd.*

views on 15 (of 16) plts., spotted, plts. & ll. detchd., some margins frayed, orig. cl., lacks spine. (S. Mar.6; 41) *Shapero.* £55

MECHEL, Chrétien de
See— PIGAGE, Nicolas de & Mechel, Chrétien de

MEDAI, D.S.
- **Vollständiges Thaler-Cabinet.** Königsberg, 1765-74. 3pts. & 3 supps. in 4 vols. Some foxing & slight browning in vol.1. cont. hf. leath. gt. (R. Apr.3; 1067) DM 1,600

MEDALLIC HISTORY OF NAPOLEON. A Collection of all Medals, Coins, & Jettons relating to his Actions & Reign
1819. 4to. 60 engraved plts., mod. hf. mor. gt. (BBA. Jul.27; 252) *The Bookroom.* £70

MEDER, Johannes
- **Quadragesimale Novum de Filio Prodigo.** Basle, Michael Furter, 1497. *2nd. Edn.* Rubricated, cont. stpd. cf. over wood bds., upr. cover decor., clasps incompl.; from Fondation Furstenberg-Beaumesnil. [H. 13629; BMC III, 785; Goff M422] (HD. Nov.16; 17) Frs. 28,000
- **[Quadragesimale] Parabola Filij Glutonis Profusi atq[ue]p[ro]digi ...** Basel, 1510. *3rd. Edn.* Poem from Seb. Brandt on title verso, 3 different printers marks, 1 lf. restored in margin, some slight browning in outer margin, 19th. C. mor. gt., gold-tooled decor. centre-piece on covers, gt. inner & outer dentelle sigd. by Rivière. (D. Nov.23; 130) DM 4,000

MEDER, Joseph
- **Dürer-Katalog.** Wien, 1932. 4to. 52 plts. & 190 text ills., lightly browned, linen, bumped & spotted. (HT. May 9; 955) DM 450
- - **Anr. Copy.** Sm. 4to. Orig. hf. linen. (H. Nov.23; 147) DM 440
- **Die Handzeichnung ihre Technik und Entwicklung.** Vienna, 1919. *1st. Edn.* Orig. roan-bkd. bds., lacks spine. (S. Oct.4; 176) *Hamery.* £50
- - **Anr. Edn.** Wien, 1932. 4to. Orig. hf. leath. (HK. Nov.12; 4733) DM 430

MEDICAL ESSAYS & OBSERVATIONS
Contribs.:– Monro, Simson, Barry, Armstrong, & others. Edinb., 1733-35. *1st. Edns.* Vols. I-III. Some dampstains, cont. cf., 2 vols. rebkd. (SG. Mar.22; 215) $150

MEDINA, Balthasar de
- **Vida ... del Invicto Proto-Martyr de el Japan San Felipe de Jesus, Patron de Mexico, su Patria, Imperial Corte de Nueva España, en el Nueve Mundo.** Madrid, 1751. *2nd. Imp.* 4to. Old vell. [Sabin 47337] (SG. Oct.20; 219) $250

MEDINA, Jose Toribio
- **Biblioteca Hispanoamericana.** Santiago de Chile, 1958-62. 7 vols. Ptd. wraps., some loose, unopened. (BG. Jan.5; 222) $300
- **La Imprenta en Guadalajara de Mexico.** Santiago de Chile, 1904. *(200).* Lge. 8vo. Ptd. wraps., unc., cl. folding case. (SG. Jan.5; 223) $110
- **La Imprenta en Manila Desde sus Origenes hasta 1810.** Santiago de Chile, 1896. *(300).* 4to. Red three-qtr. mor.; B. Mendel bkplt. (SG. Jan.5; 225) $110
- **La Imprenta en la Puebla de Los Angeles.** Santiago de Chile, 1908. *1st. Edn.* 4to. Facs., cont. qtr. cf., cl. covers, unc., ptd. wraps. bnd. in, back hinge brkn. (SG. Jan.5; 224) $200

MEDINA, Pedro de
- **Arte del navegar.** Trans.:– Vicenzo Paletino. Venice, 1554. *1st. Italian Edn.* 4to. Some foxing or soiling, few other ll. reprd., 1 lf. with reprd. tear, 19th. C. leath. in cont. style. (R. Oct.13; 2981) DM 3,500
- - **Anr. Edn.** Venice, 1609. *2nd. Italian Edn.* 4to. Title browned, old Liby stp., corner reprd., 1 text lf. with sm. margin tear, 1 sig. misbnd., late 19th C. hf. leath., spine slightly defect. (R. Apr.5; 2765) DM 3,600
- **Libro de la Verdad.** Sevilla, 1576. Fo. Vell. (DS. Oct.28; 2601) Pts. 75,000

- - **Anr. Edn.** Cuenca, 1592. Fo. Linen. (DS. Mar.23; 2183) Pts. 60,000

MEDINACELI, Duque de
- **Series de los mas importantes Documentos del Archivo y Biblioteca.** Madrid, 1915-22. Fo. Some ll. slightly spotted, cont. hf. mor., rubbed. (BBA. Feb.9; 219) *Walford.* £55

MEDLER, N.
- **Rvdimenta Arithmeticae Practicae.** Wittenb., 1550. Title lightly frayed in side margin, bds. (HK. Nov.8; 275) DM 2,200

MEDLEY, T.
- **The Shandymonian.** L., 1779. *2nd. Edn.* Cf. gt. (P. Feb.16; 266) £80

MEDWIN, Thomas
[–] **'Sydney's' Letter to the King; and other Correspondence, Connected with the Reported Exclusion of Lord Byron's Monument from Westminster Abbey.** 1828. Cont. cf., spine gt., rubbed; hf.-title inscr., 'Colonel Wildman with the Author's sincere Regards'. (BBA. Feb.9; 75) *Wise.* £85

MEE, Arthur
- **King's England Series.** Ca. 1950/70. 32 vols. Some underscoring & annots., orig. cl., d.-w.'s. (TA. Jan.19; 53) £100

MEE, Margaret
- **Flores do Amazonas.** Rio de Janiero, 1980. *(1000) numbered.* Fo. Orig. cl., s.-c.; sig. of artist on title-p. (BBA. Sep.29; 55) *Burton-Garbett.* £60

MEEHAN, Thomas
- **The Native Flowers & Ferns of the United States in their Botanical, Horticultural, & Popular Aspects.** Ill.:– after Alois Lunzer. Boston, 1878. *1st. Edn.* 2 vols. 4to. 96 full-p. chromolithos., with some ageing, some offsetting to opposing text pp., some old margin dampstains, orig. bevelled sheep & cl., gt.-lettered, some scuffing & wear to covers. (HA. Feb.24; 272) $100
- - **Anr. Edn.** Boston, 1878-80. *1st. Edn.* 1st. & 2nd. Series. 3 vols. only (of 4, lacks 2nd. Series Vol. 1). 4to. 144 chromolith. plts., buckram. (SG. Mar.22; 223) $100
- - **Anr. Edn.** Ill.:– Louis Prang after Alois Lunzer. Boston & Phila., 1879-80. Series I & II: 4 vols. 4to. 192 full-p. cold. litho. plts., very light foxing to a few plts., 1 title-p. spotted, orig. publisher's mor. gt., slightly rubbed; the Rt. Hon. Visc. Eccles copy. (CNY. Nov.18; 193) $280
- - **Anr. Edn.** Boston, 1879, Phila., 1880. 1st. & 2nd. Series: 4 vols. 192 chromolith. plts., perforated stp. on titles, liby. buckram, shelf numbers on spines; ex-liby. (SG. Mar.22; 224) $130

MEEK, A.S.
- **A Naturalist in Cannibal Land.** L., 1913. *1st. Edn.* Frontis. loose, cl., decor. gt.; copy of E.E. Selous. (SKC. Oct.26; 405) £55

MEEKE, Mrs. Mary
- **Palmira & Ermance, a Novel.** L., 1797. *1st. Edn.* 3 vols. 12mo. Some spotting, cont. cf. (S. Apr.9; 270) *Bennett.* £170

MEFFRET[H]
- **Sermones de Tempore et de Sanctis sive Hortulus Reginae.** Nürnberg, A. Koberger, 14 Feb. 1487. *1st. Nürnberg Edn.* Pt. 2 (of 3). Fo. Rubricated, some light margin spotting, especially last ll. a few ll. spotted, underlining & short marginalia in old MS., short owners mark from 1606 in upr. margin 1st. lf., 3 ll. slightly torn, cont. blind-tooled pig over wood bds., upr. cover lightly wormed, head of spine slightly defect., lr. cover rubbed, lacks clasps. [H 11004; BMCII, 431; Goff M-443] (R. Apr.3; 5a) DM 1,200

MEGERLE, Johann Ulrich
See— ABRAHAM A SANTA CLARA [i.e. Johann Ulrich Megerle]

MEGGENDORFER, Lothar
- **Always Jolly.** L., ca. 1890. 4to. 8 cold. plts. with movable pts., orig. pict. bds. (P. May 17; 393) *Glendale.* £140
- **Aus dem Leben.** Munich, n.d. *2nd. Edn.* 8 cold. moving pictures, some sections torn, some light

soiling, orig. cl.-bkd. bds., lightly rubbed & soiled. (CSK. Oct.21; 120) £110
- **Bewegliche Schattenbilder. II. Vorstellung.** München, [1886]. Lge. ob. 4to. Orig. bds., loose & rubbed. (HK. Nov.10; 2924) DM 900
- **Bubenstreiche.** München, ca. 1895. Fo. 4 chromo-litho. moving pictures, publisher's ill. bds. (HD. Feb.28; 69) Frs. 1,100
- **Gemischte Gesellschaft.** Eklingen & Munich, n.d. Lge. 4to. 8 cold. full-p. ills. with moving parts operated by thumb tags, 2 ills. cleanly torn, some parts in need of repair or lacking, margins slightly browned, orig. cl.-bkd. bds., rubbed & soiled. (CSK. Apr.27; 147) £70
- **Neue Thierbilder.** Munich, n.d. Lge. 4to. 8 cold. full-p. ills. with moving parts operated by thumb tags, 1 ill. slightly torn, 3 tags & some moving parts lacking, some margin soiling, orig. cl.-bkd. bds., worn. (CSK. Mar.23; 166) £100
- **Tiny [Tim] Prince [of Liliput].** N.d. Fo. 6 chromo-litho. movable pictures, 4 with sections detchd., section of title excised, orig. cl.-bkd. pict. bds., soiled. (CSK. Jan.13; 129) £85

MEGGENDORFER, Lothar & Feldigl, Ferd.
- **Prinz Liliput.** Stuttgart, ca. 1910. Fo. Moving picture book, separate text with further ills., loose in orig. cl.-bkd. pict. bds., corners bumped; van Veen coll. (S. Feb.28; 280) £260

MEGILLAT EICHA, Tefillot Leil Tisha Be'av Ve'Kinot Minhag Ashkenazim, Polin, Bohemia, Moravia
Mantua, 1620. Inner margin strengthened not affecting text, stained thro.-out, creased, edges frayed, leath. (S. Oct.25; 254) *Klein.* £100

MEHEUT, Mathurin
- **Etude de la Forêt.** Preface:– J. Constantin. Ed.:– L. Plantefol. Paris, [1927]. 2 vols. Lge. 4to. 110 plts. (40 mntd. & in col.), all with sm. stp. on blank versos, loose as iss. in cl.-bkd. pict. bd. folders, linen ties. (SG. Mar.22; 226) $175
- **Etude de La Mer; Faune et Flore de la Manche et de L'Océan.** Text:– P. Verneuil. Paris, ca. 1920?. *New Edn.* 2 vols. Fo. 50 col. plts., liby stp. on titles, pict. cl., shelf mark on spines. (SG. Mar.22; 225) $200
- **Etudes d'Animaux.** Paris, [1911]. Lge. fo. 52 full-p. plts., some minor soiling & chipping to plt. mounts, loose-bnd. in hf. cl. & ptd. bd. portfo., slightly worn, ties. (CBA. Jan.29; 9) $120

MEHLIS, C.
- **Bilder aus den Landschaften des Mittelrheins.** Leipzig, [1881]. 1 double-p. map, 3 plts., 98 wood-cuts, some full-p. orig. linen. (R. Oct.13; 2710) DM 400

MEID, Hans
- **Don Juan. 15 Radierungen zur Oper von Mozart ...** Berlin, 1912. *(10) De Luxe Edn. on japan.* Lge. fo. All etchings sigd. by artist, all etchings except title under guards, title lf. with sm. crease, loose in orig. hf. vell. portfo., spine & margins lightly worn. (H. May 23; 1415) DM 7,000
- **Zwanzig Radierungen zur Bibel.** Leipzig, 1916-26. *(100) on Bütten.* 4 series. Fo. Each portfo. with contents table, 5 sigd. & numbered etchings, all ll. under guards, ll. in 1st. portfo. with some light margin foxing, loose ll. in orig. hf. linen covers. (H. Nov.24; 1847) DM 6,400

MEIDNER, Ludwig
- **Septemberschrei. Hymnen, Gebete, Lästerungen.** Berlin, 1920. *1st. Edn.* 4to. Margins lightly browned, orig. bds., spine defect., slightly holed. (HK. Nov.11; 3812) DM 460
- **Strassen und Cafés.** Ill.:– after Meidner. Leiden, [1918]. *(150).* Fo. 8 plts., all under guards, loose in orig. hf. linen portfo., soiled & slightly defect.; printer's mark sigd. by artist. (H. Nov.24; 1849) DM 1,000

MEIER-GRAEFE, Julius von
- **Cézanne und Seine Ahnen.** Ill.:– Cézanne, Dela-croix, & others. Munich, 1921. *(220) numbered.* Fo. 21 matted reproductions of drawings & water-colours, loose as iss. in cl.-bkd. bd. portfo. (SG. Dec.15; 136) $150
- **Die Kunst der Gegenwart.** Ill.:– Lovis Corinth,

Max Beckman, Paul Klee & others. Munich, [1925]. *(80) specially numbered, with 6 sigd. prints.* Tall fo. 42 facs. reproductions, many cold., individually matted, sm. liby. stps. on title & limitation pp., loose as iss. in coarse-weave buckram folder, spine defect. (SG. Apr.26; 139) $12,500
– Orlando und Angelica. Ill.:– Klossowski. N.p., n.d. *De Luxe Edn., (12) on old Japan bütten.* 2 sigd. orig. aquas., hand-bnd. mor., gold-tooled cover ill., gt. spine & inner dentelle, slightly spotted, faded & worn; sigd. by author & artist. (H. Nov.24; 1707)   DM 550

MEIER-GRAEFE, J. (Ed.)
See— GANYMED

MEILAH, KINIM, MIDOT & TAMID
Commentaries:– Rashi, Tosafot, Piskei Tosafot & Maimonides. Basle, 1578. Fo. Browned, stained & creased, hf. leath. (S. Oct.25; 390) *Kimche.* £450

MEILAH, KINIM, TAMID, MIDOT & SOFRIM
Commentaries:– Rashi, Tosafot, Piskei Tosafot. Venice, 1528-29. Fo. Staining in margins, slightly foxed & creased, mod. vell. (S. Oct.25; 389) *Klein.* £950

MEILHAC, H. & Halevy, Lud
– Les Sonnettes. Comédie. Paris, 1873. *(40) on Holland paper.* Extra-ill. with over 70 orig. watercolour & ink drawings on text ll., by Guydo, many sigd., hf. mor., slightly rubbed. (LC. Oct.13; 63)   £110

MEINERTZHAGEN, Col. Richard
– Birds of Arabia. 1954. 4to. Orig. buckram, slightly bubbled, d.-w. (SKC. May 4; 1864)   £200
– – Anr. Copy. 4to. Orig. cl., d.-w. (BBA. Nov.30; 112)   *Evans.* £170
– – Anr. Edn. Edinb. & L., [1954]. *1st. Edn.* 4to. Folding map in lr. cover holder, few liby. handstps. on margin of 1 text lf. & end-papers, cl., some wear. (RO. Dec.11; 210) $325
– – Anr. Edn. 1958. 4to. Folding map in end pocket, orig. cl., d.-w., slightly soiled. (P. Oct.20; 23)   £180
– – Anr. Edn. L., 1980. *De Luxe Edn. (295).* Fo. Hf. mor. gt. (VA. Apr.26; 115)   R 820
– Kenya Diary 1902-1906. 1957. Orig. cl. (CSK. Sep.16; 49)   £60

MEINHOLD, William
– Mary Schweidler, the Amber Witch. Trans.:– Lady Duff Gordon. [L., Vale Pr.], 1903]. *(300).* Sm. fo. Linen-bkd. bds., unc. & unopened. (SG. Mar.29; 268) $120

MEIR BEN BARUCH [Maharam of Rottenburg]
– She'eilot U'Teshuvot. Cremona, 1557. *1st. Edn.* 4to. Slightly soiled, hf. leath. (S. Oct.25; 255)   *Stern.* £700
– – Anr. Copy. (*Bound with:*) MOSHE BEN YITZ-CHAK ALASHKAR – She'eilot Uteshuvot. Sabionetta, 1553. *1st. Edn.* Together 2 works in 1 vol. 4to. 1st. work sigd. by Dominico Irosolomita & Giovanni Dominico Caretto, 1628, a few words censored, 2nd. work sigd. by Carretto, 1622, Domenico Yerushalmi, 1597, & Hippolitus of Ferrara, 2 & 4 Jan. 1594, a few words censored, owners stps., margin notes in cont. hand, slight soiling, old vell., worn; Hochschule für die Wissenschaft des Judenthums stps. [Steinschneider 6323 & 6424] (SPB. Jun.26; 17) $2,250
– – Anr. Copy. 4to. Slight staining, contents loose in bdg., mod. wraps., worn. (SPB. Feb.1; 64) $850

MEIR BEN GEDALIA, of Lublin [Maharam Mi'Lublin]
– She'eilot U'Teshuvot. Venice, 1618. *1st. Edn.* Fo. Old Yiddish texts, owners' sigs. on title, some staining, creased, hf. leath. (S. Oct.25; 256)   *Ludmir.* £550

ME'IR IBN GABBAI
– Sefer Avodat ha-Kodesh [kabbala]. Salawuta, 1827. *3rd. Edn.* Sm. fo. Damp-wrinkled, title soiled, cl.-bkd. bds., extremities worn. (SG. Feb.2; 253) $200

MEISS, Millard
– De Artibus Opuscula XL: Essays in Honor of Erwin Panofsky. Contribs.:– J. Bier, W. Cook, R.

Ettinghausen, J. Held, & others. 1961. *1st. Edn.* 2 vols. Tall 4to. Cl. gt., boxed. (SG. Sep.15; 257) $110

MEISSEN
– Festschrift zur 200jährigen Jubelfeier der ältesten Europ. Porzellanmanufaktur Meissen 1710-1910. Leipzig, 1910. Fo. Orig. linen. (HK. Nov.12; 4708)   DM 900

MEISSENER MUSTERBUCH FUR HOROLDT CHINOISERIEN
Commentary:– R. Behrends. Leipzig, [1978]. *(450).* Text vol. & 2 plt. vols. Lge. fo. German, Engl., Fr. & Spanish text, 16 plts. in text & 132 cold. facs. plts. loose in box, orig. Honan silk, 2 spine medallions of Meissen porclain gt., orig. bd. s.-c. (H. May 22; 115)   DM 1,400

MEISSENER PORZELLAN
See— RUCKERT, Rainer

MEISSNER, August Gottlieb
– Historisch-Malerische Darstellungen aus Böhmen. Ill.:– A. Pucherna after F.K. Wolf & others. Prague, 1798. Ob. 4to. Engraved title with vig., 1 engraved end vig., 14 plts. in old. cold. etching, cont. hf. leath., lightly rubbed, with old aquarelle. (R. Oct.13; 3188)   DM 1,500

MEISSNER, Franz Hermann
– Max Klinger: Radirungen, Zeichnungen, Bilder and Sculpturen des Kuenstlers. Munich, 1897. Fo. 61 heliogravure plts., on India paper & mntd., hf. vell., case worn & with some hinges brkn. (SG. Nov.3; 115) $750
– – Anr. Copy. Lge. fo. Orig. linen, slightly soiled. (R. Apr.3; 819)   DM 1,250

MEISTER, P.W.
– Porzellan des 18. Jhdts. Frankfurt, 1967. 4to. Orig. linen. (BR. Apr.13; 2076)   DM 400

MEITNER, Lise
– Der Zusammenhang zwischen β und γ-Strahlen. Berlin, 1924. 'Ergebnisse der Exakten Naturwissenschaften', Vol. 3, pp. 160-81. Orig. cl., light soiling; Stanitz coll. (SPB. Apr.25; 298) $250

MEITNER, Lise & Delbrueck, Max
– Der Aufbau der Atomkerne Natürliche und Künstliche Kernumwandlungen. Berlin, 1935. *1st. Edn.* Orig. ptd. stiff wraps., slight soiling, Stanitz coll. (SPB. Apr.25; 299) $225

MEJAN, Maurice
– Recueil des Causes Celèbres. Paris, 1808-20. *2nd. Edn.* 23 vols. Browned, orig. bds., slightly worn. (S. Oct.11; 560)   *Duran.* £50

MEJER, Wolfgang
– Bibliographie der Buchbinderei-Literatur. Leipzig, 1925. 4to. Mod. cl. (BBA. Mar.7; 312)   *Quaritch.* £50
– – Anr. Edn. Leipzig, 1925-33. 2 vols. 4to. Orig. cl., spines gt.; H.M. Nixon coll., with his sig. in both vols. (BBA. Oct.6; 94)   *Oak Knoll. Books.* £220

MELA, Pomponius
– Cosmographia; sive, De Situ Orbis. Venice, 15 Nov. 1477. *2nd. Edn. Dtd. Iss.* 4to. (in 8's). Lge. copy, some paragraph marks & initial strokes supplied in red or blue, lacks 3 blanks, few repairs, mostly marginal, 19th. C. mor. gt. extra, gt. dentelles; Quaritch collation note, Charles W.G. Howard & O.O. Fisher bkplts. [BMC V, 261; H. 11015] (SG. Nov.3; 139) $2,600
– – Anr. Edn. Venice, Franciscus Renner, de Heilbronn, 1478. 4to. Some early MS. annots., some marginalia cropped, red mor.-bkd. diced russ.; David P. Wheatland bkplt., Stanitz coll. (SPB. Apr.25; 300) $1,700
– De Situ Orbis Libri Tres. Andreas Schott & others. Antw., 1582. 4to. Paper a little browned, cont. cf., jnts. reprd., ptd. pastedowns; Lamoignon copy, bkplts. of Lady Rodd & James Rennell. (BBA. Nov.30; 11)   *George's.* £95

MELANCHTHON, Philipp 'Didymus Faventinus'
– Adversus Thoman Placentinum, pro Martino Luthero Theologo Oratio. Ill.:– L. Cranach. Wittenberg, [1521]. *1st. Edn.* 4to. Upr. margin slightly

stained, hf. vell., incunable paper. (R. Oct.11; 79)   DM 1,000
– Annotationes in Johannem ... Cum Epistola commendatita M. Lutheri. [Hagenau], 1523. *Reprint of Basle, May 1523 Edn.* (*Bound with:*) AGRICOLA [ISLEBIUS], Johann – In Evangelium Lucae Annotationes. Preface:– G. Spalatin. Nümberg, 1525. Together 2 works in 1 vol. Renaissance decor. bdg.,rubbed & slightly soiled, 2 clasps. (V. Oct.1; 3774)   DM 500
– [-] Confessio ... auff dem Reichstage gehalten zu Augspurgk 1530. Ill.:– J. Jonas. Frankfurt, 1553. 2 pts. in 1 vol. Cont. pig over wood bds., roll blind-tooled. (BR. Apr.12; 880)   DM 500
– Corpus Doctrinae Christianae. Ill.:– E. Vögelin. Leipzig, Jan. 1560. *1st. Edn.* Fo. Wide margin, minimal staining, cont. style vell., incunable paper covered. (GB. Nov.3; 948)   DM 1,000
– Declamativncvla in D. Pavli Doctrinam Epistola ad Iohannem Hessum Theologum. Wittenb., 1520. 4to. Rubricated thro.-out, title with owners mark, old text annets., side margin slightly stained, last ll. slightly wormed, 18th. C. bds., spine torn; hand-painted ex-libris Otto Hupp on end-paper. (HK. May 15; 194)   DM 750
– Formae Precationvm Piarvm Collectae ex Scriptis ... Ed.:– L. Backmeistero. Wittenburg, 1559. *1st. Edn.* Title with sm. MS. note, last p. soiled, lacks last lf. blank, bds. (HK. Nov.8; 278)   DM 1,100
– Haubtartikel Christlicher Lere. –Loci Theologici, etwa von Juston Jona in Deudsche Sprach gebracht. Wittemb., 1579. 2 works in 1 vol. 4to. Cont. cf. polychrome leath. onlay decor., centre arms, faded. (D. Nov.23; 163)   DM 3,000
– Initia Doctrinae Physicae, dictata in Academia Witenbergensi. – Liber de Anima. Witenberg, 1587. 2 works in 1 vol. Cont. stpd. cf., A. von Ryffenberg arms stpd. in black on upr. cover, port. on lr. cover, slightly worn; from Fondation Furstenberg-Beaumesnil. (HD. Nov.16; 136)   Frs. 1,300
– Kirchenordnung. Wittenberg, 1554. *2nd. Edn.* (*Bound with:*) CONFESSIO oder Bekentnis des Glaubens, Durch ... Herrn Johans Hertzogen zu Sachssen, Churfürsten & c. und etliche Fürsten und Stedte, uberantwort Keiserliche Maiestat, auff dem Reichstag zu Augspurk, Anno 1530 ... Wittenberg, 1555. Lacks 2 ll., last ll. lightly margin stained. 2 works in 1 vol., cont. decor. tooled pig over wood bds., dtd. 1557, clasps defect. (R. Oct.11; 83)   DM 750
– Oratio Uber der Leich des Ehrwirdigen ... Luthers ... Trans.:– D. Casper Ceutzingen. Wittenberg, [15]46. *1st. Edn. 2nd. Printing.* 4to. 1 lf. with tear, slightly soiled thro.-out, later wraps,. (HT. May 8; 164)   DM 500
– Von der Kirchen und Alten Kirchenleren. Trans.:– J. Jonas. Wittenberg, 1540. 4to. Lightly wormed thro.-out, title restored, last ll. slightly soiled, washed, hf. vell. (R. Oct.11; 82)   DM 500
– Ware Historia. [Nuremb.], 1546. 4to. Copper engraved port on upr. end-paper, smooth cf., decor., gt. spine. (D. Nov.23; 131)   DM 440

MELANCHTHON, Philipp
See— SACROBOSCO or SACROBUSTO, J. - MELANCHTHON, Philipp

MELBOURNE
– City of Melbourne Detail Fire Survey. Melbourne, ca. 1910. Index plan, 24 lge. chromolitho. sheets, each about 22 × 22 inches, some ptd. & MS. addendum slips pasted on, some minor defects, old hf. roan, brkn. (KH. May 1; 482)   Aus. $1,700

MELLADO, F. de Paula
– Arte de Fumar y tomar Tabaco sin disgustar a las Damas. Madrid, 1833. 42 × 30mm. Miniature Book. Mosaic leath., s.-c. (DS. Dec.16; 2396)   Pts. 20,000

MELLEN, J. von
– Epistola de Antiqvis Qvibvsdam Nvmmis Germanicis Historiam Thvringicam Praecipue illustrantibus ... Jena, [1678]. *1st. Edn.* Cont. hf. leath. gt., lightly bumped, end-papers browned. (HK. Nov.9; 1940)   DM 480

MELLERIO, Andre
– Le Mouvement Idéaliste en Peinture. Ill.:– Odilon Redon H. Nocq. Paris, 1896. *(350).* MS. dedication Mellerios, lithos. on tinted vell., hf. mor., sigd., orig.

MELLERIO, Andre -Contd.

wraps. with ill. bnd. in. (GB. Nov.5; 3189)
DM 750
- Odilon Redon. Paris, 1913. *(550).* 4to. Brkn., orig. wraps., slightly torn & soiled. (S. Oct.4; 177)
Hamery. £160
- - Anr. Edn. 1913. 4to. On japan, sewed, unc. (HD. Jun.29; 141) Frs. 4,200

MELLI, Elieser
- Lakol Chefetz-Tikun Shtarot. Venice, 1552. *1st. Edn.* 4to. Staining mostly in margins, hf. leath.; 'Reishit Chochma' Soc. stp. (S. Oct.24; 46)
Yardeni. £300

MELLING, Auguste Ignace
- Voyage Pittoresque de Constantinople et des Rives du Bosphore. Paris, 1819. 2 vols. Lge. fo. Additional engraved title, port., 3 double-p. maps, 48 double-p. plts., many before letters, mntd. on guards, maps, few plts. & some text ll. spotted, cont. mor.-bkd. bds. (C. Dec.9; 101) *Elmerside.* £5,000

MELLON, Paul & Mary
- Alchemy & the Occult: A Catalogue of Books & Manuscripts, 1472-1790, from the Collection of ... given to Yale University Library. Ed.:– I. MacPhail. Essays:– R.P. Multhauf & A. Jaffe. Notes:– W. McGuire. New Haven, Spiral Pr., 1968. *(500).* 2 vols. Lge. tall 4to. Two-tone buckram, cl. box. (SG. Sep.15; 1) $300

MELMOTH, William Henry
- The Adventures of Telemachus, the son of Ulysses. L., n.d. 4to. Slight foxing thro.-out, pol. cf. gt. (LH. Sep.25; 569) $170

MELON, Jean François
- Essai Politique sur le Commerce. N.P., 1736. *New Edn.* 12mo. Cont. cf. (HD. Feb.22; 136)
Frs. 1,800

MELONIUS, J.
- Thesaurus Juris Feudalis, Ciuilis et Criminalis Novus. Dillingen, 1630. *1st. Edn.* Fo. Some browning, cont. vell. (R. Apr.3; 1194) DM 620

MELTON, Edward [i.e. G. van Broekhuizen?]
- Zeldzaame en Gedenkw. Zee– en Landreizen; door Egypten, West-Indiën, Perziën, Turkyen, Oost-Indiën en d'Aangrenzende Gewesten. Ill.:– J. Luiken &c. Amst., 1681. *1st. Edn.* 4to. Frontis. & several plts. short, some with sm. repairs, few stains, 19th. C. hf. vell., slightly worn. [Sabin 47472] (VG. Sep.14; 1112) Fls. 520

MELTZER
See— HALOANDER, Gregorius [i.e. Meltzer]

MELTZER, David – SCHENKER, Donald
- Poems. – Poetry. [San Franc., 1957]. *(25)* numbered & sigd. by both authors. Together 2 works in 1 vol., as iss. Qtr. cl., pict. bds.; inscr. by Schenker, 1967. (SG. Mar.1; 331) $130

MELVILLE, A.G
See— STRICKLAND, Hugh Edwin & Melville, A.G.

MELVILLE, Herman
- Battle-Pieces & Aspects of the War. N.Y., 1866. *1st. Edn.* Orig. cl., mor.-bkd. s.-c.; Frederic Dannay copy. (CNY. Dec.16; 231) $420
- Mardi: & a Voyage Thither. L., 1849. *1st. Edn. 1st. Iss.* 3 vols. Lacks hf.-title in Vol. 1, some margin darkening & soiling, later three-qtr. mor. & marb. bds., marb. end-papers, covers rubbed, upr. cover of Vol. 1 detchd. (CBA. Mar.3; 384) $420
- Moby Dick; Or, the Whale. N.Y., 1851. *1st. Amer. Edn.* Dampstained, heavily foxed, orig. cl., very shabby. (SG. Mar.15; 135) $600
- - Anr. Edn. Ill.:– Rockwell Kent. Chic., Lakeside Pr., 1930. *(1000).* 3 vols. 4to. Silver gt.-decor. cl., aluminium s.-c., light wear. (RO. Dec.11; 169)
$775
- - Anr. Copy. 3 vols. 4to. Silver-decor. cl., minor discoloration to 1 spine, aluminium s.-c. (SG. Nov.3; 140) $750
- - Anr. Edn. Ill.:– Barry Moser. San Franc., Arion Pr., 1979. *(250).* Fo. Mor., box. (CBA. Mar.3; 385)
$2,250

- Narrative of a Four Months' Residence among the Natives ... of the Marquesas Islands: or, a Peep at Polynesian Life. L., 1846. *1st. Edn. 1st. Iss.* With 'Pomarea' on p. 19 line 1, lacks hf.-title & advts., some slight soiling to text, faint pencil marks on title-p., later three-qtr. mor. & marb. bds., gt.-decor. ribbed spine, new fly-ll., covers rubbed, darkening, a few scuff marks to mor. (CBA. Mar.3; 386) $250
- - Anr. Edn. 1846. *1st. Edn.* Hf.-title, mod. red. hf. mor., spine gt. (BBA. Jan.19; 94)
Sons of Liberty Books. £75
- Redburn: His First Voyage. N.Y., 1949. *1st. Amer. Edn. 1st. Printing.* 10 pp. publisher's advts., some spotting, some corners torn, orig. cl., spotted. (SPB. Dec.13; 706) $175
- The Works ... L., 1922-24. *Standard Edn. (750).* 16 vols. Embossed cl., most vols. in worn d.-w.'s. (PNY. Dec.1; 17) $950

MELVILLE, Robert
[-] A Critical Inquiry Into the Constitution of the Roman Legion; with some observations on the Military Art of the Romans, Compared with that of the Moderns. Edinb., 1773. 4to. Hf.-title, mod. hf. mor.; De Peyster bkplt. (SG. Sep.22; 204) $100

MELZO, Lodovico
- Regole Militari Sopra il Governo e Servitio Particolare della Cavalleria. Antw., 1611. Fo. Some ll. browned or spotted, mod. vell. (BBA. Nov.30; 39)
Fazzi. £380

MEMENTO: A Gift of Friendship
Ed.:– C.W. Everest. N.Y., 1847. Lge. 12mo. Orig. blind-ornamental cl., minor nicking on corners; from liby. of F.D. Roosevelt, inscr. by him. (SG. Mar.15; 37) $225

MEMMIUS, Conrad
See— FRANCUS, Jacobus, ie. Conrad Memmius or Lautenbach]

MEMOIRE SUR LE DIFFEREND qui est entre M. Levesque de Tournay et les Reguliers de son Diocèse
Paris, 1672. 4to. Cont. Fr. red mor., triple gt. line-border, arms of Louis XIV on covers & fleur-de-lys at corners, spine gt. with fleur-de-lys in compartments, marb. end-papers. (S. May 10; 332)
Maggs. £260

MEMOIRES POUR L'HISTOIRE NATURELLE DE LA PROVINCE DE LANGUEDOC
Paris, 1737. 3 pts. in 1 vol. 4to. Cf. gt., rubbed. (P. Feb.16; 201) £65

MEMOIRS OF THE LIVES AND CONDUCT of Those Illustrious Heroes Prince Eugene of Savoy and John Duke of Marlborough
1742. Fo. 1 plt. torn, cont. cf., slightly worn; sig. of P.Western 1744, later Western bkplt. (BBA. Feb.9; 37) *Armstrong.* £85

MEMORIAL MILITAR Y PATRIOTICO DEL EXERCITO DE LA IZQUIERDA
[Extramadura], 1810. Nos. 1-59. (DS. Mar.23; 2184) Pts. 130,000

MENACHEM AZARIA DI FANO
- Asara Ma'amarot. Venice, 1597. *1st. Edn.* 4to. 2 ll. 17th. C. MS. notes inserted between title & 1st. p., staining, edges frayed, browned, trimmed, mod. mor. (S. Oct.25; 257) *Davidson.* £350
- - Anr. Edn. Commentary:– Moshe Ben Shlomo Ha'Levi, of Frankfurt. Amst., 1649. *3rd. Edn.* 4to. Washed, title reprd. without loss of text, staining, discold., vell., worn. (S. Oct.25; 258) *Sol.* £150
- Teshuvot. Venice, ca. 1600. *1st. Edn.* 4to. Owners' sigs. on title, slightly soiled & creased, mod. mor. gt. (S. Oct.25; 260) *Ludmir.* £400
See— MORDEKHAI YA'AKOV, of Prague

MENACHEM AZARIA DI FANO & Gallico, Shmuel
- Asis Rimonim. Mantua, 1623. *2nd. Edn.* 4to. Wormed & reprd. affecting some letters, staining, slightly discold., inner margins strengthened, blank p. with MS. glosses on Calender, hf. leath., slightly worn. (S. Oct.25; 259) *Sol.* £120

MENACHEM RECANTI
- Taamei Ha'Mitzvot U'Peirush Ha'Brachot V'Hazmirot, V'Hayotzer. Constantinople, 1543-44. *1st. Edn.* Very browned, sm. losses to title & 1st. lf., stained, mod. blind-stpd. cf. (SPB. Feb.1; 76)
$2,900

MENACHER, Th.
- Adolf Lier und sein Werk. München, 1928. Orig. linen, slightly soiled. (HK. Nov.12; 4726) DM 550

MENAGE, Gilles
- Dictionnaire Etymologique de la Langue Française. Paris, 1750. *New Edn.* 2 vols. Fo. Cont. hf. roan. (HD. Feb.22; 138) Frs. 1,900
- Dictionnaire Etymologique ou Origines de la Langue Française. 1694. Fo. Cont. glazed cf., Riquet de Caraman arms; A.L., dtd. 2 Jul. 1661. (HD. Jan.24; 36) Frs. 2,850
- Les Origines de la Langue Françoise. Paris, 1650. *1st. Edn.* 4to. L.P., ruled, cont. red mor., Du Seuil decor; 2 engraved ex-libris (including Joseph-Laurent d'Estavaye). (HD. Mar.29; 62) Frs. 45,000

MENANTES (Pseud.)
See— HUNOLD, C.F.

MENASSEH BEN ISRAEL
- Conciliador. Amst., 1641-51. *1st. Edns.* Pts. 2-4, in 1 vol. 4to. Foxed & dampstained, slightly creased, discold., vell., worn. (S. Oct.25; 261)
Prince. £1,250
- De Resurrectione Mortuorum Libri III. Amst., 1636. *1st. Edn.* Title loose, mild dampstaining, later hf. tree cf., extremities worn, spine label slightly chipped. (SG. Feb.2; 96) $850
- Mikveh Israel. Trans.:– Eliakim Ben Yakov Chazan. Amst., 1697-98. *1st. Edn. in Hebrew.* Some worming affecting some letters, browned & stained. (*Bound with:*) BENJAMIN, of Tudela - Masa'ot. Amst., 1698. *5th. Edn.* Ptd. without title, browned & trimmed. Together 2 works in 1 vol. Mod. cf. (S. Oct.25; 262) *Kings.* £270
- Nishmat Chaim. Amst., 1652. *1st. Edn.* 4to. Lacks Latin title & preface (5 ll.), title washed & mntd. without affecting text or columns, slightly soiled & discold., hf. leath., marb. paper bds. (S. Oct.25; 263) *Moriah.* £340

MENCKEN, Henry Louis
- The American Language. N.Y., 1936. With Supps. 1 (1945) & 2 (1948). Cl., d.-w.; sigd. by author, T.N.s., 1 supp. sigd. by author. (LH. Sep.25; 570) $100
[-] A Monograph of the New Baltimore Court House. [Balt., 1899]. *1st. Edn.* Ob. fo. 500 ills., orig. cl.-bkd. stiff litho. wraps., some soiling; Perry Molstad copy. (SPB. May 16; 488) $600
- A New Dictionary of Quotations on Historical Principles. 1947. *Galley Proofs.* No corrections; inscr. twice to Perry Molstad. (SPB. May 16; 495a)
$250
- Prejudices. – Selected Prejudices. N.Y., [1919-27]. 1st.-6th Series, 1st. work, 1st.-2nd. series 2nd. work, together 10 vols. Some marginal browning, orig. bdgs., some d.-w.'s, some soiling & browning; most inscr. to Perry Molstad. (SPB. May 16; 489)
$900
- Ventures into Verse. Balt., 1903. *1st. Edn.* Orig. wraps., red mor.-bkd. s.-c., 'For Review' slip tipped in; inscr. twice, to Col. N.N. Wallack & to Robert L. Weinberg; Perry Molstad copy. (SPB. May 16; 490) $2,500

MENCKEN, Henry Louis & Hirshberg, Leonard Keen
- What You Ought to Know about your Baby. N.Y., 1910. *1st. Edn.* Marginal browning, orig. cl., sigd.; Perry Molstad copy. (SPB. May 16; 494) $500

MENCKEN, Henry Louis & Nathan, George Jean
- Heliogabalus. N.Y., 1920. *1st. Edn. (200).* Advance copy, orig. wraps., browned, cl. s.-c.; inscr. to Perry Molstad by both authors. (SPB. May 16; 492) $425

MENDEL, Gregor Johann
- Versuche über Pflanzen-Hybriden. Brünn, 1866. *1st. separate Edn.* 1st. & last ll. very soiled, last with sm. hole, some spotting, sewed. (H. Nov.23; 219) DM 13,500

MENDEL, P.J. & Reding, H.
- Atlas van het Koningrijk der Nederlanden en de Overzeesche Bezittingen. 's-Gravenhage, 1841. Ob. 4to. 13 plts., 14 litho. maps, cont. hand-cold. in outl., 2 maps slightly defect., some plts. foxed, orig. hf. cf., litho. bds., slightly soiled. (VS. Dec.8; 924)
Fls. 775

MENDELSSOHN, Moses
- Jerusalem; oder, Ueber Religioese Macht und Judentum. Berlin, 1783. *1st. Edn.* 2 pts. in 1 vol. Sm. 8vo. Faint liby. stp. on title, later qtr. cl. (SG. Feb.2; 97)
$250
- Sämmtliche Werke. Budapest, 1819-25. *1st. Coll. Edn.* Cont. hf. leath. gt., slightly bumped. (HK. Nov.10; 2595)
DM 2,700
- - **Anr. Edn.** Ed.:- [Fr. Gräffer]. Ill.:- J. Stoiber after A. Graff. Wien, 1838. *1st. coll. Edn.* On vell., lacks advt. lf. at end, title & port. slightly foxed, cont. hf. leath. gt., slightly bumped. (HK. May 16; 2162)
DM 420

MENDELSSOHN, Sidney
- South African Bibliography. 1910. *(500).* 2 vols. Cl., marked. (SSA. Jul.5; 270)
R 180

MENDES, Catulle
- Hesperus. Ill.:- Carloz Schwabe. Paris, 1904. *(165). (50) on 'papier vélin'.* 4to. Art Nouveau bdg. of mor. by Salvator David, sigd. on upr. turn-in, upr. cover with col. onlaid mor. design, lr. corners framed by gt. curved lines, lr. cover with smaller onlaid cold. mor. decor., spine in 5 compartments, gt.-lettered in 2, cold. floral onlays in rest, bd. edges with double gt. fillet, turn-ins gt. with onlaid mor. gt. stars, cold. stripes & black floral silk brocade doubls. & free end-pp., marb. paper fly-ll., partly unc., spine discold. & extremities with minute wear, 1 marb. fly-lf. detchd., end-ll. browned, orig. ptd. wraps. preserved; Albert May Todd & Raphael Esmerian bkplts. (CNY. May 18; 178)
$1,500

MENDES DA COSTA, E.
- Elements of Conchology. L., 1776. Lightly browned, some plts. spotted in lr. margin, cont. leath., spine renewed. (R. Apr.4; 1761)
DM 600

MENDEZ SILVA, Rodrigo
- Población General de España ... Madrid, 1675. Fo. Vell. (DS. Mar.23; 2185)
Pts. 70,000

MENDOZA, Bernardino de
- Theorica y Pratica de Guerra. Madrid, 1595. *1st. Edn.* 4to. Vell. (DS. Apr.27; 2179)
Pts. 75,000

MENDOZA, Diego Hurtez de
- Leben des Lazarillo von Tormes. Ill.:- H. Meid. Berlin, 1924. *(150).* Hand-bnd. orig. hf. leath; Gll full-p. etchings sigd. by artist. (H. Nov.24; 1843)
DM 580

MENESTRIER, Claude François, S.J.
- L'Art des Emblèmes, ou s'enseigne la Morale par les Figures de la Fable, de l'Histoire et de la Nature. Paris, 1684. Old cf., spine decor. (LM. Mar.3; 133)
B. Frs. 10,000
- Histoire Civile ou Consulaire de la Ville de Lyon. Ill.:- Ferdinand de la Monce. Lyon, 1696. *Orig. Edn.* Fo. Cont. blind-decor. vell. (HD. Jun.18; 30)
Frs. 5,500
- La Philosophie des Images Enigmatiques. Lyon, 1694. 12mo. Lacks port. of Père de Bussières (as often), cf. gt., spine decor., by Trautz-Bauzonnet; from Yemeniz liby. (HD. Nov.9; 52) Frs. 2,400
- Le Véritable Art du Blason ou l'Usage des Armoiries. -Les Recherches du Blason. Seconde Partie de l'Usage des Armoiries. Paris, 1673. 2 vols. 12mo. Vol. II lacks frontis., cont. cf., spines decor., sm. tears to turn-ins of Vol. II. (HD. Nov.9; 51)
Frs. 1,000

MENGHI, Girolamo
- Compendio dell'arte Essorcistica, et Possibilità delle Mirabili et stupende Operationi delli Demoni, et de i malefici. Bologna, 1590. Stained, 118 torn & reprd., some stains, cont. vell., slightly discold. (SI. Dec.18; 26)
Lire 400,000

MENGIN, Ernst
- Corpus Codicum Americanorum Medii Aevi. Havniae, 1942-52. 4 vols. in 6. Fo. In Engl., Fr.,

German & Spanish, cl., slight wear. (RO. Dec.11; 213)
$175

MENNEL, Jak.
- [-] Ain Hüpsche Chronik von Heidnischen un Christen Künigen, der Teütschen und Welschen Francken. Freiburg, 1523. *1st. Edn.* 4to. Title with MS. owners monog. & number, 1 lf. in facs. on old paper, 4 ll. restored, some browning & soiling, 17th. C. vell., rebnd. (HK. Nov.8; 280)
DM 1,400

MENNIE, Donald
- The Pageant of Peking. Shanghai, 1922. *3rd. Edn.* Fo. 66 mntd. photogravure plts., pres. label at front, publisher's silk-covered bds. gt., slightly faded. (S. Nov.1; 59)
Armitage. £55

MENON
- [-] La Cuisinière Bourgeoise, suivie de l'Office. Paris, 1771. Cont. cf. (CSK. Feb.24; 118)
£90
- La Science du Maître d'Hôtel, Confiseur, à l'Usage des Officiers ... Paris, 1768. Cont. leath. gt., slightly worn. (GB. Nov.4; 1434)
DM 470
- [-] La Science du Maître d'hôtel Cuisinier. Paris, 1749. *1st. Edn.* Stp. on hf.-title, browned, foxed & soiled, cont. leath. gt., slightly defect. (R. Oct.12; 2038)
DM 460
- [-] Les Soupers de la Cour. Paris, 1778. *New Edn.* 3 vols. Cont. cf., worn. (CSK. Mar.23; 34) £280

MENPES, Mortimer
- Whistler as I knew Him. 1904. *(500) numbered & sigd.* Slight staining, cl. gt., soiled. (P. Sep.29; 7)
£65
- - **Anr. Copy.** 4to. Orig. cl., soiled. (CSK. Sep.16; 55)
£50

MENSING, Ant. W.M.
- Catalogue of the Very Valuable & Important Library. 1936-37. 2 vols. 4to. Sale catalogue, erratum & Addenda lf. loosely inserted, cl.: H.M. Nixon coll., with some MS. notes. (BBA. Oct.6; 157)
Laywood. £60

MENTELLE, Edme
See— MIRABEAU, Honoré Gabriel Riquetti, Comte de & Mentelle, Edme

MENTZEL, Albert & Roux, Albert
- Formes Nues. Ill.:- after Brassai, Man Ray, Platt Lynes, List, & others. Paris, 1935. 4to. Spiral-bnd. pict. wraps., rubbed & chipped. (SG. May 10; 97)
$300

MENZEL, Adolphe von
- Die Armee Friedrichs des Grossen in ihrer Uniformirung. Ed.:- F. Skarbina & C. Jany. Berlin, [1906-08]. 2 vols. Lge. fo. Vol. 1 lacks 1 plt. & 1 text lf., all plts. mntd. on bd.-ll., 8 plts. & several text ll. slightly foxed, some ll. lightly creased, loose ll. in orig. linen box, 1 spine torn, wear & scratches; Pres. copy with L. dtd. 4.1v.1908. (H. May 22; 431)
DM 1,600

MENZEL, C.A.
- [-] Geschichte Schlesiens. Breslau, [1808-10]. 3 pts. & supp. in 3 vols. 4to. Title with MS. dedication, 2 titles with sm. defects., 1 copper engr. mntd., 3 copper engrs. with bkd. tears, slightly foxed, mid 19th. C. marb. bds., corners bumped. (HK. Nov.8; 11i2)
DM 850

MENZIES, Sir Robert
- Winston Churchill: A Tribute ... Melbourne, 1965. *(500).* Orig. cl.; inscr. & sigd. (KH. Nov.8; 81)
Aus. $120

MENZIES, William
- Catalogue of Books, Manuscripts & Engravings. Ed.:- Joseph Sabin. N.Y., 1875. Lge. 8vo. Priced thro.-out, hf. mor., orig. wraps. bnd. in. (SG. Jan.5; 227)
$100
- The History of Windsor Great Park & Windsor Forest. L., 1864. Fo. 20 orig. mntd. photos. (including frontis.), 2 folding maps, 1 with portion torn away but present, frontis. loose & frayed, margins stained, spotted, hf. mor., worn; pres. copy. (S. Apr.10; 555)
Elliott. £70
- - **Anr. Copy.** Fo. 2 folding maps, 20 mntd. albumen photographs, some fading & foxing, especially at edges, gt.-lettered hf. leath., disbnd. (SG. Nov.10; 109)
$450

MERAY, Antony
See— NUS, Eugene & Meray, Antony

MERCATOR, Gerard
- Atlas Minor. Ca. 1630. Ob. 4to. 188 uncol. maps, no title or prelims., 24 maps with repairs, 5 with some loss of plt. surface, some dampstains, mod. bds. (P. Jul.26; 230)
£1,700
- L'Atlas on Meditations Cosmographiques de la Fabrique du Monde et Figure diceluy. Amst., J. Hondius, 1609. *1st. Edn. in Fr.* Fo. Architectural engraved title, 4 engraved sectional titles, 147 map-sheets, all but 1 double-p., hand-cold. in wash & outl., titles highlighted with gold, some mapsheets split at centrefold without loss of engraved surface, some soiling or faint browning, mostly affecting blank margins, last few index ll. frayed & detchd., orig. vell. gt., soiled, lacks ties. (S. Dec.1; 185)
Phila. Prints. £10,400
- Atlas sive Cosmographicae Meditationes de Fabrica Mvndi et Fabricati Figvra. Amst., 1613. *4th. Edn.* Fo. Lacks 1 coll. map & blank lf., map versos with text, 1 engraved sub-title bnd. inverted, engraved general title reprd. & partly bkd., 30 maps & 15 text ll. reprd. in margins, browned & lightly soiled thro.-out, cont. cf. gt., worn & bumped; F.C. Koch liby. ex-libris, Hauswedell coll. (H. May 24; 873)
DM 42,000
- - **Anr. Edn.** Amst., 1623. *5th. Edn.* Fo. A tall copy, Latin text, architectural engraved title, double port. of Mercator & Hondius, 4 engraved sectional titles & 156 mapsheets (all but 1 double-p.), some light browning, cont. cf., gt.-panel, lge. central arabesques, w.a.f. (S. May 21; 103)
Casten. £6,800
- - **Anr. Copy.** Fo. In Latin, architectural engraved title, 4 engraved sectional titles, double-p. port., 156 mapsheets, all but 1 double-p., hand-cold. in wash & outl. thro.-out, a few mapsheets damaged by green paint, affecting engraved surface, 1 or 2 creases or tears, browned thro.-out, cont. vell. gt., soiled. (S. Dec.1; 187)
Schuster. £2,700
- - **Anr. Edn.** Maps:- after Mercator, Hondius & others. Amst., Johannes Cloppenburgh, 1632. *2nd. Cloppenburgh Edn.* Ob. 4to. Latin text, engraved title, & 179 full-p. engraved maps (many sigd. by Pieter van den Keere), additional map. 'Frisia Occidentalis' at Hhh2 (p. 431) not called for in Koeman but listed in index, a few ll. browned, sm. margin wormhole touching 1 or 2 outer neat-lines, titles & last few ll. creased & slightly stained or soiled, sm. owners inscr. on front pastedown, cont. vell., worn & slightly soiled, w.a.f. (S. May 21; 104)
T. Schuster. £2,400
- Historia Mundi, or Mercator's Atlas. Ed.:- J. Hondius. Trans.:- W. S[altonstall]. L., 1635. Sm. fo. Engraved title has the second imprint of Michaell Sparke, the words 'Second Edytion' added, & dtd. 1639, lacks the maps of New England & Valesia (the former replaced with dupl.), lacks pp. 403-8 (never ptd.?) & all after 4N4, engraved title mntd., 18th. C. spr. cf. (SG. Nov.3; 101)
$2,000

MERCEREAU, Alexandre
- La Conque Miraculeuse. Ill.:- Albert Gleizes. Paris, 1921. 4to. Some foxing, leaves, wrap. (HD. Jun.13; 72)
Frs. 1,600

MERCIER, Louis Sebastien
- Tableau de Paris. Amst., 1738-88. *New Edn.* 12 vols. in 8. Later hf. roan. (HD. Feb.22; 139)
Frs. 4,200

MERCKLIN (or Mercklein), G.A.
- Tractatio Med. Curiosa, de Ortu & Occasu Transfusionis Sanguinis ... Nürnberg, 1679. *1st. Edn.* Some spotting, frontis. cut close & outer margin slightly defect., cont. vell., slightly spotted, sm. fault in upr. cover. (R. Oct.12; 1439) DM 560

MERCURE FRANCOIS (LE) ou, la Suite de l'Histoire de la Paix
Geneva, Cologne & Paris, 1619-15-37. *Mixed Edns.* Vols. I-XVIII & XX & dupl. of Vol. XVIII, together 20 vols. Some gatherings loose, some browning, Vols. I-XVIII unif. vell. gt., dupl. Vol. XVIII cf., worn, Vol. XX plain vell., some vols. a little rubbed; most. vols. with inscr. on title-p. 'A l'usage des Capucins de Pertius Donné par Mr le

MERCURE FRANCOIS (LE) ou, la Suite de l'Histoire de la Paix -*Contd.*
Baron des Bras 1881', the Phillipps copy with pressmark in ink & MHC in pencil, as a periodical, w.a.f. (S. Nov.17; 48)   *Lyon.* £700

MERCURI, Paolo
See— BONNARD, Camillo & Mercuri, Paolo

MERCURIALIS, Hieronymus
– De Arte Gymnastica. Ill.:– Cristoforo Coriolano. Venice, 1573. *2nd. Edn.* Sm. 4to. Some foxing & staining, cont. vell., spotted, some worming, soiled. (CBA. Dec.10; 321) $750
– – **Anr. Edn.** Paris, 1577. *2nd. Edn.* 4to. 23 full-p. woodcuts, blank outer corners of most ll. inkstained, mod. antique style cf., raised bands. (SG. Apr.19; 128) $350
– – **Anr. Copy.** Sm. 4to. Title lf. stpd., 2 ills. with sm. hole, some mispagination, some ll. wormed in upr. corner, 1st. 3 ll., including title, strengthened in inner margin, slightly crumpled & with sm. bkd. faults in upr. margin. (HT. May 8; 179)
                    DM 1,000
– – **Anr. Edn.** Venice, 1601. 4to. Final blank, lr. corners at end lightly stained, cont. limp vell., slightly worn & soiled. (S. May 10; 333)
                    Henderson. £240

MERCURIO, Scipione
– La Commare o Raccoglitrice ... con il Colosto ... di Pietro di Castro ... nuovamente acresiuta ... di due Tratatti cioe del Parto Settimestre, & Fascino Naturale de Faniculli da Rannutio Arragoni. Verona, 1664-54. 3 pts. in 1 vol. 4to. Cont. vell. (SI. Dec.15; 166)   Lire 480,000

MERCURIO PERUANO
[Lima], 1791. Vol. I nos. 1-17. 4to. With supplementary glossary of mineralogy (pp. 73-89) in no. 9, & the 3 ll. of additional subscribers bnd. after no. 9, Prospectus ([Lima], 1790) bnd. in, some foxing, some worming, mostly marginal, early qtr. cf., spine chipped. (SG. Oct.20; 221) $300

MERCURIUS, Trismegistus
See— HERMES, Trismegistus

MEREA, G.
– Ademaro Ovvero Corsica Liberata Poema Eroico. Ill.:– S. Merellus (frontis.). Lucca, 1723. Cont. vell.; D. de Auria ex-libris. (HD. Oct.21; 124)
                    Frs. 3,000

MEREAU, Sophie
[–] Das Blüthenalter der Empfindung. Ill.:– Dan. Chodowiecki. Gotha, 1794. *1st. Edn.* Col. papercovered bds., unc. (HK. Nov.10; 2597)   DM 700

MEREDITH, D.
– The Grasses & Pastures of South Africa. Johannesburg, 1955. *(300) numbered.* Mor. (SSA. Jul.5; 271)   R 230

MEREDITH, George
– Modern Love & Poems of the English Roadside ... L., 1862. *1st. Edn.* 12mo. Orig. cl., spine gt., some wear; author's copy, with holograph corrections & revisions, Paul Lemperly bkplt., Frederic Dannay copy. (CNY. Dec.16; 234) $1,200
– Poems. L., [1851]. *1st. Edn.* 12mo. Errata slip, sm. stain on dedication lf. & b1, orig. cl., blocked in blind; sigd. by author, Clement K. Shorter bkplt., Frederic Dannay copy. (CNY. Dec.16; 232) $600
– – **Anr. Copy.** 12mo. Errata slip, orig. cl., blocked in blind, sm. tear in spine; Newton Hall, Camb., bkplt., Frederic Dannay copy. (CNY. Dec.16; 233)
                    $280
– – **Anr. Copy.** Sm. 8vo. Hf.-title, errata slip, slightly browned, orig. cl., mor. solander case; sig. of Bayard Taylor, Perry Molstad copy. (SPB. May 16; 500) $225
[–] A Tour to the Rhine. 1825. *(25).* Lacks hf.-title, cont. mor. gt., decor., lightly rubbed, watered silk doubls., vell. end-ll. (CSK. Jan.13; 160)   £95
– The Works ... L., 1909-11. *Memorial Edn.* 27 vols. Hf. mor. (KH. Nov.9; 340)   Aus. $260

MEREDITH, Louisa Anne, née Twamley
– Notes & Sketches of New South Wales ... L., 1844. 2 pp. of advts. at end, cl.-bkd. bds. (CA. Apr.3; 85)   Aus. $150

– Our Island Home, a Tasmanian Sketchbook ... 1879. Fo. No bdg. stated. (JL. Jun.24; 99)
                    Aus. $525
– Over the Straits; A Visit to Victoria. L., 1861. Hf. leath., marb. bds. (JL. Jun.24; 131)   Aus. $220
– The Romance of Nature; The Flower-Seasons Illustrated. 1836. *2nd. Edn.* Hand-cold. ornamental title, 26 plts., cont. mor. gt., heavily rubbed on spine. (TA. Aug.18; 1)   £65
– – **Anr. Copy.** 27 hand-cold. plts., including title, mor. gt., rubbed. (P. Feb.16; 94)   £60
– Some of my Bush Friends in Tasmania. L., 1860. Fo. Chromolitho. title & 14 plts., spotted thro.-out, cont. hf. mor., rubbed. (BBA. May 3; 298)
                    Morrell. £130
– Tasmanian Friends & Foes ... L., 1880. *1st. Edn.* Sm. 4to. Weakness in sewing, orig. cl. (KH. Nov.9; 655)   Aus. $450
– – **Anr. Edn.** L., 1881. *2nd. Edn.* 4to. Slight foxing, some offsetting on to plts., orig. cl., a couple of sm. defects to cl. (KH. Nov.9; 342)   Aus. $230

MERELLO, M.
– Della Guerra dei Francesi e dei Tumulti Suscitati poi da Sampiero dalla Bastelica nella Corsica ... Genova, 1607. 4to. Cont. vell.; D. de Auria ex-libris. (HD. Oct.21; 125)   Frs. 9,500

MERELO, J., y Casademunt
– Tratado Completo de la Escrima del Sable Español. Toledo, 1862. 4 folding litho. plts., orig. mor. gt. pres. bdg., upr. cover stpd. in gt. 'Al Exceno. Sr. Marques del Duero El Autor.' (CSK. Nov.4; 134)   £75

MERIAN, Caspar
– Solemnis Electionis et Inaugurationis Leopoldi Romanor. Imperatoris Augusti Descriptio & Repraesentatio. Frankfurt a. M., Caspar Merian, 1660. Fo. Text in German & Fr., numerals on pp. 19-20 & 81-82 omitted, engr. of Emperor's crown on title, folding heraldic plt. with port. of Emperor, 7 ports. of Electors, 14 engraved plts. (mostly lge. folding), sm. repair in middle of plt. 6, plt. 9 slightly frayed at extreme outer margin, cont. vell., gt. oval central ornament, lacks ties. (S. May 10; 334)
                    Loeb. £2,600

MERIAN, Maria Sibylla
– Dissertatio de Generatione et Metamorphosibus Insectorum Surinamensium. Dissertation sur la Generation ... des Insectes de Surinam. Den Haag, 1726. Lge. fo. Wide margin, Latin-Fr. parallel text, lacks hf.-title, 18 copper engrs. with stain in upr. right corner, 8 copper engrs. browned, 5 copper engrs. & 2 text ll. loose, some brown spotting in text, cont. cf., worn, corners bumped, spine defect. (H. May 22; 180)   DM 23,000
– Erucarum Ortus, Alimentum et Paradoxa Metamorphosis. Amst., [1718]. *1st. Latin Edn.* 4to. Lacks engraved port. & 3 title copper engrs., slightly browned, some light foxing, cont. leath. gt., bumped, jnts. brkn. (R. Apr.4; 1759) DM 12,600
– Histoire Générale des Insectes de Surinam et de toute l'Europe. Ed.:– Buchoz. Paris, 1771. *3rd. Edn.* 3 pts. in 1 vol. Lge. fo. Some copper engrs. cut slightly close, vol. 1 title with erased owners mark, vol.II title with upr. corner restored, some ll. slightly stained, cont. leath. gt., spine slightly reprd. & with sm. tear, light scuffing. (D. Nov.23; 449)
                    DM 32,500
– Metamorphosis Insectorum Surinamensium. Ofte Verandering der Surinaamsche Insecten. Amst., [1705]. *Dutch Edn.* Fo. 60 uncold. engraved plts., cont. MS. astrological tables & diagrams in Russian on some plt. versos, plt. 35 with heavy Russian inscr. at foot, dampstained & soiled thro.-out, plt. 5 badly stained & frayed, plt. 29 torn across, several margin tears, stitching brkn. & text & plts. disbnd., cont. cf., very worn & defect., lacks spine, w.a.f. (S. Nov.28; 63)   *Schuster.* £2,800
– – **Anr. Copy.** Wide margin, cont. marb. cf. gt., spine & corners partly restored., Hauswedell coll. (H. May 24; 850)   DM 47,000
– Over de Voortteeling en Wonderbaerlyke Veranderingen der Surinaemsche Insecten. Amst., 1719. Fo. Hand-cold. engraved frontis., 72 hand-cold. engraved plts., some browning & spotting, mostly affecting text, 1st. plt. trimmed at fore-edge, cont. elab. gt.-panel. cf. [by Georg Christoph Stoy of

Augsburg], recently rebkd., gt. floral patterned endpapers. (S. Nov.28; 62)   *Schuster.* £8,400

MERIAN, Matthaeus
– Bybel Printen, vertoonende de Voornaemste Historien der Heylige Schrifture ... Amst., ca. 1640. 3 pts. in 1 vol. Sm. fo. 260 copper engraved figures, cont. mor., blind dentelle, decor. spine, sm. defects. (HD. Jan.30; 71)   Frs. 2,300
– La Danse des Morts, comme elle est depeinte dans la Louable et Celebre Ville de Basle ... Todten-Tanz, wie derselbe in der Löbl ... Stadt Basel ... Ill.:– J.A. Chovin after Merian. Basel, 1789. *3rd. Chovin Edn.* Sm. 4to. Engraved title dtd. 1744, verses Fr. & German, some slight browning, hand-bnd. mod. mor., leath. inlays on both covers, ex-libris inside cover, coll. stp. on prelim. lf. (H. May 22; 460)
                    DM 1,500
– Historiae Sacrae Veteris et Novi Testamenti./ Bybelische Figuren. Ed.:– P.H. Schut. Amst., Ca. 1660. 3pts. in 1 vol. Ob. 4to. Some paper excisions in plts. bkd. along lr. plt. margin, lacks 4 copperplts.; prelims., 1st. 5 ll., & approx. 10 end lr. partly bkd., soiled, 19th. C. hf. leath., clasps. (R. Oct.12; 2233)
                    DM 1,520
– Theatrum Europaeum. Ed.:– J. Ph. Abelinus,. Frankfurt, 1644-1707 & n.d. *Various Iss.* Vols. I-XVI. Fo. 16 engraved titles, 59 double-p. or folding maps, 716 (of 773) partly double-p. or folding copperplts., 361 (of 370) text copper engrs., ports., 4 genealogical plts. vol. XVI, 10 plts. with tear, 1 loose, vol. IV stained & spotted thro.-out, vol. VII with hole thro.-out in last pt., vol. I & IX some ll. with frayed margins, vol. XIV brown spot in upr. margin thro.-out, some light browning, cont. vell., slightly spotted, especially vols. III & IV, vol. XIV very browned, 2 vols. with sm. defects.; all vols. with engraved ex-libris. (H. May 22; 228)
                    DM 56,000
– Todten-Tantz, wie derselbe in der Löblichen Statt Basel ... zu sehen ist. [Frankfurt, priv. ptd., 1696]. *2nd. Edn.* 4to. Lacks pp. 1-8, some light spotting, several bkd. tears, 1 p. with sm. corner tear, last lf. pasted over in fold, cont. vell., slightly spotted; coll. stp. inside cover. (H. May 22; 459)   DM 420

MERIAN, Matthaeus (Ill.)
See— ZEILLER, Martin

MERIDA, Carlos
– Carnavales de Mexico. Mexico, 1940. *(500).* Fo. Title lf. & 10 cold. lithos., ex-liby., loose in cl.-bkd. bd. folder, linen ties. (SG. May 3; 252) $200

MERIGOT, James
– Promenade ou Itineraire des Jardins d'Ermenonville. Paris, 1788. 1 vol. 25 engraved plts., 2 engraved ll. of mus. notat. on blue paper, cont. tree cf. gt., spine extremities chipped; John Leigh Philips ex-libris. (*With:*) – Promenades ou Itineraire des Jardins de Chantilly. Paris, 1791. 1 vol. L.P., engraved folding plan, 20 plts., orig. bds., spine chipped. (C. Dec.9; 102)   *Henderson.* £450
[–] A Select Collection of Views & Ruins in Rome & its Vicinity. Ca. 1819. 4to. Engl. & Fr. text, aquatint title & 61 plts., mod. hf. cf. (CSK. Jul.6; 1) £140
– – **Anr. Edn.** N.d. 4to. Frontis., 61 tinted aquatints, bds., unc. (S. Nov.1; 80)   *Lacquaforte.* £160
– – **Anr. Copy.** 4to. Aquatint title, 61 aquatint plts. (dtd. 1797), hf. mor. gt., rubbed. (P. Jul.5; 126)
                    £130

MERIMEE, Prosper
– Carmen. Trans.:– A.E. Johnson. Ill.:– Rene Bull. L., ca. 1910. *(100) sigd. by artist.* 4to. Gt.-decor. parch., covers & contents slightly darkened. (CBA. Aug.21; 72) $140
– – **Anr. Edn.** Trans.:– Elfriede Willis. Ill.:– H. Steiner-Prag. 1920. *(430). (XXX) (here (20)) numbered special De Luxe Edn.* Orig. litho. title & 19 orig. lithos., including 11 full-p. mntd. on japan sigd. & with remarks, orig. burgundy mor., goldtooled, gt. decor., orig. s.-c., defect. (GB. May 5; 3365)   DM 1,300
– – **Anr. Edn.** Ill.:– L. Courbouleix. Paris, 1929. *(5) numbered De Luxe Edn. on Japan with various states of etchings.* 4to. Partly with remarks & col. trials, with copper plt. for 1 etching, leaves in hf. leath., cover, lightly worn, orig. wraps. (HK. May 17; 2659)   DM 550
– – **Anr. Edn.** Ill.:– Clave. Paris, 1946. Sm. 4to. On-

Arches, slight foxing, leaves, wrap., box. (HD. Mar.27; 93) Frs. 2,200
– – **Anr. Edn.** Ill.:– Barta. Paris, 1952. *(23) on japon nacré with 5 orig. gouaches & suite in bistre.* 4to. Blind-decor. red mor. by Semet & Plumelle, cf. liners, watered silk end-ll., s.-c. (HD. Jun.13; 77) Frs. 13,000
– **La Carosse du Saint-Sacrement.** Ill.:– Louis Jou. Paris, 1921. *(150) on vélin d'Arches.* 4to. 15 orig. woodcuts, mor. gt. by G. Mercier, spine decor., mor. doubls., wrap. & spine preserved, s.-c.; member's copy with separately ptd. suite on vélin d'Arches, in 3 states, bnd. in hf. mor. (HD. May 4; 358) Frs. 7,100
– **Chronique du Règne de Charles IX.** Ill.:– Edouard Morin. Paris, 1876. *(115) with added suite of ills. on japan by Toudouze for 1889 Testar Edn.* 2 vols. Mor., spine decor., wrap. preserved. (HD. Jun.13; 73) Frs. 4,200
– – **Anr. Edn.** Ill.:– Ed. Morin. Paris, 1876. *(115) numbered.* 2 vols. 4to. Red mor. by Cuzin, spine raised bands (1 defect.), wrap. preserved. (SM. Mar.7; 2181) Frs. 1,300
– – **Anr. Edn.** Ill.:– Ed. Toudouze. Paris, 1889. Cont. bradel hf. mor., decor. & mosaic spine, corners, unc., wrap. preserved, by Ch. Meunier. (HD. Feb.17; 101) Frs. 3,000
– – **Anr. Edn.** Ill.:– Joseph Hemard. [Paris], 1927. *(640) numbered on vélin de Rives.* Lge. 4to. Lev. gt., lge. onlaid arabesque on both covers, wide gt. dentelles, satin doubls. & end-ll., orig. wraps. bnd. in. (SG. Feb.16; 200) $250
– **La Double Méprise.** Ill.:– Bertrand. Paris, 1902. *(150) on Marais.* Mor. gt. by Noulhac, spine decor., silk liners & end-ll., wrap.; with A.L.s., Cannes, 4 Apr. [1869]. (HD. Jun.13; 75) Frs. 5,500
– – **Anr. Copy.** Cont. mor., decor. & mosaic spine, gt. & mosaic cover decor., inner dentelle, wrap & spine preserved, by Champs-Stroobants. (HD. Feb.17; 104) Frs. 4,000
– **Nouvelles, La Mosaïque ...** Ill.:– Aranda, Beaumont, Bramtot & others. Paris, 1887. *(100) on holland.* Mor. gt. by Kauffman-Horclois, spine decor., s.-c. (HD. Jun.13; 74) Frs. 4,200

MERIVALE, Charles
– **A History of the Romans Under the Empire.** L., 1860-62. 7 vols. Lge. 8vo. Some foxing, cf. gt. by Bickers, spines gt. (SG. Feb.16; 201) $275

MERLINUS COCAIUS (Pseud.)
See— FOLENGO, Teofilo 'Merlinus Cocaius'

MERRILL, James
– **First Poems.** N.Y., 1951. *1st. Edn. (990) numbered.* Orig. cl., d.-w.; pres. copy from author to Esther King, Frederic Dannay copy. (CNY. Dec.16; 235) $420

MERRITT, A.
– **The Face in the Abyss.** N.Y., [1931]. *1st. Edn.* Bdg. not stated, d.-w. chipped at spine, soiled to rear portion, clipped; covers lightly soiled. (CBA. Oct.29; 564) $190

MERRY, William
– **Transportation Considered in Connexion with a System of Previous Reformatory Instruction in Separate Confinement.** Reading, 1848. Disbnd. (KH. May 1; 486) Aus. $160

MERSENNE, Marin
– **Correspondance (1617-1640).** Ed.:– P. Tannery & C. de Waard. Paris, 1945-67. 10 vols. 1st. 2 vols. 8vo., rest 4to. No bdg. stated. (B. Jun.21; 398) Fls. 650

MERTENE, Edmond
– **Commentarius in Regulam S.P. Benedicti Litteralis, Moralis, Historicus.** Paris, 1690. *1st. Edn.* 4to. Cont. cf., worn. (SG. Oct.27; 217) $140

MERULA, Paulus
– **Cosmographiae Generalis Libri Tres: item Geographiae Particularis Libri Quatuor.** [Leiden], 1605. 4to. Europa map with sm. tear, some slight foxing, cont. blind-tooled pig, lacks ties. (D. Nov.23; 768) DM 1,800

MERVEILLES DES CHATEAUX DE FRANCE
Paris, v.d. 11 vols. Fo. No bdg. stated. (SPB. Nov.30; 288) $400

MERY, J.
– **Les Etoiles, Dernière Féerie.** Ill.:– Geoffroy & 'Grandville'. Paris, Leipzig, [1849]. *1st. Printing.* Polychrome & gt. decor. publishers cl., by Haarhaus. (HD. Mar.14; 44) Frs. 4,300
– – **Anr. Edn.** Ill.:– 'Grandville'. Paris, Leipzig, [1858]. Cont. hf. chagrin, decor. spine. (HD. Mar.14; 45) Frs. 2,100

MERYMAN, Richard
– **Andrew Wyeth.** Boston, 1968. *1st. Edn. (1000) numbered.* Ob. fo. Two-tone linen, d.-w., orig. shipping box. (HA. Nov.18; 92) $160
– – **Anr. Edn.** Cont. gilt inscr. at top corner of hf. title, 2-tone linen, d.-w., orig. shipping box. (HA. May 4; 336) $110

MESONERO ROMANOS, R. de
– **Manuel de Madrid.** Madrid, 1831. Linen. (DS. Apr.27; 2182) Pts. 25,000

MESUE, Johannes
– **Canones Universales ... de Consolatione Medicinarum ...** [Venice, 15 July 1513]. Name erased from title, bds. (fragment of early ptd. book); Dr. Walter Pagel copy. (S. Feb.7; 259) *Phelps.* £160

METCALF, G.L.
– **A Collection of Some of the Most Interesting Narratives of Indian Warfare in the West, Containing an Account of the Adventures of Daniel Boone.** Lexington, Kentucky, 1821. Cont. sigs. on title, some discolouration & stains, cont. sheep, spine slightly wormed & reprd. [Sabin 48166] (S. May 22; 329) *Maggs.* £400

METEREN, Emanuel Van
– **Historien der Nederlanden, Oorlogen tot 1612.** Amst., 1647. Fo. Cf., top of spine a little defect. (VG. May 3; 571) Fls. 675
– – **Anr. Edn.** Amst., 1652. Fo. Engraved title, ports. in text, faint marginal staining, sm. stain on title, cont. blind-ruled vell., worn, lacks clasps. (S. Apr.10; 326) *Jones.* £90

METEYARD, Eliza
– **Choice Examples of Wedgwood Art.** L., 1879. *1st. Edn.* Fo. 28 mntd. plts., ex-liby., rebnd. in cl. (SG. May 3; 84) $140

METHODIST HISTORY OF VICTORIA & TASMANIA
Melbourne, 1899, 1901, n.d. 3 vols. Fo. Collations uncertain, 1st. vol. with some external wear & staining, 1 other bd. a little marked. (KH. Nov.9; 343) Aus. $280

METHODIUS, Saint, attributed to
– **Revelationes.** Trans.:– W. Aytinger. Basle, 1504. 19th. C. hf. chagrin, corners; from Fondation Furstenberg-Beaumesnil. (HD. Nov.16; 137) Frs. 30,000

METIUS, Adrien
– **Arithmaticae Libri Duo: et Geometriae Libri VI.** Leyden, 1640. 4to. Cont. bdg. (HD. Apr.13; 72) Frs. 1,300

METMAN & Vaudoyer
– **Le Bronze, Le Cuivre, L'Etain, Le Plomb: Premième Album – Du Moyen Age au Milieu du XVIIIe Siècle; Deuxième Album – Du Milieu du XVIIIe au Milieu du XIXe Siècle.** Paris, ca. 1910. 2 vols.; comprising 2nd. pt. of Musée des Arts Decoratifs 'Le Metal' series. Sm. fo. 166 plts., loose as iss., cl.-bkd. bd. folder. (SG. Aug.25; 70) $175

METRONOMO (EL). Semanario Musical y Literario
Ed.:– J.A. Clavé. Barcelona, 1863-64. Nos. 1-57. Fo. Sewed. (DS. Mar.23; 2188) Pts. 100,000

METROPOLITAN IMPROVEMENTS. First (Second) Report from the Select Committee
1838. Fo. 1 engraved map & 40 litho. plans & maps, most folding, some partly hand-cold., some ll. rather soiled, disbnd. (BBA. Jun.14; 331) *Levy.* £80

METROPOLITAN MUSEUM OF ART
– **Pennsylvania German Designs: a Portfolio of Silk Screen Prints.** Ed.:– Benjamin Knotts. [N.Y.,

1943]. Sm. fo. 20 cold. plts., each liby.-stpd. on blank verso, loose in bd. folder. (SG. May 3; 277) $150

METZDORF, Robert F. (Ed.)
See— TINKER, Chauncey Brewster

METZGAR, Judson D.
– **Adventures in Japanese Prints.** Los Angeles, [Grabhorn Pr., 1943]. *1st. Edn. (300) L.P.* Sm. fo. Cl.-bkd. patterned bds., covers slightly soiled, spine label stained. (SG. Aug.4; 139) $240

METZGER, J.B.
– **Itinera Christi, of Geographische Beschryvinge van het Heilige Land.** Ill.:– Visscher (maps). Amst., 1711. 24 engraved town plans, 4 maps, cont. vell., soiled. (CSK. May 4; 43) £240

METZINGER, J.
See— GLEIZES, A. & Metzinger, J.

MEUNG, Jean de
See— LORRIS, Guillaume de & Meung, Jean de

MEUNIER, Charles
– **Cent Reliures de la Bibliothèque Nationale.** Paris, 1914. 4to. Mor.-bkd. cl., orig. wraps. preserved; H.M. Nixon coll., with his MS. notes. (BBA. Oct.6; 95) *Maggs.* £400

MEUNIER, Constantin
– **Au Pays Noir.** Ill.:– engraved by Karl Meunier. Bruxelles, n.d. Fo. 7 orig. etchings, 1 port., 4 pp. text, in sheets, 2 wraps., bds. (LM. Feb.28; 36) B.Frs. 8,500

MEURER, Noé
– **Loci Communes. Aller des Heiligen Roemischen Reichs.** Mainz, 1578. Fo. Cont. stpd. cf., blinddecor., gt.-stpd. episcopal arms (Salzburg?): from Fondation Furstenberg-Beaumesnil. (HD. Nov.16; 138) Frs. 4,200

MEURSIUS, Joannes, i.e. Nicolas Chorier
– **Creta, Cyprus, Rhodus.** Amst., 1675. 3 pts. in 1 vol. Sm. 4to. Cont. vell. bds. (S. Mar.6; 95) *Nicolas.* £110
– – **Anr. Copy.** Some slight browning, cont. vell. bds., slightly soiled. (S. Dec.13; 183) *Oneill.* £90
– – **Anr. Copy.** 3 pts. in 1 vol. 4to. Mod. cl. (CSK. Aug.5; 128) £50
– **Histoire Générale du Dauphiné.** Grenoble, 1661, Lyon, 1672. *Orig. Edns.* 2 vols. 4to. 19th. C. red mor. (HD. Feb. 29; 8) Frs. 7,500
– **Denarius Pythagoricus.** Leiden, 1631. 4to. Foxed, underscoring, cont. vell. (SG. Oct.6; 255) $100
See— FORTUNATUS, Patavinus Monachus – MEURSIUS, Joannes

MEUSNIER DE QUERLON, A.G.
– **Les Graces.** Paris, 1769. 4to. Red mor., gt.-tooled, sigd. by Delorme, box. (DS. Oct.28; 2081) Pts. 24,000

MEXICO
– **Reglamento para el Gobierno Interior de la Soberana Junta Provisional Gubernativa del Imperio Mexicano.** Mexico City, 1821. 4to. Unlettered wraps. (SG. Oct.20; 227) $150

MEXICO ET SES ENVIRONS [Mexico y sus alrededores.] Collection de Vues Monumentales, Paysages et Costumes du Pais Dessinés d'après Nature et Lithographiés par les Artistes Mexicains C. Castro. G. Rodriguez & J. Campillo ...
Mexico, 1869. *New Edn.* Fo. Folding chart & map (some repairs), litho. title, 51 litho. plts. on 47 sheets, text in Spanish & Fr., some foxing & spotting, hf. mor., rubbed, scuffed. (SPB. Dec.14; 67) $4,750

MEY
– **Maximes de Droit Public François.** Amst., 1775. *2nd. Edn.* 6 vols. 12mo. 19th. C. roan. (HD. Feb.22; 140) Frs. 1,500

MEYER, Adolf Bernard
– **Die Hirschgeweih-Sammlung im Koeniglichen Schlosse zu Moritzburg bei Dresden ... mit Allerhoechster Genehmigung und Unterstützung seiner Majestaet des Koenigs Albert von Sachsen.** Dresden, 1887. Fo. Plts. hand-stpd. in margins, minor chipping, loose in portfo. as iss., worn, ex-liby. (RO. Dec.11; 215) $110

MEYER, Alfred Richard
– Lady Hamilton oder die Posen-Emma. Ill.:– G. Grosz. Berlin, [1923]. *(50) De Luxe Edn. with all lithos. sigd. & cold. by ill., printer's mark sigd. by author.* 4to. On Bütten, orig. hf. vell. (H. May 23; 1262) DM 6,200
– – **Anr. Edn.** Ill.:– G. Grosz. [1923]. *(150) numbered De Luxe Edn.* Lge. 4to. 8 orig. lithos. sigd. by artist, slightly foxed thro.-out, orig. hf. vell. (GB. May 5; 2632) DM 4,000
– – **Anr. Copy.** Lge. 4to. Lightly foxed, orig. hf. vell., some light browning; all lithos sigd. by artist. (HK. Nov.11; 3594) DM 3,200

MEYER, B.
See— **GORLING, A., Meyer, B. & Woltmann, A.**
See— **WOLF, Joh. & Meyer, B.**

MEYER, Ernest H.F.
– Geschichte der Botanik. Königsberg, 1854-57. *1st. Edn.* 4 vols. in 2. Foxed, hf. leath. gt., orig wraps bnd. in, some wear; Hauswedell coll. (H. May 24; 846) DM 600

MEYER, Dr Hans
– Les Hautes Andes de L'Equateur. Paris, 1908. 4to. 24 chromolitho. plts., most adhering to the upr. sheet, unbnd. as iss. in orig. portfo. (CSK. Mar.9; 45) £65

MEYER, Henry Leonard
– Coloured Illustrations of British Birds & their eggs. L., 1842-50. 7 vols. 432 litho. plts., most hand-cold., a few plts. slightly shaved, some with loss of numeral, some spotting, hf. cf. (C. Mar.14; 189) *Harris.* £700
– – **Anr. Copy.** 7 vols. 432 litho. plts., most hand-cold., cont. hf. mor. gt. (C. Jun.27; 174) *Lovatt.* £650
– – **Anr. Edn.** 1853. Vol. 3 only. 60 hand-cold. plts., slight spotting, cont. hf. mor., gt.-decor. spine, spine worn. (TA. Dec.15; 171) £55
– – **Anr. Edn.** 1853-57. 7 vols. Cont. hf. mor. (SSA. Sep.21; 281) R 500
– – **Anr. Copy.** 7 vols. 4to. 432 hand-cold. plts., orig. linen, corners. (DS. Nov.25; 2130) Pts. 100,000
– Illustrations of British Birds. N.d. Plts. approx. 14½ × 10½ inches. 197 hand-cold. lithos. from fo. edn., hf. mor. gt. by Bayntun-Rivière, as a coll. of plts., w.a.f. (LC. Mar.1; 174) £1,000

MEYER, J.
[–] Description du Jubilé de Sept Cens Ans de Saint Macaire, Patron Particulier contre la Peste, qui sera célébré dans la Ville de Gand ... Ill.:– Wauters after Van Reysschoot. Gand, 1767. 4to. Cont. Russian hf. cf., decor. spine, disbnd. (HD. Dec.16; 26) Frs. 1,400

MEYER, J.F.
– Chymische Versuche zur Näheren Erkenntniss des Ungelöschten Kalchs, der Elastischen und Electrischen Materie, des Allerreinsten Feuerwesens, und der Ursprünglichen Allgemeinen Säure. Nebst einem Anhang von den Elementen. Hannover, 1770. *2nd. Edn.* Cont. hf. leath. (R. Oct.12; 1698) DM 460

MEYER, Jacob de Baillolanum
– Comment. sive Annales Rerum Flandricarum Libri XVII. Antw., 1561. Fo. Some scribbling & staining on title & in text, cont. cf., lacks ties. (VG. Sep.14; 1179) Fls. 500
– Compendium Chronicarum Flandriae. Nürnberg, Petreius, 1538. Wide margin, blind-tooled cont.-style leath. (V. Oct.1; 3763) DM 430

MEYER, Johann Daniel
– Angenehmer und Nützlicher Zeit-Vertreib mit Betrachtung Curioser Vorstellungen allerhand Kriechender, Fliegender und Schwimmender ... Tiere, als auch ... Scelete oder Bein-Körper. Nürnberg, 1748-52. 2 vols. Fo. Cont. hand-cold. engraved port. frontis., frontis., 100 cont. hand-cold. engraved plts., some slight foxing, cont. panel marb. cf., spines gt., corners slightly bumped, marb. gt. end-papers. (VS. Jun.7; 933) Fls. 4,000

MEYER, Joseph
– Europa in Bildern. Hildburghausen & N.Y., 1834. Ob. 4to. 18 steel engraved or aquatint plts., foxed, cont. bds., upr. cover with lge. ink stain. (HK. May 15; 929) DM 500
– Groschen-Atlas aller Länder und Staaten der Erde. Hildburghausen, [1859]. Ob. 4to. 154 steel engraved maps, most outl. cold., slightly foxed at beginning, some outer margins slightly soiled, cont. hf. leath. (BR. Apr.12; 45) DM 1,200
– Das Grosse Conversations-Lexicon für die Gebildeten Stände. Hildburghausen, 1840-55. 46 vols. & 6 supp. vols. Minimal browning, cont. unif. hf. leath. gt., minimal rubbing & bumping. (HT. May 8; 721) DM 16,000
– – **Anr. Edn.** Leipzig, 1905-09. 20 vols. & 1 supp. vol. Some vols. with light stains, orig. hf. leath. (D. Nov.24; 4333) DM 500
– – **Anr. Edn.** Leipzig & Wien, 1905-13. 21 vols. & 3 Supp. vols. Orig. hf. leath., spine partly slightly faded. (D. Nov.24; 4332) DM 1,300
– – **Anr. Edn.** Leipzig & Wein, 1908-20. 20 vols., continuation vol., 3 supp. vols. & 3 war supps. in 27 vols. Cont. hf. leath. gt. (BR. Apr.12; 989) DM 1,100
– Illustrationen zum Neuen Konversations-Lexikon. Porträts und Ansichten. Ed.:– H.J. Meyer. Hildburghausen, 1860. Lacks 2 steel engraved ports., foxed, cont. hf. linen, rubbed. (R. Oct.12; 2392) DM 1,200
– Konversations-Lexikon. Leipzig & Wien, 1890-92. 16 vols., 1 index & 2 supp. vols. Hf. leath. gt., corners lightly rubbed. (D. Nov.24; 4334) DM 800
– – **Anr. Edn.** Leipzig, 1895-1900. 17 vols. & 3 supp. vols. Orig. hf. leath. gt., spine lightly rubbed. (D. Nov.24; 4331) DM 850
– – **Anr. Edn.** Leipzig & Wien, 1897-1901. *5th. Edn.* 18 main & 3 supp. vols. in 21 vols. Not collated, hf. leath. gt., slightly rubbed. (R. Apr.3; 657) DM 1,200
– Universum. Hildburghausen & N.Y., 1833-60. *Various Edns.* 21 vols. in 11. 18 (of 21) engraved titles, 998 (of 999) steel-engraved plts., Vol. 2 lacks index, some foxing, heavier in early vols., marb. bds. gt. (V. Sep.29; 81) DM 7,700
– – **Anr. Edn.** Amst., 1834-41. 6pts. in 3 vols. Ob. 4to. 282 steel engraved plts., title lf. stpd., lightly foxed, cont. hf. leath. (D. Nov.23; 806) DM 2,400
– – **Anr. Edn.** Trans.:– C. ten Brink & J. Geelhoed. Amst., 1834[-41]. 6 pts. in 2 vols. Lge. ob. 8vo. 2 steel-engraved titles, 282 steel-engraved views, some foxing as usual, cont. hf. chagrin gt., slightly rubbed, 1 vol. loose. (VS. Dec.8; 809) Fls. 1,500
– – **Anr. Edn.** Trans.:– C. ten Brink & others. Amst., 1834-46. Pts. 1-4 & 6-10 only (of 10). Lge. ob. 8vo. 5 steel-engraved frontis., 422 steel-engraved views & plts., some foxing (as usual), Vols. 8 & 10 margin stained, cont. hf. cf. (VS. Dec.8; 808) Fls. 3,600
– – **Anr. Edn.** N.Y. & Amst., 1834-46. 10 vols. Lge. ob. 8vo. 471 steel-engraved views, some plts. or text ll. slightly foxed, some offsetting from text onto plts., hf. cf., slightly rubbed, spines of 2 vols. slightly defect. (B. Jun.21; 533) Fls. 3,200
– – **Anr. Edn.** Hildburghausen, 1835-36. Vols. 2 & 3. Ob. 4to. Slightly foxed, cont. hf. leath. gt., lightly rubbed. (HK. May 15; 933) DM 520
– – **Anr. Edn.** Hildburghausen, 1836. Vol. 3. Foxed, cont. hf. leath. (R. Oct.12; 2398) DM 400
– – **Anr. Edn.** Hildburghausen, 1836-37. Vol. 3 & Fragment of Vol. 4 in 1 vol. 73 steel engraved views, 25 steel engraved plts. from Vol. 4, browned & soiled, cont. hf. leath. (R. Apr.4; 2224) DM 480
– – **Anr. Edn.** Hildburghausen, 1837. Vol. 4. Ob. 4to. Lightly foxed, some plts. oxidised in margin, lightly stained in margin thro.-out, cont. bds. (HK. May 15; 934) DM 480
– – **Anr. Copy.** Vol. 3. Ob. 8vo. Lacks 1 view, slightly foxed & stained, 1 quire loose, orig. hf. cf., slightly rubbed. (VG. Mar.19; 49) Fls. 450
– – **Anr. Edn.** Ed.:– K.A. Nicander. Stockholm, 1838-41. Vols. I-IV in 4 vols. 3 (of 4) engraved titles with vig., 191 (of 192) steel engraved plts., Vol. II lacks 6 pp., 1 plt. defect. & bkd., vol. IV 5 plts. slightly cockled, some browning & slight foxing, cont. hf. leath., slightly rubbed & bumped. (HT. May 10; 2835) DM 1,100
– – **Anr. Copy.** Vols. I-IV. Ob. 4to. Lacks engraved title IV, ptd. title II & 2 pp. in III, some heavy browning, especially vol. I, 1 engr. cut to subject & loose, 1 with sm. margin tear, some plts. browned, some spotted, cont. hf. leath., very bumped & worn, lacks 1 spine, 1 spine defect. (H. Nov.23; 319) DM 1,000
– – **Anr. Edn.** Hildburghausen, 1839. Vol. 6. Foxed, cont. bds. (R. Oct.12; 2401) DM 420
– – **Anr. Edn.** Hildburghausen, 1840. Vol. 7. Foxed, cont. bds. (R. Oct.12; 2403) DM 700
– – **Anr. Copy.** Vol. 7. Engraved title & 47 steel engraved views, without vol. 7 contents list, vol. 5 & 6 contents lists bnd. in, 2 plts. loose, cont. hf. leath. (R. Apr.4; 2227) DM 620
– – **Anr. Copy.** Lacks 2 steel engraved views, foxed, cont. linen, corners bumped. (GB. Nov.3; 190) DM 540
– – **Anr. Edn.** Hildburghausen, 1842. Vol. 9. Foxed, cont. hf. leath., bumped. (R. Oct.12; 2404) DM 500
– – **Anr. Edn.** Hildburghausen, 1843. Vol. 10. Engraved title & 46 (of 48) steel engraved views, lacks 2 engrs. & 2 pp., cont. hf. linen. (R. Apr.4; 2229) DM 550
– – **Anr. Copy.** Vol. 10. Foxed, cont. hf. leath., bumped. (R. Oct.12; 2405) DM 460
– – **Anr. Edn.** Amst., 1843. Pt. 7. Ob. 8vo. Engraved title & 47 views, few plts. foxed, hf. cf. (VG. May 3; 398) Fls. 475
– – **Anr. Edn.** Stockholm, 1847. *2nd Edn.* Vol. 3. Some plts. loose, cont. hf. linen, rubbed & bumped. (R. Oct.12; 2410) DM 480
– – **Anr. Edn.** Hildburghausen, 1847. Vol. 12. Foxed, cont. hf. linen. (R. Oct.12; 2406) DM 520
– – **Anr. Copy.** Vol. 12. Engraved title & 43 (of 48) steel engraved views, lacks 5, cont. hf. leath. (R. Apr.4; 2230) DM 450
– – **Anr. Edn.** Stockholm, 1849-51. New Series Vols1 1 & 2 in 1 vol. Later hf. leath. (R. Oct.12; 2411) DM 550
– – **Anr. Edn.** Ed.:– C.A. Dana. N,Y., [1852]. Vol. I only. Ob. 8vo. Additional engraved title, 48 steel-engraved plts., foxed, gt.-decor. cl., worn. (SG. Sep.22; 205) $110
– – **Anr. Edn.** Hildburghausen & N.Y., 1856. Ob. 4to. Lacks 1 steel engraved view., cont. hf. linen, lr. cover defect. (GB. May 3; 16) DM 480
– – **Anr. Edn.** Hildburghausen, 1858. Vol. 1. Orig. linen. (R. Oct.12; 2412) DM 420
– – **Anr. Edn.** Hildburghausen, 1859. Vol. 2. Engraved title, 41 steel engraved plts., orig. linen. (GB. May 3; 181) DM 820
– – **Anr. Copy.** Vol. 3. Stained, orig. linen. (R. Oct.12; 2414) DM 400
– – **Anr. Edn.** Hildburghausen, 1859-60. Vols. 3-5. 121 steel engraved plts., some foxing, cont. linen, spotted. (D. Nov.23; 807) DM 750

MEYER, M. de
– De Volks- en Kinderprent in de Nederlanden van de 15e tot de 20e Eeuw. Antw./Amst., 1962. Fo. Hf. cl., s.-c. (VG. Mar.21; 815) Fls. 650

MEYER, Peter
See— **DUFT, Johannes & Meyer, Peter**

MEYER, Rudolf & Conrad
– Die Menschlichen Sterblichkeit unter dem title Todten-Tanz. Hamburg & Leipzig, 1759. Sm. 4to. Several ills. with light traces of col., 8 pp. misbnd., some pencil margin notes, minimal spotting, cont. cf., worn, slightly spotted; coll. stp. & ex-libris on end-paper. (H. May 22; 462) DM 3,000

MEYER, Thomas
– Blind Date. Ill.:– John Furnival. [Guildford], Circle Pr., 1979. *1st. Edn. (300) sigd.* Sq. 4to. Somerset rag-made paper, 10 full-p. etchings or embossed prints, all initialled by artist, loose folded sheets with prints inserted, as iss., laid into cl.-covered folder, the whole contents in cl.-covered s.-c., orig. card. shipping box. (HA. Feb.24; 232) $130

MEYERS, William H.
– Sketches of California & Hawaii ... Intro. & Notes:– John H. Kemble. San Franc., 1970. *(450).* Fo. Loose-woven cl. over bds. (CBA. Nov.19; 266) $125

MEYNELL, Mrs.
See— **MANSON, J.B. & Meynell, Mrs.**

MEYRICK, Samuel Rush
– A Critical Inquiry into Antient Armour as it Existed in Europe, but particularly in England. L.,

1824. *1st. Edn.* 3 vols. Fo. L.P., engraved title-vigs., additional engraved titles, 10 uncold. & 70 hand-cold. aquatint plts., hand-cold. initials heightened with gold, light offsetting, mod. hf. mor. gt., unc.; Lowther copy with bkplts. on covers. (C. Jun.27; 48) *Houle.* £450
– – **Anr. Copy.** 3 vols. 4to. Hand-cold. engraved frontis. & 80 plts. (60 hand-cold., several heightened with gold), end-papers lightly spotted, cont. hf. mor. gt., extremities rubbed. (CSK. Jun.1; 31) £350
– – **Anr. Edn.** L., 1842. *2nd. Edn.* 3 vols. Fo. Frontis., 79 (of 80) engraved plts., most hand-cold., initials illuminated in cols. & gold, red hf. mor., spines gt., jnts. very scuffed. (SG. Oct.13; 237) $425
– – **Anr. Copy.** 3 vols. Fo. 73 plts., most hand-cold., with details in gold, text initials fully illuminated, lacks plt. of 'Bavarian Jousting Armour', but with unlisted plt. 'Battle of the Locks' included, 1 plt. reprd., contents completely loose & laid into orig. red hf. mor. covers, gt. armorial device designs on spines, liby. bkplt. (SG. Jan.26; 248) $300
See— SHAW, H. & Meyrick, S.R.

MEYRICK, Samuel Rush & Smith, Charles Hamilton
– **The Costume of the Original Inhabitants of the British Islands, from the Earliest Periods to the Sixth Century** ... 1815. Fo. Hand-cold. vig. title, 24 hand-cold. aquatints, recent hf. mor. (TA. Jan.19; 227) £140
– – **Anr. Edn.** 1821. Fo. Hand-cold. aquatint title & 24 plts., cont. hf. mor., rubbed. (CSK. Jul.6; 89a) £80
– – **Anr. Edn.** L., ca. 1830. Fo. Hand-cold. & plated titles, 24 hand-cold. plts., some slight soiling, hf. mor. (GM. Dec.7; 659) £100
– – **Anr. Edn.** Ca. 1831. Fo. Hand-cold. title, 24 hand-cold. plts., no hf.-title, some spotting, hf. mor. (P. Oct.20; 119) £55

MEYRICK, William
– **The New Family Herbal, or Domestic Physician.** 1790. Engraved frontis., 14 engrs., advts., cf., rebkd. (P. Jun.7; 223) £95

MEYRINK, G.
– **Der Golem.** Ill.:– H. Steiner-Prag. Leipzig, [1915]. *1st. Ill. Edn.* 4to. Orig. pict. hf. vell., slightly bumped. (HK. Nov.11; 3994) DM 400

MIALHE, Francisco & Dandiran, F.
– **Excursion dans les Pyrenées.** Paris, [1830?]. 4to. Engraved title, 79 (of 80) litho. plts., spotted, hf. mor. gt., rubbed. (P. Nov.24; 193) *Schuster.* £280

MICALI, Giuseppe
– **Monumenti inediti a Illustrazione della Storia degli Antichi Popoli Italiani.** Firenze, 1844. Fo. Album of 60 engraved plts., some hand-cold., hf. vell. (CR. Jun.6; 54) Lire 200,000

MICHAEL
– **Botica General de Remedios Experimentados** ... Pueblo de Los Angeles, 1796. Vell. (DS. Nov.25; 2506) Pts. 32,000

MICHAILOVITCH, Grand-Duc Georges
– **Monnaies de L'Empire de Russe 1725-1894.** Trans.:– Madame Nadine Tacke. Paris, 1916. 19 pts. in 4 vols. Lge. 4to. Cont. hf. mor. (S. May 1; 480) *Spink.* £1,100

MICHAUD, Joseph
– **Histoire des Croisades.** Ill.:– Gustave Doré. Paris, 1877. *1st. Printing of ills.* 2 vols. Fo. Cont. red hf. mor. gt., spines decor. (HD. May 16; 49) Frs. 2,200

MICHAUD, Louis Gabriel
– **Biographie Universelle Ancienne et Moderne.** Paris, 1811-28. 52 vols. Some foxing, cont. hf. roan, limp decor. spines, spines faded. (HD. Jan.27; 232) Frs. 1,300

MICHAUX, François André
– **Travels to the Westward of the Allegany Mountains** ... L., 1805. Title with sm. tear, map with crease, blind-tooled leath., ca. 1840. [Sabin 48706] (HK. Nov.8; 842) DM 420

MICHAUX, François André & Nuttall, Thomas
– **The North American Sylva.** Ill.:– after the Redoutés & others. Paris, 1819. 3 vols. Lge. 8vo. Light offsetting, some foxing chiefly in text, cont. hf. mor., extremities rubbed. (SG. Mar.22; 228) $930
– – **Anr. Edn.** Ill.:– Bessin, Renard, & others, after Bessa, Redouté, & others. Phila., 1855. 3 vols. Lge. 8vo. 156 full-p. hand-cold. engraved plts., text & some plts. foxed, orig. blind-stpd. mor., worn; the Rt. Hon. Visc. Eccles copy. (CNY. Nov.18; 194) $500
– – **Anr. Edn.** Phila., 1859. 5 vols. Tall 8vo. 277 full-p. hand-cold. & hand-finished plts. (compl.), tissue guards, few plts. lightly dusted or with finger smudges in margins, text with some light foxing, orig. unif. mor., stpd. ornamental designs at all cover panels, raised bands, gt.-lettering, edges & jnts. slightly scuffed, some sm. chips at ends of backstrips, 2 vols. recently recased using orig. covers & backstrips. [Sabin 48695, 56351] (HA. May 4; 269) $650
– – **Anr. Edn.** Phila., 1865. 6 vols. in 5. Steel-engraved frontis. port., 277 hand-cold. litho. plts., three-qtr. mor. (CBA. Dec.10; 350) $600

MICHAUX, Henri
– **Exorcismes.** 1943. *Orig. Edn. 1st. Printing of ills.* (20) on vergé de Rives, with 4-col. drawing, numbered & sigd., suite in col. & suite of rejected drawings. 4to. Sewed; autograph dedication. (HD. Apr.13; 172) Frs. 3,600

MICHEL, Ad.
– **L'Ancienne Auvergne et le Velay. Histoire, Archéologie, Moeurs, Topographie.** Moulins, 1843-47. 4 vols., including Atlas. Fo. Plts., views & ports. erratically numbered, some perforation stps. in text, all plts. hand-stpd. on rectos, cont. leath., ex-liby. (RO. Dec.11; 216) $450

MICHEL, Andre
– **Histoire de l'Art.** Paris, 1905-29. 8 vols. & index in 18 vols. 4to. Some slight spotting, cl., partly unc., soiled. (S. Apr.30; 206) *Zwemmer.* £55

MICHEL, Etienne
– **Traité du Citronier, redigé par M. Etienne Michel, editeur du Nouveau Duhamel.** Ill.:– after P. Bessa. Paris, 1816. Fo. L.P., 21 stipple engraved plts. ptd. in cols., some spotting & minor discolouration, cont. gt.-lettered cl., lacks backstrip. (C. Jun.27; 177) *Schuster.* £650

MICHEL, Francisque & Fournier, Edouard
– **Histoire des Hotelleries, Cabarets** ... Paris, 1859. 2 vols. Lge. 8vo. Cont. hf. chagrin. (HD. Nov.17; 51) Frs. 2,400

MICHEL, Nicholas Leopold
– **Compte Général de la Dépense des Edifices et Bâtiments que le Roi de Pologne.** ... Luneville, 1759. *1st. Edn.* Fo. Engraved title-vig., lge. folding plan, 3 folding plts., cont. hf. cf., spine gt.; liby. stp. of Prince Starhemberg at Schloss Eferding. (C. Dec.9; 103) *Goldschmidt.* £600

MICHELET, F.G.
– **De Zangwijsen der Psalmen Davids ... met Harmonyen op't Orgel.** Amst., [1771]. Ob. 8vo. Cont. cf. (VG. Sep.14; 1011) Fls. 480

MICHELI, Pier Antonio
– **Nova Plantarum Genera iuxta Tournefortii Methodum disposita.** Firenze, 1729. 2 vols. 4to. Later bds. (SI. Dec.15; 167) Lire 1,200,000

MICHELOT, Henry & Brémond, Laurent
– **Recueil de Plusieurs Plans des Ports et Rades de la Mer Méditerrannée.** Ill.:– Starkman. Marseille, [1727-30]. Ob. 8vo. Title-frontis. & 38 plans, cont. roan, worn. (HD. Jul.2; 27) Frs. 3,500

MICHELSON, A.A.
– **Light Waves & their Uses.** Chic., 1903. *1st. Edn.* Inserted slip showing Wesley & Son to be Engl. publishers, cl., spine slightly defect. (SG. Mar.22; 230) $100

MICKS, W.L.
– **History of the Congested Districts Board.** Dublin, 1925. Royal 8vo. Cl.; inscr. by author to Marquis of Sligo. (GM. Dec.7; 442) £90

MICOLLE, Jehan
– **Elucidarius Carminum et Historiarum vel Vocabularius Poeticus.** Ca. 1500. Sm. 4to. Lacks final lf., contents slightly wormed, mod. limp vell., ties. (TA. Sep.15; 424) £70

MIDDIMAN, Samuel
– **Select Views of Great Britain.** [Plts. dtd. 1784-1813]. Ob. 4to. Engraved title, & 53 plts., text in Engl. & Fr., some light spotting, mod. cl. (CSK. Dec.2; 29) £120
– – **Anr. Edn.** L., [1792]. Ob. 4to. Engraved title, 40 plts. (dtd. 1784-92, these dates added to title in pen by early owner), text in Engl. & Fr., some foxing, old red str.-grd. mor. (SG. Sep.22; 206) £110
– – **Anr. Edn.** L., [1800?]. Album, approx. 60 engrs., hf. cf., corners. (CR. Jun.6; 225) Lire 240,000

MIDDLEMISS, G.
– **With the Northumberland ... Volunteers in South Africa, 1900-01.** Alnwick, 1902. Sm. 8vo. Some light foxing, decor. cl., recased. (VA. Apr.27; 856) R 185

MIDDLETON, Charles
[–] **Decorations for Parks & Gardens.** L., [plts. wtrmkd. 1828]. Engraved title, 55 plts., stained, pig, unc., marked, rebkd. (S. Mar.6; 296) *Henderson.* £90

MIDDLETON, Charles Theodore
– **A New & Complete System of Geography.** 1777. Fo. Frontis., 100 plts., 21 maps, some frayed, lacks 2 ll. of table, hf. cf. (P. Sep.8; 41) *Sweet.* £150
– – **Anr. Edn.** [1777-78]. 2 vols. Frontis. torn, 20 maps, many folding, 100 plts., some pp. loose, some tears, sheep, defect., as a coll. of plts., w.a.f. (P. Apr.12; 244) *Burgess.* £240
– – **Anr. Edn.** 1778. 2 vols. Fo. 85 engraved plts. & 18 folding maps only, several cleanly torn or trimmed, title of Vol. 2 lacking, some soiling, old cf., worn, w.a.f. (CSK. May 4; 35) £160
– – **Anr. Edn.** 1780. 2 vols. in 1. Fo. Frontis., 95 maps & plts., hf. cf., worn, as a collection of plts., w.a.f. (P. Sep.8; 105) *Brown.* £160

MIDDLETON, Conyers
– **Bibliotheca Cantabrigiensis Ordinandae Methodus.** Camb., 1723. Lge. 4to. Margin stains, slightly trimmed, later wraps. (SG. Sep.15; 226) $375

MIDDLETON, J.J.
– **Grecian Remains in Italy, a Description of the Cyclopian Walls & of Roman Antiquities.** L., 1820. Fo. Cont. hf. mor., corners, worn. (HD. Jun.6; 110) Frs. 2,700

MIDOLIE, Jean
– **Galerie Compositions, Ecritures Anciennes et Modernes.** Strasbourg, 1834-35. 3 pts. in 1 vol. Ob. fo. Frontis., 118 (of 120?) cold. litho. plts., some slight soiling or foxing, qtr. mor., worn. (SG. Jan.5; 230) $200

MIDRASH
– **Midrash Chamesh Megillot.** Pesaro, 1519. *1st. Edn.* Sm. fo. Song of Songs only, title in facs., margins of most ll. reprd. with loss of some text, slight staining, blind-tooled leath., slightly worn. (S. Oct.25; 265) *Halprin.* £580
– – **Anr. Copy.** Fo. Lacks title-p. (as usual), 1 lf. misbnd., slight staining, some wormholes not affecting text, 1 lf. reprd. in middle, without loss of text, owners' sigs., old sheep, crudely reprd., worn. (SPB. Feb.1; 66) $3,000
– **Midrash Chamesh Megillot Rabbata.** Saloniki, 1594. Fo. Owners' sigs. on title, edges frayed affecting some words, 2 ll. defect. & reprd., with loss of text, stained, browned, hf. mor., marb. paper bds. (S. Oct.25; 266) *Freedman.* £450
– **Midrash Ha'Mechilta.** Venice, 1545. Fo. Title mntd. with losses, slight staining & spotting, mod. cl. (SPB. Feb.1; 67) $400
– **Midrash Rabbah [English].** Ed.:– H. Freedman & M. Simon. L., Soncino Pr., 1961. 10 vols. Cl. (B. Jun.21; 221) Fls. 550
– **Midrash Rabbot.** Amst., 1777. Sm. fo. With commentaries Matnat Kehuna, Yedei Moshe, Kitsur Yefe To'ar, Mishnat Rabbi Eliezer, Zera

MIDRASH -*Contd.*

Avraham, & others, browned, minor stains on both title-pp., cont. tree cf., worn. (SG. Feb.2; 255)
$120

MIEGE, Guy
– A Relation of Three Embassies from His Sacred Majestie Charles II to the Grand Duke of Muscovie, the King of Sweden & the King of Denmark ... in the Years 1663 & 1664. 1669. *1st. Edn.* 8vo. Cl a cancel, 1st. few ll. slightly stained, mod. pol. cf., spine gt. [Wing M2025] (BBA. Jan.19; 157)
Morris. £80
– – **Anr. Copy.** Old cf., spine chipped. [Wing M2025] (CSK. Sep.30; 172)
£60

MIERIS, Frans van
– Beschrijving der Stad Leyden, haare Gelegenheid, Oorsprong, Vergrootinge ... Leiden, 1762-84. 3 vols. Fo. Engraved title vig., dedication lf., 8 double-p. views, 1 double-p. map & 22 engrs. on 15 plts., cont. mott. cf., gt. spines with 6 raised bands, spines rubbed, some wear. (CH. May 24; 50)
Fls. 4,000
– Histori der Nederlandsche Vorsten ... sedert Albert, Graaf v. Holland, tot den Dood v. Karel v. 's-Gravenhage, 1732-35. 3 vols. Fo. Cont. hf. cf., spines gt., Vol. I spine top slightly defect. (VG. Mar.19; 174)
Fls. 600
– – **Anr. Copy.** 3 vols. Fo. A few ll. loose, some staining, lacks 2 tables, cont blind-stpd. vell., slightly soiled. (VG. Mar.19; 175)
Fls. 500

MIERS, John
– Travels in Chile & La Plata. 1826. 2 vols. 22 engraved & litho. plts. & maps, lacks last lf. (blank?) in Vol. 1, mod. hf. cf., gt. spines. [Sabin 48889] (BBA. Sep.29; 56)
Steedman. £230
– – **Anr. Copy.** 2 vols. Near-cont. cf., spine faded. (CSK. Dec.16; 71)
£140

MIGER, Pierre Auguste Marie
[–] Les Ports de France Peints par Joseph Vernet et Huë. Paris, 1812. Imperial 8vo. 2 ports. & 24 etched views, some spotting, mainly of text, mod. red mor. gt. (C. Jun.27; 49)
Shapero. £90

MIHLES, Samuel
– The Elements of Surgery ... Ed.:– Alexander Reid. 1764. *2nd. Edn.* 18 folding engraved plts., some offsetting affecting plt. area, some dampstaining, cont. cf., clipped at head & foot. (CSK. Apr.6; 74)
£90

MIKHAEL, Ephraïm
– Halyartès. Ill.:– Paul Gervais. 1904. *(100).* This copy with suite in black, pink hf. mor., corners, by Meunier. (*With:*) – Le Cor Fleuri. 1889. *Orig. Edn.* No bdg. stated. (HD. May 11; 68)
Frs. 1,900

MILANO, G.
[–] Costumi Diversi di Alcune Populazioni de' Reale Domini. Ill.:– Aloja after Milano. [Naples,. 1832]. Fo. Lacks title & 1 plt., hf. cf., worn; 3 cold. plts. 'Gruppi di Napoli' by F. Kaiser bnd. at end, as a coll. of plts. w.a.f. (BBA. Jun.14; 315)
Erlini. £650

MILBERT, Jacques
– Itineraire Pittoresque du Fleuve du Hudson et des Parties latérales ... [Paris, 1828-29]. *[25?] with India proof plts.* Atlas vol. only. Ob. fo. 53 (of 54) black & white litho. views, plts. 38 & 51 before letters, lacks map & the 2 prelims., some foxing to plt. mounts & tissue guards, not affecting image, plt. 51 with printers fold across image, cont. cf.-bkd. bds., folding case. [Howes M592 (noting some copies were iss. with only 53 plts.); Sabin 48916] (PNY. Jun.6; 528)
$2,400

MILES, Edmund & Lawford
– An Epitome, Historical & Statistical, Descriptive of the Royal Naval Service of England. Ill.:– Fielding after W. Knell (plts.). L., 1841. *1st. Edn.* Tall 8vo. Text engrs. hand-cold., 16 pp. of publisher's advts., str.-grd. three-qtr. mor., by Bayntun, spine gt., orig. gt.-pict. upr. cover bnd. in. (SG. Nov.3; 141) $425

MILES, Henry Downes
– The Book of Field Sports. N.d. 2 vols. 4to. 73 litho. plts. (7 hand-cold.), cf. gt. (P. Jun.7; 216)
£270

– British Field Sports. L., ca. 1880. 4to. 4 plts. less than stated in title, mod. hf. leath. (R. Apr.4; 1927)
DM 950
– – **Anr. Edn.** N.d. 4to. Cl. (P. Mar.15; 267)
Burlington. £200
– Pugilistica: Being One Hundred & Forty-Four Years of the History of British Boxing. 1880. *1st. Edn.* 3 vols. Cont. crimson hf. mor. gt. by Hatchards. (TA. Apr.19; 591)
£90
– – **Anr. Edn.** Edinb., 1906. 3 vols. Orig. cl. gt., partly untrimmed. (TA. May 17; 631)
£95
– – **Anr. Copy.** 3 vols. Orig. cl. gt., partly untrimmed. (TA. Oct.20; 105)
£54
– – **Anr. Copy.** 3 vols. Orig. cl. (S. Oct.11; 562)
Smith. £50

MILET-DECHALES, Claude-François
[–] L'Art de Naviguer Démontré par Principes et Confirmé par Plusieurs Observations Tirées de l'Expérience. Paris, 1677. *Orig. Edn.* 4to. Folding abacus (often lacking), some sm. stains, cont. cf., spine decor.; Gargas de Maurand sig. on title. (HD. Mar.9; 108)
Frs. 2,200

MILHAUD, Darius
– Deux Poèmes de Coventry Patmore. Ill.:– John Buckland-Wright. Maastricht, 1931. *(25)* numbered on Imperial Japanese, sigd. Fo. Orig. wraps., unopened. (BBA. Oct.27; 207)
Rota. £65

MILHOLLEN, Hirst
– Etchings of Haiti. N.p., 1937. *(50) numbered.* 4to. 10 etchings, each sigd. & numbered in pencil by artist, loose as iss., slightly worn cl. portfo., ties. (SG. Jun.7; 380)
$175

MILITARY DICTIONARY
1704. *2nd. Edn.* 12mo. Engraved armorial plt. pasted on title verso, later mor., rubbed, jnts. cracked. (CSK. May 18; 81)
£120

MILITARY SKETCH-BOOK; Reminiscences of Seventeen Years in the Service Abroad & at Home; By an Officer of the Line ...
1827. *1st. Edn.* 2 vols. With hf.-title in Vol. 1 not called for by Ferguson, orig. bds., unc., 1 lr. endpaper removed. (KH. May 1; 15)
Aus. $100

MILIZIA, Francesco
– Trattato Completo, Formale, e Materiale del Teatro. Venice, 1794. 4to. Cont. limp bds. untrimmed & largely unopened. (SG. Oct.27; 222)
$225

MILL, James
– Analysis of the Phenomena of the Human Mind. Ed.:– John Stuart Mill. L., 1869. *1st. J.S. Mill Edn.* 2 vols. Some light foxing, cl., some wear, covers slightly bowed; tipped to hf.-title a pres. slip, inscr. 'From the Editor.'. (RO. Dec.11; 217) $150
– Elements of Political Economy. 1821. *1st. Edn.* Errata, publisher's advts., mod. hf. cf. gt. (P. Oct.20; 168)
£240
– – **Anr. Edn.** L., 1824. *2nd. Edn.* Cf., rebkd. (S. Oct.11; 563)
Joseph. £130

MILL, John Stuart
– Gesammelte Werke. Ed.:– Th. Gompertz. Leipzig, 1869-80. *1st. German Coll. Edn.* 12 vols. All vols. browned thro.-out, some underlining, some sigs. loose, orig. linen, vol. 12 bnd. later. (R. Apr.3; 1230)
DM 1,000
– On Liberty. L., 1859. *1st. Edn.* Sm. 8vo. 4-p. publisher's catalogue tipped in, orig. cl., spine worn, s.-c.; armor. bkplt. of Rev. Prebendary Hedgeland, & inscr. of E. Stephens, 1859. (SG. Apr.19; 303)
$260
– Principles of Political Economy. L., 1848. *1st. Edn.* 2 vols. Advt. ll. at end of each vol., orig. cl., labels worn & slightly frayed. (C. Nov.9; 100)
Thorp. £600
– – **Anr. Copy.** 2 vols. Each vol. lacks advt. lf. at end & Vol. II 1st. lf. (hf.-title?), numerous pencil & pen MS. underlinings & some notes, cont. cf., rather worn, 1 cover detchd. (S. Oct.11; 564)
Boyle. £160
– The Subjection of Women. 1869. *1st. Edn.* Hf. cf. gt. (P. Sep.8; 246)
Stone. £130
– – **Anr. Copy.** Cl., light wear & soiling; pres. copy, inscr. 'From the Author' on hf.-title. (RO. Dec.11; 218)
$345

MILLAIS, John Guille
– British Deer & their Horns. 1897. 4to. 1 photogravure wormed, minor spotting, orig. decor. cl. (TA. Nov.17; 316)
£70
– – **Anr. Copy.** Fo. Orig. cl., soiled. (SPB. Dec.13; 594)
$125
– British Diving Ducks. Ill.:– after A. Thorburn, H. Gronvold, & others. L., 1913. *(450).* 2 vols. Fo. Minor dampstain to blank margin of 1 plt. & a few text ll., orig. cl. gt., covers slightly affected by damp. (C. Nov.16; 279)
Grahame. £200
– Game Birds & Shooting-Sketches. L., 1892. Lge. 4to. Frontis., 16 chromolitho. plts., other plts. & ills., some minor spotting. cont. red hf. mor. gt., covers slightly soiled. (C. Jun.27; 175) *Hill.* £180
– – **Anr. Copy.** Fo. Plts., 16 cold., ills., slightly spotted, red hf. mor., soiled. (S. Apr.10; 559)
Russell. £130
– The Mammals of Great Britain & Ireland. Ill.:– G.E. Lodge, A. Thorburn, & Millais. 1904-06. *(1025) numbered.* 3 vols. Lge. 4to. Qtr. buckram gt. (SKC. Mar.9; 1948)
£240
– – **Anr. Copy.** 3 vols. 4to. Orig. cl. gt., spines slightly faded. (P. Apr.12; 133) *Joseph.* £150
– – **Anr. Copy.** 3 vols. Lge. 4to. Minor spotting to some plts., 2 tissue guards adhering to facing plts., orig. buckram-bkd. cl., minor tears to 1 spine. (C. Nov.16; 277)
Shapero. £130
– – **Anr. Copy.** 3 vols. Lge. 4to. Qtr. buckram gt., spines rubbed. (SKC. Nov.18; 1980)
£100
– – **Anr. Copy.** 3 vols. 4to. 273 plts., orig. cl. (SG. Oct.6; 257)
$175
– The Natural History of British Game Birds. 1909. *(550) numbered.* Fo. Orig. cl., lightly soiled, d.-w. (CSK. Jun.1; 161)
£260
– – **Anr. Copy.** Fo. Orig. cl. gt., spine faded. (C. Nov.16; 278)
Grahame. £230
– The Natural History of the British Surface-Feeding Ducks. 1902. *(600) numbered on L.P.* 4to. Orig. cl. gt., partly untrimmed, spine ends & corners rubbed. (TA. Apr.19; 135)
£280
– – **Anr. Copy.** 4to. Orig. cl. gt., partly untrimmed, corners slightly rubbed. (TA. May 17; 272) £220
– – **Anr. Copy.** 4to. Orig. cl. (SPB. Dec.13; 597)
$275
– Rhododendrons. 1917-24. *(550).* 2 vols. Fo. Cl. (P. Jun.7; 8)
£380
– – **Anr. Copy.** Vol. 1 only. Fo. Orig. cl. gt., worn. (P. Apr.12; 209)
Dartmoor. £100
– – **Anr. Edn.** Ill.:– Beatrice Parsons, Winifred Walker & others. L., 1917-24. *1st. Edns. (550) numbered.* 1st. & 2nd. Series: 2 vols. Lge. fo. 34 col. plts. & 28 collotype plts., liby. stp. on titles, gt.-lettered cl., shelf marks on spine. (SG. Mar.22; 231)
$600
– The Wildfowler in Scotland. 1901. 4to. Hf. vell., orig. d.-w. (PD. Aug.17; 140)
£75
– – **Anr. Copy.** 4to. Recent hf. parch., partly untrimmed. (TA. May 17; 270)
£65

MILLAR, Eric George
– Descriptions of an Illuminated Manuscript of the Thebaid of Statius. Oxford, priv. ptd., 1931. Fo. Errata slip, cont. cl. (BBA. Mar.7; 352)
Dawson. £80
– English Illuminated Manuscripts of the XIVth & XVth Centuries. Paris & Brussels, 1928. Fo. Orig. cl. gt., slight mark on upr. cover, d.-w. (LC. Mar.1; 15)
£110
– The St. Trond Lectionary. Oxford, Roxb. Cl., 1949. 4to. Orig. mor.-bkd. buckram, H.M. Nixon coll; pres. inscr. from Millar to Nixon. (BBA. Oct.6; 114)
Quaritch. £380

MILLAR, George Henry
– A New, Complete & Universal Body, or System of Natural History. L., [1785]. Fo. Engraved frontis., 85 plts., slightly browned & spotted, minor worming of few lr. margins, cont. hf. cf., worn. (S. Apr.10; 560)
Sanders. £90
– – **Anr. Edn.** L., [1785?]. Fo. Engraved frontis., approx. 85 plts., 2 with sm. margin tears & defects, a few plts. shaved, mod. hf. cf., spine gt. (C. Jun.27; 176)
Shapero. £110
– The New & Universal System of Geography. Ill.:– T. Kitchen. (maps). L., A. Hogg, ca. 1782. Fo. Frontis., 26 engraved maps, many folding, 94 engraved plts., advts. lf. at end, frontis. with reprd. tear, offset on title, world map creased & with short

tears, a few short tears & minor stains, cont. cf., reprd. (S. Dec.1; 268) *Noble.* £450
– – **Anr. Edn.** 1783-n.d. 2 vols. Fo. Some slight staining, orig. sheep, worn. (P. Apr.12; 275)
Antiques. £320

MILLAR, John
– **Observations concerning the Distinction of Ranks in Society.** 1771. *1st. Edn.* 4to. Hf.-title, advt. lf. at end, cont. cf.; Sir Ivar Colquhoun, of Luss copy. (CE. Mar.22; 215) £650

MILLARES, Agustin
– **Historia de la Inquisicion en las Islas Canaria.** Las Palmas, 1874. 4 vols. in 1. Cont. linen. (DS. Oct.28; 2249) Pts. 24,000

MILLAY, Edna St. Vincent
– **The Buck in the Snow & Other Poems.** N.Y. & L., 1928. *(515) numbered & sigd. by author.* Bds., cl. spine, unopened, s.-c. (defect.), light wear. (RO. Apr.23; 232) $125
– **Renascence & Other Poems.** N.Y., 1917. *1st. Edn. 1st. Iss. on Glaslan paper.* Orig. cl., d.-w., mor. s.-c.: pres. copy to Frank Crowninshield, Perry Molstad copy. (SPB. May 16; 503) $3,750
– – **Anr. Copy.** Orig. cl., d.-w., hf. mor. s.-c.; Frederic Dannay copy. (CNY. Dec.16; 237) $600

MILLER, Bertha Mahony
See— **MOORE, Anne Carroll & Miller, Bertha Mahony**

MILLER, Edgar G.
– **American Antique Furniture.** 1963. 2 vols. No. bdg. stated. (JL. Jun.24; 196) Aus. $240

MILLER, Edmund Morris
– **Australian Literature ...** Melbourne, 1940. *1st. Edn.* 2 vols. Orig. cl., d.-w.'s with a couple of spots on backs. (KH. Nov.9; 666) Aus. $190

MILLER, Edward
– **The History & Antiquities of Doncaster & its Vicinity.** [1804]. 4to. Folding map, 8 plts., 1 lf. reprd., hf. cf. (P. Jul.26; 103) £50

MILLER, Francis T.
– **The Photographic History of the Civil War.** N.Y., 1912. 10 vols. 4to. Few sigs. loosening, cl., gt.-lettered, some covers rubbed &/or spotted. (HA. Sep.16; 379) $150

MILLER, George
– **The Traveller's Guide to Madeira & the West Indies; being a Hieroglyphic Representation of Appearances & Incidents during a Voyage out & Homewards.** Haddington, 1815. *1st. Edn.* Engraved map, 9 plts., hf.-title, cont. hf. cl. (BBA. Sep.29; 57) *Brook-Hitching.* £210

MILLER, Henry
– **Black Spring.** Paris, 1936. *1st. Edn.* Sm. 4to. Orig. ptd. wraps., partly unopened, slightly worn; pres. copy. (SPB. May 17; 647) $600
– – **Anr. Edn.** Paris, [Jun. 1936]. *1st. Edn.* 1 vol. Orig. pict. wraps., worn, hf. mor. s.-c.; pres. copy, inscr. 'To Walt & Lil [Lowenfels]-from Henry, Paris 7/36. Ubiguchi', Lowenfels' name & N.Y. address written at top of p. (*With:*) – **Tropic of Cancer.** Paris, [1934]. *1st. Edn.* 1 vol. Orig. pict. wraps., covers detchd., together in box. (CNY. May 18; 126) $320
– **Book of Friends.** Santa Barbara, Capra Pr., 1976. *(26) lettered & sigd., with sigd. drawing by Miller* bnd. in. Page 134 has corrected readings 'awakening' & 'com-/plete', art mor., d.-w., cl. s.-c. (BG. Mar.1; 347) $325
– **Quiet Days in Clichy.** Ill.:– Brassai. Paris, Olympia Pr., 1956. *1st. Edn.* Photo. ills., orig. ptd. wraps. (SPB. May 17; 648) $175
– – **Anr. Edn.** Ill.:– after Brassai. Paris, 1958. 16mo. Pict. wraps., slightly loose. (SG. Nov.10; 32) $110
– **Tropic of Cancer.** Paris, 1934. *1st. Edn.* Orig. pict. wraps., slip attached to upr. cover. (SPB. May 17; 649) $2,600
– **Tropic of Capricorn.** Paris, Obelisk Pr., [1939]. *1st. Edn.* Sm. 4to. Without errata slip, orig. wraps., slightly frayed. (BBA. May 23; 116) *Maggs.* £80
– – **Anr. Copy.** Yellow errata slip, decor. wraps. (SG. May 24; 338) $350

– – **Anr. Copy.** Errata slip tipped in before title-p., three-qtr. mor., spine ends & jnts. rubbed, orig. wraps. bnd. in. (SG. Jan.12; 264) $200

MILLER, J.S.
– **A Natural History of the Crinoidea, Or Lily-Shaped Animals ...** Bristol, 1821. 4to. 49 (of 50) col. litho. plts., (lacks frontis.), publishers advt. lf. bnd. in at rear, recent hf. cf., untrimmed. (TA. Jun.21; 271) £80

MILLER, Joaquin
– **Songs of the Sun Lands.** L., 1873. *1st. Edn.* 4to. L.P., orig. cl., soiled; pres. copy from author to Ford Madox Brown, Sydney Ainsell Gimson bkplt., Frederic Dannay copy. (CNY. Dec.16; 238) $160

MILLER, John
– **Illustratio Systematis Sexualis Linnaei ... An Illustration of the Sexual System of Linnaeus.** L., [1770-]77. *1st. Edn.* Lge. fo. 2nd. iss. of subscribers list, engraved title & frontis., 4 hand-cold. plts. of leaves, 104 hand-cold. plts. of plants, without the dupl. set of 104 uncold. plts., without errata lf. (found in some copies), title & frontis. creased, the latter slightly stained, 1 plt. stained, some browning of text, slight soiling, cont. russ., very worn, lr. cover detchd. (S. Nov.28; 65)
Goldschmidt. £3,100
– **Tabulae Iconum Centum Quatuor Plantarum ad Illustrationem Systematis Sexualis Linnaeani ...** Frankfurt, 1789. Pt. 2 plt. vol. only (of 2). 4to. Slightly foxed & soiled, some plt. margins lightly defect. & some torn, cont. bds., slightly soiled & bumped. (HK. Nov.8; 638) DM 900

MILLER, John Frederick & Shaw, George
– **Cimelia Physica. Figures of Rare & Curious Quadrupeds. Birds, & c. Together with Several of the Most Elegant Plants.** L., 1796. *2nd. Edn.* Fo. 60 hand-cold. etched plts., 17 plts. have copyright line added in MS, apparently by Miller himself, MS. imprints added to some plts., tear in margin of plt. 2, repair to plt. 33, 9 (of 10) ll. (table of Linnaean classifications) ptd. on 1 side only at end (lacks lf. with descriptions of plts. 49-54), some slight discolouration, a few ll. at end stained in margins, cont. hf. mor., worn; W.H. Edwards, Illinois, bkplt. (S. Feb.1; 38) *Simpson.* £5,500
– – **Anr. Copy.** Fo. 60 hand-cold. engraved plts., slight soiling & discoloration, plt. 1 with crease in lr. inner margin, plt. 37 with split along plt.-mark, & sm. margin tear, plt. 49 with margin repair, a few other plts. with minor margin tears, tears in E1 & S2 of text, early 19th. C. gt.-& blind-tooled maroon mor., rubbed, rebkd., new end-papers. (S. Nov.28; 66) *Graham.* £1,550

MILLER, Patrick
– **Ana the Runner, a Treatise for Princes & Generals attributed to Prince Mahmoud Abdul.** Ill.:– Clifford Webb. Gold. Cock. Pr., 1937. *(150) numbered & sigd., specially bnd.* Orig. niger-bkd. bds.; from D. Bolton liby. (BBA. Oct.27; 143) *Sawyer.* £60
– **Woman in Detail.** Ill.:– after Mark Severin. Gold. Cock. Pr., 1947. *(550) numbered & sigd. by author & artist. (100) specially bnd., with suite of 5 dupl. & 3 extra ills.* Lge. 8vo. The additional suite loose in pocket in lr. cover, crushed qtr. mor. by Sangorski & Sutcliffe, s.-c., partly unc., spine darkened. (SG. Jan.12; 130) $130

MILLER, Philip
– **Dictionnaire des Jardiniers.** Paris, 1785. 8 vols. 4to. Cont. hf. cf. (LM. Oct.22; 88) B. Frs. 9,000
– **Figures of the Most Beautiful, Useful, & Uncommon Plants described in the Gardeners Dictionary.** Ill.:– after G.D. Ehret & others. L., priv. ptd., 1771. 2 vols. Fo. 300 hand-cold. engraved plts., including 1 folding, cont. hf. sheep, unc., mor.-bkd. box. (C. Nov.16; 280) *Henderson.* £3,100
– **The Gardener's & Botanist's Dictionary.** 1707. 2 vols. in 4. Fo. Some browning, hf. cf., rubbed. (P. Apr.12; 239) *Rix.* £60
– – **Anr. Edn.** 1807. 2 vols. in 4. Fo. 5 plans, 15 plts., some browning, hf. cf., rubbed. (P. Jul.26; 104) £110
– – **Anr. Copy.** 2 vols. in 4. Fo. 17 engraved plts., some spotting, cont. cf., 2 covers detchd. (S. Apr.10; 561) *Studio.* £100
– **The Gardeners Dictionary.** L., 1741. *2nd. Edn.* 3 vols. Some staining & foxing, old cf., worn & dried.

(*With:*) – **The Gardeners Kalendar.** L., 1745. 1 vol. Unif. bnd. with 1st. work as 'Vol. IV'. (RO. Sep.13; 126) $125
– – **Anr. Edn.** 1752. *6th. Edn.* Fo. Engraved frontis., 7 plts., cont. diced cf. gt. (P. Jul.26; 141) £130
– – **Anr. Copy.** Fo. Some spotting, cont. cf. (CSK. Sep.30; 1) £110
– – **Anr. Edn.** 1759. *7th. Edn.* 2 vols. in 1. Fo. Cont. cf. (CSK. Aug.19; 99) £120
– – **Anr. Copy.** Fo. Some foxing, browning, & offsetting, old cf., brkn., crudely taped. (RO. Dec.11; 222) $130
– – **Anr. Edn.** Dublin, 1764. 2 vols. 4to. A few ll. dampstained, recent qtr. cf., spines gt.-decor. (TA. Feb.16; 120) £65
– **Groot en Algem. Kruidkundig, Hoveniers en Bloemisten Woordenboek ...** Leiden, 1745. 2 vols. Fo. Text stained in margins, cont. hf. cf., rubbed. (VG. Sep.14; 936) Fls. 1,400

MILLER, Philip & Martyn, Thomas
– **The Gardener's & Botanist's Dictionary.** [1797-1804]. Pts. I-XVIII of text & nos. 1-22 of plts. only. Fo. 7 engraved plts. in text vols., 115 hand-cold. engraved plts., some ptd. in green & brown, orig. ptd. paper wraps. & bds.; Sir Ivar Colquhoun, of Luss copy, w.a.f. (CE. Mar.22; 216) £1,300

MILLER, Thomas, of Great Yarmouth, seaman
– **The Complete Modellist: shewing the True & Exact Way of raising the Model of any Ship or Vessel.** 1667. 4to. 1 plt. with sm. tear. wraps., folding case. [Wing M2036a] (BBA. Jun.14; 53)
Quaritch. £1,200

MILLER, Willium, Publisher
– **The Natural History of Shells.** L., 1810. Fo. 62 hand-cold. aquatints (wtrmkd. 1808), lacks title, later cf.-bkd. bds., as a coll. of plts., w.a.f. (PNY. Jun.6; 550) $1,250

MILLET, Jean François
– **Le Livre d'Or de. J.-F. Millet par un Ancien Ami.** Paris, n.d. *(550). (50) on Japan.* 4to. 3 plts. badly spotted, 2 slightly affected by offsetting, cont. hf. mor., spine gt., orig. wraps. bnd. in, s.-c. (S. Oct.4; 178) *Bishop.* £80

MILLIERE, P.
– **Iconographie et Description de Chenilles et Lépldoptères inédits.** 1859-74. New Series: 3 vols. text & 1 vol. atlas. Foxing, cont. hf. chagrin. (HD. Feb.29; 27) Frs. 19,000

MILLIEUS, Antonius
– **Moyses Viator.** Dillingen, 1680. Cont. German vell. gt., decor.; from Fondation Furstenberg-Beaumesnil. (HD. Nov.16; 139) Frs. 3,500

MILLIN DE GRANIMAISON, Aubin Louis
– **Antiquités Nationales.** Paris, 1790-95. *1st. Edn.* 5 vols. Lge. 4to. Approx. 250 engraved plts., ex-liby., 2 ll. of vol.4 plt. list defect., mod. buckram, unc. (SG. May 3; 255) $475
– – **Anr. Edn.** Paris, 1790-99. 5 vols. 4to. 249 engraved plts., some folding, cl.-bkd. bds. (BBA. Apr.5; 184) *Fletcher.* £200
– – **Anr. Copy.** 5 vols. 4to. Old hf. roan, bdgs. defect. (HD. Jun.29; 145) Frs. 2,300
– – **Anr. Copy.** 5 vols. Fo. Bradel marb. paper, gt. decor. spine, 1 corner worn vol. V. (HD. Dec.16; 27) Frs. 2,150
– **Atlas pour Servir au Voyage dans les Départements du Midi de la France.** Paris, 1807. 4to. 83 plts., sewed. (HD. Nov.17; 53) Frs. 1,000
– **Elemens d'Histoire Naturelle.** Paris, 1802. *3rd. Edn.* 22 engraved folding plts., cont. cf., gt. key-pattern borders on covers, gt. spine, rubbed, lr. jnt. cracked & with sm. holes. (C. Jun.27; 122)
Shapero. £50

MILLOT, Abbé Claude François Xavier
[–] **Abregé de l'Histoire Romaine.** Ill.:– Piauger (frontis.), Eisen, St Aubin, Gravelot & Bolomey. 1789. 4to. Cont. marb. cf. gt., spine decor. (HD. Apr.13; 29) Frs. 1,100

MILLS, John
– **The Life of a Foxhound.** L., 1848. *1st. Edn.* 7 engraved plts., hf.-title, lacks final blank, mod. mor. by Bayntun, Bath, orig. covers & spine preserved. (S. Oct.4; 277) *Gmur.* £130

MILLS, Samuel J. & Smith, Daniel
– **Report of a Missionary Tour through that part of the United States which lies west of the Allegany Mountains** ... Andover, 1815. *1st. Edn.* Text browned with a few spots, mod. hf. mor., rubbed. (LH. Apr.15; 342) $130

MILLS, T.B.
– **A History of the North-Western Editorial Excursion to Arkansas.** Little Rock, 1876. Cl., orig. wraps. bnd. in. (LH. Jan.15; 230) $100

MILLY, Comte de
– **L'Art de la Porcelaine.** Ill.:– N. Ransonnette. [Paris], 1771. Tall fo. Very dampstained, old leath.-bkd. bds. (SG. Oct.13; 73) $110

MILNE, Alan Alexander
– **The Chrisopher Robin Story Book.** Ill.:– E.H. Shepard. L., 1929. *1st. Edn.* Orig. cl., d.-w. (BBA. May 23; 120) *Jolliffe.* £80
– **The House at Pooh Corner.** Ill.:– E.H. Shepard. 1928. *1st. Edn.* Cf. gt.; sigd. by author on title-p. (P. Jul.5; 368) £130
– – **Anr. Copy.** Orig. cl., d.-w. (BBA. Feb.23; 330) *Randall.* £90
– – **Anr. Copy.** Sm. 8vo. Gt.-pict. cl., end-papers slightly discold., d.-w. (SG. Dec.8; 234) $170
– – **Anr. Edn.** Ill.:– E.H. Shepard. 1928. *(350) sigd. by author & artist.* Orig. cl.-bkd. bds., unopened, d.-w. (P. Jul.26; 216) £220
– – **Anr. Edn.** Ill.:– E.H. Shepard. N.Y., [1929]. *(250) numbered on Japan vell., sigd. by author & artist.* Lge. 8vo. Cl.-bkd. pict. bds., unc. & unopened, pict. box worn. (SG. Nov.3; 142) $250
– **The House at Pooh Corner. – Winnie the Pooh. – Now We Are Six. – When We Were Very Young.** L., 1928; 1926; 1927; 1924. *1st. Edns.* Together 4 vols. Unif. mor. gt. by Bayntun. (SPB. Dec.13; 549) $1,600
– – **Anr. Copy.** Together 4 vols. Sm. 8vo. 1st. vol. sigd. by Shepard, 1st. vol. with owner's sig., the 2nd. with bkplt., gt.-pict. cl., upr. cover of 1st. vol. lightly spotted, 4th. vol. with d.-w. (SG. Dec.8; 235) $300
– **Now We Are Six.** Ill.:– E.H. Shepard. 1927. *1st. Edn.* Orig. leath., d.-w. torn, orig. box. (BBA. Feb.23; 331) *Maggs.* £130
– – **Anr. Copy.** Orig. cl., d.-w. (BBA. Feb.23; 332) *Randall.* £85
– – **Anr. Edn.** Ill.:– Ernest H. Shepard. L., [1927]. *1st. Edn. (200) numbered on L.P., sigd. by author & artist.* Sm. 4to. Orig. cl.-bkd. bds., unopened, d.-w., hf. mor. s.-c.; Frederic Dannay copy. (CNY. Dec.6; 239) $350
– **Now We Are Six. – The House at Pooh Corner.** Ill.:– E.H. Shepard. L., 1927; 1928. *1st. Edns.* Together 2 vols. Orig. cl. gt., d.-w. torn; orig. roan gt., spine slightly faded. (S. Dec.20; 618) *Marks.* £50
– **Toad of Toad Hall.** [1929]. *(200) numbered on H.M.P., sigd. by author & Kenneth Grahame.* Orig. cl.-bkd. bds., unc. d.-w., torn. (P. Sep.8; 404) *Elliott.* £110
– **When I Was Very Young.** N.Y., Fountain Pr., 1930. *Ltd. Edn., sigd.* Pict. linen, s.-c.; sigd. card inserted. (P. Mar.15; 278) £85
– **When We Were Very Young.** 1924. *1st. Edn.* Orig. cl., d.-w. (CSK. Aug.19; 28) £110
– **When We Were Very Young. – The House at Pooh Corner.** 1924; 1928. *1st. Edns.* Together 2 vols. Orig. cl., 2nd. vol. soiled, 1st. with d.-w. (BBA. Aug.18; 142) *Bailey.* £80
– **Winnie-the-Pooh.** Ill.:– E.H. Shepard. L., 1926. *1st. Edn.* Orig. cl., d.-w. (BBA. May 23; 117) *Maggs.* £190
– **Winnie-the-Pooh. – Now We Are Six.** Ill.:– E.H. Shepard. L., [1926; 1927]. *1st. Edns. (350) numbered & sigd. by author & artist; (200) numbered & sigd. by author & artist.* Together 2 vols. 4to. Orig. cl.-bkd. bds., unopened, covers of 1st. work slightly discold., 1st. d.-w. defect., 2nd. d.-w. worn. (CNY. May 18; 127) $450
– **Winnie-the-Pooh. – Now We Are Six. – The House at Pooh Corner.** Ill.:– E.H. Shepard. 1926; 1927; 1928. *1st. Edns.* Together 3 vols. Orig. cl. gt., 2 vols. in orig. d.-w.'s. (LC. Mar.1; 122) £110
– – **Anr. Copy.** Together 3 vols. 1st. 2 works in orig. leath. gt., decor. spines (slightly frayed at heads), 3rd. work in orig. cl. gt., some fading. (LC. Mar.1; 123) £65
– – **Anr. Edn.** L., [1926]; [1927]; [1928]. *1st. Trade Edns.* Together 3 vols. Sm. 8vo. 1st. work little stained. Gt.-pict. cl., extremities rubbed. (SG. May 24; 118) $110

MILNE, John & Burton, W.K.
– **The Great Earthquake in Japan, 1891.** Ill.:– K. Ogawa. Yokohama, [1891]. Lge. ob. 4to. Last plt. slightly creased in margin, gt.-lettered cl., light wear & soiling. (RO. Dec.11; 223) $300

MILNER, Rev. Th. & Petermann, A.
– **The Atlas of Political Geography.** L., 1851. *Revised Edn.* Fo. 51 steel-engraved maps, some text & few maps with margin tears, orig. hf. cf., slightly defect., upr. jnt. brkn., loosening. (VG. Nov.30; 501) Fls. 450
– **A Descriptive Atlas of Astronomy & of Physical & Political Geography.** 1850. 4to. 73 maps & tables, most hand-cold. in outl., mor. gt., rubbed. (P. Mar.15; 391) *Martin.* £85

MILTON, John
– **Allegro und Penseroso.** Ed.:– Ferd. von Kobell. Trans.:– O.H. von Gemmingen. Mannheim, 1782. *1st. German Edn.* On Dutch paper, Engl. & German parallel text, brown stain thro.-out in lr. margin, slightly brittle here, most lr. margins with sm. tear, new bds., brocade covered, Hauswedell coll. (H. May 24; 1477) DM 700
– **Complete Poetical Works.** L., ca. 1870. Sm. 8vo. Some foxing, gt.-& blind-stpd. mor., fore-e. pntg. (SG. Feb.16; 203) $325
– **Comus.** Ill.:– Arthur Rackham. [1914]. 4to. On vell., no bdg. stated; sigd. by artist. (HD. Jun.26; 133) Frs. 1,600
– – **Anr. Edn.** Ill.:– Arthur Rackham. L., [1921]. *(550) numbered & sigd.* 4to. Orig. parch.-bkd. bds. gt., worn. (S. Dec.20; 578) *Roberts.* £100
– – **Anr. Edn.** Gregynog Pr., 1931. *(250) numbered.* Orig. cl.-bkd. bds., lightly soiled. (CSK. Jun.29; 166) £150
– **A Defence of the People of England.** 1692. *1st. Engl. Edn.* No imprint, blank lf. on 8, advt. lf. at end, mod. cf., gt. spine, new end-papers & fly-ll. (SKC. Jan.13; 2234) £70
– – **Anr. Copy.** Blank A1 & A7 & 'Advt. to Reader' lf., few margins slightly soiled, cont. sheep., rebkd. [Wing M 2104] (SPB. May 16; 101) $125
– **Early Poems.** Ill.:– C. Ricketts. [Vale Pr., 1896]. *(310).* 4to. Order form loose, mor. gt. by Bagguley, vell. gt. doubls., lined box; Kenneth Oldaker copy. (P. Jan.12; 10) *Sawyer.* £400
– **Four Poems** ... Ill.:– Blair Hughes-Stanton. Gregy. Pr., 1933. *(250) on Japanese vell. (25) specially bnd.* Lge. 8vo. Prospectus laid in, red lev., faded, head of spine chipped. (SG. Jan.12; 146) $200
– **The History of Britain.** L., 1670. *1st. Edn. 1st. Iss.* 4to. Engraved port., errata, marginal soiling, cont. cf., rebkd., endpapers browned; sig. of George Legh, High Legh Liby. bkplt. [Wing M2119] (SPB. May 16; 102) $375
– **The Masque of Comus.** Ill.:– Edmund Dulac. Camb., for Ltd. Edns. Cl., 1954. *(1500) numbered.* Lge. 8vo. Marb. bds., gt. vell. spine, s.-c., minimal wear. (RO. Mar.21; 79) $110
– **Le Paradis Perdu.** Notes:– Addisson. Paris, 1736. 3 vols. 12mo. Mor., Madame Victoire arms, spines decor. (SM. Mar.7; 2031) Frs. 3,800
– – **Anr. Edn.** Ill.:– Clement, Colibert, Gautier, & others, after Schall. Paris, 1792. *Engl. & Fr. Edn.* 2 vols. 4to. Plts. ptd. in col. before letters, on papier vélin, mntd. on end-paper before title in Vol. 1 is a grey ink & wash port. of Milton, by or attributed to Bonington, with sig., & in Vol. 2 a watercolour by Goustave Courtois, dtd. 1909, cont. tree cf. (C. Nov.9; 100a) *Temperley.* £820
– – **Anr. Copy.** 2 vols. Fo. 12 plts. before letters, text in Engl. & Fr., some spotting & browning, cont. tree cf. gt., rubbed. (SPB. Dec.14; 68) $550
– – **Anr. Edn.** Ill.:– after Schall. Paris, 1792. *1st. Printing of engrs.* 2 vols. Lge. 4to. In Engl. & Fr., marb. cf. (SM. Mar.7; 2030) Frs. 4,300
– **Paradise Lost.** L., 1667. *1st. Edn.* Sm. 4to. Amory's no. 1b ¶ sub-iss. (1st. title), with 7 ll. 'Printer to the Reader', 'The Argument', 'The Verse' & 'Errata' inserted, some ll. slightly stained, sm. restoration to lr. inner blank corner of title-p., purple mor. gt. by J. Clarke; Frederic Dannay copy. [Wing M 2136] (CNY. Dec.16; 241) $3,600
– – **Anr. Iss.** L., 1668. *1st. Edn.* Sm. 4to. Amory's no. 2 iss. (4th. title), containing no. 1a 1st. title bnd. at front, with 7 ll. 'Printer to the Reader', 'The Argument', 'The Verse' & 'Errata', & with a lf. at end (probably integral) with device on recto, mor. gt., sm. gt. crest of Sir Francis Freeling on covers, spine gt.-lettered, turn-ins & bd. edges gt.; 2 A.L.s. bnd. in: 1 from T.F. Dibdin, the other from John Osmond Deakin, Joseph Neald bkplt., Frederick Dannay copy. [Wing M 2139] (CNY. Dec.16; 242) $3,600
– – **Anr. Iss.** 1669. *1st. Edn.* Sm. 4to. 5th. title, with 5 line 'The Printer to the Reader' on fo. A2, title trimmed & mntd., sm. burnhole on 2 ll., a few other sm. margin tears, some ll. slightly soiled & dampstained, 18th. C. panel, cf. gt., rebkd. with orig. spine. [Wing M2142] (BBA. Sep.29; 141) *Price.* £380
– – **Anr. Iss.** L., 1669. *1st. Edn.* 4to. Fifth title-p. (Amory 3), 'Angel' in roman in imprint, errata on a4v, 'Printer to the Reader' on A2r, 'illustrious' on line 109 Book 7 & 'farr' on line 2 Vvlr, mor., gt. & blind-stpd. decor; bkplts. of Edna & Samuel F. Berger. (SPB. May 16; 103) $1,700
– – **Anr.Iss.** L., 1669. *1st. Edn.* 4to. Few stains, old MS. notes, few marginalia, panel. antique mor. by Riviere. [Wing M2143] (SG. Apr.26; 142) $950
– – **Anr. Edn.** L., 1688. *4th. Edn.* 4to. Port., 12 engraved plts., few margin annots., cf., covers detchd. (P. May 17; 187) *Bickersteth.* £160
– – **Anr. Copy.** Fo. Engraved port., 11 (of 12) plts., margin at head of title cut away, some ll. spotted or marginally stained, cont. cf., worn, covers detchd. [Wing M2147] (S. Mar.29; 942) *Sekuler.* £80
– – **Anr. Edn.** Ed.:– Richard Bentley. Ill.:– G. Vertue. L., 1732. *New Edn.* Lge. 4to. 2 engraved ports., cont. cf. (SG. Apr.19; 129) $275
– – **Anr. Edn.** Bg'ham, 1759. 4to. Some light browning, cont. panel cf. gt. (CSK. May 18; 92) £110
– – **Anr. Edn.** Bg'ham, Baskerville Pr., 1760. 2 vols. Lge. 8vo. Slight spotting, cont. cf., spines gt. (SPB. May 16; 104) $200
– – **Anr. Edn.** Ill.:– John Martin. 1827. 2 vols. Lge. 8vo. Gt.-decor. mor. by Hayday. (SKC. Mar.9; 1799) £650
– – **Anr. Copy.** 2 vols. Fo. Some browning & spotting thro.-out, ink stains on bottom centre 11 pp., hf. cf., marb. bds., worn, some browning; Joseph Ablett bkplt. (BS. May 2; 18) £580
– – **Anr. Copy.** 2 vols. Lge. 8vo. Plts. slightly spotted, cont. blind-tooled str.-grd. mor., slightly rubbed. (S. Nov.22; 336) *Tuttie.* £400
– – **Anr. Copy.** 2 vols. 23 (of 24) plts., crimson mor. gt. (P. Nov.24; 89) *Marks.* £150
– – **Anr. Copy.** Text & plt. margins foxed, mor. gt., stained. (P. Sep.8; 236) *Frankel.* £110
– – **Anr. Copy.** 2 vols. Some slight foxing or margins lightly browned, hf. leath., corners rubbed; ex-libris inside cover. (GB. May 4; 1378) DM 2,000
– – **Anr. Edn.** Ill.:– John Martin. L., 1833. A few margins slightly spotted or stained, cont. mor. gt., slightly rubbed. (S. Nov.22; 337) *Joseph.* £230
– – **Anr. Copy.** 4to. A few ills. slightly browned, cont. cf. gt., slightly rubbed. (SKC. Mar.9; 1800) £170
– – **Anr. Edn.** Ill.:– John Martin. 1838. Hf. mor. gt. (P. Sep.8; 197) *Harris.* £100
– – **Anr. Copy.** Lge. 8vo. 24 mezzotint plts., few blank margins worned, margin spotting, mod. hf. mor. (CSK. Feb.24; 110) £80
– – **Anr. Copy.** 4to. Gt.-decor. mor., worn, spine torn. (SG. Jun.7; 378) $200
– – **Anr. Edn.** Ill.:– John Martin. L., 1846. Fo. Majority of plts. marked 'Proof', spotted, cont. red mor., rubbed. (S. Nov.22; 338) *Tuttie.* £550
– – **Anr. Edn.** Ill.:– John Martin. L., 1849. 4to. 24 plts., some foxing, mor. gt. (P. Nov.24; 103) £150
– – **Anr. Edn.** Ill.:– John Martin. 1853. 4to. 1 mezzotint ill. loose, gt.-decor. mor., dentelles. (SKC. Sep.9; 1877) £110
– – **Anr. Edn.** L., 1858. 4to. Some slight foxing, cont. leath., spine renewed with old material. (GB. Nov.4; 1840) DM 1,000
– – **Anr. Edn.** Ed.:– Robert Vaughan. Ill.:– Gustave Doré. L., 1882. Sm. fo. Red mor. gt., front jnt.

defect.; from liby. of F.D. Roosevelt, inscr. by him 'James Roosevelt from his loving son, Franklin, Christmas, 1899'. (SG. Mar.15; 60) $1,500
– – **Anr. Edn.** Doves Pr., 1902. *(300).* Orig. limp vell. (BBA. Jan.19; 286) *Thomas.* £130
– – **Anr. Edn.** Ill.:– Mary Groom. Gold. Cock. Pr., 1937. *(200) numbered.* Fo. Orig. hf. pig, s.-c. (S. Nov.21; 227) *Appleton.* £460
– – **Anr. Copy.** Fo. Hf. mor. gt. by Zaehnsdorf, s.-c. (P. Sep.29; 296) *Wilton.* £290
– **Paradise Lost; Paradise Regain'd.** Ed.:– Thomas Newton. Bg'ham., 1760. 2 vols. Tall 8vo. Extra port. frontis., cont. mott. cf., gt.-decor. (TA. Feb.16; 213) £85
– **Paradise Lost; Paradise Regained, to which are added Samson Agonistes & Poems both English & Latin.** Doves Pr., 1905. *(325). (300) on paper.* 2 vols. 4to. Lge. capitals in 'Paradise Lost' supplied in red & blue by G. Hewitt & E. Johnston, a few pp. very slightly spotted, orig. limp vell., unc. (S. Nov.22; 299) *Duschness.* £350
– **Paradise Regain'd.** L., 1671. *1st. Edn.* With misprint 'loah' on p.67 line 2 uncorrected, licence lf. reprd., mor. gt. by F. Bedford; Charles Tennant bkplt., Frederic Dannay copy. (CNY. Dec.16; 243) $650
– **Poems, & c. Upon Several Occasions** ... L., 1673. *2nd. Edn.* 2 pts. in 1 vol. Advts., hole in A1, few marginal tears, old sheep. [Wing M2161] (SPB. May 16; 105) $500
– **Poems in English.** Ill.:– William Blake. L., Nones. Pr., 1926. *(1450) numbered.* 2 vols. Cf. (LH. Sep.25; 432) $160
– **The Poetical Works.** Ill.:– R. White (port.), Burghers after Medina (plts.). L., 1695. Fo. Cont. cf., brkn. (SG. Feb.9; 286) $250
– **The Poetical Works ... with a life of the author by William Hayley.** Ill.:– after Richard Westall. 1794-95. 3 vols. Fo. 30 engraved plts., some foxing affecting plts., cont. diced russ., spines gt.-decor., rubbed, spines faded; Sir Ivar Colquhoun, of Luss copy. (CE. Mar.22; 217) £380
– – **Anr. Edn.** Ill.:– after R. Westall. 1794-97. 3 vols. Fo. L.P., some foxing, owners sigs. on fly-ll., cont. str.-grd. red mor., blind- & gt.-decor. (C. May 30; 163) *Thorp.* £320
– – **Anr. Copy.** 3 vols. Fo. 4 engraved ports., 28 engrs., extra ill. with 24 mezzotints by John Martin, leath. (DS. Dec.16; 2525) Pts. 105,000
– – **Anr. Edn.** L., 1835. 6 vols. 12mo. Pol. mor., by Bayntun, covers gt. with rose cornerpieces & border. (PNY. Dec.1; 18) $300
– – **Anr. Copy.** 6 vols. 16mo. Lacks 3 hf.-titles, hf. cf., spines gt. (SG. Feb.16; 202) $150
– – **Anr. Edn.** Boston, 1836. *New Edn.* 2 vols. Some light foxing, light stain to pp. 333-380 in Vol. 2, p. 337 heavily browned, orig. blue embossed cl. [Blanck's CM pattern], lacks both spines, extremities worn, sewing separating; both vols. sigd. in pencil 'H. Melville N.Y. 1849' on fly-lf., & with his extensive pencil annots., margin notes, underlinings, check marks, asterisks, etc., 2 annots. cut away & 10 or more erased, each vol. inscr. in upr. cover 'C. Horn 1860'. (PNY. Mar.27; 45) $100,000
– **Pro Populo Anglicano Defensio.** L., 1651. Sm. 12mo. Cont. vell. (SG. Feb.9; 285) $120
– **Pro Populo Anglicano Defensio Secunda.** L., 1654. *1st. Edn.* A few headlines shaved. [Wing M2171] *(Bound with:)* **Pro se Defensio Contra Alexandrum Morum.** L., 1655. *1st. Edn.* Light stains. [Wing M2172]. Together 2 works in 1 vol. Cont. cf., rebkd. (BBA. May 3; 132) *Howes Bookshop.* £85
– **The Shorter Poems.** Ill.:– Samuel Palmer. 1889. 4to. Some margin foxing, cont. mor. gt. (P. Dec.8; 123) *Scott.* £95
– **The Works.** 1863. 8 vols. Cont. dark purple mor. gt. by Maclehose. (CSK. Aug.19; 45) £170

MILTON, Visc. William W. Fitzwilliam & Cheadle, W.B.
– **An Expedition across the Rocky Mountains into British Columbia by the Yellow Head or Leather Pass.** Priv. Ptd., [1865]. *1st. Edn.* Orig. cl. (BBA. Sep.29; 51) *Ginzberg.* £300

MINADOI, Giovanni Tommaso
– **Historia della Guerra fra Turchi et Persiani.** Venice, 1594. *2nd. Edn.* 4to. Margin worming towards end affecting a few letters of index, cont.

limp vell., lacks ties. (C. Nov.16; 135) *Wood.* £250

MINAMOTO, H.
– **The Screen Paintings of Momoyama Period.** Tokyo & Kyoto, [1935]. Ob. lge. fo. 50 plts. in colours & gold, ex-liby., accordion folded, gt. brocaded cl., folding s.-c., ivory clasps. (SG. May 3; 256) $110

MINANO, Sebastián de
– **Diccionario Geográfico-estadistico de Espâna y Portugal.** Madrid, 1826-29. 11 vols. 4to. Many engrs. hand-cold., cont. linen. (DS. Mar.23; 2383) Pts. 36,000

MINASIAN, Khatchik
– **The Simple Songs of** ... Intro.:– William Saroyan. Ill.:– V. Angelo. San Franc., Colt Pr., at the Grabhorn Pr., 1950. *(300) sigd. by Minasian & Saroyan.* Hf. cl. & decor. bds., covers slightly darkened, d.-w. slightly darkened & chipped; the V. Angelo copy. (CBA. Oct.1; 175) $130

MINER, Dorothy
– **Studies in Art & Literature for Bella De Costa Greene.** Contribs.:– L.C. Wroth, B. Berenson, G. Keynes, E.P. Goldschmidt, & others. Princeton, 1954. *1st. Edn.* 4to. Buckram. (SG. Sep.15; 149) $140
– – **Anr. Copy.** 4to. Buckram. (SG. Sep.15; 148) $120

MINER, Harriet Stewart
– **Orchids.** [Boston], 1885. 4to. 24 chromolithos., some plts. offset to text, orig. cl. gt., spine worn & rubbed. (TA. Dec.15; 180) £80
– – **Anr. Copy.** Hf. leath. & marb. bds., spine & edges nicked & rubbed. (RS. Jan.17; 477) $175

MINISTERE DE LA GUERRE [FRANÇAISE]
– **Ordonnance du Roi, du 6 Décembre 1829, sur l'Exercice et les Evolutions de la Cavalerie.** Paris, 1829. 2 vols. Fo. 130 engraved plts., 8 folding sheets of music, slight foxing, few minor tears, sheep-bkd. bds. (S. Apr.10; 371) *Browning.* £100

MINKOWSKI, Hermann
– **Raum und Zeit.** Leipzig, 1909. *1st. Edn.* No. 3, 'Physikalische Zeitschrift', Vol. 10, pp. 104-11. 4to. Slight browning, cont. hf. mor., rubbed; Stanitz coll. (SPB. Apr.25; 303) $300
– **Vorlesungen über Varationsrechnung.** Ed.:– C. Veitken. Göttingen, 1907. Stp. on front free endpaper, cont. hf. leath., slightly worn. (HT. May 8; 497) DM 800

MINORSKY, V. (Ed.)
See– BEATTY, Chester

MINSHEU, John
– **Minshaei Emendatio ... sui Ductoris in Linguas. In Nine Languages.** L., 1627. *2nd. Edn. 4th. Iss.* Fo. Art leath. [STC 17947] (SG. Oct.27; 225) $100

MIOT
[–] **Le Régime Fiscal de la Corse.** Ajaccio, 1896. Sewed. (HD. Oct.21; 128) Frs. 1,300

MIOT, Comte André François de Mélito
– **Mémoires.** 1858. *Orig. Edn.* 3 vols. Cont. hf. chagrin, covers lightly rubbed. (HD. Jun.29; 144) Frs. 1,400

MIRABEAU, Honoré Gabriel Riquetti, Comte de
– **Considerations on the Order of Cincinnatus ... as also a Letter from Turgot to Dr. Price on the Constitution of America.** L., 1785. Mod. hf. cf., gt. spine. (SG. Apr.5; 130) $150
– **Elegies de Tibulle.** Paris, 1798. 3 vols. Mor., sigd. by Zaehnsdorf. (DS. Feb.24; 2440) Pts. 36,000
[–] **Errotika Biblion.** Rome, 1783. *1st. Edn.* Cont. mott. cf., unc., rebkd. in gt. cf. (SG. Feb.9; 288) $110
[–] **Histoire Secrète de la Cour de Berlin, ou Correspondance d'un Voyageur François.** N.p., 1789. 2 pts. in 1 vol. Cont. hf. leath. gt. (GB. Nov.3; 307) DM 400
– **Système Militaire de la Prusse, et Principes de la Tactique Actuelle des Troupes les Plus Perfectionnées.** L. [i.e. Paris], 1788. 4to. 93 double-p.

engraved plts., cont. tree cf., little worn. (SG. Sep.22; 216) $200

MIRABEAU, Honoré Gabriel Riquetti, Conte de & Mentelle, Edme
– **De la Monarchie Prussienne.** L., 1788. Atlas only. Fo. 10 double-p. engraved maps, 3 partly hand-cold. in outl., 93 engraved plts., 5 double-p., hf.-title, cont. hf. cf. (BBA. Aug.18; 288)
Wenner. £120

MIRABILIS LIBER
Ca. 1520-21. *1st. Printing.* 2 vols. bnd. in 1. Some ll. a little short at head, mor., by Gruel, roulette & blind motifs decor. in Renaissance style. (HD. Dec.9; 63) Frs. 3,000

MIRBEAU, Octave
– **Dingo.** Ill.:– Pierre Bonnard. Paris, 1924. *(370) numbered. (40) on Japan de Shidzuoka, with extra suite of plts. on vergé d'Arches.* Lge. 4to. Mor., blind- & gt.-decor., watered silk doubls. & end-ll., orig. pict. wraps. bnd. in, s.-c., by G. Cretté, s.-c. rubbed. (S. Nov.21; 2) *Minou.* £1,500
– **Le Jardin des Supplices.** Ill.:– Raphaël Freida. Paris, 1927. *(15) on old japan with 5 states of etchings, orig. drawing & refused plt.* 4to. Red mor. gt. by Gilbert, mosaic decor., watered silk liners & end-ll., wrap., s.-c. (HD. Jun.13; 78) Frs. 14,600
– **Le Journal d'une Femme de Chambre.** Paris, 1900. *Orig. Edn. (200) numbered in 8vo. format, on vélin d'Arches.* Red hf. mor., corners, by Marius Magnin, unc., wrap. & spine. (HD. Jul.2; 87) Frs. 1,600
– **La 628-E8.** Ill.:– Pierre Bonnard. Paris, 1908. *De Luxe Printing. (25) numbered reimposed on japon impérial.* Sm. 4to. Marb. cf. gt., painted, unc., ill. wrap. (HD. Jul.2; 89) Frs. 4,500
– – **Anr. Edn.** Ill.:– Pierre Bonnard. Paris, 1908. *De Luxe Edn. (255).* 4to. Hf. damson chagrin, corners, decor. & mosaic spine, wrap & spine preserved. (HD. Dec.9; 157) Frs. 2,200

MIRBEAU, Octave & others
– **Cezanne.** Ill.:– Cézanne, Bonnard, Denis, Matisse, Maillol, Roussel & Vuillard. Paris, 1914. *(600) numbered.* Fo. Hf. linen with orig. bd. cover, soiled. (HK. Nov.11; 3463) DM 1,600

MIRO, Joan
– **Der Lithograph.** Preface:– R. Queneau. Genf, [1975]. Vol. 2. Lge. 4to. Orig. wraps., 1 cold. litho. (HK. Nov.11; 3821) DM 520
– – **Anr. Edn.** Preface:– J. Teixidor. Genf, [1977]. Vol. 3. Lge. 4to. Orig. linen, orig. wrap. with 1 cold. litho. (HK. Nov.11; 3822) DM 420
– **Lithographie.** N.Y. & Geneva, 1972-77. Vols. 1-3. 4to. Vol. 1 in Engl., Vols. II & III in German, orig. linen with orig. pict. wraps. (GB. Nov.5; 2818) DM 1,200
– **L'Oiseau Solaire, L'Oiseau Lunaire, Etincelles.** Text:– Patrick Waldberg. [Paris], 1967. *(150) numbered on velin de Rives paper.* Special no. of 'Derrière Le Miroir'. Sm. fo. Unbnd. in col.-pict. wraps., heavy bd. s.-c.; sigd. in pencil by Miro. (SG. Mar.29; 239) $250
– **Peintures sur Cartons.** Text:– Jacques Dupin. [Paris, 1965]. *(150) numbered on velin de Rives paper.* Special no. of 'Derrière Le Miroir'. Sm. fo. Unbnd. in col.-pict. wraps., heavy bd. s.-c.; sigd. in pencil by Miro. (SG. Mar.29; 238) $250
– **Sculptures.** Text:– Audré Balthazar & Jacques Dupin. [Paris, 1970]. *(150) numbered on velin de Lana paper.* Special no. of 'Derrière Le Miroir'. Sm. fo. Unbnd. in col.-pict. wraps., heavy bd. s.-c.; sigd. in pencil by Miro. (SG. Mar.29; 240) $300

MIRROR, The
1823-40. Vols. 1-36. All but 7 in orig. bds. (P. Feb.16; 125) £90

MIRYS, S.D.
– **Figures de l'Histoire de la République Romaine** ... Paris, priv. ptd., An VIII [1800]. 4to. Old mor., spine decor.; Alfred Piet ex-libris. (HD. May 4; 360) Frs. 2,000

MISCELLANEA CURIOSA, sive Ephemeridum Medico-Physicarum Germanicarum Academiae Imperialis ... Anni M.DC.LXXXIX
Norimbergae, 1690. 4to. Hf. title, cont. vell. (LM. Mar.3; 187) B.Frs. 12,000

MISHMERET HA'KODESH
Commentary:– Yakov Ben Joseph Rofe. Calcutta, 1895. 2 pts. in 1 vol. 12mo. 1st. title defect. & reprd., slight worming not affecting text, cl. (S. Oct.25; 270) *Gubbay.* £140

MISHNA
Commentary:– Moshe ben Maimon & others. Trans.:– Judah ben Solomon Al-Harizi. Naples, Joshua Solomon Soncino & Yosef Ibn Peso, 1 Iyyar 5252 [8 May 1492]. *1st. Compl. Edn.* Fo. Lacks 21 ll., spaces left for additional diagrams (some supplied in MS.), 1st. few & last 12 ll. with repairs to margins with browning & staining, repairs sometimes affecting sm. parts of text, some browning & staining thro.-out, margin glosses &c. in various hands, censored but not sigd., old bds., worn. [Steinschneider 1982; Goff Heb-82] (SPB. Jun.26; 19) $17,000
– – **Anr. Edn.** Commentaries:– Moshe Ben Maimon & Ovadia Bertinoro. Sabbioneta, Mantua, 1559-63. 6 vols., compl. Various sizes. Vol. I: owners sigs. on title & verso, ll. towards beginning crudely reprd. with loss of text, browned, margin glosses in 16th. C. hand, hf. leath. with marb. paper bds.; Vol. II: washed, wormed affecting some letters, lacks 4 ll. diagrams (as usual), stained, mod. blind-tooled mor.; Vol. III: worming reprd., some staining, marb. paper bds.; Vol. IV: margins of some ll. reprd. with loss of text, sigd. by censor & owner on last p., mod. blind-tooled mor.; Vol. V: slight staining, hf. leath., marb. paper bds.; Vol. VI: reprd., staining, slight worming affecting some letters, hf. leath., marb. paper bds.; s.-c., w.a.f. [Steinschneider 1985] (S. Jul.3; 142) £200

MISHNAYOT
Amst., 1633. *1st. Menasseh Ben Israel Edn.* 2 pts. in 1 vol. Sm. 8vo. Latin & Hebrew titles, Hebrew divisional titles (dtd. 1631), slightly soiled, margin tears to Latin title, final lf. remargined, old hf. leath., worn, loose. (SG. Feb.2; 263) $1,100

MISHNAYOT [with nikud]
Amst., 1646. 2 pts. in 1 vol. Hole in 1 title not affecting borders, browned, slight staining, owner's sig. on fly-lf., trimmed, vell., slightly worn. (S. Oct.25; 272) *Gillis.* £650

MISSALS [*Chronologically, irrespective of use*]
– **[Missale Ordinis Praedicatorum].** Naples, Mathias Moravus, for Franciscus Palmerus, 29 Mar. 1483. 4to. Initials supplied in red, blue or green, a few with ornamental penwork, some ll. inserted from anr. copy, many ll. stained, a few crude repairs, some fore-margins nibbled by rodents, new end-papers, cont. Northern Italian blind-stpd. cf. over wood bds., rebkd., bosses, new clasps. [BMC VI, 864; Goff M-368] (SPB. Dec.14; 24) $350
– **Missale Curiense.** Augsburg, Erhardt Ratdolt, 13 Aug. 1497. Fo. 8 ll. of 'Canon Missae' ptd. on vell., lacks 3 ll. of prelims., but with 4 ll. in last gathering not cited by Reichling or Weale-Bohatta, reprd. tears affecting text on 6 ll., a few margin tears & repairs, some stains, deleted liby. stp. on 1st. p., final blank used as pastedown, cont. Augsburg blind-stpd. cf. over wood bds., spine ends worn, central metal bosses & cornerpieces (lacks 3, 1 loose), lacks clasp. (SPB. Dec.14; 23) $2,900
– **Missale Ratisponense.** [Bamberg, Johann Pfeyl, 11 Dec. 1497]. *1st. Edn.* Fo. Lacks 1st. 6 ll., folios 23 & 24, the 12 vell. ll. with the Canon, folios 302 & 303 & all after fo. 309, short tear in fore-margin of penultimate lf., cont. German blind-stpd. pig over wood bds., worn, clasps, lacks all 10 bosses. [Goff M-687; HC 11358*] (SPB. Dec.14; 25) $300
– **Missale Praedicatorum cum suo Ordinario.** [Paris, 14.11.1519]. Later title lf. at beginning mis-titled, lacks 7 unnumbered & 2 numbered ll., initials, some ll. lighlty defect., or with sm. defects reprd., some browning or soiling, slightly stained at beginning, hf. vell. (HK. May 15; 198) DM 750
– **Missale secundum Ordinem Fratrum Praedicatorum.** Venice, 1.IV.1522. Lacks 1st. 8 unnumbered ll. & 10 numbered ll., 1st. lf. slightly soiled & with reprd. corner, 19th. C. blind-tooled leath. (HK. Nov.8; 286) DM 650
– **Missale Romanum.** Ill.:– Zoan Andrea. Venice, 1532. 4to. Lacks 1st. 8 unnumbered ll. & 8 numbered ll., 3 ll. with sm. hole, 1st. & last ll. wormed, 2 ll. reprd., some staining & soiling, 18th. C. leath., slightly wormed. (HK. Nov.8; 285) DM 400
– **Missale Insignis Ecclesie Cathalaunen.** 1543. Fo. On vell., some staining, arms on 1st. p. under miniature, 1st. p. entirely painted, including title, 5 sm., 30 medium & 2 lge. miniats., some orig., (with blank space left), some covering wood engrs., lge. illuminated engr. of canon with date 1538, nearly all lge. initials hand-painted, approx 300 decor. letters, last lf. nearly entirely remade in pen, arms on verso, La Valliere mor., mosaic decor., decor. mosaic spine, red mor doubl., semi, gt. dentelle, wtrd. silk-end-papers, mor. s.-c., by Lortic. (HD. Mar.30; G) Frs. 200,000
– **Missale Ambrosianum.** Mailand, 1548. 4to. Title stpd., 1st. & last ll. slightly soiled & wormed, some old annots., cont. blind-tooled leath. over wood bds., wormed & rubbed, spine renewed, lacks clasps. (HK. Nov.8; 284) DM 1,300
– **Missale Romanum. Ex Decreto Sacrosancti Concilii Tridentini restitutum.** Venedig, 1571. 4to. Leath., gt. decor., wormed, restored. (D. Nov.23; 83) DM 2,200
– **Missale Romanum.** Venetiis, 1572. Fo. Dampstain, cont. blind-stpd. roan over wood bds., spine renewed, clasps incompl.; from Fondation Furstenberg-Beaumesnil. (HD. Nov.16; 141) Frs. 2,500
– – **Anr. Edn.** Venice, 1597. 4to. Partly dampstained, about 40 ll. wormed, old blind-stpd. cf., worn. (SG. Oct.27; 230) $120
– – **Anr. Edn.** Antw., 1640. Fo. Engraved vig. on title, engraved capitals & full-p. ills., slight browning, few ll. cropped, cont. cf., worn, rebkd. (S. Apr.10; 327) *Pearson.* £80
– – **Anr. Edn.** Rome, 1662. Fo. Foxed, few pp. reprd., 3 later missals bnd. in, gt.-decor. cf. (CBA. Dec.10; 459) $130
– **Missale Cartusiani Ordinis ex Ordinatione Capituli Generalis.** 1679. Fo. Some foxing & soiling, old cf., rubbed. (RO. Mar.28; 126) $125
– **Missale Romanum ex Decreto Sacrosancti Concilii Tridentini Restitutum S. Pii V. Pontificis Max.** Ill.:– Orsolini. Venice, 1761. (*Bound with:*) – **Missae Propriae Sanctorum.** Salisburg, 1759. Together 2 works in 1 vol. Fo. Cont. cf., 16th. C. Aldine-style decor, clasps; from Fondation Furstenberg-Beaumesnil. (HD. Nov.16; 143) Frs. 1,700
– **Missale Romanum.** Rome, 1794. Fo. Cont. mor. gt., decor. (HD. Nov.29; 64) Frs. 1,400
– – **Anr. Edn.** Ratisbon, 1920. Fo. Red mor., gt.– & silver-decor., silver clasps, 8 (book-mark) ribbons. (B. Oct.4; 600) Fls. 800

MISSION PELLIOT EN ASIE CENTRALE
Paris, 1920-46. Vols. 2-4 only in 5. 4to. Orig. bdgs. (BBA. Mar.7; 68) *D. Loman.* £65

MISSON, François Maximilian
– **Memoirs et Observations faites par un Voyageur en Angleterre.** The Hague, 1698. *1st. Edn.* Engraved title-p. scraped with slight loss of text, 2 folding maps, 18 plts., 16 folding, title & 1st. few ll. discold., cont. cf., rebkd. (BBA. May 23; 342) *Vine.* £60

MISTRAL, Frédéric
– **Mireio.** Avignon, 1859. *Orig. Edn.* Parallel Provençal & Fr. text, some foxing, mor. by Taffin, spine raised bands (faded), wrap. preserved. (SM. Mar.7; 2520) Frs. 2,000
– **Mireille, Poème Provençal.** Ill.:– E. Burnand, M.Scott & after H.L. Pallandre. Paris, 1884. *(150) on japan paper.* Fo. Fr. trans. & orig. text, cont. hf. mor., corners, decor. spine, s.-c. (HD. Jan.30; 72) Frs. 1,700
– – **Anr. Edn.** Ill.:– Jean Droit. Paris, 1923. 2 pts. in 1 vol. Sm. 4to. On japan, separate suite of ills., mosaic mor. by Flammarion, watered silk liners & end-ll., wraps. & spines. (HD. Jun.6; 112) Frs. 2,200
– – **Anr. Edn.** Ill.:– Marianne Clouzot. Paris, 1962. *(915). (25) with suites in cols. & black & 2 aquas.* 2 vols. 4to. Unnumbered, leaves, wrap, s.-c.'s. (HD. Mar.30; 32) Frs. 1,900
– – **Anr. Edn.** Ill.:– Clouzot. 1962. 2 vols. 4to. Leaves, wraps. & bds. (HD. Jan.24; 75) Frs. 1,150

MITCHEL, Flora H.
– **Vanishing Dublin.** Dublin, 1966. *[1st. Edn.].* 4to. D.-w. & plastic outer cover; inscr by author. (GM. Dec.7; 79) £260
– – **Anr. Copy.** Sm. fo. No bdg. stated, d.-w. (GM. Dec.7; 320) £180

MITCHELL, Donald G.
– **The Works.** N.Y., 1907. *(204). (179) numbered & sigd.* 16 vols. Lev. mor., double-ruled gt. borders & decor. cornerpieces, spines in 6 compartments, gt.-panel. with sm. red mor. gt. onlays, turn-ins gt., watered silk linings, partly unc., by The Monastery Hill Bindery. (CNY. Dec.17; 582) $450

MITCHELL, John
[–] **The Contest in America between Great Britain & France, with its Consequence & Importance.** L., 1757. *[1st. Edn.].* Cont. cf. gt., sm. repair to spine, edges worn; Brocket Hall & Panshanger bkplts., the Rt. Hon. Visc. Eccles copy. [Sabin 49693] (CNY. Nov.18; 198) $600
– – **Anr. Copy.** Cont. cf., worn, covers detchd. [Sabin 49693] (SG. Oct.20; 239) $325
[–] **The Present State of Great Britain & North America.** L., 1767. *1st. Edn.* Hf.-title, hf. mor., reprd. [Sabin 49696] (S. May 22; 330) *Quaritch.* £160

MITCHELL, Margaret
– **Gone With the Wind.** N.Y., 1936. *1st. Edn. 1st. Iss.* May 1936 copyright, cl., light wear; sigd. by author on front free end-paper. (RO. Apr.23; 235) $300
– – **Anr. Copy.** Cl. (SG. May 24; 348) $100

MITCHELL, R.L.
– **Journal of an Expedition into the Interior of Tropical Australia.** L., 1848. *1st. Edn.* 12 plts., 7 engraved maps (several folding, 1 with fore-margin strengthened), a few margins slightly soiled, cont. hf. mor., rubbed. (S. May 22; 482) *Maggs.* £360

MITCHELL, Robert
– **Plans, & Views in Perspective.** 1801. Fo. 18 aquatint plts., title & text in Engl. & Fr., later hf. cf. (C. Dec.9; 104) *Glasgow.* £550

MITCHELL, Samuel Augustus
– **A General View of the United States ... also, of its Canals, Rail-Roads, Colleges, Religious Denominations, etc.** Phila., 1846. *1st. Edn.* Lge. folding map tape-reprd. at folds, later hf. leath., worn. (SG. Oct.20; 238) $120
– **Mitchell's New General Atlas.** Phila., 1860. Fo. 76 maps & plans in col., on 47 sheets, gt.-lettered cl., mor. back & tips, worn. (SG. Jun.7; 24) $250
– – **Anr. Edn.** Phila., 1864. Sm. fo. 84 hand-cold. maps on 53 sheets. orig. gt. cl., leath. spine, crudely reprd., loose in case. (SG. Dec.15; 11) $375
– – **Anr. Edn.** Phila., 1868. Fo. Hand-cold. plt., 54 hand-cold. maps, some double-p., hf. mor., defect. (P. Dec.8; 413) *Noble.* £320
– – **Anr. Edn.** Phila., 1869. Sm. fo. 96 hand-cold. maps on 63 sheets, gt. cl., leath. spine, worn. (SG. Jun.7; 27) $225
– – **Anr. Edn.** Phila., 1870. Lge. 4to. 58 hand-cold. litho. mapsheets, containing 96 maps & plans (insets numbered as separate subjects, publisher's hf. roan, worn, w.a.f. (S. May 22; 364) *Marsden.* £280
– **A New Universal Atlas.** Phila., 1849. Fo. Litho. title with lge. vig., 73 hand-cold. litho. mapsheets, 42 relating to Americas, (including town plans & individual State & Territory maps), some slight spotting, publisher's hf. roan, gt. label on upr. cover, rubbed, w.a.f. (S. May 22; 363) *Downra.* £480
[–] – **Anr. Edn.** Phila., 1850. Fo. 76 hand-cold. engraved maps, numbered 1-72 & 4 bis plts., & frontis. chart, numbered 73, a few maps from other atlases affixed to blank versos of some maps, three-qtr. leath., worn, ex-liby. (RO. Dec.11; 225) $550
– – **Anr. Edn.** Phila., 1854. Litho. title, table, 74 hand-cold. maps, 1 cleanly torn along fold, cont. hf. mor., worn. (CSK. Mar.9; 24) £320
– **Traveller's Guide Through the United States.** Phila., 1836. 12mo. Folding map hand-cold., some tears at creases to text, orig. embossed front on later bdg., cl. case. (LH. Jan.15; 358) $120

MITCHELL, Sir Thomas L.
- Journal of an Expedition into the Interior of Tropical Australia. L., 1848. *[1st. Edn.].* 7 maps, 12 plts., blind-stpd. cl., unc., rebkd. (CA. Apr.3; 87)
Aus.$850
- - **Anr. Copy.** Outer edge of 1 folding map frayed, cl., unc., worn, crudely reprd. (KH. May 1; 491)
Aus.$720
- Three Expeditions into the Interior of Eastern Australia, with Descriptions of the Recently Explored Region of Australia Felix, & of the Present Colony of New South Wales. L., 1838. *1st. Edn.* 2 vols. 2 litho. titles with vigs., folding engraved map hand-cold. in outl., 51 litho. plts., maps & charts including 6 hand-cold., titles & some plts. spotted, pres. bdg., ribbed cl., elab. arabesque interwoven panels on covers stpd. in gt., gt. vigs. on spines, by Remnant & Edmonds with their ticket; inscr. to Rt. Hon. Sir George Murray, G.C.M. (C. Jun.27; 97)
Dunsheath. £1,200
- - **Anr. Copy.** 2 vols. Litho. title, 52 plts. & maps, slight discolouration in margins of some plts., orig. blind-stpd. cl., unc., Vol. 2 unopened, 1 spine reinforced. (CA. Apr.3; 86)
Aus. $1,100
- - **Anr. Edn.** L., 1839. *2nd. Edn.* 2 vols. Orig. cl., some repairs, unc. (KH. Nov.9; 668)
Aus. $600
- - **Anr. Copy.** Lacks lge. general map & several prelims., otherwise not collated, several plts. folded or shaved, some soiling & discoloration, later binder's cl. (KH. Nov.9; 351)
Aus. $200
- - **Anr. Edn.** Adelaide, 1965. *Facs. Edn.* Orig. cl. (KH. Nov.9; 352)
Aus. $130

MITFORD, Algernon Bertram
- Tales of Old Japan. L., 1871. *1st. Edn.* 2 vols. 1 plt. reprd. & laid down, spotted, hf. mor. (S. Jun.25; 43)
Subunso. £90
- - **Anr. Copy.** 2 vols. Hf.-titles, cont. hf. cf., spines gt., slightly rubbed. (BBA. Feb.9; 96)*Brailey.* £50

MITFORD, John
- An Essay upon the Harmony of Language. 1774. *1st. Edn.* Cont. hf. cf. gt., a little worn. (BBA. Sep.29; 157)
Jarndyce. £60

MITFORD, John 'A. Burton'
- The Adventures of Johnny Newcome in the Navy. 1819. 20 hand-cold. plts., cf., hinges reprd. (P. Jun.7; 228)
£85
- [-] My Cousin in the Army; or Johnny Newcombe. L., 1822. *1st. Edn.* 16 hand-cold. aquatint plts., mor. gt. by Zaehnsdorf, partly unc. (S. Mar.20; 734)
Thorp. £260

MITFORD, Mary Russell
- Our Village: Sketches of Rural Character & Scenery. 1824-32. *1st. Edn.* 5 vols. Spotted, cont. cf., spines faded, rubbed. (BBA. Jul.27; 139)
Peter Murray Hill. £340

MITFORD, Nancy
- The Sun King. 1969. *(265) numbered & sigd.* Red mor. gt., by Zaehnsdorf, green & black overlays forming sun on upr. cover, lined s.-c. (P. Sep.29; 112)
Wolfson. £55

MIVART, St. George
- Dogs, Jackals, Wolves, & Foxes, a monograph of the Canidae. L., 1890. *[1st. Edn.].* 4to. 45 hand-cold. litho. plts., a few ll. spotted, liby. stps., orig. cl., partly unc. (S. Dec.13; 287)
Wedikind. £290
- - **Anr. Copy.** 4to. 45 hand-cold. litho. plts., few with minor margin wear, cl., disbnd., ex-liby. (SG. Oct.6; 259)
$700

MIZA ABU TALEB KHAN
- Travels. Trans.:- Charles Stewart. 1814. *2nd. Edn.* 3 vols. Engraved port., cont. cf., rubbed. (CSK. Jul.6; 56)
£65

MIZNER, Addison
- Florida Architecture of Mizner Addison. Intro.:- I.M. Tarbell. N.Y., [1929]. *1st. Edn.* Fo. Port., 184 photographic rotogravure plts., orig. linen & marb., hinges brkn. (SG. Oct.13; 244) $450

MIZRACHI, Elijah
- Mizrachi Al Ha'Torah. Cracow, 1595. *4th. Edn.* Fo. Lacks 2 ll., lr. margins of 1st. 3 ll. reprd. not affecting text, last lf. torn & reprd. with loss of some text, browned & stained, hf. leath., marb. paper bds. (S. Oct.25; 273)
Rosenfeld. £500

MOCATTA, Frederic D.
- Catalogue of the Printed Books & Manuscripts Forming the Library ... Compiler:- Reginald A. Rye. L., 1904. Sq. 8vo. 2 copies each of later acquisitions, 1905-09 & 1909-11, & a 2-p. multigraphed list of additions from Jan. through May 1926 laid in, orig. qtr. cl., rubbed of shaken. (SG. Feb.2; 25)
$250

MODA DI TUTTE LE EPOCHE (il Settecento, il Periodo Napoleonico. etc.)
Milano, 1945. *(190) numbered.* 4 portfos. 4to. 112 orig. hand-cold. plts., bds. (CR. Jun.6; 199)
Lire 320,000

MODE (La)
Text:- Balzae, E. Sue, Mme de Staël, Ch. Nodier, Benjamin Constant, D. Gay, & others. Ill.:- de Valmont, Victor Adam, 'Grandville', T. Johannot (woodcut). 3 Oct. 1829-27 Mar. 1830. Vols. 1 & 2, in 1 vol. Lge. 8vo. On vell., 38 lithos. (32 cold.), some foxing, cont. hf. roan, blind- & gt.-decor. (HD. Feb.28; 174)
Frs. 4,500

MODES (Les)
Paris, 1901-Dec. 1920. Nos. 1-200 in 17 vols., compl. Lge. 4to. On 'papier couché', hf. chagrin, wraps. (HD. Feb.28; 175)
Frs. 5,200

MODIUS, Franciscus
- Cleri totius Romanae Ecclesiae Suiecti ... Frankfurt, 1585. Sm. 4to. Interfoliated, ff. Cl - Z4 ptd. on recto only, lacks 2 ll., cf., gt. decor. (HD. Feb.22; 142)
Frs. 1,200

MODON, Shimshon
- Kol Musar. Mantua, 1725. *1st. Edn.* 4to. Some staining, hf. leath. (S. Oct.25; 278)
Sapir. £130

MODUS VACANDI BENEFICIORUM
[Rome], ca. 1500. 4to. Bds. [H. 11531] (HK. Nov.8; 287)
DM 400

MOE, Jørgen I.
See— ASBJØRNSEN, Peter Christen & Moe, Jørgen I.

MOEHSEN, Johann Carl Wilhelm
- Beschreibung einer Berlinischen Sammlung die Vorzüglich aus Gedächtnis-Münzen Berühmter Aerzte besteht ... Beiträge zur Geschichte der Wissenschaften in der Mark Brandenburg. Berlin & Leipzig, 1773-81-83. 3 vols. Vols.1-2 new bds., unc., Vol.3 old bds.; Dr. Walter Pagel copy. (S. Feb.7; 260)
Levy. £180

MOELLER, J. & Thoms, H.
- Real-Enzyklopädie der Gesamten Pharmazie. Berlin & Wien, 1904-14. *2nd. Edn.* 13 vols. & supp. vol. in together 14 vols. Orig. hf. leath. gt. (R. Apr.4; 1342)
DM 700

MOERDER, J. de
See— SIMONOFF, L. de & Moerder, J. de

MOERDYK, G.
- Kerkgeboue vir Suid Afrika. Intro.:- J.D. Kestell & Anton van Wouw. Johannesburg, 1919. Sm. 4to. Wraps. (VA. Jan.27; 289)
R. 180

MOES, Ernst Willem & others
- Nederlandsche Kasteelen en hun Historie. Amst., 1912-15. 3 vols. 4to. Orig. cl. (B. Feb.8; 659)
Fls. 450

MOEURS ET COUTUMES des Peuples, ou Collection de Tableaux Représ. les Usages ... des nations du Monde
Paris, 1811-14. 2 vols. 4to. 142 cont. hand-cold. plts., 1 extra plt., lacks index-lf. & 2 plts. in Vol. 2, cont. marb. cf. gt., crowned monog., spine-ends & corners defect., slightly rubbed. (VG. Nov.30; 524)
Fls. 1,500

MOFFATT, Elizabeth Whitney
See— GARDILANNE, Gratiane de & Moffatt, Elizabeth Whitney

MOFFET, Thomas
- Health's Improvement: or, Rules Comprizing & Discovering the Nature, Method & Manner of Preparing all Sorts of Food. L., 1655. *1st. Edn.* 4to. 1st. (licence) lf. present, later cf., spine gt. [Wing M2382] (BBA. May 3; 51)
Ximenes. £360

- The Theater of Insects ... L., 1658. Fo. Later cf. (SKC. Oct.26; 409)
£300

MOGG, Edward
- Survey of the High Roads of England & Wales. 1817. Vol. 1 (all publd.). 4to. Additional engraved title, double-p. map of England & Wales, 223 handcold. strip road maps on 112 ll., prelims. spotted, later cl., orig. spine relaid. (TA. Sep.15; 124)
£380
- - **Anr. Copy.** Vol. 1 (all publd.). Engraved title, hand-cold. general map, 223 road maps on 112 plts., cold. in outl., hf. cf., spine defect. (P. Jun.7; 339)
£300

MOHAMMED V. BAGDAD (Al Baghdadi)
- Libri del Modo di dividere le Superficie. Ed.:- J. Dee & F. Commandino. Pesaro, 1570. 4to. Some staining, cont. limp vell. (BR. Apr.12; 760)
DM 400

MOHE, Fr.
- Commentar zur Pharmacopoea Germanica. Braunschweig, 1873. *1st. single vol. Edn.* Cont. hf. linen. (BR. Apr.12; 761)
DM 550

MOHOLY-NAGY, Laszlo
- Buch Neuer Künstler. Ed.:- L. Kassak. [Wien, 1922]. *Orig. Edn. (1500).* Lge. 4to. Some margin tears pasted, bds., orig. upr. wrap. pasted on. (HK. Nov.11; 3685)
DM 900
- Malerei, Fotografie, Film. Ill.:- after Moholy-Nagy, Man Ray, Muche, & others. Munich, [1927]. *1st. Edn.* 4to. Orig. ptd. cl., d.-w. chipped. (SG. May 10; 90)
$225
- - **Anr. Edn.** München, [1929]. Orig. linen, bdg., wrap. & typography by H. Moholy-Nagy. (H. Nov.24; 1342)
DM 400
- Von Material zu Architektur. [Bauhausbücher Bd. XIV]. München, [1929]. *1st. Edn.* Orig. linen, bdg., wrap. & typography by Moholy-Nagy, wraps. slightly torn, sm. fault in spine. (H. Nov.24; 1345)
DM 560

MOIVRE, Abraham de
- Animadversiones in D. Georgii Cheynaei Tractatum de Fluxionum Methodo Inversa. L., 1704. *1st. Edn.* Some soiling & staining, 1 text lf. rubbed affecting a few letters, cont. panel. cf., lr. cover scraped; Stanitz coll. (SPB. Apr.25; 304) $200

MOLARD, Claude Pierre
See— PRONY, Gaspard, Baron de & Molard, Claude Pierre

MOLBECH, Chr.
- Briefe über Schweden im Jahre 1812. Altona, 1818-20. *1st. German Edn.* Cont. hf. leath. (R. Apr.5; 3114)
DM 480

MOLESWORTH, Robert, Viscount Molesworth
- [-] An Account of Denmark as it was in the Year 1692. 1694. *1st. Edn.* Cont. panel. cf. [Wing M2382A] (BBA. Jan.19; 174)
Vinderen Antikvariat. £75

MOLHUYSEN, P.C., Blok, P.J. & others
- Nieuw Nederlandsch Biogr. Woordenboek. Leiden, 1911-37. 10 vols. including Index. Cl. (VG. May 3; 169)
Fls. 650

MOLIERE, Jean Baptiste Poquelin, dit
- Les Fourberies de Scapin. Ill.:- Théodore Strawinsky. Paris, [1935]. *(10) on japan.* Lge. 8vo. Sewed; all drawings sigd. in pencil by artist. (HD. May 16; 101)
Frs. 1,700
- Oeuvres. Ill.:- Francois Harrewyn. Bruxelles, 1694. *New Edn.* 4 vols. 12mo. Red mor. gt. by Chambolle-Duru. (HD. Mar.19; 75)
Frs. 8,700
- - **Anr. Edn.** Ill.:- after Brissart. Paris, 1697. *Reiss. of 1st. Coll. Edn. (1682).* 8 vols. 12mo. Cont. grd. cf., decor. spine, some pieces renewed, some repairs. (HD. Jan.30; 73)
Frs. 2,200
- - **Anr. Edn.** Amst., 1704. *New Edn.* 4 vols. in 32 pts. 12mo. MS. contents list, arms ex-libris inside covers, marb. paper bds., cont. leath. box, blind-tooled. (GF. Nov.12; 744)
Sw. Frs. 950
- - **Anr. Edn.** Ill.:- Boucher. Paris, 1734. *1st. Printing, with 'Comteese' in last vol.* 6 vols. 4to. Cont. spr. cf., spines decor.; from Château des Noës liby. (HD. May 25; 55)
Frs. 33,500
- - **Anr. Edn.** Ill.:- Lepicie after Coypel (port.),

MOLIERE, Jean Baptiste Poquelin, dit -*Contd.*

Laurent Cars after Boucher. Paris, 1734. *2nd. Printing.* 6 vols. 4to. Foxing & stains on some ll., late 18th. C. tree cf., decor. spines, inner roll-stp., turn-ins restored. (HD. Sep.22; 290)   Frs. 5,800
– – **Anr. Edn.** Ill.:– Laurent Cars & others after F.E. Boucher & others. Paris, 1734. *New Edn.* 6 vols. 4to. Lacks some blanks, 3K1 in Vol. 3 reprd., some tears, foxing & browning, cont. cf., worn. (SPB. Dec.13; 783) $275
– – **Anr. Edn.** Life & Remarks:– F.M.A. d. Voltaire. Ill.:– J. Punt. Amst. & Leipzig, 1765. *New Edn.* 6 vols. 12mo. Late 19th. C. mor., gt. dentelles. (SG. Nov.3; 143) $275
– – **Anr. Edn.** Ill.:– Punt after Boucher. Amst. & Leipzig, 1765. 6 vols. Sm. 12mo. Old str.-grd. bradel mor., spines decor. (HD. May 3; 100)   Frs. 1,800
– – **Anr. Edn.** Notes:– M. Bret. Ill.:– Moreau le jeune. Paris, 1773. *1st. Printing of ills.* 6 vols. Cont. marb. cf., spines decor. (HD. May 16; 50)   Frs. 5,300
– – **Anr. Copy.** 6 vols. Cont. cf., jnts. & turn-ins renewed; from Horace Walpole liby. (HD. Apr.13; 30)   Frs. 5,000
– – **Anr. Edn.** Ed.:– Bret. Ill.:– Mignard (port.) & Moreau. Paris, 1788. *Reprint of 1773 Edn.* 6 vols. Some gatherings yellowed, sm. margin dampstains in some vols., cont. tree cf. gt., spines decor. (HD. May 3; 101)   Frs. 2,100
– – **Anr. Edn.** Ed.:– M. Bret. Ill.:– Mignard, Moreau. Paris, 1804. 6 vols. Cont. tree cf., gt.-tooled floral border. (GM. Dec.7; 686)   £80
– – **Anr. Copy.** 6 vols. Marb. cf., by Simier, decor. spines, inner roll-stp. (HD. Sep.21; 152) Frs. 2,100
– – **Anr. Copy.** 6 vols. Cont. tree cf., spines decor., slightly rubbed. (HD. Nov.29; 103)   Frs. 1,400
– – **Anr. Edn.** 1823. 6 vols. Some light spotting, cont. cf., spines gt., lightly rubbed. (CSK. Apr.6; 139)   £110
– **Oeuvres Complètes.** Paris, 1863. *(100) numbered, on L.P.* 6 vols. Lge. 8vo. Hf.-titles, errata lf., extra-ill. with about 160 engrs. inserted, red mor. gt., gt. dentelles by Claessens; J.H. Bates bkplt. (SG. Apr.26; 144) $600
– – **Anr. Edn.** Paris, 1878. 4 vols. Hf. cf. gt. (PNY. Oct.20; 187) - $125
– – **Anr. Edn.** Paris, 1879. Some plts. hand-cold., browned due to quality of paper, hf. cf., gt.-tooled-spine. (CR. Jun.6; 226)   Lire 280,000
– – **Anr. Edn.** Intro.:– Jules Janin. Ill.:– after Geoffroy & Sand. Paris, 1885. Cont. hf. mor. gt. (SKC. Nov.18; 1901)   £70
– **Remerciement au Roy.** Paris, 1663. *Orig. Edn.* 4to. Jansenist red mor., Baron de Lurde cyphers on covers; from Baron de Ruble liby. (HD. Mar.29; 63)   Frs. 102,000
– **Le Tartuffe.** Ill.:– Mariette Lydis. Paris, 1939. *(273). (15) 'ad personam', ptd. for Erica Marx.* Lge. 8vo. 7 engraved plts., including 1 folding, niger mor., by Sangorski & Sutcliffe, orig. wraps. bnd. in, s.-c. (S. Nov.21; 94)   Desk. £110
– **Théâtre Complet.** Intro.:– Jacques Scherer. Ill.:– Robert Beltz. Paris, 1964. 5 vols. 4to. On vell., chagrin, spines decor., unc., box. (HD. Jul.2; 92)   Frs. 1,300
– **Vignettes en Couleurs de Joseph Hémard.** Ill.:– Hémard. Paris, 1921. *(50) De Luxe Edn. on vell. pur fil.* Separate series of ills. in bistre & 1 orig. pen ill., hand- bnd. mor., by H. Blanchetière, cold. leath. inlays on spine & upr. cover, cold. leath. onlays inside cover, marb. M.P. doubls. & end-papers, orig. pict. wraps. bnd. in. (H. Nov.23; 1017)   DM 2,300

MOLINA Y SAAVEDRA, H. de

– **Epistola ... sobre la Recuperación de Portugal.** Colonia Agripina, 1650. 4to. Leath. (DS. Mar.23; 2179)   Pts. 40,000

MOLINER, Emile

– **Le Mobilier Francais du XVIIe et du XVIIIe Siècle.** Paris, n.d. Lge. 4to. Some faint foxing, unc., red hf. mor., spine reprd., slightly rubbed. (S. Nov.8; 555)   *Waleski.* £110

MOLINET, Claudio du

– **Historia Summorum Pontificum a Martino Vad Innocentium XI per eorum Numismata.** Paris, 1679.

Fo. Some spotting & browning, especially in margin, marb. leath. gt. (V. Sep.30; 2416)   DM 480

MOLINUS, Franciscus

– **De Maria Magdalena, Triduo Christi, et ex Tribus Una Maria, Disceptatio** ... Parisiis, 1518. *2nd. Edn.* Sm. 4to. Early notes, wormed, mod. bds. (BBA. Jun.28; 160)   *Marlborough Rare Books.* £95

MOLL, Hermann

– **Atlas Geographus. A Complete System of Geography.** 1711-14. 4 vols. only (of 5). 4to. Hand-cold. title to Vol.1, 71 hand-cold. maps, cont. cf. (P. Oct.20; 262)   £360
– – **Anr. Edn.** L., 1711-17. 5 vols. Sm. 4to. Maps in Vols. 3 & 4 hand-cold. in outl., non-unif. old panel. cf., w.a.f. [Sabin 49902] (C. Nov.16; 136)   *Burgess.* £500
– **Atlas Minor: A Set of Sixty-Two New & Correct Maps of All the Parts of the World.** N.d. *2nd. Edn.* 4to. Double-p. title, 10 folding maps, 52 double-p. maps, 2 maps with ink annots., cont. cf.-bkd. marb. bds., spine gt., slightly worn; the Hinton House copy. (LC. Oct.13; 447)   £850
– **Geographia Antiqua Latinorum Graecorum.** 1721. Sm. 4to. Engraved double-p. pict. title, 32 engraved double-p. maps, cont. leath.-bkd. bds., worn. (SKC. Sep.9; 2054)   £85
[–] **Geographia Classica: The Geography of the Ancients ... in the Greek & Latin Classicks in the Maps of the Old World** ... Dublin, 1736. *6th. Edn. [so stated].* Ob. sm. fo. 4 prelims., including rubric title on hf.-p. sheets, with untrimmed fore-edges, elab. extra engraved title, 30 (of 32) full-p. & folded black & white copperplt. maps, stains at fore-edge with folded maps affected, 1 defect. lacks portions chipped from fold, light foxing, orig. buff bds. with later cl. backing, covers worn. (HA. Feb.24; 382a) $120
– – **Anr. Edn.** L., 1755. Sm. 4to. Engl. & Latin titles, extra double-p. engraved title, 32 maps, most double-p., few folding, hf. cf., lacks spine, lr. cover loose. (S. Apr.9; 80)   *Voorhees.* £100
– **A Set of Fifty New & Correct Maps of England & Wales &c. With the Great Roads & Principal Cross-Roads** ... L., 1724. 4to. Double-p. title, 2 folding maps, 48 double-p. maps, sm. portion lacking from margin of 1 map, slight tear to anr. map, cont. cf. gt., slightly worn; the Hinton House copy. (LC. Oct.13; 448)   £750
– – **Anr. Copy.** Ob. fo. 50 engraved maps, hand-cold. in outl., including 2 folding, 1st. map with sm. tears, ptd. title stained, lr. margin frayed, cont. hf. cf., spine & corners slightly scuffed. (C. Nov.16; 137)   *Burden.* £600
– **A Set of the Thirty Two New & Correct Maps of the Principal Parts of Europe.** Ca. 1727. Ob. 4to. 32 engraved maps, 5 additional maps, by Bowen & others, bnd. in, orig. bds., worn. (CSK. May 4; 31)   £480
– **Thirty Two New & Accurate Maps of the Geography of the Ancients.** 1721. Sm. 4to. Double-p. engraved title (part of blank margin torn away), 32 double-p. or folding engraved maps, text in Latin & Engl., cont. panel. cf. (S. Nov.1; 176)   *Deane.* £110
– **The World Described; or, a New & Correct Sett of Maps.** [L.], T. Bowles, [maps dtd. 1709-20]. Narrow atlas fo. 30 double-p. folding engraved maps, hand-cold. in outl., all on guards, broadside title hinged with tape & slightly soiled, single 2 inch tears to folds of 2 maps, maps 1, 2, 28 & 29 slightly wormed extending to end-papers & paste-downs, orig. sheep, spine gt.-lettered, covers rubbed, spine & corners worn & chipped. (CNY. Nov.18; 301) $7,000
[–] – **Anr. Edn.** [1717 or later]. Fo. Collection of 14 double-p. maps extracted from Moll's General Atlas, all hand-cold. in outl., most soiled in margins, lightly wormed, 2 cleanly torn with loss, several reprd., old cf.-bkd. bds., worn, w.a.f. (CSK. May 4; 48)   £500
[–] – **Anr. Edn.** J. Bowles, T. Bowles, J. King & P. Overton, [1733 or later]. 27 lge. double-p. engraved folding maps (including 2 world maps, 6 of the Americas & general maps of Africa & Asia), variously dtd. between 1708 & 1720, folding table Geography Epitomiz'd (after A.G. Duzauzet) at end dtd. 1733, maps hand-cold. in outl., 1 or 2

---

longitudinal folds worn, others strengthened without significant loss of engraved surface, some faint stains, 1 or 2 short tears, 18th. C. hf. russ., w.a.f. (S. May 21; 127)   *Voorhees.* £4,000
– – **Anr. Edn.** L., T. Bowles, ca. 1733. Tall narrow fo. 30 lge. double-p. engraved folding maps, cont. hand-cold. in outl., ptd. title & contents lf. pasted on front pastedown, 1 or 2 longitudinal folds worn (as usual) with slight loss of engraved surface, only slight browning to some maps, some stains, 1 or 2 short tears without loss of engraved surface, cont. blind-ruled cf., worn. (S. Dec.1; 203)   *Burgess.* £4,300

MOLLER, Albin

– **Gruendlicher und Warer Bericht von dem Newen Cometstern ... Gesehen ... in October und Novemb. des M.DC. IV. Jahrs.** Eisleben, 1605. Sm. 4to. Pamphlet, dampstained, disbnd. (SG. Oct.27; 231) $120

MOLLHAUSEN, Baldwin

– **Diary of a Journey from the Mississipi to the Coasts of the Pacific** ... Intro.:– Alexander von Humboldt. Trans.:– Mrs. Percy Sinnett. L., 1858. *1st. Edn. in Engl.* 2 vols. Engraved folding map, 19 plts., bnd. without advts., pol. cf. gt., upr. cover of Vol. 1 stained, spines browned; the Rt. Hon. Visc. Eccles copy. [Sabin 49915] (CNY. Nov.18; 199) $600
– – **Anr. Copy.** 2 vols. Hf. cf., covers worn; Littell bkplt. [Sabin 49915] (LH. Sep.25; 265) $425
– **Tagebuch einer reise vom Missippi nach den Küsten der Südsee.** Intro.:– A. von Humboldt. Leipzig, 1858. *1st. Edn.* Lge. 4to. Subscribers list. title ll. stpd., orig. linen. [Sabin 49414] (GB. Nov.3; 59)   DM 3,600
– – **Anr. Copy.** 4to. 1st. Printing, subscriber list, slightly foxed, orig. linen gt., slightly eroded, spine bkd., dedication on end-paper. [Sabin 49414]. (R. Apr.5; 2771a)   DM 2,700
– – **Anr. Copy.** 4to. Very spotted & browned in places, cont. linen, spine reprd. [Sabin 49914] (H. May 22; 273)   DM 2,400
– **Wanderungen durch die Prairies u. Wüsten des Westl. Nordamerikas von Mississippi nach den Küsten der Südsee.** Ed.:– A.V. Humboldt. Leipzig, 1860. Hand-bnd. hf. leath. ca. 1900, elab gt. [Sabin 49916] (HK. May 15; 611)   DM 440

MOLLIEN, Gaspard Théodore, Comte de

– **Travels in Africa, to the Sources of the Senegal & Gambia in 1818.** 1820. Orig. paper wraps., detchd. (TA. Nov.17; 31)   £50
– **Voyage dans la République de Colombia en 1823.** Paris, 1825. *2nd. Edn.* 2 vols. Cont. wraps., unc. [Sabin 49917] (D. Nov.23; 1343)   DM 600

MOLLOY, Charles

– **De Jure Maritimo et Navali.** L., 1701. Cont. cf. (P. Dec.8; 364)   *Shaw.* £75

MOLLOY, Francis

– **Lucerne Fidelium.** Rome, 1676. *1st. Edn.* Sm. 8vo. In Gaelic, rebnd. qtr. cf. (GM. Dec.7; 363)   £200

MOLOKO KOBYLITS [The Milk of Mares]

Contribs.:– D. & N. Burliuk, Kamensky, Khleb-nikov Kruchenykh, Livshits, Mayakovsky, & Sever-yanin. Ill.:– D. & V. Burliuk. Moscow, 1914. *1st. Edn., [100].* Orig. ptd. wraps., covers reattached. (S. Nov.21; 158)   *Gheerbrant.* £300

MOLTKE, Helmuth C.B. von

– **Gesammelte Schriften und Denckwürdigkeiten des General-Feld-Marschalls.** Berlin, 1891-92. *1st. Coll. Edn.* 7 vols. Orig. hf. leath. gt., gold-tooled monog. on upr. cover, minimal bumping, 3 spines lightly worn. (HT. May 10; 2541)   DM 420

MOMMSEN, Theodor

– **Gesammelte-Schriften.** Berlin, 1905-13. *1st. Edn.* 8 vols. New hf. leath. (H. Nov.23; 547) DM 500

MOMORO, Antoine-François

– **Traité élémentaire de l'Imprimerie, ou le Manuel de l'Imprimeur.** Paris, 1793. Engraved figures mis-numbered, old marb. cf., decor. (HD. Mar.30; 25)   Frs. 5,000

MOMUS, Marmaduke
- The Jolly Jester, or The Wit's Complete Library. L., 1794. Vol. I only?. 12mo. Hf. mor. gt. (P. Jan.12; 257) £170

MONBODDO, James Burnett, Lord
See— BURNETT, James, Lord Monboddo

MONCEAU, Henri Louis Duhamel du
See— DUHAMEL DU MONCEAU, Henri Louis

MONCK, George
See— MONK, George, Duke of Albemarle

MONCK, Thomas 'M. Mason'
- Aeronautica. L., 1838. *1st. Edn.* Slightly browned & foxed thro.-out, cont. hf. leath. gt., rubbed & bumped. (R. Oct.12; 1627) DM 600

MONCRIF, François Augustin Paradis de
- Oeuvres. Ill.:– Duflos (port.), De Sève. 1751. *1st. Edn.* 3 vols. Sm. 12mo. Cont. marb. cf., spine decor. (HD. Mar.21; 58) Frs. 1,100

MONDE ELEGANT
Jan. 1881-Dec. 1882. 4to. Many plts., many cold., hf. mor., worn, as a coll. of prints, w.a.f. (BS. May 2; 66) £160

MONDONVILLE, Jean-Joseph Cassanéa de
- Pièces De Clavecin En Sonates Avec accompagnement de Violon ... Oeuvre 3e ... Paris & Lille, priv. ptd., ca. 1734. *1st. Edn.* Lge. fo. A little foxing, a little dust-stained, waxing on p. 22 slightly affecting text, mod. marb. bds. (S. May 10; 114)
Fenyves. £600

MONDRIAN, P.
- Le Neo-plasticisme. Paris, 1920. *1st. Edn.* Lge. 8vo. Browned thro.-out, orig. wraps., browned, spines torn, MS. sig. on wraps. (H. May 23; 1431) DM 540

MONETTE, John W.
- History of the Discovery & Settlement of the Valley of the Mississippi. N.Y., 1846. *1st. Edn.* 2 vols. Orig. embossed cl., rebkd. (LH. Sep.25; 266) $140

MONGAN, Agnes & Sachs, Paul
- Drawings in the Fogg Museum of Art. Cambridge, Mass., 1946. *2nd. Edn.* 2 vols. 4to. Orig. cl. (BBA. Sep.8; 53) *Makiya.* £75
– – **Anr. Copy.** 2 vols. No bdg. stated. (SPB. Nov.30; 241) $250

MONGE, Gaspard
- Description de l'Art de Fabriquer les Canons. An II [1793/94]. *[1st. Edn.].* 4to. 60 engraved folding plts., 4 tables, 2 plts. torn, 1 reprd., 1 stained, title & a few text ll. slightly spotted, hf. cf. gt. (P. Jan.12; 258) *Phelps.* £180
– – **Anr. Copy.** 4to. A little light spotting, later hf. mor. (CSK. Nov.4; 129) £120
– – **Anr. Copy.** 4to. 60 folding hand-cold. engraved plts. (colouring crude in places), 4 folding tables, some soiling, cont. tree cf., spine worn. (SPB. Dec.13; 715) $275

MONGEOT, Kienne de
- La Nudité, Belle & Vraie. Chateau d'Aigremont, 1952. *(1000) numbered for the 'Amis de Vivre'.* 4to. 36 full-p. gravure reproductions, pict. wraps. (SG. Nov.10; 120) $300

MONGEZ, Antoine
- Tableaux, Statues, Bas-Reliefs et Camées de la Galerie de Florence et du Palais Pitti. Paris, 1789-92. 4 pts. in 2 vols. Lge. fo. Engrs. on Papier-Velin Superfin de Johannot d'Annonay, cont. hf. mor. gt. (SKC. Sep.9; 1812) £110
See— VISCONTI, E.Q. & Mongez, A.

MONIER, Pierre
- The History of Painting, Sculpture, Architecture, Graving ... 1699. Publisher's advts., cont. cf., gt.-decor. spine. (TA. Aug.18; 322) £65

MONK, George, Duke of Albemarle
- Observations upon Military & Political Affairs. L., 1671. Fo. Cont. red mor. gt. extra, rubbed, soiled, restored. (SG. Sep.22; 218) $150

MONKHOUSE, William Cosmo
- The Works of Sir Edwin Landseer. Ca. 1870. 4to. Orig. blind-stpd. & gt.-decor. mor. (TA. Sep.15; 372) £50
– – **Anr. Edn.** [1879-80]. Fo. Engraved vig. title, 54 plts., ill. red mor. gt. (P. Feb.16; 144) £60
– – **Anr. Edn.** N.d. 2 vols. Fo. 44 steel engrs., red mor. gt. (PWC. May 3; 669) £105
– – **Anr. Copy.** Fo. Steel-engraved additional title & 54 plts., cont. mor., lightly stained. (CSK. Mar.23; 146) £80
– – **Anr. Copy.** Lge. 4to. Mor. gt. (PD. May 16; 206) £52

MONKHOUSE, William Cosmo (Ed.)
See— TURNER, Joseph Mallord William

MONNET, Ch.
- Etudes d'Anatomie à l'usage des Peintres. Paris, ca. 1775. Fo. Title slightly browned., some light margin soiling & spotting in lr. corner, late 19th. C. hf. leath. (R. Apr.3; 851) DM 800

MONNET, T.E.
- Description de Medailles Antiques, Grecques et Romaines ... Paris, 1808. 79 engraved plts., mod. hf. cf., corners. (CR. Jun.6; 55) Lire 220,000

MONNIER, Henri
- Moeurs Administratives. Paris, 1828. 12 lithos., each hand-cold. & reworked in pen & pencil, trimmed to border & mntd. on larger stiff paper, ptd. captions mntd. below, title-p. from anr. edn. laid in, 1 plt., some mounts & title foxed, orig. pict. wraps.; title inscr. by Monnier, plts. sigd. by the artist in ink, 1 also dtd., Charles Malherbe copy, with stps. (SG. Dec.15; 331) $600
- La Morale en Action des Fables de La Fontaine. Paris, 1828-30. Hf. mor., corners, limp spine, by Durvand. (HD. Jan.27; 240) Frs. 1,400

MONRO, Alexander
- The Structure & Physiology of Fishes. Edinb., 1785. Fo. 44 plts., some folding, title soiled, tear in plt. 2 without loss, cont. hf. cf., rebkd. (P. Mar.15; 99) *Neylon.* £130

MONRO, Robert
- Monro his Expedition with the Worthy Scots Regiment (Called Mac-Keyes Regiment). L., 1637. *1st. Edn.* 2 pts. in 1 vol. Fo. Cont. spr. cf., rebkd. (SG. Sep.22; 219) $375
- The Scotch Military Discipline learned from the valiant Swede. 1664. Fo. Title soiled, cont. cf., worn; Sir Ivar Colquhoun, of Luss copy. [Wing M 2454a] (CE. Mar.22; 220) £160

MONSTRELET, Enguerrand de
- The Chronicles. Trans.:– Thomas Johnes. Ill.:– Moses. Hafod Pr., 1809. *[Ltd. Edn.].* 4 vols. Fo. 51 hand-cold. plts., three-qtr. mor., scuffed. (SG. Nov.3; 144) $700
- Chroniques. Paris, 1572. 3 pts. in 2 vols. Fo. Cont. cf. gt., spines decor., turn-ins & corners reprd. (HD. Nov.17; 55) Frs. 4,500

MONTAGU, Lady Barbara & Scott, Mrs. Sarah
[–] A Description of Millenium Hall & the Country Adjacent ... Ed.:– [Oliver Goldsmith]. L., 1762. *1st. Edn.* 12mo. Engraved frontis, advt. lf., advts., cont. mott. cf. (SPB. May 16; 74) $125

MONTAGU, Charles, Earl of Halifax
See— PRIOR, Matthew & Montagu, Charles, Earl of Halifax

MONTAGU, George
- Testacea Britannica: or, Natural History of British Shells. L., 1803-08. *1st. Edn.* 2 vols., & Supp. 4to. 2 engraved titles, 30 hand-cold. engraved plts., titles foxed, stains, cont. diced russ., very worn, Supp. disbnd. (SG. Oct.6; 260) $225

MONTAIGNE, Michel Eyquem de
- Essais. Bordeaux, 1580. *1st. Edn.* 2 vols. in 1. Vol. 2 title a variant, with author's honorary titles omitted, 1st. title with sm. reprd. tear & 3 old ink inscrs., 1st. 2 ll. with sm. restoration, inkstain on Dd4 margin, some staining in Vol. 2, 18th. C. sheep., spine gt., corners worn, spine restored. (CNY. Dec.17; 584) $14,000
– – **Anr. Copy.** 2 vols. Sm. 8vo. Lavallière mor. by Cuzin père, fanfare decor, blind- & gt.-decor. red mor. liners, double end-ll., mor. s.-c.; from E. Daguin liby. (HD. Mar.29; 65) Frs. 175,000
– – **Anr. Edn.** Paris, 1588. *5th. Edn.* 4to. 17th. C. red mor., Marquise de Montespan cyphers; MS. name 'Pusey' on title-frontis., engraved ex-libris. (HD. Mar.29; 66) Frs. 1,000,000
– – **Anr. Edn.** Lyon, 1595. *Reprint of 5th. Edn. (Lyon, 1593).* 12mo. Some old underlinings & sm. stains, cont. cf., spine renewed. (HD. Mar.19; 78) Frs. 2,300
– – **Anr. Edn.** Ill.:– Thomas de Leu. Paris, 1611. *New Edn.* Stains at beginning, old red mor., decor., centre motif, traces of old bands. (HD. Mar.30; 12) Frs. 32,000
– – **Anr. Edn.** Paris, 1625. 4to. Mor. gt. by Rivière. (P. Oct.20; 58) £180
– – **Anr. Edn.** Paris, 1635. Fo. Cont. red mor., Du Seuil decor., Louis de Bourbon arms, spine decor.; from Bordes liby. (HD. Mar.29; 67) Frs. 95,000
– – **Anr. Edn.** Paris, 1640. Fo. Cont. marb. cf., gt. decor., decor. spine. (HD. Dec.9; 64) Frs. 1,300
– – **Anr. Edn.** Brussels & Amst., 1659. 3 vols. 12mo. 18th. C. mor. gt., rubbed. (BBA. Nov.30; 50) *Greenwood.* £160
– – **Anr. Copy.** 3 vols. 12mo. Cont. red mor. gt., spines decor. (HD. Mar.27; 24) Frs. 12,000
– – **Anr. Copy.** 3 vols. 12mo. Bradel mor., spine decor. (SM. Mar.7; 2032) Frs. 6,000
– – **Anr. Copy.** 3 vols. 12mo. Wide margins, cont. spr. cf., spines decor.; from Château des Noës liby. (HD. May 25; 56) Frs. 2,500
– – **Anr. Edn.** Ed:– Pierre Coste. Ill.:– Chereau (port.). L., 1724. *New Edn.* 3 vols. 4to. Cont. cf., many defects, spines decor. (HD. Nov.17; 56) Frs. 1,200
– – **Anr. Edn.** Notes:– Pierre Coste. Paris, 1725. *[2nd. Edn.].* 3 vols. 4to. Cont. spr. cf., spines decor.; from Château des Noës liby. (HD. May 25; 57) Frs. 6,200
– – **Anr. Copy.** 3 vols. 4to. Cont. cf., spine decor., tear at foot of 1 spine, corners worn. (HD. Nov.9; 53) Frs. 3,200
– – **Anr. Copy.** 3 vols. 4to. Some ll. yellowed, cont. Italian vell. (HD. Apr.13; 31) Frs. 3,000
– – **Anr. Edn.** Notes:– Pierre Coste. L. [Paris], 1754. 10 vols. Sm. 12mo. Cont. hf. cf., papier granite covers. (HD. Nov.9; 54) Frs. 1,200
– – **Anr. Edn.** Paris, 1783. 3 vols. Bdg. not stated. (HD. Oct.14; 114) Frs. 1,150
– – **Anr. Edn.** Paris, 1886-89. 7 vols. 12mo. Cont. hf. havanna mor., decor. spines, by Pagnant. (HD. Apr.11; 43) Frs. 1,700
- Essais ... avec les Notes de Tous les Commenteurs. Paris, 1826. 5 vols. *(Bound with:)* GRUN, A. - La Vie Publique de Michel Montaigne. Paris, 1855. Cf. gt., by Petit, decor. spines, 1 cover stained. (HD. Sep.22; 292) Frs. 2,300
- The Essayes. Trans.:– [John Florio]. L., 1603. *1st. Edn. in Engl.* 3 pts. in 1 vol. Fo. Correction slip pasted on recto B1, cont. panel. cf., gt. arabesque centre-piece with initials WL, rebkd. ca. 1810, since rejointed, mod. maroon mor.-bkd. box. [STC 18041] (S. Dec.8; 26) *Thomas.* £3,500
– – **Anr. Edn.** Trans.:– John Florio. Ill.:– William Hole (port.). L., 1613. *2nd. Edn. in Engl.* 3 pts. in 1 vol. 4to. Title-pp. soiled, several ink sigs., cont. cf., worn, covers detchd. (CBA. Dec.10; 329) $325
– – **Anr. Edn.** L., 1632. *3rd. Edn. in Engl.* Sm. fo. Slight staining, old cf., slightly worn. [STC 18043] (BS. Nov.16; 42) £130
– – **Anr. Copy.** 3 pts. in 1 vol. Fo. Lightly soiled, cont. cf. (CSK. Sep.16; 37) £85
– – **Anr. Copy.** Fo. Engraved title preceded by 'To the Beholder of this Title' lf., light browning, mod. mott. cf. by Riviere, upr. cover detchd.; Marsden J. Perry Shakespearian Liby. bkplt. (SPB. May 16; 106) $325
– – **Anr. Copy.** 3 pts. in 1 vol. Fo. Title with bkd. excision & MS. ex-libris, some lf. at rear with traces of worming, cont. vell. (D. Nov.24; 2528) DM 1,100
– – **Anr. Edn.** Trans.:– Charles Cotton. L., 1685-93-93. *1st. Edn. Vol.1, 2nd. Edns. Vols.2-3.* 3 vols. Port., spotting & browning, cont. cf., rebkd., corners renewed, new endpapers; William Congreve's copy, with sig. on each title, as an association copy, w.a.f. (SPB. May 16; 35) $600

MONTAIGNE, Michel Eyquem de -*Contd.*

– – **Anr. Edn.** Trans.:– John Florio. Boston, Riverside Pr., 1902-04. *(265) numbered.* 3 vols. Fo. Some slight foxing, buckram-bkd. mott. bds., unc. & unopened. (SG. Nov.3; 145) $300
– – **Anr. Edn.** L., Nones. Pr., 1931. *(1375) numbered.* 2 vols. Orig. mor., soiled, s.-c.; bkplt. of David Garnett. (BBA. Mar.21; 317) *Pearson.* £60
– – **Anr. Copy.** 2 vols. Cont. cf., mor. inlay, soiled. (CSK. Apr.6; 144) £55
– – **Anr. Copy.** 2 vols. Gt.-lettered niger, cover medallions, spines unif. darkened. (CBA. Nov.19; 476) $110
– – **Anr. Edn.** Intro.: André Gide. Trans.:– G.B. Ives. Ill.:– T.M. Cleland. Ltd. Edns. Cl., 1946. *(1500) numbered & sigd. by artist.* 4 vols., including 'Handbook'. Sm. 8vo. Hf. vell., spines lightly darkened. (SG. Mar.29; 213) $100
– **Journal du Voyage ... en Italie.** Ill.:– Saint-Aubin (port.). Rome & Paris, 1774. *Orig. Edn.* 4to. Cont. marb. cf., arms in centre of covers, decor. spine, many defects,. (HD. Sep.22; 291) Frs. 2,350
– – **Anr. Copy.** 3 vols. Sm. 12mo. Cont. marb. cf., spines decor. (HD. Mar.21; 59) Frs. 1,550
– **Versuche, nebst des Verfassers Leben.** Ed.:– Peto Coste. Trans.:– [J.D. Titus]. Leipzig, 1753-54. *1st. German Edn.* Lacks port., cont. hf. leath., rubbed. (R. Oct.11; 344) DM 700.

MONTALEMBERT, Charles Forbes René, Comte de
– **The Monks of the West from St. Benedit to St. Bernard.** Edinb. & L., 1861-79. 7 vols. Some light foxing, three-qtr. cf., spines gt., lightly rubbed. (RO. Sep.13; 127) $145

MONTANO, Giovanni Battista
– **La Cinque Libri di Architettura.** Rome, 1691. 5 vols. in 4. Fo. Engraved title, 5 sub-titles, 2 ports., 200 plts., some foxing in 2 vols., cont. cf., spine gt. (C. Dec.9; 105) *Weinreb.* £850

MONTANO, Lorenzo
– **Bishop San Zeno, Patron of Verona.** Verona, Bodoni Pr., 1949. *(60).* Orig. bds., d.-w., s.-c. (BBA. Oct.27; 196) *James.* £250

MONTANUS, Arnoldus
– **Atlas Chinensis** ... Trans.:– John Ogilby. L., priv. ptd., 1671. *1st. Edn. in Engl.* Fo. Engraved frontis., 41 engraved maps & plts., many double-p., rusthole in 1 text lf., cont. gt.-panel. mott. cf., spine gt., slightly rubbed, corners reprd. [Wing M 2484] (C. Nov.16; 20) *Maggs.* £680
– **Atlas Jappanensis** ... Trans.:– John Ogilby. L., priv. ptd., 1670. *1st. Edn. in Engl.* Fo. Engraved frontis., folding map, 24 double-p. or folding plts., map detchd., cont. gt.-panel. mott. cf., spine gt. [Wing M 2485] (C. Nov.16; 21) *Randall.* £950
– – **Anr. Copy.** Fo. 23 (of 26) double-p. & lge, copperplts., most plts. reprd., one badly defect., mod. cl. (SG. Dec.15; 178) $375
– **Gedenkwaerdige Gesantschappen der Oost-Indische Maetschappy in't Vereenigde Nederland aen de Kaisaren van Japan.** Amst., 1669. *1st. Edn.* Fo. Additional engraved title, lge. engraved folding map, 24 engraved double-p. or folding plts., sm. scrape on engraved title, map torn & partly reprd., 3 plts. with slight tears at folds, corner of X1 renewed, a few margin tears to text, a few ll. or plts. becoming detchd. through damp & with a few faint dampstains to upr. portions, orig. Dutch publisher's blind-stpd. vell., lr. edges worn, front end-papers renewed, w.a.f. (CNY. May 18; 129) $600

See **OGILBY, John**

MONTAUSIER, Charles de Sainte-Maure, duc de
– **La Guirlande de Julie offerte à Mlle de Rambouillet, Julie Lucine d'Angenes.** Paris, 1818. Sq. 16mo. Sm. autograph poem by Mme de Genlis bnd. in front of vol., cont. red mor., gt. decor., decor. spine. (HD. Dec.16; 28) Frs. 2,500

MONTCORBIER, Francois de
See— **VILLON, Francois [i.e. Francois de Montcorbier]**

MONTE, Guidobaldo del, Marchese
– **Le Mechaniche.** Venice, 1518. *1st. Edn. in Italian.* Sm. 4to. Cont. limp vell., rubbed & soiled; Stanitz coll. (SPB. Apr.25; 305) $650

MONTECALERIO, Joannis a
– **Chorographica Descriptio Provinciarum, et Conventuum ... S. Francisci Capucinorum.** Ill.:– J.B. Cassini, Michael Angelo Dionantensis, & others. Milan, J.P. Malatesta, 1712. Ob. fo. Engraved title, 63 engraved maps, including 1 folding, each with ptd. text lf. in decor. woodcut borders, folding map strengthened at folds, title & a few ll. slightly soiled, some slight stains touching engraved & ptd. surfaces, cont. cf., rebkd. preserving gt. spine, mod. label. (S. Dec.1; 202) *Schuster.* £1,850
– – **Anr. Copy.** Ob. fo. Some dampstains, mainly to lr. margin, cont. cf., rebkd. with orig. spine relaid. (TA. Sep.15; 66) £660

MONTECLAIR, Michel Pinolet de
– **Jephté. Tragédie tirée de l'Ecriture Sainte Mise En Musique Et Dediée A La Reyne** ... Paris, ca. 1735. *3rd. Edn.* Fo. Full score, a little browning in places, cont. mott. cf., gt. ornamental spine, corners & spine reprd., sm. hole in both covers; from Toulouse-Philidor collection? (S. May 10; 115) *Baron.* £400

MONTE-SNYDER, Johannes de
– **Metamorphosis Planetarum das ist eine Wunderbarliche Verenderung der Planeten und Metallischen Gestalten** ... Ed.:– A. Gottlob Berlich. Frankfurt & Leipzig, 1684. *1st. Edn. in German.* Bds.; Dr. Walter Pagel copy. (S. Feb.7; 265) *Janssen.* £280
– **Tractatus de Medicina Universali.** Franckfurt, 1662. *1st. Edn.* Title with old stp. & name in lr. margin, lightly browned, bds., spine restored. (R. Apr.4; 1440) DM 1,300
– – **Anr. Copy.** Title stpd. & with owners mark, browned, corners bumped, paper-covered bds. (HK. Nov.8; 662) DM 750

MONTESQUIEU, Charles Louis de Secondat, Baron de La Brè et de
– **Considerations sur les Causes de la Grandeur des Romains et de leur Décadence.** Amst., 1734. *Orig. Edn. 1st. Printing.* Sm. 8vo. Without errata lf., cont. blind-decor. cf.; from Baron de Claye liby. (HD. Mar.29; 68) Frs. 12,000
– – **Anr. Edn.** Paris, 1755. 12mo. Cont. roan, worn. (HD. Feb.22; 144) Frs. 1,600
– **De l'Esprit des Lois.** Geneva [Paris, 1748]. *2nd. Edn. Counterfeit of Orig. Edn.* 2 vols. 4to. Hf.-titles, final errata lf. in Vol. 1, cont. cf., spines gt., slightly rubbed. (S. Dec.20; 794) *Meister.* £250
– – **Anr. Copy.** 2 vols. 4to. With errata lf., some stains, cont. cf., some defects. (HD. Feb.22; 143) Frs. 2,600
– – **Anr. Edn.** Amst., 1749. *New Edn.* 3 vols. Cont. hf. cf., slightly worn. (TA. Dec.15; 496) £68
– – **Anr. Copy.** Amst., 1749. 4 vols. 12mo. Cont. cf., spines decor., Marquise de Pompadour arms. (HD. Mar.29; 70) Frs. 62,000
– **Lettres Persanes.** Amst., Pierre Brunel, 1721. *Antedated Edn.* 2 vols. 12mo. Cont. cf. (HD. Apr.13; 32) Frs. 1,900
– – **Anr. Edn.** Cologne, Pierre Martaau [Amst., J. Desbordes?], 1721 [1730?]. *Orig. 2nd. Edn.* 2 vols. Sm. 12mo. Cont. spr. roan, spined decor. (HD. Mar.21; 60) Frs. 1,550
– – **Anr. Edn.** Preface:– H. Tourneux. Ill.:– Beaumont, engraved by Boilvin. Paris, 1886. 2 vols. 12mo. On holland, red mor. gt. by Pagnant, spines decor., wraps. (HD. May 4; 363) Frs. 1,800
– **Oeuvres.** Amst. & Leipzig, 1758. 3 vols. 4to. Cont. marb. cf. gt., decor. spines. (HD. Sep.22; 298) Frs. 4,000
– – **Anr. Edn.** L., 1767. 3 vols. 4to. Port.-frontis., hf.-titles, 2 folding maps, light stain in vol. 2, cont. Fr. mott. cf., spines gt., vol. 1 spine slightly torn, some covers worn, few wormholes. (S. Apr.10; 298) *McKiernan.* £120
– – **Anr. Copy.** 3 vols. 4to. Cont. marb. cf., decor. spines, 1 cover slightly stained. (HD. Jan.30; 107) Frs. 1,310
– – **Anr. Edn.** Paris, 1822. 8 vols. Followed by 'Considérations sur l'Esprit des Lois., by Destutt de Tracy, hf. cf., spine faded. (HD. Feb.22; 145) Frs. 2,600
[–] **Le Temple de Gnide.** Ill.:– N. Le Mire after C. Eisen. Paris, 1772. *New Edn.* Lacks last lf. (ll.?), later crimson mor. gt. (TA. Aug.18; 223) £50
– – **Anr. Copy.** 4to. L.P., some light foxing, crimson mor. gt. by Lortic, slight wear to jnts., open-bkd. s.-c. (SPB. Dec.14; 70) $800
– – **Anr. Copy.** This copy before the numbers, cont. cf. gt., spines decor., hinges reprd. (HD. May 3; 104) Frs. 1,700
– – **Anr. Copy.** Before letters, slightly spotted, cont. leath., gt. spine, inner & outer dentelle, decor., upr. cover slightly wormed. (HK. Nov.10; 3090) DM 1,600
– **Complete Works.** L., 1777. *1st. Coll. Edn. in Engl.* 4 vols. Hf.-titles, early tree cf., spines gt. (SG. Feb.16; 211) $230

MONTESQUIOU-FEZENSAC, Comte Robert de
– **Les Chauues-Souris, Clairs Obscurs.** [Paris, 1892]. *Orig. Edn. (100) hors commerce.* 4to. Cont. embroidered silk, hf. mor spine, box., spine lightly faded; long autograph dedication sigd. & dtd. from author to Aurélien Scholl. (HD. Dec.9; 159) Frs. 9,800
– **Le Chef des Odeurs Suaves.** N.p., n.d. *Orig. Edn. (200) for author hors Commerce.* 4to. Cont. hf. havanna mor., decor., spine lightly faded., wrap. preserved; long autograph dedication sigd. from author to Aurélien Scholl. (HD. Dec.9; 158) Frs. 1,300
– **Paul Helleu.** 1913. *(100) on japan.* No bdg. stated. (HD. May 11; 75) Frs. 3,500
– **Roseaux Pensants.** 1897. *Orig. Edn. (10) on japan.* No bdg. stated. (HD. May 11; 77) Frs. 1,100

MONTETH DE SALMONET
– **Histoire des Troubles de la Grande Bretagne.** Paris, 1649. 4to. Cont. vell. (HD. Feb.22; 148) Frs. 2,100

MONTFAUCON, Bernard de
– **Antiquitates Graecae et Romanae.** Ed.:– J.J. Schatzio. Nuremb., 1763. 1 vol. in 2. Fo. 150 engraved plts., cont. bds., untrimmed; Prince Liechtenstein bkplt. (SG. Oct.27; 232) $225
– **L'Antiquité expliquée.** Amst., 1712. *2nd. Edn.* 5 vols. in 10. Fo. Cf. (DS. Feb.24; 2185) Pts. 125,000
– – **Anr. Edn.** Paris, 1719-24. 5 vols. in 10, & 5 vol. Supp. Fo. 1 Supp. vol. with stain at lr. margin, cont. mott. cf., some spines worn, w.a.f. (C. Dec.9; 187) *Duran.* £400
– – **Anr. Copy.** 10 vols., including 5 supps. Fo. Approx. 1,400 engraved plts., port., 2 tinted vigs., cf. (DS. Dec.16; 2375) Pts. 150,000
– – **Anr. Edn.** Paris, 1722-24. *2nd. Edn.* 10 vols. in 15, including 5 vols. supp. Fo. Some perforation stps. in titles & text, plts. hand-stpd. on versos, cont. cf., gt. spines, some chipped, ex-liby., not collated, w.a.f. (RO. Dec.11; 227) $400
– – **Anr. Edn.** Paris, 1722-57. *New Edn.* 15 vols. (5 vols. supp.). Fo. Tears & dampstains to some ll., 19th. C. hf. roan gt., last vol. covers scratched. (HD. May 21; 56) Frs. 6,100
– **Antiquity Explained, & Represented in Sculptures.** Trans.:– David Humphreys. L., 1721-25. *1st. Edn. in Engl.* 7 vols., including 5 vols. supp. in 2 vols. Fo. Perforation stps. in titles, plts. hand-stpd. on versos, old cf., worn, some covers detchd., ex-liby. (RO. Dec.11; 228) $200
– **Diarium Italicum** ... Paris, 1702. 4to. Cont. roan, spine worn. (HD. Feb.22; 147) Frs. 2,000
– **The Travels of Father Montfaucon from Paris thro' Italy.** 1712. Cont. cf. (CSK. Oct.7; 83) £65

MONTFORT, Eugène
– **La Belle-Enfant, ou l'Amour à Quarante Ans.** Ill.:– Raoul Dufy. Paris, 1930. *(390) numbered. (35) on Japon supernacré.* 4to. Mor., by P.L. Martin, matching suede doubls. & end-ll., orig. pict. wraps. bnd. in, mor.-bkd. folder & s.-c. (S. Nov.21; 72) *Minou.* £1,800

MONTFORT, Guillaume
– **Principes d'Ecriture.** Ill.:– Beaublé. Paris, ca. 1800. Fo. Light stains, some corners brkn., sewed. (HD. Mar.19; 39) Frs. 1,400

MONTGOMERY, Visc. Bernard of Alamein
- A History of Warfare. 1969. *(265) numbered & sigd.* Mor. gt., by Zaehnsdorf, red & orange overlays in design of cannon on upr. cover, lined s.-c. (P. Sep.29; 113) *Simpson.* £80

MONTGOMERY, James & others
- Poems on the Abolition of the Slave Trade. 1809. Slight foxing, hf. leath., worn. (JL. Mar.25; 379)
Aus. $120

MONTHERLANT, Henri Millon de
- Les Célibataires. Paris, 1934. *Orig. Edn. (20) on vélin d'Arches, for Les XX, sigd.* Leaves, double wrap., s.-c., box. (HD. Mar.27; 95) Frs. 1,550
- La Guerre Civile. Ill.:– P.Y. Trémois. Paris, 1965. *(200) on Rives.* Fo. 25 orig. engrs., leaves, publisher's box; sigd. autograph dedications by author & artist. (HD. May 4; 364) Frs. 4,200
- Les Jeunes Filles. Ill.:– Mariette Lydis. Paris, 1938. *(382) numbered.* 4to. 12 cold. litho. plts., cont. mor. gt., orig. wraps. bnd. in. (S. Nov.21; 92) *Roe.* £120
- Les Lepreuses. Ill.:– Kees van Dongen. Paris, 1947. *(390) on velin de Rives.* Lge. 4to. Orig. wraps. with 1 cold. litho., orig. bd. cover & s. c. (HK. Nov.11; 3825) DM 420
- Malatesta. Ill.:– Yves Brayer. Paris, 1947. 4to. 25 orig. lithos., leaves, box. (HD. Sep.22; 295)
Frs. 2,300
- Pasiphae. Le Chant de Minos. Ill.:– P.-Y. Trémois. Paris, 1953. *(245) numbered on vélin de Rives.* Lge. 4to. Leaves, wrap., box. (HD. Jun.26; 115)
Frs. 4,000
- - Anr. Copy. Fo. 29 orig. engrs., leaves, box. (HD. Sep.22; 297) Frs. 3,400
- La Petite Infante de Castille. Ill.:– Mariano Andreu. Paris, 1947. *(500) on vélin de Rives.* 4to. Leaves, box. (HD. Sep.22; 294) Frs. 1,500
- La Rédemption par les Bêtes. Ill.:– Pierre Bonnard. Paris, 1959. *(316). (160) numbered 'Normalausgabe'.* Fo. 22 orig. lithos., loose ll. in orig. wraps. in orig. linen cover in s.-c. (GB. May 5; 2220) DM 1,200
- La Rose de Sable. Ill.:– André Hambourg, Henri Renaud (title). Paris, 1967. *Orig. integral Edn. (200) numbered & some hors commerce. This 1 of (8) on japon nacré.* 2 vols. Lge. 4to. With double suite of plts. on japan nacré & on Rives, lge. orig. pastel, hf.-title, leaves, wrap., box; autograph dedication sigd. by author. (HD. Dec.16; 162)
Frs. 5,800
- La Ville dont le Prince était un Enfant, Trois Actes, Texte de 1967 ... Ill.:– Raymond Carrance. Bourg-la-Reine, 1967. 4to. Leaves, box. (HD. Jun.13; 79) Frs. 2,000

MONTHLY CHAPBOOK, The [The Chapbook]
Ed.:– Harold Munro. L., June 1919-June 1923. 38 (of 40) issues. 4to. Ills., some light browning, orig. wraps., light soiling, with dupl. issues of Nos. 31 & 33; Perry Molstad copy. (SPB. May 16; 505) $225

MONTHLY FLORA, The; or, Botanical Magazine.
N.Y., 1846. Vol. I (all publd.). Lge. 8vo. 60 col. litho. plts., 1 stained, some foxing & minor stains, cont. hf. cf. (SG. Oct.6; 261) $200

MONTIGNY, Cl. A. de Littret
- Uniformes Militaires. Paris, 1773. Title lf. a copy, sm. margin tears, 1 lge. bkd. tear, 1 copper engr. faded, some soiling, hf. vell. (GB. Nov.3; 964)
DM 1,200

MONTMORT, P.R. de
[-] Essay d'Analyse sur les Jeux de Hazard. Paris, 1713. *2nd. Edn.* Slightly foxed, some ll. slightly browned, cont. cf. gt., gt. outer dentelle, lightly rubbed, some scratches. (HT. May 10; 2708)
DM 650

MONTOJO, Patricio
- Las Primeras Tierras Descubiertas por Colon. Madrid, 1892. *1st. Edn.* Sm. fo. In Spanish & Fr., minor spotting to text, cont. mor.-bkd. dyed bds., corners worn. (SG. Oct.20; 106) $100

MONTORGUEIL, Georges [i.e. Octave Lebesque]
- Aquarelles de Job. Murat. Paris, n.d. Publisher's ill. bds. (HD. Jan.27; 72) Frs. 1,000
- Bonaparte. Ill.:– Job. Paris, 1910. Fo. In Fr.,

contents darkening, a little loose, orig. gt.-pict. cl. (CBA. Aug.21; 334) $190
- La Cantinière. France son Histoire. Ill.:– Job. Paris, [1897]. *(With:)* - France, son Histoire jusqu'en 1789. Ill.:– Job. Paris, [1910]. Together 2 albums. 4to. Publisher's ill. polychrome & gt. bds. (HD. Mar.27; 96) Frs. 1,100
- Louis XI. Ill.:– Job. 1905. 4to. Publisher's decor. cl. (HD. Jun.29; 148) Frs. 1,250
- La Tour d'Auvergne ... Ill.:– Job. 1902. 4to. Publisher's decor. cl. (HD. Jun.29; 147) Frs. 1,350
- La Vie à Montmartre. Ill.:– Pierre Vidal. Paris, 1899. 4to. On papier du Marais, light foxing, hf. chagrin, corners, spine decor., ill. wrap. & spine, unc. (HD. May 21; 135) Frs. 1,250
- - Anr. Edn. Ill.:– Pierre Vidal. Paris, [1899]. *(25) De Luxe Edn. on China.* Sm. 4to. 2nd. series of cold. lithos., some sm. spots, 2 ll. with col. spots, orig. pict. wraps.; Hauswedell coll. (H. May 24; 714) DM 580

MONTORGUEIL, Georges & Forest, Louis
- Monseigneur le Vin. Ill.:– Charles Martin, Carlegle & others. Paris, [1927]. 4 vols. Limp mor. (SG. Feb.16; 329) $175

MONTORGUEIL, Georges & Job
- Napoleon. Paris, 1921. 4to. Publisher's ill. buckram. (HD. Jan.27; 56) Frs. 3,000

MONTPENSIER, Anne-Marie-Louise Henriette d'Orleáns, duchesse de, dite La Grande Mademoiselle
- Divers Portraits. [Caen], 1659. *Ltd. Edn.* 4to. Early 18th. C. marb. roan, spine decor., Claret de La Tourette arms, with his engraved ex-libris, Lyon, 1740. (HD. Mar.29; 72) Frs. 90,000
- Mémoires. Amst., 1729. 3 vols. 12mo. Cont. red mor., spine decor. (HD. Mar.29; 73) Frs. 9,000
- - Anr. Edn. Preface:– J. Frederic Bernard. Ed.:– J. Regnault de Segrais. Ill.:– Tanjé (port.). Amst., 1735. 8 vols. 12mo. Cont. marb. cf., spines decor. (HD. Mar.21; 61) Frs. 2,000
- Les Nouvelles Françoises, ou les Agréables Divertissements de la Princesse Aurelie. Ed.:– Segrais. Paris, 1656. *Orig. Edn.* 2 vols. Sm. 8vo. 18th. C. mor., spine decor., Beatrix de Choiseul-Stainville arms; from libys. of Prince Radziwill & Comte de Behague. (HD. Mar.29; 71) Frs. 30,000

MONTRESOR, Claude de Bourdeille, Comte de
- Mémoires ... Diverses Pièces durant le Ministère du Cardinal de Richelieu. Cologne, 1664. *Orig. Edn. (With:)* - Mémoires ... et autres Pièces Curieuses, pour servir d'Eclaircissement à ce qui est contenu au Premier Volume. Leyde, 1665. Together 2 vols. 16mo. 19th. C. red mor., spines decor.; H. Chasles ex- libris. (HD. Mar.27; 25) Frs. 1,200
- Mémoires de Monsieur de Montrésor. Leyde, 1667, 1665. 2 vols. Sm. 12mo. Cont. red mor., spines decor., Jacques-Nicolas Colbert arms; from Comte de Béarn liby. (HD. Mar.29; 74)
Frs. 12,000

MONTULE, Edouard
- A Voyage to North America, & the West Indies, in 1817. L., 1821. *1st. Separate Engl. Edn.* Slightly spotted, mor.-bkd. bds., unc. [Sabin 50230] (S. Jun.25; 109) *Faupel.* £50
- - Anr. Copy. Later bdg. (LH. Jan.15; 360) $130

MOODIE, Lieut. John W.D.
- Ten Years in South Africa: Including a Particular Description of the Wild Sports of that Country. 1835. 2 vols. Prelims. spotted, cont. hf. mor., gt.-decor. spines. (TA. Nov.17; 34) £110

MOODY, T.W. (Ed.)
See IRISH HISTORICAL STUDIES

MOON, William
- A Simplified System of Embossed Reading for the Use of the Blind. L., Moon Soc., ca. 1900?. Sm. ob. fo. Mod. stiff wraps., ex-liby. (SG. Oct.6; 58)$100

MOOR, J.F.
- The Birth-Place, Home, Churches, & other Places Connected with the Author of 'The Christian Year' [i.e., J. Keble]. Ill.:– William Savage. Winchester, 1866. 4to. Photographic advt. at end of text, minor foxing, cl. gt., some wear, head of spine torn, inner jnt. brkn. (RO. Dec.11; 294) $100

MOORE, A.W.
- The Alps in 1864. A Private Journal. L., [priv. ptd.]. 1867. *1st. Edn. (100).* 10 maps, lacks 1st. lf. (?hf.-title), inscrs. on back end-papers, orig. cl., rubbed, pencil note 'Ed. Whymper's copy', loosely inserted is A.L.s. & postcard sigd. E.H. Stevens, who edited the Blackwell reprint. (BBA. May 3; 354) *Bob Finch Books.* £250

MOORE, Anne Carroll & Miller, Bertha Mahony
- Writing & Criticism: A Book for Margery Bianco. Ill.:– V. Angelo. Boston, 1951. *1st. Edn.* Bdg. not. stated, jacket lightly frayed; the V. Angelo copy, with holograph MSS. of his contrib. laid in loose, 4 A.L.s. from M. Bianco & 2 from P. Bianco, other related letters, & a review & handbill. (CBA. Oct.1; 48) $100

MOORE, Edward 'Adam Fitz-Adam' (Ed.)
See WORLD, The

MOORE, Francis
- Travels into the Inland Parts of Africa. 1738. *1st. Edn.* 2 pts. in 1 vol. Cont. cf. (SKC. Sep.9; 2055)
£140
- - Anr. Copy. Folding map reprd., few plts. lightly soiled, cont. cf., rebkd . (CSK. Dec.16; 106) £50

MOORE, Frank
- The Rebellion Record: A Diary of American Events. N.Y., 1977. *Photographic reprint of orig. 1861-68 edn.* 12 vols. Fabricoid. (HA. Sep.16; 386)
$130

MOORE, George Fletcher
- A Descriptive Vocabulary of the Language in Common Use amongst the Aborigines of Western Australia. 1842. Browned, orig. cl., soiled & faded, spine chipped; pres. copy, inscr. 'Robt. Austin To James Manning Freemantle'. (CSK. Sep.16; 206)
£130

MOORE, Henry
- Heads, Figures & Ideas. Comment:– Geoffrey Grigson. L., 1958. Fo. Linen-bkd. pict. bds., lr. edge slightly nicked, d.-w., edges torn. (SG. Jan.12; 270)
$200
- Maquetten. [München, 1978]. *(100) De Luxe Edn.* Lge. 4to. Sigd. cold. litho., orig. linen. (H. Nov.24; 1878) DM 590

MOORE, James
- A Narrative of the Campaign of the Army in Spain. L., 1809. 4to. Str.-grd. cf. gt. (P. Jun.7; 177) £50
- - Anr. Copy. 4to. Cont. diced hf. cf. (SG. Sep.22; 220) $100

MOORE, John
[-] A Treatise on Domestic Pigeons. 1765. 5 plts. wormed, soiled, cont. bds., worn; cont. engraved trade label of 'Skipman ... Buys & Sells Birds, Pigeons, Fowls, Rabbits, etc ... ' on front pastedown. (CSK. Feb.10; 53) £75

MOORE, John Hamilton
- The Practical Navigator ... [later The New Practical Navigator ...]. L., 1791. *9th. Edn.* Tape repair to inner margin of title, dampstain thro.-out, old cf., worn, lacks spine, jnts. strengthened with tape. (PNY. Mar.27; 165) $130
- - Anr. Edn. L., 1795. *11th. Edn.* Worn thro.-out, mod. mor., stp. of J. Haraden on port. verso. (PNY. Mar.27; 166) $100
- - Anr. Edn. L., 1807. *17th. Edn.* Cont. cf., worn. (PNY. Mar.27; 170) $100

MOORE, Lieut. Joseph
- [Eighteen Views Taken at & Near Rangoon]. [1825]. 1st. Series: plt. vol. only. Ob. fo. Litho. dedication, subscribers lf., 18 hand-cold. engraved aquatint plts., lacks 3pp. India subscribers, orig. upr. wrap. bnd. in. *(Bound with:)* KERSHAW, Capt. James & Daniell, William - [Views in the Burman Empire]. [1831]. Plt. vol. only. Fo. 10 hand-cold. engraved aquatint plts., lightly browned, 1 margin cleanly torn, all with vertical crease, orig. upr. wrap. bnd. in. Together 2 works in 1 vol. Mntd. on guards thro.-out, later mor. gt., lightly soiled, central oval vell. title panel, stpd. in gt., gt. inner dentelles, moire silk end-ll. (CSK. May 4; 139)
£2,000
- - Anr. Copy. 1st. Series. Fo. Litho. subscribers

MOORE, Lieut. Joseph -*Contd.*

lf., dedication, lightly stained, 3 pp. subscription in India list, 18 hand-cold. aquatint plts., 1 plt. & several margins lightly soiled, lacks title, cont. hf. mor., rubbed; with 6 hand-cold. aquatint plts. from 2nd. series, spotted or soiled, unbnd., w.a.f. (CSK. Jul.6; 46) £650

– – **Anr. Copy.** 1st. Series. Fo. Litho. dedication, subscribers lf., 3 pp. subscriptions in India list, 16 hand-cold. aquatint plts. only, 1 margin trimmed, some soiling, cont. hf. cf., worn, w.a.f. (CSK. Jul.6; 69) £400

MOORE, Marianne
– **Marriage.** N.Y., 1924. *1st. Edn. (200).* 12mo. Without Glenway Wescott 4 p. leaflet, orig, pict. wraps., worn; Frederic Dannay copy. (CNY. Dec.16; 247) $130
– **Poems.** L., Egoist Pr., 1921. *1st. Edn.* Orig. decor. wraps., stitched as iss.; Frederic Dannay copy. (CNY. Dec.16; 246) $340

MOORE, Thomas, Botanist
– **The Ferns of Great Britain & Ireland, nature-printed by Henry Bradbury.** Ed.:– John Lindley. L., 1857. Lge. fo. 62 cold. plts., cont. hf. mor. gt., slightly rubbed. (SKC. May 4; 1865) £500
– – **Anr. Copy.** Lge. fo. 51 cold. nature-ptd. plts., dampstained thro.-out at foot, also at upr. corners of last 2 plts., slight spotting, cont. hf. mor., worn. (S. Nov.28; 67) *Hagelin.* £270
– **The Floral Magazine, comprising Figures & Descriptions of Popular Garden Flowers ...** Ill.:– Walter Finch & J. Andrews. 1861-62. 2 vols. 4to. 131 col. plts., some folding, hf. cf. gt. (PD. May 16; 255) £280
– – **Anr. Copy.** Vols. 1 & 2 only, in 1 vol. Hand-cold. litho. plts., title trimmed with loss, cont. mor. gt., lightly rubbed. (CSK. Jun.29; 171) £240
– **The Octavo Nature Printed British Ferns.** L., 1859. *1st. Edn. thus.* 2 vols. 1 plt. reinserted, few plts. & pp. lightly foxed, cont. cf., gt. panels, double gt.-ruled covers. (HA. Nov.18; 284) $200

MOORE, Thomas, Botanist (Ed.)
See— FLORIST & POMOLOGIST

MOORE, Thomas, Poet 'Thomas Little'
– **The Beauties of Moore.** Ill.:– E. Finden & others. N.d. 4to. Engraved title, 48 ports., mor., worn. (P. Mar.15; 194) *Erlini.* £85
– **Irish Melodies.** Ill.:– after D. Maclise. L., 1846. 4to. Pol. mor., gt.-tooled, by Zaehnsdorf, Japanese silk ends & fly ll., spine slightly scuffed & faded, unc. (BS. May 2; 17) £100
– – **Anr. Copy.** Royal 8vo. Mor., gt.-decor., armorial motif on spine. (GM. Dec.7; 439) £70
– – **Anr. Edn.** L., 1860. Sm. 8vo. Cf. gt., spine gt., by J.B. Hawes, Camb. (SG. Feb.16; 212) $100
– **Lalla Rookh.** Ill.:– after Meadows & Corbould. L., 1842. *20th. Edn.* Cont. red mor., gt., decor., gt. inner & outer dentelle, aquarele cold. fore-e. pntg. of Picadilly Circus. (D. Nov.23; 161) DM 1,800
– – **Anr. Edn.** L., 1846. Lge. 8vo. Plts. foxed, 19th. C. purple mor. gt. extra by Martin of Calcutta, with his ticket, fore-e. pntg. (SG. Nov.17; 230) $275
– **The Life & Death of Lord Edward Fitzgerald.** L., 1831. *1st. Edn.* 2 vols. Sm. 8vo. Hf. mor., armorial motif on spine. (GM. Dec.7; 385) £130
– **The Poetical Works.** Phila., 1846. 12mo. Mor. gt., fore-e. pntg. (SG. Nov.17; 231) $275
– – **Anr. Edn.** L., 1853-54. 10 vols. Cont. cf. by Bedford, spines gt., 1 cover detchd., lacks sm. sections of 2 spines. (S. Mar.20; 783) *Booth.* £65

MOORE, William
– **The Story of Australian Art.** Sydney, 1934. *1st. Edn.* 2 vols. Some slight foxing, bdg. not stated. (JL. Mar.25; 733) Aus. $300

MOR DE FUENTES, J.
– **El Patriota.** Valencia, 1809. Nos. 1-5 (all publd.). 4to. Cl. (DS. Mar.23; 2678) Pts. 44,000

MORALEJA, Joseph
See— SANCHEZ TORTOLES, Antonie & Moraleja, Joseph

MORAND, Paul
– **Bouddha Vivant.** Ill.:– Alexeieff. Paris, 1928. 4to. On Holland, mor. by Creuzevault. (HD. Nov.17; 158) Frs. 1,900
– – **Anr. Edn.** Ill.:– Alexeieff. Paris, 1928. *(100)* on H.M.P. Pannekoek. 4to. Orig. wraps. with aquatint on upr. cover, unc. (VS. Jun.6; 204) Fls. 675
– **Fermé la Nuit.** Ill.:– J. Pascin. Paris, 1925. *1st. Ill. Edn.* 4to. On vell., red hf. mor., corners, by Huser, wraps. preserved, unc. (HD. Nov.17; 160) Frs. 1,800
– **Lewis et Irène.** Ill.:– J. Oberle. 1925. 4to. On japan, 15 orig. etchings, 15 engrs. in 3 states, 4 orig. ills., sewed, wrap. & s.-c.; from Daragnès liby. (HD. Dec.9; 46b) Frs. 1,050
– **Paris de Nuit.** Ill.:– 'Brassaï'. Paris, [1922]. *1st. Edn.* Orig. pict. wraps., spiral bnd., slightly rubbed, 2 corners crumpled. (H. Nov.24; 1923) DM 520
– – **Anr. Edn.** Ill.:– 'Brassaï'. Paris, ca. 1933. *1st. Edn.* 4to. 62 full-p. gravures, spiral-bnd. pict. wraps., corners slighlty worn & creased. (SG. Nov.10; 30) £175
– – **Anr. Edn.** Ill.:– 'Brassaï'. [Paris], ca. 1938. 4to. 62 photos, spiral-bnd. photo wraps. (PNY. Jun.6; 531) $200
– **Paysages Méditerranéens.** Ill.:– F.L. Schmied. Paris, Jun. 1983. *Orig. Edn.* Mor. by Paul Bonnet, gt.- & silver-decor., wrap. preserved, folder, s.-c. (HD. Jun.13; 80) Frs. 111,000
– **Poèmes.** Ill.:– G. Gaudion. Toulouse, 1926. *(349)* numbered on vell. d'Arches. 4to. Mor., cold. mor. onlays, suede end-papers & doubls., goat-lined wrap., orig. s.-c. with mor. borders, orig. wraps. bnd. in. (D. Nov.23; 164) DM 11,000
– **Tendres Stocks.** Ill.:– Chas. Laborde. 1924. 2 separate suites, 13 etchings, black & cold., 3 proofs, cold., sewed, wrap. & s.-c.; Daragnès copy, with dedication from Laborde. (HD. Dec.9; 35e) Frs. 1,800

MORANT, Philip
– **The History & Antiquities of ... Colchester.** 1768. *2nd. Edn.* Fo. Cont. cf. (CSK. Sep.16; 242) £100
– **The History & Antiquities of the County of Essex.** Maps.:– T. & E. Bowen. L., 1768. *[1st. Edn.].* 2 vols. Fo. 10 folding maps, 23 plts., several folding, 1 or 2 trimmed to neatlines, margin wormhole in Vol. 2 affecting 2 plts. & text, cont. cf. gt., rubbed. (S. Dec.1; 171) *Rota.* £260
– – **Anr. Copy.** 2 vols. Fo. 10 folding maps, 23 engraved plts., several folding, 'Copped Hall' plt. replaced by anr., margins of some plts. & text ll. reprd., cont. cf., rebkd. (S. Mar.6; 297) *Sanders.* £240
– – **Anr. Copy.** 2 vols. Fo. 2 plts. torn & reprd., cont. cf. gt., 2 covers detchd. (P. Apr.12; 111) *Hadland.* £220

MORANTE, J.
– **Gomez de la Cortina, Marqués de: Catalogo Librorum.** Madrid, 1854-62. 8 vols. Orig. linen. (DS. Nov.25; 2139) Pts. 70,000

MORASSI, Antonio
– **Guardi. L'Opera Completa di Antonio e Francesco Guardi.** Venezia, n.d. 2 vols. 4to. Orig. cl., wraps., s.-c. (SI. Dec.15; 214) Lire 480,000

MORAYTA, Miguel
– **Historia General de España.** Madrid, 1886. 9 vols. Fo. Linen. (DS. Oct.28; 2068) Pts. 60,000

MORAZZONI, Giuseppe
– **La Rilegatura Piemontese nel '700.** Milan, 1929. Tall 4to. Orig. wraps., H.M. Nixon coll., with his sig., acquisition note & some MS. notes. (BBA. Oct.6; 97) *Parikian.* £170

MORDECAI BEN HILLEL
– **Sefer Rav Mordecai.** Riva di Trento, 1559. *1st. Edn.* Fo. Uncensored, some sentences underlined, last lf. reprd. not affecting text, some staining, buckram. (S. Oct.25; 279) *Klein.* £600

MORDECAI COHEN
– **Rosh Mar Dror.** Venice, 1615. *1st. Edn.* 4to. Tears & holed in title affecting columns, last lf. of index in facs., discold., staining, trimmed, with loss of parts of some letters, hf. leath., marb. paper bds. (S. Oct.25; 280) *Dzialowski.* £180

MORDECHAI HALBERSTADT, of Dusseldorf
– **Ma'amar Mordechai.** Brünn, 1790. *Only Edn.* 4to. Slight soiling, browning & staining, old vell., very rubbed. (SPB. Feb.1; 69) $400

MORDEKHAI TSAHALON
– **Metsits u-Melits.** Venice, 1715. *1st. [& only] Edn.* Sm. 4to. Scattered browning, several ll. strengthened at gutters, qtr. leath. (SG. Feb.2; 264) $300

MORDEKHAI YA'AKOV, of Prague
– **Sefer Pa'amon ve-Rimmon.** Commentaries & Additions:– Mordekhai Ya'akov. Amst., 1708. Sm. 4to. Comprising Sefer Asis Rimmonim by Shmuel Gallico, Sefer Falah Rimmon by Menahem Azarya, of Fano, dampstained, some worming, margin repairs to title & folding plt., leath. antique, trimmed. (SG. Feb.2; 265) $120

MORDEN, Robert
– **Geography Rectified.** L., 1693. *3rd. Edn.* Sm. 4to. 76 maps, 1 laid down, old cf. rebkd., lr. cover detchd. (P. May 17; 423) *Whiteson.* £720
See— ATLASES

MORE, G.
– **Dresden Types.** 1895. Fo. 12 cold. litho. plts., loose as iss., orig. cl. portfo. (P. Dec.8; 84) *Walford.* £60

MORE, Sir Thomas
– **De Optimo Reip. Statv deqve Noua Insula Vtopia Libellus ... Epigrammata ... Thomae Mori pleraq è Graecis uersa. Epigrammata Des. Erasmi Roterodami.** Ill.:– A. &. H. Holbein & Urs Graf. Basel, 1518. 3 pts. in 1 vol. 4to. Some cont. underlining in red, sm. MS. notes, MS. owners mark on lr. title margin, cont. wrap. vell., vell. wrap. worn & slightly spotted, with cont. owners mark 'Lvdoff von Munchausen' on spine & covers, cont. vell. MS. lf. as front. free end-paper. (HK. May 15; 204) DM 15,000
– **Epigrammata.** Ed.:– Beatus Rhenanus. Ill.:– Hans Holbein & Urs Graf. Basle, 1520. *2nd. Edn.* 4to. Light wear, 19th. C. russ., rebkd., owner's inscr. of L. Novelli, 1564. (VG. Nov.30; 575) Fls. 950
– – **Anr. Edn.** L., 1638. *1st. Separate Edn.* 16mo. Last 'Imprimatur' lf. present, some margins shaved, later mor., spine gt. [STC 18086] (BBA. May 3; 117) *Thomas.* £210
– **Lucubrationes ab Innumersis Mendis Repurgates.** Basel, 1563. Woodcut device on title & last lf. mntd., some worming in margin, cf. gt. (P. Feb.16; 268) £110
– – **Anr. Copy.** *1st. Latin Coll. Edn.* Old owners mark on title, minimal browning, cont. limp vell., lightly cleaned. (R. Apr.3; 67) DM 1,800
– **Omnia ... Latina Omnia.** Louvain, 1566. Fo. 3 early 17th. C. inscrs. deleted, some stains, 19th. C. cf.; Evelyn copy, with inscr. dtd. 1651. (SPB. Dec.13; 716) $225
– – **Anr. Copy.** Sm. fo. Some staining, new mor., gt. inner dentelle, linen s.-c. (BR. Apr.12; 882) DM 1,400
– **Utopia.** Ed.:– T.F. Dibdin. L., 1808. *1st. Dibdin Edn.* 2 vols. in 1. Sm. 8vo. Hf. cf., spine gt. (SG. Mar.29; 243) $120
– – **Anr. Edn.** Ill.:– Eric Gill (decors.). Gold. Cock. Pr., 1929. *(500)* numbered. 4to. Orig. cl. (CSK. Mar.23; 104) £80

MOREAS, Jean
– **Les Stances, Ire et IIe Livres.** 1890. *Orig. Edn. (100)* on china. (With:) – **Les Stances, IIIe, IVe, Ve et VIe Livres.** 1901. *Orig. Edn.* (With:) – **Le Septième Livre des Stances.** 1920. *Orig. Edn.* Together 7 vols. No bdg. stated. (HD. May 11; 82) Frs. 1,000

MOREAU, Hégésippe
– **Petits Contes à ma Soeur,.** Ill.:– Cl. Bellenger after L. Dunki. Paris, 1896. *(100)* on Velin à la Cuve. Woodcuts in 2 states, all in separate pulls on China bnd. in, red mor., sigd. by Gruel, gt. decor., blue mor. onlay centre-piece, leath & flower shape multi-cold. inlays, mor. doubls gt., gt. inner & outer dentelle, silk end-papers. (D. Nov.23; 167) DM 4,000

MOREAU, Jacob Nicolas
- Les Devoirs du Prince reduits à un seul Principe ou Discours sur la Justice. Versailles, 1775. Cont. cf. (HD. Feb.22; 149) Frs. 2,500

MOREAU, Philippe
- Le Tableau des Armoiries de France. Ill.:– L. Gaultier (frontis.). 1609. *1st. Edn.* Cont. vell. (HD. Mar.21; 120) Frs. 1,500

MOREAU COLLECTION
- Meubles et Objets d'Art des XV-XVI-XVII Siècles. Ill.:– Goupil & Cie. [Paris], 1871. Fo. 57 phototype plts., some foxing thro.-out, qtr. leath., worn. (SG. May 10; 59) $175

MOREAU DE JONNES, Al.
- Monographie Historique et Médicale de la Fièvre Jaune des Antilles et Recherches Physiologiques. Paris, 1820. Cont. hf. leath. (D. Nov.23; 595) DM 400

MOREAU-NELATON, Etienne
- Les Clouet et leurs Emules. Paris, 1924. *(300).* 3 vols. 4to. Orig. wraps., unc., slightly soiled & stained. (S. Apr.30; 207) *Leicester.* £200
- – Anr. Copy. 3 vols. 4to. Cont. mor.-bkd. bds., slightly rubbed, orig. wraps. bnd. in. (S. Apr.30; 69) *Leicester.* £180
- Corot Raconté par lui-même. Paris, 1924. *(600).* 2 vols. 4to. Cont. cl. (BBA. Nov.10; 179) *Shama-Levy.* £130
- Millet Raconté par lui-même. Paris, 1921. *(100) numbered.* 3 vols. 4to. Orig. sewed. (D. Nov.23; 1839) DM 1,500
- – Anr. Edn. Paris, 1921. *(600).* 3 vols. 4to. Hf. mor., slightly faded, orig. wraps. bnd. in. (SG. Oct.13; 239) $250

MORECAMP, Arthur
- Live Boys; or Charley & Nasho in Texas. Boston, [1878]. Pict. cl. gt. (LH. Jan.15; 361) $160

MORECK, Curt [i.e. Haemmerling]
- Die Pole des Eros. Ill.:– J. Eberz. Hannover, [1918]. *De Luxe Edn., (30) numbered on heavy Flemish paper.* Printer's mark sigd. by author & artist, 7 sigd. orig. lithos., mor., gt. inner dentelle, sigd. Fanck. (GB. Nov.5; 2398) DM 650

MOREL, Frederic
- De Numerorum Historia Carmen Philosophotheologopoietikoon. Paris, 1609. *1st. Edn.* 19th. C. vell.; T.L. De Vinne bkplt. (SG. Oct.27; 233) $175

MOREL, L.F.
- Traité des Champignons du Point de Vue Botanique, Alimentaire et Toxicologique. Paris, 1865. 12mo. 18 cold. litho. plts., sm. piece cut from title, cont. decor. chagrin. (HD. Jun.22; 21) Frs. 1,000

MORELL, J.R.
- The Neighbours of Russia & History of the Present War to the Siege of Sebastopol. L., 1854. Pol. qtr. leath., mor. title-piece. (JL. Jul.15; 328) Aus. $110

MORELLY
- [–] Code de la Nature, ou le Véritable Esprit de ses Lois, de Tous Temps Négligé ou Méconnu. [Amst.], 1755. *Orig. Edn.* 12mo. 18th. C. hf. cf., corners. (HD. Mar.19; 79) Frs. 3,400

MORENO DE VARGAS, B.
- Discursos de la Nobleza de España. Madrid, 1622. *1st. Edn.* 4to. Slight worming at beginning, 1 lf. slightly torn, linen, corners. (DS. Dec.16; 2550) Pts. 60,000

MORERI, Louis
- Le Grand Dictionnaire ou le Mélange Curieux de l'Histoire Sacrée et Profane. Amst. & La Haye, 1702. 3 vols. 4to. Cont. spr. cf., spines decor.; from Château des Noës liby. (HD. May 25; 58) Frs. 1,300
- – Anr. Edn. Paris, 1725. 6 vols. Fo. Cont. spr. cf., spines decor., worn; from Château des Noës liby. (HD. May 25; 59) Frs. 2,100
- – Anr. Edn. Ill.:– Desmarets (frontis.), after de Troye (port.). Paris, 1759. 10 vols. Fo. Cont. cf., decor. spines, some turn-ins restored. (HD. Sep.22; 301) Frs. 9,600

– – Anr. Copy. 10 vols. Fo. Cont. marb. cf. (HD. Jun.29; 153) Frs. 3,000

MORESBY, Capt. John
- Discoveries & Surveys in New Guinea. L., 1876. An additional map poorly adhered to p. 17, which is loose, title soiled, hf. mor., partly unc., covers slightly rubbed. (CA. Apr.3; 88) Aus. $300
- – Anr. Copy. Defects to blank margin of 1 plt., slight wear, name erased from title-p., bdg. not stated, unc. (KH. May 1; 501) Aus. $200

MORETI, J.J.
- Historia de la Ciudad de Ronda. Ronda, 1867. 4to. Linen, mor. corners. (DS. Nov.25; 2167) Pts. 24,000

MORETUS, Theodorus
- Tractatus Physico-Mathematicus de Aestu Maris. Antw., 1665. *1st. Edn.* 4to. Lacks errata lf., blank corner torn from A1, 2 sm. holes in upr. margin of title, cont. limp vell. (S. Nov.28; 128) *Bozzolato.* £200

MORGAGNI, Joannes Baptista
- Du Sedibus et Causis Morborum per Anatomen Indagatis. Yverdun, 1779. 3 vols. 4to. Cont. stained cf., spines gt. (a little rubbed); bkplt. of Dagonet, D.M.P. (LC. Mar.1; 175) £170

MORGAN, Dale L.
- The West of William H. Ashley. Denver, 1964. *(250) numbered.* Fo. Hf. cf., cl.; sigd. by author. (LH. Sep.25; 267) $180

MORGAN, John
- The Life & Adventures of William Buckley ... Hobart, 1852. Sewing opening (but firm) at title-p., frontis. a little foxed, orig. cl., minor wear. (KH. Nov.9; 670) Aus. $110

MORGAN, John Pierpont
- Catalogue des Porcelaines Francaises. Paris, 1910. *(150) numbered.* 4to. Additional engraved pict. title & tailpiece, both in 2 states, cold. plts., red mor. gt., upr. cover detchd., lr. cover becoming so, top & bottom of spine worn, unc. (S. May 1; 634) *Sims.* £180
- Catalogue of the Morgan Collection of Chinese Porcelains. N.Y., priv. ptd., 1904. 77 cold. plts., cont. mor. gt., mor. & silk doubls., mor. free end-papers, rubbed, spine faded. (CSK. Jul.27; 79) £65
- – Anr. Edn. N.Y., priv. ptd., 1904-11. *(250).* 2 vols. Lge. 8vo. Elab. mor. gt., spines faded, some rubbing, mor. end-paper on 1st. vol., watered silk end-papers, pres. copy from Morgan, sigd. with initials. (SPB. Nov.30; 162) $2,300
- – Anr. Copy. 2 vols. Lge. 8vo. 158 col. plts., lev. gt., leath. dentelles, 2 ribs on 1 vol. gashed, moire silk end-papers. (SG. Nov.3; 146) $475
- Catalogue of the Collection of Miniatures ... of J. Pierpont Morgan. Ed.:– G.C. Williamson. L., 1906-8. *(150).* 4 vols. Fo. Hf. mor., lightly rubbed. (SPB. Nov.30; 299) $750

MORGAN, Lewis H.
- League of the Ho-De-No-Sau-Nee, or Iroquois. Rochester, 1851. *1st. Edn.* Map torn, a few ll. loose or frayed, publisher's leath., rubbed, spine torn & chipped. (RO. Jun.26; 128) $100

MORGAN, Lady Sydney Owenson
- Absenteeism. L., 1825. *1st. Edn.* 12mo. Hf. mor., armorial motif on spine. (GM. Dec.7; 375) £75
- The O'Briens & the O'Flaherty's, a National Tale. Paris, 1828. *1st. Fr. Edn.* 4 vols. 12mo. Hf.-titles, crimson hf. mor., armorial motif on spine. (GM. Dec.7; 373) £55

MORGENLAENDISCHE MOTIVE: Original-Teppiche, Stoffe und Stickereien
Plauen i. V., ca. 1930. Series I-III. Fo. 66 col. plts., loose as iss., last 26 mntd., lacks plt.-list for Series I, title indicates Series II only & has been corrected, bd. folder, spine defect. (SG. Aug.25; 377) $160

MORGENTHAU, H.
- Germany is our Problem. N.Y. & L., 1945. *1st. Edn.* Orig. linen. (BR. Apr.13; 2491) DM 1,290

MORHOF, Daniel Georg
- Polyhistor, in tres Tomos, Literium, Philosophicium et Practicum. Ill.:– J. Möllerus. Lübeck, 1708. *1st. Müller Edn.* 4to. Some light foxing, cont. vell. (R. Oct.11; 346) DM 400

MORIARTY, Henrietta Maria
- Viridarium: Coloured Plates of Greenhouse Plants ... with Concise Rules for their Culture. L., 1806. *1st. Edn.* 50 hand-cold. engraved plts., cont. cf., rubbed, rebkd., orig. spine laid down; Francis Horner Lyell (one of the subscribers) bkplt. (C. Jun.27; 178) *Phelps.* £280
- – Anr. Copy. 50 hand-cold. plts., cont. cf., rebkd., part of orig. spine relaid. (TA. Apr.19; 188) £145

MORIER, Sir James Justinian
- A Journey through Persia, Armenia, & Asia Minor to Constantinople in the Years 1808 & 1809. 1812. 4to. Lacks hf.-title, mod. hf. mor. gt.; from liby. of Luttrellstown Castle, w.a.f. (C. Sep.28; 1751) £240
- – Anr. Copy. 4to. 3 maps, plt. of inscrs., 25 views, maps foxed, repairs to pp. 114-115 without loss, diced cf., worn, crudely rebkd. (P. Mar.15; 111) *Azezian.* £200

MORIN, Jean Baptiste
- Longitudinum Terrestrium necnon Coelestium. Paris, 1634-37. *1st. Edn.* 3 pts. in 1 vol. Lightly browned, slightly stained at beginning & end, cont. vell. (R. Apr.4; 1551) DM 400
- Trigonometriae Canonicae. Paris, 1633. *1st. Edn.* 4to. Margin repair & inscr. to title, cont. cf. gt., spine worn. (SG. Oct.6; 263) $120

MORIN, Jean-Baptiste
- La Chasse Du Cerf, Divertissement Chanté Devant Sa Majesté, à a Fontainebleau le 25me jour d'Aout 1708 ... Ce Divertissement est mêlé de Plusieurs Airs à boire ... Paris, 1709. *1st. Edn.* Ob. 4to. Full score, cont. crimson mor., gt. fleur-de-lys in panels of spine, foot slightly worn, gt. arms of Comte de Toulouse on cover with triple gt. fillets, wormhole on upr. cover, a little soiled, marb. end-papers; from Toulouse-Philidor collection. (S. May 10; 117) *Macnutt.* £1,000

MORIN, Louis
- Carnavals Parisiens. Paris, n.d. On japan, red hf. mor., corners, spine decor., 2 different wraps. preserved; with prospectus. (HD. Jun.13; 81) Frs. 2,300
- Les Cousettes, Physiologie des Couturières de Paris. Ill.:– Henry Somm. Paris, 1895. *(100) on japon à la forme.* Lge. 8vo. 21 orig. dry-points, sewed bradel silk gt. by Carayon, unc., wraps. & spine preserved; extra-ill. with compl. suite of dry-points with remarks on japan & 9 artist's proofs with different remarks. (HD. May 4; 365) Frs. 2,300
- Les Dimanches Parisiens. Notes d'un Décadent. Ill.:– Louis Lepère. Paris, 1898. *(250) on vélin du Marais.* Lge. 8vo. 41 orig. etchings, bradel hf. mor., corners, by Carayon, spine decor. (slightly faded), unc., wrap. & spine preserved; Madame Ackermann's nominative copy, extra-ill. with 3 etchings. (HD. May 4; 366) Frs. 2,800

MORISON, Alexander
- Memorial of Twenty-One Year's Ministry of the Rev. Alexander Morison in the First Independent Church, Victoria. Melbourne, 1864. 12mo. Slightly chipped & loose, orig. cl.; accompanied by 2 p. MS. letter dtd. 1927 from Morison's son. (KH. Nov.9; 356) Aus. $350

MORISON, Samuel Eliot
- The Maritime History of Massachusetts. Boston, 1921. *1st. Edn. (385) numbered on L.P.* 4to. Cold. frontis., 60 plts., orig. bds., unc., corners bumped. (LH. Apr.15; 345) $170

MORISON, Stanley
- The Art of the Printer. L., 1925. *1st. Edn.* 4to. Cl. (SG. May 27; 261) $100
- The English Newspaper. Camb., 1932. 4to. Orig. cl., d.-w. (P. Apr.12; 39) *Jarndyce.* £80
- – Anr. Copy. Fo. Orig. cl. (BBA. Nov.10; 102) *Forster.* £50
- Four Centuries of Fine Printing. L., [1924]. *(390)*

MORISON, Stanley -*Contd.*

numbered. Tall fo. Cl., covers badly spotted. (SG. May 17; 260) $100
- **Fra Luca de Pacioli of Borgos Sepolcro.** N.Y., 1933. *(390) on H.M.P.* 4to. Qtr. vell. gt., s.-c. (P. Sep.8; 309) *Georges.* £320
- **German Incunabula in the British Museum.** L., 1928. *(398).* Fo. Orig. cl. (BBA. Nov.10; 99) *Hogg.* £100
- **Meisterdrucke aus Vier Jahrhunderten.** Berlin, 1924. *Ltd. Edn.* Fo. Orig. cl. (BBA. Nov.10; 98) *Forster.* £95
- **Meisterdrucke Gotischer Schrift.** 1928. *(125) numbered.* Fo. 152 plts., orig. cl., upr. cover slightly stained. (CSK. Jan.27; 188) £100
- **Modern Fine Printing: An Exhibit of Printing ... during the Twentieth Century ...** L., 1925. *(650).* Lge. fo. Three-qtr. linen & cl., covers lightly rubbed, slightly soiled. (CBA. Nov.19; 765) $100
- **Selected Essays on the History of Letter-Forms in Manuscript & Print.** Ed.:– D. McKitterick. Camb., 1981. 2 vols. 4to. Cl., d.-w.'s, cl.-covered s.-c. (*With:*) - **Typographic Design in Relation to Photographic Composition.** Intro.:– J. Carter. San Franc., 1959. *(400).* 1 vol. Sm. 4to. Marb. bds., bd. back. (SG. Sep.15; 232) $170

MORISON, Stanley (Ed.)
See— FLEURON

MORISON, Stanley & Carter, Harry
- **John Fell, the University Press & the 'Fell' Types.** Oxford, 1967. *Ltd. Edn.* Fo. Orig. cl., d.-w. (BBA. Oct.27; 208) *Howell.* £100
- - **Anr. Copy.** Fo. Orig. cl., d.-w. (BBA. Nov.10; 104) *Morton-Smith.* £85

MORISON, Stanley & Day, Kenneth
- **The Typographic Book.** L., 1963. 4to. Orig. cl., d.-w. (BBA. Feb.9; 220) *Walford.* £70
- - **Anr. Copy.** Lge. 4to. Orig. cl., d.-w. (S. May 1; 419) *Hornung.* £60

MORISON, Stanley & others
- **The History of the Times.** L., 1935-52. 4 vols. in 5. Orig. cl. (BBA. Mar.7; 242) *Blackwells.* £65

MORISON, W.F.
- **The Aldine History of South Australia ...** Sydney, &c., 1890. 2 vols. 4to. Publisher's hf. mor., rubbed & defect. (KH. Nov.9; 671) Aus. $160

MORISOT, Claude Barthelemy
- **Orbis Maritimi sive Rerum in Mari et Littoribus Gestarum Generalis Historia.** Paris & Dijon, 1643. *1st. Edn.* Fo. Slightly browned, 1st. & last lf. lightly stained, several stps., cont. cf., spotted, slightly defect. [Sabin 50723] (H. May 22; 241a) DM 780
- - **Anr. Copy.** Fo. Slightly browned, 1st. & last ll. lightly stained, several stpd., cont. cf., spotted, slightly defect. (H. Nov.23; 326) DM 550

MORITZ, Graf v. Sachsen
- **Mes Rêveries.** Ed.:– Abbé Perau. Amst. & Leipzig, 1757. 2 vols. 4to. Cont. marb. leath. gt., decor. cover, bumped. (R. Oct.12; 2304) DM 550

MORITZ, K. Ph.
- **Anthousa oder Roms Alterthümer.** Berlin, 1791. Title lf. with owner's mark, cont. hf. leath. (GB. Nov.4; 2132) DM 580
- - **Anr. Edn.** Berlin, 1796-97. *Pt. 2: 1st. Edn.* 2 vols. Slightly foxed thro.-out, cont. hf. leath., bumped & worn. (GB. May 4; 1385) DM 480
- **Götterlehre od. Mytholog. Dichtungen d. Allen.** Ill.:– J.J. Tassaert after J.A. Carstens. Berlin, 1791. *1st. Edn.* Cont. hf. leath. (HK. Nov.10; 2607) DM 1,700
- **Die Symbolische Weisheit der Aegypter.** Berlin, 1793. *1st. Edn.* Title lf. with old MS. note, approx. 3 early ll. wormed, 1 lf. near end browned, cont. bds., soiled. (GB. Nov.4; 2133) DM 700
- **Unterhaltungen mit seinen Schülern.** Berlin, 1783. Lightly browned, cont. hf. leath. gt. (GB. Nov.4; 2131) DM 600

MORLAND, Samuel
- **Elevation des Eaux par Toute Sorte de Machines ...** Paris, 1685. *1st. Edn.* 2 pts. in 1 vol. 4to. 1 plt. repeated, soiling & staining, some margin tears (no loss), cont. cf., spine gt., rebkd., orig. spine laid

down, worn; E.N. da C. Andrade bkplt., Stanitz coll. (SPB. Apr.25; 308) $1,200

MORLEY, Christopher
- **The Eighth Sin.** Oxford, 1912. *1st. Edn. (250).* 12mo. Orig. ptd. wraps., upr. cover stained, spine worn, cl. s.-c.; inscr. by author to Mark Mendoza, Frederic Dannay copy. (CNY. Dec.16; 250) $400

MORLEY, Christopher (Contrib.)
See— ROSENBACH, Dr. Abraham Simon Wolf

MORLEY, Countess of
[-] **Portraits of the Spruggins Family.** Ed.:– Richard Sucklethumkin Spruggins. 1829. 4to. Cont. panel. hf. cf. gt.; pres. copy from author to Sir Charles Bagot. (PD. Oct.19; 172) £80

MORNAND, Pierre
- **Trente Artistes du Livre.** Paris, [1945]. *(900) numbered.* 4to. Ills., ex-liby., ptd. wraps. (SG. May 17; 264) £110
- **Vingt-Deux Artistes du Livre.** Intro.:– J.-R. Thome. Paris, [1948]. *(1800) numbered.* 1 vol. 4to. Pict. wraps., s.-c. (*With:*) - **Onze Artistes du Livre.** Paris, 1938. *(400).* 1 vol. 4to. Wraps. (SG. Aug.4; 206) $140

MORNAY?
[-] **A Picture of St. Petersburgh.** L., 1815. Fo. Additional engraved title, 20 hand-cold. aquatint views, a few margins slightly soiled, some tears in text & inter ll., cont. hf. mor., covers worn & detchd. (S. May 21; 235) *Mason.* £450

MORNAY, Philippe de
- **De Veritate Religionis Christianae Liber, adversus Atheos, Judaeos, Mahumedistas et Caeteros Infideles ... Vitae Mortisque Christiana Exhortatio.** Siegeri & Herborn, 1597, 1594. (*Bound with:*) RAMUS, P. –**Commentariorum de Religione Christiana Libri IV.** Frankfurt, 1594. Together 2 works in 1 vol. Bnd. in reverse order, cont. blind-tooled pig, arms centre piece, over wood bds., slightly rubbed. (R. Apr.3; 66) DM 1,500
- - **Anr. Edn.** Herborn, 1602. 2 pts. in 1 vol. Hf. cf., rubbed. (VG. May 3; 726) Fls. 480

MORNER, H. von
- **Il Carnevale de Roma.** Rome, 1820. Lge. ob. fo. Wide margin, slightly browned & spotted, some plts. with stains, cont. hf. leath., slightly defect. (HT. May 9; 1577) DM 1,500

MORNER, K.G.H.
- **Scènes Populaires de Naples en Douze Tableaux.** Paris, 1828. Ob. fo. Lacks title, 12 lithos., some under guards, Fr. captions, margins spotted, loose in litho. orig. wraps., defect., unc.; Hauswedell coll. (H. May 23; 127) DM 2,200

MOROGUES, Bigot, Vicomte de
- **Tactique Navale, ou Traité des Evolutions et des Signaux.** Paris, 1763. 4to. Engraved vig. on title, hf.-title, 49 plts., some light spotting, cont. mott. cf., spine gt. (S. Apr.10; 372) *Pearson.* £100

MORPURGO, Shimshon, of Ancona
See— ERGAS, Joseph — MORPURGO, Shimshon, of Ancona

MORRELL, Benjamin
- **A Narrative of Four Voyages to the South Sea ... Indian & Antarctic Ocean ... 1822 to 1831 ...** N.Y., 1832. Lacks 2 ll., frontis. cut & laid down, title-p. slightly frayed, foxed, hf. mor. by Frost. (KH. May 1; 505) Aus. $100

MORRIS, B.F.
- **Memorial Record of the Nation's Tribute to Abraham Lincoln.** Wash., 1865. *[1st. Edn.].* Mor. gt., 'Captain Robert Lincoln' gold-stpd. on upr. cover, covers rubbed. (LH. Jan.15; 152) $350
- - **Anr. Copy.** Orig. mor. gt., covers scuffed. (LH. Apr.15; 346) $110

MORRIS, Beverley Robinson
- **British Game Birds & Wildfowl.** L., 1855. *[1st. Edn.].* 4to. 60 hand-cold. plts., light spotting, cont. hf. mor. (CSK. Sep.16; 145) £550
- - **Anr. Copy.** 4to. 60 hand-cold. plts., fore-edges spotted, cont. red hf. mor. gt., rubbed. (S. Nov.28; 68) *Benyon.* £540

- - **Anr. Copy.** Lge. 4to. Cont. hf. leath. gt., slightly rubbed. (R. Oct.12; 1876) DM 2,900
- - **Anr. Edn.** 1891. *3rd. Edn.* 4to. 60 hand-cold. plts., orig. cl., worn. (P. Oct.20; 105) £600
- - **Anr. Copy.** 4to. 60 hand-cold. plts., hf.-title, orig. cl. gt., worn on spine & bd. edges. (LC. Mar.1; 176) £520
- - **Anr. Edn.** Ed.:– W.B. Tegetmeier. 1895. *4th Edn.* 2 vols. Lge. 8vo. 60 double-p. hand-cold. plts., slight tears in some fore-edges of Vol. 2, orig. decor. cl. gt. (SKC. Mar.9; 1949) £240
- - **Anr. Edn.** Ed.:– W.B. Tegetmeier. 1897. *5th. Edn.* 2 vols. Lge. 8vo. 60 double-p. hand-cold. plts., minor spotting, orig. cl. gt., rubbed. (TA. Feb.16; 94) £300
- - **Anr. Edn.** L., n.d. 4to. 60 hand-cold. plts., slight spotting, crimson hf. mor. gt. (P. Sep.8; 1) *Schuster.* £480

MORRIS, Edward E.
- **Cassell's Picturesque Australasia.** 1889-90. 4 vols. in 2. Fo. Cont. hf. roan, rubbed. (TA. Dec.15; 45) £50

MORRIS, Ethel Jackson
- **The White Butterfly, & Other Fairy Tales.** Melbourne, 1921. *(250) numbered & sigd.* 4to. Orig. cl., some wear & soiling. (KH. Nov.9; 358) Aus. $100

MORRIS, Rev. Francis Orpen
- **A History of British Birds.** L., 1851-52. *1st. Edn.* 6 vols. 358 hand-cold. plts., many soiled, hf. mor. gt., spines defect. (P. Dec.8; 104) *Duran.* £240.
- - **Anr. Edn.** L., 1851-57. *1st. Edn.* 6 vols. 358 hand-cold. engraved plts., hf. mor., spines gt.-decor. (SKC. Nov.18; 1983) £380
- - **Anr. Copy.** 6 vols. 358 hand-cold. plts., some light spotting, cont. hf. cf., spines gt., lightly rubbed. (CSK. Jul.27; 23) £280
- - **Anr. Copy.** 6 vols. 358 hand-cold. plts., cont. hf. cf., lightly rubbed. (CSK. Jun.29; 66) £240
- - **Anr. Copy.** 6 vols. Plts. hand-cold., slight spotting & soiling, some plts. & ll. loose, orig. cl., discold., spines ends worn. (S. Oct.4; 278) *Shapiro.* £190
- - **Anr. Edn.** L., 1852-57. *1st. Edn.* 6 vols. 357 hand-cold. plts., 1 text lf. loose, hf. cf. gt. (P. Apr.12; 221) *Duran.* £270
- - **Anr. Edn.** L., 1860-61. Vols. 2, 3, 4 (of 6). 180 hand cold. plts., cl. gt. worn. (P. May 17; 308) *Way.* £110
- - **Anr. Edn.** L., 1862. 6 vols. Engrs. hand-cold., light browning due to quality of paper. hf. red mor., corners. (CR. Jul.6; 227) Lire 700,000
- - **Anr. Edn.** L., 1863-64. 6 vols. 358 hand-cold. plts., 1 loosely inserted, title of Vol. 5 detchd. & loosely inserted, E3 of Vol. 3 cleanly torn, orig. cl. (CSK. Nov.4; 112) £220
- - **Anr. Edn.** L., 1863-65. 6 vols. 358 hand-cold. engrs., hf. mor., gt. spines, Vol. 1 hinge brkn. (SKC. Jan.13; 2337) £300
- - **Anr. Edn.** L., 1864. 6 vols. 350 cold. plts. only, about 25 defect., lacks 2 titles, cl., worn, as a coll. of plts., w.a.f. (P. May 17; 307) *Groves.* £220
- - **Anr. Edn.** L., 1865-64-65. 6 vols. 358 hand-cold. plts., some slight spotting, orig. publisher's gt.-decor. cl. (SKC. Jan.13; 2336) £210
- - **Anr. Edn.** L., 1866. 6 vols. 358 col. plts., orig. cl. gt. (P. Sep.8; 296) *Duran.* £220
- - **Anr. Edn.** L., 1868. 6 vols. 358 hand-cold. plts., 2 text ll. in Vol. 6 creased, orig. cl. gt. (P. Apr.12; 132) *Joseph.* £300
- - **Anr. Edn.** L., 1870. *[2nd. Edn.].* 6 vols. Plts. hand-cold., orig. cl. gt. (P. Jan.12; 195e) *Steinacker.* £440
- - **Anr. Copy.** 6 vols. 365 hand-cold. plts., orig. cl., gt.- & blind-blocked. (CSK. Apr.6; 73) £400
- - **Anr. Copy.** 6 vols. 4to. 365 hand-cold. plts., some light spotting, orig. cl., lightly rubbed. (CSK. Dec.2; 122) £320
- - **Anr. Copy.** 6 vols. 365 hand-cold. engraved plts., some see-through in Vol. 6, cont. hf. mor., rubbed. (SKC. Mar.9; 1950) £300
- - **Anr. Copy.** 6 vols. Tall 8vo. 365 hand-cold. plts., minor spotting, mainly to 1st. vol., orig. cl. gt., spine ends frayed. (TA. Feb.16; 92) £240
- - **Anr. Copy.** 6 vols. 365 hand-cold. plts., few detchd. & frayed, some soiling, orig. cl., soiled & frayed. (CSK. Sep.30; 128) £220

– – **Anr. Copy.** 5 vols. only (lacks Vol. 2). 304 hand-cold. plts., some ll. slightly spotted, cont. hf. mor., spines gt., rubbed. (BBA. Dec.15; 137)

Snelling. £170

– – **Anr. Copy.** 6 vols. Sm. 4to. 365 hand-cold. plts., disbnd. (SG. Mar.22; 236) $550

– – **Anr. Copy.** 6 vols. Orig. linen gt. (R. Oct.12; 1877) DM 2,250

– – **Anr. Copy.** 4to. 358 hand-cold engrs., publishers stpd. cl. gt. (DS. Feb.24; 2345) Pts. 110,000

– – **Anr. Edn.** L., [1870?]. 8 vols. Engrs. hand-cold., publishers cl., some vols. lightly defect. (CR. Jun.6; 229) Lire 700,000

– – **Anr. Edn.** Ca. 1880. 8 vols. 358 hand-cold. plts., a few ll. in Vols. 1 & 2 detchd., orig. cl. gt., rubbed. (TA. Dec.15; 172) £145

– – **Anr. Copy.** Vols. 2-8 only. 303 hand-cold. plts., orig. cl. gt., faded, spines little worn. (TA. Nov.17; 323) £100

– – **Anr. Copy.** Vols. 5-8 only, in 2 vols. 160 hand-cold. plts., cont. hf. mor., worn, 1 cover defect. (TA. Dec.15; 173) £60

– – **Anr. Edn.** L., [1888]. 8 vols. 351 hand-cold. plts., 1 text lf. & 1 plt. loose, orig. cl. gt. (P. Apr.12; 216) *L'Affineur.* £220

– – **Anr. Copy.** 7 vols. only (of 8). 310 (of 311) cold. plts., shaken, a few loose, orig. cl., worn, hinges brkn. (S. Apr.10; 564) *Kouchak.* £170

– – **Anr. Copy.** 8 vols. Minimal foxing, cont. hf. leath., spine faded & worn. (HK. Nov.8; 769) DM 1,000

– – **Anr. Edn.** L., 1895. *4th. Edn.* 6 vols. 4to. 6 hand-cold. frontis., 388 plts., some light soiling, 1 lf. cleanly torn, orig. cl., lightly soiled & rubbed. (CSK. Jan.27; 121) £320

– – **Anr. Copy.** 6 vols. 4to. 394 hand-cold. plts., mor.-bkd. bds. (PD. Apr.18; 133) £280

– – **Anr. Edn.** L., 1895-96. *4th. Edn.* 6 vols. 4to. 394 hand-cold. plts., very slight foxing, gt.-pict. cl., spine ends torn, hinges strengthened. (SG. Nov.3; 147) $700

– – **Anr. Edn.** L., 1895-97. *4th. Edn.* 6 vols. 394 hand-cold. plts., cont. hf. cf. gt., spines slightly rubbed & faded. (S. Nov.28; 71)

Antik Koch. £280

– – **Anr. Copy.** 6 vols. 394 hand-cold. plts., 5 loose, orig. cl. gt., 2 worn. (P. Nov.24; 86)

Map House. £260

– – **Anr. Edn.** L., 1903. *5th. Edn.* 6 vols. 400 hand-cold. plts., cl. gt. (P. Mar.15; 195) £280

– – **Anr. Copy.** 6 vols. Plts. hand-cold., very loose, a no. of plts. & ll. torn or frayed, orig. cl., very worn, w.a.f. (S. Oct.4; 280) *Walford.* £170

– – **Anr. Copy.** Vols. 1, 3 & 4 only (of 6). 193 hand-cold. plts., cl. gt., soiled. (P. Nov.24; 190)

Erlini. £110

– – **Anr. Copy.** 6 vols. Publishers cl. (CR. Jun.6; 228) Lire 800,000

– – **Anr. Edn.** L., n.d. 8 vols. 358 hand-cold. plts., 1 loose, spotting, cl. gt., rubbed. (P. Jan.12; 194) *Clark.* £240

– – **Anr. Copy.** 8 vols. 358 cold. plts., some ll. slightly soiled, a few loose, orig. cl., rubbed. (BBA. May 3; 83) *Tooley.* £210

– – **Anr. Copy.** 8 vols. Plts. hand-cold., orig. blind-stpd. cl. gt. (SKC. May 4; 1867) £190

– – **Anr. Copy.** 8 vols. 358 cold. plts., Vol. 2 lacks contents lf., many ll. browned or soiled, orig. cl., worn, mostly loose. (BBA. May 3; 84)

Russell. £140

– – **Anr. Copy.** 8 vols. Publishers cl. (DS. Nov.25; 2170) Pts. 60,000

– **A History of British Birds. — A Natural History of the Nests & Eggs of British Birds.** L., 1870; 1875. *2nd. Edns.* 6 vols.; 3 vols. 1st. work: 364 hand-cold. plts., some spotting; 2nd. work: 223 cold. plts.; orig. cl. gt. (P. May 17; 222) *Haden.* £300

– – **Anr. Edn.** L., 1895-97; 1896. *4th. Edns.* 6 vols.; 3 vols. 1st. work: 394 hand-cold. plts.; 2nd. work: 248 cold. plts.; orig. cl. gt. (S. Nov.28; 70)

Antik Junk. £260

– **A History of British Butterflies.** L., 1853. 71 cold. plts., cont. mor. gt., slightly rubbed. (BBA. Nov.30; 114) *Old Hall.* £65

– – **Anr. Copy.** Stained & browned, hf. cf., corners, spine defect. (CR. Jun.6; 231) Lire 200,000

– – **Anr. Edn.** L., 1864. 71 hand-cold. plts., slight spotting, hf. mor. (SKC. Oct.26; 411) £55

– – **Anr. Edn.** L., 1870. *[5th. Edn.].* 71 col. plts., 2 plain plts., orig. cl. gt. (P. Nov.24; 169) £60

– – **Anr. Copy.** Hf. mor., spine gt. (LC. Oct.13; 204) £55

– – **Anr. Edn.** L., 1876. 4to. 72 cold. plts., advts., orig. cl. gt. (PD. Oct.19; 181) £62

– – **Anr. Edn.** L., 1891. *6th. Edn.* 72 cold. plts., a little soiling, orig. cl., slightly stained. (S. Oct.4; 279) *Edistar.* £70

– – **Anr. Edn.** L., 1895. *8th. Edn.* 4to. 79 hand-cold. plts., orig. cl., spine reprd. (SKC. Oct.26; 410) £55

– – **Anr. Copy.** 2 vols. 79 hand-cold. plts., limp mor., defect. (P. Nov.24; 159) *Rossi.* £50

– – **Anr. Edn.** L., 1908. *10th. Edn.* 4to. 79 hand-cold. plts., orig. cl. (SKC. Oct.26; 412) £50

– **A Natural History of British Moths.** L., 1872. 4 vols. 132 hand-cold. plts., cont. hf. mor. gt., spines rubbed. (SKC. May 4; 1868) £70

– – **Anr. Edn.** L., 1894. 4 vols. 132 hand-cold. engraved plts., orig. cl., lightly rubbed. (CSK. Jul.27; 117) £80

– – **Anr. Edn.** L., 1896. *5th. Edn.* 4 vols. 4to. 132 hand-cold. litho. plts., three-qtr. cf., gt.-decor. spines. (CBA. Dec.10; 348) $130

– – **Anr. Edn.** Intro.:– W.E. Kirby. L., 1903. *6th. Edn.* 4 vols. 4to. Plts. hand-cold., orig. cl. (SKC. Oct.26; 413) £55

– **A Natural History of the Nests & Eggs of British Birds.** L., 1875. *2nd. Edn.* 3 vols. 233 cold. plts., orig. cl. gt. (GM. Dec.7; 608) £90

– **A Series of Picturesque Views of the Seats of the Noblemen & Gentlemen of Great Britain & Ireland.** Ca. 1879-80. 6 vols. 4to. Orig. cl. gt. (S. Nov.1; 119) *Cavendish.* £110

– – **Anr. Copy.** 6 vols. 4to. Gt.-decor. red mor., Vols. 1-4 with Royal arms on covers, Vols. 5 & 6 with Windsor Castle, dentelles. (SKC. Sep.9; 2056) £85

– – **Anr. Copy.** 6 vols. 4to. 240 cold. plts., slightly spotted, orig. cl. (S. Mar.6; 300) *Old Hall.* £75

– – **Anr. Copy.** 6 vols. 4to. 2 vig. titles, 75 chromo-litho. plts., orig. cl. gt., spine ends frayed. (TA. Feb.16; 61) £58

– – **Anr. Copy.** 6 vols. (*With:*) – **Fac-Simile of Autographs of Subscribers to the Picturesque Views ...** Ca. 1880. 1 vol. Together 7 vols. 4to. Orig. gt.-decor. cl., spine ends slightly worn. (TA. Apr.19; 81) £58

– – **Anr. Edn.** L., [1880?]. 6 vols. 4to. 6 additional vig. title-pp., 240 col. litho. plts., some minor margin foxing, & darkening, orig. elab. gt.-blocked cl., light wear at extremities, spines slightly fading. (CBA. Aug.21; 418) $200

– – **Anr. Edn.** L., [1880?]. 6 vols. 4to. Publishers cl. gt. (CR. Jun.6; 230) Lire 260,000

– – **Anr. Edn.** N.d. 6 vols. 4to. Crimson mor. gt. (P. Mar.15; 136) *MacDonald.* £160

– – **Anr. Copy.** 6 vols. Some spotting, orig. cl., spines chipped at head & foot or lightly affected by damp. (CSK. Apr.6; 64) £90

– – **Anr. Copy.** 4to. Mor. gt. (P. Dec.8; 39)

Bailey. £50

MORRIS, Frank T.
– **Birds of the Australian Swamps.** 1978. *(500) numbered & sigd. by author & artist.* Vols. 1 & 2. Bdg. not stated. (JL. Mar.25; 657) Aus. $510

– **Impressions of Waterfowl of Australia.** 1977. *(350) numbered & sigd.* Bdg. not stated. (JL. Mar.25; 656) Aus. $140

– **Pigeons & Doves of Australia.** 1976. *(500) numbered.* Fo. Bdg. not stated. (JL. Mar.25; 658) Aus. $650

– **Robins & Wrens of Australia.** 1979. *(500) numbered & sigd. by author & artist.* Leath. (JL. Mar.25; 659) Aus. $180

MORRIS, George P.
– **The Deserted Bride.** N.Y., 1843. Elab. gt. mor., floral inlays on covers & spine, inlaid label on spine with 'Maria Walker', inlaid gt. dentelles, folding box with initials 'M.W.' on cover. (SPB. Dec.13; 550) $125

MORRIS, Henry
– **Bird & Bull Pepper Pot.** North Hills, Bird & Bull Pr., 1977. *Ltd. Edn.* 4to. Hf. mor. & decor. bds. (CBA. Nov.19; 20) $110

– **Omnibus: Instructions for Amateur Papermakers.**

Bird & Bull Pr., 1967. *(500) numbered on Green's B. & B. H.M.P.* Prospectus & specimen of 'De Schoolmester' paper laid in, qtr. mor. by Sangorski & Sutcliffe; inscr. by author. (SG. Jan.12; 39) $200

See— **TAYLOR, W. Thomas & Morris, Henry**

MORRIS, Richard
– **Essays on Landscape Gardening ...** L., 1825. *[1st. Edn.].* 4to. 2 plts. with overslips, orig. bds., unc., spine torn & slightly defect. (C. Jul.27; 139)

Weinreb. £350

– – **Anr. Copy.** 4to. 6 full-p. aquatint plts. (3 hand-cold. & 2 uncold. with overslips), incidental foxing to few text ll., later cl.-bkd. buff bds., some wear & rubbing, bkplts. at front pastedown, including early Baltimore owner, Macauley, his Mondawmin armorial bkplt. (HA. May 4; 272) $525

– **Flora Conspicua: a Selection of the Most Ornamental ... Trees, Shrubs, & Herbaceous Plants, for Embellishing Flower-Gardens & Pleasure-Grounds.** 1826. 60 hand-cold. engraved plts., including 1 double-p., slight margin staining to 4 plts., cont. hf. cf., spine gt., spine chipped & rubbed; inscr. by author. (LC. Oct.13; 205) £280

See— **BARBER, William — DEARN, T.D.W. — MORRIS, Richard**

MORRIS, Robert
– **Architecture Improved ... Lodges & other Decorations in Parks, Gardens ... Portico, Bath, Observatory.** L., 1757. 50 engraved plts., cont. cf., worn. (BBA. Dec.15; 316)

Marlborough Rare Books. £190

MORRIS, William
– **A Book of Verse.** 1980. *Facs. Edn., (300) numbered.* 4to. Vell. gt. by Rivière, cl. box. (P. Apr.12; 33) *Thorp.* £85

– **Child Christopher & Godilind the Fair.** Kelms. Pr., 1895. *(612). (600) on paper.* 2 vols. 16mo. Orig. holland-bkd. bds., unc. spines slightly soiled. (S. Dec.20; 559) *Blackwells.* £130

– **The Defence of Guenevere & Other Poems.** Kelms. Pr., 1892. *(310). (300) on paper.* 8vo. Orig. limp vell., ties; Rennell Rodd bkplt. (BBA. Dec.15; 250) *Blackwell.* £180

– **Gothic Architecture.** Kelms. Pr., 1893. *(1545). (1500) on paper.* Sm. 4to. Orig. qtr. canvas, sides a little soiled; sig. of May Morris on fly-lf. (BBA. Sep.29; 212) *Quaritch.* £70

– **Guenevere: Two Poems ...** Ill.:– D.G. Rossetti. L., Fanfrolico Pr., [1930]. *(450) numbered on Barcham Green vell.* Sm. 4to. Hf. cl., partly unc. (SG. Mar.29; 139) $140

– **A Note on his Aims in Founding the Kelmscott Press.** Kelms. Pr., 1898. *(537). (525) on paper.* Orig. holland-bkd. bds., slightly soiled. (BBA. Nov.10; 106) *Traylen.* £160

– – **Anr. Copy.** Orig. qtr. canvas, slightly rubbed. (BBA. Nov.10; 107) *Duschnes.* £120

– – **Anr. Copy.** With sm. loose errata, orig. hf. linen, slightly spotted. (HK. May 17; 2865) DM 660

– **Poems by the Way.** Kelms. Pr., 1891. *(313). (300) on paper.* Orig. stiff vell., silk ties, covers soiled; pres. copy from author to Herbert M. Ellis, Visc. Esher bkplt., Frederic Dannay copy. (CNY. Dec.16; 251) $650

– – **Anr. Copy.** Sm. 4to. Orig. vell. gt., ties. (GB. Nov.5; 2658) DM 1,200

– **Some Hints on Pattern Designing.** 1899. Orig. qtr. cl.; inscr. 'Katherine Whitaker from Jane Morris Kelmscott Nov. 1902'. (BBA. Sep.29; 214)

Thorp. £55

– **The Story of Cupid & Psyche.** Ill.:– after Edward Burne-Jones & Morris. Clover Hill Edns., 1974. *(400) roman-numbered. (130) with portfo. containing proofs of the wood engrs.* 2 vols., & portfo. Fo. Mor. gt., s.-c. & mor.-bkd. box; loosely inserted prospectus, 1st. trial proof (1 of 50 numbered copies) sigd. & dtd. 23/ix/70 by Will Carter, & other related material. (S. Nov.21; 183)

Desk. £620

– **The Story of the Glittering Plain.** Ill.:– W. Crane. Kelms. Pr., 1894. *(257). (250) on paper.* 4to. Orig. limp vell., slightly soiled, ties. (BBA. Sep.29; 213)

Forsythe. £320

– **The Sundering Flood.** [Kelms. Pr., 1897]. *(310). (300) on paper.* Linen-bkd. paper bds., spine worn. (LH. Sep.25; 406) $200

MORRIS, William -*Contd.*

- **The Well at the World's End.** Ill.:– Edward Burne-Jones. Kelms. Pr., 1896. *(358). (350) on paper*. 4to. 4 trial ll. with hand-tinted decors. between columns loosely inserted, orig. limp vell., ties; inscr. by author to W.H. Hooper. (SKC. Jan.13; 2168)
£680
– – **Anr. Copy**. 4to. Orig. cl.-bkd. bds., unc., corners bumped, label frayed; inscr. 'Arthur Morris. 19 Salisbury Road', pres. label of Mrs. William Morris, A.L.s. from author to Arthur Morris, 16 Nov. 1895, loosely inserted. (C. May 30; 189)
Nudleman. £350
- **The Wood Beyond the World.** Kelms. Pr., 1894. *(358). (350) on paper*. Orig. vell., unc. slightly soiled, linen ties defect. (SG. Jan.12; 178) $300
– – **Anr. Copy**. Wide margin, blind-tooled mor., decor. (GB. May 5; 2768)   DM 3,000

MORRIS, William (Trans.)
See— AMIS & AMILE
See— BEOWULF

MORRIS, William (Ill.)
See— SHAKESPEARE, William

MORRIS, William & Magnusson, Birikr
- **Volsunga Saga: The Story of the Volsungs & Niblungs.** L., 1870. *(12) L.P., for private circulation.* 2 pp. with hand-painted decors., those on p. 1 enclosing the initials G[eorgiana] B[urne-]J[ones], mod. mor.-bkd. patterned satin, covers frayed at outer edges, unc. (SG. Nov.17; 101) $650

MORRIS, Rev. W. Meredith
- **British Violin Makers Classical & Modern ... a Biographical & Critical Dictionary** ... L., 1904. *1st. Edn.* Foxing, cl. (PNY. Dec.1; 69) $100

MORRISON, Arthur
- **The Painters of Japan.** L. & Edinb., 1911. 2 vols. Fo. Orig. cl., partly unc., slightly soiled. (S. May 1; 601)   *Tang*. £90
– – **Anr. Edn.** N.Y., [1911]. 2 vols. Tall fo. 122 plts., some cold., lettered tissue-guards, ex-liby., cl. (SG. May 3; 259) $175
– – **Anr. Edn.** L., 1921. 2 vols. Fo. Orig. buckram, slightly rubbed & soiled. (S. Oct.4; 179)
Zwemmer. £80
– – **Anr. Edn.** Edinb., 1921. *(150) numbered & sigd. by publishers.* 2 vols. Fo. Orig. buckram, d.-w., unc. (PD. Oct.19; 256)   £80

MORRISON, Hugh Alexander (Ed.)
See— LEITER, Levi Ziegler

MORRISON, James
- **The Journal.** Intro.:– Owen Rutter. Ill.:– Robert Gibbings. Gold. Cock. Pr., 1935. *(325) numbered.* Sm. fo. Orig. cl., top of spine slightly soiled; inscr. to Alex Hyman from Robert Gibbings. (S. Nov.21; 223)   *Buzek*. £190
– – **Anr. Copy.** 4to. Two-tone cl., partly unc., unopened, minimally soiled. (SG. Mar.29; 151)
$250

MORSE, Hosea Ballou
- **The Chronicles of the East India Company Trading to China, 1635-1834.** Camb., Mass., & Oxford, 1926-29. 5 vols. Cl. (SG. Sep.22; 124) $120

MORTERA, Shaul Levi
- **Givat Shaul.** Amst., 1645. *1st. Edn.* 4to. Owner's sig. on title, stained thro.-out, edges frayed, 2 holes not affecting text, buckram. (S. Oct.25; 281)
Freedman. £150

MORTIER, Pieter
See— JAILLOT, Alexis Hubert & Mortier, Pieter

MORTIER, R.
- **Rabelais; sa Vie, son Oeuvre.** Ill.:– Marcel Jean-jean. Paris, 1933. 5 vols. 4to. On Vergé, hf. chagrin, corners, spines decor., unc., wrap. & spine. (HD. Mar.27; 103)   Frs. 1,600

MORTIMER, John
- **The Whole Art of Husbandry.** 1708. *2nd. Edn.* Cont. panel. cf., rubbed. (BBA. Jul.27; 31)
Quevedo. £65
– – **Anr. Edn.** 1721. 2 vols. Leath. (PWC. Jul.11; 542)   £54

MORTIMER, Ruth
- **French 16th. Century Books.** Camb. [Mass.], 1964. 2 vols. 4to. Buckram. (SG. Sep.15; 235)
$160
– – **Anr. Copy.** 2 vols. Lge. 4to. Buckram. (SG. Aug.4; 207) $120

MORTON, Caroline
- [–] **Heroes of Notasia; A Record of Australian Exploration.** Hobart, 1888. Sm. defects to several fore-edges, wraps., slightly chipped & frayed. (KH. May 1; 507)   Aus. $150

MORTON, John
- **The Natural History of Northampton-shire.** 1712. Fo. 1 double-p. folding map, 14 engraved plts., dampstained, cont. cf., worn. (CSK. Jan.27; 184)
£150

MORTON, Samuel George
- **Crania Americana, or a Comparative View of the Skulls of Various Aboriginal Nations of North & South America.** Phila. & L., 1839. Fo. Frontis., 77 plts., cold. map, chart, spotted, hf. mor., rubbed. (BBA. Jul.27; 44)   *Quaritch*. £210
– – **Anr. Copy.** Fo. Hand-cold. map, 79 litho. plts., spotted, orig. cl., rubbed, inscr. on front end-paper. (BBA. Feb.23; 94)   *Quaritch*. £130

MORVILLE
See— LEVRAULT, L. & others

MORYSON, Fynes
- **An Itinerary ... containing his Ten Yeares Travell through the Twelve Dominions of Germany, Bohmerland, Sweitzerland, Netherland, Denmark, Poland, Italy, Turky, France, England, Scotland, & Ireland.** L., 1617. *1st. Edn.* Fo. Some mispagination & staining, armorial cf. gt., defect. (GM. Dec.7; 486)
£180
– – **Anr. Edn.** Glasgow, 1907-08. *(100) numbered on H.M.P.* 4 vols. Vell.-bkd. cl. gt., unc. (SKC. Mar.9; 2028)   £130

MOSCHEROSCH, Joh. M.
- [–] **Wunderliche und Warhafftige Gesichte Philanders von Sittewald.** Strassburg, 1650. Title lacks printing year, title with old owner's mark, foxed & stained thro.-out, or browned, cont. vell. (HK. Nov.10; 2608)   DM 480

MOSCHETTI, Allessandro & others
- **Raccolta delle Principali Vedute di Roma.** Rome, ca. 1848. Ob. fo. Engraved title, plan, 68 engraved views, cont. red hf. mor., lr. cover dampstained. (C. Nov.16; 130)   *Bifolco*. £130

MOSCHETTI, Andreas
- **Principali Monumenti di Roma.** N.d. Ob. 4to. Cont. hf. mor., slightly rubbed. (CSK. Jul.6; 60)
£220

MOSELEY, H.N.
- **Notes by a Naturalist on the Challenger.** L., 1879. Some slight foxing, orig. cl. (CA. Apr.3; 90)
Aus. $150

MOSELEY, Henry Gwyn Jeffreys
- **The High-Frequency Spectra of the Elements.** L., 1913-14. *1st. Edn.* 2 pts., 'Philosophical Magazine' Vol. 26 no. 156 & Vol. 27 no. 160. Orig. ptd. wraps., 1st. pt. unopened, minimal wear to spines; Stanitz coll. (SPB. Apr.25; 309) $200

MOSELLY, Emile
- **La Charrue d'Erable.** Ill.:– L. Pissarro & C. Pissarro. L., Eragny Pr., Dec. 1912. *(116) numbered.* Orig. limp cf. (GB. Nov.5; 2896)DM 5,600

MOSES, Henry
- **Visit of William the Fourth, When Duke of Clarence, as Lord High Admiral, to Portsmouth.** [L., 1831]. Fo. Slightly browned, cont. hf. leath., orig. wraps. pasted on, defect. & worn. (R. Oct.12; 2320)
DM 2,200

MOSHE ALFALAS
- **Ho'il Moshe.** Venice, 1597. (*Bound with:*)
- **Va'Yakhel Moshe.** Venice, 1597. (*Bound with:*)
YEHUDA UZIEL - Bet Ha'Uzieli. Venice, 1603. Together 3 works in 1 vol. 4to. Slight staining & minor losses to a few preliminary ll., some soiling,

contents loose in bdg., old cf., worn. (SPB. Feb.1; 13) $850

MOSHE BEN MAIMON [Maimonides]
- **Iggerot le-ha-Ma'or ha-Gadol.** Venice, [1670]. *3rd.[?] Edn.* 16mo. Dampstained, mod. cl., trimmed. (SG. Feb.2; 266) $150
- **Milot Ha'Higayon.** Venice, 1550. *1st. Edn.* 4to. 2 ll. in facs., owner's sig. on title, browned & creased, few Latin margin glosses, mod. mor. (S. Oct.25; 283)   *Ludmir*. £340
- **Mishna Torah.** Constantinople, 1509. 4 vols., & the 'Abadia Peirush Hilchot Kidush Ha Chodesh' (here bnd. as Vol. II). Dupl. p. 17 in Vol. I, lacks 3 ll. in Vol. I, folios 1-3 in Vol. I & folios 96-100 in Vol. III supplied in facs., some ll. supplied from shorter copies, 1 lf. in Vol. III misbnd., traces of worming, staining & browning, extensive margin repairs with loss of text, Vol. II in vell.-bkd. bds., rest in spr. hf. cf. gt. (SPB. Feb.1; 61) $10,000
– – **Anr. Edn.** Commentaries:– Abraham Ben David, Shem Tov Gaon & Maggid Mishne. Venice, 1524-25. *5th. Edn.* 14 books in 2 vols. Fo. Mispaginated, uncensored, 3 ll. misbnd., 1st. title mntd. without loss of text, some margins reprd. not affecting text, some staining, creased, hf. leath., marb. paper bds. (S. Oct.25; 284)
Dzialowski. £3,500
– – **Anr. Edn.** Commentaries:– Abraham Ben David [Raavad], Joseph Karo & Levi Ibn Chabib. Venice, 1574-75. *7th. Edn.* 14 pts. in 4 vols. Sm. fo. Some ll. including 1st. title reprd. affecting some text, browned, staining, trimmed, cl. (S. Oct.25; 285)
Klein. £750
- **Mishne Torah or Yad Hachazaka.** Ed.:– Eliezer ben Shmuel. Soncino, Gershom ben Moshe Soncino [Menzlein Soncino], 1 Nisan 5250 [23 Mar. 1490]. Fo. Uncensored, lacks 1st. lf. & final blank, staining to a few prelim. & final ll., 2nd. lf. crudely rehinged with minor losses, a few repairs mostly to margins, sometimes affecting sm. part of text, approx. 10 ll. supplied from anr. copy, ink stain in upr. margin affecting a few quires, old vell.-bkd. bds., very rubbed. [Steinschneider 6513, 2] (SPB. Jun.26; 22)
$60,000
- **Moreh Nevuchim.** [Rome, Obadiah, Menaseh & Benjamin of Rome], ca. 1469-72. *1st. Edn.* 4to. Sigd. by censors Dominico Yerushalmi (in Latin & Hebrew) 1615, & Giovanni Antonio Costanzi, deletions on several pp., lacks 3 ll. (2 blanks), a few repairs to inner & several outer margins, final lf. mntd., staining, slight marginalia, slight trace of foxing, bds., worn; owners sig.(?) of Giuseppe Menachem(?), Hochschule für die Wissenschaft des Judenthums stps. [Steinschneider 6513, 100; Goff Heb-80] (SPB. Jun.26; 21) $120,000

MOSHE BEN MAIMON [Maimonides] & Ovadia di Bertinoro
- **[Mishna with Commentaries:] Vol. I: Zeraim.** Sabionetta, 1559. Owners' sigs. on title & verso, ll. towards beginning crudely reprd. with loss of text, browned, 16th. C. margin glosses, hf. leath., marb. paper bds. (*With:*) - **Vol. II: Moed.** Sabionetta, 1559. Lacks 4 ll. of diagrams (as usual), washed, worming affecting some letters, stained, mod. blind-tooled mor. (*With:*) - **Vol. III: Nashim.** Mantua, 1561. Worming reprd., some staining, hf. leath., marb. paper bds. (*With:*) - **Vol. IV: Nezkin.** Mantua, 1562. Some margins reprd. with loss of text, browned & stained, sigs. of censor & owner on last p., mod. blind-tooled mor. (*With:*) - **Vol. V: Kodashim.** Mantua, 1562. Slight staining, hf. leath., marb. paper bds. (*With:*) - **Vol. VI: Taharot.** Mantua, 1562-63. Reprd., staining, slight worming affecting some letters, hf. leath., marb. paper bds. Together 6 vols. Various sizes. In s.-c. (S. Oct.25; 271)   *Davidson*. £1,700

MOSHE BEN NACHMAN [Nachmanides]
- **Chidushei Baba Batra.** Venice, 1523. *1st. Edn. [2nd. Edn. of Dina Degarmei].* Fo. 2 ll. misbnd., title defect. & reprd., owner's sig. on 1st. p., slight staining, some margin glosses, hf. leath. (S. Oct.25; 286)   *Klein*. £800
- **Peirush HaTorah.** [Naples, Yosef ben Yaacov or Azriel ben Yaacov Azhkenazi (Gunzenhausen)], 13 Tanmuz 5250 [2 Jul. 1490]. Fo. Wide margins, censored (a few minor phrases only) & sigd. by Camilo Yaghel on verso of final lf., slight staining &

some soiling, a few margin notes in 16th. C. hand, cf.-bkd. bds., very rubbed. [Steinschneider 6532, 50] (SPB. Jun.26; 23) $65,000
- **Sha'ar Ha'Gemul.** Ferrara, 1556. *2nd. Edn.* 4to. Some staining, discold., 16th. C. margin glosses, mod. blind-tooled mor. (S. Oct.25; 287) *Davidson.* £850
- **Teshuvot She'eilot.** Venice, 1518-19. *1st. Edn.* 4to. Unpaginated, 2 ll. supplied in MS., title defect. & reprd. affecting some words, last lf. mntd., some worming affecting some words, slight staining, trimmed, mod. pig. (S. Oct.25; 288) *Klein.* £500
- **Torat Ha'Adam.** Venice, 1595. *2nd. Edn.* 4to. Worming thro.-out affecting text, sig. of owner & inquisitor, inscr. on blank p. at end, creased, browned, slight foxing, margin glosses, mod. blind-tooled leath. (S. Oct.25; 289) *Klein.* £320

MOSHE BEN NACHMAN [Nachmanides], attributed to
See— SHLOMO IBN ADRET [Rashba]

MOSHE BEN YAACOV, of Coucy
- **Mitzvot lo Tasse, V'Mitzvot Ase, im Peirushim Ketzarim.** Ed.:– Sebastian Munster. Basle, 1533. In Latin & Hebrew, slight staining & soiling, disbnd. (SPB. Feb.1; 70) $900
- **Sefer Mitzvot Gadol.** [Soncino], Gershom ben Moshe Soncino, 15 Tevet 5249 [19 Dec. 1488]. *2nd. Edn.* Fo. Uncensored, lacks 1 lf., repairs to 1st. lf., sm. loss to margin lr. left, slight staining & browning, a few margins frayed, margin glosses, old vell., worn; R. Akiba Eiger copy, inscr. by his son in Hebrew on fly-lf., Hochschule für die Wissenschaft des Judenthums stps. [Steinschneider 6453, 2; Goff Heb-85] (SPB. Jun.26; 20) $60,000
- **Sefer Mitzvot Gadol; Catalogus Omnium Praeceptorum Legis Mosaicae.** Trans.:– Sebastian Munster. Basle, 1533. 12mo. In Hebrew & Latin, unpaginated, some Latin margin glosses, hf. leath., marb. paper bds. (S. Oct.25; 282) *Klein.* £780

MOSHE BEN YITZCHAK ALASHKAR
See— MEIR BAR BARUCH [MAHARAM], of Rottenburg —— MOSHE BEN YITZCHAK ALASHKAR

MOSHE DE LEON
[–] **Midrash Ha'Ne'elam Ve'Zohar Shir Ha'Shirim, Eicha, Ruth & Tikunim.** Ed:– Moshe Sacuto. Venice, 1658-63. 4to. Slightly stained & creased, buckram. (S. Oct.25; 452) *Hirschler.* £140
[–] **Sefer Ha'Zohar [Genesis; Exodus; Leviticus, Numbers & Deuteronomy].** Mantua, 1558-60. *1st. Edn.* 3 vols. 4to. Vol. I: hole in title not affecting text, verso of title with names of owners in Yemen dtd. 1689, stained & browned, some creasing; Vol. II: title reprd. affecting top of arch, owners' sigs. on 1st. text lf., staining, browned, slight worming not affecting text, trimmed; Vol. III: title defect. & reprd. with loss of hf. of arch, margins at beginning & end reprd. affecting text, last lf. in facs., worming affecting text, browned, margin glosses in Yemenite script, mod. mor., trimmed. (S. Oct.25; 451) *Klein.* £2,500

MOSHE ROMI
- **Sha'arei Gan Eden.** Venice, 1589. *1st. Edn.* Pt. 1 only. 4to. Stained, edges badly frayed, some worming affecting some letters, creased, hf. leath., marb. paper bds. (S. Oct.25; 291) *Dzialowski.* £250

MOSHEIM, Joh. L. von
- **Sämmtliche Heiligen Reden über Wichtige Wahrheiten der Lehre Jesu Christi.** Hamburg, 1765. Cont. marb. leath., gt. spine, covers, inner & outer dentelle, slightly rubbed, cover slightly scratched, 1 spine with sm. defect.; Johann Carl Bohn coll., Hauswedell coll. (H. May 24; 1483) DM 1,100

MOSKOWITZ, Ira, Editor
- **Great Drawings of all Time.** N.Y., 1962. 4 vols. 4to. Orig. cl., s.-c.'s. (S. Apr.30; 208) *Cohen.* £60
– – **Anr. Copy.** 4 vols. Fo. No bdg. stated. (SPB. Nov.30; 307) $175
– – **Anr. Copy.** 4 vols. Lge. 4to. Orig. hf. linen, orig. pict. s.-c.'s. (BR. Apr.13; 1986) DM 500
– – **Anr. Edn.** N.Y., [1962]. 4 vols. Fo. Cl., s.-c.'s slightly worn. (CBA. Jan.29; 226) $190

– – **Anr. Copy.** 4 vols. Sm. fo. Two-tone buckram, cl. boxes worn. (SG. Jan.26; 252) $175

MOSLEY, S.L.
- **Illustrations of Varieties of British Lepidoptera.** L., ca. 1895. 30 col. plts., orig. cl. (SKC. Oct.26; 414) £140

MOSQUES OF EGYPT (The), from 21 H. (641) to 1365 H. (1946)
Giza, 1949. 2 vols. Fo. Plain & cold. plts., 2 folding plans & 1 index in pocket at end of Vol. 1, intro. & preface loose, orig. cl. (S. May 1; 560) *Sims.* £260

MOSS, Edward Lawton
- **Shores of the Polar Sea.** L., 1875-76. Title stpd., plt. versos stpd., orig. linen, wear, jnts. torn, corners bumped. (HK. May 15; 622a) DM 600
– – **Anr. Edn.** L., 1878. Fo. Map, 16 chromolitho. plts., slightly spotted, cont. maroon mor. gt., slightly rubbed. (S. Jun.25; 26) *Remmington.* £120
– – **Anr. Copy.** Fo. Orig. cl., soiled. (CSK. Jul.6; 49) £80
– – **Anr. Copy.** Fo. Some perforation stps. in text, plts. stpd. on versos, cl., some wear & soiling, ex-liby. (RO. Dec.11; 243) $180

MOSS, Fletcher
- **Pilgrimages to Old Homes.** 1906-20. Vols. 1 & 4-7. (*With:*) - **Pilgrimages to Old Homes Mostly on the Welsh Border.** 1903. 1 vol. (*With:*) - **Pilgrimages in Cheshire & Shropshire.** 1901. 1 vol. (*With:*) - **Folklore.** 1898. 1 vol. Together 8 vols. Cl. gt., faded. (P. Feb.16; 9) £80

MOSS, Lieut.-Col. William E.
- **Bindings from the Library of Robt. Dudley, Earl of Leicester, K.G. 1533-1588.** Priv. ptd., 1934. *(60).* 4to. 18 actual photos. mntd., orig. ptd. bds., s.-c.; pres. copy to H.M. Nixon, with very many MS. notes. (BBA. Oct.6; 99) *Maggs.* £750
- **Catalogue of the Very Well-Known & Valuable Library.** 1937. 4to. Some prices & buyers' names, cl.; H.M. Nixon coll., with many MS. annots. (BBA. Oct.6; 158) *Beres.* £140

MOSSMAN, R.C.
See— RUDMORE BROWN, R.N. & others

MOSSMANN, X.
See— LEVRAULT, L. & others

MOT (Le)
Ill.:– Cocteau, Dufy, Gleizes, Lhôte & others. Paris, 28 Nov. 1914-1 Jul. 1915. 20 facsicules, compl. Fo. Decor. folder, wraps. by Paul Iribe. (HD. Jun.6; 114) Frs. 2,500

MOTHER GOOSE
- **Mother Goose, or the Old Nursery Rhymes.** Ill.:– Kate Greenaway. [1881]. *[1st. Edn.].* Orig. decor. cl., spotted, orig. ptd. d.-w. slightly frayed at spine ends. (TA. May 17; 664) £82
– – **Anr. Copy.** 12mo. Pict. white cl., pink cl. spine, 3rd. variant, with only 'Mother Goose' on cover & salmon-cold. d.-w. (SG. Dec.8; 169) $150
– – **Anr. Edn.** Ill.:– Arthur Rackham. L., 1913. *(1130) numbered & sigd. by artist.* 4to. Orig. cl. gt., soiled, spine darkened. (CSK. Jan.27; 197) £130
– – **Anr. Edn.** Ill.:– Arthur Rackham. N.Y., [1913]. *(150) sigd. by artist.* 4to. Some black & white ills. hand-cold. with watercol. or crayon, several plts. creased, hf.-title & last index p. darkened, contents slightly darkened with mild offset, gt.-decor. buckram, covers lightly soiled, spine darkening. (CBA. Mar.3; 462) $275

MOTHER GOOSE'S MELODIES or Songs for the Nursery
Ill.:– Alfred Kappes. Boston, 1879. *1st. Edn.* 4to. Stpd. pict. cl., light wear, d.-w. (some fraying & chipping); Ken Leach coll. (RO. Jun.10; 19) $160

MOTHER HUBBARD & HER DOG
L., Read & Co., n.d. Ills. hand-cold., with moving parts operated by levers, inscr. dtd. 1866, loose in orig. cl.-bkd. bds., worn. (S. Nov.22; 442) *Matthews.* £110

MOTHER'S GIFT
1770. 16mo. Last 9 advt. pp., lacks pp. 63-66, orig. flowered bds., very worn; H.M. Nixon coll. (BBA. Oct.6; 236) *Temperley.* £80

MOTLEY, James Lothrop
- **The Rise of the Dutch Republic.** L., 1866. Sm. 8vo. Red mor. by H. & C. Treacher, Brighton, with their inscr., fore-e. pntg. (SG. Nov.17; 232) $225
- **The Rise of the Dutch Republic. — History of the United Netherlands.** 1864; 1860-67. 3 vols.; 4 vols. 1st. work with slight spotting, unif. pol. cf., spines gt.-decor., by Hopkins of Glasgow. (SKC. Sep.9; 1926) £65

MOTONO, S.
- **La Légende de la Demoiselle de Lumière.** Ill.:– Kiyoshi Hasegawa. Paris, 1933. *(150) on paper specially made in Japan.* 4to. Leaves, s.-c. (HD. Nov.17; 161) Frs. 22,000

MOTTEUX, Peter
- **Love's a Jest. A Comedy.** 1696. *1st. Edn.* 4to. Slightly stained, outer margin of last. lf. reprd., mor. by Sangorski & Sutcliffe. [Wing M2953] (BBA. Jan.19; 144) *Maggs.* £90

MOTTEVILLE, Mme de
- **Mémoires, pour servir à l'Histoire d'Anne d'Autriche, Epouse de Louis XIII.** Amst., 1723. *Orig. Edn.* 5 vols. 12mo. Late 18th. C. cf., spine decor.; from liby of J.J. de Bure l'Aîné. (HD. Mar.29; 75) Frs. 18,500
– – **Anr. Edn.** Amst., 1783. *New Edn.* 6 vols. 12mo. Cont. marb. cf., spines decor. (HD. May 21; 59) Frs. 1,800

MOTTLEY, John 'Robert Seymour'
- **A Search after the 'Comfortable'.** L., 1829. Ob. 4to. Plts. hand-cold., soiling, hf. mor., spine worn, wraps. bnd. in; bkplt. of Sir David Lionel Goldsmid-Stern-Salomons. (SPB. Dec.13; 893) $125

MOUBACH, Abraham
- **Naaukeurige Beschryving der Uitwendige Godtsdienstplichten, Kerkzeden en Gewoontens van alle Volkeren der Waereldt.** Ill.:– Picart & others. 's-Gravenhage, Amst. & Rotterdam, 1727-38. 6 vols. Fo. Vol. 6 lacks 1 plt., 1 extra plt. as usual, Vol 1 slightly stained at end, foxing, some stains, cont. hf. cf., unc. (VS. Jun.7; 968) Fls. 1,000

MOUILLARD, Lucien
- **L'Armée Française. Les Régiments sous Louis XV. (1737-1774).** Paris, 1882. 4to. 49 litho. plts., publisher's ill. bds. (HD. Jan.27; 185) Frs. 2,500

MOULE, Thomas
- **Bibliotheca Heraldica Magnae Britaniae.** Priv. ptd., 1822. 4to. L.P., spotted, cont. mor., gt. spine. (BBA. Nov.10; 109) *Marlborough Rare Books.* £75
- **The English Counties Delineated; or, a Topographical Description of England.** L., G. Virtue, 1837. 2 vols. 4to. Engraved frontis. showing William IV, 2 additional engraved titles, 52 (of 57) full-p. or folding engraved maps, plans & thematic plts., including a folding plan of L., hand-cold. in wash & outl., some cropping, cont. hf. cf., rubbed, w.a.f. (S. May 21; 36) *Ross.* £750
– – **Anr. Copy.** 2 vols. 4to. Engraved frontis., 2 additional titles, 2 plts., 58 maps, mostly lightly spotted & soiled, cont. hf. cf., lightly rubbed, w.a.f. (CSK. Dec.2; 49) £450
– – **Anr. Copy.** 2 vols. 4to. Engraved title, 7 town plans, 52 county maps some tears, soiled, cl. gt., covers detchd., w.a.f. (P. Oct.20; 2) £400
See— WESTALL, William & Moule, Thomas

MOUNIER, Jean Joseph
- **Recherches sur les Causes qui ont empêché les Français de devenir Libres.** Geneva, 1792. 2 vols. Mod. hf. vell. (HD. Feb.22; 187) Frs. 2,500

MOUNTBATTEN, Louis, Earl, of Burma
[–] **An Introduction to Polo by 'Marco'.** Foreword:– Lord Wodehouse. 1931. *(100) numbered & sigd. by Mountbatten & Wodehouse.* 4to. Orig. qtr. vell. & cl. gt., untrimmed. (SKC. May 4; 1762) £90

MOUNTENEY, B.
- Selections from the Various Authors who have Written Concerning Brazil. L., 1825. Hf. cf. (P. Dec.8; 345) *Burton Garbett.* £95

MOUNTFORD, Charles Pearcy
- Nomads of the Australian Desert. Adelaide, 1976. Bdg. not stated, d.-w. (KH. May 1; 509)
Aus. $170
- - **Anr. Copy.** Orig. cl. (KH. Nov.9; 672)
Aus. $130
- Records of the American-Australian Scientific Expedition to Arnhem Land. Melbourne, 1956. Vol. 1 only. Orig. cl., d.-w. wearing. (KH. Nov.9; 360)
Aus. $180
- - **Anr. Edn.** Melbourne, 1956-64. 4 vols. Bdg. not stated, d.-w.'s; 1st. vol. sigd. by Mountford. (KH. May 1; 516) Aus. $520
- The Tiwi: Their Art, Myth & Ceremony. 1958. *(250) for sale in Australia.* Bdg. not stated, d.-w. torn & chipped; inscr. & sigd. (KH. May 1; 512)
Aus. $160
- - **Anr. Copy.** Buckram, d.-w. chipped; sigd. by author. (KH. May 1; 511) Aus. $150

MOURADJA D'OHSSON, Ignace de
- Tableau General de l'Empire Othoman. Paris, 1787-90. Vols. 1 & 2 only (of 3). Fo. Additional engraved title with ill., dedication with engraved arms, 137 (of 138) engraved plts. on 69 ll., some folding, hf.-titles, 2 ll. of index in Vol. 2 misbnd., sm. liby. stp. at foot of ptd. titles, cont. red hf. mor., unc., jnts. & edges rubbed, w.a.f. (C. Mar.14; 69)
Kassis. £420

MOURE, Nancy Dustin Wall
- Dictionary of Art & Artists in Southern California before 1930. Los Angeles, priv. ptd., 1978. 4to. Bdg. not stated. (CBA. Jan.29; 82) $110

MOURET, Jean-Joseph
- Ariane, Tragédie En Musique ... **Représentée Pour La Première Fois, Par L'Academie Royale De Musique** ... Paris, 1717. *1st. Edn.* Ob. 4to. Full score, cont. crimson mor., gt., ornamental spine, gt. arms of Comte de Toulouse on covers in triple fillets, marb. end-papers; sigd. by composer & printer beneath ptd. note on final p., from Toulouse-Philidor coll. (S. May 10; 119) *Macnutt.* £1,000

MOURIER, P.
See— WIENER, L. — MOURIER, P.

MOURLOT, Fernand
- Braque Lithographe. Preface:– Fr. Ponge. Ill.:– Braque. [Monte Carlo, 1963]. *Ltd. Edn.* 4to. Orig. pictor. wraps. (H. May 23; 1166) DM 440
- - **Anr. Copy.** 4to. 2 col. lithos., including 1 on cover, 1 litho. title vig., many partly cold. ills., orig. pict. wraps., sewed. (H. Nov.24; 1397) DM 400
- - **Anr. Edn.** Preface:– F. Ponge. Monte Carlo, [1963]. *(4125).* 4to. 1 cold. litho. frontis., cold. litho. title vig., 146 cold. ills., cold. litho. orig. wraps., orig. bd. s.-c. (HT. May 9; 912) DM 520
- Chagall Lithograph. Monte Carlo, [1960-63]. Vols. I & II. 4to. 22 orig. lithos. (14 cold.), 375 partly cold. ills., orig. linen, cold. litho. wraps. (HT. May 9; 923) DM 3,500
- - **Anr. Edn.** Ed.:– J. Cain & Ch. Sorlier. Monte Carlo, [1960-63-69-74]. Vols. I-IV. 4to. Vol. III in Fr., orig. linen, orig. cold. pictor. wraps., 1 with sm. spot & stain. (H. May 23; 1177) DM 4,800
- - **Anr. Edn.** Monte Carlo, [1963]. Vol. II. Lge. 4to. Stained thro.-out, orig. linen, cold. pict. orig. wraps., stained. (H. Nov.24; 2462) DM 1,000
- - **Anr. Edn.** [Paris], 1969. Vol. III. 4to. 1 orig. cold. litho., orig. linen, orig. litho. wrap. (D. Nov.24; 2984) DM 500
- - **Anr. Edn.** Trans.:– [O. Baumgartner]. Monte Carlo, 1969. Vol. III. 4to. Orig. linen, cold. orig. wraps. (H. Nov.24; 2463) DM 400
- - **Anr. Edn.** Ed.:– Charles Sorlier. Trans.:– E. Weiser. Monte Carlo, 1974. Vol. IV. 4to. 2 cold. orig. l'thos (frontis. & wrap.), orig. linen, wrap. (R. Apr.3; 738) DM 510
- Chagall Lithographe. Monte Carlo, 1960-63. Vols. I & II. 4to. Vol. I in Engl., Vol. II in Fr., 22 orig. lithos., orig. linen, orig. wraps. (GB. Nov.5; 2343) DM 2,900
- - **Anr. Edn.** Ed.:– J. Cain & C. Sorlier. Monte Carlo, 1960-63-69. Vols. I-III. 4to. 22 orig. lithos.,

orig. linen, orig. pict. wrap. (mostly orig. litho.). (GB. May 5; 2274) DM 3,800
- - **Anr. Edn.** Ed.:– Julien Cain & Charles Sorlier. [Monte Carlo, 1960-63-69], N.Y., [1974]. Vols. I-IV. Lge. 4to. Vol. IV in Engl., cl., col.-pict. d.-w.'s. (SG. Mar.29; 42) $1,200
- - **Anr. Edn.** Monte Carlo, 1963. Vol. II. 4to. 11 orig. lithos. (including 6 cold.), orig. linen, cold. pict. wrap. (R. Apr.3; 737) DM 1,800
- - **Anr. Edn.** [Monte Carlo, 1963]. Vol. II. 4to. 11 lithos., including 5 cold., 376 ills., orig. pict. wraps. (H. Nov.24; 1448) DM 1,000
- - **Anr. Edn.** Ill.:– Marc Chagall. [Monte Carlo, 1963-69]. Vols. II & III only. 4to. Orig. cl., 1 d.-w. worn. (SPB. Dec.13; 788) $275
- - **Anr. Edn.** Ed.:– J. Cain. Monte Carlo, 1969. Vol. III. Lge. 4to. Orig. linen, orig. wraps., orig. cold litho. wraps., s.-c. (HK. May 17; 2649)
DM 420
- - **Anr. Edn.** [Monte Carlo, 1969]. Vol. III. 4to. 2 cold. lithos., including 1 on wraps., many partly cold. ills., orig. linen, orig. pict. wraps. (H. Nov.24; 1444) DM 500
- Joan Miró Der Lithograph I (und IV). Trans.:– U. Patzies & H.D. Ruelle. Genf/Paris, 1972-82. 4to. 18 cold. orig. lithos., orig. linen. (R. Oct.11; 894)
DM 1,100
- The Lithographs of Chagall. Trans.:– M. Jolas. 1960-63-69. Vols. I-III only (of 4). 4to. 22 full-p. lithos., including 15 in col., cl., pict. d.-w.'s. (P. Feb.16; 219) £850
- - **Anr. Edn.** N.Y., Boston or Monte Carlo, 1960-63-69-74. Vols. 1-4. 4to. Engl. text in Vols. 1, 2 & 4, a few ll. in Vol. 1 loose, orig. cl., pict. d.-w.'s. (S. Nov.21; 61) *Sims.* £880
- - **Anr. Edn.** Ed.:– Charles Sorlier. Boston, [1963-69]. Vols. II & III. Sm. fo. Cl., col. litho. d.-w.'s, glassine d.-w.'s, publisher's s.-c.'s. (SG. Mar.29; 39) $400
- - **Anr. Copy.** Vols. II & III. Sm. fo. Cl., col. litho. d.-w.'s, glassine d.-w.'s, Vol. III in publisher's s.-c (SG. Mar.29; 40) $350
- - **Anr. Edn.** Ed.:– Charles Sorlier & Julien Cain. Boston, 1969. Vol. 3. 4to. Orig. litho. frontis. & d.-w., bdg. not stated, in orig. packing box. (CBA. Jan.29; 98) $325
- - **Anr. Copy.** 4to. 1 orig. cold. litho., orig. linen, orig. litho. wrap. (D. Nov.24; 2983) DM 550
- - **Anr. Edn.** Ed.:– Julien Cain & Charles Sorlier. Boston, [1969]. Vol. 3. 4to. Frontis. orig. litho., cl., d.-w. (orig. litho.). (LH. Sep.25; 510) $170
- - **Anr. Edn.** Ed.:– Charles Sorlier. N.Y., [1974]. Vol. 4. 4to. Orig. litho. frontis. & d.-w., bdg. not stated. (CBA. Jan.29; 111) $140
- - **Anr. Copy.** Vol. 4. 4to. Frontis. orig. litho., cl., d.-w. (orig. litho.). (LH. Sep.25; 513) $130
- Picasso Lithographe. Monte Carlo, [1949-50]. *Ltd. Iss.* Vols. I & II. 4to. Orig. pict. wraps. (H. Nov.24; 1930) DM 1,700
- - **Anr. Edn.** Preface:– J. Sabartès. Monte Carlo, 1949-56. *(2500) numbered.* Vols. I-III. Orig. wraps. (HK. May 17; 3053) DM 2,000
- - **Anr. Edn.** Monte Carlo, [1949-56]. Vols. I-III. Lge. 4to. Litho. frontis., plts., ex-liby., pict. wraps. (SG. May 3; 282) $800
- - **Anr. Edn.** Monte Carlo, [1949-69]. Vols. I-IV. 4to. Orig. pict. wraps. & 2 hf. linen, slightly bumped, vols. I & II orig. wraps. (H. Nov.24; 1929)
DM 1,800
- Souvenirs et Portraits d'Artistes. Ill.:– Matisse, Braque, Miro, Picasso, Chagall, & others. Paris, [1972]. *(800) numbered.* 4to. 25 litho. plts., loose as iss. in ptd. wraps., cl. folding box. (SG. Jan.12; 272) $425

MOURLOT, Fernand (Ill.)
See— VERVE

MOUSSINAC, Léon
- Etoffes Imprimées et Papiers Peints. Paris, [1924]. *(With:)* - Etoffes d'Ameublement Tissées et Brochées. Paris, [1925]. Together 2 vols. 4to. Each vol. with 50 loose plts., several pochoir-cold., bd. folders, worn, spine detchd. (SG. Aug.25; 29)
$250

MOXO Y DE FRANCOLI, Benito M. de
- Cartas Mejicanas. Genoa, [1839]. Wormed, few other defects, mostly marginal, tree sheep. (SG. Oct.20; 241) $250

MOXON, Joseph
- Mechanik Exercises: Or, the Doctrine of Handy-Works. 1695. *2nd. Edn.* Sm. 4to. Some margin repairs & stains, recent panel. cf. (TA. Oct.20; 277) £100
- A Tutor to Astronomie & Geographie. L., 1659. *1st. Edn.* Sm. 4to. Engraved title in Latin, text woodcuts & engrs., 1st. blank reprd., 1 lf. with marginal tear, some stains, cont. cf., crudely reprd.; sigs. of M.R. & J.E. Moxon, latter dtd. 1871. (SG. Apr.26; 147) $325
- - **Anr. Edn.** L., 1670. *[2nd. Edn.].* 4to. 1 margin torn with loss of a few letters, later hf. cf. [Wing M3023] (BBA. May 3; 53) *Traylen.* £150
- - **Anr. Copy.** Sm. 4to. Slightly soiled thro.-out, some sm. tears, mostly marginal, mod. cf. gt., earlier end-papers preserved; inscr. of Franc. Buxton Magd. Oxon. (BBA. Nov.30; 115) *Demetzy.* £130
- - **Anr. Edn.** L., 1686. *4th. Edn.* 4to. Cont. cf., rebkd. & relined. (SG. Oct.6; 266) $130
See— MANDEY, Venterus & Moxon, Joseph

MOYLLUS, Damianus
- A Newly Discovered Treatise on Classic Letter Design printed at Parma by Damianus Moyllus circa 1480. Intro.:– Stanley Morison. Montagnola, Bodoni Pr., for At the Sign of the Pegasus, 1927. *Facs. Reprint, (350).* Sm. 4to. Prospectus loosely inserted, orig. vell.-bkd. bds., unc., unopened. (S. Nov.22; 267) *Quaritch.* £340

MOZART, Leopold
- Grondig Onderwys in het Behandelen der Viool. Haarlem, 1766. *1st. Edn. in Dutch.* 4to. Mus. notat., some margins stained, 19th. C. vell. gt., slightly foxed. (VG. May 3; 533) Fls. 1,700
- Gründl. Violinschule. Augsburg, 1800. 4to. Slightly foxed thro.-out, notation supp. with sm. tear & slightly crumpled, cont. leath., slightly rubbed & bumped. (HK. Nov.9; 2270) DM 950

MOZART, Wolfgang Amadeus
- L'Enlèvement Du Serail ... Clavecin arrangement:– C.G. Neefe. Bonn, ca. 1799. *Early Edn.* Ob. fo. No bdg. stated. (S. May 10; 122)
Haas. £170
- Idomeneo Rè Di Creta ... Piano arrangement:– Giov. Wenzel. Leipzig, [1796 or 1797]. *1st. Edn.* Ob. fo. Ptd. subscribers list, some cont. annots. in pencil, a few pp. with tears, no paper loss, but text affected, cont. wraps., disbnd., cont. label on outer cover. (S. May 10; 121) *Stephens.* £850
- Kurzgefasste Generalbass-Schule. Wien, [1818]. *1st. Edn.* Foxed, orig. wraps., with owners note, corners bumped. (HK. Nov.9; 2271) DM 1,400

MUCHALL-VIEBROOK, A.
- Seglers Handbuch. Berlin, 1889. *1st. Edn.* 4to. Orig. linen, worn. (HK. Nov.9; 2189) DM 420

MUDFORD, William
- An Historical Account of the Campaign in the Netherlands. Ill.:– G. Cruikshank & others. L., 1817. *1st. Edn.* Lge. 4to. 2 folding maps, 28 col. aquatints & etchings (wtrmkd. 1814-16), including 1 folding, 4 mntd. as iss., 1 map laid down, folds reprd., few repairs in text, cont. red str.-grd. mor., elab. gold- & blind-tooled, rehinged. (SG. Nov.3; 149) $600

MUDIE, James
- The Felonry of New South Wales. L., 1837. Map & some ll. foxed, pres. inscr. at head of title, orig. blind-stpd. cl., covers stained & worn. (CA. Apr.3; 91) Aus. $300

MUDIE, Robert
- The Feathered Tribes of the British Islands. L., 1835. *2nd. Edn.* 2 vols. Cont. gt. decor. hf. leath. (GB. Nov.3; 1152) DM 400
- - **Anr. Edn.** 1841. *3rd. Edn.* 2 vols. Orig. cl., spines gt.-decor. (SKC. Mar.9; 1951) £65
- Hampshire, Its Past & Present Condition. Winchester, ca. 1838. 3 vols. 3 engraved titles, 3 folding maps, 134 plts., hf. cf. (WW. Nov.23; 39) £440
- [-] The Picture of Australia. 1829. Bnd. without hf.-title & advts., frontis., title-p. & several other ll. slightly foxed, early cf. (KH. May 1; 517)
Aus. $130

MUELLER, Baron Ferdinand von

- Eucalyptographia. L., 1879-84. 10 pts. in 1 vol. 4to. 110 plts., dampstaining, hf. cf., worn; Royal Commonwealth Soc. copy. (P. Nov.24; 280)
Wheldon & Wesley. £100
- Fragmenta Phytographiae Australiae. L., 1858-81. Vols. 1-11. Hf. mor., rubbed, & orig. cl., Vol. 7 soiled; Royal Commonwealth Soc. copy. (P. Nov.24; 276) *Wheldon & Wesley.* £150
- Iconography of Australian Salsolaceous Plants. Melbourne, 1889-91. 9 pts. in 1. 4to. 90 plts., some dampstaining to upr. margin, qtr. cf., soiled; Royal Commonwealth Soc. copy. (P. Nov.24; 281) *Wheldon & Wesley.* £50
- Iconography of Australian Species of Acacia. L., 1887-88. 13 pts. in 1 vol. 4to. 130 plts., some dampstaining, hf. cf., rubbed; Royal Commonwealth Soc. copy. (P. Nov.24; 282)
Wheldon & Wesley. £80
See— BENTHAM, G. & Mueller, Baron F. von

MUELLER, Jacob

- Ornatus Ecclesiasticus. Munich, 1591. 2 pts. in 1 vol. 4to. 1st. pt. in Latin, 2nd. pt. in German, bd. covers from an early book, rather shabby. (SG. Feb.9; 290) $300

MUHAMMED IBN AHMAD, Called Ibn Rushd, or Averroes

- Kitzurei ibn Rushd. Trans.:– Moshe ibn Tibbon. Riva di Trento, Yakov Mercaria, 1560. *1st. Edn.* 12mo. Worming affecting some letters, discold., blind-tooled leath. (S. Oct.24; 75) *Jansen.* £380
- – Anr. Edn. Trans.:– Moshe ibn Tibbon. Riva di Trento, Christoforo Madruzzi, 1560. 12mo. Lacks ll. 41-47, ll. 38-40 defect., lacks 24, some mod. pencil annots. in Greek, dampstained, crude hand-drawn border on title, later cl., soiled. (SG. Feb.2; 145) $175
- Kol Mlechet Higayon. Trans.:– Jakov ibn Machir. Riva di Trento, 1559. *1st. Edn.* 12mo. Title & 1st. p. with 2 holes affecting 2 words, margin of title reprd. not affecting text, stained, owners' sigs. on title, hf. leath., marb. paper bds. (S. Oct.24; 76)
Jansen. £380
See— ARISTOTELES — ARISTOTELES & Muhammed Ibn Ahmad, called Ibn Rushd, or Averroes

MUHSAM

- Die Gläser der Sammlung Mühsam. Intro.:– R. Schmidt. Berlin, 1914 & [1926]. *(350) numbered.* 2 vols. Fo. Orig. linen. (HK. Nov.12; 4669)
DM 4,200

MUIR, John, Explorer

- The Cruise of the Corwin. L., 1917. *(550) numbered.* L.P., hand-cold. frontis., plts., hf. mor., faded. (P. Nov.24; 16) *Cavendish.* £65
- Picturesque California & the Region West of the Rocky Mountains, from Alaska to Mexico. N.Y. & San Franc., 1888. *1st. Edn.* 2 vols. Fo. Publisher's blind- & gt.-stpd. red mor., minor wear, minor fraying of extremities, buckram d.-w., inner flaps closed at top & bottom to make sealed pockets, worn; Ken Leach coll. (RO. Jun.10; 110) $575
- – Anr. Copy. 3 vols. Leath., spine & edges rubbed & scraped. (RS. Jan.17; 485) $300

MUIR, John, Explorer (Text)
See— HARRIMAN ALASKA EXPEDITION

MUIR, Percy Horace

- Points, 1866-1934. L., 1934. *(750).* 2nd. Series: 1 vol. Tall 8vo. Orig. bds. (SG. Sep.15; 237) $120
- Points, 1874-1930. - Points, 1866-1934. L., 1931, 1934. 1st. & 2nd. Series: 2 vols. Plts., orig. parch.-bkd. bds.; Fred A. Berne copy. (SPB. May 16; 175) $225
- – Anr. Edn. L., [1931], 1934. *Ltd. Edns.* 1st. & 2nd. Series: 2 vols. Qtr. vell. or art vell., marb. bds. (SG. Jan.5; 235) $130
See— CARTER, John Waynflete & Muir, Percy H.

MUIR, Percy Horace (Ed.)
See— BIBLIOGRAPHICAL NOTES & QUERIES

MUIR, Thomas [Pseud.]

- The Telegraph, a Consolatory Epistle from Thomas Muir ... [Edinb., 1796]. 4to. The names

omitted in the text of the satire supplied in cont. MS. (partly shaved through later cutting), mod. red hf. mor. gt. (C. Nov.16; 140)
Remington. £120

MUIRHEAD, George

- The Birds of Berwickshire. Edinb., 1889-95. 2 vols. Cl. gt. (PD. Dec.14; 43) £52

MUJERES ESPANOLAS, PORTUGUESAS Y AMERICANAS

Madrid, 1872-76. 3 vols. Lge. fo. Chagrin, sigd. by Zaehnsdorf. (DS. Feb.24; 2150) Pts. 200,000

MULDER, Joseph

- Vues de Gunterstein. Amst., ca. 1730. Ob. 8vo. Engraved title & 15 engrs., bds. (VG. Dec.1; 1312)
Fls. 900

MULHOUSE

- Histoire Documentaire de l'Industrie de Mulhouse et de ses Environs au XIXe Siècle. Mulhouse, 1902. Lge. 4to. Publisher's bds. (HD. Mar.21; 179)
Frs. 1,600

MULLER, Ad. H.

- Die Elemente der Staatskunst. Berlin, 1809. *1st. Edn.* 3 vols. Slightly foxed, col. paper end-papers, cont. hf. leath. (HK. Nov.10; 2610) DM 1,000

MULLER, Ad. H. (Ed.)
See— PHOBUS

MULLER, Ch.
See— REBOUX, P. & Müller, Ch.

MULLER, Elisabeth

- Le Monde en Estampes. Ill.:– after M.M. Leloir & Fossey. N.d Ob. 4to. 23 hand-cold. litho. plts., some margins dampstained or spotted, cont. cl., rebkd., worn. (CSK. Jun.1; 108) £85

MULLER, Eugène

- La Forêt. Paris, 1878. Hf. mor., decor.spine, by A. Knicht. (HD. Apr.11; 45) Frs. 1,100

MULLER, Frederic

- Catalogue of Books, Maps, Plates on America, & of a Remarkable Collection of Early Voyages ... Amst., 1872. *(25) on extra large, thick Dutch paper.* Vol. 1 (of 3) only, separate Iss., 3 facs. tipped in,. Sm. 4to. Later red qtr. mor. & marb. bds. orig. ptd. upr. wrap. bnd. in, partly unc. (SG. Apr.5; 283) $130
- – Anr. Edn. Amst., 1872; 1875; 1875. 3 facs in vol. 1, 3 vols. separately iss. On ordinary paper, vol. 1 with broadside errata lf. of De Bry's Voyages tipped in, unif. later red qtr. mor. & marb. bds., orig. wraps. bnd. in Vol. I, orig. front. wrap. bnd. in. vol. III. (SG. Apr.5; 282) $275

MULLER, Hans Alexander

- Woodcuts & Wood Engravings: How I Make Them. N.Y., 1939. *1st. Edn. (250) in portfo.* Sm. fo. Cl. folding box., with sigd. proof of self-port. (SG. Aug.4; 208) $100

MULLER, Hermann Alexander (Ed.)
See— ALLGEMEINES KUNSTLER LEXIKON

MULLER, J.

- Beschreibung d. Insel Java. Berlin, 1863. Plts. partly browned, foxed thro.-out, cont. hf. linen, slighlty rubbed. (HK. May 15; 642) DM 560

MULLER. J.G.
See— MUSAUS, Johann Karl August & others

MULLER, Johannes

- Uber die Fossilen Reste der Zeuglodonten von Nordamerika mit Rücksicht auf d. Europ. Reste aus dieser Familie. Berlin, 1849. Lge. fo. 5 plts. with sm. margin defects., 1 plt. crumpled, some foxing, orig. bd. portfo., spine defect. [Sabin 51287] (HK. Nov.8; 665) DM 500

MULLER, Johannes, Physiologist

- Ueber den Feineren Bau und die Formen der Kran-khaften Geschwülste. Berlin, 1838. *[1st. Edn.].* Pt.1. (all publd.). Fo. Title & explanation lf. at end are ptd. on different paper of different size (a wrap.?), qtr. cf.; Dr. Walter Pagel copy. (S. Feb.7; 266)
Rota. £520

– – Anr. Copy. Pt. I (all publd.). Tall fo. Mod. buckram, ex-liby. (SG. Oct.6; 267) $500
- Uber zwei Verschiedene Typen in dem Bau der Erectilen Männlichen Geschlechts-Organe bei den Straussartigen Vögeln und über die Entwicklungs-formen dieser Organe unter den Wirbelthieren Uber-haupt. Berlin, 1838. Fo. L.P., some foxing, cl.; Dr. Walter Pagel copy. (S. Feb.7; 268) *Heller.* £120

MULLER, John

- Treatise of Artillery ... 1757. Cont. cf., lightly rubbed, 2 A.L.S.'s from Muller to publisher lossely inserted, both neatly reprd. (CSK. My 18; 80)
£240

MULLER, Karl & Braun, Louis

- Die Bekleidung, Anrüstung und Bewaffnung der Königlich Bayerischen Armée von 1806 bis zur Neu-zeit. München, 1899. 2 vols. 4to. 70 lithos., leaves, publisher's bds. (HD. Jan.27; 297) Frs. 2,800

MULLER, S.
See— VETH, J. & Muller, S.

MULLER, W.Y.
See— BENDER, E. & Muller, W.Y.

MULLER, William James

- Sketches of the Age of Frances 1st. L., 1841. Lge. fo. Foxing, especially on title, pp. disbnd., publishers bdg., havanna mor. spine, worn. (HD. Feb.29; 28)
Frs. 1,400

MULLIGAN, P.

- The Independent Navigator or Mariner's Best Companion. L., 1828. Folding frontis. glued to upr. cover as iss., some browning, embossed stp. on title, cont. cf.-bkd. bds.; sig. of Augustus Sampson, Boston, 23 Feb. 1830. (PNY. Mar.27; 171) $140

MULLINER, H.H.

- The Decorative Arts in England during the late XVIIth & XVIIIth Centuries. 1923. Fo. Orig. cl. (LC. Oct.13; 65) £60

MULSANT, Etienne

- Lettres à Julie sur l'Ornithologie. Ill.:– by or after E. Traviès. Paris, [1868]. Lge. 8vo. 16 litho. plts., all cont. hand-cold. & 'gommées', orig. hf. chagrin. (VS. Dec.7; 409) Fls. 475

MUMEY, Nolie

- History of the Early Settlement of Denver. (1599-1860). Glendale, California, 1942. *(500) numbered.* Linen-bkd. bds.; sigd. by author. (LH. Sep.25; 268)
$100
- A Study of Rare Books. L., 1930. *(1000) sigd.* Facs. ills., cl.-bkd. bds. (P. May 17; 61)
Dreesmann. £70

MUMFORD, John Kimberley

- Yerkes Collection of Oriental Carpets. N.Y., 1910. *De Luxe Amer. Edn. (750) numbered.* Tall fo. 27 cold. plts., ex-liby., loose in satin folder, linen ties. (SG. May 3; 394) $375
- – Anr. Copy. Fo. 27 col. plts., loose as iss., silk folder, spine torn. (SG. Aug.25; 283) $225

MUMFORD, Lewis

- American Taste. Ill.:– [V. Angelo]. San Franc., Westgate Pr., at the Grabhorn Pr., 1929. *(500) sigd. by author & artist.* Hf. cl. & decor. bds., covers lightly rubbed; leath. bkplt. of Alfred Sutro, the V. Angelo copy. (CBA. Oct.1; 167) $130

MUMMERY, A.F.

- My Climbs in the Alps & Caucasus. L., 1895. *1st. Edn.* Lge. 8vo. A few ll. slightly spotted, orig. cl., rubbed. (BBA. May 3; 355)
Bob Finch Books. £85
- – Anr. Copy. 4to. Red hf. mor. gt. by Sangorski & Sutcliffe. (BS. Nov.16; 16) £80

MUNBY, Alan Noel Latimer

- Phillipps Studies. Camb., 1951-56. Vols. 1-4 only (of 5). Orig. cl., d.-w.'s. (BBA. Nov.10; 110)
Blackwell. £65

MUNCHENER BILDERBOGEN

Munich, n.d. Vols. 8-9 only. Sm. fo. 48 folding cold. plts., orig. bds., rebkd. (BBA. Mar.21; 35)
Wenner. £110

MUNCHHAUSEN, Baron (Pseud.)
See— **RASPE, Rudolph Erich 'Baron Munchhausen'**

MUNCHHAUSEN, O. von
- **Der Hausvater.** Hannover, 1768-75. Pts. I-VI/I (all publd.) in 6 vols. Text not collated, slightly foxed & browned, cont. bds., corners slightly bumped. (HK. May 16; 1541)   DM 1,000

MUNCHNER BLATTER FUR DICHTUNG UND GRAPHIK
Ed.:– R. Kuon. Text:– F. Wedekind, I. Goll, P. Claudel, P. Amann, E. Weiss etc. Ill.:– Paul Klee, R. Seewald, A. Kubin, M. Unold & others. München, 1919. Yr. 1, pts. 1-12 (all publd.). in 11 pts. 4to. 54 orig. ills., 1st. 3 pts. slightly crumpled & minimal browned, orig. pict. wraps., stpd., pt. 1 slightly spotted. (HT. May 9; 1969)   DM 3,300

MUNDY, Rear Admiral Sir Rodney
- **H.M.S. 'Hannibal' at Palermo & Naples, during the Italian Revolution, 1859-61. With Notices of Garibaldi, Francis II, & Victor Emmanuel.** 1863. Wood-engraved frontis., single-p. map, recent hf. mor. gt.; author's pres. copy to Maj. J.L. Cowell, with A.L.s. from author to Maj. Cowell requesting that he be allowed to present a copy of his book to Prince Alfred. (TA. Jun.21; 74)   £54

MUNDY, Talbot
- **Queen Cleopatra.** Indianapolis, [1929]. *1st. Edn. (265) sigd.* 4to. Hf. cl. & bds. (CBA. Oct.29; 598)
$150

MUNERELLE (Text)
See— **CURIOSITES ET MERVEILLES DE LA NATURE**

MUNNINGS, Sir Alfred
- **An Artist's Life.** 1950-52. *1st. Edn.* 3 vols. A few ll. slightly spotted, orig. cl., d.-w.'s. (BBA. Jun.14; 150)   *Lilburn.* £70
- **An Artist's Life; The Second Burst; The Finish.** 1950-52. 3 vols. Mod. crimson mor. gt., sporting emblems on spines. (P. Feb.16; 100)   £85
- **Pictures of Horses & English Life, with an Appeciation by Lionel Lindsey.** Ptd. in Great Britain, publd. Scribners of N.Y., 1939. Cl. (DM. May 21; 30) $175

MUNRO, Harold (Ed.)
See— **MONTHLY CHAPBOOK, The**

MUNRO-FRASER, J.P.
- **Pictorial History of California.** Ed.:– Owen C. Coy. Ill.:– after C.E. Watkins & others. Berkeley, ca. 1910?. Thick lge. 4to. 261 plts., orig. gt. hf. cf., batik bds., upr. hinge splitting; sigd. on title-p. by F.D. Roosevelt Jr. (SG. Apr.5; 34) $140

MUNSTER, Sebastian
- **Aruch Ha'Shorashot [Dictionarium Hebraicum].** [Basel], 1523. *(Bound with:)* - **Melechet Ha'Dikduk [Institutiones Grammaticae in Hebream Linguam].** [Basel], 1524. Together 2 works in 1 vol. Lacks 4 ll. from 2nd. work, margin notes in early hand, slight traces of soiling, cont. blind-stpd. pig, traces of metal clasps, rubbed; hochschule für die Wissenschaft des Judenthums stps. (effaced). (SPB. Jun.26; 24) $800
- **Cosmographie oder Beschr. alle Länder.** Basle (?), 1552. 208 × 295mm. 9 woodcut maps, with 1 fragment, 87 ll. German text, 2 maps defect., vell.-bkd. bds. (CH. May 24; 236)   Fls. 1,400
[–] - **Anr. Edn.** [Basel, 1572]. Fo. Lacks 1st. 40 ll. & 134 pp., 28 pp. probably from anr. copy (some not paginated), many ll. extended or with slits & repairs, lge. woodcut reprd. with loss, browned & soiled thro.-out, linen on wood bds., renewed near end 18th. C., worn, 2 clasps. (HK. Nov.8; 1133)
DM 1,050
– – **Anr. Edn.** Basel, 1588. Fo. 3 lge. folding views slightly crumpled, cont. blind-tooled pig over wood bds., monog. & dtd. HAP 1589, lightly rubbed, corners slightly bumped. (R. Apr.5; 2611)
DM 14,000
[– –] **Anr. Edn.** Basel, 1598. Fo. Lacks 5 ll. title & preface & 18 pp., 1st. ll. with many repairs, maps with extended corners & margin defects., sm. tears bkd., browned & soiled, mostly in margins, lr. margin frayed nearly thro.-out, some lge. defects.

reprd., mostly in margin, some lge. plts. cut close, linen. (HK. Nov.8; 1134)   DM 4,800
– – **Anr. Edn.** 1628?. 280 × 395mm. 8 woodcut maps, with 1 fragment, 246 ll. Fr. text, a few stains & other minor defects., later cf. (CH. May 24; 237)   Fls. 2,600
- **Cosmographey. Fragment der Deutschen Ausgabe.** Basel, 1598. Fo. Slightly browned & stained, some sm. worming in margins, loose & without bdg., w.a.f. (R. Oct.13; 2821)   DM 1,800
[–] **Cosmographiae Universalis Lib. VI.** [Basel, 1550]. *1st. Latin Edn.?.* Fo. Lacks title & 3 ll., several ll. loose & with margin defects., folding lf. torn & crumpled, some old annots., slightly soiled, especially at beginning & end, lightly wormed, 1 lf. with reprd. margin defects., 18th. C. leath. gt., very worn. (HK. Nov.8; 1132)   DM 6,000
- **La Cosmographie Universelle.** [Basel, 1552]. *1st. Fr. Edn.* Fo. Title woodcut, 14 double-p. woodcut maps, 38 double-p. town views or plans, many lge. & sm. text woodcuts, lacks approx. 45 ll. & last 3 blank ll., many ll. with bkd. margins, some (with text loss), corners & tears, some staining or soiling, some numbering irregular or missed, 18th. C. hf. leath., bumped. [Sabin 51397] (D. Nov.23; 769)   DM 12,000
- **Proverbia Salomonis.** [Basel, 1524?]. *2nd. Edn.* Hebrew-Latin parallel Edn., preface dtd. 18 May 1524, underlining & old MS. marginalia, old owners marks on title, 2 end ll. restored in margin, 17th. C. leath. gt., rubbed. (R. Apr.3; 68)
DM 2,200
- **Rvdimenta Mathematica.** Basel, 1551. Fo. Author's name on title & dedication defaced, lightly browned, some slight staining, folding plt. slightly frayed & crumpled, cont. blind-tooled leath., slightly worn & spotted, corners & joints partly renewed. (HK. Nov.8; 290)   DM 2,700
- **Sei Libri della Cosmografia Universale.** Basel, Henrigo Pietro, 1558. *1st. Edn. in Italian.* Fo. Ptd. title with woodcut map, port. on verso, 3 folding panoramic views, 53 double-p. woodcut maps, some slight defects affecting a few text ll., wormholes affecting front pastedown & 1st. few text ll. without loss, cont. Italian (Roman?) blind-stpd. cf., slightly worn, sm. wormholes at foot of spine, minor repairs, lacks ties. (S. Dec.1; 182)   *Israel.* £4,600
– – **Anr. Copy.** Fo. Ptd. title showing woodcut map, port. of Münster on verso (sm. inscr. at foot), 53 double-p. woodcut maps, plans & views, 3 panoramic views (bnd. as separate sheets), upwards of 900 ills. in text including maps, plans, town views, ports. & natural history subjects, device at end, errors in pagination, some faint discolouration, 1 or 2 natural flaws affecting text & 1 woodcut, vell. bds., w.a.f. (S. May 21; 84)   *Quaritch.* £4,000

MUNSTER, Sebastian & Levita, Elijah Bachur
- **Sefer Ha'Dikduk; Grammatica Hebraica.** Basle, 1525. *1st. Edn.* In Hebrew & Latin, unpaginated, mod. mor. gt. (S. Oct.25; 294)   *Landau.* £680

MUNTER, J. E. A.
- **Praktisches Handuch zur Gründlichen Kenntniss der Dampfmoschine.** Quedlinburg & Leipzig, 1831. *1st. Edn.* Title-lf. stpd., 1 plt. with clean pasted margin tear, cont. hf. leath., spine partly brkn. (R. Apr.4; 1625)   DM 850

MUNTING, Abraham
- **Waare Oeffening der Planten.** Leeuwarden, 1671. *1st. Edn.* 4to. Lacks frontis. & 2 plts., some foxing & stains in text, loosening, cont. vell., soiled. (VG. Sep.14; 1261)   Fls. 625

MURATORI, Lodovico A.
- **Annali d'Italia dal Principio dell'era Volgare fino all'Anno 1750.** Roma, 1752-54. 24 vols. Vell. (CR. Jun.6; 232)   Lire 320,000
- **Dissertazioni sopra le Antichita Italiane ... Opera Postuma data in Luce dal Proposto Gian Francesco Soli Muratori.** Milano, 1751. 3 vols. 4to. Mod. hf. cf., corners. (CR. Jun.6; 57)   Lire 220,000
- **Rerum Italicarum Scriptores ab Anno Aerae Christienae D ad MD.** Mediolani, 1723. Vols. 1 (2 vols.), 2 (2 vols.), 3 (2 vols.), 4-9 (of 28). Lge. fo. Frontis. in all vols., leath. (DS. Apr.27; 2345)   Pts. 30,000

MURE, William
- **A Critical History of the Language & Literature of Antient Greece.** L., 1854-67. 5 vols. Lge. 8vo. Cf.

gt., spines gt., by Maclaren. (SG. Feb.16; 217)
$150

MURER, P.F.H.
- **Helvetia Sancta.** Ill.:– Meyer & Haulk after J. Asper & others. Lucern, 1648. Engraved additional title, title vig. & full-p. ills., L3 cleanly torn, a few letters reprd., some browning, cont. pig, soiled & rubbed, lacks ties. (CSK. May 18; 135)   £190

MURET, E.
- **Geschichte der Französische Kolonie in Branden-burg-Preussen, unter Besonderer Berücksichtigung der Berliner Gemeinde.** Berlin, 1885. Lge. 4to. Orig. hf. linen. (GB. May 3; 258)   DM 450

MURET, Marc-Antoine
- **Orationes.** *(Bound with:)* SIGONIUS, Carolus - **Orationes Septem.** Cologne, 1592. Together 2 works in 1 vol. Cont. German stpd. pig, 2 medallions (from Nuremb.?), sig. C.H., slightly worn; from Fondation Furstenberg-Beaumesnil. [Haebler I, 167] (HD. Nov.16; 144)   Frs. 1,000
See— **CARO, Annibal – MURET, Marc-Antoine**

MURGER, Henry
- **Scenes de la Bohème.** 1851. *Orig. Edn.* 12mo. Cont. hf. cf. (HD. Apr.13; 102)   Frs. 1,000

MURNER, Thomas
[–] **An den Grossmechtigsten un[d] Durchlüchtig-ste[n] Adel Tütscher Nation das sye den Christlichen Glauben beschirmen, wyder den Zerstörer des Glaube[n]s Christi, Martinu[m] Luther.** [Strassburg], 24 Dec. 1520. *1st. Edn.* 4to. Wide margin, some ll. slightly stained, 8 ll. slightly soiled in lr. outer corner, bds. (R. Apr.3; 70)   DM 4,000

MURPHY, Bailey
- **English & Scottish Wrought Ironwork.** 1904. Fo. Orig. cl., slightly soiled. (BBA. Jul.27; 262)
Lobo. £50

MURPHY, Robert Cushman
- **Oceanic Birds of South America.** N.Y., 1936. *(1200) numbered.* 2 vols. 4to. Plts., some cold., orig. cl.; pres. copy. (S. Apr.10; 436)   *Wesley.* £100
– – **Anr. Edn.** Ill.:– F.L. Jaques & others. 1936. 2 vols. 4to. Orig. buckram, fore-edge slightly discold., orig. box. (SKC. May 4; 1870)   £55

MURR, C.G. von
- **Diplomatische Geschichte des Portugiesischen Beruehmten Ritters Martin Behaims, aus Originalurkunden.** Gotha, 1801. *2nd. Edn.* Old patterned wraps., unc. [Sabin 51478] (SG. Jan.19; 102)
$120
- **Versuch einer Geschichte der Juden in Sina. Nebst P. Ignaz Koeglers Beschreibung ihrer heiligen Buecher** ... Halle, 1806. Tall 8vo. Some browning, mod. leath., cont. ink annots. on verso of front free end-paper. (SG. Feb.2; 41) $300

MURRAY, Charles Augustus
- **Travels in North America** ... L., 1839. *1st. Edn.* 2 vols. Without hf.-title in Vol. 2, cont. hf. mor. gt., gt. spines; the Rt. Hon. Visc. Eccles copy. [Sabin 51490] (CNY. Nov.18; 204) $280
– – **Anr. Copy.** 2 vols. 1 plt. slightly torn, cont. hf. cf. & cl. (SG. Jan.19; 254) $225

MURRAY, Charles Fairfax
- **Catalogue of a Collection of Early German Books in the Library of C. Fairfax Murray.** Ed.:– H.W. Davies. L., Priv. Ptd., 1913. *Orig. Edn. (100).* 2 vols. Fo. Orig. hf. linen, corners bumped, unc.; Hauswedell Coll. (H. May 23; 480)   DM 2,800
– – **Anr. Edn.** Ed.:– Hugh William Davies. L., Holland Pr., 1962. *(250).* 2 vols. Lge. 4to. Orig. cl (CSK. Feb.24; 196)   £80

MURRAY, Rev. J.
[–] **The Travels of the Imagination, A True Journey from Newcastle to London in a Stage-Coach.** L., 1773. Cf. gt. (P. Jan.12; 259)   *Jarndyce.* £280

MURRAY, J. & Marston, G.
- **Antarctic Days.** 1913. *(280) numbered & sigd. by authors & Sir. E.H. Shackleton.* Cl. gt., d.-w. (P. Jun.7; 33)   £520
– – **Anr. Copy.** Orig. cl. gt., faded. (P. Jun.7; 34)
£260

MURRIE, Eleanore Boswell
See— DAY, Cyrus Lawrence & Murrie, Eleanore Boswell

MURTHAHA IBN AL KHAFIF
- The Egyptian History, ... Trans.:– Vattier & J. Davies. L., 1672. *1st. Edn.* 7 advt.-ll. at end, lacks blank A1, cont. sheep, spine chipped at head & foot. [Wing M3127] (S. Oct.11; 566)
Maggs. £170

MUSAEUM HERMETICUM REFORMATUM et Amplificatum
Frankfurt & Leipzig, 1749. 4to. Stained thro.-out 1st. portion, a few stains on plts. at end, cont. cf., new end-papers, hinges reprd.; Dr. Walter Pagel copy. (S. Feb.7; 274)
Rota. £380

MUSARD, A.
- Le Maître à Danser, la Polka Illustreé. Ill.:– Sorrien after Anaîs Colin. [L., 1844]. Fo. Slightly browned, 1st. lf. reprd., orig. ptd. bds., paper spine, stained, worn. (CH. May 24; 149)
Fls. 800

MUSAUS, Johann Karl August
- Contes Populaires de l'Allemagne. Trans.:– A. Cerfberr de Medelsheim. Ill.:– De Richter, G. Osterwald, & De Jordan. 1846. *1st. Printing.* 2 vols. in 1. Cont. hf. chagrin, corners. (HD. Mar.21; 180)
Frs. 1,000
- Hero & Leander. Trans.:– F.L. Lucas. Ill.:– John Buckland-Wright. Gold. Cock. Pr., 1949. *(100) numbered, specially bnd. & with extra engr.* Orig. vell., s.-c.; from D. Bolton liby. (BBA. Oct.27; 144)
Marks. £150
[–] Volksmährchen der Deutschen. Ill.:– Thönert. Gotha, 1782-87. *1st. Edn.* 5 vols. Title lf. browned, some foxing, cont. hf. leath., slightly worn & bumped; Hauswedell coll. (H. May 24; 1485)
DM 1,700
[– –] Anr. Copy. 5 pts. in 3 vols. *(Bound with:)* - Straussfedern. Berlin & Stettin, 1787. *1st. Edn.* Vol. I. Together 2 works in 1 vol., foxed & lightly browned thro.-out, some brown spotting, cont. hf. leath. gt., very rubbed. (H. May 22; 806)
DM 1,150
– – Anr. Edn. Foreword:– Fr. Jacobs. Paris, 1837. Some light browning, cont. cf., blind-tooled & gt., Hauswedell coll. (H. May 24; 1723) DM 1,150
– – Anr. Edn. Ed.:– J.L. Klee. Leipzig, 1842. *1st. Edn.* Foxed, cont. hf. leath., rubbed; Hauswedell coll. (H. May 24; 1724) DM 780
– – Anr. Copy. Hf. linen. (GB. Nov.4; 1852)
DM 580
– – Anr. Copy. Some foxing, cont. hf. leath. gt., spine worn. (R. Oct.11; 394) DM 420
– – Anr. Edn. Ed.:– J.L. Klee. Ill.:– L. Richter, R. Jordan, G. Osterwald, & A. Schrödter. Leipzig, 1842. *De Luxe Edn.* Hf. leath., romantic gt., ca. 1900. (HK. Nov.10; 2616) DM 850

MUSAUS, Johann Karl August & others
[–] Straussfedern. Berlin & Stettin, 1787-98. *1st. Edn.* 8 vols. in 3. 19th. C. hf. cf. (C. Dec.9; 271)
Quaritch. £620

MUSCATO, Yehuda
- Nefutzot Yehuda. Venice, 1588-89. *1st. Edn.* 4to. Sigs. on title, inner margin of title strengthened not affecting text, browned, staining mostly in margin, slightly creased, mod. mor.; sig. of Shimson Cohen Modon. (S. Oct.25; 293) *Davidson.* £360

MUSCHLER, R.C.
- Die Heilandin. Ill.:– F. Staeger. Leipzig, 1924. *1st. Edn. (100) numbered sigd by author & artist in printers mark.* 4to. 7 sigd. orig. etchings, orig. hf. leath. (GB. May 5; 3355) DM 400

MUSCULUS, Andreas
- Precationes ex Veteribus Orthodoxis Doctoribus. Lipsiae, 1571. 12mo. Ruled, some light foxing, cont. havanna mor., fanfare decor., limp decor. spine, some restoration. (HD. Dec.9; 77) Frs. 2,800

MUSCULUS, C. Th. & Riemer
- Inhalts- u. Namen Verzeichnisse über Sämtliche Goeth'sche Werke. Stuttgart & Tübingen, 1835. *1st. Edn.* Cont. bds., rubbed. (D. Nov.24; 2463)
DM 480

MUSEE D'ART ET D'INDUSTRIE DE MOSCOU
- Histoire de l'Ornement Russe du Xe au XVIe Siècle d'après les Manuscrits. Paris & Moscow, 1870 (cover indicates 1872). Fo. 100 chromolitho. plts., loose as iss., title, text, plt. list, & captions in Fr. & Russian, some light foxing in text & titles, cl.-bkd. bd. folder, worn. (SG. Aug.25; 315) $900

MUSEE DU LOUVRE
- Les Maîtres de la Peinture. Paris, 1899-1900. 12 pts. in 2 vols. Fo. Cold. plts., ills. in text, loose, as iss., orig. wraps., slightly soiled, orig. mor. binders, gt., slightly rubbed. (S. Apr.30; 209)
Shapero. £50

MUSEE ET ECOLE MODERNE DES BEAUX ARTS PARIS
- Annales. Paris, 1801-15. 32 vols. (of 42). Linen, corners. (DS. Oct.28; 2254) Pts. 34,000

MUSEE FRANÇAIS
Ed.:– S.C. Croze-Magnan. 1803. Vol. 1 only. Fo. Engraved title & 85 plts. only, spotted, cont. hf. mor., rubbed. (CSK. Oct.21; 146) £90
- Recueil des Plux Beaux Tableaux, Statues, et Bas-Reliefs Qui Existaient au Louvre Avant 1815. ... Ed.:– Duchesne Aine. Paris, [1829]. Vol. II only. Elephant fo. Fr. & Engl. texts, some foxing, orig. mor., ornate gt. ornamental rules, raised bands, gt. panels, some wear, light scuffing. (HA. May 4; 322) $100

MUSEE POUR RIRE
Text:– Maurice Alhon, Jouis Huart & Ch. Philippon. Ill.:– Daumier, Gavarni, Grandville, Traviès & others. Paris, 1839-40. *1st. Printing of lithos.* 3 vols. Lge. 8vo. Old hf. russ., spines decor.; extra-ill. with 4 cold. lithos. (2 by Daumier & 1 by Gavarni). (HD. May 4; 367) Frs. 6,600

MUSEE ROYAL DE NAPLES
- Peintures, Bronzes et Statues Erotiques du Cabinet Secret avec leur Explication par M.C.F. Paris, 1836. 4to. Wide margins, frontis. & 60 cold. or tinted plts., foxing, mod. hf. chagrin, corners, spine decor., unc. (HD. Jun.26; 22) Frs. 2,300

MUSELLI, Vincent
- Les Travaux et les Jeux. Ill.:– André Derain. Paris, 1929. *(111) numbered & sigd. by author & artist.* 4to. Orig. wraps., folder & s.-c. (S. Nov.21; 13) *V. & A.* £230
– – Anr. Edn. Ill.:– A. Derain. Paris, 1929. *(88) numbered on vell.* Lge. 4to. Printer's mark sigd. by author & artist, 40 orig. lithos., loose ll. sewed, in orig. box. (GB. Nov.5; 2371) DM 1,200

MUSEO DE LA INDUSTRIA
Madrid, 1869-73. 4 vols. in 2. Lge. fo. Linen. (DS. Mar.23; 2679) Pts. 150,000

MUSES FAREWELL (The) to Popery & Slavery, or, a Collection of Miscellany Poems, Satyrs, Songs, & c; A Supplement to the Collection of Miscellany Poems.
L., 1689. 2 pts. in 1 vol. 1st. 'License' lf. present, lacks last lf. (? blank), some headlines shaved, hf. cf., upr. cover detchd.; sig. of John Oldmixon. (BBA. May 3; 170) *Murray Hill.* £95

MUSEUM VERONENSE hoc est Antiquarum Inscriptionum atque ...
Verona, 1749. Fo. Hf. cf., defect. (CR. Jun.6; 58)
Lire 200,000

MUSICAL MISCELLANY
1729-31. 6 vols. Slight spotting, old cf. (BS. Nov.16; 4) £240

MUSIL, Robert
- Grigia. Ill.:– A. Zangerl. Potsdam, 1923. *1st. Edn. (100) De Luke Edn. with etchings on japan.* all etchings sigd. by artist, orig. linen, lightly browned. (H. May 23; 1437a) DM 560
- Der Mann ohne Eigenschaften. 1930-33. *1st. Edn.* Vols. I & II (of III). Orig. linen, slightly browned. (GB. May 5; 2998) DM 500
– – Anr. Edn. Berlin & Lausanne, 1930-43. *1st. Edn.* 3 vols. Orig. linen, Vol. 2 with mntd. orig. wraps. (GB. Nov.5; 2834) DM 1,800
– – Anr. Edn. Ill.:– E.R. Weiss (binding). Berlin, 1931-33, & Lausanne, 1943. *1st. Edn. (Vols. 2 &*

3), *2nd. Edn. (Vol. 1).* Orig. linen rather spotted & faded, vol.2 sewed, orig. wraps. browned & partly torn. (H. Nov.24; 1888) DM 1,400

MUSSCHENBROEK, Pieter van
- Physicae Experimentales et Geometricae. Leiden, 1729. Text browned, cont. hf. vell., cover worn. (R. Apr.4; 1552) DM 442
- Tentamina Experimentorum Naturalium Captorum in Academia del Cimento. Vienna, 1756. 4to. 32 folding engraved plts. bnd. in at end, cold. browning & foxing, cont. hf. vell., soiled. (TA. Oct.20; 386) £60

MUSSET, Alfred de
- Complete Writings. N.Y., 1905. *(58) numbered on Japan paper.* 10 vols. Engraved frontis'.s cold. & uncold., rose mor., onlaid mor. gt. Art Nouveau design on covers, spines in 6 compartments, gt., mor. gt. double, watered silk free end-pp., partly unc. (CNY. Dec.17; 551) $2,400
- La Confession d'un Enfant du Siècle. Paris, 1836. *Orig. Edn.* 2 vols. On papier vergé, wide margins, jansenist red mor. by Cuzin. (HD. May 4; 368)
Frs. 5,800
- Gesammelte Werke. Ed.:– Alfr. Neumann. München & Leipzig, 1925. 5 vols. Orig. hf. leath. (HK. Nov.11; 4246) DM 400
- Histoire d'un Merle Blanc. Ill.:– H. Giacometti, engraved by L. Boisson. Paris, 1904. Mor. by Chambolle-Duru, spine decor. (slightly faded), wrap. & spine preserved, s.-c. (HD. Jun.13; 84)
Frs. 6,900
- Lorenzaccio. Ill.:– Albert Maignan. Paris, 1895. *(115) numbered.* Mor., gold-tooled, corner fleurons, decor., inner & outer dentelle, cold. endpapers, s.-c., marb. paper covered & leath., by Creuzevault. (D. Nov.24; 2313) DM 1,000
– – Anr. Copy. Mor. gt. by Chambolle-Duru, richly decor., sewed silk end-ll., wrap., s.-c. (HD. May 4; 372) Frs. 10,800
- La Mouche. Preface:– Ch. Gille. Ill.:– Ad. Lalauze. Paris, 1892. *Numbered on vell. d'Arches.* Engrs. in 2 states, including avant-lettre with remark, cont. red mor., decor., mor. doubls., gt. & mosaic decor., double guards, pict. wrap. preserved, s.-c., by Reparlier. (HD. Feb.17; 109) Frs. 3,600
- Nouvelles. Ill.:– Barney (port.), F. Flameng & O. Cartezzo. Paris, 1887. *New Edn.* On lge. vell., jansenist red mor. by Noulhac, wrap. preserved. (HD. Jun.13; 83) Frs. 3,500
- Oeuvres. Ill.:– Pille & Eug. Lami. 1884-95. *Ltd. Edn. On holland, numbered.* 10 vols. 4to. 42 added plts., hf. mor., corners, by Guétant, spine faded. (HD. Jan.24; 76) Frs. 1,050
- Oeuvres Complètes. Paris, 1865-66. *(1000).* 10 vols. Red mor., decor., lge. sm. tool dentelle, centre arms, inner dentelle. (B. Apr.27; 632) Fls. 725
- Poésies Nouvelles 1840-49. Paris, 1850. *1st. 12mo. Edn. (partly Orig. Edn.).* Hf. mor., corners, spine decor., wrap. preserved. (HD. Jun.13; 82)
Frs. 3,400
- Un Spectacle dans un Fauteuil. 1834. *Orig. Edn.* 3 vols. Hf. mor., corners, 1st. vol. by Trautz-Bauzonnet, others in his style, wraps., unc. (HD. Apr.13; 103) Frs. 9,200
- Théâtre. Intro.:– Jules Lemâitre. Ill.:– Ch. Delort engraved by Boilvin. Paris, 1889-91. 4 vols. Hf. red mor., limp decor. spines, wraps. preserved. (HD. Dec.9; 161) Frs. 1,100

MUSSET, Alfred de & Hetzel, Pierre Julius 'Pierre Julius Stahl'
- Voyage où il Vous Plaira. Ill.:– Tony Johannot. 1843. *Orig. Edn. 1st. Printing of engrs.* Red str.-grd. mor., corners, by G. Mercier, 1935, spine decor., wrap., s.-c. (HD. Apr.13; 105) Frs. 4,500
– – Anr. Copy. Lge. 8vo. Old hf. chagrin, spine decor. (HD. May 4; 450) Frs. 1,100

MUSSET, Paul de
- The Last Abbé. Ill.:– A. Lalauze. Paris, Société des Beaux Arts, ca. 1900. *Edn. des Deux Mondes. (20) lettered on Japan vell.* 4to. Plts. & text engrs. in 3 states (plain, India-proof & cold.), all (excepting 1 state of the text engrs.) with vig. remarque, cold. lev. gt., cold. mor. inlays, elab. gt.-decor. dentelles, lev. doubls., upr. doubl. with inlaid oval hand-cold. engraved vig. on vell., moire grosgrain cl. liners, partly unc. (SG. Feb.16; 289) $1,000

MUSTER ZU ZIMMERVERZIERUNG und Ameublements
Leipzig, 1794-95. 2 pts. in 1 vol. Ob. fo. 29 plts., most old cold., str.-grd. Bradel hf. mor. by Champs-Stroobants. (HD. Nov.29; 65)　Frs. 4,000

MUTH, H.L.
- Anatomia Oculi Humani ... — Perspicilla, Augen-stärckende u. Gesicht Erhaltende Augen-Gläser. Cassel, 1730. 2nd. Edn. 2 pts. in 1 vol. Sm. 8vo. Stp. on titles, cont. gt.-decor. cf., spine & corners defect., upr. jnt. partly brkn. (VG. Sep.14; 1262)　Fls. 1,000

MUYBRIDGE, Edweard
- Animals in Motion. L., 1899. 1st. Edn. Ob. 4to. Orig. cl., rebkd., slightly marked. (S. Apr.30; 210)　Frolich. £50
- The Human Figure in Motion. L., 1907. Ob. 4to. Orig. linen. (BR. Apr.12; 783)　DM 650

MY DARLINGS ABC
[America], 1850's. 16mo. 26 hand-cold. accordion-folding plts., bds. (SG. Dec.8; 10)　$150

MYDORGE, Claude
- Examen du Livre des Récréations Mathématiques ... Paris, 1639. With 2nd. pt., margin stain, 1 p. reprd. with loss of some words, old vell., reprd. (HD. Feb.28; 70)　Frs. 4,200

MYERS, Francis
See— HUTCHINSON, Frank & Myers, Francis

MYLIUS, Karl Friedrich
- Malerische Fussreise durch das Sudliche Frankreich und einen Theil von Oberitalien. Ill.:- Bauer, H.C., A. Falger, Charles de Mangste, Wolf, & others. [Karlsruhe, 1818]. 2 vols. Fo. & ob. 4to. Cont. bds. & hf. roan. (HD. Mar.21; 180b)　Frs. 2,300

MYLLER, Angelicus Maria
- Peregrinus in Jerusalem. Fremdling zu Jerusalem, Oder, Ausführliche Reiss-Beschreibungen. Prague, 1729. 4to. Browned thro.-out, few sm. worm-holes, most marginal, last lf. loose, cont. cf., worn, lacks spine, upr. cover detchd. (BBA. Aug.18; 199)　Habibis. £65

MYLLER, Chr. H.
[-] Sammlung Deutscher Gedichte aus dem XII, XIII und XIV. Jahrhundert. [Berlin], 1784-85. 1st. Edn. Vols. I-II. (Lacks incompl. vol. III as usual.). Some MS. notes, minimal foxing, mod. hand-bnd. hf. leath., Hauswedell coll. (H. May 24; 1486)　DM 950

MYNORS, Roger Aubrey Baskerville
- Durham Cathedral Manuscripts. Oxford, 1939. (250) numbered. Fo. Orig. cl., unc. (S. Oct.4; 180)　Quaritch. £280

MYNSICHT, Adrian von
- Thesaurus Medico-Chymicvs. Hamburg, 1631. 1st. Edn. 4to. Title with owners mark, 1st. ll. slightly frayed in side margin, cont. vell. (HK. Nov.8; 669)　DM 790

MYRBACH, F. von (Ed.)
See— ARS NOVA

MYSTERY OF THE GOOD OLD CAUSE BRIEFLY UNFOLDED
L., 1660. 1st. Edn. Notes on title, title-p. reprd. with slight damage to text, 19th. C. hf. mor.; John Brand bkplt., John Burns sig. [Wing M3191] (BBA. May 3; 145)　Maggs. £70

MYTHOLOGIE EN ESTAMPES, ou Figures des Divinités Fabuleuses ... Ouvrage Utile aux Jeunes Gens des Deux Sexes
Paris, [1811]. Ob. 8vo. 1 gathering loose, orig. ptd. wrap.; van Veen coll. (S. Feb.28; 87)　£50

NABBES, Thomas
- Hannibal & Scipio. An Historical Tragedy. 1637. 1st. Edn. 4to. Lacks K4 (blank), 1 outer margin restored, mor. gt. by Rivière. [STC 18341] (BBA. Jan.19; 124)　Maggs. £200

NABOKOV, Vladimir
- Lolita. Paris, [1955]. 1st. Edn. 2 vols. 12mo. Portion of revised price label on rear cover of Vol. I, ptd. wraps. (SG. May 24; 349)　$130
- - Anr. Copy. 2 vols. 12mo. Wraps., spines cocked. (SG. Jan.12; 273)　$100
- Stikhotvoreniia. Paris, 1952. 1st. Edn. 12mo. Orig. wraps. (SPB. Dec.13; 731)　$100

NACHBAUR, A. & Ngen Joûng, W.
- Les Images Populaires Chinoises. Peking, 1926. (200). Fo. Leaves, publishers decor. bds. (HD. Mar.14; 193)　Frs. 2,300
- - Anr. Edn. Peking, [1926]. (220). Fo. Publisher's bds. (HD. Jun.6; 116)　Frs. 3,000

NACHTIGAL, G.
- Sahara und Sudan. Berlin, 1879-81. 2 vols. (of 3). Orig. linen gt. (R. Oct.13; 2919)　DM 580

NAEVE, Lady Dorina
- Romance of the Bosphorus. L., n.d. Cl.; dedication copy, inscr. by author to Winston Churchill, 12 May 1949, with his & R.S. Churchill's bkplts. (LH. Jan.15; 258)　$100

NAFTALI ASHKENAZI
- Imrei Shefer. Venice, 1601. 1st. Edn. 4to. Owners' sigs. on title, worming affecting some letters, slight staining, buckram. (S. Oct.25; 295)　Sol. £240

NAGLER, Dr. Georg K.
- Die Monogrammisten und Diejenigen Bekannten und Unbekannten Kumstler aller Schulen. Munich & Leipzig, 1879-1920 & n.d. Vols. 1-5, & general index, together 6 vols. (mixed set). Unif. hf. cl. (S. Apr.30; 211)　Zwemmer. £150
- - Anr. Edn. Nieuwkoop, 1977. Facs. Edn. 5 vols. Tall 8vo. Cl. (SG. Oct.13; 253)　$120
- Neues Allgemeines Künstler-Lexikon. Leipzig, [1924]. 25 vols. Orig. linen. (GB. May 4; 1864)　DM 1,600

NAJARA, Israel
- Zemirot Israel. Venice, 1599-60. 2nd. or 3rd. Edn. 3 pts. in 1 vol. 4to. Hebrew text with instructions in Ladino, margin of 1 title & 3 ll. torn affecting text, stained thro.-out, trimmed, mor. gt., some worming. (S. Oct.25; 296)　Toporwitch. £400

NAJERA, Antonio de
- Navegacion Especulativa, y Practica, Reformadas sus Reglas, y Tablas por las Observaciones de Ticho Braha ... Lisboa, 1628. 1st. Edn. 4to. Slightly stained, few annots., later hf. mor. (VG. Sep.14; 999)　Fls. 650

NALSON, John
- An Impartial Collection of the Great Affairs of State, From the Beginning of the Scottish Rebellion In the Year MDCXXXIX To the Murder of King Charles I. 1682-83. 1st. Edn. 2 vols. Fo. Old panel. cf., spines gt.-decor., defect.; Sir Ivar Colquhoun, of Luss copy. [Wing N 106 & 107a] (CE. Mar.22; 225)　£60
- A True Copy of the Journal of the High Court of Justice for the Tryal of K. Charles I. 1685. (Bound with:) MAIMBOURG, Louis - The History of the Crusade. Trans.:-John Nalson. 1685. Together 2 works in 1 vol. Sm. fo. Cont. cf., worn. (BBA. Jun.28; 61)　Rouse. £100

NANCE, Ernest Morton
- The Pottery & Porcelain of Swansea & Nantgarw. 1942. 4to. Orig. cl. (CSK. Sep.16; 136)　£300
- - Anr. Edn. Foreword:- R.L. Hobson. L., [1942]. 1st. Edn. 4to. Gt.-lettered cl., spine end torn. (SG. Jan.26; 134)　$400

NANI, Battista
- Historia della Republica Veneta. Venice, 1663. 2nd. Impression. 4to. Cont. mott. cf., spine gt., slightly rubbed. (BBA. Jun.28; 164)　Bailey. £50
- The History of the Affairs of Europe in this Present Age. L., 1673. Fo. Cont. cf. [Wing N151] (CSK. Feb.24; 119)　£55

NANNINI, Remigio, dit
- Orationi Militari. Venice, 1557. 1st. Edn. 4to. Cont. Italian tree cf., blind- & gt.-decor., arms, spine renewed; from Fondation Furstenberg-Beaumesnil. (HD. Nov.16; 145)　Frs. 4,200

NANSEN, Fridtjof
- Fram over Polhavet den Norske Polarfaerd 1893-1896. Oslo, 1897. 1st. Edn. 2 vols. Hf.-title in Vol. 1, ptd. wrap. bnd. at beginning of Vol. 2, folding maps, plts., (some cold.), orig. decor. cl. (S. May 22; 456)　Christensen. £200

NANTEUIL, H. de
- Collection de Monnaies Greques. Paris, 1925. 2 vols. 60 plts. loose, as iss., in orig. cl.-bkd. bd. portfo., text vol. in orig. wraps., unc. (S. May 1; 483)　Drury. £70

NAPIER, Col. Charles James
- Colonization, Particularly in Southern Australia ... 1835. No final advts., old cf., worn, front hinge brkn.; inscr. by author. (KH. May 1; 522)　Aus. $160
- Memoir on The Roads of Cefalonia. 1825. 4 plts. & charts, 1 slightly torn, some spotting, orig. bds., spine torn. (P. Sep. 29; 69)　Maggs. £130

NAPIER, Jean
- Ouvertures des Secrets de l'Apocalypse, ou Révélation de S. Iean. Trans.:– G. Thomson. La Rochelle, 1603. (Bound with:) THOMSON, G. - Quatre Harmonies sur la Révélation de S. Iean: touchant la Royauté, Prestrise, & Prophetie de Iesus Christ. 1603. Together 2 works in 1 vol. Some parts underlined, red mor., decor. spine, gt. decor., inner dentelle, by Hardy, slight wear. (B. Apr.27; 584)　Fls. 900

NAPIER, Sir William Francis Patrick
- History of the War in the Peninsula ... 1828. 6 vols. Panel. hf. cf. gt. (PD. Apr.18; 175)　£60
- - Anr. Edn. 1835-40. 3rd. Edn. 6 vols. Cf., spines gt.-decor. (SKC. Sep.9; 1928)　£85

NAPOLEON I, Emperor
- Correspondance Publiée par Ordre de l'Empereur Napoléon III. Paris, 1858-69. 32 vols. 4to. Some slight spotting, cont. hf. mor. (S. Apr.10; 392)　Edwards. £280
- Postes Imperiales. Etat General Postes et Relais de l'Empire Français. Paris, 1810. A little stained, cont. red mor., gt., Imperial arms in gt. on covers; front free end-paper inscr. 'Napoleon's own post book, ... '. (BBA. Nov.30; 79)　Shackleton. £120
[-] Tableaux Historiques des Campagnes d'Italie depuis l'an IV jusqu'à la Bataille de Marengo. Ill.:– Duplessi-Bertaux after Carle Vernet. Paris, 1806. Lge. fo. Cont. bradel bds., rubbed. (HD. Dec.9; 162)　Frs. 5,600

NAPOLEON III, Emperor
- Oeuvres. Paris, 1854-56. 4 vols. Lge. 8vo. Some foxing & wrinkling, red cf., spines gt., by Leighton, defect. (SG. Feb.16; 221)　$200

NAPOLEON'S DEFEAT
[-] A Narrative of the Grand Festival at Yarmouth. Yarmouth, 1814. Some ll. slightly spotted, entrance ticket pasted in, orig. cl. (BBA. Oct.27; 48)　Vine. £50

NARBOROUGH, John & others
- An Account of Several Late Voyages & Discoveries from the South & North, towards the Streights of Magellan, the South Seas, the Vast Tracts of Land beyond Hollandia Nova, &c. L., 1694. 1st. Edn. 2 pts. in 1 vol. Lacks 'Mapp of the Streights of Magellan', cropped, tear in folding table margin, plts. rather foxed, title washed & with very sm. wormhole reprd., mod. qtr. leath. & marb. bds. [Sabin 72185] (SG. Sep.22; 226)　$250

NARRATIVE OF THE PROCEEDINGS of his Majesty's Fleet in the Mediterranean ...
1744. Sm. 4to. Cont. red mor. gt.; pres. copy to the Marquis of Tweesdale. (P. Jun.7; 321)　£220

NARRATIVE OF THE SHIPWRECK OF THE ANTELOPE ... in the Pelew Islands
Perth, 1788. 12mo. Cont. cf. (BBA. Dec.15; 12)　Quaritch. £75

NARSHAKHI, Mukhammad
- Istoriya Bukhary [The History of Bukhara]. Tashkent, 1897. Last errata lf., few ll. slightly soiled, mod. cl. (BBA. Mar.7; 73)　D. Loman. £65

NASH, John & others
- Some Account of the Proposed Improvements of the Western Part of London ... 1814. Folding plans mostly hand-cold., orig. bds., unc., worn, soiled. (TA. Dec.15; 83) £130

NASH, Joseph
- The Mansions of England in the Olden Time. L., 1839-42. 4 vols. (Series 1-4). Atlas fo. Pict. title-pp., 100 litho. plts., tissue-guards frayed, ex-liby.; some foxing thro.-out, orig. mor.-bkd. moire cl. (SG. May 3; 261) $150
- - Anr. Edn. L., 1839-49. 4 vols. in 2. Lge. fo. Litho. titles, 90 (of 104) full-p. lithos., three-qtr. mor. & cl., marb. end-papers, covers slightly rubbed, minor foxing & light soiling, bkplts. (CBA. Jan.29; 322) $250
- - Anr. Edn. L., 1869-71. 3 vols. only. Fo. Tinted litho. extra titles & plts., all on India paper, mntd., some spotting, several detchd., cont. mor.-bkd. cl., w.a.f. (CSK. Feb.24; 25) £120
- - Anr. Edn. 1869-72. 4 vols. in 2. 4to. Col. litho. title to each pt., 100 col. litho. plts., orig. crimson mor. gt., rubbed, spines chipped at base. (TA. Dec.15; 104) £155
- - Anr. Edn. N.d. 1st.-4th. Series: 4 vols. Fo. 4 litho. titles, 100 litho. plts., some loose, some spotting, qtr. mor. gt., brkn. (P. Mar.15; 196) *Erlini.* £150

NASH, Paul
- Places. L., 1922. *(210).* 4to. Orig. pict. bds., slightly worn. (P. Nov.24; 41) *Sadler.* £90

NASH, Dr. Treadway Russel
- Collections for the History of Worcestershire. 1781-82. *1st. Edn.* 2 vols. Fo. Engraved vig. titles, 76 engraved plts., 13 engraved facs. of Domesday, 2 dedications, 25 genealogical tables, cont. tree cf., spines gt.; Sir Ivar Colquhoun, of Luss copy. (CE. Mar.22; 226) £450
- - Anr. Edn. 1799. *2nd. Edn.* 2 vols. Fo. Mod. cl. (P. Sep.8; 357) *Nichols.* £130

NASMYTH, James & Carpenter, James
- The Moon: Considered as a Planet, a World, & a Satellite. N.Y., 1885. 4to. Silver-stpd. cl. (SG. Nov.10; 113) $200

NASS, J.
- Examen Chartaceae Lutheranorum Concordiae. Ingolstadt, 1581. 4to. Some old MS. marginalia, cont. limp vell., slightly defect., Ingolstadt Jesuit liby. stp. 1626. (R. Apr.3; 72) DM 450
- Quinta Centuria ... der Evangelischen Wahrheit ... Martin Luther. Ingolstadt, 1570. *1st. Edn.* Title with large tear & slight loss, title & some text ll. with old MS. notes, 6 ll. very soiled, many pencil underlinings cont. pig over wood bds., blind-tooled, metal clasps, lacks lr. clasp, slightly defect. (HT. May 8; 188) DM 420

NATALIBUS, Petrus de
- Catalogus Sanctorum et Gestorum eorum. Lyon, 1508. Fo. Some old marginalia, wormed at beginning & end, browned, lightly soiled, cont. blind-tooled pig over wood bds., spine defect. at top, wormed, 2 clasps. (HK. Nov.8; 311) DM 650
- - Anr. Copy. Sm. fo. Cont. pig over wood bds., blind-stpd. compartments, decor. clasps brkn. (HD. Dec.2; 127) Frs. 3,800
- - Anr. Edn. Ed.:– [A. Verlus]. Ill.:– Urs Graf. Strassburg, 1513. Fo. Title slightly spotted, old name, sm. worm-hole nearly thro.-out, some sm. wormholes increasing near end, 1 lf. with sm. tear in upr. corner, cont. wood bds., blind-tooled pig spine, lightly wormed, lacks clasps, upr. cover old brkn & glued, old munich royal liby. stp. (R. Apr.3; 73) DM 1,300
- - Anr. Edn. [Lyon, Jacques Saccon, 9 Dec. 1514]. Fo. Title remargined, lacks 1 lf., old vell. (HD. Jan.30; 18) Frs. 2,700

NATALIS, Hieronymus
- Adnotationes et Meditationes in Evangelia quae in Sacrosancto Missae Sacrificio Toto Anno Leguntur ... Antw., 1594 [colophon 1595]. Fo. Plts. washed, crushed decor. red mor. gt. by Allô. (HD. Nov.9; 11) Frs. 10,500
- Evangelicae Historiae Imagines. Antw., 1593. *1st.*

Edn. Fo. Slightly soiled & browned, cont. reddish-brown mor. gt., slightly rubbed & bumped. (HK. Nov.9; 1919) DM 2,600

NATALIS, Michel
- Abrégé de la Vie et Passion de Notre Seigneur Jésus Christ ... Seconde Partie Contenant La Passion. Paris, [1663]. *1st. Printing.* Fo. Lr. margin of title restored, mod. vell. (LM. Oct.22; 256) B. Frs. 20,000

NATHAN, George Jean
See— MENCKEN, Henry Louis & Nathan, George Jean

NATHAN BEN YECHIEL, of Rome
- He'Aruch. Pesaro, 1517. *2nd. Edn.* Fo. Mispaginated & misbnd., title in facs., some ll. defect. & reprd. with loss of text, browned, some worming affecting some letters, staining, mod. mor. [Steinschneider 6632, 2] (S. Oct.25; 298) *Landau.* £800
- - Anr. Edn. [Pessaro, 1517]. Fo. Owners sigs. on title & 1st. lf., title mntd., a few minor margin repairs, slight soiling & foxing, some ll. misnumbered by printer, old blind-stpd. cf., crudely reprd., rubbed. [Steinschneider 6632, 2] (SPB. Jun.26; 25) $3,250
- - Anr. Edn. Basel, 1599. Sm. fo. Some margin dampstaining, early blind-tooled pig, stained, badly chafed, lacks clasp. (SG. Feb.2; 267) $425

NATIONAL ANTARCTIC EXPEDITION 1901-4
1908. 2 vols., including 'Album of Photographs & Sketches' & 'Portfolio of Panoramic Views'. 4to. 2 maps, 24 panoramas, 165 plts., orig. buckram-bkd. cl., ties defect. (P. Jun.7; 35) £680

NATIONAL GALLERY
- French School; Early Netherlandish School; Spanish School; Earlier Italian Schools; Dutch School. V.d. Together 7 vols. Fo. No bdgs. stated. (SPB. Nov.30; 318) $150
- National Gallery of Pictures by the Great Masters. L., 1850. 2 vols. 4to. 114 steel engrs., gt.-tooled cf. (CR. Jun.6; 300) Lire 320,000

NATIONAL GAZETTEER: A Topographical Dictionary of the British Isles
1868. 3 vols. Sm. fo. Cont. hf. mor., scuffed. (TA. Sep.15; 137) £80

NATIONAL MARITIME MUSEUM
- Catalogue of the Library. L., 1968-76. Vols. 1-5 in 7. 4to. Orig. cl., d.-w.'s. (S. May 1; 420) *Weinreb.* £90

NATIONAL PALACE MUSEUM
- The Illustrated Catalogue of Sung Dynasty Porcelain in the National Palace Museum. Taiwan, 1973-74. *(300).* 4 vols. in 8, including plt. vol. Fo. Orig. wraps. & cl., boxed. (CSK. Jun.29; 3) £1,100

NATTES, John Claude
- Scotia Depicta. Ill.:– J. Fittler after Nattes. L., 1819. Fo. Etched frontis., 48 views, some faint spotting, cont. roan-bkd. bds., unc., upr. cover detchd. (S. Mar.6; 372) *Walford.* £160

NATTIER, S.
- La Gallerie du Palais Luxembourg peinte par Rubens. Parigi, 1710. Fo. Hf.-title, 21 plts., some double-p., lacks 2 ports., lightly browned, w.a.f. (CR. Jun.6; 59) Lire 750,000

NATURA BREVIUM [French]
- La Vieux Natura Brevium. 1580. Cont. notes & underlinings, flaw in 1 lf. affecting a few words, margin wormhole & defects not affecting text, slightly stained at beginning & end, cont. cf., rebkd. [STC 18401] (BBA. Jun.14; 22) *Boswell.* £220

NATURAL HISTORY
Ill.:– after Moses Harris, George Edwards, etc. L., Harrison, ca. 1800. 3 vols. Sm. 8vo. Over 200 hand-cold. engraved plts., some dtd. 1798-99, cont. hf. cf., gt. spines. (SKC. Oct.26; 415) £55

NATURAL HISTORY OF BIRDS
Bungay, 1815. Vol. 1 only (of 2). 50 hand-cold. plts., hf. cf. (P. Sep.29; 41) £65
- - Anr. Copy. 2 vols. Hand-cold. engrs., hf. cf. (CR. Jun.6; 301) Lire 350,000

NATURE, Revue des Sciences et de leur Application aux Arts et à l'Industrie
Paris, 1873-1905. 33 vols. Cont. hf. red chagrin, decor. spines. (HD. Jan.27; 252) Frs. 3,400

NAUDE, Gabriel
- Considérations Politiques sur les Coups d'Estat. 1667. 12mo. Glazed Lavallière cf. by Petit, gt. decor., decor. spine, inner dentelle, ex-libris. (HD. Dec.9; 65) Frs. 1,100
- - Anr. Edn. N.p., 1712. 16mo. Cf., corners worn. (HD. Feb.22; 155) Frs. 1,100
- Ivgement de tovt ce qui a esté imprimé contre le Cardinal Mazarin depuis le Sixieme Ianuier, iusques à la Declaration du Premier Avril Mil Six Cens Quarante-neuf. [Paris, 1650]. Lge. 4to. L.P., ruled, cont. mor. gt., crowned cyphers of Louis XIII & Anne d'Autriche, spine decor.; from libys. of Comet de Lignerolles & Bordes. (HD. Mar.29; 76) Frs. 240,000

NAUDE, Ph.
- Gründe der Messkunst. Berlin, 1706. *1st. Edn.* 4to. Title stpd., some light browning, cont. hf. leath. gt., lightly rubbed. (HK. Nov.8; 671) DM 550

NAUMANN, E.
- Illustrierte Musikgeschichte. Berlin & Stuttgart, [1885]. *1st. Edn.* 2 vols. Some plts. cold., orig. linen, slightly worn. (H. Nov.23; 479) DM 440

NAUMANN, Johann Andreas
- Naturgeschichte der Vögel Deutschlands. Leipzig, 1822-60. 13 vols. Cont. hf. leath. gt., vol. 13 not quite unif. (R. Apr.4; 1762) DM 2,100
- Naturgeschichte der Vögel Mitteleuropas. Ed.:– C.R. Hennicke. Gera, 1897-1905. Vols. 1-5, 7, 10 & 12 only (of 12). Fo. 3 vols. orig. bds., 4 vols. orig. linen, 1 vol. orig. hf. leath., worn, w.a.f. (HK. Nov.8; 770) DM 1,900
- - Anr. Edn. Ed.:– C.R. Hennicke. Gera, ca. 1900. Vols. 2, 6 & 8 in 3 vols. Fo. 2 title ll. stpd., orig. hf. linen & 2 orig. hf. leath. (R. Oct.12; 1881) DM 900
- - Anr. Edn. Ed.:– C.R. Hennicke. Gera-Untermhaus, [1903]. Vol. 12. Fo. Orig. linen, bumped. (R. Apr.4; 1763) DM 500

NAUSEA, Fredericus, Bp. of Vienna
- Christlich Einrede in die Vermeinte New Reformation vn Kirches Ordnůg ... Mainz, 17.VIII.1532. *1st. Edn.* Some browning & staining, most margins slightly frayed, sewed; MS. ex-libris Otto Hupp. (HK. May 15; 205) DM 850
- De Praecipvo hvivs Anni post Christvm Natvm. Mainz, 1531. *1st. Edn.* 4to. Title stpd., slightly foxed, sewed. (HK. Nov.8; 293) DM 650
See— BERTHORIUS, Petrus — NAUSEA, Fredericus — GREGORIUS NYSSANUS

NAUTICAL MAGAZINE & Naval Chronicle, The
L., 1834-56. Vols. III-XXVI. Orig. hf. cf. (VG. Sep.13; 168) Fls. 1,000

NAVAL CHRONICLE
L., 1799-1816. Vols. 1-35 only (of 40). Almost 500 plts., cont. Engl. russ. gt., spines decor. (HD. Mar.9; 115) Frs. 12,500
- - Anr. Run. L., 1799-1818. Vols. 1-33, 36, 37 & 40. Last 3 vols. cont. hf. cf., marb. bds., worn, rest. unif. cont. diced cf., rebkd., spines gt.-decor. (SKC. Mar.9; 1911) £720

NAVILLE, Edouard
- The Temple of Deir el Bahari. Ill.:– after Howard Carter. L., [1896-]1908. 6 vols. Fo. 174 plts., some folding or double-p., orig. cl.-bkd. ptd. bds., worn & soiled; Alexander Cochrane bkplts. (SG. Nov.3; 153) $475

NAVORSCHER (De). Een Middel tot Gedachtenwisseling en Letterkundig Verkeer ...
Amst., 1851-1928. Years 1-77. & Index. Lge. 8vo. 15 vols. hf. cf., 32 vols. bds., 31 vols. bnd., some vols. slightly shabby, some spines defect. or reprd. (VS. Dec.7; 195) Fls. 825

NAVY & ARMY ILLUSTRATED, The
20 Dec. 1895-16 Sep. 1899. 8 vols. Fo. Unif. pict. cl. gt., sm. tear to spine of Vol. 6. (LC. Jul.5; 76) £125

NAVY RECORDS SOCIETY
- **Publications.** L., 1894-1982. 122 vols. (lacks plt. vol. 34). Plts., folding plans, little spotting, orig. buckram, few vols. slightly soiled, some unc. & unopened. (S. Apr.10; 375) *Georges.* £820
- – **Anr. Run.** 1895-1982. Vols. 1-123 (compl. set including vol. 34 'The Battle of Sole Bay'). 8vo. & fo. Orig. cl., a few earlier vols. slightly soiled. (BBA. Jun.28; 62) *Georges.* £700

NAXAGORAS, Ehrd von
- **Johann Equitis Aureum Vellus oder Gueldenes Vliss ... indem ... wahre ... Grund ... der Hermetischen Philosophiae Enthalten.** Giessen, 1715. *1st. Edn.* 56 prelims. only (all publd.?), title soiled & imprint cut into, bds., vell. spine torn; Dr. Walter Pagel copy, w.a.f. (S. Feb.7; 275) *Van Aalst.* £180

NAYLER, Sir George
- **The Coronation of his most Sacred Majesty King George the Fourth.** L., 1837. Lge. fo. Engraved hand-cold. aquatint vig. title dtd. 1824, 41 hand-cold. aquatint plts., 3 engraved plts., cont. mor. gt. by MacKenzie, jnts. reprd. (C. Mar.14; 71) *Harley-Mason.* £900

NAYLIES, M. de
- **Mémoires sur la Guerre pendant les Années 1808, 1809, 1810 et 1811.** Paris, 1817. Cont. hf. cf., corners. (HD. Jan.27; 75) Frs. 1,450

NEAL, Daniel
- **The History of New England.** L., 1720. *1st. Edn.* 2 vols. in 1. Some browning, mod. mor. [Sabin 52140] (SG. Jan.19; 261) $200
- – **Anr. Copy.** 2 vols. Some ll. browned, cont. cf. gt., corners & edges worn; the Rt. Hon. Visc. Eccles copy. (CNY. Nov.18; 206) $110

NEALE, Adam
- **Travels through some parts of Germany, Poland, Moldavia & Turkey.** L., 1818. 4to. 14 hand-cold. views on 10 sheets, title-p. torn & crudely reprd., some offset on text, hf. mor. (P. Dec.8; 94) *Edwards.* £110

NEALE, H. St. John
- **Chirurgical Institutes, drawn from Practice, on the Knowledge & Treatment of Gun-Shot Wounds** ... L., 1804. *1st. Edn.* Slight browning, cont. red str.-grd. mor. gt., slight rubbing, spine fading. (SPB. May 23; 46) $325

NEALE, John Preston
- **Views of the Seats of Noblemen & Gentlemen.** L., 1818-23. 1st. Series: 6 vols. Engraved title, 426 engraved plts., few slightly offset, some slight spotting, cont. hf. roan, unc. (S. Apr.9; 181) *Nolan.* £220
- – **Anr. Edn.** L., 1822-23-20-21. 4 vols. only. Engraved additional titles, 282 plts. only, some spotting, cont. hf. cf., spines slightly soiled, w.a.f. (CSK. Feb.10; 187) £150
- – **Anr. Edn.** L., 1822-29. 1st. Series: 6 vols., 2nd. Series: 5 vols. Extra engraved titles, 722 engraved plts., some light spotting or offsetting, cont. red str.-grd. mor. (S. Mar.6; 302) *Traylen.* £550

NEANDER, M. von Sorau
- **Chronicon.** Leipzig, 1586. (*Bound with:*) – **Historia Ecclesiae sive Populi Dei.** N.p., n.d. (*Bound with:*) – **Historia et Narratio Plane Stupenda, Prodigiosa, neque Ullo Aevo audita de Pseudo Martino Gallo.** Leipzig, 1586. (*Bound with:*) – **Orbis Terrae.** Leipzig, 1586. Together 4 works in 1 vol. Browned, cont. MS. vell., blind-tooled pig spine, slightly rubbed & bumped. (R. Apr.3; 74) DM 650

NEBEL, R.
- **Rakatenflug.** Berlin, 1932. *1st. Edn.* Last lf. bkd. in margin, orig. pict. wraps. (GB. May 3; 1178) DM 450

NEBRIJA, E. Antonio de
- **Rerum a Fernando et Elisabet Hispaniarum ... Regibus Gestarum Decades Duae, necnon Belli Navariensis Libri Duo** ... Granada, 1500. Lacks 1 lf., vell. (DS. Apr.27; 2191) Pts. 75,000

NEBRISSENSIS or LEBRIXA, Aelius Antonius or Antonio de
- **Rerum a Fernando & Elisabe Hispaniarum felicissimis Regibus Gestarum. [with 2 other works].**

Grenada, 1545. Fo. Lacks 3 ll. at end (index?), some worming & dampstains, mott. cf., rebkd. (SPB. Dec.13; 620) $100
- **Vafre dicta Philosophorum cum Glossematis.** [Salamanca, printer of Nebrissensis' Gramatica], ca. 1498. 4to. Lev. mor. by Rivière. [Goff A-911 (Hispanic Soc. copy only)] (SPB. Dec.14; 3) $4,250

NECESSARY DOCTRINE & Erudition for Any Chrystenman, Set Furth by the Kynges Maiestye of Englande ...
1543. Sm. 8vo. Title in woodcut border, relaid, some margin dampstains, later cf. (TA. Jun.21; 526) £180

NECKER, Jacques
- **De l'Administration des Finances de la France.** N.p., 1784. *[Orig. Edn.].* 3 vols. Cont. spr. roan gt., spines decor. (HD. Nov.9; 143) Frs. 3,500
- – **Anr. Copy.** 3 vols. Cont. marb. sheep gt., decor. spines, scratches on 1 cover. (HD. Sep.22; 303) Frs. 1,800
- – **Anr. Copy.** 3 vols. Vol. 1 title with owners mark, minimal worming, cont. hf. leath., decor., slightly bumped. (HK. May 15; 799a) DM 520
- **Du Pouvoir Executif dans Les Grand Etats.** [Paris], 1792. 2 vols. in 1. Browned, liby. stp. on 1st. title, cont. mott. cf., spine gt., rubbed. (BBA. Jul.27; 84) *Frognal.* £100
- – **Anr. Copy.** 2 vols. Old roan, spines decor. (HD. Nov.9; 145b) Frs. 1,550

NECKER DE SAUSSURE, Louis Albert
- **Voyage en Ecosse et aux Iles Hebrides.** Geneva, 1821. 3 vols. Cont. cf.-bkd. bds. (C. Mar.14; 72) *Blackwell.* £130

NEDDERMEYER, F.H.
- **Topographie der Freien und Hanse Stadt Hamburg.** Hamburg, 1832. Some foxing, 1 plan slightly browned, owner note on prelim. lf., cont. hf. leath., orig. litho. wraps. bnd. in, slightly worn & bumped. (H. Nov.23; 384) DM 400

NEDERLAND'S PATRICIAAT
's-Gravenhage, 1910-81. Years 1-65. Sm. 4to. 63 vols. orig. cl. gt., 2 vols. orig. bds., slightly defect. (VS. Dec.8; 740) Fls. 4,400
- – **Anr. Edn.** 's-Gravenhage, 1910-82. Years 1-66: 66 vols. Sm. 4to. Orig. cl. gt. (VG. Sep.13; 47) Fls. 3,700

NEDERLANDSCH BLOEMWERK. Door een Gezelschap geleerden
Amst., 1794. 4to. Engraved title with hand-cold. engraved vig., 53 hand-cold. engraved plts., upr. outer corners of 1st. 8 ll. damp spotted affecting 2 plts., plt. 41 cut down & inserted, cont. mott. cf., spine gt., unc., corners worn. (CNY. May 18; 147) $1,400

NEDERLANDSCHE LEEUW (De), Maanblad v.h. Genealogisch-heraldiek Genootschap
's-Gravenhage, 1883-1981. Years 1-98, 27 vols., rest in pts. 4to. 24 vols. hf. cl., 3 vols. hf. cf., rest wraps., vol. 1 slightly loose; partly from A.R.F. van Kinschot liby. (VS. Dec.8; 738) Fls. 1,600

NEDERLANDSCHE SPECTATOR (De)
Leyden, 1749-60. 12 pts. in 6 vols. Hf. cf., slight defects, unc. (B. Oct.4; 7) Fls. 500

NEDERLANDSCHE TAFEREELEN van Kunsten, Ambachten en Bedrijven, voor Kinderen
Zaltbommel, 1828-29. 2nd. & 3rd. pts. in 2 vols. Sm. 8vo. A few stains & repairs, later bds. (VG. Mar.21; 481) Fls. 1,800

NEEFE, C.G.
- **Dilettanterien.** [Bonn?], 1785. 4 ll. subscribers list, minimal browning, cont. interims wraps, unc. (R. Apr.3; 376) DM 650

NEEL, L.-B.
[–] **Histoire de Maurice, Comte de Saxe, Maréchal Général des Camps et Armées de Sa Majesté** ... 1752. 3 vols. 12mo. Cont. marb. cf. gt., spines decor., 1 turn-in torn; stp. & ex-libris of Le Tellier, Marquis de Courtanvaux. (HD. Nov.9; 148) Frs. 1,300

NEES V. ESENBECK, Christian Gottfried
- **Handbuch der Botanik.** Nürnberg, 1820-21. *1st. Edn.* 2 vols. Cont. marb. bds. (BR. Apr.12; 763) DM 450

NEESE, George M.
- **Three Years in the Confederate Horse Artillery.** N.Y. & Wash., 1911. *1st. Edn.* Sm. 8vo. Buckram, spine faded. (HA. Sep.16; 393) $140

NEFF, C.
- **Ein Köstliche Schatzkamer der Schreibkunst und Cleinott der Cantzley vnnd der Schreiber. Ein seer Zierlich Kunstreich Buchlein** ... Cölln, 1571. Title lf. with owners mark. (*Bound with:*) – **Thesavrarivm Artis Scriptoriae et Cancellariae Scribarumq[ue] Clenodium Pretiosum Libellus** ... Cölln, 1571. Together 2 works in 1 vol. Fo. Wide margin, slightly browned, spotted, sm. wormholes in margin, slight staining, cont. blind-tooled leath. over wood bds., corners slightly bumped, spine with 2 defects., 1r. cover with sm. defect. & worming; ex.-libris. Hauswedell coll. (H. May 23; 216) DM 28,000

NEGARIS DE ARATI, R.J. [Pseud.]
- **Calvinische Rotte.** Harbone, 1598. Sm. 4to. Slightly foxed & browned, approx. 60 blank ll. bnd. in MS. vell. (GB. Nov.3; 951) DM 700

NEHEMYA HIYYA HAYON
- **Divrei Nehemya.** Berlin, 1713. *1st. Edn.* Sm. 4to. Soiled & browned, running head of approbation lf. cropped, old bds., defect. (SG. Feb.2; 268) $800

NELSON, E.
- **Gestaltwandel und Artbildung erörtert am Beispiel des Orchidaceen Europas und der Mittelmeer insbesondere der Gattung Ophrys.** Chernex-Montreux, 1962. 1 text & 1 plt. vol. 8vo & Fo. Orig. linen & orig. linen box. (D. Nov.23; 451) DM 650

NELSON, Edward W.
- **Report upon Natural History Collections made in Alaska between the years 1877 & 1881.** Ill.:– R. & J.L. Ridgway, & others. Wash., 1887. 4to. Hf. leath., cl. bds. (LH. Jan.15; 366) $130

NELSON, Henry Loomis
- **The Army of the United States.** Ill.:– after H.A. Ogden. N.Y., [1888; 1907]. 3 vols. text & 2 vols. plts. Lge. fo. 48 (of 67) chromolitho. plts., qtr. cl. & gt. pict. bds., plt. vols. unbnd., vol. 3 lacks cl. ties, rather worn, 2 vols. in publishers box. (SG. Apr.5; 193) $250
- – **Anr. Edn.** Ill.:– Henry Ogden. N.Y., [1959]. *(60) numbered, specially bnd.* Tall fo. 44 cold. plts., oasis leath., spine gt., boxed. (SG. Feb.16; 9) $130

NELSON, Visc. Horatio
- **The Dispatches & Letters.** Ed.:– Sir Nicholas Harris. 1844-46. Some ll. spotted, mod. hf. cf. (BBA. Feb.9; 89) *Denison.* £200
- – **Anr. Edn.** 1845-46. 7 vols. Orig. cl., spines faded. (CSK. Jun.1; 67) £170

NELSON, John
- **The History & Antiquities of the Parish of Islington.** 1823. *2nd. Edn.* 4to. L.P., engraved folding map & 22 plts., cont. hf. mor., slightly rubbed; extra-ill. with approx. 31 engraved or litho. plts., cont. hf. mor., slightly rubbed. (BBA. Jul.27; 331) *Love.* £80

NEMEITZ, J. Chr.
- **Nachlese Besonderer Nachrichten von Italien ... zum Nutzen derjenigen ... so in Italien zu reisen gedencken.** Leipzig, 1726. 2 pts. in 1 vol. Vol. 2 title bnd. in pt. 1 prelims., cont. hf. leath., spine rubbed, jnts. brittle. (BR. Apr.12; 120) DM 600

NEPHEW KING, William
- **The Story of the Spanish-American War & the Revolt in the Philippines.** N.Y., 1899. Lge. ob. fo. Publishers cl. (DS. Jan.27; 2302) Pts. 19,000

NERCIAT, Andréa de
- **Monrose ou Suite de Felicia.** Ill.:– Queverdo(?). 1797. 4 vols. 16mo. Cont. mosaic mor., painted. (HD. Jan.24; 40) Frs. 8,500

NERESSIAN, Sirarpie Der
- **Manuscrits Armeniens Illustrés des XIIe, XIIIe et XIVe Siècles de la Bibliogthèque des Perses**

Mekhitharistes de Venise. Paris, 1937. 2 vols. Fo. Orig. wraps. & portfo. (*With:*) – **Armenian Manuscripts in the Freer Gallery of Art.** Wash., 1963. 1 vol. Fo. Orig. cl. (*With:*) – **Armenian Manuscripts in the Walters Art Gallery.** Baltimore, 1973. 1 vol. Fo. Orig. cl. (BBA. Sep.8; 19) *Saidi.* £110

NERUDA, Pablo
– **Die Höhen von Macchu Picchu.** Trans.:– R. Hagelstange. Ill.:– Hap Grieshaber. Hamburg, 1965. *Ltd. numbered Iss.* Fo. 10 orig. cold. woodcuts, including 3 double-p., orig. linen. (GB. Nov.5, 2545) DM 600
– – **Anr. Edn.** Trans.:– R. Hagelstange. Ill.:– Grieshaber. Hamburg, [1965]. With text pt.: Alturas de Macchu Picchu with orig. Spanish text. Fo. Orig. pict. linen. (D. Nov.24; 3043) DM 650
– **Ode to Typography.** [Torrance, Ca.], 1977. *(100) numbered.* Narrow fo. Ptd. wraps., cl. folding case. (SG. Mar.1; 368) $175
– **Toros.** Ill.:– Pablo Picasso. Paris, 1960. *(500).* Fo. With suppressed plt., 15 other plts., numbered in pencil, loose in orig. folder as iss. (SPB. Dec.13; 884) $175
– **We are Many.** Trans.:– Alastair Reid. Ill.:– Hans Ehrmann. [L., 1967]. *(100) numbered & sigd. by author & trans.* Sm. 4to. Bds., d.-w., die-cut wraps. by Jim Dine bnd. in, as iss. (SG. Mar.1; 369) $110

NERVAL, Gérard Labrunie, dit de
– **Contes et Facéties.** Paris, 1852. 18mo. Cont. chagrin, Far Eastern decor. hf. mor. wrap. & box by Alix; George Sand copy, inscr. by Aurore Sand. (HD. Nov.29; 106) Frs. 5,800
– **La Main Enchantée.** Preface:– Jules Marthold. Ill.:– Marcel Pille. Paris, 1901. On japan, hf. mor., corners, by Affolter, spine decor., unc., wrap. & spine preserved. (HD. May 4; 375) Frs. 1,150
– **Sylvie.** Ill.:– Pierre Laprade. Paris, 1938. *(10) on Japon nacré with suite in black.* 4to. Mor., s.-c. (HD. Nov.17; 164) Frs. 1,550
– – **Anr. Edn.** Ill.:– Michel Ciry. Paris, 1945. On vell., frontis., title vig., 44 orig. dry-points, leaves, wrap., box. (HD. Mar.27; 97) Frs. 1,450

NERVAL, Gérard de & Fleury, Arthus
– **Le Nouveau Genre ou Le Café d'un Théâtre.** 1860. *Orig. Edn.* 12mo. On thick vell., sewed; autograph dedication by Fleury. (HD. Apr.13; 106) Frs. 1,050

NESBITT, Robert
– **Ostergenie oder Abhandlung von Erzeugung der Knochen in Menschlichen Körper.** Ed.:– Chr. G. Ludwig. Trans.:– J.E. Greding. Ill.:– J.C.G. Fritzsch. Altenburg, 1753. 5 ll. spotted in margin, cont. leath. (D. Nov.23; 598) DM 410

NESSEL, Daniel de
– **Catalogus, sive Recensio Specialis omnium Codicum Manuscriptorum Graecorum.** Vienna & Nuremb., 1690. 7 pts. in 1 vol. Fo. Some ll. browned & slightly dampstained, cont. blind-stpd. vell., recased, slightly soiled. (BBA. Feb.23; 27) *Fletcher.* £200

NESSEL, Daniel de
See— LAMBECK, P. & Nessel, Daniel de

NESSEL, F.
– **Compendium der Zahnheilkunde.** Wien, 1856. *1st. Edn.* Some slight foxing, cont. hf. linen. (GB. May 3; 1024) DM 450

NESTROY, Johan
– **Freiheit in Krähwinkel.** Wien, 1849. *1st. Edn.* Light crumpling, orig. wraps., unc., spine slightly torn. (HK. Nov.10; 2618) DM 800
– **Sämtliche Werke.** Ed.:– F. Brukner & O. Rommel. Wien, 1924-30. 15 vols. End-paper stpd., orig. linen, some spotting & bumping. (HT. May 9; 1973) DM 600
– – **Anr. Edn.** Ed.:– V.F. Brukner & O. Rommel. Wien, [1924-30]. 15 vols. Red hf. leath., upr. doubl. with MS. owners mark, red hf. leath., spine faded. w.a.f. (HK. May 16; 2180) DM 950
– **Die Verhängnisvolle Faschingsnacht.** Wien, 1841. *1st. Edn.* Slightly spotted, orig. wraps., mod. bds., by Larink (Hamburg). (H. May 22; 813) DM 400

NETTO & Lehmann
– **L'Art de Tricoter.** Leipzig, 1802. *1st. Edn.* Ob. fo. 25 engraved plts., each in 2 states, 1 plain, other hand-cold., blank corner of title-p. torn, slight foxing, later bds., spine worn. (SG. Apr.26; 115) $1,900

NEUBURGER, Kurt
– **Der Tod des Herrn Tarantel.** Ill.:– J. Vennekamp. Berlin, 1967. *(101) numbered.* All woodcuts sigd. (as in 1st. 10 copies), printers mark sigd. by artist, orig. pict. sewed. (GB. May 5; 3162) DM 700

NEUCHATEL
– **Essai Statistique sur le Canton de Neuchatel.** Zurich, 1818. 12mo. Engraved title, port., hand-cold. folding engraved map, 1 hand-cold. costume plt., 7 folding or double-p. plts., orig. ptd. bds., spine slightly worn, s.-c. (S. Dec.1; 330) *Dimsdale.* £240

NEUDORFFER, A.
– **Schreibkunst.** Nürnberg, 1601. 2 vols. in 1. 54 copperplts. with lge. initials, title & some. ills. cold., some slight spotting, wear, some repairs, hf. vell., Hauswedell coll. (H. May 23; 222) DM 3,600

NEUE BILDER GALLERIE fuer Junge Soehne und Toechter
Berlin, 1805. *New Edn.* Vol. 3 only. Frontis., vig. title, 20 copperplate engrs., all hand-cold., qtr. leath. (SG. Dec.8; 242) $110

NEUE BILDERGALLERIE FUR DIE JUGEND
Gotha, 1831. Vol. 4. Ob. 4to. Lacks 24 plts., title stpd. & slightly soiled, cont. hf. leath. gt., lightly bumped. (HK. Nov.8; 939) DM 880

NEUE FARBIGE VORLAGEN FUER DIE TEXTIL-INDUSTRIE
Plauen i. V., ca. 1910?. Serie I/II. Fo. 48 loose cold. plts., 2 compl. sets, 1 set mntd., unmntd. plts. measure 47 × 31cm., cl.-bkd. bd. portfos., 1st. portfo. worn. (SG. Aug.25; 324) $325

NEUE JUGEND
Ed.:– H. Barger & Wieland Herzfelde. Contribs.:– J.R. Becher, Th. Däubler, E. Lasker-Schüler, G. Trakl, G. Landauer & others. Berlin, 1921. Pts. 7-11/12 in 1 vol. Orig. bds., spine defect. (HK. Nov.11; 3831) DM 420

NEUE RUNDSCHAU
Ed.:– O. Bie, S. Fischer, S. Saenger. Contribs.:– Benn, Brecht, Döblin, Hesse, Hofmannsthal, Mann, Rilke, Zweig & others. Leipzig, 1925-35. Years 36-46 in 22 vols. Lge. 8vo. Some light browning, hf. vell. & hf. linen. (H. May 23; 1441) DM 520

NEUER LUST-WEG ZUM ZIEL NUTZLICHER KUNSTE UND WISSENSCHAFTEN
Nürnberg, Ca. 1750. 3 pts. in 1 vol. Ills. captioned in German, Latin, Fr. & Italian, a few pp. soiled, 19th. C. bds., slightly worn; J.H. Krelage bkplt., van Veen coll. (S. Feb.28; 158) £660

NEUER ORBIS PICTUS FÜR DIE JUGEND
See— COMENIUS or KOMENSKY, John Amos

NEUES A B C BUCHLEIN DER KINDER
Nürnberg, Ca. 1730. Ills. captioned in German & Latin, soiled, cont. embossed decor. bds., backstrip slightly defect.; van Veen coll. (S. Feb.28; 159) £600

NEUES ELEGANTESTES CONVERSATIONS-LEXICON
Ed.:– O.L.B. Wolff. Leipzig, 1834-37. 4 vols. 4to. 80 steel-engraved plts., some foxing thro.-out, cont. hf. roan. (C. Nov.16; 202) *Shapero.* £110

NEUES NATIONEN-ALPHABET
Mainz, ca. 1860. 126 × 1,910mm. Panorama, 24 hand-cold. litho ills., orig. bds.; van Veen coll. (S. Feb.28; 303) £140

NEUESTER ORBIS PICTUS für die Jugend
Ill.:– after P.C. Geissler. Nuremb., 1842. Fo. Lacks 3 ll., plts. with loss, partly bkd. tears, very soiled, some pp. partly lacking, cont. hf. linen, loose, worn. (HK. Nov.10; 2937) DM 1,200

NEUJAHRS-GESCHENK FUR FORST– UND JAGDLIEBHABER auf das Jahr 1799
Ed.:– L.C.E.H.F. von Wildungen. Marburg, [1798]. Plts. slightly browned, some foxing, mod. bds., orig. wraps. bnd. in. (GB. May 4; 1981) DM 400

NEUMANN, Johann Andreas
– **Naturgeschichte der Vögel Mitteleuropas.** Gera, [1902-]1905. *Jubiläum De Luxe Edn.* Vols. 1, 8, 9, 11 & 12 only (of 12). Fo. Orig. hf. leath. (HK. Nov.8; 771) DM 1,400

NEVILE, Henry
[–] **The Isle of Pines, or, A Late Discovery of The Fourth Island near Terra Australis, Incognita.** L., 1668. Sm. 4to. Crimson mor. gt. by Rivière & Son; ptd. title with Rosebury Durdons liby. stp. [Wing N506] (P. Oct.20; 246) £550

NEVILL, Ralph
– **Old English Sporting Books.** L., 1924. *(1500).* 4to. Slightly spotted, orig. buckram gt., spine faded. (S. Mar.20; 736) *Thorp.* £90
– – **Anr. Copy.** 4to. Orig. cl., spine slightly faded. (S. May 1; 422) *Stodart.* £50
– – **Anr. Copy.** 4to. Orig. cl., sunned, some wear to head & foot of spine. (SG. Mar.15; 278) $150
– **Old English Sporting Prints & their History.** 1923. *(1500) numbered.* Lge. 4to. Plts., some mntd. & cold., orig. cl., d.-w. (CSK. Jul.13; 175) £60
– – **Anr. Copy.** 4to. Cl. gt. (P. Dec.8; 186) *Solomon.* £55
– – **Anr. Copy.** Lge. 4to. Buckram gt., spine faded. (SG. Mar.15; 277) $100

NEW & COMPLETE DICTIONARY OF ARTS & SCIENCES
L., 1763-64. *2nd. Edn.* 4 vols. in 8. No bdg. stated. (P. Nov.24; 122) *Walford.* £85
– – **Anr. Copy.** 4 vols. Lacks 1 plt., cont. cf., rebkd. (SG. Oct.6; 270) $200

NEW CYCLOPAEDIA OF BOTANY & COMPLETE BOOK OF HERBS
N.d. 2 vols. Hand-cold. engraved additional title, 98 plts., some light soiling, cont. hf. mor. (CSK. Dec.16; 173) £50

NEW DIRECTIONS in Prose & Poetry
Norfolk, Conn., or N.Y., [1937-66]. Vols. 2-4, 8-10, 12-13, 16 & 18-19. Lge. 8vo. & smaller. Cl. & bds. all but Vol. 16 in d.-w. (SG. Mar.1; 370) $225

NEW DISCOVERIES Concerning the World
L., 1778. *1st. Edn.* Cont. hf. cf. gt., brkn., covers detchd. [Sabin 52591] (SG. Sep.22; 229) $150

NEW ENGLAND MANUFACTURER'S & MECHANICS' INSTITUTE
– **Catalogue of the Art Department.** Boston, 1883. 4to. Cl., worn, covers soiled. (RO. Sep.13; 25) $200

NEW GEOGRAPHICAL DICTIONARY
L., 1759. Fo. Engraved frontis., 43 maps & plans & 88 plts. only, lacks some text, some ll. torn, staining, old sheep, defect., lacks 2 covers, as a collection of plts., w.a.f. (P. Sep.29; 198) *Sweet.* £160

NEW GUINEA
– **Annual Report on British New Guines from 1st July, 1900, to 30th June, 1901** ... Brisbane, 1902. Fo. Minor wear, bdg. not stated. (KH. May 1; 524) Aus. $200
– **Report of the Royal Commission on the Affray at Goaribari Island, British New Guinea, on the 6th of March, 1904** ... Sydney, 1904. Sm. fo. Ptd. wraps., slight wear. (KH. May 1; 527) Aus. $130

NEW HISTORICAL-SYSTEM OF GEOGRAPHY
Manchester, 1815. Fo. Frontis., 29 maps & plts., cf. gt. (P. Nov.24; 186) £75

NEW JERSEY
[–] **A Bill in the Chancery of New-Jersey, at the Suit of John Earl of Stair, & others, Proprietors of the Eastern-Division of New Jersey ... against Benjamin Bond & some other Persons of Elizabeth-Town ... To which is added the Publications of the Council of Proprietors of East New-Jersey, & Mr.**

NEW JERSEY -*Contd.*

Nevill's Speeches to the General Assembly, concerning the Riots committed in New-Jersey ... N.Y., 1747. Fo. Engraved maps reprd. & with splitting at folds of Map No. III, maps & text pp. slightly browned, donor's inscr. on title-p. & liby. stps. on title-p. & p. 80, cont. qtr. cf. & marb. paper, worn, upr. cover separated from spine. (SPB. Oct.26; 23)
$3,000

NEW MUENTZ BUECH
Munich, 1597. *1st. Edn.* 2 section titles dtd. 1596, many woodcuts hand-tinted, lacks I1 (lf. 49), loosely bnd. into vell. from a 15th. C. MS. (SG. Nov.3; 156)
$475

NEW PRINT MAGAZINE ... Picturesque Views of Beautiful Scenes
Ca. 1795. Engraved title, 58 plts., dampstained thro.-out, cont. cf., worn, upr. cover detchd. (BBA. Feb.9; 237)
Elliott. £65

NEW ROYAL PRIMER: or the Easy & Pleasant Guide to the Art of Reading
L., n.d. 24mo. Final lf. torn, stitched. (CSK. Feb.24; 166)
£150

NEW SOUTH WALES
- **Landscape Scenery, Illustrating Sydney, Paramatta, Richmond, Maitland, Windsor & Port Jackson, New South Wales.** Sydney, Melbourne & L., n.d. Ob. 4to. Steel-engraved additional title, 36 plts. only, spotted, dampstained, orig. cl., worn, disbnd., w.a.f. (CSK. Feb.10; 56)
£680
- **Photographs of New South Wales.** Sydney, Charles Potter, 1892. Ob. fo. 100 photo plts. mauve mor. gt. (P. Oct.20; 12)
£1,500

NEW SPORTING MAGAZINE, The
L., May 1831-Dec. 1847. Vol. 1 no. 1-New Series Vol. 14 no. 84, in 33 vols. Text & plts. browned, hf. cf., spines gt. in 6 compartments, by Riviere,. (CNY. Dec.17; 585)
$2,600
- - **Anr. Edn.** 1856-65. 11 vols., incompl. run. Some foxing of plts., hf. cf., worn. (PD. Aug.17; 233)
£100

NEW TESTAMENT Chippewa]
- **Kekitchemanitomenahn Gahbemahjeinnunk Jesus Christ, Otoashke Wawweendeummahgain.** Albany, 1833. 12mo. Browned & foxed, cf., rebkd., covers loose. [Sabin 12833] (S. Dec.13; 130)
Edwards. £90

NEW TESTAMENT [Dutch]
- **Dat Nieuwe Testament ... Na de Copye van Nic, Biestkens.** Amst., 1634. Sm. 4to. Initials & many capitals touched with col., inner margins of title & some ll. stained & slightly defect., cont. vell., lacks ties, new end-papers. (VG. Nov.30; 916) Fls. 600
- **Het Nieuwe Testament, mitsgaders: d'Epistelen u.h. O. Test.** Ed.:- H. vanden Leemputte. Ill.:- C. v. Sichem?. Amst., 1672. Some staining in text, few ll. defect. in margins, sm. worm-hole through 1st. & last ll., cont. blind-stpd. cf. over wood, old brass catches, rubbed, defect., lacks clasps. (VG. Sep.14; 1299) Fls. 480

NEW TESTAMENT [English]
- **The New Testament of Iesus Christ faithfully translated ... by the English College.** Antw., 1600. *2nd. Edn. of Douai version.* 4to. Sm. piece torn from lr. blank corner of a few ll., title-p. slightly stained, cont. cf., rebkd. [STC 2898; D. & M. 198] (BBA. May 3; 99) *Howes Bookshop.* £100
- **New Testament.** L., 1615. 12mo. Title in woodcut border, cont. embroidered bdg. of knotwork with blue thread overlaid with silver & gt. thread, tarnished, reprd., lacks clasps; bkplt. of G.W.F. Gregor. (SPB. May 16; 53)
£225
- **The Text of the New Testament of Iesus Christ, Translated out of the Vulgar Latine by the Papists of the Traiterous Seminaire at Rheims** ... Trans.:- William Fulke. 1617. [STC 2917] (*Bound with:*) FULKE, William - **A Defense of the Sincere & True Translation of the Holy Scripture into the English Tongue.** 1617. [STC 11431]. Together 2 works in 1 vol. Fo. Old cf., spine gt., parts reprd. (LC. Mar.1; 489)
£60
- **The New Testament.** Camb., 1628. (*Bound with:*)
- **Whole Book of Psalms** L., 1629. Together 2 works

in 1 vol. long 24 mo. 18th. C.(?) linen on bds., elab. embroidered in colours & silver thread, slightly worn or frayed. [STC 2617] (SG. Apr.19; 38)
$550
- - **Anr. Edn.** Trans.:- Engl. College in Rheims. Ill.:- Picquet & van Lochom. [Rouen?], 1633. *4th. Edn.* 4to. Errata lf., 6 (of 8) copperplts., early 19th. C. russ., rebkd., cover detchd. (SG. Feb.9; 8) $120
- - **Anr. Edn.** 1640. (*Bound with:*) PSALMS, PSALTER & PSEUMES [English] - **The Whole Book of Psalmes.** 1641. Together 2 works in 1 vol. Cont. embroidered dos-à-dos bdg., some wear. (P. Jul.5; 134)
£400
- - **Anr. Edn.** L., 1822. A few gatherings slightly sprung, mor. gt., rubbed, 2 sm. abrasions on fore-e. (SG. Mar.15; 255)
£350
- **The Rockefeller McCormick New Testament.** Ed.:- H.R. Willoughby. Chic., [1932]. 3 vols. Lge. 8vo. Portfo. of cold. miniature paintings, cl., boxed. (SG. May 3; 40)
$110
- **The New Testament.** Camb., 1939. *Reprint of Tyndale's 1534 Edn., (500) numbered.* 4to. Orig. mor., slightly soiled, s.-c. (BBA. Jan.19; 258)
Thomas. £55

NEW TESTAMENT [French]
- **Le Nouveau Testament, contenant les Quattre Evangelistes ... avec L'Apocalipse ou la Revelation.** Antw., 18 Jan. 1529. *Le Fevre's Version.* Sm. 8vo. 19th. C. cathedral-style black mor., slightly rubbed. (C. Nov.9; 40)
Thomas. £750
- **Le Nouveau Testament.** Charenton, 1668. (*Bound with:*) PSALMS, PSALTERS & PSEUMES [French] - **Pseavmes de David.** Ed.:- Cl. Marot & Th. de Bèze. Charenton, 1668. Together 2 works in 1 vol. Owners note on end-papers, cont. leath. gt., 4 chiselled silver corner bosses, 2 chiselled silver clasps, lacks ties. (HK. Nov.9; 1553) DM 650
- - **Anr. Edn.** Amst., [1716]. (*Bound with:*) PSALMS, PSALTERS & PSEUMES [French] - **Psaumes de David.** Cl. Marot & Th. de Beze. 1716. Together 2 works in 1 vol. Cont. black mor., chiselled silver & 5 chiselled heart-shaped silver bosses, 2 silver clasps. (HK. Nov.9; 1556) DM 460

NEW TESTAMENT [German]
- **Das New Testament.** Trans.:- H. Emser. Freiburg, 1534. *2nd. Freiburg Edn.* Lacks title lf., some slight spotting, slightly stained at beginning, 18th. C. hf. leath., worn & bumped. (HT. May 8; 85)
DM 1,900
- **Dat Nye Testament Jhesu Christi.** Magdeburg, 1563. Some foxing in places or browning, 1 lf. with sm. corner tear & some loss, cont. leath., rubbed & worn, leath. torn, lacks clasps. (GB. Nov.3; 933)
DM 1,600
- **Das Neue Testament.** (*Bound with:*) PSALMS, PSALTERS & PSEUMES [German] - **Die CL Psalmen Davids.** Zurich, 1752. Together 2 pts. in 1 vol. Cont. shagreen over wood bds., silver decor. cover, decor. clasps, spine worn; owners inscr. of Hans Jacob Hüni on 1st. inserted lf. (C. May 30; 46)
Lyon. £340
- **Das Ganz Neue Testament unsers Herrn Jesu Christi.** Ephrata in Pennsylvanien, 1787. Browned, stains, names on end-paper, cont. cf. over wood, reprd. (VG. Nov.30; 534) Fls. 725
- **Evangelium S. Johannis.** Trans.:- M. Luther. Ill.:- K. Nebel. Frankfurt, Kleukens Pr., 1920. *(250) numbered.* 11 orig. woodcuts, orig. bds., spine browned. (GB. Nov.5; 2684) DM 400

NEW TESTAMENT [Greek]
- **Nouvum Testamentum Graece.** Strassburg, 1524. *1st. 8vo. Edn. in Greek.* 8vo. 10 pp. Greek. MS. at front, Greek annots. thro.-out. some stains, later mor. gt. [D. & M. 4600] (BBA. Jan.19)
McKitterick. £260
- - **Anr. Edn.** Ed.:- D. Erasmus. Basel, 1543. Sm. 8vo. Cont. vell. on bds., elab. stpd. with oval ports. enclosing centre panel, 1 (of 2) metal clasp, lacks fly-ll. [D. & M. 4621] (SG. Feb.9; 3) $175
- **New Testament.** Paris, 1546-47. 16mo. Some outer margins partly excised, cont.? mor. (CSK. Feb.24; 165)
£85
- **Biblia Graeca. Novum Testamentum Graece.** Zürich, 1547. Some ll. slightly soiled, some interlinear notes in old MS., MS. owner's note on title,

cont. blind-tooled pig over wood bds., arms supralibros. stpd. on upr. cover with initial over, dated 1558 below. (R. Oct.11; 12) DM 900
- **Novum Testamentum ex Bibliotheca Regia.** Paris, 1549. 16mo. With the 2 final blanks, some margin worming, cont. German (Palatinate?) cf., flat spine gt., covers tooled, head & foot of spine reprd., later end-papers; several early 17th. C. inscrs. at beginning including copy of a Scaliger poem. [D. & M. 4620] (S. Nov.17; 50) *A. Thomas.* £660
- **Novum Testamentum.** Paris, 1549. *2nd. Estienne Edn.* 2 pts. in 1 vol. 16mo. Some slight spotting, cont. vell. wraps., slightly defect. [D. & M. 4620] (HT. May 8; 86) DM 750
- **Novum Jesu Christi D.N. Testamentum.** Paris, 15 Jun. 1550. *3rd 'Estienne' Edn. (the 'Editio Regia').* 2 pts. in 1 vol. Fo. Engl. bdg. of russ., covers panel. gt. & blind, elab. gt. decor., spine gt. in compartments, inner borders of gt. frames, dark grey end-papers (by Roger Payne), cl. box. [D. & M. 4622] (S. May 10; 368) *D. Smith.* £1,400
- **Novum Testamentum, sive Novum Foedus.** Ed.:- Th. Beza. Geneva, 1565. *Beza's 1st. Major Edn. (2nd. Edn. of Commentary).* 2 pts. in 1 vol. Fo. Tear in 2 ll., some annots. & underlinings, some stains, cont. richly blind-stpd. pig over wood, ports., soiled, some defects, lacks clasps. (VG. Nov.30; 917) Fls. 1,250
- **He Kaine Diatheke.** Leiden, 1633. Bnd. in 4 vols. 12mo. 18th. C. red mor. gt., dentelle border enclosing cruciform pattern, decor., crucific in centre & IHS with winged putti heads & 'Via Prima Salutis'. (S. Nov.17; 51) *Tzakas.* £250
- **Novum Testamentum.** Ed.:- Jo. Jac. Griesbachius. Ill.:- after G. Reni, H. Carracci, C. Screda & C. Dolci. engraved by Böhm, Rosmaesler & others. Leipzig, 1803-07. *De Luxe Edn. on vell.* Lge. 4to. Wide margin, title with old owners mark, cont. hf. leath., bumped & rubbed; Hauswedell coll. (H. May 24; 1302) DM 620

NEW TESTAMENT [Greek & Latin]
- **Novum Testamentum Omne.** Trans.:- Desiderius Erasmus. Basel, 1522. *3rd. Edn. of this trans.* Fo. Title & dedication ll. in woodcut borders, printer's device on final lf. verso, lacks H2, title slightly soiled & with inscrs., few marginal stains, mod. vell. bds. (S. Apr.10; 313) *Tile.* £800
- **Novum Testamentum, sive Novum Foedus.** Ed.:- Th. Beza. [Geneva], 1582. *Beza's 2nd. Major Edn.* 2 pts. in 1 vol. Fo. 1 lf. slightly defect. with loss of text, some staining, slightly browned thro.-out, cont. blind-stpd. & panel. pig over wood, port. of Luther on upr. cover, arms on lr. cover, worn & rubbed, lacks clasps. [D. & M. 4643] (VG. Mar.19; 205)
Fls. 500
- **Novum Jesu Christi D.N. Testamentum.** Lugduni, 1600. 16mo. Cont. bdg., gt. decor. (LM. Mar.3; 219) B.Frs. 10,000

NEW TESTAMENT [Hebrew]
See— BIBLES [Hebrew]

NEW TESTAMENT [Latin]
- **Novum Testamentum.** Ed.:- Desiderius Erasmus. 1536. A few ink annots., cont. panel. cf. gt., worn, lacks ties. (P. Dec.8; 115) *Tzakas.* £240
- - **Anr. Edn.** 1541. 17th. C. mor. gt., slightly rubbed. (P. Jan.12; 161) *Edmunds.* £140
- **Testamenti Novi** ... Trans.:- Ioannis Benedicti. [Dillingen, 1565]. Woodcut border to title-p. touched in colour, 32 woodcuts (21 full-p.), lacks last blank, cont. blind-stpd. pig., 1 (of 2) clasps, stained, lr. cover cracked. (S. Apr.10; 344) *Snelling.* £100
- **Novi Testamenti.** Zürich, 1575. Title with cont. owner's mark, last 2 ll. with slight worming, 19th. C. vell. gt., slightly rubbed. (R. Nov.8; 118)
DM 800

NEW TESTAMENT [Latin & French]
- **Le Nouveau Testament** ... Trans.:- Sacy. Ill.:- Moreau le Jeune. Paris, 1793. *1st. Printing of ills.* 4 vols. only (lacks commentary vol., as often). Cont. Bradel-Dèrôme style str.-grd. red mor. gt., richly decor., paper doubls. & end-papers. (HD. Mar.19; 81) Frs. 2,100

NEW TESTAMENT [Marra]
- **Testamenta Marra** ... Ed.:- J.G. Reuther & C. Strehlow. Tanunda, 1897. Later? cl., qtr. roan. (KH. May 1; 590) Aus. $170

NEW TESTAMENT [Peguan]
- The New Testament. Maulmain, 1847. Slightly dampstained, cont. cf. [D. & M. 9094] (BBA. Mar.7; 37)　　　　　　　　　　*D. Loman.* £120

NEW TESTAMENT [Polyglot]
- Novum Testamentum ... Syriacè, Ebraicè, Graecè, Latinè, Germanicè, Bohemicè, Italicè, Hispanicè, Gallicè, Anglicè, Danicè, Polonicè ... Ed.:– Elias Hutter. Nuremberg, 1599. Vol. 1 only (of 2). Fo. Engraved title rather damaged & reprd., last lf. very torn & crudely reprd. with sellotape, 9 prelims. loose, cont. black silk over wood bds., silver corner-pieces & central armorial shields, that on upr. cover with arms of Elector Palatine & date 1601 & that on lr. with arms of Duke of Württemberg, gt. & gauffered edges with same 2 coats-of-arms & initials O.H.P. & D.M.P. & date 1607, all in floral wreaths, piece of metal nailed to lr. cover with armorial shield (lifted & relaid down) & poor quality leath. straps. & strap-holders added in this C., w.a.f. (S. May 10; 369)　　*D. Smith.* £340
- Novum Testamentum Harmonicum. Trans.:– Elias Hutter. Nürnberg, 1602 (with new title: Amst., 1615). Sm. 4to. In Hebrew, Greek, Latin & German, some staining & browning, leath. gt., old soiling & wear, sm. faults. (V. Oct.1; 3712)
　　　　　　　　　　　　　　　　　　DM 650

NEW TESTAMENT [Tahitian]
- Te Fanfaa Api. Lonedona, 1838. 12mo. Stitching brkn., cont. sheep, worn,. [D. & M. 9081] (CSK. Feb.10; 191)　　　　　　　　　　　　£70

NEW TESTAMENTIANA [Arabic & Latin]
- [Four Gospels]. Ill.:– A Tempesta & others. Flor., 1744. Re-iss. of orig. sheets of 1591 Medicea Edn. Fo. Final p. 'Typographus lectori' dtd. 1591, sm. worm-hole in last 27 ll., a few ll. browned, cont. vell. [D. & M. II, 1643, note] (C. May 30; 9)
　　　　　　　　　　　　Sims Reed & Fogg. £480

NEW TESTAMENTIANA [English]
- Parables of Our Lord. Ill.:– Henry Noel Humphries. 1847. Contents loose due to gutta-percha bdg., papier mâché, medallions & floral decors., mor. spine. (LC. Mar.1; 92)　　£90
-- Anr. Copy. Orig. papier mâché, with medallions & floral decors., rebkd. in mor. gt., mor. s.-c. (LC. Oct.13; 144)　　　　　　　　　　£60
- The Sermon on the Mount. Ill.:– W.R. Tymms after Charles Rolt. 1861. Lge. fo. Orig. embossed cl. gt. (LC. Oct.13; 153)　　　　　　£120
- The Four Gospels of the Lord Jesus Christ. Ill.:– Eric Gill,. Gold. Cock. Pr., 1931. (500) numbered. Fo. Orig. hf. pig & buckram, spine slightly discold., covers spotted, s.-c. (S. Nov.21; 221)
　　　　　　　　　　　　Lapiccirella. £1,650
- The Second Chapter from the Gospel according to Saint Matthew. Ill.:– V. Angelo. [San Franc.], Golden Cross Pr., 1936. (100). 12mo. Title vig. & text decors. hand-cold., hand-decor. bds., covers slightly rubbed & darkened; the V. Angelo copy. (CBA. Oct.1; 139)　　　　　　　　$100
- The Stonyhurst Gospel of St. John. Ed.:– T. Julian Brown. Roxb. Cl., 1969. Orig. qtr. mor. (S. Oct.4; 245)　　　　　　　　　　*Maggs.* £110
-- Anr. Copy. Orig. qtr. mor. (S. Oct.4; 246)
　　　　　　　　　　　　　　Maggs. £100

NEW TESTAMENTIANA [German]
- Epistolae et Evengelia. Hye hebt sich an das Evengelbuch. Augsburg, Johann Schönsperger, 1495. Reprint of 1489 Edn. Fo. Woodcuts cont. cold., cont. buck over wood bds., clasps; from Fondation Furstenberg-Beaumesnil. [C. 2335] (HD. Nov.16; 7)　　　　　　　　　　　　Frs. 53,000
- Der Offenbarung Künftiger Geschicht Johannis. N.p., 1558. 4to. Cont. stpd. cf., richly decor., dtd. 1546, clasps, lacks ties; from Fondation Fürstenberg-Beaumesnil. (HD. Nov.16; 87)　　Frs. 3,200
- Die Offenbarung St. Johannis. Ill.:– Br. Goldschmitt. Hellerau, 1923. (450). (180) numbered De Luxe Edn. 4to. Printers mark sigd. by artist, 10 orig. woodcuts (9 full-p. monogrammed) & separate series (9 sigd.), orig. vell., orig. hf. vell. portfo. (GB. May 5; 2587)　　　　　　　　DM 500

NEW TESTAMENTIANA [Latin]
- Euangelia et Epistolae ... Trans.:– Desiderius Erasmus. Strassburg, 1604. 16mo. Sm. hole in title,

liby, stp., cont. cf., worn, rebkd. (S. Oct.11; 395)
　　　　　　　　　　　　　　　Maggs. £70
- Sancti Beati a Liebana in Apocalypsin Codex Gerudensis. Olten, 1962. Facs. Edn., (680). 2 vols., including text vol. Lge. fo. Text in Engl., German & Spanish, blind-tooled mor. & hf. mor. (B. Oct.4; 270)　　　　　　　　　　　　　Fls. 750
- Sanctum Evangelium secundum Matthaeum, Marcum, Lucam, Johannem. Ill.:– after Bartholomaeus di Giovanni engraved by Bruno Bramanti. Vecona, 1963. (140). Fo. Red mor., linen s.-c. (R. Oct.11; 330)　　　　　　　　　DM 3,400

NEW YORK CITY
- The Building Laws, relating to the Construction of Buildings in the City of New York. N.Y., 1891. Tall 8vo. Many advts. thro.-out, cl., ex-liby. (SG. Aug.4; 225)　　　　　　　　　　　$100
- Competition for the New York Court House, 1913. N.Y., [1913]. Atlas fo. 88 plts., each liby.-stpd. on blank verso, loose in hf. cl. folder, linen ties. (SG. May 3; 265)　　　　　　　　　　　$150
- Description of the New York Central Park. Ill.:– A.F. Bellows. N.Y., 1869. 1st. Edn. Frontis., 2 full-p. plans, many woodcut views, orig. gt. pictor. cl., spine ends slightly frayed. (SG. Apr.5; 152) $375
- First Annual Report of the Board of Commissioners of the Department of Public Parks for the Year Ending May 1, 1871. Ill.:– George C. Rockwood (photos). N.Y., 1871. 4to. Lacks 1 mntd. photo, hf. leath., rubbed & scuffed. (SG. May 10; 93)　　　　　　　　　　　　$120
-- Anr. Copy. 4to. Hf. leath., scuffed. (SG. Nov.10; 117)　　　　　　　　　　　　　$100
- A Letter from a Gentleman of the City of New-York to Another, Concerning the Troubles which happen'd in That Province in the Time of the late Happy Revolution. N.Y., 1698. Pamphlet, p. 19 misnumbered, browned, stains at inner margins not effecting text, holes from oversewing, disbnd. [Sabin 40295] (SPB. Oct.26; 17)　　$6,000
- Modest & Impartial Narrative of Several Grievances & Great Oppressions That the Peacable & most Considerable Inhabitants of Their Majesties Province of New-York in America lie under ... [Phila., 1691]. Pamphlet, browned & spotted, some ll. lightly foxed, sm. stain at inner margins of some pp., taped repair to title-p., visible holes from oversewing, disbnd.; inscr. on title-p. 'Francis Leeds ... Bought at philladellphia Tho Wost Aprill 2d. 1698 Thom bought'. [Sabin 40907] (SPB. Oct.26; 18)
　　　　　　　　　　　　　　$14,000

NEW YORK STATE
- Documents relating to the Colonial History of the State of New-York, procured in Holland, England & France by J.R. Brodhead. Ed.:– E.B. O'Callaghan. Albany, 1856-87. 15 vols. Lge. 4to. Cl., defect., lacks 1 spine, ex-liby. (SG. Aug.4; 217)　　$240
- Photographs of the Members of the Assembly of the State of New York, 1880. Albany, ca. 1880. 4to. Most photographs sigd. by the sitters, hf. leath., scuffed. (SG. Nov.10; 116)　　　　　　$150

NEW YORK TIMES
N.Y., 9 Jan. 1862-30 Jun. 1865. In 11 vols. Tall fo. Qtr. roan, worn, ex-liby., not collated, w.a.f. (SG. Aug.4; 230)　　　　　　　　　$1,900

NEW ZEALAND ASSOCIATION
- A Statement of the Objects of the New Zealand Association. L., 1837. Wraps. (P. Jul.5; 327) £85

NEWBERRY, J.S.
See– MACOMB, Capt. John N. & Newberry, J.S.

NEWBOLT, Frank
- The Etched Work of Frank Brangwyn; a Catalogue. 1908. (100) numbered. Fo. 4 orig. sigd. etchings in front pocket as called for, orig. cl.-bkd. bds., upr. cover slightly browned, unbnd. as iss. in orig. cl. portfo., lacks ties. (CSK. Feb.10; 176)　£110

NEWBURY, J.
[-] The Royal Primer; or, an Easy ... Guide to the Art of Reading. Salisbury, n.d. 12mo. Lr. margin A12 torn with slight loss, owner's inscr. dtd. 1764 on front pastedown, orig. decor. paper bds., spine worn. (CSK. Oct.7; 153)　　　　　£100

NEWCASTLE, William Cavendish, Duke of
- A General System of Horsemanship in all its Branches. L., 1743. 2 vols. Fo. 37 (of 42) double-p. engraved plts. in Vol. I, 20 engraved plts., including 2 double-p., in Vol. II, lacks 5 pp. of text in Vol. I, cont. cf., 1 cover detchd., w.a.f. (C. Nov.16; 282)　　　　　　　*Erlini.* £1,050

NEWCASTLE & CARLISLE RAILWAY BILL
- Copy of the Evidence taken before a Committee of the House of Commons. Newcastle, 1829. Cl. (P. Jun.7; 316)　　　　　　　　　　£130

NEWCOME, Rev. Peter
- The History of the Ancient & Royal Foundation called the Abbey of St. Alban. 1795. 4to. Folding map hand-cold. in outl., tree cf. gt. (P. Jun.7; 156)
　　　　　　　　　　　　　　　　　　£85

NEWELL, Peter S.
- A Shadow Show. N.Y., 1896. 1st. Edn. Ob. 8vo. Pict. bds., some wear. (RO. Mar.21; 86)　$130

NEWENHAM, Thomas
- A View of the Natural, Political & Commercial Circumstances of Ireland. L., 1809. 1st. Edn. 4to. Folding map cold. in outl., bkplt., hf. mor., armorial motif on spine. (GM. Dec.7; 433)　　　£210

NEWHALL, Charles L.
- The Adventures of Jack; or, A Life on the Wave. Southbridge, Mass., priv. ptd., 1859. 1st. Edn. 12mo. Orig. gt.-pict. cl., corners nicked, lacks front free end-paper; from liby. of F.D. Roosevelt, inscr. by him. (SG. Mar.15; 63)　　　　　$200

NEWHOFF, Friedrich von 'Frederick'
- The Description of Corsica with an Account of its Union to the Crown of Great Britain. L., 1795. Str.-grd. mor. gt.-decor. by Stoneham, spine decor.; David C. Sassoon ex-libris. (HD. Oct.21; 87)
　　　　　　　　　　　　　　Frs. 6,500

NEWHOUSE, Charles B., Engraver
- The Roadster's Album. 1845. [1st. Edn.]. Fo. Engraved title, 16 plts., all hand cold., last 4 advt. ll., some plts. loose & slightly soiled, 4 frayed, orig. cl., rubbed. (BBA. Feb.9; 236a) *Denistoun.* £1,100
-- Anr. Copy. Fo. Hand-cold. engraved title-p., 16 hand-cold. engraved plts., orig. tissue-guards, 8-p. publisher's catalogue, 3 plts. with very sm. stain on fore-edge, orig. cl., covers soiled, spine worn; pencil sig. of Burton Mansfield. (SG. Apr.26; 151)
　　　　　　　　　　　　　　$3,750

NEWMAN, Isidora
- Fairy Flowers: Nature Legends of Fact & Fantasy. Ill.:– after Willy Pogany. L., [1926]. 4to. A little soiled, orig. hf. cl. & matte bds., matching pict. s.-c. slightly rubbed. (CBA. Aug.21; 466)
　　　　　　　　　　　　　　　$100

NEWMAN, John Henry, Cardinal
- Apologia pro Vita sua. L., 1864. 1st. Edn. Orig. cl., slightly faded. (BBA. Nov.30; 260)
　　　　　　　　　　　　　Jarndyce. £60
[-] Lyra Apostolica. Derby, 1836. 1st. Edn. 12mo. Orig. cl., lacks rear free end-paper; Frederic Dannay copy. (CNY. Dec.16; 252)　　　$600
[-] Verses on Various Occasions. L., 1868. 1st. Edn. 1st. Iss. 16mo. Orig. cl., covers blistered. (SG. Apr.19; 305)　　　　　　　　　$175

NEWPORT, Maurice
- Sereniss. Principi Carolo Secundo ... Regi: Votum Candidum Vivat Rex. L., 1669. 2nd. Edn. 12mo. Errata ll., 1 with cont. mntd. ptd. corrections, sm. later ptd. slip mntd. at blank opposing title, light ageing, 19th. C. cf. & marb. bds., raised bands & gt. panels, some mild scuffing to extremities, text slightly trimmed at top edge when rebnd.; Browning's copy, with 'J.M.J. Ex Libris Rhetorum' written underneath his sig. (HA. Feb.24; 183)
　　　　　　　　　　　　　　　$180

NEWTON, Alfred Edward
- This Book-Collecting Game. L., 1931. Red cf., gt.-tooled & inlay arabesque on covers, gt.-panel. spine, by Sangorski & Sütcliffe. (SG. Feb.16; 223)
　　　　　　　　　　　　　　　$175

NEWTON, Sir Charles Thomas
- Travels & Discoveries in the Levant. L., 1865. *1st. Edn.* 2 vols. Several plts. dampstained, gt.-lettered cl., soiled, 1 spine torn, 1 gathering sprung. (SG. Sep.22; 230) $120

NEWTON, C.T. & Pullan, R.P.
- A History of Discoveries at Halicarnassus, Cnidus, & Branchidae. L., 1862. 3 vols., including Atlas. 8vo., tall fo. Some foxing, margin chipping, plts. stpd. on versos, cl., worn or brkn., ex-liby. (RO. Dec.11; 250) $125

NEWTON, Sir Isaac
[-] Analysis per Quantitatum Series, Fluxiones, ac Differentias: cum Enumeratione Linearum Tertii Ordinis. L., 1711. *1st. Edn.* 4to. Thick paper, cont. panel. cf., spine gt.; Stanitz coll. (SPB. Apr.25; 314) $2,900
- Arithmetica Universalis; sive de Compositione et Resolutione Arithmetica Liber. Camb. & L., 1707. *1st. Edn.* Hf.-title, recent cf., unc.; H. Warren's name on title, Stanitz coll. (SPB. Apr.25; 315) $1,600
- The Chronology of Ancient Kingdoms Amended. 1728. *1st. Edn.* 4to. Cont. cf., gt. spine. (SKC. Jan.13; 2237) £80
- - **Anr. Copy.** 4to. L.P., cont. spr. cf., gt.-decor. spine. (TA. Dec.15; 592) £66
- - **Anr. Copy.** 4to. Some stains & wrinkling, later hf. cf., unc. (SG. Feb.16; 224) $120
- - **Anr. Copy.** 4to. Cont. panel. cf., very worn. (SG. Oct.27; 235) $110
- - **Anr. Copy.** 4to. Cont. cf., corners worn. (HD. Feb.22; 156) Frs. 1,600
- Excerpta Quaedam e Newtoni Principiis Philosophiae Naturalis. Ed.:– [John Jebb]. Camb., 1765. *1st. Edn.* 4to. Subscriber's list, cont. cf., cover detchd. (SKC. Sep.9; 1929) £70
- The Mathematical Papers of ... Ed.:– D.T. Whiteside. Camb., 1971-74. 6 vols. 4to. Gt.-lettered cl., light wear, ex-liby. (HA. Nov.18; 368) $110
- The Method of Fluxions & Infinite Series; with its Application of the Geometry of Curve-Lines ... Ed.:– John Colson. L., 1736. 4to. L.P., interpolate lf. (pp. 143/144), errata lf. & advts., slight margin soiling, cont. panel cf., rebkd., corners renewed; Stanitz coll. (SPB. Apr.25; 316) $2,600
- Observations upon the Prophecies of Daniel, & the Apocalypse of St. John. 1733. *1st. Edn.* 4to. Cont. panel. cf., some wear to spine. (TA. May 17; 342) £80
- - **Anr. Copy.** 4to. Cont. panel. cf., spine ends chipped. (TA. Aug.18; 375) £75
- Optical Lectures read in the Publick Schools of the University of Cambridge, Anno Domini, 1669 ... L., 1728. *1st. Edn.* 13 folding plts., a few ll. slightly soiled or spotted, cont. cf., very worn, upr. cover detchd. (S. Nov.28; 129) *Quaritch.* £600
- Opticks. L., 1704. *1st. Edn.* 4to. 9 (of 19) folding plts., fly-title between Tt1 & Tt2, p.120 pt. 2 misnumbered 112, cont. panel. cf., cancelled liby. stp. of Univ. liby., Edinb. (S. Apr.10; 568) *Perceval.* £110
- - **Anr. Copy.** 4to. Errata, margin repair to 1 lf., minor soiling, old panel cf., rebkd., some rubbing; Brook Taylor's copy with his sig. on end-paper, several MS. corrections & notes in margins, Stanitz coll. (SPB. Apr.25; 317) $5,750
- - **Anr. Edn.** L., 1718. *2nd. Edn.* Lf. of advts., cont. cf. (BBA. May 3; 54) *Pickering & Chatto.* £480
- Opuscula Mathematica, Philosophica et Philologica. Ed.:– John. Castillioneus. Lausanne & Geneva, 1744. *1st. Edn.* 4 vols. 4to. A few gatherings in Vols. I & III browned, stains in lr. margins of Vols. I & III, several ll. stained in Vol. I, ll. adjacent to folding tables have lr. margins extended, cont. blind-stpd. pig, light soiling & rubbing; MS. note & sm. stp. of 'Bibliothecae Piar Scholar in Collegio Loevenburgio' on titles, Stanitz coll. (SPB. Apr.25; 318) $350
- Philosophiae Naturalis Principia Mathematica. L., 1687. *1st. Edn. 1st. Iss., with 2-line 'plures Bibliopolas' imprint.* 4to. Diagram on D3 inverted, folding engraved plt. of comet following (A)4, inserted errata lf at end, P4 a cancel as usual but with incorrect catchword 'tivi', errata corrected in early hand, lacks final blank lf., margins of 1st. 4 ll. restored, those of next 7 ll. reinforced with

sm. restorations (no loss from ptd. area), some other ll. slightly brittle at edges, some with minor tears & restorations (no loss), pieces torn from blank margins of 1 lf., lr. corner of anr. lf. reprd., inner & upr. margins of errata lf. restored (text not affected), some browning as usual, recent cf., sm gt. stp. of Athenaeum on upr. cover, mor. solander case; no. 40 in Macomber's 'Census', sig. of Matthew Maty in upr. blank margin of title, sigd. by Francis Maseres on end-paper & dtd. 4 Aug. 1780, inscr. on end-paper records gift of book to John Hellins, later in liby. of Athenaeum, Pall Mall, L., sold to Dawsons of Pall Mall at Sotheby's, 26 May 1964, Stanitz coll. [Wing N1048] (SPB. Apr.25; 319) $20,000
- - **Anr. Copy.** Wide margin, erased stp. on title verso, cont. vell. (R. Oct.12; 1699) DM 68,000
- - **Anr. Edn.** Ed.:– Roger Cotes. Camb., 1713. *2nd. Edn., approx. (750).* 4to. Light staining affecting some upr. margins, cont. diced russ., spine gt., upr. cover slightly bumped; owners inscr. of G.W. Chad, 26 June 1800, bkplt. of Sir Willoughby Jones, Bt, & his note on end-paper, Stanitz coll. (SPB. Apr.25; 320) $2,900
- - **Anr. Edn.** Amst., 1714. 4to. Slightly browned thro.-out, cont. cf., rebkd. & reprd. (BBA. Jan.19; 48) *Thomas,.* $240
- - **Anr. Edn.** Amst., 1723. 4to. Few ll. slightly torn at foot affecting few letters, some sm. margin repairs, slight staining, 2 ll. MS. notes bnd. at beginning, cont. cf., worn, rebkd. (S. Nov.1; 290) *Faurre.* £120
- - **Anr. Edn.** Ed.:– Henry Pemberton. L., 1726. *3rd. Edn.* 4to. Hf.-title (bnd. after title), Royal Privilege, lf. with Halley's Ode, Dedication to Royal Society, cont. cf., rebkd., rubbed; name of W.D. Hall on end-paper, Stanitz coll. (SPB. Apr.25; 321) $1,100
- - **Anr. Copy.** 4to. Hf.-title, Privilege & advt. ll., port., text figures, 1 lf. margin reprd., cont. cf., early rebacking. (SG. Apr.26; 152) $950
- - **Anr. Copy.** 4to. Cont. cf. (LH. Sep.25; 576) $200
- - **Anr. Edn.** Ed.:– Th. Le Seur & Fr. Jacquier. Genf., 1739-42. 3 vols. 4to. Cont. cf., gold-tooled arms supralibros sigd. (D. Nov.23; 681) DM 2,400
- Traité d'optique ... Trans.:– Coste. Ill.:– Chanfournier engraved by Herisset. Paris, 1722. *2nd. Fr. Edn.* Cont. porphyry cf., decor. spine. (HD. Dec.9; 66) Frs. 2,200
- Two Treatises of the Quadrature of Curves, & Analysis by Equations of an Infinite Number of Terms ... Trans.:– John Steward. L., 1745. *1st. Edn.* 4to. Errata & advt. lf., 4 pp. 18th. C. MS. notes laid in, minor spotting to a few ll., cont. cf., head of spine slightly rubbed; Alex Shirressi sig. on title, Stanitz coll. (SPB. Apr.25; 322) $700

NEWTON, James
- A Compleat Herbal. 1752. Port., 175 plts., no plt. 1, cf., rebkd. (P. Jun.7; 225) £80

NEWTON, John
See— COWPER, William & Newton, John

NIBBY, Antonio
- Raccolta de'Monumenti piu Celebri di Roma Antica ... Roma, [1830?]. 4to. 40 engraved plts., gt.-tooled cf. (CR. Jun.6; 236) Lire 240,000

NIBELUNGE, Die
Ill.:– J. Sattler. Berlin, 1898-1904. *(30) De Luxe Edn. on Jap.* Lge. fo. Hand-bnd. mor. by Rudolf Lang, Müchen, gt. spine, covers, inner & outer dentelles. (H. Nov.24; 1998) DM 7,000

NIBELUNGEN, Die
Ed.:– F. Keim. Ill.:– C. Czeschka. Wien & Leipzig, [1909]. *1st. Edn.* Orig. linen, slightly soiled. (HK. May 17; 2662) DM 620
- - **Anr. Edn.** Ed.:– F. Keim. Ill.:– C.O. Czeschka. Wien & Leipzig, [1920]. *2nd. Edn.* Orig. hf. linen, slightly soiled. (HK. Nov.11; 3485) DM 550
- - **Anr. Edn.** Ed.:– Fr. Keim. Ill.:– C.O. Czeschka. Wien & Leipzig, 1920. Orig. hf. linen. (GB. May 5; 2310) DM 480

NIBELUNGENLIED
Trans.:– G.O. Marbach. Leipzig, 1840 [-41]. *De Luxe Edn.* Lge. 4to. With subscriber list & owners lf. at front (name erased), cont. hf. leath. gt.,

rubbed. (*With:*) **NIBELUNGEN NOTH** Ed.:– G. Pfizer, 1843. *1st. Edn.* 4to. Some light spotting, 4 steel engrs. bnd. at front (foxed, cont. hf. leath. gt., slightly bumped & loose. (R. Apr.3; 378) DM 500
- - **Anr. Edn.** Trans.:– G.O. Marbach. Ill.:– Bendemann, Hübner, Rethel & Stilke. Leipzig, 1840 [-41]. *1st. Edn. with these ills.* Lge. 4to. Subscribers list, cont. hf. leath. gt. (GB. Nov.4; 1859) DM 470
- - **Anr. Copy.** 4to. Browned at beginning & end, cont. red mor. gt., worn & bumped; Hauswedell coll. (H. May 24; 1490) DM 400
- - **Anr. Edn.** Ed.:– H. Engels. [L. & Stuttgart, 1968]. *(500).* Facs. of MS. C from Fürstenberg Court Liby. Donaueschingen & text vol. Handbnd. orig. pig & hf. leath. (H. Nov.23; 93) DM 520

NICCOLS, Richard
- London's Artillery, Briefly Containing the Noble Practise of that Worthie Societie: With the Moderne & Ancient Martiall Excrises, Natures of Armes, Vertue of Magistrates, Antiquitie, Glorie & Chronography of this Honourable Citie. [By R.N.]. [1616]. Sm. 4to. Title a little soiled, with slight tear reprd. & presumably date cut off foot of title, headline shaved on several ll., cf. gt. [STC 18522] (LC. Mar.1; 373) £500

NICHOLLS, W.H.
- Orchids of Australia. Melbourne, 1969. *Compl. Edn.* 4to. Bdg. not stated, d.-w. slightly defect. (KH. May 1; 531) Aus. $280
- - **Anr. Edn.** Ed.:– D.L. Jones & T.B. Muir. Melbourne, 1969. *Compl. Edn.* 4to. Orig. cl., d.-w. (KH. Nov.9; 674) Aus. $230

NICHOLS, John, Publisher & author
- Bibliotheca Topographica Britannica. L., priv. ptd., 1780-90. 8 vols. only (of 10). 4to. Cont. tree cf., spines gt., w.a.f. (C. Nov.16; 22) *Traylen.* £800
- The History & Antiquities of Appleby Magna & Parva, Orton on the Hill & Norton, in the Sparkenhoe Hundred. 1810. Fo. Cl. (HBC. May 17; 327) £67
- The History & Antiquities of the County of Leicester. 1971. *Facs. of 1795-1811 Edn.* 4 vols. in 8. Fo. Orig. cl. gt. (TA. Nov.17; 182) £195

NICHOLS, John & Bowyer, William
- Literary Anecdotes of the Eighteenth Century. 1812-15. 9 vols. Some spotting, cont. gt.-panel. cf., most spines worn. (TA. Jul.19; 386) £58

NICHOLS, Thomas L.
- A Biography of the Brothers Davenport. 1865. Orig. cl.; sigd. & inscr. by Harry Houdini to Sir Arthur Conan Doyle, 10 May 1922, with Conan Doyle's ownership inscr., as an association copy, w.a.f. (S. Nov.8; 427) *Lionheart.* £190

NICHOLSON, Benedict
- Hendrick Terbrugghen. L., 1958. No bdg. stated. (SPB. Nov.30; 151) $500

NICHOLSON, Francis
- The Practice of Drawing & Painting Landscape from Nature. L., 1823. *2nd. Edn.* 4to. 17 litho. plts., including 2 hand-cold., some spotting & staining, cont. cf. gt., rubbed & crudely reprd. (S. Dec.13; 469) *Hetherington.* £60
- - **Anr. Copy.** 4to. Litho. plts., 2 hand-cold., a few spots & stains, cont. cf. gt., rubbed & reprd. (S. Apr.30; 212) *Aust. Nat. Gall.* £50

NICHOLSON, George
- Dictionnaire Pratique d'Horticulture et de Jardinage. Paris, 1892-93. 5 vols. 4to. Hf. chagrin, worn. (SM. Mar.7; 2524) Frs. 3,200

NICHOLSON, John
- The Operative Mechanic, & British Machinist ... L., 1825. *1st. Edn.* Spotting & foxing, crossings out at head of title, notes on frontis., hf. mor., worn; Frederick Brodie bkplt., Stanitz coll. (SPB. Apr.25; 328) $200

NICHOLSON, Peter
- The Carpenter's New Guide. 1808. 78 engraved plts., light foxing, bookseller's advts. bnd. in. (*With:*) - The Carpenter & Joiner's Assistant. 1822. 79 engraved plts. (6 folding). Together 2 vols.

4to. Unif. cont. tree cf., rebkd. with new spines & end-papers. (SKC. Mar.9; 1912) £75
- **A New & Improved Dictionary of the Science & Practice of Architecture Building etc** ... Ed.:– E. Lomax & T. Gunyon. [1852]. 2 vols. 4to. Cont. panel. cf. gt. (PD. Feb.15; 171) £90
[–] **The New Practical Builder, & Workman's Companion** ... L., 1823. *1st. Edn.* Lge. 4to. Some plts. & text lightly foxed or browned, diced cf., ornamental gt. rules, covers detchd. with wear & scuffing at edges, front & rear blanks detchd., backstrip intact with much wear. (HA. May 4; 324) $120

NICHOLSON, William, 1785-1845
- **The History of the Late Wars occasioned by the French Revolution.** L., ca. 1816. Fo. Frontis., cold. plts., some soiling, cf., defect., w.a.f. (S. Apr.10; 376) *Marshall.* £130
– – **Anr. Edn.** N.d. Fo. 21 hand-cold. engraved plts., 1 torn & reprd., cont. cf., worn, w.a.f. (CSK. Oct.21; 93) £100

NICHOLSON, William, Artist
- **An Almanac of Twelve Sports.** Text:– Rudyard Kipling. 1898 [1897]. *[Liby. Edn.].* 4to. Vell.-bkd. bds., soiled. (CSK. Nov.4; 63) £170
– – **Anr. Copy.** 4to. Woodcut title, 12 cold. woodcuts, orig. pict. bds., shaken. (P. May 17; 143) *Edistar.* £100
– – **Anr. Copy.** 4to. Orig. cl.-bkd. bds. (BBA. Oct.27; 185) *Primrose Hill.* £80
– – **Anr. Edn.** L., 1898. 4to. 12 cold. plts., orig. pict. bds., soiled. (P. May 17; 274) *Edistar.* £120
– – **Anr. Copy.** 4to. Some spotting, orig. pict. bds. (P. Sep.29; 13) *Edistar.* £90
– – **Anr. Copy.** 4to. Some browning, orig. bds., worn. (CSK. Jun.15; 32) £75
- **An Alphabet.** [L.], 1898 [1897]. 4to. 26 cold. plts., orig. cl.-bkd. bds., rubbed. (BBA. May 23; 226) *Nudelman.* £130
– – **Anr. Edn.** 1898. 4to. Lacks part. of end-paper, orig. bds., spine torn, soiled. (P. Sep.8; 11) *Edistar.* £160
– – **Anr. Copy.** 4to. Title, 26 plts., orig. pict. bds., soiled. (P. Oct.20; 40) £130
– – **Anr. Copy.** 4to. Orig. cl.-bkd. bds., soiled. (BBA. Oct.27; 186) *Primrose Hill.* £100
– – **Anr. Copy.** 4to. Orig. pict. hf. linen, slightly spotted, free end-paper recto browned. (GB. Nov.5; 3185) DM 750
– – **Anr. Edn.** N.Y., 1898. 4to. Pict. bds., covers slightly soiled. (RO. Dec.11; 251) $140
– – **Anr. Edn.** 1899. 4to. Orig. cl.-bkd. pict. bds.; van Veen coll. (S. Feb. 28; 12) £140
– – **Anr. Edn.** L., 1899. *3rd. Imp.* 4to. 26 cold. litho. plts., orig. cl.-bkd. bds., soiled. (CSK. Feb.24; 105) £130
- **Douze Portraits.** [Paris, 1899]. *(100).* Fo. Slightly foxed, 12 cold. woodcuts mntd. on bds., loose ll. in orig. linen portfo., rubbed. (GB. May 5; 3033) DM 1,400
- **London Types.** L., 1898. 4to. 12 plts., orig. bds., soiled. (P. Nov.24; 39) *Ayres.* £100
– – **Anr. Copy.** 4to. Orig. pict. hf. linen, end-papers browned. (GB. May 5; 3032) DM 600
- **Twelve Portraits.** N.d. *[Liby. Edn.].* Fo. 10 litho. plts. only, mntd. on bd., 1 browned, unbnd. as iss. in orig. cl. portfo., worn & soiled, w.a.f. (CSK. Jan.27; 29) £140

NICHOLSON, William, Scientist
- **An Introduction to Natural Philosophy.** L., 1782. *1st. Edn.* 2 vols. Lacks hf.-titles, outer part of 1 plt. soiled, cont. cf., spines gt., rebkd. preserving orig. spines, corners worn; Stanitz coll. (SPB. Apr.25; 327) $175

NICOL, John
- **The Life & Adventures of** ... Ed.:– John Howell. Edinb., 1822. *1st. Edn.* 12mo. Lacks hf.-title, cont. wicker pattern cf. gt., lacks 1st. compartment of spine; the Rt. Hon. Visc. Eccles copy. [Sabin 55241] (CNY. Nov.18; 208) $220
– – **Anr. Copy.** 12mo. Lacks hf.-title, sm. margin defect to port., 1 lf. detchd., old hf. cf., worn; the Rt. Hon. Visc. Eccles copy. [Sabin 55241] (CNY. Nov.18; 209) $150

NICOL, Walter
- **The Scotch Forcing Gardener ... together with Instructions on the Management to the Greenhouse,**

Hot Walls, etc ... Edinb., 1797. Some foxing, cont. hf. cf. (PD. Dec.14; 256) £90

NICOLAI, Chr. Friedrich
- **Geschichte eines Dicken Mannes worin drey Heurathen und drey Körbe nebst viel Liebe.** Ill.:– J.W. Meil. Berlin & Stettin, 1794. *1st. Edn.* 2 vols. Private red mor., gold-tooled decor., gt. inner & outer dentelle. (D. Nov.24; 2317) DM 780

NICOLAY, Jean
- **L'Art et la Manière des Maîtres Ebénistes Français du XVIIIe. Siècle.** Paris, 1956. 2 vols. 4to. Publisher's cl. (SM. Mar.7; 2188) Frs. 1,100

NICOLAY D'ARFEUILLE, Nicolas de
- **La Navigation du Roy d'Ecosse Jacques Cinquiesme ... autour de son Royaume & Iles Hebrides & Orchades.** Paris, 1583. 4to. Inserted slip with diagram, mod. cl. (BBA. Jan.19; 6) *Braunschweig.* £280.
- **Le Navigationi et Viaggi nella Turchia.** Ill.:– Antonij van Leest & others. Antw., 1577. Sm. 4to. Title slightly defect. & laid down to size, 4 ll. rehinged affecting some text of 2 ll., lacks final blank, mod. red hf. mor. (C. May 30; 39) £380
- **Les Quatre Premiers Livres des Navigations et Peregrinations Orientales.** Lyon, 1568. *1st. Edn. 2nd. Printing.* Lge. 4to. Title & 1st. ll. with lge. faults reprd., stained or soiled thro.-out, plts. partly with bkd. tear or faults, very defect., 6 costume plts. from unr. work bnd. at end, 17th. C. leath. gt., gold-tooled, lightly rubbed & spotted, slightly torn. (HT. May 8; 190) DM 850

NICOLE, Pierre
- **Pensées de Nicole, de Port-Royal.** Paris, 1806. 12mo. On vell., hf.-title, 2 ll. publisher's advt., orig. parch., unc., cont. roan-bkd. bd. pull-off case. (C. May 30; 92) *Lyon.* £100

NICOLL, Michael J.
- **Birds of Egypt.** Ed.:– Col. R. Meinertzhagen. 1930. 2 vols. 4to. Orig. cl. (CSK. Oct.7; 106) £200
– – **Anr. Copy.** 2 vols. 4to. Hf. cf. (SPB. Dec.13; 598) $125

NICOLSON, Bartholomaeus
[–] **Essai sur l'histoire naturelle de l'isle de Saint-Domingue.** Paris, 1776. Additional title, 10 folding plts., slightly spotted, cont. cf., rubbed. [Sabin 55259] (S. Jun.25; 111) *Kossow.* £300

NICOLSON, Harold
- **The English Sense of Humour.** 1947. *(550)* numbered. *(25)* sigd. & specially bnd. 4to. Qtr. vell. & buckram, unc. (HBC. May 17; 170) £70

NICOLSON, Bp. William
- **The English, Scotch & Irish Historical Libraries, giving a Short Account of Most of Our Historians, either in Print or Manuscript.** L., 1776. *New Edn.* 4 pts. in 1 vol. Lge. 4to. Very foxed & stained, cont. cf., rebkd. (SG. Sep.15; 248) $100

NIDER, Johannes
- **Consolatorium Conscientie.** [Paris], Jehan Petit, ca. 1495. Full-p. printers mark, washed, mod. black mor., gt. lined, inner dentelle, silk doubls. (VG. May 3; 495) Fls. 3,000
- **Praeceptorium Divinae Legis, sive Expositio Decalogi.** [Paris, Ulrich Gering]. not before 1483. 4to. 231 ll. (of 238, lacks initial blank & last 6 ll.), initials supplies in red or blue, sm. hole in lst. lf. with slight loss of text, margin cut away from E8 with no damage to text, a few stains, cont. marginalia, mod. qtr. sheep. [Goff N211] (S. Nov.17; 52) *Tzakas.* £180
– – **Anr. Edn.** Paris, 14.1.1515. 4to. Stained, cont. blind-tooled leath., restored, end-papers renewed. (HK. Nov.8; 295) DM 400
- **Sermones de Tempore. Sermones de Sanctis cum Quadragesimali.** Esslingen, Konrad Fyner, ca. 1477-79. Fo. Rubricated, capitals painted, many words underlined in red, cont. stpd. pig over wood bds., richly decor., cornerpieces & clasps, trace of bosses; from Fondation Furstenberg-Beaumesnil. [BMC II, 517: Goff N215] (HD. Nov.16; 24) Frs. 13,500

NIEBUHR, Carsten
- **Beschreibung von Arabien.** Kopenhagen & Leipzig, 1772. *1st. Edn.* 4to. Title with MS. owners mark, old notes on prelim. lf., 1 plt. & map with sm. tear, some margin annots., some browning & foxing, mostly in margins, cont. cf., slightly bumped & worn. (H. May 22; 282) DM 2,200
- **Beachryving van Arabie.** Amst. & Utrecht, 1774. Some stains, blank wraps., unc. (B. Jun.21; 446) Fls. 500
- **Description de l'Arabie.** Trans.:– Mourier. Kopenhagen, 1773. *1st. Fr. Edn.* 4to. Cont. leath. gt., rubbed, corners bumped, upr. jnts. brkn. (R. Oct.13, 2999) DM 750
- **Reize near Arabie en Omliggende Landen.** Ill.:– C. Philips, C.F. Fritsch, C.J. de Huyser & others. Amst. & Utr., 1776-80. *1st. Dutch Edn.* 2 vols. 4to. Engraved titles, 7 folding engraved maps, 31 folding plts. & views & 86 engraved plts., some foxing & slight margin stains cont. hf. cf., chintz on covers not cont. (VS. Jun.7; 1019) Fls. 1,100

NIECAMPIUS, Jean Lucas
- **Historia Missionis Evangelicae in India Orientali.** Trans.:– I.H. Grischovius. Halle, 1747. 4to. Browned, cont. cf., defect. (VG. Mar.19; 218) Fls. 650

NIEL, P.G.J.
- **Portraits des Personnages Français les plus Illustres du XVI Siècle.** Paris, 1848-56. 2 vols. in 1. Fo. Some ports. lightly spotted, cont. mor. gt., rubbed. (CSK. Jun.1; 28) £85

NIELSEN, Kay (Ill.)
See— ASBJORNSEN, Peter Christen & Moe, Jorgen I.

NIELSEN, Lauritz
- **Dansk Bibliografi.** Copen., 1919-35. 2 Series (1482-1550, 1551-1600) in 9 fascicules, & 2 vol. Register. Sm. fo. Ptd. wraps., unc. & unopened. (*With:*) - **Boghistoriske Studier till Dansk Bibliografi, 1550-1600.** 1923. 1 vol. 4to. Ptd. wraps., detchd. (SG. Sep.15; 249) $225
- **Dansk Biografi 1482-1600.** Kopenhagen, 1919-23. 3 vols. 4to. Private hf. mor. (D. Nov.23; 275) DM 660

NIEPELT, W.
- **Lepidoptera Niepeltiana.** Leipzig, 1914. 4to. Cl., orig. wraps. bnd. in; pres. copy from author. (SKC. Oct.26; 418) £50

NIETZSCHE, Friedrich
- **Also Sprach Zarathustra.** Leipzig, [1886-]91. 4 vols. in 2 (Vols. I-III in 1 vol.). Orig. wraps., Vol. IV loose, mor. book-box. (S. Oct.11; 570) *Rota.* £110
– – **Anr. Edn.** Ill.:– Van de Velde. Leipzig, 1908. *(100) De Luxe Edn.* Sm. fo. Ptd. title with slight offset of double title & with 3 cold stains, some foxing, orig. mor., gold-tooled vig. on upr. cover & gold-tooled spine title, corners slightly bumped, light scratching on upr. cover. (H. Nov.24; 2159) DM 3,500
– – **Anr. Copy.** Fo. Some foxing, orig. leath, gt. spine & lr. cover, slightly rubbed. (HK. Nov.11; 4037) DM 1,700
– – **Anr. Edn.** Ill.:– H. van de Vekle. Leipzig, 1908. *(530) numbered.* Fo. Orig. vell. gt., slightly rubbed. (HK. May 17; 3194) DM 1,900
– – **Anr. Edn.** Ill.:– Henry van de Velde. Leipzig, 1908. *(530) numbered on Van-Gelder-Bütten.* Fo. Light foxing in upr. & lr. margin at beginning & end, orig. vell. (R. Oct.11; 361) DM 1,200
- **The Antichrist.** Trans.:– P.R. Stephenson. Ill.:– Norman Lindsay. L., Fanfrolico Pr., [1928]. *(550) numbered on Arnold's H.M.P.* Sm. fo. Hf. mor., partly unc., rubbed. (SG. Mar.29; 140) $175
- **Le Chant de la Nuit.** Trans.:– Jacques Arnold. Ill.:– Pierre-Yves Trémois. Paris, 1977. *(166). (130) on Rives sigd. by artist.* Fo. 12 orig. ills., leaves, decor. wrap. box. (HD. Dec.16; 164) Frs. 2,350
- **Dionysos Dithyramben.** Ill.:– Van de Velde. [Leipzig, 1914]. *(130) on Bütten.* Sm. 4to. Hand-bnd. red-brown orig. mor., gold decor., gold-tooled cover ill., some light rubbing, 1 outer dentelle with sm. fault. (H. Nov.24; 2160) DM 4,100
– – **Anr. Copy.** Sm. fo. Orig. wraps., slightly foxed. (VG. Sep.13; 304) Fls. 450

NIETZSCHE, Friedrich -Contd.

- **Ecce Homo.** Ill.:– H. van de Velde. [Leipzig, 1908]. *(50) De Luxe Edn. on japan.* Sm. 4to. Orig. suede, light spotting, end-papers partly mis-cold., engraved ex-libris inside cover. (H. May 23; 1444) DM 2,200

- – **Anr. Edn.** Ill.:– Van de Velde. [Leipzig, 1908]. *(150) De Luxe Edn. on Japan.* Sm. 4to. Decor. double title, many gold vigs., chapter heads, early ll. & end-ll. gold ptd., some sm. foxing in end-ll., 1 end-lf. crumpled, ex-libris inside cover, orig. suede, gold ptd., slightly rubbed, spine faded. (H. Nov.24; 2161) DM 840

- – **Anr. Edn.** Ill.:– H. van de Velde. Leipzig, [1908]. *(1250) numbered.* Sm. 4to. Orig. hf. vell. (R. Oct.11; 362) DM 400

- **Gesammelte Werke.** München, 1922-29. *Musarion Edn. (185) numbered.* 23 vols. On Hadernpaper, orig. vell., gold decor. by Hübel & Denck, some light spotting. (R. Apr.3; 380) DM 2,300

- – **Anr. Edn.** München, [1922-29]. *Musarion Edn. (1500) numbered.* 23 vols. Orig. hf. leath., some slight rubbing, w.a.f. (HK. May 16; 2188) DM 1,600

- **Gesammelte Werke.** München, [1922-29]. *Musarion Edn. (1600) numbered.* 23 vols. Vols. 1-12 leath. by O. Dorfner, Leipzig, gt. spine, cover & inner dentelle, some corners bumped, from vol. 13 on interim bds., some spine defects. (HK. Nov.10; 2630) DM 1,300

- – **Anr. Edn.** München, 1922-29. 22 (of 23) vols., lacks vol. 16. Orig. hf. leath., rubbed. (R. Oct.11; 360a) DM 750

- **Unzeitgemässe Betrachtungen.** Leipzig, 1873-74. *1st. Edn.* 3 pts. in 1 vol. Margins slightly browned, cont. hf. leath. gt., rubbed, corners bumped. (HK. Nov.10; 2631) DM 700

- **Werke.** Leipzig, 1901-06 (vols. 8-14) & Leipzig, 1910-17. 3 pts. with 19 vols. Orig. hf. leath., spine slightly rubbed. (H. Nov.24; 1900) DM 460

NIEUHOFF, Jean

- **L'Ambassade de la Cie Orientale des Provinces Unies vers l'Empereur ou Grand Cam de Tartarie faite par les Sieurs Pieer de Coyer et Jean de Keyser.** Trans.:– Jean de Carpentier. Leiden, 1665. 2 pts. in 1 vol. Fo. 19th. C. hf. roan. (HD. Feb.22; 157) Frs. 9,000

- **L'Ambassade de la Compagnie Orientale des Provinces Unies vers l'Empereur de la Chine.** Leiden, 1665. *1st. Edn. in Fr.* 2 pts. in 1 vol. Fo. Additional engraved title, title in red & black with engraved vig., double-p. folding engraved map, 34 (only, of 35) double-p. engraved views, many engraved ills., lacks port., map browned & sm. tears at fold, minor tears & dampstain to some margins, cont. spr. cf., worn at head & foot of spine. (C. Jun.27; 51) *Campbell.* £320

- **An Embassy from the East India Company ... to the ... Emperor of China.** L., 1669. *1st. Edn. in Engl.* Fo. Lge. copy, medieval MS. sewing guards, cont. cf., slightly worn. (BBA. Sep.29; 82) *Traylen.* £470

- – **Anr. Edn.** Trans.:– John Ogilby. L., priv. ptd., 1673. *2nd. Edn. in Engl.* Fo. Engraved frontis., 22 engraved maps & plts., some double-p., cont. mott. cf., covers gt.-panel., spine gt. [Wing N 1153] (C. Nov.16; 23) *Maggs.* £700

- **Het Gezantschap der Neerlandtsche Oost-Indische Compagnie.** Amst., 1665. Fo. 2 engraved arms, engraved port., map, 34 (of 35) double-p. plts., map torn with slight loss, a few margin tears, some staining or spotting, 2 ll. at front loose, cont. cf., worn. (S. Jun.25; 45) *Browning.* £320

- – **Anr. Edn.** Antw., 1666. Fo. Additional engraved title, folding map, 32 (of 33) double-p. plts., lacks port., engraved title laid down, spotted & stained, cont. cf., rubbed, rebkd. (S. Jun.25; 44) *Schure.* £160

- **Legatio Batavia ad Magnum Tartariae Chamum Sungteium, Modernum Sinae Imperatorem.** Trans.:– G. Hornius. Amst., 1668. *1st. Latin Edn.* Fo. Cont. vell., gold-tooled decor., lge. gold-tooled centrepiece, 4 corner fleurons à la Du Seuil, gt. spine, orig. silk ties. (D. Nov.23; 858) DM 5,200

NIEUW GROOT A/B/C/ BOEK
Zutphen, ca. 1840. Sm. 8vo. Old wraps. (VG. Mar.21; 410) Fls. 500

NIGER, Franciscus

- **Ars Epistolandi.** [Augsburg, J. Schoensperger], 1499. Sm. 4to. Wide margin, mod. qtr. cf. [BMC II, 374; Goff N-252; H. 1188] (SG. Nov.3; 155) $800

NIGHTINGALE, Florence

- **Notes on Nursing: What it is, & what it is not.** L., n.d. Limp cl., minor wear; early sig. C. (?) McKie, Melbourne Hospital, sigd-pres. envelope from author tipped in. (KH. Nov.9; 371) Aus. $110

NIGNON, Edouard

- **Eloges de la Cuisine Française.** Ill.:– Pierre Courtois. Paris, [1933]. Lge. 8vo. Some slight foxing, lev., gt. borders & spine, orig. wraps. bnd. in. (SG. Feb.16; 134) $100

- **Les Plaisirs de la Table.** Preface:– R. de Flers. Ill.:– P.F. Grignon. Paris, priv. ptd., [1930]. *Orig. Edn.* Sm. 4to. On papier vergé, lightly tinted, sewed. (HD. May 16; 89) Frs. 2,050

- – **Anr. Edn.** Preface:– R. de Flers. Ill.:– P.F. Grignon. Paris, priv. ptd., 1930. *2nd. Edn.* Sewed, decor. wrap. (HD. May 4; 376) Frs. 1,000

NIGRINUS [SCHWARTZ], G.

- **Apocalypsis, das ist: Die Offenbarung S. Johannis dess Aposteln u. Evangelisten ... Erkläret u. Aussgelegt.** Frankfurt, 1593. 4to. Some staining &/or browning in text, cont. vell. (VG. Sep.14; 1346) Fls. 550

NIHELL, James
See— TISSOT, Samuel Auguste Andre – NIHELL, James

NIJHOFF, Wouter & Kronenberg, M.E.

- **Nederlandsche Bibliographie van 1500 tot 1540.** 's-Gravenhage, 1923-61. 3 vols. in 5. Hf. chagrin. (LM. Oct.22; 178) B. Frs. 11,000

- – **Anr. Edn.** 's-Gravenhage, 1923-71. 5 vols. (all publd.) Pencil underlinings, 3 vols. hf. mor. & wraps. (VG. May 3; 171) Fls. 520

- – **Anr. Copy.** Pts. I-III & V (all publd.) in 8 vols. 1st. 6 vols. hf. mor., last 2 vols. wraps. (VG. Sep.13; 560) Fls. 500

NILSSON, Sven

- **Illuminerade Figurer till Skandinaviens Fauna.** Ill.:– Magnus P. Korner. Lund, [1829-]32-40. 2 vols. 4to. 200 hand-cold, litho. plts., including 163 of birds (bnd. together at end of 2nd. vol.), some plts. slightly discold., some spotting of text, mod. hf. mor. gt., unc., orig. wraps. to the 20 pts. bnd. at end of Vol. 1. (S. Nov.28; 72) *Hagelin.* £1,900

- **Ornithologia Suecica.** Copen., 1817-21. 2 vols. 12 hand-cold. engraved plts., some text ll. browned, cl.-bkd. bds., slightly worn. (S. Apr.10; 437) *Evans.* £230

NIMROD (Pseud.)
See— APPERLEY, Capt. Charles James 'Nimrod'

NIN, Anais

- **D.H. Lawrence: An Unprofessional Study.** Paris, 1932. *(500) numbered.* Sm. 8vo. Cl., d.-w.; inscr. by author to Mrs. Mabel Scott. (SG. Mar.1; 380) $400

- – **Anr. Copy.** Sm. 8vo. This copy out-of-series, marked 'Complimentary Copy', cl., unopened, d.-w. worn. (SG. May 24; 123) $120

- **The House of Incest.** Paris, [1936]. *(249) numbered.* Lge. 8vo. Ptd. wraps.; inscr. (SG. Mar.1; 375) $150

- **Under a Glass Bell.** Ill.:– Ian Hugo. [N.Y., Gemor Pr., 1944]. *(300).* Engraved pict. bds., worn; inscr. by author, sigd. by artist. (SG. Mar.1; 384) $110

- **Winter of Artifice.** Ill.:– Ian Hugo. N.Y., [Anais Nin, 1942]. *(500).* Pict. bds.; inscr. by author to Caresse Crosby. (SG. Mar.1; 385) $500

NISBET, Alexander

- **A System of Heraldry.** Edinb., 1722-42. *1st. Edn.* 2 vols. Fo. Engraved plts., some spotting & browning, red mor., gt. (S. Apr.10; 377) *Traylen.* £110

- – **Anr. Copy.** 2 vols. Fo. 45 engraved plts., 1 plt. reprd., 1 defect., cont. cf., worn; Sir Ivar Colquhoun, of Luss copy. (CE. Mar.22; 228a) £100

- – **Anr. Edn.** Edinb., 1816. 2 vols. Fo. Some plts.

browned, cont. cf., rebkd., old spines preserved, rubbed. (CSK. May 18; 164) £55

NISSEN, Claus

- **Die Botanische Buchillustration, Ihre Geschichte & Bibliographie.** Stuttgart, 1951. 2 vols. in 1. Orig. decor. cl., slightly rubbed. (TA. Dec.15; 301) £120

- **Die Zoologische Buchillustration. Ihre Bibliographie und Geschichte.** Stuttgart, 1969-78. 2 vols. Lge. 8vo. Cl., Vol. 2 in quires as iss. (VS. Dec.7; 338) Fls. 450

NISTER, Ernest

- **What the Children Like.** L. & N.Y., n.d. Lge. 4to. 5 double-p. chromolitho. 'pop-up' plts., light soiling, orig. cl.-bkd. pict. bds., soiled, lightly rubbed. (CSK. Jan.13; 128) £110

NITSCHKE, A
See— MANN, G. & others

NITZSCHEWITZ, Herm.

- **Nouum Beatae Marie Virgis Psalterium.** N.P., ca. 1494-95. 4to. Wide margin, lacks 27 ll. (supplied in xerox, title & next 7 ll. stpd., slight margin worming, some ll. lightly browned & slight margin stains, early 19th. C. marb. bds., decor., slightly bumped. [Hain 11891. BMC III 700; Goff N260] (HK. May 15; 207) DM 21,000

NIVERNOIS (Le)
Text:– J.N. Morellet, Barat & E. Bussière. Nevers, 1838-40. 2 vols. 4to. 120 litho. plts. on china, some worm-holes, cont. hf. chagrin, spines decor., 1 turn-in slightly defect. (HD. Jun.22; 62) Frs. 4,300

NIXON, Right Rev. Francis R.

- **The Cruise of the Beacon, A Narrative of a Visit to the Islands in Bass's Straits.** L., 1857. Orig. bds. gt., covers worn & stained. (CA. Apr.3; 143) Aus. $160

- – **Anr. Copy.** Orig. cl., slightly shaken, unc. (KH. Nov.9; 372) Aus. $120

NIXON, Howard M.

- **Broxbourne Library. Styles & Designs of Bookbindings from the twelfth to the twentieth century.** 1956. *(300).* 4to. Specially bnd. for author in alumtawed pig from Hewitt's of Scotland, by Peter Waters of Gaithersburg, Maryland, 12 lines of title repeated in blind on covers over gt. rules, spine ribbed, cl. box, H.M. Nixon coll. (BBA. Oct.6; 104) *Kokoro.* £1,500

- – **Anr. Copy.** 4to. Orig. vell.-bkd. cl. (S. May 1; 424) *Dreesman.* £900

- – **Anr. Copy.** 4to. Orig. qtr. parch. (S. Oct.4; 226) *Forster.* £700

- **Sixteenth-Century Gold-Tooled Bookbindings in the Pierpont Morgan Library.** N.Y., 1971. 4to. Page proofs, heavily corrected by Nixon, plts., unbnd.; H.M. Nixon coll. (BBA. Oct.6; 105) *Goldschmidt.* £240

NOAH, Mordecai M.

- **Travels in England, France, Spain, & the Barbary States, in the Years 1813-14 & 15.** N.Y. & L., 1819. Some foxing, cont. cf., worn, upr. cover wormed. (RO. Jun.26; 134) $110

NOAILLES, Anna-Elisabeth de Brancovan, Comtesse de

- **Les Vivants et les Morts.** Paris, 1913. *Orig. Edn. (60) on holland paper.* Mor., gt. decor., decor. spine, rep doubls. & end-papers, wrap. & spine preserved, s.-c., by Franz. (HD. Dec.9; 163) Frs. 1,900

NOBBES, Robert

- **[-] The Compleat Troller.** L., 1682. [Ca. 1790]. *Facs. reprint.* 12mo. Some ll. spotted, 19th. C. cf.-bkd. cl. (BBA. May 3; 222) *Quaritch.* £170

NOBLE, Charles Frederick

- **A Voyage to the East-Indies in 1747 & 1748.** L., 1762. 11 engraved plts. (1 folding), sm. hole in O2 & Q6 slightly affecting 2 words, cont. cf., rubbed, spine ends worn. (C. Mar.14; 73) *Thorp.* £260

NOCQ, Henry

- **Le Poinçon de Paris.** Paris, 1926-31. *(600).* 5 vols., including Index. 4to. Some plts. hand-cold., orig. wraps. (VG. Sep.13; 679) Fls. 1,100

– – **Anr. Edn.** Paris, 1968. *(400) numbered.* 5 vols. 4to. Some plts. hand-cold., orig. cl. (VS. Jun.6; 102)　　　　　　　　　　　　　　　　　Fls. 825

NOCQ, Henry & Dreyfus, Carle
– Tabatières, Bôites et Etuis: Orfevreries de Paris, XVIIIe Siècle et Début du XIXe, des Collections du Musée du Louvre. Paris, 1930. Sm. fo. 88 plts., orig. wraps., disbnd. (SG. Aug.25; 340)　　　　　$120

NODDER, Frederick P.
See– SHAW, George & Nodder, Frederick P.

NODE, Pierre
– Declamation contre l'erreur Execrable des Maleficiers, Sorciers, Magiciens, Deuins, & Semblable, Obseruateurs des Superstitions. Parigi, 1579. *1st. Edn.* Light staining, 2 stps. & cancelled sig. on frontis., cont. vell., discold. (SI. Dec.15; 28)
　　　　　　　　　　　　　　　　　Lire 420,000

NODIER, Charles
– Le Bibliomane. Ill.:– F. Noel after Maurice Leloir. Paris, 1893. *(500). (150) numbered on papier de chine et japon, initialled by publisher. (80) with dupl. set of woodcuts.* This copy on japon, dupl. suite bnd. next to each ill. on a full-size sheet, str.-grd. hf. mor. gt. by Carayon, smooth spine gt.-lettered & with gt. dentelle design, unc., corners slightly rubbed, orig. ptd. wraps. & spine preserved; Robert Hoe & Raphael Esmerian bkplts. (CNY. May 18; 195)　　　　　　　　　　　$650
– – **Anr. Edn.** Ill.:– M. Leloir, wood engraved by F. Noël. Paris, 1893. *(500).* Lavallière mor. by Gruel, gt. mosaic, decor. spine, mor. doubl., watered silk end ll., wrap. preserved; from Mrs. F. Watters & F. Kettenach libys., former's cypher on upr. cover. (HD. Dec.9; 164)　　　　　　　　Frs. 3,100
– Contes ... Ill.:– Tony Johannot. Paris, 1846. *1st. Printing.* Lge. 8vo. Etchings before the letter, hf. mor., corners, by Canapé, spine decor., unc. (HD. May 4; 378)　　　　　　　　　　　Frs. 2,500
– Histoire du Roi de Bohème et de ses Sept Châteaux. Ill.:– Tony Johannot, engraved by Porret. Paris, 1830. *Orig. Edn. 1st. Printing of vigs.* Washed, cf. by Duplanil, blind– & gt.-decor. (HD. May 4; 377)　　　　　　　　　Frs. 2,600
– Journal de l'Expédition des Portes de Fer. Ill.:– Raffet, Decamps & Dauzats. Paris, 1844. Publishers bds. (HD. Dec.16; 29)　　　　Frs. 2,100
– Le Légende de Soeur Béatrix. Ill.:– Henri Caruchet. Paris, 1903. *De Luxe Edn. (150) on japan, with separate printing of engrs. in black.* Bradel hf. mor., corners, by Champs, unc., wrap. & spine preserved. (HD. Apr.26; 51)　　　Frs. 1,100
– La Seine et ses Bords. Ill.:– after Marville & Foussereau. Paris, 1836. Sm. 8vo. 4 maps, 46 engraved plts., some margin worming, cont. hf. russ., spine decor. (HD. Mar.19; 111)　Frs. 1,400
– – **Anr. Copy.** Hf. mor., corners, decor. spine. (HD. Apr.11; 48)　　　　　　　　　Frs. 1,000

NODIER, Charles [ie Jean-Charles-Emmanuel]
See– TAYLOR, Bon J., Nodier Charles & Cailleux, A. de

NOE, Comte Amédée-Charles-Henri 'Cham'
– Tribulations des Bains de Mer d'Ostende. Bruges, n.d. Lge. 4to. Romantic cl. bds. by P.G. Zilig of Brussels. (LM. Oct.22; 286)　　B. Frs. 20,000

NOE, Louis Pantaléon Jude Amédée
– Mémoires Relatifs à l'Expédition Anglaise partie du Bengale en 1800, pour Aller Combattre en Egypt l'Armée d'Orient. [Paris,], 1826. Inscr. shaved, 1 folding map torn, pol. cf., rebkd.; sigd. pres. copy. (SG. Sep.22; 231)　　　　　　　　　$175

NOEHDEN, G.H.
– Rabenhorst's Dictionary of the German & English Languages ... Part II German & English. L., 1814. 12mo. Cont. cf., rebkd., very worn; sig. of Nathaniel Bowditch, with many underlinings & MS. table of verbs & nouns in his hand. (PNY. Mar.27; 141)
　　　　　　　　　　　　　　　　　$160

NOEL, E.B. & Clark, J.O.M.
– A History of Tennis. 1924. 2 vols. 4to. Cl., unc.; pres. copy, sigd. by E.B. Noel. (BS. Nov.16; 64)
　　　　　　　　　　　　　　　　　£150

NOEL, Francois
See– COLLECTION DES MORALISTES ANCIENS

NOEL, J.N.A.
– Souvenirs Militaires d'un Officier du Premier Empire. Paris, Nancy, 1895. Hf. cf. (HD. Jan.27; 76)　　　　　　　　　　　　　Frs. 1,500

NOGARET, François Felix
– Le Fond du Sac ... Venice, 1780. 2 vols. 18mo. Cont. marb. cf. gt., spines decor. (*With:*) [–] Cantiques et Pots-pourris. Borel. L. [Paris], 1789. 6 pts. in 1 vol. 18mo. Cont. cf. (HD. May 3; 106)　　　　　　　　　　　Frs. 1,150
– – **Anr. Edn.** Ill.:– J. Garniet & Fesquet, engraved by Champollion. Rouen, 1879. *(354) De Luxe (50) on Chine.* 2 vols. 12mo. Hf. mor., by Champs, corners, wraps & spine preserved, s.-c. (HD. Dec.9; 165)　　　　　　　　　　　Frs. 1,000

NOISAY, Maurice de
– Tableaux Contemporains No. 1: Tableau des Courses. Ill.:– J.L. Boussingault. Paris, 1921. *(315) numbered.* Sm. 4to. Orig. wraps., slightly soiled. (BBA. Jun.14; 190)　　　　*Makiya.* £200

NOISETTE, Louis
– Le Jardin Fruitier. Ill.:– after P. Bessa. Paris, 1839. 2 vols., including plt. vol. 6 (of 8) uncold. engraved plts. in text vol., 152 plts. in plt. vol., all but 5 col.-ptd. & hand-finished, some plts. cropped with lose of ptd. caption, some captions supplied in MS., 1 plt. smudged, mor.-bkd. bds., spines gt. [Nissen 1451 (calling incorrectly for 216 plts.] (C. Nov.16; 283)　　　　　　　　*Shapero.* £650

NOLHAC, Pierre de
– La Dauphine Marie-Antoinette. Paris, 1896. *(1000) numbered.* 4to. Cont. cf. by Cedric Chivers, gt.-embossed. (BBA. Mar.21; 34)　*Duran.* £60
– J.H. Fragonard 1732-1806. Paris, [1904]. *(100) on Japan, with additional boxed suite of plts.* 4to. Red hf. mor., wraps. bnd. in. (PNY. Jun.6; 534)
　　　　　　　　　　　　　　　　　$160
– J.-M. Nattier, Peintre de la cour de Louis XV. Paris, 1905. 4to. On vélin de Rives, 18th. C. style mor. gt. by Durvand, spine decor., wrap. & spine. (HD. May 21; 137)　　　　　Frs. 2,700
– – **Anr. Copy.** 4to. New state, mor. gt. by Richardot, spine decor., wrap. preserved. (HD. Jun.13; 86)　　　　　　　　　　　　Frs. 2,200
– Versailles. – Les Trianons. Paris, ca. 1910. Together 3 vols. (2 + 1). Tall fo. 160 & 110 photo. plts., each liby.-stpd. on blank verso, loose in pict. bds., linen ties. (SG. May 3; 266)　　　$450

NOLLET, Abbé Jean Antoine
– L'Art des Expériences. Paris, 1770. 3 vols. 3 titles stpd., vol. 2 with margin fault bkd., cont. leath. (D. Nov.23; 682)　　　　　　　　　DM 500

NOLLI, Giambattista
– Nuova Pianta di Roma. Roma, 1746. Fo. 19 double-p. engrs., including indices & 10 plts., mod. hf. cf., corners. (CR. Jun.6; 60)　　Lire 2,100,000
– – **Anr. Edn.** N.p., 1748. *1st. Edn.* Fo. 1 plt. crudely reprd., anr. torn without loss to engr., stains, 19th. C. hf. roan; 4 added plts. (3 cold. maps, & view dtd. 1754). (HD. Apr.13; 35)　　　Frs. 2,000

NONESUCH PRESS
– The Nonesuch Century: an Appraisal, a Personal Note & a Bibliography of the first Hundred Books issued by the Press, 1923-1934. Nones. Pr., 1936. *(750) numbered.* Fo. A few pp. creased, orig. buckram, spine faded, slightly marked. (S. Nov.22; 264)　　　　　　　　　　　*Subunso.* £180
– – **Anr. Copy.** Fo. This copy unnumbered & marked 'out-of-series', orig. buckram, spine slightly faded. (S. Nov.22; 263)　　　　*Joseph.* £140
See– BIBLES [English]
See– BIBLIANA [English]
See– BLAKE, William
See– BURTON, Robert 'Democritus Junior'
See– CERVANTES SAAVEDRA, Miguel de
See– CONGREVE, William
See– DANTE ALIGHIERI
See– DARWIN, Bernard & Elinor
See– DICKENS, Charles
See– DRYDEN, John
See– EVELYN, John

See– HARVEY, Dr. William
See– HERODOTUS
See– HOMER
See– MILTON, John
See– MONTAIGNE, Michel Eyquem de
See– PLUTARCH
See– SHAKESPEARE, William
See– VANBRUGH, Sir John
See– WALTON, Isaac
See– WHITE, Gilbert

NOORTHOUCK, J.
– A New History of London, including Westminster & Southwark. L., 1773. 4to. Engraved arms on title, 4 folding maps & plans, including 2 hand-cold., 37 (of 38) plts., some folding, 1 or 2 minor tears at folds without loss of engraved surface, some browning, 19th. C. hf. cf. gt., rubbed. (S. Dec.13; 211)　　　　　　*Haddon.* £140

NOOTKA SOUND
– Official Papers Relative to the Dispute between ... Great Britain & Spain, on the Subject of the Ships Captured in Nootka Sound. L., [1790]. *1st. Edn.* Red hf. mor. by Sangorski & Sutcliffe, unc.; the Rt. Hon. Visc. Eccles copy. [Sabin 56776] (CNY. Nov.18; 210)　　　　　　　　　　$1,600

NORBERT, P. Parisot
– Memorie Storiche intorno alle Missione dell'Indie Orientali. Lucca, 1744. *1st. Italian Edn.* 4to. Some slight browning, title with old MS. owners mark, cont. vell. (D. Nov.23; 1374)　　　DM 900

NORDEN, Friderik Ludwig
[–] Drawings of Some Ruins & Colossal Statues at Thebes in Egypt ... L., 1741. 4to. Old maroon mor. (C. Nov.16; 141)　　　　　*Weinreb.* £220
– Travels in Egypt & Nubia. L., 1757. *[1st. Engl. Edn.].* 2 vols. in 1. Fo. Tall copy, hf.-title, frontis., port., 160 engraved plts. on 158 sheets, cont. hf. cf., worn. (S. May 22; 283)　　*Samiramis.* £550
– – **Anr. Copy.** 2 vols. in 1. Fo. 162 plts., engraved head & tailpieces, some offsetting, red mor., worn; Holland House bkplt. (SPB. May 17; 652)　$550
– Voyage d'Egypte et de Nubie. Paris, 1795-98. 3 vols. 4to. 3 frontis., port., 168 plts. on 165 sheets, some foxing, hf. cf., defect. (P. Dec.8; 284)
　　　　　　　　　　　　　　　　Negro. £190

NORDENSKIOLD, Adolf Erick
– Facsimile-Atlas to the Early History of Cartography with Reproductions of the Most Important Maps Printed in the XV & XVI Centuries. Stockholm, 1889. Fo. Some perforation stps., most plts. hand-stpd. in margins, cl., disbnd., lacks spine, ex-liby. (RO. Dec.11; 254)　　　　　　　$160
– – **Anr. Edn.** Trans.:– J.A. Ekelof & C.P. Markham. [N.Y.], 1961. *Facs. of Stockholm 1889 Edn.* Lge. fo. 51 double-p map reprods. & 84 text ills., orig. linen. (R. Oct.13; 2855)　　　DM 500
– Periplus: an Essay on the Early History of Charts & Sailing-Directions. Trans.:– F.A. Bather. Stockholm, 1897. *1st. Edn.* Atlas fo. Gt.-lettered cl., mor. back & tips. (SG. Jun.7; 149)　　　$450
– – **Anr. Copy.** Lge. fo. Few perforation stps., hand-stpd. on versos, cl., brkn., lacks spine, ex-liby. (RO. Dec.11; 255)　　　　　　　　$160
– – **Anr. Copy.** Lge. fo. Orig. hf. leath., worn. (R. Oct.13; 2856)　　　　　　　　　DM 800
– Voyage de la Vega, autour de l'Asie et de l'Europe. Trans.:– Ch. Rabot & Ch. Lallemand. 1883. 2 vols. Lge. 8vo. Cont. hf. chagrin, corners, spine decor. (HD. Mar.21; 181)　　　　　Frs. 1,100

NORIE, John William
– Plates Descriptive of the Maritime Flags of all Nations. L., 1824. *New Edn.* 20 engraved plts. with numerous hand-cold. figures, some ll. trimmed, cont. hf. cf., worn. (BBA. Dec.15; 336)
　　　　　　　　　　　　　　　　Burnett. £100

NORIEGA Y ALVARADO, J.
– Cartilla de la Cavalleria Militar. Madrid, 1708. Vell. (DS. Apr.27; 2193)　　　　Pts. 20,000

NORMAN, Dorothy
– Stieglitz Memorial Portfolio: 1864-1946. Contribs.:–Steichen, Strand, Weston, Cartier-Bresson, F.L. Wright, & others. N.Y., [1947].

NORMAN, Dorothy -Contd.

(1500). Fo. Loose as iss. in bd. portfo., ties, beginning to separate at some flap hinges. (SG. Nov.10; 150) $175

NORMAND, Charles

- Recueil Varie de Plans et de Facades. Paris, 1831. Fo. Prelims. stained, spotted, later hf. mor. (BBA. Apr.5; 186) *Fletcher.* £75

NORMANDIE ILLUSTREE

Texts:- R. Bordeaux, Mlle Amelie Bosquet ... Ill.:- After Fx.Benoist & Hippolyte Lalaisse. Nantes, 1852. 2 vols. Fo. Publishers hf. chagrin, corners, gt. decor. motifs. (HD. Dec.1; 76) Frs. 8.000
- - **Anr. Edn.** Text:- R. Bordeaux, Melle Amélie Bosquet & others. Ill.:- after Felix Benoist & Hippolyte Lalaisse. Nantes, 1854. 2 vols. Fo. 153 plts., publisher's chagrin gt. (HD. Mar.9; 116) Frs. 6,900

NORMANDIE MONUMENTALE ET PITTO-RESQUE

Le Havre, 1896. 10 vols. Fo. Internal defects, publisher's bds., very worn; from Château des Noës liby. (HD. May 25; 60) Frs. 3,200

NORMYX (Pseud.)

See— DOUGLAS, Norman 'Normyx'

NORR[E], E.

- Chirurgischer Wegweiser. Schwabach, Nürnberg, [1693]. *3rd. Edn.* Lacks last 3 Index ll., sm. wormhole in margin, title with date excised from lr. margin, cont. vell., spotted. (BR. Apr.12; 768) DM 550

NORRIS, Charles

- Etchings of Tenby, including Many Ancient Edifices which have been Destroyed ... 1812. Some spotting, later hf. mor. gt., rubbed. (TA. May 17; 498) £60

NORRIS, Frank

- McTeague. A Story of San Francisco. N.Y., 1899. *1st. Edn. 1st. Printing, with 'moment' last word on p. 106.* Stpd. cl., orig. cl. case, minor wear, sm. hole in edge of spine, d.-w. (light wear, minor tears, tape-repair on verso); Ken Leach coll. (RO. Jun.10; 543) $3,400
- Yvernelle. Phila., 1892. *1st. Edn.* Tall 8vo. Gt.-decor. cl., worn. (RO. Apr.23; 241) $500

NORRIS, John, Rector of Bemerton

- Letters Concerning the Love of God, between the Author of the Proposals to the Ladies & Mr. John Norris. 1695. *1st. Edn.* Cont. panel. cf., slightly worn. (TA. Nov.17; 411) £60

NORTH, Roger

- A Treatise on Fish & Fish-Ponds. Ill.:- E. Albin. L., [1832-35]. Fo. 18 hand-cold. engraved plts., a few with cont. MS. notes in ink in blank margins, cont. hf. mor., slightly rubbed. (C. Mar.14; 146) *Guinevere.* £800

NORTH, T.

- The Church Bells of Leicestershire. Leicester, 1876. 4to. Embossed cl. (HBC. May 17; 332) £52

NORTH GEORGIA GAZETTE (The), & Winter Chronicle

Ed.:- Edward Sabine. L., 1821. Nos. 1-21 (all publd.). Lge. 4to. Mod. cl. (SG. Mar.29; 289) $100

NORTHCOTE, James

- One Hundred Fables, Original & Selected. L., 1828. *1st. Edn.* Tall 8vo. Later gt.-decor. cf., s.-c., light wear. (RO. Jul.24; 201) $170
- - **Anr. Edn.** Ill.:- after William Harvey & Northcote. L., 1828-33. [1st.] & 2nd. Series: 2 vols. L.P., a few ll. very slightly spotted, hf. mor., sm. hole at foot of 1 spine. (S. Nov.22; 391) *Hirsch.* £230
- - **Anr. Copy.** Together 2 vols. L.P., a few spots in 1st. vol., mott. cf. gt. (S. Mar.20; 944) *Huntley.* £220

NORVINS, J. Marquet de, Baron de Montbreton

- Histoire de Napoléon. Ill.:- Coudre Fils, Perrot (maps & plans). Paris, 1827-28. *Orig. Edn. 1st.*

Printing of ills. 4 vols. 6 extra ills., glazed hf. cf., sigd. by Renard Fils, 1831, spines decor., unif. faded. (HD. Nov.29; 108) Frs. 1,100
- - **Anr. Edn.** Ill.:- A. Raffet. Paris, 1839. *1st. Edn. in this format & with these ills.* Lge. 8vo. Some foxing in parts, 2nd. lf. loose, cont. hf. leath., romantic gt. (GB. Nov.4; 1878) DM 400

NOSTRADAMUS, Michel

- Les Prophéties, Revues et Corrigées sur la Copie Imprimée à Lyon par Benoist Rigaud. 1568. Lyon?, 1605. 'Prédictions admirables' at end of 2nd. pt., mod. vell. gt. (LM. Mar.3; 200) B.Frs. 21,000
- Les Vrayes Centuries et Prophéties ... Revües et Corrigées suyvant les Premières Editions Imprimées en Avignon en l'An 1556 et à Lyon en l'An 1558. Amst., 1668. 16mo. Old red mor. gt., spine decor. (HD. Mar.27; 26) Frs. 3,300

NOTABLE AUSTRALIAN THOROUGHBREDS

New Zealand, 1980. *(3000)* numbered. Cl., boxed. (JL. Jul.15; 592) Aus. $150

NOTABLE NEW ZEALAND THOROUGH-BREDS

New Zealand, 1980. *(2000)* numbered. Cl., boxed. (JL. Jul.15; 593) Aus. $150

NOTITIA UTRAQUE cum Orientis tum Occidentis ultra Arcadii Honoriique Caesarum Tempora

Basle, 1552. *1st. Edn.* Fo. Some woodcuts with later crude col., later roan. (HD. Nov.17; 1) Frs. 1,500

NOTT, Stanley Charles

- A Catalogue of Rare Chinese Jade Carvings. Intro.:- Lt. Gen. Sir Sydney Lawford. Palm Beach, 1940. 4to. 44 photo. plts., cl. (SG. May 3; 269) $200
- Chinese Jade in the Stanley Charles Nott Collection. West Palm Beach, Florida, 1942. *(1000)* numbered. 4to. Col. frontis., 118 photographic plts., cl., spine rather worn. (SG. Aug.25; 213) $160
- - **Anr. Copy.** 4to. Cl. (PNY. Dec.1; 93) $100
- Chinese Jade Throughout the Ages. Intro.:- Sir Cecil Harcourt-Smith. L., [1936]. Tall 8vo. 148 plts. (39 cold.), 73 text engrs., ex-liby., cl. (SG. May 3; 268) $130

NOUGARET, P.J.B.

- Beautés de l'Histoire des Etats-Unis de l'Amérique Septentrionale. Paris, 1824. *3rd. Edn.* 12mo. Additional engraved title & 4 engraved plts., cont. mott. cf., jnts. & edges very worn; from liby. of F.D. Roosevelt, inscr. by him. (SG. Mar.15; 64) $100

NOUVEAU DICTIONNAIRE D'HISTOIRE NATURELLE, Appliquée aux Arts, Principalement à l'Agriculture et à l'Economie Rurale et Domestique

Ill.:- after de Sève. Paris, 1802. 24 vols. 236 copperengraved plts., cont. Bozerian-style tree cf. gt., spines decor. with fleurons on gt. pointillé ground. (HD. Sep.22; 259) Frs. 8,300
- - **Anr. Copy.** 24 vols. Cont. tree roan, spines decor.; from Château des Noës liby. (HD. May 25; 19) Frs. 3,800

NOUVEAU DICTIONNAIRE HISTORIQUE ou Histoire abrégée de tous les Hommes

Ed.:- Mayeul Chaudon. Caen, 1786. 8 vols. Lacks title, cont. roan, spine faded. (HD. Feb.22; 158) Frs. 2,800

NOUVEL AMBIGU MAGIQUE

Paris, 1778. Sm. 4to. Flick book, hand-cold. ills., slightly soiled, orig. decor. paper wraps., slightly worn; C. Carsten bkplt., van Veen coll. (S. Feb.28; 242) £1,000
- - **Anr. Edn.** Paris (?), ca. 1780. Sm. 4to. Hand-cold. ills., without title-p. or instructions (as iss.), slightly soiled, orig. decor. paper wraps., worn; van Veen coll. (S. Feb.28; 243) £440

NOUVELLE GALLERIE DE FIGURES, pour Servir à Connoître les Objets de la Maitre et de l'Art, les Moeurs et les Coutumes de la Vie Commune, à l'Usage des Jeunes Gens des Deux Sexes.

Ill.:- Kruger jun. after P. Haas. Berlin, ca. 1800. 151 engraved ills. on 28 plts., all but 1 hand-cold., lr. margins of text slightly dampstained, last few gatherings wormholed, errata lf. loosely inserted, cont. bds., van Veen coll. (S. Feb.28; 90) £140

NOUVELLE MAISON RUSTIQUE ou Economie Générale ...

Paris, 1721. 2 vols. 4to. Frontis. in Vol. 1, 29 engraved plts., cont. cf. (P. Mar.15; 119)
Thorp. £110
- - **Anr. Edn.** Paris, 1755. 2 vols. 4to. 1 title slightly soiled, cont. marb. cf. (HD. Dec.1; 77) Frs. 1,000

NOUVELLE METHODE D'ENSEIGNER L'A.B.C. Suite (&) 2e Suite. Abrégé de l'Histoire Sacrée

Lausanne, 1792. 4 pts. in 1 vol. Cont. bds. (VG. Mar.21; 413) Fls. 450

NOVALIS (Pseud.)

See— HARDENBERG, Friedrich Leopold von 'Novalis'

NOVERRE, Jean Georges

- Lettres sur la Danse et sur les Ballets. Stuttgart & Lyon, 1760. *Orig. Edn.* Cont. cf., decor. spine. (HD. Dec.16; 31) Frs. 3,100
- - **Anr. Edn.** L. & Paris, 1783. *2nd. Edn.* Cont. cf., spine decor., upr. turn-in & top of jnt. wormed. (HD. Nov.9; 55) Frs. 1,700

NOVIOMAGUS, Gerardus

See— SCRIVERIUS, Petrus - NOVIOMAGUS, Gerardus

NOVOTNY, Fr. & Dobai, J.

- Gustav Klimt. Salzburg, 1967. Ob. 4to. Orig. linen. (HK. May 17; 2893) DM 460
- - **Anr. Edn.** L., 1968. *(1250).* 4to. Orig. cl. gt., d.-w., s.-c. (S. Apr.30; 70) *Sims.* £130

NOWELL, Alexander

[-] Christianae Pietatis Prima Institatio. 1577. 1st. gathering repeated, erased names on title, little stained, old cf., rubbed, becoming loose. [STC 18713.5] (BBA. Jul.27; 91) *Quaritch.* £75

NOYE, Sir William

[-] A Treatise of the Principal Grounds & Maximes of the laues of this Nation. By W.N. L., 1660. *3rd. Edn.* Cont. cf. [Wing N 1454] (SG. Oct.27; 185) $125

NOZEMANN, Cornelius & others

- Nederlandsche Vogelen. Amst., J.C. Sepp, 1770-1829. *1st. Edn.* 5 vols. Lge. fo. 5 additional hand-cold. engraved titles, 250 hand-cold. engraved plts., margins of last 4 vols. sometimes marked with ink, mntd. on guards, mod. tree cf., unc. (C. Jun.27; 123) *Dreesmann.* £16,000
- - **Anr. Copy.** 5 vols. Lge. fo. Wide margin, cont. hf. leath. gt., Hauswealth coll. (H. May 24; 869) DM 63,000
- - **Anr. Edn.** Ill.:- Ch. Sepp & son. Amst., 1809. Pt. IV only. Lge. fo. Engraved title, 50 plts., hand-cold., unc., hf. cf., slightly defect. (B. Oct.4; 774) Fls. 8,000

NUCIARELLIS, Hieronymus de

[-] Opusculum Philosophiam & Medicinam Legibus praeferendam demonstrans. Venice, 1515. 4to. Margins browned, bds. (R. Oct.11; 85) DM 950

NUGENT, Thomas

- Travels through Germany ... L., 1768. *1st. Edn.* 1 folding plt. with slight tear, cont. cf. (C. Nov.9; 151) *Georges.* £260
- - **Anr. Copy.** 2 vols. Cont. cf., spines gt., slightly rubbed, jnts. strengthened. (VG. Nov.30; 851) Fls. 500

NUIX, Giovanni

- Reflexiones Imparciales sobra la Humanidád de los Españoles en las Indias. Ed.:- Pedro Varela y Ulloa. Madrid, 1782. *1st. Edn. in Spanish.* Sm. 4to. Hf.-title, errata lf., cont. Spanish mott. cf. gt. [Sabin 56309] (S. Mar.20; 806) *Blanko.* £220

NUMISMATIC CIRCULAR (THE) (SPINK & SON LTD.)

L., 1892-1982. Vols. 1-47, 63, 68, 71-90, & index to Vols. 1-20. 8vo. & fo. Vols. 1-15 in various cl. bdgs., some rubbed, rest unif. red cl. (S. May 1; 487) *Spink.* £700

NUMISMATIC CHRONICLE (THE) & Journal of the Royal Numismatic Society.

1956-60, 1961-82 in 27 vols. Vols. for 1956-60 in

orig. wraps., rest cont. cl. (S. May 1; 486)
Krown. £200

NUNEZ, Pedro
– Libro de Algebra en Aritmética y Geometría.
Amberes, 1567. Vell. (DS. Mar.23; 2193)
Pts. 100,000

NUNEZ DE LA PENA, Juan de
– Conquista y Antiguedades de las Islas de la Gran
Canaria. Madrid, 1676. *1st. Edn.* Sm. 4to. 2 advt.
ll., 2 errata ll., browned, few short tears & sm.
holes, cont. cf., spine gt. (S. Mar.20; 807)
Blanko. £280

NUR, S.F.
[–] Ausführliche Lebens-Beschreibung Karls des XII
Königs in Schweden. Frankfurt & Leipzig, 1704-
05. Pts III & IV only (of 10), in 2 vols. 12mo. Vell.
gt., spotted, slight worming. (V. Sep.29; 72)
DM 400

NUREMBERG CHRONICle
See— SCHEDEL, Hartmann

NUS: LA BEAUTE DE LA FEMME
Ill.:– after Man Ray, Platt Lynes, Hoppe, Mor-
tensen, Perckhammer, & others. Paris, [1933]. 4to.
96 full-p. gravure reproductions, ptd. wraps., laced.
(SG. Nov.10; 121) $300
– – **Anr. Copy.** 4to. Ptd. wraps., laced, lightly
rubbed. (SG. May 10; 99) $130

NUS, Eugene & Meray, Antony
– L'Empire des Légumes. Ill.:– A. Varin. Paris, n.d.
Hand-cold. engraved title, 24 hand-cold. plts., some
spotting, hf. mor., unc., orig. wraps. bnd. in. (P.
Mar.15; 104)   *Henderson.* £160

NUTCRACKER & SUGARDOLLY: A Fairy Tale
Trans.:– Charles A. Dana. Phila., 1852. *1st. Edn.*
12mo. Plts. hand-cold., 4 ll. of advts., 1 text lf. torn,
gt.-pict. cl., spine nicked. (SG. Dec.8; 253) $110

NUTT, Frederic
– The Complete Confectioner. N.Y., 1807. *1st.*
Amer. Edn. 12mo. Cont. tree cf., ex-liby. (SG.
Nov.17; 195) $100

NUTTALL, Thomas
– The Genera of North American Plants, & a Catalogue of the Species to the Year 1817. Phila., prfv.
ptd., 1818. *1st. Edn.* 2 vols. 12mo. Few dampstains,
1 lf. torn, few margins reprd., cropped, buckram.
[Sabin 56347] (SG. Mar.22; 244) $100
– The North American Sylva ... Not Described in ...
Michaux. Phila., 1842-49. *1st. Edn.* 3 vols. Lge.
8vo. 121 col. litho plts., some foxing, mainly in
text & tissue-guards, cont. hf. mor., extremities
rubbed. (SG. Mar.22; 229) $600
See— MICHAUX, François André & Nuttall,
Thomas

NYLANDT, P.
– De Nederlandtse Herbarius ... Amst., 1682. 4to.
Some slight browning, old annots., cont. hf. leath.,
slightly rubbed & bumped. (HK. May 15; 487)
DM 1,400

OAKES, Maud
See— KING, Jeff & Oakes, Maud

OAKES, William
– Scenery of the White Mountains. Boston, [1848].
Fo. Perforation stp. in title, plts. stpd. on versos,
some foxing, cl., brkn., ex-liby. (RO. Dec.11; 257)
$165

OATES, Frank
– Matabele Land & the Victoria Falls ... Ed.:– C.G.
Oates. L., 1881. *1st Edn.* Pict. cl. (VA. Apr.27;
686)   R 240

OATES, Titus
– A True Narrative of the Horrid Plot & Conspiracy
of the Popish Party Against the Life of His Sacred
Majesty, the Government, & the Protestant Religion. 1679. Fo. Imprimatur lf., some minor margin
stains, recent qtr. mor. gt. [Wing 059] (TA. Apr.19;
369)   £80

OBEY, Andre
– L'Apprenti Sorcier. Paris, 1926. 12mo. Cf. by
Marie-Jeanne Maudot, richly decor., buckskin

doubls., unc., wrap., s.-c. (HD. May 16; 98)
Frs. 4,000
– Le Joueur du Triangle: Roman. Paris, 1928. *Orig.*
Edn. 12mo. On papier d'alfa, mor. by Pierre
Legrain, richly decor., silk doubls. & end-ll., unc.,
wrap. & spine, s.-c.; author's dedication. (HD. May
16; 97)   Frs. 25,000

O'BRIEN, Capt. C. & Tennent, J.E.
– A Series of Fifteen Views in Ceylon. 1864. Fo. A
few margins soiled, text browned, orig. cl., soiled,
disbnd., w.a.f. (CSK. Jul.6; 41)   £520

O'BRIEN, Henry
– The Round Towers of Ireland. L., 1834. *2nd. Edn.*
Advt. & errata lf. at end, hf. mor., armorial motif
on spine. (GM. Dec.7; 155)   £85

O'BRIEN, Rev. Paul
– A Practical Grammar of the Irish Language.
Dublin, 1809. *1st. Edn.* Hf.-title, errata at end, cf.,
defect. (GM. Dec.7; 408)   £50

OBSOPOEUS, Vincentius
– De Arte Bibendi Libri Tres. Nürnberg, 1536. *1st.*
Edn. Cont. marginalia on title & end lf., 19th. C.
marb bds., rubbed. (R. Oct.11; 86)   DM 1,000

O'CALLAGHAN, E.B. (Ed.)
See— NEW YORK STATE

OCEAN FLOWERS & THEIR TEACHINGS
Bath, 1846. Bouquet frontis., & 38 other mntd.
specimens of sea-weeds, corallines, sponges &
zoophytes, few partly defect., some offsetting &
light foxing, orig. dark red mor. gt. extra, lge.
emblematic designs stpd. on spine & covers. (SG.
Oct.6; 274) $250

OCEAN OF STORY
Ed.:– Norman M. Penzer. Trans.:– C.H. Tawney.
Priv. ptd., 1924-28. *(1500).* 10 vols. 4to. Orig. decor.
buckram gt., unc. & unopened. (SKC. Mar.9; 1916)
£90

OCHA DE LA SALDE, Juan
– Crónica del Esforzado Príncipe y Capitán Iorge
Castrioto, Rey de Epiro o Albania. Madrid, 1597.
Fo. Vell. (DS. Nov.25; 2133)   Pts. 60,000

OCKLEY, Simon
– The Conquest of Syria, Persia, & Egypt, by the
Saracens. 1708. Errata, cont. panel. cf., spine gt.,
rubbed. (S. Nov.1; 60)   *Thorp.* £80

O'CLUNY, Thomas
– The Merry Multifleet & the Mounting Multi-
corps. Ill.:– W. Heath Robinson. L., 1904. *1st. Edn.*
Light foxing, lacks front free end-paper, ill. cl.,
covers rubbed & soiled. (CBA. Oct.29; 613) $190

O'CONNELL, Daniel
– Observations on Corn Laws, on Political
Pravity & Ingratitude, & on Clergical & Personal
Slander in the Shape of a Meek & Modest Reply
... Dublin, 1842. *1st. Edn.* Mor. gt.; Inscr. by author
to Right Rev. Whelan. (P. Sep.8; 157) *King.* £220

O'CURRY, Eugene
– Lectures on the Manuscript Materials of Ancient
Irish History. Dublin, 1878. Cl. (GM. Dec.7; 253)
£70
– On the Manners & Customs of the Ancient Irish.
L., 1873. *1st. Edn.* 3 vols. Bkplt., orig. cl. gt. (GM.
Dec.7; 441)   £160

ODDY, S.A.
– Oddy's New General Atlas of the World, Containing Maps of Empires, Kingdoms, States, Princi-
palities, & c. Engraved & Carefully Selected from
the Latest & Most Approved Authors by James
Wallis. L., S.A. Oddy, [1813]. Fo. Double-p. dou-
ble-hemisphere map & 29 (of ?) single-p. maps, all
hand-cold., title & 1st. few maps detchd., some
maps stained, cover imprint 'London: J. Wallis,
1813', ptd. bds., leath. back, disbnd. (SG. Jun.7;
34) $120

ODELL, George C.D.
– Annals of the New York Stage. N.Y., 1927-40.
Orig. Edn. 12 vols. Lge. 8vo. Cl., some wear, ex-
liby. (SG. Nov.17; 304) $275

ODELL, S.W.
– The Last War. Chic., [1898]. *1st. Edn.* Some
light foxing, orig. cl., covers soiled. (CBA. Oct.29;
614) $120

ODOLANT-DESNOS
– Mémoire Historique sur la Ville d'Alençon et sur
ses Seigneurs. Alençon, 1787. 2 vols. Cont. lavallière
hf. roan; from Château des Noës liby. (HD. May
25; 61)   Frs. 2,800

O'DONOGHUE, Freeman Marius & Hake, Henry
M.
– Catalogue of Engraved British Portraits in the
British Museum. 1908-25. *6 vols., with Supp.* Orig.
cl. (BBA. Sep.8; 35)   *Leicester Art Books.* £70
– – **Anr. Copy.** 6 vols., including Supp. & Indexes.
Cl., some wear. (SG. Aug.25; 136) $150

O'DONOVAN, Edmund
– The Mery Oasis. Travels & Adventures East of
the Caspian. 1882. 2 vols. Orig. cl., soiled. (CSK.
Jul.6; 62)   £110

O'DONOVAN, John
– Leabhar na G. Ceart, or the Book of Rights.
Dublin, 1847. *1st. Edn.* Royal 8vo. Diced cf. (GM.
Dec.7; 231)   £120
– The Martyrology of Donegal. Dublin, 1864. Cl.
(GM. Dec.7; 76)   £100

O'DONOVAN, John (Ed.)
See— ANNALS OF THE KINGDOM OF IRE-
LAND

OECHELHAUSER, A. von
– Die Miniaturen der Universitäts-Bibliothek zu
Heidelberg. Heidelberg, 1887-95. 2 vols. 4to. Orig.
hf. linen, spotted & browned, Hauswedell coll. (H.
May 23; 467)   DM 450

OEHLER, R
See— LANCKORONSKA, Maria & Oehler, R.

OERTEL, W. 'W. O.v. Horn'
See— HORN, W.O. v. [ie W. Oertel]

OESCHLAEGER, Adam
See— OLEARIUS or OESCHLAEGER, Adam

OESTERREICH, Matthias
– Beschreibung der Königlichen Bildergallerie und
des Kabinets in Sans-Souci. Potsdam, 1770. *2nd.*
Iss. (Bound with:) – Versuch einer Beschreibung
der Kaiserlich-Königlichen Schatzkammer zu Wien.
Nuremb., 1771. Together 2 works in 1 vol. Cont.
hf. cf. (C. May 30; 194)   *Parikian.* £240

OESTERREICHER, [J.] H. [O.]
– Anatomischer Atlas od. Bildliche Darstellung d.
Menschl. Körpers. München, 1845. Imp. fo. Some
plts. soiled, especially at end, some plts. with sm.
margin repairs, last plt. mntd. & bkd tear, some
slight foxing, hf. leath., ca. 1870, bumped & rubbed,
spine partly defect. (HK. Nov.8; 675)   DM 500

OEUVRE ET L'IMAGE (L'): Revue de l'Art Con-
temporain et du Livre Illustré
Paris, Nov. 1900-02. In 3 vols. 4to. Cl.-bkd. bds.,
rubbed, orig. wraps. bnd. in, light discoloration, as
a periodical, w.a.f. (SPB. Dec.13; 639) $600

OFFICE, Divine [*Chronologically, irrespective of*
use]
– Officium B. Mariae Virginis, nuper Reformatum,
et Pii V. Iussu Ed. Ill.:– J. Wierix, A. de Bruyn,
Cr. van den Broek, P. van der Borcht, & P. Huys.
Antw., 1573. Lacks last 2 ll. (blank?), some light
stains & traces of wear, 18th. c. mor. gt., spine gt.
slightly rubbed. (VG. Sep.14; 986)   Fls. 2,400
– – **Anr. Copy.** Some slight spotting, some ll. with
sm. defects last lf. mntd. (*Bound with:*)
ORATIONES SANCTAE BRIGIDAE ca. 1580.
Latin MS. on paper, lightly foxed, last ll. wormed.
Together 2 works in 1 vol. 18th. C. leath., slightly
wormed, corners lightly bumped. (HK. May 15;
208)   DM 1,500
– Officium Sacerdotis Hebdomadarii ad Usum Car-
tuisensis Ordinis. Paris, 1665. Sm. 4to. Some ll.
remargined, 17th. C. vell., partly painted in old
rose & gt. decor., limp decor. spine. (HD. Jan.30;
80)   Frs. 1,650
– Officium B. Marie Virg. Antw., 1677. Ptd. area

OFFICE, Divine [*Chronologically, irrespective of use*] -Contd.
60 × 33mm., various p. sizes between 110 × 77mm., & 83 × 47mm. L.P., some ll. lightly soiled, mod. vell., lightly soiled, mostly unc. & unopened. (CSK. Feb.10; 51) £85
– **Office de la Semaine Sainte selon la Bréviaure et Missal de Paris en Latin et en Français.** Ill.:– Bouche & Morin. Paris, 1678. Old red mor., crowned spine cypher decor., centre arms, sm. inner dentelle. (HD. Mar.30; 21) Frs. 16,000
– **Office de la Semaine Sainte.** Paris, 1715. Red mor., arms. (HD. Oct.14; 121) Frs. 1,350
– – **Anr. Edn.** 1717. Red mor., central medallion with royal arms (scratched), renewed, spine decor. (HD. Apr.13; 36) Frs. 1,200
– – **Anr. Edn.** Paris, 1726. Red mor., Marie Leczinska arms (effaced), fanfare pres. bdg., corners worn. (SM. Mar.7; 2034) Frs. 1,000
– **Office Paroissial Latin–François à l'Usage de Rome et de Paris, dédié à la Reine.** Paris, 1726-29. 4 vols. (of 8). 12mo. Old mor., gt. decor., arms sm. inner dentelle, wtrd. silk doubls. & end-papers. (HD. Mar.30; 19) Frs. 18,000
– **Office de la Semaine Sainte en Latin et en François à l'Usage de Rome et de Paris.** Ill.:– Scotin. Paris, 1728. Old red mor., gt. decor., centre arms, 2 autograph notes on end-paper. (HD. Mar.30; 23) Frs. 32,800
– **Office de la Semaine Sainte.** Ill.:– J.B. Scotin. Paris, 1729. Cont. red mor., gt. decor., centre arms, decor. spine, s.-c. (HD. Dec.9; 67) Frs. 1,050
– **L'Office de la Semaine Sainte à l'Usage de la Maison du Roy ... par M. l'Abbé de Bellegarde.** Paris, 1741. 2 ills. sigd. by Humblot, old red mor., gt. & sm. tool decor., centre arms, dentelle, sm. inner dentelle. (HD. Mar.30; 24) Frs. 14,200
– **Office de la Semaine Sainte à l'Usage de la Maison du Roy ...** Paris, 1743. Cont. red mor. gt., Louis XV arms, spines decor. (HD. May 3; 146) Frs. 2,000
– **Office de la Semaine Sainte en Latin et on François à l'Usage de Rome & de Paris.** Paris, 1746. Liby. stp. at corner of title, cont. Fr. red mor. gt. decor., arms of the Dauphine, Marie-Josephe de Saxe, Dutch gt. end-papers, head of spine slightly scuffed. (C. May 30; 93) *Benveniste.* £700
– **Office de la Semaine Sainte à l'Usage de la Masion du Roy.** Ill.:– J.B. Scotin. Paris, 1748. Cont. Fr. red mor. gt., Louis XV arms, head of spine chipped, sm. repairs at corners & head & foot of spine. (C. May 30; 94) *Greenwood.* £100
– – **Anr. Copy.** Cont. red mor., richly decor., Louis XV arms. (HD. Nov.9; 68) Frs. 6,600
– **L'Office de la Semaine Sainte, en Latin et en François, à l'Usage de Rome et de Paris.** 1751. Decor. red mor. (HD. Mar.21; 62) Frs. 1,000
– **Officium Beatae Mariae Virginis.** Ill.:– after B. Falconi. Venice, 1754. Cont. Italian purple red mor., gold & wax col. decor., arms supralibros, gt. inner & outer dentelle, gold brocade doubl. & end-papers. Ernst Kyriss monog. stp. on end-paper. (D. Nov.23; 174) DM 2,400
– **Officium Beatae Mariae. Nuper reformatum, & S. Pli V. Pontificis Maximi jussu Editum.** Antw., 1759. 4to. A few ll. slightly spotted, lightly browned. (R. Oct.12; 2234) DM 420
– **Office de la Semaine Sainte.** Ca. 1760. Red mor., royal arms. (HD. Jan.24; 42) Frs. 1,500
– **L'Office de la Semaine Sainte à l'Usage de la Maison du Roi.** Ed.:– Abbé de Bellegarde. Paris, 1766. Latin & Fr., red mor., Louis XV arms on both covers, gold-tooled border, lily stp., inner & outer dentelle, marb. end-papers, lightly rubbed. (D. Nov.23; 169) DM 2,000
– **The Office of the Holy Week, According to the Roman Missal & Breviary ...** Balt., 1810. *1st. Amer. Edn.* 12mo. In Latin & Engl., lacks rear fly-lf., old cf., reprd., new spine label; sig. of Juliana C. Van Pradelles on title, sig. of E.M. Pease on front fly-lf. & head of preface. (SG. Jan.19; 142) $125
– **The Office of the Blessed Eucharist.** Illuminator:–Julia Valerie Rowe. Easter 1865. 4to. Pict. title & 43pp. illuminated in cols. & gold lf., including 1 full-p. painting & others in text, cont. vell. decor. gt., with ornamental crosses on both covers & spine; inscr. by Rowe as present for her father, Rector of Morchard Bishop. (SKC. Jan.13; 2246) £50

OFFICE OF UNITED STATES, CHIEF OF COUNSEL FOR PROSECUTION OF AXIS CRIMINALITY
– **Nazi Conspiracy & Aggression.** Wash., 1946. *1st. Edn.* 8 vols. 6 lge. folded charts in rear pocket of Vol. VIII, few vols. with fore-edges slightly rippled, incidental dusting, buckram, backstrips faded. (HA. Feb.24; 436) $120

OFFICINA BODONI
– **Das Werkbuch einer Handpresse in den ersten sechs Jahren Ihres Wirkens.** Ill.:– Fr. Masereel. Paris, 1929. *(350).* 4to. Orig. linen. (H. Nov.24; 1824) DM 820

OFFREDI, Apollinaris, Cremonensis
– **Expositio et Quaestiones super Libros Aristotelis de Anima.** Venice, Bonetus Locatellus for Octavianus Scotus, 10 Sep. 1496. Fo. 1st. 15 ll. with outer blank margins reprd. or strengthened, rest stained & some margins brittle & slightly frayed, a few sm. wormholes at beginning, old paper bds. [BMC V, 446; Goff O59; HC 12004] (S. May 10; 372) *McKiddrick.* £400

O'FLAHERTY, Liam
– **The Informer.** L., [1925]. *1st. Edn.* Cl., d.-w., wrap. of binder's cl. (LH. Sep.25; 578) $180

OGAWA, K.
– **Costumes & Customs in Japan.** Captions:– S. Takashima. Yokohama, 1897. 1 vol. Fo. 23 hand-cold. collotypes, crepe-covered flexible bds., laced, rubbed & discold. (*With:*) – **Famous Castles & Temples of Japan.** Tokyo, ca. 1900? 1 vol. Ob. fo. 35 hand-cold. collotypes, crepe-covered flexible bds., laced. (SG. May 10; 105) $175
– **Illustrations of Japanese Life.** Captions:– S. Takashima. Ill.:– Ogawa, K. Tamamura, S. Kajima, & W.K. Burton. Yokohama, 1896. 2 vols. Sm. 4to. & ob. 4to. 98 collotypes on crepe paper, pict. crepe wraps., bnd. in the Japanese manner, laced, worn. (SG. May 10; 104) $175

OGDEN, Henry Alexander
[–] **Uniform of the Army of the United States, from 1774 to 1889.** N.p., [1890]. Fo. 44 col. litho. plts., mor. gt., spine slightly rubbed. (SG. Sep.22; 208) $650

OGDEN, James
– **Ogden on Fly Tying, etc.** Cheltenham, 1879. *1st. Edn.* No errata slip, orig. cl., soiled. (S. Oct.4; 42) *Marlborough.* £130

OGILBY, John
– **Actual Survey of the Principal Roads of England & Wales ...** Ed.:– John Senex. 1719. Vol. I only. Double-p. engraved title & dedication, 54 maps, cf., upr. bd. torn. (PD. Aug.17; 33) £90
– **Africa.** L., 1670. Fo. Engraved frontis., 47 plts., 10 hf.-p. plts. & a port. not listed in the 'Directions to Binder', cont. gt.-panel. mott. cf., spine gt., corners reprd., sm. repair to upr. jnt. [Wing O 163] (C. Nov.16; 24) *Traylen.* £850
– – **Anr. Copy.** Fo. Engraved frontis., lge. folding general map, 38 double-p. plts., 13 smaller plts. on 8 ll., lacks hf.-title, a few plts. & ll. browned, 1 or 2 sm. flaws affecting text, last lf. laid down on rear free-end-paper affecting plt.-list, cont. cf., spine gt. reprd., slightly worn; Earl of Breadalbane bkplt., the Stowe copy. [Wing O 163] (S. Dec.1; 360) *Marshall.* £620
– – **Anr. Copy.** Fo. 15 double-p. engraved maps & town plans, 43 engraved plts., 1 map torn & reprd., 1 map & 1 plt. lightly browned, a few margin annots., cont. cf. gt. (P. Oct.20; 245) £520
– **America, being the latest & most accurate description of the New World** [translated from Arnoldus Montanus]. L., priv. ptd., 1671. *2nd. Edn.* Fo. Engraved frontis., 56 engraved ports., maps & views, without the map of Virginia & Florida called for, but with additional map of Barbados not called for, cont. gt.-panel. mott. cf., spine gt. [Wing O 165] (C. Nov.16; 25) *Schuster.* £3,500
– – **Anr. Copy.** Lge. fo. Additional engraved title, 50 double-p. engraved maps & views, including 4 folding, 1st. folding map torn, vig. at p. 219 torn with slight loss, slight tears to 3 folding plts., some slight browning, cont. cf., rebkd., corners & edges

restored; the Rt. Hon. Visc. Eccles copy. [Sabin 50089; Wing O 165] (CNY. Nov.18; 212) $6,500
– **Asia.** L., priv. ptd., 1673. *1st. Edn.* Pt. 1 (all publd.). Fo. Engraved frontis., 32 engraved maps & plts., some double-p., some folding, cont. gt.-panel. mott. cf., spine gt. [Wing O 166] (C. Nov.16; 26) *Traylen.* £580
– **Britannia.** L., A. Swall & R. Morden, 1698. *2nd. Edn.* Fo. 100 double-p. engraved road maps, without the lf. 'To the Reader', 1 or 2 maps just shaved at outer neatlines, a few minor repairs without loss of engraved surface, some browning affecting text & several maps, a few creases, cont. panel. cf., rebkd., worn. (S. Dec.1; 153) *Burgess.* £1,900
– **The Entertainment of ... Charles II in his Passage ... to his Coronation.** 1662. Fo. 13 engraved plts., lacks frontis., cont. mott. cf., worn, arms on covers. (BBA. Jun.28; 65) *Bloomsbury Rare Books.* £70

OGILBY, John & Bowen, Emanuel
– **Britannia Depicta, or Ogilby Improv'd.** Ed.:– John Owen. 1720. *1st. Edn.* Title, 273 pp. engraved maps, table, 1 p. catalogue at end, new end-papers, cont. cf., rebkd. (SKC. Nov.18; 2063) £380
– – **Anr. Copy.** 252 (of 273) pp. of roadmaps, some soiled, cf., lacks lr. cover. (P. Oct.20; 256f) £320
– – **Anr. Copy.** Engraved title & 2 plts. (detchd., soiled, torn with loss), 268 pp. strip road maps only, some detchd. & cleanly torn, w.a.f. (CSK. Sep.16; 53) £130
– – **Anr. Edn.** Ed.:– I. Owen. Ca. 1720. 273 pp. of roadmaps, lacks title, cf., covers detchd. (P. Oct.20; 256g) £360
– – **Anr. Copy.** 273 road maps on 136 sheets, lacks title, some maps soiled, cf., upr. cover detchd. (P. Jul.5; 386) £330
– – **Anr. Edn.** Ed.:– J. Owen. T. Bowles & E. Bowen, 1720 [1721]. *1st. Edn. 2nd. Iss.* Engraved title, 2 ll. of engraved tables & 273 pp. of engraved county & strip road maps, some faint browning, cont. panel. cf., upr. cover detchd., w.a.f. (S. May 21; 30) *Nicholson.* £420
– – **Anr. Edn.** L., 1730. Sm. 4to. Engraved title, 2 ll. of tables, 273 engraved road maps, slight worming in outer margin, cont. cf. (P. May 17; 428) *Martin.* £400
– – **Anr. Edn.** L., 1731. *4th. Edn.* 8vo. 273 road maps on 137 ll., 4 pp. index, cont. cf., rebkd., slightly rubbed. (BBA. Dec.15; 114) *Postaprint.* £380
– – **Anr. Edn.** Ed.:– John Owen. L., T. Bowles, 1736. *4th. Edn.* Engraved title, 273 pp. of engraved county & strip road maps, 5 ll. of ptd. tables, some faint offsetting, cont. cf., rebkd., worn. (S. Dec.1; 157) *Burden.* £410
– – **Anr. Edn.** L., 1749. *4th. Edn.* Engraved title, 273 ll. of county & strip road maps, 4 ptd. index ll., title & 1st. few ll. stained, last 2 ll. torn without loss of engraved surface, some worming at inner margin not affecting engraved surface, cont. law cf., worn. (S. Dec.1; 158) *Burden.* £260
– – **Anr. Edn.** Ed.:– John Owen. L., 1759. *4th. Edn.* Engraved title, 273 road maps on 135 sheets, 1 margin trimmed, ink stain on upr. margin of first 8 ll., cont. cf., rebkd. (P. May 17; 424) *Burgess.* £260

OGILBY, John & Senex, John
– **The Roads through England Delineated.** 1762. Ob. 4to. Engraved title reprd., mod. cl. gt. (P. Sep.8; 426) *Cranbrook.* £220

OGILVIE-GRANT, William Robert & others
– **The Gun at Home & Abroad.** 1912-15. *Ltd. Edn.* 4 vols. Lge. 4to. Mor., w.a.f.; from liby. of Luttrellstown Castle. (C. Sep.28; 1779) £420

OGLE, Nathaniel
– **The Colony of Western Australia.** L., 1839. The folding map different from that called for by Ferguson, title, prelims. & plts. foxed, hf. cf., loose, covers rubbed. (CA. Apr.3; 92) Aus. $580
– – **Anr. Edn.** L., 1839. *2nd. Iss.* The folding map different from that called for by Ferguson, tear in margin of 1 appendix p., 1st. 2 sections loose, blind-stpd. cl., unc., covers slightly stained. (CA. Apr.3; 93) Aus. $620

OGLETHORPE, [Gen. James Edward]
- The Late Expedition Against St. Augustine. 1742. Engraved port. loose, folding engraved map lacks portion from centre, some ll. slightly soiled & browned, later roan-bkd. bds., worn. (BBA. Feb.9; 302) *Julian Burnett Books.* £670

O'HANLON, Canon J. & O'Leary Rev. Ed.
- History of the Queen's County. Dublin, 1907. *1st. Edn.* 2 vols. Royal 8vo. Cl. (GM. Dec.7; 303) £90

O'HARA, James
- [-] The History of New South Wales. 1818. *2nd. Edn.* Repair to title-p. without loss, some soiling, mainly marginal, 19th. C. hf. cf. by Morrell, partly unc. (KH. May 1; 538) *Aus.* $400

O'HARA, John
- Appointment in Samarra. N.Y., [1934]. *1st. Edn.* Orig. cl., d.-w. creased, mor.-bkd. s.-c., acknowledgement slip tipped in; Perry Molstad copy. (SPB. May 16; 508) $375

OHLSEN, Th.
- Durch Süd-Amerika. Hamburg & Leipzig, 1894. Fo. Plts. slightly spotted, loose ll. in orig. linen portfo., defect. (D. Nov.23; 1328) DM 750

OHM, M.
- Die Lehre vom Grössten und Kleinsten. Berlin, 1825. Slightly browned, cont. linen. (HT. May 8; 455) DM 420

OKAMOTO, K.S.
- Ancient & Modern Various Usages of Tokio. Tokyo, 1885. Orig. wraps., slightly soiled. (SG. Jan.26; 222) $140

O'KEEFE, Georgia
- Georgia O'Keefe. N.Y., [1976]. *1st. Trade Edn.* Fo. Bdg. not stated, light wear to d.-w. (CBA. Jan.29; 327) $120

O'KEEFFE, John
- Recollections of the Life of ... L., 1826. *1st. Edn.* 2 vols. Hf. mor. (GM. Dec.7; 405) £120

O'KELLY, Pat
- The Eudoxologist, or an Ethicographical Survey of the Western Parts of Ireland. A Poem, to which are Prefixed the Author's Poems on the Giants Causeway & Killarney. Dublin, 1812-08. Lists of subscribers, text cut in, bkplt., crimson hf. mor. (GM. Dec.7; 226) £230

OKEN, Lorenz
- Abbildungen zu Oken's Allgemeiner Naturgeschichte für Alle Stände. Stuttgart, 1843. Plt. vol. only. 4to. Title mntd. & with name, 6 plts. stained, 1 with sm. margin tear, later hf. linen. (R. Oct.12; 1883) DM 680
- - Anr. Copy. 3 vols. Lge. 4to. Tinted litho. & 164 litho. plts. (133 cold.), 94 ll. plt. captions, some animals erased from 19 plts., faults bkd., some cut-outs pasted back, some text foxing, some plt. browning, cont. linen, slightly rubbed & bumped, cover slightly cockled. (HK. May 15; 489) DM 550
- - Anr. Edn. Stuttgart, [1843]. plt. vol. Lge. 4to. Tinted litho. title, 164 litho. plts., (133 cold.), lacks typographic title & 64 ll. plt. captions, a few plts. foxed, 13 anatomy plts., very foxed, uncold. plts. stained, cont. hf. leath., corners slightly bumped. (HK. May 15; 490) DM 1,300
- Allgemeine Naturgeschichte für Alle Stände. Ed.:- Walchner (Vol. 1). Ill.:- Schillinger, Löffler, & others, after Knoll & others. Stuttgart, 1833-45. 7 vols. & Index; in 14 vols., 4 pt. vol. Plt. vol. fo. Some foxing, especially at beginning & end, plts. with light old spotting, especially in margin, 1 plt. defect., hf. leath. gt., lightly rubbed & bumped. (V. Sep.29; 1478) DM 1,500

OLAFSEN & Povelsen
- [-] Voyage en Islande, fait par Ordre de S.M. Danoise. Trans.:- Gaulthier de La Peyronie & Biornered. Paris, 1802. Atlas only. 4to. Cont. hf. roan, corners, worn. (HD. Jun.26; 47) *Frs.* 2,050

OLASCOAGA, Manuel J.
- Estudio Topografico de la Pampa y Rio Negro. Buenos Aires, 1880. 2 vols. including map in folder.

4to. Litho. port. & 7 plts., folding map, cont. cl. (BBA. Jun.28; 236) *Duran.* £80

OLAUS MAGNUS
- Historiae de Gentibvs Septentrionalibvs. Ed.:- C. Scribonius. Antw., ca. 1557. *1st. Edn.* Title with owner's note, 9 contents & index ll. misbnd. at end 10 ll. text defect. in 1 corner, some slight staining, gold- tooled vell., gt. oxidised. (HK. Nov.8; 300) DM 610

OLD EDINBURGH CLUB
See— BOOK OF THE OLD EDINBURGH CLUB

OLD MASTER DRAWINGS
[N.Y.], 1927 [1970]. *Reprint.* 14 vols. Orig. cl. (BBA. Apr.5; 110) *Sterner.* £90
- - Anr. Copy. 14 vols. 4to. Orig. cl. (BBA. Sep.8; 84) *Zwemmer.* £60

OLD NICK (Pseud.)
See— FORGUES, Paul Emile Daurand 'Old Nick'

OLD WATERCOLOUR SOCIETY
- [Annual]. 1950, 1968-78. Vols. 28 & 37-53. Orig. cl. (LC. Oct.13; 68) £70

OLDENBOURG, R
See— BUCHHEIT, H. & Oldenbourg, R.

OLDENBURG, Henry
See— PHILOSOPHICAL TRANSACTIONS

OLDFIELD, Otis
- A Pictorial Journal of a Voyage Aboard ... the Louise. Last of the Sailing Codfishermen ... of San Francisco. San Franc., 1969. *1st. Edn. (400).* Fo. Hf. mor. & linen, cover lightly soiled. (CBA. Nov.19; 267) $110

OLDFIELD, T.H.B.
- [-] An Entire & Complete History, Political & Personal, of the Boroughs of Great Britain. L., 1792. 3 vols. Hf.-title in Vol. 1, a few ll. trimmed, slightly browned, cont. cf., spine gt., slightly rubbed. (BBA. May 3; 223) *Hannas.* £160

OLDFIELD, Thomas
See— SCLATER, Philip Lutely & Thomas, Michael R. Oldfield

OLDHAM, James Basil
- English Blind-Stamped Bindings. Camb., 1952. *(750).* Fo. Orig. cl., slightly scuffed. (CSK. Jun.15; 143) £75
- - Anr. Copy. Fo. Orig. cl., d.-w. (BBA. Nov.10; 17) *Demetzy.* £60
- - Anr. Edn. L., 1952. Fo. Plts., cl. (P. May 17; 62) *King.* £70
- Shrewsbury School Bindings. Catalogue Raisonné. Oxford, 1943. *(200) numbered.* Fo. Pres. inscr. from author to H.M. Nixon, orig. buckram, H.M. Nixon copy, with his MS. annots., rubbing & cuttings loosely inserted. (BBA. Oct.6; 106) *Maggs.* £650
- - Anr. Copy. 4to. Orig. cl. (BBA. Nov.10; 16) *Lyon.* £250

OLDMIXON, John
- [-] Het Britannische Ryk in Amerika, zynde eene Beschryving van de Ontdekking, Bevolking, Koophandel, en Tegenwoordige Staat van Alle de Britannische Colonien ... Amst., 1721. 2 pts. in 1 vol. 4to. Lr. corner of title & 2 ll. torn off with text in MS., cont. cf., spine gt. [Sabin 57160] (VG. Sep.14; 1116) *Fls.* 800
- [-] The British Empire in America. L., 1741. 2 vols. Pages 321-336 bnd. after 352, cont. cf., worn. [Sabin 57157] (S. May 22; 331) *Faupel.* £240

OLDYS, William
- [-] The British Librarian. 1737. 6 pts. in 1 vol. Cont. cf., rebkd. (BBA. Nov.10; 111) *Forster.* £60
- - Anr. Edn. L., 1738. Mod. cf.-bkd. bds. (CSK. Feb.24; 193) £55

OLEARIUS or OESCHLAEGER, Adam
- Vermherte Newe Beschreibung der Muscowitisohen und Persischen Reyse. Schleswig, 1656. Fo. Additional engraved title, 4 ports., 27 engraved plts. & maps, most double-p. or folding, tears affecting folding maps without loss, cont. vell. bds., slightly soiled. (S. Dec.1; 321) *Baker.* £1,050
- Voyages Très Curieux et Très Rénommez faits en

Moscovie, Tartarie et Perse. Amst., 1727. 2 pts. in 1 vol. Fo. 2 ports., 38 (of 40) double-p. engraved maps & views, lacks advt. lf. at end, old cf. (RO. Dec.11; 258) $425
- - Anr. Copy. 2 pts. in 1 vol. Fo. 41 double-p. or folding plts. & maps, mod. hf. cf., corners, blind-decor., unc. (LM. Mar.3; 236) *B.Frs.* 28,000

O'LEARY, Rev. Ed
See— O'HANLON, Canon J. & O'Leary, Rev. Ed.

OLINA, Giovanni Pietro
- Vccelliera overo Discorso della Natvra, a Proprieta di Diversi Vcelli. Ill.:- after Ant. Tempesta. Rome, 1684. *2nd. Edn.* 4to. 1 lf. with sm. tear at foot reprd., 4 ll. with paste marks, minimal soiling, 19th. C. hf. leath., spine defect. (HK. Nov.8; 772) DM 2,400

OLIPHANT, Laurence
- A Journey to Katmandu (the Capital of Nepaul), with the Camp of Jung Bahadoor; including a Sketch of the Nepaulese Ambassador at Home. 1852. Cont. hf. cf. by Nutt, rebkd. (TA. Sep.15; 82) £65
- Masollam. 1886. *1st. Edn.* 3 vols. Hf.-titles, advts., orig. cl. gt. (P. Jan.12; 139) *Kossow.* £75
- Narrative of the Earl of Elgin's Mission to China & Japan. 1859. 2 vols. 19 tinted & cold. plts. only, 5 folding maps, orig. cl., lightly soiled. (CSK. May 4; 114) £80
- - Anr. Edn. 1860. *2nd. Edn.* 2 vols. Orig. cl. gt., spines faded. (P. Jun.7; 4) £60

OLIPHANT, Mrs. Margaret
- Hester. 1883. *1st. Edn.* 3 vols. Hf.-titles, advts., orig. cl. gt. (P. Jan.12; 140) *Maggs.* £75

OLIVER, William
- Eight Months in Illinois; with Information to Emigrants. Newcastle, 1843. *1st. Edn.* Orig. cl., unc., faded, head of spine worn; author's sig. on dedication p., Rt. Hon. Visc. Eccles copy. [Sabin 57214] (CNY. Nov.18; 213) $600

OLIVER HURTADO, Jose y Manuel
- Granada y sus Monumentos Arabes. Malaga, 1875. 4to. Linen, corners, orig. wraps. preserved. (DS. Dec.16; 2426) *Pts.* 20,000

OLIVEYRA, Selomoh de
- Yad Lashon.- Dal Sfataim.- Darchei Noam.- Tuv Ta'am Va'Da'at.- Ets Chaim.- Zait Ra'anan.- Ayelet Ahavim.- Charshot Gavlot. Amst., 1665-89. *1st. Edns.* 8 works in 1 vol. 12mo. Browned, some staining, trimmed, hf. leath. (S. Oct.25; 302) *Kornbluth.* £300

OLIVIER, Dr. Eugene & others
- Manuel de l'Amateur de Reliures Armoriées Francaises. Paris, 1924-38. 30 vols. 4to. Vol. XXIX on japan, leaves, wraps. (HD. May 21; 167) *Frs.* 4,200

OLIVIER, Guillaume Antoine
- Atlas pour Servir au Voyage dans l'Empire Othoman, l'Egypte et la Perse. Paris, 1800-01-07. 3 pts. in 1 vol. Lge. 4to. 49 (of 50) engraved plts. & maps, many folding, lacks hf.-title, old hf. sheep, worn. (SG. Dec.15; 12) $200
- - Anr. Edn. Paris, [1801]-07. 3 pts. in 1. vol. Fo. 50 full-p., double-p. & folded copperplt. maps, views, ports., & zoological & botanical plts., some foxing, orig. bds., cf. back bds. worn, short recent tape repairs across backstrip. (HA. May 4; 273) $175

OLIVIER, Guillaume Antoine
See— CHAMPAGNAC & Olivier, Guillaume Antoine

OLMSTED, Frederick Law
- A Journey in the Seaboard Slave States. N.Y., 1856. *1st. Edn. (With:)* - A Journey through Texas; or a Saddle-Trip on the Southwestern Frontier. N.Y., 1857. *1st. Edn. (With:)* - A Journey in the Back Country. N.Y., 1860. *1st. Edn.* Together 3 vols. Orig. cl., s.-c.'s; Littell bkplts. (LH. Sep.25; 273) $350
- A Journey through Texas. N.Y., 1857. *1st. Edn.* Advts. at end, orig. cl. (S. Jun.25; 113) *Maggs.* £200

O'LOONEY, Brian
- A Collection of Poems ... By the Clare Bards, in Honor of the Macdonnells of Kilkee & Kilone, in the County of Clare. Collected for Major Mac Donnell. Dublin, for private circulation, 1863. Sm. 8vo. Provincial mor., tooled lines & decor. (GM. Dec.7; 369) £210

OLSCHKI, Leo S.
- La Bibliografia, raccolta di Scritti sull'Arte Antica in Libri, Stampe, Manoscritti, Autografi e Legature. Firenze, 1900-25. Vols. I-XXV & 2 index vols. 4to. Hf. leath, some spines loose. (SI. Dec.18; 232) Lire 1,800,000

OLSON, Charles
- Letter for Melville. [Black Mountain, N.C.], 1951. (10) with watercolour design by author. 2 hf.-sheets, ptd. in black & hand-painted in colours, slightly worn, folded & tipped into wraps.; inscr. to 'Tessa'. (SG. Mar.1; 398) $950
- Maximus, from Dogtown, -I. Foreword:- Michael McClure. San Franc., 1961. (500). 4to. Ptd. wraps., faded; inscr. (SG. May 24; 140) $425
- - Anr. Copy. 4to. Ptd. wraps.; inscr. (SG. May 24; 141) $300
- The Maximus Poems / 1-10. Stuttgart, 1953. (50) sigd. 4to. Prospectus lf. with text by Creeley for The Maximus Poems 11-22 laid in, as iss., prospectus for present edn. also laid in, ptd. on white paper, ptd. wraps., faded; inscr. 'for Joel O'p [?].'. (SG. May 24; 137) $950
- - Anr. Edn. Stuttgart, 1953. (300). 4to. Ptd. on pale green paper, prosnectus lf. with text by Creeley for The Maximus Poems 11-22 laid in, as iss., prospectus for present edn. also laid in, ptd. wraps. (SG. May 24; 138) $175
- - Anr. Edn. N.Y., 1960. 1st. Compl. Edn. (75) numbered. Cl. (SG. May 1; 400) $425
- 'West'. L., 1966. (25) numbered & sigd. Lge. 8vo. Bds., d.-w. (SG. Mar.1; 403) $175
- Y. & X. Ill.:- Corrado Cagli. [Paris], Black Sun Pr./Caresse Crosby, 1948. Ltd. Edn., numbered. 4to. Ptd. self-wraps. (SG. Mar.1; 404) $150
- - Anr. Edn. Ill.:- Corrado Cagli. [Wash.], Black Sun Pr., [1950]. (400). 16mo. Ptd. self-wraps., soiled; inscr. by Caresse Crosby to T.S. Eliot. (SG. Mar.1; 405) $650

OMAN, Charles
- The History of the Peninsular War. Oxford, 1902-30. 1st. Edns. 7 vols. Hf. mor., spine gt., by Bayntun (Rivière). (S. Oct.4; 95) Foyles. £440
- Nelson. L., 1948. Mor., elab. gt., by Bayntun (Rivière), upr. cover inlaid with miniature hand-painted port. of Nelson, boxed, slightly worn. (S. Oct.4; 118) Joseph. £300

OMAR KHAYYAM
- Rubaiyat. Trans.:- [Edward Fitzgerald]. L., 1859. 1st. Edn. (250). Sm. 4to. Orig. ptd. wraps., faint offset from wrap. to blank margins of covers & facing blank fly-ll., folding cl. case, fitted box; Frederic Dannay copy. (CNY. Dec.16; 257) $9,000
- - Anr. Edn. Trans.:- Edward Fitzgerald. L., 1859. 1st. Edn. Misprint 'Lightning' corrected by trans. on p.4, maroon hf. mor.; London Liby. blind-stp. on title recto, cancel stps. on verson. (S. Dec.8; 119) Finch. £980
- - Anr. Copy. Sm. 4to. Bdg. filled out with 24 blank pp. at end, 19th. C. parch., doubls. & free end-pp. covered in gold paint, upr. free end-paper detchd.; letter 'n' deleted by trans. in Stanza XIV, inscr. of John Thaxter stating the book was presented by Fitzgerald to his father, Thomas Wentworth Higginson & Jahu De Witt Miller copy, with 2 letters from Thaxter to Higginson & 2 letters from Higginson to Miller tipped in, anr. related material inserted, Frederic Dannay copy. (CNY. Dec.16; 258) $1,800
- - Anr. Edn. Trans.:- Edward Fitzgerald. Ill.:- Elihu Vedder. Boston, 1884. Sm. fo. 56 full-p. reproductions of handwritten text & drawings, gt.-decor. cl., spine worn. (SG. Dec.15; 179) $175
- - Anr. Edn. Trans.:- E. FitzGerald. N.Y., Grol. Cl., 1885. (150) numbered. Lge. 8vo. Orig. decor. wraps. (SG. Sep.15; 158) $170
- - Anr. Edn. L., 1902. MS. dedication on end-paper, watered, silk end-papers, mor., decor.,

inner & outer gt. dentelle, by Hatchards. (HK. Nov.11; 3533) DM 440
- - Anr. Edn. Ill.:- Edmund Dulac. [1909]. (750) numbered & sigd. by artist. 4to. 20 mntd. cold. plts., orig. vell., lacks 1 tie. (CSK. Jun.29; 157) £190
- - Anr. Copy. Lge. 4to. 20 mntd. cold. plts., orig. vell. gt., lightly soiled, lacks ties. (CSK. Oct.21; 97) £170
- - Anr. Copy. 4to. Ex-series, gt.-decor. vell., unc., ties. (SKC. Sep.9; 1869) £90
- - Anr. Edn. Ill.:- Edmund Dulac. N.Y., [1909]. (200), for sale in the U.S. 4to. 1 sig. partially detchd., gt-decor. vell., soiled & warped. (CBA. Aug.21; 198) $120
- - Anr. Edn. Trans.:- Edward Fitzgerald. Ill.:- after F. Sangorski & G. Sutcliffe. L., [1910]. Fo. Niger mor. gt. by Sangorski & Sutcliffe, gt.-panel., upr. cover with central gt. tudor rose surrounded by rose ornament repeated 8 times in onlaid mor. with onlaid mor. gt. leaf ornaments set against open arabesque with gt. grape & vine cluster corner ornaments, title gt.-lettered above, lr. cover plain but for gt. panelling, spine in 6 compartments, gt.-panel., gt.-lettered in 2 compartments, bd. edges & turn-ins gt., single wrap. preserved, covers stained. (CNY. May 18; 201) $260
- - Anr. Edn. Ill.:- after F. Sangorski & G. Sutcliffe. L., [1911]. (550) numbered & sigd. by artists. This copy numbered '000' & inscr. 'Presentation Copy', plt. margins discold., orig. decor. vell. gt., slightly bowed, spine slightly discold. (S. Dec.20; 590) Cavendish. £110
- - Anr. Edn. Ill.:- H. Fish. L., [1922]. 4to. Some light soiling, orig. cl.-bkd. bds., soiled. (CSK. Feb.24; 181) £50
- - Anr. Edn. Ed.:- E. Heron-Allen. Trans.:- F.W.S. Rolfe. Ill.:- Hamzeh Carr. L., [1924]. Lge. 8vo. Pict. cl. (SG. Mar.1; 508) $275
- - Anr. Edn. Ill.:- Willy Pogany. [1930]. (750) numbered & sigd. by artist. 4to. 1 orig. etching sigd. by Pogany, 12 mntd. col. plts., some light spotting, orig. mor. (CSK. Mar.23; 103) £160
- - Anr. Edn. Ill.:- V. Angelo. N.Y., Ltd. Edns. Cl., 1935. (1500) sigd. by artist. Hand-illuminated, blind-stpd. mor., decor. end-papers, folder & box, both worn; the V. Angelo copy. (CBA. Oct.1; 270) $120
- - Anr. Edn. Ill.:- J. Yunge Bateman. [Waltham St. Lawrence], Gold. Cock. Pr., 1958. (75) with extra suite of plts., specially bnd,. Fo. Rose mor. gt. (SPB. Dec.13; 533) $375
- - Anr. Edn. Ill.:- E. Dulac. N.d. Ltd. Edn., sigd. by artist. 4to. Orig. vell. gt., ties. (P. Feb.16; 289) £190
- - Anr. Edn. Ill.:- after F. Sangorski & G. Sutcliffe. L., n.d. Fo. Elab. vell., gt. stpd. 'Sangorski & Sutcliffe peacock' on upr. cover, watercolour decoration to upr. cover, gt. jewelled clasps. (SPB. Dec.13; 551) $900
- - Anr. Copy. Maroon mor., gt. borders, cold. cf. & mor. gt. onlays, spine gt., turn-ins gt., cl. case, by Riviere & Son, as a bdg., w.a.f. (CNY. Dec.17; 592) $750

O'MEARA, Barry E.
- Napoleon at St. Helena. L., 1888. 2 vols. Extra-ill. with 22 engraved plts., a few hand-cold. or slightly spotted, red mor., elab. gt., by Bayntun (Rivière), upr. cover of Vol. 1 inlaid with miniature hand-painted port. of Napoleon (sigd. Duprie), boxed. (S. Oct.4; 122) Bender. £650

OMEIS, M.D.
- Gründliche Anleitung zut Teutschen Accuraten Reim-und Dicht-Kunst ... Nürnberg, 1712. 2nd. Edn. Title copper engr. with sm. worn trace, minimal browning, cont. vell. (R. Oct.11; 365) DM 730

ON THE AMBITIOUS PROJECTS OF RUSSIA in Regard to North West America ...
San Franc., 1955. (350). Lge. 8vo. Bds., spine extremities slightly darkening. (CBA. Nov.19; 6) $110

ONASSIS, Jacqueline Bouvier Kennedy & Radziwill, Lee Bouvier
- One Special Summer. N.Y., 1974. 1st. Edn. (500) sigd. by authors. 4to. Paper over bds., s.-c. (PNY. Jun.6; 418) $140

ONCKEN, W. & others.
- Allgemeine Geschichte in Einzeldarstellungen. Berlin, 1879-99. Lacks index Vols., some title ll. stpd., 31 hf. leath., not unif., 13 hf. linen, 5 not unif., some slight wear & fading, 1 defect. (H. Nov.23; 506) DM 640

O'NEILL, Eugene
- Anna Christie. Ill.:- Alexander King. N.Y., 1930. (775) sigd. Patterned bds., unc. (SG. Jan.12; 283) $100
- The Emperor Jones. Ill.:- Alexander King. N.Y., 1928. (775) sigd. Patterned bds., unc. d.-w., orig. publisher's box. (SG. Jan.12; 282) $150
- The Hairy Ape. Ill.:- Alexander King. N.Y., 1929. 1st. Separate Edn. (775) numbered & sigd. 4to. Qtr. cl., batik bds., d.-w. frayed, bkplt. removed. (SG. May 24; 352) $100
- The Plays. N.Y., [1934-35]. Wilderness Edn. (770) numbered, sigd. 12 vols. Tall 8vo. Gt.-decor. buckram. (SG. Apr.26; 155) $650
- Strange Interlude. N.Y., 1928. 1st. Edn. (750) sigd. Vell., orig. box., unc. & unopened. (SG. Jan.12; 281) $225

ONGANIA, Ferdinand, Publisher
- Calli, Canali e Isole della Laguna. Streets & Canals in Venice & in the Islands of the Lagoons. Venice, 1894-95. Fo. 100 heliogravure views, 2 titles, 4 p. plt. list in Engl., some foxing thro.-out, loose as iss. in ptd. wraps., torn & reprd., folding cl. case, with mntd. pict. title in Italian. (SG. Nov.10; 127) $600
- Early Venetian Printing Illustrated. Venice, 1895. 4to. Later buckram, orig. upr. wrap. bnd. in. (TA. May 17; 412) £50
- Streets & Canals in Venice (Calli e Canali in Venezia). Venice, 1893. Fo. 100 photogravures, some light foxing thro.-out, minor dampstain in some lr. margins, lr. margins of last few plts. wormed at edge, leath.-bkd. gt.-pict. cl., matching cl.-bkd. bd. portfo., worn, lacks ties. (SG. Nov.10; 126) $850
- - Anr. Copy. Fo. 76 (of 100) photogravures, some foxing thro.-out, especially on 1st. & last ll., some margin defects, leath.-bkd. gt.-pict. cl., worn, partially disbnd. (SG. May 10; 106) $300
- - Anr. Copy. Fo. Lightly browned due to quality of paper, slightly loose, publisher's hf. cf. (CR. Jul.6; 117) Lire 500,000

ONWHYN, Thomas & others
- Thirty-Two Illustrations to Pickwick. [L.], Ca. 1840?. Three-qtr. pol. cf. by Root & Son, orig. ptd. wraps. bnd. in, light wear. (RO. Apr.23; 129) $150

ONZE KUNST. Voortzetting v.d. Vlaamsche School
Amst., 1902-29. Years 1-25, 45 vols. only (Lacks Vol.40), in 43 vols. Lge. 8vo. Orig. cl. gt. (VS. Dec.7; 90) Fls. 675

OORT, Eduard Daniel Van
- Ornithologia Neerlandica – De Vogels van Nederland. Ill.:- after M.A. Koekkoek. 's-Gravenhage, 1922-35. 5 vols. Fo. Without index as usual, orig. hf. mor. gt., 3 spines a little discold. (VS. Jun.6; 515) Fls. 2,300
- - Anr. Copy. 5 vols. Fo. Without 1939 index vol., hf. leath. (VG. May 3; 63) Fls. 1,900

OPAL (The): A Pure Gift for the Holidays, MDCCCXLVII. - ... MDCCCXLVIII
Ed.:- Sarah J. Hale. N.Y., 1847; 1848. 2 vols. 1st. vol. foxed, orig. gt.-ornamental cl., rebkd. with orig. backstrip laid down, & gt.-pict. mor., from liby. of F.D. Roosevelt, both vols. inscr. by him. (SG. Mar.15; 39) $225
- - Anr. Copy. 2 vols. Both vols. foxed, 1st. with hand-cold. additional engraved title, tissue guards, orig. gt.-pict. mor., head of spine torn, gt.-pict. cf., extremities rubbed; from liby. of F.D. Roosevelt, both vols. inscr. by him. (SG. Mar.15; 38) $150

OPITZ, C.
See— KOCH, W. & Opitz, C.

OPITZ, Martin
- Acht Bücher, Deutscher Poematum ... Breslau, 1625. 4to. Mis-paginated, cont. cf., elab. blind-tooled, corners slightly bumped. (H. May 22; 818a) DM 5,400
- Opera Poetica. Amst., 1646 & 1645. *1st. Coll. Edn.* 3 vols. in 1. Cont. vell. (GB. Nov.4; 2144) DM 1,300
- Teutsche Gedichte. Ill.:– M. Tyroff. Frankfurt, 1746. 4 vols. 3 vols. with ex-libris. (HK. Nov.10; 2634) DM 440
- Vielgut. Breslau, 1629. *1st. Edn.* Browned, upr. corner browned thro.-out, Later bds. (R. Oct.11; 366) DM 750

OPPEN, George
- Discrete Series. Preface.:– Ezra Pound. N.Y., 1934. Sm. 8vo. Cl.; Carl Rakoski copy, sigd., inscr. to his wife Leah. (SG. Mar.1; 412) $200

OPPENHEIM, M.
See— RODER, Kurt & Oppenheim, M.

OPPENPORT, Gille Marie
- Premier [-XIme] Livre de Differents Morceaux. Paris, ca. 1725. Pts. 1-11, & Pt. 12, entitled 'Nouveau Livre de Fontaines'. 90 engraved plts. on 72 ll. *(Bound with:)* – Livre de Fragments d'Architecture. Paris, ca. 1725. 14 pts. 84 engraved plts. Together 2 works in 1 vol. Fo. A Few ll. slightly discold., early 19th. C. cf. gt. (C. Dec.9; 106) *Weinreb.* £600

OPPIANUS
- De Venatione Libri IIII. Ed.:– Joan Bodinus Andegavensus. Parigi, 1555. 4to. Light stain, cont. limp vell., 17th. C. sig. (SI. Dec.15; 29) *Lire 320,000.*
- Halieuticks, of the Nature of Fishes & Fishing of the Ancients in V. Books. Trans.:– Draper & John Jones. Oxford, 1722. *1st. Edn. in Engl.* Tall 8vo. (in 4s). Hf.-title, 7-p. subscribers list, cont. panel. cf.; pres. copy inscr. 'Tho: Keath ex Dono Authoris 1724', with handwritten note (perhaps in Jones's hand). (SG. Mar.15; 279) $300

OPUSCULUM, de Variis Judeorum et Gentilium de Christo Testimonis
Oppenheim, n.d. Sm. 4to. Sewed. (HD. Jun.29; 157) Frs. 2,600

ORANGE, James
- A Small Collection of Japanese Lacquer. Yokahama etc., 1910. *1st. Edn.* Sm. 4to. Light wear & dusting, orig. light cl. with brown & red lettering, Japanese bdg. with open cord stitching at backstrip. (HA. May 4; 313) $120

ORANGE RIVER COLONY
- Government Gazette of the Orange River Colony, Letters Patent ... Establishment of Responsible Government ... Bloemfontein, 10 Jun. 1907. Fo. 16 pp. ptd. on yellow silk, orig. bdg. (VA. Apr.27; 795) R 170

ORBELLIS, Nicolas de
- Expositio in Quattuor Sententiarum. Rouen, Martin Morin for Jean Alexandre. Ca. 1497. 4to. Red rubric., margin annots. nearly thro.-out with sig., Packs last 18 ll., old vell. [Goff 0-76] (HD. Jan.30; 19) Frs. 2,700
- Expositio Logicae. Ed.:– Petrus de Parma. Parma, Damianus de Moyllius & Johannes Antonius de Montalli, 30 Apr. 1482. *1st. Edn. [?].* 4to. Wide margin, much marginalia, some pasted over & re-written, lightly browned & slightly soiled or stained thro.-out, cont. limp vell., slightly spotted & loose. [HC. 12043; Goff 0 75; BMC VII, 940] (GT. May 8; 43) DM 3,700

ORBIGNY Alcide d'
- Voyage dans les deux Amériques. Paris, 1854. *New Edn.* Tall 4to. 2 cold folding maps, 27 cold. plts., some light foxing, cont. mor. gt., inner dentelles. (BBA. Feb.9; 276) *Howell,.* $160
- Voyage Pittoresque dans les Deux Amériques. Paris, 1836. Tall 4to. 2 folding maps, 134 plts., some foxing, sm. stp. on title, cont. mor.-bkd. bds.,

spine gt., slightly worn. [Sabin 57458] (BBA. Feb.9; 275) *Howell.* £110

ORBIGNY, Alcide de & Eyries, Jean-Baptiste Benoît
- Viaje Pintoresco a las dos Américas, Asia y Africa. Barcelona, 1842. 2 vols. Fo. 134 steel engrs., 2 folding maps, lge. format, linen. (DS. Feb.24; 2490) Pts. 30,000

ORBIGNY, Charles d'
- Dictionnaire Universel d'Histoire Naturelle. Paris, 1841-49. 13 vols. text & 3 vols. atlas. 288 cold. plts., mntd. on guards (foxing), spots & margin stains to text, unif. hf. chagrin. (HD. Jul.6; 63) Frs. 9,500
- - Anr. Edn. Paris, 1842-49. 16 vols. Lge. 8vo. Approx. 280 engraved illuminated plts., cont. hf. roan, unc. (HD. Mar.19; 84) Frs. 3,300

ORBIGNY, Charles d' (Ed.)
See— KEEPSAKE D'HISTOIRE NATURELLE. Description des Mammières

ORD, George
See— WILSON, Alexander & Ord. George

ORDENANZAS PARA EL GOVIERNO de la Labor de Monedas que se fabricaren en la Real Casa de Moneda de Mexico, y de ma de las Indias
Mexico, 1751. Fo. Stain affecting lr. margins of 1st. ll., blank fore-margin of last lf. slightly defect., disbnd. (S. May 22; 394) *Cortes.* £500

ORDNANCE SURVEY
- Maps of England & Wales. 1865-78. *1st. Edn.* 107 (of 110) hand-cold. maps, sectionalised on linen, 6 orig. s.-c.'s, worn & partly brkn. (TA. Apr.19; 72) £700
- 'Old Series'. L., 1805-24. Sheets approx. 25½ × 37½ inches, boxes 4to. 85 engraved maps (nos. 1-84 & index sheet) depicting Southern England & Wales, each in 16 sections. linen-bkd., edged in blue silk, with numbered tabs, folding into 21 mor. boxes, covers with gt. & blind-tooled borders, spines gt., slightly scuffed. (C. Jun.27; 53) *Traylen.* £1,800
- Scotland. Edinb., [1856-57]. Fo. 131 uncold. engraved map-sheets, cont. hf. bdg., worn. (PD. Apr.18; 161) £460

ORDONNANCE DE LOUIS XIV pour les Armées Navales et Arcenaux de Marine
Paris, 1689. 4to. Cont. cf., spine decor., slightly worn, some repairs. (HD. Jul.2; 28) Frs. 2,200

ORDONNANCE DU ROI, du 6 Décembre 1829, sur l'Exercise et les Evolutions de la Cavalerie
Paris, 1830. 3 vols. 12mo. Some spotting, orig. bds., orig. s.-c. (CSK. Sep.16; 184) £65

ORDONNANCE, EDICT & DECRET DU ROY sur le Faict de la Iustice Criminelle es Pays Baz
Anvers, [1570]. *1st. Edn. 2nd. Iss.* 2 pts. in 1 vol. 4to. L.P., interleaved, many cont. annots. in margins & on blank ll., few margin stains, cont. limp vell. (VG. Sep.14; 954) Fls. 650

ORDONNANTIE VAN HEER ENDE WETH DER STAD GEND
See— PHARMACOPOEA GANDAVENSIS Nobilissimi Senatus Jussu Renovata – ORDONNANTIE VAN HEER ENDE WETH DER STAD GEND

ORELLANA, Francisco J.
- Historia del General Prim. Barcelona, [1900]. 3 vols. 4to. Linen, corners. (DS. Oct.28; 2064) Pts. 26,000

ORENDI, Jul.
- Das Gesamtwissen über Antike und Neue Teppiche des Orients. Wien, 1930. *1st. Edn.* 2 vols. 1 plt. with sm. tear in margin, orig. linen. (GB. Nov.4; 1404) DM 1,200
- - Anr. Copy. 2 vols. Orig. linen, 2 jnts. torn. (BR. Apr.13; 2082) DM 800

ORFORD, Horace Walpole, Earl of
See— WALPOLE, Horace, Earl of Orford

ORIENTAL ART
1948-82. Vol. 1 - new series vol. 28 in 13 vols. & 40 orig. iss. 4to. Cont. cl. with orig. wraps. bnd. in, & orig. wraps. (CSK. Jun.29; 16) £360

ORIENTAL CERAMIC SOCIETY
- Transactions. 1923-[82]. *Some vols. Ltd. Edns.* Vols. 1-45. 4to. Orig. cl. & wraps., last vol. with d.-w. (CSK. Jun.29; 18) £450
- - Anr. Edn. 1942-76. *Ltd. Edns.* Vols. 18, 20-40. 4to. Cont. cl., soiled. (CSK. Jun.29; 102) £260
- - Anr. Edn. [L., 1951-67]. *Ltd. Edns.* Vols. 24-27 & 33-36. Tall 4to. Unif. cl. (SG. Oct.13; 74) $150

ORIGENES
- Contra Celsum et in Fidei Christianae Defensionem Libri. Trans.:– [Christophorus Persona]. Rome, Georgius Herolt, Jan. 1481. *1st. Edn.* 2 vols. Fo. & 4to. Some light foxing, quire [d] misbnd. after quire [a], cont. limp vell., torn. [BMC IV, 126; Goff 0-95; HC 12078*] (SPB. Dec.14; 28) $2,000
- Opera. Ill.:– A. Dürer. Paris, 1522. *1st. Latin Coll. Edn. 3rd. Printing.* 4 pts. in 1 vol. Fo. Pt. 1 title with slight wear, some old MS. annots., some inking, slightly stained near end, leath., ca. 1700, very bumped & rubbed, spine defect. (HK. Nov.8; 304) DM 620

ORIGIN: A Quarterly for the Creative
[Dorchester, Mass., 1951-52]. Nos. 1, 3, 4 & 6. Ptd. wraps.; no. 1 inscr. & with penciled drawings & sm. correction by Charles Olson, the others his own copies, no.6 with about 20 MS. corrections. (SG. Mar.1; 408) $275

ORLEANS, Charles d'
- Gebed om Vrede. Groningen, Priv. ptd., May 1943. *(75).* 4to. Pict. wraps., 1 corner lightly creased. (H. Nov.24; 2208) DM 1,100
- Poèmes. Ill.:– H. Matisse. Paris, 1950. *(1200) numbered & sigd. by Matisse.* Fo. Cont. pig-bkd. bds., unc., slightly soiled, orig. wraps. & spine preserved, s.-c. (BBA. Jan.19; 315) *Duran.* £300
- - Anr. Edn. Ill.:– Henri Matisse. Paris, 1950. *(1200) on Arches.* Lge. 4to. Leaves, box. (HD. Sep.22; 280) Frs. 2.500
- - Anr. Edn. Ill.:– Henri Matisse. Paris, 1950. *(1230) numbered & sigd. by artist.* Fo. Unsewn in orig. wraps., unc., folder & s.-c., the latter slightly defect. (S. Nov.21; 104) *Marks.* £420
- - Anr. Copy. Fo. Unsewn in orig. wraps., unc., litho. cover designs, worn, upr. cover stained. (S. Nov.21; 34) *Makiya.* £380
- - Anr. Edn. Ill.:– Henri Matisse. Paris, 1950. Fo. On vélin d'Arches, leaves, wrap. & s.-c.; sigd. by ill. at end. (HD. May 16; 93) Frs. 5,100
- Poésies. Grenoble, 1803. *Orig. Edn.* 12mo. Dedication from P.V. Chalvet to Barthelemy, 19th. C. hf. red chagrin, corners, unc. (HD. Dec.16; 13) Frs. 2,500

ORLEANS, Louis Philippe d'
[-] Les Associations Ouvrières en Angleterre. Paris, 1869. Hf.-title, some ll. slightly spotted, upr. margins dampstained cont. hf. cf., gt. spine; inscr. 'A Sir Robert Peel de la part de l'auteur Louis Philippe D'Orleans'. (BBA. Oct.27; 27) *Pickering & Chatto.* £90
- Description des Principales Pierres Gravés du Cabinet d'Orleans. Paris, 1780-84. 2 vols. Fo. Port., 2 vig. titles, 178 engrs., mor. gt., 1 spine defect. (P. Dec.8; 269a) *Tzakas.* £90

ORLEANS, Pierre Joseph d'
- Histoire des Revolutions d'Espagne depuis la Destruction de l'Empire des Goths jusqu'à l'Entière et Parfaite Réunion des Royaumes de Castille et d'Aragon en une Seule Monarchie. Paris, 1734. 3 vols. Fo. L.P., leath. (DS. Nov.25; 2158) Pts. 36,000

ORLERS, Jan Jansz.
- Beschrijving der Stad Leyden. Leiden, 1781. *3rd. Edn.* 3 vols. in 2. Sm. 4to. 2 plts. a little browned in Vol. 1 & 1 or 2 with sm. tears at folds, unc. mod. wraps. (CH. Sep.20; 38) Fls. 1,000
[-] Description & Representation de Toutes les Victoires des Provinces Unies du Pais-Bas sous la Conduite & Gouvernement de Prince Maurice de Nassau. Leiden, 1612. Sm. Fo. Some slight browning, cont. leath., worn, spine slightly defect. (R. Oct.13; 3132) DM 1,500
- Genealogia Illustr. Comit. Nassouiae ... ab 682 ad

ORLERS, Jan Jansz. *-Contd.*

hunc 1616. Leyden, priv. ptd., 1616. Fo. Mod. hf. vell., unc. (VG. Sep.14; 1184) Fls. 900
[–] **La Généalogie des Illustres Comtes de Nassau, nouvellement Imprimée avec la Description de Toutes les Victoires** ... Leyde, 1625. *2nd. Edn.* Sm. fo. Cont. cf. gt., slightly worn. (HD. Nov.29; 66) Frs. 3,400

ORLIK, Emil
– **Aus dem Reigen-Process 1921.** Berlin, 1921. *(150)* on Bütten. Fo. Sigd. by artist on printers mark, 14 sigd. orig. lithos., pict. bd. portfo., spine defect. (GB. May 5; 3048) DM 4,200

ORLOWSKI, G.
– **Russian Cries, in Correct Portraiture from Drawings done on the Spot by ... ; & now in the Possession of the ... Lord Kinnair.** Ill.:– J. Godby. L., 1809. Sm. fo. Engraved title with cold. vig., 8 cold. copperplts., title cut slightly close in right margin, later linen, spine defect.; Hauswedell coll. (H. May 23; 164) DM 600

ORLOWSKI, Hans
– **Amiran. Eine Georgische Sage.** Berlin, 1924. *(50) numbered.* 4to. Printers mark sigd. by artist & with MS. dedication, 4 sigd. orig. woodcuts, orig. wraps., repeated title. (GB. May 5; 3050) DM 500
– **Das Jüngste Gericht.** Berlin, 1923. *(100) numbered.* Fo. Printers mark sigd. by artist with MS. dedication, 6 orig. woodcuts sigd., some nearly full-p. hand-cold. initials, text wood engraved thro.-out, orig. hf. vell. (GB. May 5; 3051) DM 900

ORME, Edward
– **Collection of British Field Sports.** Ill.:– after orig. engraved designs by S. Howitt. [Guildford, 1955]. Ob. fo. Pict. title, pict. plt. list, & 20 plts., ptd. in col., hf. mor., slightly rubbed. (SG. Mar.15; 280) $100
– **Historic, Military & Naval Anecdotes.** L., n.d. [plts. wtrmkd. 1829]. 4to. 40 hand-cold. aquatint plts., minor stain on frontis., slight offset from some plts onto text, short tear reprd. in blank inner margin of plt. 39, with only 1 rule below Battle of Waterloo on title, cont. hf. mor., gt. spine. (C. Jun.27; 54) *Ross.* £600
– **A Picture of St. Petersburgh.** 1815. Fo. Engraved title (loose) 18 (of 20) hand-cold. plts., orig. bds., upr. cover detchd. (P. Feb.16; 159) £460
See— JENKINS, James – ORME, Edward

ORMEROD, George
– **The History of the County Palatine & City of Chester.** L., 1819. *1st. Edn.* 3 vols. Fo. Engraved map, 47 plts. (4 cold.), some spotting, cl., unc. (S. Mar.6; 497) *Coombes.* £240
– – **Anr. Copy.** 3 vols. Fo. Engraved port. & 44 plts. (2 hand-cold.), 3 maps, orig. bds., rebkd. (CSK. Jul.6; 64) £200
– – **Anr. Copy.** 3 vols. Fo. Port., 2 hand-cold. engraved maps & plts., some cold., heightened with gold, cont. russ., some covers detchd. (S. Apr.9; 182) *Kidd.* £160
– – **Anr. Edn.** L., 1882. *2nd. Edn.* 3 vols. Few ll. Vol. 1 & few plts. stained, some slight spotting, orig. cl.-bkd. bds., unc., cockled, worn. (S. Mar.6; 498) *Hepner.* £130
– – **Anr. Copy.** 3 vols. Fo. L.P., frontis. port. in Vol. 1 detchd. & frayed, orig. cl.- bkd. bds., rubbed, paper labels worn. (C. Mar.14; 74) *Chesters.* £110

ORMONDE, James, Duke of
– **The Life of** ... L., 1747. *1st. Edn.* Bkplt., cf., rubbed. (GM. Dec.7; 144) £65
– – **Anr. Edn.** Oxford, 1851. *New Edn.* 6 vols. Cf. (GM. Dec.7; 449) £180

ORNANO, Marquis d'
– **La Corse Militaire.** Paris, 1904. Lge. 8vo. Mod. marb. hf. roan, corners, wrap.; dedication from author to Princesse Pierre-Napoléon Bonaparte. (HD. Oct.21; 135) Frs. 1,700

OROSIUS, Paulus
– **Histo-Tiographi Clarissimi opus prestatissimū.** 1510. Some light dampstains, 19th. C. hf. mor. gt. (P. Jun.7; 122) £75

OROUX, Abbé
– **Histoire Ecclesiastique de la Cour de France** ... Paris, 1776-77. 2 vols. 4to. Cont. cf. gt., Louis XVI arms, cypher repeated on spines. (HD. May 21; 61) Frs. 3,100

ORR, Hiram Winnett
– **A Catalogue of the H. Winnett Orr Historical Collection & Other Rare Books in the Library of the American College of Surgeons.** Chic., 1960. Sm. 4to. Cl. gt. (SG. Sep.15; 251) $110

ORR, Louis
– **Ten Etchings of Yale University.** [1926]. Fo. Etched title, 10 etched plts., contents 1f., some foxing, loose in ptd. paper portfo. as iss., light wear; each plt. sigd. in pencil by artist. (RO. Dec.11; 264) $160

ORRERY, Roger Boyle, Earl of
– **A Treatise of the Art of War.** L., 1677. Engraved frontis.-port., 6 double-p. engraved plans, lightly damp-wrinkled, cont. panel. cf., brittle, rebkd. [Wing 0-499] (SG. Apr.19; 143) $110

ORSCHALL, Joh. Chr.
[–] **Ars Fusoria Fundamentalis et Experimentalis, das ist Gründliche und auss Erfahrenheit Stammende Schmeltz-Kunst oder Gründlicher Unterricht vom Rohschmeltzen, Rösten und Seigern.** Cassel, 1687. (*Bound with:*) – **Wunder-drey, das ist Beschreibung Dreyer dem Ansehen nach Unannehmlicher der Practic nach aber wohl Practibler Particularian.** Cassel, 1684. (*Bound with:*) – **Wunder-dreyes Continuatio, welches sind Fernere Experimenta.** Cassel, 1686. Together 3 works in 1 vol. 12mo. Minor staining in lr. hf. of vol., cont. vell. (C. May 30; 119) *Hill.* £500
– **Oeuvres Metallurgiques ... traduit de l'Allemand.** Paris, 1761. 12mo. Errata 1f., cont. mott. cf., spine gt. (C. May 30; 120) *Thorp.* £180

ORTA, Garcia da
– **Aromatum et Simplicium Aliquot Medicamentorum apud Indos Nascentium Historia.** Trans.:– C. Clusius. Ill.:– A. Nicolai after P. van der Borcht. Antw., 1567. *1st. Ill. Edn.* Sm. 8vo. Slightly browned, blank lr. margin of 1 lf. cut off, cont. limp vell. (VG. Nov.30; 773) Fls. 2,400

ORTELIUS, Abraham
– **Epitome Theatri Orteliani.** Maps:– Philip Galle. Antw., C. Plantin, 1589. Ob. 8vo. Ptd. title with sm. woodcut device: engraved trinity plt., & 94 engraved maps by Philip Galle in text, title reprd. without loss of ptd. surface, some margin staining, sm. inscr. on front pastedown, cont. vell., soiled, w. a. f. (S. May 21; 96) *T. Schuster.* £650
– **Théâtre de l'Univers.** Antw., 1572 [colophon, title-slip: 1574]. Fo. Architectural engraved title with pasted on slips, 65 hand-cold. double-p. mapsheets, comprising 50 (of 53) of the maps in the 1572 edn. & 15 (of 16) of the maps from the Fr. addition of 1574, a few mapsheets torn & reprd., some with margin repairs touching engraved surface, 1 or 2 maps with surface flaws or stains, title soiled, 19th. C. hf. vell., worn. (S. Dec.1; 179) *Burgess.* £3,800
– – **Anr. Edn.** [Antw.], 1587. *3rd. Fr. Edn.* Fo. Engraved allegorical title, port., 112 double-p. engraved maps, (36 x 50 cm.), last lf. (colophon) reprd., a little soiled, stained or margin stained in parts, 17th. C. blind- stpd. vell., rebnd.; H. Boekenoogen bookplt. (VS. Jun.7; 990) Fls. 32,000
– **Theatro d'Abrahamo Ortelio, Ridotto in Forma Piccola.** Maps:– Philip Galle. Antw., Officina Plantiniana, 1593. *1st. Italian text Edn.* Ob. 8vo. Ptd. title with device (engraved allegorical plt. on verso), 107 engraved maps, slight browning, some worming touching a few headlines, cont. vell., soiled, w.a.f. (S. May 21; 97) *T. Schuster.* £700
– **Theatro del Mondo.** Trans.:– Filippo Pigafetta. Antw., J.B. Vrients. 1608. *1st. Edn. in Italian.* 2 pts. in 1 vol. Fo. Engraved architectural title with engraved port. of Pope Clement VIII by J.B. Vrients on verso, engraved port. of Ortelius by Galle on verso, engraved epitaph incorporating miniature port. of Ortelius, 'Introduttione Mathematica nelle tavole geografiche' by Michel Coignet with 5 engraved ills. in text, & 183 maps on 127 double-p. engraved mapsheets; 'Parergon ... overa alcune tavole dell'antica geografia', ptd. title in engraved architectural border, 44 maps, views & plts. on 38 double-p. engraved mapsheets, 'Nomenclator Ptolemaicus' at end, titles, ports., ills. & maps cont. hand-cold., woodcut initials in text similarly so, sm. split at lr. centrefold of world map & map of Italy in Theatrum (1st. reprd., minimal loss of engraved surfaced), & in 1st. map of Palestine in 'Parergon', sm. natural flaw in map of Artois, some faint browning, margin stains affecting a few text ll., cont. gt.- panel. vell., split at head of spine, slightly soiled. (S. Feb.1; 40) *Burgess.* £36,000
– **Il Theatro del Mondo ... Ridotto de la Forma Grande, [Epitome].** Brescia, Compagnia Bresciana, 1598. *1st. Italian ptd. Edn.* 4to. Ptd. title with lge. woodcut device (repeated at end), 109 engraved maps inset into text, woodcut heading & initials, index at end after colophon, some spotting, cont. vell., w.a.f. (S. May 21; 99) *Witt.* £1,000
– **Theatro del Mondo ... Ridotto a Intiera Perfettione.** Venice, G.M. Turrini, 1655 [preface dated July 15]. Ptd. title with lge. woodcut device, 106 full-p. engraved maps (of 109, but including world & 4 continents), title & outer margins of 1st. few ll. reprd., faint browning, vell. bds., w.a.f. (S. May 21; 108) *Schmidt.* £440
– **Theatro de la Tierre Universal.** Antw., 1588. *1st. Spanish Edn.* Fo. Copper engraved title border, 1 full-p. port. copper engr., 100 double-p. copper engraved maps, wear & soiling in margins, some light browning & foxing, 8 plts. with tear to subject, 7 plts. with longer tears, (6 bkd.), 9 plts. with margin tears, 6 end plts. with slight worming, 1 map very browned & creased, torn & bkd., cont. leath., very rubbed & bumped, spine defect. (R. Oct.13; 2864) DM 25,500
– **Theatrum Orbis Terrarum.** Antw., A.C. Diesth, 1571. Fo. Latin text, engraved title, (defect, cut round & mntd.), 53 double-p. engraved mapsheets, browned thro.-out, several mapsheets shaved, some worming affecting some engraved surfaces, a few repairs, cont. vell., soiled, w.a.f. (S. May 21; 88) *Marshall.* £2,400
– – **Anr. Copy.** Fo. Engraved title & 35 (of 53) double-p. engraved maps, uncold., title stained, chipped, partially reprd. along upr. margin, margins of dedication & several maps also reprd., some staining & rubbing thro.-out, especially at map corners, lacks world map, maps of America, Asia, Africa, & several others, although Latin text & colophon dtd. 1571, vol. varies from Koeman's Ort 2: epigram on title verso longer than 4 lines, Catalogus Auctorum has 92 names, P. an iiijv ends 'in Sclauoniam pro-.', Map 29 is 'Bavariae olim Vindeliciae,' called for in 1571 Dutch edn. & afterwards, old cf., shabby. (SG. Jun.7; 35) $2,600
– – **Anr. Edn.** Antw., 1575. *5th. Latin Edn.* Fo. All maps in col. & partly gold heightened, engraved title reprd., 2 maps reprd. in margin, some sm. margin tears & creases, later cf. gt., spine & corners renewed, slightly rubbed & bumped; ex-libris, Hauswedell coll. (H. May 24; 875) DM 44,000
– – **Anr. Edn.** Antw., Officina Plantiniana, 1592. 2 Pts. in 1 vol. Fo. Latin text, engraved architectural title, engraved port. of Ortelius by Philip Galle, & 160 maps on 108 double-p. engraved mapsheets; Parergon, sive Veteris Geographiae aliquot tabulae, ptd. title in wood-engraved architectural border, & 28 maps & 1 view on 26 double-p. engraved mapsheets, Nomenclatur Ptolemaicus at end, both titles, port. & maps cold. by cont. hand & heightened with gold thro.-out, woodcut initials, head- &-tail pieces in text hand-cold., short split in centrefold of map of Europe without loss of engraved surface, maps of Spain, Franconia, Verona in the Theatrum, & ancient Spain in the Parergon faintly browned, 1 or 2 light creases elsewhere, cont. cf., richly gt., lge. corner & central arabesque on upr. & lr. covers, reprd., new guards & end-papers, new ties. (S. Feb.1; 39) *Israel.* £58,000
– **Theatrum Orbis Terrarum. –Parergon. – Nomenclator Ptolemaicus.** Antw., Officina Plantiniana, 1595 [Nomenclator Ptolemaicus so dtd.]. 3 pts. in 1 vol. Fo. Latin text, engraved title, port. of Ortelius, & 115 mapsheets; Parergon: ptd. title in woodcut border & 32 mapsheets; Nomenclator Ptolemaicus: ptd. title with woodcut device;

together 147 double-p. engraved mapsheets, hand-cold. in full thro.-out (engraved title heightened with gold) in cont. hand, including woodcut text initials, 1 or 2 minor repairs at centre-folds without loss of engraved surface, sm. liby. stp. erased from foot of title, a few ll. of text lightly browned, some margin soiling, vell. bds., slightly worn, w.a.f. (S. May 21; 92) *Arkway.* £18,000
– – **Anr. Edn.** Antw., Jan Baptist Vrients, 1603. 3 pts. in 1 vol. Fo. Latin text, engraved title with arms of Philip of Spain on verso, engraved epitaph plt. & port. of Ortelius, & 118 mapsheets; Parergon: engraved title, & 36 mapsheets (of 38: without the Tempe & Daphne plts.); Nomenclator Ptolemaicus: ptd. title with engraved device incorporating world map; together 154 double-p. engraved mapsheets, cont. hand-cold. thro.-out, some discolouration or slight offsetting, title & 1 or 2 mapsheets split or neatly reprd. without loss of engraved surface, some wormholes, cont. blind-stpd. cf., worn, w.a.f. (S. May 21; 102) *Marshall.* £16,000

ORTELIUS, Abraham & Vivianus, Johannes
– **Itinerarium per nonnullas Galliae Belgicae Partes ... ad G. Mercatorem.** Anvers, 1584. 12mo. Cont. vell. (HD. Dec.2; 132) Frs. 1,900

ORTH, J. Ph.
[–] **Nöthig und Nützlich-erachtete Anmerckungen über die ... Tituln ... der so genannten Erneueden Reformation der Stadt Frankfurt am Mayn.** Frankfurt, 1731-75. Main vol., 4 continuation vols. & supp. vol. in 6 vols. 4to. Some slight foxing, private hf. leath. (D. Nov.23; 1472) DM 2,250

ORTIZ, Fernando
– **Los Instrumentos de la Musica Afrocubana.** La Habana, 1952. 5 vols. 4to. Pict. wraps. (DS. Jan.27; 2660) Pts. 22,000

ORVILLE, Jacobus Phillipus de
– **Sicula, Quibus Siciliae Veteris Rudera.** Amst., 1764. 2 vols. Fo. Hf.-titles, Vol. 1 lacks 2P3-4, cont. mott. cf. (S. Oct.11; 412) *Callea.* £80
– – **Anr. Copy.** 2 vols. bnd. in 1. Fo. Hf. vell., 5 gt. decor. spine raised bands. (CR. Jun.6; 238) Lire 400,000

ORWELL, George (Pseud.)
See— BLAIR, Eric Arthur 'George Orwell'

OSANN, E.
– **Physikal.-medicinische Darstellung der Bekannten Heilquellen der vorzüglichsten Länder Europas.** Berlin, 1829-32. Vols. 1-2 (all publd.). Vol. 1 foxed, vol. 2 title verso stpd., cont. bds. (R. Apr.4; 1276) DM 1,050

OSANN, E. (Ed.)
See— JOURNAL DER PRACTISCHEN HEIL-KUNDE

OSBALDESTON, George
– **His Autobiography.** Ed.:– E.D. Cuming. 1926. *(100) with 13 extra plts.* 4to. Cl., unc. (P. Feb.16; 105) £65

OSBALDISTON, William Augustus
– **The British Sportsman.** N.d. 4to. Engraved frontis. & 40 plts. only, frontis., title & prelims. dampstained & torn with some loss. (CSK. Jun.15; 120) £110

OSBORN, Capt. Sherard
– **Quedah; Or, Stray leaves from a Journal in Malayan Waters.** 1857. Publisher's catalogue bnd. in at end, minor spotting, untrimmed, orig. cl. (TA. Sep.15; 79) £60

OSBORNE, Edward Cornelius & W.
– **Guide to the Grand Junction, or Birmingham, Liverpool, & Manchester Railway ...** Bg'ham., 1838. *2nd. Edn.* Sm. 8vo. Advts. bnd. in at end, orig. cl., rubbed. (TA. May 17; 152) £56
– – **Anr. Copy.** Sm. 8vo. Advts. bnd. in at end, engraved map partially torn along 1 fold, orig. cl., slightly frayed at spine ends. (TA. May 17; 153) £54
– **London & Birmingham Railway Guide.** Ill.:– mostly by Samuel Williams. Ca. 1838. Slight staining, orig. cl., slightly worn, lacks end-papers. (SKC. Jan.13; 2289) £60

OSBORNE, Francis
[–] **Advice to a Son; or, Directions for your Better Conduct ...** Oxford, 1656. *1st. Edn.* Sm. 8vo. 19th. C. pol. cf. gt., hinges brkn. (SG. Oct.27; 241) $275

OSBORNE, Max
– **Die Kunst des Rokoko.** Berlin, 1929. Publishers cf. (CR. Jun.6; 239) Lire 180,000

OSBOURNE, Lloyd
See— STEVENSON, Robert Louis & Osbourne, Lloyd

OSENBRÜGGEN, E.
– **Alpes et Glaciers de la Suisse.** Basel, ca. 1880. 4to. Foxed, orig. linen gt. (R. Apr.5; 3094) DM 2,100
– **Das Hochgebirge der Schweiz.** Basle, n.d. 4to. Engraved frontis., 63 plts., spotting thro.-out, cont. hf. mor. (CSK. Nov.4; 16) £300
– **Die Urschweiz.** Basel, ca. 1870. *4th. Iss.* 4to. Engraved title, 63 steel-engraved views, some spotting, slightly loose, cl., spotted, slightly defect. (B. Oct.4; 673) Fls. 1,600
– – **Anr. Edn.** Basel, ca. 1900. 4to. 64 steel-engrs., lacks 3 ills., 3 supp. plts., hf. linen. (G. Sep.15; 2295) Sw. Frs. 3,200
– – **Anr. Edn.** Ill.:– I. Huber & others. Basel, n.d. Lge. 4to. 64 steel engraved plts., orig. gold-tooled linen. (GF. Nov.16; 1149) Sw. Frs. 1,800

OSIANDER, A., the elder
[–] **Grundt und Ursach aus der Heiligen Schrifft ...** Wittenberg, 1525. Some soiling, hf. vell. (R. Oct.11; 89) DM 480
– **Vermutung von den Letzten Zeiten und dem Ende der Welt, aus der Heiligen Schrifft gerzogen.** Nürnberg, 1545. *1st. Edn.* 4to. Wraps. (R. Oct.11; 90) DM 600

OSLER, Sir William
– **Bibliotheca Osleriana: a Catalogue of Books Illustrating the History of Medicine & Science.** Oxford, 1929. *1st. Edn.* 4to. Buckram. (SG. Oct.6; 282) $250
– **Incunabula Medica. A Study of the Earliest Printed Medical Books, 1467-1480.** 1923. 4to. Orig. buckram-bkd. bds.; H.M. Nixon coll. (BBA. Oct.6; 207) *Zeitlin & Verbrugge.* £120
– **The Principles & Practice of Medicine.** N.Y., 1892. *1st. Edn. 2nd. Iss., with the 'Gorgias' reading.* Lge. 8vo. 6 & 8 pp. of advts. at end, the latter dtd. Oct. 1892, rebnd., orig. covers laid down. (SG. Oct.6; 280) $175

OSORIUS, Hieronymus
– **De Gloria Libri V.** 1580. Sm. 8vo. Cont. cf. [STC 18884.3] (BBA. Jun.14; 23) *Quaritch.* £150
– **Histoire de Portugal.** Paris, 1581. Cont. vell., wallet-edge. (SG. Apr.5; 288) $300

OSSERVATORE ROMANO. Giornale Quotidiano Politico Religioso
Città del Vaticano, [1 Jan.] 1927-[30 Jun.] 1939. 25 vols. (lacks vol. 85 (Oct.-Dec. 1935)). Lge. fo. Bnd. (B. Feb.8; 951) Fls. 475

OSSIAN
– **Die Gedichte von Ossian dem Sohne Fingals.** 'Trans.':– James Macpherson. Trans.:– Friedrich Leopold. Hamburg, 1806. *1st. Edn.* 3 vols. Wide margin, slightly foxed thro.-out, cont. gold-tooled cf., gt., floral gold decor., inner & outer dentelle, minimal rubbing, corners bumped, vol. 1 spine lightly defect. (HT. May 9; 1595) DM 700
– **Fingal, an Ancient Epic Poem ... by Ossian.** 'Trans.':– J. Macpherson. 1762. *1st. Edn. (With:)*
– **Temora, an Ancient Epic Poem ... by Ossian.** 'Trans.':– J. Macpherson 1763. Together 2 vols. 4to. Cont. spr. cf., spines gt.-decor.; Sir Ivar Colquhoun, of Luss copies. (CE. Mar.22; 205) £300
– **Ossian's Gedichte.** 'Trans.':– J. Macpherson. Trans.:– J.H. Rhode. Ill.:– Rhode. Berlin, 1800. *1st. Edn. ill. Rhode.* 3 vols. Some light foxing, cont. lf. leath. cf., slightly worn. (H. May 22; 819) DM 740

OSSIETZKY, Maud von (Ed.)
See— WELTBUHNE

OSTADE, Adrian
– **Het Compeete Etswerk van Adrian van Ostade.** Ed.:–H.P. Bremmer. Utrecht, ca. 1913. 4to. Orig. lf. leath. portlo., wear. (D. Nov.23; 1841) DM 400

OSTAIJEN, P. van
– **Bezette Stad.** Ill.:– O. Jespers. Amst., 1921. *1st. Edn. (540).* 4to. Name on hf.-title, orig. pict. wraps., back slightly worn, unc. (B. Apr.27; 968) Fls. 1,200
– **Krities Proza.** Antw., [1929-31]. *1st. Edn. (525).(25) on Pannekoek paper.* 2 vols. Orig. wraps., unc. (B. Apr.27; 971) Fls. 600

OSTWALD, W.
– **Lebenslinien. Eine Selbstbiographie.** Berlin, 1927. *1st. Edn. (100) numbered special Edn.* 3 vols. MS. name on 3 titles, orig. aqua., MS. painted tempera ill. & Farbenpartitur. with gt. monog. & border & verso Farbenpartitur, name on hf.-title, orig. aqua., orig. cf. (GB. May 5; 3054) DM 450

OTHO, Georgius
– **Palaestra Linguarum Orientalium.** Frankfurt, 1702. 4to. Title stained, some foxing, cont. hf. vell., spine worn. (SG. Feb.9; 329) $100

OTHO, Georguis
See— ALTING, Jacob – OTHO

OTTENS, Reiner & Joshua
– **Atlas [sive Geographia Compendiosa ...].** Amst., ca. 1750. Fo. 41 double-p. & folding hand-cold. maps, 3 double-p. tables, later hf. vell. (TA. Sep.15; 64) £920
– – **Anr. Edn.** [Amst.], ca. 1750. Lge. fo. 19 hand-cold. double-p. engraved maps, & 1 cont. hand-cold. double-p. engraved map of Europe, Asia & Africa from Jansson's atlas, cont. bds., slightly defect. (VS. Dec.9; 1268) Fls. 3,200
– – **Anr. Edn.** Ill.:– Munnikhuysen after Webbers (title). Amst., ca. 1790. Fo. 33 engraved maps, all but 1 double-p. & cont. hand-cold., & 1 engraved map from Engl. atlas, 1794, 19th. C. hf. cf. (VS. Dec.9; 1269) Fls. 4,200
– **Atlas van Vytegezogte Landkaarten.** Amst., ca. 1730. Lge. fo. Composite atlas, engraved general title by J. van Munnikhuysen after L. Webbers with Ottens imprint, additional engraved title to Covens & Mortier Atlas Novus (ca. 1730) by Romein de Hooghe, 4 engraved allegorical frontis. Europa, Asia, Africa & America, as sectional titles orig. publd. in Blaeu Atlas Major 1662, all but 1st. with Ottens imprint, ptd. title in red & black to Dutch text of Sanson's Inleidinge tot de Geografie followed by 20 ll. of ptd. text, double-p. MS. index listing 94 subjects (including titles & index) & full-p. MS. copy of poem Op het Toonneel des Aerdryx, ofte Nieuwe Atlas by Joost van den Vondel both written in ink, 85 maps & charts, mostly double-p. or folding, including 5 wall-maps in sheets, by various 17th. & 18th. C. mapmakers, 4 astronomical plts. by or after C. Allard, J.G. Doppel-maier & N. de Fer, 2 sheets, joined, & partly unc., of armorial playing cards by Claude Oronce Finé (1660, Caspar Specht iss. of ca. 1710) titled in MS., 2 distance tables also by Specht, 1 naval plt., 1 plt. showing naval ensigns, both by Covens & Mortier, engraved titles, maps & plts. richly illuminated & heightened with gold in cont. hand thro.-out, titles cut round & mntd., mapsheets & ptd. text mostly inlaid to lge. fo., 1 or 2 folding maps a little weak at additional folds (without significant loss of engraved surface), 1 or 2 faint stains, cont. Dutch red mor., gt.-panel., slightly worn, title on spine. (S. Feb.1; 41) *Prince.* £88,000
– **Nieuw en Accuraat Geographies Kaart-Boekje van de XVII Nederlandse Provincien.** Maps:– Jacob Kiezer. Amst., [1725-50]. Sm. 4to. Engraved title, 25 double-p. hand-cold. maps, mntd. on guards, engraved title cut round & mntd., fore-margin of 1 map soiled & frayed, cont. mor. gt., upr. cover detchd. (C. Mar.14; 75) *Ward.* £420
– **Het Verheerlykt Utrecht ...** Amst., ca. 1730. Fo. Engraved double-p. folding map, 32 views on 16 plts., cont. paper bds., upr. cover detchd. (C. Nov.16; 143) *Loose.* £550

OTTLEY, William Young
- A Collection of Fac-Similes of Scarce & Curious Prints, by the Early Masters of the Italian, German, & Flemish Schools ... L., 1826. *1st. Edn. 1st. Iss.* Fo. L.P., 100 mntd. India-proof plts., & 12 dupls. of the Niello plts. ptd. in silver, cont. vell.-bkd. cl., disbnd. & shaken. (SG. Oct.13; 268) $225
- - **Anr. Edn.** L., 1828. Fo. Additional engraved title reprd. at inner margin, plts., some margin soiling, cont. hf. mor., rubbed, rebkd., reprd. (S. Apr.30; 214) *Shapero.* £100
- - **Anr. Copy.** Fo. Title spotted, hf. vell. (P. Sep.29; 8) *Edistar.* £70
- An Inquiry into the Origin & Early History of Engraving upon Copper & Wood. L., 1816. *1st. Edn.* 2 vols. Lge. 4to. Hf-titles, tipped-in errata slip, 22 plts. including 4 prints from orig. wood-blocks of Dürer, text engrs., crude hf. cf., needs rebinding; P.E. Boissier copy. (SG. Apr.26; 156) $250
- A Series of Plates engraved after the Paintings & Sculptures of the Most Eminent Masters of the Early Florentine School. L., 1826. Lge. fo. Engl. & Fr. text, title & text ll. slightly foxed, 56 copperplts., cont. hf. leath., slightly rubbed & bumped. (HT. May 9; 981) DM 420
See— TRESHAM, Henry & others

OTTLEY, William Young & Tomkins, Peltro William
- Engravings of the Most Noble the Marquis of Stafford's Collection of Pictures, in London ... L., 1818. *1st. Edn.* 4 vols. Fo. 13 full-p. copperplt engraved architectural floor plans, 126 composite & full-p. copperplt engrs. of art works, all plts. on J. Whatman heavy H.M.P., some light to heavy foxing, orig. cf. & buff bds., Vol. I lacks upr. cover, Vol. IV bdg. brkn., covers worn with some scuffing. (HA. Feb.24; 278) $175

OTTO, Bp. of Freising
- Rerum ab Origine Mundi ap Ipsius usque Tempora Gestarum. [Strassburg, 1515]. Fo. Some tears & repairs, stained thro.-out, mod. three-qtr. mor. (SG. Feb.9; 293) $300

OTTO, Julius Conrad
- Gali Razya [Aramaic]/ Gali Razia Occultorum Detectio ... ; das ist, Entedeckung der Lehr unnd Meynung Aller Rabbinen, die vor und nach Christi Geburt von dem Messia ... Geschrieben Haben. Nuremb., 1605. 4to. In Hebrew, Latin & German, cont. vell. (SG. Feb.2; 88) $140

OTTOLANDER, K.J.W. & others
[-] Nederl. Flora en Pomona. Ill.:– after A.J. Wendel. Groningen, 1879. 2 vols. Sm. fo. 81 chromolithos., orig. pict. cl. (VG. Sep.14; 821) Fls. 600
[-] Verzameling v. Tuinsieraden, Koepels, Tuinhuizen, Prieeltjes ... Gouda, ca. 1870. Mod. cl. (VG. Mar.19; 42) Fls. 850

OTTOLENGHI, L.M.
See— BIBLIOTECA AMBROSIANA, MILAN

OTWAY, Caesar
[-] Sketches in Erris & Tyrawly. Dublin, 1841. *1st. Edn.* Bkplt., hf. mor., armorial motif on spine. (GM. Dec.7; 227) £150

OUDAAN, J.
- Uyt-breyding over het Boek der Psalmen,. Music:– Remigius Schrijver. Rotterdam, 1680-81. 2 pts. in 1 vol. Some light staining, cont. cf., spine gt. (VG. Mar.19; 168) Fls. 450

OUDERMEULEN, C. Van der
[-] Recherches sur le Commerce ou Idées Relatives aux Intérêts des Differens Peuples de l'Europe. Amst., 1778-84. 4 pts. in 2 vols. Cf., rubbed. (VG. May 3; 457) Fls. 500

OUD—HOLLAND. Tijdschrift voor Nederlandsche Kunstgeschiedenis
Amst., 1946-70. Years 61-85, in 92 pts. Lge. 8vo. Orig. wraps., some slightly defect. (VS. Dec.7; 115) Fls. 650

OUGHTRED, William
- Mathematical Recreations ... L., 1653. Folding engraved title margins torn with slight loss of plt.,

ptd. title ink-stained & outer margin trimmed, hf. cf., upr. cover detchd. (P. Jan.12; 260) *Burden.* £200

OUIDA (Pseud.)
See— RAMEE, Marie Louise de la 'Ouida'

OURADOU, Maurice
See— VIOLLET-LE-DUC, E. & Ouradou, Maurice

OURDAN, A.J.L.
- Pharmacopoea Universalis. Weimar, 1832. 2 vols. Foxed & stained, supp. misbnd., cont. hf. leath., bumped. (BR. Apr.12; 778) DM 600

OUR OLD NURSERY RHYMES. Original Tunes Harmonized by Alfred Moffat
Ill.:– H. Willebeek Le Mair. L., [1911]. Ob. 4to. Slight margin darkening, few pp. creased, lightly soiled, or with few short tears, no bdg. stated, d.-w. chipped & torn. (CBA. Aug.21; 377) $110

OUR PASTORAL PROPERTY
Adelaide, 1910. 4to. 3 or 4 short margin tears, later(?) hf. mor. gt. (KH. Nov.9; 677) Aus. $550

OUSELEY, Sir William
- Travels in Various Countries of the East. L., 1819-23. 3 vols. 4to. 3 engraved folding maps, 82 plts., many double-p., 1 plt. torn at fold, plt. numeral shaved cont. embossed cl., unc. & unopened, spines faded, 1 torn at head. (C. Nov.16; 144) *Remington.* £750
- - **Anr. Copy.** 3 vols. 4to. 3 engraved folding maps, 82 plts., many folding, lacks map 2, 1 plt. torn at fold, 2 plt. numerals shaved, orig. cl., unc. & unopened, head of 1 spine torn. (C. Mar.14; 77) *Kossow.* £380

OUSPENSKY, P.D.
- The Major Arcana of the Tarot. Ill.:– Taylor McCall. Sante Fe, 1975. *(150) numbered & sigd.* Lge. fo. Sheets loose with wrappered facs. trans. of orig. text, all as iss., three-qtr. mor. & cl. drop-leaf box, light offsetting from marb. end-papers to blank fly-lf. (CBA. Jan.29; 335) $1,000

OUSTALET, M.E.
See— DAVID, Abbé Armand & Oustalet, M.E.

OUTHWAITE, Grenbry & Rentoul, Annie R.
- Fairyland. Ill.:– Ida Rentoul Outhwaite. L., [1931]. *1st. Edn.* 4to. End-papers very slightly soiled, decor. cl., a little soiled. (CBA. Aug.21; 436) $120

OUTRAM, Lieut.-Gen. Sir James
- Persian Campaign in 1857. Priv. ptd., 1860. Orig. qtr mor; pres. copy from author to Rt. Hon. Lord Clyde. (TA. Aug.18; 47) £110

OUWEJAN, R.J.
- Zaens Skoon. Wormerveer, 1934. *(550) numbered.* Ob. 4to. Orig. cl. (CH. May 24; 151) Fls. 700

OVADIA DI BERTINORO
See— MOSHE BEN MAIMON [Maimonides] & Ovadia di Bertinoro

OVALLE, A.
- Historia Relatione del Regne di Chife, e delle Missioni e Ministerii che esercita in quelle la Compagna di Gieusu. Rome, 1646. *1st. Edn.* Sm. Fo. Slightly browned or foxed, cont. vell. [Sabin 57972]. (D. Nov.23; 1314) DM 1,800

OVER, Charles
- Ornamental Architecture in the Gothic, Chinese & Modern Taste. 1758. *1st. Edn.* Cont. cf. (BBA. Jun.14; 160) *Sims, Reed & Fogg.* £300
- - **Anr. Copy.** 54 engraved plts., a few fore-edges trimmed to plt. mark, 19th. C. hf. cf. (C. Dec.9; 107) *Henderson.* £220

OVERBEKE, Bonaventura ab
- Reliquiae Antiquae Urbis Romae. Amst., 1708. 3 vols. in 1. Lge. fo. All plts. in early imp., 2 engraved frontis., titles with engraved vig., port., double-p. plan, 144 engraved plts., including 1 double-p., cont. blind-stpd. vell., spine gt. (C. Nov.16; 27) *Traylen.* £650

- Stampe degli Avanzi dell' Antica Roma Opera. 1739. Lge. fo. Port., vig. title, double-p. map, 148 engraved plts. (1 double-p.), dedication, list of plts., cont. cf., worn. (SKC. May 4; 1816) £220

OVERBEKE, Bonaventura & Michael
- Les Restes de l'Ancienne Rome. Amst., 1709. *[2nd. (1st. Fr.) Edn].* 3 vols. Fo. Dedication or pres. copy(?), engraved frontis., engraved dedication lf. (to Queen Anne of England), port., double-p. engraved map, 146 engraved plts., slight discoloration to 1 or 2 ll., cont. Dutch mott. cf., arms of Queen Anne on covers in 2 roll-borders with the rose & thistle, corners with crown & 'AR' monog. (S. Dec.1; 347) *Libris Antik.* £1,300
- - **Anr. Copy.** 3 vols. Fo. Engraved frontis., 2 ports., 147 plts., mott. cf., worn. (P. Feb.16; 172) £230
- - **Anr. Copy.** 3 pts. in 1 vol. Lge. fo. Wide margin, a few text ll. lightly browned, cont. leath. gt., light scratching. (R. Oct.11; 786) DM 1,900

OVERHEIDE, Gebhardus
- Fünff Bücher, der Edlen Schreib-Kunst ... Braunschweig, 1665. 4to. Title with old owners mark, slightly browned, sm. margin hole reprd., stp. on lr. end-paper, late 19th. C. hf. leath.; Hauswedell coll. (H. May 23; 244) DM 800

OVERTON, Thomas Collins
- The Temple Builder's Most Useful Companion. 1766. *1st. Edn.* Engraved frontis., 50 plts., including 1 double-p., cont. cf. (C. Dec.9; 108) *Weinreb.* £400

OVIDIUS NASO, Publius
- Amorum Libri♪ Tres. Trans.:– R. Schott. [München, Marées-Gesellschaft, 1918]. *(50) on vell. De Luxe Edn.* Sm. 4to. German & Latin text, hand-bnd orig. mor., gt. decor. (H. May 22; 1068) DM 1,400
- - **Anr. Edn.** Monaco, 1918. *(240) numbered.* Publishers vell., gt.-tooled. (CR. Jun.6; 240) Lire 450,000
- Elegies. Trans.:– Christopher Marlowe & John Davies. Middlebourgh [i.e. L.], ca. 1640. Sm. 8vo. Marginal repair to F2 & 3, light browning of title & margins, mor. gt., Clawson-Locker-Lampson bkplts. [STC 18933] (SPB. May 16; 99) $900
- Epistole. Lyon, 1523. 4to. Title in woodcut border, woodcut text ills., printer's device on final lf. verso, title & 1st. few ll. frayed, some stains, 18th. C. spr. cf., splits in jnts. (S. Apr.10; 328) *Tile.* £180
- Fastorum Libri Diligenti Emendatione. 1527. Lge. 12mo. Wormhole in lr. margin affecting text, 19th. C. mor. gt. (P. Sep.29; 167) *Rix.* £55
- De Gedaant-wisselingen. Notes:– A. Banier. Trans.:– I. Verburg. Ill.:– after Picart, Lebrun, Punt, Wandelaar & others. Amst., 1732. 2 vols. Lge. fo. L.P., in Latin & Dutch, 7 text-ills. in dupl. mntd. on blank ll. in Vol. 2, a few ll. slightly foxed, cont. red mor., spine gt., slightly rubbed, corners defect. (VG. Nov.30; 609) Fls. 1,800
- - **Anr. Copy.** 2 pts. in 1 vol. Lge. fo. Cont. tree cf. gt., slightly rubbed. (VG. Sep.14; 920) Fls. 650
- Der Griecxscher Princerssen en Jonckvrouwen Clachtighe Seyndthbrieven, Heroidum ghenaemt ... Trans.:– C. van Ghistele. Antw., 1589. Sm. 8vo. Browned, some stains, upr. margins slightly short, 17th. C. blind-stpd. vell. (VG. Nov.30; 693) Fls. 950
- Lettres d'Amoureuses, Les Heriodes. Trans.:– G. Miroux. Ill.:– Manuel Orazi. Paris, 1919. *(30) on japon, with suites of ills. on Chine & japon.* 4to. Elab. blind-stpd. orange mor. by René Kieffer, s.-c. (SPB. Dec.13; 874) $125
- [English] Metamorphosis. Trans.:– George Sandys. Ill.:– after F. Cleyn. Oxford, 1632. Fo. 3 sm. spots to engraved title, cont. mott. cf., spine gt., spine & jnts. reprd., sm. loss to leath. on upr. cover; bkplt. of T. Gaisford, Frederic Dannay copy. [STC 18966] (CNY. Dec.16; 260) $220
- - **Anr. Edn.** 1717. Fo. Cf., upr. cover detchd. (P. Jul.26; 202) £100
- - **Anr. Edn.** L., 1760. Sm. 8vo. First 2 ll. & free end-paper detchd., some browning, cont. cf., rebkd.; Robert Browning copy with sig. & notes, all in pencil, Frederic Dannay copy, as an association copy, w.a.f. (CNY. Dec.16; 54) $700

– – Anr. Edn. Trans:– John Dryden, Alexander Pope & others. Ill.:– Hans Erni. Verona, Giovanni Mardersteig at Officina Bodoni for Ltd. Edns. Cl. 1958. *(1500) numbered, sigd. by printer & artist.* Lge. 8vo. Buckram, bds., orig. s.-c. (SG. May 17; 211) $175

– [French] La Métamorphose. Ill.:– Bernard Salomon. Lyons, 1564. *2nd. Edn. of this version.* Last lf. blank, fo. 5 correctly sigd., woodcuts on d3 & d4 of erotic subject damaged by ink causing tiny holes in d3, date changed in ink to 1557. *(Bound with:)* **POURTRAITS DIVERS** Lyons, 1557. *2nd. Edn.* 62 Woodcuts mostly attributed to Bernard Salomon, collected by de Tournes. Together 2 works in 1 vol. 17th. C. cf., rather worn. (S. May 10; 375)   *Marlborough.* £700

– [French] Les Métamorphoses. Paris, [1767]. *1st. Printing.* 4to. Some light foxing, cont. tree cf., spine gt. (HD. May 3; 108)   Frs. 2,200

– – Anr. Edn. Ill.:– Boucher, Gravelot, Eisen, Moreau, etc. Paris, 1767-71. 4 vols. 4to. In Fr. & Latin, lacks engraved dedication, some spotting & offsetting, red mor. gt. by Sangorski & Sutcliffe. (SPB. Dec.14; 71) $550

– – Anr. Edn. Trans:– Abbé Banier. Ill.:– Boucher, Eisen, Gravelot, Monnet, Moreau, & others. 1767-71. *1st. Printing.* 4 vols. 4to. In Latin & Fr., cont. Engl. red mor. (HD. Apr.13; 37)   Frs. 12,000

– – Anr. Copy. 4 vols. 4to. In Latin & Fr., tree cf. gt. by Bradel l'aîné. (HD. Mar.27; 28) Frs. 4,800

– – Anr. Copy. 4 vols. 4to. Cont. diced cf., spines decor., faded. (HD. Mar.21; 63)   Frs. 4,100

– – Anr. Edn. Ill.:– Le Barbier, Monsiau & Moreau. Paris, 1806. 4 vols. 4to. Figures before the letter, foxing, dampstain in Vol. IV, cont. str.-grd. red hf. mor., corners, spines decor. (HD. May 4; 381)   Frs. 1,000

– – Anr. Edn. Ed.:– Jean Rostand. Trans.:– André Berry. Ill.:– Pierre-Yves Tremois. Paris, 1968. *(190). (130) on japon nacré sigd. by author.* Lge. 4to. With suite on Arches of 3 double plts. & 2 refused plts., autograph dedication by P.Y. Tremois, sigd., with orig. ink sketch, leaves, wrap., box. (HD. Dec.16; 169)   Frs. 3,550

– Metamorphoses en Rondeaux. Ill.:– Chr. v. Hagen. Amst., 1679. Approx. 10 ll. with slight margin tear, partly bkd., cont. vell. (D. Nov.24; 2321)   DM 1,100

– [Opera] Metamorphoseon Libri Quindecim ... Venice, Oct.-Dec. 1502-Feb. 1503. *1st. Aldine Edn.* 3 vols. Title-pp. lightly soiled, sm. paper loss to corner of title of 2nd. vol. 19th. C. red mor., gt. Aldine anchor stpd. on covers, spines darkened, jnts. slightly rubbed; John Scott, of Halkshill bkplt. (SPB. Dec.14; 29) $700

– – Anr. Edn. Venice, 1516. Some light stains, pre-lims. affected by worm in lr. margin, cont. vell., soiled. (TA. Jul.19; 474)   £70

– – Anr. Edn. Ed.:– Raphael Regius, & others. Venice, 1534. Fo. Title in woodcut ornamental border, text woodcuts, some ll. browned, scattered early marginalia, minor repairs, mod. vell. (SG. Apr.19; 144) $250

– – Anr. Edn. Venice, 1574. Fo. Old. vell. (HD. Jan.30; 20)   Frs. 1,700

– Metamorphoseon, hoc est, Transformationum, libri XV; Factorum Lib. VI. Tristium Lib. V. De Ponto Lib. IIII. Lyons, 1539-46. Together 2 vols. 18th. C. cf. gt., rebkd. with orig. spines, slightly rubbed; Chatsworth bkplt. (BBA. Nov.30; 26)   *Thomas.* £70

– [Latin & Engl.] Metamorphoses. Ill.:– B. Picart & others. Amst., 1732. 2 vols. Fo. Vig. titles, engraved frontis., dedication & 130 hf.-p. plts., slight spotting, hf. cf. gt. (P. May 17; 51)   *Georges.* £240

– – Anr. Copy. 2 vols. Fo. Pol. cf., corners bumped. (LH. Sep.25; 580) $350

– [Latin & French] Les Métamorphoses. Trans.:– Abbé Banier. Ill.:– Picart. & others. Amst., 1732. 2 vols. in 1. Fo. Some spotting & foxing, cont. cf., gt. arms of Turinetti, Marquis of Prie, Italy. (SPB. Dec.13; 876) $300

– – Anr. Copy. 3 vols. 12mo. Sm. repair to title of Vol. II, decor. red mor. gt. by L. Delorme, mor. doubls., silk end-ll., unc.; Alf. Piat ex-libris. (HD. Mar.27; 27)   Frs. 3,900

– – Anr. Copy. 2 vols. in 1. Fo. Plts. slit & stained, foxing, cont. red mor., gt. decor., sm. tool spine

decor., inner dentelle. (HD. Mar.14; 67)   Frs. 2,900

– – Anr. Copy. 2 vols. in 1. Lge. fo. Cont. marb. cf., spine decor. (HD. May 3; 107)   Frs. 1,900

– – Anr. Copy. 2 pts. in 1 vol. Lge. fo. 2 cont. owners notes past on hf.-title, 2 early ll. strengthened, 1 tear bkd., 1 corner with loss, some foxing, soiling & staining, cont.-style leath. (HK. Nov.10; 3091)   DM 1,500

– Metamorphosis. Dat is die Herscheppinge oft Veranderinge. Trans.:– Johannes Florianus [i.e. J. Bloemaerts]. Ill.:– Chr. van Sichem. Hantwerpen, 1619. Sm. 8vo. Slightly browned, margins at end slightly defect., cont. vell., slightly warped. (VS. Dec.9; 1067)   Fls. 750

– Metamorphosis, oder: Wunderbarliche vnd Seltzame Beschreibung, von der Menschen, Thiern, vnd anderer Creaturen Veränderung ... Ed.:– Jörg Wickram. Ill.:– Virgil Solis. Frankfurt, 1609. 4to. Title lf. excised & mntd., stps. & sm. worm-hole, lightly browned thro.-out, cont. vell., slightly removed, loose. (H. May 22; 821)   DM 800

– Les Oeuvres Galantes. Genève, 1777. 2 vols. 18mo. Cont. red mor. gt., spines decor., later arms of Président de Viefville. (HD. May 3; 109)   Frs. 1,800

– Operum. Amst., 1735. 3 vols. Old red mor., decor., wtrd. silk doubl. & end-papers. (HD. Mar.30; 13)   Frs. 26,100

– Suite des 140 Figures et du Cut-de-lampe ... pour les Métamarphoses. Ill.:– Baquoy, Basan, Binet ... after Boucher, Eisen, Gravelot ... Paris, 1767-71. 4to. Later lf. roan. (HD. Jan.27; 256)   Frs. 1,350

– Verwandlungen. Ill.:– Benedict, Mansfeld, Stöber & others. Wien, 1791. 3 vols. Wide margin, slightly foxed thro.-out, cont. hf. leath., slightly rubbed, worn & bumped, spine slightly defect. (HT. May 9; 1603)   DM 1,000

OWEN, John (Ed.)
See— OGILBY, John & Bowen, Emmanuel

OWEN, Sir Richard
– Odontography. L., 1840-45. *1st. Edn.* 2 vols. 4to. Some light foxing to atlas, later lf. leath., slightly rubbed. (R. Oct.12; 1514)   DM 1,400

OWEN, Samuel
See— COOKE, William Bernard & Owen, Samuel
See— WESTALL, William & Owen, Samuel

OWEN, William Fitzwilliam
– Narrative of Voyages to Explore the Shores of Africa, Arabia & Madagascar. 1833. 2 vols. Folding maps mntd. on linen, sm. tear to 1st. 8 pp. of text in Vol. 2, not affecting text, cont. hf. cf. (SSA. Jul.5; 305)   R 400

OWEN, Wilfred
– Poems. Intro:– Siegfried Sassoon. L., 1920. *1st. Edn.* Sm. 4to. Orig. cl., faint foxing on covers, d.-w. chipped & soiled; Frederic Dannay copy. (CNY. Dec.16; 261) $400

OXFORD ENGLISH DICTIONARY
– A New English Dictionary. Ed.:– J.A.W. Murray. Oxford, 1888. Vols. 1-10, with Supp, in 26 vols. 4to. Hf. mor., worn. (PD. Apr.18; 119)   £50

– The Oxford English Dictionary. Oxford, 1933. 13 vols. 4to. Orig. cl., spines faded. (S. Dec.20; 869)   *Sims.* £120

– – Anr. Copy. 13 vols. with Supp. 4to. Cl., some d.-w.s. soiled. (SG. May 17; 285) $350

– – Anr. Copy. 13 vols. 4to. Buckram, d.-w.'s. (KH. Nov.9; 363)   Aus. $550

– – Anr. Edn. Ed.:– James Murray & others. Oxford, 1933-76. 15 vols,, including Supps. 4to. Orig. cl., stained, last 2 vols. in d.-w.'s. (BBA. Aug.18; 29)   *Traylen.* £110

– – Anr. Edn. Oxford, [1961]. 13 vols., including Supp. Fo. Orig. cl. (CSK. Aug.19; 147)   £170

– – Anr. Edn. Oxford, 1978-82. 16 vols. including 4 vols. supps. 4to. Orig. cl., d.-w.'s. (CSK. Jul.13; 188)   £240

– – Anr. Edn. 1980. *Compact Edn.* 2 vols. 4to. With magnifying glass, orig. cl., boxed. (TA. Sep.15; 393)   £52

OXFORD POETRY, 1923-1925, 1927
Contribs:– W.H. Auden, C. Day-lewis, Graham Greene, & others. Oxford, 1923-27. *1st. Edns.* 4

vols. Orig. parch.-bkd. bds., slightly marked. (S. Mar.20; 951)   *Hawthorn.* £55

OXFORD SHAKESPEARE CONCORDANCES
Ed.:– T.H. Howard-Hill. Oxford, 1969-71. 29 vols. only. Orig. cl., d.-w.'s. (BBA. Aug.18; 30)   *Quaritch.* £60

OXLEY, John
– Journals of Two Expeditions into the Interior of New South Wales. L., 1820. *1st. Edn.* 4to. Maps offset or slightly foxed, old pol. cf. gt., spine reinforced. (CA. Apr.3; 94)   Aus. $3,000

– – Anr. Edn. L., 1964. *Facs.* 4to. No bdg. stated. (JL. Jun.24; 97)   Aus. $200

– – Anr. Copy. 4to. Bdg. not stated. (KH. May 1; 545)   Aus. $190

– – Anr. Copy. 4to. Orig. cl., sm. snag at head of backstrip. (KH. Nov.9; 374)   Aus. $160

OZANAM, Jacques
– La Méchanique ... Paris, 1720. *1st. Edn.* Slightly browned, some staining of 1st. few ll., old owners inscrs. on title scored through, recent bds.; Stanitz coll. (SPB. Apr.25; 330) $150

[–] Méthode de Lever les Plans et les Cartes de Terre et de Mer avec Toutes Sortes d'Instruments et sans Instruments. Paris, 1750. *New Edn.* 12mo. Cont. cf., spine decor. (HD. Nov.9; 190)   Frs. 1,100

– Recréations Mathématiques et Physiques. Paris, 1725. Vols. 1, 2 & 4 only (of 4). Slightly soiled, cont. hf. leath. gt., bumped & worn, spine partly defect. (HK. Nov.8; 680)   DM 650

– – Anr. Edn. Paris, 1741. 4 vols. Lacks 4 plts. in Vol. II, cont. marb. cf., spines decor. (HD. Nov.9; 189)   Frs. 1,300

– – Anr. Edn. Paris, 1750, 1749 (Vol. 2). 4 vols. Cont. marb. leath. gt. (HK. Nov.8; 681)   DM 1,000

OZANNE, Nicolas
– Marine Militaire ou Recueil des Differens Vaisseaux qui servent à la Guerre ... Paris, priv. ptd., [1762]. *1st. Printing.* Lge. 8vo. Cont. hf. roan, spine decor. (HD. Jun.18; 32)   Frs. 7,500

– – Anr. Edn. Paris, [1775]. Title, dedication, 50 plts., faint margin spotting, cont. mott. cf., spine gt., Claret de Fleurieu bkplt. (S. May 21; 12)   *Maggs.* £377

– – Anr. Edn. Paris, priv. ptd., [1792]. Scratch on lr. margin of frontis., cont. paper bds. (HD. Jul.2; 30)   Frs. 5,000

– Nouvelles Vues Perspectives des Ports de France dessinées pour le Roi. [Paris, 1787]. Sm. ob. fo. 64 plts., lacks title & map, MS. table at end, cont. marb. roan, spine decor. (HD. Jul.2; 29)   Frs. 15,000

– Vues des Lieux Célèbres de Diverses Parties du Monde d'après les Dessins de N. Ozanne. Ill.:– Pillement, Gareau, Le Gouaz & others. Paris, ca. 1799. Sm. ob. 4to. Mod. str.-grd. hf. mor., blue paper wrap. (HD. Jun.18; 34)   Frs. 6,000

OZANNE, Pierre
– Mélanges de Vaisseaux, de Barques et de Bateaux.
– Mélanges de Vaisseaux, de Frégates et de Corvettes. – Receuil de Vaisseaux. Paris, ca. 1800. 4 suites in 1 vol. 4to. 44 engraved plts., 2 slightly faded, old hf. roan. (HD. Mar.9; 118) .Frs. 5,500

P., F. de
– Clef de la Langue Francaise ou Guide de l'Etude Pratique de Cette Langue. St. Petersh., 1849. 9 vols. & 2 folded sheets. 4to. Orig. limp cl., hf. roan folder, roan label 'A Son Altesse Imperiale Madame la Grande Duchesse Marie Nicolaevna humble hommage de l'auteur'; van Veen coll. (S. Feb.28; 91)   £90

P., J.
– The Merchants Dayly Companion. L., 1684. 12mo. Liby. stps. on title-p. & 2 other ll., lacks Al (blank), recent hf. cf. [Wing P58] (BBA. May 3; 164)   *Jarndyce.* £310

PACHECO DE NARVAEZ, L.
– Libro de las Grandezas de la Espada. Madrid, 1600. *1st. Edn.* 4to. Leath. (DS. Mar.23; 2203)   Pts. 100,000

PACIFIC RAILROAD

- Reports of Explorations & Surveys to Ascertain the Most Practicable & Economical Route for a Railroad from the Mississippi River to the Pacific Ocean ... **1853-1855.** Wash., 1855-60. *1st. Senate Iss., 1st. House Iss. of Vol. XII (in 2 vols.).* 12 vols. in 13. Lge. 4to. Orig. cl., spine extremities on most vols. frayed, 2 vols. in orig. hf. cf., spines very worn. (SG. Oct.20; 263) $950
-- **Anr. Edn.** Wash., 1855-60. *Vols. 5-8 & 11: Senate Iss., rest: House Iss.* 12 vols. only (of 13, lacks pt. 2 of Vol. 12). Lge. 4to. Some vols. orig. qtr. leath., others later leath. (shabby) or unbnd., ex-liby., w.a.f. (SG. Aug.4; 338) $650
-- **Anr. Edn.** Wash., 1855-61. *De Luxe Edn.* 12 vols. 4to. Vol. 10 with 3 extra plts. not cited by Sabin, Vol. 12 with additional plt., lacks 5 col. plts. in Vol. 2, plts. in Vol. 11 foxed, & with some maps torn at folds & general map detchd. some foxing & dampstains thro.-out, orig. mor. or sheep & bds. or blind cl., some wear. [Sabin 69946] (HA. Nov.18; 144) $1,100

PACIFICUS MAXIMUS

- **Opera.** Fano, 1506. *1st. Edn.* With last lf. blank, 19th. C. hf. leath. (SI. Dec.15; 30) Lire 450,000

PACINI, Eugene

- La Marine, Arsenaux, Navires, Equipages, Navigation, Atterages, Combats. Ill.:– after Morel-Fatio & Pauquet. Paris, 1844. *1st. Printing of plts.* Frontis., 1 cold. plt., 8 cold. & gommées plts., 22 steel-engraved plts., minimal foxing, cont. hf. chagrin, decor. spine. (HD. Sep.21; 157) Frs. 1,100

PACKE, Christopher

- Ankographia, sive Convallium Descriptio ... the Valley & Hills, Brooks & Rivers **(as an Explanation of a New Philosophical-Chorographical Chart of East Kent).** Canterbury, 1743. 4to. Errata & advt. lf. at end, cont. cf. gt. (S. Mar.6; 441) *Frankland.* £80

PADRE, A.

- L'Italia. Turin, 1834-38. 5 vols. 4to. 328 copperplts., 1 multi-folding map, slightly foxed, cont. hf. leath. (HK. May 15; 896) DM 500

PAGE, F.

- The Principle of the English Poor Laws. L., 1822. Hf. cf. gt. (P. Jan.12; 263) *Laywood.* £75

PAGEANT, The

Ed.:– C.H. Shannon & J.W. Gleeson White. Ill.:– Rossetti, Burne-Jones, Rothenstein, Whistler, & others. L., 1896, 1897. 2 vols. (all publd.). 4to. 1 lf. in 1st. vol. torn, orig. gt.-decor. cl., slightly worn, 2nd. Vol. unopened. (SG. Nov.17; 105) $200
-- **Anr. Copy.** 2 vols. (all publd.). 4to. Bkplt., gt.-decor. cl. (SG. Jan.12; 286) $150

PAGEANT of Japanese Art.

Tokyo, [1952]. 6 vols. Fo. 300 cold. mntd. plts., ills., ex-liby., cl. (SG. May 3; 217) $175
-- **Anr. Edn.** Tokyo, [1953]. 6 vols. 4to. Publisher's cl., ptd. d.-w.'s. (SM. Mar.7; 2190) Frs. 3,200

PAGES, Pierre Marie François

- Travels round the World, in the years 1767, 1768, 1769 , 1770, 1771 [& 1773 & 1776]. L., 1793-92. *2nd. Edn. in Engl.* 3 vols. Cont. cf., spines gt., heads of spines chipped, the Rt. Hon. Visc. Eccles copy. [Sabin 58171] (CNY. Nov.18; 218) $420
- Voyages autour du Monde et vers les Deux Pôles ... Paris, 1782. 2 vols. Cont. marb. roan, spines decor.; from Château des Noës liby. (HD. May 25; 63) Frs. 3,000

PAGET, Maj. Guy

- The Melton Mowbray of John Ferneley. Ptd. in Great Britain for Scribners of N.Y., 1931. Cl. gt., spine faded & nicked. (DM. May 21; 31) $100

PAGNINUS, Santes

- Kotser Otsar Leshon ha-Kodesh / Hoc est, Epitome Thesauri Linguae Sanctae. Antw., 1570. 2 errata & privilege ll. at end, some dampstaining. MS. ex-libris on title, marginalia in cont. hand, cont. hand-lettered thumb index tabs mntd., cont. dyed vell., dampwrinkled, worn, loose, lacks ties. (SG. Feb.2; 102) $100

PAILLOT DE MONTABERT

- Traité Complet de la Peinture. 1829-51. 10 vols., including atlas. 8vo. & ob. fo. Cont. hf. chagrin, corners, gt. cypher of André Weiss on spines. (HD. Mar.21; 183) Frs. 1,950

PAIN, William

- The Builder's Companion, & Workman's General Assistant. L., 1762. Fo. 102 engraved plts., some folding, title & a few margins slightly dust-soiled, qtr. cf., unc. (SG. Nov.3; 159) $400
-- **Anr. Edn.** 1765. *2nd. Edn.* Fo. Cont. cf., upr. cover detchd. (P. Oct.20; 182) £120
-- **Anr. Edn.** L., 1769. *3rd. Edn.* Fo. A few stains, mostly marginal, mod. cf., dampstained at lr. edges. (S. Oct.11; 572) *Elliott.* £70
- The Practical House Carpenter. L., 1799. *6th. Edn.* 4to. 147 engraved plts., few sm. stains, mod. qtr. cf. gt. (P. May 17; 182) *Cooper.* £130

PAINE, James

- Plans, Elevations & Sections, of Noblemen & Gentlemen's Houses, & also of ... Temples & other Garden Buildings. L., priv. ptd., 1767-83. *1st. Edn.* 2 vols. in 1. Lge. fo. 123 engraved plts., including 54 double-p., subscribers list, cont. diced cf., rebkd.; pencil note 'Presentation copy to King George the third by the author & sold by King William the 4th. ... ', with Royal Liby. dupl. stp. (C. Dec.9; 109) *Clode.* £1,100

PAINE, Thomas

- The Age of Reason. Boston, 1794. *Pt. I 1st. Amer. Edn.?.* 12mo. Slightly foxed, later crude bds. (SG. Jan.19; 282) $110
- Common Sense: Addressed to the Inhabitants of America ... Phila., 1776. *1st. Edn. 1st. Iss. [as distinguished in Gimbel].* Title-p. browned, scattered foxing thro.-out, mod. qtr. mor. & marb. paper bdg. [Gimbel CS-1; Sabin 58211] (SPB. May 23; 48) $27,000
- Examination of the Passages in the New Testament. N.Y., priv. ptd., [1807]. *1st. Edn.* 4 ll. stained, title-p. lacks corner, later crude bds.; sigd., few margin annots. by author. (SG. Jan.19; 284) $425
- A Letter Addressed to the Abbé Raynal, on the Affairs of North America ... 1791. *(Bound with:)*
- A Letter to the Earl of Shelburne, on his Speech ... Respecting the Acknowledgement of American Independence. 1791. Together 2 works in 1 vol. Both interleaved with blanks, cont. hf. cf. (TA. May 17; 533) £105
- Rights of Man. - The American Crisis. - Common Sense. - The Decline & Fall of the English System of Finance. - Agrarian Justice. L., n.d. & 1835. Together 5 works in 1 vol. Cont. str.-grd. mor. gt., by Archibald Macliesh, silk end-papers with pres. label from binder, with fore-e. pntg., mor. s.-c. worn. (S. Oct.11; 530) *Quaritch.* £350
- The Writings. Albany, 1794. Some browning & spotting, sig. on free end-paper, cont. sheep, spine lacks label. (SPB. Dec.13; 461) $250

PAINLEVE, M.P.

- Leçons sur la Théorie Analytique des Equations Différentielles professées à Stockholm [Sept.-Nov. 1895]. Paris, 1897. *1st. Edn.* 4to. Title, intro. & contents list, text MS. facs., margins slightly spotted & browned, cont. hf. leath., slightly spotted. (HT. May 8; 456) DM 600

PAINTER, William

- The Palace of Pleasure. Intro.:– Hamish Miles. Ill.:– Douglas P. Bliss. L., Cresset Pr., 1929. *(500) numbered.* 4 vols. 4to. Qtr. cl., patterned bds., partly unc. (SG. Mar.29; 94) $110

PAJON

[-] Contes Nouveaux et Nouvelles. Anvers, 1753. 12mo. Cont. red mor. gt., spine decor., 19th. C. arms of Marquis de Villeneuve; from libys. of Le Barbier de Tinan & Marigue de Champprepus. (HD. May 3; 110) Frs. 1,650

PALACHE, Hayyim

- Sefer Ateret Hayyim. Salonika, 1841. *1st. Edn.* Sm. 8vo. Artless mod. cl. (SG. Feb.2; 272) $175

PALAEOGRAPHICAL SOCIETY

- Facsimiles of Manuscripts & Inscriptions. Ed.:– E.A. Bond & E.M. Thompson. L., 1873-83. 3 vols. Fo. Perforation stps. in text, plts. hand-stpd. on

rectos, three-qtr. mor., worn, ex-liby. (RO. Dec.11; 266) $350

PALAFOX Y MENDOZA, Juan de, Bp.

- The History of the Conquest of China by the Tartars. 1671. *1st. Edn. in Engl.* 8vo. 3 pp. advts., mor. by Sangorski & Sutcliffe. [Wing P200] (BBA. Jan.19; 160) *Quaritch.* £180

PALATIIS, Laurus de

- Aureus Tractatus super Statuto quod Extantibus Masculis Femine non succedant. Pavia, Giovanni Andrea Bosco & Michele Garaldi, IX kal. ian [24 Dec.] 1495. *1st. Edn.* Fo. Stained at outer portion with margins frayed & torn, not affecting text, vell. (lge. lf. of 13th. C. Italian MS.). [H. 12272] (S. May 10; 374) *Quaritch.* £880

PALATINO, Giouambattista.

- Libro Nuovo d'imparare a scrivere tutte sorte Lettere. 1540. Vell. (G. Sep.15; 2296) Sw. Frs. 380

PALATIUS, J.

- Fasti Ducales ab Anafestoi ad Silvestrum Valerium. Venice, 1696. 4to. Owner's inscr. on title, slight spotting, cont. bds., rubbed, rebkd. with cf. (S. May 1; 489) *Rebecchi.* £100

PALAU Y DULCET, Antonio

- Manual del Libreo Hispano-Americano. Barcelona, 1923-27. *[1st. Edn.].* 7 vols. 4to. Cont. parch.-bkd. bds., rubbed. (BBA. Feb.9; 224) *Fazzi.* £160
-- **Anr. Copy.** 7 vols. Cf., wraps. (DS. Nov.25; 2087) Pts. 60,000
-- **Anr. Edn.** Barcelona, 1924-27. *1st. Edn.* 7 vols. Lge. 8vo. Browned & brittle, some ll. sprung & chipped, buckram. (SG. Jan.5; 243) $250
-- **Anr. Edn.** Barcelona, 1948-77. Vols. 1-28 (A-Z, without later vol. of addenda etc.). Wraps., some a little dusty. (BBA. Sep.29; 58) *Duran.* £480
-- **Anr. Copy.** 28 vols. 4to. Orig. wraps. (DS. Feb.24; 2149) Pts. 250,000

PALESTINE EXPLORATION FUND

- Quarterly Statement. 1869-80. 11 vols. Liby, stps. to prelims. & labels pasted in upr. covers, orig. cl., Vol. 1 brkn. on spine, rubbed. (TA. Mar.15; 39) £62

PALFYN, Jean

- Description Anatomique des parties de la Femme, qui Servent à la Génération; avec un Traité des Monstres. Leiden, 1708. *1st. Edn.* Sm. 4to. Engraved frontis., 11 plts., including 6 folding, 3 with short tears, some stains & soiling, 2 sm. holes in H2 affecting engr., cont. vell., soiled. (S. Nov.28; 130) *Studd.* £400
-- **Anr. Copy.** 3 pts. in 1 vol. 4to. Title-p. soiled, some stains, plt. Cl pasted over dupl. of that on B3r, lacks frontis., hf. cf.; Dr. Walter Pagel copy. (S. Feb.7; 282) *Colombo.* £180
-- **Anr. Copy.** Sm. 4to. Cont. cf., decor. spine. (HD. Sep.22; 306) Frs. 9,300
- Heelkonstige Ontleeding van 's Menschen Lichaan. Leyden, 1733. *2nd. Printing.* Lacks frontis. (?), stains & wear, last ll. reprd., bnd. (VG. May 3; 695) Fls. 550

PALI CANON

- Auswahl aus den Pali-Kanon. Trans.:– P. Dahlke. Ill.:– M. Behmer. [Berlin, 1922]. *(225) on Bütten.* 4to. Hand-bnd. orig. vell. gt., leath. inlays, by P.A. Demeter, Hellerau. (H. Nov.24; 1364) DM 1,300

PALISOT DE DEAUVOIS, A.M.F.J.

- Flore d'Oware et de Benin, en Afrique. Paris, 1804. Fo. Part of Vol. 1 only, comprising pp. 1-50, 30 hand-finished col.-ptd. plts., some spotting & offsetting, mainly affecting text, cont. mor.-bkd. bds., rubbed. (S. Nov.28; 73) *Varekamp.* £200

PALLADIO, Andrea

- Architecture. L., 1715. 2 pts. only (of 4). Fo. Engraved port. & frontis., 92 engraved plts., titles & text in Engl., Italian & Fr., subscribers list, cont. cf., w.a.f. (C. Dec.9; 188) *Connolly.* £180
-- **Anr. Edn.** Ed.:– Giacomo Leoni. 1715[-20]. Fo. pts. in 5 vols. Fo. Engl., Fr. & Italian titles & text, subscribers list, minor worming to some blank margins of Vol. I, 1 plt. torn, cont. panel. cf.,

rubbed, 1 cover detchd. (C. May 30; 5)
Quaritch. £950
– – **Anr. Edn.** Ed.:– Giacomo Leoni. Ill.:– Picart, v.d. Gucht, & others. L., 1721. *2nd. Edn.* Fo. Port. frontis., engraved title, 230 engraved plts., few folding, subscribers list, privilege lf. loose, some mild browning, owner's sig. on divisional titles & front pastedown, cont. blind-panel. cf., worn. (SG. Oct.13; 270) $600
– – **Anr. Edn.** Ed.:– Giacomo Leoni. L., 1721; n.d. *2nd. Edn. (Vol.1).* 2 vols. Tall fo. Ptd. & engraved titles, port., 165 engraved plts., licensing lf. & subscribers' list in vol.1, ex-liby., cont. panel. cf., rebkd., vol.1 wormed. (SG. May 3; 271) $750
– – **Anr. Edn.** Trans.:– Ware. L., 1738. 4 pts. in 1 vol. Fo. 4 engraved titles, 205 plts., cf., slightly rubbed, jnts. defect. (B. Oct.4; 690) Fls. 1,600
– – **Anr. Edn.** Ed.:– G. Leoni. Notes:– I. Jones. L., 1742. *3rd. Edn.* 2 vols. Lge. fo. Minimal spotting, cont. cf., lightly rubbed, jnts. brkn. (H. May 22; 69) DM 2,200
– **L'Architettura.** Venice, 1642. Fo. Dampstains, vell. (GM. Dec.7; 641) £140
– **Le Fabriche e i Disegni[-Le Terme dei Romani].** Ed.:– Ottavio Bertotti-Scamozzi. Venice, 1796-97. 5 vols. 4to. 2 engraved ports., 235 engraved plts., cont. cf.-bkd. bds. (C. Dec.9; 110)
Harcourt-Williams. £500
– **Five Orders of Architecture.** Ed.:– Colin Campbell. L., 1729. Fo. Engraved title & 34 plts. only (of 36), some plt.-marks cropped at outer edge, some soiling, cont. panel. cf., rebkd. & reprd., new end-papers. (S. May 1; 562) *Hood.* £120
– **Lantichita di Roma.** Venice, 1554. Old bds. (H. May 22; 295) DM 600
– **Les Quatre Livres de l'Architecture.** Paris, 1650. *1st. Fr. Edn.* Fo. Title soiled & slightly torn, stains, 1 plt. detchd., cf. (HD. Feb.22; 159) Frs. 5,500
– – **Anr. Copy.** 4 pts. in 1 vol. Fo. Roan, worn. (SM. Mar.7; 2036) Frs. 4,800
– – **Anr. Copy.** Fo. Cont. cf., worn. (HD. Dec.15; 26) Frs. 4,500
– **I Quattro Libri dell'Architettura.** Venice, 1570. *1st. Coll. Edn.* Sm. fo. Many margins shaved, slightly affecting ptd. area, a few spots & stains, early 18th. C. diced cf., gt. dentelle border & centrepiece, spine gt.; inscr. of Richard Boyle, 3rd. Earl of Burlington dtd. 1727/8, ex-libris of Laurence Sterne. (C. Dec.9; 111) *Weinreb.* £3,000
– – **Anr. Edn.** Venice, 1581. *2nd. Edn.* 4 pts. in 1 vol. Fo. Lacks final blank, most inner margins strengthened or reprd., 4R1 loose, some staining, margins cut close just touching a few headlines & p. numerals, 18th. C. Engl. panel. cf., worn, lacks end-papers. (S. Nov.17; 53) *Cox.* £550
– – **Anr. Copy.** 4 vols. in 1. Fo. Engraved titles, woodcut ills., many full-p., 1st. title frayed & reprd., affecting border, some tears, 3C2 badly frayed & reprd., some staining, some ll. loose, inner margins cut close, mod. hf. mor. (S. May 1; 563)
Callea. £350
– **Traité des Cinq Ordres de l'Architecture.** Trans.:– Le Muet. Paris, n.d. Sm. sq. 8vo. Hf. bdg. (HD. Dec.15; 27) Frs. 1,250

PALLAS, Peter Simon
– **Characteristik der Thierpflanzen.** Ed.:– J.F.W. Herbst. Trans.:– C.F. Wilkens. Nürnberg, 1787. 2 pts. in 1 vol. 4to. Cont. hf. leath., jnts. brkn. (R. Apr.4; 1767) DM 1,600
– **Reise durch Verschiedene Provinzen des Russischen Reichs.** St. Petersb., 1771-76. *1st. Edn.* 4 vols. in 3. 4to. 4 lge. engraved folding maps, 104 (of 110) folding plts. & maps, 1 lightly shaved, cont. cf. (C. Nov.16; 145) *Hannas.* £120
– **Travels Through the Southern Provinces of the Russian Empire in the Years 1793-94.** 1802. *[1st. Edn.].* 2 vols. 4to. 52 hand-cold. aquatint plts., most folding, folding maps, hand-cold. vigs., etc., recent qtr. cf. gt. (TA. May 17; 70) £400
– – **Anr. Copy.** 2 vols. 4to. Plts. & vigs., many cold. or folding, hf.-cf., worn, covers loose. (SPB. May 17; 655) $375
– – **Anr. Edn.** L., 1802-03. 2 vols. 4to. 55 engraved plts. & maps (some folding, most cold.), cold. ills. in text, some offsetting from plts. & spotting, minor repairs to fore-margin of 2nd. title, qtr. cf. (S. May 21; 236) *Enzler.* £400
– – **Anr. Copy.** 2 vols. 4to. Cont. hf. russ., w.a.f.;

from liby. of Luttrellstown Castle. (C. Sep.28; 1754) £350
– – **Anr. Edn.** Ill.:– G. Geisler. L., 1812. *2nd. Edn.* 2 vols. 4to. 1 plt. & 1 lf. slit without loss, cont. La Vallière hf. cf., corners. (HD. Dec.16; 54)
Frs. 2,400
– **Voyages ... en Différentes Provinces de Russie et dans l'Asie Septentrionale.** Trans.:– Gauthier de la Peyronie. 1788. 5 vols., lacks Atlas. 4to. Cont. marb. roan. (HD. Apr.13; 38) Frs. 2,000
– – **Anr. Copy.** 5 vols. – Gauthier de la Peyronie. Paris, 1788-93. *1st. Fr. Edn.* 5 vols. & plt. vol. 4to. & fo. Title ll. & text lightly browned in places, plt. vol. lightly spotted at end, 1 margin very browned, cont. marb. cf. gt., lightly worn, corners lightly bumped. (H. May 22; 302) DM 1,350
– **Voyage en Plusieurs Provinces de l'Empire de Russie et dans l'Asie Septentrionale.** Ed.:– Lamarck & Langlès. Trans.:– Gauthier de la Peyronie. Paris, an II [1793/94]. *New Edn.* 8 vols. & Atlas vol. Lge. 8vo. & Fo. Mod. bds., unc. (D. Nov.23; 1107) DM 7,500

PALLIOT, Pierre
– **La Vraye et Parfaite Science des Armoiries.** Dijon, Paris, 1661. *Reprint of 1st. Edn.* Fo. Lacks frontis., title-lf. in facs., 18th. C. cf., spine decor. (HD. Mar.21; 121) Frs. 2,600

PALMA, Giacomo
– **Regole per Imparar a Disegnar i Corpi Humani.** Venice, 1636. 4to. 2 pict. titles, 63 engraved plts., 1 detached, some mntd., some stains or wear, early cf., very worn. (SG. Feb.9; 294) $140

PALMA VIRTUTUM
See— DIOGENES LAERTIUS – PALMA VIR-TUTUM – DEL BEN VIVER DE LE DONNE MARIDAD CHIAMATO GLORIA MULIERUM

PALMER, Alfred Herbert
– **The Life & Letters of Samuel Palmer.** 1892. *(150)* L.P. Fo. Orig. maroon mor. gt., partly unc., worn. (LC. Jul.5; 82) £55
– – **Anr. Edn.** L., 1892. Orig. cl. gt. (P. Nov.24; 166) *Craddock & Barnard.* £85
– – **Anr. Copy.** 4to. Port. frontis., orig. etched plt., photogravures & other ills., errata slip, single advt. lf. bnd. in at rear, some spotting, orig. cl. gt., untrimmed, rubbed on corners. (TA. Jun.21; 513)
£74
– – **Anr. Copy.** Minimal foxing, orig. linen, slightly bumped, spine burst. (HT. May 9; 1139) DM 420

PALMER, Arnold
– **More Than Shadows. A Biography of W. Russell Flint.** 1945. Orig. cl.; inscr. by W. Russell Flint. (LC. Mar.1; 91) £70

PALMER, E. & Pitman, N.
– **Trees of Southern Africa.** Cape Town, 1972. *De Luxe Edn. (200)* sigd. 3 vols. 4to. Qtr. leath., d.-w.'s. (VA. Apr.27; 874) R 350
– – **Anr. Edn.** Cape Town, 1972. 3 vols. 4to. Orig. bdgs., d.-w.'s. (VA. Oct.28; 536) R 240

PALMER, George
– **Kidnapping in the South Seas; being, A Narrative of a Three Months' Cruise of H.M.S. Rosario.** Edinb., 1871. *1st. Edn.* Cl., worn, hinges crudely reprd. (SG. Sep.22; 274) $125

PALMER, Joel
– **Journal of Travels Over the Rocky Mountains, to the Mouth of the Columbia River.** Cinc., 1847. *1st. Edn. 1st. Iss.* Without errata slip (found in some copies), orig. upr. wrap. & new lr. wrap. & spine, portion of orig. spine laid down, s.-c. [Sabin 58358] (LH. Apr.15; 350) $750
– **Journal of Travels in the United States of North America.** L., 1818. *[1st. Edn.].* Folding maps, hand-cold. in outl., 1 torn, some stains, hf. cf., hinges worn. (P. May 17; 82) *Ruddell.* £90
– – **Anr. Copy.** Folding engraved map hand-cold. in outl., slight tear at inner margin of map reprd., some spotting, hf. mor. gt., head of spine chipped, partly unc.; the Rt. Hon. Visc. Eccles copy. [Sabin 58360] (CNY. Nov.18; 219) $260

PALMER, Samuel, Artist
– **Sketch-Book, 1824.** Trianon Pr., for the William Blake Trust, 1962. *Facs. Edn.* 2 vols. Ob. 8vo. Orig. cl., s.-c. (P. Oct.20; 240) £90
– – **Anr. Copy.** 2 vols. Ob. 8vo. Orig. cl., s.-c. (BBA. Jun.28; 300) *Viney.* £85

PALMERIN OF ENGLAND: The First Part [Second Part] of the no lesse rare, then excellent & stately history
L., 1639. 2 pts. in 1 vol. Sm. 4to. (in 8's). 1st. title reprd. at inner & lr. margins & tipped in, some upr. margins reprd. affecting a few headlines, repair to R2 in pt. 2 affecting catchword, mor. gt., by Bedford, inner gt. dentelles. [STC 19164] (C. Nov.9; 102) *Howes.* £160

PALOU, Francisco
– **Relación Historica de la Vida y Apostolics Tareas del Venerable Padre Fray Junipero Serra, y de las Misiones que fundo en la California Septentrional, y nuevos establecimientos de Monterey.** Mexico, 1787. *1st. Edn.* Iss. with 'A Expensas de Don Miguel Gonzalez Calderon' on title before the imprint. Sm. 4to. 2nd. iss. of the folding map, with the words 'Mar Pacifico', slight red ink stain to extreme edges of a few ll. at end, cont. limp vell., with knots & ties, 1 tie defect. [Sabin 58392] (CNY. Nov.18; 302) $950

PALQUERA, Shem Tov
– **Tzari Hayagon.** Cremona, 1557. *1st. Edn.* 4to. Slight staining & browning, old wraps., worn. (SPB. Feb.1; 74) $1,000

PALUCCHINI, R.
– **La Pittura Veneziana del Settecento.** Venezia & Roma, 1960. 4to. Orig. cl., wraps. (SI. Dec.15; 216)
Lire 550,000

PAMANS, Geesje
– **Egt Verhaal van Geestlyke Bevindingen.** Zwolle, 1775. Title soiled, cont. hf. cf., slightly rubbed. (VG. Nov.30; 976) Fls. 825

PAN
Ill.:– O. Eckmann, P. Haln, Heine, E. Kirchner, M. Klinger, M. Liebermann, F. Rops, Steinlen, F. Vallotton, A. Zorn & others. Berlin, 1895-96. Fo. Lacks cold. litho. by Toulouse-Lautrec, some plts. slightly browned, 2 plts. slightly brittle in margin, hf. leath. (HK. Nov.11; 3849a) DM 1,400
– – **Anr. Edn.** Ill.:– Klinger, Kollwitz, Liebermann & others. Berlin, 1895-1900. Years 1-5 (all publd.), in 21 vols. & 1 pt. No. Approx. 100 partly cold. orig. ills., lacks 6 orig. ills., hf. leath. & hf. linen (2), hf. leath. spine defect. & worn, orig. wraps. bnd. in, 1 orig. wraps., all vols. with liby. stp. struck thro. (HK. Nov.11; 3849) DM 5,800

PANCIROLUS, Guido
– **Noticia Utraque Dignitatum, cum Orientis, tum Occidentis ...** Lugduni, 1608. Fo. Cont. decor. roan, Duc d'Orleans-Longueville arms. (HD. Mar.29; 77) Frs. 25,000

PANCKOUCKE, André Joseph
– [–] **L'Art de Désopiler la Rate ...** [Lille, 1756-57]. *2nd. Edn.* 2 vols. 12mo. Cf. gt. by Petit (successor of Simier), spines decor, slight worming to covers; Jules Bobin MS. ex-libris. (HD. Mar.27; 29)
Frs. 1,500

PANCKOUCKE, Charles Louis Fleurie
– **L'Ile de Staffa et Sa Grotte Basaltique.** 1831. Fo. Engraved title, partly col. double-p. map, 12 plts., slight spotting, orig. bds., spine worn. (P. Jun.7; 64)
£65

PANOFSKY, Erwin
See— MEISS, Millard

PANTOMINE PICTURES
Intro:– F.E. Weatherly. L., [1895]. 4to. 5 double-p. col. pop-up plts., 1 slightly defect. but operational, a few text ll. loose, cl.-bkd. pict. bds. (SG. Dec.8; 277) $130

PANVINIUS, Onuphrius
– **De Ludis Circensibus Libri II. De Triumphis Liber Unus ...** Padova, 1642. Fo. Some light staining, mod. hf. leath. (SI. Dec.15; 53) Lire 650,000
– **Fasti et Triumphi Roma, a Romulo Rege usque ad**

PANVINIUS, Onuphrius -*Contd.*

Carolum V. Venice, 1557. *1st. Edn.* Fo. Light stains at few fore-edges, mod. antique-style cf. (SG. Feb.9; 295) $175

PAOLO MASINI, A. di
- **Bologna perlustrata** ... Bologne, 1666. 3 pts. in 2 vols. Sm. 4to. Title frontis. lacks 1 corner, cont. marb. roan. (HD. Dec.2; 134) Frs. 1,600

PAPELIER, G.
- **Leçons sur les Coordonnées Tangentielles.** Paris, 1894/95. 2 vols. Private hf. linen. (HT. May 8; 457) DM 520

PAPIN, Denis
- **Fasciculus Dissertationum de Novis Quibusdam Machinis.** Marburg, 1695. *1st. Edn.* Sm. 8vo. Margins trimmed, affecting a few catchwords, mod. vell.-bkd. bds.; Stanitz. coll. (SPB. Apr.25; 331) $700

PAPINI, Giovanni
- **Saint Augustine.** Trans.:– Mary Prichard. Agnetti. N.Y., [1929]. Square 8vo. Pre-publication sheets, title & 9-330 ll., ptd. on recto only, wraps., stitched, worn; Christopher Morley's sigd. & inscr. copy. (RO. Apr.23; 248) $150

PAPWORTH, John Buonarotti
- **Hints on Ornamental Gardening.** 1823. Hand-cold. frontis., 1 plain plt., 26 hand-cold. plts., some offsetting, hf. cf. (P. Mar.15; 149) *Walford.* £180

PAPWORTH, John Buonarotti & others
- **Poetical Sketches of Scarborough.** 1813. *1st. Edn.* 21 hand-cold. aquatint plts., some spotting & offsetting, 2 plts. reprd., mod. hf. cf., unc. (S. Nov.1; 110) *Thorp.* £120
- - **Anr. Copy.** 21 hand-cold. aquatint plts., spotted thro.-out, few margin tears, cont. hf. cf., rebkd. (BBA. Aug.18; 87) *Solomons.* £85
- - **Anr. Copy.** 21 hand-cold. aquatint plts., light foxing, mod. three-qtr. crushed maroon mor. & marb. bds., untrimmed, marb. end-papers, upr. bd. detchd., boxed. (CBA. Aug.21; 570) $180
- - **Anr. Copy.** 1st. 3 ll. loose, lightly foxed, cont. hf. leath. gt., corners bumped, spine defect. (HK. Nov.10; 3105) DM 550
- **Rural Residences consisting of a Series of Designs for Cottages etc.** 1818. Sm. fo. 27 hand-cold. aquatints. advt. ll bnd. in, mod. red hf. mor. gt. (BBA. Sep.29; 121) *Fletcher.* £420

PARACELSUS, Philip Aureol Theophrastus Bombast von Hohenheim
- **Alchymia Vera das ist der Waren.** N.p., ca. 1610-20. Woodcut on fo. 8v hand-cold., flaw in D7, little margin worming, old vell.; Dr. Walter Pagel copy. (S. Feb.7; 293) *Klingsor.* £780
- **Archidoxa** ... **De Tinctura Physicorum, Tesaurus Tesaurorum, Manuale, Occulta Philosophia** ... Ed.:– [Michael Toxites]. Strassburg, 1574. Engraved port. inserted, some stains, title soiled, some worming, lr. blank corner 3 torn, bds., rebkd.; Dr. Walter Pagel copy. (S. Feb.7; 288) *Quaritch.* £420
- **Aurora Thesaurusque Philosophorum** ... **accessit Monarchia physica per Gerardum Dornaeum in Defensionem Paracelsicorum principiorum** ... Basle, 1577. (*Bound with:*) - **Schreiben von den Frantzosen in IX Bucher Verfasset** ... Basle, 1577. A few stains. Together 2 works in 1 vol. Limp vell.; Dr. Walter Pagel copy. (S. Feb.7; 290) *Klingsor.* £880
- **Chirurgische Buecher und Schrifften.** Strassburg, 1605. 4 pts. & Appendix, in 1 vol. Fo. Sm. strip cut from blank margin fo. 4, name in lr. margin of title partly erased, very browned thro.-out, liby. stp., cont. vell.; Dr. Walter Pagel copy. (S. Feb.7; 292) *Colombo.* £820
- **Erster [-dritter] Theyl der grossen Wundartzeney.** Frankfurt, ca. 1563. *2nd. Edn.* 4to. 1st. title with sm. tear, 72 ll. stpd., lightly browned nearly thro.-out, some slight staining, end-papers with old entries, cont. leath.-bkd. wood bds., very defect., lacks clasps. (H. Nov.23; 247) DM 4,400
- **Etliche Tractat.** Strassburg, 1582. Cont. vell., slightly browned. (GB. May 3; 1027) DM 1,500
- **Fünffter Theil der Bücher vnd Schrifften.** Ed.:– I. Huserus. Basel, 1589. *1st. German Coll. Edn.* 2

vols. in 1. 4to. Main pt. lacks 48 ll. index, woodcut port. cold. later, title with sm. stp., margin frayed, 1st. & last sigs. stained, some cold. lining, lightly browned thro.-out. cont. vell., browned. (H. Nov.23; 247a) DM 1,000
- **The Hermetic & Alchemical Writings.** Ed.:– A.A. Waite. L., 1894. 2 vols. 4to. Cl.; Dr. Walter Pagel copy. (S. Feb.7; 299) *Carmichael.* £140
- **Onomastica II. I. Philosophicum, Medicum, Synonymum ex Variis Vulgaribusque Linguis. II. Theophrasti Paracelsi, hoc est earum vocum quarum in Scriptis ejus solet esse** ... Ed.:– [Michael Toxites]. Strassburg, 1574. 2 colophon ll., some worming, 1 section very bad, limp vell.; Dr. Walter Pagel copy. (S. Feb.7; 287) *Quaritch.* £320
- **Opera, Bücher und Schriften.** Strassburg, 1603. 2 pts. in 1 vol. Fo. Index, pp. 109-122 from shorter copy, discold., cont. blind-stpd. pig. on oak bds., 2 clasps, hinges reprd., new spine label; Dr. Walter Pagel copy. (S. Feb.7; 291) *Klingsor.* £920
- - **Anr. Copy.** Fo. Lightly browned thro.-out, cont. vell., soiled. (GB. Nov.3; 1036) DM 5,500
- **Opera Omnia Medico-Chemico-Chirurgica.** Ed.:– Frid. Bitiskius. Geneva, 1658. 3 vols. in 2. Fo. Few stains, tears in fo. 4 Vol.2, bdg. not stated; Dr. Walter Pagel copy. (S. Feb.7; 294) *Colombo.* £1,000
- **Opus Chirurgicum. Wund und Artzney Buch Darinnen Begriffen** ... Frankfurt, 1566. Lacks pp. 682-704, 17th. C. cf., spine gt. (*With:*) - **Chyrurgia minor quam alias Bertheoneam Initulavit ex versione Gerardi Dorn.** [Basle], 1573. Lacks last blank lf., title supplied in photo facs., paper discold., old wraps. Together 2 vols. Fo. Dr. Walter Pagel copies. (S. Feb.7; 283) *Nadob.* £300
- **Pharmacandi Modus.** Strassburg, 1578. *1st. Edn.* Lacks 2 blank ll. at end, lightly browned, upr. margin cut close, new hf. vell. (H. Nov.23; 247b) DM 800
- - **Anr. Edn.** Strassburg, 1578. *2nd. Edn.* Minimal browning, new hf. vell. (R. Apr.4; 1351) DM 2,100
- **Philosophiae Magnae** ... Cologne, 1567. (*Bound with:*) - **Des Hocherfahrnesten Medici** ... N.p., 1567. *Orig. Edn.* (*Bound with:*) - **Das Buch Meteorum.** Cologne, 1566. *Orig. Edn.* (*Bound with:*) - **Astronomica et Astrologica.** Cologne, 1567. Together 4 works in 1 vol. Cont. stpd. hf. pig over wood bds., decor., monog. 'P.v.P.', clasps; Paulus von Praun sig. on end-paper, from Fondation Furstenberg-Beaumesnil. (HD. Nov.16; 146) Frs. 32,000
- **Pyrophilia Vexatio-Numque liber** ... Basle, 1568. Colophon lf. at end, new bds.; Dr. Walter Pagel copy. (S. Feb.7; 285) *Quaritch.* £350
- **Sämtliche Werke.** Jena, 1926-32. Vols. 1-4 (all publd.). Buckram; Dr. Walter Pagel copy. (S. Feb.7; 295) *Radziowsky.* £120
- - **Anr. Edn.** Ed.:–J. Strebel. St. Gallen, 1944-49. *(750) numbered.* 8 vols. Bds., leath. spine; Dr. Walter Pagel copy. (S. Feb.7; 300) *Quaritch.* £200
- **Sämtliche Werke, Medizinische, Naturwissenschaftliche und Philosophische Schriften. - Theologische und Religionsphilosophische Schriften.** Munich & Berlin, 1929-33-23-60. 14 vols.; 2 vols., including Register. Cl., 2nd. work not unif., bds., cl. spine; Dr. Walter Pagel copies. (S. Feb.7; 296) *Klausner.* £300
- **Vom Ursprung der Pestilentz und ihren Zufallenden Kranckheiten.** Ed.:– Bartholomaeus Scultetus. Basle, 1575. Cont. blind-stpd. pig., rebkd., recased; bkplt. of Baron Johann Georg Picheltorff & Altenburg(?), Dr. Walter Pagel copy. (S. Feb.7; 289) *Colombo.* £500

PARADIN, Claude
- **Les Devises Héroiques de M. Claude Paradin** ... Antw., 1563. 16mo. Lacks E4, some headlines cropped or shaved, late 18th. C. cf. gt., rubbed. (S. Dec.20; 761) *Erasmus.* £90

PARADIN, Guillaume
- **Chronique de Savoie.** Lyon, 1561. Fo. No bdg. stated. (HD. Oct.14; 123) Frs. 2,550
- **De Antiquo Statu Burgundiae** ... Lugduni, 1542. *Orig. Edn.* 4to. Blind-stpd. cf. by Pralon of Dijon. (HD. Jun.29; 159) Frs. 2,900
- **Historiarum Memorabilium ex Genesi Descriptio.** Lyon, 1558. *1st. Edn.* Sm. 8vo. Lacks all of sig. e,

some stains, few cuts with Fr. text added by early owner, crude bds. (SG. Feb.9; 297) $100

PARATUS
- **Sermones Parati de Tempore et de Sanctis [1st. Part].** [Passau, Johann Petri], ca. 1487-88. *1st. Edn.* (*With:*) - **Sermones Parati de Sanctis [2nd. Part].** [Passau, Johann Petri], ca. 1485. *1st. Edn.* Together 2 vols. Fo. 2nd. vol. rubricated, 1st. vol. title & last lf. remntd., dampstains, mod. vell.; from Fondation Furstenberg-Beaumesnil. [HC 12405; BMC II, 615 & 616] (HD. Nov.16; 40) Frs. 4,600

PARBONI, Achille
- **Albumetto.** Roma, 1824. 20 × 13cm. Album, 70 engrs., lacks bdg. (CR. Jun.6; 245) Lire 200,000

PARCERISA, F.J.
- **Recuerdos y Bellezas de España.** Text: P. Piferrer, Quadrado etc. Ill.:– Parcerisa. 1839; 1842; 1844; 1850; 1853. 7 vols. Cont. grd. roan, limp decor. spines, scratched. (HD. Dec.9; 126) Frs. 7,800
- - **Anr. Edn.** Text:– P. Piferrer. 1882. *1st. Edn.* Fo. Orig. stpd. linen gt., chromolitho. wraps. (DS. Feb.24; 2419) Pts. 65,000

PARDIELLAN, Commandant
- **Récits Militaires d'Alsace.** Ill.:– Frédéric Gegamey. Strasbourg, 1905. 4to. Hf. chagrin, corners, wrap. (HD. Jan.27; 77) Frs. 1,800

PARDIES, Ignace Gaston
- **La Statique ou la Science des Forces Mouvantes.** Paris, 1674-76. *2nd. Edn.* (*Bound with:*) - **Deux Machines Propres à Faire les Quadrans avec Très Grande Facilité.** Paris, 1674-76. *2nd. Edn.* Together 2 works in 1 vol. 12mo. Old cf. (RO. Dec.11; 268) $170

PARDOE, Julia
- **The Beauties of the Bosphorus.** Ill.:– after W.H. Bartlett. 1838. 4to. Additional engraved title, port., 79 plts., including full-p. map, some spotting, cont. cf. gt. (S. Nov.1; 97) *Clegg.* £110
- - **Anr. Copy.** 4to. Steel-engraved port., additional title, 1 map, 78 plts., some light spotting, orig. mor. gt., upr. cover detchd. (CSK. Sep.16; 115) £55
- - **Anr. Edn.** [1838]. 4to. Engraved vig. title, map, 85 plts., some spotting, hf. cf. (P. Sep.8; 167) *Aspin.* £70
- - **Anr. Edn.** 1839. 4to. Port., engraved title, map, 78 plts., mor. gt. (P. Jul.26; 200) £95
- - **Anr. Edn.** L., [1839]. 4to. Port., engraved title, map, 84 engraved views, hf. cf. gt. (P. Nov.24; 37) *Traylen.* £75
- - **Anr. Edn.** Ill.:– after W.H. Bartlett. L., 1843. 1 vol. in 2. 4to. Cont. embossed cl. gt. (C. Nov.16; 146) *Irani.* £150
- - **Anr. Edn.** Ill.:– W.H. Bartlett. N.d. 8 orig. pts. Cl. gt. (PD. Aug.17; 234) £220
- - **Anr. Copy.** 1st. 3 divisions only of 'The Bosphorous & the Danube'. 4to. Orig. cl. gt. (LC. Mar.1; 227) £60
- **Louis the Fourteenth & the Court of France in the 17th Century.** 1886. 3 vols. (*With:*) - **The Court & Reign of Francis the First, King of France.** 1887. 3 vols. (*With:*) - **The Life of Marie de Medicis, Queen of France.** 1890. 3 vols. Together 9 vols. Hf. mor. by Bumpus Ltd., gt.-decor. spines; partly untrimmed. (TA. Sep.15; 297) £54
See— **BEATTIE, William - PARDOE, Julia**

PARDONI, Pietro
- **I Celebri Frieschi di Gaspare Possino.** Rome, 1810. Ob. fo. Some light soiling, cont. hf. mor., worn; 8 plts. by Raphael bnd. in, w.a.f. (CSK. Jun.29; 178) £140

PARE, Ambroise
- **Les Oeuvres.** Paris, 1585. *4th. Edn.* Fo. Some foxing & staining, cont. spr. cf., decor. spine, scratched. (HD. Dec.9; 68) Frs. 30,100
- - **Anr. Edn.** Paris, 1607. *6th. Edn.* Fo. Some browning, cont. vell. bds., soiled, lacks ties. (S. Nov.28; 131) *Pickering & Chatto.* £600
- **The Workes.** [1665]. 2 pts. in 1 vol. Fo. Lacks title-p., spotted, 2nd. pt. bnd. 1st., later cf., slightly rubbed. [Wing P350?] (BBA. Jul.27; 45) *Demetzy.* £220

PARENT, A.
- **Industries et Accessoires du Vêtement (Exposition Internationale de Bruxelles).** Paris, 1910. 4to. On holland, dedication, hf. roan, corners, by Durvand, spine richly decor., wrap. & spine. (HD. Feb.28; 182)   Frs. 1,150

PARIS
- **Collection de Vues de Paris Prises au Daguerreotype.** Ill.:– [Claude-Hilaire-Alphonse?] Chamouin. [Paris], ca. 1842? Ob. 4to. Engraved title, 25 plts., some worming, cont. bds.; Jules Asselin exlibris. (HD. Mar.19; 112)   Frs. 3,100
- **La Grande Ville. Nouveau Tableau de Paris, Comique, Critique et Philosophique.** Paris, 1842-43. 2 vols. Lge. 8vo. Cont. hf. mor., spines gt., unc. (HD. Mar.19; 96)   Frs. 2,800
- **Panorama Intérieur de Paris.** Paris, n.d. Ob. fo. Folding panorama, 16 litho plts., cold. & 'gommées', publisher's cl., spine reprd. (HD. May 4; 382)   Frs. 2,700
- **Paris.** Ill.:– Josefa Simy. [Prague, 1927]. *(120) numbered & sigd. by artist.* Fo. 18 hand-cold. etchings, loose as iss. in pict. wraps., torn. (SG. Jan.12; 315) $150
- **Paris à travers les Ages.** Text:– A. Bonnardot, J. Cousin, E. Drumont & others. Ill.:– M.F. Hoffbauer. Paris, 1885. *2nd. Edn.* 14 pts. in 2 vols. Fo. 92 chromolitho. plts., publisher's hf. chagrin gt., Paris arms, spines decor. (HD. May 21; 139)   Frs. 4,100
- **Paris au XIXème Siècle.** Text:– Albéric Second & others. Ill.:– Victor Adam, Gavarni, Daumier, Bouchot, Bourdet, & others. Paris, 1839. *1st. Edn.* Lge. 4to. 48 plts., light foxing, hf. chagrin, spine decor., slight wear. (LM. Oct.22; 320)   B.Frs. 11,000
- **Paris Comique.** Ill.:– Daumier &c. Paris, [1844]. Lge. 4to. Lacks title & hf.-title, cont. hf. roan. (HD. May 4; 383)   Frs. 4,800
- – **Anr. Copy.** 4to. Some foxing, 1 margin tear, cont. hf. corinthian roan, limp decor. spine, lightly scratched. (HD. Dec.9; 167)   Frs. 2,200
- **Paris – Croquis.** Ill.:– Henri Boutet. Paris, 6 Oct. 1888-20 Jul. 1889. Nos. 1-22 in 1 vol. 4to. 28 orig. dry-points, hf. mor., corners, by Bretault (not sigd.), spine gt., wrap.; 12 orig. dry-points ('Types de Parisiennes') by Boutet bnd at end. (HD. Jun.22; 64)   Frs. 1,800
- **Paris et ses Environs.** 1855. Ob. 4to. Litho. title, 20 cold. litho. plts., orig. cl., covers detchd. (P. Sep.8; 396)   *Tzakas.* £110
- – **Anr. Copy.** Ob. 4to. 20 cold. litho plts., margin dampstain on some plts., publisher's bds., covers detchd. (HD. Nov.17; 60)   Frs. 2,200
- **Paris-guide par les Principaux Ecrivains et Artistes de la France.** Contribs.:– V. Hugo, Renan, Sainte-Beuve, Littré, Michelet, Th. Gautier, Viollet-le-Duc, George Sand. Paris, 1867. 2 vols. Sm. 8vo. Cont. hf. mor. (HD. Mar.19; 114) Frs. 1,400
- **Paris Moderne et ses Environs.** Ill.:– Charles Rivière. Paris, ca. 1860. Ob. sm. fo. 24 litho. plts., some foxed, orig. cl.-bkd. & gt.-lettered bds., cover loose. (SG. Sep.22; 236) $100
- **Paris Moderne Grand Album** ... Ill.:– after Rivière, Jacottet, Benoist, & others. Paris, ca. 1860. Ob. 4to. Tinted litho. title, 40 hand-finished cold. litho. plts., 1 spotted, orig. cl. gt., rubbed. (C. Nov.16; 149)   *Weissert.* £400
- **Paris qui crie. Petits Métiers.** Notices:– Albert Arnal, Henry Spencer Ashbee, Claretie & others. Trans.:– Henri Beraldi. Ill.:– Pierre Vidal. Paris, 1890. Mor. gt. decor., spine decor. (faded), wrap. preserved. (HD. Jun.13; 87)   Frs. 2,100
- – **Anr. Edn.** Notice:– A. Arnal, H. Spencer Ashbee, J. Claretie & others. Trans.:– Henri Béraldi. Ill.:– Pierre Vidal. Paris, 1890. *(120).* Str.-grd. bradel mor. by Champs, unc., wrap. & spine preserved; Henri Meilhac copy. (HD. May 4; 384)   Frs. 4,300
- **Plan de Paris, avec Détails Historiques de ses Agrandissements et de ses Embellissements, depuis Jules César jusqu'à ce Jour** ... Paris, ca. 1810. 4to. Cont. bds., spine & corners defect. (SM. Mar.7; 2526)   Frs. 1,200
- **Principales Vues de Paris et de ses Environs.** Ill.:– Martens, after Schmidt & others. Paris, 1832. Ob. 8vo. Engraved title with aquatint vig., 55 aquatint views, cont. mor.-bkd. bds. (C. Nov.16; 148)   *Shapero.* £320

- **Revolutions de Paris.** Ed.:– Louis-Marie Prudhomme. 12 Apr. 1790-94. Nos. 40-225 in 14 vols. (Lacks 6 issues). Qtr. cf., worn, as a periodical, w.a.f. (P. Apr.12; 304a)   *S. Dupré.* £170
- **Les Types de Paris.** Text:– E. de Goncourt, A. Daudet, E. Zola, G. de Maupassant, P. Bourget, J.K. Huysmans, & others. Ill.:– Jean-François Raffaëlli. Paris, [1889]. 4to. Publisher's buckram, decor. cover & spine. (HD. Sep.21; 158)   Frs. 2,500
- **Vues de Paris et ses Environs.** Ill.:– after Charles Fichot & others. [Paris,], ca. 1855. Ob. 4to. 30 hand-cold. litho. views, rather foxed, 1 margin tear, orig. gt.-lettered cl., dampstained. (SG. Sep.22; 238) $110

PARIS, François Edmond
- **Souvenirs de Jérusalem.** Paris, [1862]. Atlas fo. Litho. title with cold. mntd. plan, 2 tinted & 12 chromolitho. views, cont. hf. mor., spine ends worn. (C. Mar.14; 78)   *Walford.* £380

PARIS, John Ayrton
[–] **Philosophy in Sport made Science in Earnest.** Ill.:– Cruikshank. 1827. *1st. Edn.* 3 vols. Orig. bds., worn; H.M. Nixon coll. (BBA. Oct.6; 237)   *Quaritch.* £70

PARIS, Matthew
- **Angliae Historia Maior, a Guilielmi Conquaestore.** Zurich, 1589. Fo. Cont. cf., 17th. C. MS. note on rear free end-paper. (BBA. Feb.23; 11)   *Thorp.* £80

PARISH-WATSON COLLECTION
- **Mohammadan Potteries.** N.Y., 1922. *(500) numbered.* Fo. Orig. cl., d.-w. (CSK. Sep.16; 251)   £120
- – **Anr. Copy.** Fo. This copy unnumbered, cl. (SG. Jan.26; 140) $150
- – **Anr. Copy.** Fo. Mntd. cold. frontis., 94 plts., many cold., ex-liby., cl. (SG. May 3; 88) $130

PARTIUS, Georg Heinrich
[–] **Gründliche Anweisung zur Schreib-Kunst** ... **Current– und Cantzley– ... Fractur und Lateinische** ... Nürnberg, 1709. Title browned & with owners mark, 1st. & last ll. bkd. in outer margin, slight spotting, mod. bds.; Hauswedell coll. (H. May 23; 260)   DM 600
- **Gründliche Handleitung zur Schreib-Kunst** ... Nürnberg, 1703. Mod. bds.; Hauswedell coll. (H. May 23; 255)   DM 600

PARIVAL, Jean
- **The History of this Iron Age.** 1656. *1st. Edn. in Engl.* 4to. Browned thro.-out, stained on upr. margin, cont. cf., upr. cover detchd., 1 corner reprd., rubbed. (BBA. Jun.28; 68)   *Coupe.* £50

PARK, John James
- **The Topography & Natural History of Hampstead.** L., 1818. Folding map (slightly torn), 10 engraved plts., 3 extra plts. bnd. in, 2 folding tables, cont. hf. cf., split in upr. hinge. (BBA. Mar.21; 122)   *Levy.* £75

PARK, Lawrence
- **Gilbert Stuart an Illustrated Descriptive List of his Works.** N.Y., 1926. 4 vols. 4to. Orig. cl. (S. Apr.30; 72)   *Alcaz.* £200
- – **Anr. Copy.** 4 vols. Lge. 4to. Advt. & 2 prospectuses laid in Vol. 1, cl., s.-c. (SG. Oct.13; 336) $550

PARK, Mungo
- **Travels in the Interior Districts of Africa.** L., 1799. *1st. Edn.* 4to. Port., 3 folding maps, 5 plts., 2 music ll., slight offsetting, cont. cf., rebkd. (S. Mar.6; 12)   *Beale.* £90
- – **Anr. Copy.** Lge. 4to. Subscribers list, lacks port. & 2 mus. plts., crude bds. (SG. Sep.22; 5) $125
- – **Anr. Edn.** L., 1799. *2nd. Edn.* 4to. Cont. cf. gt. (C. Nov.16; 28)   *Scott.* £70
- – **Anr. Copy.** 4to. 7 engraved plts., 2 folding, 2 folding maps, 1 torn & reprd., 2 ll. of music with margins reprd., soiled & browned thro.-out, mod. hf. cf. (BBA. Jun.28; 237)   *Swanson.* £55
- – **Anr. Edn.** 1799. *3rd. Edn.* 4to. Cont. cf., worn. (CSK. Jul.6; 74)   £70
- – **Anr. Edn.** L., 1816-15. 2 vols. 4to. 10 engraved plts. & maps (2 slightly torn), a few folding, engraved lf. of music, hf.-titles, spotted, cont. cf. gt., rebkd., slightly rubbed. (BBA. Dec.15; 35)   £70

PARKER, Dorothy
- **Not So Deep As a Well: The Collected Poems of Dorothy Parker.** Ill.:– V. Angelo. N.Y., 1936. *1st. Edn. (485) sigd. by author & artist.* Faint offset from decors., hf. cl. & bds., box rubbed & bumped; the V. Angelo copy. (CBA. Oct.1; 327) $110

PARKER, Capt. H. & Bowen, Frank C.
- **Mail & Passenger Steamships of the Nineteenth Century.** 1928. *[1st. Edn.].* 4to. Orig. cl., soiled. (CSK. Jan.13; 191)   £105
- – **Anr. Copy.** 4to. Orig. cl. (BBA. Sep.8; 85)   *Green.* £75
- – **Anr. Copy.** 4to. Cl., soiled. (SG. Aug.25; 274) $250

PARKER, J.T. & Mathey, J.
- **Antoine Watteau. Catalogue Complet de son Oeuvre Dessiné.** Paris, 1957. 2 vols. 4to. No bdg. stated. (SPB. Nov.30; 72) $900

PARKER, Samuel
- **Journal of an Exploring Tour beyond the Rocky Mountains.** Ithaca, 1838. *1st. Edn.* Lge. 12mo. Map wrinkled, orig. cl.; ex-liby. (SG. Jan.19; 286) $200

PARKHOUSE, T.A.
- **Reprints & Papers Relating to the Autochthones of Australia.** Woodville, ca. 1933-35. 2 vols. bdg. not stated; 1 p. A.L.s. from author to Charles Glover loosely inserted, carbon typescript reply & 2 or 3 sm. pieces of ephemera. (KH. May 1; 550)   Aus. $110

PARKINSON, John
- **Paradisi in Sole Paradisus Terrestris.** 1629. *1st. Edn.* Fo. I1 + 2Z2 torn, hole to 3E2, some browning, cf., upr. cover detchd., w.a.f. (P. Dec.8; 157)   *Symonds.* £300
- – **Anr. Edn.** L., 1656. *2nd. Edn.* Fo. Woodcut title, woodcut garden plan, 109 full-p. woodcuts, sm. repair to woodcut title, sm. tear in *5 just touching text, minor worming through a few lr. margins, cont. sheep, slightly rubbed, recased & reprd. [Wing P495] (C. Jun.27; 125) *Segal.* £750
- – **Anr. Copy.** Fo. Minor staining & foxing, few cont. marginalia, 19th. C. cf., covers detchd. (SG. Nov.3; 161) $550
- – **Anr. Copy.** Fo. Lacks engraved title & last 5 ll. of index, old hf. cf., marb. bds. rebkd. with mor.; Frances Parkinson Keyes bkplt. (SG. Mar.22; 254) $300
- – **Anr. Edn.** 17th. C. Fo. 103 full-p. woodcuts, lacks title & all ll. before **3, lacks ll. of Index, some staining, a few ll. torn, disbnd., w.a.f. (P. Jun.7; 212)   £260
- **Theatrum Botanicum: the Theater of Plants, or, an Herball.** L., 1640. *[1st. Edn.].* Fo. Engraved title, upwards of 2,700 woodcuts in text, engraved title shaved at foot, some dampstaining, last 2 ll. of index reprd. at lr. edges, just touching text in 1 case, final errata with upr. & lr. corners torn away & lacking a few letters of text, cont. cf., recased & reprd. [STC 19302] (C. Jun.27; 124)   *Houle.* £800
- – **Anr. Copy.** Fo. 2F1-2F6 wear to margins, hole to 2B6 & 3P6 with loss of 1 letter, lacks 3N3-3N4, panel. cf., hinges reprd., w.a.f. (P. Feb.16; 204)   £400
- – **Anr. Copy.** Fo. Lacks engraved & ptd. titles & 1 prelim., prelims. very frayed with some loss, some ll. of table also frayed, partially browned thro.-out, cont. cf., worn, upr. cover detchd. (TA. May 17; 320)   £170
- – **Anr. Copy.** Fo. Lacks ll. G2 & G5, dupls. of ll. C2 & C5 mistakenly bnd. in their place, old cf., disbnd. [STC 19302] (RO. Dec.11; 270) $375
- – **Anr. Copy.** Fo. Lacks some index ll. at end, frontis. defect. & reprd., mod. hf. cf. (SI. Dec.15; 170)   Lire 1,100,000

PARKINSON, Richard
- **A Tour in America ... & a particular account of the American system of agriculture.** L., 1805. 2 vols. Hf. cf. (S. Jun.25; 114)   *Quaritch.* £70

PARKINSON, Sydney
– **A Journal of a Voyage to the South Seas in His Majesty's Ship, the Endeavour.** 1773. *1st. Edn.* Lge. 4to. Engraved frontis. & 27 plts., front free end-paper loose, cont. spr. cf., spine gt., slightly rubbed; bkplts. of Marquiss of Donegal with Bibliotheca Lindesiana. (BBA. Jul.27; 270) *Arnold.* £1,250
– – **Anr. Copy.** Port., engraved map, 26 engraved plts., port. foxed, title offset, light offsetting from some plts., hf. mor., rebkd. (CA. Apr.3; 95) Aus. $2,800
– – **Anr. Edn.** L., 1784. Lge. 4to. Engraved frontis. port., double-p. engraved chart, engraved map, 26 engraved plts., errata lf., engraved crest mntd. on title verso, without the 4 pp. of letters & poem, 2 plts. slightly spotted, some offset to a few ll., sm. stain to blank margin of 2 ll., 19th. C. hf. cf., inner hinges strengthened. (C. Nov.16; 150) *Foyle.* £1,000
– – **Anr. Edn.** Adelaide, 1972. *Facs. Edn.* 4to. Bdg. not stated. (KH. May 1; 551) Aus. $110

PARKMAN, Francis
– **The California & Oregon Trail; being, Sketches of Prairie & Rocky Mountain Life.** N.Y., 1849. *1st. Edn. 2nd. Printing.* Cl., loose, spine torn. (SG. Jan.19; 287) $150
– **The Discovery of the Great West.** Boston, 1870. *1st. Edn. (75) numbered on L.P.* Sm. 4to. Orig. cl. gt., covers dampstained, spine ends frayed; inscr. by publisher to W.W. Appleton. (SG. Jan.19; 288) $100
– **History of the Conspiracy of Pontiac.** L., 1851. *1st. Engl. Edn.* 2 vols. 3 folding maps, extra-ill. with 17 plts., some hand-cold., mor. gt. by Bayntun (Rivière). (S. Oct.4; 96) *Sawyer.* £90
– **The Old Regime of Canada.** Boston, 1874. *1st. Edn. (75) numbered on L.P.* 1 vol. (*With:*) – **Montcalm & Wolfe.** Boston, 1885. *1st. Edn. (75) numbered on L.P.* 2 vols. Together 3 vols. Sm. 4to. Unif. cl. gt., covers dampstained, 1 spine snagged, unopened; 2nd. work inscr. by publisher (J. Murray Brown) to W.W. Appleton. (SG. Jan.19; 137) $120
– **The Oregon Trail. Sketches of Prairie & Rocky-Mountain Life.** Ill.:– Frederic Remington. Boston, 1892. *1st. Remington Edn. 1st. Iss., without list of ills.* Decor. cl. gt., light wear, decor. d.-w. (frayed, rather darkened); Ken Leach coll. (RO. Jun.10; 203) $250

PARKS, Mrs. Fanny P.
– **Wanderings of a Pilgrim in Search of the Picturesque during Four-and-Twenty Years in the East.** 1850. 2 vols. 4to. 49 (of 50) litho. plts., some hand-cold., folding panorama loosely inserted, some spotting, mod. hf. cf., orig. cl. upr. covers preserved. (BBA. Sep.29; 68) *Bauman.* £50

PARKYNS, George Isham
– **Monastic & Baronial Remains ... in England, Wales, & Scotland.** 1816. 2 vols. 100 plts., str.-grd. mor. gt. (P. Jun.7; 68) £85

PARLEY, Peter (Pseud.)
See— **GOODRICH, Samuel Griswold 'Peter Parley'**

PARLIAMENT
[*Arranged in Chronological Order*]
– **Another Declaration from both Houses of Parliament Sent to his Majesty, March 22nd, 1641.** 1641. Title & 5 pp. text, hf. mor. gt. (P. Feb.16; 180) £60
– **An Act for erecting & establishing a Post-Office.** [1660]. Fo. Pp. 129-[144], slightly soiled, disbnd. (BBA. Sep.29; 228) *Pickering & Chatto.* £95
– **An Act for preventing the Frequent Abuses in Printing Seditious, Treasonable, & Unlicensed Books & Pamphlets** ... 1662. Fo. Pp. [2], 425-438, 435-[446], last blank lf., slightly soiled, margin stains, disbnd. (BBA. Sep.29; 227) *Quaritch.* £150
– **An Act Declaring the Rights & Liberties of the Subject, & Settling the Succession of the Crown [caption title].** L., 1689. *1st. Printing?.* Sm. fo. Bnd. with 43 other acts covering 23 Feb. 1688[-27 Jan. 1689], cont. cf. (SG. Oct.27; 184) $750
– **Act of Parliament for Erecting a Bank in Scotland. Edinburgh, July 17. 1695.** Edinb., 1695. Fo. Slightly soiled, folded as iss., mod. cl. folder. [Wing S1128] (BBA. May 3; 177) *Drury.* £100
– **Acts.** L., 1695-1759. 36 vols. Fo. Some browning, & staining, cont. cf., worn. (S. Oct.11; 573) *Prichard-Jones.* £1,450
– **An Act for the Preservation of White & other Pine-Trees growing in Her Majesties Colonies of New Hampshire, the Massachusets-Bay ... in America, for the Masting Her Majesties Navy.** 1711. Fo. Pp. [2], 387-388, margin tears, disbnd. [Sabin 42780] (BBA. Sep.29; 264) *Bauman.* £130
– **An Act for the Preserving all such Ships, & Goods thereof, which shall happen to be forced on Shore, or Stranded upon the Coasts of this Kingdom ... – An Act for enforcing the Laws against Persons who shall steal or detain Shipwrecked Goods: & for the Relief of Persons suffering Losses thereby.** 1714; 1753. Together 2 acts. Fo. Pp. [2], 337-382, stained; pp. [2], 303-[312]; disbnd. (BBA. Sep.29; 235) *Bauman.* £50
– **An Act for Preventing Tumults & Riotous Assemblies & for the more speedy & Effectual Punishing the Rioters.** 1715. Fo. Pp. [2], 243-248, spotted, disbnd. (BBA. Sep.29; 234) *Bauman.* £65
– **An Act for securing certain Powers & Privileges intended to be granted by His Majesty by Two Charters for Assurance of Ships & Merchandizes at Sea, & for lending Money upon Bottomry; & for restraining several Extravagant & Unwarrantable Practices therein mentioned.** 1720. Fo. Pp. [2], 363-382, disbnd. (BBA. Sep.29; 248) *Pickering & Chatto.* £150
– **An Act for Establishing an Agreement with Seven of the Lords Proprietors of Carolina, for the Surrender of their Title & Interest in that Province to His Majesty.** 1729. Fo. Pp. [2], 543-562, slightly browned, small margin wormholes, disbnd. [Sabin 87355] (BBA. Sep.29; 265) *Bauman.* £360
– **An Act to prevent the Exportation of Hats out of any of His Majesty's Colonies or Plantations in America, & to restrain the Number of Apprentices taken by the Hat-makers ... & for the better Encouraging the Making Hats in Great Britain.** 1732. Fo. Pp. [2], 379-[384], disbnd. (BBA. Sep.29; 266) *Bauman.* £100
– **An Act for restraining & preventing several unwarrantable Schemes & Undertakings in His Majesty's Colonies & Plantations in America.** 1741. Fo. Pp. [2], 683-688, disbnd. (BBA. Sep.29; 249) *Pickering & Chatto.* £95
– **An Act for giving a Publick Reward to such Person or Persons, His Majesty's Subject or Subjects, as shall discover a North-West passage through Hudson's Streights, to the Western & Southern Ocean of America.** 1745. Fo. Pp. [2], 483-486, disbnd. (BBA. Sep.29; 276) *Bauman.* £310
– **An Act to Amend & Render more Effectual, in His Majesty's Dominions in America, an Act passed in this present Session of Parliament, intituled 'An Act for Punishing Mutiny & Desertion, & for the better Payment of the Army & their Quarters'.** 1765. Fo. Pp. [2], 579-596, disbnd. (BBA. Sep.29; 267) *Bauman.* £358
– **An Act for restraining & prohibiting the Governor, Council, & House of Representatives, of the Province of New York, until Provision shall have been made for furnishing the King's Troops with all the Necessaries required by Law, from passing or assenting to any Act of Assembly, Vote, or Resolution, for any other Purpose.** 1767. Fo. Pp. [2], 891-894, disbnd. (BBA. Sep.29; 268) *Bauman.* £400
– **An Act to incorporate Certain Persons therein named, & their Successors, with proper Powers for the Purpose of establishing One or more Glass Manufactories within the Kingdom of Great Britain; & for the more effectually supporting & conducting the same upon an Improved Plan, in a Peculiar Manner, calculated for the Casting of large Plate Glass.** 1773. Fo. Pp. [2], 739-758, disbnd. (BBA. Sep.29; 259) *Marlboro' Rare Books.* £65
– **An Act for the better providing Suitable Quarters for Officers & Soldiers in His Majesty's Service in North America.** 1774. Fo. Pp. [2], 1251-1252, disbnd. (BBA. Sep.29; 274) *Bauman.* £160
– **An Act for the better regulating the Government of the Province of Massachuset's Bay, in New England.** 1774. Fo. Pp. [2], 1047-1062, disbnd. (BBA. Sep.29; 273) *Bauman.* £290
– – **Anr. Copy.** Mod. cf.-bkd. bds. (BBA. Mar.21; 213) *Goldman.* £220
– **An Act for the Impartial Administration of Justice on the Cases of Persons questioned for any Acts done by them in the Execution of the Law or for the Suppression of Riots & Tumults, in the Province of the Massachuset's Bay, in New England.** 1774. Fo. Pp. [2], 991-998, disbnd. (BBA. Sep.29; 272) *Bauman.* £250
– – **Anr. Copy.** Fo. Mod. cf.-bkd. bds. (BBA. Mar.21; 212) *Goldman.* £200
– **An Act to discontinue, in such Manner, & for such Time as therein mentioned, the Landing & Discharging, Lading or Shipping of Goods ... at the Town, & within the Harbour, of Boston ...** 1774. Fo. Pp. [2], 515-522, 3 ll. browned, disbnd. [Sabin 94142] (BBA. Sep.29; 271) *Bauman.* £280
– – **Anr. Copy.** Fo. Browned, mod. cf.-bkd. bds. [Sabin 94142] (BBA. Mar.21; 211) *Goldman.* £200
– **15 George III cap. 10. An Act to Restrain the Trade & Commerce of the Provinces of Massachuset's Bay .. in North America, to Great Britain ... & to Prohibit such Provinces ... from Carrying on any Fishery on the Banks of New Foundland ...** L., 1775. Fo. Mod. cf.-bkd. bds. (BBA. Mar.21; 215) *Goldman.* £100
– **15 George III cap. 15. An Act to Amend & Render more Effectual in H.M.'s Dominions in America an Act ... intituled An Act for Punishing Mutiny & Desertion & for the better Payment of the Army & their Quarters ... to His Majesty's Marine Forces in America.** L., 1775. Fo. Mod. cf.-bkd. bds. (BBA. Mar.21; 214) *Goldman.* £80
– **15 George III cap. 18. An Act to Restrain the Trade & Commerce of the Colonies of New Jersey ... to Great Britain ... under certain Conditions & Limitations.** L., 1775. Fo. Mod. cf.-bkd. bds. [Sabin 53039] (BBA. Mar.21; 216) *Goldman.* £100
– **16 George III cap. 6. An Act for giving a Publick Reward unto such Person ... as Shall Discover a Northern Passage for Vessels by Sea between Atlantic & Pacific Oceans** ... L., 1776. Fo. Disbnd. (BBA. Mar.21; 218) *Goldman.* £200
– **An Act to prohibit all Trade & Intercourse with the Colonies of New Hampshire, Massachuset's Bay, ... during the Continuance of the present Rebellion within the said Colonies respectively; for repealing an Act made in the Fourteenth Year of the Reign of His Present Majesty to Discontinue the Landing & Discharging, Lading or Shipping of Goods, Wares, & Merchandize, at the Town & within the Harbour of Boston** ... 1776. Fo. Pp. [2], 215-244, disbnd. [Sabin 52780] (BBA. Sep.29; 275) *Bauman.* £410
– – **Anr. Copy.** Fo. Disbnd. [Sabin 52780] (BBA. Mar.21; 217) *Goldman.* £350
– **22 George III cap. 10. An Act for the Better Detaining & more easy Exchange, of American Prisoners brought into Great Britain.** L., 1782. Fo. Mod. cf.-bkd. bds. (BBA. Mar.21; 219) *Goldman.* £80
– **22 George III cap. 46. An Act to enable His Majesty to conclude a Peace or Truce with certain Colonies in North America therein mentioned.** L., 1782. Fo. Mod. cf.-bkd. bds. (BBA. Mar.21; 220) *Goldman.* £180
– **An Act to remove Doubts respecting the Function of Juries in Cases of Libel.** 1792. Fo. Pp. [2], 979-980, disbnd. (BBA. Sep.29; 260) *Bowers.* £50
– **An Act to prevent Unlawful Combination of Workmen.** 1799. Fo. Pp. [653-]662, disbnd. (BBA. Sep.29; 241) *London Univ. Library.* £65
– **An Act for the Abolition of the Slave Trade.** 1807. Fo. Pp. [317]-[328], last blank lf., disbnd. (BBA. Sep.29; 244) *Bauman.* £110
– **An Act for the more effectually detaining in Custody Napoleon Buonaparte. — An Act for regulating the Intercourse with the Island of Saint Helena, during the Time Napoleon Buonaparte shall be detained there** ... 1816. Together 2 acts. Fo. Pp. [209]-216; disbnd. (BBA. Sep.29; 245) *Sawyer.* £80
– **An Act to vest the Elgin Collection of Ancient Marbles & Sculpture in the Trustees of the British Museum for the Use of the Public.** 1816. Fo. Pp. [865]-[868], disbnd. (BBA. Sep.29; 246) *Quaritch.* £65
– **Abstract of the Answers & Returns Made Pursuant to an Act, Entitled, an Act for Taking an Account of the Population of Great Britain.** 1831. 3 vols. Fo. Cont. hf. cf., rubbed. (BBA. Jun.28; 1) *Drury.* £50

– An Act for the Better Regulation of Chimney Sweepers & their Apprentices together with the Minutes of Evidence taken before the Lords Committees. 1834. Fo. 'Index to Minutes' loosely inserted, cont. hf. cf., cover detchd., lacks part spine. (SKC. Nov.18; 1923) £80
– An Act to provide for the Government of British Columbia. 1858. Fo. Pp. [798]-800, disbnd. (BBA. Sep.29; 282) *Baldwin.* £100
– An Act for the Union of Canada, Nova Scotia, & New Brunswick, & the Government thereof ... 1867. Fo. Pp. [9]-[48], disbnd. (BBA. Sep.29; 283) *Baldwin.* £110
– [A Collection of Acts & Ordinances]. L., 1648 [-53]. In 2 vols. Fo. About 280 items, including 90 broadsides, slight browning, few short tears, cont. cf., upr. covers wormed, rebkd., as a collection, w.a.f.; Earl of Roden bkplt. (S. Dec.8; 307) *Quaritch.* £4,000
– An Exact Collection of all Remonstrances, Declarations, Votes ... between the King ... & his High Court of Parliament. L., 1643. 2nd. Edn. 4to. Cont. spr. cf.; from John Evelyn's Liby., with his pressmark 0.2 (deleted), inscr. & motto. [Wing E 1533] (S. Dec.8; 308) *Seibu.* £160

PARLIAMENTARY GAZETTEER OF IRELAND
Dublin, 1846. 9 vols. only (lacks Vol. 7). Royal 8vo. Bkplt., cl. (GM. Dec.7; 288) £50

PARLIAMENTARY PAPERS
– Copies or extracts of correspondence relative to the discovery of gold in the Fraser's River District, in British North America. L., 1858. Fo. Crease mark on title, wraps. (S. Jun.25; 116) *Faupel.* £160
– Further Papers relative to the Mutinies in the East Indies. L., 1857-60. 14 papers in 1 vol. Fo. 1 paper browned & 1 p. with sm. tears, cl., rubbed, upr. cover detchd. (S. Jun.25; 47) *Maggs.* £300

PARNASSE SATYRIQUE DU XIXe SIECLE
1856. 3 vols. 12mo. On holland, frontis. in double state, 8 autograph facs., cont. jansenist red mor. (HD. May 4; 385) *Frs. 1,700*

PARNELL, Sir Henry
– A Treatise on Roads. L., 1833. 1st. Edn. 7 folding plts., orig. cl. (P. May 17; 275) *Congleton.* £140

PARNELL, Thomas
See– GOLDSMITH, Oliver & Parnell, Thomas

PARNY, Evariste Desiré de Forges, vicomte de
– Oeuvres Choisies. Paris, 1827. Some foxing, hf. mor. by Kochler, corners, decor. spine, from Comte de la Beroyère liby.; A.L. from author. (HD. Jan.27; 261) *Frs. 2,100*

PAROISSIEN ROMAIN d'après les Imprimés Français du XVe Siècle
1858. 12mo. 15th. C. style russ. gt. by Gruel, crowned cypher, gt. bronze studs & clasp, silk end-ll. (HD. Jun.29; 170) *Frs. 1,250*

PARR, Richard
– The Life of the Most Rev. Father in God, James Usher ... of Armagh. L., 1686. 1st. Edn. Fo. Bkplt., orig. cf. (GM. Dec.7; 97) £100

PARR, Samuel
– Bibliotheca Parriana. A Catalogue of the Library of the Late Reverend & Learned Samuel Parr, LL.D. 1827. (40). (5) with the 4 cancelled ll. The 4 ll. substituted for cancelled ll. bnd. at end, hf. vell. gt.; Sir Francis G.M. Boileau bkplt. (LC. Mar.1; 18) £140
– A Discourse on Education & Plans Pursued in Charity-Schools. 1786. 4to. Title slightly soiled, wraps., unc. (P. Mar.15; 330) £260

PARRA, Antonio
– Descripcion de Diferentes Piezas de Historia Natural las mam del Ramo Martimo. Havana, 1787. Sm. 4to. 75 engraved plts., including 1 folding, errata lf. spotted, owners' stps., cont. cf. (SPB. Dec.13; 599a) $850

PARRISH, Maxfield & Guerin, Jules
[–] A Collection of Colour Prints [cover title]. Cleveland, [1917]. 4to. 45 col. plts. each separately mntd. in border & captioned, 1 mount foxed, hf.

buckram & cl. portfo. foxed, cl. ties. (CBA. Aug.21; 445) $200

PARRY, J.
– Extraordinary Characters of the Nineteenth Century. L., 1805. 1st. Edn. 4to. Frontis. & 18 cold. plts., engraved thro.-out, some stains, cont. hf. cf. (BBA. May 23; 214) *Quaritch.* £130

PARRY, Robert Williams
– Cerddi. L., Gregy. Pr., 1980. (215). 4to. Prospectus loosely inserted, orig. mor.-bkd. cl., unc. (BBA. Mar.21; 310) *Maggs.* £55

PARRY, Sir William Edward
– Journal of a Voyage for the Discovery of a North-West Passage from the Atlantic to the Pacific, 1819-20, in H.M.S. Hecla & Griper. L., 1821. 1st. Edn. Lge. 4to. Errata slip, some foxing, disbnd. (SG. Sep.22; 37) $175
– – **Anr. Edn.** L., 1821. 2nd. Edn. 4to. Mod. hf. mor. gt.; from liby. of Luttrellstown Castle, w.a.f. (C. Sep.28; 1755) £200
– – **Anr. Copy.** 4to. Some margin spotting, recent hf. mor. (TA. Apr.19; 58) £55
– – **Anr. Copy.** With Appendix. 4to. Some foxing, cont. leath., gold & blind-tooled decor., rubbed, spine renewed, tooled liby. stp. on upr. cover. [Sabin XIV, 58860] (D. Nov.23; 1348) DM 820
– Journal of a Second Voyage for the Discovery of a North-West Passage. L., 1824. 4to. Some foxing, linen. [Sabin XIV, 58864] (D. Nov.23; 1349) DM 560
– Journal of a Third Voyage for the Discovery of a North-West Passage from the Atlantic to the Pacific. Phila., 1826. 1st. Amer. Edn. Folding frontis. map torn, three-qtr. leath., rubbed, spine slightly chipped. (RO. May 22; 137) $110

PARSONS, Sir L.
– Observations on the Bequest of Henry Flood, Esq. to Trinity College, Dublin. Dublin, 1795. Hf.-title, bkplt., crimson hf. mor. (GM. Dec.7; 216) £60

PARSONS, Robert
[–] An Answere to the Fifth Part of Reports Lately Set Forth by Sir Edward Cooke ... by a Catholicke Diuyne. L., 1606. Iss. with reading 'Kinges' on title-p. 4to. Margins cut a little close, some stains & underlinings, later cf. [STC 19532] (BBA. May 3; 96) *Parsons.* £130

PARSONS, Robert, Rowlands, R. & others
– A Conference About the Next Succession to the Crowne of Ingland. [Antw.], 1594 [1595]. 1st. Edn. 2 pts. in 1 vol. Lge. folding genealogical table, mntd., torn in 1 fold, sm. wormhole through several ll., some headlines shaved, lightly browned, 19th. C. mor. gt. [STC 19398] (BBA. May 3; 97) *Maggs.* £150
– – **Anr. Copy.** Lacks folding plan & last (?blank) lf., upr. margin trimmed, mod. cf. [STC 19398] (BBA. Mar.21; 163) *Parsons.* £100

PARTERRE DE FLORE
Paris, n.d. 12mo. Hand-cold. vig. title, 11 plts., cf. gt. (P. Oct.20; 22) £85
– – **Anr. Copy.** 18mo. Cont. str.-grd. mor. gt., richly decor., stain on 1 cover. (HD. Nov.17; 5b) *Frs. 2,000*

PARTINGTON, Charles Frederick
– National History & Views of London. L., 1834. 2 vols. A few plts. slightly offset, some slight spotting, cont. hf. cf. (S. Jun.25; 334) *Quaritch.* £140
– – **Anr. Edn.** 1837. 2 vols. in 1. 2 engraved titles, 2 frontis., plts. on 11 sheets, hf. mor., rubbed. (P. Jul.5; 205) £55

PARTO DE LOS MONTES
Barcelona, 1864. Prospectus & 13 issues (complete). Fo. (DS. Mar.23; 2207) *Pts. 40,000*

PARTRIDGE, Frank
– Ralph Wood Pottery: Mr. Frank Partridge's Collection. L., n.d. Ltd. Edn., numbered. Tall 8vo. 31 plts., gt.-decor. cl. (SG. Oct.13; 77) $100

PARUTA, Paolo
– Discorsi Politici ... Aggiontovi un suo Soliloquio. Venice, 1599. 1st. Edn. 4to. Cf., spine gt., corners worn. (BBA. Jan.19; 9) *Maggs.* £95

– Historia Vinetiana. Venice, 1605. 1st. Edn. 2 pts. in 1 vol. 4to. Partly dampstained, old vell.; Earl of Galloway armorial bkplt. (SG. Oct.27; 247) $175

PARZER-MUHLBACHER, A.
– Das Moderne Benzin–Automobil. Wien & Leipzig, 1907. Orig. linen. (R. Apr.4; 1576) DM 460

PAS, Jan
– Mathematische of Wiskundige Behandeling der Schryfkonst Behelzende een Manier om alle de Gemeene Letteren van het Regt-en Schuin Romeins; Curcyf; Italiaansch; Nederduitsch; en Fractuur ... Amst., 1737. 1st. Edn. Fo. Sigd. by author on A2v, 51 (of 52) engraved plts. of calligraphy, 2 letters cold. in outl. in blue crayon, text in Dutch & Fr., cont. Dutch vell. gt., arms on covers, slightly stained. (S. Nov.17; 54) *Tzakas.* £200

PASCAL, Adrien
– Histoire de l'Armée et de tous les Régiments depuis les Premiers Temps de la Monarchie jusqu'à nos Jours. Ill.:– after Philippoteaux, Charpentier, Bellangé & others. Paris, 1847-50. 4 vols. (lacks Vol. V). Frontis. (disbnd.) & 121 plts. (of 125) including 103 cold., cont. hf. cf., spines decor., worn. (HD. May 21; 96) *Frs. 2,100*

PASCAL, Blaise
– Pensées sur l'Homme et Dieu. Ill.:– A. Gleizes. Paris, 1950. Orig. Edn. (200) numbered. Fo. 57 orig. etchings, loose ll. in orig. wraps., orig. box, slightly defect. (GB. Nov.5; 2518) DM 1,800
– Pensées ... sur la Religion et sur quelques autres Sujets... Paris, 1670. [1st. Edn.]. Vell., soiled. (P. Jan.12; 262) *Greenwood.* £85
– – **Anr. Copy.** 12mo. Wide margins, ruled, cont. red mor., Du Seuil compartments, spine decor.; cont. MS. ex-libris 'Montecler' on title. (HD. Mar.29; 78) *Frs. 300,000*
– – **Anr. Copy.** Wide margin, some light staining in lr. margin, slight browning, cont. leath. (D. Nov.25; 4816) DM 5,000
– – **Anr. Edn.** Amst., 1699. New Edn. 12mo. Sm. stain on text, cont. cf., spine decor., sm. old repairs. (HD. Mar.19; 131) *Frs. 1,100*
– Les Provinciales. Cologne, Pierre de la Vallée [i.e. Amst., Elzevier], 1657. 1st. Elzevier Edn. 1st. Iss., without the 18th. letter. 12mo. Mod. bds. (SG. Oct.27; 91) $130
– – **Anr. Edn.** Cologne, [Leiden], 1659. Cont. vell. (HD. Feb.22; 161) *Frs. 2,200*
– – **Anr. Edn.** Ed.:– G. Wandrock. N.p., 1733. New Edn. 3 vols. 12mo. Cf. (HD. Feb.22; 162) *Frs. 1,800*
– Traitez de l'Equilibre des Liqueurs, et de la Pesanteur de la Masse de l'Air. Paris, 1663. 1st. Edn. Sm. 12mo. Some worming, mostly marginal but affecting some text & 1 plt., cont. cf.; sig. of Darminy on title, Stanitz coll. (SPB. Apr.25; 332) $1,100
– – **Anr. Copy.** 12mo. Cont. spr. cf., spine decor., L.-C. de Cremeaux arms; from M. Escoffier liby. (HD. Mar.29; 79) *Frs. 15,000*

PASCH, G.
– De Novis Inventis. Leipzig, 1700. 2nd. Edn. 4to. Cont. vell. (R. Oct.12; 1536) DM 440

PASCOLI, Alessandro
See– BAGLIVI, Giorgio – PASCOLI, Alessandro

PASQUIER, Etienne
– Oeuvres contenant ses Recherches de la France. Amst., 1723. 2 vols. Fo. Cf. (HD. Feb.22; 163) *Frs. 2,100*

PASQUIN, Peter (Pseud.)
See– PYNE, William Henry 'Peter Pasquin'

PASS or PASSE, Crispin van der, the Younger
– [Hortus Floridus] Jardin de Fleurs contenant en Soy le plus Rares et plus Excellentes Fleures ... Utrecht & Arnheim, 1614-16. 4 pts. only (of 5). Ob. 4to. 4 garden plts., 99 plts. of flowers, all but 1 with Latin text on verso, without the plt. of garden ornaments, extra tulip plts. & the engraved Latin general title, title & next 2 ll. defect., 1 garden plt. torn & reprd., 3 plts. wormed, 2 plts. discold., inserted from anr. copy, 18 plts. torn out just

PASS or PASSE, Crispin van der, the Younger - *Contd.*
affecting ptd. area on 4 plts., all reinserted, penultimate plt. with outer margin eaten away, cont. limp vell., worn, w.a.f. (C. Mar.14; 191)
Marsden. £2,800
– – **Anr. Edn.** Cresset Pr., 1928-29. *(30) numbered.* 2 vols. Orig. vell., stained, s.-c.'s. (CSK. Jun.1; 63)
£110

PASSAVENT, J.D.
[–] **Ansichten über die Bildenden Künste u. Darstellung des Ganges derselben in Toscana.** Heidelberg & Speier, 1820. *1st. Edn.* Slightly foxed, cont. hf. leath. gt., worn. (HK. Nov.9; 2009) DM 420

PASSEBON, Henri Sbonki de
– **Plan de plusieurs Bâtiments de Mer, avec leurs Propositions.** Ill.:– Randon. Paris, ca. 1690. Fo. Cont. red mor., Du Seuil decor, Duc du Maine arms, spine decor. (HD. Jun.18; 35) Frs. 210,000

PASSERI, Giovanni Battista
– **Picturae Etruscorum in Vasculis nunc primum in Unum collectae.** Rome, 1767-75. 3 vols. Fo. Vol. 1 title lf. & 1 lf. dedication partly loose, vol. 2 dedication loose, cont. hf. leath., gt. spine, rubbed & bumped. (D. Nov.23; 1983) DM 4,000

PASSIO DOMINI NOSTRI JESU CHRISTI
Ill.:– Eric Gill. Gold. Cook. Pr., 1926. *(250) numbered.* 4to. Orig. cl., soiled, d.-w., with label 'Exhibition Copy of a Golden Cockerel Press Book ... '; unopened. (S. Nov.21; 216) *Liechti.* £220

PASTEUR, Louis
– **Etudes sur la Bière ... avec une Théorie Nouvelle de la Fermentation.** Paris, 1876. *1st. Edn.* Hf.-title, 4 pp. publisher's advt., faint dampstain at corner to front & end ll., orig. wraps., unc. & unopened. (C. May 30; 121) *Benveniste.* £140
– **Etudes sur le Vin.** 1873. *2nd. Edn.* Some light spotting, mod. mor.-bkd. bds., orig. front wrap. bnd. in. (CSK. Jun.1; 142) £110

PASTON, George
– **Social Caricature in the Eighteenth Century.** 1905. Fo. Slightly spotted, orig. cl.-bkd. bds.; bkplt. of Bibliotheca Lindesiana. (BBA. Nov.10; 222)
Traylen. £55

PASTOR, Ludwig
– **Storia dei Papi dalla Fine del Medio Evo.** Rome, 1910-34. Vols. i-XVI & 1 supp. vol. bnd. in 21 vols. Vol. 2. i-X hf. vell., rest in orig. ptd. wraps. (SI. Dec.15; 122) Lire 500,000

PATAS
– **Sacre et Couronnement de Louis XVI.** Paris, 1775. 4to. LP. holland, cont. mor., gt. decor., centre arms, decor. spine, stains, faded. (HD. Dec.9; 70)
Frs. 9,000
– – **Anr. Copy.** 4to. On holland, lacks plan of Rheims & 1 costume plt., old cf. gt., spine decor., covers stained, corners worn. (HD. May 3; 111)
Frs. 1,600

PATCHEN, Kenneth
– **Before the Brave.** N.Y., [1936]. Cl., d.-w. (SG. Mar.1; 417) $250
– **The Dark Kingdom.** N.Y., [1942]. *(75) numbered & sigd. Out-of-Series copy.* Lge. 8vo. 4 pp. partly browned, ptd. wraps., with lge. pict. overslip painted by author & mntd. on upr. cover, ptd. s.-c.; inscr. by author to 'Margaret'. (SG. Mar.1; 421)
$375
– – **Anr. Edn.** N.Y., [1942]. *(75) numbered & sigd.* Lge. 8vo. Ptd. wraps., with lge. pict. overslip painted by author & mntd. on upr. cover, unopened, ptd. s.-c. (SG. Mar.1; 422) $175
– **The Famous Boating Party.** [N.Y., 1954]. *(50) numbered with covers painted by author.* Sm. 4to. Few ll. discold., cl., hand-painted bds., partly unopened, unlettered acetate d.-w.; author's autograph colophon sigd. on lr. pastedown. (SG. May 24; 162) $175
– **First Will & Testament.** [N.Y., 1948]. Cl.; long T.L.s. from author to Louis Untermeyer tipped in. (SG. Mar.1; 419) $175
– **Glory Never Guesses.** [Palo Alto, Ca., Kenneth Patchen, 1955]. *(200).* Lge. 4to. 13 (of 18) ll.,

picture-poems serigraphed on H.M.P., some hand-cold. by author, leaves laid in serigraphed folding-case, as iss.; lf. [1] stpd. 'Specimen copy'. (SG. Mar.1; 431) $225
– **Hurrah for Anything.** Highlands [N.C.], 1957. *(100) prepared & painted by author, with autograph MS. colophon on lr. end-paper.* Pict. bds., hand-painted by author, acetate d.-w. (SG. Mar.1; 432) $325
– **Orchards, Thrones & Caravans.** Ill.:– David Ruff. [San Franc.?, Greenwood Pr., for Print Workshop, 1952]. *'Engraver's Edn.'. (90) numbered & sigd. by author & artist.* Sm. 4to. Art vell. wraps., numbered & sigd. etching mntd. on upr. wrap. (SG. Mar.1; 428) $225
– – **Anr. Edn.** [San Franc.?, Greenwood Pr., for Print Workshop, 1952]. *'Vell. Edn.'. (120) numbered & sigd.* Sm. 4to. Art vell. wraps., unc. (SG. Mar.1; 429) $225
– **Panels for the Walls of Heaven.** N.p., 1946. *'Painted Edn.', (150). Out-of-Series Over-Run copy.* Sm. 4to. Cl., pict. bds., bds., lr. pastedown, title-p. & all edges painted by author. (SG. Mar.1; 426) $225
– **Poem-Scapes.** Highlands, N.C., 1958. *1st. Authorized Edn.,. Painted Iss., (35) numbered, painted by author, with sigd. autograph colophon on lr. pastedown.* Qtr. cl., bds., spine & covers painted by author. (SG. Mar.1; 435) $325
– – **Anr. Edn.** Highlands, N.C., 1958. *1st. Authorized Edn. 'Gold & Gray' Iss., (42) numbered, with autograph poem & sigd. autograph colophon on lr. pastedown,.* Sm. 8vo. Bds. (SG. Mar.1; 434) $175
– – **Anr. Edn.** Highlands, N.C., 1958. *(75) numbered with covers painted by author.* Sm. 8vo. Qtr. cl., bds., spine & covers painted by author; author's autograph colophon sigd. on lr. end-paper. (SG. May 24; 164) $250
– **Red Wine & Yellow Hair.** N.Y., [1949]. *(108) numbered & sigd.* 4to. Decor. bds., painted by author. (SG. Mar.1; 427) $250
– **Sleepers Awake.** [N.Y., 1946]. *(75) numbered & sigd.* Lge. 8vo. Cl., with lge. pict. overslip painted by author & mntd. on upr. cover. (SG. Mar.1; 425) $250
– – **Anr. Copy.** Lge. 8vo. Cl. (SG. May 24; 156) $120
– **CCCLXXIV Poems.** N.p., ca. 1950. *1st. Coll. Edn.* Cl., d.-w. (SG. May 24; 157) $110
– **To Say if You Love Someone.** Prairie City, Ill., [1948]. *[Approx. 180]. 2nd. State. (With:)*
– **Fables.** Karlsruhe, 1953. *(450). (With:)*
– **Wonderings.** [N.Y., 1971]. *(100).* Together 3 vols. 16mo. & 8vo. Bds.; wraps.; & cl. (SG. May 24; 158) $275
– **Two Poems for Christmas.** [N.p., 1958]. Sm. 4to. Leaflet unbnd.; laid in lf. inscr. 'Holiday greetings/Miriam & Kenneth Patchen', probably by Miriam Patchen. (SG. May 24; 165) $300
– **When we Were Here Together.** [Norfolk, Conn., 1957]. *(75) numbered & sigd., with autograph colophon on lr. end-paper.* Lge. 8vo. Qtr. cl., 4to. bds., spine & covers painted by author. (SG. May.1; 433) $200

PATER, Walter H.
– **Studies in the History of the Renaissance.** L., 1873. Mor. gt.; John A. Spoor bkplt. (designed by Emery Walker). (LH. Sep.25; 581) $110

PATERSON, A.B.
– **Song of the Wheat.** Ill.:– G.D. Nicol. 1925. Bdg. not stated, boxed. (JL. Mar.25; 456) Aus. $525

PATERSON, A.T.
[–] **The Thirty-Ninth: The History of the 39th Battalion Australian Imperial Force ...** Melbourne, 1934. Bdg. not stated. (KH. May 1; 552)
Aus. $130

PATHELIN, Pierre
– **Maistre Pierre Pathelin de Nouveau Reveu, & mis en son Naturel avec le Blason & Loyer des Faulses et Folies Amours.** Paris, 1564. 12mo. Headlines on 2 ll. shaved, faint dampstain in a few margins, 19th. C. pink mor. gt. by Niedré. (C. May 30; 96)
Lyon. £1,000

PATHINA, Carla Caterina
– **Pitture Scelte e Dichiarate.** Cologne, 1691. Fo. Engraved title, 40 engraved plts., many double-p. or folding, cont. vell., soiled. (TA. Jul.19; 471)
£160
– – **Anr. Copy.** Fo. Additional engraved title, ptd. title with engraved vig., 40 engrs., many double-p., cf., worn. (P. Jul.5; 264) £130

PATINUS, Carolus
– **Imperatorum Romanorum Numismata ex Aere Mediae et Minimae Formae.** Amst., 1697. Fo. Cont. leath., slightly worn. (GB. Nov.3; 921) DM 800

PATMORE, Coventry
[–] **Odes.** [L., priv. ptd., 1868]. *1st. Edn. (250).* Sm. 8vo. Orig. ptd. wraps., upr. cover creased; pres. copy from author to Denis Florence MacCarthy, envelope from author to MacCarthy laid in, Frederic Dannay copy. (CNY. Dec.16; 265) $800
– **Poems.** L., 1844. *1st. Edn.* 12mo. Lacks final blank, hf. cf. *(With:)* – **Odes.** L., [1868]. *1st. Edn.* Sm. 8vo. Orig. ptd. wraps. Together 2 vols. Frederic Dannay copies, w.a.f. (CNY. Dec.16; 266) $200

PATON, Lucy Allen
– **Selected Bindings from the Gennadius Library.** Camb., 1924. 4to. Frontis., 38 col. plts., slight foxing, cl. (SG. Sep.15; 54) $300

PATRICK, R.W.
– **Early Records relating to Mining in Scotland ...** Edinb., 1878. *(350) numbered.* 4to. Hf. mor. (PD. May 16; 166) £62

PATRICK, Saint
– **Opuscula.** Ed.:– Sir James Ware. L., 1656. *1st. Edn.* Cont. panel. cf., cover detchd. (SG. Oct.27; 248) $175

PATTE, Pierre
– **Mémoires sur les Objets les plus Importants de l'Architecture.** Paris, 1769. *1st. Edn.* 4to. Hf.-title, dampstains, 1 plt. torn, cont. cf., worn. (SM. Mar.7; 2037) Frs. 1,000
– **Monumens Erigés en France à la Gloire de Louis XV.** Paris, 1765. *1st. Edn.* Fo. 57 engraved plts., owner's inscr. on title, cont. mott. cf., spine gt. (C. Dec.9; 112) *Marlborough.* £380
– – **Anr. Copy.** Tall fo. 57 copperplates, some folding, a few misbnd., some spotting, mod. hf. cf., spine very worn. (SG. Nov.3; 163) $300
– – **Anr. Copy.** Fo. Red mor. by Derome le jeune with his label, spine decor. (HD. Jun.18; 36)
Frs. 16,200
– – **Anr. Edn.** Ill.:– Boucher, Marvye & Patte. Paris, 1767. Fo. Unc., spr. roan. (HD. Dec.1; 79)
Frs. 2,200

PATTERSON, Samuel
– **Narrative of the Adventures & Sufferings ... experienced in the Pacific Ocean, & many other Parts of the World, with an Account of the Feegee, & Sandwich Islands.** Palmer, [Mass.,], 1817. *1st. Edn. 2nd. Iss.* 12mo. Lacks top margin of title, browned & stained, several tears, orig. sheep, worn. (SG. Sep.22; 239) $300
– – **Anr. Edn.** Palmer, Massachussetts, 1817. *1st. Edn.* 12mo. Margin repairs to title & a few ll. slightly affecting a few words, some spotting, minor stains, liby. blind-stp. at head of title, cont. hf. cf., upr. cover detchd. (C. Jun.27; 98)
Remington. £100

PATTERSON, William
– **A Narrative of Four Journeys into the Country of the Hottentots & Caffraria.** 1789. 4to. Page 61 torn through centre, orig. bds., spine frayed. (SSA. Jul.5; 311) R 440

PATTISON, John
[–] **New South Wales; Its Past, Present & Future Condition ...** 1849. Bnd. without book advts., some light discoloration, later buckram. (KH. May 1; 553) Aus. $120

PATTISON, Mark
– **The Estiennes.** Intro.:– Robert Grabhorn. San Franc., [Grabhorn Pr.], 1949. *(390).* Fo. With 3 orig. ll. ptd. by the Estiennes, end-papers mildly darkening, slight staining to front end-papers, hf.

cl. & gt.-decor. bds., d.-w. slightly soiled, edges creased & slightly torn. (CBA. Nov.19; 220) $100

PAUL, Sir James Balfour
The Scots Perage Founded on Wood's Edition of Sir Robert Douglas's Peerage of Scotland. Edinb., 1904-14. 9 vols., including Index. Cl. gt.; 2 A.L.s. to publishers. (PD. Dec.14; 104) £145

PAUL, J.B. & others
– **Registrum Magni Sigilli Regum Scotorum: The Register of the Great Seal of Scotland** ... Edinb., 1882-97. 8 vols. (covering the period 1424-1651). 4to. Orig. cl., soiled. (PD. May 16; 122) £52

PAUL, Jean (Pseud.)
See— RICHTER, Jean Paul Friedrich 'Jean Paul'

PAUL, Sir John Deane
[–] **Journal of a Party of Pleasure to Paris in the Month of August 1802.** L., 1802. *1st. Edn.* 13 sepia aquatint plts., little light staining, cont. hf. cf., worn. (BBA. May 23; 227) *Quaritch.* £55

PAUL, William
– **The Rose Garden.** L., 1848. 14 (of 15) cold. plts., 1 slightly trimmed, orig. cl., worn. (S. Apr.10; 571) *Nolan.* £160

PAULHAN, Jean
– **Braque le Patron.** Ill.:– Georges Braque. Geneva & Paris, 1947. *(25) numbered on Arches sigd. by author & artist with orig. cold. litho. numbered & sigd. by Braque.* 4to. Orig. wraps., cl.-bkd. bd. folder, s.-c. (BBA. Jun.14; 191) *Makiya.* £850
– – **Anr. Edn.** Geneva, [1947]. *(65) on Bütten.* 4to. Printers mark sigd. by artist, orig. wraps. with cold. litho., sm. tears, hf. linen portfo., unc. (H. May 23; 1167) DM 600
– **Les Paroles Transparentes.** Ill.:– Georges Braque. Paris, Bibliophiles de l'Union Française, 1955. *(132) numbered & sigd. by author, artist & President of the Soc.* Fo. Unsewn in orig. pict. wraps., folder & s.-c.; unc.; this copy no. 28, for Marcel Sautier. (S. Nov.21; 5) *Rota.* £600

PAULIAN, Aimé-Pierre
– **Dictionnaire de Physique, Dédié à Monseigneur le Duc de Berry.** Avignon, 1761. 3 vols. 4to. Cont. marb. cf., decor. spines, sm. loss from 1 turn-in. (HD. Sep.22; 308) Frs. 1,150

PAULIN, G.
– **Atlas Complet du Manuel du Sapeur Pompier.** Paris, 1838. Some foxing, orig. sewed, worn. (D. Nov.24; 4044) DM 700

PAULINUS, F.
– **Centum Fabulae ex Antiquis Scriptores acceptae, et Graecis Latinisque Tetrastichis Senariis Explicatae.** Venice, 1587. *1st. Edn.* Title with 2 sm. bkd. holes, cont. vell. (R. Oct.11; 92) DM 1,000

PAULITSCHKE, Ph.
– **Beiträge zur Ethnographie und Anthropologie der Somàl, Galla und Hararî.** Leipzig, 1886. *1st. Edn.* Fo. Some light foxing, orig. leath., gold-tooled, slightly worn; MS. dedication of author to Prince Ferdinand von Sachsen-Coburg-Gotha. (HK. Nov.8; 805) DM 540

PAULLI, Simon
– **A Treatise on Tobacco, Tea, Coffee & Chocolate.** Trans.:– Dr. James. 1746. Hf.-title, cont. cf. (BBA. Jun.14; 71) *Bickersteth.* £280

PAULLINI, Christian Franz
– **Heilsame Dreck-Apotheke.** Frankfurt, 1699. *3rd. Edn.* Title with owner's mark, browned, cont. vell., slightly soiled. (HK. Nov.8; 684) DM 1,400
– **Neu-vermehrte, Heilsame Dreck Apotheke. – Flagellum Salutis.** Frankfurt, 1699 & 1698. *1st. Edn.* 2 works in 1 vol. Cont. hf. leath. (D. Nov.23; 657) DM 3,000

PAULS-EISENBEISS, E.
– **German Porcelain of the 18th. Century.** Preface:– P.W. Meister. Trans.:– D. Imber. L., 1972. 2 vols. Lge. 4to. Orig. linen. (R. Apr.3; 880) DM 420

PAULUS, Nicoletti, Venetus
– **Expositio in Analytica Posteriora Aristotelis.** Venice, Guilelmus Anima Mia, Tridinensis. 11

Aug. 1486. Fo. Capital spaces, a few margin annots, some sm. wormholes, old paper bds; sig. of Gaspardus Clanlardi (?) 1535. [BMC V, 410; Goff P214; H. 12512] (S. May 10; 376) *Maggs.* £580

PAULUS DIACONUS
– **Historiae Miscellae ... à Land. Sagaci auctae ... Libri XXIII.** Basel, 1569. Title with owners mark, 1st. & last ll. slightly wormed, cont. pig, gold-tooled arms supralibras on upr. cover (Joh. Crato), slightly spotted & wormed; Joh. Crato v. Craffthein coll. (HK. May 15; 212) DM 520

PAULUS DE MIDDELBURG
– **Ain fast Nutzlich Büchlin zu dieser Zeit zulesen, Von dem Sindtfluss** ... [Augsburg, 1524]. 4to. Wide margin, bds. (HK. Nov.8; 308) DM 520

PAUQUET, Hippolyte & Polydor
– **Modes et Costumes Historiques.** Paris, ca.1865. Lge. 4to. 96 hand-cold. engraved plts., orig. qtr. mor. (SG. Sep.22; 112) $225
– **Modes et Costumes Historiques Etrangers.** Paris, 1864. Fo. 61 (of 96) hand-cold. full-p. engrs., some margins shaved, portfo. (DS. Feb.24; 2115) Pts. 40,000
– – **Anr. Edn.** Paris, n.d. 4to. 96 hand-cold. litho. plts., cont. hf. mor., rubbed. (CSK. Jul.6; 26) £170
– **Modes et Costumes Historiques Français.** Paris, 19th. C. Fo. Publishers cl. (DS. Mar.23; 2209) Pts. 150,000

PAUSANIAS
– **The Description of Greece.** Trans.:– [Thomas Taylor]. L., 1824. *New Edn.* 3 vols. Tall 8vo. Cont. hf. mor. gt. & marb. bds. (SG. Nov.17; 305) $120
– **Pausaniae Veteris Graeciae Descriptio.** Trans.:– Romulus Amasaeus. Flor., 1551. *2nd. Edn. in Latin.* Fo. Upr. margins dampstained, lr. part of title mntd., 18th. C. marb. roan, spine decor., scratches; from Fondation Furstenberg-Beaumesnil. (HD. Nov.16; 147) Frs. 1,400
– **Pausanias, ou Voyage Historique de la Grèce.** Paris, 1731. 2 vols. 4to. Cont. cf. (CSK. Sep.30; 171) £110

PAVIERE, Sydney H.
– **A Dictionary of Flower, Fruit & Still Life Painters, 15th Century-1885.** Leigh-on-Sea, 1962-64. 3 vols. in 4. 4to. Orig. cl., d.-w.'s. (S. Nov.8; 561) *Larson.* £70

PAVLOV, Ivan Petrovitch
– **The Work of the Digestive Glands.** Trans.:– W.H. Thompson. L., 1902. *1st. Edn. in Engl.* 32 p. publisher's catalogue dtd. 20/7/03 at end, rebnd. in buckram, ex-liby. (SG. Oct.6; 287) $200

PAXTON, Joseph
– **Magazine of Botany.** L., 1834. Vols. 1-2 (of 16). 77 cold. plts., some folding, 1 detchd. & slightly frayed, few shaved, some spotting, hf. mor. (S. Apr.10; 572) *Walford.* £150
– – **Anr. Run.** L., 1834-38. Vols. 1-6 only (of 16). Approx. 170 hand-cold. engraved plts., many double-p., cont. hf. mor., as a periodical, w.a.f. (C. Mar.14; 192) *MacInnes.* £420
– – **Anr. Run.** Ill.:– after F.W. Smith, S. Holden, others. L., 1834-49. 16 vols. 717 hand-cold. engraved or litho plts., a few plt. captions chopped, some slight staining, minor tears to a few folding plts., cont. hf. mor. gt., w.a.f. (CNY. Dec.17; 586) $1,300
– – **Anr. Run.** L., 1836. Vol. 2. Minimal spotting, cont. leath. gt., rubbed. (R. Oct.12; 1886) DM 400
– – **Anr. Copy.** Vol. II (of 16). Engrs. hand-cold., cf., tooled, w.a.f. (CR. Jun.6; 246) Lire 320,000
– – **Anr. Run.** 1837. Vol. 3. Cont. leath. gt., rubbed. (R. Oct.12; 1887) DM 400
– – **Anr. Run.** 1838. *1st. Edn.* Vol. 4. Sm. 4to. 1 col. litho. plt., 42 full-p. & folded engraved plts. with cont. hand-colouring, 2 plt. lists for the cold. plts., 1 plt. with sm. tear at upr. edge, few text cracks, recent cl., new end-papers. (HA. Feb.24; 281) $300
– – **Anr. Copy.** Vol. IV & IX (of 16). Hf. cf., corners, as a collection of plts., w.a.f. (CR. Jun.6; 247) Lire 500,000
– – **Anr. Copy.** Vol. V (of 16). Engrs. hand-cold.,

hf. cf., as a collection of plts., w.a.f. (CR. Jun.6; 249) Lire 350,000
– – **Anr. Run.** 1838. Vol. 5. Lacks title & 1 lf., cont. hf. leath. gt., worn. (R. Oct.12; 1890) DM 400
– – **Anr. Edn.** L., 1838-44. Vols. I-VI-XI (of 16). Engrs. hand-cold., hf. cf., corners, as a collection of plts., w.a.f. (CR. Jun.6; 248) Lire 850,000
– – **Anr. Run.** L., 1841. Vol. 8. Minimal foxing, cont. hf.-leath. (R. Apr.4; 1768) DM 550
– – **Anr. Run.** L., 1841-53. Vols. 1-10 only (of 16). 459 cold. plts., some double-p., a few trimmed, hf. mor., Signet arms on covers, rubbed or worn, w.a.f. (S. Nov.28; 75) *Burden.* £720
– – **Anr. Run.** 1843. Vol. 10. Cont. hf. leath. (R. Oct.12; 1891) DM 580
– – **Anr. Run.** 1848-49. Vols. 14 & 15 (of 16) in 1 vol. 88 hand-cold. plts., hf. mor. (P. Sep.8; 300) *Blake.* £180
– – **Anr. Run.** 1849. Vol. 16 only. 24 hand-cold. plts., 6 with light foxing, hf. cf. gt. (P. Feb.16; 93) £65

PAXTON, Sir Joseph & Lindley, John
– **Flower Garden.** 1850-52. Vols. 1 & 2 only (of 3). 4to. 72 hand-cold. plts., hf. cf. & orig. cl., defect. (P. Sep.29; 329) *Erlini.* £130
– – **Anr. Edn.** 1852-53. Vols. 1 & 3 only (of 3). 4to. 72 hand-finished plts., orig. cl., spines torn. (P. Oct.20; 16) £200
– – **Anr. Edn.** 1882-84. 3 vols. 4to. 108 cold. plts., Vol. I lacks text to plts. 33 & 34, text to plts. 31 & 32 repeated, 1 plt. detchd. & frayed, few plts. trimmed, orig. cl., slightly worn & marked, w.a.f. (S. Nov.1; 282) *Wedekind.* £160

PAYNE, Albert Henry
– **Berlin & its Treasures, Being a series of Views from the Royal Picture Gallery.** Leipzig & Dresden, ca. 1850. 4to. Engraved title, 108 (of 109) steel engraved plts., foxed, cont. leath. gt. (R. Oct.12; 2521) DM 1,500
– **Berlin und seine Kunstschätze. Die Königlichen Museen in Berlin.** Leipzig & Dresden, ca. 1850. Engraved title & 99 steel engraved plts., some light foxing, cont. hf. leath. gt., very rubbed. (R. Oct.12; 2519) DM 1,450
– **Book of Art, with the Celebrated Galleries of Munich. Being a Selection of Subjects Engraved after Pictures by Old & Modern Masters, with Descriptive Text together with a History of Art.** Dresden, ca. 1850. 3 vols. 4to. Approx. 100 engraved plts., slight foxing, crimson three-qtr. mor., backs richly gt. (SG. Jun.7; 384) $170
– – **Anr. Copy.** 3 vols. in 1. 4to. Some slight foxing, cont. mor. gt. (R. Oct.12; 2255) DM 1,000
– – **Anr. Edn.** N.d. 3 vols. 4to. Hf. mor., spines gt., some scuffing. (LC. Mar.1; 93) £150
– – **Anr. Copy.** 3 vols. 4to. Some spotting, cont. hf. cf., worn, 1 cover detchd., w.a.f. (CSK. Aug.19; 106) £140
– **Les Galeries et les Monuments d'art de Berlin.** Leipzig & Dresden, ca. 1850. 4to. Engraved title, 99 steel engraved plts., some foxing, cont. hf. leath. gt. (R. Oct.12; 2524) DM 1,400
– **Universum.** L., ca. 1840. 4to. Engraved title with vig., 59 (of 63) steel engraved plts., foxed, cont. hf. leath. gt., defect. (R. Apr.4; 2239) DM 540
– – **Anr. Edn.** Leipzig, [1843-49]. Vols. 1-8 in 8 vols. Vol. 2 lacks title lf., vol. 8 lacks 7 pp., slightly foxed, unif. hf. leath. gt., 2 spines defect. (R. Oct.12; 2423) DM 3,000
– – **Anr. Edn.** Ed.:– Ch. Edwards. L., ca. 1845. Vols. 1-3. 4to. Slightly foxed, cont. leath. gt. (R. Oct.12; 2172) DM 1,000
– **Anr. Edn.** L. & Leipzig, 1845 [-49]. Vols. 4-8 (5 vols). Ob. 4to. Some foxing, 1 p. with ink stain in 6th. vol., vol. 8 2 pp. & 1 plt. with col. & damp spots, anr. later plt. with light stain at head, cont. linen, lightly rubbed & bumped. (HK. May 16; 1771) DM 1,100
– **Anr. Edn.** Leipzig & Dresden, ca. 1850. Vol. 1. 4to. Fr. text, engraved title, 62 steel engraved plts., 1 plt. defect., foxed, cont. hf. leath. (R. Apr.4; 2238) DM 630
– **Universum und Buch der Kunst.** Leipzig & Dresden, ca. 1860-65. New Series, Vols. I, II & IV. 4to. Some heavy foxing & browning, 2 cont. linen & 1 cont. hf. linen, spines faded, 2 spines slightly defect., slightly bumped & spotted. (H. Nov.23; 321) DM 1,700

PAYNE, Albert Henry, Publisher
See— GORLING, Adolph

PAYNE, T., Publisher
- Egypt. Ill.:– J. Powell & others. Ca. 1810. Lge. fo. Map, double-p. aquatint of 'Phyla', 23 soft-ground etched plts., many double-p., no title (called for?), hf. cf., worn, rebkd., as a collection of plts., w.a.f. (LC. Oct.13; 264) £240

PAYNE, Thomas, Bookseller
- Catalogue for the Year 1766. L., 1766. Head of final 2 pp. cropped slightly affecting text, mod. cl. (S. Oct.11; 472) *Blackwell's.* £160

PAYNE, Thomas & Foss, Henry
- Catalogues. L., 1799-1840. 26 in 9 vols. 19th. C. hf. cf., labels loose or missing; Vol. 4 with sig. of Rev. E.C. Hawtrey, Vol. 2 sigd. W. Hawtrey, Vol. 9 sigd. Dr. Hawtrey. (S. Oct.11; 473) *Quaritch.* £1,050

PAYNE-GALLWEY, Sir Ralph
- The Book of Duck Decoys. 1886. 4to. 14 cold. plts., ills., orig. cl., rubbed. (BBA. May 23; 304) *Roberts.* £160
- The Fowler in Ireland. L., 1882. *1st. Edn.* Bkplt., cl. (GM. Dec.7; 38) £50

PAZAUREK, Gustav E.
- Deutsche Fayence– und Porzellan-Hausmaler. Leipzig, 1925. *1st. Edn.* 2 vols. Tall 4to. 34 plts., cl., spine ends frayed. (SG. Jan.26; 141) $300
-- **Anr. Copy.** 2 vols. 4to. Orig. bds. (H. May 22; 116) DM 800
- Die Glaesersammlung des Nordboehmischen Gewerbe-Museums in Reichenberg. Leipzig, 1902. Fo. 40 plts. (3 cold.), text ills., each plt. liby.-stpd. on blank verso, loose in hf. cl. folder. (SG. May 3; 273) $175
- Kunstgläser d. Gegenwart. Leipzig, 1925. 4to. Orig. linen. (HK. Nov.12; 4670) DM 420

PEABODY, George
- Proceedings at the Reception & Dinner in Honor of George Peabody ... Ill.:– [Winslow Homer]. Boston, 1856. *1st. Edn.* 4to. Steel-engraved frontis., 17 duotone lithos., margin dampstaining to some plts., especially at beginning & end, orig. stpd. gt.-decor. cl., spine darkening, extremities rubbed. (CBA. Jan.29; 238a) $110

PEACHAM, Henry
- The Compleat Gentleman. L., 1661. *3rd. Edn.* 2 pts. in 1 vol. Sm. 4to. Engraved title torn with slight loss of ills. & mntd., 4 ll. torn slightly affecting text, slightly browned & soiled thro.-out, 19th. C. cf., rebkd. with orig. gt. spine, slightly rubbed; Edward Gilbertson & N.D. Livesay bkplts. [Wing P943] (BBA. Nov.30; 197) *Matthews.* £120
- The Compleat Gentleman ... with the Art of Limming & other Additions. L., 1634. 2 pts. in 1 vol. 4to. Part 2 with variant imprint 'for I.M. & to be sold by Francis Constable', 2 ll reprd. with some loss of text, later cf.; sig. of P. Le Neve on title (partially defaced), Joseph Haslewood. (BBA. May 3; 111) *Maggs.* £95

PEACOCK, Francis, of Aberdeen
- Sketches Relative to the History & Theory ... to the Practice of Dancing. Aberdeen, 1805. Advt. lf., some browning & pencilling, orig. bds., defect. (PD. Oct.19; 281) £90

PEACOCK, George
- A Collection of Examples of the Applications of the Differential & Integral Calculus. - Collection of Examples of the Application of the Calculus of Finite Differences. — Examples of the Solutions of Functional Equations. Camb., 1820, [1820]; 1820. Together 3 works in 1 vol. Some spotting, 19th. C. hf. cf., rubbed, scuffed; Stanitz coll. (SPB. Apr.25; 334) $450
- A Collection of Examples of the Application of the Differential & Integral Calculus. - A Treatise on Algebra. Camb., 1820; 1830. Together 2 vols. Errata slip in 2nd. vol., some spotting & foxing, mostly to 1st. work, cont. bds., rubbed, some chipping, shaken; sigs. of Osborne Gordon & Oswald Hunter on end-paper of 1st. vol., Stanitz coll. (SPB. Apr.25; 335) $125

PEACOCK, Lucy
[–] The Adventures of the Six Princesses of Babylon, in their Travels to the Temple of Virtue. L., priv. ptd., 1785. *1st. Edn.* Sm. 4to. 18 p. list of subscribers, qtr. cf., rubbed; sigd. by author. (SG. Dec.8; 260) $175

PEACOCK, Thomas Love
[–] Crotchet Castle. 1831. *1st. Edn.* Hf.-title, orig. bds. (BBA. Feb.23; 199) *Quaritch.* £220
-- **Anr. Copy.** Prelim. advt. lf., street no. of publisher erased from title, orig. bds., spine slightly worn. (C. Nov.9; 103) *Maggs.* £200
-- **Anr. Copy.** Old cl., title & Neptune figure stpd. on spine. (BBA. Sep.29; 177) *Finch.* £95
[–] Gryll Grange by the author of 'Headlong Hall'. 1861. *1st. Edn.* 4pp. advts. at end, orig. cl. (SKC. Jan.13; 2238) £60
[–] The Misfortunes of Elphin. 1829. *1st. Edn.* Margins browned, orig. bds., front end-paper torn. (BBA. Feb.23; 198) *Thorp.* £120
-- **Anr. Copy.** Mod. hf. mor. (BBA. Sep.29; 176) *Quaritch.* £75
-- **Anr. Edn.** L., Gregy. Pr., 1928. *(250) numbered.* Orig. buckram-bkd. cl., slightly soiled; bkplt. of David Garnett. (BBA. Mar.21; 308) *Palace Books.* £75
[–] Sir Hornbook; or, Childe Launcelot's Expedition. L., 1817. *4th. Edn.* Sq. 16mo. Ptd. wraps., spine slightly torn. (SG. Dec.8; 261) $425

PEAKE, Mervyn
- Titus Groan. L., 1946. *1st. Edn.* Orig. cl., d.-w.; pres. copy. (S. Apr.9; 275) *Whiteson.* £50

PEAKE, Richard Brinsley
[–] The Characteristic Costume of France. L., n.d. 4to. 19 hand-cold. plts., hf. mor., rubbed. (P. Feb.16; 155) £240

PEARCE, Sir Edward Lovett
See— VANBRUGH, Sir John & Pearce, Sir Edward Lovett

PEARL (THE): a Journal of Facetiae & Voluptuous Reading
L., 1879. 3 vols. 36 plts., hand-cold., some loose, cont. hf. mor. gt. (BBA. May 3; 239) *S. Finch.* £340

PEARSE, Geoffrey Eastcott
- Eighteenth Century Architecture in South Africa. L., 1957. Fo. Orig. bdg., d.-w. (VA. Apr.26; 73) R 180
-- **Anr. Edn.** Pretoria, 1960. Lge. 4to. Orig. bdg. (VA. Oct.28; 540) R 180
-- **Anr. Edn.** Pretoria, 1960. *De Luxe Edn., (50) sigd.* Lge. 4to. Errata slip, publisher's leath. (VA. Oct.28; 218) R 200

PEARSON, Edwin
- Banbury Chap Books & Nursery Toy Book Literature [of the XVIII & Early XIX Centuries]. Ill.:– T. & J. Bewick, Blake, & others. L., 1890. *(50) L.P.* 4to. Pict. bds., mor. back & tips, some cover soiling & scuffing. (RO. Dec.11; 271) $120

PEARY, Robert E.
- The North Pole. 1910. *(500) numbered & sigd. by Peary & R.A. Bartlett.* Lge. 4to. This copy unnumbered, some plts. mntd., 1 folding cold. map, orig. cl., lightly soiled. (CSK. Nov.4; 71) £90

PECHSTEIN, Max
- Reisebilder: Italien-Suedsee. Berlin, 1919. *(800).* Ob. 4to. 25 lithos. (only?), lacks title & possibly other ll., loose as iss., orig. cl. folder. (SG. Dec.15; 180) $400
-- **Anr. Copy.** Ob. fo. Orig. linen, little worn; printer's mark sigd. by artist. (GB. Nov.5; 2882) DM 1,000

PECK, Francis
- Academia Tertia Anglicana; or, the Antiquarian Annals of Stanford. L., priv. ptd., 1727. Fo. 32 engraved plts. (2 folding), a few ll. slightly soiled, cont. cf., slightly worn. (BBA. Dec.15; 102) *Scott.* £85
- Desiderata Curiosa: Or, A Collection of Divers Scarce & Curious Pieces (Relating Chiefly to Matters on English History ...). 1732-35. *1st. Edn. (250).* 2 vols. Fo. Frontis. port., 9 engraved plts.,

cancel title for Vol. I & contents ll. bnd. at end of Vol. II, cont. spr. cf. gt., worn & scuffed. (LC. Mar.1; 376) £60
-- **Anr. Edn.** L., 1779. 2 vols. in 1. 4to. Cont. cf., rebkd.; Edmond Malone's copy, with bkplt., 2 pp. of autograph notes & engraved port. tipped in, some autograph corrections & annots. (S. Dec.8; 55) *Pickering & Chatto.* £200

PECK, George Wilbur
- Peck's Bad Boy & His Pa. Chic., 1883. *1st. Edn.* With text ending at p.196, without 'A Card from the Author', advts., lightly soiled, owner's inscr. & date, orig. decor. cl., decor. endpapers, spine frayed, lr. cover little soiled; Fred A. Berne copy. (SP. May 16; 336) $150

PEEL, Rt. Hon. Robert
- Substance of the Speech ... in the House of Commons, on Thursday, March 9th, 1826, on moving for Leave to bring in a Bill for the Amendment of the Criminal Law ... 1826. Later cl. (KH. May 1; 557) Aus. $100

PEET, T. Eric
- The Great Tomb-Robberies of the Twentieth Egyptian Dynasty. Oxford, 1930. 2 vols. Tall 8vo. & atlas fo. 39 plts., ex-liby., cl. (SG. May 3; 274) $175

PEETS, Elbert
See— HEGEMANN, Werner & Peets, Elbert

PEGUY, Charles
- Presentation de la Beauce à Notre-Dame de Chartres. Ill.:– Alfred Manessier. Paris, 1964. *(178) numbered.* Lge. ob. fo. Unsewn in orig. pict. wraps., decor. case slightly soiled; unc. (S. Nov.21; 101) *Makiya.* £420

PELAYO, Orlando
- La Vida de Lazarillo de Tormes. Madrid, 1975. *(225) with text. (5) special copies.* Lge. format, 11 etchings, publishers cl. portfo. (DS. Oct.28; 2053) Pts. 30,000

PELBARTUS DE THEMESVAR
- [Pomerium Sermonum Quadragesimalium]. – Pomerium Sermonum de Beata Virgine. Lyon, 1509. 2 works in 1 vols. Sm. 4to. Rubricated, 1st. work lacks title, late 16th. C. German blind-stpd. cf., decor.; from Fondation Furstenberg-Beaumesnil. (HD. Nov.16; 148) Frs. 1,000
- Sermones Pomerii Fratris Pelbarti de Themeswar Divi Ordinis Sancti Fra[n]cisci de Tempore Incipiunt feliciter. [Haguenau, Heinrich Gran for Johannes Rynman, 6 Aug. (27 Jul.) 1498]. Sm. 4to. Lacks last lf. blank, some light stains & sm. wormholes, inscrs. on title & old margin annots., vell. [HC. 12551; Goff P-254] (HD. Jan.30; 21) Frs. 4,100

PELLERIN, Joseph
- Recueil de Medailles. Paris, 1762-78. *1st. Edns.* 12 vols. in 9. 4to. 1st. 8 vols. in cont. mott. cf., last in cont. pig, gt. spines; Ragley Hall bkplt. (S. May 1; 491) *Spink.* £650

PELLETIER, Jacques
- L'Art Poëtique de Iaques Peletier du Mans. De Parti an Deus Livres. Lyon, 1555. *Orig. Edn.* Slightly short, affecting some margin notes, slight scratch on title, slightly stained on verso, jansenist red mor. by Thibaron Joly. (HD. Mar.21; 65) Frs. 9,000

PELLICO, Silvio
- Mes Prisons. Trans.:– Comte H. de Messey. Ill.:– after Gerard-Seguin, d'Aubigny, Steinhell & others. Paris, 1844. *1st. Printing of ills.* Lge. 8vo. Cont. mor. finish hf. roan, spine decor. (HD. May 4; 388) Frs. 1,000

PELOTARI, El
1893. Nos. 1-63. Fo. Cl. (DS. Dec.16; 2042) DM 80,000

PELT LECHNER, A.A. van
- Oologia Nederlandica. De Eieren der in Nederland Broedende Vogels. 's-Gravenhage, 1910[-14]. *(250). (150) in Dutch.* 2 vols. 191 plts., some light foxing, hf. cl.; inscr. by publisher to printer. (B. Feb.8; 856) Fls. 1,350

PEMBERTON, Henry
- A View of Sir Isaac Newton's Philosophy. 1728. *1st. Edn.* 4to. Subscribers list, rebnd. in bds., worn. (SKC. Jan.13; 2239) £80
- - **Anr. Copy.** 4to. Subscribers list, cont. mott. cf. (S. Oct.11; 576) *Feingold.* £55
- - **Anr. Copy.** 4to. Subscribers list, a few margin tears (no loss of text), some light soiling, name erased from title, sig. Ddd repeated, mod. hf. mor., cl. s.-c.; Stanitz coll. (SPB. Apr.25; 325) $200
- - **Anr. Copy.** 4to. Cont. cf., brkn. (SG. Mar.22; 242) $150

PEMBROKE, Henry Herbert, Earl of
- A Method of Breaking Horses & Teaching Soldiers to Ride. L., 1761. *1st. Edn.* Cont. cf., slightly rubbed. (BBA. Nov.30; 226) *Sutherland.* £100
- Military Equitation ... 1793. *4th. Edn.* Hf. cf., a little worn. (BBA. Sep.29; 160) *Maggs.* £65

PEMBROKE, Thomas, Earl of
- Numismata Antiqua in Tres Partes divisa. L., 1746. 4 pts. in 1 vol. (Dupl. of Pt. 3 bnd. in). Fo. Engraved title & 357 engraved plts., cont. tree cf., rubbed; Baron Northwick bkplt. (S. May 1; 492) *Drury.* £150

PENA, Juan Antonio de la
- Vera Relatione delle Feste Reali a Giuochi di Canni o Caroselle ... Milan, 1623. 4to. Unevenly inked, traces of orig. folding, patterned bds.; the Chatsworth copy. (S. Dec.20; 784) *Mediolanum.* £100

PENA MONTENEGRO, Alonso de
- Itinerario para Parochos de Indios. Antw., 1698. Sm. 4to. Minor wormholes, mainly in margins, a few light stains, cont. cf. [Sabin 59624] (S. Dec.1; 288) *Baldwin.* £280
- - **Anr. Edn.** Amberes, 1754. 4to. Linen. (DS. Feb.24; 2464) Pts. 75,000

PENHALLOW, Samuel
- The History of the Wars of New-England, with the Eastern Indians; or, A Narrative of their Continued Perfidy & Cruelty. Boston, 1726. *1st. Edn.* Sm. 8vo. Advt. lf. at end, some 15 ll. with sm. margin repairs to tears or paper flaws, S1 with reprd. tear to text, some spotting, browning, front & rear pastedowns with early ink drawings of Indians, cont. unlettered cf., scuffed, tear in spine reprd., free endll. replaced; laid in is a receipt dtd. 21 Oct. 1706 (Possibly sigd. by Penhallow). [Sabin 59654] (CNY. Nov.18; 303) $2,500

PENN, Irving
- Momenti: Otto Saggi in Immagini e Parole. Milan, [1960]. *1st. Italian Edn.* Fo. Cl., d.-w. & pict. s.-c., lightly scuffed. (SG. May 10; 108) $150
- Moments Preserved: Eight Essays in Photographs & Words. N.Y., [1960]. *1st. Edn.* Tall 4to. Cl., orig. d.-w. & pict. s.-c., lightly scuffed. (SG. Nov.10; 130) $300
- - **Anr. Copy.** Tall 4to. Cl., orig. d.-w. & pict. s.-c., lightly scuffed. (SG. May 10; 107) $275

PENN, William
- An Account of W. Penn's Travails in Holland & Germany, Anno MDCLXXVII. For the Service of the Gospel of Christ, by way of Journal. L., 1695. *'2nd. Imp.'.* 16mo. 8 pp. printer's advts., some foxing & light browning spaced thro.-out, few cont. margin ink notations, recent red cf. & cl., raised bands, gt. panels, trimmed, light wear at corners & edges. (HA. Feb.24; 428) $200
- [-] Recuil de Diverses Pièces Concernant la Pennsylvanie. The Hague, 1684. 12mo. Marb. wraps., worn, spine defect. [Sabin 60445] (BBA. Jan.19; 87) *Sawyer.* £220

PENNANT, Thomas
- [-] Arctic Zoology. Ill.:- P. Mazell. L., 1784-85. *1st. Edn.* 2 vols. 4to. L.P., engraved vig. titles, 23 full-p. engraved plts., scattered light spotting, cont. cf., rebkd., corners worn; the Rt. Hon. Visc. Eccles copy. (CNY. Nov.18; 221) $480
- The British Zoology. Class I. Quadrupeds II. Birds. L., [1761-]66. *1st. Edn.* Lge. fo. Some plts. with wide margin, cont. cf. gt., spine reprd., bumped, some scratches, Hauswedell coll. (H. May 24; 870) DM 30,000
- [-] - **Anr. Edn.** Ill.:- P. Marzel, after P. Paillon &

others. L., [1761-]66. *3rd. Iss., without Preface, but with additional plt.* Lge. fo. Title & dedication ptd. in red & black, 133 hand-cold. etched plts., some offsetting affecting text & plts., slight graze on plt. of female Black Game, sm. smudge on plt. of Sheldrake, cont. russ. gt., reprd., sm. bird tool in compartments of spine. (S. Feb.1; 42) *Parker.* £12,500
- - **Anr. Edn.** Ill.:- mostly after Peter Paillou by Peter Mazell. L., 1766. *1st. Edn.* 2 pts. in 1 vol. Fo. Title ptd. in red & black, 132 hand-cold. engraved plts., minor offsetting, plt. 104 bnd. inverted & with ptd. caption partially erased, insignificant tear to p. 1 of text reprd., mod. cf.-bkd. bds. gt. (C. Jun.27; 126) *Quaritch.* £9,000
- - **Anr. Edn.** L., 1776-77. *3rd. Edn.* 4 vols. Additional engraved titles with vigs., 278 engraved plts., 1 folding engraved plt. of music, no ptd. title to Vol. IV, cont. vell. gt.; John Anderson, M.D. copy, his sig. on engraved titles. (C. Jun.27; 127) *Hill.* £280
- - **Anr. Edn.** Warrington, 1776-77. *4th. Edn.* 4 vols. 4to. 274 engraved plts., including additional titles, cont. spr. cf., spines gt.; Sir Ivar Colquhoun, of Luss copy. (CE. Mar.22; 236) £450
- - **Anr. Copy.** 4 vols. Last lf. in Vol. 1 reprd. (*With:*) - History of Quadrupeds. L., 1781. 3 vols. Together 6 vols. 4to. Some slight spotting or soiling, hf. cf., spines gt., faded, rubbed. (S. Mar.20; 784) *Thorp.* £130
- - **Anr. Copy.** 4 vols. 4to. Engraved titles & plts., few slightly spotted or offset, lacks ptd. title of Vol. 4, cont. cf. (S. Apr.10; 574) *Foster.* £105
- - **Anr. Copy.** 4 vols. Lge. 8vo. Additional engraved titles, 338 (of 339) plts., buckram, ex-liby. (SG. Mar.22; 255) £140
- - **Anr. Edn.** L., 1812. *New Edn.* 4 vols. 294 copperplt. engrs., some offset to text, cont. hf. cf., rubbed. (TA. Apr.19; 184) £90
- - **Anr. Copy.** 4 vols. Cf., spines slightly defect. (CR. Jun.6; 250) Lire 250,000
- [-] The History of Hindoostan. L., 1798. 2 vols. 4to. Folding map, 2 frontis., 19 plts., including 1 handcold., few mildly foxed, early cf., worn, covers & 1st. gathering in Vol. I detchd. (SG. Sep.22; 242) $120
- History of London, Westminster & Southwark. L., 1814. 2 vols. 4to. Extra-ill. with extra engraved titles & 150 plts., some spotting, mod. hf. sheep., w.a.f. (S. Mar.6; 395) *Jacksonn.* £130
- History of Quadrupeds. L., 1781. *1st. Edn.* 4to. 52 engraved plts., some spotting, cont. hf. cf., covers detchd. (TA. Jul.19; 241) £50
- The History of the Parishes of Whiteford & Holywell. 1796. 2 pts. in 1 vol. Lge. 4to. L.P., 2 plts. in 2 states, 1 folding, engraved port. of author inserted, some ll. slightly spotted or offset, cont. hf. mor., partly unc.; William Beckford copy with his & Hamilton's mottoes. (BBA. Sep.29; 122) *Vine.* £120
- Indian Zoology. L., 1790. *2nd. Edn.* 4to. Engraved hand-cold. title, 16 hand-cold. plts., Aikin's trans. of J.R. Forster's 'An Essay on India' & the list 'The Indian Fanula' bnd. at end, cont. hf. mor. (C. Nov.16; 285) *Junk.* £220
- A Tour in Wales. 1810. 3 vols. Hf. mor. gt.; extra-ill. with 354 plts. &c., some hand-cold., w.a.f. (P. Apr.12; 215) *Williams.* £260
- A Tour of Scotland, MDCCLXIX. Chester, 1771. Some light spotting, cont. cf., worn; fly-lf. inscr. 'The Gift of the Author 1771', 1 lf. annotated by Sir Roger Mostyn. (CSK. Dec.16; 211) £120

PENNECUIK, Alexander
- [-] A Geographical, Historical Description of the Shire of Tweeddale ... by A.P. 1715. 4to. Lacks map, old hf. cf.; Sir Ivar Colquhoun, of Luss copy. (CE. Mar.22; 239) £50

PENNELL, Joseph & Elizabeth Robins
- Lithography & Lithographers: Some Chapters in the History of the Art. Ill.:- Whistler, Legros, Strang, Shannon, Lunois, Hamilton, & Way (lithos.). N.Y. & L., 1898. *'Special Edn. for America', numbered on Japan vell.* Fo. Ptd. bds., slightly worn. (SG. Nov.3; 164) $350

PENNSYLVANIA GAZETTE, The
Phila., 5 Jan. 1764-26 Dec. 1765. Nos. 1828-1931 (lacks nos. 1837, 1853, 1866-69, 1896 & 1905),

with Supps. to nos. 1840, 1844, 1845 & 1925, together in 1 vol. Fo. Ragged stubs present for all lacking nos. except 1853 (never present?), 1st. 2 nos. creased & with some wear to gutter, browned & with some faint mildew stain thro.-out, some other stains from pressed flowers, 2nd. sheet of 1887 defect., 1923 slightly cropped at foot, cont. hf. cf. & marb. bds., covers worn with leath. & marb. paper lost from upr. cover; Shippen family copy, as a newspaper, w.a.f. (CNY. May 18; 160) $3,800

PENOT, B.G.
- Theophrastisch Vade Mecvm. Trans.:- Ioh. Hippodamus. Magdeburg, 1597. 4to. Some annots. & sm. ills. in old MS., lightly wormed at beginning, very browned, cont. vell., soiled, spine wormed. (HK. Nov.8; 686) DM 560

PENROSE ANNUAL
L., 1905-72. 24 vols. only. 4to. Orig. cl., d.-w.'s. (BBA. Apr.5; 243) *C. Cox.* £95

PENTAMERONE
- Stories from the Pentamerone. Ill.:- Warwick Goble. 1911. *De Luxe Edn., (150).* 4to. Orig. vell., gt.-decor., untrimmed, lacks ties. (SKC. Mar.9; 1779) £90

PENTHER, Johann Friedrich
- Ausführliche Anleitung zur Bürgerlichen Baukunst. Augsburg, 1744. Pt. 1 (of 4). Fo. Cont. hf. vell., defect. (D. Nov.23; 1913) DM 400
- Praxis Geometriae. Augsburg, 1738. Sm. fo. Stain thro.-out, lightly spotted, sm. margin slit, cont. leath., rubbed & worn. (GB. May 3; 1065) DM 680
- - **Anr. Edn.** Augsburg, 1761. *6th. Edn.* 2 pts. in 1 vol. Fo. Minimal foxing, cont. vell., slightly spotted. (GB. May 3; 900) DM 780

PENZER, Norman M.
- An Annotated Bibliography of Sir Richard Francis Burton. L., 1923. *(500) sigd.* 4to. Orig. cl., soiled. (S. May 1; 425) *Dawson.* £80
- - **Anr. Copy.** 4to. Orig. cl., unc. (S. Dec.13; 173) *Jongsma.* £50
- Paul Storr, The Last of the Goldsmiths. L., 1954. *1st. Edn.* 4to. Orig. buckram, d.-w., torn. (S. Nov.8; 562) *Thorp.* £60

PEOPLES GALLERY of Engravings
L., 1844. 3 vols. 4to. 193 steel engrs., red mor., gt.-tooled. (CR. Jun.6; 302) Lire 350,000

PEPYS, Samuel
- Diary. Ed.:- Lord Braybrooke & John Smith. L., 1825. *1st. Edn.* 2 vols. 4to. Mod. maroon str.-grd. mor. gt. by Bayntun. (S. Dec.8; 27) *Sotheran.* £200
- - **Anr. Copy.** 2 vols. Lge. 4to. 13 engraved plts. (1 dbl.-p.), 1 lf. stained, some spotting, orig. drab bds., unc., minor repairs to jnts., cl. folding boxes; Perry Molstad copy. (SPB. May 6; 511) $900
- - **Anr. Edn.** Ed.:- Henry B. Wheatley. N.Y., [1892-99]. *(1500).* 17 vols. only (of 18). Three-qtr. lev. mor., gt.-decor. spines. (CBA. Dec.10; 366) $160
- - **Anr. Edn.** 1893-99. *(250) L.P.* 10 vols., including Index & Pepysiana. Orig. vell.-bkd. cl., lightly soiled. (CSK. Jul.27; 90) £90
- - **Anr. Edn.** Ed.:- H.B. Wheatley. 1920. 10 vols. Mod. hf. cf. gt. (P. Sep.8; 281) £65
- - **Anr. Edn.** 1928. 10 vols. Orig. cl. gt. (P. Sep.29; 140) *Thorp.* £50
- - **Anr. Edn.** Ed.:- R. Latham & W. Matthews. 1970. 10 vols. & Index. Bdg. not stated. (PWC. May 3; 683) £62
- - **Anr. Edn.** Ed.:- Robert Latham & W. Matthews. L., 1970-72. 1st. 7 vols. Buckram, d.-w.'s (1 torn, several chipped). (KH. Nov.9; 384) Aus. $110
- Memoirs Relating to the State of the Royal Navy of England. Ill.:- Robert White. L., 1690. *1st. Edn. 1st. Iss.* Engraved port., folding sheet of accounts, D6 browned, MS. marginalia inked out in some places, cont. cf., rebkd.; sold stp. & bkplt. of Trinity College Camb., early book-label of John Laughton, MA. [Wing P1449] (SPB. May 16; 109) $475
- - **Anr. Edn.** L., 1690. Lacks folding table (supplied in photostat) & B7, upr. margin of title-p.

PEPYS, Samuel -*Contd.*

reprd., recent cf.; Henry Pepys, Bp. of Winchester, bkplt. [Wing P1450] (BBA. May 3; 174)
Bookroom. £60

PERACHYA BEN DAVID LIDA (Ed.)
See— **BIBLIANA [Hebrew]**

PERCEAU, Louis
- Bibliographie du Roman Erotique du XIXe Siècle. Paris, 1930. *(1050) numbered.* 2 vols. Orig. wraps., spines slightly torn. (BBA. Nov.10; 112)
Duran. £60

PERCIER, Charles & Fontaine, Pierre François Léonard
- Choix des plus Belles Maisons de Plaisance de Rome et de ses Environs. Paris, 1809. Fo. 76 plts., cont. hf. roan. (HD. Apr.13; 109) Frs. 1,900
– – **Anr. Copy.** Lge. fo. 28 text pp., with engraved captions & culs-de-lampe (stained, wear), 61 engraved plts., incompl., leaves, 2 pt. wraps. preserved, worn. (HD. Feb.29; 29) Frs. 1,000
– – **Anr. Edn.** Paris, 1824. *2nd. Edn.* Fo. 77 engraved plts. (numbered 1-75 & 39 bis.), without engraved title (not called for), but with additional unnumbered plt., mod. hf. cf. (C. Dec.9; 113)
Weinreb. £300

PERCIVAL, Capt. Robert
- An Account of the Cape of Good Hope. L., 1804. *1st. Edn.* 4to. Last 2 advt. ll., cont. cf., worn. (BBA. Dec.15; 56) *Quevedo.* £180
- An Account of the Island of Ceylon. L., 1803. 4to. Cont. cf. (C. Nov.16; 151) *Obeyesekera.* £120
– – **Anr. Edn.** 1805. *2nd. Edn.* 4to. Folding engraved map & 3 charts, 5 engraved plts., cont. hf. cf., hinges reprd. (SKC. Jan.13; 2385) £90

PERCIVAL, Thomas
- Essays Medical, Philosophical, & Experimental. Warrington, 1788-89. *4th. Edn.* 2 vols. Lightly damp-wrinkled, early owner's sigs., few liby stps., mod. qtr. mor. (SG. Mar.22; 257) $150

PERCY, Sholto & Reuben
[-] London. L., 1826 or later. 3 vols. in 5. 12mo. Inlaid to lge. 4to. & extra-ill. with over 700 subjects, including plans & views, ports. & ephemera, mostly engraved, a few mezzotint & aquatint, several wood-engraved, a few cold., some dustsoiling thro.-out, a few torn, 19th. C. bds., defect., w.a.f. (S. Dec.1; 169) *Talbot.* £700

PERCY, Bp. Thomas
[-] Reliques of Ancient English Poetry. 1765. *1st. Edn.* 3 vols. Frontis. in Vol. I, hf.-titles in Vols. II & III, some spotting, cont. cf., gt. rules. (BBA. Jul.27; 121) *Thorp.* £170
– – **Anr. Copy.** 3 vols. Hf.-titles in vols. 2 & 3, preliminary blank lf. in vol.1, engraved music lf. in vol.2, final errata & advts. in vol.3, some worming & staining, cont. cf., slightly worn, cl. folder, s.-c.; pres. copy. (SPB. May 16; 110) $600
– – **Anr. Copy.** 3 vols. Frontis. in vol.1, hf.-title in vol.2 only, vigs. thro.-out, cont. spr. cf., rebkd. (SG. Apr.19; 146) $130

PERECYVELLE
- Syr Perecyvelle of Gales. Kelms. Pr., 1895. *(358).* *(350) on paper.* Orig. qtr. cl., slightly soiled, bkplt. removed. (BBA. Oct.27; 167) *Fletcher.* £160

PEREGRINUS, Peter
- Epistle of Peter Peregrinus of Maricourt to Sygerus of Foncaucourt, Soldier concerning the Magnet. L., 1902. *(240).* 4to. Rubricated, orig. cl.-bkd. bds.; Stanitz coll. (SPB. Apr.25; 338) $325

PEREIRA, A. Marques
- As Alfandegas Chinesas de Macau. Macau, 1870. Wood-engraved plt. & litho. map, hand-cold. outl., 1 clean tear, orig. wraps., upr. cover & front free end-paper cleanly torn with loss, w.a.f. (CSK. Jul.6; 53) £320

PERELLE, Adam
- Recueille des plus Belles Vues des Maisons Royale de France. Paris, ca. 1670. Ob. 4to. 271 plts. & 8 titles, several plts. remargined, cont. marb. cf., spine decor. (reprd.); 2nd. proof of 5 plts. in 1st. printing

added, 1 title & 10 plts. in various printings bnd. at end. (HD. Jun.18; 37) Frs. 52,000
– – **Anr. Edn.** Paris, ca. 1680. Ob. fo. 106 (of 138?) copperplts., minimal spotting & staining, some pencil margin notes, hf. vell., slightly bumped. (H. May 22; 70) DM 2,600
– – **Anr. Edn.** Paris, ca. 1690. *Early Iss., with centre cartouche of title blank & plts. unnumbered.* Ob. fo. Engraved title, engraved plan (mntd. to size), 107 plts., cont. cf., panel. in blind, rebkd. (C. Dec.9; 115) *Bemberg.* £1,200
– – **Anr. Copy.** Ob. fo. Engraved title, 95 plts., a few discold., late 18th. C. mott. cf. gt., as a coll. of plts., w.a.f. (C. Dec.9; 114)
Craddock & Barnard. £700
– – **Anr. Edn.** Paris, n.d. Ob. fo. Mod. hf. marb. roan. (HD. Dec.9; 71) Frs 7,500

PERELLE, Gabriel, Nicholas & Adam
[-] Les Délices de Paris, et de ses Environs. Paris, 1753. Fo. Title with engraved ill., 224 engraved plts. on 210 ll., 1 with tear, slightly affecting engraved area, cf.-bkd. cont. bds. (C. Dec.9; 116)
Hammond. £900

PERERIO, B.
- De Magia, de Observatione Somniorum et de Divinatione Astrologica. Cologne, 1598. Some staining, vell. (P. Jan.12; 264) *Georges.* £85

PERET, Benjamin
- La Brébis Galante. Ill.:– M. Ernst. [Paris, 1949]. *(300) on Grand Velin d'Arches.* Lge. 8vo. Orig. pict. wraps., corners slightly bumped. (H. May 23; 1214) DM 2,000
- Le Gigot, sa Vie et son Oeuvre. Ill.:– Toyen (frontis.). Paris, [1 Aug.] 1957. *Orig. Coll. Edn. (56).* Lge. 8vo. On tinted vélin de Rives, frontis. with artist's autograph sig. & justification, sewed, d.-w. & s.-c. (HD. Nov.17; 167b) Frs. 1,500

PERETZ BEN YITZHAK COHEN, of Gerona
- Ma'arechet Ha'elohut. Commentary:– Yehuda Chayat. Mantua, 1558. *2nd. Edn.* 4to. Several outer margins reprd. not affecting text, last lf. defect. affecting text, lightly stained, vell., w.a.f. (S. Jul.3; 158) £400

PEREYRA, Carlos
- Historia de América Española. Madrid, 1920-26. 8 vols. in 4. 4to. Publishers cl. (DS. May 25; 2114) Pts. 32,000

PEREZ, Antonio
- Las Obras y Relaciones de ... Génova, 1631. Leath. (DS. Apr.27; 2704) Pts. 50,000

PEREZ BAYER, Francisco
- De Numis Hebrae Samaritanis. Valencia, 1781. Fo. Cont. mor. (DS. Mar.23; 2215) Pts. 70,000
- Numorum Haebraeo Samaritanorum. Valencia, 1790. Fo. L.P., leath. (DS. Mar.23; 2686) Pts. 70,000

PEREZ DE GUZMAN, F.
- Comiença la Cronica del Serenissimo Rey Don Juan el Segundo. Ed.:– [L. Galindoz de Carvajal]. Logroño, 1517. *1st. Edn.* Fo. Light soiling nearly thro.-out in margins, some spotting, title old mntd., 1 lf. torn at foot, 1 lf. bkd. in lr. margin, 3 sm. top corner tears extended, lacks 3 ll. & completed in old MS. 18th. C. leath., cont. style spine, renewed with gt. (R. Apr.3; 76) DM 2,100

PEREZ DE VALENTIA, Jacobus
- Centum ac Quinquaginta Psalmi Davidi, cum Diligentissima etiam Titulorum Expositione ... — Cantica Canticorum Salomonia cum Expositione ... Ed.:– Jodocus Ascensius. Ill.:– Guillaume II Leroy. Lyon, 1517. 2 pts. in 1 vol. 4to. 1st. title slightly rubbed, defect. & reprd. in upr. outer corner, with loss of text on verso, antique-style panel. gt. & blind-stpd. mor., spine raised bands, copper clasps. (C. May 30; 42) *Snelling,.* £320

PEREZ DE VILLA-AMIL, Genaro
- España Artistica y Monumental: Vistas y Descripción de los Sitios y Monumentos mas Notables de España ... Texto Redactado por Patricio de la Escosura. Paris, 1842. *1st. Edn.* Vol. 1 only (of 3). Tall fo. Text in Spanish & Fr., 47 litho. plts., scattered foxing, variously affecting roughly hf. the

plts., hf. pig, chafed, spine darkened. (SG. Jun.7; 385) $800
– – **Anr. Edn.** Paris, 1842-50. *1st. Edn.* 3 vols. Tall fo. Text in Spanish & Fr., 144 litho. plts., some foxing, marginally affecting plts., sm. liby. stps. at foot of titles, hf. leath. (SG. Nov.3; 165) $3,500

PEREZ GALDOS, Benito
- Episodios Nacionales. Ill.:– E. & A. Melida & others. Madrid, 1885. 10 vols. 4to. Publishers cl., stpd. (DS. Apr.27; 2451) Pts. 42,000

PERGER, A.R. von
- Die Kunstschätze Wien's in Stahlstich. Triest, 1861. 4to. Lightly browned & slightly stained, engraved title & 107 steel engraved plts., cont. hf. leath., slightly rubbed. (HT. May 9; 984) DM 480

PERGOLESI, Michel Angelo
- Original Designs of Vases ... L., [plts. dtd. 1777-92]. Fo. 66 plts., including the dedication to the Duchess of Buccleugh, engraved dedication to Hugh Percy, Duke of Northumberland bnd. with plt. 56, no ptd. title or text, orig. ptd. sheet 'Proposals for Publishing' with cont. MS. corrections mntd. in place of title, a few plts. with minor dampstaining in blank margins, mod. maroon hf. mor. gt. by Sangorski & Sutcliffe. (C. Nov.16; 152) *Harris.* £600

PERKINS, Charles C.
See— **CHAMPLIN, John Denison & Perkins, Charles C.**

PERKINS, John
- A Profitable Booke ... Treating of the Lawes of England. L., 1567. Sm. 8vo. Sig. & notes on title of Thomas Emylie, cont. MS. margin notes (of Emylie?), stain to lr. inner margin of 1 gathering, some soiling to end-papers, cont. cf., spine & corners rubbed, some worming to spine, clasps renewed. [NSTC 19635.5] (SPB. Dec.13; 701) $350
– – **Anr. Edn.** L., 1609. 12mo. Few marginalia, old sheep, rebkd., hinge brkn.; from the Lincoln's Inn Liby. [STC 19642] (SG. Oct.27; 188) $100

PERKINS, William
- A Treatise Tending unto a Declaration, Whether a Man bee in thee State of Damnation, Or in the Estate of Grace ... 1591. Sm. 8vo. Top margin of title reprd., lacks A2?, 19th. C. panel. cf. gt., rubbed. [STC 19753] (TA. Jun.21; 527) £85

PERNAU, F.A.
- Gründliche Anweisung alle Arten Vögel zu Fangen. Nuremb., 1754. 46 plts., many folding, 3 crudely reprd., cont. hf. cf. (S. Apr.10; 445) *Koch.* £260
[-] – **Anr. Copy.** Cont. bds. (R. Apr.4, 1957) DM 2,300

PERNEDER, Andreas
- Institutiones. Ingolstadt, 1573. Fo. Title slightly soiled & with owners mark, 17th. C. vell., 4 ties. (HK. May 15; 214) DM 1,600

PERNETY, Antoine Joseph D.
[-] The History of a Voyage to the Malouine (or Falkland) Islands, made in 1763 & 1764. L., 1771. *1st. Engl. Edn.* 4to. 16 maps & plts., including 8 folding, cont. cf. [Sabin 6870] (S. Dec.1; 289)
Cavendish. £520

PERON, A.
See— **LOCARD & Cotteau — PERON, A.**

PERON, François Auguste & Freycinet, Louis
- Voyage de Découvertes aux Terres Australes ... Atlas par MM. Lesueur et Petit. [Paris, 1807-11]. Atlas vol. only. Fo. Engraved title, 40 plts., numbered 2-41, many hand-cold., cont. roan-bkd. bds., unc. (C. Nov.16; 153) *Burgess.* £2,100

PERONDIUS, P.
- Magni Tamerlanis Scytharum Imperatoris Vita. [Amberg], 1597. *1st. Amberg Edn.* 12mo. Cont. owners mark on title, slightly browned, early 19th. C. red mor., gold-tooled, inner & outer dentelle, engraved ex-libris. (HT. May 8; 193) DM 400

PEROTTUS, Nicolaus.
- Cornucopiae. Lyon, 2.VI.1501. *Early Edn.* Fo. Title & last lf. with MS. entry, 2 ll. with lr. corner

torn off & slight loss, some slight browning or staining, cont. limp vell., bumped & soiled, lacks ties. (HK. Nov.8; 310) DM 620
- Queste Son Le Regule de Perotto. Milan, ad impensas domini Lazari de Turate, 23 Dec. 1499. 4to. Some very sm. wormholes, mainly marginal, long wormhole through el-8 & fo. 1 affecting letters, cont. oak bds., cf. spine, lacks clasps. (S. May 10; 382) *Quaritch.* £6,200
- Rudimenta Grammaticae. Rome, 1493. 4to. 167 ll. (of 168), decorative woodcut initials, rubricated in yellow, lf. h8 renewed at margins, few ll. stained, some discoloration thro.-out, hf. sheep. [H. 12685] (SPB. May 17; 656) $850

PERRAULT, Charles
- La Belle-au-Bois-Dormant; La Barbe Bleue; Cendrillon. Ill.:– H. Lemarié. Paris, 1948-50. 3 vols. On Rives, leaves, wraps., ill. box. (HD. Mar.27; 100) Frs. 12,300
- La Belle au Bois Dormant; Cendrillon. Ill.:– Arthur Rackham. N.d. Together 2 vols. 4to. On vell., no bdg. stated; sigd. by artist. (HD. Jun.26; 141) Frs. 1,400
- La Belle au Bois Dormant et Quelques Autres Contes de Jadis. Preface:– Edmond Pilon. Ill.:– Edmund Dulac. Paris, [1910]. *(400) numbered on Japan vell., sigd. by artist.* 4to. Three-qtr. mor. by Babin, orig. wraps. bnd. in. (SG. Nov.3; 66) $225
- – Anr. Edn. Ill.:– Edmund Dulac. [1910]. 4to. Cf. by Lagorse, painted decor. (HD. Jan.24; 77) Frs. 1,700
- Le Cabinet des Beaux-Arts. Ill.:– Le Brun (vig.), Coypel, Boulogne l'Ainé, Friquet, Bonnard, J.B. & N. Corneille, & others (engrs.). 1695. Ob. 4to. Much foxing, some tears without loss of text, cont. silk over bds., gold silk doubls. (HD. Mar.21; 66) Frs. 1,500
- Les Contes. Ill.:– Gustave Doré. Paris, 1862. *1st. Printing.* Fo. Minimal foxing, publisher's decor. buckram. (HD. May 4; 390) Frs. 5,000
- – Anr. Edn. Ill.:– Edouard de Beaumont. Paris, 1888. Fo. 4 orig. etchings, with special engraved text, 2 A.L.s.'s, mor., mosaic decor., inner mosaic border, embroidered silk doubls. & end-papers, s.-c., by Marius Michel; from Descamp-Scrive liby. (HD. Dec.9; 168) Frs. 65,000
- Contes des Fées. Paris, 1781. 2 pts. in 1 vol. Lacks frontis., cont. red mor., gt. inner & outer dentelles, ex-libris in cover, slightly reprd., mod. hf. leath. box; Hauswedell coll. (H. May 24; 1728) DM 3,600
- Les Contes des Fées en Prose et en Vers. Intro.:– Ch. Giraud. Ill.:– Annedouche (port.), Rebel after Eisen (vig.), Rebel after Gerlier (frontis.). Lyon, 1865. *2nd. Edn.* Maroon mor. by Smeers, 18th. C. style gt. dentelle, spine decor. (HD. Mar.27; 99) Frs. 2,300
- Contes du Tempe Passé ... Intro.:– M.E. de La Bedollière. Ill.:– Pauquet, Marvy, Jauron, Jacque & Beaucé. Paris, 1842-43. Lge. 8vo. Some light foxing, blind-decor. hf. chagrin by Curmer, spine decor. (HD. May 4; 389) Frs. 4,000
- [–] Courses de Festes et de Bague. Paris, 1670. Imp. fo. Some plts. with text below ill. & on verso, lacks text ll., last 2 plts. with slight tear in lr. margin, some slight foxing, title & last plt. verso stpd., cont. reprd. leath., gt. & gold-tooled arms supralibros. (D. Nov.24; 2323) DM 3,800
- The Fairy Tales. Intro.:– Thomas Bodkin. Ill.:– Harry Clarke. L., [1922]. *1st. Edn.* 4to. Lacks front free end-paper, gt.-decor. cl. (SG. Dec.8; 116) $130
- Festiva ad Capita Annulumque Decursio, a Rege Ludovico XIV. Ill.:– Sylvestre & Chauveau. Paris, 1670. Fo. Title with engraved royal arms, additional engraved title, 30 engraved ills., including 1 double-p., 55 engraved heraldic plts. on 10 ll., 11 double-p. engraved plts. on 7 ll., hf.-title, minor dampstain to margins of a few ll. & plts., 2 plts. slightly shaved at margin, cont. hf. cf., spine gt.; Victorien Sardou bkplt. (C. Dec.9; 117) *Weinreb.* £900
- Histoire ... ou les Contes de ma Mère l'Oye. The Histories, or the Tales of Mother Goose. L., Bruxelles, 1785. 2 vols. Sm. 8vo. Fr. & Engl. parallel text, a few ll. slightly stained, 1 blank corner torn off, late 19th. C. bds., unc. (VG. Mar.21; 465) Fls. 1,100

- Les Hommes Illustres qui ont Paru en France Pendant ce Siècle. Paris, 1696-1700. *1st. Edn.* 2 vols. in 1. Fo. Port. of author, frontis., 97 (of 98) plts., privilege lf., cont. cf. gt., a composite remboîtage, crudely rebkd. with old spine laid down. (SG. Oct.27; 251) $160
- – Anr. Edn. Paris, 1696-1700. 2 vols. Engraved frontis., 103 engraved ports. (with ports. of Thomassin & Du Cange instead of suppressed plts. of Arnauld & Pascal), 2 engrs. pasted to a4 of Vol. 1, 1 plt. stained. (*With:*) - Les Illustres Modernes; ou Tableau de la vie privée des principaux personnages des deux sexes. Paris, 1788. 2 vols. in 1. Engraved title to Vol. 1, ptd. hf.-title to Vol. 2, 100 engraved ports., some slight dampstaining, mostly to margins. Together 3 vols. Fo. 18th. C. Fr. red mor. gt., covers gt.-stpd. with arms of Cardinal Fleury, & with his stps. on spines, linings & end-papers renewed, new label on 3rd. vol. which has been recased, some slight wear, w.a.f. (CNY. May 18; 161) $950
- [–] Labyrinte de Versailles. Ill.:– Sébastien le Clerc. The Hague, 1724. *2nd. Edn.* Sm. ob. 4to. Engraved frontis., 40 plts., cont. cf. gt. (C. Dec.9; 118) *D'Arcy.* £300
- Popular Tales. Ed.:– Andrew Lang. Ill.:– Ulysse-Roy (watercolour) & A. Lalauze & others (engrs.). Oxford, 1888. 4to. Mor. gt. extra, elab. dentelles, by R. Ruban, Japanese-style end-papers. (SG. Dec.8; 265) $150
- Tales of Mother Goose. Intro. & Critical Text:– Jacques Barchilen. N.Y., 1956. *Facs. of the dedication MS. of 1695. (250) numbered with ills. handcold.* 2 vols. Cl.-bkd. patterned bds., tissue jackets, cl. box. (SG. Dec.8; 267) $100

PERRAUT, Claude
- [–] Memoirs for a Natural History of Animals. L., 1701. *2nd. Engl. Edn.* Fo. Engraved frontis., 35 plts., some dampstaining, a few margins frayed, title browned & with upr. margin trimmed, cont. cf., rebkd. & reprd. (S. Nov.28; 76) *Shapero.* £170
- Ordonnances des Cinq Espèces de Colonnes selon la Méthode des Anciens. Paris, 1683. (*Bound with:*) SCAMOZZI, Vincent - Les Cinq Ordres d'Architecture. Paris, 1685. 2 works in 1 vol. Fo. Cont. cf. (HD. Dec.15; 30) Frs. 3,000
- A Treatise of the Five Orders of Columns in Architecture. Trans.:– John James. 1708. Fo. Engraved title, frontis., dedication lf., 6 plts., cont. cf., rebkd. (P. Jul.26; 118) £160

PERRET, Claude
- Exercitatio Alphabetica Nova et Vtilissima, variis expressa Lingvis et Characteribus: raris Ornamentis, Vmbris, & Recessibus, Picture, Architecturaeque ... Ill.:– C. de Hooghe. Brussels, 1569. *1st. Edn.* Ob. fo. Lacks typographic printers privilege for Chr. Plantin & 1 plt., plts. 10-12 cut to plt. margin & mntd., some plts. at beginning & end with sm. margin holes, all with folds & margin fraying & spotted, hf. leath., ca. 1850, bumped, spine defect. (HK. May 15; 215) DM 800

PERRET, Jean Jacques
- L'Art du Coutelier. Paris, 1772. Pts. 1 & 2: from the 'Description des Arts et Metiers' series. Tall fo. Pt. 1: comprising plts. 73-122, no title or text, Pt. 2: comprising plts. 123-172 & text pp. 375-527, bnd. at end is de Bondaroy's 'L'Art du Coutelier en Ouvrages Communs': comprising 54 text pp., lacks plts., mod. qtr. cf., cont. cf.-bkd. bds. (SG. Oct.6; 291) $300
- – Anr. Copy. Pt. 1: from the 'Description des Arts et Metiers' series. Tall fo. Comprising plts. 73-122 & text pp. 241-374, old bds., leath. back, unc. (SG. Oct.6; 292) $110

PERREZ, Luis
- Del Can y del Caballo. Sevilla, 1888. *(50) on rag paper.* 4to. Linen. (DS. Mar.23; 2214) Pts. 35,000

PERRIER, Franciscus
- Segmenta Nobilium Signorum et Statuarum quae Temporis dentem invidium evasere urbis aeternae ruinis cvasere. Rome, 1638. *Iss. with subscription 'A Paris, chez la veufue de defunt Perrier'.* Fo. Engraved dedication lf., 100 engraved plts (2 double-p), 1st. lf. dust-stained, some (mainly margin

stains, hf. cf., worn, spine brkn. (BBA. Jan.19; 13) *Callea.* £95
- – Anr. Edn. Rome, 1638. Fo. Engraved dedication lf., 99 (of 100) engraved plts. (2 double-p.), 2 index ll., pen & ink drawing loosely inserted, cont. vell., slightly worn. (BBA. Mar.21; 18) *Shapiro.* £75

PERRIN, Mrs. H.
See— BOULGER, Prof. George S. & Perrin, Mrs. H.

PERRINET D'ORVAL, J.C.
- [–] Essay sur les Feux d'Artifice pour le Spectacle et pour la Guerre. Paris, 1745. *1st. [& only] Edn.* 13 engraved plts., owner's inscrs., cont. mott. cf. gt. (SG. Oct.6; 293) $170

PERRON, E.
- Het Land van Herkomst. Amst., 1935. *1st. Edn.* Cont. cl.; autograph dedication by author, dtd. Paris 27 May '35. (VS. Jun.6; 355) Fls. 1,200
- De Smalle Mens. Amst., 1934. *1st. Edn.* Cont. cl.; autograph dedication by author dtd. Paris Oct. '34. (VS. Jun.6; 353) Fls. 500

PERRONET, Jean Rodolphe
- Description des Projets et de la Construction des Ponts De Neuilly, de Mantes, d'Orléans & autres. Ill.:– German & others after E. de St. Far & others. Paris, 1782/83. 2 vols. only (without Supp.). Lge. fo. Some old spotting & wear, leath gt., spine bumped, sm. defects. (V. Sep.30; 1561) DM 500

PERROT, Ferdinand
- Vues de Saint–Pétersbourg et deses Environs. Ill.:– C. Pohl. N.p., n.d. Ob. fo. 20 2-tones lithos., Russian & Fr. captions, light foxing, cont. hf. chagrin, corners. (HD. Feb.29; 30) Frs. 6,000

PERROT, Georges & Chipiez, Charles
- Histoire de l'Art dans l'Antiquité. Paris, 1882-1914. 10 vols. Lge. 8vo. Vols. I-IX hf. chagrin, corners, spines decor., Vol. X sewed. (LM. Mar.3; 88) B. Frs. 10,000

PERROTT, Sir John
- The History of ... L., 1728. *1st. Edn.* Mott. cf., spine rubbed. (GM. Dec.7; 393) £55

PERRY, George
- Conchology, or the Natural History of Shells. L., 1811. *1st. Edn.* Fo. 61 hand-finished cold. aquatint plts., slight offsetting from text onto plts., cont. gt.- & blind-panel. purple mor., rubbed. (S. Nov.28; 77) *Schuster.* £720

PERRY, Capt. John
- An Account of the Stopping of Daggenham Breach. Map:– H. Moll. L., 1721. Folding map reprd., sm. portion torn from fore-edge, spotted, mor.-bkd. cont. bds. (S. Mar.6; 443) *Frankland.* £100
- The State of Russia, under the Present Czar. Map:– H. Moll. 1716. *1st. Edn.* Folding engraved map slightly torn, some ll. slightly browned or soiled, cont. cf. (BBA. Sep.29; 90) *Quevedo.* £100

PERRY, Matthew Calbraith
- [–] Narrative of the Expedition of an American Squadron to the China Seas & Japan, Performed in 1852-1854. Wash., 1856. 3 vols. Lge. 4to. Handcold. zoological plts., lacks nude bathing plt. but with photographer plt., orig. cl., spine ends worn, corners slightly frayed. (SG. Jan.19; 298) $350
- – Anr. Copy. 2 vols., mixed set. 4to. Vol II with 33d Congress, 2d Session, House Executive Document 97 title, 80 full-p. toned & cold. lithos., in Vol. I, plus 2 folded & 1 full-p. cold facs. of Japanese woodblock prints, several folded maps, many black-&-white text engrs., 18 full-p. handcold. lithos., plus 4 col. & 5 black-&-white litho. plts. in Vol. II, plus folded map, 16 engraved charts, & 14p. facs. of orig. treaty at rear, few plts. foxed or lightly stained in margins, some with light foxing & some ageing & staining, later cl. or orig. mor. & cl., gt. lettering, covers slightly worn. (HA. May 4; 404) $325

PERS, D.P.
- [–] Bellerophon of Lust tot Wysheyd. Amst., 1614. *1st. Edn.* 4to. Mor. gt., rebnd. (VG. Nov.30; 724) Fls. 500

PERS, D.P. -Contd.

- **– – Anr. Edn.** Amst., ca. 1635. *4th. Edn.* Sm. 8vo. Cont. vell. (VG. Nov.30; 725) Fls. 450

PERSE, St. John [i.e. Marie René Auguste Alexis Saint-Leger]

- **Amers.** Ill.:– André Marchand (lithos.) & Robert Blanchet (title-p. & initials). Les Bibliophiles de Provence, 1962. *(250) numbered. (150) reserved for members of the soc.* Fo. Text & plts. unsewn in separate orig. wraps., fitted cases, unc. (S. Nov.21; 102) *Makiya.* £200
- **Eloges.** 1911. Ltd. Orig. Edn. on papier vergé. No bdg. stated. (HD. May 11; 167) Frs. 2,900

PERSIUS FLACCUS, Aulus

See — JUVENALIS, Decimus Junius & Persius Flaccus, Aulus
See — MARTIALIS, Marcus Valerius — PERSIUS FLACCUS, Aulus

PERU

- **Constitucion Politica de la republica Peruana.** Lima, ca. 1823. Fo. Slightly soiled, sm. hole in 1st. 3 ll., stitched as iss. [Sabin 61098] (BBA. Mar.21; 99) *Quaritch.* £120

PERUCCI, Francesco

- **Pompe Funebri di tutte le Natione del Mondo.** Verone, 1639. Fo. Some ll. stained, cont. limp vell., slightly disbnd. (HD. Jan.27; 267) Frs. 1,600

PERUGINI, G.

- **Album ou Collection Complète et Historique des Costumes de la Cour de Rome des Ordres Monastiques, Religieux et Militaires et des Congrégations Séculières des Deux Sexes.** Ed.:– P. Hélyot. Paris, 1862. *2nd. Edn.* 4to. Minimal foxing, cont. hf. leath. (D. Nov.24; 4356) DM 700

PERZYNSKI, F.

- **Japanische Masken Nô und Kyôgen.** Berlin, 1925. 2 vols. 4to. Orig. linen. (R. Oct.11; 900) DM 400

PESTALOZZI, Johann Heinrich

- **[–]** **Anschauungslehre der Zahlenverhältnisse.** Tübingen, 1803. *1st. Edn.* 2 vols. Title lf. with old stp., cont. bds. (GB. May 4; 1546) DM 650
- **Meine Lebensschicksale als Vorsteher meiner Erziehungsinstitute in Burgdorf und Iferten.** Leipzig, 1826. *1st. Edn.* Wide margin, some light soiling, cont. bds., unc., slightly worn, spine defect., many cont. entries in upr. cover. (R. Oct.11; 521) DM 600

PETERMANN, A.

See — MILNER, Rev. T. & Petermann, A.

PETERMANN, V.

- **Jagd-Büchlein.** Erfurt, ca. 1875. Orig. wraps., unc. (R. Oct.12; 2065) DM 460

PETERMANN, Wilhelm Ludwig

- **Deutschlands Flora mit Abbildungen Sämmtlicher Gattungen auf 100 Tafeln.** Leipzig, 1849. Sm. 4to. Title & end-papers stpd., brown spotted, cont. hf. leath., spine faded, slightly rubbed. (H. May 22; 202) DM 400

PETERS, Dewitt C.

- **Kit Carson's Life & Adventures** ... Hartford, 1873. Orig. gt. decor. cl. (SG. Apr.5; 44) $140

PETERS, Harry T.

- **America on Stone.** Garden City, 1931. *(751) numbered.* Lge. 4to. 154 plts. (18 cold.), other plts. tipped on text ll., ex-liby., linen. (SG. May 3; 278) $250
- **California on Stone.** Garden City, 1935. *1st. Edn.* 4to. Laminated linen, s.-c. (LH. Sep.25; 275) $425

PETERS, J.

- **[–]** **Civitates Hungariae Turic ereptae.** Antw., [1692]. Ob. 4to. 3 plts. with slight margin slits & loss, slightly browned & soiled, hf. leath. using old material, gt. spine. (D. Nov.23; 808) DM 1,700

PETERS, James Lee

- **Checklist of Birds of the World.** Camb., Mass., 1931-79. 14 vols. Orig. cl. (S. Apr.10; 446) *Evans.* £150

PETHERICK, John

- **Egypt, the Soudan & Central Africa.** 1861. Publishers catalogue at end, orig. cl., spine faded; pres. copy from author to Lady Ashburton. (TA. Nov.17; 16) £58

PETIOT, Dr. M.

- **Le Hasard Vaincu. Les Lois des Martingales, Application à tous Jeux dits 'de Hasard' Courses, Roulette, Loterie Nationale** ... Paris, 1946. *Orig. Edn.* 4to. Facs. of MS., sewed. (HD. Feb.28; 74) Frs. 1,400

PETIT, Jean Louis

- **Abhandlung von denen Kranckheiten derer Knochen am Menschlichen Leibe** ... Berlin, 1725. *1st. German Edn.* 2 pts. in 1 vol. Old liby. stp. on title-lf. & several text ll., lacks plt. 1, cont. vell., slightly soiled. (GB. Nov.3; 1037) DM 750
- **L'Art de Guérir les Maladies des Os.** Paris, 1705. Cf. (P. Jan.12; 265) *Phillips.* £360

PETIT, Victor

- **Architecture Nouvelle: Recueil de Constructions Modernes Executées en France, en Angleterre, en Allemagne, en Italie.** Paris, ca. 1850. Fo. 50 litho. plts., some light foxing, mainly marginal, orig. cl. gt., extremities worn, ex-liby. (SG. Jan.26; 264) $250
- **Bagnères de Luchon et ses Environs.** Paris, ca. 1860. Ob. 4to. Publisher's buckram bds., gt. motif. (HD. Feb.17; 16) Frs. 1,150
- **Châteaux de la Vallée de la Loire des XVe et XVII Siècles.** Ill.:– Victor Petit. 1861. 2 vols. in 1. Lge. fo. Table & 100 litho. plts. on tinted ground, all mntd. on guards & on vell., hf. red chagrin, corners. (HD. Feb.29; 31) Frs. 6,800
- **Souvenirs des Pyrénées.** Pau, ca. 1860. 5 pts. in 1 vol. Fo. Chromolitho. ports., vigs., 6 pp. text lithos., 39 tinted lithos. (1 folding), linen. (DS. Mar.23; 2496) Pts. 46,000

PETIT FABULISTE

Paris, ca. 1840. 25 x 18mm., miniature book. Orig. red mor. gt.; van Veen coll. (S. Feb.28; 194) £110

PETIT NECESSAIRE OU ALMANACH POUR L'ANNEE 1781

Amst., [1780]. 69 x 34mm., miniature book. Cont. cf., covers gt. & painted; van Veen coll. (S. Feb.28; 195) £200

PETITE HISTOIRE DE PIERROT

Paris, ca. 1820. 51 x 72mm., miniature book. Engraved pict. title & 7 plts. hand-cold., orig. embossed pict. bds., lr. cover rubbed; van Veen coll. (S. Feb.28; 196) £70

PETITE VOLIERE

Paris, ca. 1820. 56 x 40mm., miniature book. Engraved pict. title-p. & 6 plts. hand-cold., text slightly spotted, orig. ptd. bds., similar decor. s.-c., worn; van Veen coll. (S. Feb.28; 198) £310

PETITES HISTOIRES

Paris, ca. 1820. 4 vols. 70 x 48mm., miniature book. 4 hand-cold. engraved plts., spotted, orig. embossed wraps., case, former owner's name written on 1 side; van Veen coll. (S. Feb.28; 199) £70

PETITS MONTAGNARDS, Année 1822

Paris, [1821]. 27 x 18mm., miniature book. Soiled, orig. red mor. gt.; van Veen coll. (S. Feb.28; 200) £130

PETIVER, James

- **Gazophulacii Naturae & Artis Decas Prima [only].** L., 1702. Fo. 30 engraved plts. (1st. 20 with facing text pasted to versos & ptd. dedication in lr. margin), advt. lf. facing title, old wraps., worn & soiled; cont. bkplt. of Dr. H.T. Baron of Paris, w.a.f. (BBA. May 3; 57) *Quaritch.* £170

PETRARCA OR PETRARCH, Francesco

- **Le Cose Volgari.** Venice, Jul. 1501. *1st. Aldine Edn. 2nd. Iss.* Lacks 1st. & last ll., a2 slightly soiled & with minor flaw affecting a few letters of text, piece torn from lr. fore-corner of ul with slight loss of text, 17th. C. spr. sheep; cont. sig. 'Mellini Sangelasii'. (S. Nov.17; 56) *Quaritch.* £110
- **– – Anr. Edn.** Venice, 1501. Mod. mor. gt. (LC. Jul.5; 371) £160

– De los Remedios contra Próspera y Adversa Fortuna M.D.XXX.III. Sevilla, 1534. Fo. Orig. vell. (DS. Nov.25; 2149) Pts. 160,000
- **Opera Latina.** Basle, Johann Amerbach, 1495. *1st. Coll. Edn.* Sm. fo. Minor rust-stain affecting a few letters on a7v, single wormhole through last 74 ll. slightly affecting text, 13 lines of Latin verse in 17th. C. hand on recto of last lf., 18th. C. Fr. red mor., gt. spine with fleurons in compartments, triple gt. fillet, inner gt. dentelles; 16th. C. motto & sig. of Bellosier on title-p., Marquess of Crewe bkplt. [BMC III, 757; Goff P365; HC 12749] (S. Nov.17; 55) *Maggs.* £2,050
- **[Opera] Librorum Francisci Petrarchae Basilae Impressorum Annotatio.** Basle, Amerbach, 1496. *1st. Edn.* Fo. 17th. C. buckram, spine partly defect.; from Fondation Furstenberg-Beaumesnil. [HC 12749; BMC III, 757; Goff P365] (HD. Nov.16; 16) Frs. 11,000
- **Le Opere Volgari** ... **Cioe, Sonetti et Canzoni in Laude di Madonna Laura.** Venice, Nov. 1511. 12mo. Last lf. loose & with sm. hole, 18th. C. Fr. mott. sheep, worn. (S. Nov.17; 57) *Lurie.* £490
- **Il Petrarca** ... Commentary:– Alessandro Vellutello. Venice, 1528. *2nd. Edn. of Commentary.* With lf. 165 (often lacking), some sonnets erased & washed, 1 lf. removed & reinserted, 2 dampstains, MS. Spanish Inquisition certificate dtd. 1622 at beginning & end, cont. Venetian mor., blind- & gt.-decor.; from Fondation Furstenberg-Beaumesnil. (HD. Nov.16; 149) Frs. 7,000
- **– – Anr. Copy.** With lf. 165 (often lacking), dedication on verso of title, 1st. 12 ll. remargined, end-papers renewed, cont. mor. gt.; from Fondation Furstenberg-Beaumesnil. (HD. Nov.16; 150) Frs. 2,800
- **– – Anr. Edn.** Commentary.:– Alessandro Vellutello. Venice, 1532. *3rd. Edn. of Commentaries.* Decor. mor., ca. 1860, Andre Weiss cypher on spine. (HD. Mar.21; 67) Frs. 3,000
- **– – Anr. Edn.** Commentary:– Alessandro Velutello. Venice, 1545. Last part very defect., 16th. C. Venetian mor., richly blind- & gt.-decor.; from Fondation Furstenberg-Beaumesnil. (HD. Nov.16; 162) Frs. 3,200
- **– – Anr. Edn.** Lyons, 1551. 18mo. Erased sigs. on title, 2 ll. replaced in old MS., 16th. C. Lyonnais cf., vari-cold. wax & gt. decor. (HD. Mar.30; 17) Frs. 16,500
- **Le Rime.** Ed:– Lod. Castelvetro. Ill.:– Cristoforo Zapata de Cisneros. Venise, 1756. 2 vols. 4to. Engraved dedication lf., cont. hf. red mor., limp decor. spines. (HD. Jan.27; 269) Frs. 1,600
- **Soneti, Canzoni e Triomphi.** Commentary:– Bernardino Daniello de Lucca. Venice, 1549. 4to. Old Persian mor., decor., mor. doubls., spine & end-papers renewed; from Fondation Furstenberg-Beaumesnil. (HD. Nov.16; 151) Frs. 3,500
- **Trionfi.** Venice, Bernardino [Rizo] de Novara, 18 Apr. 1488. *1st. Ill. Edn.* Pt. 1 only. Fo. Capital spaces, most with guide-letters, very sm. hole in 1st. lf. reprd., slightly affecting a few letters, sm. hole in inner blank margin of a few ll. (from fo. 112) reprd., slit in woodcuts no. 2 & no. 6 reprd. in lr. margin hardly affecting woodcut, tear in inner lr. corner of h4 reprd., old wood bds., rebkd. with sheep, lacks clasps. [BMC V, 401; Goff P383; H. 12787] (S. May 10; 381) *Duran.* £800
- **– – Anr. Edn.** Ed:– Bernardo Glicino. Venetia, Pelegrino di Pasquali & Domenico Bertocho, 1488. Fo. Lacks 1st. lf. blank & anr. lf., some old margin notes, mod. bds. [H. 12788] (CR. Jun.6; 252) Lire 1,200,000

PETRASANCTA, Silvestro

- **De Symbolis Heroicis Libri IX.** Antw., 1634. 4to. Last imprint lf., some stains, affecting text on 10 ll., 18th. C. cf., rebkd. & reprd., rubbed. (BBA. Feb.23; 15) *Thorp.* £120

PETRIE, George

- **The Ecclesiastical Architecture of Ireland.** Dublin, 1845. *2nd. Edn.* Royal 8vo. Mor., armorial motif on spine. (GM. Dec.7; 436) £160

PETRINI, A.F.

- **Gli Aborigeni dell'Australia.** Arezzo, 1888. Corrigenda slip, ptd. wraps.; author's(?) inscr. (KH. May 1; 561) Aus. $400

PETRONIO, Alessandro Traiano
- De Victu Romanorum et de Sanitate Tuenda.
Rome, 1581 [1582]. *1st. Edn.* Fo. Margin stains,
limp vell., soiled; Dr. Walter Pagel copy. (S. Feb.7;
306)   *Colombo.* £240

PETRONIUS ARBITER, Titus or Gaius
- Satyricon. Ill.:– Norman Lindsay. L., 1910. *(250)*
numbered & sigd. by artist & printer. 4to. In
Latin & Engl., liby. bkplt., blind-stps. on limitation
lf. & title-p., accession no. at foot of p. 1, purple
crushed three-qtr. mor., partly unc. (SG. Jan.12;
242) $200
- - Anr. Edn. Ill.:– André Derain (drawings), Baudier (engrs.). Paris, priv. ptd., 1951. *(30) with suite*
on vélin d'Arche. Fo. 36 orig. drawings, 44 engrs.,
leaves, box; extra-ill. with sigd. orig. pen drawing
by Derain on indigo paper. (HD. Sep.22; 231)
                                              Frs. 4,200
- The Complete Works. Trans.:– Jack Lindsay.
Ill.:– Norman Lindsay. L., Fanfrolico Pr., 1927.
Bdg. not stated, cover stained. (JL. Jul.15; 569)
                                              Aus. $220
- - Anr. Edn. Trans.:– Jack Lindsay. Ill.:– Norman
Lindsay. L., Fanfrolico Pr., [1927]. *(650) num-*
bered & sigd. by trans. Sm. fo. Hf. vell. (SG.
Mar.29; 141) $250
- - Anr. Edn. Trans.:– Jack Lindsay. Ill.:– Norman
Lindsay. L., Fanfrolico Pr., n.d. *(100) numbered,*
for Australia. Bdg. not stated; pres. copy, inscr. by
artist, Harry F. Chaplin copy. (JL. Jul.15; 250)
                                              Aus. $280

PETRUS, Galatinus
- Opus toti Christiane Republice Maxime Utile, de
Arcanis Catholice Veritatis, contra Obstinatissimum
Judeoru[m] ... ex Talmud, aliisque Hebraicis Libris
... 1518. *1st. Edn.* Fo. On last lf. dedication letter
Pope Leo X, 9 Apr. 1518 to author old mntd., sm.
hole at head, title with pale old liby. stp., 18th. C.
leath. gt. (R. Oct.11; 27)   DM 3,500

PETRUS LOMBARDUS
- Sententiarum Libri IV, cum Conclusionibus Hen-
rici Gorichem. Basle, Nicolas Kesler, 23 May 1487.
Fo. Rubricated, cont. stpd. roan over wood bds.,
richly decor., brass corners & centre, clasps
incompl.; from Fondation Furstenberg-Beaumesnil.
[H. 10194; BMC III, 764; Goff P490] (HD. Nov.16;
10)   Frs. 25,000

PETTER, Nicolaes
- Klare Onderrichtinge der Voortreff. Worstel-
Konst ... en Alle Aengrepen, Borst-stooten, Vuyst-
slagen ... Ill.:– Rom. de Hooghe. Amst., 1674. *1st.*
Edn. 4to. Some margin dampstaining at end, cont.
hf. cf. (VG. Sep.14; 1024)   Fls. 1,800

PETTERSON, Carl Anton
- Lappland. Stockholm, 1866. Ob. fo. Lge. folding
map, 20 chromolitho. views on India paper mntd.,
collation & other details inserted by cont. hand,
unbnd. in cont. (publisher's) cl. portfo. (S. Dec.1;
311)   *Quaritch.* £420

PETTIGREW, Thomas Joseph
- History of Egyptian Mummies. Ill.:– George
Cruikshank. 1834. *[1st. Edn.].* 4to. 13 engraved &
litho. plts. (dampstained), hf.-title, last errata lf.,
soiled, mod. mor.-bkd. cl. (BBA. Feb.9; 198)
                                              Museum Books. £65
- - Anr. Copy. Sm. fo. Hf.-title, errata lf., 5 p.
subscribers list, some plts. misbnd., mod. three-qtr.
mor., orig. cover label, noting this as a 'Subscription
Copy, Two Guineas', mntd. on blank fly-lf. (SG.
Mar.29; 246) $225

PETTUS, Sir John
- Fodinae Regales. Or the History ... of the Chief
Mines & Mineral Works in England, ... L., 1670.
1st. Edn. Fo. Corrigenda lf. present, sm. hole in Xl
affecting a few letters, 1 lf. torn, cont. cf., a little
rubbed. [Wing P1908] (BBA. May 3; 58)
                                              Cavendish Rare Books. £320

PETTY, William
- Hiberniae Delineatio. L., 1685 or later. Fo. Port.
frontis., double-p. engraved title & contents lf.
(2nd. state, with wording 'Our Privilegio Regis'
added), 37 maps on 36 mapsheets, including 27
double-p. & 6 folding, lr. left corner of the map of
Cork restored using portion of the 1875 restrike, 1

or 2 additional folds strengthened (as usual), mod.
hf. vell. (S. Dec.1; 150)   *Burgess.* £5,600
- The Petty Papers. L., 1927. 2 vols. No bdg. stated.
(With:) - Calendar of State papers, Ireland & Domestic, 1625-1681. L., 1900 & 1921. 2 vols. Royal
8vo. No bdg. stated. *(With:)* - Calendar of Documents Relating to Ireland, 1171-1284. L., 1875-77.
2 vols. Royal 8vo. No bdg. stated. (GM. Dec.7;
109)   £60
- The Political Anatomy of Ireland, to which is
Added Verbum Sapienti. L., 1691. *1st. Edn.* Sm.
8vo. Rebnd. cf., by Rivière. [Wing P1931] (GM.
Dec.7; 337)   £1,350

PETZENDORFER, L.
- Schriftenatlas Neue Folge: Eine Sammlung von
Alphabeten, Initialen und Monogrammen. Stuttgart,
ca. 1900. Fo. 141 col. plts., cl. (SG. Aug.25; 38)
                                                   $100

PEU, Philippe
- La Pratique des Acouchemens. Paris, 1694. *Only*
Edn. Cont. mott. cf., richly gt., rubbed, extremities
slightly worn, liby. bkplt., few stps. (SG. Mar.22;
248) $475

PEUCER, Daniel
See— GESSNER, C.F. — PEUCER, Daniel —
LESSER, F.C.

PEUCHET, J.
- Dictionnaire Universel de la Géographie Commer-
cante. Paris, 1798-1800. 5 vols. 4to. Some spotting,
cont. tree cf. (TA. Aug.18; 272)   £92
- Statistique Elementaire de la France. Paris, 1805.
Hf. roan. (HD. Feb.22; 164)   Frs. 2,300

PEURBACH, G.
See— PTOLEMAEUS, Claudius — PEURBACH,
G.

PEYER, Johann Conrad
- Parerga Anatomica et Medica Septem; Exerci-
tatio Anatomico-medica de Glandulis Intestinorum.
Schaffhausen, 1677. 1st. pt. lacks 1 lf., slightly
spotted, pt. 2 very stained, cont. vell., very spotted.
(H. Nov.23; 248)   DM 660

PEYRE, Marie Joseph
- Oeuvres d'Architecture. Paris, 1795. Fo. Cont. hf.
roan, worn. (HD. Dec.2; 140)   Frs. 3,000

PEYSSONEL
- Situation Politique de la France et ses Rapports
Actuels avec toutes les Puissances de l'Europe.
Neuchatel, 1790. 2 vols. in 1. Roan, corners. (HD.
Feb.22; 165)   Frs. 1,200

PEZAY, M., Marquis de
- Cartes Géographiques, Topographiques, Plans, des
Marches, Campemens, Villes, Sièges, Batailles ...
en Italie 1745 & 1746 par les Armées combinées
de France et d'Espagne. [Paris], 1775. Lge. fo. 1
engraved title lf. & 70 engraved maps (3 double-
p.), cont. marb. leath., gold decor., gt. spine, slightly
rubbed & bumped. (D. Nov.23; 772)   DM 790

PEZZI, Lorenzo
- La Vigna del Signore. Venice, 1589. Sm. 4to.
Lacks Ll, old vell., soiled, ties (1 brkn.). (CSK.
Jul.13; 72)   £100

PFANNSTIEL, Arthur
- Modigliani. Preface:– Louis Latourrettes. Paris,
[1929]. Lge. 8vo. 6 cold. plts., ills., liby. buckram.
(SG. May 3; 258) $200

PFEIFFER, Carl
- Systematische Anordnung und Beschreibung
Deutscher Land-und Wasser-Schnecken. Cassel,
1821. 8 hand-cold. engraved plts. *(Bound with:)* -
Naturgeschicte Deutscher Land– und Süsswasser-
Mollusken. Weimar, 1821-28. 3 pts. 16 hand-cold.
engraved plts., pts misbnd., some foxing. Together
4 pts. in 1 vol. 4to. Cont. diced russ. gt., rebkd. (C.
Jun.27; 128)   *Needham.* £170

PFEIFFER, Ida
- Reise nach Madagaskar. Wien, 1861. *1st. Edn.* 2
vols. Cont. bds., mntd. orig. wraps. (R. Apr.5; 2709)
                                              DM 800
- - Anr. Copy. 2 vols. Bds., orig. upr. cover wraps.

pasted on, lightly soiled. (HK. Nov.8; 808)
                                              DM 420

PFEIFFER, M.A.
[-] Berichte aus der Staatlichen Porzellan Man-
ufaktur Meissen. Ill.:– Scheurich, Langer, Marcks,
Scheibe & Niemeyer. [Leipzig, 1920]. *(250).* Lge.
4to. Hf. vell. (H. May 22; 117)   DM 1,400

PFEUFER, B.
- Beyträge z. Bambergs Topograph. u. Statist. so
wohl älteren als Neueren Gesch. Bamberg, 1791.
Cont. hf. vell. (HK. Nov.9; 1334)   DM 460

PFINZING, Melchior
- Der Aller–Durchleuchtigste Ritter, oder ... Gross-
Thaten ... dess Heldens Maximiliani I ... unter
dem Nahmen Theur-Danck. Ill.:– L. Beck, H.
Burgkmair, H. Schäufelein & others. Augsburg,
before 1688. *9th. Edn.* Fo. Lacks supp. 58 pp.
'Lebensbeschreibung', frontis., title & dedication
with restored corner tear at top with slight loss,
18th. C. vell. (R. Apr.3; 77)   DM 2,200
[-] Die Geuerlicheiten vnd eins Teils der Geschichten
des Lobliche[n] Streitbaren vnd Hochberumbten
Helds vnd Ritters Tewrdannckhs. Augsburg, 1519.
2nd. Edn. 2nd. Printing. Lacks 1 blank lf., some
spotting, some sm. repairs, 18th. C. cf., gt. decor.
spine, covers, inner & outer dentelle, slightly
rubbed & bumped, upr. jnt. partly torn; Hauswedell
coll. (H. May 24; 1167)   DM 18,000

PFISTER, Kurt
- Deutsche Graphiker der Gegenwart. Ill.:– L.
Corinth, Kollwitz & Liebermann, Barlach, Beckmann, Heckel, Klee, Kubin, Kokoschka, Meidner &
others. Leipzig, 1920. 4to. 23 orig. ills., approx. 5
ll. slightly loose with slight margin tears, hf. linen,
orig. pict. wraps. mntd. (GB. May 5; 3088)
                                              DM 5,000
- - Anr. Copy. 4to. 23 orig. ills., 1 text lf. with
margin tear, orig. hf. linen, worn & spotted. (R.
Apr.3, 868)   DM 3,820

PFNOR, Rudolphe
- Monographie du Château d'Aret ... Paris, 1867. 4
pts. in 1 vol. Lge. fo 58 engraved plts. (2 cold.),
cont. hf. mor., spine defect. *(With:)* - Monographie
du Palais de Fontaine-bleau. Paris, 1863. Vol. 1
only. Lge. fo. 70 engraved plts. (1 cold. & 3 folding),
cl. (SKC. Mar.9; 1990)   £60
- Monographie du Palais de Fontainebleau Accom-
pagnée d'un Texte Historique et Descriptif par M.
Champollion-Figeac. Paris, 1863. 2 vols. Lge. fo.
Some light spotting, orig. hf. mor. gt. (LC. Mar.1;
19)   £55
- - Anr. Copy. 2 vols. Fo. 150 plts. engraved on
Chine, mntd., on guards, some double plts. count
as 2, 5 cold. plts., hf. red chagrin, decor. spine.
(HD. Feb.29; 32)   Frs. 2,500
- - Anr. Edn. Paris, 1863, 1863, 1885. 3 vols. Atlas
fo. 280 plts., many text ills. & decors., ex-liby., red
hf. mor. (SG. May 3; 279) $550

PFORZHEIMER, Carl H.
- The Carl Pforzheimer Library: English Literature
1475-1700. Ed.:– William A. Jackson. Designer:–
Frederic Warde. N.Y., Priv. Ptd., 1940. *(150) num-*
bered. 3 vols. 4to. Orig. cl. gt., partly unc.; frontis.
port. sigd. by Pforzheimer. (CNY. Dec.17; 573)
                                              $3,000

PHARMACOPOEA BORUSSICA
Berlin, 1846. *6th Edn.* Hf. leath., some old spotting & wear. (V. Sep.29; 1485)   DM 950

PHARMACOPOEA GANDAVENSIS Nobilissimi
Senatus Jussu Renovata
Gandavi, 1786. Errata lf. *(Bound with:)* ORDON-
NANTIE VAN HEER ENDE WETH DER STAD
GEND. Gend, n.d. Together 2 works in 1 vol. 4to.
Hf. cf. (LM. Mar.3; 188)   B.Frs. 8,500

PHARMACOPOEA GERMANICA
Berlin, 1882. *2nd. Edn.* Hf. linen. (D. Nov.23, 658)
                                              DM 1,250
- - Anr. Copy. Some slight spotting, cont. hf. leath.
(R. Apr.4; 1357)   DM 1,240

PHARMACOPOEIA COLLEGII REGALIS LON-DINI
1682. 12mo. Early sig. etc. on fly-lf., cont. panel cf., lacks 1 clasp. (BS. May 2; 58) £50

PHELPS, Elizabeth Stuart
[-] **Kitty Brown Series.** Phila., [1851-53]. *1st. Edn.* 4 vols. 12mo. Blind- & gt.-stpd. cl., light wear, orig. publisher's box, worn: Ken Leach coll. (RO. Jun.10; 2) $110

PHELPS & Ensign
See— UNITED STATES OF AMERICA

PHILADELPHIA
- **The Hospital of the Protestant Episcopal Church in Philadelphia: Its Origin, Progress, Work, & Wants.** Phila., 1869. *1st. Edn.* Sm. 8vo. Some yellowing to plts., orig. cl., gt. cover vig., covers slightly chipped, short tears to spine ends. (HA. Dec.16; 211) $120
- **Philadelphia Circulating Business Directory.** Ed.:– J.R. Savage. Phila., [1838]. 4to. Some foxing, orig. marb. bds., linen back; N.Y. Historical Soc. dupl., not collated, w.a.f. (SG. Oct.20; 64) $475

PHILADELPHIA MINERVA
Phila., 14 Mar. 1795-24 Dec. 1796. Nos. 6-99. Lge. 4to. Foxed, partly dampstained, approx. 8 nos. impft., later qtr. leath., cl., unc. (SG. Jan.19; 278) $250

PHILADELPHIA PHOTOGRAPHER, The
Ed.:– Edward L. Wilson. Phila., 1865-71, 1875, 1879, 1881. Vols. II-VIII, XII, XVI & XVIII, & 13 miscellaneous monthly issues, 1869-88. Tall 8vo. Not collated, various bdgs., some disbnd., 1 ex-liby., individual issues in orig. ptd. wraps., rubbed & chipped. (SG. May 10; 112) $1,900

PHILALETHA, Irenaeus [i.e. George Starkey]
- **Chymie oder Erklaerung der Natur und Vertheidigung Helmonts als ein Kurtzer ... Weg zu einem Langen und Gesunden Leben ...** Nuremb., 1722. 12mo. Stp. removed from title with slight damage, old bds., spine defect.; Dr. Walter Pagel copy. (S. Feb.7; 350) *Quaritch.* £150

PHILBY, Harry St. John Bridges
- **The Background of Islam.** Alexandria, 1947. *(500)* sigd. Orig. cl.-bkd. bds., d.-w.; pres. copy to Nina Hutton. (S. Apr.9; 47) *Loman.* £170

PHILIDOR, A.D.
- **Analysis of the Game of Chess.** 1777. *New Edn.* Some browning, cont. cf., worn. (CSK. Jun.15; 81) £60

PHILIP, John D.D., Missionary 1775-1851
- **Researches in South Africa.** L., 1828. 2 vols. Ill. & errata lf. at end of Vol. 2, some foxing, hf. cf., slightly rubbed. (VA. Oct.28; 222) R 210

PHILIPON, Ch.
- **Les Cent et un Robert Macaire.** Ill.:– after H. Daumier. Paris, 1839-40. *1st. Book Edn.* 2 pts. in 1 vol. 4to. Lacks 1 plt., 1 plt. in dupl., lr. margin slightly stained, hf. mor. gt. (VG. May 3; 374) Fls. 3,000
See— ALHOY, Maurice, & others

PHILIPON, Ch. (Ed.)
See— CARICATURE [POLITIQUE], Morale, Religieuse, Litteraire et Scenique

PHILIPON DE LA MADELAINE, V.
- **L'Orléanais.** Ill.:– Baron, Français, C. Nanteuil & Rouargue. Paris, 1845. *1st. Printing of engrs.* Lge. 8vo. Lacks errata & anr. lf., hf. mor., corners, by Champs, wrap. (HD. May 4; 393) Frs. 2,800

PHILIPOTT, Thomas
- **Villare Cantianum, or Kent Surveyed & Illustrated.** 1659. *1st. Edn.* Cf., rebkd. preserving orig. label. (PWC. Jul.11; 584) £740
- - **Anr. Copy.** Fo. Folding map reprd., few sm. holes along fold, cont. cf., spine reprd. [Wing P1989] (S. Mar.6; 444) *Frankland.* £550
- - **Anr. Edn.** Map:– R. Blome. Kings Lynn, 1786. Fo. Double-p. engraved map in cont. outl. hand-col., hf. cf., slightly worn. (S. Mar.6; 445) *Councer.* £140

PHILIPPE, Charles Louis
- **Bûbu vom Montparnasse.** Ill.:– Frans Masereel. München, 1920. *1st. Edn.* Orig. hf. linen. (D. Nov.24; 3133) DM 2,500
Bubu de Montparnasse. Ill.:– André Dunoyer de Segonzac. Paris, 1929. *(130) numbered with extra suite of plts.* 4to. Loose as iss. in orig. wraps., vell. portfo., s.-c.; pres. copy inscr. by ill. to Percy Turner. (BBA. Jun.14; 204) *Makiya.* £1,800

PHILIPPS, Henry
- **A Treatise Enumerating the Most Illustrious Families of England who Have Been Raised to Honour & Wealth by the Profession of the Law.** L., 1686. *1st. Edn.* 2 pts. in 1 vol. Sigs. irregular in 2nd. pt., cont. owner's inscr. of Thomas Thoroton inserted on front free end-paper, recent hf. mor. [Wing P2023] (BBA. May 3; 168) *Meyer-Boswell.* £90

PHILIPPSON, Johanes 'Sleidanus'
- **Commentariorvm de Statv Religionis et Reipvblicae, Carolo Quinto Caesare, Libri XXVI ... M. Bevtheri ... Commentariorvm de Rebvs in Evropa et aliis quibusdam Orbis Terrarum Illustrioribus Regnis, eodem Carolo V. Imperatore gestis Libri VIII ... M. Delio ... interprete ...** Strassburg, 1568. 2 pts. in 1 vol. Fo. Title with deleted owners mark, creased, stained in upr. margin thro.-out, cont. blind-tooled pig over wood bds., slightly spotted & with sm. defects., 2 clasps, defect. (HK. May 15; 242) DM 600
- - **Anr. Edn.** Strassburg, 1576. Cont. stpd. pig over wood bds., decor., ports. of Charles V & Johann Friedrich, Elector of Saxony, clasps; from Fondation Furstenberg-Beaumesnil. (HD. Nov.16; 171) Frs. 1,300

PHILIPS, C.
[-] **Verzaameling van alle de Huizen en Prachtige Gebouwen langs de Keizers en Heere-Grachten der Stadt Amsteldam.** Amst., [1768-71]. Fo. Title, subscribers list, 24 double-p. plts., some stains, a few sm. margin wormholes, bds., back defect. (B. Apr.27; 523) Fls. 1,900

PHILIPS, John [Pseud.?], Midshipman
- **An Authentic Journal of the late Expedition Under the Command of Commodore Anson.** L., 1744. *1st. Edn.* Inner margin of title-p. torn, sm. hole in F7, a few inner margins dampstained, cont. cf. gt., worn; the Rt. Hon. Visc. Eccles copy. [Sabin 62548] (CNY. Nov.18; 223) $100

PHILIPS, John, poet, 1676-1709
[-] **Cyder a Poem.** 1708. Cont. cf.; Evelyn Liby. bkplt. (CSK. Jun.15; 95) £70
- - **Anr. Edn.** L., 1791. Cont. cf. gt. (P. Nov.24; 257) *Fletcher.* £50

PHILIPS, Katherine
[-] **Poems.** L., 1664. *1st. Edn. [Unauthorised].* Imprimatur lf., errata, sigs. on endpapers, cont. sheep., some worming to spine. [Wing 2032] (SPB. May 16; 111) $300

PHILISTINE (The): A Periodical of Protest
East Aurora [N.Y.], 1895-1915. Vols. 1-41 no. 2, bnd. in 32 vols., & Young's Index to Vols. 1-20. Qtr. chamois, some wear, orig. wraps. bnd. in. (SG. Mar.29; 247) $225

PHILLIP, Capt. Sir Arthur
- **The Voyage of Governor Phillip to Botany Bay ...** L., 1789. *1st. Edn.* 4to. Engraved title with vig., 3 ports., 7 folding maps & charts, 44 engraved plts., cont. tree cf., spine gt. (C. Nov.16; 30) *Burgess.* £2,400
- - **Anr. Copy.** 4to. Engraved title, port. & 53 plts., plans & charts (1 with short tear), subscribers list, errata & advt. ll., repair to margin of Kangaroo plt. without loss, 1 or 2 prelims slightly loose, cont. mott. cf., worn. (S. May 22; 485) *Hammond.* £1,050
- - **Anr. Copy.** 4to. Port., engraved vig. title, 53 plts. & maps, hole in 1 plt., map torn & reprd. & 1 plt. torn lacking margins & laid down, hf. cf., reprd. (P. Feb.16; 151) £900
- - **Anr. Copy.** 4to. Engraved title slightly soiled, 45 (of 53) plts., plans & charts, errata & advt. ll., lacks port. frontis. & subscribers list, some stains, short tears, errata lf. inscr. in early hand 'a few of

the earliest impressions have H. Webber inv. on the Vignette in the title page; – as in this copy', mod. hf. mor., s.-c., w.a.f. (S. May 22; 484) *Smith.* £420
- - **Anr. Copy.** 4to. Port. frontis., vig. title, 50 (of 55) engraved maps & plts., some folding & linen-bkd., 1 hand-cold., subscribers list, some spotting, recent spr. & panel. cf., gt.-decor. spine. (TA. Aug.18; 49) £400
- - **Anr. Copy.** 4to. Cold. copy, the text on wove paper, the plts. on laid & wtrmkd. paper, corner defect to a folding chart, some mild foxing & offsetting, mod. crimson mor. (KH. May 1; 566) Aus. $4,000
- - **Anr. Copy.** 4to. 54 engraved maps & plts., 1 map with sm. tear at fold, title & a few plts. foxed, offsetting from some plts., hf. cf. gt., covers worn. (CA. Apr.3; 98) Aus. $2,000
- - **Anr. Copy.** 4to. Engraved title, 55 engraved maps & plts., title & frontis. foxed, sm. tears to plt. 12, plt. 19 torn & reprd., pp. 187 & 189 with margin reprd., top edge of plts. at end stained, some offsetting showing, rebnd. hf. mor. (CA. Apr.3; 133) Aus. $1,800
- - **Anr. Edn.** L., 1790. *2nd. Edn.* 4to. Text does not contain the 'History of New Holland' & ends at p. 1xxiv (as in the 1st. Edn.), catchword 'HIS' at foot of p. 1xxiv tallies with following advt. lf., natural history plts. hand-cold., 1 bnd. inverted, foxing & offsetting (not major), early tree cf., rebkd. (KH. Nov.9; 678) Aus. $3,300

PHILLIPPS, Sir Thomas
- **Catalogus Manuscriptorum in Bibliothecis Angliae, Cambriae, Scotiae, et Hiberniae, 1833 ...** 1833-37. Fo. 24 pp., sheets loose, stitching brkn.; Stanitz coll. (SPB. Apr.25; 339) $300

PHILLIPS, Edward
- **The New World of Words.** Ed.:– [John Kersey]. 1706. *6th. Edn.* Fo. 1p. advts. at end, slight browning, cont. panel. cf., gt. spine. (SKC. Jan.13; 2292) £50

PHILLIPS, Henry
- **Floral Emblems.** 1825. Hand-cold. title-p., 18 hand-cold. plts., orig. cl. (P. Sep.8; 206) *Hollingsworth.* £85

PHILLIPS, John, Surveyor
- **A General History of Inland Navigation.** L., 1793. *1st. Edn.* 4to. Engraved folding map laid down, some margin staining, Mm1 torn, cont. cf., crudely rebkd. (S. Mar.6; 311) *Walford.* £240
- - **Anr. Copy.** 4to. Folding map laid down, some margin dampstaining, Mm1 torn, cont. cf., crudely rebkd. (S. Jun.25; 336) *Walsh.* £90

PHILLIPS, John C.
- **A Natural History of the Ducks.** Ill.:– Frank W. Benson & others. Boston, 1922-26. *[1st. Edn.].* 5 vols. Lge. 4to. 102 plts. (74 cold.), 118 maps, hf. linen. (SG. Apr.26; 158) $1,200
- - **Anr. Copy.** 4 vols. 4to. Orig. cl.-bkd. bds., partly unopened, some soiling. (SPB. Dec.13; 880) $850

PHILLIPS, Philip
- **The Forth Bridge in its Various Stages of Construction, & Compared with the Most Notable Bridges of the World.** Edinb., ca. 1890. Ob. fo. Orig. cl. gt., faded, some wear, recased. (TA. Jul.19; 106) £54
- - **Anr. Edn.** Edinb., N.d. *2nd. Edn.* Ob. fo. Orig. cl., soiled, lightly rubbed. (CSK. Jul.27; 152) £70

PHILLIPS, Philip A.S.
- **Paul de Lamerie, Citizen & Goldsmith of London.** L., 1935. *(200).* Fo. Orig. buckram, slightly rubbed & soiled. (S. May 1; 689) *Robinson.* £200
- - **Anr. Edn.** 1935. *(250).* Fo. Some spotting, orig. cl. gt., some discolouring. (LC. Mar.1; 20) £130
- - **Anr. Edn.** L., Holland Pr., 1968. *Facs. Edn. (500).* Fo. Cl., d.-w. frayed. (SG. Oct.13; 182) $225

PHILLIPS, Philip Lee
- **A List of Geographical Atlases in the Library of Congress.** Wash., 1909. *1st. Edn.* Vols. 1 & 2 (of 4). Sm. 4to. Cl. (SG. Aug.4; 249) $100

PHILLIPS, Sir Richard
[–] **Modern London, being the History & Present State of the Metropolis.** 1805. Folding frontis., 1 folding plan (loose), 31 hand-cold. plts., 20 (of 52) plain plts. (spotted), lacks map, bds., defect., as a coll. of plts., w.a.f. (P. Jan.12; 49) *Orde.* £200
– – **Anr. Copy.** 4to. Folding frontis., engraved town plan (torn along fold & frayed at edges), 21 engraved plts., & 31 hand-cold. plts. of 'Itinerant Traders', lacks pp. 153-168, some margin dampstains & minor tears, cont. cf., old reback. (TA. Oct.20; 69) £180
– – **Anr. Copy.** Lge. 4to. Hf. red mor. gt. in cont. style, unc. (HK. Nov.8; 1039) DM 1,800
– **New Voyages & Travels.** [1819-23]. 9 vols. Some ll. detchd., cont. hf. cf., rubbed, w.a.f. (CSK. Jul.6; 107) £450
– – **Anr. Edn.** L., [1820-23]. Vols. 1-8 only (of 9). 202 engraved maps & plts., including 5 hand-cold., many folding, 2 maps torn, some folding plts. creased, some staining, cont. red hf. mor. gt., spines worn; the Rt. Hon. Visc. Eccles copy; w.a.f. (CNY. Nov.18; 224) $850

PHILLIPS, Tom
– **Ein Deutsches Requiem, after Brahms.** Tetrad Pr., 1972. *(50).* 4to. This copy marked 'a/p' & inscr. by Phillips 'for Ronald & Peggy Kinsey', each litho. sigd., with prospectus, loose as iss. in orig. folder, soiled, box. (S. Nov.21; 208) *Tyson.* £300

PHILLIPS, Watts
– **The Coast in Danger!!! A Laugh at the Threatened Invasion.** N.d. 6 × 91½ inches. Hand-cold. engraved concertina fold-out in 11 sections, some light spotting, orig. pict. bds., soiled. (CSK. Jun.1; 72) £120

PHILLPOTTS, Eden
– **A Dish of Apples.** Ill.:– Arthur Rackham. L., 1921. *(500) numbered & sigd. by author & artist.* 4to. Orig. cl. gt., 3 sm. red stains on upr. cover. (S. Nov.22; 355) *Appleby.* £210
– – **Anr. Copy.** 4to. Orig. cl. (SPB. Dec.13; 889) $200

PHILLY, John
[–] **Newes out of the East, ... or, a True Account of the Tryals & Sufferings, Jeopardies & Tortourings, which John Philly & William Moore passed through of late.** 1664. *1st. Edn.* 4to. Later cl.-bkd. bds. [Wing P2128 & N1035] (BBA. Jan.19; 154) *Jarndyce.* £90

PHILOBIBLON
Wien & Leipzig, 1929-40. Yrs. I-XII in 10 vols. & 5 pts. Linen, orig. wraps. bnd. in & 5 orig. wraps. (H. Nov.23; 112) DM 860
– – **Anr. Edn.** Ed.:– E.L. Hauswedell. Hamburg, 1957-79. Years I-XXIII (lacks Year VIII, pt. 3 & Year XXII, pt. 1). Orig. wraps. (H. May 22; 51) DM 620
– – **Anr. Edn.** Ed.:– E.L. Hauswedell. Hamburg, 1957-82. Yrs. I-XXVI in 103 pts. Orig. wraps. in s.-c.'s. (H. Nov.23; 113) DM 620

PHILOPATRIS
– **All for the Better; or, the World turn'd Up-side Down, being the History of the Head-Longs & the Long-Heads.** L., 1720. *1st. Edn.* Disbnd.; autograph dividend warrant laid in, sigd. by Lord Paisley & Burrell, 12 Apr. 1722. (SG. Feb.9; 336) $250

PHILOPONUS, Johannes
– **In Libros Priorum Resolutiorum Aristotelis Commentariae Annotatationes.** Venice, 1541. *(Bound with:)* – **Commentaria ... in Libros Posteriorum Aristotelis.** Venice, 1542. *(Bound with:)* – **In Posteriora Resolutoria Aristotelis Commentarium.** Venice, 1534. Together 3 works in 1 vol. Fo. A few ll. spotted, some early notes & pen sketches of horses on title of 1st. work, 19th. C. vell. bds., Stanitz coll. (SPB. Apr.25; 341) $1,200
– **In Primos Quatuor Aristotelis de Naturali Ausculatione Libros Commentaria (Greek).** Venice, 1535. *1st. Edn.* Fo. Lge. copy, title reprd. at inner margin, early margin annots., sm. liby stp. on verso of title, old hf. vell. over bds.; Stanitz coll. (SPB. Apr.25; 340) $850

PHILOSOPHICAL TRANSACTIONS
Ed.:– Henry Oldenburg. L., 6 Mar. 1664-65. *1st. Edn.* Vol. 1, no. 1. 4to. Light browning, 1st. p.

soiled, strip added along inner margin of title, cont. MS. note on title, disbnd., some chipping along inner margin, red mor.-bkd. folding box; Stanitz coll. (SPB. Apr.25; 342) $250
– **A General Index ... from the First to the End of the Seventieth Volume.** Ed.:– Paul Maty. L., 1787. *1st. Edn.* Some spotting & light browning, mod. mor., orig. wraps. bnd. in, mostly unopened; Stanitz coll. (SPB. Apr.25; 343) $200

PHILOSTRATUS, Flavius
– **De la Vie d'Apollonius Thyanéen en VIII Livres.** Ill.:– B. de Vigenère. Paris, 1611. 2 vols. in 1. 4to. Glazed cf. gt., Louis XVIII arms, fleurs-de-lys, spine slightly wormed, lr. cover slightly rubbed; Bibliothèque Prytanée stp. on title, stp. of Bibliothèque du Roi, Saint-Cloud. (SM. Mar.7; 2448) Frs. 5,000
– **Les Images ou Tableaux de Platte Peinture ...** Ill.:– Antoine Caron, Jasper Isaac & others. Paris, 1614. Lacks 4 ll. (including figure of fisherman), cont. red mor. gt., Du Seuil decor, arms of Lefevre de Caurmartin, spine decor., turn-ins reprd., w.a.f. (HD. May 3; 116) Frs. 7,000
– – **Anr. Edn.** Trans.:– Blaise de Vigenère. Ill.:– Th. de Leu, Gaultier & others. Paris, ca 1615. Fo. Front. & 68 soft-points, some stains & tears, old cf., defect. (HD. Jan.30; 77) Frs. 2,250
– – **Anr. Edn.** Ed.:– A. Thomas Sieur d'Embry. Trans.:– B. de Vigrières. Paris, 1629. *3rd. Edn.* Wide margin, some light browning, some ll. with sm. tears in margin, cont. leath., spine renewed, partly restored. (R. Oct.11; 186) DM 600

PHILOTHEUS (Pseud.)
See– LUDWIG, Karl, Elector Palatine of the Rhine 'Philotheus'

PHIPPS, Constantine John
– **Reise nach dem Nordpol ... unternommen im Jahr 1773 ... aus dem Englischen.** Bern, 1777. 2 vols. in 1. 4to. Engraved dedication, 5 folding engraved maps, 6 plts., mod. cf.-bkd. bds. (C. Jun.27; 129) *Koch.* £250
– **A Voyage towards the North Pole ... 1773.** 1774. *1st. Edn.* 4to. Hf. cf. (P. Jun.7; 36) £300
– – **Anr. Copy.** 4to. Some spotting, cf., defect. (P. Nov.24; 21) *Scott.* £260

PHIPPS, Joseph
– **A System of Military Discipline for His Majesty's Army.** 1777. 8 plts., 1 torn. *(Bound with:)* FORTUNE, T. – **The Artillerist's companion.** 1778. Together 2 works in 1 vol. Cont. cf. gt. (P. Jan.12; 267) *Maggs.* £100

PHOBUS. Ein Journal für die Kunst
Ed.:– H. v. Kleist & A.H. Müller. Dresden, Feb. 1808. Yr. 1, pt. 2. 4to. Wide margin, title stpd., minimal foxing, orig. wraps. with 2 outline etchings in bd. box, partly loose. (HK. May 16; 2127) DM 2,100

PHOKYLIDES
– **Poema Nutheticon.** Trans.:– Jac. Locher. [Augsburg, Froschauer, after 5.IV.1500]. *1st. Edn. in Latin.* 4to. Title with sm. note & stp., slightly browned, margins foxed, bds. [H. 12984; BMC II 399; Goff P629] (HK. Nov.8; 312) DM 850

PHOTO CLUB DE PARIS
– **Première [Deuxième] Exposition d'Art Photographique.** 1894-95. *(500). (30) on japan.* 2 vols. Fo. Sewed, spines brkn. with losses. (HD. Mar.21; 186) Frs. 4,500

PHOTOGRAPHIE
Ill.:– Moholy-Nagy, Man Ray, Cartier-Bresson, Steichen, Beaton & others. Paris, 1930-40. 9 vols. only (lacks 1938). Lge. 4to. Orig. wraps. (VG. Nov.29; 183) Fls. 900
– – **Anr. Edn.** Ill.:– after Man Ray, Sougez, Tabard, Blumenfeld, & others. N.Y., for 1937 & 1938. 2 vols. 4to. Spiral-bnd. ptd. wraps., chipped, 1st. vol. with minor repair. (SG. May 10; 117) $100

PHUI CHAMBERLAIN, Traurige 'Helden' im Lichte der Karikatur
Berlin, [1903]. Pict. paper bds., cl. back. (VA. Apr.27; 879) R 200

PIACENZA, Francesco
– **L'Egeo Redivivo.** Modena, 1688. Sm. 4to. Lacks 3 folding maps, cont. vell., edges worn. (C. Mar.14; 79) *Nicholas.* £550
– – **Anr. Copy.** Sm. 4to. Port. frontis., additional engraved title, 63 maps, including 3 folding, 3 gatherings inserted from anr., smaller, copy (last 2 ll. defect. in margins), flaws affecting text of L15, Oo7 & Qq3, some slight worming, 1 or 2 stains, cont. vell. (S. Dec.1; 346) *Noble.* £500

PIAZZETTA, Giovanni Battista
– **Studi di Pittura.** Ill.:– M. Pitteri & F. Bartolozzi. Venice, 1760. *1st. Edn.* Ob. fo. Lacks 2 copperplts., some plts. loose, cont. limp interim bds., partly loose, unc. (R. Apr.3; 870) DM 620

PIBRAC, Guy du Faure de
[–] **La Belle Vieillesse ou les Anciens Quatrains des Sieurs de Pibrac, du Faure et Matthieu ... Remarks:–** Abbé de la Roche. Paris, 1746. *New Edn.* 12mo. Cont. cf., spine decor. (HD. Nov.9; 58) Frs. 2,200
– **Les Quatrains ... Ensemble les Plaisirs de la Vie Rustique.** Paris, 1667. Sq. 8vo. Cont. roan, spine decor., slightly worn. (HD. Nov.9; 57) Frs. 1,000

PIC DE LA MIRANDOLE, J.
– **Opera qua exstant Omnia ...** Basilae, 1601. 2 vols. Fo. Foxing, 17th. C. cf., bdg. defect. (HD. Jun.29; 166) Frs. 2,300

PICARD, E.
– **Traité d'Analyse.** Paris, 1901-08. *2nd. Edn.* 3 vols. Unif. cont. hf. leath., sm. scratches. (HT. May 8; 458) DM 640

PICART, Bernard
– **Cérémonies et Coutumes Religieuses des Peuples Idolatres.** 1723-28. 3 vols. Fo. 127 engraved plts., cf., defect., as a coll. of plts., w.a.f. (P. Mar.15; 159) £110
– **Cérémonies et Coutumes Religieuses de Tous les Peuples du Monde, Représentées par des Figures ...** Amst., 1723-43. 8 vols. in 9. *(With:)* – **Superstitions Anciennes et Modernes Préjugés Vulgaires qui ont induit les Peuples à des Usages et à des Pratiques contraires à la Religion.** Amst., 1733-36. 2 vols. Together 11 vols. Fo. 266 plts., lacks frontis. (as often), cont. marb. cf. gt. (HD. May 3; 12) Frs. 6,500
– – **Anr. Edn.** Ill.:– Bernard Picart. Amst. & Paris, 1789. *Nouvelle Edn.* 4 vols. in 2. Lge. fo. About 260 engraved plts., some folding, early cf. (SG. Apr.26; 159) $850
– **The Ceremonies & Religious Customs of Various Nations of The Known World.** 1733-34. 4 vols. only. Fo. Cont. mott. cf. gt. (P. Sep.8; 84) *Shapero.* £340
[–] **Histoire des Ordres Monastiques Religieux et Militaires.** Paris & Douai, 1714-19. 8 vols. 4to. Cont. vell., slightly worn, w.a.f. (BBA. Feb.23; 35) *Thorp.* £220
– **Histoire des Religions et des Moeurs de tous les Peuples du Monde.** 1816, 1819. 6 vols. 4to. Cont. bds. (HD. Jun.29; 165) Frs. 3,600
– **Histoire Générale des Cérémonies ... de tous les Peuples du Monde.** Paris, 1741. 6 vols. Fo. Some browning & slight foxing, cont. mott. cf. gt., as a coll. of plts., w.a.f. (SPB. Dec.13; 882) $200
– **Naaukeurige Beschryving der Uitwendige Godtsdienst-Plichten, Ker-Zeden en Gewoontens van alle Volkeren der Waereldt.** Trans.:– A. Moubach. Ill.:– B. Picart. Amst., Den Haag & Rotterdam, 1727-38. 6 vols. Fo. Some stains, some ll. lightly browned, cont. vell. (H. May 22; 513) DM 2,200
– – **Anr. Copy.** 6 vols. Fo. Lacks 1 plt., some staining in 1 vol., few quires slightly foxed, cont. hf. cf., spines gt. (VG. Sep.14; 1348) Fls. 1,600
– **Neueröffneter Musen-Tempel.** Preface:– Chr. G. Stockman. Amst. & Leipzig, 1754. Lge. fo. Wide margin, 1 lf. with sm. ink stain, some light foxing or browning, cont. leath. gt., worn & bumped. (HK. Nov.9; 2029) DM 1,000
– **Recueil de Lions, dessinez d'après Nature par Divers Maitres.** Ill.:– after Durero, Rembrandt & Le Brun. Amst., 1729. *1st. Edn.* Ob. 4to. 2-cold. port. with vig., frontis., 42 etchings, linen. (DS. Nov.25; 2138) Pts. 32,000
– **Le Temple des Muses.** Amst., 1733. *[1st. Edn.].* 1 vol. Fo. Most ll. browned, cont. mott. cf., rubbed. *(With:)* – **Numismata aerea selectiora maximi**

PICART, Bernard -*Contd.*

moduli e Museo Pisani. Venice, ca. 1750. 1 vol. Fo. Orig. limp bds., worn. (BBA. Feb.23; 44)
Weston. £160
- - **Anr. Copy.** Fo. Linen, corners. (DS. Oct.28; 2152)
Pts. 85,000
- - **Anr. Copy.** Lge. fo. Leath., defect. (DS. Feb.24; 2145)
Pts. 80,000

PICASSO, Pablo

- **Carnet Picasso Paris 1900.** Intro:– R.M. Subirana. Barcelona, 1972. *(1040) numbered.* 2 vols. 8vo. & 12mo. Spanish, Fr. & English text, s.-c. (DS. Oct.28; 2143)
Pts. 34,000
- **Eaux-fortes Originales pour des Textes de Buffon.** Paris, 1942. *(226) numbered on vélin de Vidalon.* Fo. Crushed mor., partly unc., gt. doubls. & endpapers, cf.-lined mor.-edged s.-c. (C. May 30; 192)
Sims & Reed. £3,200
- - **Anr. Copy.** Lge. fo. 31 etchings, wtrmrkd. paper, wraps., s.-c. (DS. Oct.28; 2123)
Pts. 850,000
- **Le Gout du Bonheur.** N.Y., Abrams, [1970]. *(105) numbered, on pure rag Velin d'Arches, with proof etching sigd. in pencil.* Sm. fo. 71 plts. from orig. drawings, some cold., heavy linen, unbnd., matching linen folding-case, cf. clasp. (SG. Apr.26; 161)
$1,400
- **Grace et Mouvement.** Ed.:–Louis Grosclaude. Zurich, [1943]. *(250) numbered on velin paper, sigd. by ed.* Sm. fo. Unbnd. as iss., ptd. wraps., veil.-bkd. s.-c., box worn; inscr. by ed. to Erica Van der Hoeft, 1947, inscr again to Hoeft on box. (SG. Jan.12; 292)
$110
- **Linogravures.** Paris, 1962. *1st. Edn.* Fo. 45 linocuts, publishers cl., s.-c. (DS. Feb.24; 2117)
Pts. 90,000
- **Picasso 347.** N.Y., [1970]. 2 vols. Ob. 4to. Cl.-bkd. decor. bds., cl. folding case. (PNY. Jun.6; 542)
$250
- **Quarante Dessins en Marge du Buffon.** Paris, 1957. *(226) on vell. d'arches numbered.* Fo. 1 orig. lino-cut, many plts., orig. wraps., box; sigd. (DS. Feb.24; 2120)
Pts. 200,000
- **Sueño y Mentira de Franco.** N.p., [colophon: 'autorisé par l'artiste en date de 9 juin 1939']. *MS. Facs. Edn., (1000) numbered. (850) on vergé.* Ob. fo. Transcript in Spanish & Fr., unsewn in orig. wraps., folder & s.-c. (S. Nov.21; 37) *Sims.* £800
- **30 Eaux-fortes Barrées pour les Métamorphoses d'Ovide.** 1931. *(100) numbered on vélin de Rives.* 4to. Leaves, wrap. (HD. May 21; 140) Frs. 3,800
See— GUILLEN

PICCOLOMINI, Aeneas Sylvius
See— PIUS II, Pope, Aeneas Sylvius Piccolomini

PICCOLOMINI, Alessandro

[-] **De la Sfera del Mondo.** Venice, 1540. *1st. Edn.* 4to. 2 title-pp. with lge. circular devices, 47 woodcut maps, 2-lf. errata & register, 1st. errata badly defect., some marginal foxing, cont. vell., worn & stained, no flyll. (SG. Apr.26; 162)
$750
- - **Anr. Copy.** 2 pts. in 1 vol. Sm. 4to. 20 ll. misbnd. between sigs. P & V of 2nd. pt., some staining, last 2 ll. detchd., cont. limp vell., worn & stained, sm. portion of cover gnawed, inner bdg. brkn. with slight tear to title-p. (CNY. May 18; 162) $400

PICENI, E. & others
- **Boldini.** (I Grandi Maestri dell'800). Milan, n.d. *(800).* Fo. Leath. (SPB. Nov.30; 84) $250

PICERLI, Silverio
- **Specchio Primo di Musica** ... Naples, 1630. Sm. 4to. Title-lf. with cont. owners entry, some foxing in places, cont. brocade paper. (GB. Nov.4; 1507)
DM 800

PICHETTE, Henry
- **Dents de Lait, Dents de Loup.** Ill.:– Jacques Villon. Paris, 1949. *Orig. Edn. 1st. Printing, (211). (50) on lge. vélin de Rives with suite on Arches of plts. on double p.* Lge. 4to. Leaves, ill. wrap., box. (HD. May 21; 141)
Frs. 2,200
- - **Anr. Edn.** Ill.:– Jacques Villon. Paris, 1959. *(211) numbered. (3) on japon nacré, sigd. by author, artist & publisher, with double-p. copper engr., bon-à-tirer for anr. ill., sigd. by artist, 2 double-p. ills. & wrap. on vell., & 2 suites on old japan &*

vélin d'Arches. Leaves, orig. wrap., unc., box. (SM. Mar.7; 2361)
Frs. 24,000

PICHON, Thomas Jean & Gobet, Nicolas
- **Le Sacre et Couronnement de Louis XVI.** Ill:– Patas. Paris, 1775. 4to. L.P., 2 engraved titles, folding plan, 49 plts., including 10 double-p., cont. marb. cf. gt., spine gt. (C. Dec.9; 119)
Meister. £400
- - **Anr. Copy.** Marb. mor., by Rivière, gold-tooled decor. (D. Nov.24; 4357)
DM 920

PICKERING, Charles
- **The Races of Man.** Boston, 1848. Vol. IX of Wilkes's 'United States Exploring Expedition'. 4to. Double-p. engraved col. map, 12 engraved col. plts., orig. cl., rebkd. (SG. Oct.6; 299)
$175

PICKERING, Joseph
- **Inquiries of an Emigrant: The Narrative of an English Farmer, 1824-1830, during which Period he Traversed the United States & Canada.** L., 1832. *3rd. Edn.* Sm. 8vo. Lacks map (?), mod. cf. gt. (SG. Jan.19; 306)
$200

PICKERING, William
[-] **The Tale of the Basyn & the Frere & the Boy: Two Early Tales of Magic Printed from Manuscripts preserved in the Public Library of the University of Cambridge.** Preface:– Thomas Wright. L., 1836. 16mo. Orig. qtr. gt. mor., rose bds., unc.; from liby. of F.D. Roosevelt, inscr. by him. (SG. Mar.15; 65)
$225

PICO DELLA MIRANDOLA, Giovanni Francesco or Johannes
- **Cabalistarum Selectiora, Obscuriora' que Dogmata.** Ed.:– A. Burgonovensus. Venice, 1569. *1st. Edn.* Light staining near end, 8 ll. cut close, a little offsetting in margin, mod. blind-tooled, pig. (R. Oct.11; 95)
DM 950
[-] **Disputationes adversus Astrologos.** Bologna, Bened. Hector, XVI. Jul. 1495 [1496]. Fo. Lacks title lf. & last 3 ll. including 1 blank & privilege, 3 ll. partly bkd. in margin, stained, hf. vell. (H. 12992; Goff P632] (HK. May.15; 218) DM 1,100
- **Hymni Heroici Tre, una cum Commentariis.** Strassburg, 1511. Fo. Title-p. reprd., browned, cont. blind-stpd. cf. over wood boards, rebkd., edges restored. (SPB. Dec.13; 722)
$475
- **Libro detto Strega; o, Della Illusioni del Demonio.** Bologna, Apr. 1524. *1st. Edn. in Italian.* 4to. Title in woodcut border, woodcut device at end, ex-liby., little foxed, qtr. cl. (SG. Apr.26; 163)
$700
- **Opera Omnia.** Basle, 1557. Fo. Bkplt. removed from title-p. with damage to imprint, sm. hole in 1st. few ll., sig. on title dtd. 1576, 17th. C. cf., spine gt., device in compartment; Dr. Walter Pagel copy. (S. Feb.7; 308)
Janssen. £380

PICOT, Emile
- **Catalogue des Livres composant la Bibliothèque de Feu M. le Baron de Rothschild.** Paris, 1884-1920. *1st. Edn. (400).* 5 vols. 4to. On rag paper, wraps., cl. (DS. Oct.28; 2261)
Pts. 78,000

PICTURE BOOKS OF OLD MASTERS [spine title]
N.p., ca. 1895. 3 vols. Lge. 8vo. Preliminary text in Japanese, plts. captioned in Japanese, decor. wraps., bnd. with string, some minor soiling, cl. s.-c. fading round edges. (CBA. Jan.29; 267) $110

PICTURE LESSONS in Natural History
Ill.:–A.T. Elwes. L., [Bacon & Co., 1896-97]. Lge. fo. Inscr. by G.W. Bacon to F.W. Payne, with additional material relating to the production of the book, including 4 rough pencil & watercolour designs by Payne, some typed notes for text, & 6 A.L.s. from Elwes to Payne, 43 double-p. cold. plts., mntd. on stubs, folding table, 1 plt. lacks sm. corner portions, anr. loose, cont. cl. (S. Dec.20; 628)
Shapero. £160

PICTURES FOR GROUPING. The Realm of the Queen of Flowers
N.d. *(7th Edn.).* 4to. Fr., German & Engl. text, 4 pp. unbnd. hand-cold. litho. cards & 50 loose flower cutouts, orig. cl.-bkd. portfo., lightly stained, lacks ties. (CSK. Jun.1; 176)
£210

PICTURESQUE AMERICA
See— BRYANT, William Cullen

PICTURESQUE BEAUTIES OF ENGLAND & WALES
Ill.:– N. Whittock & H. Gastineau. 1829. 4to. Engraved vig. title, 53 plts., spotting, hf. cf., worn, upr. cover detchd. (P. Sep.29; 216)
£90

PICTURESQUE CANADA
Ca. 1870. 6 orig. divisions. 4to. Steel engraved frontis to Vol. 1, vig. title to each, orig. gt.-decor. cl., rubbed on spines & some covers dampspotted. (TA. Jun.21; 54)
£66

PICTURESQUE DESCRIPTION OF NORTH WALES
1823. Ob. 4to. Hf.-title, 19 hand-cold. aquatints (of 20), ptd. label on upr. pastedown, cont. hf. roan. (S. May 21; 73)
Rowles. £150

PICTURESQUE EUROPE
Ca. 1870. 5 vols. 4to. Mor. gt., rubbed. (P. Jul.5; 127)
£140
- - **Anr. Edn.** L., ca. 1875. 5 vols. Lge. 4to. 5 engraved titles, 58 (of 60) steel engraved plts., many wood engrs., some full-p., some foxing, cont. hf. leath., spine defect., worn, loose. (R. Oct.13; 3082)
DM 500
- - **Anr. Edn.** Ed.:– Bayard Taylor. N.Y., [1875-79]. 3 vols. Lge. 4to. Orig. hf. mor., worn. (SG. Sep.22; 243)
$125
- - **Anr. Copy.** 4to. 3 engraved titles & 60 steel engraved views, many wood engraved ills., some full-p., some text ll. slightly torn in upr. margin, hf. leath. (R. Oct.13; 3083)
DM 400
- - **Anr. Edn.** L., ca. 1875. Vols. 1,2,4,8 & 9 (of 10) in 5 vols. Lge. 4to. Engraved title & 30 steel engraved views, many text woodcuts, some full-p, orig. linen, partly loose. (R. Apr.5; 2932) DM 420
- - **Anr. Copy.** Vols. 3-5 in 3 vols. Lge. 4to. 3 engraved titles & 36 steel engraved views, many full-p. woodcuts, cont. hf. leath., worn, cover loose. (R. Apr.5; 2933)
DM 400
- - **Anr. Edn.** Ca. 1880. Vols. I-V. 4to. 60 steel engrs., cont. hf. mor., gt.-decor. spines. (TA. Nov.17; 80)
£75
- - **Anr. Copy.** Vols. I-V. 4to. 5 engraved titles, 60 steel engraved plts., many wood cut ills., some full-p., some light browning, cont. hf. leath., defect. (HT. May 10; 2785)
DM 720
- - **Anr. Edn.** Ed.:– Bayard Taylor. N.Y., 1880. 3 vols. 4to. Approx. 60 steel engraved plts., many text wood engrs., cont. cf., blind-stpd. (CR. Jun.6; 298)
Lire 420,000
- - **Anr. Edn.** L., 19th. C. 5 vols. Fo. 5 frontis., many steel engraved plts., linen. (DS. Feb.24; 2184)
Pts. 75,000
- - **Anr. Edn.** N.d. 5 vols. 4to. Qtr. mor., rubbed. (P. Apr.12; 195)
£150

PICTURESQUE TOURIST (The)
N.Y., 1844. *1st. Edn.* Sm. 12mo. Engraved title & 12 engraved plts., including 5 maps & plans (1 folding & partially hand-cold.), foxed, orig. gt.-pict. cl., very worn; from liby. of F.D. Roosevelt, inscr. by him. (SG. Mar.15; 62)
$175

PICTURESQUE VIEWS of the Principal Seats of the Nobility & Gentry in England & Wales
L., 1786-88. Ob. 4to. Engraved title, 100 views, some slight spotting & offsetting from plts., cont. hf. cf., worn. (S. Mar.6; 313) *Buckingham.* £210
- - **Anr. Edn.** Ill.:– Middiman, Walker, & others, after Courbould, Dayes, & others. L., [1788]. Ob. 4to. Engraved title, 99 (of 100) engraved plts., some text ll. cropped, 19th. C. hf. mor. (C. Dec.9; 120)
Clegg. £240

PIEPENBRING, G.H.
- **Deutschlands Allgemeines Dispensatorium.** Erfurt, 1801-03. *1st. Edn.* 2 vols. (of 3) in 1 vol. Bds., spine brown spotted & bumped. (D. Nov.23; 659)
DM 400

PIER'ANTONIO PACIFICO
- **Breve Descritzione Corografica del Peloponneso o'Moreä** ... Venezia, 1704. 4to. Lge. cold. folding map, cont. vell. (HD. Jun.29; 101) Frs. 4,200

PIERS, Harry
- Robert Field, Portrait Painter in Oils, Miniature & Water-colours & Engraver. N.Y., 1927. *(325)*. Sm. 4to. Mod. cl.-bkd. bds. (CSK. Feb.24; 209) £95

PIETERS, Charles
- Annales de l'Imprimerie Elsevirienne, ou Histoire de la Famille de Elsevier. 1851. Hf. mor. (P. May 17; 106) *Maggs.* £55

PIETRA SANTA, Prosper de
- La Corse et la Station d'Ajaccio. Paris, 1864. Some foxing, cont. Bradel hf. cl. (HD. Oct.21; 139) Frs. 1,200

PIEYRE DE MANDIARGUES, André
- Jacinthes. Ill.:– Alexandre Bonnier. Paris, 1967. *(85) numbered & sigd. by author & artist*, with suite of the etched plts. ptd. in black, each numbered & sigd. by artist. Sm. 4to. Orig. cf., lge. panel on upr. cover blocked in blind, s.-c., unc. (S. Nov.21; 55) *Christine.* £160

PIFERRER, P. (Text)
See— RECUERDOS Y BELLEZAS DE ESPANA

PIGAGE, Nicolas de & Mechel, Chrétien de
- La Galerie Electorale de Dusseldorff ou Catalogue Raisonné et Figuré de ses Tableaux. Basle, 1778. 6 pts. in 1 vol. Ob. fo. Some browning, early 19th. C. cf. gt., rebkd. with orig. spine preserved; bkplt. of Joseph Strutt. (S. Nov.17; 58) *Tumarkin.* £200

PIGANIOL DE LA FORCE, Jean Aymar
- Les Délices de Versailles de Trianon et de Marly. Amst., 1717. 2 vols. Some plts. lightly crumpled or slightly torn, lightly browned, cont. leath. gt., rubbed. (GB. May 3; 902) DM 1,000
- Description de Paris, de Versailles, de Marly, de Meudon, de St-Cloud, de Fontainebleau, et de Toutes les Autres Belles Maisons & Châteaux des Environs de Paris. Ill.:– Scotin. Paris, 1742. 8 vols. 12mo. Engraved folding plan of Paris (heightened), 73 plts., many folding, cont. cf., some jnts. strengthened. (HD. Mar.19; 122) Frs. 2,300
- Nouvelle Description des Châteaux et Parcs de Versailles et de Marly. Ill.:– Scotin l'Ainé after Sébastien Le Clerc. Paris, 1713. *3rd. Edn.* 2 vols. Sm. 8vo. Cont. jansenist red mor., Comte de Toulouse arms; pres. copy, from N ... liby. (HD. Jun.18; 38) Frs. 22,000
- – Anr. Edn. Paris, 1751. 2 vols. 12mo. Cont. marb. cf., decor. spines. (HD. Dec.1; 81) Frs. 2,550

PIGNA, Giovanni Battista
- Carminum Lib. Quatuor ... his Adiunximus C. Calcagnini ... Venice, 1553. *1st. Combined Edn.* Sm. 8vo. 19th. C. qtr. mor., spine gt. (SG. Feb.9; 300) $200

PIGOT, James & Co.
- British Atlas. Ca. 1834. Fo. 3 cold. folding maps, 43 hand-cold. country maps, 3 frayed at margins, hf. cf., defect. (P. Oct.20; 256c) £440
- National Commercial Directory of the Whole of Scotland, & of the Isle of Man. 1837. 2 pts. in 1 vol. Lge. 8vo. Each pt. with folding map, offset to title, orig. binder's cl., backstrip & upr. cover detchd. (TA. Jun.21; 177) £58
- Royal National & Commercial Directory & Topography of The Counties of Berkshire, etc. 1844. 13 hand-cold. folding maps on linen, cl.gt. (P. Oct.20; 4) £160

PIGOTT, Charles
- [-] The Jocky Club; or a Sketch of the Manners of the Age Pt. I-III. The Female Jocky Club ... L., 1793-94. 4 pts. in 2 vols. Extra ill. with approx. 75 port. engrs., later hf. mor. gt. (PNY. Oct.20; 273) $150

PIKE, Zebulon Montgomery
- An Account of a Voyage up the Mississippi River from St. Louis to its Source ... [Wash.?, 1807?]. *1st. Edn.* Without map (possibly not iss. with all copies), last 2 ll. in facs. by Lakeside Pr., some browning & spotting, liby. stp. on title, later plain paper wraps., cl. case; Littell bkplt. (LH. Apr.15; 352) $300
- Exploratory Travels Through the Western Territories of North America: Comprising a Voyage From

St. Louis, On the Mississippi, to the Source of That River ... L., 1811. *1st. Engl. Edn.* 4to. Bnd. without hf.-title, map offset onto title, cont. pol. cf. gt., rebkd. preserving orig. gt.– & blind-tooled spine; the Rt. Hon. Visc. Eccles copy. [Sabin 62837] (CNY. Nov.18; 227) $800
- – Anr. Edn. L., 1811. 4to. Hf.-title, 2 engraved maps (1 folding), cont. hf. cf. [Sabin 62836] (S. May 22; 332) *M. Mason.* £650

PILCHER, P.W.
See— OLDHAM, James Basil & Pilcher, P.W.

PILES, Roger de 'François Tortebat'
- Historie und Leben der Berühmtesten Europäischen Mahler ... Hamburg, 1710. Some browning in parts, cont. hf. leath. gt. (GB. Nov.3; 897) DM 400

PILKINGTON, Matthew
- Poems on Several Occasions ... Ed.:– Rev. Dr. Swift. L., 1731. S3-4 cancelled (as in all copies?), cont. cf. gt. (C. Nov.9; 152) *Ximenes.* £220

PILLARS OF THE STATE
Ca. 1760. Ob. 8vo. 1 plt. repeated, some staining, wraps., defect. (P. Apr.12; 293) *Vine.* £55

PILLEAU, H.
- Sketches in Egypt. 1845. Fo. Some light spotting or soiling, cont. hf. cf., rubbed. (CSK. Jul.6; 43) £220
- – Anr. Copy. Fo. 11 (of 12) litho. plts., 1 torn & reprd., orig. cl., worn. (P. Sep.29; 194) *Shapiro.* £130

PILLET, Roger
- Les Oraisons Amoureuses de Jeanne-Aurelie Grivolin Lyonnaise. Ill.:– Yan B. Dyl. Paris, 1926. *(500) numbered.* 4to. This copy with extra etching bnd. in, cont. mor., inner borders gt., woven silk doubls. & end-ll., orig. wraps. bnd. in. (S. Nov.21; 73) *Greenwood.* £65

PILLIUS
- Opus, seu Ordo, de Civilium Criminalium Causarum Iudiciis ... Ed.:– J. Goblerus. Basel, 1543. *1st. Edn.* Lightly browned, some light stains, 19th. C. hf. leath. (R. Oct.11; 96) DM 1,050

PILON, E. (Trans.)
See— ASBJØRNSEN, Peter Christen & Moe, Jørgen

PIM, Cdr. Bedford
- The Gate of the Pacific. L., 1863. 3 publisher's catalogues at end (28 pp.), orig. cl., upr. cover & spine gt., by Westley's, with their ticket, slight horizontal tear at foot of spine; the Rt. Hon. Visc. Eccles copy. [Sabin 62872] (CNY. Nov.18; 228) $150

PIMENTEL, Juan
- Sermon, que en la Solemne Fiesta que Celebro al Humano Seraphin. Mexico City, 1683. Sm. 4to. Unbnd. (SG. Jan.19; 244) $110

PIMPINELLO, V.
- Ain Oration oder Rede vor Rö. Kaiserl. Mai. Carolo V., Churfürsten etc. des Heyligen Röm. Reichs. Augsburg, 1530. 4to. End-lf. with sm. hole & ink mark, wraps. (R. Oct.11; 97) DM 520

PINARGENTI, Simon
- Isole, Che son da Venetia nella Dalnatia, et per Tutto l'Arcipelago, fino a Constantinopoli. Venice, priv. ptd., 1573. 4to. Engraved architectural title, 54 full-p. engraved maps & battle plans, 12 of which are sigd. by G.F. Camocio, several variously dtd. between 1568 & 1572, slight soiling or staining mostly in margins, cont. cf. gt., slightly worn, arms of Mitte de Chevrieres on covers; sm. owners inscr. of Paolo Bombini dtd 1637 & of 'Herrn Johann Freyhr Eigenhandtn' dtd. Mantua 7 Aug., 1630, w.a.f. (S. May 21; 145) *Hillman.* £10,000

PINCHART, Alexandre
- Histoire de la Tapisserie dans les Flandres. Paris, 1878-85. Fo. 25 mntd. 'photoglyptie' plts., some light foxing, three-qtr. mor., loose in bdg. (SG. Aug.25; 367) $160

PINCIO, Giano Pirro
- Annali, overo Croniche di Trento. Trento, 1648. *1st. Edn.* Fo. With last errata lf., cont. vell. (SI. Dec.15; 54) Lire 400,000

PINCKARD, G.
- Notes on the West Indies. L., 1806. 3 vols. Hf.-title in Vol. 1, hf. cf. [Sabin 62893] (S. Jun.25; 117) *Scott.* £140

PINDAR
- Carmina Olympica. Ed.:– G.B. Wheeler. Dublin, 1840. Cl., 2pp. of notes in Daniel O'Connell's hand, sigd. Daniel O'Connell, Dublin, initialled D.O'C. in 3 places. (GM. Dec.7; 131) £140
- Odes of Victory. Ill.:– John Farleigh. Stratford & N.Y., Shakes. Hd. Pr., 1929. *(250). (100) for the U.S.* 2 vols. 4to. Cl.-bkd. bds., worn, bkplts.; 2 autograph poems inscr. on fly-ll. of Vol. 1 by Padraic Colum. (PNY. Jun.6; 549) $110

PINDAR, Peter (Pseud.)
See— WOLCOT, John 'Peter Pindar'

PINDER, Ulrich
- Speculu[m] Patie[n]tie cum Theologycis Consolationibus Fratris Joannis de Tambaco. Nuremb., Aug. 1509. *1st. Edn.* 4to. Slightly browned & spotted thro.-out., old MS. marginalia, 1st & last ll. very stained, 2 end ll. with loss, sm. upr. corner extended up to lf. 8, title with bkd. side tear & sm. fault, mod. hf. vell., incunable paper cover. (R. Apr.3; 78) DM 1,800

PINDER, Wilhelm
- Die Deutsche Plastik des Vierzehten [Funfzehnten] Jahrhunderts. Munich, 1925-24. 2 vols. 4to. Orig. cl. (BBA. Nov.10; 256) *Quaritch.* £60

PINE, John
- The Procession & Ceremonies ... at the Time of the Installation of the Knights Companion of the ... Order of the Bath ... L., 1730. *1st. Edn.* Lge. fo. Vig. titles, 20 engraved plts., all but 1 double-p., partly hand-cold., text in Engl. & Fr., subscribers list, mod. hf. cf. (S. Dec.8; 319) *Dupre.* £200
- The Tapestry Hangings of the House of Lords: representing the Engagements between the English & Spanish Fleets in 1588. Ill.:– Gravelot & Lemprière after Pine. L., 1753. *2nd. Edn.* Lge. fo. Cont. hf. cf., rubbed. (VG. Mar.19; 187) Fls. 5,000

PINEL, Honoré
- ABC du Sportsman. Paris, 1869. 3 vols. only. Litho. plts. hand-cold., orig. bds. (CSK. Feb.10; 44) £75

PINELLI, Bartolommeo
- Avventure di Telemaco. Rome, 1828. Lge. ob. fo. Cont. hf. vell. (SI. Dec.15; 124) Lire 500,000
- Don Quichotte, album. Roma, 1833. 45 × 42cm. 65 engraved plts., cont. hf. cf. (CR. Jun.6; 64) Lire 450,000
- Gruppi Pittoreschi Modellati in Terra-Cotta ed Incisi all'Acquaforte. Rome, 1834. Fo. Self-port at beginning, cont. sewed, engraved orig. wraps. on upr. cover. (HK. Nov.9; 2031) DM 750
- Il Meo Patacca o vero Roma in Festa nei Trionfi di Vienna ... Roma, 1823. *2nd. Edn.* 40 × 25cm. Album, 52 engrs., hf. cf., lacks spine. (CR. Jun.6; 254) Lire 650,000
- Nuova Raccolta di Cinquanta Costumi de' Contorni di Roma. Rome, 1823. Ob. fo. Wide margin, a few plts. with some sm. spots, cont. hf. leath., slightly worn & bumped. (H. May 22; 391) DM 1,200
- Nuova Raccolta di Cinquanta Costumi Pittoreschi. Rome, 1816. Ob. 4to. Engraved title, 50 etched plts., title & some margins slightly stained, cont. bds., rubbed & worn. (C. Mar.14; 127) *Bifolco.* £280
- – Anr. Copy. Ob. 4to. Engraved title, 49 (of 50) plts., some spotting, hf. cl., worn. (P. Sep.29; 230) *L'Aquaforte.* £230
- – Anr. Copy. Album. 43 × 25cm. 50 engrs., lightly browned, lacks wraps. (CR. Jun.6; 65) Lire 1,000,000
- – Anr. Edn. Rome, 1817. Sm. ob. 4to. Engraved title, 50 uncold. plts., dampstains, mostly to margins, cl., soiled. (P. Mar.15; 103) £200

PINELLI, Bartolommeo -Contd.

− − **Anr. Copy.** Sm. ob. 4to. Some browning, hf. cf., upr. cover detchd. (P. Apr.12; 238) *Shapiro.* £190

− − **Anr. Copy.** 24 × 18cm. Album, light browning, hf. cf., marb. bds., slightly defect. (CR. Jun.6; 255) Lire 650

− **Raccolta di Cinquanta Costumi Pittoreschi.** Rome, 1809. Ob. 4to. Engraved title, 50 numbered etched plts., some lightly foxed, hf. leath., worn. (SG. Dec.15; 184) $450

− **Raccolta de' Costumi di Roma.** Rome, 1819. Ob. fo. 50 etched plts., some spotted or stained, some corners creased, title soiled & torn, sewn as iss. with vestige of lr. wrap. remaining. (S. Apr.30; 146) *King.* £250

− **Raccolta di N. 100 Soggetti li piu Rimarchevoli dell'istoria Greca** ... Roma, 1821. 21 × 30cm. Album, hf. cf., defect. (CR. Jun.6; 256) Lire 330,000

− **A Series of Plates with Descriptive Particulars, of the Most Interesting Facts Connected with the Life of the Celebrated Brigand Chief, Massaroni** ... 1823. Ob. fo. 11 engraved plts., cont. cl.; the Hinton House copy. (LC. Oct.13; 451) £50

− **Twenty Five Views in Rome, & its Vicinity.** L., 1827. 4to. Album, hf. cf., spine defect. (CR. Jun.6; 257) Lire 400,000

PINETTE, Giuseppe

− **Physical Amusements & Diverting Experiments** ... L., 1784. Hf.-title, spotted, 1st. & last few ll. stained, cl. (S. Dec.20; 682) *Huber.* £500

PINETTI DE WILLEDAL, Joseph

See— DECREMPS, Henry — PINETTI DE WILLEDAL, Joseph

PINGRET, Edouard

− **Voyage de S.M. Louis-Philippe 1er, roi des Français au Château de Windsor.** Paris & L., 31 Jan. 1846. Fo. 25 litho. plts., most in 2 tones, 1 in cols. on Chine, mntd., some foxing, publishers cl., spine lacks 1 piece. (HD. Feb.29; 33) Frs. 2,300

PINHAS HAI ANAV

− **Tosefet Bikkurei Katsir.** Venice, 1715. Sm. 4to. Title secured to front end-paper, qtr. leath., spine badly worn. (SG. Feb.2; 275) $300

PINKERTON, John

− **A General Collection of the Best & Most Interesting Voyages & Travels.** 1808-14. 17 vols. 4to. Vol. 3 lacks title, Vol. 4 lacks title & contents lf., Vol. 6 lacks all before B4, some browning, cont. pol. cf., worn, lacks 4 covers, w.a.f. (CSK. Jan.13; 108) £300

[−] **The Medallic History of England to the Revolution.** L., 1790. 4to. Later hf. cf. (S. May 1; 494) *Spring.* £70

− **A Modern Atlas.** 1815. Fo. 61 hand-cold. double-p. engraved maps, mod. hf. mor., orig. bds. (CSK. Jul.6; 65) £800

− − **Anr. Copy.** Lge. fo. Hand-cold. double-p. engraved maps, old bds., rebkd. & recornered with mor.; from liby. of Luttrellstown Castle, w.a.f. (C. Sep.28; 1757) £700

− − **Anr. Copy.** Fo. 60 double-p. maps, hand-cold. in outl., 1 map damaged in margin with loss & sm. loss of plt. surface, cf., defect. (P. Apr.12; 325) *Burgess.* £580

− **Modern Geography: A Description of the Empires, Kingdoms, States, & Colonies, with the Oceans, Seas, & Isles, in All Parts of the World.** L., 1802. *1st. Edn.* 2 vols. 4to. 45 engraved maps, including 3 folding, scattered foxing, cont. tree cf., extremities worn. (SG. Sep.22; 245) $200

PINO, P.B.

− **Noticias Historicas y Estadisticas de la Antigua Provincia del Nuevo-Mexico.** Ed.:− A. Barreiro & J.A. de Escudero. Mexico, 1849. Several margin notes & corrections (probably in his hand), cf., ptd. wraps. bnd. in; inscr. by Escudero. (SG. Oct.20; 284) $250

PINSKER, Leo

[−] **'Autoemancipation!' Mahnruf an seine Stammesgenossen von einem Preussischen Juden.** Berlin, 1882. *1st. Edn.* Tall 8vo. Binder's buckram. (SG. Feb.2; 136) $900

PINTHUS, K. (Ed.)

See— GENIUS Zeitschrift für Alte und Werdende Kunst

PIOSSENS, Charles de

[−] **Mémoires de la Régence de S.A.R. Mgr le Duc d'Orléans durant la Minorité de Louis XV.** La Haye [Rouen], 1729. *1st. Edn.* 3 vols. 12mo. Cont. cf., spines decor. (HD. Nov.9; 152) Frs. 1,250

PIOZZI, Hesther Lynch

− **Anecdotes of the Late Samuel Johnson, LL.D. During the Last Twenty Years of his Life.** L., 1786. *2nd. Edn. [so stated].* Sm. 8vo. Some light foxing, 20th. C. pol. cf. & marb. bds. by W. & G. Boyle, raised bands, slight wear. (HA. Feb.24; 208) $100

− **Letters to & from the late Samuel Johnson,.** L., 1788. *1st. Edn.* 2 vols. A few ll. spotted, later hf. cf., slightly rubbed. (BBA. Nov.30; 237) *Scott.* £110

− − **Anr. Copy.** 2 vols. Extra-ill. with 70 engraved ports. & views (20 cold.), crushed lev. mor., covers elab. decor., gt.-panel. spines in 6 compartments, upr. doubls. set with miniature ports. of Johnson & Piozzi in mor. gt. panels, watered silk linings, silk markers, by Bayntun, fleece-lined cl. box; A.L.s. from Piozzi to Samuel Lysons tipped in, w.a.f. (CNY. Dec.17; 587) $2,800

− − **Anr. Copy.** 2 vols. Errata slip in vol.1, some spotting, bds., unc. (SPB. May 16; 89) $200

PIOZZI, Hester Lynch & others

[−] **The Florence Miscellany.** Flor., 1785. *1st. Edn.* Pasted slips on pp.9, 20, 27, 68 bearing additional lines & on p.215 a pasted slip correcting a line, also on p.110 blank space for slip, 3-pp. engraved music, slight soiling, cont. cf., rebkd., orig. spine laid down; Isham copy. (SPB. May 16; 112) $650

PIPER, H. Beam

− **Four-Day Planet.** N.Y., [1961]. *1st. Edn.* Bdg. not stated, d.-w. lightly rubbed & creased; sigd. (CBA. Oct.29; 654) $200

PIPER, John

− **Brighton Aquatints.** Intro.:− Lord Alfred Douglas. L., 1939. *(55) numbered with the plts. hand-cold. by artist, sigd. by artist.* Ob. fo. Orig. buckram-bkd. bds., fitted case with mor. centrepiece with arms of Maj. Abbey. (S. Nov.21; 198) *Desk.* £700

PIPER VERLAG

− **Dem Verlag R. Piper & Co. zum 19 Mai 1924.** Ill.:− M. Beckmann, K. Hofer, W. Kandinsky, A. Kubin & others. München, [1923]. *(60).* Sm. 4to. 8 ills. sigd., orig. hf. vell. (H. Nov.24; 1934) DM 6,000

PIRANESI, Francesco

− **Monumenti degli Scipioni.** 1785. Lge. fo. Bds. (DS. Feb.24; 2143) Pts. 34,000

PIRANESI, Francesco & Pietro

− **Antiquités d'Herculanum.** Text:− S.E. Ph. Chaude. Ill.:− engraved by Th. Piroli. Paris, 1804-06. 26 pts. in 4 vols. 19th. C. bds., pt. wraps. preserved. (HD. Mar.19; 133) Frs. 1,900

PIRANESI, Giovanni Battista

− **Antichita Romane de'Tempi della Repubblica, e de'primi Imperatori.** Rome, [1748]. *1st. Edn.* Lge. ob. fo. Minimal soiling, 1 slight margin tear restored, cont. hf. leath., blind-tooled decor., cold paper cover, sm. faults & defects. (HK. Nov.8; 1085) DM 7,000

− **Della Magnificenze ed Architettura de Romani.** Rome, 1761-65. 3 pts. in 1 vol., including Supp. 'Osservazioni ... sopra la lettre de M. Mariette' bnd. at end. Lge. fo. 3 engraved titles, port., 41 engraved plts. (29 full-p., 8 double-p., 4 double-p. & folding), including the 3 plts. of friezes 'Essais de differentes frises' in Supp., but without the 6 unnumbered plts. usually found in the section 'Parere su l'Architettura' of supp., cont. marb. paper bds., spine ends chipped, slightly rubbed. (C. Mar.14; 15) *Guinevere.* £1,200

− − **Anr. Edn.** Rome, 1761[-65]. 1 vol. & the supps. 'Osservazione' & 'Della Introduzione', together 3-vols. in 1. Lge. fo. Italian & Latin engraved titles, port., 38 engraved plts., some double-p. or folding, 'Osservazione' with engraved title & 6 plts., 'Introduzione' with 3 engraved plts., some margin stains & soiling, disbnd. (S. Dec.1; 344) *Sims, Reed & Fogg.* £650

− **Diverse Maniere d'Adornare i Cammini ed Ogni Altre Parte degli Edifizi.** Rome, 1769. Fo. Double-p. engraved dedication, 1 sm. plt. (with text on verso), 3 larger plts., 66 full-p. plts., without the additional plt. 38A called for by Focillon, title & text in Italian, Engl. & Fr., mod. hf. cf. (C. Dec.9; 122) *Quaritch.* £1,900

− **Lapides Capitolini.** Rome, 1762. Hf.-title, folding plt. reprd., blank portion of last lf. cut away. (*Bound with:*) − **Antichita di Cora.** [Rome, 1764]. Hf.-title, lacks 3 plts. (*Bound with:*) − **Le Rovine dell Castello dell'Acqua Giulia.** Rome, 1761. Hf.-title, lacks 6 plts. Together 3 works in 1 vol. Fo. Some light browning or discoloration, mod. hf. parch. over marb. bds. (SPB. Dec.14; 77) $700

− **Opere Varie di Architettura Prospettive Grotteschi Antichita.** Rome, 1750 [1761]. The 'Grotteschi' or 'Capricci' plts. in early states without nos., & with the address on plts. 2-4, title with engraved vig., engraved frontis., 2 double-p. plans, 15 (of 16) full-p. engraved views, 10 hf.-p. engraved views, the 4 double-p. 'Grotteschi' plts. bnd. separately. (*Bound with:*) − **Trofei di Ottaviano Augusto.** [Rome, 1780]. Engraved title, 10 plts., some double-p., including plt. 34 from the 'Vedute di Roma' & view of the Arco di Aosta. Together 2 works in 1 vol. Fo. Unif. mod. hf. cf. by Sangorski & Sutcliffe. (C. Nov.16; 155) *Weinreb.* £4,500

− − **Anr. Copy.** Fo. Title with engraved vig., engraved frontis., double-p. plan & double-p. plt., 10 hf.-p. engraved views, 16 full-p. engraved views, without the 4 'Groteschi' plts. (as usual), unc., cont. vell.-bkd. paper bds. (C. Dec.9; 123) *Quaritch.* £1,100

− **Roman Architecture, Sculpture & Ornament.** Ed.:−William Young. L., 1900. 2 vols. Lge. fo. 200 facs. plts., plt. list, each plt. stpd. on blank verso, liby. buckram. (SG. May 3; 283) $250

− **Vedute di Roma.** Rome, ca. 1750. 2 vols. Lge. fo. Engraved title, & 124 plts. (of up to 138), mostly in Hind's state I or II, & with 2 plts. from Trofeo di Ottaviano Augusto in addition, fleur-de-lys in double-circle wtrmks., some faint spotting in a few margins, cont. cf.; Roger Peyrefitte bkplt. (S. May 21; 237) *Hammond.* £29,000

PIRANESI, Giovanni Battista & Francesco

− **[Collected Works].** Rome, 1750-84-n.d. In 21 vols. Fo., lge. fo. & lge. ob. fo. Etched prelims., including full-p. titles, dedications, etc., over 800 etched plts., some double-p. or folding, some slight spotting, a few stains, some plts. torn, 1 text lf. & 2 plts. patched in margin, orig. bds., parch. spines & corners, 1 cover stained, 1 backstrip defect. (*With:*) **PIRANESI, Francesco & others** − **[A Collection of 14 Etchings].** Rome, 1709-91. 1 vol. Atlas ob. fo. Wide margins, 14 etchings on 19 sheets, some folding, extreme edges of the larger sheets dust-soiled, cont. wraps., stabbed & stitched, untrimmed, upr. wrap. torn, edges frayed. Together in 22 vols. Baron Carl Bonde bkplts., gift of Gustavus III or IV, Kings of Sweden, thence by descent, as a coll., w.a.f. (CNY. Dec.17; 615) $170,000

− **Differentes Vues de Quelques Restes de Trois Grands Edifices qui Subsistent Encore dans le Milieu de L'Ancienne Ville de Pesto** ... [Rome, 1778]. Lge. fo. Etched frontis. (with title), 20 etched plts., cont. cf.-bkd. bds. (C. Dec.9; 121) *Hammond.* £15,000

PIRANESI, Giovanni Battista & others

− **Collection of Il Engraved Views of Italy & Switzerland.** Ill.:− G.G. Endner after Piranesi (3), Liebe, after P. Colson & W.F. Gmelin (3). N.p., 1792-94. Ob. fo. Rather dampstained & soiled, later cl.-bkd. bds. (BBA. Sep.29; 108) *Finch.* £55

− **Varie Vedute di Roma Antica, Moderna, disegnate e intagliate da Celebri Autori.** Ill.:− Piranesi, Bellicard, Duflos, & others. Rome, 1748. Ob. 4to. Etched title, 84 plts. (many dtd. 1750), of which 45 are sigd. Piranesi, early 19th. C. mor.-bkd. bds., spine gt., s.-c.; inscr. on fly-lf. from Count Sforza Mar. 1948, as a coll. of plts., w.a.f. (C. Mar.14; 78a) *Craddock.* £660

PIRATAS DE LA AMERICA y Luz a la Defensa de las Costas de las Indias Occidentales ...

Madrid, 1793. 4to. Cf. (DS. Mar.23; 2220) Pts. 40,000

PIRKEI AVOT
Commentaries:– Shlomo Yitzhaki [Rashi] & Moshe Ben Maimon [Maimonides]. Trans.:– Shmuel Ibn Tibbon. Mantua, 1560. Fo. Slight staining, mod. mor. (S. Oct.25; 309)
Ludmir. £480

PIRKEI RABBI ELIESER
Venice, 1608. *5th. Edn.* 4to. Mispaginated, owner's sig. on title, slight staining & worming, mod. mor. gt. (S. Oct.24; 48) *Toporwitch.* £220

PIROLI, Tommaso
– Le Antichita di Ercolano. Rome, 1789-97. 6 vols. 4to. 314 engraved plts., bds., some defects. (CR. Jun.6; 68) Lire 380,000

PIRON, Alexis
– Oeuvres Complettes. Paris, 1776. 9 vols. 16mo. Lacks port., cont. marb. roan gt., spines decor. (HD. Mar.27; 31) Frs. 2,200

PISA, Francisco de
– Descripción de la Imperial Ciudad de Toledo. Toledo, 1617. Fo. Vell. (DS. Mar.23; 2221)
Pts. 140,000

PISO, Gulielmus & Marcgraf de Liebstad, George
– De Indiae Utriusque Re Naturali et Medica. Amst., 1658. Fo. Engraved title-p., lge. text woodcuts, very sm. wormhole on lr. margin of text ll., old cf. [Sabin 63029] (SG. Apr.26; 165) $2,000
[–] Historia Naturalis Brasiliae. Leiden, 1648. Fo. Some discoloration. mott. vell., reprd. (S. Dec.1; 290) *Maggs.* £1,000

PISTOFILO, Bonaventura
– Oplomachia di ... del Maneglio e dell'Uso delle Armi ... Pica, d'alabarda e di Moscheto. Siena, 1621. Ob. 4to. Vell. (DS. Dec.16; 2643)
Pts. 90,000

PISTOLESI, Erasmo
– Il Vaticano. Rome, 1829-38. 8 vols. Fo. Hf.-title, cont. decor. vell. (SI. Dec.15; 125) Lire 750,000
– – Anr. Copy. 8 vols. Fo. Hf. vell., some spines defect. (CR. Jun.6; 260) Lire 550,000
– – Anr. Edn. Rome, 1838. 8 vols. Fo. Cont. vell. bds. gt., slightly rubbed; Richard Champernowne bkplt. (S. Dec.13; 472) £230

PISTORIUS, Johannes Nidanus
– Artis Cabalisticae. Basle, 1587. Fo. Discold. or browned in places, 18th. C. mott. cf. gt., spine gt., hinges worn; from coll. of Stanislas de Guaita, with his notes, Dr. Walter Pagel copy. (S. Feb.7; 309)
Ritman. £650

PIT, A. & others
– George Hendrik Breitner. Indrukken en Biographische Aanteekeningen. Amst., ca. 1902. Lge. fo. 90 plts. & ills., cont. hf. cf. gt., slightly soiled, spine slightly rubbed, 1 jnt. partly brkn. (VS. Dec.7; 23)
Fls. 500

PITMAN, N.
See– PALMER, E. & Pitman, N.

PITON, Camille
– Le Costume Civil en Frances du XIIIe au XIXe Siècle. Paris, [1926]. Lge. 8vo. Gt.-pict. bds. (SG. Mar.29; 92) $110

PITTMAN, Benn
– The Assassination of President Lincoln & the Trial of the Conspirators. N.Y., 1865. *1st. Edn.* Maroon mor. gt. (LH. Apr.15; 353) $170

PITTMAN, Philip
– The Present State of the European Settlements on the Mississippi. L., 1770. *1st. Edn.* 4to. Lacks hf.-title, 2 maps slightly split along a fold, some foxing, 19th. C. qtr. mor.; L'pool. Liby. bkplt. & stps., the Rt. Hon. Visc. Eccles copy. [Sabin 63103] (CNY. Nov.18; 229) $1,400

PITT-RIVERS, Gen. Augustus H.L. Fox
– Antique Works of Art from Benin. L., priv. ptd., 1900. 4to. Ptd. wraps. (S. Dec.13; 473)
Leicester. £70
– Excavations in Cranbourne Chase, near Rushmore, on the borders of Dorset & Wilts. L., priv. ptd., 1887-97. 4 vols. 4to. 1 or 2 plts. loose, publisher's

cl. gt., slightly worn & dampstained. (S. Dec.13; 215) *Salisbury.* £200

PIUS II, Pope, Aeneas Sylvius Piccolomini
– Commentariorvm de Concilio Basileae celebrato Libri duo ... [Basel], ca. 1525. *1st. Edn.* Fo. Title soiled, lightly browned, margins stained, especially at end & lightly frayed, 19th. C. vell., spine paper-covered. (HK. Nov.8; 314) DM 900
– Opera quae extant Omnia ... accessit Gnomologia. Basel, 1551. *1st. Coll. Edn.* Old MS. margin annots., some heavy browning at beginning, a few restored margin tears, cont. pig over wood bds., roll-stpd., dtd. 1578, rubbed & soiled, clasps brkn. (D. Nov.23; 134) DM 3,800

PLACCAET-BOEK VAN VLAANDEREN
– Placcaet-Boek van Vlaanderen. Ghendt, 1639, 1683-84; Brussel, 1740; Ghendt, 1727. *1st. pt. 2nd. Printing. (With:)* – Generalen Index ... der Materien Begrepen in de Vyf Placcaet-Boeken van Vlaenderen. Gend, 1767. Together 13 vols. Fo. Old cf., spines gt., some vols. worn. (LM. Oct.22; 138)
B.Frs. 40,000

PLACCIUS, Vincentius
– Theatrum Anonymorum et Pseudonymorum, ex Symbolis et Collatione Virorum per Europam Doctissimorum ac Celeberrimorum ... Ed.:– L.F. Vischer. Hamburg, 1708. *2nd. Edn.* Fo. 4 ll. with reprd. hole & few words supplied in old MS., cont. hf. vell. (VG. Sep.13; 565) Fls. 500

PLACE, Victor
– Ninive et l'Assyrie. Paris, 1867-70-67. 3 vols., including Atlas of plts. Fo. Perforation stps. in titles, plts. stpd. on versos, cl., brkn. or crudely taped, lacks spines, ex-liby. (RO. Dec.11; 276)
$300

PLACENTINIO, G.
– Epitome Graecae Palaeographiae ... Rome, 1735. 4to. Hf. cf. (HD. Dec.2; 142) Frs. 2,850

PLAKAT (Das): Elfter Jahrgang, 1920
Berlin, 1920. 4to. Many ills. mntd., several ll. loose, pict. cl., spine crudely taped, shaken, orig. pict. wraps. bnd. in, uncollated, w.a.f. (SG. Aug.25; 294)
$250

PLANCHE, James Robinson
– A Cyclopaedia of Costume or Dictionary of Dress. L., 1876-79. *1st. Edn.* 2 vols. Tall 4to. Mor., rubbed, 1 cover detchd., ex-liby. (RO. Nov.30; 151) $100
– Lays & Legends of the Rhine. 1827. Vol.1 only (of 2). 4to. Vig. title, 8 plts., cl.-bkd. bds. (P. Dec.8; 281) *Schuster.* £50

PLANCK, Max
– Das Princip der Erhaltung der Energie. Leipzig, 1887. *1st. Edn.* Pencillings & notes, browning, cont. hf. mor., corner-pieces removed, rubbed; Stanitz coll. (SPB. Apr.25; 345) $375
– Vorlesungen über Thermodynamik ... Leipzig, 1897. *1st. Edn.* Ptd. end-papers (some spotting), orig. cl., spotted; Stanitz coll. (SPB. Apr.25; 346) $200
– Zur Theorie des Gesetzes der Energieverteilung im Normalspectrum. — Ein Vermeintlicher Widerspruch des Magnetooptischen Faradayeffectes mit der Thermodynamik.— Ueber ein Verbesserung der Wein'schen Spectralgleichung. — Ueber das Sogenannte Wein'sche Paradoxon. — Deduction der Strahlungsentropie aus dem Zweiten Hauptsatz der Thermodynamik. Leipzig, 1900. *1st. Edn.* In 'Verhandlungen der Deutschen Physikalischen Gesellschaft im Jahre 1900', 2nd. Year. Hf. cl., marb. bds.; Stanitz coll. (SPB. Apr.25; 348) $2,100

PLANISCIG, L.
– Andrea Riccio. Wien, 1927. 4to. Orig. hf. leath. (R. Apr.3; 872) DM 1,300
– Die Bronzeplastiken Statuetten, Reliefs, Geräte und Plaketten. Vienna, 1924. 4to. Orig. cl., d.-w. (S. May 1; 691) *Sims.* £210
– Venezianische Bildhauer der Renaissance. Vienna, 1921. 4to. Liby. stps., some slight dampstaining, orig. cl., rubbed. (S. May 1; 690) *Larte.* £220

PLANS DES HOPITAUX ET HOSPICES CIVILS DE LA VILLE DE PARIS
Paris, 1820. Fo. 29 cont. cold. double plts. (1

folding), cont. decor. roan, loss from spine. (HD. Mar.21; 189) Frs. 8,000

PLANS DES PRINCIPAUX PORTS DE FRANCE
N.d. Ob. 8vo. Title & 29 plts., hand-cold., str.-grd. decor. mor. by Bozérian, watered silk liners. (HD. Jun.18; 39) Frs. 11,000

PLANS ET PROFILS DE L'EGLISE DU CHATEAU ROYAL DES INVALIDES
N.p., late 17th. C. Lge. fo. Lacks title, coll. of 14 lge. engraved plts. in soft-point, multi-folding, cont. old red mor., dentelle, royal arms, decor. spine with royal monogs. (HD. Dec.1; 82) Frs. 2,350

PLAT, Sir Hugh
– The Jewel House of Art & Nature. 1653. *2nd. Edn.* Sm. 4to. Paper loss at edges on p. 107, slight browning thro.-out. MS. sigs. in ink on title-p., old cf., worn, jnts. & corners reprd. (BS. May 2; 39)
£90

PLATEA, Franciscus de
– Opus Restitutionum. Venice, Johannes de Colonia & Johannes Manthen, 22 Jan. 1477. *Reprint of 1474 Edn.* [BMC V, 227; Goff F-758; HC 13038] *(Bound with:)* ANTONINUS, Saint, Archbp. of Florence – De Censuris. Venice, Johannes de Colonia & Johannes Manthon, 10 May 1480. *Reprint of 1474 Edn.* [BMC V, 236; Goff A-777; HC 1270] Together 2 works in 1 vol. 4to. Decor. cf., spine gt.; from Fondation Furstenberg-Beaumesnil. (HD. Nov.16; 64) Frs. 7,300

PLATH, Sylvia
– The Colossus. L., 1960. *1st. Edn.* Orig. cl., d.-w.; Frederic Dannay copy. (CNY. Dec.16; 269) $700
– Crystal Gazer & Other Poems. Ill.:– Ted Hughes. L., Rainbow Pr., 1971. *(400) numbered. (80) numbered, specially bnd.* 4to. Red cape mor., gt. dentelles, partly untrimmed, by Zaehnsdorf, cl. s.-c. (SG. Mar.1; 453) $150
– Lyonnesse: Poems. L., Rainbow Pr., 1971. *(10) numbered.* Sm. fo. Vell., partly unc., by Zaehnsdorf, cl. folding case. (SG. Mar.1; 455) $325
– Pursuit. Ill.:– Leonard Baskin. [L., Rampant Lions Pr., for] Rainbow Pr., 1973. *(100) numbered, with sigd. & numbered etching laid in.* Sm. fo. Cf., gt. dentelles, partly unc., by Zaehnsdorf, cl. s.-c. (SG. Mar.1; 456) $325
– Uncollected Poems. Turret Books. 1965. *(150).* Orig. wraps. (BBA. Nov.30; 286) *Belanske.* £70

PLATINA, or SACCHI, Bartholomaeus
– De Vitis Maxi. Ponti Historia Periocunda. Venice, 1518. Fo. Woodcut ill. on title, woodcut initials, title & last lf. remargined, some ll. frayed, lacks final (?blank) lf., last few ll. stained, later vell. bds. (S. Apr.10; 330) *Tile.* £90
– Historia della Vite de Sommi Pontefici. Venice, 1622. 4to. Cont. leath. (D. Nov.23; 136) DM 800
– Vitae Pontificum. Nuremb., Anton Koberger, 11 Aug. 1481. Fo. Wide margin, sm. stain on some ll., margin repair tp last lf., cont. pig over wood bds., blind stpd., clasps brkn. [HC 13047; Goff P-769] (H.D. Jan.30; 22) Frs. 4,100

PLATO
– Le Banquet ou de l'Amour. Ill.:– L. Lebègue. Paris, 1911. *(500). (26) numbered De Luxe Edn.* Double series of ills., monog. on printers mark, 1 cold. orig. ill, pold. cf., orig. wraps. bnd. in, gt. vig., corner-pieces, gt. decor., wtrd. silk doubls. & endpapers. (GB. May 5; 3099) DM 550
– Le Banquet de Platon. Trans.:– Jean Racine & Madame de Mortemart. Paris, 1732. *Orig. Edn.* 12mo. Cont. red mor. by Anguerrand, Du Seuil decor.; bnd. for President de Lamoignon, with his ptd. ex-libris & stp. (HD. Mar.29; 82) Frs. 40,500
– De Republica, sive de Justo. Ed.:– Edmund Massey. Camb., 1713. *1st. Engl. Edn.* 2 vols. In Greek & Latin, cont. panel. cf., slightly worn. (SG. Feb.9; 301) $100
– The Dialogues. Trans.:– B. Jowett. Oxford, 1892. *3rd. Edn.* 5 vols. Lge. 8vo. Crushed three-qtr. lev., spines gt., by Zaehnsdorf. (SG. Feb.16; 234) $275
– – Anr. Copy. 5 vols. Cl. over bevelled bds., a few sm. markings. (KH. Nov.9; 397) Aus. $170
– Opera; ... adjectis ad eius Vitae & Operum Enarrationem ab Rudolpho Agricola & Alcyone ab Augustino Dacho tralatis. Trans.:– Marsilius

PLATO *-Contd.*

Ficinus. [Paris, 13 Sep. 1522]. Fo. Sm. paper flaw in margin of Y1 with MS. entry at end recording baptism of Ranuccio Farnese on 28 Aug. 1530, cont. Roman mor., covers panel. blind, tool at inner corners of 2 frames surrounding central ornament, spine reprd. at top & bottom, lacks ties; woodcut armorial bkplt. of Ludovicus Momanus, from Jean Fürstenberg coll. with his bkplt. (S. May 10; 383) *Maggs.* £900

– **Opera quae extant omnia.** Ed.:– Ioannis Serranus. [Paris], 1578. 3 vols. Fo. Latin & Grk. text, wide margin, 3 ll. slightly defect., browned & spotted, vol. II with some staining, 18th. C. red mor., gt. spine, cover, inner & outer dentelles decor., slightly rubbed, 1 cover a little scratched, 20th. C. gold-tooled supralibros on covers; Hauswedell coll. (H.May 24; 1134) DM 3,000

– **The Phaedo.** Ill.:– Eric Gill. Gold. Cock. Pr., 1930. *(500)* numbered. 4to. Orig. cl., faded. (BBA. Oct.27; 162) *Primrose Hill.* £55

– – **Anr. Copy.** Sm. 4to. Gt.-decor. cl., unc., faded, spine label chafed. (SG. Jan.12; 131) $100

– **The Republic.** 1898. 2 vols. Mor. gt. (P. Jul.26; 177) £90

– **Timaeus sive de Natura Dialogus.** Paris, 1532. *1st. Separate Edn. in Greek.* Sm. 4to. A few slight wormholes, qtr. cf., spine torn. (S. May 10; 384) *McKiddrick.* £280

– **Tou Theiou Platonos Apanta ta Sozomena/Divini Platonis Opera Omnia Quae Exstant.** Trans.:– Marsilio Ficino. Lyon, 1590. Fo. Greek & Latin text, printer's device on title, initials, some light staining, slight marginal worming, early owner's inscrs. on title, early vell., worn & soiled. (SG. Apr.19; 150) $275

– **Tres Epistolae.** Trans.:– Helene Simon-Eckardt. [Berlin, Officina Serpentis, 1926]. *(340)* on Bütten. Fo. German & Greek parallel text, hand-bnd. mor. gt., by Hans Glökler, Berlin. (H. Nov.24; 1216) DM 800

– **The Works.** Trans.:– Floyer Sydenham & Thomas Taylor. L., priv. ptd., 1804. *1st. Edn.* 5 vols. Lge. 4to. Wide margin, hf.-titles, later hf. mor. (SG. Nov.17; 308) $600

PLATT LYNES, George

– **New York City Ballet: Photographs from 1935 through 1955.** Afterword:– Glenway Wescott. N.Y., 1957. *1st. Edn.* 4to. Pict. wraps. (SG. Nov.10; 134) $110

PLATTES, Gabriel

– [–] **A Collection of Scarce & Valuable Treatises upon Metals, Mines & Minerals.** 1740. *2nd. Edn.* 12mo. Old cf., worn; Sir Ivar Colquhoun, of Luss copy. (CE. Mar.22; 243) £150

– **A Discovery of Subterranean Treasure viz. all Manner of Mines & Minerals.** L., ca. 1712. Sm. 4to. Browned, cont. hf. cf., worn. (BBA. Nov.30; 121) *Gurney.* £95

PLAUTUS, A.

– **Ex Fide atque Auctoritate Complurium Liberorum Manuscriptorum Opera Dionys Lambini Monstroliensis.** Geneva, 1622. Sm. 4to. Cont. cf., repeated crowned L decor., centre Louis XIII arms, decor. spine. (HD. Dec.9; 72) Frs. 6,500

PLAUTUS, Titus Maccius Accius

– **Comédies.** Trans.:– Gueudeville. Leide, 1719. 10 vols. Sm. 8vo. Cont. marb. cf., spine decor., jnts. of 2 vols. wormed; D.D. Le Tellier de Courtanvaux stp. & ex-libris. (HD. Nov.9; 60) Frs. 1,700

– **Comoediae Latine.** [Strasburg], 1605. *1st. Taubman Edn.* 4to. Cont. vell., decor., Brunswick-Lüneburg arms; Philippus Sigismondus copy, with his MS. ex-libris on title, from Fondation Fürstenberg-Beaumesnil. (HD. Nov.16; 153) Frs. 2,500

– **Comoediae Viginti.** Commentaries:– Bernardus Saracenus & Johannes Petrus Valla. 1518. Fo. Top corner of title reprd., last 4 ll. slightly damp-frayed on outer edge, old cf., upr. cover detchd. (TA. Feb.16; 351) £165

PLAW, John

– **Rural Architecture or Designs from the Simple Cottage to the Decorated Villa.** L., 1802. 4to. Some margin staining, mod. qtr. cf. gt. (P. Nov.24; 219) *Bookroom.* £80

PLAYFAIR, P.

– **A New General Atlas.** L., 1814. Fo. 43 engraved double-p. maps, mostly spotted, cont. hf. cf., bds. detchd. (BBA. Dec.15; 125) *Jeffery.* £190

PLAYFORD, Henry

– **Harmonia Sacre: or Divine Hymns & Dialogues with a Through-Bass for the Theorbo-Lute, Bass-Viol, Harpsichord, or Organ. Composed by the Best Masters of the Last & Present Age** ... L., 1703 & 1714. *2nd. Edn.* 2 vols. Fo. Title-p. bears advt., lacks pp. 32-36 in 1st. vol., some paper-loss on title-p. of 1st. vol., orig. cf. bds., a little scuffed, a little stained & wormed. (S. Nov.17; 151) *Jeffrey.* £80

PLEMPIUS, Vopiscus Fortunatus

– **Fundamenta Medicinae ad Scholae Acribologiam** ... Ill.:– T. Mather after I. Backer (port.). Louvain, 1644. Fo. Hole in margin pp. 381-383, names on title scribbled out, vell., soiled; Dr. Walter Pagel copy. (S. Feb.7; 311) *Gurney.* £300

PLENK, Joseph Jacob

– **Doctrina de Morbis Oculorum.** Vienna, 1777. Lightly foxed, owner's stp. on title, old tree cf., worn, covers loose, liby. bkplt. (SG. Mar.22; 266) $225

PLEYDELL, J.C.

– **An Essay on Field Fortification, Intended Principally for the Use of Officers of Infantry. Translated from the Original Manuscripts of an Officer of Experience in the Prussian Service.** Ill.:– T. Jefferys. L., 1768. Disbnd. (SG. Sep.22; 247) $100

PLEYTE, W.

– **Leiden, vóór 300 Jaren en Thans.** Leiden, 1874. *(200)*. Fo. Orig. vell., soiled. (VG. Mar.21; 1035) Fls. 650

PLIMSOLL, Samuel

– **Our Seamen: An Appeal.** L., 1873. *1st. Edn.* 4to. Cl. (SG. Mar.29; 334) $100

PLINIUS, Gaius Secundus, the Elder

– **Commentarii in Librum Secundum Historiae Mundi C. Plinii Conscripti a Jacobo Milichio Professore Mathematum in Schola Vuittenbergensi.** Haganoae, 1535. Sm. 4to. Some cont. marginalia, cont. blind-stpd. pig, clasps, soiled, new end-papers. (TA. Sep.15; 421) £160

– **Historia Naturalis.** Ed.:– Philippus Beroaldus & Hieronymus Bononius. Treviso, Michael Manzolus, 25 Aug. 1479 [but not before 13 Oct. 1479]. *Reprint of Parma, 1476 Edn.* Fo. Pius II's abbreviation of Blondus' Decades of Roman History bnd. at end, sheet l2 in dupl., capital spaces with guide letters, cont. marginalia, 2 sm. wormholes in 1st. few ll., 1 affecting text, repairs to blank margins of 1st. ptd. lf., lr. inner margins of last few ll. stained, 18th. C. vell.; Stanitz coll. [BMC VI, 888; Goff P791] (SPB. Apr.25; 349) $2,000

– – **Anr. Edn.** Ed.:– [Philippus Beroaldus]. Venice, Raynaldus de Novimagio, 6 Jun. 1483. Fo. Margins lightly spotted, old MS. marginalia on some ll., 1 lf. with corner tear at foot, old owners mark dtd. 1600 on 1 lf. verso at foot, cont. leath. over wood bds., decor., clasps brkn., early 19th. C. spine renewed in same style, defect. [HC 13095; BMC V, 257; Goff P-794]. (R. Apr.3; 6) DM 3,800

– – **Anr. Edn.** Venice, Bartholomaeus de Zanis, 12 Dec. 1496. Fo. Capitals supplied in red or blue (blue sometimes oxidized with damage to paper), a few ll. stained, wormed towards end, 18th. C. vell., soiled; 19th. C. bkplt. of Rev. Prebendary Hedgeland, sm. Penzance Liby. stps. on 1st. & last ll., Stanitz coll. (SPB. Apr.25; 350) $1,000

– – **Anr. Edn.** Ed.:– Hermolaus Barbarus, revised by Jo. Baptista Palmarius. Venice, Joannes Aluisius, 18 May 1499. Fo. Capital spaces, many with guide letters, many 16th. C. margin annots., 9-line quotation on blank verso of colophon lf., minor repair to blank margin of title slightly affecting a few words of text on verso, dampstain to upr. margin of 1st. 10 ll., sm. wormhole to 1st. 35 ll., sm. hole at V5 slightly affecting a few letters, 3 ll. browned, 16th. C. vell., head of spine frayed. [HC 13104; BMC V, 572; Goff P800] (C. May 30; 122) *Fletcher.* £620

– – **Anr. Edn.** Ed.:– J. Harduin. Paris, 1723. *2nd. Edn.* 2 vols. in 3. Fo. Some slight brown spotting,

cont. leath. gt., jnts. & corners restored. (R. Apr.4; 1419) DM 550

– – **Anr. Edn.** Ed.:– Joannes Harduinus. Paris, 1741. 2 vols. Fo. Cont. marb. cf. gt., spines decor., covers rubbed, corners rounded. (HD. Jun.26; 24) Frs. 1,100

– – **Anr. Edn.** Ed.:– Gabriel Brotier. Ill.:– after Marillier (frontis.). Paris, 1779. 6 vols. 12mo. Cont. mott. cf. gt. (SG. Mar.22; 267) $100

– **Historiae Mvndi Libri XXXVII.** Frankfurt, 1599. Fo. Title with owners mark, slightly browned, cont. blind-tooled pig over wood bds., slightly spotted, rubbed & wormed, 2 clasps, brkn. (HK. May 15; 221) DM 520

– **The Historie of the World.** Trans.:– Philemon Holland. 1601. 2 vols. Fo. A few ll. lightly stained, later cf.-bkd. bds., rubbed. [STC 20029] (CSK. Jan.27; 33) £180

– **Naturae Historiarum Libri XXXVII.** Ed.:– H. Barbarus, [J.B. Palmarius], J. Camertis. Hagenau, Nov. 1518. 2 pts. in 1 vol. Fo. Title with 2 old names 1553 & 1634 & sm. corner tear at foot, index lacks last lf., cont. blind-tooled pig over wood bds., lightly worn & soiled, clasps, lacks 1 hasp. (R. Oct.11; 100) DM 1,000

– **Naturalis Historiae Libri XXXVII.** Paris, [1516]. Fo. 1st. few ll. stained & frayed, some worming, crude hf. leath., reprd. (SG. Feb.9; 303) $150

PLINIUS, Gaius Caecilius Secundus, the Younger

– **Epistolarum, Libri X.** Ed.:– M. Ritchie & J. Sammells. L., 1790. Sm. 8vo. Errata lf., cont. red mor., spine gt. (SG. Feb.9; 304) $200

– **Opera quae Supersunt; Omnia.** Glasgow, 1741. 4to. Cont. cf., spine gt.-decor.; Sir Ivar Colquhoun, of Luss copy. (CE. Mar.22; 121) £140

PLOMER, Henry R.

– **Wynkyn de Worde & his Contemporaries from the Death of Caxton to 1535.** 1925. 4to. Orig. buckram-bkd. bds.; H.M. Nixon coll., with his sig. & a few MS. notes. (BBA. Oct.6; 110) *Hellinga.* £55

PLOMLEY, Norman James Brian

– **Friendly Mission: the Tasmanian Journals & Papers of George Augustus Robinson 1829-34.** 1966, 1971. *1st. Edn.* 2 vols. including Supp. No bdgs. stated. (JL. Jun.24; 92) Aus. $160

– – **Anr. Copy.** Orig. cl. (KH. Nov.9; 398) Aus. $120

PLON, Eugene

– **Leone Leoni et Pompeo Leoni.** Paris, 1887. Orig. mor.-bkd. cl. (BBA. Apr.5; 64) *Leicester Art Books.* £80

– – **Anr. Copy.** 4to. Orig. mor.-bkd. cl. (BBA. Sep.8; 249) *Sims, Reed & Fogg.* £65

PLOT, Robert

– **The Natural History of Oxfordshire, being an Essay Toward the Natural History of England. [By R.P.].** Oxford, 1677. Fo. Title with engraved vig., folding map, 16 engraved plts., map with tear reprd., lr. inner corners dampstained thro.-out, later hf. roan, foot of spine defect. [Wing P2586] (C. Jun.27; 56) *Shapero.* £160

– – **Anr. Copy.** Fo. Engraved title, 16 plts., 1 folding map cleanly torn along line of previous repair, cont. cf., rubbed. (CSK. Jan.27; 183) £150

– – **Anr. Edn.** Oxford, 1705. *2nd. Edn.* Fo. Cold. folding map, 16 hand-cold. engraved plts., map slightly defect. mntd., a few ll. browned or slightly stained, sm. hole in Ss4, cont. panel. cf., corners worn, rebkd. (S. Nov.28; 78) *Burgess.* £150

– **The Natural History of Staffordshire.** Ill.:– J. Browne & others. Oxford, 1686. *1st. Edn.* Fo. Lge. folding map on thick paper, engraved plts., without 'Armes omitted' lf., sm. repair to title margin, few rust holes, cont. panel. cf., worn. (S. Apr.10; 577) *Kohler.* £300

PLOTHO, C. von

– **Der Krieg in Deutschland und Frankreich i.d. Jahren 1813 u. 1814.** Berlin, 1817. 2 vols. Slightly foxed, cont. hf. linen. (D. Nov.24; 3567) DM 400

PLOTINUS

– **Opera.** Trans.:– Marsilius Ficinus. Flor., Antonio di Bartolommeo Miscomini, 9 May 1492. *1st. Edn.*

PLU

Fo. 18th. C. vell.; from Fondation Furstenberg-Beaumesnil. [HC 13121; BMC VI, 640; Goff P815] (HD. Nov.16; 26) Frs. 42,000

PLUCHE, Noël-Antoine
- Histoire du Ciel où l'on recherche l'Origine de l'Idolâtrie ... Paris, 1757. 2 vols. Decor. red mor., Madame Adelaïde arms, spine decor.; Baron Double ex-libris. (SM. Mar.7; 2038) Frs. 7,000
[-] Schau-Platz der Natur. Frankfurt & Leipzig, 1760-64. Lacks 4 copperplts., cont. marb. leath. gt. (HK. Nov.8; 693) DM 450
[-] Schouwtoneel der Natuur ... Trans.:– P. Le Clercq. Ill.:– P. Yver & others. Amst., Dordrecht, 1739-84. 16 vols. Sm. 8vo. 7 engraved frontis., 202 engraved plts., many folding, cont. pol. cf., vols. 15 & 16 not quite unif., spines gt. (VS. Dec.9; 1323) Fls. 1,100
[-] Spectacle de la Nature: or, Nature Display'd. Trans.:– S. Humphreys. L., 1744-43. 4 vols. 12mo. Margin paper flaw to 1 text lf., cont. cf. gt. (C. Nov.16; 31) Scott. £140
[-] Spectacle de la Nature, ou Entretiens de l'Hist. Naturelle. Paris, 1745-51. New Edn. 8 pts. in 9 vols. 9 frontis., 205 maps & plts., mod. hf. cf. (VG. May 3; 696) Fls. 475

PLUMART DE DANGEUL
- Remarques sur les Avantages et les Desavantages de la France et de la Grande Bretagne par Rapport au Commerce. La Haye, 1754. 2nd. Edn. 12mo. Cont. cf. (HD. Feb.22; 166) Frs. 1,200

PLUMBE, John
- Sketches of Iowa & Wisconsin, Taken during a Residence of Three Years in those Territories. St. Louis, 1839. 1st. Edn. Lge. folding map slightly wrinkled, front fly-lf. removed, orig. cl.-bkd. ptd. wraps., light wear affecting 4 letters on lr. cover, a few minor stains, hf. mor. folding case; the Rt. Hon. Visc. Eccles copy. [Sabin 63444] (CNY. Nov.18; 230) $2,200

PLUMTRE, Anne
- Narrative of a Residence in Ireland, ... L., 1817. 1st. Edn. 4to. Hf. cf., upr. cover detchd.; Castletown copy. (GM. Dec.7; 63) £150

PLUQUET, François André Adrien
- Traité Philosophique et Politique sur le Luxe. Paris, 1786. 2 vols. 12mo. Cont. cf. (HD. Feb.22; 167) Frs. 1,500

PLUTARCH
- De Cohibenda Ira cun Dia. Löwen, 1531. Title with sm. stp., slightly browned, 19th. C. bds., spine defect. (HK. Nov.8; 315) DM 550
- Graecorum Romanorumque Illustrium Vitae. Venice, Apr. 1538. Fo. Lge. printer's woodcut device on title & final lf. verso, initials, many histor., lightly damp-wrinkled, early inscrs. on title, mod. vell. (SG. Apr.19; 151) $250
- The Lives of the Noble Grecians & Romaines. Trans.:– Sir Thomas North. L., 1612. 2 pts. in 1 vol. Fo. Lacks 1st. lf. (?blank), light staining, later cf., rebkd.; bkplt. of David Garnett. [STC 20069] (BBA. Mar.21; 168) Museum Bookshop. £85
– – Anr. Copy. Sm. fo. Separate title-p. for 'Lives of Epaminondas' dtd. 1610, lacks A1 or A2, title laid down with some blank portions lacking, some stains, later cf.; pict. bkplt. of W. Jaggard. (SG. Oct.27; 267) $130
– – Anr. Edn. Trans.:– Sir Thomas North. Camb., 1676. Fo. Some light stains, later hf. cf., slightly rubbed. [Wing P2634] (TA. Jul.19; 379) £60
– – Anr. Copy. 2 pts. in 1 vol. Fo. Margins lightly soiled, mod. cf. (CSK. Feb.24; 11) £55
– – Anr. Edn. L., 1703. 5 vols. Cont. panel. cf., tooled borders. (GM. Dec.7; 675) £55
– – Anr. Edn. Ed.:– Francis Wrangham. Trans.:– John & William Langhorne. L., 1813. 2nd. Edn. 6 vols. Str.-grd. mor., spines gt.; armorial bkplt. of Arthur, Earl of Castlestewart. (SG. Feb.16; 236) $140
– – Anr. Edn. Ed.:– A.C. Clough. 1874. 5 vols. Cont. tree cf. gt., spines gt., some covers scuffed. (CSK. Jul.27; 108) £55
– – Anr. Edn. Ill.:– Thomas Lowinsky. Shakes. Hd. Pr., 1928. (500) numbered. 8 vols. 8vo. Orig. cl. (BBA. Dec.15; 253) Bennett & Kerr. £60
– – Anr. Copy. 8 vols. Orig. buckram, a trifle

marked, partly unc. (S. Oct.11; 456) Bookroom. £55
– – Anr. Copy. 8 vols. Edges yellowed, orig. cl., 1 or 2 trivial markings, unc. (KH. Nov.9; 399) Aus. $220
– – Anr. Edn. L. & N.Y., Nones. Pr., 1929-30. (1550). 5 vols. Buckram. (PNY. Dec.1; 78) $120
– – Anr. Edn. Ed.:– Roland Baughman. Trans.:– Thomas North. Designer:– W.A. Dwiggins. Ltd. Edns. Cl., 1941. (1500) numbered & sigd. by ed. & designer. 8 vols. Cl. (SG. Mar.29; 216) $100
- Oeuvres. Ill.:– after Maréchal, Monet, Myris, Borel, & others. Paris, 1801-05. 25 vols. Cont. tree sheep, decor. spines,. (HD. Sep.22; 312) Frs. 2,500
- Les Oeuvres Morales et Meslées. Trans.:– Jacques Amyot. 1572. 1st. Fr. Trans. of 'Oeuvres Meslées'. Fo. Ruled, cont. decor. cf., jnts. & spine reprd. (HD. Mar.21; 69) Frs. 2,500
– – Anr. Edn. Trans.:– [Jacques Amyot]. Paris, 1574. 2nd. Edn. of this trans. 6 vols. Lacks title for Tome I, Vol.3 & 1 prelim. in Tome I, Vol.1, dupl. of one title-p. laid in, general title reprd., early mor. gt. (SG. Feb.9; 305) $150
– – Anr. Edn. Trans.:– J. Amyot. Paris, 1575. 3rd. Edn. of this trans. 2 vols. Fo. 17th. C. cf., Duc de Richelieu arms in centre of covers, decor. spines, turn-ins restored. (HD. Sep.22; 311) Frs. 4,200
– – Anr. Edn. 1582. (With:) - Les Vies des Hommes Illustres Grecs et Romains. Trans.:– Jacques Amyot. 1583. Lacks 1 lf. Together 2 vols. Fo. Several ll. dampstained, cont. blind-stpd. vell. (HD. Nov.17; 61) Frs. 3,500
– – Anr. Edn. Trans.:– J. Amyot. Genf, 1614. New Edn. 2 pts in 1 vol. Fo. Some light foxing, last text ll. pt. 2 & index slightly stained in margins, cont. style vell. (R. Oct.11; 101) DM 500
- Parallela. Venice, Aug. 1519. 1st. Aldine Edn. Fo. In Greek, title-p. lightly dust-stained, a few margins slightly defect. or reprd., some early Greek annots., 4 binder's blanks at beginning, 5 at end (watermark of an angel surmounted by a star, same as pastedowns), cont. Venetian bdg. 'alla Graeca' mor. over wood bds., edges cut flush & grooved, raised headcaps, covers with blind rolls & scroll ornament, central panel of maltese cross tool, flat back similarly decor., title lettered in ink on lr. edge, lacks clasps, spine (including humps) worn & upr. jnt. patched; Mark Pattison copy. (BBA. Nov.30; 13) Breslauer. £12,500
- Plutarchi Chaeronensis omnium quae exstant Operum ... Paris, 1624. 2 vols. Fo. In Latin & Greek, old vell., lightly rubbed, lacks ties. (CSK. Jul.13; 77) £80
- Summi et Philosophi et Historici Parallela, id est, Vitae Illustrium Vivorum Graecorum et Romanorum. Frankfurt, 1580. Fo. Woodcut device on title & recto of final lf., woodcut text ills., margins cropped affecting sidenotes & few headlines, all after 4Z2 badly frayed, some browning, few stains, rough parch., worn. (S. Apr.10; 331) Snelling. £90
- Les Vies des Hommes Illustres Grecs et Romains. Paris, 1567. 3rd. Edn. 6 vols. (With:) - Oeuvres Morales et Meslées. Paris, 1574. 2nd. Edn. of this trans. 7 vols. Lacks title to Vol. 7. Together 13 vols. 17th. C. Fr. red mor. gt. (P. Feb.16; 111) £880
– – Anr. Edn. Trans.:– J. Amyot. 1583. Lge. fo. Cont. cf. gt., decor., reprd., spine renewed. (P. Nov.29; 69) Frs. 1,050
- Vitae Virorum Illustrium. Ed.:– Gerard de Vercel. Paris, 1514. Fo. Lacks blank last lf., title-lf. remntd., late 18th. C. hf. roan, corners, worn; from Fondation Furstenberg-Beaumesnil. (HD. Nov.16; 154) Frs. 1,300

PLUVINEL. Antoine de
- L'Instruction du Roy, en l'Exercice de monter à Cheval. Paris, 1625. Ob. fo. Lacks text & ports., internal defects, old roan, very worn; from Château des Noës liby. (HD. May 25; 68) Frs. 7,000
– – Anr. Edn. Paris, 1627. 2nd. Edn. Fo. Lacks 2 ports., 1 plt. unnumbered, lacks 2 repeated plts., 1 plt. crumpled & holed, lr. margin partly stained, especially at beginning, minimal wear, cont. vell., spotted, lacks ties. (HK. May 16; 1787) DM 3,000

POE

PLYMLEY, Peter (Pseud.)
See— SMITH, Rev. Sydney 'Peter Plymley'

PLYMOUTH COLONY
- A Patent for Plymouth in New-England. To which is annexed, Extracts from the Records of that Colony, etc. etc. Boston, 1751. Sm. 4to. Edges slightly frayed, several ink emendations in hand of Josiah Cotton, Register & Keeper of Records, self-wraps., sewed as iss. [Sabin 59034] (SG. Oct.20; 285) $350

POCCI, Franz Graf von
- Kasperlkomödien. Ill.:– A. Woelfle. Berlin, 1922. (100) De Luxe Edn. on Bütten. 4to. Hand-bnd. orig. mor. by W. Hacker, Leipzig, gt. spine, covers, inner & outer dentelles; full-p. lithos. sigd. by artist. (H. Nov.24; 1227) DM 560

POCCI, Franz Graf von (Ill.)
See— BLUMEN-LIEDER FUR KNABEN UND MADCHEN

POCCIANTI, M.
- Catalogus Scriptorum Florentinorum. Flor., 1589. 1st. Edn. Some staining, cf., spine rubbed. (P. Jan.12; 270) Quaritch. £440

POCHHAMMER, P.
- Ein Dantekranz aus Hundert Blättern. Ill.:– F. Stassen. Berlin, 1905. 4to. 1 Supp., hf. vell., orig. vell. wraps. bnd. in. (GB. Nov.5; 3192) DM 400

POCOCK, Mrs. Rose R.
- The Longleat Views. Bristol, ca. 1840. Ob. fo. 6 tinted litho. plts., orig. limp cl., mor. backstrip, spine ends frayed. (TA. Jul.19; 105) £125

POCOCKE, Richard
- A Description of the East. L., 1743-45. 3 pts. in 2 vols. Fo. Engraved dedication lf., 179 engraved maps & plts., several folding, slight discoloration affecting a few ll., cont. cf., spines slightly worn. (S. Dec.1; 356) Trotter. £440
– – Anr. Copy. Fo. Engraved dedication lf., 172 (of 178) maps & plts., cont. cf., rebkd., w.a.f. (P. Mar.15; 156) £250

POE, Edgar Allan
- The Bells & Other Poems. Ill.:– Edmund Dulac. L., n.d. Ltd. Edn., sigd. by artist. 4to. Orig. vell. gt., lacks ties. (P. Apr.12; 310) Joseph. £150
– – Anr. Copy. 4to. Some offset from headpieces, free end-papers darkened, elab. gt.-decor. vell., slightly yawning, ribbon ties. (CBA. Aug.21; 195) $250
- Eureka: a Prose Poem. N.Y., 1848. 1st. Edn. Spotted, orig. cl., worn. (BBA. May 23; 39) Leaves of Grass. £85
- The Fall of the House of Usher. Ill.:– Alastair. Paris, 1928. (300) on Van Gelder Bütten. Sm. 4to. Ills. mntd. on silver paper, some margins slightly discold., bds., orig. wraps., slightly spotted; Franz Goldstein ex-libris on end-paper. (H. Nov.24; 1315) DM 520
- Histoires Extraordinaires. — Nouvelles Histoires Extraordinaires. — Aventures d'Arthur Gordon Pym. — Eureka. — Histoires Grotesques et Sérieuses. Trans.:– Charles Baudelaire. Paris, 1856; 1857; 1858; 1864; 1865. Orig. Edns. 5 vols. 12mo. Mor., sigd. by Noulhac, wraps. & spines. (HD. May 16; 8) Frs. 31,000
- König Pest u.a. Novellen. Trans.:– G. Etzel. Ill.:– A. Kubin. München, 1911. (50) numbered on Bütten. Orig. vell. gt. (HK. May 17; 2935) DM 650
– – Anr. Edn. Trans.:– Gisela Etzel. Ill.:– A. Kubin. München, 1911. (1000). Orig. hf. vell. (HK. Nov.11; 4166) DM 400
- Manuscrit Trouvé dans une Bouteille. Trans.:– Charles Baudelaire. Ill.:– Pierre Falke. Paris, 1921. (500) numbered on velin. 4to. Mott. cf., gt. rules enclosing mor. panel, cold. pict. wraps. bnd. in. (SG. Feb.16; 239) $100
- The Mask of the Red Death. Ill.:– Federico Castellon. Baltimore, Aquarius Pr., 1969. (500) numbered & sigd. by artist. Tall fo. Two-tone cl., boxed. (SG. Jan.12; 57) $250
- Mesmerism 'In Articulo Mortis'. L., 1846. 1st. Separate Edn. 12mo. Slightly discold., stitched as iss., cl. folder; Prescott copy. (SPB. May 17; 658) $475

POE, Edgar Allan -Contd.

[-] **The Narrative of Arthur Gordon Pym.** L., 1838. *1st. Engl. Edn.* Slightly soiled thro.-out, orig. cl., worn, lacks spine. (BBA. May 23; 38)
Ferret Fantasy. £110

- **Quinze Histoires d'Edgar Poë.** Trans.:- Charles Baudelaire. Ill.:- Louis Legrand. Paris, 1897. 15 etchings ptd. on japan in double state, jansenist decor. mor. by Chambolle-Duru, red mor. liners, s.-c., wrap.; Madame Tarah-Haggin copy, Edouard Rahir ex-libris. (HD. Jun.13; 88)   Frs. 38,000

- **The Raven.** Ill.:- Gustave Doré. N.Y., 1884. *1st. Amer. Edn.* Tall fo. Black- & gt.-decor. pict. cl., light wear, publisher's decor. box, worn; Ken Leach coll. (RO. Jun.10; 59) $260

- **The Raven & Other Poems.** N.Y., 1845. *1st. Edn. (750).* 12mo. 12 pp. advts., hf.-title & few fore-edges foxed, orig. ptd. wraps., spine slightly worn, mor.-bkd. s.-c.; Prescott copy. (SPB. May 17; 659) $8,500

- - **Anr. Copy.** 12mo. Cont. inscrs., faint staining thro.-out, orig. ptd. wraps., unc., rebkd., most of orig. spine preserved, hf. mor. folding case; Frederic Dannay copy. (CNY. Dec.16; 272) $4,000

- **Tales.** Ill.:- W.A. Dwiggins. Chic., Lakeside Pr., 1930. *(1000).* Mor., by Donnelley, of Chic., covers inlaid; 1 p. A.L.s. from artist to Guy Littrell & autograph MS. of the 'Illustrator's Note' sigd. with initials. (SPB. Dec.13; 553) $400

- **Tales of Mystery & Imagination.** Ill.:- Harry Clarke. L., [1919]. 4to. Red hf. mor., decor. paper bds., s.-c., spine discold. (LH. Sep.25; 583) $120

- - **Anr. Edn.** Ill.:- Harry Clarke. N.Y., 1933. 4to. Orig. cl., a few marks, d.-w. worn. (KH. Nov.8; 231)   Aus. $120

- - **Anr. Edn.** Ill.:- A. Rackham. L., 1935. 4to. Orig. cl. gt., d.-w. torn. (P. Sep.8; 403)   £65

- - **Anr. Copy.** 4to. Orig. rexine gt., decor. end-papers, a little damp spotted, orig. d.-w., slightly frayed at top & bottom of spine. (TA. Mar.15; 423)   £64

- **Tales & Poems ... with Biographical Essay.** Ed.:- John H. Ingram. Phila., ca. 1895-1905. *'Commemorative' Edn.* (5) numbered on Japan paper, ptd. for Warren R. Fales. 6 vols. Plts. in 3 printings, 1 on Japanese etching paper, in black, 1 on Dutch H.M.P., in bistre & 1 on Whatman drawing-paper, finished in watercolours, crushed lev. mor., spines in 5 compartments, mor. gt. ornament, mor. gt. doubls. with lge. gt. panel of onlaid mor. gt. & gt. ornament in gold frame, satin free end-pp., matching velvet-lined buckram s.-c.'s. (CNY. Dec.17; 588) $2,200

- **Vingt Histoires Extraordinaires.** Trans.:- Charles Baudelaire. Ill.:- Lobel Riche. Paris, 1927. *(217).* 4to. On vélin d'Arches, 41 orig. etchings (20 plts.), plts. in 4 states including pure etching, leaves, box. (HD. May 4; 396)   Frs. 2,600

- **The Works.** Ed.:- J.H. Ingram. L., 1899 [1900]. *[Standard Edn.].* Vol. I only. Diced cf. gt. extra, fore-e. pntg. after A. Rackham on each edge, sigd. with monog. MF. (SG. Nov.3; 167) $1,200

- - **Anr. Edn.** Ed.:- R.H. Stoddard. N.Y., 1900. *Fordham Edn.* 6 vols. Maroon three-qtr. mor., spines gt. with fleurons. (SG. Feb.16; 238) $375

- **The Complete Works.** Intro.:- Charles F. Richardson. Ill.:- Frederick Simpson Coburn. N.Y., [1902]. *Eldorado Edn. (1050) numbered.* 10 vols. Lge. 8vo. Etched port., gravure plts. on Japan vell., lettered pict. guards, additional pict. titles, publisher's three-qtr. mor., gt.-panel. backs, spines a little worn & discold. (SG. Mar.15; 138) $500

- **The Works.** Ed.:- E.C. Stedman & G.E. Woodberry. Ill.:- after A.E. Sterner & others. N.Y., 1903. *Bibliophile's Edn.* (10) numbered & sigd. by eds. 10 vols. Ills. in 2 states, hand-cold. gravure plts. & mntd. India-proofs, tissue-guards, crushed hf. mor., gt.-panel. backs, moiré silk bds. & end-ll., partly unc.; extra-ill. with 12 watercolours, bkplt. of R.C. Durant, Los Angeles. (SG. Apr.26; 167) $650

POE, Edgar Allan (Contrib.)

See— **GIFT (The); A Christmas & New Year's Present ...**
See— **GRAHAM'S MAGAZINE**
See— **IRVING OFFERING; A Token of Affection, for 1851**

POELLNITZ, Carl Ludwig von

- **Amusemens des Eaux d'Aix-la-Chapelle.** Amst., 1736. *1st. Edn.* 3 vols. Some slight spotting, especially multi-folding view with bkd. tears. (R. Oct.13; 2665)   DM 1,100

POESTE per l'Ingresso Solenne di ... Gio. Antonio Gabriel

Venice, [1785]. Sm. fo. Thick paper, early 19th. C. blind-tooled cl. (C. Dec.9; 161)   *Lyon.* £320

POETE DE L'ENFANCE 1845

Paris, [1844]. 25 × 17mm., miniature book. Loose in orig. red mor. gt.; van Veen coll. (S. Feb.28; 201)   £140

POETS

- **The Works of the British Poets.** Preface:- Robert Anderson, M.D. L., 1795. 13 vols. Lge. 8vo. Three-qtr. cf. by Root, spines gt. (SG. Feb.16; 44) $400

- - **Anr. Edn.** Ed.:- Thomas Park. 1808, 1809. 42 vols., & 6 vol. Supp. (*With:*) **JOHNSON, Dr. Samuel** - **Lives of the English Poets.** 1805-06. 6 vols. in 3. Together 51 vols. 16mo. Unif. cf. gt. (LC. Oct.13; 370)   £420

- **The Works of the English Poets.** Ed.:- Samuel Johnson. L., 1790. 75 vols. 12mo. 1 section loose, cont. cf., spines gt. (S. Dec.13; 418)   *Samia.* £340

- - **Anr. Edn.** 1810. 21 vols. Cont. red str.-grd. mor. gt., worn. (BS. Nov.16; 65)   £360

POET'S TRANSLATION SERIES

Ed.:- Richard Aldington. Trans.:- H.A. Aldington & others. [L., 1915-16]. Series 1: nos. 1-6, & 1st. & 2nd. prospectuses. Sq. 12mo. Self-wraps. (SG. Mar.1; 2) $150

POICTEVIN, Francis.

- **Heures.** Paris, 1892. *Orig. Edn.* Sq. 12mo. On Whatman, Jansenist mor., wrap.; dedication & L. from author. (HD. Jan.30; 78)   Frs. 1,300

POINCARE, Henri

- **Electricité et Optique. I. Les Théories de Maxwell et la Théorie Electromagnétique de la Lumière. II. Les Théories de Helmholtz et les Expériences de Hertz.** Paris, 1890-91. *1st. Edn.* 2 pts. in 1 vol. Cont. mor.-bkd. marb. bds. (*With:*) - **Théorie Analytique de la Propogation de la Chaleur.** Paris, 1895. *1st. Edn.* Buckram. (*With:*) - **Théorie des Tourbillons** ... Paris, [1893]. *1st. Edn.* Mod. cl.-bkd. marb. bds. (*With:*) - **Cinématique et Mechanismes. Fotentiel et Méchanique des Fluides.** Paris, 1899. *1st. Edn.* Mor.-bkd. bds. Together 4 vols. Slight browning, some rubbing to bdgs.; Stanitz coll. (SPB. Apr.25; 352) $600

POINCY, Louis de

See— **ROCHEFORT, Charles de & Poincy, Louis de**

POINSETT, Joel R.

- **Notes on Mexico.** L., 1825. Folding map cl.-bkd., & loose & stained, orig. bds., defect. (P. Dec.8; 347)   *Burton Garbett.* £85

POINT OF VIEW, The

Ill.:- after Alphonse Mucha & others. L., 1905. *(25) numbered.* 4to. Some ills. &c. hand-cold., extra-ill. with watercolour drawings in margins, cont. mor. gt. by Stikeman, gt.-tooled cf. doubls., watered silk end-ll., lr. cover marked & defect. (S. Dec.20; 505)   *Crete.* £130

POIRET

See— **CHAUMETON, Fr. P. & Poiret**

POISSON, Michel

- **Cris de Paris.** Ill.:- Poisson, Godin & Beurlier. Paris, [1769-75]. 4to. Engraved title, 73 etchings, Fr. captions, all plts. mntd. in old borders, minimal spotting, cont. red pol. mor., gt. spine, decor. covers & gt. inner & outer dentelles, cover slightly worn, spine lightly bumped; Hauswedell coll. (H. May 23; 97)   DM 3,800

POISSON, Simeon-Denis

- **Théorie Mathématique de la Chaleur.** Paris, 1835. *1st. Edn.* 4to. Hf.-title, slight foxing, cont. cf.-bkd. bds., spine gt.; pres. copy, inscr. by author on hf.-title (inscr. cropped), Stanitz coll. (SPB. Apr.25; 353) $275

- **Traité de Méchanique.** Paris, 1811. *1st. Edn.* 2

vols. Hf.-title & errata lf. in each vol., some spotting & browning, 1 plt. torn & reprd. with some discoloration but no loss, cont. qtr. cf., spines gt., spine ends worn; Stanitz coll. (SPB. Apr.25; 354) $600

POITIERS, Diane de

- **Lettres Inédites ...** Paris, 1866. Red mor. gt. by Hardy, D. Borelli arms, spine decor. (HD. May 4; 398)   Frs. 1,300

POLACK, Joel Samuel

- **Manners & Customs of the New Zealanders.** L., 1840. *1st. Edn.* 2 vols. Title of Vol. 1 browned, inscr. on front fly-lf., orig. cl. gt. (PNY. Oct.20; 274) $150

- **New Zealand, Being a Narrative of Travels & Adventures During a Residence in that Country Between the Years 1831 & 1837.** L., 1838. *1st. Edn.* 2 vols. Folding engraved map hand-cold. in outl., 6 engraved plts., 4pp. publisher's advt., cont. cl.-bkd. bds., rubbed. (C. Jun.27; 99)   *Dunsheath.* £150

POLAIN, Louis

- **Catalogue des Livres Imprimés au Quinzième Siècle des Bibliothèques de Belgique.** Bruxelles, 1932. *Orig. Edn. Numbered on Holland.* 4 vols. Lge. 8vo. Cl. (LM. Oct.22; 180)   B.Frs. 9,000

POLDO D'ALBENAS, J.

- **Discours Historial de l'Antique Cité de Nismes.** Lyons, 1559. *1st. Edn. 1st. Iss.* Fo. Fore-margin of d1 restored with neat-line executed in pen, a few light margin stains, 17th. C. cf., arms on covers of Gedeon Tallemant des Peaux & crest in compartments on spine, repairs to head & tail of spine; owner's inscr. relating to Jean Baptiste Debrize(?), Conseillor du Roy. (S. May 21; 239)   *Fletcher.* £950

POLEHAMPTON, Edward & Good, John M.

- **Gallery of Nature & Art.** L., 1821. 6 vols. Cont. Engl. cf., lge. orig. pen ill. in sepia, washed, gold-tooled corners, spine reprd. (D. Nov.23; 171)   DM 2,800

POLENI, Giovanni, Marquis

- **De Castellis per quae derivantvr Flvviorvm Aquae Habentibvs Latera Convergentia Liber.** Padua, 1718. *1st. Edn.* 4to. Final license & colophon ll., cont. Engl. cf., spine gt., wear; Marquess of Bute copy, Stanitz coll. (SPB. Apr.25; 356) $325

- **De Motv Aqvae Mixto Libri Dvo.** Padua, 1717. *1st. Edn.* Sm. fo. Final 2 ll. of Approbation & errata, slight margin staining, cont. cf. gt., lr. corners reprd., cl. s.-c.; Stanitz coll. (SPB. Apr.25; 357) $300

- **Utriusque Thesauri Antiquitatum Romanarum Graecarumque nova Supplementa congesta.** Venezia, 1737. 5 vols. Fo. Cont. vell. (SI. Dec.15; 83)   Lire 450,000

POLI, Xavier

- **Histoire Militaire des Corses au Service de la France.** Ajaccio, Bastia, 1898-1900. 2 vols. (all publd.). Cont. hf. chagrin, spines decor., turn-ins restored. (HD. Oct.21; 141)   Frs. 1,500

POLIDORI, John William

- **The Vampyre; a Tale.** L., 1819. *1st. Edn.* Mildly foxed or stained, three-qtr. cf. & marb. bds., leath. scuffed, marb. end-papers; copy of Rev. Charles Lutwidge Dodgson, his initials on verso of front free end-paper. (CBA. Oct.29; 673) $750

- - **Anr. Copy.** Hf.-title (slightly torn), 20 pp. advts., red hf. mor., decor. bds., unc. (SG. Feb.16; 241) $300

POLITE REPOSITORY OR POCKET COMPANION ...

L., 1786. 32mo. Cont. vell. gt., miniature in cols. on upr. bd. & in sepia on lr. bd.; Sir David Salomons bkplt. (PNY. Dec.1; 25) $250

- - **Anr. Edn.** L., 1797. 32mo. 8 pp. of diary entries cut away, red mor. gt., lozenge-pattern onlays, matching s.-c.; Sir David Salomons bkplt. (PNY. Dec.1; 24) $125

POLITIANUS, Angelus

- **Epistolarum Libri Duodecim.** Basle, 1522. Cont. blind-stpd. cf., turn-ins reprd., traces of clasps; from

Fondation Furstenberg-Beaumesnil. (HD. Nov.16; 155) Frs. 1,000
- **Omnia Opera.** Ed.:– [Alexander Sartius]. Venice, Aldus Manutius, Jul. 1498. *1st. Coll. Edn.* Fo. Capital spaces with guide letters, lr. outer blank corners of last 2 ll. restored, some margin dampstaining, mostly at front & back, a few ll. browned, a few spotted, some early ink margin notes, str.-grd. mor. by Whitman Bennett, blind-tooled borders & spine, gt.-lettered, qtr. mor. box; Arthur E. Neergaard & Alexandre P. Rosenberg bkplts., Thomas B. Stevenson copy. [BMC V, 559 (IA 24475); Goff P-886; HC 13218] (CNY. May 18; 84) $2,200
- – Anr. Copy. Fo. Cont. German blind-stpd. cf., richly decor., traces of clasps; from Fondation Furstenberg-Beaumesnil. (HD. Nov.16; 78) Frs. 18,600
- **Opera, quae Quidem Extitere Hactenus** ... Basle, 1553. *(Bound with:)* FLORIDI, Francisci – Opera. Basle, 1540. 2 pts. in 1 vol. Some cont. marginalia. Together 2 works in 1 vol. Fo. Old vell., soiled. (TA. Oct.20; 308) £82
- **Le Stanze.** Parma, 1792. 4to. Cont. spr. cf., gt.-decor. spine. (TA. Aug.18; 341) £55

POLITISCHES TASCHENBUCH
Ed.:– F.J. Wit named von Döring. Trans.:– Speckter after J.P.T. Lyser. Hamburg, 1831. Year II. Sm. 8vo. Some slight spotting, orig. pictor. bds., ill. inner covers, browned, sm. spine tear & defect. (H. May 22; 589) DM 480

POLITZER, Adam
- **Lehrbuch der Ohrenheilkunde.** Stuttgart, 1878-82. *1st. Edn.* 2 vols. in 1. Cont. hf. leath. (R. Apr.4; 1349) DM 460

POLK, James K.
- **The Diary During his Presidency, 1845 to 1849.** Ed.:– Milo M. Quaife. Intro.:– Andrew C. McLaughlin. Chic., 1910. *1st. Edn. (500).* 4 vols. Lge. 8vo. Qtr. cl., bds., spines shelf-darkened, 1 label worn; from liby. of F.D. Roosevelt, inscr. & sigd. & 'given to the President July 27/41' by Frederic A. Delano, & inscr. 'Franklin D. Roosevelt Hyde Park', Delano bkplt., underlinings & margin pencil marks by Roosevelt. (SG. Mar.15; 67) $1,400

POLLARD, Alfred Frederick
- **Henry VIII.** L., 1902. *(1050) numbered on fine paper.* 1 vol. in 2. Lge. 4to. Crimson three-qtr. mor., spines elab. gt.; extra-ill. with over 100 engraved ports., historical scenes, etc. inlaid to size, each vol. with handwritten title 'Extra Illustrated by Caroline & Craig Wright, 1935', W.D.C. Wright bkplt. (SG. Nov.17; 263) $200

POLLARD, Alfred William
- **Books about Books.** L., 1893-94. *1st. Edns.* 6 vols. (compl.). Unif. gt.-lettered buckram, spines slightly faded. (SG. Sep.15; 265) $175
- **An Essay on Colophons with Specimens & Translations.** Chic., Caxton Cl., 1905. *(252) on Fr. H.M.P.* Bds., gt.-lettered paper parch. back, unc., light wear. (RO. Dec.11; 277) $150
- **Odes from the Greek Dramatists.** Trans.:– Oscar Wilde, A.E. Housman & others. L., David Stott, 1890. *1st. Edn. (50) numbered on L.P., for presentation.* 4to. Orig. parch., slightly soiled, inscr. by ed. & publisher to Oscar Wilde, Perry Molstad copy. (SPB. May 16; 550) $650

POLLARD, Alfred William, Redgrave, G.R. & others
- **Short-Title Catalogue of Books Printed in England, Scotland, & Ireland & of English Books Printed Abroad, 1475-1640.** L., 1926. *1st. Edn.* Tall 4to. Qtr. linen; the A.A. Houghton Jnr. copy. (SG. Sep.15; 301) $130
- – Anr. Edn. Ed.:– W.A. Jackson, F.S. Ferguson, & K.F. Pantzer. L., 1976. *2nd. Edn.* Vol. 2 (all publd.). Tall 4to. Cl., d.-w. (SG. Sep.15; 302) $170

POLLARD, Edward E.
- **Observations in the North: Eight Months in Prison & on Parole.** Richmond, 1865. Hf. cf. (SG. Oct.20; 114) $130

POLLARD, Eliza F.
- **Greuze & Boucher.** L., 1904. Sm. sq. 8vo. Lev. mor., elab. gt. decor., each cover with miniature port. on ivory, gt. spine in 6 compartments, gt.-tooled turn-ins, watered silk linings, partly unc., binder's name erased from free end-paper, spine worn, fleece-lined cl. s.-c.; Phoebe A.D. Boyle bkplt. (CNY. Dec.17; 589) $550

POLLARD, Graham
See— CARTER, John Waynflete & Pollard, Graham

POLLARD, Graham & Ehrman, Albert
- **The Distribution of Books by Catalogue ... based on Material in the Broxbourne Library.** Camb., Roxb. Cl., 1965. Fo. Orig. mor.-bkd. cl.; pres. inscr. from Ehrman to H.M. Nixon. (BBA. Oct.6; 116) *Maggs.* £1,100
- – Anr. Copy. Fo. Orig. qtr. mor. (S. Oct.4; 239) *Maggs.* £1,000
- – Anr. Copy. Orig. hf. leath; Hauswedell Coll. (H. May 23; 401) DM 4,400

POLLARD, Hugh Bertie Campbell
See— SOUTHGATE, Frank & Pollard, Hugh B.C.

POLLARD, Hugh Bertie Campbell & Barclay-Smith, Phyllis
- **British & American Game-Birds.** Ill.:– Philip Rickman. L., 1945. *(125) numbered, with orig. pencil sketch by artist.* 4to. Orig. qtr. pig, spine faded. (S. Dec.13; 290) *Laywood.* £60

POLLEY, J.
See— TIELEMAN VAN DER HORST & Polley, J.

POLLOCK, Benjamin
- **Characters & Scenes in Oliver Twist.** Ca. 1878. Ob. 4to. 23 hand-cold. plts., cf. gt. by Zaehnsdorf; from Norman Tarbolton liby. (P. Apr.12; 10) *Jarndyce.* £110

POLLUX, Julius
See— STEPHANUS BYZANTIUS — POLLUX, Julius — HESYCHIUS

POLO, Marco
- **Le Livre de Marco Polo.** Ill.:– Mariette Lydis. Paris, 1932. *(111). (10) numbered, ptd. for the artist, with suite of 7 plts. in uncold. state.* 4to. 9 etched hand-cold. plts., including 2 folding maps sigd. by artist, vell. by Birdsall, inside borders gt., unc., orig. wraps. bnd. in. (S. Nov.21; 93) *Desk.* £220

POLONSKI, Vyacheslav
- **Russki Revoluzionni Plakzt.** Moskau, 1925. 4to. Lightly foxed at beginning, orig. pict. hf. linen, corners bumped. (GB. Nov.5; 2899) DM 2,000

POLWHELE, Richard
- **History of Devonshire.** Ill.:– Cary. 1797. 3 vols. in 1. Fo. Engraved map, port cut out & lafd down on map verso, 21 engraved plts. only, some staining thro.-out, hf. mor., brkn., title & map loose in bdg., w.a.f. (BS. May 2; 19) £55

POLYBIUS
- **Histoire.** Ed.:– de Folard. Trans.:– Dom Vincent Thuillier. Paris, 1727-30. 6 vols. 4to. Cont. marb. cf., decor. spines. (HD. Sep.22; 314) Frs. 3,300
- – Anr. Edn. Ed.:– Folard. Trans.:– V. Thuillier. Amst., 1753. *New Edn.* 6 vols. & 1 vol. Supp. 4to. Cont. hf. roan. (HD. Feb.22; 171) Frs. 4,200
- – Anr. Edn. Ed.:– J. Ch. de Folard. Trans.:– V. Thuillier. Amst., 1759. *3rd. Edn.* 7 vols. 4to. Some foxing, cont. hf. cf., slightly rubbed. (VG. Mar.19; 161) Fls. 450
- **Historiarum Libri qui Supersunt.** Trans.:– Isaac Casaubon. [Frankfurt], 1609. 2 pts. in 1 vol. Fo. Title & text in Greek & Latin, late 18th./early 19th. C. Engl.(?) red str.-grd. mor., flat spine & covers ornately gt., inner gt. dentelles, a few scuff-marks on lr. cover, chemise & s.-c. (S. Nov.17; 59) *Fletcher.* £230

POMARIUS, J.
- **Christlicher Junger Herren, Junger Gesellen und Jüngling Ehrenschild.** Magdeburg, 1582. 12mo. Browned thro.-out, cont. vell., slightly soiled, lacks ties. (GB. Nov.4; 2152) DM 1,900

POMBAL, Seb.-Jos. de Carvalho, Marquis de
- **Memoires.** Trans.:– Gattel? Lisbonne & Bruxelles, 1784. 4 vols. in 2. Cont. cf., spines decor. (HD. Nov.9; 153) Frs. 1,500
- – Anr. Copy. 2 vols. 12mo. Cont. roan. (HD. Feb.22; 172) Frs. 1,600

POMET, Pierre
- **A Compleat History of Drugs.** 1712. 2 vols. in 1. 4to. 86 plts., a few browned, cont. cf., upr. cover detchd. (P. Jul.5; 192) £190
- **Histoire Générale des Drogues, Traitant des Plantes, des Animaux, & des Mineraux.** Paris, 1694. *1st. Edn.* 4 pts. in 1 vol. Fo. Hf.-title, privilege lf., 32 pp. insert in 1st. section, 16 pp. Remarques at end (not in 1st. imp.), hf.-title & last lf. torn without loss of text, old liby stps., some foxing, ink stains &c., old cf., brkn. (SG. Mar.22; 259) $500

POMIS, David de
- **Zemach David.** Venice, 1587. *1st. Edn.* Fo. In Hebrew, Latin & Italian, worming affecting some letters, staining, mod. blind-tooled mor. (S. Oct.25; 315) *Klein.* £320
- – Anr. Copy. Fo. Vell. (DS. Mar.23; 2222) Pts. 100,000

POMMEREUL, F.R.J.
- [–] **Histoire de l'Isle de Corse.** Berne, 1779. 2 vols. Cont. marb. cf., spines decor. (HD. Oct.21; 142) Frs. 5,200

POMOLOGICAL MAGAZINE, The
Ed.:– John Lindley. Ill.:– S. Watts & W. Clark, after Mrs. Withers & C.M. Curtis. L., 1828-29-30. 3 vols. in 1. 152 hand-cold. engraved plts., a few folding, some offsetting onto text, mor. gt. by J. Clarke. (S. Nov.28; 79) *Henderson.* £1,700

POMPADOUR, Jeanne Antoinette Poisson Marquise de
- **Catalogue des Livres de la Bibliothèque de Feue Madame la Marquise de Pompadour.** Paris, 1765. Cont. marb. cf., prices marked. (HD. Jun.6; 124) Frs. 2,700

PONCELET, Jean Victor
- **Applications d'Analyse et de Géométrie, qui ont servi de Principal Fondement au Traité des Propri-etes Projectives des Figures.** 1862. *Orig. Edn.* 2 vols. Cont. bradel hf. buckram. (HD. Apr.13; 75) Frs. 1,000
- **Mémoire sur les Roues Hydrauliques à Aubes Courbes, Mues par-dessous** ... Metz, 1827. *2nd. Edn.* 4to. Hf.-title, spotting & margin soiling, orig. wraps., mostly unopened, rubbed, spine worn; Stanitz coll. (SPB. Apr.25; 358) $250
- **Traité de Méchanique appliqueé aux Machines.** Liege, 1845. 2 vols. Some browning or spotting, cont. bds., rebkd. with mod. mor.; Stanitz coll. (SPB. Apr.25; 359) $100
- **Traité des Proprietés Projectives des Figures.** Paris, 1822. *Orig. Edn.* 4to. Mod. cont. style hf. cf. (HD. Apr.13; 74) Frs. 2,000
- – Anr. Copy. 4to. Wide margin, especially 1st. & last ll. slightly browned, cont. private hf. leath. (HT. May 8; 400) DM 820

PONCELET, Polycarpe
- [–] **Chémie du Gout et de l'Odorat.** Ill.:– B. Audran. Paris, 1755. Wide margin, minimal browning, cont. leath. gt., spine slightly split. (R. Apr.4; 1933) DM 700

PONCELIN DE LA ROCHE-TILHAC, J.-Ch.
- [–] **Campagnes de Louis XV, ou Tableau des Expéditions Militaires sous le Dernier Règne** ... Ill.:– Nattier, Lepicié, Rigaud, La Tour, Van Loo, & others. Priv. ptd., 1788. Fo. Sewed, unc. (HD. Mar.21; 70) Frs. 2,500

PONS, F.
- **Topographia Europae. In Vier Gespräch ... Sitten, Gebräuchen, Regierungen** ... Basel, 1689. Parallel German, Fr., Italian & Latin text, cont. leath. gt., upr. jnt. rubbed. (BR. Apr.12; 174) DM 500

PONS, Joseph Sebastien
- **Concert d'Eté, Poèmes.** Ill.:– A. Maillol. Paris, 1945. *(200) numbered on Lana.* Lge. 4to. Rough ll. in orig. wraps., orig. hf. linen cover & bd. s.-c., slightly bumped. (HK. Nov.11; 3766) DM 800

PONTANUS, Joannes Jovianus

- **Rerum Danicarum Historia.** Amst., H. Hondius, 1631. Fo. Engraved allegorical title, port., 4 engraved folding maps (Bibliotheca Danica calls for only 3), hf.-title, maps with 1 or 2 margins out close, strengthened at some folds, slight discoloration of text, cont. panel. cf. gt., worn. (S. Dec.1; 309) *Israel.* £260
- – **Anr. Copy.** Fo. Hf.-title, engraved allegorical title, port. of author, 4 engraved folding maps (of 5), 1 or 2 margins cut close, some folds strengthened, some browning in text, cont. panel. cf. gt., worn. (S. May 21; 240) *Charles.* £250
- **Rerum et Urbis Amstelodamensium Historia.** Amst., 1611. *Orig. Edn.* Sm. fo. Slightly foxed, sm. repair to 1 plt., blank outer margins of some quires slightly defect., cont. vell. (VG. Mar.19; 251) Fls. 2,500
- – **Anr. Copy.** 2 pts. in 1 vol. Sm. fo. Title defect. & mntd., p. 2/3 restored with loss of text, view of Exchange very defect., old sm. map mntd., old cf., corners slightly defect., w.a.f. (VG. Sep.14; 1189) Fls. 700
See— BRACELLUS, J. & Pontanus, Joannes Jovianus

PONTE, Lorenzo da

- **Memorie.** N.Y., 1829. *2nd. [partly Orig.] Edn.* 3 vols. 16mo. Cont. hf. roan, spines decor. (HD. Mar.9; 112) Frs. 1,100

PONTIANI, Ottavio

- **Poesie Nella Creatione e Coronatione di Papa Urbano Ottavo.** Rome, 1623. *1st. Edn.* Cont. limp vell., lge. arms gt. on covers, dedication copy. (BBA. May 23; 330) *Parikian.* £240

PONTICUS, Ludovicus Virunius

- **Britannicae Historiae Libri Sex [etc.].** L., 1585. 3 pts. in 1 vol. Continuous sigs. & pagination, blank D6, wormhole in a few ll., not affecting text, slight browning, 18th. C. cf. [STC 20109] (S. Oct.11; 578) *Georges.* £110

PONTIFICALE ROMANUM An. Dom. 1726

Ill.:– Sébastien Lonca. Vatican, 1726. Fo. Cont. richly decor. red mor., unidentified archiepiscopal arms. (HD. Mar.21; 71) Frs. 1,600

PONTING, Herbert George

- **The Great White South.** 1921. Cl. gt., d.-w. (P. Jun.7; 37) £240

PONTOPPIDAN, Erich

- **The Natural History of Norway.** L., 1755. 2 pts. in 1 vol. Fo. Engraved folding map, 28 plts., cont. cf. (C. Nov.16; 32) *Steedman.* £550
- – **Anr. Copy.** 2 pts. in 1 vol. Fo. Folding map cleanly torn & reprd., old cf., worn. (CSK. Sep.16; 170) £110
- – **Anr. Copy.** 2 pts. in 1 vol. Fo. Cont. cf., rebkd., rubbed. (VG. Sep.14; 1118) Fls. 600

POOL, Robert & Cash, John

- **Views of the most Remarkable Public Buildings ... in City of Dublin.** Dublin, 1780. 4to. Engraved title, 2 folding plans, 29 plts., including 1 folding, owner's inscr. on title, cont. hf. cf. (C. Dec.9; 124) *Weinreb.* £450

POOLE, Joshua

- **The English Parnassus: or, a Helpe to English Poesie.** L., 1657. *1st. Edn.* Iss. with title in red & black. Lacks A1 & Qq7, some headlines shaved, title & last lf. laid down, a few stains, cont. cf. [Wing P2814] (BBA. May 3; 138) *Thomas.* £50

POOLE, Matthew

- [–] **A Model for the Maintaining of Students of Choice Abilities at the University.** L., 1658. 4to. Recent vell.-bkd. bds. [Wing P2842] (BBA. May 3; 141) *Jarndyce.* £220

POOR LAWS

1724. Sm. 8vo. Recent spr. cf. (TA. Dec.15; 459) £70

POOT, Herbert Cornelisson

- **Het Groot Natuur- en Zederkundigh Werelttoneel of Woordenboek van meer dan 1200 Aeloude Egiptische, Grieksche en Romeinsche Zinnebeelden of Beeldenspraek.** Ill.:– F. Ottens & J.C. Philips. Delft,

1743-50. *1st. Compl. Edn.* 3 vols. Fo. Some light soiling or foxing, 2 ll. slightly torn, mod. hf. linen, unc. (R. Apr.3; 181) DM 1,100
- – **Anr. Copy.** 3 vols. Fo. L.P., 1st. 6 emblems hand-cold., few ll. of Vol. 1 foxed, cont. blind-tooled vell. (VG. Nov.30; 610) Fls. 1,800

POPE, Alexander

- [–] **The Dunciad.** L., 1729. *1st. Compl. Edn. 1st. Iss., without addenda lf.* 4to. Mod. paper-bkd. marb. bds., unc., orig. wraps. preserved, upr. wrap. stained; John Drinkwater bkplt., Frederic Dannay copy. (CNY. Dec.16; 274) $250
- [–] – **Anr. Edn.** L., 1729. *1st. Compl. Edn.* 4to. Engraved title cropped, cont. cf., rather worn. (BBA. May 3; 196) *Bickersteth.* £70
- [–] – **Anr. Copy.** 4to. Minor repairs to engraved title, mod. mott. cf., spine gt., partly unc. (SPB. May 16; 113) $300
- **An Essay on Man.** L., [1733-34]. *1st. Edns.* Pts. 1-4 in 1 vol. Fo. Hf.-titles to pts. 2-3, advt. lf. in pt. 4, maroon str.-grd. mor. (SPB. May 16; 114) $2,000
- – **Anr. Copy.** Pts. 1-4. Fo. Title in facs., dedication lf. reprd., lacks hf.-title, later engraved port. bnd. in, mod. mor. gt. (SG. Apr.19; 153) $250
- – **Anr. Edn.** Intro.:– Maynard Mack. Oxford, Roxb. Cl., 1962. 4to. Orig. qtr. mor., covers a little marked. (S. Oct.4; 240) *Traylen.* £140
- – **Anr. Copy.** Fo. Crushed qtr. mor.; the A.A. Houghton Jnr. copy. (SG. Sep.15; 295) $225
- **The First Satire of the Second Book of Horace, Imitated in a Dialogue between Alexander Pope of Twickenham in Com. Midd. Esq.; on the one Part, & his Learned Council on the Other.** L., 1733. *1st. Edn. 1st. Iss., without comma after 'Pope', comma after 'virtuti'.* Fo. Mod. three-qtr. mor., worn; H. Buxton-Forman bkplt. laid in before title-lf. (RO. Apr.23; 253) $100
- **Lockenraub.** Trans.:– Luisen Adelgunden Victorien Gottsched. Leipzig, 1744. *1st. German Edn.* 4to. Title verso & 1 p. stpd., browned, several end sigs. with lr. margin worming, 19th. C. bds. (HK. Nov.10; 2649) DM 400
- [Of False Taste] **An Epistle to ... Burlington.** L., 1731. *1st. Edn. 1st. Iss.* Fo. Hf.-title, advts., short margin tears, few stains mostly marginal, hf. mor.; Hagen-Clawson copy. (SG. Feb.9; 308) $300
- [Of the Knowledge & Characters of Men] **An Epistle to ... Cobham.** L., 1733 [1734]. *1st. Edn.* Fo. Hf.-title, advts., 2 early marginalia, spr. cf. gt., dentelles gt., by R. Wallis, cl. s.-c. (SG. Feb.9; 309) $200
- **Oeuvres Complètes.** Ill.:– Kneller & Marillier. Paris, 1779. *New Edn. 1st. Printing.* 8 vols. Cont. cf. gt., decor. spines, inner roll-stp. (HD. Sep.22; 315) Frs. 4,000
- **Opyt o cheloveke [Essay on Man].** Ill.:– J. Punt. Moscow, 1757. *1st. Russian Edn.* A few ll. spotted, cont. mor., slightly rubbed. (BBA. Feb.9; 135) *Quaritch.* £70
- **The Poetical Works.** Glasgow, 1785. 3 vols. Fo. Orig. bds. (P. Jun.7; 88) £230
- **Sämtliche Werke.** Altona, 1758-64. *1st German Coll. Edn.* 5 vols. in 3. Engraved frontis. & vig. title to each, cont. cf. gt., a little rubbed. (TA. Jun.21; 324) £100
- – **Anr. Copy.** 5 vols. in 3. Foxing cont. leath. gt., decor., 2 vols. slightly wormed. (HK. May 16; 2197) DM 500
- **The Temple of Fame: A Vision.** L., 1715. *1st. Edn.* Hf.-title & 'Proposals', a few stains, spr. cf. gt., gt. dentelles, by Riviere. (SG. Feb.9; 307) $275
- **The Works.** L., 1717-35. *1st. 4to. Edn. Vol. 1: 1st. Iss.* 2 vols. Directions to binder, lacks frontis. (With:) – **Letters.** L., 1737. *1st. Authorized Edn. 1st.? Iss.* 1 vol. 1st. imp. of gathering B. Together 3 vols. 4to. Early mott. cf. gt. extra, 1 cover scraped. (SG. Feb.9; 311) $130
- [Collected Works]. L., 1717-1807. 6 vols. 4to. Frontis.-port., ports., lacks 'Directions to Binder' lf., lacks some hf.-titles, some ll. misbnd., some browning & spotting, cont. red mor. gt., some jnts. reprd., soiling, scuffing, w.a.f. (SPB. May 16; 117) $700
- **The Works.** Ed.:– William Warburton. 1751. 9 vols. Cont. mott. cf.; Sir Ivar Colquhoun, of Luss copy. (CE. Mar.22; 246) £320

- – **Anr. Edn.** 1766. 9 vols. Cont. cf. (SKC. Nov.18; 1903) £60
- – **Anr. Edn.** Ed.:– Owen Ruffhead. L., 1769-1807. *Partly Orig. Edn.* 6 vols. 4to. Cont. hf. cf., corners. (HD. Apr.13; 40) Frs. 2,700
- – **Anr. Edn.** Ed.:– William Roscoe. L., 1847. 8 vols. Lge. 8vo. Early tree cf., mod. rebacking, covers worn. (SG. Feb.16; 242) $200

POPE, Alexander & others

- **Miscellanea in two Volumes. Never before published. Viz. I. Familiar letters written to Henry Cromwell Esq; by Mr. Pope, [etc.].** L., 1727 [i.e. 1726]. 2 vols. Variant of Vol. 2 containing in 2nd hf. 'Laus Ululae the praise of Owls ... translated by a Canary Bird', cont. cf., trifle worn, bkplt. removed from 1st. vol. (BBA. Nov.30; 212) *Hannas.* £380
- [–] **Miscellaneous Poems & Translations, by Several Hands.** L., 1712. *1st. Edn.* Engraved frontis., hf.-title, 4 ll. advts., cont. panel. cf., spine gt.; lge. engraved cont. bkplt. of Maurice Johnson, antiquary, Gerald E. Slater copy. (SPB. May 16; 115) $1,300

POPE, Arthur Upham

- **A Survey of Persian Art.** L., 1938-39. 6 vols. 1,482 plts. (With:) BESTERMANN, Theodore – **Index.** L., 1958. 1 vol. Together 7 vols. Fo. Buckram, ex-liby. (SG. May 3; 284) $1,900

POPE, Dr. Walter

- **The Wish ... with a short life of the author by Mr. Beverly Chew.** Jamaica, Long Island, Marion Pr., 1897. *(120) numbered.* 4to. Hf. cf.; Beverly Chew bkplt., with 10 A.L.s from F. Hopkins Chew & 1 A.L.s. from E.C. Stedman. (SG. Sep.15; 90) $140

POPE-HENNESSY, John

- **An Introduction to Italian Sculpture.** 1955, 1958, 1963. 3 pts. in 5 vols. 4to. No bdg. stated. (SPB. Nov.30; 117) $225

POPE-HENNESSY, Una

- **Early Chinese Jades.** L., 1923. *[1st. Edn.].* 4to. Orig. cl., rubbed. (TA. Jun.21; 457) £56
- – **Anr. Copy.** 4to. 64 plts., cl. (SG. Aug.25; 214) $125

POPHAM, Arthur Ewart

- **Italian Drawings exhibited at the Royal Academy.** L., 1930. 4to. Mor., gt. decor. in Renaissance style, gt. decor. inner dentelle, inner jnt. strengthened. (GB. May 4: 1884) DM 400

POPLIMONT, Ch.

- **La Belgique Héraldique.** Paris, 1863-67. 11 vols. Some foxing, bnd. by Sky. (LM. Mar.3; 150) B.Frs. 9,000

POPOLO D'ITALIA

Founder:– Benito Mussolini. Milano, [1 Jun.] 1927-[11 May] 1940. 37 vols. Fo. Bnd., 2 vols. in pts. (B. Feb.8; 953) Fls. 1,600

POPPEL, Johann

- **Malerische Ansichten aus Nurnberg, Picturesque Views of Nuremberg.** L., ca. 1840. Lge. 8vo. Steel-engraved title, 21 plts., orig. cl. gt. (C. Nov.16; 155a) *D'Arcy.* £500

POPPEL, J. (Ill.)
See— LANGE, Ludwig

POPPEL, J. & Kurz, M.

- **Salzburg u. s. Umgebungen.** Ed.:– R. Löser. München, ca. 1840. 24 steel-engraved plts., lightly foxed, orig. linen. (HK. Nov.9; 1164) DM 1,250

PORCACCHI, Thomaso da Castiglione.

- **Funerali Antichi di Diversi Popoli et Nationi.** Venice, 1574. *1st. Edn.* 4to. Wormhole at title & 2 ll., repair to 1 lf. of Table, liby. stp. on title, erased at margin, 18th. C. vell., short tear at head of spine, some worming at hinges. (C. May 30; 44) *Thomas.* £200
- **L'Isole Piu Famose del Mondo.** Maps:– Girolamo Porro. Venice, Heredi di Simon Galignani, 1590. *3rd. Edn.* 4to. Engraved architectural title, 47 maps inset in text, faint browning or staining mostly affecting text, a few MS. annots. in ink in cont. hand in latter, cont. limp vell., spine lettered in ink,

slightly soiled, w.a.f. [Sabin 64150] (S. May 21; 148) *Schuster.* £750

PORCHER, Cdr. E.A
See— SMITH, Capt. R. Murdoch & Porcher, Cdr. E.A.

PORCHER, F.P.
- Prize Essay ... :Illustrations of Disease with the Microscope; Clinical Investigations. Charleston, S.C., 1861. *1st. Edn.* Pt. 1 (all publd.). Lge. 8vo. Foxed, few ll. slightly stained, ptd. wraps., extremities chipped, upr. wrap. soiled. (SG. Jan.19; 159) $850

PORCUPINE, Peter (Pseud.)
See— COBBETT, William 'Peter Porcupine'

PORRI, Alessio
- Vaso di Verità nel quale si contengono dodeci Resolutioni vere ... intorno all'Origine ... e Morte dell'Antichristo. Ill.:– Girolamo Porro. Venezia, 1597. *1st. Edn.* Sm. 4to. Some stains, mod. mod. covers, orig. vell. spine, soiled. (SI. Dec.15; 32) Lire 380,000

PORT, Célestin
- Dictionnaire de Maine et Loire. Angers, [1880]. 4to. Cont. hf. chagrin, decor. spine. (HD. Dec.9; 170) Frs. 3,000

PORT OF LONDON
- The Several Plans & Drawings referred to in the Third Report from the Select Committee upon the Improvement of the Port of London. L., 1800. Lge. fo. 21 lge. engraved or aquatint-engraved double-p. or folding plts., plans, diagrams & elevations, some hand-cold. in wash & outl., orig. bds., back-strip defect. (S. Mar.6; 396) *Weinreb.* £380
– – Anr. Copy. Lge. fo. 20 (of 21) folding plts., including 5 hand-cold., 4 stained in lr. margin, few slight tears, orig. wraps., defect. (P. Sep.8; 188a) *Burgess.* £95

PORT PHILIP GAZETTE, The
Mona Vale, 1979. *Facs. Edn. (285) numbered.* 5 vols. Fo. Bdg. not stated. (KH. May 1; 580) Aus. $140

PORTA, Johannes or Giovanni Baptista
- Coelestis Physiognomiae. Naples, 1603. 4to. MS. on 17 ll. at end, sigd. 'Matthaeus Hc. fecit Hieronymus Massa, Patritius Salernitanus 24 July 1685', vell.; Dr. Walter Pagel copy. (S. Feb.7; 315) *Phelps.* £200
- De Humana Physiognomonia. Frankfurt, 1608. Cont. vell. (D. Nov.23; 610) DM 740
– – Anr. Edn. Frankfurt, 1618. 2 human figures inked over in parts, sm. hole in 2 text ll., some browning, cont. leath. gt., slightly spotted, spine restored. (R. Oct.12; 1456) DM 450
- Magia Naturalis, oder: Hauss–, Kunst– und Wunder-Buch. Trans.:– Chr. Peganius ('Rautner'). Nuremb., 1713. 4to. Old MS. marginalia, slightly stained thro.-out, from p. 1001 to end stained in lr. corner with some slight loss of text or ills., & in some upr. corners, lacks free end-papers, cont. leath. gt., rubbed & spine torn. (D. Nov.24; 4445) DM 2,600
– – Anr. Copy. 4to. 3 ll. torn, cont. vell. (R. Oct.12; 2069) DM 1,500
– – Anr. Copy. 4to. Title with tear & margin defect. reprd., lacks frontis. & 8 pp. copper engrs., chaps. 1-12 spotted, especially in early margins, cont. vell., spotted. (HK. May 15; 504) DM 1,050

PORTAL, Baron Antoine
- Histoire de l'Anatomie et de la Chirurgie. Paris, 1770-73. 6 vols. in 7. Hf.-titles, cont. Fr. cf., worn; Dr. Walter Pagel copy. (S. Feb.7; 316) *Goodrich.* £350

PORTALIS, Baron Roger
- Danloux Peintre de Portraits et son Journal durant l'Emigration. Paris, 1910. *(36) numbered special copies.* Fo. This copy for Emile Picot, orig. wraps., slightly soiled. (BBA. Nov.10; 223) *Leicester Art Books.* £110
- Honoré Fragonard, sa Vie et son Oeuvre. 1889. 2 vols. 4to. Decor. mor. by Chambolle-Duru, wraps., upr. cover of 1st. vol. reprd. (HD. Apr.13; 110) Frs. 3,500

PORTALIS, Baron Roger & Beraldi, Henri
- Les Graveurs du Dix-Huitième Siècle. Paris, 1880-82. *(500).* 3 vols. Orig. linen. (GB. Nov.5; 1376) DM 400

PORTER, Arthur Kingsley
- Romanesque Sculpture of the Pilgrimage Roads. Boston, ca. 1923. *1st. Edn.* 10 vols. (1 text & 9 plt. vols.). Orig. linen (text) & orig. linen s.-c.'s (plts.). (HT. May 9; 1161) DM 1,600
– – Anr. Edn. Boston, 1923. *(500) numbered.* Text vol. & 9 plt. vols., together 10 vols. Each plt. liby.-stpd. on blank verso, cl. & loose in matching s.-c.'s. (SG. May 3; 286) $475
- Spanish Romanesque Sculpture. Flor. & Paris, 1928. 2 vols. 4to. Orig. hf. mor. (BBA. Sep.8; 299) *Leicester Art Books.* £80

PORTER, George Richardson
- The Nature & Properties of the Sugar Cane. 1830. Orig. cl. (PD. Dec.14; 254) £78

PORTER, Katherine Anne
- A Christmas Story. Ill.:– Ben Shahn. N.Y., [1967]. *(500) numbered, with special frontis., sigd. by author & artist.* Sq. 12mo. Cl., cl. s.-c. (SG. Mar.1; 458) $110

PORTER, Sir Robert Ker
[–] Costumes of Russia. L., n.d. 4to. Engraved title-p. & 26 hand-cold. aquatint plts. only, new marb. wraps. (SPB. May 17; 660) $100
- Travelling Sketches in Russia & Sweden. L., 1809. *[1st. Edn.].* 2 vols. 4to. 28 plts. hand-cold., cont. hf. cf., rubbed. (BBA. Dec.15; 74) *Hannas.* £110
– – Anr. Copy. 2 vols. in 1. 4to. 41 plts., including 28 cold. costume plts., 2nd. title remargined, some foxing, some offsets in text, hf. cf. (SG. Sep.22; 248) $225
– – Anr. Edn. 1813. *2nd. Edn.* 2 vols. in 1. 4to. 41 plts., including 28 hand-cold. & 3 folding, lacks hf.-titles, some faint offsetting, sm. tear affecting 1 plt. reprd., sm. hole affecting 1 lf. in Vol. 1, later hf. cf. gt. (S. Nov.1; 82) *Thorp.* £120
- Travels in Georgia, Persia, Armenia, Ancient Babylonia ... L., 1821-22. *1st. Edn.* 2 vols. 4to. Maps & plts., some folding, slightly browned & stained, hf. cf., worn, marb. bds. (SPB. May 17; 661) $375
– – Anr. Copy. 2 vols. 4to. 91 (of 92) engraved & aquatint plts., some folding, 1 letterpress chart inserted, scattered light foxing, some offsetting, cont. cf. gt., rebkd. (SG. Sep.22; 249) $350

PORTER, William Ogilvie
[–] Sir Edward Seaward's narrative of his shipwreck ... Ed.:– Jane Porter. L., 1832. *2nd. Edn.* 3 vols. Cont. cf., spines gt.; 4 p. A.L.s. from Miss Porter loosely inserted. (BBA. Dec.15; 14) *Remington.* £50

PORTER, William Sydney 'O. Henry'
[–] Complete Writings. Ill.:– Gordon Grant. N.Y., 1917. *Memorial Edn. de Luxe, (1075).* 14 vols. Hf. mor. gt. (SPB. Dec.13; 555) $600

PORTFOLIO, The, an Artistic Periodical
Ed.:– Philip Gilbert Hamerton. Ill.:– A. Brunet-Debaines or H. Toussaint. L., 1880. Vol. XI. Fo. Orig. sheep & marb. bds. (HA. Nov.18; 59) $130

PORTFOLIO, The, or a Collection of State Papers
Ed.:– [David Urquhart]. 1836-37. 5 vols. 3 partly hand-cold. engraved plts., orig. cl., rubbed. (BBA. Feb.9; 136) *Parsloe.* £80

PORTHAISE, Jean
- Cinq Sermons ... Paris, 1594. 2 pts. in 1 vol. 19th. C. pink mor. gt. by Koehler, pink mor. doubls.; Charles Nodier bkplt. (C. May 30; 98) *Henner.* £500

PORTLOCK, J.E.
- Report of the Geology of the County of London-derry, & of Parts of Tyrone & Fermanagh. Dublin, 1843. *1st. Edn.* Lge. folding frontis. map & folding plans hand-cold., unopened, cl. (GM. Dec.7; 244) £70

PORTLOCK, Capt. Nathaniel
- A Voyage round the World ... L., 1789. *1st. Edn.* 4to. 20 engraved ports., plts. & folding maps, cont.

tree cf., spine gt. [Sabin 64389] (C. Nov.16; 33) *Brooke-Hitching.* £900
– – Anr. Copy. 4to. Engraved port. frontis., 6 folding maps, 13 engraved plts., including 5 hand-cold., 1st. folding map bkd. with linen, lf. M2 torn across, some pencil margin annots., cont. tree cf., rebkd., corners reprd., corners worn, end-papers renewed; the Rt. Hon. Visc. Eccles copy. (CNY. Nov.18; 232) $1,000

PORTLOCK, Capt. Nathaniel & Dixon, Capt. George
[–] A Voyage Round the World, in the years 1785, 1786, 1787, & 1788. Preface:– C[hristopher] L[ogie]. L., R. Randal, 1789. Cont. spr. sheep, corners worn; Bryan Edwards bkplt., the Rt. Hon. Visc. Eccles copy. [Sabin 100817] (CNY. Nov.18; 233) $1,800

PORTLOCK, William Henry
- A New Complete & Universal Collection of Authentic & Entertaining Voyages & Travels to All the Various Parts of the World. [1794]. Fo. Lacks frontis. & World chart, 1 ill. torn, cont. pol. cf., Ralph Shedley arms, rebkd., new end-papers. (SKC. Mar.9; 2030) £130

PORTUGAL
- Ordenacoes e Leis do Reino de Portugal. Recopiladas per Mandado do Muito Alto Catholico, & Poderoso Rei Dom Phillippe I. Lisboa, 1603. Fo. Some dampstains, some ll. reprd. in margins, many early MS. glosses in margins, later cf., rebkd., some wear. (RO. Dec.11; 278) $170

POSADA, Jose Guadalupe
- Illustrador de la Vida Mexicana. Mexico, 1963. Fo. No bdg. stated. (SPB. Nov.30; 128) $125

POSNIKOV, S.P.
- Bibliografiya Russkoi revolyutsii [Bibliography of the Russian Revolution & Civil War 1917-21]. Prague, 1938. Cont. cl., rubbed, orig. wraps. preserved. (BBA. Feb.9; 137) *Edwards.* £75

POSSANNER, B.
- Chemische Technologie jener Industrien. Wien, 1893. 4 pts. in 1 vol. 4to. 2 plts. torn, hf. linen with orig. wraps. (D. Nov.24; 4130) DM 480

POSSEVINUS, Antonius
- Moscovia. Antw., 1587. *2nd. Edn.* Some ll. lightly foxed, cont. limp vell. (R. Oct.11; 102) DM 700

POSTER, The
Ill.:– after Beardsley, Bradley, Mucha, Cherot, Steinlen, & others. L., Jun. 1898-Aug. 1900. Nos. 1-10, 12, 13 & 21-25 only (of 33). Orig. wraps., some covers detchd., 1 no. lacks covers. (S. Dec.20; 512) *Till.* £170

POSTES IMPERIALES. Etat General des Postes et Relais de l'Empire Francais ... pour l'An 1810
Paris, 1810. Cont. str.-grd. red mor. gt., Napoleon I arms, spine decor., watered silk end-ll. & doubls. (HD. May 4; 400) Frs. 14,500

POSTLETHWAYT, Malachy
- The Universal Dictionary of Trade & Commerce. L., 1751-55. 2 vols. in 4. Fo. Engraved frontis., 2 vig. titles, 24 folding maps, some staining, hf. cf., rubbed. (P. Mar.15; 197) £240
– – Anr. Copy. 2 vols. Fo. 23 folding engraved maps (some closely cropped & slightly wormed), folding tables, cont. spr. cf. (TA. Aug.18; 286) £95
– – Anr. Edn. L., 1757. *2nd. Edn.* 2 vols. Fo. Some staining, margin fraying, foxing, old cf., worn, jnts. brkn. (RO. Dec.11; 279) $240

POTERIUS, Petrus
- Pharmacopoeia Spagirica. Bologna, 1622. Limp vell.; Dr. Walter Pagel copy. (S. Feb.7; 317) *Quaritch.* £440

POTHIER
- Traité des Contrats de Bienfaisance. — Traité des Obligations. Paris, 1766. 2 vols. & 2 vols. 12mo. Cont. cf. (HD. Feb.22; 173) Frs. 1,700

POTOCKI, Count Joseph
- Sport in Somaliland. L., 1900. *(200) numbered.* 4to. Orig. cl., soiled. (BBA. Dec.15; 36) *Trophy Room books.* £420

POTT, Joseph Holden
- Chymische Untersuchungen. Berlin, 1757. 3 pts. in 1 vol. Title with MS. owners mark, 3 ll. pasted, some browning, cont. hf. vell., slightly rubbed, spine pasted over. (HT. May 8; 253)   DM 410

POTTER, Beatrix
- Ginger & Pickles. 1909. *1st. Edn.* Sm. 4to. Orig. bds., slightly soiled. (BS. May 2; 83)   £50
- Peter Rabbit's Painting Book. L., [1911]. 4to. Orig. bds., spine & edges slightly worn; pres. copy, inscr. to Mary Kynaston 'from Miss Potter & Peter Rabbit ... July 11. 11', 2nd. & 3rd. outl. ills. hand-cold. (but of a much higher standard than would be expected from the recipient, & may be by Beatrix Potter herself). (S. Nov.22; 398)   *Quaritch.* £550
- The Roly-Poly Pudding. 1908. *1st. Edn.* Sm. 4to. Orig. cl. bds. (BS. May 2; 81)   £90
- The Story of a Fierce Bad Rabbit. 1906. *1st. Edn.* 16mo. 2 sections creased, orig. cl. wallet-style bdg., slightly rubbed, van Veen coll. (S. Feb.28; 14)£90
- The Tailor of Gloucester. L., Dec. 1902. *1st. Edn., [500].* 16mo. Orig. ptd. bds., cl. case. (S. Nov.22; 395)   *Steedman.* £920
- The Tale of Benjamin Bunny. L., 1904. *1st. Edn.* Orig. bds., covers lightly rubbed, spine chipped at head; Joe E. Brown bkplt., Marymount College copy. (CBA. Mar.3; 446) $110
- The Tale of the Flopsy Bunnies. L., 1909. *1st. Edn.* 16mo. With the notice board on p. 14, orig. bds., spine faded. (BS. May 2; 82)   £55
- - Anr. Copy. Bds., spine faded, ill. end-papers. (CBA. Aug.21; 476) $105
- The Tale of Mrs. Tittlemouse. L., 1910. *1st. Edn.* A few sm. finger marks, orig. bds., covers lightly rubbed, slightly soiled; Joe E. Brown bkplt., Marymount College copy. (CBA. Mar.3; 449) $150
- The Tale of Peter Rabbit. [Oct. 1902]. *1st. Edn.* 16mo. Frontis. reinserted, orig. cl., leaf-pattern end-papers. (BBA. Oct.27; 88)   *Elkin Mathews.* £70
- - Anr. Edn. L., ca. 1902. *1st. Edn. 5th. Printing.* Hf.-title clipped, some light soiling, 1st. state bdg. of grey bds., with dotted 'O', & pict. label on upr. cover, double-p. ill. end-papers (corresponding to neither Linder's 5th. nor 6th. printing). (CBA. Aug.21; 480) $120
- - Anr. Edn. L., ca. 1904. Ink inscr. to frontis. recto, bds., covers with dotted 'O', later state of double-p. end-papers, glassine wrap. chipped. (CBA. Aug.21; 481) $150
- The Tale of Pigling Bland. L., 1913. *1st. Edn.* 16mo. Slightly soiled, orig. bds., slightly worn; pres. copy, inscr. 'with kind regards from Beatrix Potter in remembrance of Sawrey Sept. 1920'. (S. Nov.22; 399)   *Steedman.* £260
- The Tale of Squirrel Nutkin. L., 1903. *1st. Edn.* Orig. bds., slightly loose, covers rubbed; Joe E. Brown & Marymount College bkplts. (CBA. Mar.3; 451) $150
- The Tale of Timmy Tiptoes. L., 1911. *1st. Edn.* 16mo. Orig. bds. (BS. May 2; 84)   £55
- - Anr. Copy. Orig. bds., slightly loose, covers lightly rubbed, a few sm. finger marks; Joe E. Brown & Marymount College bkplts. (CBA. Mar.3; 453) $150
- The Tale of Tom Kitten. L., 1907. *1st. Edn.* 16mo. Orig. bds., slightly rubbed. (BBA. May 23; 126)   *S.C. Smith.* £55
- - Anr. Copy. Orig. bds., covers lightly rubbed; Joe E. Brown & Marymount College bkplts. (CBA. Mar.3; 452) $110

POTTER, Robert
- Observations on the Poor Laws, on the Present State of the Poor, & on Houses of Industry. 1775. Stitched as iss. (LC. Mar.1; 531)   £150

POTTER, Thomas Rossell
- The History & Antiquities of Charnwood Forest. L., 1842. 4to. Embossed cl. (HBC. May 17; 310)   £60

POUCHKINE, Aleksandr Sergyeevich
See— PUSHKIN or POUCHKINE, Aleksandr Sergyeevich

POUCHOT, François
- Memoir upon the Late War in North America, between the French & English. Trans.:– Franklin B. Hough. Roxbury, 1866. *1st. Edn. in Engl. (50)*

L.P. 2 vols. 4to. Light liby. mark, red hf. mor., rubbed. (SG. Apr.5; 170) $300

POULENC, Francis
- Sonates pour Instruments à vent [piano reduction]. L., 1925. *1st. Edn.* Slightly dust-stained; inscr. on fly-lf. 'au cher Diaghilev avec mon affection Fr. Poulenc 1925', Serge Lifar Coll. (S. May 9; 185)   £200
- Suite pour Piano. L., 1920. *1st. Edn.* Slightly dust-stained; inscr. on 1st. p. of music 'a Serge de Diaghilev en temoinage de gratitude F. Poulenc', Serge Lifar Coll. (S. May 9; 187)   £200

POULLAIN DE SAINT-FOIX, Germain François
[-] Catalogue des Chevaliers, Commandeurs et officiers de l'ordre du Saint Esprit. Ill.:– after Boucher (frontis), Gravelot. Paris, 1760. Fo. Cont. cf., gt. decor., crowned H in corners, centre emblem, decor. spine, scratched, corners defect. (HD. Dec.9; 73)   Frs. 1,100

POULLIN DE LUMINA, E.J.
- Histoire de la Guerre Contre les Anglois. Geneva, 1759-60. *1st. Edn.* 2 pts. in 1 vol. Hf.-titles, mod. hf. mor. [Sabin 64720] (SG. Nov.3; 170) $550

POULSON, George
- The History & Antiquities of the Seigniory of Holderness in the East-Riding of the County of York ... Hull, 1840-41. 2 vols. 4to. Some foxing, old hf. mor. (KH. Nov.9; 405)   Aus. $150

POUNCY, John
[-] [Dorset Photographically Illustrated]. [Dorchester & L.], n.d. Pt. 2 only. Ob. fo. 20 tinted photolitho. plts., light spotting, orig. cl., faded. (CSK. Aug.19; 113)   £120

POUND, Ezra
- Antheil & the Treatise on Harmony. Paris, Three Mountains Pr., 1924. *[600].* Orig. wraps., unopened. (BBA. Nov.30; 293)   *Duschnes.* £150
- Cathay. L., 1915. *1st. Edn. [1000].* Slightly spotted, orig. wraps., soiled, loose; inscr. to Sara [Teasdale] from Dorothy [Pound]. (BBA. Nov.30; 288)   *Belanske.* £90
- - Anr. Copy. 12mo. Advt. lf. laid in as iss., orig. ptd. wraps., partly unopened, fore-corners creased; Frederic Dannay copy. (CNY. Dec.16; 277) $160
- Cavalcanti Poems. Verona, Bodoni Pr. [for James Laughlin], a New Directions Book, 1966. *(200) numbered. (190) on Pescia paper, sigd.* 4to. Orig. vell.-bkd. bds., s.-c. (S. Nov.22; 269)   *Henderson.* £420
- Drafts & Fragments of Cantos CX-CXVII. L., 1968. *(310) sigd.* Fo. Errata slip loosely inserted, orig. cl., s.-c. (S. Apr.9; 276)   *Henderson.* £95
- - Anr. Edn. [N.Y.], Stone Wall Pr., [1968]. *(310) numbered & sigd.* Sm. fo. Errata slip laid in, cl., unc., s.-c. (SG. Mar.1; 460) $275
- Hugh Selwyn Mauberley. L., Ovid Pr., 1920. *1st. Edn., (200). (165) numbered.* Tall 8vo. Orig. cl.-bkd. bds., unopened, a few light stains on upr. cover & spine; Frederic Dannay copy. (CNY. Dec.16; 281) $2,600
- Imaginary Letters. Paris, Black Sun Pr., 1930. *(300) numbered on Navarre paper.* Sm. 4to. Ptd. wraps.; Clifton Waller Barrett bkplt. (SG. Mar.1; 461) $110
- Indiscretions. Paris, Three Mountains Pr., 1923. *1st. Edn. (300) numbered.* Orig. cl.-bkd. bds., slightly soiled. (BBA. Nov.30; 292)   *Belanske.* £300
- - Anr. Copy. Bi-fo. Orig. 4 ptd. sheets, unfolded & unbnd., minor wear & soiling. (RO. Apr.23; 254) $350
- Lustra. [L., 1916]. *1st. Edn. 1st. Imp. (200) numbered.* Orig. cl., soiled. (BBA. Nov.30; 289)   *Belanske.* £110
- - Anr. Copy. Orig. cl., cover stained, cl. d.-w.; Harry & Caresse Crosby bkplt., Frederic Danny copy. (CNY. Dec.16; 278) $380
- - Anr. Edn. L., 1916. *1st. Edn.* Orig. cl., spine slightly soiled. (BBA. Aug.18; 33)   *Bell, Book & Radmall.* £60
- Lustra ... with Earlier Poems. Ill.:– Gaudier-Brzeska. N.Y., 1917. *1st. Amer. Edn. 1st. Imp., (60) numbered.* Hf.-title with advt. on verso excised, orig. cl.; Frederic Dannay copy. (CNY. Dec.16; 279) $320

- - Anr. Edn. N.Y., 1917. *1st. Amer. Edn. 2nd. Imp.* Orig. bds., unopened, d.-w.; Frederic Dannay copy. (CNY. Dec.16; 280) $220
- - Anr. Copy. Ptd. bds., defect.; Louis Zukofsky copy, with later MS. bkplt. (SG. Mar.1; 462) $175
- Personae. L., 1909. *1st. Edn. 1st. Iss., [1000].* Orig. bds., spine reprd. (BBA. Nov.30; 287)   *Belanske.* £85
- - Anr. Edn. L., 1909. *1st. Edn., (500).* 12mo. Orig. bds. [1st. bdg.], unopened; Frederic Dannay copy. (CNY. Dec.16; 276) $320
- - Anr. Edn. L., 1909. 12mo. Bds. (SG. Mar.1; 463) $175
- Poems 1918-21. N.Y., 1921. *1st. Edn.* Orig. bds., unopened, d.-w. (BBA. Nov.30; 291)*Jolliffe.* £160
- Quia Pauper Amavi. L., [1919]. *1st. Edn. (500).* Slightly spotted, orig. cl.-bkd. bds., very slightly rubbed. (BBA. Nov.30; 290)   *Belanske.* £110
- Redondillas, or Something of that Sort. [N.Y., Grabhorn-Hoyem, for] New Directions, [1967]. *(100) sigd.* 4to. Errata slip, qtr. linen, unlettered d.-w. (SG. Mar.1; 465) $550
- The Seafarer. Ill.:– Oskar Kokoschka. Frankfurt, 1965. *(195) numbered. (25) lettered.* 4to. Title sigd., with author's port., sigd. orig. litho., loose ll. in orig. bd. portfo., spine rubbed. (GB. May 5; 2821)   DM 1,200
- Umbra. The Early Poems. L., 1920. *1st. Edn.* Sm. 4to. Orig. holland-bkd. bds., spine slightly soiled. (BBA. Aug.18; 34)   *F. Edwards.* £60

POUPÉE MODEGELE, Journal des Petites Filles, 4th & 5th Année.
Paris, Nov. 1866-Oct. 1868. 24 pts. in 2 vols. 4to. 3 hand-cold. engraved plts. (1 folding), 2 pts. misbnd., cont. hf. roan, slightly rubbed, orig. wraps. but for 2 pts. bnd. in; van Veen coll. (S. Feb.28; 97)   £170

POUQUEVILLE, François Charles Hughes Laurent
- Grèce. Paris, 1835. 2 folding maps, 62 engraved plts. (*Bound with:*) ARTAUD, Chevalier – Italie. Paris, 1835. (*Bound with:*) LASALLE, M. de. – Sicile. Paris, 1835. Together 3 works in 1 vol. Hf. roan. (HD. Mar.19; 56)   Frs. 1,000
- Histoire de la Régénération de la Grèce. 1824. *Orig. Edn.* 4 vols. Some slight foxing, hf. roan. (HD. Jun.29; 103)   Frs. 3,000

POURTRAITS DIVERS
See— OVIDIUS NASO, Publius — POURTRAITS DIVERS

POVELSEN
See— OLAFSEN & Povelsen

POWELL, John Wesley
- Exploration of the Colorado River of the West & its Tributaries. Explored in 1869, 1870, 1871, & 1872. Wash., 1875. *1st. Edn.* 4to. Three-qtr. mor., light wear. (RO. May 29; 156) $110

POWELL, Lawrence Clark
- Heart of the Southwest. Los Angeles, 1955. 1 vol. Linen-bkd. bds. (*With:*) - A Southwestern Century. California, 1958. *(500) ptd. by Carl Hertzog.* 1 vol. Cl.-bkd. bds.; inscr. by Hertzog to DeWitt O'Kieffe. (LH. Sep.25; 277) $130
- Robinson Jeffers: The Man & his Work. Ill.:– Rockwell Kent. Los Angeles, Primavera Pr., 1934. *(750).* 1 vol. Lge. 8vo. Cl., d.-w.; inscr. (*With:*) - Robinson Jeffers: A Lecture. [Los Angeles], 1951. 1 vol. 8vo. Ptd. wraps.; author's compliments slip laid in. (SG. Mar.1; 199) $175

POWELL, Thomas
[-] Humane Industry. L., 1661. *1st. Edn.* Title slightly stained, paper discold., short tear in C8 margin, cont. cf., corners worn, rebkd., new end-papers. [Wing P3072] (S. Apr.10; 578)   *Phelps.* £200

POWELL, William H. & Shippen, Edward
- Officers of the Army & Navy (Regular) Who Served in the Civil War. Phila., 1892. *1st. Edn.* 1 vol. in 2 pts. Tall 4to. Oval photographic ports. of approx. 500 entries, few corners dog-eared, later cl. wraps., with mild wear. (HA. Sep.16; 405) $130

POWELL-COTTON, Percy Horace Gordon
- A Sporting Trip through Abyssinia ... L., 1902. Sm. 4to. Hf. mor. (VA. Apr.27; 692)   R 310

POWNALL, Thomas
[–] A Memorial, Most Humbly Addressed to the Sovereigns of Europe on the Present State of Affairs, between the Old & New World. L., 1780. *1st. Edn.* A few ll. at end foxed, hf. mor. by Sangorski & Sutcliffe; the Rt. Hon. Visc. Eccles copy. [Sabin 64826] (CNY. Nov.18; 235) $220

POWYS, Llewelyn
- The Book of Days. Ed.:– J. Wallis. Ill.:– E. Corsellis. Gold. Cock. Pr., 1937. *(300) numbered.* 4to. Qtr. mor. gt. (P. Sep.29; 297)   *Thorp.* £55
– – **Anr. Edn.** Ed.:– John Wallis. Ill.:– Elizabeth Corsellis. Gold. Cock. Pr., 1937. *(300) numbered. (50) on Batchelor H.M.P., sigd. by artist, with extra set of the plts.* Fo. Orig. mor., partly untrimmed, spine faded, soiled. (TA. Oct.20; 169)   £74
- Glory of Life. Ill.:– Robert Gibbings. Gold. Cock. Pr., 1934. *(277) numbered.* Fo. Specially bnd. for G. McNeil Esq., pig, gt. fillets, s.-c.; from D. Bolton liby. (BBA. Oct.27; 145)   *Monk Bretton.* £280

POWYS, Thomas Littleton, Baron Lilford
See— LILFORD, Thomas Littleton Powys, Baron

POYER, John
- The History of Barbados. L., 1808. *1st. Edn.* 4to. Errata lf., spotted, cont. cf., rubbed, rebkd. (S. Jun.25; 118)   *Hunt.* £200

POYNTING, Frank
- Eggs of British Birds – with an Account of their Breeding Habits, Limocolae. 1895-96. *Ltd. Edn., for subscribers.* 4to. Slight spotting, cont. hf. mor., wraps. of orig. 4 pts. bnd. in. (SKC. Jan.13; 2340)   £70
– – **Anr. Copy.** 4to. 54 col. plts., hf. mor. gt., rubbed, orig. wraps. bnd. in. (P. Nov.24; 36) *Graham.* £60

POZZO, Andrea
- Perspectiva Pictorum et Architectorum. Rome, 1764-58. 2 vols. Fo. Frontis. & text in Latin & Italian, cont. hf. vell., spine wormed. (SI. Dec.15; 171)   Lire 1,300,000
- Rules & Examples of Perspective proper for Painters & Architects. Trans.:– John James. L., ca. 1715. Fo. Engraved frontis. & title dedication, 103 engraved plts., text in Latin & Engl., lacks Latin title & subscribers list, few plts. frayed, cont. hf. cf., worn. (C. Dec.9; 190)   *Wood.* £100

PRACTICA DER PFAFFEN
- Anfangk unnd Auszganck desz gantzen Bapstumbs, auss Alten Practicken und Propheceyen, mer dann vor. CCC. Jaren her also Trewlichen Abcontrafait, der Jetzigen Welt zu Gut unnd Besserung ... [Strassburg], ca. 1535. 4to. 1 lf. with sm. hole with slight loss, slight worming in margin, vell., blind-tooled decor.; from Karl Friedr. von Nagler liby., with sm. stp. on title. (HK. Nov.8; 318)   DM 1,600

PRAGMATICA SANCTIO
[Lyon, Nicolaus Philippi, 6 Sep. 1488]. 4to. Lacks last lf. blank, old vell. [Goff C-211] (HD. Jan.30; 23)   Frs. 5,900

PRATT, Anne
- The Flowering Plants, Grasses, Sedges & Ferns of Great Britain. L., ca. 1873. 6 vols. Cold. plts., hf. cf. gt. (P. May 17; 38)   *Gilbert.* £90
– – **Anr. Edn.** [1873]. 6 vols. Qtr. mor. gt., 1 spine defect. (P. Apr.12; 131)   *Perham.* £60
– – **Anr. Edn.** L., [1880?]. 3 vols. (of 4). Publishers cl., as a collection of plts., w.a.f. (CR. Jun.6; 265)   Lire 320,000
– – **Anr. Edn.** 1889. 4 vols. A few plts. lightly spotted, orig. cl. (CSK. Mar.9; 52)   £90
– – **Anr. Edn.** 1891. 4 vols. Orig. cl. gt., 1 cover faded. (P. Mar.15; 230)   *MacDonald.* £85
– – **Anr. Copy.** 4 vols. Most plts. cold., a few ll. slightly spotted, orig. cl., rubbed. (BBA. Jun.28; 275)   *Erlini.* £60
– – **Anr. Edn.** L., 1899. 4 vols. Publishers cl. (CR. Jun.6; 263)   Lire 280,000
– – **Anr. Copy.** 4 vols. Cl. (CR. Jun.6; 264)   Lire 220,000

– – **Anr. Edn.** L., 1899-1900. 4 vols. Plts., mostly cold., hf.-titles, cont. hf. mor., spines gt. (BBA. May 23; 286)   *Randall.* £100
– – **Anr. Edn.** L., n.d. 1 plain plt., 318 cold. plts., orig. cl. gt. (P. Dec.8; 34)   *Symonds.* £100
– – **Anr. Copy.** 6 vols. Orig. gt.-decor. cl. (SKC. May 4; 1871)   £65

PRAYER BOOKS
[Arranged Chronologically by Language]

PRAYER BOOKS [English]
- The Book of Common Prayer. Ill.:– Hollar, Faithorne, & others. L., 1661[-1660]. Fo. Engraved coat-of-arms frontis., 25 engraved plts., 1 full-p. engraved ill. in text, crudely hand-cold., a few plts. mntd., slight browning, owner's inscr. erased from title, cont. red mor. gt. [Wing B3620] (S. Oct.11; 493)   *Snelling.* £75
- The Book of Common Prayer ... with the Psalter. Oxford, ca. 1681. Fo. Rubricated thro.-out, lr. corner stained &, at beginning, defect., cont. Engl. restoration-style red mor., decor. with strapwork, pointillé tools & cold. onlays, spine similarly gt. (but lacks onlay), [by Queen's binder 'A': William Nott?], slightly worn, w.a.f.; H.M. Nixon coll. (BBA. Oct.6; 225)   *Finch.* £120
- The Book of Common Prayer. Ill.:– John Sturt. 1717. Engraved thro.-out, ills., decor. borders, rubricated thro.-out, sm. part of 1st. lf. adhering to 2nd. lf., some margins close shaved, cont. velvet, white metal clasps, corner- pieces & central panels, worn. (CSK. May 18; 122)   £85
– – **Anr. Edn.** Camb., 1760. Marriage gift of 1784, with inscr., cont. gt.-decor. red mor.,. (BBA. Oct.27; 28)   *Fletcher.* £380
- Abridgement of the Book of Common Prayer, & Administration of the Sacraments, & other Rites & Ceremonies of the Church, According the Use of the Church of England ... Ed.:– Benjamin Franklin & Sir Francis Dashwood, Lord Le Despencer. L., 1773. Minor foxing to a few pp., cont. red mor., elab., scuffed, upr. cover separating from spine, cl. case; Theodore Broadhurst bkplt. (SPB. May 23; 37) $2,000
- The Book of Common Prayer. Camb., 1782. Cont. mor., gt. extra, rubbed, fore-e. pntg. (PNY. Dec.1; 50)
- Book of Common Prayer [with] A New Version of the Psalms of David by Brady & Tate. Oxford, 1793. 2 pts. in 1 vol. 12mo. Mor. gt., fore-e pntg. (SG. Feb.16; 37) $250
- The Book of Common Prayer. 1794. 2 vols. 4to. Cont. panel. mor. gt.; extra ill. with engrs., etc. (TA. Dec.15; 591)   £105
- The Book of Common Prayer ... with Psalter or Psalms of David. L., 1796. Cont. black mor., with fore-e. pntg. of Windsor Castle, as a fore-e. pntg., w.a.f. (SPB. May 17; 729) $300
- The Book of Common Prayer. Oxford, 1838. 16mo. Cont. red mor. gt., gt.-panel. spine, fore-e. pntg. (SG. Nov.17; 224) $225
- The Order for the Administration of the Holy Communion . Ill.:– Evelyn Lambert. 1867. Fo. Orig. watercol. ills. & illuminated initials, some margins soiled, mor.-bkd. wood bds., upr. cover with carved & inlaid borders, jnts. strengthened with gt. metal strip. (CSK. Mar.9; 156)   £85
- Book of Common Prayer. L., ca. 1870. Ecaille bdg., completely decor. & heightened with chiselled silver plaques, crowned monog. AB on upr. cover, together 19 pieces & chain linking 2 covers at top, slit in spine écaille, velours inner frame, watered silk doubls. & end-papers with silver decor., clasps, with engraved inscr. 'G.J. Appels Anno 1717'. (HD. Jan.30; 90)   Frs. 2,200
- Book of Common Prayer ... Use of Protestant Episcopal Church in the U.S., together with the Psalter. Ed.:– D.B. Updike. Ill.:– B.G. Goodhue. N.Y., De Vinne Pr., 1893. *Ltd. Edn., on Amer. H.M.P.* Fo. 4 p. leaflet by Updike laid in, orig. vell., elab. gt.-stpd. on upr. cover & spine, 2 metal clasps, partly unc., spine & upr. cover soiled; certified on title verso with sigs. of Henry C. Potter, J. Pierpont Morgan, Samuel Hart, & others, pres. copy from Hart to Frank B. Gray, with A.L.s. (SG. Feb.9; 94) $550
– – **Anr. Copy.** Fo. 4 p. leaflet by Updike laid in, orig. vell., elab. gt.-stpd. on upr. cover & spine, 2

metal clasps, partly unc., very soiled. (SG. Feb.9; 95) $200
- The Book of Common Prayer [Prayer Book of Edward VII]. Ill.:– W.H. Hooper & Clemence Housman, after C.R. Ashbee. Norwood, Mass., 1904. Lge. 4to. Folded sheet 'A Key to the Principle Decorations in the Prayer Book of King Edward VII' [Essex House Pr., 1903] unbnd. & loosely inserted, dark pink mor. gt., lge. armorial centerpiece surrounded by 4 crowned fleur-de-lis & border of repeated 'E's' & 'VII's' in frame, crowned monogs. at corners, suede doubls., watered silk end-ll., designed by M. Walter Dunne specially for this end. (S. Nov.22; 292)   *Joseph.* £100
- The Order for the Administration of the Lord's Supper, or Holy Communion. [U.S.A.?, 1932]. 8vo. (in 4's). On vell., about 30 capitals supplied in gold, red mor. (SG. Aug.4; 325) $180
- The Book of Common Prayer. N.d. Cont. velvet, gt. metal clasp, cornerpieces & monog., silk doubls. (CSK. Feb.10; 162)   £75
- Book of Common Prayer [with] A New Version of the Psalms of David by Brady & Tate. Oxford, n.d. 2 pts. in 1 vol. 16mo. Red mor., fore-e. pntg. (SG. Feb.16; 38) $325

PRAYER BOOKS [French]
- Livre de Prières Tissé d'après les Enlumineurs des Manuscrits du XIVe au XVIIe Siècle. Lyon, 1886-87. *(50) or (60).* Sm. 4to. 25 woven silk ll., orig. mor. by Kauffmann-Horclois, box. (HD. Nov.9; 198)   Frs. 9,200

PRAYER BOOKS [German]
- Echte und Catholice Form zu betten in Gemein und in Sonderheit ... N.p., ca. 1560. Sm. 8vo. On vell., 'Préface au lecteur chrétien' & 'calendrier chrétien' bnd. at end, 19th. C. vell.; from Fondation Furstenberg-Beaumesnil. (HD. Nov.16; 119)   Frs. 37,500
- Allzeit Erinnendes Andacht-Feur, das ist Catholische Gebett zu Gott und seinen Heiligen an den Feyr-und Fest-tagen dess jahrs. Ill.:– J.B. Wening & others. [Augsburg], ca. 1700?. 16mo. Approx. 90 engraved text ll., each facing a full-p. engraved port., many with emblematic details, some light stains, mod. mor.; few text ll. sigd. by Anton Birckhart. (SG. Apr.19; 56) $200

PRAYER BOOKS [Hebrew]
- Machzor [Roman rite. Minhag Rome with commentary Kimcha D'Avishana by Jochanan of Treves]. Bologna, 1540-41. 2 vols. Fo. Some ll. supplied from a shorter copy, 1 title mntd., repairs thro.-out, staining & browning, traces of worming, some loss of text, mod. hf. mor. (SPB. Feb.1; 57) $2,500
- Mahzor [Roman rite]. Bologna, [1541]. 2 pts. in 1 vol. Fo. Some worming, not affecting text, many ll. remargined, 1st. title & 1 other lf. secured with cellotape, 2nd. title cropped, early Hebrew marginalia, many ostensibly Anti-Christian passages inked over, final 29 ll. supplied from anr., smaller, copy, early cf., rebkd., shabby. (SG. Feb.2; 229) $2,200
- Machzor [Ashkenazic rite]. Cremona, 1560. 4to. Pages 196-392 only, on blue paper, crudely reprd. thro.-out, worming, some staining, mod. cl., w.a.f. (SPB. Feb.1; 58) $550
- Kinot ve-Tsiunim. Venice, 1599. 12mo. Title remargined, margin repair to last lf., scattered stains, few ink marginalia, pol. cf. antique, blind-tooled. (SG. Feb.2; 279) $1,300
- Seder ha-Tefillot [Sefardi rite]. Amst., 1726. Some browning, a few ll. (*Bound with:*) BELMONTE, Mosseh de Joseph – Kalendario Hebrayco, que contiene los novilunios, Fiestas y Ayunos, Las Parasihot que se juntan ... desde al Ano 5485 [1724] hasta el de 5700 [1940]. Amst., 5485 [1724]. Together 2 works in 1 vol. Elab. gt.-tooled early leath., gt.-tooled mor. doubls. stpd. 'ANNO 5507' [1747], silver clasps, extremities worn, spine ends chipped. (SG. Feb.2; 284) $225
- Seder Berakhot [Ashkenazi rite]. Mantua, 1777. Some mild browning, later wraps., worn, lacks spine. (SG. Feb.2; 282) $175

PRAYER BOOKS [Hebrew & English]
- Siddur Divrei Tsaddikim ... / The Book of Daily Prayers ... Ed.:– Isaac Leeser. Phila., 5608 [1848].

PRAYER BOOKS [Hebrew & English] -Contd.

Lge. 8vo. Crushed mor. antique. (SG. Feb.2; 287)
$800
- Siddur Siftei Tsaddikim / ... The Form of Prayers according to the Custom of the Spanish & Portuguese Jews. Ed.:- Isaac Leeser. Phila., 5617 [1857]. Vol. 1st.: Daily Prayers. 2 gatherings loose, cont. leath. gt. extra, extremities worn, owner's name gt.-stpd. on upr. cover, owner's labels on upr. & lr. pastedown recording parents' deaths. (SG. Feb.2; 289)
$250

PRAYER BOOKS [Hebrew & German]

- Seder Tefillot. Offenbach, 1806. Tall 8vo. Hebrew text, German instruction & trans. in Hebrew characters, last part, Seder Tehillim, has separate title dtd. 1802, mild browning, cont. str.-grd. leath., back gt., elab. latticework cast silver clasp, extremities worn. (SG. Feb.2; 285)
$300
- Siddur Safa Berura. Roedelheim, Heidenheim, 1829. Tall 8vo. Last pt., Sefer Tehillim, has separate title dtd. 1826, with Tehillim & Tehinot for women, recased in cont. leath., worn, silver floral cornerpieces & silver star ornaments centred on upr. & lr. covers. (SG. Feb.2; 288)
$300

PRAYER BOOKS [Hebrew & Old Yiddish]

- Seder Hatefilot Mikol Hashana Keminhag Ashkenaz im ... Tehilim v'Techinot. Amst., 1804. Some soiling to margins, slight staining, a few inner margins reprd., cont. gt.-stpd. cf., silver cornerpieces, centre medallions & clasps, leath. very rubbed, lacks 1 clasp guard, 1 clasp detchd. (SPB. Feb.1; 78)
$500

PRAYER BOOKS [Hebrew & Spanish]

- Seder Berakhot / Orden de Benediciones. Amst., 5447 [1687]. 1st. Edn. in Hebrew & Spanish, 6th. Edn. of Hebrew text. 12mo. Initial ll. crudely remargined with some text loss, later cl., rebkd., worn & discold. (SG. Feb.2; 281)
$200

PRAYER BOOKS [Hebrew, Spanish & Portuguese]

- Seder me'a Berachot. Amst., 1687. Hand-cold. engraved frontis., cont. blind-stpd. mor., clasps, slight wear. (SPB. Jun.26; 27)
$5,500

PRAYER BOOKS [Hebrew & Yiddish]

- [Mahzor. Ashkenazi rite; prayers for Passover, Sukkot, Shavu'ot, with Yiddish trans.]. Amst., 1750. 4to. Some browning, old blind-tooled leath., extremities worn, lacks clasps. (SG. Feb.2; 230)
$250

PRAYER BOOKS [Manx]

- Book of Common Prayer, translated into Manks. Ramsey, Isle of Man, 1769. Lacks some blanks, browned, bds., early MS. notes on inner bds. & last lf. (P. Apr.12; 159)
King. £75

PRAYER BOOKS [Spanish]

- Liturgia Inglesa. [1623]. 1st. Edn. in Spanish. Sm. 4to. 19th. C. vell. bds.; cont. sigs. 'H. Slingesby' & 'W. Wingfelde' on title, bkplt. of J.P.P. Lyell. [STC 16434] (S. Oct.11; 385)
Georges. £150
- - Anr. Copy. Sm. 4to. Lacks final blank, slight dampstaining, sm. wormhole, sometimes affecting catchwords, early 19th. C. str.-grd. mor. (S. Oct.11; 384)
Fletcher. £70
- La Liturgia Ynglesa, o el Libro de Oración Commún ... [Book of Common Prayer]. Trans.:- D. Felix Anthony de Alvarado. 1707. Sm. part of 1 corner torn away, affecting a few words, cont. red mor. gt., spine rubbed; Robert Sherard bkplt. [D. & M. II, 8482, note] (C. May 30; 15)
Quaritch. £120

PRAZ, Mario

- Studies in Seventeenth-Century Imagery. Rome, 1974-75. 2nd. Edn. 2 vols. Tall 8vo. Orig. ptd. wraps., unc. & mainly unopened. (TA. Apr.19; 306)
£56

PRECHTL, Johann Joseph

- Grundlehren der Chemie in Technischer Beziehung. Wien, 1813-15. 1st. Edn. Some light browning, cont. hf. leath. gt. (GB. Nov.3; 1092)
DM 1,000

PREDICATIE tegen 't Danssen

See- VOET, Gisbert - PREDICATIE tegen 't Danssen

PREDL, F.X.

- Erinnerungen aus Griechenland. Würzburg, 1836. Map browned & slightly crumpled, cont. hf. leath., spine & corners rubbed. (HK. Nov.8; 1033)
DM 620

PREECE, Louisa

See- SYMONDS, Mary & Preece, Louisa

PREETZ BEN YITZHAK COHEN, of Gerona

- Ma'arechet Elohut. Commentary & Intro.:- Yehuda Chayat. Perrara, 1558. 1st. Edn. 4to. Title torn & reprd. affecting some letters, staining, browned, hf. leath. (S. Oct.25; 307) Alex. £1,250

PREIRA BRACAMONTE, Domingo

- Banquet que Apolo hizo a los Embaxadores del Rey de Portugal Don Juan Quarto. Lisboa, 1642. 4to. Vell. (DS. Dec.16; 2043) Pts. 35,000

PREISLER, Johann Martin & Ihle, Johann Eberhard

- Gründliche Zeichenkunst für Junge Leute und Liebhaber aus allen Standen nach Originalzeichnungen. Nürnberg, 1795-1802. Pts. 1-9 (of 10) & 2 supps. Fo. Dampstained, orig. wraps., unc.; van Veen coll. (S. Feb.28; 164)
£50

PRELIMINARY ARTICLES OF PEACE between His Britannick Majesty, the Most Christian King, & the Catholick King.

L., 1762. 4to. [Sabin 65044] (Bound with:) DEFINITIVE TREATY (THE) ... Concluded at Paris, the 10th Day of February, 1763 L., 1763. [Sabin 19275] Together 2 works in 1 vol., some margin annots. in cont. hand, device on final lf. of 1st. cropped, qtr. cf. (S. May 22; 300)
Maggs. £350

PRENTICE, Andrew N.

- Renaissance Architecture & Ornament in Spain. L., [1893]. Tall fo. 60 plts., ex-liby., gt.-pict. cl., linen ties, loose. (SG. May 3; 288)
$130

PRESCOTT, William Hickling

- History of the Conquest of Mexico. N.Y., 1843. 1st. American Edn. 3 vols. Orig. cl., some spine tears. (SG. Apr.5; 171)
$110
- History of the Conquest of Peru, 1524-1550. Intro.:- Samuel Eliot Morison. Ill.:- Everett G. Jackson. Mexico City, Ltd. Edns. Cl., 1957. (500) numbered & sigd. by artist & printer. Fo. Marb. leath., box; out-of-series copy, for Morison, initialled by him & with long inscr. to his wife dtd. 22 Jul. 1957 on front blank, a few pencil & ink notes by Morison in margins, 1 p. T.L.s. from Patrick A. Hill to Morison & an orig. 4 p. L.E.C. Newsletter laid in. (HA. Nov.18; 279)
$150
- Complete Works. L., 1884. (25), for sale in the U.S. 15 vols. Three-qtr. red mor., gt.-decor. spine. (CBA. Dec.10; 372)
$160
- The Works. L., [1896-97]. Liby. Edn. 12 vols. Hf. mor., spines faded, unc. (S. Oct.11; 579)
Traylen. £65
- - Anr. Edn. L., n.d. Liby. Edn. 12 vols. Cont. cf., spines gt. (S. Mar.20; 788) Booth. £100

PRESS & TRIBUNE DOCUMENTS FOR 1860. No. 3 Proceedings of the National Republican Convention ...

Chic., 21 May 1860. Front & back pp. lightly foxed, box. (LH. Apr.15; 334)
$400

PREST, Thomas Pecket

- The Hebrew Maiden: or The Lost Diamond. L., 1851. Contents darkened, mild marginal dampstaining to early pp. bdg. not stated, covers rubbed & mildly stained. (CBA. Oct.29; 678)
$200

PREVOST, F.

See- KNIP, Madame Antoinette Pauline Jacqueline & others

PREVOST, Pierre

- Du Calorique Rayonnant. Paris & Geneva, 1809. 1st. Edn. Hf.-title, errata, some light spotting, cf.-bkd. bds., slightly crude style, light rubbing; A.

Norsa stp. on spine, Stanitz coll. (SPB. Apr.25; 360)
$225
- Recherches Physico-Méchaniques sur la Chaleur. Geneva, priv. ptd., 1792. 1st. Edn. Orig. wraps., unc. & unopened, minor rubbing; pres. copy, inscr. on end-paper by author & recipient, Charles Bonnet, Stanitz coll. (SPB. Apr.25; 361)
$300

PREVOST D'EXILES, L'Abbé Antoine François

- Histoire de Manon Lescaut. Ill.:- J. Chauvet. Paris, 1867. (2) on parch. Port. & 15 orig. ink drawings on vell., slight spotting or soiling, lev. mor. gt. by Rivière, gt.-decor. spine. (SPB. Dec.13; 886)
$800
- - Anr. Edn. Paris, 1867. (342). (20) De Luxe Edn. On China, extra ill. several 19th. C. series ills, 1 with 6-8 states of each ill., MS. artists annots., some slight foxing, mor., gt. rococo style stp., gold-tooled decor. outer dentelles, gold-tooled decor. inner dentelle, cold embroidered wtrd. silk end-papers & doubl., sigd. M. Michel. (D. Nov.24; 2327)
DM 5,800
- - Anr. Edn. Ill.:- after Leloir. Paris, 1885. Ltd. Edn. 4to. A few ports. added, some foxing, mor. gt. by Rousselle, s.-c. (S. Oct.11; 414) Maggs. £120
- - Anr. Copy. 4to. On vell., cont. hf. mor., decor. spine, corners, unc., wrap. & spine preserved, by Champs. (HD. Feb.17; 111) Frs 1,100
- - Anr. Edn. Ill.:- L. Monzies. Paris, 1878. 12mo. Triple state of engrs., mor. gt. by Petit & Trioullier, spine decor. (HD. May 4; 402) Frs. 1,300
- Histoire de Marguerite d'Anjou, Reine d'Angleterre. Amst., 1740. Orig. Edn. 4 pts. in 2 vols. 12mo. Cont. marb. cf., spines decor. (HD. Nov.9; 62)
Frs. 1,300
- Histoire Générale des Voyages. N.p., [1746]. Atlas vol. 4to. 74 maps (66 folding), 1 map reprd., hf. roan. ca. 1800, spine decor., worn. (HD. Apr.13; 65)
Frs. 2,000
- Oeuvres Choisies. Ill.:- Marillier. Amst., 1783-85. 39 vols. Cont. tree cf. gt., decor. spines. (HD. Sep.22; 316)
Frs. 5,500

PRICE, Charles Matlack

- Poster Design. N.Y., 1922. New Edn. 4to. Cl., spine ends frayed; lacks rear free end-paper. (SG. Aug.25; 295)
$100

PRICE, Edward

- Norway. Views of Wild Scenery. L., 1834. 4to. 21 aquatint plts., some ll. spotted or slightly soiled, orig. cl.-bkd. bds., rubbed. (BBA. May 3; 334)
Cavendish Rare Books. £95
- - Anr. Copy. 4to. Cont. bds., linen backstrip, worn. (TA. Nov.17; 56)
£84

PRICE, Elizabeth

- The New, Universal, & Complete Confectioner. L., ca. 1780. 12mo. Leaves browned & brittle thro.-out, crude mod. cl., ex-liby. (SG. Nov.17; 196)
$120

PRICE, Frederic Newlin

- Etchings & Lithographs of Arthur B. Davies. N.Y. & L., 1929. Lge. 4to. Port., 205 plts., ex-liby., cl., partly unc. (SG. May 3; 129)
$120

PRICE, George

- A Treatise of Fire & Thief-Proof Depositories & Locks & Keys. L., 1856. 1st. Edn. Index, 50 pp. advts., some foxing, new cl. (SG. Oct.6; 237) $225
- - Anr. Copy. 32 p. publisher's catalogue at end, cont. cl. (SG. Oct.13; 277)
$150

PRICE, Julius M.

- Dame Fashion: Paris-London. N.Y., 1913. 1st. Amer. Edn. 53 plain plts., 155 col. plts., slight margin tears to a few plts., foxing, hf. mor. & buckram, slightly rubbed & soiled. (CBA. Dec.10; 210)
$130

PRICE, O.

See- RUSSELL, P. & Price, O.

PRICE, Richard

- Observations on Reversionary Payment; On Schemes for Providing Annuities for Widows, & for Persons in Old Age ... & on the National Debt. 1783. 4th. Edn. 2 vols. Cont. spr. cf.; Signet Liby. copy. (TA. Nov.17; 392)
£50

PRICHARD, James Cowles
- **The Natural History of Man** ... Ed.:– Edwin Norris. L., 1855. *4th. Edn.* 2 vols. 60 (of 62) cold. port. engrs., plts. 12 & 13 bnd. as frontis., hf.-titles, orig. embossed cl., worn & spotted. [Sabin 65475] (PNY. Jun.6; 543) $200
- **Researches into the Physical History of Mankind.** L., [1836-47]. 5 vols. Partly hand-cold. folding map, 22 plts., including 9 hand-cold., cont. cf., rebkd., rubbed; William Packe bkplt. (BBA. Nov.30; 122) *Matthews.* £60

PRICHARD, K.S.
- **The Black Opal.** L., n.d. *1st. Edn.* 1 vol. Orig. cl.; inscr. & sigd., 2 p. A.L.S. tipped in. (*With:*) – **Working Bullocks.** L., n.d. *1st. Edn.* 1 vol. Orig. cl; inscr. & sigd. (KH. Nov.9; 409) Aus. $120

PRIERIO, Silvestro
- **Malleus in falsas Assumptiones Scoti côtra diuum Thomas in Primo Sententiar[um].** Bologna, Sep. 1514. Sm. 4to. Cold. capitals, mod. tooled decor. cf. (SI. Dec.15; 34) Lire 900,000

PRIEST, Cecil D.
- **The Birds of Southern Rhodesia.** 1933-36. 4 vols. Orig. cl., spines faded, covers marked. (LC. Mar.1; 179) £120
- – **Anr. Copy.** 4 vols. Lge. 8vo. Cold. folding map, 40 cold. plts., map torn, tear in last index lf. in Vol. 2, orig. cl., rubbed & stained, liby. labels removed from upr. covers. (S. Dec.13; 293) *Bateleur.* £90
- – **Anr. Copy.** 4 vols. Cl.; pres. copy, inscr. 'To Maxwell Arnot with the author's compliments ... '. (SSA. Jul.5; 321) R 280

PRIESTLEY, Joseph
- **Experiments & Observations on Different Kinds of Air.** 1774-77. *1st. Edn.* 3 vols. 6 engraved plts., 4 pp. of errata & advts. at end of Vol. 1, 4 pp. advts. at end of Vols. 2 & 3, mod. cf. (BBA. Jul.27; 47) *Sons of Liberty Books.* £370
- – **Anr. Edn.** 1775. *2nd. Edn.* 2 vols. 'Philosophical Empiricism containing remarks on a Charge of Plagiarism respecting Dr. [Bryan] H[iggins]', 1775, bnd. in at end of Vol. 1, cont. cf., worn. (CE. Sep.1; 69) £190
- – **Anr. Edn.** B'gham., 1790. 3 vols. 6 pp. publisher's advt., without port. & hf.-titles to Vols. 2 & 3, short tear at blank margin of Vol. 3 title reprd., later hf. cf. (C. Nov.9; 104) *Waterfield.* £100
- – **Anr. Copy.** 3 vols. Some light soiling, some ll. with stp., cont. leath., recased, spine renewed, cover worn. (HK. Nov.8; 697) DM 480
- **Heads of Lectures on a Course of Experimental Philosophy.** 1794. *1st. Edn.* Cont. cf. (BBA. Jul.27; 48) *Waterfield.* £160
- **Historical Account of the Navigable Rivers, Canals, & Railways, throughout Great Britain.** L., 1831. 4to. Engraved map & folding partly hand-cold. plan, some ll. spotted or soiled, orig. cl., worn, loose, partly unopened. (BBA. May 23; 287) *Quaritch.* £75

PRIESTLEY, R.E.
- **Antarctic Adventure, Scott's Northern Party.** 1914. *1st. Edn.* Some slight spotting, orig. pict. cl. (P. Jun.7; 38) £150

PRINT: A Quarterly Journal of the Graphic Arts
New Haven, 1940-53. Vols.1-7. Sm. 4to. Pict. wraps. (SG. Jan.5; 256) $125

PRINT COLLECTOR'S QUARTERLY
N.Y., Feb. 1911-Apr. 1942. Vol. 1 no. 1-Vol. 29 no. 2 only, together 30 vols. (Vol. 1 in 2 vols.). Unif. cl. (SPB. Nov.30; 331) $475

PRIOR, H.
See— BERTARELLI, A. & Prior, H.

PRIOR, Matthew
- **Poems on Several Occasions.** L., 1718. Fo. Engraved frontis., vig. on title & headpieces, subscribers' list, some light margin stains, cont. cf., rebkd., document sigd. by Prior & other commissioners for Trade & Plantations loosely inserted. (SPB. May 16; 118) $175
- **Poetical Works.** L., 1779. *1st. Coll. Edn.* 2 vols. Sm. 8vo. Hf.-titles, port., crushed lev., triple gt. fillet borders, spines gt., gt. dentelles, by Chambolle-Duru. (SG. Apr.19; 156) $200

PRIOR, Matthew & Montagu, Charles, Earl of Halifax
- [–] **The Hind & Panther Transvers'd.** L., 1687. *1st. Edn.* Sm. 4to. Mod. maroon mor.-bkd. cl. [Wing P3511] (S. Dec.8; 28) *Pryor.* £140

PRIP-MOLLER, J.
- **Chinese Buddhist Monasteries.** Copen., 1937. Fo. Orig. parch.-bkd. bds., soiled. (BBA. Nov.10; 296) *Quaritch.* £160

PRISCIANUS
- **Prisciani Grammatici Caesariensis Libri Omnes.** Venice, 1527. *1st. Aldine Edn.* 4to. Some repairs, cont. blind-stpd. mor., decor.; from Fondation Furstenberg-Beaumesnil. (HD. Nov.16; 156) Frs. 4,500

PRISSE D'AVENNES, Achille Constant T. Emile
- **L'Art Arabe.** Paris, 1877. 4 vols. (3 plts.+ 1 text). Atlas fo; lge. 4to. 334 plts., many cold., ex-liby., later three-qtr. mor. (SG. May 3; 292) $2,600
- – **Anr. Edn.** Beirut, n.d. *Reprint of 1877 Edn.* 1 text vol. & 3 plt. vols. Fo. Qtr. mor. gt. (PD. Oct.19; 148) £82
- **La Décoration Arabe.** Paris, 1885. *1st. Edn.* Fo. 110 plts., mainly chromolitho., some heightened with gold, mor.-bkd. bds., worn. (PNY. Oct.20; 276) $475
- – **Anr. Edn.** Paris, 1885. Fo. 110 chromolitho. plts., leath.-bkd. bds. (SG. Aug.25; 120) $250
- **Esquisses sur Navarre.** Rouen, 1839. 4to. Frontis. & lithos. on india, linen. (DS. Feb.24; 2462) Pts. 36,000

PRIMITIFS FLAMANDS
Brussels, v.d. 20 vols. only (of 23), including 2 dupl. vols. No bdg. stated. (SPB. Nov.30; 139) $425

PRIN, Alice
- [–] **Kiki's Memoirs.** Intro.:– Ernest Hemingway. Ill.:– Man Ray, Foujita, & others. Paris, 1930. *(1000).* Sm. 4to. Pict. wraps., bumped, ptd. wrap-around paper band, s.-c. worn. (SG. May 24; 80) $150

PRINCE, John
- **Danmonii Orientales Illustres: Or, the Worthies of Devon.** Exeter, 1701. Fo. Mod. cl. (RO. Nov.30; 156) $100

PRINCE, Thomas
- **A Chronological History of New-England.** Boston, 1736. *[1st. Edn.].* Vol. 1 only: 3 pts. in 1 vol. Few ll. just trimmed, cont. (Amer.?) cf., worn. (BBA. Jan.19; 88) *Angle Books.* £180
- – **Anr. Copy.** Vol. 1 (all publd.). Sm. 8vo. Slight browning, 1 lf. loose, cont. panel. sheep, very worn, covers detchd. (SG. Jan.19; 312) $150
- [–] **The Vade Mecum for America; or, A Companion for Traders & Travellers.** Boston, 1732. *2nd. Edn.* 12mo. Cont. leath. over wood bds., defect.; early owners' sigs. on end-papers. (SG. Jan.19; 311) $250

PRINGLE, Sir John
- **Observations on the Diseases of the Army.** Notes:– Benjamin Rush. Phila., 1812. Some foxing, cont. tree cf., spine worn. (SG. Oct.6; 303) $120

PRINSEP, James
- **Benares Illustrated, in a Series of Drawings.** Ill.:– L. Haghe, J.D. Harding, G. Scharf, W. Walton & others. Calcutta, 1831. Fo. 28 mntd. litho. plts., & 5 engraved plts., staining or spotting on surrounds of most litho. plts., 1 engraved plt. badly foxed, hf. mor., corners bumped, slightly rubbed. (LC. Mar.1; 230) £200
- – **Anr. Edn.** Ill.:– L. Haghe, J.D. Harding, G. Scarf, W. Walton, & others. Calcutta, 1833. Fo. 6 engraved plts., 28 mntd. litho. plts., spotting or staining to surrounds of some litho. plts., cont. gt.-& blind-decor. cf. by R. MacCulloch, Calcutta, with his ticket, rubbed. (LC. Jul.5; 224) £340

PRITT, Thomas Evan
- **The Book of the Grayling.** Leeds, 1888. *1st. Edn.* L.P., folding plt. with very sm. tear. (*With:*) – **An Angler's Basket.** Manchester & L., 1896. *1st. Edn.* Together 2 vols. Orig. cl., 1st. slightly marked. (S. Oct.4; 47) *Bishop.* £60
- **Yorkshire Trout Flies.** Leeds, 1885. *1st. Edn.* 1

vol. Hf.-title inscr. 'Copy No 12', 12 plts., loose (gutta-percha perished). (*With:*) – **North-Country Flies.** 1886. *2nd. Edn.* 1 vol. 12 plts., loose, slight soiling, stps. on title & hf.- title, orig. cl., slightly marked. (S. Oct.4; 46) *Angle.* £160

PRIVATE EYE. A Fortnightly Lampoon
1963-73. 4to. Orig. ptd. wraps. (TA. May 17; 575) £52

PRIVATE LIBRARIES ASSOCIATION
- **Private Press Books.** Middlesex, for 1959-76. 18 vols. Wraps. (SG. Sep.15; 273) $100

PROCEEDINGS AT THE UNVEILING of the Statue of William E. Dodge
N.p., priv. ptd., 1886. Moderate wear, piece clipped from blank corner of title, cl.; sig. of Theodore Roosevelt. (RO. Feb.29; 143) $100

PROCLUS
- **De Sphaera Liber I. Cleomedis de Mundo ... Libri II ..., una cum Ioan. Honteri ... de Cosmographiae Rudimentis Duplici Editione.** Basilea, 1585. 5 pts. in 1 vol. Latin & Greek text, some light stains in margins, mod. hf. vell. (SI. Dec.15; 172) Lire 750,000

PROCOPIUS, of Caesarea
- **Arcana Historia.** Ed.:– Nic. Alemannus. Lyons, 1623. *1st. Edn.* Fo. In Greek & Latin, title-p. reprd., cont. vell. (BBA. Nov.30; 15) *Mundy.* £70

PROCTER, Bryan Waller 'Barry Cornwall'
- **Dramatic Scenes & Other Poems.** L., 1819. *1st. Edn.* 12mo. Errata slip, orig. bds., unc., corners slightly worn, cl. folding box; pres. copy from author to Sir John E. Swinburne, Frederic Dannay copy. (CNY. Dec.16; 283) $600

PROCTOR, Percival & others
- **The Modern Dictionary of Arts & Sciences.** B'gham., n.d. 4 vols. Cont. suede. (LC. Jul.5; 74) £85

PROCTOR, Robert
- **An Index to the Early Printed Books in the British Museum.** Ed.:– Frank Isaac. L., 1898-1938. *(350).* 5 vols., including Supp. 4to. & 8vo. Cont. mor.-bkd. cl., some jnts. split; A.L.s. from ed. loosely inserted. (BBA. Mar.7; 338) *Maggs.* £65
- **The Printing of Greek in the Fifteenth Century.** 1900. 4to. Orig. buckram-bkd. bds.; H.M. Nixon coll. (BBA. Oct.6; 190) *Blackwell.* £95

PROKESCH V. OSTEN, A.
- **Denkwürdigkeiten u. Errinnerungen aus den Orient.** Ed.:– E. Münch. Stuttgart, 1836-37. 3 vols. Cont. hf. leath., lightly rubbed; from Prinz Luitpold v. Bayern liby. (HK. Nov.8; 876) DM 650

PROMENADE D'UN FRANCAIS DANS LA GRANDE BRETAGNE
Dublin, 1797. *1st. Edn.* Vol.3 only. Bkplt., tree cf. (GM. Dec.7; 391) £90

PROMINENT MEN OF THE GREAT WEST
Chic., 1894. Lge. 4to. Mor., stpd. & gt., corners bumped, hinges reprd. (LH. Jan.15; 373) $110

PRONTI, Domenico
- **Nuova Raccolta Delle Vedutine Moderne Antichi Della Città di Roma e Sue Vicinanze.** Rome, ca. 1795. 4to. 59 plts., cont. tree cf., spine gt.-decor., rubbed. (TA. Feb.16; 27) £75
- – **Anr. Edn.** N.d. 2 vols. in 1. 2 engraved titles, 170 engrs. on 85 sheets, hf. mor., defect. (P. Nov.24; 203) *Rossi.* £80

PRONY, Gaspard, Baron de
- **Leçons de Mécanique Analytique données à l'Ecole Royale Polytechnique.** Paris, 1815. *1st. Edn.* 2 pts. in 1 vol. Sm. 4to. Sm. wormhole at lr. margins not affecting text, 19th. C. hf. cf. over marb. bds., rebkd., orig. spine laid down; Stanitz coll. (SPB. Apr.25; 362) $125
- **Nouvelle Architecture Hydraulique.** Paris, 1790-96. 2 vols. Lge. 4to. Errata, advts., worming in Vol. I, affecting some text but mostly marginal, some spotting & browning to a few gatherings, cont. gt. mor.-bkd. marb. bds.; Stanitz coll. (SPB. Apr.25; 363) $500
- **Rapport ... sur les Projets ... pour Remplacer la**

PRONY, Gaspard, Baron de -*Contd.*

Machine de Marly. Paris, 15 Vendemiaire, An III [1794]. *1st. Edn.* 4to. Lacks hf.-title (?), new marb. bds.; Stanitz coll. (SPB. Apr.25; 365) $450

PROPERTIUS, Sextus Aurelius.
- Elégies. Ill.:– Marillier. Paris, 1802. *New Edn.* 2 vols. Mor. gt. by Visinand, spines decor. (HD. May 4; 403) Frs. 1,050
- Opera. Ed.:– Antonii Mureti. Venice, Aldine Pr., 1558. 3rd. Pt. only. Sm. 8vo. Printer's device on title, 19th. C. blind-tooled leath. (SG. Apr.19; 6) $250
See– CATULLUS, Gaius Valerius, Tibullus, Albius & Propertius, Sextus Aurelius

PROPIAC, M. le Chevalier de
- Les Merveilles du Monde, ou les Plus Beaux Ouvrages de la Nature et des Hommes, repandus sur toute la Surface de la Terre. Paris, 1823. *3rd. Edn.* 2 vols. 12mo. Engraved frontis.'s & 14 plts. hand-cold., orig. wraps., unc., backstrip slightly worn; van Veen coll. (S. Feb.28; 98) £60

PROPYLAEN-KUNSTGESCHICHTE
Berlin, 1923-30. 16 vols. & 1 supp. vol. 4to. Orig. decor. hf. leath., some light wear. (HT. May 9; 1192) DM 1,300
– – Anr. Edn. Berlin, 1923-31. Vols. I-XVI. Vol. III lacks 1 plt., orig. hf. mor., a few spine heads torn. (S. Oct.4; 189) *Sofer.* £300

PROSE, e Versi per onorare la Memoria di Livia Doria Caraffa Principessa del S.R.Imp. e della Rocella di alcuni Rinomati Autori
Ill.:– R. Morghen & S. Bianchi. Parma, 1784. *Ltd. Edn.* 4to. Wide margin, some slight foxing, some ll. worse, several ll. loose in fold., mod. marb. bds. (H. May 22; 617a) DM 400
– – Anr. Edn. Ill.:– Morghen (ports.) & Bossi (vigs. &c.). Parma, 1784. 4to. 1st. & last ll. slightly soiled, early 19th. C. pol. blind- stpd. cf., back gt., inside dentelle. (VG. Sep.13; 383) Fls. 900
– – Anr. Edn. Parma, 1793. Lge. 4to. Slightly soiled, early 19th. C. hf. russ., back gt., foot of spine slightly defect. (VG. Sep.13; 384) Fls. 1,100

PROSPER AQUITANUS
- Epigrammata de Viciis et Virtutibus ex Dictis Augustini. Mainz, Peter von Friedberg, 1494. 4to. Initials painted in red & extended in margins, lr. margins wormed, early 19th. C. bds. unc.; from Fondation Furstenberg-Beaumesnil. [HC 13422; BMC I, 47; Goff P1014] (HD. Nov.16; 30) Frs. 4,200

PROSSER, George Frederick
- Select Illustrations of Hampshire. L., 1833. *1st. Edn.* 4to. Litho. title, 56 plts. (?46 only called for), some spotting & browning, cont. hf. mor., slightly worn. (S. Mar.6; 314) *Marlborough.* £190

PROTEAN FIGURE (The) & Metamorphic Costumes
L., 1811. Aquatint cut-out figure & 11 cut-out costumes, each with 4-8 articles of clothing or accessories, hand-cold., each costume in separately folded sheets with engraved label, mntd. on stubs, 'Directions' lf. pasted in upr. cover, lacks 1 boot (& maybe more, but owing to difficulty of collation impossible to determine), 1 foot of figure supplied in facs., orig. s.-c. split & worn, hand-cold. engraved pict. cover label. (S. Nov.22; 446) *Hirsch.* £350

PROUDHON, Pierre Joseph
- Système des Contradictions Economiques, au Philosophie de la Misère. Paris, 1846. *1st. Edn.* 2 vols. Minimal foxing, some slight margin defects., unc., orig. wraps, in 1 linen box. (HK. Nov.9; 2164) DM 2,200
- Die Widersprüche der National-Oekonomic oder die Philosophie der Noth. Trans.:– W. Jordan. Leipzig, 1848. 2 vols. Cont. bds. (R. Oct.11; 1215) DM 600

PROUST, A. (Text)
See– TYPES DE PARIS

PROUST, Marcel
- A la Recherche du Temps Perdu. Paris, 1913-27. *1st. Edn. 1st. Iss. of Vol. 1, with imprint of Bernard Grasset 1914 on title & yellow wraps. dtd. 1913.* 8 vols. in 13. Sm. 4to. (Vols. 1 & 2) & 8vo. All except 1st. 2 vols. ltd. to 800 (later 1200) 'exemplaires reservés aux amis de l'edition originale', some foxing in Vols. 3-6, hf. mor. gt. by Creuzevault, all with orig. ptd. paper wraps. & spines bnd. in, unc. (*With:*) – Chroniques. Paris, 1927. *1st. Edn.* 1 vol. Unif. bdg., orig. wraps. bnd. in. (C. Nov.9; 179a) *Cavendish.* £2,000
- A la Recherche du Temps Perdu. Du Côté de chez Swann. Paris, 1914. *Orig. Edn.* 12mo. 1st. state, with imprint 8 Nov. 1913 on verson of p. 523, but lacks some corrected faults, 1920's old hf. mor., corners, blind-decor, spine raised bands, wrap. & spine. (HD. May 16; 95) Frs. 3,200
- A l'Ombre des Jeunes Filles en Fleurs. Ill.:– Laboureur & Boullaire. Paris, 1946. 2 vols. 4to. Sewed, s.-c. (HD. Nov.17; 173) Frs. 1,300
– – Anr. Edn. Ill.:– J.E. Laboureur & Jacques Boullaire. 1946-48. *(502).* 2 vols. Lge. 8vo. On vélin de Lana, 50 orig. engrs., sewed, folders, s.-c.'s. (HD. May 4; 404) Frs. 2,250
– – Anr. Edn. Ill.:– J.E. Laboureur. (& Jacques Boullaire). Paris, 1948. 2 vols. On vell., sewed, box. (HD. Dec.16; 173) Frs. 1,500
- Oeuvres Complètes. Paris, 1929-36. *1st. Coll. Edn.* 18 vols. Hf. chagrin, corners, spines slightly faded, wraps. preserved. (HD. Sep.22; 317) Frs. 4,200
- Les Plaisirs et les Jours. Ill.:– Madeleine Lemaire. Paris, 1896. *1st. Edn.* 4to. Orig. ill. wraps., unc., cl. box. (C. May 30; 99) *Maas.* £140

PROUT, John Skinner
- The Castles & Abbeys of Monmouthshire. 1838. Fo. Lr. margins stained thro.-out, light spotting, cont. mor.-bkd. cl., soiled, w.a.f. (CSK. Dec.16; 125) £130
- Picturesque Antiquities of Bristol. Ca. 1830. 2 vols. Fo. Engraved title, dedication, 29 litho. plts. on India paper, cont. qtr. mor., rubbed. (TA. Dec.15; 106) £55
- Sydney Illustrated 1842-3. *(750)* numbered & *sigd. by publisher.* No bdg. stated. (JL. Jun.24; 51) Aus. $140

PROUT, Samuel
- Facsimiles of Sketches made in Flanders & Germany. Ill.:– Hullmandel. L., [1833]. Lge. fo. Litho. title & dedication, 50 lithos., dedication & some margins foxed, cont. hf. cf., spine ends worn. (C. Dec.9; 191) *Schuster.* £1,500
– – Anr. Edn. Ill.:– Hullmandel. L., [1838]. Fo. Litho. title & dedication, 50 litho. views on light grey paper, litho. title & dedication spotted & stained, hf. roan, corners rubbed, backstrip detchd. (C. Mar.14; 79a) *Dupont.* £1,700
- Illustrations of the Rhine, Drawn from Nature & on Stone. [Some plts. dtd. 1822]. 5 orig. pts. Fo. Title, 25 plts., orig. wraps., slightly torn & soiled. (P. Oct.20; 9) £500
– – Anr. Edn. L., 1853. Lge. fo. Litho. title 1 contents lf, 30 tinted lithos, wide margin, orig. hf. leath., worn. & loose. (R. Oct.13; 2724) DM 2,900
- Series of Views of Rural Cottages in the North of England. L., 1821. Fo. 11 etched plts., slightly spotted, later wraps., rebkd., soiled. (BBA. May 23; 228) *Marlboro' Rare Bks.* £70

PROVIS, W.A.
- An Historical & Descriptive Account of the Suspension Bridge constructed over the Menai Strait ... under the direction of Thomas Telford. L., 1828. Lge. fo. 17 engraved plts. including 3 aquatint views, facs. of the Irish petition, all on India paper, some slight spotting, sm. stain affecting margins of last plts., advt. slip, roan-bkd. bds, unc., worn. (S. May 21; 74) *Leggett.* £1,100
– – Anr. Copy. Lge. fo. Engraved facs., 17 engraved plts., including 3 aquatint views, all on India paper, advt. slip before hf.-title, some stains, 1 folding plt. reprd. in folds with tape, others with creases, cont. hf. cf., unc., worn; inscr. on hf-title 'To Davies Gilbert ... with the Author's respectful compliments'. (S. Dec.1; 384) *Weinreb.* £600

PRUDENTIUS CLEMENS, Aurelius
- Liber Historiarum. Leipzig, 1505. Some spotting, inscr. & stp. on end-paper, later cf., gt. rule, little rubbed. (BBA. Jun.28; 170) *Quaritch.* £90

PRYCE, William
- Archaeologia Cornu-Britannica; Or, An Essay to Preserve the Ancient Cornish Language; Containing the Rudiments of that Dialect, in a Cornish Grammar ... Sherbourne, 1790. 4to. Some minor margin dampstains, cont. spr. cf., backstrip deficient. (TA. Jun.21; 191) £90
- Mineralogia Cornubiensis. L., priv. ptd., 1778. Fo. Frontis. port. slightly stained, early 19th. C. hf. cf. (C. Nov.9; 106) *Quaritch.* £450

PRYER, H.
- Rhopalocera Nihonica, A Description of the Butterflies of Japan. Yokohama, 1886-89. 3 pts. in 1 vol. (all publd.). 4to. 10 col. plts., text in Engl. & Japanese, cont. hf. mor. (SKC. Oct.26; 420) £110

PRYNNE, William
- Anti-Arminianisme. Or the Church of Englands Old Antithesis to New Arminianisme. 1630. *2nd. Edn.* Sig. on title-p., ¶2 a cancel, light stains, a few blank margins defect. [STC 20458] (*Bound with:*) – God, no Impostor, nor Deluder. 1630. Light stains, lacks final blank. [STC 20461] Together 2 works in 1 vol. 4to. Cont. cf., slightly rubbed. (BBA. Jun.14; 26) *Duffield.* £50
- The Antipathie of the English Lordly Prelacie, both to Regall Monarchy, & Civil Unity. 1641. *1st. Edn.* 2 pts. in 1 vol. 4to. 'Dedication to Parliament' & lf. 'to the reader' present, lacks ¶2, rust hole, 1 margin torn, cont. cf., slightly worn; sig. of John Washington. [Wing P3891 & 4074] (BBA. Jun.14; 28) *Coupe.* £60
- A Moderate Apology against a Pretended Calummy. 1644. *1st. Edn.* [Wing P4010]. (*Bound with:*) – The False & Scandalous Remonstrance of the Inhumane & Bloody Rebells of Ireland. 1644. [Wing F343] Together 2 works in 1 vol. 4to. Errata lf. present in 2nd. work, errata corrected in ink, hf. cf. by Rivière, spine gt. (BBA. Jun.14; 30) *Waterfield.* £70
- A True & Perfect Narrative of what was Done, Spoken by & between Mr. Prynne ... 1659. 4to. Title & verso of last lf. dust-stained, recent hf. mor., unc. [Wing P4113] (BBA. Jun.14; 32) *Bondy.* £50
- The Unlovelinesse, of Love-Lockes. L., 1628. *1st. Edn.* 4to. Title & last 3 ll. frayed or torn, lacks 1st. lf. (blank?) few stains, hf. cf., covers loose, lacks part of spine. (S. Mar.20; 954) *Smallwood.* £50
– – Anr. Edn. L., 1628. *1st. Edn. 2nd. Iss.* Sm. 4to. With 'needs' reading on D2r line 2, lacks sig. A1, later hf. mor., marb. bds.; mod. bkplt. of George H. Yenowine. [STC 20477] (SG. Apr.19; 157) $130

PSALMANAZAAR, George
- Description de l'ile Formosa en Asie. Amst., 1705. 12mo. Folding map, 17 plts., cf. (P. Dec.8; 348) *Shapero.* £100
– – Anr. Copy. Cont. leath., worn, spine with defect. (D. Nov.24; 2328) DM 400
- An Historical & Geographical Description of Formosa. L., 1704. *1st. Edn.* Slight dampstain to title & some ll., minor worming to inner blank margins of title & preface, sm. rusthole at F3, cont. panel. cf. (C. Nov.9; 107) *Armstrong.* £110

PSALMS, PSALTERS & PSEUMES
[*Arranged Chronologically, under Language*]

PSALMS, PSALTERS & PSEUMES [Dutch]
- Souter Liedekens. Trans.:– W. van Zuylen van Nyevelt. Music:– Clemens non Papa & Tilman Susato. Antw., 1584. Sm. 8vo. 1st. 2 letters on title erased, cont. blind-stpd. panel. cf., orig. clasps. (VG. Nov.30; 733) Fls. 3,000
- Het Boeck der Psalmen. Wt der Hebreïsscher Sprake. Trans.:– Ph. van Marnix van Sint Aldegonde. Haarlem, Enschedé, 1928. *(150) in 16th. C. type.* Lge. 8vo. Orig. hf. vell. (VG. Sep.13; 301) Fls. 550

PSALMS, PSALTERS & PSEUMES [English]
- The Whole Booke of Psalmes ... Ed.:– Tho. Sternhold, Jo. Hopkins & others. 1637. 24mo. A few headlines shaved, cont. decor. needlework bdg., buckram box. (C. May 30; 165) *Quaritch.* £500
– – Anr. Edn. L., 1733. Foxed, cont. mor. gt. extra, covers gt.-panel, fore-e. pntg. (SG. Nov.17; 236) $225

– **Psalms of David in Metre.** 1764. Cont. ?Scottish bdg. of red mor. gt., gt.-panel. spine. (P. Mar.15; 290) *Quaritch.* £120
– **A Selection of Psalms & Hymns.** 1832. 12mo. Cont. mor., lightly rubbed, fore-e. pntg. (CSK. Jul.27; 33) £95
– **Illustrations of Old Testament History in Queen Mary's Psalter, by an English Artist of the Fourteenth Century.** Ill.:– N.H.J. Westlake & W. Purdue. L. & Oxford, ca. 1850?. 4to. Captions in Fr. & Engl., qtr. cf., covers detchd.; sigd. inscr. by Westlake. (SG. Feb.9; 137) $125
– **Psalms of David. Illuminated.** Illumination:– O. Jones. [1861]. Fo. Orig. embossed cf. (P. Apr.12; 83) *Thorp.* £150
– – **Anr. Copy.** Fo. Pages loose, cont. blocked papier-mâché bds. (P. Sep.29; 19) *Henderson.* £120
– – **Anr. Edn.** Ill.:– Owen Jones. [1862]. Fo. Prelims. slightly spotted, orig. relievo leath., spine slightly rubbed. (TA. Dec.15; 590) £75
– **The Book of Psalms.** Ill.:– V. Angelo. N.Y., Ltd. Edns. Cl., 1960. *(1500) sigd. by artist.* Blind-stpd. persimmon mor., spine gt., decor. folder, s.-c. slightly worn; the V. Angelo copy, with initials & publisher's pres. blind-stp. (CBA. Oct.1; 259) $150
See— **NEW TESTAMENT [English] – PSALMS, PSALTERS & PSEUMES [English]**

PSALMS, PSALTERS & PSEUMES [French]
– **Les Pseavmes de David Mis en rime Françoise.** Sedan, 1636. Miniature book. Approx. 2½ x 1½ inches. Title slightly soiled, slight tears to last few ll., black mor., clasp & catch lacking. (LC. Jul.5; 356) £100
– – **Anr. Edn.** Trans.:– Clément Marot & Théodore de Bèze. Charenton, 1662. 12mo. Over 300 pp. mus. notat., cont. mor., gt. filigrain motif decor., metal corners, worked metal clasp. (HD. Jan.30; 69) Frs. 3,000
See— **NEW TESTAMENT [French] – PSALMS, PSALTERS & PSEUMES [French]**

PSALMS, PSALTERS & PSEUMES [German]
– **Das Kleine Davidische Psalterspiel der Kinder Zions.** Germantown (Pennysylvania), 1764. *3rd. Edn.* Sm. 8vo. Owner's inscr. on end-paper, cont. cf. over wood, 1 clasp (of 2). (VG. Nov.30; 535) Fls. 625
– **Die Psalmen.** Trans.:– M. Luther. Ill.:– F.W. Kleukens. [Leipzig, Ernst Ludwig Pr., 1911]. *(10) De Luxe Edn. on vell.* Lge. 4to. Orig. red hand-bnd. pol. mor. gt., by Carl Sonntag jun., Leipzig. (H. Nov.23; 1029) DM 8,000
– – **Anr. Edn.** Darmstadt, Ernst Ludwig Pr., 1911. *(440) on Bütten.* Fo. Orig. bds, worn. (HK. May 17; 2744) DM 400
– – **Anr. Edn.** Ill.:– Martin Luther. Ernst Ludwig Pr., 1911. *(500).* Orig. wrap. & s.-c. (GB. May 5; 2462) DM 550
– **Der Psalter Deudsch.** Ed.:– Carl von Kraus. Trans.:– M. Luther. Ill.:– A. Simons. Müchen, Bremer Pr., 1929. *(18) De Luxe Edn. on vell.* Sm. fo. Initials hand gilded, hand-bnd. orig. mor., gold decor. spine, covers, inner & outer dentelles, vell. doubls. & end-papers, by Frieda Theirsch. (H. Nov.23; 945) DM 7,000
See— **NEW TESTAMENT [German] – PSALMS, PSALTERS & PSEUMES [German]**

PSALMS, PSALTERS & PSEUMES [Hebrew]
– **Tehilim.** Commentary:– David Kimchi. Isny, 1542. Fo. Sigd. by censors but not censored, lacks 2 unpaginated ll. & Latin lf. 'Cum Privilegio', top margin of title reprd. without text loss, slightly stained, no bdg. stated. [D. & M. 5089] (S. Oct.24; 111) *Alex.* £500
– – **Anr. Edn.** Latin Intro.:– Hieronimus Opitius. Wittenberg, 1566. 12mo. Verso of title with Lives from Adam to Methuselah in 17th. C. square Hebrew MS., title mntd., slightly soiled & browned, hf. leath., marb. paper bds., trimmed. (S. Oct.24; 112) *Alex.* £260
– – **Anr. Edn.** Commentaries:– Rashi & Elieser Ha'levi Murwitz, & Ma'amadot of Aron of Apta. Zhitomir, 1856. Hf. leath., w.a.f. (S. Oct.25; 168) £130

PSALMS, PSALTERS & PSEUMES [Hebrew & Spanish]
– **Las Alabancas de Santidad.** Trans.:– Yakov Yehuda Leon Templo. Amst., 1671. 4to. Slightly creased, cl. (S. Oct.24; 113) *Moriah.* £180
– – **Anr. Edn.** Approbation:– Yitshak Aboab, Moshe Rephael de Aquilar, Shlomo de Oliveira, & others. Spanish Trans.:– Ya'akov Yehuda Leon. Amst., 5431 [1671]. *1st. Edn.* Lacks final lf. (pt. of index), scattered stains, old leath., defect. (SG. Feb.2; 162) $550

PSALMS, PSALTERS & PSEUMES [Latin]
– **Psalterium.** Mainz, Joh. Fust & Peter Schöffer. 1457. *1st. Edn.* Fo. On paper, 5 incompl. single ll., bds., ca. 1830. corners bumped. [H. 13479; BMC I, 18f.; Goff P1036] (HK. May 15; 223) DM 28,000
– – **Anr. Edn.** Nuremb., Friedrich Creussner, ca. 1477. 4to. Capitals supplied in red thro.-out, larger capitals heightened with blue & with cold. penwork, rubricated, lacks folios 8, 9, 16 & 159 of text & 1st. & last blank ll., some worming to inner margins, some soiling, a few slight margin repairs, cont. annots., some painted over but still legible, cont. Nuremb. bdg. of blind-tooled pig over wood bds., upr. cover with floral diaper, lr. cover with scroll stps., brass bosses & cornerpieces, brass clasps & catches, leath. tabs. at fore-edges, head of spine slightly defect., end-papers renewed. [Goff P-1041; H. 13474 (CNY. May 18; 163) $440
– **Incipit Liber Psalteri** ... Seville, 1629. Lge. fo. Ptd. in 2 cols., leath., bronze clasps. (DS. Dec.16; 2167) Pts. 20,000
– **Psalmi Penitentiales.** Kelms. Pr., 1894. *(300).* According to note loosely inserted this copy was bnd. ready for tooling but Cobden-Sanderson objected to leath. & tore it off. (BBA. Dec.15; 255) *Marlborough Rare Books.* £70

PSEUDO-ARISTOTELES
– **Mechanica Graeca.** Commentary:– Henricus Monantholius. Paris, 1599. 4to. Greek & Latin text, sm. margin wormhole in 1st. 2 ll., some minor spotting, cont. vell.; John D. Stanitz coll. (SPB. Apr.25; 20) $850
See— **GABIROL, Schlomo Ibn & Pseudo-Aristoteles**

PSEUDO-BONAVENTURA
See— **HANAPIS, Nicolaus de**

PTOLEMAEUS, Claudius
– **Almagestum.** Venice, 1515. *1st. Compl. Edn.* (*Bound with:*) **PEURBACH, G. – Tabulae Eclypsium. Tabula Primi Mobilis Joannis a Monteregio.** Wien, 1514. *1st. Edn.* lacks 2 loose ll. as usual, 2 works in 1 vol. Fo. Wide margin, old MS. marginalia, cont. blind-tooled pig over wood bds., foot of spine slightly defect from old erased painted over sig., brass clasps. (R. Apr.3; 84) DM 7,500
– – **Anr. Edn.** Trans.:– George of Trebizond. Venice, 1528. *1st. Latin Trans. from orig. Greek.* Fo. Wide margins, some margin worming & stains, a few ll. lightly browned, title-p. loosening, old cf., rebkd.; owners inscr. of Marques de Alegrete on title-p., Stanitz coll. (SPB. Apr.25; 368) $1,800
– **La Geographia.** Ed.:– Sebastian Munster. Trans.:– Pietro Andrea Mattialus. Venice, 1548. [Colophon: Oct. 1547]. *1st. Italian Edn.* Woodcut title border, 1 half-p. & 7 schematical text woodcuts, 60 double-p. copper engraved maps, many woodcut initials, repeated woodcut printers mark, cont. limp vell., creased, upr. jnt. broken, spine loose, lacks ties. [Sabin 66502] (D. Nov.23; 773) DM 15,500
– – **Anr. Edn.** Trans.:– Bilibald Pirckheymer.& Gioseppe Moleto. Maps:– after Gastaldi. Venice, 1562. 4to. Latin text, Woodcut device on title, 27 maps of ancient world, 37 of mod. world, woodcut diagrams in text, some faint discolouration, a few MS. side notes in ink in cont. hand in text, vell. bds., soiled, w.a.f. [Sabin 66489] (S. May 21; 82) *King.* £1,100
– – **Anr. Copy.** 3 pts. in 1 vol. 4to. Ptd. title with lge. woodcut device, 63 double-p. engraved maps (of 64: lacks map 9 of mod. France), woodcut diagrams in text, title & index ll. slightly soiled or stained, sm. piece torn from head of title without loss of ptd. surface, a few ms. annots in ink on latter & in lr. margin of 1 map, cont. limp vell., slightly soiled, w.a.f. [Sabin 66489] (S. May 21; 85) *Schuster.* £900
– – **Anr. Edn.** Ed.:– G. Malombra. Trans.:– G. Ruscelli. Venice, G. Ziletti, 1574. *3rd. Italian Edn.* 3 pts. in 1 vol. 4to. Woodcut devices on 2 titles, 27 maps of ancient world, 38 of modern world, all double-p. & engraved, woodcut diagrams in text, some browning or margin. staining, mostly affecting text vell-bkd. bds., w.a.f. [Sabin 66505] (S. May 21; 90) *Schuster.* £800
– – **Anr. Copy.** 4to. 65 uncold. maps, 4 text ll. badly browned, vell., some wear. (P. Mar.15; 394) *Franks.* £700
– – **Anr. Edn.** Ed.:– G.A. Magini. Trans.:– L. Cernoti. Maps:– after Mercator, Ortelius & others. Venice, G.B. & G. Galignani, 1598. 2 pts. in 1 vol. 4to. Italian text, ptd. titles with engraved vigs., & 27 maps of ancient world, 37 of mod. world, most maps inset into text, some wormholes in text & touching 1 or 2 plts., cont. north Italian mor., gt. & blind-ruled, central & corner arabesques on covers, head & foot of spine worn, w.a.f. [Sabin 66506] (S. May 21; 93) *Traylen.* £1,200
– – **Anr. Edn.** Ed.:– G. Rosaccio. Trans.:– G. Ruscelli. Venice, Heirs of Melchior Sessa. 1598-99. *5th. Italian Edn.* 4to. 27 maps of the ancient world, 42 maps of the mod. world, including 2 twin-hemispherical world maps, ptolemaic world map punctured by over-sewing affecting engraved surface, some browning, mostly affecting text, title soiled, liby. & owners' stps. at foot, a few margin MS. ink annots. in cont. hand, 19th. C. vell. bds., preserving mor., soiled. [Sabin 66507] (S. Dec.1; 184) *Delmre.* £850
– – **Anr. Edn.** Trans.:– Girolamo Ruscelli. Maps:– after Gastaldi, Ortelius & others. Venice, Heirs of Melchior Sessa, 1599. *5th. Italian Edn.* 3 pts. in 1 vol. 4to. Ptd. title, 69 double-p. engraved maps (including 3 mod. world maps), woodcut ills. in text, some margin wormholes (1 or 2 just touching plt.-marks), title & a few ll. at end slightly browned, cont. vell., spine lettered in ink, w.a.f. (S. May 21; 101) *King.*£850
– – **Anr. Edn.** Ed.:– I.A. Magini. [Köln], 1608. *3rd. Magini Edn.* Sm. 4to. Maps from 1596 & 1597 Edn., with world map, lacks 28 ll. index at end, both title borders cut, some with fault, lightly browned, leath., with old cover. [Sabin 66495] (HK. Nov.8; 891) DM 1,600
– **Geographia Vniversalis, vetvs et nova, complectens ... Libros VIII.** Basel, 1540. Fo. Wide margin, plts. strengthened with paper strips, cont. blind-tooled pig-bkd. wood bds., 1 clasp (of 2); Hallswedell coll. (H. May 24; 974) DM 25,000
– – **Anr. Edn.** Basle, 1545. Fo. Lacks 2nd. pt. with all maps, rubricated, piece torn from margin of 1 lf., late 19th. C. cf., strapwork decor. in grolieresque-style, gt. name across centre of covers, [by Hagué], rather worn; bkplt. & accession no. of J.R. Abbey, the Quaritch copy, H.M. Nixon coll. (BBA. Oct.6; 239) *Beres.* £650
– **Geographiae Claudii Ptolemaei Alexandrini.** Trans.:– Bilibald Pirckheymer. Basel, 1552. *4th. Sebastian Münster Latin Edn.* Fo. Woodcut port. of Ptolemy on verso of title, 27 maps of ancient world & 27 of mod. world, woodcut device on verso of last map, all maps with text on versos, mod. world map 'Typus Universalis' revised version of 1550, sm. wormhole affecting 1st. few ll. without loss of ptd. surface. vell. bds., w.a.f. [Sabin 66488] (S. May 21; 83) *Tooley.* £3,000
– **Geographicae Enarrationis Libri Octo.** Ed.:– Michael Villanovanus [Servetus]. Trans.:– Bilibald Pirchheymer. Lyons, Melchoir & Gaspar Trechsel, 1535. *1st. Servetus Edn.* Fo. Tall copy, 27 double-p. maps of the ancient world, 22 double-p. maps of the mod. world, & 1 full-p. map of Lotharingia on verso of map 46, all woodcut, most with text on verso in elab. woodcut borders, index & errata at end, slight margin worming of title & 1st. few text ll., some soiling, sm. piece cut from head of title, sm. owner's ink inscr. at foot & liby. stp. at foot on verso, 18th. C. cf-bkd. bds. gt., spine & sm. device on upr. cover dtd. 1787, slightly worn. [Sabin 66483] (S. Dec.1; 178) *Burgess.* £6,600
– – **Anr. Edn.** Ed.:– Michael Villanovanus [Servetus]. Trans.:– Bilibald Pirckheymer. Lyons & Vienne, 1541. *2nd. Servetus Edn.* Fo. Ptd. title with

PTOLEMAEUS, Claudius -*Contd.*

lge. woodcut device, 27 double-p. maps of ancient world, 22 double-p. maps of mod. world, 1 full-p. map of Lotharingia on verso of map 46, most with text on versos, headline running title of map 37 just shaved, title reprd. without loss of ptd. surface, some faint discolouration, 18th. C. hf. cf., spine gt., head & tail of spine slightly wormed, w.a.f. [Sabin 66485] (S. May 21; 81) *Franks.* £4,000
- **Geography.** Intro.:– Joseph Fischer. Trans.:– Edward Luther Stevenson. N.Y., 1932. *(250) numbered on H.M.P.* Tall fo. Sm. perforated stp. on title, hf. cf., shelf mark on spine. (SG. Jun.7; 151) $375
- **Harmonicorum Libri Tres.** Ed.:– Johannes Wallis. Oxford, 1682. 4to. In Greek & Latin, cont. panel. cf. (TA. Oct.20; 274) £160
- **In hoc Opere haec Continentur Geographiae Cl. Ptolemaei.** Ed.:– Johannes Cotta. Trans.:– Jacobus Angelus. Rome, Bernardinus Venetus de Vitalibus, 1508 [Colophon 8 Sep. 1507]. Fo. Elab. woodcut initial 'I' on ptd. title, woodcut diagrams & initials in text, full-p. woodcut diagram at N1, text 108 & 34 ll. (including blank at 08), & 34 engraved maps on 68 conjugate ll. (27 of ancient world, 7 of mod. world), Johannes Ruysch's 'Universalior Cogniti Orbis Tabula ex Recentibus Confecta Observationibus' apparently in State II for both halves, lf. Gl mis-sigd. Hl, full-p. diagram & neatline of 1 or 2 maps just shaved, wormholes affecting margins of a few ll. at end, some slight surface dirt, 1 or 2 minor repairs without loss of text, vell. bds., spine lettered in ink; bkplt. of Charles Casimir de Dolomieu, that of Joseph du Merteau on front free endpaper with sm. inscr. in ink, & inscr. in same hand on rear pastedown dtd. 1759, w.a.f. [Sabin 66476] (S. May 21; 80) *Niewodniczanski.* £22,000
- **Ioannis Antonii Magini ... Geographiae, tum Veteris, tum Novae.** Ed.:– Gaspar Ens. Trans.:– Magini. Arnhem, Joannes Janssonius, 1617. *4th. Magini Edn.* Vol. 2: 2 pts. in 1 vol. 4to. Engraved title, ptd. title to pt. 2 in elab. engraved border, ptolemaic world map on verso, 27 full-p. maps of the ancient world, 37 maps of the mod. world, including the double-p. twin-hemispherical world map, 1 or 2 text ll. detchd., unif. browning (as usual), a few cont. MS. ink annots., mod. limp vell. bds. [Sabin 66496] (S. Dec.1; 186) *Tooley's.* £680
- **Orbis Antique Tabulae Georgraphicae.** Amst., R. & J. Wetstenios & G. Smith, 1730. Fo. Engraved additional allegorical title, ptd. title with sm. vig., 28 double-p. engraved maps, engraved title & maps hand cold. in wash & outl., hf.-title, 1 or 2 margin stains, some creasing or slight browning, cont. owner's inscr. on ptd. title verso & on front free end-paper, mod. hf. cf. (S. Dec.1; 200) *Cope.* £900
- – **Anr. Copy.** Fo. Additional engraved titles, 28 hand-cold. double-p. engraved maps, hf.-title, minor margin dampstains, recent hf. mor. (TA. Sep.15; 65) £620
- – **Anr. Copy.** Fo. Slightly dampstained, l lf. & 12 maps lined with thin paper, mod. hf. mor., rebnd. & washed. (VG. Sep.14; 1073) Fls. 820
- **Theatri Geographiae Veteris.** Ed.:– P. Bertius. Ill.:– Mercator, Ptolomaeus, Ortelius. Amst., J. Hondius, 1618. Fo. 1 map hand-cold., some maps slightly browned, cont. vell., some spine restorations. (SI. Dec.15; 55) Lire 2,700,000

PUCKLE, Edward

- **The Eglinton Government** ... Ill.:– after J.H. Nixon. Colnachi & Puckle, 1843. 21 col. plts. with col. engraved frontis., slightly browned & torn, hf. cf. portfo. (PD. Aug.17; 141) £120

PUCKLER-MUSKAU, H. von

- **Südöstlicher Bildersaal.** Stuttgart, 1840-41. *1st. Edn.* 3 vols. Some ll. foxed or stained, cont. linen. (GB. Nov.4; 2154) DM 600

PUDLICH, Robert

- **Von dem Fischer un Syner Frau.** Düssoldorf, 1957. Fo. 9 cold. lithos. on 8 sigd. plts., orig. wraps. (V. Oct.1; 4391) DM 450

PUFENDORF, Samuel, Baron von

- **Commentariorum de Rebus Suecicis Libri XXVI.** Utrecht, 1686. *1st. Edn.* Fo. 1st. 13 ll. with bkd.

margin tears, some slight browning, cont. spr. vell. gt., gold-tooled, rubbed. (HT. May 10; 2551a) DM 650
- – **Anr. Copy.** Lge. fo. Copper engraved title, typographical title & text stpd., cont. leath. gt. (HK. Nov.9; 1288) DM 440
- **Le Droit de la Nature et des Gens.** Trans.:– J. Barbeyrac. Amst., n.d. 2 vols. 4to. Cont. cf. (HD. Feb.22; 175) Frs. 2,500
- **Introduction à l'Histoire des Principaux Royaumes & Etats ... dans l'Europe.** Leiden, 1710. 4 vols. Cont. cf. gt. extra. (SG. Oct.27; 271) $100
- **Introduction à l'Histoire Générale et Politique de l'Univers.** Amst., 1721. *New Edn.* 6 vols. Sm. 8vo. Cont. vell. (VG. Nov.30; 856) Fls. 450
- **Of the Law of Nature & Nations.** Oxford, 1703. *1st. Edn. in Engl.* Fo. Cont. panel. cf., worn. (SG. Oct.27; 270) $250
- **Sieben Bucher von Denen Thaten Carl Gustavs Konigs in Schweden.** Nuremb., 1697. *[1st. German Edn.].* Fo. Frontis., 2 ports., 112 double-p. or folding engraved maps & views, 1 torn at fold, slight discoloration at beginning & end, a few plts. loose, cont. cf., w.a.f. (S. Dec.1; 318) *Baker.* £900
- – **Anr. Copy.** Fo. Additional engraved title, port., 89 double-p. engraved views, maps & plans, 1 plt. defect. & detchd., title remargined, some dampstaining, mainly marginal, old blind-stpd. vell. over wood bds., worn, spine defect., w.a.f. (C. Nov.16; 156) *Hart.* £300
- – **Anr. Copy.** Fo. Some plts. restored, cont. cf., decor. spine. (HD. Sep.22; 318) Frs. 14,000
- – **Anr. Copy.** Fo. Some plts. with light defects., 1 lge. view with light defects. in fold, a few tears bkd., lightly browned thro.-out, some slight spotting, cont. marb. cf. gt., slightly rubbed, upr. cover loose. (HT. May 10; 2845) DM 4,000

PUGET DE LA SERRE, Jean

- **Het Graf der Wereltse Vermakingen.** Trans.:– J. D[ullaart]. *2nd. Printing. (Bound with:)* – **Gedachtenisse der Eeuwigheyt.** Trans.:– J. v.d. Schuere. *(Bound with:)* – **De Spiegel die niet Vleyd.** Trans.:– J.H. Glazemaker. Together 3 works in 1 vol. Sm. 8vo. Amst., 1666-67. Cont. vell. (VG. Nov.30; 557) Fls. 500
- **The Mirrour which Flatters not.** L., 1639. *1st. Edn. in Engl.* Slight browning & soiling, cont. cf., soiled, rebkd. [STC 20490] (S. Oct.11; 580) *Waterfield.* £100

PUGH, David

See— HUGHSON, David [i.e. David Pugh]

PUGH, Edward

[–] **Cambria Depicta: A Tour Through North Wales.** 1816. 4to. Hand-cold. engraved aquatint frontis. & 70 plts., title reprd. & laid down, H2 cleanly torn, cont. hf. cf., lightly rubbed, rebkd. (CSK. May 4; 107) £380

PUGIN, Augustus Charles

See— BRITTON, John & Pugin, Augustus Charles

PUGIN, Augustus Welby Northmore

- **Designs for Gold & Silversmiths.** L., 1836. 4to. Pict. title, 27 plts., some light foxing, cl., spine worn. (SG. Aug.25; 301) $160
- **Glossary of Ecclesiastical Ornament & Costume.** 1844. 4to. Col. title, 72 col. plts., slight spotting, cl., rebkd. (P. Feb.16; 11) £130

PUGIN, Augustus Welby Northmore & Heath, Charles

- **Paris & its Environs.** L., 1829-31. 2 vols. 4to. 200 views on 100 steel-engraved plts., some light spotting, cont. mor. (CSK. Nov.4; 190) £95
- – **Anr. Copy.** 2 vols. 4to. 2 engraved titles, 202 views on 101 sheets, hf. cf., lacks 1 spine. (P. Sep.8; 29) *Tzakas.* £70
- – **Anr. Edn.** 1831. 2 vols. in 1. 4to. Engraved additional titles, 202 views on 101 plts., some light staining, cont. hf. mor., rubbed. (CSK. Jan.27; 34) £110
- – **Anr. Copy.** 2 vols. in 1. 4to. Engraved extra titles, 101 plts. with 2 views on each, spotted, bds., soiled, hinges reprd. (S. Apr.9; 50) *Traylen.* £75
- – **Anr. Copy.** 2 vols. in 1. 4to. Extra engraved titles, 202 views on 101 plts., most spotted, cf.-bkd. bds., worn. (S. Apr.9; 49) *Jeffery.* £65
- – **Anr. Copy.** 2 vols. 4to. 200 views on chine

appliqué, cont. chagrin gt., spines richly decor. (HD. Nov.17; 63) Frs. 2,200
- – **Anr. Edn.** Parigi, 1831. 2 vols. bnd. in 1. 4to. 200 engrs., browning, lacks bdg. (CR. Jun.6; 267) Lire 250,000

PULLAN, R.P

See— NEWTON, C.T. & Pullan, R.P.
See— TEXIER, Charles & Pullan, R.P.

PULMAN, George P.R.

- **Vade Mecum of Fly-Fishing for Trout.** Axminster, 1841. *1st. Edn.* Slight spotting, cl., slightly worn & faded. (S. Oct.4; 48) *Head.* £70

PULSIFER, John S.

- **[The Phonal Depot].** Orwigsburg, Aug. 1848-Jun. 1849. *1st. Edn.* Vol. 1 nos. 1-12, in 1 vol. 4to. Pres. bdg.? of cont. roan, the Aubaot title stpd. on upr. cover & painted in gold, edges worn; 2 ptd. ll. 'Presented to the Franklin Institute', stp. & bkplt. of the Franklin Institute Liby. (CNY. May 18; 164) $1,400

PUNCH

Ill.:– Richard Doyle, Furniss, Tenniel, Leech, Partridge, Sambourne, Phil May, etc. L., Jul. 1841-Jun. 1899. Vols. 1-115, in 33. Not collated, apparently compl., some light foxing, orig. publisher's bdgs., slightly faded in places. (CBA. Aug.21; 486) $325
- – **Anr. Edn.** L., 1843-1940. Vols. 4, 7-11, 14, 57, 61, 69, 77-193 & 198 only in 128 vols. 4to. Few ll. torn or lacking from early vols., vols. before 157 in cont. hf. cf. or cf.-bkd. bds., some spines worn, rest in cl. (BBA. Mar.21; 267) *G. Jeffery.* £100
- – **Anr. Edn.** L., 1845-91. Vols. 9-100, in 23 vols. 4to. Cont. red mor. gt. (TA. Aug.18; 406) £54
Jan. 1925-Dec. 1940, Jan. 1942-Jun. 1949. 47 vols. 4to. Orig. cl. gt., 2 spines faded. (TA. Jul.19; 312) £100

PUNIN, N.N.

- **Pervyi Tsikl Letsii: Sovremenroe Iskussive [First Circle of Lectures: Contemporary Art].** Petrograd, 1920. *1st. Edn.* Orig. wraps., cold. litho. cover designs by Malevich, slight ink mark from rubber stp. on upr. cover, sm. rust stain on lr. cover. (S. Nov.21; 162) *Baum.* £500
- **Russian Placards, Placard Russe, 1917-22.** Ill.:– Lebedev. Petersburg, 1923. *(1700).* 4to. Tissue guards captioned in Engl. & Fr., orig. wraps., with design on upr. cover, backstrip worn. (S. Nov.21; 160) *Marks.* £260
- – **Anr. Edn.** Ill.:– V. Lebedev. Petersburg, 1923. 4to. Tissue guards captioned in Engl. & Fr., 2 lithos. dampstained, orig. wraps., with design on upr. cover, slightly worn. (S. Nov.21; 173) *Sims.* £220

PUNT, Jan

- **Afbeelding van de Zaal Praalbed Waar op het Lyk van ... Willem Karel Hendrik Friso ... ten toon is Gesteld Geweest.** Amst., 1752. Fo. 41 double-p. engraved plts., including 1 hand-cold., double-p. view of the procession with numbered key inserted at end (headline trimmed), qtr. cf., slightly worn. (S. Dec.1; 328) *Baker.* £140

PURBACH, George

- **Opus Algorithmi Iucundissimů.** [Leipzig], 1503. *3rd. Edn.* 4to. Wide margin, red & blue rubricated, 4 wormholes in side margin, sewed. (HK. Nov.8; 320) DM 750

PURCELL, Henry

- **The Indian Queen.** [L.], early or mid-18th. C. *1st. Edn.* Fo. Orig. marb. bds., worn. (S. Nov.17; 154) *Maggs.* £280
- **Orpheus Britannicus.** L., 1706 & 1712. *2nd. Edn.* 2 vols. Fo. Cont. cf. bds., stained, upr. cover detchd. (S. Nov.8; 483) *Knill.* £200
- **The Vocal & Instrumental Musick of the Prophetess, or the History of Dioclesian.** L., priv. ptd., 1691. *1st. Edn.* Overall browning, some dampstaining, some paper loss not affecting text, a few pp. trimmed affecting text, title-p. detchd., a few MS. annots. in cont. hand, cont. marb. bds., upr. cover detchd., spine defect. (S. Nov.17; 153) *Lubrano.* £300
See— HANDEL, Georg Friedrich - PURCELL, Henry

PURCELL, Henry & others
- The Catch Club or Merry Companions. Ed.:-
C.I.F. Lampe. L., ca. 1765. 2 vols. in 1. Some
spotting, orig. marb. bds., cont. MS. label. (S.
Nov.8; 461) *Quaritch.* £110

PURCHAS, Samuel
- Hakluytus Posthumus or Purchas his Pilgrimes.
L., 1625. *1st. Edn. Earlier iss. of Vol. 1, with
'Hondius his Map ... ' at p. 65 before cancellation & with pp. 703-706 before reprinting.* 4 vols.
H2 in Vol. 1 torn, sm. wear holes to map of
Germany at 6L3 & 6Q1 torn & reprd. in Vol. 2,
4F3 torn & sig. 4Z stained in Vol. 3, folding map
of Virginia restored at edges & margin repair &
some lr. margins dampstained in Vol. 4. [NSTC
20509; Sabin 66682] *(With:)* - Purchas his Pilgrimage. L., 1626. *4th. Edn. Iss. with the dedication
to King Charles I.* 1 vol. S4 & 5 with rust holes,
map of East India at 2T5 stained, sm. hole to 4N2.
[NSTC 20508.5; Sabin 66686] Together 5 vols. Fo.
Engraved title in 1st. vol. incorporating 2 world
maps & port., ptd. titles, 7 double-p. engraved
maps, 89 maps & plts. in text, cont. cf., rebkd.; the
Rt. Hon. Visc. Eccles copies. (CNY. Nov.18; 236)
$6,500
– – **Anr. Edn.** 1625. 4 vols. *(With:)* - Purchas his
Pilgrimage or Relations of the World & the Religions. 1626. 1 vol. Together 5 vols. Fo. Lacks
maps & numerous ill. ll., several ill. reprd., some
margins lightly strained, later vell., soiled, 1 cover
detchd., w.a.f. [STC 20509; 20508] (CSK. May 4;
46) £160
– – **Anr. Edn.** Glasgow, 1905-07. *(100) numbered.*
20 vols. Plts. & maps on Japan paper, orig. vell.-
bkd. cl., lightly soiled. (CSK. Jan.13; 6) £380

PURMANNUS, Matthaeus Gothofredus
- Chirurgia Curiosa ... to which is added Natura
Morborum Medicatrix ... by Conrade Joachim
Sprengell. 1706. Fo. Title & pp. 337/8 reprd.,
margins browned, cont. panel. cf., rebkd. (TA. May
17; 383) £180
– – **Anr. Copy.** Fo. 5 folding copperplt. engrs., titled
stained & reprd., pp. 337/8 reprd., lacks contents
lf., some spotting, cont. panel. cf., rebkd. (TA.
Jun.21; 376) £90

PUSHKIN, Alexandre Sergeevich
- La Dame de Pique. Trans.:- Prosper Merimée.
Ill.:- Antoine Clave. Editions du Pré aux Clecs,
1946. *(300) numbered. (10) with 2 extra suites of
ills. in sepia & black.* 4to. Unsewn in orig. wraps.,
folder & s.-c., unc. (S. Nov.21; 11) *Duran.* £130
- The Golden Cockerel. Ill.:- Edmund Dulac. N.Y.,
Ltd. Edns. Cl., n.d. *(1500) numbered & sigd. by
artist.* Lge. 4to. Orig. cl. (CSK. Jan.27; 111) £50
- Ruslan und Ludmilla. Trans.:- J.v. Guenther. Ill.:-
after W. Masjutin. München, 1922. Fo. Orig. hf.
linen, worn, spine defect. (R. Apr.3; 326) DM 410
- The Tale of Tsar Saltan ... Trans.:- L. Zellikoff.
Ill.:- I. Bilibin. Moscow, [1921]. Ob. 4to. Upr.
margin stained, cold. orig. pict. wraps. (GB. May
5; 2211) DM 550

PUTNAM, George Haven
- Books & their Makers During the Middle Ages.
N.Y., 1962. 2 vols. Royal 8vo. No bdg. stated, s.-
c. (GM. Dec.7; 605) £55

PUTZOLA, A. & others
- La Corsica nella sua l'Italianita a Cura della
Rivista Mediterranea. Cagliari, [1939]. Lge. 8vo.
Sewed, wrap. (HD. Oct.21; 66) Frs. 1,400

PUYSEGUR, Jacques François de Chastenet
See— CHASTENET DE PUYSEGUR, Jacques
François de

PYE, Henry J.
[-] The Democrat; or, Intrigues & Adventures of
Jean Le Noir, from his Inlistment as a Drummer in
General Rochembeau's Army. N.Y., 1795. *1st. Edn.*
2 vols. in 1. 12mo. Slightly foxed, cont. mott. cf.,
lacks front free end-paper. (SG. Jan.19; 313) $200

PYLE, Howard
- The Merry Adventures of Robin Hood. N.Y.,
1883. *1st. Edn.* 4to. Orig. blind-stpd. leath., shaken.
(SPB. May 17; 669) $225
– – **Anr. Copy.** Some mild foxing or staining, orig.

tooled cf., rebkd., scuffed, edges & corners worn,
new end-papers. (CBA. Aug.21; 492) $150
– – **Anr. Edn.** L., 1883. *1st. Engl. Edn. (510).* Lge.
8vo. Pict. cl., corners frayed, spine worn. (SG.
Dec.8; 289) $180
- Otto of the Silver Hand. N.Y., 1888. *1st. Edn.*
Advt. for 'Robin Hood' facing hf.-title, & 16 pp.
of advts. at end, orig. leath.-bkd. pict. cl., spine
rubbed, chipped at ends, cl.-covered s.-c. (SG.
Dec.8; 290) $110
- Pepper & Salt, or Seasoning for Young Folk.
N.Y., 1886. *1st. Edn.* 4to. Decor. cl., light wear,
lacks part of front free end-paper, d.-w., worn; Ken
Leach coll. (RO. Jun.10;85) $160
- The Rose of Paradise. N.Y., 1888. *1st. Edn.*
Margin darkening, ink owner's name on front free
end-paper, orig. cl., corners & spine ends bumped &
slightly frayed, spine leaning, bkplt.; long inscr. by
author defending book on dedication p., initialled
'H.P.'. (CBA. Aug.21; 493) $250

PYNE, James Baker
- The Lake Scenery of England. [1859]. Orig. cl.
(CSK. Sep.16; 246) £75
– – **Anr. Copy.** 4to. Tinted litho. title, 24 plts., some
detchd., orig. cl. (CSK. Dec.16; 225) £55
– – **Anr. Edn.** Ca. 1870. Sm. fo. Tinted litho. title &
plts. (25 in all), some spotting, contents loose in
orig cl. gt., rubbed, a few ll. slightly frayed at
edges. (TA. Jun.21; 175) £260

PYNE, William Henry 'Peter Pasquin'
- The Costume of Great Britain. L., 1804. Fo. Hand-
cold. vig. on title, 60 hand-cold. aquatint plts.,
maroon hf. mor., rubbed. (S. May 21; 62)
Schmidt. £520
- Etchings of Rustic Figures. L., 1815. Sm. 4to. 60
engraved plts., many slightly cropped, some loose,
spotted, cont. hf. cf., defect. (S. Jun.25; 440)
Shapiro. £70
- The History of the Royal Residences of Windsor
Castle, St. James's Palace, Carlton House, Kensington Palace, Hampton Court, Buckingham
House, & Frogmore. L., 1819. 3 vols. 4to. 100 cold.
aquatint plts., old marb. bds., rebkd. & recornered
with red mor., unc. (C. Jun.27; 57)
Weinreb. £1,700
– – **Anr. Copy.** 3 vols. 4to. 100 hand-cold. aquatint
plts. (wtrmkd. 1812-16), 1 slightly creased, some
ll. slightly spotted or browned, cont. hf. cf., rebkd.
with orig. gt. spines. (BBA. Sep.29; 123)
Old Hall Books. £680
– – **Anr. Copy.** 3 vols. 4to. 100 aquatint plts., all
but 1 uncold., sky of some plts. ptd. in blue, cont.
hf. roan, spines & corners rubbed. (C. Jun.27; 58)
Ross. £550
– – **Anr. Copy.** Vols. 1 & 2 only (of 3). 4to. 2 partly
cold. frontis., 64 plain plts., bds., spines crudely
reprd. (P. Sep.29; 222) £100
- Lancashire Illustrated. 1831. 4to. Additional
engraved title with vig., 49 plts. on India paper,
some faint staining affecting few plts., few ll. loose,
cont. hf. roan, worn. (S. Nov.1; 120) *Kidd.* £85
- Microcosm. [1802]. Ob. fo. Engraved title, 116
plts., some staining, wraps., worn, as a coll. of plts.,
w.a.f. (P. Feb.16; 157) £460
– – **Anr. Edn.** 1803. Vol. 1 only. Ob. fo. 60 aquatint
plts. only, light soiling thro.-out, cont. hf. cf., worn,
covers detchd., w.a.f. (CSK. Oct.7; 163) £220
– – **Anr. Edn.** 1808. 2 vols. Ob. 4to. 118 (of 120)
plts., some foxing & a few tears in Vol. 1, red mor.,
rubbed, w.a.f. (P. Jan.12; 171) £420
- Picturesque Groups for the Embellishment of
Landscape. L., 1845. Vol. 1 (of 2). Fo. 61 aquatint
plts., including frontis., slight spotting, a few margin
stains, roan-bkd. cl., worn, w.a.f. (S. Apr.30; 219)
Shapero. £120

QUAD, Matthias
- Europae Totius Terrarum Orbis Partis ...
Descriptio. Ill.:- Johann Bussemecher, Heinrich
Nagel & Quad. Cologne, Johann Bussemecher,
1596. 4to. Ptd. title with engraved port. on verso,
engraved allegory of Europa, 67 double-p. maps,
many embellished with port. vigs., apparently lacks
an engraved title, some browning, 1 or 2 maps
hand-cold., title reprd., limp vell., w.a.f. (S. May
21; 176) *Reiss.* £3,000

QUADRADO (Text)
See— RECUERDOS Y BELLEZAS DE ESPANA

QUADRI, Antonio
- Il Canal Grande di Venezia. Ill.:- Dionisio Moretti.
Venice, 1828. *1st. Edn.* 2 pts. in 1 vol. Ob. fo.
Engraved map, 47 plts. (title calling for 60, but
compl.), all hand-cold., mod. hf. vell., orig. ptd.
wraps. with MS. captions bnd. in. (C. Dec.9; 126)
Hildebrand. £1,600

**QUADRUM. Revue Internationale d'art Moderne.
Internat. Zeitschrift für Moderne Kunst**
Brussels, 1956[-1967]. Yrs. 1-20 (all publd.). 4to.
Orig. bds. (BR. Apr.13; 1998) DM 1,200

QUAIN, Jones
- The Muscles of the Human Body. L., 1836.
(With:) QUAIN, Jones & Wilson, W.J.E. - The
Vessels of the Human Body. L., 1837. *(With:)* - The
Nerves of the Human Body. L., 1839. *(With:)* - The
Bones & Ligaments of the Human Body. L., 1842.
Together 4 vols. Fo. 169 plts., most cold. (except
in last work), some foxing & staining, a few plts.
loose, orig. cl., stained & faded. (S. Nov.28; 132)
Phillips. £280

QUAIN, Jones & Wilson, Erasmus
- A Series of Anatomical Plates ... illustrating the
Structure of the Different Parts of the Human Body.
1842. 5 pts. in 2 vols. Fo. 197 (of 200) cold. &
uncold. litho. plts., some ll. loose & slightly frayed
at edges, cont. hf. mor. (TA. Oct.20; 292) £72

QUAIN, Richard
- The Anatomy of the Arteries of the Human Body
with its Applications to Pathology & Operative
Surgery. Ill.:- J. MacLise. 1844. Atlas vol. only.
Lge. fo. 87 mntd. col. litho. plts., some with slight
staining & fraying to borders, contents loose in
gutta-percha bdg., cont. hf. mor. gt., worn. (LC.
Oct.13; 210) £140

QUARITCH, Bernard
- Catalogue of English & Foreign Bookbindings.
1921. 4to. Cl.; H.M. Nixon coll., with his MS.
notes. (BBA. Oct.6; 171) *Quaritch.* £65

QUARLES, Francis
- Divine Fancies, Digested into Epigrams, Medita-
tions, & Observations. L., 1675. 2 sm. rust holes,
cont. cf., a little worn; sig. of Charles Cholomon-
deley, 1695. [Wing Q68] (BBA. May 3; 156)
Ximenes. £65
- Emblems. L., 1663. 2 pts. in 1 vol. Some ll. torn,
rather soiled & dampstained thro.-out, cont. mor.,
slightly worn. [Wing Q80] (BBA. Mar.21; 190)
Baldwin. £70
- A Feast for Wormes, set Forth in a Poeme of the
History of Jonah. 1620. 4to. Lacks 'Pentelogia'
(N1-02) at end, old vell., lightly soiled, lacks ties;
stp. of Bibliotheca Lambethana. (CSK. Sep.30; 60)
£85

QUASIMODO, Salvatore
- Giorgio De Chirico. Napoli, 1968. *De Luxe Edn.
(1,526).* Fo. 40 plts., 1 photolitho., cf. (CR. Jun.6;
241) Lire 600,000

QUATRE FILS AYMON
- Histoire des Quatre Fils Aymon. Ill.:- Eugène
Grasset. Paris, 1883. *(100) on japon.* 4to. Orig.
decor. cl., soiled. (SPB. Dec.13; 774) $600
– – **Anr. Edn.** Ill.:- Eugène Grasset. Ch. Gillet
(engrs.). Paris, 1883. 4to. Bradel hf. mor., chagrin
cl. covers, incrusted decor., unc., pict wrap & spine
preserved, s.-c., by Ch. Meunier. (HD. Feb.17; 78)
Frs. 3,400

QUATRE SAISONS
Paris, ca. 1820. 4 vols. Miniature book, 66 × 45
mm., 4 hand-cold. engraved plts., text spotted, orig.
embossed wraps., case, rubbed; van Veen coll. (S.
Feb.28; 203) £160

**IV CENTENARIO DE LA FUNDACION DEL
MONASTERIO LE SAN LORENCO EL REAL.
El Escorial, 1563-1963: Historia - Literature;
Arquitectura - Arte**
Madrid, 1963. 2 vols. Fo. No bdg. stated. (SPB.
Nov.30; 176) $325

QUAYLE, T.
- General View of the Agriculture & Present State of the Islands on the Coast of Normandy ... 1815. Cf., reprd.; from the Farmers' Club. Liby. (P. Jul.5; 48) £70

QUEEN SUMMER, or the Journey of the Lily & the Rose
Ill.:– Walter Crane. 1891. *(250) numbered L.P.* Publishers advt. lf. to rear, orig. bds., vell. backstrip, rubbed & soiled. (TA. Jun.21; 584) £60

QUEEN VICTORIA'S JUBILEE GARLAND
Ill.:– Kate Greenaway. L., 1887. *1st. Edn.* Ob. 12mo. Pict. wraps., lightly soiled, blue ribbon. (SG. Dec.8; 177) $120

QUEENY, Edgar M.
- Prairie Wings: Pen & Camera Flight Studies. Explanatory Sketches:– Richard E. Bishop. N.Y., 1946. *1st. Edn.* 4to. Cl., d.-w. slightly worn. (SG. Mar.15; 284) $175

QUEIROZ, José
- Ceramic Portugueza. Lisbon, 1907. *(50) numbered & inscr. special copies.* 4to. Slightly browned, some ll. slightly affected by damp, cont. cf. gt. (BBA. Nov.10; 284) *Zwemmer.* £75

QUENSTEDT, F.A.
- Handbuch der Petrefaktenkunde. Tübingen, 1852. *1st. Edn.* Cont. hf. leath., jnts. partly brkn. (BR. Apr.12; 688) DM 450

QUERCETANUS, Joseph (Pseud.)
See– DU CHESNE, Joseph 'Joseph Quercetanus'

QUEVEDO VILLEGAS, Francisco de
- La Caída para levantarse, el Ciego para dar Vista, el Montante de la Iglesia, en la Vida de San Pablo Apóstol ... Lisboa, 1648. *2nd. Edn.* 12mo. Leath. (DS. Apr.27; 2263) Pts. 30,000
- The Comical Works. 1707. *1st. Engl. Edn.* Some ll. slightly soiled, cont. cf., rebkd. (BBA. Oct.27; 21) *Bickersteth,* £55
- Pablo de Ségovie el Gran Tacano. Trans.:– J.H. Rosny. Ill.:– D. Vierge. Paris, 1902. *(455) numbered sigd. by artist.* Lge. fo. Red mosaic mor., wrap. preserved, mosaic front free end-papers, silk guards, case, sigd. Franz 1908. (DS. Nov.25; 2195) Pts. 65,000
- The Visions. Trans.:– Roger L'Estrange. 1671. License lf., rust hole in 1 lf., tear in anr. lf., slightly spotted at end, cont. cf. (BBA. Jun.14; 55) *Quaritch.* £75

QUILLER-COUCH, Sir Arthur
- In Powder & Crinoline, Old Fairy Tales retold by Sir Arthur Quiller-Couch. Ill.:– Kay Nielsen. L., [1913]. 4to. Orig. cl.-bkd. pict. bds., slightly worn. (S. Nov.22; 342) *Subunso.* £150
-- Anr. Copy. 4to. Some light foxing, cl.-bkd. pict. bds., orig. box. (SG. Dec.8; 252) $300
-- Anr. Copy. 4to. Qtr. cl. gt., pict. bds., rubbed. (SG. Jan.12; 275) $130
-- Anr. Edn. Ill.:– Kay Nielsen. [L., 1913]. *(500) sigd. by artist.* 4to. Slight edge darkening, end-papers foxed, gt.-decor. vell., slightly bowing. (CBA. Aug.21; 431) $750
-- Anr. Edn. Ill.:– Kay Nielsen. N.d. *(500) numbered & sigd. by ill.* 4to. 1st. few ll. lightly dampstained, some light browning, orig. stained vell. gt., affected by damp, lr. corner of upr. cover chewed, lacks ties. (CSK. Oct.21; 52) £160
- The Sleeping Beauty & Other Fairy Tales from the Old French. Ill.:– Edmund Dulac. L., [1910]. *1st. Dulac Trade Edn.* 4to. Some foxing to prelims., last pp., top & fore-e's, gt.-decor. cl. (CBA. Aug.21; 202) $110
-- Anr. Edn. Ill.:– Edmund Dulac. [1910]. *(1000) sigd. by artist.* 4to. A few corners lightly creased, orig. mor., worn. (CSK. Jan.27; 165) £65
-- Anr. Copy. Gt.-decor. mor., spine ends worn. (SKC. Mar.9; 1773) £55
-- Anr. Copy. Mor. gt. by Zaehnsdorf. (SPB. Dec.13; 524) $425
-- Anr. Edn. Ill.:– Edmund Dulac. N.d. 4to. Orig. decor. mor. gt., orig. box; C.C. Beausire bkplt. (LC. Mar.1; 97) £60

QUILLIVIC, R.
- Douze Gravures Originales de Finistère sur Bois de Fil. N.p., ca. 1920. *(50).* Fo. Leaves, folder; justified & sigd. (HD. Jun.6; 126) Frs. 3,200

QUIN, E.
- An Historical Atlas. 1830. *1st. Edn.* Fo. (408 × 333mm.). Engraved title, 21 engraved maps, hand-cold., outer margins of title & few text ll. slightly frayed, new end-papers, publisher's bds., rebkd. (S. Nov.1; 183) *Marlboro Rare Bks.* £60
-- Anr. Edn. L., 1846. Ob.fo. 21 engraved & fully hand-cold. maps (7 folding), few tears, some slight spotting, publisher's bds., defect. (S. Apr.9; 81) *Traylen.* £80

QUIN, Edwin, 3rd. Earl of Dunraven
See– DUNRAVEN, Edwin Quin, 3rd. Earl of

QUINBY, Jane (Ed.)
See– HUNT, Rachel McMasters Miller

QUINCY, Charles Sevon, Marquis de
- Histoire Militaire du Regne de Louis Le Grand, Roy de France. – Maximes et Instructions sur l'Art Militaire. Paris, 1726. *1st. Edn. (2nd. work).* Together 8 vols. (7 + 1). 4to. 1st. work, port., folding maps & tables, 2nd. work, folding tables & plans, sm. holes in title margin, unif. cont. Fr., mott. cf., spines gt. (S. Apr.10; 300) *Quaritch.* £160

QUINN, David Beers
See– HULTON, Paul & Quinn, David Beers

QUINONES, Juan de
- Tratado de las Langostas. Madrid, 1620. 4to. Leath. (DS. Mar.23; 2236) Pts. 35,000

QUINTANA, Manuel Josef
- Vidas de Españoles Célebres. Madrid, 1807-30-33. *1st. Edn.* 3 vols. Cf. (DS. Dec.16; 2084) Pts. 20,000

QUINTILLIANUS, Marcus Fabius
- Institutiones Oratoriae. [Treviso, Joannes Rubeus], ca. 1480-85. Fo. Rubricated, initials painted in red or blue, ex-libris 'Bibliothecae Weissenau' & painted blazon in lr. margin of 1st. text lf., mod. cont.-style stpd. cf. over wood bds., clasps; from Fondation Furstenberg-Beaumesnil. [H. 13644] (HD. Nov.16; 56) Frs. 9,000
-- Anr. Edn. Paris, Feb. 1531-Nov. 1530. 2 pts. in 1 vol. Fo. Upr. margins of title & following few ll. reprd., cont. blind-stpd. cf., roll-tool borders, a little worn. (S. Oct.11; 415) *Robert-Shaw.* £100
- Oratoriae Institutiones. Declamationes. Paris, 1520. *2nd. Edn.* 2 pts. in 1 vol. 4to. 1st. pt. lacks last 4 ll., cont. MS. annots., cont. stpd. roan over wood bds., decor., clasps; from Fondation Furstenberg-Beaumesnil. (HD. Nov.16; 157) Frs. 1,400

QUIROZ, José Maria Silva y Angel
- Codigo Civil de la Republica del Salvador en Centro-America Redactado ... N.Y., 1860. *1st. Edn.* Tall 4to. Orig. gt.– & blind-stpd. cl., soiled & slightly shaken. (SG. Oct.20; 145) £100

QUIZ (Pseud.)
See– ROWLANDSON, Thomas 'Quiz'

RAA. F.J.G. ten
- De Uniformen v.d. Nederl. Zee– en Landmacht hier te Lande en in de Koloniën. 's-Gravenhage, 1900. Text vol. & plt. vol. Lge. fo. Some plts. slightly foxed, 1 plt. torn, reprd., orig. gt. & pict. cl., 1 spine slightly defect. (VG. Mar.21; 531) Fls. 1,200

RAABE, Wilh.
- Hollunderblüthe. Eine Erinnerung aus dem Hause des Lebens. Ill.:– H. Steiner-Prag. Weimar, 1925. *(300) numbered.* 8 sigd. orig. lithos., dedication on end-paper, orig. bds., paper cover slightly loose. (GB. May 5; 3366) DM 550
- Die Schwarze Galeere. Ill.:– B. Goldschmitt. München, 1920. *(50) numbered on very heavy Bütten.* Lge. 4to. All woodcuts monogrammed by artist, printers mark sigd., orig. pict. vell., gt. inner dentelle. (HK. Nov.11; 3579) DM 460
-- Anr. Edn. Ill.:– B. Goldschmitt. München, 1920. *(250).* 4to. On Bütten, printers mark sigd. by artist,

orig. hand-bnd. hf. vell., cover ill. (H. Nov.24; 2485) DM 400

RABADAN, Mahomet
- Mahometism Fully Explained. L., 1723. 2 vols. Last advt. lf. in Vol. 2, lacks last (blank?) lf. in Vol. 1, few ll. slightly soiled, cont. cf., slightly worn. (BBA. Mar.21; 207) *Yapp.* £50

RABANUS MAURUS
- De Sacramento Eucharistiae. Cologne, 1551. *1st. Edn.* Some ll. lightly soiled at beginning, 17th. C. leath. gt., spine restored, re-cased, bumped. (R. Oct.11; 103) DM 800
-- Anr. Copy. Many old MS. marginalia & notes, 19th. C. leath., bumped & slightly worn. (R. Apr.3; 86) DM 520

RABELAIS, François
- La Chronique de Gargantua. Ed.:– Paul Lacroix. Paris, 1868. *(12) numbered on China.* Text of 1532 Edn. with 1533 variant, title-lf. of 1st. Lyon Edn., cont. mor., sigd. by Petit, gt. decor. in Le Gascon style, gt. inner & outer dentelle, marb. paper end-papers; & J. Bullrich ex-libris. (D. Nov.24; 2547) DM 750
- Les Cinq Livres. Ed.:– P. Chéron. Ill.:– Emile Boilvin. Paris, 1876-77. 5 vols. 12mo. 11 orig. etchings, cont. hf. mor., corners, sigd. by Canapé, spines gt., wraps. & spines. (HD. May 16; 96) Frs. 1,700
- Gargantua. Ed.:– Abel Lefranc. Ill.:– Barta. Fontenay-aux-Roses, 1934. 4to. Some foxing, recovered vell. by Lavaux, each cover decor. with painting by Barta, orig. watercols. on liners & end-ll., folder, s.-c.; with 2 letters (1 about cost of bdg.). (HD. Jun.13; 89) Frs. 4,000
- Gargantua et Pantagruel. Ill.:– Louis Icart. Paris, 1936. *(900) numbered on specially wtrmkd. velin d'Arches.* 5 vols. 4to. 76 cold. plts., maroon lev., gt.-decor., orig. wraps. bnd. in. (SG. Feb.16; 244) $475
-- Anr. Edn. Ill.:– Henry Lemarié. Paris, ca. 1940. 3 vols. On vélin d'Arches, leaves, wrap., box. (HD. Mar.27; 104) Frs. 2,500
-- Anr. Edn. Ill.:– Dubout. Paris, [1957]. *Ltd. Iss.* 2 vols. Sm. 4to. Hand-bnd. rust red mor., decor. spine, covers, inner & outer dentelles, by Schroth, Basel, orig. pictor. wraps. bnd. in; Hauswedell coll. (H. May 24; 760) DM 940
- Les Horribles et Espovantables Faictz et Prouesses du très Renommé Pantagruel. Ill.:– André Derain. Paris, [1943]. *(200) on Vell d'Arches.* Lge. 4to. Printers mark sigd. by artist, loose ll. in orig. wraps., bd. cover & s.-c.; Hauswedell coll. (H. May 24; 597) DM 18,500
-- Anr. Edn. Ill.:– André Derain. Paris, 1943. *(275) numbered & sigd. by artist.* 4to. Cf. by Y. Chartier, vari-col. mor. onlays, orig. pict. wraps. bnd. in, hf. mor. folder & s.-c. (S. Nov.21; 15) *Minou.* £4,100
-- Anr. Copy. Fo. Loose as iss. in orig. wraps., bd. folder; pres. copy with inscr. & sketch by Albert Skira to Anthony Zwermer. (BBA. Jun.14; 201) *Sims, Reed & Fogg.* £2,200
- Les Oeuvres. Lyons, Jean Martin, 1558 [i.e. after 1600]. 24mo. Lacks front fly-lf., some foxing, etc., cont. vell. (SG. Oct.27; 272) $225
-- Anr. Edn. Lyon, 1596. 12mo. 2 mod. sigs. on title-p., cont. vell., spine worn, lacks ties; sig. of Ryndesay (?) 1 May 1619. (S. May 10; 392) *Quaritch.* £560
-- Anr. Edn. N.p., 1596. *(With:)* – Le Cinquiesme et Dernier Livre des Faits et Dits Héroiques du Bon Pantagruel. Lion, 1596. Together 2 vols. 16mo. Mod. recovered vell. (HD. Apr.13; 42) Frs. 4,200
-- Anr. Edn. N.p., 1659-69 [i.e. 1669]. 2 vols. 12mo. Qtr. mor. (SG. Feb.9; 317) $100
-- Anr. Edn. 1725. 5 vols. Cf. (DS. Feb.24; 2453) Pts. 38,000
-- Anr. Edn. 1732. 6 vols. in 5. Dampstains, cont. roan, worn. (HD. Jan.24; 45) Frs. 1,500
-- Anr. Edn. Ill.:– Folkema (frontis), Picart & Du Bourg. Amst., 1741. 3 vols. 4to. Red mor. gt. by Hardy-Mennil, spines decor.; from Docteur Danyau liby. (HD. May 3; 119) Frs. 7,800
-- Anr. Copy. 3 vols. 4to. Some ll. lightly foxed, 19th. C. mor. gt., decor. spines, inner roll-stp.; from Henry Hope Edwards & Archibald Philip of Rosebery libys. (HD. Sep.22; 319) Frs. 4,000
-- Anr. Copy. 3 vols. 4to. Some foxing, cont. spr.

cf., spines decor., slightly worn. (HD. Nov.9; 63)
Frs. 3,500
– – **Anr. Copy.** 3 vols. 4to. Some light browning, cont. hf. leath., slightly faded, sm. worm-holes, engraved ex-libris inside cover; Hauswedell coll. (H. May 24; 1503) DM 1,250
– – **Anr. Edn.** Remarks:– Le Motteux. Trans.:– César de Missy. Paris, An VI [1797]. 3 vols. 4to. On vell., figures before the letter, cont. tree cf., spines decor. (HD. May 3; 120) Frs. 4,200
– – **Anr. Edn.** Ill.:– Thompson after Desenne (port.), after Adam fils. Paris, 1820. 3 vols. in 1. 18mo. Port. on china, mor. gt. by Trautz-Bauzonnet, spine decor., Vicomte de Jansé arms. (HD. Mar.27; 34)
Frs. 1,150
– – **Anr. Edn.** Notes:– Le Duchat, Bernier, Le Motteux, Abbé de Marsy, Voltaire, & others. Commentary:– Esmangart & Eloi Johanneau. Ill.:– Devéria. 1823-26. 9 vols. Cont. hf. cf., corners. (HD. Mar.21; 192) Frs. 2,200
– – **Anr. Edn.** Ed.:– P.L. Jacob (i.e. Paul Lacroix). Ill.:– G. Doré. Paris, 1854. *1st. Doré Edn.* 4to. Mor., sigd. by Marcus Michel, gold-tooled, gt. outer dentelle, border inside cover, marb. paper endpapers & doubls., orig. cold. wraps. bnd. in; Jules Noilly monog. ex-libris & port. bnd. in (sigd. oval etching). (D. Nov.24, 2263) DM 3,500
– – **Anr. Copy.** Lge. 8vo. Old hf. chagrin. (HD. May 4; 405) Frs. 2,100
– – **Anr. Edn.** Ill.:– after Gustave Doré. Paris, 1873. *1st. Printing.* 2 vols. Fo. Publisher's decor. cl., minor defects. (HD. May 4; 406) Frs. 1,800
– – **Anr. Copy.** 2 vols. Fo. Publishers decor. buckram. (HD. Dec.9; 173) Frs. 1,800
– – **Anr. Edn.** Ed.:– Pierre Jannet. Ill.:– Albert Robida. Paris, [1885-86. *1st. Printing.* 2 vols. Lge. 8vo. Some ll. foxed, publisher's cl. bds., special blue & gt. tools. (HD. Mar.27; 102) Frs. 2,200
– – **Anr. Edn.** Paris, 1912-22. *(28) De Luxe Edn. on Japan.* Vols. 1-IV. Sm. 4to. Hand-bnd. rust cold mor. gt., 1 vol. spotted, a few sm. nail marks, 1 jnt. defect from worming; Hauswedell coll. (H. May 24; 759) DM 1,000
– – **Anr. Edn.** Ill.:– Gustave Doré. Paris, n.d. 2 vols. Lge. 4to. Plts., text ills. & vigs., hf. leather, worn, orig. wraps. bnd. in. (SG. Apr.19; 215) $130
– **Oeuvres Publiées sous le Titre de Faits et Dits du Géant Gargantua et de son Fils Pantagruel avec la Prognostication Pantagrueline ...** N.p., 1732. *New Edn.* 6 vols. in 5. Sm. 8vo. Cont. cf. gt., crowned monog. of Jacques-François Léonor de Goyon, MS. ex-libris 'Le Prince de Monaco, 1732' on titles. (HD. Mar.27; 33) Frs. 16,500
– **La Plaisante et Joyeuse Histoyre de Grand Géant Gargantua ...** Late 16th./early 17th. C. *Counterfeit of 1547 edn.* 3 pts. in 1 vol. 16mo. 3 blank ll. (of 5?) at end of 1st. pt., owner's stp. & MS. ex-libris on titles, 19th. C. red mor., blind– & gt.-decor. (HD. Mar.27; 32) Frs. 15,100
– **Works.** Trans.:– Samuel Putnam. Ill.:– Jean de Bosschère. N.Y., 1929. *(1300).* 3 vols. Fo. Three-qtr. mor. & buckram. (CBA. Dec.10; 375) $150

RABETT, Lieut. George W.
– **Proposed Substitute for a Ships Rudder at Sea, When Carried away, Choked in Action or Otherwise Useless.** L., 1830. Pres. copy from author to Lord Marlborough, orig. wraps. (P. Jan.12; 272)
Henderson. £90

RACCOLTA D'AUTORI che trattano del Moto dell'Acque
Florence, 1723. 3 vols. 4to. Some light foxing, sm. liby. stps. on titles, cont. vell. bds.; Stanitz coll. (SPB. Apr.25; 369) $300

RACHEL, L.
– **Illustrierter Atlas d. Königreichs Württemberg.** Stuttgart, 1872. Ob. fo. Orig. hf. linen, orig. litho. wraps. bnd. in. (HK. Nov.8; 903) DM 11,500

RACINAIS, Henry
– **Les Petits Appartements des Roys Louis XV et Louis XVI au Château de Versailles.** Paris, [1950]. 2 vols. 4to. 1 vol. sewed, folder, s.-c. (SM. Mar.7; 2208) Frs. 1,300

RACINE, Jean Baptiste
– **Athalie, Tragedie.** Paris, 1691. *1st. Edn.* 4to. Some slight browning, cont. cf., spine gt., head of spine chipped. (C. May 30; 100) *Spinoit.* £500

– **Bajazet, Tragédie.** Paris, 1672. *1st. Edn.* 12mo. Some light browning, cont. vell. (S. Nov.17; 61)
Tzakas. £400
– **Cantique Spirituel.** Ill.:– Jacques Villon. Paris, 1945. *On vell. d'Arches, sigd. by artist.* Fo. Leaves, wrap., box. (HD. Mar.14; 145) Frs. 1,800
– **Idylle sur la Paix.** 27 Jun. 1685. *Orig. Edn.* Sm. 4to. Jansenist red mor. by Lortic, mor. liners, watered silk end-ll.; from Rattier liby. (HD. Mar.29; 80) Frs. 28,000
– **Mémoires sur la Vie de Jean Racine.** Lausanne & Genève, 1747. 2 vols. 12mo. Cont. mor., spine decor., arms of Madame Victoire, with her armorial ex-libris. (HD. Mar.29; 83) Frs. 45,000
– **Mithridate.** 1673. *Orig. Edn.* 12mo. Margins slightly short, jansenist red mor. by Godillot. (HD. Apr.13; 43) Frs. 3,500
– **Oeuvres.** Paris, 1702. 2 vols. 12mo. Ruled, cont. blind-decor. mor., red mor. liners, Madame de Chamillart arms & cypher; from libys. of Comte de Lignerolles & Bordes. (HD. Mar.29; 81)
Frs. 430,000
– – **Anr. Edn.** Ill.:– Daullé (frontis.), de Sève, Tardieu, Le Mire, & Bacquoy, after de Sève. Paris, 1760. 3 vols. Cont. cf. gt., decor. spines, inner roll-stp. (HD. Sep.22; 321) Frs. 11,000
– – **Anr. Copy.** 3 vols. 4to. Margin slightly browned or spotted, marb. cf. gt., very worn, corners bumped. (GB. May 4; 1406) DM 900
– **Oeuvres Complètes.** Ill.:– Le Barbier. Paris, An IV-1796. 4 vols. Lge. 8vo. On vell., slight loss from 1 p., red mor., spines decor. (SM. Mar.7; 2040)
Frs. 7,800
– – **Anr. Copy.** 4 vols. Cont. marb. cf. gt., spines decor., slightly worn. (HD. May 3; 122) Frs. 1,700
– – **Anr. Edn.** Paris, 1807. 7 vols. Some light spotting, cont. cf., spines gt., lightly rubbed. (CSK. Jan.27; 44) £120
– – **Anr. Edn.** Ed.:– Aignan. Paris, 1824. 6 vols. Hf. cf., decor. spines, corners. (HD. Feb.22; 178)
Frs. 1,800

RACINET, Auguste
– **Le Costume Historique.** 1876. 20 pts. 4to. 492 cold. & camaïeu plts. (of 500), losses from text, dampstains, leaves, publisher's lace folders, cl. spine. (HD. Jul.6; 70) Frs. 2,400
– – **Anr. Edn.** Paris, [1876-88]. 5 vols. Fo. Not collated, approx. 456 chromolitho. plts., highlighted in gold & silver, some plts. slightly soiled, loose-bnd. in hf. cl. & ptd. bds., covers worn, ties brkn. (CBA. Jan.29; 134) $600
– – **Anr. Copy.** Livraisons 1-13 only (of 20). Fo. Gt.-lettered cl., worn, w.a.f. (SG. Jan.26; 268)
$400
– – **Anr. Edn.** Paris, [1876-]88. *Racinet 'Petite Edn.'(?).* 5 (of 6?) vols. Sm. 4to. Over 350 litho. plts., several double-p., leath.-bkd. bds., worn, 1 vol. disbnd., uncollated, w.a.f. (SG. Aug.25; 302)
$275
– – **Anr. Edn.** Paris, 1888. 6 vols. Fo. 300 chromolitho. plts., 200 litho. plts., some light spotting, cont. hf. mor. (CSK. Aug.19; 51) £580
– – **Anr. Copy.** 6 vols. Lge. fo. 500 plts., including 300 chromolithos. in colours, gold & silver, ex-liby., mod. three-qtr. mor. (SG. May 3; 297) $900
– – **Anr. Copy.** 6 vols. Fo. 300 chromolitho. plts. & 200 plts. 'en camaieu', hf. mor. by S. David, ribbon bookmarks. (SG. Apr.26; 168) $850
– – **Anr. Copy.** 6 vols. 4to. 500 plts. (200 'en camaieu' & 300 in cols., silver & gold), some repairs, mostly to prelims., hf. mor. gt., slight rubbing, as a coll. of plts., w.a.f. (SPB. Dec.14; 78)
$350
– – **Anr. Copy.** 6 vols., including text vol. Fo. 500 plts., disbnd., not collated, w.a.f. (SG. Oct.13; 279)
$200
– **L'Ornement Polychrome.** Paris, [1875; 1885]. *2nd. Edn. (1st. Series).* 1st. & 2nd. Series, each 2 vols. together 4 vols. Tall fo. 220 plts. in colours, gold & silver, ex-liby., mod. red hf. mor. (SG. May 3; 296) $1,100
– – **Anr. Edn.** Paris, n.d. 1st. & 2nd. series. 220 chromolitho. plts., some light spotting, cont. hf. mor. (CSK. Aug.19; 52) £400
– **Polychromatic Ornament.** L., 1873. Fo. 100 gt. & chromolitho. plts., title faintly dampstained, gt.-decor. cl., spine ends frayed, ex-liby. (SG. Jan.26; 269) $200

– **Das Polychrome Ornament.** Plauen, n.d. Fo. 100 chromolitho. plts., orig. portfo. (CSK. Feb.24; 111) £130

RACKHAM, Arthur
– **Book of Pictures.** Intro.:– Sir Arthur Quiller-Couch. 1913. *1st. Edn.* 4to. Orig. cl. gt., rubbed, stain on upr. cover. (TA. Jun.21; 595) £50
– – **Anr. Edn.** L., [1913]. *(1030) numbered, sigd.* 4to. 44 cold. plts., orig. cl. gt., slightly soiled. (P. May 17; 377) *Steenson.* £150
– – **Anr. Copy.** 4to. Orig. cl. gt., slightly soiled. (S. Dec.20; 572) *Russell.* £120
– – **Anr. Edn.** Intro.:– Sir Arthur Quiller-Couch. N.Y., n.d. 4to. Cl., some shelf-wear, covers & spine chewed at edges. (RO. Jul.24; 379) $135
– **L'Oeuvre de A. Rackham.** [1900-13]. *(60) on japan, sigd. by artist.* 4to. No bdg. stated. (HD. Jun.26; 126) Frs. 2,000
– **The Peter Pan Portfolio.** L., [1912]. *(500) numbered.* Lge. 4to. 3 (of 12) lge. cold. plts., orig. hf. parch. folder, orig. box worn. (S. Dec.20; 569)
James. £190
– – **Anr. Edn.** L., [1912]. *(500) numbered & sigd. by publisher, engraver & printer.* Atlas fo. Liby. blind-stp. on title, gt.-lettered cl., bd. back & tips, slightly soiled, spine laced with linen ties, two-piece box, defect., lacks ties. (SG. Nov.3; 171) $950
– – **Anr. Edn.** N.Y., 1914. *1st. Amer. Edn. (300) numbered.* Tall fo. 12 mntd. col. plts., 3 plts. matted, mntd. to bds. & loosely inserted, lacks 2 tissue guards, corners of a few plts. creased, gt.-lettered silk moiré, cl. back & tips, moderate wear, covers lightly stained, lacks silk ties. (RO. Jul.24; 235)
$525

RACKHAM, Arthur (Ill.)
See– AESOP
See– ANDERSEN, Hans Christian
See– ARNOUX, Alexandre
See– BARHAM, Rev. Richard Harris 'Thomas Ingoldsby'
See– BARRIE, Sir James Matthew
See– DICKENS, Charles
See– DODGSON, Rev. Charles Lutwidge 'Lewis Carroll'
See– ES WAR EINMAL
See– EVANS, Charles Seddon
See– GOLDSMITH, Oliver
See– GRAHAME, Kenneth
See– GRIMM, Jacob Ludwig Carl & Wilhelm Carl
See– GUYOT, Charles
See– HAWTHORNE, Nathaniel
See– IBSEN, Henrik
See– IRVING, Washinmpton
See– LAMB, Charles & Mary
See– LA MOTTE FOUQUE, Friedrich Heinrich Karl, Baron de
See– MALORY, Thomas
See– MILTON, John
See– MOTHER GOOSE
See– PERRAULT, Charles
See– PHILLPOTTS, Eden
See– POE, Edgar Allan
See– RUSKIN, John
See– SHAKESPEARE, William
See– SOME BRITISH BALLADS
See– STEEL, Flora Annie
See– STEPHENS, James
See– SWINBURNE, Algernon Charles
See– WAGNER, Richard
See– WALTON, Isaac & Cotton, Charles

RACKHAM, Bernard
– **Catalogue of Italian Maiolica, Victoria & Albert Museum.** L., 1940. *1st. Edn.* 2 vols. 4to. Cl., rubbed. (SG. Jan.26; 148) $150
See– HANNOVER, Emil & Rackham, Bernard
See– HOBSON, Robert Lockhart & others

RACKHAM, Bernard (Ed.)
See– BEIT, Otto

RADCLIFFE, Ann, née Ward
– **The Italian, or the Confessional of the Black Penitents: a Romance.** L., 1797. *1st. Edn.* 3 vols. Ink holograph notation to fly-lf. of Vol. 1, darkening to prelims., marb. end-papers, period gt.-ruled mott. cf., gt.-decor. spine, covers rubbed & worn, upr. cover Vol. 3 detchd. (CBA. Oct.29; 687) $325

RADCLIFFE, Ann, née Ward -Contd.

- The Mysteries of Udolpho, a Romance. L., 1794. *1st. Edn.* 4 vols. Orig. hf.-titles, moderately stained & soiled, several sigs. detchd. or nearly so, lacks fly-lf. 1st. vol. (all end-papers & fly-ll. apparently glued during bdg.), period hf. cf. & marb. bds., leath. corners, vol. 2 brkn. in half along spine, bkplts. (CBA. Oct.29; 688) $475
- - **Anr. Copy.** 4 vols. Hf.-titles, cont. cf., some repair to spines & jnts. (SPB. May 16; 119) $225

RADCLYFFE, Charles W.

- Memorials of Charterhouse. 1844. Fo. Some spotting, hf. mor. gt. (P. Sep.29; 223) *Angle.* £50
- Memorials of Rugby. 1843. Fo. Slightly spotted, mor., gt. decor., slightly rubbed; S.L. Courtauld bkplt. (S. Nov.1; 121) *Thorp.* £130
- Views in Birmingham & its Vicinity. Bg'ham, n.d. Ob. 4to. Soiled or stained, orig. wraps., soiled, w.a.f. (CSK. Jul.6; 92) £100

RADEMAKER, Abraham

- Alle de Voornaamste Gesigten van de Wydberoemde Steeden Alknaar, Delft en Dordregt. Amst., 1736. Fo. 67 engraved plts. on 34 ll., cont. hf. cf.; ex-libris of J.L. Beraud. (C. Dec.9; 39) *Goldschmidt.* £950
- Cent Vues de Perspective de la Fameuse Rivière de Buyten-Amstel depuis Amsterdam ... [Amst.], ca. 1730. Fo. 100 engrs. on 50 ll., 1 with tear reprd., cont. marb. bds. unc. (C. Dec.9; 40) *Weinreb.* £750
- Hollands Arcadia of the Vermaarde Rivier Den Amstel. Amst., 1730. Fo. Lacks title, cont. hf. roan, unc., slightly worn. (VG. Nov.30; 1053) Fls. 900
- Kabinet van Nederlandsche Outheden, in Gezichten. Amst., 1731. 2 vols. in 1. 4to. Text beneath engrs. in Dutch, Fr. & Engl., some foxing, cont. cf. gt. (SG. Nov.3; 172) $950
- Rhynlands Fraaiste Gezichten Vertoonende alle Deszelfs Lustplaatzen Heerenhuizen en Dorpen van halfwegen Haarlem en Leyden ... Amst., 1732. *1st. Edn.* Fo. Engraved title vig., 100 plts. on 50 ll., cont. roan-bkd. bds. (C. Dec.9; 41) *Goldschmidt.* £1,200
- Spiegel van Amsterdams Zomer Vreugd ... Miroir des Délices dans la Belle Saison d'Amsterdam. Amst., n.d. Ob. 4to. Ink stain in outer margin of 1st. 6 ll., not affecting engrs., cont. wrap. (LM. Oct.22; 289) B. Frs. 10,000

RADER, Matthaeus

- Bavaria Sancta. Ill.:– R. Sadeler after M. Kager. München, 1615. *1st. Edn.* Pt. 1 only (of 4). Fo. Title with struck thro. cont. MS. owner's note & pasted over MS. owners note, hf. leath., ca. 1870, spine worn. (HK. Nov.9; 1455) DM 580

RADICKE, F.W.G.

- Handbuch der Optik. Berlin, 1839. *1st. Edn.* 2 vols. in 1. 1 title lf. stpd., cont. linen gt. (R. Oct.12; 1708) DM 400

RADIGUET, Raymond

- Le Diable au Corps. Ill.:– Maurice de Vlaminck. Paris, 1926. *(345) numbered, ptd. for Romain Arents.* 4to. This copy with further suite of the etching & 10 lithos. on chine (normally found only with the 25 copies on japon), crimson mor. by Henry Mercher, 1964, onlaid with scarlet mor., black tooling, orig. wraps. bnd. in, s.-c.; Maj. Abbey bkplt. (S. Nov.21; 42) *Desk.* £1,250
- Les Pélican. Ill.:– Henri Laurens. Paris, 1921. *(112) numbered & sigd. by author & artist.* Fo. Prospectus lf. loosely inserted, orig. pict. wraps., unc. (S. Nov.21; 28) *Desk.* £2,500

RADLOFF, V.V.

- Opyt Slovarya Tyurkskikh Narechii ... Versuch eines Wörterbuches der Türk-dialekte. Moscow, 1968. *Reprint of St. Petersb., 1893-1911 edn.* 4 vols. in 8. 4to. Orig. cl. (BBA. Mar.7; 61) *E.J. Brill.* £55

RADNOR, Helen Matilda Bouverie, Countess of & Squire, W.D.

- Catalogue of The Picture in The Collection of The Earl of Radnor. Chiswick Pr., 1909. *(200) numbered.* 2 vols. Fo. Orig. cl. gt., slightly worn & soiled. (P. Nov.24; 97) *Marlboro'.* £50

RADOS, L.

See— JACOB, N.H. & Rados, L.

RADZIWILL, Lee Bouvier

See— ONASSIS, Jacqueline Bouvier Kennedy & Radziwill, Lee Bouvier

RADZIWILL, Prince M.K.

- Hierosolymitana Peregrinatio. Brunsberg, 1601. *1st. Edn.* Sm. fo. Sm. hole in 201 affecting 1 or 2 letters, early owner's inscr. on title (shaved at foot), some stains, later hf. cf. (S. Dec.1; 359) *Israel.* £480

RAEMAEKERS, Louis

- The Great War. A Neutral's Endictment. 1916-17-19. *De Luxe Edns., Vols. 1 & 2 (1050), Vol. 3 (1030).* 4to. Orig. hf. cl. gt., partly untrimmed, orig. boxes, brkn.; Vols. 2 & 3 sigd. by artist. (TA. Apr.19; 556) £65

RAESFELD, F. von

- Das Deutsche Weidwerk. Ill.:– after K. Wagner. Berlin, 1914. *1st. Edn.* Orig. linen. (R. Apr.4; 1936) DM 140

RAESIDE, Jules

- Golden Days, being Memoirs & Reminiscences of the Goldfields of Western Australia ... 1929. Cl., slightly marked. (KH. May 1; 583) Aus. $160

RAFF, M.

- Abrégé d'Histoire Naturelle pour l'Instruction de la Jeunesse. Trans.:– M. Perrault. Ill.:– B.F. Leizel. Strasbourg & Paris, 1786. 2 vols. 1 plt. with short tear, 4 with upr. margins dampstained, cont. hf. roan, unc., rubbed; van Veen coll. (S. Feb.28; 100) £80

RAFFAELE, G.

- Ostreticia Teoricopratica. Naples, 1841-43. 2 pts. in 1 vol. Lge. fo. Wide margins slightly foxed, cont. hf. leath., slightly rubbed & bumped, spine with sm. defect. (HT. May 8; 540) DM 900

RAFFALD, Elizabeth

- The Experienced English Housekeeper, for the Use & Ease of Ladies, Housekeepers & Cooks, & c. L., 1773. *3rd. Edn.* Sigd., 3 folding engraved plts., (1 torn), final advt. lf., some spotting, cont. cf., reprd. & brkn. (S. Oct.4; 283) *Traylen.* £80

RAFFLES, Lady Sophia

- Memoir of the Life & Public Service of Sir Thomas Stamford Raffles. L., 1830. 2 pts. in 1 vol. 4to. 11 plts. & maps, some folding, 1 torn, some ll. loose & soiled, orig. cl., unc., worn, loose. (BBA. May 3; 308) *Remington.* £100
- - **Anr. Copy.** 4to. Orig. bds., unc., rebkd. (PD. Feb.15; 137) £90

RAFFLES, Sir Thomas Stamford

- Antiquarian, Architectural, & Landscape Illustrations of the History of Java. 1844. Plts. only. 4to. Folding map, 89 engraved plts., including 8 hand-cold., cont. cl., spine faded. (TA. Oct.20; 36) £135
- The History of Java. L., 1817. *1st. Edn.* 2 vols. 4to. Folding engraved map hand-cold. in outl., 65 plts. including series of hand-cold. aquatint costume, frontispieces foxed, cont. cf., rebkd. preserving spines. (S. May 22; 447) *Nevill.* £950
- - **Anr. Copy.** 2 vols. 4to. Hf.-titles, loosely inserted folding engraved map, 56 engraved & aquatint plts., & 10 hand-cold. aquatint plts. of costume, folding map discold., sm. tears at fold, 1 lf. of dedication detchd., later mor.-bkd. bds., spines slightly faded. (C. Jun.27; 59) *Remington.* £600
- - **Anr. Copy.** 2 vols. 4to. 1 folding map, hand-cold. in outl., 66 engraved & aquatint plts., including 10 hand-cold., some light soiling, map lightly offset, cont. hf. cf., rebkd. (CSK. Dec.2; 50) £520
- - **Anr. Copy.** 2 vols. 4to. 66 engraved plts. (10 hand-cold.), some imprints cropped, lacks map, slight soiling, margin pencil scoring, erasure from title-p. Vol.1, hf. cf., spines gt. (S. Mar.6; 42) *Waterloo.* £340
- - **Anr. Copy.** 2 vols. 4to. 2 frontis., 1 map, 62 (of 63) aquatint & etched plts., lacks lge. map (as often), cont. tree cf., foot of 1 spine slightly defect. (VS. Dec.8; 854) Fls. 700

RAFFLES, Sir Thomas Stamford & Crawfurd, John

- Descr. Géogr., Hist. et Commerciale de Java et des Autres Iles de l'Archipel Indien. Trans.:– Marchal. Bruxelles, 1824. 4to. Some foxing & margin staining towards end, cont. panel. cf., some repairs. (VG. Nov.29; 149) Fls. 600

RAFN, Carl Christian

- Antiquitates Americanae sive Scriptores Septentrionales Rerum ante-Columbianarum in America. Copen., 1837. Lge. & thick paper, 18 plts. & maps, some double-p. or folding, 3 tables, some foxing and staining, later hf. vell., unc., orig. wraps. preserved. [Sabin 67470] (BBA. Feb.9; 225) *Johnsen.* £220
- - **Anr. Copy.** Fo. L.P., 17 maps & plts., several double-p., some stains affecting text, orig. wraps., unc. & mostly unopened, spine slightly defect. [Sabin 67470 (calling for an engraved title & a further plt.)] (S. Dec.1; 291) *Baker.* £150

RAGUSE, Marechal, Duc de

- Voyages. Paris, 1837-38. 6 vols., including plt. vol. 8vo. & 4to. Plt. vol. with port., 28 engraved plts., including 8 folding maps, some stained, hf. cf. & marb. bds., spines gt.-decor. (SKC. May 4; 1817) £100

RAHIR, Edouard

- La Bibliothèque. Paris, 1930-31. 2 vols. 4to. Sale catalogue, orig. wraps., spines worn; H.M. Nixon coll., with many MS. annots., newspaper cuttings loosely inserted. (BBA. Oct.6; 160) *Quaritch.* £85
- Livres dans de Riches Reliures des Seizième, dix-septieme, dix-huitième et dix-neuvième Siècles. Paris, 1910. Fo. Cont. hf. mor.; H.M. Nixon coll., with his sig., note & some annots. (BBA. Oct.6; 172) *Laywood.* £180

RAILROADS

- Copies or Extracts of Correspondence between Her Majesty's Government, The Colonial Authorities, & Parties proposing to construct Railways in Ceylon, Trinidad, British Guiana, & New Brunswick. 1847. Fo. Folding maps hand-cold. in outl., slightly soiled, disbnd. (BBA. Jan.19; 90) *Faupel.* £85

See— PACIFIC RAILROAD

RAILWAY COMMISSIONERS OF IRELAND

- Atlas to accompany the Second Report of the ... L., 1838. Lge. atlas fo. 6 maps, including 1 handcold., cl., as an atlas, w.a.f. (GM. Oct.5; 483) £180

RAILWAY ENGINEER, The

Jan. 1927-Dec. 1934. Vols. 48-55. 4to. Cl.; the Eighth Earl Poulett copy. (LC. Oct.13; 461) £50

RAILWAY GAZETTE & NEWS, The

Jan. 1935-Dec. 1969. Vols. 62-123, & 3 special nos. 4to. Cl., spines gt.; the Eighth Earl Poulett copy. (LC. Oct.13; 462) £280

RAILWAY TIMES

L., 1854. 4to. Cont. linen, spine renewed. (BR. Apr.12; 640) DM 650

RAIMON, A.

- Soies et Tissus de Soie (Exposition de 1908). St. Denis, 1909. 4to. On holland, sewed. (HD. Feb.28; 188) Frs. 2,000

RAIMUND, Ferdinand

- Das Mädchen aus der Feenwelt oder der Bauer als Milionär. Ill.:– Oskar Laske. Wien, 1923. *(420) numbered. (20) roman numbered De Luxe Edn.* Printers mark sigd. by artist, 7 full-p. orig. cold. lithos., red orig. leath., gt. cover vig. (GB. May 5; 2861) DM 750
- Sämtliche Werke. Ed.:– F. Brukner & E. Castle. Wien, [1924-34]. 6 pts. in 7 vols. Ob. 4to. Red hf. leath. gt. (HK. Nov.10; 2657) DM 950

RAINSFORD, Marcus

- An Historical Account of the Black Empire of Hayti. [L.], 1805. *[1st. Edn.].* 4to. 2 engraved folding maps, 9 plts., 3 pp. of facs., spotted towards beginning & end, upr. margins stained, hf. cf., rubbed. (S. Jun.25; 119) *Duval.* £130
- - **Anr. Copy.** 4to. Lacks port. of Toussaint l'Ouverture, some ll. browned, old hf. cf. gt. extra,

extremities chafed. [Sabin 67531] (SG. Jan.19; 181) $150

RAISON, Théo
See— RONE, Alfred & Raison, Théo

RALEIGH, Sir Walter
- The Cabinet-Council. L., 1658. *1st. Edn.* Sm. 12mo. Lacks engraved port., later cf., disbnd.; armorial bkplt., marked in pencil 'Hollis copy'. [Wing R 156] (SG. Apr.19; 158) $100
- A Declaration of the Demeanor & Cariage of ... L., 1618. *1st. Edn. 1st. Iss.* Sm. 4to. Title with crudely shaved foreedge & soiled, last p. supplied in MS., later hf. roan, marb. bds. [STC 20652.5] (SG. Apr.19; 159) $120
- The History of the World. Ill.:– W. Hole. L., 1614. *1st. Edn.* Fo. Engraved frontis., 8 double-p. maps & plans, 2 shaved, 4 strengthened or reprd., hole in 2 plts. reprd., frontis. & 'The Minde of the Front' lf. cut down & mntd., 4 prelims. strengthened, some slight staining, rust hold in DD6, later hf. cf., worn. (S. Apr.9; 51) *Voorhees.* £280
- – **Anr. Copy.** Fo. Some dampstains, mod. hf. mor. (P. Sep.29; 231) *Tooley.* £90
- – **Anr. Edn.** 1617 [1621]. Fo. Lacks title, old tree cf., rebkd. [STC 20638a] (TA. Sep.15; 68) £75
- – **Anr. Edn.** 1634 [engraved title dtd. 1614]. Fo. Engraved & port. titles defect. & laid down, old spr. cf., spine gt.; Sir Ivar Colquhoun, of Luss copy. [NSTC 20641] (CE. Mar.22; 249) £140
- – **Anr. Edn.** L., 1634. Fo. 8 double-p. maps, engraved titles frayed & laid down, lacks lf. 'The Minde of the Front', last lf. of Index defect., few minor wormholes & tears, cont. cf., reprd., rebkd. preserving orig. backstrip. [STC 20641] (BBA. Mar.21; 169) *Blair.* £180
- – **Anr. Copy.** Fo. Some margin worming, tears, many due to paper flaws, sig. & note on title, engraved title attached to title, old cf., reprd. (SPB. Dec.13; 727) $325
- – **Anr. Edn.** L., 1652. Fo. The lf. 'the minde of the front' facing additional engraved title, sm. burnhole to 1 double-p. map, cont. cf. (C. Nov.9; 25) *Burgess.* £220
- – **Anr. Copy.** Fo. Engraved frontis., lf. of explanation, 8 double-p. maps, port. on title, maps & 2 other ll. loose, title & frontis. frayed & with sm. tears, latter crudely reprd., some maps torn at fold, 2 reprd., little wormed & stained, later cf., worn, backstrip defect. [Wing R-162] (BBA. Jul.27; 99) *Holdorf.* £110
- Judicious & Select Essayes & Observations. Ill.:– Robert Vaughan. L., 1650. *1st. Edn.* 4 pts. Sm. 8vo. Title-p. to each pt., engraved port., disbnd. [Wing R170] (SG. Apr.19; 160) $120
- The Prerogative of Parliaments in England. Midelburge [i.e. L.], 1628. Sm. 4to. D3v, line 17 ending with 'none' in roman, port. crudely hand-cold. & oxidized, blank corner of A4 defect., browned, title stained, wraps.; Frederic Dannay copy. [NSTC 20649.7] (CNY. Dec.16; 284) $130

RAMAL, Walter (Pseud.)
See— DE LA MARE, Walter 'Walter Ramal'

RAMAZZINI, Bernardinus
- The Abyssinian Philosophy Confuted. L., 1697. Title-p. repeated after preface to reader, new cf.; Dr. Walter Pagel copy. [Wing R 199] (S. Feb.7; 320) *Gurney.* £280
- Opera Omnia, Medica et Physiologica. Genf, 1717. Sm. 4to. Slightly stained thro.-out in upr. margin, some slight browning & foxing, cont. leath. gt., lightly worn. (HT. May 8; 571) DM 700
See— TORTI, F. - RAMAZZINI, B.

RAMBAUD, A.
See— LAVISSE, Ernest & Rambaud, A.

RAMBERG, Joh. Heinr.
- Kriegskalender für Gebildete Leser aller Stände. Leipzig, 1809. 1st. Yr. 12mo. Caricature ll. lightly foxed, orig. bds., gold-tooled decor., spine defect., 2 ex-libris. (D. Nov.24; 2329) DM 700

RAMBLERS MAGAZINE
1822. Vol. 1 (all publd.?). Frontis., 12 plts., mor. gt. by Wallis, unc. (P. Mar.15; 332) *Cavendish.* £200

RAMEAU, Jean Philippe
- Démonstration du Principe de l'Harmonie Servant de Base à Tout l'Art Musical Théorique et Pratique. Paris, 1750. *Orig. Edn.* Cont. marb. cf. gt., spine decor. (HD. Nov.9; 64) Frs. 4,900
- Les Indes Galantes. Balet, reduit à quatre Grands Concerts. Paris, [1736]. *1st. Edn.* Lge. ob. 4to. Stained nearly thro.-out, mostly in margin, 1 lf. torn, some light foxing, cont. marb. leath. gt., rubbed & bumped, lr. cover worn. (HK. Nov.9; 2280) DM 1,400
- Nouveau Système de Musique Théorique ... Paris, 1726. *Orig. Edn.* (*Bound with:*) GERVAIS, M. - Méthode pour l'Accompagnement du Clavecin. Paris, 1733. *Orig. Edn.* Together 2 works in 1 vol. 4to. Cont. roan, a little worn. (HD. Dec.16; 34) Frs. 3,000
- Observations sur notre Instinct pour la Musique et sur son Principe. Paris, 1754. *Orig. Edn.* Cont. marb. cf. gt., spine decor. (HD. Nov.9; 65) Frs. 3,900
- A Treatise of Musick, Containing The Principles of Composition ... L., 1752. 4to. Extensively annotated in cont. hand, apparently that of David Ironmonger, errata sheet, some foxing, mod. marb. bds., hf. cf., unc. (S. May 10; 145) *Maggs.* £80

RAMEE, Marie Louise de la 'Ouida'
- Folle-Farine. 1871. *1st. Edn.* 3 vols. Hf.-titles, orig. cl. gt., slight wear. (P. Jan.12; 147) *Jarndyce.* £95

RAMELLI, Agostino
- Schatzkammer Mechanischer Künste. Leipzig, 1620. *2nd. (1st. German) Edn.* Fo. Browned thro.-out, cont. blind-stpd. pig; Stanitz coll. (SPB. Apr.25; 370) $2,300
- – **Anr. Copy.** Lge. 4to. Lacks 2 plts., title with lge. bkd. tear & cut at foot, old MS. entry on recto, slightly browned, minimal soiling, last lf. with slight crumple, cont. vell., slightly soiled. (HK. Nov.8; 700) DM 3,100

RAMIRO, Erastène (Pseud.)
See— RODRIGUES, Eugène 'Erastène Ramiro'

RAMSAY, Alexander
- A Series of Plates of the Heart, Cranium & Brain in Imitation of Dissections. Edinb., 1813. *2nd. Edn.* 4to. 15 orig. copper-engraved plts., including 2 foldouts, holograph inscr. opposite title indicates these as the proof imps. for the edn., contents darkening, with some offset, three-qtr. gt.-ruled mor. & bds., covers worn, stitching visible at lr. cover. (CBA. Mar.3; 378) $275

RAMSAY, Allan
- The Ever Green. Edinb., 1724. *1st. Edn.* 2 vols. Proposals leaf-receipt sigd., cont. mott. cf.; bkplt. of Charles Visc. Bruce dtd. 1712. (SPB. May 16; 120) $175
- The Gentle Shepherd, a Pastoral Comedy. Ill.:– David Allan. Glasgow, 1788. Aquatint frontis. port., 12 plts., hf.-title, 18 pp. of engraved music bnd. at end, cont. tree cf., spine gt.; Sir Ivar Colquhoun, of Luss copy. (CE. Mar.22; 123) £320
- Poems. Edinb., 1721-28. *1st. Edn.* 2 vols. 4to. Engraved port. in each vol., subscribers' list, soiling & staining, 1 port. creased, cont. cf., not unif., some wear, one spine reprd.; pres. copy, bkplt. & inscr. of Robert Lumsdaine of Innergelly. (SPB. May 16; 121) $700
- – **Anr. Edn.** 1800. 2 vols. Port. foxed, cont. mott. cf., spines gt.; Sir Ivar Colquhoun, of Luss copy. (CE. Mar.22; 250) £80

RAMSAY, Andrew Michel, dit le Chevalier de
[–] Histoire du Vicomte de Turenne. Paris, 1735. *[1st. Edn.].* 2 vols. 4to. Hf.-titles, engraved port., 13 double-p. plans & vigs., cont. cf., spines gt. (S. Apr.10; 378) *Tile.* £100
- – **Anr. Copy.** 2 vols. 4to. Cont. marb. cf., spines decor. (HD. Mar.21; 74) Frs. 2,200
[–] The Travels of Cyrus. L., 1730. *4th. Edn.* 4to. Subscribers list misbnd., old pol. spr. cf. gt. (SG. Oct.27; 273) $110

RAMSAY, David
- Histoire de la Révolution d'Amérique, par rapport à la Caroline Meridionale. L. & Paris, 1787. *1st. Fr. Edn.* 2 vols. Hf.-titles, errata ll., 5 engraved folding maps, 4-pp. advts., few spots, cont. tree cf., spines gt. & wormed. (S. Apr.9; 52) *Burden.* £100
- The History of the Revolution of South-Carolina, from a British Province to an Independent State. Trenton, 1785. *1st. Edn.* 2 vols. Hf.-titles, a few maps with light browning, 1 with blank corner chipped, cont. tree cf., spine darkened, light wear at extremities: the Rt. Hon. Visc. Eccles copy. [Sabin 67691] (CNY. Nov.18; 237) $800
- – **Anr. Copy.** 2 vols. Hf.-titles, cont. cf. spines, lightly rubbed, spine ends slightly chipped; the Rt. Hon. Visc. Eccles copy, pres. inscr. from 'the author's nephew, John Ramsay' on both fly-ll. [Sabin 67691] (CNY. Nov.18; 238) $600
- – **Anr. Copy.** 2 vols. Hf.-titles, cont. cf.; Lord Northwick armorial bkplts. (SG. Nov.3; 173) $475
- – **Anr. Copy.** 2 vols. Some browning & foxing thro.-out, gt.-stpd. cf., worn, covers detchd., ex-liby. [Sabin 67691] (SPB. Dec.13; 464) $275

RAMSAY, David & Smith, S.S.
- History of the United States, from their First Settlement as English Colonies in 1607, to the Year 1808. Phila., 1818. *2nd. Edn.* 3 vols. Cont. tree cf., spines badly worn; from liby. of F.D. Roosevelt, inscr. in each vol., cont. sig. of John B. Bibb, 1819. (SG. Mar.15; 68) $400

RAMSDEN, Charles
- Bookbinders of the United Kingdom (Outside London) 1780-1840. Priv. ptd., 1954. *(500).* 4to. Orig. cl.; H.M. Nixon coll., with a few MS. notes. (BBA. Oct.6; 112) *Maggs.* £190
- French Bookbinders 1789-1848. Priv. ptd., 1950. 4to. Orig. cl.; H.M. Nixon coll., with 1 MS. note, pres. inscr. (BBA. Oct.6; 111) *Parikian.* £110
- – **Anr. Copy.** Sm. 4to. Orig. cl., slightly soiled. (BBA. Apr.5; 268) *Hannas.* £85
- – **Anr. Copy.** Plts., cl. (P. May 17; 63) *Droesmann.* £70
- London Bookbinders 1780-84. 1956. 4to. Orig. decor. cl.; H.M. Nixon coll., with some MS. notes, other cuttings & photostats loosely inserted, pres. inscr. (BBA. Oct.6; 113) *Maggs.* £160
- – **Anr. Copy.** 4to. Orig. cl. gt., d.-w. slightly soiled. (TA. May 17; 442) £80

RAMSEY, Stanley C.
- Small Houses of the Late Georgian Period. 1924. 2 vols. No bdgs. stated. (JL. Jun.24; 212) Aus. $240

RAMUS, Petrus
- Arithmeticae Libri Tres. Paris, 1555. *1st. Edn.* Title with excision bkd., verso stpd. (*Bound with:*) THEODOSIUS TRIPOLITA - Sphaericorum, Libri Tres, numquam antehae Graece excusi. Trans.:– J. Pena. Paris, 1558. *1st. Edn. in Greek & Latin.* (*Bound with:*) HENISCH, G. – Arithmetica Perfeta et Demonstrata, ... Augsburg, 1609. Together 3 works in 1 vol. 4to. Minimal soiling, 18th C. vell., spine renewed with old vell. (HK. Nov.8; 701) DM 900
See— MORNAY, Philippe de - RAMUS, P.

RANDOLPH, Thomas
[–] Cornelianum Dolium, Comoedia Lepidissima ... L., 1638. *1st. Edn.* 12mo. Engraved title, lacks A1 & a12 blanks, later blindstpd. cf.; bkplt. of John Kershaw. [STC 2069] (SPB. May 16; 122) $175

RANKIN, F.Harrison
- The White Man's Grave. 1836. 2 vols. 12mo. Cf., rebkd.; pres. copy from author. (P. Jul.5; 163) £75

RANKINE, William J.M. Macquorn
- A Manuel of Civil Engineering. L., 1862. *1st. Edn.* 2 vol. title-pp. at end, spotting on hf.-title, orig. cl., light soiling, rubbing; Stanitz coll. (SPB. Apr.25; 371) $175

RANKING, Boyd Montgomery Maurice & Tully, Thomas K. (Text)
See— GREENAWAY, Kate & Crane, Walter

RANKING, John
- Historical Researches on the Conquest of Peru, Mexico, Bogota, Natches, & Talomeco, in the Thirteenth Century, by the Mongols. L., 1827. *1st. Edn.* Orig. bds., cl. back, unc., paper label chipped & darkened, some wear, upr. jnt. brkn. (RO. Dec.11; 283) $160

RANLETT, William H.
- The Architect: a Series of Original Designs for Domestic & Ornamental Cottages & Villas. N.Y., 1847-51. 2 vols. Fo. Port. frontis., 120 plans & tinted litho. views, prelims. to Vol. 1 reprd., Vol. 1 rebnd. in buckram, Vol. 2 in reprd. cl., cover detchd., ptd. wraps. (3rd. edn.) bnd. in Vol. 1, ex-liby. (SG. Jan.26; 270) $325

RANSOM, Ernest
- Histoire d'Ardres depuis son Origine Jusqu'en 1891. Ill.:– Amédée Bodart. Saint-Omer, [1891]. Orig. Edn. Lge. 8vo. Hf. chevrette, spine decor. (HD. Mar.19; 137) Frs. 2,200

RANSOM, Will
- Private Presses & Their Books. N.Y., Lakeside Pr., 1929. (1200). Lge. 8vo. Cl. (SG. Sep.15; 282) $160
- Selective Check Lists of Press Books. N.Y., 1945-50. 12 pts. in 9 vols. Ptd. wraps. (SG. Sep.15; 283) $150

RANSOME, Arthur
- Aladdin & his Wonderful Lamp. Ill.:– T. Mackenzie. Ca. 1920. (250) sigd. by artist. 4to. Orig. cl. gt., soiled. (P. Jul.26; 44) £95

RANTZAU, Heinrich de
- Tractatus Astrologicus de Genethliacorum Thematum Indiciis pro Singulie Nati Accidentibus. Frankfurt, 1615. Cont. vell. (HD. Nov.17; 64) Frs. 1,750

RAOUL-ROCHETTE, D.
- Monumens Inédits d'Antiquité figurée, Grecque, Etrusque et Romaine. Paris, 1883. Lge. fo. Some slight foxing, cont. hf. leath. (R. Apr.3; 693) DM 400

RAPHAEL, Sanzio
- Vita Inedita di Raffaello da Urbino. Illustrata con Note da Angelo Comolli. Rome. 1790. 1st. Edn. Lge. 4to. Cont. vell. gt. (SG. Oct.13; 280) $110

RAPIN, Henri
- La Sculpture Décorative Moderne. Paris, [1925-29]. 3 vols. (Series 1, 2 & 3). Tall fo. 96 photo. plts., each liby.-stpd. on blank verso, loose in pict. bd. folders, linen ties. (SG. May 3; 299) $225

RAPIN DE THOYRAS, Paul
- Atlas. Ca. 1740. Fo. Ports., plts., 60 folding town & battle plans & maps, many torn at folds, cf., defect. (P. Oct.20; 64) £180
- Histoire d'Angleterre. The Hague, 1724-36. 13 vols., including 3 vol. continuation. 4to. Cont. sheep, spines gt., worn. (S. Mar.20; 790) Booth. £110
- – Anr. Edn. La Haye, 1727. 13 vols. 4to. Cont. cf., arms on upr. cover, decor. spines. (HD. Sep.22; 322) Frs. 2,100
- – Anr. Edn. Ill.:– E.M. La Cave (frontis.). La Haye, 1727-36. 2nd. Edn. 13 vols. 4to. Frontis. dtd. 1723, cont. spr. cf., spines decor. (HD. Mar.21; 75) Frs. 2,500
- [History of England]. [1732-56]. Collection of 66 maps & 34 ports. extracted from Rapin's History of England, several trimmed, some lightly browned, disbnd., w.a.f. (CSK. May 4; 49) £480
- – Anr. Edn. 1733-45. Vols. 2-4 only. Fo. Ports., 71 maps & town plans, 5 loose, cont. cf. gt. (P. Oct.20; 65) £420
- – Anr. Edn. Continuation:– N. Tindal. 1743-47. 3rd. Edn. 4 vols. in 5. Fo. Spr. cf., spines gt., a few minor stains; Sir Ivar Colquhoun, of Luss copy. (CE. Mar.22; 251) £420
- – Anr. Edn. L., 1751 & 1743. 3 vols. 2nd. Edn., 2 vols. 3rd. Edn. 5 vols., including N. Tindal's Continuation. Fo. Cont. cf., worn, lacks upr. cover of Vol. 1. (S. Oct.11; 581) Shapiro. £250

RAPPARINI, G.M.
- [-] La Monarchia Risoluta. Düsseldorf, 1696. (With:) [-] La Nascita del Diamante. Düsseldorf, 1697. Together 2 vols. 4to. Marb. wraps. (SG. Nov.17; 163) $150

RASPE, Rudolph Erich 'Baron Munchhausen'
- Des Berühmten Freiherrn von Munchhausen höchst Wunderbare Reisen. Renhingen, early 19th. C. 12mo. Cont. hf. roan. (HD. Mar.21; 179b) Frs. 1,250

[-] De Verrezen Gulliver ... Avonturen v.d. Baron van Munchhausen. Huaheine, 1790. 1st. Edn. Sm. 8vo. A few stains, later hf. vell. (VG. Mar.21; 467) Fls. 450

RASTELL, John
[-] An Exposition of certaine Difficult & Obscure Words, & Termes of the Lawes of this Realm. [1579]. Last blank lf., lacks 2 ll. of index, dampstained, some ll. wormed, affecting text in places, cont. cf. [STC 20707] (BBA. Sep.29; 137) Bauman. £100

RATCLIFF, John & Son
[-] [Brass-Founder's Pattern Book]. Ca. 1832 [wtrmkd. 1831 or earlier]. Ob. fo. 14 folding engraved plts., 211 full-p. engraved ills. on 108 ll., plt. nos. & prices added in ink, index lf. with p. nos. in ink, slight tears to 2 plts., lr. portion of plt. no. 46/47 cut out, cont. hf. leath., worn & loosening, covers detchd. (LC. Oct.13; 22) £1,600

RATELBAND, Johannes
- Kleyne en Beknepte Atlas of Tanneel des Oorlogs in Europa ... Amst., 1735. Ob. 4to. Wide margin, title creased, maps loose, minimal spotting, cont. hf. leath., worn & bumped. (HK. May 15; 664) DM 3,800

RATHBORNE, Aaron
- The Surueyor. L., 1616. 1st. Edn. Fo. Lacks port. on recto of A4, some stains, old vell. bds., slightly soiled, rebkd. [STC 20748] (S. Oct.11; 582) Eckert. £110

RATIONARIUM EVANGELISTARUM
Text:– Pierre Rosenhelm (Simler). [Pforzheim], 1510. Reprint of 'Ars Memorandi'. 4to. Wide margins, jansenist black mor. by Lortic fils. (HD. Mar.21; 76) Frs. 14,500

RATISBONNE, Marie de
[-] Zu disem Buchlein seind begriffen die Wunderbarlichen Zaychen beschehen zu Regensburg zu der Schönen Maria der Mutter Gottes. Ratisbonne, 1519. Sm. 4to. Mod. hf. cf. (HD. Dec.2; 117) Frs. 2,000

RATTA, Cesare
- Gli Adornatori del Libro in Italia. Bologna, 1923-27. Ltd. Edn. 9 vols. Fo. Orig. wraps., unc. (SI. Dec.15; 234) Lire 1,600,000
- L'Arte del Libro e della Rivista nei Paesi d'Europa e d'America. Bologna, 1927. (750). 2 vols. Fo. Orig. decor. bds. (SI. Dec.15; 233) Lire 260,000

RATTI, C.G.
See— SOPRANI, R. & Ratti, C.G.

RATTRAY, Lieut. James
- The Costumes of the Various Tribes, ... & Interior of the Cities & Temples of Afghaunistaun. L., 1848. Lge. fo. Additional hand-cold. litho. title, 29 hand-cold. lithos. on 25 sheets, dedication, list of subscribers, errata slip, advt. lf. at end, sm. repairs to margins of additional title, light stain affecting inner margins of a few plts., some faint discolouration, publisher's hf. mor. gt., rebkd., corners rubbed. (S. Feb.1; 43) Wheless. £3,200
- – Anr. Copy. Lge. fo. Additional hand-cold. litho. title loose & with fore-margin chipped, 29 hand-cold. lithos. on 25 sheets, errata slip, advt. lf. at end, light stain affecting inner margins of a few plts., hf. mor. by Hering, rebkd. (S. May 22; 448) Shapiro. £1,900
- Scenery, Inhabitants, & Costumes, of Afghaunistan. L., 1848. Lge. fo. Additional hand-cold. litho. title, 29 hand-cold. litho. plts. on 25 ll., orig. red hf. mor., green moiré cl. bds., by Hering. (C. Nov.16; 157) Hart. £1,350

RATTRAY, Sylvester (Ed.)
See— THEATRUM SYMPATHETICUM ...

RATZEBURG, J.T. Chr.
- Die Forst - Insecten. Berlin, 1837-44. 1st. Edn. 3 vols. & supp. 4to. All plt. versos stpd., cont. hf. leath. (R. Oct.12; 1897) DM 950
- – Anr. Copy. 3 vols. Some slight browning, vol. 1 with lge. stain, cont. hf. leath. gt., vol. 3 hf. leath., bumped. (R. Apr.4; 1776) DM 800

RAUCAT, Thomas
- L'Honorable Partie de Campagne. Ill.:– Foujita. Paris, 1927. (357). 4to. On Arches, jansenist mor., wrap. & spine preserved, s.-c., by Gruel. (HD. Dec.9; 175) Frs. 7,200
- – Anr. Edn. Ill.:– T. Foujita. Paris, 1929. (20) numbered on japon impérial. Lge. 8vo. 29 orig. cold. etchings, sewed. (HD. May 16; 85) Frs. 4,800

RAULIN, Joannes
- Itinerarium Paradisi. Lione, 18 Dec. 1518. 4to. Lge. stain at end, later limp vell. (SI. Dec.15; 35) Lire 700,000

RAULIN, V.
- Description Physique de l'Ile de Crète. Paris, 1869. 3 vols., including Atlas. 8vo. & 4to. 18 litho. plts., 3 engraved folding maps & plans (cleanly torn at folds), 2 hand-cold., orig. wraps., atlas vol. unbnd. as iss., soiled. (CSK. Dec.16; 20) £220

RAUNIE, Emile
- Histoire Générale de Paris. Paris, 1890-1918. 4 vols. Fo. Publisher's bradel bds. (HD. Jun.6; 127) Frs. 1,200

RAUTENSTRAUCH, Joh.
[-] Schwachheiten der Wiener. Wien & Leipzig, 1784. 3 colls. in 1 vol. Some staining, cont. sewed, soiled, spine defect. (GB. Nov.3; 135) DM 500

RAVAISSON-MOLLIEN, Ch.
- Les Manuscrits de Leonardo de Vinci. Paris, 1881-91. 6 vols. Lge. fo. Some slight spotting, liby. hf. linen, slightly spotted, wear. (HT. May 9; 1072) DM 3,100

RAV KAHANA, attributed to
[-] Pesikta Rabbati. Prague, 1655? 1st. Edn. 4to. Outer margins of title reprd. without loss of text, browned, edges trimmed with some partial loss of letters, hf. leath., marb. paper bds. (S. Oct.24; 47) Bragadin. £370

RAVENSTEIN, Ernst Georg
- Martin Behaim, his life & his globe. L., 1908. (510) numbered. Lge. 4to. Chromolitho. facs. of the gores in pocket at end, orig. bds., slightly soiled; many MS. notes by G.R. Crone loosely inserted. (S. Jun.25; 300) Tooley. £110
- – Anr. Copy. Fo. Qtr. linen, armorial bds. (SG. Jan.5; 23) $120

RAVILIOUS, Eric
- Wood Engravings. Lion & Unicorn Pr., 1972. Fo. Orig. cl., spine lightly soiled, s.-c. (CSK. Sep.16; 144) £110
- – Anr. Copy. Fo. Plts., orig. cl. (CSK. May 18; 73) £80

RAWLINGS, Marjorie Kinnan
- The Yearling. Ill.:– after N.C. Wyeth. N.Y., 1939. 1st. Edn. (770) numbered & sigd. by author & artist. Lge. 8vo. Cl., s.-c. (SG. Dec.8; 311) $275
- – Anr. Copy. Few pp. lightly foxed, gt.-decor. cl. (CBA. Aug.21; 679) $190

RAWLINS, Thomas
- Familiar Architecture. L., 1768. 1st. Edn. Fo. 60 engraved plts., subscribers list & lf. of 'References to the Apparatus' at end, some slight spotting, cont. cf., spine gt., rubbed; sig. of author on title below ptd. notice 'No copy of this work is authentic ... '; bkplt. of Thomas Boswall of Blackadder. (S. Dec.8; 388) Weinreb. £310

RAWSTORNE, Lawrence
- Gamonia: or, the Art of Preserving Game. L., 1837. 1st. Edn. 15 hand-cold. plts., without errata slip, slight offsetting, few gatherings slightly sprung, publisher's bdg. of mor. gt. (SPB. May 27; 672) $700

RAY, John
- A Collection of Curious Travels [by Leonhart Rauwolff, etc.] ... L., 1693. 1st. Edn. 2 pts. in 1 vol. Some browning, cont. cf., spine ends worn. [Wing R 385] (C. Nov.16; 158) Quaritch. £260
- – Anr. Copy. 3 pts. in 1 vol. Lacks 1st. licence lf., some ll. slightly browned, mod. cf. [Wing R385] (BBA. Mar.21; 70) M.D. Cox. £60
- A Collection of English Proverbs. Camb., 1670.

1st. Edn. Port. laid down, diced cf. [Wing R 386] (P. Mar.15; 333) *Bickersteth.* £90
- **A Compleat Collection of English Proverbs.** L., 1742. *3rd. Edn.* 2 pts. in 1 vol. Cancelled titles, a few ll. slightly soiled, 19th. C. cf., spine gt., rubbed. (BBA. May 3; 202) *Quaritch.* £85
- **A Collection of English Words not Generally used.** 1691. *2nd. Edn.* Some dampstaining, cf., worn. (P. Mar.15; 335) *Jarndyce.* £85
- **Historia Insectorum.** L., 1710. *1st. Edn.* 4to. Cont. cf., spine decor. gt. (SKC. Oct.26; 422) £170
- **Miscellaneous Discourses Concerning the Dissolution & Changes of the World.** L., 1692. *1st. Edn.* 1st. 'Imprimatur' lf. present, cont. cf., spine gt. [Wing R397] (BBA. May 3; 62) *Ximenes.* £200
- **Select Remains, with his Life by W. Derham.** 1760. *1st. Edn.* Errata slip, mod. mor. gt. (BBA. Feb.23; 180) *Wise.* £70
- **The Wisdom Manifested in the Works of Creation in Two Parts.** Glasgow, 1758. Cont. spr. cf.; Sir Ivar Colquhoun, of Luss copy. (CE. Mar.22; 124) £220

RAY, Man
- **Les Mains Libres.** Paris, 1937. *(675) numbered.* Lge. 4to. Orig. wraps., slightly bumped. (HK. Nov.11; 3891) DM 850
- **Photographies 1920-1934.** Text.:– André Breton, Paul Eluard, Rose Selavy, Tristan Pzara, & Man Ray. Hartford, [1934]. *2nd. Edn.* 4to. Port., 104 gravure reproductions, text in Fr. & Engl., spiral-bnd. pict. wraps., upr. portion of spiral casing brkn. & reprd. with tape. (SG. Nov.10; 106) $450
- **Man Ray Photographs, 1920-1934, Paris.** Essays:– André Breton, Paul Eluard, Rose Selavy, Tristan Tzara, & Man Ray. Hartford, [1934]. *2nd. Edn.* 4to. Title in Engl. & Fr., essays in Engl., Fr. & German, spiral-bnd. pict. wraps., a few very minor scuffs. (SG. May 10; 86) $450
- – **Anr. Copy.** 4to. Essays in Engl., Fr. & German, spiral-bnd. pict. wraps., rubbed, lightly chipped; Berenice Abbott copy. (SG. May 10; 85) $350

RAY, Patrick Henry
- [–] **Report of the International Polar Expedition to Point Barrow.** Wash., 1885. Lge. 4to. Few ll. loose, hf. leath. (SG. Sep.22; 15) $150

RAYBAUD, M.
- **Mémoires sur la Grèce** ... 1824. 2 vols. Hf. chagrin. (HD. Jun.29; 104) Frs. 1,500

RAYLEIGH, John Strutt, Baron
- **The Becquerel Rays & the Properties of Radium.** L., 1904. *1st. Edn.* Advts., orig. cl., spine slightly faded; Stanitz coll. (SPB. Apr.25; 374) $175

RAYMOND, Jehan
- **Le Cuir: Compositions Decoratives.** Paris, ca. 1910. Sm. fo. 48 col. plts., with outl. designs on lettered tissue-guards, loose in gt.-lettered imitation snakeskin, lacks spine. (SG. Aug.25; 37) $325

RAYMOND, John
- **An Itinery Contayning a Voyage made through Italy in the Yeare 1646 & 1647.** 1648. 12mo. Spotting, mor. (P. Jan.12; 273) *Marlboro. Rare Bks.* £150

RAYMUND, Alexandre
- **Alttuerkische Keramik in Kleinasien und Konstantinopel.** Ed.:– Karl Wulzinger. Munich, 1922. Atlas fo. 40 cold. plts., each liby. stpd. on blank verso, pict. bds., d.-w. (SG. May 3; 86) $375

RAYNAL, Abbé Guillaume François Thomas
- [–] **Histoire Philosophique et Politique des Etablissemens & du Commerce des Européens dans les Deux Indes.** Ill.:– C.P. Marillier. Genf, 1775. 3 vols. Title ll. & end-papers vols. II & III slightly foxed, some ll. lightly browned Vol. I, 4 pp. Vol. III with light stain, cont. leath., gold-tooled, lightly rubbed & bumped, sm. worm-holes. [Sabin 68080] (HT. May 10; 2754) DM 420
- – **Anr. Edn.** Ill.:– Cochin, Moreau. Genève, 1780. 5 vols. including atlas. 4to. Lacks 23 statistic tables, cont. marb. cf. gt. decor., decor. spine. (HD. Jan.27; 294) Frs. 2,800
- – **Anr. Copy.** 10 vols. (lacks Atlas). With arrêt de la cour du parlement condemning the work 'à etre lacéré et brûlé par l'Executeur de Haute Justice', (HD. Jun.29;

cont. cf. gt. decor. spines, inner roll-stp. (HD. Sep.22; 324) Frs. 2,100
- – **Anr. Edn.** Ill.:– Moreau le Jeune. Geneva, 1781. 10 vols. (lacks atlas vol.). Hf.-titles, errata ll., port., 9 plts., cont. Fr. cf., gt., flat spines gt., some corners worn, 1 defect., some spines worn. (S. Apr.10; 301) *Diaz.* £90
- – **Anr. Edn.** Geneva, 1782. 10 vols. (lacks atlas vol.). Liby. stps. on titles, cont. mott. sheep., spines gt., 1 spine defect., liby. stps. on spine labels. (S. Mar.20; 791) *Booth.* £65
- – **Anr. Edn.** Ill.:– Bovinet & others after Moreau Le jeune. Paris, an III [1794]. 10 vols. & Atlas. Engraved port. vol. 1, 9 title copper engrs. & 50 double-p. copper engraved maps in atlas, some light browning, cont. leath. gt., atlas not quite unif., spine partly restored. (R. Apr.5; 2786) DM 1,200
- – **Anr. Edn.** Paris, 1820. 12 vols. & atlas. Hf. roan, spine vol. 1 & Atlas with loss. (HD. Feb.22; 179) Frs. 3,800
- **A Philosophical & Political History of the Europeans in the East & West Indies.** L., 1776. *2nd. Edn.* 5 vols. Spotting, cont. cf., rebkd., old spine laid down, mod. spine labels. (CSK. Feb.24; 106) £120
- – **Anr. Edn.** Trans.:– J.O. Justamond. L., 1788. 8 vols. Cont. tree cf. gt., spines gt. (C. Nov.9; 155) *Traylen.* £340
- – **Anr. Copy.** 1 folding map worn, mott. cf. (P. Jul.5; 162) £130
See— **BONNE, Pugobert (Atlas Vol.).**

RAYNAL KEENE, R.
- **Reclamación ... a las Cortes contra la Arbitariedad del ... Ministerio de La Gobernación de Ultramar.** Madrid, 1820. 4to. Sewed. (DS. Nov.25; 2412) Pts. 24,000

RAZOUMOWSKY, Comte de
- **Histoire Naturelle du Jorat et de ses Enviroms, et celle des Trois Lacs de Neufchâtel, Morat et Bienne.** Lausanne, 1789. Old hf. parch., corners. (HD. Nov.17; 65) Frs. 2,200

RAZUK SHIMSHON
- **Shir Yedidut.** L., 1870. 4to. 1 sheet ptd. on 1 side, lightly stained, cl., reprd., w.a.f. (S. Oct.25; 153) £140

RE, Vincenzo
- **Narrazione delle Solenni Reali Feste ... in Napoli ... Filippo Real Principe delle due Sicilie.** Ill.:– Carlo Gregori, Giuseppe Vasi, & others, after Re. Naples, 1749. Lge. fo. Title with engraved ill., engraved frontis., 15 double-p. plts., 2 ll. rehinged, some plts. reprd., cont. red mor., covers with gt. panel enclosing gt. Royal Arms of Naples, spine gt. (C. Dec.9; 127) *Weinreb.* £2,800

REA, John
- **Flore, – seu De Florum Cultura. Or, a Complete Florilege** ... L., 1676. *2nd. Edn.* Fo. 1 lf. with tear, cont. cf. (GM. Dec.7; 636) £70

READ, Charles Hercules & Dalton, Ormonde Maddock
- **Antiquities of the City of Benin.** L., 1899. Atlas fo. 32 plts., text ills., ex-liby., cl.-bkd. ptd. bds. (SG. May 3; 300) $475

READE, Aleyn Lyell
- **Johnsonian Gleanings.** L., 1909-1952. *(350) (1st. 2 vols.)* 11 vols. Some sm. marks & bds. of 1st. vol. spotted; 1st. pt. with author's inscr. & A.L.s. set down, some cuttings laid in. (KH. Nov.8; 273) Aus. $140

READE, Charles
- **The Cloister & the Hearth.** L., 1861. *1st. Edn.* 4 vols. Orig. cl., covers discold. & faded. (LH. Sep.25; 586) £180

REAL-ENCYKLOPADIE FUR PROTESTANTISCHE THEOLOGIE UND KIRCHE
Hamburg, 1854-68. *1st. Edn.* 22 vols., including Supp. & Gesamtregister. Vols. 5 & 8 lack pp. 401-416, some spotting, especially at beginning & end, hf. leath., 1 spine with sm. fault, 1 vol. rubbed & bumped. (V. Sep.30; 2210) DM 440

REALLEXIKON FUR ANTIKE UND CHRISTENTUM
Ed.:– Th. Klauser. Stuttgart, 1950-83. Vol. I-XII. 1st. 7 vols. hf. mor., rest in pts., 4 vols. with orig. wraps. (B. Jun.21; 280) Fls. 1,000

REALLEXIKON ZUR DEUTSCHEN KUNSTGESCHICHTE
Ed.:– O. Schmitt, E. Gall & L.H. Heydenreich (from vol. III). Stuttgart, 1937-58. Vols. I-IV in 4 vols. Orig. linen. (R. Apr.3; 889) DM 850

REAL LIFE IN LONDON
See— **EGAN, Pierce**

REAUMUR, René Antoine Ferchault de
- **L'Art de Convertir le Fer Forgé en Acier et l'Art d'Adoucir le Fer Fondu.** Paris, 1722. *1st. Edn.* 4to. Cont. mott. cf., spine gt. (C. May 30; 123) *Hill.* £450
- **Art de Faire Eclore et d'Elëver en Toute Saison des Oiseaux Domestiques de Toutes Espèces, soit par le Moyen de la Chaleur du Fumier, soit part le Moyen de Celle du Feu Ordinaire.** Paris, 1749. *1st. Edn.* 2 vols. Few margins soiled or stained, some stains, cont. mott. cf. gt., spines. (TA. Nov.17; 337) £60
- **Fabrique des Ancres.** Ed.:– H.L. Duhamel du Monceau. [Paris], 1764. *Orig. Edn.* Fo. Old hf. roan. (HD. Mar.9; 119) Frs. 1,700
- **Mémoires pour servir a l'Histoire des Insectes.** Paris, 1734-42. *1st. Edn.* 6 vols. 4to. 267 folding engraved plts., some margin tears in Vol. 1, some dust soiling, cont. cf. gt., badly worn, backs brkn. (CNY. May 18; 148) $300

REBELL, Hughes
- **Les Nuits Chaudes du Cap Français.** Ill.:– Hermine David. 1927. Orig. aqua sigd. with sigd. autograph dedication from David to Willy Michel, hf. mor. (HD. Dec.9; 21c) Frs. 1,150

REBOULET, Simon
- **Histoire du Règne de Louis XIV.** Avignon, 1744. 3 vols. 4to. Cont. marb. cf., spines decor. (HD. Nov.9; 154) Frs. 2,700

REBOUX, P.
- **La Maison de Danses.** Ill.:– Lobel-Riche. [Paris], 1928. *De Luxe Edn., (250). (9) on Japon.* 2 vols. 4to. Series of etchings in 1st. state without remarks, series ptd. in black on vell, series in black with remarks series in bistre with remarks & series ptd. in red, 2 sigd. prelim. ills., orig. wraps., bd. s.-c., worn, 1 slightly defect. (HK. Nov.11; 3741) DM 2,300

REBOUX, P. & Müller, Ch.
- **A la Manière de** ... Paris, 1908; 1910-25. *Orig. Edn.* 4 vols. 12mo. Vol. III on imitation japan, Vol. IV on 'pur fil', sewed; 2 sigd. autograph dedications & 1 letter. (HD. Feb.28; 126) Frs. 1,000

REBULLOSA, Jayme
- **Descripcion de todas las Provincias, Estados y Ciudades ... del Mundo, Sacades de las Relaciones Toscanas de Juan Botero Benes** ... Gerona, 1748. 4to. Vell. (DS. Feb.24; 2528) Pts. 20,000

RECANATI, Menachem
- **Piskei Halachot.** Bologna, 1538. *1st. Edn.* 4to. Owners' sigs. & inscr. on title, last lf. reprd. not affecting text, stained & browned, hf. leath. (S. Oct.25; 317) *Klein.* £1,000
- **Ta'amei Ha'Mitzvot.** Intro. & Afterword:– Jacob Luzatto. Basel, 1581. *2nd. Edn.* 4to. Owners sig. on title, slight staining & soiling, some worming, reprd., sometimes affecting a few letters, cl. [Steinschneider 6363, 2] (SPB. Jun.26; 26) $1,000

RECHPERGER, W.
- **Astrolabium.** Augsburg, 1611. 4to. Mod. hf. vell. (R. Apr.4; 1559) DM 1,050

RECHT, Camille
- **Die Alte Photographie.** Preface:– Ivan Goll. Paris & Leipzig, [1931]. 4to. Separate pamphlet of captions laid in at rear, gt.-pict. cl. (SG. May 10; 119) $100

RECKE, Elise von der & Schwarz, Sophie (née Becker)
- **Elisens und Sophiens Gedichte.** Ed.:– I.L.

RECKE, Elise von der & Schwarz, Sophie (née Becker) -*Contd.*
Schwarz. Berlin, 1790. *1st. De Luxe Edn. on Bütten. (Not for Sale?).* Later bds. gt. (GB. May 4; 1409)   DM 500

RECORD, Robert
- The Castle of Knowledge. L., 1556. *1st. Edn.* Fo. With reading 'Caste' on verso of title-p., sm. deficiencies in 2 blank margins, title a little dust-stained, some mainly light, stains, later panel. cf. [STC 20796] (BBA. May 3; 63) *Thomas.* £2,300

RECUEIL CHOISI DE CHANSONS ET DE POESIES MACONNES
Ca. 1780. 12mo. Cont. bradel bds., unc. (HD. May 3; 56)   Frs. 1,200

RECUEIL D'ESTAMPES REPRESENTANT LES DIFFERENTS EVENEMENTS DE LA GUERRE ...
Paris, ca. 1874. Sm. fo. L.P., 16 engraved plts., without separate title-p., as iss., some foxing, cont. mott. cf., s.-c. [Sabin 68421] (LH. Sep.25; 181) $800

RECUEIL DE QUELQUES PIECES NOUVELLES ET GALANTES ...
Cologne, 1667. *3rd. Elzevir Edn.* 2 pts. in 1 vol. Sm. 12mo. Ruled, cont. red mor., spine decor., red mor. liners. (HD. Mar.29; 84)   Frs. 11,000
– – **Anr. Edn.** Text:– Abbé Tallemant, Abbé de Montrouil, Boileau, Furetière, & La Fomtaine. Cologne [Amst.], 1667. 2 pts. in 1 vol., 18mo. Mor. gt. by Niedrée, 1847, spine decor.; Viollet Le Duc ex-libris. (HD. Mar.27; 35)   Frs. 1,300

RECUEIL DES FETES ET SPECTACLES donnés devant sa Majesté à Versailles, à Choisy et à Fontainebleau pendant l'Anmée 1771
Paris, 1771. Cont. marb. cf. gt., Louis XVI arms, spine decor.; Madame de Rougemont ex-libris. (HD. May 3; 123)   Frs. 1,700

RECUEIL DES MEILLEURS CONTES EN VERS
Ill.:– Duplessi-Bertaux?. L. [Paris], 1778. 4 vols. 18mo. Cont. marb. cf. gt., spines decor. (HD. May 3; 124)   Frs. 1,600

RECUEIL DES PLUS BEAUX VERS de Messieurs de Malherbe, Racan, Montfuron ...
Paris, 1627. *Orig. Edn.* Ruled, some ll. transposed at end, cont. red mor. by Boyet, spine decor.; from Comte de Lignerolles liby. (HD. Mar.29; 85)   Frs. 28,000

RECUEIL VAN VERSCHEYDE PLACATEN, Ordonnantien, Resolutien, instructien, & c. Betr. de Saacken v.d. Oorlogh, te Wozer en te Lande
's-Gravenhage, [1716-]70. 5 vols. 4to. Cont. vell., ties. (VG. Sep.14; 1192)   Fls. 750

REDDING, Cyrus
- A History & Description of Modern Wines. 1833. Orig. cl. (BBA. Aug.18; 120)   *Shaw.* £55
– – **Anr. Edn.** L., 1851. 4to. Publishers cl. (DS. Apr.27; 2568)   Pts. 35,000

REDEL, August Casimir
- Annus Symbolicus, Emblemmatica et versu Leoninó ad Animum Pie Recreandum Oblatus. Augsburg, ca. 1695. Slightly spotted, mod. cold. paper covered bds. (R. Oct.11; 187)   DM 480

REDFERN, William Beales
- Royal & Historic Gloves & Shoes. L., 1904. 4to. Some slight spotting, orig. cl.; A.L. from author inserted. (S. May 1; 657)   *Quaritch.* £85

REDGRAVE, G.R.
See— POLLARD, Alfred William, Redgrave, G.R. & others

REDI, Francesco
- Opere. Napoli, 1687. 3 vols. Hf.-titles, some stains & browning, cont. leath., decor. spines, rubbed. (SI. Dec.15; 174)   Lire 350,000
- Osservazioni Intorno agli Animali Viventi. Flor., 1684. *1st. Edn.* Title with engraved device, 26 plts. (2 folding), extra plt. numbered 'Nona', hf.-title, lacks port., cont. vell.; Dr. Walter Pagel copy. (S. Feb.7; 324)   *Heller.* £180

REDING, H.
- Atlas van het Koningrijk der Nederlanden en de Overzeesche Bezittingen. Text:– P.J. Mendel. 's-Gravenhage, 1841. Ob. sm. fo. 13 hand-cold. maps, frontis. slightly defect., cont. hf. mor., defect. (VG. Mar.19; 10)   Fls. 750
See— MENDEL, P.J. & Reding, H.

REDOUTE, Pierre Joseph
- Les Liliacées. Ill.:– Langlois, de Gouy, Lemercier, Lemaire, & others, after Redoute. Paris, priv. ptd., 1802-16. 8 vols. Fo. Lge. copy, engraved port., 487 plts., numbered 1-486 + 428 bis (misnumbered 427, plt. 429 misnumbered 428), all but 1 plt. col.-ptd. & hand-finished, hf.-titles, tables of plants in Fr. & Latin, plts. 154, 155 & 463-468 misbnd., a few plts. in Vol. 7 with very slight offsetting from text, 2 plts. in Vol. 8 slightly spotted, 3 plts. loose, cont. Fr. red mor.-bkd. bds., covers gt.-tooled, spines gt.- unc., some corners rubbed, others with repairs, mod. red cl. s.-c.'s; A.N.s of author pasted at front of Vol. 1. (C. Nov.16; 286) *Papp.* £58,000
– – **Anr. Copy.** 8 vols. Fo. Engraved port., 486 plts. (plts. 370/371 constituting 1 lge. folding plt.), all but 1 col.-ptd. & hand-finished, most plt. numbers intact, some foxing & offsetting in Vols. 1-3, slight margin staining at beginning of Vol. 3, sm. piece torn from lr. margin of plt. 42 & a similar piece from upr. margin of plt. 77, a few other minor margin tears & repairs, cont. mor.-bkd. bds., 3 covers detchd. (S. Nov.28; 80) *Robinson.* £28,000
– – **Anr. Edn.** Paris, 1802-16. *(200).* 8 vols. Fo. 485 etched plts., including plt. 427 (bis): 'Narcissus laetus', but lacks plts. 469-470, all but plt. 372 ptd. in col. & hand-finished, plts. 370/371 constitute 1 double-p. plt., plts. 471-474 without nos. in plt. (inserted from anr. copy, at point where text is mis-paginated), other plt. nos. intact, port. of Redouté in Vol. I loosely inserted, plt. 6 Vol. I soiled, Vol. III with crease in plt. 143 & slight staining at end to margins, plt. 295 Vol. V foxed, some browning in Vols. VII & VIII, cont. Fr. str.-grd. red mor.-bkd. bds., gt. borders, flat spines richly gt. with floral emblems, slightly rubbed & marked, entirely unc.; Decrés bkplt. (S. Feb.1; 44)   *Robinson.* £45,000
– – **Anr. Edn.** Ill.:– Langlois, de Gouy, Lemercier, Lemaire, & others, after Redouté. Paris, priv. ptd., 1805-16. 8 vols. in 4. Fo. Plt. 95 in 2nd. state, engraved port., 486 plts., all but 1 plt. col.-ptd. & hand-finished/hf.-titles, tables of plants in Fr. & Latin, without the ptd. dedication to Chaptal & the additional 'Narcissus Laetus' plt. (428bis), all but 9 plt. numerals intact (of these, 5 plts. with other numbers added), plts. 75 & 76 misbnd., hf.-title & title to Vol. 7 spotted, some other minor spotting affecting a few plts. & text ll., mainly in Vols. 1, 7 & 8, 19th. C. dark red hf. mor., spines gt. in 6 compartments. (C. Mar.14; 193)   *Mitchell.* £40,000
- Les Roses. Text:– Cl. Ant. Thory. Paris, 1817 & 1821. *De Luxe 1st. Edn. (100).* Vols. 1-2 [of 3]. Lge. fo. With subscribers prospectus, minimal spotting, cont. red hf. mor. gt., slightly rubbed & bumped; ex-libris, Hauswedell coll. (H. May 24; 861)   DM 112,000
– – **Anr. Edn.** Ill.:– Bessa, Bessin, Chapuy, Charlin, Coutant, Langlois, Lemaire, Talbot (Talbaux), Tiellard, & Victor, after Redouté. Paris, 1817-24. *1st. Edn.* 3 vols. Fo. L.P., engraved port. of Redouté, 170 plts. (including wreath frontis.), ptd. in col. & hand-finished, tear reprd. in pp. 71/72 Vol. I, some spotting of text, plt. of Rosa muscosa at p. 39 Vol. I stained in lr. outer margin, 1st. plt. (Rosa Gallica latifolia) in Vol. III foxed, some light spotting & offsetting, purple hf. mor. gt. by Simiar, his ticket in Vol. I, ornately blind-stpd. spines, partly unc., slightly rubbed & faded; from liby. at Longleat House. (S. Feb.1; 45)   *Robinson.* £68,000
– – **Anr. Edn.** Ed.:– C.A. Thorny. Paris, 1824. *2nd. Edn.* 1 vol. Some heavy browning, especially text in 2nd. half, plts. only slightly, late 19th. C. hf. leath. gt., endpapers renewed, s.-c. (R. Oct.12; 1897a)   DM 23,000
– – **Anr. Edn.** Paris, 1824[-26]. *2nd. (1st. 8vo.) Edn.* 40 pts. in 1 vol. On vell., 160 plts., cont. hf. cf., spine decor. (LM. Oct.22; 90)   B. Frs. 380,000

REDTENBACHER, F.
- Die Gesetze des Lokomotiv-Baues. Mannheim, 1855. 4to. Some foxing, later hf. linen. (R. Oct.12; 1604)   DM 450

REED, Walter & others
- Report on the Origin & Spread of Typhoid Fever in U.S. Military Camps during the Spanish War of 1898. Wash., 1904. *1st. Edn.* 2 vols. 4to. & ob. 4to. Liby. stp. on titles, orig. cl., shaken, spine ends worn, shelf labels. (SG. Mar.22; 273) $100

REES, Abraham
- The Cyclopaedia, or Universal Dictionary of Arts, Sciences & Literature. 1819. 45 vols., including 6 vols. of engraved plts. & maps. 4to. Cont. diced cf. gt., very worn, few jnts. crudely reprd. (BBA. Aug.18; 297)   *Jeffreys.* £160
– – **Anr. Edn.** L., 1820. 6 vols. of plts. only. 4to. Engraved plts., folding maps, most double-p., some spotting, cont. hf. cf., worn, some jnts. split. (BBA. May 23; 288)   *Jeffrey.* £120

REEVE, Emma
- Character & Costume in Turkey & Italy. Ill.:– T. Allom. Paris, [1839]. Fo. Litho. title, 20 tinted litho. plts., 1 loose, some dampstaining, mor. gt., upr. cover detchd. (P. Oct.20; 81)   £90
– – **Anr. Edn.** Ill.:– T. Allom. L., n.d. Fo. Additional litho. title, 20 litho. plts., orig. block mor., gt.-tooled decor. (GM. Dec.7; 660)   £170

REEVE, Mrs. S.
- The Flowers at Court. 1809. 10 orig. watercolours, 1 loose, mor. gt. (P. Jun.7; 320)   £130

REEVES, R.S.
See— WEYER, J.C. & Reeves, R.S.

REEVES, William
- The Life of St. Columba. Dublin, 1857. 4to. Cl. (GM. Dec.7; 69)   £65

REFAEL MI-NORZI
- Orah Hayyim. Venice, 1579. *1st. Edn.* Sm. 4to. Mild foxing & dampstaining, mostly marginal, 2 ll. misbnd., early annots. in Hebrew & Ital. on final lf., later cl., soiled, spine defect. (SG. Feb.2; 291) $200

REGA, Henri
- Catalogus Librorum ... quos reliquit ... Henr. Jos. Rega. Lovanii, 1755. *(Bound with:)* - Catalogus Librorum/Dominus Guillielm Ant. Van Dieven. Lovanii, 1755. *(Bound with:)* - Catalogue d'un Belle Collection de Tableaux de Feu Monsieur Henri Réga. Louvain, 1839. Together 3 works in 1 vol. Hf. bdg. (LM. Oct.22; 173)   B.Frs. 15,000

REGINO, Abbas Prumensis
- Annales. Ed.:– Seb de Rotenhan. Mainz, Aug. 1521. Fo. Title with old MS. owner's note in margin, cont. blind-tooled leath., restored, spine renewed. (R. Oct.11; 104)   DM 1,900

REGIOMONTANUS, Johannes
- Epytoma in Almagestum Ptolomaei. Venice, Johannes Hamman, 31 Aug. 1496. *1st. Edn.* Fo. Wide margins, lacks final blank & Abiosus letter (as usual), woodcut & initials highlighted with brown col. with some seepage, sm. margin wormholes to a few ll., 1 lr. blank corner torn away, some light spotting or staining, a few diagrams just shaved, 19th. C. tree sheep, covers with blind-stpd. borders & gt. centrepiece, panel. spine, lr. corner slightly scuffed; Stirling-Maxwell copy, lge. bkplt., Stanitz coll. (SPB. Apr.25; 376) $4,750
- In Ptolemaei Almagestum Libri Tredecim. Nuremb., 1550. Fo. (in 6's). Lge. marginal woodcut devices, 1ge. pict. initials. [*bound with:*] SCHRECKENFUCHS, Erasmus Oswald - Commentaria, in Nouas Theoricas Planetarum G. Purbachii. Basel, 1556. Lge. title-p. ill., lge. woodcut diagrams, 8 sm. woodcut plts. bnd. in, many tables, cont. inscr. on title & marginalia by Johannes Fusolini of Basel, 1560, old hf. vell., marb. bds., spine defect., upr. cover loose. (SG. Apr.26; 170) $1,700

REGNARD, Jean François
- Oeuvres. Ed.:– Garnier. Ill.:– after Rigaud (port.); Moreau Le Jeune. Paris, 1789-90. *New Edn.* 4 vols.

Tree cf. gt. by Mouillé, spines decor.; from Vieil-Castel liby. (HD. May 3; 125) Frs. 1,700
– – **Anr. Edn.** Notes:– Garnier. Paris, 1820. *New Edn.* 6 vols. Cont. glazed cf. gt., spines decor., sm. repair to 1 cover, slightly faded. (HD. Nov.29; 111)
Frs. 1,300

REGNAULT, Nicolas François
– **La Botanique Mise à la Portée de Tout le Monde** ... Ill.:– after N.F. & G. de N. Regnault. Paris, 1774. 3 vols. Fo. 1 (of 3) hand-cold. engraved title, 421 (of 472) hand-cold. etched plts., lacks engraved dedication, 1 text lf. with sm. hole, a few ll. with minor stain in blank margins, recent hf. roan, w.a.f. (C. Nov.16; 287) *Shapero.* £2,800

REGNAULT, Noël (S.J.)
– **Les Entretiens Physiques d'Artiste et d'Eudoxe.** Paris, 1745. *7th. Edn.* Vols. 1-4 (of 5?). Title stpd., some foxing, cont. leath., very rubbed, lacks leath. in parts. (D. Nov.23; 684) DM 550

REGNAULT-WARIN, J.J.
– **Les Prisonniers du Temple.** Paris, 1800. 3 vols. Darkening, three-qtr. cf. & bds., covers darkening slightly with mild staining & scuffing. (CBA. Oct.29; 697) $140

REGNIER, Henri de
– **Le Miracle du Fil. Seize Sonnets de Henri de Regnier.** Ill.:– Yan-B. Dyl. Paris, n.d. *(350). (334)* on papier Canson Montgolfier. Fo. 16 col. plts., leaves, box. (HD. Sep.22; 325) Frs. 1,450
– **Les Rencontres de M. de Bréot, Roman.** Ill.:– Robert Bonflis. Paris, 1919. Hf. mor., wrap. & spine preserved. (HD. Jun.13; 90) Frs. 1,000
– – **Anr. Edn.** Ill.:– George Barbier. [Paris], 1930. *(847)* numbered on papier de Rives. Three-qtr. lev., pict. wraps. bnd. in. (SG. Feb.16; 253) $100
– **Scènes Mythologiques.** Ill.:– Andre-E. Marty. Paris, 1924. *(300)* numbered on Van Gelder Holland paper. Vell., covers & spine hand-painted by G.G. Levitzky, pict. wraps. bnd. in, bd. s.-c. (SG. Feb.16; 250) $550
– – **Anr. Copy.** 40 orig. etchings, supp. orig. etching with 3 line dedication from artist, sigd. mosaic mor., cold. mor. inlay, gold tooled, mor. doubl., silk & double gt. paper end-papers, hf. mor. wrap., lacks s.-c.; etched ex-libris, with 5 ll. orig. etchings. (D. Nov.23; 173) DM 3,000

REGNIER, L. Sieur de la Planche
[–] **Du Grand et Loyal Devoir, Fidelité et Obéissance de Messieurs de Paris envers le Roy et Couronne de France.** N.p., 1656. *Orig. Edn.* Slight foxing, old red mor., gt. decor., limp decor. spine. (HD. Dec.9; 75) Frs. 2,100

REGNIER, Mathurin
– **Les Satyres, et Autres Oeuvres.** Paris, 1642. 18mo. Havanna mor., decor., inner dentelle, by Bretault. (HD. Mar.30; 15) Frs. 3,500

REIBISCH, Fr. M. von
– **Der Rittersaal.** Stuttgart, 1842. Ob. 4to. Text & some plts. lightly foxed, 1 plt. more foxed, some margin browning, cont. hf. leath., slightly rubbed & bumped. (HT. May 10; 2633) DM 950

REICHARD, Gladys A.
– **Sandpaintings of the Navajo Shooting Chant.** Ill.:– F.J. Newcomb. N.Y., [1937]. 4to. 35 cold. plts., ex-liby., lettered tissue-guards, cl. (SG. May 3; 12) $175

REICHEL, Anton
– **The Chiaroscurists of the XVI-XVII-XVIII Centuries.** Camb., n.d. Fo. Orig. cl. (BBA. Sep.8; 91) *Sims, Reed & Fogg.* £121

REICHENBACH, Heinrich Gustav Ludwig & G.H.
– **Icones Florae Germanicae et Helveticae.** Leipzig, 1837[1870]. Vols. I-XXII (of 25) in 17 vols. 4to. Vol. XXI lacks title, some slight foxing, cont. unif. hf. mor., gold-tooled, lightly spotted & rubbed. (HT. May 8; 310) DM 16,000
– – **Anr. Edn.** N.d. – 1909. Vol. 19, pt. 2, sections 1-25, & Vol. 24, sections 1-22. Unbnd. in 46 folders. (WW. Nov.23; 132) £100

REICHENBACH, Joh. Fr. J. & others
[–] **Allgemeines Küchenlexikon für Frauenzimmer.** Leipzig, 1794. *1st. Edn.* 2 vols. Cont. hf. leath., slightly rubbed. (HK. Nov.9; 1690) DM 800

REICHENOW, Anton
– **Histoire Naturelle des Perroquets.** Trans.:– Faucheux. Ill.:– G. Muetzel. Paris, 1879-80. Fo. 33 col. litho. plts., MS. plt.-list bnd. in, lacks title & prelims., hf. leath., extremities worn, ex-liby. (SG. Oct.6; 312) $350
– **Vogelbilder aus Fernen Zonen.** Ill.:– Fischer after G. Mutzel. 1878-83. Fo. Some plts. spotted, 1 lightly dampstained, orig. cl.-bkd. bds., soiled. (CSK. Sep.16; 125) £340

REICHENTHAL, Ulrich von
– **Das Concilium. So zu Constanz Gehalten ist Worden des Jars ... M.ccc.xIII Jar. Mit allen Handlungen in Geystlichen vn Weltlichen Sachen** ... Augsburg, 1536. *2nd. Edn.* Fo. Woodcut on title-p. & 44 woodcuts in text, 1160 woodcut coats-of-arms (20 cut out & crudely reprd.), some lge., some left blank, title-p. damaged & crudely reprd. at margins, fore-margin of following lf. reinforced, several tears & margin defects, worst being at a5, c6, & e6, some staining, bds., covered with lf. of a 17th. C. antiphoner. (S. Nov.17; 63)
L'Aquaforte. £600

REID, Arthur
– **Those Were the Days.** Perth, 1933. 4to. Orig. cl., a few spots. (KH. Nov.9; 414) Aus. $160

REID, John Eaton
– **History of the County of Bute, & Families Connected Therewith.** Ill.:– Thomas Annan. Glasgow, 1864. 4to. Some foxing thro.-out, minimal edge fading to plts., cl., worn, shaken. (SG. May 10; 4) $150

REID, Capt. Mayne
– **The Headless Horseman: A Strange Tale of Texas.** L., [1866]. *1st. Edn. in Book Form.* 2 vols. Hf. mor. & marb. bds. by Bayntun, orig. cl. covers bnd. in at end of each vol. (LH. Jan.15; 377) $200

REID, Thomas, Clock-maker
– **Treatise on Clock & Watch Making.** Edinb., 1826. *1st. Edn.* 20 folding engraved plts., hf.-title, some ll. rather soiled, cont. cf., rebkd., reprd. (BBA. Apr.5; 212) *Crisford.* £80
– – **Anr. Edn.** Glasgow, 1845. *2nd. Edn.* Lge. 8vo. Some edges frayed, three-qtr. cf. gt. (SG. Mar.22; 163) $175

REID, Thomas, Surgeon, 1791-1825
– **Two Voyages to New South Wales & Van Diemen's Land.** L., 1822. Text stained, rough edges, slightly soiled, bkplt., orig. cl. & leath. (JL. Nov.13; B57) Aus. $200

REID, W.H. & Wallis, James
– **The Panorama; or Travellers Instructive Guide.** [1820]. 12mo. Engraved additional title, contents lf., 53 hand-cold. maps, cont. hf. mor. (CSK. Dec.16; 119) £100

REIL, Joh. Chr.
– **Ueber die Erkenntnisse und Cur der Fieber.** Halle, 1797-1802. 4 vols. (Vol. 5 publd. later). Cont. hf. leath. (D. Nov.23; 616) DM 500

REILLE, Baron Karl
– **La Vénerie Française Contemporaine.** Paris, 1914. *(600).* 4to. Some light foxing, publisher's decor. cl. bds.; nominative copy with orig. watercol., from Château des Noës liby. (HD. May 25; 70)
Frs. 18,000

REILLY, Franz Johann Joseph von
– **Grosser Deutscher Atlas.** Wien, 1796. Lge. fo. Double-p. engraved frontis., index, 22 (of 28) double-p. cold. copper engraved maps, 1 map with sm. holes, lr. right corner soiled thro.-out, later hf. leath. (R. Oct.13; 2869) DM 1,000
– **Schauplatz der fünf Theile der Welt.** Wien, 1789. Pts. 1 & 2, section 1, in 2 vols. Lge. 4to. Maps sm. ob. fo., engraved title, 4 unnumbered & 233 (of 240) partly cold. numbered copper engraved maps, cont. hf. leath., spine defect. (R. Oct.13; 2870) DM 11,000

– – **Anr. Edn.** Ill.:– Ignatz Albrecht. Wien, 1791-1806. 2 pts. in 6 vol. Ob. fo. 6 engraved titles & hf.-title, 4 outl. & border cold. maps, 823 (of 826) numbered border & outl. cold. copper engraved maps, 16 (of 48) arms copper engrs., many maps with pencil or col. annots., written index in lr. map margin, some slight spotting, lacks 3 maps, cont. leath., worn, vol. 1 lacks spine, cover loose. (D. Nov.23; 774) DM 31,000

REINERS, H.
– **Das münster unserer Lieben Frau zu Konstanz.** Konstanz, 1955. Sm. 4to. Orig. linen. (R. Apr.3; 892) DM 880

REINHARDT, Johann Christian
– **A Collection of Swiss Costumes in Miniature.** L., 1822. Lge. 8vo. A tall copy, text in Engl. & Fr., 30 hand-cold. plts., hf. cf., rebkd., portion of orig. ptd. label on upr. cover. (S. May 21; 251) *Schumman.* £2,400
– – **Anr. Copy.** 4to. 30 hand-cold. plts., text in Engl. & Fr., few plts. slightly soiled in margins, title & 1 plt. loose, hf. mor., spine torn. (P. Sep.8; 164) *Tzakas.* £980

REINICK, Robert
[–] **Lieder eines Malers mit Randzeichnungen seiner Freunde.** Contribs.:– A. Achenbach, A. Rethel, Schrödter, etc. Düsseldorf, 1838. *De Luxe Edn.* on heavy card. 4to. Cont. hf. leath., corners slightly worn, orig. litho. wraps. bnd. in. (GB. May 4; 1416) DM 500

REIS DOOR HOLLAND IN HET JAAR 1806 [1807-12]. Amst., [1806-12]. 3 vols. Engraved titles, hf.-title to Vol. 3, 57 plts. (including 20 hand-cold. engraved costume plts.), some faint staining or spotting, sm. liby. stp. at foot of titles, 19th. C. cl. gt., soiled. (S. May 21; 242) *Biesebroecx.* £240

REISCH, Gregorius
– **Margarita Philosophica cum Additionibus Novis.** Basel, 1508. *3rd. Edn.* 4to. Some woodcuts old cold. in, lacks title & 8 ll., lacks world map as usual, wormed thro. out, many cont. marginalia, 17th. C. leath. over wood bds., remains of old gt., reprd., spine extended. [STC 7231] (BR. Apr.12; 887) DM 3,200
– – **Anr. Edn.** [Basle, 1508]. *[3rd. Edn.].* Sm. 4to. Lacks title, E2, 3, 5 & 6, P5 or 7, N1 & 2 supplied in a cont. MS. hand, dampstained, mod. old-style cf., w.a.f. (CSK. Nov.4; 168) £160

REISER, H.
– **Die Fünf Wetteile.** 4 vols. Cont. linen. (D. Nov.23; 809) DM 2,050

REISET, Marie Antoine, Vicomte de
– **Marie-Caroline Duchesse de Berry.** Paris, 1906. *(800)* on Bütten. 4to. Mor., gold-tooled arms supra-libros on both covers, gold-tooled decor., corner fleurons, gt. inner & outer dentelle, orig. wraps. bnd. in. (D. Nov.23; 156) DM 1,200

REISSNER, Adam
– **Ierusalem.** Ill.:– Virgil Solis. Frankfurt, 1563. 2 pts. in 1 vol. Some light browning or ll., some spotting, 1 corner tear reprd., pt. 1 lacks title lf., (with xerox of 1565 Edn.) & 1 map, 1 view repeated, (1 washed & reprd.), cont. blind-tooled pig. bkd. wood bds., clasps. (R. Oct.13; 3033) DM 2,200
– – **Anr. Copy.** 2 pts. in 1 vol. Lacks 1 folding woodcut plt., slightly foxed, cont. blind-tooled pig. (D. Nov.23; 1394) DM 1,200

REITTER, Edmund
– **Fauna Germanica. Die Käfer des Deutschen Reiches.** Ed.:– K.G. Lutz. Stuttgart, 1908-16. 5 vols. Orig. linen, defect. (R. Apr.4; 1778) DM 420

REITZ, Joannes Fredericus
[–] **Oude en Nieuwe Staat van't Russische of Moskov. Keizerryk.** Ill.:– J.C. Phillips. Utrecht, 1744. 4 pts. in 2 vols. 4to. Vol. 1 slightly dampstained, cont. vell. (VG. Sep.14; 1119) Fls. 550

REIZENSTEIN, Wolf Ehrenfried zu
– **Der Vollkommene Pferde-Kenner, welcher nicht nur alle Schönheiten, Fehler und Verschiedene Landes-Arten der Pferde mit Schönen Kupfern zu**

REIZENSTEIN, Wolf Ehrenfried zu -Contd.

Erkennen Giebt, Sondern auch Anweiset ... Uffenheim, 1764. *1st. Edn.* 2 pts. in 1 vol. Sm. 4to. Engraved frontis., 28 plts., margins of a few plts. very slightly shaved, cont. cf., spine gt. (C. Jun.27; 131)　　　*Campbell.* £320

RELAND, Adrian
- **Palaestina en Monumentis Veteribus Illustrata.** Utrecht, 1714. 2 pts. in 1 vol. 4to. Additional engraved title, folding port., 4 folding maps (1 torn) & 6 others, 2 folding plts., folding engraved pedigree, folding ptd. table, few plts. foxed, cont. panel. vell. (SG. Feb.2; 105)　　　$425

RELATION DE LA CAPTIVITE DE LA MERE ANGELIQUE de Saint-Jean, Religieuse de Port-Royal des Champs
N.p., 1711. 12mo. Mor. by Smeers, spine decor.; from D. Borelli liby. (HD. May 3; 66) Frs. 2,400

RELATION OF THE ENGAGEMENT OF HIS MAJESTY'S FLEET WITH THE ENEMIES, on the 11th of August, 1673
L., 1673. Sm. fo. Pamphlet, 12pp., unc. & stitched as iss., suede-lined buckram box. [Wing R827] (C. Jun.27; 50)　　　*Houle.* £70

RELLSTAB, Ludwig
- **Berlin und Seine Nächsten Umgebungen** ... Ill.:– Rohbock. Darmstadt, G.C. Lange, 1854. Steel-engraved title, 54 plts., orig. cl. gt. (C. Nov.16; 159)　　　*Weissert.* £1,100

REMARKS ON THE COMPARATIVE MERITS of Cast Metal & Malleable Iron Railways
Newcastle, 1827. Cl.-bkd. bds. (P. Jun.7; 317)　　　£450

REMBOWSKI, Alexandre
- **Sources Documentaires concernant l'Histoire du Régiment des Chevau-légers de la Garde de Napoléon ler Enrichi de Gravure et de Fac-similé.** Varsovie, 1899. 4to. In Fr. & Polish, hf. chagrin. (HD. Jan.27; 197)　　　Frs. 3,200

REMBRANDT VAN RIJN, Harmensz
- **L'Oeuvre Complet de Rembrandt.** Ed:– Dutuit. Paris, 1883. *(500) unnumbered.* 2 vols. Fo. On Bütten, margins with sm. tears, some brown spotting, orig. wraps., very defect., vol. 1 lacks spine & with pasted strips. (H. May 22; 120a)　DM 1,900
- **Oeuvres.** Paris, ca. 1880?. 5 vols. Atlas fo. Many mntd. heliogravure reproductions, all liby.-stpd. on blank versos, no text, uncollated, 1 vol. mod. marb. bds., others loose in cl. folders, w.a.f. (SG. May 3; 301)　　　$325
- **Original Drawings.** Ed.:– F. Lippmann & others. The Hague, 1900-20. *(150) numbered (2nd, 3rd & 4th Series).* 4 Series in 10 vols. (complete set). Lge. fo. 500 mntd. plts., each liby.-stpd. on blank verso, loose in cl. folders, linen ties. (SG. May 3; 304)　　　$950
- **Rembrandts Handzeichnungen ... zu Amsterdam, Berlin, Dresden.** Ed.:– Kurt Freise, Karl Lilienfeld, Heinrich Wichmann. Parchim i. M., 1922-25. 3 vols. 4to. Mor.-bkd. cl.; each vol. inscr. by W. Russell Flint 'from my dear brother's library'. (S. Apr.30; 79)　　　*Leicester.* £160

REMINGTON, Frederic
- **Crooked Trails.** N.Y., 1898. *1st. Edn.* Decor. cl., slight wear, d.-w., advts. on back, lacks lr. part of spine; Ken Leach coll. (RO. Jun.10; 475)　　　$310
- **John Ermine of Yellowstone.** N.Y., 1902. Cl., unc., moderate wear, pres. copy, sigd. & inscr. by author. (RO. Feb.29; 145)　　　$110

REMMELIN, Johann
- **Kleiner Welt Spiegel.** Ulm, 1661. *2nd. German Edn.* Lge. fo. Sm. tear in title side margin bkd., sm. liby stp. in ptd. title with MS. sig., some slight text browning, mor. gt. (R. Oct.12; 1464)　　　DM 7,000

RENAN, Ernst
- **History of the People of Israel.** 1888. Orig. cl.; Sir Arthur Conan Doyle's copy, inscr. & dtd. 1916 ('Annus irae'), annots. by Conan Doyle thro.-out, as an association copy, w.a.f. (S. Nov.8; 425)　　　*Sawyer.* £160

RENARD, Jules
- **Poil de Carotte** ... Ill.:– Lobel-Riche. Paris, 1911. *(350). (150)* on japan or holland with 3 states of engrs. *(1 with remarks).* 4to. 52 orig. etchings, bordeaux mor. by Rainsford, blind- & gt.-decor., watered silk doubl. & end-ll., unc., wrap. & spine preserved, s.-c.; extra-ill. with watercol. dedicated & sigd. by artist on end-lf. (HD. May 4; 411)　　　Frs. 4,200

RENAUDOT, Eusebius
- **A General Collection of Discourses of the Virtuosi of France upon questions of all sorts of Philosophy, & other Knowledge; Another Collection of Philosophical Conferences** ... Trans.:– G. Havers & J. Davies. 1664, 1665. *1st. Edns.* 2 vols. Fo. Minor margin worming in Vol. 1, mod. mor. [Wing R 1034 & 1033a] (BBA. Jan.19; 155)　　　*Bickersteth.* £220

RENDLE, J.J.
See— McMINN, G.R. & Rendle, J.J.

RENGER-PATZSCH, Albert
- **Baeume.** Essay:– Ernst Juenger. Ingelheim am Rhein, 1962. *1st. Edn.* Fo. Cl. (SG. May 10; 120)　　　$275
- **Die Halligen.** Berlin, [1927]. *1st. Edn.* 4to. Cl. (SG. May 10; 122)　　　$110
- **Die Welt Ist Schoen.** Text:– Carl Georg Heise. Munich, [1928]. *1st. Edn.* 4to. Flexible cl., extremities rubbed, spine faded. (SG. May 10; 123) $225
- – **Anr. Copy.** 4to. Orig. linen, orig. wraps., orig. s.-c. (GB. May 5; 2524)　　　DM 400

RENGGER, J.R. & Longchamps, M.
- **The Reign of Doctor Joseph Gaspard Roderinck de Francia in Paraguay.** 1827. Cont. cf., slightly scuffed, spines gt. (CSK. Jun.1; 64)　　　£50

RENNELL, James
- **Memoir of a Map of Hindoostan; or the Mogul Empire** ... L., 1793. *3rd. Edn.* 4to. Offsetting from maps, light foxing on a few pp., mor. gt. pres. bdg.; inscr. by author to George Washington, & sigd. by Washington. (SPB. May 23; 50)　　　$12,000

RENNEVILLE, Mme. de
- **Education de la Poupée, ou Petit Dialogues Instructifs et Moraux, a la Portée du Jeune Age.** Paris, 1822 [1823 on upr. cover]. Ob. 8vo. Slightly spotted, orig. pict. bds.; van Veen coll. (S. Feb.28; 103)　　　£60

RENNIE, Sir John
- **The Theory, Formation & Construction of British & Foreign Harbours.** L., 1854. 2 vols. Fo. Mezzotint port., 122 engraved plts., a few ll. slightly spotted or soiled, cont. hf. mor., spines gt., rubbed. (BBA. Nov.30; 123)　　　*Weinreb.* £650

RENOU, Jean de
- **A Medical Dispensatory, containing the Whole Body of Physick.** Trans.:– Richard Tomlinson. 1657. *1st. Edn. in Engl.* Sm. hole in 1 lf. affecting a few words. [Wing R1037] *(Bound with:)* – **A Physical Dictionary ... Published for the more Perfect Understanding of Mr. Tomlinson's Translation of Rhaenodaeus Dispensatory.** 1657. *1st. Edn.* Together 2 works in 1 vol. Fo. Mod. mor. by Sangorski & Sutcliffe. (BBA. Jan.19; 49)　　　*Thomas.* £800

RENSHAW, Richard
- **Voyage to the Cape of Good Hope & Up the Red Sea.** Manchester, 1804. Cont. hf. cf. (SSA. Sep.21; 331)　　　R 200

RENTOUL, Annie R.
- **Fairyland.** Ill.:– Ida Rentoul Outhwaite. Melbourne, 1926. *(1000) numbered & sigd.* 51 mntd. plts., 1 margin torn. *(With:)* – **Elves & Fairies of Ida Rentoul Outhwaite.** Melbourne, n.d. Some light spotting. Together 2 vols. Fo. Orig. cl., 1st. vol. with spine holed, s.-c.'s. (CSK. Feb.24; 19) £650
See— OUTHWAITE, Grenbry & Rentoul, Annie R.

RENUCCI, F.O.
- **Storia di Corsica.** Bastia, 1833-34. 2 vols. in 1. Cont. hf. roan, decor. spine. (HD. Oct.21; 151)　　　Frs. 5,500

RENVERSEMENT de la Morale Chretienne ... Omstootinge der Christelyke Zeden
Ill.:– R. de Hooghe (frontis.), J. Gole after C. Dusart (mezzotints). [Holland,], ca. 1685. 2 pts. in 1 vol. 4to. Etched folding frontis., 50 mezzotint caricatures, text in Fr. & Dutch, some slight stains, cont. vell. (VG. Nov.30; 553)　　　Fls. 900
- – **Anr. Edn.** [Holland], ca. 1695. *1st. Edn.* 2 pts. in 1 vol. Sm. 4to. Title & text in Fr. & Dutch, a few light spots & stains, sm. rust-hole in K2, 18th. C. Fr. mor. gt. in Derome style, inner hinges reprd., head & foot of spine & 2 corners slightly rubbed. (S. Nov.17; 64)　　　*Chapponiere.* £1,000

REPERTOIRE DU THEATRE FRANÇAIS, ou Receuil des Tragédies et Comédies Restées au Théâtre depuis Rotrou
Ed:– Petitot. Ill.:– after Perin. Paris, 1803-04. 23 vols. Cont. tree cf., decor. spines. (HD. Sep.22; 326)　　　Frs. 2,500

REPERTOIRE GENERAL DU THEATRE FRANÇAIS
Paris, 1821-23. 147 vols. 32mo. Cont. roan, some bdgs. defect. (SM. Mar.7; 2209)　　　Frs. 3,600

REPERTORY OF ARTS & MANUFACTURES (THE): Consisting of Original Communications, Specifications of Patent Inventions ...
1795[-1802]. Vols. III-XVI. 198 engraved plts., Vol. XVI lacks title, cont. tree cf., gt.-decor. spines. (TA. Mar.15; 378)　　　£60
- – **Anr. Copy.** Vols. III-XVI. 198 engraved plts. (many folding), Vol. XVI lacks title, cont. cf., spines gt. decor. (TA. Feb.16; 225)　　　£50

REPORT FROM THE SELECT COMMITTEE ON TRANSPORTATION
L., 1837. 2 pts. in 1 vol. Fo. 6 folding maps of Australia, some partly hand-cold., some ll. slightly soiled, cont. cl.-bkd. bds., worn, loose. (BBA. May 3; 299)　　　*Kelly.* £180

REPORT UPON THE CLAIMS of Mr. George Stephenson relative to the Invention of His Safety Lamp
Newcastle, 1817. Wraps. (P. Jul.26; 209)　　　£90

REPRESENTATION DES FETES DONNEES par la Ville de Strasbourg pour la Convalescence du Roi
Ill.:– Le Bas after Weis. Paris, 1745. Fo. Engraved title, port., 2 lge. vigs., 11 double-p. plts., sm. liby. stp. on title, text ll. slightly wormed, cont. mott. cf., arms of Louis XV gt.-stpd. on covers, gt. spine with repeated royal cypher, by Pandeloup, with his engraved ticket, upr. cover almost detchd., lr. cover scuffed. (C. Dec.9; 94)　　　*Weinreb.* £850

REPTON, Humphry
- **Designs for the Pavilion at Brighton.** 1808. *[1st. Edn].* Fo. 12 hand-cold. or sepia plts., 2 double-p., 6 with overslips, title-p. lightly soiled, a few light dampstains, mod. hf. mor. on orig. bds., with orig. label, hf. mor. s.-c. (P. Mar.15; 203) *Conn.* £1,550
- – **Anr. Copy.** Fo. 9 cold. or sepia plts. & plans, including 2 double-p., 5 plts. & 2 text ills. with hinged overslips, old hf. cf., rebkd. (C. Dec.9; 131)　　　*Harcourt-Williams.* £950
- – **Anr. Copy.** Lge. fo. Wide margin, on Bütten, lf. with pasted tear, folding plt. with sm. tear, frontis. bkd. in margin, some spotting & margin browning, new linen, pasted on. orig. wrap. title (from later edn.). (H. May 22; 176a)　　　DM 3,200
- **An Enquiry into the Changes of Taste in Landscape Gardening.** L., 1806. Cont. spr. cf., rebkd. (C. Dec.9; 128)　　　*Heneage.* £300
- **Observations on the Theory & Practice of Landscape Gardening.** 1803. *1st. Edn.* Engraved port., 27 hand-cold. or tinted plts., 14 with hinged overslips, bdg. not stated. (GT. Jun.28; 358)　　　£1,150
- – **Anr. Copy.** 4to. Port., 12 cold. plts., (mostly aquatints & 9 of these with overlays), 15 uncold. plts. (3 with overlays), ills. in text (2 with overlays), short tear in 1 folding plt., cont. russ., rebkd. preserving orig. spine. (S. May 21; 63)　　　*Sheiry.* £900
- – **Anr. Edn.** 1805. *2nd. Edn.* 4to. Port., 27 plts., hand-cold. & sepia, 14 with overslips, some light offsetting, crimson mor. gt. (P. Mar.15; 204)　　　*Hannas.* £1,350

- - **Anr. Copy.** 4to. Engraved port., 27 cold. or tinted aquatint & engraved plts. & plans (1 folding, 1 double-p.), 12 plts. & 2 text ills. with hinged overslips, title tipped in, 3 engraved plts. foxed & partly stained, 1 overslip detchd., tear in double-p. plt. reprd. with tape, tear in folding plt. reprd. with sm. loss of wash border, old liby. stp. on title verso, later hf. mor. gt. (C. Mar.14; 80) *Walford.* £700
- **Odd whims; & Miscellanies.** 1804. 2 vols. in 1. Hf.-title & vig. title to each pt., 9 (of 10) hand-cold. aquatints, cont. cf., rebkd. with orig. gt.-decor. spine relaid. (TA. Mar.15; 369) £55
- **The Red Books of Humphry Repton.** Ed.:– E. Malins. 1976. *Ltd. Edn.* 4 vols. Ob. 4to. & fo. Red qtr. mor., s.-c. (P. Apr.12; 82) *Hannas.* £160
- **Sketches & Hints on Landscape Gardening.** [1794]. Ob. fo. 16 aquatint plts., including 4 double-p., many with hinged overslips, hf. cf. (C. Dec.9; 132) *Henderson.* £2,300

REPTON, Humphrey & John Adey
- **Fragments on the Theory & Practice of Land-scape Gardening.** L., 1816. 4to. 42 aquatint plts., some double-p., 14 plts. & 2 text ills. with hinged overslips, lacks hf.-title, mod. hf. cf., unc. (C. Dec.9; 130) *Weinreb.* £1,200

RERESBY, Sir John
- **The Travels & Memoirs.** 1813. 39 plts., including 10 hand-cold., cont. diced cf., spine cracked. (SKC. Nov.18; 2015) £50
- - **Anr. Edn.** L., 1813. *L.P. Extra-Ill. Edn.* 4to. 40 plts., of which 2 are ports., & 8 are wtrcol. land-scapes, in grisaille, old catalogue entry tipped in vol. attributes wtrcol. scenes to 'John Smith' – possibly John Warwick Smith?, cf., partially lacking spine. (SG. Jun.7; 386) $500

RESEN, Peder Hansoen
- **Inscriptiones Haffnienses.** Copen., 1668. *1st. Edn.* 4to. Natural paper flaw in 3H1, with loss of few letters, hf. roan; bkplt. & supralibros of J. Gomez de la Cortina. (SG. Oct.27; 38) $250

RESTA, Sebastiano
- [–] **The True Effigies of the Most Eminent Painters.** L. [Antw.], 1694. Fo. Later cf., worn, covers detchd. [Wing R1174] (CSK. Dec.16; 142) £150

RESTIF DE LA BRETONNE, Nicolas Edme
- **La Découverte Australe par un Homme Volant ou le Dédale Français.** Paris, n.d. *Orig. Edn.* 4 vols. in 2. 12mo. Mor. gt. by Petit-Simier, spines decor. (HD. May 3; 127) Frs. 14,500
- **La Dernière Avanture d'un Homme de Quarante-cinq Ans.** Ill.:– Binet. Genève & Paris, 1783. *Orig. Edn.* 2 vols. 12mo. Cont. marb. roan, spines decor. (HD. May 3; 129) Frs. 3,500
- **Le Drame de la Vie contenant un Homme tout Entier.** Paris, 1793. 5 pts. in 2 vols. Mispaginated, lacks 1 lf., corners of 2 ll. torn with loss of text, old hf. roan, worn, defect. (HD. Nov.9; 69) Frs. 2,700
- **La Malediction Paternelle.** Leipzig, 1780. *1st. Edn.* 3 vols. Vell. (DS. Dec.16; 2387) Pts. 35,000
- [–] **Le Ménage Parisien, ou Déliée et Sotentout.** La Haye, 1773. *Orig. Edn.* 2 pts. in 1 vol. 12mo. Cont. marb. cf., decor. spine, worn & reprd. (HD. Dec.16; 35) Frs. 2,200
- **Monsieur Nicolas.** Ill.:– Sylvain Sauvage. Paris, 1924-25. 4 vols. Tall 8vo. Hf. cf., spines gt., cold. inlays, orig. wraps. bnd. in. (SG. Feb.16; 79) $110
- [–] **Monument du Costume Physique et Moral ...** Ill.:– Moreau & Freudenberg. Neuwied sur le Rhin, 1789. Lge. fo. 26 engraved plts., mntd. on mod. guards thro.-out, red mor. gt. by Pagnant, spine gt., in chemise. (C. Nov.9; 108) *Dreesman.* £2,000
- [–] **Le Nouvel Abailard, ou Lettres de Deux Amans qui ne se sont jamais vus.** Neufchâtel & Paris, 1778. *Orig. Edn.* 4 vols. 12mo. Washed, old bds. (HD. May 3; 128) Frs. 1,000
- **Les Nuits de Paris ou le Spectacle Nocturne.** Ill.:– Binet. L. & Paris, 1788-94. *Orig. Edn.* 16 pts. in 8 vols. 12mo. Lacks port. (?), cont. spr. hf. roan, corners, spines decor. (HD. May 3; 133) Frs. 27,100
- **Les Parisiennes.** Ill.:– Binet?. Neufchâtel & Paris, 1787. *Orig. Edn.* 4 vols. 12mo. Cont. marb. cf., spines decor., slightly rubbed, jnt. reprd. (HD. May 3; 132) Frs. 3,500
- - **Anr. Copy.** 4 vols. Some light soiling, 1 plt.

slightly defect in margin, 19th. C. hf. mor. (R. Oct.11; 389) DM 520
- **Le Paysan et la Paysanne Pervertis.** Ill.:– Binet. La Haye, 1784. 16 pts. in 4 vols. 12mo. Cont. hf. cf., corners, spines decor. (rubbed). (HD. May 3; 130) Frs. 8,000
- **Le Quadragenaire ou l'age de renoncer aux Passions.** Ginebra, 1777. 2 vols. in 1. Linen. (DS. Oct.28; 2150) Pts. 40,000
- **La Vie de mon Père.** Neufchatel & Paris, 1788. Cont. str.-grd. red mor., spine decor. (HD. Mar.29; 87) Frs. 58,000

RESTORATION OF THE BEAUCHAMP CHAPEL at St. Mary's Collegiate Church, Warwick, 1674-1742
Ed.:– Sir William Dugdale. Roxb. Cl., 1956. 4to. Orig. qtr. mor. (S. Oct.4; 241) *Traylen.* £180

RETROSPECTIVE REVIEW, The
L., 1820-28. 1st. Series: Vols.1-14, 2nd. Series: Vols. 1 & 2. Cf. gt. by White, splits in jnts., some spines chipped. (S. Mar.20; 792) *Booth.* £75

RETHEL, A.
- **Das Luther-Lied. Ein' Feste Burg ist unser Gott.** Ill.:– A. Gaber after A. Rethel. Dresden, [1851]. Lge. fo. Orig. wraps., some slight defects. & spotting. (HK. Nov.10; 2661) DM 400

RETURN OF OWNERS OF LAND, 1873
1875. 7 Vols. Fo. Vol. 1 title & some ll. stained, hf. cf., spines gt., some scuffing. (LC. Mar.1; 536) £80

RETZIUS, Gustav
- **Das Gehoerorgan der Wirbelthiere. Morpholo-gisch-Hisologische Studien.** Stockholm, 1881-84. *1st. Edn.* 2 vols. Fo. Few perforation stps., three-qtr. vell., worn & soiled, ex-liby.; sigd. pres. copy from author. (RO. Dec.11; 285) $210

REUCHLIN, Joannes
[–] **De Rudimentis Hebraicis Liber Primer [–tertius].** [Pforzheim, 6. IV. 1506]. *1st. Edn.* Fo. 606 (of 620) pp., with supp. ll., pp. 589/90, lacks pp. 607-20 & both end ll., some old annots., lightly browned, several ll. very spotted with margin defects., especially at beginning & end, no bdg. stated. (HK. May 15; 226) DM 600

REULEAUX, Franz
- **Lehrbuch der Kinematik: Theoretische Kinematik. Grundzüge einer Theorie des Maschinenwesens [Vol. I].** Braunschweig, 1875. *1st. Edns.* (With:) – **Die Praktischen Beziehungen der Kinematik zu Geometrie und Mechanik [Vol. II].** Braunschweig, 1900. *1st. Edn.* Together 2 vols. Errata in 2nd. vol., some spotting, mor.-bkd. marb. bds., rubbed, new spines, cl. corners; stps. of Staatl. Verein. Maschinenbau-schulen Köln & Gewerbliche Fachschulen der Stadt Köln on titles, Stanitz coll. (SPB. Apr.25; 379) $375

REULEAUX, Franz (Ed.)
See— **BUCH DER ERFINDUNGEN, GEWERBE UND INDUSTRIEN**

REUMONT, A. von
[–] **Römische Briefe von einem Florentiner.** Leipzig, 1840-44. *1st. Edn.* 4 vols. Title stpd., browned & foxed, cont. hf. linen. (R. Oct.13; 3155) DM 650

REUSNER, Chr.
- **Contrafacturbuch. Ware vnd Lebendige Bild-nussen etlicher Weitberhümbten vnnd Hochgelehrten Männer in Teutschland.** Ill.:– T. Stimmer. Strass-burg, 1587. *1st. Edn.* Interleaved, lacks 2 plts., title, 1 lf. & last plt. defect., some plts. misbnd. at end, some old annots., browned, some staining & foxing, cont. vell., blind-tooled pig spine, sm. defects. (HK. Nov.8; 322) DM 1,800

REUSNER, Nikolaus
- **Icones aive Imagines Virorum Literis Illustrium.** Ill.:– T. Stimmer. Strassburg, B. Jobinus, 1587. Interleaved, 22 port. woodcuts cont. cold., some browning, a little offsetting, 38 entries in Latin, Greek & Hebrew (from 1589-96), mostly on blank ll., blind-tooled decor. vell., age darkened, slightly bumped. (V. Oct.1; 3772) DM 1,800
- - **Anr. Edn.** Strassburg, 1590. Slightly foxed, loose in cont. vell. (HK. Nov.8; 324) DM 1,300

REUTER, Fritz
- **Hanne Nüte un de Lütte Pudel.** Ill.:– K. Rössing. Hellerau, [1923]. *(330).* Orig. hand-bnd. hf. leath., by P.A. Demeter, spine slightly faded; printer's mark sigd. by artist. (H. Nov.24; 1982) DM 400

REUVEN HOSHKI KATZ
- **Yalkut Reuveni Al Ha'Torah.** Prague, ca. 1660. *1st. Edn.* 4to. Unpaginated, owners' sigs. & stp. on title, badly stained, browned, trimmed, blind-tooled mor. mntd. on wood, worn, lacks clasps. (S. Oct.25; 318) *Rosenfeld.* £260

REVERDY, Pierre
- **Ancres.** Ill.:– after Modigliani, Picasso, Juan Gris, Braque, Leger, Matisse, & others. Paris, 1977. *(1000).* Fo. Sigs. in wraps. & cl. folding case. (PNY. Oct.20; 278) $175
- **Braque [Une Aventure Méthodique].** [Paris], 1949-50. *(15)* roman-numbered & sigd. by Reverdy & Braque, not for sale. Tall fo. Loose in ptd. wraps. as iss., cl. folding case. (SG. Nov.3; 29) $650
- **Coeur de Chêne.** Ill.:– Manolo. Paris, 1921. *Orig. Edn. (112).* Sm. 4to. On Hollande Van Gelder, sigd. by author & artist, 8 orig. wood engrs., sewed. (HD. Dec.9; 176) Frs. 3,200

REVERE, Joseph Warren
- **A Tour of Duty in California Including a Description of the Gold Region** ... N.Y. & Boston, 1849. *1st. Edn.* 12mo. Advts., orig. blind-stpd. cl., spine darkened & ends chipped; the Rt. Hon. Visc. Eccles copy. [Sabin 70182] (CNY. Nov.18; 240) $150

REVETT, Nicholas
See— **STUART, James, Architect & Revett, Nicholas**

REVISTA ANDALUZA
1841-42. 4 vols. Linen. (DS. Mar.23; 2246) Pts. 130,000

REVOLUCION DE SEPTIEMBRE
Madrid, 1870-71. Nos. 1-10. Fo. Bds. (DS. Dec.16; 2051) Pts. 50,000

REVUE DE L'EDUCATION NOUVELLE, Journal des Mères et des Enfants
Paris, Dec. 1848-Oct. 1853. 5 vols. 4to. Each vol. with 12 hand-cold. double-p. litho. plts., cont. roan-bkd. bds., slightly worn; van Veen coll. (S. Feb.28; 105) £60

REVUE FRANÇAISE D'ORNITHOLOGIE [later l'Oiseau et la Revue Francaise d'Ornithologie]
[Paris], 1926-83. Plts., some cold., last 13 years orig. wraps., rest cl. or cl.-bkd. bds., w.a.f. (S. Apr.10; 448) *Wesley.* £320

REVUE INTERNATIONALE D'ORNITHO-LOGIE
See— **ALAUDA**

REWALD, John
- **Aristide Maillol: The Woodcuts. A Complete Catalogue.** N.Y., [1943]. *(55) numbered & specially bnd.* Lge. 8vo. Cf.-bkd. pict. linen by Gerhard Gerlach, jnts. scuffed. (SG. Jan.12; 250) $175
See— **DORRA, Henri & Rewald, John**

REXROTH, Kenneth
- **The Spark in the Tinder of Knowing.** Camb., Mass., Pym-Randell Pr., 1968. *(26) lettered & sigd.* Sm. 4to. Ptd. wraps. (SG. Mar.1; 483) $110

REY, Guido
- **The Matterhorn.** 1907. 4to. Hf. mor. gt. by San-gorski & Sutcliffe. (BS. Nov.16; 15) £70

REYBAUD, Louis
- **Jérôme Paturet à la Recherche de la Meilleure des Républiques.** Ill.:– J.-J. Grandville. Paris, 1846. *1st. Ill. Edn. 1st. Printing.* Foxing, publisher's decor. cl. (HD. Jun.26; 25) Frs. 1,100
- **Jérôme Paturot à la Recherche d'une Position Sociale.** Ill.:– after J.J. Grandvillé. Paris, 1846. *1st. Ill. Edn. 1st. Printing.* Lge. 8vo. Frontis., 31 plts., str.-grd. hf. mor., corners, by Blanchetière, spine decor., ill. wraps. & spine; André Villet ex-libris. (HD. Nov.29; 113) Frs. 5,100
- - **Anr. Copy.** Some foxing, publishers bds, gt. &

REYBAUD, Louis -*Contd.*

polychrome decor., decor. spine. (HD. Mar.14; 42)
    Frs 2,900
– – **Anr. Copy.** Cont. hf. chagrin. (*With:*) – **Jérôme Paturot à la Recherche de la Meilleure des Républiques.** Tony Johannot. 1849. *1st. Printing.* 1 vol. Publisher's gt. ill. bds. (HD. Jan.24; 22)
    Frs. 1,300

REYES, Matias de los
– **Para algunos de** ... Madrid, 1640. 4to. Vell. (DS. Dec.16; 2650)
    Pts. 30,000

REYNARD THE FOX
– **The Most Delectable History of Reynard the Fox.** L., 1681-1701. 3 pts. in 1. 1st. title lf. slightly soiled, sm. margin repair, minimal spotting, hand-bnd. hf. mor., monog E.B.; Hauswedell coll. (H. May 24; 1178)
    DM 2,000
– **De Olde Reynike Voss.** Ill.:– J. Amman. Hamburg, 1660. Browned, cut slightly close in places, pagination uncertain, vell. gt.; Hauswedell coll. (H. May 24; 1175)
    DM 1,300
– **Reineke de Voss.** Ill.:– J. Amman. Hamburg, 1604. *1st. Hamburg Edn.* Brown spotted, some stains, mis-paginated, cont. pig-bkd. wood bds., blind-tooled, 2 clasps; Hauswedell coll. (H. May 24; 1174)
    DM 8,200
– **Reineke Fuchs.** Trans.:– D.W. Soltau. Ill.:– F.W. Kleukens. Darmstadt, 1929. *(150) numbered, sigd. by artist.* 4to. Orig. hf. vell. (R. Oct.11; 294)
    DM 560
– **Von Reinicken Fuchss.** Ill.:– Virgil Solis. Frankfurt, 1608. Title reprd., some brown spotting, sm. margin defects., old MS. vell., soiled; Hauswedell coll. (H. May 24; 1177)
    DM 1,200

REYNARDSON, Charles Thomas Samuel Birch
– **'Down the Road', or Reminiscences of a Gentleman Coachman.** 1875. *2nd. Edn.* Additional col.-ptd. title, 12 chromolitho. plts., 1 with margin stain, orig. cl. gt., slightly worn. (LC. Oct.13; 78) £60

REYNMANN, L.
[–] **Von Warer Erkan[n]tnus dess Wetters.** Ill.:– Hans Burgkmair. Augsburg, ca. 1510. 4to. Title with old MS. owners note, slightly browned, especially upper right corner, old MS. marginalia, MS. on last lf. blank, mod mor., blind-tooled decor., s.-c. (D. Nov.23; 380)
    DM 3,400

REYNOLDS, Helen Wilkinson
– **Dutch Houses in the Hudson Valley Before 1776.** Intro.:– Franklin D. Roosevelt. Ill.:– Margaret D.M. Brown. N.Y., 1929. *1st. Edn. (250) numbered.* Lge. 4to. Folding map in rear sleeve, gt.-lettered buckram; from liby. of F.D. Roosevelt, inscr. 'For Franklin D. Roosevelt Jr. from his affectionate Father, Franklin D. Roosevelt'. (SG. Mar.15; 69)
    $700

REYNOLDS, J.N.
– **Voyage of the United States Frigate Potomac, under the Command of Commodore John Downes, during the Circumnavigation of the Globe 1831-1834.** N.Y., 1835. *1st. Edn.* Some plts. torn or frayed, foxed, cl., top of spine torn away. (RO. Aug.23; 57)
    $105

REYNOLDS, Joshua
– **Engravings from the Works of** ... L., [1833-39]. *1st. Edn.* 3 vols. Fo. Engraved titles, engraved plt. lists, 299 uncold. engraved plts. on stiff stock, lacks plt. of 'The Nativity', never bnd. in (as usual), plt. lists ageing, light foxing at some margins, later pencil annots. in margins or lr. captions, orig. crimson mor. & marb. bds., elab. gt.-stpd. panel. backstrips. (HA. Nov.18; 78)
    $125
– – **Anr. Edn.** L., 1836. 3 vols. Fo. 300 acquatints, light browning due to quality of paper, hf. red mor., gt.-tooled spines, slightly defect. (CR. Jun.6; 271)
    Lire 700,000

REYNOLDS, Osborne
– **Papers on Mechanical & Physical Subjects.** Camb., 1900-01-03. 3 vols. Fo. Liby. stp. with cancel on title, slight spotting, mostly of fore-edges, orig. cl., some rubbing, sm. paper tags on spines; from Charles E. Smith liby., Stanitz coll. (SPB. Apr.25; 380)
    $175

REZNIKOFF, Charles
– **Going To & Fro & Walking Up & Down.** N.Y., [1941]. Sm. 8vo. Cl., d.-w.; inscr. to David Meltzer. (SG. Mar.1; 487)
    $200
– **Separate Way.** N.Y., [1936]. Sm. 8vo. Cl., d.-w.; inscr. to David Meltzer. (SG. Mar.1; 490)
    $110

REZNIKOFF, Sarah, Nathan & Charles
– **Family Chronicle: Early History of a Seamstress; Early History of a Sewing-Machine Operator; Needle Trade.** N.Y., [1963]. Bds., d.-w.; inscr. to David Meltzer. (SG. Mar.1; 491)
    $700

RHASES
– **Liber Nonus ad Almansorum cum Expositione Sillani de Nigris. Receptae Petri de Tussignano supra Nonum ad Almansorem.** Venice, Bernardinus Stagninus, de Tridino, 30 Mar. 1483. Fo. Capital spaces, some sm. wormholes, wood bds., rebkd. with cf., lacks clasps. [BMC V, 364; Goff R182; H. 13895] (S. May 10; 394)
    Rota.£1,500

RHEAD, George Woolliscroft
– **History of the Fan.** 1910. *[1st. Edn.].* (450). 4to. Orig. cl. gt. (P. Apr.12; 144)   *Henderson.* £280
– – **Anr. Copy.** 4to. Gt.-decor. buckram, unc. (PD. Oct.19; 141)
    £230
– – **Anr. Copy.** Lge. 4to. 127 plts. (27 cold.), text ills., ex-liby., gt.-decor. buckram. (SG. May 3; 307)
    $300
– – **Anr. Copy.** 4to. This copy unnumbered, cl., d.-w. reprd. (SSA. Jul.5; 335)   R 340

RHEAD, Louis
– **A Collection of Book Plate Designs.** Boston, 1907. Mntd. port., 22 plts., ills., pict. bds., cl.-back; sigd., inscr. & sigd. by Truesdell to Hugh McLellan. (SG. May 17; 47)
    $100

RHEEDE VAN DRAAKESTEIN, Hendrik Adrian van & Caesarius, J.
– **Hortus Indicus Malabaricus, cont. Regni Malabarici apud Indos Celeberrimi Omnis Generis Plantas Rariores.** Ed.:– A. Syen. Amst., 1678. Vol. I only (of 12). Fo. Linnean names in MS. in blank lr. margins of plts., cont. vell. (VG. Sep.14; 1268)
    Fls. 500

RHEGIUS, Urbanus
– **Unterricht, wie ain Christenmensch Got seinem Herren teglich beichten soll.** Augsburg, 1521. *1st. Edn.* Sm. 4to. Bds. [STC 738] (BR. Apr.12; 888)
    DM 420

RHEINHABEN, G.W. v.
– **Poetische Ubersetzungen und Gedichte.** Weimar, 1711. Title with 2 MS owners entries & verso stpd., lightly browned, cont. hf. vell., very worn & bumped. (R. Oct.11; 391)   DM 650

RHENANUS, Joannes
– **Solis et Puteo Emergentis sive Dissentationis Chymiotechnicae** ... Frankfurt, [1613]. *1st. Edn.* 3 pts. in 1 vol. Engraved title defect. & mntd., the lr. outer section lacking, rough repair to margins of 3 following ll. (*Bound with:*) BASILIUS VALENTINUS – Azoth sive Aureliae Occultae Philosophorum Materiam ... Georgio Beato. Frankfurt, 1613. Together 2 works in 1 vol. 4to. Some stains & discolouration of poor paper, new cf.; Dr. Walter Pagel copy. (S. Feb.7; 327)   *Ritman.* £720

RHODES, Alexander de, S.J.
– **Divers Voyages et Missions en la Chine & Autres Royaumes de l'Orient.** Paris, 1653. Sm. 4to. Additional outl. cold. folding map of China by Sanson & sm. world map by Du Val bnd. in, sm. tear in fold of lge. folding map, cancelled liby. stp. on title, mod. mor.-bkd. bds. (C. Nov.16; 160)
    Blackwells. £240
– **Relazione de' Felici Successi della Compagnia di Giesu nel Regno di Tunchino.** Rome, 1650. *1st. Edn.* 4to. 10 ll. wormed, 4 tiny blank spots in map wormed, title defect. & laid down, few stains, early limp vell., stained. (SG. Sep.22; 256) $250

RHODES, Ebenezer
– **Peak Scenery, or Excursions in Derbyshire.** 1818. 4 pts. in 1 vol. 4to. 28 engraved plts., cont. cf. gt. (P. Dec.8; 14)   *Burden.* £75
– – **Anr. Edn.** 1818-22. Pts. 1-3 only (of 4). 4to.

L.P., some spotting, orig. bds., unc., 2 spines defect. (LC. Jul.5; 425)   £55
– – **Anr. Edn.** 1818-23. 4 pts. in 1 vol. 4to. Slight spotting to some plts., hf. mor. gt., some slight scuffing. (LC. Jul.5; 424)   £105

RHYME OF A RUN
Ill.:– Florence Harrison. L., ca. 1915. Ob. 4to. Very slight margin darkening, orig. gt.– & col.-decor. cl., some soiling. (CBA. Aug.21; 293) $100

RICARD DE MONTFERRAND, Auguste
– **Plans et Details du Monument Consacré à la Mémoire de l'Empereur Alexandre.** Paris & St. Petersb., 1836. *1st. Edn.* Lge. fo. Vig. title, 41 lithos., hf.-title, a few margins frayed, title & some ll. foxed, loose as iss. in cont. hf.-cl. portfo., orig. ptd. wrap. mntd. on upr. cover. (C. Dec.9; 192)
    Weinreb. £500

RICARDO, David
– **On the Principles of Political Economy & Taxation.** L., 1817. *1st. Edn.* Lightly stained thro.-out, cont. hf. sheep, worn & shaken. (S. Dec.8; 380)
    Lewis. £1,800

RICAULT, Paul
– **Histoire de l'Etat Present de l'Empire Ottoman.** Trans.:– Briot. Paris, 1670. 4to. Cont. cf. (HD. Feb.22; 193)   Frs. 5,800

RICAULT, Paul & others
[–] **Der Neu-eröffn. Ottomanischen Pforten, Forts** ... Ill.:– Kilian & others after J.A. Thelot. Augsburg, 1700. Fo. 179 copper engrs., 20 engraved vigs., lacks supp., frontis. & 3 ll. preface, lightly soiled, cont. vell. over wood bds., defect. (HK. Nov.9; 1304)   DM 700

RICCARDI, Pietro
– **Biblioteca Matematica Italiana dalla Origine della Stampa ai Primi Anni del Secolo XIX.** Milano, [1952]. 2 vols. 4to. Cl., some wear. (RO. Dec.11; 286) $170

RICCARDI PRESS
See— AURELIUS, Marcus Antoninus, Emp.
See— HOUSMAN, Alfred Edward

RICCHI, Immanuel Chai
– **Hon-Ashir.** Amst., 1731. *1st. Edn.* With 2 pp. of Kabalistic poems & sheet of music (lacking in most copies). (*With:*) – **Aderet Eliyahu.** Livorno, 1742. *1st. Edn.* Pts. I & II in 1 vol. (*With:*) [–] **Haskamot.** Livorno, 1742. Together 3 vols. 4to. Some browning & soiling, some worming, various bdgs., worn. (SPB. Feb.1; 77) $700

RICCI, Bartolommeo
– **Vita D.N. Jésu Christi ex Uerbis Evangeliorum** ... Romae, 1607. Old red mor. gt., spine decor. (HD. May 3; 136)   Frs. 1,700

RICCI, Elisa
– **Antiche Trina Italiane.** Bergamo, [1920?]. 4to. Publishers cl. (CR. Jun.6; 273)   Lire 260,000
– **Old Italian Lace.** L. & Phila., 1913. *(300) numbered, for England.* 2 vols. Sm. fo. Photo. ills., many mntd. in text, ex-liby., gt.-decor. buckram. (SG. May 3; 308) $275

RICCI, James V.
– **The Development of Gynaecological Surgery & Instruments.** Phila., 1949. (*With:*) – **The Genealogy of Gynaecology, 2000 B.C.-1800 A.D.** Phila., 1950. *2nd. Edn.* Together 2 vols. Lge. 8vo. Cl., rubbed & shaken, ex-liby. (SG. Mar.22; 249) $175

RICCIOLI, Giovanni Battista
– **Geographiae et Hydrographiae Reformatae.** Bologna, 1661. *1st. Edn.* Fo. Engraved armorial plt., many text diagrams, fore-edge of title-p. torn away affecting 3 words, old vell., soiled. (SG. Apr.19; 161) $150
– – **Anr. Edn.** Venice, 1672. Fo. Cont. panel. cf., rebkd., rubbed. (TA. May 17; 381)   £70
– – **Anr. Copy.** Fo. Some light browning, pig over wood bds., blind-tooled, brass clasps. (D. Nov.23; 417)   DM 850

RICCOBONI, Louis
– **Histoire du Théâtre Italien.** Paris, 1728. Cf., worn, hinges worn. (P. Sep.29; 178)   *L'Acquaforte.* £80

RICE, D.G.
- **Rockingham Ornamental Porcelain.** 1965. No bdg. stated. (JL. Jun.24; 211) Aus. $300

RICH, E.
- **Germany & France; a popular History of the Franco-German War.** L., ca. 1875. 2 vols. 4to. Some slight foxing, cont. hf. leath. (BR. Apr.12; 334) DM 1,500

RICH, Obadiah
- **Bibliotheca Americana Nova.** L., 1835; 1846. 2 vols. Later qtr. linen; inscr. (SG. Jan.5; 275) $100
- – **Anr. Edn.** 1846. 2 vols. Cont. cf., gt. spines, rubbed. [Sabin 70876] (BBA. Sep.29; 40) *Bauman.* £75

RICHARD, A.
- **Types de l'Ile Maurice.** Port-Louis, n.d. Lge 4to. 16 lithos, including 12 in cols., some light foxing, publishers buckram. (HD. Dec.9; 177) Frs. 4,800

RICHARD, Abbe René
- **Description Historique et Critique de l'Italie.** Dijon & Paris, 1766. 6 vols. 12mo. Cont. marb. cf., spine decor.; cont. ex-libris 'Francisci Josephi Menage de Mondesir'. (HD. Nov.9; 70) Frs. 2,000

RICHARDS, Lysander Salmon
- **Breaking Up.** Boston, 1896. *1st. Edn.* End-papers darkening affecting adjacent pp. including title-p., some foxing or staining to contents, several margin ink indications, bdg. not stated, covers lightly rubbed. (CBA. Oct.29; 707) $130

RICHARDS, T. Addison
- **American Scenery, Illustrated.** Ill.:– W.H. Bartlett & others. N.Y., [1854]. *1st. Edn.* Sm. 4to. 31 (of 32) full-p. engraved plts., light ageing to some plt. margins, orig. gt.-decor. cl., applied col. ill. of roses at front panel (mostly lacking), covers worn. (HA. Nov.18; 234) $175

RICHARDS, Walter
- **Her Majesty's Army.** L., [1888-91]. 3 vols. 4to. Additional cold. vig. titles, 44 cold. plts., red mor.-bkd. bds., spines gt., slightly rubbed, stain on 1 cover. (S. Dec.20; 875) *Browning.* £120
- – **Anr. Copy.** 3 vols. 4to. 3 additional cold. titles with vigs., 44 cold. plts., some spotted, 1 lf. lacks corner of text, orig. cl., spines faded, slightly worn. (S. Oct.11; 584) *Schuster.* £70
- – **Anr. Edn.** Ca. 1890. 3 vols. 4to. Orig. cl. gt., rubbed. (TA. May 17; 142) £100
- – **Anr. Edn.** L., n.d. 3 vols. 4to. 3 cold. litho. frontis., 3 additional title vigs., 41 plts., some light soiling, 1 plt. detchd., orig. cl., stitching slightly shaken. (CSK. Feb.24; 109) £140
- – **Anr. Copy.** 3 vols. 4to. Cold. additional titles & plts., orig. cl., spines faded. (CSK. May 18; 83) £120
- – **Anr. Copy.** 2 vols. 4to. Cold. vig. titles, 29 cold. litho. plts., orig. cl., rubbed. (*With:*) - **Her Majesty's Territorial Army.** R. Caton Woodville. L., n.d. 4 vols. 4to. Orig. cl., worn & loose. (BBA. Dec.15; 339) *Snelling.* £75

RICHARDSON, B.H
See— COLLIVER, E.J. & Richardson, B.H.

RICHARDSON, C.
- **Memoirs of ... Louisa, Queen of Prussia.** L., 1847. Extra-ill. with 14 engraved plts., a few hand-cold., very slightly spotted, 1 lf. reprd., mor. gt., mor cover inlaid with hand-painted port. of Louisa, Queen of Prussia, by Rose, boxed. (S. Oct.4; 119) *Joseph.* £260

RICHARDSON, George
- **A Book of Ceilings.** L., 1776. Fo. Engraved dedication, 48 hand-cold. engraved plts., including 1 folding, title & text in Engl. & Fr., subscribers list, 1 plt. inverted, cont. cf., rebkd., corners reprd. (C. Dec.9; 134) *Henderson.* £700
- – **Anr. Copy.** Fo. In Fr. & Engl., lacks 1st. blank, hf. cf., worn. (P. Oct.20; 199) £170
- **New Designs in Architecture.** L., 1792. Fo. Aquatint title, engraved dedication, 44 aquatint plts., title & text in Engl. & Fr., subscribers list, minor foxing to a few margins, mod. hf. cf. (C. Dec.9; 135) *Heneage.* £800
- **The New Vitruvius Britannicus.** L., 1802-08. 2 vols. Lge. fo. 115 aquatint plts., several double-p., titles & text in Engl. & Fr., contents lf. in Vol. 2, subscribers list, a few text ll. slightly spotted, cont. hf. cf., rebkd., unc. (C. Dec.9; 136) *Weinreb.* £2,200

RICHARDSON, Sir John
- **Arctic Searching Expedition: a Journal of a Boat-Voyage through Rupert's Land & the Arctic Sea.** L., 1851. *1st. Edn.* 2 vols. Folding map cold. to show geology, 10 chromolitho. plts., ills. in text, orig. cl. [Sabin 71025] (S. May 22; 456) *Kossow.* £380
- – **Anr. Copy.** 2 vols. Folding map, 10 chromolitho. plts., slight defect to a contents lf. by adhesion to map verso, orig. cl. [Sabin 71025] (S. Jun.25; 27) *Traylen.* £300
- – **Anr. Copy.** 2 vols. Folding map, 10 chromolitho. plts., map with short tear reprd., cont. cf. [Sabin 71025] (S. Jun.25; 28) *Bonham.* £240
- **Fauna Boreali-Americana, or, The Zoology of the Northern Parts of British America.** L., 1829-31. *1st. Edn.* 2 vols. 4to. 28 uncold. engraved plts. of quadrupeds, 50 hand-cold. litho. plts. of birds, hf.-titles, errata slip, 2 cold. plts. with reprd. tears at margin, minor foxing to margins of some plts., orig. cl., unc.; the Rt. Hon. Visc. Eccles copy. (CNY. Nov.18; 241) $1,100
- **Ichthyology of the Voyage of H.M.S. Erebus & Terror, under the Command of Captain Sir James Clark Ross ...** 1844-48. 4to. Mod. hf. mor., buckram, covers slightly marked. (KH. May 1; 592) Aus. $900

RICHARDSON, Samuel
- **Clarissa. or, the History of a Young Lady.** 1748. *1st. Edn.* 7 vols. 12mo. Mostly 1st. state but E10 in Vol. VI a cancellans, cont. cf., 2 covers detchd. (C. May 30; 167) *Service.* £100
- – **Anr. Copy.** 7 vols. 12mo. 1st. state of vols. 3 & 4 with preface in vol.4, folding music plt. cont. sigs. on titles & endpp., R1 in vol.4 torn, cont. cf., rebkd., orig. labels laid down, A.Edward Newton/ Fred A.Berne copy. (SPB. May 16; 340) $225
- – **Anr. Edn.** Trans.:– L. Th. Kosegarten. Leipzig, 1790-93. 8 vols. Title & end-paper stpd., ex-libris, cont. bds. (GB. Nov.4; 2164) DM 500
- **Clarissa. - Letters & Passages Restored from Original Mss. of the Moral & Instructive Sentiments ... Contained in the History ...** L., 1748; 1751. *1st. Edn.* 7 vols. & 1 vol. 1st. work, 3 ll. of 'Editor to the Reader' in vol.3, with 'allowed' on p.149, vol.4, browning & spotting, unif. bnd. in cont. hf. cf., 3 covers detchd. (SPB. May 16; 123) $300
- [–] **Clarissens Schicksale.** Trans.:– L.T. Kosegarten. Ill.:– D. Chodowiecki. Leipzig, 1796. Some margins lightly spotted, hand-bnd. burgundy mor. gt., gt. decor. (H. Nov.23; 741) DM 1,350
- **Correspondence.** Ed.:– Anna Laetitia Barbauld. L., 1804. *1st. Edn.* 6 vols. 2 engraved ports., 3 aquatint frontis. (2 cold., 1 folding), hf.-titles, folding facs., orig. bds., unc., 2 vols. soiled. (SPB. May 16; 124) $225
- **The History of Sir Charles Grandison.** 1754. *1st. Edn.* 7 vols. Browned & spotted, 1 lf. loose, cont. cf., rubbed. (BBA. Jun.14; 72) *J. Price.* £190
- – **Anr. Copy.** 7 vols. Advt. lf., some marginal worming, sm. hole in imprint vol.4, few short marginal tears, cont. mott. cf. gt., 1 spine reprd., lacks front free end-papers from few vols. (SPB. May 16; 125) $325
- [–] **Lettres Angloises, ou Histoire de Miss Clarissa Harlove.** Ill.:– Sysang & Fritzech after Eisen & Pasquier. Dresden, 1751-52. 12 pts. in 6 vols. Some slight browning or spotting, cont. vell. (HK. Nov.10; 3100) DM 420
- [–] **The Life & Heroic Actions of Balbe Berton, Chevalier de Grillon.** L., 1760. *1st. Edn. 1st. Iss.* 2 vols. 12mo. Stain on E4 & K3, in vol.1, some soiling of fore-e., mod. mor.-bkd. bds., unc. (SPB. May 16; 126) $300
- **Novels.** Oxford, Shakes. Hd. Pr., 1929-31. 18 vols. Some fore-e. foxing, buckram, partly unc., largely unopened. (KH. Nov.9; 420) Aus. $290
- **Works.** 1811. 19 vols. Lightly spotted, cont. hf. cf., slightly rubbed, rebkd. (CSK. Jan.27; 11) £120

RICHARDSON, Thomas Miles
- **Sketches in Italy, Switzerland, France, & c.** L., [1837]. Fo. Tinted litho. title, 25 tinted litho. views, dedication with 'list of subjects' on verso, some spotting, cont. mor.-bkd. cf., upr. cover gt.-lettered. (C. Nov.16; 161) *Dupont.* £700

RICHARDSON, William
- **The Monastic Ruins of Yorkshire ...** Historical Descriptions:– Rev. Edward Churton. York, 1843. 2 vols. Lge. fo. L.P., cold. litho. dedication, 82 plts., including 32 full-p. & 26 hf.-p. cold. views, & uncold. or tinted plans & details, titles & most cold. plts. mntd., the plts. without titles or sigs., cont. red hf. mor. gt. (C. Mar.14; 81) *Marlborough.* £1,400
- – **Anr. Copy.** 2 vols. Fo. Litho. title, dedication, 82 litho. plts. including 32 full-p. & 26 hf.-p. views, some margin foxing & staining, a few plts. slightly shaved, lacks map, cont. red hf. mor. gt., rubbed. (C. Jun.27; 60) *Shapero.* £200

RICHE, J.M.L.
- **Vues des Monumens Antiques de Naples.** [Paris], 1827. 12 pts. in 1 vol. 4to. Light spotting thro.-out, cont. bds., rebkd. (CSK. Dec.16; 144) £150

RICHELET, Pierre
- **Dictionnaire de la Langue Française, Ancienne et Moderne.** Lyon, 1759. 3 vols. Fo. Cont. cf. (HD. Feb.22; 194) Frs. 1,900
- **Les plus Belles Lettres des Meilleurs Auteurs François avec des Notes.** Amst., 1690. 12mo. Ruled, cont. red mor., spine decor.; from libys. of La Roche-Lacarelle & H. de Becker. (HD. Mar.29; 89) Frs. 10,500

RICHELIEU, Armond Jean du Plessis, Cardinal de
- **Instruction du Chrestien.** Poictiers, 1620. *Orig. Edn.* Sm. 8vo. (*Bound with:*) - **Les Principaux Poincts de la Foy de l'Eglise Catholique, deffendus contre l'Esprit, addressé au Roy par les Quatre Ministères de Charenton.** Paris, 1618. *Orig. Edn.* (*Bound with:*) - **Harangue pronocée en la Sale du Petit Bourbon, le XXIII Février 1615. À la Closure des Estats tenus à Paris.** Paris, 1615. *Orig. Edn.* Together 3 works in 1 vol. Cont. decor. red mor., Richelieu arms, silk ties; author's MS. margin notes corrections, from Comte de Mosbourg liby. (HD. Mar.29; 90) Frs. 82,000
- **Maximes d'Etat ou Testament Politique.** Paris, 1764. *1st. Authentic Edn.* 2 vols. Cont. marb. cf. gt., spines decor.; stp. & ex-libris of Le Tellier de Courtanvaux on titles. (HD. Nov.9; 155) Frs. 3,100

RICHENTHAL, Ulric von
- **Das Concilium. So zu Constanz gehalten.** Meersburg, 1936. *Facs. of Augsburg 1536 Edn.* Sm. fo. Orig. vell. gt. (R. Apr.3, 624) DM 500

RICHEOME, Louis
- **Plainte Apologetique ... Contre le Libelle ... Intitulé Le Franc et Veritable Discours & c.** Bordeaux, 1603. Cont. cf., worn, upr. cover detchd.; arms of Thomas Wentworth, Earl of Strafford & an autograph inscr. on an end-paper 'A Orleans, pt. 2F. (?) Qui nimis notus omnibus ignotus moritur sibi Tho. Wentworth'. (S. Oct.11; 417) *Smallwood.* £80

RICHEPIN, Jean
- **Paysages et Coins de Rues.** Preface:– Georges Vicaire. Ill.:– Auguste Lepère. Paris, 1900. Mor. by Noulhac., elab. La Vallière decor, blind-decor. mor. liners, silk end-ll., wrap.; Beraldi copy. (HD. Jun.13; 92) Frs. 25,000

RICHER, Adrien
- **Vies des plus Célèbres Marins.** 1789. *1st. Coll. Edn.* 13 vols. in 7. 18mo. Cont. marb. cf. (HD. Apr.13; 45) Frs. 2,500

RICHER, Paul
See— CHARCOT, Jean Martin & Richer, Paul

RICHTER, Prof. Dr. E.
- **Die Erschliessung der Ostalpen.** Berlin, 1893-94. 3 vols. 4to. Orig. cl. gt. (TA. Oct.20; 27) £80

RICHTER, Gisela

- **The Portraits of the Greeks.** L., Phaidon Pr., [1965]. 3 vols. 4to. Cl., d.-w. (LH. Sep.25; 588) $140
- **Red-Figured Athenian Vases in the Metropolitan Museum.** Ill.:– L.F. Hall. New Haven, 1936. *(500).* 2 vols. Sm. fo. 83 drawings, 181 collotype plts., exliby., pict. cl. (SG. May 3; 87) $600

RICHTER, J. & Geissler, C.G.H.

See— GRUBER, J.C. & Geissler, C.G.H. – RICHTER, J. & Geissler, C.G.H.

RICHTER, J.W.O.

- **Bilder aus dem Westlichen Mitteldeutschland.** Leipzig, [1883]. Title verso stpd., 1 map torn, orig. linen. (R. Oct.12; 2579) DM 620

RICHTER, Jean Paul Friedrich 'Jean Paul'

- [–] **Biographische Belustigungen unter der Gehirnschale einer Riesen.** Berlin, 1796. *1st. Edn.* 'Erstes Bändchen' (all publd.). Cont. bds., spine gt. (C. Dec.9; 311) *Hoffman.* £380
- **Clavis Fictiana seu Leibgeberiana.** Erfurt, 1800. *1st. Edn.* Title with monog. some slight foxing, 1 brown stain, 2 pp. with sm. hole, slight loss, cont. bds. gt., corners lightly bumped. (H. Nov.23; 684) DM 460
- **Grönlandische Prozesse oder Satirische Skizzen.** Berlin, 1783. *1st. Edn.* 2 vols. in 1. Title verso & end-paper with owners mark, slightly browned, cont. bds., corners bumped. (GB. May 4; 1343) DM 3,200
- **Kleine Bücherschau.** Breslau, 1825. *1st. Edn.* 2 vols. Minimal brown spotting, cont. hf. leath., slightly spotted & rubbed; Hauswedell coll. (H. May 24; 1404) DM 640
- **Der Komet, oder Nikolaus Marggraf.** Berlin, 1820-22. *1st. Edn.* 3 vols. in 2. Lightly foxed thro.-out, cont. hf. leath., slightly spotted & worn, corners reprd. (H. Nov.23; 687) DM 520
- **Leben des Quintus Fixlein.** Bayreuth, 1796. *1st. Edn.* 1 vol. Sm. 8vo. Sm. old liby. stp. on title, cont. hf. cf. (With:) – **Museum.** 1814. *1st. Edn.* 1 vol. Sm. 8vo. Slight dampstaining thro.-out, old marb. bds., worn; sig. of Mendelssohn Bartholdy on title. (C. Dec.9; 249) *Hoffman.* £380
- **Sämmtliche Werke.** Berlin, 1826-28. *1st. Coll. Edn.* 60 vols. in 30. Cont. hf. cf., 1 spine defect., 1 lacking. (C. Dec.9; 250) *Bender.* £190
- – **Anr. Edn.** Ed.:–[R.O. Spazier & H. Förster]. Berlin, 1826-38. *1st. Coll. Edn.* 65 pts. in 26 vols. All titles stpd. & with MS. numbers in upr. right corner, 2 pp. pt. 53 with defect. in lr. corner with loss & lge. tear, some foxing or browning, cont. hf. leath. gt., spine slightly worn, corners lightly bumped. (HK. Mar.16; 2109) DM 2,300
- – **Anr. Copy.** 65 vols. Slightly foxed, cont. marb. sewed, unc. (GB. May 4; 1342) DM 1,260
- **Sämmtliche Werke, – Literarischer Nachlass.** Ed.:– R.O. Spazier & E. Förster. Berlin, 1826-38. *1st. Coll. Edn. De Luxe Edn. on vell.* 60 vols. & 5 vols., together in 24 vols. 1 added engraved port. vol. I, some slight spotting, cont. bds., gt. spine, slightly defect., 2 spines torn, rubbed; Hauswedell coll. (H, May 24; 1400) DM 1,400
- **Titan.** Berlin, 1800-03. *1st. Edn.* 4 vols. Vol 1 cont. bds., lr. cover & spine very defect., Vols. 2-4 later hf. leath. gt., rubbed & bumped, lr. spine with pasted paper strips, vol. 4 lr. spine defect. (D. Nov.24; 2500) DM 450
- **Die Unsichtbare Loge.** Berlin, 1793. *1st. Edn.* 2 vols. 2 ll. of errata at end Vol. 2, cont. hf. cf. (C. Dec.9; 247) *Hoffman,.* £400

RICHTER, Joh. Solomon

- **Leipziger National Trachten.** Leipzig, [1791]. 48 numbered & cold. etchings, nos. 1-37 sigd. in plt., 1 lf. sigd. by author, some slight spotting, hand-bnd. red mor., gt. decor. spine & decor. covers; Hauswedell coll. (H. May 23; 33) DM 3,000

RICHTER, Ludwig

- **Landschaften.** Text:–H. Lücke. Leipzig, 1875. *1st. Edn.* Ob. fo. Plts. loose, some slight foxing, orig. hf. linen, very defect. & stained. (D. Nov.24; 2335) DM 1,000

RICHTER, L. (Ill.)

See— DEUTSCHE JUGENDKALENDER

RICHTHOFEN, Karl von

- **Untersuchungen über Friesische Rechtsgeschichte.** Berlin, 1880-86. Pts. I-III, 1 (all publd), 3 vols. in 4. No bdgs. stated, unc. (B. Feb.8; 749) Fls. 480

RICKENBACKER, Capt. Edward V.

- **Seven Came Through.** Garden City, 1943. *1st. Edn.* Orig. cl., d.-w., mor.-bkd. s.-c.; inscr. to Mrs. Marjorie Wiggin Prescott, orig. plane ticket laid in. (SPB. May 17; 673) $175

RICKETT, Harold William

- **Wild Flowers of the United States.** N.Y., 1966-70. Vols. I-IV in 9 vols. Lge. tall 4to. Orig. prospectus for Vols. III & IV, cold. buckram, orig. stiff bd. s.-c.'s. (HA. May 4; 481) $110

RICKETTS, Charles (Ill.)

See— MARLOWE, Christopher & Chapman, George
See— PAGEANT, The
See— WILDE, Oscar

RICKMAN, John

- [–] **Journal of Captain Cook's Last Voyage to the Pacific Ocean on Discovery.** L., 1785. *2nd. Edn.* Folding chart, 10 plts. (1 folding), lacks E4 & E5 of prelims., chart torn, cf., back split, w.a.f. (P. Jun.7; 276) £140

RICKMERS, W. Rickmer

- **The Duab of Turkestan.** 1913. *1st. Edn.* 4to. Orig. cl., rubbed. (BBA. Jun.14; 295) *Makiya.* £90

RICO, Juan

- **Reales Excquias, que por el Fallecimiento del Señor Don Carlos III, Rey de España y de las Indias** ... Lima, 1789. *1st. Edn.* Fo. Sm. liby stp. in corner of title-p., cont. vell. (SG. Jan.19; 317) $250

RIDDELL, Robert

- **The Carpenter & Joiner Stair Builder & Hand-Railer.** N.d. Fo. Hf. cf., reprd. (P. Apr.12; 86) *Axel.* £55

RIDER, Cardanus

- **British Merlin.** 1756. 12mo. Cont. cottage style red mor. wallet, gt., Dutch flowered end-papers with pockets, white metal clasps. (CSK. May 18; 187) £90
- – **Anr. Edn.** 1789. 12mo. Partly interleaved, cont. red mor., elab. gt., silver clasps with retaining pin, floral end-papers with pockets. (BBA. Feb.23; 185) *Maggs.* £85

RIDER, G. de

- **Catalogue et Description Bibliographique de Livres à Gravure sur les Costumes Militaires. Autriche-Hongrie.** Paris, 1928. Hf. chagrin, wrap. (HD. Jan.27; 337) Frs. 1,600

RIDER, William

See— BRADSHAW, T. & Rider, William

RIDGWAY, Robert

See— BAIRD, Spencer F. & others

RIDGWAY, Robert & Friedmann, H.

- **The Birds of North & Middle America.** Wash., 1901-50. 11 vols. (all published). Plts., vols. 1-6 hf. mor., rest cl.-bkd. bds. (S. Apr.10; 449) *Dawson.* £140

RIDING, Laura

- **Laura & Francisca.** Deya, Malloroa, Seizin Pr., 1931. *(200) numbered & sigd.* 4to. Qtr. cl., pict. bds., glassine d.-w.; inscr. by Robert Graves to Ruthven Todd. (SG. Mar.1; 496) $350
- **The Life of the Dead.** Ill.:– R.J. Beedham after John Aldridge. L., [1933]. *(200) numbered & sigd. by author & artist.* Lge. 4to. Ptd. stiff wraps. (SG. Mar.1; 497) $160
- **Love as Love, Death as Death.** L., Seizin Pr., 1928. *(175) numbered & sigd.* Cl. (SG. Mar.1; 499) $425
- **The Second Leaf** [caption title]. Deya, 1935. 4to. 1st. recto ptd., 'By / Laura Riding', seems to be awaiting title, unsewed & unbnd., opened. (SG. May 24; 180) $225

RICHTER, L. (Ill.)

- **Though Gently.** Deya, Majorca, 1930. *(200) numbered, sigd.* 4to. Hf. buckram, abstract pict. bds. (SG. May 24; 355) $175

RIDINGER, Johann Elias

- [–] **Entwurf einiger Thiere.** [Augsburg], ca. 1745. 33 ll. from series, margins mostly foxed, 19th. C. cf., very worn. (H. Nov.23; 282) DM 3,200
- **Lehrreiche Fabeln aus dem Reiche der Thiere.** Augsburg, 1744 [after 1767]. Fo. Ptd. title, 20 engraved plts., some light foxing, cont. hf. cf. (S. May 10; 397) *Ant Koch.* £1,000
- **Zu den besonderen Ereignissen und Vorfallenheiten bey der Jagd.** Ill.:– Martin Ridinger after Johann Elias Ridinger. [Augsburg, 1778]. Fo. Lacks title-p., 45 engraved plts. (all a little spotted), cont. hf. cf., rubbed. (S. May 10; 398) *Ant Koch.* £1,800

RIDOLFI, Carlo

- **Le Maravighe dell'Arte.** Venice, 1648. *1st. Edn.* 4to. Vol. 1 frontis. cut to margin, slightly browned in places, 18th. C. leath., rubbed & bumped, spine renewed, Charles de Tolnay MS. ex-libris. (D. Nov.23; 1847) DM 2,400

RIECKE, V.A

See— BERGE, F. & Riecke, V.A.

RIEDEL, Gottlieb Friedrich

- **Naturhistorische Abbildungen.** Ill.:– Riedel. Augsburg, N.d. Ob. fo. Approx. 15 plts. with brownstain at top right, light soiling, hf. leath., spine defect. (V. Sep.30; 1564) DM 500

RIEDEL, Wilh.

- **Die Grasmücken u. Nachtigallen in Europa.** Nördl., 1833. Title with old MS. name, plt. 7 with sm. hole, orig. bds., rubbed & bumped. (HK. May 15; 559) DM 1,050

RIEDERER, Friedrich

- **Spiegel der Waren Rhetoric.** Freiburg, Riederer, [11 Dec.] 1493. *1st. Edn.* Fo. Wide MS. margin, owner's mark in inner cover & on title, some light soiling, foxing & staining, cont. blind-tooled leath. over wood bds., torn, spine slightly defect., jnts. brkn., bumped, lacks clasps. [HC. 13914; BMC III, 696; Goff R 197] (HK. May 15; 228) DM 12,000

RIEDL, A. v.

- **Reise Atlas von Bajern od. Georg.-geometr. Darstellung aller Bajirischen Haupt-u. Landstrassen.** Müchen, 1796[-1806]. *Ltd. Iss.* 4to. Engraved title, 62 cold. copper engraved maps, including 1 folding & 1 double-p. folding, 1 added multi-folding cold. copper engraved map, maps numbered in ink, upr. end-paper cut away, cont. hf. leath. gt. (HK. Nov.9; 1458) DM 7,200

RIEDLIN, V.

See— HELLWIG, Chr. von –RIEDLIN, V.

RIEFENSTAHI, Leni

- **Schoenheit im Olympischen Kampf.** Berlin, 1936. *1st. Edn.* Lge. 4to. Gt.-lettered buckram, slightly bowed, pict. d.-w. chipped. (SG. May 10; 126) $550

RIEFSTAHL, R. Mayer (Ed.)

See— PARISH-WATSON COLLECTION

RIEGLIN, Susanna Dorothea

- **Neu-Erfundenes Modelbuch zum Naehen, Stricken, Wuérk und Weben** ... Nuremb., 1761. *1st. Edn.* Ob. sm. fo. Title in elab. border, engraved dedication, 5 engraved section titles, 45 engraved plts. very stained & worn, old bds., shabby. (SG. Apr.26; 116) $1,200

RIEMANN, Bernhard

- **Gesammelte Mathematische Werke und Wissenschaftlicher Nachlass.** Ed.:– R. Dedekind & H. Weber. Leipzig, 1876. *1st. Edn.* Slight margin browning, cont. red hf. mor., rubbed; Stanitz coll. (SPB. Apr.25; 378) $500

RIEMER

See— MUSCULUS, C. Th. & Riemer

RIEMER, Jacob de

- **Beschryving van 'sGraven-hage.** Delft & The Hague, 1730-29. 3 vols. Fo. L.P., engraved frontis., 2 dedication ll., 57 plts. & views, many double-p.

or folding, a few minor tears in folds, margin wormhole in parts of Vol. 2, not affecting text or plts., some browning in Vol. 3, cont. mott. cf., decor., city arms in centre of covers, spines gt. (C. Dec.9; 137) *Goldschmidt.* £950
– – **Anr. Edn.** Delft, 1730-39. 2 pts. in 3 vols. Fo. Some plts. with sm. tears in folds or reprd., cont. cf., spines richly gt. rubbed, some defects. (VG. Sep.14; 1196) Fls. 2,400

RIENITS, Rex & Thea
– **Early Artists of Australia.** Sydney, 1963. Bdg. not stated, d.-w. slightly worn. (KH. May 1; 593)
Aus. $170

RIEPEL, Jos.
– **Anfangsgründe zur Musicalischen Setzkunst.** 1752-65. *1st. Edn.* 4 pts. in 1 vol. Fo. Title Vol. 1 with sm. repair, Vol. 3 title with old MS. owners mark, lightly soiled, cont. hf. leath., rubbed & bumped, sm. defects. (HK. Nov.9; 2281)
DM 2,000

RIESBECK, J.K.
– **Briefe eines Reisenden Franzosen über Deutsch-land an seinen Bruder au Paris.** [Zürich], 1785. 2 vols. Some slight staining & foxing, cont. bds. (BR. Apr.12; 335) DM 450

RIESE, Adam
– **Rechenbüchlein, Auff der Linien und Federn, in allerley Handthierung, Geschefften und Kauff-mannschafften gestellet.** Erfurt, 1615. *Later Edn.* Browned, & slightly stained near end, some sm. wormholes, last lf. with long wormhole, cont. leath. over wood bds., head of spine slightly defect., lacks clasps. (R. Oct.12; 1710) DM 650

RIESENTHAL, Otto von
– **Die Raubvögel Deutschlands u. d. Angrenz. Mittel-europas.** Kassel, 1894. Fo. Title & upr. cover stpd., orig. hf. linen, corners slightly worn. (HK. May 15; 560) DM 900
– – **Anr. Copy.** Fo. Lr. margins soiled, orig. hf. linen, slightly spotted, lr. cover defect. (BR. Apr.12; 844) DM 600
– **Das Waidwerk.** Berlin, 1880. *1st. Edn.* Title lightly soiled, with old erased name, orig. hf. leath., spine defect. (R. Oct.12; 2082) DM 420

RIETSTAP, Johannes B.
– **Wapenboek v.d. Nederlandschen Adel.** Groningen, 1883-87. Lge. fo. Orig. hf. mor., richly gt. (VG. Mar.21; 1043) Fls. 1,700

RIGA
– **De Expugnatione Civitatis Rigensis Livoniae Metropolis.** Riga, 1622. Sm. 4to. Letterpress key pasted on sides of folding engraved plan, short splits & some wear in folds, cont. vell. bds. (S. Dec.1; 317) *Israel.* £320

RIGAUD, Jacques
– **[Recueil Choisi de Plus Belles Vues des Palais, Chateaux et Maisons Royales de Paris et des Envi-rons].** Paris, [Some plts. sid. 1752, a few 1730]. Ob. fo. 125 engraved plts., in various numbered series, red mor.-bkd. bds. by Simier, spines gt., 3 with fleur-de-lys, crowned gt. monog. of the Duchaese de Berry on upr. cover. (C. Dec.9; 138)
Weinreb. £8,500

RIGENERAZIONE DELL'OLANDA, Specchio a Tutti Popoli Rigenerati
Venice, 1799. Fo. Engraved title, 19 engraved cari-cature plts., ptd. in red & bistre, 1 sepia aquatint, text in Fr. & Italian, a few margins lightly stained, orig. ptd. limp bds., slightly rubbed & stained, buckram s.-c.; John A. Saks copy. (S. May 10; 399)
A.K.H. £240

RIGHT OF THE BRITISH LEGISLATURE to Tax the American Colonies Vindicated
L., 1774. *1st. Edn.* Unbnd.; pres. copy to Gov. Glen. (P. Jun.7; 313) £280

RITS, Rev. H.U.
– **Grammatical outline & Vocabulary of the Oji-Language** ... Basle, 1854. Dampstained, cont. mor.-bkd. bds. (BBA. Mar.7; 33)
Merrion Book Co. £55

RILING, Ray
– **The Powder Flask Book.** New Hope, Pa., 1953. *1st. Edn.* Tall 4to. Orig. pres. bdg. of buckram gt., stpd. with owner's name; sigd. pres. copy inscr. by author & publisher to L.A. Heinrich, also sigd. on p. 450 by Riling, Heinrich & 5 others. (SG. Aug.4; 114) $100

RILKE, Rainer Maria
– **Die Aufzeichnungen des Malte Laurids Brigge** ... Leipzig, 1910. *2nd. Iss.* 2 vols. Orig. cf. (*With:*)
– **Das Buch der Bilder** ... Berlin, n.d. *2nd. Edn.* 1 vol. Orig. bds., spine defect. Together 3 vols. 12mo. Each work inscr. by author to Stina Frisell, w.a.f. (CNY. Dec.17; 443) $600
– **Ausgewählte Gedichte aus den Jahren 1902-1917.** Ill.:– after M. Slevogt. [Priv. ptd., 1931]. *(60) DeLuxe Edn. with sigd. etching by Slevogt.* Sm. 4to. Hand-bnd. orig. vell., by Frieda Thiersch, with introduction to origination history of work. (H. May 23; 1515) DM 4,800
– **Das Buch der Bilder.** [Leipzig, Ernst Ludwig Pr., 1913]. *(50) De Luxe Edn. on japan.* Lge. 8vo. Dedication copy, hand-bnd. orig. mor., gold-tooled vig., engraved ex-libris inside cover. (H. May 23; 1472) DM 5,200
– **Les Cahiers de Malte Lauride Briggs.** Ill.:– Her-mine David. 1942. *(100) on vergé de Hollande ptd. in name of J.G. Daragnès.* 4to. Separate suite of 38 etchings, anr. of 25, ptd. in bistre, 2 others, incompl., with refused plts. & 30 bons à tirer sigd. by David, including 3 with corrections, A.L.s from David to Daragnès, sewed. (HD. Dec.9; 21g)
Frs. 1,050
– **Duineser Elegien.** Leipzig, 1923. *1st. Edn. (300) numbered.* Mor., decor. (R. Oct.11; 398)
DM 4,300
– – **Anr. Copy.** Sm. 4to. Hand-bnd. orig. mor., gt. decor., sm. red leath. onlays, gold-tooled, red striped end-papers, spine lightly faded. (H. Nov.24; 1961) DM 3,200
– – **Anr. Copy.** 4to. Hf. mor., mor. corners, slightly worn. (R. Apr.3; 405) DM 1,910
– **Gesammelte Gedichte.** Ill.:– A. Maillol, E. Gill. Leipzig, Cranach Pr., 1930-34. *(20) De Luxe Edn. on Japan.* Sm. 4to. Without 2nd. title lf., orig. hand-bnd. mor., decor. spine, inner & outer dentelles, by Gerhard Prade, Leipzig, spine slightly faded, minimal rubbing, vol. 2 inside cover slightly spotted; Hauswedell coll. (H. May 24; 735) DM 6,200
– – **Anr. Edn.** Ill.:– A. Maillol (initials), E. Gill (title ill.). Leipzig, Cranach Pr., 1930-34. *(200) on Maillol-Kesslerschem Bütten.* 4 vols. Sm. 4to. Orig. hand-bnd. hf. vell., by Gerhard Prade, Leipzig. (H. Nov.23; 983b) DM 4,400
– **Gesammelte Werke.** Leipzig, 1927. *1st. Coll. Edn.* 6 vols. Orig. hf. leath., spine vol. 6 slightly faded. (HK. May 17; 3077) DM 420
– **Ohne Gogenwart.** Berlin, 1898. *1st. Edn.* Orig. sewed, spine slightly rubbed. (GB. May 5; 3138)
DM 1,000
– **Lettres à Une Amie Venetienne.** Ill.:– M. Vellani-Marchi. Mailand, Officina Bodoni, 1941. *1st. Edn. (350) numbered.* 4to. Orig. vell. (HK. Nov.11; 3837) DM 850
– – **Anr. Edn.** Ill.:– M. Vellani-Marchi. [Verona, Officina Bodoni, 1941]. *1st. Edn. (350) on Bütten.* Orig. vell. (H. Nov.24; 1971) DM 1,150
– **Les Roses.** Ill.:– Imre Reiner. Paris, [1959]. *(105) numbered.* 4to. Loose ll. in hf. linen portfo., bd. s.-c., defect. (HT. May 9; 1999) DM 550
– **Sämtliche Werke.** Wiesbaden & Frankfurt, 1955-66. 6 vols. Orig. limp leath. (HK. Nov.11; 3899)
DM 460
– **Die Sonette an Orpheus.** [Leipzig], 1923. *1st. Edn. (300) De Luxe Edn. on Bütten.* Hand-bnd. orig. cf. by H. Sperling, gold decor. covers, inner & outer dentelle, decor. end-papers, spine slightly faded. (H. Nov.24; 1966) DM 1,800
– **Das Stundenbuch.** [Leipzig, Insel Pr., 1921]. *(440) on Bütten.* Sm. 4to. Hand-bnd. orig. mor. by F.A. Enders, gold-tooled, spine lightly darkened, slightly soiled. (H. Nov.24; 1967) DM 620
– – **Anr. Copy.** Orig. vell., slightly rubbed, unc. (GB. May 5; 3141) DM 410
– **Die Weisse Fürstin.** Berlin, 1920. *1st. Edn. (30) on Zanders Bütten.* Sm. 4to. Hand-bnd. orig. mor., faded. (H. Nov.24; 1962) DM 480

RILKE, Rainer Maria (Contrib.)
See— NEUE RUNDSCHAU

RILLIET, F.J.L. & others
– **Soldats Suisses au Service Etranger.** Genève, 1903-19. 8 vols. Hf. chagrin. (HD. Jan.27; 199)
Frs. 3,000

RIMBAUD, Arthur
– **Les Illuminations.** Ill.:– Blaise Monod after Roger de La Fresnaye. Paris, 1949. *(126). (110) numbered on papier velin d'Arches.* Perspex sides over abstract ptd. design of irregular lattice pattern of black on light yellow & continuing to light yellow on black, set in oval shape round central black & yellow-on-black oval, repeated in reverse on lr. cover & crossing smooth light yellow mor. spine where tooled in black, title lettered vertically down spine on onlaid cf. strip, partly unc., orig. wraps. & spine preserved, by Henri Mercher, sigd. on onlay on upr. doubl., dtd. '1957' on lr. doubl. (CNY. May 18; 191) $1,200
– – **Anr. Edn.** Preface:– Henry Miller. Ill.:– F. Leger. Lausanne, [1949]. *(275) numbered on hand-made vélin teinte, sigd. by artist & publisher.* 4to. Loose in ptd. wraps. as iss., s.-c. worn. (SG. Nov.3; 122) $950
– – **Anr. Edn.** Preface:– Henry Miller. Ill.:– Fer-nand Leger. Lausanne, [1949]. *(395) numbered & sigd. by artist & publisher.* 4to. 14 lithos., unsewn as iss. in paper bds., s.-c. (LH. Jan.15; 380) $900
– – **Anr. Edn.** Paris, 1967. *(200) on Rives.* Fo. Sigd. by artist, leaves, box. (HD. Nov.29; 144)
Frs. 1,050
– – **Anr. Edn.** Ill.:– Carzou. Genève, 1969. *(225) sigd. by artist. This 1 of (5) on japan nacré.* Lge. 4to. Triple suite of lge. engrs. in black, cols. or sanguine, copper engr. & orig. ink ill., sigd., by Carzou, leaves, wrap., relief decor., box. (HD. Dec.16; 181) Frs. 10,000
– – **Anr. Copy.** Fo. 2 suites, leaves, orig. decor. wrap., unc., box; annotated copy with drawing at foot of each lf., prospectus & specimen in separate portfo. (SM. Mar.7; 2311) Frs. 6,000
– **Poèmes, les Illuminations, une Saison en Enfer.** Notice:– Paul Verlaine. Paris, 1892. Red hf. mor., wrap. & spine preserved; added port. (HD. Jun.13; 93) Frs. 3,000
– **Poésies Complètes.** Preface:– Paul Verlaine. Ill.:– Verlaine. Paris, 1895. *Partly Orig. Edn.* 12mo. Red hf. mor., corners, by Semet & Plumelle, decor. spine, wraps. preserved. (HD. Sep.22; 329)
Frs. 3,800
– **Reliquaire. Poésie.** Preface:– R. Darzens. 1891. *Orig. Edn.* 16mo. Sewed. (HD. Jun.29; 175)
Frs. 5,000
– **Une Saison en Enfer.** The Hague, 1949. *(19) numbered, with extra suite of lithos. sigd. by Louis Favre.* 4to. Unsewn as iss. in orig. wraps., portfos., s.-c. (BBA. Jan.19; 317) *Duran.* £70
– **Une Saison en Enfer. Les Déserts de l'Amour. Les Illuminations.** Ill.:– Germaine Richier. Lausanne, [1951]. *(118).* Fo. Printers mark sigd. by artist, loose ll. in orig. wraps., hf. vell. & s.-c., bumped & torn; Hauswedell coll. (H. May 24; 685)
DM 1,300

RIMBAULT, E.F.
See— HOPKINS, Edward L. & Rimbault, E.F.

RIMMER, Alfred
– **Ancient Streets & Homesteads of England.** Ill.:– J.D. Cooper after Rimmer. L., 1877. Lge. 8vo. 150 wood engrs., extra-ill. with 25 hand-cold. steel engrs. of the early 1840's, crushed lev., lge. gt. design on covers & spine, gt. dentelles, by Bayntun; R.H. Hoskins bkplt. (SG. Sep.22; 257) $100

RINDER, Frank
– **D.Y. Cameron: An Illustrated Catalogue of His Etched Work.** Glasgow, 1912. *(700).* 4to. Some offsetting, gt.-lettered cl., slightly soiled. (SG. Oct.13; 49) $130
– – **Anr. Edn.** Glasgow, 1932. *2nd. Edn. (600) num-bered.* 4to. 500 reproductions, ex-liby., cl. (SG. May 3; 71) $200

RINEHART, F.A.
– **Rinehart's Indians.** [Omaha, 1899]. Sm. 4to. Minor stains & tears to a few plt. margins, plts.

RINEHART, F.A. -Contd.

dampwrinkled, pict. wraps., laced, covers dampwrinkled. (SG. Nov.10; 136)　　$225

RINGELNATZ, Joachim [i.e. H. Bötticher]
- Geheimes Kinder-Spiel-Buch. Potsdam, 1924. 1st. Edn. 4to. Some foxing & browning, orig. bds., cold. ill., spine browned, ex-libris; end-paper sigd. by author. (HK. Nov.11; 3906)　　DM 520
- Kinder Verwirr-Buch. Berlin, 1931. 1st. Edn. Orig. pict. bds., cover slightly browned. (HK. Nov.11; 3908)　　DM 460
- Weitab von Lappland. [Berlin, 1922]. 1st. Edn. (50). 4to. Orig. bds.; port. sigd. by author & artist. (H. Nov.24; 1980)　　DM 1,000

RINGELNATZ, Joachim [i.e. H. Bötticher] & Seewald, R.J.M.
- Die Schnupftabaksdose. München, [1912]. 1st. Edn. Endpaper & title with MS. entry, orig. wraps., light wear. (HK. Nov.11; 3913)　　DM 440

RIO DE LA PLATA
- El Virrey de las Provincias del Rio de la Plata presenta ... un Examen de la Situación Política y Militar de España ... Montevideo, 1811. 4to. Sewed. (DS. Oct.28; 2565)　　Pts. 36,000

RIOLAN, Jean, the Younger
- Anthropographia et Osteologia Omnia Recognita. Ill.:– Crispin de Pas & M. Lasne. Paris, 1626. 4to. Privilege & errata ll., 2 unpaginated ll. between 4d4 & EEee1, no sig. 5T (correct), few letters strengthened in ink, some margin worming, few corners stained, cont. sheep, 1 corner defect.; Dr. Walter Pagel copy. (S. Feb.7; 330)
　　Goldschmidt. £420
- Comparatio Veteris Medicinae cum Nova, Hippocraticae cum Hermetica Dogmatice cum Spagyrica; Examen Animadversionum Baucyneti e Harveti. Paris, 1605. 1st. Edn. 2 pts. in 1 vol. 12mo. Cut in sig. G6-7, new cf., wraps. bnd. in; Dr. Walter Pagel copy. (S. Feb.7; 329) Nat. Lib. of Medicine. £480
- Les Oeuvres Anatomiques. Trans.:– Pierre Constant. Ill.:– Crispin de Pas. Paris, 1628-29. 2 vols. in 1. Lacks ptd. title to Vol.1, some prelims. misbnd., pp. 775-778 folding & torn, some worming, cont. cf., very torn; bkplt. of Frederic Wood Jones, Dr. Walter Pagel copy. (S. Feb.7; 332)　　Colombo. £70
- Opuscula Anatomica Nova. Ed.:– Joannis Wallaei. L., 1649. 4to. Title stained & margin slightly scraped, sm. margin tear in Ee2, some margin worming, some stains, cont. vell., upr. hinge torn; Dr. Walter Pagel copy. [Wing R 1524] (S. Feb.7; 333)　　Gurney. £270

RIORDAN, Roger
- A Score of Etchings. Ill.:– P.G. Hamerton, F.S. Haden, A. Legros, & others. N.Y., ca. 1880. Fo. Minor dampsoiling to upr. & lr. margins of text, not affecting plts., gt.-pict. cl., soiled, hinges shaken. (SG. Oct.13; 287)　　$150
-- Anr. Edn. Ill.:– Haden, Legros, Hamerton, Herkomer, & others. N.Y., ca. 1885. Fo. 20 etchings, most sigd. in plt., gt.-pict. cl., faded & discold. (SG. Jun.7; 387)　　$120

RIRE
Paris, 1894-1900. Series I : Vols. 1-2 & 4-6. 4to. 2 ll. Vol. V defect. with loss, cl. (B. Apr.27; 613)
　　Fls. 600

RIS PAQUOT
- Dictionnaire Ency. des Marques et Monogrammes, Chiffres, Lettres Initiales, Signes ... Paris, n.d. 2 vols. Fo. Linen, corners. (DS. Oct.28; 2316)
　　Pts. 19,000

RISSO, J. Antoine
- Histoire Naturelle des Orangers. Ill.:– after A. Poiteau. Paris, 1818. 1st. Edn. Fo. Some slight foxing, some plts with slight crumples, cont. hf. mor., slightly rubbed. (D. Nov.23; 454) DM 7,000
- Ichthyologie de Nice, ou Histoire Naturelle des Poissons du Département des Alpes-Maritimes. Paris, 1810. Cont. hf. vell., corners. (HD. Nov.17; 69)　　Frs. 1,500

RIST, Johann
- Starker Schild Gottes Wider die Gifftigen Mordpfeile falscher und verleümderischer Zungen [etc]. Hamburg, 1644. 1st. Edn. Hf. vell. (GB. Nov.4; 2166)　　DM 1,100

RITCHIE, Anne Thackeray
- Alfred, Lord Tennyson & His Friends. Intro.:– H.H.H. Cameron. Ill.:– after J.M. & H.H.H. Cameron. L., 1893. (400) numbered. Fo. Faint spot of dampstaining along some lr. margins, not affecting plts., orig. gt.-pict. cl., worn & stained, spine reprd., recased. (SG. Nov.10; 37)　　$170
- The Village on the Cliff. Ill.:– Frederick Walker. 1867. 1st. Edn. Orig. cl. (LC. Jul.5; 381)　　£140

RITCHIE, Leith
- Travelling Sketches in the North of Italy, the Tyrol, & on the Rhine. Ill.:– after Clarkson Stanfield. 1832. 1 vol. Engraved frontis. & additional engraved vig. title 'Heath's Picturesque Annual for 1832' (both stained), & 25 other engraved plts., some margin staining, orig. red mor. gt., rubbed. (With:) - Travelling Sketches on the Rhine, & in Belgium & Holland. 1833. 1 vol. Engraved frontis. & additional engraved vig. title, 25 engraved plts., 1 loose, some staining, orig. red mor. gt., stained. (LC. Mar.1; 232)　　£60
- Wanderings by the Loire. -- Wanderings by the Seine. Ill.:– after Turner. L., 1833-34. Together 2 vols. 41 steel-engraved plts., cont. hf. chagrin, corners, spines decor. (HD. Nov.17; 70) Frs. 1,100

RITSON, Joseph
- Robin Hood, A Collection of all the Ancient Poems, Songs & Ballads. Ill.:– after Thomas Bewick. L., 1885,. (500) numbered. 4to. Orig. parch.-bkd. cl., spine slightly soiled. (S. Dec.20; 634)　　Cavendish. £60
-- Anr. Edn. Ill.:– Thomas Bewick & others. L., 1887. 2 vols. Lge. 8vo. L.P., 80 vigs. on mntd. China paper from orig. blocks used in 1832 edn., engraved port., 9 plts. on Japan vell., orig. gt.-pict. qtr. roan, cl., spotted. (SG. Apr.19; 207)　　$100

RITTER, C.
- Die Erdkunde in Verhältnis zur Natur und zur Geschichte des Menschen, oder Allgemeine, Vergleichende Geographie. Berlin, 1822-59. Pts. 1-19 in 21, & Index to pts. 2-11. Foxing, hf. leath., spines defect. (B. Feb.8; 563)　　Fls. 700

RITTER, L.
- Malerische Ansichten aus Nürnberg. Text:– R. Dohme. Berlin, [1876]. Lge. fo. Lightly stained at head, orig. pict. linen. (HK. Nov.9; 1437) DM 750
-- Anr. Edn. Text:– R. Dohme. Berlin, ca. 1880. Fo. 25 etchings & wood engraved ills., cl. (VG. May 3; 406)　　Fls. 1,100

RITTERHAUS, E. & Mannfeld, B.
- Rheinlands Sang Und Sage. Bonn, 1898. 4to. Title loose, orig. pict. cl. gt. (P. Dec.8; 271)
　　Tzakas. £95
-- Anr. Edn. Bonn, [1898]. 4to. Title, 19 plts., orig. pict. cl. gt., head of spine slightly torn. (P. Mar.15; 11)　　Cullen. £170

RITZ, Philip
- Letter upon the Agricultural & Mineral Resources of the North-Western Territories ... [Wash., 1868]. 1st. Edn. Orig. ptd. wraps., tied as iss., slightly creased, lr. wrap. slightly soiled, qtr. mor. s.-c. (LH. Apr.15; 361)　　$120

RIVERA, Diego
- Frescoes. N.Y., [1933]. Tall fo. 19 cold. plts., individually matted, text ills., each mat liby.-stpd. on blank verso, loose in orig. portfo. (SG. May 3; 311)　　$200
-- Anr. Copy. Tall fo. Unbnd. in linen-bkd. ptd. bds., covers slightly soiled; sigd. by Rivera on title-p. (SG. Jan.12; 303)　　$175

RIVERS, Gen. Augustus H.L. Fox Pitt
See— PITT-RIVERS, Gen. Augustus H.L. Fox

RIVERS, W.H.R.
- The History of Melanesian Society. Camb., 1914. 2 vols. Orig. cl., spines rubbed. (BBA. May 3; 309)
　　Quaritch. £95

RIVIERE, Georges
- Le Maitre Paul Cezanne. Paris, 1923. 4to. Hf. mor., unc., spine rubbed, orig. upr. pict. wrap. bnd. in. (S. Apr.30; 83)　　Scott. £50

RIVOIRA, Giovanni Teresio
- Le Origini dell'Architettura Lombarda. Roma, 1901-07. 2 vols. 4to. Publishers mor., corners, gt. monog. decor. spines, orig. wraps. preserved. (CR. Jun.6; 274)　　Lire 500,000

RIZZI ZANNONI, Giovanni Antonio
- Atlas Géographique. Paris, 1762. 12 x 14cm. Hand-cold. frontis., hand-cold. title, 1 plain & 30 hand-cold. double-p. maps, a few pencil markings, slight dampstaining, mor. gt., rubbed. (P. Nov.24; 318)　　Knight. £100
- Atlas Géographique et Militaire ou Théâtre de la Guerre Présente en Allemagne. France, 1761. 2 works in 1 vol. 12mo. Engraved title & 17 hand-cold. engraved maps, cont. red mor., arms, spine decor., watered silk liners & end-ll., lr. cover stained. (HD. Jun.18; 50)　　Frs. 4,500
- Atlas Historique de la France Ancienne et Moderne. Ed.:– Desnos. Ill.:– after Eisen. Paris, 1765. 4to. Engraved frontis., engraved title & dedication, 2 engraved multi-folding maps & 57 double-p. cold. maps, red mor., gt. decor., gt. inner & outer dentelle, gold-tooled arms supralibros. (D. Nov.23; 779a)　　DM 8,000
- Carte de la Pologne. N.p., 1772. Fo. Double-p. engraved & cold. title, engraved dedication lf., 1 engraved plan, 23 engraved & cold. double-p. maps, some spotting, last map margin stained, cont. leath., defect. (D. Nov.23; 780)　　DM 3,700

ROBAUT, Alfred
- L'Oeuvre de Corot: Catalogue Raisonné et Illustré. Paris, 1905. (400). (25) on Japan Shizuoka. 5 vols. Fo. Port., ills., 3,221 reproductions, ex-liby., three-qtr. mor. (SG. May 3; 106)　　$1,200
-- Anr. Edn. Paris, 1965. (500) numbered. 5 vols. Lge. 4to. Cont. cl., slightly soiled, orig. wraps. bnd. in. (S. Apr.30; 84)　　Mackinnon. £320

ROBBE-GRILLET
- Jealousy. Ill.:– Michèle Forgeois. Kentfield, California, Allen Pr., 1971. (140). 4to. Paper bds. (LH. Sep.25; 311)　　$425
-- Anr. Copy. 4to. Ill. bds., orig. acetate wrap. (CBA. Nov.19; 7)　　$250

ROBERT, J.B.M.
- Adresse aux Chambres. La Police sous MM. les Ducs de Cazes, Comte Angles et Baron Mounier. Paris, 1821. 2nd. Edn. 2 vols. Hf. chagrin cf. (HD. Feb.22; 168)　　Frs. 1,800

ROBERT, Philippe
- Feuilles d'automne. Preface:– Ph. Godel. Ill.:– Philippe Robert & E. Grasset. Biel, 1909. Ltd. De Luxe Edn. on light grey Bütten. Lge. fo. Orig. linen, orig. bd. s.-c. (BR. Apr.13; 1775) DM 400

ROBERT DE VAUGONDY, Gilles & Didier
- Atlas Universel. Paris, 1757. Fo. Engraved title (lr. margin slightly torn with loss), & 108 double-p. engraved maps, hand-cold. in outl., several slightly shaved, 1 reprd., cont. cf., worn. (CSK. May 4; 40)　　£5,800
-- Anr. Copy. fo. 24 (of 108) double-p. engraved maps, mostly France & Russian empire, outl. hand-cold., title dust-soiled, cont. cf., defect. (S. Nov.1; 177)　　Schwedt. £160
-- Anr. Copy. Lge. fo. Engraved frontis., 108 double-p. maps engraved & cont. cold. outl., linen. (DS. Dec.16; 2097)　　Pts. 225,000
-- Anr. Edn. Paris, 1757 [1758 or later]. Fo. Engraved allegorical title, ptd. advt. lf. & 20 ll. ptd. text, 108 double-p. engraved maps variously dtd. between 1749 & 1758, hand-cold. in outl., 1 or 2 split at centre-fold, a few outer margins torn, frayed or strengthened, a few creases, some soiling or staining affecting mostly the European maps, 19th. C. mor. gt., worn, w.a.f. (S. May 21; 129)
　　Burgess. £1,300
-- Anr. Edn. Paris, 1757 [1783 or later]. Fo. Pict. engraved title, 18 ll. of text, 108 mostly double-p. engraved maps variously dtd. between 1750 & 1783, hand-cold. in outl., worming affecting margins & centre-folds of a few maps (mostly of

France), 1 or 2 tears touching engraved surfaces, some faint browning, cont. bds., worn, w.a.f. (S. May 21; 128)   *Harris*. £2,000
– – **Anr. Edn.** Paris, Delmarche, [1793]. Fo. Engraved title, 4 double-p. engraved geographical tables, 112 (of 113) double-p. engraved maps, hand-cold. in outl., some light foxing & creasing, a few margin tears & slight margin dampstaining towards end, 1 map foxed, anr. torn at central fold, cont. cf.-bkd. bds., worn, spine defect. (C. Mar.14; 82)
                                                       Burgess. £1,600
[–] **Nouvel Atlas Portatif.** Paris, 1778 [or later]. 31 double-p. engraved maps & astronomical diagrams (1 folding), hand-cold. in outl., some light soiling, qtr. cf. (S. Jun.25; 272)   *Faupel*. £240

ROBERTS, Austin
– **The Mammals of South Africa.** Johannesburg, 1951. *(500)*. 4to. Hf. cf., d.-w. (SSA. Sep.21; 346)
                                                                R 220
– – **Anr. Edn.** Johannesburg, 1951. *De Luxe Edn., (500) sigd.* 4to. Errata slip, orig. hf. leath. (VA. Oct.28; 239)   R 290

ROBERTS, David
– **Egypt & Nubia.** Intro.:– H.D. Schneider. Aalsmeer, ca. 1980. *Facs. of 1846-49 Edn.* Lge. fo. Mor. gt. (VG. Mar.21; 629)   Fls. 600
   The Holy Land, Syria, Idumea, Arabia... L., 1842[-45]. 20 orig. pts. in 18. Fo. Port., 2 litho. titles, 60 full-p. & 60 smaller litho. plts., all on India paper, hand-cold. & mntd. on card (without any foxing or cockling), 4 pp. advts., 2 publisher's notices to the subscribers loosely inserted, each pt. loose in publisher's limp cl. covers, gt. designs on upr. covers, roan spines. (S. May 22; 287)
                                                       Beistejhi. £51,000
– – **Anr. Edn.** 1842-49. 3 vols. in 2. Lge. fo. 3 litho. titles, port., map, 120 tinted litho. plts., some spotting, cont. red hf. mor., spines & corners rubbed. (CH. Sep.20; 10)   Fls. 11,000
– – **Anr. Edn.** Ill.:– Louis Haghe after Roberts. L., 1843. Vol. II only. Some foxing, cont. Engl. bordeaux hf. mor., decor. spine. (HD. Mar.14; 74)   Frs. 10,200
– – **Anr. Edn.** L., ca. 1870. 2 vols. in 1. 4to. 120 tinted litho. plts., some minor spotting, cont. hf. mor. gt., a little rubbed. (TA. May 17; 30) £260
– **The Holy Land, Syria, Idumea, Arabia...; Egypt & Nubia.** L., 1842-49. 6 vols. Lge. fo. 6 litho. titles with vigs., 241 litho. plts., uncold. port. of David Roberts on India paper, 2 engraved maps, list of subscribers, titles & plts. hand-cold. & mntd. on card, plts. & text on linen guards thro.-out, some very faint offsetting onto interleaving, cont. red hf. mor., richly gt. (S. Feb.1; 46)   *Egee*. £78,000
– – **Anr. Copy.** 6 vols. Lge. fo. Litho. port. of Roberts, engraved map of Egypt & Nubia, 7 cold. litho. titles, 241 litho. plts., hand-cold. & mntd. on card, on linen guards, Holy Land bnd. without Vol. III title, map, list of subscribers & lf. of description for title-p. vigs. to Vols. II & III, missing Vol. III title replaced by dupl. of Vol. II 'Baalbec from the Fountain' with numeral altered in MS., title to Vol. II Egypt & Nubia replaced by dupl. of Vol. I 'Entrance to the Great Temple of Aboo Simble, Nubia', Vol. II title 'Great Gateway, leading to the Temple of Karnac-Thebes' (with minor pencil scribble) bnd. at end of Vol. III, 3 titles slightly spotted, 2 plts. with minor tear at margin, a few blank margins slightly soiled, embossed liby. stp. thro.-out in blank margin of plts. sometimes touching plt., sm. ptd. stp. at corner of some plts., cont. maroon mor., gt.-panel. covers, Holy Land with gt. vig. of armorial ensigns of Jerusalem, Egypt & Nubia with title gt.-stpd. in Egyptian mythological figures, by A. Tarrant, rubbed, a few surface tears, short split at foot of 1 jnt. (C. Jun.27; 62)   *Bernard*. £42,000
– – **Anr. Copy.** 6 vols. Lge. fo. Engraved port. of Roberts, 2 engraved maps, 6 tinted litho. titles, 241 tinted litho. plts., including 121 full-p., on thick paper, mntd. on guards thro.-out, without subscribers list, minor spotting to some text ll., 3 titles & a few plt. margins, cont. red hf. mor., corners rubbed, Vol. II covers slightly warped. (C. Jun.27; 63)   *Davidson*. £9,500
– – **Anr. Copy.** 6 vols. Fo. 6 pict. litho. titles, port. on India paper in 1st. work, 2 engraved maps, 241 tinted litho. views, including 121 full-p., some

spotting, slight defects or staining affecting a few outer margins, cont. purple hf. mor. gt., rubbed, slight soiling, 3 orig. pt. wraps. to 2nd. work bnd. in. (S. Dec.1; 354)   *Oberman*. £7,500
– – **Anr. Edn.** L., 1855-56. 6 vols. in 3. 4to. 250 litho. plts. (including port., titles, & 2 maps), some spotting, cont. mor. gt., slightly rubbed. (S. May 22; 286)   *Zouein*. £700
– – **Anr. Copy.** 6 vols. in 2. 4to. 6 vig. titles, port. frontis. in 1st. work, 2 maps, 241 litho. plts., some spotting, cont. elab. gt. red mor., slightly rubbed. (S. Dec.1; 355)   *Du Pont*. £620
– – **Anr. Copy.** 6 vols. in 3. 4to. Tinted litho. ports., titles & 241 plts. only, 2 maps, some spotted, cont. mor. gt., disbnd., w.a.f. (CSK. Jul.6; 76)   £600
– – **Anr. Copy.** 6 vols. in 3, as iss. 4to. Port., 6 vig. titles, 2 engraved maps, 241 tinted litho. plts., qtr. mor. gt., Vol. I disbnd., text not collated, as a collection of plts., w.a.f. (SG. Sep.22; 258) $750
– – **Anr. Copy.** 6 vols. in 3. 4to. Litho. port., 6 litho. titles, 2 engraved maps & 241 litho. plts., cont. leath. gt., gt. arms supralibros on all covers. (R. Apr.5; 2859)   DM 4,700
– **Picturesque Sketches in Spain.** 1837. Fo. Tinted litho. title, 22 (of 25) plts., some spotting, especially to 1st. & last plts., cont. qtr. mor., worn, backstrip defect. (TA. Jul.19; 52)   £310
– **Views in Spain.** L., 1836. Fo. 2 frontis., 40 etchings, linen. (DS. Feb.24; 2173)   Pts. 225,000

ROBERTS, Col. David
[–] **The Military Adventures of Johnny Newcome.** Ill.:– T. Rowlandson. L., 1815. *1st. Edn.* 15 handcold. aquatint plts., some imprints cropped, a few captions shaved, 2 text ll. reprd., mod. hf. mor., spine gt. (C. Mar.14; 83)   *Solomons*. £130
[–] – **Anr. Edn.** Ill.:– Thomas Rowlandson. L., 1816. *2nd. Edn.* 15 hand-cold. aquatint plts., sm. hole in Y1, cf. gt. by Root. (S. Apr.9; 228)   *Elliott*. £75

ROBERTS, Emma
See— **ELLIOT, Robert & Roberts, Emma**

ROBERTS, Henry
– **Calliope, or English Harmony.** 1739. Vol. 1. Cont. cf. (P. Feb.16; 269)   £320

ROBERTS, Lewis
– **The Merchants Map of Commerce.** Ill.:– Ph. Chetwind. L., 1677. *3rd. Edn.* Sm. fo. 4 folding maps (1666), cf., new gt. spine. (VG. May 3; 460)
                                                                Fls. 1,500

ROBERTS, P.
See— **CALVERT, F. & Roberts, P.**

ROBERTS, W.
– **An Account of the First Discovery, & Natural History of Florida.** Ill.:– Maps:– T. Jeffreys. 1763. *1st. Edn.* 4to. 7 folding maps (1 hand-cold.), cf. [Sabin 71926] (S. May 22; 333) *Robinson*. £1,300

ROBERTS, William of Florida
See— **WARD, Thomas Humphrey & Roberts, William**

ROBERTSON, Archibald
– **A Topographical Survey of the Great Road from London to Bath & Bristol.** L., 1792. 2 vols. Cont. diced cf., rebkd.; from liby. of Luttrellstown Castle, w.a.f. (C. Sep.28; 1759)   £260
– – **Anr. Copy.** Vol. 1 only. 6 maps, 32 (of 33) plts., mor. gt. (P. Dec.8; 285)   *Burgess*. £150

ROBERTSON, David
– **A Tour through the Isle of Man** ... 1794. Some offset foxing from map, cont. diced russ., gt.-decor. spine; Sir Ivar Colquhoun, of Luss copy. (CE. Mar.22; 254)   £220

ROBERTSON, Edward Graeme
– **Early Buildings of Southern Tasmania.** 1970. 2 vols. No bdg. stated. (JL. Jun.24; 172) Aus. $130
See— **CRAIG, Clifford & others**

ROBERTSON, Edward Graeme & Craig, Edith N.
– **Early Houses of Northern Tasmania** ... Melbourne, 1964. *Orig. Edn. Numbered & sigd.* 2 vols. Bdg. not stated, d.-w.'s. (KH. May 1; 596)
                                                                Aus. $260
– – **Anr. Copy.** 2 vols. 2 or 3 early ll. in Vol. 1 with sm. stain, orig. cl., d.-w.'s slightly chipped. (KH. Nov.9; 689)   Aus. $250

– – **Anr. Edn.** 1966. Bdg. not stated, d.-w. (KH. May 1; 597)   Aus. $100

ROBERTSON, John Parish & W.P.
– **Letters on Paraguay.** 1838. 2 vols. Liby. stps. on titles, orig. cl., soiled. (BBA. Jun.28; 244)
                                                       Rudge. £55

ROBERTSON, John
– **Francis Drake & other Early Explorers along the Pacific Coast.** Ill.:– V. Angelo & others. San Franc., Grabhorn Pr., 1927. *(1000)*. 4to. Rear section partially detchd., hf. parch. & bds., darkened, some cracking to spine, s.-c. worn; the V. Angelo copy. (CBA. Oct.1; 170) $150

ROBERTSON, William, Architect
– **Designs in Architecture.** L., 1800. *1st. Edn. Early Iss., with plts. & text wtrmkd. 1797.* Lge. ob. 4to. Col. engraved vig. dedication lf., 24 cold. aquatint plts., some light foxing & offsetting, thumbed, cont. bds., worn, rebkd., partly unc. (SG. Nov.3; 174)
                                                                $1,800

ROBERTSON, William, Historian
– **L'Histoire de l'Amérique.** Trans.:– Suard. Paris, 1778. *1st. Fr. Trans.* 2 vols. 4to. Cont. marb. cf., spines decor., some repairs. (HD. May 21; 66)
                                                       Frs. 1,000
– **An Historical Disquisition concerning the Knowledge which the Ancients had of India.** 1791. *1st. Edn.* 4to. Cont. spr. cf., spine gt.; Sir Ivar Colquhoun, of Luss copy. (CE. Mar.22; 255) £100
– **The History of America.** 1777-96. *1st. Edn.* 10 books in 3 vols. 4to. Hf.-titles, cont. cf., spines gt.; Sir Ivar Colquhoun, of Luss copy. (CE. Mar.22; 256)   £280
– – **Anr. Edn.** Maps:– Kitchin. L., 1783. *4th. Edn.* 3 vols. Hf.-titles, cont. tree cf. gt., lacks 1 spine label. (SG. Jan.19; 318) $175
– – **Anr. Edn.** Maps:– Ill.:– Thomas Kitchin. 1800. *9th. Edn.* 4 vols. Cont. mott. cf. (TA. Nov.17; 68)
                                                                £54
– **The History of the Reign of Emperor Charles V.** L., 1769. *1st. Edn.* 3 vols. Lge. 8vo. Hf.-titles, errata lf., cont. cf., spines gt. with fleurons. (SG. Feb.16; 256) $130
– **The History of Scotland** ... 1759. *1st. Edn.* 2 vols. 4to. Advt. lf. in 1st. vol., cont. spr. cf., wormholes in 1 hinge of 2nd. vol.; Sir Ivar Colquhoun, of Luss copy. (CE. Mar.22; 257)   £130

ROBERTSON, William, Lexicographer
– **Sha'ar o Petah Leshon ha-Kodesh / A Gate or Door to the Holy Tongue.** L., 1653[-54]. 2 pts. in 1 vol. Pt. 1 comprises a general title [like Wing R1612 but without 'part I'] & 5 other prelims, & a title for pt. 1 [Wing R1611] & text, pt. 2 is [Wing R1618], qtr. vell., mod. bds. (SG. Feb.2; 109)
                                                                $550

ROBERTUS REMENSIS
– **Bellum Christianorum Principum ... Christophorus Colom de Prima Insularum ...** Basle, 1533. Fo. Sm. margin repair to 1 lf., a few light margin stains, margin annots. in 2 early hands, mod. old-style panel. cf. [Sabin 72023] (S. Dec.1; 292)
                                                       Baker. £450

ROBIDA, Albert
– **Les Vieilles Villes du Suisse.** Paris, 1879. *1st. Edn.* Slightly foxed, cont. hf. leath., very rubbed. (R. Apr.5; 3097)   DM 400
– – **Anr. Edn.** Paris, 1879. Lge. 4to. Linen. (G. Sep.15; 2316)   Sw.Frs. 550
See— **UZANNE, O. & Robida, Albert**

ROBILLARD DE BEAUPAIRE
– **Caen Illustré. Son Histoire, ses Monuments.** Ill.:– Paulin Carbonnier. Caen, 1896. *(400)*. Sm. fo. Hf. chagrin, corners, unc., wrap.; from Château des Noës liby. (HD. May 25; 71)   Frs. 1,100

ROBINS, Benjamin
– **Mathematical Tracts ... Containing his New Principles of Gunnery ...** L., 1761. *1st. Edn.* 2 vols. Hf.-titles, tear in 1 lf., some browning of end-papers, cont. cf., spine gt., some chipping, upr. cover of Vol. 2 bumped; Stanitz coll. (SPB. Apr.25; 381)
                                                                $550

ROBINS, Benjamin -*Contd.*

– – **Anr. Copy.** 2 vols. Blind-ruled cf.; Royal Institution crest on title-p. & handwritten pres. statement to verso. (CBA. Dec.10; 299) $170
– **Neue Grundsätze der Artillerie.** Trans.:– Leonhard Euler. Berlin, 1745. *1st. Edn. in German.* Slight browning, old tree cf., rebkd.; Stanitz coll. (SPB. Apr.25; 166) $425
– **New Principles of Gunnery.** L., 1742. *1st. Edn.* Errata, mod. hf. mor.; Stanitz coll. (SPB. Apr.25; 382) $550

ROBINSON, Charles N.
– **Old Naval Prints, their Artists & Engravers.** L., 1924. *(1500) numbered.* 4to. Orig. cl. (BBA. Apr.5; 154) *Thorp.* £55
– – **Anr. Copy.** Lge. 4to. 96 plts. (24 cold.), mntd., ex-liby., cl. (SG. May 3; 312) $175
– – **Anr. Copy.** Lge. 4to. 96 plts., gt.-lettered cl. (SG. Sep.22; 260) $150
– – **Anr. Edn.** L., 1924. *Ltd. Edn.* 4to. Some spotting, orig. cl., d.-w. (BBA. Jun.28; 302) *T. Parsons.* £85

ROBINSON, Edwin Arlington
– **The Children of the Night.** Boston, 1897. *1st. Edn., (500). (450) on Batchworth paper.* 12mo. Orig. pict. cl., hf. mor. s.-c.; Frederic Dannay copy. (CNY. Dec.16; 288) $250
– **The Torrent & the Night Before.** Gardiner, Maine, 1896. *1st. Edn. (312).* 12mo. Orig. ptd. wraps., lacks most of spine, cl. s.-c.; pres. copy from author (name of recipient eradicated), Frederic Dannay copy. (CNY. Dec.16; 287) $950

ROBINSON, I.C.
– **The Treasury of Ornamental Art.** Ill.:– F. Bedford. Day & Son, ca. 1870. Vell. gt., fore-e. pntg. (P. Sep.8; 288) £180

ROBINSON, John
– **Proof of a Conspiracy Against All the Religions & Governments of Europe, carried on in the Secret Meetings of Free Masons** ... Edinb., 1797. *1st. Edn.* Lf. of corrections. *(Bound with:)* – **Postscript to the Second Edition of Mr. Robinson's Proof of a Conspiracy** ... 1797. Together 2 works in 1 vol. Cont. cf., spine gt.; Sir Ivar Colquhoun, of Luss copy. (CE. Mar.22; 259) £140
– – **Anr. Edn.** L., 1798. *4th. Edn.* Cont. cf. (CBA. Dec.10; 381) £160

ROBINSON, Michael Strang
– **A Pageant of the Sea: The Macpherson Collection of Maritime Prints & Drawings.** L., 1950. *1st. Edn.* 4to. Gt.-decor. moiré cl. (SG. Sep.22; 261) $100

ROBINSON, Robert
– **Thomas Bewick, his Life & his Times.** Newcastle, 1887. 4to. Orig. cl. (BBA. Apr.5; 155) *Thorp.* £55

ROBINSON, Rev. Stanford F.H.
– **Celtic Illuminative Art.** Dublin, 1908. Fo. Orig. buckram gt. (GM. Dec.7; 328) £110
– – **Anr. Copy.** 4to. Orig. cl. gt. (BBA. Mar.7; 354) *Blackwell.* £55

ROBINSON, Vincent J.
– **Eastern Carpets.** Ill.:– E. Julia Robinson. 1893. 2nd. Series. Lge. fo. Orig. cl., rubbed. (TA. Dec.15; 314) £52

ROBINSON, W. (Ed.)
See— FLORA & SYLVA

ROBINSON, William Davis
– **Memoirs of the Mexican Revolution** ... L., 1821. *1st. Edn.* 2 vols. Lacks hf.-titles, hf. cf., gt. spines. (SG. Apr.5; 123) $300

ROBINSON, William Heath
– **Bill the Minder.** L., 1912. *1st. Edn.* Slight margin darkening, gt.-decor. cl., spine & edges darkened, light foxing to end-papers. (CBA. Aug.21; 558) $200

ROBINSON, William Heath (Ill.)
See— ANDERSEN, Hans Christian
See— KIPLING, Rudyard

ROBISON, R.
– **A Short Statement of the Case of R. Robison ... The Sentence of Court-Martial Against Him on the Charges of Lieut.-General Ralph Darling** ... 1834. Lacks title-p. or title-wrap., some discoloration. (KH. May 1; 598) *Aus.* $100

ROBSON, George Fennell
– **Picturesque Views of the English Cities.** Ed.:– J. Britton. L., 1828. Lge. 4to. Cont. leath. gt., blind-tooled, lightly bumped. (HK. Nov.8; 1043) DM 480
– **Scenery of the Grampian Mountains.** L., 1819. Fo. 41 aquatint plts., folding partly hand-cold. engraved map (creased), some ll. slightly soiled, cont. hf. cf., very worn, upr. cover from anr. book, loose. (BBA. Mar.21; 328) *Shapiro.* £160

ROBSON, Joseph
– **An Account of Six Years Residence in Hudson's Bay.** L., 1752. *1st. Edn.* 3 folding plts. (2 maps & a plan), advt. lf. before title, cont. cf. [Sabin 72259] (S. May 22; 334) *Traylen.* £380
– – **Anr. Copy.** 1st. map creased, folding engraved plt. of plans cropped at outer edge, lr. margins of a few ll. stained, old hf. mor. gt., worn, upr. jnt. brkn.; the Rt. Hon. Visc. Eccles copy. (CNY. Nov.18; 242) $550

ROBSON, Mary
[–] **The Ivy Wreath. By Mrs. Hughs.** Ill.:– John Sartain. Phila., [1849]. Lge. 12mo. Additional chromolitho. title-p. & 5 aquatint plts., orig. gt.-floral cl., corners nicked; from liby. of F.D. Roosevelt, inscr. by him, cont. inscr. to George Henry Leonard, Leonard bkplt. (SG. Mar.15; 70) $130

ROCA, Vicente
– **Hystoria en la qual se trata del Origen y Guerras que nan tenido los Turcos** ... Valencia, 1555. Fo. Vell. (DS. Nov.25; 2131) Pts. 80,000

ROCHE, Maria
– **The Children of the Abbey.** Ill.:– Lafitte. Paris, 1807. *New Edn.* 5 vols. Darkening, some mild staining, red mor., covers mildly rubbed, extremities rubbed, most corners showing; bkplts. of Chateau de Spy, end-papers foxed. (CBA. Oct.29; 710) $130

ROCHEFORT, Charles de & Poincy, Louis de
[–] **Histoire Naturelle et Morale des Iles Antilles de l'Amérique** ... Rotterdam, 1665. *2nd. Edn.* 4to. Additional engraved title, 3 folding plts., 46 text engrs. (Sabin counting only 44), slight tear to 1st. folding plt., Nn4-6 with tears affecting about 8 lines with slight loss, some slight spotting, cont. Dutch blind-stpd. vell. over bds.; the Rt. Hon. Visc. Eccles copy. [Sabin 72316] (CNY. Nov.18; 243) $750

ROCHEFORT, Henri
– **Fantasia.** Ill.:– Caran d'Ache, T. Bianco (aquas). Paris, 1888. *Orig. Edn. (20) on japan imperial sigd. by author & artist.* 2 orig. pen ills. & 2 orig. aquas., Jansenist pink mor., decor. spine, wrap & spine preserved, by Wendling, spine lightly faded. (HD. Dec.9; 179) Frs. 2,000

ROCHESTER, [John Wilmot], Earl of
– **Poems [& c.].** L., 1696. *4th. Edn.* Later cf., rebkd., rubbed; Ditton Park bkplt. [Wing R1757] (BBA. Nov.30; 203) *Finch.* £70

ROCHETTE, Desiré, Raoul dit & Engelmann
– **Lettres sur la Suisse.** Ill.:– Villeneuve. Paris, 1823-26. 2 vols. Fo. 14 litho. views., hf. leath. (G. Sep.15; 2316) *Sw.* Frs. 11,000

ROCHLING, C. & others
– **Die Königin Luise in 50 Bildern für Jung und Alt.** Berlin, 1896. Ob. 4to. Publisher's ill. bds. (HD. Jan.27; 84) Frs. 1,100

ROCKHAUS, F.A.
– **Allgemeine Deutsche Real-Encyklopädie für die gebilkdeten Stände. Conversations-Lexikon.** Leipzig, 1843-48. 15 vols. Foxed, cont. hf. leath. gt. decor. (BR. Apr.12; 963) DM 1,000

ROCKSTROH, Dr. Heinrich
– **Die Kunst mancherlei Gegenstände aus Papier zu formen. Eine bereits anerkannte nützliche und angenehme Beschäftigung für junge Leute.** Leipzig,

1810. *1st. Edn.* 4to. 20 engraved plts. (ll partly hand-cold.), 19th. C. cl.-bkd. bds.; van Veen coll. (S. Feb.28; 165) £240

ROCQUE, John
– **An Exact Survey of the Cities of London & Westminster** ... [1746]. Fo. Engraved vig. title in Engl. & Fr., map of L. on 16 double-p. engraved sheets, orig. hand-colouring of roads, borders, water, cartouches, etc., cont. hf. cf., marb. bds., rubbed, spine chipped, marb. paper partly torn; subscriber's copy of the Earl of Cardigan. (LC. Jul.5; 225) £640
– – **Anr. Copy.** Fo. 16 double-p. engraved maps, margins lightly browned, later mor.-bkd. cl. (CSK. Nov.4; 11) £420
– **A Topographical Survey of the County of Berks.** L., 1761. Fo. 18 engraved mapsheets, most double-p., hand-cold. in outl., ptd. index, lacks general index map, 1 or 2 sheets torn & reprd. with tape, some creases & stains, cont. bds., defect. (S. Jun.25; 352) £150

RODENBACH, Georges
– **Bruges-la-morte.** [1892]. *Orig. Edn.* No bdg. stated; dedication to Alfred Stevens. *(With:)* – **Le Règne du Silence.** 1891. *Orig. Edn.* No bdg. stated. (HD. May 11; 106) Frs. 2,600

RODENWALDT, Gerhart
– **Die Akropolis.** Ill.:– after Walter Hege. Berlin, 1930. *1st. Edn.* 4to. Partially foxed, gt.-pict. cl., spine age-darkened, d.-w. & s.-c. defect. (SG. May 10; 62) $100

RODER, Kurt & Oppenheim, M.
– **Das Höchste Porzellan auf d. Jahrtausend-Ausstellung in Mainz. 1925.** Mainz, 1930. Lge. 4to. Orig. linen. (HK. Nov.12; 4712) DM 1,100

RODES, N.F.B. de
[–] **Herra Georg Psalmanazaara.** Trans.:– Philipp Georg Hübner. Frankfurt & Leipzig, 1716. *1st. German Edn.* Slightly browned or foxed thro.-out, cont. vell., spine slightly slit, clasps. (GB. Nov.3; 82) DM 900

RODIGAS, Em.
See— LINDEN, J. & Lucian & others

RODIN, Auguste
– **L'Art.** Ed.:– Paul Gsell. 1911. *Orig. Edn.* On japon imperial, sewed, unc.; Rodin's visiting card & c. (HD. Apr.13; 173) Frs. 2,000

RODING, Johann Heinrich
– **Allgemeines Wörterbuch der Marine.** Hamburg, n.d. Vols. 2-4 only (of 4). 4to. 115 engraved plts., cont. cf., rubbed. (CSK. Dec.2; 68) £55

RODRIGO, Francisco Javier G.
– **Historia Verdadera de la Inquisición.** Madrid, 1876. 3 vols. in 1. 4to. Vell., orig. wraps. (DS. Dec.16; 2500) Pts. 30,000

RODRIGO, N.
– **Reglas para torear a Caballo.** Madrid, 1894. *(25).* Cf. (DS. Mar.23; 2250) Pts. 36,000

RODRIGUES, Eugène Erastène Ramiro
– **Catalogue Descriptif et Analytique de l'Oeuvre gravé de Felicien Rops.** Paris, 1887. 2 vols., including 'Supplément au Catalogue', Paris, 1895. 4to. Hf. leath. (SPB. Nov.30; 68) $250
– **L'Oeuvre Lithographié de Félicien Rops.** Paris, 1891. 4to. Dedication copy, lr. margin slightly stained, cont. hf. leath., orig. wraps. bnd. in *(With:)* – **Supplement au Catalogue de l'oeuvre gravé de Félicien Rops.** 1895. 4to. *(500) numbered on vell.,* slight stain in lr. margin at beginning & end, cont. hf. leath., with anr. orig. etching. (R. Apr.3; 900) DM 620

RODRIGUEZ, A., Dramatist
[–] **Colecció Generál de los Trages que en la Actualidád se usan en España: Principiada en el Año 1801.** Madrid, ca. 1801. 87 (of 112) hand-cold. engraved costume plts., lacks 76 & all after 88, captions added in Engl. in cont. hand, lr. corners of title & a few plts. reprd. without loss of engraved surface, later cl. (S. May 21; 243) *Faupel.* £380

RODRIGUEZ, F.
- Relación ... de dos Victorias que el Governador de Larache tuvo ... Sevilla, 1617. Fo. Bds. (DS. Apr.27; 2582) Pts. 35,000

RODRIGUEZ DE MONFORTE, P.
- Descripción de las Honras qve se hicieron a la Catholica Magd. de D. Phelippe Quarto Rey de las Españas ... Madrid, 1666. *1st. Edn.* 4to. 4 copper engrs. with pasted tears, 3 with sm. margin tears, engraved title cut close, old name on verso, some slight browning or soiling, newer vell. (H. May 22; 649) DM 1,000

RODRIGUEZ Y FERNANDEZ, Idelfonso
- Historia de Medina del Campo. Madrid, 1903-04. 2 pts. in 1 vol. 4to. Linen. (DS. Feb.24; 2229) Pts. 35,000

ROE, Frederick Gordon
- Sea Painters of Britain. Leigh-on-Sea, 1947-48. *(500).* 2 vols. 4to. Orig. cl. (S. Apr.30; 85) *Mackinnon.* £60

ROEMER, Johann Jakob
- Genera Insectorum Linnaei et Fabricii Iconibus illustrata. Ill.:– J.R. Schellenberg. Winterthur, 1789. 4to. Ptd. title with hand-cold. engraved vig., 37 engraved plts., all but 1 hand-cold., title & text slightly spotted, old hf. cf. gt., spine & corners slightly worn. (CNY. May 18; 149) $600

ROESBRUGGE, V.M. van
- Veelderhande Schrituerlijcke Liedekens ghecompneert uyt den Ouden ende Nieuwen Testamente. Leyden, 1609. *3rd. Edn.* (*Bound with:*) EXEMPLEN DES GHELOOFS Leyden, 1609. Together 2 works in 1 vol. Sm. 8vo. Stp. erased from titles, some minor margin stains, 18th. C. hf. roan. (VS. Dec.9; 1121) Fls. 1,000

ROESSLIN, Eucharius
[–] Kreutterbuch. Frankfurt, 1542. Sm. fo. Lacks 1st. 6 ll. & 4 others, browned & stained, repairs thro.-out, many old MS. annots., 19th. C. hf. linen. (HK. Nov.8; 705) DM 1,050

ROETHEL, Hans Konrad
- Kandinsky. Das Graphische Werk. [Köln, 1970]. *Ltd. numbered Iss.* 4to. Orig. linen, wraps., s.-c., slightly defect. (HT. May 9; 1034) DM 640

ROETHKE, Theodore
- Open House. N.Y., 1941. *1st. Edn.* Orig. cl., d.-w.; pres. copy from author to Viola Surferson, Frederic Dannay copy. (CNY. Dec.16; 290) $480

ROETHLISBERGER, Marcel
- Claude Lorraine, the Drawings. Berkeley & Los Angeles, 1968. 2 vols. 4to. Orig. cl. (BBA. Apr.5; 114) *Leicester Art Books.* £75
- - **Anr. Copy.** 2 vols. 4to. Orig. cl. (S. Apr.30; 86) *Hetherington.* £60
- - **Anr. Copy.** 4to. Orig. linen. (H. Nov.23; 171) DM 520
- - **Anr. Copy.** 2 vols. Lge. 4to. Orig. linen. (HT. May 9; 1082) DM 400

ROFFERIO, Angelo
- Antica e Nuova Grecia. Scene Elleniche. Torino, 1844-46. 2 vols. 4to. Some staining, cont. hf. leath., slightly loose. (SI. Dec.15; 98) Lire 380,000

ROGER, père & fils
- Le Champ du Repos ou le Cimetière Mont-Louis, dit du Père Delachaise. Paris, Sept. 1816. *Orig. Edn.* 2 vols. Port., folding plan, 38 folding engraved plts., cont. paper bds., unc. (HD. Mar.19; 125) Frs. 1,600

ROGER-MARX, Claude
- Bonnard Lithographe. Paris, 1952. Fo. Catalogue, orig. wraps., case. (SPB. Nov.30; 15) $130
- - **Anr. Edn.** Monte-Carlo, 1952. 4to. 98 lithos. in col. & black, sewed, pict. wrap., box. (HD. Dec.16; 77) Frs. 1,350
- Les Lithographies de Renoir. Monte Carlo, [1951]. *(3000).* 4to. Three-qtr. cl. & marb. bds., covers lightly rubbed, orig. wraps. bnd. in. (CBA. Jan.29; 389) $150
- L'Oeuvre Gravé de Dunoyer de Segonzac. Paris, 1937. *(90) on vélin d'Arches (text)* & *Hollande (engrs.).* 4to. 3 orig. paraphed etchings by Dunoyer

de Segonzac, leaves, publisher's portfo. (HD. May 16; 82) Frs. 1,700
- L'Oeuvre Gravé de Vuillard. Ill.:– Mourlot Frères (col.-ptd. lithos.). Monte Carlo, [1948]. *(2500) numbered.* 4to. 67 plts., col. pict. wraps., some chipping. (SG. Aug.25; 399) $100
- Simili. Ill.:– Pierre Bonnard. Paris, 1930. *(310) numbered.* Sm. 4to. Orig. wraps., unc. & unopened. (S. Nov.21; 3) *Makiya.* £160
- - **Anr. Edn.** Ill.:– Pierre Bonnard. 1930. *Orig. Edn. 1st. Printing of ills. (30) on holland,* with *suite of engrs. on japan.* Sm. 4to. 7 orig. dry-points, sewed. (HD. Apr.13; 174) Frs. 2,200
- - **Anr. Edn.** Ill.:– Pierre Bonnard. Paris, [1930]. *(310), (280) numbered on Vélin Lafuma.* Sm. 4to. Orig. sewed, unc. (GB. May 5; 2221) DM 800

ROGER-MILES, Léon
- Catalogue des Tableaux de Rosa Bonheur. Paris, 1900. 1st. vol. Fo. In Fr. & Engl., cl., disbnd. (SG. Aug.25; 60) $300

ROGERS, A.N.
- Communication Relative to the Location of the U.P.R.R. Across the Rocky Mountains through Colorado Territory. Central City, 1867. *1st. Edn.* Orig. ptd. wraps., qtr. mor. s.-c. (LH. Apr.15; 362) $300

ROGERS, Fairman
- A Manual of Coaching. L., 1900. *Ltd. Edn.* Frontis., plts., orig. cl. gt. (P. May 17; 281) *Quaritch.* £190

ROGERS, John
- A Dissertation on the Knowledge of the Ancients in Astronomy & Optical Instruments. L., 1755. *1st. Edn.* Cont. pol. cf., rebkd. & relined. (SG. Oct.6; 314) $250

ROGERS, Maj. Robert
- A Concise Account of North America. L., 1765. *1st. Edn.* Cont. cf. [Sabin 72723] (S. May 22; 335) *Nebenzahl.* £380
- - **Anr. Copy.** Cont. cf., slight wear, bkplt. in cover. (SG. Nov.3; 175) $750
- - **Anr. Copy.** Cont. cf., rebkd., corners slightly worn; the Rt. Hon. Visc. Eccles copy. [Sabin 72723] (CNY. Nov.18; 244) $550
- Journals of ... Containing An Account of the Several Excursions he Made ... during the late War. L., priv. ptd., 1765. *1st. Edn.* Hf.-title, 2 advt. ll. at end, cont. cf., spine ends chipped; the Rt. Hon. Visc. Eccles copy. [Sabin 72725] (CNY. Nov.18; 245) $800
- - **Anr. Copy.** Some browning, cont. cf., worn, covers detchd.; bkplt. of James Veitch, Lord Eliock. [Sabin 72725] (SPB. Dec.13; 465) $400

ROGERS, Samuel
- Italy. Ill.:– Finden, Goodall, Allen & others. L., 1838. 4to. L.P., wide margin, slightly foxed, heavier in places, cont. mor., gt. cover vig., slightly bumped & worn, several scratches. (H. Nov.23; 744) DM 400
- The Pleasures of Memory. L., 1810. 12mo. Cont. mor. gt., double fore-e. pntg. (SG. Nov.3; 176) $700

ROGERS, Samuel
- Poems. 1838. (*With:*) - Italy, a Poem. 1838. Together 2 vols. 4to. Some spotting, later mor. gt. by Hayday. (TA. Sep.15; 340) £60
- The Poetical Works. Ill.:– after Turner & Stothard. L., 1869. *New Edn.* Sm. 4to. Some spotting, cont. red mor. gt., fore-e. pntg. (S. Dec.20; 837) *Cavendish.* £90

ROGERS, Capt. Woodes
- A Cruising Voyage Round the World. 1712. *[1st. Edn.].* 1 map lightly soiled pasted at fold, later cf., lightly rubbed, rebkd. (CSK. Jul.6; 55) £130
- - **Anr. Copy.** Browning & spotting, cont. cf., spine worn. [Sabin 72753] (SPB. Dec.13; 466) $500
- - **Anr. Edn.** 1718. *2nd. Edn.* Appendix, some mild discoloration, several liby. stps., mod. hf. mor. [Sabin 72754] (KH. May 1; 599) Aus. $500
- - **Anr. Edn.** L., 1726. 5 folding engraved maps, 2 folding plts., cont. cf., rebkd. (S. May 22; 486) *Cavendish.* £360

ROGISSART, Le Sieur de & Havard, Abbé
- Les Délices de l'Italie. Paris, 1707. *[2nd. Edn.].* 4 vols. 12mo. Cont. cf. gt. (SG. Oct.27; 167) $140
- - **Anr. Copy.** 4 vols. 12mo. 144 plts., many folding, lacks paper from 2 plts., sm. margin stains in Vol. II, marb. hf. cf. (HD. Mar.19; 140) Frs. 3,700
- - **Anr. Edn.** Amst., 1743. 6 vols. 12mo. Cont. marb. cf., spines decor., last 2 vols. not quite unif.; from Château des Noës liby. (HD. May 25; 72) Frs. 3,000

ROH, Fr. & Techichold, J.
- Foto-Auge, Oeil et Photo. Photo-eye. Ill.:– Baumeister, Max Ernst, G. Grosz, & others. Stuttgart, 1929. *Orig. Edn.* 4to. Title-lf. lightly soiled, orig. pict. wraps., Lissitzky's self-port. on upr. wrap. (GB. Nov.5; 2479) DM 700
- - **Anr. Edn.** Ill.:– M. Ernst, A. Feininger, J. Heartfield, Hannah Höch, L. Moholy-Nagy, Man Ray & others. Stuttgart, [1929]. 4to. Tri-lingual text, orig. bds., photo montage on upr. cover by El Lissitzky, slightly spotted. (H. Nov.24; 1925) DM 820

ROHAN, Henri, Duc de
- Mémoires. N.p., 1644. *Orig. Edn.* 2 pts. in 1 vol. Sm. 12mo. Cont. vell.; from liby. of Charles de Baschi, Marquis d'Aubais. (HD. Nov.9; 156) Frs. 1,750
- A Treatise of the Interest of the Princes & States of Christendome. Paris, 1640. *1st. Edn.* No licence-lf., a few MS. notes. [STC 21253] (*Bound with:*) BUCKINGHAM, G. Williams, Duke of – His Speech to the King in Parliament April 4.1628. L., 1641. *1st. Edn.* [Wing B5334] (*Bound with:*) LEICESTER, R. Dudley, Earl of – Leycesters Common-wealth. L., 1641. *1st. Edn.?* Lacks final blank? [Wing L968] Together 3 works in 1 vol. 4to. Slight browning, cont. spr. cf. (S. Oct.11; 586) *Coupe.* £70

ROHAULT DE FLEURY, Georges
- La Toscane au Moyen Age. Paris, 1873. 2 vols. Tall fo. Approx. 140 engraved plts., text engrs., ex-liby., cont. red hf. mor., spines gt. (SG. May 3; 317) $175

ROHBOCK, Ludwig & Cooke, W.J.
- Düsseldorf dargestellt in Malerischen Original-Unsichtten. Darmstadt, 1856 [but ca. 1960]. *Facs. (500).* 7 cold. mntd. plts. & text in folder, s.-c. (S. Apr.9; 53) *Nolan.* £50

ROHDE, Eleanour Sinclair
- The Old English Herbals. 1922. Mod. hf. mor. gt. (CSK. May 18; 180) £50

ROHIFS, G.
- Quer durch Afrika. Leipzig, 1874-75. Cont. linen. (R. Oct.13, 2927) DM 850

ROHLEDER, Wittich
- Tage. Sieben Gedichte. Ill.:– K. Fussmann. Karlsruhe, 1980. *(90) numbered.* 4to. 8 orig. lithos., including 2 monogrammed, orig. bds. & s.-c.; printer's mark sigd. by author & artist. (GB. Nov.5; 2498) DM 500

ROHRBACH, P.
- Dernburg und die Südwestafrikaner. Berlin, 1911. Wraps., unopened. (VA. Oct.28; 569) R 170

ROINE, Jules Edouard
- The Lincoln Centennial Medal. Presenting the Medal of Abraham Lincoln ... N.Y. & L., 1908. *Unnumbered Edn., with the bronze medal.* Orig. pict. cl. gt. (LH. Apr.15; 364) $170

ROJAS, Fernando de
- La Celestina. Veneccia, 1553. Lacks glossary, vell. (DS. Mar.23; 2049) Pts. 80,000

ROLAND LE VIRLOY, M.C.F.
- Dictionnaire d'Architecture. Paris, 1770. 3 vols. in 4. 4to. 101 plts., text in Fr., Latin, Italian, Spanish, Engl. & German, marb. cf., spine decor. (LM. Mar.3; 7) B.Frs. 14,000

ROLANDO, Guzman
- The Modern Art of Fencing. L., 1822. Hand-cold. frontis., 22 plts., ink notes on hf.-title, some soiling, 1 tissue guard with pencil tracings, contents detchd. from covers, cont. cf. gt. (CBA. Dec.10; 384) $160

ROLEVINCK, Werner
- **Fasciculus Temporum.** Strassburg, 1488. Fo. Some old MS. marginalia & owners entries, later hf. vell., slightly rubbed. [HC 6937; G. R-274] (D. Nov.23; 139) DM 4,000

ROLFE, Frederick W.S. 'Baron Corvo'
- **Chronicles of the House of Borgia.** L., 1901. *1st. Edn.* Cl. (LH. Sep.25; 518) $140

ROLFE, R.A.
See— LINDEN, J. & Lucian & others.

ROLFINCIUS, Guernerus
- **Chimia in Artis Formam Redacta.** Jena, 1662. *1st. Edn.* 4to. Vell., 2 clasps; Dr. Walter Pagel copy. (S. Feb.7; 335) *Quaritch.* £280

ROLLAND, Leon
- **Atlas des Champignons de France, Suisse et Belgique.** [1910, 1906]. Text vol. & atlas. Lge. 8vo. Hf. chagrin, spine raised bands (browned). (HD. Jul.6; 74) Frs. 1,250

ROLLAND sieur du PLESSIS, N.
- [–] **Remontrances très Humbles au Roy de France et de Pologne.** Henry Troisièerze de ce Nom ... N.p., 1588. *Orig. Edn.* Janseniot red mor., inner dentelles s.-c., by Hardy, spine slightly faded. (HD. Dec.9; 79) Frs. 1,000

ROLLIN, Charles
- **The Ancient History of the Egyptians, Carthaginians** ... 1738-40. *2nd. Edn.* 10 vols. Cont. cf.; Sir Ivar Colquhoun, of Luss copy. (CE. Mar.22; 261) £150
- **Histoire Ancienne des Egyptiens, des Carthaginois, des Assyriens, des Babyloniens, des Mèdes et des Perses, des Macédonieans, des Grecs.** Ill.:– after Coypel (frontis.), Le Bas. Paris, 1740. 6 vols. 4to. Cont. cf., decor. spines, title labels renewed, turn-ins. restored. (HD. Sep.22; 330) Frs. 2,600
- **Histoire Romaine, depuis la Fondation de Rome jusqu'à la Bataille d'Actium.** Paris, 1752. 8 vols. 4to. Cont. marb. cf., decor. spines. (HD. Sep.22; 331) Frs. 1,400
- **The History of the Arts & Sciences of the Antients.** L., 1737-39. *1st. Edn. in Engl.* 4 vols. 52 folding copper engrs., 2 reprd. with adjacent stains, mod. cl., blind-stps. of Cedric Gibbons. (CBN. Dec.10, 385) $110
- **The Method of Teaching & Studying the Belles Lettres.** L., 1769. *6th. Edn.* 3 vols. Cont. cf., spines gt., rubbed. (RO. Oct.18; 121) $140

ROLLIN, Charles & others
- **The Roman History.** 1739-50. 16 vols. Non-unif. cont. cf., spines gt.; Sir Ivar Colquhoun, of Luss copy. (CE. Mar.22; 260) £150

ROLT, John
- **On Moral Command.** 1836. Cont. crimson mor., emblematically gt., fore-e. pntg. of military figures with view of RMA Woolwich in cols.; pres. copy, inscr. to Lord Melbourne. (BBA. Oct.27; 60) *Cavendish.* £140

ROMAINS, Jules
- **Mort de Quelqu'un.** Ill.:– Maurice Asselin. Paris, 1927. *Ltd. Edn.* Sm. 4to. Orig. wraps., upr. cover warped, s.-c.; pres. copy inscr. to Vicomte Carlow. (BBA. Jun.14; 183) *Diluia.* £60

ROMAN, Adriaen
- [–] **Samen-spraeck, tusschen Waermondt & Gaergoedt, nopende de Opkomste en Ondergangh v. Flora.** Haerlem, 1637. (*Bound with:*) - **Tweede Samenspraeck.** Haerlem, 1637. (*Bound with:*) - **Register van de Prijsen der Bloemen.** Haerlem, 1637. Together 3 works in 1 vol. Sm. 4to. Few light stains, mod. hf. cf. (VG. Nov.30; 651) Fls. 900

ROMAN, Jeronimo
- **Cronica de la Orden de los Ermitanos del Gloriosos Padre Sanco Augustin** ... Salamanca, 1569. Fo. Owners' sigs. & near-cont. annots. thro-out, some stains & tears, lacks leaf *6 (table of authors), 17th. C. panel. sheep, stained, upr. cover stitched on, spine worn. (SPB. Dec.13; 729) $125

ROMAN DE RENARD
Text:– Maurice Genevoix. Ill.:– Paul Jouve. 1958. *(198). (45) on Rives with suite & double plt. sigd.*

by *M. Genevoix, P. Jouve & J. Beltrand.* 2 vols. 4to. Leaves, box. (HD. May 4; 415) Frs. 1,400

ROMANA, Marqués de la
- **Representación del Excmo. Sr** ... a la Suprema Junta Central. Sevilla, 1809. Fo. Sewed. (DS. Apr.27; 2586) Pts. 30,000

ROME
- **Antiquae Urbis Splendor.** Ill.:– J. Lauri. Rome, 1612 [1641]. Ob. fo. 167 soft-point plts., cont. vell., gt. decor. (HD. Dec.1; 84) Frs. 1,500
- **Les Merveilles et Antiquités de la Ville de Rome.** Liége, 1631. Approbation lf., mod. hf. roan, worn. (LM. Mar.3; 160) B. Frs. 10,000
- **Nuova Collezione di Vedute di Roma, Antiche e Moderne** ... Roma, [1820?]. Album, frontis., 1 folding map & 50 engrs., loose. (CR. Jun.6; 237) Lire 320,000
- **Nuova Raccolta delle piu Belle Vedute di Roma.** 1761. Ob. 4to. 42 engraved views, hf. cf. (P. Oct.20; 10) £90
- **Nuova Raccolta di Cento Principali Vedute Antiche e Moderne dell'alma Città' di Roma e delle sue Vicinanze.** Rome, 1796. Ob. 4to. Vig. title, 100 etched plts., some margin foxing, 2 plts. soiled & creased, vell.-bkd. bds. (SG. Jan.26; 209) $225
- **Nuova Raccolta di 25 Vedute Antiche e Moderne di Roma** ... Ill.:– after G.B. Piranesi, F. Morelli, G.B. Cipriani, & others. [Rome], ca. 1800. Ob. 4to. Engraved title, 24 views, cont. paper wraps., worn. (C. Mar.14; 126) *Bifolco.* £190
- **Raccolta di No. 40 Vedute Antiche e Moderne della Citta di Roma.** Rome, 1860. Ob. fo. Engraved title & 40 engraved plts., cl., worn. (BS. Jun.27-28) £190
- **Raccolta di No. 60 Vedute e Antiche, e Moderne della Citta di Roma e sue Vicinanze.** Rome, n.d. Engraved title, 60 engraved plts., old title soiling, minimal foxing, especially in margin, later bd. wraps. (V. Sep.29; 122) DM 400
- **Raccolta di Vedute Antiche e Moderne della Citta di Roma.** Ill.:– S. Rossi. F. Morel, A. Parboni & others. Rome, [1816]. Ob. fo. Some slight foxing, cont. sewed. (GB. May 3; 125) DM 600
- **Raccolta di ... Veduti si antiche che moderne della Citta di Roma.** Rome, ca. 1810. Ob. 4to. 320 views on 80 plts., cont. hf. cf., marb. sides, slightly worn. (BBA. Jun.14; 318) *Erlini.* £200
- **Raccolta 320 Ansichten des Alten und Neuen Rom in Kupfer.** Rome, Ca. 1800. Ob. 4to. Bds. (G. Sep.15; 2305) Sw. Frs. 380
- **Roma Antica e Moderna o sia Nuova Descrizione** ... Roma, 1765. 3 vols. 12mo. Parch. (SM. Mar.7; 2045) Frs. 1,900
- **Rome dans sa Grandeur.** Paris, 1870. 3 vols. Fo. Bdg. not stated. (HD. Oct.14; 135) Frs. 6,350
- **Select Collection of Views & Ruins in Rome & its Vicinity** ... 1798. 4to. Sepia aquatint frontis., 62 plts., orig. bds., mor. backstrip, some wear, unc. (TA. Sep.15; 69) £95
- – – **Anr. Edn.** N.d. 4to. 62 aquatint plts. (dtd. 1796-98), cont. hf. cf. (SKC. May 4; 1819) £130

ROMIER, Lucien
- **Les Origines Politiques des Guerres de Religion.** Paris, 1913-14. 2 vols. Hf. chagrin, spines faded. (HD. Feb.22; 198) Frs. 1,000

ROMME, Nic. Ch.
- **L'Art de la Marine.** La Rochelle, 1787. 4to. Cont. marb. cf., spine reprd. (HD. Mar.9; 122) Frs. 1,300
- **L'Art de la Voilure.** [Paris], 1781. Fo. Old hf. roan. (HD. Mar.9; 121) Frs. 1,450
- **Description de l'Art de la Mâture.** [Paris], 1778. Fo. Old hf. roan. (HD. Mar.9; 120) Frs. 1,100
See— CHAPMAN, Frederic - ROMME, Nic. Ch.

RONALDS, Alfred
- **Companion to Alfred Ronalds' fly Fisher's Entomology.** [Bg'ham., after 1862]. 47 artificial flies in vell. pockets with accompanying descriptions, 4 vell. envelopes at end for inserting additional specimens, orig. leath. wallet with strap, slightly worn. (S. Oct.4; 51) *Maggs.* £420
- – – **Anr. Edn.** L., ca. 1900. 12mo. Interleaved thro-out (as iss.?) with vell. stock-book ll. & with white felt bifolium at centre, about 100 flies are inserted in these ll., burlap folding-case, w.a.f. (SG. Mar.15; 287) $425

- **The Fly-Fisher's Entomology.** L., 1836. *1st. Edn.* 19 hand-cold. plts., 2 ll. carelessly opened, slight browning & spotting, orig. cl., stained, rebkd.; bkplt. of Bibliotheca Piscatoria Lynnians. (S. Oct.4; 50) *Angle.* £120
- – – **Anr. Edn.** 1877. *8th. Edn.* 20 hand-cold. plts., publisher's catalogue bnd. in at end, orig. cl., rubbed. (TA. May 17; 291) £65
- – – **Anr. Edn.** L., 1913. *(270) numbered.* 2 vols. 4to. Frontis., 20 plts., 48 artificial flies on sunken mounts, mor. gt., spines tooled with fishes onlaid in mor., slightly discold. (S. Oct.4; 52) *Joseph.* £650
- – – **Anr. Edn.** L'pool., 1913. *De Luxe 11th. Edn. [250].* 2 vols. 4to. 21 plts., 14 hand-cold., 48 artificial flies mntd., orig. mor.-bkd. cl. (BBA. Oct.27; 322) *Joseph.* £380

RONALDS, Hugh
- **Pyrus Malus Brentfordiensis.** Ill.:– Hullmandel after E. Ronalds. L., 1831. 4to. 42 hand-cold. litho. plts., hf. mor., spine gt. (C. Nov.16; 288) *Grahame.* £950
- – – **Anr. Copy.** 4to. 42 col. plts., some foxing, hf. mor. gt., slightly rubbed. (P. Nov.24; 258) *Traylen.* £680

RONGEAT, A.
- **An Amusing & Instructive Geography.** N.d. 12mo. 10 litho. cards ptd. with 20 hand-cold. maps & views. lightly soiled, unbnd. as iss. in orig. s.-c., rubbed. (CSK. Jun.15; 202) £160

RONSARD, Pierre de
- **Les Amours.** Ill.:– Emile Bernard. Paris, 1915. *(325) numbered.* 4to. 16 etched plts., unsewn in orig. wraps., unc. & unopened, etchings separately mntd. & in s.-c. (S. Nov.21; 1) *Rota.* £180
- **Choix de Sonnets.** Ill.:– E. Pissarro after L. Pissarro. L., Eragny Pr., 1902. *(226).* Flowered bds., upr. end of spine chipped. (SG. Aug.4; 108) $150
- **Discours de Misères de ce Temps.** Ill.:– Decaris. Paris, 1930. 4to. Recovered vell. by Lavaux, wrap., s.-c. (HD. Jun.13; 95) Frs. 3,100
- **Florilège des Amours.** Ill.:– Mourlot Frères after Henri Matisse. Paris, 1948. *(320) on Arches wove paper, sigd. by artist & publisher. (20) numbered with extra suite of 12 initialled 'pierres refusées' lithos. on japon imperial.* Fo. Title & frontis. offset (as usual), some minimal offsetting thro-out, 'irradiante classique' bdg. of rose-red lev. mor. by Paul Bonet, sigd. on upr. turn-in, dtd. '1966' on lr. turn-in, covers, elab. decor. & gt.-lettered, lr. cover similarly gt. in reverse without lettering, thin untooled strip at hinges, designs cross smooth spine turn-ins ivory cf. begin, doubls. & free end-pp. of 'cardinal rouge', end-pp. lightly framed in ivory cf., partly unc., orig. wraps. preserved, matching rose-red hf. mor. chemise with gt.-lettered backstrip, backstrip discold., matching mor.-edged s.-c. (CNY. May 18; 174) $42,000
- **Les Oeuvres** ... Paris, 1610. *2nd. Coll. Edn.* 11 pts. in 5 vols. 12mo. A few minor brown spots, lev. mor. gt. by M. Duru; sig. of Charles Augustin Sainte-Beuve, 9 sm. slips of paper with his notes laid in, Thomas B. Stevenson copy. (CNY. May 18; 166) $850
- – – **Anr. Edn.** 1623. 2 vols. Fo. Old hf. roan. (HD. Jun.29; 177) Frs. 3,800
- **Les Poèmes.** Ill.:– E. Othon Friesz. Paris & Lausanne, 1934. *(99). (20) numbered & sigd. by artist & publisher.* 2 vols. 4to. Extra suite of plts. in various states sigd. by artist & publishers, loose as iss. in orig. wraps., vell.-bkd. bds., s.-c. brkn. (BBA. Jun.14; 210) *Diluia.* £350

RONSE, Alfred & Raison, Theo
- **Fermes-Types et Constructions Rurales en West-Flandres.** Bruges, 1918. 2 vols. Lge. 4to. Many cold. plts. mntd. on art paper, text ills., many mntd., ex-liby., pict. wraps., unc. (SG. May 3; 318) $120
- – – **Anr. Copy.** 2 vols. Lge. 4to. Owner's stps., sewed. (LM. Oct.22; 139) B. Frs. 13,000

RÖNTGEN, Wilhelm Conrad
- **Eine Neue Art von Strahlen.** Würzburg, 1896. *1st. Edn.* Orig. wraps., box. (R. Oct.12; 1711) DM 2,000

ROOD KAPJE
s'Gravenhage, ca. 1860. Moving picture book, 8 ills. hand-cold., sections lifting to form 3-dimensional

view, 2 tapes brkn., orig. cl.-bkd. pict. bds.; van Veen coll. (S. Feb.28; 286) £130

ROORDA-SMIT, J.A.
– De Zoeloe-Kaffers. N.p., [1878?]. Sm. 8vo. Sm. hole in middle of last lf., wraps., frayed, part of lr. wrap. missing, bottom right hand corners frayed. (VA. Jan.27; 396) R. 180

ROOSES, Max
– Le Musée Plantin Moretus, contenant la Vie et l'Oeuvre de Christophe Plantin. 1914. *Ltd. Edn.* Cont. hf. mor., worn. (BBA. May 23; 255) *Vine.* £90
– L'Oeuvre de P.P. Rubens. Ill.:– Joes Maes. Anvers, 1886-92. 5 vols. Lge. 4to. Hf. chagrin, corners. (LM. Mar.3; 93) B. Frs. 31,000

ROOSEVELT, Franklin D.
– D-Day Prayer from the White House, June 6, 1944, Here Printed for his Friends at Christmastide 1944. [Wash., 1944]. *1st. Edn. (100) numbered.* 4to. Qtr. vell., marb. bds., spine slightly soiled on extremities, glassine d.-w. frayed; from liby. of F.D. Roosevelt, inscr. (as President) 'For Franklin Jr. & Ethel … '. (SG. Mar.15; 73) $3,200
– Inaugural Addresses. Wash., 1943. *1st. Edn. (100) numbered.* 4to. Qtr. vell., marb. bds., glassine d.-w., s.-c.; from liby. of F.D. Roosevelt, inscr. (as President) 'For Franklin & Ethel … '. (SG. Mar.15; 74) $2,200
– Whither Bound?. Boston, 1926. *1st. Edn.* Lge. 8vo. L.P., blind pict. cl.; from liby. of F.D. Roosevelt, inscr. 'For my son & namesake, Franklin D. Roosevelt, Jr., from his affectionate Father, Franklin D. Roosevelt Senior'; on front free end-paper & sigd. by author on title-p. (SG. Mar.15; 72) $3,000

ROOSEVELT, Franklin D. & Churchill, Sir Winston Leonard Spencer
– Addresses. Wash., 1942. *1st. Edn. (100) numbered.* 4to. Qtr. vell., marb. bds., glassine d.-w. frayed over spine, s.-c.; from liby. of F.D. Roosevelt, inscr. by him (as President) 'For Franklin Jr. & Ethel … '. (SG. Mar.15; 75) $3,400
– Wartime Correspondence. Intro. & Explanatory Notes:– Myron C. Taylor. N.Y., 1947. *1st. Edn.* Sm. 4to. Gt.-ornamental vell., glassine d.-w., vell. s.-c., spine ends darkened, d.-w. frayed over spine; from liby. of F.D. Roosevelt, inscr. 'To Mr. & Mrs. Franklin D. Roosevelt (Junior) … Myron C. Taylor, … '. (SG. Mar.15; 76) $375

ROOSEVELT, Robert B.
– Five Acres Too Much: a Truthful Elucidation of the Attractions of the Country. Ill.:– [Thomas Worth]. N.Y., 1869. *1st. Edn.* Sm. 8vo. Orig. cl., corners frayed; long sigd. pres. inscr. to Mr. Young from author; from liby. of F.D. Roosevelt, inscr. by him. (SG. Mar.15; 77) $175

ROOSEVELT, Theodore
– Complete Writings. Phila., 1902-03. *'Author's Edn.'. (26) numbered.* 22 vols. Engraved plts. in 2 forms, mntd. & unmntd., red mor., gt. borders, presidential eagle corner ornaments, spines in 6 compartments, ornament in 4 compartments, turnins gt., mor. gt. doubls. with author's monog. as gt. ornaments on decor. gt. ground, silk markers. (CNY. Dec.17; 596) $1,300
– – **Anr. Edn.** Phila., 1903. *Author's/Uniform Edn. (26).* 22 vols. Plts. in 2 states, elab. red mor. gt., gt. dentelles & mor. gt. doubls. (SPB. May 27; 750) $1,200
– Outdoor Pastimes of an American Hunter. N.Y., 1905. *(260) sigd.* Slightly spotted, orig. hf. pig, soiled, upr. hinge brkn., unc. (S. Mar.20; 745) *Herring.* £100
– [Works]. Ill.:– Remington, Bicknell, Zogbaum, W. Crawford, & others. Phila., Gebbie & Co., 1902-03. *Uniform Edn.* 22 vols. Cf. gt. extra, dentelles &c. cf. doubls. super gt. extra; 1 vol. inscr. 'To A.R. Keller Esq. from Theodore Roosevelt Jan 5th 1903', similarly inscr. in same vol. by Henry Cabot Lodge, 2 limitation ll. sigd. by Keller & G. Gebbie, a unique set 'specially made for, and under the personal supervision of, the President of this Company', with calligraphed limitation ll., watercolour plt.-lists & lettered guard ll. in each vol., 90 plts., each in India proof (of which 36 sigd. by

artists), Japan vell. & finished (usually cold.) states, extra-ill., with 126 inserted watercolours (54 sigd. 'OHJ'), many pen & ink drawings in text by D. Garber, & 4 inserted mntd. autograph pieces, about 12 watercolours browned. (SG. Nov.3; 177) $2,600

ROOT, George Frederic
– The Story of a Musical Life. Chic., [1891]. *1st. Edn.* Cl.; inscr. with 2 bars of music & 'yes we'll rally round the flag boys!', sigd. & dtd. Dec. 1894; Eugene Field & John Gribbel bkplts. (PNY. Dec.1; 70) $125

ROPS, Felicien
– Dix Eaux-Fortes pour illustrer les Diaboliques de J. Barbey– D'Aurevilly. Paris, 1886. Loose in orig. hf. linen portfo. (H. Nov.23; 748) DM 520
– Das Erotische Werk. [Germany], 1905. *(500) numbered.* Fo. 42 mntd. etchings, some cold., in portfo., brkn. (SI. Dec.18; 126) Lire 800,000
– Das Weib [cover title]. Vienna, ca. 1900. Fo. 30 plts., no text, loose in cl.-bkd. pict. bds. (SG. Mar.29; 116) $110

ROQUES, Joseph
– Histoire des Champignons, Comestibles et Vénéneux. Atlas. Paris, 1841. *2nd. Edn.* Lge., 4to. 24 cold. copperplts., slightly foxed, orig. hf. linen, spotted. (R. Apr.4; 1774) DM 1,300
– – **Anr. Edn.** Paris, [1864]. 4to. Minimal spotting, orig. bds., linen spine. (H. Nov.23; 271)DM 1,150
– Phytographie Medicale. Paris, 1845. Atlas of plts. only. 4to. 149 (of 150) plts., partly col.-ptd. & hand-finished, title & list of plts. stained, a few plts. spotted, cont. purple mor.-bkd. bds. (C. Nov.16; 289) *Harris.* £700

ROSA, Salvator
– [Figurine Series]. N.p., 18th. C. 4to. 32 etched plts., scattered light foxing, 19th. C. hf. mor., extremities rubbed. (SG. Jun.7; 389) $100

ROSACCIO, Giuseppe
– Teatro del Cielo e della Terra. Treviso, Francesco Righettini, 1674. Woodcut oval world map on title (repeated in text), ll continental & regional maps in text, lf. B1 (pp. 17-18) misbnd., slight browning, vell.-bkd. bds., w.a.f. (S. May 21; 111) *Niewodniczanski.* £400

ROSARIO DE VIRTU Extracta da Multi Philosophi. Theologi, et altri Excellenti Authori. Opera Utilissima per Sequitare Virtute
Naples, 20 Mar. 1521. 16mo. (in 4's). Later marb. bds. (SG. Feb.9; 321) $150

ROSARIO DELLA GLORIOSA VIRGINE MARIA
[Rome?], preface dtd. 1521. Sm. 4to. Some dampstains & minor margin defects, old vell., worn. (TA. May 17; 507) £70

ROSCIO, Giulio & others
– Ritratti et Elogii di Capitani Illustri. Rome, 1646. *1st. Edn.* 4to. Old vell., soiled. (SG. Nov.3; 179) $200

ROSCOE, S.
– Thomas Bewick A Bibliography Raisonné. L., 1953. Orig. cl., d.-w. (CSK. Nov.25; 194) £90

ROSCOE, Thomas
– The Tourist in Italy. L., 1830-33. 4 vols. 4 engraved titles with vigs., 100 steel engraved plts., plts. foxed, some stains, leath. gt. (BR. Apr.12; 132) DM 420
– – **Anr. Edn.** Ill.:– after S. Prout & J.D. Harding. L., 1831-33. 3 vols. 3 engraved titles with vigs., 75 steel engraved plts. on China, some slight foxing, cont. leath., blind-tooled, decor. spine, inner & outer dentelles, slightly worn. (HK. May 15; 904) DM 600
– The Tourist in Spain. L., 1835-36-37-38. 4 vols. 4 engraved frontis. & vigs., 80 full-p. steel engrs., romantic leath. (DS. May 25; 2348b) Pts. 95,000
– The Tourist in Switzerland & Italy. – Tourist in Italy. 1830; 1831. Together 2 vols. 1st. work: engraved title, 25 plts.; 2nd. work: engraved title, 25 plts., some dampstaining; cf. gt. (P. Oct.20; 75) £60
– Views of Cities & Scenery in Italy, France &

Switzerland. Trans.:– A. Sosson. Ill.:– after S. Prout & J.D. Harding. L., Paris, N.Y., ca. 1835. 3 vols. 4to. 135 steel-engraved plts., text in Engl. & Fr., some foxing, publisher's buckram, decor. with special blind & gt. tools, decor. mor. spines. (HD. Mar.19; 156) Frs. 2,400
– – **Anr. Edn.** 1838. 3 vols. 4to. 3 engraved titles, 132 engraved views, text in Engl. & Fr., slight spotting. (P. Sep.8; 192) *Georges.* £170
– Wanderings & Excursions in South Wales & North Wales. 1854-53. 2 vols. Hf. mor., rubbed, orig. cl. gt. (P. Jun.7; 181) £100

ROSCOE, William
– The Life of Lorenzo de'Medici, called the Magnificent. 1796. *2nd. Edn.* 2 vols. 4to. Cont. tree cf. gt., spines gt.-decor.; Sir Ivar Colquhoun, of Luss copy. (CE. Mar.22; 258) £300

ROSE, Rev. Hugh James
– A New General Biographical Dictionary. L., 1850. 12 vols. Cont. tree cf., spines gt., some wear. (S. Mar.20; 746) *Wade.* £60

ROSE, Thomas
– Vues Pittoresques des Comtés de Westmoreland, Cumberland, Durham et Northumberland. Trans.:– J.F. Gerrard. Ill.:– after T. Allom. G. Pickering & others. L., ca. 1833. 3 vols. 4to. 1 engraved title & 215 steel engrs. on 109 plts., minimal foxing, cont. hf. leath. (HK. May 15; 851) DM 600
– Westmoreland, Cumberland, Durham & Northumberland Illustrated. 1832. 2 vols. 4to. Vig. title to Vol. 1, 200 engraved views on 101 sheets, cf. gt. (P. Sep.8; 385) *Edistar.* £130
– – **Anr. Copy.** 4to. Engraved title with vig., 180 views on 90 plts. only, most spotted & stained, cont. hf. mor., rubbed. (S. Jun.25; 337) *Price.* £110
– – **Anr. Copy.** 2 vols. 4to. 165 steel-engraved views on 85 plts., minor spotting, cont. hf. cf., gt.-decor. spines. (TA. Nov.17; 157) £80
– – **Anr. Edn.** 1832[-35]. 4to. Engraved title, 216 views on 109 sheets, slight spotting, hf. mor. gt., rubbed. (P. Jul.26; 212e) £100
– – **Anr. Edn.** 1833. 4to. Vig. title, 214 engraved views on 108 sheets, some foxing, cf., upr. cover detchd. (P. Sep.8; 380) *Kidd.* £110
– – **Anr. Edn.** Ill.:– after T. Allom & others. L., ca. 1835. 4to. 109 (of 110) engraved plts., lacks engraved title, some slight spotting, bdg. defect. (material not stated). (S. Mar.6; 320) *Kidd.* £90
– – **Anr. Edn.** Ill.:– Thomas Allom, George Pickering, & others. 1838. 4to. Additional engraved title-p., 5 full-p. & 210 half-p. engrs., some slight spotting, cont. hf. mor., rubbed. (SKC. Mar.9; 1992) £120

ROSE OF SHARON: A Religious Souvenir for 1844. – … 1851. – … , 1854
Ed.:– Sarah C. Edgarton & Mrs. C.M. Sawyer. Boston, 1844; 1850; 1854. Lge. 12mo. Orig. gt.-floral & blind-ornamental red leath., worn, spine of 3rd. vol torn & portion of front fly-lf. clipped; from liby. of F.D. Roosevelt, each vol. inscr. by him. (SG. Mar.15; 44) $250

ROSEL VON ROSENHOF, A.J.
– Historie der Polypen und Kleiner Wasserinsecten. [Nuremb.], ca. 1757-59. Vol. II (compl.) of 'Monatlich-herausgegebenen Insecten-Belustigung'. Some slight browning, cont. leath. gt., gold-tooled arms supra-libris, slightly worn, with 3 plts. from Vol. III. (HT. May 8; 612) DM 550
– Der Monatlich herausgegebenen Insecten Belustigung. Nuremb., 1755. Pt. 3 (of 4). 4to. Cont. leath. gt., lr. part of spine defect. from water damage. (HK. May 15; 391) DM 2,200
– – **Anr. Edn.** Ed.:– D.F.C. Kleemann. Nuremb., 1771. With continuation: KLEEMANN, Ch. F.- Beiträge zur Natur-und Insectengeschichte. [1776]. 4to. Pp. 1-344 of continuation & plts. 1-40, lacks end of text with 4 plts., most plts. slightly browned, cont. leath., worn & slightly bumped. (R. Oct.12; 1901) DM 1,600
– De Natuurlyke Historie der Insecten. Haarlem & Amst., 1764-68. 4 vols. in 8. 4to. 3 hand-cold. engraved frontis., engraved port., 356 hand-cold. engraved plts. on 288 ll., cont. hf. cf., gt. spines, slightly scuffed, minor tears & repairs to heads of spines. (C. Jun.27; 132) *Dillon.* £2,500

ROSEL VON ROSENHOF, A.J. -Contd.

– – **Anr. Edn.** Ed.:– C.F.C. Kleemann A. Abrahamsz v. Moerbeek (index). Haarlem & Amst., [1764-68]. 4 vols. in 8, including index. 4to. 4 frontis. & 287 engraved plts. cont. hand-cold., some plts. loose, 3 plts. slightly defect. at top of spines, cont. hf. cf. gt., unc. & partly unopened. (VS. Jun.7; 934) Fls. 8,600
– – **Anr. Copy.** 4 vols. 3 frontis., 288 plts. (3 folding), all hand-cold., port., some light stains, later hf. cf., slightly worn, 1 vol. slightly defect. (B. Feb.8; 863) Fls. 8,200
– – **Anr. Copy.** 8 pts. in 4 vols. 4to. 3 engraved titles, 288 plts., some folding, all cont. hand-cold., cont. hf. cf., spines gt. (VG. Nov.30; 776) Fls. 5,800
– – **Anr. Edn.** Haarlem & Amst., Ca. 1764-70. Fragment only bnd. in 10 vols. 4to. 170 hand-cold. engraved plts. & small part of text only, cl.-bkd. bds. & wraps., w.a.f. (CH. May 24; 43) Fls. 1,500

ROSEN, G.

[–] **Christliches Gemüths-Gespräch von dem Geistlichen u. seligmachenden Glauben** ... Ephrata, 1769. Very browned & soiled, cont. leath., worn. (HK. Nov.9; 1524) DM 600

ROSENBACH, Abraham Simon Wolf

– **The Collected Catalogues.** N.Y., Arno reprint, [1967]. Vols. I-X, compl. Cl. (LH. Sep.25; 591) $110
– **Early American Children's Books; with Bibliographical Descriptions of the Books in his Private Collection.** Foreword:– A. Edward Newton. Portland, 1933. *(585) numbered on Worthy Aurelian paper, sigd.* 4to. Unnumbered review copy, mor.-bkd. pict. bds., slightly discold., s.-c. (SG. Dec.8; 317) $140
– **An Introduction to Herman Melville's Moby Dick.** N.Y., 1924. *(250) numbered.* Bds. (SG. Sep.15; 288) $100
– **To Dr. R.: Essays Here Collected & Published in Honor of the Seventieth Birthday of Dr. A.S.W. Rosenbach, July 22, 1946.** Contribs.:– L.C. Wroth, E. Wolf II, C. Morley, & others. Phila., 1946. *1st. Edn.* Tall 8vo. Cl.; engraved card of P.H. Rosenbach inserted. (SG. Sep.15; 291) $100

ROSENBACH, Dr. Abraham Simon Wolf (Ed.)
See— WIDENER, Harry Elkins

ROSENBERG, Isaac

– **Poems.** Ed.:– Gordon Bottomley & Laurence Binyon. L., 1922. *1st. Edn.* Hf.-title, last lf. blank but for imprint on recto, orig. cl., slightly marked, d.-w. (S. Mar.20; 956) *Hawthorn.* £60
– – **Anr. Copy.** Hf.-title, orig. cl., slightly marked, d.-w. (S. Oct.11; 360) *Sherington.* £55

ROSENBERG, Dr. Marc

– **Der Goldschmiede Merkzeichen.** Frankfurt & Berlin, 1922-28. *3rd. Edn.* 4 vols. Orig. cl., d.-w.'s. (CSK. Sep.16; 97) £120
– – **Anr. Copy.** 4 vols. Gt.-lettered cl. (SG. Jan.26; 279) $225
– – **Anr. Edn.** Berlin, 1922-28. 4 vols. Cl., d.-w. (BS. May 2; 96) £75
– – **Anr. Edn.** Frankfurt, 1922-28. 4 vols. Orig. linen. (BR. Apr.13; 2031) DM 500
– – **Anr. Edn.** Frankfurt [Hofheim in Taunus, Schmidt & Guenther], 1922-28 [but later]. *Reprint.* 4 vols. Tall 8vo. Cl., d.-w.'s. (SG. Oct.13; 183) $150

ROSENFELD, Margarethe Johanne

[–] **Vollst. u. Genaue Anleitung alle Gattungen von Backwerk, Krem's, Sulzen ... zu verfertigen.** By R.M.J. Brünn, 1832. Foxed, cont. bds., rubbed. (HK. Nov.9; 1695) DM 400

ROSENMULLER, Fr. K.

– **Ansichten von Palästina.** Ill.:– after L. Mayer. Leipzig, ca. 1815. 3 pts. Ob. fo. 36 cold. copperplts., Pt. II & III loose, some slight spotting & browning. cont. wraps., loose, spine slightly defect. (H. May 22; 287) DM 1,750

ROSENTHAL, Leonard

– **Au Royaume de la Perle.** Ill.:– Edmund Dulac. Paris, [1920]. 4to. Pres. lf. facing title unfilled, silver-patterned wraps., spine ends chipped. (SG. Dec.8; 144) £125

– **The Kingdom of the Pearl.** Ill.:– E. Dulac. 1920. *(100) sigd. by artist.* 4to. Orig. vell.-bkd. bds., soiled. (P. Mar.15; 368) *Henderson.* £150
– – **Anr. Edn.** Ill.:– Edmund Dulac. L., [1920]. *(675) numbered.* 4to. Somewhat spotted, orig. cl.-bkd. bds., d.-w. slightly worn. (S. Nov.22; 322) *Joseph.* £80
– – **Anr. Copy.** Fo. 10 mntd. cold. plts., leath.-bkd. lacquered bds., upr. cover with painted & mother-of-pearl inlay view & borders, mntd. pearls on corners, a few inlays lacking, cl. folding box. (SG. Feb.16; 100) $425
– – **Anr. Copy.** 4to. Slight foxing thro-out, gt.-decor. hf. cl. & decor. bds., corners slightly bumped. (CBA. Aug.21; 197) $150
– – **Anr. Edn.** Ill.:– Edmund Dulac. N.d. *(675) numbered.* 4to. Light spotting, orig. cl.-bkd. bds., d.-w., publisher's box. (CSK. Dec.16; 30) £140

ROSEN-ZEITUNG

Ed.:– P. Lambert. Frankfurt, 1898-1905. Yrs. 13-20 in 2 vols. 4to. Hf. leath. (R. Apr.4; 1780) DM 600

ROSIS, Angelo

[–] **Racolta di Vari Schizi.** Venice, 1747. Fo. 24 engraved plts., including title, a few ll. slightly stained in blank margin, cont. mott. sheep, spine gt. (C. Dec.9; 139) *Marlborough.* £1,400

ROSMASLER, F.H.W.

– **Hamburgs Bürger-Bewaffnung, in Fünf und Dreisig Figuren Dargestellt.** Hamburg, 1816. Square 4to. 22 cold. plts., mod. hf. mor., corners. (HD. Jan.27; 299) Frs. 11,500

ROSNEL, P. de

[–] **Le Mercure Indien.** Paris, 1667. 2 vols. in 1. Red ruled, insert fo. 15 in Vol. 2, cont. red mor. gt., slightly rubbed. (BBA. Sep.29; 73) *Rota.* £120

ROSS, Alexander, 1591-1654

– **Arcana Microcosmi.** L., 1652. *2nd. Edn.* Wormhole in middle of p. thro.-out most of book, light stain at end, hf. cf. gt.; Dr. Walter Pagel copy. [Wing R 1947] (S. Feb.7; 337) *Goodrich.* £100
– **The Philosophicall Touch-Stone: or Observations upon Sir Kenelm Digbie's Discourses of the Nature of Bodies, & of the Reasonable Soule** ... L., 1645. *1st. Edn.* Sm. sq. 8vo. Compl., few sm. spots at last pp., old stabholes at gutters, few sm. letters inked at bottom corner of title, some cont. owner's sigs. at front & rear blanks, 18th. C. cf. & bds., trimmed, covers detchd., backstrip & label worn & chipped. (HA. Feb.24; 433) $150

ROSS, Alexander, 1783-1856

– **Adventures of the First Settlers on the Oregon or Columbia River.** L., 1849. *1st. Edn.* Orig. cl., recased with spine & corners reprd.; the Rt. Hon. Visc. Eccles copy. [Sabin 73326] (CNY. Nov.18; 246) $300
– **The Fur Hunters of the Far West.** L., 1855. *1st. Edn.* 2 vols. Orig. cl. *(With:)* – **The Red River Settlement.** 1856. *1st. Edn.* Orig. cl. [Sabin 73327, 73328] (S. May 22; 336) *Maggs.* £480
– – **Anr. Copy.** 2 vols. in 1. Without the 2 advt. ll., Edinb. Institute prize bdg. of cont. pol. cf. gt., edges slightly rubbed; the Rt. Hon. Visc. Eccles copy. [Sabin 73327] (CNY. Nov.18; 247) $420

ROSS, Andrew

– **Old Scottish Regimental Colours** ... Edinb. & L., 1885. Fo. Publisher's buckram. (HD. Jan.27; 203) Frs. 1,400
– – **Anr. Edn.** Edinb., 1885. *Ltd. Edn.* 4to. Orig. cl. gt. (PD. Apr.18; 219) £55

ROSS, Frederick

– **The Ruined Abbeys of Britain.** Ill.:– after A.F. Lydon. L., ca. 1885. Fo. Some foxing not affecting plts., orig. gt.-pict. cl., wear to extremities. (CBA. Aug.21; 566) $110

ROSS, Sir John

– **Appendix to the Narrative of a Second Voyage in Search of a North-west Passage.** 1835. 4to. Engraved port. (spotted), 19 litho. plts. (13 hand-cold.), some ll. spotted, a few ll. loose & margin torn, title torn with loss of text, orig. cl., lacks spine, covers detchd. (BBA. Jan.19; 72) *Simper.* £90
– **Narrative of a Second Voyage in Search of the**

North West Passage. 1835. 4to. Folding hand-cold. map, 29 charts & plts., orig. cl. (P. Sep.29; 318) £150
– – **Anr. Copy.** 4to. 1 folding chart mntd. on linen, orig. cl.-bkd. bds. (CE. Sep.1; 78) £90
– – **Anr. Copy.** Lge. folding outl. cold. map, 30 full-p. engraved or litho. plts. or charts, including 9 hand-cold., errata lf., minor spotting to a few ll., new end-ll. [Sabin 73381] *(With:)* – **Appendix to the Narrative of a Second Voyage in Search of a North-West Passage.** L., 1835. *1st. Edn.* Frontis. port., 19 engraved or litho. plts. or diagrams, including 9 hand-cold., frontis. spotted, soiled, new end-papers. [Sabin 73384] Together 2 vols. Lge. 4to. Unc., orig. cl., gt. spines, recased, 1st. vol. rebkd. preserving most of orig. spine; the Rt. Hon. Visc. Eccles copies. (CNY. Nov.18; 249) $550
– – **Anr. Copy.** Lge. 4to. L.P., 29 (of 30) full-p. black & white engraved plts. & maps or cont. hand-cold. litho. plts., including lge. folded map with col. highlights at rear, moderate foxing & some browning & margin stains thro.-out, later patterned cl., buckram backstrip, recent end-papers. (HA. Feb.24; 310) $350
– – **Anr. Copy.** Lge. 4to. Some foxing & dampstains, hf. art mor. (SG. Sep.22; 38) $250
– – **Anr. Copy.** Lge. 4to. Wide margin, some steel-engraved plts. lightly foxed, cont. linen, unc.; ex-libris. [Sabin 73381] (GB. Nov.3; 27) DM 1,200
– **A Voyage of Discovery & Research in the Southern & Antarctic Regions.** L., 1847. *1st. Edn.* 2 vols. 16 plts. & charts (some folding, 1 or 2 with slight damage by adhesion), cont. hf. cf. (S. May 22; 458) *Bonham.* £420
– **A Voyage of Discovery ... for the Purpose of Exploring Baffin's Bay.** L., 1819. *1st. Edn.* 4to. 3 engraved folding maps, 25 engraved plts., some folding, 4 folding engraved tables, errata slip, maps with light offsetting, a few margins slightly soiled, gtr. cf., slightly worn. (S. Dec.1; 293) *Crete.* £400
– – **Anr. Copy.** 4to. 3 engraved folding maps, 10 engraved plts., including 3 folding, 15 hand-cold. aquatint plts., including 3 folding, 4 engraved meteorological tables, light offsetting from several plts., title slightly soiled, several plts. lightly soiled or foxed, mod. hf. mor. gt., unc.; the Rt. Hon. Visc. Eccles copy. [Sabin 73376] (CNY. Nov.18; 248) $750
– – **Anr. Copy.** Lge. 4to. 33 plts., views & charts, many folding, many hand-cold., cont. mott. cf., jnts. slightly worn. (SG. Mar.29; 339) $600

ROSS, John Dix

[–] **Lions: Living & Dead, or Personal Recollections of the Great & Gifted.** L., 1854. *2nd. Edn.* 1 vol. in 2. Lge. 4to. Extra-ill. with 240 ports., mostly 19th. C. engrs., three-qtr. mor., spines gt. (SG. Feb.16; 258) $300

ROSS, Martin (Pseud.)
See— MARTIN, Violet Florence 'Martin Ross'

ROSS, Metcalf & Hair, T.H.

– **A Series of Views of the Collieries in the Counties of Northumberland & Durham.** Ill.:– after Hair. L., 1844. Fo. Additional engraved title, 42 engraved plts. on India paper, cont. roan-bkd. bds. (C. Nov.16; 164) *Steedman.* £700

ROSS, Robert

– **Aubrey Beardsley.** L., 1909. A few dampstains, mainly marginal, gt.-pict. cl., faded, slightly stained; 2 A.L. from Beardsley (1 sigd.) mntd. on front free end-paper. (SG. Jan.12; 31) $225

ROSS, Thomas
See— MacGIBBON, David & Ross, Thomas

ROSS, W.A.

– **A Yacht Voyage to Norway, Denmark & Sweden.** 1848. *1st. Edn.* 2 vols. Some ll. slightly soiled, orig. cl. (BBA. Sep.29; 109) *Congleton.* £75

ROSSBERG, Chr. Gottlob

[–] **Systematische Anweisung zum Schönschreiben.** [Dresden & Leipzig, 1793 & 1806]. 2 pts. in 1 vol. Ob. 4to. Wide margin, mod. bds., Hauswedell coll. (H. May 23; 314) DM 660

ROSSELLI, Giovanni

[–] **Epulario il quale tratta del Modo di cucinare ogni Carne, Uccelli, et Pesci d'Ogni Sorta.** Venezia &

Bassano, ca. 1675. 12mo. Frontis. & last p. badly reprd. with slight loss, stain, mod. bds. (SI. Dec.15; 175) Lire 280,000

ROSSETTI, Christina
- **Goblin Market & Other Poems.** Ill.:– W.J. Linton after Dante Gabriel Rossetti. Camb. & L., 1862. *1st. Edn.* 12mo. Orig. cl., blocked in gt. & blind; Frederic Dannay copy. (CNY. Dec.16; 294) $300
- – **Anr. Edn.** Ill.:– D.G. Rossetti, E. Cotton. L., 1862. Frontis. & title vig., extra-ill. with many pen & ink sketches & decors., some spotting, orig. cl., slightly rubbed. (BBA. May 23; 229)
Nudelman. £170
- – **Anr. Edn.** Ill.:– Laurence Housman. L., 1893. 12mo. Title, plts. & ills. hand-cold. by (?) Gloria Cardew, orig. cl., blocked in gt. from design by Housman. (CSK. Nov.25; 133) £260
- **Poems.** Ed.:– Walter de la Mare. Gregy. Pr., 1930. *(300) numbered.* Orig. cf.-bkd. bds., slightly soiled. (BBA. Oct.27; 165) *Rota.* £80
- **The Prince's Progress & Other Poems.** Ill.:– W.J. Linton after Dante Gabriel Rossetti. L., 1866. *1st. Edn.* 12mo. Orig. cl., gt.-blocked, slightly soiled; autograph quotation sigd. by author pasted to inside upr. cover, Frederic Dannay copy. (CNY. Dec.16; 295) $600
- **Verses ... Dedicated to Her Mother.** L., Gaetano Polidori. 1847. *1st. Edn.* 12mo. Lf. 74 a cancel, title stained, orig. unbnd. gatherings, unopened, hf. mor. folding box; inscr. by William Michael Rossetti to Alfred T. Rake, Frederic Dannay copy. (CNY. Dec.16; 293) $3,600

ROSSETTI, Dante Gabriel
- **Ballads & Narrative Poems.** Kelms. Pr., 1893. *(310).* 8vo. Orig. limp vell., ties, unopened. (BBA. Dec.15; 251) *Fletcher.* £210
- **Ballads & Sonnets.** L., 1881. *1st. Edn.* Orig. cl., gt.-blocked after design by Rossetti; pres. copy from Theodore Watts[-Dunton] to Lady Jane Swinburne, Frederio Dannay copy. (CNY. Dec.16; 298) $650
- **Hand & Soul.** Hammersmith, Kelms. Pr., 1895. *Ltd. Edn.* Orig. vell. (HK. Nov.11; 3686)
DM 1,000
- **Poems.** L., 1870. *1st. Edn.* Crushed lev. mor. by the Doves Bindery, sigd. at end 'THE DOVES BINDERY 18 c-s 99', covers with single gt.-ruled border enclosing dense pattern of Tudor rose, leaf sprays & triple- headed tulip sprays, mostly gt. over mor. onlays in gt.-dotted ground, lge. lozenge space in centres with triple-headed flower spray of mor. gt. onlay framed by 2 thin oval wreaths with leaf & dot ornaments, spine in 6 compartments, gt.- lettered in 1, Tudor rose ornament, dots & leaves in rest, bd. edges & turn-ins gt., qtr. mor. gt. box, worn; Henry John & Minnie Caroline Bell bkplt., Thomas B. Stevenson copy. (CNY. May 18; 181) $4,800
- – **Anr. Copy.** Orig. gt.-blocked cl., after design by Rossetti, lr. fore- corners worn; pres. copy from author to Seymour Kirkup, Frederic Dannay copy. (CNY. Dec.16; 296) $700
- **Sonnets & Lyrical Poems.** Kelms. Pr., 1894. *(310).* Orig. limp vell., ties, qtr. mor. box; from Norman Tarbolton liby. (P. Apr.12; 21)
Ayres. £220

ROSSI, Domenico de
- **Gemme Antiche Figurate** ... Rome, 1707-09. *1st. Edn.* 4 vols. Tall 4to. 419 copperplates, cont. heavy vell., some soiling; sigd. 'The Duchess of Sussex' on titles. (SG. Oct.13; 290) $500
- **Raccolta di Statue Antiche Moderne.** Roma, 1704. 4to. Old hf. vell. (HD. Jun.29; 178) Frs. 2,100

ROSSI, Filippo
- [–] **Descrizione di Roma Antica.** Rome, 1697. Few margin stains, cont. vell. (SG. Oct.27; 281) $150

ROSSI, Giovanni Battista de
- **La Roma Sotterranea Christiana.** Rome, 1864-77. 6 vols. in 3. Lge. 4to. Spotted, cont. hf. cf., worn, ex-liby. (S. Dec.13; 475) *Fenton.* £80
- – **Anr. Edn.** Rome, 1865-77. 3 vols. 4to. Plts., plans & c. bnd. in at end of each vol., cont. crimson mor. gt. (TA. Feb.16; 297) £120

ROSSI, Giovanni Gherardo de
- **Scherzi Poetici e Pittorici.** Ill.:– Giuseppe Tekeira. Rome, priv. ptd., 1794. 4to. Engraved pict. title, 40 plts., all ptd. in yellow & black, cont. purple str.-grd. mor., gt.-& blind-tooled, slightly rubbed. (C. Nov.9; 110) *Lyon.* £220
- – **Anr. Edn.** Rome, [but Parma], 1794. [but 1795]. 4to. Line-engraved title & 40 plts., hand-cold. in black & yellow, lacks final colophon lf., some light spotting, near-cont. purple str.-grd. mor., ruled & tooled in gt. & blind, slightly rubbed. (CSK. Mar.23; 139) £280
- – **Anr. Copy.** 4to. Most plts. lightly foxed, 19th. C. hf. leath. (R. Oct.11; 151) DM 500

ROSSI, Giovanni Giacomo de
- **Le Fontane di Roma ... – Le Fontane delle Ville di Frascati, nel Tusculano ... – Le Fontane ne'Palazzi et ne'Giardini dii Roma ... – Le Fontane del Giardino Estense in Tivoli ...** Ill.:– G.B. Falda & G.F. Venturi. Roma, 1691. 4 pts. in 1 vol. Ob. 4to. 4 engraved titles, 4 dedication ll. & 104 plts. (of 107, lacks 3 plts. in 3rd. pt.), 48 plts. in proof before the numbers, washed, mod. vell., ties. (HD. Jun.18; 41) Frs. 8,000
- **Insignium Romae Templorum Prospectus exteriores interioresque a Celebrioribus Architectis Inventi.** Roma, 1684. Fo. 72 engraved plts., including 1 plt. reprd. hf. cf., spine defect. (CR. Jun.6; 26) Lire 800,000
- – **Anr. Copy.** Lge. fo. 72 engraved plts., slightly browned or foxed, cont. hf. leath., slightly rubbed. (GB. May 3; 906) DM 1,800
- **Veteres Arcus Augustorum Triumphis Insignes.** Rome, 1690. Lge. fo. 47 (of 52?) copper engrs. (24 folding), old reverse cf., slightly worn; Delapre Abbey bkplt. (SKC. May 4; 1820) £70

ROSSI, Giovanni Giacomo & Domenico de
- **Mercurio Geografico overo Guida Geografica in Tutte le Parti del Mondo.** Ill.:– Maps.:– Cantelli da Vignola, Sanson & others. Rome, D. de Rossi & heirs of G.G. de Rossi, [1693 or later]. 2 pts. in 1 vol. Lge. fo. 2 engraved pict. titles, 128 engraved maps (double-p. sheets counted as 2 in ptd. index, which lists 155 subjects), variously dtd. between 1668 & 1693, mostly hand-cold. in outl., some slight surface dirt, mod. cf.-bkd. bds., w.a.f. (S. May 21; 113) *Hillman.* £4,800

ROSSI, Matteo Gregorio
- **Il Nuovo Splendore delle Fabriche in Prospettiva di Roma Moderna.** Rome, ca. 1686-1750. Ob. 4to. Port. of Benedict XIII pasted to verso of title, some views cut close & pasted to versos, late 18th. C. hf. vell., as a coll. of plts. w.a.f. (BBA. Jun.14; 319) *Weinreb.* £1000

ROSSIGNOL, Louis
- **Art d'Ecrire Nouvellement mis au Jour sur les Differens Caractères les plus Usitez d'après Rossignol.** Paris, ca. 1770?. Tall fo. 39 (of 40) engraved plts., three-qtr. vell., marb. bds. (SG. May 17; 53) $275

ROSSING, Karl
- **Mein Vorurteil gegen diese Zeit.** Berlin, 1932. *1st. Edn.* 4to. Orig. linen. (GB. Nov.5; 2940) DM 460

ROSSINI, Luigi
- **Le Antichita Romane Ossia Raccolta delle piu Interessamti Vedute di Roma Antica.** Rome, 1829. Lge. fo. 101 engraved views, margins of title & 2 plts. stained, tears reprd., cont. portfo. with ties, rebkd. (C. Jun.27; 65) *Weinreb.* £2,400
- – **Anr. Copy.** Ob. fo. 67 (of 101) engraved plts., 44 stained, 23 loose, hf. cf., defect., as a coll, of plts., w.a.f. (P. Oct.20; 14) £750

ROSSLER, B.
- **Speculum Metallurgiae Politissimum.** Dresden, 1700. *1st. Edn.* Fo. Slightly browned & spotted, cont. leath., rubbed. (H. Nov.23; 217) DM 1,700

ROSSLIN, E.
- [–] **Der Schwanngeren Frawen und Hebammen Rosegartten.** Augsburg, 6 Aug. 1528. 4to. Title crumpled, lacks. 2 ll. (end of dedication preface), old MS marginalia & underlining, writing on verso last blank lf. 19th. C. hf. vell. (R. Oct.12; 1465)
DM 4,800

ROSSMAESLER, W.H.
- **Preussen, in Landschaftlichen Darstellungen, nach eigenen Zeichnungen in Stahl gestochen.** Berlin, 1841[-1843]. 4to. 20 steel engraved plts., cont. hf. linen. (GB. Nov.3; 324) DM 1,000

ROSSO, Joseph del
- **Guide de Fiesole et ses Environs.** Flor., 1846. In Fr. & Italian, cont. hf. cf. (HD. Mar.9; 89)
Frs. 1,400

ROSTAGNY, de
- **Traité de Primerose sur les Erreurs Vulgaires de la Médecine avec des Additions très Curieuses.** Lyon, 1689. *Orig. Edn.* Cont. red mor. gt., decor., later arms. (HD. Nov.29; 71) Frs. 1,250

ROSTAND, Edmond
- **Cyrano de Bergerac.** Ill.:– Bernard, Flameng, Albert Laurens, Léandre, Adrien Moreau, Thevenot. Paris, 1899. *(40) on old japan with 4 states of woodcuts.* 4to. Jansenist red mor. gt. by Bretable, mor. liners, wrap & spine preserved, s.-c. (H. Jun.13; 96) Frs. 4,800
- – **Anr. Edn.** Trans.:– L. Fulda. Ill.:– E. Oppler. Berlin, [1923]. *(300) on Zanderabütten.* 4to. Hand-bnd. cherry red mor. gt., by Br. Scheer. Berlin; all etchings sigd. by artist. (H. Nov.24; 1910)
DM 620
- **Cyrano de Bergerac. – L'Aiglon.** Paris, 1898-1900. *Orig. Edns.* 2 vols. 2nd. work on japan, sewed. (HD. May 4; 416) Frs. 1,450
- **La Princesse Lointaine.** Ill.:– Georges Desvalliers. [Paris], 1920. *(150). (100) numbered for members of the Société du Livre.* 4to. Mor. by Madeleine Noulhac, sigd. on upr. turn-im, covers with lge. panels of double gt. rules enclosing linked chain decor. set vertically & horizontally to from 8 rectangular panels with sm. squares of onlaid mor. at intersections, linked chain decor. wrapping round spine at head & foot, lge. circular cornerpiece ornaments of onlaid cf. surrounded by onlaid mor. with mor. gt. circlets & gt. dots, central panels filled with stylized Art Nouveau flower in 2 col. mor. gt. with 3 blooms on green ground, framed by bread circular border of alternating col. onlaid mor. gt. circles & gt. dots, also on green ground, spine in 6 compartments, gt.-lettered in 1, mor. onlaid circle & gt. dots in rest, bd. edges with double gt. fillet, mor. doubls. with black stripe three-qtr. border enclosing inner border of gt. fillets, gt. dots & dotted flower ornaments, silk free end-pp., marb. paper fly-ll., partly unc., orig. ptd. wraps, & spine preserved, matching mor.-edged s.-c., repairs to jnts. & case, 1 corner slightly bruised; the copy of A. de Fleuriau, with his ink initials on fly-lf. (CNY. May 18; 196) $2,000

ROSTAND, Jean
- **Le Bestiaire d'Amour.** Ill.:– P.Y. Tremois. Paris, priv. ptd., 1958. *Orig. Edn., (175).* Fo. 22 orig. ills., leaves, box. (HD. May 4; 418) Frs. 4,100

ROSTINI, C.
- **Mémoires (1715-1740).** Ed.:– P. & L. Lucciana. Trans.:– Abbé Letteron. Bastia, 1882. 2 vols. Cont. hf. chagrin, spines decor. (HD. Oct.21; 157)
Frs. 2,000

ROSTOVTZEFF, Mikhail I.
- **Iranians & Greeks in Southern Russia.** Oxford, 1922. 4to. Orig. cl. (BBA. Aug.18; 299)
Museum. £55

ROTBARTH, Christopher
See– BROTOFFER, Ratichs [i.e. Christopher Rotbarth?]

ROTE ERDE
Ed.:– K. Lorenz. Ill.:– Tegetmeier & others. Hamburg, 1922. *Ltd. Edn.* 2nd. Series, 1st. Book. 4to. 30 orig., all etchings sigd. by artists, orig. by. linen, slightly faded, worn, corners bumped. (H. May 23; 1485) DM 500

ROTH, Abraham
See— ADAM, Eugen & Roth, Abraham

ROTH, H. Ling (Trans.)
See— CROZET

ROTH, J.
See— SCHUBERT, Gotthill Heinrich & Roth, J.

ROTH, Joseph
- Panoptikum, Gestalten und Kulissen. Ill.:– R. Lindner. München, 1930. *1st. Edn.* Orig. linen, cold. orig. pict. wraps. (GB. Nov.5; 2950) DM 450

ROTH, Walter E.
- Ethnological Studies Among the North-West-Central Queensland Aborigines. Brisbane, 1897. Cancelled liby. stp. on title-p., bdg. not stated; Thomas Gill bkplt., sig. of A.J. Norman. (KH. May 1; 604) Aus. $130

ROTHELIN, Abbé Charles d'Orléans de
- Catalogue des Livres. Ed.:– G. Martin. Ill.:– Tardieu after Coypel (port.). Paris, 1746. MS. prices in margin, cont. marb. cf. gt., rubbed. (VG. Sep.13; 457) Fls. 500

ROTHENBURG, F.R. von
- Schlachten-Atlas. Wien, 1840. *1st. Edn.* Sm. ob. fo. Old stp. on title, some slight foxing or staining, cont. hf. leath., rubbed & slightly worn. (GB. May 3; 190) DM 1,400

ROTHENSTEIN, Sir John
- Victor Hammer: Artist & Craftsman. – Victor Hammer: Artist & Printer. Boston; Lexington, Godine; Anvil Pr., [1978], 1981. *Edn. C. (50) special roman-numbered sets ptd., by Martino Marderstwig at Stamperia Valdonega, Verona.* Together 2 vols. Tall 8vo. Ills., with envelope with orig. print by Hammer & 4 specimens of his printing, also, orig. prospectus, mor., linen covers. (SG. May 17; 119) $275
- William Rothenstein: Portrait Drawings 1889-1925, An Iconography ... Preface:– Max Beerbohm. N.Y., 1927. *(520) numbered.* Sm. fo. This copy unnumbered, 101 plts., cl. (SG. Aug.25; 312) $100

ROTHESAY, Stuart de, Lord
- Catalogue of the Valuable Library. [L., 1855]. Sm. 4to. L.P., each text p. ruled with red ledger lines & priced with name of each buyer, later gt. red qtr. mor. & mar: bds., orig. painted wraps. bnd. in, partly unc.; inscr. & sigd. on upr. wrap. (SG. Apr.5; 314) $110

ROTHLISBERGER, M.
- Claude Lorrain. The Paintings. New Haven, 1961. 2 vols. 4to. Orig. linen. (HK. Nov.12; 4636) DM 500

ROTHSCHILD, A. de
- Histoire de la Poste aux Lettres depuis ses Origines les plus Anciennes jusqu'à nos Jours. Paris, 1873. *2nd. Edn.* 12mo. Red mor. gt. by R. Petit, arms of George I of Greece, pres. copy. (HD. May 21; 169) Frs. 1,700

ROTHSCHILD, Edouard de
- Bernard Palissy et Son Ecole (Collection Edouard de Rothschild). Text:– Germaine de Rothschild & Serge Grandjean. Paris, [1952]. *(300) numbered on Grand Vélin d'Arches.* Tall fo. 42 plts., facs. lf., loose as iss. in decor. wrap., box, soiled. (SG. Jan.26; 139) $100

ROTHSCHILD, Ferdinand de, Baron
- Livre d'Or. Ed.:– James Pope-Henessy. L., Roxb. Cl., 1957. 4to. Orig. qtr. mor. (S. Oct.4; 242) *Thomas.* £270

ROTHSCHILD, James de, Baron
- Catalogue des Livres composant la Bibliothèque. Paris, 1884-1920. *(400) on vergé.* 5 vols. Hf. mor., corners, by Vermorel, unc., last vol. slightly faded. (HD. Jun.6; 131) Frs. 4,000
- – Anr. Edn. N.p., n.d. *New Edn.* 5 vols. 4to. Publishers cl. (DS. Dec.16; 2358) Pts. 26,000

ROTHSCHILD, James A. de
- The James A. de Rothschild Collection at Waddesdon Manor. Ed.:– Sir Anthony Blunt. Fribourg, 1968-75. 6 vols. 4to. Orig. cl., wraps., s.-c. (CSK. Mar.9; 112) £550

ROTHSCHILD, Lionel Walter, Baron
- Extinct Birds. L., 1907. *(300) sigd.* Fo. 4 uncold. & 45 cold. plts., on guards, a few plts. with minor margin spotting, some pencil annots., mod. hf. mor. (C. Nov.16; 290) *Grahame.* £950

ROTHSCHILD, Philippe de
- A l'Aube d'une Guerre. Ill.:– Mario Avati. Paris, 1950. *(141) numbered.* Fo. Unbnd. in orig. wraps., unc. (S. Nov.21; 50) *Rota.* £310

ROTHSCHILD, Baron Victor
- Rothschild Library: A Catalogue of the Collection of Eighteenth Century Printed Books & Manuscripts ... Ed.:– N.M. Shawyer & others. Camb., priv. ptd., 1954. 2 vols. Sm. 4to. 60 plts., two-tone cl. (SG. Sep.15; 294) $300
- – Anr. Edn. 1969. *Reprint.* 2 vols. Tall 8vo. Orig. cl., slightly rubbed. (TA. Dec.15; 291) £95

ROTHSCHILD, Walter
- A Monograph of the Genus Casuarius. Ed.:– W.P. Pycraft. Ill.:– J.G. Keulemans. L., [1900]. 4to. Extract from Zoological Society Transactions, vol. XV, pp. 109-290, 18 hand-cold. litho. plts., 4 other plts., 2 maps, hf. mor. gt. (S. Apr. 10; 451) *Evans.* £420

ROTHSCHILD, Hon. Walter & Jordan, Karl
- A Revision of the Lepidopterous Family Sphingidae. L., 1903. 2 vols. 4to. 67 plts., folding diagrams, hf. mor. (SKC. Oct.26; 424) £240

ROTONCHAMP, Jean de
- Paul Gauguin. 1906. *(300).* 4to. Mor. by Durvand, decor. by Séguy, wrap. & spine preserved, s.-c. (HD. Jun.29; 179) Frs. 30,000

ROTTH, A. Chr.
- Vollständige Deutsche Poesie. Leipzig, 1688. *1st. Edn.* Probably lacks 3 blank ll. 4 page nos. omitted, cont. vell., lr. cover worn, lacks lr. end-paper, old owners marks; Hauswedoff coll. (H. May 24; 1189) DM 1,400

ROTZ, John
- The Maps & Text of the Boke of Idrography, Presented ... to Henry VIII. Ed.:– Helen Wallis. Roxb. Cl., 1981. Lge. fo. Orig. hf. mor. (S. Oct.4; 243) *Traylen.* £450

ROUAULT, Georges
- Divertisement. Paris, 1943. *(1270).* Fo. Elab. mor. & cf. gt., sigd. by F.L. Valencia, Encuaderno. (SPB. Dec.13; 560) $450
- Souvenirs Intimes. [1927]. 4to. Sewed. *(With:)*
- Miserere. [1951]. Publisher's cl.; pres. inscr. (HD. Jun.29; 181) Frs. 3,000
- Visages. Text:– Pierre Courthion. Paris, 1969. *(500) on vell. (50) numbered, not for sale.* Fo. Leaves, box. (HD. Mar.27; 108) Frs. 1,100

ROUCH, W.A.
See— COATEN, Arthur W. & Rouch, W.A.

ROUCHER, Jean Antoine
- Les Mois, Poème en Douze Chants. Ill.:– Cochin, Marillier & Moreau. Paris, 1779. 2 vols. Lge. 4to. Cont. marb. cf. gt., spines decor. (HD. May 3; 138) Frs. 1,350

ROUGET DE LISLE, Claude Joseph
- La Marseillaise. Ill.:– Eugène Grasset. Lyon, ca. 1915?. *(300) numbered.* 4to. Set of 4 ll. ptd. on silk, each matted on bd. in tricolor silk border, also ptd. title-p. on bd., fabric wrinkled, loose. (SG. Dec.15;190) $150

ROUIT, H.
- La Mode Feminine à Travers les Ages. Paris, ca. 1920. *Ltd. Edn., numbered & sigd.* Sm. fo. Col.-pict. title-p., 54 partly engraved & partly ptd. hand-cold. plts., edges of 1st. 2 ll. slightly brittle, unbnd. in orig. hf. cl. folder, ties, spine frayed; inscr. & sigd. by Rouit on front pastedown. (SG. Mar.29; 259) $110

ROULLION-PETIT, F.
- Campagnes Mémorables des Francais. Paris, 1817. 2 vols. Fo. 42 engraved views, slight spotting, margin tear in 1 plt., cont. bds., unc., spines detchd. (lacks 1). (S. May 21; 13) *Harris.* £400

ROUPELL, Arabella E.
- [–] Specimens of the Flora of South Africa. L., 1849. Fo. Engraved hand-cold. title, 8 hand-finished plts. & hand-cold. vig., pp. loose, mor. gt., rubbed, ex-libris. (P. Nov.24; 259) *Hammond.* £1,500
- – Anr. Copy. Fo. Cold. frontis., 8 litho. plts., some foxing, orig. cl., spine partially lacking, recased; Alpheus F. Williams bkplt. (SSA. Jul.5; 345) R 2,500

ROUSSEAU, Jean Jacques
- La Botanique. Ill.:– P.J. Redouté. Paris, 1822. Fo. 65 hand-cold. plts., some light staining on outer margins, text slightly spotted, hf. mor. gt., spine faded. (P. Sep.8; 86) *Tzakas.* £1,150
- Citoyen de Genève à Mr. d'Alembert ... sur son Article Genève dans le VIIme Volume de l'Encyclopedie ... sur le Projet d'establir un Théâtre de Comédie en cette Ville. Amst., 1758. *1st. Edn.* Cont. leath. gt., gt. outer dentelle, corners slightly bumped. (D. Nov.24; 2554) DM 600
- – Anr. Copy. Note for printer, errata & publisher's catalogue, cont. marb. cf., spine decor., cont. ex-libris 'bibliothecae M.I. Theodori Baron ... '. (HD. Nov.9; 75) Frs. 3,000
- Collection Complète des Oeuvres. Ed.:– [Paul mouttou & du Peyrou]. Gerf, 1780-82. 24 vols. & 6 supp. vols. Lacks 1789 supp., cont. bds., 1 spine with sm. fault. (D. Nov.24; 2207) DM 800
- – Anr. Edn. Geneva, 1782. Vols. 1-12 (of 15, lacks supp.). 4to. Cont. Fr. mott. cf., spines gt., corners worn. (S. Apr.10; 302) *Goldbaum.* £150
- – Anr. Copy. 25 vols. Title multi stpd., cont. hf. leath. gt., slightly rubbed, w.a.f. (HK. May 17, 2470) DM 700
- – Anr. Edn. Ill.:– Moreau le Jeune. Ginebra, 1782-90. 17 vols. 4to. Cf. (DS. May 25; 2249) Pts. 140,000
- Collection Compléte des Oeuvres ... – Supplement à la Collection des Oeuvres. - Second Supplement ... Deux-Ponts & Geneva, 1782-83; 1782-84; 1789. 24 vols. in 12; 6 vols. in 3; 3 vols. 12mo. Cont. hf. roan, spines slightly worn. (HD. Feb.22; 199) Frs. 4,000
- Collection Complète des Oeuvres. – [Oeuvres Posthumeas]. Neuchâtel, 1785. [Genève, 1781-82]. 12 vols.; 8 vols. Cont. marb. cf., decor. spines. (HD. Sep.22; 333) Frs. 3,700
- Les Confessions. Geneva, 1782. 2 vols. Hf.-titles, some soiling of fore-edges, names cut from titles in upr. corners, orig. bds., unc., rebkd. (SPB. May 16; 127) $250
- – Anr. Edn. [Genève], 1782. 2 vols. 12mo. Hf.-titles, cont. cf., spines gt., covers partly detchd.; Edward Gibbon copy, bkplt. of Edward Cheney, each vol. inscr. by Henry Edward Fox. (SG. Feb.9; 322) $850
- – Anr. Edn. Ill.:– after Moreau Le Jeune. 1798. 4 vols. Cont. roan, retinted. (HD. Apr.13; 46) Frs. 1,200
- – Anr. Edn. Preface:– Jules Claretie. Ill.:– M. Leloir. Paris, 1889. 2 vols. 4to. Cont. hf. mor., decor. spines, corners, unc., pict. wrap. upr. cover preserved. (HD. Feb.17; 115) Frs. 2,200
- The Confessions with the Reveries of the Solitary Walker. 1783. 2 vols. Cont. qtr. cf., gt. spines. (SKC. Jan.13; 2245) £55
- Discours sur l'Origine & les Fondements de l'Inégalité Parmi les Hommes. Amst., 1755. *1st. Edn.* 12mo. Cont. cf.-bkd. bds., slightly rubbed. (S. Dec.20; 786) *Crete.* £90
- – Anr. Edn. Amst., 1755. *Pirated Edn.?.* Cont. marb. roan, spine decor. (HD. Nov.9; 74) Frs. 1,450
- Emile, ou de l'Education. 1762. 4 vols. in 2. Hf.-titles, cont. red hf. mor., unc., covers rubbed, von Veen coll. (S. Feb.28; 107) £120
- – Anr. Copy. 4 vols. Cont. cf. gt., decor. spines. (HD. Sep.22; 332) Frs. 4,500
- – Anr. Edn. Amst., 1762. *[Mixed Edn.?].* 4 vols. 12mo. Vols. II-IV title ll. different from vol.I, (changed vig.), other sm. variances, cont. cf., gt. spine. (D. Nov.24; 2555) DM 1,200
- Emilus; or, A Essay on Education. Ill.:– Schley. 1763. 2 vols. *(With:)* - Eloisa; or, A Series of Original Letters. 1764. *3rd. Edn.* 4 vols. 12mo. Hf.-titles. Together 6 vols. Cont. spr. cf., spines gt.; Sir Ivar Colquhoun, of Luss copies. (CE. Mar.22; 262) £300

– Geständnisse. Nebst den Selbstbetrachtungen des Einsameen Naturfreundes. Riga, 1782. *1st. German Edn.* 2 pts. in 2 vols. Cont. bds. (GB. Nov.4; 2170)
DM 1,000
– Lettres de Deux Amans Habitans d'une Petite Ville au Pied des Alpes.[La Nouvelle Héloïse]. Ill.:– Gravelot. Amst., 1761. *Orig. Edn.* 6 vols. 12mo. Lacks 4 errata ll. & catalogue, cont. cf. gt., spines decor. (HD. May 3; 139)
Frs. 4,800
– – Anr. Edn. Ill.:– Cochin, engraved by Longueil (frontis.); Gravelot. Neufchâtel, Paris, 1764. 4 vols. Cont. marb. roan, spines decor., arms. (HD. Mar.21; 84)
Frs. 2,150
– – Anr. Edn. Ill.:– Martinet. Amst., 1772. *3rd. Edn.* 6 pts. in 3 vols. Cont. cf. gt., spines decor. (HD. May 21; 67)
Frs. 1,000
– – Anr. Edn. Ill.:– Moreau, engraved by Delvaux. L. [Paris], 1781. 7 vols. 18mo. Cont. marb. roan, spines decor. (HD. Mar.21; 85)
Frs. 2,700
– Oeuvres Complettes. Ill.:– after Marillier. Paris, 1793. *New Edn.* 37 vols. (Lacks supp. vol. 38). Sm. 8vo. Lacks 1 plt., 4 vols. with light browning, cont. marb. cf., spine, cover, unner & cuter dentelle, slightly bumped, 2 vols torn in jnt., some sm. wormholes & spots, vol. IV very rubbed & stained. (H. May 22; 852)
DM 820
– – Anr. Copy. 37 vols. 18mo. Lacks 2 figures, cont. marb. roan gt., spines decor. (HD. Jun.6; 132)
Frs. 3,000
– – Anr. Edn. Basle, 1795. 34 vols. in 17. Cont. cl. (PD. May 16; 1)
£62

ROUSSEAU, Samuel
[–] The Flowers of Persian Literature. L., 1805. Lge. 8vo. Persian & Engl. text, disbnd., covers present; William Morris's copy, with Kelmscott House book-label. (SG. Apr.19; 311)
$120

ROUSSELET, Cl.
– Epigrammata. Lugduni, 1537. 4to. Lacks blank lf., red mor. by Koehler. (HD. Jun.29; 182)
Frs. 1,700

ROUSSELET, Louis
– L'Inde des Rajahs. Paris, 1875. 4to. Stained thro.-out, orig. cl., worn & reprd. (CSK. Jun.1; 186)
£55
– – Anr. Copy. 4to. Spotted, orig. decor. cl., upr. hinge brkn. (S. Dec.13; 151)
Scott. £50

ROUSSET, François
– Ysterotomotokias id est Caesarei partus assertio historiologica ... Paris, 1590. Errata lf. (*Bound with:*) **– Dialogus Apologeticus pro Caesareo Partu.** Paris, 1590. Together 2 works in 1 vol. Cont. limp vell.; sig. of Andrew Fletcher, [of Saltoun] on both title-pp., Dr. Walter Pagel copy. (S. Feb.7; 336)
Clemence. £480

ROUSSET, Jean
– Les Intérêts Présents des Puissances de l'Europe fondés sur les Traités. Conclus depuis la Paix d'Utrecht. La Haye, 1734-36. 17 vols. 12mo. Cf. (HD. Feb.22; 200)
Frs. 3,500

ROUSSIN, Albin René
– Derrotero de Las Costas de la América Meridional. Trans.:– D.J. Doy y Carbonell. Barceiona, 1844. Stained & browned thro.-out, Cont. leath gt. [Sabin XVIII,31] (D. Nov.23; 1337)
DM 600

ROUVEYRE, Edouard
– Connaissances Nécessaires à un Bibliophile. Paris, [1899]. *5th. Edn.* 9 vols. only (of 10). Lge. 8vo. Vell. gt., orig. wraps. bnd. in. (SG. Feb.16; 259)
$110

ROUX, Albert
See— MENTZEL, Albert & Roux, Albert

ROUYER, Eugène & Barcel, Alfred
– L'Art Architectural en France. Paris, 1867; 1866. 2 vols. Fo. 200 engrs., ex-liby., red hf. mor. (SG. May 3; 320)
$140

ROVILLIUS, G.
– Historia Generalis Plartarum. Lugduni, 1586. 2 vols. Fo. Some lf. yellowed, mod. vell. (HD. Dec.9; 80)
Frs. 4,600

ROVINSKI, Dmitri
– L'Oeuvre Gravé de Rembrandt. – Supplement. – Catalogue Raisonné. St. Petersb., 1890; 1914; 1890.

3 vols., 1 vol., 1 vol. Lge. fo. & 8vo. 1st. work, 1001 reproductions, full-p. or mntd. in groups, each liby. stpd. on blank verso, 2nd. work, Russian & Fr. text, 94 plts., 3rd. work, Fr., German, Engl. & Russian text, 4 vols. leatherette, last vol. limp cl. (SG. May 3; 302)
$1,200

ROWAN, Mrs. Ellis
– A Flower Hunter in Queensland & New Zealand. Sydney, 1898. Some generally pale foxing thro.-out, orig. cl., & little worn, unc. (KH. Nov.9; 427)
Aus. $190
– The Flower Paintings of ... Intro.:– Margaret Hazzard. 1982. Fo. S.-c. (JL. Jun.24; 140)
Aus. $140
– Wild Flowers: Facsimiles of Water Colours. N.Y., 1899. Sm. fo. Orig. papered bds., qtr. buckram, spine gt., covers slightly rubbed. (KH. May 1; 605)
Aus. $750

ROWE, George
– A Picturesque Illustration of the Isle of Wight. Cowes, n.d. 4to. Some spotting, cont. hf. mor., rubbed. (CSK. Jul.6; 112)
£110

ROWLANDS, R.
See— PARSONS, Robert, Rowlands, R., & others

ROWLANDSON, Thomas 'Quiz'
– The Grand Master or Adventures of Qui Hi? in Hindostan . 1816. Hand-cold. engraved aquatint frontis., title & 26 plts., text slightly browned, cont. cl., lightly soiled. (CSK. Jun.1; 62)
£110
– Hungarian & Highland Broad Sword. L., 1799. Ob. fo. Cold. aquatint title, 23 cold. aquatint plts. in grey borders, mod. maroon hf. mor. gt. (C. Mar.14; 85)
Harley-Mason. £700

ROWLANDSON, Thomas (Ill.)
See— ACKERMANN, Rudolph
See— ANGELO, Henry Charles William
See— BUNBURY, Henry William 'Geoffrey Gambado'
See— COMBE, William
See— EGAN, Pierce
See— ENGELBACH, L.
See— ROBERTS, Col. David
See— WIGSTEAD, Henry

ROWLEY, George
– Ambrogio Lorenzetti. Princeton, 1958. 2 vols. 4to. No bdg. stated. (SPB. Nov.30; 111)
$225

ROWLEY, George Dawson
– Ornithological Miscellany. Ill.:– J.G. Keulemans & others. L., [1875-]78. 3 vols. 4to. 3 maps, 135 plts., most cold. or tinted, some spotting, cl., soiled, orig. wraps. bnd. in. (S. Nov.28; 81)
Head. £750

ROXBURGH, William
– Flora Indica, or, Descriptions of Indian Plants. L., 1832. Slight spotting, cl. gt., unc., spines defect; Royal Commonwealth Soc. copy. (P. Nov.24; 285)
Weldon & Wesley. £80

ROXBURGHE, John Ker, Duke of
– A Catalogue of the Library of the Late John Duke of Roxburghe. – A Supplement to the Catalogue. – The Prices of the Roxburghe Library. L., 1812. 3 pts. in 1 vol. Prelims. spotted, prices & buyers marked in margins by cont. hand, cont. red mor. gt., slightly rubbed. (S. May 1; 429)
Dawson. £220
– – Anr. Copy. 3 pts. in 1 vol. Some prices & buyers written in cont. hand, a few ll. spotted, 1 lf. defect., mor.-bkd. cl. (S. Oct.11; 474)
Marlborough Rare Books. £170

ROY, William
– The Military Antiquities of the Romans in Britain. 1793. *[1st. Edn.].* Lge. fo. 50 engraved plts. (6 double-p.), table, str.-grd. mor., covers elab. gt.-decor. & including the arms of Riddel, spine gt. in 6 compartments, slightly rubbed; Sir Ivar Colquhoun, of Luss copy. (CE. Mar.22; 263) £800
– – Anr. Copy. Fo. 51 engraved plts., some spotted, liby. stps. on plt. versos & in text, hf. cf., unc., rubbed. (S. Jun.25; 338)
Elliott. £50

ROYAL ACADEMY OF ARTS
– The Exhibition of the Royal Academy. L., [1769-1849]. Vols. 1-81 in 7. 4to. 19th. C. hf. cf.; Richard

Gough-Dawson Turner set with catalogues for 1835-39 extra ill. from cont. periodicals & annot, by him & daughters, bnd. in is Joseph Baretti's Guide through the Royal Academy [1781], Charles Westmacott's Annual Descriptive & Critical Catalogue of the Exhibition [1825], Charles Rosenberg's Critical Guide to the Exhibition [1847] & Guide to the Exhibition [1848]. (SG. Apr.26; 171)
$7,000

ROYAL AUSTRALIAN HISTORICAL SOCIETY
– Journals & Proceedings. 1945-70/71. Vols. 31-56 in 13. A few indices, & c., not collated, cl. gt. (KH. May 1; 606)
Aus. $100

ROYAL BOTANIC GARDEN OF CALCUTTA
– Annals. L., 1891-1911. 24 orig. pts., not a run. 12 pts. in orig. portfo., as a periodical, w.a.f.; Royal Commonwealth Soc. copy. (P. Nov.24; 288)
Weldon & Wesley. £550

ROYAL COMMISSION ON ANCIENT & HISTORICAL MONUMENTS & CONSTRUCTION OF SCOTLAND
– Fife, Kinross & Clackmanan ... 11th. Report. 1935. *New Edn.* 4to. Cl. (PD. Oct.19; 106) £50

ROYAL COMMISSION ON HISTORICAL MANUSCRIPTS
– First-Ninth Reports. 1870-84. 7 vols., including Appendices & Indexes. Fo. Cont. cf., old reback, some wear. (TA. Feb.16; 445)
£75

ROYAL COMMISSION ON HISTORICAL MONUMENTS
– Essex. L., 1916-23. 4 vols. 4to. Liby. stp. on titles, orig. cl. (S. Mar.6; 244)
Lord. £70

ROYAL GEOGRAPHICAL SOCIETY
– Journal. Ca. 1872. Vol. 41. Bdg. not stated, some wear. (KH. May 1; 607)
Aus. $100

ROYAL HORTICULTURAL SOCIETY
– Transactions. 1820-48. 1st. Series:Vols. I-VII. 2nd. Series:Vols. I-III. 4to. Many plts. ptd. in col. & hand-finished, cont. hf. cf., spines gt., last 2 vols. rebnd. to match; from liby. of Luttrellstown Castle, w.a.f. (C. Sep.28; 1781)
£4,800

ROYAL IRISH ACADEMY
– A Biological Survey of Clare Island in the County of Mayo, Ireland, & of the Adjoining District. Dublin, 1911-15. 3 vols. (compl.), pts. 1-68. Royal 8vo. Cl. (GM. Dec.7; 80)
£500
– Transactions. Dublin, 1825. Vol. XIV only. 4to. Engraved vig. on title, 10 single-p. maps & plts. & 3 lge. folding plts. cold., hf. cf., armorial motif on spine. (GM. Dec.7; 274)
£200

ROYAL MILITARY ACADEMY
– Records. Woolwich, 1851. 4to. 4 plts. hand-cold., orig. cl., stained. (CSK. Jun.1; 33)
£55

ROYAL SOCIETY
– Philosophical Transactions. L. & Oxford, 1667-83. Vols.2-3, 5-11 & 13-14 only, in 6 vols. Sm. 4to. 75 engraved plts. only, some folding, a few torn, 1 defect., lacks fo. 4R1 in Vol. 3 & fo. 5X4 in Vol. 7, rather soiled & stained thro.-out, few tears, mod. hf. cf. (BBA. Mar.21; 62)
N. Phillips. £480

ROYAL SOCIETY OF ANTIQUARIES OF IRELAND
Dublin, ca. 1858-1930. Approx. 50 vols. Orig. wraps. & some bnd. vols., as a periodical, w.a.f. (GM. Dec.7; 192)
£550

ROYAUMONT, Nicolas Fontaine, Sieur de
– L'Histoire du Vieux et du Nouveau Testament. Ill.:– Duflos. Paris, 1723. 2 pts. in 1 vol. Fo. Cont. cf., gt. decor., decor. spine. (HD. Mar.14; 12)
Frs. 3,500
– The History of the Old Testament & the New ... Trans.:– Richard Blome. 1690-88. 2 vols. in 1. Fo. Ruled in red thro.-out, cont. reversed cf. (TA. Apr.19; 255)
£100
– – Anr. Edn. Ill.:– Van Hove & others. L., 1701. [Appendix 1700]. *2nd. Edn.* Fo. 5 double-p.maps, 250 copperplts., 2 plt. appendix, disbnd. (SG. Feb.9; 138)
$175

ROYE, Jean de
[–] **Chronique Scandeleuse ou Histoire des Estranges Faictis Arrivez soubs le Règne de Louis XI depuis l'An 1460 jusques à 1483.** 1620. 4to. Cont. spr. cf. gt., decor. spine, arms. (HD. Nov.9; 157)
Frs. 1,850

ROYEN, J.F. von & Eyck, P.N. von
– **Over Boekkunst en de Zilverdistel.** Den Haag, 1916. *(125).* Ptd. in red & black, woodcut printers mark at end. orig. vell., gold-tooled silver thistle on upr. cover, MS. dedication on end-papers. (HK. Nov.11; 4085)
DM 400

ROYLE, John Forbes
– **Illustrations of the Botany & other Branches of the Natural History of the Himalayan Mountains & of the Flora of Cashmere.** 1839. 2 vols. Fo. Cold. engraved frontis., cold. plan, 100 plts., 97 hand-touched cold. litho. plts., hf.-titles, cont. hf. cf. (SKC. Nov.18; 1985)
£1,300
– – **Anr. Copy.** 2 vols., including plt. vol. 4to. Plts. vol. with litho. frontis., 2 plans, 94 (of 98) further litho. plts., lacks plts. 7, 13, 66, plt. 79 replaced by mntd. hand-drawn copy in an amateur hand, some browning, later two- toned cl., spines gt. (LC. Mar.1; 181)
£60

ROYLLET
– **Les Nouveaux Principes de l'Art d'ecrie.** Paris, 1731. Fo. Foxing & some sm. stains, old hf. vell., some defects. (HD. Dec.9; 81)
Frs. 1,900

ROZIER, Abbé François
– **Cours Complet d'Agriculture Théorique, Pratique, Economique et de Médecine Rurale et Vétérinaire.** Paris, 1781-1805. 12 vols., including 2 vol. Supp. 4to. 1st. 10 vols. cont hf. roan, arms on spines, last 2 vols. sewed. (HD. Nov.9; 193)
Frs. 3,700
– – **Anr. Copy.** 12 vols. including supp. 4to. Hf. roan, spine decor., worn, some losses from spines. (HD. Jul.6; 76)
Frs. 3,050
– **Mémoire sur la Meilleure Manière de Faire et de Gouverner les Vins ...** Paris, 1772. *Orig. Edn.* Cont. hf. roan, arms, unc. (HD. Nov.9; 187)
Frs. 1,500

ROZIER DE LA CHASSAGNE
– **Manuel des Pulmoniques ... On y a Joint une Nouvelle Methode de Reconnoitre ces Mêmes Maladies par la Percussion du Thorax, traduite du Latin d'Auenbrugger.** Paris, 1770. *1st. Fr. Edn.* 2 pts. in 1 vol. Blank corner of 2nd. title torn away, cont. Fr. mott. cf., gt. spine, some wear. (S. Nov.28; 105)
Quaritch. £350

RUBAKIN, N.A.
– **Sredi Knig [Amongst Books].** Moscow, 1911. *2nd. Edn.* 3 pts. in 1 vol. Slightly browned, cont. cf.-bkd. cl., rubbed. (BBA. Feb.9; 142) *Edwards.* £55

RUBEIS, Dominicus de
See— ROSSI, Domenico de

RUBEIS, Jacobus de
See— ROSSI, Giovanni Giacomo de

RUBENS, Albert
– **De Re Vestiaria Veterum, Praecipue de Lato Clamvo Libri Duo.** Antw., 1665. 4to. Cont. vell. gt., arms. (TA. Apr.19; 361)
£80

RUBENS, Philip
– **Electorum Libri II.** Antw., 1608. *1st. Edn.* (*Bound with:*) RUBENS, Albert – **De Re Vestiaria Veterum.** Antw., 1665. *1st. Edn.* 2 pts. Folding engraved plt. torn. Together 2 works in 1 vol. 4to. A few ll. slightly soiled. Cont. cf., slightly worn. (BBA. Nov.30; 37)
Quaritch. £350

RUBENS, Pieter Paul
– **La Gallerie du Palais du Luxembourg.** Ill.:– Audran. Picart & others. after Rubens. Paris, 1710. Lge. fo. Port. frontis., 24 plts., including 3 double-p., cont. mott. cf., spine defect. (C. Dec.9; 193)
Duran. £350
– – **Anr. Copy.** Lge. fo. Engraved title, 1 (of 4) ports., 21 plts., advt., hf. russ., worn. (SPB. Dec.13; 890)
$200
– **Palazzi Antichi di Genova.** Antw., 1663. Vig. title, 72 engraved plts. & ground plans. (*Bound with:*)
– **Palazzi Moderni di Genova ...** Antw., 1663. Vig. title, 67 engraved plts. & ground plans. Together 2

works in 1 vol. Lge. 4to. some light margin stains, cont. gt.-panel. cf., some wear. (TA. Mar.15; 451)
£380
– **Palazzi di Genova.** [Antw., 1622]. *1st. Edn.* 2 pts. in 1 vol. Fo. 138 (of 139) plts., including 15 double-p., lacks 1 plt. from 1st. pt., plts. in 2nd. pt. (not by Rubens?) mntd. on guards, outer margin renewed at time of bdg., last 7 plts. defect., anr. plt. torn with with sm. losses, cont. cf., crudely reprd. (HD. Apr.13; 47)
Frs. 9,500
– **Théorie de la Figure Humaine Considérée dans ses Principes, soit en Repos ou en Mouvement.** Paris, 1773. 4to. Hf.-title, mod. hf. cf., gt. spine, partly unc. (S. Nov.17; 65)
Quaritch. £320

RUBIE, G.
– **The British Celestial Atlas.** L., 1830. 4to. 16 engraved plts., (2 with together 6 volvelles), 2 volvelle mountings slightly defect., slight foxing & offsetting, hf. c cf. antique, marb. bds., orig. ptd. label laid down. (SG. Apr.26; 172)
$600

RUBYS, Claude de
– **Histoire Véritable de la Ville de Lyon contenans ce qui a été omis par Maistres S. Champier, Paradin et Autres ...** Lyon, 1604. Fo. Cont. roan, rubbed. (HD. Nov.9; 135)
Frs. 1,350

RUCHAT, Abraham. [i.e. G. Kypseler]
– **Etat et Délices de la Suisse.** ca. 1750. Sm. ob. 4to. 52 copper plts., including maps, 19th. C. hf. leath., rubbed. (R. Oct.13; 3280)
DM 6,400

RUCKERT, Friedrick
– **Lieder und Sprüche der Minnesinger.** Darmstadt, Ernst Ludwig Pr., 1924. *(30) Deluxe Edn. on Japan.* Orig. mor., decor. spine, cover & inner & outer dentelle, by Ernst Rehbein, bd. s.-c., lightly bumped. (HK. May 17; 2746)
DM 900
– **Morgen ländische Sagen und Geschichten.** Ill.:– L. Corinth. Berlin, 1919. *(20) numbered.* All etchings sigd. by artist, 4 full-p. orig. etchings, orig. cold. pict. bds., unc., with subscriber list. (GB. May 5; 2292)
DM 1,200

RUDBECK, Gustaf
– **Broderade Bokband fran Aldre Tid.** Stockholm, 1925,. *(800).* 4to. Orig. wraps., spine chipped, H.M. Nixon coll. (BBA. Oct.6; 119)
Maggs. £100

RUDBECK, Johannes
– **Svenska Bokband undern Yare Tiden.** Stockholm, 1912-14. 3 vols. in 1. Fo. Cont. hf. cf., gt. spine, faded. (BBA. Nov.10; 120)
Laywood. £130

RUCKERT, Rainer
– **Meissener Porzellan.** München, 1966. 4to. Orig. bds. (BR. Apr.13; 2072)
DM 1,700
– – **Anr. Copy.** 4to. Orig. wraps. (D. Nov.23; 2018)
DM 900

RUDDIMAN, Thomas & others
– **A Catalogue of the Library of the Faculty of Advocates, Edinburgh.** Edinb., 1742-76. 2 vols. Fo. Cont. spr. cf., spines gt.; Sir Ivar Colquhoun, of Luss copy. (CE. Mar.22; 264)
£480
– – **Anr. Copy.** 2 vols. Fo. Few ll. slightly soiled, cont. cf., gt. spines, worn, jnts. brkn. (BBA. Mar.7; 339)
Maggs. £60

RUDDIMAN'S WEEKLY MAGAZINE
Edinb., 3 Jul. 1777-23 Dec. 1778. Vols. 1-3, with indexes to Vols. 1 & 2, in 2 vols. 8vo. & 4to. Cont. cf.-bkd. bds., unc.; Sir Ivar Colquhoun, of Luss copy. (CE. Mar.22; 265)
£260

RUDMORE BROWN, R.N. & others
– **The Voyage of the 'Scotia'.** 1906. Orig. cl., rubbed; pres. copy from William S. Bruce (the leader of the expedition) to the Marquis of Tullibardine, T.L.s. inserted. (P. Jun.7; 46)
£120

RUDOLPH, J.K.
– **Die Hausmaurerkunst.** Kassal, 1827. *1st. Edn.* 4to. Cont. style lf. leath. (R. Oct.12; 1770)
DM 500

RUELLIUS, Joannes
– **Veterinariae Medicinae Libri II.** Paris, 1530. *Orig. Edn.* Fo. Wide, margins, some light staining, a few pencil annots., cont. limp vell., slightly soiled, loosening. (VG. Mar.19; 274)
Fls. 1,650

RUFF, J.
– **Hebammen Buch.** Frankfurt, 1580. *1st. Edn.* 4to. Old copper engraved ex-libris pasted on title verso, lightly browned, some slight margin foxing, limp vell. (R. Oct.12; 1465a)
DM 2,400

RUGE, Arnold
– **Anekdota zur Neuesten Deutschen Philosophie und Publicistik von Bruno Bauer, Ludwig, Feuerbach, Friedrich Köppen, Karl Nauwerck, Arnold Ruge und Einigen Ungenannten.** Zürich & Winterthur, 1843. 2 vols. in 1. Some light browning, cont. bds, slightly rubbed. (R. Oct.11; 1221) DM 2,800

RUGENDAS, Joh. M.
– **Malerische Reise in Brasilien.** Paris & Mühlhausen, 1835. Lge. fo. On vell, wide margin, litho. hf. title & title, 100 litho. plts., all lithos on China, captions Fr., text partly browned & spotted, some plt. margins very spotted, a few lithos. with sm. spots, cont. lf. leath., bumped & spotted. [Sabin 73934] (H. May 22; 274)
DM 18,500

RUINI, Carlo
– **Anatomia et Medicina Equorum Noua.** Trans.:– P. Uffenbach. Frankfurt, 1603. *1st. German Edn.* 2 pts. in 1 vol. Fo. 1st. ll. with margin defects., several ll. with tears, worming in margins, very browned thro.-out & slightly stained. cont. vell., very defect. (HT. May 10; 2588a) DM 430
– **Dell'Anatomia, e dell'Infermita del Cavallo.** Bologna, 1598. *1st. Edn.* Pt. 1 only (of 2). Fo. Lacks title & probably 1st. blank, 2 dedication ll. defect., several following ll. frayed, some browning, some margin worming, mor. by Sangerski & Sutcliffe. (S. Dec.13; 308)
Rix. £100

RUKEYSER, Muriel
– **Theory of Flight.** Foreword:– Stephen Vincent Benet. New Haven, 1935. *1st. Edn.* Orig. cl., d.-w. a little spotted; inscr. by author to Mr & Mrs. Frederic Dannay. (CNY. Dec.16; 300)
$110
– **Wake Island.** Garden City, 1942. *1st. Edn. 1st. Bdg.* 12mo. Orig. pict. bds.; inscr. by author to Mr. & Mrs. Frederic Dannay. (CNY. Dec.16; 301)
$380

RULES & ARTICLES for the better Government of his Majesties Land-Forces; An Abridgement of the English Military Discipline
1685. Together 2 works in 1 vol. 18th. C. cf., gt., rubbed. [Wing R2239; A105] (BBA. Sep.29; 145)
Trotman. £160

RULES & REGULATIONS for the Sword Exercise of the Cavalry
L., 1796. Cont. bds., worn. (CSK. Sep.16; 196)
£60
– – **Anr. Copy.** 4to. 28 (of 29) copper engrs., some hand-cold., 1 torn, some staining & foxing, new end-papers, 19th. C. three-qtr. cf., rebkd. with orig. spine leath., glazed. (CBA. Dec.10; 325) $130

RULHIERE, Claude Carloman de
– **Histoire de l'Anarchie de Pologne et du Démembrement de Cette République.** Paris, 1807. 4 vols. Roan, decor. spines. (HD. Feb.22; 201) Frs. 3,500
– – **Anr. Copy.** 4 vols. Cont. tree sheep, decor. spines. (HD. Sep.22; 335)
Frs. 1,400

RUMANN, A.
See— LANCKORONSKA, Maria & Rümann, A.

RUMORR, C.F. von
– **Geist der Kochkunst.** Stuttgart & Tübingen, 1832. *2nd Edn.* Most margins lightly brown spotted, later bds., worn, spine faded. (H. May 22; 385)
DM 400

RUMPF, Andreas
– **Chalkidische Vasen.** Berlin & Leipzig, 1927. Text & 2 plt. vols. in 3 vols. 4to. Orig. linen. (R. Apr.3; 695)
DM 480

RUMPF, J.D.F.
– **Beschreibung der Königlichen Schlösser in Berlin, Chearlottenburg, Schönhausen in und bey Potsdam.** Berlin, 1794. *1st. Edn.* Cont. bds., unc. (GB. Nov.3; 325)
DM 1,700

RUMPH, Georg Eberhard

- D'Amboinsche Rariteitkamer ... Amst., 1741. Fo. Some foxing, cont. cf., rubbed, spine reprd. (VG. Nov.30; 778) Fls. 1,800

RUMPOLT, Markus

- Eln New Kochbuch. Ill.:– J. Amman, V. Solis, H. Weiditz. Frankfurt, 1587. *2nd. Edn.* Fo. Title & last lf. slightly pale & spotted, title with sm. margin fault & MS. owner's note, 1630, cont. vell., soiled, slightly worn, lacks ties. (HK. Nov.8; 327a) DM 29,000

RUNAU, D.

- Historia und Einfeltige Beschreibung des Grossen Dreizehenjerigen Kriegs in Preussen, im Jar 1454 angefangen, und im 66 geendet samt Kurtzer Historien des Kleinen Zweyjerigen Kriegs ... Wittenberg, 1582. 4to. Slightly browned, last 6 ll. partly restored in margins, hf. vell. (R. Oct.11; 107) DM 950

RUNGE, Heinrich

- Die Schweiz in Original-Ansichten. Darmstadt, 1863. Very foxed thro.-out, cont. hf. leath., rubbed. (GB. Nov.3; 140) DM 4,800
- – – **Anr. Edn.** Darmstadt, 1867-69. *De Luxe Edn.* 3 vols. 4to. 3 engraved titles with vigs., 195 steel engraved plts., on China in lge. format, slightly foxed, unc., 66 orig. pt. wraps. (R. Oct.13; 3282) DM 15,000
- La Suisse. Darmstadt, 1870. Cont. blind-tooled leath., slightly rubbed. (GB. Nov.3; 139) DM 4,600

RUNGE, Philipp Otto

- Von dem Fischer un Syner Frau. Ill.:– M. Behmer. Berlin, 1914. *(12) De Luxe Edn.* Printers mark sigd. by artist, hand-bnd. rust cold. mor., gt. spine, covers & inner dentelles, by O. Dorfner, Weimar; Hauswedell coll. (H. May 24; 582) DM 10,400

RUPERT, Charles G.

- Apostle Spoons: Their Evolution from Earlier Types, & the Emblems Used by the Silversmiths for the Apostles. L., 1929. *1st. Edn.* 4to. L.P., 135 photographic reproductions on 23 plts., buckram gt., spotted. (SG. Oct.13; 327) $100

RUPERT V. DEUTZ, Tuitiensis

- Ruperti Abbatis Tuitiensis Commentariarum in Evangelium Ioannis Libri XIIII. Nuremb., 1526. *1st. 8vo. Edn.* Cont. German stpd. roan over wood bds., gt.- & silver-decor., clasps incompl.; from Fondation Furstenberg-Beaumesnil. (HD. Nov.16; 168) Frs. 1,500

RUPPANER, Antoine

- Hypodermic Injection in the Treatment of Neuralgia, Rheumatism, Gout, & Other Diseases. Boston, 1865. *1st. Edn.* Sm. 8vo. Liby. stp., orig. cl., rebkd. (SG. Oct.6; 318) $325

RUPPELL, Wilhelm Peter Eduard Simon

- Atlas zu der Reise im Nördlichen Afrika. Frankfurt, 1826-28. 5 pts. in 3 vols. Fo. General title, 119 litho. plts., including 114 hand-cold., cont. cf.-bkd. bds., spines a little wormed. (C. Jun.27; 133) *Quaritch.* £1,200

RUPPRECHT PRESS

See— VOSS, Johann Heinrich

RUPRICH-ROBERT, V.

- Flore Ornamentale. Paris, [1866]-76. 2 pts. in 1 vol. Fo. Hf.-title, engraved title & 156 plts, (151 called for) including 4 dupls. & 1 additional plt., spotted, mor.-bkd. cl. (S. Apr.30; 221) *Thomas.* £110

RURAL CYCLOPEDIA (THE), or a General Dictionary of Agriculture

Ed.:– J.M. Wilson. Edinb., 1847-50. 4 vols. Engraved plts., a few hand-cold., cont. hf. mor., covers soiled & rubbed, upr. bd. of Vol. 4 cracked. (CSK. Apr.27; 112) £65

RUSCA, Louis

- Recueil des Dessins de Differens Batimens construits à Saint-Pétersbourg, et dans l'Interieur de l'Empire de Russie. Ill.:– Thierry & Normand after Rusca. Saint-Pétersbourg [Paris], 1810. 2 pts. in 1 vol. Fo. Fr. & Italian text, cont. hf. chagrin, spine

decor., bdg. defect., loss from spine. (HD. Jun.18; 42) Frs. 23,000

RUSCELLI, Girolamo 'Alexis de Piedmont'

- De' Commentarii della Lingua Italiana. Venice, 1581. *1st. Edn.* 4to. Early vell., loose. (SG. Oct.27; 283) $120
- Le Imprese Illustri. Venice, 1584-83. 4 pts. in 1 vol. 4to. 4 engraved title-pp., engraved emblems thro.-out, last lf. blank, defect. in inner upr. corner & upr. margins at beginning & end, also some lr. inner & outer corners affecting text, some head-lines shaved, 2 double-p. engrs. shaved, bad inkstains on p.5 pt.IV, dampstained at beginning, paper wraps. (S. Apr.10; 333) Rix. £125
- Kriegs und Archeley Kunst ... Frankfurt, 1620. *1st. German Edn.* 2 pts. in 1 vol. Fo. Wide margin, some light browning, cont. vell., ties. (HK. Nov.9; 1906) DM 2,200
- Precetti della Militia Moderna, Tanto per Mare, Quanto per Terra. Venice, 1595. Sm. 4to. Cont. limp vell. (BBA. Jun.28; 172) *Dilua.* £100

RUSCONI, Giovanni Antonio

- Della Archiettura Libri Dieci. Venice, 1690. Sm. fo. Title & dedication lf. facs, some slight spotting, bds. (D. Nov.23; 1918) DM 1,200
- I Dieci Libri d'Achitettura. Venice, 1660. Fo. Title slightly spotted, stp removed from left margin, slightly defect., last plt. verso stpd., cont. style hf. leath. (D. Dec.23; 1917) DM 2,400

RUSHWORTH, John

- Historical Collections. 1721. *2nd. Edn.* 8 vols. Fo. Cont. panel. cf., spines decor.: Sir Ivar Colquhoun, of Luss copy. (CE. Mar.22; 266) £280

RUSKIN, John

- The Elements of Drawing. 1857. *1st. Edn.* 1 vol. Cl. gt. (*With:*) - **Pre-Raphaelitism.** 1851. *1st. Edn.* 1 vol. Orig. bds. (*With:*) - **Lectures on Architecture & painting.** 1854. *1st. Edn.* 1 vol. Hf. mor. gt. (P. Oct.20; 167) £55
- The Harbours of England. Ill.:– Thomas Lupton after J.M.W. Turner. 1856. Fo. 12 mezzotint plts., orig. cl. gt. (LC. Oct.13; 286) £50
- – – **Anr. Edn.** Ill.:– T. Lupton after J.M.W. Turner. 1877. *New Edn.* Fo. 12 uncold. mezzotint type plts., contents loose in orig. cl. gt., rubbed. (TA. Jun.21; 209) £75
- The King of the Golden River. Ill.:– Arthur Rackham. L., 1932. *(570) numbered & sigd. by artist.* Slightly spotted, orig. parch. gt. (S. Dec.20; 579) *Antique.* £110
- – – **Anr. Copy.** Limp vell., unc., s.-c. (brkn.), light wear & soiling. (RO. Mar.21; 102) $200
- The Nature & Authority of Miracle. N.p., '1873' [i.e. before 1890]. *Wise Forgery.* Red mor. gt., by Doves Bindery, dtd. 19 C-S 04, mor. solander case; Perry Molstad copy. (SPB. May 16; 557) $550
- The Nature of Gothic. A Chapter of the Stones of Venice. [Hammersmith, Kelms. Pr., 1892]. *(500).* Sm. 4to. Gt.-lettered vell., unc., bowed, lightly soiled, linen ties. (SG. Mar.29; 174) $200
- [-] Poems by J.R. [L.], 1850. *1st. Edn.* 12mo. Cont. hard-grain mor. gt., spine & corners worn; Frederic Dannay copy. (CNY. Dec.16; 303) $550
- The Stones of Venice. 1851-53. *1st. Edn.* 3 vols. Hf. vell. gt., soiled. (P. Dec.8; 268) *Newell.* £50
- Unto this Last. Doves Pr., 1907. *(300).* Niger mor. by Doves Bindery, [1919]. (BBA. Oct.27; 161) *Sawyer.* £170
- Works. Boston, [1898]. *St. Mark's Edn., (1000) numbered on L.P.* 27 vols., including J.A. Hobson's 'John Ruskin, Social Reformer'. Lge. 8vo. Buckram. (SG. Nov.17; 113) $250
- – – **Anr. Edn.** L., 1903-12. *(2062).* 39 vols. Lge. 8vo. Liby. stp. on verso of each title, orig. cl. gt., unc., faded on spines & somewhat rubbed. (TA. Jun.21; 318) £380
- – – **Anr. Copy.** 39 vols. 4to. Orig. roan-bkd. cl., liby. stp. on front free end-papers. (S. Oct.11; 361) *M. Wais.* £200
- – – **Anr. Copy.** 39 vols. Buckram. (KH. Nov.9; 429) Aus. $450

RUSKIN, John (Ed.)

See— DAME WIGGINS OF LEE, & her Seven Wonderful Cats

RUSSELL, Alex

- The Natural History of Aleppo. L., 1756. Lge. fo. Leath. (DS. May 23; 2255) Pts. 150,000

RUSSELL, Sir Bertrand

- The Queen of Sheba's Nightmare. Ill.:– Hans Erni. Zurich, 1970. *MS. Facs. Edn. (267) numbered & sigd. by author & artist.* Fo. Cover sigd. by artist & dtd. 19.10.72., unbnd. in orig. wraps., ptl. in blind high relief, fitted case. (S. Nov.21; 75) *Makiya.* £550

RUSSELL, Charles E.

- English Mezzotint Portraits & their States. 1926. 2 vols., including plt. vol. 8vo. & 4to. Hf. pig. gt. (P. Mar.15; 199) *Sims, Reed & Fogg.* £140
- – – **Anr. Edn.** 1926. *(625) numbered.* 2 vols. Fo. & 4to. Orig. hf. mor. gt., spines slightly worn. (TA. May 17; 400) £105

RUSSELL, George William

- [-] Homeward Songs by the Way, A.E. Dublin, 1894. *1st. Edn.* 12mo. Orig. ptd. wraps., hf. mor. s.-c.; Arthur B. Spingarn bkplt., Frederic Dannay copy. (CNY. Dec.16; 304) $100

RUSSELL, John Scott

- On the Nature, Properties & Applications of Steam, & on Steam Navigation. Edinb., 1841. Some spotting, a few tears along folds, orig. cl., faded, some soiling & rubbing; Stanitz coll. (SPB. Apr.25; 384) $100

RUSSELL, Kenneth Fitzpatrick

- British Anatomy, 1525-1800; A Bibliography. Melbourne, 1963. *(750) numbered & sigd.* Buckram, card. s.-c. (KH. May 1; 609) Aus. $130

RUSSELL, P. & Price, O.

- England Displayed. Ill.:– J. Rocque, T. Kitchen, G. Rollos, & T. Bowen. L., 1769. 2 vols. Fo. Engraved allegorical frontis., vig. title, 54 maps (Chubb listing 52 only), 81 plts. of views, list of subscribers, 1 or 2 plts. folded, faint margin staining or some wormholes, cont. qtr. cf., worn. (S. Dec.1; 156) *Marrell.* £450

RUSSELL, Thomas

- Sonnets & Miscellaneous Poems. Oxford, 1789. *1st. Edn.* 4to. Lacks 1st. & last blank ll., title stained, mod. marb. bds.; Frederic Dannay copy. (CNY. Dec.16; 305) $150

RUSSELL, William

- The History of America. 1778. 2 vols. 4to. Some light spotting, cont. hf. cf., 1 cover detchd. (CSK. Sep.16; 213) £220

RUSSELL, William Howard

- The Atlantic Telegraph. Ill.:– R. Dudley. [1865]. 4to. Orig. cl. gt., slight wear. (P. Apr.12; 36) £140
- The Prince of Wales Tour: A Diary in India. 1877. Fo. Mntd. woodburytype frontis., 30 engraved plts., 1 cold. map, cont. hf. mor., rubbed. (CSK. Mar.23; 48) £55

RUSSELL, William Howard & Dudley, Robert

- A Memorial of the Marriage of H.R.H. Albert & H.R.H. Alexandra. N.d. Fo. Cold. title, 40 (of 41) litho. plts., some loose & frayed, orig. cl. gt. (P. Sep.8; 132) £55

RUSSIAN CRIES

Ill.:– G. Orlowski. 1809. Fo. Hand-cold. engraved title, 8 hand-cold. plts., hf. mor., upr. cover detchd., as a coll. of plts., w.a.f. (P. Mar.15; 165) £280

RUSSOLI, F.

- Modigliani. L., 1959. (*With:*) - **Modigliani Drawings.** L., 1969. Together 2 vols. No bdgs. stated. (SPB. Nov.30; 116) $100

RUST, Margaret

- The Queen of the Fishes, an Adaptation in English of a Fairy Story of Valois. Ill.:– Lucien Pissarro. Eragny Pr. 1894. *(150) initialled by artist.* Orig. limp cf., spine faded, slightly rubbed; van Veen coll. (S. Feb.28; 18) £580

RUTHERFORD, Sir Ernest

- Radioactive Substances & their Radiations. Camb., 1913. *1st. Edn.* Slight browning, mostly to end-papers, orig. cl., extremities rubbed; stp. & sig.

RUTHERFORD, Sir Ernest -Contd.

of Edward Beattie Stephenson, Stanitz coll. (SPB. Apr.25; 387) $100

– – **Anr. Copy**. Text extended in old MS., orig. linen gt. (D. Nov.23; 686) DM 600

– **Radio Activity**. Camb., 1904. *1st. Edn*. Slight browning, title & dedication lf. creased & supplied from anr. copy, orig. cl. gt.; Stanitz coll. (SPB. Apr.25; 385) $425

– – **Anr. Edn**. Camb., 1905. *2nd. Edn*. Orig. cl.; Stanitz coll. (SPB. Apr.25; 386) $175

RUTHERFORD, Sir Ernest & others

– **Radiations from Radioactive Substances**. Camb., 1930. *1st. Edn*. Spotting of fore-edges, orig. cl., d.-w. (minor wear, Stanitz coll. (SPB. Apr.25; 388) $100

RUTHERSTON, Albert

– **Sixteen Designs for the Theatre**. Oxford, 1928. *(475) numbered*. Fo. 16 plts. (10 hand-cold.), orig. cl. (CSK. Feb.10; 119) £75

RUTHERSTON, Albert

See— DRINKWATER, John & Rutherston, Albert

RUTLAND, John Henry Manners, Duke of

[–] **A Tour through Part of Belgium & the Rhenish Provinces**. L., 1822. 4to. Pencil scribbles on 4 text ll., cont. hf. mor. (C. Nov.16; 131) *Hannas*. £100

RUTLIDGE, C.S.

– **Guide to Queensland** ... L., ca. 1899. Orig. cl., minor soiling; inscr. by author. (KH. Nov.9; 691) Aus. $130

RUTLINGER, Caspar

– **Neüw Zugerichte Schreibkunst ... Allen Secretarien, Schreibern/Kouff= vnd handelsleüten** ... Zürich, 1648. Lge. 4to. Wide margin, plts re-cased & reprd., some spotting, hf. vell., Hauswedell coll. (H. May 23; 234) DM 5,400

– **Neuw Zugerichte Schreibkunst: Von Capital vnd sonst allerhand Nutzlichen Alphabeten ... Alles von Freyer Hand mit der Feder auffs Kupffer gebracht** ... Zurich, 1605. Title & dedication margin defect., 1 tear, partly reprd., very stained in lr. margin, (*Bound with:*) **Calligraphia Nova** 1605. Margin worming, 1 tear. Together 2 works in vol. Ob 4to. old MS. vell., slightly defect., upr. cover brkn., Hauswedell coll. (H. May 23; 224) DM 3,600

RUTTER, John

– **Delineations of Fonthill & its Abbey**. L., priv. ptd., 1823. *[1st. Edn.]*. 4to. L.P. subscribers copy, frontis., additional title & 1 plt. in 2 states, hand-cold. aquatint & etching on India paper, folding litho. plan, 12 etched plts. on India paper with 5 in additional proof state, title vig. & head & tail-pieces etched on India paper, orig. engraved bds., rebkd. in mor.; ex-libris of Duke of Bedford. (C. Dec.9; 142) *Quaritch*. £300

– – **Anr. Copy**. Lge. 4to. L.P., additional hand-cold. aquatint engraved title, 12 plts., including 2 hand-cold., hf.-title, subscribers list, some faint spotting, cont. hf. roan gt., rubbed; Henry Cunnington bkplt. (S. Nov.1; 127) *Campbell*. £140

– – **Anr. Copy**. 4to. folding litho. map, 13 engraved plts., including 3 hand-cold., some light foxing & staining, orig. bds., worn. (S. Oct.11; 442) *Quaritch*. £80

RUTTER, Owen

– **We Happy Few**. Gold. Cock. Pr., 1946. *(100) numbered*. Orig. cl.-bkd. bds. (BBA. Jul.27; 194) *Keegan*. £50

RUXNER, Georg

[–] **Anfang, Urspru[n]g und Herkomen des Thurniers inn Teutscher Nation**. Simmern, 1532. *2nd. Edn*. Fo. Slightly stained in margins nearly thro.-out, especially title & some text ll., 1st. 60 ll. in upr. inner corner & last 20 ll. in lr. outer corner restored, title with several old owners marks, 17th. C. leath. gt., gt. royal arms on upr. cover, slightly rubbed, defect., spine partly reprd. (R. Apr.3; 87) DM 3,000

[–] **Thurnierbuch**. Ill.:– J. Amman. Frankfurt, 1578. *2nd. Frankfurt Edn*. 2 pts. in 1 vol. Fo. Title with owner's note, 2 sigs. reversed, some slight browning & worming, slight staining in side margin

near end, 2 pp. with pen scribble, cont. blind-tooled pig. gold-ptd. (HK. Nov.8; 327) DM 3,200

RUYSCH, Frederik

– **Observationum Anatomico-Chirurgicarum Centuria; accedit, Catalogus Rariorum quae in Museo Ruyschiano Asservantur**. Amst., 1691. *1st. Edn*. Lge. 4to. Cont. cf., covers detchd. (SG. Mar.22; 277) $350

– **Thesaurus Anatomicus**. Amst., 1737-39. 43 pts. in 2 vols. 4to. Title & 1st. 3 ll. torn & creased at lr. margin with loss of 1 letter, 1 or 2 plts. loose, slightly browned cont. sheep worn, loose. (CH. May 24; 44) Fls. 1,400

RYCAUT, Sir Paul

– **The History of the Present State of the Ottoman Empire**. L., 1675. *4th Edn*. 3 pts. in 1 vol. 1 plt. torn, some faint browning, cont. cf., slightly worn. [Wing 2402] (S. Mar.6; 18) *Azezian*. £150

– **The History of the Turkish Empire**. L., 1680. *1st. Edn*. 2 pts. in 1 vol. Fo. Mod. cl. [Wing R 2406] (SG. Oct.27; 284) $130

RYCQUIUS, J.

– **De Capitolio Romano Commentarius**. Ghent, 1617. Fo. 16th. C. Engl. bdg. of cf., gt. to a corner & centrepiece pattern, spine partly defect., upr. cover detchd. (BBA. Jun.28; 173) *King*. £85

RYDE, H.T.

– **Illustrations of the New Palace of Westminster**. 1849-65. 1st. & 2nd. Series: 2 vols. 4to. 1 plt. torn, few spotted orig. cl., spines faded. (S. Nov.1; 123) *Woodruff*. £50

RYE, Reginald Arthur (Compiler)

See— MOCATTA, Frederic D.

RYFF, Walther Hermann 'Q. Apollinaris'

– **Der Furnembsten, Notwendigsten, der Gantzen Architectur Angehoerigen Mathematischen und Mechanischen Kuenst, Eygentlicher Bericht**. Nuremb., 1547. *1st. Edn*. Fo. Lacks title, 4 other prelims. & ll. 3a7 & 2C4, stains, &c., later vell. (SG. Mar.22; 279) $250

– **Kurtzs Handtbüchlein unnd Experiment Viler Artzneyen**. Strassburg, 1583. *18th. Edn*. Cont. style leath. (R. Oct.12; 1466) DM 1,500

– **Recht Gründtliche Bewerte Cur des Steins, Sandt und Griesz, in Nieren, Blasen und Lenden**. Strassburg, [1543]. *1st. Edn*. 4to. 2 ll. with old MS. annots., some browning, hf. vell. (D. Nov.23; 620) DM 1,700

RYLEY, Arthur Beresford

– **Old Paste**. L., [1913]. Lge. 4to. Col. frontis., 28 plts., gt.-decor. cl., spine crudely taped. (SG. Aug.25; 230) $110

RYMILL, John

– **Southern Lights, The Official Account of the British Graham Land Expedition 1934-1937**. 1938. Upr. blank cut away, slight spotting, cl., slightly soiled, d.-w. torn. (P. Jun.7; 41) £150

RYUKYU FURU-BINGATA

Kyoto, Showa 43 [1968]. 2 vols. Lge. 4to. 100 col. plts., orig. cl., cl. folding case, publisher's corrugated-bd. box. (SG. Jan.26; 223) $150

RYVES, Sir Thomas

– **Historia Navalis Antiqua**. L., 1633. Lge. folding plt. of 5 woodcuts, damp-wrinkled, little wormed, cont. vell. gt., soiled, MS. exlibris, bkplts. [STC 21475] (SG. Apr.26; 174) $300

– **Historia Navalis Mediae**. L., 1640. Cont. vell. gt., loose, lacks ties; Phillipps copy. [STC 21476] (SG. Apr.26; 175) $225

S., I.

– **A Brief & Perfect Journal of the Late Proceedings & Successe of the English Army in The West Indies, ... by I.S. an eyewitness**. 1655. *1st. Edn*. 4to. Lacks last lf., mor. by Sangorski & Sutcliffe. [Wing S35, Sabin 74616] (BBA. Jan.19; 148) *Remington*. £500.

S., M.

– **Manners & Customs of the French**. L., 1893. *Facs. of 'Letters from France, by M.S.', (1815)*. *(250) numbered & sigd. by publisher*. Red mor.,

spine & covers with gt. fleur-de-lys, spine reprd. (SG. Feb.16; 193) $110

SA'ADYA GA'ON, Sefer ha-Emunot ve-ha-De'ot

Trans.:– Yehuda ibn Tibbon. Amst., 1648. *2nd. Edn*. *[Menaasseh Ben Israel Edn.]*. Sm. 4to. Dampstained, slight margin worming, text mostly unaffected, title & few other ll. remargined, 2 ll. loose, lacks 2nd. (approbation?) lf., later qtr. leath., shabby. (SG. Feb.2; 294) $100

SAAR, Joh. J.

– **Ost-Indianische Funfzehen-Jährige Kriegs-Dienste** ... Nürnberg, 1672. *2nd. Edn*. Fo. Title vero stpd., prelim. lf. with MS. owners mark, 1812, 2nd. sm. copper engr. with note to binder, some light browning & foxing. (H. May 22; 283) DM 1,600

SAAVEDRA FAJARDO, Diego

– **Idea Principis Christiano Politici**. Köln, Münich, 1650. Slightly soiled & stained, cont. vell. (GB. Nov.3; 923) DM 600

SAAZ, Johannes von

[–] **Der Ackermann und der Tod**. Trans.:– [A. Berntl.]. [Leipzig, 1919]. *Facs. Edn., (320)*. 4to. Orig. hf. vell., 1 corner bumped, coll. stp. inside cover. (H. May 22; 454) DM 420

SABA, Abraham

– **Zeror Ha'Mor**. Venice, 1567. *3rd. Edn*. Fo. Margins of title & 5 ll. reprd. with loss of text, some staining, trimmed, cl. (S. Oct.25; 323) *Klein*. £250

SABACHNIKOFF, T.

– **I Manoscritto di Leonardo da Vinci della Reale Biblioteca di Windsor. Dell'Anatomia**. Paris, 1898. *(400) numbered (vol. 2.)*. Codices A & B. Fo. Italian & Fr. text, lightly browned, liby. stp., bds., slightly spotted. (HT. May 9; 1073) DM 1,400

SABARTES, Jaime

– **A los Toros mit Picasso**. Ill.:– Picasso. Monte Carlo, 1961. Ob. 4to. Orig. pict. linen, pict. s.-c. (D. Nov.24; 3169) DM 600

– – **Anr. Edn**. [Monte Carlo, 1961]. Lge. ob. 4to. Orig. pict. linen, orig. bd. s.-c., lightly bumped. (HK. May 17; 3054) DM 750

– – **Anr. Copy**. 4 orig. lithos. (1 in 24 cols.) & 103 ills. & plts. (1 cold.), orig. pict. linen, orig. pict. bd. s.-c. (HT. May 9; 1979) DM 540

– – **Anr. Edn**. Trans.:– U.R. Hemmerich. [Monte Carlo, 1961]. Ob. 4to. Orig. pict. linen, orig. pict. s.-c. (H. Nov.24; 2548) DM 460

– **Dans l'Atelier de Picasso**. Ill.:– Picasso. Paris, [1957]. *(200) on thick Bütten*. Lge. fo. Printers mark sigd. by artist, 6 lithos., (4 cold., including 2 on wraps.), 30 ills (21 cold.), loose in orig. wraps. & linen box. (H. May 23; 1459) DM 2,200

SABATINI, Raphael

– **The Writings**. Ill.:– Brook & others. Boston & N.Y., Riverside Pr., 1924-36. *'Autograph' Edn.,. (750) numbered & sigd*. Vols. 1-33 only (of 34). Red mor., covers gt.-panel., mor. gt. onlays, spines gt. in 6 compartments, gt.-panel. turn-ins, mor. doubls., watered silk free end-pp., partly unc., w.a.f. (CNY. Dec.17; 598) $850

SABBATHIER, François

– **Recueil de Planches pour le Dictionnaire de l'Intelligence des Auteurs Classiques** ... 1773-74. 8 pts. in 2 vols., bnd. in 1. 199 plts., lacks text, bds. (HD. Jan.24; 46) Frs. 1,700

SABBATINI, Luigi Antonio

– **La Vera Idea delle Musicali Numeriche Segnature**. Venice, 1799. *1st. Edn*. 4to. Wormed, cont. hf. leath. & bds., worn. (SG. Nov.17; 319) $125

SABELLICUS, Marcus Antonius

– **Degl' Istorici delle Cose Veneziane**. 1718. 11 vols. 4to. Vols. 1 & 2 affected by damp, cont. vell. gt., bkplt. of 6th. Duke of Portland. (P. Oct.20; 218) £65

SABIN, Joseph

– **A Bibliographical Catalogue of the Waltonian Library belonging to ... Robert W. Coleman**. N.Y., 1866. *(75)*. Hf. leath. (SG. Mar.15; 311) $100

– **A Dictionary of Books Relating to America**. Amst., 1961-62. 29 vols. in 15, as iss. Cl. (SG. Jan.5; 279) $450

– – **Anr. Edn.** Amst., 1961-62. *Reprint of 1868 Edn.* 29 vols. in 15. Cl., 1 vol. not quite unif. (VS. Dec.7; 356) Fls. 775

– **Reprints.** N.Y., 1865. *L.P. 4to. Edn. (50) numbered.* Nos. I-X in 1 vol. 4to. Hf.-title torn, lacks 1st. hf.-title, gt.-lettered hf. mor., worn; ex-liby., several limitation ll. initialed by Sabin. (SG. Jan.19; 320) $375

SABINUS, O.

– **Poemata et Nvmero Librorvm et Aliis Additis avcta** ... [Leipzig, 1563?]. Title with sm. margin defects., old underlining, lightly browned & some slight spotting, lacks end-papers, cont. blind-tooled pig, worn & slightly soiled. (HK. Nov.8; 328) DM 460

SABOUREUX DE LA BONNETERIE

– **Traduction d'Anciens Ouvrages Latins Relatifs à l'Agriculture et à la Médecine Vétérinaire avec des Notes.** Paris, 1771. 6 vols. Cont. hf. roan, unc., arms. (HD. Nov.9; 163) Frs. 1,300

SACCHI, Bartholomaeus

See— **PLATINA or Sacchi, Bartholomaeus**

SACERDOTALE ROMANUM

Venice, 1585. 4to. Cont. stpd. pig., gt.-decor., from Fondation Furstenberg-Beaumesnil. (HD. Nov.16; 169) Frs. 1,400

SACHER-MASOCH, L.

– **Contes Juifs. Récits de Famille.** Ill.:– Gerardin, Alph., E. & H. Lévy, Loevy, etc. Paris, 1888. *(125) on japan. This 1 of (25) with suite of 27 heliogravures before the letter on japan & orig. aqua. ill., dtd. [18]88 & sigd. Loevy.* 4to. Hf. mor., by Champs, corners, decor. spine gt., wrap. & spine, unc. (HD. Dec.16; 183) Frs. 3,500

SACHS, Edwin O.

– **Modern Opera Houses & Theatres.** L., 1897-98. 3 vols. Atlas fo. Over 200 plts., over 1000 text ills., ex-liby., buckram, worn, partly loose. (SG. May 3; 322) $2,400

SACHS, Hans

– **Ausgewählte Worke.** Ed.:– P. Merker. Ill.:– after H.S. Beham, Jost Amman, A. Dürer & others. Leipzig,. 1911. *(200) numbered De Luxe Edn.* 2 vols. Orig. pig. (HK. May 16; 2225) DM 580

– **Ain Dialogus und Argument der Romanisten wider das Christich Heuflein, den Geytz und ander offentlich Laster betreffend.** [Augsburg, 1524]. *1st. Edn. 2nd. Printing.* 4to. Dedication L., washed, later blind-tooled leath. (R. Oct.11; 108) DM 1,700

– **Der Genta Haussrat.** Nuremb., 1553. 4to. Browned & slighly foxed, especially title-lf., without bdg., unc.,. (HT. May 8; 202) DM 1,300

[–] **Eyn Wunderliche Weyssagung von dem Babstumb** ... [Nuremb.], 1527. *1st. Edn.* 4to. Some light foxing, mor., gt. spine, cover, inner & outer dentelles. (HK. May 15; 232) DM 8,500

– **Zwölf Fastnachtspiele.** [München, 1922]. Orig. pig, bd. s.-c., spine slightly faded. (HK. May 17; 2849) DM 700

SACHS, Paul

See— **MONGAN, A. & Sachs, Paul**

SACHSE, L.

– **Das Preussische Heer unter Friedrich, Wilhelm IV.** Berlin, 1843-45. Lacks 1 plt., 7 plts. with margin tears bkd., 2 plts. soiled, slightly browned thro.-out, cut slightly close, later hf. linen, rubbed & bumped. (R. Oct.12; 2308) DM 2,700

SACK, Baron Albert von

– **Beschreibung einer Reise nach Surinam und des Aufenthaltes ... sowie von des Verfassers Rückkehr nach Europa über Nord-Amerika.** Berlin, 1818. *1st. German Edn. De Luxe Edn., on vell.* 2 pts. in 1 vol. Lacks 1 copperplt., some light foxing, cont. red hf. chagrin, gt. decor., inner & outer dentelles, gt. spine; Karl v. Preussea liby. stp. on engraved title. [Sabin 74749] (GB. Nov.3; 64) DM 3,800

– **Beschreibung einer Reise nach Surinam in 1805-07.** Berlin, 1821. 2 vols. Lge. 4to. Orig. bds., unc., 1 slightly defect. [Sabin 74749] (VG. Nov.30; 861) Fls. 650

SACKVILLE-WEST, Victoria

– **Collected Poems.** L., Hogarth Pr.,. 1933. *(150) numbered & sigd.* Vol. 1 only. Vell.-bkd. cl. (SG. Jan.12; 309) $325

– **Nursery Rhymes.** 1947. *(550) numbered. (25) sigd. & specially bnd.* 4to. Qtr. vell. & buckram, d.-w. (HBC. May 17; 178) £115

SACRABUSTO, Joannes de

See— **SACROBOSCO or SACRABUSTO, Joannes de**

SACRAMENTO, Fr. Leando do

– **Memoria Economica sobre a Plantacao Cultura e Preparacao do Cha.** Rio de Janeiro, 1825. Mod. wraps., partly unopened. (SG. Apr.5; 332) $300

SACRE DE LOUIS XV, Roy de France et du Navarre dans l'eglise de Reims.

Ill.:– Audran, Beaivais, Cochin pèrem Desplaces, Duchange, Dupuis, Larmessi, Tardieu, Ulin. [Paris], 1723. Lge. fo. Engraved thro.-out. 1 margin, slight foxing, mainly in margin, cont. black mor., decor., fleurs-de-lis, royal monog., Louis XV arms in centre, decor. spine, inner fleurs de lis border, 2 corners worn. (HD. Feb.29; 41) Frs. 33,500

– – **Anr. Copy.** Lge. fo. 28 costume plts. only, lacks final table lf., cont. red mor., Du Seuil decor, Louis XV arms. (HD. Apr.13; 48) Frs. 20,000

SACRED GEOGRAPHIE. Or Scriptural Mapps

See— **LANGEREN, Jacob van - SACRED GEOGRAPHIE. Or Scriptural Mapps**

SACRED SCRIPT (A)

1971. *(250) numbered.* Sq. fo. Hebrew script, title, limitation lf. & 27 ll., loose as iss. in orig. cl. portfo. (BBA. Jan.19; 321) *Silber.* £50

SACROBOSCO, Joannes de

– **Libellvs, de Sphaera ... [de Anni Ratione].** Preface:– Ph. Melanchthon. Wittenberg, 1538. 2 vols. 49(of 52) ll., old marginalia thro.-out, additions on 2 inserted ll. in pt. 1, pt. 2 with added entries, browned & spotted, wraps. (HK. May 15; 233) DM 420

– – **Anr. Edn.** Preface:– Ph. Melanchthon. Wittenberg, 1558. (*Bound with:*) **MELANCHTHON, Philipp – Examen Eorum qui audiuntur ante Ritum Publicae Ordinationis, qua commendatur eis Ministerium Evangelii.** Wittenberg, 1556. 2 works in 1 vol. Blind-tooled pig over wood bds., dtd. 1559, 2 brass clasps. (R. Oct.11; 109) DM 850

– **Liber de Sphera. Addita est Praefatio in eundem Librum Philippi Melanch. ad Simonem Grynaeum.** [Wittenberg, 1534]. Last 2 blank ll. with cont. annots., slightly wormed at foot, wraps. (HK. Nov.8; 329) DM 600

– **Sphaera Emendata ... Eliae Vineti Santonis Scholia in eamdem Sphaeram, ab ipso Authore restituta. Adiunximus huic Libro Compendium in Sphaeram, per Pierium Valerianum Bellunensem ... ex postrema impressione Lutetiae.** Venice, 1546. Cont. vell., ties, slightly defect. (GB. Nov.3; 1094) DM 400

– **Sphaera Mundi.** (*With:*) **GERARD OF CREMONA – Theorica Planetarum.** Venice, Franciscus Renner, de Heilbron, 1478. *1st. Ill. Edn.* Together 2 works in 1 vol. 4to. 1 woodcut hand-cold. in red & green, anr. in red, light soiling to 1st. few ll., sm. margin wormhole through a few ll., 18th. C. mor., 'fanfare' decor, traces of orig. gt., rebkd.; Dyson Perrins copy, Stanitz coll. [BMC V, 195; Goff J402] (SPB. Apr.25; 389) $4,000

– – **Anr. Edn.** Venice, Erhard Ratdolt, 6 Jul. 1482. 4to. Some ills partly hand-cold. in green or yellow, some light browning, mostly minor but affecting yellow col. on 1 lf., 1st. lf. strengthened at inner margin, mod. mor., mor. inlays of arms & monog. on covers; Stirling-Maxwell copy, Stanitz coll. [BMC V, 286; Goff J405] (SPB. Apr.25; 390) $2,500

– – **Anr. Edn.** Venice, Erhard Ratdolt, [before 4 Nov.] 1485. 4to. 7 diagrams partly ptd. with cols., 1st. initial cont. hand-cold., sm. hole in 2nd. lf. affecting a few letters of text & a sm. portion of diagram, short tear in blank margin of 1st. lf. reprd., slight browning, cont. MS. annots. & underlinings, cont. limp vell., lacks 1 tie. [BMC V, 290; Goff J-406; HC 14111] (C. Nov.9; 111) *Thomas.* £850

– – **Anr. Edn.** Venice, [B. Locatellus] for O. Soctus, 4 Oct. 1490. 4to. A few woodcuts hand-cold., lacks 4 ll. (1 blank), some light staining, limp bds., covered with lf. from an Italian MS.; the Walter Goldwater copy. [BMC V, 438; Goff J-409] (SG. Dec.1; 205) $650

– – **Anr. Edn.** Venice, Dec. 1519. Sm. 4to. A few sm. stains, later vell. (BBA. Nov.30; 16) *Fazzi.* £280

– – **Anr. Copy.** Sm. 4to. Rust stains to a few ll., inner margin of A8 strengthened, patterned bds. (C. Nov.9; 112) *Pickering.* £220

– **Textus Sphaerae ... , Exposition Sphaerae Eximii Artium & Medicinae Doctoris Domini Fraciaci Capuani de Manfredonia. Annotationes Nonullae eiusde Bartholomei Vespucii hic ide itersertae. Jacobi Franbri Stapulensis Commentarii** ... Venice, 1508. 2 pts. in 1 vol. Fo. Cont. marginalia, old vell., worn. (TA. Sep.15; 420) £220

SACUT, Moshe

– **She'eilot U'Teshuvot.** Venice, 1760-61. *1st. Edn.* 4to. Owner's stp. on title, staining mostly in margins, trimmed with loss of parts of some letters, leath., slightly worn. (S. Oct.25; 324) *Riemer.* £120

SADE, Donation Alphonse François, Marquis de

– **Die Hundertzwanzig Tage von Sodom oder Die Schule der Ausschweifung.** Trans.:– K. v. Haverland. Ill.:– K.M. Diez. Leipzig, 1909. *1st. Compl. German Edn. (650) numbered.* 2 vols. 4to. Minimal wear, orig. red mor., gt. spine & upr. cover. (HK. Nov.9; 2116) DM 600

– **Les 120 Jourées de Sodome ou l'Ecole du Libertinage.** Ed.:– Maurice Heine. Paris, 1931-35. *(300) on vell.* 3 vols. 4to. Sewed. (SM. Mar.7; 2222) Frs. 1,000

– **Historiettes, Contes et Fabliaux,.** Ed.:– Maurice Heine. Paris, 1926. *Orig. Edn. (170) on vell.* 4to. Leaves, s.-c.; ptd. for Robert Desnos, prospectus added. (SM. Mar.7; 2219) Frs. 1,200

– **Oeuvres Complétes.** Ed.:– G. Lely. Paris, 1973. 16 vols. in 8. Orig. leatherette. (GB. Nov.5; 2957) DM 750

– **La Philosophie dans le Boudoir.** Londres (Paris), 1795. *1st. Edn.* 2 vols. Orig. mor., corners. (DS. Jan.27; 2573) Pts. 70,000

SADELER, Aegidus

– **Vestigi delle Antichita di Roma, Tivoli, Possuolo et Altri Luochi.** Prague, priv. ptd., 1606. Ob. fo. Engraved title & 50 plts., including dedication, a few plts. with unobtrusive vertical creases, cont. vell.; Charles Chauncy bkplt. (C. Jun.27; 66) *Sims & Reed.* £420

SADELER, Marco

– **Vestigi delle Antichita di Roma Tivoli Pozzuolo et Altri Luochi.** Rome, [1660]. Ob. fo. Engraved architectural title, dedication & 49 architectural views of Rome, dampstain to blank fore-margins, 19th. C. hf. cf. (C. Jun.27; 67) *Zanzotto.* £250

SADLEIR, Michael

– **The Evolution of Publisher's Binding Styles 1770-1900.** L. & N.Y., 1930. *(500).* Orig. parch.-bkd. bds.; Oliver Brett bkplt., H.M. Nixon coll., with his sig., acquisition note & a few MS. notes. (BBA. Oct.6; 121) *Knuf.* £130

– **XIX Century Fiction. A Bibliographical Record.** 1951. *(1025).* 4to. Orig. cl. (BBA. Nov.10; 121) *Traylen.* £150

– – **Anr. Edn.** 1951. *Ltd. Edn.* 2 vols. 4to. Orig. cl. gt., d.-w.'s. (P. Sep.8; 256) *Quaritch.* £160

– – **Anr. Edn.** N.Y., 1969. 2 vols. 4to. Orig. cl. (TA. Dec.15; 294) £95

SADLEIR, Thomas U. & Dickinson, Page L.

– **Georgian Mansions in Ireland.** Dublin, 1915. *(700).* 4to. Orig. cl. (GM. Dec.7; 87) £120

SADOLET, Jacques

– **Interpretatio in Psalmum Miserere Mei Deus.** Lyon, 1528. *Orig. Edn.* Mod. vell. (HD. Apr.13; 49) Frs. 1,300

SADYK PASHA

– **The Moslem & the Christian.** L., 1855. 3 vols. Litho. frontis., a few ll. in Vol. 1 loose, orig. cl., rubbed; David Sassoon bkplt. (BBA. May 3; 331) *Cavendish Rare Books.* £50

SAENGER, S.
See— NEUE RUNDSCHAU

SAFA BERURAH
Reggio?, 1820?. Hebrew-Italian glossary, slight staining, buckram. (S. Oct.24; 49) *Ny.* £150

SAGE, Mr.
- **Arte de ensayar Oro y Plata.** Madrid, 1785. 4to. Cf. (DS. Mar.23; 2259) Pts. 20,000

SAINCTONGE, Mme de
- **Poésies Galantes.** 1696. *Orig. Edn.* 12mo. Decor. red mor. by Capé. (HD. Mar.21; 87) Frs. 2,000

SAINT-ANGE, Walter de
- **Metallurgie Pratique du Fer. Atlas des Machines, Appareils et Outils Actuellement Employés.** Ill.:– Le Blanc. Paris, 1835-38. 2 pts. in 1 vol. Ob. fo. Some foxing, leath.-bkd. bds., orig. upr. wraps. bnd. in, worn, spine torn. (RO. Dec.11; 289) $100

SAINT-AUBIN, Gabriel de
- **Catalogues de Ventes et Livrets de Salons.** Intro.:– Emile Dacier. 1909. *(125).* 11 vols. in 6. Lge. 8vo. Cont. hf. mor., corners. (HD. Mar.21; 196) Frs. 8,200

ST. BARBE BAKER, Richard
- **Famous Trees.** Ill.:– S.R. Badmin. 1952. *(999) numbered. (53) sigd. by author & artist, specially bnd.* Lge. 8vo. Cf., d.-w. (HBC. May 17; 224) £52

SAINT-EVREMOND, Charles Margotelle de St. Danys
- **Oeuvres.** L., 1709. 3 vols. 4to. Cf. (DS. Feb.24; 2305) Pts. 19,000

SAINT-EXUPERY, Antonine de
- **Courrier Sud.** Paris, 1929. *Orig. Edn.* 12mo. Sewed; sigd. autograph dedication to Marcelle Tinayre. (HD. Jun.26; 147) Frs. 2,100
- **Oeuvres Complètes.** Ill.:– Georges Feher & author. Paris, 1963. *(4091) numbered. (5) on japon nacré, with 2 suites of lithos. on japon nacré & vell., progressive proofs for 2 lithos., watercol. drawings for 2 lithos., & 2 prelim. drawings, all. sigd. by artist.* 8 vols. 4to. Leaves, orig. wrap., unc., box., suites & drawings in separate portfo., box. (SM. Mar.7; 2325) Frs. 7,000
- **Le Petit Prince.** N.Y., 1943. *Orig. Edn.* Sm. 4to. Bds., ill. in col. (HD. Mar.27; 109) Frs. 1,300
- **Terre des Hommes.** Paris, 1939. *Orig. Edn. (130) on Lafuma Navarre.* Sewed. (HD. Apr.13; 175) Frs. 2,080
- **Vol de Nuit.** Preface:– André Gide. Paris, 1931. *Orig. Edn.* 12mo. Sewed; sigd. autograph dedication. (HD. Jun.26; 148) Frs. 2,300

SAINT-GELAIS, Octavien de & La Vigne, André de
- **Le Vergier Doneur nouvellement Imprimée** ... [Paris], ca. 1500. 4to. Slit reprd in last lf., 2 next last ll. re-made (zincograph reproduction), mor., blind decor., decor. spine, gt. inner dentelle, by Duru 1847; J. Copinger ex-libris. (HD. Dec.16; 37) Frs. 28,100
- – **Anr. Copy.** 4to. 19th. C. pol. mor., gt. inner & outer dentelle, by Duru, 1847. [Copinger 5992; Goff 5-18]. (R. Apr.3; 8) DM 16,000

ST. GEORGE GRAY, Harold
See— BULLEID, Arthur & St. George Gray, Harold

SAINT GERMAIN, Christopher
- **The Dialogue in English, between a Doctor of Divinitie, & a Student in the Lawes of England.** L., 1593. 16mo. Some headlines shaved, slightly browned, velvet, worn. [STC 21576] (S. Mar.20; 835) *Boswell.* £120

SAINT-HILAIRE, Emile, Marco de
- **Histoire Anecdotique, Politique et Militaire de la Garde Impériale.** Ill.:– H. Bellangé, E. Lamy, Ch. Vernier etc. Paris, 1847. *1st. Printing.* Bradel hf. red chagrin, ca.1890, unc. (HD. Feb.17; 18) Frs. 3,100

SAINT-HYACINTHE
- [-] **Historiettes Galantes, tant en Prone qu'en Vers.** La Haye, 1730. *2nd. Edn.* Decor. mor. by L. Poullet,

slight defect. to lr. cover. (HD. Mar.21; 88) Frs. 1,100

SAINT IGNY, Jean d'
- **Elemens de Pourtraiture ou la Méthode de Representer & Pourtraire toutes les Parties du Corps Humain.** Paris, [1630]. Engraved title & divisional title, 30 plts. only, lacks D4 & E1, several margins defect. & crudely reprd., cont. spr. cf., rebkd. (S. Dec.20; 800) *Milton.* £70

SAINTIN, C.
- **Nouvel Atlas des Enfans et des Commençans ou les Premiers Elémens de la Géographie, mis à la Portée du plus Jeune Age.** Paris, 1811. 2 engraved plts. & 8 maps, hand-cold., cont. cf. gt., lge. prize stp. on covers; certificate to D. Gurloss, van Veen coll. (S. Feb.28; 108) £90

SAINTINE, X.B.
- **Le Chemin des Ecoliers, Promenade de Paris à Marly-le-Roy en suivant les Borde du Rhin.** Ill.:– G. Doré, Forster & others. Paris, 1861. *Orig. Edn.* Hf. mor., spine richly decor., wrap. & spine preserved, sm. repair to wrap. (HD. Jun.13; 97) Frs. 3,500
- – **Anr. Copy.** Cont. hf. chagrin, spine gt. (HD. Jun.22; 34) Frs. 1,500

ST. JOHN, J. Allen
- **The Face in the Pool: A Faerie Tale.** Chic., 1905. *1st. Edn.* 4to. Pict. cl., covers mildly rubbed & soiled, lr. front, corner creased. (CBA. Oct.29; 799) $200

ST. JOHN, Spencer
- **Life in the Forests of the Far East.** 1862. 2 vols. Cl., rebnd. (PD. Feb.15; 138) £50
- – **Anr. Edn.** 1863. *2nd. Edn.* 2 vols. Some spotting, orig. cl., gt.-decor. spine. (TA. Oct.20; 19) £120
- – **Anr. Copy.** 2 vols. Orig. decor. cl. gt., slightly soiled, hinges weak or brkn. (SKC. Mar.9; 2032) £60

ST. JOSEPH, E. de
- **Le Ministère du Confesseur en Pratique.** Liège, 1718. 2 vols. Cont. red mor. gt. (S. Oct.11; 419) *Booth.* £85

SAINT-LAMBERT, Jean François, Marquis de
- **Les Saisons.** Ill.:– Choffard. Amst., 1775. Mor. gt. à la fanfare, gt. inner & outer dentelle sigd. Niédrée, ca. 1880, A.L.s. from author to printer; Leon Rattier ex-libris. (D. Nov.24; 2344) DM 3,200
- – **Anr. Edn.** Ill.:– Chaudet. Paris, An IV [1796]. 4to. Some light foxing, cont. cf. gt., spine decor., sm. defects. (HD. May 3; 140) Frs. 1,200

SAINT-LEGER, Marie René Auguste Alexis
See— PERSE, St. John [i.e. Marie René Auguste Alexis Saint-Leger]

ST. LOUIS
- **Report of the Celebration of the Anniversary of the Founding of St. Louis.** 1847. Foxed, orig. ptd. wraps., soiled & chipped, cf.-bkd. folding case. (LH. Jan.15; 390) $150

SAINT-MARTIN, Jean de
- **L'Art de faire des Armes reduit à ses Vrais Principes.** Wien, 1804. Sm. 4to. Cont. leath. gt., slightly rubbed. (GB. Nov.4; 1545) DM 600

SAINT-NON, Jean-Claude Richard, Abbé de
- **Voyage Pittoresque à Naples et on Sicile.** Paris, 1829. *New Edn.* Atlas of plts. only: 3 vols. in 2. Lge. fo. 558 engraved views & ills. on 280 plts., no titles & no plt. 135 (the latter never issued?), cont. mor.-bkd. bds., rubbed, some orig. wraps. bnd. in. (C. Mar.14; 86) *La Fenice.* £1,700
- – **Anr. Edn.** 1876. *New Edn.* Atlas 1st. pt. only (Naples). Fo. 125 (of 138) plts., some foxing, cont. cf., romantic decor. spine, wrap. covers preserved. (HD. Feb.29; 42) Frs. 3,500
- **Voyage Pittoresque ou Description des Royaumes de Naples et de Sicile.** Ill.:– after Fragonard & others. Paris, 1781-86. *1st. Edn.* 4 vols. in 5. Fo. Wide margins, engraved vig. titles, engraved dedication lf. in Vol. 1, 13 maps (5 double-p.), 305 engraved plts. (1st. iss. of nos. 84, 85, 87 & 88 in Vol. 3), hf.-titles, lacks phallus plt. (as usual), a few plts. with offsetting, plt. 45 with slight staining,

minor margin staining to a few other plts., stained cf., spines gt., worn & scuffed. (LC. Jul.5; 426) £2,100
- – **Anr. Copy.** 4 vols. Fo. 305 plts., including 12 maps, 1 plan, phallus plt. & the 14 additional plts. of medals, plts. 84, 87 & 88 of Vol. III of the 1st. printing, only 2 (of 3) additional ll. following p. 112 of Vol. III, some light browning, cont. stained cf., some scuffing. (SPB. Dec.14; 79) $5,000
- – **Anr. Copy.** 5 vols. Fo. With all plts., cont. bds., spines slightly defect. (HD. Dec.9; 82) Frs. 29,000
- – **Anr. Copy.** 4 vols. in 5. Fo. Plts. 84 to 88 numbered 24, 24bis, 11, 12 & 13, lacking phallus plt. in facs., slight tear to 2 pp. in Vol. 3, cf., worn. (SM. Mar.7; 2048) Frs. 22,000
- – **Anr. Copy.** 5 pts. in 4 vols. Fo. 284 plts., 6 maps, 1 topographical ill., 14 plts. of medals, light staining in last vol., cont. marb. cf., gt.-tooled spines, spines & some covers lightly scratched. (CR. Jun.6; 280) Lire 9,000,000

ST. PAUL, Charles de & Sanson, Nicolas
- **Geographia Sacra.** Ed.:– Luca Holstenius. Amst., 1704. 3 vols. including atlas. Fo. Dedication p., browning, 4 maps hand-cold., some browning & staining, cont. hf. leath., decor. spines, some slight defects. w.a.f. (SI. Dec.18; 86) Lire 700,000

ST. PETERSBURG
- **Nouvelle Collection de Quarante Vues de Saint-Petersbourg et de ses Environs.** St. Petersb., 1825. Ob. 4to. 23 (of 40) hand-cold. lithos., title of 1 plt. erased, some dampstains, few pp. loose, hf. mor., defect., as a coll. of plts., w.a.f. (P. Apr.12; 193) *Elliott.* £200

ST. PETERSBURG IMPERIAL ACADEMY OF ARTS & SCIENCES
- **Plan de la Ville de Saint-Petersbourg avec ses Principales Vües.** St. Petersbourg, 1753. Fo. Cont. decor. limp cf. (HD. Jun.18; 43) Frs. 52,000

ST. PETERSBURG IMPERIAL ACADEMY OF SCIENCES
- **Commentarii Academiae Scientiarum Imperialis Petropolitanae.** Petropoli, 1728-35. 4 vols. 4to. Plts. bnd. in at end of each vol., later cl., some wear. (TA. Apr.19; 485) £50

SAINT-PIERRE, Jacques-Henri Bernardin de
- **Etudes de la Nature.** Ill.:– Moreau. Paris, 1788. *Partly Orig. Edn.* 4 vols. 12mo. Cont. marb. roan. spines decor. (HD. May 3; 141) Frs. 1,900
- **Paul et Virginie.** Ill.:– after Lafitte, Girodet, Gerard, Moreau, Prudhon, & Isabey. Paris, 1806. 4to. Hf.-title, mosaic bdg. of crushed lev. mor. by Marius Michel, sigd. on upr. doubl., covers with elab. panel borders incorporating interlaced strapwork head, foot & side ornaments of oval form & lge. central oval medallion, all of onlaid mor. gt., heightened by lge. swirling Art Nouveau flower ornaments emanating from centre of medallion at head & foot & curling to lge. corner ornaments, all of onlaid mor. gt., spine in 6 compartments, gt.-lettered in 1, alternative panels of 2 onlaid mor. stylized flower designs in onlaid mor. strapwork borders in rest, bd. edges with double gt. fillet, mor. doubls. with broad gt.-ruled borders incorporating intertwined gt. foliage pattern with mor. gt. onlay, gold brick-stitched silk free end-pp., marb. paper fly-ll., mor. pull-off case (slightly rubbed); extra-ill. with 8 orig. drawings (1 unpubld.) by Pierre E.A. Hedouin for the Lemerre edn. of 1878, charcoal, heightened with chalk, all but 2 sigd., & suites of the 7 publd. engrs. for that edn. in 3 states (before aquatint, after aquatint, after aquatint on blue paper), last 2 with artist's monog. ptd. in lr. margins, René Descamps Scrive & Maj. J.R. Abbey bkplts. (CNY. May 18; 194) $12,000
- – **Anr. Edn.** Ill.:– Isabey, Johannet etc. Paris, 1838. Some plts. foxed, shaved, hf. mor., corners. limp decor. spine with gt. plaque; Charles Monselet ex-libris. (HD. Jan.30; 95) Frs. 1,600
- – **Anr. Edn.** Pforzheim, 1840. Some spotting, orig. hf. roan; inscr. to Clara Schumann by Johannes Brahms, as an association copy. (S. Nov.17; 91) *Young.* £2,000
- – **Anr. Edn.** Notes:– 'Anatole France'. Ill.:– Pierre E.A. Hodouin. Paris, 1878. *(100), sigd. by publisher. (50) numbered on Whatman paper.* Plts.

in 2 states (before & after aquatint), crushed jansenist lev. mor. by Marius Michel, sigd. on upr. doubl., spine in 5 compartments, gt.-lettered in 2, bd. edges with double gt. fillet, turn-ins gt., mor. doubls. diapered in gt. & decor. with overall alternating pattern of lge. & sm. Art Nouveau flowers of onlaid cf. gt. climbing from onlaid cf. gt. leaves, watered silk free end-pp., marb. paper fly-ll., partly unc., orig. wraps. preserved; exhibition label of the Exposition Universelle, Paris, 1900. (CNY. May 18; 193) $650
– – **Anr. Copy.** Sm. 8vo. Lev. gt. by Smeers Engel, spines gt. with sm. red mor. onlays, gt. dentelles orig. wraps. bnd. in. (SG. Feb.16; 261) $110
– – **Anr. Edn.** Ill.:– A. Lalauze. Paris, 1879. 12mo. On holland, etchings in 3 states, mor. gt. by Marius Michel, spine decor., wraps. (HD. May 4; 421) Frs. 2,100
– **Paul et Virginie. La Chaumière Indienne.** Paris, 1828. 2 works in 1 vol. Some copper engrs. on China, 6 (of 7) copper engrs. in 4 states, 7th. engr. in 3 states, engraved title in 2 states, extra pull of title vigs., slightly foxed, 1st. sig. loose, lacks both hf.-titles, cont. red long-grd. mor., gt. spine, cover & inner dentelle; Konigl. Bibliothek in Neuilly stp. on end-paper. (R. Apr.3; 421) DM 650
– – **Anr. Edn.** Ill.:– after T. Johannot & others. Paris, 1838. Lge. 8vo. 7 ports., 29 wood-engraved plts., all in mntd. proof state on China paper, slight foxing, cont. gt.– & blind-tooled mor., spine elab. gt., gt. dentelles, orig. wraps. (dtd. 1839) bnd. in. (SG. Nov.3; 180) $475
– – **Anr. Edn.** Ill.:– after Tony Johannot, Maroille, Isabey, etc. Paris, 1838. *1st. Printing.* Engrs. before letter, some foxing, red mor. by David, gt. decor., decor. spines, inner dentelle. (HD. Dec.9; 182) Frs. 2,100
– – **Anr. Edn.** Ill.:– Pierre Falké & J. Saude. Paris, 1927. *(135). (25) on japan nacré.* 4to. 3 suites of ills. on japan in cols., in black (without map) 7 orig. full-p. aquas., sewed, with suites, box. (HD. Dec.16; 184) Frs. 2,800
[–] **Voyage à l'Isle de France, à l'Isle de Bourbon, au Cap de Bonne-Espérance** ... Amst. & Paris, 1773. 2 pts. in 1 vol. Plt. 2 torn, slightly foxed & stained, cont. hf. leath., rubbed & bumped. (HK. Nov.8; 1008) DM 440

SAINT-POL ROUX
– **Les Reposoirs de la Procession.** 1893. *Orig. Edn.* Vol. I. No bdg. stated; 4 ll. MS. article by author, sigd. 'Jean Royère'. (HD. May 11; 113) Frs. 1,050

SAINT-REAL, Abbé Vischard de
[–] **La Conjuration des Espagnols contre la République de Venise en l'Année 1618.** Paris, 1674. *Orig. Edn.* 12mo. Cont. cf., spine decor., Comte d'Hoym arms. (HD. Mar.29; 91) Frs. 6,500
– **Les Oeuvres.** Paris, 1745. *New Edn.* 3 vols. 4to. Cont. red mor., gt. decor., limp decor. spines. (HD. Dec.9; 83) Frs. 3,200

SAINT-SIMON, Louis de Rouvroy, Duc de
– **Die Memoiren des Herzogs von Saint-Simon.** Trans.:– H. Floerke. 1913-17. *(150) numbered De Luxe Edn. on Bütten.* 3 vols. Orig. leath. gt. (R. Apr.3; 363) DM 1,000
– **Mémoires Complete et Authentiques sur le Siècle de Louis XIV et la Régence.** Paris, 1829-30. *Partly Orig. Edn.* 21 vols. Cont. hf. roan, spines decor., worn. (HD. May 21; 98) Frs. 1,300
– – **Anr. Edn.** Paris, 1840-44. 40 vols. in 20 vols. Linen. (DS. Feb.24; 2454) Pts. 27,000
– – **Anr. Edn.** 1856. 20 vols. Port. of author in facs., extra ill. with 183 steel engrs., cont. hf. chagrin. (HD. Mar.21; 197) Frs. 5,500
– – **Anr. Edn.** Preface:– Sainte-Beuve. Paris, 1856-58. *Partly Orig. Edn.* 20 vols. Some foxing, cont. hf. chagrin, spine raised bands, cypher, lightly rubbed. (HD. May 16; 52) Frs. 2,350
– – **Anr. Edn.** Paris, 1873-75. 19 vols. only (of 22, lacks 2 vols. tables & supp.). Some ll. disbnd., cont. hf. cf., decor. spines. (HD. Feb.17; 38) Frs. 1,600
– – **Anr. Edn.** Ed.:– A. de Boislisle. Paris, 1923-30. *Partly orig. Edn.* 42 vols. Hf. chagrin, corners, decor. spines, slight defects. (HD. Jan.27; 311) Frs. 3,300

SAINT-VENANT, Adhemar Jean C. Barre de
– **Mémoire sur la Torsion des Prismes. avec des Considerations sur leur Flexion ainsi que sur l'Equilibre Intérieur des Solides Elastiques en Général** ... [Paris, 1855]. *1st. Edn.* 4to. Removed from 'Mémoires des Savants Etrangers', pp. 233-560, spotting, hf. cf., rubbed, faded, rebkd., orig. spine laid down, corners renewed; Robert W. Webb sig. on end-paper, Stanitz coll. (SPB. Apr.25; 391) $175

SAINT VICTOR, J.B. de
– **Tableau Historique et Pittoresque de Paris.** Paris, 1809. 3 vols. 4to. Plans, plts., titles of vols. 2 & 3 browned, some spotting & browning in some margins, red hf. mor. gt. (S. Apr.10; 303) *Greenwood.* £180

SAINTE BEUVE, Charles Augustin
– **Port Royal.** Paris, 1860. *2nd. Edn.* 5 vols. Hf. chagrin. (HD. Feb.22; 202) Frs. 8,000

SAINTE CROIX
– **Histoire des Progrèe de la Puissance Navale de l'Angleterre.** Yverdon, 1783. 2 vols. 12mo. Some plts. defect., roan, corners worn. (HD. Feb.22; 203) Frs. 2,200

SAINTE MARIE MADELAINE, Pierre de
– **Traité d'Horlogiographie.** Paris, 1701. *New Edn.* Title with excision in upr. margin, slightly foxed, cont. leath. gt., corners reprd., bumped. (HK. Nov.8; 733) DM 460

SAKS, Herzog Zu Braunschweig und Luneburg
– **Von Gottes Gnaden.** Oct. 28, 1751. 4to. Wide margins, 2 ll., cl., w.a.f. (S. Oct.25; 30) £110

SALA, George Augustus
– **The Great Exhibition: 'Wot is to Be'.** 1850. 5½ × 218 inches. Engraved concertina foldout in 23 sections, orig. bds., lr. cover detchd., lacks spine. (CSK. Jun.1; 105) £60
– **The Great Glass House Opend; the Exhibition wot is.** 1851. Ob. 8vo. Hand-cold. title, 22 hand-cold. plts. (1 folding), hf. mor. gt. (P. Apr.12; 73) *Argyll Etkin.* £85

SALAMAN, Malcolm C.
– **The Etchings of Sir Francis Seymour Haden.** 1923. *(200) numbered.* Fo. Orig. cf.-bkd. cl., soiled. (CSK. Jun.1; 44) £50
– **The Etchings of James McBey** ... 1929. 4to. Orig. cl. gt. (PD. Aug.17; 71) £65
– – **Anr. Edn.** L., 1929. *(100) numbered & sigd. by McBey.* 4to. Orig. etched frontis. sigd., orig. vell.-bkd. cl., slightly soiled. (BBA. Apr.5; 158) *Loader.* £90

SALAME, Abraham
– **A Narrative of the Expedition to Algiers.** 1819. *[1st. Edn.].* Cf., rebkd., rather worn. (BBA. Jun.14; 288) *Makiya.* £110
– – **Anr. Copy.** 1 folding plt. hand-cold., cont. spr. cf., gt. spine, jnts. reprd. (SKC. Sep.9; 2059) £100
– – **Anr. Copy.** 4 engraved plts., spotted, cont. hf. cf. (S. Apr.9; 54) *Scott.* £50

SALAZAR Y LAREGUI, Jose
– **Datos de Los Trabajos Astronomicos y Topograficos, Dispuestos en Forma de Diario.** Mexico, 1850. *1st. Edn.* Qtr. cf., boxed. (LH. Sep.25; 281) $550
– – **Anr. Copy.** Collectors' stps. on maps & end-papers, cont. cf.-bkd. bds., slightly rubbed. (LH. Apr.15; 366) $300

SALAZAR Y OLARTE, Ignacio
– **Historia de la Conquista de Mexico, Poblacion, y Progresos de la America Septentrional, Conocida por el Nombre de Nueve España. Segunda Parte.** Madrid, 1786. Fo. Cf. (LH. Sep.25; 282) $350

SALCHER, P.
See— MACH, Ernst & Salcher, P.

SALDIAS, Adolfo
– **Historia de la Confederación Argentina.** Buenos Aires, 1892. *2nd. Edn.* 5 vols. Sm. liby. stp. on title-pp., mor.-bkd. bds. (BBA. Feb.9; 285) *Walford.* £60

SALE, Sir Robert Henry
– **The Defence of Jellalabad.** L., ca. 1845. Fo. Litho. port., title, double-p. plan, 21 plts., sm. stains in margins, some spotting, text & plts. detchd., few margins slightly frayed, orig. mor.-bkd. cl., worn. (S. Mar.6; 44) *Walford.* £180

SALERNO
– **Regimen Sanitatis Salerni.** Trans.:– T. Paynelle. L., 1575. *2nd. Edn. in Engl.* [STC 21601] (*Bound with:*) – **The Englishmans Doctor; or, The School of Salerne.** Sir John Harington. L., 1612. *5th. Imp.* Together 2 works in 1 vol. Lacks 2nd. A2(?) & C8 (blank?), few minor margin defects, 2nd. work with natural paper fault in 1 lf., cf. antique. (SG. Nov.3; 181) $550

SALERNO SCHOOL
[–] **L'Art de Conserver sa Santé, Composé par l'Ecole de Salerno.** Petit-Bourg, 1888. Sm. 12mo. Cont. str.-grd. red mor., spine decor. (HD. May 4; 258) Frs. 1,400

SALLANDER, H.
– **Bibliotheca Walleriana.** Stockholm, 1955. 2 vols. Orig. linen. (R. Oct.11; 777) DM 420

SALLIETH, M.
See— DE JONG, Dirk & Sallieth, M.

SALLUSTIUS CRISPUS, Gaius
– **Die Catilinarischen Unruhen.** Ed.:– F. Homeyer. [Berlin, Maximillan-Gesellschaft, 1929]. *(400) on Bütten.* 4to. German-Latin parallel text, hand-bnd. mor., by Hans Glökler, Berlin, gold decor. (H. Nov.23; 1173) DM 400
– **De Coniuratione Catilinae. Eiuedom de Bello Jugurthino [& other works].** Venice, Apr. 1509. *1st. Aldine Edn.* Capital spaces with guide letters, a few cont. ink annots. in red, cont. Venetian mor. gt., covers elab. decor. in gt. & blind, flat spine in 4 compartments, diapered in blind with triple fillets, sm. repairs to extreme upr. & lr. corners of upr. jnt. & to each corner, spine slightly rubbed, end-papers renewed (at an early date?), lacks ties, gt.-lettered mor. box; J. Renard & Henri Beraldi bkplts., Thomas B. Stevenson copy. (CNY. May 18; 88) $3,600
– **Opera.** Venice, Johannes de Colonia & Johannes Manthen, 23 Mar. 1474. Fo. Wide margins, capital spaces with guide letters, Cataline's oration bnd. at end, light margin stains, scattered wormholes, 18th. C. mott. vell.; John Scott, of Halkshill bkplt. [BMC V, 229; Goff S-56; HC 14201] (SPB. Dec.14; 30) $1,000
– – **Anr. Edn.** Lyon, 1519. Lge. 8vo. Many headlines shaved, some worming, lacks a3-6, hf. cf. (SG. Feb.9; 324) $225
See— CURTIUS RUFUS, Quintus – SALLUSTIUS CRISPUS, Caius

SALLUSTIUS CRISPUS, Caius & Florus, Lucius Annaeus
– **Histories.** Bg'ham., 1773. 4to. Lacks 1st. section title, cont. red mor., gt., extremities lightly rubbed. (CSK. Nov.25; 88) £55
– – **Anr. Edn.** Bg'ham, Baskerville Pr., 1773. 4to. Hf.-title, cont. red mor. gt., spine gt. (SPB. May 16; 7) $225
– **Opera.** Bg'ham, Baskerville Pr., 1774. 12mo. Cont. cf., rebkd. (SG. Apr.19; 20) $100

SALM, A.
– **Java, naar Schilderijen en Teekeningen ... op Steen gebracht** ... Ill.:– J.C. Gneve. Amst., ca. 1860. Lge. fo. Title & 24 litho. plts., ptd. in cols. & hand-finished, each laid at edges on to blank sheets, orig. decor. cl., gt. (CH. May 24; 52) Fls. 4,000

SALMON, André
– **Le Manuscrit trouvé dans un Chapeau.** Ill.:– Pablo Picasso. Paris, 1919. *Ltd. Edn.* 4to. Orig. wraps. (BBA. Jun.14; 243) *Sims, Reed & Fogg.* £90
– **Rive Gauche: Quartier Latin, Plaisance Montparnasse, Les Quais Saint-Germain-des-Prés.** Ill.:– Maurice de Vlaminok. Paris, priv. ptd., 1951. *(300) numbered, with self-port. sigd. by artist.* 4to. Unsewn in orig. pict. wraps., unc., folder & fitted case. (S. Nov.21; 41) *Marks.* £450
– **Venus dans la Balance.** Ill.:– Pascin. [1926]. *Orig.*

SALMON, André- *contd.*

Edn. (25) on japan with 4 autograph verses. Orig. engr., sigd. in pencil, leaves. (HD. Apr.13; 176)
Frs. 2,100

SALMON, Thomas
- **Modern History: or the Present State of all Nations.** Ill.:– Herman Moll. L., 1739. *2nd. L. Edn.* 3 vols. 4to. Liby. stps. on titles, cont. cf., worn. (BBA. May 3; 275) *Yapp.* £640
- - **Anr. Copy.** 3 vols. 4to. 41 engraved folding maps, 63 other engraved plts., cont. cf., worn. (SKC. Jan.13; 2247) £600
- - **Anr. Copy.** Vol. 3 only. 4to. Engraved plts. & folding maps, a few loose, cont. cf., worn. (BBA. May 3; 276) *Burton.* £240
- **A New Geographical & Historical Grammar ...** 1749. 22 folding engraved maps, cont. cf. gt., worn. (LC. Mar.1; 541) £60
- **Lo Stato Presente di tutti I Paesi e Popoli del Mondo.** Venezia, 1731-65. 7 vols. Some tears, stains & other slight defects., cont. bindings, not unif., w.a.f. (SI. Dec.15; 87) Lire 500,000

SALMON, William, Dr., 1644-1713
- **Botanologia. The English Herbal: or, History of Plants.** L., 1710. *1st. Edn.* Fo. Without the 'Index morborum' (found in some copies), some ll. browned, slight margin staining, a few minor tears & sm. holes slightly affecting text, cont. panel. cf., gt. spine, rather worn. (S. Nov.28; 82) *Traylen.* £340
- - **Anr. Copy.** Fo. Some worm in margins, few ll. dampstained, lacks 2 ll. of index at end, vell., worn, w.a.f. (P. Sep.8; 301) *Edmunds.* £220
- - **Anr. Copy.** Fo. Frontis. cut to plt. margin & mntd., some ll. with sm. margin tears at foot, some light staining or spotting from pressed plants, cont. leath., partly restored, cont. style renewed spine. (R. Oct.12; 1904a) DM 2,000
- - **Anr. Copy.** Fo. Leath. (G. Sep.15; 2327) Sw. Frs. 1,300
- - **Anr. Copy.** Fo. Very browned & stained, hf. cf., defect., as a collection of plts., w.a.f. (CR. Jun.6; 279) Lire 750,000
- **The Family Dictionary; or Household Companion.** 1696. *2nd. Edn.* Light soiling, cont. cf. [Wing S429] (CSK. Aug.19; 98) £160
- - **Anr. Edn.** L., 1710. *4th. Edn.* Mod. mor. (C. Nov.9; 113a) *Traylen.* £160
- **Pharmacopeia Londinensis.** L., 1682. *2nd. Edn.* Sm. 8vo. Some foxing, etc., old crude hf. cf. (SG. Oct.6; 319) $130
- **Polygraphice; or the Art of Drawing, Engraving, Etching, Limning, Painting, Washing, Varnishing, Colouring & Dying.** L., 1672. *1st. Edn.* Some browning, cont. sheep; sig. of Robert Eastchurch, 1604, on recto of frontis. [Wing S444] (BBA. May 3; 153) *Quaritch.* £600

SALMON, William, Builder, Fl. 1745.
- **Palladio Londinensia.** 1734. *1st. Edn.* 3 pts. in 1 vol. 4to. 2 pp. advts. at end, front end-paper & fly-lf. loose, cont. cf. (SKC. Nov.18; 1824) £120
- - **Anr. Edn.** 1773. *8th. Edn.* 4to. Cf., upr. cover detchd. (P. Apr.12; 74) *Jarndyce.* £60

SALMON & TROUT MAGAZINE: Journal of the Salmon & Trout Association.
Dec. 1910-Mar. 1975. Nos. 1-203, & 3 subject index. 4to. Iss. nos. 1-151 in buckram with general indices, rest unbnd. in orig. pts. (PD. Oct.19; 197) £270

SALT, Sir Henry
- **Twenty-Four Views Taken in St. Helena, the Cape, India, Ceylon, Abyssinia & Egypt.** Ill.:– Havell & Bluck, after Salt. L., 1809. Without text vol. Lge. fo. On thick paper, wide margins, lge. copy, sepia aquatint title incorporating dedication, 24 hand-cold. aquatint views, interleaved thro.-out, orig. bds., worn, rebkd. in cf. gt.; Lonsdale copy with Lowther Castle bkplt. (S. Feb.1; 47) *Dew.* £7,200
- - **Anr. Copy.** Plt. vol. only. Lge. fo. Uncold. aqua-tint title, dedication, 24 hand-cold. aquatint plts., hf. buckram, spine gt.-lettered. (C. Nov.16; 167) *Hosain.* £2,000
- **A Voyage to Abyssinia.** 1814. 2 vols. Lge. 4to. 7 maps, 5 folding, 1 hand-cold., 27 engraved plts.,

some light spotting, cont. cf. (CSK. Aug.19; 20) £220
- - **Anr. Copy.** 4to. 27 engraved plts., 7 maps, some folding, 1 hand-cold. (cleanly torn), cont. cf. gt., rubbed. (CSK. Jan.27; 156) £170

SALTER, Robert
- **The Modern Angler.** Oswestry, priv. ptd., 1811. 12mo. Little foxing or offsetting. three-qtr. mor., rubbed. (SG. Mar.15; 290) $150

SALVAGE, Jean Galbert
- **Anatomie du Gladiateur Combattant, applicable aux Beaux-Arts.** 1812. Fo. Sm. margin stains, 19th. C. hf. long-grd. mor., restored. (HD. Feb.29; 43) Frs. 2,500

SALVIANI, Hippolyte
- **Aquatilium Animalium Historiae.** Rome, 1554[-58]. *1st. Edn.* Fo. Wide margin, title bkd., some old underlining, minimal soiling, hf. leath. (HK. Nov.8; 555) DM 5,000

SALVIN, Francis Henry & Brodrick, William
- **Falconry in the British Isles.** L., 1873. *2nd. Edn.* 4to. 28 hand-cold. litho. plts., mor. gt., gt. figure on upr. cover, silk liners. (C. Mar.14; 147) *Foyle.* £800

SALVIN, Osbert
See— GODMAN, Frederick du Cane & Salvin, Osbert
See— SCLATER, Philip Lutley & Salvin, Osbert

SALVINI
[-] **Giustificazione della Revoluzione di Corsica.** Corte, 1764. Cont. vell. (HD. Oct.21; 159) Frs. 7,000

SALVIO, Alessandro
- **Trattato dell' Inventione et Arte Liberale del Gioco di Scacchi.** Naples, 1604. *1st. Edn.* 4to. Errata/imprimatur lf., corner off A2, V3 reprd., foxed, cont. vell., relined, soiled. (SG. Nov.3; 182) $600

SALWEY, Charlotte M.
- **Fans of Japan.** L., 1894. 4to. 10 cold. plts., errata slip, orig. decor. cl., soiled. (BBA. Mar.7; 24) *H. Landry.* £110

SALZBURGISCHES KOCHBUCH
[Salzburg], ca. 1750. 4 pts. in 1 vol. 4to. Lacks title & 89 pp. pt. 1, lacks some index ll. at end. lacks 20 engraved pp., minimal soiling, cont. bds. (HK. Nov.9; 1677) DM 1,300

SALZMANN, Christian Gotthilf
- **Gymnastics for Youth, or a Practical Guide to Healthful & Amusing Exercises for the Use of Schools.** L., 1800. Frontis. torn & spotted, browned, cont. cf., upr. cover detchd. (S. Nov.22; 392) *Agassi.* £130
- - **Anr. Edn.** Ill.:– after W. Blake. Phila., 1802. *1st. Amer. Edn.* Sm. 8vo. Some text ll. dampsoiled, cont. tree cf., head of spine frayed. (SG. Aug.4; 145) $225

SAMAIN, Albert
- **Xanthis, ou La Vitrine Sentimentale.** Ill.:– Gustave Adolphe Mossa & Eugène Charpentier. Paris, 1920. *(775) numbered on beau vélin d'Arches.* Ills. hand-cold., maroon three-qtr. lev., by Affolter. spine gt., cold. pict. wraps. bnd. in. (SG. Feb.16; 262) $190

SAMBUCUS, J.
- **Emblemata et Aliquot.** Antw., 1584. 12mo. M.S. initials in ink on title-p., cf., worn, re-bkd. (BS. May 2; 35) £120
- - **Anr. Copy.** 12mo. Lacks title-lf., some slight staining, cont. leath. (D. Nov.23; 108) DM 800
- **Veterum Aliquot ac Recentium Medicorum Philosophorumq[ue] Icones.** [Antw.], 1603. Fo. Engraved title (border with space for letterpress left blank), 67 engraved ports., few minor margin tears, cont. limp vell. (SPB. Dec.13; 735) $150

SAMETZKY, C.W.
- **Lehrbuch der Kochkunst.** Berlin, 1819. *1st. Edn.* 2 vols. Slightly browned thro.-out, orig. bds., worn. (GB. Nov.4; 1441) DM 630

SAMIGA, Joseph
- **Mikraei Kodesh.** Venice, 1586. *1st. Edn.* 4to. Owners' sigs. on title, corners reprd. not affecting text, title & last lf. washed, some staining, hf. leath., marb. paper bds. (S. Oct.25; 325) *Ludmir.* £360
- **Porat Joseph.** Venice, 1590. *1st. Edn.* Pt. I only. 4to. Owner's sig. on title, worming affecting some letters, margins crudely reprd., browned, edges frayed from burning, mod. mor. gt. (S. Oct.25; 326) *Sol.* £260

SAMMES, Aylett
- **Britannia Antiqua Illustrata.** L., 1676. *1st. Edn.* Vol.1 (all publd.). Fo. Short tear in R4, cont. cf., worn. (S. Mar.6; 323) *Bloomsbury.* £80

SAMMONICUS, Q. Serenus
See— CELSUS, Aureluis Cornelius– SAMMONICUS, Q. Serenus

SAMPERI, Placido
- **Iconologia della Gloriosa Vergine Madre de Dio Maria Protettrice di Messina.** Messina, 1739. Fo. Frontis., 76 copper-engraved plts., sm. loss from 1 plt., some foxing, old vell. (HD. Mar.9; 125) Frs. 2,100

SAMUEL, Rabbi
- **Epistola Rabbi Samuelis Israelite missa ad Rabbi Ysaac ... Annexa est ... Pontii Pilati ... Epistola ad Tiberium Imperatorem.** Nurenberg, Caspar Hochfeder, 19 Mar. 1498. 4to. Slight traces of worming, slight soiling, mod. vell. [Goff S-113; HC 14270*] (SPB. Feb.1; 7) $3,250

SAMUEL PEPYS CLUB
- **Occasional Papers Published for the Members of the Samuel Pepys Club.** L., 1917 & 1925. *(250).* Vol. I, 1903-14: Vol. II, 1917-23. Cl., qtr. buckram, 1st. with backstrip rather dull. (KH. Nov.9; 388) Aus. $230

SAN BLAS
- **[Printed Copy of the Provisional Regulations for the Infantry Company of the Port of San Blas, Comprising Thirty-Five Articles Including Rates of Pay.]** Mexico, 23 Nov. 1790. Fo. 8 pp., disbnd. (S. May 22; 306) *Cortes.* £500

SANCHEZ, Franciscus
- **De Multum Nobili.** Frankfurt, 1618. Few head-lines shaved, discold. in places, vell.; Dr. Walter Pagel copy. (S. Feb.7; 338) *Quaritch.* £120

SANCHEZ TORTOLES, Antonio & Meraleja, Joseph
- **El Entrenido.** Madrid, 1673 & 1741. *1st. Edn.* Pts. 1 & 2 (compl.). 4to. Frontis. strengthened, slightly worn, cont. leath. (DS. Dec.16; 2100) Pts. 48,000

SANCTORIUS, S.
- **Medecina Statica.** Trans.:– John Quincy. 1723. *3rd. Edn.* Later cf. gt. (BBA. Jul.27; 53) *Thorp.* £70

SAND, George (Pseud.)
See— DUPIN, Amandine Aurore Lucie, Baronne Dudevant 'George Sand'

SAND, Maurice (Pseud.)
See— DUDEVANT, Maurice 'maurice Sand'

SANDBURG, Carl
- **Abraham Lincoln. The War Years.** N.Y., [1939]. *Deluxe 1st. Edn. (515) numbered.* 4 vols. Cl., s.-c.; sigd. (LH. Sep.25; 283) $210
- **Chicago Poems.** N.Y., 1916. *1st. Edn.* Orig. cl., d.-w.; inscr. by author to John Valentine, Frederic Dannay copy. (CNY. Dec.16; 307) $1,600
- **Smoke & Steel.** N.Y., [1920]. cl., some wear; sigd. pres. copy, 8-line poem in author's hand. (RO. Sep.13; 165) $110

SANDBY, Paul
- **The Virtuosi's Museum.** L., 1778 [but 1778-81]. Ob. 4to. Engraved title, 108 views, some slight spotting, few plts. stained in margin, hf. cf., slightly worn. (S. Mar.6; 324) *Loveday.* £260
- - **Anr. Edn.** 1778. Ob. 4to. Engraved title & 80 plts. only. cont. hf. mor. (CSK. Dec.16; 175) £170

SANDEMAN, Fraser
- **By Hook & by Crook.** L., 1892. *1st. Edn. (100) sigd.* 4to. 16 plts., some cold., slightly spotted, orig. cl., soiled. (S. Apr.10; 582) *Head.* £100

SANDER, August
- **Antlitz der Zeit.** Intro.:– Alfred Doeblin. Munich, [1929]. *1st. Edn.* 4to. Orig. cl. over flexible bds., lightly rubbed, spine faded. (SG. May 10; 129) $475
- – **Anr. Copy.** 4to. Orig. linen. (H. May 23; 1455) DM 530

SANDER, Henry Fredk. Conrad
- **Reichenbachia. Orchids Illustrated & Described.** St. Albans & L., 1892-94. *2nd. Series.* 2 vols. Lge. fo. 35 plts & text ll. pasted & defect., vol. II 1 plt. pasted to text lf., some margins with staining, & spotting, hf. leath., very defect., lacks 1 spine., loose. (H. May 22; 204) DM 2,600

SANDERUS, Antonius
- **Chorographia Sacra Brabantiae, siva Celebrium Aliquot in ea Provincia Abbatiarum, Coenobiorum Monasteriorum ... Descriptio.** The Hague, 1726-27. 3 vols. Fo. Engraved port., engraved title vigs., 66 engraved plts., cont. pol. cf., gt.-panel. spines. (CH. Sep.20; 12) Fls. 2,900
- **Flandria Illustrata.** Maps:– after Hondius, Blaeu & others. Cologne [Amst.], Cornelis van Egmont (Johannes Blaeu), 1641-44. *1st. Edn.* 3 pts. in 2 vols. including supps. Fo. Hf.-titles, engraved armorial titles, 37 double-p. maps, plans & views, 7 full-p. plts., including ports., & upwards of 270 ports., plans, views & elevations in text, 1 or 2 tears touching engraved surfaces, some light creasing or faint browning, cont. gt.-panel. vell., soiled, new ties; cont. owner's inscr. of Cistercian abbey at Roosendaal in ink on both engraved titles. (S. May 21; 245) *Harris.* £4,000
- **Presbyteri Chorographia Sacra Brabantiae.** Hagae Comitum, 1726. 3 vols. Lge. fo. Lacks view of Averbode & Tongerloo abbeys, spr. cf., spine decor., turn-ins & corners slightly worn. (LM. Oct.22; 97) B.Frs. 60,000

SANDFORD, Francis
- **A Genealogical History of the Kings of England & Monarchs of Great Britain.** L., 1677. Fo. Later mor. gt., soiled. (S. Mar.20; 836) *Page.* £140

SANDRART, Joachim von
- **L'Academia Tedesca della Architettura, Scultura et Pittura, oder Teutsche Academie der Edeln Bau-Bild- und Mahlerkunst.** Nuremb., Leipzig, 1675-80. *1st. Edn.* 3 vols. in 4. Fo. 1 plt. spotted, cont. roan, spine blind-stpd.; from Fondation Fursten-berg-Beaumesnil. (HD. Nov.16; 170) Frs. 7,000
- **Iconologia Deorum, oder Abbildung der Götter welche von den Alten Verchret worden.** Ill.:– Collin (port.): Joachim Sandrart, engraved by Eimmart, Johann Sandrart & Suzanna Maria Sandrart. Nuremb., 1680. Fo. Port. dtd. 1679, cont. German marb. roan, covers richly decor. (HD. Mar.21; 89) Frs. 2,050
- **Sculpturae Veteris Admiranda.** Ill.:– R. Collin & others. Nuremb., 1680. *1st. Edn.* Tall fo. Title vig., port., 68 (of 70) copperplts., some double-p., hf.-title, old cf., rebkd., worn; armorial bkplt. of Earl Fitzwilliam. (SG. Feb.9; 325) $150
- **Teutsche Academie der Bau Bildhaeuer und Maler-Kunst.** [Nuremb., 1768-75]. Vol. 2 only (of 8?). Fo. Engraved title, engraved frontis., 283 plts., lacks covers, as a collection of plts., w.a.f. (P. Sep.29; 236) *L'Aquaforte.* £100

SANDS, John
- **New Atlas of Australia.** 1886. Fo. Poor, no bdg. stated. (JL. Jun.24; 152) Aus. $340
- – **Anr. Edn.** Sydney, ca. 1887. South Australian section. Fo. Bds., brkn. (KH. May 1; 613) Aus. $100

SANDS, John & Kenny, Thomas
- **Victoria Illustrated.** Melbourne & Sydney, 1857. *(750).* Ob. 4to. Orig. decor. cl. (TA. Aug.18; 51) £200
- – **Anr. Edn.** Melbourne, ca. 1857. 1st. Series. Ob. 4to. Engraved title-p. & 45 plts. (compl.), some generally pale foxing thro.-out, recased in orig. bds.,

new backstrip, minor wear. (KH. Nov.9; 432) Aus. $750

SANDYS, Sir Edwin
[–] **Europae Speculum or a View or Survey of the State of Religion in the Westerne Parts of the World.** 'Hagae Comitis' [L.], 1629. *1st. Authorised Edn.* 4to. A few stains, limp vell. [STC 21718] (BBA. May 3; 109) *Howes Bookshop.* £70
- – **Anr. Edn.** The Hague, [for M. Sparke, L.], 1629. 4to. Margin defects in F2, corner off N3, slight worming, mostly marginal, few ll. partly dampstained, old vell. (SG. Oct.27; 285) $100

SANDYS, George
[–] **A Relation of a Journey Begun An Dom. 1610. Foure Bookes, containing a Description of the Turkish Empire; of Aegypt, of the Holy Land, of the Remote Parts of Italy & Ilands adjoyning.** L., 1627. Sm. fo. Foxed & stained, old cf., worn & loose. (SG. Sep.22; 266) $325
- – **Anr. Edn.** L., 1632. *3rd. Edn.* Fo. Engraved title, folding view & ills., foot of title shaved, slightly soiled towards beginning & end, a few dampstains, cont. cf., rubbed. [STC 21729] (C. Jun.27; 68) *McManmon.* £120
- – **Anr. Edn.** L., 1670. Fo. Some browning & spotting, mod. hf. sheep. (S. Mar.6; 45) *Coupe.* £130

SANGUINETI, A.
- **La Serrurerie au XIXe Siècle.** Paris, ca. 1880. 4 pts. in 1 vol. Ob. fo. Slightly foxed, folding plts. with tears, cont. hf. linen, bumped. (HK. May 17; 3476) DM 400

SANNAZARO, Jacopo
- **Arcadia.** [Venice, 1514]. Sm. 8vo. Vell. (LH. Sep.25; 307) $200
- – **Anr. Edn.** Venezia, Sep. 1514. Stain on frontis. & last p., mod. vell. (SI. Dec.15; 38) Lire 350,000

SAN NICOLAS, Lorenzo de
- **Segunda Parte del Arte y Uso de Architectura ...** Madrid, 1663. Fo. Lacks 2 pp., vell. (DS. Apr.27; 2595) Pts. 35,000

SANSON D'ABBEVILLE, Nicolas
- **Atlas Nouveau, Contenant Toutes les Parties du Monde.** Paris, H. Jaillot, 1692 [1694]. 2 vols. Lge. fo. Engraved architectural title to Vol. 2, ptd. title to Vol. 1, top corner torn away with some loss, contents lf. to each vol., 99 hand-cold. engraved maps, mostly double-p., 1 folding, a few minor repairs without loss, some slight browning or offsetting, cont. gt.-panel. cf., rebkd. with orig. spines relaid. (TA. Jun.21; 92) £5,200
- – **Anr. Edn.** Paris, Hubert Jaillot, [1692-]96. 2 vols. Fo. 2 hand-cold. engraved architectural titles, 2 ptd. 'tables des cartes' pasted in engraved pict. hand-cold. borders, 123 engraved maps (28 single-p., 95 double-p. mntd. on guards), all but 1 hand-cold. in outl., accompanied by engraved geographical tables & gazetteers, 31 uncold. engraved plts. of sm. town plans & views, a few maps with tears & repairs at centrefold, lr. margin of 1 map slightly shaved, cont. Dutch mott. cf., covers gt.-panel., gt. central ornament, spines chipped, corners reprd. (C. Mar.14; 87) *Burgess.* £9,000
- – **Anr. Edn.** Paris, H. Jaillot, 1693. Lge. fo. Architectural engraved title, contents lf. border, ptd. title in red & black, MS. contents list, 98 mostly double-p. engraved maps, dtd. between 1691 & 1696, (mostly 1692, including Michalet's map of Egypt & Moll's map of environs of L. (ca. 1700)), maps hand-cold. in outl., title & contents border fully so, 1 or 2 splits at centre-folds reprd. without loss of engraved surface, sm. portion of 1 map torn with loss of engraved border, some faint offsetting or creasing, mod. blind-panel. cf., spine gt., w.a.f. (S. May 21; 115) *Burgess.* £4,200
- – **Anr. Edn.** Paris, H. Jaillot, 1696. Lge. fo. Additional engraved architectural title, engraved lf. 'Table des Cartes', 112 engraved maps, hand-cold. in outl., most double-p., some accompanied by engraved geographical tables, mntd. on guards, the centre blank without the ptd. table, minor stain & some spots in a few blank margins, cont. blind-

stpd. cf., rubbed & worn. (C. Nov.16; 208) *Burgess.* $5,200
- **Description de tout l'Univers.** Ill.:– A. de Winter. Amst., François Halma, 1700. 6 pts. in 2 vols., including Supps. 4to. Double-p. engraved additional title, 74 double-p. maps, 15 plts., including 11 folding, in Bion's supp., 1 or 2 minor stains, cont. spr. cf., spines gt. (S. Dec.1; 198) *Map House.* £1,500
- **L'Europe.** Paris, 1665. 4to. Text ll. rearranged & remargined, mod. vell. (VG. Sep.14; 1075) Fls. 740

See— CAESAR, Gaius Julius – SANSON D'ABBE-VILLE, Nicolas
See— ST. PAUL, Charles de & Sanson d'Abbeville, Nicolas

SANSON D'ABBEVILLE, Nicolas, the Elder & the Younger
- **L'Europe; L'Asie; L'Affrique; L'Amérique.** Paris, [1648]; 1657; [1656]; [1657]. 4 vols. 4to. Double-p. engraved title in 1st. vol., ptd. titles in others, 60 double-p. engraved maps (only, of 62, lacks maps of Syria & Turcomanie), hand-cold. in outl. thro.-out, a few in 1st. vol. with additional wash col., engraved title defect. with loss, a few short tears without loss of engraved surface, some soiling, owners' inscrs. on front free end-papers, cont. cf., spines gt., worn. (S. Dec.1; 190) *McCall.* £1,000

SANTA CLARA, Abraham a
See— ABRAHAM A SANTA CLARA [i.e. Ulrich Megerle]

SANTAYANA, George
- **The Works.** N.Y., 1936. *(940) sigd.* 15 vols. Orig. cl.-bkd. bds., some soiling to spines & labels, several boxes worn. (SPB. Dec.13; 562) $400
- – **Anr. Edn.** N.Y., 1936 & 1940. *Triton Edn. (940) numbered & sigd.* 15 vols., including the later publd. final vol. Lge. 8vo. Linen-bkd. bds. gt., partly unc. & unopened, orig. s.-c.'s. (SG. Nov.3; 183) $550
- – **Anr. Copy.** 15 vols. Lge. 8vo. Frontis.-ports., linen-bkd. bds., partly unc. & unopened, s.-c's. (SG. Apr.26; 176) $400
- – **Anr. Copy.** 15 vols. Cl.-bkd. bds., s.-c.'s. (PNY. Jun.6; 458) $320

SANTEE, Ross
- **The Bubbling Spring.** N.Y., 1949. *1st. Edn.* Cl., d.-w. soiled & torn; inscr. by author, with ink sketch. (LH. Jan.15; 381) $140

SANTINI, P.
- **Atlas Universel, dressé sur les Meilleures Cartes Modernes.** Maps:– after d'Anville, Bellin, Janvier, the Roberts de Vaugondy, Rizzi-Zannoni, Homann & others. Venice, 1776. *1st. Edn.* 2 vols. in 1. Fo. Engraved allegorical title, contents ll., 124 engraved double-p. mapsheets, map of Gibralter not called for in contents list, hand-cold. in outl. thro.-out, 1 or 2 maps detchd., faint margin stains at end, cont. blind-ruled cf., spine gt., slightly wormed, w.a.f. (S. May 21; 133) *Traylen.* £3,200

SANTOS, D. de los
- **Vocabulario de la Lengua Tagala.** Manila, 1835. Fo. Vell. (DS. Apr.27; 2598) Pts. 50,000

SANTOS, Francisco de los
- **Canonis Missae Interpretatio.** Salamanca, [printer of Nehrissensis' Gramatica] for Peter Manuel de Madrigal, 20 Feb. 1495. 4to. Some capital spaces filled in with brown ink, MS. marginalia cropped, some spotting, vell. [Goff S-164] (SPB. Dec.14; 31) $2,100
- **Descripción breve del Monasterio de S. Lorenzo el Reál del Escorial.** Madrid, 1657. *1st. Edn.* Fo. Engraved port., 10 plts., most folding, some dampstains, few short tears in text & plts., cont. limp vell., soiled; bkplts. of Joseph Sedgwick, 1723 & W.C. Mylne. (S. Mar.20; 808) *Baldwin.* £170
- – **Anr. Copy.** Fo. Vell. (DS. Oct.28; 2134) Pts. 50,000
- – **Anr. Edn.** Madrid, 1681. Fo. Leath., superlibris. (DS. Mar.23; 2717) Pts. 40,000

SAPPHO
- **Carmina [Graece].** Ill.:– R. Sintenis & E.R. Weiss. München, 1921. *(185) numbered.* Sm. 4to. Orig. bds. (GB. Nov.5; 3015) DM 2,800
- – **Anr. Copy.** 4to. In Grk., printers mark sigd. by artist, & Weiss, red hf. leath. (HK. May 17; 3130) DM 2,400
- – **Anr. Copy.** Sm. 4to. 12 orig. etchings, orig. bds., spine & cover partly faded. (GB. May 5; 3327) DM 1,800
- – **Anr. Copy.** 4to. Printers mark sigd. by artists, orig. bds., some fading, especially spine. (HK. Nov.11; 3975) DM 1,200
- **Songs of Sappho [Greek].** Ill.:– A. Simons. [München, Bremer Pr., 1922]. *(14) De Luxe Edn. on vell. with title in gold.* Sm. 4to. Orig. hand-bnd. mor., gold decor., by Frieda Thiersch. spine slightly discold. (H. Nov.23; 936) DM 7,200

SAPPINGTON, John
- **The Theory & Treatment of Fevers.** Ed.:– Ferdinando Stith. Arrow Rock, priv. ptd., 1844. *1st. Edn.* 12mo. Dampstained thro.-out, new leatherette. (SG. Oct.6; 320) $130

SARASIN, Jean-Francois
- **Les Oeuvres.** Paris, 1656. *Orig. Edn.* 2 pts. in 1 vol. 4to. Cont. blind-decor. mor., Crémeaux d'Entragues arms. (HD. Mar.29; 92) Frs. 21,000

SARGENT, Charles Sprague
- **The Silva of North America: A Description of Trees which Grow Naturally in North America Exclusive of Mexico.** Ill.:– P. & E. Picart after Charles Edward Faxon. Boston, 1890-1902. *Orig. Edn.* 14 vols., including 2 Supp. vols. Fo. Sm. perforated liby. stp. on titles, ptd. bds., unc., shelf mark on spines. (SG. Mar.22; 280) $900
- **Trees & Shrubs: Illustrations of New or Little Known Ligneous Plants ... chiefly from Material at the Arnold Arboretum.** Ill.:– Charles Edward Faxon. Boston, 1905-13. *1st. Edn.* 2 vols. Sm. fo. 200 plts., hf. buckram, slightly rubbed. (SG. Mar.22; 282) $275

SARGENT, John S.
See— MANSON, J.B. & Meynell, Mrs.

SARLANDIERS, Jean Baptiste
- **Systematised Anatomy or Human Organography** ... Trans.:– W.C. Roberts. N.Y., 1837. Ob. fo. Liby. stp. on title & plt. versos, hf. cf., some wear. (TA. Nov.17; 595) £68

SAROYAN, William
- **Contes.** Ill.:– Henri Laurens. Paris, 1953. *(147). (47) numbered.* 4to. Sigd. by artist with extra suite of plts., loose as iss. in orig. wraps., orig. fibre folder & s.-c. (BBA. Jun.14; 224) *Makiya.* £320
- **The Daring Young Man on the Flying Trapeze.** N.Y., Random House, 1934. *1st. Edn.* Some slight margin darkening, cl., cover edges darkened, d.-w. soiled, chipped & darkened at spine & edges, tears reprd. with paper tape on verso, foil wraparound band; pres. copy, inscr. 'To 'Val' Valenti Angelo ... with good wishes William Saroyan Dec. 1934'. (CBA. Oct.1; 428) $150
- **The Fiscal Hoboes.** Ill.:– V. Angelo. N.Y., Pr. of Valenti Angelo, 1949. *(250) sigd. by Saroyan & Angelo.* Bds., lightly soiled; the V. Angelo copy. (CBA. Oct.1; 394) $225
- – **Anr. Copy.** Bds., end-papers mildly darkening, lightly soiled & rubbed, spine fading; the V. Angelo copy, newspaper article & A.L.s. by Don Freeman laid in loose. (CBA. Oct.1; 395) $150
- **Harlem as Seen by Hirschfeld.** N.Y., [1941]. *(1000) numbered.* Fo. 23 (of 24) tipped-in plts., 3 plts. lightly creased, 1 also slightly soiled, pict. cl., soiled & dampstained. (SG. Jan.12; 158) $110

SARPI, Paolo
- **Histoire du Concile de Trante.** Trans.:– De La Motto-Josseval. Amst., n.d. 4to. Hf. roan. worn. (HD. Feb.22; 205) Frs. 1,500
- [–] **The History of the Inquisition.** Trans.:– R. Gentilia. 1639. *1st. Edn. in Engl.* 4to. License lf., some catchwords cropped or shaved, rust hole in 1 lf., mod. cf.-bkd. bds. [STC 21765] (BBA. Jun.14; 37) *A. Stewart.* £75

SARRATT, J.H.
- **The Works of Damiano, Ruy-Lopez & Salvio, on the Game of Chess.** L., 1813. Hf.-title, last advt. lf., some ll. slightly browned, orig. bds., unc., slightly worn; bkplt. of David Garnett. (BBA. Mar.21; 253) *Weininger.* £50

SARRE, Friedrich & Trenkwald, Hermann
- **Altorientalische Teppiche.** Ed.:– Osterr. Museum f. Kunst u. Industrie. Wien & Leipzig, 1926-28. Imp. fo. Hf. leath., spine slightly worn. (HK. Nov.12; 4814) DM 4,800
- **Old Oriental Carpets.** Vienna, 1926-29. Fo. 120 plts., including 7 double-p., errata slip tipped in, prospectus laid in, few tissue guards torn, 2 reprd., orig. cl., rebkd., old spines laid down. (SG. Nov.3; 185) $2,200

SARTON, George
- **Introduction to History of Science.** Balt., 1950-48. 3 vols. in 5. Orig. cl.; Dr. Walter Pagel copy. (S. Feb.7; 339) *Goldschmidt.* £110

SARTORIUS, G.F.
- **Urkundliche Geschichte des Ursprungs der Deutschen Hanse.** Ed.:– J.M. Lappenberg. Hamburg, 1830. 4to. Foxed, cont. hf. leath., bumped, 1 spine reprd. (R. Apr.3; 1040) DM 420

SARTRE, Jean-Paul
- **Visages. Précédé des Portraits Officiels.** Ill.:– Wols. 1948. *Orig. Edn.* 12mo. On Crevecoeur du Marais, sewed. (HD. Apr.13; 177) Frs. 4,500
- – **Anr. Edn.** Ill.:– Wols. [Paris, 1948]. *(916).(900) numbered on Crevecoeur du Marais.* 4 orig. etchings, orig. wraps. (GB. Nov.5; 3133) DM 1,200

SASSOON, Siegfried 'Saul Kain'
- **Counter-Attack & Other Poems.** 1918. *1st. Edn.* 1 vol. Sm. 8vo. Light spotting. Orig. wraps.; sigd. by author. (*With:*) - **The War Poems.** 1919. *1st. Edn.* 1 vol. Sm. 8vo. Orig. cl.; sigd. by author. (SKC. Jan.13; 2248) £80
- **The Daffodil Murderer by Saul Kain.** 1913. Hf.-title, light foxing, orig. wraps.; sigd. by author. (SKC. Jan.13; 2249) £85
- **Memoirs of a Fox-Hunting Man.** L., [1928]. *1st. Edn. 1st. Iss.* Misprint on last line, p. 365, cl., d.-w., crimson qtr. lev. s.-c. (SG. May 24; 357) $130
- **Memoirs of an Infantry Officer.** 1930. *1st. Edn.* (*With:*) - **Sherston's Progress.** 1936. *1st. Edn.* Together 2 vols. Orig. cl., d.-w.'s.; sigd. by author. (SKC. Jan.13; 2251) £100
- – **Anr. Edn.** Ill.:– Barnett Friedman. L., 1931. *(320) numbered & sigd. by author & artist.* Orig. bds., d.-w., s.-c. (BBA. Nov.30; 295) *Maggs.* £130
- – **Anr. Copy.** Orig. bds., d.-w., s.-c. (BBA. Aug.18; 88) *Ingrams.* £75
- **To My Mother.** Ill.:– Stephen Tennant. L., 1928. *(338) numbered on L.P., sigd. 'Ariel Poems' no.14.* Orig. bds., unc. (S. Mar.20; 958) *Maggs.* £50
- **The Old Huntsman & Other Poems.** 1917. *1st. Edn.* Hf.-title, orig. bds.; sigd. by author. (SKC. Jan.13; 2253) £110
- **Orpheus in Diloeryum.** L., 1908. *1st. Edn. (50).* Orig. ptd. wraps.; pres. inscr. from Sassoon to E.L. Guilford, & with an A.L.s. from Sassoon to Guilford. (C. Nov.9; 181) *Browning.* £750
- **Poems.** L., priv. ptd., 1906. *1st. Edn. (50).* Orig. ptd. wraps., upr. cover slightly discold.; pres. inscr. 'To E.L. Guilford ... from Siegfried Sassoon, Xmas 06'. (C. Nov.9; 180) *Henderson.* £1,000
- **Sonnets.** L., priv. ptd., 1909. *1st. Edn. (50).* 4to. Orig. bds.; pres. copy from author, with note loosely inserted ' ... given to me by him with corrections in his own writing', autograph corrections in pencil. (C. Nov.9; 182) *Quaritch.* £820
- **Vigils.** Ill.:– Sigrist, frontis. by Stephen Gooden. 1934. *Ltd. Edn., numbered & sigd.* Orig. cl.-bkd. bds. (SKC. Jan.13; 2255) £75

SATTLER, Josef
- **Ein Moderner Totentanz in 16 Bildern.** Berlin, 1912. *2nd. Edn., (100).* Fo. Orig. linen, coll. stp. inside cover. (H. May 22; 465) DM 420

SATYRE MENIPEE de la Vertu du Catolicon d'Espagne et de la Tenue des Etats de Paris ...
Ratisbonne, 1726. 3 vols. Sm. 8vo. Bordeaux mor. by Petit, spines decor. (SM. Mar.7; 2049) Frs. 2,100

SAUERBRUCH, F.
- **Die Willkürlich bewegbare Künstliche Hand.** Ed.:– G. Ruge, W. Felix & A. Stadler. Berlin, 1916. *1st. Edn.* Orig. wraps., unc. (GB. Nov.3; 1044) DM 900

SAUERWEID, A.
- **L'Armée Saxonne.** Ill.:– engraved by Granicher, cold. by Botticher. Dresden, 1810. Sm. fo. 31 plts., including 1 dupl., some disbnd., lacks title, hf. mor. (HD. Jan.27; 302) Frs. 7,500
- **Uniformes de l'Armée Royale de Westphalie.** N.p., [1810]. 4to. Reprint (ca. 1900) of cold. plts., publisher's hf. bdg. (HD. Jan.27; 210) Frs. 1,000

SAULT, Richard
See— LEYBOURN, William

SAUNDERS, Edmund
- **Les Reports ... des Divers Pleadings et Cases.** L., 1686. *1st. Edn.* Sm. fo. In Latin & Law Fr., licence lf. starting, R2 & 3 loose, marginalia, owner's sig. on title, later hf. mor., slightly worn, rehinged. [Wing S 743] (SG. Oct.27; 189) $100

SAUNDERS, Howard
- **An Illustrated Manual of British Birds.** 1899. 1 vol. in 4. Hf. mor. gt. by Bickers, spines gt.-tooled; extra-ill. with 218 hand-cold. plts. from Donovan's 'History of British Birds' & 148 plts. from Hewitson's 'Illustrations of the Eggs of British Birds'. (SKC. May 4; 1872) £650

SAUNDERS, James
- **The Compleat Fisherman** ... 1724. *1st. Edn.* 12mo. Some browning, cf. gt., rebkd. preserving old spine. (S. Oct.4; 53) *Quaritch.* £280

SAUNDERS, Louise
- **The Knave of Hearts.** Ill.:– Maxfield Parrish. Racine, Wisconsin, [1925]. Square 4to. Spiral-bnd. wraps., some minor soiling, slight foxing to inside. (CBA. Aug.21; 444) $200

SAUNDERS, Richard (Pseud.)
See— FRANKLIN, Benjamin 'Richard Saunders'

SAUNDERSON, Nicholas
- **The Method of Fluxions applied to a Select Number of Useful Problems** ... L., 1756. Advts., errata, some spotting, sheep-bkd. marb. bds., spine & extremities worn, rubbed; circulating liby. label of John Nicholson, Camb., Stanitz coll. (SPB. Apr.25; 392) $175

SAUNIER, Baudry de & others
- **Histoire de la Locomotion Terrestre.** Paris, 1936. Fo. Cold. plts., ills., cl.-bkd. bds., worn. (P. May 17; 284) *Allan.* £55

SAUNIER, Charles
- **Auguste Lepère (1849-1918), Peintre et Graveur, Décorateur de Livres.** Ill.:– A. Lepère. Paris, 1931. *(150) numbered on Madagascar paper.* 4to. Some foxing, sewed, spine cut. (HD. Dec.16; 144) Frs. 1,700

SAUNIER, Jean & Gaspard de
- **La Parfaite Connoissance des Chevaux.** The Hague, 1734. *1st. Edn.* Fo. Title & margins soiled, 4 plts. browned, later [late 19th. early 20th. C.?] mor. (TA. Aug.18; 285) £290
- – **Anr. Copy.** Some plts. browned, some margins soiled, later mor., rubbed. (CSK. Jun.1; 132) £260

SAUR, Abraham
- **Fasciclvs Ivdiciarii Ordinis Singvlaris. Reichs Stätten Reformationen** ... Frankfurt, 1588 [Colophon 1589], Mainz, 1589. 2 pts. in 1 vol. Fo. Pts. with separate pagination, Fürstl. Reuss j. L. Schloss-Bibliothek stp. inside cover & on 1st. title lf., cont. blind-tooled pig, arms in centre. (H. Nov.23; 592) DM 1,200
- **Güldiner Ausszug vnd Fluss Von Erbschafften dero**

Right column entries:

- – **Anr. Copy.** 3 vols. Sm. 8vo. Cont. marb. cf., spines decor.; from Château des Noës liby. (HD. May 25; 75) Frs. 1,200
- – **Anr. Edn.** Ratisbonne, 1752. *Latest Edn.* 3 vols. Cont. marb. cf., spines decor. (HD. May 21; 68) Frs. 1,100

Erbaigen vnnd Lehen, Güter, wie die nach Art Allgemeiner beschriebenen Keyserl., auch vieler Besondern Landt vnd Stätt Rechten, etc. ohne Testament, vnd ab Intestato vererbt vnd verstellt werden ... Frankfurt, 1580. *1st. Edn.* Fo. Lightly browned & slightly stained, bds. (HK. Nov.8; 333)   DM 900
– **Theatrum Urbium.** Frankfurt, 1595. Title with bkd. tear & slit, blank lr. qtr. part of end-lf. bkd., slightly browned, some slight spotting, cont. vell. (R. Oct.12; 2434)   DM 6,500

SAURET, Andre
– **Grand Prix des Meilleurs Romans.** Paris, n.d. *(3000).* 59 vols. Wraps., s.-c.'s. (SSA. Jul.5; 348)   R 200

SAURIN, Jacques & Beausobre, M.C.S. de
– **Discours Historiques du Vieux & Nouveau Testament.** Ill.:– after Hoet, Houbraken & Picart. La Haye, 1728-39. 6 vols. Lge. Fo. L.P., some ll. frayed & loose, some wormholes, some slight foxing, cf., very defect. (VG. May 3; 705) Fls. 600

SAUSSURE, Horace Benedict de
– **Essais sur l'hygrométrie.** Neuchâtel, 1783. *1st. Edn.* 4to. Wide margin, minimal foxing, some light spotting in upr. inner corner, hf. leath. gt., corners slightly bumped. (R. Apr.4; 1562)   DM 650

SAUTER, J.N.
– **Anweisung, die Beinbrüche der Gliedmassen ... zu heilen.** Konstanz, 1812. *1st. Edn.* Title with stp. visible from verso. some light browning, cont. bds. (HT. May 8; 577)   DM 400

SAUVAN, Jean Baptiste Balthazar
– **Picturesque Tour of the Seine from Paris to the Sea.** L., 1821. 4to. Hand-cold. vig. on title & at end, engraved map, 24 hand-cold. aquatints, orig. cl., jnts. slightly worn. (S. May 21; 246)
Traylen. £1,350
See— LISKENNE, Ch. & Sauvan, Jean Baptiste Balthazar

SAUZEY, Col. Camille
– **Les Allemands sous les Aigles Francaises (1806-1814).** Paris, 1902-12. 7 vols., including Atlas. Hf. chagrin. (HD. Jan.27; 211)   Frs. 1,600
– – **Anr. Edn.** Ed.:– R. Sereau. Baden, 1953. Hf. chagrin, wrap. preserved. (HD. Jan.27; 94)   Frs. 1,600

SAVAGE, J.R. (Ed.)
See— PHILADELPHIA

SAVAGE, Richard
– **The Works ... with an account of the Life & Writings of the Author, by Samuel Johnson.** 1775. *1st. Edn.* 2 vols. Hf.-titles, cont. spr. cf.; Sir Ivar Colquhoun, of Luss copy. (CE. Mar.22; 268) £300

SAVAGE, William
– **A Dictionary of the Art of Printing.** L., 1841. *1st. Edn.* Hf.-title, cont. hf. cf., hinges split. (BBA. Mar.7; 377)   *C. Cox.* £70
– **Practical Hints on Decorative Printing.** L., 1822 [1823]. *1st. Edn.* 4to. 48 (of 50) plts., many tinted or cold., subscribers list, slight staining in blank inner margins, 19th. C. blind-stpd. cf. (S. Dec.8; 390)   *Henderson.* £400

SAVARY DES BRUSIONS, Jacques
– **Dictionnaire Universel de Commerce.** Amst., 1726-32. *2nd. Edn.* 2 vols & 2 supps. in 3 vols. 4to. Cont. leath. gt., gold arms supralibros on upr. cover, faded on vol. 1, lightly rubbed & soiled. (R. Apr.3; 1240)   DM 1,000

SAVILLE-KENT, William
– **The Great Barrier Reef of Australia; its Products & Potentialities.** 1893. 4to. Orig. cl. gt. (TA. Sep.15; 17)   £65
– – **Anr. Copy.** 4to. Orig. cl. gt., top of spine replaced. (TA. Sep.15; 18)   £60

SAVIN, Jacques
See— BERRIN, Emille & Savin, Jacques

SAVONAROLA, Girolamo
– **Confessionale pro Instructione Confessorum.** Venice, 11 Feb. 1520. Ruled in red & rubricated, mod. cf., blind panel. in cont. style. (S. May 10; 405)   *Frers.* £280

– **De Simplicitate Vite Christiane.** Venice, 12 Jan. 1512. Sm. 8vo. Lacks F2, old bds. (SG. Feb.9; 326) $175

SAVOY COCKTAIL BOOK
Ill.:– G. Rumbold. N.Y., 1930. H. Craddock's MS. dedication, orig. pict. hf. linen, slightly rubbed. (GB. May 5; 3196)   DM 460

SAWYER, Charles J. & Darton, F.J. Harvey
– **English Books 1475-1900.** L., 1927. 2 vols. Orig. cl. (BBA. Dec.15; 306)   *Morris.* £50

SAXE, Maurice de
– **Lettres et Mémoires choisis parmi les Papiers Originaum ... Campagne de Flandre.** Paris, 1794. 5 vols. Hf. cf. (HD. Feb.22; 207)   Frs. 3,000
– **Mes Rêveries.** Ed.:– Abbé Perau. Amst. & Leipzig, 1757. 2 vols. 4to. L. P., Cont. cf., vol. 1 corners worn, slight loss. (HD. Feb.22; 206)   Frs. 3,100

SAXTON, Christopher
– **An Atlas of England & Wales.** 1979. *Facs. of 1579 edn., (500).* Fo. Qtr. cf. gt., s.-c. (P. Apr.12; 332)   *Burgess.* £130

SAXTON, Christopher & Lea, Philip
– **The Shires of England & Wales.** Maps:– Saxton, Lea, John Seller, William Morgan. Ca. 1693. Fo. Engraved title, ptd. gazetteer lf., 41 double-p. or folding regional & county maps, including 30 by or after Saxton, 7 by Lea, 3 by John Seller, & 1 by William Morgan, 1 map (Yorkshire) hand-cold. in outl., 1 or 2 short tears without significant loss of engraved surface, 1 or 2 minor repairs, some faint stains or dust soiling, 19th. C. hf. cf., worn, w.a.f. (S. May 21; 26)   *Tooley.* £9,000

SAY, Jean-Baptiste
– **Ausführliches Lehrbuch der Praktischen Politischen Oekonomie.** Trans.:– Max Stirner (i.e. J.K. Schmidt). Leipzig, 1845-46. 4 vols. in 5. Some slight foxing, vol. 4 stained, orig. wraps, slightly defect. (R. Apr.3; 1241)   DM 600
– **Traité d'Economie Politique.** Paris, 1819. *4th. Edn.* 2 vols. Old MS. notes, hf. roan, spines faded. (HD. Feb.22; 209)   Frs. 2,000

SAY, Thomas
– **American Entomology, or Descriptions of the Insects of North America.** Phila., 1824-28. Vols. 1 & 3 only (of 3). Engraved frontis., 35 (of 36) hand-cold. plts., plt. 47 stained, plt. 39 inserted from a shorter copy, Vol. 1 browned, bds., unc., worn, rebkd. (S. Nov.28; 83)   *Danckers.* £380

SAYER, Robert
– **Athen's Ruinen nebst anderen Merkwürdigen Alterthümern Griechenlands.** Ed.:– G.C. Kilian. Ill.:– G.C. Kilian. Augsburg & Leipzig, 1825. Fo. 12 folding copperplts., Some slight foxing, cont. bds. (R. Oct.13; 3145)   DM 1,300
– **An English Atlas.** Maps:– Kitchin & Jefferys. 1787. 4to. Engraved vig. title, hand-cold. folding general map, 48 hf.-p. col. maps, index lf., folding table of distances, cont. hf. cf. gt. (F. Feb.16; 294)   £720

SAYGER, C. & Desnarnod, A.
– **Album d'un Voyage en Turquie fait par Ordre de sa Majesté Empereur Nicolas I en 1829 at 1830.** Paris, n.d. Fo. 51 litho. plts., spotted, cont. bds., worn (BBA. Jun.28; 246)   *Martinos.* £280

SAYRE, Eleanor
– **Late Caprichos of Goya: Fragments from a Series.** N.Y., 1971. *(125) numbered.* 4to. Suite of 6 engraved plts. (ptd. from Goya's orig. plts.) loose as iss., limitation no. defaced, qtr. mor., matching folding box. (SG. Jan.26; 201) $400

SCALA, A. von
– **Illustrations of Turkish, Arabian, Persian, Central Asiatic & Indian Metal Ware.** Vienna, 1895. Sm. fo. 50 loose plts., title & notes in Engl. & German, title-p. torn, cl.-bkd. bd. folder, worn. (SG. Aug.25; 258) $180

SCALE, Bernard
– **An Hibernian Atlas; or General Description of the Kingdom of Ireland.** L., 1 Feb. 1788. *2nd. Edn.* 4to.

Engraved title with lge. vig., dedication, 37 hand-cold. maps (with imprint of Robert Sayer, a variant), dedication lf. reprd. with tape, cont. bds., defect. (S. Jun.25; 433)   £380

SCALIGER, Joseph Justus
– **Cyclometria Elemento duo, Messalabium, Appendix ...** Leiden, 1594. *1st. Edn.* 3 pts. in 1 vol. Fo. Woodcut device on title-pp., diagrams ptd. in red, errata, vell. (S. Apr.10; 583)   *Poole.* £240
– **De Emendatione Temporum.** Frankfurt & Basel, 1593. Fo. 2 sm. wormholes thro.-out, cont. hf. pig, roll blind-tooled, copper engraved port. in upr. inner cover, corners bumped. [STC 782] (BR. Apr.17; 890)   DM 1,000
– **Opus de Emendatione Temporum. Addita Veterum Graecorum Fragmenta Selecta.** Genevae, 1629. Fo. Old vell., worn. (RO. Mar.28; 152) $105
– **Poemata Omnia.** Leiden, 1615. *1st. Coll. Edn.* 3 pts. in 1 vol. 16mo. Cont. vell. (SG. Feb.9; 327) $110

SCAMMON, Charles M.
– **The Marine Mammals of the North-Western Coast of North America.** San Franc., 1874. *1st. Edn.* Lge. 4to. 27 litho. plts., text engrs., some foxing thro.-out, gt.-pict. cl., vertical crease at spine, some wear. (SG. Apr.26; 177) $950

SCAMOZZI, Ottavie Bertotti
– **Il Forestiere Istruito delle Cose piu'rare di Architettura e di Alcune Pitture ... di Vicenza.** 1761. 4to. Cont. bds. (HD. Dec.15; 34)   Frs. 3,100

SCAMOZZI, Vincenze
– **L'idea della Architettura Universale.** Venice, 1615. *1st. Edn.* Fo. 19th. C. hf. bdg. (HD. Dec.15; 35)   Frs. 2,100
– **Oeuvres d'Architecture.** Trans.:– A. Ch. d'Aviler & S. du Ry. Leide, 1713. Fo. Hf. cf., defect. (B. Oct.4; 691a)   Fls. 850
– – **Anr. Edn.** Trans.:– A. Ch. d'Aviler. La Haye, 1736. Fo. Cont. cf. (HD. Dec.15; 36)   Frs. 1,400
– **Het Voorbeelt der Algemeene Bouwkunst.** Amst., 1658. 2 pts. in 1 vol. Fo. Engraved title dtd. 1661, printed titles misbnd., lacks 2 prelims., some stains, 1st. 26 ll. loose & frayed, no bdg. (B. Oct.4; 691)   Fls. 550

SCARPA, Antonio
– **Traité Pratique des Hernies, ou Mémoires Anatomiques et Chirurgicaux sur ces Maladies.** Paris, 1812. Fo. 11 engraved plts. (10 in 2 states), additional Dutch MS. descriptions inserted, hf. cf. gt. (P. Jul.26; 102)   £95

SCARRON, Paul
– **Oeuvres.** Paris, n.d. *New Edn.* 7 vols. Cont. marb. cf. gt., decor. spines, inner roll-stp. (HD. Sep.22; 339)   Frs. 1,100
– **Le Roman Comique.** Ill.:– Lemire (port.), Le Barbier, engraved by Baquoy, Dambrun, Duclos, & others. Paris, [1796]. 3 vols. Cf. gt. by P. Grandin, monog., spines decor. (HD. Mar.27; 37) Frs. 2,600
– – **Anr. Copy.** 3 vols. Cont. marb. cf. gt., spines decor. (HD. May 3; 144)   Frs. 2,300
– **Virgile Travesti, en Vers Burlesques.** Paris, 1752. 3 vols. Sm. 12mo. Cont. marb. cf., Madame d'Epinay arms, spines decor. (HD. Mar.29; 93) Frs. 15,000

SCHADEN, Adolph von
– **Neuestes Taschenbuch f. Reisende durch Bayerns u. Tyrols Hochlande, dann durch Berchtesgadens u. Salzburge Romantische Gefilde.** Ill.:– G. Kraus. München, 1833. *1st. Edn.* 1 outl. etching, 6 folding lithos., lacks map slightly foxed, orig. pict. bds., lightly bumped. (HK. Nov.9; 1460)   DM 420

SCHAEFER, Ernst
– **Dach der Erde: Durch das Wunderland Hochtibet.** Berlin, [1938]. Cl.-bkd. bds., very worn; sig. of Heinrich Himmler beneath a secretarial inscr. in German. (SG. Sep.29; 125) $125

SCHAEFFER, A.
– **Lene Stelling.** Ill.:– A. Kubin. Berlin, 1923. *(300) numbered.* 4to. Printer's mark sigd. by author, orig. pict. bds. (HK. Nov.11; 4176)   DM 500
– **Die Marien-Lieder.** Leipzig, 1924. *1st. Edn. Ltd. Iss.* Hand-bnd. pol. orig. mor., gt. spine, cover & inner dentelle, by E.A. Enders. (H. Nov.24; 2002)   DM 540

SCHAFFER, D.F.
- **Der Weltumsegler.** Berlin, 1805-20. Vols. 1-6 only (of 7). 4to. Vols. 1-4 & 6 lack 1 lf., Vol. 5 lacks 2 ll., title defect. & reprd., some slight spotting, most on bluish paper, 1 lf. loose, cont. hf. leath. gt., bumped & rubbed, spine vol. 1 loose. (HK. Nov.10; 2974) DM 1,000

SCHAFFER, J.G.
- **Geschichte des Grauen Staares und der Neuen Operationen solchen durch Herausnehmen der Crystallinse zu heylen.** Regensburg, 1765. Sm. 4to. Copper engrs. cut slightly close, mod. leath. (GB. Nov.3; 1045) DM 780

SCHAFFER, Jacob Christian
- **Abhandlungen von Insekten.** Regensburg, 1764. *1st. Edn.* Vols. 1 & 2 (of 3). 4to. Cont. hf. leath. gt., slightly bumped. (R. Oct.12; 1905) DM 1,300
- **Elementa Entomologica cum adpendice.** Ratisbone, 1780. *3rd. Edn.* 4to. 140 hand-cold. engraved plts. on 72 sheets, most ptd. on recto & verso, text in Latin & German, slight stain to plts. 60 & 61, cont. Spanish cf. gt., upr. cover with lge. central gt. stp. of the arms of the Marquis of Stafford, spine & corners worn. (CNY. May 18; 151) $550
- **Neue Versuche u. Müster dae Pflanzenreich zum Papiermunchen u.a. Sachen Wirtschaftanutlich zu gebrauchen.** Regensburg, 1766-67. *1st. Edn.* Pts. 2 & 3 only (of 3), in 1 vol. (*Bound with:*)
- **Wiederholte Versuche auf Ordentlichen Papiermühlen aus allerhand Pflanzen u. Holzarten Papier zu Machen.** Regensburg, 1771. *1st. Edn.* Together 2 works in 1 vol. 4to. Cont. leath. (HK. Nov.9; 2003) DM 4,000

SCHALTENBRAND, C.
- **Die Locomotiven.** Berlin, 1876. 2 vols. 8vo. & 4to. Some plts. slightly foxed, cont. hf. leath., rubbed, atlas spine reprd. (R. Oct.12; 1605) DM 920

SCHANGE, J.M.A.
- **Précis sur le Redressement des Dents.** Paris, 1841. *1st. Edn.* MS. numbering thro.-out in upr. corner, mod. bds. (R. Oct.12; 1518) DM 500

SCHARMANN, Hermann B.
- **Overland Journey to California from the Pages of a Pioneer's Diary.** [N.Y.], priv. ptd., [1918]. *1st. Edn. in Engl. (50).* Sm. 8vo. Cl. (LH. Jan.15; 382) $160

SCHATZGER, Casp.
- **Von dem Hayligsten Opffer der Mess.** [Augsburg], 1525. *1st. Edn.* 4to. Wide margins, lacks last lf. blank, stained, old annots., lightly browned, early margins lightly frayed, 1st. 2 ll. with repairs, 19th. C. bds.; title with Otto Hupp owners mark. (HK. May 15; 237) DM 550

SCHAUB & Gallieur, E.H.
- **La Suisse Historique, Politique et Pittoresque.** Genève, 1856. Pt. 2. Hf. leath. (G. Sep.15; 2330) Sw. Frs. 380

SCHAUBACH, A.
- **Die Deutschen Alpen. E. Handbuch für Reisende.** Jena, 1845-47. *1st. Edn.* 5 vols. Vol. 4 with supp. by Emmrich, cont. linen gt., w.a.f. (HK. Nov.8; 820) DM 400

SCHAUER, Georg Kurt
- **Deutscher Buchkunst.** Hamburg, 1963. 2 vols. (text & plts.). 4to. Orig. linen. (D. Nov.23; 321) DM 800
- - **Anr. Edn.** Hamburg, 1963. *Ltd. Iss.* Text & plt. vol. 4to. Orig. linen. (HK. May 17; 3399) DM 680

SCHAUER, Georg Kurt (Ed.)
See— IMPRIMATUR

SCHAUPLATZ D. KRIEGES IN ITALIEN
Leipzig, 1702. 66 engraved plts., some folding, 2 folding tables, leath., gt. arms on cover, restored. (V. Sep.29; 67) DM 900

SCHEDEL, Hartmann
- **Das Buch der Cronicken.** Trans.:– Georg Alt. Ill.:– Wohlgemuth & Pleydenwurff. Nuremb., Anton Koberger, 23 Dec. 1493. *1st. Edn. in German.* Fo. Tall copy, lr. blank margin of double-p. map slightly trimmed, margin tears in map reprd.

with slight loss to text in lr. border, & 2 sm. holes in centre, title reprd. in inner blank margin, early 19th. C. russ. gt. [BMC II, 437; Goff S-309; H. 14510] (C. Mar.14; 88) *Bender.* £10,000
- - **Anr. Edn.** Ill.:– Wohlgemuth & Pleydenwurff. [Nuremb., A. Koberger, 23 Dec. 1493]. Fo. 136 (of 297) ll., many ll. loose & detched., a few tears, some browning, cont. blind-stpd. pig over wood bds., clasps & bosses, worn & wormed, w.a.f. (S. Nov.17; 67) *Jaenson.* £1,200
- - **Anr. Copy.** Fo. Many woodcuts, world map, about 20 ll. stained, few ll. torn without loss, few marginal defects, cont. South German pig. elab. tooled in blind, worn, lacks clasp, thumbed. [Goff S307] (SG. Apr.26; 154) $13,000
- - **Anr. Edn.** Nuremb., 1493. *Ltd. Iss.* Fo. Orig. hf. vell. (GB. May 3; 21) DM 680
- - **Anr. Edn.** [Augsburg, Schönsperger, 1496]. *2nd. German Edn.* Fo. Lacks 26 ll., 1 lf. verso completely bkd., 1 lf. lacks lr. corner, 2 ll. torn in upr. margin with slight loss, unregularly & misnumbered (some double), some woodcuts cold. in, some staining, some repairs, cut slightly close at side, wood bds., ca. 1550, blind-tooled pig cover, 2 brass clasps. [H. 14511; Goff S 310] (HK. Nov.8; 336) DM 7,200
- - **Anr. Edn.** Leipzig, 1933. *Facs. of Nuremb. 1493 Edn.* Lge. fo. Orig. hf. leath. (R. Apr.3; 627) DM 800
- - **Anr. Copy.** Lge. fo. On Hadernbütten (special for this book), orig. linen, by Sperling, Leipzig. (D. Nov.23; 358) DM 420
- - **Anr. Copy.** Fo. On Hadernbütten, orig. hf. leath. (H. Nov.23; 75) DM 400
- **Das Buch der Chroniken. Fragment.** Nuremb., 1493. *1st. Edn.* Fo. 165 ll. (of 326), some soiling, slightly defect., some ll. with lengthy tears, loose, without bdg., w.a.f. (R. Oct.13; 2829) DM 4,500
- **Liber Chronicarum.** Ill.:– Wohlgemuth & Pleydenwurff. Nuremb., A. Koberger, 12 Jul. 1493. Fo. 326 ll. (the last blank), xylographic title, upwards of 1800 (including repeats) woodcuts, including the double-p. ptolemaic world map & the map of central Europe after Münzer at end, 3 ll. blank (folios 259-261) except for headline & foliation, anr. before fo. 267, without woodcut before title, title & a few ll. slightly soiled or stained, sm. hole in fo. 101, a few tears elsewhere without loss of ptd. surface, 1 or 2 headlines shaved, vell. bds., spine gt., slightly soiled. [BMC II, 437; Goff S307: HC 14508] (S. May 21; 168) *Arpass.* £8,400
- - **Anr. Copy.** Fo. Lacks last blank, title-p. trimmed & mntd. affecting some ptd. flourishes, folios 26 & 27 supplied from anr. copy & trimmed & mntd., world map supplied from anr. copy & trimmed & stained, 2 ll. guarded, folios 68 & 149 with reprd. tears, corner of 2nd. index lf. torn away, minor wormhole to text of 20 ll., 18th. C. mor. gt., spine gt. [BMC II, 437; Goff S-307: HC 14508] (CNY. Dec.17; 600) $9,000
- - **Anr. Copy.** 2nd. unnumbered lf. & last lf. & lf. 267 with gold & cold. initials, lf. 1 with decor. border in left & lr. margin, 2 ll. with decor. cold initials, rubricated, lacks 1 text lf., 5 unnumbered ll. & last blank lf. bnd. between ll. 266 & 267, lr. outer corner soiled thro.-out, several ll. at beginning & end stained & browned, 1st. ll. slightly wormed, reprd. tears & margin defects., some loss, 2 ll. with heavy loss in lr. half, old MS. annots., pig, 2 clasps. [H. 14508; BMC II, 437; Goff S 307]. (HK. May 15; 238) DM 46,000
- - **Anr. Copy.** Lge. fo. Painted initial at beginning, (slightly oxidised & rubbed), title lf. slightly defect. from stp. on verso, last 3 numbered ll. bkd. in margins partly, minimal margin soiling, 6 ll. misbnd., 18th. C. stp., 18th. C. marb. cf., slightly rubbed & worn, jnts. brkn. [H. 14508; BMC II, 437; Goff S 307] (HT. May 8; 46) DM 37,000
- - **Anr. Copy.** Fo. Rubricated, painted initials, 1 (of 2) double-p. maps & approx. 1650 (of 1808) woodcuts, including repeats, lacks 47 ll. including 6 blank ll., lacks 4 lge. plts., lacks half of 1 lge. plt. & anr. plt., some light margin soiling, 1st. 2 ll. very browned & soiled, 1 plt. very soiled, 1 browned, 1 full-p. woodcut with hole, old vell. (R. Oct.13; 2828) DM 18,000
- - **Anr. Copy.** Fo. Lacks 22 ll., many ll. from other copies, stains & other defects, 17th. C. marb. cf.,

spine decor., worn, w.a.f. [HC 14508; BMC II, 437; Goff S307] (SM. Mar.7; 2452) Frs. 48,000
- - **Anr. Copy.** Fo. 20 ll. only, woodcuts, margins & some ll. wormed, no bdg. stated. (LM. Mar.3; 41b) B.Frs. 15,000
- - **Anr. Edn.** Ill.:– after Wohlgemuth & Pleydenwurff. Augsburg, Johann Schoensperger, 1497. Fo. Lacks b1 & 3, double-p. map cropped at foot, title torn with loss of text on verso, sm. corner torn from a5 with loss of text, sm. hole in h1, early owner's inscr. on title, 17th. C. Engl. owner's inscrs. & notes at beginning & end, old cf., later gt.-tooled spine, w.a.f. [BMC II, 370; Goff S-308; H. 14509] (C. Mar.14; 89) *Marshall.* £2,200
- **Nuremberg Chronicle.** Nuremb., 1492-93. Fo. 60 ll. from Latin & German edns., most in woodcuts, some hand-cold., some double-p., occasional staining, tears, as a coll. of plts., w.a.f. (SPB. Dec.13; 873) $850
- - **Anr. Edn.** N.Y., [1979]. *Reduced Facs. of German Edn.* Fo. Orig. leath. in orig. bd. s.-c. (HT. May 8; 745) DM 480

SCHEEN, Pieter A.
- **Lexicon Nederlandse Beeldende Kunstenaars, 1750-1950.** The Hague, 1969-70. 2 vols. 4to. Cl. (SG. Oct.13; 300) $100

SCHEERBART, D.
- **Von Zimmer zu Zimmer.** Berlin, 1921. *1st. Edn. (99)* with sig. of Anna Scheerbart. Orig. bds. (GB. May 5; 3212) DM 420

SCHEFFELT, M.
- **Pes Mechanisus Artificialis.** Ulm, 1718. *2nd. Edn.* 4to. Title stpd., cont. leath., spine defect. (R. Oct.12; 1713) DM 500

SCHEFFER, John
- **The History of Lapland.** Oxford, 1674. *1st. Edn.* in Engl. Fo. Mott. cf. [Wing S851] (BBA. May 3; 264) *Maggs.* £350
- - **Anr. Copy.** Sm. fo. Cont. cf., rebkd. (P. Oct.20; 243) £320

SCHEINER, Christoph
- **Oculus.** Innsbruck, 1619. *1st. Edn.* 4to. Old owners mark on title, cont. vell., head of spine lightly defect., upr. cover wormed. (R. Apr.4; 1563) DM 4,600

SCHELLENBERG, Johann Rudolph
- **Freund Heins Erscheinungen in Holbeins Manier.** Winterthur, 1785. *1st. Edn.* Later cf. gt. (C. Dec.9; 277) *Schwing.* £400

SCHELLING, Friedrich Wilhelm Joseph
- **Bruno oder über das Göttliche und Natürliche Princip der Dinge, Ein Gespräch.** Berlin, 1802. *1st. Edn.* Sub-title after title-p., bds., cl. spine with gt. stp. Freder, Bibl. Univers. & crest; Dr. Walter Pagel copy. (S. Feb.7; 343) *Van Aaltst.* £220
- **Ideen zu einer Philosophie der Natur.** Ill.:– Rosmaesler after Schnorr. Leipzig, 1797. *1st. Edn.* Some foxing, cont. bds., slightly spotted. (GB. Nov.4; 2173) DM 440
- **System des Transcendentalen Idealismus.** Tübingen, 1800. *1st. Edn.* Errata & colophon lf., 19th. C. cf. antique; Dr. Walter Pagel copy. (S. Feb.7; 341) *Weiner.* £160
- **Ueber die Möglichkeit einer form der Philosophie überhaupt.** Tübingen, 1795. *1st. Edn.* Browned thro.-out, sewed, unc. (R. Oct.11; 530) DM 1,300
- **Zeitschrift für Spekulative Physik.** Jena & Leipzig, 1800-01. 4 pts. in 1 vol. Slightly foxed, cont. hf. leath. gt. (HK. Nov.10; 2685) DM 1,000

SCHENK, E. (Ed.)
See— FLORA VON DEUTSCHLAND

SCHENK, Pierre
- **Délices de Mer, Terre et de Rivières ...** Ill.:– A. Van der Laan. Amst., ca. 1720. Ob. 4to. 16 plts. mntd. on guards, early 19th. C. str.-grd. red mor. gt., spine decor., liners, watered silk end-ll.; 2 extra suites (each 16 plts.) by Van der Laan after Van der Meulen mntd. at end. (HD. Jun.18; 44) Frs. 45,000
- **Hecatomopolis sive Totius Orbis Terrarum Oppida.** [Amst.], 1702. Ob. fo. Engraved title, contents lf., 97 full-p. engraved plts. showing town views (of 100: lacks plts. 39, 78, & 79), hand-cold.,

some staining or dust-soiling, 1 or 2 plts. creased, margin annots. in ink on a few plts., cont. cf.-bkd. bds., worn., w.a.f. (S. May 21; 116) *Reiss.* £3,300
– – **Anr. Edn.** [Amst., 1702]. Lacks frontis. (port), copper engraved title, engraved plt. index & 9 plts., poor imprs. of some copper engrs., stain in upr. inner corner, especially last plts., cont. bds., later leath., corners & spine, defect. & loose. (R. Oct.13; 2830) DM 21,500

SCHENKER, Donald
See— MELTZER, David – SCHENKER, Donald

SCHENKLING, S.
See— HORN, W. & Schenkling, S.

SCHERER, Dr. A.N.
See— LAVOISIER, Antoine Lourent de – SCHERER, Dr. A.N.

SCHERER, Christian
– **Die Braunschweiger Elfenbeinsammlung: Katalog der Elfenbeinbildwerke des Herzog Anton Ulrich-Museums.** Leipzig, 1931. 4to. 71 plts., pict. cl., soiled. (SG. Aug.25; 210) $160

SCHERZ, Johann Georg
– **Glossarium Germanicum Medii Aevi, potissimum Dialecti Suevicae.** Ed.:– J.J. Oberlinus. Strassburg, 1781-84. *1st. Edn.* 2 vols. in 1. Fo. Cont. hf. vell. (SG. Oct.27; 288) $150

SCHETKY, J. & Manners, Lord J.
– **Sketches & Notes of a Cruise in Scotch Waters.** L., 1850. Fo. Publisher's bds. (HD. Jun.6; 137) Frs. 5,000

SCHEUCHZER, Hans Jacob
– **Geestelyke Natuurkunde.** Amst., 1735-39. Pts. 4-6 & 12-15 only (of 15), in 3 vols. Fo. 1 plt. loose, some stpd. in lr. margin, cont. spr. leath. gt. (HK. Nov.9; 1572a) DM 1,700
– **Helvetiae Historia Naturalis.** Ill.:– J.M. Füssli. Zürich, 1716-18. 3 vols. Sm. 4to. Lightly foxed, cont. vell. (R. Oct.13; 3283) DM 5,000
– **Herbarium Diluvianum.** Leiden, 1723. *2nd. Edn.* Fo. Title with vig., additional engraved title with vig., port., 14 engraved plts., cont. cf., worn, covers detchd. (C. Mar.14; 194) *Wheldon & Wesley.* £100
– **Kupfer-Bibel in Welcher die Physica Sacra oder Geheiligte Natur-Wissenschaft derer in Heil. Schrifft Vorkommenden Natürlichen Sachen Deutlich Erklärt ... in Künstlichen Kupfer-Tafeln ausgegeben ... Johann Andreas Pfeffel.** Ill.:– J.D. Preisler, T. Lamb after L.H. Heidegger, J.A. Corvinus, G.W. Knorr, J.G. Pintz, C. & H. Sperling & others. Augsburg & Ulm, 1731-35. 4 vols. Fo. Engraved frontis., mezzotint port., 760 engraved plts., hf.-title in Vol. I only (apparently not called for in other vols.), lacks 1 port. (Nissen calls for a 3rd., possibly an error or repeat), list of plts. in each vol. (misbnd.), cont. cf., rebkd. (S. May 10; 407) *Watson.* £2,000
– – **Anr. Copy.** 4 vols. in 5. Fo. 1 port. slightly spotted & cut close at side, cont. leath. gt., rubbed, spine partly defect. (R. Oct.12; 2237) DM 7,500
– **Physique Sacrée, ou Histoire Naturelle de la Bible.** Ill.:– C. Sperlingum, F.M. Regenfus, L.A. Corvinus, & others. Amst., 1732-37. 8 vols. Fo. Engraved port., mezzotint port., frontis., 758 (of 759) engraved plts., Vols. 3 & 6 without hf.-titles, 1 plt. reprd., 1 text lf. with tear, cont. mott. cf., rebkd. preserving orig. spines, worn, some tears, w.a.f. (C. Mar.14; 142) *Fletcher.* £1,600
– – **Anr. Copy.** Fo. 10 supp. plts., cont. leath. gt., jnts. burst, worn. (R. Oct.12; 2238) DM 5,000
– **Piscium Querelae et Vindiciae.** Zürich, 1708. Plts. with sm. tears, 1 plt. defect., foxed thro-out, cold. paper covered bds., slightly bumped, spine defect., engraved ex-libris. (D. Nov.23; 486) DM 700

SCHEUREN, Caspar
– **Vom Deutschen Rhein.** Köln, ca. 1870. Ob. fo. Some tears, browning in margin, some lithos. rubbed from pasting together, orig. linen, soiled & defect. (GB. May 3; 214) DM 600
– – **Anr. Edn.** Düsseldorf, [1880]. Ob. fo. Orig. linen, & gold-tooled upr. cover, defect., loose. (R. Oct.13; 2731) DM 710

SCHEURICH, P.
– **Der Rosenkavalier.** Berlin, 1920. *(100) numbered.* Lge. fo. Slightly foxed, orig. hf. linen portfo. (HK. Nov.11; 3931) DM 480

SCHICKFUSS, Jacob
– **New Vermehrte Schlesische Chronica ...** Jena, [1625]. *1st. Edn.* Sm. fo. Light browning & sm. stain, marginalia, leath., sm. faults, slightly rubbed. (V. Oct.1; 3776) DM 2,500

SCHICKH (Ed.)
See— WIENER ZEITSCHRIFT FUR KUNST, THEATER UND MODE

SCHIDLOF, Leo
– **La Miniature en Europe aux 16e, 17e, 18e et 19e siècles.** Graz, 1964. 4 vols. No bdg. stated. (SPB. Nov.30; 300) $200

SCHIEBELHUTH, H.
– **Der Hakenkreuzug. Neo-dadaistische Ungedichte.** Ill.:– V.J. Kuron. Darmstadt, 1920. *1st. Edn. (500).(100) hand-cold.* 3 line dedication, orig. wraps., slightly crumpled. (HT. May 9; 2013a) DM 740

SCHIEFLER, Gustav
– **Die Graphik Ernst Ludwig Kirchners.** Berlin, 1924-26. *(620) numbered.* This copy unnumbered, 52 orig. woodcuts, orig. linen. (GB. Nov.5; 2665) DM 4,000

SCHIELE, Egon
– **Handzeichnungen.** Wien, Prag & Leipzig, 1920. *(500).* Lge. fo. Title ll. foxed, tear in printers mark (without number), publishers stp. & sig., title lf. torn & reprd., hf. linen portfo. (HK. Nov.11; 3933) DM 1,200
– **Watercolours & Drawings.** L., 1970. *(400) numbered.* Fo. Orig. cl., s.-c. (CSK. Sep.16; 143) £100
– – **Anr. Copy.** Lge. fo. Canvas bds. (KH. Nov.9; 693) Aus. $190
– **Zeichnungen.** Wien, 1917. *(400) numbered.* Fo. Printer's merk sigd., plts. lightly foxed, 2 plts. with sm. margin defects. orig. hf. linen portfo. (HK. Nov.11; 3934) DM 1,800

SCHIESTL, Rudolf
– **Der Tod von Basel.** Berlin, n.d. *(600) numbered.* Ob. 4to. Orig. hf. vell. (V. Oct.1; 4411) DM 550

SCHIFF, Mortimer L.
– **A Catalogue of Early Italian Majolica in [his] Collection.** Ed.:– Seymour De Ricci. N.Y., 1927. *(250) numbered.* 4to. 111 plts., three-qtr. mor., chipped. (SG. Jan.26; 152) $375
– **Catalogue of a Selected Portion of the Famous Library.** Mar.-Dec. 1938. 3 vols. 4to. Sale catalogue, later cl.; H.M. Nixon coll., with many MS. notes, some cuttings & a rubbing loosely inserted. (BBA. Oct.6; 162) *Beres.* £580
– **French Signed Bindings in the Mortimer L. Schiff Collection.** N.Y., 1935. 4 vols. Lge. square 4to. Bradel cl. bds. (HD. Jun.6; 128) Frs. 6,800

SCHILLER, Johann Christoph Friedrich von
– **An die Freude.** Ill.:– Ernst Barlach. Berlin, 1927. Ob. 4to. Slightly foxed, orig. bds. (D. Nov.24; 2940) DM 520
– **Don Karlos Infant von Spanien.** Ill.:– H. Schmidt after Tischbein (title copper engr.), W. Böhm after F. Catel (copperplts.). Leipzig, 1802. *De Luxe Edn.* Some foxing, MS. entry, cont. red mor., gt. decor. green leath. borders, cornerpieces, green leath. strips & gt. on spine, a few spots, gt. inner & outer dentelles, silk doubls. & end-papers; Paul Hirsch ex-libris, Hauswedell coll. (H. May 24; 1541) DM 8,500
– – **Anr. Copy.** Some foxing, watered silk end-papers. cont., red mor. gt., gold-tooled decor., sigd. by I.N. Muller. (HK. Nov.10; 2693) DM 1,400
– **Gedichte.** Ill.:– W. Böhm. Leipzig, 1800-03. *1st. Edn.* 2 vols. Some slight browning & spotting, especially in II, 1 lf. with margin repair, cont. cf. gt., cold. decor. end-papers; from R. Daetsch-Benziger liby; Hauswedell coll. (H. May 24; 1539) DM 3,400
– – **Anr. Edn.** Ill.:– after Piloty, Ramberg, Schwind, etc. 1859-62. *Jubiläums Edn.* 4to. Orig. leath., blind-tooled, 3 brass bosses on spine & 8 brass burls on covers. (GB. Nov.4; 1936) DM 530

– – **Anr. Edn.** Ed.:– R.A. Schröder. [München, Brenner Pr., 1926]. Orig. mor. gt., decor., by R. Oldenbourg, München. (HK. May 17; 2625) DM 500
– **Der Geisteresher.** Ill.:– E. Oppler. Berlin, [1922]. *(100) De Luxe Edn. on Bütten.* Sm. 4to. All etchings sigd. by artist, hand-bnd. orig. mor., gt., lr. outer dentelle & corners lightly rubbed. (H. Nov.24; 1911) DM 680
– **Geschichte des dreyssigjährigen Kriegs.** Leipzig, 1802. *1st. separate Edn.* Title stpd., cont. hf. leath. gt., corners bumped, cold. paper end-papers; liby. label on upr. cover. (HK. May 16; 2243) DM 420
– **Neue Thalia.** Leipzig, 1792-93. *1st. Edn.* 12 pts. in 4 vols. Title lf. with owners mark, a little spotting & browning, cont. bds., marb. covers; Hauswedell coll. (H. May 24; 1535) DM 1,800
[–] **Die Räuber.** Frankfurt & Leipzig, [Stuttgart], 1781. *1st. Trade Edn. (800).* Wide margin, error in 4th Act not corrected, title with sm. etching over erased stp. in lr. margin, lightly browned & some slight foxing, light creasing at beginning & end, cont. hf. leath., worn, jnts. slightly brittle, slightly split at foot, marb-paper end-papers. (HK. May 16; 2246) DM 16,000
– – **Anr. Edn.** Ill.:– L. Corinth. Hellerau, 1923. *(280) numbered. Printers mark sigd. by Corinth in pencil.* Fo. Orig. hf. vell., bd. s.-c., defect. (HK. May 17; 2656) DM 750
– **Sämmtliche Werke.** Stuttgart & Tübingen, 1835-36. 12 vols. Cont. hf. roan, spines gt. (C. Dec.9; 329) *Wenner.* £370
– – **Anr. Copy.** 12 vols. Some spotting, cont. cf. gt., lacks few spine labels. (CSK. Dec.16; 161) £75
– – **Anr. Copy.** 12 vols. Plts. slightly foxed as usual, cont. hf. cf. gt. & blind-tooled. (BR. Apr.12; 1516) DM 2,700
– – **Anr. Copy.** 12 vols. Cont. hf. leath. gt., new tooled initials. lightly rubbed, some wear, engraved ex-libris. (H. May 22; 859) DM 1,550
– – **Anr. Copy.** 12 vols. Steel engrs. slightly spotted or browned, some ll. defect. in margin, later hf. leath., spine faded, partly bumped. Hauswedell coll. (H. May 24; 1530) DM 660
– – **Anr. Edn.** Stuttgart & Tübingen, 1838. 12 vols. Hf. leath. (V. Oct.1; 3876) DM 850
– – **Anr. Edn.** München (Berlin from Vol. 16), 1910-26. 22 vols. Orig. linen gt., w.a.f. (HK. Nov.10; 2690) DM 580
– – **Anr. Copy.** 22 vols. Orig. linen, spine lightly faded, 2 spines slightly spotted. (GB. May 5; 3217) DM 500
– – **Anr. Edn.** München & Leipzig, [1910-26]. *(250) De Luxe Edn.* 22 vols. A few ll. slightly browned, orig. mor. gt., by Hübel & Denck, Leipzig, spines vols. 16-22 faded, w.a.f. (HK. May 16; 2240) DM 1,600
– – **Anr. Edn.** Leipzig, ca. 1926. Orig. limp cf., wraps., s.-c. (D. Nov.24; 2214) DM 420
– **Thalia.** Leipzig, 1787-91. *1st. Edn.* 12 pts. in 3 vols. (all publd.). With mus. supp. in 2nd. pt., cont. hf. red leath. gt., corners lightly bumped, jnt. slightly torn. (GB. May 4; 1448) DM 1,900
[–] **Der Venuswagen.** [Stuttgart, 1781]. Bds. (HK. May 16; 2247) DM 500
– **Wallenstein.** Tübingen, 1800. *1st. Edn.* 2 vols. Cont. bds. (C. Dec.9; 281) *Quaritch.* £320
– – **Anr. Copy.** Lightly browned, some foxing & brown spotting, several ll. pasted in margin, new hf. leath. gt., slightly worn; Hauswedell coll. (H. May 24; 1540) DM 1,100
– – **Anr. Copy.** 2 pts. in 1 vol. Minimal spotting, cont. hf. leath., slightly rubbed & bumped. (HT. May 9; 1646) DM 420
– – **Anr. Edn.** Ill.:– H. Meid. [Berlin, 1915-18]. *(300) on Bütten.* 4to. Hand-bnd. mor., gold decor. spine, covers, inner & outer dentelles, by Hans Glökler, Berlin. (H. Nov.24; 1844) DM 1,800
– **Werke.** Ed.:– A.W.Heymel; Harry Grof Kessler & Emery Walker. Leipzig, 1905-06. *1st. Edn.* 6 vols. Orig. Limp red leath., gt. spine & upr cover. (HK. May 16; 2238) DM 460
– **Wilhelm Tell.** Tübingen, 1804. *1st. Edn.* 12mo. 3 hand-cold. engraved plts., advt. lf. at end, mid-19th. C. hf. cf. gt. (C. Dec.9; 282) *Quaritch.* £550
– – **Anr. Copy.** Wide margin, 1 lf. advts., minimal foxing, cont. cf. gt., slightly worn; Hauswedell coll. (H. May 24; 1542) DM 3,400
– – **Anr. Copy.** Wide margin, title cut slightly close,

SCHILLER, Johann Christoph Friedrich von -
Contd.
sm. owner's monog. pasted on verso, no bdg. stated.
(HK. Nov.10; 2698)   DM 2,800
- **Works.** Boston, [1901]. *(1000).* 10 vols. Three-qtr. mor., gt.-decor. spines. (CBA. Dec.10; 391)
$150

SCHILLER, Friedrich von (Ed.)
See— HOREN

SCHIMMELPENNINCK, Mary Anne, of Bristol
- **Theory on the Classification of Beauty & Deformity, & their Correspondence with the Physiognomonic Expression** ... 1815. *1st. Edn.* 4to. 38 col. plts., 2 folding tables, title & some margins dust soiled, recent hf. mor. gt. (TA. Mar.15; 402)
£60

SCHINDLER, Karl Friedrich
- **L'Armée Prusienne sous l'Empereur Gyullaume.** Berlin, ca. 1872. 4to. Title & contents list in Fr., plt. captions German, loose ll. in orig. hf. linen portfo., rubbed. (GB. May 3; 319)   DM 1,300
- - **Anr. Edn.** Berlin, ca. 1880. Fo. Orig. hf. linen portfo., spine renewed, bumped. (HK. Nov.9; 1907)
DM 850

SCHINKEL, Karl Friedrich
- **Lebenswerk.** Ed.:- Paul O. Rave, G. Grundmann. Berlin, 1941. Vol. V: 'Schlesien'. Fo. Orig. linen, orig. wraps. (GB. Nov.4; 1352)   DM 460
- **Möbel-Entwürfe, welche bei Einrichtung Prinzlicher Wohnungen in den Letzten Zehn Jahren ausgeführt werden.** Ed.:- Ludwig Lohde. Berlin, 1835-37. *1st. Compl. Edn.* Ob. fo. Loose ll. in portfo. (GB. May 3; 908)   DM 5,000
- - **Anr. Copy.** Pts. 1[-4]. Ob. fo. Slightly foxed thro.-out, some margin defects., hf. linen portfo. with 4 upr. end-papers of orig. wraps. mntd. on linen, some cockling & foxing. (HK. Nov.9; 2076)
DM 2,200
- **Sammlung Architektonischer Entwürfe.** Berlin, 1828. Ob. fo. Some foxing in parts, cont. hf. leath. (GB. Nov.3; 902)   DM 2,000
- **Troja. Ergebnisse Meiner Neuesten Ausgrabungen.** Preface:- A.H. Sayce. Leipzig, 1884. *1st. Edn.* Bds., orig. wraps. mntd. (GB. Nov.3; 904)
DM 850

SCHINZ, H.
- **Deutsch-Südwest-Afrika Forschungsreisen** ... **1884-1887.** Oldenburg, [1891]. Pict. cl., spines slightly faded. (VA. Apr.26; 526)   R 330

SCHINZ, Heinrich Rudolf
- **Naturgeschichte und Abbildungen der Menschen und der Säugethiere.** Ill.:- J. Honegger. Zurich, 1840. *2nd. Edn.* Sm. fo. Litho. titles, 184 (of 186) litho. plts., some foxing, plt. 1 torn with loss of text, a few minor tears & surface abrasions to plts., cont. russ.-bkd. bds., worn. (C. Jun.27; 183)
Burden. £320
- **Naturgeschichte und Abbildungen der Saeugethiere.** Ill.:- C.I. Brodtmann. Zurich, 1824-29-[40?]. 2 vols. 4to. 81 (of 177) litho. plts., 2 stained, portion (pp. 187-417) of what is presumably additional (& later) edn. of text bnd. in Vol. II, cont. hf. roan, not unif., rubbed, jnts. brkn., w.a.f. (C. Jun.27; 182)   *Burden.* £140
- **Naturgeschichte und Abbildungen der Vögel.** Zurich, [1824]. Fo. Litho. title, 143 (of 144) plts., spotted thro.-out, cont. cf.-bkd. bds., slightly worn. (BBA. Dec.15; 139)   *Erlini.* £160
- - **Anr. Edn.** Zurich, [1835?]. Fo. Browned due to quality of paper, hf. cf., corners. (CR. Jun.6; 285)
Lire 800,000

SCHIPPERUS, P.A.
See— CRAANDIJK, J. & Schipperus, P.A.

SCHKUHR, Chr.
- **Botanisches Handbuch.** Wittenberg, 1807. Pts. 21-30 in 1 vol. Bnd. in pt. titles with MS., lacks text, some spotting, cont. bds., very bumped & worn. (H. Nov.23; 262)   DM 400

SCHLAGINTWEIT, E.
- **Indien in Wort und Bild.** Leipzig, 1880. 2 vols. Fo. Orig. pict. linen. (R. Oct.13; 3022)   DM 400

SCHLECHTENDAL, Diedrich Franz Leonhard von
- **Abbildung und Beschreibung aller in der Pharmacopoea Borussica Aufgefuehrten Gewaesche.** Ed.:- F. Guimpel. Berlin, 1833-37. Vols. 2 & 3 only (of 3). 4to. 95 (of 100) & 94 (of 108) hand-cold. copperplates, cont. qtr. leath., very worn, lacks spines, as a collection of plts., w.a.f. (SG. Oct.6; 323) $225

SCHLECHTENDAL, D.F.L. v. (Ed.)
See— FLORA VON DEUTSCHLAND

SCHLEGEL, August Wilhelm von
- **Essais Littéraires et Historiques.** Bonn, 1842. *1st. Edn.* Wide margin, cont. mor., gt. spine, cover & outer dentelles, gt. decor.; slightly shabby, ex-libris in cover, anr. ex-libris; dedication copy, Hauswedell coll. (H. May 24; 1547)   DM 3,200
- **Sämmtliche Werke.** Ed.:- E. Böcking. Leipzig, 1846-47. *1st. Coll. Edn.* 12 vols. Minimal spotting, cont. bds., gt. spine; Eduard Erdmann ex-libris, Hauswedell coll. (H. May 24; 1545)   DM 1,200
- **Ueber Dramatische Kunst und Litteratur.** Heidelberg, 1809-11. *1st. Edn.* 2 vols. in 3. Title to Vol. 3 bnd. in Vol. 2, owners inscrs. on title, cont. hf. russ., spines gt. (C. Dec.9; 284)   *Kaldewey.* £380

SCHLEGEL, August Wilhem von & Tieck, Ludwig
- **Musen-Almanach für das Jahr 1802.** Contribs.:- A.W. & Fr. von Schlegel, Tieck & others. Tübingen, 1802. *1st. Edn.* Minimal spotting, cont. style hand-bnd. hf. leath.; Hauswedell coll. (H. May 24; 1549)   DM 460

SCHLEGEL, Friedrich von
- **Lucinde.** Berlin, 1799. *1st. Edn.* Slightly foxed, cont. hf. leath., bumped, end-papers renewed. (HK. May 16; 2254)   DM 800
- **Philosophie des Lebens. in Funfzehn Vorlesungen gemalten zu Wien im Jahre 1827.** Wien, 1828. *1st. Edn.* Cont. bds. (BR. Apr.12; 1290)   DM 550
- **Philosophische Vorlesungen insbesondere über Philosophie der Sprache und des Wortes.** Wien, 1830. Some light foxing, hf. leath. gt., owners mark on end-paper. (GB. May 4; 1600)   DM 700
- **Sämmtliche Werke.** Wien, 1822-25. *De Luxe 1st. Coll. Edn.* 10 vols. Some spotting or browning to title, margins & end-papers, later hf. leath., blind-tooled, gt. spine, ex-libris; Hauswedell coll. (H. May 24; 1551)   DM 2,600
- - **Anr. Copy.** 10 vols. in 5. On Dutch paper, some slight foxing, hf. mor., ex-libris. (GB. May 4; 1598)
DM 1,000
- - **Anr. Copy.** 10 pts. in 5 vols. Slightly spotted, minimal margin browning, ex-libris, hf. leath. ca. 1890, spine with gt. leatherette, w.a.f. (R. Nov.10; 2704)   DM 520
- **Ueber die Sprache und Weishert der Indier.** Heidelberg, 1808. *1st. Edn.* Some spotting, cont. cf., gt. spine, gt. decor. covers, slightly worn, upr. cover with sm. wormhole, Hauswedell coll. (H. May 24; 1553)   DM 800

SCHLEGEL, Hermann
See— BONAPARTE, Prince Charles Lucien & Schlegel, Hermann

SCHLEGEL, Hermann & Verster van Wülverhorst, A.H.
- **Traité de Fauconnerie.** Ill.:- J.B. Sonderland, & J. Dillmann, Wendel, & W. van Wouw, after Joseph Wolf & others. Leiden & Düsseldorf, 1844-53. Lge. fo. Tinted litho. title on India paper containing 11 vigs., 16 plts. (14 hand-cold.), title & 2 plain plts. slightly spotted in margins, sm. tear in margin of 1 plt., some browning of text, cont. red hf. mor., gt., royal monog. on spine, rubbed. (S. Feb.1; 48)
Graham. £14,500

SCHLEMMER, Oskar
- **Die Bühne im Buhnen.** Contribs.:- Moholy-Nagy, M. Breuer, K. Schmidt. Ill.:- L. Moholy-Nagy. München, [1924]. *1st. Edn.* MS. owner's note on end-paper, orig. pict. bds. (GB. Nov.5; 2987)
DM 700
- - **Anr. Copy.** Orig. pict. bds. (GB. May 5; 3220)
DM 500

SCHLEY, Frank
- **American Partridge & Pheasant Shooting.** Frederick, Md., 1877. *1st. Edn.* Orig. pict. cl. (LH. Jan.15; 383) $100

SCHLIEMANN, Dr. Henry
- **Ithaque le Péloponnèse Troie. Recherches Archéologiques.** Paris, 1869. *1st. Fr. Edn.* Minimal foxing, mod. bds. (D. Nov.23; 1985)   DM 450
- **Mycenae; A Narrative of Researches & Discoveries at Mycenae & Tiryns.** Preface:- W.E. Gladstone. 1878. Publisher's catalogue bnd. in at end, orig. cl. gt., rubbed. (TA. Feb.16; 2)   £80
- - **Anr. Copy.** Publishers advts. bnd. in at rear, some spotting of prelims., ex-liby. with stp. on end-papers only, orig. gt.-decor. cl., rubbed. (TA. Jun.21; 1)   £66
- **Trojanische Alterthümer.** Leipzig, 1874. *1st. Edn.* Hf. title with MS. dedication, some slight foxing, cont. hf. linen, 1 corner excised. (H. Nov.23; 421)
DM 400
- **Troy & its Remains; A Narrative of Researches & Discoveries Made on the Site of Ilium** ... 1875. Folding map, 2 folding plans, sm. liby. stp. on title only, cont. hf. mor., rubbed. (TA. Mar.15; 37)
£62

SCHLUMBERGER, Gustave
- **Soldats de Napoléon. Journal de Route du Capitaine Robinaux, 1803-1832.** Paris, 1908. Hf. roan, wrap. (HD. Jan.27; 97)   Frs. 1,000

SCHMALEN, J.C.H. v.
- **Accurate Vorstellung der Sämtlichen Koeniglich Preussischen Armee** ... Nuremb., 1759. *1st. Edn.* Cont. marb. leath., gt. spine & outer dentelle, slightly rubbed. (HK. Nov.9; 1908)   DM 10,500
- - **Anr. Edn.** Nürnberg, 1762. *New Edn.* Copper engrs. heightened by gold & silver, all copper engrs. with erased stp. partly painted over, 1 with sm. repair, some slight soiling. (*Bound with:*) SEYFART, J.F.S. - **Kurzgefassete Geschichte aller Königlichen Preussischen Regimenter [by J.F.S.S.].** 1762. *3rd. Edn.* Together 2 works in 1 vol. Mod. hand-bnd. hf. leath. (H. May 22; 434)   DM 6,800

SCHMELLER, J. Andr.
- **Bayer. Wörterbuch.** Stuttgart & Tübingen, 1827. 4 vols. Slightly foxed, hf. leath., ca. 1860. (HK. Nov.9; 1462)   DM 750

SCHMIDT, Arno
- **Abend mit Goldrand.** Frankfurt, 1975. *1st. Edn.* De Luxe Edn., (350) numbered & sigd. Fo. Orig. hf. vell., s.-c. (V. Oct.1; 4412)   DM 800
- **Aus dem Leben eines Fauns.** Hamburg, [1953]. *1st. Edn.* Orig. linen, orig. pict. wraps. (HT. May 9; 2026)
- **Leviathan.** Hamburg, Stuttgart, Berlin, 1949. *1st. Edn.* Orig. bds. (D. Nov.24; 2874)   DM 550
- **Die Miniaturen des Gerokodex.** Leipzig, 1924. Fo. Orig. hf. linen. (R. Apr.3; 628)   DM 420
- **Das Steinerne Herz.** Karlsruhe, 1956. *1st. Edn.* Orig. linen. (D. Nov.24, 2879)   DM 550
- **Zettel's Traum.** Stuttgart, 1963-69. *1st. Edn.* Fo. Printers mark sigd., orig. linen. (HK. May 17; 3115)   DM 800

SCHMIDT, F.A.
- **Mineralienbuch.** Stuttgart, 1850. 4to. Cont. hf. leath. gt. (GB. Nov.3; 1095)   DM 750
- **Petrefactenbuch.** Stuttgart, 1850. 4to. Cont. hf. leath. gt. (GB. Nov.3; 1096)   DM 600

SCHMIDT, Isaac Jacob
- **Grammatik der Tibetischen Sprache.** St. Petersb. & Leipzig, 1839. 4to. Few ll. slightly soiled or spotted, orig. wraps., unc., torn & soiled. (BBA. Mar.7; 57)   *Hoseins Books.* £420

SCHMIDT, Johann Georg
- **Curiöse Speculationes bey Schlaflosen Nächten.** Chemnitz & Leipzig, 1707. *1st. Edn.* Frontis. with sm. margin slit, lightly browned thro.-out, cont. vell., slightly spotted. (GB. May 4; 1451)
DM 1,200

SCHMIDT, Max
- **Aus unserem Kriegsleben in Südwestafrika.** Berlin, 1907. Orig. bdg. (VA. Oct.28; 579)   R 220

SCHMIDT, Rob.
- **Die Gläser der Sammlung Mühsam.** Berlin, 1914. *(250) numbered.* Fo. This copy not numbered, orig. linen, corners & spine defect. (R. Apr.3; 779)
DM 1,700

SCHMIED, François-Louis
- Catalogue des Livres de F.-L. Schmied exposés en Mars 1927 chez A. Seligmann à New-York. Suivi du Catalogue Général des Livres de F.-L. Schmied ... 1927. 4to. Sewed. (HD. Dec.16; 187) Frs. 4,200
- La Creation. Trans.:– Mardrus. Paris, 1928. *Ltd. Edn., sigd. in both vols.* 2 vols. Fo. Plts. in 2 states, vol. 1 with text & cold. woodcut ills., 12 full-p., vol. 2 with extra suite of uncold ills., loose in wraps. & s.-c.'s as iss. (SPB. May 17; 676) $1,900
- Peau-Brune. De St Nazaire à la Ciotat. Journal de Bord. 1931. *(135) sigd. by artist on vell. de Hollande.* 4to. Orig. aqua. sigd. with initials on 1st. lf. blank, mor., by G. Cretté, blind & gt. decor. spine, hemp doubls. & end-papers, double end-papers, wrap., s.-c.; autograph dedication. (HD. Dec.16; 186) Frs. 14,000

SCHMIEDEL, K. Chr.
- Erz Stüffen und Berg Arten. Nuremb., 1753. *1st. Edn.* 4to. Lacks 16 pp. German text, 16 pp. Latin text & 16 plts., text near end browned, some plts. slightly foxed or soiled, cont. leath. gt. (HK. Nov.8; 457) DM 1,700

SCHMITT, A.
See— DEGENHART, B. & Schmitt, A.

SCHMITT, O. (Ed.)
See— REAL LEXIKON ZUR DEUTSCHEN KUNSTGESCHICHTE

SCHMITZ, H.
- Berliner Eisenkunstguss. München, 1917. *1st. Edn.* 4to. Orig. hf. linen. (GB. May 4; 1918) DM 1,100

SCHMOLDER, Bruno
- Neuer Praktischer Wegweiser fur Auswanderer nach Nord-Amerika ... Mainz, 1849. *1st. Edn.* 3 vols. in 1. Folding maps in facs., some foxing, orig. cl., covers loose. (LH. Apr.15; 368) $200

SCHMUCK, F.W.
- Fasciculus Admirandorum Naturae. Ill.:– J.A. Seupel. Strassburg, 1679-82. 4 pts. in 1 vol. 4to. 1 title verso & all plt. versos lightly stpd., last 2 plts. sigd. or initialled, later vell., head of spine slightly defect. (R. Oct.12; 1472) DM 650

SCHNEEDE, Uwe
- Max Ernst. Stuttgart, 1972. *De Luxe Edn., (15) numbered.* 1 sigd. orig. cold. etching, cold. orig. wraps. (GB. Nov.5; 2424) DM 1,300

SCHNEIDER, A.G.
See— WEIGEL, Christoph & Schneider, A.G.

SCHNEIDER, J.
- Naturhistorisch-Topographisch-Statistische Beschreibung des Hohen Röhngebirges, seine Vorberge und Umgebungen. Fulda, 1840. Foxed & stained thro.-out, bds. (D. Nov.23; 1480) DM 680

SCHNITZLER, Arthur
- Die Hirtenflöte. Ill.:– F. Schmutzer. Wien, 1912. *1st. Book Edn. (400).* Etched ex-libris inside cover, end-papers slightly discold., hand-bnd. orig. mor. gt., by Wiener Werkstätte, corners & spine slightly rubbed; with ptd. map. (H. Nov.24; 2021) DM 820
- Reigen. Zehn Dialoge. [Wien], priv. ptd., 1896/97. *1st. Edn. (200) numbered, dedication on 2nd. lf.* MS. facs., MS. sig. dtd. 6.2.1901, cont. hf. leath. gt., leath. corners. (R. Oct.11; 406) DM 4,700
- – Anr. Edn. Ill.:– Margit Gaal. Berlin & Wien, 1923. *Jubilee Edn. Ltd. Iss.* Printers mark sigd. by artist, 11 orig. aqua. pencil ills., 1 sigd., orig. red brown mor., sigd. H. Fikentscher, Leipzig, 1923, gt. decor. gt. inner dentelles. (GB. May 5; 3230) DM 1,300

SCHOBERL or SHOBERL, Frederic
- A Historical Account ... of the House of Saxony. L., 1816. Lge. 8vo. 4 ll. of advts. at end, ports. foxed, scarlet str.-grd. mor. gt. super extra, by Hering, gt. dentelles, fore-e. pntg. (SG. Nov.17; 233) $300
- The World in Miniature: Africa. L., 1821. 4 vols. Engraved title with cold. vig., 2 cold. maps, 43 cold. copperplts., 1 engraved supp., slightly browned, some light foxing. (R. Oct.13; 2930) DM 560

– – Anr. Edn. L., [1821]. 4 vols. Orig. bds., worn. (BBA. Jun.28; 249) *Swanson.* £75
- The World in Miniature: Austria. L., [1823]. 2 vols. in 1. 12mo. Cl., worn, rebkd., orig. spine laid down. (SG. Jun.7; 335) $120
- The World in Miniature: Hindoostan. N.d. 6 vols. 12mo. 103 hand-cold. plts., some folding, some ll. slightly spotted, blind liby. stp. on some ll., cont. cf., spines worn or lacking, some covers detchd. (BBA. Sep.29; 70) *Macfarlane.* £75
- The World in Miniature: Switzerland. L., 1827. 12mo. 18 cold. aquatint plts., frontis. cut slightly close, some light browning, later hf. leath. gt. (R. Apr.5; 3099) DM 950

SCHOELLHORN, F.
- Bibliographie des Brauwesens. Einsiedeln, 1928. Orig. linen. (BR. Apr.13; 2100) DM 430

SCHOENE, A. (Ed.)
See— EMBLEMATA ...

SCHOEPFF, J.D.
- Historia Testudinum Iconibus illustrata. Erlangen, 1792 [ff]. *1st. Latin Edn.* 4to. Title & some text ll. slightly foxed, 19th. C. hf. linen. (R. Oct.12; 1915) DM 1,400

SCHOEPFLIN, Joannes Daniel
- Vindiciae Typographicae. Strassburg, 1760. *1st. Edn.* 2 pts. in 1 vol. 4to. 7 engraved plts. (6 folding), cont. cf., spines gt., worn. (BBA. Mar.7; 378) *W. Forster.* £65

SCHOLEM, Gershon
See— CHAYUN, Nechemia — ERGAS, Joseph — SCHOLEM, Gershon

SCHOLTE, H. (Ed.)
See— FILMLIGA

SCHOLZ, J., Publisher
- Der Kindheit Lust und Freude. Mainz, n.d. 11 hand-cold. lithos., orig. bds., soiled. (P. Jun.7; 332) £190

SCHOMBURCK, Sir Robert Herman
- Twelve Views in the Interior of Guiana. Ill.:– after Charles Bentley. L., 1841. Fo. Additional hand-cold. litho. title, engraved map, 12 hand-cold. litho. views, fore-margin of litho. title slightly soiled, cont. red hf. mor. (S. Dec.1; 295) *Van Hunersdorf.* £1,250

SCHONGAUER, Martin
- Oeuvre de Martin Schongauer. Text:– George Duplessis. Paris, 1881. Tall fo. Mounts slightly soiled, loose in orig. cl. portfo., worn, ties. (CBA. Jan.29; 406) $750

SCHOOLCRAFT, Henry Rowe
- Archives of Aboriginal Knowledge. Ill.:– S. Eastman &c. Phila., 1857, 1860. 6 vols. 4to. Vol. II supplied from earlier edn. (1853-57), cl., various, some repairs, ex-liby., plts. unstpd. [Sabin 77839 & 77855] (SG. Jan.19; 323) $650
- [–]The Indian Tribes of the United States. Ed.:– Francis S. Drake. Phila., 1884. 2 vols. 4to. 100 plts., some cold. including ethnographical map, hf. mor. [Sabin 77854] (S. May 22; 337) *Robinson.* £380
- Information Respecting the History, Condition & Prospects of the Indian Tribes of the United States. Ill.:– S. Eastman &c. Phila., 1853. *Imperial 8vo. Edn.* Pts. [Vols.] I-III (of 5). Lge. 8vo. Gt.-pict. cl., chipped, ex-liby., plts. unstpd. [Sabin 77855] (SG. Jan.19; 322) $400
- Journal of a Tour into the Interior of Missouri & Arkansaw. L., 1821. *1st. Edn.* Margin tear to folding map reprd., hf. cf. [Sabin 77858] *(With:)* – Narrative Journals of Travels through the North-Western Regions of the United States. Albany, 1821. *1st. Edn.* Errata slip, folding map with a few minor tears, some foxing, cont. hf. cf., upr. cover detchd. [Sabin 77862] Together 2 vols. The Rt. Hon. Visc. Eccles copies, w.a.f. (CNY. Nov.18; 250) $350
- Narrative Journal of Travels through the North-Western Regions of the United States. Albany, 1821. *1st. Edn.* Added engraved title, map, 8 plts., lacks errata slip. foxed. early owners sigs., pencil marginalia, early cf., rather worn, lacks free end-papers. (SG. Apr.5; 178) $110

- A View of the Lead Mines of Missouri. N.Y., 1819. *1st. Edn.* Foxed, cl.-bkd. bds., worn. (RO. Aug.23; 62) $135

SCHOONEBEEK, Adriaan
- Histoire des Ordres Religieux. — Courte Description des Ordres des Femmes & Filles Religieuses. Amst., priv. ptd., 1695 & n.d. 2 vols. Sm. 8vo. 7 frontis., 235 etchings & some vigs., all cont. hand-cold. & heightened with gold, unif. cont. cf. gt. (VG. Mar.19; 133) Fls. 2,600

SCHOONHOVIUS, F.
- Emblemata Partim Moralia, Partim etiam Civilia. Leiden, 1626. *2nd. Edn.* 4to. Engraved title, port., 74 emblems, cont. vell., rebnd., warped, few stains. (VG. May 3; 473) Fls. 600

SCHOOTEN, Franciscus A.
- Exercitationvm Mathematicarum Libri Quinque ... Quibus accedit Christiani Hugenii Tractatus, de Ratiociniis in Alae Ludo. Leiden, 1657-56. *1st. Edn.* 5 pts. in 1 vol. 4to. Final errata lf., some spotting & browning, early 18th. C. hf. cf., spine gt., slight wear; Stanitz coll. (SPB. Apr.25; 394) $425

SCHOPENHAUER, Arthur
- Kan Menneskets Frie Villie Bevises af dets Selbevidsthed? Trondheim, 1840. *1st. Edn.* 4to. Vol. 3, pt. 2 in German, only title & preface Norwegan, bnd in F.M. Bugges's 'Den Constitutionelle Statsform', orig. wraps., unc., bd. s.-c. (R. Oct.11; 537) DM 400
- Sämtliche Werke. Ed.:– Grisebach & others. Ill.:– E. Gill. [1912-13]. *(200) numbered De Luxe Edn. on Dutch paper.* 2 vols. Margin slightly browned, orig. red leath. gt., corners rubbed. (GB. May 5; 3232) DM 460
- Die Welt als Wille und Vorstellung. Leipzig, 1819. *1st. Edn. (750).* Lge. 8vo. Some ll. with pencil notes, light browning, some slight spotting, cont. style hf. leath., gt. (H. May 22; 872) DM 4,600

SCHOPENHAUER, Johanna
- Sämmtliche Schriften. Leipzig & Frankfurt, 1830-31. *1st. Coll. Edn.* 24 vols. in 12. 12mo. Orig. cl. (C. Dec.9; 285) *Braecklein.* £170

SCHOPPER, Hartmann
- De Omnibus Illiberalibus sive Mechanicis Artibus ... Ill.:– after Jost Amman. Frankfurt, 1574. 12mo. Last ll. lightly foxed, old cf., decor. spine. (HD. Mar.14; 77) Frs. 19,000
- Specvlvm Vitae Avlicae. Ill.:– J. Amman. Frankfurt, 1574 [1575]. *2nd. Latin Edn.* 12mo. Pagination jumps from p. 145-156 & 369-380, 1 end-paper with old entries, minimal spotting, old vell.; Hauswedell coll. (H. May 24; 1173) DM 1,600
- – Anr. Edn. Ill.:– Jost Amman. Frankfurt, 1584. Slightly browned thro.-out, title-lf. & inner cover wormed & stained, cont. vell., very browned & cockled. (GB. Nov.4; 1987) DM 550

SCHOTANUS, J.
See— GEULINCX, A. — SCHOTANUS, J. — LE GRAND, Anthony

SCHOTANUS A STERRINGA, B.
- Uitbeelding der Heerlijkheit Friesland. Ill.:– J. & C. Luyken & others. [Leeuwarden], 1718. Fo. Double-p. general map, hand-cold., few maps with annots. in mod. MS., 19th. C. leath., very rubbed. (VG. Sep.14; 1199) Fls. 4,000

SCHOTT, Gasper
- Cursus Mathematicus. Würzburg, 1661. *1st. Edn.* Fo. Browned & stained, 2 prelim. ll. loose, cont. blind-stpd. pig, ties & clasps; inscr. on end-paper recording gift of book from Domenico Ricci to San Vincenzo di (?) Strastesio Liby., bkplt. & release stp. of St. Mary's College, Bg'ham., Stanitz coll. (SPB. Apr.25; 395) $450
- Physica Curiosa, sive Mirabilia Naturae et Artis Libris XII. comprehensa. Nürnberg, 1667. *2nd. Edn.* 2 vols. in 1. 4to. Arms on title verso, some ll. torn, some pasted, engraved & ptd. title loose, former with sm. bkd. tear, cont. vell., slightly spotted, very worn, new ex-libris inside cover. (H. May 22; 220) DM 1,500
- Technica Curiosa, aive Mirabilia Artis. Würzburg, 1644. 2 pts. in 1 vol. 4to. 2 plts. numbered 16, plt. 36 after plt. 9, 1 folding plt. torn, a few

SCHOTT, Gasper -*Contd.*

plts. worn at margins, some spotting, cont. vell., sides made from old antiphoner lf.; Stanitz coll. (SPB. Apr.25; 396) $800

SCHOTT, P.

- De Mensuris Syllabarum. Strassb., J. Schott, 24.XII.1500. *1st. Edn.* 4to. Wormed, sm. margin defects., misbnd., bds. [H. 14525; BMC I, 167; Goff S 322] (HK. Nov.8; 337) DM 1,000

SCHOTTELIUS, J. Gg.

- Ausführliche Arbeit von der Teutschen Haubt Sprache ... Braunschweig, 1663. *1st. Edn.* 4to. German & Latin title ll., cont. vell.; engraved Earl of Marchmont ex-libris, Hauswedell coll. (H. May 24; 1192) DM 4,000

SCHOUTEN, Wouter

- Oost-Indische Voyagie. Amst., 1676. *1st. Edn.* 2 pts. in 1 vol. 4to. Tear in 3 plts. reprd., 1 lf. misbnd., mod. hf. mor. (VG. Mar.19; 253) Fls. 1,100

SCHRAMM, Albert

- Der Bilderschmuck der Frühdrucke. Leipzig, 1920-43. 23 vols. Fo. Mod. hf. leath. in orig. style. (R. Oct.11; 759) DM 8,200

SCHRAMM, C.C.

- Hist. Schauplatz, in welchem die Merkwürdigsten Brücken aus Allen Theilen d. Welt, insonderheit die Dresdner Elb-Brücke ... vorgestellet werden. Ill.:- after I.A. Richter. Leipzig, 1735. Fo. Lacks 2 plts.?, cont. cf., richly gt., spine defect., rubbed, thick floral end-papers. (VG. Mar.19; 116) Fls. 8,500

SCHRAUD, F. von

- Historia Pestis Sirmiensis Annorum 1795 et 1796. Buda, 1802. 3 vols. in 1. 4to. Later hf. cf. (D. Nov.23; 623) DM 480

SCHRECKENFUCHS, Erasmus Oswald
See— REGIOMANTANUS, Johannes

SCHREIBER, A.W.
See— VOGT, N. & Schreiber, A.W.

SCHREIBER, Lady Charlotte

- Catalogue of English Porcelain, Earthenware, Enamels & Glass ... presented to the [Victoria & Albert] Museum in 1884. L., 1928-30-24. 3 vols. Tall 8vo. 1st. vol. in wraps., rest in cl., spine ends rubbed or chipped. (SG. Jan.26; 153) $130
- Journals ... Ed.:- Montagu J. Guest. L., 1911. 2 vols. Orig. cl. (KH. Nov.9; 694) Aus. $180

SCHREIBER, Johann Georg

- Atlas selectus von allen Königreichen und Ländern der Welt. Leipzig, ca. 1750. Sm. 4to. Engraved cold. title, 1 contents lf., 35 old cold. double-p. copper engraved maps, lacks Germany map, added mile scale, all maps strengthened on side margin, margins slightly soiled, newer hf. vell. (R. Oct.13; 2874) DM 3,300

SCHRENCK VON NOZING, Jacob

- Augustissimorum Imperatorum, Regum atque Archiducum, Ilustrissimorum Principum, necnon Comitum, Baronum ... quorum Arma in Ambrosianae Arcis Armamentario conspiciuntur. Ill.:- Dom. Custodis after J.A. Fontana. Oeniponti [Innsbruck], 1601. Lge. fo. Title-p. & last plt. reprd., late 18th. C. hf. vell., corners. (HD. Mar.21; 91) Frs. 2,500

SCHREVELIUS, Theodor

- Harlemias, of Eerste Stichting der Stad Haarlem. Ill.:- R. de Hooghe, Spilman, & Luiken. Haarlem, 1754. *2nd. Printing.* 4to. Few plts. slightly foxed, light margin staining towards end, unc., cont. hf. roan. (VG. Sep.14; 1200) Fls. 1,200

SCHRÖDER, Johannes

- Pharmacopoeia Medico-Chymica, sive Thesaurus Pharmacologicus. Frankfurt, 1669. *6th. Edn.* Vell., lightly browned. (V. Sep.29; 1484) DM 1,300
- Pharmacopeia Universalis. Nuremb., 1748. Vol. 3 only (of 3). Lacks 8 pp. & 1 copper engr., 1st. 4 ll. with slight margin tears, some browning & soiling, cont. hf. leath., spine defect., cover pasted with white paper. (HK. Nov.8; 721) DM 420

- Trefflich-Versehene Medicin-Chymische Apotheke. Ed.:- J.U. Müller. Nürnberg, 1686. *2nd. German Edn.* 4to. Lacks frontis., ptd. title slightly defect. inner margin, browned & foxed, cont. vell., spine slightly defect., end-papers renewed. (R. Oct.12; 1473) DM 1,250

SCHRODER, Rudolf Alex

- Audax Omnis Perpeti. Gedichte. Leipzig, [1922]. *(150) numbered.* Red mor., gt. decor., by Heinrich & Scheffel, Leipzig, some light scratches. (HK. Nov.11; 3953) DM 440
- Empodocles. Ill.:- H. Vogeler. [Leipzig, 1900]. *1st. Edn. (50).* 1st. ll. lightly soiled, some slight foxing, orig. hf. vell., corners bumped, spine slightly soiled. (H. Nov.24; 2033) DM 560
- Lieder und Elegien. Ill.:- H. Vogeler. [Leipzig, 1911]. *(100) on Bütten.* Sm. 4to. Orig. hf. vell. (H. Nov.24; 2034) DM 400
- Widmung und Opfer. Ill.:- A. Simons. München, Bremer Pr., 1925. *(150) on Bütten.* 4to. Hand-bnd. orig. vell. (H. Nov.23; 940) DM 620

SCHROEDINGER, Erwin

- Abhandlungen zur Wellenmechanik. Leipzig, 1927. *1st. Edn.* Light browning of title & final lf., orig. wraps., faded, some wear to spine, chipping; K. Wickland sig. on title, Stanitz coll. (SPB. Apr.25; 393) $200

SCHROETER, Johann Heironymus

Lilienthalische Beobachtungen der Neu Entdeckten Planeten Ceres, Pallas, und Juno. Goettingen, 1805. *1st. Edn.* Lge. 8vo. Instructions to binder, errata, orig. bds., reprd., unc. & unopened; Herschel copy, few margin notes in his hand in preface & on p. 8. (SG. Mar.22; 283) $325

SCHROTER, Casp.

- Rares Koch-Condir- u. Distillir-Buch. Frankfurt & Leipzig, 1712. Lacks index, title with pasted tear, browned thro.-out, side margin wormed, marb. bds. (HK. Nov.9; 1702) DM 500

SCHROTER, J.F.

[-] Allgemeine Geschichte der Länder und Völker von Amerika. Preface:- S.J. Baumgarten. Halle, 1752-53. *1st. Edn.* 2 vols. 4to. Vol. 2 lacks 7 plts., 16 supp. plts., frontis. with sm. pasted bkd. tear, mod. hf. vell. in cont. style. (R. Apr.5; 2790) DM 1,300

SCHUBART, Chr. Fr. D.

- Gedichte. Ed.:- L. Schubart. Frankfurt, 1802. *1st. Edn.* 2 vols. Some light browning, cont. hf. leath., rubbed & spotted. (H. May 22; 873) DM 520

SCHUBERT, Franz

- Erlkönig. [1821]. *1st. Edn.* Some staining consistent with use, some spotting, sigd. on title-p. 'Gessinger', mod. fitted case; sigd. (with paraph) & numbered by composer, sig. slightly trimmed. (S. Nov.17; 166) MacNutt. £2,200
- Complete Works. N.Y., [1965]. *Breitkopf & Haertel Critical Edn. of 1884-97.* 19 vols. Sm. fo. Unif. cl., 16 vols. with d.-w. (SG. Nov.17; 322) $150

SCHUBERT, Dr. Gotthilf Heinrich von

- Naturgeschichte der Säugethiere in Bildern zum Anschauungs-Unterricht für die Jugend. Stuttgart & Esslingen, [1860]. *2nd. Edn.* Fo. Cold. litho. pict. title-p. & 30 hand-finished double-p. plt., margins slightly soiled & discold., cont. cl.-bkd. bds., slightly worn; van Veen coll. (S. Feb.28; 166) £70
- Naturgeschichte des Pflanzenreichs. Esslingen, n.d. Fo. 54 double-p. cold. plts., hand finished, margins lightly browned, orig. hf. cf., soiled, rubbed. (CSK. May 18; 51) £65
- Naturgeschichte des Tierreichs für Schule und Haus. Esslingen, ca. 1880. *8th. Edn.* 4to. 4 pp. pt 2 with corner tear reprd., cont. leath. gt., restored. (R. Oct.12; 1918) DM 440

SCHUBERT, Dr Gotthilf Heinrich von & Roth, J.

- Album des Heiligen Landes./Album of the Lands of the Bible./Album de la Terre Sainte. Ill.:- J.M. Bernath. Stuttgart & Leipzig, L., Paris, [1855]. Ob. 4to. Some slight foxing, cont. hf. leath. gt., spine slightly spotted. (R. Oct.13; 3035) DM 450

SCHUBERT, Walter F.

- Die Deutsche Werbegraphik. Berlin, 1927. Fo. Orig. linen. (HK. Nov.11; 4058) DM 660
- - Anr. Copy. Fo. Some slight foxing, orig. linen, stpd. (D. Nov.24; 3187) DM 440

SCHUBLER, Johann Jakob

- Deutlicher Unterricht von Heizersparenden Stuben-Oefen nach allen ihren Theilen ... Beschrieben. Nuremb., 1789. Sm. fo. Engraved frontis., 29 plts., some stained at upr. outer corner, 19th. C. paper bds. (C. Dec.9; 194) Henderson. £320
- Erste [-Achtzehende] Ausgabe Seines Vorhabenden Wercks. Augsburg, ca. 1724? 19 pts. (1, 1 bis-18) in 1 vol. Fo. 114 engraved plts., a few tears reprd. with sellotape, 1st. title creased with 1 repair, blank corner torn from last plt., mod. spr. cf., spine gt. (C. Dec.9; 143) Henderson. £650
- Gründlicher und Deutlicher Unterricht zur Verfertigung der Vollständigen Saülen-Ordnung, wie man sie in der heutigen Civil-Bau-Kunst zu gebrauchen pflegen. Nuremb., [1723-24]. *1st. Edn.* 2 pts. in 1 vol. Fo. Lightly foxed, mostly text ll., cont. bds.; spine pasted over & recent defect. (R. Apr.3; 698) DM 820
- Nützliche Anweisung zur Unentbehrlichen Zimmermanne Kunst. Nuremb., 1749. Some heavy staining, some slight spotting, title lf. foxed with old MS. owners entries, plt. margins slightly crumpled, cont. hf. vell., defect. (HT. May 8; 655) DM 400

SCHUBRING, Konrad
See— GALENUS, Claudius — SCHUBRING, Konrad

SCHUCKING, Christoph B. Levin

- Der Rhein. Ill.:- Fourmois, Lauters & Stroobant. Brüssel, Gent & Leipzig, ca. 1860. Fo. Cont. gold-tooled linen. (R. Oct.13; 2734) DM 4,700
- Der Rhein von Mains bis Köln. Ill.:- Fourmois, Lauters & Stroobant. Brüssel, Leipzig, Gent, n.d. Fo. Some foxing, 1 plt. heavily foxed, orig. hf. leath. (V. Sep.29; 97) DM 3,400

SCHUCKING, Christoph B. Levin & Freiligrath, F.

- Das Malerische und Romantische Westphalen. Paderborn, 1872. *2nd. Edn.* Some plts. foxed & lightly browned, cont. hf. leath., bumped. (R. Oct.13; 2735) DM 2,500
- - Anr. Edn. Ed.:- L. Brungert. Paderborn, 1890. Lge. 8vo. 20 steel engraved plts. (including title), 15 plts., 100 text woodcuts, browned, some brown spotting & soiling, 6 ll. loose, orig. linen gt., slightly bumped, some light spots. (H. May 22; 353) DM 1,500
- - Anr. Copy. Engraved title, 19 steel engraved plts., 15 (of 16) chiaroscuro plts., 100 text ills., slightly foxed, hf. linen. (D. Nov.23; 824) DM 1,200
- - Anr. Edn. Ed.:- L.L. Schücking. Paderborn, 1898. *4th. Edn.* Engraved title, 21 steel engrs., 13 plts., 131 text woodcuts, orig. linen gt. (R. Oct.13; 2736) DM 1,550

SCHUDT, Johann Jacob

- Juedische Merckwuerdigkeiten, Vorstellende Was sich Curieuses und denckwuerdiges ... mit denen in alle IV. Theile der Welt ... zerstreuten Juden zugetragen. Sammt einer vollstaendigen Franckfurter Juden-Chronik, darinnen der zu Frankfurt am Mayn wohnenden Juden ... merckwuerdigste Begebenheiten enthalten. Frankfurt, 1714. *1st. Edn.* 3 (of 4) pts. in 1 vol. Sm. 4to. Text in German (in Hebrew characters), Hebrew & Latin, browned, hf. leath., extremities quite worn, rehinged, bkplt. removed from front pastedown, ex-liby. (SG. Feb.2; 111) $425

SCHUETTE, Marie

- Gesticte Bildteppiche und Decken des Mittelalters. Leipzig, 1927-30. 2 vols., & 2 vols. text. Fo. 114 plts., 32 cold., loose as iss. in orig. cl. portfo.'s, text vols. in orig. wraps., some slight soiling. (S. May 1; 659) Heneage. £520
- Spitzen von der Renaissance bis zum Empire. Leipzig, 1929. *(300).* Lge. fo. Orig. hf. linen. (HK. Nov.12; 4801) DM 500
- - Anr. Edn. Leipzig, 1929. Fo. Orig. cl. gt. (CH. May 24; 160) Fls. 600

SCHULT, F.
- **Ernst Barlach.** Hamburg, [1958]. Lge. 4to. Orig. linen. (HK. May 17; 2559) DM 1,000

SCHULTES, Joannes
See— SCULTETUS [or SCHULTES], Joannes

SCHULTZ, Christian
- **La Peyrouse Reise um die Welt; I.G. Stedman's Reisen in Surinam.** Berlin, ca. 1820. 2 vols. Each vol. with engraved frontis., pict. title-p. & 3 plts. hand-cold., liby. stps. on title-p. & versos on other plts. in 2nd. vol., orig. bds., slightly worn; van Veen coll. (S. Feb.28; 167) £50

SCHULTZE, Benjamin
- **Hymnologia Damulica.** Tranquebar, 1723. Sm. 8vo. Titles in Latin & Tamil, index in German, text in Tamil with German headings, cont. red mor. gt. (C. May 30; 49) *Ad Orientem.* £650
See— FRITZ, J.H. & Schultze, Benjamin

SCHULZ, G.
- **Descripción Geosnóstica del Reino de Galicia ...** Madrid, 1835. 4to. Wraps. (DS. Apr.27; 2601) Pts. 28,000

SCHULZ, H.C.
- **A Monograph on the Italian Choir Book ...** Ill.:– V. Angelo. San Franc., David Magee, [at the Grabhorn Pr.], 1941. *(75). (27) sigd. by artist & inscr. by Magee, with orig. gold-heightened col. lf.* Fo. Initials hand-illuminated in red, blue & gold, hf. linen & cl., covers lightly rubbed, spine lightly faded; the V. Angelo copy. (CBA. Oct.1; 173) $800

SCHULZE, Max
- **Die Orchidaceen Deutschlands, Deutsch-Osterreichs und der Schweiz.** 1894. 4to. Publisher's hf. chagrin, corners, spine browned. (HD. Jul.6; 80) Frs. 1,550

SCHUMANN, K.
- **Blühende Kakteen.** Neudamm, [1900 ff.]. Pts. 1-11 only (of 45). Lge. 4to. Orig. hf. linen portfo., slightly soiled. (HK. Nov.8; 612) DM 420

SCHUMANN, Robert
- **Second Symphony.** Leipzig, [1847]. *1st. Edn.* Some foxing & staining in margins, title-p. stained, mor. bds.; autograph pres. inscr. to Moscheles, sigd. by Schumann. (S. May 10; 153) *Haas.* £1,700

SCHUNKE, Ilse
- **Die Einbände der Palatina in der Vatikanischen Bibliothek.** Vatican City, 1962. 3 vols. Cont. buckram, orig. wraps. preserved; H.M. Nixon coll., with a few MS. notes. (BBA. Oct.6; 125) *Quaritch.* £140
- **Leben und Werk Jakob Krauses.** Leipzig, 1943. 4to. Orig. cl.-bkd. bds.; H.M. Nixon coll., with his sig., acquisition note & loosely inserted notes. (BBA. Oct.6; 123) *Maggs.* £280
- – **Anr. Copy.** 4to. 31 plts. (1 cold.), orig. cl.-bkd. bds. (BBA. Mar.7; 313) *Zeitlin & Verbrugge.* £180

SCHURMANN, C.W.
See— TEICHELMANN, C.G. & Schürmann, C.W.

SCHUT, Pieter H.
- **Toneel der Voornaamster Bybelsche Historien.** Amst., ca. 1740? Ob. 16mo. 330 copperplts., cont. vell., loose. (SG. Feb.9; 143) $200

SCHUTZ, C.
- **Historia Rerum Prussicarum.** Leipzig, 1599. *2nd. Edn.* Fo. Cont. vell., some old MS. annots. in margin, slightly browned & foxed. (D. Nov.24; 3808) DM 2,650
- – **Anr. Edn.** [Eisleben], 1599. Fo. Sm. hole affecting last ll., including a few letters & the device, later cf., spine gt. (S. Dec.1; 323) *Werner.* £650

SCHUYLER, Eugene
- **Turkistan, Notes of a Journey on Russian Turkistan, Khokand, Bukhara, & Kuldja.** L., 1876. 2 vols. Cont. hf. cf., corners. (HD. Mar.21; 199) Frs. 1,400

SCHUYLKILL FISHING COMPANY
- **History of the Schuylkill Fishing Company of the State in Schuylkill.** Phila., 1889-1932. 2 vols. Cont. hf. mor. gt.; pres. copy from publishers. (CSK. Nov.25; 81) £50

SCHWAB, Gustav Benjamin
- **Die Argonauten.** Ill.:– R. Seewald. 1923. *(300) numbered. De Luxe Edn. (100) with all full-p. orig. lithos. & 4 sm. lithos. sigd. by artist.* 4to. This copy unnumbered with sigd. full-p. lithos. & 4 sm. sigd. lithos., orig. pict. hf. leath., spine rubbed. (GB. May 5; 3312) DM 550
- **Die Deutschen Volksbücher für Jung und Alt wieder erzählt.** Ill.:– H. Bürkner after W. Camphausen, O. Pletsch & others. Stuttgart, 1859. *1st. Ill. Edn.* Some foxing in parts, orig. hf. leath., gold-stpd. spine. (GB. Nov.4; 1943) DM 600
- **Die Schweiz in ihrer Ritterburgen u. Bergschlössern historisch dargestellt von Vaterländischen Schriftstellern.** Ill.:– E. Rauch (frontis.), F. Hegi (copper engr.), C. Naumann (pen ills.) & R. Iselin (aquatints). Bern, 1828, or 1839. 3 vols. 1 engraved frontis., 1 copper engr., 4 pen lithos. & 4 aquatints, minimal foxing, sewed. (GF. Nov.16; 310) Sw.Frs. 400
- **Wanderungen durch Schwaben.** Leipzig, ca. 1838. *1st. Edn.* 29 (of 30) steel engrs, title & 2 ll stpd., lightly browned or spotted in places, cont. hf. leath., very worn & bumped. (H. May 22; 310) DM 1,800
- – **Anr. Edn.** Leipzig, ca. 1840. *1st. Edn.* Plts. washed, text partly foxed, cont. hf. leath., worn, spine sprung at top. (R. Oct.12; 2479) DM 2,150

SCHWABE, J.J. & others
- **Allgemeine Historie der Reisen zu Wasser und zu Lande.** Leipzig, 1747-74. 21 vols. 4to. 251 engraved maps. some multi-folding, many ills. on 401 copperplts., 3 maps torn some pp. lightly browned, some light spotting, cont. marb. cf. gt., heavy wear, sm. defect. & tears. (HT. May 10; 2853) DM 7,200
- – **Anr. Edn.** Leipzig, 1748. Vols. I & II in 1. 4to. Engraved frontis. & vig., 34 engraved maps & 47 copperplts., some folding, vell., slightly soiled. (V. Sep.29; 93) DM 800
- – **Anr. Edn.** Leipzig, 1748, 1774. Vols. I & XXI. 4to. 1 (of 2) engraved maps & 13 (of 15) copperplts., 1 copper engr. vol. XXI torn, 2 text ll. torn, several ll. bumped, cont. cf., bumped, vol. XXI cover with defects & worming. (H. May 22; 278) DM 800
- – **Anr. Edn.** Leipzig, 1749-50. Vols. V & VI. 4to. Vol. VI lacks 2 copper engrs, 2 maps & 2 copper engrs. torn, some foxing, cont. cf., 1 spine defect., very bumped. (H. May 22; 279) DM 850
- – **Anr. Edn.** Leipzig, 1750. Vol. VI. 4to. 1 plt. with bkd. tear, minimal light spotting & browning, cont. leath., end-papers renewed. (HK. May 15; 1087) DM 400

SCHWABE, K.
- **Die Deutschen Kolonien.** Berlin, ca. 1912. 2 vols. Fo. Hand-bnd. suede, silver & gold arms on upr. cover, gt. inner dentelle, silk end-papers & doubls., orig. box, slightly defect. (H. Nov.23; 311) DM 520
- **Der Krieg Deutsch-Südwestafrika 1904-06.** Berlin, 1907. Lge. 8vo. Some foxing, pict. cl., bottom of spine reprd., slightly shaken. (VA. Apr.27; 909) R 170

SCHWAN, Christian Fridrich
- **Abbildungen derjenigen Ritter-Orden welche eine eigene Ordenskleidung haben.** Mannheim, 1791. 4to. 57 hand-cold. engraved plts., cont. cf., rubbed & reprd. (C. Mar.14; 143) *Rheinbuch.* £300

SCHWANDNER, Johann Georg
- **Dissertatio Epistolaris de Calligraphiae Nomenclatione, Cultu, Praestantia, Utilitate.** Wien, 1756. Fo. Wide margin, 1 text lf. torn, 2 text ll. wormed in fold, MS. owners mark & stp., cont. cf., gt. spine, wormed, loose, worn; Hauswedell coll. (H. May 23; 287) DM 4,500

SCHWARTZ, G.
See— NIGRINUS [SCHWARTZ], G.

SCHWARZ, A.Z.
- **Die Hebräischen Handschriften der Nationalbibliothek in Wien.** Leipzig, 1925. Lge. fo. Stained thro.-out, orig. linen, worn. (R. Oct.11; 762) DM 450

SCHWARZ, H.A.
- **Gesammelte Mathematische Abhandlungen.** Berlin, 1890. *1st. Edn.* Some slight browning, orig. linen, slightly spotted & bumped. (HT. May 8; 477) DM 460

SCHWARZ, Ign.
- **Wiener Strassenbilder im Zeitalter des Rokoko.** Ed.:– R.H. Bartsch. Wien, 1914. *(300) numbered.* Fo. Orig. sewed, unc., bd. s.-c. (R. Oct.13; 3220) DM 680
- – **Anr. Edn.** Wien, 1914. 4to. Orig. red mor. gt., orig. s.-c. (D. Nov.23; 1082) DM 1,900

SCHWARZ, Karl
- **Das Graphische Work von Lovis Corinth.** Berlin, 1917. *1st. Edn. Ltd. Iss., not numbered.* Margins slightly browned, orig. bds., browned & slightly defect. (H. Nov.24; 2472) DM 600
- – **Anr. Edn.** Berlin, 1922. *2nd. Edn. De Luxe Edn.* on Bütten, with 2 etchings sigd. by artist. Sm. 4to. Orig. pict. hf. vell.; ex-libris Thomas Corinth inside cover etched & sigd. by Charlotte Berend-Corinth. (H. May 23; 1185a) DM 2,000
- – **Anr. Edn.** Berlin, 1922. *2nd. Edn.* Slight tear on hf. title, orig. cold. pict. bds. (D. Nov.23; 1809) DM 1,100

SCHWARZ, Sophie (née Becker)
See— RECKE, Elise von der & Schwarz, Sophie (née Becker)

SCHWATKA, Frederick
- **Nimrod in the North or Hunting & Fishing Adventures in the Arctic Regions.** N.Y., 1885. *1st. Edn.* 4to. Decor. cl., worn. (RO. May 29; 171) $105

SCHWEINFURTH, Dr. Georg
- **Im Herzen von Afrika. Reisen und Entdeckungen im Centralen Aequatorial-Afrika während der Jahre 1868 bis 1871.** Leipzig, 1874. *1st. Edn.* 2 vols. Title I with sm. repair, 2nd. title mntd., folding map creased., linen, slightly worn, spine vol. I slightly defect. (H. May 22; 248) DM 600
- – **Anr. Copy.** 2 vols. Vol. 2 lacks 1 lf. hf.-title & 32 pp., cont. hf. leath., rubbed. (R. Oct.13; 2933) DM 520

SCHWEITZER, Christopher
See— FRYKE or FRICK, Christopher & Schweitzer, Christopher

SCHWENCKFELD, C.
- **Ain Liebliche Tröstung für die so umbs Herzen Christi unnd seiner Warhait Willen Creutz und Verfolgung Leiden.** N.p., ca. 1550. 12mo. Later wraps. (HT. May 8; 209) DM 420
- [–] **Trostbüchlein.** N.p., 1546. 12mo. Margins slightly foxed, later wraps. (HT. May 8; 208) DM 650
- **Von der Götlichen Kindtschaft, vnd Herrlichait des Ganntzen Sones Gottes Jesu Christi erst Büchlen ...** N.p., 1555. Slightly soiled, incunable paper covered bds. (HK. Nov.8; 338) DM 1,000

SCHWENTER, D.
- **Deliciae Physice-mathematicae.** Nuremb., 1636. *1st. Edn.* Title stpd., some slight soiling, old MS. notes on end-paper, cont. blind-tooled vell., slightly spotted. (HT. May 8; 479) DM 2,500

SCHWERDT, Charles Francis George Richard
- **Hunting, Hawking, Shooting Illustrated in a Catalogue of Books, Manuscripts, Prints & Drawings.** L., priv. ptd., 1928-37. *(300) numbered.* 4 vols. 4to. Vol. 4 unnumbered, mor. by Kelly & Sons, partly unc., trifle marked or faded. (S. Nov.28; 100) *Hagelin.* £1,550

SCHWITTERS, Kurt
- **Anna Blume.** Hannover, 1919. Margin slightly browned, orig. pict. bds., lightly browned. (GB. Nov.5; 3003) DM 520
- **Die Scheuche.** Hannover, [1925]. *1st. Edn.* Ob.

SCHWITTERS, Kurt -*Contd.*

4to. Browned, sm. margin tear thro.-out, orig. wraps., slightly discold., sm. spot & tears. (H. Nov.24; 2039) DM 920

SCHWITTERS, Kurt & Steinitz, Käthe
- Das Märchen vom Paradies. Hannover, 1924. *1st. Edn.* Vol. 1 (all publd.). Sm. 4to. Orig. bds., orig. pict. wraps., loose, slightly spotted; Hauswedell coll. (H. May 24; 703) DM 2,000
- – Anr. Copy. Vol. I (all publd.). 4to. Slightly browned, orig. pict. sewed, margins slightly browned & slit, spine very defect., photo. pasted inside cover. (H. May 23; 1498) DM 1,000

SCHWOB, Marcel
- Vies Imaginaires. Ill.:– Georges Barbier, engraved by Pierre Bouchet. Paris, 1929. *(120).* Square 8vo. Mor. gt. by Semet & Plumelle, mor. liners, wrap. & spine preserved, s.-c.; G. Canapé copy. (HD. Jun.13; 98) Frs. 30,000

SCHYNVOET, Simon
- Voor Beelden der Lusthof-Cieraaden Zynde Vaasen, Pedastellen, Orangie Bakken, Blompotten en andere Bywerken. Amst., ca. 1704. 2 vols. in 1. Fo. 54 engraved plts., including titles & dedication ll., few plts. lightly stained, 19th. C. roan-bkd. bds., unc. (C. Dec.9; 144) *Marlborough.* £500

SCIENCE DES HIEROGLYPHIQUES
La Haya, 1736. 4to. Sewed. (DS. Feb.24; 2441) Pts. 26,000

SCLATER, Philip Lutley
- A Monograph of the Jacamars & Puff-Birds. Ill.:– J.G. Keulemans. L., priv. ptd., [1879-]82. 4to. Title with wood-engraved vig., 55 hand-cold. litho. plts., subscribers list supplied in facs., mod. hf. mor. (C. Nov.16; 291) *Walford.* £1,400

SCLATER, Philip Lutley & Salvin, Osbert
- Exotic Ornithology, Containing Figures & Descriptions of New or Rare Species of American Birds. Ill.:– Joseph Smit. L., [1866-]69. *(15) L.P.* Fo. 100 hand-cold. litho. plts., some light spotting, mainly affecting protective guards, maroon mor. by Bickers, gt. borders & panel, spine richly tooled with ornaments including crowns between raised bands, slightly faded; Lord Braybrooke bkplt. (S. Feb.1; 50) *Hill.* £14,500

SCLATER, Philip Lutley & Thomas, Michael R. Oldfield
- The Book of Antelopes. Ill.:– J. Smit & J. Wolf. L., 1894-1900. 4 vols. Lge. 4to. 100 col. litho. plts., three-qtr. mor. gt., ex-liby.; the Zoological Soc. of Phila. copy. (SG. Nov.3; 186) $4,500
- – Anr. Copy. 4 vols. 4to. 100 cold. litho. plts., few ll. loose, cl., spines slightly worn. (SG. Apr.26; 179) $3,000

SCLATER, William Lutley
See— JACKSON, Sir Frederick John & Sclater, William Lutley

SCLATER, William Lutley & Stark, A.
- The Birds of South Africa. 1900-06. 4 vols. Cl., bdgs. weak. (SSA. Sep.21; 395) R 290

SCOBELL, Henry
- A Collection of Acts & Ordinances. 1658. In 2 pts. Fo. Old cf., spine defect. (P. Sep.29; 374) *Parsloe.* £50

SCORESBY, William, 1789-1859
- Journal of a Voyage to the Northern Whale-Fishery. Edinb., 1823. *1st. Edn.* Hf.-title, 12 ills. on 5 plts., 2 folding maps, 1 plan, hf. cf., unc. (S. May 22; 461) *Bowes.* £210

SCOT or SCOTT, Reginald
- The Discoverie of Witchcraft. L., 1584. *1st. Edn.* Corners of title-p. reprd., sm. repairs to last lf., mor. gt. by Ramage. [STC 21864] (P. Mar.15; 205) *Fletcher.* £1,450
- – Anr. Edn. L., 1651. *2nd. Edn. 2nd. Iss.* 4to. Title supplied from anr. copy, a few sm. holes & tears, stained, cont. cf., rebkd. & recovered; Roland Winder bkplt., & his inscr. to Tom Morley. [Wing S 943] (S. Dec.20; 683) *Dawson.* £280
- Ontdecking van Tovery. Trans.:– Th. & G. Basso.

Beverwyck, 1638. Sm. 8vo. Slight margin staining or soiling, cont. vell. (VS. Dec.9; 1393) Fls. 475

SCOTLAND
- Scotland Illustrated in a Series of 80 Views ... Descriptive text:– Prof. Wilson. 1863. 4to. Mor. gt. (PD. May 16; 134) £52

SCOTS LAW TIMES
Edinb., 1952-81. 30 vols. Orig. cl. (PD. Aug.17; 11) £230

SCOTT, Baron
See— ESSUILE, Comte d' — SCOTT, Baron

SCOTT, Capt. A.N.
- Sketches in India; taken at Hyderbad & Secunder-abad. L., 1862. 101 orig. mntd. photos., some slight spotting, frontis. & front end-ll. loose, orig. cl., worn. (S. Mar.6; 46) *Browning.* £360

SCOTT, Alexander Walker
- Australian Lepidoptera & their Transformations. Ill.:– Harriet & Helena Scott. 1864. Orig. 3 pts. Fo. Hf. mor., slightly rubbed, wraps. bnd. in. (KH. May 1; 615) Aus. $800
- – Anr. Edn. Ill.:– Harriet & Helena Scott. L. & Sydney, 1864-90. 2 vols., bnd. from the orig. 8 pts. Fo. 1899 reprinted title to Vol. 1, 21 uncold. litho. plts., title stained & slightly wormed at lr. margin, margin tears to final plt., mor. gt., some orig. wraps. bnd. in. (CA. Apr.3; 146) Aus. $700

SCOTT, John, Engraver, 1774-1827
- The Sportsman's Repository. L., 1845. 4to. Engraved additional title, 37 plts., engraved title dampstained, lightly soiled, cont. cf.-bkd. bds. (CSK. Nov.4; 47) £190

SCOTT, John, of Berwick-upon-Tweed
- Berwick-upon-Tweed ... the History of the Town & Guild. 1888. Lge. 4to. Mor.-bkd. bds., unc. (PD. May 16; 158) £55

SCOTT, John, Poet, 1730-83
- Amwell, a Descriptive Poem. Ill.:– Godfrey. L., 1776. *1st. Edn.* 4to. Hf.-title, mod. qtr. parch. & marb. bds.; Frederic Dannay copy. (CNY. Dec.16; 310) $100

SCOTT, John A.
- The Defense of Gracchus Babeuf, before the High Court of Vendome. Ill.:– Thomas Cornell. Northampton, Gehenna Pr., 1964. *(300) numbered, sigd. by Leonard Baskin.* Lge. 4to. 21 etched ports., embossed titles, 20 ptd. on pale blue laid paper, sigd. in pencil by artist, blind-ruled crushed mor., unbnd. as iss., unopened, matching mor.-bkd. cl. folding-case. (SG. May 17; 93) $175

SCOTT, Joseph
- The United States Gazetteer, containing an Authentic Description of the Several States. Phila., 1795. *1st. Edn.* Sm. 12mo. Engraved title & 18 (of 19) folding maps, lacks last few ll. of text after Williamsburg, some foxing, stains, 1 map separated at fold, mod. bds., w.a.f. (SG. Jun.7; 37) $350

SCOTT, Kathleen L.
- The Mirroure of the Worlde. Roxb. Cl., 1980. Fo. Roxb. Cl. menu loosely inserted, orig. mor.-bkd. cl.; H.M. Nixon coll. (BBA. Oct.6; 118) *Maggs.* £110

SCOTT, Peter
- Morning Flight. L., [1935]. *(750) sigd.* 4to. Orig. cl. gt., d.-w., torn & soiled. (P. Dec.8; 149) *Traylen.* £60
- Wild Chorus. L., 1938. *(1250) numbered, sigd.* 4to. 88 plts. (24 cold.), ills., orig. buckram, unc., d.-w., s.-c. (S. Apr.10; 586) *Quaritch.* £220
- – Anr. Edn. L., [1938]. *(1250) numbered & sigd.* 4to. Orig. cl., some soiling. (CSK. Mar.9; 134) £65
- – Anr. Copy. 4to. Orig. cl. (SPB. Dec.13; 606) $125

SCOTT, Reginald
See— SCOT or SCOTT, Reginald

SCOTT, Capt. Robert Falcon
- The Voyage of the 'Discovery'. L., 1905. *1st. Edn.* 2 vols. Lacks maps in pockets at end, orig. cl.; pres.

copy to Sir Allen Young from E.H. Shackleton, Sep. 1907. (S. Mar.6; 66) *Quaritch.* £240
- – Anr. Copy. 2 vols. Cl. gt., rubbed; pres. copy from author to Miss. Adelaide Stickney, May 1907, Adelaide Livingstone bkplt. by Rex Whistler. (P. Jun.7; 43) £190
- – Anr. Copy. 2 vols. Lacks 2 pocket maps, orig. cl., rubbed; pres. copy to Sir Allen Young from E.H. Shackleton, Sep. 1907. (CSK. May 4; 67) £90
- – Anr. Copy. 2 vols. Cl. gt., rubbed & shaken. (P. Jun.7; 44) £50
- – Anr. Edn. L., 1905. *2nd. Imp.* 2 vols. Some foxing, bdg. not stated. (KH. May 1; 617) Aus. $160

SCOTT, Mrs. Sarah
See— MONTAGU, Lady Barbara & Scott, Mrs. Sarah

SCOTT, Thomas
[-] An Experimental Discoverie of Spanish Practises, or the Counsell of a Well-Wishing Souldier; A Second Part of Spanish Practises, or a Relation of more Particular Wicked Plots. 1623, 1624. *1st. Edn.* 2 pts. in 1 vol. 4to. Mod. mor.-bkd. cl. [NSTC 22077.5 & 22078.5; Sabin 78363 & 78364] (BBA. Jan.19; 121) *Quevedo.* £110
- Robert Earle of Essex his Ghost, Sent from Elizian: To the Nobility, Gentry & Communaltie of England. L.?, 1624. *1st. Edn. 1st. Iss.* 2 vols. in 1. Sm. 4to. Date on Vol. 2 title reading '1642' & with 'parti' reading on A2r, 1st. title-p. slightly frayed, some text soiling, later hf. roan, marb. bds. [STC 22084; Wing P3025] (SG. Apr.19; 168) $150

SCOTT, Dr. Thomas
See— SMITH, G. — SCOTT, Dr. Thomas

SCOTT, Sir Walter
- The Border Antiquities of England & Scotland. L., 1814. 2 vols. 4to. Engraved title, 91 plts., red str.-grd. mor. gt. (P. May 17; 8) *Cavendish Rare Books.* £85
- – Anr. Edn. L., 1814-17. 2 vols. in 1. 4to. Copperplt. engrs. (compl. as listed), later hf. mor. gt. (TA. Jun.21; 195) £56
- – Anr. Copy. 2 vols. 4to. Additional steel-engraved titles, 94 steel engrs., cont. hf. cf., gt.-stpd. with initials 'A' & 'E' & crown, leath. corners, gt.-decor. spines. (CBA. Dec.10; 397) $140
[-] The Fortunes of Nigel. Edinb., 1822. *1st. Edn.* 3 vols. 12mo. 6 pp. advts., orig. drab bds.; Fred A. Berne copy. (SPB. May 16; 343) $150
- Ivanhoe. Edinb., 1820. *1st. Edn.* 3 vols. 12mo. Hf.-titles (state 2), light spotting, orig. bds., unc., vol. 2 spine torn; cont. inscr. 'Kilravock Castle 1820'. (SPB. May 16; 129) $300
- Kenilworth. Edinb., 1821. *1st. Edn. 2nd. State.* 3 vols. 12mo. Sig. erased on hf.-titles, light spotting, orig. bds., mor.-bkd. s.-c.; A.L.s., Borowitz copy. (SPB. May 16; 130) $225
- The Lay of the Last Minstrel: a Poem. L., 1809. *10th. Edn.* Mor. gt., end-papers discold., fore-e. pntg. (SG. Feb.16; 267) $150
- Marmion: a Tale of Flodden Field. Edinb., 1811. *7th. Edn.* Mor. gt., fore-e. pntg. (SG. Feb.16; 268) $200
- Novels & Tales. 1819. 12 vols. Crimson hf. mor. (GM. Dec.7; 672) £80.
- Novels, Tales & Romances. Edinb., 1822-33. 41 vols. Cont. cf., spines gt.; Sir Ivar Colquhoun, of Luss copy. (CE. Mar.22; 269) £350
- Novels. — The Poetical Works. Ca. 1829; Edinb., 1861. 48 vols. cf. & 12 vols. 12mo. Hf. mor., spines gt. (LC. Oct.13; 378) £150
- Oeuvres. Trans.:– M. Defaucompret. 1863-72. 30 vols. Cont. hf. cf., some slight scratches. (HD. Dec.9; 183) Frs 2,200
- The Poetical Works. Paris, 1827. Cont. cf. gt., as a fore-e. pntg., w.a.f. (SPB. May 17; 739) $350
- – Anr. Edn. Edinb., 1833-34. 12 vols. 12mo. Bkplt., hf. mor. (GM. Dec.7; 376) £75
- – Anr. Edn. Ill.:– Corbould. L., 1862. Sm. 8vo. Loose in bdg., elab. blind-stpd. mor., fore-e. pntg. (SG. Nov.17; 234) $120
- Sämmtliche Werke. Danzig, 1825-29. 26 vols. (of 73). 12mo. 1 title not compl., cont. hf. leath. gt., slightly worn. (D. Nov.24; 2219) DM 800
- Tales of the Crusaders. Edinb., 1825. *1st. Edn.* 4

vols. Hf.-titles, light spotting, bds.; inscr., sig. of Henry Mackenzie in vols. 2-4. (SPB. May 16; 132) $600
[–] **Waverley; or, 'Tis Sixty Years Since.** Edinb., 1814. *1st. Edn.* 3 vols. Hf.-titles, later hf. cf., slightly rubbed. (BBA. Jun.28; 82) *Hannas.* £220
[–] – **Anr. Copy.** 3 vols. Hf.-titles, browned thro.-out, mod. hf. mor. (BBA. Jun.28; 83)
Hannas. £110
– – **Anr. Copy.** 3 vols. 12mo. A4 vol. 1, & A2 vol. 2, cancels, vol. 3 I7 with margin tear, light offsetting, orig. bds., unc., jnts. worn; Hugh Rose-Stockhausen copy. (SPB. May 16; 133) $6,250
[–] – **Anr. Copy.** 3 vols. 12mo. Hf.-titles, final imprint ll. in vols. 1 & 2, cont. cf., spines gt., rebkd., orig. spines preserved; Fred A. Berne copy. (SPB. May 16; 348) $175
– **Waverley Novels.** Edinb., 1818-32. *1st. Edns.* 61 vols. only (of 74). Vol. 3 of 'Tales of My landlord, Third Series' with quotation & not advts. on hf.-title verso, lacks 2 hf.-titles & 1 errata slip, 1 vol. lacks advts., slight spotting, unc., 32 vols. in orig. bds., others recased in later bds. (S. Dec.8; 120)
Lewis. £300
– – **Anr. Edn.** Edinb., 1822-25. 52 vols. Hf. cf. gt., a few vols. slightly rubbed. (P. Jun.7; 116) £160
– – **Anr. Edn.** Edinb., 1823-33. 48 vols. Engraved frontis. & additional 113 engraved plts., from imps. as iss. in pts. in 1842, mor. gt. by Kerr & Richardson, Glasgow. (PD. Aug.17; 154) £200
– – **Anr. Edn.** Edinb., 1829-33. 48 vols. 12mo. Cont. hf. mor. (CSK. Jul.27; 92) £220
– – **Anr. Copy.** 48 vols. Hf. cf. (PD. Aug.17; 22) £150
– – **Anr. Edn.** 1829-33. 50 vols. Crimson hf. cf. gt. (P. Nov.24; 124) £320
– – **Anr. Edn.** 1830-33. 48 vols. Hf. cf. gt. (P. Dec.8; 246) £120
– – **Anr. Edn.** Edinb., 1860. 48 vols. Hf. cf., spines gt.; the Hinton House copy. (LC. Oct.13; 467) £160
– – **Anr. Copy.** 48 vols. Hf. cf. gt., slightly rubbed. (P. Jun.7; 211) £80
– – **Anr. Edn.** Edinb., 1871. *Centenary Edn.* 25 vols. Cont. hf. cf., spines gt. (CSK. Jan.27; 3) £140
– – **Anr. Edn.** Edinb., 1876-77. *Liby. Edn.* 25 vols. 1 plt. detchd., gt.-ruled cf., elab. gt.-decor. spines, inner stpd. dentelles. (CBA. Dec.10; 404) $100
– – **Anr. Edn.** 1897. *Victoria Edn.* 25 vols. Gt.-panel. hf. cf. (PD. Feb.15; 54) £100
– **[Waverley Novels]. — The Poems & Ballads.** Boston, 1893-94; 1900. *'Edn. de Grande Luxe'.* *(500) numbered.* 48 vols.; 6 vols. Lge. 8vo. Unif. qtr. roan gt., partly unc., trifle rubbed. (SG. Mar.15; 141) $275
– **The Waverley Novels. — The Prose Works. — The Poetical Works.** 1829-33; 1834-36; 1833-34. 48 vols.; 28 vols.; 12 vols. 12mo. Orig. hf. cf., slightly worn. (BS. Nov.16; 104) £280
– **Works.** Edinb., 1821-25. 41 vols. only (of 42?). Cont. hf. mor.; from liby. of Luttrellstown Castle, w.a.f. (C. Sep.28; 1844) £280
– – **Anr. Edn.** Edinb., 1830-36. Approx. 81 vols. Sm. 8vo. Cont. hf. russ.; from liby. of Luttrellstown Castle, w.a.f. (C. Sep.28; 1845) £550
– – **Anr. Edn.** 1830-36. 30 vols. Hf. cf. gt. (P. Nov.24; 123) £120
– – **Anr. Edn.** 1830-80. 42 vols. Unif. hf. cf. gt. (PD. Oct.19; 182) £68
– – **Anr. Edn.** Edinb., 1877-79. *Ill. Edn.* 48 vols. some spotting, cont. hf. cf. (S. Oct.11; 364)
Findlay. £220

SCOTT, William Henry (Pseud.)
See— LAWRENCE, John 'William Henry Scott'

SCOTTI, R.
– **Helvetia Profana. Helvetia Sacra.** Macerata, 1642. 4to. Cont. leath., gt. inner & outer dentelle. (D. Nov.23; 1164) DM 450

SCOTTISH NATIONAL DICTIONARY
Ed.:– W. Grant. Edinb., n.d. *(2000) numbered.* 10 vols. 4to. This copy unnumbered, cl. (PD. Aug.17; 94) £175

SCOTTISH REGISTER: or General View of History, Politics, & Literature
Edinb., 1794-96. Vols. 1-6. Cont. cf., spines gt.; Sir

Ivar Colquhoun, of Luss copy. (CE. Mar.22; 270) £320

SCRATCHLEY, Sir Peter
– **Australian Defences & New Guinea** ... Ed.:– C. Kinloch Cooke. L., 1887. Frontis. a little foxed & lightly offset, orig. cl., slightly soiled. (KH. Nov.9; 696) Aus. $180

SCRIBE, Eugène
– **Oeuvres Complètes.** Ill.:– A. & T. Johannot & others. Paris, 1854. *New Edn.* 17 vols. 181 plts., most browned in margins, bds., red mor. spines gt. (S. Apr.10; 304) *Wade.* £130

SCRIBLERUS SECUNDUS (Pseud.)
See— FIELDING, Henry

SCRIBONIUS, Wilhelm Adolphus
– **Idea Medicinae** ... Lemgo, 1584. *1st. Edn.* Mod. bds. (R. Oct.12; 1475) DM 480

SCRIBONIUS LARGUS
– **De Compositio Medicamentorum Liber** ... Ed.:– Jo. Ruellius. Basel, 1529. *2nd. Latin Edn.* Prelims. lightly stained, last lf. slightly wormed in lr. corner, title stpd. in lr. margin, cont. limp vell., spine renewed with leath., very defect. (R. Oct.12; 1476) DM 400

SCRIPPS, John Looke
– **1860 Campaign. Life of Abraham Lincoln.** Foreword & Notes:– M.L. Houser. [Peoria, Illinois, Edward J. Jacob, 1931]. Mor.; Jacob's copy, sigd. by Houser. (LH. Apr.15; 371) $200
[–] **Life of Abraham Lincoln. Chapter 1. Early Life.** Chic., 1860. *1st. Printing, with advts. on p. 32 in double columns.* Bdg. not stated, s.-c. & box. (LH. Apr.15; 369) $1,200

SCRIPTORES HISTORIAE AUGUSTAE
– **Vitae Caesarum quarum Scriptores hi.** Ed.:– Erasmus. Basle, 1546. Fo. Cont. cf., decor., some scratches, jnts. reprd.; from Fondation Furstenberg-Beaumesnil. (HD. Nov.16; 128) Frs. 1,600
See— SUETONIUS TRANQUILLUS, Gaius & the Scriptores Historiae Augustae

SCRIPTORES REI MILITARIS
Rome, Eucharius Silber, 24 Oct. & 3 Nov. 1494. 5 pts. in 1 vol. 4to. Some spaces with guide letters, sm. wormhole in upr. margin not affecting text, vell. bds. by Henderson & Bisset; Stanitz coll. [BMC IV, 116; Goff S344] (SPB. Apr.25; 397) $850
[–] **Flavi Vegeti Renati ... De Re Militari ... Accesserunt Sex. Iuli Frontini Strategematon** ... Leiden, 1592. 2 pts. in 1 vol. Title-p. lightly soiled, few headlines cropped in index, cf.-bkd. bds., some wear; Stanitz coll. (SPB. Apr.25; 398) $250

SCROPE, William
– **The Art of Deer-Stalking; Illustrated by a Narrative of a Few Days' Sport in the Forest of Atholl** ... 1838. Tall 8vo. Some light foxing to prelims., cont. panel. cf. gt. (TA. Feb.16; 124) £95
– – **Anr. Edn.** L., 1839. *New Edn.* Additional engraved vig. title, 12 litho. plts., maroon str.-grd. mor. gt., emblematically tooled at corners & in compartments of spine, orig. cl. covers bnd. in. (S. Oct.4; 99) *Sawyer.* £210
– – **Anr. Copy.** Tall 8vo. Engraved frontis., vig. & ptd. titles, 11 tinted litho. plts., 1 relaid, cont. hf. mor., rubbed. (TA. Jun.21; 261) £60
– **Days & Nights of Salmon Fishing in the Tweed.** L., 1843. *1st. Edn.* 13 tinted or cold. litho. plts., including additional engraved title, mor. gt. by Rivièdre; Schwerdt bkplt. (S. Oct.4; 54)
Sawyer. £340
– – **Anr. Copy.** Some lithos. hand-cold., orig. gt.- & blind-decor. cl. (SKC. May 4; 1765) £150

SCUDDER, Samuel Hubbard
– **The Butterflies of the Eastern United States & Canada, with Special Reference to New England.** Camb. [Mass.], priv. ptd., 1889. *1st. Edn.* 3 vols. 4to. Sm. liby. stp. on title, maroon three-qtr. mor. gt., spines slightly worn, shelf mark on spines. (SG. Mar.22; 285) $400

SCULPTURA HISTORICO-TECHNICA
1770. *4th. Edn.* Sm. 8vo. Cont. spr. cf., spine slightly worn. (TA. Apr.19; 338) £50

SCULTETUS [or SCHULTES], Joannes
– **Armentarium Chirurgicum.** Venice, 1665. *5th. Edn.* Some slight foxing, cont. vell. (D. Nov.23; 627) DM 1,850

SEABY, B., Ltd.
– **Coin & Medal Bulletin.** 1962, 1964-81. 19 vols. Cont. cl. (S. May 1; 499) *Spink.* £160

SEAMAN, William (Trans.)
See— HOJAH EFFENDI, Sa'd Al-Din

SEARLE, Mark
– **Turnpikes & Toll-bars.** L., n.d. *(500) numbered.* 2 vols. 4to. Orig. hf. mor., d.-w.'s. (CSK. May 4; 50) £110
– – **Anr. Copy.** 2 vols. Plts., ills., hf. mor., scuffed, d.-w. (P. May 17; 285) *Allan.* £100
– – **Anr. Copy.** 2 vols. 4to. Orig. cl., d.-w.'s. (BBA. Dec.15; 340) *Vine.* £75

SEAVER, James E.
– **A Narrative of the Life of Mrs. Mary Jemison** ... Canandaigua, 1824. *1st. Edn.* 16mo. Title reprd. with a few letters in pen facs., mor. by Sangorski & Sutcliffe. (LH. Apr.15; 372) $160

SEAWARD, Sir Edward
– **Narrative of his Shipwreck.** Ed.:– J. Porter. 1831. 3 vols. Cl. (P. Oct.20; 149) £70

SEBA, Albert
– **Locupletissimi Rerum Naturalium Thesauri Accurata Descriptio.** Ill.:– F. de Bakker, A. van Buysen Jnr., De la Croix, & others; & P. Tanjé after L.F. Dubourg (engraved frontis.), J. Houbraken after J.M. Quinkhard (port.). Amst., 1734-65. 4 vols. Fo. Hand-cold. engraved frontis., hand-cold. port. of Seba, 449 hand-cold. etched plts. (175 double-p.), text in Latin & Dutch, titles ptd. in red & black with cold. vig., sm. flaw in plt. 36 Vol. I, plt. 23 Vol. III stained, some browning of text, cont. Dutch mott. cf., gt. floral borders & shaped panel enclosing lge. central ornament, gt. spines, slightly worn; each vol. inscr. on 1st. plt. by colourist 'J[oh] Fortuyn F. Hagae Com[itum]', loosely inserted in 1st. vol. orig. wash drawing for frontis., & uncold. imps. of frontis. & port. of Seba. (S. Feb.1; 51)
Wheless. £41,000
– – **Anr. Copy.** 4 vols. Fo. 449 plts. (many double-p.), plts. in 1st. 2 vols. cold. later, text in Fr., Latin & Dutch, cont. cf. (HD. Apr.13; 50)
Frs. 7,000
– – **Anr. Edn.** Amst., 1735. *1st. Edn.* Vol. II only. Fo. Cold. engraved title, 114 cold. engraved plts., including 40 double-p., text in Latin & Dutch, hf.-title, 2 plts. marginally stained, few plts. laid down, few margin repairs, faint pencil annots. on a few plts., partly erased inscr. on hf.-title, old red mor. gt. extra, worn; stps. of the Royal Entomological Soc. (SG. Nov.3; 188) $4,250

SECKENDORF, Veit Ludwig von
– **Commentarius Historicus et Apologeticus de Lutheranismo, sive de Reformatione Religionis Ductu Martini Lutheri.** Frankfurt, 1692. 3 pts. in 1 vol. Fo. Lacks frontis. & ports., cont. cf., spine worn at foot, ex-liby. (SG. Oct.27; 289) $150

SECOND, Albéric & Delord, Taxile
– **Les Métamorphoses du Jour.** Ill.:– 'J.J. Grand-ville'. Paris, not before 1854. *New Edn.* Lge. 8vo. Wood-engraved vig. title, 71 cold. wood-engraved plts., hf.-title, some foxing, qtr. cf. gt. extra, marb. bds., ptd. wraps. bnd. in. (S. Nov.3; 90) $450
– – **Anr. Edn.** Ill.:– 'J.J. Grandville'. Paris, [1865?]. Engrs. hand-cold., cl., as a collection, w.a.f. (CR. Jun.6; 170) Lire 700,000
– – **Anr. Edn.** Ed.:– C. Blanc. Ill.:– 'J.J. Grandville'. Paris, 1869. Col. frontis., 70 hand-cold. plts., qtr. mor. gt. (P. Nov.24; 47) *Finch.* £200
– – **Anr. Copy.** Frontis., 70 cold. plts., most on thick paper, sm. stains on 2 ll., cont. hf. chagrin, spine decor. (HD. Nov.29; 94) Frs. 2,500
– – **Anr. Copy.** Some stains at end, hf. red chagrin. (HD. Apr.11; 29) Frs. 1,800
– – **Anr. Copy.** Lge. 8vo. 70 cold. plts., cont. hf. chagrin, corners, spine decor. (HD. Mar.21; 156)
Frs. 1,200
– – **Anr. Copy.** Lge. 8vo. 70 col. plts., foxing, trace of old dampstain, publisher's hf. chagrin. (LM. Oct.22; 258) B. Frs. 9,000

SEDAINE, Michel Jean
[–] La Tentation de Saint-Antoine. Le Pot-pourri de Loth. Ill.:– Borel, engraved by Elluin. L., 1781. 2 pts. in 1 vol. Cont. spr. roan gt., spine decor. (HD. May 3; 145) *Frs. 1,900*

SEDDON, William
– Coal Mining Made Easy, Safe & Healthy. 1887. 4to. Orig. cl. gt., some wear. (P. Dec.8; 290) *Mallet. £70*

SEDENO, Juan
– Summa de Varones Illustres en la qual se contienen Muchas Sentencias y Grandes Hazañas ... Famosos Emperadores, Reyes y Capitanes. Toledo, 1590. Fo. Linen, corners. (DS. Dec.16; 2058) *Pts. 35,000*

SEDER, Anton
– The Plant in Creative & Industrial Art. Vienna, n.d. Fo. 82 plts., many repairs to margins, liby. stps. on title & plts., mod. cl. gt. (P. Mar.15; 43) *Walford. £95*

SEDER LESHALOSH REGALIM KE'MINHAG CARPENTRAS
Amst., 1759. Title in facs., lacks 3 p. special supp. for Lislois (as usual), margins frayed, browned, some staining & soiling, MS. poem on last lf. (blank), mod. blind-tooled leath. (S. Oct.25; 332) *Bragadin. £200*

SEDER MA'AMADOT
Venice, 1606. *1st. Edn. with commentary of Avraham Saraval.* 16mo. Soiled, margins trimmed close, affecting title border & running heads, 13, 51 & 10 lacking, other minor defects, early blind-stpd. cf., shabby, loose. (SG. Feb.2; 295) *$350*

SEDER [ME'AH] BERACHOT; Orden de Bendiciones
Amst., 1687. 12mo. In Hebrew & Spanish, lacks 1st. engraved title, slight staining, creased, red mor., elab. gt.-tooled, s.-c. (S. Oct.25; 333) *Moriah. £300*

SEDER OLAM ZUTAH. Chronicon Breve et Capita R. Mose ben Maiemon de Rebus Regis Messie ...
Paris, 1572. In Latin & Hebrew, some staining & spotting, vell.-bkd. bds.; Hochschule für die Wissenschaft des Judenthums stp. [Steinschneider 5873, 13] (SPB. Jun.26; 28) *$1,100*

SEDER TEFILAT HA'MINCHA EREV ROSH CHODESH
Venice, 1794. Last lf. torn & reprd. affecting 1 word, creased & soiled, inscr. on blank fly-lf., hf. leath., marb. paper bds., slightly worn. (S. Oct.25; 337) *Bragadin. £140*

SEDER TEFILOT LI'YEMEI SIMCHAT TORAH VE'CHUPAT HE'URIM ... Kefi Minhagei Anshe Shinigali-Cochin
Amst., 1769. *2nd. Edn.* Slightly soiled, hf. leath. (S. Oct.25; 342) *Jansen. £850*

SEDER TEPHILOT MINHAG ASHKENAZI
Venice, 1776-77. 24mo. Browned, cont. mor. gt., silver clasps. (S. Oct.25; 338) *Halprin. £360*

SEDLEY, Charles
– A Winter in Dublin. A Descriptive Tale. L., 1808. *1st. Edn.* 3 vols. 12mo. Hf.-titles, hf. cf. (GM. Dec.7; 366) *£150*

SEDULIUS, F. Henricus
– Historia Seraphica Vitae B.P. Francisci Assisiatis ... Ill.:– C. Galle, Collaert, de Mallery, & others, after P. de Jode. Antverpiae,. 1613. Fo. Title frontis. remntd., cont. monastic blind-stpd. vell., wood bds. (LM. Mar.3; 157) *B.Frs. 10,000*

SEEBASS, L. Alex
– Prakt. Anweisg. z. Behandlung u. Reparatur d. Thurmuhren. Quedlinburg & Leipzig, 1846. *1st. Edn.* Text slightly foxed & stained, plts. rather browned, cont. hf. linen. (HK. Nov.8; 752) *DM 620*

SEEBOHM, Henry
– The Geographical Distribution of the Family Charadriidae. L., [1887-88]. 4to. Some spotting, orig. cl. (SPB. Dec.13; 607) *$225*

SEETZEN, U.J.
– Reisen durch Syrien, Palästina, Phönicien, die Transjordan-Länder, Arabia, Petrarea u. Unter-Agypten. Ed.:– Fr. Kruse. Berlin, 1854-59. *1st. Edn.* 4 vols. in 2. 6 litho. plts., 3 folding litho. maps, cont. hf. linen. (BR. Apr.12; 204) *DM 430*

SEEWALD, R.J.M.
See— RINGELNATZ, Joachim [i.e. H. Bötticher] & Seewald, R.J.M.

SEFER HA-SHORASHIM IM NIGZARIN / Dictionarium Hebraicum ... ab ... Sebastiano Munstero recognitum, & ex Rabinis, prassertim ex Radicibus David Kimhi, auctum & locupletatum
Basel, 1539. Sm. 8vo. Cf. gt., worn, unidentified armorial gt. supralibros, spine restored at head, cover loose; Wilberforce Eames sig., Adolf Lewisohn copy. (SG. Feb.2; 90) *$600*

SEFER HATARAT NEDARIM, Mesirat Moda'ah, Seder Tashlich
Verona, 1827. Folding plt. of Shlomo Aron Cohen emblem (usually missing), short tear, staining, hf. leath., marb. paper bds., s.-c. (S. Oct.25; 343) *Maggs. £360*

SEFER HA-YASHAR/Or the Book of jasher; referred to in Joshua & Second Samuel
Trans.:– [Mordecai Manuel Noah]. N.Y., 1840. *1st. Edn.* Tall 8vo. Orig. cl., worn, spine chipped at head, end-papers browned. (SG. Feb.2; 6) *$350*

SEFER TEHILLIM
Venice, 1598. 32mo. 94 ll. (Habermann, di Gara calling for 86 only), 2 ll. torn at lr. corner with slight loss, mod. leath. (SG. Feb.2; 258) *$1,600*

SEGALEN, Victor
– Stèles. Pékin [Paris, 1914]. Elongated 8vo. Folding accordion text, 2 wood covers, joined by 2 ribbons. (HD. May 16; 99) *Frs. 1,800*

SEGAR, Sir William & Edmondson, Joseph
– Baronagium Genealogicum. L., [1764-]84. 6 vols., including supp. Fo. Vol. 1 lacks plt. 75, some browning & spotting, cont. mott. cf. gt., some wear, last vol. not unif. (S. Dec.8; 320) *Ferres-Walker. £380*

SEGARD, Sir William & Testard, F.M.
– Picturesque Views of Public Edifices in Paris. 1814. 4to. 20 hand-cold. circular aquatint plts., orig. bds., worn, rebkd. (CSK. Dec.16; 146) *£170*

SEGOING, Charles
– Armorial Vniversel contenant les Armes des Principales Maisons Estatz et Dignitez des plus Considerables Royaumes de l'Europe. Paris, 1679. Sm. fo. Wide margin, some slight spotting or browning, cont. leath., gt. spine & outer dentelle, bumped & slightly spotted. (HK. May 16; 1503) *DM 400*

SEGUIN, Lisbeth Gooch
– A Picturesque Tour in Picturesque Lands. 1881. *(300) on H.M.P.* 4to. 72 proof plts. on Japan paper, qtr. vell., defect. (P. Dec.8; 303) *Martinos. £160*
– – **Anr. Edn.** 1881. *(600) numbered.* Fo. Plts. & ills. on india paper, mntd., orig. parch., worn. (CSK. Jun.29; 50) *£55*
– Rural England. Ill.:– J.E. Millais, Arthur Hughes, Helen Allingham, & others. [1881]. *De Luxe Edn., (600) on H.M.P. with proofs of ills. on Japanese paper.* Lge. 4to. Orig. vell., elab. decor., mor. inlays, unc. (SKC. Jan.13; 2174) *£50*

SEGUR, Jos. Alex.
– Women: their Condition & Influence in Society. L., 1803. *1st. Engl. Edn.* 3 vols. Browned, cont. hf. cf. (BBA. May 23; 10) *Quaritch. £90*

SEGUY, E.-A.
– Bouquets et Frondaisons: 60 Motifs en Couleur. Paris, ca. 1925. Sm. fo. 20 pochoir-cold. plts., loose as iss. in cl.-bkd. pict. bd. folder, spine edges frayed, linen ties. (SG. Nov.3; 189) *$250*
– Papillons. Paris, ca. 1925. Sm. fo. 20 pochoir-col. plts., loose as iss., 1 plt. stpd. on recto, cl.-bkd. pict. bds., soiled. (SG. Aug.25; 325) *$600*
– Suggestions pour Etoffes et Tapis. Paris, ca. 1925. Fo. 20 pochoir-cold. plts., captions in Fr. & Engl., Loose as iss. in cl.-bkd. bd. folder, cl. ties. (SG. Aug.25; 326) *$250*

SEIDA UND LANDENSBERG, Franz Eugen Fhr. von
– Denkbuch der Franzoesischen Revolution ... 28 Apr. 1789 ... den 21 Januar. 1793; ... 21ten Januar 1793 ... den 9ten November 1799. Mermingen, [1815?]. 2 vols. in 1. Ob. 4to. Engraved titles & 82 plts., a few torn & reprd., spotted, cont. hf. cf., worn, w.a.f. (CSK. Mar.23; 89) *£130*

SEIDEL, H.
– Neuer Orbis Pictus in sechs Sprachen, oder Unterhaltendes und Belehrendes Bilderbuch für Kinder von jedem Alter. Nürnberg, 1821. *6th. Edn.* Ob. 16mo. 40 hand-cold. engraved plts., slightly cropped affecting some ills., 19th. C. bds., slightly worn; J.H. Krelage bkplt., van Veen coll. (S. Feb.28; 168) *£300*

SEIDEL, W.
– Yali und sein Weisses Weib. Ill.:– M. Pechstein. Berlin, ca. 1925. *(220) numbered.* Lge. 4to. Wide margin, some foxing, orig. hf. vell., cold. litho. paper, lightly bumped, worn & soiled, sm. scratches on covers, lr. cover paper torn. (HK. Nov.11; 3854) *DM 4,400*

SEIDL, J.G.
– Wanderungen durch Tyrol und Steiermark. Leipzig, n.d. 2 vols. Cont. hf. mor. (CSK. Dec.16; 72) *£110*

SEIDLITZ, Woldemar von
– Allgemeines Historisches Porträtwerk. Ed.:– H.A. Lier. München, 1884-90. 12 pts. in 5 vols. Lge. 4to. Some old spotting, orig. hf. leath., spines lightly bumped. (V. Sep.30; 2233) *DM 2,100*

SEILERN, Antoine
– Flemish Paintings & Drawings at 56 Princes Gate. L., 1955. 6 vols. 4to. Orig. cl., s.-c. (SI. Dec.15; 221) *Lire 480,000*

SEIROKU, Noma
– The Arts of Japan. Tokyo, [1975 & 1970]. 2 vols. Sm. fo. Bdg. not stated, 2nd. d.-w. lightly rubbed, 1st. vol. in orig. s.-c. (CBA. Jan.29; 269) *$100*

SEITZ, A.
– Die Gross-Schmetterlinge der Erde. Stuttgart, 1906-27. Lge. 4to. Some plts. stained & with sm. tears, loose in part wraps. (BR. Apr.12; 806) *DM 4,200*

SEITZ, Don Carlos
– Writings by & about James Abbott McNeill Whistler, a Bibliography. Edinb., 1910. *(350).* Orig. cl., slightly soiled. (BBA. Apr.5; 304) *Dawson. £60*

SEIXAS, James
– Manual [of] Hebrew Grammar for the Use of Beginners ... Andover, 1834. *2nd. Edn.* Tall 8vo. Mildly browned, orig. cl.-bkd. bds. (SG. Feb.2; 5) *$300*

SEIZ, Johann Christian
– Het Derde Jubeljaar der Uitgevondene Boekdrukkonst. Haarlem, 1740. Engraved title, 5 engraved plts. (1 folding), hf.-title, last errata lf., slightly browned, cont. vell. (BBA. Mar.7; 379) *Questor Books. £150*

SEJOUR DES MUSES (Le) ou la Cresme des Bons Vers
Rouen, 1627. *Orig. Edn.* Decor. red mor. by Capé. (HD. Mar.21; 93) *Frs. 4,000*

SELAVY, Rose (Text)
See— RAY, Man

SELBY, Prideaux John
See— JARDINE, Sir William & Selby, Prideaux John

SELCHOW, Felix [i.e. J.H. Meynier]
– Europa's Länder und Völker. Ein Lehrreiches Unterhaltungsbuch für die Gebildete Jugend. Berlin, 1827-28. *2nd. Edn.* 3 vols. in 2. 2 engraved frontis., pict. title-pp. & 28 plts., all hand-cold., 8 p. catalogue at end of Vol. 3, orig. ptd. bds., backstrips slightly soiled & worn; van Veen coll. (S. Feb.28; 156) *£320*
– – **Anr. Edn.** Berlin, 1828. 2 pts. in 1 vol. Minimal spotting, bds. (R. Nov.10; 2985a) *DM 520*

- - **Anr. Edn.** Stuttgart, 1832. *New Edn.* 3 pts. in 1 vol. Orig. bds., lacks spine, rubbed, old soiling. (V. Oct.1; 3967) DM 400

SELDEN, John
- **The Priviledges of the Baronage of England, When they Sit in Parliament.** 1642. Title reprd., some dampstaining, recent traditional-style cf. by Grace Bindings, Devon. (TA. Aug.18; 370) £50
- **Table-Talk.** 1689. *1st. Edn.* 4to. Disbnd. (TA. Oct.20; 299) £85

SELDWYLA PRESS
See— MARCHEN VON DEM FISCHER UN SYNER FRU

SELECT & IMPARTIAL ACCOUNT of the Lives, Behaviour & Dying-Words of the Most Remarkable Convicts ...
L., 1745. *2nd. Edn.* 3 vols. 12mo. Cont. mott. cf., rather blistered & worn. (SG. Feb.6; 72) $110

SELICHA KE'MINHAG ASHKENAZIM SHE'BE' ITALIA
Venice, 1712. *3rd. Edn. of epistle by Shlomo Alami Ibn Lachmish.* 4to. Title & 1st. 3 ll. from anr. copy, title worn & reprd., staining thro.-out, slightly creased, hf. leath., marb. paper bds. (S. Oct.25; 346) *Abramsky.* £200

SELICHOT LE'LEILEI ELLUL AD YOM HA'-KIPURIM MINHAG FERRARA
Pisa, 1780. 12mo. 8 ll., edges frayed, staining, discold., mod. bds. (S. Oct.25; 352) *Bragadin.* £140

SELICHOT MIKOL HA'SHANA MINHAG ASH-KENAZIM
Venice, 1548. 4to. Hebrew text with Old Yiddish instructions, censored but legible, sig. of censor on title, title defect. & reprd., some staining, discold., 2 prayers written on blanks, mod. blind-tooled mor. (S. Oct.25; 344) *Klein.* £650

SELIG, G.
- **Kurtzer u. Gründliche Anleitung zu einer Leichten Erlernung der Jüdischdeutschen Sprache.** Leipzig, 1767. *(Bound with:)* CALLENBERG, J.H. **-Jüdischdeutsches Wörterbüchlein** ... Halle, 1736. Together 2 works in 1 vol. Foxed & slightly stained, cont. hf. leath., lightly rubbed & bumped. (HK. Nov.9; 1807) DM 750

SELIGMAN, G. Saville & Hughes, Talbot
- **Domestic Needlework; its Origins & Customs throughout the Centuries.** L., [1926]. *(500) numbered.* Fo. Frontis. with minor margin repair, gt.-decor. cl., spine rather worn, shaken. (SG. Aug.25; 327) $150

SELIGMANN, Johann Michael
- **Sammlung Verschiedene Ausländischer und Seltener Vögel.** Nuremb., 1749-51. *1st. Edn.* Pts. 1 & 2 (of 9) in 2 vols. Fo. Pt. 2 lacks 1 plt., 1 plt. pt. 1 with short bkd. tear in lr. right corner, 6 plts. pt. 2 slightly stained, cont. leath. gt., restored. (R. Oct.12; 1919) DM 10,000
- - **Anr. Edn.** Trans.:– [Georg Leonhard Huth]. Ill.:– after Mark Catesby & George Edwards. Nuremb., 1749-64. 6 pts. only (of 9), in 2 vols. Fo. 2 additional engraved titles, port., hand-cold. folding map, 288 hand-cold. engraved plts., lacks plt. 5 in pt. 2 & plts. 57 & 75-105 in pt. 6, 1 engraved title with vertical crease, cont. hf. cf., slightly rubbed. (C. Nov.16; 294) *Davidson.* £5,000
- - **Anr. Copy.** 6 vols. bnd. in 3. Fo. 3 engraved frontis., 1 folding engraved map & 321 engraved plts. all cont. hand-cold., some foxing or browning, cont. panel marb. cf., spines gt., top & foot of spines a little defect., covers slightly rubbed, some jnts. weak, marb. gt. end-papers. (VS. Jun.7; 935) Fls. 25,000
- - **Anr. Edn.** Ill.:– after Mark Catesby & George Edwards. Nuremb., 1749-76. Fo. Collection of 120 hand-cold. plts. (36 from pt. 1, 34 from pt. 2, & 50 from pts. 6-9), no title or text, cont. vell. bdg., disbnd., as a collection of plts., w.a.f. (C. Nov.16; 295) *Davidson.* £1,800

SELLER, John
- **Atlas Coelestis.** Ca. 1677. 16mo. Engraved title, 15 double-p. celestial charts only, 13 plts. & tables, 1 torn with loss, lacks frontis. & all after I4, old cf., rubbed, w.a.f. (CSK. May 4; 44) £140
- **Atlas Minimus or a Book of Geography.** L., [1679]. 12mo. Frontis., engraved title-p., 53 maps, 1 folding, tears in 2 ll., last gathering a little loose, cont. cf., spine gt., worn; inscr. by Francis Sherwood, Oct. 1719. [Wing S2465?] (BBA. May 3; 250) *Archway.* £900

SELMA UNION HIGH SCHOOL
- **The Magnet.** Selma, Ca., 1928-31. Vols. XXI-XXIV. 4to. Containing 11 poems by William Everson, art leath. (SG. Mar.1; 132) $2,400

SELNECCER, N.
- **Theophania. Comoedia Nova, et Elegans, de Primorvm Parentvm Conditione, et Ordinvm sive Gradvvm in Genere Hvmano Institvtione.** Wittenburg, 1560. *1st. Edn.* Some old annots., stained, sewed. (HK. Nov.8; 339) DM 400

SEMANARIO CRISTIANO POLITICO DE MALLORCA
Palma, 1813. Nos. 26-57. 4to. Linen. (DS. Nov.25; 2610) Pts. 60,000

SEMANARIO DE AGRICULTURA Y ARTES. Por Marcelino Calero y Portocarrero
L., n.d. 1 vol. 4to. Linen. (DS. Mar.23; 2039) Pts. 150,000

SEMANARIO LITERARIO DE CARTAGENA
1787. Nos. 27-52, with 27 supps. 4to. Vell. (DS. Apr.27; 2661) Pts. 50,000

SEMEDO, Alvarez
- **Historie Universelle de la Chine.** Lyons, 1667. 4to. Hf.-title, last privilege lf., slightly browned thro.-out, fo. P1 torn, liby. stp. on title, cont. cf., worn. (BBA. Feb.23; 23) *Browning.* £65

SEMPERE Y GUARINOS, Juan
[–] **Descripción de los Ornatos Publicos con que la Corte de Madrid.** Ill.:– Marti & Giraldo, after Fontana de Vargas & others. Madrid, 1789. Sm. fo. 11 folding engraved plts., owner's inscr. on title, cont. cf., spine gt. (C. Dec.9; 145) *Quaritch.* £2,200
- **Historia del Lujo y de las Leyes Suntuarias de España.** Madrid, 1788. 2 vols. in 1. Linen. (DS. Mar.23; 2269) Pts. 32,000

SEMPLE, Miss
- **The Costume of the Netherlands.** L., 1817. 4to. Engraved title, 30 hand-cold. aquatint plts., some light spotting, cont. hf. mor., upr. cover detchd. (CSK. Sep.30; 158) £140
- - **Anr. Copy.** Fo. Mostly on paper wtrmkd. Whatman 1816, some light foxing, marb. end-papers, cont. hf. mor. gt., slightly worn & bumped. (HK. Nov.9; 1849) DM 1,600

SENATOR: or Clarendon's Parliamentary Chronicle ...
1790-1818. Vols. I-XXVII & a vol. of engraved ports. Unif. cont. tree cf., spines gt.; Sir Ivar Colquhoun, of Luss copy. (CE. Mar.22; 271) £280

SENCKENBURG, J. Chr. von
- **Stiftungs-Briefe zum Besten der Artzneykunst und Armenpflege** ... [Frankfurt], 1770. Lge. 4to. Some pp. slightly browned, cont. hf. linen, lightly rubbed & bumped. (HT. May 8; 580) DM 410

SENEBIER, Jean
- **Recherches sur l'Influence de la Lumiére Solaire pour métamorphoser l'air Fixe en Air Pur par la Végetation.** Genf, 1783. *1st. Edn. (Bound with:)* HUBER, F. & Senebier, J. **-Mémoires sur l'Influence de l'Air et de Diverses Substances Gazeuses dans la Germination de Differentes Graines.** Genf, an Ix [1801]. *1st. Edn.* 2 works in 1 vol. Cont. hf. leath., spine rubbed. (R. Oct.12; 1715) DM 900

SENECA, Lucius Annaeus
- **Oeuvres.** Trans.:– La Grange. Paris, 1795. 6 vols. Cont. marb. cf., decor. spines. (HD. Sep.22; 341) Frs. 1,400
- - **Anr. Copy.** 6 vols. Liby. stp. on frontis., tears, cont. spr. cf., decor. (SI. Dec.15; 89) Lire 450,000

- **Opera quae Extant Omnia.** Lyons, 1555. Little scoring, cont. elab. blind-stpd. pig, stained & a little worn, minor repair. (BBA. Jun.28; 176) *Spencer.* £125
- **Philosophi Opera quae existant omnia.** Ed.:– Iustus Lipsius. Antw., 1652. *4th. Edn.* Fo. Cf., corners worn, Mazarin arms. (HD. Feb.22; 210) Frs. 1,500
- **Sittliche Zuchtbücher.** Trans.:– Michael Herr. Strassburg, 1536. *1st. German Edn.* Fo. Minimal light browning, slight margin soiling, lf. with sm. tear at foot, cont. blind-tooled pig over wood bds., clasps. (R. Oct.11; 112) DM 1,900
- **Tragoediae Pristinae Integritati Restitutae.** Ed.:– D. Erasmus & others. [Paris, 1514]. Fo. Title restored & mntd. with loss of decor., margins of several ll. restored, last few ll. mntd. with loss of several words, including colophon, upr. margin trimmed, stained, cf.; bkplt. of W. Constable. (BBA. Jun.28; 175) *Whitby.* £75

SENEX, John
- **An Actual Survey of the the Principal Roads of England & Wales** ... N.d.-1742. *4th. Edn., 2nd. Edn.* 2 vols. in 1. Ob. fo. Engraved title & dedication, engraved map, 100 engraved road maps on 50 ll., some creasing to map edges, particularly towards end of Vol. 2, cont. limp leath., with folding flap; the Hinton House copy. (LC. Oct.13; 469) £130
[–] **Modern Geography: or All the Known Countries in the World.** T. Bowles, J. Bowles, & R. Sayer, [1760?]. Tall fo. 33 engraved maps & 1 plt. showing Solar System, including several on 2 sheets, joined & folding, MS. contents list in ink on front pastedown, maps hand-cold. in outl., several frayed or torn affecting engraved surface, some dust-soiling, cont. bds., defect., w.a.f. (S. May 21; 130) *Franks.* £850
- **A New General Atlas.** D. Browne & others, 1721. Fo. Ptd. title in red & black with inset engraved vig., 34 double-p. engraved maps & town plans, 13 full-p. plts. showing arms of subscribers, maps hand-cold. in outl., 1 or 2 short splits at centre-folds without loss of engraved surface, some discolouration, some ll. & maps detchd., cf.-covered bds., w.a.f. (S. May 21; 121) *Quaritch.* £2,000
- **The Roads Through England Delineated.** 1757. Engraved title, general map, 101 road maps on 51 sheets, 8 pp. preface & index, mod. hf. cf. gt. (P. Feb.16; 295) £240
See— OGILBY, John & Senex, John

SEPP, Jan Christian Andreas
- **Beschouwing der Wonderen Gods, in de Minstgeachte Schepzelen van Nederlandsche Insecten.** Amst., priv. ptd., 1728-1842. 1st. Series, Vols. I-VI only (of 8). Sm. 4to. 6 hand-cold. engraved titles, 300 hand-cold. engraved plts., cont. hf. cf., Vol. VI not quite unif. (C. Jun.27; 135) *Parkway.* £2,600
- - **Anr. Edn.** Amst., 1762. Vol. 1 only (6 pts.). 4to. 46 hand-cold. engraved folding plts., lacks additional engraved title, str.-grd. mor. gt., w.a.f. (C. Nov.16; 297) *Perceval.* £170
- - **Anr. Copy.** Vol. 1 (in 5 pts.). 29 hand-cold. copper-engraved plts., cont. mott. cf., spine worn. (CSK. Dec.2; 204) £130
- - **Anr. Edn.** Amst., 1762-1843. 6 vols. only (of 8, being 1st. Series: Vols. 1-6). 4to. 6 additional hand-cold. engraved titles, 300 hand-cold. folding plts., some heightened with silver or gold, mod. cf.-bkd. bds., unc. (C. Nov.16; 296) *Dillon.* £2,200
- - **Anr. Edn.** Amst., Priv. ptd., [1762-1860). *1st. Series.* 8 vols. 4to. Vol. 2 collation incorrect., 6 engraved frontis., 2 litho. frontis. & 300 engrs. & 100 litho. plts., all in cont. hand-col. but for vol. 8) on folding ll., 19th. C. hf. cl., spines defect. (VS. Jun.7; 936) Fls. 12,000
- **Nieuwe Geographische Nederlandsche Reise- en Zakatlas.** Amst., 1773. 74 cont. hand-cold. engraved maps, a little soiled or stained in places, cont. hf. cf. (VS. Jun.7; 992) Fls. 1,300
See— NOZEMANN, Cornelius & others

SEPT PECHES CAPITAUX
Ill.:– Detôuche. Lge. 4to. On vell. du Marais, 8 orig. etchings in col., hf. red mor., by Yseux Sr. de Thierry-Simier, corners, decor. spine, wrap., s.-c. (HD. Jan.30; 96) Frs. 1,450

SEPULVEDA, Juan Ginés de
– Historia de la Vida y Hechos [del] ... **Cardenal Don Gil de Albornoz** ... **Fundador de** ... **Colegio de S. Clemente de los Españoles de Bolonia.** Bolonia, 1612. 4to. Vell. (DS. Mar.23; 2719) Pts. 35,000

SERARIUS or SERRURIER, P.
– De Vertredinge des Heyligen Stadts, ofte Bewijs van 't Verval der Eerste Apostolische Gemeente. Mitsg. Chr. Entfelders Bedenckinge over de Veelderley Scheuringen. Amst., 1659. 2 pts. in 1 vol. 4to. Hf. vell. (VG. Nov.30; 904) Fls. 1,000

SERIYES
[–] Voyage de Dimo et Nicolo Stephanopoli en Grèce ... [1800]. 2 vols. Hf. chagrin, corners, by Loisellier, some scratches. (HD. Jun.29; 105) Frs. 1,600

SERLE, Percival
– A Bibliography of Australasian Poetry & Verse ... Melbourne, 1925. (250) numbered. Bds., qtr. cl., slightly marked. (KH. May 1; 622) Aus. $190

SERLIO, Sebastiano
– Il Primo [–quinto] Libro d'Architettura. Venice, 1551. 5 pts. in 1 vol. Fo. 2nd. pt. without title, owner's inscr. on 1st. title, some ll. badly frayed or torn, affecting text & plts., some dampstaining, vell. bds., rubbed. (S. May 1; 568) Weinreb. £150
– Livres I à V et Livre Extraordinaire. Venice, 1566. 4to. Some stains, mod. vell. (HD. Dec.15; 39) Frs. 1,100
– Regole Generali di Architettura ... Venice, 1544. Fo. (Bnd. at end:) – Il Terzo Libro ... 1 vol. Fo. 1 sig. detchd., cont. vell. (HD. Dec.15; 37) Frs. 3,000
– Tutte L'Opere Architettura et Prrospetiva [sic]. Venice, 1600. 2nd. Edn. 7 pts. in 1 vol. 4to. Cont. limp vell., lacks ties; from liby. of Earl Fitzwilliam. (C. Dec.9; 146) Harcourt-Williams. £800
– Von der Architectur Fünff Bücher ... Basel, 1608-09. 1st. German Edn. 5 pts. in 1 vol. Fo. Few sm. margin repairs, parch. (B. Oct.4; 692a) Fls. 2,300

SERMONES QUADRAGESIMALES (qui Anima Fidelis Inscribuntur) ...
[Venice, 1505]. Sm. 8vo. 1st. initial of table rubricated, lr. blank edge of colophon cut away, cont. blind-stpd. mor., very shabby; MS. bkplt. of 'Andreas 15 Sept. 1511'. (SG. Feb.9; 331) $150

SERMONES THESAURI NOVI DE TEMPORE
Strasburg, Martin Flach, 1497. Fo. Painted initials, 1st. initial painted in blue & red, lacks 4 corners, cont. stpd. roan over wood bds., richly decor., studs, turn-ins. defect.; from Fondation Furstenberg-Beaumesnil. [HC 5420] (HD. Nov.16; 54) Frs. 8,000

SERPENTIS PRESS
See— FONTANE, Theodor

SERRADIFALCO, Domenico lo Faso Pietrasanta, duca di
– Le Antichita della Sicilia. Palermo, 1834-36. 3 vols. only (of 5). Fo. 99 maps & plts., lacks 5 plts. in Vol. III, some with partial hand-colouring, orig. ptd. bds., rebkd. with mor., w.a.f. (C. Jun.27; 69) Shapero. £160

SERRANUS, J.
– Synonymorum Libellus. Nuremb., 1555. Lacks 1 lf. & last lf. (blank?), last 2 ll. with sm. hole, with loss of a few letters, stained in places, expecially at beginning & end. (HT. May 8; 210) DM 400

SERRE, Olivier de
– Le Théâtre d'Agriculture et Mesnage des Champs. Paris, 1804-05. 2 vols. 4to. Cont. hf. cf., some defects. (HD. Mar.19; 145) Frs. 2,200

SERRE DE RIEUX, J. de
– Les Dons des Enfans de Latone : la Musique et la Chasse du Cerf. Ill.:– Le Bas after Oudry. Paris, 1734. Minimal foxing, ex-libris, cont. style leath., ca. 1860, gt. spine & outer dentelle. (HK. Nov.10; 3108) DM 520

SERRES, Olivier de
– Le Théâtre d'Agriculture et Mesnage des Champs ... Genève, 1651. Latest Edn. 4to. Cont. vell. (HD. Nov.9; 194) Frs. 3,300
– – Anr. Edn. Ill.:– after Maréchal & Marillier. An

XII-XIV (1804-05). 2 vols. 4to. Hf. roan, spines faded. (HD. Jul.6; 81) Frs. 1,950

SERRURE, R.
See— ENGEL, A. & Serrure, R.

SERRURIER, P.
See— SERARIUS or SERRURIER, P.

SERUSIER, P.
– A.B.C. de la Peinture. 1921. Orig. Edn. Sewed; dedicated to Mme Druet. (HD. Jun.29; 187) Frs. 1,000

SERVANDONY, Chevalier
– Description des Fêtes Données par la Ville de Paris ... les Vingt-neuvième et Trentième Août Mil Sept Cent Trente-neuf. Ill.:– J.F. Blondel after Servandony. Paris, n.d. Tear in 1 plt. restored, in sheets, cont. red mor. gt. decor., Paris arms on covers, spines decor., stains restored. (LM. Oct.22; 144) B.Frs. 38,000

SESTINI, Dominique
– Voyage dans la Grèce Asiatique. Paris, 1789. 1st. Edn. (Bound with:) SHERLOCK, M. – Lettres d'un Voyageur Anglois. 1780. Together 2 works in 1 vol. Cont. cf.-bkd. paper bds., rubbed. (BBA. Jun.28; 248) Martinos. £240

SETHUS, Simeon
– Syntagma per Literarum Ordinem, de Cibariorum Facultate. Trans.:– Lilio G. Giraldi. Basel, 1538. Sm. 8vo. In Greek & Latin, title margin partly cut away, mod. vell. (SG. Oct.27; 291) $275

SETON, Ernest Thompson
– Studies in the Art Anatomy of Animals ... L., 1896. 1st. Edn. Tall 4to. 1 text crack, light foxing, orig. gt.-stpd. cl., covers lightly worn & scuffed at edges. (HA. May 4; 286) $120

SEUME, Johann Gottlieb
– Mein Sommer 1805. [Leipzig], 1806. 1st. Edn. Title slightly spotted, cont. marb. paper wraps., unc., corners lightly bumped. (HK. Nov.10; 2715) DM 400
– Sämmtliche Werke. Leipzig, 1826-27. 1st. Coll Edn. 12 vols. Cont. bds., bumped, some light defects., w.a.f. (HK. May 16; 2260) DM 400
– Spaziergang nach Syrakus. Braunschweig & Leipzig, 1803. 1st. Edn. Cont. hf. cf. gt. (C. Dec.9; 286) Kaldewey. £420
– – Anr. Edn. Ill.:– Böhm after Schnorr v. Carolsfeld. Braunschweig & Leipzig, 1805. 2 pts. in 1 vol. On vell., title with MS. owners mark, some slight foxing, later linen gt. (GB. May 4; 1455) DM 450

SEURE, Georges
– Monuments Antiques Relévés et Restaurés par les Architectes Pensionnaires de l'Academie de France à Rome. Paris, ca. 1910. 2 vols. Tall fo. 177 heliogravure plts., each liby.-stpd. on verso, loose in cl. folders, linen ties. (SG. May 3; 330) $100

SEUSS, Dr.
– The Seven lady Godivas. N.Y., [1939]. 1st. Edn. 4to. Godiva bookmark laid in, pict. cl., d.-w. (SG. Dec.8; 324) $100

SEUTTER, Matthias
– Atlas Novus indicibus instructus oder neuer mit Wort Registern versehener Atlas. Vienna, 1736. Fo. Double-p. dedication, maps hand-cold., 2 maps with light defects. in outer margin, 1 map torn & reprd., cont. leath., bumped. (SI. Dec.15; 90) Lire 4,800,000
– Taschenatlas. Augsburg, ca. 1740. Late 19th. C. bds. (HK. May 15; 669) DM 550

SEVERINUS, Marcus Aurelius
– Vipera Pythia. Patavii, 1651. 4to. Bordeaux mor., by Montserat, mosaic decor., decor. spine, s.-c. (HD. Dec.9; 84) Frs. 4,000

SEVIGNE, Marie de Rabutin Chantal, Marquise de
– The Letters. Intro.:– A. Edward Newton. Phila., 1927. 'Carnavalet' Edn. (1550). 7 vols. Lev. mor., gt. borders, upr. covers with Sevigne arms, gt. spines in 4 compartments, gt. turn-ins, partly unc. (CNY. Dec.17; 601) $380
– Lettres. Paris, 1806. New Edn. 8 vols. Near-cont.

mor. gt., spine lightly faded. (CSK. Jan.27; 43) £180
– Lettres de Madame de Sévigné, de sa Famille, de ses Amis. Ill.:– Deveria. Paris, 1823. 12 vols. Cont. hf. sheep, decor. spines. (HD. Sep.22; 342) Frs. 1,500
– Lettres Nouvelles de Madame la Marquise de Sévigné à Madame la Comtesse de Grignan, sa Fille. 1754. Reprint of 1734 Edn. 2 vols. 12mo. Cont. red mor., later arms of Alexandre de La Rochefoucauld. (HD. Apr.13; 52) Frs. 3,000
– Recueil des lettres à Madame la Comtesse de Grignan, sa Fille. Ill.:– Cheveau & Petit. Paris, 1738. New Edn. 6 vols. 12mo. Sm. wormholes, cont. cf., gt. decor., decor. spines. (HD. Dec.9; 85) Frs. 2,000
– – Anr. Edn. Paris, 1763. 8 vols. Sm. 12mo. Cont. marb. cf., spines decor. (HD. Mar.19; 147) Frs. 1,300
– – Anr. Edn. Paris, 1774. 8 vols. 12mo. Cont. marb. cf., spines decor., several corners & turn-ins worn; from Château des Noës liby. (HD. May 25; 77) Frs. 2,600
– – Anr. Edn. Paris, 1785. 9 vols. 12mo. Lacks hf.-titles of Vols. 8 & 9, cont. cf., spines gt., lacks 5 vol. no. labels. (S. Mar.20; 811) Blanko. £100

SEWARD, Anna
– Letters Written between the Years 1784-1807. Edinb., 1811. 6 vols. Cont. mott. hf. cf. (BBA. Jul.27; 135) Quaritch. £60

SEWEL, Willem
– Volkomen Woordenboek der Nederduitsche en Engelsche Taalen. Ed.:– E. Buys. Amst., 1766. 2 vols. 4to. Browned, cont. hf. cf. (VG. Sep.14; 1059) Fls. 500

SEXTON, Anne
– Selected Poems. L., 1964. Cl., pict. postcard mntd. on upr. pastedown; inscr., with autograph correction & annot. (SG. Mar.1; 516) $275

SEXTON, J.J. O'Brien
See— BINYON, Robert Lawrence & Sexton, J.J. O'Brien

SEXTON, R.W.
– American Commercial Buildings of Today. N.Y., [1928]. 1 vol. Lge. 4to. Cl., spine ends worn, shaken. (With:) – American Apartment Houses, Hotels & Apartment Hotels of Today. N.Y., [1929]. 1 vol. Lge. 4to. Cl., spine ends worn. (With:) – The Logic of Modern Architecture. N.Y., [1929]. 1 vol. Lge. 4to. Cl. (SG. Aug.25; 328) $130

SEYBOLD, Johann Georg
[–] Versuch eines Elementarbuches für Kinder durch Abbildung der Merkwürdigsten Dinge. Nürnberg, 1770. Ills. captioned in German, Latin, Fr. & Italian, some ll. slightly browned, cont. cf., lacks most of backstrip, paper added to covers, upr. jnt. reprd.; van Veen coll. (S. Feb.28; 170) £450

SEYD, Ernest
– California & its Rescources. L., 1858. 1st. Edn. 2 engraved folding maps, 22 plts. on 18 sheets, orig. cl. gt., rubbed; the Rt. Hon. Visc. Eccles copy. (CNY. Nov.18; 251) $240

SEYMOUR, Edward
See— STREET, George Edmund & Seymour, Edward

SFORNO, Ovadiah
– Be'ur Al Hatorah. – Be'ur Shir Ha'Shirim Ve'Kohelet. Venice, 1567. 1st. Edns. 2 works in 1 vol. 4to. 2nd. title in facs., owners' stps. on 1st. title, edges frayed, staining, browned, some worming affecting some letters, last lf. of 2nd work reprd., trimmed, mod. mor. (S. Oct.25; 357) Klein. £200
– Be'ur Al Sefer Tehilim. Venice, 1586. 1st. Edn. 4to. Some inner margins reprd. with loss of words, staining, trimmed, hf. leath., marb. paper bds. (S. Oct.25; 358) Klein. £800

SGRILLI, Bernardo Sansone
– Descrizione della Regia Villa ... di Pratolino. Ill.:– Stefano della Bella. [Flor., 1742]. Fo. Folding plan, 6 double-p. plts. (in early state, with nos. added by hand), faint margin dampstain, orig.

wraps., Prince of Liechtenstein ex-libris. (C. Dec.9; 147) *Hedworth.* £2,200

SHABTAI BASS
- **Siftei Chachamim.** Frankfurt, 1712. *1st. Edn.* 4to. Lightly stained, trimmed, vell., w.a.f. (S. Jul.3; 174) £130

SHABTAI COHEN
- **Siftei Cohen.** Cracow, 1647. *1st. Edn.* 1 vol. only. Fo. Lacks title-p., slight traces of worming, some browning, cont. stpd. cf. over bds., very rubbed, traces of clasps. (SPB. Feb.1; 35) $700

SHACKLETON, Sir Ernest Henry
- **The Antarctic Book, Winter Quarters 1907-1909.** 1909. *(300) sigd. by all members of the shore party.* 4to. Some slight spotting, orig. hf. vell. gt. (P. Jun.7; 47) £580
- **The Heart of the Antarctic, being the Story of the British Antarctic Expedition 1907-1909.** L., 1909. 2 vols. 2 ll. of sigs. of members of the expedition, folding maps in pocket (not included in known edns.), vell. gt.; pres. copy from author to P. Brocklehurst 'in remembrance of all his help on the Expedition', Nov. 1909, Brocklehurst bkplt. (P. Jun.7; 48) £700
- - **Anr. Copy.** 2 vols. 3 folding maps & panorama in pocket at back Vol. 2, orig. cl., spines soiled. (CSK. Feb.10; 182) £55
- - **Anr. Copy.** 2 vols. Orig. cl., marb. end-pp., some wear. (JL. Jul.15; 351) Aus. $110
- - **Anr. Edn.** Phila., 1909. *1st. Amer. Edn.* 2 vols. Bdg. not stated, backstrips worn & wrinkled, sewing weakening. (KH. May 1; 624) Aus. $140
- **South, the Story of Shackleton's Last Expedition, 1914-17.** 1919. *1st. Edn.* Cl., d.-w. (P. Jun.7; 51) £280

SHACKLETON, Sir Ernest Henry (Ed.)
See— SOUTH POLAR TIMES, The

SHADWELL, Thomas
- **The Amorous Bigotte.** L., 1690. *1st. Edn.* 4to. Title torn & reprd. with slight loss of text, mod. mor. by Sangorski & Sutcliffe. [Wing S2835] (BBA. May 3; 175) *Rhys Jones.* £75
- **Bury-Fair, a Comedy.** L., 1689. *1st. Edn.* 4to. Mod. hf. lev. mor., new end-papers. (CBA. Dec.10; 408) £110
- **Epsom-Wells. A Comedy.** 1673. *1st. Edn.* 4to. Epilogue lf., a few upr. margins shaved, mor. by Sangorski & Sutcliffe. [Wing S2843] (BBA. Jan.19; 133) *Sutherland.* £100
- **The Humorists, a Comedy.** 1671. *1st. Edn.* 4to. Lacks A1 (blank), some stains, mor. by Sangorski & Sutcliffe. [Wing S2851] (BBA. Jan.19; 132) *Maggs.* £140
- **The Scowrers. A Comedy.** 1691. *1st. Edn.* 4to. Advt. lf., mod. red hf. mor. [Wing S2872] (BBA. Jan.19; 136) *Maggs.* £80
- **The Squire of Alsatia.** L., 1688. *1st. Edn.* Sm. 4to. Some staining, mod. cf.-bkd. marb. bds. [Wing S2874] (S. Dec.8; 29) *Sutherland.* £140
- **The Volunteers, or the Stock-Jobbers. A Comedy.** 1683. *1st. Edn.* 4to. Natural flaw affecting a few letters, lr. margins shaved, mor. by Sangorski & Sutcliffe. [Wing S2885] (BBA. Jan.19; 137) *Maggs.* £85
- **The Woman-Captain: A Comedy.** 1680. *1st. Edn.* 4to. Mod. mor.-bkd. cl. [Wing S28887] (BBA. Jan.19; 134) *Maggs.* £140

SHAFFER, Ellen
- **Nuremberg Chronicle: A Pictorial World History from the Creation to 1493. A Monograph.** Los Angeles, 1950. *(300) numbered, with an orig. lf. from the Augsburg 1497 Edn.* Sm. fo. Publisher's advertising leaflet laid in, pict. cl. (SG. Sep.15; 250) $280
- - **Anr. Edn.** Los Angeles, Plantin Pr., for Dawson's Book Shop, 1950. *(300) numbered, sigd. by author & Dawson's proprietors.* 4to. Reproductions, lf. from original Augsburg Latin edn. of 1497 tipped to hf.-title, pict. cl. (SG. May 17; 277) $200

SHAFTESBURY, Anthony Ashley Cooper, Earl of
- **Characteristicks of Men, Manners, Opinions, Times.** B'gham., 1773. 3 vols. Cont. tree cf. gt.;

Charles Ramus bkplt. (S. Dec.13; 395) *Temperley.* £170
- - **Anr. Edn.** B'gham., 1773. '5th. Edn.'. 3 vols. Cont. cf., spines gt., slightly rubbed. (BBA. Nov.30; 231) *Weininger.* £120

SHAKESPEARE, Sir Geoffrey
- **Let Candles Be Brought In.** L., [1949]. Cl., slightly scuffed; pres. copy from author to Winston Churchill, with his & R.S. Churchill's bkplts. (LH. Jan.15; 257) $100

SHAKESPEARE, William
[Separate Pieces]
- **Antony & Cleopatra.** Ill.:– Paul Avril. Paris, Société des Beaux Arts, ca. 1900. *Edn. des Deux Mondes. (20) lettered on Japan vell.* 4to. Plts. & text engrs. in 3 states (plain, India-proof & cold.), all (excepting 1 state of the text engrs.) with vig. remarque, orig. lev. gt., cold. mor. inlays, elab. gt.-decor. dentelles, lev. doubls., upr. doubl. with inlaid oval hand-cold. engraved vig. on vell., moire grosgrain cl. liners, partly unc. (SG. Feb.16; 290) $900
- - **Anr. Edn.** Ill.:– M. Ludwig. München, 1923. *(146) on Bütten.* 4to. Printers mark sigd. by artist, hand-bnd. orig. vell., gt. spine, cover & inner dentelle. (H. Nov.24; 1854) DM 420
- - **Anr. Edn.** Ill.:– Mary Grabhorn. San Franc., Grabhorn Pr., 1960. *(185).* 1 vol. Fo. Paper bds. (*With:*) - **The Tempest.** Ill.:– Mary Grabhorn. San Franc., Grabhorn Pr., 1951. *(160).* 1 vol. Fo. Linen-bkd. decor. paper bds. (LH. Sep.25; 391) $350
- - **Anr. Edn.** Intro. Essay:– Keith Please. Ill.:– Ronald King. [Guildford], Circle Pr., 1979. *1st. Edn. (300) numbered sigd. by artist.* Fo. On Velin Cuve Rives Blanc paper, unsewn loose folded sheets, as iss., untrimmed, all laid into cl.-covered fold-down box, mor. side edges & interlocking cover, orig. card. shipping box. (HA. Feb.24; 234) $120
- **As You Like It.** Ill.:– H. Thomson. N.d. *Ltd. Edn., sigd. by artist.* 4to. Vell. gt., lacks ties. (P. Apr.12; 309) *Joseph.* £55
- - **Anr. Copy.** 4to. Orig. vell. gt., lacks ties. (P. Feb.16; 288) £50
- - **Anr. Copy.** 4to. Vell., minor soiling, lacks ties. (KH. Nov.8; 246) Aus. $100
- **The Comedie of Errors.** [1632]. Extracted from the 2nd. Fo. Edn. Fo. Mod. panel. cf. gt. (P. Apr.12; 59) *Chelsea Rare Books.* £100
- **Hamlet.** Ill.:– S. Frank. [Berlin, 1920]. *(35) De Luxe Edn.* 4to. Printers mark sigd., on Bütten, orig. hand-bnd. vell., gt. spine, cover & inner dentelle, etched end-papers & doubls., orig. pict. vell. s.-c., copperplt. inset. (H. Nov.24; 1510) DM 900
- - **Anr. Edn.** Ed.:– J. Dover Wilson. Ill.:– E.G. Craig. Weimar, Cranach Pr., 1930. *Engl. Edn. (7) trade De Luxe Edn. on vell. with 3 supp. sigd. woodcuts on white & yellow Jap. & on vell.* Fo. Some ll. from series on yellow Jap. with light spots, hand-bnd. burgundy mor., mor. portfo., decor. spine, covers, inner & outer dentelles, vell. doubl., by W.H. Smith & Son Ltd.; Hauswedell coll. (H. May 24; 734) DM 67,000
- - **Anr. Edn.** Ed.:– J. Dover Wilson. Ill.:– Eric Gill (title) & E.G. Craig (wood engrs.). Weimar, Cranach Pr., 1930. *(300).* Fo. Gt.-lettered hf. holland & bds., notes separately bnd. in wraps. & laid in pocket on rear pastedown, box; T.L.s from Harry Kessler & Emery Walker laid in, announcements for this & an earlier (cancelled) edn. laid in. (CBA. Nov.19; 110) $4,000
- [-] - **Anr. Edn.** Ill.:– V. Angelo. Mount Vernon, Peter Pauper Pr., n.d. 4to. Hf. cl. & decor. bds., box lightly rubbed, spine slightly faded; the V. Angelo copy, with his sig. on colophon. (CBA. Oct.1; 343) $130
- **Hamlet Prinz von Dänemark.** Ill.:– O. Wirsching. Dachau, [1920]. *(70) numbered on Bütten.* Orig. leath., spine slightly faded. (HK. May 17; 2702) DM 440
- **Hamlet. — Othello. — The Merchant of Venice.** L. & N.Y., 1895; 1896; n.d. 3 vols. 12mo. Orig. limp leath., cl. folding case; 1st. & 3rd. vols. sigd. by Ellen Terry, with deletions, corrections & stage directions in portions of each vol. in Terry's hand, silk playbill including scene from Merchant of Venice to be performed by Terry & Henry Irving & 3 other playbills laid in case. (PNY. Dec.1; 120) $300

- **King Lear.** Ill.:– Oscar Kokoschka. Ganymed, 1963. *(279) numbered & sigd. by artist, with an additional sigd. litho.* Fo. This copy unnumbered, prospectuses for this book, 'Saul & David', 'The Odyssey', & 'Hellas & Apulia' loosely inserted, orig. vell., unc., s.-c. (S. Nov.21; 27) *Rota.* £320
- **Lucrece.** L., Doves Pr., 1915. *(175).* Vell. (P. May 17; 56) *Sawyer.* £150
- **Macbeth.** Ill.:– Mary Grabhorn. San Franc., Grabhorn Pr., 1952. *(180).* 1 vol. Fo. Cf.-bkd. decor. paper bds. (*With:*) - **Julius Caesar.** Ill.:– Mary Grabhorn. San Franc., Grabhorn Pr., 1954. *(180).* 1 vol. Fo. Red mor.-bkd. decor. paper bds. (LH. Sep.25; 394) $300
- - **Anr. Copy.** Fo. 2nd. plt. sigd. by artist, prospectus & cancelled print loosely laid in, light soiling & offset to end-papers, hf. mor. & decor. bds., slight rubbing, head of spine torn. (CBA. Nov.19; 232) $200
- - **Anr. Edn.** Ill.:– M. Gromaire. Paris, 1958. *(200) numbered & sigd. by artist.* Fo. Loose as iss. in orig. wraps., cl.-bkd. bd. folder, s.-c. (BBA. Jun.14; 217) *Makiya.* £230
- - **Anr. Edn.** Ill.:– Ronald King. Circle Pr., 1970. *(150) numbered & sigd. by artist.* Lge. fo. Each print captioned & initialled by artist, unbnd. as iss. in orig. folder & s.-c. (S. Nov.22; 333) *Temperley.* £130
- **A Midsummer-Night's Dream.** Ill.:– A. Rackham. L. & N.Y., 1908. *1st. Edn. ill. Rackham. Ltd. Iss.* 4to. Printer's mark sigd. by aritist, orig. vell., defect. (H. Nov.24; 1950) DM 820
- - **Anr. Edn.** Ill.:– Arthur Rackham. 1908. 4to. Cont. hf. cf., by Bayntun, gt.-decor. spine, partly untrimmed. (TA. Oct.20; 182) £75
- - **Anr. Copy.** 4to. Orig. gt.-decor. cl., slightly soiled. (SKC. Mar.9; 1805) £65
- - **Anr. Copy.** 4to. Cl. gt. (HBC. May 17; 142) £52
- - **Anr. Edn.** Ill.:– W. Heath Robinson. 1914. 4to. Cl., d.-w. (P. Mar.15; 370) *Henderson.* £80
- - **Anr. Copy.** 4to. Orig. decor. cl., unopened. (SKC. Mar.9; 1809) £50
- - **Anr. Copy.** L.P., minor soiling to title, lacks front free end-paper, hf. buckram & cl., lightly soiled, corners worn, upr. portion of d.-w. laid in loose. (CBA. Aug.21; 562) $110
- - **Anr. Edn.** Ill.:– Arthur Rackham. L., [1919]. Some slight foxing & darkening, ink inscr. on front free end-paper, gt.-decor. cl., rubbed, corners bumped, gt. fading. (CBA. Aug.21; 527) $150
- **Othello.** Ill.:– Mary Grabhorn. San Franc., Grabhorn Pr., 1956. *(185).* 1 vol. Fo. Red mor.-bkd. decor. paper bds. (*With:*) - **King Lear.** Ill.:– Mary Grabhorn. San Franc., Grabhorn Pr., 1959. *(180).* 1 vol. 4to. Linen-bkd. decor. cl. bds. (LH. Sep.25; 393) $450
- **Romeo & Juliet.** Ill.:– J. Wagrez & Louis Titz. Paris, Société des Beaux Arts, ca. 1900. *Edn. des Deux Mondes. (20) lettered on Japan vell.* 4to. Plts. & text engrs. in 3 states (plain, India-proof & cold.), all (excepting 1 state of the text engrs.) with vig. remarque, orig. lev. gt., cold. mor. inlays, elab. gt.-decor. dentelles, lev. doubls., upr. doubl. with inlaid oval hand-cold. engraved vig. on vell., moire grosgrain cl. liners, partly unc. (SG. Feb.16; 291) $950
- **Seven Ages of Man.** Ill.:– Henry Alken. L., 1824. Ob. 4to. Plts. hand-cold., orig. wraps., some spotting & creasing, spine carefully reprd. (SPB. Dec.13; 769) $150
- **Ein Sommernachtstraum.** Trans.:– A.W. v. Schlegel. Frankfurt, Kleukens Pr., 1923. *(250) numbered on Bütten.* 4to. Orig. vell., gt. outer dentelle. (HK. May 17; 2890) DM 850
- **Le Songe d'une Nuit d'Été.** Ill.:– Arthur Rackham. 1909. 4to. On japan, no bdg. stated. (HD. Jun.29; 129) Frs. 1,200
- **The Taming of the Shrew.** Ill.:– Valenti Angelo. Palo Alto, Grabhorn Pr., 1967. *(375).* 1 vol. Fo. Decor. linen. (*With:*) - **The First Part of Henry the Fourth.** Mary Grabhorn. San Franc., Grabhorn Pr., 1961. *(180).* 1 vol. Fo. Linen-bkd. decor. paper bds. (LH. Sep.25; 390) $275
- - **Anr. Copy.** Fo. Decor. linen. (CBA. Nov.19; 268) $120
- **The Tempest.** Ill.:– Edmund Dulac. [1908]. *(500) sigd. by artist.* 4to. Vell. gt., lacks ties. (P. Dec.8; 369) *Joseph.* £180

SHAKESPEARE, William -*Contd.*

- - **Anr. Edn.** Ill.:- Edmund Dulac. [1908]. *(550) numbered & sigd. by artist.* 4to. Some foxing, orig. gt.-decor. vell., partly untrimmed, soiled on spine, lacks ties. (TA. Mar.15; 416) £80
- - **Anr. Edn.** Montagnola di Lugano, Jul. 1924. *(224) on Bütten.* Fo. Orig. vell., spine slightly faded, orig. bd. s.-c., lightly bumped. (HK. Nov.11; 3838) DM 2,900
- - **Anr. Edn.** Ill.:- Arthur Rackham. 1926. 4to. Orig. cl. gt., slightly damp spotted, orig. d.-w. slightly soiled. (TA. Mar.15; 421) £64
- - **Anr. Copy.** 4to. Orig. cl. gt., slightly soiled d.-w. (TA. Jun.21; 593) £54
- - **Anr. Edn.** Ill.:- Willi Baumeister. Stuttgart & Calw, 1946-47. *De Luxe Edn., (100) numbered.* Fo. Sigd. orig. litho., printer's mark sigd. by artist, orig. pict. linen. (GB. Nov.5; 2267) DM 800
- - **Anr. Edn.** Ill.:- W. Baumeister. Stuttgart & Calw, [1947]. *1st. Edn. (90) with sigd. litho.* Fo. Printers mark sigd. by artist, lightly browned, orig. hf. linen, 2 sm. faults in spine with sm. tear. (H. Nov.24; 1350) DM 770
- - **Anr. Edn.** Ill.:- E. Dulac. N.d. *(500) numbered & sigd. by artist.* 4to. Vell. gt., slightly soiled, lacks ties. (P. Mar.15; 364) *Marks.* £180
- - **Anr. Copy.** 4to. 40 mntd. cold. plts., orig. vell., lightly soiled, lacks ties. (CSK. Oct.21; 90) £170
- **La Tempête.** Trans.:- André du Bouchet. Ill.:- after Léonor Fini. Paris, 1965. *(200) numbered. (50) on vélin de Rives, sigd. by trans. & artist, with suite of ills.* Fo. Leaves, orig. ill. wrap., unc., box. (SM. Mar.7; 2326) Frs. 6,000
- **Twelfth Night.** Ill.:- W. Heath Robinson. L., [1908]. *(350) numbered & sigd. by artist.* 4to. This copy numbered '0000', orig. vell. gt., partly unc., slightly discold., lacks ties. (S. Dec.20; 587) *Rosenblatt.* £150
- - **Anr. Copy.** 4to. Vell. (SSA. Jul.5; 359) R 260
- **Venus & Adonis.** L., 1602 [but 1608?]. *9th. Edn.* Sm. 8vo. 27 ll., lacks final blank, 19th. C. hard-grd. mor. by Hatton of Manchester, Earl of Macclesfield arms gt. on upr. cover; Macclesfield crest blind-stpd. on title & A2, Viscount Parker copy. [STC 22360a] (C. May 30; 170) *Maggs.* £120,000
- - **Anr. Edn.** Paris, Harrison, [1930]. *(20) numbered on iridescent Japan vell.* Tall 8vo. Three-qtr. mor. & silvered bds. by G. Huser, Paris, boxed. (SG. Mar.29; 164) $110

[Poems, Songs & Sonnets] (*Arranged Chronologically*)
- **Poems.** Ill.:- William Marshall after Martin Droeshout. L., 1640. *1st. Coll. Edn.* Sm. 8vo. Dtd. & undtd. title-pp. with woodcut printer's device, 2nd. title-p. from a shorter copy & restored affecting ptd. surfaces, faint early owner's inscr. on frontis. recto, some light browning or spotting to a few ll., cf. gt. by F. Bedford, mor. solander case; Frederic Dannay copy. [STC 22344] (CNY. Dec.16; 314) $9,000
- - **Anr. Edn.** Ed.:- F.S. Ellis. Ill.:- Wm. Morris. L., Kelms. Pr., 1893. *(500).* Orig. limp vell., lacks some. (GB. May 5; 2769) DM 1,600
- - **Anr. Edn.** Essex House Pr., 1899. *(450) numbered.* Sm. 4to. Woodcut initials, pencil inscr. on front end-paper disclaiming responsibility for Venus & Adonis woodcut, sigd. by F.S.E. (Ellis?), orig. vell., rather soiled, ties. (BBA. May 23; 195) *Vine.* £80
- **Sonette.** Trans.:- E. Ludwig. [Berlin, Officina Serpentis, 1923]. *(175).* Sm. 4to. Some light browning, hand-bnd. vell., gold decor., by H. Glökler, Berlin. (H. Nov.24; 1217) DM 420
- **The Sonnets.** Preface:- Robert Graves. Ill.:- C. Hutton. Swallow Press, 1975. *(300) numbered & Sigd.* 4to. Prospectus loosely inserted, orig. mor. gt., s.-c. (BBA. Dec.15; 264) *Friedlaender.* £75

[Collected Works] (*Arranged Chronologically*)
- **Comedies, Histories & Tragedies.** Ill.:- Droeshout (port.). L., 1632 [after 1640]. *2nd. Fo. Edn. 2nd. Iss.* Fo. Hinman's state III of port., lacks last lf., supplied in ptd. facs., 1st. lf. 'To the Reader' cut down to text area & mntd., title defect., reprd. & mntd., hole in G1, about 15 ll. with short tears or sm. holes, some browning, early 20th. C. red mor. gt. by Maltby, Oxford. [NSTC 22274e.3] (S. Dec.8; 30) *Holdstock.* £3,200

- - **Anr. Edn.** L., 1685. *4th. Edn. 1st. Iss.* Fo. Port. frontis. laid down, some ll. with tears reprd. or sm. holes, crimson lev. mor. gt., elab. decor. gt. spine, inner gt. dentelles, by Bedford. [Wing S 2915] (C. Nov.9; 113) *Joseph.* £3,800
- - **Anr. Edn.** 1685. *4th. Fo. Edn.* Fo. Frontis. & last 2 ll. in facs., 2 ll. supplied from a shorter copy, cont. panel. cf., rejointed. [Wing S 2961] (P. Mar.15; 206) *Burgess.* £1,900
- **The Works.** Ed.:- Alexander Pope. 1725. Vols. 1-6 only (of 7). 4to. Some ll. stained & soiled, cont. cf., rebkd., worn. (BBA. Aug.18; 35) *Quaritch.* £350
- - **Anr. Edn.** Ed.:- L. Theobald. 1733. 7 vols. Sm. worm hole in some pp., cont. cf., rebkd. (BBA. Aug.18; 36) *Quaritch.* £320
- - **Anr. Edn.** L., 1747. 9 vols. 18mo. Cont. cf., spines gt., some wear. (SG. Feb.16; 272) $175
- **Comedies, Histories & Tragedies.** Ed.:- Edward Capell. [1767-68]. 10 vols. Few ll. slightly spotted, cont. cf., rebkd. & reprd. (BBA. Aug.18; 37) *Quaritch.* £300
- **The Plays.** Ed.:- Samuel Johnson. 1768. 8 vols. Hf.-titles, cont. cf., spines gt., slightly worn, 1 cover loose. (BBA. Aug.18; 38) *Quaritch.* £160
- **Works.** 1771. 7 vols. in 13. Cont. vell., lightly rubbed. (CSK. Jun.1; 127) £170
- **Schauspiele.** Ed.:- Joh. Joach. Eschenburg. Ill.:- S. Gessner. Zürich, 1775-82. *1st. Edn.* 13 vols. Minimal worming, cont. marb. cf., gt. spine, 1 cover with slight worm trace; from Fürstl. Starhomberg' schen Bibliothek; Hauswedell coll. (H. May 24; 1561) DM 5,000
- **[Oeuvres] Shakespeare Traduit de l'Anglais.** Trans.:- Pierre Le Tourneur. Paris, 1776-82. *Orig. Edn.* 20 vols. 4to. L.P., cont. cf., spines gt. (HD. Mar.19; 149) Frs. 3,100
- **The Plays & Poems.** 1790. 11 vols. with Commentary vol. by Malone. Some ll. spotted, 8 ll. in Vol. 2 mntd., cont. cf., slightly worn. (BBA. Oct.27; 36) *Peace.* £80
- **The Plays.** Ed.:- E. Malone. 1790-86. 7 vols. Hf.-titles, few ll. slightly spotted, cont. cf. (BBA. Aug.18; 39) *Quaritch.* £300
- - **Anr. Edn.** Ed.:- Samuel Johnson & George Steevens. L., 1793. *4th. Edn.* Vols. 1-13 only (of 15). Lge. 8vo. Tree cf., spines gt., some wear. (SG. Feb.16; 273) $175
- **The Dramatic Works.** Ed.:- Rowe. Braunschweig, 1801. *1st. Engl. Edn. publd. in Germany.* 8 vols. Cont. bds., slightly bumped. (BR. Apr.12; 1529) DM 550
- - **Anr. Edn.** Ed.:- George Steevens. 1802. 9 vols. Lge. fo. Some foxing, diced russ. gt., spines gt. in 6 compartments, minor chips at foot of a few spines, faded; Sir Ivar Colquhoun, of Luss copy. (CE. Mar.22; 273) £300
- - **Anr. Copy.** 8 vols. Fo. Cf. gt., rubbed. (P. Jul.5; 276) £140
- - **Anr. Copy.** 9 vols. 4to. Some stains, cont. Engl. long-grd. mor., decor., some vols. slightly loose. (SI. Dec.15; 130) Lire 320,000
- **The Dramatic Works, with Life.** Ed.:- Dr. Johnson. L., 1815. 7 vols. 32mo. Cont. stained cf., spines gt., some wear. (SG. Feb.16; 274) $140
- **Dramatische Werke.** Ed.:- Ludwig Tieck. Trans.:- A.W. von Schlegel. Berlin, 1825-33. 9 vols. Cont. hf. cf. (C. Dec.9; 287) *Lindsay.* £190
- - **Anr. Copy.** 9 vols. Cont. cf.-bkd. marb. bds., spines worn. (C. Dec.9; 288) *Braecklein.* £150
- **The Plays.** L., 1826. 8 vols. Port. spotted, cont. cf. gt. by C. Smith, spines soiled. (S. Mar.20; 794) *Ghani.* £100
- **The Works.** Ed.:- T. Bowdler. 1827. 8 vols. Cf. gt., Trinity College Dublin arms on covers, Vol. 7 scuffed. (P. Jan.12; 1) *Jarndyce.* £110
- **The Dramatic Works.** 1838. 8 vols. 16mo. Orig. cl. gt., orig. box, glass front, gt.-lettered. (SKC. Nov.18; 1908) £70
- **Oeuvres Complètes.** Trans.:- François-Victor Hugo. Paris, 1859-66. *1st. Victor Hugo Edn.* 18 vols. Some foxing, hf. chagrin by Adriaensen. (HD. Jul.2; 102) Frs. 1,050
- **Comedies, Histories, & Tragedies.** Southampton, 1862. *Photo-Zincographic Facs. of the 1st. Fo. Edn.* Tall fo. Gt.-tooled leath. by Rivière; cont. pres. bkplt. from the Rt. Hon. the Secretary of State for War to Earl de Grey & Ripon, bkplt, &

release stp. of the Folger Shakespeare Liby. (SG. Nov.10; 143) $225
- - **Anr. Copy.** Tall fo. Gt.-tooled leath. by Riviere, rubbed; cont. pres. bkplt. from the Rt. Hon. the Secretary of State for War to Lieut.-Gen. Sir E. Lugard, release stp. of the Folger Shakespeare Liby. (SG. May 10; 130) $140
- **Works.** Ed.:- C. Knight. Ca. 1865. 2 vols. Fo. Crimson mor. gt. (P. Feb.16; 224) £110
- **Comedies, Histories & Tragedies.** [1866]. *Facs. of 1623 Edn.* Fo. Some ll. slightly soiled, cont. cf. (BBA. Aug.18; 46) *Quaritch.* £50
- **The Works.** Ed.:- Alexander Dyce. L., 1866-67. *2nd. Edn.* 9 vols. Lge. 8vo. Three-qtr. cf., spines gt. (SG. Feb.16; 277) $275
- **The Family Shakespeare.** Ed.:- Thomas Bowdler. L., 1874. Cont. red mor. gt., with fore-e. pntg., as a fore-e. pntg., w.a.f. (SPB. May 17; 730) $325
- **Works.** Ed.:- Alexander Dyce. L., 1880-81. *4th. Edn.* 10 vols. Lge. 8vo. Tree cf., spines gt. (SG. Feb.16; 278) $225
- - **Anr. Edn.** Ed.:- Staunton. 1881. *(1000) numbered.* 15 vols. Orig. cl. (CSK. Feb.10; 32) £85
- - **Anr. Copy.** 15 vols. 4to. Ills. on India paper, some ll. slightly spotted, orig. cl. (BBA. Sep.29; 211) *Howell.* £55
- - **Anr. Edn.** 1890. *Henry Irving Edn.* 8 vols. 4to. Cont. lev. mor. gt. by Zaehnsdorf, inner silk doubls., rubbed; pres. inscr. from Irving to Sir Edward Russell in Vol. 1. (BBA. Feb.23; 216) *Bailey.* £120
- **The National Shakespeare.** Ill.:- J. Noël Paton. L., ca. 1890. *Facs. of 1st. Fo. Edn.* 3 vols. Fo. On H.M.P., 20 India-proof plts., partly unc., orig. mor. over wood bds., richly gt.- & blind-tooled, corners & spine-ends slightly rubbed. (B. Oct.4; 416) Fls. 500
- **[Works].** Phila., [1895]. *Variorum Edn.* 23 vols. Hf. mor. (LH. Sep.25; 594) $525
- - **Anr. Edn.** Ed.:- Israel Gollancz. L., 1899-1900. *(500) on H.M.P.* 12 vols. Hf. mor. gt. (PNY. Oct.20; 188) $325
- - **Anr. Edn.** Ed.:- W.E. Henley. L., 1901-04. *(1000) sigd. by publisher (Grant Richards).* Fo. Extra-ill., many plts., mostly engraved, many hand-cold., a little light spotting in 3 vols., mor. gt. by Bayntun (Rivière). (S. Oct.4; 100) *Cavendish.* £1,650
- **Comedies, Histories & Tragedies.** Oxford, 1902. *Facs. of 1623 Edn. (1000) numbered & sigd. by Sidney Lee.* Fo. Census loosely inserted, orig. reversed cf., ties. (BBA. Aug.18; 47) *Quaritch.* £120
- - **Anr. Edn.** 1904. *Facs. of 1685 Edn.* Fo. Orig. cl.-bkd. bds. (BBA. Aug.18; 51) *Quaritch.* £50
- **The Works.** 1904-33. *Arden Edn.* 39 vols. Orig. cl. (BBA. Aug.18; 41) *Quaritch.* £65
- **Comedies, Histories & Tragedies.** 1905. *Facs. of 1664 Edn.* Fo. Orig. cl.-bkd. bds. (BBA. Aug.18; 50) *Quaritch.* £50
- **The Works.** Ed.:- W.E. Henley. Edinb., [1906]. *'Anne Hathaway' Edn. (50) numbered.* 20 vols. Fo. Extra-ill. with inserted plts. & marginal & textual decoration in watercolour & gold in Art Nouveau style, mor., elab. gt.-decor., onlaid mor. ornaments, lge. gt.-stpd. & red cont-of-arms, gt. spines in 6 compartments, turn-ins gt., watered silk linings, partly unc., w.a.f. (CNY. Dec.17; 603) $4,600
- **Werke.** Ed.:- Fr. Gundolg. Ill.:- M. Lechter. Berlin, 1908-18. *1st. Gundolg Edn.* 10 vols. 4to. Orig. mor. gt., spine browned & worn. (HK. Nov.11; 3730) DM 420
- **Comedies, Histories & Tragedies.** 1909. *Facs. of 1632. Edn.* Fo. Orig. cl.-bkd. bds. (BBA. Aug.18; 49) *Quaritch.* £50
- **Works.** Ed.:- William G. Clark & William A. Wright. Ill.:- after Boydell. Phila., Ca. 1915. *Interlinear Edn. (500) numbered, on Japanese vellum.* 16 vols. Two-toned semi-limp mor., single-rule gt. spine boxes & cover borders, each spine stpd. with gt. vigs. of Shakespeare, Bottom, & group of 4 characters from 1 play, marb. end-papers, linen hinges, minimum shelf wear & rubbing. (HA. May 4; 222) $650
- **Sämtliche Werke.** Ed.:- L.L. Schücking & E. von Schubert. München, 1925-29. Orig. hf. leath. (H. Nov.24; 1269) DM 640
- **Dramatische Werke.** Trans.:- A.W. v. Schlegel.

Berlin, 1925-33. *1st. Edn.* 9 vols. Cont. hf. leath. gt. (R. Oct.11; 415) DM 1,050
- **The Works** ... L. & N.Y., Nones, Pr., 1929. *(1600).* 7 vols. Niger goat, spines slightly darkened. (PNY. Dec.1; 21) $275
– – **Anr. Edn.** N.Y., Nones, Pr., 1929-32. *(1050).* 7 vols. Cf. gt. (LH. Sep.25; 434) $475
– – **Anr. Edn.** Nones. Pr. 1929-33. *(1600) numbered.* 7 vols. Orig. mor., lightly stained. (CSK. Jul.27; 89) £300
– – **Anr. Copy.** 7 vols. Orig. mor., slightly stained. (BBA. Sep.29; 220) *Old Hall Books.* £210
– – **Anr. Edn.** Nones. Pr., 1929-33. *Ltd. Edn.* 7 vols. Mor. gt., partly unc., w.a.f.; from liby. of Luttrellstown Castle. (C. Sep.28; 1835) £800
– – **Anr. Edn.** Ed.:– Herbert Farjeon. Nones. Pr., 1929-33. *(1050) numbered.* 7 vols. Orig. niger mor., spines & some covers darkened & rubbed; each vol. with Samuel Kahn bkplt., designed by Eric Gill, that in 1st. vol. sigd. by Gill. (S. Nov.22; 262) *Fletcher.* £150
- **The Complete Works.** Preface:– Christopher Morley. Ed.:– William Aldis Wright. Ill.:– Rockwell Kent. Garden City, 1936. *(750) numbered & sigd. by artist.* 2 vols. Lge. 4to. Buckram, s.-c., partly unc., rubbed. (SG. Jan.12; 185) $450
– – **Anr. Copy.** 2 vols. 4to. Cl.; sigd. by artist. (LH. Sep.25; 411) $290
– – **Anr. Copy.** 2 vols. 4to. Decor. buckram, slight rubbing to covers; Joe E. Brown & Marymount College bkplts. (CBA. Mar.3; 315) $170
- **Comedies, Histories & Tragedies.** Ed.:– Herbert Farjeon. Designed:– Bruce Rogers. Ill.:– Arthur Rackham & others. N.Y., Ltd. Edns. Cl., 1939-41. 37 vols. Sm. fo. Ills., many cold., qtr. cl., patterned bds., partly unc., lacks case. (SG. Apr.26; 180) $540
- **Complete Works.** Nones. Pr., 1953. *Coronation Edn.* 4 vols. Orig. cl. (BBA. Aug.18; 41) *Quaritch.* £70
- **The National Shakespeare.** L., n.d. *Facs. reprint of 1st. fo. of 1623.* 3 vols. Fo. Plts. spotted, orig. cl., gt. (S. Apr.10; 395) *Diaz.* £90
– – **Anr. Copy.** 3 vols. Fo. Mntd. frontis.'s & plts., orig. mor. gt., lightly rubbed. (CSK. Jun.29; 55) £65

SHAKESPEARIANA
- **Shakespeare.** Ed.:– Louis Aragon. Ill.:– Pablo Picasso. N.Y., [1965?]. *(1000) numbered.* Fo. 12 plts., facs. paper-guards, ptd. bds., d.-w. soiled. (SG. Apr. 26; 160) $175

SHAKESPEARE HEAD PRESS
See— BEDE, The Venerable
See— FROISSART, Sir John

SHAKESPEAREAN SHOW BOOK
1884. Ob. 8vo. Advts., Bank Order form for Chelsea Hospital for Women, mor.-bkd. bds. retaining orig. cover, spine gt. (LC. Oct.13; 400) £70

SHANKS, Edward
- **Images from the Progress of the Seasons.** Ill.:– Charles Berry. 1947. *(450) numbered. (50) sigd. by author & artist, specially bnd.* Mor., d.-w. (HBC. May 17; 205) £50
- **Universal War & the Universal State.** 1946. *(550) numbered. (25) sigd. & specially bnd.* Qtr. vell. & buckram, unc., d.-w. (HBC. May 17; 192) £52

SHANNON, Charles Hazlewood (Ed.)
See— PAGEANT, The

SHARPE, Edmund
- **Architectural Parallels. — Supplement.** L., 1848. *1st. Edn.* 3 vols. Atlas fo. 181 litho. plts., ex-liby., later hf. mor., supp. cl.-bkd. bds. (SG. May 3; 331) $200

SHARPE, Richard Bowdler
- **An Analytical Index to the works of the late John Gould, F.R.S.** L., 1893. *(100) L.P.* Fo. Lacks port., orig. cl. (C. Mar.14; 172) *Davidson.* £240
- **Monograph of the Paradiseidae, or Birds of Paradise, & Ptilonorhynchidae, or Bower-Birds.** Ill.:– J. Gould, W. Hart, & J.G. Keulemans. L., 1891-98. 2 vols. Fo. 79 hand-cold. plts. (some plts. appear to be ptd., possibly by photo-lithography, on mod. paper, colouring also appears to be mod.), mor. gt. by Sotheran. (S. Feb.1; 54) *Vischer.* £4,800

– – **Anr. Copy.** 2 vols. Lge. fo. 79 hand-cold. litho. plts., cont. mor. gt., spines & extreme edges renewed to match, 8 orig. upr. ptd. wraps. bnd. at end of Vol. 2. (CNY. May 18; 153) $5,600

SHARPE, Richard Bowdler & Wyatt, Claude
- **A Monograph of the Hirundinidae or Family of Swallows.** 1885-94. 2 vols. Lge. 4to. 129 cold. litho plts. & maps, cont. hf. mor., spines gt. (SKC. Nov.18; 1986) £2,000

SHAW, G.F.
- **The Panorama of Nature.** 1817. 4to. 2 uncold. plts., 78 hand-cold. plts., 2 bnd. inverted, cont. cf., gt. fillets & spine, slightly rubbed. (SKC. Jan.13; 2343) £70

SHAW, George
- **General Zoology.** L., 1800-06. Vols. I-VI only, in 12 vols. Lge. 8vo. Some foxing & dampstaining, liby. stps., early bds., mod. cf. back, 1 hinge reinforced with tape; sig. of William Clarke in each vol. (3 obscured by liby. stp.). (SG. Oct.6; 329) $150
– – **Anr. Edn.** L., 1800-26. 14 vols. in 28, including General Index. Imperial 8vo. Cont. red hf. mor., unc., spines gt., last 4 vols. rebnd. to match, w.a.f.; from liby. of Luttrellstown Castle. (C. Sep.28; 1782) £2,400
– – **Anr. Copy.** 14 vols. in 28. Cont. hf. cf., rubbed, lacks some spines, 1 bd. detchd., w.a.f. (CSK. Mar.9; 154) £200
– – **Anr. Edn.** Ed.:– J.F. Stephens. L., 1815-19. 5 part vols. (Birds). Vols. 9, I/II; 10, II & 11,I/II. Title ll. stpd., foxed, cont. hf. leath. gt., rubbed, 1 cover loose. (BR. Apr.12; 847) DM 600
- **Zoological Lectures.** 1809. 2 vols. Engraved additional titles, 167 plts., cont. hf. cf., rubbed, 1 spine slightly chipped. (CSK. Apr.6; 32) £55
See— MILLER, John Frederick & Shaw, George

SHAW, George & Nodder, Frederick P.
- **Vivarium Naturae, or The Naturalist's Miscellany.** [L., 1789]. Vol. I only. 36 (of 37) hand-cold. engraved plts., 1 folding plt. with sm. tear, Latin dedication detchd., cont. leath., covers detchd., spine chipped, ex-liby. (SG. Oct.6; 331) $150
– – **Anr. Edn.** [1789-1808]. Vols. 1-20 in 10. Engraved dedication & 871 hand-cold. plts. only, lacks 5 plts., some light spotting, cont. cl.-bkd. bds., rubbed, w.a.f. (CSK. Jun.1; 74) £1,900
– – **Anr. Edn.** L., ca. 1790. 2 vols. 134 col. plts., 2 torn, many soiled, no titles, cf., worn, w.a.f. (P. Nov.24; 212) *Shapero.* £170
– – **Anr. Edn.** L., 1790[-1813]. *1st. Edn.* 24 vols., bnd. from the orig. pts. Tall 8vo. 1064 hand-cold. copperplates, text in Latin & Engl., old tree cf., disbnd. (SG. Nov.3; 191) $3,200
– – **Anr. Edn.** L., 1790-1813. 24 vols. in 12. Engraved dedication in Vol. I, 1064 hand-cold. engraved plts., some folding, titles, dedications & text in Engl. & Latin, general indexes bnd. at end of Vol. 24, 3 plts. with sm. tear at fold, a few plts. slightly shaved, owner's stp. on titles & dedication, cont. cf. gt., a few covers detchd. (C. Nov.16; 298) *Junk.* £2,400

SHAW, George Bernard
- **Cashel Byron's Profession.** [L.], The Modern Pr., 1886. *1st. Edn.* 2 ll. slightly soiled, orig. wraps., mor.-bkd. s.-c.; Perry Molstad copy. (SPB. May 16; 514) $400
- **John Bull's Other Island & Major Barbara.** Leipzig, [1907]. Hf.-title, orig. ptd. wraps., cl. box; inscr. & slip pasted on spine inscr., Perry Molstad copy. (SPB. May 16; 515) $175
- **Saint Joan.** L., 1924. Orig. cl., mor.-bkd. s.-c.; pres. copy to Sam Pickles, inscr. by Sybil Thorndike & 2 other members of the cast, Perry Molstad copy. (SPB. May 16; 518) $350
- **Shaw Gives Himself Away.** [Newton, Mon.], Gregy. Pr., 1939. *(300) numbered.* Lge. 8vo. Wood engraved port., orig. mor., mor. inlays, designed by Paul Nash, s.-c.; Perry Molstad copy. (SPB. May 16; 520) $275
- **Statement of the Evidence in Chief ... before Joint-Committee on Stage Plays (Censorship & Theatre Licensing).** L., Priv. ptd., July 1909. *1st. Edn.* Sm. 8vo. Orig. ptd. wraps., orig. publisher's vell. box slightly warped, mor.-bkd. box; Barton

Currie/Perry Molstad copy. (SPB. May 16; 521) $275
- **This is the Preachment. On Going to Church.** East Aurora, N.Y., Roycroft Printing Shop, 1896. *1st. Edn. (26) on japan vell., initialled by Elbert Hubbard.* Sm. 8vo. Orig. watercolour decors. in margins of 13 pp., orig. limp vell., ties, mor.-bkd. s.-c.; Perry Molstad copy. (SPB. May 16; 522) $900
- **Widower's Houses.** L., 1893. *1st. Edn.* Orig. cl., unc., cl. case; full-p. autograph inscr. dtd. Nov. 1929, Perry Molstad copy. (SPB. May 16; 525) $750
– – **Anr. Copy.** Title & hf.-title browned, ports. pasted to endpapers & hf.-title verso, orig. cl., cl. folding case; inscr. to Jules Magny, Perry Molstad copy. (SPB. May 16; 524) $275
- **The Works.** L., 1930-32. *(1025) numbered.* Vols. 1-30. Orig. cl. (S. Oct.11; 366) *Mangold.* £150
– – **Anr. Edn.** L., 1930-38. *1st. Coll. Edn., (1025).* 33 vols. Lge. 8vo. Orig. cl., spines slightly discold., d.-w.'s; Vol. 1 inscr. on hf.-title 'to Beatrice & Sidney Webb/George Bernard Shaw ... 26 July 1930'; inscr. on front free end-paper of Vol. 1 'George M. Booth ... from the Webb Sale'. (S. Dec.8; 256) *Sotheran.* £1,050

SHAW, Henry
- **Alphabets Numerals & Devices of the Middle Ages.** L., 1845. *[1st. Edn.].* Sm. 4o. 48 plts., most hand-cold. or ptd. in cols., spotted, orig. cl., new end-papers, rebkd., slightly worn. (S. Mar.1; 433) *Quaritch.* £50
– – **Anr. Copy.** Slight darkening, 1 tissue guard detchd. but present, orig. cl., spine gt., corners & spine ends lightly bumped, lge. bkplt., partially defaced. (CBA. Aug.21; 589) $110
- **The Decorative Arts, Ecclesiastical & Civil, of the Middle Ages.** L., 1851. *1st. Edn.* 4to. 41 plts., hf.-title detchd., bds., spine crudely taped. (SG. Aug.25; 332) $170
- **Details of Elizabethan Architecture.** 1839. 4to. Engraved title, 60 plts., including 3 hand-cold., some ll. slightly soiled, cont. cl.-bkd. bds. (BBA. Nov.10; 260) *Philip Morris Books.* £60
- **Dresses & Decorations of the Middle Ages.** L., 1843. *[1st. Edn.].* 2 vols. Hand-cold. litho. & chromolitho. plts. & ills., red mor. gt. by Hayday, gt. spines, chemises & s.-c.'s. (S. Oct.11; 592) *Henderson.* £520
– – **Anr. Copy.** 2 vols. Fo. Additional title, plts., ills. & initials all hand-cold., plain ills., some pp. spotted (mainly Vol. 1), cont. mor. gt. gt. by J. Clarke, jnts. slightly rubbed. (S. Apr.30; 222) *Quaritch.* £350
– – **Anr. Copy.** 2 vols. Fo. L.P. 93 engraved or litho. plts. only, most hand-cold., some light spotting, cont. cl., rubbed, spines faded, disbnd., w.a.f. (CSK. Jun.15; 139) £140
– – **Anr. Copy.** 2 vols. in 1. 4to. Hand-cold. additional title & 94 cold. plts. (several hand-cold.), some staining & spotting, cont. hf. mor., rubbed. (CSK. Jun.1; 42) £110
– – **Anr. Copy.** 2 vols. 4to. Engraved titles (1 cold.), 94 hand-cold. engraved plts., some ll. spotted, orig. cl., rubbed, spines torn. (BBA. Feb.23; 253) *Subunso.* £80
– – **Anr. Copy.** 2 vols. 4to. 94 col. litho. plts., most partly hand-cold., cont. hf. mor. gt. & cl. (SG. Oct.13; 301) $200
– – **Anr. Copy.** 2 vols. Tall 4to. 94 plts., most hand-cold., many text ills. & initials hand-cold., some light foxing, disbnd. (SG. Aug.25; 331) $150
– – **Anr. Copy.** 2 vols. Lge. 4to. 94 cold. plts., many cold. text engrs. & pict. initials, ex-liby., mod. buckram. (SG. May 3; 332) $110
– – **Anr. Edn.** 1858. 2 vols. Fo. 94 plts. (2 double-p.), some foxing, cont. red mor. gt., upr. covers slightly faded. (BBA. Jan.19; 334) *Blundell.* £150
– – **Anr. Copy.** 2 vols. 4to. 93 col. plts., slight spotting, qtr. cf. gt., rubbed. (P. Feb.16; 31) £85

SHAW, Henry & Madden, Sir Frederick
- **Illuminated Ornaments Selected from Manuscripts & Early Printed Books.** L., 1833. 4to. Extra pict. title, 59 hand-cold. plts., buckram, disbnd. (SG. Aug.25; 329) $220

SHAW, Henry. & Meyrick, S.R.
- **Specimens of Ancient Furniture.** L., 1836. Fo. Additional hand-cold. engraved title & plts.,

SHAW, Henry. & Meyrick, S.R. -*Contd.*

slightly spotted, cont. roan-bkd. cl., rubbed. (S. May 1; 720) *Sims.* £140

SHAW, James
- Sketches of the History of the Austrian Netherlands. 1786. Vell., pink end-papers, covers with gt. border on blue ground, & inner decor. border, upr. cover with monochrome painting of figure of Fame & putto holding gt. tablet with title, lr. cover with painting of putto & drape with arms of Poulett per pale with Shergold, spine gt.-tooled, with blue bands, vell. cords partly exposed, fore-e, pntg., orig. mor. gt. s.-c., by the 'Edwards of Halifax' bindery. (LC. Oct.13; 434) £1,500

SHAW, Norton
- Royal Illustrated Atlas. L., n.d. Fo. Maps mostly frayed at edges, defect., loose, disbnd. (BBA. Mar.21; 136) *M. Cassidy.* £120

SHAW, Ralph R. & Shoemaker, Richard H.
- American Bibliography: A Preliminary Checklist for 1810[-1819]. N.Y., 1961-66. 13 vols., including 3 vols. of Indexes, etc. Cl. (*With:*) **SHOEMAKER, Richard H.** - A Checklist of American Imprints for 1822 [& 1826-1830]. Metuchen, N.J., 1967-73. 8 vols., including 2 vols. of Indexes for 1820-1829. Cl., some vols. in both sets ex-liby. (SG. Aug.4; 285) $175

SHAW, T.E. (Pseud.)
See— LAWRENCE, Thomas Edward 'T.E. Shaw'

SHAW, Thomas
- Travel or Observations relating to ... Barbary & the Levant. Oxford, 1738. 2 pts. in 1 vol., including Supp. Fo. 34 maps & plts., cont. cf. gt., rubbed. (P. Mar.15; 102) *Azezian.* £240
- - Anr. Copy. Fo. 26 engraved plts. & maps, several lightly stained, cont. cf., worn. (CSK. May 4; 73) £160
- - Anr. Copy. Fo. 32 engraved plts. & maps, including 5 folding, hf.-title, without supp., cont. cf., rebkd., worn. (S. Dec.13; 149) *Scott.* £110
- - Anr. Edn. 1757. 2nd. Edn. 2 pts. in 1 vol. 4to. A few pp. wormholed, cont. cf. (SKC. Jan.13; 2389) £80
- - Anr. Copy. 38 copper engrs., most folding, sm. liby. stp. to title-p., later hf. mor. (CBA. Dec.10; 473) $150
- - Anr. Copy. 3 vols. in 1. 4to. 6 maps with sm. tears, 2 margins slightly browned & creased, some slight foxing, MS. purchase & owners mark on prelim lf., dtd. 1819, cont. cf. gt., slightly worn & bumped. (H. May 22; 249) DM 780
- Voyages dans Plusieurs Prov. de Barbarie et du Levant ... Alger, Tunis, la Syrie, l'Egypte et l'Arabie Petrée. La Haye, 1743. 3 pts. in 1 vol. 4to. Cont. cf., spine gt. (VG. Nov.30; 866) Fls. 570

SHAW, W.
- A Defence of the Wesleyan Missionaries in Southern Africa. L., 1839. Wraps. (VA. Oct.28; 256) R 320

SHAW, Rev. William
- A Galic & English Dictionary, Containing all the Words in Scotch & Irish Dialects of the Celtic, ... Old Books & Manuscripts. L., 1780. 2 vols. 4to. Tree cf. (GM. Dec.7; 627) £130

SHAW, W.H.
- Calendar of Treasury Books Preserved in the Public Record Office. 1904-57. 62 vols. various. Orig. cl., most in d.-w.'s. (CSK. Feb.10; 171) £120

SHAW MASON, William
- A Statistical Account or Parochial Survey of Ireland. Dublin, 1814. 1st. Edn. 3 vols. Cl.-bkd. bds. (GM. Dec.7; 65) £210

SHAWYER, N.M. (Ed.)
See— ROTHSCHILD, Lord

SHE'EILOT U'TESHUVOT HA'GEONIM [Response]
Prague, [1590]. 3rd. Edn. 4to. Few glosses in margins, unpaginated, few wormholes affecting some letters, stained, hf. cl., w.a.f. (S. Oct.25; 157) £450

SHEERES, Sir Henry
[-] A Discourse Touching Tanger: in a Letter to a Person of Quality. 1680. 1st. Edn. 4to. Some stains, cont. cf., rebkd. [Wing D1621 & S3057] (BBA. Jan.19; 166) *Lawson.* £80

SHEFFIELD PLATE & SILVER MANUFACTURER'S PATTERN BOOK
Ca. 1820's. Ob. fo. Engraved title, 2 engraved ll. of measurements, 127 engraved plts., prices & some additional information added in ink, lacks corner of 1 plt., anr. plt. torn, some slight spotting, hf. cf., orig. bds. retained; sig of Charles Thompson. (LC. Mar.1; 24) £1,200

SHELDON, George William
- Artistic Country-Seats: Types of Recent American Villa & Cottage Architecture. N.Y., 1886. 5 vols. Tall fo. 100 mntd. photogravure plts., liby. stp. on ptd. titles, loose as iss. in leath.-bkd. lettered bds., brkm., bkplts. (SG. May 10; 8) $325

SHELDON, Col. Harold P.
- Tranquility Revisited. Ill.:– A.L. Ripley. Derrydale Pr., [1940]. (485) numbered. 4to. Gt.-pict. cl., trivial tapestains on end-papers. (SG. Mar.15; 237) $225

SHELDRAKE, Timothy
- Botanicum Medicinale. L., [1759]. Fo. 108 (of 118?) ll. with hand-cold. figure of a plant surrounded by engraved text, hf.-title, & title in MS., some staining, hf. mor., worn, as a collection of plts., w.a.f. (P. Nov.24; 260) *Shapero.* £720

SHELEKHOV, Gregori Ivanovich
[-] [The Voyage of ... from Okhotzk, on the Eastern Ocean, to the Coast of America ... & His Return to Russia]. Trans.:– Rev. W. Tooke. L., 1795. 1st. Edn. in Engl. From Vol. 2 of 'Varieties of Literature', pp. 1-42, in 2 vols. Cont. tree cf., spines gt., head of 1 spine chipped; the Rt. Hon. Visc. Eccles copy. (CNY. Nov.18; 252) $900

SHELLEY, Capt. George Ernest
- A Handbook to the Birds of Egypt. Ill.:– Keulemans. L., 1872. Lge. 8vo. 14 cont. hand-cold. litho. plts., mod. hf. chagrin. (VS. Dec.8; 663) Fls. 550

SHELLEY, Mary Wollstonecraft
- Frankenstein. L., 1833. 1st. Amer. Edn. 2 vols. 12mo. Hf.-titles, 4-pp. advts. vol.1, 24-pp. advts. vol.2, pp. 13-34 vol.1 misbnd., marginal loss from p.25, vol.2, some browning & spotting, buckram, soiled; Perry Molstad copy. (SPB. May 16; 526) $750
- The Last Man. L., 1826. 1st. Edn. 3 vols. Lacks some blanks, 1st. & last ll. & end-papers glued at inner margin & slightly creased, some spotting, near-cont. cl., lightly rubbed. (SPB. Dec.13; 738) $750
- - Anr. Copy. 3 vols. in 2. Title-pp. reinforced on verso with linen, darkening, some foxing & staining, some ink notations in margins, darkening, lending liby. bkplts., three-qtr. cf. & bds., end-papers irregularly darkening, covers scuffed & worn; A.N.s. breakfast invitation from Shelley. (CBA. Oct.29; 749) $600

SHELLEY, Percy Bysshe
[-] An Address to the People on the Death of the Princess Charlotte. By the Hermit of Marlow. 1843? Reprint. Slightly soiled, early 20th. C. hf. mor., spine gt., slightly soiled; Charles Stewart Rolls bkplt. (BBA. Jan.19; 228) *Thomas.* £160
- Adonais, an Elegy on the Death of John Keats. Pisa, 1821. 1st. Edn. 4to. Lacks 1st. & last blank ll., orig. ptd. wraps., unc., rebkd. & restitched, lr. wrap. defect. with upr. area & backstrip restored, edges of wraps. strengthened, cl. box with copy of T.J.Wise's facs. edn. laid in; Frederic Dannay copy. (CNY. Dec.16; 322) $3,200
- - Anr. Edn. Camb., 1829. 1st. Engl. Edn. Orig. wraps., stitched as iss., unc., slight stain on upr. cover, hf. mor. s.-c.; Mary Elizabeth Hudson bkplt., Frederic Dannay copy. (CNY. Dec.16; 323) $1,000
- - Anr. Edn. Ill.:– C.R. Ashbee (frontis.). [Essex House Pr., 1900]. (50) numbered on vell. Hand-cold. engraved frontis., pen, ink & wash initials, orig. parch., lightly soiled. (CSK. Oct.21; 27) £110

- The Cenci, A Tragedy in Five Acts. Italy [Leghorn], 1819. 1st. Edn. 8vo. Later hf. cf., slightly rubbed. (BBA. Jan.19; 226) *Thomas.* £400
- - Anr. Copy. Lacks 1st. & last blanks, late 19th. C. red mor. gt., gt. inside borders. (S. Dec.8; 128) *Swales.* £300
- - Anr. Edn. L., 1821. 2nd [1st. Engl.] Edn. 1 vol. Hf. leath. (*Bound with:*) - Essays, Letters from Abroad [etc.]. L., 1840. 1st. Edn. 2 vols. Orig. cl. (BBA. Dec.15; 191) £190
- The Daemon of the World. L., priv. ptd., 1876. 1st. Edn. (50). 16mo. Orig. imitation vell. bds., unc., soiled; Hugh Walpole's copy, Brackenburn bkplt., Frederic Dannay copy. (CNY. Dec.16; 324) $150
[-] Epipsychidion. 1821. [100]. Some ll. slightly soiled, mod. mor., gt. spine, by F. Bedford. (BBA. Oct.27; 52) *Blackwell.* £1,300
- Laon & Cythna. L., 1818. 1st. Edn. 2nd. state, without fly-lf. & advt. lf., at front, errata lf., red mor. gt. by Sangorski & Sutcliffe partly unc.; Frederic Dannay copy. (CNY. Dec.16; 319) $480
- Miscellaneous Poems. 1826. 12mo. Some ll. spotted & slightly soiled, orig. bds., rubbed, spine worn, upr. cover detchd. (BBA. Jan.19; 227) *Jarndyce.* £50
- Poems. Hammersmith, Doves Pr., 1914. (12) on vell. Sm. 4to. Crushed lev. mor., covers elab. gt.-decor., spine in 6 compartments, gt.-panel., turnins gt., sigd. 'Doves Bindery 19 C-S 14', mor. solander case; bkplt. of H. Alfred Fowler, as a bdg., w.a.f. (CNY. Dec.17; 555) $4,200
- The Poetical Works. L., 1892. 2 vols. Lev. mor. gt., each upr. cover with oval miniature port., Vol.1 of Shelley, Vol.2 of Mary, spines in 6 compartments, watered silk linings, silk markers, fleecelined folding cl. boxes, by Bayntun, as a bdg., w.a.f. (CNY. Dec.17; 531) $1,500
- - Anr. Edn. Ed.:– H. Buxton Forman. L., 1908-10. Aldine Edn. 5 vols. Sm. 8vo. Maroon three-qtr. mor., gt.-panel. spines, by Hatchard. (SG. Feb.16; 279) $225
- Prometheus Unbound. L., 1820. 1st. Edn. 1st. state, misprint 'Misellaneous' in list of 'Contents', hf.-title, lacks advt. lf., some slight foxing, old str.-grd. mor. gt.; bkplt. of Robert Alfred Potts, Frederic Dannay copy. (CNY. Dec.16; 320) $700
- - Anr. Edn. L., 1820. 1st. Edn. 2nd. state, 'Miscellaneous' correctly spelt in list of 'Contents', hf.-title, advt. lf., some foxing, orig. bds., unc., rebkd. with facs. label, sides stained, edges worn, cl. folding box; Frederic Dannay copy. (CNY. Dec.16; 321) $250
- - Anr. Edn. [Den Haag], 1917. (125). Orig. vell.; Hauswedell coll. (H. May 24; 777) DM 460
- Queen Mab; a Philosophical Poem. L., Ptd. by P.B. Shelley, 1813. 1st. Edn. With the dedication (usually removed) 'Too Harriet & the imprint on title & verso of last lf. intact, slight browning, orig. bds., unc., early 20th. C. velvet-lined lev. mor. gt. box. (S. Dec.8; 127) *Joseph.* £4,000
- - Anr. Copy. Dedication lf. & imprints on title & verso of final lf. intact, title & last page a little dust-soiled, early 19th. C. diced russ. gt., rebkd. with orig. backstrip laid down, corners worn, qtr. mor. gt. s.-c.; Frederic Dannay copy. (CNY. Dec.16; 317) $2,000
- - Anr. Edn. 1821. 1st. Publd. Edn. Lacks publisher's advt. lf., disbnd. (P. Sep.8; 248) *Finch.* £55
- - Anr. Edn. 1829. Orig. bds., unc. (P. Jul.5; 194) £60
- The Sensitive Plant. Ill.:– Charles Robinson. L. & Phila., [1911]. [1st. Robinson Edn.]. 4to. Elab. gt.-decor. cl., d.-w., s.-c., light wear. (RO. Jul.24; 288) $130

SHELVOCKE, Capt. George
- A Voyage Around the World. L., 1726. [1st. Edn.]. Cont. cf., rebkd., worn, Stuart de Rothesay arms & 'Foreign Office' stp. on covers; Bute bkplt. on verso of title. (BBA. Dec.15; 15) *Quaritch.* £360
- - Anr. Copy. Vig. on title, folding twin hemisphere map (strengthened in fold), 4 engraved plts. (2 folding), cf., rebkd. [Sabin 80158] (S. May 22; 487) *Cavendish.* £340
- - Anr. Copy. Cont. leath., gold decor., jnts-brkn. (D. Nov.23; 906) DM 2,500

SHEM TOV IBN SHEM TOV
- **Drashot Ha'Torah.** Venice, 1547. *1st. Edn.* Fo. Owner's stp. on title & many ll., edges frayed, margin of title reprd. not affecting text or engr., slight staining not affecting text, mod. blind-tooled mor. (S. Oct.25; 359) *Davidson.* £650
- **– Anr. Edn.** Padua, 1567. *3rd. Edn.* Fo. Slight soiling & staining, a few minor margin repairs, old bds., rubbed. (SPB. Feb.1; 82) £1,000
- **Sefer Ha'Emunot.** Ferrara, 1556. *1st. Edn.* (*Bound with:*) ALASHKAR, Moshe – Hasagot Al Ma Shekatav Rabbi Shem Tov. Ferrara, 1557. *1st. Edn.* Unpaginated, Together 2 works in 1 vol. 4to. Mod. blind-tooled mor. (S. Oct.25; 360) *Stern.* £1,000

SHEM TOV MELAMED
- **Keter Shem Tov.** Venice, 1596. *1st. Edn.* Fo. Owner's sig. on title, some worming not affecting text, index pp. shorter than rest of text, last 2 ll. defect. & reprd., staining, creased, blind-tooled leath., worn. (S. Oct.25; 361) *Ludmir.* £400

SH'EN CH'ING KU CHIEN
N.p., [1908]. 40 vols. in 24, including 2 vol. Supp. Lge. 8vo. Wraps., bnd. Chinese-style with silk thread, some light markings to wraps., minor light foxing. (CBA. Jan.29; 367) $150

SHEPHERD, Thomas Hosmer
- **Modern Athens! Displayed in a Series of Views: Or, Edinburgh in the Nineteenth Century.** 1829. 4to. Some spotting, recent hf. mor. gt. (TA. Sep.15; 131) £92
- **– Anr. Copy.** Lge. 4to. 100 steels engrs. on 48 plts., some slight foxing, cont. mor., richly gt., slightly rubbed. (VG. Mar.21; 1071) Fls. 450
- **– Anr. Edn.** 1829-30. 21 orig. pts., & additional pt. 22 of Jones' Views of Edinburgh, together 22 pts. Engraved title. 92 engraved views on 44 plts., some dampstaining to plts. in pt. 1, wraps. (PD. Oct.19; 269) £60
- **– Anr. Edn.** 1831. 4to. Engraved title, 98 views on 47 sheets, slight spotting, orig. cf.-bkd. bds. (P. Sep.8; 253) *Macdonald.* £75
- **The World's Metropolis, or Mighty London.** L., ca. 1851. 4to. Engraved title, 2 ports., hand-cold. folding map, 147 engraved views, including 1 dupl., some foxing, cont. hf. cf. (S. Dec.1; 172) *Edmonds.* £700
- **– Anr. Edn.** L., ca. 1852. 4to. Dampstained thro.-out affecting lr. hf. of text & plts., cont. hf. cf. (PD. Dec.14; 24) £80

SHEPHERD, Thomas Hosmer & Elmes, James
- **London & its Environs in the Nineteenth Century.** 1829. 4to. 188 views on 80 proof plts., orig. cl., spine torn. (P. Sep.29; 256) *Woodall.* £80
- **– Anr. Edn.** [1830-31]. 4to. Vig. title, 180 ills. on 75 sheets, hf. mor. gt. (P. Sep.8; 19) *Willis.* £110
- **– Anr. Edn.** L., n.d. Engraved vig. title, 80 plts., some spotting, cont. hf. cf., worn. (BBA. Mar.21; 126) *Bowers.* £130
- **Metropolitan Improvements or London in the Nineteenth Century.** 1827. Fo. L.P., steel-engraved title, 78 plts., all on India paper, mntd., margins spotted, cont. hf. mor., rubbed. (CSK. Jan.13; 38) £170
- **– Anr. Copy.** 4to. Vig. title, plan, 154 engraved views on 77 sheets, foxing thro.-out, 1 plt. reprd., cf., defect. (P. Jul.5; 202) £110
- **– Anr. Copy.** 4to. Additional title, map, 78 engrs., hf. cf., spine gt. (SKC. Mar.9; 1993) £80
- **– Anr. Copy.** 4to. Hf. cf. (P. Sep.8; 258) *Elliott.* £60
- **– Anr. Edn.** 1828. 4to. 2 additional engraved titles (dtd. 1827 & 1829), engraved plan, 163 engrs. on 81 plts. (dtd. 1827-30), cont. red hf. mor., spine gt. (C. Dec.9; 148) *Levy.* £190
- **– Anr. Copy.** 4to. Engraved title, plan, 150 views on 75 sheets, diced cf. gt. (P. Oct.20; 28) £80
- **– Anr. Copy.** 2 pts. in 1 vol. 4to. Engraved titles, map, 162 views on 81 India paper plts. only, spotted thro.-out, cont. hf. cf., worn. (BBA. Feb.23; 123) *Elliott.* £60
- **– Anr. Edn.** 1829. 4to. 2 additional engraved titles, 79 plts., some spotting or browning, publisher's bds., unc., soiled & worn. (S. Nov.1; 128) *Vine.* £70
- **– Anr. Copy.** 2 vols. 4to. 2 frontis. & engraved titles, 156 plts., foxing, hf. mor., corners. (SM. Mar.7; 2535) Frs. 1,000
- **– Anr. Edn.** L., 1830. 4to. Some foxing, three-qtr. cf. (RO. Dec.11; 297) $100
- **– Anr. Edn.** L., 1831. 4to. Some spotting, cont. mor. (S. Mar.6; 399) *Sanders.* £80
- **Metropolitan Improvements. – London & its Environs in the Nineteenth Century.** L., 1827; 1829. 2 vols. 4to. 2 engraved titles, 388 views on 210 sheets, hf. cf., spines torn. (P. Dec.8; 2) *Nicholson.* £200
- **– Anr. Copy.** 2 vols. 4to. 2 engraved titles (1 torn & reprd.), 349 views on 159 sheets, hf. cf., 1 spine defect. (P. Dec.8; 3) *Finney.* £170
- **– Anr. Edn.** L., 1828; n.d. 2 works in 1 vol. 4to. 1 (of 2) engraved titles, 302 views on 139 sheets, hf. mor., gt., as a collection of plts., w.a.f. (P. Oct.20; 29) £190
- **– Anr. Edn.** L., 1829. Together 2 works in 1 vol. 4to. 1st. work: engraved vig. title, engraved views on 79 sheets; 2nd. work: engraved vig. title, engraved plan, engraved views on 79 sheets; some discoloration & a few sm. stains, hf. cf., rubbed. (S. Dec.13; 222) *Salinas.* £120
- **– Anr. Edn.** L., n.d.; 1892. Together 2 vols. 4to. 1st. work: engraved plan, engraved views on 79 India paper sheets, no engraved title, some discoloration & stains; 2nd. work: engraved vig. title, engraved views on 79 sheets, some discoloration & stains, cont. cf., rubbed. (S. Dec.13; 221) *Elliott.* £75

SHEPPARD, William
- **The Touch-stone of Common Assurances.** 1648. *1st. Edn.* Sm. 4to. Lacks blank ll. 27-8, slightly soiled thro.-out, mod. cf. [Wing S3214] (BBA. Jun.14; 49) *Cavendish Rare Books.* £220

SHERATON, Thomas
- **Appendix to the Cabinet-Maker & Upholsterer's Drawing-Book; An Accompaniment to the Cabinet-Maker & Upholsterer's Drawing-Book.** 1802. 4to. 52 engraved plts., slightly browned & soiled, cont. cf.-bkd. bds., worn. (BBA. Jun.28; 304) *Demetzy Books.* £100

SHERER, John
- **Europe Illustrated.** L., ca. 1850. 1st. series vol. 2 only. Lge. 4to. Engraved title & 62 steel engrs., lightly stained thro.-out, cont. hf. leath., defect., upr. cover loose. (R. Oct.13; 2738) DM 800
- **– Anr. Edn.** L., [1876-79]. 1st. Series: 2 vols. Some spotting, cont. red hf. mor., rubbed. (S. Dec.13; 176) *Chancery.* £130
- **– Anr. Copy.** 2 vols. 4to. 120 steel-engraved plts., light plt. offset, three-qtr. cf. & cl., covers rubbed, spine ends worn; Marymount College copy, with some markings. (CBA. Mar.3; 204) $180
- **The Gold-Finder of Australia** ... L., ca. 1853. Plt. at p. 73 with variant title (but correct so?), a few ll. soiled, some staining, 1 plt. trimmed at fore-e., bdg. not stated, recased, new backstrip, bds. soiled. (KH. Nov.9; 699) Aus. $170
- **Rural Life Described & Illustrated, in the Management of Horses, Dogs, Cattle, Sheep, Pigs, Poultry etc** ... 1860. Sm. fo. Some margin dampstains, cont. mor., slightly worn. (TA. Apr.19; 178) £95
- **– Anr. Edn.** Ca. 1870. Lge. 8vo. Index incompl., some foxing, cont. cf., worn, covers & backstrip detchd. (TA. May 17; 256) £85
- **– Anr. Copy.** 4to. Three-qtr. leath., worn. (RO. Jun.26; 177) $100

SHERIDAN, Richard Brinsley
- **[-] The Rivals.** L., 1775. *1st. Edn.* Sm. 4to. Hf.-title, mor. gt. by Macdonald. (P. Oct.20; 206) £190
- **– Anr. Edn.** L., 1775. *2nd. Edn.* Sm. 4to. Hf.-title, mor. gt. by Macdonald, some staining. (P. Jan.12; 129) *Cavendish.* £60

SHERIDAN, Thomas
- **British Education.** L., 1756. *1st. Edn.* Hf.-title, cont. cf., splits in jnts., lacks part of label. (S. Mar.20; 683) *Drury.* £85
- **The Life of the Rev. Dr. Jonathan Swifte.** L., 1784. *1st. Edn.* Vol. 1. Bkplt., cf. (GM. Dec.7; 453) £70

SHERINGHAM, Hugh Tempest
- **An Angler's Hours.** L., 1905. (*With:*) – **Elements of Angling.** L., 1908. (*With:*) – **An Open Creel.** L., 1910. (*With:*) – **Coarse Fishing.** L., 1912. (*With:*) – **Trout Fishing: Memories & Morals.** L., [1920]. Slight spotting. (*With:*) – **Fishing: its Cause, Treatment, & Cure.** L., 1925. Together 6 vols. Cl., last rebnd. (S. Oct.4; 55) *Angle.* £60

SHERLOCK, M.
See— SESTINI, Dominique – SHERLOCK, M.

SHERLOCK, William
- **A Practical Discourse concerning Death.** Glasgow, 1761. Cont. spr. cf., spine gt.; Sir Ivar Colquhoun, of Luss copy. (CE. Mar.22; 125) £340

SHERLOCK HOLMES JOURNAL
Ed.:– James E. Holroyd & Philip Dalton. L., 1952-80. Vols. 1-15, No. 1 (lacks vol. 11, No. 1), together 54 (of 55) numbers. Lge. 4to. Ills., pict. wraps., stapled, inserted in 5 unif. cl. binders. (SG. Apr.19; 279) $150

SHERMAN, Stuart C.
- **The Voice of the Whaleman. With an Account of the Nicholson Whaling Collection.** Providence, Stinehour Pr., 1965. *1st. Edn.* 4to. Two-tone blind-pict. cl., d.-w. (SG. Sep.15; 346) $150

SHERWOOD, Mrs. Mary Martha
- **[Collected Works].** L., 1835-51 & n.d. *Mixed Edns.* 48 vols. 12mo. & 8vo. Cont. hf. cf. or roan; many vols. inscr. by members of her family, as a coll., w.a.f. (S. Dec.8; 130) *Quaritch.* £500

SHIEL, Matthew Phipps
- **Prince Taleski.** Boston, 1995. *1st. Amer. Edn.* Darkening, spine darkening, bdg. not stated, light stain to covers, extramities bumped & slightly rubbed. (CBA. Oct.29; 755) $130

SHILLINGLAW, John J.
- **... Copies of Certain Recently Discovered Historical Records Respecting the First Survey & Subsequent Settlement of Port Phillip Heads** ... Melbourne, 1878. *(775).* Sm. fo. Later? bds. & qtr. cl., spotted. (KH. Nov.9; 448) Aus. $210
- **– Anr. Edn.** 1879. Folding chart strengthened, some foxing, limp cl.; inscr. (KH. May 1; 628) Aus. $170
- **A Narrative of Arctic Discovery.** 1851. Some spotting, orig. cl. (P. Jun.7; 53) £75

SHIMON, of Cairo
- **Halachot Gedolot.** Venice, 1548. *1st. Edn.* Fo. Owner's stp. on verso of title, slight staining, some worming in margin, browned, mod. blind-tooled mor. (S. Oct.25; 362) *Klein.* £600
- **– Anr. Copy.** Fo. Slight staining & soiling, minor margin repair, sigd. by censors Fra. Hippolitus, 1601 & Camillo Yaghel, 1601, bds., rubbed; Hochschule für die Wissenschaft des Judenthums stps. [Steinschneider 7211, 1] (SPB. Jun.26; 30) $1,700

SHIMON BAR YOCHAI
- **Sifri.** Venice, 1546. Fo. Slight soiling & staining, traces of worming, early margin notes, mod. cl.; owner's note in Sefardic script of Eliezer Marzliach. (SPB. Feb.1; 83) $750

SHIMON BEN YOCHAI, attributed to
See— MOSHE DE LEON

SHIMON BEN ZEMACH DURAN
- **Ohev Mishpat, Mishpat Zedek.** Venice, 1589-90. *1st. Edn.* Fo. Some worming affecting some letters, slight staining mostly in margins, slightly creased, mod. blind-tooled mor. (S. Oct.25; 364) *Dzialowski.* £420
- **Tashbatz [Responsa].** Amst., 1738-41. 4 pts. in 1 vol. Fo. Lacks titles to pts. II & III, lightly browned, shaved, mod. cf., w.a.f. (S. Oct.25; 158) £180

SHIMON DARSHAN, of Frankfurt
- **Yalkut Shimoni.** Venice, 1566. *2nd. Edn.* 2 vols. Fo. Vol. I: title in facs., 1st. lf. torn & reprd. without loss of text, censor's sig. on 1st. lf., owner's sig. on 2nd. lf., some staining, slightly browned, hf. leath., marb. paper bds.; Vol. II: slight staining in margins, sig. of 'Ish Ger' [Abraham Joseph Shlomo Graziano] on last lf., blind-tooled mor. (S. Oct.25; 363) *Klein.* £800

SHIN BIJUTSU KAI
Kyoto, 20th. C. Vols. 1-7 & 15. Ptd. wraps., ex-liby. (SG. Jan.26; 224) $175

SHIPP, Horace
- **Edward Seago, Painter in the English Tradition.** 1952. *(85) numbered, sigd. by artist.* Fo. Orig. mor.-bkd. cl., s.-c. (S. Apr.30; 89) *Way.* £180

SHIPPEN, Edward
See— POWELL, William H. & Shippen, Edward

SHIRLEY, Henry
- **The Martyr'd Souldier.** 1638. *1st. Edn.* 4to. Lacks K4 (blank), mod. mor. by Rivière; title-p. sigd. 'Stamford 1683' (?Thomas Grey, 2nd. Earl of Stamford). [STC 22435] (BBA. Jan.19; 125) *Sutherland..* £180

SHIRLEY, James
- **The Dukes Mistris.** L., 1638. *1st. Edn.* Sm. 4to. Sm. hole in most ll. affects text, printing flaw in B4, some ll. browned, 19th. C. cf., worn, upr. cover detchd. (STC 22441). *(With:)* - **The Maides Revenge.** L., 1639. *1st. Edn.* Sm. 4to. Browned thro.-out, some margin tears, wraps., worn. [STC 22450] (BBA. May 3; 118) *Maggs.* £100
- **The Maides Revenge. A Tragedy.** T.C[otes] for William Cooke, 1639. *1st. Edn.* 4to. 2nd.? version of imprint, little margin worming, later cf.-bkd. bds. [STC 22450] (BBA. Jan.19; 126) *Maggs.* £240
- **Poems.** L., 1646. *1st. Coll. Edn.* Engraved port., initial & D8 blanks, lacks final blank, some stains, second D3 flawed, cont. sheep., jnts. reprd., bkplts. of Graham Pollard & Thomas Bramston of Skreens. [Wing S3481] (SPB. May 16; 136) $400

SHLOMO BEN AVRAHAM IBN ADERET of Barcelona
- **Teshuvot She'elot.** Rome (?), [1469-72]. *1st. Edn.* 4to. Uncensored, lacks 20 ll., 1 lf. inserted in reverse, 4 ll. misbnd., slight margin, staining, mostly in margins, trace of worming to inner & outer margins, some margin notes in later Sephardic hands, cl.-bkd. bds., rubbed; owners sigs. including Eliahu Chazan & Shmuel Chakim. [Steinschneider 6891, 24; Goff Heb-95] (SPB. Jun.26; 32) $26,000

SHLOMO BEN ZEMACH DURAN
- Ed.:– Shmuel Chagis. Venice, ca. 1596. 4to. Unpaginated, inner margins strengthened, foxed, edges slightly frayed, trimmed, mod. blind-tooled leath. (S. Oct.25; 379) *Davidson.* £400

SHLOMO IBN ADRET [Rashba]
- **Avodat Ha'Kodesh.** Venice, 1602. *1st. Edn.* 4to. Mispaginated, some margins badly frayed & reprd. not affecting text, stained buckram. (S. Oct.25; 368) *Davidson.* £320
- **Chidushei Brachot.** Venice, 1523. *1st. Edn.* 4to. Owners' sigs. on title, title mntd., slight staining, worming affecting some letters, buckram. (S. Oct.25; 369) *Jansen.* £700
- **Chidushei Chulin.** Venice, 1523. *1st. Edn.* 4to. Title mntd., some worming affecting some letters, some staining, slightly creased, hf. leath., marb. paper bds. (S. Oct.25; 370) *Toporwitch.* £620
- **Chidushei Gitin.** 1523. *1st. Edn.* 4to. Owner's sig. on title, staining, slightly creased, hf. leath. (S. Oct.25; 371) *Sunlight.* £850
- **She'eilot U'Teshuvot.** Hanau, 1610. *5th. Edn.* 4to. Title defect. & reprd. with loss of lr. part of engr., owners' sigs. on title, browned, slight foxing, trimmed, hf. leath., worn. (S. Oct.25; 372) *Toporwitch.* £280
- **Torat Ha'Bayit.** Cremona, 1565. 4to. Sigd. by censor Domenico Irosomitano (?), 1598, some soiling & staining, vell.-bkd. bds.; Hochschule für die Wissenschaft des Judenthums stp. [Steinschneider 6891, 33] (SPB. Jun.26; 31) $1,100
- **Torat Ha'bayit He'aruch.** Venice, 1608. *1st. Edn.* Fo. Title defect. not affecting text, 1st. 5 ll. lr. margins frayed affecting text, hf. leath., w.a.f. (S. Jul.3; 178) £260

SHLOMO IBN MELECH
- **Michol Yofi.** Constantinople, 1549. *1st. Edn.* Fo. Unpaginated, title reprd. without loss of text, owner's sig. on title, worming affecting some letters,

browned, slight staining, mod. mor. (S. Oct.25; 374) *Thomas.* £1,500

SHLOMO IBN VERGA
[-] **Shevet Yehuda / Tribus Judae ... complectens ... Res Judaeorum Ab everso Hierosolymorum Templo ad haec fere tempora usque ... De Hebraeo in Latinum versa a Georgio Gentio.** Amst., 1680. 4to. Cl.-bkd. card., unc. & unopened. (SG. Feb.2; 112) $200

SHLOMO ROCCA
- **Kavanot Shlomo.** Venice, 1670. *1st. Edn.* 4to. Leath., w.a.f. (S. Jul.3; 182) £160

SHMUEL
- **Maftechot Ha'zohar.** Ed.:– Israel Berechia Funtanella. Venice, 1744. *1st. Edn.* 2 pts. in 1 vol. 4to. Bds., w.a.f. (S. Jul.3; 185) £100

SHMUEL ABOAB
- **Dvar Shmuel.** Venice, 1702. Fo. Cl., w.a.f. (S. Jul.3; 186) £300

SHMUEL BEN JOSEPH, of Cracow
- **Olat Tamid.** Amst., 1681. Fo. Worming affecting some words, browned, creased, corners of upr. margins reprd. without loss of text, mod. bds. (S. Oct.25; 381) *Dzialowski.* £120

SHMUEL BEN ZADOK
- **Tashbatz.** Cremona, 1556-61. *1st. Edn.* 4to. Owners' stps. on title, trimmed with loss of parts of some letters, mod. mor. (S. Oct.25; 382) *Alex.* £550

SHMUEL FEIVISH KAHANA
- **Leket Shmuel.** Venice, 1694. *1st. Edn.* Fo. Owners' sigs. on title, discold., stained & creased, cl. (S. Oct.25; 380) *Hirschler.* £130

SHMUEL GALLICO
See— MORDEKHAI YA'AKOV, of Prague

SHMUEL TSARTSA
- **Sefer Mekor Hayyim.** Mantua, 1559. *1st. Edn.* Sm. fo. Last lf. reprd., scattered dampstaining & annots in ink, title remargined, later hf. cl., marb. bds., crude paper spine label. (SG. Feb.2; 300) $250

SHOBERL, Frederic
See— SCHOBERL or SHOBERL, Frederic

SHOEMAKER, Richard H.
- **A Checklist of American Imprints for 1820-29.** N.Y. & L., 1964-73. 12 vols., including 2 Indexes. Cl., slight wear. (RO. Dec.11; 299) $110

SHOEMAKER, Richard H.
See— SHAW, Ralph R. & Shoemaker, Richard H.

SHOIB, Joel Ibn
- **Olat Shabat.** Venice, 1576. Fo. Defect. & reprd., 3 ll. shorter than rest, some edges slightly frayed, some staining, worming affecting some letters, mod. mor. (S. Oct.25; 383) *Toporwitch.* £280

SHOP SIGNS OF PEKING
Preface:– H.J. Fung. Peking, [1931]. *(100).* Ob. fo. 18 hand-cold. plts., orig. decor. bds., upr. cover silk. (BBA. Nov.10; 297) *Han Shan Tang.* £110

SHORT INTRODUCTION OF GRAMMAR, A
1642. 12mo. Old sheep. (LC. Oct.13; 380) £100

SHORT VIEW OF THE DISPUTE Between the Merchants of London, Bristol, & Liverpool ... Concerning the Regulation of the African Trade
L., 1750. Lr. right-hand corner of title reprd., not affecting text, disbnd. (P. Sep.8; 94) *Bickersteth.* £90

SHUSHAN, Isachar Ben Mordecai Ibn
- **Ibur Shanim. Pe'ulat Isachar.** Venice, 1578-79. *2nd. Edn.* 4to. 1 hole in title not affecting border, title washed, some worming affecting some letters, staining, trimmed, hf. leath., marb. paper bds. (S. Oct.25; 384) *Davidson.* £300

SIBBALD, Sir Robert
- **A Collection of Several Treatise in Folio concerning Scotland, As it was of Old, & also in later Times.** Edinb., 1739. Fo. Cont. panel. cf.; Sir Ivar Colquhoun, of Luss copy. (CE. Mar.22; 275) £600

- **Scotia Illustrata sive Prodromus Historiae Naturalis ...** Edinb., 1684. Lge. 4to. 17 engraved plts., cont. cf. gt., worn. (PD. May 16; 162) £150

SIBERUS, Adamus
- **Lvdus Literarvm apud Chemnicvm Misniae, qva Ratione administretur. Item, Praecepta Morvm, ac Vitae Isocratis ad Demonicum ...** Strassb., 1549. Minimal spotting, bds. (HK. Nov.8; 341) DM 520
- - **Anr. Edn.** Trans.:– Andreae Sidelii. Leipzig, 1559. Sm. 8vo. Partly Greek & Latin text, ?lacks last lf. (blank?), slight browning & soiling, 19th. C. hf. cf. (S. Mar.20; 809) *Poole.* £55

SIBLY or SIBLEY, Ebenezer
- **The Medical Mirror.** L., n.d. *New Edn.* Engraved title, port., 13 plts. (1 double-p.), some light spotting, mod. hf. cf. (CSK. Feb.24; 5) £75
- **A New & Complete Illustration of the Occult Sciences or the Art of Foretelling Future Events ...** L., 1790. *1st. Edn.* 4to. Mod. hide. (CBA. Dec.10; 358) $150

SIBYLLINA ORACULA: Oracula Magica Zoroastris ... ; Oracula Metrica Iovis ...
Paris, 1607. 3 pts. in 1 vol. Cont. blind-stpd. cf., rebkd. (BBA. Mar.21; 14) *Poole.* £70

SICHEM, Christoffel van
- **Bybels Lusthof, ofte Twee Hondert en Veertig, zoo Historien als Leeringen des Bybels.** Amst., 1754. 4to. Old bds., badly worn. (SG. Feb.9; 144) $175

SICKLER, J.V.
- **Der Teutsche Obstgärtner.** Weimar, 1794-1802. Vols. 1-2, 11-14, 17-18 (lacks Vol. 12, pt. 6 & Vol. 13, pts. 1 & 3), in 41 pts. Wide margin, slightly stained in upr. margin, ptd. orig. wraps., unc. (R. Apr.4; 1716) DM 5,000
- - **Anr. Edn.** Weimar, 1800. Vol. 14 in 6 pts. Some slight foxing, orig. wraps. (R. Oct.12; 1842) DM 1,050
- - **Anr. Edn.** Weimar, 1801. Vol. 15 in 6 pts. Some slight foxing, orig. wraps. (R. Oct.12; 1843) DM 1,500
- - **Anr. Edn.** Weimar, 1802. Vol. 17 in 6 pts. Orig. wraps. (R. Apr.4; 1719) DM 1,200
- - **Anr. Edn.** Weimar, 1803. Some slight foxing, orig. wraps. (R. Oct.12; 1844) DM 1,500
- - **Anr. Edn.** Weimar, 1804. Vol. 22 in 6 pts. Some slight foxing, orig. wraps. (R. Oct.12; 1845) DM 1,500

SIDNEY, Algernon
- **Discourses Concerning Government.** 1698. *1st. Edn.* Fo. Cont. spr. cf., spine gt., rubbed. (BBA. Jun.28; 87) *Hannas.* £150
- - **Anr. Copy.** Fo. Cont. panel. cf. (TA. Aug.18; 378) £60
- - **Anr. Edn.** 1704. *2nd. Edn.* Sm. fo. Cont. cf., spine gt., slightly rubbed. (BBA. Jun.28; 88) *Bloomsbury Rare Books.* £80
- - **Anr. Copy.** Fo. Cf., corners reprd. (HD. Feb.22; 212) Frs. 1,800

SIDNEY, Sir Philip
- **L'Arcadie de la Comtesse de Pembrok.** Ill.:– Crispin de Passe, Michael von Lochom &c. 1625. 3 vols. Title-pp. of Vols. 2 & 3 torn, former with sm. loss of letters, 19th. C. vell. (HD. Apr.13; 53) Frs. 1,600
- **The Countess of Pembrokes Arcadia.** 1598. *3rd. Edn.* Sm. fo. With initial blank, title & blank rehinged, repair to final lf., cont. Engl. panel cf. gt., rebkd., orig. spine preserved, sm. repair to foot of upr. cover, lacks ties; cont. inscr. at head of title, sig. of Bernard Mearne, 17th. C. sig. of Robert Kemp. [STC 22541] (C. May 30; 6) *Quaritch.* £450
- - **Anr. Edn.** Ed.:– H. Oskar Sommer. 1891. *Facs. of orig. 4to. edn.*-Orig. blind-stpd. cf. by Fazakerley, partly untrimmed. (TA. May 17; 331) £55

SIDNEY, Samuel
- **The Book of the Horse.** Ca. 1885. 4to. 25 chromolithos., cont. hf. cf., recased. (TA. May 17; 244) £90
- **The Three Colonies of Australia.** L., 1851. Some ll. slightly soiled, orig. cl., rebkd. with orig. cl., slightly rubbed. (BBA. Dec.15; 29) *Stodart.* £70

- - **Anr. Edn.** 1852. *1st. Edn.* 8vo. Frontis. & title-p. slightly loose & spotted, orig. decor. cl. gt. (BBA. Jan.19; 79) *Simper.* £50

SIDUR MI'BRACHA MINHAG ITALIANI [with passover Haggadah]
Ferrara, 1693. 12mo. 1st. lf. torn & reprd. not affecting text, some staining, trimmed, hf. leath., marb. paper bds. (S. Oct.25; 385) *Herzfeld.* £300

SIEBER, F.W.
- **Reise nach d. Insel Kreta.** Leipzig, 1823. 2 vols. Slightly browned or foxed, cont. hf. leath., lightly rubbed or bumped. (HK. Nov.8; 1031) DM 950

SIEBMACHER, Johann
- **Allgemeines Grosses und Vollständiges Wappenbuch.** Nuremb., 1777. 6 vols. & 12 supps., in 5. Fo. Cont. bds., worn, spines defect. (C. May 30; 195) *Goldschmidt.* £700
[-] **Das Erneuerte Teutsche Wappenbuch: in Welchem dess H. Römische Reichs Potentaten, Fürsten, Herre, Edlen, Stände und stätte Namen; Wappen, Schilde, Helm, Kleinodion etc. abgebildet.** Nuremb., 1657-[68]. 5 pts. & supp. to 5 pts. in 3 vols. Ob. 4to. 4 (of 5) engraved titles, vol. 1 hf. title loose, pt. 1 plt. 140 to end stained increasingly in lr. corner, some copper engrs. cold in, general index bnd. in vol. 1, 2 arms excised vol. 1, foxing, cont. leath., rubbed, spine slightly defect. (D. Nov.24; 4193) DM 3,500
[-] **Das Gueldne Vliese, oder das Allerhoechste ... Kleinod ... in Welchem die ... Materia Prima ... Frucht des Philosophischen Steins ... Dargethan.** Nuremb., 1737. Lf. 'Lapis philosophorum' misbnd., instruction to binder at N4 cut into, new cf.; Dr. Walter Pagel copy. (S. Feb.7; 348) *Janssen.* £380
- **New Wappenbuch.** Nuremb., 1605. *1st. Edn.* Ob. 4to. 1 plt. with margin repair, lacks 1 corner, a few tears in lr. margin, minimal soiling, cont. vell., slightly soiled. (HK. Nov.9; 1729) DM 650
[-] **Newes Modelbuch in Kupffer Gemacht, darinnen Allerhand Arth Newer Model von Duen, Mittel, und Dick Aussgeschnidener Arbeit ...** Nuremb., 1604. Ob. 4to. Engraved & pict. titles, 58 numbered engraved plts., old vell. (SG. Apr.26; 117) $3,600

SIEBOLD, Philipp Franz von
- **Nippon.** Würzburg & Leipzig, 1897. 2 vols. Sm. 4to. Orig. decor. linen. (V. Sep.30; 2001) DM 400
- **Open Brieven uit Japan.** Desima, 1861. Orig. bds. (VG. Sep.14; 902) Fls. 1,900

SIEGEMUNDIN, Justina
- **Königl. Preussische und Chur-Brandenburgische Hof-Wehe-Mutter.** Berlin, 1752. 4to. Margins slightly foxed or soiled at beginning, cont. leath., corners worn, lacks ties. (GB. May 3; 1036) DM 2,500

SIEGFRIED
- **Illustrierter Kalender für 1887.** Ed.:– P.F. Krell.' Ill.:– Frz. v. Stuck. Stuttgart, [1886]. 4to. Bds., orig. cold. pict. wraps., wraps. stpd. & slightly browned, spine brittle. (HK. Nov.11; 4005) DM 440

SIEMSEN, Hans
- **Das Tigerschiff.** Ill.:– Renée Sintenis. Frankfurt, 1921. *(250).* 4to. Printers mark sigd. by author & artist, 9 (of 10) sigd. orig. etchings, loose, title-lf. mntd., lacks a hf.-title, orig. hf. leath., endpapers foxed. (GB. May 5; 3329) DM 1,000

SIEYES, E.
- **Politische Schriften ... nebst zwei Vorreden über Sieyès Lebensgeschichte ...** Trans.:– K.F. Oeisner. [Leipzig], 1796. *1st. German Edn.* 2 vols. Lacks engraved port., mod. bds. (R. Oct.11; 1226) DM 600

SIGAUD DE LA FOND, Jean René
- **Précis Historique et Experimental des Phenomènes Electriques ...** Ill.:– Sellier. Paris, 1781. *1st. Edn.* Hf.-title, privilege lf., 9 folding copperplates, some foxing, cont. mott. cf., spine elab. gt. (SG. Oct.6; 332) $130

SIGNA CHIMICA cum eorum Explicatione ex varys Authoribus collecta
[Germany, 18th Century]. 4to. Vell. bds. (S. May 10; 250) *Frers.* £180

SIGNAAL. Speciale Uitgave van de 'Berliner Illustrierte Zeitung'
1940-45. Years I-VI, 5 (all publd.), lacks 1 pt. of Vol. III. Fo. Mainly Dutch text, a few pts. in German or Engl., some defects, 4 vols. bnd. in 8, rest in pts. (B. Feb.8; 985) Fls. 1,500

SIGNATURE: A Quadrimestrial of Typography & Graphic Arts
Ed.:– Oliver Simon. L., 1935[-52]. Orig. Series: Nos. 1-18, New Series: Nos. 1-15 (all publd.), in 22 vols. Sm. 4to. Orig. wraps., or orig. wraps. laid in publisher's qtr. cl. & patterned bds., or cl. with orig. wraps. bnd. in. (SG. Sep.15; 303) $325
- - **Anr. Edn.** Ed.:– Oliver Simon. L., 1950-54. New Series nos. 10-18. Orig. wraps., in 3 orig. cl.-bkd. bd. folders. (S. May 1; 434) *Marks.* £60

SIGONIUS, Carolus
See— MURET, Marc-Antoine – SIGONIUS, Carolus

SIGOURNEY, Lydia Howard, nee Huntley
- **Moral Pieces in Prose & Verse.** Hartford, 1815. *1st. Edn.* Orig. ptd. bds., unc., upr. cover stained; Frederic Dannay copy. (CNY. Dec.16; 326) $110

SILBERSCHLAG
- **Théorie des Fleuves.** Paris, 1769. (*Bound with:*) BOSSUT & Viallet –Recherches sur la Construction la plus Avantageuse des Digues. Paris, 1764. Together 2 works in 1 vol. 4to. Cont. marb cf. decor. spine. (HD. Jan.27; 325) Frs. 1,500

SILBERT, J.P.
- **Gelobte sei Jesus Christus!** Wien, ca. 1840. Cont. mor., gt. cover, inner & outer dentelle, 2 sm. defects. on upr. cover. (HK. Nov.9; 1526) DM 520

SILESIO, Mariano
[-] **The Arcadian Princesse.** Trans.:– R. Brathwait. L., 1635. *1st. Edn.* Sm. hole in G2, some browning, cont. cf., rebkd.; David & Lulu Borowitz bkplt. [STC 22553] (S. Dec.8; 32) *Lawson.* £300

SILLIMAN, Dr. Benjamin
- **A Tour to Quebec in the Autumn of 1819.** L., 1822. Later cf.-bkd. cl., unc. (BBA. Dec.15; 50) *Maquire.* £130

SILTZER, Capt. Frank
- **The Story of British Sporting Prints.** 1929. *2nd. Edn.* 4to. Cl., slightly worn. (BS. Nov.16; 59) £75
- - **Anr. Edn.** 1929. *(1000).* Cl. gt., spine slightly worn. (DM. May 21; 28) $140

SILVA, Theodor Machado Freire Pereira da
- **Reforma do Estado Servil.** Rio de Janeiro, 1871. *1st. Edn.* Title-p. brittle on inner margin, mod. wraps., unc. (SG. Apr.5; 326) $150

SILVER, J.M.W.
- **Sketches of Japanese Manners & Customs.** 1867. Sm. 4to. Chromolitho. additional title & 27 plts., some margins spotted, orig. cl., disbnd., w.a.f. (CSK. Mar.23; 208) £260

SILVESTRE, Armand
- **Floréal.** Music:– Jules Massenet. Ill.:– Georges Cain. Paris, n.d. *Ltd. Iss. numbered.* 4to. Orig. aqua. port. sigd., 2 extra suites of ills., publishers bds. (DS. Feb.24; 2025) Pts. 36,000

SILVESTRE, Israël
- **Recueil de Planches sur les Châteaux de France.** N.d. Lge. ob. fo. 44 plts., some double or triple-p., stp. cf. 'Musées Nationaux Calcographie du Louvre,' hf. red chagrin. (HD. Feb.29; 44) Frs. 3,100

SILVESTRE, Joseph Balthasar
- **Alphabetum-Album. Collection de Soixante Feuilles d'Alphabets ...** Paris, 1843. Atlas fo. Additional engraved title, 59 engraved plts., a few hand-cold., some spotting, cont. hf. mor., top part of backstrip defect., covers detchd. (TA. Jul.19; 419) £110
- **Paléographie Universelle ...** Paris, 1841. *1st. Edn.* 4 vols. Fo. Additional engraved titles, 295 plts., many col.-ptd. or hand-cold. & heightened with gold, cont. red hf. mor. gt., scuffed. (C. Nov.9; 29) *Quaritch.* £1,600

SIM, Thomas Robertson
- **The Forests, Forest Flora of the Colony of the Cape of Good Hope.** Aberdeen, 1907. 4to. Title-p. foxed, cl. (SSA. Jul.5; 363) R 360

SIMLER, Josias
- **La République des Svisses.** Paris, 1578. *2nd. Fr. Edn.* Title with owner's note & reprd. margins, stained, cont. limp vell., lacks ties. (HK. Nov.8; 343) DM 2,400

SIMMS, Frederick Walter
- **Public Works of Great Britain.** 1838. Lge. fo. Vig. title, 2 uncold. aquatint plts., 153 engraved plans & diagrams, errata slip bnd. in at end, hf. cf. (TA. Oct.20; 291) £460

SIMON, André L.
- **Bibliotheca Vinaria: A Bibliography of ... Wines & Spirits.** L., 1913. *1st. Edn. (180)* numbered. Sm. 4to. Margin marks thro.-out, most in pencil, orig. cl., worn. (SG. Sep.15; 304) $220
- **The History of the Wine Trade in England.** 1906-09. 3 vols. Some ll. spotted, orig. cl. gt. (BBA. Aug.18; 121) *Price.* £190

SIMON, H.E. & others
- **In Memoriam Walther Rathenau 24 Juni 1922.** Ill.:– A. Maillol (initials), E. Gill (titles). Weimar, Cranach Pr., (1925). *(50)* on Maillol-Kessler-Bütten. Sm. 4to. Some foxing, MS owners name inside cover, with newspaper cutting, wraps. (H. Nov.24; 2552) DM 1,100

SIMON, O. (Ed.)
See— FLEURON

SIMON DE TROYES, M.E.T.
- **Choix de Poésies.** 1786. 2 vols. 16mo. Cf. gt., slightly worn. (BS. May 2; 36) £68

SIMOND, Charles (Pseud.)
See— CLEEMPUTTE, Paul Adolphe van 'Charles Simond'

SIMONET, J.F.
- **Lettres sur la Corse.** Paris, 1821. Some ll. yellowed, mod. hf. cl. (HD. Oct.21; 161) Frs. 1,800

SIMONETAE, Johannis
- **Commentarios Rerum Gestarum Francisci Sphortiae. Libri XXXI.** Mediolanum [Milan], Antonius Zarotus, [1479]. Narrow fo. Hand-cold. initials, very light spotting to 1st. & last few ll., early ink notations in some margins, 19th. C. pol. goat with interior bevels, gt.-lettered, some wear & scuffing at corners. [H. 14753] (HA. Nov.18; 355) $525

SIMONOFF, L. & Moerder, J. de
- **Les Races Chevalines avec une Etude Spéciale sur les Chevaux Russes.** Paris, [1894]. 4to. Cont. red hf. leath. gt., slightly worn. (HK. Nov.9; 2023) DM 420
- - **Anr. Edn.** Paris, n.d. Mor. gt., orig. wraps. bnd. in. (P. Apr.12; 183) *Shapiro.* £90

SIMONS, Anna
- **Title u. Initialen für die Bremer Presse.** München, Bremer Pr., 1926. *(220).* Lge. fo. 20 plts., orig. hf. linen portfo. (HK. Nov.11; 3451) DM 420

SIMONSON, George A.
- **Francesco Guardi.** 1904. Fo. Few ll. slightly spotted, orig. cl., slightly soiled. (BBA. Nov.10; 185) *Zwemmer.* £50

SIMPLE DIRECTIONS IN NEEDLE-WORK & CUTTING OUT; ... for the use of the National Female Schools of Ireland
Dublin, 1862. 4to. Orig. samples sewn in, no bdg. stated, as a coll., w.a.f.; bkplt. of Eliza Murphy Model School Parsonstown. (GM. Dec.7; 247) £140

SIMPLICIUS, of Silicia
- **Commentarii in Quatuor Aristotelis Libros de Coelo.** Venice, Jan. 1526. Fo. In Greek, some lr. margins lightly stained, outer margins of last few ll. reprd., cont. limp vell., reprd. (BBA. Nov.30; 17) *Poole.* £400
- - **Anr. Edn.** Venice, 1526. *1st. Edn.* Fo. Greek text, lacks prelim. blank, Engl. 18th. C. diced russ., probably by Roger Payne; Stanitz coll. (SPB. Apr.25; 399) $1,150

SIMPSON, Christopher
- A Compendium o Practical Musick. L., 1678. *3rd. Edn.* 5 pts. in 1 vol. Mus. notat. thro.-out, title-p. soiled, lacks port., later hf. cf., marb. bds., upr. cover loose. [Wing S53811] (SG. Apr.19; 170)
$110

SIMPSON, James H.
- Report of Explorations across the Great Basin of the Territory of Utah ... Wash., 1876. *1st. Edn.* Lge. 4to. Orig. cl.; ex-liby. with minimal marks. (SG. Apr.5; 181)
$110

SIMPSON, Thomas
- A New Treatise of Fluxions ... L., 1737. *1st. Edn.* (*With:*) - Essays upon Several Curious & Useful subjects, in Speculative & Mixed Mathematicks. L., 1740. *1st. Edn.* Together 2 vols. 4to. 1st. vol. cont. paper-bkd. bds., rubbed, soiled, spine worn, 2nd. vol. cont. tree cf., spine gt.; bkplt. & sig. of William Fyers in 2nd. vol., Stanitz coll. (SPB. Apr.25; 400)
$300

SIMPSON, William
- The Seat of War in the East. L., 1855. 1st. Series only. Fo. Hand-cold. litho. title, 39 cold. plts., some tissues with ptd. keys, some spotting, last 2 plts. with margins dustsoiled or slightly defect., cont. qtr. roan, covers slightly soiled. (S. Dec.1; 352)
Vittorio. £300
- - Anr. Copy. 1st. Series only: 1 vol. Fo. Col. litho. vig. title, litho. dedication, 35 (of 39) plts., soiling, vig. title & dedication dampstained, cont. hf. mor., worn, w.a.f. (CSK. Sep.30; 109)
£170
- - Anr. Copy. Lacks 5 plts., browning due to quality of paper, hf. cf., corners lacks spine, as a collection of plts., w.a.f. (CR. Jun.6; 291)
Lire 700,000
- - Anr. Edn. L., 1855-56. 1st. & 2nd. Series: 2 vols. Fo. 2 litho. titles with cold. vigs., 79 hand-cold. lithos., explanatory keys on tissues, light spotting affecting titles, dedication spotted, 2nd. title & a few outer margins in Vol. 2 stained, cont. red hf. mor. gt. (S. Dec.1; 351)
Vittorio. £1,000
- - Anr. Copy. 1st. & 2nd. Series: 2 vols. Lge. fo. 2 tinted litho. titles, dedication, 79 tinted litho. plts., some with engraved 'key' on tissue, margins of title & a few plts. spotted, cont. red mor., covers blind- & gt.-decor. (C. Nov.16; 171)
Maggs. £400
- - Anr. Copy. 1st. & 2nd. Series: 2 vols. in 1. 81 tinted litho. plts., including vig. title to each as listed, some minor spotting, a few ll. slightly loose, orig. hf. mor. gt., rubbed. (TA. Mar.15; 61) £240
- - Anr. Copy. 1st. & 2nd. Series: 2 vols. in 1. Fo. Litho. titles with vigs., 79 lithos., most plts. spotted & detchd., a few tissues torn, cont. red hf. mor., worn. (S. Mar.6; 47)
Quaritch. £220
- - Anr. Copy. 1st. & 2nd. Series: 2 vols. in 1. Fo. Tinted litho. titles, 79 plts., some slightly spotted, some loose, marginally soiled & frayed, cont. hf. mor. (BBA. Sep.29; 91)
Maggs. £190
- - Anr. Copy. 2 vols. in 1. fo. Tinted litho. titles, dedication, 79 plts., some spotting, some ll. detchd., cont. hf. mor., worn, upr. cover detchd., w.a.f. (CSK. Dec.16; 171)
£120

SIMPSON, Sir W.G.
- The Art of Golf. 1887. *1st. Edn.* Edg. not stated. (PD. Jul.13; 33)
£480

SIMROCK, Karl
- Das Maler. u. Romant. Rheinland. Leipzig, ca. 1840. 61 steel-engraved plts., some supp. plts., foxed, bumped & worn, cont. hf. leath. gt. (HK. Nov.9; 1200)
DM 1,500
- - Anr. Edn. Leipzig, [1841]. *1st. Edn.* Some slight foxing, some ll. loose, cont. hf. leath. gt. (GB. May 3; 214a)
DM 1,800
- - Anr. Edn. Leipzig, 1851. *New Edn.* 60 steel engrs., slightly foxed, mostly only in plt. margins, 1 with bkd. tear, cont. hf. linen, slightly spotted. (R. Oct.13; 2739)
DM 1,850
- - Anr. Copy. 53 (of 60) steel engraved plts., minimal spotting, cont. linen, blind-tooled, spine faded, lr. jnts. split. (HK. May 15; 1023) DM 950
- Rheinland. Leipzig, 1847. Das Malerische u. Romantische Deutschland Vol. VIII. Lightly foxed thro.-out. cont. linen, spotted. (H. Nov.23; 412)
DM 1,200

SIMS, Richard
- A Manual for the Genealogist, Topographer, Antiquary & Legal Professor. 1856. Orig. cl.; 2 A.L. from author on end-papers. (LC. Jul.5; 96)
£80

SINCERUS, Alex.
- Der Wohlerfahrne Salpeter Sieder u. Feuerwerker. Frankfurt & Leipzig, 1755. 2 pts. in 1 vol. Penultimate lf. with hf.-p. text excision, last lf. with bkd. margins, browned, bds. (HK. Nov.8; 554)
DM 480

SINCERUS [Zinzerling], J.
- Itinerarum Galliae ... cum Appendice de Burdigala. Amst., 1649. 12mo. Slightly browned or foxed, cont. leath., defect. (D. Nov.23; 834) DM 500
- - Anr. Edn. Amst., 1655. 12mo. Title stpd., end-paper & frontis. cleaned, cont. vell. (R. Oct.13; 3104)
DM 750
- - Anr. Copy. 12mo. Copper engraved title, 21 (of 22) folding copperplts., stained at beginning, wormed at end, slight loss, cont. vell., rubbed, spine with paper remains, lacks ties. (HT. May 10; 2794)
DM 440

SINCLAIR, Mrs. Francis
- Indigenous Flowers of the Hawaiian Islands. L., 1885. [*1st. Edn.*]4to. Sm. tear in intro. lf., 43 (of 44), col. plts., hf. mor. gt., rubbed. (P. Nov.24; 261)
Walford. £200
- - Anr. Copy. Perforation stp. on title, each plt. with light liby. hand-stp. on face, cl., worn. (RO. Dec.11; 304)
$575

SINCLAIR, George
- Hortus Gramineus Woburnensis: Or, an Account of the Results on the Produce & Nutritive Qualities of Different Grasses & Other Plants. L., 1825. *2nd. Edn.* 60 hand-cold. botanical plts., mod. hf. leath., some wear. (RO. Dec.11; 303)
DM 120
- The Hydrostaticks: or, the Weight, Force, & Pressure of Fluid Bodies ... Edinb., 1672. *1st. Edn.* Sm. 4to. Additional engraved title, folding plt. of arms, 7 folding plts., without lf. Pp4 (longitudinal title), a few plts. just trimmed, sm. repairs to border of ptd. title & margin of engraved title, cont. cf., spine rubbed; the Hopetoun House copy, with purchase note of John Hope. [Wing S 3845] (S. Nov.28; 134)
Phelpe. £420

SINCLAIR, Sir John
- The Code of Health & Longevity. Edinb., 1807. *1st. Edn.* 4 vols. Orig. bds., unc. (PD. Dec.14; 213)
£75
- The Statistical Account of Scotland, drawn up from the Communications of the Ministers of the Different Parishes. Edinb., 1791-99. [*1st. Edn.*]. 21 vols. Cont. cf., spines gt.; Sir Ivar Colquhoun, of Loss copy. (CE. Mar.22; 277)
£800
- - Anr. Copy. 21 vols. Hf.-titles, sm. liby. stps. on titles or hf.-titles, hf. cf., spines rubbed. (S. May 21; 77)
Weinreb. £360
- - Anr. Copy. Vols. 1-7 & 9-21, & dupl. Vol. 15. Most vols. in orig. hf. cf., worn. (PD. May 16; 184)
£160

SIND, Baron J.B. von
- Vollständiger Unterricht in den Wissenschaften eines Stallmeisters mit eines Lehrbegrif der Pferde-arzneikunst. Göttingen, 1775. *New Edn.* Some browning of text, cont. bds., spine worn. (S. Oct.4; 286)
Way. £160

SINGER, Charles Joseph
- Studies in the History & Method of Science. Intro.:– William Osler. Oxford, 1917-21. 2 vols. 4to. Cl. (SG. Oct.6; 334)
$140

SINGER, Hans Wolfgang
- Die Moderne Graphik. Ill.:– Manet, Slevogt & others. Leipzig, 1914. (*200*) numbered De Luxe Edn. Lge. 4to. 4 orig. etchings, orig pold. mor., gold-tooled decor., cover vig.; ex-libris inside cover. (GB. May 5; 3323)
DM 800
See— MULLER, Hermann Alexander & Singer, Hans Wolfgang

SINGER, Hans Wolfgang (Ed.)
See— ALLGEMEINES KUNSTLER-LEXIKON

SINGER, Hans Wolfgang & Springer, J.
- Rembrandts sämtliche Radierungen. München, ca. 1920. (*50*) De Luxe Edn. 3 portfos. Lge. fo. 312 ills. on plts., loose in 2 orig. bd. portfos. & 1 hf. leath. portfo., defect. & spotted. (H. Nov.23; 201)
DM 400

SINGER, Isaac Bashevis & Shub, Elizabeth
- Zlateh the Goat & Other Stories. Ill.:– Maurice Sendak. [N.Y., 1966]. *1st. Edn.* (*500*) numbered & sigd. by Singer & Sendak at colophon p. Andora wtrmkd. laid paper, coarse linen with mntd. black-&-white cover ill., gt.-stpd., backstrip slightly rubbed, orig. lightly marb. bd. s.-c., some rubbing. (HA. May 4; 285)
$160

SINISTRARI, Ludovico Maria
- Demoniality. Intro. & Notes:– M. Summers. Trans.:– M. Summers. L., [1927]. (*90*) sigd. by Summers. Vell. (SG. Nov.17; 203)
$100

SINJOHN, John (Pseud.)
See— GALSWORTHY, John 'John Sinjohn'

SINSABAUGH, Art & Anderson, Sherwood
- 6 Mid-American Chants, 11 Midwest Photographs. Highlands, North Carolina, 1964. *1st. Edn.* (*1550*). Ob. 8vo. Spiral-bnd. pict. wraps. (SG. May 10; 131)
$375

SIQUEIROS, David Alfaro
- No Hay Mas Ruta que la Nuestra ... Mexico, 1945. Ptd. wraps., spine chipped & faded; inscr. by author. (SG. Oct.13; 331)
$150

SIRE, Petrus
- Hanswick ende het Wonderdadigh Beeldt van de Alder-heylighste Magget ende Moeder Godts Maria ... Termonde, 1738. 12mo. Hf. roan. (HD. Dec.2; 161)
Frs. 1,050

SIREN, Osvald
- Chinese Painting: Leading Masters & Principles. Part I: The First Millenium. N.Y., [1956]. 3 vols., including plt. vol. Lge. 4to. 388 plts., cl., s.-c.'s. (SG. Oct.13; 103)
$150
- Chinese Sculpture from the Fifth to the Fourteenth Century. L., 1925. 4 vols. Sm. fo. 623 collotype plts., ex-liby., gt.-decor. buckram. (SG. May 3; 334)
$750
- A History of Early Chinese Art. L., 1929-30. 4 vols. Fo. Orig. buckram, spines slightly faded. (S. Oct.4; 193)
Llama. £250
- - Anr. Copy. 4 vols. 4to. Orig. cl. (BBA. Nov.10; 298)
Short. £100
- - Anr. Copy. 4 vols. Lge. 4to. 476 plts., ex-liby., buckram. (SG. May 3; 337)
$325
- - Anr. Copy. 4 vols. Lge. 4to. Buckram, spine ends nicked. (SG. Aug.25; 349)
$250
- A History of Early Chinese Painting. L., 1933. [*Medici Soc.*]. (*525*) numbered. 2 vols. Fo. Orig. buckram. (S. Oct.4; 194)
Llama. £200
- - Anr. Copy. 2 vols. Sm. fo. Buckram, shaken. (SG. Oct.13; 102)
$275
- - Anr. Copy. 2 vols. Lge. 4to. 228 plts., ex-liby., buckram. (SG. May 3; 338)
$200
- A History of Later Chinese Painting. L., 1938. (*525*) numbered. 2 vols. Fo. Orig. buckram. (S. Oct.4; 195)
Llama. £350
- The Imperial Palaces of Peking. Paris & Brussels, 1926. 3 vols. Sm. fo. 12 drawings, 2 maps, 274 collotype plts., ex-liby., buckram, shaken. (SG. May 3; 335)
$475
- The Walls & Gates of Peking. L., 1924. (*800*). 4to. Orig. cl.-bkd. bds., slightly rubbed. (S. May 1; 604)
Tang. £170
- - Anr. Edn. N.Y., [1924]. (*800*) numbered. 4to. Some light soiling, orig. cl.-bkd. bds., soiled. (CSK. Sep.16; 252)
£220
- - Anr. Copy. Sm. fo. 109 photogravure plts., 50 drawings, ex-liby., buckram-bkd. marb. bds. (SG. May 3; 333)
$350

SIRIGATTI, Lorenzo
- La Pratica di Prospettiva. Venice, 1596. *1st. Edn.* Fo. Tall copy, engraved title, 65 plts., some dampstains, few plts. misbnd., cont. vell., worn, lack ties. (SG. Oct.27; 300)
$1,000

SITGES, J.B.
- Les Mujeres del Rey Don Pedro I de Castilla. Madrid, 1910. 4to. Wraps. (DS. Mar.23; 2314)
Pts. 50,000

SITGREAVES, Lorenzo
- Report of an Expedition down the Zuni & Colorado Rivers. Wash., 1853. *1st. Edn. 1st. Iss.* Tall 8vo. Cont. cf. (SG. Jan.19; 324) $200

SITWELL, Edith
- The Mother & Other Poems. Oxford, 1915. *1st. Edn. (500).* Sq. 12mo. Some pp. a little foxed, orig. ptd. wraps., one of the two spine stitching threads partly loose; pres. copy from author to John Freeman, Frederic Dannay copy. (CNY. Dec.16; 327) $450

SITWELL, Sir George
- On the Making of Gardens. Ill.:– John Piper. 1949. *(1000) numbered. (100) sigd. by artist & O. Sitwell,* specially bnd. Mor., d.-w., case. (HBC. May 17; 216) £170
- - **Anr. Edn.** Ill.:– John Piper. 1949. *(1000) numbered.* Buckram, d.-w. (HBC. May 17; 218) £85
- - **Anr. Copy.** Buckram, d.-w. (HBC. May 17; 217) £70

SITWELL, Maj.-Gen. Hervey Degg Wilmot
- Crown Jewels & Other Regalia in the Tower of London. Ed.:– Clarence Winchester. L., Dropmore Pr., [1953]. Fo. Cl., spine faded. (SG. Oct.13; 211) $110

SITWELL, Osbert
- Autobiography. L., 1945-50. *1st. Engl. Edns.* 5 vols. Orig. cl., 2 vols. slightly soiled; pres. copies to C.H. Wells, Vol. 2. also inscr. by dedicatee, Maynard Holingworth. (S. Mar.20; 963)
Waterfield. £50

SITWELL, Sacheverell & Madol, Roger
- Album of Redouté. 1954. *Ltd. Edn.* Lge. fo. 25 facs. cold. plts., cl.-bkd. ptd. bds.; from liby. of Luttrellstown Castle, w.a.f. (C. Sep.28; 1799) £170
- - **Anr. Copy.** Fo. Orig. bds. (P. Nov.24; 128) £60

SITWELL, Sacheverell & others
- Fine Bird Books, 1700-1900. 1953. *(2000).* Fo. Hf. cl. (P. Jan.12; 51) *Maggs.* £180
- - **Anr. Copy.** Fo. 74 plts. (38 col.), cl., marb. bds. (HBC. May 17; 458) £155
- - **Anr. Copy.** Fo. Orig. cl. (SPB. Dec.13; 608) $400
- - **Anr. Copy.** Fo. Hf. cl. (VS. Dec.7; 367) Fls. 625
- Great Flower Books, 1700-1900: a Bibliographical Record. L., 1956. Fo. Orig. hf. cl. (S. Nov.28; 85) *Wilson.* £250
- - **Anr. Copy.** Fo. Orig. hf. cl., lightly soiled, lr. cover scuffed. (CSK. May 18; 123) £180
- - **Anr. Copy.** Tall fo. Bds., cl. back & tips, moderate wear, d.-w. torn & frayed. (RO. May 22; 159) $300

SIX SKETCHES IN LITHOGRAPHY: Representing the Common Actions of the Horse
Ill.:– after R.F.R. Day & Haghe, 1842. Fo. 6 litho. plts., orig. paper covers. (LC. Mar.1; 543) £180

SKELLETT, Edward
- A Practical Treatise on the Breeding Cow & Extraction of the Calf. Ill.:– after Kirtland & Mogdridge. 1807. Tall 8vo. 13 hand-cold. folding engraved plts., orig. cl.-bkd. bds., label slightly defect. (SKC. Nov.18; 1987) £60

SKELTON, Joseph
- Engraved Illustrations of the Principal Antiquities of Oxfordshire. Ill.:– after F. MacKenzie. Oxford, 1823. Fo. Cont. gt.-embossed mor.; subscription copy. (HBC. May 17; 369) £95
- - **Anr. Copy.** 4to. Engraved frontis., engraved title, map, 49 engraved plts., staining & spotting to some plts., leath.-bkd. bds., worn, scuffed. (LC. Jul.5; 228) £70
- Etchings of the Antiquities of Bristol from Original Sketches by the Late Hugh O'Neill. Ca.1830. 4to. 53 engraved plts., cont. hf. mor., some wear. (TA. Dec.15; 107) £50

SKELTON, Raleigh Ashlin
- James Cook Surveyor of Newfoundland. San Franc., Grabhorn Pr., 1965. *(365).* 2 vols. Fo. Orig. wraps., canvas book-box. (BBA. Jun.14; 278)
Quaritch. £75

SKELTON, Raleigh Ashlin & Summerson, John
- A Description of Maps & Architectural Drawings in the Collection made by William Cecil, First Baron Burghley, now at Hatfield House. Roxb. Cl., 1971. Fo. Orig. qtr. mor., covers stained. (S. Oct.4; 244)
Traylen. £220

SKENE, Sir John
- The Lawes & Acts of Parliament, maid be King James the First & His Successours ... Edinb., 1597. Fo. Initial lf. with list of publications, slightly shaved, old panel. cf., rubbed; Sir Ivar Colquhoun, of Luss copy. [NSTC 21877] (CE. Mar.22; 279) £280
- Regiam Majestatem, The Avld Lavves & Constitutions of Scotland faithfvllie collected ... Edinb., 1609. Fo. Title-p. strengthened & some stains, old spr. cf., spine gt.; Sir Ivar Colquhoun, of Luss copy. [STC 22626] (CE. Mar.22; 278) £180
- - **Anr. Copy.** Fo. Limp. vell. [STC 22626] (P. Jan.12; 277) *Smallwood.* £110

SKENE, W.F. & others
- The Historians of Scotland ... Edinb., 1875-80. 10 vols. Orig. cl. gt. (PD. May 16; 79) £50

SKETCH OF A TOUR in the Highlands of Scotland through Perthshire, Argyleshire & Inverness-Shire in Sept/Oct 1818
1819. Rebnd., cl.; ex-liby. (PD. Jun.13; 220) £50

SKIFF, F.J.V
See— DAWSON, Thomas F. & Skiff, F.J.V.

SKINNER, Andrew
See— TAYLOR, George & Skinner, Andrew

SKINNER, Sgt. H.M.
See— DOLLMAN, Lieut.-Col. M. & Skinner, Sgt. H.M.

SKINNER, Joseph
- The Present State of Peru. 1805. 4to. 16 (of 20), cold. plts. tear in 1 margin just affecting text, sm. liby. stp. on title-p., cont. cf. gt., jnts slightly weak. (BBA. Feb.9; 292) *Waggett.* £70
- - **Anr. Edn.** [L., 1805]. 4to. Slightly soiled or foxed, leath. [Sabin 81615] (D. Nov.23; 1332) DM 900

SKINNER, Liam C.
- Politicians by Accident. Dublin, 1946. *1st. Edn.* Mor., spine defect.; sigd. & inscr. by author, also inscr. by all of Cabinet of 1945. (GM. Dec.7; 333) £75

SKIRA, Albert
- Historie de la Peinture. Priv. ptd., 1950-62. 14 vols. Sm. 4to. Publisher's cl. (SM. Mar.7; 2231)
Frs. 2,600
- Les Tresors de la Peinture Française. Text:– Aragon, Ponge, Soupault, Tzara & others. Genève, priv. ptd., 1942-49. 38 vols. Lge. 4to. Publisher's bds. (SM. Mar.7; 2232) Frs. 1,900

SKLODOWSKA, Marie
See— CURIE, Mme Marie, née Sklodowska

SKODA, Joseph
- Abhandlung über Perkussion und Auskultation. Wien, 1839. *1st. Edn.* Fo. Cont. bds., corners slightly bumped. (R. Oct.12; 1479) DM 1,600
- - **Anr. Copy.** Hf.-title, last ll. & end-papers lightly foxed, light browning. cont. hf. leath., spine rubbed. (GB. May 3; 1037) DM 1,300

SKOGMAN, Carl Johan Alfred
- Fregatten Eugenies Resa Omkring Jorden Aren. 1851-1853. Stockholm, [1854-55]. *1st. Edn.* 2 vols. in 1. 3 folding maps, 20 cold. plts., sm. liby. stp. on title-p., orig. hf. cf. gt. (BBA. Feb.9; 269)
Edwards. £120
- - **Anr. Copy.** 2 pts. in 1 vol. Lge. 8vo. 18 col. & 2 tinted litho. plts., 6 wood-engraved plts., 3 partly tinted folding litho. maps, errata lf., hf. mor. gt. (SG. Sep.22; 270) $750

SKUES, George Edward Mackenzie
- The Way of a Trout with a Fly. L., 1921. *1st. Edn.* Bkplt. of Col. Keith Rollo. *(With:)* - Minor Tactics of the Chalk Stream. L., 1924. *3rd. Edn. (With:)* - Side-Lines, Side-Lights & Reflections. L., [1932]. *1st. Edn. (With:)* - Nymph Fishing for Chalk Stream Trout. L., 1939. *1st. Edn.* Together 4 vols. Orig. cl. (S. Oct.4; 57) *Inge.* £75

SLABBER, M.
- Natuurkundige Verlustigingen ... Microscopise Waarneemingen v. In- & Uit-landse Water- en Land-dieren. Ill.:– R. Muys, after author or P.M. Brasser. Haarlem, [1769]-78. 18 pts. in 1 vol. 4to. 18 cont. hand-cold. plts., cont. hf. cf. (VG. Nov.30; 780) Fls. 1,000
- - **Anr. Copy.** 4to. 18 hand-cold. plts., bds., defect. (VG. May 3; 697) Fls. 700

SLAUERHOFF, J.
- Het Leven op Aarde. Rotterdam, 1934. *1st. Edn.* Orig. cl. gt., spine discold., autograph dedication by author dtd. Paris Jan. '35. (VS. Jun.6; 370)
Fls. 1,300

SLAVE TRADE
- Abstract of the Evidence ... for the Abolition of the Slave-Trade. L., 1791. Folding map, plt., orig. bds., partly unopened, spine torn. (P. May 17; 163)
Bickersteth. £75

SLEATER, Rev. M.
- ... Civil & Ecclesiastical Topography & Itinerary of Counties of Ireland. Dublin, 1806. *1st. Edn.* List of subscribers, orig. bds., unc. (GM. Dec.7; 147) £80

SLEE, Sophie
[-] A Hermit's Tale. 1787. *1st. Edn.* 4to. Hf. cf. (P. Jul.26; 145) £200

SLEEMAN, William Henry
- Rambles & Recollections of an Indian Official. 1844. 2 vols. Browned & lightly soiled, orig. cl., rebkd., old spine preserved, damp-affected. (CSK. Sep.30; 31) £70

SLEIDANUS, Johannes (Pseud.)
See— PHILIPPSON, Johannes 'Johannes Sleidanus'

SLEIGH, John
- A History of the Ancient Parish of Leek, in Staffordshire; Including Horton, Cheddleton, & Ipstones. Ca. 1890. *2nd. Edn. Ltd. Subscribers' Edn., numbered & sigd. by publishers.* 4to. Orig. decor. cl., spine rubbed, unc. (TA. Apr.19; 100) £58

SLESSOR, Kenneth
- Earth Visitors. Ill.:– Norman Lindsay. L., Franfrolico Pr., 1926. *(425) numbered.* Bdg. not stated; 2 A.L. from author, inscr. by Jack Lindsay, Harry F. Chaplin copy. (JL. Jul.15; 249) Aus. $210

SLEVOGT, Max
- Der Gelernte Jäger. Berlin, [1924]. *(100) numbered.* Fo. 13 lithos. on China under passepartout, mntd, all lithos. sigd. by artist, lacks double-p. ptd. title with imprint, lf. 1 slightly foxed, loose in orig. hf. vell. portfo. (R. Oct.11; 421) DM 850
- Randzeichnungen zu Mozarts Zauberflöte. Berlin, Pan Pr., 1920. *(100). (90) for sale.* Fo. All etchings sigd., 47 etchings, 8 ll. in litho., under guards, with double lf., creased in lr. margin, loose lf. in bd. box, torn. (H. Nov.24; 2087) DM 10,000
- Zeichnungen zu Kinderliedern, Tierfabeln und Maerchen. Berlin, 1920's?. *(600) numbered & sigd.* 4to. Parch.-bkd. pict. bds., soiled. (SG. Mar.29; 261) $175

SLEVOGT, Max (Ill.)
See— ARABIAN NIGHTS

SLEZER, Capt. John
- Theatrum Scotiae, containing the Prospects of their Majesties Castles & Palaces. 1693. *1st. Edn.* Fo. Cont. mott. cf., spine gt., reprd. (PD. Jun.13; 142) £980
- - **Anr. Edn.** 1718. *2nd. Edn.* Fo. Vig. title, 57 double-p. engraved plts., 2 plts. torn at centrefold affecting engraved area, cont. cf., worn; Sir Ivar Colquhoun, of Luss copy. (CE. Mar.22; 280) £480

SLICHTENHORST, Arend van
- XIV Boeken van de Geldersse Geschiedenissen. Arnhem, 1653. 2 pts. in 1 vol. Fo. Some stains, tears in 3 plts. reprd., hole in 1 plt., mod. wraps. (B. Oct.4; 739)   Fls. 2,400

SLIMAN ben Ibrahim Baamer
- La Vie de Mohammed Prophète d'Allah. Ill.:– E. Dinet & Mohamed Racim. Paris, 1918. (925). 4to. Seived, partly detchd. (HD. Dec.9; 124) Frs. 3,600

SLIMAN BEN IBRAHIM, S.
- Khadra, Danseuse Ouled Nail. Ill.:– Etienne Dinet, decor.:– Mohammed Racim. Paris, 1926. Sm. 4to. On vell., sewed, pict. wrap., box. (HD. Dec.16; 111)   Frs. 1,600
- Rabiâ el Kouloub ou le Printemps des Coeurs. Ill.:– E. Dinet. 1902. On vélin de Rives, mosaic mor. by Lortic, silk doubls. & end-papers, wrap., spine faded. (HD. Jan.24; 85)   Frs. 3,600

SLOAN, Samuel
- City & Suburban Architecture. Phila., 1859. 1st. Edn. Sm. fo. 136 litho. plts., some foxing, orig. gt.-pict. cl., lacks backstrip. [Sabin 82161] (SG. Oct.13; 333) $275
- Sloan's Constructive Architecture. Ill.:– L.N. Rosenthal after Sloan. Phila., 1859. 4to. 66 litho. plts., 29 tinted or cold., 1 folding, 1 double-p., some light soiling, orig. cl., soiled, spine chipped at extremities. (CSK. May 18; 3)   £75

SLOANE, B.L.
See— WHITE, A. & Sloane, B.L.

SLOANE, Sir Hans
- An Account of a Most Efficacious Medicine for Soreness, Weakness, & Several Other Distempers of the Eyes. L., ca. 1750. 2nd. Edn. Mod. qtr. cl. (SG. Oct.6; 335) $150

SLOANE, William Milligan
- Life of Napoleon Bonaparte. N.Y., 1896. 8 vols. Very lge. 4to. Extra-ill. with hundreds of plts., many hand-cold. & some folding or double-p., with approx. 170 letters & documents, all extra ills. & autograph pieces keyed in pencil to the appropriate text p., crushed armorial red mor. gt. extra, by Bayntun, Napoleon arms stpd. on covers, gt. inner dentelles, moire silk doubls. & free end-papers, cl. s.-c.'s. (SG. Nov.3; 151) $9,500
- – Anr. Edn. N.Y., 1906. 8 vols. Fo. Extra-ill. with many plts., many engraved & inlaid, some hand-cold., including a few folding or double-p. views after L. Mayer, C. Vernet, & from R. Bowyer's ill. 'Record of Important Events in the Annals of Europe', a little light spotting, red mor. gt. by Bayntun (Rivière), boxed. (S. Oct.4; 101)
                              Traylen. £1,250
- – Anr. Copy. 4 vols. 4to. Cont. mor. gt. (SKC. May 4; 1605)   £75

SLONIMSKY, Hayyie Zelig
- Sefer Toledot ha-Shamayim. Zhitomir, 1866. 2nd. Edn. Tall 8vo. Mod. leath., orig. wraps. bnd. in. (SG. Feb.2; 302) $150

SLUYTERMAN, K.
See— MOES, Ernst Willem & others

SMALL, James
- A Treatise on Ploughs & Wheel Carriages. Edinb., 1784. Orig. bds., unc. worn. (BBA. May 3; 66)   Jarndyce. £190

SMALLEGANGE, Matthias
- Nieuwe Cronyk van Zeeland. Middelburg, 1696. Pt. 1 (all publd.). Fo. Engraved title, 90 maps, plts. & plans, including extra 'Oostersteijn', some sm. tears & repairs, few wormholes, cf., slight defects, new end-papers. (B. Oct.4; 740) Fls. 4,000
- – Anr. Copy. Vol. I (all publd.). Fo. Lacks general map & 2 plts., few plts. slightly creased, some with sm. margin tears, cont. blind-stpd. vell. (VG. Sep.14; 1201)   Fls. 3,300

SMALLEY, George W.
- London Letters. L., 1890. 2 vols. Cl., worn; pres. copy from author to Lady Randolph Churchill, with bkplts. of Randolph S. & Winston Churchill. (LH. Jan.15; 259) $100

SMART, Christopher
- Poems on Several Occasions. Ill.:– Grignion & Worlidge. L., 1752. 1st. Edn. 4to. Frontis. & title stained, cont. cf., upr. cover detchd., upr. free end-paper detchd., piece torn from 1st. fly-lf.; Frederic Dannay copy. (CNY. Dec.16; 328) $120

SMEATON, John
- An Experimental Enquiry concerning the Natural Powers of Water & Wind to turn Mills & other Machines, Depending on a Circular Motion. L., 1760. Blank K4 present. (Bound with:) – An Account of Some Experiments upon a Machine for Measuring the Way of a Ship at Sea. [L.], 1754. Together 2 works in 1 vol. 4to. Minor spotting, cont. sheep-bkd. marb. bds., rebkd., rubbed; armorial bkplt. of Delamere House Liby., Northwick, Cheshire, Stanitz coll. (SPB. Apr.25; 401) $700
- A Narrative of the Building of the Edystone Lighthouse with Stone. L., 1791. Fo. Lge. engraved vig. on title, 23 engraved maps & plts. (1 short tear in fold), a few margins slightly dust-soiled, hf. cf., rebkd. (S. May 21; 18)   Fisher. £280
- – Anr. Edn. 1793. Fo. Rebnd. in recent hf. mor. (LA. Nov.29; 94)   £200
- – Anr. Edn. 1813. 2nd. Edn. Fo. Engraved vig. title, 23 plts. & plans (1 folding), title lightly spotted, cont. hf. mor., worn, covers detchd., w.a.f. (CSK. Apr.6; 2)   £190
- Reports made on Various Occasions, in the Course of his Employment as a Civil Engineer. L., 1812. [1st. Coll. Edn.]. 3 vols. 4to. 72 engraved plts., hf.-title in Vol. 2, no port., spotted & soiled thro-out, liby. stps. on titles, unc., later cl.-bkd. bds., worn. (BBA. Nov.30; 124)   Demetzy. £150
- – Anr. Copy. 3 vols. Browning & spotting, liby. buckram; Liby. of Congress dupl. with stps., Stanitz coll. (SPB. Apr.25; 402) $275

SMELLIE, William
- The Philosophy of Natural History. Edinb., 1790. 1st. Edn. 4to. Cont. owner's sig. on title, old hf. cf. (CE. Sep.1; 44)   £50
- – Anr. Edn. Edinb., 1790-99. 1st. Edn. 2 vols. 4to. Cont. tree cf., spines gt.; Sir Ivar Colquhoun, of Luss copy. (CE. Mar.22; 282)   £300

SMIDS, Ludolph
- Schatkamer der Nederl. Oudheden. Notes:– P. Langendyk. Ill.:– J. Schynvoet after J. Rochman. Haarlem, 1737. 2nd. Printing. Hf. cl., unc. (B. Jun.21; 489)   Fls. 650

SMILES, Samuel
- Self-Help. 1859. 1st. Edn. Various notes & letters loosely inserted, orig. cl., spotted & slightly worn. (BBA. Oct.27; 66)   Pickering & Chatto. £190

SMITH, Adam
- An Inquiry into ... Wealth of the Nations. 1793. 7th. Edn. 3 vols. Cf., worn. (P. Oct.20; 153)   £85
- – Anr. Edn. 1805. 11th. Edn. 3 vols. Cf. (P. Jul.5; 169)   £160
- – Anr. Edn. L., 1819. 3 vols. Cont. cf. gt., jnts. & spines worn. (SG. Feb.16; 281) $100
- – Anr. Edn. Edinb., 1828. 4 vols. Some spotting, lending liby. stp. partly removed from each title, bds., unc., rebkd., some soiling. (SPB. Dec.13; 740) $275
- Recherches sur la Nature et les Causes de la Richesse des Nations. Trans.:– Germain Garnier. Ill.:– Prévost (port.). Paris, 1802. New Edn. 5 vols. Cont. cf., decor. spines. (HD. Sep.22; 345)   Frs. 1,400

SMITH, Adolphe
- Street Incidents: A Series of Twenty-One Permanent Photographs ... Ill.:– after J. Thomson. L., 1881. 4to. Title & last p. of text age-darkened, gt.-pict. cl., a few minor stains, rubbed. (SG. Nov.10; 158) $2,000

SMITH, Albert
- The Story of Mont Blanc. 1853. Orig. cl., soiled. (BS. Nov.16; 18)   £75

SMITH, Sir Andrew
- Illustrations of the Zoology of South Africa. Johannesburg, Winchester Pr., 1977. Facs. Edn. (350) numbered. 3 vols. 4to. Orig. leath. gt. (S. Nov.28; 86)   Hill. £250

SMITH, Bradley
- Japan. A History in Art. N.Y., 1964. (500) numbered. 4to. Silk-covered bds., Paulownia box; pres. copy from author. (LH. Sep.25; 472) $130
- – Anr. Copy. Sm. fo. Silk brocade, with family crests in gold, paulownia wood box with hand-lettered title. (SG. Jan.26; 225) $100

SMITH, Charles
- New English Atlas. 1804. Fo. Engraved title, contents lf., 46 hand-cold. maps, some torn, cont. limp cf. (CSK. Feb.10; 19)   £450
- – Anr. Edn. L., priv. ptd., 1808. 2nd. Edn. Fo. Engraved title & contents list, 42 maps on 46 double-p. engraved mapsheets, neatly wash & outl. cold. by hand, subscribers list, some dust-soiling or faint discolouration, cont. hf. russ., defect., w.a.f. (S. May 21; 34)   Walford. £450
- New General Atlas. 1808. Fo. 45 hand-cold. engraved maps, cont. hf. cf., rather worn. (BBA. Jun.14; 260)   New York Public Library. £240
- – Anr. Copy. Sm. fo. (396 × 325mm). Engraved title, 43 engraved maps, including 2 double-p., hand-cold. in wash & outl., title & few maps dust-soiled, some slight margin staining, cont. hf. cf., defect. (S. Nov.1; 181) Marlboro Rare Bks. £130
- – Anr. Edn. 1816. 4to. 48 hand-cold. maps, cont. hf. mor., backstrip defect., covers detchd. (TA. Jan.19; 33)   £110

SMITH, Charles Hamilton
- Selections of the Ancient Costume of Great Britain & Ireland, from the Seventh to the Sixteenth Century ... 1814. Fo. Hand-cold. vig. title, 63 hand-cold. aquatints (3 plts. in 2 states), cont. str.-grd. hf. mor., rubbed. (TA. Jan.19; 226)   £330
- – Anr. Copy. Fo. Engraved title & 60 plts., all hand-cold., some ll. slightly soiled or spotted, mod. hf. mor. (BBA. May 23; 232)   Hanna. £120
See— MEYRICK, Samuel Rush & Smith, Charles Hamilton

SMITH, Charles Roach
- Collectanea Antique, Etchings & Notices of Ancient Remains, Illustrative of the Habits, Customs & History of Past Ages. Priv. ptd., 1848-80. 7 vols. Some plts. hand-cold., unif. cont. cf., gt.-decor. spines, Vol. 1 very rubbed. (TA. Nov.17; 221)   £110

SMITH, Charlotte
- Ethelinde, or the Recluse of the Lake. 1789. 1st. Edn. 5 vols. Cont. hf. cf., very worn, covers loose. (BBA. Aug.18; 90)   Jarndyce. £65
- Ethelinde, or the Recluse of the Lake. – Emmeline. The Orphan of the Castle. 1789. 1st. Edn; 3rd. Edn. 5 vols. & 4 vols. 12mo. Hf.-titles, unif. cont. cf. gt., decor. oval centre panels; the Minton House copies. (LC. Oct.13; 472)   £300
- Rural Walks, in Dialogue; Intended for the Use of Young Persons. Phila., 1795. 2 vols. in 1. 12mo. Owner's sig. on title clipped, early cf., worn. (SG. Dec.8; 325) $175

SMITH, Daniel
See— MILLS, Samuel J. & Smith, Daniel

SMITH, David Eugene
- Rara Arithmetica. Boston & L., 1908. (151) numbered. 2 vols. Gt.-decor. vell., unc., light wear & soiling. (RO. Dec.11; 306) $160
- – Anr. Edn. Camb., Mass., 1908. (150) numbered De Luxe Edn. Orig. vell. gt. (R. Oct.11; 765)
                              DM 450
- – Anr. Edn. L., 1908-39. 2 vols., including Supp. Orig. cl. & orig. wraps. (BBΛ. Mar.7; 260)
                              Maggs. £65

SMITH, David Nichol
See— COURTNEY, William Prideaux & Smith, David Nichol

SMITH, Edgar W. (Ed.)
See— BAKER STREET JOURNAL

SMITH, Elizabeth
- The Compleat Housewife. L., 1742. 11th. Edn. Engraved frontis., folding engraved plts., frontis. loose, 1 plt. torn, slight browning, cont. panel. cf., worn. (S. Apr.9; 230)   Vince. £100
- – Anr. Edn. 1753. Some worm at lr. corner of 1st. few ll., cf., worn. (P. Jul.26; 49)   £80

– – **Anr. Edn.** 1766. *17th. Edn.* 1 lf. torn, some soiling, MS. longitudinal title on D1, cont. sheep, worn. (BBA. Jun.14; 73)
Cavendish Rare Books. £70

SMITH, Garden G.
See— HILTON, Harold H. & Smith, Garden G.

SMITH, George
[–] **The Angler's Magazine, or, Necessary & Delightful Store-House.** L., 1754. *1st. Edn.* Lacks 2 folding tables. (*Bound with:*) SCOTT, Dr. Thomas [–] **The Anglers. Eight Dialogues in Verse.** L., 1758. *1st. Edn.* Printing flaw on last lf. Together 2 works in 1 vol. 12mo. Cont. cf. gt. (S. Oct.4; 58)
Simpson. £100

SMITH, George, Upholsterer
– **The Cabinet-Maker & Upholsterer's Guide** ... 1826. 4to. (in 2's). Additional engraved title, 144 (of 153?) plts., many hand-cold., slight foxing & offsetting, contents detchd., early hf. cf. (KH. May 1; 633)
Aus. $180

SMITH, Grafton Elliot & Dawson, Warren R.
– **Egyptian Mummies.** N.d. 4to. Orig. cl., d.-w. (CSK. Dec.16; 162)
£55

SMITH, Harry B.
– **A Sentimental Library.** N.p., priv. ptd., 1914. *1st. Edn.* 4to. L.P., 56 plts., qtr. vell. gt. (SG. Sep.15; 305)
$100

SMITH, James
– **The Cyclopedia of Victoria** ... Melbourne, 1903-4. 3 vols. 4to. Not collated, 1 vol. water-damaged (largely externally), publisher's hf. roan. (KH. Nov.9; 450)
Aus. $200

SMITH, Sir James Edward
– **Fifteen Views Illustrative of a Tour of Hafod, in Cardiganshire, the seat of Thomas Johnes.** Ill.:– J.C. Stadler. L., 1810. Lge. fo. 15 lge. aquatints, 1 slightly defect. in margin & with tear reprd., soiled & stained, mod. bds. (S. Apr.9; 186)
Williams. £150
– **A Grammar of Botany, Illustrative of Artificial, as well as Natural, Classification, with an Explanation of Jussieu's System.** 1821. Some staining & discoloration, mod. bds., qtr. cf., unc. (KH. May 1; 634)
Aus. $130

SMITH, Sir James Edward & Sowerby, James
– **English Botany.** 1790-1800. Vols. 1-10. 719 handcold. plts., lacks plt. 436 & text for 437, hf. cf., defect., as a coll. of plts., w.a.f. (P. Dec.8; 37)
Hildebrandt. £320
– – **Anr. Edn.** L., 1790-1814. *1st. Edn.* 36 vols. 2,592 hand-cold. engraved plts., some minor spotting in a few vols., cont. russ. gt., rebkd., spines gt. (C. Mar.14; 195)
Harcourt-Williams. £2,200
– – **Anr. Copy.** 36 vols. (without the Supp. vols.). 2,592 cold. engraved plts., 'General Indexes' (1814) bnd. at end of Vol. 36, a few plts. in Vol. 1 stained, some foxing & offsetting, mainly affecting text, a few plts. slightly trimmed, cont. tree cf., spines gt., some slightly worn, jnts. of last vol. reprd., w.a.f.; Lindsay Fleming bkplt. (S. Nov.28; 87)
Symonds. £1,650
– – **Anr. Copy.** 36 vols. in 19, including Index, without Supp. vols. 2,592 hand-cold. engraved plts., in genus order but not numerical sequence, 1 plt. inverted, 1 text lf. detchd. & torn, cont. pol. cf., covers with blind-stpd. & gt. rule panel, spines rubbed, w.a.f. (C. Mar.14; 117)
Hildebrandt. £1,200
– – **Anr. Copy.** Vols. 1-7, 13-24, 26-36, & Index. Many plts. soiled, cf., mostly worn & defect., as a coll. of plts., w.a.f. (P. Oct.20; 185)
£480
– – **Anr. Copy.** 36 vols. Cont. hf. leath. gt. (28 vols.) & cont. style hf. leath. (8 vols.). (D. Nov.23; 457)
DM 11,000
– – **Anr. Edn.** L., 1790-1805, 1831-34. 22 vols., including 2 supp. vols. Lge. 8vo. Over 2,800 handcold. plts., index, cont. qtr. cf., marb. bds. (HBC. May 17; 457)
£820
– – **Anr. Edn.** L., 1790-1843. *1st. Edn.* Vols. 1-36 & 3 supp. vols. (of 5) in 21 vols. A few plts. slightly foxed or browned, cont. hf. leath., very rubbed & bumped, 1 cover loose. (R. Apr.4; 1798)
DM 8,000

– – **Anr. Edn.** 1794-96. Vols. 3-5 only. 227 handcold. engraved plts., a few with some spotting, old cf. gt., rubbed, rebkd. with cl., w.a.f. (LC. Jul.5; 160)
£150
– – **Anr. Edn.** L., [1832-]40. *2nd. Edn.* Vols. 1-7 only (of 12). Approx. 1,580 hand-cold. engraved plts., a few trimmed, some slight browning or spotting, identifications added in pen where omitted, cf., rebkd., w.a.f. (S. Nov.28; 89)
Schmull. £400
– – **Anr. Edn.** L., [1832-]42. *2nd. Edn.* Vols. 1-9 only (of 12). 1,901 hand-cold. engraved plts., including dupls. of plts. 194-198, 594, 707, 784 & 785, & 1,486* lacks plt. 706, cont. scored cf. gt., spines rubbed. w.a.f. (S. Nov.28; 88)
Schuster. £500
– – **Anr. Edn.** L., [1832-]46. *2nd. Edn.* 12 vols. 2,757 partly hand-cold. engraved plts., 1 torn, some ll. spotted & slightly soiled, a few ll. of text torn & loose, cont. hf. cf., worn, some covers detchd., 6 vols. lack spine. (BBA. Feb.23; 103)
Duran. £480
– – **Anr. Edn.** Ed.:– J.T. Boswell Syme. L., 1863-66. Vols. 1-6 (of 12). Some slight foxing or soiling, orig. linen, partly loose. (BR. Apr.12; 818)
DM 1,700
– – **Anr. Edn.** 1863-72. Vols. 1-6 & 8-11 only. 4to. 1,681 hand-cold. plts. only, 1 cleanly torn, orig. cl., lightly soiled, 1 spine chipped, disbnd., w.a.f. (CSK. Dec.16; 156)
£180
– – **Anr. Edn.** Ed.:– John T. Boswell Syme. L., 1863-73. *3rd. Edn.* Vols. II, IV, V, VII & X. Lge. 4to. 632 hand-cold. plts., various bdgs., brkn., w.a.f. (SG. Mar.22; 291)
$200
– – **Anr. Edn.** Ed.:– John T. Boswell Syme [& N.E. Brown (Vol. 12)]. L., 1863-86. *3rd. Edn.* 12 vols. Approx. 1,939 hand-cold. plts., cont. hf. mor. gt., w.a.f. (C. Mar.14; 196)
Symonds. £520
– – **Anr. Copy.** 12 vols. 1,936 col. plts., hf. mor. gt. (P. Jun.7; 239)
£320
– – **Anr. Copy.** 12 vols. Lge. 8vo. 1,891 (of 1,939) col. plts., some ll. detchd. & slightly frayed at edges, orig. cl., spines gt.-decor., some wear. (TA. Apr.19; 150)
£200
– – **Anr. Copy.** 12 vols. 4to. Engrs. hand-cold., publishers cl., slightly loose, some spines torn, as a collection of plts., w.a.f. (CR. Jun.6; 294)
Lire 1,600,000
– – **Anr. Edn.** L., 1863-99. 12 vols. & 1 supp. vol. Some plts. with sm. tears, margins slightly browned, some slight foxing, end-papers renewed, orig. linen, gold & blind-tooled, bumped. (HK. Nov.8; 735)
DM 2,300
– – **Anr. Edn.** Ed.:– J.T. Boswell Syme. 1873. Vols. 1-11, lacks Supp. 1,824 hand-cold. plts., cont. hf. mor. gt., partly untrimmed. (TA. Aug.18; 7)
£240
– – **Anr. Edn.** Ed.:– J.T. Boswell Syme. 1873-92. *3rd. Edn.* 13 vols., including Supp. 4to. 1,939 handcold. plts., including plt. 1,834* (often lacking), mor. gt., Vol. 12 rebkd. preserving orig. spine. (SKC. May 4; 1877)
£540
– – **Anr. Edn.** 1899. *3rd. Edn.* 12 vols. & Supp. Lge. 8vo. 1,922 col. plts., cont. qtr. mor., rubbed; from G.W.R. Mechanics' Institution, stp. on most plts. (TA. Apr.19; 149)
£85
– – **Anr. Copy.** 13 vols., including Supp. Lge. 8vo. 1,922 col. plts., perforated liby. stp. on titles, cl. gt., spines shelf-numbered. (SG. Mar.22; 292)
$275

SMITH, James Thorne, Jnr.
– **Dream's End.** N.Y., 1927. *1st. Edn.* Bdg. not stated, d.-w. lightly worn & soiled, white specks to cover. (CBA. Oct.29; 775)
$130

SMITH, John, Artist
– **Select Views in Italy.** William Byrne & John Emes. 1792-96. 2 vols. Ob. fo. 72 engraved plts., cont. hf. russ., w.a.f.; from liby. of Luttrellstown Castle. (C. Sep.28; 1761)
£240
– – **Anr. Edn.** 1796. 4to. Engraved dedication, 72 plts., cf. gt. (WW. Nov.23; 15)
£190
– – **Anr. Copy.** Ob. fo. Engraved dedication lf. with vig., 1 engraved map, 69 (of 72) copperplts., margin browned, cont. leath. gt., slightly rubbed. (R. Oct.13; 3162)
DM 1,100

SMITH, John, Clockmaker
– **The Art of Painting in Oyl.** 1705. '4th. Imp.'. 12mo. 4 pp. of advts. at end, mor. gt.; Paul Jodrell bkplt. (LC. Oct.13; 86)
£150

SMITH, John, Dealer in Pictures
– **A Catalogue Raisonné of the Works of the Most Eminent Dutch, Flemish, & French Painters.** [L., 1908]. *Facs. Reprint of the orig. 1829-42 edn., (1250).* 9 pts., including Supp. 4to. Cl., spines faded, a few spine labels chipped. (SG. Jan.26; 289)
$150

SMITH, John, Fellow of Queen's College, Cambridge
– **Select Discourses.** L., 1660. *1st. Edn.* Sm. 4to. Maroon mor., by MacDonald, gt. dentelles, silk doubls. (SG. Oct.27; 301)
$120

SMITH, John, Merchant
– **England's Improvement Reviv'd: In a Treatise of all Manner of Husbandry & Trade by Land & Sea.** 1673. 4to. Imprimatur lf., some cont. annots., some margin dampstains, recent panel cf. (TA. Apr.19; 363)
£90

SMITH, Capt. John
– **The Generall Historie of Virginia, New-England & the Summer Isles.** L., 1627. *1st. Edn. 4th. Iss.* Fo. Engraved title, 4 folding maps laid down, 1 map in facs., mor. gt., gt. dentelles by Pratt for Stevens & Son, 1889, free endpaper & flylf. loose; J.H. Bates bkplt., A.L.s. by Joseph Sabin tipped in. [Sabin 82827] (SG. Apr.26; 183)
$6,500

SMITH, John Russell
– **Bibliotheca Cantiana.** L., 1837. Foxed, cf. (S. Mar.6; 449)
Baker. £70

SMITH, John Thomas
– **Antiquities of London & its Environs.** 1791. 4to. 96 engraved plts., title & prelims. frayed at edges, some margin dampstains, cont. hf. cf., rubbed. (TA. Dec.15; 78)
£64
– **Antiquities of Westminster; The Old Palace, St. Stephen's Chapel** ... 1807. 2 vols. 4to. 36 engraved plts. (some hand-cold.), in litho. & copper states, cont. str.-grd. hf. mor., spine gt.-decor., rubbed. (TA. Feb.16; 63)
£75
– – **Anr. Copy.** Vol. 1 only (of 2). 4to. 37 (of 38) plts., some hand-cold., cf., hinges reprd. (P. Apr.12; 185)
£55
– – **Anr. Edn.** 1807[-09]. 2 pts. in 1 vol. 4to. 100 engraved & aquatint plts., some hand-cold., some tinted, cont. diced cf., rebkd., gt.-decor. spine. (TA. Dec.15; 77)
£130
– **The Cries of London.** Ed.:– Francis Douce. L., 1839. 4to. On vell., wide margin, engraved port. (loose), 30 cold. etchings, hand-bnd. cf., gt. spine, covers, inner & outer dentelles, by Root & Sons, wear, jnts. partly torn; Hauswedell coll. (H. May 23; 74)
DM 1,600
– **Etchings of Remarkable Beggars, Itinerant Traders & other Persons of Notoriety in London & its Environs.** L., 1815[-16]. Lge. 4to. On L.P. vell., etched title with cold. arms, 48 etchings, some slight spotting, later hf. leath., romantic gt. spine; Hauswedell coll. (H. May 23; 56)
DM 1,800
– **Vagabondia; or Anecdotes of Mendicant Wanderers** ... **of London.** 1817. 4to. Cont. hf. mor., rubbed; pres. copy to Samuel Forster from Duchess of Marlborough. (CSK. Jul.6; 28)
£100

SMITH, Joseph, Mormon
– **The Book of Mormon.** Palmyra, N.Y., 1830. *1st. Edn.* Testimony lf., damp-wrinkled, some stains, cont. sheep., worn, cover detchd. [Sabin 83038] (SG. Apr.26; 184)
$2,600

SMITH, Patti
– **Ha! Ha! Houdini!** N.Y., 1977. *1st. Edn. (26) lettered & sigd.* 1 vol. Stabbed as iss., pict. wraps., sm. lock & key; inscr. by author on limitation lf. (*With:*) – **A Useless Death.** N.Y., n.d. *1st. Edn. (300) numbered & sigd.* 1 vol. Pict. self-wraps., glassine d.-w. (SG. Jan.12; 318)
$125

SMITH, Capt. R. Murdoch & Porcher, Cdr. E.A.
– **History of the Recent Discoveries at Cyrene.** 1864. Fo. 86 plts., prelims. slightly spotted, orig. cl. gt., slightly soiled. (SKC. Mar.9; 2034)
£160

SMITH, Robert
– **Compleat System of Opticks.** Camb., 1738. *1st. Edn.* 2 vols. 4to. At end J. Jurin 'Essay on Distinct & Indistinct Vision', some plts. slightly browned, cont. leath., gt. spine & outer dentelle, worn & bumped. (HK. Nov.8; 731)
DM 1,800

SMITH, Robert, Rat-catcher
- The Universal Directory for Taking Alive & Destroying Rats. L., 1768. 6 plts. (4 folding), some offsetting, ptd. slip on title verso, cont. cf., rebkd. cl. (S. Apr.10; 588) *Ramer.* £85

SMITH, Samuel
- The History of the Colony of Nova Caesaria, or New-Jersey. Burlington, N.J., 1765. *1st. Edn. (600).* State with uncommaed imprint date, with all corrected readings, except p. 188 line 1 'would' for 'could', browned, few stains, orig. cf. gt., rubbed, rebkd; cont. MS. ex-libris of Jabez Maud Fisher, dtd. 1765, later ex-libris. (SG. Apr.5; 139) $550
-- **Anr. Copy.** 1st. iss. of the title-p. with commas in the date, some of the errata corrected, slightly browned thro.-out, orig. cf. gt., worn; inscr. on upr. paste-down 'For the Honble. Thomas Penn Esqr.', Bibliotheca Lindesiana bkplt., the Rt. Hon. Visc. Eccles copy. [Sabin 83981] (CNY. Nov.18; 254) $420

SMITH, Rev. Samuel Stanhope
- An Essay on the Causes of the Variety of Complexion & Figure in the Human Species ... Edinb., 1788. *New Edn.* 1 advt. lf. bnd. in at end, cont. spr. cf. (TA. Feb.16; 230) £95
See— RAMSAY, David & Smith, S.S.

SMITH, Rev. Sydney 'Peter Plymley'
- Letters on the Subject of the Catholics to my Brother Abraham who Lives in the Country. Richmond, 1809. Title reprd., later cl. (PNY. Dec.1; 104) $100

SMITH, Sydney Ure
See— URE-SMITH, Sydney

SMITH, T.
- South Africa Delineated. L., 1850. Some foxing, embossed cl. (VA. Oct.28; 266) R· 230

SMITH, Sir Thomas
- The Commonwealth of England, & the Maner of Gouernment Thereof. L., 1609. 4to. Lacks last lf. (? blank), light stains, later cf. [STC 22862] (BBA. May 3; 100) *Rhys-Jones.* £130

SMITH, Thomas W.
- A Narrative of the Life, Travels & Sufferings ... Boston, 1844. 12mo. (in 4's). Some light foxing, mod. cl. (KH. May 1; 638) Aus. $190

SMITH, William
[-] A Brief State of the Province of Pennsylvania. L., 1755. *1st. Edn.* Hf.-title, hf. cf., unc.; the Rt. Hon. Visc. Eccles copy. [Sabin 84589] (CNY. Nov.18; 255) $200
- The History of the Province of New York. L., 1757. *1st. Edn.* 4to. Short tear in 2C3 affecting 1 or 2 letters, cont. cf.-bkd. bds. [Sabin 84566] (S. May 22; 339) *Quaritch.* £280
-- **Anr. Copy.** 4to. Lge. & thick paper, the folding plt. of 'The South View of Oswego on Lake Ontario' inlaid & inserted from a sm. paper copy, a few ll. slightly dust-soiled, unc., crimson lev. mor. gt., sigd. on front turn-in 'Bound by W. Pratt for H[enry] Stevens 1883', long scrape mark on lr. cover, slight wear at edges; bkplt. & stpd. monog. of Robert Hoe, the William E. Benjamin copy. [Sabin 84566] (CNY. Nov.18; 304) $3,200

SMITHWICK, Noah
- The Evolution of a State or Recollections of Old Texas Days. Austin, [1900]. *1st. Edn.* Cl., s.-c., cover slightly soiled. (LH. Sep.25; 285) $140

SMOLLETT, Tobias
[-] Ferdinand Count Fathom. L., 1753. *1st. Edn.* 2 vols. Cont. spr. cf., trifle worn; Hon. Charles Agar bkplt. (BBA. Nov.30; 220) *Maggs.* £240
[-] The History & Adventures of an Atom. L., 1749 [1769]. *1st. Edn.* 2 vols. 12mo. Cont. cf., spines gt. (C. Nov.9; 159) *Blackwells.* £280
[-] – **Anr. Edn.** L., 1769. *1st. Edn.* 2 vols. 12mo. With corrected date, hf.-titles, some light spotting & browning, vol.2 lacks final blank, cont. blindstpd. cf., rebkd. (SPB. May 16; 141) $150
- Humphry Clinker. 1671 [1771]. *1st. Edn.* 3 vols. 12mo. Hf.-titles, with final blank in Vol. II, cont. cf., spines gt., rubbed. (C. May 30; 171) *Maggs.* £130

[-] – **Anr. Edn.** L., [1771]. *1st. Edn.* 3 vols. 12mo. Rothschild's variant (A4), cont. cf., spines gt. (C. Nov.9; 158) *Blackwells.* £1,100
[-] – **Anr. Copy.** 3 vols. Cont. cf. (BBA. Nov.30; 221) *Bookroom.* £90
[-] – **Anr. Copy.** 3 vols. 12mo. Few gatherings sprung, slight browning, cont. cf., spine worn, vol. 2 wormed. (SPB. May 16; 140) $325
[-] – **Anr. Copy.** 3 vols. 12mo. Rothschild's variant A4, but with p.vi in vol. 1 so numbrd., hf.-titles & final blank in vol. 2, tear reprd., some soiling, cont. cf., spines worn, 2 jnts. brkn.; Fred A. Berne copy. (SPB. May 16; 351) $175
[-] – **Anr. Edn.** 1772. *2nd. Edn.* 3 vols. Cf. gt. (P. Sep.29; 130) *Scott.* £95
[-] Peregrine Pickle. L., priv. ptd., 1751. *1st. Edn.* 4 vols. 12mo. L12 in Vol. 3 a cancel as usual, cont. cf., spines gt. (C. Nov.9; 157) *Kinross.* £1,100
[-] – **Anr. Copy.** 4 vols. L12 in Vol. 3 in 2nd. state, cont. cf., spines crudely reprd.; Cliveden bkplt. (BBA. Nov.30; 219) *Matthews.* £190
-- **Anr. Copy.** 4 vols. 12mo. L12 in cancelled state, some browning, lacks final blanks, mott. cf. by Riviere, upr. cover detchd. 1 vol. (SPB. May 16; 138) $200
-- **Anr. Copy.** 4 vols. Cont. mott. cf., gt.-decor. spines. (CBA. Dec.10; 418) $160
- Reise durch Frankreich und Italien. Leipzig, 1767. *1st. German Edn.* Hf. leath. gt. (R. Oct.13; 3105) DM 620
- Roderick Random. L., 1748. *1st. Edn.* 2 vols. 12mo. Lf. 19 uncancelled, vol. 1 margin of N gathering stained, vol. 2 D7 torn, cont. cf. with arms of Stuart de Rotheray in blind on covers. (SPB. May 16; 139) $425
- Travels through France & Italy. L., 1766. *1st. Edn.* 2 vols. Cont. cf., spines gt. (C. Nov.9; 160) *Blackwells.* £400
- Works. Ed.:– John Moore, M.D. Ill.:– George Cruikshank. L., 1797. 8 vols. Hand-cold. port., 18 hand-cold. plts. inserted, cont. cf., jnts. very worn. (SG. Apr.19; 172) $175
-- **Anr. Edn.** 1890. *New Edn.* 6 vols. Hf. cf. gt. by Bickers. (PD. Dec.14; 326) £78
-- **Anr. Edn.** Ill.:– Frank Richards. 1895. *(150) numbered.* 12 vols. L.P., red mor. gt., by Morrell, dentelles, spines decor. gt. (SKC. Jan.13; 2260) £220
-- **Anr. Edn.** N.Y., 1902. *'Handmade' Edn. (150) numbered.* 12 vols. Frontis.'s cold. & uncold., engraved plts. in 2 states, mor., triple gt.-ruled borders, onlaid mor. gt. ornaments, gt. spines in 6 compartments, turn-ins gt., maroon mor. doubls., watered-silk free end-pp., partly unc. (CNY. Dec.17; 604) $950
See— HUME, David — SMOLLETT, Tobias

SMYTH, B.
- History of the Lancashire Fusiliers. Dublin, 1903. 2 vols. Plts., several cold., cont. red mor. gt., by Galwey & Co., gt. inner dentelles, silk end-papers. (CSK. May 18; 85) £180

SMYTH, C. Piazzi
- Life & Work at the Great Pyramid. Edinb., 1867. 3 vols. Orig. cl. (BBA. Apr.5; 172) *C. Cox.* £60
- Teneriffe, an Astronomer's Experiment. 1858. Liby stp. on some pp., cl., worn. (P. Apr.12; 186) *Duran.* £80

SMYTH, Henry de Wolf
- A General Account of the Development of Methods of using Atomic Energy for Military Purposes under the Auspices of the United States Government 1940-45. Wash., 1945. *1st. Edn. for general distribution.* Stapled as iss., orig. ptd. wraps., upr. wrap. dtd. 'Aug. 1945', sig. of Nathan A. Conn on wraps. (LH. Jan.15; 388) $180

SMYTH, Sir James Carmichael
- Precis of the Wars in Canada, from 1755 to the Treaty of Ghent in 1814. L., [priv. ptd.], 1824. *1st. Edn.* Dedication copy to the Duke of Wellington, cont. hf. cf.; the Rt. Hon. Visc. Eccles copy. (CNY. Nov.18; 257) $500

SMYTH, John Ferdinand Dalziel
- A Tour in the United States of America. L., 1784. *1st. Edn.* 2 vols. Hf.-titles, errata lf. in Vol. 1, cont. cf., a few corners slightly worn; the Rt. Hon. Visc.

Eccles copy. [Sabin 85254] (CNY. Nov.18; 256) $380

SMYTH, Robert Brough
- The Aborigines of Victoria ... Melbourne, 1878. *1st. Edn.* 2 vols. 4to. 6 or 7 ll. a little foxed, short tear in each map, orig. cl., sm. defects. & split reprd. in 1 lr. jnt. (KH. Nov.9; 705) Aus. $220
-- **Anr. Copy.** Liby. stps., some erased, bdg. not stated, marked & shaken. (KH. May 1; 642) Aus. $160
-- **Anr. Copy.** 2 vols. 4to. A few ll. with spotted foxing, 1 folding map torn & largely defect., 1st. vol. shaken in sewing, orig. cl. (KH. Nov.9; 451) Aus. $140
-- **Anr. Edn.** Melbourne, 1972. *Facs. Edn.* 2 vols. Bdg. not stated. (KH. May 1; 641) Aus. $100

SMYTHIES, Bertram E.
- The Birds of Borneo. Edinb. & L., 1960. *1st. Edn.* Plts., some cold., folding map, orig. cl. (S. Apr.10; 355) *Ant of the Orient.* £110
-- **Anr. Copy.** Orig. cl. (LC. Mar.1; 186) £70
-- **Anr. Copy.** Cl., inscr. on front end-paper, d.-w. (CA. Apr.3; 103) Aus. $130
- The Birds of Burma. 1953. *2nd. Edn.* Orig. cl., d.-w. (LC. Mar.1; 187) £80
-- **Anr. Copy.** Orig. cl., untrimmed, spine rubbed. (TA. Feb.16; 100) £60

SNAPE, Andrew
- The Anatomy of a Horse. L., priv. ptd., 1683. *1st. Edn.* Fo. 44 plts. only (of 49, port. & plts. 1 & 6 supplied in facs., 1 image in anr. plt. also supplied in facs., completely lacks 2 plts.), buckram. (SG. Mar.22; 288) $120

SNELL, James
- A Practical Guide to Operations on the Teeth: & A Historical Sketch of the Rise and Progress of Dental Surgery. Phila., 1832. Some foxing, cont. sheep, worn, covers loose; Asbell bkplt. (SG. Mar.22; 94) $110

SNELLEN VAN VOLLENHOVEN, S.C.
- Pinacographia. Afbeeldingen van Meer van 1000 Soorten van Noord-West-Europeesche Sluipwespen. 's-Gravenhage, 1880. 4to. 45 hand-cold. litho. plts., text in Dutch & Engl., slightly loose, cl., jnts. defect. (B. Oct.4; 776) Fls. 825

SNELLING, Thomas
- Snelling on the Coins of Great Britain, France & Ireland, & c. 1763-69. Fo. 70 engraved plts. & cuts, port. by J. Thane pasted in opposite title, cont. spr. cf.; Sir Ivar Colquhoun, of Luss copy. (CE. Mar.22; 283) £200
[-] A View of the Silver Coin & Coinage of England. L., 1762-63. *1st. Edn.* 4to. Minor dampstaining. (Bound with:) - A View of the Gold Coin & Coinage of England. L., 1762-63. *1st. Edn.* Minor dampstaining. Together 2 works in 1 vol. Later sheep, some wear. (RO. Dec.11; 308) $120

SNELLING, William J. 'Solomon Bell'
- Tales of Travel West of the Mississippi. Boston, 1830. *1st. Edn.* 16mo. 2 prelims. tipped in, cl.-bkd. bds. (SG. Dec.8; 326) $300

SNOW, W.R.
- Sketches of Chinese Life & Character. N.d. 3 pts. in 1 vol. Fo. 17 hand-cold. tinted litho. plts. only, lacks 1 plt. in 2nd. pt., margins lightly soiled, 3 with clean tears, orig. front wraps. bnd. in, spotted mod. hf. mor., lacks 1 end-paper. (CSK. Jul.6; 86) £600

SNOW, William Parker
- A Two Years Cruise of Tierra del Fuego, The Falkland Islands ... 1857. *1st. Edn.* 2 vols. Orig. cl. (SKC. Nov.18; 2017) £100

SNOW-FLAKE (The); A Christmas, New-Year, & Birthday Gift, for MDCCCLII
Phila., 1852. Sm. 8vo. Orig. gt.-ornamental mor., rubbed, 3 cont. sigd. on both front end-papers; from liby. of F.D. Roosevelt, inscr. by him (as President). (SG. Mar.15; 45) $275

SNOWMAN, A. Kenneth
- Eighteenth Century Gold Boxes of Europe. Boston, 1966. 4to. Orig. cl., d.-w. (BBA. Sep.8; 253) *Winter Palace.* £100

SNYDER, Gray
- Riprap. [Ashland, Mass.], Origin Pr., 1959. *1st. Edn.* Orig. decor. wraps., sewn as iss.; Frederic Dannay copy. (CNY. Dec.16; 329) $180

SOANE, Sir John
- Description of the House & Museum on the North Side of Lincoln's Inn Fields. 1835. *(150) sigd.* 4to. Title lightly browned, qtr. mor. gt. (P. Sep.8; 200) *Quaritch.* £200
- Plans, Elevations & Sections of Buildings. L., 1788. Lge. fo. L.P., 47 engraved plts. (dtd. 1789), subscribers list, margin repair to 1 plt. & text lf., faint spotting to 1 plt., cont. gt.-panel. cf.; the Prince Starhemberg copy. (C. Dec.9; 149) *Henderson.* £620

SOBY, James Thrall
- Ben Shahn: His Graphic Art. N.Y., 1957. *(250) numbered & sigd. by Soby & Shahn.* 4to. With serigraph ptd., hand-cold. & sigd. by Shahn, hf. cl., nicked & faded. (SG. Jan.12; 312) $200
- The Prints of Paul Klee. N.Y., 1945. *1st. Edn. (1000).* 4to. 16-pp. ill. text, plt. list, 40 plts. (8 stencil cold.), each plt. liby.-stpd. on blank verso, loose in cl. folder. (SG. May 3; 225) $150

SOCCUS [Conrad, of Brundelsheim]
- Sermones de Tempore. Augsburg, Anton Sorg, 1476. Fo. Rubricated, ptd. initials, heightened with red, 2 lge. 1st. initials painted in various cols. with floral decor. continued in margin, 16th. C. stpd. hf. pig; from Fondation Furstenberg- Beaumesnil. [H. 14827; BMC II, 343; Goff S587] (HD. Nov.16; 4) Frs. 7,500

SOCIAL DEMOCRAT, The
1897-1909. Vols. 1-13 only, in 79 vols. Vols. 1-7 in cont. bdgs., others orig. wraps., slightly torn & soiled, lacks 1 wrap. (BBA. Feb.9; 144) *Koffler.* £210

SOCIEDAD ESPANOLA DE AMIGOS DEL ARTE
- Catalogo de la Exposicion de Retratos de Niño en España. Madrid, 1925. Fo. 50 plts., some in col., publishers bds. (DS. Nov.25; 2166) Pts. 22,000

SOCIETE ANONYME DES PRODUITS FRED BAYER et cie, editors
- La Teinture des Tissus Mi-Soie ... à L'aide des colorants. 1904. *(With:)* - Les Couleurs pour Mordants des Farbenfabriken. 1902. *(With:)* - La Teinture de la Mi-Laine evec les Colorants. [1911]. Together 3 vols. 90 ll. of mntd. cl. samples, ills., some light staining, orig. cl., slightly soiled. (CSK. Mar.23; 12) £150

SOCIETE DE L'HISTOIRE DE FRANCE
- Mémoires, Chroniques, Lettres, Oeuvres ... 1836-1912. 63 vols. Some foxing, old hf. roan, spine decor. slightly varies. (HD. Dec.9; 185) Frs. 4,500

SOCIETE DES BIBLIOPHILES BRETONS
- L'Imprimerie en Bretagne au XVe Siècle: Etude sur les Incunables Bretons. Nantes, 1878. *(400) numbered.* Hf. cf., worn. (SG. Jan.5; 183) $110

SOCIETE DES SCIENCES HISTORIQUES ET NATURELLES DE LA CORSE
- Bulletin. Bastia, 1881-87. 4 vols. Hf. chagrin, spines decor. (HD. Oct.21; 47) Frs. 3,100

SOCIETY FOR THE DIFFUSION OF USEFUL KNOWLEDGE
- Complete Atlas. 1874. Fo. 169 col. maps., 50 plans & 6 star charts, hf. cf., upr. cover detchd. (P. Apr.12; 327) *Martin.* £320
- Maps. Chapman & Hall, 1844. 2 vols. Fo. 212 engraved maps & plans, several with inset vigs. (of 218: lacks astronomical charts), hand-cold. in outl., some light spotting, disbnd. as loose sheets in mod. buckram s.-c.'s., w.a.f. (S. May 21; 134) *Cassidy.* £380
- - Anr. Copy. Vol. 2 only. Fo. 49 maps, 49 plans & 6 star charts, all partly cold., hf. cf., upr. cover detchd. (P. Apr.12; 326) *Martin.* £340
- - Anr. Copy. 2 vols. in 1. Lge. fo. 214 (of 218) engraved cold. maps, a few sm. tears, bdg. defect., as an atlas, w.a.f. (GM. Oct.5; 478) £180
- - Anr. Edn. 1845-46. Lge. 4to. Hand-cold. engraved maps & town plans, contents of Vol. 1 loose due to gutta-percha bdg., orig. hf. cf., worn. (LC. Mar.1; 546) £320
- - Anr. Edn. 1849. 4to. 134 engraved maps, some double-p., many loose, mod. cl., soiled. (BBA. Feb.9; 252) *Argosy Bookstore.* £170
- Penny Cyclopaedia. 1833-44. 27 vols. 4to. Orig. cl., some spines faded, w.a.f.; from liby. of Luttrellstown Castle. (C. Sep.28; 1818) £160
- A Series of Maps, Modern & Ancient. L., 1829-32. Pts. 1-35 only (of 54). Fo. 70 full-p. engraved maps & plans, hand-cold. in outl., some soiling, publisher's ptd. wraps. (S. Mar.6; 112) *Cassidy.* £100

SOCIETY FOR PROMOTING CHRISTIAN KNOWLEDGE
- Phenomena of Nature. 1849. 4to. 30 hand-cold. vigs., cl. (P. Apr.12; 97) *Shapiro.* £60
- Plates Illustrative of Natural History. Ca. 1870. Ob. fo. 108 hand-cold. plts., with descriptive text below, a few margin repairs, 1 plt. relaid, orig. cl. (TA. Mar.15; 281) £100
- Prints Illustrative of Natural History, with Descriptions. Ca. 1850. 2 vols. Ob. fo. 180 hand-cold. plts., 1 plt. in Vol. 2 defect., a few other plts. with margin tears, title-pp. creased, some slight staining, cl., slightly worn, spines faded. (S. Nov.1; 294) *Eisler.* £300
- Rules & Regulations of the District Committee of the Society for Promoting Christian Knowledge, Established in New South Wales, 1826 ... Sydney, 1826. Mod. hf. cf., wraps. bnd. in. (KH. May 1; 644) Aus. $290
- Thirty Plates Illustrative of Natural Phenomena. Ill.:– after Whymper. 1846. Lge. 4to. 30 hand-cold. wood-engraved plts., orig. cl., rebkd., old spine laid down. (CSK. Jul.27; 154) £90

SOCIETY ... GRADUAL ABOLITION OF SLAVERY
- Report on the Slave Trade. Second Report of the Committee of the Society ... Gradual Abolition of Slavery. 1825. Folding plt. laid down on linen, mod. cl. (P. Jan.12; 279) *Maggs.* £55

SOCIETY OF ANTIQUARIES
- Vetusta Monumenta. L., 1747-1815. Vols. 1-4 only (of 6), in 2 vols. Fo. Cf. gt. (P. Nov.24; 168) *Garratt.* £85

SOCIETY OF ANTIQUARIES OF LONDON
- Archaeologia: or Miscellaneous Tracts Relating to Antiquity. L., 1773-1973. Vols. 1-104 in 130, excluding 2 index vols. 4to. Plts. & plans, some offset, some cold., cont. cf., rubbed, rebkd., 1 cover & 1 spine detchd., & orig. cl., some spines worn; ex-Lincoln's Inn Liby. set with their stps. (S. Apr.30; 223) *Loudry.* £580

SOCIETY OF ANTIQUARIES OF SCOTLAND
- Proceedings ... 1855-n.d. Vols. 1-35 & catalogue & index vols. Hf. mor. gt., later vols. in orig. bds. (PD. May 16; 118) £240

SOCIETY OF FRIENDS
- Transactions of the Central Relief Committee ... during the Famine in Ireland 1846 & 1847. Dublin, 1852. Hf. mor., armorial motif on spine; pres. copy to Marquis of Sligo. (GM. Dec.7; 224) £90

SOCRATES
See— EUSEBIUS PAMPHILIUS, Bp. of Caesarea & others

SÖDDY, Frederick
- Radio-Activity: An Elementary Treatise, from the Standpoint of the Disintegration Theory. L., 1904. *1st. Edn.* Advts., slight browning, mostly marginal, orig. cl., slight rubbing & darkening; bkplt. & stp. of William M. Baker, Stanitz coll. (SPB. Apr.25; 403) $125

SOFT PORCELAIN OF SEVRES, The
Historical Intro.:– Edouard Garnier. L., 1892. Fo. 50 col. plts., decor. cl., worn. (SG. Jan.26; 156) $140

SOHR, K. & Handtke, F.
- Vollst. Universal-Handatlas du neueren Erdbeschreiben über alle Theile d. Erde. Glogau, 1859. Ob. fo. Title & 1st. 2 maps creased, 3 maps frayed in side margin to ill., 3 maps defect., slightly foxed & soiled, cont. hf. leath., defect., w.a.f. (HK. May 15; 670) DM 400

SOLA, A.E.
- Klondyke, Truth & Facts of the New Eldorado. [1897]. Orig. cl. gt. (P. Jun.7; 197) £50

SOLANDER, Daniel
- The Natural History of Many Curious & Uncommon Zoophytes, collected from Various Parts of the Globe by the Late John Ellis. L., 1786. Lge. 4to. Some light foxing, cont. leath. gt., very rubbed & worn, cover loose. (GB. Nov.3; 1164) DM 540

SOLANO DE FIGUEROA Y ALTAMIRANO, J.
- Historia Eclesiastica de la Ciudad y Obispado de Badajoz. Badajoz, 1929-35. *1st. Edn.* 8 vols. in 4. 8vo. Cl., wraps. (DS. Apr.27; 2365) Pts. 20,000

SOLAR, Felix
- Catalogue de la Bibl. de. Paris, 1866. 3 vols. in 1. 4to. Orig. linen. (DS. Nov.25; 2171) Pts. 26,000

SOLGER, K.W.F.
- Philosophische Gespräche. Berlin, 1817. *1st. Edn.* Before title MS. letter from author with sig., 1 p., 11 lines, old end-paper pasted in upr. cover with MS dedication, later hf. leath. (R. Oct.11; 542) DM 1,650
- Vorlesungen über Aesthetik. Ed.:– K.W.L. Heyse. Leipzig, 1829. *1st. Edn.* 1 errata lf., cont. marb. bds., slightly rubbed. (R. Oct.11; 543) DM 420
- - Anr. Copy. Slightly foxed, cont. marb. bds. gt. (HK. May 16; 2265) DM 400

SOLINUS, Gaius Julius
- Delle Cose Maravigliose del Mondo. Trans.:– G.V. Belprato. Venice, 1559. 1st. lf. browned, 19th. C. cl. (BBA. Nov.30; 18) *George's.* £55
- Pomponii Malae de Orbis ... Polyhister. Basle, 1576. 31 maps, some margins trimmed, 1 map & some text pp. affected by termites, cont. vell. (P. May 17; 425) *Franks.* £220

SOLIS, Antonio
- Historia de la Conquista de México, Población, y Progressos de la America Septentrional, conocida por el Nombre de Nueva España. Brussels, 1704. *3rd. Edn.* Fo. 19th. C. cf. gt. [Sabin 86448] (SG. Jan.19; 325) $300
- - Anr. Copy. Fo. Cf. (DS. Apr.27; 2305) Pts. 70,000

SOLIS, Virgil
- Biblische Figuren dess Alten (u. Newen Testaments). Frankfurt, 1565. 2 pts. in 1 vol. Ob. 4to. Lacks 9 ll., excision in title bkd., sm. tears or worming in margin mostly bkd., some sm. tears & repairs in margin, cut slightly close at top, last 8 ll. very defect. with tears, worming & margin bkd., 17th. C. bds., lacks ties, slightly worn, soiled. (HK. Nov.8; 344) DM 800
- Libellvs Scvtorvm ... Wappenbüchlein. Zu Ehren der Römischen Kay. vnd Kü. Nuremb., 1555. *2nd. Edn.(?).* 4to. Lacks hf.-title, Latin title with old owners note, title with Purchase note, 1576, ll. numbered in same hand, 1st. 8 ll. ruled, late 16th. C. MS. 8 p. index at end, 4 ll. with slight repaired faults, some browning, soiling, staining & ink marks, late 16th. C. vell., ca. 1900; Ida Schoeller ex-libris. (HK. Nov.8; 345) DM 1,500
- Wappenbüchlein zu Ehren der Römischen Kay, und Kü. mit, auch Bäbstlicher Heyligkeit [etc.]. Nuremb., 1555. Sm. 4to. 50 (of 51) engraved ll., lacks section title (as often), monog. HB & date 1574 in calligraphic script in lr. margin of Nuremb. arms, soiled thro.-out in margins, especially spotted near end, cont. style mod. leath., cover with old slightly defect. leath., s.-c. (R. Oct.11; 112a) DM 2,800

SOLLEYSEL, Jacques, Sieur de
- The Compleat Horseman. 1696. *8th. Edn. [1st. Edn. in Engl.].* 4to. Port. (reprd.), additional engraved title for Part 2, cont. panel. cf., rebkd. with new end-papers. (SKC. Mar.9; 1957) £120
- - Anr. Copy. Fo. Additional engraved title to pt. 2, 6 folding engraved plts., lacks port. frontis. & all before 3rd. p. of preface, rebnd. in mod. cf., lacks sm. piece at head of spine. (SKC. May 4; 1766) £55

SOLLEYSEL, Jacques, Sieur de -*Contd.*

- **Le Parfait Maréchal qui enseigne à Connoistre la Beauté, la Bonté et les Defauts des Chevaux** ... Paris, 1664. *1st. Edn.* 4to. Cut short, slight defect to 7 plts., cont. marb. cf. gt., spine decor. (HD. Nov.9; 195) Frs. 2,200
-- **Anr. Edn.** Paris, 1676. *4th. Edn.* 2 vols. in 1. 4to. Some sm. stains, old vell. (HD. Dec.9; 86) Frs. 1,000

SOLOMON, King of Israel

- **Canticum Canticorum.** Berlin, 'Gannymed', 1921/22. *Archetype Edn.* (220) numbered. 4to. Orig. hf. vell. (D. Nov.23; 349) DM 400
-- **Anr. Edn.** München, Marées-Gesellschaft, 1922. *(400). (80) numbered De Luxe Edn.* Sm. fo. Orig. vell. (GB. May 5; 2261) DM 800
-- **Anr. Edn.** Berlin, 1922. *(100) Engl. Edn.* 4to. Orig. vell., cockled; Hauswedell coll. (H. May 23; 441) DM 660
-- **Anr. Edn.** Ill.:- E. Gill. [Leipzig, Cranach Pr., 1931]. *(60) De Luxe Edn. on Japan.* Sm. 4to. Last ll. with slight spotting, hand-bnd. orig. mor., gold decor., by O. Dorfner, Weimar. (H. Nov.23; 983d) DM 5,600
-- **Anr. Copy.** 11 orig. woodcuts & 18 woodcut initials, hand-bnd. orig. red mor., sigd. O. Dorfner, Weimar, gold decor., end-papers with some light foxing. (GB. May 5; 2296) DM 4,800
-- **Anr. Copy.** Sm. 4to. Orig. hand-bnd. red mor., gt. decor., by O. Dorfner, Weimar, lr. cover with 3 sm. nail holes, 2 light scratches. (H. May 22; 993) DM 4,000
- **Canticum Canticorum [Basque].** Trans.:- Jose A. de Uriarte. L., 1858. *(250).* Fo. Cl. (DS. Dec.16; 2660) Pts. 35,000
- **Le Cantique des Cantiques.** Trans.:- J. de Bonnefon. Ill.:- F. Kupka. Paris, 1905. *(500) on Hollande à la forme.* Fo. Mod. hf. leath., orig. pict. wraps bnd. in. (R. Oct.11; 311) DM 1,600
-- **Anr. Edn.** Ill.:- Clark Fay. N.p., 1930. *(100) numbered, with extra suite of 6 plts.* Fo. Loose in orig. wraps., s.-c. brkn. (BBA. Jan.19; 301) *Marks.* £50
-- **Anr. Edn.** Ill.:- E. Gill. Weimar, Cranach Pr., 1931. *(100) numbered on papier de Monval.* Tall 4to. 10 orig. woodcuts, red mor. gt. (GB. Nov.5; 2366) DM 3,600
-- **Anr. Edn.** Ill.:- Eric Gill. Weimar, Cranach Pr., 1931. *(158) roman-numbered. (50) on japon.* Orig. red lev. mor., unc. (S. Nov.21; 190) *Appleton.* £1,250
-- **Anr. Edn.** Ill.:- Barta. Paris, 1936. 4to. Text etchings not ptd., but replaced with orig. watercols., mor. by Sebely, richly decor., wrap., folder, s.-c.; artist's copy with suite of 15 refused plts., extra-ill. with suite of plts. on japan. (HD. Jun.13; 14) Frs. 7,500
-- **Anr. Edn.** Commentaries:- Saint Theresa of Avila. Ill.:- Michel Ciry. Paris, 1946. *(143) numbered on Vélin d'Arches.* 4to. 15 orig. dry-points, leaves, wrap., folder & s.-c. (HD. May 16; 65) Frs. 1,500
- **Das Hohe Lied von Salomo.** Ed.:- Rud. A. Schröder. Trans.:- E. Kautzsch. Ill.:- F.W. Kleukens. Leipzig, Ernst Ludwig Pr., 1909. *(300).* On Japan, orig. cf., partly faded, slightly worn, some scratches. (HK. May 17; 2731) DM 1,250
-- **Anr. Edn.** Trans.:- M. Luther. Ill.:- L. Corinth. Berlin, Pan Pr., 1911. *(250) on Japan.* Fo. Last 2 pp. & end-papers browned, margins lightly spotted, ex-libris, orig. silk, spine bumped. (H. Nov.24; 1456) DM 2,000
-- **Anr. Copy.** Fo. Some slight soiling & light browning, end-papers slightly foxed, orig. linen, spotted & defect. (H. Nov.24; 2469) DM 900
-- **Anr. Edn.** Ill.:- L.v. Hofmann. [Berlin, 1921]. *(350), ((50) not for sale) on Zandersbütten.* Orig. hf. vell. (HK. May 17; 2834) DM 600
-- **Anr. Edn.** 4to. 11 orig. woodcuts, orig. hf. vell., slightly spotted. (GB. May 5; 2702) DM 530
-- **Anr. Edn.** Ill.:- L. von Hofmann. [Berlin, 1921]. *(300) on Bütten.* Sm. 4to. Orig. hf. vell., slightly faded. (H. Nov.24; 1612) DM 760
-- **Anr. Edn.** Trans.:- M. Luther. Ill.:- E. Gill. [Leipzig, Cranach Pr., 1931]. *(50) De Luxe Edn. on Japan.* Some light browning & foxing, hand-bnd. red orig. mor., decor. spines, covers, inner &

outer dentelle, by O. Dorfner, Wien; Hauswedell coll. (H. May 24; 736) DM 8,000
- **Shir Ha'Shirim im Targum Jonathan Ben Uziel.** Bombay, 1862. In Hebrew, Aramaic & Judaeo-Arabic, some worming affecting a few letters, browned, marb. paper bds. (S. Oct.24; 118) *Hebrew.* £100
- **The Song of Solomon.** Ill.:- Ronald King. Circle Pr., 1968. *(150) numbered & sigd. by artist.* Fo. 2 prospectuses loosly inserted, unsewn in orig. buckram folder gt., s.-c. (S. Nov.21; 177) £210
- **Song of Songs.** Ill.:- O. Jones. 1849. Embossed relievo leath. by O. Jones. (P. Apr.12; 85) *Thorp.* £70
-- **Anr. Edn.** Ill.:- W. Russell Flint. L., Medici Soc., 1909. *(500) numbered on Riccardi H.M.P.* 4to. Orig. vell., partly unc., linen ties; Sir Francis Danson armorial bkplt. (SG. Nov.3; 78) $325
-- **Anr. Edn.** Ill.:- Eric Gill. Gold. Cock. Pr., 1925. *(750) numbered.* 4to. Orig. cl., unc., d.-w. spotted. (S. Nov.21; 212) *Joseph.* £250
-- **Anr. Copy.** 4to. Orig. cl., unc. (S. Nov.21; 213) £220
-- **Anr. Copy.** 4to. Orig. cl., unc. (S. Nov.21; 189) *Liechti.* £130
-- **Anr. Copy.** 4to. Some light offset from ills., buckram, gt.-lettered spine, covers lightly soiled, free end-papers darkened. (CBA. Mar.3; 224) $300
-- **Anr. Edn.** Ill.:- L. Sandford. Gold. Cock. Pr., 1936. *(65) numbered on Batchelor H.M.P., with 6 extra sigd. plts.* Fo. Lacks 2 of the extra plts., orig. hf. mor., slightly soiled. (BBA. Jan.19; 293) *Pickford.* £80

SOLON, Louis Mark Emanuel

- **The Ancient Art Stoneware of the Low Countries & Germany.** L., 1892. *(300) numbered & sigd.* 2 vols. Fo. Orig. wraps., unc., soiled. (S. May 1; 640) *Tropper.* £80
-- **Anr. Copy.** 2 vols. Fo. Some light spotting, orig. wraps., soiled. (CSK. Oct.7; 175) £70
-- **Anr. Copy.** 2 vols. Fo. 25 etched plts., a few lightly foxed, some discoloration from tissue guards, ptd. wraps., chipped, disbnd. (SG. Jan.26; 159) $150
- **The Art of the Old English Potter.** 1883. Lge. fo. L.P., subscribers' list, maroon hf. mor., rubbed & stained. (S. Nov.8; 572) *Thorp.* £80
-- **Anr. Edn.** L. & Derby, 1883. *(250) numbered & sigd. by publishers.* Fo. Orig. pict. cl., soiled. (CSK. Jun.1; 45) £65
- **Ceramic Literature.** L., 1910. 4to. Later hf. pig. (BBA. Apr.5; 208) *Thorp.* £85
-- **Anr. Copy.** 4to. Buckram. (SG. Jan.26; 70) $150
- **A History & Description of Italian Majolica.** 1907. *(750) numbered.* Lge. 8vo. Cont. crimson mor. gt. by Simson & Co. Ltd., Hertford. (TA. May 17; 405) £92

SOLORZANO PEREIRA, Joannes de

- **Emblemata Centum, Regio Politica.** [Madrid], n.d. Fo. Later hf. cf., worn, covers detchd., mod. box; inscr. 'Mary Scott 26th Jany. 1838'. (CSK. Jul.13; 85) £145
- **Politica Indiana.** Madrid, 1648. Fo. Without frontis., port. laid down, tear in 2F6 reprd., some light stains, sm. liby. stp. on title, later mott. cf. (S. Dec.1; 296) *Fenton.* £400

SOLVYNS, Frans Baltasar

- **A Collection of Two Hundred & Fifty Coloured Etchings: Descriptive of the Manners, Customs & Dresses of the Hindoos.** Calcutta, 1796. 12 pts. in 1 vol. Fo. General title, 6 section titles only, 207 plts. only (10 folding), some hand-cold. or partly hand-cold., all mntd. with MS. captions & numerations, few slightly torn, few soiled, cont. cf., worn, loose; proof copy?, arabic sig. of Joseph Francis Fearon on title. (BBA. Mar.7; 80) *T.P. Engineer.* £1,900
-- **Anr. Edn.** Calcutta, 1799. 12 pts. in 1 vol. Fo. General title, some pt. titles & all ll. of descriptive text supplied in MS. in neat hand, 209 (of 250) hand-cold. etched plts., all trimmed to borderline & inlaid with double ruled borders, old bds., rebkd. & recornered preserving orig. spine, as a coll. of plts., w.a.f. (C. Jun.27; 70) *Marks.* £750

SOMAIZE, Antoine Baudeau de

- **Le Grand Dictionaire des Pretieuses** ... — **La Clef du Grand Dictionaire Historique des Pretieuses.** Paris, 1661. *1st. Edn.* 3 vols. in 1. 12mo. Frontis. (usually lacking) from anr. copy, early 18th. C. red mor., spine decor. (HD. Mar.29; 94) Frs. 18,000

SOME BRITISH BALLADS

Ill.:- Arthur Rackham. L., [1919]. *(575) numbered & sigd. by artist.* 4to. Corner of 1 plt. creased, orig. parch.-bkd. bds. gt., slightly worn. (S. Dec.20; 581) *Roberts.* £100

SOMEREN, J. van

- **Uyt-spanning der Vernuften, Best. in Geestelijcke & Wereltlijcke Poësy.** Nymegen, 1660. *1st. Edn.* 4to. Slightly stained, cont. vell. (VG. Sep.14; 1060) Fls. 725

SOMERVILLE, Edith Oenone

- **Slipper's ABC of Fox Hunting.** 1903. 4to. Pict. cl. (BS. Nov.16; 95) £80

SOMERVILLE, Edith Oenone & Martin, Violet Florence 'Martin Ross'

- **Sporting Works.** Foreword:- Harry Worcester Smith. Ill.:- E.O.E. Somerville. Derrydale Pr., 1927. *Hitchcock Edn. (500) numbered.* 7 vols. Sm. 4to. Unif. gt.-armorial cl., labels slightly brittle; sigd. by Somerville. (SG. Mar.15; 240) $300

SOMERVILLE, Thomas

- **The History of Political Transactions & of Parties from ... Charles the Second, to ... King William.** 1792. *(With:)* - **The History of Great Britain during the Reign of Queen Anne.** 1798. Together 2 vols. 4to. Hf.-titles, unif. spr. cf., spines gt.; Sir Ivar Colquhoun, of Luss copies. (CE. Mar.22; 284) £150

SOMERVILLE, William

- **The Chace. A Poem.** 1735. *[1st. Edn.].* 4to. Errata, disbnd. (BBA. Jul.27; 117) *Howes.* £50
-- **Anr. Copy.** 4to. Errata lf., slightly wormed, 2 slight margin tears & some slight staining, orig. wraps., unc., spine defect.; Frederic Dannay copy. (CNY. Dec.16; 330) $250
-- **Anr. Edn.** Ill.:- Thomas Bewick after John Bewick. L., 1796. 4to. Cont. str.-grd. mor. gt., gt.-ruled border & ruled panel, elab. gt.-tooled spine in 6 compartments, turn-ins gt., silk doubls. & free end-paper, by Henry Walther, with his ticket, slightly worn, slight score to lr. cover; bkplt. of Howard Pease, Thomas B. Stevenson copy, as a bdg., w.a.f. (CNY. Dec.17; 611) $380

SOMMARIA DELLE VITE de gl'Imperatori Romani, da C. Giulio Cesare sino a Ferdinando II

Rome, 1637. Sm. 4to. Slight browning, last p. scraped at foot affecting text, limp bds., spine worn. (S. Dec.20; 787) *Fenton.* £50

SOMMER, Frederick

- **1939-1962 Photographs.** [Millerton, 1963]. *1st. Edn.* 4to. Ptd. cl., rubbed. (SG. May 10; 132) $100

SOMMERFELD, Armond

- **Atombau und Spektrallinien.** Braunschweig, 1919. *1st. Edn.* Light margin browning, spotting, orig. cl.-bkd. bds., light wear, d.-w., publisher's box, worn; sig. & bkplt. of Heinrich Hirschfeld, Stanitz coll. (SPB. Apr.25; 404) $500

SOMMERING, S. Th.

- **Abhandlung über die Schnell und langsam tödtlichen Krankheiten der Harnblase und Harnröhre bey Männer im Hohen Alter.** Frankfurt, 1809. Cont. bds., soiled. (D. Nov.23; 631) DM 420

SOMNER, William

- **The Antiquities of Canterbury.** L., 1640. *1st. Edn.* 4to. Errata lf., sm. tears or repairs, prelims. faintly browned, cont. cf.; Daniel Fleming copy. [STC 22918] (S. Mar.6; 450) *Maggs.* £100
-- **Anr. Edn.** Ed.:- Nicholas Batteley. Ill.:- W. Hollar, J. Kip, & others. L., 1703. *2nd. Edn.* 2 pts. in 1 vol. Fo. 23 engraved plts., some folding or double-p., some offsetting, cont. russ., rebkd. (S. Mar.6; 451) *Potts.* £240
- **A Treatise of Gavelkind.** L., 1660. *1st. Edn.* 4to. Title stained, rust-hole in Y4, imprint cut into,

some spotting, minor worming, mod. cf. [Wing S4668]. (S. Mar.6; 452) *Coulter.* £70
- **A Treatise of the Roman Ports & Forts in Kent.** Oxford, 1693. *[1st. Edn.].* 2 pts. in 1 vol. Sm. 8vo. Cont. cf., rebkd., spine gt.-decor. (TA. Feb.16; 80) £84
-- **Anr. Copy.** 2 pts. in 1 vol. Cf., rebkd. (P. Sep.29; 102) *Blackwells.* £50
-- **Anr. Copy.** 12mo. Some slight browning, some foxing, early owner's ink block sig. at top margin of title, cont. cf., front panel detchd., heavy wear, stpd. borders & corner ornaments faintly visible, bkplt. removed from front pastedown. (HA. May 4; 446) $100

SONCINO GESELLSCHAFT
- **Soncino-Blaetter.** Berlin, 1925-26, Jul. 1929, n.d. Vol. 1, Vol. 3 no. 1, Vol. 3 nos. 2-4. (*With:*)
- **Festschrift fuer Aron Freimann.** Berlin, 1935. 1 vol. Together 4 vols. Sm. fo. Orig. wraps. (SG. Feb.2; 26) $250

SONCINO PRESS
See— HAGGADAH

SONCINUS, Faustus
- **Defensio Animadversionum in Assertiones Theologicae Collegii Posnaniensis de Trino & Uno Deo, adversus Gabrielem Eutropium.** Racow, 1618. *1st. Edn.* Sm. 8vo. Errata lf. at end, cont. vell., bdg. partly detchd. from stitching. (C. May 30; 62) *Quaritch.* £500
- **Disputatio de Adoratione Christi, habita inter Faustum Soncinum & Christianum Francken.** Racow, 1618. *1st. Edn.* Sm. 8vo. Tear in blank inner margin of title, 2 headlines slightly shaved, 18th. C. bds. (C. May 30; 63) *Quaritch.* £220
- **Responsio ad Libellum Jacobi Wuieki ... De Divinitate Filii Dei & Spiritus Sancti.** [Racow], 1624. *1st. Edn.* (*Bound with:*) - **Fragmenta Duorum Scriptorum Fausti Socini Senensis.** Racow, 1619. *1st. Edn.* (*Bound with:*) - **Brevis Discursus de Causa ob quam creditur aut non creditur Evangelio Jesu Christi.** Racow, 1614. Together 3 works in 1 vol. Sm. 8vo. Cont. vell. (C. May 30; 65) *Quaritch.* £520

SONG OF ROLAND (The)
[Camb., Mass., Riverside Pr., 1906]. *(220) numbered.* Fo. Hand-cold. ills., vell.-bkd. decor. paper bds. (LH. Sep.25; 444) $375
-- **Anr. Copy.** Tall fo. Decors. hand-cold., vell.-bkd. patterned bds., soiled & smudged. (SG. Aug.4; 271) $300

SONGS FOR THE PEOPLE: comprising, National, Patriotic, Sentimental, Comic & Naval Songs
Ed.:– Albert G. Emerick. Ill.:– Croome & others. Phila., 1848. Lge. 8vo. Additional pict. title frayed on fore-e., foxed, lacks front free end-papers & end-paper at rear, orig. gt.-pict. cl., worn & soiled; from liby. of F.D. Roosevelt, inscr. by him (as Governor). (SG. Mar.15; 78) $300

SONNERAT, Pierre
- **Voyage aux Indes Orientales et à la Chine.** Paris, 1782. 2 vols. 4to. 140 engraved plts., plans & tables, numeration on some plts. shaved, some ll. in Vol. 1 lightly dampstained, cont. cf., rebkd. (CSK. Jan.27; 96) £340

SONNETS ET EAUX-FORTES
Text:– J. Aicard, Th. De Banville, Th. Gautier & others. Ill.:– G. Doré, C. Nanteuil, Corot & others. Paris, 1869. Lge. Fo. Each sonnet ill. with orig. etching, mor. finish cf. by Lafesse. watered silk liners & end-ll. (HD. Jun.13; 99) Frs. 25,000

SONNINI, Charles Sigisbert
- **Voyage dans la Haute et Basse Egypte.** Paris, 1799. 3 vols. (lacks Atlas). Cont. marb. cf., decor. spines. (HD. Sep.22; 346) Frs. 1,100
- **Voyage en Grèce et en Turquie ... An IX [1801].** 2 vols. & atlas. 8vo & 4to. 1 lge. cold. folding map, cont. roan & publisher's bds. (HD. Jun.29; 107) Frs. 3,800
See— BUFFON, George Louis Leclerc, Comte de & Sonnini, C.S.

SONNTAG, Carl
- **Kostbare Bucheinbände des XV bis XIX Jahrhunderts. (C.G. Berner Catalogue 21).** Leipzig, n.d. Fo.

Later cl.; H.M. Nixon coll. (BBA. Oct.6; 173) *Oak Knoll Books.* £180
-- **Anr. Copy.** 4to. 52 plts. (9 cold.), mod. bds. (BBA. Mar.7; 314) *Quaritch.* £150

SOPHOCLES
- **Antigone.** Ill.:– Victor Steward, hand-cold. by D. Allen. Greenbrae, 1978. *(130).* 4to. Bds., acetate wrap., orig. shipping box. (CBA. Nov.19; 8) $325
- **Tragaediae Septum cum Commentariis.** Venice, Aug. 1502. *1st. Edn.* In Greek, stained, vell.; Joseph Smith & John Scott of Holkshill bkplts. (SPB. Dec.14; 32) $900
- **Tragodiai Hepta ...** Ed.:– Aldus Manutius. Venice, Aug. 1502. *1st. Edn.* Capital spaces with guide letters, 1st. & last ll. stained, the 1st. with sm. hole & wear to 2 letters, some staining near margins at front & back, some early ink annots., 18th. C. Fr. red mor. gt., flat spine gt. in 8 compartments, bd. edges & turn-ins gt., marb. end-papers, qtr. pig box; Mortimer L. Schiff & Henri Burton bkplts., Thomas B. Stevenson copy. (CNY. May 18; 86) $1,200
- **Tragoediae, cum Veterum Grammaticorum ...** Ed.:– Brunck. Strasbourg, 1786. 2 vols. Lge. 4to. Mor. gt., mor. linings. (LH. Sep.25; 598) $325
- **Die Trauerspiele.** Trans.:– Fr. Hölderlin. Frankfurt, 1804. *1st. Edn. Ltd. Iss. on Bütten.* 2 vols. in 1. Some sm. tears, I with slight loss. cont. hf. leath. gt., slightly bumped; Eduard Erdmann ex-libris; Hauswedell coll. (H. May 24; 1384) DM 10,500

SOPRANI, R. & Ratti, C.G.
- **Vite de'pittori, Scultori e Architetti Genovesi.** Genova, 1768-69. 2 vols. 4to. Cf., gt.-tooled spine. (CR. Jun.6; 293) Lire 650,000

SORBIERE, Samuel
- **Relation d'un Voyage en Angleterre.** Paris, 1664. *1st. Edn.* 12mo. Some stains, cont. cf. gt., rebkd. with orig. spine laid down. (SG. Oct.6; 339) $425

SOREL, Charles
[-] **The Comical History of Francion.** L., 1655. *1st. Edn. in Engl.* Fo. Sig. of Seth Ward inserted, margins of title-p. frayed, browned & spotted, recent leath. [Wing S4702] (BBA. May 3; 134) *Maggs.* £70
[-] **De la Connoissance des Bons Livres.** Paris, 1671. *1st. Edn.* 12mo. Cont. cf. gt., spine ends worn. (SG. Sep.15; 308) $260

SORIO, Balthaser
- **Mariale.** Tortosa, 7 Jan. 1538. 4to. Rather browned, short tear in margin of B7, some worming in inner margins of some ll. in middle, light dampstain at end, sm. cancel strip pasted over a few lines on R3v col. 1, sm. slit in blank corner of S1 reprd., 19th. C. cf. gt., stain on upr. cover. (S. May 10; 410) *Quaritch.* £450

SORLIER, Charles
See— MOURLOT, Ferrand & Sorlier, Clarles

SORREGUIETA, Tomas de
- **Semana Hispano-Bascongada, la Unica de la Europa, y la Mas Antigua del Orbe. Con dos Suplementos de Otros Ciclos, y Etimologias Bascongadas.** Pamplona, 1804. 2 pts. in 1 vol. 4to. Cont. pol. tree sheep. (SG. Aug.4; 28) $130

SOSA, J. de
- **Noticia de la Gran Casa de los Marqueses de Villafranca.** Napoles, 1676. 4to. Lacks genealogical tree, cf. (DS. Apr.27; 2609) Pts. 50,000

SOSTHENNAJAI BOZHESTVENNAJA LITURGIA ... / Avodat Adonai ha-Kedosha al pi Avinu ha-Kadosh Yohanan Siftei ha-Zahav
St. Petersb., 1846 [?]. 4to. Titles & text in Russian & Hebrew, some dampstaining & foxing, owner's stp. on title, cl.-bkd. card., unc. & partially unopened. (SG. Feb.2; 113) $100

SOTERAS, J. Pijoan y
See— COSSIO, M.B. & Soteras, J. Pijoan y

SOTHEBY, Samuel Leigh
- **Principia Typographica.** 1858. *Ltd. Edn., not for sale.* 3 pts. in 1 vol. Fo. Some ll. spotted, cont. hf. mor.; enlarged specimen with pres. inscr. by author. (BBA. Nov.10; 130) *Marlborough Rare Books.* £220

-- **Anr. Edn.** L., 1858. 3 vols. Fo. Some ll. spotted, cont. hf. mor., worn. (BBA. Mar.7; 380) *W. Forster.* £70
- **Ramblings in the Elucidation of the Autograph of Milton.** L., 1861. Lge. fo. 2 mntd. albumen photos., 27 plts., ills., mor. by J. Wright, lge. countersunk panels on covers, worn. (SG. May 17; 317) $110

SOTHEBY, William
- **A Tour through Parts of Wales, Sonnets, Odes, & Other Poems.** Ill.:– J. Smith. 1794. 4to. Some margin dampstains, cont. hf. mor. (TA. Feb.16; 64) £85

SOTHEBY PARKE BERNET & CO.
- **Art at Auction.** N.Y., 1966-82. 16 vols. 4to. No bdg. stated. (SPB. Nov.30; 200) $425

SOTO, Domingo de
- **Relectio Fratris Dominici ... de Ratione Tuendi Secretum.** Salamanca, 1557. 4to. Vell. (DS. Mar.23; 2273) Pts. 60,000

SOUBEIRAN, E.
- **Handbuch der Pharmaceutischen Praxis.** Trans.:– Fr. Schödler. Heidelberg, 1839. *1st. German Edn.* Title lf. stpd., some spotting, cont. hf. leath. gt. (GB. May 3; 1039) DM 450

SOULAGES, Gabriel
- **Le Malheureux Petit Voyage.** 1926. Sm. 4to. Sewed, wrap. & s.-c. (HD. Dec.9; 11b) Frs. 1,100

SOULE, Frank & others
- **The Annals of San Francisco.** N.Y., 1855. Prelims. spotted, orig. mor. gt., new end-papers. (TA. Sep.15; 111) £64

SOURIRE
Ill.:– Morin, Radiguet, Villemot, Alix, Iribe, Laborde, Hemard, Bofa, Brunelleschi & others. Paris, 1899-1911. 12 vols. 4to. Cont. hf. roan. (HD. Dec.9; 49) Frs. 3,000

SOUSA, Luis de
- **Plans Elevations Sections & Views of the Church of Batalha.** 1795. Fo. Several ll. spotted, cont. hf. cf. (CSK. Jun.1; 69) £85

SOUTH AFRICA
- **The Gold & Diamond Fields, Transvaal.** [1910?]. Ob. 4to. Pict. cl. (SSA. Jul.5; 155) R 800
- **Photographic Scenery of South Africa.** Cape Town, 1878. 4to. Port., 108 plts., some warping, foxing, some plts. rubbed, black bdg. (SPB. Dec.13; 881) $375

SOUTH AUSTRALIA
- **Votes & Proceedings of the Legislative Council, during the Second Session.** Adelaide, 1856. Fo. 8 litho. maps & plans, sm. liby. stps. on title, mod. hf. cf. gt. (S. Mar.6; 13) *Orientum.* £100

SOUTH AUSTRALIAN GRAPHIC ADVERTISER
Adelaide, 1892. No. 1. Lge. 4to. Ptd. wraps., a few sm. defects. (KH. May 1; 161) Aus. $2,100

SOUTH POLAR TIMES
1907. *(250) numbered.* Vols. 1 & 2 only. End-papers & 1st. few ll. lightly spotted, orig. cl., d.-w.'s. (CSK. Jul.6; 50) £1,100
-- **Anr. Edn.** Ed.:– Sir E.H. Shackleton, & A. Cherry-Garrard. 1907-14. *Vols. 1 & 2: (250), Vol. 3: (350).* 3 vols. 4to. Cl. ğt., Vols. 1 & 2 with d.-w., torn. (P. Jun.7; 54) £1,700
-- **Anr. Copy.** 3 vols. 4to. Orig. ribbed cl. gt. with cold. ill. on upr. covers. (C. Jun.27; 71) *Dunsheath.* £1,500

SOUTHERNE, Thomas
- **The Fatal Marriage: or, The Innocent Adultery, a Play.** 1694. *1st. Edn.* 4to. Some staining, later cf. [Wing S4756] (BBA. Jan.19; 141) *Maggs.* £110

SOUTHEY, Robert
- **History of the Peninsular War.** 1823-27-32. *1st. Edn.* 3 vols. Cont. hf. mor., spine gt. in compartments. (SKC. May 4; 1607) £110
-- **Anr. Copy.** 3 vols. 4to. Recent hf. cf. (TA. Mar.15; 295) £50
- **Letters Written during a Short Residence in Spain & Portugal.** Bristol, 1797. *1st. Edn.* Single

SOUTHEY, Robert -Contd.

advt. lf. for Joan of Arc tipped in at end, cont. bds., unc., worn. (BBA. Nov.30; 243) *Bickersteth*. £65
- **The Poetical Works.** L., 1859-60 & n.d. 10 vols. Cf., spines gt. (S. Mar.20; 795) *Aschan*. £80
See— COLERIDGE, Samuel Taylor & Southey, Robert

SOUTHGATE, Frank & Pollard, Hugh B.C.
- **Wildfowl & Waders. Nature & Sport in the Coastlands.** 1928. *(950)* numbered. 4to. Minor spotting, orig. bds., vell. backstrip, rubbed. (TA. Feb.16; 98) £54

SOUTHOUSE, Thomas
- **Monasticon Favershamiense in Agro Cantiano.** L., 1671. *1st. Edn.* 12mo. Cont. cf., rebkd. [Wing S4772] (S. Mar.6; 454) *Frankland*. £170

SOUVENIR DE LA SUISSE en Vues Pittoresques
Darmstadt, ca. 1840. Lge. ob. 8vo. Steel engraved title & 68 plts., several with 2 or more views, gt. cl., loosening, some foxing. (VG. May 3; 414) Fls. 4,800
- - **Anr. Edn.** Basle, ca. 1850. Ob. fo. Engraved title with vig., 98 steel-engraved plts., some margins spotted, stain affecting lr. margin of title & 1st. view, orig. cl., contents slightly loose. (S. May 21; 254) *Hochwacht*. £2,900

SOUVESTRE, Emile
- **Le Foyer Breton.** Ill.:– Mme. T. Johannot & others. Paris, [1844]. *1st. Printing.* Hf. mor., by Champs-Stroobants, corners, decor. spine, wrap. & spine preserved; autograph dedication sigd. from author. (HD. Dec.9; 186) Frs. 2,800
- **Le Monde tel qu'il sera.** Ill.:– Bertall, O. Penguilly, & St Germain. [1846]. *1st. Printing of ills.* Lge. 8vo. Foxing, publisher's buckram bds. (HD. Mar.21; 201) Frs. 2,600

SOVIET CINEMA
Ed.:– [A. Arossev]. Ill.:– V. Stepanova & A. Rodchenko. Moskau, 1935. Sm. 4to. Transparent plt. torn, orig. linen, cover ill. photo montage, slightly rubbed, lacks upr. end-paper. (H. Nov.24; 2567) DM 580

SOWERBY, George B.
- **A Conchological Manual.** L., 1852. *4th. Edn.* 29 hand-cold. plts., few plt. headlines shaved, old hf. leath. gt., rubbed, covers slightly discold. (SG. Mar.22; 290) $130

SOWERBY, James
See— SMITH, Sir James Edward & Sowerby, James

SOWERBY, James de Carle & Lear, Edward
- **Tortoises, Terrapins, & Turtles.** 1872. Fo. 61 plain lithos., 2 plts. spotted, cl. soiled. (P. Oct.20; 123) £180

SOWERBY, John Edward & Johnson, Charles Pierpoint
- **British Wild Flowers Illustrated.** Supp.:– J.W. Salter & J.E. Sowerby. 1894. 2 uncold. plts., 1,780 hand-cold. figures on engraved plts., orig. cl. gt. (LC. Mar.1; 164) £65

SOWJET-ENZYKLOPADIE
Moskau, 1970-81. *Destalinised Edn.* 30 in 31 vols. & 1 index vol. Sm. 4to. Orig. bdgs. (H. Nov.23; 104) DM 700

SOYER, Alexis
- **The Gastronomic Regenerator – a Simplified & Entirely New System of Cookery.** 1846. *2nd. Edn.* Orig. cl.; *(with:)* - **The Pantropheon, or History of Food & its Preparation.** 1853. Orig. cl. gt. (PD. Aug.17; 253) £135

SPACH, E.
- **Histoire Naturelle de Végétaux, Phanérogames, Atlas.** Paris, 1846. 152 numbered & most cold. steel engraved plts., cont. decor. hf. leath., gold-tooled. (HT. May 8; 313) DM 600

SPAIN IN THE WEST SERIES
Cleveland & Glendale, 1914-77. Vols. I-XII. Cl. (LH. Sep.25; 287) $250

SPALLANZANI, Lazzaro
- **Dissertations relative to the Natural History of Animals & Vegetables.** 1784. 2 vols. Cont. cf.-bkd. bds., vell. corners; slightly rubbed; Cholmondeley Liby. bkplts. (BBA. Jul.27; 55) *Gurney*. £80
- - **Anr. Edn.** Trans.:– Thomas Beddoes. L., 1789. 2 vols. Few ll. Vol. 1 loose, cf., rebkd., corners reprd.; Dr. Walter Pagel copy. (S. Feb.7; 355) *Quaritch*. £110
- - **Anr. Copy.** 2 vols. Lge. 8vo. Buckram, ex-liby. (SG. Mar.22; 293) $175
- **Expériences sur la Circulation.** Trans.:– J. Tourdes. Paris, [An] 8, [1800]. *1st. Fr. Edn.* Cont. hf. leath. (D. Nov.23; 632) DM 400
- **Tracts on the Natural History of Animals & Vegetables.** Trans.:– John Graham Dalvell. Edinb., 1803. *2nd. Edn.* 2 vols. Engraved hf.-titles & 11 folding plts., wormed, cont. tree cf. (BBA. Jul.27; 57) *Gurney*. £50
- **Travels in the Two Sicilies.** 1798. *1st. Edn.* 4 vols. 11 folding engraved plts., some browning & spotting, last 2 plts. in Vol. 4 stained, L8 misbnd. before L1 in Vol. 2, cont. cf., rebkd., corners reprd, rubbed. (BBA. Jul.27; 56) *Quaritch*. £190

SPAMER, O.
- **Illustriertes Konversations-Lexikon.** Leipzig, 1893. *2nd. Edn.* 8 vols. 4to. Cont. hf. linen, new spine. (R. Oct.12; 2176) DM 1,300
- - **Anr. Copy.** Vols. 1-2 & 4-8 in 7 vols. 4to. Orig. hf. leath., bumped. (R. Oct.12; 2177) DM 800

SPAMPANI, G.B. & Antonini, C.
- **Il Vignola Ilustrato.** Ill.:– C. Antonini after F. Smuglewicz. Rome, 1770. *1st. Edn.* Fo. Some slight text foxing, only some plt. margins, 2 prelim ll. with sm. bkd. hole with slight loss in 3 contents lines, 19th. C. hf. leath. (R. Oct.11; 794) DM 620

SPANHEIM, Ezekiel
- **Dissertationes de Praestantia et Usu Numismatum Antiquorum.** L. & Amst., 1706 & 1717. 2 vols. Fo. Some browning & spotting, liby. stps. on titles, cont. mott. cf., rubbed. (S. May 1; 517) *Drury*. £50

SPANHEIM, Friedrich
- **Histoire de la Papesse Jeanne.** Cologne, 1695. 12mo. Old vell., soiled. (SG. Feb.9; 313) $275

SPANN, M.J. (Ed.)
See— ZUKOFSKY, Louis

SPARLING, Henry Halliday
- **The Kelmscott Press & William Morris.** 1924. Orig. linen-bkd. bds., unc. (P. Jul.26; 41) £75

SPARLING, Marcus
- **Theory & Practice of the Photographic Art including its Chemistry & Optics ...** L., 1856. *1st. Edn.* Cl. gt. (PNY. Dec.1; 100) $300

SPARRMAN, Anders
- **Voyage au Cap de Bonne-Espérance et autour du Monde avec le Capitaine Cook, et principalement dans les Pays des Hottentots et des Caffres.** Paris, 1787. *1st. Fr. Edn.* 3 vols. Cont. marb. cf., spine decor., turn-ins torn out, corners rounded (1 corner reprd.). (HD. Jun.26; 48) Frs. 1,350
- - **Anr. Copy.** 3 vols. Cont. cf. (SSA. Sep.21; 392) R 220
- **A Voyage round the World.** Ill.:– Peter Barker-Mill. Gold. Cock. Pr., 1944. *(350)* numbered. Sm. fo. Orig. buckram gt. (S. Nov.21; 229) *Libris*. £390
- - **Anr. Copy.** Sm. fo. Orig. buckram gt., untrimmed. (SKC. Sep.9; 1889) £210
- - **Anr. Copy.** Sm. fo. Buckram, slight markings. (KH. Nov.8; 105) Aus. $500
- - **Anr. Copy.** Sm. fo. Buckram. (KH. May 1; 652) Aus. $380
- - **Anr. Edn.** Ill.:– Peter Barker-Mill. Gold. Cock. Pr., 1944. *(50)* numbered, specially bnd. Sm. fo. Prospectus loosely inserted, orig. mor. gt., s.-c.; from D. Bolton liby. (BBA. Oct.27; 148) *Joseph*. £500
- **A Voyage to the Cape of Good Hope ...** 1785. 2 vols. Cf., upr. covers loose. (SSA. Jul.5; 370) R 420

SPARROW, Walter Shaw
- **Angling in British Art through Five Centuries.** 1923. *1st. Edn.* 4to. Minor spotting to prelims., orig. cl. gt., spine little faded. (TA. Sep.15; 389) £50
- - **Anr. Edn.** L., 1923. *(125)* numbered, & sigd., with orig. etching by Norman Wilkinson. 4to. Orig. buckram, partly unc., slightly soiled. (S. Oct.4; 59) *Marks*. £70
- **A Book of British Etching, from Francis Barlow to Francis Seymour Haden.** L., [1926]. 4to. Cl., soiled. (SG. Aug.25; 356) $110
- **A Book of Sporting Painters.** L., 1931. Cl. gt., slight fraying at bottom of spine. (DM. May 21; 29) $130
- **George Stubbs & Ben Marshall.** 1929. *(250)* numbered. 4to. Buckram. (BS. May 2; 119) £65
- **Henry Alken.** L., 1927. *(With:)* - **George Stubbs & Ben Marshall.** L., 1929. Together 2 vols. in series The Sport of Our Fathers, 4to. orig. cl., 2nd. faded, d.-w.'s. (S. Apr.30; 90) *Morris*. £90

SPECHT, R.L.
See— MOUNTFORD, C.P. & Specht, R.L.

SPECIMAN DAYS
Intro.:– Alfred Kazin. Boston, 1971. 4to. Cl., with mntd. photographic reproduction, d.-w. (SG. May 10; 153) $100

SPECIMENS OF MODERN MASTERS
1835. Fo. Steel-engraved dedication & 96 plts. only, all on India paper, mntd., mostly ports. & continental views, several margins spotted, cont. hf. mor., rubbed. (CSK. Apr.27; 13) £75

SPEE, Friedrich von
- **Trvtz Nachtigal.** Cöllen, 1649. *1st. Edn.* 12mo. Lacking last verse line completed in MS., title with old partly erased owners marks, end-paper & doubl. with MS. notes, slightly browned & soiled thro.-out, some staining, cont. vell., slightly defect., Hauswedell coll. (H. May 24; 1193) DM 5,800

SPEECHES OR ARGUMENTS of the Judges, the Court of King's Bench ... in April 1769; In the cause Millar against Taylor, For printing Thomson's Seasons ...
Leith, 1771. Cont. hf. cf.; Sir Ivar Colquhoun, of Luss copy. (CE. Mar.22; 285) £120

SPEECHLY, William
- **A Treatise on the Culture of the Vine.** York, 1790. *1st. Edn.* 4to. Subscribers list, some offsetting from plts., slight stain to corner of a few ll., hf. cf., rubbed, spine torn; Charles Meigh bkplt. (LC. Jul.5; 428) £220
- - **Anr. Copy.** 4to. 1 lf. torn, hf. cf., rubbed. (P. Jan.12; 280) *Cole*. £110

SPEEDE, John
- **England, Wales, Scotland & Ireland Described & Abridged ...** George Humble, 1627. Engraved title (lr. margin slightly trimmed), 63 maps (2 folding). *(Bound with:)* - **A Prospect of the Most Famous Parts of the World.** N.d. 20 engraved maps, 2 trimmed, 1 with loss, lightly soiled & dampstained, lacks title. Together 2 works in 1 vol. Ob. 8vo. Old cf., rubbed. (CSK. Mar.9; 4) £1,000
- - **Anr. Edn.** Ill.:– [Pieter Van den Keere]. [1632]. Sm. ob. 8vo. 61 (of 63) engraved maps, lacks A1-5, A6 detchd., 1 map torn without loss, anr. with lr. margin torn away, minor margins dampstained, some maps with points of compass inked in margin, some marginalia to text, cont. cf., worn, upr. cover detchd. (TA. Dec.15; 93) £640
- - **Anr. Edn.** L., 1666, 1668. Engraved title-p., 1 folding map (of 2), 61 full-p. maps, lr. portion of title-p. reprd., missing ptd. area supplied in facs., sm. hole in S1, browned. *(Bound with:)* - **A Prospect of the Most Famous Parts of the World.** L., 1668. [Wing S4884]. Together 2 works in 1 vol. Ob. 8vo. Cont. cf., reprd. & rebkd.; 17th. C. sig. of Edwin Norris, as an atlas, w.a.f. (BBA. May 3; 249) *Ingol Maps*. £950
- **An Epitome of Mr. John Speed's Theatre of the Empire of Great Britain & of his Prospect of the most famous Parts of the World.** Ed.:– P. van de Keere. 1676-75. 2 pts. in 1 vol. Ob. 8vo. Theatre with 59 engraved maps only (2 soiled with loss), prospect with 22 engraved maps only (1 trimmed

with loss), lacks F7-H8, lr. margins soiled thro.-out, old bds., worn, w.a.f. (CSK. Jul.6; 66) £800
- **The Historie of the Great Britaine.** 1623. *2nd. Edn.* Fo. Browned, cont. mott. cf., rubbed. (BBA. Jul.27; 95) *Shapiro.* £80
- - **Anr. Edn.** L., 1627. *2nd. Edn.* Lge. fo. Lacks Books I-IV, engraved title mntd. with hinge repairs, port. inserted, sm. liby. stp. on title, 18th. C. crimson mor., elab. gt. ornaments on covers, spine gt. [STC 23048] (SG. Feb.9; 337) $100
- - **Anr. Edn.** L., 1631. *3rd. Edn.* Fo. Slight stains, cont. cf., rebkd. (S. Mar.6; 327) *Bloomsbury.* £130
- - **Anr. Edn.** L., 1650. *3rd. Edn.* Lge. fo. Lacks port., some margin stains, early cf., gt. arms on covers, very worn, rebkd. (SG. Oct.27; 304) $100
- **The Theatre of the Empire of Great Britaine.** L., John Sudbury & Georg Humble, 1611. *1st. Edn.* 4 pts. in 1 vol. Fo. Engraved architectural title, engraved or woodcut Royal arms & ptd. titles to each pt., 67 double-p. maps, Engl. text on verses, mntd. on guards, some worming at central fold thro.-out, wormhole in outer portion of later ll., some 6 maps with outer margins slightly shaved, old cf., reprd., rebkd. preserving orig. backstrip. [STC 23041] (C. Nov.16; 176) *Burgess.* £7,000
- - **Anr. Edn.** L., Basset & Chiswel, 1676. Atlas fo. 96 double-p. maps, lacks engraved title & frontis., title-p. for 'Prospect' bnd. after main title, all ll. rehinged, early 19th. C. elab. gt.-tooled crimson str.-grd. mor., sm. liby. bkplt. (SG. Nov.3; 196) $23,000
- - **Anr. Edn.** 1743. Fo. 55 (of 58) double-p. outl. cold. maps, Berks. & Channel Islands foxed, hf. cf., worn. (P. Jan.12; 321) *Burgess.* £4,000
- **Theatrum Imperii Magnae Britanniae.** Trans.:- Philemon Holland. Ill.:- Jodocus Hondius after Christopher Saxton, John Norden, William Smith, & others. Thomas Snodham for Sudbury & Humble, 1616. *Latin text Edn.* Fo. Engraved allegorical title, royal achievement, 4 woodcut royal arms & those of Speed, & 67 double-p. regional & county maps, cont. hand-cold. in full thro.-out, a few minor repairs without loss of engraved surface, some browning mostly affecting margins, new guards thro.-out, cont. vell., gt.-panel., slightly soiled, new ties, w.a.f. (S. May 21; 20) *Robinson.* £13,500

SPELTZ, Alexander
- **The Coloured Ornament of All Historical Styles.** Leipzig, [1914-15]. 3 vols. Sm. fo. 180 plts. in colours & gold, text pamphlet laid in, ex-liby., loose in cl. folder. (SG. May 3; 342) $100

SPENCE, Joseph
- **Polymetis.** 1747. Fo. Engraved port. & 42 plts., including 1 additional plt. trimmed & mntd., cont. red mor., gt. inner dentelles. (CSK. Apr.27; 11) £60

SPENCE, Thomas
[-] **The Real Reading-Made-Easy.** Newcastle, 1782. Orig. cf., worn. (P. Jun.7; 326) £440

SPENCER, Sir Baldwin
- **Guide to the Australian Ethnological Collection Exhibited in the National Museum of Victoria ...** Melbourne, 1922. Bds., qtr. cl.; sigd. & inscr. by author. (KH. May 1; 653) Aus. $100
- **Native Tribes of the Northern Territory of Australia.** 1914. Bdg. not stated; Will Sowden copy. (KH. May 1; 654) Aus. $170
- **Report on the Work of the Horn Scientific Expedition to Central Australia ...** Melbourne & L., 1896. 4 vols. 4to. (in 8's). 1 plt. with slight adhesion damage, cl., lightly worn. (KH. May 1; 658) Aus. $1,600
- **Scientific Correspondence ...** Ed.:- R.R. Marrett & T.K. Penniman. Oxford, 1932. Bdg. not stated. (KH. May 1; 657) Aus. $200
- **Wanderings in Wild Australia.** L., 1928. Vols. I & II. Cl., d.-w.'s. (JL. Nov.13; B551) Aus. $200
- - **Anr. Copy.** 2 vols. Lacks 1 lf. of plts., anr. in dupl., bdg. not stated. (KH. May 1; 655) Aus. $190

SPENCER, Baldwin & Gillen, F.J.
- **Across Australia.** L., 1912. *1st. Edn.* 2 vols. Orig. cl. gt. (BBA. Mar.21; 80) *J. Brailey.* £110

- - **Anr. Copy.** 2 vols. Bdg. not stated, slightly marked. (KH. May 1; 659) Aus. $230
- - **Anr. Copy.** 2 vols. Orig. blind-stpd. cl., covers slightly rubbed, sig. on front end-papers. (CA. Apr.3; 105) Aus. $160
- **The Arunta ...** L., 1927. 2 vols. Orig. cl. (KH. Nov.9; 710) Aus. $350
- - **Anr. Copy.** 2 vols. Bdg. not stated, slight wear. (KH. May 1; 660) Aus. $150
- **The Native Tribes of Central Australia.** 1899. Buckram, largely unopened, slightly marked. (KH. May 1; 661) Aus. $220

SPENCER, E.
- **The King's Racehorses.** 1902. *(50) numbered on Japanese vell., sigd.* 4to. Hf. vell. gt. (P. Dec.8; 220) *Way.* £55

SPENCER, Earl & Dobson, Christopher
- **Letters of David Garrick & Georgiana Countess Spencer, 1759-1779.** Roxb. Cl., [1960]. 4to. Orig. qtr. mor., a trifle marked. (S. Oct.4; 236) *Traylen.* £80

SPENCER, Edmund
- **Travels in Circassia, Krim Tartary.** 1837. 2 vols. Some foxing, orig. cl., reprd. (P. Jul.5; 138) £70

SPENCER, G., Third Duke of Marlborough
See— MARLBOROUGH, G. Spencer, Third Duke of

SPENCER, Nathaniel
- **The Complete English Traveller.** L., 1772. Fo. 3 maps (2 torn & detchd.), 56 full-p. plts., 1st. few text ll. & index torn or frayed, cont. hf. cf., defect., w.a.f. (S. Mar.6; 328) *Kidd.* £130

SPENCER, Stephen
- **Twenty Poems.** Oxford, 1930. *1st. Edn., (135). (75) numbered & sigd.* 12mo. Prospects, orig. ptd. wraps., lr. cover little soiled, cl. s.-c.; Frederic Dannay copy. (CNY. Dec.16; 332) $450

SPENCER, S. & Hockney, David
- **China Diary.** L., 1982. *(1000) numbered & sigd. by author & artist & with orig. litho. sigd. by Hockney in folder.* Orig. cl. (S. Apr.30; 91) *Burwood.* £55

SPENSER, Edmund
[-] **The Faerie Queene.** L., 1590-96. *1st. Edn.* 2 vols. 4to. With both cancellans quire 2Q4 & cancellanda 2P6-7 & blank spaces for Welsh words on p.332 of vol.1, first title in facs., several repairs, mainly marginal, early marginalia on 2Q4v, red lev. gt. by Rivière for Pickering; J.H. Bates bkplt. [STC 23080-82] (SG. Apr.26; 186) $1,000
- - **Anr. Edn.** 1751. 3 vols. 4to. Cont. cf. gt., rebkd., corners reprd. (P. Jun.7; 94) £75
- - **Anr. Copy.** 3 vols. Lge. 4to. 32 engraved plts., title-pp. foxed, cont. gt. decor. cf., disbnd.; early armorial bkplt. of Thomas Hutton. (SG. Apr.19; 173) $130
- - **Anr. Edn.** Ed.:- Thomas J. Wise. Ill.:- Walter Crane. L., 1897-95-94-96. 6 vols. 4to. Lev. mor., triple gt. borders, upr. covers with lge. panels gt.-decor., gt. panel. spine in 6 compartments, turnins gt., orig. ptd. wraps. preserved, by Bates of Leicester. (CNY. Dec.17; 605) $1,200
- **The Faerie Queene [& other works].** 1609-11. *1st. Coll. Edn. Early Iss., with 1609 title.* 12 pts. in 1 vol. Sm. fo. Without general title & dedication, title & 2 ll. rehinged, short tear to B2 & Cl, sm. hole to B5, mod. cf., spine gt., slightly rubbed; Diocese of Southwark copy. (C. May 30; 135) *Aspin.* £200
- **The Faerie Queen. The Shepherds Calendar.** L., 1611. *1st. Coll. Edn.* 4to. Woodcut border to title, woodcut initials & head & tail-pieces, mor. gt. (P. May 17; 173) *Finch.* £220
- **The Faerie Queen: The Shepheards Calendar: Together with Other Works ...** L., 1611-09-11. *1st. Coll. Edn. Early Iss., without 'Prosopopoia' & 'Mother Hubberds Tale'.* 5 pts. in 1 vol. Fo. Some ll. browned, few sm. repairs to inner margins in sig. A, some slight staining to few ll. in first 2 pts., 18th. C. panel. cf., spine reprd., worn, qtr. mor. s.-c.; Frederic Dannay copy. [NSTC 23083.3] (CNY. Dec.16; 333) $450
- - **Anr. Edn.** L., 1611. *1st. Coll. Edn. 2nd. Iss.* Fo. Woodcut title border, many woodcut devices &

head & tail pieces, some browning, lacks 2 blanks, 18th. C. cf., rebkd., slightly worn; Mark Masterman Sykes' copy with arms stpd. in blind on covers & notat. on endpaper. [STC 23084] (SPB. May 16; 143) $475
- - **Anr. Edn.** L., 1611. *(Bound with:)* BEAUMONT, Joseph – Psyche: or Loves Mysterie in XX Canto's ... L., 1648. Together 2 works in 1 vol. Some dampstaining, margin worming & annots., cont. cf., worn. (PNY. Dec.1; 105) $250
- - **Anr. Edn.** L., 1617-12-11. *2nd. Coll. Edn.* 3 vols. Fo. Interleaved copy, with many MS. annots. by John Callander, 1749, early 18th. C. cf.-bkd. bds. [STC 23085] (C. Nov.9; 161) *Henderson.* £260
[-] **The Shepheardes Calendar.** L., [1581]. *2nd. Edn.* 4to. Title in typographical border, 12 lge. woodcut ills., woodcut capitals, title & prelims. mended with pt. of title & a little text restored in facs., other defects mainly marginal, early marginalia, old cf., worn, brkn.; early MS. bkplt. of Brian Tailer, anr. struck out. [STC 23090] (SG. Apr.26; 185) $9,500
- **The Works.** Ill.:- Hilda Quick. Shakes. Hd. Pr., 1930-31. *(375) numbered.* 8 vols. 4to. Mor.-bkd. paper-covered bds., unc. & unopened. (SKC. Mar.9; 1815) £160
- - **Anr. Edn.** Oxford, Shakes. Hd. Pr., 1930-32. *(375) numbered.* 8 vols. Sm. fo. Bds., qtr. cf. (KH. Nov.9; 462) Aus. $350

SPERBER, Julius, V.H.
- **Mysterium Magnum das ist das Allergroesseste Geheimbnus von Gott, von Seinem Sohne und von der Seele des Menschen.** Amst., 1660. Vell., soiled; Dr. Walter Pagel copy. (S. Feb.7; 351) *Janssen.* £380

SPERONE, Carlo
- **Real Grandeza dela Serenissima Republica de Genova.** Madrid, 1665, Genova, 1669. Fo. In Spanish & Italian, cont. vell. (HD. Oct.21; 164) Frs. 3,200

SPIEGHEL or SPIGELIUS or VAN DEN SPIEGHEL, Adrianus
- **Opera Quae Extent, Omnia.** Ed.:- T.A. van der Linden. Amst., 1645. Engraved port. frontis., engraved title (reprd. & stained), 117 engraved plts., all but 1 full-p., some soiling & staining, cont. cf., reprd. (GM. Dec.7; 661) £1,000

SPIELMANN, Marion Harry & Layard, George Somes
- **Kate Greenaway.** L., 1905. *De Luxe Edn., (500) numbered & sigd. by John Greenaway, with orig. pencil drawing laid in.* 4to. Gt.-lettered cl., lightly soiled. (SG. Dec.8; 179) $550
- - **Anr. Copy.** 4to. Orig. cl., some soiling. (SPB. Dec.13; 830) $325
- - **Anr. Edn.** 1905. Orig. cl., spine faded. (LC. Oct.13; 87) £50

SPIELMANN, Percy Edwin
- **Catalogue of the Library of Miniature Books.** 1961. *(500) numbered.* Orig. cl.-bkd. bds.; H.M. Nixon coll., with his sig. & MS. notes, others loosely inserted. (BBA. Oct.6; 126) *George's.* £160
- - **Anr. Copy.** Cl.-bkd. patterned bds., d.-w. (SG. Sep.15; 229) $170

SPIELWARREN; Blech und Zinnspiele
Ill.:- F. Scharrer or A. Kolb. [Nürnberg?], ca. 1877. 2 vols. Ob. fo. 175 hand-cold. litho. plts., pencil & ink annots., MS. indexes pasted inside upr. covers, slightly soiled, few short tears, orig. cl., van Veen coll. (S. Feb.28; 172) £18,500

SPIESS, B.
- **Wanderbüchlein durch die Rhön.** Meiningen, 1854. Lightly foxed, orig. wraps., unc. (HK. Nov.8; 1059) DM 420

SPIGELIUS, Adrianus
See— SPIEGHEL or SPIGELIUS or VAN DEN SPIEGHEL, Adrianus

SPIKER, S.H.
- **Berlin u. seine Umgebungen im 19. Jhdt.** Berlin, 1833. 4to. Slightly spotted thro.-out, cont. hf. leath. gt., slightly rubbed & bumped. (HK. May 15; 727) DM 4,400

SPIKER, S.H.
See— BRUHL, Graf Carl & Spiker, S.H.

SPILL
– Tratado llamado El Desseoso ... Ill.:– Simon de Portonaris. Salamanca, 1574. Vell. (DS. Nov.25; 2459) Pts. 20,000

SPILLE, Henrick
– Beschryving van een Nieuwe Manier om Molen-assen en Molen-Roeden ... Amst., 1779. *1st. Edn.* Slight margin soiling, mod. mor., unc.; Stantiz coll. (SPB. Apr.25; 407) $350

SPILLER, Burton L.
– Firelight. Ill.:– Lynn Bogue Hunt. Derrydale Pr., [1937]. *(950) numbered.* 4to. Gt.-decor. cl., cold. medallion on cover, unc. & unopened. (SG. Mar.15; 242) $140
– Grouse Feathers. Ill.:– Lynn Bogue Hunt. Derrydale Pr., [1935]. *(950) numbered.* 4to. Gt.-decor. leatherette, cold. medallion by Dr. Edgar Burke on cover. (SG. Mar.15; 241) $175

SPILSBURY, Francis B.
– Picturesque Scenery in the Holy Land & Syria Delineated. During the Campaigns of 1799 & 1800. L., 1819. *2nd. Edn.* Fo. Dedication, 19 hand-cold. aquatint plts., some slight margin soiling, mod. hf. mor. (S. Feb.1; 55) *Hatch.* £2,600
– – Anr. Edn. L., 1823. 4to. 18 (of 19) cold. aquatints, orig. hf. cf. on marb. bds., worn. (SG. Sep.22; 277) $375

SPINNIKER, Adrian
– Leerzaame Zinnebeelden. – Vervolg der Leerzaame Zinnebeelden. Ill.:– V. v.d. Vinne (1st. work) & J.C. Philips (2nd. work). Haarlem, 1756-58. *1st. work: 2nd. Edn.; 2nd. work: 1st. Edn.* Together 2 vols. in 1. 4to. Some foxing, antique-style cf., spine gt. (VS. Dec.9; 1150) Fls. 600

SPINO, P.
– Historiae della Vita, et Fatti dell'Eccellentissimo Capitano di Gverra Bartolomeo Coglione. Venice, 1569. *1st. Edn.* 4to. 1st. state title 'con privilegio', title cut to subject margin & mntd., 19th. C. vell. gt. (HK. Nov.8; 348) DM 600

SPINOLA, W. Th. J.
– Handbuch der Speciellen Pathologie u. Therapie für Thierärzte. Berlin, 1858. 2 vols. in 4. Main title, preface & contents vol. 1 bnd. before vol. 4, cont. hf. leath. (BR. Apr.12; 837) DM 500

SPINOZA, Benedictus (Baruch) de
[–] Opera Posthuma. [Amst.], 1677. *1st. Edn.* Name on title, vell., blind-tooled decor., slight spotting. (V. Oct.1; 3779) DM 2,800
– Opera quae supersunt omnia. Ed.:– H.E.G. Paulus. Jena, 1802-03. *1st. critical coll. Edn.* 2 vols. Some slight browning, some pencil underlining, cont. hf. leath., gold-tooled, rubbed, jnts. partly sprung. (HT. May 10; 2298) DM 500
– Réflexions Curieuses d'un Esprit Dés-interessé sur les Matières les plus Importantes au Salut. Cologne, 1678. *(Bound with:)* FENELON, François de Salignac de la Motte & others – Refutation des Erreurs de Benoît de Spinoza. Bruxelles, 1731. Together 2 works in 1 vol. Sm. 12mo. 18th. C. red mor. (by Derome?); from libys of Comte de La Bédoyère & Baron de La Roche-Lacarelle. (HD. Mar.29; 95) Frs. 14,000
– Sämmtliche Werke. Trans.:– Berthold Auerbach. Stuttgart, 1841. *1st. Edn.* 5 vols. Some foxing, blind-tooled orig. linen gt., slightly soiled. (GB. Nov.4; 2189) DM 400
– Tractatus Politicus (1677). Hilversun, 1928. *(125) with De Roos 'Meidoorn' characters.* On H.M.P., vell., little warped. (B. Apr.27; 824) Fls. 460
[–] Tractatus Theologico-politicus. Hamburg, 1670. *1st. Edn. 1st. Iss.?.* Sm. 4to. P. 104 misptd. as 304, errata lf. at end & errata uncorrected, 1 letter of headline shaved, lacks final blank Gg2, cont. cf., spine gt.; Prof. A.G. Wernham copy. (C. May 30; 128) *Drury.* £2,200
[–] –Anr. Edn. Hamburg [Amst.], 1670. *1st. Edn. 2nd. Iss. (no. B).* 4to. Some margin stains & sm. wormhole thro.-out, cont. tree cf. (VG. Sep.14; 1357) Fls. 1,500
– Tractatus Theologico-politicus. Traitté des Cérémonies Superstitieuses des Juifs tant Anciens que

Modernes. Amst., 1678. *1st. Fr. Edn.* 12mo. Lacks last ll. blank. 19th. C. burgundy mor., gt. inner & outler dentelle, marb. paper end-papers. (D. Nov.25; 4825) DM 2,200

SPIX, Johann Baptist von
– Animalia Nova sive Species Novae Lacertarum quas in Itinere per Brasiliam ... Suscepto. Munich, 1825. 4to. 30 hand-cold. litho. plts., later red hf. mor., jnts. slightly rubbed. (C. Jun.27; 184) *Phelps.* £600

SPIX, Johann B. von & Martius, Karl F.P. von
– Reise in Brasilien. Munich, 1823. *1st. Edn.* 3 vols., without Atlas. 4to. The supp. 'Brasilianische Volkslieder' loosely inserted in orig. ptd. wraps. at end of Vol. 3, some foxing, hf. cf. (S. Dec.1; 297) *Israel.* £380

SPON, Jacob
– Histoire de Genève. Ill.:– Daudet & others. Geneva, 1730. 2 vols. 4to. Titles with engraved vig., lge. double-p. folding map, 2 folding engraved panoramic views, 13 engraved plts. & maps, hf.-titles, cont. cf., spines gt., rubbed; sig. of Erasmus Philipps. (C. Mar.14; 16) *Chaponniere.* £350
– – Anr. Edn. Geneva, 1780. 2 vols. 4to. 2 lge. folding panoramas, both torn & reprd., many plts. & ills., some spotting or browning, vell.-bkd. bds., worn. (S. Apr.9; 55) *Robinson.* £50
– The History of the City & State of Geneva. 1687. *1st. Edn.* 4to. Cont. cf. (P. Sep.8; 225)*Dupre.* £80
See— WHELER, Sir George & Spon, Jacob

SPONDE, H. de
– Annales Sacri A Mundi Creatione ad eiusdem Reparationem. Paris, 1660. Fo. Cont. roan, wide dentelle, fleurs de lys semé, centre arms, fleurs de lys on spine, repairs. (HD. Jan.30; 83) Frs. 1,500

SPONSEL, Jean Louis
– Das Moderne Plakat. Dresden, 1887. Hf. leath., rubbed. (D. Nov.23; 2078) DM 1,500

SPORSCHIL, Joh.
– Der Dreissigjährige Krieg. Ill.:– after F.W. Pfeifer. Braunschweig, 1843. Some staining, cont. hf. leath. gt., rubbed. (BR. Apr.13; 2372)DM 450

SPORTING MAGAZINE, The
L., Oct. 1792-Jun. 1845. 102 vols., & 1 early dupl. Most plts. with orig. tissue guards, a few soiled or foxed, few vols. stained & mildewed, three-qtr. old cf., worn, 15 with one or both covers loose, some lack a cover; many vols. with armorial bkplt. of Francis Brooks, most with ink. sig. of Edward Brooks. (CBA. Dec.10; 419) $1,300
– – Anr. Edn. 1792-1870. 157 vols., including Index. Hf. cf. gt., panel. spines, many with orig. wraps. bnd. in, as a periodical, w.a.f. (P. Dec.8; 199) *G. Stewart.* £6,500
– – Anr. Edn. 1793-1842. Vols. 1-100 only (of 157). Hf. cf., 2 upr. covers detchd., as a periodical, w.a.f. (P. Oct.20; 102) £1,750
– – Anr. Edn. 1818-28. *New Series.* Vol. 1, no. 4 - vol. 21 in 10 vols. 16 engraved titles & 205 plts. only, a few torn & defect., soiled thro.-out, some ll. torn, defect. & misbnd., cont. cf., rubbed, 2 spines worn, w.a.f. (BBA. May 23; 306) *Shapiro.* £220

SPORTING REPOSITORY, The
L., 1904. 22 hand-cold. plts., cl. gt. (P. May 17; 288) *Bailey.* £80

SPRAT, Thomas
– The History of the Royal-Society of London. 1702. *2nd. Edn.* Cont. inscrs. on title, cont. panel. cf., rubbed. (BBA. Jul.27; 113) *Thorp.* £55

SPREAT, W.
– Picturesque Sketches of the Churches of Devon. L., 1842. Ob. 4to. Litho. title, 71 plts., hf. mor. gt., slightly rubbed. (P. Nov.24; 194)*Temperley.* £220

SPRENGER, J. & Institoris, H.
– Malleus Maleficarum. [Speyer, P. Drach], ca. 1490-91. *2nd. Edn.* Fo. Red painted versals & initials, a little worming at end, 4 ll. with paper corners added, late 19th. C. vell. [HC 9239; Goff I-164; BMC II, 498] (BR. Apr.12; 873) DM 9,500

SPRINGER, J.
See— SINGER, Hans Wolfgang & Springer, J.

SPRINGER, Rob.
– Berlin, Ein Führer durch die Stadt u. ihre Umgebungen. Leipzig, 1861. 110 text woodcuts, 1 outl. plan. 1 cold. litho., folding plan, stained at beginning, orig. pict. wraps., slightly defect., unc. (BR. Apr.12; 245) DM 600

SPURLING, J. & Lubbock, B.
– Sail The Romance of the Clipper Ships. [1930-36]. *Vol. 1 3rd. Edn., Vol. 2 2nd. Edn., Vol. 3 1st. Edn.* 3 vols. 4to. Prospectus Vol. 3 loosely inserted, orig. cl. (CSK. May 4; 120) £380

SPURZHEIM, Johann Caspar G.
– A View of the Elementary Principles of Education. Edinb., 1821. *1st. Edn.* Orig. bds., unopened. (P. May 17; 17) *Kossow.* £170

SQUIER, Ephraim George
– Travels in Central America particularly in Nicaragua. N.Y., 1853. 2 vols. Orig. cl., lightly soiled. (CSK. Jul.6; 11) £130
– – Anr. Copy. 2 vols. Some light spotting, cont. cf. (CSK. Dec.16; 160) £90

SQUIRE, W.B
See— RADNOR, Helen Matilda Bouverie, Countess of Squire, W.B.

STAAL, Marguerite Jeanne, Cordier de Launay, Baroone de
– Mémoires. Londres, 1755. *Orig. Edn.* 4 vols. in 2. 12mo. Cont. marb. cf., spines decor. (HD. Mar.21; 94) Frs. 1,100
– – Anr. Edn. Paris, 1890. *(20) on china.* Mor. by Meunier, mosaic decor., silk liners & end-ll., wrap., s.-c. (HD. Jun.13; 100) Frs. 2,000

STABY, W.
See— HELMHOLTZ, R. & Staby, W.

STACE, Machell
[–] Cromwelliana. Westminster, 1810. Fo. Extra-ill. with 94 engraved & mezzotint plts. (2 folding), some spotted, mod. hf. cf. (BBA. Jan.19; 215) *Blundell.* £75

STACE, Publius Papinus
– Opera quae extant. Antw., 1607. Cont. cf., completely fleurdelisé (covers & spine), centre arms, ties brkn. (HD. Jan.30; 98) Frs. 2,200

STADLMAYER, Marie
– Was uns freut. Leipzig, [1924]. Lge. ob. 4to. Title with owners number & stp. removed, orig. cold. pict. hf. linen. (HK. Nov.10; 2989) DM 560

STADTBIBLIOTHEK FRANKFURT AM MAIN
– Katalog der Judaica und Hebraica. Compiler:– [Aron Freimann]. Frankfurt, 1932. Vol. 1: 'Judaica' (all publd.). 4to. Binder's cl., orig. spine & upr. wrap. laid down. (SG. Feb.2; 27) $200

STAEGER, Ferdinand
– 7 Signierte Orig.-Radierungen zu Josef von Eichendorff. Aus dem Leben eines Taugenichts. München, [1919]. 7 sigd. orig. etchings, all etchings mntd. on japan, with sm. remarks & under guards, orig. bd. portfo., corners rubbed. (GB. May 5; 3352) DM 650

STAEL-HOLSTEIN, Anna Louise Germaine de Necker, Baronne de
– Considérations sur les Principaux Evènements de la Révolution Française. Paris, 1818. *Orig. Edn.* 3 vols. Hf. cf., decor. spines. (HD. Feb.22; 192) Frs. 4,900
– – Anr. Copy. 3 vols. Cont. marb. sheep gt., decor. spines. (HD. Sep.22; 350) Frs. 1,400
– Corinne ou l'Italie. Paris, 1807. *Orig. Edn.* 2 vols. Cont. sheep; Albertine de Stael ex-libris. (HD. Sep.22; 348) Frs. 5,000
– De l'Allemagne. Paris, 1814. *2nd. [Orig. Fr.] Edn.* 3 vols. Cont. sheep. (HD. Sep.22; 349) Frs. 1,200
– De la Littérature Considérée dans ses Rapports avec les Institutions Sociales. Paris, An 8 [Apr. 1800]. *Orig. Edn.* 2 vols. Quire 15 reprinted, cont. hf. roan, sm. corners. (HD. Mar.19; 152) Frs. 1,500

- **Lettres.** N.p., 1789. *Counterfeit Edn.* Roan. (HD. Mar.19; 151) Frs. 1,100
- **Oeuvres Complètes.** Ill.:– Müller (port.). Paris, 1820-21. 17 vols. Cont. hf. mor., corners, spines richly decor., spines unif. faded; Lord Gwydyr ex-libris. (HD. Nov.17; 80) Frs. 3,300

STAELPAERT VAN DER WIELEN, J.
- **Extractum Catholicum, tegen Alle Gebreken, van Verwarde Harsenen.** Louvain, 1631. *1st. Coll. Edn.* Sm. 8vo. Cont. vell. (VG. Mar.19; 171) Fls. 2,500

STAENTZL DE CRONFELS, A.L.
- **Piscinarium od. Teicht Ordnung.** Olmütz, 1690. Title & end-papers with several MS. owners marks, cont. vell., gold-tooled arms supralibros, spine slightly worn, 2 clasps. (HK. Nov.9; 1645) DM 700

STAFFORD, Elizabeth, Marchioness of
See— SUTHERLAND, Elizabeth, Duchess of [formerly Marchioness of Stafford]

STAFFORD, Thomas
- **Pacata Hibernia, Ireland Appeased & Reduced.** L., 1633. *1st. Edn.* Fo. 2 engraved ports., 16 folding & other maps & plans, lacks general map, but cont. Speede map loosely inserted, orig. cf., spine defect. (GM. Dec.7; 485) £200
- **Anr. Edn.** Dublin, 1810. 2 vols. Royal 8vo. 2 ports. (rebkd.), 2 lge. folding maps, 16 folding plans, plts., etc., hf. mor., armorial motif on spine. (GM. Dec.7; 463) £150

STAHL, Pierre Julius (Pseud.)
See— HETZEL, Pierre Jules 'P.J. Stahl'
See— MUSSET, Alfred de & Hetzel, Pierre Julius 'Pierre Julius Stahl'

STAHLIN, K.
- **Geschichte Russlands.** Stuttgart, 1923-39. 4 vols. in 5. Orig. hf. linen. (R. Oct.11; 1041) DM 900

STAIR, Sir James Dalrymple, Earl of
- **The Decision of the Lords of Council & Session.** Edinb., 1683-87. 2 vols. Fo. Old cf., spines decor.; Sir Ivar Colquhoun, of Luss copy. [Wing S 5175-6] (CE. Mar.22; 289) £140
- **The Institutions of the Law of Scotland.** Edinb., 1681. *1st. Edn.* 2 pts. in 1 vol. Fo. Partly interleaved with blanks, title lf. slightly defect., old cf., rubbed; Sir Ivar Colquhoun, of Luss copy. [Wing S 5177] (CE. Mar.22; 290) £300

STALDER, F.J.
- **Fragmente über Entlebuch. Nebst einigen Beylagen allgemeinen Schweizerischen Inhalts.** Ill.:– I.H. Meyer & D. Beyel. Zürich, 1797 or 1798. 2 vols. 2 etchings., orig. sewed. (GF. Nov.16; 1173) Sw. Frs. 1,400

STANDING, Percy Cross
- **Cricket of Today & Yesterday** ... L., n.d. *Subscription Ill. Edn.* 2 vols. 4to. Orig. cl., some little wear & looseness; sigs. of members of England & Australia teams in 1928 Test Series in Vol. I. (KH. Nov.9; 712) Aus. $400
- **Anr. Edn.** L., n.d. 2 vols. 4to. Orig. cl., spine frayed. (CSK. Sep.16; 118) £100

STANFIELD, Clarkson
- **Coast Scenery.** L., 1836. 4to. Extra engraved title, frontis. (loose), 38 plts., some spotted, orig. cl., spine worn. (S. Mar.6; 329) *Besley.* £70
- **Anr. Copy.** 4to. Additional vig. title, 39 engraved plts. on India paper, some margin stains, cont. mor. gt., head of spine worn. (TA. Oct.20; 87) £58
- **Promenade d'un Artiste, Bords du Rhin, Hollande & Belgique.** Paris, ca. 1850. Some foxing, orig. red hf. mor., spine gt. (VG. Sep.14; 825) Fls. 600
- **Sketches on the Moselle, the Rhine & the Meuse.** L., 1838. Lge. fo. 30 tinted litho. views, including title, foxed, mostly in margin, orig. hf. leath., bumped, spine worn & slightly torn. (R. Oct.13; 2714) DM 4,800

STANFORD, Edward
- **London Atlas of Universal Geography.** L., 1887. *1st. Edn.* Fo. 90 cold. litho. mapsheets, mostly double-p., few detchd. from guards, publisher's hf. mor. gt., soiled. (S. Mar.6; 113) *Charles.* £90

- **Anr. Copy.** Fo. 90 litho. mapsheets, mostly double-p., few loose, publisher's hf. mor., slightly soiled. (S. Apr.9; 83) *Charles.* £80
- **Anr. Edn.** L., 1904. *3rd. Edn.* Fo. 110 double-p. cold. litho. mapsheets, publisher's hf. mor. gt. (S. Mar.6; 114) *Nicholas.* £70

STANGE, Alfred
- **Deutscher Malerei der Gotik.** München & Berlin, 1951-60. Vols. 4-11. Orig. linen, orig. wraps. (V. Sep.30; 1890) DM 650

STANGEFOL, H.
- **Opus Chronologicum et Historicum Circuli Wes[t]phalici in quatuor libros congestum.** Köln, 1656. 4 pts. in 1 vol. 4to. Genealogical plt. with lengthy pasted tear, cont. vell., spine defect. (R. Oct.13; 2741) DM 1,000

STANHOPE, John Spencer
- **Olympia; or, Topography Illustrative of the Actual State of the Plain of Olympia.** 1824. Fo. Dampstained thro.-out, orig. bds., worn. (BBA. Jun.28; 251) *Shapiro.* £90

STANHOPE, Philip Dormer, Earl of Chesterfield
See— CHESTERFIELD, Philip Dormer Stanhope, Earl of

STANHOPE, Philip Henry. Lord Mahon
- **History of England.** L., 1858. 7 vols. Sm. 8vo. Cf. gt., spines gt. (SG. Feb.16; 192) $200

STANLEY, Arthur Penrhyn
- **Historical Memorials of Westminster Abbey.** L., 1882. Lge. 8vo. Mor. gt., fore-e. pntg. after Thomas S. Boys. (SG. Nov.17; 235) $175

STANLEY, Henry Morton
- **A travers le Continent Mystérieux.** Trans.:– H. Loreau. 1879. *2nd. Edn.* 2 vols. Cont. hf. chagrin. (HD. Mar.21; 202) Frs. 2,300
- **In Darkest Africa.** 1890. *1st. Edn.* 2 vols. Orig. pict. cl. (P. Jun.7; 195) £60
- **Anr. Copy.** 2 vols. 4 maps (3 folding), 38 plts. & ills., liby. stp. on titles, few ll. spotted, orig. cl. gt. (S. Apr.9; 56) *Scott.* £55
- **Anr. Edn.** N.Y., 1890. *1st. Amer. Edn.* 2 vols. Pict. cl. gt. (SG. Sep.22; 6) $150
- **Anr. Edn.** L., 1890. *'Edition de Luxe', (250) numbered on L.P.,* sigd. 2 vols. 4to. 6 etched plts. sigd. in pencil by G. Montbard, 2 folding maps mntd. on cl., some light browning, orig. hf. mor., lightly rubbed & soiled; owner's inscr. of Peter Mackinnon. (CSK. Oct.21; 44) £270
- **How I Found Livingstone.** L., 1872. *1st. Edn.* Photo. frontis., 5 maps, (1 folding), 28 plts. & text ills., few ll. spotted, orig. decor. cl., slightly worn, 1 hinge split. (S. Apr.9; 57) *Scott.* £55

STANNUS, Hugh
- **Alfred Stevens & His Work.** 1891. *(150) numbered & sigd. by publisher.* Lge. 4to. 2 liby. stps., hf. leath. gt. (SKC. Mar.9; 1730) £50

STAPHORST, N.
- **Historia Ecclesiae Hamburgensis Diplomatica, das ist Hamburgische Kirchengeschichte.** Hamburg, 1723-29. 4 vols. (of 5). 4to. With partly low German text, lacks port., lightly browned, some spotting, 2 title ll. with liby. stp., cont. vell., darkened & slightly spotted, 1 spine defect. (H. May 22; 326) DM 400
- **Anr. Edn.** Hamburg, 1723-31. Vol. 1, pts. 1, 2 & 4 in 3 vols. 4to. Cont. vell. (D. Nov.23; 1670) DM 1,200

STAPLEY, Mildred
See— BYNE, Arthur & Stapley, Mildred

STAPP, William Preston
- **The Prisoners of Perote.** Phila., 1845. 12mo. Orig. ptd. wraps. (LH. Jan.15; 392) $425

STARK, A.
See— SCLATER, William Lutley & Stark, A.

STARK, James
- **Scenery of the Rivers of Norfolk.** 1834. Fo. Engraved vig. title (stained), 24 plts., some dampstains, mor. gt., rubbed & loose. (P. Apr.12; 268) *Shapiro.* £70

STARK, Robert M.
See— WHITE, Adam & Stark, Robert M.

STARKEY, George
See— PHILALETHA, Irenaeus [i.e. George Starkey]

STARLING, T.
- **Geographical Annual or Family Cabinet Atlas.** L., 1832. Engraved title, 46 engraved maps, 4 tables of comparative geography, hand-cold. thro.-out, publisher's cl., worn. (S. Jun.25; 273) *Quaritch.* £130

STATEMENTS & DOCUMENTS RELATIVE TO THE ESTABLISHMENT OF STEAM NAVIGATION IN THE PACIFIC
L., 1838. *1st. Edn.* Sm. 8vo. Slight offsetting to maps, ptd. wraps., slightly soiled & chipped. [Sabin 90775] (SG. Jan.19; 329) $110

STATIUS, Publius Papinius
- **Opera.** Leyden, 1671. 18th. C. red mor. gt., decor., tie; W. Burrell bkplt. (P. Jan.12; 281) *Maggs.* £150
- **Sylvarum Libri Quinque Thebaidos Libri Duodecim Achilleidos Duo. - Orthographia.** Venice, Aldine Pr., Aug., 1502. *1st. Aldine Edn.* Lf. a2v of lst. work illuminated with arms of Julius de Medici as Pope Clement VII, a3r with initial Q & floral border, painted in gold, red, blue, green & silver, few margin stains, 19th. C. russ. gt., cl. folding-case. (SG. Apr.19; 9) $550

STATUTA or STATUTES
[Arranged Chronologically]
- **Statuta Ordinis Cartusiensis.** Ill.:– after Urs Graf. Bâle, 1510. *1st. Edn.* 6 pts. in 1 vol. Fo. Orig. cf. over wood bds., covers blind-decor., sm. piece missing from spine & part of jnts., traces of paste-ons & clasps, vell. end-papers from MSS. (HD. Nov.9; 12) Frs. 19,000
- **Anno XXI, Statuta ad Rem Spectantia ..., An Act Concerning the King's Generall Pardon.** 1551? Fo. Bdg. not stated. [STC 9367] (P. Mar.15; 314) £75
- **At the Parliament holden at Westminster the xii. of January, in the fyfth Yeere of the Raigne of our Soueraigne Lady Elizabeth.** 1563. 2 pts. in 1 vol. Fo. Last blank lf. to each pt., slight stains, sm. wormhole thro. text, mod. cf.-bkd. bds. [STC 9466] (BBA. Sep.29; 296) *Bauman.* £240
- **Ordinancie, Statuyt ende Gebot Provisionnael ... des Conincx, Aengaende de Printers, Boekvercoopers ende Schoelmeesters.** Brussel, 1570. 4to. Sm. tear, slightly stained, few annots., bds. (VG. Sep.14; 868) Fls. 1,000
- **Statuta Provisionesq. Ducales Civitatis Tarvisii.** Venice, 1574. *1st. Edn.* 2 pts. in 1 vol. Sm. fo. Most margins & a few ll. slightly browned or stained, late 17th. or early 18th. C. vell., browned. (S. May 10; 423) *Hatchwell.* £160
- **Statuti, Ordine e Porta ... Concernent il Benefico, & Buon Governo della ... Territorio Veronese.** Verona, 1613. Sm. fo. Woodcut title device hand-cold., Gl lr. margin cleanly torn affecting catchword, blank margins of title & lst. few ll. lightly wormed, lightly dampstained, cont. Northern Italian red mor., elab. ruled & tooled in gt. & blind, spine wormed with loss to head & foot. (CSK. Nov.4; 167) £130
- **Statuti dell'Ordine di Cavalieri di Sto Stephano.** Ill.:– Jacques Callot (frontis.). Flor., 1665. 4to. Frontis. in 2nd. state, cont. Italian vell., richly decor., painted Medici arms (reprd.); from Fondation Furstenberg-Beaumesnil. (HD. Nov.16; 172) Frs. 5,500
- **The Statutes of the Colledge of Physicians London.** 1693. Index notes & corrections in ink, cont. cf. (P. Feb.16; 272) £60
- **Statuts et Règlements de la Communauté des Maîtres Perruquiers, Barbiers, Baigneurs et Etuvistes de la Ville ... de Lyon.** Lyon, 1763. Cont. mor. gt., Jean-Baptiste Lacour arms, spine decor., lacks spine label. (HD. Nov.9; 136) Frs. 3,100
- **Statutes of the Realm.** 1810-28. 11 vols. in 12 including 2 vols. Index. Fo. Cont. hf. cf., slightly rubbed. (BBA. Jul.27; 133) *Blackwood.* £550
- **Halsbury's Statutes of England.** 1948-69. *2nd. Edn.* 50 vols., including 2 vol. Cumulative Supp. Lge. 8vo. Orig. cl. gt. (TA. Jul.19; 274) £70

STATUTA or STATUTES -Contd.

- Le Livre des Statuts et Ordonnances de l'Ordre et Milice du Benoist Sainct Esprit, estably par le Très-chrestien Roy de France et de Pologne Henry Trois-ieme de ce Nom. N.p., n.d. 4to. Cont. mor. gt. by Eve Atelier, Henri III arms on covers, crowned cypher at each corner, rebkd. gt., lacks ties; owners inscr. of Antoine de Ruze on pastedown of lr. cover, Lucien Graux bkplt. (C. May 30; 90)
Spinoit. £3,800

STAUFFER, David McNeely
- American Engravers upon Copper & Steel. N.Y., Grol. Cl., 1907. *(350).* 2 vols. Lge. 8vo. 43 plts., qtr. buckram., unc., bd. jackets. (SG. Jan.5; 154)
$250

STAUNTON, George Leonard
[-] An Authentic Account of an Embassy ... to the Emperor of China. L., [plts. dtd. 1796]. Atlas vol. only. Fo. 44 engraved maps, plts. & views, some double-p., cont. tree cf., spine gt. (C. Mar.14; 90)
Kossow. £850
- - Anr. Copy. Atlas vol. only. Fo. 42 engraved maps & plts., many double-p. or folding, 1 torn, some soiled, cont. hf. cf., worn. (S. Apr.9; 59)
Shapiro. £650
- - Anr. Copy. Atlas vol. only. Fo. 44 engraved maps, charts, plts. & views, some double-p., cont. bds., lacks spine, upr. cover detchd., covers scuffed. (C. Nov.16; 179)
Davidson. £550
- - Anr. Edn. 1797. 3 vols., including Atlas. 4to. & fo. Engraved frontis.'s, 44 engraved plts., some folding. 4 torn & mntd., a few ll. slightly browned. cont. diced cf., gt. spines, rebkd., atlas cont. cf.-bkd. bds., all rubbed. (BBA. Sep.29; 83)
Traylen. £740
- - Anr. Copy. 2 vols. only (lacks Atlas). 4to. cont. tree cf. gt., spines gt., slightly rubbed. (C. Nov.16; 34)
Traylen. £450
- - Anr. Copy. 2 vols. (without atlas). 4to. Frontis. ports., cont. cf.-bkd. bds., worn, unc. (S. Apr.9; 58)
Remington. £180
- - Anr. Copy. 2 text vols. only. 4to. Cf., rebkd. (P. Mar.15; 72)
Maggs. £110
- - Anr. Copy. 3 vols. 1 folding map torn with loss & reprd., some spotting, cont. cf., rubbed. (S. Jun.25; 51)
Scott. £70
- - Anr. Copy. 3 vols., including Atlas. 4to. & fo. 2 port. frontis., Atlas with 44 maps & plts., including 7 folding or double-p., some foxing, cont. tree cf., worn, rebkd., covers detchd. (SG. Nov.3; 197)
$1,100
- - Anr. Copy. 3 vols., including Atlas. 4to. & fo. 47 engraved plts. & maps, some spotting, tears on folding maps, cont. mor. gt., Atlas in cf.-bkd. marb. bds. (SPB. Dec.13; 468)
$700
- - Anr. Edn. L., 1798. 2nd. Edn. 3 vols. Engraved title, 5 folding maps (3 slightly torn), 21 plts., 1 caption cropped, a few spots, cont. hf. russ. (S. Mar.6; 48)
Quaritch. £100
- Reis van Lord Macartneij naar China. Ill.:- R. Vinkeles. Amst., 1798-1801. 1st. Dutch Edn. 7 vols. 46 engraved ports., plts., maps & views, some foxing, slight margin staining in last vol., cont. hf. cf.; J.W. Six bkplt. (VS. Dec.9; 1298)
Fls. 675
- Voyage dans l'Intérieur de la Chine et en Tartarie. Ar XII [1804]. Atlas vol. only. 4to. 4 folding maps, 37 plts., slight stains, cont. hf. long-grd. mor., decor. spine. (HD. Feb.29; 26)
Frs. 3,000

STAVERN, Augustino van
- Auctores Mythografi Latini. Leyden & Amst., 1742. 4to. Cont. diced cf. gt. (TA. Sep.15; 344)
£60

STAVORINUS, John S.
- Voyage par le Cap de Bonne-Esperance à Batavia ... Paris, 1798. 1st. Fr. Edn. Mod. mor. gt. (P. Dec.8; 317)
Shapero. £120

STEARNS, Samuel
- The American Herbal. Walpole, 1801. 1st. Edn. 12mo. 13 p. subscribers list, many margin tears, some repairs, very foxed, old cf., very worn, ex-liby., w.a.f. (SG. Oct.6; 342)
$200

STEBBING, Henry
- The Christian in Palestine. Ill.:- Bartlett [1847]. 4to. Engraved title, map, 78 plts., spotting, hf. cf., worn. (P. Jul.5; 156)
£60
- - Anr. Edn. Ca. 1850. 4to. Additional vig. title, map, 73 (of 78) engrs., cont. diced cf. gt. (TA. Dec.15; 64)
£50
- - Anr. Edn. Ill.:- after Bartlett. N.Y., ca. 1850. 80 steel-engraved plts., some foxing, gt.-decor. & blind-stpd. mor., covers lightly rubbed, liby. no. on spine; Marymount College label & ex-liby. stps. (CBA. Mar.3; 20)
$120

STEDMAN, Charles
- The History of the Origin, Progress & Termina-tion of the American War. L., 1792. 1st. Edn. 2 vols. 4to. 15 plts. & maps, most folding, some tears, some foxing & spotting, cont. cf., spines gt., rebkd. (SPB. Dec.13; 469)
$700
- - Anr. Edn. L., priv. ptd., 1794. 1st. Edn. 2 vols. 4to. 15 engraved maps & plans, most folding, hf.-titles, a few maps & plans with light foxing, 1 with minor tear, cont. cf.; the Rt. Hon. Visc. Eccles copy. [Sabin 91057] (CNY. Nov.18; 259) $1,200
- - Anr. Edn. L., 1794. 2 vols. 4to. Some water spotting at lr. right-hand corners of last 20 pp. of each vol., some browning & offsetting on maps, taped repairs to several of the larger folding plts., cont. paper-back bds., worn, with later gt.-stpd. mor. spines; inscr. of Arthur Foulks. [Sabin 91058] (SPB. Oct.26; 24)
$600

STEDMAN, Capt. John Gabriel
- Narrative of a Five Years' Expedition, against the revolted Negroes of Surinam. N.Y., 1796. 1st. Edn. 2 vols. 4to. Cont. hf. leath., spine worn. [Sabin 91075] (HK. Nov.8; 850)
DM 950
- - Anr. Edn. L., 1806. 2nd. Edn. 2 vols. 4to. Sm. piece torn from title with loss of 1 letter, titles a little foxed, owners stp. on fly-ll., old bds., paper spine, rubbed. (CH. May 24; 45)
Fls. 800

STEEDMAN, Andrew
- Wanderings & Adventures in the Interior of Sou-thern Africa. 1835. 2 vols. Plts. foxed, cont. cl. (SSA. Jul.5; 376)
R 390

STEEL, David
[-] The Elements & Practice of Rigging & Seaman-ship. 1794. 1st. Edn. 2 vols. 4to. Engraved frontis., 90 engraved plts., moveable pts. in Vol. 2 loose, cont. mott. cf., rebkd., old spines preserved, new end-papers. (SKC. Jan.13; 2364)
£500
- - Anr. Copy. 2 vols. 4to. 93 plts. (1 double-p. & 5 folding), hf. cf., corners. (HD. Mar.9; 127)
Frs. 3,500
- Naval Chronologist of the War. L., n.d. *(Bound with:)* - Prize Pay-lists. L., n.d. *(Bound with:)* - Supplement. L., n.d. *(Bound with:)* LOSACK, William - The Nautical Nomenclator. L., n.d. Last advt. lf. Together 4 works in 1 vol. Sm. 4to. Cont. cf.-bkd. bds., worn, sig. of Capt. Fothergill. (BBA. Dec.15; 230)
Edwards. £110

STEEL, Flora Annie
- English Fairy Tales. Ill.:- Arthur Rackham. 1918. *(500) numbered & sigd. by artist.* 4to. Orig. parch. gt., soiled. (CSK. Mar.9; 133)
£150
- - Anr. Copy. 4to. Orig. vell., scuffed, base of spine torn with slight loss. (CSK. Jan.27; 198)
£100
- - Anr. Copy. 4to. Fore-e.'s lightly foxed, gt.-decor. vell., very light soiling. (CBA. Aug.21; 530)
$425

STEELE, John
- In Camp & Cabin: Mining Life & Adventure, in California during 1850 & later. Lodi, 1901. 1st. Edn. Ptd. wood-grain wraps. (SG. Nov.3; 198)
$225

STEELE, Sir Richard
See— ADDISON, Joseph & Steele, Sir Richard

STEELE, Robert
- The Revival of Printing. A Bibliographical Cata-logue of Works issued by the Chief Modern English Presses. 1912. *(350) numbered.* Orig. holland-bkd. bds., slightly soiled. (BBA. Nov.10; 132)
Quaritch. £50

STEENSEN, Nicolas
See— STENO [or Steensen], Nicolas

STEERWELL, J.
- The Little Traveller ... N.d. Hand-cold. wood-engraved frontis. & ills., orig. wraps., soiled, back-strip torn with loss. (CSK. Jun.1; 84)
£50

STEFFENS, Heinrich (Henrik)
- Schriften. Breslau, 1821. 1st. Edn. 2 vols. Cont. marb. bds. (GB. May 4; 1604)
DM 800

STEGMAN, Fr. L.
- Lehrbuch der Variationsrechnung und Ihrer Anwendung bei Untersuchungen über das Maximum und Minimum. Kassel, 1854. 1st. Edn. 1 text lf. bnd. in dupl., cont. hf. linen. (HT. May 8; 501)
DM 400

STEICHEN, Edward
- A Life in Photography. Garden City, 1963. 1st. Edn. 4to. Gt.-lettered bds., d.-w. (SG. May 10; 135)
$100

STEIDELE, R.J.
- Lehrbuch v. der Hebammenkunst. Wien, 1784. Plts. soiled, creased & with margin defects, cont. bds., spotted & very bumped. (HK. May 15; 536)
DM 500

STEIGERWALD, F. von
- Lebensbeschreibung Herrn Götzens von Berlich-ingen. Ed.:- W.F. Pistorius. Nuremb., 1731. 1st. Edn. Title copper engr. completely bkd. with sm. fault & tear, slightly browned or soiled, cont. vell. (HK. Nov.10; 2458)
DM 700

STEIN, D.C. & G.D.
- Neuer Atlas der Ganzen Welt. Ill.:- after J. Boreux, F.W. Streit & others. Leipzig, 1823. 5th. Edn. Sm. ob. fo. (430 × 480mm.). 18 engraved mapsheets, outl. hand-cold., ptd. text., some dust-soiling & creasing, outer margins frayed, publi-sher's ptd. paper wraps. (S. Nov.1; 182)
Palmer. £100

STEIN, Gertrude
- Dix Portraits. Trans.:- Georges Hugnet & Vergil Thomson. Ill.:- Picasso & others. Paris, [1930]. *(25) on hollande van Gelder, sigd. by author & trans.* 4to. Orig. wraps. (SPB. Dec.13; 742) $400
- - Anr. Edn. Ill.:- Picasso, Tchelitchef, & others. Paris, [1930]. *(65) numbered on vélin d'Arches, sigd. by author & translators, & containing the 10 plts.* Tall 8vo. Ptd. wraps., unc. & unopened, buckram s.-c. (SG. May 24; 363)
$300
- Have They Attacked Mary. [West Chester, Pa., 1917]. *(200) numbered.* Sm. 4to. Ptd. wraps., chipped. (SG. May 24; 205)
$200
- Portrait of Mabel Dodge at the Villa Curonia. [Flor., 1912]. 1st. Edn., *(300), with printer's imprint at foot of p. [12].* Sm. 4to. Wall-paper wraps., label stained. (SPB. Dec.13; 745) $800
- - Anr. Edn. [Flor., 1912]. *(300).* Sm. 4to. Orig. decor. wraps.; pres. copy inscr. to Madeleine Lucette Ryley. (C. May 30; 180)
Hellenic. £550
- - Anr. Copy. Orig. floral wraps. (P. May 17; 130)
Rota. £340
- - Anr. Copy. Orig. floral wraps. (P. May 17; 129)
Rota. £260
- A Primer for the Gradual Understanding of ... Ed.:- Robert Bartlett Haas. Los Angeles, Black Sparrow Pr., 1971. *(60) numbered, with cut sig. mntd. on colophon lf.* Qtr. cl., pict. bds., acetate d.-w., marb. bd. s.-c. (SG. Mar.1; 558)
$150
- Three Lives. N.Y., 1909. 1st. Edn. *(700).* 12mo. Bkplt., gt.-lettered cl., slightly soiled. (SG. Jan.12; 321)
$475
- Unpublished Writings. New Haven, 1951-58. Vols. 1, 3-5 & 7-8 only (of 8). Lge. 8vo. Cl., d.-w.'s. (SG. Mar.1; 563)
$150
- A Village are you Ready Yet not Yet. Ill.:- Elie Lascaux. Paris, 1928. *(90) on Arches, sigd. by author & artist.* 4to. Orig. wraps., unc. (SPB. Dec.13; 748)
$450
- What are Masterpieces. Los Angeles, 1940. *(60) sigd. (10) special copies, for author.* Orig. cl., d.-w. discold. (SPB. Dec.13; 749)
$400
- The World is Round. Ill.:- Clement Rurd. N.Y., [1939]. *[1st. Edn.].* *(350) sigd. by author & artist.* 4to. Bds., s.-c. worn. (SG. Mar.1; 547)
$300

– – Anr. Copy. Sm. 4to. Bds., spine faded. (SG. Nov.3; 199) $175

STEIN, K. Ph. C.
– Handbuch des Zubereitens und Aufbewahrens der Thiere aller Classen ... Frankfurt, 1802. *1st. Edn.* 2 sm. wormholes at beginning, cont. hf. leath. gt. (R. Oct.12; 2070) DM 520

STEIN, Sir Marc Aurel
– Innermost Asia: Detailed Report of Explorations in Central Asia, Kan-Su & Eastern Iran ... Oxford, 1928. *1st. Edn.* 4 vols., including plt. vol. & portfo. of maps. 4to. Gt.-lettered buckram, 1st. 3 vols. in d.-w.'s, slightly soiled & chipped, maps loose as iss. in folding cl. case. (SG. Mar.29; 344) $2,600
– Sand-Buried Ruins of Khotan. 1904. Orig. decor. cl., untrimmed. (TA. Oct.20; 3) £70
– The Thousand Buddhas. L., 1921. 2 vols. Tall fo. & atlas fo. 48 plts., many cold. (33 linen-bkd.), liby. buckram. (SG. May 3; 344) $950

STEINBECK, John
– The Bulletin From Johnny Cake Hill. 1965. Wraps.; inscr. in pencil on upr. cover 'For Phillip from John Steinbeck'. (PNY. Jan.24; 84) $150
– Cup of Gold. A Life of Sir Henry Morgan, Buccaneer. N.Y., [1936]. *1st. Edn. 2nd. Iss.* Cl., 'Covici Friede' on spine, d.-w., light wear. (RO. Apr.23; 265) $265
– East of Eden. N.Y., 1952. *1st. Edn. (1500) numbered & sigd.* Lge. 8vo. Cl., spine slightly rubbed, s.-c. rubbed. (SG. May 24; 366) $300
– – Anr. Copy. Cl., corner bumped. (SG. Jan.12; 322) $175
– The Grapes of Wrath. Intro.:– Joseph Henry Jackson & Thomas Craven. Ill.:– Thomas Hart Benton. N.Y., Ltd. Edns. Cl., 1940. *(1146) numbered, designed by George Macy, sigd. by artist.* 2 vols. 4to. Hf. rawhide, coarse-weave buckram, orig. s.-c., bdg. note laid in. (SG. May 17; 223) $375
– – Anr. Copy. 2 vols. 4to. Sigd. by artist, hf. rawhide & 'grass cl.', glassine wraps. creased & chipped, box worn. (CBA. Aug.21; 48) $250
– Of Mice & Man. N.Y., [1937]. *1st. Edn. 1st. Iss.* With bullet between 8's on p.88, orig. cl., d.-w.; pres. copy to A.T. Barham?, Fred A. Berne copy. (SPB. May 16; 333) $750
– The Red Pony. N.Y., 1937. *(699) sigd.* Fo. Orig. cl., unc., publisher's box; Fred A. Berne copy. (SPB. May 16; 354) $500

STEINBERG, Saul
– Le Masque. Text:– Michel Butor & Harold Rosenberg. [Paris, 1966]. *1st. Edn. (300) numbered, with sigd. & numbered black & white litho. laid in.* Lge. ob. 4to. Col.-pict. wraps. over plain bds., glassine d.-w., s.-c. (SG. Mar.29; 263) $200

STEINER, J.
– Systematisches Entwicklung der Abhängigkeit Geometrischer Gestalten von einander ... Berlin, 1832. *1st. Edn.* Pt. 1 (all publd.). Slightly browned, cont. hf. leath., sm. scratches. (HT. May 8; 404) DM 500

STEINERT, Otto
– Subjektive Fotografie: Ein Bildband Moderner Europaeischer Fotografie; Subjektive Fotografie 2: Ein Bildband Moderner Fotografie. Bonn, [1952], Munich, [1955]. *1st. Edns.* 2 vols. 4to. Text & captions in 3 languages, cl., d.-w.'s, s.-c. (SG. May 10; 136) $300

STEINGRUBER, Johann David
– Architectionisches Alphabet. Schwabach, 1773-75. 2 vols. Engraved additonal title, 32 plts. including 2 double-p., faint dampstain to text at beginning of Vol. 2, cont. marb. wraps. (C. Dec.9; 150) *Lustenberger.* £2,600

STEINITZ, Käthe
See— SCHITTERS, K. & Steinitz, Käthe

STEINLEN, Théophile Alexandre
– Des Chats images sans Paroles. Paris, ca. 1900. 4to. Orig. pict. bds., soiled. (P. Jul.5; 189) £160
– – Anr. Edn. Paris, n.d. Fo. 26 plts., orig. cl.-bkd. bds. (CSK. Feb.24; 120) £90
– Dans La Vie. Preface:– C. de Sainte-Croix. Paris, 1901. *1st. Printing. (100) De Luxe Edn. on Japan.*

MS. dedication from author on his port., hand-bnd. hf. mor., cold. orig. pict. wraps. bnd. in, by Blanchetière-Bretault, spine slightly faded, Hauswedell coll. (H. May 24; 706) DM 740

STEINMANN, Ernst
– Die Sixtinische Kapelle. Munich, 1901-05. 2 vols. Lge. 4to. Orig. cl. gt., recased. (S. May 1; 571) *Marlborough.* £160

STEINMANN, J.
– Souvenirs de Rio de Janeiro. [Basel], 1836. Ob. 4to. Pict. title, 10 (of 12?) lithos., tipped at corners to pp. with identical pict. borders, title foxed, stained & reinforced on verso, 4 lithos. torn at corners, cl., worn. (SC. Apr.26; 187) $800

STEINSCHNEIDER, M.
– Catalog der Hebräischen Handschriften in der Stadtbibliothek zu Hamburg und der sich anschliessenden in anderen Sprachen. Hamburg, 1878. Foxed, cont. linen, defect., upr. cover loose. (R. Oct.11; 1114) DM 400

STELLA, Jacques & Claudine Bouzounet
– Les Ieux et Plaisirs de l'Enfance. Paris, priv. ptd., 1657. Ob. 4to. Engraved title, 50 engraved plts., some margins slightly soiled, 19th. C. pol. cf., slightly defect.; Andres Rourg mor. bkplt. (VS. Dec.9; 1010) Fls. 1,300

STELLWAG v. CARION, C.
– Die Opthalmolgie vom Naturwissenschaftlichen Standpunkte ... Freiburg, 1853-58. *1st. Edn.* Hf.-title & title stpd., cont. hf. leath. (R. Oct.12; 1342) DM 1,400

STENDHAL, M. de (Pseud.)
See— BEYLE, Henri 'M. de Stendhal'

STENGER, Erich
– The History of Photography: Its Relation to Civilization & Practice. Trans.:– Edward Epstean. Easton, [priv. ptd., by the] Mack Printing Co., 1939. 4to. Ptd. 'Notice' laid in, cl. (SG. Nov.10; 147) $225
– – Anr. Copy. 4to. Ptd. notice laid in, cl., lacks portions of d.-w. (SG. May 10; 137) $175

STENO [or Steensen], Nicolas
– De Solido intra Solidum Naturaliter contento Dissertationis prodromus. Flor., 1669. *1st. Edn.* 4to. Some slight foxing, some spotting in lr. margin, cont. vell., minimal spotting. (HT. May 8; 258) DM 11,000

STENZ, C.
See— DIEPENBACH, W. & Stenz, C.

STEP, Edward
– Favourite Flowers of the Garden & Greenhouse. 1896-97. 4 vols. 312 cold. plts., hf. mor., rubbed. (BBA. Jul.27; 59) *Gupta.* £130

STEPHANIE, J.
– Abbildungen der K.K. Oesterreichischen Armee, durch alle Waffengattungen Enthael ... Wienn, 1815 or 1820?. Fo. Title, dedication, 6 litho. tables, 36 mntd. cold. plts., hf. chagrin gt., corners; C.F. Koch ex-libris. (HD. Jan.27; 307) Frs. 10,000

STEPHANOPOLI, D. & N.
[–] Voyage ... en Grèce Pendant les Années V & VI. Paris, An VIII. 2 vols. Mod. hf. cl. (HD. Oct.21; 167) Frs. 1,700

STEPHANUS, Charles
See— ESTIENNE or STEPHANUS, Charles

STEPHANUS, Henricus
See— ESTIENNE, Henri

STEPHANUS Byzantius
– De Urbibus. Flor., 1521. In Greek. (*Bound with:*) POLLUX, Julius - **Vocabularium.** Flor., 1521. In Greek, with final register/colophon lf. (*Bound with:*) HESYCHIUS - **Dictionarium.** Hagenau, 1521. In Greek, title-p. torn & reprd., a few stains. 3 works in 1 vol. Fo. 18th. C. cf., rebkd. (S. Nov.17; 68) *Quaritch.* £680

STEPHANUS, Saint
– Liber Sententiarum. – Maximes et Enseignements. Paris, 1704. 2 vols. 12mo. Cont. blind-decor. red

mor., arms of Godet des Marais, Bp. of Chartres. (HD. May 3; 43) Frs. 1,900

STEPHENS, James
– Crock of Gold. Ill.:– Wilfred Jones. N.Y., 1922. Orig. decor. cl., mor.-bkd. s.-c.; pres. copy with 4-line verse, Perry Molsted copy. (SPB. May 16; 530) $150
– Irish Fairy Tales. Ill.:– Arthur Rackham. L., 1920. *(520) sigd. by artist.* 4to. Hf. vell. (LH. Sep.25; 443) $225

STEPHENS, James Francis
– General Zoology: ... Commenced by the Late George Shaw. L., 1815-26. 6 vols. only (lacks Vol. X pt. 1, Vol. XIII pt. 1, & Vol. XIV pt. 2), & General Index, in 10 vols. Some light foxing, cont. qtr. leath. gt., ex-liby. (SG. Oct.6; 330) $225

STEPHENS, J.F.
See— SHAW, George & Stephens, J.F.

STEPHENS, John
– The History of the Rise & Progress of the New British Province of South Australia. L., 1839. *2nd. Edn.* Plts. stained, some margin notes, orig. blind-stpd. cl. gt., unc., loose, spine faded. (CA. Apr.3; 106) Aus. $270
– – Anr. Copy. Some foxing, bdg. not stated, unc., recased, reinforced with mor. at corners & head & foot of backstrip; Coles copy. (KH. May 1; 666) Aus. $180
[–] The Land of Promise, being an Authentic & Impartial History of ... South Australia. L., 1839. Bnd. without advts., sm. section torn from blank margin of 1 plt., some mild foxing, later hf. cf. (KH. Nov.9; 713) Aus. $180
– The Royal South Australian Almanack & General Directory for 1846. Adelaide, ca. 1846. Bnd. without wraps. or advts., corner of final lf. a little damaged, old hf. roan, sm. defect. at head of backstrip. (KH. Nov.9; 716) Aus. $150

STEPHENS, John Lloyd
– Incidents of Travel in Central America, Chiapas, & Yucatan. Ill.:– F. Catherwood. N.Y., 1841. *1st. Edn.* 2 vols. Gt.-pict. cl., jnts. & spine ends very worn. (SG. Aug.4; 298) $160
– – Anr. Copy. 2 vols. MS. owner's entry on title, orig. linen, gold-tooled. [Sabin 91297] (R. Oct.13; 2985) DM 850
– – Anr. Copy. 2 vols. Some slight foxing, map with tear in margin, cont. hf. leath. gt., bumped. [Sabin 91297] (HK. Nov.8; 852) DM 700
[–] Incidents of Travel in Greece, Turkey, Russia, & Poland. N.Y., 1838. *1st. Edn.* 2 vols. Tall 12mo. Spotted, orig. blind-patterned cl., corners slightly nicked. (SG. Mar.29; 345) $150
– Incidents of Travel in Yucatan. N.Y., 1843. *1st. Edn.* 2 vols. Some slight foxing, cont. hf. leath. gt., bumped. [Sabin 91299] (HK. Nov.8; 853) DM 650
– – Anr. Edn. Ill.:– F. Catherwood. N.Y., 1848. Lge. 8vo. Foxed, gt.-pict. cl., extremities frayed, lacks free end-papers. (SG. Jan.19; 331) $110

STEPHENS, Robert
– Letters of Sr Francis Bacon. 1702. 4to. Cont. cf. (CSK. Feb.10; 133) £100

STEPHENS, William
[–] A State of the Province of Georgia, Attested upon Oath in the Court of.Savannah, November 10, 1740. L., 1742. *1st. Edn.* Hf.-title, hf. mor.; the Rt. Hon. Visc. Eccles copy. [Sabin 27113] (CNY. Nov.18; 260) $220

STEPHENSON, John & Churchill, James Morse
– Medical Botany. L., 1831. 4 vols. 185 hand-cold. engraved plts., cont. hf. cf., rebkd. (C. Nov.16; 300) *Blackwells.* £550
– – Anr. Copy. 4 vols. 185 cold. engraved plts., including 6 double-p., hf.-title to Vol. 1, plts. slightly cropped, affecting engraved surface of 3 plts., some staining to 3 plts., slight margin staining to some 20 other plts., a few ll. slightly stained, cont. diced cf. gt., 1 spine loose. (LC. Oct.13; 218) £340

STERLING, C. & Adhemar, H.
– Musée National du Louvre. Peintures Ecole Français, XIXe Siècle. Paris, 1958. 4 vols. 4to. No bdg. stated. (SPB. Nov.30; 69) $200

STERN, Bernhard
- Illustrierte Geschichte der Erotischen Literatur aller Zeiten u. Völker. Wien & Leipzig, 1908. 2 vols. Orig. limp linen. (HK. May 16; 1870)
DM 650

STERN, Daniel (Pseud.)
See— AGOULT, Marie de Flavigny, Contesse d' 'Daniel Stern'

STERN, Frederick Claude
- A Study of the Genus Paeonia. 1946. 4to. Orig. cl. gt. (P. Sep.8; 213) *Ashwell.* £65

STERN, Jtzig Feitel (Pseud.)
See— HOLZSCHUHER, Johann Friedrich Siegmund von 'Jtzig Feitel Stern'

STERNAUX, L. (Ed.)
See— STYLE, Blätter für Mode ...

STERNBERG, K. von
- Umrisse einer Geschichte der Böhmischen Bergwerke. Prag., 1836-38. 2 vols. in 3. Some light foxing, cont. hf. leath. gt., rubbed & bumped. (R. Apr.4; 1474) DM 610

STERNE, Laurence
[-] Das Leben und die Meynungen des Herrn Tristram Shandy. Trans.:– [J. Bode.]. Berlin, 1774. Some foxing & slight browning, cont. hf. leath., gt. spine, rubbed; Hauswedell coll. (H. May 24; 1572)
DM 880
[-] Letters from Yorick to Eliza. L., 1773. *1st. Edn.* Sm. 8vo. Cont. spr. cf., rebkd. (SG. Apr.19; 175) $300
- Letters ... to His Most Intimate Friends ... L., 1775. *1st. Edn.* 3 vols. Engraved frontis., F1 in vol. 2 stained, some soiling, orig. wraps., spine reprd. (SPB. May 16; 145) $475
- A Sentimental Journey Through France & Italy. 1768. *1st. Edn.* 2 vols. in 1. Hf.-titles, later red mor., rebkd., slightly rubbed. (BBA. Jun.28; 96)
T. Scott. £170
- - Anr. Copy. 2 vols. Lacks 'advt.' lf., some browning, cont. cf., some worming to Vol.2 spine, reprd. (SPB. Dec.13; 751) $325
- - Anr. Copy. 2 vols. Sm. 8vo. Rothschild's variant 2, hf.-titles, without 'Advt.' lf., cont. qtr. cf., spines worn, reprd., 1 lr. cover detchd.; Fred A. Berne copy. (SPB. May 16; 356) $125
- - Anr. Copy. 2 vols. Long subscriber list at beginning vol. 1, (with asterisks for Imp. paper), cont. Engl. leath., spine & jnts. restored, hf. mor. box. (D. Nov.24; 2574) DM 3,200
- - Anr. Copy. 2 vols. Some slight browning, especially 1st. & last ll., vol. II mis-paginated, cont. hf. leath., bumped & jnts. partly brkn.; Hauswedell coll. (H. May 24; 1569) DM 1,400
- - Anr. Edn. Ill.:– J.E. Laboureur. Gold. Cock. Pr., 1928. *(500) numbered.* Orig. cl., d.-w. (BBA. Jan.19; 290) *Spencer.* £75
- - Anr. Edn. Ill.:– Denis Tegetmeier. Hague & Gill for Ltd. Edns. Cl., 1936. *(1500) numbered, sigd. by Gill & artist.* Tall 4to. 8 etchings, patterned buckram, moiré cl. s.-c. (SG. May 17; 225) $225
[-] The Sermons of Mr. Yorick. L., [1760]-69. *1st. Edn.* 7 vols. Engraved port., subscribers' list, no advts. in vol. 4, cont. cf. gt. (SPB. May 16; 147)
$250
[-] Tristram Shandy. L., 1760-67. *1st. Edn.* 9 vols. Sm. 8vo. Collates as Rothschild 1970, with hf.-titles, engraved frontis. in vol. 3, lf. marb. paper in vol. 3, vols. 5, 7 & 9 sigd., vol. 7 in 1st. state with errata on title verso, unif. cont. spr. cf., spines gt., most vols. rebkd. with orig. spines preserved; Fred A. Berne copy. (SPB. May 16; 355) $1,700
- - Anr. Edn. Ill.:– William Hogarth. L., 1760-67. *2nd. Edn. vols. 1-2, 1st. Edn. vols. 3-9.* 9 vols. 2 plts., frontis. plt. from vol. 3 misbnd. in vol. 4, vol. 4 lacks hf.-title, some pencil notats., some spotting & soiling, cont. cf., few jnts. reprd., 3 vols. sigd. (SPB. May 16; 146) $350
- - Anr. Edn. L., 1761-67. *Mixed Edns.* 9 vols. Vol. 2 stained in margins, cont. cf., some slight wear; 3 vols. sigd. (S. Mar.20; 964) *Sott.* £180
- - Anr. Edn. Ill.:– J.E. Laboureur. Berkshire, Gold. Cock. Pr., 1929-30. *(500) numbered.* 3 vols. Cl. (LH. Sep.25; 367) $100
- Voyage Sentimental. Essay:– J. Janin. ill.:– T. Johannot & Jacque. Paris, [1841]. *1st. Edn.* Wide

margin, woodcut plts. on China, supp. series of woodcut plts. on China, hf.-title & frontis. loose, some slight foxing; Hauswedell coll. (H. May 24; 1577) DM 800
- - Anr. Copy. 4to. Wide margin, last lf. (contents) restored, cont. hf. leath., Romantic gt., spine slightly faded. (GB. Nov.4; 1816) DM 400
- - Anr. Edn. Trans.:– E. Blemont. Ill.:– M. Leloir. Paris, 1884. *De Luxe Edn. (100) on Whatman.* Double series of photogravures before letter & with sigd. & dtd. orig. aqua. on hf.-title, etched & dtd. (1888) ex-libris, hand-bnd. burgundy mor., gt. decor., inner & outer dentelles, decor., orig. pict. wraps. bnd. in, by Chambelle-Duru. (H. Nov.23; 701a) DM 1,200
- Voyage Sentimental, suivi des Lettres d'Yorick à Eliza ... Ill.:– after Monsiau. Paris, Amst., An VII [1799]. 3 vols. 18mo. Foxing, cont. cf., spines decor. (HD. May 21; 69) Frs. 1,400
- - Anr. Copy. 2 vols. in 1. Lge. 4to. On vell., in Engl. & Fr., some foxing, old hf. cf., spine blind-decor. (HD. May 3; 148) Frs. 1,250
- The Works ... Ill.:– after Hogarth & others. 1788. 10 vols. Cont. mott. cf., panel. spines; Sir Ivar Colquhoun, of Luss copy. (CE. Mar.22; 291) £480

STERNHEIM, C.
- Fairfax. Ill.:– Fr. Masereel. Berlin, 1922. *1st. Edn. (50) De Luxe Edn. on white Bütten.* 4to. Printers note sigd. by author & artist, all lithos. sigd., orig. hf. vell., worn, loose. (H. Nov.24; 1827) DM 1,650
- Gauguin und van Gogh. Berlin, 1924. *1st. Edn. (150). (10) numbered A Edn. on japan Bütten.* Fo. Orig. mor., sigd. HD (=Hübel & Denck), spine slightly faded, lge. gold cover vig., double inner dentelle decor. (GB. May 5; 3042) DM 500

STEUART, Sir James
- An Inquiry into the Principles of Political Oeconomy. L., 1767. *1st. Edn.* 2 vols. 4to. Errata lf. at end of Vol. 2, cont. cf. (C. Nov.9; 162)
Kossow. £1,700

STEUR
- Ethnographie des Peuples de l'Europe avant J.C. ou Essai sur les Nomades de l'Asie ... Bruxelles, Paris, L., 1872-73. 3 vols. Hf. cl. (HD. Feb.22; 214)
Frs. 1,300

STEVENS, Bertram
See— URE SMITH, Sydney & Stevens, Bertram

STEVENS, George Alexander
- A Lecture on Heads. Ill.:– Thomas Rowlandson after G.M. Woodward. L., 1808. *1st. Edn.* Hand-cold. fold-out frontis., 24 plts., faint offset from plts., some light foxing, period gt.-decor. cf., gt. dentelles, spotted & chipped, corners showing, marb. end-papers, bkplt. (CBA. Aug.21; 571)
$140

STEVENS, Henry
- Historical Nuggets: Bibliotheca Americana, or, A Descriptive Account of my Collection. L., 1862. 2 vols. Sm. 8vo. Orig. cl., unc. (SG. Jan.19; 332)
$250

STEVENS, Wallace
- Harmonium. N.Y., 1923. *1st. Edn. (500).* Orig. cl.-bkd. bds. [1st. bdg.]; Frederic Dannay copy. (CNY. Dec.16; 335) $180
- Three Academic Pieces. [Cummington, Cummington Pr.], 1947. *1st. Edn. (250).* Sewn bds., ties. (SPB. May 17; 682) $350

STEVENS-NELSON PAPER CORPORATION
- Specimens: a Stevens-Nelson Paper Catalogue. [N.Y.], ca. 1950. Lge. 4to. Over 100 specimens, revised price list July 1953 laid in, qtr. lev., marb. bds., s.-c.; hand-lettered pres. from G.A. Nelson to T.M. Black. (SG. Jan.5; 244) $100
- - Anr. Edn. [N.Y., 1953]. Lge. 4to. Over 100 specimen sheets, qtr. mor. & marb. bds., July 1953 & 21 Oct. 1957 price sheets laid in. (SG. May 17; 288) $150
- - Anr. Edn. N.Y., n.d. 4to. Price-list & 3 pieces of ephemera loosely inserted, orig. mor.-bkd. bds., s.-c. (BBA. Nov.10; 133) *Blackwell.* £75

STEVENSON, Allan (Ed.)
See— HUNT, Rachel McMasters Miller

STEVENSON, David
- Sketch of the Civil Engineering of North America. L., 1838. *1st. Edn.* Engraved folding map, plan, & 13 plts. (2 folding), 1 more plt. than called for by Howes S976, cont. hf. cf., marb. bds., rebkd. with cf., hinges reinforced; from liby. of F.D. Roosevelt, inscr. by him. (SG. Mar.15; 79) $175

STEVENSON, Edward Luther
- Facsimiles of Portolan Charts Belonging to the Hispanic Society of America. N.Y., 1916. *Ltd. Edn., numbered.* Atlas fo. Each plt. rubberstpd. on blank verso, loose in orig. buckram, linen ties. (SG. Jun.7; 152) $130
- Terrestrial & Celestial Globes. New Haven, 1921. *1st. Edn.* 2 vols. Lge. 8vo. Cl., partly unopened. (SG. Jan.5; 292) $140

STEVENSON, Robert Louis
- The Black Arrow. Ill.:– N.C. Wyeth. N.Y., 1916. *1st. Wyeth Edn.* Slight margin darkening, orig. cl.; inscr. & sigd. by artist. (CBA. Aug.21; 681) $500
- A Child's Garden of Verses. L., 1885. *[1st. Edn.].* Sm. 8vo. Orig. cl., unc., cl. s.-c.; Perry Molstad copy. (SPB. May 16; 533) $325
- - Anr. Copy. 12mo. Orig. cl., variant with apostrophe shaped like a 7 on spine, partly unc.; Frederic Dannay copy. (CNY. Dec.16; 337) $250
- - Anr. Copy. 12mo. Owner's sig. on hf.-title, cl., partly unc., qtr. mor. folding case. (SG. Dec.8; 331) $225
- Dr. Jekyll & Mr. Hyde. L., 1886. *1st. Edn.* Orig. wraps., reprd., cl. folder, mor.-bkd. cl. s.-c. (S. Dec.8; 131) *Segal.* £190
- - Anr. Copy. Hf.-title, 1 p. of advts., cf.-bkd. cl., orig. wraps. bnd. in. (S. Dec.13; 401)
Steinfeld. £140
- - Anr. Copy. Lacks advt. lf., cont. hf. cf. gt. (PD. Aug.17; 80) £50
- - Anr. Copy. Sm. 8vo. Hf.-title, advt. lf., maroon lev. gt., gt. dentelles, by Bayntun (Riviere). (SG. Feb.16; 301) $225
- The Novels & Tales ... N.Y., 1911-17. 27 vols. Red hf. mor., lightly worn. (PNY. Jun.6; 459)
$300
- On the Thermal Influence of Forests. 'Edinb., 1873'. Orig. wraps., edges slightly frayed, cl. folder, hf. mor. book-form s.-c. (P. Apr.12; 31)
Jarndyce. £150
- La Porte de Maletroit. Ill.:– Ray Bethers (decors.). Cagnes-Sur-Mer, [Allen Pr.], 1952. *(300).* Wraps., s.-c. (LH. Sep.25; 312) $250
- Treasure Island. L., 1883. *1st. Edn.* Early iss. points, '7' stpd. on p. 127, 'dead man's chest' on pp. 2 & 7, '8' dropped from p. 83, 'worse' for 'worst' on p. 197, 'a' missing on p. 63, period lacking on p. 178, frontis.-map in 3 cols., advts. dtd. '5R 1083', orig. cl., spine gt., mor.-bkd. s.-c.; Walter Preston-E.E. Taylor-Prescott copy. (SPB. May 17; 683)
$3,750
- - Anr. Copy. Advts. dtd. 5 G-783, 'dead man's chest' on pp. 2 & 7, '7' missing on p. 127, 'worse' instead of 'worst', period missing on p. 178, '8' present in p. 83, battered type on first words of last two lines on p. 40, hf.-title, frontis.-map, light spotting, orig. cl., tear along lr. hinge; Fred A. Berne copy. (SPB. May 16; 360) $500
- - Anr. Copy. Many early iss. points, including '7' stpd. in pagination of p. 127, but with the 8 pp. of advts. dtd. '5R-1083', map detchd., cl., soiled, sm. stain on lr. fore-edge. (SG. Dec.8; 332) $475
- - Anr. Edn. Ill.:– Rowland Hilder. L., [1929]. Gt.-ruled pol. cf. by Bayntun, gt.-decor. spine, inner dentelles, marb. end-papers; Marymount College copy. (CBA. Mar.3; 509) $120
- Weir of Hermiston. L., 1896. *1st. Publd. Edn.* Sm. 8vo. Hf.-title, 32 p. catalogue dtd. Mar. 1896, cf. gt. by Riviere, spine gt. with fleurons, gt. dentelles, orig. buckram bdg. bnd. in. (SG. Feb.16; 302) $140
- The Works. 1904-07. *Pentland Edn. (1550).* 20 vols. Buckram, unc. (PD. Feb.15; 62) £60
- - Anr. Edn. 1906-07. *Pentland Edn. (1550) numbered.* 20 vols. Cont. hf. mor. by Maclehose, some light dampstains. (CSK. Jan.13; 123) £250
- - Anr. Copy. 20 vols. Orig. buckram. (GM. Dec.7; 680) £110

– – Anr. Edn. 1911-12. *Swanston Edn. (2060).* 25 vols. Hf. mor. (CSK. Jan.27; 169) £320
– – Anr. Edn. N.Y., 1919. 25 vols. Sm. 8vo. Red three-qtr. mor., spines gt. (SG. Feb.16; 303) $550
– – Anr. Edn. 1922-23. *Valima Edn. (1060) numbered.* 26 vols. Orig. buckram gt. (SKC. Nov.18; 1911) £140
– – Anr. Edn. 1924-25. *Waverley Edn.* 26 vols. Unif. cl., spines gt. (LC. Mar.1; 398) £50

STEVENSON, Robert Louis & Osbourne, Lloyd.
– The Ebb Tide. A Trio & Quartette. Chic. & Camb., 1894. *1st. Edn.* 12mo. Decor. cl., spine gt., unc., light wear, d.-w., minor wear; Ken Leach coll. (RO. Jun.10; 279) $700

STEVENSON, Robert Louis & others
[–] An Object of Pity, or, The Man Haggard; A Romance. Amst., ca. 1892. *1st. Edn. (100).* Unsigd. inscr. (Apia, 1893), orig. wraps., slightly chipped & loose, hf. mor. s.-c. (KH. May 1; 670) Aus. $320

STEVENSON, Robert & Son
– Report Relative to Granton Harbour. 1834. Fo. Folding charts hand-cold., orig. wraps. (P. Mar.15; 339) *Weinreb.* £60

STEVENSON, William Bennett
– A Historical & Descriptive Narrative of Twenty Years' Residence in South America. 1825. *1st. Edn.* 3 vols. 6 engraved plts. only, lacks folding frontis., stained, liby. stps. on titles, later cf., rubbed. (BBA. Jun.28; 252) *Rudge.* £55

STEVIN, Simon
– Les Oeuvres Mathématiques. Leiden, 1634. 2 pts. in 1 vol. Fo. Hf.-title, slight browning, cont. vell. bds.; Stanitz coll. (SPB. Apr.25; 409) $1,200
– – Anr. Copy. 6 pts. in 1 vol. Fo. Lacks 2 pp., some stains, cont. hf. roan, rubbed. (VG. Mar.19; 276) Fls. 900

STEWART, Basil
– Subjects Portrayed in Japanese Colour-Prints. L., 1922. Fo. Orig. qtr. cl., slightly scuffed & soiled. (SKC. Jan.13; 2119) £100
– – Anr. Copy. Fo. Cl.-bkd. bds. (SG. Aug.25; 225) $160
– – Anr. Copy. Lge. 4to. End-papers creased, no bdg. stated, spine crudely reprd., some staining, edges rubbed, corners bumped. (RS. Jan.17; 498) $125

STEWART, Douglas
– Shipwreck: A Poetic Drama. L., 1948. *De Luxe Iss., (100) with added plts. sigd., by Norman Lindsay & Stewart.* 4to. Mor. (KH. Nov.9; 466) Aus. $250

STEWART, Dugald
– Outlines of Moral Philosophy, for the use of students, in the University of Edinburgh. Edinb., 1793. *1st. Edn.* Orig. bds.; Sir Ivar Colquhoun, of Luss copy. (CE. Mar.22; 293) £350

STEWART, James Lindsay
– Golfing Miscellanea. 1887. *1st. Edn.* Bdg. not stated. (PD. Jul.13; 34) £300

STEWART, John
– Conseils aux Acheteurs de Chevaux. Paris & Brussels, 1861. Bradel bds. (HD. Jan.27; 333) Frs. 1,100

STEWART, Dr. Matthew
– The Distance of the Sun from the Earth determined by the force of gravity. Edinb., 1763. *1st. Edn.* Slight spotting, orig. bds., paper-covered spine, unc., slightly worn. (SKC. May 4; 1749) £75

STIBBE, D.G. (Ed.)
See— ENCYCLOPAEDIE VAN NEDER-LANDSCH–INDIE

STIEGLITZ, Alfred
See— NORMAN, Dorothy

STIEGLITZ, Christian Ludwig
– Plans et Dessins Tirés de la Belle Architecture. Paris, 1801. Fo. 105 engraved plts., including 8 double-p. & 1 folding, 2 p. preface, 19th. C. red mor., gt.-panel with crest of Duke of Devonshire, inner dentelles, by C. Lewis, upr. cover detchd., spine faded. (C. Dec.9; 151) *Waldersee.* £650

– Zeichnungen ausder Schönen Baukunst. Leipzig, 1805. *2nd. Edn.* Fo. Title lf. foxed, some general foxing, cont. style hf. leath. (GB. May 3; 910) DM 2,200
– – Anr. Copy. Fo. 105 copper plts. (9 double-p.), title lf. brown spotted, a little spotting, mostly in margins, sm. stains, cont. hf. leath., worn & bumped, spines partly pasted with leath. (H. May 22; 72) DM 1,600

STIELER, A.
– Hand Atlas. 1868. Fo. 63 partly cold. maps, hf. roan, upr. cover loose. (P. Feb.16; 296) £55

STIELER, C. & others.
– Italia, Viaggio pittoresco dall'Alpi all'Etna. Milan, 1876. Fo. Some light stains, orig. cl., loose. (SI. Dec.15; 131) Lire 250,000

STIELER, K., Wachenhusen, H. & Hackländer, F.W.
– Rheinfahrt von den Quellen des Rheins bis zum Meere. Stuttgart, [1875 ff.]. In 2 vols. Fo. 29 (of 60) tinted woodcut plts., approx. 250 text woodcuts, some slight foxing, hf. leath., rubbed, spine defect. (R. Apr.4; 2544) DM 700
– – Anr. Edn. Stuttgart, ca. 1880. In 2 vols. Fo. 60 tinted woodcut plts., minimal foxing, orig. linen. (HK. Nov.9; 1202) DM 1,100
– – Anr. Copy. Fo. Plts. & opposite pp. mostly foxed, orig. gold-tooled linen, lightly bumped, jnts. partly defect. (GB. May 3; 216) DM 750
– – Anr. Edn. Ill.:– after Achenbach, Püttner, & others. Stuttgart, ca. 1880-85. Fo. 60 woodcut plts., orig. linen. (V. Sep.29; 101) DM 1,400
– The Rhine from its Source to the Sea. Trans.:– G.C.T. Bartley. L., ca. 1875. Fo. 60 woodcut plts. & 365 text woodcuts, orig. linen gt. (R. Oct.13; 2742) DM 1,000
– – Anr. Edn. Trans.:– G.C.T. Bartley. 1878. 4to. 60 plts., orig. cl. gt. (P. Oct.20; 94) £300
– – Anr. Copy. Fo. 60 woodcut plts., 365 text woodcuts, orig. gold-tooled leath., upr. cover loose, spine defect. (R. Apr.4; 2545) DM 800
– – Anr. Copy. Bdg. not stated, but edges & spine rubbed. (RS. Jan.17; 457) $200

STIFTER, Adalbert
– Bunte Steine, Ein Festgeschenk. Pesth, 1853. *1st. Edn.* 2 pts. in 1 vol. Pt. 1 hf.-title lightly cut at foot, 1 litho. lf. for owner's mark bnd. in pt. 1 after typographic title, margins stained, cont. blind-tooled linen, spine slightly faded. (HK. Nov.10; 2729) DM 500

STIFTER, Adalbert (Ed.)
See— WIEN UND DIE WIENER, IN BILDERN AUS DEM LEBEN

STIGAND, Capt. Chauncy Hugh
– The Game of British East Africa. 1913. *2nd. Edn.* 4to. Commercial advts. bnd. in at end, some spotting, orig. cl. gt., spine worn. (TA. Sep.15; 43) £50
– Hunting the Elephant in Africa. Intro.:– T. Roosevelt. L., 1913. Orig. bdg. (VA. Oct.28; 268) R 260

STIGLIANI, T.
– Del Mondo Nvovo. Venti Primi Canti. Piacenza, 1617. *1st. Edn.* Margins slightly frayed at beginning & end, lightly browned, some staining, bds. [Sabin 91728] (HK. Nov.10; 3109) DM 440

STILLINGFLEET, Edward, Bp. of Worcester
[–] Answer to Mr. Locke's Letter Concerning Some Passages Relating to his Essay. L., 1697. *1st. Edn.* 2-pp. advts., cont. inscr. on title, cont. cf., spine defect. (S. Apr.10; 345) *Drury.* £65

STILLMAN, Jacob D.B.
– The Horse in Motion. Boston, 1882. *[1st. Edn.].* Hf. leath., edges & spine nicked & rubbed. (RS. Jan.17; 500) $190
– – Anr. Copy. Lge. 4to. Orig. gt.-pict. cl., spine ends & extremities worn. (SG. May 10; 92) $120

STILTZER, F.
– The Story of British Sporting Prints. L., [1925]. Some MS. ll. bnd. in, orig. linen. (R. Apr.3; 675) DM 540

STIMMER, Tobias
– Novae Sacrorum Bibliorum Figurae ... Strassburg, 1590. Sm. 8vo. Engraved title in cols. & gold, lacks some 10 ll. & all of sig. D, some foxing & soiling, vell., dtd. 1596; sig. & annots. of Johann Heinrich Ammianus, of Schaffhausen on title & end-paper, w.a.f. (SG. Feb.9; 147) $250

STIRLING, A.W.M.
– Coke of Norfolk & his Friends. L., 1908. 4 vols. Extra-ill. with many plts., some hand-cold., spotted, mor. gt. by Bayntun (Rivière). (S. Oct.4; 102) *Walford.* £210

STIRLING, James
– Lineae Tertii Ordinis Neutonianae, sive Illustratio Tractatus D. Neutoni de Enumeratione Linearum Tertii Ordinis. Oxford, 1717. *1st. Edn.* Subscribers list including Newton, light margin soiling, cont. panel cf., some chipping & wear; Stanitz coll. (SPB. Apr.25; 410) $550
– Methodus Differentialis: sive Tractatus de Summatione et de Interpolatione Serierum Infinitarum. L., 1730. *1st. Edn.* Slight spotting at beginning & end, 18th. C. mott. sheep, spine gt.; Stanitz coll. (SPB. Apr.25; 411) $550

STIRLING, William Alexander, Earl of
– Recreations with the Muses. L., 1637. *1st. Edn.* Fo. Without the port. sometimes found, lacks initial & final blanks, title creased & stained with short tear across centre, tears in G3 & G4 with loss of 1 word, cont. cf. [STC 347] (C. Nov.9; 126) *Aberdeen.* £100

STIRRUP, Thomas
– Horometra: or the Compleat Diallist. L., 1652. *1st. Edn.* 4to. Piece cut from title-p. without loss of text, names on frontis., a little dust-stained, cont. cf., spine gt., rebkd. [Wing S5688] (BBA. May 3; 68) *Sherlock.* £160

STISSER, F.U.
– Forst- und Jagd-Historie der Teutschen. Ed.:– H.G. Francke. Leipzig, 1754. *3rd. Edn.* Some light browning, title lf. lightly creased, cont. hf. leath. gt., slightly rubbed, jnts. brittle. (R. Apr.4; 1949) DM 1,800

STOCK, Bp. J.
[–] A Narrative of What Passed at Killala in the County of Mayo, by an Eye Witness. Dublin, 1800. *1st. Dublin Edn.* 1 lf. torn, bkplt., hf. cf. (GM. Dec.7; 395) £70

STOCKDALE, F.W.L.
– Etchings from Original Drawings of Antiquities in the County of Kent. 1810 [1811]. *1st. Edn.* Fo. Hf. cf., worn. (P. Sep.29; 103) *Fancycrest.* £80
– – Anr. Edn. 1811. 4to. Vig. title, 39 plts., orig. cf.-bkd. bds. (P. Feb.16; 118) £85

STOCKDALE, John
– A Geographical, Historical & Political Description of the Empire of Germany, Holland ... & Sardinia. L., 1800. *[1st. Edn.].* 4to. Key map, 3 folding maps, 23 town plans, hf. cf., covers worn & detchd. (P. Nov.24; 242) *Noble.* £260
– – Anr. Copy. 4to. Engraved frontis. map, 3 folding maps, 22 (of 23) engraved plans, orig. bds., unc., loose. (PD. Dec.14; 206) £170
– – Anr. Copy. 4to. Engraved index map, 3 double-p. folding engraved maps, 23 plans (2 folding), maps torn at fold, a few ll. & 1 plan spotted, cont. russ., covers with marb. paper panel, head of spine worn. (C. Mar.14; 118) *Hildebrandt.* £150
– Map of England & Wales. 1809. Fo. Engraved title, 19 sectional maps, hf. cf. (P. Oct.20; 266) £65

See— CARY, John & Stockdale, John

STOCKHOLM
– Album Pittoresque de Stockholm. Ill.:– Baerentzen, after Billing, Wollander, & Heinemann. [Stockholm], ca. 1840. Ob. fo. Map, 10 litho. views, cont. hf. roan, lettered on upr. cover, worn. (S. Dec.1; 314) *Koch.* £250

STOCKLEIN, J.
– Allerhand so Lehr- als Geist-reiche Brief, Schrifften u. Reis-Beschreibungen, Welche v. denen Missionariis der Ges. Jesu ... Augsburg & Graz,

STOCKLEIN, J. -*Contd.*

1726. *1st. Edn.* Pts. 1-4, in 1 vol. Fo. 2 copperplts., 6 copper engraved maps, including 4 folding, frontis. verso & title recto stpd., slightly foxed, cont. leath. gt., slightly rubbed. [Sabin 91981] (HK. Nov.9; 1294) DM 550

STOCKMANN, J.A.
- **Pinacotheca Mariana.** Augsburg, 1760. 4 vols. Cont. red mor., gold-tooled decor., 4 corner fleurons. (D. Nov.24; 2357) DM 3,500

STODART, Robert Riddle
- **Scottish Arms.** 1881. *(300) numbered.* 2 vols., including plt. vol. Fo. Cl. gt., soiled. (P. Sep.29; 24) *McEwan.* £65
- - **Anr. Edn.** 1881. 2 vols. Fo. Orig. cl. gt., soiled. (P. Jun.7; 93) £70

STODDARD, Richard Henry
- **Abraham Lincoln. An Horation Ode.** N.Y., [1865]. *1st. Edn.* Red hf. mor., marb. paper bds. (LH. Apr.15; 375) $110

STODDART, Thomas T.
- **The Death Wake.** Edinb. & L., 1831. *1st. Edn.* 12mo. Orig. cl., unc.; long note by former owner 'T.H.' on front fly-lf., Frederic Dannay copy. (CNY. Dec.16; 338) $280

STOEFFLER, Johann
- **Calendarium Romanum Magnum.** Oppenheym, 1518 (at end). *Orig. Edn.* Fo. Lacks 1 prelim., many MS. margin annots., cont. blind-stpd. vell., spine decor., slight wear. (HD. Nov.29; 74) Frs. 2,900
- **Elucidatio Fabricae Ususque Astrolabii.** Parigi, 1564. Mark on frontis., folding plt. torn, some stains, cont. limp vell. (SI. Dec.15; 178) Lire 240,000
- **In Procli Diadochi ... Sphaeram Mundi, Omnibus Numeris longe Absolutissimus Commentarius.** Tubingen, 1534. *1st. Edn.* Fo. Last lf. (with port.) slightly soiled & mntd., slight staining, margin repair to title, old owners' inscrs., cont. limp vell. [Sabin 91983] (S. Nov.28; 138) *Bozzolato.* £400

STOKER, Bram
- **Dracula.** L., 1897. *1st. Edn.* Some spotting, mostly endpapers, sig. on hf.-title, orig. cl., soiled; Fred A. Berne copy. (SPB. May 16; 362) $850
- - **Anr. Copy.** Advt. lf., some ll. creased, orig. cl., soiled, mor.-bkd. s.-c.; Perry Molstad copy. (SPB. May 16; 534) $650
- **Under the Sunset.** Ill.:- W. Fitzgerald & W.V. Cockburn. L., 1882. *2nd. Edn.* Slight darkening, some margin staining, gt.-decor. imitation vell., covers mildly foxed & rubbed, edges & spine darkening; sigd., inscr. & dtd. by author. (CBA. Oct.29; 809) $275

STOKES, George Gabriel
- **Mathematical & Physical Papers.** Camb., 1880-1905. *1st. Edn.* 5 vols. 1 port. inserted from anr. publication, slight spotting of fore-e. & end-papers, slight creasing of Vol. 3 fore-e., orig. cl., slight rubbing; Stanitz coll. (SPB. Apr.25; 412) $250

STOKES, Isaac Newton Phelps
- **The Iconography of Manhattan Island.** N.Y., 1915-28. *1st. Edn. (360) on Engl. or Holland H.M.P.* 6 vols. Lge. 4to. Plts., some cold., many folding, orig. unif. hf. vell., gt.-armorial cl., cl. d.-w.'s., cl. s.-c.'s.; inscr. to Mr. Hewitt. (SG. Apr.26; 189) $2,800
- - **Anr. Copy.** 6 vols. 4to. Orig. mott. cf. gt., partly untrimmed, worn some hinges brkn. (SG. Nov.3; 200) $1,900

STOKES, Isaac Newton Phelps & Haskell, Daniel C.
- **American Historical Prints, Early Views of American Cities** ... N.Y., 1932. 4to. Gt.-lettered cl., light wear. (RO. May 22; 169) $190
- - **Anr. Edn.** N.Y., 1933. 4to. Cl. (SG. Jan.19; 334) $175

STOKES, Cdr. John Lort
- **Discoveries in Australia with an Account of the Coasts & Rivers ... Voyage of H.M.S. Beagle.** L., 1846. *1st. Edn.* 2 vols. & Atlas. 8 folding maps, 26 plts., Vol. 1 frontis. partly detchd., title to Vol. 1 slightly foxed, 1 map foxed & offset, sm. hole in fold of 1 chart, hf. cf. gt., partly unc. (CA. Apr.3; 107) Aus. $2,400

STOLBERG, Chr. zu
- **Gedichte.** Hamburg, 1782. *1st. Edn.* Minimal spotting, cont. cf., gt. spine, monog. B.C.U.S.; Hauswedell coll. (H. May 24; 1579) DM 600

STOLBERG, Frederic Leopold, Count
- **Travels through Germany, Switzerland, Italy. & Sicily.** L., 1796-97. *1st. Engl. Edn.* 4to. Engraved folding map, 19 plts., 4 ll. of music, prelims. misbnd. into Vol. 2, orig. bds., unc., slightly soiled. (S. Jun.25; 177) *Jud & Co.* £180

STOLK, A.P. van
[-] **Flor de Pascua.** Ill.:- M.C. Escher. Baarn, 1921. Sm. 4to. Orig. litho. wraps. by author, slightly worn, loose. (VG. Nov.29; 205) Fls. 5,500

STOLL, Caspar
- **Représentation Exactement Colorée d'Après Nature des Cigales et Punaises, qui se Trouvent dans les Quatres Parties du Monde, l'Europe, l'Asie, l'Afrique et l'Amérique.** 1780-88. 2 vols. in 1. 4to. 2 hand-cold. engraved frontis., additional ptd. title in Vol. 1, titles & text in Dutch & Fr., 70 hand-cold. engraved plts., all bnd. at end, cont. hf. cf., worn, head of spine torn. (C. Jun.27; 134) *Seymour.* £500
- - **Anr. Edn.** Amst., 1787-88. 3 vols. 4to. 2 additional hand-cold. titles, 100 hand-cold. engraved plts., titles & text in Dutch & Fr., without hf.-title to 1st. vol. & 2nd. ptd. title to 3rd. vol. called for by Landwehr, 1 plt. numeral shaved, unif. cont. red str.-grd. mor. gt., spines gt.-tooled. (C. Mar.14; 197) *Quaritch.* £3,600
See— CRAMER, Pieter — STOLL, Caspar

STONE, Edmund
- **The Construction & Principal Uses of Mathematical Instruments** ... L., 1758. *2nd. Edn.* 2 pts. in 1 vol., including Supp. Fo. 30 engraved plts., last 4 with margins frayed, title worn & laid down, browned thro.-out, mod. mor. (PNY. Mar.27; 175) $840

STONE, Elizabeth
[-] **Chronicles of Fashion, from the time of Elizabeth to George IV.** L., 1845. 2 vols. in 5. Fo. Titles, text & plts. cut round & inset in wide margins, extra-ill. with approx. 700 engraved, aquatint & mezzotint ports. & plts. after Westall, Cruikshank, Rowlandson, & others, several hand-cold., & 2 orig. water-colour drawings, crushed mor. gt. by Zaehnsdorf, spines gt. (C. Nov.16; 180) *Traylen.* £4,500

STONE, Herbert L. & Loomis, Alfred F.
- **Millions for Defense: A Pictorial History of the Races for the America's Cup.** Derrydale Pr., [1934]. *(950) numbered.* 4to. Orig. cl. (SG. Mar.15; 243) $110

STONE, Reynolds
- **Engravings.** Appreciation:- Kenneth Clark. L., [1977]. *(150) numbered & sigd., with a sigd. engr. laid in.* Tall 8vo. Buckram, marb. bd. s.-c. (SG. Jan.12; 325) $275
- **Wood Engravings of Thomas Bewick.** L., 1953. *(1000) numbered & sigd.* 4to. Orig. cl., d.-w. (BBA. May 23; 198) *Adam Mills Rare Bks.* £60

STONEHOUSE, John Harrison
- **The Story of the Great Omar bound by F.L. Sangorski.** 1933. *(75) sigd.* 4to. Orig. buckram gt., d.-w., s.-c. (P. Sep.29; 299) *Henderson.* £120

STONER, Frank
- **Chelsea, Bow, Derby Porcelain Figures.** Newport, 1955. *1st. Edn.* No bdg. stated. (JL. Jun.24; 206) Aus. $130

STONEY, Capt. H. Butler
- **A Residence in Tasmania: with a Descriptive Tour through the Island.** L., 1856. Frontis. detchd. with fore-e. slightly tattered, light browning & spotting, orig. cl., lightly soiled. (CSK. Feb.10; 190) £85
- - **Anr. Copy.** No bdg. stated. (JL. Jun.24; 130) Aus. $320

- - **Anr. Copy.** 4to. Some little foxing of plts., no bdg. stated, unc., shaken, label removed from upr. bd. (KH. Nov.9; 468) Aus. $140

STONHAM, Charles
- **The Birds of the British Islands.** Ill.:- Lilian M. Medland. L., 1906-11. *(1) with all bird plts. hand-cold. by Martin W. Woodcock, & sigd. by him.* 5 vols. 4to. Inserted before hf.-title in each vol. is additional title-p. certifying this to be the only copy of its kind, mor. gt. by Zaehnsdorf. (C. Mar.14; 198) *Quaritch.* £6,200
- - **Anr. Edn.** Ill.:- Lilian M. Medland. L., 1906-11. 5 vols. 4to. 2 folding cold. maps, 318 litho. plts., some light spotting, lr. margin of title & prelims. to Vol. 5 dampstained, cont. hf. mor., spines gt., lightly rubbed. (CSK. Apr.6; 134) £280
- - **Anr. Copy.** 5 vols. 4to. Slight spotting thro.-out, orig. cl., 3 spines torn. (P. Mar.15; 20) *Erlini.* £170
- - **Anr. Copy.** 5 vols. Fo. Some ll. detchd., light spotting thro.-out, orig. buckram, rubbed, spines faded, ex-liby., w.a.f. (CSK. Jan.13; 103) £130

STOPENDAAL, Daniel
[-] **De Vechtstrom.** Ill.:- Van der Laan after Lairesse. [Amst.], ca. 1725? Fo. Engraved allegorical title, 102 views on 51 plts., old vell.-bkd. bds. (C. Dec.9; 43) *Weinreb.* £800
- **Verscheyde Schoone en Evrmaakelyke Gezigten in de Hofstede van Clingendaal.** [Amst.], ca. 1700. Ob. 4to. Engraved title, 32 plts., cont. hf. cf. (C. Dec.9; 152) *Goldschmidt.* £1,000

STOPS, Mr. [Pseud.]
- **Punctuation Personified.** 1824. 16 hand-cold. plts., orig. wraps., slight wear. (P. Sep.29; 392) *Greer.* £220

STORACE, Stephen
- **The Haunted Tower.** L., [1780]. *2nd. Edn. Bound with:*) KELLY, Michael – Blue Beard. L., 1798. *1st. Edn.* Together 2 works in 1 vol. Ob. fo. Longman & Broderip catalogue; later sigd. with initials by Kelly, in vocal score. (S. May 10; 51) *Wise.* £180

STORER, James Sargent
- **A Description of Fonthill Abbey.** L., 1812. 4to. Cont. hf. cf., slightly rubbed. (S. Jun.25; 340) *May & May.* £110

STORER, James Sargent & Henry Sargent & Brewer, James Norris
- **Delineations of Gloucestershire.** 1824. Engraved title, 48 plts. all on India Paper, some spotting, cont. hf. mor., rubbed. (BBA. Feb.9; 338) *Abra Bks.* £170

STORER, James Sargent & Greig, J.
[-] **Antiquarian & Topographical Cabinet.** 1807-11. 10 vols. Sm. 8vo. Cont. str.-grd. mor., gt.-& blind-tooled covers & spines; from liby. of Luttrellstown Castle, w.a.f. (C. Sep.28; 1849) £300
- - **Anr. Copy.** 10 vols. Sm. 8vo. Vig. title to each vol. but for Vol. 2, 480 engraved plts., cont. tree cf., some covers detchd. (TA. Jun.21; 212) £50

STORIA POLITICA DELL'ANNO 1781
Modena, 1782. 4to. Linen. (DS. Mar.23; 2275) Pts. 250,000

STORK, William
[-] **A Description of East-Florida, with a Journal Kept by John Bartram of Philadelphia, Botanist to His Majesty for the Floridas.** L., 1769. *3rd. Edn.* 4to. 3 folding engraved maps, 1 torn & frayed at edge, disbnd. [Sabin 92222] (C. Jun.27; 72) *Davidson.* £550

STORM, Thedor
- **Immensee.** Darmstadt, Ernst Ludwig Pr., 1909. *(180).* Orig. vell., gold-tooled cover vig. (HK. May 17; 2749) DM 460
- **Der Schimmelreiter.** Berlin, 1888. *1st. Book Edn.* Some slight foxing, title verso with collector stp., orig. linen. (GB. May 4; 1465) DM 630
- - **Anr. Copy.** Orig. linen. (BR. Apr.12; 1536) DM 600

STORRS, Sir Ronald
See— HART, Capt. Liddell & Storrs, Sir Ronald

STORY, George
- An Impartial History of the Wars of Ireland. L., 1693. (*Bound with:*) – A Continuation of the Impartial History of the Wars of Ireland. L., 1693. *1st. Edn.* Together 2 vols. in 1. Sm. 4to. 1 folding plt. reprd., some foxing, rebnd. hf. mor. [Wing S5749 & S5748] (GM. Dec.7; 242) £260

STORY, Robert
- The Poetical Works. L., 1857. Lge. 8vo. Cont. crimson mor. gt., fore-e. pntg. (SG. Nov.17; 237) $200

STORY OF POOR TRICKET THE GAMESTER
... & How Lastly, his Gaming was the Occasion of his being transported as a Convict to Botany Bay ...
Late 18th. C. Disbnd. (KH. May 1; 17) Aus. $350

STOSCH, Philippe de
- Pierres Antiques Gravées. Trans.:– M. de Limiers. Ill.:– B. Picart. Amst., 1734. Fo. Cont. red mor. gt., spine decor. (HD. May 3; 149) Frs. 5,200

STOTHARD, Charles Alfred
- The Monumental Effigies of Great Britain. L., 1817-32. 4to. Frontis. in cols. & gold, 147 etched plts., many partly hand-cold., some slight spotting, cont. hf. mor., worn. (S. Mar.6; 333)
Bennett. £100

STOTHARD, Thomas (Ill.)
See— DEFOE, Daniel
See— ROGERS, Samuel

STOW, John
- The Annales or Generall Chronicle of England ... 1615. Fo. 17th. C. cf. gt., royal arms, rebkd. in later cf. (SKC. Mar.9; 1884) £300
– – **Anr. Edn.** Ed.:– Edmund Howes. L., 1631 [colophon dtd. 1632]. Fo. Title defect. & laid down, cf.-bkd. marb. bds.; Sir Ivar Colquhoun, of Luss copy. [NSTC 23340] (CE. Mar.22; 295a) £100
– – **Anr. Copy.** Sm. fo. Title in panel. border, some margins defect., some stains, early cf., worn. (SG. Apr.19; 176) $100
- A Survey of the Cities of London & Westminster. L., 1720. 2 vols. Fo. 8 extra plts. in Vol. 1, cont. cf., upr. covers detchd. (P. Jul.5; 236) £420
– – **Anr. Copy.** 2 vols. Fo. Lge. folding plan slightly torn on fold, cont. panel. cf. gt. (P. Sep.8; 182)
Map House. £360
– – **Anr. Copy.** 2 vols. Fo. 43 (of 68) engraved plts. & plans, including 21 double-p., 19th. C. gt.-panel. russ., w.a.f. (C. Nov.16; 178) *Willis.* £250
– – **Anr. Edn.** Ed.:– John Strype. L., 1754-55. 2 vols. Fo. Lacks 1 plt., old cf., rubbed & worn, cover detchd., w.a.f. (C. Mar.14; 129)
Burgess. £750
- The Survey of London. L., 1633. *[4th. Edn.].* Fo. Prelim. & 3 ll. reprd., cf., rebkd. (P. Apr.12; 76)
Robertshaw. £130
– – **Anr. Copy.** Fo. Cf., defect., lr. cover & last 3 ll. detchd. (P. Mar.15; 131) *Rix.* £55

STOW, J.P.
- South Australia; Its History, Productions & Natural Resources ... Adelaide, 1883. With 3 unlisted plts., but lacks 1 plt. which is called for, a few sm. defects to several ll., cl., marked. (KH. May 1; 672)
Aus. $120

STOWE, Harriet Beecher
- Dred; A Tale of the Great Dismal Swamp. L., 1856. *1st. Engl. Edn.* 2 vols. Orig. cl., spines blistered; inscr. by author to the Lord Chief Baron Pollock. (SG. Nov.17; 126) $225
- Uncle Tom's Cabin. Boston, 1852. *1st. Edn. 1st. Iss.* 2 vols. Spotted, orig. cl., rubbed, spines reprd. (BBA. Jun.14; 17) *Bertram Rota.* £95
– – **Anr. Copy.** 2 vols. Hobart & Robbins slug on copyright pp., some browning & spotting, few gatherings sprung, orig. cl., 'J.P. Jewett & Co.' on spines, spines reprd.; pres. copy to Mr. Fleece with autograph quotation laid in, Prescott copy. (SPB. May 17; 684) $5,500
– – **Anr. Copy.** 2 vols. Hobart & Robbins slug on title versos, spotting & browning, orig. cl., 'J.P. Jewett & Co.' on spines & spines & corners worn,

mor.-bkd. s.-c.; Perry Molstad copy. (SPB. May 16; 535) $600
– – **Anr. Copy.** *1st. Edn.* 2 vols. Printer's slug of Hobart & Robbins on copyright pp., some light foxing, orig. gt.-stpd. cl., with 'J.P. Jewett & Co.' at foot of spines, covers lightly rubbed, corners slightly bumped, spine ends chipped, spines leaning, mod. two-part hf. mor. folding s.-c.; Marymount College copy. (CBA. Mar.3; 512) $400
– – **Anr. Edn.** Boston, 1852. *1st. Edn.* 2 vols. Pol. cf. gt. by Bayntun, orig. cl. covers bnd. in. (LH. Sep.25; 601) $325
– – **Anr. Copy.** 2 vols. 12mo. Foxed, cuttings mntd. on final blank & end-papers, orig. cl., spines cocked, extremities worn. (SG. Nov.17; 125) $225
– – **Anr. Edn.** Ill.:– George Cruiksbank. L., 1852. *1st. Engl. Edn.* Orig. 13 pts. Frontis.-port., 27 wood-engraved plts., slight soiling, orig. ptd. wraps., mor. solander case; with 1-p. autograph quotation, sigd., & envelope with artist's sig., Perry Molstad copy. (SPB. May 16; 536) $850

STOWER, Caleb
- The Printer's Grammar. L., 1808. Sm. 8vo. Later hf. mor. (SG. Jan.5; 293) $225

STOY, Johann Sigmund
- Manuel pour l'Instruction de la Jeunesse. Ill.:– after Chodowiecki, Schellenberg & Penzel. 1817. Plt. vol. Ob. 4to. 2 tears, 1 crudely reprd., cont. roan-bkd. bds., slightly rubbed; van Veen coll. (S. Feb.28; 109) £120

STOY, Peter
- Formular Buch von Allerhand Wolgebreüchlichen Teütschen und andern Zierschrifften. Leipzig & Nuremb., 1639. Sm. ob. fo. Title frayed, lacks upr. corner with much loss, slightly soiled nearly thro.-out, many old MS. notes, mostly on versos, notes on dedication lf., endpapers & doubls., some numeric notes, some ll. loose, cont. vell., slightly cockled, spotted, foot of spine defect., lacks ties. (HK. Nov.9; 2088) DM 540

STRABO, P.
- De Situ Orbis. Venice, 1502. Fo. Folio 68 repeated & lacks fo. 69, some slight stains, mor.-bkd. bds. (GM. Dec.7; 622) £75
– – **Anr. Edn.** Ed.:– Conrad Heresbach. Trans.:– Guarinus Veronesi & Gregorius Trifernate. Basel, 1549. Fo. Greek & Latin parallel text, title lf. with old MS. owners mark, cont. pig, roll-tooled, sm. port. medals, blind-tooled arms centre-piece on upr. cover, centre-piece on lr. cover, monog. stp., corners slightly bumped, 2 brass clasps. (D. Nov.23; 145) DM 1,450
- Geographia. [Venice], Joannes (Rubeus) Vercellensis, 24 Apr. 1494. Fo. Capital spaces, MS. marginalia, 1st. title mntd., sm. hole in last lf. affecting 4 words, blank lr. outer corners of several ll. renewed, some spotting & staining, old bds., new cf. back & corners; Paolo Giovio's copy, with his margin annots. & those of his brother Benedetto, note dtd. 1790 on front end-paper by Count G.B. Giovio, Stanitz coll. (SPB. Apr.25; 413) $1,100
- Rerum Geographicarum Libri XVII. Notes:– Casaubonus. Ill.:– Hübertz. Amst., 1707. 2 vols. Fo. Margins of 1st. 5 ll. in Vol. II slightly defect., cont. vell. gt. (HD. Nov.29; 75) Fls. 1,000
– – **Anr. Edn.** Ed.:– Th. Falconer. Oxford, 1807. 2 vols. Fo. L.P., bluish paper, MS. entry on 1st. lf. Vol. I, cont. cf., gt., gt. arms, slightly bumped & worn, sm. spine tear, 1 upr. cover loose, several sm. scratches. (H. Nov.23; 777) DM 500

STRADA, Famiano
- De Bello Belgico. Rome, 1632-47. 2 vols. Fo. Engraved titles, 30 engraved plts., hf.-titles, some browning in text, vell. bds., spines gt. (S. May 21; 250) *Quaritch.* £950
– – **Anr. Edn.** [Rome, 1640-47]. 2 vols. Fo. Engraved titles, 30 copperplts., some spotting & stains, crude old cf., worn. (SG. Feb.9; 341) $450
– – **Anr. Edn.** L., 1650. *1st. Edn. in Engl.* 3 pts. in 1 vol. Fo. Errata & advts. at end, old cf., worn, hinge brkn. (SG. Sep.22; 280) $110
– – **Anr. Edn.** Frankfurt, 1699. 4to. Some plts. creased & slightly frayed, lightly browned thro.-out, cont. leath. gt., worn, gt. oxidised. (HK. May 15; 721) DM 1,500
– – **Anr. Copy.** Text slightly browned, cont. leath.

gt., gold-tooled supralibros arms, slightly rubbed. (D. Nov.24; 3823) DM 600

STRAFFORDE, Sir Thomas Wentworth, Earl of
- Letters & Despatches, with an Essay towards his Life by Sir George Radcliffe. 1739. *1st. Edn.* 2 vols. Fo. Minor dampstain affecting a few ll., cont. mott. cf., spines gt.-decor.; Sir Ivar Colquhoun, of Luss copy. (CE. Mar.22; 328) £90

STRAHAN, Edward
- Mr. Vanderbilt's House & Collection. Boston, [1883-84]. *(1000) numbered on Holland.* 10 vols. Fo. Pict. wraps., spines crudely taped, 1st. vol. worn, disbnd. (SG. Aug.25; 396) $100

STRAHLENBERG, P.J. von
- Das Nord und Ostliche Theil von Europa und Asia, in so weit solches das Gantze Russische Reich mit Siberien. Stockholm, 1730. *1st. Edn.* Sm. 4to. Lge. folding woodcut plan, folding table, 10 engraved plts. (numbered erratically, as usual), slight worming affecting margin of title & dedication lf., faint liby. stp. on title, cont. cf., gt. device on upr. cover. (S. May 21; 248) *Morrell.* £300

STRAHLHEIM, C.
- Die Wundermappe. Frankfurt, 1834-36. Vol. 1 (in 3 pts.) in 3 vols. 162 (of 163) copper & steel engrs., some slight foxing, cont. bds., slightly bumped. (R. Apr.5; 2982) DM 600
– – **Anr. Edn.** Frankfurt, 1835. Vol. 1 pt. 2. Some spotting, cont. hf. leath., rubbed & bumped. (R. Oct.13; 3175) DM 450
– – **Anr. Edn.** Frankfurt, 1836. Vol. 7: Die Schweiz. Slightly foxed, some text ll. browned, cont. bds. (R. Apr.5; 3100) DM 1,500

STRAND MAGAZINE
L., Jan. 1891-Dec. 1903. 26 vols. Lge. 8vo. Cl., leath.-bkd. (gt. extra), some light wear to spine ends or extremities. (SG. Mar.15; 149) $300

STRANGE, Edward F.
- Chinese Lacquer. L., 1926. *(600) numbered. (100) specially bnd.* 4to. Orig. pig, head & tail of spine slightly rubbed. (S. May 1; 605) *Tang.* £110
– – **Anr. Edn.** L., 1926. 4to. No bdg. stated. (SPB. Nov.30; 165) $375
- The Colour-Prints of Hiroshige. L., [1925]. *(250).* 4to. Vell. gt., boxes. (S. May 1; 607)
Forster. £110

STRAPAROLA, Giovanni Francesco
- Les Facecievses Nvicts. Trans.:– Iean Louueau [& P. Delariney]. Lyon, 1596. 2 pts. in 1 vol. Slightly stained, end-paper defect., cont. vell., 1 (of 4) ties. (HK. Nov.10; 3110) DM 400

STRASSMAN, F.
See— HAHN, Otto & Strassman, F.

STRATICO, S.
[–] Bibliografia di Marina nelle varie Lingue dell' Europa. Milan, 1823. 4to. 1st. 12 & last ll. torn & reprd., spotted, later cl.-bkd. bds., lightly soiled. (CSK. Feb.24; 222) £50

STRATILAT, Pheoder
[–] Slavonisch-russisches Heiligthum mitten in Deutschland; das ist der Grosse Heilige und Martyrer, Pheodor Stratilat, oder Theodorus Dux ... vorgesteller von Jo. Alex. Doderlein. Nuremb., 1724. Sm. 4to. Old bds. (HD. Dec.2; 162) Frs. 1,500

STRATTON, Arthur
See— GARNER, Thomas & Stratton, Arthur

STRATTON, Ezra M.
- The World on Wheels. N.Y., 1878. *1st. Edn.* Ills., cl. gt. (P. May 17; 289) *Joseph.* £75
– – **Anr. Copy.** Lge. 8vo. Some margins frayed, crude hf. linen, ex-liby. (SG. Mar.15; 190) $100

STRAUSS, Dav. Friedr.
- Gesammelte Schriften. Ed.:– Ed. Zeller. Bonn, 1876-78. *1st. Coll. Edn.* 12 vols. Cont. linen gt., spine lightly faded, w.a.f. (HK. Nov.10; 2732) DM 900

STRAUSS, Ralph
- Carriages & Coaches. L., 1912. Plts., cl.; T.L.s. inserted. (P. May 17; 290) *Quaritch.* £55

STRAUSS, Ralph -Contd.

- **The Unspeakable Curll.** L., 1927. (535). Plts., cl. gt. (P. May 17; 98) *Blackwell*. £50

STRAUSS, Richard

- **Josephslegende [piano score].** Paris, 1913. 2 vols. Fo. Some pp. stpd. 'Als Manuscript Gedruckt', p. 56 torn, bds. & paper wrap.; sigd. by Mikhail Fokine in upr. cover of 1st. vol., with some pencil annots., mostly indicating deletions to music, presumably in Fokine's hand, some also apparently in Diaghilev's hand, inscr. on upr. cover of 1st. vol. by Serge Lifar 'Ballet russes de Diaghilev Joseph', Serge Lifar Coll. (S. May 9; 215) £550
- **Krämerspiegel. Zwölf Gesänge von Alfred Kerr für eine Singstimme mit Klavierbegleitung ... Opus 66.** Ill.:– M. Fingeston. Berlin, 1921. *Numbered on Zanderbütten.* Fo. Sigs. of author & artist, some plts. slightly browned in margin & soiled, orig. hf. vell., wear, 2 faults. (D. Nov.24; 3202) DM 880
- **Salome.** Piano extract with text:– Otto Singer. Trans.:– H. Lachmann. Berlin, 1905. *1st. Edn.* Lge. 4to. Title with MS. mus. notat. & sigd., Berlin, 13.11.1907, title foxed, margin slightly soiled, hf. linen, orig. wraps. mntd. (GB. May 5; 3372) DM 1,400
- **Sechs Lieder nach Gedichten von Cl. Brentano.** Op. 68. Ill.:– F. Christophe. Berlin, [1919]. *1st. Edn. De Luxe Iss.,* (60) *numbered on H.M.P.* Lge. fo. MS. name of composer on 1st. etching, orig. hf. leath., lge. cold. ill. on upr. cover. (GB. Nov.5; 2354) DM 1,300

STRAWBERRY HILL PRESS
See— GRAY, Thomas
See— HENTZNER, Paul
See— HERBERT, Lord Edward, of Cherbury
See— LUCANUS, Marcus Annaeus
See— WALPOLE, Horace, Earl of Orford

STREET, George Edmund & Seymour, Edward
- **The Cathedral of the Holy Trinity ... Christ Church, Dublin.** 1882. Fo. Cont. vell. gt., soiled. (P. Oct.20; 203) £110

STREETER, Burnett Hillman
- **The Chained Library.** L., 1931. 4to. Orig. cl., d.-w. (BBA. Mar.7; 265) *Maggs.* £55

STREETER, Thomas Winthrop
- **Bibliography of Texas. 1795-1845.** Camb., 1955. Pt. I: 'Texas Imprints', 2 vols. Cl., d.-w. (LH. Sep.25; 290) $275
- – **Anr. Edn.** Camb., 1955-60. *1st. Edn.* (600). 3 pts. in 5 vols. Cl., light wear, d.-w.'s. (RO. Dec.11; 315) $700
- – **Anr. Copy.** 5 vols. Lge. 8vo. Cl., 1 vol. without d.-w. (SG. Sep.15; 320) $550
- **The Celebrated Collection of Americana.** N.Y., 1966-70. 8 vols., including Index. Orig. cl. (BBA. Nov.10; 38) *Blackwell.* £170
- – **Anr. Copy.** 8 vols., including Index. Sm. 4to. Ills., bds., 6 vols. with glassine d.-w. (SG. Apr.26; 191) $400
- – **Anr. Copy.** 7 vols. & Index. Tall 8vo. A Seven Gables copy, with prices & buyers written in margins, bds., worn, 1 cover detchd., others shaken. (SG. Sep.15; 321) $325
- – **Anr. Copy.** 8 vols., including Index. Vol. 1 defect., some pp. stuck together, orig. bds. (SPB. Dec.13; 470) $250
- – **Anr. Copy.** Vols. I & V-VIII only (of 8). Sm. 8vo. Bds. gt., 3 vols. in glassine d.-w. (SG. Sep.15; 322) $160

STREETON, Arthur
- **The Art of Arthur Streeton.** Sydney, 1919. (1500). Square 4to. Bds., qtr. cl., a little minor wear. (KH. Nov.9; 469) Aus. $110

STREHLOW, T.G.H.
- **Songs of Central Australia.** Sydney, 1971. Bdg. not stated, d.-w. (KH. May 1; 674) Aus. $300

STREICH, T.F. & Gerstenberg, K. von.
- **Arbeitsstätten & Werkzeuge der Wichtigsten Handwerker.** Esslingen, 1875. 4to. Slightly foxed, orig. pict. hf. linen, loose. (R. Oct.12; 2216) DM 2,500
- – **Anr. Edn.** Esslingen & Munchen, n.d. Fo. Some

soiling, orig. cl.-bkd. bds., soiled & rubbed. (CSK. Jun.15; 105) £340

STRELETZ [The Archer]
Ed.:– Alexander Belenson. Ill.:– D. & V. Burliuk, Rosanova, Annenkov, Kul'bin, Chagall, & others. Petersburg, 1915-16-22. Nos. 1-3 (compl.). 4to. Buckram-bkd. bds., unc., no. 2 largely unopened, slightly soiled & frayed, orig. wraps. bnd. in; unnumbered & inscr. to Victor Iretski. (S. Nov.21; 166) *Makiya.* £450

STRICKLAND, Agnes
- **Lives of the Queens of England.** 1844-48. 12 vols. Hf. mor. (BS. Nov.16; 70) £95
- – **Anr. Edn.** L., 1851-52. 8 vols. Cf. gt. extra by Tout, upr. cover of Vol. VI detchd. (PNY. Oct.20; 189) $175
- – **Anr. Edn.** L., 1864-66. *New Edn.* 8 vols. Sm. 8vo. Mor. & marb. bds., raised bands, gt. panels, light shelf wear, light edge wear; Charles H. Swan bkplts. (HA. May 4; 447) $180

STRICKLAND, Hugh Edwin & Melville, A.G.
- **The Dodo & its Kindred** ... Ill.:– after Savery & others. L., 1848. *1st. Edn.* 4to. Cold. litho. frontis., 17 plts. (1 cold.), orig. cl., slightly worn. (S. Apr.10; 457) *Ralph.* £190

STRICKLAND, Walter G.
- **A Dictionary of Irish Artists.** Dublin & L., 1913. *[1st. Edn.].* 2 vols. Imperial 8vo. Cl.; from liby. of Luttrellstown Castle, w.a.f. (C. Sep.28; 1722) £240
- – **Anr. Copy.** 2 vols. Royal 8vo. Bkplt., cl. (GM. Dec.7; 279) £170

STRIXNER, N.
- **Albrecht Dürers Christlich-mythologische Handzeichnungen.** Ill.:– N. Strixner after Dürer. [München, 1808]. *1st. Edn.* Title & approx. 15 plts. lightly foxed, cont. hf. leath., bumped, spine defect. (R. Oct.11; 832) DM 1,500

STROHL, H.G.
- **Heraldischer Atlas.** Stuttgart, 1899. Fo. Hf. mor. gt. (P. Nov.24; 133) *Traylen.* £55

STROMAYR, Caspar
- **Die Handschrift des Schnitt- und Augenarztes Caspar Stromayr in Lindau im Bodensee.** Ed.:– Walter von Brunn. Berlin, [1925]. *1st. Printing.* 4to. 169 col. plts., medieval-style blind-stpd. vell., light wear. (SG. Oct.6; 346) $120

STROMER VON AURBACH, Heinrich
- **Adversus Pestilentiam Observationes.** [Strassburg, 7 Sep. 1518]. Sm. 4to. Little worming in last 2 ll., qtr. vell.; Dr. Walter Pagel copy. (S. Feb.7; 357) *Goldschmidt.* £350

STRONG, Sandford Arthur
- **Reproductions of Drawings by Old Masters in the Collection of the Duke of Devonshire at Chatsworth.** L., 1902. (98) *numbered.* Fo. Mor. gt., rubbed. (S. Apr.30; 93) *Marlborough.* £90

STROUSE, Norman H.
- **The Passionate Pirate.** North Hills, Bird & Bull Pr., 1964. (200) *numbered.* Prospectus (in wraps.) laid in, qtr. mor. (SG. Jan.12; 41) $375

STROZZI, Giulio
- **La Venitia Edificata.** Ill.:– Valesio after Castillo. Venise, 1624. Fo. Sewed. (HD. Jan.27; 334) Frs. 1,700

STRUCK, Hermann
- **Die Kunst des Radierens.** Berlin, [1919]. 3 (of 5) etchings, 1 litho., lacks Liebermann & Munch ills., mod. linen. (D. Nov.23; 2064) DM 500
- – **Anr. Copy.** Sm. 4to. 6 orig. ills., name on title, hf. linen. (HK. May 17; 3165) DM 460
- – **Anr. Copy.** 6 orig. ills., many plts. & ills., orig. bds., spine with 2 tears, lr. cover scratched, ex-libris inside cover. (H. Nov.24; 2121) DM 440
- – **Anr. Edn.** Berlin, 1920. 5 orig. etchings & 1 orig. litho, orig. bds., rebkd. (BBA. Feb.9; 204) *Quaritch.* £210
- – **Anr. Copy.** 5 orig etchings & 1 orig. litho., orig. bds. (GB. May 5; 3373) DM 500
- – **Anr. Edn.** Berlin, 1923. *5th. Edn.* Lge. 8vo. 4

orig. ills., orig. pict. linen. (H. May 23; 1532) DM 540

STRUTT, Jacob George
- **Sylva Britannica; or, Portraits of Forest Trees.** L., 1826. Fo. Additional etched title, 49 etched plts., title slightly spotted, cont. hf. mor. gt., rubbed. (S. Nov.28; 90) *Wheldon & Wesley.* £520

STRUTT, Joseph
- **Angleterre Ancienne, ou Tableau des Moeurs, Usages Armes ... des Anciens Habitans de l'Angleterre.** Paris, 1789. 2 vols., including atlas. 4to. Cont. spr. leath., decor. spines, lightly bumped. (SI. Dec.15; 91) Lire 260,000
- **A Biographical Dictionary; containing ... all the Engravers from the Earliest Period ...** L., 1785-86. *1st. Edn.* 2 vols. 4to. 2 engraved frontis., 18 plts. (2 hand-cold.), hf.-titles, cont. spr. cf., faded; Sir Ivar Colquhoun, of Luss copy. (CE. Mar.22; 296) £300
- – **Anr. Copy.** 2 vols. 4to. L.P., hf.-titles, a few MS. notes, spotted, a few tears (1 reprd.), print faint on p. 162 of Vol. 2, mod. hf. cf., unc. (S. Apr.30; 148) *Agasi.* £50
- **A Complete View of the Dress & Habits of the People of England.** L., 1796-99. *1st. Edn.* 2 vols. in 1. 4to. Hand-cold. engraved frontis. to each vol., 151 plts., titles & few plts. slightly spotted, cont. red str.-grd. mor. ruled in blind. (S. Apr.9; 189) *Quaritch.* £240
- – **Anr. Copy.** 2 vols. 4to. 153 hand-cold. plts., slightly browned, cont. cf., rubbed, jnts. split. (BBA. May 23; 233) *Quaritch.* £150
- – **Anr. Edn.** L., 1842. 2 vols. 153 col. plts., hf. cf. gt. (P. Feb.16; 30) £200
- – **Anr. Copy.** 2 vols. Lge. 4to. 153 hand-cold. plts., frontis.'s with margin chipping, 1 frontis. loose, disbnd. (SG. Aug.25; 362) $150
- **Glig-Gamena Angel-Deod, or Sports and Pastimes of the People of England.** Ca. 1785. 4to. Engraved frontis., 39 plts., all hand-cold., cont. russ., worn, covers detchd. (BBA. Feb.9; 244) *Vitale.* £55
- – **Anr. Edn.** L., 1810. *2nd. Edn.* 4to. 40 hand-cold. plts., cf., scuffed. (P. Nov.24; 130) *Walford.* £75
- **Horda Angel-Cynnann.** L., 1774-76. *1st. Edn.* 3 vols. 4to. 157 copper engrs., later three-qtr. mor., gt.-decor. ribbed spines. (CBA. Dec.10; 94) $275
- **The Regal & Ecclesiastical Antiquities of England.** L., 1777. *1st. Edn.* 4to. 60 engraved plts., cont. cf., spine gt. (S. Apr.9; 188) *Scott.* £50

STRUVE, Burcard Gotthelf
- **Bibliotheca Historica.** Ed.:– C.G. Buderus & J.G. Meuselius. Leipzig, 1782-95. Vols. 1-8 (of 11). Cont. leath. gt., rubbed. (R. Apr.3; 1045) DM 950
- **Corpvs Historiae Germanicae a Prima Gentis Origine ad Annvm vsque MDCCXXX ... Praemittitvr Chr. G. Bvderi Bibliotheca Scriptorvm Rervm Germanicarvm.** Jena, 1730. *1st. Edn.* 2 pts. in 1 vol. Sm. fo. Mispagination, some light browning or foxing, 1 lf. with corner tear, some cont. annots. on end-paper & in text, cont. vell., lightly spotted. (HT. May 10; 2566) DM 400
- **Introductio in Notitiam Rei Litterariae et Usum Bibliothecarum.** Frankfurt & Leipzig, 1754. Cont. vell. (BBA. Mar.7; 266) *Quaritch.* £200

STRUVE, G.A.
- **Juris-Prudenz.** Merseburg, 1689. *1st. Edn.* Some brief old marginalia, cont. vell. (R. Oct.11; 1291) DM 480

STRUYS, J.J.
- **Sehr Schwere, Wiederwetige und Denckwürdige Reysen durch Italien, Griechenland, Lifland ... Ost-Indien, Japan und Unterschiedliche Andere Länder.** Amst., 1678. Fo. 19 double-p. views (1 torn), double-p. map of Caspian Sea, a few stains, tears affecting title & dedication lf. (including loss of corner from title with letters), sm. liby. stp. at foot of title, cf., arms of Maria Elizabeth Stenbock on covers. (S. May 21; 170) *Crete.* £520

STRYIENSKI, C.
- **Mesdames de France, Filles de Louis XV.** Paris, 1910. 4to. On vélin d'Arches, numbered, red mor. gt. by Durvand, arms, fleurs-de-lys on spine, unc., wrap. (HD. May 21; 151) Frs. 3,600

STRZELECKI, Paul Edmund de
- **Physical Description of New South Wales & Van Diemens Land.** 1845. *1st. Edn.* Hand-cold. folding map, 22 litho. plts., 32pp. publishers advts., orig. cl., faded, rebkd., old spine preserved. (CSK. Sep.30; 77) £260
- – **Anr. Copy.** Early cf., slightly rubbed. (KH. May 1; 221) Aus.$620
- – **Anr. Copy.** Folding map with long reprd. tear & a few margin defects, slight minor foxing, cl., unc., faded & slightly rubbed. (KH. May 1; 220) Aus.$320

STUART, Alexander
- **Dissertatio de Structura et Motu Musculari.** 1738. 4to. 1 plt. partly hand-cold., cont. cf. (C. May 30; 125) *Pickering.* £160

STUART, Gilbert
- **A View of Society in Europe, in its progress from rudeness to refinement.** Edinb., 1778. *1st. Edn.* 4to. Hf.-title, lf. of corrections, cont. cf., gt.-decor. spine, slightly rubbed; Sir Ivar Colquhoun, of Luss copy. (CE. Mar.22; 297) £280

STUART, James & Revett, Nicholas
- **Les Antiquités d'Athènes.** Trans.:– L.F. F[euillet]. Paris, 1808-22. 4 vols. 2 titles with engraved port., 191 engraved views, charts & plans, some double-p., hf.-titles, sm. owner's stp. at head of titles & lr. margins of final plts. (*With:*) – **Les Antiquités Inédités de l'Attique.** Trans.:– J.J. Hittorff. Paris, 1832. 1 vol. 60 engraved plts., hf.-title. Together 5 vols. Fo. Cont. bds., unc., sm. hole in lr. cover of Vol. 1, Vol. 5 lacks backstrip. (C. Mar.14; 92) *Martinos.* £600
- – **Anr. Edn.** Paris, 1822? *Reprint?* Plt. vol. only. Fo. 242 full-p. engraved views, maps & diagrams, including 7 folding, some foxing, old hf. leath., worn, rehinged. (SG. Oct.13; 337) $300
- **The Antiquities of Athens.** L., 1762-87. Vols. 1 & 2 only (of 5). Lge. fo. Vig. titles, engraved frontis., port. in Vol. 2, 148 engraved plts., including 4 double-p., few plts. spotted, cont. cf., reprd., spines worn. (C. Dec.9; 195) *Dupont.* £300
- – **Anr. Edn.** L., 1762-87-94-1816-30. 5 vols., including Supp. Fo. Plts. stpd. on versos, perforation stps. in titles, disbnd., ex-liby. (RO. Dec.11; 316) $900
- – **Anr. Edn.** Ed.:– William Kinnard. L., 1825-27-30. *Vols. 1-3: 2nd. Edn., Supp. Vol.: 1st. Edn.* 3 vols. & Supp. vol., in 2 vols. Lge. fo. 2 engraved ports., vig. titles, 191 engraved plts., hf.-titles, errata lf. in Vol. 3, 3 p. subscribers list in Vol. 4, a few plts. foxed, mainly at beginning & end of the 2 vols., later gt.-ruled hf. mor. & marb. cl., partly unc.; pencil note on front pastedown indentifying this as the Lord Portman set. (SG. Jan.26; 291) $1,100

STUART, John, LL.D.
- **Sculptured Stones of Scotland.** Aberdeen, 1856, Edinb., 1867. 2 vols. 4to. Rebkd. cf., s.-c. (PD. Dec.14; 102) £100

STUART, John McDouall
- **Explorations Across the Continent of Australia** ... Melbourne, 1863. Spotting, slight wear & staining, tear in folding map, stiff ptd. wraps. (KH. May 1; 676) Aus. $350
- – **Anr. Copy.** Margin of title age-stained, some light foxing, orig. cl.-bkd. bds. (CA. Apr.3; 108) Aus. $320
- **Explorations in Australia, the Journals of John McDouall Stuart During the Years 1858, 1859, 1860, 1861, & 1862.** Ed.:– William Hardman. Ill.:– George Angas. L., 1864. *1st. Edn.* Hf.-title, engraved map, mntd. sepia photographic frontis. port., 12 engraved plts., mod. cf.-bkd. bds.; tipped-in is folding engraved linen-bkd. map of Stuart's discoveries, from 2nd. Edn. (C. Jun.27; 101) *Traylen.* £200
- – **Anr. Copy.** Minor spotting, cont. cf., rebkd. (TA. Aug.18; 53) £170
- **Mr. Stuart's Exploration in South Australia.** Melbourne, 1858. Sm. fo. Lge. folding map with slight margin defects, mod. bds. (KH. May 1; 677) Aus. $260

STUART, John Sobieski Stolberg & Charles Edward [i.e. John Carter & Charles Manning Allen, afterwards John Hay & Charles Stuart Hay Allan]
- **The Costume of the Clans.** Edinb., 1845. 2 vols. Fo. 36 plts., 1 cut round & mntd., spotted, stained in lr. margins, mor. (S. Apr.10; 379) *Schuster.* £60
- – **Anr. Edn.** Edinb., 1892. Atlas fo. Ptd. & illuminated titles, cold. frontis., 36 plts., most tinted lithos., ex-liby., cl., red mor. back & tips, loose. (SG. May 3; 120) $175

STUART, Martinus
- **De Mensch zoo als hij Voorkomt op den bekenden Aardbol.** Ill.:– Portman after J. Kuyper. Amst., 1802-07. 6 vols. Frontis. in Vol. 1, engraved titles with cold. pict. vig., engraved folding plt., 41 cold. plts., orig. paper bds., spines defect. & stitching partly brkn. (C. Mar.14; 94) *Blackwell.* £220
- – **Anr. Copy.** 6 vols. Hand-cold. frontis., titles & 41 plts., 2 folding uncold. plts., lacks final lf. (plt.-list) from Vol. 1, some light spotting, cont. hf. cf., worn, w.a.f. (CSK. Oct.21; 66) £170
- – **Anr. Edn.** Ill.:– Portman after Jacques Kuyper. Amst., 1805, Zalt-Bommel, 1818. *Vol. V: 1st. Edn., rest: Zalt-Bommel Edn.* 6 vols. 6 engraved titles with cold. vigs., 41 cold. stipple-engraved plts., 1 folding plt., cont. hf. sheep or cf. or bds., unc. & largely unopened, rebkd. (SG. Sep.22; 281) $300

STUART-WORTLEY, Col. H.
- **Tahiti: A Series of Photographs.** L., 1882. 4to. Bkplt., gt.-pict. cl. (SG. Nov.10; 153) $300

STUBBE, Henry
- **Horae subecivae: seu Prophetiae Jonae et Historiae Susannae.** L., 1651. Old marb. wraps., pasted to A1r (blank but for sig. in decor. frame) & D4v (blank), spine bit worn. [Wing S6047] (BBA. Oct.27; 14) *Sanders.* £50

STUBBS, George
- **The Anatomy of the Horse.** L., 1853. Fo. 24 double-p. plts., disbnd. (P. May 17; 27a) *Saunders.* £140

STUDER, G.
- **Berg- und Gletscher-Fahrten.** Zürich, 1859. Bds. (G. Sep.15; 2463) Sw.Frs. 460

STUDER, Jacob H.
- **The Birds of North America.** N.Y., 1888. Lge. 4to. Port., 119 chromolitho. plts., orig. leath., needs rebdg., ex-liby., unstpd. (SG. Mar.22; 295) $250
- – **Anr. Copy.** 4to. 119 chromolitho. plts., front free end-paper & fly-lf. detchd., gt.-decor. buckram, covers soiled & stained, spine with remnants of mor. labels. (CBA. Dec.10; 340) $170

STUDIA IMPRESSIONISTOV [The Studio of the Impressionists]
Contribs.:– D. & N. Burliuk, V. Khlebnikov, N. Kul'bin, & others. Ill.:– Kul'bin, Vaschenko, & Shmit-Ryzhova. Petersburg, 1910. *1st. Edn.* 4to. Orig. wraps., cover designs by Shmit-Ryzhova, frayed, repair at foot of upr. cover. (S. Nov.21; 165) *Davies.* £80

STUDIO: An Illustrated Magazine of Fine & Applied Art
Ill.:– after Beardsley, Crane, Forbes, & others. L., 1894. Vol. 4. 4to. Some light foxing, orig. gt.-decor. cl., rubbing & fading to covers. (CBA. Jan.29; 428) $120
- – **Anr. Run.** 1894-1915. Vols. 3-11, 14, 17-29, 31-47 & 49-63. Fo. 14 vols. in hf. mor., rest in cl. (SSA. Jul.5; 383) R 300
- – **Anr. Run.** Ill.:– Bonnard, Burne-Jones, Crane, Fischer, & others. L., 1897. Vol. 9. 4to. Orig. gt.-decor. cl., rubbing & fading, end-papers darkened, some light foxing. (CBA. Jan.29; 430) $110
- **The Year Book of Decorative Art.** 1902-26. 15 vols. only. 4to. Orig. cl. & wraps. (P. Feb.16; 110) £200
- – **Anr. Run.** 1906-21. 15 vols. only (lacks 1911). 4to. Cl. or orig. paper wraps. (PD. Feb.15; 221) £75
- – **Anr. Run.** L., 1906-30. Vols. 1-25. Sm. fo. Orig. cl., ex-liby. (B. Oct.4; 586) Fls. 1,300

STUDY, E.
- **Geometrie der Dynamen.** Leipzig, 1903. *1st. Edn.* Cont. private hf. leath. (HT. May 8; 405) DM 420

STUKELEY, William
- **The Medallic History of Marcus Aurelius Valerius Carausius.** L., 1757. 2 vols. in 1. 4to. Some slight browning & spotting, later pol. panel. cf. (S. May 1; 500) *Spink.* £110
- **Stonehenge. A Temple Restor'd to the British Druids.** 1740. *1st. Edn.* Engraved frontis. port., 35 engraved plts. (9 folding), index, spotting to most plts. (*Bound with:*) – **Abury, A Temple of the British Druids.** 1743. *1st. Edn.* 40 engraved plts. (4 folding), margin spotting to most plts. Together 2 works in 1 vol. Fo. Hf. mor., spine gt., worn, lacks some marb. paper. (LC. Mar.1; 238) £210

STUMPF, Johan
- **Gemeiner Loblicher Eydgnoschafft** ... Zürich, 1548. *1st. Edn. 1st. Printing.* Vol. II only. Lge. fo. Cont. stpd. pig over wood bds., decor., initials 'S.N.' & 'Z.L.', dtd. 1562, clasps incompl.; from Fondation Furstenberg-Beaumesnil. (HD. Nov.16; 173) Frs. 7,800

STURGE, J. & Harvey, T.
- **The West Indies in 1837.** L., 1838. *1st. Edn.* Spotted, orig. cl., spotted. (S. Apr.9; 61) *Bishop.* £80

STURGEON, William
- **Scientific Researches.** 1850. Orig. cl., slightly bumped. (CSK. May 18; 181) £90

STURM, Der
Ed.:– Herwarth Walden. Ill.:– Bauer, Molzahn, Heermakerck, Herzog, Topp, & others, after Chagall, Kandinsky, Klee, etc. Berlin, 1919-20. 12 iss. in 1 vol. Sm. fo. Cl., orig. wraps. bnd. in. (S. Nov.21; 118) *Terech.* £60

STURM, A.
- **Taschen–Globus.** Ill.:– J. Tritschler. Wien, ca. 1820. Globus & text pt. Text pt. slightly foxed, orig. pict. bd. s.-c. (R. Oct.13; 2842) DM 500

STURM, Jacob
- **Flora von Deutschland in Abbildungen nach der Natur.** Ed.:– K.G. Lutz. Stuttgart, 1900-07. 15 vols. Orig. linen, 3 vols. slightly different. (BR. Apr.12; 824) DM 500

STURM, Joh. Chr.
- **Collegium Experimentale, sive Curiosa in quo Primaria Seculi Superioris Inventa et Experimenta Physico-Mathematica ... exhibita.** Nürnberg, 1701-15. *2nd. Edn.* 2 pts. & 2 supps. in 1 vol. 4to. Title with owners mark, lacks last lf. blank, little spotting, 19th. C. hf. leath., upr. cover & spine loose, worn. (H. May 22; 212) DM 950

STURM, L.C.
- **Durch einen Grossen Teil von Teutschland und den Niederlanden biss nach Paris gemachte Architectonische Reise-Annmerckungen.** Augsburg, 1719. Fo. Cont. style mod. hf. leath. (R. Apr.3; 700) DM 1,200
- – **Anr. Copy.** Fo. Slightly foxed & soiled or stained, later hf. leath. (D. Nov.23; 1926) DM 510
- [–] **Volstandige Anweisung aller Arten von Bürgerlichen Wohn-Häusern wohl anzugeben.** Augsburg, 1721. Fo. Cont. bds. (R. Oct.11; 795) DM 800
- **Vollstandige Mühlen Baukunst.** Augsburg, 1718. Fo. Title slightly spotted, old stp. erased, cont. hf. vell., rubbed & slightly spotted. (R. Apr.4; 1624) DM 1,350

STURT, Capt. Charles
- **Narrative of an Expedition into Central Australia, Performed under the Authority of Her Majesty's Government during the Years 1844-6, together with a Notice of the Province of South Australia, in 1847.** L., 1849. *1st. Edn.* 2 vols. Some minor spotting, later hf. cf., gt.-decor. spines, a little rubbed. (TA. Mar.15; 10) £540
- – **Anr. Copy.** 2 vols. Publisher's advts. bnd. in at rear of each, orig. blind-stpd. cl. gt., unc., worn on spines. (TA. Mar.15; 9) £520

STURT, Capt. Charles *-Contd.*

-- **Anr. Copy.** 2 vols. Folding map, 16 plts. (4 cold.), some minor foxing, cont. cf. (S. May 22; 489) *Hammond.* £445
-- **Anr. Copy.** 2 vols. Folding engraved map, 16 plts., some cold., some tinted, publisher's advts. at end & 2 inserted advt. slips, a few plts. slightly spotted, orig. blind-stpd. cl., recased; Geoffrey C. Ingleton bkplt. (C. Jun.27; 102) *Traylen.* £350
-- **Anr. Copy.** 2 vols. With advt. ll. not mentioned by Ferguson, 1 tipped in advt. slip (varying as usual from his description), bdg. not stated, unc. & largely unopened, a few spots. (KH. May 1; 678) Aus. $980
-- **Anr. Copy.** 2 vols. 1 folding map, 16 plts., titles lightly foxed, some sections loosening, orig. blind-stpd. cl., unc., spines chipped. (CA. Apr.3; 110) Aus. $580
-- **Anr. Edn.** Adelaide, 1965. *Facs. Edn.* 2 vols., with map folder. Orig. cl. (KH. Nov.9; 470) Aus. $160
- **Two Expeditions into the Interior of Southern Australia.** L., 1833. *1st. Edn.* 2 vols. Hf.-titles, 2 engraved maps (1 folding & laid on linen), 13 plts. (4 cold.), cont. cf., slightly rubbed. (S. May 22; 490) *Hammond.* £420
-- **Anr. Copy.** 2 vols. Uncold. folding engraved map, single-p. chart, 14 litho. plts., some cold., publisher's advts. bnd. in at rear of Vol. 2, some minor spotting, orig. cl., unc., backstrips deficient. (TA. Mar.15; 7) £400
-- **Anr. Copy.** 2 vols. Folding map, chart, 13 engraved plts. (4 hand-cold.), tears in fold of map, old cf. gt., rebkd. (CA. Apr.3; 134) Aus. $600
-- **Anr. Edn.** 1834. *2nd. Edn.* 2 vols. Partly cold. folding map, single-p. uncold. chart, 14 litho. plts., some cold., later hf. cf. gt.; inscr. by author to Mr. Hammersley. (TA. Mar.15; 8) £560
-- **Anr. Copy.** 2 vols. A few sm. marks, early hf. cf., slightly rubbed. (KH. May 1; 680) Aus. $800
-- **Anr. Copy.** 2 vols. Folding map loosely inserted, 1 plt. frayed in margin & lacking sm. corner portion, bdg. not stated, unc., 1st. vol. with lr. cover stained & end-papers discold., 2nd. vol. recased & with sm. repairs. (KH. May 1; 679) Aus. $500

STUTZ, A.
- **Mineralogisches Taschenbuch. Enthaltend eine Oryctographie von Unterösterreich zum Gebrauche Reisender Mineralogen.** Ed.:- J.G. Megerle v. Mühlfeld. Wien, 1807. *1st. Edn.* 12mo. Slightly foxed thro.-out, cont. hf. leath., slightly rubbed. (HT. May 8; 250) DM 460

STYL. Blätter für Mode u. die Angenehmen Dinge d. Lebens.
Ed.:- L. Sternaux. Contribs.:- Fr. Blei, M. v. Boehn, K. Edelschmid, & others. Berlin, 1922. Year I pts. 2-10, in 6 pts. Lge. 4to. Pt. 3 lacks plt. 2, pts. 5/6 lack plt. 7, many cold. supps., loose in orig. wraps., some slightly crumpled. (HK. Nov.11; 4006) DM 520
-- **Anr. Run.** Ed.:- R.L. Leonard & L. Sternaux. Berlin, 1922-24. Years. I-III in 17 pts. (all publd.). Sm. 4to. & 4to. Orig. wraps. in orig. box, spine faded, slightly bumped. (H. Nov.24; 2126) DM 5,600

SUARES, André
- **Hélène chez Archimède.** Ill.:- Pablo Picasso, engraved by Georges Aubert. Paris, 1955. *(240) on vélin de Rives.* Fo. 2 compl. extra suites of plts. on blue & cream vell., wrap., box. (HD. Mar.27; 112) Frs. 1,800
- **Le Livre de l'Eméraude.** Ill.:- A. Brouet. Paris, 1927. *(40) on japon impérial with state with remark & definitive state of etchings.* 4to. Sewed, box. (HD. Jun.13; 126) Frs. 2,800

SUCHET, Louis Gabriel
- **Mémoires.** 1828. Atlas only. Fo. 1 view, 15 maps & plans, qtr. roan, rubbed. (P. Dec.8; 302) *Maddock.* £180
-- **Anr. Copy.** Atlas only. Fo. 1 view, 15 maps & plans, qtr. roan, rubbed, as a coll. of plts., w.a.f. (P. Jul.26; 101) £160

SUCKLING, Sir John
- **Fragmenta Aurea.** L., 1646. *1st. Edn.* Variant with 1st. line of title in even Roman capitals & with line below date, engraved frontis. port. inserted, few headline numerals & catchwords shaved, sm. hole in C1, minor worming on last 44 ll., few ll. browned, cont. blind-tooled sheep., spine reprd., sm. patch to leath. on lr. cover, some slight wear & repair to covers. [Wing S6126] (CNY. Dec.17; 607) $360
-- **Anr. Copy.** With 1st. line of title in upr. & lr. case & without line under date, engraved port., lacks blank A1, marginal tear on C1 'Aglaura', sm. inkmarks, slight offsetting & discoloration, cont. cf., reprd.; Stockhausen copy with sigs. of Alice & Thomas Coke with note laid in. (SPB. May 16; 151) $300

SUDEK, Josef
- **Fotografie.** Text:- Lubomira Linharta. Prague, 1956. *1st. Edn.* Lge. 8vo. 232 gravure plts., linen, d.-w. lightly rubbed & chipped. (SG. May 10; 140) $325
- **Janacek-Hukvaldy.** Preface:- Jaroslav Seda. Prague, [1971]. *1st. Edn.* 4to. Ills. captioned in 3 languages, gt.-lettered cl., outer corners bumped, d.-w. chipped. (SG. Nov.10; 155) $100

SUDERMANN, D.
- **Hohe Geistreiche Lehren, vnd Erklärungen.** Franckfurt, 1622. *1st. Edn.* Fo. Title lf. with typographic border, slightly browned & foxed, last lf. with sm. repair, new hf. vell. (H. May 22; 901) DM 3,400

SUDHOFF, Karl
- **Beiträge zur Geschichte der Chirurgie im Mittelalter.** Leipzig, 1914. Lge. 8vo. 94 plts., bds., cl. spine; Dr. Walter Pagel copy. (S. Feb.7; 356) *Quaritch.* £120

SUE, Eugène
- **Die Geheimnisse von Paris.** Trans.:- A. Diezmann. Ill.:- Hosemann. Berlin, 1843. *1st. German Edn.* 8 pts. & Supp. in 4 vols. Some slight foxing, 8 repeated wrap. ills., pt. 5 with sm. tear, cont. linen gt., lightly spotted. (GB. May 4; 1338) DM 650
-- **Anr. Copy.** 8 pts. & Supp. in 4 vols. Vols. 3 & 4 hf.-title with sm. tear, some foxing, cont. linen gt. (HK. Nov.10; 2737) DM 460
- **Histoire de la Marine Française.** Paris, 1855-57. 5 vols. Lge. 8vo. Some slight foxing, cont. decor. hf. chagrin. (LM. Mar.3; 184) B.Frs. 8,500
- **Le Juif Errant.** Ill.:- Gavarni. Paris, 1845. *1st. printing of ills.* 4 vols. Lge. 8vo. Old red bradel hf. mor., spines decor., wraps. preserved, sm. repairs to Vol. I & IV wraps. (HD. May 4; 432) Frs. 1,050

SUEDERICUS, J.
- **Collectaniolum de Religiosorum Origine.** [Dresden], 1525. 4to. Lightly browned thro.-out, sm. wormhole in lr. right margin thro.-out. later paper wraps. (HT. May 8; 214) DM 600

SUETONIUS TRANQUILLUS, Gaius
- **De La Vie des XII Cesars.** Trans.:- Georges de la Boutière. Lyon, 1556. 4to. Lacks last lf. blank with printers mark on verso, mor., by Hardy Menil, decor. spine, gt. centre motif. (HD. Jan.27; 335) Frs. 1,750
- **De Vita XII Caesarum.** Commentary:- Antonius Sabellicus. Venice, Damianus de Mediolano, 29 Mar. 1493. Fo. Foxing, stp. cut away in margin of last lf., vell., spine renewed in 18th. C.; from Fondation Furstenberg-Beaumesnil. [HC 15124; BMC V, 543; Goff S824] (HD. Nov.16; 73) Frs. 4,000
-- **Anr. Edn.** Venice, 1510. Old mott. cf. gt., slightly worn. (SG. Apr.19; 177) $300
- **Vitae XII Caesarum.** [Venice], Nicolaus Jenson. 1471. *3rd. Edn.* 4to. Lge. copy, spaces for Greek words, old marginalia & annots. very faded, a few minor margin paper losses & careful repairs, vell.; John Scott, of Halkshill bkplt. [BMC V, 170; Goff S-817; H. 15117] (SPB. Dec.14; 33) $2,500
- **The Lives of the XII Caesars.** 1717. 2 vols. Cont. gt.-panel. red mor. (TA. Dec.15; 463) £50
- **[Opera].** Utrecht, 1672. 2 pts. in 1 vol. 4to. Cont. Dutch vell., lacks ties; John Locke copy. (BBA. Nov.30; 53) *Pickering & Chatto.* £500
-- **Anr. Edn.** Commentary:- Samuel Pitisci. Leovardiae, 1714-15. 2 vols. 4to. Vell. (LH. Jan.15; 397) $120
-- **Anr. Copy.** 2 vols. 4to. Vell. (LH. Sep.25; 603) $110
- **Suetonius cum Commento.** Commentary:- Antonius Sabellicus. [Venice, Baptista de Tortis, 15 Feb. 1490]. *1st. Edn. of Commentary.* Sm. fo. Mispaginated, lacks colophon lf. & following blank, dampstains, 19th. C. hf. chagrin. (HD. Nov.9; 12b) Frs. 2,500
- **XII Caesares; Eutropius, De Gestis Romanorum [& other works].** Venice, May 1521. Margin annots. & underlinings, title-p. & anr. reprd. without loss of text, later vell. (BBA. Nov.30; 19) *Thomas.* £50

SUETONIUS TRANQUILLUS, Gaius & the Scriptores Historiae Augustae
- **Omnia quam Antehae e Emendatiora.** Ed.:- Erasmus & Egnatius. Basle, Jul. 1533. Fo. Last gathering reprd. at inner margin, a few fore-margins lightly stained, cont. Basle blind-stpd. pig over wood bds., title in gt. on upr. cover, clasps, blue painted edges by Cesare Vecellio, with medallion ports. of 12 Caesars; the Bonaccorso Grino, Giovanni Grino, Odorico Pillone copy. (S. May 10; 411) *Thomas.* £1,800

SUGDEN, Nan V. & Edmondson, John L.
- **A History of English Wallpaper 1509-1914.** L.,[1925]. 4to. Orig. buckram gt., slightly rubbed & faded. (S. Dec.13; 478) *Traylen.* £160
-- **Anr. Copy.** 4to. Orig. cl. gt., slightly dampstained. (P. Nov.24; 213) *Potterton.* £140

SUHR, Chr.
- **Der Ausruf in Hamburg.** Hamburg, 1808. *1st. Edn.* With plt. 46, minimal plt. foxing, cont. leath., gold-tooled cover decor., gt. spine, sm. tear. (D. Nov.23, 1693) DM 14,000
-- **Anr. Copy.** Engraved title, 119 cold. aquatint etchings, 1 cold. litho., pagination jumps from 50 to 57, later red hf. leath., romantic gt. spine, cover loose & slightly bumped; Hauswedell coll. (H. May 23; 22) DM 8,600
- **Hamburgische Trachten.** Berlin, 1908. *Facs. of Hamburg 1838 Edn. (15) De Luxe Edn. on Japan.* Fo. 50 cold. plts., orig. hf. leath., spine faded, slightly rubbed; Hauswedell coll. (H. May 24; 794) DM 500

SUHR, P. & Chr.
- **Ansichten von Hamburg und der Umgebend.** Hamburg, ca. 1835. Ob. 4to. 47 (of 50?) litho. views, litho title of 2nd. pt. as title-lf., cont. leath. gt., bumped & worn. (R. Oct.12; 2606) DM 4,700

SUIDAS
- **Lexicon.** Ed.:- Demetrius Chalcondylas. Milan, Joannes Bissolus & Benedictus Mangius for Demetrius Chalcondylas, 15 Nov. 1499. *1st. Edn.* Fo. 3A8 & A1 slightly defect. with missing text supplied from anr. edn. (pasted on), most top margins stained, a few early marginalia, 18th. C. mor. gt. [Goff S829] (S. Nov.17; 69) *Harper.* £1,450

SULLIVAN, Edward
- **Rambles & Scrambles in North & South America.** L., 1852. Title-p. foxed, orig. embossed cl. gt., chipped. (LH. Jan.15; 398) $100

SULLIVAN, Louis H.
- **A System of Architectural Ornament.** N.Y., 1924. No bdg. stated, edges rubbed, stained cover. (RS. Jan.17; 501) $140

SULLY, Maxmilien de Bethune, duc de
- **Mémoires des Sages et Royales Oeconomies d'estat, domestiques, politiques et Militaires de Henry le Grand.** Amst., [1638]. *1st. Edn.* 2 vols. Fo. Vol. 1 with some slight worm traces, last 30 ll. near end increasingly slightly stained, cont. vell. (R. Apr.3; 245) DM 3,200
-- **Anr. Edn.** L., 1767. *Reprint of 1747 Edn.* 8 vols. 12mo. Cont. marb. cf., spines decor., some turn-ins reprd. (HD. Jun.6; 144) Frs. 1,600
- **Memoirs** ... L., 1763. *4th. Edn.* 6 vols. 12mo. Cont. cf., chipped; letter from Public Library of Victoria concerning this edn. loosely inserted. (KH. Nov.9; 472) Aus.$110

SULPICIUS SEVERUS
- **Historiae Sacrea a Mundi Exordio.** Cologne, 1573. *Bound with:)* **HAYMO, Bp. of Halberstadt**

- Historiae Sacrae Epitome. Cologne, 1573. Together 2 works in 1 vol. Cont. Fr. red mor., bnd. for J.A. de Thou, bachelor arms of de Thou in gt. on sides, spine gt. with IADT monog., de Thou press-mark on upr. cover & paste-down. (C. May 30; 47) *Lyon.* £400

SULZER, Johann Georg
- Allgemeine Theorie der Schönen Künste. 1777. 2 vols. in 4. Preface misbnd. in vol. 1, title, spine & upr. cover with liby. label, cont. marb. bds. (BR. Apr.12; 1539) DM 500

SULZER, Johann Heinrich
- Die Kennzeichen der Insekten nach Karl Linnaeus. Preface:– Johannes Gessner. Ill.:– J.R. Schellenburg. Zürich, 1761. *1st. Edn.* Sm. 4to. Slight foxing in places, title with faded cont. name, cont. hf. vell., slightly rubbed, spine with slight slits. (GB. Nov.3; 1166) DM 4,500
- – Anr. Copy. Sm. 4to. Wide margin, some staining in lr. part, some light text foxing, 2 plts. slightly browned, cont. hf. leath. gt., slightly worn, spine slightly wormed & with 2 sm. defects reprd. (HK. May 15; 392) DM 2,200

SUMMERS, Rev. Montague (Trans.)
See– MALEUS MALEFICARUM

SUMMERSON, John
See– SKELTON, Raleigh Ashlin & Summerson, John

SUMNER, Heywood
- The Ancient Earthworks of Cranborne Chase. Ill.:– Emery Walker (reproduction of plans). Chiswick Pr., 1913. *(200) numbered & sigd. by author, with the map hand-cold.* 4to. Orig. decor. cl., untrimmed, d.-w. (SKC. Sep.9; 2060) £100

SUMNER, Thomas H.
- A New & Accurate Method for Finding a Ship's Position at Sea ... Boston, 1857. *4th. Edn.* Frontis., 5 folding plts. (apparently compl.), cl. gt. (PNY. Mar.27; 176) $100

SUMOWSKI, Werner
- Drawings of the Rembrandt School. Trans.:– Walter L. Strauss. N.Y., [1979-81]. 5 vols. Tall 4to. Cl. (SG. Jan.26; 274) $225

SUPERVIELLE, Jules
- La Fable du Monde. Ill.:– Jean Lurcat. Lausanne, 1959. *(190) numbered & sigd. by artist & publisher.* Fo. The 5 double-p. col. lithos. with further hand-colouring by artist, unsewn in orig. decor. wraps., folder & s.-c., the latter defect. (S. Nov.21; 91) *Makiya.* £180

SUPREME COURT OF THE UNITED STATES
- Proceedings of the Bar & Officers of ... in Memory of Benjamin Nathan Cardozo, November 26, 1938. Wash., 1938. Sm. 4to. Wraps.; laid in is a sigd. studio photographic port. of Cardozo. (SG. Feb.2; 37) $250

SURIUS, Laur.
- Kurtze Chronick od. Beschreibung d. Vornembsten Händeln u. Geschichten, so sich beide in Religions u. Weltlichen Sachen ... zugetragen ... Trans.:– H. Fabricius Aquensem. Köln, 1568. *1st. German Edn.* Fo. Printer's mark cold. in, title stpd., sm. excision in upr. margin, 1st. 4 ll. supplied in neat cont. hand, slightly foxed & some staining, lacks lr. end-paper, cont. blind-tooled pig over wood bds., 2 clasps. (HK. Nov.8; 352) DM 800

SURIUS, Père B.
- Le Pieux Pélerin ou Voyage de Jérusalem ... Bruxelles, 1666. *Orig. Edn.* 4to. Cont. vell. (HD. May 21; 70) Frs. 3,000

SURTEES, Robert, Antiquary
- The History & Antiquities of the County Palatine of Durham. L., 1816-40. 4 vols. Fo. 82 engraved plts., hf. mor. gt. (P. May 17; 166) *Georges.* £260
- – Anr. Copy. 1816-40. 6 pts. in 4 vols., including Taylor's Memoir. Fo. 83 engraved plts. (only 81 called for), some faint spotting, few light pencilled margin annots., cont. cf. gt., spines worn. (S. Nov.1; 130) *Turton.* £115
- – Anr. Edn. 1972. *Facs. of 1816-40 Edn.* 4 vols. Fo. Orig. cl., d.-w.'s. (TA. Nov.17; 183) £70

SURTEES, Robert Smith
- [–] The Analysis of the Hunting Field. Ill.:– Henry Alken. L., 1846. *1st. Edn. 1st. Iss., with single-p. preface dtd. Oct. 1846.* Plts. hand-cold., sm. blank corner of plt. 1 renewed, some staining to plts. & text, str.-grd. mor. gt., orig. cl. covers & spine preserved at end. (CNY. May 18; 154) $150
- [–] – Anr. Iss. L., 1846. *1st. Edn. 2nd. Iss.* Cont. cf. gt., panel. spine. (P. Dec.8; 236a) *Jarndyce.* £160
- [–] – Anr. Edn. Ill.:– Henry Alken. L., 1846. *1st. Edn.* Ill.:– H. Alken. 2 ll. of advts. at end, a few sm. tears reprd., red hf. mor. by Bayntun (Riviere). (S. Dec.13; 317) *Traylen.* £220
- [–] – Anr. Copy. Hand-cold. title, 6 plts., 5 lightly browned, hf. mor. gt. (P. Dec.8; 227) *Head.* £190
- – Anr. Edn. Ill.:– H. Alken. L., 1903. *(500).* Title, 12 plts., hand-cold., red mor. gt. by Bayntun (Riviere), cold. pict. onlay of hunters & hounds on upr. cover. (S. Oct.4; 104) *Head.* £210
- – Anr. Copy. Orig. gt.-decor. cl. (SKC. May 4; 1767) £50
- [–] Handley Cross: or Mr. Jorrock's Hunt. Ill.:– John Leech. L., 1854. 17 hand-cold. engrs., three-qtr. leath. gt. (DM. May 21; 26) $225
- [–] Jorrock's Jaunts & Jollities. Ill.:– Henry Alken. L., 1843. *2nd. Edn.* Ptd. & hand-cold. engraved title-pp., 14 hand-cold. engraved plts., later hf. mor., marb. bds., by Grieve; armorial bkplts. of Charles F.S. Chambers & Herbert R. Pyne, & A.N.s. by Chambers & mntd. portion of orig. cl. spine on front blank. (SG. Apr.26; 192) $500
- [–] – Anr. Edn. Ill.:– Henry Alken. L., [1869]. *New Edn.* Additional title & plts. hand-cold., some slight spotting, mostly marginal, later red hf. mor. (S. Oct.4; 289) *Old Hall.* £50
- [–] – Anr. Edn. Ill.:– H. Alken. L., 1874. *4th. Edn.* Litho. title, 15 plts., hand-cold., red str.-grd. mor. gt. (S. Oct.4; 103) *Chelsea.* £140
- Mr. Facey Romford's Hounds. Ill.:– John Leech & H.K. Browne. L., n.d. Gt.-embossed leath. (DM. May 21; 25) $140
- [Sporting Novels]. Ill.:– after John Leech & H.K. Browne. L., ca. 1865 & 1870. 4 vols. 'Plain or Ringlets' lacks frontis., plt. 1 bnd. in as frontis., cont. hf. leath. gt., slightly worn & bumped. (HK. Nov.10; 2738) DM 400
- [–] [–] Anr. Edn. Priv. ptd., ca. 1870. 6 vols. Plts. hand-cold., unif. hf. cf. gt. by Bayntun, partly untrimmed. (TA. Aug.18; 26) £125
- [–] [–] Anr. Edn. Ca. 1880-90. 4 vols. Unif. hf. cf. gt. (TA. Aug.18; 27) £50
- – Anr. Edn. Ca. 1900. *Ltd. Edn.* 11 vols. Hf. cf. gt., unc., rubbed. (P. Jul.5; 102) £90
- – [–] Anr. Edn. Ill.:– after John Leech. L., priv. ptd., ca. 1900? 5 vols. Titles with hand-cold. vigs., 74 hand-cold. plts., hf.-titles, mod. red hf. mor. by Bayntun, gt., spines tooled in compartments with ornaments. (S. Oct.4; 287) *Walford.* £190
- [–] [–] Anr. Edn. L., n.d. 8 vols. Some plts. hand-cold., some light spotting, cont. hf. mor. (CSK. Nov.4; 54) £160
- – Anr. Copy. 8 vols. Hf. cf. gt., spines decor. (P. Jul.5; 280) £120
- – Anr. Edn. N.d. 6 vols. Hf. mor. gt., rubbed. (P. Jul.5;249) £65
- Works. N.d. 8 vols. 6 vols. crimson hf. mor. gt., spines decor., 2 others similarly bnd. (P. Apr.12; 141) *Cavendish.* £220

SUSEMIHL, J.C. & E.
- [–] Teutsche Ornithologie. Ed.:– Borkhausen. Darmstadt, 1800-11. *1st. Edn.* Pts. 1-20 in 11 vols. Fo. Wide margin, some foxing, especially in margins, some slight margin tears, cont. bds., unc., orig. wraps. bnd. in, slightly defect.; Hauswedell coll. (H. May 24; 871) DM 19,000

SUSLOV, W.
- Monuments de l'Ancienne Architecture Russe. St. Petersb., 1895-1901. 7 vols. Tall fo. Text in Russian, plt. lists & descriptive text engraved on plts. in Russian & Fr., 115 mntd. engraved plts., each liby.-stpd. on blank verso, loose in cl.-bkd. pict. bds., linen ties. (SG. May 3; 349) $1,300

SUSPIRO, El
Zaragoza, 1845. Fo. Sewed. (DS. Dec.16; 2279) Pts. 34,000

SUSSEX
- Excursions in the County of Sussex ... 1822. Sm. 8vo. 1 plt. reprd., some minor spotting, cont. diced cf. gt., slightly rubbed. (TA. Apr.19; 98) £58

SUSSMILCH, J.P.
- Die Göttliche Ordnung in den Veränderungen des Menschlichen Geschlechts aus der Geburt, dem Tode und der Fortpflanzung desselben erwiesen. Berlin, 1765. 2 vols. Minimal browning, cont. hf. leath., slightly rubbed. (HT. May 10; 2361) DM 400
- – Anr. Edn. Berlin, 1798. 3 vols. Cont. bds. (SG. Oct.6; 350) $250

SUTCLIFFE, Matthew
- The Practice, Proceedings, & Lawes of Armes. L., 1593. *1st. Edn.* 4to. Title dust-soiled, early inscrs., early 19th. C. mor. gt., slightly soiled. [STC 23468] (SG. Sep.22; 284) $450

SUTCLIFFE, Thomas
- [–] The Earthquake of Juan Fernandez, as occurred in the Year 1835. Manchester, 1839. Orig. wraps., soiled. (CSK. Jul.6; 100) £90

SUTHERLAND, Alexander & others
- Victoria & its Metropolis, Past & Present. Melbourne, 1888. 2 vols. 4to. No bdg. stated. (KH. Nov.9; 474) Aus. $400
- – Anr. Copy. 2 vols. 4to. 1 hf.-title & frontis. bnd. in dupl., publisher's leath., some wear, a few corners stained. (KH. Nov.9; 473) Aus. $350
- – Anr. Copy. 2 vols. 4to. Bdg. opened at title-p. of 1 vol. & crude repair attempted, publisher's roan or mor., rubbed & with vermin damage. (KH. Nov.9; 725) Aus. $240

SUTHERLAND, Capt. David
- A Tour up the Straits from Gibraltar to Constantinople. 1790. Cont. mor. gt. (CSK. Jul.6; 52) £190
- – Anr. Copy. Cont. cf. (CSK. Sep.30; 73) £60

SUTHERLAND, Elizabeth, Duchess of [formerly Marchioness of Stafford]
- Views in Orkney & on the North Eastern Coast of Scotland ... 1807. Fo. Etched title, 31 etched plts. & text vigs., cont. inscr. on title, cont. hf. cf., worn. (PD. Feb.15; 252) £95

SUTTON, Thomas
- The Danielle Artists & Travellers. L., 1954. *(150) numbered.* Mor. gt. (P. May 17; 72) *Randall.* £130

SUZUKI, D.T. & Herrigel, Eugen
- [–] Le Tir à l'Arc. Ill.:– Georges Braque. Paris, 1960. *(165) roman-numbered.* Loose as iss., orig. fitted silk case & folder. (S. Nov.21; 7) *Makiya.* £780

SVININE, Paul
- [–] Sketches of Russia. 1814. *1st. Edn.* Orig. bds., spine brkn. & defect. (BBA. Jun.14; 323) *Quaritch.* £150

SWAIN, Charles
- [–] An Account of a Voyage For the Discovery of a North-West Passage by Hudson's Streights, to the Western & Southern Ocean of America ... L., 1748. *1st. Edn.* 2 vols. in 1. Lacks 1 folding chart, 3 other charts torn & reprd., cont. panel. cf., rebkd., corners worn; the Rt. Hon. Visc. Eccles copy, w.a.f. [Sabin 20808] (CNY. Nov.18; 261) $320

SWAINSON, William
- Zoological Illustrations. L., 1822-23. Vol. 3: 'Entomology' pts. I-III. 35 hand-cold. engraved plts. with corresponding uncold. plts., hf. mor. (SKC. Oct.26; 443) £70

SWAMMERDAM, Jan
- Bibel der Natur ... Ill.:– J.C.G. Fritzsch. Leipzig, 1752. *1st. German Edn.* Fo. Some light crumples, lightly browned & slightly soiled, cont. leath. gt., slightly worn & bumped. (HK. Nov.8; 546) DM 900

- Bybel der Natuure, of Historie der Insecten. Trans.:– H.D. Gaubius. Leiden, 1737-38. *1st. Edn.* 3 vols. Fo. Dutch & Latin text, 2 plts. remtd., some margin stains, later cf. (B. Apr.27; 573) Fls. 3,400
- – Anr. Copy. 2 vols. Fo. L.P., 53 plts. (52 folding), Dutch & Latin text, cont. vell., slightly dust-soiled. (B. Feb.8; 863a) Fls. 2,700

SWAMMERDAM, Jan -Contd.

- Historia Insectorum Generalis, ofte Algemeene Verhandeling van de Bloedelose Dierkens. Utrecht, 1669. *1st. Edn.* 2 pts. in 1 vol. 4to. Cont. vell. (VG. Nov.30; 782) Fls. 2,700
- - Anr. Edn. Ed.:- Henricus Christopher Henninus. Leiden, 1685. 4to. Hf.-title, instructions to binder at end, stp. on title, cont. cf.; Dr. Walter Pagel copy. (S. Feb.7; 358) *Israel.* £200

SWAN, Abraham

- Book of Architecture. L., 1750. *2nd. Edn.* Lacks part of title-p., some foxing, bdg. not stated. (JL. Mar.25; 396) Aus. $170
- A Collection of Designs in Architecture. L., 1757. 2 vols. in 1. Fo. 120 engraved plts., text to 1st. vol. slightly spotted, cont. reversed cf., worn. (S. May 1; 573) *Marlborough.* £150

SWAN, Joseph

- Select Views of Glasgow & its Environs. Ed.:- J.M. Leighton. Glasgow, 1828. 4to. Minor foxing, cont. mor. gt. by Carss. (CE. Sep.1; 95) £50

SWANN, Harry Kirke

- A Monograph of the Birds of Prey. Ed.:- A. Wetmore. L., 1930-45. 2 vols. 4to. 56 plts., slight spotting of text in Vol. 1, hf. roan, slightly rubbed. (S. Nov.28; 91) *Wakeling.* £290

SWANSTON, G.H.

- The Companion Atlas to the Gazetteer of the World. A. Fullarton, n.d. 9 pts. Fo. 48 col. maps, 1 defect., orig. wraps. (P. Mar.15; 393) £200

SWARBRECK, Samuel D.

- Sketches in Scotland. 1839. Fo. 25 tinted litho. plts., including pict. title, 1 loose, orig. mor.-bkd. cl., slightly soiled. (SKC. Jan.13; 2391) £450
- - Anr. Copy. Fo. Orig. frontis.'s & 22 plts. only, some foxing & staining, orig. mor.-bkd. bds., worn. (PD. Jun.13; 121) £145

SWAYNE, Capt. H.G.C.

- Seventeen Trips through Somaliland. A Record of Exploration & Big Game Shooting, 1885-93. 1895. *1st. Edn.* 4to. 2 folding maps reprd., single advt. lf. bnd. in at rear, recent hf. cf. gt. (TA. Jun.21; 43) £52

SWAYSLAND, Walter

- Familiar Wild Birds. 1883. *1st. Edn.* 4 vols. Hf. cf. (PD. Feb.15; 93) £65
- - Anr. Edn. L., 1883[-88]. *1st. Edn.* 4 vols. Vol. 1 slightly spotted, cont. hf. leath. gt., corners lightly worn. (HK. May 15; 561) DM 440
- - Anr. Edn. N.d. 4 vols. Crimson hf. mor. gt. (P. Sep.29; 33) £90
See— BLAKSTON, W. & others

SWEDBURG, J.D.

- Dissertatio Gradualis de Svionum in America Colonia. Ed.:- P. Elvius. Uppsala, [1709]. Foremargins of title & 1st. ll. shaved slightly affecting letters, later bds. [Sabin 94037] (S. Dec.1; 299) *Sawyer.* £160

SWEET, Robert

- The British Flower Garden. L., 1823-38. 1st. Series: Vols. I-III, 2nd. Series: Vols. I-IV. 712 hand-cold. engraved plts., some folding, cont. hf. mor., spines gt. (C. Nov.16; 301) *Walford.* £2,300
- - Anr. Edn. L., 1838. Vol. 1 only (of 7). Linen. (HK. May 15; 540) DM 1,000
- The Florist's Guide, & Cultivator's Directory. 1827-29. Vol. 1 only. 91 hand-cold. engraved plts. only (of 100), some light browning, mod. cl. (CSK. Apr.27; 6) £450
- Geraniaceae, or Natural Order of Geraniums. Ill.:- after E.D. Smith. L., 1820-21. Orig. pts. nos.1-24 only (of 125). 96 hand-cold. engraved plts., as iss. in orig. grey ptd. paper wraps., unc., w.a.f. (C. Jun.27; 185) *Marsden.* £480
- - Anr. Edn. 1820-22. Vol. 1 & part of Vol. 2 only. 145 hand-cold. engraved plts., few lightly affected by offsetting, cont. hf. cf., worn, covers detchd., w.a.f. (CSK. Feb.10; 137) £350

SWETNAM, J.
See— ZWETNAM or SWETNAM, J.

SWIFT, Jonathan

[-] A Complete Collection of Genteel & Ingenious Conversation. 1738. *1st. Engl. Edn.* Advt. lf. before title, no bdg. stated. (P. Jan.12; 282) *Way.* £95
- Le Conte du Tonneau, contenant Tout ce que les Arts et les Sciences ont de plus Sublime et de plus Mystérieux ... La Haye, 1732. 2 vols. (*With:*)
- Traité des Dissensions entre les Nobles et le Peuple ... l'Art de Ramper en Poésie ... pour servir de Suite au Conte du Tonneau. Lausanne & Genève, 1742. 1 vol. Together 3 vols. 12mo. Cont. cf., spines decor., not quite unif. (HD. Mar.19; 157) Frs. 2,000
- Conseila aux Domestiques. Ill.:- Gus Bofa. 1921. 12mo. Sewed. (HD. Dec.9; 7d) Frs. 1,800
- Des Capitain Lemuel Gullivers Reise in das Land derer Houyhnhnms. Ill.:- R. Janthur. Berlin, 1919. *(150) numbered.* 2nd. Series. Fo. Printer's note sigd. by artist, orig. woodcut hf.-title, 11 orig. lithos., orig. pict. hf. linen. (GB. Nov.5; 2634) DM 420
[-] Des Capitains Lemuel Gulliver Reisen in Unterschiedliche Entfernte und Unbekannte Länder. Hamburg, 1727-28. *1st. German Edn.* Tears in 2 pp. reprd. with slight loss, browned, a little spotting, cont. cf., very worn; Hauswedell coll. (H. May 24; 1582) DM 4,200
- Gulliver's Reise ins Land der Riesen. Eine Reise nach Brobdingnag. Ill.:- L. Corinth. Berlin, 1922. *(400) numbered.* 4to. 25 mntd. orig. lithos., with side numbers & some MS. corrections, MS. text addition, some soiling, linen. (GB. Nov.5; 2361) DM 1,500
- - Anr. Copy. 4to. Printers mark sigd. by artist, 25 orig. lithos., slightly foxed at beginning, orig. hf. mor. gt. (GB. May 5; 2293) DM 1,100
- - Anr. Copy. Lge. 4to. Printer's mark sigd. by artist, minimal foxing, orig. hf. leath. (HK. Nov.11; 3481) DM 900
- Gullivers Reisen in Unbekannte Länder. Ed.:- A. Lewald after W. Scott. Trans.:- F. Kottenkamp. Stuttgart, 1839. 2 vols. in 1. Slightly foxed, cont. hf. linen gt., slightly rubbed. (R. Apr.3; 226) DM 450
[-] Gulliver's Travels. L., 1726. *1st. Edn. 1st. Iss. [Teerinck's 'A' Edn.].* 2 vols. Totally unsophisicated L.P. copy, engraved port. in 1st. state, p. no. in pt. IV p. 62 ptd. correctly (differing from Teerinck/Scouten copy) lf. 2E8 not a cancel, orig. blank ll. at beginning & end of each vol., some slight traces of spotting in lr. margins of some ll. in Vol. 2, early owner's inscr. on fly-lf. of both vols., & note on front end-paper of Vol. 1, cont. cf., spines gt., lacks labels, spines worn. (C. Nov.9; 116) *Lyon.* £8,500
[-] - Anr. Edn. L., 1726. *1st. Edn. [Teerinck's 'AA' Edn.].* 4 pts. in 2 vols. Antique-style cf. gt. (C. Nov.9; 117) *Blackwells.* £600
[-] - Anr. Copy. 2 vols. Few stains, cont. cf., cover detchd. (SG. Feb.9; 347) $225
[-] - Anr. Edn. L., 1726. *1st. Edn. [Teerinck's 'B' Edn.].* 2 vols. Plts. 4 & 5 with double imps., spotted, 19th. C. cf. (BBA. Mar.21; 208) *Thorp.* £140
[-] - Anr. Copy. 2 vols. Engraved port. in vol. 1 with legend round frame, 4 maps, 2 plans, some spotting & browning, similar panel. mott. cf., jnts. & spine of vol. 1 worn, vol. 2 spine lightly wormed & chipped. (SPB. May 16; 153) $300
[-] - Anr. Copy. 2 vols. With 2nd. edn. (1727) titles in Vol. II, partly stained, cont. cf., rebkd.; Richard Gimble Foundation bkplts. (SG. Oct.27; 313) $275
[-] - Anr. Edn. L., 1726. *1st. Edn.* 2 vols. Prelims. of Vol. 2 Teerink 'AA' edn., text 'B', engraved port. slightly torn & laid down, browned & soiled, cont. cf., rebkd., slightly rubbed. (BBA. Dec.15; 161) *Snelling.* £100
[-] - Anr. Edn. L., 1727. *2nd. Edn.* 2 vols. Slight browning & soiling, cont. mott. cf., rebkd. (S. Dec.13; 425) *Hannas.* £50
[-] - Anr. Edn. Ill.:- David Jones. Gold. Cock. Pr., 1925. *(480) numbered.* 2 vols. 4to. Some ills. hand-cold., orig. hf. cl., unc., unopened, s.-c. (S. Nov.21; 214) *Busek.* £300
[-] - Anr. Copy. 2 vols. 4to. Some ills. hand-cold., orig. hf. cl., unc., slightly soiled. (S. Nov.21; 215) *Joseph.* £220

[-] - Anr. Copy. 2 vols. Orig. hf. cl., scuffed, spines soiled. (CSK. Jun.1; 163) £140
[-] - Anr. Copy. 2 vols. 4to. Some ills. hand-cold., hf. buckram & bds., Vol. 2 unopened, minor scuff on lr. edge of upr. & lr. covers of 1 vol. (SG. Mar.29; 152) $325
[-]The Hibernian Patriot. Dublin/L., 1730. *[1st. Edn.].* Partial liby. stp. on base of title & stp. on verso, recent qtr. mor. gt. (TA. Jun.21; 356) £62
[-] -Anr. Edn. L., 1730. *[1st. L. Edn.].* Cont. panel. cf., rubbed. (LC. Mar.1; 551) £80
- The History of the Four Last Years of the Queen. L., 1758. *1st. Edn.* Sm. holes & repairs to title, not affecting text, slight browning, later mott. cf.; bkplts. of Sir Winston & Randolph S. Churchill. (S. Oct.11; 370) *Taylor.* £100
- - Anr. Copy. Cont. cf. (CSK. May 18; 91) £60
- - Anr. Copy. 1st. state, cont. cf., worn; bkplt. of Gouverneur Morris. (SG. Oct.27; 312) $300
- Letters Written by the Late Jonathan Swift, D.D. Ed.:- Deane Swift. Dublin, 1786. 3 vols. 12mo. Advt. lf. Vol. 1, Vols. I & III lack front & end blanks, cf. (GM. Dec.7; 364) £55
- Memoirs ... Ed.:- Sir W. Scott. Paris, 1826. *1st. Edn.* 2 vols. 12mo. No bdg. stated. (GM. Dec.7; 362) £60
- Miscellaneous Poems. Ill.:- Robert Gibbings. Waltham St. Lawrence, Gold. Cock. Pr., 1928. *(375) numbered & sigd. by artist.* 4to. Orig. parch.-bkd. bds., d.-w., s.-c. (BBA. Jul.27; 193) *Blackwell's.* £60
- Miscellanies in Prose & Verse. L., 1711. *1st. Edn. 2nd. Iss.* G6 & 7 cancelled, title-p. a little spotted, cont. cf., spine gt., slightly worn; Earl of Denbigh bkplt. (BBA. May 3; 182) *Hannas.* £100
- - Anr. Edn. L., 1711. *1st. Edn.* 2nd. state, with cancellans G6 (=A8) & with G7 cancelled, 4-pp. advts. at end, dampwrinkled, some stains, cont. panel. cf., rebkd. (SG. Feb.9; 343) $150
- - Anr. Edn. L., 1728-27-32-32. 4 vols. Cont. cf. (CBA. Dec.10; 425) $120
- On Poetry: A Rhapsody. Dublin & L., 1733. *1st. Edn.* Fo. Sm. repair to blank margin of title, few ll. faintly spotted, mod. mor. gt.; Frederic Dannay copy. (CNY. Dec.16; 340) $150
[-] Some Remarks upon a Pamphlet. L., 1711. *1st. Edn.* Few p. numbers, catchwords & 'FINIS' shaved, wraps. (SG. Feb.9; 344) $110
[-] A Tale of a Tub. L., 1704. *1st. Edn.* 2nd. state, with blank space at p. 320 line 10, advt. lf., sm. natural paper fault in L1, short margin tear in M2, early sig., lev. gt. extra, gt. dentelles, by Rivière. (SG. Nov.3; 202) $650
- - Anr. Copy. Some brown spotting & stains, cont. cf., gold decor., spine restored, hand-bnd. mod. mor. box; Schocken coll.; Hauswedell coll. (H. May 24; 1580) DM 2,000
- A Tale of a Tub. — The History of the Four Last Years of the Queen. L., 1704; 1758. *1st. Edns.* Together 2 vols. 1st. work: advt. lf., cont. panel. cf., rebkd.; 2nd. work: cont. cf., armor. bkplt. of Henry Brouncker. (SPB. May 16; 152) $700
- A Voyage to Lilliput; A Voyage to Brobdingnag. N.Y., Ltd. Edns. Cl., 1950. *(1500) numbered, designed & initialed by Bruce Rogers.* 2 vols. 32mo. & tall fo. Decorative titles & initials, map frontis., cl. spines, maps on bd. covers, specially-designed s.-c. (SG. May 17; 227) $120
- - Anr. Copy. 2 vols. Fo. & 64mo. Bdg. not stated, together in s.-c., light wear to covers & case; bequest of Joe E. Brown to Marymount College, with their bkplt. (CBA. Mar.3; 467) $110
- Voyages de Gulliver. Trans.:- Abbé Desfontaines. Paris, 1727. *Orig. Edn.* 2 vols. (*With:*) - Le Nouveau Gulliver ou Voyage de Jean Gulliver, Fils du Capitaine Gulliver. Trans.:- Abbé Desfontaines. Paris, 1730. *Orig. Edn.* 2 vols. in 1. Together 3 vols. 12mo. Jansenist red mor. by Pagnant & Dupré, spines decor. (not quite unif.). (HD. May 3; 150) Frs. 4,400
- - Anr. Copy. 2 vols. 12mo. Cont. cf., decor. spines. (HD. Jan.24; 338) Frs. 1,450
- - Anr. Edn. Ill.:- Lefevre, engraved by Masquelier. Paris, An V, 1797. 4 pts. in 2 vols. 12mo. On vell., figures before the letter, cf. gt. by Thouvenin, spines decor. (slightly faded). (HD. May 3; 151) Frs. 3,000
- - Anr. Edn. Ill.:- Brévière (frontis.) & 'Grand-ville'. Paris, 1838. *New Trans. 1st. Printing.* 2 vols.

Some slight foxing, sm. splits at beginning, cont. red mor. gt., spines decor. (HD. May 4; 433)
Frs. 2,000
– – **Anr. Edn.** Paris, 1838. 2 vols. Some scattered foxing, cont. glazed cf., blind- & gt.-decor.; from libys. of Octave Uzanne & Henri Houssaye with their ex-libris. (HD. May 16; 53) Frs. 5,800
– – **Anr. Copy.** 2 vols. Some foxing, 1st. ll. vol. II very browned, cont. hf. leath., gt. spine, faded; Hauswedell coll. (H. May 24; 1584) DM 720
– – **Anr. Edn.** Ill.:– Gus Bofa. 1929. 2 vols. 4to. Vell. de Hollande, sewed, wraps. & s.-c.'s. (HD. Dec.9; 7l) Frs. 3,500
– – **Anr. Edn.** Ill.:– Poirson. Paris, n.d. 4to. L.P., elab. decor. mor. by Ruband, s.-c., wrap. preserved; publisher's copy on japan. (SM. Mar.7; 2237)
Frs. 2,400
[–] **Voyages du Capitaine Gulliver en Divers Pays Eloignés.** The Hague, 1773. 3 vols. in 2. 12mo. Text slightly browned & spotted, cont. mott. cf., spines gt.; van Veen coll. (S. Feb.28; 126) £100
– **The Works.** Ill.:– J.S. Muller. 1755-54-55. 12 vols. Cont. cf. (SKC. Jan.13; 2263) £60
– – **Anr. Edn.** Ed.:– J. Nichols. L., 1801. *New Edn.* 19 vols. Hf. cf. (GM. Dec.7; 132) £130
– – **Anr. Copy.** 19 vols. Russian cfs., spines faded. (HD. Feb.22; 215) Frs. 2,300
– – **Anr. Edn.** Ed.:– Thomas Sheridan & John Nicols. 1808. 19 vols. Cont. diced russ. gt. (SKC. Mar.9; 1861) £160
– – **Anr. Edn.** Ed.:– Sir Walter Scott. Edinb., 1814. 19 vols. Some ll. stained or spotted, cont. cf., spines gt., some jnts. split. (S. Mar.20; 968) *Wade.* £160
– – **Anr. Copy.** 19 vols. Some spotting, cont. hf. mor., lightly rubbed, 1 spine reprd. (CSK. Jan.27; 8) £150
– – **Anr. Edn.** Ed.:– Sir Walter Scott. Edinb., 1824. 19 vols. Cont. cf. gt. (P. Sep.29; 358) *Nolan.* £50
– **The Works & Letters** ... Ill.:– Muller. L., 1755-79. 11 vols. only (of 14). 4to. Diced cf. (GM. Dec.7; 462) £100

SWINBURNE, Algernon Charles
– **Atalanta in Calydon.** L., 1865. *1st. Edn.* Sm. 4to. Cl. gt., a little soiled, unc.; Maurice Baring's copy, with bkplt. & sig., J. Wyndham's sig., C.L. Shadwell bkplt. (LC. Mar.1; 401) £90
– – **Anr. Copy.** 4to. Carte-de-visit photograph of author pasted in, orig. cl., soiled. (BBA. Oct.27; 68) *Spencer.* £80
– – **Anr. Copy.** 4to. Some foxing, orig. buckram, gt.-decor. upr. cover designed by Dante Gabriel Rossetti, stained, corner reprd.; Frederic Dannay copy. (CNY. Dec.16; 341) $120
– – **Anr. Edn.** [Hammersmith, Kelms. Pr.], 1894]. *(258). (250) on Bütten.* Sm. 4to. Wide margin, orig. vell., ties, lacks 2, slightly spotted. (H. May 22; 1056) DM 1,000
– **Grace Darling.** L., Ptd. for Private Circulation [a T.J. Wise piracy ptd. by R. Clay & Sons]. 1893. *1st. Edn., (33). (3) on vell.* 4to. Crushed lev. mor., unc., slightly bowed; Frederic Dannay copy. (CNY. Dec.16; 344) $600
– **Hymn to Proserpine.** Ill.:– John Buckland-Wright. Gold. Cock. Pr., 1944. *(50) numbered, with extra engr., specially bnd.* Orig. mor. gt., s.-c.; from D. Bolton liby. (BBA. Oct.27; 150) *May.* £180
– **Laus Veneris.** Ill.:– John Buckland-Wright. Gold. Cock. Pr., 1948. *(100) numbered, with extra engr., specially bnd.* Orig. mor., gt.-decor.; from D. Bolton liby. (BBA. Oct.27; 151) *Quaritch.* £140
– **Pasiphaë, A Poem.** Ill.:– John Buckland-Wright. Gold. Cock. Pr., 1950. *(100) numbered, with extra engr., specially bnd.* Orig. stained vell., gt.-decor.; from D. Bolton liby. (BBA. Oct.27; 152)
Quaritch. £120
– **Poems.** 1912. 6 vols. *(With:)* – **Tragedies.** 1912. 5 vols. Together 11 vols. Unif. cf., rubbed, spines gt. (CSK. Jun.15; 125) £90
– **Poems & Ballads.** L., 1866. *1st. Edn. 1st. Iss.* 1st. Series. 12mo. Orig. uncancelled state of each sig. & the 24 errors uncorrected (except for [N3], as usual), with earliest iss. of 8-pp. Moxon advts. inserted, title & following dedication lf. trimmed, few ll. lightly foxed, orig. cl., unc., cl. folding case; Frederic Dannay copy. (CNY. Dec.16; 342) $650
– – **Anr. Edn.** L., 1878. *1st. Edn.* 2nd. Series. Sm. 8vo. Orig. cl., shaken; pres. copy from author, inscr. 'For the much tried Downey ... Capheaton', Letitia

Mary Swinburne bkplt., Frederic Dannay copy. (CNY. Dec.16; 343) $210
– **Siena.** 1868 [but after 1890]. 12mo. Mor. gt. by Rivière, orig. wraps. bnd. in. (P. Apr.12; 27) £90
– **The Springtide of Life.** Ill.:– Arthur Rackham. L., 1918. *(765) numbered & sigd. by artist.* 4to. Orig. parch.-bkd. bds. gt., slightly worn. (S. Dec.20; 582) *Bowes.* £70
– – **Anr. Edn.** Ill.:– Arthur Rackham. Phila., 1918. *1st. Amer. Edn.* Tall 8vo. Gt.-lettered cl. (SG. Jan.12; 301) $130
– **Tristram of Lyonesse & Other Poems.** Portland, Maine, 1904. *(4) numbered on vell., sigd. by publisher.* 4to. Lev., linen s.-c. (SG. Jan.12; 329) $650
– **Two Unpublished Manuscripts: De Monumentis Epilaphiisque Mortuorum & Limits of Experience** – **Written during his College Years at Oxford.** Ill.:– V. Angelo. San Franc., [for Herbert L. Rothchild, at the Grabhorn Pr.], 1927. *(50) sigd. by artist.* 4to. Specially bnd. in orig.? gt.-ruled & lettered mor., spine lightly faded, s.-c. rubbed; the V. Angelo copy. (CBA. Oct.1; 177) $250
– **Under the Microscope.** 1872. *1st. Edn.* Pages 41/42 a cancel as usual, errata slip, late 19th. C. mor. gt. (BBA. Oct.27; 69) *Joseph.* £80
– **[Works].** 1905-13. 16 vols., various. Some light browning, cont. red hf. mor. by Zaehnsdorf, spines gt., a few lightly rubbed. (CSK. Mar.9; 209) £180

SWINBURNE, Henry, Judge, 1560-1623
– **A Briefe Treatise of Testaments & Last Wills.** L., 1635. 4to. Cont. cf., rebkd. [STC 23530] (BBA. May 3; 112) *Frognall.* £150

SWINBURNE, Henry, Traveller, 1743-1803
– **Travels in the Two Sicilies ... in the Years 1777 [to] 1780.** L., 1783-85. *1st. Edn.* 2 vols. 4to. Folding engraved map (torn, reprd. & loose), folding ptd. table (with a short tear), 22 plts. & plans, including 2 folding, hf.-title in Vol. II, some light browning & offsetting, cont. tree cf., slightly worn. (S. Oct.11; 443) *Erlini.* £180
– **Travels Through Spain in the Years 1775 & 1776.** 1779. 4to. 1 plt. tipped in cover, some light soiling, cont. hf. cf. (CSK. Sep.30; 72) £100

SWIRE, Herbert
– **The Voyage of the Challenger.** Gold. Cock. Pr., 1938. *(300) numbered.* 2 vols. Sm. fo. Orig. cl., spines gt., s.-c.; from D. Bolton liby. (BBA. Oct.27; 153) *Quaritch.* £370
– – **Anr. Copy.** 2 vols. Fo. Orig. cl., linen backstrips, spines gt.-decor., untrimmed, s.-c. (TA. Feb.16; 367) £280

SWITZER, Stephen
– **A Universal System of Water & Water-Works, Philosophical & Practical, Vol. 1.** L., 1734. *2nd. Edn.? (Bound with:)* – **An Introduction to a General System of Hydrostaticks & Hydraulicks, Philosophical & Practical. Vol. II.** L., 1729. *1st. Edn.?* Together 2 works in 1 vol. Frontis. & title of 1st. work bkd. & browned, 1 lf. reprd., repair on verso of 1 plt., lacks blanks, some browning & spotting, cont. tree cf.; William Balston-Boies Penrose copy with bkplts., Stanitz coll. (SPB. Apr.25; 414) $475

SWITZERLAND
– **Guide through Switzerland.** [Paris, Glaginani]. ca. 1825. Sm. 8vo. Lge. folding litho. hand-cold., cont. hf. cf., worn. (S. Mar.6; 87) *Locker.* £55
– **Suisse Illustrée, Description et Histoire de ses 22 Cantons.** 1851. 2 vols. in 1. 71 steel engrs., 20 plts. in col. & 2 double-p. cold. maps., cont. hf. havanna chagrin, decor. spine, decor. cl. covers. (HD. Feb.29; 45) Frs. 9,200

SYDENHAM, E.A.
– **Historical References on Coins of the Roman Empire.** L., 1911. Later mor.; extra-ill. with 191 ills. of Roman coins taken from major sales catalogues. (S. May 1; 501) *Dreesman.* £70

SYKES, Sir Mark Masterman
– **A Catalogue of the Highly Valuable Collection of Prints.** 1824. 5 pts. in 1 vol. 4to. MS. prices, cont. hf. cf. (BBA. Nov.10; 231) *Peters.* £110
– – **Anr. Copy.** 5 pts. in 1 vol. 4to. Priced & with buyer's names thro.-out, cont. cf., lacks bds. (BBA. Apr.5; 161) *Lister.* £85

SYLBURGIUS, F.
– **Catalogue Codicum Graecorum M.SS. Olim in Bibliotheca Palatina, Nunc Vaticana Asservatorum.** Frankfurt, 1701. 2 pts. in 1 vol. 4to. Cont. vell. gt. (SG. Sep.15; 325) $170

SYLLOGE NUMMORUM GRAECORUM DEUTSCHLAND
Ed.:– G. Kleiner. Berlin, 1957-62. Pts. 1-4 & 7 only. Lge. 4to. Orig. wraps. (HK. Nov.9; 1942)
DM 750

SYLVAN. Ein Jahrbuch für Forstmänner, Jäger und Jagdfreunde auf das Jahr 1814
Ed.:– C.P. Laurop & V.F. Fischer. Ill.:– Susemihl. Marburg & Kassel, 1814. Slight staining, cont. hf. leath. (GB. May 4; 1985) DM 400

SYME, J.
– **Nine Years in Van Diemen's Land** ... Dundee, 1848. Bdg. not stated, unc., backstrip faded. (KH. May 1; 687) Aus. $130

SYMES, Michael
– **An Account of an Embassy to the Kingdom of Ava, sent by the Governor-General of India in the Year 1795.** 1800. 4to. 2 folding maps (1 reprd. along creases), 26 engraved plts., cont. panel. cf. gt., old reback, some wear to top & bottom of spine. (TA. Mar.15; 15) £85
– – **Anr. Copy.** 4to. 2 folding engraved maps (1 torn & reprd.), 25 plts., lacks hf.-title, some ll. slightly soiled or dampstained, cont. hf. cf., head of spine torn. (BBA. Oct.27; 310) *Scott.* £65

SYMMONS, Edward
– **A Vindication of King Charles: or, a Loyal Subjects Duty.** 1648 [1647]. *1st. Edn.* 4to. Sm. hole in 1 lf. affecting a few letters, cont. cf., part of spine defect., rubbed. [Wing S6350] (BBA. Jun.14; 44)
R. Parsons. £60

SYMONDS, Mary & Preece, Louisa
– **Needlework through the Ages.** L., 1928. *[1st. Edn.].* 4to. Orig. parch.-bkd. cl., very slightly rubbed & soiled; sigd. by authors. (S. Oct.11; 595) *Traylen.* £100
– – **Anr. Copy.** 4to. 104 plts., some cold., orig. hf. vell., bkplt. removed. (SG. Apr.26; 118) $325

SYMONDS, Robert Wemyss
– **English Furniture from Charles II to George II.** L., 1929. *(1000).* 4to. Orig. buckram. (S. Oct.4; 203) *Woodruff.* £60
– **Furniture-Making in 17th. & 18th. C. England.** Connoisseur 1955. No bdg. stated. (JL. Jun.24; 194) Aus. $400
– **Masterpieces of English Furniture & clocks.** 1940. *(750).* 4to. Hf. cf., gt. spine; pres. copy, inscr. by author. (SKC. Jan.13; 2120) £90
– **Thomas Tompion, his Life & Work.** L., 1951. *(350) numbered & sigd.* 4to. Orig. hf. mor., s.-c. (S. May 1; 696) *Sawyer.* £85
– – **Anr. Edn.** L., [1951]. *(350) numbered & sigd.* Orig. hf. mor., s.-c.; A.L.s., dtd. 5 Dec. 1949. (CSK. Jun.1; 7) £110
– – **Anr. Copy.** 4to. Cont. hf. mor., s.-c. (CSK. Sep.16; 43) £95

SYMONS, Alphonse James Albert
– **The Quest for Corvo An Experiment in Biography.** 1934. *1st. Edn.* Orig. cl., orig. d.-w.; inscr. by author to John Wyndham, Oct. 1935. (LC. Mar.1; 405)
£80

SYMONS, Alphonse James Albert (Ed.)
See— **BOOK COLLECTOR'S QUARTERLY**

SYMONS, Arthur
– **Days & Nights.** L., 1889. *1st. Edn.* Endpapers foxed, orig. cl.; pres. copy from author to Coventry Patmore, Frederic Dannay copy. (CNY. Dec.16; 345) $2,200

SYMSON, Capt. William
– **A New Voyage to the East Indies.** 1715. Advt. lf. before title, cont. cf., little worn. (BBA. Sep.29; 32)
Brook-Hitching. £370

SYNESIUS, Bp. of Cirene
– **Opera que extant Omnia.** Trans.:– Dionysius Petavius. Pris, 1612. *1st. Edn.* 2 pts. in 1 vol. Fo. Last blank lf., lacks fo. 2N6 (blank), rather browned

SYNESIUS, Bp. of Cirene -*Contd.*

thro.-out, a few ll. stained, some marginalia, cont. cf., rebkd., slightly rubbed. (BBA. May 23; 328) *West.* £70

SYNGE, Patrick M.
See— HAY, Roy & Synge, Patrick M.
See— SITWELL, Sacheverell & others

SYREITSCHIKOFF, N.P. & Treneff, D.K.
- **Ornements sur les Monuments de l'Ancien Art Russe.** Moscow, 1904. Fo. 25 col.-ptd. plts., loose as iss., title & notes in Russian & Fr., ptd. bds., spine defect. (SG. Aug.25; 316) $160

SYSTEM OF CAMP-DISCIPLINE
L., 1757. *2nd. Edn.* 2 pts. in 1 vol. 22 engraved plts. & maps, a few partly hand-cold., folding table slightly torn, cont. cf., worn, upr. cover detchd. (BBA. May 3; 206) *Bookroom.* £65

SYSTEM OF SIGNALS. Combining a Method Commonly Used in the British Navy, of Making the Signals from Fixed Places of the Masts or Rigging, with a Numerary Method, By Which the Flags are Shewed Where they May be Best Seen, so as to Gain the Advantages of Both those Methods ...
N.p., 1787. Fo. Index, parts of margins of some ll. cut out & ills. of flags stuck to tabs to form thumb index arranged by flags, cont. leath.-bkd. bds., 'S-23' in gt. on spine. (LC. Mar.1; 552) £650

SZYK, Arthur
- **Ink & Blood: a Book of Drawings.** Prefatory Text:– Struthers Burt. N.Y., 1946. *(1000) sigd.* Sm. fo. 75 plts., upr. third of limitation lf. cut away, mor., spine very worn. (SG. Jan.12; 331) $130

TABANELLI, M.R.
- **Edgar Chahine. Catalogue de l'Oeuvré Gravé.** Ill.:– E. Chahine. Milan, 1977. *(100) first copies numbered.* 4to. Pict. cl., box. (HD. Dec.16; 92) Frs. 1,700

TABERNAEMONTANUS, Jacobus Theodorus
- **New Vollkommentlich Kräuter-Buch.** Ed.:– H& C. Bauhin. Basel, 1664. *4th. Edn.* 3 pts. in 1 vol. Fo. 1 title lf. soiled & with sm. hole, slight loss, tear in lr. margin, lacks 2 ll. prelims., lightly browned thro.-out, cont. blind-tooled leath., browned, spine & upr. cover reprd. (R. Oct.12; 1925) DM 3,400
- **New Wasserschatz.** Frankfurt, 1605. Slight browning, cont. MS. vell. (R. Oct.12; 1353) DM 2,500

TABLEAU DE LA CROIX Présenté dans les Cérémonies de La Sainte Messe
Ill.:– J. Collin, G. de Geyn & J. Durant. Paris, 1651. Jansenist black mor. by Bauzonnet-Trautz, blind-decor. (HD. May 3; 153) Frs. 1,900

TABLEAUX HISTORIQUES DE LA REVOLUTION FRANÇAISE
Ill.:– after Duplessis-Bertaux, Fragonard fils, Delvaux, Ozanne. Paris, 1791-96. Vol. 1 only. Fo. 55 (of 58) plts., some sm. margin stains, bds. (HD. Jan. 30; 75b) Frs. 2,100
- - **Anr. Edn.** Paris, 1797-1804. 5 vols. Fo. 202 (of 222) engraved plts., lacks the 3 title-pp. & the final parts of text with royal ports., cont. mott. cf., spines gt., slightly rubbed, w.a.f. (C. Mar.14; 95) *Bifolco.* £200
- - **Anr. Edn.** Paris, 1817. 2 vols. Fo. Hf. cf. (P. Sep.29; 324) *Edmunds.* £220

TABLEAUX HISTORIQUES des Campagnes d'Italie
Paris, 1806. Fo. Some foxing in margins, hf. cf. gt. (P. Sep.29; 325) *Erlini.* £220

TACHARD, Guy
[-] **A Relation of the Voyage to Siam.** L., 1688. *1st. Engl. Edn.* Engraved title, 30 plts., some folding, some worming, foxed, lacks hf.-title(?), cf., slightly worn. (S. Mar.6; 49) *Waterloo.* £180

TACHENIUS, O.
See— EBEQUE, J.C. de - TACHENIUS, O.

TACITUS, Publius or Gaius Cornelius
- **The Annales ... ; The Description of Germanie.** [L.], 1604, [1605]. *1st. Combined Edn. in Engl.* 2 pts. in 1 vol. Fo. Sidenotes cropped, mott. cf. antique. [STC 23645] (SG. Feb.9; 348) $110
- **De Situ Moribus et Populis Germaniae qui Fertur Libellus.** Trans.:– R. Borchardt. Ill.:– Anna Simons. Bremen, Bremer Pr., 1914. *(250) on Bütten.* Sm. 4to. Hand-bnd orig. mor., by Bremer Binderei F. Th[iersch], spine faded; trace of erased ex-libris inside cover; Hauswedell coll. (H. May 24; 724) DM 1,600
- - **Anr. Copy.** Sm. 4to. Orig. hand-bnd. vell. (H. Nov.23; 924) DM 780
- - **Anr. Copy.** Sm. 4to. Latin & German text, hand-bnd. mor., lr. cover with sm. stain, by W. Hacker, Leipzig. (H. May 22; 985) DM 440
- **De Vita et Moribus Iulii Agricolae Liber.** Hammersmith, Doves Pr., 1900. *(230). (5) on vell.* Sm. 4to. Orig. limp vell., spine gt.-lettered, unc., qtr. mor. gt. s.-c.; John A. Saks bkplt., Thomas B. Stevenson copy. (CNY. May 18; 102) $1,800
- **Germania.** [Nuremb., Friedrich Creussner], ca. 1473-74. Fo. Lge. letter at beginning & initial strokes supplied in red, sm. margin repairs to folios 1 & 2, minute wormholes in same ll. not affecting text, 19th. C. red mor., darkened & rubbed; John Scott, of Halkshill bkplt. [BMC II, 447; Goff T-10; HC 15224*] (SPB. Dec.14; 34) $4,500
- **Les Oeuvres.** Trans.:– Nicolas Perrot. Paris, 1688. 3 vols. 12mo. Cont. blind-decor. mor., red mor. liners, Madame de Chamillart arms. (HD. Mar.29; 96) Frs. 4,800
- **Opera.** Paris, 1826. *De Luxe Edn., (80).* 4 vols. Fo. On vell., some foxing, cont. str.-grd. red hf. mor., spines decor. (HD. May 21; 99) Frs. 2,300

TACQUET, Andreas
- **Opera Mathematica.** Antw., 1669. *1st. Coll. Edn.* 3 pts. in 1 vol. Fo. Cont. cf., spine gt., rubbed, some wear at foot of spine; Stanitz coll. (SPB. Apr.25; 415) $650
- - **Anr. Copy.** Fo. Some foxing & browning, old cf., very worn. (SG. Mar.22; 300) $200

TAFFIN, J.
- **De Boetveerdicheyt des Levens ...** Amst., 1609. *4th. Printing.* Title & some margins reprd., a few stains & other slight defects, recent vell. (B. Jun.21; 523) Fls. 750

TAGART, Edward
- **A Memoir of the Late Captain Peter Heyward, R.N. ...** 1832. Bnd. without errata slip, early qtr. roan, corners slightly rubbed. (KH. May 1; 689) Aus. $240

TAGLIACOZZI, Gaspare
- **Cheirurgia Nova.** Frankfurt, 1578. *1st. German Edn.* Dampstained, few other stains, old vell., soiled, lettering-piece defect. (SG. Nov.3; 204) $2,800

TAILLARD, Constant
See— A., L.N. & Taillard, Constant

TAINE, Hippolyte A.
- **History of English Literature.** Trans.:– H. Van Laun. Edinb., 1873-74. 4 vols. Three-qtr. cf., spines gt., by Bayntun. (SG. Feb.16; 307) $100
- **Voyage aux Pyrénées.** Ill.:– Gustave Doré. Paris, 1860. *3rd. (1st. 8vo.) Edn. Partly 1st. Printing of ills.* Publisher's decor. cl. (HD. May 4; 434) Frs. 2,100

TAISNIER, Joannes
- **Opvs Mathematicvm Octo Libros complectens.** Köln, 1583. Fo. Some old annots., slightly browned thro.-out, some margin worming near end, cont. blind-tooled pig. slightly rubbed, lr. cover wormed, corners bumped. (HK. Nov.8; 354) DM 750

TAITATZAK, Joseph
- **Lechem Starim.** Venice, 1608. *1st. Edn.* 4to. Slightly stained & soiled, trimmed, blind-tooled leath., slightly worn. (S. Oct.25; 387) *Ludmir.* £550

TAK, P.L. (Ed.)
See— KRONIEK

TAJIMA, Shichi
- **Shim-bi- Taik-wan: Selected Relics of Japanese Art.** Foreword: E.F. Fenollosa. Tokyo, 1899-1908. 20 vols. Tall fo. Plts., some cold., rest collotype, each with text lf. in Japanese & Engl., three-qtr.

mor., orig. patterned wraps. bnd. in thro.-out. (SG. Apr.26; 98) $325

TAKENOBU, Y. & Kawakami, K.
- **History of the Japanese Arts, compiled by the Imperial Museum under Control of Baron R. Kuki.** Tokio, ca. 1915. Lge. fo. Orig. silk, orig. silk-covered bd. box, 2 clasps. (HK. Nov.12; 4765) DM 1,000

TALBO, John
- **Travels through Spain.** L., 1780. 4to. Cf. (DS. Nov.25; 2148) Pts. 100,000

TALBOT, Catherine
[-] **Essays on Various Subjects.** 1772. *1st. Edn.* 2 vols. Cont. cf., rubbed; sig. of John Dalziel. (BBA. Jun.28; 97) *Hannas.* £85

TALBOT, Edward Allen
- **Cinq Années de Séjour au Canada ...** Paris, 1825. *1st. Edn. in Pr.* 3 vols. Cont. (orig.?) plain stiff wraps., unc., rebkd. in cl.; the Rt. Hon. Visc. Eccles copy. [Sabin 94228] (CNY. Nov.18; 263) $170
- **Five Years' Residence in the Canadas.** 1824. *[1st. Edn.].* 2 vols. Some spotting, bds., defect. (P. Dec.8; 351) *Way.* £80
- - **Anr. Copy.** 2 vols. Cont. cf. gt., spines slightly scuffed; the Rt. Hon. Visc. Eccles copy. [Sabin 94229] (CNY. Nov.18; 262) $150

TALES OF MAGIC & MYSTERY
Camden [N.J.], Dec. 1927-Apr. 1928. Vol. 1 nos. 1-5 (compl. run). Darkening slightly, pict. wraps., lightly rubbed, corners creasing, year pencilled in, spine reinforced with tape, all except 1st. with cover versos taped. (CBA. Oct.29; 825) $225

TALLEMANT DES REAUX, Gédéon
- **Les Historiettes. Mémoires pour Servir à l'Histoire du XVIIe Siècle.** Ed.:– Monmerqué. Paris, 1834. *Orig. Edn.* 6 vols. Cont. hf. cf., decor. spines; Baron de Nervo Liby. (HD. Sep.22; 354) Frs. 1,400

TALLEYRAND-PERIGORD, Charles Maurice, Duc de
- **Memoirs.** Ed.:– Duc de Broglie. Intro.:– W. Reid. L., Grol. Soc. ca. 1910. *(26) De Luxe Edn.* 5 vols. On Bütten, ills. in 2 states, col. on Bütten & uncold. on Jap., title lf. on Japan, partly unc., hand-bnd. mor., gt. spine, covers, inner & outer dentelles, red leath. onlays with gold Napoleon I insignia, gt. Napoleon I arms on red mor. doubls., spine slightly faded, corners slightly bumped, silk end-papers. (H. Nov.23; 1018) DM 1,200

TALLIS, John
- **History & Description of the Crystal Palace.** L., [1851]. 3 vols. in 2. 4to. Extra cold. title, frontis., 146 engraved plts., frontis. torn, some staining & spotting, cont. cf. (S. Mar.6; 402) *Quaritch.* £60
- **Views in London.** Ca. 1840. 42 (of 88) folding plans, a few titles cropped, text tipped in, facs. title, mod. mor., s.-c., as a coll. of plts., w.a.f. (P. Apr.12; 77) *Thomas.* £180

TALLIS, John
See— GASPEY, William

TALMUD
- **Babylonian Talmud.** Ed.:– Isaac M. Wise. Trans.:– Michael L. Rodkinson. Boston, 1918. *2nd. Edn.* 20 vols. in 10. Hf. leath., few spines defect. (SG. Feb.2; 119) $190
- **The Babylonian Talmud Seder Nezikin.** Trans.:– I. Epstein. Soncino Pr., 1935. *(1000).* 8 vols. Orig. cl., lightly soiled. (CSK. Sep.30; 84) £85
- **Babylonische Talmud.** Trans.:– L. Goldschmidt. Berlin, 1930-36. 12 vols. Cl. (B. Jun.21; 224) Fls. 700
- **Der Babylonische Talmud; mit Einschluss der Vollstaendügen Misnah.** Ed.:– Lazarus Goldschmidt. Berlin, [etc.], 1899-1922. *1st. Edn. with the Hebrew text.* 8 vols. 4to. Hebrew text surrounded by German trans., variae lectiones in Hebrew & notes in German, orig. leath., rubbed. (SG. Feb.2; 118) $400
- **The Living Talmud: The Wisdom of the Fathers & its Classical Commentaries.** Trans.:– Judah Goldin. Ill.:– Ben Zion. N.Y., Ltd. Edns. Cl., 1960. *(1500)*

numbered, sigd. by artist. Sm. fo. 12 full-p. drawings, lettered tissue-guards, hf. vell., buckram, orig. s.-c. (SG. May 27; 228) $110
– **Masekhet Eruvin**. Commentaries:– Rashi & the Tosafists. Venice, 1522. *1st. Edn.* Sm. fo. Title remargined, some other repairs, some dampstaining, scattered Hebrew marginalia in ink, later hf. leath., worn, spine badly chafed, extremities rubbed. (SG. Feb.2; 306) $1,900
– **[Talmud Bavli]**. Commentaries:– Rashi & Tosafiats, Rabbenu Asher, Rabbenu Nissim, Shimshon of Sens, commentary of Rambam on the Mishna. Amst., 1644-48. 12 vols. 4to. Few ll. remargined, few torn, scattered Hebrew marginalia in ink, some soiling or dampstaining, negligible worming, cont. blind-tooled pol. sheep, worn, spine ends chipped, mostly lacks metal clasps. (SG. Feb.2; 303) $2,600
– **Talmud Yerushalmi**. Venice, 1523-24. *1st. Edn.* 4 pts. in 1 vol. Fo. Lacks 1st. engraved title, pt. 4 misbnd. after pt. 1, some soiling & staining, a few margins frayed or with minor repairs, final lf. mntd., sig. on 1st. lf., cl., rubbed; Hochschule für die Wissenschaft des Judenthums stp. [Steinschneider 2309] (SPB. Jun.26; 33) $2,500

TALON, Abbé Jean Crasset de
– **The History of the Church of Japan**. L., 1705-07. 2 vols. in 1. 4to. Some sm. tears, mostly marginal, soiled & browned, cont. rebkd. sheep, worn. (BBA. May 23; 1) *Quaritch*. £120

TAMURA, Jitsuzo & Kabayashi, Yukia
– **Tombs & Mural Paintings of Ch'ing-Ling**. Kyoto, 1953-2. *(200)*. 2 vols. Fo. Orig. cl. (CSK. Jun.29; 2) £85

TANNER, Matthias
– **Societas Jesu apostolorum Imitatrix, sive Costa Praeclara et Virtutes Eorum**. Ill.:– Kilian. Prague, 1694. Fo. A few sm. rust-holes & other minor imperfections, 19th. C. red mor. gt., inner gt. dentelles, by Mackenzie; Huth copy. (S. Nov.17; 70) *A. Thomas*. £260

TANS'UR, William
– **Melodia Sacra: Or The Devout Psalmist's New Musical Companion**. [St. Neots?], priv. ptd., 1768. *1st. Edn.* Ob. 8vo. Unpaginated, etched music, ptd. text, engraved port. of Tans'ur on fly-lf., apparently compl., sheets ptd. 1 side only, some ptd. sections pasted in, price '3s.6d.' added in brown ink on fly-lf., ptd. price of 2s. 6d. on title-p. altered to 3s.6d., traces of offsetting, impressions of 2 engraved plts. of music on inside covers of bdg., cont. cf., worn; owner's inscr. of William White, Apr. 5 1769. (S. May 10; 167) *Haas*. £600

TAPLIN, Rev. George
– **The Folklore, Manners, Customs & Languages of the South Australian Aborigines** ... Adelaide, 1879. Ink markings to 1 plt., bdg. not stated, slightly worn. (KH. May 1; 694) Aus. $320
– **The Folklore, Manners, Customs & Languages of the South Australian Aborigines** ... – **Grammar of the Narrinyeri Tribe**. Adelaide (1st. work), 1879; 1878. Together 2 works in 1 vol. 1st. work: some pale foxing, mounting card (only) of frontis. cracked; 2nd. work: continuously paginated 4-p. Index to the combined works; pres.(?) mor.; Henry L. White bkplt. (KH. Nov.9; 727) Aus. $480
– **The Narrinyeri; An Account of the Tribes of South Australian Aborigines** ... Adelaide, 1874. *1st. Edn.* Semi-limp cl. (KH. May 1; 693) Aus. $300

TAPLIN, George & others
– **The Native Tribes of South Australian** ... **With an Introductory Chapter by J.D. Woods**. 1879. Early hf. mor. (KH. May 1; 695) Aus. $290

TAPLIN, William
– [–] **The Sportsman's Cabinet, or a Correct Delineation of the Canine Race**. 1803-04. *1st. Edn.* 4to. Cont. cf., jnts. reprd. (SKC. Nov.18; 1990) £240

TARDIEU, Ambroise
– **Galerie des Uniformes des Gardes Nationales de France** ... Paris, 1817. 2 vols. 1 frontis., 27 cold. engraved plts., extra frontis. by Canu, plts. mntd. on guards, hf. chagrin, wrap. preserved. (HD. Jan.27; 311) Frs. 2,000
– **Grand Dictionnaire Historique, Généalogique et**

Biographique de la Haute Marche (Dept. de la Creuse). Priv. ptd., 1894. 4to. Sewed. (HD. Mar.21; 125) Frs. 1,000

TARKAVACHASPATI, T.
– **Sabdastoma Mahanidhi** ... **a Sanskrit Dictionary**. Calcutta, New Sanskrit Pr., 1869-70. 5 pts. in 1 vol. 4to. Ptd. in Sanskrit thro.-out, Middle Hill bds., w.a.f. (S. Mar.6; 50) *Koster*. £120

TARKINGTON, Booth
– **The Gentleman from Indiana**. N.Y., 1899. *1st. Edn.* 3rd. state, inscr. by author. (*With:*) – **The Magnificent Ambersons**. N.Y., 1918. *1st. Edn.* Inscr. by author. (*With:*) – **Alice Adams**. N.Y., 1921. *1st. Edn.* 1st. state, sigd. by author. Together 3 vols. Orig. cl., slightly rubbed. (SG. Jan.12; 334) $300
– **The Works**. Garden City, 1922. *Seawood Edn. (1075) numbered & sigd.* 27 vols. Port. & limitation ll. loose in Vol. I, cl.-bkd. bds., spine dust soiled, partly unc. & unopened. (SG. Mar.15; 150) $175
– – **Anr. Edn.** Garden City, 1922-28. *Seaward Edn. (1075) numbered & sigd. by author & publisher.* Vols. 1-21. Cl.-bkd. bds., liby. bkplt. (SG. Nov.17; 332) $110

TARLETON, Sir Banastre
– **A History of the Campaigns of 1780 & 1781, in the Southern Provinces of North America**. Ill.:– W. Faden. L., 1787. *1st. Edn.* Lge. 4to. Each map partly hand-cold. in outl., 1 map slightly wrinkled & slightly frayed on blank lr. edge, anr. map with sm. tear at inner margin, cont. mott. cf. gt. [Sabin 94397] (SG. Nov.3; 205) $800

TARTAGLIA, Niccolo
– **Nova Scientia**. Venice, 1537. *1st. Edn.* Sm. 4to. A4 blank, colophon lf., slight browning in inner margins, cont. paper bds., soiled; Stanitz coll. (SPB. Apr.25; 418) $4,250
– **Quesiti, et Inventioni Diverse**. Venice, 1546. *1st. Edn.* 4to. Lacks folding plt. (as usual), some spotting at end, mod. mor. by Lakeside Press; Stanitz coll. (SPB. Apr.25; 417) $1,200

TARTAGNUS, A. de Imola
– **In primam et secundam ff. novi Partem cum Apostillis Doctissimoque Doctorum Domini Francesci de Curte et Bernardini de Laudriano et cum Aliis Innumeris Additionibus per Dominium Antonium Franciscum de Doctoribus Patavinum noviter editis**. Venice, 1514. Fo. Slightly stained at head thro.-out, cont. wood bds., blind-tooled cf. spine, clasps brkn., jnts. reprd.; Hans Fürstenberg ex-libris. (R. Apr.3; 93) DM 4,400
– **Tabula super Prima et Secunda Parte ff. Novi**. Venice, 1514. Lge. fo. Cont. stpd. hf. cf. over wood bds., spine renewed, clasps incompl., chain; from Fondation Furstenberg-Beaumesnil. (HD. Nov.16; 174) Frs. 3,200

TARTINI, G.
[–] **Trattato di Musica seconds la Vera Scienza dell'Armoria**. Padua, 1754. *1st. Edn.* 4to. Some slight spotting, most in margin, many pencil entries, some in blue pen, 1 copperplt. misbnd., cont. bds., very worn & defect. (HK. Nov.9; 2286) DM 650

TASCHENBIBLIOGRAPHIEN FUR BUCHER-SAMMLER
Stuttgart, [1924-26]. Vols. 1-4 in 4 vols. Orig. linen. (R. Apr.3; 679) DM 750
– – **Anr. Edn.** Stuttgart, [1924-27]. 5 vols., compl. Orig. linen, 1 spine faded. (H. May 22; 7) DM 750

TASCHEN KALENDER DER NEUESTEN FRANZOSISCH UND ENGLISCHEN MODEN FUR DAS 1793 JAHR.
Frankfurt, [1792]. 94 × 61 mm., miniature book. Engraved frontis., pict. title-p. & 17 plts. handcold., 1 other plt., lacks most of anr. folding plt., orig. bds., slightly worn & soiled; van Veen coll. (S. Feb.28; 205) £70

TASMAN, Abel Janszoon
– **Journal of his Discovery of Van Diemen's Land & New Zealand in 1642** ... Amst., 1898. Fo. Bds., qtr. vell., minor wear. (KH. Nov.9; 728) Aus. $280

TASMANIA
See— VAN DIEMEN'S LAND

TASSIN, Nicolas
– **Les Plana et Profile de Toutes les Principales Villes et Lieux Considerables de France** ... Paris, 1636. Pt. 2 only. Ob. 4to. 20 engraved titles & tables, approx. 190 maps, plans & views, cont. cf., w.a.f. (C. Nov.16; 209) *Shapero*. £350
– – **Anr. Copy**. 2 vols. Ob. 8vo. Folding plan, 415 copper-engraved plts., cont. vell. (HD. Sep.22; 356) Frs. 19,000
– – **Anr. Edn.** Paris, 1644. *1st. Printing*. 2 vols. Ob. 8vo. Title renewed, cont. cf., spines decor. (HD. Jun.18; 45) Frs. 18,000

TASSO, Torquato
– **Aminta, Favola Boschereccia**. Bodoni Pr., 1789. *(50) on laid paper*. 4to. Lightly browned, hf. cf., defect. (CR. Jun.6; 15) Lire 400,000
– – **Anr. Edn.** Crisopoli [Parma], 1789. 4to. Wide margin, on Bütten, lacks blank ll. at beginning & end & Avis lf. at end, (not present in all copies), a few ll. with slight foxing, later red mor., gt. decor. spine, slightly bumped. (H. May 22; 618) DM 1,400
– – **Anr. Edn.** Parma, 1796. *(100) on vell.* 4to. Upr. endpaper with stp., minimal foxing, cont. hf. dark red mor., gt., decor., minimal wear. (HK. Nov.10; 3114) DM 600
– – **Anr. Edn.** Ill.:– Ruger after Prudhon. Parma, 1796. Some slight foxing, cont. cf. gt., gold-tooled decor., gt. inner & outer dentelle. (D. Nov.24; 2578) DM 850
– – **Anr. Edn.** Ill.:– Prudhon &c. Parigi, 1813. (*Bound with:*) – **L'Aminte** ... **imitée en Vers Français**. Trans.:– Baour de Lormian. Ill.:– Desenne & c. Paris, n.d. Together 2 works in 1 vol. 12mo. On vell., figures before the letter, cont. violet stp.-grd. mor., blind– & gt.-decor. (HD. May 4; 435) Frs. 2,500
– **L'Aminte** ... **imitée en Vers Français**. Trans.:– Baour de Lormian. Ill.:– Desenne. Paris, [1813]. Sm. 12mo. On vell., ills before the letter, cont. str.-grd. mor. gt., richly decor., cypher of Augusta Amalia of Bavaria, watered silk doubls. & end-ll. (HD. May 4; 436) Frs. 2,900
– **La Gerusalemme di Torquato Tasso**. Notes:– Giuilio Guastavini. Ill.:– Bernardo Castello. Genova, 1617. Sm. fo. Cont. Italian red mor., richly decor. (HD. Nov.9; 81) Frs. 4,700
– **La Gerusalemme Liberata**. Genoa, 1617. Sm. fo. Cont. cf., rebkd. (BBA. Jun.28; 180) *Dilua*. £200
– – **Anr. Copy**. Fo. P. 29 reprd., mod. hf. cf. (P. Sep.8; 345) *Duran*. £90
– – **Anr. Edn.** Venetia, 1673. Sm. 4to. Title strengthened, 2 ll. remargined, dampstains in upr. margins, old blind-decor. cf. (HD. May 3; 154) Frs. 1,300
– – **Anr. Edn.** 1724. 2 vols. Cont. mor. gt. (CSK. Jun.15; 92) £500
– – **Anr. Copy**. 2 vols. 4to. Cont. porphyry cf., decor. spine, sm. defects, Talleyrand heraldie ex-libris & device in each vol. (HD. Jan.30; 101) Frs. 2,000
– – **Anr. Edn.** Ill.:– Giambattista Piazzetta. Venice, 1745. Fo. List of subscribers, slight spotting on 1 lf., cont. mott. sheep, gt. spine, covers & spine wormed, rubbed; Starhemberg copy. (SPB. Dec.14; 83) $2,100
– – **Anr. Copy**. Fo. Decor. initials & end-pieces, hf.-title, cont. decor. marb. cf., slightly loose. (SI. Dec.15; 92) Lire 5,000,000
– – **Anr. Edn.** Paris, 1784-86. *1st. Edn.* 2 vols. 4to. Lacks frontis., cont. leath. gt., gold-tooled decor. & inner dentelle, cover loose. (GB. Nov.4; 2205) DM 500
– – **Anr. Edn.** Ill.:– after Cochin. Paris, [1785-86]. *2nd. Edn.* 2 vols. 4to. Frontis. & a few plts. spotted, some text ll. browned, cont. roan gt. (S. May 30; 102) *Thorp*. £400
– – **Anr. Edn.** Firenze, 1820. 2 vols. Fo. Cf., gt.-tooled decor. (CR. Jun.6; 76) Lire 600,000
– – **Anr. Copy**. 2 vols. Fo. Cont. bds. (CR. Jul.6; 297) Lire 450,000
– **La Jérusalem Délivrée**. Trans.:– L.P.M.F. Baour-Lormian. Ill.:– Cochin. Paris, 1796. 2 vols. 4to. Some foxing, cont. mor. finish hf. roan, spines decor., unc. (HD. May 3; 155) Frs. 1,500
– **Scielta delle Rime. Parte Prima, Parte Seconda.**

TASSO, Torquato -*Contd.*

Ferrara, 1582. Herzog Alfons II arms on title, vell. (D. Nov.24; 2579)   DM 700

TASSONI, Alessandro
- **La Secchia Rapita.** Modena, 1744. 4to. 2 folding maps, folding facs., 12 plts., including 1 folding, all ptd. in blue, folding ptd. genealogical table, hf.-title, last lf. with the woodcut, 19th. C. mor. gt., spine faded. (S. Nov.17; 71)   *Henderson.* £270

TATE, Allen
- **The Hovering Fly, & Other Essays.** Ill.:- Wightman Williams. [Cummington, Mass.], Cummington Pr., 1948 [1949]. *(93) numbered & sigd. by author & artist.* Qtr. vell., decor. bds. (SG. Mar.1; 582) $900

TATTERSALL, C.E.C.
See— KENDRICK, A.F. & Tattersall, C.E.C.

TATTET, E.
- **Journal d'un Chirurgien de la Grande Armée (L.V. Lagmeau) 1803-1815.** Paris, 1913. Hf. cf. (HD. Jan.27; 87)   Frs. 1,200

TAUBERT, Sigfrid
- **Bibliopola: Pictures & Texts about the Book Trade.** Designed:- Herman Zapf. Hamburg, [1966]. *1st. Edn.* 2 vols. Sm. fo. In Engl., Fr. & German, linen. (SG. Jan.5; 295) $226
- - **Anr. Copy.** 2 vols. 4to. In Engl., Fr. & German, bdg. not stated, card. s.-c. (CBA. Nov.19; 836) $110

TAULER, Johannes
- **Predigten. Sermon des Grossgelarten.** Leipzig, Conrad Kachelofen. 1498. 4to. Rubricated in red & blue, cont. stpd. cf. over wood bds., richly gt., spine renewed, traces of clasps; from Fondation Furstenberg-Beaumesnil. [HC 15346; BMC III, 628; Goff T48] (HD. Nov.16; 29)   Frs. 48,100

TAULLARD, A.
- **Plateria Sudamericana.** Buenos Aires, 1941. *(800) numbered.* Lge. 4to. Pict. bds. (SG. Aug.25; 343) $110

TAUNT, Henry W.
- **A New Map of the River Thames from Oxford to London.** L., 1873. *2nd. Edn.* Ob. 8vo. 24 litho. maps ill. with 78 mntd. photographs, orig. cl. (CSK. Aug.5; 25)   £85

TAUNTON, Thomas H.
- **Portraits of Celebrated Racehorses of the Past & Present Centuries.** L., 1887-88. 4 vols. 4to. Crimson hf. mor. gt. by Sangorski & Sutcliffe. (P. Nov.24; 101)   *Marks.* £420
- - **Anr. Copy.** 4 vols. 461 plts., qtr. mor. gt. (P. May 17; 31)   *Allen.* £320
- - **Anr. Copy.** 4 vols. 4to. Some ll. loose in 3 vols., orig. red mor.-bkd. cl. gt., spine rubbed. (LC. Mar.1; 554)   £220

TAUSIN, H.
See— CHASSANT, A. & Tausin, H.

TAUT, Br.
- **Alpine Architektur.** Hagen, 1919. 5 pts. Fo. Title & margins slightly browned, orig. sewed, spine slightly faded, 1 tear & sm. faults. (H. Nov.24; 2133)   DM 1,600

TAVANNES, Gaspard de Saulx, Seigneur de
- **Memoires.** [Lugny, 1653]. *1st. Edn.* 2 pts. in 1 vol. Fo. Cont. mott. cf. gt. (SG. Oct.27; 315) $175

TAVERA, Don Juan
- **Constituciones Synodales del Arzobispado de Toledo hechas por el Illustrissimo Señor Don Juan Tavera.** Alcala de Henares, 1536. Fo. Mod. vell. (DS. Nov.25; 2182)   Pts. 175,000

TAVERNER, Eric & others
- **Salmon Fishing.** L., 1931. *Lonsdale Liby. Edn. (275) numbered & sigd.* This copy unnumbered, 7 artificial flies in sunken mount under perspex at end (mount slightly warped), orig. mor. gt., spine & little faded. (S. Oct.4; 61)   *Joseph.* £190
- - **Anr. Copy.** 7 artificial flies in sunken mount under perspex at end, orig. mor. gt. (S. Nov.28; 102)   *Head.* £150

- **Trout Fishing from all Angles.** L., 1929. *Lonsdale Liby. Ltd. Edn. (375) numbered & sigd.* 30 artificial flies in sunken mount under perspex at end, orig. mor. gt.; inscr. 'To Scott [Atkinson] ... From The Greenwell Club'. (S. Oct.4; 60)   *Atkinson.* £240
- - **Anr. Copy.** 30 artificial flies in sunken mount under perspex at end, orig. mor. gt. (S. Nov.28; 103)   *Head.* £150

TAVERNIER, Jean Baptiste
- **Collections of Travels through Turky into Persia, & the East-Indies.** L., 1684. 6 pts.: 2 vols. in 1. Fo. Some browning & dampstaining, a few ll. slightly defect., buckram. [Wing T250-254] (SG. Sep.22; 285) $175
- **Les Six Voyages en Turquie, en Perse et aux Indes.** Amst., 1678. 2 vols. Both title versos stpd., vol. 1 title with lr. corner cut off, text & plts. very slightly spotted, cont. vell., some browning. (HK. May 15; 651)   DM 480
- - **Anr. Edn.** Paris, 1679-81. *Elzevir Edn.* 3 vols. 12mo. Cont. spr. cf., spines decor. (HD. May 3; 156)   Frs. 3,900
- - **Anr. Edn.** La Haye, 1718. 3 vols. 12mo. Cont. cf. (HD. Apr.13; 55)   Frs. 3,500
- **The Six Voyages of ... through Turkey into Persia & the East Indies ...** L., 1678. *2nd. Edn.* 3 pts. in 1 vol. Fo. Title & 1 plt. supplied in facs., cont. cf., rebkd. [Wing T 256] (PNY. Jun.6; 552) $120
- **Vierzig-jährige Reise-Beschreibung. Durch Turkey, Persien, Indien ...** Nürnberg, 1681. 3 pts. in 1 vol. Fo. Title & some text ll. torn, some ll. very browned, especially in lr. margin, 2 pp. pt. 1 defect., with slight loss, some browning, foxing or spotting, cont. vell., spine slightly defect. (R. Oct.13; 3054)   DM 1,250
See— VALLE, Pietro della– TAVERNIER, Jean Baptiste

TAYLOR
- **Lettres Politiques, Commerciales et Littéraires sur l'Inde; ou Vues et Intérêts de l'Angleterre.** Paris, 1801. Cont. cf., decor. spine. (HD. Feb.22; 216)   Frs. 1,300

TAYLOR, Bayard
- **Eldorado; or, Adventures in the Path of Empire: Comprising a Voyage to California ...** Ill.:- Sarony & Major, after Taylor. L., 1850. *1st. L. Edn. (issued simultaneously with the Amer. Edn.).* 2 vols. Orig. blind-stpd. cl., heads of spines slightly worn; the Rt. Hon. Visc. Eccles copy. [Sabin 94440] (CNY. Nov.18; 264) $140

TAYLOR, Bayard (Ed.)
See— PICTURESQUE EUROPE

TAYLOR, Bon J., Nodier, Ch. & Cailleux, A. de
- **Voyages Pittoresques et Romantiques dans l'ancienne France. La Normandie.** Ill.:- Atthalin, Fragonard, Isabey, Vernet, etc. Paris, 1820-25. 2 vols. (of 3) as usual. Fo. Vol. 1 with hf.-title, vol. II lacks 2 plts., 2 supp. plts., stains vol. II, 1 plt. reprd. in margin, cont. hf. chagrin, slits. (HD. Dec.9; 188)   Frs. 4,100
- **Methodus Incrementorum Directa et Inversa.** L., 1715. *1st. Edn.* 4to. Errata lf., spotting & browning, cont. cf.-bkd. marb. bds., some wear; Stanitz coll. (SPB. Apr.25; 419) $700

TAYLOR, Frederick Winslow
- **The Principles of Scientific Management.** L. & N.Y., 1911. *1st. Edn. 1st. Iss.* Cl. gt. (PNY. Jun.6; 553) $375

TAYLOR, G.
- **With Scott: The Silver Lining.** 1916. *1st. Edn.* Orig. cl., rubbed. (P. Jun.7; 56)   £110

TAYLOR, G.L.
See— CRESY, Edward & Taylor, G.L.

TAYLOR, George & Skinner, Andrew
- **Maps of the Roads of Ireland.** L., 1778. *1st. Edn.* Royal 8vo. Folding frontis. map (torn & reprd.), engraved title, 288 engraved maps, bkplt., hf. cf., rubbed. (GM. Dec.7; 447)   £180
- - **Anr. Copy.** Engraved title with vig., folding map, 288 pp. of engraved road maps, folding map torn & reprd., cont. red mor. gt., gt.-lettered on

upr. cover 'Fred. Trench Esq. Heywood ... '. (C. Nov.16; 181)   *Henderson.* £130
- - **Anr. Edn.** L. & Dublin, 1778. Engraved title, dedication, folding map of Ireland, 288 road maps, cont. hf. cf., w.a.f.; from liby. of Luttrellstown Castle. (C. Sep.28; 1723)   £160
- - **Anr. Copy.** Engraved title with vig., dedication, folding general map (torn), 288 full-p. road & regional maps ptd. recto & verso, index & subscribers' list, some faint soiling, cont. roan-bkd. bds., worn. (S. Apr.9; 156)   *Franks.* £110
- - **Anr. Copy.** Engraved title, dedication, 288 road maps on 144 ll., lacks folding map, title & 1st. few ll. soiled, cont. marb. cf. (CSK. Aug.5; 143)   £70
- - **Anr. Edn.** L., 1783. *2nd. Edn.* Engraved title, 289 engraved maps, lacks folding general map, cf., rubbed. (GM. Dec.7; 440)   £160
- - **Anr. Edn.** L., n.d. 289 engraved maps, lacks title & index, hf. cf., w.a.f. (GM. Oct.5; 141)   £120

- **Survey & Maps of the Roads of North Britain, or Scotland.** 1776. Engraved folding title, folding map, 61 strip road maps (dtd. 1775) on 31 folding sheets, 2 torn, cont. sheep; Sir Ivar Colquhoun, of Luss copy. (CE. Mar.22; 304)   £190
- - **Anr. Copy.** Ob. fo. Engraved title, 62 maps, (1 folding & torn), title & few plts. browned, some creasing, cont. limp cf. (S. Mar.6; 375)   *Korn.* £120
- - **Anr. Copy.** Ob. 4to. Engraved title, 59 road maps on 30 ll., all folding, general map cleanly torn, some light soiling, cont. travelling cf., lacks ties. (CSK. May 4; 42)   £85
- **Survey of the Roads of Scotland.** 1800. Engraved title, 178 road maps on 89 sheets, 8 pp. of index at end, orig. bds., rebkd. (P. Oct.20; 267)   £90

TAYLOR, Isidore Justin Séverin, Baron
- **Voyages Pittoresques et Romantiques dans l'Ancienne France.** Dauphiné, 1854. 2 vols. Lge. fo. On vell., title-frontis., title vig., 173 litho. plts., most on tinted ground, all pp. mntd. on guards, cont. hf. mor., corners, decor. spine. (HD. Feb.29; 46)   Frs. 23,500

TAYLOR, J.H.
- **On Golf.** 1902. Bdg. not stated. (PD. Jul.13; 8)   £70

TAYLOR, Rev. Jeremy
- **A Choice Manual. Containing what is to be Believed, Practised, & Desired or Praied for.** 1674. 12mo. Later cf. gt., little rubbed. [Wing T219a] (BBA. Jun.28; 98)   *Quaritch.* £110
- **The Great Exemplar of Sanctity & Holy Life ...** L., 1653. 3 pts. in 1 vol. 4to. Title-p. vigs., 14 copper engrs., some folding & double-p., new end-papers, later cf., rebkd. with mod. cf. (CBA. Dec.10; 464) $200
- **The Whole Works ... with a Life of the Author ... by Reginald Heber.** 1822. 15 vols. Cont. cf. gt. (LC. Mar.1; 556)   £70

TAYLOR, John, the Water Poet
- [-] **Verbum Sempiternum [Salvator Mundi].** L., [1693]. *2nd. Edn.* 32mo. Licence lf. with sig. 'A' only on recto, hf.-title 'The Bible', blank A3 & S8, a few headlines & letters in outer margin lightly shaved, 18th. C. str.-grd. mor. gt., metal clasp. [Wing T526] (C. May 30; 172)   *Quaritch.* £290
- - **Anr. Edn.** Ed.:- John Taylor. Providence, ca. 1768. 55 × 40mm. Miniature Book. Lacks 1st. 2 sigs., 1st. 2 ll. in 3rd. sig. & last 2 blank ll. in final sig., C3 & 4 mutilated with loss of text, leath. disbnd. (SG. Dec.8; 335) $475

TAYLOR, Joseph H.
- **Sketches of Frontier & Indian Life on the Upper Missouri & Great Plains.** Pottstown, priv. ptd., 1889. *1st. Edn.* Orig. hf. leath., moderate wear, lacks front end-paper. (RO. May 22; 176) $180

TAYLOR, Matthew
- **England's Bloody Tribunal.** L., 1771. 4to. Tear to frontis. reprd. with tape, some foxing, ink names to front end-papers, cont. cf. (CBA. Dec.10; 379) $250

TAYLOR, Capt. Meadows
- **Confessions of a Thug.** L., 1839. 3 vols. 12mo. Orig. cl.; A. Edward Newton copy. (LH. Sep.25; 604) $100

TAYLOR, Paul S.
- **An American Exodus.** Ill.:– after Dorothea Lange. N.Y., [1939]. 1st. Edn. 4to. Minor foxing to 1st. & last ll., as usual, gt.-lettered cl., d.-w. chipped. (SG. Nov.10; 99) $110

TAYLOR, Samuel
- **Angling in all its Branches.** 1800. 3 pts. in 1 vol. 6 advt. pp., cont. pig. (P. Dec.8; 119) *Nolan.* £55

[TAYLOR, Silas &] Dale, Samuel
- **The History & Antiquities of Harwich & Dover-court.** 1732. 2nd. Edn. 4to. Cont. hf. cf., rebkd. (CSK. Sep.16; 121) £75
- – **Anr. Copy.** 4to. 14 plts., some folding, mod. hf. cf. gt. (P. Jun.7; 165) £55

TAYLOR, Thomas, 1758-1835
- [–] **A Dissertation on the Eleusinian & Bacchic Mysteries.** Amst. [i.e. L., 1790]. 1st. Edn. Mod. cl. (SG. Apr.19; 180) $225

TAYLOR, Thomas, fl. 1715
- **The Principality of Wales Exactly Described.** L., 1718. Ob. 8vo. Engraved title, 10 full-p. maps, some shaved, title reprd., some faint stains, 19th. C. cf.-bkd. bds., worn. (S. Mar.6; 340) *Korn.* £160

TAYLOR, W. Thomas & Morris, Henry
- **Twenty-One Years of Bird & Bull: A Bibliography, 1958-1979.** [North Hills, Pa.], Bird & Bull Pr., 1980. 1st. Edn. (350) numbered on Roma V.E. H.M.P. De Luxe Iss., with cl. folder containing ll. of ephemera. Tall 8vo. Mor.-bkd. patterned bds., cl. folding box. (SG. Aug.4; 36) $180
- – **Anr. Edn.** [Austin], Bird & Bull Pr., 1980. (350) numbered. Lge. 8vo. Qtr. mor., pict. bds. (SG. Jan.5; 39) $140
- – **Anr. Copy.** Lge. 8vo. Patterned bds., mor. back & tips, unc. (SG. Jan.12; 42) $120

TCHAIKOVSKY, Pietr Il'yich
- **The Sleeping Princess [piano score].** Paris, n.d. Some tears reprd. with tape, some additional pp. tipped in & laid down, bds.; annots. in pencil & black ink by Diaghilev, many sigd. with initials, additions from other works by Tchaikovsky, dancers' names, details of scenario (some of these in other hands), with annots. to music by Stravinsky, including autograph p. tipped in between pp. 44 & 45, inscr. by him on outer cover 'Spashchaya krasa-vista La belle au bois dormant', fly-lf. inscr. & sigd. by Serge Lifar 'Collaboration de Diaghilev avec Stravinsky Bakst pour la Réalisation de la Belle au Bois dormant à Londres – Theatre Alhambra de 1921 ... ', Serge Lifar Coll. (S. May 9; 227) £10,000

TCHEMERZINE, Avenir
- **Bibliographie d'Editions Originales et Rares d'Auteurs Français des XV, XVI, XVII et XVIII Siècles.** Paris, 1927. 1st. Edn. 10 vols. 4to. 600 facs., publishers cl. (DS. Jan.27; 2550) Pts. 60,000
- – **Anr. Edn.** Paris, 1927-33. Orig. Edn. (800) numbered on papier surglacé. 10 vols. Lge. 8vo. Qtr. mor., marb. bds. (SG. Jan.5; 296) $800
- – **Anr. Edn.** Paris, 1927-33. 10 vols. Hf. cl. bds. (HD. Jun.6; 147) Frs. 2,900
- – **Anr. Copy.** 10 vols. Cont. hf. chagrin. (VG. Sep.13; 585) Fls. 1,000

TCHERNYKOV, Jacob
- **Arkhitekturnye Fantazii [Architectural Fictions].** Leningrad, 1933. 1st. Edn. 4to. 101 cold. plts., title-pp. in Russian, German, Fr. & Engl., orig. cl. (S. Nov.21; 167) *Garmey.* £800

TEASDALE, Sara
- **Stars To-Night: Verses New & Old for Boys & Girls.** Ill.:– Dorothy P. Lathrop. N.Y., 1930. 1st. Edn. Cl., d.-w. frayed; sigd. inscr. on front free end-paper 'For Margaret Conklin from Sara ... November 10, 1930', inscr. & sigd. by Conklin to Mrs. Lyon, an A.L.s. & 2 handmade C'mas & Easter cards, inscr. from Conklin to Mrs. Lyon, inserted. (SG. Jan.12; 337) $140

TECHENER, J. & L.
- **Histoire de la Bibliophilie. Reliures.** Paris, 1861. Lge. fo. MS. note on front fly-lf., sigd. 'W.S.M.' re non-iss. of title & table of contents due to publisher's bankruptcy before completion, title & table made up from pt. wraps., cont. red str.-grd. mor., Stirling Maxwell arms blind-stpd. on covers, rebkd.; H.M. Nixon coll. (BBA. Oct.6; 128) *Maggs.* £600

TEELING, Charles H.
- **Personal Narrative of the Irish Rebellion of 1798.** L., 1828. 1st. Edn. Bkplt., hf. cf., rubbed. (GM. Dec.7; 383) £70

TEERINK, Dr. Hermann
- **Jonathan Swift: A Bibliography of the Writing in Prose & Verse.** The Hague, 1937. 1st. Edn. (315) numbered. Sm. 4to. Gt.-ornamented cl.; sigd. by author. (SG. Sep.15; 324) $110
- – **Anr. Edn.** Ed.:– Arthur H. Scouten. 1963. 2nd. Edn. Orig. cl., slightly rubbed. (TA. Dec.15; 393) £62

TEESDALE, Henry
- **New British Atlas.** Ca. 1830. Fo. 48 hand-cold. maps (3 folding), hf. mor. gt., worn. (P. Jun.7; 335) £340
- – **Anr. Edn.** 1831. Fo. Engraved title, 3 col. folding maps, 45 hand-cold. double-p. county maps, hf. mor. gt. (P. Jul.5; 390) £360
- – **Anr. Edn.** 1842. Fo. Engraved title, general key map, 3 folding maps, 45 col. double-p. county maps, cont. mor. gt. (P. Jul.5; 376) £350

TEICHELMANN, C.G. & Schürmann, C.W.
- **Outlines of a Grammar, Vocabulary, & Phraseology of the Aboriginal Language of South Australia** ... Adelaide, 1840. 1st. Edn. 2 or 3 ll. & wraps. slightly chipped at edges, stabbed, disbnd. (KH. May 1; 701) Aus. $170

TEIXERA, Jose
- **The Strangest Adventure that ever happened ...** Trans.:– A. Munday. 1601. 1st. Edn. in Engl. Sm. 4to. Sm. stain on title, a few p. numerals shaved, 18th. C. mott. cf. gt., foot of spine torn; Penrose bkplt. [STC 23864] (C. May 30; 174) *Quaritch.* £620

TELESCOPIO POLITICO.
Cádiz, 1820. Nos. 1-18. 4to. Sewed. (DS. Dec.16; 2061) Pts. 36,000

TELFER, Comm. J. Buchan
- **The Crimea & Transcaucasia.** L., 1876. 2 vols. in 1. Orig. cl., rubbed. (BBA. May 3; 332) *Cavendish Rare Books.* £75

TELFORD, Thomas
- **The Charts & Plans, referred to in the Report from the Committee appointed to examine into Mr. Telford's Report & Survey, relative to the Communication between England & Ireland by the North-West of Scotland.** L., 1809. Lge. fo. Drophead title, 16 double-p. or folding maps & plans, some slight discolouration, orig. wraps., worn, new backstrip. (S. May 21; 19) *Fisher.* £480
- **Life of Thomas Telford Civil Engineer.** 1838. Atlas vol. only. Fo. Engraved port., 82 maps & plts., margins dampstained thro.-out, cont. hf. cf., rebkd., old spine preserved. (CSK. Aug.5; 56) £380

TEMMINCK, C.J.
See— KNIP, Madame Antoinette Pauline Jacqueline & others

TEMPLE, R.
- **Eight Views of the Mauritius comprising the positions of the British Army** ... Ill.:– I. Clark after Temple. L., [1813]. Ob. fo. 8 hand-cold. aquatints, some margins very slightly soiled, cl. (S. Dec.1; 369) *Dutroberville.* £950

TEMPLE, Sir William
- **Miscellanea.** 1680. 1st. Edn. Cont. cf., spine gt.-decor.; Sir Ivar Colquhoun, of Luss copy. [Wing T 646] (CE. Mar.22; 31a) £160
- **The Works.** Ill.:– after Lely (frontis.). 1750. 2 vols. Fo. Cont. cf., spines reprd., 18th. C. heraldic bkplt. (SKC. Mar.9; 1862) £65

TEMPLO, Yehuda Leon
- **Tavnit Heichal.** Amst. 1650. 1st. Edn. in Hebrew. 4to. Mispaginated, lacks plts. (as usual), owners' sigs. on both titles, few wormholes not affecting text, edges frayed, browned, mod. leath. (S. Oct.25; 394)
(S. Oct.25; 394) *Davidson.* £140

TEMPSKY, G.F. von
- **Mitla, a Narrative of ... Adventures on a Journey in Mexico, Guatemala & Salvador.** 1858. Lr. margin of title slightly shaved, cont. cf. gt. (CSK. May 4; 133a) £170

TENAC, Charles van
- **Histoire Générale de la Marine Comprenant les Naufragres Célébres, l'Histoire des Pirates, Corsairs et Négriers** ... Ill.:– Morel-Fatio & Pauquet. Paris, n.d. 4 vols. Cold. frontis., 1 cold. plt., 8 cold. & gommées plts., 14 other plts., some foxing, cont. hf. cf., decor. spines. (HD. Sep.21; 146) Frs. 1,100

TENCH, Capt. Watkin
- **A Narrative of the Expedition to Botany Bay.** L., 1789. 1st. Edn. Hf.-title slightly soiled, mod. hf. cf (CA. Apr.3; 111) Aus.$2,200
- – **Anr. Edn.** Dublin, 1889. (Bound With:) KAETE, G.–An Account of the Pelew Islands. L., 1788, Together 2 works in 1 vol., bnd in reverse order, slightly browned & foxed thro.-out, hf. leath., rubbed & bumped. (D. Nov.23; 1407) DM 850

TENIERS, David
- **Theatrum Pictorium.** Antw., [1684]. Fo. Mostly wide margin, lacks & plts., lightly soiled & foxed, ex-libris., cont. vell., soiled & slightly worn. (HK. Nov.9; 2205) DM 400

TENINT, W.
See— CHALLAMEL, A. & Tenint, W.

TENKENGOPP
- **Costumes Militaires Russes.** Paris, [1890]. Fo. Mod. hf. chagrin. (HD. Jan.27; 312) Frs. 1,100

TENNENT, James Emerson
- **Letters from the Aegean.** L., 1829. 1st. Edn. 2 vols. Sm. 8vo. Cont. hf. cf. & marb. bds., outer corners bruised. (SG. Mar.29; 346) $200

TENNENT, J.E.
See— O'BRIEN, Capt. C. & Tennent, J.E.

TENNEY, Mrs. Sanborn
- **Pictures & Stories of Animals for the Little Ones at Home.** N.Y., 1868. 1st. Edn. 6 vols. 12mo. Blind-stpd. cl., spines gt., light wear, orig. publisher's box, worn; Ken Leach coll. (RO. Jun.10; 5) $110

TENNIEL, Sir John (Ill.)
See— AESOP
See— DODGSON, Rev. Charles Lutwidge 'Lewis Carroll'
See— PUNCH

TENNYSON, Alfred Lord
- **The Charge of the Light Brigade.** N.p., [8 Aug., 1855]. 1st. Separate Edn. 4to. 4-p. leaflet ptd. on 3-pp., 2 ll. with creases, reprd. in few places, red mor., jnts. reprd.; pres. copy to Maj. M'Crea. (SPB. May 17; 686) $9,000
- **English Idyls; The Princess, & Maud; In Memoriam; Idylls of the King.** Glasgow, 1905. 4 vols., with continuous register. 32mo. Limp mor., fore-e. pntg. in each vol., solander case; Wilbur M. Stone bkplts. (SG. Nov.3; 206) $650
- **Enoch Arden.** L., 1865. 12mo. Gt.-tooled mor. by S. Style, fore-e. pntg. (SG. Nov.17; 238) $175
- **Idylls of the King.** L., 1869. Sm. 8vo. Old red mor., Rowlandsonesque double fore-e. pntg. (SG. Nov.17; 239) $175
- **Life & Works.** L., 1898-99. 'Edn. de Luxe'. (1050). 12 vols. Lge. 8vo. Lev. gt., partly unc. (SG. Feb.16; 309) $350
- **Poems.** L., 1842. 1st. Edn. 2 vols. Sm. 8vo. 8 pp. inserted advts., orig. bds., unc., worn, hf.-mor. s.-c.: E. Hubert Litchfield bkplt., Frederic Dannay copy. (CNY. Dec.16; 348) $220
- – **Anr. Edn.** Ill.:– after Edward Lear. L., 1889. 1st. Edn. (100) sigd. 4to. Frontis. tissue guard loose, orig. hf. mor., fore-corners worn; Frederic Dannay copy. (CNY. Dec.16; 349) $500

TENNYSON, Alfred Lord -*Contd.*

- **Prolusiones Academicae** ... Camb., 1829. *1st. Edn.* Sm. margin tear in title & following lf., orig. wraps., partly unc., re-stitched, most of spine chipped away; Frederic Dannay copy. (CNY. Dec.16; 347) $280
- **The Sailor Boy.** L., Emily Faithfull [T.J. Wise]. 1861 [1890s]. Sm. 8vo. Lev. gt., ptd. wraps. (state '25 copies for the Author's Use') bnd. in; the Henry William Poor copy. (SG. Mar.15; 151) $450
- **Viviane.** Trans.:– F. Michel. Ill.:– Gustave Doré. Paris, 1868. *1st. Printing.* Fo. Publisher's buckram. (HD. May 4; 438)   Frs. 1,300
- **Works.** L., 1872-73. 6 vols. Lge. 8vo. Tree cf. gt., spines gt., worn. (SG. Feb.16; 308) $225
- - **Anr. Edn.** L., 1894. Mor. gt., with fore-e. pntg., as a fore-e. pntg., w.a.f. (SPB. May 17; 740) $600
- - **Anr. Edn.** Ed.:– William J. Rolfe. Boston, 1895-98. *Edition De Grande Luxe. (1000) numbered on L.P.* 12 vols. Lge. 8vo. Titles & plts. on Japan vell., cont. red three-qtr. mor. & marb. bds., gt.-panel. spines, unc. (SG. Feb.16; 310) $250
- **The Poetic & Dramatic Works.** Ill.:– Charles S. Olcott. Boston & N.Y., 1929. *(500) numbered on L.P.* 7 vols. Red mor., gt.-decor., inlaid mor. doubls., inner dentelles, watered silk liners, light wear; A.L.s from author, with orig. mailing envelope, inlaid in Vol.1 end-paper. (RO. Dec.11; 318) $395

TENNYSON, Alfred Lord & Charles

[–] **Poems by Two Brothers.** L., 1827. *1st. Edn.* 12mo. Sm. paper copy, mor., partly unc.; William Marchbank bkplt., Frederic Dannay copy. (CNY. Dec.16; 346) $550

TENNYSON, Frederick

[–] **Poems.** N.p., n.d. *Page proofs.* 12mo. Corrected page proofs of poems 'Halcyone' & 'Aeson', with pagination but without sigs., cont. hf. cf. & marb. bds., gt. spine, gt.-lettered 'Unpub./Poems/By/ F.T.'; Mary Boyle bkplt., Frederic Dannay copy. (CNY. Dec.16; 352) $2,800

TENTZEL, Andreas

- **Medicina Diastatica ... Beneficio Mumialis Transplantationis Operationem ... Commentarii in Tractatum Tertium de Tempore seu Philosop. D. Theoph. Patacelei.** Jena, 1629. *1st. Edn.* 12mo. Lacks engraved frontis., paper wraps.; Dr. Walter Pagel copy. (S. Feb.7; 301)   *Colombo.* £70

TE'OMIM, Jonah, of Prague

- **Kikayon De'Jonah.** Hanau, 1712. *2nd. Edn.* Fo. Foxed & creased, buckram. (S. Oct.25; 395)   *Klein.* £100

TERENTIUS AFER, Publius

- **Andria oder das Mädchen von Andros.** Trans.:– F. Mendelssohn-Bartholdy. Ill.:– F. Kredel after A. Dürer. Verona, 1971. *(160) on Bütten.* 4to. Orig. hf. vell., s.-c. (D. Nov.24; 3206)   DM 520
- **The Brothers.** Ill.:– Albrecht Durer. Kentfield, California, Allen Pr., 1968. *(145).* Fo. Cl.-bkd. ill. paper bd., s.-c. (LH. Sep.25; 313) $350
- **Le Comedie Volgari.** Venice, 1546. Sm. 8vo. Some smudging, lr. margin of title clipped away, early vell. (SG. Feb.9; 161) $225
- **Les Comédies.** Trans.:– Abbé Le Monnier. Ill.:– Cochin. Paris, 1771. 3 vols. Latin & Fr. parallel text, cont. cf., spines decor. (HD. May 3; 157)   Frs. 1,250
- **A Comedy called Andria.** Trans.:– Richard Bernard. Ill.:– Fritz Kredel after Albrecht Durer. Verona, Bodoni Pr., 1971. *(170) numbered.* Fo. Orig. parch.-bkd. bds., s.-c. (S. Nov.22; 272)   *Duschness.* £280
- **Comicorum Elegantissimi Comoediae a Guidone Juvenale perq. Litterato familiariter explanatae ...** Mailand, 1523. Sm. fo. Old MS. annots. on title, some browning & soiling, end-papers partly renewed, 17/18th. C. leath., worn & bumped. (GB. May 3; 931)   DM 700
- **Comoedia.** Ed.:– Richard Bentley. Amst., 1727. *2nd. Edn.* Lge. 4to. Text browned, cont. vell., upr. cover soiled. (SG. Feb.9; 355) $100
- **Comoediae.** Commentary:– Aelius Donatus. [Paris, 1489]. Sm. fo. Initials supplied in red ink, capitals in yellow thro.-out, fore-margin of 1 lf. strengthened, sm. wormholes in 1st. 11 ll. slightly affecting a few letters, minor stain to 1 lf., 18th. C.

cf., rubbed; sig. of Erasmus Philipps. [C. 5744] (C. May 30; 48)   *Quaritch.* £1,700
- - **Anr. Edn.** Ed.:– Aelius Donatus. Toscolano, 1526. 4to. 1 lf. with sm. tear, 1 with margin hole, some browning & spotting, some MS. annots., 18th. C. cf., ex-libris in cover. (H. May 22; 571)   DM 660
- - **Anr. Edn.** Paris, 1529. Fo. Some ll. misnumbered, slight spotting, cf., reprd. (P. Mar.15; 107)   *Fletcher.* £85
- - **Anr. Edn.** Paris, 1552 [colophon: 1551]. Fo. Title & few ll. lightly soiled, later hf. mor. (CSK. Aug.5; 116)   £110
- - **Anr. Edn.** Paris, 1642. Fo. Hf.-title, some minor spotting, 18th. C. Fr. red mor., gt. spine, wider border round covers, royal arms, head & foot of spine chipped; sig. of Ja: Stuart. (S. Nov.17; 72)   *Maggs.* £140
- - **Anr. Copy.** Fo. Wide margin, 6 engraved initials, cont. leath. gt., decor., lge. gold-tooled arms supra-libros Ludwig XIV in centre covers, jnts. defect., upr. cover with 2 sm. reprd. defects.; from Freund-Deschamps, Lytton Strachey & Roger Senhouse coll. (BR. Apr.12; 1544)   DM 600
- - **Anr. Edn.** Ed.:– Danielis Heinsii. Romae, 1767. 2 pts. in 1 vol. Fo. Light margin dampstains, mor., covers detchd., lacks part of spine; pres. copy from headmaster of Eton to Antonio Panizzi. (RO. Dec.11; 319) $120
- - **Anr. Copy.** 2 vols. in 1. Elephant fo. Some stains in lge. bottom margin of most of 1st. book, early mor., raised bands, very ornate gt. panels & cover borders, gt. dentelles, some wear. (HA. May 4; 291) $110
- - **Anr. Edn.** Bg'ham, 1772. 4to. Cont. red mor. gt., gt. inner dentelles. (CSK. May 18; 93)   £150
- - **Anr. Copy.** 4to. Cont. tree cf., slightly marked, spine reprd. (S. Apr.9; 232)   *Lord.* £55

TERNISIEN D'HAUDRICOURT, F.

- **Fastes de la Nation Française.** Paris, ca. 1812. 3 vols. Fo. Some ll. slightly spotted, cont. hf. mor., rebkd. with orig. gt. spines. (BBA. Oct.27; 344)   *Archdale.* £130

TERRASSE, Charles

- **Bonnard.** Paris, 1927. *(200) numbered on Japan vell., with extra plt., dupl. inp. in bistre of the orig. etching, & an orig. dry-point.* 4to. Cold. pict. wraps.; unc. & unopened. (SG. Nov.3; 21) $550

TERRET, Victor

- **La Sculpture Bourguignonne aux XII et XIII Siècles.** Autun & Paris, 1914-25. 3 vols. Fo. Cont. cl., soiled, orig. wraps. bnd. in. (CSK. Jan.27; 18)   £170

TERRY, Michael

- **Hidden Wealth & Hiding People.** N.d. 1 vol. Bdg. not stated, d.-w. (*With:*) - **Untold Miles** ... N.d. 1 vol. Not collated, some wear & marking, bdg. not stated; inscr. (KH. May 1; 703)   Aus. $180
- **Sand & Sun** ... 1937. (*With:*) - **Across Unknown Australia** ... 1925. Together 2 vols. Slight wear, bdgs. not stated. (KH. May 1; 704)   Aus. $180

TERTULLIANUS, Quintus Septimus Florens

- **The Address ... to Scapula Tertullus Proconsul of Africa.** Trans.:– Sir David Dalrymple [later Lord Hailes]. Edinb., 1790. Cont. (Scottish?) red mor., gt. spine, rubbed; prex. copy from Dairymple to Edmund Burke. (BBA. Nov.30; 239) *Maggs.* £160
- **Opera.** Ill.:– A. Holbein. Basel, 1521. *1st. Coll. Edn.* Fo. 2 ll. misbnd., sm. stain thro.-out, slightly soiled at beginning, some ll. with marginalia, 6 ll. with brown mark, cont. clab. blind-tooled pig, spotted, partly bumped, lacks clasps. (GB. May 3; 932)   DM 1,800
- - **Anr. Edn.** [Basel, July 1521]. Fo. Wide margins, very wormed at beginning & end, cont. stiff vell., elab. blind-stpd., episcopal arms on covers, 2 metal clasps. (SG. Feb.9; 356) $450

TERTULLIANUS, Quintus Septimus Florens

See— **LACTANTIUS, Lucius Coelius Firminianus**

TERWEN, J.L.

- **Het Konigrijk der Nederlanden.** Ill.:– Cooke, Rohbock & others. Gouda, [1862]. 3 vols. Lge. 8vo. 3 steel-engraved titles, 136 steel-engraved views, some foxing, cont. cl., gt. & blind-stpd., richly

decor., spine lettering slightly faded. (VS. Dec.8; 954)   Fls. 5,000

TESAURO, Emanuel

- **Del Regno d'Italia sotto i Barbari Epitome.** Notes:– Abbot D. Valeriano Castiglione. Turin, 1664. 4 pts. in 1 vol. Fo. Some ll. disbnd., traces of dampstains, cont. vell. (HD. Jun.26; 28)   Frs. 3,400

TESORO DELLE GIOLE: Trattato Curioso, nel quale si Dichiara Brevemente le Virtu, Qualita, a Proprieta delle Gioie

Venice, 1676. 12mo. Old vell. (SG. Oct.27; 125) $175

TESTAMENT OF THE TWELVE PATRIARCHS

Trans.:– R. Grostete. L., 1677. A3 slightly cropped, some spotting, cf., worn. (P. Mar.15; 340)   *King.* £70

TESTARD, F.M.

See— **SEGARD, Sir William & Testard, F.M.**

TEUPKEN, J.F.

- **Beschrijving Hoedanig de Koninklijke Nederlandsche Troepen ... - Vervolg van de Beschrijving Hoedanig de Koninklijke Nederlandsche Troepen ... met eene Nieuwe Uitgave van ... Platen.** The Hague & Amst., 1823-26. Together 2 vols. Fo. Additional engraved title, 69 engraved plts., all but 3 hand-cold., blank corner out from 1st. title, some very minor staining, orig. bds., spines torn; sig. of author on versos of titles & sm. authentication stps. on titles. (CH. Sep.20; 59)   Fls. 6,000

TEUSCHER, F.A.

- **Die Deut[s]chen Eisenbahnen in Hinsicht ihres Abganges, ihrer Ankurft und der Preise der Plaetze.** Leipzig, 1848. *[2nd. Edn.].* Slightly spotted, orig. wraps. (R. Apr.4; 1486)   DM 500

TEUTSCHEN ACADEMIE, Der

- [**Der Architectur oder Bau-Kunst**]. [Nuremb.]. 1677 on later. Vol. 2 pt. 1 only. Fo. Engraved frontis., engraved title, folding plan, 70 plts., several double-p., many irregularly numbered, faint margin browning, cont. cf., worn, defect., w.a.f. (S. Dec.13; 238)   *Levy.* £130

TEUPKEN, J.F.

- **Beschrijving Hoedanig de Koninklijke Nederlandsche Troepen ... — Vervolg van de Beschrijving Hoedanig de Koninklijke Nederlandsche Troepen ... met eene Nieuwe Uitgave van ... Platen.** The Hague & Amst., 1823-26. Together 2 vols. Fo. Additional engraved title, 69 engraved plts., all but 3 hand-cold., blank corner cut from 1st. title, some very minor staining, orig. bds., spines torn; sig. of author on versos of titles & sm. authentication stps. on titles. (CH. Sep.20; 59)   Fls. 6,000

TEUSCHER, F.A.

- **Die Deut[s]chen Eisenbahnen in Hinsicht ihres Abganges, ihrer Ankunft und der Preise der Plaetse.** Leipzig, 1848. *[2nd. Edn.].* Slightly spotted, orig. wraps. (R. Apr.4; 1486))   DM 500

TEX, J. den

- **Oldenbarnevelt.** Haarlem/Groningen, 1960-72. 5 vols. Cl. (VG. Sep.13; 31)   Fls. 450

TEXAS

- **El Gebernader del Estado de Coahuila y Tejas, a Todos sus Habitantes Sabed: Que el Congresso del Mismo Estado Ha Decretado lo Siguiente.** [Dtd. at Monclova, 26 Apr. 1834]. Fo. Few marginalia, disbnd. (SG. Oct.20; 348) $130

TEXIER, Charles

- **Description de l'Arménie, la Perse et la Mésopotamie.** Paris, 1842. 2 vols. Fo. Cont. hf. cl. (HD. Jun.18; 46)   Frs. 17,000

TEXIER, Charles & Pullan, R.P.

- **Byzantine Architecture.** L., 1864. *1st. Edn.* Tall fo. 70 litho. plts., many in colours & gold, rest tinted, text wood engrs., some foxing, ex-liby., gt.-pict. cl., loose in bdg. (SG. May 3; 353) $425

TEXTOR, J. (Pseud.)
See— WINCKLER, G.E. 'J. Textor'

THACHER, James
- **American Medical Biography.** Boston, 1828. *1st. Edn.* 2 vols. in 1. 1 plt. loose, spotted cl., jnts. worn. (BBA. Jul.27; 61)   *Sons of Liberty Books.* £100
- – **Anr. Copy.** 2 vols. in 1, as iss. 8vo. Hf.-title, subscribers list, three-qtr. lev., rubbed. (SG. Mar.22; 209) $175

THACKERAY, William Makepeace 'M.A.Titmarsh'
- **The Adventures of Philip.** L., 1862. *1st. Edn.* 3 vols. Orig. cl., covers discold. (LH. Sep.25; 608) $100
- **The Book of Snobs.** 1848. *1st. Edn.* Advt. lf., gt.-panel, cf., by Zaehnsdorf, rectangular cf. bordered inlay to bds., white washed silk end-papers, gt. binders stp., slight fading to spine, orig. pict. wraps. bnd. in. (PD. Aug.17; 180)   £50
- **Comic Tales & Sketches.** ... 1841. *1st. Edn.* 2 vols. Advt. lf. Vol. 2, some slight foxing, gt.-panel. cf., rectangular cf. bordered inlay to bds., white washed silk end-papers, gt. binders stp., by Zaehnsdorf, slight fading to spines, orig. cl. bnd. in. (PD. Aug.17; 177)   £90
- **Doctor Birch & his Young Friends.** 1849. *1st. Edn.* Advt. lf., gt.-panel. cf., rectangular cf. bordered inlay to bds., white washed silk end-papers, gt. binders stp., by Zaehnsdorf, slight fading to spine, orig. pict. wraps. und. in. (PD. Aug.17; 181)   £80
- **The Four Georges: Sketches of Manners, Morals, Court, & Town Life.** L., 1861. 8vo., inlaid to fo. Orig. ll., bnd. with about 80 additional engraved parts., etc., some hand-cold., red mor. by Rivière, spine gt. in compartments, inner dentelles. (RO. Dec.11; 320) $250
- **The Great Hoggarty Diamond.** N.Y., 1848. *1st. Edn. 1st. Iss.* Unc., orig. ptd. wraps., worn. (SG. Nov.3; 207) $2,000
- **The History of Henry Esmond.** L., 1852. *1st. Edn.* 3 vols. Orig. cl., corners bumped, shaken. (LH. Sep.25; 610) $100
- **The History of Pendennis.** 1848-50. *1st. Edn. in pts.* 23/24 pts. in 2 vols. Many advts. & slips, some browning, gt.-panel. cf., rectangular cf. bordered inlay to bds., white washed silk end-papers, gt. binders stp., by Zaehnsdorf, slight fading to spines, orig. wraps. bnd. in (error in upr.-wrap. Pt.13). (PD. Aug.17; 182)   £150
- – **Anr. Copy.** Orig. 23/24 pts. Ills., many of the advts. called for, orig. wraps., some soiling, reprd., mor. solander case. (SPB. May 16; 154) $250
- – **Anr. Copy.** Orig. 23/24 pts. Most advts. & slips called for, plts., some foxing & fraying, orig. ptd. wraps., some repair to spines, soiled, mor. solander cases; Clawson/Perry Molated copy. (SPB. May 16; 538) $200
- – **Anr. Edn.** L., 1849-50. *1st. Edn.* 2 vols. Some slight foxing, hf. leath. (D. Nov.24; 2362)   DM 700
- – **Anr. Edn.** 1863. 1 vol. (*With:*) - **The Virginians.** 1863. 1 vol. (*With:*) - **Irish Sketch Book.** 1863. 1 vol. (*With:*) - **Vanity Fair.** 1861. 1 vol. (*With:*) - **Henry Esmond.** 1858. 1 vol. (*With:*) - **The Newcomes.** 1860. 1 vol. (*With:*) - **Miscellanies.** 1861-60. 4 vols. Together 10 vols. Unif. hf. mor. gt. (CSK. Aug.19; 3)   £110
- **Irish Sketch Book.** 1843. *1st. Edn.* 2 vols. Gt.-panel. cf., rectangular cf. bordered inlay to bds., white washed silk end-papers, gt. binders stp., by Zaehnsdorf, slight fading to spines, orig. cl. bnd. in. (PD. Aug.17; 178)   £100
- **The Kickleburys on the Rhine.** 1850. *1st. Edn.* Hf.-title, advt. lf. at end, gt.-panel. cf., rectangular cf. bordered inlay to bds., white washed silk end-papers, gt. binders sto., by Zaehnsdorf, slight fading to spine, orig. wraps. bnd. in (washed). (PD. Aug.17; 183)   £80
- **The Newcomes.** 1853-55. *1st. Edn. in Pts.* Orig. 24 monthly pts. in 23, in 2 vols. Newcomes advertiser & advts., some foxing, gt.-panel. cf., rectangular cf. bordered inlay to bds., white washed silk end-papers, gt. binders stp., by Zaehnsdorf, slight fading to spines, orig. wraps. bnd. in. (PD. Aug.17; 185)   £160
- – **Anr. Copy.** Orig. 23/24 pts. Ills., most advts. & slips called for, some slight spotting, orig. ptd.

wraps., few spines reprd., lightly soiled; bkplts. of Albert M. Cohn & Herbert Brenon, Fred A. Berne copy. (SPB. May 16; 366) $350
- – **Anr. Copy.** Orig. 23/24 pts. Most advts. & slips called for, ills., few plts. spotted, orig. wraps. (SPB. May 16; 155) $275
- **Our Street.** 1848. *1st. Edn.* Advt. lf., gt.-panel. cf., rectangular cf. bordered inlay to bds., white washed silk end-papers, gt. binders stp., by Zaehnsdorf, slight fading to spine, orig. pict. wraps. bnd. in. (PD. Aug.17; 179)   £90
- **The Paris Sketch Book.** 1840. *1st. Edn.* 2 vols. Gt.-panel. cf., rectangular cf. bordered inlay to bds., white washed silk end-papers, gt. binders stp., by Zaehnsdorf, slight fading to spines, orig. cl. bnd. in. (PD. Aug.17; 175)   £80
- **The Rose & the Ring.** 1855. *1st. Edn.* 16 pp. catalogue, gt.-panel. cf., rectangular cf. bordered inlay to bds., white washed silk end-papers, gt. binders stp., by Zaehmsdorf, slight fading to spine, orig. pict. wraps. bnd. in. (PD. Aug.17; 186)   £92
- – **Anr. Copy.** Sm. 4to. Last 8 advt. ll., later mor., orig. wraps. preserved. (BBA. Feb.9; 92)   *Jaradyce Books.* £60
- **Die Rose und der Ring.** Trans.:– Clarisse Meitner. Ill.:– E. Ballin-Wolterreck. Stuttgart, Phaidon, 1924. *(80) on Japan.* Printers mark sigd. by artist, hand-bnd. mor. gt. (H. Nov.24; 1285)   DM 580
- **The Second Funeral of Napoleon ... & the Chronicle of the Drum.** 1841. Advt. lf., gt.-panel. cf., rectangular cf. bordered inlay to bds., white washed silk end-papers, gt. binders stp., by Zaehnsdorf, slight fading to spine, orig. wraps. bnd. in. (PD. Aug.17; 176)   £160
- **Vanity Fair.** L., 1847-48. *1st. Edn.* Orig. 19/20 pts. Page 1 with heading in rustic type, p.336 with woodcut of Marquis of Steyne, p.453 with reading 'Mr. Pitt', inserted advts., some spotting, orig. pict. wraps., pt. 19/20 lacks lr. cover, pt.11 with lr. cover in facs., with orig. loosely inserted, pt.12 with upr. cover torn, few spines defect., few covers, plts. & ll. loose. (S. Dec.8; 137)   *Lewis.* £500
- – **Anr. Edn.** L., 1848. *1st. Edn. in Book Form.* Browned, slight offsetting, hf. mor., jnts. cracked; pres. copy to J.W. Parker. (S. Mar.20; 971)   *Sawyer.* £340
- – **Anr. Edn.** 1848. *1st. Edn. 1st. Iss.* 1 advt. lf. bnd. in at front, later mor. gt. by Zaehnsdorf. (TA. Feb.16; 368)   £68
- – **Anr. Edn.** L., 1848. *1st. Edn. in Book Form. 1st. Iss., with reading 'Mr. Pitt' at p. 453 line 31 & woodcut of the Marquis of Styne at p. 336.* Some foxing, mod. red mor. by Bayntun. (CBA. Dec.10; 433) $130
- **The Virginians.** Nov. 1857-Oct. 59. *1st. Edn. in Pts. 1st. Iss.* Orig. 24 monthly pts. in 2 vols. Misprint on p. 207, 'actresses' for 'ancestresses', 1 misnumbering of Chaps 47 & 48 Vol. 1, each pt. with Virginians advertiser, advts. & slips, some minor foxing, gt.-panel. cf., rectangular cf. bordered inlay to bds., white washed silk end-papers, gt. binders stp., by Zaehnsdorf, slight fading to spines, orig. wraps. bnd. in. (PD. Aug.17; 187)   £320
- – **Anr. Copy.** Orig. 24 pts. Advts., orig. wraps., mor.-bkd. box; from Norman Tarbolton liby. (P. Apr.12; 14)   *Jarndyce.* £240
- – **Anr. Copy.** In orig. 24 pts. Plts., text engrs., with 'Virginians Advertiser' in each pt. & other advts., pict. wraps., some spines reprd., unc., hf. lev. solander s.-c. (SG. Apr.26; 194) $650
- – **Anr. Copy.** Orig. 24 pts. Plts., ills., most advts. called for including 'Dickens & his Publishers' lf., with 'actresses', some spotting, orig. ptd. wraps., some repairs to spines, lightly soiled; Fred A.Berne copy. (SPB. May 16; 367) $325
- – **Anr. Copy.** Orig. 24 pts. With 'actresses' on line 33, p.207, pt. 7, advts., plts., foxing, orig. wraps. soiled, some tears, red mor. solander cases. (SPB. May 16; 156) $225
- – **Anr. Copy.** Orig. 24 pts. Most advts. & slips alled for, some soiling, orig. ptd. wraps., some repairs & soiling; A.Edward Newton/Perry Molstad copy. (SPB. May 16; 539) $200
- **Works.** Leipzig, 1848-73. *Copyright Edn.* In 18 vols. 16mo. Three-qtr. cf., spines gt. (SG. Feb.16; 312) $425
- – **Anr. Edn.** L., 1869. 24 vols. Hf. mor. (SPB. Dec.13; 567) $225

- – **Anr. Copy.** 22 vols. Three-qtr. pol. cf., elab. gt.-decor. spines. (CBA. Dec.10; 436) $130
- – **Anr. Edn.** L., 1877-78. *(1000) numbered.* 26 vols. in 52. Tall 4to. All plts. & text ills. on mntd. India-proof sheets, unif. later mor. & marb. bds., raised bands, gt. spine lettering, light shelf wear, incidental wear to a few vols. (HA. Feb.24; 215) $750
- – **Anr. Edn.** L., 1878. *(1000).* 26 vols. Fo. Hf. mor., spines gt. (SPB. Dec.13; 568) $600
- **The Complete Works.** L., 1878-86. 26 vols. in 52. Lge. 8vo. L.P., extra-ill., specially ptd. title-pp. on Japan paper, full-p. plts. & text ills. on India paper mntd., a few inserted watercolour drawings as frontis.'s, elab. gt.-panel. sides with onlaid red mor. ornaments, gt.-panel. spines in 6 compartments, turn-ins gt., crimson mor. gt. doubls., watered silk free end-pp., silk markers; A.L.s. from author to Chapman & Hall tipped in, w.a.f. (CNY. Dec.17; 608) $3,500
- – **Anr. Edn.** 1878-86. *(1000) numbered.* 26 vols. 4to. Orig. buckram. (PD. Apr.18; 214)   £55
- – **Anr. Copy.** 26 vols. in 52. Cf. gt., gt. dentelles, by Zaehnsdorf, slightly rubbed, spines faded. (SG. Feb.16; 313) $700
- – **Anr. Edn.** 1883-86. 26 vols. Cont. hf. mor. (CSK. Feb.10; 21)   £180
- – **Anr. Edn.** 1899. *Biographical Edn.* 13 vols. Hf. cf. gt. (PD. Feb.15; 53)   £145
- – **Anr. Edn.** L., 1904-02. *Biographical Edn.* 13 vols. Cont. cf., spines gt. (CSK. Feb.24; 16)   £110
- – **Anr. Edn.** L., 1911. *Harry Furniss Centenary Edn.* 20 vols. Orig. cl. gt. (BS. Nov.16; 76)   £55

THAER, A.
- **Leitfaden zur Allgemeinen Landwirtschaftlichen Gewerbs-Lehre.** Berlin, 1815. *1st. Edn.* Cont. hf. leath. (R. Oct.11; 1318)   DM 400

THARAUD, Jérôme & Jean
- **L'An Prochain à Jérusalem.** Ill.:– André Sureda, engraved by G. Beltrand. Paris, 1929. *De Luxe Edn. (23) numbered on japan,* with orig. gouache & 3 separate cold. suites of engrs. Lge. 4to. Publisher's box. (HD. Apr.26; 272)   Frs. 3,200
- **La Semaine Sainte à Séville.** Ill.:– Polat & Raynolt. Paris, [1927]. *1st. Edn. (30) numbered on japon imperial.* 6 orig. etchings (including 2 ports.), many engraved initials & vigs., mor., geometric decor., gold-tooled, double with leath. inlay, silk end-papers, by Gruel. (D. Nov.23; 175) DM 1,200

THAYER, William M.
- **Character & Public Services of Abraham Lincoln.** Boston, 1864. Sm. 8vo. Orig. pict. wraps., lightly foxed & faded, s.-c. (LH. Apr.15; 379) $190

THEATER ARTS MAGAZINE
N.Y., 1916-33. Vols. 1-15 & 17, in 25 vols. 4to. Binder's cl., worn. (SG. Nov.17; 339) $225

THEATRE OF THE PRESENT WAR in the Netherlands & Upon the Rhine
L., 1745. Cf., rebkd. (P. Sep.8; 193)   *Dupre.* £65

THEATRICAL PICTURE-BOOK
England?, 19th. C. 4to. Each of the 4 sections with col. plt. which lifts to reveal a 4-layered scene, some minor repairs & tears, pict. bd. corner, minor chipping, disbnd. (SG. Dec.8; 279) $250

THEATRUM SYMPATHETICUM Auctum Exhibens Varios Authores de Pulvere Sympathetico quidem: Digbaeum, Straussium, Papinium et Mohyum de Unguento vero armario ...
Ed.:– Sylvester Rattray. Nuremb., 1662. 4to. Cont. cf., rebkd.; Dr. Walter Pagel copy. (S. Feb.7; 360)   *Quaritch.* £360

THELLER, Edward Alexander
- **Canada in 1837-38.** N.Y., 1841. *1st. Edn.* 2 vols. 12mo. Orig. cl.; ex-liby. (SG. Jan.19; 140) $110

THEOBALD, Lewis
- **Double Falshood; or, the Distrest Lovers. Written originally by W. Shakespeare, & now revised & adapted to the stage by Mr. Theobald.** L., 1728. *1st. Edn.* Three-qtr. mor. (SG. Oct.27; 298) $175

THEOCRITUS
- **Idylles.** Trans.:– J.-B. Gail. Ill.:– Barbier & Boichot. Paris, priv. ptd., 1794. 2 vols. 4to. On vell.,

THEOCRITUS -*Contd.*

Greek & Fr. parallel text, some sm. foxing, cont. mor. gt., decor. spines, inner roll-stp., stain on 1 cover. (HD. Sep.22; 358)　　　　Frs. 3,500
– – **Anr. Edn.** Trans.:– J.B. Gail. Ill.:– Boichot, Fragonard fils, Bovinet, Lempereur & others. Paris, An IV [1796]. (*Bound with:*) – **Les Amours de Léandre et de Héro** ... Paris, An IV. Together 2 works in 2 vols. 4to. Greek & Fr. text (2nd. work has Latin text also), cont. tree cf. gt., spines decor. (HD. May 3; 159)　　　　Frs. 1,400
– – **Anr. Edn.** Ill.:– Henri Laurens. Paris, 1945. *(220) numbered & sigd. by artist.* 4to. Loose as iss. in orig. wraps., cl.-bkd. bd. folder, s.-c. (BBA. Jun.14; 225)　　　*Sims, Reed & Fogg.* £260
– **Idylles et autres Poésies.** Trans.:– Gail. Paris, 1792. Fr., Greek & Latin text, cont. red mor. gt., spine decor. (HD. May 3; 158)　　　　Frs. 1,200
– **Idyllia-Scholia.** [Rome], 15 Jan. 1516. *1st. Edn. of the Scholia.* 2 pts. in 1 vol. Title & last lf. slightly soiled, 18th. C. red mor. gt., slight wear to extremities, bdg. slightly loose, qtr. mor. box; Thomas B. Stevenson copy. (CNY. May 18; 169)　　　　£700
– **Oeuvres.** Trans.:– Paul Desjardins. Ill.:– Arnaud Berton. Paris, 1910. Mor. by Blanchetière, bronze medallion by Mouchon on upr. cover, watered silk liners & end-ll., wrap. & spine preserved, s.-c., spine slightly faded. (HD. Jun.13; 104) Frs. 2,000
– **Opera** [Greek]. Rome, 1516. Some old annots., some ll. with sm. partly reprd. wormholes in lr. margin, mor., ca. 1800, gt. spine, cover, inner & outer dentelle, browned, slightly worn, corners bumped. (HK. Nov.8; 357)　　　　DM 1,000
– **Sixe Idyllia.** Ill.:– Anthony Cross. Clover Hill Edns. 1971. *(417) sigd. by artist. (12) with orig. drawing, a set of proofs in 1st. state (including 2 discarded etchings) & a set in final state.* Fo. Prospectus loosely inserted, orig. mor. gt., mor.-bkd. box, s.-c. (S. Nov.21; 184)　*Appleton.* £240

THEOCRITUS
See— ANACREON & others – THEOCRITUS

THEODOR I, King of Corsica
– **History Containing Genuine & Impartial Memoires of his Private Life, & Adventures in France, Spain, Holland, England** ... L., 1743. 12mo. Mod. Bradel bds., wrap. (HD. Oct.21; 170)　　　　Frs. 1,400

THEODORUS, Gaza
– **Introductionis Grammaticae.** Basle, 1529. In Greek & Latin, cont. italian black mor., spine worn, extra gilding & Apollo & Pegasus medallion added in 19th. C.; H.M. Nixon coll., with his pencil note on fly– lf, 'a Bologna fake'. (BBA. Oct.6; 242)　　　　*Quaritch.* £350

THEODOSIUS TRIPOLITA
See— ARCHIMEDES – APOLLONIUS PERGAEUS – THEODOSIUS
See— RAMUS, P. – THEODOSIUS TRIPOLITA – HENISCH, G.

THEOPHRASTUS
– **History of Stones.** Ed.:– J. Hill. L., 1746. *1st. Edn.* In Greek & Engl., slightly browned, cont. hf. cf., rebkd., slightly rubbed. (BBA. May 23; 4)　　　　*Lyon.* £220
– – **Anr. Edn.** Ed.:– Sir John Hill. L., 1774. *2nd. Edn.* 19th. C. hf. cf., worn. (S. Apr.10; 590)　　　　*Phelps.* £180
See— ARISTOTELES & Theophrastus – THEOPHRASTUS

THEOPHYLACTUS, Archbp. of Achrida
– **Paideia Basiliske ... Institutio Regia.** Paris, 1651. *1st. Edn.* 4to. In Greek & Latin, mod. qtr. mor. (SG. Oct.27; 316)　　　　$300

THESAURUS EXORCISMORUM ATQUE, CONIURATIONUM TERRIBILIUM ...
Cologne, 1626. Browned thro.-out, cont. blind-stpd. pig over wood bds., with clasps, rubbed. (S. Dec.20; 790)　　　　*Brown.* £90

THEURIET, André
– **Fleurs de Cyclamens.** Ill.:– Ch. Coppier. Paris, 1899. *(115).* Sm. 4to. Red mor., decor. gt. & col. mor., wtrd. silk end-papers, wrap preserved, by

Mercier; Lacroix Laval ex-libris. (HD. Feb.17; 120)　　　　Frs. 5,300

THEVENOT, Melchisedek
– **The Art of Swimming.** 1699. 12mo. Lacks 1st. lf. (imprimatur?), title soiled, 2 plts. affected by printing flaws, cont. sheep, worn. [Wing T 888] (CSK. Sep.16; 54)　　　　£180
– – **Anr. Edn.** 1764. *2nd. Edn.* 12mo. Old cf., worn. (P. Feb.16; 275)　　　　£160
– **Relations de divers Voyages Curieux.** Paris, Thomas Moette, 1696. 5 pts. in 2 vols. Fo. 7 double-p. or folding engraved maps, 15 folding plts. & tables, many errors, in pagination & sigs., lacks gathering 4H in pt. 1, & 1st. lf. in pt. 2 & apparently 3 ptd. titles, map of Australia with compass rose & rhumb-lines partly erased, 1 or 2 short tears in folding maps without loss of engraved surface, some browning, cont. cf., rebkd. preserving labels. (S. Dec.1; 263)　　　　*Arkway.* £2,050

THEVET, André
– **La Cosmographie Universelle.** Paris, Pierre l'Huillier, 1575. 2 vols. Fo. Lacks? 2 blank ll., browned thro.-out (as usual), 17th. C. mott. cf., spines gt., reprd. (S. Dec.1; 266)　　　　*Burgess.* £4,000
– **Les Singularitez de la France Antarctique.** Paris, 1558. *1st. Edn. 2nd. Iss.* Sm. 4to. Incorrectly numbered p. 135, some minor stains, sm. hole in lf. m1 affecting woodcut & 1 letter, mod. cf. [Sabin 95339] (C. Nov.9; 118)　　　　*Ramer.* £4,000
– **Les Vrays Pourtraits et Vies des Hommes Illustres.** Paris, 1584. *1st. Edn.* 2 vols. in 1. Fo. Lacks title, A6 & last ll. from table to end, major dampstains with some losses, roan, worn. (HD. Mar.27; 38)　　　　Frs. 1,800

THIBAULT, Anatole François
See— FRANCE, Anatole [i.e. Anatole François Thibault]

THIBAULT, Girard
– **Academae de l'Espée.** Leiden, 1628. Imp. fo. Engraved title reprd., browned, cont. leath., blind-tooled, lr. cover defect. (R. Apr.4; 2154)　　　　DM 12,000

THIBAUT I, King of Navarre
[–] **Les Poésies.** 1742. 2 vols. 12mo. Cf. by Petit (successor of Simier), spines decor. (HD. Mar.21; 95)　　　　Frs. 1,000

THIEBAULT, Baron
– **Mémoires du Général publiés sous les Auspices de sa Fille, d'après le Manuscrit Original par Fernand Calmettes.** Paris, 1908. *1st. Edn.* 5 vols. Hf. chagrin. (HD. Jan.27; 88)　　　　Frs. 1,100

THIEBAULT, Dieudonné
– **Friedrich der Grosse.** Leipzig, 1828. *1st. German Edn.* Some light browning, cont. bds. bumped. (H. May 22; 509)　　　　DM 420

THIEME, Dr. Ulrich & Becker, Dr. Felix
– **Allgemeines Lexikon der Bildendes Künstler.** Leipzig, 1907-50. 37 vols. (mixed set). All but 5 vols. hf. mor., others various, rubbed, a few worn, a few covers detchd.; Otto Beit bkplt. (S. Apr.30; 226)　　　　*Sims.* £750

THIERRY, Augustin
– **Premier Récit des Temps Mérovingiens.** Paris, 1881. Lge. fo. Bdg. not stated. (HD. Oct.14; 156)　　　　Frs. 1,100

THIERS, J.B.
See— LEBRUN, Pierre & Thiers, J.B.

THIERS, Louis Adolphe
– **Histoire de la Révolution Française. – Histoire du Consulat et de l'Empire.** Paris, 1845-65. 30 vols. & 2 atlases. Cont. hf. chagrin, spines decor., 'Révolution' atlas in 4 pts., bds.; from Château des Noës liby. (HD. May 25; 78)　　　　Frs. 1,800
– **The History of the French Revolution.** Trans.:– Frederick Shoberl. L., 1838. 3 vols. 41 steel-engraved ports., three-qtr. cf., spines gt. with fleurons. (SG. Feb.16; 314)　　　　$200

THILENIUS, M. Gerh.
– **Medicinische und Chirurg. Bemerkingen.** Frankfurt, 1809-14. 2 vols. Both titles multi-stpd., cont.

hf. leath., spine slightly defect., partly reprd. (HK. May 15; 542)　　　　DM 400

THIOLLET, M. & others
– **Nouveau Recueil de Menuiserie et de Decorations Intéérieures et Extérieures** ... Liège, 1848. Fo. 60 litho. plans, some light soiling, hf. cf., worn. (CSK. May 18; 1)　　　　£80

THIVET, M.
– **Traité Complet de Bandages et d'Anatomie.** Paris, 1840. *1st. Edn.* Cont. hf. leath., slightly rubbed. (R. Oct.12; 1486)　　　　DM 540

THOINAN, Ernest
– **Les Relieurs Francâis (1500-1800).** Paris, 1893. *(650) numbered.* Cont. hf. mor.; H.M. Nixon coll., with a few MS. notes. (BBA. Oct.6; 129)　　　　*Quaritch.* £240

THOMAS, Auguste H.
– **Formes et Couleurs.** Paris, ca. 1925. Fo. 20 cold. plts., ex-liby., each plt. stpd. on blank verso, loose in bd. folder, linen ties. (SG. May 3; 24)　　　$325
– – **Anr. Edn.** Paris, 1920's. Fo. 20 pochoir-cold. plts., loose as iss., bd. folder, worn. (SG. Aug.25; 25)　　　　$210
– – **Anr. Copy.** Fo. 16 (of 20) pochoir-cold. plts., lacks title, bd. folder, spine worn. (SG. Dec.15; 125)　　　　$150

THOMAS, Arthur Hermann & Thornley, I.D.
– **The Great Chronicle of London.** 1938. *(500) numbered.* 4to. Mor. gt. by Zaehnsdorf. (P. Sep.8; 328)　　　　*Traylen.* £60

THOMAS, Dylan
– **Collected Poems.** L., 1952. *1st. Edn. (65) numbered on mould-made Paper, sigd. (60) for sale.* Orig. mor., orig. cellophane d.-w.; Frederic Dannay copy. (CNY. Dec.16; 355)　　　　$1,100
– **18 Poems.** L., [1934]. *1st. Edn. 1st. Iss., (250).* Orig. cl., d.-w., hf. mor. s.-c.; Frederic Dannay copy. (CNY. Dec.16; 353)　　　　$480
– **Portrait of the Artist as a Young Dog.** L., 1940. *1st. Edn.* Orig. cl.; pres. copy from author, Frederic Dannay copy. (CNY. Dec.16; 354)　　　　$550
– **Under Milk Wood.** L., 1954. *1st. Edn.* Orig. cl., d.-w. (S. Mar.20; 972)　　　　*Matthews.* £50

THOMAS, Edward
– **Lafcadio Hearn.** L., 1911. Proof copy, with autograph corrections & alterations by author in some 16 places, inscr. by author on hf.-title to A.D. Williams, & with A.L. (sigd. 'ET') to Williams inserted, paper wraps., detchd., as an association copy, w.a.f. (S. Dec.8; 260)　　　*Swales.* £580
– **Six Poems by Edward Eastaway.** Flansham, Sussex, ptd. by James Guthrie at the Pear Tree Pr., [1916]. *Ltd. 1st. Edn., numbered & sigd. by printer.* 4to. Eckert's 1st. state, with 2 extra blank ll., the author's copy, unnumbered & unsigd., with 2 MS. corrections by Thomas?, & sig. of his wife, proofs of title, 1 text lf. & 2 ills. loosely inserted, mod. mor.-bkd. bds., orig. wraps. preserved, upr. cover with orig. paper label, mor.-edged buckram s.-c. (S. Dec.8; 261)　　　　*Jolliffe.* £2,600

THOMAS, Henry
– **Early Spanish Bookbindings XI-XV Centuries.** [L., Bibliographical Soc.], 1939. 4to. Orig. buckram-bkd. bds.; H.M. Nixon coll. (BBA. Oct.6; 217)　　　　*Quaritch.* £80
– – **Anr. Edn.** L., Bibliographical Soc., 1939. 4to. Orig. cl.-bkd. bds., lightly soiled. (CSK. Feb.24; 204)　　　　£50

THOMAS, Isaiah
– **The History of Printing in America.** Worcester, 1810. *1st. Edn.* 2 vols. Some foxing, liby. stps. on titles, 1 plt. loose & split at folds, few early inked notes on title, mod. buckram. (RO. Dec.11; 323)　　　　$190

THOMAS, J.
– **Un Régiment Rhénan sous Napoléon Premier. Historique du Régiment de Cavalerie du Grand-Duché de Berg.** Liège, 1928. 4to. Hf. chagrin, wrap. preserved. (HD. Jan.27; 218)　　　　Frs. 1,700

THOMAS, Joh. Bapt.
– **Un An à Rome et dans ses Environs.** Paris, [1823]. *1st. Edn.* Fo. Title with erased date, some plts.

browned, some slight foxing, hf. leath., corners bumped. (D. Nov.23; 844) DM 4,400

THOMAS, Michael R. Oldfield
See— SCLATER, Philip Lutley & Thomas, Michael R. Oldfield

THOMAS, Philip Edward
- Collected Poems. Foreword:– Walter de la Mare. 1920. *1st. Edn.* 1 vol. Orig. bds.; printer's proofs of Preface, with corrections in de la Mare's hand, loosely inserted. (*With:*) – In Pursuit of Spring. after Ernest Hazelhurst. 1914. *1st. Edn.* 1 vol. Orig. cl. gt. (*With:*) – The Country. 1913. *1st. Edn.* 1 vol. Orig. cl. gt. (LC. Mar.1; 412) £110

THOMAS, W.
See— BURROW, J.C. & Thomas, W.

THOMAS, William
- Antiquitates Prioratus Majoris Malverne. L., 1725. L.P., folding map, 2 engraved folding plts., diced russ. gt., corner ornaments, decor. panel. in gt. rule, mor. inr. hinges, bnd. by Roger Payne for Sir Richard Colt Hoare, ca. 1790. bdr.'s orig. account tipped in; from collections of Sir Richard Colt Hoare, William Loring Andrews-Cortland F. Bishop & Emery L. Ferris. (SPB. May 16; 108) $600

THOMASE, E.
- Tratado de Esgrima a Pie y a Caballo. Barcelona, 1823. 4to. Cl. (DS. Apr.27; 2615) Pts. 25,000

THOMASIUS, Christian
- Kurtze Lehr-Saetze von dem Laster der Zauberey ... Ed.:– Johann Reichen. Halle, 1704. 2 pts. in 1 vol. 4to. Hf. vell., marb. sides, spine worn, sig. on fly-lf.; Dr. Walter Pagel copy. (S. Feb.7; 362) *Klingsor.* £180

THOMASON, George
- Catalogue of the Pamphlets, Books, Newspapers & Manuscripts, relating to the Civil War, the Commonwealth, & Restoration, 1640-1661. 1908. 2 vols. Orig. cl.; H.M. Nixon coll., with his sig. in both vols. (BBA. Oct.6; 130) *Quaritch.* £100

THOMASSIN, Simon
- Recueil des Figures, Groupes, Thermes, Fontaines, Vases et Autres Ornaments tels qu'ils se voyent à Présent dans le Château et Parc de Versailles. Ill.:– engraved by Le Comte, Guerin, Jouvenet, J. de Boulogne & others. Priv. ptd., 1694. 1 engr. cut out without loss, hf. russ., ca. 1830, spine decor. (HD. Mar.21; 97) Frs. 1,200

THOME, Prof.
- Flora von Deutschland, Osterreich und der Schweiz. N.d. 4 vols. Sm. 4to. Publisher's hf. chagrin, corners, spines browned. (HD. Jul.6; 85) Frs. 2,300

THOMPSON, Benjamin (Trans.)
See— GERMAN THEATRE, The

THOMPSON, C.
- Travels through Turkey in Asia, the Holyland, Arabia, Egypt. 1767. *3rd. Edn.* 2 vols. 12mo. Cont. cf. gt. (P. Sep.8; 324) *Azezian.* £60

THOMPSON, Francis
- Sister Songs. 1895. Sm. 4to. Lacks title & dedication lf., spotted, cont. mor. [by Monica Meynell], slightly worn; 12 pencil alterations in author's hand, front free end-paper inscr. 'Alice Meynell from Francis Thompson', & by the former to Monica, A.L.s. from C.W. Saleeby to Mrs. Meynell loosely inserted. (BBA. Feb.23; 304) *Sawyer.* £700

THOMPSON, George
- Travels & Adventures in Southern Africa. 1827. *[2nd. Edn.].* 4to. Cont. bds., orig. spine label, upr. hinge brkn. (SSA. Jul.5; 397) R 620
- - Anr. Copy. 2 vols. Liby stps. on title-pp. with reprd. backing, some marks on plt. edges, lacks 1 vig., cf., edges rubbed. (VA. Apr.27; 700) R 260
- - Anr. Copy. 2 vols. Edges slightly browned, hf. cf. (VA. Oct.28; 605) R 200

THOMPSON, George Alex.
- The Geographical & Historical Dictionary of America & the West Indies. L., 1812-15. 5 vols.

4to. Orig. cl.-bkd., rubbed & soiled. (BBA. Dec.15; 44) *Remington.* £75

THOMPSON, Sir Henry
- A Catalogue of Blue & White Nankin Porcelain. Ed.:– Murray Marks. Ill.:– James Whistler. L., 1878. *(220), (100) for private circulation.* 4to. 26 Autotype plts., ex-liby., embossed bds. gt., newspaper clippings pasted on front endpapers. (SG. May 3; 89) $500
- - Anr. Edn. 1878. *(220).* 4to. Loose, orig. cl. gt., slightly rubbed & soiled. (S. Nov.8; 576) *Sims.* £120
- - Anr. Copy. 4to. Loose, in orig. decor. gold cl. (S. May 1; 642) *Sims.* £100

THOMPSON, Henry Yates
- A Lecture on Some English Illuminated Manuscripts. Chiswick Pr., 1902. *(50).* Tall 8vo. Orig. cl., partly untrimmed, rubbed; pres. copy to M.R. James, sigd. on hf.-title & numbered. (TA. Jun.21; 442) £62

THOMPSON, J.
- Simple Stories for Little Children. Bg'ham., 1792. Wraps. (P. Nov.24; 299) *Temperley.* £55

THOMPSON, M.
- The New Style Silver Coinage of Athens. N.Y., 1961. 2 vols. Orig. cl. (S. May 1; 502) *Spink.* £50

THOMPSON, Ruth Plumly
- Handy Mandy in Oz. Ill.:– John R. Neill. Chic., [1937]. *1st. Edn.* Cl., pict. d.-w., edges chipped. (SG. Dec.8; 42) $140
- Ozoplaning with the Wizard of Oz. Ill.:– John R. Neill. Chic., [1939]. *1st. Edn.* Cl., d.-w. chipped. (SG. Dec.8; 44) $120
- The Silver Princess in Oz. Ill.:– John R. Neill. Chic., [1938]. *1st. Edn.* Cl., d.-w. chipped. (SG. Dec.8; 43) $140
- The Wishing Horse of Oz. Ill.:– John H. Neill. Chic., [1935]. *1st. Edn.* Lge. 8vo. Cl., spine slightly cocked, d.-w. (SG. Dec.8; 41) $140
- - Anr. Copy. Cl., lightly discold. (SG. Mar.29; 57) $110
- The Yellow Knight of Oz. Ill.:– John R. Neill. Chic., [1930]. *1st. Edn.* Cl. (SG. Dec.8; 40) $125

THOMPSON, William
- The English Flower Garden of Hardy & Half-Hardy Plants. 1855. 2 vols. in 1. 4to. 23 hand-cold. litho. plts., no title or prelims. to Vol. 2, as iss.?, some slight spotting, orig. cl. gt., spine & corners reprd. (LC. Jul.5; 166) £90

THOMPSON, Winfield M.
- The Holy Land, Egypt, Constantinople, Athens. [1862?]. 4to. 47 (of 48) photographic plts., stain in lr. margin thro.-out, orig. cl. gt. (P. Sep.8; 398) £80

THOMS, H.
See— MOELLER, J. & Thoms, H.

THOMSON, Arthur S.
- The Story of New Zealand: Past & Present-Savage & Civilised. 1859. *1st. Edn.* 2 vol. Some ll. in Vol. 2 stained, liby stps., cont. cf. gt., rebkd. (BBA. Jan.19; 80) *Scott.* £55

THOMS, William
- A New Treatise on the Practice of Navigation at Sea ... N.Y., 1867. *8th. Edn.* Worn, cont. sheep, worn, drawing on front fly-lf. (PNY. Mar.27; 178) $120

THOMSON, Basil
See— AMHURST, Lord, of Hackney & Thomson, Basil

THOMSON, James, Naturalist
- Arcana Naturae ou Receuil D'Histoire Naturelle. Paris, 1859. Vol. 1 (all publd.). Fo. Engraved frontis., 13 plts. (11 partly hand-cold.), unbnd. as iss. in orig. wraps., slightly frayed. (CSK. Apr.6; 38) £85

THOMSON, James, Poet, 1700-48
[-] Alfred, a Masque. 1740. *1st. Edn.* Hf. mor. by Macleish. (BBA. Sep.29; 152) *Pickering & Chatto.* £60
- The Castle of Indolence. L., 1748. *1st. Edn.* 4to.

Advt. lf., cf. gt., gt. dentelles, by Rivière, spine defect. (SG. Feb.9; 357) $130
- Les Saisons. Ill.:– Baquoy after Eisen. Paris, 1759. *1st. Printing of ills.* Sm. 8vo. Cont. cf. gt., spine decor. (HD. Nov.9; 82) Frs. 1,200
- - Anr. Edn. Ill.:– Le Barbier. Paris, 1795. Hf.-title, light foxing, str.-grd. red mor. (by Thouvenin?), ca. 1830, gold- & blind-decor, corners worn, covers lightly rubbed. (SM. Mar.7; 2453) Frs. 1,000
- - Anr. Edn. Ill.:– Le Barbier. Paris, 1796. *(300)* on vell. Figures before the letter, cont. cf. gt., decor. mor. spine. (HD. May 3; 162) Frs. 1,400
- The Seasons. Ill.:– Bartolozzi & Tomkins, after Hamilton. L., 1797. Lge. fo. Short tear in title reprd., mod. hf. cf., spine gt. (S. Dec.8; 62) *Nolan.* £130
- - Anr. Copy. Fo. Some foxing on title & plts., cont. Engl. russian cf., wide dentelle, gt. decor., decor. spine. (HD. Dec.16; 38) Frs. 2,800
- - Anr. Edn. Ill.:– Thomas Bewick. 1805. Cf., spine gt., by Morrell. (S. Mar.20; 756) *Thorp.* £50
- - Anr. Edn. Ill.:– Bartolozzi & Tomkins after Hamilton. L., 1807. *De Luxe Edn.* Fo. L.P., mor., sigd. by Ramage, gold-tooled decor., stp. in corners, gt. spine, decor. stps., gt. inner & outer dentelle, slight wear. (D. Nov.24; 2363) DM 2,000
- The Seasons & the Castle of Indolence. L., 1841. Mor. gt., with fore-e.pntg., as a fore-e.pntg., w.a.f. (SPB. May 17; 741) $400
- The Seasons ... together with a life of the author ... by Robert Heron. Perth, 1793. 4to. Cont. russ., faded; Sir Ivar Colquhoun, of Luss copy. (CE. Mar.22; 309) £150
- Winter. A Poem. L., 1726. *1st. Edn.* Fo. Last page soil-marked, disbnd.; Frederic Dannay copy. (CNY. Dec.16; 357) $2,500

THOMSON, John, Cartographer
- The Atlas of Scotland. Edinb., L. & Dublin, 1832. Lge. fo. 29 lge. engraved county & regional maps on 54 mapsheets, several joined or folding, index map & 2 comparative views, hand-cold. in outl., the views fully so, gazetteer at end, a few tears reprd., some dust-soiling or slight browning, 1 or 2 creases, mod. cl., spine defect., w.a.f. (S. May 21; 35) *Marsden.* £420
- - Anr. Copy. Fo. 2 folding engraved cold. charts & Index map, 58 engraved cold. maps & plans, hf. mor., defect. (PD. Dec.14; 292) £220
- - Anr. Copy. Fo. 2 engraved folding cold. charts, index map, 58 engraved cold. maps & plans, some staining to last maps, cont. hf. cf., worn & detchd. (PD. May 16; 264) £110
- A General Atlas. 1819. 4to. 41 col. maps, hf. cf., upr. cover detchd. (P. Apr.12; 329) *Burgess.* £180
- A New General Atlas. Edinb., 1817. Lge. fo. Engraved armorial dedication, folding engraved plt., engraved view, 58 (of 74) hand-cold. engraved maps in wash borders, title defect. & laid down, some folds reprd., a few creases, cont. hf. cf. (C. Mar.14; 96) *Burgess.* £500
- - Anr. Copy. Fo. 40 engraved maps only, most frayed, all dampstained, loose, disbnd. (BBA. Dec.15; 126) *Jeffery.* £170
- - Anr. Edn. [Edinb., 1817]. Fo. 22 double-p. engraved maps only, hand-cold. (some in outl.), cont. hf. cf., worn, lacks spine loose. (BBA. Jan.19; 68) *Faupel.* £50
- - Anr. Edn. Edinb., 1828. Fo. Engraved dedication, 76 maps on 85 double-p. engraved mapsheets, hand-cold. in wash & outl., 2 folding tables, some slight offsetting, 1 or 2 faint creases, last index lf. torn & soiled, cont. hf. cf., defect. (S. Dec.1; 210) *Burgess.* £640

THOMSON, John, F.R.G.S.
- Illustrations of China & its People ... 1873-74. *[1st. Edn.].* 4 vols. Fo. 96 plts., minimal foxing on title-pp., orig. pict. cl. gt., slight paint mark on upr. cover of Vol. 1. (PD. Apr.18; 210) £1,250
- - Anr. Copy. 4 vols. Fo. 96 plts. containing 200 autotype reproductions, titles slightly soiled, sm. liby. blind-stp. on most plts., affecting only margins or corners of image, front end-papers & fly-ll. creased, orig. gt.-pict. cl., worn. (SG. Nov.10; 157) $1,900

THOMSON, Joseph John
- **Conduction of Electricity through Gases.** Camb., 1903. *1st. Edn.* Perforated liby. stp. on title, 'withdrawn' stp. on end-paper, orig. cl., slight wear; Stanitz coll. (SPB. Apr.25; 423) £125
- **The Discharge of Electricity through Gases.** L., 1898. *1st. Engl. Edn.* Orig. cl., slightly rubbed; Stanitz coll. (SPB. Apr.25; 425) £300
- **A Treatise on the Motion of Vortex Rings.** L., 1883. *1st. Edn.* 1 p. torn along inner margin, not affecting text, slight margin browning, orig. cl., slight fading & rubbing of spine, some soiling; Stanitz coll. (SPB. Apr.25; 429) £175

THOMSON, Thomas
- **Travels in Sweden during the Autumn of 1812.** 1813. *[1st. Edn.].* 4to. Margin tear to plt. XII, cont. cl., old reback. (TA. Sep.15; 106) £90
- **– Anr. Copy.** 4to. Some foxing, old bds., cf. back & tips, upr. jnt. reprd. (RO. Dec.11; 324) £150

THOMSON, William Rodger
- **The Kafir Wars & the British Settlers in South Africa.** Ill.:– after T.W. Bowler. 1865. Fo. 20 tinted litho. plts., slight spotting, 1 plt. loose, orig. cl. gt., corner of upr. cover with slight stain. (LC. Jul.5; 429) £560
See— BOWLER, Thomas William & Thomson, W.R.

THORBURN, Archibald
- **British Birds.** 1915-18. 5 vols. including supp. 4to. Orig. cl. or wraps. (CSK. Jun.29; 64) £460
- **– Anr. Copy.** 4 vols. & Supp. 4to. 80 cold. plts. & Supp. with 2 cold. plts., minor spotting in Vol. 4, orig. cl., Supp. in ptd. wraps. (C. Mar.14; 199) *Sotheran.* £250
- **– Anr. Edn.** 1917-18. *Vols. 1 & 2: 3rd. Edn., Vols. 3 & 4: 2nd. Edn.* 4 vols. 4to. Orig. cl. gt. (SKC. Mar.9; 1960) £180
- **– Anr. Edn.** L., 1925-26. *(205).* 4 vols. Orig. cl. (C. Mar.14; 200) *Old Hall.* £280
- **– Anr. Edn.** L., 1925-26. *New Edn.* 4 vols. Preface in Vol. 1 with autograph sig. of author, 4 related A.L.s. from Thorburn to Veronica Coverdale loosely inserted, orig. cl., 1 corner of Vol. 1 chewed, Vol. 3 damp-affected. (CSK. Dec.2; 176) £170
- **– Anr. Copy.** 4 vols. Orig. cl., some fading. (P. Jul.5; 160) £95
- **– Anr. Copy.** 4 vols. Cl. (PD. Dec.14; 313) £75
- **– Anr. Copy.** 4 vols. 192 cold. plts., orig. cl. (S. Apr.10; 458) *Grahame.* £60
- **– Anr. Edn.** 1925-31. *New Edn.* 4 vols. Orig. cl., spines slightly faded. (TA. Oct.20; 158) £52
- **British Mammals.** L., 1920-21. *(155) numbered on L.P.* 2 vols. Fo. 50 cold. plts., orig. cl., discold. (S. Nov.28; 92) *Graham.* £380
- **– Anr. Edn.** 1920-21. 2 vols. in 1. Orig. cl., lightly soiled. (CSK. Jun.29; 63) £260
- **– Anr. Copy.** 2 vols. 4to. 50 cold. plts., orig. cl. (C. Mar.14; 202) *Old Hall.* £200
- **– Anr. Copy.** 2 vols. in 1. 4to. Lr. edge of some pp. slightly defect., not affecting text, orig. cl., d.-w. (SKC. Nov.18; 1993) £90
- **Game Birds & Wild-Fowl of Great Britain & Ireland.** 1923. Fo. Orig. cl., rubbed. (BBA. Jun.28; 283) *Benyon.* £300
- **– Anr. Copy.** Lge. 4to. Sig. of author on title, some light spotting, orig. cl., lightly affected by damp. (CSK. Dec.2; 177) £260
- **A Naturalist's Sketch Book.** L., 1919. 4to. 60 plts., orig. cl. (C. Mar.14; 201) *Hawker.* £140
- **– Anr. Copy.** 4to. 60 plts., including 24 cold., most with margin stains, mod. hf. mor. gt. (P. Dec.8; 77) *Mar.* £60

THOREAU, Henry David
- **The Maine Woods.** Boston, 1864. *1st. Edn. 1st. Iss.* Advts. dtd. Apr. 1864, 1 lf. Atlantic Monthly advt. at end, cl. gt., worn, end-paper slightly defect., sm. piece torn from mor. corner. (RO. Apr.23; 279) £170
- **Walden.** Boston, 1854. *1st. Edn.* Last 4 advt. ll. dtd. May 1854, some ll. dampstained, mod. hf. cf. (BBA. Feb.9; 91) *Sons of Liberty Books.* £160
- **– Anr. Copy.** Map, advts. dtd. Apr. 1854, minor foxing, orig. cl., slightly spotted, mor.-bkd. s.-c.; Perry Molstad copy. (SPB. May 16; 540) $1,000
- **– Anr. Copy.** Map, advts. dtd. Sept. 1854, few

gatherings sprung, orig. cl., spine slightly frayed, mor.-bkd. s.-c.; Fred A. Berne copy. (SPB. May 16; 370) $800
- **– – Anr. Edn.** Intro.:– Henry Seidel Canby. Ill.:– Edward Steichen. N.Y., Ltd. Edns. Cl., 1936. *(1500) numbered, sigd. by artist.* Tall 8vo. Full-p. photos., cl.-bkd. pict. bds., orig. s.-c. (SG. May 17; 230) $275
- **– – Anr. Copy.** 4to. Partly unopened, cl.-bkd. patterned bds., box. (SG. Nov.10; 146) $150
- **A Yankee in Canada.** Boston, 1866. *1st. Edn.* Orig. cl., spine slightly frayed; Fred A. Berne copy. (SPB. May 16; 371) $300

THORESBY, Ralph
- **Ducatus Leodiensis.** L., 1715. *1st. Edn.* Fo. Engraved folding map, 12 plts. (some shaved), some browning & spotting, cont. panel. cf., jnts. split, spine & corners worn. (S. Mar.6; 341) *Drury.* £80

THORLEY, John
- **An Enquiry into the Nature Order & Government of Bees.** L., 1774. *4th. Edn.* Bkplt., cf. (GM. Dec.7; 688) £100

THORN, Maj. William
- **Memoir of the Conquest of Java.** Ill.:– J. Jeakes & others. L., 1815. *1st. Edn.* 4to. 35 engraved plts., maps & charts, including 16 aquatints, hf.-title, slight offsetting & spotting, cont. cl.-bkd. bds., defect. (S. Mar.6; 51) *Morrell.* £400
- **– Anr. Copy.** 4to. Some spotting, foxing & browning, mod. hf. mor. (SPB. Dec.13; 471) $400

THORNBURY, George Walter & Walford, Edward
- **[–] Old & New London.** L., n.d. 6 vols. 4to. Cont. hf. cf., lightly rubbed. (CSK. Dec.2; 173) £60

THORNDIKE, Lynn
- **A History of Magic & Experimental Science.** N.Y., 1923-58. 8 vols. Orig. cl.; Dr. Walter Pagel copy. (S. Feb.7; 369) *Simmonds.* £200
- **– Anr. Copy.** 8 vols. Orig. linen. (R. Apr.3; 680) DM 700
- **– Anr. Copy.** 8 vols. Orig. linen. (R. Oct.11; 773) DM 500

THORNHILL, Richard B.
- **The Shooting Directory.** N.d. 4to. Spotted, cont. cf., rubbed, reprd. (BBA. Jul.27; 177) *Way.* £160

THORNLEY, Iris D.
See— THOMAS, Arthur Hermann & Thornley, I.D.

THORNTON, Robert John
- **Botanical Extracts or Philosophy of Botany.** L., 1810. 3 vols., including plt. vol. Fo. Port., 79 plts., spotting, liby. stp. on titles, mor. gt., scuffed, upr. cover Vol. 1 detchd. (P. Nov.24; 262) *Burden.* £120
- **Elements of Botany.** 1812. 2 vols. Some light spotting, cont. cf., rubbed; 39 extra plts. (not called for by Nissen). (CSK. Jun.29; 138) £60
- **Illustrations of the School-Virgil.** L., 1814. Unc., cf.-bkd. bds. (S. Dec.20; 637) *Korn.* £130
- **A New Family Herbal.** Ill.:– Thomas Bewick. 1810. *1st. Edn.* L.P., prelims. slightly spotted, later crimson mor. gt., partly untrimmed. (TA. Dec.15; 129) £95
- **– Anr. Copy.** Spotting, cf. (P. Jan.12; 284) *Cavendish.* £75
- **A New Illustration of the Sexual System of Linnaeus.** L., [1799-1810]. Fo. Engraved title, frontis., port. of Queen Charlotte, plt. of Cupid & others honouring bust of Linnaeus, 58 engraved plts. & tables, etc., 22 plts. containing ports., unc., mod. hf. cf. gt., w.a.f. (S. Oct.4; 290) *Crossley.* £250
- **The Philosophy of Botany** ... L., [1799-1810]. 2 pts. in 1 vol. Fo. 2 engraved titles (the 1st. on 2 ll.), frontis., port., plt. of Cupid, 24 port. plts., 70 engraved plts. & tables, dedication lf., slight spotting & discoloration, unc., cont. bds., spine worn, w.a.f. (S. Dec.13; 299) *Hagelin.* £110
- **The Temple of Flora.** Ill.:– Caldwell, Stadler, Earlom, & others, after Henderson, Reinagle & others. [plts. dtd. 1798-1812, wtrmkd. 1804-10]. Lge. fo. Buchanan's 'A' version of plts. 9, 11, 12, 14 & 24 are present, engraved title & contents lf., aquatint frontis. 'The Universal Power of Love', mezzotint port., 30 hand-finished col.-ptd. plts.,

without the plt. 'Flora dispensing her favours ... ' called for in the list of contents, replaced with plt. 'Cupid inspiring plants with love', 3 plts. detchd. from bdg., hf. cf., due to uncertainties of collation, w.a.f. (C. Mar.14; 119) £19,000
- **– – Anr. Edn.** L., 1799-[1807]. Fo. 4 engraved calligraphic ll., including title, port. of Linnaeus in 'Lapland dress' & cold. frontis. of 'Cupid inspiring Plants with Love', 28 (of the possible 32) floral plts. ptd. in cols., mostly hand-finished, mostly early states, including signs of zodiac showing in sky on Roses plt., lacks a few ll. of text, some browning, mostly to text, hf. cf., rebkd., rubbed, some chipping, as a coll. of plts., w.a.f. (SPB. Dec.14; 84) $30,000
- **– – Anr. Edn.** Ill.:– Caldwell, Stadler, Earlom, Warner, & others, after Henderson, Reinagle & others. L., 1799[-1812]. Lge. fo. 6 engraved ll. (contents, title on 2 ll., dedication to Queen Charlotte on 2 ll., & hf.-title 'Select Plants'), ptd. hf.-title 'Part third' & title 'Picturesque Botanical Plates, illustrative of the Sexual System of Carolus von Linnaeus', 31 plts. engraved in aquatint, mezzotint, stipple or line, ptd. in cols. & hand-finished, plts. 9,11,12,14 & 24 are Buchanan's 'A' plts., plt. 21 is engraved by Earlom, most. plts. in Buchanan's 2nd. or 3rd. state (other than those found in 1 state only), cold. mezzotint port. of Linnaeus in his Lapland dress loosely inserted, text slightly foxed, cont. red mor., elab. tooled in gt. & blind, rubbed. (S. Feb.1; 57) *Kraus.* £27,000
- **– – Anr. Edn.** L., [1811-]1812. Fo. Lightly browned, cont. leath. gt., spine renewed, cover worn. (R. Apr.4; 1802) DM 5,500
- **– – Anr. Edn.** 1951. *(250) numbered & sigd. by eds.* Fo. Few ll. spotted, orig. hf. mor., s.-c. (BBA. Oct.27; 234) *Marks.* £50
- **– – Anr. Edn.** 1951. Some foxing, hf. bnd., d.-w. (JL. Mar.25; 684) *Aus.* $100

THORNTON, Col. Thomas
- **A Sporting Tour through the Northern Parts of England.** 1804. 4to. Hf.-title, cont. tree cf. (BBA. Sep.29; 136) *Old Hall Books.* £80
- **Sporting Tour through Various parts of France.** L., 1806. 2 vols. 4to. Extra engraved titles with vigs., port., engraved plts. including aquatint, some folding, 1 plt. cut down & mntd., hf. cf., defect., lacks bdg. from 1 vol. (S. Apr.9; 64) *Ayres.* £85
- **– Anr. Copy.** 2 vols. 4to. Frontis. relaid, some dampstaining, Vol. 1 margins wormed thro.-out, cont. hf. cf., rebkd. (TA. Apr.19; 34) £55

THOROTON, Robert
- **The Antiquities of Nottinghamshire.** L., 1677. *1st. Edn.* Fo. Without licence lf., cont. mott. cf., spine gt. (C. Nov.16; 35) *Traylen.* £400

THOROUGHBRED BROODMARE RECORDS
1951-52, 1956-71, 1973. 19 vols. Cf. gt., w.a.f. (P. Dec.8; 202) *Way.* £280

THORPE, Thomas B.
- **The Hive of 'The Bee-Hunter',** ... **including Peculiar American Character, Scenery, & Rural Sports.** N.Y., 1854. *1st. Edn.* 12mo. Some foxing, blind-stpd. cl. gt. (SG. Jan.19; 339) $200

THORPE, William Arnold
- **A History of English & Irish Glass.** 1929. *[1st. Edn.]. (500) numbered.* 2 vols. 4to. Orig. cl., lightly soiled. (CSK. Nov.4; 206) £75
- **– Anr. Copy.** 4to. Orig. buckram, spines slightly faded, some light foxing, bkplts. (CBA. Jan.29; 216) $200

THORY, Claude Antoine
See— REDOUTE, Pierre Joseph

THOU, Jacques Auguste de
- **Histoire Universelle.** L., 1734. *1st. Fr. Trans.* 16 vols. 4to. Cont. marb. cf. gt., decor. spines, crowned cypher on spine & corner of covers, some defects. (HD. Sep.22; 359) *Frs.* 5,000
- **– Anr. Copy.** 16 vols. 4to. Lacks 1 plt., 1 lf. torn & reprd., cont. cf., spines decor., turn-ins slightly worn, some scratches. (HD. May 21; 71) Frs. 2,100
- **– – Anr. Edn.** La Haye, 1740. 10 vols. 4to. Hf.-title, marb. cf., spines decor. (SM. Mar.7; 2050) Frs. 2,800

– – Anr. Edn. Basel, 1742. 11 vols. Lge. 4to. Later hf. cf., worn. (SG. Oct.27; 318) $130

THOUIN, Gabriel
– Plans Raisonnés de Toutes les Espèces de Jardins. Ill.:– C. Motte after Thouin. Paris, 1820. Fo. Wide margin, some plts. lightly browned, cont. hf. leath., gt., bumped; Hauswedell coll. (H. May 24; 849) DM 2,600
– – Anr. Edn. Paris, 1828. *3rd. Edn.* Fo. Hf. linen, spine defect., upr. cover loose. (D. Nov.23; 1928) DM 1,600

THREE MOUNTAINS PRESS
See— POUND, Ezra

THROSBY, John
– The History & Antiquities of the Ancient Town of Leicester. Leicester, priv. ptd., 1791. 4to. Hf. cf. & marb. bds., slightly rubbed. (SKC. May 4; 1795) £65
– Select Views in Leicestershire from Original Drawings. Leicester, 1789, L., 1790. 2 vols., including Supp. 4to. Cont. diced cf., not quite unif. (C. Nov.16; 182) *Chesters.* £120
– – Anr. Copy. 2 vols., including Supp. 4to. Cf. (HBC. May 17; 337a) £155
– – Anr. Copy. 2 vols., including Supp. 4to. Qtr. cf. (HBC. May 17; 314) £140

THRUPP, George A.
– The History of Coaches. L., 1877. *1st. Edn.* Plts., orig. cl. gt. (P. May 17; 291) *Quaritch.* £80

THUCYDIDES
– De Bello Peloponnesiaco Libri VIII. Trans.:– L. Valla. [Geneva], 1588. Fo. In Greek & Latin, 3 MS. notes on fly-lf. sigd. with 5 fermé, cont. mor. elab. gt., central panel decor., gt. spine, arms of Jacques-Elione Turgot added in centre covers, here to denote ownership of Jesuit College, Tours (his bequest), 18th. C. title label added to spine, some wear, lacks ties; A. Eyre of Grove bkplt. (BBA. Nov.30; 20) *George's.* £750
– – Anr. Edn. Ed.:– C.A. Dukerus. Amst., 1731. Fo. In Greek & Latin, cont. cf. gt. (BBA. Jan.19; 19) *Primrose Hill Books.* £95
– Eight Bookes of the Peloponnesian Warre ... Trans.:– Thomas Hobbes. 1629. Fo. Some light soiling, old cf., rubbed. [STC 24058] (CSK. Jun.1; 47) £140
– – Anr. Edn. Trans.:– Thomas Hobbes. L., 1634. *1st. Hobbes Edn. 2nd. Iss.* Fo. Engraved pict. title, 2 (of 3?) double-p. maps, 2 plts., few ll. torn, some stains, early armorial cf., worn. [STC 24059] (SG. Feb.9; 358) $110
– – Anr. Edn. Trans.:– Thomas Hobbes. 1634. Sm. fo. Engraved title & 5 plts. & maps, some double-p., 1 loose, extra map of Scottish roads inserted, title holed, some dampstains, later mott. hf. cf. (BBA. Jun.28; 342) *Rix.* £55
– The History of the Peloponnesian War. Trans.:– Benjamin Jowett, M.A. Chelsea, Ash. Pr., 1930. *(260) on paper.* Fo. Vell. (LH. Sep.25; 318) $1,100
– Rede des Perikles für die Gefallenen. Trans.:– R. Binding. Frankfurt, Kleukens Pr., 1920. *(250) numbered on Bütten.* Hand-bnd. orig. vell., gt. decor., gt. outer dentelle, decor. inner dentelle. (GB. May 5; 2810) DM 430
– Works. Trans.:– B. Jowett. Oxford, 1881. *1st. Edn. of this trans.* 2 vols. Lge. 8vo. Vell., college arms on covers, spines gt.; inscr. on fly-lf. awarding the set as the 1st. Jeff Prize, Original Latin Verse, Election 1891. (SG. Feb.16; 315) $110

THUILE, J.
– La Céramique Ancienne à Montpellier. Paris, 1843. 4to. Publisher's decor. bds. (HD. Jun.29; 198) Frs. 2,100

THUILIER
See— VUILLEMIN, Thuilier & Lacoste, C.

THUMMEL, M.A. von
– Reise in die Mittäglichem Provinzen von Frankreich im Jahr 1785 bis 1786. Leipzig, 1810. 10 vols. in 5. Cont. marb. bds., rubbed. (BR. Apr.12; 1546) DM 450

THUNBERG, Carolus Petrus
– Flora Japonica. Leipzig, 1784. 39 plts., some folding, some browning, cf. (P. Jan.12; 285) *Han Shan.* £950
– Reisen in Afrika und Asien. Ed.:– J.R. Forster. Trans.:– K. Sprengel. [Berlin, 1792]. *1st. German Edn.* Cont. style hf. leath. (R. Oct.13; 3042) DM 450

THURAH, Laurids de
[–] Hafnia Hodierna. Ill.:– M. Keyl, De Lode, & others. Copen., 1748. *1st. Edn.* 4to. Engraved frontis., 100 plts., including folding panorama, cont. Danish cf., spine gt. (C. Dec.9; 153) *Goldschmidt.* £1,000
[–] Vitruvius Danicus ... Copen., 1746-49. *1st. Edn.* 2 vols. Fo. Engraved frontis., 281 plts. & plans, some folding or double-p., text in Danish, Fr. & German, cont. cf., spines gt., foot of 1 spine reprd. (C. Nov.16; 183) *Papp.* £3,000
[–] – Anr. Copy. 2 vols. Fo. Engraved frontis., 281 plts., text in Danish, Fr. & German, 3 plts. shaved, faint dampstain in upr. part of plts., more so in Vol. 1, cont. panel. cf., spine gt. (C. Dec.9; 154) *Lyon.* £2,400

THURBER, James
– The Last Flower: a Parable in Pictures. N.Y., 1939. Ob. 4to. Pres. inscr. dtd. C'mas 1939 on front free and-paper, sigd. & dtd. ink drawing on front pastedown, pict. bds., d.-w. slightly torn. (SG. Nov.3; 210) $650
– The Thurber Carnival. N.Y., 1944. *Page Proofs for 1st. Edn. of 'Merry-Go-Round'.* Sm. 4to. 'Merry-Go-Round' on title crossed out & changed in pencil to 'Carnival' ptd. on one side of p. only, neither hf.-title nor fly-title changed, some marginal browning, orig. wraps. with corrected title written in pencil across front, probably by author, light soiling; Perry Molstad copy. (SPB. May 16; 541) $450

THURLOE, John
– A Collection of the State Papers of ... 1762. 7 vols. Fo. Cont. cf.-bkd. bds., spines gt.-decor., rubbed; Sir Ivar Colquhoun, of Luss copy. (CE. Mar.22; 311) £220

THUROCZ, Joh. de
– Chronica Hungarorum. Augsburg, Ratdolt for Feger in Budapest, 1488. *2nd. Edn.* 4to. Variant C, lacks 1st. 2 ll. as usual (with 2 woodcuts), 2 blank ll. & 2 other ll. from anr. copy, anr. lf. from a further copy wormed, last lf. blank defect. & extended, some sm. reprd. defects. some browning & spotting, old MS. annots., incunable paper covered bds. (HK. Nov.8; 360) DM 17,000

THYRAEUS, Petrus
– Daemoniaci cvm Locis Infestis et Terricvlamentis Noctvrnis ... Köln, 1604. 4to. Title with owner's mark, lightly browned, 19th. C. hf. leath. gt., rubbed, corners bumped. (HK. Nov.9; 1980) DM 440

TIBULLUS, Albius
– Elegiae. Ed.:– E. Hiller. Ill.:– A. Simons. Leipzig, 1885, Tölz, 1920. *Bremer Pr., (270) on Bütten.* 4to. Hand-bnd. orig. vell., gold decor., by Frieda Thiersch. (H. Nov.23; 927) DM 850
– Elégies. Trans.:– Mirabeau. Ill.:– Borel & Marillier. Paris, An VI, 1798. 3 vols. Fr. & Latin parallel text, cont. marb. cf. gt., spines decor. (HD. May 3; 163) Frs. 1,300
See— CATULLUS, Caius Valerius, Tibullus, Albius & Propertius, Sextus Aurelius

TIECK, Johann Ludwig
– Der Aufruhr in den Cevennen. Berlin, 1826. *1st. Edn.* Pts. 1 & 2 (all publd.). Prelim. lf. with old owners mark, cont. red. hf. leath. gt. (H. May 22; 909) DM 540
– Gedichte. Dresden, 1821-23. *1st. Edn.* 3 vols. Lightly browned, some slight spotting, cont. hf. mor. gt., lightly rubbed. (HK. Nov.10; 2747) DM 660
– Gesammelte Novellen. Breslau, 1838-42. 14 pts. in 7 vols. Red hf. leath. gt., ca. 1860, by W. Nutt, w.a.f. (HK. Nov.10; 2745) DM 850
– Minnelieder aus dem Schwäbischen Zeitalter.

Berlin, 1803. *1st. Edn.* Cont. marb. bds., spine slightly chipped. (C. Dec.9; 290) *Schwing.* £400
– Phantasus. Berlin, 1812-16. *1st. Edn.* 3 vols. Cont. hf. cf.; Label of C. von Bülow. (C. Dec.9; 291) *Quaritch.* £340
– – Anr. Copy. 3 vols. Some foxing or browning, cont. bds., spine slightly bumped, sm. split; Maximilian 2. Herzog v. Leuchtenberg ex-libris; Hauswedell coll. (H. May 24; 1595) DM 1,000
– – Anr. Copy. 3 vols. Some slight foxing, later hf. leath. (GB. May 4; 1472) DM 900
– – Anr. Copy. 3 vols. Some light foxing, vol. II browned in upr. margin, later hf. leath. (H. Nov.23; 779) DM 620
– – Anr. Edn. Ed.:– K.G. Wendriner. Ill.:– Moritz Melzer. Berlin, 1911. *De Luxe Edn., (100) numbered.* 3 vols. 12 sigd. full-p. orig. etchings, a few ll. with sm. stain, orig. leath., slightly rubbed. (GB. Nov.5; 3074) DM 400
– Romantische Dichtungen. Leipzig, 1799-1800. *1st. Coll. Edn.* Slight browning, cont., style bds., ca. 1900. (GB. Nov.4; 2209) DM 840
– – Anr. Copy. 2 vols. Slightly foxed, some heavy browning, later linen, end-papers renewed, ex-libris inside cover. (H. May 22; 910) DM 420
– Schriften. Berlin, 1828-46. *1st. Coll. Edn.* 20 vols. Cont. hf. cf., later vols. not quite unif. (*With:*)
– Gesammelte Novellen. Berlin, 1852-54. 12 vols. in 6. Vols. 5-12 with additional title stating that they are Vols. 21-28 of the 'Schriften', cont. bds. (C. Dec.9; 292) *Wohler.* £240
– – Anr. Copy. Some browning, cont. hf. leath., gt. spine, last 5 vols. slightly different, slightly rubbed, 1 upr. cover with sm. nail mark; Hauswedell coll. (H. May 24; 1590) DM 3,600
– – Anr. Edn. Berlin, 1828-54. *1st. Coll. Edn.* 28 vols. Vol. 3 lacks part of title, Vol. 19 without title, Vol. 28 stained near end, most vols. lack upr. or lr. orig. wraps., some lack both. (HK. Nov.10; 2744) DM 1,500
[–] Volksmährchen. Ed.:– Peter Leberecht. Ill.:– W. Jury. Berlin, 1797. *1st. Edn.* 3 vols. Foxing & browning, cont. bds., bumped. spine darkened, 1 spine with sm. tear; Hauswedell coll. (H. May 24; 1591) DM 1,200
See— MUSAUS, Johann Karl August & others
See— SCHLEGEL, A.W. von & Tieck, Ludwig
See— WACKENRODER, W.H. & Tieck, Ludwig

TIEDEMANN, Fr.
– Tabulae Arteriarum Corporis Humani. Karlsruhe, 1822. Imp. Fo. 2 ll. with sm. tears, hf. leath., defect. (D. Nov.23; 635) DM 1,800

TIELENBURG, G.
– Gezichten der Steeden Jorck en Lancaster, en andere omliggende Plaatzen. Amst., ca. 1740. Double-p. ptd. title, & 51 double-p. engraved plts. (including 6 maps, 8 town plans & 37 views), ptd. index lf. at end, cont. bds., worn. (S. May 21; 64) *Kidd.* £200

TIES, F.
See— WEGELER, F.G. & Ties, F.

TIETZE, H. & Tietze-Conrat, E.
– The Drawings of the Venetian Painters in the 15th. & 16th. Centuries. N.Y., 1944. 4to. Orig. cl. (SI. Dec.15; 223) Lire 240,000

TIFFANY, Louis C.
– The Art Work of ... Garden City, 1914. *(492) on Japan vell., for private distribution.* Sm. fo. Sigd. pres. copy from Tiffany, calligraphically inscr. to Jersey City Free Public Liby., & dtd. Jun. 1916, hf.-title & frontis. detchd., patterned bds. gt. (SG. Aug.25; 385) $650
– – Anr. Copy. 4to. Embossed gold lacquer; pres. inscr. from Tiffany, dtd. 1 Jan. 1915. (VA. Apr.26; 113) R 500

TIGHE, Mary
[–] Psyche; or, the Legend of Love. L., Priv. ptd., 1805. *1st. Edn., (100).* Some light foxing & soiling, elab. tooled gt.-decor. mor. by George Bullen, gt. dentelles, end-papers possibly made from earlier bdg. cl., covers rubbed at jnts. & edges, some sm. stains at rear, spine darkened; sigd. pres. copy, inscr. by author to Rev.J. Kearney, with A.L.s. from author to Kearney (short tear). (CBA. Mar.3; 530) $275

TIGHE, Mary -*Contd.*

- **Psyche, with other Poems.** L., 1812. *4th. Edn.*
Gt.-decor. str.-grd. mor., covers lightly soiled, spine
darkened, erasure from front fly-lf., some foxing to
end-papers, fore-e. pntg. in blue-grey & green, a
col. copy of the fore-edge scene & 1 other (possibly
the orig.) laid in at end. (CBA. Mar.3; 208) $375

TIGHE, Sir William
[-] **Statistical Observations Relative to the County
of Kilkenny.** Dublin, 1802. *1st. Edn.* Hf. cf. (GM.
Dec.7; 137)   £130

TIJOU, John
- **A New Booke of Drawings.** Ed.:– J. Starkie
Gardner. L., 1896. Tall fo. Title-p. & text reproduced from 1693 edn., ex-liby., vell.-bkd. bds.,
soiled. (SG. May 3; 354) $110

TILIANO, G. Morellio
- **Tabula Compendiosa de Origine, Successione,
Aetate, et Doctrina Veterum Philosophorum ...**
Basle, 1530. Slightly browned, later mor., spine
slightly worn. (TA. Nov.17; 538)   £52

TILLEY, Frank
- **Teapots & Tea.** Newport, 1957. *(1000).* No bdg.
stated. (JL. Jun.24; 207)   Aus. $170

TILLIER, Claude
- **Mon Oncle Benjamin.** Ill.:– F. Siméon. 1926. *(30)
on japan, with decomposition of all ills. on china.*
Mosaic mor. by Massénat. (HD. Jan.24; 88)
                                                Frs. 3,000

TILLY, Alexandre, Comte de
- **Mémoires ... pour Servir à l'Histoire des Moeurs
de la Fin du 18e Siècle.** Paris, 1828. 3 vols. Cont.
hf. sheep, decor. spines. (HD. Sep.22; 360)
                                                Frs. 1,300

TIMES, The
- **The Times History of 1785-1948.** 1935-52. 4 vols.
in 5. Cl. gt., d-w. (P. Mar.15; 238)   *Thorp.* £85
- **The Times History of the War in South Africa.**
Ed.:– L.S. Amery. L., 1900-09. *2nd. Edn.* 7 vols.
Orig. cl., spines slightly faded, slightly soiled. (S.
Oct.4; 72)   *Dax.* £170

TIMLIN, William M.
- **The Ship that sailed to Mars, A Fantasy.** L.,
[1923]. *[1st. Edn.]* 4to. Cold. plts. & decors. all
tipped-in, orig. parch-bkd. bds. (BBA. May 23;
236)   *Thorpe.* £380
- - **Anr. Copy.** 4to. Lacks front end-lf., orig. parch.-
bkd. bds., covers rubbed. (S. Nov.22; 363)
                                              Demetzy. £220
- - **Anr. Copy.** 4to. 48 mntd. cold. plts. & 48 pp.
calligraphic text, each plt. & text-p. mntd. on grey
paper, bds., gt.-pict. vell. spine. (SG. Apr.26; 196)
                                                      $600
- - **Anr. Edn.** N.Y., [1923]. *1st. Amer. Edn.* 4to.
Hf. gt.-decor. vell. & bds., sm. tear to upr. bd.,
spine foxed & darkened. (CBA. Aug.21; 630)
                                                      $375
- - **Anr. Edn.** N.Y., [1923]. *1st. U.S. Edn., from
British plts.* Lge. 4to. Few text ll. smudged, few
edges of art paper chipped, cont. ink gift inscr. at
bottom of 2nd. lf. (dedicatory p.), orig. paper vell. &
buff bds., gt.-lettered with pict. design on spine,
spine ends very chipped & lacks some lettering,
some wear, rubbed. (HA. May 4; 293) $175
- - **Anr. Edn.** N.d. 4to. 47 (of 48) col. plts., qtr.
vell., d-w., w.a.f. (P. Jan.12; 294)   *Ayres.* £130

TIMMERMANS, Felix
- **Beatrix. Eine Brabantische Legende.** Trans.:–
F.M. Huebner. Ill.:– Felix Timmermanns. (1921).
(310). (50) De Luxe Edn. on Bütten. 4to. 6 orig.
etchings, orig. hf. vell. (GB. May 5; 3398)
                                                    DM 500
- **Het Kindeken Jezus in Vlaanderen.** Amst., [1917].
(25) numbered on holland. Unc., orig. parch. (B.
Oct.4; 88)   Fls. 550
- **Pieter Brueghel.** Brussel, [1928]. *1st. Printing,
(207). (10) on Auvergne vergé, sigd. by author,
printer & publisher.* 4to. Slightly foxed, unc., orig.
wraps., browned, slightly defect. (B. Oct.4; 90)
                                                    Fls. 600
- **De Zeer Schoone Uren van Juffrouw Symforosa,
Vegijntjem.** Brussel & Bussum, 1918. *1st. Printing.*

(6) on chine, sigd. Slightly foxing, unc., orig. wraps.
(B. Oct.4; 91)   Fls. 1,100

TIMPERLEY, Charles H.
See— **WRIGHT, Rev. George Newnham [& Timperley, Charles H.]**

TIMAN, Jean de
- **La Petite Jeanne Pâle.** Ill.:– Ed. Chimot. Paris,
1922. *(15) numbered on japan, with 3 states of
engrs. (including cold.).* 4to. 8 orig. etchings, orig.
bdg. (HD. Apr.26; 64)   Frs. 1,700

TING, Walasse
- **One Cent Life.** Ill.:– Alechinsky, Karel Appel,
Jorn, Oldenburg, Riopelle, Ting, Warhol, & others.
Bern, 1964. *(2100).* Fo. Orig. iithos., leaves, portfo.,
cl., d-w.'s, cl. box. (B. Feb.8; 388)   Fls. 800

TINKER, Chauncey Brewster
- **The Tinker Library. A Bibliographical Catalogue.**
New Haven, 1959. 4to. Plts., orig. cl.; Fred A.
Berne copy. (SPB. May 16; 177) $100
- - **Anr. Edn.** Ed.:– R.F. Metzdorf. New Haven,
[1959]. *(500).* Sm. 4to. Cl. (SG. Sep.15; 329)
                                                      $130

TINTO, Giovanni Francesco
- **La Nobilita di Verona.** Verona, 1590. 4to. 1 lf.
crudely reprd., cont. red mor., blind– & gt.-decor.,
painted medallion, turn-ins renewed; from Fondation Furstenberg-Beaumesnil. (HD. Nov.16; 175)
                                                Frs. 3,300

TIPHAIGNE DE LA ROCHE, Charles-François
[-] **Giphantie.** A Babylone [i.e. Paris], 1760. *1st.
Edn.* 2 pts. in 1 vol. Cont. cf., worn. (SG. Nov.10;
159) $110

TIPPING, H. Avray
- **English Homes.** L., 1920-34. 9 vols. Fo. Orig. cl.,
very slightly rubbed. (S. May 1; 579)
                                              Henderson. £780
- - **Anr. Edn.** L., 1921-28. Periods 1-6 in 8 vols.
Tall fo. Photo. ills., ex-liby., cl. (SG. May 3; 355)
                                                    $1,200
- - **Anr. Edn.** L., 1921-37. *Mixed Edns.* 9 vols. Fo.
Orig. cl., 1 vol. shaken, some soiled. (S. Mar.6;
342)   *Weinreb.* £850
- - **Anr. Edn.** L., 1926-29. 6 vols. only (of 9). Fo.
Orig. cl., 4 in d-w.'s. (S. Mar.6; 343)
                                            Chamberlain. £280
- - **Anr. Edn.** 1928-29. 3 vols. only. Fo. Orig. cl.,
spines slightly faded. (CSK. Sep.30; 95)   £100
- - **Anr. Edn.** L., 1929-37. 3 vols. only (of 9). Fo.
Orig. cl. (S. Mar.6; 344)   *Weinreb.* £180
- - **Anr. Edn.** L., 1937-29. Periods 1 and 2, Vol. 2,
Period 2, Vol 1, Period 3, Vol 1. Orig. cl., slightly
rubbed. (BBA. Dec.15; 318)   *Fletcher.* £120
- **Grinling Gibbons & the Woodwork of his Age.**
L., 1914. *[1st. Edn.].* Fo. Orig. cl.-bkd. bds., worn.
(S. Oct.4; 126)   *Blackwells.* £80
- - **Anr. Copy.** Fo. Qtr. buckram, edges slightly
worn. (SKC. May 4; 1575)   £65
- - **Anr. Copy.** Fo. Port., 234 text ills., ex-liby., orig.
hf. cl. (SG. May 3; 177) $150

TIRABOSCHI, Girolamo
- **Riflessioni su gli Scrittori Genealogici.** Padua,
1789. *1st. Edn.* Cont. cf. gt., arms of Charles IV
of Spain on covers, later end-papers, head of spine
slightly worn; liby. stps. of Luigi Amoroso & Principe Pietro Amoroso d'Aragona, latter's bkplt.,
bkplt. of Benjamin Disraeli. (S. May 10; 418)
                                              Maggs. £200

TIRION, Isaak
- **Nieuwe en Beknopte Hand-Atlas.** Maps:– after de
l'Isle, de la Caille, Cruquius, Bolstra, Hattinga &
others. Amst., [1769 or later]. Fo. Ptd. title & index
lf., 109 engraved mapsheets (3 folding), variously
dtd. between 1730 & 1769, hand-cold. thro.-out in
cont. hand, many cartouches fully so, 3 maps on 2
sheets (counted as 2 nos. in index), cont. hf. cf.,
spine gt., slightly worn, w.a.f. (S. May 21; 131)
                                              Traylen. £3,500

TISSANDIER, Gaston
- **Histoire des Ballons et des Aéronautes Célèbres.**
Paris, 1887-90. 2 vols. 4to. Hf. chagrin, wraps.;
from Château des Noës liby. (HD. May 25; 79)
                                                Frs. 2,400

TISSOT, Dr. Samuel Auguste
- **Advice to People in General with Regard to their
Health.** Edinb., 1766. 2 vols. Cont. spr. cf.; Sir Ivar
Colquhoun, of Luss copy. (CE. Mar.22; 312) £50
- **De la Santé des Gens de Lettres.** Lausanne, 1768.
1st. Edn. (Bound with:) **NIHELL, James**
- **Observations Nouvelles et Extraordinaires, sur la
Prediction des Crises par le Pouls.** Paris, 1748. *1st.
Fr. Edn.* Together 2 works in 1 vol. Cont. mott. cf.,
very rubbed, spine chipped at foot. (SG. Oct.6; 360)
                                                      $250
- **Von den Krankheiten Vornehmer und Reicher Per-
sonen.** Trans.:– J.L. Drechsler. Frankfurt &
Leipzig, 1771. A few MS. margin annotats., some
slight foxing, bds. (D. Nov.23; 636)   DM 580

TITELMAN, Fr.
- **Naturalis Philosophiae Compend., sive de Consi-
deratione ... Libri XII.** Louvain, 1566. *(Bound with:)*
CICERO, Marcus Tullius – **De Officiis Libri III;
De Amicitia; De Senectute; Paradoxa; De Somnio
Scipionis.** Lyon, 1554. Together 2 works in 1 vol.
Cont. blind-stpd. pig over wood, dtd. 1569, monog.,
lacks ties; from Bibl. Collegii Societ. Jesu Land-
sperge. (VG. Sep.14; 1362)   Fls. 550

TITEUX, Eugène
- **Histoire de la Maison du Roi (1814-1830).** Paris,
1890. 2 vols. 4to. 84 cold. plts., red hf. mor., corners.
(HD. Jan.27; 220)   Frs. 8,000
- **Historiques et Uniformes des Régiments de Cava-
lerie, Cuirassiers, Dragons, Chasseurs, Hussards,
Spahis, Chasseurs d'Afrique.** Paris, [1895]. Fo.
Cont. red hf. mor., corners. (HD. Sep.21; 170)
                                                Frs. 2,400

TITI, Fil.
- **Studio di Pittura, Scoltura e Architettura nella
Chiese di Roma.** Rome, 1675. 16mo. Cont. vell.
(HD. Dec.15; 42)   Frs. 1,000

TITMARSH, M.A.
See— **THACKERAY, William Makepeace 'M.A.
Titmarsh'**

TITTMANN, E.
- **Gründliche Nachricht wegen des ohnweit der Stadt
Meissen, bey dem Dorff Gasern, im vorigen 1714
Jahr gefundenen ... Gesundheit-Wassers oder viel-
mehr Sauer-Brunnens.** Dresden, [1715]. Cont. bds.,
cover loose. (D. Nov.23; 522)   DM 400

TIZAC, H. d'Ardenne de
- **Animals in Chinese Art.** L., 1923. *(250).* Fo. A
few plts. slightly spotted, orig. cl. gt., stained &
faded. (S. Dec.13; 426)   *Marton.* £60

TOBLER, C.
- **Aventuras de Filipinas, Album Humoristico.** 1874.
4to. 24 litho. plts., in orig. folder, soiled. (P. Sep.8;
140)   *Tzakas.* £220

TOBLER, T.
- **Zwei Bücher Topographie von Jerusalem und
seinen Umgebungen.** Berlin, 1853-54. 2 vols.
Slightly foxed, cont. hf. leáth., slightly rubbed. (R.
Apr.5; 2843)   DM 450

TOCQUEVILLE, Alexis de
- **L'Ancien Régime et la Revolution.** 1856. *Orig.
Edn.* Cont. hf. chagrin; Antoine d'Orléans ex-libris.
(HD. Apr.13; 122).   Frs. 2,200

TOCQUOT, J.F.
- **The Royal Pocket Dictionary.** L., 1808. 32mo.
Mor., fore-e.pntg., as a fore-e.pntg., w.a.f. (SPB.
May 17; 742) $300

TODA Y GUELL, E.
- **Bibliografia Espanyola d'Italia dels Origens de la
Imprempta fins a l'any 1900.** Castell de San Miquel
d'Escornabou [Barcelona], 1927-31. 5 vols. 4to.
Leath., orig. wraps. (DS. Oct.28; 2120)
                                              Pts. 75,000

TOFINO DE SAN MIGUEL, V.
- **Derrotero de las Costas de España.** Madrid, 1787.
2 vols. in 1. Sm. 4to. Cont. hf. cf., rubbed. (BBA.
Jun.28; 253)   *Brook.* £120

TOKYO FINE ART SCHOOL
- **One Hundred Masterpieces of Japanese Pictorial
Art.** Tokyo, 1909. 2 vols. Fo. 1 title spotted, orig.

decor. cl., in orig. cl. portfos., lacks 1 ivory fastener. (S. Oct.4; 205) *Hollander.* £60

TOLEDO
– Relación Breve de lo que se ha hecho en ... San Juan de los Reyes de Toledo ... el Dia de la Limpissima Concepción ... Gran Procession ... y el gran adorno ... Toledo, 1615. 4to. Sewed. (DS. Nov.25; 2413)
Pts. 26,000

TOLEDO, Revista
1889. 18 nos. (complete). Fo. Pict. linen. (DS. Apr.27; 2617) Pts. 30,000

TOLETUS, D. Franciscus
– Commentaria Una cum Quaestionibus in Tres Libros Aristotelis. Cologne, 1583. Sm. 4to. Cont. German cf. gt., richly decor., slightly worn; from Fondation Furstenberg-Beaumesnil. (HD. Nov.16; 177) Frs. 1,300

TOLKIEN, John Ronald Reuel
– Farmer Giles of Ham. L., 1949. *1st. Edn.* Orig. cl., d.-w.; pres. copy. (SPB. May 17; 705) $800
– The Hobbit. L., 1937. *1st. Edn.* Hf.-title, advt. lf. at end, orig. decor. cl., d.-w. with MS. correction 'Dodgeson', short tear in spine, reprd. (S. Dec.8; 263) *Joseph.* £780
– – **Anr. Copy.** Hf.-title, advt. lf. at end, orig. decor. cl. (S. Dec.8; 268) *Halmer.* £300
– – **Anr. Copy.** Orig. cl., slightly worn & soiled. (P. Sep.8; 254) *Wilton.* £190
– – **Anr. Copy.** Orig. cl., slightly soiled. (BBA. May 23; 128) *Burton Garbett.* £150
– – **Anr. Copy.** Orig. cl., d.-w. (SPB. May 17; 707) $1,000
– The Lord of the Rings. L., 1953-54. 3 vols. Proof copy, hf.-titles, folding map for Vol. 1 loosely inserted, (other vols. without maps), Vol. 3 with paste-up for p. 403, Vol. 1 with MS. note & a typescript label, Vol. 2 with typescript labels, the title & deleted MS. note, letter from Rayner Unwin, dtd. 10 Nov. 1953, to Raymond Winter of Clarke & Satchell Ltd. loosely inserted, Winter's sig. on hf.-titles of Vols. 1 & 2, orig. plain brown wraps. (S. Dec.8; 262) *Quaritch.* £1,950
– – **Anr. Edn.** L., 1954-55. *1st. Edn.* 3 vols. Orig. cl., d.-w.'s. (BBA. Nov.30; 324) *Quaritch.* £650
– – **Anr. Copy.** 3 vols. Orig. cl., d.-w.'s. (BBA. Jul.27; 213) *Demetzy.* £500
– – **Anr. Copy.** 3 vols. Hf.-titles, orig. cl., slight stain at foot of Vol. 3. (S. Dec.8; 269)
Burton Garbett. £260
– – **Anr. Copy.** 3 vols. Orig. cl., d.-ws. (SPB. May 17; 710) $5,250
– – **Anr. Edn.** L., 1954-55. *Vols. 1 & 3: 1st. Edn., Vol. 2: 2nd. Imp.* 3 vols. Orig. cl. (S. Dec.8; 265) *Burton Garbett.* £50
– – **Anr. Edn.** 1954-55. 2 vols. (of 3, lacks The Fellowship of the Rings). Orig. cl., d.-w.'s. (BBA. Jul.27; 214) *Burton Garbett.* £100
– The Return of the King. Being the Third Part of The Lord of the Rings. 1955. *1st. Edn.* Folding map bnd. in at end, orig. cl., d.-w. (frayed). (*With:*)
– The Hobbit. 1946. 1 ill. cold. by amateur hand., orig. decor. cl.; sigd. by author on front end-paper & frontis verso. (TA. Apr.19; 400) £55

TOLLIUS, Jacobus
– Epistolae Itinerariae. Amst., 1700. *1st. Edn.* Extra engraved title, 16 plts. (4 folding). (*Bound with:*)
– Insignia Itinerarii Italici. Utrecht, 1696. *1st. Edn.* Together 2 works in 1 vol. 4to. 18th. C. tree cf. gt., upr. cover detchd. (S. Mar.20; 812) *Poole.* £70

TOLMER, A.
– Mise en Page, the Theory & Practice of Lay-Out. 1931. 4to. Orig. cl.-bkd. bds., s.-c., slightly rubbed. (S. May 1; 437) *Sims.* £60

TOLNAY, C. de
– Michelangelo. Princeton, 1943-50. 5 vols. 4to. No bdg. stated. (SPB. Nov.30; 113) $175
– – **Anr. Edn.** Princeton, 1943-60. 5 vols. 4to. Orig. cl., Vol. 1 rubbed & faded. (S. Apr.30; 22)
Mangold. £50

TOLSTOI, Leo Nikolayevich
– Works. 1929-37. *Centenary Edn.* Later cl. (CSK. Sep.16; 232) £80

TOM THUMB'S PLAY-BOOK: To teach Children their Letters as soon as they can speak
Boston, [1764]. 32mo. Browned & soiled, top fifth of 3rd. lf. torn away, 1st. & last 2 ll. & ill. paper covers partially separated at spine. (SPB. May 23; 49) $6,000

TOMASINUS, J.F.
– Bibliothecae Venetae Manuscriptae Publicae et Privatae. Udine, 1650. 4to. Vell. (P. Mar.15; 341)
Quaritch. £190

TOMBLESON, William & Fearnside, William Gray
– Eighty Picturesque Views on the Thames & Medway. 1834. 4to. Engraved title, dedication lf., folding map, 79 plts., orig. cl. (BBA. Oct.27; 287)
Bailey. £220
– – **Anr. Edn.** [1834]. Additional engraved title with vig., engraved folding map, 79 full-p. plts., lacks ptd. title, map creased, some spotting, cont. hf. cf. gt., defect. (S. Nov.1; 134) *Kidd.* £250
– – **Anr. Copy.** 4to. Engraved title, 79 engraved views, few slightly spotted, cf., spine defect. (P. Sep.8; 48) *Martin.* £230
– – **Anr. Edn.** Ca. 1840. Engraved title, 78 engraved views, many foxed, mor. gt., worn. (P. Mar.15; 1) *MacDonald.* £250
– – **Anr. Edn.** Ca. 1845. 4to. Engraved title, 79 engraved views, mor. gt. (P. Oct.20; 213) £220
– Rhein Ansichten. L., ca. 1830. 68 steel engrs., 1 folding engraved panorama, some slight plts. foxing, orig. blind-tooled linen gt. (BR. Apr.12; 400) DM 950
– – **Anr. Edn.** L., [1832]. Vol. 1 (of 2). Engraved title with vig., 68 steel engraved plts., 1 engraved folding panorama, title soiled & with MS. owners mark, slightly browned, cont. linen gt., lightly spotted & worn. (HK. May 15; 1026) DM 500
– Thames. L., ca. 1840. 4to. Fr. text, steel engraved title, lge. folding steel-engraved map, 79 steel engraved views in Romantic borders, some slight foxing, cont. hf. chagrin, plasticised. (VS. Jun.7; 856) Fls. 525
– Upper Rhine. L., [1832]. Engraved cold. title, 1 folding cold.map, 69 cold. steel engraved views, some foxing, cont. hf. leath gt., rubbed. (R. Oct.12; 2481) DM 2,200
– – **Anr. Copy.** Folding engraved map, 69 steel-engraved plts., steel-engraved title & a few plts. lightly foxed, map slightly crumpled, 1 margin tear, cont. leath., gt. spine, cover, inner & outer dentelle, decor., lightly bumped & rubbed. (HK. Nov.9; 1206) DM 1,400
– – **Anr. Copy.** Steel-engraved title, 69 steel engraved plts., lacks engraved plt., plt. margins slightly soiled, minimal foxing, hf. leath. gt., end-papers renewed. (HK. May 15; 1027) DM 1,350
– – **Anr. Copy.** 1 engraved title, 69 steel engraved plts., 1 multi folding map, orig. linen. (D. Nov.23; 823) DM 1,100
– – **Anr. Edn.** L., 1834. Engraved title, 1 folding map (margin tear) & 69 steel engraved views, slightly browned, orig.wraps. mod. hf. leath. box. (R. Apr.4; 2311) DM 1,900
– – **Anr. Edn.** Ca. 1840. Engraved title, folding panorama, 69 steel engrs., some minor spotting, cont. hf. mor., rubbed. (TA. Jul.19; 19) £260
– – **Anr. Edn.** N.d. Engraved title, folding pan-orama, 68 engraved plts., text in Fr., mor. gt. (P. Mar.15; 94) £300
– – **Anr. Copy.** Engraved title (marginally torn), folding map (torn), 69 plts., slightly dampstained, later cl. (BBA. Oct.27; 252) *Bailey.* £230
– The Upper Rhine. – Views on The Rhine. [1834]; 1832. 2 vols. 2 engraved titles, 2 folding panoramas, 137 engraved views, hf. mor. gt. (P. Oct.20; 6) £500
– Views of the Rhine. L., 1832. Engraved title with vig., folding panorama, 68 plts., panorama with reprd. tear, some slight spotting or browning, cont. hf. cf. gt. (S. Dec.1; 326) *Baker.* £270
– – **Anr. Copy.** Engraved title, folding panorama & 67 views, hf. cf. crudely reprd. (P. May 17; 140)
Bailey. £220
– – **Anr. Copy.** 4to. Vig. title, folding panorama, 67 steel engrs., some spotting, mainly to margins, later cl., untrimmed, worn on spine. (TA. Jun.21; 29) £190
– – **Anr. Copy.** Engraved vig. title, 67 engraved

plts., stains, mor. gt. defect., as a coll. of plts., w.a.f. (P. May 17; 89) *Bailey.* £140
– – **Anr. Copy.** Engraved title, folding panorama map & 68 steel engrs., some slight foxing, mod. vell., ties. (R. Oct.13; 2745) DM 1,100
– – **Anr. Copy.** Engraved title, folding panorama map, 68 steel engraved views, foxed, cont. hf. leath. gt., rubbed. (R. Apr.4; 2261) DM 1,000
– – **Anr. Edn.** Ed.:– W. G. Fearnside. L., [1832]. Engraved title, folding panorama map, 68 steel engraved views, some slight foxing, most plts. stained in 1 corner, cont. linen, spine renewed. (R. Apr.4; 2547) DM 1,000
– – **Anr. Edn.** Ed.:– W.G. Fearnside. L., ca. 1832. Engraved title, 68 steel engraved views, 1 multi folding engraved panorama, minimal spotting, cont. linen, slightly defect. (HT. May 10; 2970)
DM 850
– – **Anr. Edn.** L., ca. 1840. Steel-engraved title, lge. steel-engraved map, 68 steel-engraved views, text in German, some foxing, cont. blind-stpd. cl., spine gt. (VS. Dec.8; 784) Fls. 850
– Vues Pittoresque du Rhin. ca. 1840. *Coll. vol.* Engraved title from Bulwer-Lyttons 'Pilgrims of the Rhine', 1 folding litho. map, 36 steel engrs. from author's 'Views of the Rhine', slightly browned & foxed, stained near end, cont. bds., rubbed & soiled. (R. Oct.13; 2746) DM 480
– – **Anr. Edn.** Ill.:– Clark, Howe & others. L., n.d. Engraved title with vig., 68 (of 69) engraved plts, some old soiling, especially in margins, 1 text lf. defect., orig. hf. linen. (V. Sep.29; 96) DM 1,300

TOMES, John
– A Course of Lectures on Dental Physiology and Surgery. L., 1848. *Only Edn.* Orig. cl., rehinged, worn, loose; Robert Arthur MS. ex-libris, & his extensive MS. annots. on 5 pp. & end-paper, a few other marks & notes, Asbell bkplt. (SG. Mar.22; 95) $250

TOMES, Robert
– The War with the South. N.Y., 1862. 3 vols. 4to. Orig. block mor. (GM. Dec.7; 640) £55

TOMKINS, Peltro William
See— OTTLEY, William Young & Tomkins, Peltro William
See— TRESHAM, Henry & others

TOMLINS, Thomas E.
– Yseldon. A Perambulation of Islington. 1858. 4to. L.P., cont. hf. cf., rebkd.; extra-ill. with approx. 30 engraved maps & plts., a few tipped in. (BBA. Jul.27; 332) *Ralph.* £80

TOMLINSON, Charles
– Cyclopedia of Useful Arts, Mechanical & Chem-ical, Manufactures, Mining, & Engineering. L., 1854. 2 vols. 40 plts., hf. mor., worn. (SG. Mar.22; 302) $110
– Rudimentary Treatise on the Construction of Locks. 1853. Orig. limp cl., frayed at spine ends. (TA. Oct.20; 127) £52

TOMS, W., Jnr.
– Thirty Six New Original & Practical Designs for Chairs, Adapted for the Drawing & Dining Room, Parlour & Hall. Bath, n.d. 4to. Litho. title-p. & 36 plts., orig. cl.-bkd. ptd. bds., worn. (S. May 1; 724)
Sims. £130

TOMS, W.H.
See— BADESLADE, T. & Toms, W.H.

TONE, Wolfe William Theodore
– Life of ... Wash., 1826. *1st. Edn.* 2 vols. Titles & port. foxed, hf. cf., armorial motif on spine. (GM. Dec.7; 451) £70

TONSBERG, Niels Christian
– Billedar af Norges Natur Og Folkeliv. 1873. 24 col. litho. plts. loose with text & orig. wraps. (P. Oct.20; 138) £80
– – **Anr. Edn.** Christiana, 1875. Ob. 4to. Orig. linen, rubbed, loose, some soiling. (D. Nov.23; 1192)
DM 500
– Norske Folkelivsbilleder. Christiana, 1854. Ob. fo. 12 cold plts. hf. roan gt. (P. Apr.12; 272)
Marks. £130

TONSTALL, Cuthbert
- De Arte Supputandi Libri Quattuor. Paris, 1538. *3rd. Edn.* 4to. Slight worming to blank corners of a few ll., cont. blind-stpd. cf., rebkd.; Stanitz coll. (SPB. Apr.25; 430) $1,400

TOOKE, Thomas
- Considerations on the State of the Currency. L., 1826. *1st. Edn.* Orig. bds., unc. (P. May 17; 18) *Kossow.* £180
- Thoughts & Details on the High & Low Prices of the Last Thirty Years. L., 1823. Pt. 1: 'On the Alterations in the Currency'. Unopened, orig. bds., soiled, spine slightly torn. (S. Oct.11; 596) *Maas.* £120

TOOKE, William
- [-] Accounts & Extracts of the Manuscripts in the Library of the King of France. L., 1789. 2 vols. Cont. cf. gt. (SG. Sep.15; 211) $175

TOOKER, William
- Charisma sive Donum Sanationis. Seu Explicato ... de Solenni & Sacra Curatione Strumae. 1597. *1st. Edn.* 4to. 19th. C. hf. mor. [STC 24118] (BBA. May 3; 70) *Frognall.* £140

TOOLEY, Ronald Vere
- My Head is a Map. Ed.:– H. Wallis & S. Tyacke. L., 1973. *(30) numbered, sigd.* Ills., hf. mor. gt., by Sangorski & Sutcliffe. (P. May 17; 67) *Forster.* £60
- Printed Maps of Australia, being a Catalogue of a Collection. 1970-72. 6 pts. in 1 vol. 4to. Some prices in pencil, red hf. mor., orig. wraps. preserved. (BBA. Jan.19; 349) *Simper.* £60

TOOLEY, Ronald Vere (Ed.)
See— MAP COLLECTORS' CIRCLE

TOPFFER, Rodolphe
- Les Amours de Mr Vieux-Bois. Paris, 1860. *'1st. Edn.'?* Ob. 4to. Publisher's cl. bds., decor. with special tools on upr. cover. (LM. Oct.22; 64) B.Frs. 8,000
- Premiers Voyages en Zigzag ... Ill.:– after Calame & Töpffer. Paris, 1855. *4th. Edn.* Lge. 8vo. Publisher's bds., Lenegre decor; from Château des Noës liby. (HD. May 25; 80) Frs. 1,400
- [-] Voyages et Aventures du Docteur Festus. Genève, Paris, 1840. *Orig. Edn.* Jansenist mor., wrap. & spine preserved. (HD. May 4; 439) Frs. 3,800

TORFFAEUS, Thormodus
- Orcades seu Rerum Orcadensium Historiae Libri Tres. Copen., 1697. Some ll. margin wormed. *(Bound with:)* IMHOFF, Jacob Wilhelm – Regum Pariumque Magnae Britanniae Historia Genealogica. Nuremb., 1690. Hf.-title, without 6 appendix ll. publd. in 1691. Together 2 works in 1 vol. Fo. Browned, some ll. stained, cont. cf., worn. (BBA. May 3; 269) *Vine.* £70
See— IMHOFF, Jacob Wilhelm – TORFFAEUS, Thormodus

TORI DE LA RIVA Y HERRERO, Torquato
- Arte de Escribir. Madrid, 1802. *2nd. Edn.* Engraved title, 58 plts., a few ll. slightly browned, cont. bds., slightly rubbed, rebkd. with mod. cf. (BBA. Nov.30; 78) *Bloomsbury Rare Books.* £140

TORQUEMADA, Antonio de
- Hexameron. Rouen, 1610. 12mo. Long-grd. mor., gt. decor., limp decor. spine, by Bozerian jeune; ex-libris. (HD. Dec.9; 87) Frs. 2,400

TORQUEMADA, Juan de
- Primera [Segunda, Tercara] Parte de los Veinte y un Libros Rituales y Monarchia Indiana. Madrid, 1723. *2nd. Edn.* 3 vols. 4to. Vell. (LH. Sep.25; 291) $1,600

TORRENS, Robert
- Colonization of South Australia. L., 1835. Pencilled marginalia in hand of Sir Charles Napier, early bds. & qtr. mor., backstrip lettered 'Pamphlets on the Colonies:3:Torrens'; Henry L. White bkplt. (KH. Nov.9; 730) Aus. $780

TORRENTE, Mariano
- Historia De La Revolución Hispano-Americana. Madrid, 1829-30. 3 vols. 4to. 15 plts., 2nd. title-p. with variant imprint in Vol. 1, explanation of Battle of Ayacucho in Vol. 3, some foxing, orig. cf. gt.; pres. inscr. by author. [Sabin 96235] (BBA. Feb.9; 277) *Brook.* £200

TORRENTINUS, H.
- [-] Elucidarius Carminum et Historiarum. Strassburg, 1510. *2nd. or 3rd. Edn.* 4to. 2 extracts at end, slightly browned & wormed, bdg. loose due to removed supp., bds., ca. 1800. (HK. Nov.8; 365) DM 400

TORRES DE CASTILLA, Alfonso
- Historia de las Persecuciones Políticas y Religiosas ocurridas en Europa desde la Edad Media hasta nuestros Dias. Barcelona, 1863. 6 vols. 4to. Linen. (DS. Nov.25; 2050) Pts. 36,000
- – Anr. Copy. 6 vols. 4to. Linen. (DS. Apr.27; 2286) Pts. 32,000

TORES RUBIO, D. de
- Arte y Vocabulario de la Lengua Quichua General de los Indios del Perú. Ed.:– P. Juan de Figueredo. Lima, 1754. Linen vell. (DS. Feb.24; 2474) Pts. 90,000

TORRES VILLARROEL, Diego de
- El Gran Piscator de Salamanca para ... 1753. Sevilla, 1753. Sewed. (DS. Apr.27; 2621) Pts. 25,000

TORRIANO, Giovanni
- The Italian Reviv'd. L., 1689. *2nd. Edn.* Sm. 8vo. Cont. cf. [Wing T1922-23] (SG. Feb.9; 359) $120

TORRICELLI, Evangelista
- Lezioni Accademiche. Flor., 1715. 4to. Hf.-title, imprimatur lf., few margin dampstains, cont. limp bds., stained. (SG. Nov.3; 211) $700
- Opera Geometrica ... Flor., 1644. *1st. Edn.* Prelim. blank lf. present, browned, cont. vell., mor. solander case; Stanitz coll. (SPB. Apr.25; 431) $1,300

TORTI, Francesco
- Therapeutice Specialis ad Febres. ... Modena, 1712. (Bound with:) RAMAZZINI, B. –Ad Criticam Dissertationem de Abusu Chinae Chinae. ... Modèna, 1715. Together 2 works in 1 vol. 4to. Some foxing, slight wormhole, cont. vell., slightly rubbed. (D. Nov.23; 637) DM 400

TORY, Geofroy
- Champfleury. Paris, [28 Apr. 1529]. *Orig. Edn.* Sm. fo. Orig. blind-decor. cf.; MS. ex-libris of Jehan Viard, 1556. armorial ex-libris of Louis Chefd'hostel, from libys. of Lormier & Bordes. (HD. Mar.29; 97) Frs. 625,000

TOSCANA, Leopoldo di
- Saggi di Naturali Esperienze fatte nell Accademia del Cimento. Flor., 1666. Fo. Some dampstains, slightly wormed at lr. margins, old marb. bds., backstrip defect. (TA. Oct.20; 387) £120

TOTT, François de
- Mémoires sur les Tures et les Tartares. Amst., 1785. 2 vols. 4to. Cont. hf. leath. gt., slightly bumped & rubbed. (HK. May 15; 652) DM 750

TOTTEN, George Oakley
- Maya Architecture. Wash., Maya Pr., [1926]. Tall fo. 104 full-p. ills. (8 cold.), ex-liby., gt.-pict. cl., slightly shaken. (SG. May 3; 250) $175

TOUBEAU, Jean
- Les Institutes du Droit Consulaire ou les Eléments de la Jurisprudence des Marchands. Bourges, 1682. 4to. Dedication copy, cont. red mor. gt., Jean-Baptiste Colbert arms, spine decor. (HD. Nov.9; 93) Frs. 24,000

TOUCHARD-LAFOSSE, Georges
- La Loire Historique, Pittoresque, et Biographique. Tours, 1851. 5 vols. Lge. 8vo. Qtr. leath., 1 spine defect. (SG. Sep.22; 289) $250
- – Anr. Copy. 5 vols. Lge. 8vo. 3 maps, 62 steel-engrs., hf. roan. (LM. Mar.3; 31) B. Frs. 9,000

TOUCHSTONE, S.F.
- History of Celebrated English & French Thorough-Bred Stallions & French Mares. 1890. *(520).* Ob. 4to. Mor.-bkd. cl. gt. (P. Feb.16; 98) £190

TOUDOUZE, Georges Gustav
- François Ier (Le Roi Chevalier). Ill.:– A. Robida. Paris, 1909. 4to. Some darkening, end-paper edges fading, orig. gt.-pict. cl., light rubbing & soiling. (CBA. Aug.21; 547) $130
- Henri Rivière Peintre et Imagier. Paris, 1907. *Orig. Edn.* 4to. Hf. chagrin, corners, spine raised bands, wrap. (HD. Jun.22; 70) Frs. 1,800
- Le Roi Soleil. Ill.:– M. Leloir. Paris, 1904. *Orig. Edn. 1st Printing, (50) on japan.* Fo. Leaves, decor. buckram portfo. (HD. Dec.9; 189) Frs. 1,300
- – Anr. Edn. Ill.:– after Leloir. Paris, 1908. Fo. Darkening, end-papers fading, orig. gt.-pict. cl., light soiling, corners fraying. (CBA. Aug.21; 390) $160

TOULET, Paul-Jean
- La Jeune Fille Verte. Ill.:– Hermine David. 1928. *(225).* On japan, sewed; extra suite of ills. (HD. May 4; 441) Frs. 2,000
- – Anr. Edn. Ill.:– Hermine David. 1928. Japan, added separate suite in smaller format with 1st. engr. in 8 proofs, sewed, wrap., s.-c. (HD. Dec.9; 21d) Frs. 1,350
- Le Mariage de Don Quichotte; Roman. Paris, [1902]. *Orig. Edn.* 12mo. Hf. mor., corners, by R. Aussourd, spine raised bands, unc., wrap. & spine; sigd. pres. inscr. on hf.-title (recipient's name erased), A.L.s. (to André Gide?) dtd. Nov. 1898, bnd. at beginning. (HD. May 16; 102) Frs. 1,600
- Les Trois Impostures. Ill.:– J.E.Labourcur. Paris, 1946. *(250) on Rives.* Leaves, wrap., box. (HD. Dec.16; 193) Frs. 1,250

TOULOUSE-LAUTREC, Henri de
- Soixante-dix Reproductions. Ed.:– M. Joyant. Ill.:– Maurice Joyant. Paris, 1883. *Orig. Edn.* Fo. Leaves, portfo. (HD. Dec.9; 190) Frs. 2,100

TOUR DU MONDE. Nouveau Journal des Voyages Paris, 1860-1902. 42 vols. 4to. Hf. red chagrin, decor. spines. (HD. Jan.27; 349) Frs 6,000

TOURNEFORT, Joseph Pitton de
- Beschr. van eene Reize naar de Levant. Trans.:– P. Le Clerzq. Amst., 1737. 2 pts. in 1 vol. 4to. 88 (of 89) maps & plts., over 40 ills., stained, some repairs, mod. hf. vell. (VG. May 3; 677) Fls. 700
- – Anr. Copy. 2 pts. in 1 vol. 4to. 89 maps, plts. & views, some folding, cont. cf., spine gt., slightly rubbed, jnts. reprd. (VG. Nov.30; 874) Fls. 500
- Relation d'un Voyage du Levant. Paris, 1717. *Orig. Edn.* 2 vols. 4to. 152 engraved maps, views & botanical ills., including 5 folding, cont. mott. cf., gt. spines, some wear. (SKC. May 4; 1824) £680
- – Anr. Copy. 2 vols. 4to. Hf. chagrin, corners, by Loisellier. (HD. Jun.29; 102) Frs. 3,900
- – Anr. Copy. 2 vols. 4to. Most. plts. detchd., cont. marb. cf., w.a.f. (HD. Jun.29; 168) Frs. 3,600
- – Anr. Edn. Amst., 1718. 2 vols. in 1. 4to. Maps, plts., some browning & offsetting, slight staining, cf., covers detchd. (SPB. May 17; 657) $425

TOUSSAINT, Franz
- The Garden of Caresses. Trans.:– Christopher Sandford. Ill.:– Gertrude Hermes. Gold. Cock. Pr., 1934. *(275) numbered. [Special Iss.] with extra suite of 6 sigd. plts., specially bnd.* Sm. 4to. Orig. vell., slightly soiled. (BBA. Jan.19; 292) *Pickford.* £75

TOWN PLANNING REVIEW, The Apr. 1910-Autumn 1943. Vols. 1-19 pt. 1. Orig. wraps., as a periodical, w.a.f. (P. Mar.15; 172) £160

TOWNSEND, Rev. Horatio
- A General & Statistical Survey of the County of Cork. Cork, 1815. *2nd. Edn.* 2 vols. Bdg. not stated, w.a.f. (GM. Oct.5; 155) £140

TOWNSEND, J.
- Monthly Selection of Parisian Costumes. L., [1829]. Bnd. from orig. pts., hand-cold. engraved plts., lacks (?) individual title-pp., later hf. roan, worn, covers slightly soiled, blistered. (SG. Jun.7; 336) $130
- – Anr. Edn. L., 1835-6-7. 4to. 130 hand-cold. plts., hf. mor. gt., as a collection of plts., w.a.f. (P. Nov.24; 84) *Walford.* £220

TOWNSEND, Leonard
- An Alphabetical Chronology of Remarkable Events ... Ill.:– J. Archer. Ca. 1860. Cont. hf. cf., backstrip defect. (TA. Nov.17; 165) £62

TOWNSHEND, George, Lord Visc.
See— WINDHAM, William & Townshend, George, Lord Visc.

TOWNSON, Robert
- Travels in Hungary. 1797. 4to. Folding hand-cold. map, 16 engraved plts., folding table, sm. clean tear at map fold, some spotting, cont. cf., rebkd.; Arpad Plesch bkplt. (CSK. Sep.16; 204) £100

TOWSONTOWN
- Specifications of Sundry Works to be done in the Erection & Completion of the Court House ... to be built at Towsontown, in Baltimore County, Maryland ... Jul. 1854. 16mo. Orig. semi-limp cf. (HA. Nov.18; 134) $160

TOYE, Nina & Adair, A.H.
- Petits et Grands Verres. Choix des Meilleurs Cocktails. Ill.:– Laboureur. 1927. *Orig. Edn. (225) on vélin Montgolfier.* 12mo. Sewed. (HD. Apr.13; 178) Frs. 3,300

TRAGICUM THEATRUM ACTORUM. CASUUM TRAGICORUM LONDINI PUBLICE CELEBRATORUM.
Amst., 1649. 2 ll. inserted, a few ll. browned, 19th. C. mor., slightly rubbed. (BBA. Jan.19; 14) *Sawyer.* £95

TRAILL, Catherine Parr
- Canadian Wild Flowers. Ill.:– A.Fitzgibbon. Toronto, 1895. *Ltd. 4th. Edn.* Lge. 4to. Litho. title with floral border & 10 plts., all hand-cold., title dtd. 1869, cont. hf. mor.; sigd. (BBA. Jul.27; 18) *Bowes.* $220

TRANI, Moshe di [Mabit]
- Bet Elohim. Venice, 1576. *1st. Edn.* Fo. Owners' sigs. on title, some margins reprd. without loss of text, some worming in margins, creased, discold., cl. (S. Oct.25; 399) *Klein.* £520
- She'eilot U'Teshuvot. Venice, 1629. *1st. Edn.* Fo. Owners' inscr. & stp. on title, holes in title & 1st. lf. reprd. not affecting text, staining, creased, hf. leath., marb. paper bds. (S. Oct.25; 400) *Klein.* £450

TRANSFORMATIONS COMIQUE, Jean Qui Rit, Jean Qui Pleure, etc
Pont-Mousson, 1867. Sm. 4to. 8 hand-cold. litho. ills., 7 divided into 2 sections, orig. embossed bds. gt., rebkd.; van Veen coll. (S. Feb.28; 290) £210

TRANSVAAL WAR (The)
[1881]. Reprinted from 'Natal Mercury'. Fo. Seems to lack title or prelim. lf. 'The Convention ... ', pp. 445-450, & maps & plts. as given by S.A.B., cl. (VA. Jan.27; 478) R. 150

TRATADO DE PAZ, Amistad y Limites entre la Republica Mexicana y los Estados-Unides de Norte America ...
Queretaro, 1848. *1st. Edn.* In Engl. & Spanish, orig. ptd. wraps., unc. & unopened, cont. note on upr. cover, hf. mor. s.-c. (LH. Apr.15; 316) $750

TRATTINICK, Leop
- Oesterreichs Schwämme. Wien, 1805. *1st. Edn.* 6 pts. in 1 vol. 4to. Text foxed thro.-out, some plts. slightly soiled, hf. linen, ca. 1890, slightly rubbed. (HK. Nov.8; 691) DM 1,050

TRAVAUX D'ULYSSE, (Ecole de FONTAINE-BLEAU) desseignez par Le Sieur de Sainct Martin (le Primatice), de la Façon qu'ils se voyent dans la Maison Royddale de Fontainebleau.
Ill.:– Nicolas [dell'Abbate] copper engraved by Théodore von Tulden. Paris, 1639. Ob. fo. 4 ll. text, 1 lf. dedication to Duc de Liancourt with arms, 58 engrs., some sm. margin old ink captions, 19th. C. hf. red mor. (HD. Jan.30; 48) Frs. 1,850

TRAVIES, C.J.
- Album Travies, 20 Lithographies, Moeurs Commerciales et Industrielles, Paraphrase de La Bruyère ... 1843. Ob. fo. Litho. title & 20 hand-cold. lithos.,

cl.; from Esmerian coll. (S. May 10; 421) *Marks.* £350

TRAVIES, Edouard
- Les Oiseaux les plus Remarquables par leurs Formes et leurs Couleurs, Scènes Variées de leurs Moeurs & de leurs Habitudes. Paris & L., ca. 1857. Lge. fo. This copy with 1 plt. of butterflies, 75 (of 79) hand-cold. litho. plts., some light foxing, no text, orig. ptd. wrap. used as title, cont. hf. mor. gt. (S. Feb.1; 58) *Lester.* £18,000

TREATIES
- Recueil des Traitez de Paix, de Triève, de Neutralité ... DXXXVI jusqu'en MDCC. Amst., 1700. 4 vols. fo. Cont. spr. cf., some slightly worming. (CE. Sep.1; 53) £80

TREGEAR, Edward
- The Maori-Polynesian Comparative Dictionary. Wellington, N.Z., 1891. *1st. Edn.* Cl.; pres. copy, inscr. by author to Lord Islington. (SKC. Mar.9; 1923) £55

TREITZSAURWEIN, Marx
- Der Weiss Kunig. Eine Erzehlung vor den Thaten Kaiser Maximilian des Ersten. Ill.:– Hans Burgkmair, H. Schauffelein, H. Springingklee, L. Beck & others. Vienna, 1775. *1st. Edn.* Fo. 237 woodcut plts., plt. 234 (opposite p. 214) & plt. 183 (opposite p. 2345) torn across & crudely reprd. with sellotape, several tears in margins, 1, in 3H2, affecting text, slightly browned thro.-cut, red mor. gt. by Belz-Niedrée, covers a little scuffed, unc. (S. May 10; 422) *Benda.* £2,900

TREKKERS GIDS
Paarl, 1894. Sm. 4to. Slightly frayed, edges browned, orig. ptd. wraps. (VA. Oct.28; 284) R 190

TRENCH, Lieut.-Col. Frederick William
- Royal Palaces; & Hints for other Improvements in the Metropolis. 1852. 4to. Orig. cl. (P. Apr.12; 45) *Woodruff.* £130
– – Anr. Edn. N.d. 4to. Orig. cl., lightly affected by damp, spine chipped. (CSK. Aug. 5; 148) £75

TRENCK, Friederic von der
- Merkwürdige Lebengeschichte. Berlin, 1787. 2 vols. Cont. hf. leath. gt., bumped. [H. G. VII, 686] (BR. Apr.12; 1551) DM 400
- Sammlung Vermischter Gedichte welche in s. Zehnjähr. Gefängnis in Magdeburg geschrieben wurden. Frankfurt & Leipzig, [1767]. *1st. Edn.* Some slight browning or spotting, cont. cf., gt. decor., by C.W. Vogt, label inside cover. (HK. Nov.10; 2751) DM 520

TREND (THE): A Forecasting of the Mode for Spring & Summer 1925, from the Angles of Fabric, Silhouette, Color, & Detail, with Editorial Interpretation of the American Trend. – ... for Fall & Winter, 1925-26
[Passaic, N.J., 1925]. *Ltd. Edns.* 2 vols. Fo. 24 col. fashion plts., 72 fabric samples tipped in, qtr. cl., gt.-lettered cl. covers. (SG. Jun.7; 337) $175

TRENEFF, D. K.
See— SYREITSCHIKOFF, N.P. & Treneff, D.K.

TRENEL, J.L.
- Francfort sur le Main et ses Environs ou le Guide de l'Etranger à Francfort. Trans.:– J.H. Ludewig. Frankfurt, [1845]. 10 steel engraved plts., 1 multifolding plan, some slight browning, orig. bds., lightly bumped, slightly spotted. (IIT. May 10; 2909) DM 720

TRENKWALD, Hermann
See— SARRE, Friedrich & Trenkwald, Hermann

TRESHAM, Henry & others
- The British Gallery of Pictures ... N.d. Fo. 20 engrs., some spotting, qtr. mor., rubbed. (P. Apr.12; 196) *Davidson.* £110

TRESOR DE NUMISMATIQUE ET DE GLYPTIQUE. Ou Recueil Général de Medailles, Monnaies, Pierres Gravées, Bas-Reliefs, etc.
Ed.:– Paul Delaroche, Henriquel Dupont, & Charles Lenormant. Ill.:– Achille Collas. Paris,

1858. 20 vols. Fo. All plts. stpd. on versos, perforation stps. in titles, hf. mor., worn, few covers detchd., ex-liby. (RO. Dec.11; 331) $600

TREVIRANUS, Gottfried Reinhold
- Biologie. Göttingen, 1802-22. Cont. hf. leath. gt. (D. Nov.23; 638) DM 600

TREVISANUS, Bernardus
See— BERNARDUS TREVISANUS, Count della Maria di Treviso

TREW, Abdias
- Summa Geometriae Practicae, worinnen erstlich B. Cantzlers ... Bericht vom Feldmessen ... zum Zweiten ... Nüttzliche Annotationens auch Arithmeticae, Trigonometricae, Graphicae, Geographicae Nauticae ... zum Dritten, ein Neuer Anhang enthalten, in welchem das Feldmessen vorgestellet wird von J.G. Doppelmayr. Nürnberg, 1718. Lacks frontis. (*Bound with:*) WOLFF, Chr. – Zu der Trigonometrie und Ausziehung der Wurzeln nöthige Tafeln Halle, 1711. Together 2 works in 1 vol. Cont. style leath. (BR. Apr.12; 830) DM 400

TREW, Christoph Jakob & Ehret, Georg Dionysius
- Plantae Selectae. Ill.:– J.J. & J.E. Haid, after Ehret. [Nuremb.], 1750-73. 10 pts. in 1 vol. Fo. 10 engraved titles, hand-cold. in red, black & gold, 100 hand-cold. plts., without general title, ports. & supp., found in some copies, 2 plts. shaved, cont. hf. cf., spine gt. (C. Nov.16; 303) *Papp.* £7,600

TRIALS
- Case of the Somers' Mutiny : Defence of Alexander Slidell Mackenzie, Commander of the U.S. Brig Somers, before the Court Martial held at the Navy Yard, Brooklyn. N.Y., 1843. *1st. Edn.* Foxed, mod. qtr. mor., cl. covers; from liby. of F.D. Roosevelt, inscr. by him. (Sabin 43421) (SG. Mar.15; 66) $250
- A Complete Collection of State Trials & Proceedings for High-Treason & other Crimes & Misdemeanours. L., 1730-35. *2nd. Edn.* Vols. 1-6 & Supps. for Vols. 7-8, together 8 vols. Fo. Cont. cf., rubbed; Grosvenor bkplts. (S. Dec.20; 823) *Professional Books.* £300
– – Anr. Edn. 1730-66. *2nd. Edn.* 10 vols. Fo. Cf. (P. Sep.29; 237) *Axe.* £110
- Notable English Trials. V.d. [ca. 1911-30]. 27 vols. Cl. (P. Jul.26; 136) £320
- Report from the Committee of Secrecy [Touching the Tryals of these Eminent Persons that Suffered in the Famous Rebellion of 1798]. L., 1798. Fo. Hf. cf., rubbed. (GM. Dec.7; 470) £90
- Supreme Court of the District of Columbia, No. 14056: the United States v. Charles J. Guiteau. [Wash., 1881]. *1st. Printing.* Cont. hf. mor. & marb. bds. (SG. Apr.5; 77) $130
- The Trial of John Peter Zenger, of New-York, Printer ... L., 1765. Scattered foxing, mor., covers & spine gt. [Sabin 106311] (SPB. May 23; 53) $550
- The Tryal of Mary Blandy, Spinster; for the Murder of her Father ... at the Assizes held at Oxford ... 29 February 1752. L., 1752. Sm. fo. Title reset on a stub, later hf. cf., marb. bds., spine defect., sig. & bkplt. of Edward Ellice of Glenquoich, 1856 & cont. sig. of Henrietta Hanbury. (SG. Apr.19; 130) $130

TRICASSE, Patrizio
- La Chiromance. Paris, 1641. Some stains, later vell. (SI. Dec.15; 181) Lire 280,000

TRIEFHS, Paul
- McHamlet Hys Handycap. 1922. *1st. Edn.* Bdg. not stated. (PD. Jul.13; 35) £50

TRIER, J.W.
- Einleitung zu der Wappen-Kunst. Ill.:– J.G. Krügner. Leipzig, 1714. *1st. Edn.* Frontis. with owners mark, browned, cont. vell., lightly rubbed. (HK. May 16; 1507) DM 480

TRIGGS, Henry Inigo
- Formal Gardens in England & Scotland. L., 1902. 1 vol. only (of 2). Fo. Hf. mor., soiled. (S. Oct.4; 206) *Woodruff.* £80
– – Anr. Copy. 4to. Some spotting, crimson mor. gt. by Ramage, partly untrimmed, slightly rubbed; subscriber's copy. (TA. May 17; 438) £54

TRIMEN, R. & Bowker, J.H.
- South African Butterflies: A Monograph of the Sub-Tropical Species. L., 1887-89. 3 vols. Lge. 8vo. Some light foxing, orig. bdgs., spines slightly faded. (VA. Oct.28; 285) R 300

TRIMMER, Sarah
- The Guardian of Education. 1802-06. 5 vols. Cont. cf. gt. (P. Oct.20; 56) £130

TRINITY COLLEGE APOCALYPSE (THE)
Intro. & Description:– Peter H. Brieger. Eugrammia Pr., 1967. *(600) numbered.* 2 vols. (text & facs.). Fo. Orig. cf. gt., s.-c., & orig. bds. (text). (S. May 1; 440) *Smith.* £220
- - Anr. Copy. 2 vols. Fo. Cold. facsimiles heightened with gold, separate text, orig. cf. gt., s.-c. (S. Apr.30; 228) *Quaritch.* £120

TRINKET, (The), A Novel by a Lady
L., 1774. *1st. Edn.* 12mo. Rather browned, cont. cf. (SG. Feb.9; 360) $225

TRIOLET, Elsa
- La Mise en Mots. Ill.:– Marc Chagall. Geneva, 1969. *(175) numbered with orig. cold. litho. numbered & sigd. by Chagall.* 4to. Loose as iss. in orig. wraps., orig. vell.-bkd. bd. folder, s.-c. (BBA. Jun.14; 195) *Barrie Marks.* £800

TRIPP, F.E.
- British Mosses. 1874. 2 vols. 4to. 39 cold. etched plts., orig. cl. (SKC. Jan.13; 2350) £50

TRISSINO, Giovanni Giorgio
- La Sophonisba. Li Retratti. Epistola. Oratione. Venice, 1549. Woodcut on title-p., lacks last blank, recent hf. cf. (BBA. May 23; 318) *Quaritch.* £60

TRISSMOSIN, Salomon
- Aureum Vellus oder Guldin Schatz und Kunstkammer ... Rorschach am Bodensee, 1598[-99]. *1st. Edn.* 3 pts. in 1 vol. Sig. EE in pt.3 supplied in photostat facs., vell., gt. centrepiece (that on upr. cover oxidised), soiled; Dr. Walter Pagel copy. (S. Feb.7; 366) *Klingsor.* £1,150
- Eröffnete Geheimnisse des Steins der Weisen oder Schatzkammer der Alchymie ... Hamburg, 1718. 4to. Port. frontis. repeated on p.90, paper browned or discold., some stains, sm. hole to 'Splendor Solis' in 3C4 & 5D2, cont. cf., spine gt.; Dr. Walter Pagel copy. (S. Feb.7; 364) *Ritman.* £950

TRISTRAM, W.Outram
- Coaching Days & Coaching Ways. L., 1888. Ills., hf. mor. gt. (P. May 17; 293) *Marks.* £90

TRISTAN THE HERMIT
- Poésies Galantes et Héroïques. Ill.:– Du Guerrier. 1662. *1st. Coll. Edn.* 4to. Frontis. & port. dtd. 1648, cf. by Koehler, stpd. blind & gt. Du Seuil decor, rubbed. (HD. Mar.21; 99) Frs. 2,000

TRISTRAM, Ernest William & Bardswell, Monica
- English Medieval Wall Painting. Oxford, 1944. 1 vol. only: 'The Twelfth Century' (of 3). 4to. Orig. cl. (S. Oct.4; 207) *Zwemmer.* £130

TRITHEMIUS, Johann
- Institutio Vite Sacerdotalis. [Mainz, P. v. Friedberg, after 22.X.1494]. *1st. Edn. Variant Iss.* 4to. Rubricated, some underlining, slightly wormed & foxed, ds. [H. 15622; Goff T440] (HK. Nov.8; 368) DM 1,300

TROEMER, Johann Christian
- [-] Die Avantures von Deutsch Francoos. Ill.:– Richter, engraved by Boetius & Bosch. [Dresden, Leipzig, Vienne, Prague, Nuremb.], 1745. 4to. Cont. roan, spine decor. (HD. Nov.16; 178) Frs. 2,800
- [-] Jean Chretien Toucement des Deutsch François Schrifften. Leipssigck, priv. ptd., 1736. *1st. Compl. Edn.* Frontis. & 1 plt. with moveable parts, browned thro.-out, some foxing, 1st. ll. more heavily spotted, cont. bds., defect. & spotted, old entries inside cover. (H. May 22; 915) DM 500
- - Anr. Edn. Nuremb., [1772]. *Vol.2; 1st. Edn.* 2 vols. Some plts. with overslips, cont. cf., spines gt. (C. Dec.9; 293) *Reiss.* £320

TROESCHER, G.
- Die Burgundische Plastik des Ausgehenden Mittelalters und Ihre Wirkungen auf die Europäische Kunst. Frankfurt, 1940. 4to. Orig. hf. linen. (R. Apr.3; 928) DM 1,200

TROIL, Uno von
- Letters on Iceland ... L., 1780. *1st. Engl. Edn.* Unc., cont. paper-bkd. bds., spine slightly frayed, jnts. worn. (C. Nov.16; 186) *Quaritch.* £170

TROILI, U.
See— SCHEELE, F. von & Troili, U.

TROILI DI SPIN LAMBERTO, G.
- Paradossi per pratticare la Prospettiva senza saperla, Fiori, per facilitare l'intelligenzia, Frutti, per non operare alla Cieca. Bologna, [1672-83]. *1st. Compl. Edn.* 3 pts. in 1 vol. Fo. 4pp. pt. 3 with reprd. tear, later hf. vell. (D. Nov.23; 2050) DM 1,800

TROIS REGNES DE LA NATURE
Text:– E. Le Maout, P.A. Cap & P. Gervais. Ill.:– after Freeman, Deubigny, Louis Marvy & others. Paris, 1853-55. 5 vols. Lge. 8vo. 247 plts. (108 cold.), publisher's buckram, some defects. (HD. Jun.22; 74) Frs. 3,500

TROJA, Michael
- Neue Beobachtungen und Versuche über diue Knochen. Ed.:– J.J.A. v. Schönberg. Erlangen, 1828. *1st. german Edn.* 4to. Cont. bds. (D. Nov.23; 639) DM 500

TROLLOPE, Anthony
- An Autobiography. 1883. *2nd. Edn.* 2 vols. Orig. cl., spines faded. (P. Jul.26; 39) £50
- Barsetshire Novels. Ed.:– Michael Sadleir. Ill.:– Charles S. Olcott. Oxford, Shakes. Hd. Pr., 1929. *(525) numbered.* 14 vols. Photogravure plts., red three-qtr. mor. (SG. Apr.26; 197) $1,000
- - Anr. Edn. Ed.:– Michael Sadleir. Oxford & Boston, 1929. 14 vols. Plts. in 2 states, cold. & plain, three-qtr. mor., spines gt. in compartments; 6 line MS. fragment in author's hand Laid in Vol. 1. (RO. Dec.11; 328) $700
- The Claverings. Ill.:– M.E. Edwards. L., 1867. *1st. Edn. in Book Form.* 2 vols. Lge. 8vo. Orig. gt.- & blind-stpd. cl., extremities worn, shaken. (SG. Nov.17; 135) $275
- Hunting Sketches. 1865. *1st. Edn.* Chapman & Hall's 32 pp. Catalogue dtd. May 1865 at end, orig. cl. gt.; from George Meredith liby. (SKC. Mar.9; 1864) £130
- The Lady of Launay. N.Y., 1878. *1st. Edn.* 16mo. Ptd. wraps., chipped, buckram folding case. (SG. Nov.17; 136) $275
- The Last Chronicle of Barset. Ill.:– G.H. Thomas. 1866-67. *1st. Edn.* Orig. 32 pts. Lacks 5 advts., orig. wraps., hf. mor. box; from Norman Tarbolton liby. (P. Apr.12; 15) *Joseph.* £320
- Novels. 1872-78. 22 vols. Cont. hf. cf., spines gt., not unif. (LC. Mar.1; 415) £260
- Orley Farm. Ill.:– J.E. Millais. 1862. *1st. Edn.* 2 vols. Orig. cl. gt., worn. (P. Jul.26; 38) £50
- The Prime Minister. L., 1876. *1st. Edn.* 4 vols. Slight spotting, orig. cl.; Michael Sadleir's bkplts., Fred A. Berne copy. (SPB. May 16; 368) $950
- - Anr. Copy. 4 vols. in 8 pts. 8 hf.-titles, advts. bnd. in, thumbed, orig. cl., spines cocked & worn at ends, pict. wraps. bnd. in. (SG. Nov.17; 132) $475
- [-] The Small House at Allington. [L., 1862-64]. *1st. Edn.* Bnd. from the orig. pts. Hf. leath., sunned. (SG. Nov.17; 133) $130
- [Works]. Leipzig, 1858-80. *Tauchnitz Edn.* 19 vols. only. Later hf. mor., spines gt., 2 spines slightly chipped, a few lightly rubbed. (CSK. Jan.13; 122) £150
- - Anr. Edn. N.Y. & Chic., ca. 1900. *Parliament Edn., (250) numbered.* 30 vols. Persian three-qtr. mor., spines gt., some rubbing. (RO. Apr.23; 289) $425
- - Anr. Edn. N.Y. & Chic., ca. 1920. *'Parliament Edn.'. (250) numbered.* 30 vols. Sm. 8vo. Persian mor. & marb. bds., raised bands, gt.-stpd. spines, minimal wear. (HA. Feb.24; 216) $650

TROMBELLI, Giovan-Crisostomo
- Arte di conoscere l'Eta de Codici Latini, e Italiani. Bologna, 1756. *1st. Edn.* 4to. Hf.-title, cont. vell., reprd. (BBA. May 23; 348) *Lurie.* £50

TROMSDORFF, J.B.
- Chemische Receptirkunst. Erfurt, 1797. *1st. Edn.* Some light browning, defect., cont. bds. (HT. May 8; 584) DM 450
- Handb. d. Pharmaceutischen Warenkunde. Wien, 1808. Very foxed & some browning, cont. bds., soiled & bumped. (HK. Nov.8; 750) DM 460
See— BUSCH, G.C.B. & Trommsdorff, J.B.

TRONCON, Jean
- [-] L'Entrée Triomphante de leurs Maiestez Louis XIV. Roy de France et Navarre et Marie Thérèse d'Austriche son Espouse ... Paris, 1662. *1st. Edn.* Fo. Engraved frontis., port., dedication, 20 plts., many double-p., foremargin of frontis. strengthened, sm. hole in final plt., some margin staining, old mott. cf., spine ends chipped. (C. Nov.9; 119) *Sims & Reed.* £440
- - Anr. Copy. Fo. Some light soiling or spotting, wormed at beginning in lr. inner margin, cont. leath., spotted, bumped, spine defect. (R. Apr.4; 1984) DM 1,400

TROPFKE, J.
- Geschichte der Elementar-Mathematik in Systematischer Darstellung. Leipzig, 1902/03. *1st. Edn.* Margins lightly browned, cont. hf. linen. (HT. May 8; 487) DM 440

TROSTER, Johann
- Alt und Neu Teutsche Dacia. Nürnberg, 1666. *1st. Edn.* Cont. hf. leath. gt, slightly rubbed. (GB. Nov.3; 153) DM 680

TROTSKY, Leon
- Verratene Revolution. Antw., [1936]. *1st. Edn.* Orig. wraps. (GB. Nov.4; 1524) DM 470

TROTTER, John B.
- Walks Through Ireland, in the Years 1812, 1814 & 1817. L., 1819. *1st. Edn.* Bkplt., hf. mor., armorial motif on spine. (GM. Dec.7; 450) £180

TROTTER, William Edward
- Select Illustrated Topography of Thirty Miles Around London. 1839. Some spotting, cl. gt., rubbed. (P. Jan.12; 58) £65

TROUGHTON, Thomas
- [-] Barbarian Cruelty ... with Supplement. L., 1751. *1st. Edn.* 2 pts. in 1 vol. Cf., rebkd., new corners & end-papers. (SPB. Dec.13; 473) $550

TROWER, H.F.
See— LONGMAN, W. & Trower, H.F.

TROYAT, H.
- Tant que la Terra Durera. — Le Sac et la Cendre. — Etrangers sur la Terre. Paris, 1947-50. *Orig. Edn. (40) numbered on Crèvecoeur du Marais.* Together 5 vols. Orig. bdgs. (HD. Apr.26; 283) Frs. 1,500

TRUE ACCOUNT OF THE LATE BLOODY ... CONSPIRACY AGAINST HIS HIGHNESS THE LORD PROTECTOR
1654. Hf. cf., unc, rubbed. (P. Apr.12; 53) *Robertshaw.* £50

TRUENO GORDO, Periodico de Pólvora y Petróleo
Madrid, 1872. Nos. 1-43, lacks 14,21,26. Lge. fo. (DS. Dec.16; 2065) Pts. 50,000

TRUMBULL, Benjamin
- A Complete History of Connecticutt. Ill.:– A. Doolittle. Hartford, 1797; New Haven, 1818. *1st. Edns.* Vols. I & II. Lacks port. in Vol. II, Vol. I disbnd., Vol. II old mott. cf., worn. (SG. Aug.4; 311) $100

TRUSLER, John
- The Habitable World. L., 1787-97. 20 vols. 2 frontis., 19 (of 20) additional engraved titles, 146 plts., 61 folding maps, cont. qtr. cf., vell. tips. (SG. Sep.22; 290) $175
- Honours of the Table. L., 1788. *1st. Edn.* Some browning & spotting, lr. end-paper loose, sheep.-bkd. bds. (SPB. Dec.13; 655) $175

[–] **Proverbs Exemplified, & Illustrated by Pictures from Real Life.** Ill.:– John Bewick. L., 1790. *1st. Edn.* 12mo. A few margins torn, contents loose in bdg., early cl. (SG. Dec.8; 49) $130

TSBIKOV, G. Ts.
– Buddhist Palomnik u Svytyn Tibeta [The Bhuddist Pilgrim at the Holy Places of Tibet]. Petrograd, 1918. 4to. Orig. wraps., slightly torn & loose. (BBA. Mar.7; 58) *D. Loman.* £170

TSCHICHOLD, Jan
See— ROH, Franz & Tschichold, Jan

TSIOLKOVSKY, Konstantin Eduardovich
– Izsledovanie Mirovykh Prostranstv Reaktivnymi Priborami (dopolnenie k I i II chasti truda togo-zhe nazvaniya) [Exploration of Planetary Space with Reactive Equipment (Supplement to parts I & II of the Works of the same Title)]. Kaluga, priv. ptd., 1914. *1st. Edn.* Pres. copy, inscr. in Russian on lr. cover 'From the author to the editors of the review & the workers in Kaluga', a few margin tears, orig. ptd. wraps., rather torn & faded. (S. Nov.28; 135) *Quaritch.* £3,500
– Kosmicheskaya Raketa. Opitiaya Podgotovka [The Cosmic Rocket. Experimental Study]. Kaluga, 1927. *1st. Edn.* As issued without wraps. (S. Nov.28; 136) *Quaritch.* £560
– Kosmicheskie Raketii Poezda [Cosmic Rocket Trains]. Kaluga, 1929. *1st. Edn.* Orig. ptd. wraps., rebkd. (S. Nov.28; 137) *Quaritch.* £600

TSUJI, S.
– Etude Historique de la Cuisine Française. Tokyo, 1977. *(1250)* numbered. Sm. fo. In Japanese, Fr. & Engl., buckram, d.-w., s.-c. (SG. Nov.17; 197) $425

TUBERINUS, Joh.
– De Orgijs Christi publici Assertoris. deq Supplicationib. et [vt aiũt] Processionib.: que oppido Lipsico taliu Sacrorum Luce peraguntur. [Leipzig], ca. 1511. 4to. Cont. MS. commentary between wide spaced lines & ptd. margin annots., minimal soiling, bds. (HK. Nov.8; 370) DM 800

TUCHOLSKY, Kurt
– Deutschland, Deutschland ueber Alles. Ein Bilderbuch. Ill.:– John Heartfield. Berlin, 1929. *1st. Edn.* Orig. linen with montage, newspaper excerpt pasted inside cover. (GB. May 5; 2660) DM 580
– – **Anr. Copy.** 4to. Orig. pict. linen. (HK. Nov.11; 4032) DM 520
– Die Vormerkung aus 1179 BGB und Ihre Wirkungen. Leipzig, 1915. *1st. Edn.* Title & margins slightly spotted, linen. (H. Nov.24; 2147) DM 1,050

TUCKER, Andrew G.C.
– Ornithologia Danmoniensis. Ill.:– after W.R. Jordan. L., 1809. Vol. 1 (all publd.). 4to. 7 engraved & aquatint plts., all but 1 in 2 states, 1 state hand-cold., later maroon hf. mor., ptd. wraps. to orig. 2 pts. bnd. at end. (C. Mar.14; 205) *Old Hall.* £400

TUCKER, Rev. Josiah, Dean of Gloucester
– A Series of Answers to Certain Popular Objections, against Separating from the Rebellious Colonies. Gloucester, 1776. Mod. mor.-bkd. cl. (BBA. Jul.27; 303) *Waterfield.* £50

TUCKEY, Capt. James Kingston
– Narrative of an Expedition to Explore the River Zaire, Usually Called the Congo, in South Africa in 1816. 1818. 4to. 1 plt. hand-cold., a few plts. slightly foxed, cont. diced cf. gt., rebkd. (SKC. Mar.9; 2036) £140
– – **Anr. Copy.** 4to. Folding map, 13 engraved plts., including 1 hand-cold., cont. cf., worn, upr. cover detchd. (TA. Nov.17; 21) £95
– – **Anr. Copy.** 4to. 1 plt. hand-cold., some spotting, later qtr. mor., dampspotted & slightly wormed. (TA. Sep.15; 39) £65

TUDOR CRAIG, Sir Algernon
– Armorial Porcelain of the Eighteenth Century. 1925. *(1000)* numbered. 4to. Orig. cl. (BBA. Nov.10; 288) *Zwemmer.* £65
– – **Anr. Copy.** 4to. Unc., orig. cl., d.-w. torn. (BBA. Sep.8; 232) *Price.* £60

– – **Anr. Copy.** Cl., partly unc., spine faded. (SG. Jan.26; 78) $130

TUER, Andrew W.
– The Follies & Fashions of our Grandfathers. L., Leadenhill Pr., 1886-87. *1st. Edn.* 4to. 37 plts., many hand-cold. & gold & silver heightened, some fore-edges chipped, slight margin darkening, decor. cl. end- papers, hf. suede & bds., embroidered spine & ribbon marker, corners & spine ends defect. (CBA. Aug.21; 381) $180
– – **Anr. Edn.** L., 1886-87. *(250)* L.P., sigd. 4to. Pres. copy, many plts. hand-cold., unc., orig. bds., rubbed. (S. Dec.20; 887) *Male.* £85
– History of the Horn-Book. L., 1896. *[1st. Edn.].* 2 vols. 4to. 7 facs. horn-books & battledores in pockets, partly unc., gt.- stpd. vell. (SG. Dec.8; 345) $450
– – **Anr. Copy.** 2 vols. Sm. 4to. Few text cracks, foxing to frontis. tissue guards, orig. vell. over bds., gt.-stpd., orig. linen reinforced hinges, untrimmed, 7 facs. hornbooks in front pockets, covers lightly worn & yawning, ex-liby. precise inked nos. at base of spines, sm. paper stickers at rear end-papers; inscr. & sigd. by author, laid in 3 sigd. secretary-written letters from Tuer, on Leadenhall Pr. letterheads, to D. Croal Thomson. (HA. May 4; 158) $425
– – **Anr. Copy.** 2 vols. 4to. 7 facs. horn-books set in compartments at front end-papers, gt.-decor. vell., covers yawning slightly, slight rubbing & soiling; Marymount College copy. (CBA. Mar.3; 536) $350
– – **Anr. Edn.** L., 1897. 4to. 3 facs. hornbooks in pocket in lr. cover, pict. bds. (SG. Nov.3; 213) $150
– 1000 Quaint Cuts. Leadenhall Pr., [1896]. *Ltd. Edn.* 4to. Wood engraved title & plts., later vell., browned, orig. wraps. bnd. in. (CSK. May 18; 76) £85

TUFTS, James
[–] A Tract Descriptive of Montana Territory ... N.Y., 1865. *1st. Edn.* Lge. 8vo. Sm. margin repair to last lf., unbnd. as iss., self-wraps. (LH. Apr.15; 384) $140

TUGNY, F.M.G.T. de
– Histoire Naturelle des Insectes. Ed.:– F.E. Guerin. Paris, 1828. *3rd. Edn.* 10 vols. Sm. 12mo. Approx. 100 cold. engraved plts., cont. hf. chagrin, spines decor. (HD. Jun.22; 38) Frs. 1,150

TUINMAN, C.
– Joh. Kalvijns Onderrichting tegen de Vrygeesten ... Middelburg, 1712. *(Bound with:)* – De Heilloze Gruwelleere der Vrygeesten. Middelburg, 1714. Together 2 works in 1 vol. Cont. vell., soiled. (VG. Nov.30; 991) Fls. 450

TULL, Jethro
[–] The Horse-Hoeing Husbandry ... [A Supplement to the Essay on the Horse-Hoeing Husbandry]. 1733-36. *[1st. Edns.].* 2 pts. in 1 vol. Fo. Supp. title & preface misbnd., some spotting, cont. cf., worn. (CSK. Aug.5; 140) £300
– – **Anr. Copy.** 2 pts. in 1 vol. Fo. Title of 1st. pt. reprd. at inner hinge, title of supp. misbnd., dampstained, old cf.-bkd. bds., rebkd., section of orig. spine laid down. soiled, w.a.f. (CSK. Apr.27; 53) £240

TULLIAN, Lipps
– Des Bekannten Diebes, Moerders und Raeubers Lips Tullians, und seiner Complicen Leben und Uebelthaten. [Leipzig?], 1726. 2 pts. in 1 vol. 4to. Foxed, hf. sheep, spine & corners chafed. (SG. Feb.2; 120) $130

TULLY, Richard
– Narrative of a Ten Years' Residence at Tripoli in Africa. 1816. *1st. Edn.* 4to. Cont. hf. cf. (SKC. Mar.9; 2037) £140
– – **Anr. Edn.** 1817. *2nd. Edn.* 4to. 7 hand-cold. engraved aquatint plts., folding map, cont. cf., rebkd., old spine laid down. (CSK. May 4; 135) £85

TULP, Nicholas
– Observationes Medicae. Amst., 1652. *1st. Edn.* Lacks engraved port., cont. vell., lightly soiled. (GB. Nov.3; 1055) DM 500

TUNNICLIFF, William
– A Topographical Survey of the Counties of Stafford, Chester & Lancaster. Nantwich, 1787. Unc., orig. bds., worn. (P. Dec.8; 163) *Nicholson.* £65

TUNSTALL, Cuthbert
– De Arte Supputandi Libri Quatuor. Paris, 1538. Sm. 4to. Vig. title, slightly spotted, cont. limp vell. gt., new end-papers. (BBA. Jul.27; 63) *Sokol.* £260

TUPPER, Ferdinand Brock
– The Life & Correspondence of Major-General Sir Isaac Brock. L., 1845. 12mo. Orig. cl., slightly rubbed, faded; 4 p. A.L.s. from ed. tipped in. (BBA. Dec.15; 45) *Browning.* £90

TUPPER, Martin F.
– Proverbial Philosophy. L., 1857. Red blind-stpd. mor. gt., with fore-e.pntg., as a fore-e. pntg., w.a.f. (SPB. May 17; 743) $325

TURGAN, J.
– Die Luftballone und das Reisen durch die Luft. Weimar, 1851. *1st. Edn.* 1 plt. with bkd. tear, cont. bds., orig. pict. wraps. bnd. in. (R. Oct.12; 1636) DM 420

TURGENEV, Ivan
– The Novels ... Trans.:– Constance Garnett. L., 1920. 17 vols. Bds., qtr. cl. (KH. Nov.9; 487) Aus. $380
– The Novels & Stories. Trans.:– Isabel F. Hapgood. N.Y., 1903-04. *(204)* numbered on Ruisdael H.M.P. 16 vols. Three-qtr. mor. by Stikeman, spines gt. in compartments, slight stain on side Vol. I. (RO. Dec.11; 330) $850
– Sämtliche Werke. Ed.:– O. Buek & K. Wildhagen. Berlin & München, [1910-]31. 12 vols. Orig. hf. linen. (H. May 22; 1110) DM 520

TURGOT, Michel Etienne
– Plan de Paris Commencé l'Année 1734. Ill.:– Louis Bretez. Paris, 1739. Lge. 4to. Lacks general index sheet, a few creases, some light soiling, cont. cf., covers detchd. (TA. Apr.19; 41) £340
– – **Anr. Copy.** Fo. Plan, 20 double-p. plts., mntd. on guards, cont. red mor., richly decor., Paris arms. (HD. Mar.19; 120) Frs. 27,000
– – **Anr. Copy.** Fo. Plan & 20 plts. mntd. on guards, cont. red mor., fleurs-de- lys dentelle, decor. corners, centre arms, fleurs-de-lys spine, inner dentelle. (HD. Dec.1; 78) Frs. 16,000
– – **Anr. Edn.** Paris, 1739. *Reprint of Louvre engr.* Fo. 19th. C. hf. chagrin. (HD. Apr.13; 57) Frs. 4,500

TURIN
– La Sontuosa Illuminazione della Citta di Torino. Ill.:– Charles de Prenner, Bielmondo & others. Turin, 1737. 2 pts. in 1 vol. Fo. Engraved frontis., 14-double-p. or folding plts., text in Italian & Fr., cont. cf., gt. panel., arms of King of Sardinia, gt. spine (reprd.), worn. (C. Dec.9; 155) *Weinreb.* £1,100

TURNBULL, C.
See— BUESST, T. & Turnbull, C.

TURNBULL, John
– A Voyage round the World in the Years 1800-04. L., 1813. *2nd. Edn.* 4to. Some slight foxing, orig. bds., unc., writing on upr. cover, piece cut from head of front end-paper. (CA. Apr.3; 114) Aus. $950
– – **Anr. Copy.** 4to. Minor foxing, bds., unc., spine label slightly defect. (KH. May 1; 713) Aus. $700

TURNBULL, William
– Disputatio Jurica ad lib. I. tit. xviii digest. de Officio Praesidis. Edinb., 1832. Sm. 4to. On vell., pres. inscr. from author, silk end-papers & liners, cont. diced cf., elab. gt.-& blind-stpd., inner dentelles, rebkd. (C. Nov.9; 120) *Quaritch.* £110

TURNER, Austin
– Villas on the Hudson. N.Y., 1860. Ob. fo. 31 photolitho. views, 21 litho. plans, some lightly tinted, in gt. borders, title creased, some spotting, orig. hf. mor. (SPB. Dec.13; 837) $850

TURNER, C., publisher
- **Six Sketches in Lithography, representing the Common Actions of the Horse.** N.d. [plts. dtd. 1842]. Fo. Litho. title & 6 tinted litho. plts., a few margins lightly soiled, orig. wraps., backstrip torn. (CSK. Mar.23; 145) £250

TURNER, Sir James
- **Pallas Armata: Military Essayes of the Ancient Grecian, Roman, & Modern Art of War.** L., 1683. *1st. Edn.* Fo. Lacks advt. lf., old cf., restored. (SG. Sep.22; 291) $200

TURNER, Joseph Mallord William
- **An Antiquarian & Picturesque Tour Round the Southern Coast of England.** 1849. *[1st. Edn.].* 4to. 50 full-p. steel engrs. & ills. to text, orig. gt.-decor. cl., rebkd. (TA. Jun.21; 176) £280
- **– Anr. Copy.** 4to. 84 steel-engraved plts., slight foxing & darkening, affecting some plts., three-qtr. mor. & marb. bds., covers rubbed. (CBA. Jan.29; 465) $130
- **Liber Fluviorum, or River Scenery of France.** 1853. Engraved title, 60 plts., orig. cl. gt., worn. (P. Mar.15; 257) *Peterson.* £70
- **– Anr. Copy.** Engraved title, 61 plts., 1 loose, many foxed, orig. cl. gt. (P. Dec.8; 19) *Tsakis.* £50
- **Picturesque Views in England & Wales.** L., 1873. 3 vols. 4to. 96 plts., cl. gt. (P. May 17; 9) *Sambos.* £60
- **Picturesque Views on the Southern Coast of England.** 1826. 2 vols. in 1. Fo. 38 engraved plts. only, lacks title to Vol. 1 & 7 prelims., some margins slightly browned, cont. hf. mor., rubbed, w.a.f. (CSK. Mar.9; 165) £140
- **– Anr. Copy.** 2 vols. in 1. 4to. 47 full-p. engraved plts., some light foxing or offsetting, old russ., worn, rebkd. with tape, ex-liby. (SG. Dec.15; 194) $250
- **– Anr. Copy.** 2 vols. in 1. Fo. Engraved port., 58 steel engrs., 32 vigs., chagrin. (DS. Oct.28; 2271) Pts. 70,000
- **[–] The Rivers of France.** L., 1837. *1st. Edn.* Sm. 4to. Engraved title, 61 steel-engraved plts., few plts. rather foxed, cont. hf. mor. gt., extremities very rubbed. (SG. Sep.22; 292) $110
- **– Anr. Edn.** Ca. 1835. 4to. Engraved vig. title, 60 engraved plts., some light foxing, hf. mor. gt. (P. Jul.5; 277) £50
- **The Southern Coast of England.** L., 1892. *(500) numbered.* Fo. Vig. title, 39 engraved plts., all on India paper, some spotting, contents loose, publisher's hf. mor. gt., rubbed. (S. Dec.13; 229) *Sephton.* £130
- **– Anr. Copy.** Fo. Partly untrimmed, orig. hf. mor., worn. (TA. Oct.20; 50) £56
- **The Turner Gallery.** Ed.:– W.C. Monkhouse. Ca. 1870. 3 vols. 4to. Port., 89 engraved plts., many loose, cl. (P. Jul.5; 244) £190
- **– Anr. Edn.** Ed.:– R.N. Wornum. 1875. Fo. Hf. mor. gt. (P. Sep.29; 376) *Erlini.* £200
- **– Anr. Copy.** Lge. fo. Port., 60 engraved views on India paper, orig. hf. mor. gt. (P. Jul.5; 207) £140
- **– Anr. Edn.** Ed.:– W. Cosmo Monkhouse. N.Y., ca. 1875. 2 vols. Lge. 4to. 120 engrs., ex-liby., hf. mor. (SG. May 3; 357) $200
- **– Anr. Edn.** Text:– W. Cosmo Monkhouse. Ca. 1880. 3 vols. in 2. Fo. Engraved title, 120 steel engrs., cont. panel. mor. gt., rubbed. (TA. Feb.16; 298) £240
- **– Anr. Copy.** 2 vols. Fo. 120 engraved plts., foxed thro.-out, especially prelims., three-qtr. gt.-decor. mor. & cl., moiré end-papers, covers rubbed, especially extremities. (CBA. Mar.3; 537) $250
- **– Anr. Edn.** Ed.:– W. Cosmo Monkhouse. N.d. 3 vols. 4to. Port., 120 engraved plts., mor. gt., slightly rubbed. (P. Mar.15; 120) £340
- **– Anr. Copy.** Fo. Engraved port. & 60 plts., some margins lightly spotted, cont. mor., rubbed, w.a.f. (CSK. Jul.6; 131) £190
- **– Anr. Copy.** Fo. Some dampstaining, cont. hf. mor., very worn, upr. cover detchd. (S. Apr.30; 96) *Erlini.* £137
- **Views in Sussex** ... Ill.:– W.B. Cooke after Turner. L., 1819. Pt. 1 (all publd.). Fo. Engraved map, 5 plts., slight spotting in margins, orig. ptd. paper wraps. (splitting at fold) & outer roan-bkd. bds., with orig. engraved label, spine defect., lacks ties, mod. cl. box; Signet Liby. bkplt. (C. Mar.14; 96a) *Marlborough.* £550

TURNER, Joseph Mallord William & Girtin, Thomas
- **River Scenery.** 1827. 4to. 17 (of 18) plts., spotting, hf., cf., defect. (P. Jan.12; 60) *Goodey.* £80

TURNER, Joseph Mallord William & Huish, M.B.
- **The Seine & the Loire.** 1886. Fo. 60 engrs. on India paper, hf. cf. gt., worn. (P. Mar.15; 200) *Ayres.* £80

TURNER, Laurence
- **Decorative Plasterwork in Great Britain.** L., 1927. Fo. Orig. cl., d.-w. (S. May 1; 580) *Potterton.* £50

TURNER, Richard
- **A View of the Earth.** 1766. Sm. fo. Cont. hf. cf. (P. Mar.15; 344) *Bickersteth.* £60

TURNER, Capt. Samuel
- **An Account of an Embassy to the Court of the Teshoo Lama, in Tibet.** L., 1806. *2nd. Edn.* 4to. Engraved folding map, 13 plts. (1 folding), cont. cf., rebkd. (S. Mar.6; 52) *Georges.* £160
- **Ambassade au Thibet et au Boutan.** Paris, 1800. 8vo & 4to. Untrimmed, orig. wraps, chipped. (SG. Sep.22; 293) $375

TURNER, William
- **Sound Anatomiz'd, in a Philosophical Essay on Musick.** L., 1724. *1st. Edn.* Sm. 4to. Ptd. mus. notat. thro.-out, folding engraved mus. plt., foxed, later hf. cf., marb. bds., spine very worn, unc. (SG. Apr.19; 183) $275

TURNER, William
- **The Ceramics of Swansea & Nantgarw.** 1897. 4to. Author's copy, orig. cl., soiled. (BBA. Sep.8; 233) *Hereage.* £80

TURNOR, Edmund
- **Collections for the History of the Town & Soke of Grantham.** 1806. 4to. Roan-bkd. bds., unc., rubbed. (SKC. Mar.9; 1994) £75

TURNOR, Hatton
- **Astra Castra Experiments & Adventures in the Atmosphere.** 1865. *1st. Edn. Early iss., without vig. on dedication.* 4to. Orig. cl., very worn. (LC. Mar.1; 192) £70
- **– Anr. Edn.** L., 1865. *[1st. Edn.].* 4to. 40 photo-zincographed plts., mod.hf. cf. (CSK. Nov.25; 74) £75
- **– Anr. Copy.** 4to. Some ll. loose, orig. cl., worn. (BBA. Jun.28; 255) *Demetzy Books.* £55

TURPIN DE CRISSE, Comte Lancelot
- **Commentaires sur les Memoires de Montecuculi** ... Paris, 1769. 3 vols. & 1 vol. Atlas. 4to. Hf. roan, worn, spine vols. 2 & 3 with lacks. (HD. Feb.22; 219) Frs. 1,000
- **Essai sur l'Art de la Guerre.** Ill.:– F. Boucher. 1754. 2 vols. 4to. Cont. marb. roan. (HD. Apr.14; 58) Frs. 1,700
- **Souvenirs du Golfe de Naples recueillis en 1808, 1818, 1824** ... Ill.:– Lemercier. Paris, 1828. Fo. Some foxing, violet str.-grd. hf. mor., corners, lightly rubbed. (HD. May 4; 442) Frs. 3,100

TURRECREMATA, Joannes de
- **Expositio Psalterii.** Augsburg, 1472. Fo. Decorated red & green initials, linen; ex-libris. [HC 15696; BMC II,329] (DS. Dec.16; 2125) Pts. 200,000
- **Questiones Evangelicorum de Tempore et de Sanctis.** Nuremb., Friedrich Creussner, 1478. [H. 15711; BMC II, 450; Goff T546]. (*Bound with:*) **CARACCIOLUS, Robert – Sermones de Timore Divinorum Judiciorum.** Nuremb., Friedrich Creussner, 1479. [HC 4469; BMC II, 451; Goff C186] Together 2 works in 1 vol. Fo. Rubricated, some margin browning & damp-stains, cont. sptd. pig over wood bds., richly decor., clasps incompl.; from Fondation Furstenberg-Beaumesnil. (HD. Nov.16; 33) Frs. 7,500
- **– Anr. Edn.** Strasbur, [Georg Husner], ca. 1487. (*Bound with:*) **CORONA BEATAE MARIAE VIR-GINIS** Strasbur, [Georg Husner] ca. 1487. Together 2 works in 1 vol. Fo. Rubricated, cont. stpd. cf., richly decor.; from Fondation Furstenberg-Beaumesnil. [H. 5746; BMC I, 136] (HD. Nov.16; 46) Frs. 9,000

TURRILL, Charles B.
- **California Notes.** San Franc., 1876. Vol. 1. 12mo. Gt.-lettered cl., light wear, d.-w. (rather chipped & tattered, affecting lettering); pres. copy from author to L. Vernon Briggs, & from Briggs to Californial Historical Society, Ken Leach coll. (RO. Jun.10; 8) $110

TURSELLINUS, Horatius
- **De Vita Francisci Xaverii.** Rome, 1594. Slightly yellowed, old vell., soiled. (TA. Feb.16; 356) £180

TUSOLI, François Carcopino Tusoli
See— **CARCO, Francis (ie François Carcopine Tusoli**

TUSSAC, F. Richard de
- **Flora Antillarum, seu Historia Generalis, Botanica, Ruralis, Oeconomica.** Paris, 1808. Vol. 1 only. Fo. 30 hand-cold. plts., liby. stp. on title, some text spotted, hf. cf., spine & corners defect., as a collection of plts., w.a.f. (P. Nov.24; 263) *Heald.* £600

TUSSER, Thomas
- **Five Hundred Points of Good Husbandry.** 1931. *Ltd. Edn.* Cf. gt. (P. Oct.20; 57) £55

TUTT, J.W.
- **A Natural History of the British Lepidoptera.** L., 1899-1914. Vols. I-V & VIII-XI (all publd.). All but 1 in cl. (SKC. Oct.26; 445) £160

TUTTIETT, Miss Mary Gleed 'Maxwell Gray'
- **The Silence of Dean Maitland.** L., 1886. 3 vols. Orig. cl., s.-c.; 2-pp. A.L.s. from author to Dr. Dabbs; Alfred Tennyson & A. Edward Newton bkplts. (LH. Sep.25; 605) $190

TUVIA BEN ELIESER, of Greece [Byzantium]
- **Midrash Pesikta Zutaratei.** Venice, 1546. *1st. Edn.* Fo. Browned, some staining, mod. blind-tooled mor. (S. Oct.25; 402) *Davidson.* £520

TWAIN, Mark (Pseud.)
See— **CLEMENS, Samuel Langhorne 'Mark Twain'**
See— **MEREDITH, Louisa Anne, née Twamley**

TWEEDIE, Maj. Gen. William
- **The Arabian Horse, His Country & People.** 1894. Fo. Pict. cl. (HBC. May 17; 292) £280
- **– Anr. Copy.** Orig. cl. gt. (P. Dec.8; 242) *Remington.* £240

TWICE A YEAR: A Semi-Annual Journal of Literature, the Arts, & Civil Liberties
Ed.:– Dorothy Norman. N.Y., 1938-47. Nos. I-XV in 9 vols., & 2 dupls. of double no. XIV/XV. Orig. ptd. wraps. & bds., rubbed & chipped, lacks 1 cover, anr. detchd. (SG. May 10; 145) $250

TWINING, Elizabeth
- **Illustrations of the Natural Order of Plants.** L., 1855. Lge. fo. Cont. hf. leath. (R. Oct.12; 1926) DM 650
- **– Anr. Edn.** 1868. 2 vols. Tall 8vo. 160 col. plts., cont. qtr. mor., gt.-decor. spines, rubbed. (TA. May 17; 303) £125

TWINING, W.J.
See— **CAMPBELL, Archibald & Twining, W.J.**

TWISS, Richard
- **A Tour in Ireland in 1775.** L., 1776. *1st. Edn.* Cf. (GM. Dec.7; 424) £135
- **Travels Through Portugal & Spain.** Ill.:– after M.A. Rooker, S.H. Grimm & Cipriani (engraved Bartolozzi). 1775. 4to. Folding map hand-cold. in outl., 5 engraved plts. & 1 vig., other ills. & cont. cuttings pasted on fly-ll., hf.-title creased, lacks an end-paper, cont. gt.-decor. red mor., rubbed; author's copy, with annots. in his hand. (SKC. Jan.13; 2394) £120

TWISS, Travers
- **The Oregon Question Examined, in Respect to Facts & the Law of Nations.** L., 1846. *1st. Edn.* Inscr. on front end-paper 'F. Hammond from the author', 32 pp. publisher's catalogue dtd. Oct. 1845 at end, orig. cl., slight wear; the Rt. Hon. Visc. Eccles copy. [Sabin 97544] (CNY. Nov.18; 270) $160

TWITCHELL, Ralph Emerson
- The Leading Facts of New Mexican History. Cedar Rapids, 1911-12. 2 vols. Cl. (*With:*) - The Spanish Archives of New Mexico. Cedar Rapids, 1914. 2 vols. Cl. (LH. Sep.25; 292) $375

TWOPENY, Richard Ernest Nowell
- Town Life in Australia. L., 1833. Hf. cf. (CA. Apr.3; 115) Aus. $170

TWO WORLDS MONTHLY
Ed.:- Samuel Roth. N.Y., 1926-27. Vol. I, No. 1-Vol. III, No. 3 (all publd.). Contains James Joyce's 'Ulysses', ptd. wraps. (SG. May 24; 314) $130

TWYCROSS, Edward
- The Mansions of England & Wales. 1846-47. 2 vols. Fo. Cold. litho. plts., loose, some spotting, orig. mor.-bkd. cl., worn. (BBA. Jun.28; 256)
Shapiro. £350

TWYNE, Joannis
- Joannis Twini Bolingdunensis, De Rebus Albionicis, Britannicis, atque Anglicis, Commentariorum ... Ed.:- T. Twyne. L., 1590. M2 blank, sm. portion removed from title. [STC 24407] (*Bound with:*).
- LLYWD, Humphry - Commentarioli Britannicae Descriptionis Fragmentum. Cologne, 1572. *1st. Edn.* Together 2 works in 1 vol. Bdg. not stated. (P. Dec.8; 44) *Stewart.* £80

TYAS, Robert
- The Sentiment of Flowers. 1842. 29 hand-cold. plts., text & plts. loose, mor. gt., worn. (P. Sep.29; 53) *Marks.* £60

TYERMAN, Rev. Daniel & Bennet, George
- Journal of Voyages & Travels. Ed.:- James Montgomery. 1831. 2 vols. 2 or 3 ll. with sm. margin stains, early hf. cf., slightly rubbed. (KH. May 1; 498) Aus. $150

TYNDALE, Walter
- An Artist in Egypt. N.d. 4to. Cl. gt. bdg. (PWC. May 3; 667) £70

TYNDALL, John
- Essays on the Floating-Matter of the Air in Relation to Putrefaction & Infection. L., 1881. *1st. Edn.* A few ll. slightly spotted, orig. cl., rebkd., rubbed. (BBA. Nov.30; 126) *Hubbard.* £60
- The Glaciers of the Alps. L., 1860. *1st. Edn.* Slightly spotted, orig. cl., spine faded, slightly worn; bkplt. of John Barrow & H.J. Gladstone, MS. notes of Mrs. Barrow's ascents in the Alps on front endpapers. (S. Jun.25; 179) *Sarmani.* £95

TYPES DE PARIS
Text:- Ed. de Goncourt, A. Daudet, E. Zola, A. Proust, Maupassant, Hüysmans, Mallarmé, Mirbeau. Ill.:- J.F. Raffaëlli. Paris, [1889]. *Orig. Edn. (40) on japan paper.* 4to. No hf.-title with dedication on verso, but replaced by lge. supp. etching, red mor., mosaic upr. cover, sigd., inner dentelle, silky paper guards, decor., pict. wrap. & spine, by R. Raparlier. (HD. Mar.14; 154) Frs 7,500

TYPOTIUS, Jacobus
- Symbola. Ill.:- Aeg. Sadeler. Prag, 1600-03. *1st. Edn.* 3 pts. in 1 vol. Fo. Title pt. 1 excised & mntd., 2 copper engrs. pt. 2 with corrections pasted over, cont. limp vell. (HK. Nov.9; 1633) DM 2,200

TYRRELL, James R.
- Old books, Old Friends, Old Sydney. Sydney, 1952. No bdg. stated; inscr. (JL. Jun.24; 159)
Aus. $100

TYSKIEWICZ, Comte Joseph
- Histoire du 17ème Régiment de Cavalerie Polonaise. Cracovie, 1904. 4to. Sewed. (HD. Jan.27; 221) Frs. 1,000

TYSON, Edward
- 'Vipera Caudi-Sona Americana, or the Anatomy of a Rattle-Snake'. Ill.:- M. Burghers. Oxford, 10 Feb. 1682/83. *1st. Edn.* In 'Philosophical Transactions', no. 144. 4to. Mod. red hf. mor., gt.-lettered spine; the Rt. Hon. Visc. Eccles copy. (CNY. Nov.18; 271) $400

TYSSOT DE PATOT, Simon
- [-] Voyages et Avantures de Jaques Masse. Bordeaux, 1710 [i.e. The Hague, ca. 1714]. *1st. Edn.*

[Rosenberg's 'A' Edn.]. 12mo. Later bds. (KH. Nov.9; 732) Aus. $140

TYTLER, Alexander, Lord Woodhouselee
See— WOODHOUSELEE, Alexander Tytler, Lord

TYTLER, James
- Experiments made Dec. 1769 on Waters in & near Newcastle upon Tyne. 1769. Wraps. (P. Jul.5; 320) £70

TZARA, Tristan
- De Mémoire d'Homme. Ill.:- Pablo Picasso. Paris, 1950. *(350) numbered & initialled by author.* 4to. Unc., orig. wraps. (S. Nov.21; 36) *Makiya.* £220
- - **Anr. Edn.** Ill.:- Picasso. Paris, 1950. *(350). (30) on Holland numbered.* Fo. Sigd. by author & artist, 9 orig. lithos., including port., suite of lithos. on Japan, vell. (DS. Nov.25; 2135) Pts. 250,000
- De nos Oiseaux. Ill.:- Arp. Paris, ca. 1929. Orig. pict. wraps., prelim. lf. with dedication Jul. 1929. (H. May 23; 1128) DM 1,300
- Parler Seul. Poème. Ill.:- Joan Miró. [Paris], 1948-50. *(200) on Bütten.* Fo. Printers mark sigd by author & artist, orig. wraps., bd. cover, s.-c., s.c. torn. (H. May 23; 1420a) DM 3,800

TZARA, Tristan (Text)
See— RAY, Man

U.S.P.R.R.
- Birds of America. America, n.d. Hand-cold. engrs., some pp. torn, no bdg. stated. (RS. Jan.17; 503) $200

UBALDINI, Petruccio
- Descrittione del Regno di Scotia. Antw.[but L.], 1588. *1st. Edn.* Sm. fo. 19th. C. hf. cf. [STC 24480] (SPB. Dec.13; 474) $150
- Le Vite delle Donne Illustri del Regno d'Inghilterra & del Regno di Scotia. L., 1591. *1st. Edn. 2nd. Iss.* 4to. Cancellans title & dedication to Queen Elizabeth, margin repairs, few pp. soiled, 19th. C. mor. gt. by J. Clarke. [STC 24488] (SG. Feb.9; 361) $200

UBALDUS, Guidus
- Mechanischer Kunst-Hammer, Erster Theil. Frankfurt, 1629. Fo. Additional engraved title, 42 engraved plts., some dampstains, margins affected by worm, vell., soiled. (TA. Jul.19; 472) £80

UBER LAND UND MEER. Allgemeine Illustrirte Zeitung
Stuttgart, 1866-69. Vols. 17 & 21. Fo. Cont. hf. leath. (BR. Apr.12; 366) DM 750
- - **Anr. Edn.** Stuttgart, 1886. Vols. 55 & 56. Fo. Some ll. with tears reprd., cont. hf. leath. gt. (BR. Apr.12; 367) DM 450

UCEDA, Shmuel
- Midrash Shmuel. Venice, 1585. *2nd. Edn.* 4to. Owner's sig. on title, title & 1st. 5 ll. reprd. with loss of some text, discold., staining, trimmed, mod. mor. (S. Oct.25; 403) *Dzialowski.* £270

UDALL, William
- The Historie of the Life & Death of Mary Stuart Queene of Scotland. L., 1636. 12mo. 3 margins reprd., 19th. C. red mor. gt. by Mackenzie. [STC 24510] (BBA. May 3; 114)
Howes Bookshop. £130

UFANO, Diego
- Tratado de la Artilleria. Bruselas, 1613. 4to. No bdg. stated. (DS. Mar.23; 2283) Pts. 125,000

UGARIT-FORSCHUNGEN. Internationales Jahrbuch für die Altertumskunde Syrien-Palästinas
Ed.:- K. Bergenhof, M. Dietrich. Kevelaer, 1969-77. Vols. 1-9. 4to. Cl. (B. Jun.21; 56) Fls. 900

UHLAND, Ludwig
- Gedichte. Stuttgart & Tübingen, 1815. *1st. Edn.* Later hf. vell. gt. (C. Dec.9; 294) *Bender.* £160

UHLE, Max
- Kultur und Industrie Suedamerikanischer Voelker. Ill.:- A. Stuebel, W. Reiss & B. Koppel. Berlin, 1889-90. 2 vols. Fo. Perforation stps, in titles, all plts. hand-stpd. in lr. margin, three-qtr. mor., exliby. (RO. Dec.11; 334) $150

UILENBROEK, Gosuinus
- Bibliotheca Uilenbroukiana ... Amst., 1729. 3 pts. in 1 vol. Cont. hf. vell. (VG. Sep.13; 463) Fls. 500

UILKENS, J.A.
- Handb. v. Vaderl. Landhuishoudkunde. Zwolle, 1836. *2nd. Edn.* Prelims. margin stained, cont. bds., unc. (VG. Nov.29; 2) Fls. 500

U LARICIU, Rivista Trimestriale di Litteratura e Arti Regionalisti Corsi
Ed.:- C. Giovoni. Marseglia, [1931-34]. Nos. 16-27. Hf. roan. (HD. Oct.21; 171) Frs. 1,200

ULLOA, Antonio de & Juan y Santacilla, Jorge
- Historische Reisebeschreibungvan Geheel Zuid-America. Goes, 1771-72. 2 vols. 4to. Cont. hf. leath. [Sabin 36804] (D. Nov.23; 1322) DM 1,000
- Mémoires Philosophiques ... concernant la Découverte de l'Amérique. Paris, 1787. 2 vols. 4to. Leath., by Ramage, London. (DS. Apr.27; 2355)
Pts. 28,000
- Noticias Americanas:Entretenimientos Phisicos-Historicos, sobre la America Meridional, y la Septentrianal Oriental ... Madrid, 1772. *1st. Edn.* Sm. 4to. Some foxing, end-papers renewed, cont. vell. [Sabin 97687] (HK. Nov.8; 855) DM 440
- - **Anr. Edn.** Madrid, 1792. *2nd. Edn.* Sm. 4to. Cont. cf., shabby. (SG. Apr.5; 191) $325
- Noticias Secretas De America. 1826. 2 pts. in 1 vol., sm. liby. stp. on title-p., cont. hf. mor., corners worn. [Sabin 36807] (BBA. Feb.9; 274)
Quaritch. £250
- Observaciones Astronomicas y Phisicas de las quales se Deduce la Figura y Magnitud de la Tierra, y se aplica a la Navegación. Madrid, 1773. *2nd. Edn.* Lge. 4to. Folding copperplts. numbered 1-8, unnumbered selenographic map, very wide folding map numbered 21, old hf. cf., reprd. (SG. Sep.22; 175a) $110
- Relación Historica del Viaga a la America Meridional. Madrid, 1748. *1st. Edn.* Vol. I & II, Pt. 1-4 in 4 vols. 4to. A few plts. lightly foxed, cont. leath., gold-tooled decor., gt. spine. (D. Nov.23; 1340) DM 2,000

ULPIANUS
- Commentarioli in Olynthiacas Philippicasque Demosthenis Orationes. [Venice, Oct. 1503]. *1st. Edn.* Fo. Greek letter thro-out, last lf. blank, some sm. wormholes in margins nearly thro-out, hardly affecting text, hf. leath. worn, spine defect. at top & bottom, label torn. (S. May 10; 424) *Maggs.* £500

ULSTADT, Philip
- Coelum Philosophicum, seu Secreta Naturae ... quinta Essentia. Paris, 1544. Sm. stp. on title, cont. cf. gt., worn, spine reprd.; bkplt. Le Tellier de Courtanvaux, Dr. Walter Pagel copy. (S. Feb.7; 373) *Klingsor.* £400

ULYANOV, Vladimir Ilych
See— LENIN, Vladimir Ilych [i.e. Vladimir Ilych Ulyanov]

UMFREVILLE, Edward
- The Present State of Hudson's Bay. L., 1790. *1st. Edn.* Hf.-title, advt. lf. at end, plt. foxed, foxed at beginning & end, cont. cf., rebkd. preserving orig. spine, corners slightly worn; the Rt. Hon. Visc. Eccles copy. [Sabin 99702]. (CNY. Nov.18; 272) $1,300

UNDERHILL, Ruth (Contrib.)
See— BOOK OF SPORT

UNDERWOOD, George C.
- History of the Twenty-Sixth Regiments of the North Carolina Troops in the Great War 1861-'65. Goldsboro, [1901]. Orig. cl., spotted. (SG. Oct.20; 117) $175

UNDERWOOD, Paul A.
- The Kariye Djami. N.Y. & Princeton, 1966-75. 4 vols. 4to. Orig. cl., 3 vols. with d.-w.'s. (BBA. Sep.8; 202) *Zwemmer.* £90
- - **Anr. Edn.** 1967. 3 vols. 4to. Cl., d.-w.'s, s.-c. (P. Dec.8; 160) *Leicester.* £60

UNDERWOOD & Underwood
- Japan Through the Stereoscope. Ca. 1920. Sm. 4to. 100 stereoscopic photos, cl.-bnd. book box, soiled. (TA. May 17; 1) £78

UNGEWITTER, G.G.
- Vorlegeblätter für Holzarbeiten. 1851. 4to. Hf. mor., orig. wraps. bnd. in. (P. Dec.8; 299)
Tzakas. £75
- - Anr. Copy. 4to. Hf. mor., orig. wraps. bnd. in. (P. Feb.16; 186) £50

UNITED NATIONS EDUCATIONAL, SCIENTIFIC & CULTURAL ORGANISATION
- Australia: Aboriginal Paintings, Arnhem Land. Intro.:– Sir Herbert Read. N.Y., ca. 1954. Fo. Bdg. not stated, d.-w. (KH. May 1; 717) Aus. $100

UNITED STATES OF AMERICA
- American Archives: a Collection of Authentick Records ... Ed.:– P. Force. Wash., 1843-53. 4th. Series: Vols. 4-6 (of 6), 5th. Series: Vols. 1-3 (all publd.). Fo. Hf. leath., very worn, ex-liby. (SG. Aug.4; 124) $200
- The Constitutions of the Several Independent States of America ... Phila., 1781. *(200).* Sm. 8vo. Lacks upr. right-hand corner of title-p., with a typographical error introduced in its restoration, pp. lightly browned with minor scattered foxing, cont. leath., scuffed, owner's sig. on rear end-paper, qtr. mor. case. [Sabin 16086] (SPB. May 23; 33) $1,200
- - Anr. Edn. L., 1783. *2nd. L. Edn.* Cont. cf. gt.; Syston Park copy. (SG. Oct.20; 123) £130
- Constitutions des Treize Etats-unis de l'Amérique. Notes:– B. Franklin. Trans.:– Duc de la Rochefoucault. Phila., 1783. *(600).* Orig. paper wraps., unc., buckram box. (C. May 30; 129) *Drury.* £320
- Flags of the Army of the United States, Carried during the War of the Rebellion, 1861-1865 ... Phila., 1887. Fo. 88 chromolitho. plts., orig. gt.-lettered cl., spine ends worn. (SG. Jan.19; 149) $275
- Phelps & Ensign's Traveller's Guide Through the United States. N.Y., 1838. 12mo. Folding map hand-cold., map torn at creases & soiled, stitching brkn., orig. embossed cl. (LH. Jan.15; 371) $200
See— AMERICA, Confederate States of
See— AMERICAN CIVIL WAR

UNITED STATES ARMY
- Index Catalogue of the Library of the Surgeon-General's Office, Authors & Subjects. Washington, 1880-95. Series 1, 16 vols. 4to. Light wear, not collated, orig. linen, loose & bumped. (HT. May 8; 757) DM 400
- Regulations for the Uniform of the Army of the United States. Baltimore, n.d. Cl., spine cracked, edges rubbed. (RS. Jan.17; 495) $175
- Uniform of the Army of the United States, 1882. Ill.:– Thomas Hunter. N.p., not before 1882. Sm. ob. fo. Litho. title, 9 litho. & 10 chromolitho. plts., title & free end-papers loose, orig. cl. (SG. Oct.20; 353) $120

UNITED STATES COAST SURVEY
- Report of the Superintendent of the Coast Survey ... during the Year 1854. Wash., 1855. Lge. 4to. Shaken, cl., worn, ex-liby. (SG. Aug.4; 340) $180

UNITED STATES CONGRESS
- Proceedings at the Ceremony in Commemoration of the One Hundred & Fiftieth Anniversary of the Commencement of the First Congress of the United States under the Constitution at a Joint Session in the House of Representatives, March 4,1939. Wash., 1939. *1st. printing,.* Sm. 4to. Gt.-lettered leath. (spotted), silk doubls.; from liby. of F.D. Roosevelt, inscr. by him (as President) 'FDR Jr. from FDR, 1939'. (SG. Mar.15; 81) $450

UNITED STATES GEOGRAPHICAL SURVEY
- Report upon United States Geographical Surveys West of the One Hundredth Meridian. Wash., 1875-79. Vols. II-VII (of 7). Lge. 4to. Cl., lacks some spines, ex-liby. (SG. Aug.4; 339) $120

UNITED STATES GEOLOGICAL SURVEY
- Atlas to Accompany Monograph XXXII on the Geology of the Yellowstone National Park by Arnold Hague. Wash., 1904. Fo. 24 litho. maps, orig. cl., spines cut in several places. (SG. Dec.15; 15) $100

UNITED STATES MILITARY ACADEMY
- ... Song of the Graduates 1852. Music:– [A.] Apelles. Words:– [J. Watts Robinson]. Ill.:– James Abbott McNeill Whistler. [N.Y., 1852]. Sm. fo.

Extracted from bnd. vol. of other music, pict. upr. wrap. with litho. of 2 cadets, lacks blank rear wrap., title on upr. wrap. shaved. (SG. Jun.7; 321) $325

UNITED STATES SENATE
- Executive Document No. 1, 33d Congress, 2d Session. Message from the president ... to the Two Houses of Congress ... Part III. Wash., 1854. Lge. 4to. 45 litho. maps, plans, charts, etc., some minor foxing, orig. gt. & blind-stpd. cl. (SG. Dec.15; 16) $150

UNITED STATES TREASURY DEPARTMENT
- Vignettes & Portraits, U.S. Treasury Department Specimens. Ill.:– Bureau of Engraving & Printing. Wash., n.d. End-papers loose, cf., spine rubbed. (RS. Jan.17; 504) $225

UNIVERS. Histoire et Description de tous les Peuples.
Paris, 1835-60. 13 vols. 24 maps & 741 steel engraved plts., 2 orig. wraps., 1 hf. leath., 10 cont. linen, not collated, w.a.f. (R. Oct.13; 2832) DM 700

UNIVERS PITTORESQUE (L')
Contribs:– F. Hoefer, F. Lacroix, P. d'Avezac & others. Paris, ca. 1835-50. 47 vols. 1,000 engraved maps & views, cont. hf. roan. (HD. May 16; 54)
Frs. 7,100
- - Anr. Edn. Paris, 1837-49. Section IV. 5 vols. 405 (of 408) plts., some slight text foxing, cont. leath., 2 vols. slightly loose, slightly rubbed. (D. Nov.23; 868) DM 800

UNIVERSAL HISTORY from the Earliest Account of Time to the Present
1736-50. 8 vols. in 9, including Supp. Fo. Some light soiling, cont. cf., some covers detchd. (CSK. Sep.16; 223) £110
- - Anr. Copy. 9 vols., including Supp. Fo. Old cf., defect. (P. Nov.24; 56) *Shapero.* £65
- - Anr. Edn. 1747-48-54. 21 vols. Cont. tree cf., spines gt.; Sir Ivar Colquhoun, of Luss copy. (CE. Mar.22; 317) £420

UNIVERSIDAD DE SEVILLA
- Libro que contiene todo lo que toca y pertenece la Real Universidad de Sevilla. Sevilla, 1695. Fo. Vell. (DS. Mar.23; 2158) Pts. 50,000

UNIVERSITY OF VIRGINIA BIBLIOGRAPHICAL SOCIETY
- Papers of ... Studies in Bibliography. Charlottesville, 1948-74. Vols. 1-27. 1st. 3 vols. orig. wraps., rest orig. cl. (BBA. Aug.18; 56) *Price.* £170

UNTERMEYER, Irwin
- Untermeyer Collection: Chelsea & other English Porcelain, Pottery & Enamel. Text:– Yvonne Hackenbroch. Camb., Mass., 1957. *1st. Edn.* Sm. fo. Cl.-bkd. patterned bds. (SG. Jan.26; 160) $100
- Untermeyer Collection: Meissen & other Continental Porcelain; Chelsea & other English Porcelain, Pottery & Enamel; English Furniture; English & other Needlework; Bronzes; English & other Silver. Text:– Yvonne Hackenbroch. L., 1956-63. 6 vols. 4to. No bdgs. stated. (SPB. Nov.30; 352)
$400
- - Anr. Copy. Vols. 1-3 & 5-6 only. 4to. Orig. buckram-bkd. bds., d.-w.'s, some tears. (S. Dec.13; 481) *Heneage.* £230

UNZER, Johann August
- Medicinisches Handbuch. Leipzig, 1776. 2 pts. in 1 vol. Some light soiling, cont. hf. leath., rubbed & bumped. (R. Apr.4, 1393) DM 500

UNZER, Johann August (Ed.)
See— ARZT, Der ...

UPDIKE, Daniel Berkeley
- Printing Types. Camb., 1937. 2 vols. Orig. linen. (D. Nov.23; 345) DM 450

UPMARK, Gustaf
- Guld och Silversmeder i Sverige, 1520-1850. Stockholm, [1925]. *1st. Edn.* Sm. 4to. Cont. three-qtr. cf. gt. & marb. bds., orig. wraps. bnd. in. (SG. Oct.13; 185) $275

UPTON, Florence K. & Bertha
- The Adventures of Two Dutch Dolls & a 'Golliwogg'. L. & N.Y., [1895]. *1st. Edn.* Ob. 4to. Cl.-bkd. col.-pict. bds., slight wear; inscr on title 'To Dollywogg from Golliwogg & Florence, March 19, 1917'. (SG. Dec.8; 354) $425

URBANUS BELLUENSIS
- Grammaticae Institutiones ad Graecam Linguam. Venice, 1560. Sm. 8vo. Late 18th. C. red mor., wide gt. borders with Aldine anchor on both covers, spine elab. gt.; Syston Park bkplt. (SG. Feb.9; 159)
$450

URBINO, Shlomo Ben Abraham
- Ohel Moed. Venice, 1548. *1st. Edn.* 4to. Inner margins reprd. not affecting text, some staining, discold., hf. mor. with marb. paper bds., slightly worn; stp. of Etz-Haim Synagogue (Amsterdam) on title. (S. Oct.25; 404) *Ludmir.* £280

URE-SMITH, Sydney & Stevens, Bertram
- The Art of J.J Hilder. Sydney, 1918. No bdg. stated. (JL. Jun.24; 186) Aus. $220
- The Pen Drawings of Norman Lindsay. Sydney, 1918. Special no. of 'Art in Australia'. 55 plts. tipped in, hardback, d.-w.; sigd. by Lindsay. (JL. Nov.13; B481) Aus. $240

URFE, Honoré de
- L'Astrée. Rouen & Paris, 1647. 5 vols. Cont. roan, rubbed, vol. 5 not unif. (HD. Feb.22; 221)
Frs. 1,500

URQUHART, David (Ed.)
See— PORTFOLIO, The, or a Collection of State Papers

URSINS, Juvenal des
- Histoire de Charles VI Roy de France ... Augmentée ... par Denys Godefroy Conseiller et Historiographe du Roy. 1653. Fo. Cont. cf., spine decor. (HD. Mar.21; 101) Frs. 1,600

URSTISIUS, Christianus
- Germaniae Historicorum Illustrium quorum Plerique ab Henrico IIII Imperatore usque ad Annum Christi 1400. Frankfurt, 1585. 2 vols. in 1. Fo. Cont. cf., silver-decor., worn; from Fondation Furstenberg-Beaumesnil. (HD. Nov.16; 179)
Frs. 1,300

URUGUAY
- Two Letters ... on the Withdrawal of the British Intervention from the River Plate Question. Monte Video, 1847. Self-wraps., untrimmed & unopened. (SG. Oct.20; 352) $150

USSHER, James, Archbp. of Armagh
- Gravissimae Quaestionis, de Christianarum Ecclesiarum. L., 1613. *1st. Edn.* Sm. 4to. Interleaved, with extensive MS. revisions & additions thro.-out (taken from the author's papers?, written in preparation of a new edn.?), some browning & soiling, old cf., lettered 'opus integru ab autore auctum at recognitum MSS/[Andrew] Gifford', restored, old spine preserved. (S. Dec.8; 383)
Lewis. £820

USHER, James Ward
- An Art Collector's Treasures. Priv. ptd., 1916. *(300).* Fo. Some browning & light soiling, orig. cl., spine affected by damp & holed. (CSK. Jun.29; 44)
£55
- - Anr. Copy. Fo. Few ll. slightly soiled, orig. mor. gt. (BBA. Nov.10; 366) *Shama-Levy.* £50

USSIEUX, Louis d'
- Les Nouvelles Françoises. Ill.:– Gaucher & others. Paris, 1783. 3 vols. Tall 8vo. Foxed & soiled, cont. vell., spines gt. (SG. Feb.9; 362) $100

UTICA DIRECTORY: to which is added a brief Historical, Topographical & Statistical Account of the Village & its Neighbourhood.
Utica, 1828. *1st. Edn.* 12mo. Later hf. mor., spine rubbed & chipped on head. (SG. Apr.5; 194) $110

UYTENBOGAERT, J. & Dwinglo, B.
[-] Oorspronck ende Voortgangck der Nederl. Kerckelijcke Verschillen, tot op het Nationale Synodus van Dordrecht. Verhael van 't ghene sich toedraeghen Heeft binnen Dordrecht in 1618 en

1619. [Amst.], 1623. *1st. Edn.* 2 pts. in 1 vol. Fo. Cont. vell. (VG. Nov.30; 981) Fls. 500

UZANNE, Octave
- L'Art dans la Décoration Extérieure des Livres en France et à l'Etranger. Les Couvertures Illustrées; les Cartonnages d'Editeurs; la Reliure d'Art. Paris, 1898. *Orig. Edn. 1st. Printing.* Lge. 8vo. Numbered copy on vell., cont. hf. chagrin, corners, ill. wrap. (HD. Jul.2; 110) Frs. 1,300
- L'Eventail. Ill.:– Paul Avril. Paris, 1882. Cont. red mor. gt., onlays, orig. silk wraps. bnd. in, rebkd., orig. spine preserved; sigd. by artist. (S. Mar.20; 751) £120
- The Fan. Ill.:– Paul Avril. L., 1884. (*With:*) - The Sunshade. Ill.:– Paul Avril. L., 1884. Together 2 vols. 4to. Lev. by Maclehose, partly unc. (SG. Feb.16; 319) $130
- La Française du Siècle. Modes, Moeurs, Usages. Ill.:– after Albert Lynch. Paris, 1886. *(100) numbered on Japan.* Sewed, pict. wrap., gt. (HD. Feb.17; 123) Frs. 1,200
- Le Livre Moderne du Monde Litteraire et des Bibliophiles Contemporains. Ill.:– Robida, Bouquet, Gavarni, & others. Paris, 1890-92. *(1000).* 5 vols. Hf. cf. (CR. Jun.6; 305) Lire 300,000
- La Locomotion à Travers l'Histoire et les Moeurs. Paris, 1900. *Ltd. Edn.* Ills., folding plts., hf. mor., worn. (P. May 17; 294) *Blackwells.* £85
- Les Modes de Paris. Ill.:– François Courboin. 1898. *Orig. Edn. 1st. Printing.* 4to. On special vell., mod. hf. mor., spine decor. (HD. Apr.13; 124) Frs. 1,800
- L'Ombrelle, le Gant, le Manchon. Ill.:– Paul Avril. 1883. *Orig. Edn.* Hf. mor., corners, by Barbance, wrap. (HD. Jan.24; 89) Frs. 1,550
- Son Altesse la Femme. Ill.:– F. Rops, A. Moreau, & others. Paris, 1885. *1st. Edn.* 4to. Orig. cold. pict. wraps. in orig. hf. linen portfo., slightly defect., unc., silk ties. (GB. Nov.4; 1967) DM 400
- – Anr. Copy. Lge. 8vo. Mod. hf. roan, spine decor. (HD. Apr.13; 125) Frs. 1,150
- – Anr. Copy. (*With:*) - La Française du Siècle. Modes, Moeurs, Usages. Ill.:– after A. Lynch. Paris, 1886. *Orig. Edn.* Together 2 vols. Sewed, ill. wraps., Japanese decor. bds., silk ribbons. (HD. Jul.2; 109) Frs. 1,050

UZANNE, Octave & Robida, A.
- Contes pour les Bibliophiles. Paris, 1895. *Orig. Edn. 1st. Printing.* Lge. 8vo. On vell., lacks plt. after Fragonard (as usual), hf. roan, corners, spine decor., unc., ill. wrap. (HD. Jul.2; 111) Frs. 1,400

VACHER, Sydney
- Fifteenth Century Italian Ornament, chiefly taken from Brocades [etc.]. 1886. Fo. Orig. parch.-bkd. bds., d.-w., s.-c. (BBA. Nov.10; 368) *Goldschmidt.* £70
- – Anr. Copy. Lge. fo. Orig. vell.-bkd. bds., spine torn. (CSK. Feb.24; 223) £60

VACHON, Marius
- Les Arts et les Industries du Papier en France 1871-1894. Paris, 1894. Fo. Title verso stpd., orig. linen, slightly spotted & bumped. (HK. Nov.9; 2007) DM 640

VACQUIER, J.
- Le Style Empire. Paris, 1920. 5 vols. Fo. Cl., soiled. (SPB. Dec.13; 822) $100

VADE, Jean Joseph
- Oeuvres Possardes. Ill.:– Monsiau. Paris, 1796. *(100) on L.P.* 4to. 4 plts. ptd. in colours, slight marginal soiling, bds. (SPB. May 17; 711) $225

VAENIUS, Otto
See— VEEN, Otto van

VAERNEWIJCK, Marcus van
- Die Historie van Belgis Diemen anders Namen mach Spieghel der Nederlantscher Audtheyt. Ghendt, 1574. *2nd. Printing.* Fo. Slight defect to 1 lf. restored, light worming, old vell. (LM. Oct.22; 296) B.Frs. 27,000

VAILLANT, Jean Foy
- Nummi Antiqui Familiarum Romanarum. Amst., 1703. 2 vols. Fo. Engraved vigs. on titles, frontis., & 152 engraved plts., Vol. 1 with hf.-title, some slight

---

spotting, cont. hf. roan, rubbed. (S. May 1; 521) *Spring.* £100

VALCARCEL, Domingo & Malo, Felix Vanancio
- Reales Exequias de ... Dona Ysabel Farnecio, Princesa de Parma y Reyna de las Españas: ... Mexico City, 1767. 4to. Light margin dampstains, cont. vell., loose. (SG. Jan.19; 249) $350

VALDES, Antonio
- Noticia del Reél Instituto Asturiano. Oviedo, 1795. 4to. Mor., sigd. by Ginesta. (DS. Mar.23; 2723) Pts. 50,000

VALE PRESS
See— CENTAUR, The, & the Bacchante
See— MILTON, John
See— VAUGHAN, Henry Silurist

VALENCIA
- Actas y Estatutos del Capítulo Provincial celebrado en la Ciudad de Xativa 10/mayo/1687 ... Valencia, 1687. 4to. Sewed. (DS. Nov.25; 2409) Pts. 26,000
- Archivo de Arte Valenciano. 1915-25. 17 vols. (lacks year 1, no. 2). Fo. Sewed. (DS. Mar.23; 2015) Pts. 35,000

VALENCIA, Carlismo
[–] La Corneta Carlista ... Valencia, 1871. Nos. 1-4, all publd. Fo. (DS. Dec.16; 2012) Pts. 40,000

VALENTIA, George Annesley, Visc.
- Voyage & Travels to India, Ceylon, the Red Sea, Abyssinia & Egypt. L., 1809. *[1st. Edn.].* 3 vols. 4to. Cont. hf. cf., gt. spine. (SKC. Jan.13; 2395) £280
- – Anr. Copy. 3 vols. 4to. 67 (of 69) plts., lacks final text lf. or ll. in Vol. 2, some offsetting of plts. to text, recent cl. (TA. Feb.16; 18) £55
- – Anr. Copy. 3 vols. 4to. 67 (of 69) maps & plts., including 9 folding, hf.-titles, foxed, 2 plts. torn, orig. red hf. mor., gt.-armorial red mor. centrepieces with author's arms, worn, covers detchd.; MS. ex-libris of Alexander Knox, Kofoid bkplts. (SG. Sep.22; 19) $200

VALENTINER, Wilhelm R.
- A Catalogue of Early Italian Paintings Exhibited at the Duveen Galleries, New York, April to May 1924. [1924]. Fo. No bdg. stated. (SPB. Nov.30; 121) $200
See— BERENSON, B. & Valentiner, Wilhelm R.

VALENTINI, G.W. von
- Die Lehre vom Krieg. Berlin, 1820-22. 3 pts. in 4 vols. Lightly browned, cont. hf. leath., corners bumped. (GB. May 3; 966) DM 480

VALENTINI, Michael Bernhard
- Corpus Juris Medico-Legale. Frankfurt, 1722. 2 pts. in 1 vol. Fo. Some slight browning, cont. blind-tooled pig over wood bds., clasps brkn., 10 vell. tabs. (R. Apr.4; 1394) DM 660

VALENTINUS, J. St.
- Sacri Rosarii Virginis Mariae ab Haereticorum Calumniis Decensio una cum Musteriis et Bullis Romanorum Pontificum. Rome, 1584. 4to. Cont. vell. (HD. Dec.2; 164) Frs. 1,500

VALENTINUS, P.P.
[–] Enchiridion Medicum. Dat is: Kort Begrijp vanden Gantschen Loop der Medicine. Utrecht, 1619. (*Bound with:*) WIRTZ or WUERTZ, F. - Practica der Chirurgie. Ed.:– A.L. Vos & E. Theunisz. Amst., 1621. Together 2 works in 1 vol. 4to. Cont. limp vell., worn, warped & stained. (VG. Sep.14; 1277) Fls. 900

VALENTYN, François
- Verhandelinge der Zee-Horenkens en Zee-gewassen in en omtrent Amboina ... Dordrecht & Amst., 1726. Fo. A few wormholes, upr. margin stained thro-out, cf., slight defects., rebkd. (B. Oct.4; 777) Fls. 500

VALERIANI, Domenico
- Atlante Monumentale del Basso e dell'Alto Egitto. Flor., 1837. 2 vols. in 1. Fo. 159 engraved or aquatint plts., maps, plans & views, several hand-cold., some double-p., cont. hf. mor. gt., rubbed. (S. Dec.1; 357) *Walford.* £480

VALERIANO BOLZANI, Giovanni Pierio
- Hieroglyphica. Lyon, 1610. Fo. Some light foxing & staining, later leath., slightly worn & bumped. (HT. May 9; 1330) DM 480
- Les Hiéroglyphiques. Lyon, 1615. Fo. Hf. title & title remntd., some ll. stained, 19th. C. cf., decor. spine. (HD. Jan.24; 358) Frs. 1,200

VALERIUS FLACCUS, Gaius
- Argonautica. Venezia, 9 Jul. 1501. 4to. Stained, 19th. C. hf. vell. (SI. Dec.15; 41) Lire 450,000

VALERIUS MAXIMUS, Gaius
- Dictorum Factorumque Memorabilium Libri IX. Lyon, 1613. 12mo. (in 8's). Minor worming on 1st. few ll. reprd., early red mor., wide gt.-tooled borders enclosing arms of Alphonsus Palavicinus (upr. cover) & Vincentius Costaguta (lr. cover), smooth spine gt.-tooled & panel., worn, lacks ties. (SG. Apr.19; 37) $200
- Facta et Dicta Memorabilia. Commentary:– Oliverius Arzignanensis. Venice, Guilelmus Anima Mia, Tridinensis, 12 Aug. 1491. Fo. Spaces for capitals with guide letters, some sm. wormholes at beginning & end, title lf. reprd. in inner margin & a few sm. holes reprd., inkstain on x2v & x3, some worming in inner margins affecting letters in about 10 ll. towards end, blind-stpd. cf., rather defect. & laid down on new cf. bdg., new end-papers. [BMC V, 412; Goff V39; H. 15791] (S. May 10; 426) *Fletcher.* £450

VALERY, M.
- Voyages en Corse, à l'Ile d'Elbe et en Sardaigne. Paris, 1837. 2 vols. Foxed, cont. hf. roan, spines blind-decor. (HD. Oct.21; 172) Frs. 1,100

VALERY, Paul
- Le Cimetière Marin. 1920. *Orig. Edn. (500) on Mittineague-mill.* Sewed; author's autograph dedication & card. (HD. Apr.13; 179) Frs. 2,800
- Douze Poèmes. Ill.:– Jean Cocteau. Paris, 1959. *Orig. Edn. (200) on vélin satiné d'Auvergne.* 4to. 13 orig. lithos., leaves, box. (HD. Sep.22; 363) Frs. 1,350
- Gedichte. Trans.:– R.M. Rilke. Ill.:– E. Gill. Leipzig, Cranach Pr., 1925. *1st. Edn. (50) De Luxe Edn. on Japan.* Sm. 4to. 1 lf. with slight margin stain, hand-bnd. orig. mor., spine faded, slight offset on upr. cover. (H. Nov.23; 983) DM 2,200
- Maîtres et Amis. Ill.:– Jacques Beltrand. 1927. 4to. Suite of ports. in 3 & 4 states, mor. by Y. Ollivier, blind- & gt.-decor., s.-c. (HD. Mar.21; 226) Frs. 1,300
[–] Portrait. Ill.:– Andre Szekely de Doba. Paris, [1926]. *(44) numbered on imperial Japan vell.* 4to. Ptd. wraps., unc. & unopened; this copy ptd. for Serge Sandberg, sigd. by Valery. (SG. May 24; 373) $110
- Présence de Paris. Ill.:– Pedro Flores. Paris, n.d. *(525) numbered.* Lge. fo. Portfo. (DS. Oct.28; 2247) Pts. 20,000
- Villon et Verlaine. Maestricht, Halcyon Pr., 1937. *Orig. Edn. (10) De Luxe Edn. on Japan.* Lge. 4to. Hand-bnd. mor., spine bumped, ex-libris; Hauswedell coll. (H. May 24; 743) DM 540

VALIN, R.J.
- Nouveau Commentaire sur l'Ordonnance de la Marine du Mois d'Aôut 1681. La Rochelle, 1760. 2 vols. 4to. Cont. mott. roan, 2 turn-ins worn. (HD. Mar.9; 130t) Frs. 1,000

VALLA, Laurentius
- De Dialectica Libri III. Paris, 1530. Title stained & reprd., later vell.-bkd. paper bds., soiled. (BBA. Jun.28; 183) *Poole.* £70
- Elegantiarum Latinae Linguae Libri Sex. Ed.:– Ioannes Raenerius. Lyon, 1548. 17th. C. Spanish pig, sm. gold-tooled medal with monog., gold-tooled, leath. decor., gold-tooled pointillé, gt. outer dentelle, some fading, marb. end-papers. (D. Nov.23; 148) DM 1,800

VALLE, Genaro del
- Anales de la Inquisición. Madrid, 1868. 4to. Linen wraps. (DS. Dec.16; 2102) Pts. 30,000

VALLE, Giovanni Battista della
[–] Vallo Libro Côtinente appartenentie ad Capitanii ... Venice, 11.III.1524. *Early (2nd.?) Edn.* Lacks last lf. blank, slightly stained & foxed, minimal

VALLE, Giovanni Battista della -*Contd.*

worming, 19th. C. hf. leath. gt. (HK. Nov.8; 371)
DM 520

VALLE, Pietro della
- Reiss-Beschreibung in Unterschiedlichen Theile der Welt, nemlich in Turckey, Egypten, Palestina, Persien, Ost-Indien ... Genf, 1674. *1st. German Edn.* 4 vols. in 1. (*Bound with:*) TAVERNIER, Jean Baptiste -Beschreibung der Sechs Reisen ... Türckey, Persien, Indien. Genf, 1681. *2nd. German Edn.* 3 pts. & 2 supps. Lacks all copper engrs., text compl. Together 2 works in 1 vol. Fo. Cont. vell. (R. Oct.13; 3061) DM 2,600
- - **Anr. Copy.** 4 pts. in 1 vol. Fo. 2 port. copper engrs., 27 (of 28) copperplts., 1st. 12 ll. wormed & defect., slightly browned, cont. leath., worn & bumped, slightly torn. (HK. Nov.9; 1309)
DM 850
- The Travels ... into East-India & Arabia Deserta, in which the Several Countries ... Are Faithfully Described, whereunto is added, A Relation of Sir Thomas Roe's Voyage into the East-Indies. Trans.:- [G. Havers]. L., 1665. *1st. Edn. in Engl.* Fo. Imprimatur lf., old cf., neatly rebkd. [Wing V47] (SG. Sep.22; 294) $325
- - **Anr. Edn.** Trans.:- [G. Havers]. L., 1665. Fo. Imprimatur lf., sm. margin stains, slight worming, 1st. text. lf. dust-soiled, cf. [Wing V48A] (S. Nov.1; 62) *Edwards.* £160

VALLEMONT, Pierre Le Lorrain de, Abbé de
- Der Heimliche und Unerforschliche Natur-Kuendiger oder: Accurate Beschreibung von der Wünschel-Ruther darinnen enthalten der besondere Nutz bey Entdeckung der Wasser-Quellen, Metallen ... Nuremb., 1694. *1st. German Edn.* Cont. vell., red hf. mor. box. (D. Nov.24; 4452) DM 4,500

VALLEY, Leon (Ed.)
See— COURTIERS & FAVOURITES of Royalty

VALLOTTON, Felix
- Crimes et Chatiments. Paris, 1902. *1st. Edn.* In Special iss. (no. 48) of 'L'Assiette au Beurre'. 4to. 23 orig. lithos., pict. wraps., boxed. (LH. Sep.25; 612) $375

VALMIER, Georges
- Album No. 1. Paris, 1920's. From 'Collection Decors et Couleurs'. Fo. 20 plts., pochoir-cold. by Saude, loose as iss., cl.-bkd. decor. bd. folder. (SG. Aug.25; 320) $550

VALMONT DE BOMARE, Jacques Christophe
- Algemeen en Beredenerent Woordenboek der Natuurlyke Historie. — Historie en Beschryving der Enkele Drogeryen, welke de Drie Ryken Opleveren. Dordrecht, 1767-70. 3 vols., including Supp. 4to. Hf. cf., spine ends defect., unc. (B. Oct.4; 778)
Fls. 450
- Dictionnaire Raisonné, Universelle d'Histoire Naturelle. Paris, 1765. 5 vols. Some stains, cont. leath., gold-tooled decor., gt. spine. (D. Nov.23; 386) DM 400
- - **Anr. Edn.** Ill.:- Boily (frontis). Lyon, 1791. 15 vols. Cont. spr. cf., decor. spines, sm. wormhole on 1 cover. (HD. Sep.22; 364) Frs. 1,350

VALTURIUS, Robertus
- De Re Militari. Paris, Jul. 1532. *1st. Fr. Edn.* Fo. Title-p. soiled, some browning & foxing, mod. hf. cf. over marb. bds.; sigs. on title-p. (1 dtd. 1843) of Thomas Ewbank, Stanitz coll. (SPB. Apr.25; 433) $1,000
- - **Anr. Edn.** Paris, 1534. Fo. Stained, some worming, cont. limp vell., lacks ties. (SPB. Dec.13; 755) $300

VALVASOR, Johann Meichard
- Topographia Archiducatus Carinthiae ... Nuremb., 1681. Fo. Engraved frontis., folding panoramic view, folding map, 227 engraved views, some creases to panoramic view, early 19th. C. paper bds. (S. Dec.1; 338) *Quaritch.* £1,900

VANBRUGH, Sir John
- Complete Works. Nones. Pr., 1927-28. (*1300*) *numbered.* 4 vols. Orig. cl.-bkd. bds., spines faded. (CSK. Aug.19; 83) £50

VANBRUGH, Sir John & Pearce, Sir Edward Lovett
- Architectural Drawings in the Library of Elton Hall. Ed.:- Howard Colvin & Maurice Craig. Roxb. Cl., 1964. 4to. Orig. qtr. mor. (S. Oct.4; 231)
Weinreb. £290

VANCOUVER, George
- Reisen nach dem Nördlichen Theile der Südsee. Trans.:- F.W. Herbst. Berlin, 1799-1800. *1st. German Edn.* 2 vols. Cont. hf. leath., rubbed. [Sabin 98444] (R. Oct.13; 2997) DM 1,000
- Voyage de Découvertes à l'Océan Pacifique du Nord et autour du Monde ... An VIII [1800]. 3 vols. (lacks atlas). 4to. Old hf. chagrin. (HD. Jun.29; 201) Frs. 3,300
- - **Anr. Edn.** Trans.:- P.F. Henry. Ill.:- Tardieu, the elder. Paris, an X [1802]. 5 vols. Cont. hf. cf. (HD. Dec.16; 57) Frs. 3,550
- A Voyage of Discovery to the North Pacific Ocean. L., 1801. *[2nd. Edn.].* 6 vols. 17 folding plts., 6 engraved charts on 2 folding sheets, cont. hf. cf. (S. May 22; 491) *Traylen.* £460
- - **Anr. Copy.** 6 vols. 17 (of 19) folding engraved plts., soiled & stained thro.-out, cont. hf. cf., not unif., worn. (BBA. Mar.21; 76) *McNaul.* £100
- - **Anr. Copy.** 6 vols. 1st. chart reprd., some foxing, old tree cf., rebkd. (CA. Apr.3; 116) Aus. $880

VAN DALE, A.
- De Oraculis Ethnicorum Dissertationes Duae. Amst., 1700. *2nd. Edn.* 4to. Outer margins stained, cont. vell. (SI. Dec.15; 57) Lire 220,000

VAN DE PUT (Ed.)
See— BEIT, Otto

VAN DE WOESTYNE, Karel
- Christophorus. Ill.:- Jozef Cantré. Antw., 1926. (*110*). (*100*) numbered on Van Gelder. 4to. Publisher's cl. (LM. Oct.22; 326) B.Frs. 10,000
- De Gulden Schaduw. 1910. 1 vol. Sm. 4to. Browned parch. gt., margin untrimmed. (*With:*)
- Het Zatte Hart. Haarlem, 1926. (*190*). 1 vol. Lge. 8vo. Bdg. not stated; Joh. Enschedé en Zonen archive copy. (LM. Oct.22; 325) B.Frs. 10,000

VAN DEN KEERE, Petrus
- England Wales Scotland & Ireland Described. [G. Humble, 1627 or later]. Ob. 8vo. 60 (of 63) miniature engraved county & regional maps, map of Hertfordshire pasted over a dupl. copy of Cambridgeshire map, wanting title & some text ll., 1 or 2 maps shaved, some staining, cont. cf., rebkd., very worn, w.a.f. (S. May 21; 22) *Nicholson.* £500
- - **Anr. Edn.** [1627 or 1632]. Welsh pt. only. Ob. 8vo. 8 engraved maps, some stains, later hf. mor., some wear. (TA. Jun.21; 198) £105

VAN DEN SPIEGHEL, Adrianus
See— SPIEGHEL or SPIGELIUS or VAN DEN SPIEGHEL, Adrianus

VAN DER BURG, A.R. & P.
- School of Painting for the Imitation of Woods & Marbles. L., 1887. *2nd. Edn.* Fo. 36 litho. plts., including cold. examples, spotted, stained at head towards end, orig. cl.-bkd. ptd. bds., worn. (S. Apr.30; 232) *Williams.* £300

VAN DER LAAN, A.
- Zee Land en Stroom. Lust. Amst., ca. early 18th. C. Ob. 8vo. Engraved title, 21 plts., slight staining & foxing, mor.-bkd. bds., worn, spine defect., as a coll. of plts., w.a.f. (SPB. May 17; 712) $1,200

VANDERMAELEN, Ph.
- Atlas Universal de Géographie Physique, Politique, Statistique et Minéralogique. Ill.:- H. Ode after Vandermaelen. Brüssel, 1827. 6 vols. Fo. 391 double-p. outl. cold. litho. maps, some maps completed from anr. edn., browned in lr. margin, vol. 6 map 12 lacks left part., title & 43 pp. statistics stained in outer margin, vols. 2-6 title slightly stained or foxed, cont. hf. leath. (D. Nov.23; 777)
DM 12,000
See— GERARD, P. & Vandermaelen, Ph.

VANDERPYL, F.R.
- Voyages. Ill.:- Vlaminck. 1920. *Orig. Edn.*, (*105*) on holland. 4to. Hf. chagrin, wraps. (HD. Jun.29; 202) Frs. 8,700

VAN DIEMEN'S LAND
- Proclamations, Government Orders, & Notices, Issued ... during the Year 1840. Hobart, 1841. Fo. Faint margin browning, sm. stain not affecting text, mod. hf. cf. gt. (S. Nov.1; 46) *Maggs.* £55
- A Scheme of Taxation for Tasmania. Hobart, 1871. Title wraps. (KH. Nov.8; 7) Aus. $190

VAN DUZER, H.S.
- A Thackeray Library. N.Y., 1919. (*175*) sigd. by author & Edward Turnbull. 4to. Orig. cl., partly unc. (S. May 1; 441) *Sawyer.* £60

VANE, Sir Henry
- The Retired Mans Meditations or the Mysteris & Power of Godlines. L., 1655. *1st. Edn.* Sm. 4to. Slight browning, some MS. side-linings at end, cont. cf. gt.; sigs. of Thomas Vane & Christopher Vane. [Wing V75] (S. Oct.11; 598) *Dann.* £140

VANEGAS, Alejo
- Primera Parte de las Differencias de Libros que ay en el Universo. Toledo, 1540. *1st. Edn.* 4to. Last lf. defect. & mntd., margin paper losses to title & prelims, crudely reprd., browned, 19th. C. cf.-bkd. bds. (SPB. Dec.13; 756) $600

VAN EVEN, Edward
- Louvain Monumental ou Description Historique et Artistique de Tous les Edifices Civils et Religieux de la Dite Ville. Louvain, 1860. 4to. 112 plts., foxing, hf. chagrin, corners, spine decor., some wear. (LM. Mar.3; 177) B.Frs. 14,000

VAN HASSELT, André
- Cérémonies et Fêtes qui ont Lieu à Bruxelles du 21 au 23 Juillet 1856 à l'Occasion du 25e Anniversaire de l'Inauguration de Sa Majesté le Roi Léopold 1er. Ill.:- Helbig, Simonau & Gerlier. Bruxelles, 1856. Lge. fo. Port. on china, plts. heightened with cols. 'à la gomme', some foxing, dampstain on last 7 plts., publisher's bds., worn. (LM. Mar.3; 19)
B.Frs. 11,000

VANITY FAIR
Ill.:- 'Ape', 'Spy', & others. Nov. 1868-Dec 1873. Vol. 1 pts. 3-10, in 9 vols. Sm. fo. 230 plts., orig. cl. gt. (PD. Apr.18; 213) £300
- - **Anr. Run.** Ill.:- 'Ape' & others. 1872-75. 3 vols. various. 4to. 78 cold. plts., lacks 1 title, orig. cl., soiled, w.a.f. (CSK. Aug.19; 112) £120
- - **Anr. Run.** Ill.:- 'Ape'. L., 1874. 6th. Series. Fo. Not collated, minor edge soiling, gt-decor., disbnd. (CBA. Jan.29; 472) $130
- - **Anr. Run.** Ill.:- 'Spy' & others. L., 1877. 9th. Series. Fo. Some minor soiling to edges, gt.-decor. cl., disbnd. (CBA. Jan.29; 473) $200

VANITY FAIR ALBUM (THE)
Ill.:- 'Ape'. 1874. Vol. 6 only. 4to. 52 cold. plts., orig. cl., worn, disbnd., w.a.f. (CSK. Apr.27; 9) £120
- - **Anr. Edn.** 1900. Vol. 32 only. Fo. 51 cold. plts., several detchd. orig. cl., worn, w.a.f. (CSK. Apr.27; 46) £240

VAN MARLE, Raimond
- The Development of the Italian Schools of Painting. N.Y., 1970. 19 vols. Orig. cl. (S. Apr.30; 233) *Mansueto.* £180
- - **Anr. Edn.** [N.Y., 1970]. Facs. Reprint of The Hague, 1923-38 edn. 19 vols. Orig. cl. (BBA. Apr.5; 88) *Zwemmer.* £80

VAN MIERIS, Frans
- Histori der Nederlandsche Vorsten. Gravenhage, 1732-35. 3 pts. in 1 vol. Fo. Gt.-decor. marb. cf., some wear. (LM. Oct.22; 282) B.Frs. 13,000

VAN NOOTEN, Berthe Hoola
- Fleurs Fruits et Feuillages Choisis De L'île de Java. Bruxelles, [1880]. *3rd. Edn.* Fo. 40 col. litho. plts., text in Fr. & Engl., liby. stp. on end-papers, orig. cl.-bkd. bds., torn & soiled. (P. Nov.24; 264) *Shapiro.* £1,050

VAN NOSTRAND, Jean
- San Francisco, 1806-1906 in Contemporary Paintings, Drawings & Watercolors. San Franc., 1975. (*500*). 4to. 53 plts., decor. cl. (CBA. Nov.19; 80) $150
- - **Anr. Copy.** 4to. Prospectus laid in, cl. (SG. Mar.29; 18) $100

VANNUCCI, A.
- Tableau Topographique et Medical de l'Ile de Corse. Bastia, 1838. Sewed. (HD. Oct.21; 173)
Frs. 1,100

VAN OFFEL, Horace
- Contes. Ill.:– Jean Brusselmans, Louis Buisseret, Anto-Carte, & others. Bruxelles, 1935. *(15)* numbered on 'japon blanc nacré', with suite of engrs. 4to. Proofs sigd. by artists, leaves, wrap., publisher's bd. s.-c. (LM. Mar.3; 40) B.Frs. 120,000

VAN PRAET, Joseph
- [–] Catalogue de Livres Imprimés sur Vélin. Paris, 1924-28. *(200).* 4 vols. Hf.-titles, later vell.-bkd. bds. (BBA. Mar.7; 267)
Folchi-Vici d'Arcevia. £70

VAN REGEMORTER, Berthe
- Oriental Bindings in the Chester Beatty Library. Dublin, 1961. 4to. Orig. cl.; H.M. Nixon coll. (BBA. Oct.6; 132) *Randall.* £70

VAN RENSSELAER, Mrs. John King
- The Devil's Picture Books. A History of Playing Cards. L., 1892. Three-qtr. mor.; 3 p. A.L.s. from author tipped to front end-paper. (RO. Dec.11; 335) $150

VAN RIEBEECK SOCIETY
- [Publications]. Cape Town, 1918-69. 1st. Series: Vols. 1-50. Cl. (SSA. Sep.21; 446) R 1,100

VAN URK, J.B.
- The Story of American Foxhunting. Derrydale Pr., 1940-41. *Ltd. Edn.* 2 vols. 4to. Orig. cl. gt. (P. Feb.16; 99) £140

VANVITELLI, Luigi
- [–] Dichiarazione dei Disegni del Reale Palazzo di Caserta. Naples, 1756. Lge. fo. Engraved title, 14 double-p. plts., mntd. on guards, old mott. cf. (C. Dec.9; 156) *Giunta.* £700

VAN VOGT, Alfred Elton
- Slan. Sauk City, 1946. *1st. Edn.* Slight darkening, bdg. not stated, d.-w. darkening, extremities rubbed; sigd., dtd. & inscr. to Ross Rocklin by author, 1976 Christmas card from Van Vogt sigd. & with A.N.s. laid in loose. (CBA. Oct.29; 861) $275
- - Anr. Copy. Bdg. not stated, d.-w. darkening, extremities rubbed & wearing, spine darkened, vol. extremities lightly rubbed. (CBA. Oct.29; 862)
$130

VAN WYK, P.
- Bome van die Nasionale Krugerwildtuin. Johannesburg, 1973. 2 vols. 4to. Orig. bdgs., d.-w.'s. (VA. Oct.28; 619) R 170
- Trees of the Kruger National Park. Cape Town, 1972. 2 vols. Orig. bdgs., d.-w.'s. (VA. Oct.28; 620)
R260
- - Anr. Copy. 2 vols. 4to. Orig. bdgs., d.-w.'s. (VA. Apr.27; 938) R 220

VARDY, John, Publisher
- Some Designs of Mr. Inigo Jones & Mr. Wm. Kent. L., 1744. Fo. Engraved title, 2 lf. engraved plt.-list, 53 plts., few slightly creased, 1 with sm. repair, anr. with sm. hole, cont. cf., rebkd. (C. Dec.9; 157) *Wood.* £450
- - Anr. Copy. Fo. Engraved pict. title-p., 53 engraved plts. (only 50 listed in the table of ills.), faint dampstains in a few margins, cont. cf., covers detchd.; 3 bkplts., including that of Prince Frederick Duleep Singh. (SKC. Sep.9; 1816) £250

VARENIUS, Bernhard
- Geographia Generalis ... Ed.:– Isaac Newton. Camb., 1681. *2nd. Edn.* Cont. panel. cf. (TA. Jan.19; 301) £76
- - Anr. Copy. Some margin dampstains, old cf., worn. (TA. Apr.19; 237) £52

VARGAS PONCE, J. de
- [–] Relación del Ultimo Viaje al Estrecho de Magallanes de la Fragata de S.M. Santa Maria de la Cabeza en los anos de 1785 y 1786. 1788-93. 2 vols. 4to. Titles reprd., cont. cf., slightly rubbed. (BBA. Jun.28; 258) *Brook.* £140

VARIGNON, Pierre
- Eclaircissemens sur l'Analyse des Infiniment Petits. Paris, 1725. *1st. Edn.* 4to. Cont. cf., spine gt., slight scuffing; Stanitz coll. (SPB. Apr.25; 434) $150
- Nouvelle Méchanique ou Statique. Paris, 1725. *1st. Edn.* 2 vols. 4to. Browned, cont. vell.; Liechtenstein bkplts., Stanitz coll. (SPB. Apr.25; 437) $325
- Nouvelles Conjectures sur la Pesanteur. Paris, 1690. *1st. Edn.* 12mo. Final blank lf. present, 2 ll. of Privilege & errata, cont. mott. cf., spine gt., some wear; pres. copy, inscr. 'ex dono authoris' on end-paper, Stanitz coll. (SPB. Apr.25; 435) $400
- Projet d'une Nouvelle Méchanique, avec un Examen de l'Opinion de M. Borelli, sur les Propriétez des Poids Suspendus par des Cordes. Paris, 1687. *1st. Edn.* 4to. 2 plts. dust-soiled, cont. mott. cf., spine gt., slight wear; Stanitz coll. (SPB. Apr.25; 436) $500
- Traité du Mouvement, et de la Mésure des Eaux Coulantes et Jaillissantes ... Ed.:– Abbé Pujol. Paris, 1725. *1st. Edn.* 4to. Slightly browned thro.-out, cont. Engl. spr. cf., spine gt., worn; from Marquess of Bute liby., early bkplt. of John Earl of Bute, Stanitz coll. (SPB. Apr.25; 438) $275

VARILLAS, Antoine de
- Histoire de Henry III. Paris, 1694. 4to. Old cf., decor. (HD. Feb.17; 13b) Frs. 1,520
- Histoire de Louis XII. Paris, 1688. 3 vols. 4to. Mor., Madame Victoire arms. (SM. Mar.7; 2052)
Frs. 5,000

VARIN, A. & E.
- L'Architecture Pittoresque en Suisse. Paris, 1861. Fo. 48 plts., some foxing, mod. crimson hf. mor. gt. (P. Jan.12; 190) *Nolan.* £100

VARNHAGEN, Francisco Adolpho de, Visconde de Porto Seguro
- [–] Historia Geral do Brazil. Rio de Janeiro, 1854-57. *1st. Edn.* 2 vols. 28 plts., maps, plans & facs., few folding, 3 p. 'Post Editum' & errata lf. at end Vol. I, lacks 1st. hf.-title, some foxing. *(Bound with:)* - Examen de Quelques Points de l'Histoire Géographique du Bresil. Paris, 1858. Qtr. mor., shelfmark on spines. (SG. Oct.20; 358) $250

VARRO, Marcus Terentius
- Opera Omnia. Dordrecht, 1619. 17th. C. cf. gt., gt. arms of Gedeon Tallemant des Reaux, 1619-92 on covers, spine a little defect. (BBA. Mar.21; 15)
Poole. £70

VARTHEMA, Ludovico di
- Itinerario ... nello Egitto ... Isole Nuouamente Trouate. Venice, [1550?]. Sm. 8vo. Mor. gt., by Lortic. [Sabin 98647] (S. May 21; 171)
Maggs. £1,300

VARTY, Thomas, Publisher
- Graphic Illustrations of Animals. Ca. 1850. Ob. fo. Title & list of plts., 21 hand-cold. plts., loose, 2 with margin tears, cl., worn. (P. Oct.20; 210)
£440

VASARI, Giorgi
- Die Lebensbeschreibungen d. beruhmtesen Architekten, Bildhauer u. Maler. Trans.:– Gottschewski, Gronau & others. Strassburg, 1904-27. 7 vols. in 9. Orig. hf. linen. (V. Sep.30; 1908) DM 500
- Lives of the Most Eminent Painters, Sculptors & Architects. Trans.:– G. de Vere. L., 1912-15. 10 vols. 4to. Buckram gt., untrimmed. (SKC. Mar.9; 1732) £240
- - Anr. Copy. 10 vols. 4to. Orig. cl. (BBA. Nov.10; 188) *Howes.* £100
- - Anr. Copy. 10 vols. Orig. cl., some light rubbing or marking. (KH. Nov.9; 491) Aus. $110
- - Anr. Edn. Ltd. Edns. Cl., 1966. *(1500)* numbered & sigd. by G. Mardersteig. 2 vols. 4to. Monthly newsletter laid in, buckram, d.-w.'s. (SG. Mar.29; 225) $150
- Le Vite de'piu Eccellenti Pittori, Scultori et Architetti. Bologna, 1647. Vols. I & II pt. 3 only, in 3 vols. 4to. 2 hf.-titles, lacks ptd. title in Vol. I, mod. qtr. cf., w.a.f. (S. Dec.13; 483)
Hetherington. £140
- - Anr. Edn. Milan, 1807-11. 16 vols. Hf. vell. gt.,

spines slightly dusty. (BBA. Jan.19; 362)
Duran. £60
- - Anr. Copy. 16 vols. Hf. vell. (CR. Jun.6; 306)
Lire 500,000

VASCONCELLOS, Antonio
- Anacephalaeoses id est, Summa Capita Actorum Regum Lusitaniae. Antw., 1621. 4to. Some staining, 18th. C. cf., gt. spine, new end-papers. (S. Oct.11; 423) *Hamery.* £130

VASI, Giuseppe A.
- Delle Magnificenze di Roma Antica e Moderna. Roma, 1753-56. Vols. 3-7 only (of 10), bnd. in 2. Fo. 5 frontis. with engrs., 124 engrs., light browning. hf. vell., 2 bd. covers reprd. (CR. Jun.6; 307)
Lire 3,500,000
- Itineraire Instructif de Rome Ancienne et Moderne. Rome, 1786. *5th. Edn.* 2 vols. 12mo. Cont. cf., 1 spine worn. (S. Dec.13; 181)
King. £50
- - Anr. Edn. Rome, priv. ptd., 1804. 2 vols. 12mo. On pale green paper, hf.-title, red bradel hf. mor. (SM. Mar.7; 2112) Frs. 1,300
- Itinerario Instruttivo diviso in Otto Giornate ... di Roma. Rome, 1777. 2 folding maps, 14 plts., 45 text engrs., some spotting, vell. (P. Apr.12; 189)
£85
- [–] Nuova Raccolta di Cento Principali Vedute Antiche e Moderne dell alma Citta di Roma. Rome, 1818. Ob. 4to. Engraved title & 100 plts., later hf. mor., worn, upr. cover detchd. (CSK. Jul.6; 115)
£140
- Raccolta della piu Belle Vedute Antiche e Moderne di Roma. Rome, priv. ptd., 1786. *[2nd. Edn.].* 2 vols. Fo. Engraved title vigs., 202 plts., including 1 dupl., plts. irregularly numbered, cont. hf. cf.; Castle Goring ex-libris. (C. Dec.9; 158)
Hammond. £2,800
- - Anr. Copy. 2 vols. Ob. 4to. 2 frontis. & 214 engraved plts., cont. bds. (CR. Jun.6; 308)
Lire 8,000,000

VASSAL, C. de
- Généalogies des Principales Familles de l'Orléanais. Table Analytique des Manuscrits d'Hubert. Orléans, 1862. Sewed. (HD. Mar.21; 126)
Frs. 1,100

VATTEL, Emerich von
- Le Droit des Gens ou Principes de la Loi Naturelle, appliqués à la Conduite et aux Affaires des Nations et des Souverains. L., 1758. *Orig. Edn.* 2 vols. 4to. Cont. roan. (HD. Feb.22; 224) Frs. 4,700
- - Anr. Copy. 2 vols. in 1. 4to. Lr. margin stained, cont. mott. cf., spine gt. (VS. Dec.9; 1175)
Fls. 475

VAUBAN, Sebastien le Prestre de
- De l'attaque et de la Defense des Places. Den Haag, 1737. *1st. Edn.* Early 19th. C. hf. leath., slightly bumped, jnts. partly brkn. (R. Apr.4; 2128)
DM 1,050
- Mémoires sur la Navigation des Rivières de France, Fragment des Mémoires de ... Pour être joint à la Carte des Rivières et Canaux ... Ed.:– Dupin-Triel. Map:– Dupin-Triel. Paris, 1781. *Orig. Edn. 1st.* Printing of Map. 4to. Map partly cold., mntd., cont. vell., cont. paper bd. s.-c., slightly worn. (HD. Nov.29; 77) Frs. 1,500
- Nouvelle Manière de fortifier. Paris, 1692. 2 pts. in 1 vol. 4to. In Fr. & German, linen, corners. (DS. Oct.28; 2161) Pts. 30,000
- Oeuvres. Amst., Leipzig, 1771. 3 vols. 4to. Cont. roan, scratched, decor. spines. (HD. Mar.14; 79)
Frs. 2,200
- Veritable Manière de bien Fortifier. Ed.:– Du Fay & Cambray. Amst., 1702. 1 or 2 clean tears, cont. cf., rubbed. (BBA. Nov.30; 58) *Duran.* £70

VAUCAIRE, Michel
- Barres Parallèles. Ill.:– T. Foujita. Paris, 1927. 4to. 5 orig. etchings, hf. pink mor., corners, wrap. (HD. Apr.11; 23) Frs. 7,800

VAUDOYER
See— METMAN & Vaudoyer

VAUGHAN, Henry, Silurist
- Poems. 1924. *(500). Our-of series copy.* Orig. ptd. bds., linen backstrip, untrimmed, slightly rubbed on corners. (TA. Jun.21; 602) £55

VAUGHAN, Henry, Silurist -*Contd.*

- **The Sacred Poems** ... Vale Pr., 1897. *(210).* Orig. cl., untrimmed, slightly soiled. (TA. Jun.21; 604) £55

VAUGONDY, Gilles Robert de & Didier Robert de
See— **ROBERT DE VAUGONDY, Gilles & Didier**

VAUX, James Hardy
- **Memoirs** ... L., 1819. 2 vols. (*Bound with:*) – **A New & Comprehensive Vocabulary of the Flash Language.** Bnd. at end of Vol. II of 1st. work. Together 2 works in 2 vols. 12mo. Cont. hf. cf. (C. Jun.27; 103) *Maggs.* £170
- – **Anr. Copy.** 2 vols. 12mo. Orig. bds., unc., slightly chipped, lacks part of 1 backstrip. (KH. May 1; 721) Aus. $160

VECELLIO, Cesare
- [–] **Corona delle Nobili et Virtuose Donne.** Venice, 1592. Pts. 1-3 in 1 vol. Ob. 4to. Ptd. title & dedication lf. to each pt., 80 woodcuts, cont. vell., linen ties. (SG. Apr.26; 119) $2,600
- [–] – **Anr. Edn.** Venice, 1625. Pts. 1-4 in 1 vol. Ob. 4to. Woodcut title & dedication lf. in each pt., 108 woodcut plts., some light wrinkling & foxing, cont. vell., sm. gt. device on cover, linen ties defect. (SG. Apr.26; 120) $3,000
- [–] – **Anr. Copy.** Pts. 1-4 in 1 vol. Ob. 4to. Woodcut title & dedication lf. in each pt., 108 woodcut plts., some light wrinkling & foxing, carelessly trimmed, cont. vell., sm. gt. device on cover, shabby, linen ties. (SG. Apr.26; 121) $950
- **Costumes Anciens et Modernes.** Paris, 1860. 2 vols. Cont. hf. chagrin, spines decor. (HD. Feb.28; 198) Frs. 1,250
- – **Anr. Copy.** 2 vols. On Chine, hf. mor., by Champs, unc., orig. wraps. bnd. in. (SI. Dec.15; 133) Lire 280,000
- **De Gli Habiti Antichi, et Moderni di Diverse Parti del Mondo Libri Due.** Venice, 1590. *1st. Edn.* 2 pts. in 1 vol. 19th. C. Jansenist red mor., gt. inner & outer dentelle, sigd. Trautz-Bauzonnet. (D. Nov.23; 149) DM 6,000
- [–] **Habiti Antichi et Moderni di Tutto il Mondo.** [Venice, after 1590]. Text & tables in Italian & Latin, 453 (of 456?) full-p. woodcut plts., lacks 3 ll. & at least 1 lf. before table, 3 ll. with sm. tears, some minor worming mostly in margins, a few repairs to margins, recent vell., spine gt., w.a.f. (C. May 30; 51) *Duran.* £480
- – **Anr. Edn.** Venice, [1598]. *[2nd. Edn.].* In Italian & Latin, lacks last 3 ll., title with early crude col. wash, some staining, 2 headings of title cropped, a few woodcut borders of ports. slightly cropped, hf. mor., rubbed, w.a.f. (P. Mar.15; 164) £680
- – **Anr. Copy.** Ills. with 1 text lf. in Italian & Latin, title with sm. holes & mntd., lr. margin extended, also 20 other ll. extended in margin, some spotting, wear & offsetting, cont. note, later vell. (H. Nov.23; 462) DM 2,000
- – **Anr. Edn.** Paris, 1860. 3 vols. Cl. (CR. Jun.6; 309) Lire 380,000

VEEN or VAENIUS, Otto van
- **Amoris Divini Emblemata.** Antw., 1614. Sm. 4to. 59 engraved plts., some carelessly numbered in ink in margin, cont. vell., soiled. (TA. Sep.15; 425) £90
- **Amorum Emblemata.** Antw., 1608. *1st. Edn.* Lightly browned in parts, 2 ll. with sm. margin tears, 1 lf. with long side margin tears, 18th./19th. C. leath., gt. inner dentelle. (R. Oct.11; 190) DM 1,700
- – **Anr. Copy.** Ob. 8vo. 18th. C. decor. mor., corners slightly worn. (LM. Mar.3; 134) B.Frs. 26,000
- **Emblemata, sive Symbola a Principibus, Viris Ecclesiasticis, ac Militaribus, Alisque Usurpanda.** Bruxellae, 1624. 4to. Trace of old dampstain, red hf. mor., corners, spine decor. (LM. Oct.22; 132) B.Frs. 10,500
- **Le Spectacle de la Vie Humaine.** Ed.:– Jean Le Clerc. Trans.:– Ph. von Zesen. Den Haag, 1755. 4to. Explanations in Dutch & Fr. (& German), cont. leath. gt. (D. Nov.23; 109) DM 1,500
- **Le Théâtre Moral ou la Vie Humaine.** Brüssel, 1678. *2nd. Edn. in Fr.* Fo. Light staining, slightly

browned, lacks supp. folding plt., cont. leath. gt., slightly worn & bumped, spine slightly defect. (R. Apr.3; 185) DM 440
- [–] **Theatro Moral de la Vida Humana.** Brussels, 1672. 3 pts. in 1 vol. Fo. Port., 103 copperplts, hf.-title, some foxing & light stains, disbnd. (SG. Feb.9; 363) $150
- [–] – **Anr. Edn.** Antw., 1701. Fo. Hf.-title, cont. spr. cf., gt. spine, head & foot of spine & corners worn. (S. Nov.17; 74) *Quaritch.* £300
- **Zinnebeelden, getrokken uit Horatius Flaccus.** Amst., 1683. Sm. 4to. Slightly browned thro.-out, cont. vell., soiled. (BBA. Feb.23; 24) *Weston.* £220

VEER, Gerrit de
- **Eersta Schip-vaert der Hollanderen nae de Oost-Indien door de Waygats, By-Noorden.** Amst., 1648. 4to. 2 double-p. maps, 6 double-p. plts., 19th. C. hf. leath., spine gt. (VG. Nov.30; 889) Fls. 950
- **Tre Navigationi fatti dagli Olandesi e Zelandesi al Settentrione.** Venice, 1599. Sm. 4to. Margin repairs to title & 1st. ll., without loss, lacks last blank, few stains, slightly browned, cont. vell. (VG. Sep.14; 1126) Fls. 1,200

VEGA, Cristobal de
- **Liber Prognosticorum Hippocratis coi Medicorum omnium faci le principis** ... Salamanca, 1552. *2nd. Edn.* Fo. Final (errata) lf. is hf.-p., no colophon (differing from Palau in both instances), some early annots. in margins & underlining in ink, disbnd., due to variations mentioned above, w.a.f. (C. Mar.14; 206) *Quaritch.* £150

VEGA CARPIO, Lope de
- **Las Comedias del Famosa Poeta** ... **recopiladas por Bernardo Grassa.** Milan, 1619. Vell. (DS. Nov.25; 2061) Pts. 120,000
- – **Anr. Copy.** Vell. (DS. Apr.27; 2287) Pts. 110,000
- **Isidro, Poema Casteliano en que se escrive la Vida del Bienaventurado Isidro, Labrador de Madrid y su Patron Divino.** Madrid, 1602. *2nd. Edn.* 12mo. 19th. C. mor., gt. decor., decor. spine. (HD. Dec.2; 115) Frs. 2,550
- **Pastores de Belen, Prosas y Versos Divinos.** Brussels, 1614. *5th. [1st. Brussels] Edn.* 12mo. With penultimate licence-lf. & final blank, some worming, few headlines shaved, corner torn from 2B1, cont. cf., rebkd.; Edward Wrey Whinfield bkplt. (S. Mar.20; 814) *Quaritch.* £190

VEGETIUS, Flavius Renatus
- **Fl. Vegetii Renati Viri Illustris de Militari Libri Quator** ... Paris, 1553. 4to. With the Charles Perier imprint, device of Christien Wechel on title & final pp., title-p. soiled & slightly stained, 2 sm. holes in margins, repair at foot, several ink notations, faintly discold. from damp thro.-out, ink marginalia on pp. 72-73, 18th./19th. C. panel. cf., gt.-stpd. with crest of the Earl of Ilchester, new end-papers, covers rubbed & scuffed. (CBA. Mar.3; 545) $550
- **De Re Militari Libri Quatuor, S. Julii Frontini de Strategematis Libri Totidem. Aeliani de Instruendis Aciebus Liber Unus. Modesti de Vocabulis Militaris. Liber Unus** ... Paris, 1535. *2nd. Edn.* Fo. 2 printers marks, some slight staining, cont. limp vell. (D. Nov.23, 150) DM 3,600

VEHSE, Eduard
- **Preussische Hofgeschichten.** Ed.:– H. Conrad. Ill.:– P. Renner. 1913. *(150) numbered De Luxe Edn. on Dutch Bütten.* 4 vols. Orig. red-brown mor., gt.-decor. (GB. Nov.5; 3095) DM 1,500
- – **Anr. Copy.** 4 vols. Orig. leath. gt., slightly rubbed & spotted. (H. Nov.24; 1292) DM 540

VEIGA, M. da
- **Relaçam Geral do Estado da Christiandade de Ethiopia** ... Lisboa, 1628. Vell., stained, slightly defect. (VG. Nov.30; 890) Fls. 800

VELAZQUEZ Y SANCHEZ, J.
- **Annales del Toreo.** Ed.:– Cuchares. Ill.:– T. Aramburu. Sevilla, 1868. Lge. fo. Linen. (DS. Mar.23; 2289) Pts. 100,000

VELDE, C.W.M. van de
- **Narrative of a Journey through Syria & Palestine in 1851-52.** 1854. 2 vols. Cont. hf. cf., spines rubbed. (TA. May 17; 21) £130

- **Le Pays d'Israel.** Paris, 1857. Lge. fo. Map & 100 litho. views (62 cold.), some plts. slightly foxed, 2 with some margin damage, orig. red hf. mor. (VG. Mar.19; 56) Fls. 5,600

VELDE, Jan van den
- **Exemplar-Boec.** Amst., 1607. Cold. & gold-heightened copper engraved title with figure cartouche, 24 (of 25) copperplts., title bkd. in margin, mod. hf. vell.; Hauswedell coll. (H. May 23, 228) DM 5,200
- **Spieghel der Schrijfkonste.** Rotterdam, 1605[-09]. *1st. Edn.* 3 pts. in 1 vol. Ob. fo. Some slight spotting, some ll. bkd. & reprd. in margins & gold, newer vell., ex-libris; Hauswedell coll. (H. May 23; 227) DM 6,200

VELIUS, Th.
- **Chronyk van Hoorn.** Ill.:– Goeree & Pool after Pronk, & others. Hoorn, 1740. *4th. Printing.* 4to. L.P., lacks port. of author & 2 plans, cont. marb. cf., spine gt., rebkd. (VS. Dec.9; 1299) Fls. 625

VELLOSO, Jose Marianno da Conceicao
- **Florae Fluminensis Icones nunc Primo Eduntur. editit Antonius da Arrabida.** Paris, 1827-35. 11 vols. Elephant fo. 11 litho. titles, 1,640 litho. plts., without text as usual, cf. (C. Jun.27; 187) *Studio Books.* £9,000

VELTHEM, L. van
- **Spiegel Historiaal, of Rym-spiegel; zynde de Ned. Rym-Chronyk.** Ed.:– I. Le Long. Amst., 1727. Fo. Cont. vell. (VG. Sep.14; 1064) Fls. 600

VENEGAS, Miguel
- [–] **Histoire Naturelle et Civile de la Californie.** Paris, 1767. 3 vols. 12mo. Hf.-titles, privilege lf. at end of Vol. 3, cont. wraps., unc. [Sabin 98843] (S. Dec.1; 301) *Sneyd.* £220
- **A Natural & Civil History of California.** L., 1759. *1st. Edn. in Engl.* 2 vols. Cont. cf., Vol. 1 rehinged, spines & extremities rubbed; the Rt. Hon. Visc. Eccles copy. [Sabin 98845] (CNY. Nov.18; 276) $150
- **Noticia de la California, y de su Conquista** ... **Hasta el Tiempo Presente. Sacade de la Historia Manuscrita.** Madrid, 1757. *1st. Edn.* 3 vols. 4to. 1 map bkd. with heavy paper, cont. mott. cf., gt. spines, 1 jnt. reprd.; the Rt. Hon. Visc. Eccles copy. [Sabin 98848] (CNY. Nov.18; 275) $800

VENICE
- **Il Gran Teatro di Venezia, Ovvero Raccolta delle Principali Vedute e Pitture che in essa si Contengono.** Ill.:– Zucchi & others, after Tiepolo, Manaigo, & others. [Venice, 1720]. 2 vols. Fo. 63 (of 65) views, 55 (of 57) engrs., titles defect., cf., covers detchd., as a coll. of plts., w.a.f. (P. Sep.8; 230) *Burgess.* £2,900
- **Itinerario Interno e delle Isole della Citta di Venezia.** Ill.:– A. Lazzari. [Venice], 1832. *2nd. Edn.* Ob. 8vo. Engraved additional title, frontis., 32 sepia aquatint views, some spotting affecting text, publisher's bds., upr. cover detchd. (S. Jun.25; 169) *Callea.* £120
- **Mémoire de Alcune Fabbriche e Situazioni di Venezia.** 1831. Sm. ob. 8vo. Hf. mor., wrap. preserved. (SM. Mar.7; 2113) Frs. 2,300

VENN, Thomas
- **Military & Maritine [sic] Discipline.** Ill.:– Faithorne (armorial frontis.). L., 1672. *1st. Edn.* 3 pts. in 1 vol. Fo. Slight margin worming, cont. cf., partly eroded, spine reprd. [Wing V192] (SG. Sep.22; 295) $600
- – **Anr. Copy.** Fo. Engraved frontis., additional title, 15 plts., upr. margin of frontis. neatly reprd., sm. section of 2 blank margins torn, cont. hf., rebkd. (CSK. Mar.9; 151) £320
- **Military Observations, or the Tacticks put into Practice, Collected & Composed for the Exercise both of Horse & Foot, to our Present Mode of Discipline.** 1672. Several pts. in 1 vol. Fo. Engraved frontis., additional engraved title, various separate title-pp. to the pts., 10 folding & 4 other engraved plts., 1 cropped, slight worming to inner margins thro.-out, cont. cf., very worn. (LC. Mar.1; 418) £90

VENNE, Adrian van de
– **Tafereel van de Belachende Werelt en desselfs Geluckige Eeuwe ... op de Haegsche Kermis.** Ill.:– D.v. Bremden & P. de Jode, after Venne. 's-Gravenhage, priv. ptd., 1635. 4to. Slightly browned (as usual), some minor margin stains, 19th. C. hf. vell.; Emile van Heurck bkplt. (VS. Dec.9; 1086)
Fls. 850
– – **Anr. Copy.** Sm. 4to. A few edges slightly dampstained, cont. vell. (CH. May 24; 31)
Fls. 800
– – **Anr. Copy.** 4to. Later hf. chagrin. (LM. Mar.3; 208)
B.Frs. 15,000

VENTENAT, Etienne Pierre
– **Choix de Plantes, done la plupart sont cultivées dans le Jardin de Cels.** Paris, 1803[-08]. Lge. fo. Some slight foxing, most in margin, stpd., cont. bds., bumped, spine & upr. cover loose, unc. (BR. Apr.12; 835)
DM 4,500

VENTOUILLAC, L.T.
– **Paris & its Environs.** Ill.:– Pugin & Heath. 1831. 4to. 2 vig. titles, 202 views on 101 sheets, hf. mor. gt. (P. Mar.15; 262)
Bookroom. £70

VENTURI, Giovanni Battista
– **Experimental Enquiries concerning the Principle of the Lateral Communication of Motion in Fluids.** L., 1799. 1st. Edn. in Engl. Cf.-bkd. bds.; E.N. da C. Andrade copy with bkplt., Stanitz coll. (SPB. Apr.25; 440)
$400
– **Recherches Expérimentales sur le Principe de la Communication Latérale du Mouvement dans les Fluides.** Paris, 1797. 1st. Edn. Upr. blank part of title-p. torn away & replaced, light foxing, mod. bds.; Stanitz coll. (SPB. Apr.25; 439)
$500

VENTURI, Lionello
– **Les Archives de l'Impressionisme.** Paris, 1939. (1000). 2 vols. Tall 8vo. Orig. wraps., untrimmed. (SG. Oct.13; 353)
$225
– **Cezanne: Son Art, Son Oeuvre.** Paris, 1936. (1000) numbered. 2 vols. Lge. 4to. 406 plts., ex-liby., ptd. wraps. (SG. May 3; 90)
$2,200
– **Jacques Villon.** Paris, 1962. (175) numbered on vélin d'Arches. Ob. 4to. 8 orig. cold. lithos., all sigd. by Villon, publisher's cl. bds. (HD. Jun.26; 161)
Frs. 12,000

VENUSWAGEN. Eine Sammlung Erotischer Privatdrucke.
Ed.:– A.R. Meyer. Ill.:– L. Corinth & others. 1919-20. (700) numbered. 1st. Series: Vols. 1-9 (all publd.). 4to. Printers marks sigd. by artist, 1 vol. sigd. by Meyer, 75 orig. ills., orig. hf. vell. (GB. May 5; 3427)
DM 3,600
– – **Anr. Edn.** Ed.:– A.R. Meyer. Ill.:– L. Corinth, O. Schoff, R. Janthur, & others. Berlin, [1919-20]. 1st. Series: Vols. I-IX (all publd.). 4to. All printers marks sigd. by artist, 72 partly cold. orig. ills., orig. hf. vell., minimal wear (With:) – **Prospektbuch.** Ill.:– L. Corinth. Berlin, 1919. Sm. 4to. Slightly spotted, 3 ll. loose, orig. wraps. (H. May 22; 1111a)
DM 4,000

VENUTI, Ridolfino
– **Accurata e Succinta Descrizione Topografica delle Antichita di Roma.** Ill.:– G.B. Piranesi & others. Rome, 1763. 1st. Edn. 2 pts. 4to. Titles with engraved ills., lge. folding map, 96 etched views, cont. marb. paper bds., partly unopened, unc., slightly rubbed, spines faded. (C. Mar.14; 17)
Pampaloni. £480
– – **Anr. Copy.** 2 vols. in 1. 4to. Hf.-titles, engraved vigs. on both titles, lge. folding plan, 96 plts., papal licence at end, short tear in folding map without loss of engraved surface, cont. cf., rebkd. (S. May 21; 249)
Lacquaforte. £320
– – **Anr. Copy.** 2 pts. in 1 vol. 4to. Hf.-title, roan, worn. (SM. Mar.7; 2053)
Frs. 5,000
– – **Anr. Edn.** Ill.:– after Piranesi, Duflos & others. Rome, 1803. 2nd. Edn. 2 vols. 4to. 1 lf. in Vol. 1 torn without loss, some stains, old decor. bds., linen backstrips, untrimmed, soiled & worn. (TA. Sep.15; 71)
£90
– – **Anr. Copy.** 2 vols. 4to. 65 engraved plts., staining, hf. cl., worn. (CR. Jun.6; 310)
Lire 850,000
– **Accurata e Succinta Descrizione Topografica e Istorica di Roma Moderna.** Ill.:– G.B. Piranesi &

others. Rome, 1766. 2 pts. 4to. Titles with engraved ill., 54 etched views, Vol. 1 with short tear to A3 & sm. hole to A4, M & Gg1, slightly affecting a few words, cont. marb. paper bds., partly unopened, unc., spines faded & with short tear to head. (C. Mar.14; 18)
Pampaloni. £600
– – **Anr. Edn.** Ill.:– G.B. Piranesi & others. Rome, 1767. 2 vols. in 4. 54 folding engraved plts., margin wormhole in Vol. 2, dampstain in Vol. 4, cont. vell., upr. cover of Vol. 1 stained. (C. Nov.16; 189)
Galleria Etching. £250
– **Collectanea Antiquitatum Romanarum ... exhibet A. Borioni.** Rome, 1736. Fo. Lacks 1 plt., slightly foxed, cont. vell., bumped & soiled, spine defect. (HK. Nov.9; 1500)
DM 520

VERA Y FIGUEROA, J.A. de
– **El Fernando o Sevilla restaurada.** Milán, 1632. 4to. Vell. (DS. Apr.27; 2632)
Pts. 50,000

VERANI, C.F.
– **Philosophia Universa Speculativa Peripatetica Principiis, ac Formalitatibus Metaphysicis Disputata.** Munich, 1684-86. 1st. Edn. 4 vols. in 2. Fo. Pts. 3 & 4 some light margin spotting, cont. blindtooled pig over wood bds., clasps. (R. Apr.3; 592)
DM 520

VERANTIUS, F.
[–] **Dictionarium Quinque Nobilissimarum Europae Linguarum, Latinae, Italicae, Germanicae, Dalmatiae, & Ungaricae.** Venice, 1595. 1st. Edn. 4to. Some ll. lightly browned, cont. limp vell., spine defect., lr. cover loose. (R. Apr.3; 97)
DM 900

VERCEL, Roger
– **Jean Villemeur.** Ill.:– Charles Fouqueray. Paris, 1946. (45) on vélin d'Arches. 4to. Suite of ills. in cols., 1 plt. in double state not repeated, leaves, wrap., box; with 2 orig. watercolours by Fouqueray. (HD. Mar.27; 116)
Frs. 2,100

VERDET, André
– **Pour un Nouveau Printemps de Pablo Picasso.** Nice, 1963. (79) with orig. Picasso col. litho. Picasso col. litho., sigd. & numbered. Loose as iss. in bdg. of grass paper over bds., leath. onlays; pres. copy from author, with an orig. sketch, photograph of Picasso by Andre Villiers. (SPB. Dec.13; 885)
$900

VERDIZOTTI, Giovanni Mario
– **Cento Favole Morali. De i piu antichi et Moderni Autori Greci e Latini.** Venice, 1577. 2nd. Edn. 4to. Some slight browning, 2 pp. missed in pagination, 18th. C. leath. gt., rubbed & slightly bumped. (R. Apr.3; 98)
DM 1,000

VERE, de
– **Petite Magie Blanche ...** Paris, ca. 1880. 16mo. Sewed, ill. wrap. (With:) – **Prestidigitation Moderne; Recueil de Tours de Physique Amusante.** Paris, ca. 1880. 12mo. Sewed. (HD. Feb.28; 93)
Frs. 1,500

VEREA Y AGUIAR, José
– **Historia de Galicia.** Ferrol, 1838. 4to. Cont. linen, corners. (DS. Apr.27; 2204)
Pts. 26,000

VERELIUS, Olaus (Ed.)
See— HERRAUDS OCH BOSA SAGA ...

VERFASSUNG DES DEUTSCHEN REICHS. Vom 11. August 1919
Ill.:– A. Simons. München, Bremer, Pr., 1929. (24) De Luxe Edn. on vell. Lge. 4to. Hand-bnd. orig. mor. gt. by Frieda Thiersch, decor., gt. decor. inside covers, vell. doubls. & end-papers. (H. Nov.23; 946)
DM 3,600

VERGA, Joseph Ibn
– **She'eirit Joseph.** Mantua, 1593. 2nd. Edn. 4to. Browned, slight staining, cl. (S. Oct.25; 407)
Berlin. £200

VERGE, W.G.
– **John Verge, his Ledgers & Clients.** Sydney, 1962. (250). No bdg. stated. (JL. Jun.24; 159b)
Aus. $170

VERGILIUS, Polydorus
– **Les Mémoires et Histoires de l'Origine, Invention et Autheurs des Choses ...** Trans.:– François de Bellefrest. Paris, 1682. Sm. 8vo. 18th. C. cf. gt.,

Prondre de Guermantes arms & cypher. (HD. Nov.29; 78)
Frs. 1,700
– **Proverbiorum Libellus.** Venice, 10 Apr. 1498. 1st. Edn. 4to. Lacks 1 lf. & last lf. blank, some slight spotting, some old MS. marginalia, later hf. leath. gt. [Goff V-147] (D. Nov.23; 152)
DM 1,300

VERGILIUS MARO, Publius
– **Aenis, Translated into Scottish Verse ... To which is added A Large Glossary Explaining the Difficult Words ... [by Thomas Ruddiman].** Edinb., 1710. Fo. Cont. panel. cf., rubbed; Sir Ivar Colquhoun, of Luss copy. (CE. Mar.22; 320)
£200
– – **Anr. Copy.** Fo. Title reprd., few margin repairs, mor. (SG. Apr.19; 72)
$175
– **Antiquissimi Virgiliani Codicis Fragmenta et Picturae ex Bibliotheca Vaticana.** Rome, 1741. Engraved title reprd., margins slightly dampstained, cont. vell., rubbed. (CSK. Jan.13; 222)
£95
– **Bucolica. Ecloga I-X.** Ill.:– R. Seewald. München, 1919. (300) numbered. Lge. fo. Minimal foxing, orig. bds., lightly bumped, spine defect. (HK. Nov.11; 4274)
DM 400
– **Bucolica et Georgica.** Ed.:– John Pine. L., 1774. Vol. 1 only. Ill., slight offsetting, cont. cf. gt., jnts. cracked & reprd., spine worn; James Boswell's copy with sig. & date 'London 1790', sig. of Thomas Nelson Page & bkplt. of Alfred Sutro. (SPB. May 16; 15)
$550
– **Bucolica, Georgica, Aeneis.** Commentaries:– Servius. Venice, 1507. Sm. 4to. Lf. AA present, several woodcuts crudely cold., 1 lf. in Aeneis torn with loss of letters, many cont. MS. annots., cont. stpd. pig, decor., traces of clasps; from Fondation Furstenberg-Beaumesnil. (HD. Nov.16; 181)
Frs. 2,200
– – **Anr. Edn.** Bg'ham., 1757. 1st. Baskerville Edn. 4to. On fine writing paper, earliest list of subscribers with only 4 names added, cont. cf. (C. Nov.9; 166)
Brooke-Hitching. £380
– – **Anr. Copy.** 4to. With 24 additional subscribers, few ll. slightly foxed, cont. red mor., covers with gt. border & cornerpieces, spine in 6 compartments; Thomas B. Stevenson copy. (CNY. Dec.17; 529)
$750
– – **Anr. Copy.** 4to. 1st. state. With only 4 additional subscribers, Gaskell's 'usual' cancels, 'arferae' on p. 134 unaltered & title with 'M' slightly damaged, extra-ill. with approx. 70 engrs. mntd. or inserted, lacks 1st. blank, early red str.-grd. mor. gt., dentelles. (SG. Apr.26; 15)
$550
– – **Anr. Edn.** Bg'ham., 1757. 2nd. Baskerville Edn. 4to. Browning, later crimson str.-grd. mor., ruled & tooled in gt. & blind; bkplt. of Sir Henry Campbell-Bannerman. (CSK. Aug.19; 40)
£50
– – **Anr. Edn.** Glasgow, Foulis Pr., 1778. 2 vols. in 1. Fo. Vell. gt. (P. May 17; 175)
Georges. £150
– – **Anr. Copy.** 2 vols. in 1. Sm. fo. Hf.-titles, early 19th. C. red mor.; armorial bkplt. of Earl of Cromer. (SG. Apr.19; 188)
$325
– **Bucolica, Georgica et Aeneis ex Cod. Mediceo-Laurentiano descripta ab Antonio Ambrogi Florentino ...** Rome, 1763. 3 vols. Fo. Hf.-titles, later 18th. C. Etruscan bdg. of black- & gt.-stpd. cf., worn. (S. Dec.20; 791)
Brown. £160
– **Bucolica zü Tütsch das Hirten vnnd Buren Werck der x. Eglogen.** Trans.:– [Joh. Adelphus, gen. Mülich]. [Strassburg], ca. 1510. 1st. German Edn. Fo. Lacks 2 ll. with 1 woodcut, title stpd., wormed, slightly stained & browned, 18th. C. hf. leath., rubbed & wormed, upr. cover defect. (HK. Nov.8; 373)
DM 5,500
– **Bucolics.** Ill.:– André Beaudin. Paris, 1936. (110) numbered & sigd. by artist. 4to. Loose as iss. in orig. wraps., bd. folder, s.-c. (BBA. Jun.14; 185)
Greenwood. £60
– **Die Eclogen.** Trans.:– R.A. Schroeder. Ill.:– Eric Gill & Aristide Maillol. Weimar, Cranach Pr., 1926. (250). Fo. Some pp. lightly foxed, bds., vell. tabs, ptd. paper wrap. darkened at edges. (CBA. Nov.19; 112)
$1,200
– – **Anr. Copy.** Lge. 4to. Some light foxing, handbnd. orig. red mor. gt., by O. Dorfner, spine faded; Hauswedell coll. (H. May 24; 733)
DM 6,800
– – **Anr. Edn.** Trans.:– R.A. Schroeder. Ill.:– A. Maillol & E. Gill. [Leipzig, Cranach Pr., 1926]. (36) roman-numbered on Kessler-Maillol Seiden-Bütten. (25) for Trade. 4to. With 2nd. series of

VERGILIUS MARO, Publius -Contd.

woodcuts ptd. red on old China in hf. vell. portfo., title woodcut monog. by Maillol, minimal brown spotting, hand-bnd. orig. red mor. gt. by O. Dorfner, Weimar, orig. hf. vell. portfo. (H. May 22; 1001)
DM 12,000

- **The Eclogues in the Original Latin with an English Prose.** Trans.:– J.H. Mason. Ill.:– A. Maillot & E. Gill (woodcuts). Weimar, Cranach Pr., 1927. *(225) numbered on MK-Bütten. (25), not for sale.* Lge. 4to. Orig. hf. linen, spine slightly darkened, unc. (HK. Nov.11; 3767)
DM 2,100

- **L'Eneide.** Trans.:– Annibal Caro. Ill.:– after Zocchi. Paris, 1760. *[1st. Edn.].* 2 vols. In Italian, errata lf., last privilege lf. in Vol. 2, lacks last blank in Vol. 1, some browning, cont. hf. cf., worn. (BBA. Mar.21; 22)
Soave. £70

- **– – Anr. Copy.** 2 vols. Lge. 8vo. Lge. copy, cont. stained mott. cf. gt., spines elab. gt., some wear; armorial bkplt. of Prince Talleyrand's Château de Valencay. (SG. Nov.3; 216)
$200

- **Georgicorum Libri quatuor. The Georgicks of Virgil.** Trans.:– John Martyn. 1741. 4to. Cold. ptd. botanical plts., hand-cold. maps & charts etc. (13 in all), cont. mott. cf., rebkd., gt.-decor. spine. (TA. Jun.21; 375)
£95

- **Les Georgiques.** Trans.:– Abbé Jacques Delille. Ill.:– Aristide Maillol. Paris, 1933-43 [1950]. *(750).* 2 vols. 4to. In Latin & Fr., some spotting, loose in orig. wraps. as iss., folders, publisher's boxes, some soiling of folders & boxes. (SPB. Dec.14; 65) $800

- **– – Anr. Edn.** Trans.:– Abbé Jacques Delille. Ill.:– Maillol. Paris, 1937-43. 2 vols. 4to. In Latin & Fr., vell. gt., decor., wraps. preserved, s.-c.'s. (HD. Nov.17; 199)
Frs. 7,800

- **– – Anr. Edn.** Trans.:– Abbé Jacques Delille. Ill.:– Aristide Maillol. Paris, 1937-50. *(750) numbered.* 2 vols. 4to. In Latin & Fr., unsewn in orig. wraps., unc., parch.-bkd. folders & s.-c.'s. (S. Nov.21; 99a)
Duschness. £520

- **– – Anr. Edn.** Trans.:– Michel de Marolles. Ill.:– A.D. d. Segonzac. Paris, 1947. *(250) numbered. (50) with extra suite of the etchings on velin de Rives in matching folder & case.* 2 vols. Fo. A few ll. spotted, unsewn in orig. wraps., unc., folders & s.-c.'s; inscr. by artist to J.F. Paulsen. (S. Nov.21; 116)
Rota. £2,500

- **– – Anr. Copy.** 3 vols., including plt. vol. Fo. 119 etchings, Vols. I & II foxed (plt. vol. not affected), leaves, wraps., box. (HD. Mar.27; 124)
Frs. 49,500

- **Les Oeuvres** ... Trans.:– M. L'Abbé des Fontaines. Ill.:– Cochin fils, engraved by Cochin père & fils. Paris, 1743. 4 vols. Cancel ll., some light spotting, browning & soiling, single wormhole through inner margin of Vol. I, cont. red mor. gt., decor. covers & spine, some soiling & rubbing. (SPB. Dec.14; 85)
$400

- **Opera.** [Venice], Antonio di Bartolommeo de Bologna (Miscomini), 1486 [but 1476]. Fo. Rubricated, initials painted in red, lacks last blank lf., some cont. MS. annots., cont. stpd. cf. over wood bds., decor., clasps incompl.; ex-libris of various periods on end-papers, including 'Charles par la divine clemence Empereur des Rommains', from Fondation Furstenberg-Beaumesnil. [BMC V, 240; Goff V167] (HD. Nov.16; 62)
Frs. 23,000

- **– – Anr. Edn.** Venice, 1519. Fo. Lacks title, all before a1 & 3f2-7, some slight dampstaining, a few headlines shaved, holes & repairs in 3f8 & a1 with loss of text, later hf. cf., rubbed. (S. Dec.20; 770)
Rix. £300

- **– – Anr. Edn.** Ed.:– John Ogilvy. Ill.:– W. Hollar & others. 1658. Fo. Map cleanly torn, dampstained thro.-out, a few clean tears, margins of last few ll. wormed, old cf., worn, w.a.f. (CSK. Jul.13; 55)
£150

- **– – Anr. Edn.** Commentary:– Carolus Ruaeus. Parisiis, 1675. 4to. Cont. red mor. gt., spines decor. (HD. May 3; 164)
Frs. 1,100

- **– [-] Anr. Edn.** Amst., 1744. 16mo. Str. grd. mor., gt. tooled spine & covers, corners slightly bumped, by Simier. (BS. May 2; 34)
£85

- **– – Anr. Edn.** Ed.:– Gilbert Wakefield. L., 1796. 2 vols. Lge. 8vo. L.P., maroon mor., gt.-tooled borders & spine; 3 1/8 p. MS. by Christopher Wordsworth, sigd. & dtd. 1825, bnd. in. (SG. Feb.9; 366)
$200

- **– – Anr. Edn.** Ed.:– C.G. Heyne. Lipsia, 1800. 6 vols. Some browning & staining, unc., cont. long-grd. red mor., spine recent decor. (SI. Dec.15; 135)
Lire 400,000

- **Opera Omnia.** L., Medici Soc., 1912. *(525) numbered.* 2 vols. Vell., ribbon ties, s.-c. (LH. Sep.25; 568)
$150

- **L'opere ... cioe la Buccolica, Georgica & Eneida** ... Venice, 1586. Headpiece & device on title, many woodcut text ills., few stains, damp-wrinkled, mod. vell. (SG. Apr.19; 184)
$220

- **The Pastorals.** Ed.:– R.J. Thornton. Ill.:– W. Blake. 1821. *3rd. Edn.* 2 vols. 6 plts., 3 maps, 221 woodcuts, title of 1 plt. obscured by bdg., some spotting & offsetting from plts., mod. mor. gt. (P. Feb.16; 191)
£1,400

- **Publii Vergilii Maronis Opera, Bucolica, Georgica, Aeneis.** Ill.:– Graily Hewitt. Chelsea, Ash. Pr., 1910. *(48). (40) on Japanese paper.* 4to. Initial capitals in gold, red & blue, many blue & red paragraph marks, orig. vell., untrimmed, leath. ties; Mrs. Miles Hornby copy. (CNY. Dec.17; 528)
$2,200

- **Die Twaelf Boecken van Aeneas, ghen. Aenidos.** Trans.:– Cornelis van Ghistele. Antw., 1583. *1st. Compl. Edn.* Margins of 3 ll. defect., 2 with loss of text, inner margins of last ll. reprd., some stains, cont. vell.; V. de la Montagne bkplt. (VG. Nov.30; 704)
Fls. 1,000

- **Vergilius [Opera].** Venice, Apr. 1501. *1st. Aldine Edn.* Capital spaces with guide letters, slight worming to 1st. 5 & last 2 ll. (the holes filled), affecting some 30 letters, some staining from early pen flourishes thro.-out, some dampstaining & other stains, slight sealing wax spots between H4v & H5, N2v & N3, & O8v & Pl, G6v with stains & 2 minor abrasions affecting 4 words, g8 torn & reprd., mor. gt. by C. Kalthoeber, with his ticket, spines gt. & gt.-lettered in 6 compartments, marb. linings; George John, 2nd. Earl Spencer & Michael Wodhull copy, with sig. & notes of the latter on 1st. fly lf., Brayton Ives & Junius Spencer Morgan bkplts. (CNY. May 18; 85)
$60,000

- **The Works.** Trans.:– John Ogilby. L., 1654. Fo. Port.-frontis., extra frontis., double-p. map, 105 plts., a few minor repairs & stains, early qtr. cf., worn. (SG. Feb.9; 367)
$300

- **– – Anr. Edn.** Trans.:– John Ogilby. Ill.:– Lombart after Cleyn. L., priv. ptd., 1668. *2nd. Edn.* Fo. 100 full-p. copperplts., title mntd., some plts. trimmed & inlaid, last lf. inlaid, mod. mott. cf., gt. centrepiece, gt.-panel. spine, gt. dentelles, by Bayntun, w.a.f. (SG. Feb.16; 320)
$275

- **– – Anr. Edn.** Trans.:– John Dryden. L., 1698. *'2nd. Edn.'.* Fo. Engraved frontis. (trimmed), 101 engraved plts., slightly browned & soiled thro.-out, a few margin tears, mod. hf. mor. [Wing V617] (BBA. Nov.30; 205)
Snelling. £110

- **– – Anr. Copy.** Fo. Stained, hf. cf., corners, cont. fore-e. pntg. of Bay of Naples. (CR. Jun.6; 214)
Lire 800,000

VERGNAUD, N.

- **L'Art de créer les Jardins.** Priv. ptd., 1835. Fo. Foxing, hf. russ. (HD. Jun.6; 151)
Frs. 2,200

VERHAEREN, Emile

- **Belle Chair.** Ill.:– Volti. Paris, 1964. *Numbered on vélin de Hollande.* Lge. 4to. Leaves, ill. wrap., box. (HD. Jun.26; 165)
Frs. 1,700

- **James Ensor.** Bruxelles, 1909. *Orig. Edn.* No bdg. stated. (HD. May 11; 127)
Frs. 1,000

- **Les Plaines.** Ill.:– H. Cassiers. Paris, 1934. *(100) numbered on japon impérial with double state of ills.* Sm. 4to. Vermillion hf. mor. gt., corners, by Randeynes, unc., ill. wrap. & spine. (HD. Jun.26; 163)
Frs. 1,800

VERHEIDEN, Jacobus

- **Praestantium Aliquot Theologorum, qui Rom. Antichristum praecipuè oppugnarunt, Effigies.** Ill.:– H. Hondius. The Hague, 1602. Lge. 8vo. An incompl. work bnd. at end, cont. vell. (VG. Nov.30; 996)
Fls. 550

VERHEYEN, Phil.

- **Anatomiae Corporis Humani.** Köln, 1713. 2 pts. in 1 vol. 4to. Title stpd., minimal browning, cont. vell. (HK. May 15; 547)
DM 1,400

VERINI, Giovanbattista

- **Luminario, Seu de Clementis Libri IV.** N.p., n.d. *1st. Edn.* 4to. Cut close in places, some spotting & wear, old cf., reprd.; Hauswedell coll. (H. May 23; 211)
DM 8,400

VERLAINE, Paul

- **Amour.** Paris, 1888. *1st. Edn. (600).* Sm. 8vo. Hf. mor. & marb. bds., spine gt., partly unc., orig. ptd. wraps., including spine, preserved, by Gemet & Plumelle; Frederic Dannay copy. (CNY. Dec.16; 361)
$120

- **La Bonne Chanson.** Ill.:– E. Carlègle. Paris, 1927. *(12) numbered & monogrammed on China.* With supp. series of ills., long-grd. mor., by Paul Bonet, gold & silver decor., hand-made paper end-papers, silver spr., s.-c., orig. wraps. bnd. in. (D. Nov.23; 177)
DM 4,500

- **Choix de Poësies.** Ill.:– Eugene Carrière (port.). Paris, 1891. *(10) on Japon.* Mor. gt. by G. Levitsky, mosaic decor., mor. doubls., painted silk end-ll., edges untrimmed, wrap. & spine, box. (HD. Nov.29; 123)
Frs. 8,200

- **Epigrammes.** Paris, 1894. *Orig. Edn.* Hf. mor., corners, wrap. preserved. (HD. Jun.13; 106)
Frs. 1,400

- **Femmes; Hombres.** Ill.:– Michael Ayrton. Douglas Cleverdon, 1972. *(100) numbered & sigd. by artist.* 1 vol. Orig. mor.-bkd. marb. bds.; inscr. by Cleverdon 'For Ronald & Peggy Kinsey, prospectus & an invitation to a private view loosely inserted. *(With:)* AYRTON, Michael – **Fifteen Etchings Illustrating Femmes/Hombres by Paul Verlaine.** Douglas Cleverdon, [1972]. *(20) roman-numbered with sigd. proof plts. on white japon.* 1 vol. Ob. fo. Unbnd. as iss. in unif. mor.-bkd. portfo., both vols. together in s.-c. (S. Nov.21; 175)
Desk. £850

- **Fêtes Galantes.** Paris, 1869. *Orig. Edn. (350) on papier vergé de Hollande.* 16mo. Without blank ll., red hf. mor., corners, by Huser, wraps. preserved. (HD. Sep.22; 365)
Frs. 2,400

- **– – Anr. Edn.** Paris, 1920. *Facs. Edn.* Sm. 4to. 18th. C. style red mor. gt. by Franz, spine decor., watered silk liners & end-ll., wrap., hf. mor. folder, s.-c.; 26 orig. watercols. by Louis Icart, autograph poeme by Louis Icart, sigd. & dtd. 3 Sep. 1929, on last lf., Madame Fanny Icart ex-libris. (HD. May 21; 160)
Frs. 42,000

- **– – Anr. Edn.** Ill.:– P. Laprade. Paris, 1928. Sm. fo. On vell. de Rives, 3 orig. pen sketches, sewed. (HD. Mar.14; 157)
Frs. 2,000

- **– – Anr. Edn.** Corvinus Pr., Oct. 1944. *Fr. Edn. (37) numbered.* Qtr. cf., case. (HBC. May 17; 204)
£75

- **Jadis et Naguère. Poésies.** Paris, 1884. *Orig. Edn.* 12mo. Glazed cf., gt. inner decor., wtrd. silk doubl. & end-papers, unc., wrap. & spine, hf. cf. s.-c. & box, by Franz; sigd. autograph dedication from author. (HD. Mar.14; 156)
Frs. 4,600

- **Odes en son Honneur.** 1893. *Orig. Edn.* 12mo. Cont. hf. mor., corners. (HD. Apr.13; 140)
Frs. 1,600

- **Oeuvres Complètes.** Ill.:– Berthold Mahn. Paris, 1932. 8 vols. 4to. Hf. chagrin, corners, wraps. preserved. (HD. Nov.17; 187)
Frs. 2,150

- **Parallèlement.** Ill.:– Edouard Chimot. Paris, 1931. *(40) on japon impérial, with etchings in 3 states & orig. sketch.* 4to. Jansenist red mor. gt. by Semet & Plumelle, wrap. preserved, s.-c.; extra-ill. with 2nd. drawing in col. pencils & copper engr. inserted in s.-c. (HD. Jun.13; 108)
Frs. 12,800

- **– – Anr. Edn.** Ill.:– Edouard Chimot. Paris, 1931. *(110) on vélin de Rives.* 4to. 23 orig. eaux-fortes, each in 2 states, 1 cold., elab. plum mor., decor. gt. & black, slight fading of spine, open-bkd. s.-c.; pres. copy to Madame Paul Boyer from Chimot, with orig. charcoal drawing by Chimot bnd. in. (SPB. Dec.14; 56)
$2,100

- **– – Anr. Edn.** Ill.:– M. Vertès. Paris, 1954. *Edition De Grand Luxe, (119). (12) on japon nacré, with orig. drawing sigd. by artist, 2 suites in black & bistre, & 1 suite of 26 'rejected' plts.* Lge. 4to. 30 orig. lithos., publisher's box, d.-w., s.-c. (HD. Apr.26; 292)
Frs. 4,000

- **– – Anr. Edn.** Ill.:– Leonor Fini. Paris, 1969. *Numbered on vélin de Rives, sigd. by publisher & artist.* Lge. 4to. Leaves, ill. parch. wrap., box. (HD. Jun.26; 166)
Frs. 4,100

– – **Anr. Edn.** Ill.:– Lobel-Riche. N.p., n.d. 4to. On vell. d'Arches, leaves, wrap., s.-c. (HD. Dec.1; 53)
Frs. 1,500

– – **Anr. Edn.** Ill.:– Lobel-Riche. Paris, n.d. *De Luxe Edn., (230) numbered.* Fo. Double series of etchings on Jap., series on vell., both with remarks, 1 sigd. sanguine prelim. ill., printers mark numbered & sigd. by artist, his MS. dedication on title, orig. wraps., bd. s.-c., defect. (HK. Nov.11; 3742)
DM 2,500

– **Poèmes Saturniens.** Paris, 1866. *1st. Edn. (491).* Sm. 8vo. Hf. mor. & marb. bds., unc., orig. ptd. wraps. preserved, by V. Champs; Leon Vanier copy, with sig., Frederic Dannay copy. (CNY. Dec.16; 360)
$650

– **Poésies.** Ill.:– Robert Bonfils, Drovart, Quint, Paul Baudier, Picart Ledoux & others. 1914-27. *(50) on japan, with suite 'au trait' (except 'La Bonne Chanson': (500) on vell.).* 18 vols. Sewed. (HD. Apr.13; 146)
Frs. 1,850

– **Sagesse.** Paris, Bruxelles, 1881. *Orig. Edn.* Lacks 2 blank ll., jansenist maroon mor., by Alix, gt. inner dentelle, wrap., s.-c.; autograph dedication. (HD. Dec.16; 198)
Frs. 7,000

– – **Anr. Edn.** Ill.:– Hermine David. Paris, 1943. *(50) with suite in black & suite in col., & orig. sketch.* Cf. by Creuzevault, mosaic ills. after watercol. by Hermine David, watered silk liners & end-ll., folder, s.-c.; extra-ill. with orig. watercol. (HD. Jun.13; 107)
Frs. 15,800

– – **Anr. Copy.** Leaves, pict. wrap., box. (HD. Dec.16; 202)
Frs. 1,050

– – **Anr. Edn.** Ill.:– Hermine David. Paris, 1943. 4to. On Arches, suite in cols., old pink mor. gt., silk end-ll., s.-c. (HD. Nov.17; 191)
Frs. 1,250

VERLAINE, Paul (Contrib.)
See— GIL BLAS ILLUSTRE

VERNE, Jules
– **Bekannte u. Unbekannte Welten. Abenteuerliche Reisen.** Wien etc., 1874-83. *De Luxe Edn.* Pts. 1-3, 6-10, 17-21, 24-25 & 27-40, in 21 vols. Foxed, orig. linen (2) & hf. linen, ca. 1900 (19), w.a.f. (HK. Nov.10; 3006)
DM 800

– **Novelas.** 19th. C. 8 vols. Fo. Cl., orig. wraps. (DS. Apr.27; 2416)
Pts. 24,000

– **Voyages et Aventures du Capitaine Hatteras au Pôle Sud. Michel Strogoff.** Ill.:– Riou (1st. vol.), Ferrat (2nd. vol.). Paris, ca. 1907 & 1909. 2 vols. Publishers polychrome bds. (HD. Dec.9; 192)
Frs. 1,400

– **Voyages Extraordinaires.** Paris, ca. 1919-26. *Hetzel Edn.* 28 vols. Lge. 8vo. Orig. decor. cl. gt., spines faded, a few vols. slightly soiled. (S. Dec.20; 638)
Fletcher. £110

– – **Anr. Edn.** Paris, n.d. 7 vols. Some vols. foxed, polychrome bds., 6 'au portrait' collé & 1 ptd. 'au portrait', lighthouse spine. (HD. Mar.14; 171)
Frs. 1,550

– **Works.** Ed.:– Charles F. Horne. N.Y., [1911]. *Edition de L'Académie. (300).* 15 vols. Imitation leath., gt.-ruled, partly untrimmed, minor cover nicks, mainly to spine ends; some plts. sigd. by aquatinter. (CBA. Oct.29; 871)
$150

– – **Anr. Edn.** Ed.:– Charles F. Horne. N.Y. & L., n.d. & 1911. *'Edition Couronnee'. (50) numbered.* 15 vols. Lev. mor., covers with triple gt.-ruled borders & red onlaid mor. gt. ornaments, gt. onlaid spines in 6 compartments, turn-ins gt., watered silk linings, partly unc. (CNY. Dec.17; 610) $2,200

VERNET, Carle
– **Campagnes des Français sous le Consulat et l'Empire.** Paris, ca. 1840. Fo. Lacks frontis., some stains, publisher's buckram, imperial arms, lr. cover stained. (HD. Feb.29; 48)
Frs. 2,700

– – **Anr. Edn.** Ill.:– after Vernet & Swebach. Paris, n.d. 60 plts., in sheets, publisher's cl. bds., special tools, faded. (LM. Mar.3; 32)
B.Frs. 22,000

– **Cris de Paris.** Paris, [1820-22]. *1st. Edn.* Fo. Wide margin, lacks 1 ptd. title lf. (?), 100 lithos. & added series in col., all plts. sigd. & numbered in stone, 2 misnumbered ll. corrected in MS. in 1st. suite, a few short pasted margin tears, some light browning & spotting, cont. red hf. mor., gt., rubbed, corners bumped; Hauswedell coll. (H. May 23; 105)
DM 14,500

– **Vernet's Horses, Containing a Selection of Forty Interesting Subjects. In Lithography by E. Purcell.**

L., 1822. Ob. 4to. 40 litho. plts., foxing, browning & some spotting, red hf. mor., scraped, rubbed. (SPB. Dec.14; 86)
$500

VERNET, Horace
– **Voyage ... en Orient.** Ed. & Ill.:– Goupil-Fesquet. Paris, [1843]. Some foxing, cont. hf. chagrin, spine decor. (HD. May 4; 445)
Frs. 1,500

VERNEUIL, Ad. & M.-P.
– **Kaleidoscope: Ornements Abstraits ...** Paris, 1920's. Fo. 20 plts., loose as iss., pochoir-cold. by Saude, cl.-bkd. bd. folder. (SG. Aug.25; 321) $320

VERNIER, Charles
– **Costumes de l'Armée Française.** Paris, [1845]. Ob. 4to. 60 litho. plts., 'gommées', hf. roan. (HD. Jan.27; 316)
Frs. 2,500

VERNIER, Emile
– **La Bijouterie et la Joaillerie-Egyptiennes.** Cairo, 1907. Sm. fo. 25 plts., 200 text ills., ex-liby., red hf. mor. (SG. May 3; 367)
$325

VERNON, Robert
– **The Vernon Gallery of British Art.** [1850-51]. *Subscriber's Edn.* Vols. 1 & 3 only. 48 ports. & steel engrs., all on India paper, most sigd. in pencil to margin by engravers, each with blind stp. of Printsellers Association, some spotting, cont. hf. mor. gt. (TA. Aug.18; 291)
£150

VERONA
– **Descrizione di Verona e della sua Privincia.** Verona, 1820-21. 2 vols in 1. 33 (of 35) engraved plts. (1 folding), some ll. spotted, later hf. mor., rubbed. (BBA. Feb.9; 322)
Erlini. £80

VERSCHAFFELT, A.
[–] **Nouvelle Iconographie des Camellias.** Ill.:– G. Severeys. [Gand, 1850]. 48 old cold. litho. plts., old pencil numbered, lr. end-paper with MS. index, lightly browned, cont. hf. leath., lightly rubbed & bumped. (HT. May 8; 317)
DM 1,900

VERSTEGEN, Richard
[–] **Theatrum Crudelitatum Haereticorum Nostri Temporis.** Ill.:– J. Wiericx. Antw., 1587. 4to. Outer margins slightly short, sometimes affecting ptd. marginalia, 19th. C. mor. by Hayday & Mansell. (VG. Nov.30; 997)
Fls. 650

VERSTER VAN WULVERHORST, A.H.
See— SCHLEGEL, Hermann & Verster van Wül-verhorst, A.H.

VERTES, Marcel
– **Dames Seules.** Preface:– Carco. Paris, 1932. *(52) with 15 orig. lithos.* Fo. Orange hf. mor., corners. (HD. Nov.17; 194)
Frs. 2,500

– **L'Heure Exquise.** Paris, 1920. *(200) numbered & sigd. by artist.* 4to. 20 sigd. orig. etchings, orig. hf. linen portfo., ties. (GB. May 5; 3433)
DM 950

VERTOONINGEN
Leyden, [1864]. 4to. Moving picture book, 8 hand-cold. ills., 1 sm. tear reprd. with tape, orig. cl.-bkd. pict. bds.; D. Wouter bkplt., van Veen coll. (S. Feb.28; 291)
£210

VERTOT, René Aubert de
– **Histoire des Chevaliers Hospitaliers de S. Jean de Jerusalem.** Paris, 1726. 4 vols. 4to. Engraved frontis., 6 maps & plans, 70 port. plts., some ll. discold. or a bit spotted, cont. cf., somewhat worn, spines gt. (S. Oct.11; 424)
Booth. £260

– – **Anr. Copy.** 4 vols. 4to. Added port. of Saint Anne de Geneuillac, cont. cf., arms in centre of covers, decor. spines. (HD. Sep.22; 366)Frs. 3,100

– – **Anr. Copy.** 4 vols. 4to. Some slight foxing, cont. spr. cf., decor. spine, some defects. (HD. Dec.9; 88)
Frs. 2,800

– **The History of the Knights of Malta.** L., 1738. 2 vols. Fo. Largest paper (Lowndes states that only 25 copies were ptd.), engraved frontis. port., 2 plans, 3 lge. folding maps, 70 engraved ports., cont. panel. cf. (C. Nov.9; 165)
Marlborough. £650

– **The History of the Revolutions in Spain.** Trans.:– J. Morgan. L.,1724. 5 vols. Cont. panel. cf. (*With:*)
– **The History of the Revolution in Sweden ...** Glasgow, 1750. 1 vol. 12mo. Cont. spr. cf. (*With:*)
– **The History of the Revolutions of Portugal.** Glasgow, 1750. 1 vol. Cont. cf., spine gt. Together

7 vols. Sir Ivar Colquhoun, of Luss copies. (CE. Mar.22; 318)
£150

VERTUE, George, Editor
– **A Catalogue & Description of King Charles the First's Capital Collection of Pictures, Limnings, Statues ...** L., 1757. 4to. Some gatherings detchd. from bdg., cont. cf., defect. (S. Apr.30; 97)
Heneage. £110

[–] **Description of the Works of the most Ingenious Delineator & Engraver Wenceslaus Hollar.** L., 1745. *1st. Edn.* 4to. All engrs cut to plts., 5 with sm. margin slits, some slight foxing, 19th. C. mor. gt., slightly rubbed & loose. (R. Apr.4; 1987)
DM 430

– **Medals, Coins, Great Seals, & other works of Thomas Limon: engraved & described.** 1780. *2nd. Edn.* 4to. Engraved dedication, 40 engraved plts., cont. tree cf., spine gt.; Sir Ivar Colquhoun, of Luss copy. (CE. Mar.22; 319)
£200

VERULAM, Sir Francis Bacon, Baron
See— BACON, Sir Francis, Baron Verulam

VERVE, Revue Artistique et Literaire
Paris, 1937-38. Nos. 1-3. Tall 4to. Cold. pict. wraps. (SG. Jan.12; 346)
$140

– – **Anr. Run.** Ill.:– after Chagall, Derain, Klee, Leger, Matisse, Miro, & others. 1937-38. Nos. 1-4. Fo. Engl. text, orig. decor. wraps. (S. Nov.21; 128)
Eliopoulos. £140

– – **Anr. Run.** Paris, 1937-39. Nos. 1, 3 & 5/6. Tall 4to. Cold. pict. wraps. (SG. Jan.12; 347)
$150

– – **Anr. Run.** Ill.:– after Leger, Miro, Rattner, Borès, Kandinsky, Masson, Chagall, Klee, Derain, Matisse. 1937-43. Nos. 1-7 & 9, together 7 vols. Fo. Orig. wraps., 1st. 4 in cl.-bkd. folder & s.-c., last 3 slightly worn. (S. Apr.30; 234)
O'Neill. £240

– – **Anr. Run.** Ill.:– Bonnard, Braques, Chagall, Kandinsky, Klee, Matisse, Miro, Rouault & others. Paris, 1937-48. Nos. 1-22 (lacks no. 10) in 16 vols. 4to. Orig. bdgs., some defects. (BR. Apr.13; 1896)
DM 6,000

– – **Anr. Run.** Ill.:– by or after Bonnard, Braque, Chagall, Derain, Leger, Matisse, Miro, Picasso, & others. Paris, 1937-60. Nos. 1-38 (compl.), in 26 vols. 4to. Engl. text in nos. 1, 3, 4, 5/6, 8, 31/32 & 35/36, nos. 9-12 bnd. in 1 cl. vol. as iss., with decor. wraps. bnd. in, rest in orig. wraps. or bds. (S. Nov.21; 126)
Grandini. £4,500

– – **Anr. Run.** Ill.:– Kandinsky, Masson, Chagall, Miro, Klee, Matisse, & Derain (lithos.). Paris, Mar.-Jun. 1938 & Jan.-Mar. 1939. Nos. 2-4. Fo. Engl. & Fr. text, some margin darkening, some light water damage to some margins & upr. cover, cl., covers slightly rubbed, orig. upr. wraps. bnd. in. (CBA. Jan.29; 477)
$200

– – **Anr. Run.** Ill.:– after Chagall, Braque, Matisse, Giacometti, Leger, Miro & others. Paris, 1951. Nos. 27 & 28. Fo. Orig. pict. bds., spine darkened. (HT. May 9; 2078)
DM 980

– – **Anr. Edn.** Ill.:– Braque, Matisse, Laurens, Masson, Léger, Miro, Chagall. Paris, [1952]. Nos. 27 & 28. Fo. Orig. pict. bds. (HK. May 17; 3201)
DM 1,100

– – **Anr. Edn.** Text:– Camus & others. Ill.:– Braque & others. Paris, [1953]. Nos. 27 & 28. 4to. Margins lightly browned, orig. pict. bds., browned, margin tears. (H. May 23; 1545)
DM 1,800

– – **Anr. Run.** Ill.:– Picasso. Paris, 1954. No. 29/30. 4to. Orig. bds. (BBA. Apr.5; 92)
Callea. £80

– – **Anr. Copy.** Nos. 29 & 30. Fo. Orig. pict. bds. (GB. May 5; 3095)
DM 650

– – **Anr. Run.** N.d. & 1939. Nos. 3, 5 & 6. 4to. Orig. pict. wraps. (P. Apr.12; 35)
Frankel. £70

– **Carnets intimes de G. Braque.** Paris, 1955. No. 31/32. (*With:*) – **Dernières Oeuvres de Matisse, 1950-1954.** Paris, 1958. No. 35/36. Together 2 vols. Fo. Orig. decor. bds. (SPB. Nov.30; 356)
$300

– **Les Très Riches Heures du Duc de Berry.** Paris, [1943]. No. 10. Fo. Mor., orig. paper covers trimmed & bnd. in. (LH. Sep.25; 614)
$325

VESALIUS, Andreas
– **De Humani Corporis Fabrica.** Lugduni, 1552. Books I & II only, in 1 vol. Sm. 16mo. Cont. vell., detchd. (LM. Oct.22; 268)
B.Frs. 22,000

– – **Anr. Copy.** Ill.:– Jean de Calcar. Basle, 1555.

VESALIUS, Andreas -*Contd.*

3rd. [2nd. Ill.] Edn. Fo. Port. of author dtd. 1542, late 18th. C. roan, spine decor., slightly worn. (HD. Mar.21; 102) Frs. 100,000
- **Icones Anatomicae.** Ill.:– J. Lehnacker. München, Bremer Pr., [1932-35]. *(615).* Fo. Woodcuts on H.M.P., text on Hadernpapier by J.W. Zanders, hand-bnd. orig. hf. pig. (H. Nov.23; 954) DM 3,000

VESPUCCI, Amerigo
- **The Letter of ... describing his Four Voyages to the New World.** Intro.:– Oscar Lewis. Ill.:– V. Angelo. San Franc., [Grabhorn Pr.], 1926. *(250). (5?) specially bnd.* 4to. Gt.-ruled orange mor., s.-c. lightly worn, spine slightly faded; the V. Angelo copy, sigd. by him. (CBA. Oct.1; 181) $600
- **– Anr. Edn.** Ill.:– Valenti Angelo. San Franc., [Grabhorn Pr.], 1926. *(250).* 4to. Title-p. hand-cold., limp vell., discold., warped affecting text, s.-c. worn & brkn. (CBA. Nov.19; 244a) $120

VESSAUX, D. de Sainct Julien
- **Thresor d'Arithmetique.** Montbeliard, 1608. Cont. limp. vell., slightly spotted. (D. Nov.23; 496) DM 780

VESTA. TASCHENBUCH FUR GEBILDETE
1931-36. 6 vols. lacks title-p. & 1 plt., orig. cold. bds., 1833 vol. lacks upr. cover. (P. Apr.12; 190) £80

VETERAN & VINTAGE MAGAZINE
1956-68. Vols. 1-12. 4to. Advts., orig. cl. (TA. Oct.20; 113) £75

VETERUM MATHEMATICORUM ... OPERA
Paris, 1693. In Latin & Greek, some browning, title-p. & following lf. loose, old cf., rebkd.; Stanitz coll. (SPB. Apr.25; 442) $950

VETH, J. & Muller, S.
- **Albrecht Dürers Niederländische Reise.** Berlin & Utrecht, 1918. 2 vols. Fo. Some ll. slightly foxed, orig. pig. (R. Oct.11; 833) DM 950

VIALAR, Paul
- **La Grande Meute.** Ill.:– P.Y. Trémois. Paris, 1945. Fo. Leaves, orig. wrap., unc., box. (SM. Mar.7; 2351) Frs. 7,500
- **– Anr. Copy.** Fo. On vélin de cuve de Lana, Bordeaux mor., corners, wrap. preserved. (HD. Nov.17; 196) Frs. 6,300
- **– Anr. Edn.** Ill.:– P.Y. Tremois. 1945. *(387). (310) on vélin de cuve de Lana with autograph dedication sigd. by author & artist, & pen sketch on hf.-title.* Lge. 4to. Leaves, box. (HD. May 4; 446) Frs. 4,600
- **– Anr. Edn.** Ill.:– P.Y. Trémois. Lyon, 1945. 4to. Leaves, box. (HD. Jun.13; 109) Frs. 4,000

VIALARDI, A.L.
- **La Photographie au Percement des Alpes.** Paris, 1868. Ob. 4to. Some plts. slightly faded, orig. limp cl. wraps., worn. (SG. Nov.10; 161) $175

VIALART, Charles
- [–] **Geographica Sacra ... notae et animadversiones Lucae Holdtenii.** Amst., F. Halma, 1703. Fo. Additional engraved title, engraved dedication lf., 10 double-p. engraved maps, light stain affecting title & 1st. text ll., cont. blind-stpd. vell. (S. Dec.1; 195) Cope. £300

VIALE, Salvatore
- **Dionomachia Poemetto Eroi-Comico.** Parigi, 1823. *2nd. Edn.* Foxed, sewed, unopened. (HD. Oct.21; 174) Frs. 1,500

VIALLET
See— **BOSSUT & Viallet**

VIAUD, Louis Maris Julien
See— **LOTI, Pierre [i.e. Louis Maris Julien Viaud]**

VICAIRE, Georges
- **Manuel de l'Amateur de Livres du XIXe Siècle.** Paris, 1894-1920. 8 vols. including table vol. Lge. 8vo. On vell., marb. hf. cf., wraps. (HD. Jun.6; 153) Frs. 2,800

VICO, Aenea
- **Ex Gemmis et Cameis Antiquorum Aliquot Monumente.** Roma & Paris, n.d. 4to. Engraved title, 33 plts., inscrs. on plts., some ll. slightly spotted, cont. cf., rubbed. (BBA. Nov.30; 57) Lyon. £170
- **Le Imagini delle Donne Auguste ... Libro Primo.** Venice, 1557. *1st. Edn. 2nd. Iss.* 4to. Engraved title, 63 full-p. engrs., a few stains, sm. ink stains on pp. 73-76, vell. (S. Dec.20; 767) King. £180
- **– Anr. Edn.** Vinegia, 1557. Vol. 1 (all publd.). 4to. Lacks last lf., some repairs & dampstains, title remntd. & bkd. with privilege, 16th. C. Venetian cf. gt. decor. (HD. May 21; 72) Frs. 1,200

VICO, Giambattista
- **Grundzüge einer Neuen Wissenschaft über die Gemeinschaftliche Natur der Völker.** Trans.:– W.E. Weber. Leipzig, 1822. *1st. German Edn.* Sm. stp. on title verso, a few pencil linings, cont. bds. (R. Oct.11; 549) DM 530
- **Principi di Scienza Nuova, d'Intorno alla Comune Natura delle Nazioni.** Naples, 1744. *3rd. Edn.* 2 vols. in 1. Cont. vell. (SG. Feb.9; 368) $175

VICTOR, Benjamin
- **The History of the Theatres of London & Dublin.** L., 1761. *1st. Edn.* 2 vols. Hf.-titles, slightly soiled, cont. cf., worn, covers detchd. (BBA. Nov.30; 227) Quaritch. £140

VICTORIA, Queen of England
- **Leaves from the Journal of our Life in the Highlands from 1848 to 1861.** Ed.:– A. Helps. 1868. *1st. Edn.* Orig. cl. gt.; pres. copy to Miss Murray Macgregor, from Norman Tarbolton liby. (P. Apr.12; 20) Badcock. £100
- **– Anr. Edn.** 1868. *2nd. Edn.* Mor. gt., clasps, leath. d.-w.; pres. copy from Queen Victoria to Charles Kingsley, dtd. Mar. 1868. (BS. Nov.23; 22) £170
- **– Anr. Copy.** 1st 4 ll. loose, gt., pict. cl., upr. cover creased; sigd. pres. copy, inscr. 'Pour Madame de Morinni [?] ... Balmoral, 3 d' Octobre 1891'. (SG. Sep.29; 263) $325

VICTORIA & ALBERT MUSEUM
See— **RACKHAM, Bernard**
See— **SCHREIBER, Lady Charlotte**

VICTORIA COUNTY HISTORIES
- **Berkshire.** 1906-24. Vols. I-IV. Fo. Orig. cl. gt., partly unc. (LC. Oct.13; 289) £70
- **Kent.** Ed.:– William Page. 1908-26. 2 vols. 4to. Cl. gt. (PWC. Jul.11; 570) £50
- **Leicestershire.** 1907-58. 4 vols. 4to. Orig. cl. gt. (SKC. May 4; 1799) £90
- **Surrey.** 1902-14. Vols. 1-3 only (of 4), & Index. 4to. Orig. cl. gt. (BBA. Sep.29; 125) Thorp. £65
- **Collected Series.** 1900-79. *Some vols. in reprint.* 169 vols. (lacks 12 vols.), including General Intro. & Index vols. 4to. Orig. cl. gt., Berkshire in hf. mor., w.a.f. (C. Jun.27; 75) George's. £3,200

VICTORIA ... REPORT ON CENTRAL MINE DEPOT
Melbourne, 1900. Last lf. stained, bdg. not stated. (KH. May 1; 768) Aus. $180

VICTORIUS, Petrus
- **Commentarii in VIII. Libros Aristotelis de Optimo Statu Civitatis ...** Flor., 1576. Sm. fo. Lge. woodcut printers mark on title & last lf., cont. blind-tooled pig, decor., roll-stpd. ports., monog. on both covers, slightly rubbed & spotted, sm. scratch on lr. cover, lacks ties; from Ferdinand Hoffman liby., full-p. A. Eilian ex-libris on upr. inner cover. (HT. May 8; 74a) DM 500

VIDA, Marcus Hieronymus, Bp. of Alba
- **De Arte Poetica [& other Poems].** Rome, May 1527. *1st. Edn. of this coll.* Sm. 4to. Title browned & with show-through from early ink inscr. on verso, some other slight staining, 1st. gathering loose, 18th. C. mott. cf., spine gt., top compartment of spine renewed, lr. jnt. worn, qtr. mor. box; Thomas B. Stevenson copy. (CNY. May 18; 170) $500

VIDAL, Emeric Essex
- **Picturesque Illustrations of Buenos Ayres & Monte Video.** L., 1820. *1st. Edn.* Fo. 24 cold. aquatint views (4 double-p.), orig. embossed cl.,

rebkd. preserving orig. gt. backstrip. (C. Mar. 14; 97) Foyle. £3,500

VIDAL, Pierre [i.e. Marie-Louis Pierre]
- **Les Heures de la Femme à Paris.** Paris, [1903]. *(250). (220) on vell. de Cuves du Marais.* 2 vols. 2nd vol. with suites hors-texte, in 3, 4 or 5 states, with remarks & culs-de-lampe, hf. mor., by Champs, corners, decor. spines, wrap preserved. (HD. Dec.9; 193) Frs. 4,600

VIEILLEVILLE, Fr. de Scepeaux, Maréchal de
- **Mémoires Contenant Plusieurs Anecdotes des Règnes de François Ier, Henri II, François II et Charles IX, Composés par Vincent Carloix, Secrétaire du Maréchal.** Paris, 1757. *1st. Edn.* 5 vols. 12mo. Cont. cf., spines decor. (HD. Nov.9; 162) Frs. 1,550

VIELLOT, Louis Jean Pierre
- **Histoire Naturelle des plus Beaux Oiseaux Chanteurs de la Zone Torride.** Ill.:– Louis Bouquet after J.G. Pretre. Paris, 1805[-09]. Lge. fo. 72 hand-cold. plts., hf.-title, some spotting, mod. hf. mor. gt., unc. (C. Nov.16; 304) Monk Bretton. £2,500
See— **AUDEBERT, Jean Baptiste & Viellot, Louis Jean Pierre**

VIEN, Joseph-Marie
- **Caravanne du Sultan à la Mecque.** Paris, [1749]. Fo. Hand-cold. title, 31 hand-cold. plts., sm. liby. stps. on plt. versos, qtr. mor., rubbed. (P. Mar.15; 16) Hague. £1,100

VIER JAARGETIJDEN
Dordrecht, ca. 1825. 4 vols. Miniature book, 69 × 57 mm., 4 hand-cold. litho. frontis., slightly discold., orig. ptd. wraps., s.-c.; van Veen coll. (S. Feb.28; 208) £160

VIERI, Francesco de'
- **Trattato ... nel quale si contengono i tre Primi Libri delle Metheore.** Fiorenza, 1582. Stain on last p., cont. limp vell. (SI. Dec.15; 182) Lire 320,000

VIETZ, Ferdinand Bernhard
- **Icones Plantarum Medico-Oeconomicotechnologicarum.** Vienna, 1800-22. In 5 vols. only (of 6). 4to. 938 (of 1,153?) hand-cold. engraved plts., arranged alphabetically & renumbered in MS. 216-1153, no titles or text, red mor.-bkd. bds., as a coll. of plts., w.a.f. (C. Mar.14; 207) Walford. £2,700

VIEUSSENS, Raymond
- **Experiences et Reflexions sur la Structure et l'Usage des Viscères suivi d'une Explication Physico-Mechanique de la Plupart des Maladies.** Paris, 1755. 12mo. Hf.-title, cont. Fr. cf., spine gt.; Dr. Walter Pagel copy. (S. Feb.7; 371) Gurney. £180
- **Nevrographia Universalis.** Ill.:– Beaudeau. Lugduni, 1684. 4to. Cont. spr. cf., spine decor.; from Château des Noës liby. (HD. May 25; 82) Frs. 27,000
- **– Anr. Edn.** Lyons, 1716. *Latest Edn.* Fo. Some plts. separated at folds, some worming towards end, browned, cont. cf. (SG. Mar.22; 240) $650

VIEWS IN FRANCE, Switzerland & Italy
Ca. 1840. Fo. 63 plts. (55 litho., 6 aquatint, 2 engraved), spotted, cont. hf. cf., worn, w.a.f. (CSK. Aug.5; 146) £850

VIEWS OF THE ISLANDS OF GUERNSEY & JERSEY
L., 1829-30. Ob. 4to. 34 litho. views, 1 slightly torn, lacks title, some spotting, hf. mor. gt., as a collection of plts., w.a.f. (P. Nov.24; 192) Edwards. £420

VIGEVANO, Attilio
- **La Fine dell'esercito Pontificio.** Roma, 1925. 4to. Hf. cf. (CR. Jun.6; 312) Lire 220,000

VIGNANCOURT, E.
- [–] **Poésies Bearnaises.** Pau, 1827. *1st. Coll. Edn.* Red mor. gt., by Thivet, spine decor. (HD. Nov.29; 124) Frs. 2,100

VIGNIER, Nicolas
- **La Bibliothèque Historiale.** Paris, 1587. 3 vols. Fo. Old mott. cf., rubbed. (P. Mar.15; 158) £50
- **Histoire de la Maison de Luxembourg. Où sont Plusieurs Occurrences de Guerres et Affaires tant d'Afrique et d'Asie que d'Europe.** Paris, 1619. 4to.

Cont. red mor. gt. 'à la Duseuil', decor. spine. (HD. Sep.22; 367) Frs. 1,100

VIGNOLA, Giacomo
See— **BAROZZI called VIGNOLA, Giacomo**

VIGNY, Alfred Victor, comte de
- **Cinq-Mars, ou une Conjuration sous Louis XIII.** Paris, 1826. *Orig. Edn.* 2 vols. Cont. hf. roan, decor. spines gt. (HD. Dec.16; 40) Frs. 2,650
- **Les Destinées. Poèmes Philosophiques.** Paris, 1864. *Orig. Edn.* Cont. hf. chagrin, corners, spine decor. (HD. Nov.9; 103) Frs. 2,800
- – **Anr. Edn.** Ill.:– G. Bellenger, engraved by Eugene Froment. Paris, 1898. Red mor. gt. by Canape, mosaic spine, wrap. & spine preserved; pres. copy ptd. for Edmond Ouivet. (HD. May 4; 447) Frs. 2,100
- **Eloa ou la Soeur des Anges. Mystère.** Paris, 1824. *Orig. Edn.* Str.-grd. red hf. mor. by Semet & Plumelle, spine decor. (HD. Jun.13; 111) Frs. 4,000
- **La Maréchale d'Ancre.** Ill.:– Tony Johannot (frontis.). 1831. *Orig. Edn.* Mod. hf. mor., corners, spine decor., wrap. & spine, unc., from libys. of Victor Mercier, Laurent Meeus & A. Chauveau. (HD. Apr.13; 126) Frs. 7,100

VILJOEN, B.J.
- **Under the Vierkleur, A Romance of a Lost Cause.** Boston, 1904. Pict. cl.; inscr. by author & sigd. by P.A. Cronje. (VA. Oct.28; 624) R 300

VILLA & COTTAGE ARCHITECTURE
L., 1868. Fo. Hf. cf. (P. Dec.8; 296) *Bookroom.* £80
- – **Anr. Edn.** 1874. Fo. 80 litho. plts. (a few stained), hf.-title, cont. hf. leath., spine gt. (rubbed). (LC. Mar.1; 563) £50
- – **Anr. Edn.** L., 1876. Fo. 80 engraved plts., some faint spotting, cont. hf. mor. (S. Mar.6; 347) *M. Scott.* £70

VILLAIN, Abbé Etienne François
[–] **Histoire Critique de Nicolas Flamel.** Paris, 1761. Cont. pol. cf. gt. (SG. Oct.6; 367) $230

VILLALON, Cristobal de
- **Provechoso Tratado de Cambios y Contrataciones d'Mercadores y Reprovacion de Usura. Exortacion a la Confesion.** Valladolid, 1546. 2 pts. in 1 vol. 4to. Browned, loose in bdg., later vell. (SPB. Dec.13; 762) $550

VILLAMENA, Fr.
- **Römische Kaufrufe.** Ill.:– C. David. Early 17th. C. Fo. 6 etchings, sigd. in plt., ll. stpd. recto & verso with crease, margins with light stain, marb. bds.; Hauswedell coll. (H. May 23; 132) DM 3,200

VILLANI, Giovanni
- **Croniche.** [Venice, 1537]. Fo. Title & 1st. few ll. lightly wormed, some dampstaining, old hf. roan, worn. (CSK. Nov.4; 170) £95

VILLANI, Matteo
- **Historia ... Il Quale continua l'Historie di Giovani Vittani.** Venice, 1562. 4to. Title & 1st. few ll. wormed with a little loss, title laid down, old vell., soiled, upr. hinge split. (CSK. May 18; 128) £50

VILLAT, Louis
- **La Corse de 1768 à 1789: 1) la Reduction à l'Obéissance; 2) le 'Despotisme Eclairé' et le Don de la Corse à la France.** Besançon, 1924-25. 2 vols. Hf. roan, corners, wrap. & spine preservcd. (HD. Oct.21; 176) Frs. 1,800

VILLAUT, Nicolas
- **A Relation of the Coasts of Africk called Guinée.** L., 1670. 12mo. Advt., cf. (P. Dec.8; 352) *Lawson.* £200

VILLAVICENCIO, J.J. de
- **Vida, y Virtudes de el Venerable, y Apostolico Padre Juan de Ugarte ... Missionero de las Islas Californias, y Uno de sus Primeros Conquistadores.** Mexico, 1752. Sm. 4to. Sm. owner's stp. in lr. margin of title & at end, cont. limp. vell. [Sabin 99694] (S. May 22; 343) *Cortes.* £3,500

VILLE, Antoine de
- **Descriptio Portus et Urbis Polae.** Venice, 1683. (*Bound with:*) BARPO, G.B. – **Descrittione di Cividal di Belluno.** Belluno, 1690. (*Bound with:*) COCARELLA, B. – **Cronica Istoriale di Trenti ...** Venice, 1606. Together 3 works in 1 vol. 4to. Cont. cf., spine decor. (HD. Mar.9; 90) Frs. 2,300
- **Les Fortifications ...** Lyon, 1628. *Orig. Edn.* Fo. Frontis. dtd. 1629, 1636 edn. title pasted over orig. title, worming in middle, cont. cf., spine decor., slightly worn. (HD. Nov.29; 79) Frs. 3,800

VILLE, L.
- **La Lutte et les Lutteurs; Traité Pratique; Histoire des Saltimbanques ...** Ill.:– Photos.:– Nadar. Paris, 1891. Lge. 8vo. Hf. chagrin, corners, by Dubois d'Enghien, spine richly decor., wrap. (HD. Feb.28; 94) Frs. 2,200

VILLEFOSSE, René Heron de
- **L'Ile de France.** Ill.:– Segonzac. Paris, 1966. (*314*). Fo. Orig. wrap., unc., box; unique copy on japon nacré sigd. by author, artist & publisher, with decomposition of 2 cold. ills., bon-à-tirer for 1 ill. sigd. by Segonzac, decomposition of same ill., suite of ills. in silhouette, & suite on vélin d'Arches. (SM. Mar.7; 2346) Frs. 9,000

VILLEGAS, S.V.
- **Suma de todo lo que contiene el Arte de Cantollano.** Sevilla, 1604. 4to. Leath. (DS. Mar.23; 2293) Pts. 150,000

VILLEHARDOUIN, Geoffroy de
- **Histoire de l'Empire de Constantinople sous les Empereurs François ...** Paris, 1657. 2 vols. in 1. Fo. Cont. spr. cf. (HD. Jun.6; 154) Frs. 4,600

VILLETTE
- **Histoire de Notre-Dame de Liesse.** Ill.:– Thomassin after Stella. Laon, Renesson & Paris, 1708. Cont. roan, decor. spine. (HD. Dec.2; 167) Frs. 1,000

VILLIERS DE L'ISLE-ADAM, Auguste de
- **Akédysseril.** 1886. *Orig. Edn., (250) on japan.* Frontis. in 3 states, vig. & tail-piece in 2 states, hf. chagrin, corners. (HD. May 11; 135) Frs. 1,200
- **L'Eve Future.** Paris, 1886. *Orig. Edn.* 12mo. Lavalliere hf. cf., corners, Japanese style decor. paper bds., spine decor., unc., wrap. & spine preserved. (HD. May 4; 448) Frs. 2,050

VILLON, François [i.e. François de Montcorbier]
- **Autres Poésies de Maistre François Villon & de son Ecole.** Ill.:– Lucien Pissaro. L., Eragny Pr., 1901. (*226*). Sm. 4to. Slightly soiled, paper-bkd. bds. (LH. Sep.25; 363) $170
- – **Anr. Copy.** Sm. 8vo. Final ll. foxed, crushed mor. gt., floral cornerpieces, gt.-panel. spine, extremities badly chafed. (SG. Jan.12; 98) $150
- **Les Ballades du Grand Testament.** Ill.:– Léon Courbouleix. N.p., n.d. Lge. 4to. Vell. d'Arches, engraved thro.-out, orig. pencil ill., bradel marb. vell., unc. (HD. Dec.9; 16) Frs. 1,400
- **Les Ballades du Testament, les Poésies Diverses et la France de François Villon et de ses Compagnons.** Preface:– Pierre Champion. Ill.:– Barta. Paris, 1931. 4to. Vell., decor. with paintings by Barta, s.-c. (HD. Jun.13; 113) Frs. 4,000
- **Le Grand Testament.** Ill.:– Jacques Villon. Paris, 1963. (*148*) numbered & sigd. by publisher. Fo. This copy unnumbered, & with 2 extra suites of the lithos. (1 in black on Japon ancien & 1 in col. on Japon nacré), unsewn in orig. wraps., unc., cl. case. (S. Nov.21; 132) *Rota.* £850
- – **Anr. Edn.** Ill.:– Jacques Villon. Paris, 1963. (*148*) numbered. This 1 of (30) on vell. de Rives. Fo. With double suite of ills. in black & cols. on old japan & japan nacré, leaves, wrap., box. (HD. Dec.16; 204) Frs. 5,800
- **Les Oeuvres ...** Paris, 1532. *2nd. Edn.* 16mo. Title torn & reprd. slightly affecting 2 letters on verso, 19th. C. pink mor. by Koehler. (C. May 30; 103) *Quaritch.* £2,500
- – **Anr. Edn.** Paris, 1723. *1st. Critical Edn.* 12mo. Cont. cf., spine decor.; 18th. C. ex-libris 'Fr. Jos. Menage de Mondesir'. (HD. Nov.9; 84) Frs. 2,100
- – **Anr. Copy.** Sm. 8vo. Cont. marb. cf., decor. spine. (HD. Sep.22; 368) Frs. 1,900
- – **Anr. Edn.** Ill.:– Emile Bernard. Paris, 1918.

(250) on papier de cuve. 4to. 15th. C. style stpd. & decor. cf., spine decor., wrap. preserved (slightly wormed), s.-c. (HD. Jun.13; 112) Frs. 7,500
- – **Anr. Edn.** Ill.:– H. Leymarie. Paris, 1943. On vell. d'Arches, leaves, wrap., s.-c. & box. (HD. Mar.14; 177) Frs. 2,500
- – **Anr. Copy.** On vell. d'Arches, leaves, pict. wrap., s.-c., box. (HD. Dec.16; 203) Frs. 2,400

VILLON, Jacques
- **Cent Croquis 1894-1904.** Paris, 1959. Lge. 4to. Unsewn, orig. wraps., folder, s.-c. defect. (S. Apr.30; 98) *Aus. Nat. Gall.* £75

VIMONT, Joseph
- **Traité de Phrenologie.** 1832-36. 2 text vols., Atlas. & vol. of plt. expanations. Some spotting, cont. unif. hf. cf.; Vol. 2 sigd. by author on title. (TA. Dec.15; 595) £110

VINCENT, Augustine
- **A Discoverie of Errours in the First Edition of the Catalogue of Nobility.** L., 1622. *1st. Edn.* Fo. Woodcut coats-of-arms, slight browning, title reprd., cont. cf., rebkd., lacks ties; bkplt. of Tho. Drake Tyrwhitt, sigd. by ?J. Tyrwhilt, engraved bkplt. of Francis North, Baron of Guildford, & sigd. by him. (S. Mar.20; 752) *Thorp.* £70

VINCENT, William
- **The Voyage of Nearchus from the Indus to the Euphrates.** L., 1797. Fo. Linen. (DS. Mar.23; 2294) Pts. 25,000

VINCENT DE LA CHAPELLE
- **Le Cuisinier Moderne, qui apprend à donner toutes Sortes de Repas ...** La Haye, priv. ptd., 1742. *2nd. Edn.* 5 vols. Cont. marb. cf., spines decor.; from Chateau des Noës liby. (HD. May 25; 83) Frs. 22,500

VINCENT FERRER, Saint
- **Sermones de Tempore. Pars Estivalis, [– Pars Hyemalis].** [Strasbourg, 1503.]. Together 2 pts. in 1 vol. Sm. fo. Title of 1st. pt. stained, some other slight stains & wear, few sm. repairs, few cont. annots. on title of 1st. pt., new fly-ll., orig. blind-stpd. cf. over wood, catches preserved, spine very defect., some wormholes in covers & spine, rubbed. (VG. Sep.14; 1368) Fls. 550

VINDEL, Francisco
- **Manual Grafico Descriptivo del Bibliófilo Hispanoamericano.** Madrid, 1930-34. 12 vols., including supps. XV-XVII. Fo. 3682 facs., cl./bds. (DS. Dec.16; 2078) Pts. 100,000

VINS, FLEURS ET FLAMMES
Ed.:– Georges Duhamel. Contribs.:– 'Mac Orlan', Colette, Valery, & others. Ill.:– Brianchon, Dufy, Derain, Cocteau, Foujita, Jacob, & others. Paris, 1956. (*380*) numbered. (*20*) with extra suite of the 30 plts. & a numbered & sigd. etching by Berrin. Fo. Unsewn in orig. wraps., with cover design by Villon, pict. folder & s.-c. (S. Nov.21; 19) *Marks.* £60

VIO, Th. de Cajetano
- **Apologia ... de Co[m]parata Auctoritate Pape et Ecclesie.** Rome, 1513. Sm. 4to. Some light browning, 19th. C. sewed. (HT. May 8; 218) DM 420

VIOLET, Fabius
- **La Parfaicte et Entière Cognoissance de Toutes les Maladies du Corps Humain Causées par Obstruction.** Paris, 1635. Errata lf., few corners slightly wormed, last few ll. stained on corners, new vell.; Dr. Walter Pagel copy. (S. Feb.7; 372) *Gurney.* £100

VIOLIER DES HISTOIRES (Le) Rommaines sur les Nobles Gestes, Faictz Vertueulx et Anciennes Cronicques ...
Paris, 1521. *1st. Fr. Trans.* Fo. On vell., rubricated, all engrs. illuminated, capitals decor., Béthune arms on title, lacks 9 ll., 18th. C. roan, spine decor.; from Fondation Furstenberg-Beaumesnil. (HD. Nov.16; 180) Frs. 80,000

VIOLLET-LE-DUC, Eugène Emmanuel
- Dictionnaire Raisonné de l'Architecture Française du XIe au XVIe Siècle. 1854. 10 vols. Cont. hf. chagrin. (HD. Mar.21; 212) Frs. 1,800
- - **Anr. Edn.** Paris, 1854-68. 10 vols. Some spotting, cont. hf. cf., scuffed. (TA. Nov.17; 243) £95
- - **Anr. Edn.** Paris, 1858-75. 10 vols. Tall 8vo. Some foxing, unif. sheep & cl., raised bands, gt. lettering, scuffing to edges & backstrips. (HA. May 4; 334) $170
- - **Anr. Edn.** Paris, 1875-76. 10 vols. Hf. roan. (HD. Dec.16; 205) Frs. 2,600
- Dictionnaire Raisonné du Mobilier Français. Paris, [1858-75]. 6 vols. Hf. cf. (CR. Jun.6; 313) Lire 350,000
- Peintures Murales des Chapelles de Notre-Dame de Paris. Paris, 1870. Fo. 60 plts. ptd. in cols. & gold, cont. mor.-bkd. bds., slightly rubbed. (S. May 1; 581) Sims. £200

VIRCHOW, Rudolf
- Der Cellularpathologie in Ihrer Begründung auf Physiologische und Pathololologische Gewebelehre. Berlin, 1858. 1st. Edn. Title foxed, lacks hf. title, slightly browned in margins thro.-out, cont. hf. leath., worn, upr. jnt. reprd. (R. Apr.4; 1401) DM 2,200

VIRGILIUS MARO, Publius
See— VERGILIUS MARO, Publius

VIRTUE, George
- The Picturesque Beauties of Great Britain ... Kent. L., 1832. 4to. Extra engraved title, folding map, 126 views on 63 (of 64) plts., spotted, bdg. not stated, covers detchd., worn. (S. Mar.6; 348) Walford. £120
- - **Anr. Copy.** 4to. Extra engraved title, 125 views on 63 plts., slightly spotted, 1 lf. loose & frayed, orig. roan-bkd. ptd. bds., spine worn. (S. Mar.6; 460) Frankland. £110
- - **Anr. Edn.** L., n.d. 4to. Engraved title, folding map, 126 views on 63 sheets, hf. cf. gt. (P. Nov.24; 72) Parry. £150
- Switzerland & the Bavarian Highlands. N.d. 4 vols. Fo. A few ll. detchd., orig. cl. gt., lightly soiled. (CSK. Apr.6; 60) £280

VISCONTI, E.Q. & Mongez, A.
- Iconographie Ancienne ... Iconographie Grecque. Ill.:- after Laguiche, Montagny, Bouillon & others. Paris, 1808. 2 pts. in 3 vols. (With:) - Iconographie Romaine. Paris, 1817-26. 4 vols. Together 7 vols. Fo. Title of 'Iconographie Grecque' Vol. III erroneously replaced with title of 'Iconographie Romaine', 1 plt. ink-stained, some foxing, red mor. gt. by Gruel, spines decor. (HD. May 21; 73) Frs. 12,000

VISCONTI, Gaspare
- Di Paulo e Daria Amanti. Milan, Philippus de Mantegatiis, 1 Apr. 1495. 1st. Edn. 4to. Margin worming, repairs slightly affecting a few side-notes, 16th. C. vell. [BMC VI, 787; Goff V266] (C. May 30; 52) Rosenthal. £2,700

VISIT TO TEXAS
N.Y., 1836. 2nd. Edn. Sm. 12mo. Final ll. loosening, 1 final lf. frayed on inner margin, orig. cl., lr. hinge brkn. (SG. Jan.19; 338) $200

VISSCHER, Nicolaas
- Atlas Minor sive Totius Orbis Terrarum Contracta Delinea(ta). Ca. 1700. Fo. Composite atlas, engraved allegorical title by G. de Lairesse, & 28 double-p. or folding engraved mapsheets, including Visscher's twin-hemispherical world map, 4 by P. Schenk, 2 by J. Cailloüé (1 with D. Mortier), & 1 each by R. Morden & C. Browne, F. de Wit, & M. Skynner, map by Morden & Christopher Browne in 1st. state (ca. 1695) of 'A New Map of the English Empire in America', cont. hand-cold. in full thro.-out, 1 or 2 splits at centre-folds without loss of engraved surface, some light creasing or slight soiling, 18th. C. hf. mor. gt., rubbed, w.a.f. (S. May 21; 119) Traylen. £3,300
- - **Anr. Copy.** Fo. Hand-cold. title, 85 hand-cold. maps, all badly wormed in upr. & lower centre fold, 9 with tears, Palestine frayed & stained, no text, old sheep, worn. (P. Apr.12; 325a) Burgess. £3,000
- - **Anr. Edn.** Maps:- Visscher, de Wit, P. Schenck,

Jaillot, De la Feuille, & others. Amst., ca. 1710. Lge. fo. Engraved title, 49 hand-cold. double-p. or folding maps, MS. index, hf. roan. (B. Feb.8; 558) Fls. 16,500
- Theatrum Biblicum hoc est Historiae Sacrae Veteris et Nova Testamenti Tabulis. [Amst.], 1674. 3 pts. in 1 vol. Ob. fo. Approx. 465 plts., including titles, a few plts. cut round & mntd., some faint stains, 18th. C. cf., rebkd., worn. w.a.f. (S. May 22; 289) Erlini. £600

VITA ADAE ET EVAE
[Rome, Stephan Plannck], ca. 1487. 4to. Disbnd.; the Walter Goldwater copy. [BMC IV, 88; Goff A-44] (SG. Dec.1; 1) $250

VITAL, Hayyim
- Hok le-Yisrael. Egypt [Cairo], 1740. 1st. Edn. Vol. 2 only (of 2). Sm. 4to. Title & last lf. reprd., scattered worming & dampstaining, mod. cl., rubbed. (SG. Feb.2; 307) $275

VITE E RITRATI DI ILLUSTRI ITALIANI
Ill.:- Longhi (port.), Michele Bisi. Padova, 1812. Fo. Orig. mor. gt., Napoleon's cypher in corners, rubbed, loose. (SKC. Nov.18; 1818) £50

VITROLLES, Eugene François Auguste d'Armaud, Baron de
- Mémoires et Relations Politiques du Baron de Vitrolles. Paris, 1884. 3 vols. Hf. chagrin. (HD. Feb.22; 226) Frs. 1,800

VITRUVIUS POLLIO, Marcus
- Abrégé des Dix Livres d'Architecture. [C. Perrault]. Paris, 1674. Old bds., lacks spine, upr. cover detchd. (SG. Oct.13; 355) $110
- - **Anr. Copy.** Cont. leath. (D. Nov.23; 1933) DM 600
- Architectura. Ed.:- Perrault. Trans.:- Müller. Nuremb., Würzburg, Prag, 1757. Cont. style bds. (D. Nov.23; 1936) DM 550
- Architecture ou Art de bien bastir. Trans.:- Jean Martin. [Genève], 1618. Latest Fr. Edition. Sm. 4to. With commentary by Guillaume Philandrier, many wood engrs. from Lyon 1552 Edn. (2 lge. format folding, inscr. on title, vell. (HD. Jan.30; 104) Frs. 1,800
- - **Anr. Edn.** Coligny, 1618. 4to. Tear, dampstain, mor., arms of Henri II de Bourbon-Condé, fleurs-de-lys on spine (trace of worming). (SM. Mar.7; 2055) Frs. 4,000
- L'Architettura ... 1790. Fo. Cont. hf. vell., worn. (HD. Jun.29; 206) Frs. 1,000
- Baukunst. Trans.:- A. Rode. Leipzig, 1796. 2 vols. 4to. 19th. C. hf. leath., bumped, unc. (D. Nov.23; 1938) DM 400
- De Architectura Libri Decè. Commentary:- Caesare Cesariano. Trans.:- Bono Mauro da Bergamo & Benedetto Jovio da Comasco. Ill.:- Cesariano & others. Como, 1521. 1st. Edn. in Italian. Fo. 1 woodcut repeated, title & errata lf. reprd. at blank margins, a few hinges reprd. at front & end, tears in 4 ll. reprd., mod. vell.; sm. woodcut armorial stp. of Dom. Salviata at blank margin of title, faint stp. in margin of anr. lf. (C. May 30; 53) Thomas. £4,000
- - **Anr. Edn.** Flor., 1522. 2 pts. in 1 vol. Woodcut ills., last 3 ll. of register, blank & imprint, lacks f. E6, some ll. soiled, cont. marginalia, mod. cf.-bkd. bds. (BBA. May 23; 310) Rox. £130
- - **Anr. Edn.** Ed.:- G. Philandrus. Strassburg, 1550. 4to. Some light browning, light staining in lr. margin near end, MS. notes in upr. cover, cont. blind-tooled pig, with initials B.S.V. & 1550 on upr. cover, spine restored; Abraham Gotthelf Kaestner copy. (R. Oct.11; 796) DM 1,700
- - **Anr. Edn.** Notes:- Philander. Ill.:- Petit Bernard(?), &c. Lyon, 1552. 1st. Tournes Edn. 4to. Fo. slip-proof, cont. cf., decor.; from Fondation Furstenberg-Beaumesnil. (HD. Nov.16; 182) Frs. 4,000
- - **Anr. Edn.** Amst., 1649. Fo. Cont. leath. (D. Nov.23; 1931) DM 1,600
- - **Anr. Copy.** Fo. Lacks copper engraved title, cont. vell., 1st. & last pp. wormed. (D. Nov.23; 1932) DM 1,200
- - **Anr. Edn.** Leipzig, 1807-08. 3 vols. Foxed & browned, cont. style hf. leath. (D. Nov.23; 1939) DM 600
- - **Anr. Edn.** Romae, 1836. 4 vols. Fo. Perforation

stps. on titles, plts. stps. on versos, minor foxing, old bds., worn, ex-liby. (RO. Dec.11; 343) $100
- I Dieci Libri dell'Architettura. Trans.:- D. Barbaro. Venise, 1629. Cont. vell. (HD. Dec.15; 55) Frs. 2,300
- Les Dix Livres d'Architecture. Ed.:- Perrault. Ill.:- S. Le Clerc, engraved by Scotin (frontis.); Edelinck, Scotin, Gantrel & others. 1673. 1st. Edn. 1st. Printing of ills. Fo. Dampstain at foot of 1st. 70 ll., cont. cf., spine & jnts. reprd. (HD. Apr.13; 60) Frs. 1,500
- - **Anr. Edn.** Ill.:- Le Pautre, Scotin & others. Paris, 1684. 2nd. Edn. Fo. Cont. spr. cf., spine decor.; from Château des Noës liby. (HD. May 25; 84) Frs. 5,200
- - **Anr. Copy.** Fo. Cont. spr. cf. (HD. Jun.29; 205) Frs. 3,300
- - **Anr. Copy.** Fo. Cont. cf. (HD. Dec.15; 58) Frs. 2,500
- - **Anr. Copy.** Fo. 1p. with excision in right margin (without text loss), cont. leath., spine defect, both covers loose. (D. Nov.23; 1934) DM 900
- M. Vitruvius per Iocundum Solito Castigatior Factus cum Figuris ... Venice, 22 May 1511. 1st. Ill. Edn. Fo. Lacks final blank, lacks O4 (a dupl. of O3 bnd. in its place), margins of 1st. few ll. frayed, title-p. dust-soiled, some browning & staining, later 16th. C. blind-stpd. cf., worn, some repairs, lacks ties. (S. Nov.17; 75) Quaritch. £550
- Vitruvius Teutsch ... Zehn Bücher. Trans.:- H. Ryff. Ill.:- P. Flötner, V. Solis, G. Pencz & H. Brosamer. Nuremb., 1548. 1st. German Edn. Sm. fo. Title lf. extended in photocopy, some slight browning or staining, 17th. C. vell., slightly spotted. (GB. May 3; 911) DM 3,800

VITRY, Paul
- La Cathédrale de Reims: Architecture et Sculpture. Paris, [1919]. 2 vols. Fo. 225 photogravure plts. in sepia, cont. gt.-ruled mor. by Atelier Bindery for Charles Scribner. (SG. Jan.26; 299) $110
- Hôtels & Maisons de la Renaissance Française. Paris, ca. 1912. 3 vols. Lge. fo. 300 photogravure plts., each liby.-stpd. on blank verso, text ills., loose in cl. folders, linen ties. (SG. May 3; 368) $110

VIVALDUS DE MONTE REGALI, Johannes Ludovicus
- Aureum Opus de Veritate Cotritionis. 4 Oct. 1510. Cont. Parisian blind-stpd. cf., lge. panel of God the Father or Charlemagne on both covers surrounded by figures of the 3 Magi, the Virgin Mary, Octavian, & Sybil & Herod & the Massacre of the Innocents, in a roundel at foot binder's initials GG, rebkd. & reprd., with some loss of border, spine worn, lacks clasps, cl. box. (S. Nov.17; 76) A. Thomas. £210
- - **Anr. Edn.** Paris, 4.VII.1522. Cont. entry on last p., some staining, some margins lightly frayed, cont. blind-tooled leath.-bkd. wood bds., spine & corners renewed, lacks clasps. (HK. Nov.8; 377) DM 500
- Opus Regale. Saluzzo, 1507. 1st. Edn. 2 pts. in 1 vol. Fo. Some minor staining, tear in 1 lf. without loss of text, a few other margin tears, cont. painted vell., jnts. reprd.; bkplts. of Dyson Perrins & Broxbourne Liby. (C. May 30; 54) Thomas. £5,400
- - **Anr. Edn.** Ed.: [A. de Soncino]. Lyon, 1512. 4th. Edn. Some lengthy worm-holes, with some loss, 1st. & last lf. re-hinged, title & end-leaf discold. in margins, old owners mark, 1 lf. duplicated & pasted to 1st. lf., later old vell. gt., spine wormed & bkd. (R. Apr.3; 105) DM 380

VIVANT, Dominique, Baron Denon
See— DENON, Dominique Vivant, Baron

VIVES, Juan Luis
- Ad Sapientiae Introduccio. Salamanca, 1572. Cf. (DS. Mar.23; 2296) Pts. 50,000

VIVIAN, George
- Spanish Scenery. L., 1838. Tinted litho. title, 23 (of 28) tinted litho. plts., list of plts. spotted. (Bound with:) - Scenery of Portugal & Spain. L., 1839. Tinted litho. title, 29 (of 31) plts., including head- & tail-piece. Together 2 works in 1 vol. Fo. A few ll. detchd., cont. hf. gt., stained, lr. cover torn, w.a.f. (C. Nov.16; 191) Schuster. £600

VIVIAN, Lieut.-Col. J.L.
- The Visitations of Cornwall, Comprising the Heralds' Visitations of 1530, 1573 & 1620. Exeter, 1887. 4to. Cont. hf. mor. (TA. Aug.18; 66) £100

VIVIANI, Vincenzo
- Discorso al Serenissimo Cosimo III ... Interno al Difendersi da'Riempimenti, dalle Corrosioni de'Fiumi applicato ad Arno in Vicinanza della Citta di Firenze. Flor., 1688. 4to. Slight foxing, liby. stp. on verso of title, cont. vell.; Stanitz coll. (SPB. Apr.25; 447) $450

VIVIANUS, Johannes
See— ORTELIUS, Abraham & Vivianus, Johannes

VIVIEN, Renée
- Haillons. 1910. Orig. Edn. (50) on japan. No bdg. stated. (HD. May 11; 138) Frs. 1,250
- Sillages. 1908. Orig. Edn. (31) on old japan. No bdg. stated. (HD. May 11; 139) Frs. 1,150
- Le Vent des Vaisseaux. 1910. Orig. Edn. (50) on japan. No bdg. stated, unc.; from Lucien Graux liby. (HD. May 11; 137) Frs. 1,250

VIVIEN DE SAINT-MARTIN, Louis
- Histoire de la Géographie et des Decouvertes Géographiques. Paris, 1875; 1874. 1 vol., accompanied by Atlas vol. Lge. 8vo.; Atlas fo. Hf. mor., ex-liby.; Atlas vol.: 13 maps on 12 double-p. sheets, loose in ptd. bd. folder, ties, each map rubberstpd. on blank verso. (SG. Jun.7; 38) $225

VIZCAINO, Sebastian
- The Voyage of ... to the Coast of California ... December 28, 1602. San Franc., [Grabhorn Pr.], 1933. (240). Cl.-bkd. paper bds. (LH. Sep.25; 335) $110

VLACQ, Adrian
- Trigonometria Artificialis. Ed.:– Henry Briggs. Gouda, 1633. 1st. Edn. 2 pts. in 1 vol. Fo. Text diagrams, some spotting, cont. panel. rough cf., worn, rebkd. (SG. Apr.19; 189) $130

VLAMINCK, Maurice de
- En Noir et en Couleur. Paris, 1962. (298) numbered. 4to. Unc., unsewn in orig. pict. wraps., folder & s.-c. (S. Nov.21; 44) Makiya. £210
- La Tête Tournée. Paris, 1956. (350) numbered & sigd. by author & publisher. 4to. Orig. pict. wraps., folder & s.-c., unc. (S. Nov.21; 43) Marks. £160
- Tournant Dangereux. Paris, 1930. (275) numbered. 4to. Slightly spotted, orig. wraps., bd. folder, s.-c. brkn. (BBA. Jun.14; 250) Barrie Marks. £200

VLORA, A.K.
- Indicazioni di Bibliografia Sulla Corsice. Bari, 1941. Sewed, unopened. (HD. Oct.21; 177) Frs. 1,100

VOCABULARIUS JURIS UTRIUSQUE
[Basle, Michael Wenssler, ca. 1475]. Fo. Rubricated, rubricator's sig. 'ffrater Thomas Liwerwelder' at end of last 2 ll., many lines underlined in red, initial spaces left blank, mod. hf. cf. over wood bds.; from Fondation Furstenberg-Beaumesnil. [BMC III, 722; Goff V335] (HD. Nov.16; 8) Frs. 9,000

VOCHS, Johannes
- Opusculum Praeclarum de Omni Pestilentia ... per Dryandrum Novissime Repurgatum. [Cologne], Aug. 1537. Outer blank margins at beginning a little smudged, old rough bds., spine defect.; Dr. Walter Pagel copy. (S. Feb.7; 377) Goldschmidt. £420

VOET, Gisbert
- Een Kort Tractaetjen van de Danssen ... Utrecht, 1644. Margin stained, title reprd. (Bound with:) PREDICATIE tegan 't Danssen Rotterdam, 1643. Slightly browned. Together 2 works in 1 vol. 12mo. Mod. hf. cf. (VG. Nov.30; 585) Fls. 650

VOET, Johann Eusebius
- Beschreibungen und Abbildungen Haartschaaligter Insekten. Trans.:– G.W. Fr. Panzer. Erlangen, 1793-1802. 4to. Some pp. very browned, 19th. C. cf., gold & blind-tooled, slightly rubbed; Hauswedell coll. (H. May 24; 852) DM 3,600
- Catalogus Systematicus Coleopterorum. Ill.:–

Kleeman & others. Den Haag, 1806. 1 vol. only (of 2). 4to. In Latin, Fr. & Dutch, hf. linen. (V. Sep.29; 1530) DM 520

VOEUX DE FRANCE (Les) pour l'heureux Anniversaire du IX août ...
1831. On tricold. paper (pink, white & blue), litho. port. of Louis-Philippe on white paper, text with border, old hf. mor. tricold. red, cream & blue, gt. decor. spine, unc., pink paper wrap. (HD. Dec.9; 32) Frs. 1,000

VOGEL, Friedrich
- Die Alten Chroniken der Stadt und Landschaft Zürich. Zürich, 1845. 4to. Hf. leath. (G. Sep.15; 2492) Sw. Frs. 550

VOGEL, Lucien
- Gazette du Bon Ton, Art-Modes & Frivolités. Ill.:– Lepage, Brissand, Barbier & others. 1913. Vol. 2 nos. 7-12. 60 cold. plts., some finished by hand, orig. vell., slightly spotted. (CSK. Jun.29; 163) £700

VOGEL, Matth.
- Erste u. Fürnehmste Weiss dem Heiligen Mess-Opffer ... beyzuwohnen ... mit Erweckung Verschied. Tugends-Ubungen. Ill.:– P.A. Kilian & J.G. Wissger. Mannheim, 1752. 4to. Lacks 1 frontis., slightly soiled & some foxing, cont. red mor. gt., slightly worn & bumped. (HK. Nov.9; 1528) DM 500

VOGELER, H.
- Aus den Osten. 60 Kriegs-Zeichnungen aus dem Kriegsgebiet Karpathen ... Berlin, ca. 1916. De Luxe Edn., (100) numbered on Japan. Fo. Title with dedication, orig. leath., corners bumped; printers mote sigd. by author. (GB. Nov.5; 3101) DM 400

VOGELLIUS, H.
- Het Hoogt-Liedt Salomons, door Christelyke Gesang-Digthen Eenighsins Verklaert. Amst., 1625. 4to. Soiled & defect., cont. vell. (VS. Dec.9; 1129) Fls. 500

VOGLER, H.
- Die Märchen. Text:– E.R. Löwenwarter. Münster, [1924]. 4to. 7 (of 6) orig. etchings. orig. wraps., etched title. (GB. May 5; 3442) DM 3,700

VOGT, N. & Schreiber, A.W.
[–] Voyage Pittoresque sur le Rhin. Ill.:– Gunther. Frankfurt, 1805-07. 3 vols. Folding plan, 32 engraved plts., some light foxing, cont. str.-grd. mor. gt. (C. Nov.16; 192) Davidson. £480

VOGTHERR, Heinrich & Burgkmair, Hans
- Augsburger Geschlechter Buch. (Bound with:) ZIMMERMANN, Wilhelm Peter – Der Ander Theil ... [Augsburg], 1618? Together 2 works in 1 vol. Fo. Lacks 5 plts., about 10 with some staining, some torn & reprd., mostly in blank margin, old bds., covered with vell. from old MS., w.a.f. (C. May 30; 55) Beres. £2,600

VOIGHT, Hans Henning 'Alastair'
- Fifty Drawings. Intro.:– Carl Van Vechten. N.Y., 1925. (1025). 4to. A few plts. loose, a few gatherings starting, cl.-bkd. patterned bds., extremities slightly worn. (SG. Jan.12; 2) $130
- Forty-three Drawings by Alastair. Ed.:– R. Ross. L. & N.Y., 1914. (500). 4to. On Bütten, some margins slightly browned, 1 plt. with sm. margin tear, 1st. & last ll. reprd., end-papers renewed, orig. pict. linen, margins & spine slightly discold.; Franz Goldstein ex-libris inside cover. (H. Nov.24; 1308) DM 460

VOIGTEL, Nicolas
- Geometria Subterranea, oder Marckscheide-Kunst. Eisleben, 1686. 1st. Edn. Lacks last lf. (Bound with:) SCHONBERG, A. von
- Ausführliche Berg-Information. Leipzig, 1693. Together 2 works in 1 vol. Fo. Slightly browned, last ll. & inner cover wormed, cont. cf., short tear at head. (H. May 22; 172) DM 850

VOIGTLANDER, R.
- Album des Nahe Thales. Ill.:– G. & F. Wiessner. Kreuznach, ca. 1860. Ob. 4to. Slightly foxed thro.-out, especially margins, orig. pict. hf. linen, slightly spotted & bumped. (H. Nov.23; 414) DM 3,500

VOISENON, Abbé de
- Contes. Avec une Notice bio-bibliographique par Octave Uzanne. Ill.:– Gery Bichard. Paris, 1878. Added separate suite of frontis. & 5 plts., mor., by Allo, gt. decor., gt. inner dentelle, wrap. (HD. Dec.16; 206) Frs. 1,000

VOISIN, G.
- Quelques Morceaux de Vie Folle. Poèmes. Ill.:– C.G. Beverloo 'Corneille'. 1977. (50) sigd. by author & artist. Sm. fo. 8 orig. lithos., numbered & sigd. by artist, leaves, box, cl. (B. Feb.8; 369) Fls. 950

VOLATERRANUS, Raphael Maffei
- Commentariorum ... Basel, 1559. Fo. Wide margins, wormhole affecting last 12 ll., hf. cf. (SG. Jan.19; 216) $175

VOLBACH, W.F.
See— WULFF, O. & Volbach, W.F.

VOLBACH, W.F. & Kuehnel, Ernst
- Late Antique, Coptic & Islamic Textiles of Egypt. L., 1926. Lge. 4to. 100 plts., many cold. & mntd. on art paper, ex-liby., gt.-decor. cl. (SG. May 3; 370) $450
- – Anr. Copy. Tall 4to. 100 plts., cl., head of spine chipped. (SG. Aug.25; 376) $350

VOLCK VON WERTHEIM, Heinrich
- Auf Neue Manier Abgefasster und Allzeit Fertiger Brief-Steller ... Trans.:– Bernhard Dietrich von Scharffenberg. Chemnitz, 1741. Sm. 8vo. Frontis., mod. red mor. (SG. Apr.19; 190) $120

VOLKMANN, H. von
- Afrika. Studien und Einfälle eines Malers. Leipzig, 1895. Lge. ob. 4to. Orig. cold. pict. hf. linen. (R. Apr.3; 537) DM 460

VOLKMANN, J.J.
- Histor.-krit. Nachrichten von Italien. Ill.:– Geyser. Leipzig, 1770-77. 1st. Edn. pts. 2 & 3. 3 vols. Engraved frontis. & 3 engraved title vigs., pts. 2 & 3 with excised name in upr. margin, lightly browned thro.-out, cont. hf. leath., pts. 2 & 3 partly bumped, vol. 3 with old material pasted at top, gt. spine, vols. 2 & 3 faded, vol. 1 not unif. (HK. May 15; 908) DM 2,400

VOLLARD, Ambroise
- Catalogue Complet des Editions Ambroise Vollard, Exposition du 15 Décembre 1930 au 15 Janvier 1931 au Portique. Ill.:– Raoul Dufy & after A. Renoir. Paris, 1930. (625) numbered. (125) with etching ptd. in brown. Lge. 4to. Cont hf. mor., spine slightly faded, orig. wraps. bnd. in, unc., s.-c. (S. Nov.21; 71) Desk. £500
- Dégas. Paris, 1914. (800) numbered. Fo. Orig. wraps., unc.; pres. copy, inscr. by Vollard. (S. Apr.30; 99) Dreesman. £110
- – Anr. Edn. Paris, 1914. (800) numbered. (100) on papier vergé. Fo. Cont. hf. mor., lightly rubbed, orig. wraps. bnd. in. (CSK. Jan.27; 14) £55
- Paul Cezanne. Paris, 1914. (200) velin à la forme, with Paul Cezanne wtrmrk. Lge. 4to. Three-qtr. mor., spine slightly scuffed, orig. pict. wraps. bnd. in, unc. (SG. Oct.13; 84) $350
- – Anr. Edn. Paris, 1915. (650) numbered on tinted paper. 4to. With orig. etching, suede, orig. pict. wraps. bnd. in. (GB. Nov.5; 2334) DM 950
- La Vie et l'Oeuvre de Pierre-Auguste Renoir. Paris, 1919. (1000) numbered. Fo. Cont. hf. mor., rubbed, orig. wraps. bnd. in. (CSK. Jan.27; 13) £280
- – Anr. Edn. Paris, 1919. (375) on vélin d'Arches. Fo. No bdg. stated. (SPB. Nov.30; 64) $1,600

VOLMARIUS, M.
- Newe Zeitung vom Schrecklichen Erdbidm, den 15. nach dem Newen, aber den 5. Tag Septembris, nach der Alien Calender des 1590. Jars, zu Wien in Oesterreich geschehen ... N.p., 1591. 4to. Slightly foxed or browned, later hf. vell. (D. Nov.23; 60) DM 610

VOLNEY, Constantin François, Chasseboeuf de
- Oeuvres. Paris, 1852. 4to. Hf. cf. (HD. Feb.22; 227) Frs. 1,000
- Tableau du Climat et du Sol des Estats-Unis D'Amérique. Paris, 1803. 1st. Edn. [Sabin's 'B'

VOLNEY, Constantin François, Chasseboeuf de - *Contd.*

Iss.,] with the *'vocabulaire de langue des Miamis'* paged separately 1-8. 2 vols. Slight tear to 1 map, near-cont. cats-paw pol. cf. gt. by Hering, with his ticket, extremities rubbed; the Castle Howard & Rt. Hon. Visc. Eccles copy. [Sabin 100692] (CNY. Nov.18; 277) $480
- **Travels through Syria & Egypt** ... 1788. *2nd. Edn.* 2 vols. Cont. cf., worn. (SKC. Sep.9; 2064) £70

VOLLSTANDIGE VOLKERGALLERIE, in Getreuen Abbildungen aller Nationen ...
Meissen, [1830-39]. 3 vols. in 4. 4to. 1 engraved & 2 litho. frontis., 244 old cold. lithos with 487 ills., vol. 1. pt. 1 lacks ptd. title, no litho. title publd. for vol. 1, pt. 2. vol. 2 pts. 1-2 (in 1 vol.) with litho. title, vol. 3 with litho. title, some foxing, cont. hf. leath. (BR. Apr.12; 220) DM 1,300

VOLTAIRE, François Marie Arouet de
- **Candide.** Trans.:- Ralph. [Amst.], 1759. *1st. Edn.* Mod. spr. cf.; bkplt. of David, Earl of Buchan, taken from the earlier bdg. (S. May 10; 427) *Adams.* £360
- - **Anr. Edn.** Trans.:- Dr. Ralph. 1759-61. 2 vols. Cont. cf. gt. (P. Jun.7; 318) £190
- - **Anr. Copy.** 12mo. Cont. marb. bds. (D. Nov.24; 2593) DM 400
- - **Anr. Edn.** Ill.:- Georges Jeanniot. Paris, Lausanne, 1936. Jansenist red mor. by Semet & Plumelle, mor. liners, watered silk end-ll., wrap. preserved, s.-c.; unique copy with 4 states of engrs., 2 added orig. copper engrs. & 40 orig. drawings bnd. in 1 vol., 4to., red hf. mor. by Semet & Plumelle. (HD. Jun.13; 114) Frs. 7,200
- - **Anr. Edn.** Ill.:- Paul Klee. N.Y., [1944]. *(625)* numbered. *(50) with 2 extra sets of the ills. in envelope in lr. cover, specially bnd.* 4to. Orig. mor.-bkd. cl., s.-c. (S. Nov.21; 26) *Duschness.* £85
- **Collection Complète des Oeuvres.** Ill.:- Gravelot. Genève, 1768-77. *1st. Printing of ills.* 30 vols. 4to. Cont. cf. gt., decor. spines. (HD. Sep.22; 371) Frs. 10,500
- - **Anr. Edn.** 1780-81. 57 vols. Cont. tree cf. gt., 5 covers detchd., some spines rubbed. (P. Apr.12; 227) *Duran.* £110
- **Elémens de la Philosophie de Neuton.** Ill.:- Dubourg, Folkema, Picart & others. Amst., 1738. *1st. Edn.* Slightly spotted, port., frontis. & ptd. title washed, cont. leath., bumped, spine sprung & reprd. crudely. (R. Apr.3; 480) DM 640
- - **Anr. Edn.** L. [Paris], 1738. *2nd. Edn.* Hf.-title, errata lf., late 18th. C. cf. gt., arms of Simon-Pierre Merard de Saint-Just, hf. mor. s.-c.; inscr. on fly-lf. from Voltaire to Abbé Prevost, Lucien-Graux bkplt. (C. May 30; 104) *Quaritch.* £2,500
- [-] **La Henriade.** Ill.:- De Longueil after Ch. Eisen. Paris, [1769-]70. *New Edn.* 2 vols. Minimal browning, some slight foxing, cont. marb. cf., decor. gt. spine, cover & outer dentelle, slightly bumped, jnts. partly a little torn. (HK. May 17; 2499) DM 520
- - **Anr. Edn.** Ill.:- after Gerard. Paris, 1819. Sm. fo. L.P., 2 engraved plts., mod. tree cf., unc. (SG. Apr.19; 323) $140
- **Histoire de Charles XII, Roi de Suède.** Bâle [Rouen], 1731. *Orig. Edn.* 2 vols. 12mo. Lacks errata ll. (as often), cont. glazed spr. cf., spine decor. (H. Nov.9; 85) Frs. 2,400
- [-] **Histoire du Parlement de Paris par l'Abbé Big** ... Amst., 1769. *Orig. Edn.* 2 vols. 19th. C. hf. roan. (HD. Feb.22; 228) Frs. 1,200
- [-] **Kandide oder die Beste Welt.** Trans.:- [W. Chr. S. Mylius]. Ill.:- Chodowiecki. Berlin, 1778. Mininal spotting, cont. bds., slightly spotted; Hauswedell coll. (H. May 24; 1612) DM 600
- - **Anr. Edn.** Ill.:- Paul Klee. Munich, 1920. 4to. Orig. cl.-bkd. bds., slightly worn. (S. Nov.21; 25) *Rota.* £120
- **Lettres à l'Abbé Moussinot, son Trésorier.** La Haye & Paris, 1781. *Orig. Edn.* Cont. marb. cf. gt., spine decor. (HD. Nov.9; 88) Frs. 2,850
- **Lettres Philosophiques.** Amst., 1734. *Orig. Edn.* 12mo. Cont. spr. cf., Marc-Pierre de Voyer arms, spine decor. (HD. Mar.29; 99) Frs. 19,000
- **La Mérope Française.** Ill.:- Delatour, Duflos after Boucher, Fessard. Paris, 1744. *1st. Edn.* *(Bound with:)* - **Lettres à M. Norberg.** L. [Paris], 1744.

1st. Edn. Together 2 works in 1 vol., cont. bds. (D. Nov.24; 2368) DM 400
- **Le Micromegas.** L., 1752. *1st. Edn.* 12mo. Few ll. slightly browned, cont. cf., slightly worn. (BBA. Mar.21; 21) *Thorp.* £120
- **Oeuvres.** Amst. [Rouen?], 1740. *Pirated Edn.?.* 4 vols. 12mo. Cont. Italian cf. gt., arms of Antonio Ottaviano, Count de Collato on covers, gt. end-pp., bkplts. (PNY. Jun.6; 443) $275
- - **Anr. Edn.** N.p., 1756. 17 vols. Cont. cf.; Deneys Reitz copy. (SSA. Jul.5; 420) R 230
- - **Anr. Edn.** [Geneva], 1775. 40 vols. Lacks 1 frontis., 1 figure in 'Théâtre' & figures in 'La Pucelle', cont. marb. cf., spines decor., bdgs. not quite unif. (HD. Jun.6; 156) Frs. 6,500
- - **Anr. Edn.** Ill.:- after Moreau la Jeune. [Kehl], 1785-89. 70 vols. Cont. spr. cf. gt., spines gt., w.a.f.; from liby. of Luttrellstown Castle. (C. Sep.28; 1850) £2,600
- - **Anr. Edn.** Paris, 1809-18. 23 vols. 12mo. Bkplt., hf. mor. (GM. Dec.7; 578) £120
- **Oeuvres Complètes.** Notes:- Condorcet. Ill.:- Moreau le Jeune. Kehl, 1781 & 1785-89. 70 vols. Unopened, bds., worn. (LM. Mar.3; 239)
B. Frs. 13,000
- - **Anr. Edn.** Ill.:- Moreau. 1784. 70 vols. Cont. tree cf. gt., spines decor., some vols. dampstained. (HD. May 21; 74) Frs. 10,000
- - **Anr. Copy.** 70 vols. Cont. tree cf., decor. spines; La Rochefoucauld ex-libris. (HD. Sep.22; 372)
Frs. 8,000
- - **Anr. Edn.** Ill.:- after Moreau le Jeune. Kehl, 1784-89. 70 vols. Lge. 8vo. Some browning or foxing, cont. marb. leath. gt., Vol. 1 8vo. & not unif. (GB. Nov.4; 2215) DM 4,000
- - **Anr. Edn.** Ill.:- Baquoy & others after Moreau. Kehl, 1784-89. 68 vols. only (of 70). Cont. tree cf. gt., most vols. slightly rubbed, some spine ends worn. (S. Dec.20; 792) *Fenton.* £140
- - **Anr. Edn.** [Kehl], 1784-89. 69 vols. only (of 70). Vol.1 with cont. engraved port. laid onto fly-lf., mod. cf. in cont. style., gt.-decor. spines. (CBA. Dec.10; 479) $850
- - **Anr. Edn.** Gotha [Basel], 1784-90. 71 vols. 2 vols. with slight margin browning, some light foxing, cont. hf. leath. gt., lightly faded, slightly bumped, 8 vols. with margin tears. (H. May 22; 923) DM 2,400
- - **Anr. Edn.** Ill.:- Boquoy Delaunay Duclos, Langlois, Masquelier, Simonet & others after Moreau le Jeune. [Kehl] & Paris, 1784-89 & 1808. 70 vols. & 2 supp. vols. L.P., cont. marb. cf., decor. gt., bumped, wear. (H. Nov.23; 789) DM 3,400
- - **Anr. Edn.** Ill.:- after Moreau le Jeune. [Kehl], 1785-89. 70 vols. Cont. cf. gt. decor. by Bozérian, sigd. at foot. (C. May 30; 105) *Traylen.* £4,000
- **La Philosophie de l'Histoire.** Amst., [Genf.], 1765. *1st. Edn.* Old MS. notes on hf. title verso, slightly browned & spotted, mod. cf. gt. (D. Nov.24; 2595) DM 1,200
- **La Princesse de Babylone.** Ill.:- F. Heubner. München, 1922. *(34) De Luxe Edn.* 4to. On Bütten, 2 loose added series of etchings, hand-bnd. orig. vell. & box, orig. vell. s.-c.; printers mark & added etchings sigd. by artist. (H. Nov.24; 1856) DM 640
- [-] **Das Privatleben des Königs von Preussen, oder Nachrichten zum Leben des Herrn von Voltaire von ihm selbst geschrieben.** [Leipzig], 1784. *1st. German Edn.* Hf.-title stpd., slightly browned, cont. sewed, soiled. (GB. Nov.3; 263) DM 480
- [-] **La Pucelle d'Orléans** ... Paris, 1755. *1st. Edn.* 12mo. Title soiled, cont. cf., slightly worn; inscr. 'To Mr. White, un petit gage d'amitié Robt. Burns'. (BBA. Mar.21; 230) *Bauman.* £150
- - **Anr. Copy.** Most plts. loose, cont. red mor. gt., spine decor. (HD. May 3; 167) Frs. 3,400
- - **Anr. Edn.** Ill.:- Gravelot. Ginebra, 1762. *1st. Edn.* Cf. (DS. Oct.28; 2228) Pts. 25,000
- - **Anr. Copy.** Some browning or foxing, cont. leath., corners worn. (GB. Nov.4; 2216) DM 460
- - **Anr. Copy.** Some light browning & slight spotting, cont. hf. leath., worn, slightly bumped, lacks sm. piece at foot of spine. (HK. May 17; 2502) DM 420
- - **Anr. Edn.** Ill.:- Duplessi-Bertaux, Marillier-De Launay (frontis.). L., 1780. 2 vols. bnd. in 1. L.P., vigs. in double state before letter, wtrd. silk endpapers, mor. gt. decor., decor. spine, lavallière mor.

doubls., dentelle à l'oiseau, s.-c., by Cuzin. (HD. Dec.9; 91) Frs. 20,000
- - **Anr. Copy.** 18mo. Ills. loose, mor. gt. by A. Bertrand, spine decor. (HD. May 3; 168)
Frs. 4,200
- - **Anr. Copy.** 2 vols. in 1. 18mo. Sm. stain on frontis., mor., gt. decor., decor. spine, by Cuzin from Bayard Rives & Francis Kettanch libys. (HD. Dec.9; 90) Frs. 2,900
- - **Anr. Edn.** Ill.:- after Lebarbier & others. Paris, An VII [1789-99]. 2 vols. Port., 21 plts., 21 additional inserted plts. after Moreau le jeune, some light spotting, panel. spr. cf., by Mansell, spines gt. (SPB. Dec.13; 910) $200
- - **Anr. Edn.** Ill.:- Duplessi-Bertaux engraved by Loizelet. Rouen, 1880. *(354). (150) on Whatman with state of engrs. on China.* 2 vols. Hf. havanna mor., by Champs, corners, decor. spines, wraps. & spine preserved, s.-c. (HD. Dec.9; 196) Frs. 1,200
- **Romans et Contes.** Ill.:- Cathelin after La Tour (port.), Monnet, Marillier & Martini. 1778. *1st. Printing of ills.* 3 vols. Vol. 3 has instructions to binder (usually lacking), cont. mor.; from Zierer liby. (HD. Apr.13; 62) Frs. 7,000
- - **Anr. Copy.** 3 vols. Cont. marb. cf., spines decor., 1 turn-in defect. (HD. Mar.19; 159) Frs. 2,000
- - **Anr. Copy.** Red mor. gt. by Marius Michel, spines decor. (HD. May 3; 165) Frs. 1,500
- **Suite des 117 Figures ... pour les Oeuvres.** Ill.:- Moreau le Jeune, engraved by Simmonet, de Ghendt, Nicolet etc. Paris, 1802. Sewed. (HD. Jan.27, 372) Frs. 1,250
- **Suite des 80 Figures par Desenne ... pour l'edition des Oeuvres Complètes.** Paris, 1827-29. Fo. 80 figures on Chire appliqué in 2 states, ie. 160 figures, added ports., some margin foxing, later hf. red chagrin, corners, decor. spine; Emanuel Martin ex-libris. (HD. Jan.27; 370) Frs. 1,700
- **Théâtre Complet.** Lausanne, 1772. (L., 1774-80 last 2 vols.). 10 vols. Stains on last ll. 1 vol., cont. red mor., gt. decor., inner roulette, slight wear. (B. Apr.27; 589) Fls. 600
- **Thérèse, a Fragment** ... Ed.:- Desmond Flower. Roxb. Cl., 1981. 4to. Orig. qtr. mor. (S. Oct.4; 247)
Traylen. £80
[-] **Vie de Molière, avec des Jugemens sur ses Ouvrages.** Paris, 1739. *Orig. Edn.* 12mo. Cont. cf., Du Butay arms, spine decor. (HD. Mar.29; 100)
Frs. 10,000
- **La Vie Privée du Roi de Prusse, ou Mémoires pour servir à la Vie de Mr. de Voltaire, écrits par lui-même.** Amst., 1784. *Reprint.* 12mo. Mor. by Derome, spine decor.; from libys. of Pixerécourt & Edouard Rahir. (HD. Mar.29; 101) Frs. 4,500
- **Zadig oder das Geschick.** Trans.:- E. Hardt. Ill.:- M. Behmer. Berlin, 1912. *(80) De Luxe Edn. on Bütten.* Lge. 4to. Orig. vell.; printers mark sigd. by artist. (H. Nov.24; 1370) DM 4,400
- - **Anr. Copy.** Lge. 4to. Printers mark sigd. by artist, some light foxing, orig. vell. gt. cover vig., slight spotting, spine with pasted part & sm. tear. (H. May 23; 1151) DM 2,200
- - **Anr. Edn.** Trans.:- E. Hardt. Ill.:- M. Behmer. 1912. *(170) numbered on Amer. Japan.* Lge. 4to. Orig. etchings, orig. linen. (GB. Nov.5; 2281)
DM 1,400
- **Zadig ou La Destinée. Histoire Orientale.** [Paris, Rouen], 1748. *1st. Compl. Edn.* 12mo. Red mor. by Reymann. (HD. Apr.13; 64) Frs. 2,800
- - **Anr. Edn.** Ill.:- J. Garnier, F. Rops & A. Raubaudi engraved by Gaujeans. Paris, 1893. *(50) for members of Amis des livres, with the 29 proofs of plts. by Gaujeans.* Lge. 8vo. This copy for Germain Bapst, sm. stabmark affecting pp. between front end-paper & title, elab. mor., lattice work & greenery designs inlaid on covers, by E. Caravon, some darkening of spine, rubbing. (SPB. Dec.14; 87) $400
- **The Works.** Trans.:- T. Smollet. L., 1761-63. Vols. 1-30 only (additional vols. publd. later). Cont. cf. gt. (P. Sep.29; 360) *Axe.* £75

VON DER GEBRAUCH der Heiligen Horwirdigen Sacramenten
See— CATECHISMUS oder Kinder Predig – VON DER GEBRAUCH der Heiligen Hochwirdigen Sacramenten – KIRCHEN ORDNUNG im Churfurstenthum der Marcken zu Brandemberg

VONDEL, Joost. van den
- **Verzamelde Werken.** Ill.:– Saedeler, Gerards. 1636-1716. *Partly 1st. Edn.* 11 vols. 4to. Some margin browning & staining, 18th. C. blind-stpd. vell., spines gt., 1 spine slightly torn. (VS. Jun.7; 920) Fls. 1,700
- **Vorstelijcke Warande der Dieren.** Ill.:– Marcus Gheeraerts & [Ph. Galle?]. Amst., 1617. *1st. Edn.* 4to. Washed(?), tear in lf. reprd., margins of 2 ll. strengthened, mod. vell. (VG. Sep.14; 911) Fls. 3,400

VON HAGEN, Victor Wolfgang
- The Aztec & Maya Papermakers. Intro.:– Dard Hunter. N.Y., 1943. *1st. Edn. (220) in 14-point type.* Sm. fo. Mntd. frontis., 32 plts., ills., ex-liby., cl. (SG. May 17; 290) $200

VONK, L.C.
- **Geschiedenis der Landing v.h. Engelsch-Russisch Leger in Noord-Holland, 1799.** Haarlem, 1801. 2 vols. Hand-cold. folding map & 6 folding plts., unc., cont. hf. cf., spines gt. (VG. Nov.30; 1070) Fls. 520

VOORN, Henk
- **Old Ream Wrappers: an Essay on Early Ream Wrappers of Antiquarian Interest.** North Hills, Pa., Bird & Bull Pr., 1969. *(375) numbered, on the Press's H.M. coarse laid paper.* Tall 8vo. Ills., red hf. mor., marb. bds., by Kurt Gabel & Sons, Holland, Pa., prospectus laid in, with folder of 2 engrs. 'pulled from the orig. plts.' for the paper-makers C. & I. Honig. (SG. May 17; 35) $175

VORAGINE, Jacobus de
- **Golden Legend.** Ed.:– Frederick S. Ellis. Trans.:– William Caxton. [Hammersmith, Kelms. Pr., 1892]. 3 vols. 4to. Linen-bkd. bds., covers rubbed & lightly soiled. (LH. Sep.25; 405) $400
- **[Der Heiligen Leben].** [Augsburg, Johann Schönsperger, 1485?]. Vol. I only (of 2). Fo. Lacks 1st. 7 ll. (including table) & last 3 ll., most replaced with MS. copies of various periods, some ll. remargined, 19th. C. cf. over wood bds., richly decor., clasp; from Foundation Furstenberg-Beaumesnil. [H. 9978; Goff J162] (HD. Nov.16; 5) Frs. 28,000
- **Legenda Aurea Sanctorum.** Ulm, Johann Zainer, not after 1478. Fo. Rubricated, lacks 6 ll., some wormholes & stains, old stpd. pig over wood bds., worn, lacks clasps; armorial bkplt. of Robert Proctor, the Walter Goldwater copy. [BMC II, 529; C. 6390; Goff J-91] (SG. Dec.1; 192) $800
- – **Anr. Edn.** Basle, Michael Wenssler, 1490. 4to. Rubricated, 18th. C. vell.; from Fondation Furstenberg- Beaumesnil. [BMC III, 733; Goff J125] (HD. Nov.16; 14) Frs. 5,000
- – **Anr. Edn.** Nuremb., Anton Koberger, 6 Nov. 1492. Fo. 1st. initial in cols. & gold, other initials rubricated, lacks 1st. blank, quite heavily browned & stained, old vell., torn; the Walter Goldwater copy. [BMC II, 435; C. 6457; Goff J-130] (SG. Dec.1; 193) $700
- – **Anr. Edn.** Trans.:– R. Benz. Jena, 1917-21. *(1500).* 2 vols. 4to. Many hand-painted initials, blind-tooled pig, by Heyne Ballmüller, slightly rubbed. (HK. May 17; 2691) DM 400
- – **Anr. Edn.** Trans.:– R. Benz. Jena, 1917-21. *Ltd. Iss.* 2 vols. 4to. Hand-bnd. mor. by W. Hacker, Leipzig, blind-tooled, leath. inlays gt. (H. Nov.23; 1125) DM 470
- **Passional oder Leben der Heiligen.** Augsburg, Johann Schönsperger, 5 Aug. 1499. Vol. II only. Sm. fo. 157 ll. (of 269, lacks all before EE3, all after gg8 & a few other ll. in between), text woodcuts cold. by cont. hand, numerous defects, mostly involving loss of text or woodcuts, most crudely reprd. with strips of white tissue paper, mostly rather stained thro.-out, a few wormholes, 16th. C. German blind-stpd. cf., rebkd., w.a.f. [Goff J166] (S. Nov.17; 37) *Tzakas.* £850
- **Quadragesimales.** [Lyon, Johannes Trechsel. Mar. 1494]. 4to. Without De Tempore & De Sanctis, lacks 4 index ll., printers mark ptd. in red on verso of 1 lf., old limp vell., spine reinforced. [Copinger 6524. Goff J-199] (HD. Jan.30; 15) Frs. 2,300
- **Sermones de Sanctis et Quadragesimales.** Pavia, Jacobus de Paucis Drapis, 2 Sep. 1499. 4to. Heavily dampstained in part, old sheep, with orig. panel. cf.

covers mntd., very worn; the Walter Goldwater copy. [BMC VII, 1019; C. 6526; Goff J-201, III] (SG. Dec.1; 194) $250
- – **Anr. Edn.** Pavia, Jacobus de Paucis Drapis, 8 Jan. 1500. Pt. 2 only. Margin dampstains, 5 outer margins scorched, covers from early vell. MS.; the Walter Goldwater copy. [BMC VII, 1019; C. 6526; Goff J-201, II] (SG. Dec.1; 195) $250
- **Sermones de Sanctis per Anni Circulum.** Venetiis, Simon de Luere impensis Lazari de Soardis, 1497. 4to. Some slight worming, hf. vell. [Copinger II, 6525, 2] (CR. Jun.6; 16) Lire 800,000
- **Sermones Dominicales de Tempore et de Sanctis. Quadragesimales.** Pavia, Jacobus de Paucis Drapis, 14 Nov. 1499, 8 Jan. 1500, 2 Sep. 1499. 3 vols. in 1. (Vol. III misbnd. before Vol. II). Lacks final blank in Vol. I & III, sm. wormhole in 1st. 2 ll. slightly affects text & woodcut, last 3 or 4 ll at fore-margin of Vol. I & III, sm. wormhole in 1st. 2 ll. slightly affects text & woodcut, last 3 or 4 ll at fore-margin, lr. corner of gg2 torn away with slight loss of text, some spotting & staining, cont. Northern Italian blind-stpd. cf. over wood bds., lacks clasps, some repairs to spine but head & foot of spine worn, later end-papers; erased cont. owner's inscr. of Monastary of the BMV Cortemaggiore. [Goff J201] (S. Nov.17; 38) *A. Thomas.* £450

VORSTERMAN VAN OYEN, A.A.
- **Stam- en Wapenboek van Aanzienlijke Nederlandsche Familiën.** Groningen, 1885-90. 3 vols. Fo. 104 chromolitho. plts., lacks index (as often), orig. hf. chagrin, richly gt., spines & corners reprd., slightly loose as usual. (VS. Dec.8; 748) Fls. 750

VOS, Martin de
- **Oraculum Anachoreticum.** Ill.:– John Baptist Cavazza after de Vos. 1644. 4to. Engraved title & 16 plts. only, cut down & mntd. in 19th. C. album, cl.-bkd. bds., slightly soiled. (CSK. Jun.15; 101) £90

VOSBURGH, Walter S.
- **Cherished Portraits of Thoroughbred Horses from the Collection of William Woodward.** N.Y., Derrydale Pr., 1929. *1st. Edn. (200) on Japan vell.* Fo. 68 photogravure plts., red mor. gt. by Sangorski & Sutcliffe, minor spotting to covers; inscr. & sigd. by Woodward. (LH. Apr.15; 300) $900
- – **Anr. Edn.** Derrydale Pr., 1929. *(200).* 4to. 52 plts., red mor. gt. by Sangorski & Sutcliffe, orig. box defect.; pres copy from Woodward to E.C. Potter. (P. Dec.8; 207) *Way.* £700
See— HERVEY, John & Vosburgh, Walter S.

VOSMAER, Arnout
- **Description d'un Recueil Exquis d'Animaux Rares.** Amst., 1804 [separate titles dtd. 1767-1805]. 4to. Col.-ptd. frontis., 35 hand-cold. engraved plts., cont. cf., head of spine frayed. (C. Mar.14; 208) *Franklin.* £600

VOSS, Johann Heinrich
- **Des Publius Virgilius Maro Werke.** Braunschweig, 1799. *1st. Edn.* 3 vols. Cont. leath., gt marb. covers, decor. (HK. Nov.10; 2761) DM 400
- **Luise.** Ill.:– Kohl, Henne & Guttenberg after Chodowiecki. Königsberg, 1795. *1st. Edn.* Cont. style cf. gt. (D. Nov.24; 2598) DM 900
- – **Anr. Edn.** [Müchen, Rupprecht Pr., 1918]. *(200) on Bütten.* Hand-bnd. cf., by O. Dorfner, slightly bumped. (H. Nov.24; 1245) DM 440

VOSSIUS, M.
- **Annalium Hollandiae Zelandiaeque Libri V[– XX].** Amst., 1635-46. *1st. Compl. Edn.* 4 vols. 4to. Cont. vell. (VG. Sep.14; 1206) Fls. 600

VOYAGES IMAGINAIRES, Songes, Visions, et Romans Cabalistiques
Ed.:– Charles George Thomas Garnier. Ill.:– Marillier. Paris, 1787-89. 36 vols. (of 39). 70 plts., hf.-titles, cont. mott. cf., spines gt., vol. 36 spine slightly defect., as a collection, w.a.f. (S. Apr.10; 308) *Quaritch.* £640

VOYSIN, Joseph de
- **Disputatio Cabalistica R. Israel Fillii R. Mosis de Anima ... ex Doctrina Platonis Convenere.** Paris, 1635. Paper browned, sm. tear in c2 Hebrew section, cont. cf., arms of an Archbp. of Canterbury on sides, rebkd.; Dr. Walter Pagel copy. (S. Feb.7; 378) *Ritman.* £460

VREDEMAN DE VRIES, J.
- **Hortorum Viridariorumque Elegantes & Multiplicis Formae.** Köln, 1615. Ob. 4to. Engraved title & 14 copperplts. mntd. on bd. ll., loose. (R. Apr.3; 770) DM 1,800

VREDIUS or DE VREE, Olivario
- **Historiae Comitum Flandrae Libri Prodromi Duo.** Brügge, 1650. Vol. 2, pt. 1 in 1 vol. (of 2). Sm. 4to. Lacks ptd. title, some ll. mispaginated, 2 ll. with sm. fault, 1 lf. with bkd. tear, cont. leath., defect. (HT. May 10; 2575a) DM 460
- **De Seghelen der Graven van Vlaenderen ende Hunne Brieven Histori-wys Uyt-gheleyt.** Brugge, 1640. Fo. Cont. blind-stpd. vell. (VG. Sep.14; 1216) Fls. 2,200
- – **Anr. Copy.** Fo. Frontis., map, 111 plts., tear in 3 ll., blank corner of 1 plt. torn off, lr. margin of 1st. 64 plts. stained, later hf. vell., unc. (B. Oct.4; 730) Fls. 1,200

VRIES, Simon de
- **Curieuse Aenmerckingen der Bysonderste Oost en West-Indische Verwonderenswaerdige Dingen.** Ill.:– Romeyn de Hooghe. Utrecht, 1682. 4 vols. 4to. 46 etchings & 15 maps, lacks 19 plts., cont. vell. (VG. May 3; 682) Fls. 550
- **De Doorlughtige Weereld; voorstellende den zeer Nette Genealogische, Historische en Politische Beschrijvingh.** Amst., 1700. 3 vols. Sm. 8vo. Engraved frontis., title-vigs., 15 plts., 9 full-p. ills. of coats of arms, etc. & text ills., all hand-cold., many heightened in gt., very sm. area of worming through a few margins in Vol. 1, 1 or 2 minor tears, cont. cf., covers elab. tooled, gt.-decor., gt.-panel. spines (worn); MS. note on fly- lf. traces provenance to Antony Radcens (?) of Middelburg, 1770. (CH. Sep.20; 45) Fls. 700

VRIES, S. de
See— GOTTFRIED, Johann Ludwig & Vries, S. de

VRYER, A. de
- **Histori van John Churchill, Hertog van Marlborough en Prins van Mindelheim.** Ill.:– A. v.d. Laan & others. Amst., 1738-40. Sm. 8vo. Cont. cf., spines gt., 2 jnts. slightly wormed. (VS. Dec.9; 1220) Fls. 450

VUILLEMIN, Thurlier & Lacoste, C.
- **Nouvel Atlas Illustré la France et ses Colonies.** Paris, 1890. Fo. 106 hand-cold. maps, qtr. mor. (P. Feb.16; 298) £80

VUILLIER, Gaston
- **La Danse.** Paris, 1898. *[1st. Edn.].* Fo. Some spotting, orig. gt.-decor. str.-grd. mor. (TA. Oct.20; 316) £50
- – **Anr. Copy.** Sm. fo. Sm. liby. stp. on verso of last lf., three-qtr. mor., spine gt., tips worn. (SG. Nov.17; 162) $120
- – **Anr. Copy.** Fo. Publishers leath. (DS. Mar.23; 2728) Pts. 65,000
- **Les Iles Oubliées. Les Baléares, la Corse, la Sardaigne.** Paris, 1893. 4to. Cont. red hf. mor., corners. (HD. Oct.21; 178) Frs. 2,000

VVV. Poetry, Plastic Arts, Anthropology, Sociology, Psychology
Contribs.:– André Breton, Marcel Duchamp, Max Ernst, & others. N.Y., 1942. Nos. 1-4 in 3 pts. (all iss.), bnd. in 1 vol. 4to. Index, cl., lr. cover of no. 2/3 (a ready-made by Duchamp) bnd. in. (S. Nov.21; 130) *Baum.* £110

WACE, Alan John Bayard
- **Mediterranean & Near Eastern Embroideries from the Collection of Mrs. F.H. Cook.** L., 1935. 2 vols. 4to. Title of text vol. slightly spotted, orig. cl., s.-c. (S. May 1; 660) *Sims.* £620

WACHENHUSEN, K.S.H
See— STIELER, Karl, Wachenhusen, K.S.H. & Hacklander, F.W.

WACHSTEIN, Bernhard
- **Die Grabschriften des Alten Judenfriedhofes in Eisenstadt.** Vienna, 1922. *1st. Edn. (With:)*
- **Urkunden und Akten zur Geschichte der Juden in Eisenstadt und den Siebengemeinden.** Vienna. 1926. *1st. Edn.* Together 2 vols., forming Vols. 1 & 2 (all

WACHSTEIN, Bernhard *-Contd.*

publd.) of 'Eisenstaedter Forschungen'. Lge. 8vo. Text in German & Hebrew, hf. cl., slightly rubbed, bumped. (SG. Feb.2; 123) $225
– **Die Inschriften des Alten Judenfriedhofes in Wien.** Vienna, 1912, 1917. *1st. Edn.* 2 vols. 4to. In German & Hebrew, ptd. wraps., partially unopened, soiled, 2nd. vol. disbnd. (SG. Feb.2; 122) $300

WACHTER, J.G.
– **Glossarium Germanicum continens Origines et Antiquitates Linguae Germanicae Hodiernae.** Leipzig, 1727. *1st. Edn.* MS. owners entries, on title verso dtd. 1727 J.G. Hamann, on title dtd. 1732 Hagedorn & on inner cover B. v. Münchhausen, with sale note from auction of liby. of Zimmermann 1767, cont. vell. (BR. Apr.12; 1075) DM 400

WACKENRODER, Wilhelm Heinrich & Tieck, Ludwig
– **Herzensergiessungen eines Kunstliebenden Klosterbruders.** Berlin, 1797. *1st. Edn.* Wide margin, partly unc., cont. bds. (R. Oct.11; 457) DM 850
– – **Anr. Copy.** Some slight foxing, newbds., old cover paper, Hauswedell coll. (H. May 24; 1616) DM 480
– **Phantasien über die Kunst, für Freunde der Kunst.** Hamburg, 1799, *1st Edn.* Wide margin, minimal spotting, later hf. leath., spine torn, slightly bumped. (H. May 22; 911) DM 680

WADE, William Richard
– **A Journey in the Northern Island of New Zealand** ... Hobart, 1842. 12mo. Possibly lacks final lf. of botanical appendix, some foxing, old hf. cf., worn. (KH. Nov.9; 495) Aus. $100

WAFER, Lionel
– **A New Voyage & Description of the Isthmus of America.** L., 1704. *2nd. Edn.* Plts. torn, 2 reprd., stained, cont. panel. cf., spine ends chipped, corners reprd., w.a.f.; the Rt. Hon. Visc. Eccles copy. [Sabin 100940] (CNY. Nov.18; 278) $280
– – **Anr. Copy.** Some foxing, few gatherings badly browned, lacks text lf. H8, A2 reprd., 19th. C. cf. (SPB. Dec.13; 475a) $125

WAGENAAR, Jan
– **Amsterdam in Zyne Opkonst** ... Amst., 1760-67. 3 vols. Fo. L.P., engraved frontis., title vig., 2 ports., 132 plts., many double-p., some dampstaining, mod. hf. cf., unc. (C. Dec.9; 165) Weinreb. £1,200
– – **Anr. Copy.** 3 vols. Fo. L.P., frontis. 2 ports., 6 folding maps & plans, 72 views (26 folding), other plts. (*Bound with:*) **'t Verheugd Amsterdam ter Gelegenheld v.h. Bezoek (van) Willem (V) en Fredrica Sophia van Pruissen.** Amst., 1768. Together 2 works in 1 vol. Fo. Hf. cf., spine ends slightly defect. (B. Apr.27; 526) Fls. 1,400
– – **Anr. Edn.** Amst./Harling, 1760-1802. 4 vols. Fo. L.P., frontis., 4 ports., 6 maps & plans, 84 plts. & views, many double-p., hf. cf. (VG. May 3; 602) Fls. 3,000
– – **Anr. Edn.** Amst., 1760-1820. 4 vols. Fo. Frontis. to Vol. 1, 94 engraved plts., ports. & maps, 19th. C. hf. cf., Vol. IV rebkd. (CH. Sep.20; 47) Fls. 2,200
– **'t Verheugd Amsterdam, t.g.v. het Plegtig Bezoek hunner Doorl. en Kon. Hoogheden, Willem, Prinse v. Oranje en zyne Gemaalinne, den 30 May, 1768.** Ill.:– S. Fokke & R. Vinkeles. Amst., 1768 [1772]. Lge. fo. L.P., some stains &c., cont. hf. cf., slightly defect. (VG. Nov.30; 1071) Fls. 750
– **'t Verheugd Amsterdam, t.g.v. het Bezoek v. Willem v. Oranje.** Ill.:– Vinkeles. Amst., 1768. Fo. Frontis., 11 (lf 14) plts., elab. gt. & marb. cf. 'mirror-binding', spine slightly defect., loosening. (VG. May 3; 605) Fls. 550
– **Vaderlandsche Historie.** Ill.:– Amst.,. 1749-59. 21 vols. 12 extra ports., cont. hf. cf. (VG. Sep.14; 1208) Fls. 1,400
– – **Anr. Copy.** 21 vols. Frontis., approx 130 ports., maps & plts., hf. cf. (VG. May 3; 606) Fls. 1,300
– **Vaderlandsche Historie. – Byvoegsels en Aanmerkingen.** Amst., 1749-96. 21 vols.; 20 pts in 4 vols., together 25 vols. Some stains, hf. cf., some defects. (B. Oct.4; 729) Fls. 950

WAGENSEIL, Johann Christoph
– **Belehrung Der Juedisch-Teutschen Red und Schreibart.** Koenigsberg, 1699. *1st. Edn.* Sm. 4to. Includes ptd. notice from author, early vell., bowed, loose in bdg. (SG. Feb.2; 125) $150
– [–] **Sota. Hoc est: Liber Mischnicus de Uxore Adulterii Suspecta, Una cum Libri en Jacob Excerptis Gemarae Versione Latina, & Commentario perpetuo.** Altdorf, 1674. *1st. Edn.* Sm. 4to. Hebrew text & Latin trans., later bds. (SG. Feb.2; 126) $200

WAGNER, Daniel
– **Pharmaceutisch-Medicinische Botanik.** Ill.:– after Ignaz Strenzl. Vienna, 1828. 2 vols. Fo. 248 (of 249) hand-cold. litho. plts., mntd. on guards, title to plt. vol. laid down, text title stained, slight spotting & minor staining affecting about 6 plts., lacks text for 16 plts. (supplied in MS.), cont. hf. roan gt., recornered, w.a.f. (C. Jun.27; 188) Fritz. £13,500

WAGNER, Henry Raup
– **The Earliest Documents of el Pueblo de Nuestra Señora la Reina de Los Angeles.** Los Angeles, ptd. for the Zamorano Cl., 1931. *(65).* Cl.; tipped-in T.L.s. from Wagner; Littell bkplt. (LH. Sep.25; 294) $100
– **Sir Francis Drake's Voyage around the World: Its Aims & Achievements.** San Franc., 1926. *1st. Edn.* 4to. Cl., spine faded. (SG. Sep.22; 296) $125
– **Spanish Explorations in the Strait of Juan de Fuca.** Santa Ana, California, 1933. *1st. Edn.* 4to. Orig. cl. (LH. Sep.25; 296) $225
– **Spanish Voyages to the Northwest Coast of America in the Sixteenth Century.** San Franc., 1929. *1st. Edn.* Cl. (LH. Sep.25; 297) $275

WAGNER, Joh. Chr.
– **Interiora Orientes detecta.** Augsburg, 1686. Fo. Title lf. with old stp., ex-libris, cont. vell., lacks ties. (GB. Nov.3; 86) DM 500

WAGNER, P.S.
– [–] **Gründliche Nachricht von Ankunfft, Gepräge und Werth derer in Sachssen, Thüringen und Meissen gemüñzten Groschen.** Wittenberg, 1728. 4to. Title stpd., lightly browned, cont. brocade paper covered bds., slightly bumped. (R. Oct.11; 1070) DM 550

WAGNER, Richard
– **L'Anneau du Nibelung.** Ill.:– Arthur Rackham. Paris, [1909-10]. *(300) on vélin à la forme.* 2 vols. 4to. 2 frontis., 62 col. plts., publisher's bradel parch. gt., unc. (HD. Apr.26; 236) Frs. 3,500
– **Das Judenthum in der Musik.** Leipzig, 1869. *1st. Edn. in Book Form.* Tall 8vo. Ptd. wraps., nearly disbnd., spine chipped, wraps. soiled. (SG. Feb.2; 127) $100
– **L'Or du Rhin et la Valkyrie ... Siegfried et le Crépusoule des Dieux.** Trans.:– A. Ernst. Ill.:– Arthur Rackham. [1910-11]. 2 vols. 4to. On japan, no bdg. stated. (HD. Jun.26; 130) Frs. 3,800
– **Parsifal.** Ill.:– Willy Pogany. 1912. *(525) numbered & sigd. by artist.* 4to. Orig. gt.-decor. vell., unc. (SKC. Mar.9; 1804) £90
– **The Rhinegold & the Valkyrie.** Ill.:– Arthur Rackham. 1910. *(1150) numbered & sigd. by artist.* 4to. Orig. vell., lightly soiled. (CSK. Aug.19; 9) £160
– – **Anr. Copy.** Orig. vell., soiled, lacks ties. (CSK. Sep.30; 163) £75
– – **Anr. Copy.** Lge. 4to. Mod. crushed mor., spine gt., orig. gt.-pict. vell. cover label preserved, partly unc. (SG. Mar.29; 256) $325
– **The Rhinegold & the Valkyrie. – Siegfried & the Twilight of the Gods.** Ill.:– Arthur Rackham. L., 1910; 1911. *(1150) numbered & sigd. by artist.* Together 2 vols. 4to. A few ll. slightly browned, orig. parch. gt., worn. (S. Dec.20; 584) Bowes. £220
– **Der Ring des Niebelungen.** Ill.:– Arthur Rackham. Frankfurt, 1910. *(100).* 2 vols. 63 col. plts., publisher's hf. parch., decor. spines, d.-w.'s. (HD. Sep.22; 374) Frs. 1,500
– – **Anr. Edn.** Ill.:– Arthur Rackham. Frankfurt, 1910-11. *De Luxe Edn., (100) on Bütten, sigd. by artist.* 2 vols. 64 col. plts., vell, partly unc. (B. Feb.8; 632) Fls. 1,100
– – **Anr. Edn.** Ill.:– Arthur Rackham. Frankfurt,

1910-11. 2 vols. 4to. Vell.-bkd. bds. gt. (SKC. Jan.13; 2171) £60
– **The Ring of the Nibelung.** Trans.:– Margaret Armour. Ill.:– Arthur Rackham. 1910-11. 2 vols. 4to. Orig. gt.-decor. cl., damp-affected. (TA. Mar.15; 425) £84
– **Siegfried & the Twilight of the Gods.** Ill.:– Arthur Rackham. L., 1911. *(1150) numbered & sigd. by artist.* 4to. Orig. parch. gt., spotted, lacks ties. (S. Nov.22; 351) Ayres. £130
– – **Anr. Copy.** 4to. Cont. vell., soiled, lacks ties. (P. Jan.12; 295) Ayres. £100
– – **Anr. Copy.** Orig. vell., soiled, lacks ties. (CSK. Sep.30; 162) £50
– – **Anr. Copy.** Lge. 4to. Mod. crushed mor., spine gt., orig. gt.-pict. vell. cover label preserved, partly unc. (SG. Mar.29; 257) $325
– **Tannhauser.** Ill.:– Willy Pogany. L., 1911. *(525) numbered & sigd. by artist.* 4to. Prospectus loosely inserted, orig. blind-stpd. mor., orig. box. (S. Nov.22; 346) Hirach. £220
– – **Anr. Copy.** 4to. Cf. (P. Sep.8; 414) Primrose. £60
– **Wieland der Schmiedt.** Leipzig, Ernst Ludwig Pr., [1911]. *(15) on vell. De Luxe Edn.* Lge. 8vo. Orig. red crushed mor., gt. cover ill., gold fillets, gt. inner dentelle, upr. fold slightly torn with light paste traces, lr. cover with 3 sm. nail marks. (H. May 22; 1018a) DM 5,200
– – **Anr. Edn.** Ill.:– F.W. Kleukens. Darmstadt, Ernst Ludwig Pr., [1911]. *(225). (160).* On Van Gelder Bütten, orig. cf., lge. cover vig., gold decor., gt. inner dentelle, spine slightly faded. (GB. May 5; 2467) DM 800

WAHLEN, Auguste
– **Usi e Costumi, Sociali, Politici e Religiosi, di Tutti i Popoli del Mondo (Volume I, Asia; Volume II. Ocenaia; volume III Africa & America; Volume IV, Europe.).** Trans.:– Luigi Cibrario. Turin, 1844-47. 4 vols. Tall 4to. Authorship credited on title-pp. to N. Dally, 229 (of 245) hand-cold. wood engrs., few plts. lightly foxed in margins, some foxing in text, leath.-bkd. bds., worn, 2 vols. disbnd. (SG. Aug.25; 114) $200

WAHLSTEDT, Jacobus J.
– **Iter in America.** Ed.:– O. Celsiue. Uppsala, [1725]. Slight discoloration, later bds. [Sabin 100960] (S. Dec.1; 302) Anderson. £140

WAIBLINGER, W.
– **Vier Erzählungen aus der Geschichte des Jetzigen Griechenlands.** Ludwigsburg, 1826. *1st. Edn.* Foxed, cont. hf. leath. gt., lightly rubbed; ex-libris. (HT. May 9; 1702) DM 800

WAIN, Louis
– **Big Dogs, Little Dogs, Cats & Kittens.** Ca. 1900. Fo. Orig. decor. bds., rubbed. (TA. May 17; 663) £135
– **Pa Cats, Ma Cats & Their Kittens.** N.d. 4to. Orig. pict. cl. (P. Sep.8; 401) £85

WAIT, Benjamin
– **Letters from Van Dieman's Land, written during Four Years Imprisonment for Political Offences committed in Upper Canada.** Buffalo, 1843. *1st. Edn.* 12mo. Staining in gutter-margin of 1st. few ll., old. bds., leath. back, worn. (RO. May 29; 194) $125
– – **Anr. Copy.** Perforated liby. stp. on title-p., early bds., qtr. roan, slightly rubbed; sigd. pencil inscr. by author. (KH. May 1; 729) Aus. $110

WAKEFIELD, Edward
– **An Account of Ireland, Statistical & Political.** L., 1812. *1st. Edn.* 2 vols. 4to. Hf.-titles, bkplt., cont. cf., tooled border. (GM. Dec.7; 473) £250

WAKEFIELD, Edward Gibbon 'Robert Gouger'
– [–] **The New British Province of South Australia.** L., 1834. 12mo. Folding engraved map, wood-engraved frontis., 3 charts, 1 text ill., sm. erasure on title, orig. cl., soiled. (S. Apr.9; 67) Maggs. £75
– **South Australia in 1837, in a Series of Letters, with a Postscript as to 1838.** Ca. 1838. *2nd. Edn.* Bdg. not stated, unc. (KH. May 1; 307) Aus. $190
– **A View of the Art of Colonization** ... 1849. *1st. Edn.* Early hf. roan, unc., slightly rubbed. (KH. May 1; 732) Aus. $150

WAKELY, Andrew & Atkinson, James
- The Mariner's Compass Rectified. 1738. Hf.-title, advts. on verso, cont. cf., rebkd., covers reprd. (SKC. Mar.9; 1926) £50

WAKEMAN, Geoffrey
- English Hand Made Papers Suitable for Bookwork. [Loughborough], The Plough Pr., 1972. *(75) numbered.* Fo. Orig. qtr. mor., untrimmed. (SG. Sep.15; 341) $220
See— CAVE, R. & Wakeman, Geoffrey

WAKOSKI, Diane
- The Wandering Tattler. Ill.:– Ellen Lanyon. Driftless, Wis., Perishable Pr., 1974. *(5) numbered & sigd., specially bnd.* Narrow fo. Qtr. mor., cl. covers, unc., cl. s.-c. (SG. Mar.1; 591) $300

WALCH, Garnet
- Victoria in 1880. Melbourne, [1880]. 4to. Orig. cl., slightly marked. (S. Jun.25; 20) *Bonham.* £60

WALCH, J.E.I.
- Das Steinreich Systematisch entworfen. Halle, 1769 & 1764. *1st. Edn.* pt. 2. 2 pts. in 1 vol. Pt. 1 title stpd., lightly foxed & stained, 2 plts. soiled in side margin, corners lighly bumped, cont. leath. gt., lr. cover slightly wormed. (HK. Nov.8; 658) DM 540

WALCH, J.G.
- Philosophisches Lexicon ... mit e. Kurzen Krit. Geschichte der Philosophie ... v. J.C. Hennings. Leipzig, 1775. 2 vols. Lightly foxed, cont. leath. gt., decor., slightly bumped & rubbed. (HK. Nov.9; 2227) DM 420

WALCOT, Dr.
- The History & Adventures of Little Henry. L., 1830. *11th. Edn.* 16mo. 7 aquatint cut-out figures, 1 (of 4) hats & interchangeable head, all handcold., orig. decor. wraps., with s.-c. for 'Little Fanny'. (S. Nov.22; 444) *Demetzy.* £70

WALDEMAR VON PREUSSEN, Frederick Willem, Prince
- Zur Erinnerung an die Reise des Prinzen Waldemar ... nach Indien in den Jahren 1844-46, Vorwort Alexander von Humboldt. Ill.:– Bellermann & others. Berlin, 1853. 2 vols. Fo. Additional litho. titles, litho. ports., 9 engraved maps & plans on 6 ll., some cold. in outl., 101 tinted litho. plts., lacks 3 plts. & letterpress to plt. IX at end of Vol. II, 1 plt. & a few ll. loose, a few ll. stained, some foxing to most plts., orig. cl. gt., rubbed, Vol. I covers detchd., w.a.f. (C. Jun.27; 77) *Sotheran.* £700

WALDMANN, Emil
- Edouard Manet. Berlin, 1923. 4to. With 2 etchings by Manet, orig. hf. parch. (S. Nov.21; 31) *Desk.* £170

WALDSTEIN, Albrecht von
- [–] The Relation of the Death of that great Generalissimo (of his Imperiall Maiestie) the Duke of Meckleburg [i.e. Wallenstein]. 1634. *1st. Edn.* 4to. Recent cl. [STC 24956] (BBA. Jun.14; 34) *Sokol.* £120

WALFORD, Edward
See— BRAYLEY, Edward Wedlake & Walford, Edward

WALFORD, Edward
See— THORNBURY, George Walter & Walford, Edward

WALKER, A.H.
- Atlas of Bergen County. Reading, Pa., [1876]. Lge. 4to. A few ll. slightly soiled & frayed, few repairs, hf. mor., decor. cl., rebkd. in buckram. (SG. Apr.5; 140) $275

WALKER, Adam, Philosopher
- A System of Familiar Philosophy. Priv. ptd., 1799. 4to. 47 engraved plts., some folding, lacks hf.-title, some light spotting, near-cont. hf. cf., rubbed. (CSK. Jul.27; 107) £65

WALKER, Adam, of U.S. Infantry
- A Journal of two campaigns of the Fourth Regiment of U.S. infantry. Keene, N.H., priv. ptd., 1816. 12mo. Some tears reprd. & margins strengthened,
some spotting, paper-bkd. bds. (S. Jun.25; 128) *Maggs.* £200

WALKER, Annie F.
- Flowers of New South Wales. Sydney, 1887. 4to. Plts. in col., mod. pol. cf., orig. cl. upr. cover (spotted) bnd. in at end. (KH. May 1; 734) *Aus.* $1,200

WALKER, George
- The Voyages & Cruises of Commodore Walker during the late Spanish & French Wars. L., 1760. *1st. Edn.* 2 vols. 12mo. Cont. cf., spines gt. [Sabin 101044] (C. Nov.16; 36) *Maggs.* £500

WALKER, George, Artist
- The Costume of Yorkshire. L., 1813-14. Fo. L.P., 41 plts., in 2 states (hand-cold. aquatint in wash border & plain etching), no uncold. version of plt. 5 (an orig. drawing substituted), no. 6 a sm. plt. on L.P., border of plt. 11 uncold., interleaved with tissues, mntd. on guards, without title or text, 19th. C. red hf. mor. (C. Nov.16; 194) *Foyle.* £1,400
- – Anr. Edn. L., 1814. 4to. Hand-cold. frontis., 40 hand-cold. plts., text in Engl. & Fr., hf. mor. gt. by Roger De Coverly & Sons. (P. Oct.20; 241) £1,200
- – Anr. Copy. Fo. 40 hand-cold. aquatint plts., titles & text in Engl. & Fr., lacks frontis., cont. str.-grd. mor., covers gt.– & blind-panel., spine gt. (C. Nov.16; 195) *Davidson.* £620
- – Anr. Edn. 1814 [wtrmkd. 1811-15]. Fo. Hand-cold. aquatint frontis., 40 plts., titles, contents lf. & text in Engl. & Fr., some light spotting, mod. cf. (CSK. Aug.19; 88) £850

WALKER, Rev. George
- A True Account of the Siege of London-Derry. L., 1689. *3rd. Edn.* Sm. 4to. Bkplt., hf. cf. [Wing W353] (GM. Dec.3; 236) £85

WALKER, Sir Hovenden
- A Journal, or Full Account of the late Expedition to Canada. L., 1720. *1st. Edn.* Cont. mott. cf., spine worn; Sir Clement Cottrell bkplt. [Sabin 101050] (SPB. Dec.13; 476) $450
- – Anr. Copy. Cont. panel. cf., spine gt., spine ends worn; the Rt. Hon. Visc. Eccles copy. [Sabin 101050] (CNY. Nov.18; 280) $350

WALKER, James
See— ATKINSON, John Augustus & Walker, James

WALKER, John Prof., 1731-1803
- An Economical History of the Hebrides & Highlands of Scotland. Edinb., 1808. 2 vols. Hf. cf. (PD. Dec.14; 148) £120

WALKER, John & Charles
- British Atlas. [1837]. Fo. 45 engraved maps only, lacks title, lightly stained, margins soiled, old bds., disbnd., w.a.f. (CSK. Nov.4; 12) £250
- Hobson's Fox-Hunting Atlas. L., [1850]. Fo. 42 litho. county maps hand-cold. in outl. to indicate hunt boundaries, some faint spotting, some maps loose or torn without loss of ptd. surface, publishers hf. roan gt., worn, w.a.f. (S. May 21; 38) *Shapiro.* £220

WALKER, Judson Elliott
- Campaigns of General Custer in the North-West, & the Final Surrender of Sitting Bull. N.Y., 1881. *1st. Edn.* Ptd. wraps., slightly chipped. (SG. Oct.20; 367) $200

WALKER, Robert, Architect
- The City of Cork, How it May be Improved. Cork, 1883. *1st. Edn.* Royal 8vo. Pres. copy to Arthur Hugh Smith Barry P.C. Fota from author, with Smith Barry bkplt., errata slip, hf. mor. (GM. Dec.7; 445) £95

WALL, Thomas
- [–] The Voyage of Sir Nicholas Carewe to the Emperor Charles V ... 1529. Ed.:– R.J. Knecht. Roxb. Cl., 1959. 4to. Orig. qtr. mor. (S. Oct.4; 248) *Traylen.* £260
- – Anr. Copy. 4to. Orig. qtr. mor. (S. Oct.4; 249) *Traylen.* £220
WALLACE, Alfred Russel
- The Malay Archipelago. L., 1869. *2nd. Edn.* 2 vols. Orig. cl. decor. gt. (SKC. Oct.26; 448) £100

WALLACE, H. Frank
- A Stuart Sketch Book, 1542-1746. Ill.:– Wallace & Lionel Edwards. 1933. *(50) numbered & sigd. by Wallace & Edwards.* 4to. Qtr. vell. gt. (SKC. May 4; 1650) £60
See— EDWARDS, Lionel & Wallace, H.F.

WALLACE, Robert
- [–] Characteristics of the Present Political State of Great Britain. 1758. *1st. Edn.* Cont. spr. cf., spine gt.; Sir Ivar Colquhoun, of Luss copy. (CE. Mar.22; 321) £300

WALLER, Edmund
- Poems, &c. L., 1645. *3rd. Edn.* Sm. 8vo. Some ll. washed & re-inserted, cont. cf., rebkd., hf. mor. s.-c.; Harold Greenhill bkplt., Frederic Dannay copy. (CNY. Dec.16; 366) $100
- The Second Part of ... Poems ... L., 1690. *1st. Edn.* License lf., sm. hole in G6, cont. cf., gouge on lr. cover; bkplts. of John Colbatch & Pickford Waller. [Wing W521]. (SPB. May 16; 157) $100
- Works. 1729. 4to. Title offset, red mor. gt., spine faded. (BS. Nov.16; 44) £130

WALLER, Dr. Erik
- Bibliotheca Walleriana. Ed.:– Hans Sallander. Stockholm, 1955. 2 vols. Cl. (P. May 17; 94) *Georges.* £65

WALLING, Henry F.
- Atlas of the Dominion of Canada. Montreal, 1875. Tall fo. 50 full-or double-p. maps, perforation stp. in title, some maps hand-stpd. on face, some margin stains, cl., covers crudely taped, ex-liby. (RO. Dec.11; 346) $150

WALLIS, Henry
- Egyptian Ceramic Art. N.p., 1900. *(200) numbered.* 4to. This copy unnumbered, two-tone cl., bumped, lightly soiled. (SG. Jan.26; 84) $150

WALLIS, Henry (Ed.)
See— GODMAN COLLECTION

WALLIS, James
- New British Atlas. L., S.A. Oddy, 1812 [i.e. 1813]. Sm. fo. Engraved title, 43 full-p. regional & county maps, hand-cold. in wash & outl., title torn & laid down, 1 or 2 maps soiled or stained, some faint browning, mod. cl. bds., worm. (S. Dec.1; 161) *Burgess.* £310
- New Pocket Edition of the English Counties or Travellers Companion. [1810]. 12mo. Hand-cold. engraved title, address lf. & 44 maps, cont. hf. mor., rebkd. in cl., rubbed. (CSK. May 4; 63) £140
- – Anr. Edn. [1811]. Col. title, dedication, 44 col. maps, hf. cf., worn. (P. Jul.5; 379) £100
See— REID, W.H. & Wallis, James

WALLIS, Capt. James
- An Historical Account of the Colony of New South Wales & its Dependent Settlements ... L., 1821. *[1st. Edn.].* Fo. Map, 12 engraved views (6 full-p., 6 double-p.), some minor foxing, 3 views split & reprd. at lr. centre fold, cont. cf., covers elab. blind-tooled, upr. cover reprd., sm. abrasions on lr. cover, corners rubbed. (C. Mar.14; 98) *Franklin.* £7,000
- – Anr. Copy. Fo. 9 (of 12) engraved views, including 4 double-p., sm. tears in folds & margins, some staining, 4 plts. loose, hf. cf., defect. (P. Nov.24; 50) *Remington.* £2,100

WALLIS, John
- Operum Mathematicorum Pars Prima [et Altera]. Oxford, 1656 [partly 1655]-57. *1st. Coll. Edn.* 2 pts. with 7 sectns. in 1 vol. 4to. Cont. vell. (R. Oct.12; 1723) DM 1,500
- A Treatise of Algebra, both Historical & Practical ... L., 1685. [Wing W613]. *1st. Edn.* (Bound with:) CASWELL, John – A Brief Account of the Doctrine of Trigonometry. L., 1685. [Wing C1252] *1st. Edn.* Together 2 works in 1 vol. Fo. Some browning, mostly marginal, margin stain at front, cont. cf., rebkd., corners renewed, rubbed; Stanitz coll. (SPB. Apr.25; 449) $500

WALLIS, John
- A New Atlas of France: Comprising Maps of the Eighty-Three Departments ... 1794. Ob. fo. 85 hand-cold. engraved maps, orig. bds., slightly worn, unc.; the Hinton House copy. (LC. Oct.13; 477)
£380
- - **Anr. Copy.** 4to. 85 cold. maps, cont. cf., corners worn. (BBA. Feb.9; 249) *Kentish.* £95

WALLIS, N.
- The Carpenter's Treasure, a Collection of Designs for Temples, With Their Plans, Gates ... in the Gothic Taste. L., n.d. 16 engraved plts., 1 loose, slight spotting, wraps. (P. Jan.12; 288)
Word. £360

WALLIS, Samuel
- Struggles & Escapes of Captain Wallis & his Crew, & their various Conflicts with the Natives of Otaheite ... N.d. Lacks? frontis., mod. qtr. mor. (KH. May 1; 737) Aus. $100

WALLRAF-RICHARTZ MUSEUM
- Kunst der Sechziger Jahre: Sammlung Ludwig im Wallraf-Richartz Museum. Köln, 1970. *4th. Edn.* 4to. In German & Engl., embossed clear plastic, covers slightly rubbed. (CBA. Jan.29; 357) $110

WALPOLE, Lieut. Hon. Frederick
- Four Years in the Pacific. 1849. *1st. Edn.* 2 vols. Cont. cf. gt. (P. Sep.8; 111) *Maggs.* £65

WALPOLE, Horace, Earl of Orford
- Aedes Walpolianae: or, a Description of the Collection of Pictures at Houghton-Hall in Norfolk ... 1752. *2nd. Edn.* 4to. Folding MS. plan of the gallery bnd. in at end, cont. cf.-bkd. bds., unc., rubbed; Sir Ivar Colquhoun, of Luss copy. (CE. Mar.22; 322) £180
- Anecdotes of Painting in England [with a Catalogue of Engravers ... from the MSS. of Mr. George Vertue]. Stawberry Hill, 1762-63. *1st. Edn.* Vols. 1-3 only (of 4) & the 'Catalogue ... '. 4to. Some offsetting, cont. diced russ. gt., rebkd. (SKC. May 4; 1578) £80
- - **Anr. Copy.** Vols. 1-3 only (of 4) & the Catalogue ... ' in 2 vols. 4to. Cont. diced cf., gt.-decor., covers. detchd., spines worn, Vol.1 slightly loose. (SKC. Sep.9; 1817) £50
- - **Anr. Edn.** L., 1762-63-71. *1st. Edn.* 5 vols. 4to. Cont. tree cf., flat spines gt.; A.N. to Lieut.-Col. Colquhoun, accompanying an A.L.s. to Sir James Colquhoun replying to his request for a copy of Vol. IV of the 'Anecdotes', both bnd. before title in Vol. IV, the Sir Ivar Colquhoun of Luss copy. (C. Nov.9; 167) *Franklin.* £2,600
- - **Anr. Copy.** Together 5 vols. 4to. 109 engraved ports., advt. lf. in vol.2, some offsetting, tooled cont. cf., gt., spines gt., unif., some jnts. reprd. (SPB. May 16; 158) $250
- - **Anr. Edn.** Ed.:- James Dallaway. L., 1828. 4 vols. only (of 5, without the 'Catalogue of Engravers'). 64 engraved plts., crimson three-qtr. mor., spines gt. (SG. Oct.13; 357) $110
- [-] The Castle of Otranto. L., 1765. *1st. Edn.* Slight margin browning, some faint margin stains, cont. cf., rebkd., corners worn; sig. of Adam Roxburgh. (SPB. May 16; 159) $1,200
- - **Anr. Edn.** Parma, 1791. *6th. Edn. (300).* Sm. 4to. Hf.-title, hf. mor. gt. by Sangorski, trimmed, bkplt. (PNY. Jun.6; 461) $100
- - **Anr. Edn.** 1796. *Jeffrey's Edn. On vell.* 7 cold. plts. ptd. on silk, gold margins, some ll. soiled, mod. spr. cf. (BBA. Sep.29; 161) *Bennett.* £260
- [-] - **Anr. Edn.** 1796. Cont. diced russ., spine gt.; Sir Ivar Colquhoun, of Luss copy. (CE. Mar.22; 323) £350
- - **Anr. Edn.** Ill.:- Mrs. Clarke. 1800. Some browning, orig. bds., worn; pres. copy from Shakespeare (W.H.) Ireland to his father. (BBA. Sep.29; 162) *Quaritch.* £85
- [-] Catalogue of the Classic Contents of Strawberry Hill. 1842. *[1st. Edn.].* 4to. Engraved frontis. & additional title, commission advt., orig. auctioneer's card. covers (soiled), later cl. backstrip. (SKC. Mar.9; 1733) £120
- - **Anr. Copy.** 4to. Hf. roan, gt. spine. (SKC. May 4; 1578) £80
- Catalogue of the Royal & Noble Authors of England. L., Straw. Hill Pr., 1758. *(300).* 2 vols. Sm.

8vo. Cont. cf., upr. jnts. split. (CSK. Feb.24; 206)
£65
- - **Anr. Edn.** L., 1806. 5 vols. Plts., some spotting, mod. cl. (P. May 17; 119) *Feingold.* £55
- Correspondence. Ed.:- W.S. Lewis. New Haven, 1937-61. *Yale Edn.* Vols. 1-22 & 28-31. Orig. cl., a few d.-w.'s marked or torn; 1st. vol. inscr. & sigd. by Wilmarth Lewis. (KH. Nov.9; 498) Aus. $110
- Hieroglyphic Tales. Montagnola, Bodoni Pr., for Elkin Matthews, 1926. *(250).* Orig. bds., slightly rubbed, unopened. (S. Nov.22; 266)
Parikian. £210
- Journal of the Printing-Office at Strawberry Hill. 1923. *(650).* 4to. Unc., orig. cf.-bkd. bds., s.-c. (BBA. Nov.10; 147) *Howes.* £55
- [-] A Letter to the Editor of the Miscellanies of Thomas Chatterton. Straw. Hill Pr., 1779. *1st. Edn., (200).* Mod. mor. gt.; misprints on p. 22 corrected in ink by author. (P. Apr.12; 46)
Chelsea Rare Books. £170
- - **Anr. Copy.** Misprint on p. 22 corrected in ink, wraps. (SKC. May 4; 1700) £110
- [-] - **Anr. Edn.** L., Straw. Hill Pr., 1779. *1st. Edn.* Hf.-title, red mor. gt. by Riviere, partly unc.; misprint on p.22 corrected by author, Borowitz copy. (SPB. May 16; 160) $375
- Letters. Ed.:- Peter Cunningham. 1857. 9 vols. Hf.-titles, armorial tree cf. gt. by Hayes of Oxford. (LC. Oct.13; 385) £55
- - **Anr. Edn.** Ed.:- Mrs. Paget Toynbee. Oxford, 1903-25. 19 vols., including 3 Supps. Orig. cl.; A.L.s. from author tipped in. (BBA. Dec.15; 233)
Fiske. £60
- - **Anr. Edn.** 1906. 9 vols. Hf. cf. gt. (P. Apr.12; 139) *Way.* £95
- Memoires of the Last Ten Years of the Reign of George II. L., 1822. *1st. Edn.* 2 vols. Lge. 4to. Some foxing & offsetting, later three-qtr. cf., gt.-decor. spine. (CBA. Dec.10; 111) $150
- The Works. 1798. 5 vols. 4to. Extra-ill. with many plts. & plans, light spotting, later hf. mor. (CSK. Oct.7; 64) £95
- - **Anr. Copy.** 5 vols. 4to. Some staining, mod. hf. cf. gt. (P. Jun.7; 98) £65
- - **Anr. Edn.** L., 1798-1822. 8 vols. 4to. Engraved vigs. on 6 titles, a plts. few offset, some spotting, cont. hf. cf., spines gt., soiled, last 2 vols. dampstained. (S. Mar.20; 796) *Elliott.* £95
- - **Anr. Edn.** L., 1798-1825. 9 vols. 4to. Engraved port. & plts., many folding, offsetting onto text, some spotting, cont. cf., spines gt. (S. Apr.10; 396)
Wade. £120
- - **Anr. Edn.** 1806-51. *Various Edns.* 29 vols. Unif. cont. cf., spines gt., lightly rubbed. (CSK. Jan.27; 5) £280

WALPOLE SOCIETY
- Note Book. [Portland, 1952-62]. *Each (40) for members of the Anthoensen Pr. (excluding Check List).* 11 vols., & 'Check List & Index ... 1910-1955'. Tall 8vo. Cl.-bkd. marb. bds., last title in cl.; 1st. vol. sigd. by 21 (of the 29 listed) members. (SG. Sep.15; 342) $200
- Prints Pertaining to America: A List of Publications; & A Checklist of Prints. N.p., Walpole Soc., ptd. at the Anthoensen Pr., 1963. *(1000).* Cl.-bkd. floral bds., unopened; inscr. to Lloyd Hyde from Charlie & Florence [Montgomery?]. (SG. Oct.13; 358) $100

WALPOOLE, George Augustus
- The New British Traveller. A. Hogg, [1782]. Fo. Engraved frontis., 57 plts. & 1 map only, old cf., rebkd. (CSK. Oct.7; 40) £150
- - **Anr. Edn.** Ca. 1785. Fo. 37 maps on 18 ll., plus 3 folding maps (1 torn & frayed), 148 copperplt. views on 86 ll., subscribers list, cont. panel. mor. (TA. Feb.16; 90) £270
- - **Anr. Edn.** L., ca. 1790. Fo. Frontis., engrs., folding map defect., hf. cf. worn, as a coll. of plts., w.a.f. (P. May 17; 353) *Hadland.* £370
- - **Anr. Copy.** Allegorical frontis., 23 maps, some folding, 86 (of 88) plts., 1 cut round & laid down, few imprints shaved, little spotting, slightly browned, lacks pp.149-156, hf. leath. (S. Mar.6; 350) *M. Cox.* £260
- - **Anr. Copy.** Fo. Engraved frontis., 18 maps, 80 plts., frontis. detchd., 1 map torn, some spotting or staining, cont. reversed cf., worn. (S. Jun.25; 343)
Kidd. £230

- - **Anr. Copy.** Fo. Frontis. 4 folding maps, 19 maps, 89 views, 1 folding map reprd. with tape, cont. cf., worn. (PNY. Jun.6; 557) $180

WALSER, Rob.
- Gedichte. Ill.:- Karl Walser. Berlin, [1909]. *1st. Edn. (300) on Bütten.* Printers mark sigd. by author & artist, 1 etching ptd. inverted, some slight browning, orig. pict. cold. bds., lightly bumped & spine slightly rubbed. (HK. May 17; 3219)
DM 1,400
- Seeland. Ill.:- K. Walser. Zürich, 1919. *1st. Edn. (500).* Printers mark sigd. by artist, orig. hf. linen, spine faded. (H. Nov.24; 2189) DM 1,050

WALSH, Peter
- [-] A Prospect of the State of Ireland from the Year of the World 1756 to the Year of Christ 1652. 1682. *1st. Edn.* Cont. mott. cf., spine gt.; pres. inscr. by author on front free end-paper, Evelyn book label. [Wing W640] (BBA. Jan.19; 168) *Lyon.* £230

WALSH, Rev. Robert
- Constantinople & the Scenery of the Seven Churches of Asia Minor. Ca. 1839. 2 vols. in 1. 4to. 2 engraved titles, 1 map, 94 engraved views, diced cf. gt. (P. Sep.29; 186) *Campbell.* £120
- - **Anr. Copy.** 2 vols. 4to. 2 engraved titles, 1 map, 93 engraved views, hf. cf. gt. (P. Sep.8; 393)
Sambos. £85
- - **Anr. Copy.** 2 vols. in 1. 4to. 2 vig. titles, 2 maps, 94 engrs., some foxing, hf. cf. gt. (P. Dec.8; 22)
Walford. £55
- - **Anr. Copy.** 2 vols. (1st. & 2nd. series). 4to. Extra engraved titles & 94 full-p. black-&-white engraved plts., tissue guards, some foxing to all plts. & extra titles, orig. red sheep & marb. bds., covers worn & scuffed. (HA. May 4; 294) $120
- - **Anr. Edn.** Ill.:- Thomas Allom. Ca. 1840. 2 vols. 4to. 2 engraved titles, 2 maps, 95 plts., some staining, hf. mor., worn. (P. Jan.12; 181)
Azezian. £160
- - **Anr. Edn.** L., n.d. 2 vols. in 1. 4to. Steel-engraved extra titles, 1 map, 94 plts., few plts. badly spotted, cont. hf. mor. (CSK. Feb.24; 101) £65
- - **Anr. Copy.** 2 vols. in 1. 4to. Engraved titles, 2 maps (1 folding), 93 plts., some ll. slightly spotted, cont. hf. mor., rubbed. (BBA. Dec.15; 58)
Primrose Hill Books. £60
See— **WARBURTON, John, of Dublin, Whitelaw, Rev. J., & Walsh, Rev. R.**

WALSINGHAM, Francis
- A Search made into Matters of Religion. [Saint-Omer], 1609. *1st. Edn.* Sm. 4to. Cf., rubbed. [STC 25002] (P. Jan.12; 289) *Georges.* £110

WALT DISNEY PRODUCTIONS
- The 'Pop-Up' Minnie Mouse. N.Y., [1933]. 3 double-p. col. pop-up plts., pict. bds. (SG. Dec.8; 135) $350

WALTER, Casp.
- Architectura Civilis. Augsburg, 1704. Fo. Lacks frontis., slightly foxed & soiled, cont. bds., bumped. (HK. Nov.9; 2228) DM 750

WALTER, Johann Ernst Christian
- Nordisk Ornithologie eller Trovaerdige efter Naturen Egenhaendig Tegnede, Stukne og Colorerede Afbildninger af Danske, Faerøiske, Grønlandske og Islandske Fugle. Copen., 1828-[41]. 3 vols. Fo. Text in Danish & German, 240 (of 288) hand-cold. engraved plts., some minor staining, 1 plt. with sm. surface damage, cont. hf. russ., gt. spines. (C. Jun.27; 136) *Howard.* £7,000

WALTER, Johann Gottlieb
- Observationes Anatomicae; Historia Monstri Bicorporis Duobus Capitibus, Tribus Pedibus, Pectore Pelvique Concreti. Ill.:- after J.B.G. Hopffer. Berlin, 1775. *1st. Edn.* Fo. Liby. stps., old mott. qtr. sheep, extremities slightly worn. (SG. Mar.22; 234) $325

WALTER, W.
- Das Preussische Heer in Bildern. Berlin, 1834. 25 hand-cold. plts., orig. pict. bds. (P. Mar.15; 96)
Maggs. £1,000

WALTERS, Alfred & Son
- Catalogue of Saddle, Harness & Horse Clothing. L., ca. 1880. Title, 69 (of 70) plts., orig. cl., worn. (P. May 17; 295) *Quaritch.* £150

WALTERS, Henry
- Incunabula Typographica: a Descriptive Catalogue of the Books Printed in the Fifteenth Century (1460-1500) in the Library of ... Baltimore, priv. ptd., 1906. 4to. Antique-style cf. (SG. Sep.15; 183) $125

WALTERS, Henry Beauchamp
- Select Bronzes, Greek, Roman, & Etruscan, in the British Museum. L., 1915. Lge. 4to. 73 plts., cl., spine end chipped. (SG. Aug.25; 68) $100

WALTERS, William T.
- The Collection of ... Text & Notes:- S.W. Bushell. N.Y., 1897. *(500).* 4 vols. Fo. 116 col. plts., all inlaid on Japan vell., lacks? 1 section hf.-title, a few tissue guards torn, a few text ll. with slight margin repairs, liby. stp. on plt. versos, a few stpd. in recto margin, loose as iss. in pict. cl. portfos., jnts. torn. (SG. Nov.3; 157) $650

WALTHER, E.
- Geographische Charakterbilder. Esslingen, 1891. Fo. 23 (of 24) double-p. chromolithos., plts. with sm. tears, some wear, orig. hf. linen, cover defect. (V. Sep.29; 142) DM 400

WALTHER VON DER VOGELWEIDE
[-] Agathon. Leipzig, 1773. De Luxe 1st. Edn. Minimal spotting, cont. leath., gt. spine & outer dentelle, corners lightly bumped. (HK. Nov.10; 2778) DM 1,150
- Gedichte. Ed.:- K. Simrock & W. Wackernagel. Trans.:- K. Simrock. Berlin, 1833. *1st. Edn.* Title verso stpd., cont. hf. leath. gt. (HK. Nov.10; 2769) DM 400
- Lieder. München, 1910. 4to. On Hundertbütten, hand-bnd. orig. red mor., gt. spine, cover, inner dentelle, by Carl Sonntag jun., Leipzig; Hauswedell coll. (H. May 24; 745) DM 3,200

WALTON, Elijah & Bonney, T.G.
- The Bernese Oberland: Twelve Scenes Among its Peaks & Lakes. Ill.:- after Walton. L., 1874. *1st. Edn.* Fo. Adhesion damage to 1 plt., some light foxing, heavier on title-p., elab. gt.-lettered & ruled moire cl., spine faded, to ends & corners worn. (CBA. Aug.21; 651) $110
- Flowers from the Upper Alps. 1869. 4to. 12 mntd. col. plts., some spotting, plts. & text loose, orig. cl. gt., soiled. (P. Mar.15; 233) *Walford.* £65
- Peaks & Valleys of the Alps. Ill.:- Elijah Walton. 1867. Fo. Hf. mor. gt. (P. Sep.29; 245) *Traylen.* £170

WALTON, Isaac
- The Life of Mr. Rich. Hooker. 1665. *1st. Edn.* License & errata ll., some light staining, later cf., rebkd. [Wing W670] (BBA. Jun.14; 52) *Hannas.* £60
- Works. Nones. Pr., 1929. *Ltd. Edn.* Mor. gt., partly unc., w.a.f.; from liby. of Luttrellstown Castle. (C. Sep.28; 1836) £200

WALTON, Isaac & Cotton, Charles
- The Complete Angler. Ed.:- Sir John Hawkins. L., 1760. *1st. Hawkins Edn.* Slight browning, cont. cf., worn. (S. Oct.4; 64) *Banks.* £80
- - Anr. Edn. 1775. 2 pts. in 1 vol. Cont. cf., rubbed. (CSK. Jun.29; 174) £65
- - Anr. Edn. 1815. Spotted, cont. cf. (CSK. Aug.19; 31) £50
- - Anr. Copy. Spr. cf., triple gt. fillet borders, back gt. with angling devices, gt. dentelles, by Morrell; armorial bkplt. of George Gordon Massey. (SG. Mar.15; 305) $110
- - Anr. Edn. L., 1824. Engraved plts., india proofs, mntd., woodcut vigs., few spots, late 19th. C. red mor. by Zaehnsdorf, gt., few scratch marks. (S. Apr.10; 594) *Buchhandlung.* £120
- - Anr. Edn. 1860. 2 vols. 61 mntd. plts. on India paper, hf. mor. gt., spines slightly faded. (P. Oct.20; 220) £65
- - Anr. Edn. L., 1888. *(500).* 2 vols. Lge. 4to. 54 photogravures & numerous woodcuts, each on India paper, light browning & offsetting, mostly on end-papers, orig. cl., some soiling, some wear to spine

ends, paper labels browned. (SPB. Dec.14; 88) $550
- - Anr. Edn. Ed.:- R.B. Marston. L., 1888. *Lea & Dove Edn., (250) sigd. by ed.* 2 vols. Lge. 4to. Owners' stps., unc., mor. gt., worn. (SPB. Dec.13; 613) $350
- - Anr. Edn. Ill.:- H.G. Webb. Caradoc Pr., 1905. *(364). (14) numbered on vell.* Mor. gt. by Bayntun (Rivière), covers & spine emblematically tooled, upr. cover inlaid with miniature hand-painted port. of Walton [by Stanley Hardy], watered silk linings, partly unc., cl. box. (S. Oct.4; 67) *Way.* £950
- - Anr. Edn. Ed.:- John Major. Ill.:- Damman. L., priv. ptd. for Navarre Soc. 1925. *Ltd. Edn. on specially-made paper, with etchings on Japon vell.* Lge. 8vo. Mor. by Ramage, gt. designs of fish, creels, etc., unif. back gt. (SG. Mar.15; 307) $175
- - Anr. Edn. Ill.:- Arthur Rackham. L., 1931. 4to. Mor. gt. by Bayntun (Rivière), blue & green onlays of fish & stylised water-lily leaves, upr. cover inlaid with miniature hand-painted port. of Walton, boxed. (S. Oct.4; 120) *Joseph.* £480
- - Anr. Copy. 4to. Leath. gt. (P. Sep.29; 391) *Blackwells.* £65
- - Anr. Edn. Ill.:- Arthur Rackham. L., 1931. *(775) numbered & sigd. by artist.* 4to. Orig. vell. gt., partly unc.; bkplt. of J.A. Radcliffe. (S. Oct.4; 66) *Joseph.* £210
- - Anr. Copy. 4to. Frontis. loose, orig. parch. gt., worn. (S. Nov.22; 357) *Long.* £170
- - Anr. Copy. 4to. Prelims., last pp., & end-papers with some foxing, gt.-decor. vell., slightly foxed & soiled. (CBA. Aug.21; 533) $300
- - Anr. Edn. Ill.:- Arthur Rackham. 1931. *(750) numbered & sigd. by artist.* Orig. vell. gt., spine slightly darkened. (BBA. Jan.19; 309) *Ayres.* £140
- - Anr. Edn. Ill.:- Arthur Rackham. Phila., [1931]. 4to. Ink gift pres. at front end-paper, cl., gt.-stpd., orig. d.-w. with col.-plt. reproduced at centre & orig. lettering designed by Rackham at front panel, worn, partly chipped, especially at top. (HA. May 4; 279) $150
- The Complete Angler, The Lives of Donne, Wotton ... Ed.:- Geoffrey Keynes. Ill.:- Thomas Poulton & Charles Sigrist. Bloomsbury, Nones. Pr., 1929. *(600) numbered.* Sm. 8vo. Port., ills., niger mor., marb. bd. s.-c. (SG. May 17; 274) $110

WALTON, J.
See— FIELDING, Theodore Henry & Walton, J.

WALTON, William
- The Army & Navy of the United States, from the Period of the Revolution to the Present Day. Phila., (1889-95). *De Luxe Edn.* 2 vols. Fo. Few text ll. stained, mor., warped, defect. (RO. Mar.28; 185) $190

WALTON, William, of Hayti, 1784-1857
- Present State of the Spanish Colonies. L., 1810. 2 vols. Few spots. cont. hf. cf., jnts. split, slightly worn, liby. stp. on covers. (S. Mar.6; 62) *Garbett.* £260

WALWUTKAR, Elijah Shalom
- Selichot Im Hatarat Nedarim Ve'Tashlich. Bombay, 1891. 4to. In Hebrew & Marathi, corner torn with loss of text, inner margins strengthened, browned, trimmed, hf. cl. (S. Oct.25; 348) *Freedman.* £100

WANCKEL, N.
[-] Ein Kurtze Vermerckung der Heyligen Stet des Heyligen Landts, in und umd Jerusalem. Nuremb., 20 May 1517. 4to. Title & margins slightly browned, old name on title struck out, 18th. C. wraps. (R. Apr.3; 106) DM 1,500

WANG NGEN JOUNG
See— NACHBAUR, A. & Wang Ngen Joung

WANSEY, Henry
See— BARTRAM, William — WANSEY, Henry

WAP, Johannes Jacobus Franciscus
- De Stad Utrecht. Utrecht, 1859-60. Lge. 8vo. Some slight foxing, later hf. cl., orig. covers pasted on. (VG. Mar.19; 59) Fls. 1,250

WAPENHERAUT (De). Maandblad gewijd aan Geschiedenis, Geslacht-, Wapen-, Oudheidkunde ...
Ed.:- D.G. v. Epen. 's-Gravenhage, 1897-1920. Years 1-24 (all publd.), in 23 vols. Fo. & lge. 8vo. Orig. cl.; A.R.F. van Kinschot copy. (VS. Dec.8; 750) Fls. 1,200

WARBURTON, John, of Dublin, Whitelaw, Rev. J., & Walsh, Rev. R.
- History of the City of Dublin. L., 1818. *1st. Edn.* 2 vols. Lge. 4to. 1 engraved frontis., 26 folding & other plts., charts & facs., including 2 hand-cold., cf., tooled borders. (GM. Dec.7; 490) £320
- - Anr. Copy. 2 vols. 4to. Engraved maps, some folding, & views, slightly discold., cont. cl.-bkd. bds., 1 spine worn. (S. Apr.9; 191) *Nolan.* £140

WARBURTON, Col. Peter Egerton
- Journey Across the Western Interior of Australia. L., 1875. *1st. Edn.* With 40 (not 24) pp. of book advts., clean tear in folding map, a few ll. foxed, some rubbing & slight looseness in sewing, orig. cl. (KH. Nov.9; 501) Aus. $500
- - Anr. Copy. Folding map strengthened with tape, slight foxing & light rubbing, some looseness & a few signs of use, bdg. not stated. (KH. May 1; 739) Aus. $400

WARD, C.S.
- Hints on Driving. L., 1870. *1st. Edn.* Frontis., photo.-port., cl. (P. May 17; 296) *Quaritch.* £50

WARD, H.C.
- Wild Flowers of Switzerland by H.C.W. 1883. 4to. Cold. frontis., 16 cold. plts., diagrams, loose, few edges slightly frayed, orig. cl. gt. (SKC. Jan.13; 2352) £75

WARD, Harriet
- Five Years in Kaffirland; With Sketches of the Late War in that Country ... 1848. 2 vols. Orig. cl., hinges brkn. (TA. Oct.20; 1) £52

WARD, Henry George
- Mexico in 1827. 1828. *[1st. Edn.].* 2 vols. 1 plt. hand-cold., spotted, mod. hf. mor.; William, Earl Jowitt & Lesley, Lady Jowitt bkplt. (CSK. Jan.27; 72) £170
- - Anr. Copy. 2 vols. Folding litho. frontispieces of views, 2 folding maps, litho. plt., 10 aquatint plts. (1 hand-cold.), some foxing to most plts., hf. mor., spines gt., by Wippell, Yeovil, leath. scuffed. (LC. Mar.1; 564) £90
- - Anr. Edn. L., 1829. 2 vols. A Tall copy, 2 folding frontis., 2 folding maps, 11 plts. (1 cold., 5 double-p.), cont. cl. [Sabin 101303] (S. May 22; 407) *Remmington.* £240

WARD, Humphrey
See— WARD, Thomas Humphrey & Roberts, W.

WARD, Robert
- Animadversions of Warre. 1639. *1st. Edn.* 2 pts. in 1 vol. Fo. Tear on 2nd. folding plt., some wear, old cf. [STC 25025] (BS. May 2; 44) £320
- - Anr. Edn. L., 1639. *1st. Edn. 2nd. Iss.* 2 pts. in 1 vol. Fo. Cont. spr. cf. [STC 25025] (SG. Oct.27; 330) $450
- - Anr. Copy. 2 pts. in 1 vol. Fo. Additional engraved title, many plts., 11 full-p. & 2 (of 3) folding, cont. spr. cf. [STC 25025] (SG. Apr.19; 191) $225

WARD, Rowland
- Records of Big Game with their Distribution, Characteristics, Dimensions, Weights, & Horn & Tusk Measurements. 1914. *7th. Edn.* 4to. Unused notebook contained in rear pocket, orig. cl., decor. end-papers, rubbed & soiled. (TA. Jan.19; 2) £80

WARD, Thomas Humphrey & Roberts, W.
- Romney, a Biographical & Critical Essay. 1904. 2 vols. 4to. Orig. cl., lightly soiled, spine slightly torn; pres. copy inscr. by Humphrey & Mary Ward, 3 p. letter from Mary Ward loosely inserted. (CSK. Dec.16; 174) £50
- - Anr. Copy. Fo. Leath.-bkd. bdg. (SPB. Nov.30; 8) $325
- - Anr. Edn. L., 1904. *(350) numbered on Japanese paper.* 2 vols. 4to. Cont. red lev. mor. by Bickers & Son. (BBA. Apr.5; 93) *Sims, Reed & Fogg.* £130

WARDE, John

- Captain Jorgensen's Life Boat The Storm King; An Account of the Boat, & of her Voyage from England to Australia ... Melbourne, ca. 1890. Title wraps., some foxing, minor wear. (KH. May 1; 741) Aus. $220

WARDEN, A.J.

- Angus or Forfarshire, the Land & People Descriptive & Historical. Dundee, 1880-85. 5 vols. 4to. Orig. cl. gt. (PD. Jun.13; 221) £72

WARDER, T.B. & Catlett, James M.

- Battle of Young's Branch: or, Manassas Plain. Fought July 21, 1861. Richmond, 1862. 16mo. 2 folding maps, ptd. wraps., slightly chipped, lr. wrap. detchd. (SG. Oct.20; 118) $275

WARE, Isaac

- A Complete Body of Architecture. L., 1756. *1st. Edn.* Fo. Plts. in 1st state, title with engraved vig., engraved frontis., 114 engraved plts., a few folding, with uncorrected plt. 70-71 & dupl. plt. 13 with inserted slip, anr. slip inserted between p. 24 & plt. 3, directions to binder lf. bnd. at end, without additional 6 pp. of text at end, minor repairs to inner blank corner or margin of 4 ll., cont. diced russ., covers gt.-decor., spine gt., slightly rubbed. (C. Dec.9; 166) *Weinreb.* £450
- - **Anr. Edn.** L., 1768. *1st. Edn.* Fo. Engraved frontis., 105 plts., some folding, slight browning, cont. spr. cf.; bkplt. of Thomas Boswall of Blackadder. (S. Dec.8; 391) *Thomas.* £200

WARE, Sir James

- The Antiquities & History of Ireland. L., 1705. Fo. Some pp. misnumbered or lacking, hf. cf. (GM. Dec.7; 321) £55

WARE, William Rotch

- The Georgian Period. N.Y., 1923. 6 vols. Tall fo. Text ills., 454 plts., each liby.-stpd. on blank verso, qtr. cl. & bd. folders, linen ties. (SG. May 3; 373) $250
- - **Anr. Copy.** 1 text & 5 plt. vols. Fo. Cl. & bds. (HA. Nov.18; 88) $100

WARING, John Burley

- Art Treasures of the United Kingdom. 1858. Fo. Some ll. loose, orig. cf. gt. with entwined onlay decor., rubbed. (LC. Mar.1; 29) £100
- - **Anr. Copy.** 4to. 82 col. plts., cont. cf. gt., rebkd. (P. Jun.7; 89) £70
- Masterpieces of Industrial Art & Sculpture at the International Exhibition, 1862. 1863. 3 vols. Fo. Some plts. slightly spotted, cont. hf. mor., gt. spines. (BBA. Nov.10; 267) *Traylen.* £200
- - **Anr. Copy.** 3 vols. Fo. Liby. stps., cont. hf. mor., worn. (S. Apr.30; 236) *Tropper.* £130
- - **Anr. Copy.** 3 vols. Lge. fo. Extra illuminated titles, 301 chromolitho. plts., text in Engl. & Fr., hf. leath. (S. Nov.3; 218) $550

WARING, John Burley & MacQuoid, T.R.

- Examples of Architectural Art in Italy & Spain. L., 1850. Fo. Litho. title, 64 plts., some spotted, cont. mor.-bkd. cl., rubbed. (S. Dec.13; 484) *Shapero.* £110

WARING, Edward Scott

- A Tour to Sheeraz. L., 1807. 4to. Title slightly spotted, cont. hf. cf., rebkd.; 'Bibliotheca Lindesiana' bkplt. (S. Mar.6; 19) *Georges.* £160
- - **Anr. Copy.** 2 pts. in 1 vol. 4to. Some faint browning or spotting, cont. hf. roan gt., rubbed. (S. Dec.1; 363) *Massan.* £150

WARING, Thomas

- A Treatise on Archery, or the Art of Shooting, with the Long Bow. 1814. *1st. Edn.* Cont. bds., spine defect., rubbed. (BBA. Jul.27; 137) *Quaritch.* £55

WARMHOLTZ, C.G.

- Bibliotheka Historica Sueo-gothica. Uppsala, 1782-1889. *Orig. Edn.* 15 vols. & 1 index vol. Mod. private hf. mor., marb. papers. (D. Nov.23; 226) DM 400

WARNER, Miss

- Herbert Lodge; a New Forest Story. 1808. 3 vols. 12mo. Bds. (P. Mar.15; 347) *Hannas.* £240

WARNER, Charles Dudley

See— CLEMENS, Samuel Langhorne 'Mark Twain' & Warner, Charles Dudley

WARNER, Sir George Frederick

- Queen Mary's Psalter. L., 1912. 4to. Hf. mor. (S. Oct.4; 133) *Georges.* £100

WARNER, Pelham Francis

- Imperial Cricket. 1912. Hf. leath., cover worn. (JL. Mar.25; 901) Aus. $200

WARNER, Ralph

- Dutch & Flemish Flower & Fruit Painters of the XVIIth & XVIIIth Centuries. 1928. 4to. Orig. cl., soiled. (BBA. Sep.8; 183) *St. George's Gallery.* £80
- - **Anr. Copy.** 4to. Orig. cl., d.-w. (S. Apr.30; 100) *Kapusi.* £70

WARNER, Robert & others

- The Orchid Album. Ill.:– after John Nugent Fitch. L., 1882-97. 11 vols. 4to. 528 litho. plts., most handcold., some col.-ptd., orig. cl. gt., rebkd. with cf., edges reprd. (C. Mar.14; 209) *D'Arcy.* £3,800
- - **Anr. Copy.** Vols. I & II only (of 11). 4to. 47 hand-cold. lithos., 48 col.-ptd. plts., together 95 (of 528) plts., cont. mor., gt. foliate scroll panel on covers, not quite unif., spines gt., inner dentelles. (C. Nov.16; 306) *Sotheran.* £550
- - **Anr. Edn.** L., 1886. Vol. 5. 4to. Wide margin, 47 (of 48) cold. litho. plts., some sm. margin tears, lacks bdg., loose. (R. Apr.4; 1765) DM 1,400

WARNKOENIG, L.-A.

- Histoire de la Flandre et de ses Institutions Civiles et Politiques jusqu'à l'Année 1385. Ed.:– A.F. Gheldolf. Bruxelles/Paris, 1835-64. 5 vols. Lge. 8vo. Hf. chagrin, corners. (LM. Oct.22; 140) B. Frs. 10,000

WARNOD, André

- Les Peintres mes Amis. Preface:– Pierre Brisson. Paris, 1965. *(250) numbered.* Fo. Loose ll. in orig. wraps. in orig. linen box. (GB. May 5; 3468) DM 3,000
- Trois Petites Filles dans la Rue. Ill.:– Pascin. Paris, 1925. *Orig. Edn.* 4to. Hf. chagrin, corners, by Bernasconi, wraps. preserved. (HD. Nov.17; 201) Frs. 2,000

WAROQUIER DE COMBLES

- Tableau Généalogique Historique de la Noblesse. Nyon, 1786-89. 9 vols. 12mo. Hf. chagrin, corners, by Capé, spines decor. (HD. Mar.21; 127) Frs. 3,500

WARREN, Arthur

- The Charles Whittinghams, Printers. N.Y., Grol. Cl., 1886. *(385).* Tall 8vo. Separately iss. Index ptd. at Chiswick Pr., 1898, laid in, slight foxing, orig. hf. mor., worn. (SG. Jan.5; 155) $110

WARREN, Edward

- An Epitome of Practical Surgery, for Field & Hospital. Richmond, 1863. *1st. Edn.* 12mo. Orig. bdg., extremities chafed. (SG. Oct.20; 119) $500

WARREN, Robert Penn

- At Heaven's Gate. N.Y., [1943]. *1st. Edn.* Cl., d.-w. minimally worn. (SG. May 24; 375) $130

WARTENBURG, M.

- Napoleon als Feldherr. Berlin, 1887. *2nd. Edn.* 2 vols. Red mor. gt., by Hatchards. (R. Apr.3; 1027) DM 520

WARTON, Rev. Thomas

- Poems on Several Occasions. L., 1748. *1st. Edn.* Bnd. with Richer's 'Life of Maecenas,' cont. sheep, worn. (BBA. Nov.30; 216) *Pickering & Chatto.* £85

WASER, Maur.

- Illustrierte Schweizer Geographie. Einsiedeln, 1899. 180 woodcuts, partly full-p., 1 cold. litho. plt., 1 cold. litho. folding map, orig. linen. (BR. Apr.12; 201) DM 460

WASHBURNE, Hon. E.B.

- Abraham Lincoln, His Personal History & Public Record. Speech delivered in the U.S. House of Representatives, May 29, 1860. N.d. Bdg. not stated, box. (LH. Apr.15; 387) $120

WASHINGTON, Booker T.

- Working with the Hands. Ill.:– after Francis B. Johnston. N.Y., 1904. *1st. Edn.* Bkplt., cl., spine ends worn. (SG. Nov.10; 94) $175

WASHINGTON, George

- The Journal of Major George Washington, sent by the Hon. Robert Dinwiddle, Esq; His Majesty's Lieutenant-Governor, & Commander in Chief of Virginia, to the Commandant of the French Forces on Ohio. L., 1754. *1st. Engl. Edn.* Iss. of the map with legend ' ... The Shawanons are the same with ye Senekas ... ', some offsetting on map, portion of left margin of map reinforced, text pp. slightly browned, disbnd., s.-c. [Sabin 101710] (SPB. Oct.26; 25) $20,000

WASMUTH, G. & others

- Lexikon der Baukunst. Berlin, 1929-32. 4 vols. Lge. 4to. Orig. hf. leath. gt. (HK. May 17; 3486) DM 500
- - **Anr. Edn.** Berlin, 1929-37. 4 vols. & supp. vol. in 5 vols. 4to. Orig. hf. leath., worn & spine defect., end-papers slightly foxed. (R. Apr.3; 933) DM 600

WASSEBOURG, Richard de

- Premier –Second Volume des Antiquitez de la Gaule Belgicque. Royaume de France, Austrasie et Lorraine. [Paris, Verdun], 1549. *Orig. Edn.* 2 vols. Fo. Inscr. on 1st. title, 19th. C. bds. (HD. Mar.19; 160) Frs. 2,100

WASSERMANN, Jacob

- Donna Johanna von Castilien. Ill.:– H. Meid. München, Pan Pr., [1914]. *(25) De Luxe Edn. on Japan.* Sm. 4to. Hand-bnd. orig. vell., by H. Fikentscher, Leipzig; printers mark sigd. by artist. (H. Nov.24; 1846) DM 1,200

WASSON, Robert Gordon

- Soma: Divine Mushroom of Immortality. N.Y., 1968. *(680) numbered.* Sm. fo. Orig. qtr. mor., s.-c. (S. Dec.13; 302) *Danckers.* £110
See— HEIM, Roger & Wasson, Robert Gordon

WASSON, Valentina P. & Robert Gordon

- Mushrooms, Russia & History. N.Y., 1957. *Ltd. Edn.* 2 vols. 4to. Orig. cl., s.-c. (BBA. Dec.15; 142) *Sons of Liberty Books.* £320

WATELET, Claude H.

- L'Art de Peindre. Poème. 1760. *Orig. Edn. 1st. Printing.* 12mo. Cont. mosaic mor. (HD. Jan.24; 53) Frs. 4,500

WATERHOUSE, George Robert

- A Natural History of the Mammalia. L., 1846-48. 2 vols. Lge. 8vo. 45 engraved plts., including 22 hand-cold., few plts. foxed, cl., disbnd., ex-liby. (SG. Oct.6; 370) $100

WATERING PLACES OF GREAT BRITAIN & Fashionable Directory

Ca. 1833. 54 engrs. on 52 sheets, no title, text misbnd. & lacking, spotting, cl., worn, as a collection of plts., w.a.f. (P. Sep.29; 215) *Shapero.* £130
- - **Anr. Copy.** 4to. 51 plts. only, lacks title, text incompl., some spotting, hf. cf., as a collection of plts., w.a.f. (P. Sep.29; 214) £125

WATERLOO, Antoine

- Suite de Quatre-Vingt-Huit Paysages de Differentes Grandeurs, Composés et Gravés à l'Eau Forte. Paris, n.d. Tall fo. Engraved title & 88 etchings on 49 plts., orig. ptd. wraps., spine & edges frayed, lr. wrap. reprd., unc. (SG. Nov.3; 219) $1,400

WATERTON, Charles

- Wanderings in South America. L., 1825. *1st. Edn.* 4to. Engraved port. offset onto title, some spotting, later cf. (S. Apr.9; 68) *Elliott.* £80
- - **Anr. Copy.** 4to. Some light spotting, cont. hf. cf., rubbed. (CSK. Jun.29; 62) £55
- - **Anr. Copy.** 4to. Frontis., title, & end-ll. foxed, mod. hf. cl. (SG. Sep.22; 299) $200

WATKINS, George

- The Complete English Brewer or, The Whole Art & Mystery of Brewing. L., n.d. Hf. cf. gt. (P. Jan.12; 290) *Shaw.* £85

WATSON, Douglas S.
- California in the Fifties. Fifty Views of the Cities & Mining Towns ... Drawn on Stone by Kuchel & Dresel & other Early San Francisco Lithographers. San Franc., 1936. Ob. fo. Cl. (LH. Sep.25; 299) $130

WATSON, Frank John Bagolt
- [The Wrightsman Collection]. N.Y., 1966-70. 4 vols. only (of 5). 4to. No bdg. stated. (SPB. Nov.30; 362) $325

WATSON, John Forbes
- The Textile Manufactures & the Costumes of the People of India. 1866. Fo. Hf. cf., spine gt., spine faded & scuffed. (LC. Jul.5; 241) £220

WATSON, John Forbes & Kaye, J.W.
- The People of India. L., 1868-75. 8 vols. 4to. Lacks 1 photo, some ll. disbnd., 1 text lf. cut out & remntd., publisher's decor. buckram gt. (HD. Jun.26; 40) Frs. 18,000

WATSON, William
- Experiments & Observations Tending to Illustrate the Nature & Properties of Electricity. 1746. 2nd. Edn. Recent qtr. mor., untrimmed. (TA. May 17; 359) £80
- Experiments & Observations ... of Electricity. - A Sequel to the Experiments. 1746. 3rd. Edn. Together 2 works in 1 vol. Title-p. defect., hf. cf. (CE. Sep.1; 70) £70
- - Anr. Copy. Together 2 vols. Cl. (SG. Oct.6; 371) $175

WATT, Robert, of Glasgow
- Bibliotheca Britannica. 1824. 4 vols. 4to. Cont. diced cf., rebkd. (BBA. Nov.10; 149) Shackleton. £130
- - Anr. Copy. 4 vols. 4to. Spotting, hf. cf., rebkd. (P. Sep.29; 172) Cresswell. £85

WATTEAU, Antoine
- Figures de Differents Caractères de Paysage, et d'Etudes. Paris, ca. 1740. 2nd. Edn. Fo. Frontis., port., 187 (of 213) plts., lacks last 4 cahiers, hf. cf. on marb. bds., spine gt. (SPB. Dec.13; 912) $700

WATTS, William
- The Seats of the Nobility & Gentry. Ill.:– after Sandby, Malton, Repton, & others. L., 1779. Ob. 4to. Engraved title, 84 plts., some spotting onto text, cont. cf. gt., worn. (S. Jun.25; 345) Shapiro. £160
- - Anr. Edn. L., 1779[-86]. Ob. 8vo. Engraved title, 84 engraved views, 4 pp. subscribers list, cont. tree cf. gt. (C. Nov.16; 37) Cavendish. £950
- - Anr. Copy. Ob. 8vo. Engraved title, 84 engraved plts., subscribers list, some foxing & offsetting, cont. red mor. gt., spine gt. (C. Nov.16; 193) Walford. £150
- - Anr. Copy. Ob. 4to. Engraved title, 84 plts., some light spotting, 1st. plt. creased, cont. red mor. gt., slightly worn, lr. cover detchd. (S. Jun.25; 346) Shapiro. £130
- - Anr. Copy. Ob. 4to. Engraved title & 84 plts., some spotting, cont. russ., rebkd. (S. Apr.9; 192) Russell. £100
- Select Views ... in the Cities of Bath & Bristol. 1819. Ob. 4to. 15 engraved plts., some foxing, mainly in margins, cont. hf. cf., worn, some press cuttings pasted on end-paper. (SKC. May 4; 1800) £140

WAUGH, Arthur
- The Square Book of Animals. Ill.:– William Nicholson. 1900 [1899]. 4to. Orig. cl.-bkd. pict. bds. (C. May 30; 191) Henderson. £130
- - Anr. Edn. Ill.:– William Nicholson. L., 1900. 4to. Qtr. cl., pict. bds., extremities slightly worn. (SG. Dec.8; 249) $300

WAUGH, Evelyn
- Basil Seal Rides Again. L., 1953. 1st. Edn. (750) sigd. 4to. Orig. cl. (S. Mar.20; 980) Henderson. £90
- Black Mischief. 1932. 1st. Edn. Light spotting on fore-edge & at ends, orig. cl., d.-w. (SKC. May 4; 1704) £60
- - Anr. Copy. Frontis., orig. cl., d.-w. (S. Apr.9; 282) Duschness. £55
- - Anr. Edn. 1932. (250) numbered on L.P., sigd.

Orig. cl., faded. (BBA. Feb.23; 338) Parsons. £110
- The Holy Places. Ill.:– Reynolds Stone. Queen Anne Pr., 1952. (950) numbered. Buckram, d.-w. (HBC. May 17; 231) £60
- - Anr. Edn. Ill.:– Reynolds Stone. Queen Anne Pr., 1952. (950) numbered. (50) sigd. by author & artist, specially bnd. Red mor., d.-w. (HBC. May 17; 230) £270
- - Anr. Copy. Red mor., spine gt.-lettered, d.-w. rubbed & soiled, splitting at spine; Marymount College bkplt. (CBA. Mar.3; 550) $300
- Love Among the Ruins. 1953. 1st. Edn. (350) numbered & sigd. Orig. cl. (CSK. Nov.25; 171) £90
- Scoop. L., 1938. 1st. Edn. Orig. cl., d.-w. torn. (S. Mar.20; 982) Sherlock. £75
- Selection of the Sermons of Monsignor Knox. 1949. (550) numbered. (50) sigd. & specially bnd. 4to. Cf., d.-w. (HBC. May 17; 186) £155
- Wine in Peace & War. Ill.:– Rex Whistler. L., [1947?]. (100) numbered & sigd. Sheep. (SG. Mar.1; 597) $650

WAY, Thomas R.
- The Lithographs by Whistler. N.Y., 1914. (400). Lge. fo. 166 photogravure & litho. plts., ex-liby., later buckram. (SG. May 3; 382) $300
- - Anr. Copy. Fo. Over 150 plts., loose as iss., folding cl. case, ties, soiled. (SG. Dec.15; 197) $150
- - Anr. Copy. Sm. fo. 166 plts., loose as iss., cl. portfo., soiled, text in ptd. wraps., torn. (SG. Aug.25; 406) $100
- Mr. Whistler's Lithographs ... L., 1896. (140) numbered & sigd. Vell.-bkd. ptd. bds.; A.L.s. from Way to Dr. Williamson. (SG. Aug.25; 408) $175

WEALE, John
- Divers Works of Early Masters in Christian Decoration ... with Examples of Ancient Painted & Stained Glass. L., 1846. 2 vols. Fo. 2 extra pict. titles, & some 50 plts., most cold. lithos., several folding, 1 plt. separated at fold, some foxing, qtr. leath., disbnd. (SG. Aug.25; 403) $150
- Quarterly Papers on Architecture. 1844-45. 4 vols. 4to. 242 plans & plts., cf. gt. (P. Feb.16; 5) £190

WEALE, William Henry James
- Bookbindings & Rubbings in the National Art Library. 1898-94. 2 vols. in 1. Later hf. mor.; H.M. Nixon coll., with his sig. & MS notes. (BBA. Oct.6; 134) Beres. £220

WEATHERLEY, Frederic E.
- A Happy Pair. Ill.:– Beatrix Potter. Ca. 1890. 16mo. 7 ll., orig. pict. wraps., slightly soiled, spine torn. (BBA. Aug.18; 58) Quaritch. £1,700
- - Anr. Edn. Ill.:– Beatrix Potter. N.d. 16mo. Orig. pict. wraps., slightly soiled & spotted, backstrip rubbed & with sm. ½-inch tear at foot. (CSK. Apr.27; 99) £2,300
- Twilight Hours. Ill.:– M. Ellen Edwards, John C. Staples & Jane M. Dealy. Ca. 1890. 6 vols. Sm. 4to. Orig. cl.-bkd. bds., fitted case, slightly worn; van Veen coll. (S. Feb.28; 22) £190

WEAVER, John
- An Essay Towards an History of Dancing. 1712. 1st. Edn., with dedication. Cont. panel. cf., worn, defect. (PD. Oct.19; 274) £110

WEAVER, Sir Lawrence
- English Leadwork, Its Art & History. 1909. 4to. Orig. cl. gt. (P. Apr.12; 143) Potterton. £85
- Houses & Gardens by E.L. Lutyens. L., 1913. Fo. Orig. buckram-bkd. bds. (C. Mar.14; 149) Hinton. £80
See— BENSON, Arthur Christopher & Weaver, Sir Lawrence

WEBB, John
- An Historical Essay ... that the Language of China is the Primitive Language. 1669. 1st. Edn. Later spr. cf., spine gt., slightly rubbed. (BBA. Jul.27; 107) Ad Orientem. £140

WEBB, Peter
- The Erotic Arts. Ill.:– Allen Jones, David Hockney, & others. L., [1975]. (126). (100) numbered for sale. 4to. Lev.; sigd. etching by David Hockney. (SG. Jan.12; 159) $775

WEBER, Carl J.
- Fore-Edge Painting. Irvington, N.Y., 1966. Orig. cl., d.-w., torn; H.M. Nixon coll., with some MS. notes, notes for & copies of his T.L.S. review loosely inserted. (BBA. Oct.6; 136) Ralph. £140
- Das Ritter-Wesen und die Templer, Johannita und Marianer oder Deutsch-Ordens-Ritter. Stuttgart, 1836-37. 2nd. Edn. 3 vols. Cont. hf. linen. (R. Oct.11; 1168) DM 750
- A Thousand & One Fore-Edge Paintings. Waterville, 1949. (1000). Orig. cl., d.-w., defect.; H.M. Nixon coll., with a few notes, MS. draft of his review loosely inserted. (BBA. Oct.6; 135) Ralph. £240
- - Anr. Copy. Orig. cl. (BBA. Mar.7; 269) Zeitlin & Verbrugge. £90
- - Anr. Edn. L., 1949. Plts., buckram, cl., d.-w. reprd. (P. May 17; 68) Sawyer. £80

WEBER, E.H. & W.E.
- Wellenlehre auf Experimente gegründet. Leipzig, 1825. 1st. Edn. Title lf. stpd., minimal browning & spotting, mod. hand-bnd. mor. (H. May 22; 213) DM 1,250

WEBER, H.
[-] Wegweiser durch die Wichtigsten Technischen Werkstaatten der Residenz Berlin. Berlin & Leipzig, 1819-20. Pts. 1 & 2 in 2 vols. Some slight foxing, cont. bds., spotted. (GB. May 3; 340) DM 1,050
- - Anr. Copy. Pts. I & II. Some spotting, cont. bds., spotted & worn. (H. Nov.23; 370) DM 400

WEBER, J.M.E.
- Praktisches Konditorei-Kunst. Dresden, [1926]. Lge. 4to. Lacks recipe book quoted on title & moulds, orig. linen. (GB. May 4; 1965) DM 420

WEBER, Johann Carl
- Die Alpen-Pflanzen Deutschlands und der Schweiz. München, [1845-56]. 1st. Edn. 3 vols. Orig. gold-tooled linen. (R. Apr.4; 1804) DM 1,900
- - Anr. Edn. München, 1872. 4 vols. 12mo. 400 cold. plts., Vol. 4 loose, orig. cl., gt.-decor. (SKC. Nov.18; 1994) £170
- - Anr. Copy. Vols. 2-4 (of 4). Some light foxing, 2 orig. linen, loose, vol. 3 without bdg. (R. Oct.12; 1930) DM 550
- - Anr. Edn. München, 1880. 4 vols. 12mo. Vol. 1 hf.-title with owners note, orig. linen gt., slightly bumped. (HK. Nov.8; 778) DM 900

WEBER, Victor Frederic
- 'Ko-ji Ho-ten': Dictionnaire à l'Usage ... Objets d'Art Japonais et Chinois. Paris, 1923. (585) numbered, sigd. 2 vols. Lge. fo. 75 plts. (75 cold.), over 2000 text ills., ex-liby., mor.-bkd. cl. (SG. May 3; 376) $700

WEBSTER, Benjamin (Ed.)
See— WINDSOR CASTLE

WEBSTER, John, Puritan
- Metallographia, or, An History of Metals. L., 1671. 1st. Edn. Sm. 4to. 2 sm. holes in title, text stained, some margin ink annots., mod. qtr. cf. gt. (P. Dec.8; 262) Tzakas. £70
- Untersuchung der Vermeinten u. so Genannten Hexereyen. Halle, 1719. 4to. Title with owner's mark, some text underlining, slightly browned, cont. vell. (HK. Nov.9; 1981) DM 950

WEBSTER, Malcolm R.
See— CESCINSKY, Herbert & Webster, Malcolm R.

WEBSTER, Noah
- An American Dictionary of the English Language. N.Y., 1828. 1st. Edn. 2 vols. 4to. Frontis. stained in margins, titles reprd., 1 text lf. defect. & reprd., early bds., later hf. buckram. (SG. Nov.3; 220) $1,500
- - Anr. Copy. 2 vols. 4to. Frontis.-port., mildly damp-wrinkled, some slight browning, cont. owner's sigs., mod. crushed hf. mor. (SG. Apr.26; 201) $800
- A Brief History of Epidemic & Pestilential Diseases ... Hartford, 1799. 1st. Edn. 2 vols. Heavily dampstained, few repairs, etc., mod. leatherette, ex-liby. (SG. Oct.6; 373) $150

WECKHERLIN, G.R.
See— HULSEN, E. von – WECKHERLIN, G.R.

WEDDELL, James
- A Voyage towards the South Pole ... **1822-24.**
1825. *1st. Edn.* Hand-cold. frontis., 14 maps &
plts., some folding, some spotting, hf. cf., scuffed.
(P. Jun.7; 57) £400
– – **Anr. Copy.** Hand-cold. frontis., 2 folding coastal
profiles, 7 engraved maps, most folding, 4 other
plts., errata slip, short tear to frontis., 1 map with
reprd. tear, hf. mor. (S. Dec.1; 269) *Frers.* £350

WEDEKIND, Frank
- Die Büchse der Pandora. Ill.:– 'Alastair'. Munich,
n.d. *(500) numbered.* 2 vols. 4to. Orig. cl.-bkd.
patterned bds., d.-w.'s., orig. fitted box. (SKC.
Jan.13; 2178) £160
– – **Anr. Edn.** Ill.:– 'Alastair'. Munich, n.d. *(550)
numbered.* 4to. Hf. suede, patterned bds., slightly
rubbed. (SKC. May 4; 1651) £90

WEDEKIND, F. (Text)
See— MUNCHNER BLATTER FUR DICH-
TUNG UND GRAPHIK

WEEGE, Fritz
- Etruskische Malerei. Halle, 1921. Tall 8vo. 101
plts., 89 text ills., ex-liby., loose in bd. folder, gt.
cover design. (SG. May 3; 377) $100

WEEGEE (Pseud.)
See— FELLIG, Arthur 'Weegee'

**WEEKLY FREEMAN CARTOONS, forming an
illustrated History of Ireland, for ... 1889**
Dublin, 1889. Lge. atlas fo. Orig. wraps. (GM.
Dec.7; 179) £80

WEEKLY MAGAZINE, or Edinburgh Amusement
Edinb., 1768-78. Vols. 1-42 in 27. Cf.-bkd. marb.
bds., spines gt.; Sir Ivar Colquhoun, of Luss copy.
(CE. Mar.22; 327) £500

WEGELER, F.G. & Ties, F.
- Biographische Notizen über Ludwig van Beethoven. Koblenz, 1838. Sm. tear in 1 lf. reprd., title
verso stpd., cont. bds. (HK. Nov.9; 2237)
DM 1,300

WEHRS, G.F.
- Vom Papier ... Halle, 1789. Cont. sewed, defect.,
spine brkn. (R. Apr.3; 668) DM 600

WEIBEL, Salomon
[–] Voyage Pittoresque de l'Oberland. Paris, 1812.
4to. Additional engraved title, map, 14 engraved
views, all hand-cold., some slight spotting, unc.,
cont. bds., spine worn. (S. Dec.1; 329)
Germundson. £2,500

WEICKHARD, A.
- Pharmacia Domestica. Frankfurt, 1628. 4to.
1st. & last ll. with sm. margin defects., slightly
browned, cont. vell., soiled, lacks upr. end-paper.
(HK. Nov.8; 781) DM 900

WEIDMANN, Franz Carl
- Panorama v. Wien. Ill.:– Prixner. Wien, 1832.
Ob. 12mo. Frontis. & 52 copperplts., plt. margins
with light soiling & sm. wormholes, orig. bds.,
slightly soiled, spine lightly defect., lacks end-ll.
(HK. Nov.9; 1177) DM 1,000

WEIERSTRASS, K.
- Mathematische Werke. Berlin & Leipzig, 1894-
1924. *1st. Coll. Edn.* 7 vols. 4to. Wide margin,
cont. hf. leath., partly unc. (HT. May 8; 505)
DM 3,600

WEIGEL, Christoph
- Biblische Augen- u. Seelen-Lust. Augsburg, 1696.
Frontis. worn, lightly browned, cont. leath., partly
restored, spine slightly brittle. (HK. Nov.9; 1573)
DM 520
- Ethica Naturalis. Nürnberg, [1690/1700]. *1st.
Edn.* 4to. 2 plts. with bkd. tear, 1 with sm hole,
some sm. brown stains in margins, specially at top,
title soiled & with several old names, cont. leath.,
bumped, spine defect. (R. Oct.11; 191) DM 950
– – **Anr. Edn.** Ill.:– Jan & Casper Luyken. Nuremb.,
ca. 1700. 4to. Cont. panel cf. gt., label chipped. (C.
May 30; 56) *Lyon.* £480

- Historiae Celebriores Novi Testamenti Iconibus
Representatae. Ill.:– Jan & Caspar Luyken.
Nuremb., ca. 1710. Tall fo. Engraved title, 108
engraved plts. each with engraved text in Latin &
German, later crude hf. mor. (SG. Apr.19; 192)
$350
– – **Anr. Edn.** Nuremb., 1712. 2 pts. in 1 vol. Fo.
Dampstain to upr. margin of some plts., cont. vell.,
slightly soiled; liby. stp. in blank margin of 1st. plt.
(C. May 30; 57) *Snelling.* £240
– – **Anr. Copy.** Title & plt. 1 with writing on verso,
lacks 2 plts., soiled thro.-out in lr. & side margin,
some sm. margin tears, most at foot & 4 bkd., 19th.
C. Hf. leath., bumped, spine defect. (R. Oct.12;
2242) DM 500
- Passio Domini nostri Iesu Christi; Neo-Coelatis
Iconibus Expressa ... Neu-Ersonnen und Gezeichnet
von Johann Jacob von Sandrart. Augsburg, 1693.
19th. C. vell. gt. (BBA. Nov.30; 21)
Snelling. £160

WEIGEL, Hans
- Habitus Praecipuorum Populorum. Ill.:– after
Amman. Nürnberg, 1577. Fo. Fragment, 149 (of
219) old cold. woodcuts, nearly all plts. with several
tears old bkd., approx. half of plts. with lge. defects.,
some faults or tears, 6 plts. only fragments, all plt.
versos stpd., cont. blind-tooled pig, dtd. 1582, worn,
spine defect. & reprd. (R. Apr.4; 2031) DM 6,300

WEIGEL, Johann Christoph
- Atlas Portatilis, oder Compendieuse Vorstellung
der Ganzen Welt. Nuremb., 1745. *[3rd. Edn.].*
Double-p. title ptd. in red & black, 31 double-p.
engraved maps & diagrams, hand-cold. in full, some
spotting affecting text, cont. cf., rebkd., w.a.f. (S.
May 21; 120) *Cope.* £500
– – **Anr. Copy.** 31 double-p. cold. copper engraved
maps, text lightly browned or foxed, cont. leath.
(R. Oct.13; 2880) DM 2,100
See— HOFMANN, Johann Baptiste & Weigel,
Joh. Chr.

WEIL, Yakov [Mahari Weil]
- She'eilot U'Teshuvot. Venice, 1549. *1st. Edn.* 4to.
Title defect. & reprd. affecting some letters, owner's
stp. on title, some ll. including index reprd. affecting
some words, stained, trimmed, mod. blind-tooled
mor. (S. Oct.25; 410) *Davidson.* £380

WEILAND, C.F.
[–] Allgemeiner Hand-Atlas. Weimar, [1850]. Fo.
49 double-p. engraved maps only, hand-cold. in
outl., cont. cf.-bkd. bds., lightly rubbed. (CSK. May
4; 27) £90
See— KIEPERT, H. & Weiland, C.F.

WEILER, Milton C.
- Classic Shorebird Decoys: a Portfolio of Paintings. Text:– W.J. Mackey, Jr.: Foreword:– Ed
Zern. N.Y., 1971. *(975) numbered & sigd.* Tall fo.
24 plts. in full col., laid into upr. cover, buckram
covers, art leath. back, boxed. (SG. Mar.15; 312)
$200

WEILL, Kurt
- Liebeslied. [From Die Dreigroschenoper]. Vienna,
1928. *1st. Iss.* Fo. Title-p. foxed, no bdg. stated;
sigd. & dtd. by composer. (S. Nov.17; 215)
Simeone. £360

WEINBAUM, Stanley Grauman
- Dawn of Flame & other Stories. Foreword:– Lawrence Keating. [Milwaukee, 1936]. *1st. Edn. (250)
bnd.* Frontis. roughly torn out but present, limp
fabricoid, covers lightly rubbed, end-papers
darkening. (CBA. Oct.29; 899) $300

WEINBUCHLEIN
Leipzig, 1535. Last sig. lacks last 4 ll., some old
annots., browned, upr. margin slightly stained &
wormed, bds. (HK. Nov.8; 380) DM 850

WEINMANN, Johann Wilhelm
- [Phytanthoza Iconographia] Duidelyke Vertoning
Eeniger Duizend in alle Vier Waerelds Deelen wassende Bomen, Stammen, Kuriden, Bloemen, Vrugten
... Amst., 1736-48. 4 vols. (without the 4 vols. of
Dutch text). Fo. Titles in Dutch with engraved
vigs., allegorical mezzotint plt., mezzotint port. of
author, 1025 engraved plts., many col.-ptd., all
hand-finished, including 14 double-p., lacks port. of

Bieler, owner's stp. in upr. blank margin of titles &
1 plt., cont. cf., spine ends chipped. (C. Nov.16;
307) *Davidson.* £15,000

WEINTHAL, Leo
- The Story of the Cape of Cairo Railway & River
Route, from 1887 to 1922. L., [1923]. 5 vols.,
including Map Supp. 4to. Publisher's hf. mor. gt.
(S. Dec.13; 159) *Blackwells.* £100

WEIS, J.M.
- Représentation des Fêtes données par la Ville de
Strasbourg pour la Convalescence du Roi. Ill.:– Le
Bas after Weis. Paris, [1745]. Imp. fo. Plts. with
sm. margin tear, 1 plt. with sm. stain, cont. cf. gt.,
gold-tooled decor., gt. corner fleurons inner & outer
dentelle, gold-tooled arms supralibros on both
covers, corners bumped. (D. Nov.24; 2370)
DM 6,600

WEISKE, H.A.
- Die Dresdener Gallerie. Leipzig, 1885. *3rd. Edn.*
4to. Orig. gold-tooled linen, rubbed. (R. Oct.12;
2258) DM 650

WEISS, Erich 'Harry Houdini'
- The Adventurous Life of a Versatile Artist. [N.Y.,
1922]. Sigd. inscr. from author to Mrs. Charles
Boynton, decor. wraps., spine reprd. (PNY. Dec.1;
111) $120
- Die Feuerprobe. Ill.:– L. Meidner. Berlin, 1923.
C. Edn. (675)(575) numbered. Orig. bds., spine &
lr. cover faded, spine slit. (HK. May 17; 3003)
DM 460
- A Magician Among the Spirits. N.Y., 1924. *1st.
Edn.* Inscr. by author to Clark Brown, sigd. & dtd.
10 Aug. 1921 (sic), orig. cl., d.-w. worn. (PNY.
Dec.1; 115) $275
- 'Margery' the Medium Exposed: Joaquin Maria
Argamasilla the Spaniard with X Ray Eyes. N.Y.,
[1927]. Inscr. 'to my friend Harzhof', sigd. & dtd.,
decor. wraps. chipped, spine taped. (PNY. Dec.1;
112) $100
- The Unmasking of Robert Houdin. N.Y., 1908.
Inscr. by author, 18 Jul. 1916, photo of Houdini &
Theodore Roosevelt pasted to front fly, orig. decor.
cl. (PNY. Dec.1; 114) $300
– – **Anr. Copy.** Inscr. by author to Mr. Harzhof,
sigd. & dtd. 14 Jul. 1916, orig. decor. cl. (PNY.
Dec.1; 113) $180

WEISS, H.M.
- Li. Ill.:– E. Orlik. Berlin, ca. 1924. *(1000) num-
bered.* Orig. linen gt., printers mark sigd. by artist.
(D. Nov.24; 3158) DM 480
– – **Anr. Edn.** Ill.:– Emil Orlik. Berlin, ca. 1925. *De
Luxe Edn.,. (125) numbered.* Sm. 4to. Orig. leath.,
partly unc.; printer's mark sigd. by artist. (V. Oct.1;
4455) DM 850

WEISS, Harry B. (Ed.)
See— AMERICAN BOOK COLLECTOR, The

WEISSMANN, Adolf
- Der Klingende Garten. Ill.:– Michel Fingesten.
Berlin, 1920. *(200). (9) numbered De Luxe Edn.*
4to. 10 sigd. orig. etchings mntd. on Japan in 1st. &
2nd. state, orig. hf. vell., slightly soiled. (GB. May
5; 2529) DM 1,700
– – **Anr. Edn.** Ill.:– M. Fingesten. Berlin, 1920.
(150). 4to. On Bütten, orig. hand-bnd. hf. vell.,
lightly faded; all etchings sigd. by artist. (H.
Nov.25; 1502) DM 420

WELBY, Adlard
- A Visit to North America & the English Settlements in Illinois, with a Winter Residence at Philadelphia. Ill.:– Rowney & Forster, after G. Harley.
L., 1821. *1st. Edn.* Slip of errata & directions for
binder at end, orig. bds., upr. cover detchd., most
of spine chipped away, unc., cl. box; the Rt. Hon.
Visc. Eccles copy. [Sabin 102515] (CNY. Nov.18;
281) $550

WELCH, Charles
- Modern History of the City of London. 1896. Lge.
4to. L.P., orig. cl. gt., covers stained & marked.
(LC. Oct.13; 292) £55

WELCH, D'Alte A.
- A Bibliography of American Children's Books
Printed before 1821. Worcester, Mass., 1963-68.

1st. Separate Iss. 6 pts. Holdings of Free Liby. of Phila. noted in MS. thro.-out, ptd. wraps.; inscr. 3 times. (SG. Jan.5; 311) $225

WELD, Charles Richard
- A History of the Royal Society. 1848. 2 vols. Hf. cf. gt., scuffed. (P. Feb.16; 148) £60

WELD, Isaac
- Statistical Survey of the County of Roscommon. Dublin, 1832. *1st. Edn.* Hf.-title, cl. (GM. Dec.7; 168) £125
- Travels through the States of North America, & the Provinces of Upper & Lower Canada. 1799. *1st. Edn.* 4to. Folding map hand-cold. in outl., 15 maps, plans & views, errata pastedown on p. viii, some slight discolouration, cont. cf. [Sabin 102541] (S. May 22; 344) *Maggs.* £320
- – **Anr. Copy.** 4to. Folding engraved map hand-cold. in outl., without the erratum slip for plt. facing p. 52 (present in some copies) & the 8 pp. of advts., plts. spotted & offset to text, Ee3 torn, cont. diced russ. gt. by C. Hering, gt.-stpd. Royal arms on covers, with his ticket, upr. cover detchd., spine worn; the Rt. Hon. Visc. Eccles copy. [Sabin 102541] (CNY. Nov.18; 282) $400
- – **Anr. Edn.** 1799. *2nd. Edn.* 2 vols. Folding outl.-cold. map (sm. tear in margin), 15 other folding maps, plans & plts., cont. spr. cf., spine gt.; Samuel Enderby bkplt. (LC. Oct.13; 293) £260
- – **Anr. Edn.** 1800. *3rd. Edn.* 2 vols. No advts., some spotting, hf. cf. (P. Dec.8; 353) *Faupel.* £100

WELLCOME INSTITUTE of the History of Medicine
- Catalogue of Western Manuscripts on Medicine & Science. Ed.:– S.A.J. Moorat. L., 1962-73. 3 vols. (*With:*) - Catalogue of Printed Books ... before 1850. Ed.:– F.N.L. Poynter & H.R. Denham. L., 1962-76. Vols. 1-3 (all publd. to date). Together 6 vols. 4to. Orig. cl.; Dr. Walter Pagel copies. (S. Feb.7; 380) *Simmonds.* £200

WELLER, C.H.
- Diätetik für Gesunde und Schwache Augen. Berlin, 1821. *1st. Edn.* Some slight browning, owners stp. on title sig., cont. bds., rubbed & worn. (GB. May 3; 1048) DM 450

WELLESLEY, Richard Colley, Marquis
[-] Notes relative to the late Transactions in the Marhatta Empire. Fort William, 1803. 2 pts. in 1 vol., including Appendix. Sm. fo. Pres. inscr. from author to the Duke of York, 5 hand-cold. folding engraved maps & plans, 1 folding MS. plan in ink & cols. of the battle of Delhi, errata lf. at end, cont. red mor. gt., rubbed. (S. Dec.1; 373) *Kossow.* £500

WELLING, Georg von 'Gregorius Anglus Sallwigt'
- Opus Mago cabbalisticum et Theosophicum. Homburg, 1735. *1st. Edn.* 4to. Title with 2 margin holes & fully bkd., cont. leath. gt., slightly rubbed; 39 pp. cont. MS. bnd. in: 'Anonymi Philalethae Commentaruis in Epistolam Georgie Ripiaei; trans. Johann Lange, 1685. (R. Apr.4; 1450) DM 1,800
- – **Anr. Edn.** Frankfurt & Leipzig, 1784. 4to. 15 folding plts., lf. with instructions for binder, cont. bds. gt.; Dr. Walter Pagel copy. (S. Feb.7; 381) *Janssen.* £360

WELLINGTON, Arthur Wellesley, Duke of
[-] The Funeral Procession of Arthur Duke of Wellington. Ill.:– H. Alken & G.A. Sala. L., [1853]. Ob. fo. Panorama of 56 engraved plts., some plts. at beginning reprd., publisher's decor. buckram, s.-c. (HD. May 4; 452) Frs. 1,500

WELLS, Edward
- A New Sett of Maps both of Antient & Present Geography. Ill.:– M. Burghers, R. Spofforth, & Sutton Nicholls. Oxford, at the Theatre, 1700. *1st. Edn.* Lge. ob. fo. L.P., 41 maps, all on thick paper, contents lf., lge. stain on verso of 1 map, some faint staining, edge bnd., cont. mott. panel. cf., gt., worn. (S. Dec.1; 199) *Burgess.* £1,350
- – **Anr. Copy.** Fo. 41 double-p. engraved maps, lacks title, some light soiling, 1 margin reprd., cont. cf.-bkd. bds. (CSK. Oct.7; 25) £1,000
- – **Anr. Edn.** 1718. Fo. 41 maps, some hand-cold., hf. cf., worn. (P. Oct.20; 265) £800

- Oikoumenis Periegesis. L., 1718. *3rd. Edn.* Engraved vig. title, text in Greek & Latin, 16 full-p. maps, cont. cf., upr. cover detchd., worn. (S. Dec.13; 1) *Eisler.* £90
- The Young Gentleman's Astronomy. 1712. *1st. Edn.* 3 pts. in 1 vol. 24 engraved plts., 1 torn, cont. cf. (P. Sep.8; 241) *Bickersteth.* £80

WELLS, Herbert George
- The Croquet Player. 1936. *1st. Edn.* Orig. cl., slightly soiled; dedication copy, inscr. by author to Moura Budburg. (BBA. Feb.23; 308) *Maggs.* £140
- The Door in the Wall & other Stories. Ill.:– after Alvin L. Coburn. N.Y., 1911. *(600). (300) with the plts. ptd. in photogravure.* Fo. Some staining from plts. to facing pp., cont. owner's inscr., gt.-lettered cl.-bkd. bds., worn & scuffed. (SG. Nov.10; 47) $450
- – **Anr. Edn.** Ill.:– A.L. Coburn. N.Y., 1911. *(600).* Fo. Some offsetting of gravures, cl.-bkd. bds., faded. (PNY. Jun.6; 558) $300
- The Invisible Man. L., 1897. *1st. Edn.* Orig. cl., with orig. full-p. pen sketch sigd. by Wells, inscr. to Ralph Straus 1910, Fred A. Berne copy. (SPB. May 16; 375) $1,100
- The Island of Dr. Moreau. 1896. *1st. Edn.* Advts. at end, orig. pict. cl., slightly soiled. (LC. Jul.5; 413) £50
- Love & Mr. Lewisham. L. & N.Y., 1900. *1st. Edn.* Advts., slightly browned & spotted, mostly endpapers, orig. cl.; inscr., Fred A. Berne copy. (SPB. May 16; 376) $100
- New Worlds for Old. L., 1908. *1st. Edn.* Orig. cl., cl. s.-c.; pres. copy to Joseph Conrad, Perry Molstad copy. (SPB. May 16; 545) $850
- The Time Machine. L., 1895. *1st. Edn. 1st. Bdg.* Darkening, grey cl. with purple stamping [Currey's 'B1' bdg.], covers mildly soiled & stained, spine darkening, extremities bumped & rubbed, endpapers foxing, bottom edge rough cut, other edges untrimmed; sigd. & dtd. 1937. (CBA. Oct.29; 911) $400
- – **Anr. Edn.** L., 1895. *1st. Edn.* Orig. ptd. wraps., upr. cover detchd.; Fred A. Berne copy. (SPB. May 16; 378) $175
- – **Anr. Edn.** N.Y., 1895. *1st. Amer. Edn.* 12mo. Cl., partly unc., rubbed. (SG. May 24; 378) $450
- Works. 1924-27. *Atlantic Edn. (620) numbered of British Edn.* 28 vols. Orig. cl. gt., partly unc., spines a little faded, some covers discold. near bd. edges; Clement W. Parish bkplt. (LC. Mar.1; 423) $520
- – **Anr. Edn.** N.Y., 1924-27. *'Atlantic' Edn. (1050) numbered & sigd.* 28 vols. Hf. mor. gt., spines gt. in 3 compartments, partly unc. (CNY. Dec.17; 612) $3,600
- – **Anr. Copy.** 28 vols. Hf. mor. gt. by Stikesman. (SPB. May 17; 751) $1,500

WELLSTED, James Raymond
- Travels to the City of the Caliphs ... L., 1840. 2 vols. 6 pp. publisher's advts., short tear at fold of map, hf. mor. by Sangorski. (C. Nov.16; 196) *Jaidah.* £450

WELTBUHNE
Ed.:– Maud v. Ossietzky & H. Leonhard. Contribs.:– Kästner, H. Mann, E. Rowohlt & others. Berlin, Jun. 1946-1950. Pts. 1-26 (all publd. ?), in 8 vols. Hf. linen, various, most with orig. wraps. (V. Oct.1; 4457) DM 600

WELTY, Eudora
- One Time, One Place. N.Y., 1971. *(300).* Cl., boxed. (SG. Mar.1; 598) $250

WELWOOD, William
- An Abridgement of all Sealawes. L., 1636. *2nd. Edn.* Ink stain on lr. margins, few minor paper losses, mor., gt. line-tooled, by C. Hering. [STC 25238] (SPB. Dec.13; 764) $275

WENDEL, Gottfried
- Leges Salicae Illustratae, illarum Natale Solum Demonstratum; cum Glossario Salico Vocum Advanticarum. Antw., 1649. Fo. Some margins wormed, old vell. (SG. Oct.27; 190) $110

WENTWORTH, Lady Judith Anne Dorothea Blunt-Lytton
- The Authentic Arabian Horse & his Descendants. 1945. *1st. Edn.* 4to. Orig. cl. gt., rubbed. (TA. Apr.19; 173) £75
- Thoroughbred Racing Stock. L., 1938. Bdg. not stated, col. pict. d.-w. with some wear. (DM. May 21; 41) $150
- – **Anr. Edn.** [1938]. 4to. Orig. cl. gt., d.-w. (P. Dec.8; 210) *Burton Garbett.* £65

WENTWORTH, Sir Thomas, Earl of Strafforde
See— STRAFFORDE, Sir Thomas Wentworth, Earl of

WENTWORTH, William Charles
- A Statistical Account of the British Settlements in Australasia. L., 1824. *3rd. Edn.* 2 vols. Dupl. map of Van Diemen's Land in Vol. 1, sm. tear in 1 map, all maps slightly foxed, other slight foxing, cf. gt., rebkd. (CA. Apr.3; 121) Aus. $300
- – **Anr. Copy.** 2 vols. Slight foxing, no bdg. stated. (JL. Nov.13; B70) Aus. $200
- A Statistical, Historical & Political Description of the Colony of New South Wales ... L., 1819. *1st. Edn.* 2 pp. of advts. bnd. in before hf.-title, some foxing on early ll., sig. on title & front end-paper, orig. bds., unc., stained. (CA. Apr.3; 120) Aus. $120
- – **Anr. Edn.** L., 1820. *2nd. Edn.* Some slight soiling, sm. inscr. at head of title, hf. cf. (S. Jun.25; 21) *Dunsheath.* £120
- – **Anr. Copy.** Folding map laid down, some foxing, later hf. mor., 1 backstrip panel replaced. (KH. May 1; 743) Aus. $170

WENZEL, Johann de
- Traité de la Cataracte. Paris, 1786. *1st. Edn.* Cont. hf. vell. (R. Oct.12; 1347) DM 500

WERKMANN, Hendrik Nicolaas
- Hommage à Werkmann. [Stuttgart, 1957/58]. 4to. Cl.-bkd. decor. bds. (SG. Sep.15; 344) $170

WERLICH, R.
- Orders & Decorations of All Nations Ancient & Modern, Civil & Military. Wash., Quaker Pr., 1965. Lge. 4to. Orig. linen. (V. Sep.30; 2511) DM 20,000

WERNER, F.
- Dom von Mainz ... Stadt ... Mainz, 1827-36. 3 vols. All titles with liby. stp., slightly foxed, later hf. leath., worn. (R. Oct.13; 2709) DM 420

WERTH, Leon
- Eloge de Albert Marquet. Paris, 1948. *(200) numbered.* 4to. Orig. wraps., unc. (S. Nov.21; 33) *Marks.* £150
- Eloge de Pierre Bonnard. Ill.:– P. Bonnard. [Paris, 1946]. *(20) with 2nd. series of lithos. on Japan. De Luxe Edn.* 4to. On vell. d'Arches, hand-bnd. orig. mor., orig. upr. wraps. bnd. in, rubbed. (H. May 23; 1163) DM 2,000

WERVELWIND, Der
L., 1942. Nos. 1-6 in 1 vol. 16mo. Fly-lf. with sigs. of P.S. Gerbrandy & 9 other members of the production team, hf. mor., orig. wraps. bnd. in. (S. Dec.20; 746) *Power.* £120

WESLEY, Samuel
- The Life of our Blessed Lord & Saviour Jesus Christ, An Heroic Poem. 1693. *1st. Edn.* Fo. 3 pp. advts. at end, old. panel cf., spine gt., slightly worn. (SKC. Mar.9; 1761) £70

WESSELSKI, A.
- Deutsche Märchen vor Grimm. Ill.:– Fritz Kredel. Brünn & Leipzig, 1938. With col. of De Luxe Edn. (100), but not on Bütten, many hand-cold. ills., orig. hf. linen (GB. May 5; 2828) DM 500
- – **Anr. Edn.** Ill.:– F. Kredel. Brünn & Leipzig, [1938]. *(100) De Luxe Edn. on Bütten.* Hand-bnd. hf. vell. (H. May 23; 1337) DM 880

WEST, James
- Bibliotheca Estiana: A Catalogue of the Curious & Truly Valuable Library. L., 1773. Priced in ink thro.-out, title & last lf. remargined, mod. qtr. cf. (SG. Apr.26; 203) $350

WEST, John, 1809-73
- The History of Tasmania ... Launceston, 1852. 2 vols. Sigs. bleached from title-pp., bdg. not stated, unc., 1st. vol. brkn. & opened. (KH. May 1; 744)
Aus. $100

WEST, John, 1778-1845
- The Substance of a Journal ... Red River Colony, British North America. 1824. Errata lf. at end, Frontis. foxed, bds., spine renewed. (P. Oct.20; 52)
£100

WEST, Stanley
- The Book of Dogs. N.d. 4to. Cont. mor. gt., s.-c. (CSK. Feb.10; 121)
£60

WEST, William, Bookseller
[-] Fifty years' Recollections of an Old Bookseller. L., 1837. Some ll. slightly soiled, orig. cl., rebkd., reprd. (BBA. Mar.7; 270)   Questor Books. £65
- The History, Topography & Directory of Warwickshire. Bg'ham., 1830. Hand-cold. folding map, 16 engraved plts., cont. diced cf. (TA. Nov.17; 164)
£70

- Picturesque Views & Descriptions of Cities, Towns, Castles, Mansions ... in Staffordshire & Shropshire. Ill.:– after Frederick Calvert. L., 1830-31. 2 vols. in 1. 4to. Engraved titles & 71 plts., spotted thro.-out, cont. hf. cf., rubbed. (BBA. May 3; 320)   Ingol Maps. £90

WESTALL, Richard
- Victories of the Duke of Wellington. L., 1819. 4to. Title with lge. woodcut vig., 12 cold. aquatint plts., recent cf. gt. (C. Jun.27; 78)   Ross. £140
- - Anr. Copy. Fo. 12 hand-cold. plts., slight offsetting, mod. hf. cf. by Bayntun. (S. Dec.8; 326)
Gratsos. £120

WESTALL, William
- Drawings. Ed.:– T.M. Perry & D.H. Simpson. 1962. [1st. Edn.]. Fo. Folding map in pocket, orig. cl. (S. Nov.1; 47)   Marlboro Rare Bks. £50
- - Anr. Copy. Fo. Bdg. not stated. (KH. May 1; 745)   Aus. $130
- The Mansions of England. L., ca. 1830. 2 vols. 146 hand-cold. aquatint plts., stained, hf. mor., slightly worn, hinges brkn. (S. Jun.25; 347)
Shapiro. £300

WESTALL, William & Moule, Thomas
- Great Britain Illustrated. 1830. 4to. Slight staining, hf. mor., top of spine defect. (P. Sep.29; 208)   £120
- - Anr. Copy. 4to. Extra engraved title, 56 plts., (of 59) spotted, cont. hf. roan, strip torn from lr. cover. (S. Mar.6; 301)   Besley. £90
- - Anr. Copy. 4to. Engraved title, 59 engraved plts., some foxing thro.-out, qtr. cf. with embossed cl., bds. (PD. Aug.17; 100)   £70
- - Anr. Edn. Ill.:– W. Westall. L., 1833. 4to. Extra engraved title, 59 plts., some spotting, bdg. defect. (S. Apr.9; 180)   Daveney. £110

WESTALL, W. & Owen, Samuel
- Picturesque Tour of the River Thames. L., 1828. 4to. Hand-cold. vigs. on title & at end, folding engraved map, 24 hand-cold. aquatint views, cont. hf. mor. (S. May 21; 76)   Weinreb. £1,700
- - Anr. Copy. 4to. 2 hand-cold. aquatint vigs., 1 folding engraved map, 24 plts., some light spotting affecting 1st. & last ll., mod. red hf. mor., extremities rubbed. (CSK. Dec.2; 38)   £1,100
- - Anr. Copy. 4to. Vig. title, folding engraved map, 24 hand-cold. aquatint engraved plts., stained in margins thro.-out, some offsetting, cont. red str.-grd. mor. gt., soiled & defect. (S. Mar.6; 354)
Solomons. £500

WESTERBAEN, J.
- Alle de Gedichten. 's-Gravenhage, 1672. 3 vols. Cont. vell.; J.H.W. Unger stp. (VS. Dec.9; 1093)
Fls. 500

WEST INDIES
- A Letter to a Member of Parliament, Concerning the Importance of Our Sugar-Colonies to Great Britain. L., 1745. 1st. Edn. Sm. 8vo. Mod. hf. lev. mor.; the Rt. Hon. Visc. Eccles copy. [Sabin 40397] (CNY. Nov.18; 283) $160

WESTLAKE, Nathaniel Hubert John
- A History of Design in Painted Glass. L. & Oxford, 1881-94. 4 vols. in 2. Sm. fo. Many text engrs., ex-liby., three-qtr. mor. (SG. May 3; 380)
$250
- - Anr. Copy. 4 vols. in 2. Fo. Three-qtr. mor. (RO. Dec.11; 348) $220

WESTMACOTT, Charles Malloy
- The English Spy. 1825-26. 2 vols. 71 hand-cold. plts. & 1 plain plt., mor. gt. by Morrell. (P. Apr.12; 81)   Solomon. £600

WESTMAN, G.A.
- Itinera Priscorum Scandianorum in Americam. Ed.:– Peter Kalm. Abo (Turku), [1757]. Sm. 4to. Later bds. [Sabin 103033] (S. Dec.1; 303)
Rowes. £150

WESTON, Edward
- Fifty Photographs. Texts:– Merle Armitage, R. Jeffers, D. Bear, & Weston. N.Y., [1947]. (1500) numbered. 4to. 1 plt. creased, cl.-bkd. ptd. bds., d.-w. rubbed & chipped; Weston's initials tipped in. (SG. May 10; 149) $225
- - Anr. Copy. 4to. Cl.-bkd. ptd. bds., rubbed & chipped, a few minor stains; initials of Weston tipped in. (SG. Nov.10; 164) $150

WESTWOOD, John Obadiah
- Arcana Entomologica & Illustrations of New, Rare & Interesting Insects. L., 1841-45. Royal 8vo. 96 hand-cold. litho. plts., mod. hf. mor. gt. (SKC. Oct.26; 454)   £650
- The Butterflies of Great Britain & their Transformations. 1855. 1st. Edn. 4to. Additional hand-cold. title, 2 plain plts., 19 hand-cold. plts., cont. hf. cf., gt. spine, rubbed. (SKC. May 4; 1880)   £200
- - Anr. Edn. L., 1860. Hand-cold. title, 19 hand-cold. plts., cl., reprd. (P. Nov.24; 160)
Graham. £55
- Palaeographia Sacra Pictoria. L., 1843-45. Lge. 4to. 50 cold. plts., many gt., hf. mor. (SG. Jan.5; 312) $100
- - Anr. Edn. L., 1853-55. 1st. Edn. 4to. 50 chromo-litho. plts., some heightened in gold, red mor. gt. extra. (PNY. Oct.20; 289) $100
- - Anr. Edn. N.d. Lge. 4to. Litho. additional title, 50 hand-cold. plts., liby. stp. on additional title, 1st. lf. of text & front free end-paper, cont. hf. mor. (CSK. Nov.4; 64)   £95
- - Anr. Copy. 4to. Chromolitho. hf.-title, 49 plts., some partly hand-cold., title & prelims. slightly soiled & creased, cont. hf. mor., rubbed. (CSK. May 18; 152)   £80
See— HUMPHREYS, Henry Noel & Westwood, John Obadiah

WETMORE, Helen Cody
- Last of the Great Scouts. The Life Story of Col. William F. Cody 'Buffalo Bill'. Duluth, [1899]. (500) numbered. Pict. cl.; limitation card sigd. by W.F. Cody pasted in upr. cover. (LH. Jan.15; 419)
$170

WETZLER, J.E.
- Ueber Gesundbrunnen und Heilbäder ... Mainz, 1822. New Edn. Cont. style bds., some light foxing, unc. (R. Apr.4; 1278)   DM 800

WEY, Francis
- La Haute Savoie Recits de Voyage et d'Histoire. Ill.:– H. Terry. Paris, 1866. Fo. Some foxing, plts. stpd. on versos, cl., brkn., lacks spine, ex-liby. (RO. Dec.11; 349) $470

WEYER, J.C. & Reeves, R.S.
- Thoroughbreds I Have Known. 1973. (72). 4to. Maroon mor. gt., qtr. mor. box. (P. Dec.8; 208)
£180

WEYER, J.P.
- Sammlung v. Ansichten öffentlicher Plätze Merkwürdiger Gebäude u. Denkmäler in Köln. Ill.:– Wünsch. Köln, 1827. 26 litho. plts., some misbnd., some light old spotting, hf. leath., lightly bumped. (B. Sep.30; 3015)   DM 2,000

WEYERMAN, Jacob Campo
- De Leven-Beschryvingen der Nederlandsche Konst-Schilders en Konst-Schilderessen. Ill.:– J. Houbraken. The Hague, 1729. Dordrecht, 1769. 4

vols., including the later publd. Vol. 4. 4to. Cont. pol. cf. gt. extra. (SG. Oct.13; 360) $200
- - Anr. Copy. 4 vols. 4to. Frontis., folding port., 40 plts. with 102 ports., many ills., lacks 1 port. & 1 plt., slightly browned, vell., a little soiled. (VG. May 3; 484)   Fls. 750

WEYL, H.
- Gruppentheorie und Quantenmechanik. Leipzig, 1928. 1st. Edn. Orig. linen. (HT. May 8; 507)
DM 460

WEYLER, General Valeriano
- Mi Mando en Cuba [... 1897]. Madrid, 1910-11. 5 vols. 4to. Linen. (DS. May 25; 2244)Pts. 30,000

WEZEL, Johann Karl
[-] Ueber Sprache, Wissenschaften und Geschmack der Teutschen. Leipzig, 1781. 1st. Edn. Some light browning, cont. bds., bumped, slightly soiled, lr. end-paper lacks cover. (HK. Nov.10; 2776)
DM 1,650

WHARTON, Edith
- Italian Villas & their Gardens. Ill.:– Maxfield Parish. N.Y., 1904. 1st. Edn. Decor. cl., lightly worn at extremities. (PNY. Jun.6; 560) $120
- - Anr. Edn. Ill.:– Maxfield Parrish & others. N.Y., 1905. Sm. 4to. 44 plts., gt.-pict. cl., ex-liby. (SG. Jan.12; 288) $100
- Quartet: Four Stories. Kentfield, 1975. (140). 4to. Hand-blocked cl., orig. packing box. (CBA. Nov.19; 10) $275
- - Anr. Edn. Kentfield, Calif., Allen Pr., 1975. (140) ptd. in Van Krimpen's Romance type on St. Cuthberts Mill all-rag paper. Fo. 4 full-p. ills., Fortuny print over bds., cl. spine prospectus laid in. (SG. May 17; 9) $275

WHATELY, Rev. Richard, attributed to
[-] Account of an Expedition to the Interior of New Holland. Ed.:– Lady Mary Fox. L., 1837. 16 pp. of book advts. bnd. in before hf.-title, orig. bds., unc. (CA. Apr.3; 50)   Aus. $180

WHEAT, Carl I.
- Books of the California Gold Rush. San Franc., Grabhorn Pr., 1949. (500). Cl.-bkd. decor. paper bds. (LH. Sep.25; 375) $125
- Mapping the Transmississippi West. San Franc., Institute for Historical Cartography, [at the Grabhorn Pr.], 1957-63. (1000). 5 vols. in 6. Sm. fo. Announcement & prospectus laid in, leatherette-bkd. buckram. (SG. Nov.3; 222) $1,200
- - Anr. Copy. Vols. 1-4 only (of 5 in 6). Fo. Hf. buckram & cl. (CBA. Nov.19; 251) $650
- - Anr. Edn. San Franc., Institute for Historical Cartography, [at the Grabhorn Pr.], 1959-60. (1000). Vols. 3 & 4 only (of 6). Sm. fo. Leatherette-bkd. buckram, untrimmed. (SG. Oct.20; 378)
$400

WHEATLEY, Henry B.
- The Historical & the Posthumous Memoirs of Sir Nathaniel William Wraxall, 1772-1784. 1884. 5 vols. Crimson hf. mor. gt. by Zaehnsdorf. (P. Mar.15; 25)   Thorp. £60
- Remarkable Bindings in the British Museum. 1889. (150) numbered. 4to. Orig. mor.-bkd. cl.; Aldenham House bkplt., H.M. Nixon coll., with his sig. & a few notes. (BBA. Oct.6; 138)
Goldschmidt. £150

WHEATLEY, Hewett
- The Rod & Line ... L., 1849. 1st. Edn. 9 hand-cold. plts., 32 p. publisher's catalogue, slight offsetting onto text, orig. cl. by Remnant & Edmonds. (S. Oct.4; 69)   Angle. £55

WHEATLEY, Phillis
- Poems on Various Subjects. L., 1773. 1st. Edn. Sm. 8vo. Foxed, cont. cf., upr. cover almost detchd. (LH. Sep.25; 618) $700

WHEELER, George M.
- Report Upon Geographical & Geological Explorations & Surveys West of the One Hundredth Meridian. Ill.:– Ridgway. Wash., 1875. Vol. V.: 'Zoology'. Lge. 4to. 45 litho. plts., many cold., including 15 hand-cold. bird plts., cl., brkn. (RO. Dec.11; 350) $120

WHEELER, Stephen
- History of the Delhi Coronation. 1904. *(250) numbered.* Fo. Orig. vell. gt., lightly rubbed & soiled. (CSK. Nov.4; 105) £60

WHELER, Sir George
- A Journey into Greece ... L., 1682. *1st. Edn.* Fo. Cont. cf., spine gt. (C. Nov.16; 197)
Blackwells. £300
-- Anr. Copy. Fo. Engraved folding map, 8 plts., map with tear, some spotting, cont. cf., spine reprd., rubbed. (S. Jun.25; 181) *Martinos.* £200
-- Anr. Copy. Fo. 18th. or early 19th. C. russ. gt. (SKC. May 4; 1827) £180
-- Anr. Copy. Fo. Cont. mott. cf., rebkd., badly worn; J.R. Wheeler bkplt. [Wing W1607] (SG. Sep.22; 302) $300
-- Anr. Copy. Fo. Folding map torn, slight foxing, cf., rebkd. (JL. Nov.13; B72) Aus. $340
- Voyage de Dalmatie, de Grèce et du Levant ... 1689. 2 vols. 12mo. Lacks frontis., cont. marb. cf. (HD. Jun.29; 108) Frs. 1,800

WHELER, Sir George & Spon, Jacob
- Italiänische, Dalmatische Griechische und Orientalische Reise-Beschreibung. Nuremb., 1690. *2nd. German Edn.* 2 pts. in 1 vol. Fo. Engraved frontis., 7 copper plts., 1 folding, 8 text copper engrs., 6 text woodcuts, 1 plt. with pasted tears in lr. margin, cont. leath., spine partly reprd. (R. Oct.13; 3173)
DM 420
- Voyage d'Italie, de Dalmatie, de Grèce, et du Levant. Lyons, 1678. *1st. Edn.* 3 vols. 12mo. Lacks port. frontis., cont. cf. (SKC. May 4; 1823) £80
-- Anr. Copy. 3 vols. 12mo. Cont. cf. (HD. Mar.9; 126) Frs. 2,200

WHISTLER, James Abbott McNeill
- The Gentle Art of Making Enemies. L., 1890. *1st. Edn. (250) numbered.* 4to. Cl.-bkd. bds., cover worn, bumped. (LH. Sep.25; 619) $140
-- Anr. Edn. L., 1892. Cl.-bkd. decor. bds., worn, buckram folding case; pres. inscr. in Whistler's hand, sigd. with butterfly monog. & dtd. Jun. 1893. (PNY. Jun.6; 561) $360
- L'Oeuvre ... au Palais de l'Ecole Nationale des Beaux-Arts. Intro.:- L. Bénedite. Paris, 1905. *(500) numbered.* Fo. 40 plts., disbnd. (SG. Aug.25; 407) $100

WHISTLER, Laurence & Fuller, Ronald
- The Work of Rex Whistler. 1960. 4to. Orig. buckram, gt.-decor.; T.L.s. from author to Ralph Edwards loosely inserted. (SKC. Jan.13; 2121) £140
-- Anr. Copy. 4to. Orig. cl., d.-w. (CSK. Dec.16; 27) £120
-- Anr. Copy. 4to. Orig. cl. (BBA. Nov.10; 191)
Bayley. £80

WHISTLER, Rex
- The Konigsmark Drawings. 1952. *(1000) numbered.* 4to. Orig. cl., s.-c. (CSK. Jun.1; 9) £55

WHISTON, William
- A New Theory of the Earth. L., 1696. *1st. Edn.* 2 ll. advts. & errata, a few letters on N1r supplied in pen, short tear in P1, cont. panel. cf., rebkd. [Wing W1696] (S. Oct.4; 292) *Henry.* £150

WHITAKER, Thomas Dunham
- The History & Antiquities of the Deanery of Graven in the County of York. L., 1812. *2nd. Edn.* Fo. Many plts. in 2 states, including cold. & uncold. aquatint views, cont. diced russ. gt., rebkd. (C. Nov.16; 198) *Old Hall.* £325
- An History of Richmondshire, in the North Riding of the County of York ... 1823. 2 vols. Tall fo. Some spotting, liby. stp. on verso of some plts., cont. gt.-decor. panel. cf., spine ends slightly worn; 8 extra ills. & hand-painted armorials in margins. (TA. Jul.19; 92) £350
-- Anr. Copy. 2 vols. Fo. 4 aquatint & 42 engraved plts., some light soiling, cont. cf., worn, w.a.f. (CSK. Jan.13; 200) £130

WHITE, A. & others
- The Succulent Euphorbiae (South Africa). Pasadena, U.S.A., 1941. 2 vols. 4to. Orig. bdgs., spines slightly faded. (VA. Apr.27; 944) R 250

WHITE, A. & Sloane, B.L.
- The Stapelieae. Pasadena, 1937. *2nd. Edn.* 3 vols. 4to. Errata slip, orig. bdgs. (VA. Oct.28; 634)
R 170

WHITE, Adam & Stark, Robert M.
- The Instructive Picture Book. 1857. *1st. Edn.* Vol. 1 (all publd.?). Fo. 30 hand-cold. double-p. engraved plts., cl. (LC. Oct.13; 169) £70
-- Anr. Edn. L., 1858. 4to. 30 hand-cold. double-p. plts., 1 with margin torn, orig. pict. bds., spine torn, worn. (P. May 17; 373) *Maggs.* £85

WHITE, Lieut George Francis
- Views in India, chiefly Among the Himalaya Mountains. Ed.: [Emma Roberts]. L. & Paris, 1838,. 4to. Some spotting, orig. mor. gt. (CSK. Feb.10; 205) £80
-- Anr. Copy. 4to. Steel-engraved frontis. & extra title, 35 plts., some stains, some light spotting, 1 badly spotted, cont. mor. gt. (CSK. Feb.24; 127) £55
-- Anr. Edn. N.d. 4to. 37 steel-engraved views, some margins slightly foxed, hf. mor., reprd. (S. Nov.1; 63) *Primrose.* £55

WHITE, Gilbert
- The Natural History & Antiquities of Selborne in the County of Southampton. L., 1789. *1st. Edn.* 2 pts. in 1 vol. 4to. Ptd. general title, pt. titles with engraved vigs., 7 plts., folding frontis. with sm. tear at fold, mor. gt. by Riviere. (C. Jun.27; 189)
Dunsheath. £900
-- Anr. Copy. 4to. Errata lf. at end, cont. tree cf. gt. (BBA. Sep.29; 159) *Brook-Hitching.* £520
-- Anr. Copy. Sm. 4to. Hf.-title, errata lf. at end, 2 prelim. advt. ll. slightly foxed, folding view spotted slightly, cont. cf., rebkd. preserving orig. gt. spine; John Ellis bkplt. (C. Nov.9; 121)
Thorp. £380
-- Anr. Copy. 4to. 7 plts. (2 folding), 2 vigs., errata lf., 3 plts. trimmed, some spotting, marginal repair to 2G1, cont. cf., jnts. split. (S. Apr.10; 595)
Bickersteth. £200
-- Anr. Edn. L., 1813. 4to. Extra title with engraved vig., engraved folding frontis., 8 plts. (1 hand-cold.), tail-piece & vig. on title of Antiquities, spotted, tree cf., spine gt. (S. Apr.10; 596)
Henderson. £120
-- Anr. Copy. 4to. 9 engraved plts., including 1 folding (laid down) & 1 hand-col., mott. cf., gt. spine, upr. cover detchd. (S. Oct.4; 293)
Walford. £50
-- Anr. Edn. Notes:- Frank Buckland. 1876. 2 vols. Fo. 24 mntd. photographs, hf. mor. gt. (LC. Oct.13; 222) £50
- The Works in Natural History. 1802. 2 vols. in 1. Cont. cf., w.a.f.; pres. copy to Luke White 'with the editor & publisher's best respects' inscr. on blank before frontis., from liby. of Luttrellstown Castle. (C. Sep.28; 1784) £300
- The Writings. L., Nones. Pr., 1938. *(850). Out-of-series copy.* 2 vols. Orig. cl. gt.; bkplt. of David Garnett. (BBA. Mar.21; 320) *Sherlock.* £160

WHITE, H. Kirke
- The Remains. Glasgow, 1825. Sm. 12mo. Burgundy str.-grd. mor., as a fore-e. pntg., w.a.f. (SPB. Dec.13; 529) $225

WHITE, Henry
- Catalogue of the Valuable & Extensive Library of Printed Books & Illustrated & other Important Manuscripts. 1902. Sm. 4to. Later cl.; H.M. Nixon coll., with a few MS. notes. (BBA. Oct.6; 164)
Quaritch. £50

WHITE, Isaac
- The Privateer's Man; The True Story of a Sailor: being, Incidents in the Life. Ed.:- Charles W. Denison. Boston, 1845. *1st. Edn.* 12mo. Foxed, later marb. bds.; from liby. of F.D. Roosevelt, inscr. by him. (SG. Mar.15; 83) $300

WHITE, John
- An Essay on the Indigenous Grasses of Ireland. Dublin, 1803. Hf. cf. (GM. Dec.7; 457) £90

WHITE, John, Pioneer, fl. 1585-90
- The American Drawings of John White 1577-1590. British Museum & University of North Carolina, 1964. *(600) numbered.* 2 vols. including 1 vol. plts. Fo. Orig. cl., s.-c. (CSK. May 4; 124) £120

WHITE, John, Surgeon
- Journal of a Voyage to New South Wales ... L., 1790. *1st. Edn.* Plts. hand-cold. *(Bound with:)* GILBERT, Thomas - Voyage from New South Wales to Canton in the Year 1788 ... L., 1789. *1st. Edn.* Some foxing of folding plts. Together 2 works in 1 vol. 4to. Early spr. cf., rebkd. (KH. Nov.9; 744) Aus. $5,400
-- Anr. Copy. 4to. With orig. uncancelled lf. at Hh4, natural history plts. on superior paper & hand-cold., later hf. cf., rebkd., slightly bumped & chipped. (KH. May 1; 754) Aus. $4,600
-- Anr. Copy. 4to. 65 hand-cold. engraved plts., 1 plt. dampstained in margin, old sig. at head of title, blind-stpd. cf. gt., rebkd., covers worn. (CA. Apr.3; 125) Aus. $3,500
-- Anr. Edn. L., 1790. 4to. 65 hand-cold. engraved plts., lacks advt. ll. at end, title & early ll. foxed, hf. cf., covers worn; Dame Mabel Brookes bkplt. (CA. Apr.3; 135) Aus. $3,000

WHITE, John
See— NASH, John & others

WHITE, John, of Wellington, N.Z.
- The Ancient History of The Maori, his Mythology & Traditions. 1887. 5 vols. Orig. cl., liby. stps. on spines, faded. (P. Apr.12; 211)
Vine. £55

WHITE, Joseph William Gleeson (Ed.)
See— PAGEANT, The

WHITE, Stanford
- Sketches & Designs. Ed.:- L. Grant White. N.Y., 1920. Tall fo. Cold. frontis., 56 plts., text ills., ex-liby., cl. (SG. May 3; 383) $450

WHITEFIELD, George
- A Journal of a Voyage from London to Savannah in Georgia. - A Continuation of the Journal from his Arrival at London ... - A Continuation ... during the Time he was Detained in England by the Embargo. - The Answer to the Bishop of London's last Pastoral Letter with the Supplement. L., 1739. *1st. work 3rd. Edn.* 4 works in 1 vol. 1st. work with advt. lf., mod. hf. cf., unc. [Sabin 103534; 103538; 103540; 103577] (C. Jun.27; 76) *Quaritch.* £90

WHITEHEAD, John
- The Exploration of Mount Kina, Balu, North Borneo. L., 1893. Fo. 32 litho. plts. (14 cold.), ills., prelims. slightly spotted, orig. pict. cl. (S. Apr.10; 462) *Grahame.* £440

WHITELAW, Rev. J.
See— WARBURTON, John, of Dublin, Whitelaw, Rev. J. & Walsh, Rev. R.

WHITELOCK, Sir Bulstrode
[-] Monarchy Asserted. 1660. Old cf. [Wing W1988] (P. Feb.16; 277) £75

WHITELOCK, Dorothy
- The Will of Aethelgifu, a Tenth Century Anglo-Saxon Manuscript, Translated & Examined ... Roxb. Cl., 1968. Fo. Orig. qtr. mor. (S. Oct.4; 250)
Traylen. £80

WHITELOCKE, Lieut. Gen. John
- The Proceedings of a General Court Martial ... for the Trial of Lieut. Gen. Whitelocke. 1808. Cont. cf., rubbed, Vol. 1 spine defect. (BBA. Jun.28; 260)
Archer. £50

WHITMAN, Walt
- As a Strong Bird on Pinions Free, & Other Poems. Wash., D.C., 1872. *1st. Edn.* Advts., light marginal browning, orig. cl., spine slightly frayed; pres. copy to Mrs. Wilson Eyre, Fred A. Berne copy. (SPB. May 16; 380) $600
- Complete Poems & Prose. Phila., 1888. *1st. Coll. Edn. (600) numbered & sigd.* Lge. 8vo. Hf. cf., partly unc.; Frederic Dannay copy. (CNY. Dec.16; 375) $320
- Drum-Taps. N.Y., 1865. *1st. Edn. 2nd. Iss.* 12mo.

WHITMAN, Walt -*Contd.*

Orig. cl., hf.-mor. s.-c.; Frederic Dannay copy. (CNY. Dec.16; 373) $140
- **Grashalme.** Ill.:– W. Jaeckel. Berlin, 1920. *(65) numbered on Bütten.* 4to. 13 sigd. lithos., orig. mor., upr. cover gt., spine slightly faded & worn. (HK. Nov.11; 3647) DM 650
[–] **Hymn on the Death of Lincoln.** Ill.:– C.R. Ashbee. [L.], Essex House Pr., [1900]. *(125) numbered, on vell.* Frontis., initials, all hand-cold., orig. vell., unc.; mor. bkplt. of Alexander L. Wyant. (SG. May 17; 86) $250
[–] **Leaves of Grass.** N.Y., 1855. *1st. Edn. 1st. Iss.* Sm. fo. Orig. cl. gt., decor. in blind, spine worn, hf. mor. folding case; sm. label of Fowler, Wells & Co. pasted in upr. cover, E.A. Bigelow-Walter P. Chrystler, Jnr. bkplts., Frederic Dannay copy. (CNY. Dec.16; 367) $5,800
- – **Anr. Copy.** Engraved port. with orig. tissue guard, title & few ll. foxed, slight offsetting, orig. cl., gt. & blind-stpd., spine reprd., mor. solander case; Prescott copy. (SPB. May 17; 714) $3,600
- – **Anr. Edn.** Brooklyn, 1856. *2nd. Edn.* 12mo. Foxed, orig. cl., Emerson's gt.-lettered greeting at foot of spine; Frederic Dannay copy. (CNY. Dec.16; 368) $750
- – **Anr. Edn.** Boston, 1860-61. *3rd. Edn. 1st. Iss.* Orig. heavily embossed cl., stpd. in gt. & blind; Frederic Dannay copy. (CNY. Dec.16; 369) $220
- – **Anr. Edn.** Wash., 1872. Black– & gt.-stpd. cl., worn. (RO. Apr.23; 371) $140
- – **Anr. Edn.** Camden, 1876. *Author's Edn.* 'Intercalations' ptd. in text, cf., rubbed, crudely rebkd. preserving most of orig. spine, worn; sigd. by author. (RO. Apr.23; 372) $310
- – **Anr. Edn.** Ill.:– Hollyer. Phila., 1888. *7th. Edn. Special Re-Iss.*, including 'Sands at Seventy'. Tall 8vo. L.P., orig. cl., mostly unopened, hf. mor. s.-c.; 2 autograph postcards sigd. by author, proof slips or offprints of 3 poems & 10 ports. on Japan vell. inserted, Frederick W. Skiff & Byron Price bkplts., letter from Alfred F. Goldsmith to Skiff tipped in, Frederic Dannay copy. (CNY. Dec.16; 370) $2,200
- – **Anr. Edn.** [Phila., 1889]. *'Birthday [8th. Separate] Edn.'.* (300) sigd. 12mo. Frontis.-photo. & 5 other inserted ports., orig. limp mor., wallet-style with tongue & strap & inner pocket at rear; name 'W.A. Ferguson' written on title by Whitman, Frederic Dannay copy. (CNY. Dec.16; 371) $700
- – **Anr. Edn.** Phila., 1891-92. *'Death-Bed [9th. Separate] Edn.'. 2nd. Iss.* Orig. wraps., unopened, split in front outer joint, hf. mor. s.-c.; pres. copy to Warren Fritzinger, by Horace L. Traubel for Whitman, Frederic Dannay copy. (CNY. Dec.16; 372) $2,400
- – **Anr. Edn.** Ill.:– V. Angelo. N.Y., Random House, at the Grabhorn Pr., 1930. *(400) sigd. by artist. (5) specially bnd. out-of-series copies for members of the Pr.* Fo. Slight foxing to 4 pp. & a few fly-ll., rebnd. in red niger, spine gt.-stpd., orig. fly-ll. & end-papers, boxed; sigd. trial proof of title-p. & several following pp. laid in, the V. Angelo copy. (CBA. Oct.1; 184) $1,200
- – **Anr. Edn.** Ill.:– Boyd Hanna. Mount Vernon, N.Y., Peter Pauper Pr., [1950]. *(100) numbered.* Fo. With publisher's prospectus, qtr. leath. & paper bds., s.-c. (LH. Sep.25; 441) $180
[–] **Two Rivulets, including Democratic Vistas, Centennial Songs, & Passage to India.** Camden, Author's Edn., 1876. *1st. Edn.* Hf. cf., photographic frontis. sigd. by author. (SG. Mar.15; 160) $350
- – **Anr. Copy.** Later three-qtr. leath., rebkd., rubbed; photo frontis. laid in, sigd. by author & dtd. 1881. (RO. Apr.23; 377) $300

WHITNEY, Geffrey

- **A Choic[e] of Emblemes.** Leiden, 1586. 2 pts. in 1 vol. 4to. Soiled & dampstained thro.-out, title & some ll. soiled with slight loss, lr. margins lightly wormed, old vell., w.a.f. [STC 25438] (CSK. Aug.5; 92) £120

WHITTELL, Hubert Massey

- **The Literature of Australian Birds.** Perth, 1954. 4to. Cl., covers slightly worn, sig. on front endpaper. (CA. Apr.3; 126) Aus. $220

WHITTINTON, Robert

[–] **De Octo Partibus Orationis.** L., Wynkyn de Worde, 15 Oct., 1522. 4to. Printer's full-p. woodcut device at end, woodcut capitals, lacks title, little wormed, lightly stained, marginal repairs with loss of few sidenotes, corner of B1 reprd. with about 20 letters in facs., 19th. C. qtr. roan, patterned bds.; J.H. Bates bkplt. (SG. Apr.26; 204) $650

WHITTLE, James

See— LAURIE, Robert & Whittle, James

WHITTOCK, Nathaniel

- **The Decorative Painters & Glaziers Guide.** 1827. 4to. 85 plts., including 31 hand-cold., spotting, cont. hf. cf., worn. (CSK. Sep.30; 151) £140

WHITWORTH, Charles, Lord

- **An Account of Russia as it was in** ... **1710.** Strawberry-Hill, 1758. *1st. Edn.* Errata-lf. at end, slight browning, cont. cf., spine gt., rebkd., old spine preserved. (S. Oct.11; 601) *Byrne.* £160

WHO'S WHO

L., for 1922. *[Ltd. Edn.?].* 65 × 42mm. Miniature Book. Orig. cl., d.-w. slightly worn, tear reprd. (S. Dec.20; 622) *Sawyer.* £150

WHOLE DUTY OF A WOMAN, The; or, A Guide to the Female Sex, from the Age of Sixteen to Sixty, written by a Lady

L., 1695. *1st. Edn.* 12mo. D.Poplar's license on title verso, 1st. & last ll. much reprd., some stains, old cf., rebkd. (SG. Feb.9; 371) $425

WHYMPER, Edward

- **Scrambles Amongst the Alps in the Years 1860-69.** 1871. *1st. Edn.* Orig. cl. gt. (P. Jun.7; 307) £160

WHYTE-MELVILLE, George John

- **Works.** N.d. 25 vols. Hf. cf. gt. (P. Apr.12; 140) *DeMetzy.* £110

WHYTT, Robert

- **Observations on the Nature, Causes, & Cure of those Disorders which have been commonly called Nervous, Hypochondriac, or Hysteric.** Edinb., 1765. *2nd. Edn.* Lacks lf. before title (?blank), cont. cf. gt. (S. Oct.4; 295) *Laywood.* £110

WICH, I.P.

- **Lese-Schule für Kinder-Stuben.** Ill.:– Carl Buchner. Stuttgart & Esslingen, [foreword dtd. 1852]. Lge. ob. 4to. 15 hand-cold. litho. plts., text spotted, orig. cl.-bkd. bds., slightly worn & stained; van Veen coll. (S. Feb.28; 173) £800
- – **Anr. Edn.** Stuttgart & Esslingen, [1852]. *1st. Edn.* Lge. ob. 4to. Lacks plt. 6, text foxed & stained, soiled at foot, cont. hf. linen, orig. pict. upr. wrap. excised & pasted on, bumped & slightly spotted. (HK. Nov.10; 3015) DM 1,100

WICKES, Charles

- **Illustrations of the Spires & Towers of the Mediaeval Churches of England.** 1858-69. 3 vols. in 1, including Supp. Fo. Slight spotting, orig. cl., spine reprd. (P. Sep.8; 354) £110

WICQUEFORT, Abraham de

- **L'Ambassadeur et ses Fonctions.** The Hague, 1680-81. *1st. Edn.* 2 vols. 4to. Cont. mott. cf. gt. (SG. Oct.27; 332) $200
- – **Anr. Edn.** Cologne, 1715. 2 vols. 4to. Vell. (HD. Feb.22; 230) Frs. 3,800

WIDDER, J.G.

- **Versuch einer Vollständige Geographisch-historischen Beschreibung der Kurfürstl. Pfalz am Rheine.** Frankfurt & Leipzig, 1786-88. 4 vols. 4 engraved title vigs., title stpd., some pencil underlining, slightly browned, cont. hf. leath., some wear. (HT. May 10; 2974a) DM 1,800

WIDEKINDI, J.

- **Thet Swenska i Ryszland tijo ahrs Krijgz-Historie.** Stockholm, 1671. Sm. 4to. Engraved plan with reprd. tear & splits & creases in folds, some stains, cont. cf., slightly worn. (S. Dec.1; 316) *Anderson.* £350

WIDENER, Harry Elkins

- **A Catalogue of the Books & Manuscripts of** ... Ed.:– A.S.W. Rosenbach. Phila., priv. ptd., 1928. *1st. Edn.* 2 vols. Tall 4to. L.P., cl.; inscr. & sigd. by Rosenbach. (SG. Sep.15; 289) $220
- **A Catalogue of Some of the More Important Books, Manuscripts & Drawings in the Library of Harry Elkins Widener.** Phila., 1910. *(102).* 4to. Hf. mor. (PNY. Dec.1; 39) $300
- **Robert Louis Stevenson: A Catalogue of the Books & Manuscripts in the Library of the late** ... Memoir:– A.S.W. Rosenbach. Phila., priv. ptd., 1913. *(150) numbered on L.P.* Lge. tall 4to. This copy out-of-series, crushed three-qtr. mor. gt. by H. Zucker. (SG. Sep.15; 318) $120

WIDMANN, Georg Rudolf

- **Erster [Der Ander, Der Dritte] Theil** ... **Sünden und Lastern** ... **D. Johannes Faustus** ... Hamburg, 1599. *1st. Edn.* 3 pts. in 1 vol. 4to. Lightly browned, some light soiling, old name on 1st. title old deleted, cont. vell., blind-tooled pig spine & corners, monog. HVK & date 1600, very rubbed; Hans Fürstenberg ex-libris inside cover. (R. Apr.3; 40) DM 6,600
- – **Anr. Copy.** 3 pts. in 1 vol. 4to. Cont. stpd. hf. pig, corners, vell. covers, initials 'VK' & date 1600, worn; from Fondation Furstenberg-Beaumesnil. (HD. Nov.16; 122) Frs. 8,000

WIDOWSON, Henry

- **Present State of Van Diemen's Land** ... L., 1829. *1st. Edn.* Folding map with 1 coarse repair, & a little foxed, some weakness in sewing, bds., qtr. cl., minor wear. (KH. Nov.9; 737) Aus. $220

WIEGLEB, Johann Christian

- **Die Natürliche Magie.** Ed.:– G.E. Rosenthal. Berlin & Stettin, 1786-1804. Vols. 1-18 (of 20) in 18 vols. Vols. 8-13 with sub-title: 'J.N. Martius, Unterricht in der Natürlichen Magie', some light foxing, vol. 1 lacks end of index, cont. hf. leath., vol. 1 cont. bds., slightly rubbed, some light bumping. (R. Apr.4; 1451) DM 3,200

WIELAND, Christoph Martin

- **Agathon.** Ill.:– Geyser after Mechau. Leipzig, 1853-58. *2nd. Edn.* 4 vols. in 2. Some slight brown spotting, cont. hf. leath., slightly worn & rubbed. (H. May 22; 935) DM 420
- **Auszug aus Lucians Nachrichten vom Tode des Peregrinus.** Ill.:– Rud. Schlichter. Heidelberg, 1920. *(150).* Lge. 4to. Printers mark sigd. by artist, 10 orig. lithos., orig. bds., spine renewed, corners rubbed. (GB. May 5; 3225) DM 750
- **Der Goldne Spiegel.** Leipzig, 1772. *1st. Edn.* 4 vols. in 2. Cont. hf. leath., bumped. (R. Apr.3; 490) DM 560
- **Die Grazien.** Leipzig, 1770. *1st. Edn.* Lightly foxed, cont. leath. gt., spine rubbed, corners bumped. (HK. Nov.10; 2780) DM 420
- **Musarion ou la Philosophie des Grâces.** Trans.:– M. de Laveaux. Ill.:– Saint Quentin, engraved by Holzhalb. Basle, 1780. On holland, figures before the letter, cont. spr. cf. gt., spine decor. (HD. May 3; 170) Frs. 1,400
- **Sämmtliche Werke.** Leipzig, 1794-1801. *1st. Coll. Edn.* 42 vols., including 6 Supp. vols. Vols. 1-30 cont. cf., others cont. hf. cf. (C. Dec.9; 300) *Bender.* £260
- – **Anr. Edn.** Leipzig, 1794-1801. *Definitive Edn. De Luxe Edn. on vell.* 36 vols. & 6 supp. vols. Minimal spotting, cont. mor., decor., minimal rubbing; engraved Louis Gontard ex-libris; Hauswedell coll. (H. May 24; 1621) DM 17,500
- – **Anr. Edn.** Leipzig, 1794-1802. 36 vols. & 6 supp. vols. 4to. Minimal rubbing & foxing, cont. cf., gt. spine, blind-tooled cover decor., gt. inner & outer dentelles; Hauswedell coll. (H. May 24; 1620) DM 22,000
- – **Anr. Edn.** Leipzig, 1794-1811. 45 vols. in 45, including 6 Supp. vols. Sm. 8vo. Cont. hf. cf., 8 spines very defect., w.a.f. (C. Dec.9; 301) *Bender.* £130
- – **Anr. Copy.** 45 vols. 1st. & last ll. slightly browned, cont. hf. leath. gt., lightly rubbed & bumped, spine partly split, ex-libris, w.a.f. (HK. May 16; 2311) DM 2,600
- – **Anr. Edn.** Ed.:– J.G. Gruber. Leipzig, 1818/23. 49 vols. On thin vell., bds., spine darkened. (V. Oct.1; 3905) DM 450
- – **Anr. Edn.** Ed.:– J.G. Grüber. Leipzig, 1818-28. 53 vols. Sm. 8vo. Some light browning & sm. spots,

cont. hf. leath., slightly bumped, spine very faded & rubbed. (H. May 22; 933) DM 650
– – **Anr. Edn.** Leipzig, 1853-56. *4th. Coll. Edn.* 36 vols. in 18. Some pp. slightly foxed, cont. linen gt., blind-tooled, 1st. 5 vols. (vols. 1-10) slightly different col. (R. Oct.11; 461) DM 550

WIEN UND DIE WIENER, IN BILDERN AUS DEM LEBEN
Ed.:– A. Stifter. Pesth, 1844. Ill. title, 12 sm. vigs. 30 etched plts., title stpd., 1 lf. browned, later hf. leath., gt. spine, re-cased; Hauswedell coll. (H. May 23; 153) DM 2,000

WIENER, A.F.
See— BLAKSTON, W. & others

WIENER, L.
– Recherches sur l'Industrie Cartière en Lorraine. Nancy, 1884. (*Bound with:*) MOURIER, P. – Recherches sur la Fabrication des Cartes à Jouer à Angoulême. 1904. *(100)*. Together 2 works in 1 vol. Lge. 8vo. Bradel, wrap. (HD. Feb.28; 99) Frs. 1,500

WIENER, Samuel
– Bibliographie der Oster-Haggadah, 1500-1900. St. Petersb., 1902. 4to. Cl.-bkd. bds., worn. (SG. Feb.2; 28) $150

WIENER ZEITSCHRIFT FÜR KUNST, THEATER UND MODE
Ed.:– J. Schickh. Wien, Jan.-Jun. 1829. Pts. 1-78 in 2 vols. 24 (of 26) copper engrs., plts., browned, light stain thro.-out, orig. wraps. (R. Oct.12; 2218) DM 410

WIER, Joannes
– De Praestigiis Daemonum, et Incantationibus ac Veneficijs, Libri IV. Basel, 1566. Title old restored, old hf. vell. [STC 913- HG III, 255] (BR. Apr.12; 896) DM 1,200
– – **Anr. Edn.** Basle, 1568. Title stained, sm. wormhole through last portion, cont. blind-stpd. pig., with panels (that on upr. cover very worn), 2 clasps; Dr. Walter Pagel copy. (S. Feb.7; 382)
Colombo. £450
– – **Anr. Copy.** Lacks corner of title-lf., cont. stpd. pig, arms of Holy Roman Empire & Augustus, Elector of Saxony, initials 'G.A.N.' & date 1579 blind-stpd. on upr. cover; from Fondation Furstenberg-Beaumesnil. (HD. Nov.16; 183) Frs. 6,000

WIERUSZOWSKI
– Europa in Serenissima Leczyniorum Domo Sanguine & Affinitate. Per Orientis et Occidentis Imperatores: Per Absolutas Monarchas: Per Omnes pere Poloniarum Reges. Frankfurt, 21 Jun. 1725. 12mo. Elab. decor. mor. by Padeloup, with his label, Stanislas Lesczynski arms on upr. cover, Catherine Opalinska arms on lr. cover, spine decor., red mor. liners, gt. paper end-ll. (HD. Mar.29; 55)
Frs. 170,000

WIESENER
– Le Régent, l'Abbé Dubois et les Anglais d'après les Sources Britanniques. Paris, 1891-99. 3 vols. Hf. chagrin. (HD. Feb.22; 231) Frs. 1,300

WIET, G.
See— HAUTECOEUR, L. & Wiet, G.

WIGHT, John
[–] Sunday in London. Illustrated in Fourteen Cuts, by George Cruikshank, & a Few Words by a Friend of His; with a Copy of Sir Andrew Agnew's Bill. 1833. Later pol. cf. gt. by J.B. Hawes. (TA. Jun.21; 367) £54

WIGHT, Robert
– Illustrations of Indian Botany. Madras, 1840. Vol. 1 only. 4to. 103 litho. plts., including 99 hand-cold. & 2 folding, dampstained, browned, some ll. detchd., bdg. not stated. (CSK. Oct.21; 142) £55

WIGSTEAD, Henry
– Remarks on a Tour to North & South Wales in the Year 1797. Ill.:– Thomas Rowlandson. 1800. Engraved title, 21 (of 22) plts., cf. gt., rebkd. (P. Oct.20; 33) £100

WILBUR, Richard
– A Bestiary. Ill.:– Alexander Calder. N.Y., 1955. *1st. Edn., (825). (750) numbered & sigd. by author & artist.* 4to. Orig. cl., publisher's box worn; Frederic Dannay copy. (CNY. Dec.16; 380) $130
– – **Anr. Edn.** Ill.:– after Alexander Calder. N.Y., [1955]. *(25) lettered for review, sigd. by Wilbur & Calder.* 4to. Silver-decor. cl., s.-c. worn. (SG. Jan.12; 52) $225
– Complaint. N.Y., 1968. *(26) lettered & sigd.* Ob. sm. 8vo. Unlettered wraps., marb. d.-w. (SG. Mar.1; 602) $275

WILD, Cdr. F.
– Shackleton's Last Voyage. 1923. Orig. cl. gt. (P. Jun.7; 58) £120
– – **Anr. Copy.** Orig. cl., d.-w. chipped. (KH. Nov.9; 443) Aus. $260

WILD, John James
– Bookbinding in the Library of All Souls. N.p., 1880. Lr. margin lightly stained, loose in orig.ptd. wraps.; H.M. Nixon coll. (BBA. Oct.6; 139)
Maggs. £95

WILDE, Oscar
– The Ballad of Reading Gaol. L., 1898. *1st. Edn., (830). (30) numbered on japan vell.* Orig. vell.-bkd. cl., partly unc.; Frederic Dannay copy. (CNY. Dec.16; 381) $1,600
– – **Anr. Edn.** L., 1898. *1st. Edn., (830). (800).* Orig. cl., unopened, orig. tissue d.-w.; Frederic Dannay copy. (CNY. Dec.16; 382) $900
– – **Anr. Edn.** L., 1898. *1st. Edn. (800) on H.M.P.* Orig. cl., slightly soiled; Fred A. Berne copy. (SPB. May 16; 381) $375
– – **Anr. Copy.** Tall 8vo. Two-tone cl., lightly soiled. (SG. Jan.12; 358) $200
– – **Anr. Edn.** L., 1898. *1st. Edn. (830).* Lightly soiled, orig. cl., unc., recased, soiled; Wildmerding/ Perry Molstad copy. (SPB. May 16; 547) $100
– – **Anr. Edn.** L., 1898. *3rd. Edn. (99) numbered & sigd.* Hf.-title, a few spots, partly unc. cont. red mor., covers & spine gt.-tooled, by the Hampstead Bindery, repair to corner of upr. cover, rebkd., old spine preserved. (S. Dec.8; 156) *Hever.* £500
– – **Anr. Edn.** Ill.:– R. Schlichter. [München, 1923]. *(125).* Hand-bnd. orig. hf. vell., worn & slightly spotted; 1st. etching sigd. by artist. (H. Nov.24; 2014) DM 750
– – **Anr. Edn.** Ill.:– Frans Masereel. Mandruck Pr., 1925. *1st. Engl. Edn. with these ills. (450) numbered.* Lge. 8vo. Orig. linen-bkd. bds., unc., orig. d.-w.; bkplt. of Henry Wade. (LC. Oct.13; 408) £50
– Ballade des Zuchthauses zu Reading. Trans.:– A. Holitscher. Ill.:– O. Pankok. Berlin, 1923. *(300) numbered.* Fo. Printers mark sigd. by artist, orig. hf. vell., slight wear. (HK. May 17; 3228) DM 700
– The Birthday of the Infanta. Ill.:– 'Alastair'. Paris, Black Sun Pr., 1928. *(100) numbered on Hollande Van Gelder Zonen paper.* 4to. Ptd. wraps., bd. s.-c., cracked. (SG. Jan.12; 4) $500
– Der Geburtstag der Infantin und andere Märchen. Ill.:– L. Kainer. Berlin, 1922. *(100) De Luxe Edn. On Bütten.* 4to. Hand-bnd. red-brown orig. mor., gt. spine, cover, & inner dentelles, by W. Hacker, Leipzig; all full-p. lithos. sigd. by artist. (H. Nov.24; 2219) DM 700
– The Happy Prince. Ill.:– Walter Crane & Jacomb Hood. L., 1888. *1st. Edn. (75) on L.P. sigd. by author & publisher.* 4to. Orig. decor. bds., unc., slightly soiled, mor.-bkd. s.-c.; Perry Molstad copy. (SPB. May 16; 548) $1,900
– The Happy Prince & Other Tales. Ill.:– Charles Robinson. L., 1913. *(260) numbered & sigd. by artist.* 4to. Unc., orig. parch. gt., s.-c., defect. (S. Dec.20; 585) *Greer.* £280
– Die Heilige Buhlerin. La Sainte Courtisane oder das Weib mit den Edelsteinen. Ill.:– M. Behmer. Berlin, 1921. *Hors commerce.* Monog., mor. by Bruno Scheer after M. Behmer, gold-tooled, decor., gt. inner & outer dentelles; M. Behmer ex-libris, his MS. in printer's mark 'unverstählt Probe-Druck'. (HK. Nov.11; 3419) DM 7,900
– – **Anr. Edn.** Ill.:– M. Behmer. Berlin, 1921. *(450).* Printers mark sigd. by artist, hand-bnd., orig. mor. with vig., spine slightly discold. & bumped light wear. (H. May 23; 1151a) DM 1,750

– – **Anr. Copy.** Orig. bds., slightly discold. (H. Nov.24; 1372) DM 440
– A House of Pomegranates. Ill.:– Charles Ricketts & Charles Shannon. L., 1891. *1st. Edn.* 4to. Two-tone cl., pict. end-papers, orange & gt. design by Ricketts, spine ends rubbed, mor.-bkd. folding case. (SG. Jan.12; 357) $450
– – **Anr. Edn.** Ill.:– Jessie M. King. L., [1915]. *1st. King Edn.* 4to. Foxed, slightly affecting some plts., owner's name on hf.-title, orig. decor. cl., covers bumped, spine faded. (CBA. Aug.21; 353) $110
[–] An Ideal Husband. L., 1899. *1st. Edn. (100) numbered, on L.P., sigd.* 4to. Orig. cl.; Fred A. Berne copy. (SPB. May 16; 382) $800
– The Importance of Being Earnest. 1899. *1st. Edn (1000) numbered.* Sm. 4to. Orig. decor. cl. gt., unc. (SKC. Mar.9; 1867) £120
– Lady Windermere's Fan. 1893. *1st. Edn.* Sm. 4to. 15 pp. advts. at end, orig. decor. cl. gt. (SKC. Mar.9; 1869) £120
– – **Anr. Copy.** 4to. Orig. cl. gt., unc., mor.-bkd. s.-c.; pres. copy to Edmund Gose, Prescott copy. (SPB. May 17; 715) $6,250
– Lord Arthur Savile's Crime & Other Stories. L., 1891. *1st. Edn.* 1 vol. Orig. bds., soiled. (*With:*)
– An Ideal Husband. L., 1891. *1st. Edn. (1000).* 1 vol. Orig. cl. gt., soiled. (BBA. Dec.15; 225)
Nudelman. £70
– – **Anr. Copy.** Sm. 8vo. Bds., cover design by Charles Ricketts, rubbed. (SG. Jan.12; 356) $140
– – **Anr. Edn.** L., priv. ptd., ca. 1904. *Pirated Edn. (300) numbered.* Sm. 8vo. Orig. wraps., unc., spine slightly torn. (S. Mar.20; 987) *C. Heller.* £50
– Newdigate Prize Poem: Ravenna ... Oxford, 1878. *1st. Edn.* Sm. 8vo. Ptd. wraps., cl. folding case. (SG. Jan.12; 355) $700
– – **Anr. Copy.** Orig. ptd. wraps., University arms on cover, split on spine, mor.-bkd. s.-c.; Perry Molstad copy. (SPB. May 6; 552) $250
– The Nightingale & the Rose. Priv. ptd., 1961. *Ltd. Edn., for private circulation.* Orig. gt.-decor. bds.; sigd. by Rigby Graham. (TA. Feb.16; 378) £60
– The Picture of Dorian Gray. L., N.Y. & Melbourne, [1891]. *1st. Edn. 1st. Iss.* Some fore-edges & few pp. foxed, orig. parch.-bkd. bds., d.-w. frayed, mor.-bkd. s.-c.; Prescott copy. (SPB. May 17; 716) $2,500
– – **Anr. Edn.** L., [1891]. *(250) on L.P., sigd.* 4to. Elab. mor. by Morley for Sotheran; Fred A. Berne copy. (SPB. May 16; 384) $1,300
– – **Anr. Edn.** Paris, 1908 [1910]. *1st. Ill. Edn.* 4to. Publication slip tipped in, orig. hf. parch., slightly rubbed. d.-w., torn. (BBA. May 23; 132)
Bell, Book & Radmall. £65
– – **Anr. Edn.** Ill.:– Jim Dine. L., 1968. *(200) B Edn.* On Arches paper, With supp. separ. series of 4 sigd. etchings, printers mark & each lf. of separate series sigd., orig. velvet, silver ptd., orig. s.-c.; Hauswedell coll. (H. May 24; 598) DM 4,000
– Poems. 1892. *(220) sigd.* Orig. decor. cl. gt., unc., faded, slightly worn. (P. Jul.5; 200) £600
– Salome. Trans.:– Lord Alfred Douglas. Ill.:– Aubrey Beardsley. L. & Boston, 1894. *1st. Edn. in Engl. (100) L.P., with ills on Japon vell.* 4to. Publisher's advt. at end, browning, mor. gt. by Harcourt Bindery. (SPB. Dec.13; 570) $700
– – **Anr. Edn.** Ill.:– Aubrey Beardsley. L., 1894. *[1st. Engl. Edn.]. (500).* Sm. 4to. 10 full-p. ills., orig. cl.; Perry Molstad copy. (SPB. May 16; 553) $350
– – **Anr. Copy.** Sm. 4to. A few ll. & plts. loose, orig. gt.-decor. cl., extremities rubbed, red hf. mor. s.-c.; Curt von Faber du Faur bkplt. (SG. Jan.12; 29) $250
– – **Anr. Copy.** Owners mark on hf.-title (& crease), orig. linen, cover vig., spine slightly faded. (H. Nov.24; 2448) DM 1,150
– – **Anr. Edn.** Ill.:– V. Angelo. [San Franc., Grabhorn Pr., 1927]. *(195).* Sm. 4to. Some edge darkening, specially bnd. in gt.-ruled & lettered red mor., s.-c.; frontis. sigd. & numbered 1/200 by artist, unnumbered dupl. fo. frontis. & uncold. trial proof, both sigd., laid in, the V. Angelo copy. (CBA. Oct.1; 187) $200
– – **Anr. Copy.** Sm. 4to. Hf. cl. & decor. parch., covers darkening with mild staining, yawning, end-papers darkening, box irregularly faded; frontis.

WILDE, Oscar -Contd.

sigd. & numbered 51/190 by artist, the V. Angelo copy. (CBA. Oct.1; 188) $130
- **Salomé.** Ill.:– Manuel Orazi. Pierre Bouchet (wood engrs.). Paris, 1930. *(149) on vell. de Rives.* 4to. Unc., mor., silver & gt. port. on upr. cover, wrap. (HD. Dec.16; 208) Frs. 6,200
– – **Anr. Edn.** Ill.:– Lobel-Riche. Paris, 1930. *(185) numbered. (90) on vell d'Arches.* 4to. Etchings in 2 states, 1 with remarks, leaves, ptd. wrap. (HD. Mar.30; 34) Frs. 1,400
– – **Anr. Edn.** Ill.:– André Derain. Paris, Ltd. Edns. Cl., 1938. *(1500) numbered & sigd. by artist.* 4to. Orig. wraps., s.-c. slightly worn. (S. Nov.21; 14)
V. & A. £180
- **Salomé. [French]. – Salome. [English].** Trans.:– Lord Alfred Douglas (2nd. work). Ill.:– André Derain; Aubrey Beardsley. N.Y., Ltd. Edns. Cl., 1938. *(1500) numbered, sigd. by Derain.* Together 2 vols. Tall 8vo. Fr. text ill. with gouache drawings on black paper, pochoir-reproduced by Saude, ptd. wraps. & gt.-pict. cl., orig. s.-c. (SG. May 17; 237) $100
- **Salome. [German].** Trans.:– H. Lachmann. Ill.:– M. Behmer. 1903. *1st. Edn. ill. Behmer.* Slightly foxed, hf. leath. gt., orig. wraps. (GB. May 5; 2189)
DM 540
– – **Anr. Edn.** Trans.:– Hedwig Lachmann. Ill.:– Beardsley. Leipzig, 1907. *On Japan.* Sm. 4to. Without printers mark, orig. suede, silk end-papers; Hauswedell coll. (H. May 24; 576) DM 800
- **Some Letters to Alfred Douglas.** Ed.:– A.S.W. Rosenbech. San Franc., 1924. *(225).* Fo. Frontis.-port., 26 facs. letters tipped in, orig. vell.-bkd. bds., s.-c.; Perry Molstad copy. (SPB. May 16; 554) $200
- **The Sphinx.** Ill.:– Charles Ricketts. L., 1894. *1st. Edn. (200).* 4to. Browned, orig. vell., gt.-decor.; Perry Molstad copy. (SPB. May 16; 555) $425
– – **Anr. Edn.** Ill.:– 'Alastair'. L., 1920. *1st. Edn. thus. (1000).* 4to. With 2 additional plts. not in plt.-list, ptd. initials hand-cold. in blue, ink inscr. to fly, gt.-decor. buckram, slightly soiled. (CBA. Aug.21; 4) $250
– – **Anr. Copy.** 4to. Partly untrimmed, gt.-stpd. pict. cl., cover design by Charles Ricketts, light wear. (HA. Nov.18; 325) $100
– – **Anr. Edn.** Ill.:– Alastair. L. & N.Y., 1920. *Ltd. Iss.* 4to. 2 supp. full-p. plts. not in ill. index, MS. artist name inside cover, some discol., 1 plt. with sm. stain, 1 guard-lf. torn, orig. pict. linen, soiled, spine faded; dedication & Franz Goldstein ex-libris. (H. Nov.24; 1317) DM 460
- **A Woman of No Importance.** 1894. *1st. Edn. (500).* Sm. 4to. Orig. decor. cl. gt., fly-lf. removed. (SKC. Mar.9; 1870) £100
- **The Works.** L. & Paris, 1908. *1st. Coll. Edn. (1000) on H.M.P.* 14 vols. (without Vol. 15, sometimes present). Hf.-titles, a few spots, orig. buckram, partly unc., slightly soiled. (S. Mar.20; 989) *Demetzy.* £140
– – **Anr. Copy.** 13 vols. only. Some light spotting, orig. cl., lightly soiled. (CSK. Jan.13; 78) £110
– – **Anr. Edn.** 1908-22. *(1000).* 15 vols. Orig. cl., spines faded, several with d.-w.'s. (CSK. Feb.10; 27) £320
– – **Anr. Edn.** 1909. 13 vols. Hf. mor. gt., panel spine. (P. Apr.12; 137) *Simon.* £180
- **The Writings.** L., 1911. *Cherwell Edn., (240).* 14 vols. Burgundy hf. mor. gt., light fading. (SPB. Dec.13; 571) $700
– – **Anr. Edn.** N.Y., 1925. *L.P. Edn., (575) numbered.* 12 vols. Red three-qtr. mor. by Stikeman, few covers detchd. (SG. Nov.17; 147) $200

WILDE, Sir William R.
- **Lough Corrib, its Shores & Islands.** Dublin, 1867. *1st. Edn.* Cl. (GM. Dec.7; 169) £80

WILDENSTEIN, George
- **The Paintings of Ingres.** L., 1954. *Compl. Edn.* 4to. No bdg. stated. (SPB. Nov.30; 50) $275
See– JAMOT, Paul & Wildenstein, Georges

WILDER, Thornton
- **The Angel that Troubled the Waters.** N.Y., 1928. *(775) numbered & sigd. [25 hors commerce?].* Bds., unc., unopened., d.-w. (SG. Mar.1; 603) $120
- **The Bridge of San Luis Rey.** Ill.:– Rockwell Kent. N.Y., 1929. *(1100) numbered & sigd. by author &*

artist. Tall 8vo. Pict. cl., soiled. (SG. Jan.12; 186) $150

WILDERMANN, Hans
- **Ein Pfingstschrein.** Regensburg, 1924. *Ltd. numbered Iss.* Fo. Orig. woodcuts, Lacks 1 passepartout, orig. hf. vell. portfo. (GB. Nov.5; 3122) DM 750

WILDMAN, Thomas
- **A Treatise on the Management of Bees.** 1778. *3rd. Edn.* Cont. cf. (PD. Dec.14; 215) £90

WILHELM, Georg Tenner
- **Unterhaltungen aus der Naturgeschichte.** Augsburg, 1794. 'Amphibien', 'Fische' Pt.2. in 2 vols. Text very foxed, some plts. lightly foxed, title lf. vol. I with sm. tear, last index lf. vol. II loose, cont. leath., slightly defect. (HT. May 8; 616) DM 460
– – **Anr. Edn.** Augsburg, 1795. *1st. Edn.* Pts. 4/5 'Vögel', in 2 vols. Title with MS owners mark, 3 copper engrs. Vol. 1 loose, Vol. 2 lacks 1 copperplt., 1 plt. torn, most plt. margins crumpled, slightly soiled, cont. hf. leath. gt., rubbed & bumped. (HK. Nov.8; 774) DM 720
– – **Anr. Edn.** Augsburg, 1796-97. *1st. Edn.* Pts. 6/7 'Insecten', Vols. 1-2 only (of 3). Title with MS. owners note, Pt. 2 lacks 2nd. plt., pt. 1 with many MS. annots. on blank ll. to which the plt. edges pasted, some plts. loose, most plts. crumpled in side margin, some soiling, cont. hf. leath., gt., rubbed & slightly bumped. (HK. Nov.8; 547) DM 420
– – **Anr. Edn.** Augsburg, 1796-98. *1st. Edn.* Pts. 6/7 'Insecten'in 3 vols. Lightly foxed or browned, cont. hf. leath., slightly rubbed. (R. Apr.4; 1805) DM 1,300
– – **Anr. Edn.** Augsburg, 1799-1800. *1st. Edn.* Pts. 9/10 'Fische' in 2 vols. Lacks 1 plt. vol. 2, text foxed, cont. hf. leath. gt., 1 spine restored. (R. Apr.4; 1711) DM 1,200
– – **Anr. Copy.** Pts. 9/10 'Fische', 2 vols. Title with MS. owners note, text in vol. 2 slightly stained, some plts. slightly browned & slightly crumpled in side margin, cont. hf. leath. gt., slightly rubbed & bumped. (HK. Nov.8; 556) DM 950
– – **Anr. Edn.** Augsburg, 1800. Pt. 10 'Fische'. 12mo. 52 full-p. hand-cold. composite & view plts., some foxing, early cf. & marb. bds., scuffing at edges of covers & jnts. (HA. Feb.24; 259) $110
– – **Anr. Edn.** Augsburg, 1810-20. *1st. Edn.* Pts. 16-24 'Pflanzenreich', Vols. 1-9 only (of 10). Vol. 8 browned thro.-out in lr. margin, faults & tears, affecting plts., cont. hf. leath. gt., spine Vols. 7-8 slightly dark, rubbed & bumped. (HK. Nov.8; 786) DM 1,200
– – **Anr. Edn.** Augsburg, 1811-21. *1st. Edn.* Pts. 18, 19, 21, 25 'Pflanzenreich', Vols. 3, 4, 6 & 10 only (of 10). Some slight text soiling, vol. 3 lacks 2 plts., hf. leath., ca. 1850. (HK. Nov.8; 787) DM 540
– – **Anr. Edn.** Wien, 1813. Pt. 1, 'Wurmer'. 48 hand-cold. plts., cont. hf. cf., rubbed. (SKC. Jan.13; 2353) £50
– – **Anr. Edn.** Wien, 1818-21. Pts. 7-9 'Pflanzenreich', in 3 vols. Cont. hf. leath. (R. Oct.12; 1933) DM 700
– – **Anr. Edn.** Augsburg, 1828. Pts. 26 & 27. 'Mineralreich' in 2 vols. Cont. hf. leath., gt., cover renewed, spine slightly rubbed. (HK. May 15; 481) DM 850
- **Unterhaltungen unter den Menschen.** Vienna, 1819. 3 vols. Most plts. hand-cold., some light browning, cont. hf. cf., rubbed. (CSK. Jul.13; 117) £115

WILKES, Benjamin
- **One Hundred & Twenty Copper-Plates of English Moths & Butterflies.** L., priv. ptd., 1773. 4to. Subscribers list (2pp.), 120 hand-cold. engraved plts., 3 plts. slightly spotted, cont. tree cf., rubbed, worn, upr. cover detchd. (C. Jun.27; 190)
Campbell. $2,500

WILKES, Charles
- **Narrative of the United States Exploring Expedition.** Phila., 1845. *1st. Publd. Edn., (1000).* 6 vols. Lge. 8vo. 5 folding maps, 9 maps & charts, 64 steel-engraved plts., orig. gt.-pict. cl., worn, loose, ex-liby. (SG. Sep.22; 305) $800
– – **Anr. Edn.** Phila., 1845. 5 vols. Foxed, orig. spr. pol. sheep. (SG. Mar.29; 351) $175
– – **Anr. Copy.** 5 vols. Without list of ills., as iss.,

some foxing, orig. spr. pol. sheep, gt. emblems on covers, rather worn. (SG. Sep.22; 307) $125
– – **Anr. Edn.** Phila., 1849. 5 vols. 4to. 2 port. frontis.'s, 12 folding maps, 63 full-p. plts., some light browning, Vol. 4 badly dampstained, several ll. with sm. tears, & loose in bdg., orig. sheep, devices on covers, spines gt., worn, 1 cover loose. (SG. Mar.29; 352) $400
- **Voyage Round the World, Embracing the Principal Events of the Narrative of the United States Exploring Expedition,** ... Phila., 1849. *1st. Edn. thus.* Some light foxing, cont. cf. & marb. bds., raised bands, light wear at extremities. (HA. Feb.24; 313) $120

WILKES, Charles
See– PICKERING, Charles

WILKES, George
- **The History of Oregon, Geographical & Political** ... N.Y., 1845. *1st. Edn.* Folding map bnd. inverted, paper loss to title & next 2 ll., not affecting text, some light spotting, mod. three-qtr. mor. (LH. Apr.15; 391) $550
- **Proposal for a National Rail-Road to the Pacific Ocean, for the purpose of obtaining a short route to Oregon & the Indies.** N.Y., 1847. *4th. Edn.* Some light browning & offsetting, orig. ptd. wraps., upr. wrap. slightly wrinkled, qtr. mor. s.-c. (LH. Apr.15; 392) $250

WILKIE, David
- **Etchings.** L., 1824. Fo. Inscr. by author to Robert Peel, dtd. 3 Feb. 1825, dampstained, cont. hf. roan, orig. ptd. cover label, worn. (S. Dec.20; 598)
Sims. £70
- **Sketches in Turkey, Syria & Egypt.** 1843. Fo. 1 plt. cleanly torn, 2 soiled, some light spotting & soiling, cont. hf. cf., rubbed. (CSK. Jul.6; 42)
£450
- **The Wilkie Gallery.** Ca. 1850. 4to. Prelims. spotted, minor foxing, cont. hf. mor. (TA. Sep.15; 371) £52
– – **Anr. Copy.** 4to. Prelims. spotted, minor foxing, cont. hf. mor. (TA. Aug.18; 292) £50

WILKIE, William
- **Fables.** Edinb., 1768. *1st. Edn.* Hf.-title, some slight offsetting, cont. spr. cf., spine gt., rubbed; Sir Ivar Colquhoun, of Luss copy. (CE. Mar.22; 329)
£170

WILKINS, David
- **Leges Anglo-Saxonicae Ecclesiasticae & Civiles.** 1721. *1st. Edn.* Fo. Subscribers list, cont. cf., gt., rubbed. (BBA. Jun.28; 108)
Marlborough Rare Books. £60

WILKINS, John, Bp. of Chester
[-] **A Discourse concerning a New World & Another Planet.** 1640. 2 pts. in 1 vol. Map & engraved title soiled, old cf., slightly worn. [STC 25641] (BS. Nov.16; 33) £130
- **Mathematicall Magick; or the Wonders that may be performed by Mechanical Geometry** ... L., 1619. *4th. Edn.* Sm. 8vo. A few margins trimmed, cont. cf., rebkd., rubbed; Stanitz coll. (SPB. Apr.25; 451) $125
– – **Anr. Edn.** 1648. Cf., worn. [Wing W 2198] (BS. Nov.16; 23) £280
– – **Anr. Edn.** L., 1680. *3rd. Edn.* Browned & stained, tear in K6 reprd., few sm. rust-holes, cont. cf., rebkd. [Wing W2200] (S. Mar.6; 505)
Elliott. £80
- **The Mathematical & Philosophical Works.** L., 1708. 3 works in 5 pts. in 1 vol. Port., many text ills. & diagrams, early panel. cf., spine gt.; C.A. George Newmann's copy, with bkplt. & stps. (SG. Apr.19; 196) $225
[-] **Mercury, or the Secret & Swift Messenger.** 1641. Lacks 1st. blank, old cf., rebkd. (BS. Nov.16; 32) £95

WILKINS, William
- **The Antiquities of Magna Graecia.** Camb., 1807. Fo. Title with engraved vig., 73 plts., including 21 sepia aquatint views, some minor spotting, last 4 plts. stained, mod. hf. mor., unc. (C. Mar.14; 99)
Tzakas. £350

WILKINSON, George
- Practical Geology & Ancient Architecture of Ireland. L., 1845. *1st. Edn.* Royal 8vo. Bkplt., cl., defect. (GM. Dec.7; 459)   £55

WILKINSON, George Blakiston
- South Australia: Its Advantages & its Resources ... L., 1848. 12mo. A couple of very sm. defects to bds.; the Hobill Cole copy. (KH. Nov.9; 738)
                                                    Aus. $140

WILKINSON, Henry
- Sketches of Scenery in the Basque Provinces of Spain with a Selection of National Music. L., 1838. Sm. fo. Engraved mus., 12 tinted litho. plts., some browning & spotting, hf. mott. cf., spine & corners worn; w.a.f. (BS. May 2; 9)   £300

WILKINSON, Sir John Gardner
- The Manners & Customs of the Ancient Egyptians. Ed.:– Samuel Birch. N.Y., 1879. *New Edn.* 3 vols. Lge. 8vo. Red three-qtr. mor., rubbed. (SG. Sep.22; 133) $110

WILKINSON, Robert
- Atlas Classica. 1808. 4to. Engraved title, 46 cold. maps, hf. cf., covers detchd. (P. Oct.20; 260) £90
- A General Atlas ... of the World. Ca. 1800. 4to. 48 hand-cold. maps, hf. cf., worn, spine defect. (BBA. Jun.14; 261)   *Cassidy.* £160
- – Anr. Edn. 1805. 4to. Engraved title (frayed at edges), 48 hand-cold. engraved maps (2 double-p.), cont. cf., worn, covers detchd. (TA. Apr.19; 46)
                                                    £110
- – Anr. Edn. 1809. *2nd. Edn.* 4to. 48 hand-cold. maps, a few just trimmed, hf. cf., worn. (BBA. Jun.14; 262)   *Cassidy.* £120
- – Anr. Copy. 4to. Engraved title, 48 col. maps, title stained, 2 maps worn, hf. cf., defect. (P. Jul.5; 391)   £90
- – Anr. Edn. 1812. 4to. Engraved title, 48 cold. maps, 1 with tear in fold, hf. cf., covers detchd. (P. Oct.20; 261)   £140
- Londina Illustrata. L., 1819; 1825. *1st. Edn.* 2 vols. Sm. fo. Engraved title, 206 engraved plts., ex-liby., hf. mor., jnts. crudely reprd. (SG. May 3; 385) $375

WILKINSON, Tate
- Memoirs of his Own Life. York, 1790. 4 vols. 12mo. K3 Vol. 1 & B11 Vol. 3 cancels as called for, the latter sigd. B9, cont. mor. gt., covers decor., spine in 6 sections with onlaid red-mor. false bands, other sections decor., gt. inner dentelles; Frances Mary Richardson Currer armorial bkplt. (CSK. Jan.27; 39)   £750

WILLDENOW, C.L. & Hayne, Fr. G.
- Abbildung der Deutschen Holzarten für Forstmänner und Liebhaber der Botanik. Ed.:– Fr. Guimpel. Berlin, 1815-20. 2 vols. 4to. 216 old cold. copperplts., some slight spotting, text slightly browned, cont., mor. gt., slightly rubbed, corners bumped. (HT. May 8; 324)   DM 3,000

WILLEMENT, Thomas
- Heraldic Notices of Canterbury Cathedral. L., 1827. 4to. L.P., cont. mor. gt. by J. Mackenzie. (S. Mar.6; 462)   *Marlborough.* £120

WILLET, A.
[–] Historia Fanaticorum. Danzig, 1664. Slightly browned, early 18th. C. vell. (HK. Nov.9; 2232)
                                                    DM 500

WILLETTE, Auguste
- Feu Pierrot. Paris, 1919. Sm. 4to. Orig. sigd. aqua. on hf.-title, with caption & autograph dedication, hf. mor., wrap. (HD. Apr.11; 68) Frs. 2,300

WILLIAMS, Ben Ames
- The Happy End. Foreword:– Kenneth Roberts. Ill.:– Churchill Ettinger. Derrydale Pr., [1939]. *(1250) numbered.* Two-toned cl., inscr. by author. (SG. Mar.15; 247) $110

WILLIAMS, Gardner F.
- The Diamond Mines of South Africa. N.Y., 1905. 2 vols. Cont. mor. (SSA. Jul.5; 438)   R 210
- – Anr. Copy. 2 vols. Mor. gt. (VA. Oct.28; 636)
                                                    R 180

WILLIAMS, H. Noel
- Queen Margot: Wife of Henry of Navarre. N.Y., 1907. 1 vol. in 2. Tall 8vo. 16 photogravure plts., extra-ill. with 32 engraved ports., mor. gt. by Taffin, spines gt. with fleur-de-lis, gt. dentelles, covers slightly discold. (SG. Nov.17; 349) $100

WILLIAMS, Hugh William
- Select Views in Greece. 1829. 2 vols. 4to. Cl., soiled. (P. Dec.8; 315)   *Burr.* £200
- – Anr. Copy. 2 vols. 4to. 64 engraved plts., cont. hf. mor. (CSK. Nov.4; 33)   £130
- – Anr. Copy. Vol. 2 only. Some plts. loose & spotted, cont. hf. mor., rubbed. (BBA. Feb.23; 127)
                                                Dimakarakos. £50
- – Anr. Copy. 2 vols. in 1. Lge. 8vo. 64 plts., hf.-titles, scattered foxing, chiefly marginal, cont. red mor. gt. extra, gt. arms of Trinity College, Dublin. (SG. Sep.22; 308) $250

WILLIAMS, James Leon
- The Home & Haunts of Shakespeare. Intro.:– Horace H. Furness. N.Y., 1892. *1st. Edn.* Fo. 5 (of 15) tipped in full-p. col. plts., 39 (of 45) full-p. sepia-toned photogravures, the lacking plts. appear never to have been bnd. in, sm. ink no. at upr. edge of 1st. text lf., lacks rear end-paper, cont. mor. & pebbled cl., gt.-lettered, covers with moderate wear & light scuffing at extremities. (HA. Dec.16; 218) $120

WILLIAMS, John
- An Account of some Remarkable Ancient Ruins lately discovered in the Highlands & Northern Parts of Scotland in a Series of Letters to G.C.M. Esq ... Edinb., 1777. Cf., worn, upr. bd. detchd. (PD. Jun.13; 165)   £60

WILLIAMS, John Jay
- The Isthmus of Tehuantepec. N.Y., 1852. Folding litho. map, folding chart, diagram, 14 tinted litho. plts., 1 plt. margin stained, some light foxing, mod. qtr. cf., marb. bds. (SC. Oct.20; 382) $175

WILLIAMS, Jonathan
- Elegies & Celebrations. Highlands, N.C., 1962. *(750).* Sm. 8vo. Pict. wraps.; inscr. to Kenneth [Patchen?] from author. (SG. May 24; 170) $200
- Four Stoppages. Stuttgart, 1953. *(200).* Fo. Accordion-fold self-wraps.; inscr. to Kenneth & Miriam [Patchen]. (SG. Mar.1; 605) $1,400
- Riposts. Ill.:– William Katz. Stuttgart, [1968]. *(50) numbered for sale, sigd. by author & artist.* Sm. 4to. Ptd. wraps., ptd. folding case. (SG. Mar.1; 606) $110

WILLIAMS, Loloa
- Early English Watercolours. L., 1952. *1st. Edn.* 4to. No bdg. stated. (JL. Jun.24; 33)   Aus. $170

WILLIAMS, Roger
- The Bloudy Tenent, of Persecution, for cause of Conscience, discussed, in A Conference betweene Truth & Peace. [L.], 1644. *1st. Edn.* 4to. The 1st. iss. according to the Church Catalogue, the 2nd. iss. according to Sabin, errata on p. 247, pp. slightly browned at margins, lr. margins of sig. B cut close shaving a side-note & catchwords, sig. on title, gt.-tooled mor., rubbed at hinges & corners. [Church 467; Sabin 105332] (SPB. May 23; 51) $8,000
- A Key into the Language of America: Or, An help to the Language of the Natives in that part of America, called New-England ... L., 1643. Sm. 8vo. Lacks sig. K (pp. 121-136), apparently never bnd. into this copy, cont., red mor. case; sigs. of Charles Nevill & Susanna Walley, bkplts. of Hershel V. Jones & Albert Edgar Lownes. [Sabin 104339] (SPB. Oct.26; 26) $1,500

WILLIAMS, Tennessee
- A Streetcar Named Desire. [N.Y., 1947]. Bds., d.-w.; sigd. (SG. Mar.1; 608) $550

WILLIAMS, William, of Llandegai
- Oxonia Depicta. Oxford, [1733]. Fo. 64 copper engrs., mod. three-qtr. mor. (CBA. Dec.10; 361)
                                                    $650

WILLIAMS, William Carlos
- The Clouds, Aigeltinger, Russia, etc. [Aurora, N.Y.], Wells Coll. Pr. & Cummington Pr., 1948. *(250) numbered.* Cl. (SG. Mar.1; 613) $130

- The Great American Novel. Paris, Three Mountains Pr., 1923. *(300) numbered.* Tall 8vo. Hf. cl., spine ends bumped, label soiled, slightly worn. (SG. May 24; 382) $225
- Paterson. N.Y., 1946-58. *1st. Edns.* Books 1-5. Orig. cl., d.-w.'s, Frederic Dannay copy. (CNY. Dec.16; 384) $450
- – Anr. Edn. [N.Y., 1958]. Book 5. Cl., d.-w.; inscr. to 'Ruth'. (SG. Mar.1; 615) $325
- The Tempers. L., 1913. *1st. Edn.* 18mo. Orig. bds., covers soiled; Frederic Dannay copy. (CNY. Dec.16; 383) $160

WILLIAMSON, Charles
- Description of the Genesee Country. Ill.:– Gideon Fairman & De Witt. Albany, 1798. *1st. Edn.* Sm. 4to. Folding frontis., 2 folding maps, plts. little foxed, later hf. mor. & marb. bds., partly unc. (SG. Apr.26; 206) $1,600

WILLIAMSON, George Charles
- Andrew & Nathaniel Plimer, Miniature Painters. 1903. *(110) numbered. (75) with hand-cold. plts.* 4to. 2 prospectuses loosely inserted, some very slight spotting, orig. cl. faded, bkplt. of Cuthbert A. Williamson. (S. Apr.30; 110)   *Gerino.* £250
- The Book of Famille Rose. L., 1927. *(750).* 4to. Orig. cl., d.-w., spine faded; note reading 'to Cuthbert (Williamson) with much love from Daddy, 10 March 1927' loosely inserted. (S. Apr.30; 116)   *Tropper.* £90
- – Anr. Copy. 4to. Orig. cl. (BBA. Sep.8; 234)
                                                    Lyon. £85
- Catalogue of the Collection of Miniatures, the property of J. Pierpont Morgan. L., Priv. Ptd., Chis. Pr., 1906-8. *(150).* 4 vols. Fo. On Bütten, hf. mor. gt. (D. Nov.23; 2098)   DM 3,100
- English Conversation Pictures. 1931. *(350) numbered.* 4to. Orig. cl. gt. (SKC. Mar.9; 1734)   £50
- George J. Pinwell & his Works. L., 1900. Orig. cl., slightly soiled; Williamson's bkplt., orig. photograph proofs pasted in, prospectus & letters to author loosely inserted, including 5 from J.W. North, T.L.'s from author loosely inserted, photograph of Pinwell with Gilbert Dalziel pasted in at beginning of text, some MS. notes in margins. (S. Apr.30; 112)   *Sims.* £80
- The History of Portrait Miniatures. 1904. *(520).* 2 vols. Fo. Orig. cl. gt., slightly soiled. (BBA. Jun.14; 148)   *St. George's Gallery.* £60
- – Anr. Copy. 2 vols. Fo. Orig. cl. gt., slightly rubbed & soiled. (S. Dec.13; 486)   *Jameson.* £50
- – Anr. Copy. 2 vols. Lge. fo. Over 100 collotype plts., lettered tissue-guards, ex-liby., gt.-pict. buckram, soiled. (SG. May 3; 487) $175
- The Imperial Russian Dinner Service. 1909. *(300).* 4to. Orig. parch.-bkd. cl. gt., embossed port. medallion of Wedgwood on upr. cover; publisher's liby. copy. (LC. Mar.1; 30)   £100
- – Anr. Edn. 1909. *(310).* 4to. Orig. parch.-bkd. cl., soiled. (CSK. Aug.5; 47)   £85
- John Russell. 1894. *(4) on vell.* Fo. Some slight foxing, orig. cl. (discold.), partly unc.; note in author's hand concerning other 3 copies. (LC. Mar.1; 31)   £110
- Katalog einer Sammlung von Bildnisminiaturen im Besitze seiner Könglicher Hoheit des Herzog von Cumberland. L., Chis. Pr., Priv. Ptd., 1914. *(150) on Bütten.* 4to. Orig. linen, s.-c. (D. Nov.23; 2102)
                                                    DM 400
- Life & Works of Ozias Humphry, R.A. L., 1918. *(400).* 4to. Orig. parch.-bkd. bds., slightly soiled; Letter to author from W.R.M. Lamb at Royal Academy & pres. slip loosely inserted. (S. Apr.30; 113)   *Alcaz.* £70
See— MANNERS, Lady Victoria & Williamson, G.C.
See— MORGAN, John Pierpont

WILLIAMSON, George C. & Engleheart, Henry L.D.
- George Engleheart 1750-1829, Miniature Painter to George III. L., 1902. *(53) with hand-cold. plts.* 4to. 2 prospectuses loosely inserted, orig. cl., slightly soiled; inscr. by (Williamson?) on fly-lf. '2 extra plts. in this copy, only these 2 were painted, there are no other copies of them in existence'; Williamson bkplt. (S. Apr.30; 109)   *Gerino.* £250
- – Anr. Edn. 1902. *(360).* 4to. Orig. cl. (BBA. Sep.8; 189)   *Lawson.* £60

WILLIAMSON, Peter
- The Travels of ... Among the Different Nations & Tribes of Savage Indians in America. Edinb., priv. ptd., 1768. *1st. Edn.* 3 pts. in 1 vol. 1 plt. margin cut close, sm. piece chipped from 1 margin, mod. hf. mor., spine faded, partly unc.; the Rt. Hon. Visc. Eccles copy. [Sabin 104492] (CNY. Nov.18; 287) $950

WILLIAMSON, Capt. Thomas & Blagdon, Francis William
- The European in India. Ill.:- J.H. Clark & C. Dubourg, after Charles D'Oyley. L., 1813. 4to. 20 cold. aquatint plts. with pink & grey wash borders, without hf.-title, cont. str.-grd. mor., covers gt.- & blind-tooled, spine gt. (C. Jun.27; 29)
Cavendish. £500

WILLIAMSON, Capt. Thomas & Howitt, S.
- Oriental Field Sports. L., 1807. Ob. fo. Hand-cold. additional engraved title creased, 40 hand-cold. aquatint views, some foxing, mod. cf. gt. (S. May 22; 445) *Nevill.* £2,700
- - **Anr. Copy.** 2 vols. 4to. A tall copy, frontispieces, 40 hand-cold. plts. (1 with repair in margin), hf. mor., partly unc. (S. May 22; 444) *Nevill.* £650
- - **Anr. Edn.** 1808. 2 vols. 4to. 2 engraved frontis., 40 engraved plts., some faint spotting or browning mostly affecting text, cont. cf. gt., worn, 1 cover detchd. (S. Nov.1; 64) *Marlboro Rare Bks.* £110
- - **Anr. Edn.** L., 1819. *2nd. Edn.* 2 vols. 4to. Cont. mor. gt., carefully rebkd. (SPB. Dec.13; 613a) $500
- - **Anr. Edn.** N.d. 4to. 39 (of 40) hand-cold. plts., 2 ll. reprd., some spotting, str.-grd. mor. gt., worn. (P. Feb.16; 153) £280

WILLINCK, Daniel
- Amstellandsche Arkadia, of Beschryving van Amstellandt. Ed.:- G. Schoemaker. Ill.:- J. Punt, after Pronk & others. Utrecht, 1773. *2nd. Printing.* Hand-cold. engraved frontis., 12 hand-cold. folding engraved views, slight margin staining, 19th. C. hf. cf. gt. (VS. Dec.9; 1300) Fls. 875

WILLIS, Bailey
- El Norte de la Patagonia. N.Y., 1914. 2 vols. including maps. 4to. Orig. cl., slightly rubbed. (BBA. Jun.28; 261) *Cavendish.* £50

WILLIS, Nathaniel Parker & Bartlett, William Henry
- American Scenery. L., 1840. 2 vols. 4to. Engraved title, port., map & 117 plts., cont. hf. cf., spines gt. (BBA. May 3; 294) *Stacey.* £350
- - **Anr. Copy.** 2 vols. 4to. Orig. embossed cl. gt., slightly worn & stained, w.a.f.; from liby. of Luttrellstown Castle. (C. Sep.28; 1768) £320
- - **Anr. Copy.** 2 vols. 4to. Port. frontis. to Vol. 1, vig. title to each, 117 steel engrs., map, cont. mor. gt., rubbed, some wear to top & bottom of spines. (TA. Jun.21; 94) £240
- - **Anr. Copy.** 2 vols. 4to. Port., 2 engraved titles, partly cold. map, 117 views, slight spotting, panel. cf. gt. (P. Oct.20; 242) £220
- - **Anr. Copy.** 2 vols. in 7 orig. pts. 4to. 2 vig. titles, port., map, 118 engraved plts., some foxing, orig. pict. bds. (P. Dec.8; 18) *Perham.* £200
- - **Anr. Copy.** Vol. 1 only. 4to. Cont. cf. gt., rubbed. (BBA. Jun.14; 282) *Saunders.* £120
- - **Anr. Copy.** Vol. I only. 4to. Port. frontis., additional vig. title, map, 64 steel engrs., some foxing, cont. hf. cf., gt.-decor. spine, rubbed. (TA. May 17; 68) £90
- - **Anr. Copy.** Vol. 2 only (of 2). 4to. Vig. title, 52 engraved plts., qtr. mor. gt. (P. Dec.8; 17) *Elliott.* £55
- - **Anr. Copy.** 2 vols. Lge. 4to. Port., map, 119 steel-engraved plts., all hand-cold., orig. hf. leath., spines ornately gt., slight wear. (SG. Nov.3; 3) $1,200
- - **Anr. Copy.** 2 vols. 4to. Port., 2 engraved titles, map in Vol. 1, 117 engraved plts., a few plts. with slight foxing, orig. publisher's maroon mor., covers elab. gt.-blocked, spines gt., very slightly rubbed. (CNY. Nov.18; 306) $250
- - **Anr. Edn.** [L., 1840]. Fo. Port., map, 119 India paper proofs before letters on guarded fo. sheets, pencil notes to each plt., foxed thro.-out, later hf. mor. (SPB. Dec.13; 433) $450

- - **Anr. Edn.** Ill.:- after W.H. Bartlett. L., 1849-52. 2 vols. 4to. 2 additional engraved vig. titles, port., map, 117 plts., very slight foxing, orig. gt.-pict. cl. (SG. Nov.3; 223) $750
- - **Anr. Edn.** 1852. 2 vols. 4to. Vig. titles, port., map, 117 engrs., orig. cl. gt. (P. Dec.8; 68) *Morrell.* £240
- - **Anr. Edn.** L., 1860. Pp. stained, cf., edges & spine rubbed & nicked. (RS. Jan.17; 506) $425
- - **Anr. Edn.** Ill.:- after Bartlett. N.d. 2 vols. 4to. Engraved additional titles & 117 plts., 1 map, cont. mor. gt., spines slightly faded. (CSK. Jul.6; 40) £280
- - **Anr. Copy.** Vol. 1 only. 4to. Steel-engraved additional title & 68 plts., some light spotting, bnd. with 5 plts. from Carne's Syria, cont. hf. cf., lightly rubbed, w.a.f. (CSK. May 4; 109) £100
- American Scenery - Canadian Scenery. [1840; 1842]. 2 works in 13 orig. pts. 4to. 1st. work: steel-engraved port., 2 added titles & 115 plts. only, 1 map; 2nd work: steel-engraved titles & 115 plts. only, 1 map, some spotting, orig. mor.-bkd. bds., worn, several covers detchd., w.a.f. (CSK. Jul.6; 15) £600
- Canadian Scenery. 1842. 2 vols. in 1. 4to. 2 engraved titles, map, 117 views, hf. mor. gt. (P. Jun.7; 207) £450
- - **Anr. Copy.** 2 vols. 4to. Engraved additional titles, 1 map, 117 plts., some light spotting, cont. cf. (CSK. Sep.30; 173) £360
- - **Anr. Copy.** 2 vols. in 1. 4to. 2 engraved vig. titles, port., map, 117 plts., spotted thro.-out, cont. mor. gt., slightly rubbed. (BBA. Sep.29; 53) *Bauman.* £310
- - **Anr. Copy.** 3 vols. 4to. 191 engraved plts., including 11 titles & many dupls., mostly loose, cl. & cf., as a collection of plts., w.a.f. (P. Sep.29; 189) *Peterson.* £260
- - **Anr. Edn.** Ill.:- after Bartlett. N.d. 2 vols. Steel-engraved additional titles, 1 map, 117 plts., some light soiling, mostly marginal, orig. cl., frayed, rebkd., old spines preserved. (CSK. Sep.30; 108) £350
- Das Malerische und Romantische Nordamerika. Ill.:- A.H. Payne after W.H. Bartlett. Leipzig, ca. 1840. 75 steel engraved views, 48 plts. including engraved titles, romantic hf. leath. gt. (R. Apr.5; 2802) DM 650

WILLIS, Nathaniel Parker & Coyne, Joseph Stirling
- The Scenery & Antiquities of Ireland. L., 1841. 2 vols. in 1. 4to. Engraved title, 118 plts., lacks port., some ll. spotted, cont. mor., upr. hinge brkn. (BBA. Mar.21; 116) *M. Ayres.* £65
- - **Anr. Edn.** Ill.:- after W.H. Bartlett. [1841]. 2 vols. 4to. 120 engrs., hf. cf., slightly worn. (BS. Nov.16; 90) £95
- - **Anr. Copy.** 2 vols. 4to. Spotted & stained, hf. cf. (S. Jun.25; 349) *Sephton.* £80
- - **Anr. Edn.** Ill.:- W.H. Bartlett. L., ca. 1845. 2 vols. 4to. 120 steel-engraved plts., foxed, elab. gt.-decor. moire cl., worn. (SG. Dec.15; 127) $225
- - **Anr. Edn.** L., n.d. 2 vols. 4to. Port. frontis., 2 engraved additional titles, map, 118 engraved plts., some spotting, mor., gt.-decor., armorial motif on spine, sigd. R. Stagg. (GM. Dec.7; 437) £160
- - **Anr. Copy.** 2 vols. 4to. Port. frontis., 2 engraved vig. titles, engraved map, 118 plts., some stains, diced mor. (GM. Dec.7; 309) £145

WILLIS, Robert
[-] An Attempt to Analyse the Automaton Chess Player of Mr. De Kempelen. L., 1821. Cl., worn. (P. Nov.24; 214) *Henderson.* £240

WILLIS, Prof. Robert & Clark, John Willis.
- The Architectural History of the University of Cambridge. Camb., 1886. *(120) L.P.* 4 vols., including vol. of plts. 4to. Orig. bds. (P. Oct.20; 188) £120
- - **Anr. Edn.** Camb., 1886. 4 vols. Orig. buckram-bkd. cl. gt., partly unc.; inscr. by author. (LC. Jul.5; 245) £75

WILLIS, Tomas
- Diatribe duae Medico-Philosophicae. Amst., 1663. 24mo. Slightly soiled, no bdg. stated. (BBA. Jul.27; 67) *Bertram Rota.* £55
- The London Practice of Physick. L., 1685. *1st.*

Edn. Last errata lf., disbnd. [Wing W2838] (BBA. Mar.21; 66) *N. Phillips.* £300

WILLKOMM, E.
- Wanderungen an der Nord– und Ostsee. Leipzig, 1850. Slightly foxed, partly loose, brkn., spine defect. (R. Oct.12; 2632) DM 1,900
- - **Anr. Copy.** 2 pts. in 1 vol. 28 steel engraved plts., Pt. I lacks 2 plts., slightly browned & stained thro.-out, cont. hf. leath., slightly defect. (HT. May 10; 2951) DM 1,500

WILLMOTT, Ellen
- The Genus Rosa. Ill.:- after Alfred Parsons. L., 1914. 2 vols. Fo. 132 cold. plts., mor.-bkd. cl., orig. wraps. bnd. in. (S. Nov.28; 96) *Wilson.* £550
- - **Anr. Copy.** 2 vols. Fo. 132 cold. plts., a few plts. adhering to tissue guards, a few sm. margin tears, hf. mor. gt., orig. wraps. bnd. in, by Sotheran, spines faded. (S. Nov.28; 95) *Symonds.* £400

WILLOCK, John
- Voyages to Various Parts of the World, & Remarks on Different Countries in Europe, Africa & America ... Penrith, priv. ptd., [1789?]. *1st. Edn.* Slight margin chipping to a few ll., some foxing, mod. plum hf. mor., unc.; the Rt. Hon. Visc. Eccles copy. [Sabin 104535] (CNY. Nov.18; 286) $550

WILLOX, John
- Practical Hints for Emigrants to our Australian Colonies. L'pool., 1858. Orig. pict. wraps. (P. Jun.7; 325) £100

WILLS, William John
- A Successful Exploration Through the Interior of Australia, from Melbourne to the Gulf of Carpentaria. L., 1863. *1st. Edn.* Hf.-title, folding engraved map, engraved frontis. & port., 32pp. publisher's advt. with engraved ill., short tear reprd. at corner of map, orig. cl., rubbed. (C. Jun.27; 105) *Dunsheath.* £300
- - **Anr. Copy.** Sm. tears in map reprd., old cf. gt., piece cut from upr. cover, lacks label. (CA. Apr.3; 127) Aus. $420

WILLSFORD, Thomas
- Natures Secrets, or The Admirable & Wonderfull History of the Generation of Meteors. 1658. Margins trimmed, cf., rubbed, mod. end-papers. [Wing 2875] (CSK. Jun.1; 35) £200

WILLSHIRE, William Hughues
- The Aborigines of Central Australia ... 1891. Stapled. (KH. May 1; 763) Aus. $600

WILLSHIRE, Dr. William Hughes
- A Descriptive Catalogue of Playing & other Cards in the British Museum. L., 1876. 23 plts., slight spotting, orig. cl. gt., unopened, worn. (P. May 17; 361) *Renard.* £75

WILLY (Pseud.)
See— COLETTE, Sidonie Gabrielle 'Willy'

WILLYAMS, Rev. Cooper
- Voyage up the Mediterranean. L., 1802. *1st. Edn.* Fo. Engraved dedication, folding map, 41 tinted aquatint plts., some browning & staining thro.-out, cont. cf. gt., worn, upr. cover loose; Sir Jacob Astley bookplt. (BS. May 2; 8) £800
- - **Anr. Copy.** Fo. L.P., engraved dedication with cold. arms, double-p. hand-cold. chart, 42 cold. aquatint plts., mod. red hf. mor. (C. Nov.16; 200) *Foyle.* £450
- - **Anr. Copy.** 4to. Engraved dedication p., aquatint double-p. chart, 41 aquatint plts., title-p. creased, cont. hf. cf. (SKC. Jan.13; 2365) £280
- - **Anr. Copy.** 4to. Engraved dedication, 42 tinted aquatint plts. & maps (1 folding), cont. hf. cf., worn. (BBA. Mar.21; 331) *Martinos.* £240
- - **Anr. Copy.** Fo. Engraved dedication lf., folding map, 40 tinted aquatint views, 1st. few ll. slightly soiled, sm. repairs to margins of a few ll. at end, cf., slightly rubbed. (S. May 21; 253) *Marshall.* £220
- - **Anr. Copy.** 4to. 39 tinted litho. plts. only, lacks title & engraved dedication lf., soiled, cont. cf., rebkd., old spine laid down, w.a.f. (CSK. Jan.13; 149) £130

WILMOT, John, Earl of Rochester
See— ROCHESTER, [John Wilmot], Earl of

WILMSEN, F.P.
- Euphrosyne oder Deutsches Lesebuch zur Bildung des Geistes und Herzens für die Schule und das Haus. Ill.:– L. Meyer after L. Wolf. Berlin, 1828. *2nd. Edn.* 2 vols. in 1. Square 12mo. Engraved frontis.'s, vig. title-pp. & 12 plts., hand-cold., few slight stains, cont. bds., van Veen coll. (S. Feb.28; 174) £140

WILSON, Prof. (Text)
See— SCOTLAND

WILSON, Adrian
- Printing for the Theater. Ill.:– Nuiko Haramaki. San Franc., 1957. *(250).* Fo. 2 C'mas. greetings from A. & J. Wilson laid in loose, 17 'Interplayers' announcements & brochures loose in rear endpaper pocket, 20 orig. announcements & programmes for the 'Interplayers' & photo of Joyce Lancaster by Minor White tipped in, a few loose programmes with creases, mild darkening to edges, untrimmed, Hamlet programmes as end-papers, decor. linen, covers slightly askew, lightly soiled & darkened. (CBA. Nov.19; 606a) $425

WILSON, Alexander & Bonaparte, Charles Lucien
- American Ornithology; or, the Natural History of the Birds of the United States. Ed.:– George Ord. Ill.:– Alexander Lawson, G. Murray, B. Tanner & J.G. Warnicks, after Wilson, cold. by A. Rider. Phila., Bradford & Inskeep, 1808 [1809]-14. *1st. Edn. Vol. 1: 1st. Iss.* 9 vols. Fo. 76 plts., heavy offsetting from plts. onto text, some plts. slightly foxed, plt. 68 trimmed & a few other plts. cut close, sm. tears in margins of plts. 67, 70 & 72, tears in P1 & 2N1 Vol. 8, cont. red hf. roan, spines worn (1 brkn.), 2 vols. reprd., preserved in 3 red qtr. mor. cases. (S. Feb.1; 59) *Park.* £8,800
– – **Anr. Edn.** Phila., 1808-14. *1st. Edn.* Vols. 1-8 only (of 9), in 2 vols. 4to. 70 (of 72) hand-cold. engraved plts., lacks hf.-titles, some plts. slightly trimmed, sm. tear in plt. 68, some browning & offsetting thro.-out, hf. cf., worn. (S. Nov.28; 97) *Schuster.* £400
– – **Anr. Edn.** Ed.:– Sir W. Jardine. L., 1832. 3 vols. Port., 96 hand-cold. engraved plts. (of 97), 1 frayed, slight soiling & offsetting, vol. 3 lacks hf.-title, stitching brkn. in places, cont. hf. mor. (S. Apr.10; 463) *Burden.* £240
– – **Anr. Edn.** L., 1870's? 3 vols. Port. frontis., 103 chromolitho plts., qtr. mor., spines gt., some wear, 3rd. vol. rebkd. (SG. Mar.22; 314) £140
– – **Anr. Edn.** L., 1876. 3 vols. Port. frontis., 103 hand-cold. engraved plts., orig. gt.-pict. qtr. cf., ex-liby. (SG. Oct.6; 380) $500
– – **Anr. Edn.** Ca. 1880. 3 vols. Cont. hf. mor., spines gt.-decor., rubbed. (TA. Apr.19; 158) £80
– – **Anr. Edn.** L., Cassell, Petter & Galpin, n.d. 3 vols. Orig. gt.-pict. qtr. cf., ex-liby. (SG. Oct.6; 381) $300
– – **Anr. Copy.** Vols. 1 & 3 only (of 3). 62 (of 103) chromolitho. plts., orig. qtr. leath. gt., worn. (SG. Dec.15; 199) $275

WILSON, Sir Charles
- Picturesque Palestine, Sinai & Egypt. Ca. 1870. 5 vols., including Supp. 4to. Orig. decor. cl. gt. (SKC. Nov.18; 2021) £100
– – **Anr. Edn.** Ca. 1880. 4 vols. 4to. Cont. hf. mor. gt., recased. (TA. Jul.19; 1) £62
– – **Anr. Copy.** 4 vols. 4to. Vig. title to each, steel engrs., orig. decor. cl., dampstained & rubbed. (TA. Jun.21; 16) £50
– – **Anr. Edn.** 1880-84. 4 vols. 4to. Some foxing, hf. mor. gt. (P. Jun.7; 3) £120
– – **Anr. Edn.** Ca. 1880-84. 5 vols., including Supp. 4to. Vig. titles, maps, 42 engraved plts., some loose, orig. cl. gt., lr. cover of Supp. dampstained. (P. Sep.8; 106) *Kassis.* £70
– – **Anr. Edn.** [1880-84]. 5 vols., including Supp. 4to. Orig. cl. gt., little worn & shaken. (P. Dec.8; 267) *Kassis.* £85
– – **Anr. Copy.** 4 vols. 4to. Publisher's hf. mor. gt., slightly rubbed. (S. Nov.1; 65) *Broekema.* £80
– – **Anr. Copy.** 4 vols. 4to. Cl. gt., soiled. (P. Apr.12; 191) *Russell.* £65
– – **Anr. Edn.** L., [1880-84]. *1st. Edn.* 4 vols. 4to.

2nd. & 3rd. vols. in orig. cl., other 2 rebnd. (SG. Feb.2; 106) $200
– – **Anr. Edn.** N.d. 4 vols. 4to. Cont. cf., lightly rubbed. (CSK. Jul.6; 77) £110
– – **Anr. Copy.** 5 vols., including supp. 4to. Orig. decor. cl. gt. (SKC. Mar.9; 1997) £90
– – **Anr. Copy.** 10 orig. pts. 4to. 2 folding maps, 38 plts., few ll. slightly soiled, orig. wraps., slightly torn & soiled. (BBA. Aug.18; 207) *Museum Bookshop.* £50

WILSON, Edmund
- Three Reliques. N.p., n.d. Decor. wraps.; inscr. (SG. Mar.1; 624) $150

WILSON, Erasmus
- On Diseases of the Skin. Phila., 1857. 2 vols. Liby. stps., orig. blind-stpd. decor. cl. (CBA. Dec.10; 319) $100

See— QUAIN, Jones & Wilson, Erasmus

WILSON, George
- Reports of the Cases Argued & Adjudged in the King's Court at Westminster. Dublin, 1792. Vols. 1 & 3 only. Law sheep, worn; Vol. 1 title inscr. 'Bought of Christopher Tompkins by Stephen T. Logan', sigd. thrice by Logan on front free endpaper, newspaper advts. for Logan & Lincoln, & for B.S. Prettyman pasted in, Vol. 3 inscr. by Logan on front free end-paper & sigd. on both titles. (LH. Jan.15; 153) $275

WILSON, Hardy
- The Cow Pasture Road. 1920. *(600).* No bdg. stated. (JL. Jun.24; 121) Aus. $140
- Grecian & Chinese Architecture ... Melbourne, 1937. *(100) numbered.* Fo. Bds., qtr. imitation vell. (KH. May 1; 766) Aus. $720
– – **Anr. Copy.** Fo. No bdg. stated. (JL. Jun.24; 175) Aus. $700
- Old Colonial Architecture of NSW & Tasmania. Sydney, 1924. *(1000) numbered & sigd.* Fo. No bdg. stated. (JL. Jun.24; 176) Aus. $950
– – **Anr. Copy.** Fo. Bds., qtr. imitation vell., some spotted foxing to backstrip, d.-w. worn. (KH. May 1; 767) Aus. $800
– – **Anr. Copy.** Fo. Parch.-bkd. decor. bds. gt., unc., covers worn, torn & stained. (CA. Apr.3; 144) Aus. $580
– – **Anr. Copy.** Fo. Bds., qtr. imitation vell (heavily foxed). (KH. Nov.8; 516) Aus. $350

WILSON, Harry
- Fugitive Sketches in Rome, Venice ... 1838. Fo. Some spotting in margins, 1 litho. view loose, qtr. mor. gt. (P. Sep.8; 189) *Erlini.* £90

WILSON, Harry Leon
- Merton of the Movies. N.Y., 1922. *1st. Edn. 1st. Iss.* With 'colout' spelling, orig. cl., d.-w., mor.-bkd. s.-c.; pres. copy to Harold Davis, Perry Molstad copy. (SPB. May 16; 556) $200

WILSON, Henry
See— ATKINSON, James & Wilson, Henry

WILSON, Sir John
- The Royal Philatelic Collection. L., 1952. Fo. Red mor., embossed with Royal arms, case. (HBC. May 17; 237) £185
– – **Anr. Copy.** Fo. Orig. crimson mor. gt. (TA. Oct.20; 340) £68
– – **Anr. Edn.** [1952]. Fo. Orig. mor. gt., s.-c. (CSK. Apr.6; 19) £120
– – **Anr. Copy.** Fo. Mor. gt., s.-c. slightly worn. (KH. Nov.9; 519) Aus. $350

WILSON, John
See— ARNOTT, James A. & Wilson, John

WILSON, Mona
See— BLAKE, William – WILSON, Mona

WILSON, Owen S.
- The Larvae of the British Lepidoptera & their Food Plants. Ill.:– Elinora Wilson. L., 1880. Royal 8vo. Orig. cl. gt. (SKC. Oct.26; 331) £60

WILSON, Romer
- Red Magic. Ill.:– Kay Nielsen. L., 1930. Orig. cl., rubbed. (BBA. May 23; 238) *May.* £60

WILSON, S.B. & Evans, A.H.
- Aves Hawaiienses: the Birds of the Sandwich Islands. L., 1890-91. Pts. 1 & 2 (of 8) bnd. in 1 vol. 4to. 17 hand-cold. litho. plts., 3 diagramatic plts., slight spotting, hf. cl., orig. wraps. bnd. in. (S. Apr.10; 464) *Burden.* £220

WILSON, William, Topographer
[-] The Post Chaise Companion. Dublin, ca. 1796. Hf. cf. (GM. Dec.7; 222) £60

WILSON, W.J
See— DE RICCI, Seymour & Wilson, W.J.

WILSON, William
- A Missionary Voyage to the South Pacific Ocean ... in the Ship Duff. L., 1799. *1st. Edn.* 4to. Lge. copy, 13 plts. & maps, subscribers list, cont. hf. cf., emblem gt. spine, a little worn. (BBA. Sep.29; 33) *Brook-Hitching.* £480
– – **Anr. Copy.** 1799. 4to. Engraved plts., folding maps & charts, general map slightly wormed, 1 plt. cold. by amateur hand, some dampstains, cont. hf. cf. (TA. Jun.21; 52) £90
– – **Anr. Copy.** 4to. Title & other ll. reprd. on outer edges, some minor margin dampstains, recent hf. cf. (TA. Apr.19; 57) £75
– – **Anr. Copy.** 4to. Lacks at least 1 plt. & not collated, worn & soiled, bdg. not stated. (KH. Nov.9; 518) Aus. $100

WILSON, William Bender
- History of the Pennsylvania Railroad Company. Phila., 1899. 2 vols. Red hf. mor., gt. (LH. Sep.25; 303) $100

WILSON, William Rae
- Travels in Norway, Sweden, Denmark, Hanover, Germany. 1826. 1 vol. *(With:)* - Travels in Russia. 1828. 2 vols. *(With:)* - Records of a Route through France & Italy. 1835. 1 vol. Together 4 vols. Plts. foxed, cont. unif. cl., unc. & partly unopened. (S. Nov.1; 86) *Hannas.* £100

WIMPHELING, Jacob
[-] Oratio Querolosa contra Inuasores Sacerdotum. [Augsburg, Froschauer], ca. 1496-1500. 4to. Wide margin, old MS. numbers in upr. corner, margins minimal browned, slightly ink-stained at foot, bds. [H. 16194(=12027); BMC II, 400; Goff W-45] (HK. Nov.8; 383) DM 1,050

WINCHESTER, Elhanan
- An Oration on the Discovery of America. Delivered in London, October the 12th, 1792 ... L., [1792]. *2nd. [1st. Ill.] Edn.* Folding map torn & reprd., stabbed & rebnd. in cf. antique; the Rt. Hon. Visc. Eccles copy. [Sabin 104728] (CNY. Nov.18; 288) $220

WINCHILSEA, Anne Finch, Countess of
[-] Miscellany Poems, on Several Occasions. L., 1713. *1st. Edn.* Williams variant A title-p., ll. E8, C1 & 2 are cancels, final lf. Cc4 blank, Y8 slightly defect., cont. panel. cf., rebkd.; Frederic Dannay copy. (CNY. Dec.16; 386) $220

WINCKELMANN, Johann Joachim
- Briefe an seine Freunde in der Schweiz. Ill.:– S. Gessner. Zürich, 1778. *1st. Edn.* Title slightly foxed, long cont. MS. entry on end-paper, ex-libris in cover, cont. hf. leath., slightly spotted; Jacob Grimm's copy, with his MS. entries on p. 197 & lr. end-paper. (GB. Nov.4; 2229) DM 2,000
[-] Gedanken über die Nachahmung der Griechischen Werke in der Malerey und Bildhauerkunst. Dresden & Leipzig, 1756. 4to. Foxing, some underlining, cont. leath., rubbed & very bumped. (H. Nov.23; 797a) DM 500
- Geschichte der Kunst des Altertums. Dresden, 1764. *1st. Edn.* 2 pts. in 1 vol. *(Bound with:)* - Sendschreiben von den Herculanischen Entdeckungen. 1762. *1st. Edn. (Bound with:)* - Abhandlung von der Fähigkeit der Empfindungen des Schönen in der Kunst, und dem Unterrichte in derselben. 1763. *1st. Edn. (Bound with:)* - Nachrichten von den Neuesten Herculanischen Entdeckungen. 1764. *1st. Edn.* Together 4 works in 1 vol. 4to. Some foxing, bds. (B. Oct.4; 592) Fls. 750
– – **Anr. Edn.** Preface:– Fr. Just Riedel. Wien, 1776.

WINCKELMANN, Johann Joachim -Contd.

2 pts. in 1 vol. 4to. Wide margin, on Bütten, ex-libris, cont. leath., spotted & bumped. (H. Nov.23; 798) DM 580
- Oeuvres Complètes. Paris, [1794-]1803. 2 vols. in 3. 4to. Mor.-bkd. bds., rubbed. (SPB. Nov.30; 359) $300
- Sämtliche Werke. Ed.:– J. Eiselein. Donauösch-ingen, 1825-29 & 1835. 12 text vols. & 2 plt. vols. in 1. 8vo. & fo. Some slight browning or foxing, plt. vol. with stains & soiling also, cont. hf. leath., spine faded, rubbed. (H. May 22; 937) DM 1,800
[–] Sendschreiben von den Herculanischen Entdeckungen. Dresden, 1762. 1st. Edn. 4to. Wide margin, slightly spotted & browned, old engraved ex-libris inside cover, mod. vell. (H. Nov.23; 799) DM 400

WINCKLER, E.
See— LICHTENSTEIN, H. & Winckler, E.

WINCKLER, G.E. 'J. Textor'
- Nassauische Chronik. Herborn, 1617. 1st. Edn. 4to. Lacks port., some sm. holes in title, partly reprd., holes in 2 ll. of prelims. with loss of some text, foxed & browned thro.-out, cont. hf. cf., rubbed. (VG. Sep.14; 1204) Fls. 900

WINDELER, Bernard
- Sailing Ships & Barges. Ill.:– E. Wadsworth. 1926. (450) numbered & sigd. by author & artist. Engraved additional title, 3 vigs., 1 map, 17 plts., 2 vigs. & 16 plts. hand-cold., orig. cl., s.-c.; pres. copy, inscr. by author. (CSK. Aug.5; 137) £110

WINDHAM, William & Townshend, Lord George
- A Plan of Discipline Composed for the Use of the Militia of the County of Norfolk. L., 1759. 1st. Edn. 4to. Some spotting & soiling, cont. cf., rebkd., worn. (SPB. Dec.13; 766) $200
- - Anr. Edn. 1768. Sm. 4to. 5 folding charts, 52 engraved plts., cont. cf., rebkd., orig. backstrip preserved. (BBA. Feb.23; 181) Morton-Smith. £110

WINDSOR CASTLE
- The Series of Dramatic Entertainments Performed ... at Windsor Castle, 1848-9 ... Ed.:– B. Webster. N.d. [200]. Light soiling, orig. cl. gt., soiled. (CSK. Aug.5; 26) £60

WINDSOR PARK
- Lodges in Windsor Great Park. Day & Haghe, n.d. Ob. fo. 8 hand-cold. plts., 8 plain plans, hf. mor., defect. (P. Oct.20; 121) £850

WINDUS, John
- Reise nach Mequinetz. Hannover, [1726]. Title with sm. excision, cut with loss of date, browned, folding copper engr. slightly crumpled, cont. hf. leath., spine extremities slightly split. (R. Oct.13; 2940) DM 400

WINES, E[noch] C.
- Two Years & a Half in the Navy. Phila., 1832. 1st. Edn. 2 vols. 12mo. 36pp. publisher's advts., foxing, some old stains, pencil markings to pre-lims. & end-papers Vol. I, orig. muslin, sm. tears or fraying at jnts. & spine tips. [Sabin 104776] (HA. Nov.18; 165) $120

WING, Donald
- Short-Title Catalogue of Books Printed in England ... 1641-1700. N.Y., 1945-48. Vols. 1 & 2 only. 4to. Orig. cl., hinges split. (BBA. Apr.5; 313) Col. O'Neill. £60

WINGATE, Edmund
[–] Justice Revived. 1661. 1st. Edn. 12mo. Hf.-title, cont. sheep, rebkd., rubbed. (BBA. Jul.27; 102) Blackwell's. £250

WINGFIELD, W. & Johnson, G.W.
- The Poultry Book. Ill.:– Leighton Bros. after Harrison Weir. 1853. 4to. Cold. additional title & 21 plts., ptd. in cols., a few with sm. sections of tissue guards adhering, some soiling, cont. hf. cf., rubbed, front inner hinge reprd. (CSK. Apr.27; 126) £60

WINKLE, H. & B.
- Architectural & Picturesque Illustrations of the Cathedral Churches of England & Wales. 1860. 3 vols. 3 engraved titles, 185 plts., 1 torn & a few loose, hf. mor. gt. (P. Sep.29; 219) £65

WINKLER, Edward
- Getreue Abbildung aller in den Pharmacopöen Deutschlands aufgenommenen Officinellen Gewächse. Leipzig, [1846-47]. 4to. Lacks title & text, some slight browning or spotting, col. slightly smudged in approx. 10 plts., cont. hf. leath. gt. (R. Apr.4; 1808) DM 2,100

WINKLER, Friedrich
- Die Zeichnungen Albrecht Dürers. Berlin, 1936-39. [1st. Edn.]. 4 vols. 4to, upr. cover of vol. 4 slightly worn. (S. Apr.30; 102) Cohen. £120
- - Anr. Copy. 4 vols. 4to. Some slight spotting, orig. cl., slightly rubbed. (S. Nov.8; 587) Sims. £90
- - Anr. Copy. 4 vols. Fo. 949 ills., most full-p., 96 plts., 1 plt. vol. 1 & 1 lf. Vol. IV crumpled, orig. linen. (HT. May 9; 956) DM 520

WINNECKE, Charles
- Journal of the Horn Scientific Exploring Expedition, 1894. Adelaide, 1897. 2 vols. with atlas. Slightly soiled thro.-out, text disbnd., maps in bds., worn. (BBA. May 3; 300) Morrell. £250

WINSLOW, Jacques Berugrie
- Abhandlung von dem Bau u. der Zergliederung des Menschl. Leibes ... Trans.:– Albinus. Basel, 1754. 5 pts. in 2 vols. Slightly foxed, cont. leath.-bkd. wood bds. gt., 2 clasps. (HK. Nov.8; 789) DM 560

WINSOR, Justin
- Narrative & Critical History of America. Boston, [1884-89]. 8 vols. Lge. 8vo. Three-qtr. mor. gt. (SG. Jan.19; 351) $100

WINSTANLEY, William
[–] The Lives of the most famous English Poets. 1687. Some ll. trimmed, later roan, rubbed. [Wing W3065] (BBA. Jun.14; 63) Hannas. £85

WINTERBOTHAM, William
- An Historical, Geographical, Commercial, & Philosophical View of the American United States, & of the European Settlements in America & the West Indies. L., 1795. 1st. Edn. 4 vols. 2 engraved plans, 9 folding maps, 22 plts., 77 p. appendix (as opposed to the 54 pp. called for by Howes), list of subscribers in Vol. 1, no 'Directions for the Binder' in Vol. 4, but extra lf. P2 from Vol. 3 inserted between PP. 54 & 55 of appendix to Vol. 4, a few maps with minor repairs to versos, etc., cont. tree cf., gt.-decor. spines, light wear, head of 1 spine bumped. [Sabin 104832] (RO. Dec.11; 354) £550
- - Anr. Copy. 4 vols. 4 ports., 17 engraved plts., 8 folding maps, 3 engraved plans (1 folding), folding tables, stains & spotting, tears in folding plts., cont. hf. cf., worn. [Sabin 104831] (S. Apr.9; 71) Burden. £120
- - Anr. Edn. L., 1799. 2nd. Edn. 4 vols. 4 engraved port. frontis., 11 maps & plans, including 9 folding, 19 plts. of views, etc., 4 folding ptd. table ll., subscribers list, lacks contents list in Vol. 1, unc., orig. bds. (S. Dec.13; 142) Faupel. £240

WINTER VON ADLERFLUGEL, G.S.
- Stuterey, das ist Neue Wohlbestellte Fohlenzucht. Nuremb., 1687. 4to. Leath. (G. Sep.15; 2505) Sw. Frs. 1,900
- Tractatio Nova de Re Equaria ... Nurcmb., 1672. 1st. Edn. Fo. 2 ll. torn, 1 copper engr. with tears & some loss, 1 plt. torn, very stained thro.-out, cont. vell., lacks 4 ties. (HK. Nov.9; 2024) DM 750

WINTHER, H.T.
- Anweisung auf drei Verschiedenen Wegen Licht-bilder ... auf Papier hervorzubringen und festzuhalten. Christiania, 1845. 2 ll. soiled, lightly browned, orig. wraps., spine defect., unc. (H. Nov.23; 266) DM 520

WINTTER, Raphael
- Lithographirte Thierzeichnungen als Bildliche Darstellungen der Fabeln Classischer Dichter. München, [1816]. 4to. Lithos. on vell., text &

lithos. slightly different in format, orig. wraps., unc. (GB. May 4; 1496) DM 1,100

WINTZENBERGER, D.
- Warhafftige Geschichte, und Gedenckwirdiger Händel, so von den 1500. Jar an, bis auff dis 1583. Jar ergangen. Dresden, 1583. 4to. Browned, some soiling, several ll. restored in margins, lacks last lf. on verso present last lf. Printer's mark & Psalm, cont. hf. leath., paper cover renewed later, re-cased. (R. Oct.11; 118) DM 1,300

WIRSUNG, Christopher
- The General Practice of Physicke. Trans.:– Jacob Mosan. L., 1617. 3rd. Edn. in Engl. Fo. 19th. C. panel. cf., rebkd. preserving orig. spine. [STC 25865] (C. Nov.9; 122) Finch. £200
- Ein New Artzney Buch. Ed.:– J. Th. Taberna-emontanus. Ill.:– Jost Amman. Neustadt, 1584. Fo. Title stpd. with old MS owners mark, slightly foxed, some worming in upr. & lr. margin, soiled at beginning, cont. blind-tooled pig over wood bds., lacks upr. end-paper, lr. corners reprd. with newer linen, slightly worn & bumped, 2 clasps, lacks lr. clasp. (HK. May 15; 571) DM 2,800

WIRT, Mrs. Elizabeth W.
- Flora's Dictionary. Ill.:– Ann Smith. Balt., after 1837. 4to. 58 hand-cold. litho. plts., including pict. title at front & pict. section-title between pp. 20 & 21, some foxing thro.-out, some stains from pressed leaves & flowers, orig. gt.-stpd. mor., upr. jnt. crudely strengthened with glue, corners slightly bruised; sig. of Mrs. Gardiner Greene Howland. (CNY. May 18; 155) $1,200

WIRTH, J.G.A.
- Die Rechte des Deutschen Volkes. Nancy, 1833. 1st. Edn. 12mo. Slightly crumpled, orig. bds., spine very worn. (HT. May 10; 2515a) DM 1,000

WIRTZ, F.
See— VALENTINUS, P.P. - WIRTZ or WUERTZ, F.

WISE, Lieut. Henry A.
- Los Gringos ... N.Y., 1849. 1st. Edn. (With:)
- Tales for the Marines. By Harry Gringo. Boston, 1855. 1st. Edn. Together 2 vols. Orig. blind-stpd. cl., hf. mor. s.-c. (LH. Jan.15; 423) $160

WISE, John
- A System of Aeronautics, Comprehending its Earliest Investigations & Modern Practice & Art. Phila., 1850. 1st. Edn. 12mo. Errata slip, crude hf. linen, worn, ex-liby. (With:) - Through the Air, a Narrative of Forty Years' Experience as an Aeronaut. Phila., 1873. 1st. Edn. 8vo. Pict. cl., shabby, ex-liby. (SG. Mar.22; 8) $130

WISE, Thomas James
- The Ashley Library: A Catalogue of Printed Books, Manuscripts & Autograph Letters. L., 1922. 1st. Edn. (200), for private circulation. 11 vols. 4to. Gt.-decor. buckram. (SG. Sep.15; 15) $600
- - Anr. Edn. L., 1922-30. 10 vols. (lacks last vol.). 4to. Publisher's cl. bradel bds. (HD. Jun.6; 159) Frs. 1,600
- A Bibliography of ... George Gordon Noel, Baron Byron. L., 1932-33. (180), for private circulation. 2 vols. 4to. Orig. cl. (BBA. Sep.8; 27) Clegg. £70.
- - Anr. Copy. 2 vols. 4to. Gt.-ornamented cl. (SG. Sep.15; 352) $130
- A Brontë Library. 1929. (120). Orig. cl. gt., slightly faded. (P. Feb.16; 210) £50
- A Byron Library. L., 1928. (30) on H.M.P. 4to. Orig. buckram, spine faded, partly unc.; inscr. to R.W. Clapman. (S. Oct.4; 229) Wise. £130
- A Conrad Library. 1928. (180). Cl. gt. (P. Mar.15; 170a) Ingleton. £85

WISTAR, Isaac Jones
- Autobiography. Phila., 1914. 1st. Edn. (250). 2 vols. 4to. Cl. (LH. Sep.25; 304) $170

WISZGRILL, Fr. K.
- Schauplatz des landsässigen Nieder-Oesterreich. Adels vom Herren- und Ritterstande. Wien, 1794-1804. Vols. I-V (all publd.). 4to. Some wormholes, old owner's name erased from titles, cont. marb. cf., spines gt., jnts. of 1 vol. partly bkrn. (VG. Mar.19; 258) Fls. 850

WIT, Frederick
- Atlas. [Amst., 1680?]. Fo. 51 double-p. engraved maps & 16 ll. letterpress, mntd. on guards, 1 map hand-cold., some minor margin staining, cont. vell., re-cased & reprd. (CH. May 24; 47) Fls. 12,000
- - Anr. Copy. Lge. fo. Maps outl. cold., decor. cartouches & arms cold., engraved title bkd., sm. tears or paper defects. (from col.) reprd., some bkd. with silk, cont. vell. gt., spine reprd., sm. defect., end-papers & ties renewed; Hauswedell coll. (H. May 24; 877) DM 21,000

WITHER, George
- Speculum Speculativum: Or, A Considering-Glass; Being an Inspection into the Present & Late Sad Condition of these Nations ... 1660. Sm. 8vo. 2 dupl. ll. (pp. 163-6) bnd. in at rear, containing variations to main text, generally browned, last lf. reprd., later hf. mor., rubbed. (TA. Mar.15; 515) £135
- - Anr. Copy. Sm. 8vo. Cont. sheep, rebkd. [Wing W3192] (TA. Jun.21; 524) £65

WITSEN, Nicolaas
- Noord en Oost Tartaryen ... Amst., 1785. 3rd. Edn. 2 vols. Fo. 19th. C. hf. leath., 1 cover loose. (GB. May 3; 70) DM 2,400

WITH, K.
- Jizo. Ill.:– M. Kogan. Düsseldorf, 1922. (48). 4to. Printers mark sigd. by author & artist, 12 sigd. orig. woodcuts, orig. silk, orig. linen box. (GB. May 5; 2819) DM 3,400

WITHERBY, Harry Forbes & others
- British Birds. 1930-68. Vols. 24, 27-49 & 50-61. Vols. 50-61 in orig. wraps., rest in publisher's cl. gt. (SKC. May 4; 1881) £130
- The Handbook of British Birds. 1938-41. 1st. Edn. 5 vols. Some ll. slightly spotted, orig. cl., d.-w.'s. (BBA. Feb.23; 107) Jackson. £80
- - Anr. Copy. 5 vols. Orig. cl., d.-w.'s. (CSK. Oct.7; 95) £55
- - Anr. Edn. 1945. 5 vols. Orig. cl., d.-w.'s. (P. Feb.16; 91) £55
- - Anr. Edn. 1949. 6th. Imp. 5 vols. Sm. 4to. Orig. cl. (TA. Feb.16; 103) £66

WITHERING, William
- Miscellaneous Tracts. L., 1822. 2 vols. Lacks port. & facs. letter, hf. cf. (S. Apr.10; 599) Shaftel. £90

WITKAMP, Pieter Harme
- Amsterdam in Schetsen. Amst., 1862. 2nd. Printing. Vol. 1 (of 2). Some foxing (as usual), orig. cl. gt. (VG. Mar.19; 60) Fls. 820
- Beschrijving van Duitschland. Amst., 1843. 4to. Some light browning, cont. hf. linen, slightly defect. (R. Oct.12; 2442) DM 1,900

WITSEN, Nicolaas
- Noord en Oost Tartaryen. Amst., 1785. 2nd. Edn. 2 vols. Fo. Cont. hf. leath., unc. (GB. Nov.3; 88) DM 2,800

WITT, John de
See— COURT, P. de la & Witt, John de

WITTE, C. (Text)
See— FROMMEL, C.

WITTE, H.
- Flora. Afbeeldingen en Beschrijvingen van Boomen, Heesters, Eenjarige Planten, enz., voorkomende in Ned. Tuinen. Groningen, [1868]. Fo. Chromolitho. frontis., 79 chromolitho. plts., some stains, slightly loose, orig. cl., stained. (B. Oct.4; 229a) Fls. 700

WITTGENSTEIN, Ludwig
- Logisch-Philosophische Abhandlung. Leipzig, 1921. Annalen der Naturphilosophie vol. 14, Heft 3 & 4 pp. 185-262. Orig. ptd. wraps.; from liby. of Ludwig Hänsel with ptd. slip on title. (S. May 10; 431) Steiner. £1,100

WITTKOWER, R.
See— BRAUER, H. & Wittkower, R.

WITTLIEB
[–] Histoire des Révolutions de l'Isle de Corse et de l'Elevation de Théodore Ier. La Haie, 1738. 32mo. Mod. chagrin. (HD. Oct.21; 180) Frs. 2,000

[–] Storia della Rivoluzioni dell'Isola di Corsica della Esaltazione de Téodoro I. L'Haya, 1739. 12mo. Old bds. (HD. Oct.21; 181) Frs. 2,300

WITTMAN, William
- Travels in Turkey, Asia Minor, Syria ... into Egypt ... L., 1803. 1st. Edn. 4to. Engraved folding frontis., folding map & facs., 20 (of 21?) plts., including 16 hand-cold., map & facs. torn at fold, few ll. lightly spotted, cont. tree cf., rebkd. (S. Apr.9; 72) Wood. £260

WITTON, Lieut. George R.
- Scapegoats of the Empire; The Story of the Bushveldt Carbineers. Melbourne, 1907. Slight foxing, bdg. not stated, soiled & dull. (KH. May 1; 770) Aus. $140

WODEHOUSE, Pelham Grenville
- Psmith Journalist. L., 1915. 1st. Edn. Hf.-title, little spotting, orig. pict. cl. (S. Mar.20; 991) Hawthorn. £50
- The White Feather. Ill.:– W. Townend. 1907. Some minor spotting, mostly to margins, orig. pict. cl., a little rubbed & soiled. (TA. Jun.21; 543) £240

WODROW, Rev. Robert
- The History of the Suffering of the Church of Scotland, from the Restauration to the Revolution. Edinb., 1721-22. 1st. Edn. 2 vols. Fo. Cont. panel. cf.; Sir Ivar Colquhoun, of Luss copy. (CE. Mar.22; 330) £170

WOHLBEWAHRTE Fischgeheimnisse oder Deutlicher Unterricht von der Grossen Nutzbarkeit der Fischerey
Nuremb., 1758. 1st. Edn. Last 2 index ll. possibly from anr. copy, hf. mor. gt.; from Denison coll., Dr. Walter Pagel copy. (S. Feb.7; 121) Radziewoski. £160

WOILLEZ, Dr Eug.-J.
- Archéologie des Monuments Religieux de l'Ancien Beauvoisis pendant la Métamorphose Romane. Paris, 1839-49. Fo. Bds. (HD. Dec.2; 169) Frs. 4,100

WOLCOT, John 'Peter Pindar'
- Odes of Importance. Dublin, 1792. Unbnd., orig. paper wrap. (BS. Nov.16; 85) £80

WOLF, Edwin
See— KEYNES, Geoffrey & Wolf, Edwin

WOLF, Edwin (Contrib.)
See— ROSENBACH, Dr. Abraham Simon Wolf

WOLF, Joh. & Meyer, B.
- Naturgeschichte der Vögel Deutschlands. Nürnberg, 1805[-10]. Lge. fo. Wide margin, on yellowish paper, title lf. crumpled, German & Fr. text, MS. names, last 5 copper engrs. with spotting & creasing, 4 copper engrs. with light margin stain, some text ll. browned or slightly foxed, cont. hf. leath., bumped. (H. May 22; 222) DM 3,600

WOLF, Johann
[–] Neues Buchstabir- und Lesebuch zur Beförderung der Entwickelung des Verstandes für niedere besonders aber für Landschulen. Nürnberg, 1799. 1st. Edn. Fo. 21 hand-cold. engraved plts., plts. & text in sheets, loose in portfo.; van Veen coll. (S. Feb.28; 175) £600

WOLF, Joh. Chr.
- Neues Leipziger Koch-Buch. Frankfurt & Leipzig, 1800. Some staining, plts. partly defect., cont. bds., bumped, lacks spine, new linen box. (BR. Apr.12; 1176) DM 400

WOLF, W.L.
- Das Abracadabra des 19ten Jahrhunderts oder Hahnemann's Homöpathie. Trans.:– [D.R.] Warburg. Hamburg, 1836. 1st. Edn. Title verso & 1 text lf. stpd. in lr. margin, cont. bds. (R. Oct.12; 1422) DM 420

WOLFART, C. Chr.
[–] Guntha ein Altteutsch Mährlein Schauspiel. Ill.:– R. Hundeshagen. Frankfurt, 1809. Title stpd., orig. litho. wraps., sm. spine defect. (HK. Nov.10; 2788) DM 400

WOLFE, Rev. P.
- Irish Names & Surnames. Dublin, 1923. 1 vol. No bdg. stated. (With:) – Dysert-Diarmada, or Irish Place Names. Dublin, 1919. 1 vol. No bdg. stated. (GM. Dec.7; 430) £55

WOLFE, Richard J.
- Jacob Bigelow's American Medical Botany. North Hills, Pa., Bird & Bull Pr., 1979. ('approx. 300') numbered. Tall 8vo. 2 plts., 1 cold., lev.-bkd. flowered bds., prospectus laid in. (SG. May 17; 36) $175

WOLFE, Thomas
- Look Homeward, Angel. N.Y., 1929. 1st. Edn. With lr. case 'g' in 'greek' p.308, 't' missing in 'stationed' on p. 506, some browning of endpaper, orig. cl., d.-w. with port.; Fred A. Berne copy. (SPB. May 16; 385) $800
- - Anr. Copy. Orig. cl., 1st. state of d.-w. with slight tears & repairs, s.-c.; Perry Molstad copy. (SP. May 16; 559) $750

WOLFF, Chr.
- Anfangs-Gründe aller Mathematischen Wissenschaften. Halle, 1775. 4 vols. including index. Hf. leath., spines gt., some corners bumped. (B. Jun.21; 425) Fls. 850
- Ubrige Theils noch gefundene Kleine Schriften und einzelne Betrachtungen zur Verbesserung der Wissenschaften. Halle, 1755. 1st. Edn. Some slight browning, free end-paper stpd., cont. leath., gt., gold-tooled. (HT. May 10; 2308) DM 850
See— TREW, A. - WOLFF, Chr.

WOLFF, Fr.
- Album von Ost-Asien. Düsseldorf/München-Gladbach, 1865. Fo. Dedication copy, sigd. by ed., 30 orig. photos, hand-cold. & heightened with gold & silver, text in German, Engl. & Fr., end-papers of Oriental ornaments ptd. in gold, orig. gold-stpd. cf., decor., 4 corner ornaments partly gone. (VG. Nov.30; 531) Fls. 6,000

WOLFF, H.
- Zeichnungen von Max Liebermann. Dresden, 1922. (200) numbered De Luxe Edn. with sigd. orig. etching. 4to. Orig. mor. gt., corners rubbed. (GB. May 5; 2889) DM 1,400

WOLFF, Oscar Ludwig Bernhard
- Naturgeschichte des Deutschen Studenten. Von Plinius dem Jüngsten. Leipzig, [1847]. 3rd. Edn. Some foxing, late 19th. C. hf. leath. (HK. Nov.9; 2199) DM 500

WOLFF, O.L.B. (Ed.)
See— NEUES ELEGANTESTES CONVERSA-TIONS-LEXICON

WOLFF, Oscar Ludwig Bernhard & Doerling, H.
- The German Tourist. Ill.:– after A.G. Vickers. L., 1837. Cont. leath., defect., cover loose. (R. Oct.12; 2444) DM 750
- - Anr. Edn. Trans.:– H.E. Lloyd. Ill.:– A.G. Vickers. L. & Berlin, [1837]. Publisher's mor. (RO. Dec.11; 357) $200
- - Anr. Copy. Some foxing, publisher's mor., spine tips slightly chipped. (RO. Dec.11; 356) $180

WOLFFHART, Conrad
See— LYCOSTHENES [ie. Conrad Wolffhart]

WOLFGANG, H.
- Hye habet sich an das Leben und Legend des Himelfuersten um Heyligen Peichtigers Sand Wolfgangs ... Landshut, 1516. 51 full-p. woodcuts cold. by cont. hand, sm. fault in lr. blank margin of title lf. bkd., title lf. with 2 red stamp Prints, monog. & date [1516], some offsetting, some slight soiling, cont. blind-tooled pig over wood bds., slight scratches, 2 brass clasps, hf. mor. box, gt. spine; MS. name Martin Luther in upr. part of title lf., slightly obscured. (D. Nov.23; 126a) DM 33,000

WOLFSKEHL, K. & Leyen, Friedrich von der
- Alteste Deutsche Dichtungen. [Leipzig], 1909. 1st. Edn. Orig. vell; Hauswedell coll. (H. May 24; 720a) DM 500

WOLFSKRON, Adolf Ritter von
– Die Bilder de Hedwigslegende nach einer Handschrift vom Iahre 1353. Vienna, 1846. Fo. Some spotting, cl., orig. decor. upr. wrap. bnd. in. (BBA. Jun.28; 185)   *Marlborough Rare Books.* £120

WOLLASTON, Francis
– A Portrait of the Heavens. L., 1811. *1st. Edn.* Atlas fo. 10 double-p. engraved plts., cont. marb. bds., covers detchd. (SG. Apr.26; 208) $275
– A Specimen of a General Astronomical Catalogue. L., 1789. *1st. Edn.* Atlas fo. Cont. marb. cf., spine & jnts. worn, gt.-stpd. Signet arms on covers. (SG. Apr.26; 207) $275

WOLLSTONECRAFT, Mary
– A Vindication of The Rights of Woman. L., 1792. *1st. Edn.* Vol. 1 (all publd.). Cont. cf., upr. cover detchd., spine torn. (P. Sep.8; 247) *Traylen.* £260
– – **Anr. Copy.** Inkstain on outer margins of last 130 pp., cont. red str.-grd. mor. (SG. Nov.3; 224) $550

WOLTERS, Fr.
– Herrschaft und Dienst. Ill.:– M. Lechter. Berlin, Einhorn Pr., 1909. *1st. Edn.* (10) *De Luxe Edn on vell.* Fo. Decor, double title & initials, printers mark monog. & numbered by Lechter, hand-bnd. orig. pig, gold-tooled cover vig, some scratches, slightly spotted, ex-libris inside cover. (H. May 23; 1566)   DM 4,000
– – **Anr. Edn.** Ill.:– M. Lechter. Berlin, Einhorn Pr., 1909. *1st. Edn.* Fo. Orig. pig. gold-tooled cover ill., orig. linen box, moiré silk lined, slightly spotted & bumped; printer's mark monog. by artist. (H. Nov.24; 1771)   DM 4,400
– – **Anr. Edn.** Ill.:– M. Lechter. Berlin, Einhorn Pr., 1909. *(500) monogrammed & numbered by artist.* Fo. On unbleached paper, orig. hf. vell. with inset gold-stpd. sig. on vell. (GB. Nov.5; 2732) DM 400

WOLTMANN, A.
See– GORLING, A., Meyer, B. & Woltmann, A.

WOLTMANN, A. & Meyer, B.
– Deutschlands Kunstschätze. Ill.:– French, Payne, Merkel & others. Leipzig, 1871-72. 4 vols. Lge. 4to. 228 (of 240) steel engrs., 80 ports., cont. hf. cf., slightly rubbed. (VG. Mar.19; 65)   Fls. 750

WOOD, Anthony A.
– Athenae Oxoniensies. Ed.:– P. Bliss. L., 1813-20. 4 vols. Some ll. slightly spotted, cont. hf. mor., rubbed. (BBA. May 3; 231)
Howes Bookshop. £130

WOOD, Casey A.
– An Introduction to the Literature of Vertebrate Zoology ... 1931. 4to. Orig. cl.; inscr. (LC. Jul.5; 109)   £85
– – **Anr. Copy.** 4to. Cl., moderate wear. (RO. May 22; 199) $160

WOOD, J. Medley & Evans, M.S.
– Natal Plants. L., 1897-1909. 6 vols. 4to. Qtr. mor., defect., & cl.; Royal Commonwealth Soc. copy. (P. Nov.24; 273) *Weldon & Wesley.* £100

WOOD, John George
– The Principal Rivers of Wales Illustrated. 1813. 2 pts. in 1 vol. Lge. 4to. 48 litho. plts., 4 hand-cold. double-p. maps, bnd. with 16pp. text & 7 litho. plts. on the Rivers Wye & Lugg, (n.d., but plts. dtd. 1813-17) later hf. mor., lightly rubbed. (CSK. May 4: 134)   £190
– The Principles & Practices of Sketching Landscape Scenery from Nature. 1820. *3rd. Edn.* 4 pts. in 1 vol. Ob. fo. 64 litho. plts., a few ll. slightly spotted, cont. hf. cf., worn. (BBA. Jan.19; 364)
Jarndyce. £60

WOOD, Nicholas
– A Practical Treatise on Rail-Roads. L., 1825. *1st. Edn.* Slightly soiled thro.-out, sig. on title-p. & some marginalia, cont. hf. cf. (BBA. Mar.21; 59)
Thorp. £120

WOOD, Robert
– An Essay on the Original Genius & Writings of Homer. Ill.:– Bartolozzi. L., 1775. *1st. Publd. Edn.* Lge. 4to. Cont. mott. cf., rebkd. with elab. gt. design; bkplt. of Wilberforce Liby. (SG. Feb.9; 373) $200

[–] The Ruins of Balbec. L., 1747. *1st. Edn.* Tall fo. 47 engraved plts., some double-p., ex-liby., some foxing & stains, mod. leatherette. (SG. May 3; 389) $400
– – **Anr. Edn.** 1757. Lge. fo. Engraved cut of facs. & 44 plts. on 45 sheets (10 folding or double-p.), title & a few plts. lightly foxed, hf. cf., unc.; Sir Ivar Colquhoun, of Luss copy. (CE. Mar.22; 332)   £800
– – **Anr. Edn.** Ill.:– after Borra. L., 1767. Fo. Cont. str.-grd. mor., minor defects. (HD. Jun.29; 109)
Frs. 4,500
– The Ruins of Palmyra, otherwise Tedmor in the Desart. 1753. *[1st. Edn.].* Lge. fo. 3 engraved facs. & 57 plts. on 59 sheets, hf. cf., unc.; Sir Ivar Colquhoun, of Luss copy. (CE. Mar.22; 333)£750
– – **Anr. Copy.** Fo. 59 engraved plts. (numbered 1-57), the 3 sheets of the panorama inserted individually, faint traces of damp in margins of a few plts., 2 plts. lightly foxed, cont. cf., blind-stpd. arms of Earl of Darnley on covers, gt. spine. (C. Dec.9; 170)   *D'Arcy.* £260
– – **Anr. Copy.** Lge. fo. 3 engraved plts. of inscrs., 59 engraved plts., engraved double-p. frontis. inserted, without hf.-title, cont. diced russ., upr. cover detchd. (C. Dec.9; 196)   *Kassis.* £155
– – **Anr. Copy.** Atlas fo. Lge. folding panoramic view, 56 engraved plts., mod. liby. buckram. (SG. May 3; 390) $500
– The Ruins of Palmyra & Balbec. L., 1827. *1st. Pickering Edn.* Elephant fo. 57 & 46 full-p., double-p. & folded black-&-white copperplts., some liby. in text, sm. ink handstp. at bottom margin of all plts., orig. cl. & early (orig.?) mor., gt.-lettered, slight wear, slight peeling of cl. (HA. May 4; 296) $260
– – **Anr. Copy.** Fo. Plts. stpd. in margins, three-qtr. leath., worn, spine shipped, ex-liby. (RO. Dec.11; 358) $160

WOOD, Shakspere
– The New Curiosum Urbis: A Guide to Ancient & Modern Rome. L., 1875. Cl., covers warped, endpapers dampstained; inscr. 'Mary Lincoln 1878'. (LH. Jan.15; 151) $375

WOOD, William, F.R.S.
– Index Entomologicus, or A Complete Illustrated Catalogue ... of the Lepidopterous Insects of Great Britain. L., 1839. Incompl., 128 pp. text & 28 handcold. plts., subscribers' list, cf., gt. spine. (SKC. Oct.26; 457) $50
– – **Anr. Edn.** Ed.:– J.O. Westwood. 1854. *New Edn.* 59 hand-cold. engraved plts., hf. mor., spine gt. (LC. Oct.13; 225)   £110
– – **Anr. Copy.** 59 hand-cold. plts., cont. hf. mor., gt.-decor. spine, rubbed. (TA. May 17; 306)   £70
– Zoography; or, the Beauties of Nature Displayed ... with Additions from the Mineral Kingdom. Ill.:– William Daniell. 1807. 3 vols. 60 uncold. plts., later hf. cf. (BBA. Jan.19; 42)   *Bickersteth.* £100
– – **Anr. Copy.** 3 vols. Royal 8vo. Cont. pol. cf., 1 cover detchd. (SKC. Sep.9; 2011)   £85

WOOD, William, Jnr.
– A Series of Twenty-Eight Panoramic Views of Calcutta, Extending from Chandpaul Ghaut to the End of Chowringhee Road, together with the Hospital, the Two Bridges, & the Fort. 1833. Tall fo. Some minor margin stains, not affecting plts., orig. bds., mor. backstrip, a little soiled & worn. (TA. Mar.15; 60)   £400

WOODALL, John
– The Surgeons Mate or Military & Domestique Surgery. L., 1639. *2nd. Edn.* Fo. 1 plt. in dupl. (mntd.), without the port. of Charles I on horseback, some staining, mainly marginal, cont. panel. cf. gt., rebkd., upr. cover detchd., arms of Michael Wodhull. [STC 25963] (S. Nov.28; 141)
Quaritch. £1,020

WOODARD, David
– The Narrative of Captain ... Woodard & Four Seamen, who Lost their Ship while in a Boat at Sea. 1804. Engraved frontis., 2 plts. & 2 folding maps, browned & spotted, later hf. cf., rubbed, spine chipped. (CSK. Mar.9; 143)   £55

WOODCROFT, Bennet
– A Sketch of the Origin & Progress of Steam Navigation from Authentic Documents. 1848. *[1st. Edn.].* Some spotting, orig. cl. gt., spine defect. (P. Sep.8; 71)   *Maggs.* £120
– – **Anr. Copy.** Advts. at end, spotting, orig. cl., gt. ship on upr. cover, faded, some ink marks, extremities frayed; pres. copy from author to Augt Ord (?), Stanitz coll. (SPB. Apr.25; 453) $125
– – **Anr. Copy.** Sm. 4to. 16-p. publisher's catalogue at rear, some wear, ex-liby., moderate markings, sm. handstps. at margin of extra title, 2 stps. at verso of title, orig. blind cl., blind & gt. vigs, at covers, recent crimson tape serving as backstrip, covers worn at edges, corners showing. (HA. May 4; 461) $110

WOODCUT, The
1927-30. Vols. 1-4 (all publd.). 4to. Orig. cl.-bkd. bds., some worming. (P. Apr.12; 261)
Stillwell. £70

WOODHOUSE, Robert
– The Principles of Analytical Calculation. Camb., 1803. *1st. Edn.* 4to. Some spotting & overall light browning, various paper stocks. 1 inner margin stained, hf. mor., rubbed, corner bumped; Stanitz coll. (SPB. Apr.25; 455) $200
– A Treatise on Isoperimetrical Problems & the Calculus of Variations. Camb., 1810. *1st. Edn.* Later hf. leath., lge. leath. corner-pieces. (HT. May 8; 504)   DM 700

WOODHOUSELEE, Alexander Tytler, Lord
– Memoirs of the Life & Writings of the Honourable Henry Home of Kames. Edinb., 1807. *1st. Edn.* 2 vols. 4to. Cont. spr. cf., extremities slightly worn. (SG. Nov.17; 142) $120

WOOD-MARTIN, W.G.
– The Lake Dwellings of Ireland. Dublin, 1886. *1st. Edn.* Inscr. by author, orig. cl., soiled. (GM. Dec.7; 46)   £110

WOODS, John
– Two Years' Residence in the Settlement on the English Prairie, in the Illinois Country, United States. L., 1822. *1st. Edn.* Hf.-title, errata slip, cont. cf., spine & corners slightly worn; the Rt. Hon. Visc. Eccles copy. [Sabin 105125] (CNY. Nov.18; 289) $320

WOODVILLE, William
– Medical Botany. [1790–]94. 4 vols., including Supp. 4to. 272 hand-cold. plts. only, Vol. 1 lacks title, upr. margins Vols. 3 & 4 heavily browned with some loss, cont. hf. cf., worn, lacks 1 cover, w.a.f. (CSK. Oct.7; 56)   £240
– – **Anr. Edn.** 1810. *2nd. Edn.* 4 vols. 4to. 273 (of 274) hand-cold. plts., a few slightly soiled, orig. cl. gt. (P. Oct.20; 124)   £240
– – **Anr. Copy.** 4 vols. 4to. 1 plt. double numbered, 1 plt. misbnd., 1 plt. defect & reprd., cont. cf., slightly worn & bumped, spine reprd. (H. May 22; 206)   DM 3,000
– – **Anr. Edn.** L., 1821-22. 2 (of 4) vols. Port., 137 (of 138) hand-cold. plts., plus repeat of plt. 118, some spotting, hf. cf., defect., as a collection of plts., w.a.f. (P. Nov.24; 265)   £220

WOODWARD, Bernard Bolingbroke
– Windsor Castle, Picturesque & Descriptive ... A Series of Photographic Views ... L., [1870]. Fo. Frontis. & margins of other plts. dampstained, qtr. leath. (SG. Nov.10; 168) $150

WOODWARD, E.L. (Ed.)
See– DOCUMENTS OF BRITISH FOREIGN POLICY ...

WOODWARD, John
– Fossils of all Kinds, Digested into a Method, Suitable to their Mutual Relation & Affinity. 1728. *1st. Edn.* Some margin stains, cont. cf., some wear. (TA. Feb.16; 113)   £125

WOOLF, Virginia
– Flush, A Biography. N.Y., 1933. *1st. Amer. Edn.* Orig. cl.; sigd. (BBA. Jul.27; 219)
Blackwell's. £50
– A Room of One's Own. N.Y., 1929. *(492) numbered & sigd.* Cl. (SG. Mar.1; 632) $275

– Street Haunting. San Franc., [Grabhorn Pr. for] Westgate Pr., 1930. *(500) numbered & sigd.* Sm. 8vo. Qtr. mor., spine faded, s.-c. (SG. May 24; 235) $300
– The Waves. L., Hogarth Pr., 1931. *1st. Edn.* Sm. 8vo. Orig. cl., d.-w., back dark & chipped. (SG. Jan.12; 366) $110
– The Years. L., Hogarth Pr., 1937. *1st. Edn.* Orig. cl., d.-w. by Vanessa Bell, slightly spotted. (S. Mar.20; 994) *Maggs.* £60

WOOLLEY, Sir Charles Leonard & others
– Ur Excavations. L., 1927-65. Plt. vols. 1-5, 8-10 in 9, text vols. 1, 3, 6 & 8 in 6, together 15 vols. 4to. Ex-liby., cl.-bkd. ptd. bds. (SG. May 3; 391) $850
– Palestine Exploration Fund, 1914: The Wilderness of Zin. 1915. 4to. Orig. cl.-bkd. bds., corners worn. (BBA. Jul.27; 220) *Clark.* £80
– – **Anr. Edn.** [1915]. 4to. Orig. cl.-bkd. bds. (BBA. May 23; 136) *Maggs.* £130

WOOLNOUGH, C.W.
– The Whole Art of Marbling as Applied to Paper Book-Edges. L., 1881. 38 examples of marb. paper, detchd. from bdg., slightly soiled, orig. cl., worn. (S. Apr.30; 241) *Wakeman.* £300

WOOSTER, David
– Alpine Plants. 1872-74. 2 vols. 108 cold. plts., lr. margins of Vol. 1 slightly dampstained., orig. cl. (CSK. Jan.27; 153) £120
– – **Anr. Copy.** 1st. & 2nd. Series: 2 vols. Tall 8vo. 108 col. plts., some light spotting, orig. cl. gt. (TA. May 17; 301) £100
– – **Anr. Copy.** 1st. & 2nd. Series: 2 vols. Tall 8vo. Orig. cl. gt., not unif., rubbed. (TA. Apr.19; 199) £75
– – **Anr. Edn.** 1874. *Vol. 1: 2nd. Edn.* 1st. & 2nd. Series: 2 vols. 4to. Some ll. Vol. 2 slightly loose, orig. cl. (BBA. Sep.29; 110) *Trocchi.* £130
– – **Anr. Copy.** 1st. & 2nd. Series: 2 vols. Orig. cl. (BBA. Oct.27; 235) *Brailey.* £95
– – **Anr. Edn.** 1874. 2 vols. Orig. cl. gt. (P. Mar.15; 223) *Symonds.* £85
– – **Anr. Copy.** 2nd. Series only: 1 vol. 1 cold. plt. detchd., orig. cl. (CSK. Sep.30; 64) £70

WORDSWORTH, Christopher
– Greece: Pictorial, Descriptive, & Historical. 1839. Lge. 8vo. Vig. title, 2 single-p. maps, 25 steel engrs. & ills. to text, some spotting, cont. hf. mor., gt. decor. spine, rubbed. (TA. Jun.21; 22) £80
– – **Anr. Edn.** 1840. Tall 8vo. Frontis., vig. & ptd. titles, 24 steel engrs., 2 maps, minor spotting, cont. red mor., rubbed. (TA. Mar.15; 32) £85
– – **Anr. Edn.** L., 1844. *[2nd. Edn.].* Vig. title, 27 engraved views & maps, mor. gt. (P. Nov.24; 87) *Whiteson.* £85
– – **Anr. Copy.** Tall 8vo. Advts. bnd. in at end, some spotting, orig. cl., backstrip defect., untrimmed. (TA. Apr.19; 21) £54
– – **Anr. Copy.** Cf. gt., worn. (WW. Nov.23; 11) £50
– – **Anr. Edn.** 1853. 4to. Slight foxing, cont. pol. cf., gt.-decor. (SKC. Nov.18; 2022) £60
– – **Anr. Copy.** Tall 8vo. Additional vig. title, map, 24 steel engrs., orig. cl. gt. (TA. Jul.19; 50) £52
– – **Anr. Edn.** 1859. Some spotting, mor. gt. (P. Jul.5; 170) £60
– – **Anr. Edn.** 1882. *New Edn.* Lge. 8vo. Vig. title, single-p. maps, 12 steel engrs. & ills. to text, some minor spotting, mainly marginal, cont. school prize gt.-decor. cf., rubbed on spine. (TA. Jun.21; 23) £65

WORDSWORTH, William
– An Evening Walk. L., 1793. *1st. Edn.* 4to. Errata lf., title, final page & pp. 24-25 stained, some inner blank margin repairs thro.-out, mostly to stitching holes. hf. mor. gt.; Frederic Dannay copy. (CNY. Dec.16; 389) $4,500
– Yarrow Revisited. L., 1835. *1st. Edn.* Advt. ll., 12-p. cat. dtd. Apr.1835, hf.-title, orig. drab bds., Fred A. Berne copy. (SPB. May 16; 387) $125
– The Poetical Works. L., 1832. *New Edn.* 4 vols. 16mo. Former owner's sig. in each vol., orig. cl., worn; pres. set to Lady Townshend Farquhar. (SG. Apr.19; 326) $350
– – **Anr. Edn.** L., 1856. *New Edn.* 7 vols. Red str.-grd. three-qtr. mor., spines gt.; lge. armorial bkplt.

of Sir W.D. Pearson, Visc. Cowdray. (SG. Feb.16; 330) $300
– The Poetical Works ... Ed.:– E. de Selincourt. Oxford, 1940-49. 5 vols. Orig. cl., d.-w.'s. (KH. Nov.9; 522) Aus. $160
– Poetical Works. – Poems Chiefly of Early & Late Years. 1841; 1842. 6 vols.; 1 vol. Together 7 vols. in unif. cl.; Vol. 1 of 1st. work inscr. & sigd. by author. (WW. Nov.23; 58) £280
– The Prelude. Doves Pr., 1915. *(165). (155) on paper.* 4to. Orig. limp vell., upr. cover slightly marked. (S. Nov.22; 305) *Houle.* £130
– – **Anr. Copy.** 4to. Untrimmed, orig. vell., soiled. (TA. Oct.20; 171) £76
– The Sonnets. L., 1838. *1st. Edn.* Cont. cf., upr. jnt. reprd., upr. hinge split; inscr. by author. (S. Mar.20; 995) *Quaritch.* £200
– The Waggoner, a Poem. To which are added, Sonnets. 1819. *1st. Edn.* (*Bound with:*) **– Peter Bell, a Tale in Verse.** 1819. *2nd. Edn.* Together 2 works in 1 vol. Later cl. (slightly stained), spine gt., some staining to front end-papers. (LC. Mar.1; 426) £70
– The White Doe of Rylstone. 1815. 4to. Cont. cf. gt. by S. Tyson, with his ticket; pres. copy, inscr. by author to George Gee & with Gee's bkplt. (BBA. Sep.29; 165) *Maggs.* £940

WORDSWORTH, William & Coleridge, Samuel Taylor
[–] Lyrical Ballads. L., 1798. *1st. Edn. 2nd. Iss.* Sm. 8vo. Advt. lf., few stains, slightly browned, cont. tree cf., rebkd. with parts of orig. backstrip laid down; Washington Allston copy, with sig., Frederic Dannay copy. (CNY. Dec.16; 392) $550
– – **Anr. Edn.** L., 1798; 1800. *1st. Edns. Vol.1. 2nd. Iss., vol 2 1st. Iss.* 2 vols. Errata ll., vol.1 title reprd., slight offsetting, mod. mor. by Zaehasdorf; Fred A. Berne copy. (SPB. May 16; 388) $800
– – **Anr. Edn.** L., 1800. *Vol.1: 2nd. Edn., Vol.2: 1st. Edn., 2nd. Iss.* 2 vols. Sm. 8vo. Leaves 01-2 in Vol. 2 in orig. state with 15 lines omitted from 'Michael', errata lf. uncancelled, cont. tree cf., spines gt., backs worn, sm. loss of leath. to lr. cover of Vol.2, Vol.1 with end-paper detchd., folding cl. box; Frederic Dannay copy. (CNY. Dec.16; 393) $600

WORKER'S CRY
1891. Nos. 1-20 (all publd.). Cont. cl., rubbed. (CSK. Jul.13; 94) £60

WORLD, The ...
Ed.:– Edward Moore 'Adam Fitz-Adam'. L., [1753-56]. 209 issues in 2 vols. Fo. Yearly title-pp., p.799 misbnd., cont. cf. with arms of George Granville Leveson, Duke of Sutherland; armorial bkplts. of Gower Earl Gower & Carlton R. Richmond. (SPB. May 16; 107) $300

WORLD DISPLAYED: or, A Curious Collection of Voyages & Travels, Selected from the Writers of All Nations
Dublin, 1788. 20 vols. in 10, lacks Supp. 21st. vol. (Cook's Last Voyage). Old tree cf. (SG. Sep.22; 311) $140

WORLD OF FASHION
L., 1823. 63 hand-cold. plts., browned, hf. cf., corners. (CR. Jun.6; 321) Lire 380,000
– – **Anr. Edn.** L., 1827; 1832. Vols. 4 & 9, each compl. with monthly nos. Hand-cold. engrs., 1st. vol. in crude hf. cl., 2nd. disbnd., both defect., w.a.f. (SG. Jun.7; 338) $250
– – **Anr. Edn.** 1832-36. 5 vols. 4to. 193 hand-cold. plts., hf. cf. (P. Dec.8; 29) *Demetzy.* £300
– – **Anr. Edn.** L., 1839. Vol. 16. Sm. 4to. Engraved title, frontis., 59 hand-cold. & 9 plain engraved plts., spotted (mostly plain plts.), a few shaved or reprd., slightly stained, hf. cf., upr. cover detchd., defect. (S. Oct.11; 457) *Elliott.* £60
– – **Anr. Copy.** 68 hand-cold. engrs., browning, hf. cf., corners. (CR. Jun.6; 320) Lire 420,000
– – **Anr. Edn.** L., 1839-43. 4 vols. 234 hand-cold. & 44 plain plts., hf. cf. gt. (P. Nov.24; 83) *Walford.* £380
– – **Anr. Edn.** L., 1841. Vol. 18. Sm. 4to. Engraved title, frontis., 60 hand-cold. & 11 plain engraved plts., spotted (mostly plain plts.), slightly stained, hf. cf., worn, covers detchd., spine defect. (S. Oct.11; 524) *Elliott.* £60

– Anr. Edn. 16th August 1941. [Isafjoerdhur, Iceland, 1941]. *(100) numbered.* Tell 8vo. 42 pp. photographic ills., cl.; inscr. & sigd. by Maj.-Gen. H.O. Curtis; from liby. of F.D. Roosevelt, inscr. by him (as President) ' ... For F.D.R. Jr.'. (SG. Mar.15; 84) $2,200

WORLIDGE, John
[–] Systema Agriculturae; The Mystery of Husbandry Discovered. 1675. *2nd. Edn.* 3 pts. in 1 vol. 4to. Browned & spotted, cont. cf., rubbed, very rubbed. (BBA. Jul.27; 32) *Honeyfield.* £220
– Vinetum Britannicum: or a Treatise of Cider ... to which is Added, a Discourse Teaching the Best Way of Improving Bees. 1678. *2nd. Edn.* 2 pts. in 1 vol. Later mott. cf. by Riviere, head of spine & jnts. slightly rubbed. [Wing W3608] (CSK. Jan.27; 38) £320

WORLIDGE, Thomas
– A Select Collection of Drawings from Curious Antique Gems. L., 1768. 2 vols. 4to. Foxed, some offset to tissue guards, later elab. gt.-decor. red mor., inner gt. dentelles. (CBA. Dec.10; 18) $190
– – **Anr. Copy.** 4to. Some foxing, gt.-ruled cf. bds., mod. cl. reback. (CBA. Dec.10; 19) $140

WORNUM, Ralph Nicholson (Ed.)
See— TURNER, Joseph Mallord William

WORRALL, John
– Bibliotheca Legum. L., 1756. 12mo. Slightly soiled, mod. hf. cf. (BBA. Mar.7; 275) *Marlborough.* £90

WORSLEY, Edward
[–] Truth Will Out: or, a Discovery of Some Untruths Smoothly Told by Dr Jeremy Taylor in his Disswasive from Popery. L., 1665. *1st. Edn.* 4to. Fore-e.'s a little brittle, cont. cf., rebkd. [Wing W3618] (BBA. May 3; 150) *Molloy.* £50

WORSLEY, Sir Richard
– The History of the Isle of Wight. 1781. *[1st. Edn.].* 4to. Folding engraved map hand-cold. in outl., vig. on title, 31 (of 32?) engraved plts., later hf. cf., hinges brkn. (SKC. Jan.13; 2397) £140
– – **Anr. Copy.** 4to. Engraved folding map, hand-cold. in outl., 31 plts., some double-p., some browned, slight spotting & offsetting, cont. cf., rebkd. (S. Mar.6; 358) *Coombes.* £110
– – **Anr. Copy.** 4to. Vig. title, folding engraved map hand-cold. in outl., 32 engraved plts., including 12 double-p. views, some light stains, mostly to upr. margins, cont. cf., upr. cover detchd. (TA. Jan.19; 39) £68

WORSNOP, Thomas
– History of the City of Adelaide ... Adelaide, 1878. Clean tear in folding map, fore-e.'s of a couple of ll. frayed, orig. cl. (KH. Nov.9; 743) Aus. $120

WORTHINGTON, Greville
– A Bibliography of the Waverley Novels. 1931. *(500).* Some ll. slightly spotted, orig. vell.-bkd. bds. (BBA. Nov.10; 153) *Wise.* £70

WORTHINGTON, J.
– City of Manchester, New Town Hall. [1868]. Fo. Cl. gt.; inscr. by author. (P. Mar.15; 24) £95

WORTLEY, Lady Emmeline Stuart
– Travels in the United States, etc., During 1849 & 1850. L., 1851. *1st. Edn.* 3 vols. Orig. cl.; the Rt. Hon. Visc. Eccles copy. [Sabin 93221] (CNY. Nov.18; 290) $110

WOTTON, Edward
– De Differentiis Animalium Libri Decem. Paris, 1552. *1st. Edn.* Fo. Lacks final blank, some browning, a few wornholes at end, 17th. C. Spanish red mor. gt., arms on upr. cover of Felipe Ramirez de Guzman, Duke of Medina de las Torres, impaled with those of his 2nd. wife Anna Caraffa, lr. cover slightly stained, spine slightly wormed; sig. of Sir William Godolphin on title, the Earl of Jersey (Osterley Park) copy. (S. Nov.28; 99) *Antik Junk.* £960

WOTTON, Sir Henry
– Reliquiae Wottonianae. Or, a Collection of Lives, Letters, Poems. 1651. *1st. Edn.* 12mo. Margin of

WOTTON, Sir Henry -Contd.

1 port. shaved, 1 corner reprd., cf. [Wing W3648] (BBA. Jun.14; 50)   *Stuart Bennett.* £80

WOTTON, William
- **Reflections upon Ancient & Modern Learning, with a Dissertation by Dr. Bentley on the Epistles of Phalaris** ... **& Aesop's Fables.** L., 1697. *2nd. Edn.* 2 pts. in 1 vol. Cont. panel. cf., cover detchd. [Wing W 3659] (SG. Feb.9; 374) $250

WOUDE, C. van der
- **Kronyk van Alkmaar. Met zyn Dorpen.** Ill.:– A. Rademaker. Amst. & Alkmaar, 1743. *2nd. Edn.* 4to. Liby. stp. erased from title, cont. vell. (VS. Dec.9; 1302)   Fls. 1,300

WOUVERMANS, Philippe
- **Oeuvres de Philippe Wouvermans, Hollandais, gravées d'après ses Meilleurs Tableaux qui sont dans les plus Beaux Cabinets de Paris et ailleurs.** Ill.:– C. de Vischer, de Lajoue & Wouvermans. Paris, 1737. Ob. fo. 89 plts. (of 100), ink stain in margin of 1 plt., 19th. C. hf. mor., corners. (HD. Jul.2; 36)   Frs. 41.000

WOYT, J.J.
- **Gazophylaicum Medico-Physicum.** Ed.:– J.E. Hebenstreit. Ill.:– G.P. Trautner. Leipzig, 1767. 4to. Title with MS. note, cont. vell., lacks upr. end-paper. (HK. Nov.8; 791)   DM 600

WREE, Olivier
See— VREDIUS or WREE, Olivarius or Olivier

WREECH, C.F. von
- **Warhaffte und Umstandliche Histoire von denen Schwedischen Gefangegen in Russland und Siberien.** Sorau [Prussia], 1725. Slight discoloration thro.-out, fore-margin of 2H7 trimmed, cont. cf. (S. Dec.1; 319)   *Anderson.* £200

WREN, Sir Christopher
- **Sir Christopher Wren, His Life & Work.** Bicentenary Memorial Volume published under the auspices of the Royal Institute of British Architects. 1923. 4to. Orig. cl. gt., d.-w. slightly frayed & soiled. (TA. May 17; 428)   £50

WREN SOCIETY
- **[Publications].** Oxford, 1924-40. Vols. 1-17. Lge. 4to. Orig. qtr. cl., slightly defect. (SG. Jan.26; 302) $425
- **– Anr. Edn.** Oxford, 1924-43. Vols. I-XX (all publd.). 4to. Holland-bkd. bds. (S. Dec.13; 230)   *Leicester.* £200
- **– Anr. Edn.** L., 1931-43. Vols. 8-20. 4to. Orig. cl.-bkd. bds. (BBA. Apr.5; 188)   *Weinreb.* £80
- **– Anr. Edn.** Oxford, 1933-43. Vols. 10-20. 4to. Orig. cl.-bkd. bds., soiled. (BBA. Nov.10; 233)   *Howes.* £80

WRIGHT, Edgar W.
- **Lewis & Dryden's Marine History of the Pacific Northwest.** Portland, 1895. 4to. Maroon mor gt., spine worn, hinges reprd. (LH. Jan.15; 424) $100

WRIGHT, Edward
- **Certain Errors in Navigation detected & corrected** ... L., 1657. *3rd. Edn.* 3 pts. in 1 vol. Sm. 4to. Advt. lf. 2Y4, lacks the 2 folding maps, slight dampstaining, a few ll. shaved, mod. hf. mor. [Wing W 3689] (S. Dec.20; 768)   *Turner.* £130

WRIGHT, F. von
See— M., W. & Wright, F. von

WRIGHT, Frank Lloyd
- **Genius & the Mobocracy.** Ill.:– after L.H. Sullivan. N.Y., [1949]. *1st. Edn.* 4to. 39 monochrome plts., cl., spine darkened & with sm. tears at head, d.-w. chipped; sigd. by author. (SG. Oct.13; 366) $250

See— WENDINGEN

WRIGHT, Rev. George Newnham
- **China.** Ill.:– Thomas Allom. L., 1843. 4 vols. 128 plts. (including engraved titles?), orig. mor. gt. (LA. Mar.22; 171)   £190
- **– Anr. Copy.** 4 vols. 4to. Engraved titles, 123 (of 124) plts., 3 cut down & mntd., stained, spotted,

cont. hf. roan, worn, 1 bdg. detchd., w.a.f. (S. Mar.6; 54)   *Kentish.* £150
- **– Anr. Edn.** L., [1843]. 4 vols. in 2. 4to. 4 engraved titles, 124 plts., hf. cf. gt. (P. Sep.8; 395)
     Map House. £230
- **– Anr. Copy.** 4 vols. 4to. 4 engraved titles, 124 views, spotting, cont. hf. mor. gt. (P. Oct.20; 223a)
     Waterloo. £170
- **– Anr. Copy.** 4 vols. in 2. 4to. Extra engraved titles, 124 plts., 2nd. vol. spotted, cont. mor. & hf. cf. (S. Mar.6; 53)   *Waterloo.* £170
- **– Anr. Copy.** 3 vols. only (of 4). 4to. 2 engraved titles, 104 plts., some stain, hf. cf. gt., as a collection of plts., w.a.f. (P. Sep.29; 188)   *Sweet.* £150
- **– Anr. Edn.** Ill.:– after Thomas Allom. L., ca. 1845. 4 vols. in 2, as iss. 4to. 168 plts., elab. gt.-pict. stpd. mor., spines gt., jnts. & spine ends worn. (SG. Mar.29; 298) $320
- **– Anr. Edn.** N.d. 4 vols. in 2. 4to. 4 engraved titles, 124 engraved views, some foxed, hf. cf. gt. (P. Jul.5; 246)   £270
- **– Anr. Copy.** 4 vols. 4to. 4 engraved vig. titles, 122 (of 124) plts., hf. mor. gt. (P. Mar.15; 202)
     Peterson. £170
- **The Chinese Empire.** Ill.:– after Thomas Allom. L., ca. 1860. 2 vols. in 1, with the supplementary 'Overland Route to China' & 'The History of China'. 4to. 4 additional engraved titles with vigs., 3 folding outl.-cold. engraved maps, 158 engraved views & costume plts., sm. margin stains affecting 1 or 2 plts., cont. hf. cf. (S. Dec.1; 378)
     Harris. £320
- **– Anr. Copy.** 2 vols. Lge. 4to. Additional engraved titles, 3 folding maps, over 150 steel engrs., gt.-pict. cl., leath. spines & tips, worn. (SG. Sep.22; 95)
     $375
- **– Anr. Copy.** 2 vols. 4to. 3 frontis., 3 additional pict. titles, 2 double-p. outl. cold. maps, 142 plts., hf. leath. (SG. Sep.22; 312) $350
- **France Illustrated.** Ill.:– after T. Allom. L., [1845-47]. 4 vols. in 3. 4to. 4 engraved titles, 128 (of 140) engraved plts., some text misbnd., mor. gt., as a collection of plts., w.a.f. (P. Sep.29; 187)
     Peterson. £120
- **– Anr. Copy.** 3 vols. only (of 4). 4to. Additional engraved titles with vigs., frontis.'s, 90 steel-engraved plts., some slight spotting, cont. decor. cl. gt., spines slightly chipped. (S. Nov.1; 89)
     Shapiro. £60
- **– Anr. Edn.** Ill.:– after T. Allom. L. & Paris, ca. 1850. 3 vols. 4to. 3 engraved titles, 93 steel engraved plts., some foxing, cont. hf. leath. (HK. May 15; 822)   DM 650
- **– Anr. Edn.** N.d. 4 vols. in 2. 4to. 4 engraved titles, 143 plts., few stains in margins of Vols. 3 & 4, mor. gt., slightly rubbed. (P. Apr.12; 220)
     Shapiro. £100
- **Ireland Illustrated.** L., 1829. 4to. Engraved title, 44 views on 22 plts., lacks some letter press, hf. cf. (GM. Dec.7; 466)   £55
- **– Anr. Edn.** Ill.:– after Petrie, Bartlett, & others. L., 1831. 4to. Additional engraved title, 80 views on 40 plts., orig. str.-grd. mor. gt., w.a.f. (GM. Oct.5; 261)   £110
- **– Anr. Edn.** 1833. 4to. Engraved vig. title, 80 views on 40 sheets, some spotting, liby. stp. on plt. versos, cl., rebkd. (P. Jun.7; 221)   £80
- **The Rhine, Italy & Greece.** Ill.:– Col. Cockburn, Maj. Irton, Bartlett, Leitch & Wolfensberger. L. & Paris, [1841]. 2 vols. in 1. 4to. 73 steel engrs., surface scratch on 1 plt., margin soiling on anr., hf. mor. gt., loose. (SG. Sep.22; 313) $475
- **– Anr. Edn.** N.d. 2 vols. in 1. 4to. 2 engraved titles, 71 plts., 1 engraved title with stp., hf. cf. (P. Jul.5; 271)   £180
- **– Anr. Copy.** 2 vols. 4to. 2 engraved titles, 2 frontis., 69 plts., some spotting, cl. (WW. Nov.23; 17)   £150
- **The Shores & Islands of the Mediterranean.** Ill.:– Sir Grenville Temple, W.L. Leitch, Maj. Irton, & Lieut. Allen. L., 1840. *1st. Edn.* 4to. Additional engraved title, folding map, 63 steel-engraved plts., cont. gt.-ornamental red mor., cover loose; Francis Gray Smart armorial bkplt. (SG. Sep.22; 314)
     $110
- **– Anr. Edn.** Ca. 1840. 4to. Folding map, 64 steel engrs., some minor spotting, cont. str.-grd. crimson mor. gt., a little worn at head of spine, inner hinges strengthened. (TA. Jun.21; 14)   £105

- **– Anr. Copy.** 4to. Engraved title foxed, hf. mor. gt. (P. Sep.29; 307)   *Angle.* £85
- **– Anr. Edn.** Ca. 1842. 4to. Engraved title, 58 engraved plts., hf. cf. gt. (P. Sep.8; 31)
     Tzakas. £120
- **– Anr. Edn.** N.d. 4to. Steel-engraved additional title & 63 plts., folding map, cont. hf. cf. (CSK. Jul.6; 2)   £140
- **– Anr. Copy.** 4to. Vig. title, folding map, 63 engraved plts., cont. mor. gt., slightly rubbed. (P. Mar.15; 4)   *MacDonald.* £120
- **– Anr. Copy.** No bdg. (DS. Oct.28; 2225)
     Pts. 24,000

WRIGHT, George Newnham & Buckingham, L.F.A.
- **Belgium, the Rhine, Italy, Greece & the Shores & Islands of the Mediterranean.** Ill.:– after T. Allom & others. L., ca. 1851. 2 vols. in 1. 4to. Additional engraved titles & 152 engraved views, cont. hf. cf., rubbed. (C. Jun.27; 79)   *Martinos.* £220
- **– Anr. Edn.** L., n.d. 2 vols. 4to. Engraved title in Vol. 1 & 151 plts. only, lacks title & frontis. in Vol. 2, folding map, some ll. spotted, a few loose, cont. mor., gt. rubbed. (BBA. May 3; 326)
     Dimakarakos. £240

WRIGHT, Rev. George Newnham [& Timperley, Charles H.]
- **The Gallery of Engravings.** N.d. 3 vols. 4to. Hf. cf., spines gt., slightly scuffed. (LC. Mar.1; 104)
     £55

WRIGHT, James
- **The History & Antiquities of the County of Rutland.** L., 1684. *[1st. Edn.].* Fo. Title with sm. hole & old sigs., 4 text ll. with tears in lr. margin, some dampstains, cont. cf., recornered, rebkd. preserving orig. spine. [Wing W3696] (C. Mar.14; 100)
     Chesters. £130
- **– Anr. Copy.** Fo. Browned & soiled, sm. rust-hole in a few ll., cont. sheep, rebkd., slightly worn. (BBA. Dec.15; 108)   *Schein.* £80

WRIGHT, John
- **The Fruit Grower's Guide.** Ca. 1880. 6 divisions. 4to. Orig. cl. gt. (TA. Sep.15; 487)   £165
- **– Anr. Edn.** L., [1891-94]. 6 vols. 4to. 3 extra cold. pict. titles, 43 cold. plts., those in vol. 4 loose & lacks upr. end-lf., ills., orig. cl. (S. Apr.10; 601)
     Perham. £280
- **– Anr. Copy.** 4to. Orig. decor. cl. (SKC. Nov.18; 1996)   £160
- **– Anr. Copy.** 3 vols. in 6. 4to. 3 cold. titles, 43 cold. plts., some soiling & spotting, pt. 5 lacks front free end-paper, orig. cl., worn, 1 inside hinge brkn. (S. Dec.13; 306)   *Shapero.* £110
- **– Anr. Edn.** L., n.d. 3 vols. 4to. 3 col. titles, 43 col. plts., orig. cl. gt. (P. Nov.24; 266)
     Whiteson. £260
- **– Anr. Copy.** 3 vols. 4to. Cont. hf. mor., slightly rubbed. (BBA. May 23; 291)   *Gilbert's.* £240
- **– Anr. Copy.** 3 pts. only. 4to. Light spotting, orig. cl., lightly soiled & rubbed. (CSK. Jan.13; 75)
     £70

WRIGHT, John Martin Frederick
- **A Commentary on Newton's Principia. With a Supplementary Volume.** L., 1833. 2 vols. Lge. 8vo. Last gathering of 1st. vol. misbnd. & with additional lf. headed 'Problems', cont. pol. cf. prize bdg. by Carrs & Co., Glasgow, rebkd.; Lord Kelvin's copy, presented to him by his father in 1838, Glasgow University prize label in each vol., Stanitz coll. (SPB. Apr.25; 326) $275

WRIGHT, Lewis
- **The Illustrated Book of Poultry.** L., 1885. 4to. 50 hand-cold. plts., hf. mor. gt. (P. May 17; 48)
     Perham. £240
- **– Anr. Edn.** 1890. 4to. Col. frontis., 4 uncold. plts., 49 col. plts., orig. cl. gt., hinges worn. (P. Jul.5; 284)   £360
- **– Anr. Edn.** Ill.:– after J. Ludlow. N.d. 4to. 50 chromolitho. plts., some spotting, orig. cl. (CSK. Apr.27; 69)   £150

WRIGHT, Magnus, W. & F. von
- **Svenska Faglar after Naturen och pa sten Ritade.** Text:– E. Lönnberg. Stockholm, [1917-]1929. *2nd.*

Edn. 3 vols. Fo. Orig. hf. leath gt. (R. Oct.12; 1937)
DM 2,000
– – **Anr. Edn.** Text:– Einar Lonnberg. Stockholm, 1924-29. 3 vols. Fo. 364 cold. litho. plts., hf. pol. cf. gt., marb. bds., marb. end-papers. (SKC. May 4; 1882) £680
– – **Anr. Copy.** 3 vols. Fo. Orig. cf. gt., slightly rubbed. (D. Nov.23; 738) DM 2,300
– – **Anr. Copy.** 105 pts. Fo. 54 orig. wraps., some defect. (D. Nov.23; 739) DM 1,000
– – **Anr. Edn.** Text:– E. Lönnberg. Stockholm, 1927-29. *2nd. Edn.* 3 vols. Fo. Orig. linen, gold-tooled decor., minimal rubbing. (HT. May 8; 619)
DM 2,300

WRIGHT, Michael
– **An Account of His Excellence Roger Earl of Castlemaine Embassy.** L., 1688. Fo. Frontis., port., 14 (of 16) engraved plts., including 1 lge. folding plt. loose, qtr. roan, defect. (P. May 17; 297)
Lyon. £55

WRIGHT, Thomas, Antiquary
– **The History & Antiquities of London.** Ill.:– T. Allom. L., 1839-37. 5 vols. Some discoloration, hf. vell., lacks several labels. (S. Dec.13; 239)
Haddon. £55
– **The History & Topography of the County of Essex, compr. its Ancient & Modern History.** Ill.:– after W. Bartlett. L., 1836. 2 vols. Lge. 4to. Wide margin, 2 engraved titles with vigs., 1 engraved map, 98 steel engraved plts., minimal foxing, cont. linen, blind-tooled, 1 spine slightly defect. at head, corners bumped. (HK. May 15; 852) DM 520
– **The History of Ireland.** L., n.d. 3 vols. Royal 8vo. Mor. gt. (GM. Dec.7; 435) £65
– **The Picturesque Beauties of Great Britain: Essex.** 1834. 4to. Engraved title, folding map, 96 views on 49 plts. only, all on India paper, some ll. spotted, orig. cl., recased, worn. (BBA. Feb.9; 354)
Bowers. £240
– – **Anr. Copy.** 4to. Folding map, 96 engrs. on 49 sheets, hf. cf., worn, as a coll. of plts., w.a.f. (P. Sep.29; 217) *Clark.* £120
– **The Picturesque Beauties of Great Britain: Kent.** G. Virtue, 1828. Engraved vig. title, folding map, 127 engrs. on 64 sheets, some spotting. (*Bound with:*) GASTINEAU, Henri – **Wales Illustrated.** 1830. Engraved vig. title, 90 engrs. on 45 sheets, & 4 ports., spotting. Together 2 works in 1 vol. 4to. Cl., as a collection of plts., w.a.f. (P. Sep.29; 212)
Angle. £160
– – **Anr. Edn.** G. Virtue, n.d. 4to. Hf. cf. (P. Sep.29; 104) *Angle.* £120

WRIGHT, Thomas, Antiquary & Jones, Rev. Harry Longueville
– **Memorials of Cambridge.** Ill.:– John Le Keux. 1841-42. 2 vols. Some foxing, hf. cf. gt. (P. Jul.26; 212h) £160
– – **Anr. Edn.** Ill.:– John Le Keux. 1847. 2 vols. Orig. cl., worn. (P. Jul.5; 238) £150

WRIGHT, Thomas, of Durham
– **Louthiana, or, An Introduction to the Antiquities of Ireland.** L., 1748. 4to. Engraved frontis., 66 plts., mor. (GM. Dec.7; 311) £170
– – **Anr. Edn.** L., 1758. 4to. Engraved frontis., 66 plts., cf. (GM. Dec.7; 310) £90
– **The Universe & the Stars: an Original Theory on the Visible Creation.** Ed.:– C.S. Rafinesque. Phila., 1837. *1st. Amer. Edn.* Hf.-title, crude hf. buckram, ex-liby. (SG. Oct.6; 304) $150

WRIGHT, Thomas, Theatrical Machinist
– **The Female Vertuoso's. A Comedy.** 1693. *1st. Edn.* 4to. A few lr. margins shaved, mor. by Sangorski & Sutcliffe. [Wing W3711] (BBA. Jan.19; 140) *Maggs.* £80

WRIGHTE, William
– **Grotesque Architecture.** L., 1767. *1st. Edn.* Engraved frontis., 28 plts., outer margin of frontis. creased, MS. list on verso, owners inscrs., hf. cf. (C. Dec.9; 172) *Rota.* £300
– – **Anr. Edn.** L., 1790. Last advt. lf. (*Bound with:*)
– **Ideas for Rustic Furniture proper for Garden Seats, Summer Houses, Hermitages, Cottages, & c.** N.d. Together 2 works in 1 vol. Cont. spr. cf., lr. cover holed. (BBA. Jun.14; 161)
Sims, Reed & Fogg. £300

WRISBERG, Henricus Augustus
– **Observationum de Animalculis Infusoriis Satura.** Goettingen, 1765. *1st. Edn.* Cont. wraps.; Dr. Walter Pagel copy. (S. Feb.7; 383) *Phelps.* £90

WRONSKI, Hoëné de
– **Introduction à la Philosophie des Mathématiques, et Technie de l'Algorithmie.** 1811. *Orig. Edn.* 4to. Cont. str.-grd. mor. gt., spine decor., watered silk doubls. (HD. Apr.13; 77) Frs. 3,800

WROTH, Lawrence C.
– **A History of the Printed Book.** N.Y., Ltd. Edns. Cl., 1938. *1st. Edn. (1800).* 4to. Orig. buckram. (SG. Jan.5; 321) $175

WROTH, Lawrence C. (Contrib.)
See– MINER, Dorothy
See– ROSENBACH, Dr. Abraham Simon Wolf

WUERTH, Louis A.
– **Catalogue of the Etchings of Joseph Pennell.** Intro.:– Elizabeth R. Pennell. Boston, 1928. *1st. Edn. (450) numbered on L.P., with proof etching from orig. 1921 plt.* Tall 4to. Over 800 reproductions, ex-liby., cf.-bkd. buckram. (SG. May 3; 275) $350
– **Catalogue of the Lithographs of Joseph Pennell.** Intro.:– Elizabeth R. Pennell. Boston, 1931. *(425) numbered.* Tall 4to. 621 reproductions, ex-liby., cf.-bkd. buckram, boxed. (SG. May 3; 276) $375

WUERTZ, F.
See– VALENTINUS, P.P. — WIRTZ or WUERTZ, F.

WULFF, Jeune
– **Ruines de Paris, 1871.** [Paris], ca. 1872. Ob. 4to. 20 mntd. albumen photographs, ptd. list of plts., some light foxing to plts., gt.-lettered tooled cl., rubbed. (SG. Nov.10; 169) $150

WULFF, O. & Volbach, W.F.
– **Spätantike und Koptische Stoffe aus Agyptischen Grabfunden.** Berlin, [1926]. Lge. 4to. Orig. linen, slightly holed. (H. Nov.23; 209) DM 550

WUNDERBAR, R.J.
– **Biblisch-Talmudische Medicin oder Pragmatische Darstellung der Arzneikunde der alten Israeliten.** Riga, 1850-60. 8 pts. in 2 vols. bnd. in 1. Tall 8vo. Text in German, numerous scriptural captions in Hebrew, cont. leath.-bkd. bds., extremities worn. (SG. Feb.2; 95) $120

WURFEL, A.
– **Historische Nachrichten von der Juden-Gemeinde welche ehehin in der Reichstadt Nürnberg angericht gewesen.** Nuremb., 1755. 4to. 46 incunable supps., partly in Hebrew, light lf. stpd., light browning, cont. bds., spotted & bumped, 1 end-paper with old MS. notes. (H. Nov.23; 447) DM 920

WYATT, A.J. (Trans.)
See– BEOWULF

WYATT, Claude
See– SHARPE, Richard Bowdler & Wyatt, Claude

WYATT, Sir Matthew Digby
– **The Industrial Arts of the Nineteenth Century.** L., 1851-53. 2 vols. Fo. Chromolitho. titles, 158 chromolitho. plts., some minor spotting, cont. hf. mor., spines gt. (C. Nov.9; 123) *Crisford.* £300
– **Metal-Work & its Artistic Design.** Ill.:– F. Bedford. L., 1852. *1st. Edn.* Tall fo. 50 chromolitho. plts., hf. mor., brkn., lacks most of spine, ex-liby. (SG. Oct.13; 367) $110
– **Notices of Sculpture in Ivory; & a Catalogue of Specimens of Ancient Ivory-carvings by Edmund Oldfield.** Ill.:– J.A. Spencer. L., 1856. 4to. Liby. buckram. (SG. Aug.25; 211) $120

WYATT, Sir Thomas
– **Penitential Psalms.** Corvinus Pr., Mar. 1945. *(30) numbered.* 4to. Qtr. vell. & cl., case. (HBC. May 17; 169) £75

WYBARNE, Joseph
– **The New Age of Old Names.** 1609. Sm. 4to. Hf. cf. gt. (P. Dec.8; 87) *Lawson.* £60

WYCHERLEY, William
– **Love in A Wood, or, St. James's Park. A Comedy.** 1694. 4to. 2 lr. margins defect., just affecting text, mod. crimson mor. [Wing W3748] (BBA. Jan.19; 142) *Maggs.* £50
– **Miscellany Poems.** L., 1704. *1st. Edn. 1st. Iss.* Fo. L.P., mezzotint port., errata lf., inner margin of port. torn, few corners stained, cont. cf., gt. panel., rebkd., corners reprd.; lge. armorial bkplt. of Earl of Derby, 1702. (SPB. May 16; 162) $500

WYETH, Andrew
See– MERYMAN, Richard

WYLD, James
– **A General Atlas.** Edinb., n.d. 4to. Engraved title, 41 maps, hand-cold. in outl., 2 tables, cont. hf. cf. (CSK. Feb.10; 12) £140
– **A New General Atlas.** [1842]. Fo. 40 engraved maps, hand-cold. in outl., cont. cl., worn, upr. cover detchd. (CSK. Oct.7; 23) £350
– – **Anr. Edn.** Ca. 1845. Lge. fo. 59 (of 60) engraved maps, hand-cold. in outl., 3 maps with crude additional col., 5 other engraved plts., some soiled in margins, cont. hf. leath., worn, hinges brkn. (SKC. Nov.18; 2065) £270

WYLD, Samuel
– **The Practical Surveyor.** N.d. *2nd. Edn.* Cont. cf. (CSK. Dec.16; 63) £50

WYLD, W. & Lessore, E.
– **Album Venitien Composé de Douze Vues.** Venise, 1837. Ob. fo. 12 cold. lithos. mntd., slight margin spotting, hf. cl., engraved pict. bds., worn. (SKC. Jan.13; 2399) £190

WYLIE, Elinor
– **Nets to Catch the Wind.** N.Y., 1921. *1st. Edn. 1st. Printing.* 12mo. Orig. cl.-bkd. bds., d.-w. slightly soiled, cl. s.-c.; inscr. by Amy Lowell in 1922 to [Alice?] Farwell Brown, Frederic Dannay copy. (CNY. Dec.16; 396) $350

WYNTOUN, Andrew
– **De Orygynale Cronykil of Scotland** ... Notes, etc.:– David Macpherson. 1795. *1st. Edn.* 2 vols. 4to. L.P., hf.-titles, lf. of corrections, cont. tree cf., spines gt.-decor.; Sir Ivar Colquhoun, of Luss copy. (CE. Mar.22; 334) £500

WYSZYNSKI, Stefan
– **Kreuzweg. Meditationen von Stefan Kardinal Wyszynski.** Ill.:– Hap Grieshaber. Berlin, [1967]. *(3000) numbered.* Fo. Orig. linen, orig. pict. wraps. (D. Nov.24; 3046) DM 580

WYTFLIET, Cornelis
– **Histoire Universelle des Indes Orientales et Occidentales.** Douai, François Fabri, 1605. *1st. Edn. in Fr.* 2 pts. in 1 vol. Sm. fo. Engraved title with pasted on slips, 23 maps on 21 mapsheets, most double-p. or folding, including the 4 smaller maps in Magini's supp., pen & colouring marks on title, 1 or 2 plts. trimmed to plt.-mark, unif. browning thro.-out, a few inkstains affecting text, some creasing, 18th. C. mott. cf., spine gt., slightly worn. [Sabin 105699] (S. Dec.1; 181) *Burgess.* £3,300

WYTSMAN, Philogene
– **Genera Avium.** Brussels, 1905-14. 26 orig. pts. 4to. 43 cold. plts., some slightly soiled, orig. wraps. (BBA. Nov.30; 127) *Walford.* £200
– – **Anr. Copy.** 26 orig. pts. Fo. (R. Apr.4; 1812)
DM 900

XENOPHON
– **La Cyropaedie, ou l'Histoire de Cyrus.** Trans.:– Charpentier. La Haye, 1732. 2 vols. in 1. 12mo. Cont. red mor., arms of Grand Dauphin, spine decor. (HD. Mar.29; 103) Frs. 20,000
– **Las Obras de.** Trans.:– Diego Gracián. [Salamca]. 1552. Fo. Slightly browned, vell. (DS. Oct.28; 2154)
Pts. 70,000
– **Opera, partim Graecorum Exemplarium Collatione recognita, partim a viris Doctiss. iam Primum Latinitate Donata.** Ill.:– Hans Holbein. Basel, 1534. Fo. 1 woodcut border & many woodcut initials, title reprd., 1st. ll. stained & with margin slits, 2 ll. bkd., some sm. wormholes, old hf. vell. (BR. Apr.12; 897) DM 600
– **Opera quae quidè Graecè extant ... nunc Primùm**

XENOPHON -Contd.

à Seb. Castalione ... repurgata ... Basel, [1545-50]. 2 vols. Some spotting, vol. 2 with some MS. marginalia, 18th. C. red leath., gt. spine, cover decor., inner & outer dentelle, slightly worn, lightly spotted, some scratches. (HK. May 15; 260a)
DM 900

XERES, Francisco de
- **Conquista del Peru: Verdadera Relación de la Conquista del Peru & Provincia del Cuzco llamada la Nueva Castilla. Conquistada por Francisco Pizarro** ... Salamanca, 1547. Fo. Lacks final blank, some stains, 2 margins reprd., later vell. (SG. Oct.20; 383) $1,200
- **Libro Primo de la Conquista del Peru.** Venecia, 1535. *2nd. Edn.* 4to. Bds. [Sabin 10572]. (DS. Dec.16; 2388) *Pts. 40,000*

XIMENES, Leonardo
- **Piano di Operazioni Idrauliche per ottenere la Massima Depressione del Lago di Sesto o sia di Bientina.** Lucca, 1782. 4to. Cont. vell. (SI. Dec.15; 183) *Lire 400,000*

YA'AKOV SASPORTAS
See— AHARON, of Pesaro — YA'AKOV SASPORTAS

YA'AKOV YOSEF, of Polonnoye
- **Sefer ben Porat Yosef.** Korets, 1781. *1st. Edn.* Sm. fo. Title & last lf. remargined, several ll. slightly torn at lr. corner, 2 with minimal loss, some mild browning, later cl.-bkd. bds., rubbed. (SG. Feb.2; 310) $900

YA'ARI, Avraham
- **Bibliografya shel Haggadot Pesah.** Jerusalem, 1961. Fo. Facs. of 1st. ptd. Haggada laid in, linen, d.-w. (SG. Feb.2; 29) $110
- **Diglei ha-Madpisim ha-Ivriyim.** Jerusalem, 1943. *(300).* Lge. 8vo. Text in Hebrew, Engl. title & intro. at end, cl. (SG. Feb.2; 30) $300

YAKOV BEN ASHER
- **Arbah Turim.** [Soncino], Shlomo ben Moshe Soncino, [1490]. 4 vols. in 1. Fo. Uncensored, 1st. lf. mntd., 1st. 7 ll. & last lf. reprd. with some loss of text, 1 lf. with margin repairs affecting sm. parts of border, some staining & browning to some ll., cf.-bkd. bds. [Steinschneider 5500, 2] (SPB. Jun.26; 13) $75,000
- **Anr. Edn.** Ill.:– Holbein. Augsburg, 1540. *7th. Edn.* 4 pts. in 1 vol. Fo. Lacks 2 ll., 1st. pt. heavily censored with loss of some text, outer margins of 1st. 13 & last 3 ll. reprd. with loss of text, some worming, stained & creased, browned, hf. leath. (S. Oct.25; 412) *Halprin.* £1,300
- **Anr. Edn.** Riva di Trento, 1560. *9th. Edn.* 4 pts. in 1 vol. Fo. On blue paper, lr. margins of 1st. 30 ll. reprd. with loss of some words, worming affecting some letters, some staining, trimmed, hf. leath., marb. paper bds. (S. Oct.25; 414) *Landau.* £1,600
- **Peirush Ha'Torah.** Constantinople, 1514. *1st. Edn.* 4to. Misbnd., wormed thro.-out & reprd. affecting some letters, foxed, trimmed, mod. blind-tooled leath. (S. Oct.25; 419) *Halprin.* £2,300
- **Tur Choshen Mishpat.** Commentary:– Joseph Karo. Sabbioneta, 1559. *9th. Edn. [1st. Edn. of Karo's commentary].* Fo. Owners' sig. & stps. on title, trimmed with loss of parts of some letters, staining, discold., mod. blind- & gt.-tooled mor. (S. Oct.25; 416) *Thomas.* £700
- **Tur Orach Chaim.** Commentary:– Joseph Caro. Venice, 1563. Fo. Some foxing, slight staining, bds., rebkd., worn, loose at hinges. (SPB. Feb.1; 87) $450
See— YISRAEL ISSERLEIN — YAKOV BEN ASHER

YAKOV BEN MOSHE HA'LEVI MOLIN [Maharil]
- **Maharil.** Ed.:– Shlomo, of St. Goar. Sabionetta, 1556. *1st. Edn.* 2 ll. in facs., owners' sigs. on title, edges frayed, some staining, discold., blind-tooled leath., slightly worn. (S. Oct.25; 421) *Ludmir.* £420

YAKOV BEN SHLOMO MATALON
- **She'eirit Yakov.** Saloniki, 1597. Pt. 1 only. Fo. Owners' sigs. on title, short tears in margins, soiled,

1 lf. defect. & reprd. with loss of most text, staining, trimmed, blind-tooled leath., slightly worn. (S. Oct.25; 422) *Davidson.* £300

YACOV HEILPERUN
- **Nachlat Yacov.** Padua, 1622. *1st. Edn. (With:)* JOSEF BEN MOSHE, of Kremnitz – Biur al Sefer Mitzvat Gadol (Semag). Venice, 1605. *Only Edn.* Together 2 vols. 4to. Slight staining & soiling, bds., rubbed. (SPB. Feb.1; 47) $1,200

YAKOV RABEINU TAM, attributed to
See— ZERACHIA, of Greece

YARAMENKO, A.V.
- **Nicholai Konstantinovich Roerich: His Life & Creations during the past Forty Years 1889-1929.** N.Y., 1931. *(500) numbered & sigd.* Lge. 4to. Port. frontis., 119 tipped-in plts., 2-tone pict. cl. (SG. Aug.25; 311) $125

YARRELL, William
- **A History of British Birds.** L., 1843. *1st. Edn.* 3 vols. Hf. mor., gt.-tooled spine. (GM. Dec.7; 595) £140
- **Anr. Edn.** 1856. *3rd. Edn.* 3 vols. Mor. gt. *(With:) -* **A History of British Fishes.** 1859. *3rd. Edn.* 2 vols. Unif. mor. gt. (CSK. Aug.19; 24) £100
- **A History of British Fishes.** Ed. (Supp.):– Sir John Richardson, 1836, Supp. 1860. *1st. Edn.* 2 vols. plus Supp. Sm. 4to. Cont. hf. cf., gt.-decor. spines, by Bumpus. rubbed. (TA. Jun.21; 241) £52

YASHIRO, Yukio
- **Sandro Botticelli.** L., 1925. *Ltd. Edn.* 3 vols. Lge. 4to. Orig. buckram, slightly soiled. (BBA. Apr.5; 95) *Sachs.* £120
- **Anr. Edn.** L. & Boston, Medici Society, 1925. 3 vols. Sm. fo. Mntd. cold. frontis., 291 plts., lettered tissue-gds., ex-liby., buckram. (SG. May 3; 57) $250

YAZDANI, G.
- **Ajanta: the Colour & Monochrome Reproductions of the Ajanta Frescoes based on Photography.** Intro.:– Laurence Binyon. L., 1930-55. 4 text vols. & 4 plts. vols. Atlas fo. & fo. 245 plts. (68 cold.), each liby.-stpd. on blank verso, text vols. buckram, plts. loose in matching buckram folders, linen ties. (SG. May 3; 393) $750
- **Bidar its History & Monuments.** 1947. 4to. Orig. cl. (BBA. Sep.8; 204) *Randall.* £65

YEATS, Jack Butler
- **Life in the West of Ireland.** Dublin, 1915. *New Edn.* 4to. Orig. decor. cl. (GM. Dec.7; 284) £120

YEATS, William Butler
- **The King's Threshold.** N.Y., ptd. for private circulation [for John Quinn], 1904. *1st. Edn. (100) numbered on Italian H.M.P., sigd.* Hf.-title, orig. bds., partly unc., s.-c. (S. Dec.8; 280) *Haims.* £350
- **Mosada. A Dramatic Poem.** Dublin, 1886. *1st. Edn.* Orig. ptd. wraps., sewn as iss., a few spots on upr. cover, maroon hf. mor. s.-c.; pres. copy from author to Prof. Edward Dowden, Robert P. Esty & Frederic Dannay copy. (CNY. Dec.16; 397) *Lyon.* $30,000
- **Plates to Accompany Reveries over Childhood & Youth.** Cuala Pr., 1915. 4 plts. (1 col.), no text, linen-bkd. bds. (P. Mar.15; 281) *Maggs.* £55
- **Poems.** Ill.:– H.G. Fell (title). 1895. *1st. Edn.* Orig. cl., gt.-blocked from design by Fell, lightly soiled; bkplt. & owner's inscr. of John Drinkwater. (CSK. Oct.7; 144) £80
- **Anr. Edn.** L., 1949. *Definitive Edn. (375) numbered & sigd.* 2 vols. Lge. 8vo. Orig. buckram, publisher's box; John Kobler bkplt., Frederic Dannay copy. (CNY. Dec.16; 400) $550
- **Stories of Michael Robartes & his Friends.** – Some Passages from the Letters of AE to W.B. Yeats. Dublin, Cuala Pr., 1931; 1936. *1st. Edns. (450); (300).* Together 2 vols. Linen, ptd. bds., unc. (SG. May 17; 69) $120
- **Stories of Red Hanrahan.** Dundrum, Dun Emer Pr., 1904 [1905]. *1st. Edn. (500).* Orig. linen-bkd., bds., unc., slightly soiled; J.B. Yeats' copy, inscr. to him by Lolly Yeats, 20 Apr. 1905. (C. May 30; 181) *Bennett.* £70
- **Anr. Edn.** Dublin, Cuala Pr., 1904. *(500).* Orig.

cl.-bkd. bds. soiled. (BBA. May 23; 137)
Greenwood. £50
- **The Tower.** L., 1928. *1st. Edn.* Orig. cl. gt. (BBA. Nov.30; 299) *Maggs.* £50
- **The Trembling of the Veil.** L., 1922. *1st. Edn. (1000) sigd.* Some light spotting, orig. bds., unc., slightly soiled. (S. Mar.20; 1000) *Norrie.* £60
- **The Variorum Edition of the Poems.** N.Y., 1957. *(825) numbered with lf. sigd. by Yeats.* Qtr. cl., cl. covers. (SG. May 24; 240) $225
- **A Vision.** 1925. *1st. Edn. (600) numbered & sigd.* Orig. bds., unc., d.-w. slightly soiled. (BBA. Feb.23; 341) *Edrich.* £110
- **The Wanderings of Oisin & Other Poems.** L., 1889. *1st. Edn. (500).* Sm. 8vo. Orig. cl., variant with 'Paul, Trench, Trubner & Co.' on spine & without publisher's monog. on lr. cover; inscr. by Lily Yeats to L.M. Elton, Frederic Dannay copy. (CNY. Dec.16; 398) $1,000
- **Anr. Copy.** Sm. 8vo. Owner's inscr. on title-p., orig. cl.; Frederic Dannay copy. (CNY. Dec.16; 399) $700
- **Anr. Copy.** Sm. 8vo. Cl. (SG. Apr.26; 210) $650
- **Words for Music Perhaps & other Poems.** Cuala Pr., 1915. *Ltd. Edn.* Orig. linen-bkd. bds. (P. Mar.15; 282) £70
- **The Collected Works in Verse & Prose.** Stratford-on-Avon, Shakes. Hd. Pr., 1908. 8 vols. Orig. vell.-bkd. cl. gt., partly unc. (C. Nov.9; 187)
Quaritch. £360
- **Anr. Copy.** 8 vols. Some ll. slightly stained, orig. vell.-bkd. bds., soiled, few covers worn; bkplt. of David Garnett. (BBA. Mar.21; 321)
Palace Books. £50
- **Anr. Copy.** 8 vols. A few margin tears, red hf. mor., light rubbing, 1 spine slightly chipped at head. (SPB. Dec.13; 565) $600
See— ELLIS, J.E. & Yeats, William Butler

YECHIA, Don Joseph
- **Torah Or.** Bologna, 1538. *1st. Edn.* 4to. Slight worming affecting a few letters, title margin reprd. not affecting text, slight staining, mod. blind- & gt.-tooled mor. (S. Oct.25; 424) *Herzfeld.* £1,000

YECHIEL ASHKENAZI, of Jerusalem
- **Heichal Ha'Shem.** Tracts:– Moshe de Leon & Yitzhak Luria Ari. Venice, 1596-1606. 4to. Some worming affecting some letters, browned, staining, trimmed with loss of parts of some letters, elegy in 17th. C. oriental hand on last lf., hf. leath., marb. paper bds. (S. Oct.25; 425) *Sol.* £200

YEDAIAH BEN ABRAHAM HA'PENINI, of Bediers
- **Bechinat Olam.** Commentaries:– Moshe Ibn Chabib & Joseph Frances. Ferrara, 1551-52. *4th. Edn. [1st. Edn. with commentaries].* Last lf. in facs., title defect. & reprd. with loss of parts of border, staining, browned, slightly creased, vell. (S. Oct.25; 427) *Halprin.* £700
- **Leshon ha-Zahav.** Venice, 1599. *1st. Edn.* 2 pts. in 1 vol. Sm. 4to. Mod. cl. (SG. Feb.2; 311) $400

YEHUDA ARYE MODENA
[–] **Der Belehrte und Bekehrte Spieler: Das ist Ein annehmliches Tractaetlein, Darinnen zwey Juedische Studenten ... disputiren: Was vom Spiel zu halten sey?** Ed.:– August Pfeiffer. Leipzig, 1683. Sm. 8vo. Additional Hebrew title, text in Hebrew & German, browned, bds., cl. back & tips, worn, covers loose. (SG. Feb.2; 130) $300

YEHUDA ASA'EL
- **Sefer Kis'ot le-Veit David.** Verona, 1649. *1st. Edn.* Sm. 4to. Some browning & dampstaining, handwriting in Hebrew on title, scattered Hebrew marginalia, later bds., soiled, spine defect., loose in bdg. (SG. Feb.2; 312) $140

YEHUDA BEN SHMUEL CHASID
- **Sefer Chasidim.** Bologna, 1538. *1st. Edn.* 4to. Last lf. in facs., owners' sigs. on title, owner's stp. on 2nd. lf., slightly discold., mod. blind-tooled mor. (S. Oct.25; 428) *Gottesman.* £1,200
- **Anr. Edn.** Basle, 1581. *2nd. Edn.* 4to. Some worming affecting some letters, stained, trimmed, owners' sigs. on fly-lf., title & last p., leath., worn. (S. Oct.25; 429) *Kimche.* £350
- **Anr. Edn.** Cracow, 1581. *3rd. Edn.* 4to. Last lf.

reprd. without loss of text, lightly stained, slight worming, marginal glosses in late 16th. C. hand, bds., detchd., w.a.f. (S. Oct.25; 165) £750

YEHUDA HA'LEVI
- **Kuzari.** Trans.:– Yehuda Ibn Tibbon. Venice, 1547. *2nd. Edn.* 4to. Some margins reprd. affecting some letters, staining, browned, trimmed, blind-tooled leath., slightly worn. (S. Oct.25; 430)
Freedman. £400
– – **Anr. Edn.** Commentary:– Yehuda Muscato. Trans.:– Yehuda ibn Tibbon. Venice, 1593-94. *3rd. Edn. [1st. Edn. of commentary].* 4to. Some worming affecting some letters, browned, creased, edges frayed thro.-out, hf. vell., patterned paper bds. (S. Oct.25; 431) *Goldberg.* £240
- **Anr. Edn.** Commentary:– Yehuda Muscato. Trans.:– Yehuda ibn Tibbon. Venice, 1594. *3rd. Edn. [1st. Edn. of commentary].* 4to. Margin dampstaining, handwriting in ink at foot of last lf., negligible scattered worming, early blind-tooled leath., crude paper spine label, shabby. (SG. Feb.2; 313) $400
See— **BECHAYEI BEN JOSEPH IBN PAKUDA — YEHUDA HA'LEVI**

YEHUDA LEIB BEN JOSEPH ROFE NANTUA
- **Kol Yehuda.** Prague, 1641. *1st. Edn.* Fo. Owners' stps. on title, browned, few wormholes not affecting text or borders, worming in outer margins of 1st. few ll. not affecting text, tears affecting some letters, MS. Hebrew poem on 2nd. lf., blind-tooled leath., slightly worn. (S. Oct.25; 432) *Rosenfeld.* £260

YEHUDA LEIB BEN OVADYA
- **Sefer Minhat Yehuda.** Constantinople, 1654. Sm. fo. Dampstained, remargined thro.-out at top edge, with some loss to running heads, other cellotape repairs not impairing legibility, mod. two-toned cl. (SG. Feb.2; 314) $450

YEHUDA LIWA BEN BEZALEL [Maharal, of Prague]
- **Tiferet Israel.** Venice, 1599. *1st. Edn.* Fo. Staining, slight worming in margins not affecting text, trimmed, hf. vell. with marb. paper bds., worn. (S. Oct.25; 434) *Klein.* £520

YEHUDA UZIEL
See— **MOSHE ALFALAS — YEHUDA UZIEL**

YEHUDAI GAON
See— **SHIMON, of Cairo or YEHUDAI GAON**

YELLOW BOOK, The
Ill.:– Aubrey Beardsley & others. L., 1894-95. Vols 1-5. 4to. Orig. pict. cl., spines darkened & worn. (S. Dec.20; 513) *Rutten.* £50
– – **Anr. Run.** Ill.:– Aubrey Beardsley & others. L., 1894-97. Vols. 1-13 (compl.). 4to. Orig. pict. cl., 2 spines slightly faded, 1 corner & 1 spine slightly defect. (S. Nov.22; 308) *Baldur.* £260
– – **Anr. Copy.** 13 vols. Sm. 4to. Some ll. rather spotted, orig. cl., soiled. (BBA. Nov.30; 326)
Finch. £120
– – **Anr. Copy.** 13 vols. Square 8vo. Some foxing to plts., pict. cl. (HA. Nov.18; 331) $225
– – **Anr. Copy.** 13 vols. Sm. 4to. Largely unopened, pict. cl., spines soiled & nicked. (SG. Jan.12; 30) $175
– – **Anr. Copy.** 13 vols. Sm. 4to. Pict. cl., Vols. 12 & 13 without '5/– Net' on spines, some wear, some cover soiling & minor stains, tips of a few spines with minor tears or fraying, 1 or 2 inner jnts. brkn. (RO. Dec.11; 361) $160

YEPES, Fr. Diego de
- **Vida, Virtudes y Milagros de ... Teresa de Jesus.** Madrid, 1615. *2nd. Edn.* 4to. Vell. (DS. Mar.23; 2339) Pts. 65,000

YERKES, Charles T.
- **Yerkes Collection Catalogue of Paintings & Sculpture.** N.Y., 1904. *(250) numbered.* 2 vols. Lge. 4to. Mntd. plts., orig. mor. gt., lightly rubbed. (CSK. Jun.29; 45) £75

YERUCHAM BEN MESHULAM
- **Toldot Adam Ve'Chava.** Constantinople, 1516. *1st. Edn.* Fo. Title & 1st. 4 ll. from anr. copy, margin glosses, slight worming mostly in margins,

browned, staining, mod. blind-tooled mor. (S. Oct.25; 435) *A. Stein.* £2,900
– – **Anr. Copy.** Fo. 14 ll. of index bnd. before 1st. pt., colophon mntd., slight staining & traces of worming, slight browning to some ll., a few margins reprd., a few ll. reprd. with portions of ll. cut from anr. copy, late 18th. C. diced panel. russ., rubbed, upr. portion of spine restored, fore-e. pntg.,mod. mor.-bkd. folding box. (SPB. Feb.1; 88) $5,250

YISRAEL ISSERLEIN
- **Terumot Hadeshen.** Venice, 1545. *(Bound with:)* **YAKOV BEN ASHER – Pirush Hatorah.** Venice, 1544. Together 2 works in 1 vol. 4to. 1 title crudely reprd. with sm. loss to upr. corner, browning, staining, a few other minor repairs, bdg. not stated. (SPB. Feb.1; 49) $600

YITSHAK IBN SHANGI
- **Sefer Be'er Yitshak.** Salonika, 1735. *1st. Edn.* 2 pts. in 1 vol. Sm. fo. Dampstained, margins trimmed close with loss to some ll., scattered worming, liby. blind-stp. on title, qtr. sheep, shabby. (SG. Feb.2; 320) $120

YITSHAK YESHURUN
- **Panim Hadashot.** Venice, 1651. *1st. Edn.* Sm. 4to. Title lf. torn, dampstained, early blind-tooled cf., shabby, lacks ties, crudely rebkd. (SG. Feb.2; 321) $200

YITZCHAK BEN MOSHE IBN ARROYO
- **Tanchumot El.** Saloniki, 1578. Fo. *1st. & final ll.* frayed with loss of text, stained thro.-out, disbnd. (SPB. Feb.1; 89) $1,200

YITZCHAK LEMGO, of Gronigen
[–] **Likutei Zvi.** Amst., 1809. Slight browning, margins slightly frayed at front, disbnd. (SPB. Feb.1; 53a) $175

YITZHAK, of Dueren
- **Sha'arei Dura-Issur Ve'Heter.** Venice, 1564. *5th. Edn.* 4to. Owners' sig. & stp. on title, slight worming affecting some letters, discold., slightly soiled, bnd. with 5 ll. late 16th. C. MS., mod. mor. gt. (S. Oct.25; 438) *Davidson.* £550
See— **LURIA, Shlomo [Maharshal] & Yitzhak, of Dueren**

YITZHAK BEN ABBA-MARI
- **Ha'Itur.** Venice, 1608. *1st. Edn.* Fo. Wormhole on last lf. affecting 3 letters, foxed, staining, hf. leath., slightly worn. (S. Oct.25; 437) *Klein.* £320
– – **Anr. Copy.** 108 (of 110) ll., some dampstaining & foxing, sm. repairs to title & last lf., mod. cl.-bkd. bds., crude paper spine label, worn. (SG. Feb.2; 318) $325

YITZHAK BEN ELIA SHANI
- **Me'ah She'arim.** Saloniki [Soncino], 1543. *1st. Edn.* 4to. Unpaginated, lacks 6 folios, some staining, no bdg. stated. (S. Oct.25; 439)
Davidson. £780

YITZHAK BEN SHMUEL ADARBI
- **Divrei Rivot.** Venice, 1586-87. *2nd. Edn.* Fo. Owners' sigs. on title, reprd. affecting some letters, slight staining, worming affecting some letters, corners frayed, mod. mor. (S. Oct.25; 441)
Klein. £300

YITZHAK LEON BEN ELIESER IBN ZUR
- **Megillat Esther.** Venice, 1592. *1st. Edn.* 4to. Some margins torn & reprd. with loss of some words, discold., mod. mor. gt. (S. Oct.25; 440)
Hirschler. £260

YOKOYAMA, Ibaraki
- **Kinten-Shu.** Kyoto, Showa 42 [1967]. Vol. 1 only (of 3). Fo. 88 tipped in col. plts., colophon slip mntd. on lr. pastedown, native hf. cl., with calligraphic title, extremities rubbed. (SG. Jan.26; 229) $150

YONEZAWA, Yoshiho
See— **AKIYAMA, Terukazu & others**

YONGE, Charlotte Mary
[–] **The Instructive Picture Book. Or Lessons from the Vegetable World.** Edinb., ca. 1870. *5th. Edn.* Fo. 31 double-p. col. plts., some spotting & some partially split along centrefold, orig. decor. bds.,

linen backstrip, soiled & worn. (TA. Jun.21; 257) £50

YORKE, James
- **The Union of Honour.** 1641. Sm. fo. Title torn & reprd., some pp. ink-stained, old cf., slightly worn. (BS. Nov.16; 37) £60

YOSEF IBN VERGA
- **Sefer She'eirit Yosef.** Mantua, 1593. *2nd. Edn.* Sm. 4to. With index (not present in 1st. Edn.), title remargined, 1 lf. reprd. with cellotape, mild dampstaining, some worming minimally affecting text, mod. binder's cl. (SG. Feb.2; 322) $150

YOSEF TZARFATI
- **Yad Yosef.** Amst., 1700. Fo. With engraved title (often lacking), slight spotting, staining & browning, old stpd. cf., worn, spine perished. (SPB. Feb.1; 86a) $175

YOSHUA HA'LEVI
- **Halichot Olam.** Venice, 1545. *3rd. Edn.* 4to. Slight staining, trimmed, 16th. C. margin glosses thro.-out, owner's stp. on title, trimmed, hf. cl., slightly worn. (S. Oct.25; 442) *Sol.* £140

YOSY, A.
- **Switzerland as now divided into Nineteen Cantons.** L., 1815. 2 vols. Hf.-titles, 50 hand-cold. costume plts., 2 engraved ll. of music, some foxing of text, cont. hf. mor. (S. May 21; 252)
Schumman. £2,000
– – **Anr. Copy.** 2 vols. in 1. 50 hand-cold. plts., some slight marginal stains of text, hf. cf. gt., rebkd. (P. May 17; 357) *B.Marshall.* £950
– – **Anr. Copy.** 2 vols. in 1. 41 (of 50) hand-cold. plts., hf. mor. gt. (P. Jan.12; 167) *Nolan.* £620

YOUNG, Sir Allen
- **Cruise of the 'Pandora'.** L., 1876. Folding map (torn from guard), 12 orig. mntd. photos., 2 loose, few ll. spotted, orig. cl., spine slightly worn; pres. copy to B. Ball. (S. Mar.6; 68) *Hitching.* £680
- **The Two Voyages of the 'Pandora'.** L., 1879. *1st. Edn.* 2 lge. folding maps in pockets (sm. tears at folds). 9 plts., minor staining in margins, a few loose, orig. cl., slightly worn; pres. copy to B. Ball. (S. Mar.6; 67) *Hitching.* £340

YOUNG, Arthur
[–] **The Farmer's Letter to the People of England.** 1767. *1st. Edn.* 1st. & last ll. browned, cont. cf., rebkd. (TA. Dec.15; 525) £75
- **The Farmer's Tour through the East of England.** 1771. 4 vols. Slight spotting, bds., worn, unc. & unopened. (P. Apr.12; 192) *Traylen.* £110
[–] **Observation on the Present State of the Waste Lands of Great Britain.** 1773. Disbnd. (P. Jun.7; 314) £340
- **Political Arithmetic.** 1754. *1st. Edn.* Slightly browned & spotted, cont. spr. cf., rubbed. (BBA. Jul.27; 70) *Frognal.* £290
[–] **A Six Months Tour through the North of England.** 1770. 4 vols. 28 plts. (some folding), 6 folding tables, cf., defect., lacks covers to Vol. 4; from the Farmers' Club Liby. (P. Jul.5; 27) £75
- **A Tour in Ireland.** 1780. *2nd. Edn.* 2 vols. Cont. cf., rubbed. (CSK. Jul.6; 75) £50
- **Travels [in France] 1787 [-89].** Bury St. Edmunds, 1792-94. *Vol. 1: 1st. Edn., Vol. 2: 2nd. Edn.* 2 vols. 4to. Slight spotting, cont. cf., rubbed, rebkd. (S. Nov.1; 90) *Thorp.* £50
– – **Anr. Edn.** L. & Bury St. Edmunds, 1794. *2nd. Edn.* 2 vols. 4to. 1 folding map hand-cold., cont. spr. hf. cf., rebkd. (TA. Feb.16; 21) £115
[–] **View of the Agriculture of Oxfordshire.** 1809. Hand-cold. folding map, 27 plts., hf. cf. gt. (P. Jan.12; 293) *Magna.* £110

YOUNG, Edward
- **The Complaint & the Consolation, or Night Thoughts.** Ill.:– William Blake. L., 1797 [paper wtrmkd. 1794]. Lge. 4to. Tall copy, a few outer margins slightly shaved, minor staining in upr. margin of pp. 41-42, cont. panel cf. gt. decor. in style of Edwards of Halifax. (C. May 30; 183)
Maggs. £4,500
– – **Anr. Edn.** 1817. 12mo. Cont. mor., elab. ruled & tooled in gt., double fore-e. pntg., later box. (CSK. Jul.27; 30) £220
- **Poetical Works.** L., 1813-11. 4 vols. in 2. 12mo.

YOUNG, Edward -*Contd.*

Cont. crimson mor., covers blind- & gt.-tooled, spines gt., fore-e. pntg. in each vol. (C. Nov.9; 71) *Chelsea.* £320

YOUNG, John
- **A Series of Portraits of the Emperors of Turkey from the Foundation of the Monarchy to the Year 1815.** [1815]. *1st. Edn.* Lge. fo. Additional mezzotint title, 29 (of 30) col.-ptd. hand-finished mezzotint ports., titles & text in Engl. & Fr., 2 ll. reprd., some browning of text & staining in margins, cont. hf. cf., covers detchd. (SKC. May 4; 1652) £4,000

YOUNG, Thomas
- **An Account of some Recent Discoveries in Hieroglyphical Literature and Egyptian Antiquities.** L., 1823. Hf.-title, last 3 advt. ll. slightly spotted, mod. cl.-bkd. bds., unc. (BBA. Dec.15; 345) *Quaritch.* £55
- **A Course of Lectures on Natural Philosophy & the Mechanical Arts.** 1807. *1st. Edn.* 2 vols. 4to. 43 engraved plts. in vol. Vol. 1 (2 hand-cold.), 15 in Vol. 2, liby. stp. on verso of title-pp., cont. russ., Vol.1 lacks spine, covers detchd., Vol. 2 spine defect. (SKC. Mar.9; 1929) £240

YOUNG ANGLERS' COMPANION (The)
[L.], ca. 1830. 12mo. Three-qtr. mor., rubbed, ptd. wraps. bnd. in. (SG. Mar.15; 314) $150

YOUNG LADY'S COMPANION (The), in Cookery & Pastry, Preserving, Pickling, Candying L., 1734. 12mo. Some ll. slightly soiled, cf. gt. (P. Jan.12; 292) £300

YOUNGER, J., Shoemaker of St. Boswells
- **River Angling for Salmon & Trout.** Kelso & Edinb., 1864. 1 vol. Orig. cl. gt., slight wear. (*With:*) - **Autobiography.** Kelso, 1881. 1 vol. Orig. cl., slightly rubbed & soiled; 3 A.L.s. to William Brockie, dtd. 1841, 1852 & 1856, loosely inserted. (S. Oct.4; 71) *Marlborough.* £160

YOUNGHUSBAND, George & Davenport, Cyril
- **The Crown Jewels of England.** L., 1919. *(1400) numbered.* 4to. Frontis., 18 mntd. col. plts., cl., spine badly worn. (SG. Aug.25; 231) $130

YOUSOUF KAMAL, Prince
- **Monumenta Cartographica Africae et Aegypti.** [Leiden], 1951. Vol. 5 pts. 1 & 2: Additamenta (naissance et evolution de la cartographie moderne). Lge. fo. Publisher's cl. gt., w.a.f. (S. May 22; 412) *Robinson.* £580

YOUTH'S FRIEND, The
Phila., 1833. 12mo. Marb. bds., rebkd.; sig. & bkplt. of Franklin D. Roosevelt. (PNY. Jun.6; 428) $140

YSENDYCK, J.J. Van
- **Documents Classés de l'Art dans les Pays-Bas du XIème au XVIIIieme Siecle.** Antw., [1880-]89. 1st., 2nd. & 3rd. Series: 3 vols., 1 vol., 1 vol. Tall fo. Many plts., ex-liby., new hf. mor. (SG. May 3; 395) $250

YUAN-PIEN, Hsiang
- **Noted Porcelains of Successive Dynasties.** Peiping, 1931. Fo. Orig. limp cl., boxed. (CSK. Jun.29; 5) £240
- - **Anr. Copy.** Fo. Orig. limp silk gt., orig. silk covered case, very slightly stained. (S. May 1; 645) *Tang.* £160

YU-CHIH WU-TI CH'ING WEN-CHEN [The Ching Dynasty Lexicon in Mancu, Tibetan, Mongol, Uighur & Chinese]
L., 1957. 3 vols. Lge. 8vo. Orig. cl. (BBA. Mar.7; 13) *Ad Orientem.* £65

YVIA-GROCE, H.
- **Anthologie des Ecrivains** ... Preface:- P. Graziani. Ajaccio, 1929-31. 2 vols. Sewed. (HD. Oct.21; 182) Frs. 2,500

YVON, P.
- **Leere van den H. Doop en desself Suyere Bedieninge.** Notes:- D. Koelman. Amst., 1683. *1st. Dutch Edn.* Sm. 8vo. Some slight fraying & soiling, cont. vell., slightly soiled. (VS. Dec.9; 1382) Fls. 500

ZABARELLIS, F. de, Cardinal of Florence
- **Super Primo [-Quinto] Decretalium.** Venice, 1502. 5 pts. in 2 vols. Fo. Some wormholes, Vol. II stained, cont. hf. pig. over wood, rubbed. (VG. Nov.30; 1002) Fls. 800

ZACHARIA, A.W.
- **Die Elemente der Luftschwimmkunst.** Wittenb., 1807. *1st. Edn.* Foxed, cont. hf. leath., lightly rubbed. (R. Oct.12; 1641) DM 460

ZACHARIA, of Plungian
- **Sefer Zechirah Ve'inyenei Segulot.** Hamburg, 1709. *1st. Edn.* 12mo. Lightly browned, hf. leath., w.a.f. (S. Jul.3; 211) £105

ZACUTO, Abraham ben Samuel
- **Sefer Yuchasin.** Cracow, 1580-81. *2nd. Edn.* 4to. Sigd. by censor Luigi da Bologna, 1600, a few words & 1 phrase deleted, owners sigs. on title, some soiling & browning, margin repairs to a few ll., bds.; Hoschule für die Wissenschaft des Judenthums stps. [Steinschneider 4303, 3] (SPB. Jun.26; 34) $2,500

ZAGLADA ZYDOSTWA POLSKIEGO: Album Zdjec / ... Extermination of Polish Jews: Album of Pictures
[Lodz, 1945]. Ob. 4to. Intro. & captions in Polish, Russian, Engl., Fr., Yiddish & Hebrew, ptd. wraps., worn, loose. (SG. Feb.2; 79) $200

ZAHALON, Yakov
- **Margaliot Tovot.** Venice, 1665. *1st. Edn.* 12mo. Some ll. short, edges frayed, discold., staining, buckram. (S. Oct.25; 444) *Sol.* £140

ZAHN, J.F.A.
[-] **Historisches Bilderbuch für die Jugend, enthaltend Vaterlandsgeschichte.** Leipzig, 1797-1816. 12 vols. Vol. 12 with supp. title, lightly browned or slightly foxed, vol. 2 lacks plts. 1-3 & 5, cont. hf. leath. gt. (R. Oct.11; 665) DM 1,400

ZAHN, L.
See— HAJOS, E.M. & Zahn, L.

ZAHN, Otto
- **On Art Binding. A Monograph.** Memphis, Tennessee, 1904. *(1075). (1000)* on *Strathmore Deckle Edge, sigd.* Lev. mor., gt.-decor., red mor. onlays, spine in 6 compartments, gt.-decor., turn-ins gt., watered silk linings, partly unc., by Monastery Hill Bindery, sigd. on upr. turn-in & with SL stp. (St. Louis?) on lr. turn-in, s.-c., as a bdg., w.a.f. (CNY. Dec.17; 583) $360

ZAMACOIS, M.
- **Dernière Lettre Persane mise en Français.** Ill.:- E.G. Benito. Paris, ca. 1930. 4to. Leaves, publisher's pict. portfo. (HD. Dec.1; 38) Frs. 5,200

ZANETTI, Anton Maria
- **Ancient Statues Greek & Roman.** 1800. Fo. 89 engraved plts. only, some light spotting, cont. cf., rubbed. (CSK. Jul.13; 97) £80
- - **Anr. Copy.** Fo. 89 engraved plts. only, some light spotting, cont. cf., rubbed. (CSK. Apr.6; 43) £70
- **Delle Antiche Statue Greche e Romans obe nell'antisala della Libreria de San Marco** ... Venezia, 1740. 2 vols. in 1. Fo. Cf., loose, defect. (CR. Jun.6; 80) Lire 280,000
- - **Anr. Edn.** Ill.:- Faldoni & others. Venice, 1740-43. 2 vols. in 1. Fo. Cont. hf. cf. gt., marb. paper panel, head of spine worn. (C. May 30; 58) *Quaritch.* £600

ZANGWILL, Israel
- **The Works.** L., 1925. *Edn. de Luxe, (1000) sigd.* 14 vols. Orig. hf. mor. (S. Dec.13; 419) *Davis.* £110

ZANNONI, Giovanni Antonio Rizzi
See— RIZZI-ZANNONI, Giovanni Antonio

ZANOTTO, Francesco
- **Pinacoteca della Imp. Reg. Accademia Veneta.** Venice, 1830-34. 2 vols. Lge. fo. 100 copperplts. & 55 copper engraved vigs. (ports.), lightly browned & spotted, some margins defect., cont. hf. vell., gold-tooled, bumped, 1 spine burst. (HT. May 9; 982) DM 460

ZAPATA, D.M.
- **Dissertacion Medico-Theologica.** Madrid, 1733. Old name on title, leath. gt. (D. Nov.23; 650) DM 400

ZAPF, Hermann
- **Typographic Variations.** Prefaces:- P. Standard, G.K. Schauer, & C. Peignot. N.Y., 1964. *(500).* Tall 4to. Sigd. by Zapf, vell.-bkd. bds., d.-w. (SG. Sep.15; 361) $200

ZARAGOZA
- **Estutatos de la ... Universidad y Estudio Gral. de Zaragoza establecidos por ... Fernando VI.** Zaragoza, 1753. Fo. Cf. (DS. Oct.28; 2496) Pts. 28,000

ZARAGOZA, J.
- **Noticias Historicas de la Nueve España.** Madrid, 1878. 4to. Qtr. tree sheep. (SG. Oct.20; 385) $150

ZARLINO, Gioseffo
- **Le Istitutioni Harmoniche. — Dimostrationi Harmoniche.** 1558; 1571. *1st. Edns.* Together 2 works in 1 vol. Fo. MS. sigs. on titles, 3 ll. reprd., a few end-ll. defect., old cf., brkn. (BS. May 2; 3) £900

ZASIUS, Ulrich
[-] **Nüwe Stattrechten und Statuten der Loblichen Statt Fryburg im Pryssgow gelegen.** Ill.:- Holbein. [Basel], 1.1.1520. *1st. Edn.* Fo. Stained & browned thro.-out, cont. marginalia, cont. limp vell., very worn, lacks 4 ties. (HK. Nov.8; 185) DM 500

ZAUBER-BILDERBUCH
[Germany], ca. 1880. Flick book, title-p. & instructions in 3 languages, separate sheet with Dutch version loosely inserted, litho. frontis. & ills. hand-cold., orig. cl.-bkd. pict. wraps., stitching defect.; van Veen coll. (S. Feb.28; 247) £150

ZAVALA, L. de
- **Manifesto del Gobernador del Estado de Mexico.** Tlalpam, 1829. Disbnd. (S. May 22; 408) *Quaritch.* £160

ZDANEVICH, Ilya 'Eli Elganbyuri' or 'Ilyazd'
- **Natalia Goncharova, Mikhail Larionov.** Moscow, 1913. *(525).* 4to. Orig. wraps., unc., rebkd. (S. Nov.21; 169) *Phillips.* £500

ZEEUS, Jakob
- **Gedichten ... Tweede Druk.** Amst., 1737. 4to. Added engraved title, 6 engraved divisional titles, port. & many vigs., crushed mor. panel. in blind, gt. decor., by The Club Bindery; Robert Hoe's leather bk.-label. (SG. Apr.19; 200) $150

ZE'EV WOLF BEN YEHUDA LEIB OF RUZHANY
- **Sefer Gefen Yehidit.** Amst., 1722. 16mo. Some browning, title soiled, remargined with slight loss on verso, mod. cl. (SG. Feb.2; 260) $175

ZEILLER, Martin
- **Itineraruim Germaniae Nov-antiquae.** Strassburg, 1632. *1st. Edn.* Fo. Lightly browned, cont. vell. (R. Oct.12; 2446) DM 1,100
- - **Anr. Copy.** Fo. Title slightly browned & verso stpd., cont. vell., bumped. (GB. May 3; 206) DM 800
- **Topographia Bavariae.** Ill.:- M. Merian. Frankfurt, 1654. *2nd. Edn.* 1 copper engr. very browned, 1 torn, 2 ptd. weakly, some double plts. cut close with frayed margins, 6 supp. plts., lacks 2 plts. (*Bound with:*) - **Topographia Palatinatus Rheni Sampt einer Zugabe.** Frankfurt, 1645 [1720]. *3rd. Edn.* 3 plts. weakly ptd., 2 plts. browned, 1 folding plt. very spotted, lacks 1 plt. Together 2 works in 1 vol. Fo. hf. vell. (R. Oct.12; 2385) DM 28,000
[-] **Topographia Circuli Burgundici.** Ill.:- M. Merian. [Frankfurt, 1659?]. Fo. Wide margin, lacks title & text, some foxing, cont. vell. (HK. Nov.8; 932) DM 4,300
- **Topographia und Eigentl. Beschreibung der Stäte etc. in derien Herzogthümern Braunschweig und Lüneburg.** Ill.:- M. Merian. Frankfurt, 1654[1660]. *2nd. Edn.* Fo. Some light browning, some double plts. cut close, some margins frayed, 2 plts. very browned & with some loss & bkd., 1 lr. margin defect, anr. browned & torn, with 2 new plts. not in index, cont. hf. vell. (R. Oct.12; 2386) DM 20,500

– Topographia Galliae. Ill.:– M. Merian. Frankfurt, 1655-61. *1st. Edn.* 13 pts. in 4 vols. Fo. 305 (of 306) mostly folding or double-p. copperplts., 18 double-p. or folding copper engraved maps, some plts. misbnd., 1 plt. replaced, minimal browning, cont. vell. (HK. Nov.8; 999) DM 6,500
– – Anr. Copy. Fo. 115 plts. (92 double-p. & 4 folding), & 2 loose plts., some minor defects., cont. cf. (HD. Mar.19; 73) Frs. 13,000
– – Anr. Edn. Ill.:– M. Merian. Frankfurt, 1657-61. Pts. 5-13 in 1 vol. Fo. Pt. 6 lacks text, but for 1 lf., 12 double-p. copper engraved maps, 126 views on 92 plts., most folding, some multi-folding, cont. hf. vell. (R. Oct.13; 3097) DM 2,760
– – Anr. Copy. Pts. 7-13 in 1 vol. 3 engraved titles, 8 double-p. copper engraved maps & 101 views on 78 copperplts., comprising 7 folding, 60 double-p. & 11 full-p., sm. tear in fold of 1 plan, cont. leath. gt., slightly rubbed, head of spine restored. (R. Apr.5; 2937a) DM 1,800
– Topographia Germaniae. Ill.:– M. Merian. Frankfurt, 1643-75. 4to. Orig. bds. (HT. May 8; 742) DM 750
– Topographia Germaniae-Inferioris vel Circuli-Burgundici das ist Beschreibung vnd Abbildung der Fürnembsten Orter in den Niederländischen XVII Provincien. Ill.:– M. Merian. Frankfurt, [1659]. *2nd. Edn.* Fo. Variant title (horses), crumpled, sm. tears, 106 (of 107) copperplts. & 1 supp. copperplt. (name deleted in index), 3 plts. creased with corrections & spotting, 2 ll. dedication bnd. at end, spotted & browned thro.-out, 2nd. half with ink stain in upr. margin, more near end & lr. margin stain, 5 ll. & 3 plts. with margin repair, old entry, red mor., gt. Ludwig XIII arms on covers, spine gt., slightly spotted & worn. (H. May 22; 229) DM 4,800
– – Anr. Edn. Ill.:– M. Merian. Frankfurt, ca. 1680. *3rd. Edn.* Fo. Engraved title, 12 double-p. copper engraved maps, 92 copper engraved plans on 71 plts., 67 copper engraved views on 36 partly folding plts., cont. hf. vell. (R. Oct.13; 3130) DM 4,000
– Topographia Hassia, et Regionum Vicinerum. Ill.:– M. Merian. Frankfurt, 1655. *2nd. Edn.* With Supp. Fo. Engraved ill. title, 3 double-p. engraved maps, 58 (of 59) engraved plts., including 21 double-p., lacks 1 text lf., some text ll., 1 folding map & some plts. restored in old MS., only some subjects defect., 1 plt. very cut, some spotting & staining, mostly in margin, leath., old wear, sm. defects. (V. Sep.29; 79) DM 16,000
– Topographia Helvetiae, Rhaetiae, et Valesiae. Frankfurt, 1654. *3rd. Edn.* Fo. 2 double-p. copper engraved maps, 103 views on 79 copperplates, most double-p., lge. tears in copper-engraved title & 2 views, slightly foxed, upr. margin lightly stained, some sm. repairs, cont. vell. (HK. Nov.9; 1263) DM 31,000
– – Anr. Edn. Ill.:– M. Merian. [Frankfurt, 1654]. 2 pts. in 1 vol. Engraved title, dtd. 1642, 2 folding maps (torn), 78 plts., 45 torn & 6 with portions of plt. lacking, some pp. of text & most plts. loose, no bdg. stated, w.a.f. (P. Oct.20; 66) £4,600
– Topographia Italiae. Ill.:– Matthew Merian. Frankfurt, 1688. *1st. Edn.* Fo. Copper engraved title, 9 double-p. copper engraved maps, 44 copperplts. (4 folding), stained at side thro.-out, cont. leath. gt., gt. outer dentelle, jnts. split & reprd., slightly rubbed & bumped. (HK. May 15; 909) DM 5,300
– Topographia Palatinatus Rheni et Vicinarum Regionum. Ill.:– M. Merian. [Frankfurt], 1645. *2nd. Edn.* 2 pts. in 1 vol. Fo. Engraved title, 1 engraved title vig., 3 double-p. copper engraved maps, 51 copperplts. (most double-p., 1 multi-folding) with 99 views, cont. leath. gt., lightly bumped, minimal wear. (HT. May 10; 2973a) DM 16,000
– Topographia Provinciarum Austriacaru[m]. Ill.:– M. Merian. Frankfurt, J.A. Cholin, 1678. 3 pts. in 1 vol., including Supps. 1 & 2. Fo. Engraved title, 100 (of 120) plts., most double-p., including 8 (of 10) double-p. maps & a lge. folding panorama, 1 or 2 text ll. supplied in later MS., a few ll. & plts. at beginning wormed with some loss of engraved surface, a few short tears without loss, some creases & faint browning, cont. vell., soiled. (S. Dec.1; 337) *Studio Vaduz.* £2,200
– – Anr. Edn. Ill.:– M. Merian. Frankfurt, [1736].

Latest Edn. With Supp. Fo. 6 double-p. copper engraved maps, 87 (of 88) partly folding or double-p. copperplts., some double plts. cut close & bnd. in upright, slits in lr. margin, 2 extending to ill., lacks 2 plts. (1 not in index), cont. hf. vell. (R. Oct.13; 3201) DM 12,000
– Topographia Provinciarum Austriacarum. — Topographia Bohemiae, Moraviae et Silesiae. Ill.:– M. Merian. Frankfurt, 1650. *1st. Edns.* Together 2 works in 1 vol. Fo. Engraved title, 6 double-p. copper engraved maps & 87 (of 88) partly folding or double-p. copperplts., lacks 2 plts., some plts. cut close, some crumpling & tears, some bkd., margin defects., 1 corner extended, minimal foxing, cont. vell., spine defect. (R. Oct.13; 3202) DM 17,000
[–] Topographia Saxoniae Inferiores ... Nider Sächss. Crayss. — Topographia Superioris Saxoniae, Thuringiae, Misniae, Lusatiae. Ill.:– M. Merian. Frankfurt, 1653 [1720]; 1650 [1690]. *3rd. Edn.; 2nd. Edn.* Together 2 works in 1 vol. Fo. Lacks 1 copper engrs., some sm. tears bkd., 4 supp. engrs., cont. hf. pig. (R. Oct.12; 2388) DM 10,500
– – Anr. Copy. Fo. 1 plt. torn, land plt. browned, 2 double-plts. with 2 views cut apart & bnd. separately, some slight spotting or crumpling, cont. hf. vell. (R. Oct.12; 2387) DM 7,000
– – Anr. Copy. Fo. Engraved title, 4 copper engraved maps, 53 views on 36 copperplts., 2 plts. cut through between ills., some plts. cut very close at margin, minimal spotting, mod. hf. leath. (HT. May 10; 2950a) DM 6,000
– Topographia Superioris Savoniae, Thungiae, Misniae, Lusatiae. Ill.:– M. Merian. Frankfurt, 1650 [ca. 1690]. *2nd. Edn.* Fo. 1 plt. weak, 5 supp. plts. some plts. with light crumples, 2 torn, 1 bkd., 1 folding plt. cut close at side, cont. vell. (R. Oct.12; 2389) DM 5,000
– – Anr. Copy. Fo. Some copper engrs. weak, 1 plt. very spotted, some crumpling & sm. tears, lacks 1 plt., cont. hf. vell. (R. Oct.12; 2390) DM 2,500
– Topographia Westphaliae. Ill.:– M. Merian. [Frankfurt, 1647]. Fo. Engraved title, 1 engraved double-p. folding map, 48 (of 50) engraved plts., including 32 double-p., lacks coll. view, some lge. plts. cut close, newer bds. (V. Sep.29; 80) DM 17,000

ZEISING, Heinrich
– Theatrum Machinarum. Leipzig, 1708. *2nd. Edn.?* 6 pts. in 1 vol. Ob. 4to. Lacks 4 plts., browned, a few ll. stained, a few ll. cropped at head affecting engraved area, old bds., mor.-bkd. folding box; Stanitz coll. (SPB. Apr.25; 457) $500

ZEITSCHRIFT FUR HISTORISCHE WAFFEN–UND KOSTUMKUNDE
Berlin, 1923-43. New Series:Vols. I-VIII (all publd.), in 70 pts. 4to. Orig. sewed. (GB. Nov.3; 992) DM 400

ZELLER, F.J.B.
– Die Molken-Kur in Verbindung der Mineral-Brunnenkur. Würzburg, 1828. Old light soiling, more at beginning, unc., orig. sewed. (V. Sep.29; 119) DM 400

ZENKER, F.G.
– Theoretisch-praktische Anleitung z. Kunztbäckerey. Wien, 1818. *1st. Edn.* Cont. marb. bds. gt. (HK. May 16; 1481) DM 750
– Der Zuckerbäcker f. Frauen Littlerer Stände. Wien & Prag, 1824. Slightly foxed, cut slightly close, cont. leath., blind-tooled decor. (HK. Nov.9; 1712) DM 550

ZENKER, Rudolf
– Farbiger Decken– und Wandschmuck im Geiste Fruehgermanischer Kunst. Plauen i. V., ca. 1910? Fo. 22 chromolitho. plts., loose as iss., cl.-bkd. bd. folder, spine worn. (SG. Aug.25; 323) $225

ZERACHIA, of Greece
– Sefer Ha'Yashar. Cracow, 1586. *3rd. Edn.* 4to. Inner margins wormed affecting some letters, browned, some staining, cl. (S. Oct.25; 447) *Rosenfeld.* £320

ZERELLA Y YCOAGA, Manuel de
– Tratado General y Matematico de Reloxeria. Madrid, 1791. 4to. Vell. (DS. Mar.23; 2369) Pts. 34,000

ZERVOS, Christian
– L'Art de la Crète Néolithique et Minoenne. Paris, 1956. Fo. No bdg. stated. (SPB. Nov.30; 262) $125
– Pablo Picasso, Oeuvres. Paris, 1942-66. 17 vols. in 18. 4to. Sewed, wraps. (HD. Jun.6; 161) Frs. 44,000
– – Anr. Edn. Paris, 1942-78. *Vol. 1:* (500), *Vol. 2:* (700) Vols. 1-33 in 34 vols. (all publd.). 4to. Orig. wraps., 1 pasted. (H. Nov.24; 1933) DM 18,500

ZESEN, Philipp von
– Beschreibung der Stadt Amsterdam. Amst., 1664. 4to. 66 folding litho. views, some foxing & browning, sm. tears in folds of some plts., some worming, cont. vell., rebnd. (VG. Nov.30; 1084) Fls. 1,600

ZETEL, P.
– Philosophia Sacra sive Vita divi Stanislai Kostka, Soc: Jesu ... Ill.:– J.U. Kraus. Dillingen, [1715]. *1st. Edn.* Sm. 4to. Slightly browned thro.-out, 19th. C. leath., worn, 1 jnt. brkn. (HT. May 9; 1333) DM 420

ZEUSS, I.C.
– Grammatica Celtica. Berlin, 1871. *2nd. Edn.* Hf. mor. (GM. Dec.7; 64) £70

ZICHY, Michael von
– Liebe [spine title]. N.p., not after 1906. 4to. 40 plts., hf. mor., spine gt.-lettered, cover detchd.; 1st. plt. sigd. by Zichy. (SG. Mar.29; 122) $110

ZIEGLER, Jacobus
– In C. Plinii de Natvrali Historia Librvm Secvndvm Commentarivs ... Item, G. Collimitii, et J. Vadiani, in eundes secundum Plinii Scholia quaedam ... Basel, Aug. 1531. *1st. Edn.* Fo. Wide margin, slightly stained at beginning & end in margin, a few ll. browned, title with sm. pasted tear & last p. slightly soiled, bds. (HK. Nov.8; 385) DM 540

ZIEGLER, Johann
See— JANSCHA, Lorenz & Ziegler, Johann

ZIEGLER, Wilhelm
– Ein Dokumentenwerk ueber die Englische Humanitaet. Berlin, ca. 1935? Fo. Cl. (SG. Sep.22; 66) $100

ZIMMERMANN, Joh. Georg
– Uber die Einsamkeit. Leipzig, 1784/85. *1st. Edn.* 4 pts. in 4 vols. Slightly browned thro.-out, cont. hf. leath., gold-tooled, rubbed & bumped. (HT. May 9; 1713) DM 520
– Von der Einsamkeit. Wien, 1803. *De Luxe Edn.* Fo. On vell., wide margin, slight foxing, cont. red mor., gt. spine, covers, inner & outer dentelle, slightly rubbed & spotted, spine faded; Hauswedell coll. (H. May 24; 1627) DM 4,000

ZIMMERMAN, Matthaeus
– Unda Jordanis Fabariana. Pfaeffeserischer Jordan oder ... Entwurff des ... Pfaeffers Bads in der Oberen Schweitz Wuerckung. Einsiedeln, 1682. 12mo. Vell.; Dr. Walter Pagel copy. (S. Feb.7; 384) *Quaritch.* £350

ZIMMERMANN, Wilhelm Peter
See— VOGTHERR, Heinrich & Burgkmair, Hans — ZIMMERMANN, Wilhelm

ZIMMERMAN, William
– Waterfowl of North America. Louisville, [1974]. (1000) numbered & sigd. Ob. fo. 42 col. plts., cf.-bkd. cl. bds. (LH. Jan.15; 428) $250

ZIMRA, David Ibn [Radbaz]
– She'eilot U'Teshuvot. Venice, 1745-49. *2nd. Edn.* 2 pts. in 1 vol. Fo. Sm. holes not affecting text, stained & creased, buckram. (S. Oct.25; 450) *Klein.* £140

ZINCKE, G.H.
[–] Allgemeines Oeconomisches Lexicon. Leipzig, 1731. *1st. Edn.* 2 pts. in 1 vol. Some light browning, cont. leath., rubbed. (R. Oct.12; 2133) DM 750

ZINCKE, G.H. -*Contd.*

-- **Anr. Edn.** Ed.:– J.J. Volkmann. Leipzig, 1780. 2 vols. Hf. leath., old wear. (V. Sep.29; 1544)
DM 480

ZINZERLING, J.
See— **SINCERUS, [Zinzerling] J.**

ZOCCHI, Giuseppe
- Vedute delle Ville e d'Altri Luoghi della Toscana. Flor., 1757. Ob. fo. Engraved title, 50 plts., cont. hf. cf., later label on spine. (C. Dec.9; 174)
D'Arcy. £11,000

ZOCCHI, Giuseppe & others
- Pitture del Salone Imperiale del Palazzo di Firenze. Ill.:– Faucci & others. Flor., 1751. *1st. Edn.* Lge. fo. Engraved title, engraved dedicatory plt., 27 plts., including 8 double-p., minor repair to title, cont. hf. cf. (C. Dec.9; 173) *Weinreb.* £2,000

ZOEGA, Georg
- De Origine et Usu Obeliscorum. Rome, 1797. Fo. Cont. vell., slightly soiled. (R. Apr.3; 703)
DM 1,000
-- **Anr. Copy.** Fo. On Bütten, wide margin, title lf. spotted, with sm. holes, 2 bkd., & stpd., some browning & foxing. later hf. vell. (H. Nov.23; 484)
DM 450

ZOHAR [Hebrew] ... ; seu, Specimen Theologiae Soharicae ... versione latina ac necessariis adnotationibus illustratas ... studio et opera Gottofr. Christophori Sommeri
Gotha, 1734. *1st. Edn.* Sm. 4to. Some browning, cont. vell., loose in bdg. (SG. Feb.2; 89) $100

ZOLA, Emile
- L'Assomoir. Ill.:– Bellanger, Clairin, Renoir & others. Paris, [1878]. *1st. Ill. Edn.* Sm. 4to. Hf. mor., corners, by Maylander, spine gt. (HD. Jul.6; 126)
Frs. 9,000
-- **Anr. Edn.** Ill.:– André Gill, G. Bellanger, Clairin, etc. Paris, [1878]. *(130) numbered on Hollande.* 4to. With suite on Chine of all figures, hf. mor., corners, by Bretault, unc.; A.N. from Jeannot. (HD. Dec.16; 209)
Frs. 2,300
- Nana. Ill.:– André Gill, Bertall, G. Bellander, etc. Paris, 1882. *1st. Pict. Edn. (100) numbered on Holland.* 4to. Suite on Chine, before the letter of all figures, hf. mor., corners, wrap., by Bretault, unc. (HD. Dec.16; 210)
Frs. 2,700
-- **Anr. Edn.** Ill.:–Chas Laborde. Paris, 1929. *(170) on vell., with set of 43 etchings in black.* 2 vols. 4to. Hf. mor. by Fonsèque, spines decor., wraps. preserved. (HD. Nov.17; 202)
Frs. 2,700
-- **Anr. Edn.** Ill.:– Chas. Laborde. 1929. 2 vols. 4to. With added proof of 1 figure, black on old japan, leaves, wrap., s.-c.'s. (HD. Dec.9; 35q)
Frs. 1,550
- Nouveaux Contes à Ninon. Ill.:– Ed. Rudaux. Paris, 1886. *(500). (150) on japan.* 2 vols. in 1. Mandarin mor. by Meers Engel, spine decor., s.-c. (HD. Jul.6; 127)
Frs. 7,200
-- **Anr. Edn.** Ill.:– Ed. Rudaux. Paris, 1886. On japan, mor. gt. decor. by Marius Michel, spine decor. (slightly defect.); dedication to Paul Gallinard. (HD. Jun.13; 116)
Frs. 7,000
- Le Rêve. Ill.:– Carloz Schwabe & L. Methivet. Paris, [1892]. *1st. Ill. Edn. (30) on japan.* Decor. mor. by Charles Meunier, 1898, 1900 style plaques, mosaic spine, Comtesse Czaikowska arms, embroidered silk liners & end-ll., wraps. & silk box preserved, folder-s.-c.; letter by artist on hf.-title, 5-p. A.L.s. dtd. Barbizon, 28 Sep 1895. (HD. Jun.13; 115)
Frs. 60,000
- Rougon-Macquart. Phila., n.d. *(1000) on Japanese vell., ptd. for Subscribers only.* 12 vols. Etched plts. in 2 states, sepia & black, before & after sigs., purple mor. gt., covers with Art Nouveau gt. borders & mor. gt. onlays, spines in 6 compartments with gt.-panel. onlays, turn-ins gt., silk damask linings, partly unc., w.a.f. (CNY. Dec.17; 614)
$1,200
- Thérèse Raquin. Paris, 1882. Hf. chagrin, corners, unc., wrap. & spine preserved. (HD. Apr.26; 297)
Frs. 1,000
- Les Trois Villes: Lourdes, Rome, Paris. Paris, 1894, 1896, 1898. *Orig. Edns.* 3 vols. 12mo. On

holland, cont. hf. chagrin, spines decor., unc. (HD. May 4; 453)
Frs. 1,600
- Les Trois Villes: Rome. Paris, 1896. *Orig. Edn.* 12mo. Bradel, cl., by P. Vie, unc., wrap.; author's autograph dedication to Octave Mirbeau. (HD. Mar.27; 126)
Frs. 2,200

ZOLA, Emile (Contrib.)
See— **GIL BLAS ILLUSTRE**

ZOLA, Emile (Text)
See— **TYPES DE PARIS**

ZOMEREN, C. van
- Beschryvinge der Stadt Gorinchem en Landen van Arkel ... Ed.:– T. Hoorneer. Ill.:– J.C. Philips. Gorinchem, 1755. Fo. Some pp. reprd., lacks end-papers, cont. hf. cf., reprd., slightly loose. (VS. Dec.9; 1303)
Fls. 725

ZOMPINI, Gaetano
- Le Arti Che Vanno Per Via Nella Citta Di Venezia. Venice, 1785. Fo. Hand-cold. frontis., engraved title, 59 (of 60) hand-cold. plts., 1 torn & reprd., 3 with slight tears in lr. margin, slight spotting, ink stain on upr. margin of title, hf. mor. gt. (P. Mar.15; 17)
£1,150
-- **Anr. Copy.** Fo. Hand-cold. frontis., engraved title, 59 (of 60) hand-cold. plts., 1 torn & reprd., 3 with slight stains in lr. margin, slight spotting, ink stain on upr. margin of title, hf. mor. gt. (P. Jul.5; 248)
£700

ZONARES, Joh.
- Compendium Historiarum. Basel, 1557. 3 pts. in 1 vol. Fo. Wide margin, some lge. initials, title with some cold. pencil underlinings, front free end-paper torn out, some slight spotting, pig over wood bds., blind-tooled, metal clasps, lr. clasp defect., sm. faults, slight browning & scratching. (HT. May 8; 222)
DM 400

ZONCA, Vittorio
- Novo Teatro di Machine et Edificii per varie et Sicure Operationi. Padova, 1607. *1st. Edn.* Fo. Cont. vell. (R. Apr.4; 1658)
DM 6,000
-- **Anr. Edn.** Padua, 1621. Sm. fo. Mod. red mor., s.-c. (D. Nov.25; 4663)
DM 4,200
-- **Anr. Edn.** Padua, 1656. Fo. Lacks 2 ll., some browning & soiling, old bds., worn, w.a.f. (CSK. Nov.4; 127)
£260
-- **Anr. Copy.** Fo. Sm. hole in blank area of title-p., washed, 19th. C. mott. sheep, spine gt., slightly rubbed; Bibliothèque de Sailly bkplt., Stanitz coll. (SPB. Apr.25; 458)
$800

ZOOLOGICAL SOCIETY OF LONDON
- Catalogue of the Library. L., 1902. *5th. Edn.* Cl. (SG. Sep.15; 362)
$125
- Collection of Extracts from its Transactions & from Other Works. Ill.:– E. Lear, J. & E. Gould, W. Daniell, A. Pelletier, & others. L., 1819?-36? 4to. 39 plts., most hand-cold., few text ll. & several uncold. plts. foxed or stained; James Smith MS. ex-libris on 1st. fly-lf., w.a.f. (SG. Mar.22; 318)
$250

ZORGDRAGER, Correlius Gisbert
- Alte und Neue Gronlandische Fischerei und Wallfischfang. Leipzig, 1723. *1st. Edn.* Sm. 4to. Frontis., 6 engraved maps, 6 engraved plts., including 1 folding, hf.-title, vell. bds. [Sabin 106373] (S. Dec.1; 306)
Hannes. £640
-- **Anr. Copy.** Slightly foxed, cont. leath., bumped & very worn, spine defect. (HK. Nov.9; 1647)
DM 1,400

ZORN, Johannes
[-] Amerikanische Gewächse nach Linneischer Ordnung. Zweites Hundert. Nürnberg, 1786-87. 6 ll. & 50 old cold. copperplts., cont. hf. leath. (GB. Nov.3; 1172)
DM 1,400
[-] Icones Plantarum Medicinalium Centuria V. Abbildungen von Arzneygewächsen. Fünftes Hundert. Nürnberg, 1784. *1st. Edn.* Cont. leath. gt. (GB. Nov.3; 1171)
DM 850

ZOUCH, Richard
[-] The Sophister, A Comedy. 1639. *1st. Edn.* 4to. Fore-e. of title cropped, later hf. mor. gt., slightly rubbed. [STC 26133] (BBA. Jan.19; 127)
Sutherland. £170

ZSCHOKKE, Heinrich
- Die Klassischen Stellen der Schweiz und deren Hauptorte. Ill.:– H. Winkles & others, after G.A. Müller. Karlsruhe & Leipzig, 1836. *1st. Edn.* 2 vols. Wide margin, pict. title, 85 steel-engraved plts., minimal spotting, hf. leath. gt., worn, sm. spine defect. (V. Sep.29; 126)
DM 1,700
-- **Anr. Edn.** Ill.:– H. Winkles & others, after G.A. Müller. Karlsruhe & Leipzig, 1836-38. *1st. Edn.* 2 pts. in 1 vol. Engraved title with vig., 85 steel-engraved plts., foxed, cont. hf. leath., rubbed, lr. cover loose. (BR. Apr.12; 202)
DM 2,000
-- **Anr. Copy.** 2 pts. in 1 vol. 82 (of 85) steel-engraved plts., slightly foxed, cont. hf. leath., bumped. (HK. Nov.9; 1274)
DM 1,300
-- **Anr. Edn.** Ill.:– H. Winkles after G.A. Müller. Karlsruhe, 1836[-38]. 2 pts. in 1 vol. 74 (of 85) steel-engraved plts., lacks engraved title, 2 ll. title & pp. 393-423 with 11 steel engrs., stained at outer edge, cont. linen. (R. Apr.5; 3108)
DM 1,110
-- **Anr. Edn.** Ill.:– H. Winkles after G.A. Müller. Karlsruhe & Leipzig, 1838. 2 pts. in 1 vol. Engraved title, 85 steel-engraved views, some foxing & browning, annots. on end-papers, cont. hf. leath. (B. Oct.4; 673a)
Fls. 1,500
[-] Der Schriftstellerteufel. Ill.:– Bolt. Berlin, 1791. *1st. Edn.* Lightly browned, cont. wraps., spotted & torn, unc. (H. May 22; 939)
DM 520
- Schweiz. Stockholm, 1861. 72 steel-engraved views, cont. hf. leath. gt. (GF. Nov.16; 1152)
Sw.Frs. 1,500
-- **Anr. Edn.** Ed.:– C.M. Ekbohrn & C.J. Backman. Stockholm, [1861]. Lacks 16 pp., some light foxing, cont. hf. leath., worn & bumped, spine defect. (H. Nov.23; 364)
DM 1,200

ZUALLARDO or ZUALLART, Giovanni or Jean
- Il Devotissimo Viaggio di Gerusalemme. Rome, 1587. *1st. Edn.* Sm. 4to. Engraved ill. on fo. Z1 with faded imp., tears on 3 ll., sm. margin wormholes on a few ll., some ll. browned or spotted, 8 stained, cont. limp vell., rubbed, upr. hinge brkn. (BBA. Nov.30; 32)
Snelling. £400
-- **Anr. Copy.** 4to. Title lf. with name excision in upr. margin, 1st lf. slightly stained, vell. (D. Nov.23; 864)
DM 3,800
- Le Trèsdévot Voyage de Jerusalem, Avecq les Figures des Lieux Saincts, & Plusieurs Autres, Tirées au Naturel. Antw., 1608. *1st. Edn. in Fr.* 4 pts. in 1 vol. 4to. Approbation lf., some foxing & stains, 19th. C. hf. leath. (SG. Sep.22; 316) $750

ZUBIAUR Y AYZAGA, Manuel
- Arithmetica Práctica para instruir a la Juventud. Bilbao, 1718. Vell. (DS. Dec.16; 2298) Pts. 20,000

ZUBLER, Leonard
- Fabrica et Usus Instrumenti Chorographici ... Basel, 1625. 4to. Minimal foxing, mod. limp leath. (R. Apr.4; 1659)
DM 1,800
- Novum Instrumentum Geomethikum ... Trans.:– Caspar Wasenus. Basel, 1607. *1st. Latin Edn.* 4to. Wraps. (R. Apr.4; 1661)
DM 1,600
-- **Anr. Edn.** Basel, 1625. Slight soiling & some foxing, 19th. C. hf. vell. (R. Apr.4; 1660)
DM 1,800

ZUCCARO, Taddeo
- Illustri Fatti Farnesiani ... Ill.:– G.C.v. Prenner & G.V.d. Corleone, after T., F. & O. Zuccaro & G.B.d. Vignola. Rome, 1748. Fo. Port., engraved title, engraved dedication lf. & plt.-list, 41 plts., including 15 double-p., 19th. C. cf. gt. super extra. (SG. Nov.3; 226)
$750

ZUCCHI, G.M.
See— **LE SUEUR, Eustache — ZUCCHI, G.M.**

ZUCCHI, Niccolo
- Nova de Machinis Philosophia. Rome, 1649. *2nd. Edn.* Sm. 4to. Faded circular liby. stp. on title-p., browned, cont. limp vell.; owners inscr. of Gabrel Martorell on title-p., Stanitz coll. (SPB. Apr.25; 459)
$275

ZUGASTI, Julian de
- El Bandolerismo. Madrid, 1876. *2nd. Edn.* 10 vols. Linen. (DS. Mar.23; 2419) Pts. 20,000

ZUKOFSKY, Louis
- An Analytical & Descriptive Catalogue of the Manuscripts & Letters in the Louis Zukofsky

Collection at the University of Texas at Austin. Ed.:– M.J. Spann. [Austin], 1969. 4to. Qtr. cl., stiff wraps.; typescript approbation lf., sigd. by William B. Todd & others, bnd. in, inscr. by Spann to Celia & Louis Zukofsky, inscr. by Zukofsky. (SG. Mar.1; 649) $100
– **Anew.** Prairie City, Ill., [1946]. 12mo. Cl., d.-w. chipped; inscr. (SG. May 24; 244) $275
– – **Anr. Copy.** (*With:*) – **Ferdinand; including, It Was.** L., [1968]. Sigd. Together 2 vols. 12mo. Cl. & bds. (SG. Mar.1; 650) $140
– **55 Poems.** Prairie City, Ill., [1941]. Bds.; inscr. (SG. May 24; 242) $375
– **First Half of 'A'-9.** N.Y., 1940. *(55) numbered & sigd.* 4to. Reproduced from author's typescript with a few MS. insertions, some typescript additions, typewritten wraps. (SG. Mar.1; 639) $1,500
– **I Sent Thee Late.** [Camb., Mass., 1965]. *(20) numbered & sigd.* Ob. 32mo. Wraps. (SG. Mar.1; 641) $120
– **It Was.** [Ashland, Mass.], 1961. *(50) numbered & sigd.* Sm. 8vo. Cl., unlettered glassine d.-w. (SG. May 24; 252) $120

ZUNIGA Y ONTIVEROS, M.
– **Calendario** ... **y Guía de Forasteros en Mexico.** 1797. Mor. (DS. Apr.27; 2636) Pts. 30,000

ZUNNER, A.
[–] **Gündliche Unterweisung zu Fractur- Cantzley- und Current Schrifften** ... Nürnberg, ca. 1713. Minimal spotting, hf. vell; Hauswedell coll. (H. May 23; 267) DM 800
– **Kunstrichtige Schreib-Art, welche allerley Teutsche Current- Cansley- Fractur- und auch Lateinische Schrifften, mit ihren Fundamenten.** Nürnberg, 1709. Ob. 4to. 2 plts. with sm. holes in margin, some plts. spotted, browned, cont. vell., cockled; Hauswedell coll. (H. May 23; 262) DM 600
[–] **Kurtze Anweisung zu Teutsch- und Loteinischen Schrifften** ... Nürnberg, 1701. Minimal spotting,

mod. bds.; Hauswedell coll. (H. May 23; 254) DM 600

ZURNER, A.F.
– **Atlas von der Ganzen Welt für Junge Leute.** Nuremb., after 1792. Ob. 4to. Wide margin, 31 old cold. copper engraved maps, some margin foxing, orig. ptd. wraps. (R. Oct.13; 2882) DM 2,800

ZUR WESTEN, W. von
– **Berlins Graphische Gelegenheitskunst.** Berlin, 1912. *(350).* 2 vols. 4to. Orig. hf. vell. (HK. Nov.12; 4840) DM 520
– **Vom Kunstgewand der Höflichkeit.** Ill.:– M. Behmer & others. Berlin, 1921. *(550) numbered.* 4to. Orig. hf. vell. (HK. Nov.11; 3420) DM 560

ZURLAUBEN, B.F.A., Baron de & Laborde, J.B. de
– **Tableaux Topographiques, Pittoresques, Physiques, Historiques, Moraux et Politiques de la Suisse.** Ill.:– after Le Barbier, Chatelet, Bertaux, & Perignon. Paris, 1780-86. 2 vols. in 4. Fo. Engraved frontis., engraved titles in each plt. vol., engraved ports. of authors on hf.-title verso in 1st. plt. vol., engraved hf.-title in 2nd. plt. vol., 3 pp. dedication with headpiece, 440 plts., numbered to 278, some double-p., 3 views with captions supplied in MS., 1 double-p. plt. bnd. inverted, cont. tree cf. gt., spines gt., spine ends & corners slightly rubbed, owing to the difficulty of collation, w.a.f. (C. Nov.16; 203) *Rheinbuch.* £13,000

ZWEIG, Max
– **Saul und David in der Höhle.** Ill.:– Hans Fronius. Wien, ca. 1974. *1st. Serapion Edn., (200).* Fo. 5 sigd. full-p. orig. lithos., orig. pict. bds. (GB. May 5; 2544) DM 450

ZWEIG, Stefan
– **Die Augen des Ewigen Bruders.** Ill.:– Fritz Heubner. Hellerau, 1924. *(250) numbered.* 10 orig.

etchings, of which 9 full-p. sigd. by artist & author, silk. (R. Oct.11; 466) DM 430
– **Die Gesammelte Gedichte.** Leipzig, 1924. *1st. Coll. Edn.* Mor., gt., inner & outer dentelle. (HK. May 17; 3237) DM 560

ZWEIG, Stefan (Contrib.)
See— NEUE RUNDSCHAU

ZWINGLI, Ulrich
– **Verwenung der Disputatz zü Zürich.** [Augsburg, 1523]. *1st. Edn.* Wide margin, end-lf. lightly browned, old vell., end-papers renewed with old paper. (R. Apr.3; 107) DM 4,400

ZWINNER, E.
– **Blumen-Buch des Heiligen Lands Palestina, in drey Bücher abgetheilt.** München, 1661. 4to. 4 defect. maps & 1 folding plt. with sm defects mntd., 2 folding plts. with lge. loss mntd., 1 plt. with tear at side with loss, 2 pp. with corner tears with slight text loss, lightly foxed thro.-out, cont. red mor. gt., gold decor., corner & centre fleurons rubbed, light worming, lacks ties. (R. Apr.5; 2845) DM 1,500
– – **Anr. Copy.** 4to. Title with old owners note, 3 copper engrs. with faults & partly bkd., foxed or soiled, cont. red mor., gold-tooled, slightly rubbed & wormed, lacks clasps. (HK. Nov.8; 882) DM 620

ZYL, Johannes van
– **Theatrum Machinarum Universale, of Groot Algemeen Moolen-Boek.** Amst., [1790]. *2nd. Edn.?* 2 vols. in 1. Fo. Hf.-title with verse on verso (blank part restored but no loss of text), engraved dedication lf. (supplied?), old cf.-bkd. bds., rubbed; Stanitz coll. (SPB. Apr.25; 460) $750

Part II

Printed Maps, Charts & Plans

AA, Pieter van der
- **Le Duché de Luxembourg.** [1712]. 225 × 300mm. Copper engraved map, figure cartouche, decor. borders ptd. from separate plt., cut at head to border, sm. crumple at foot to border. (R. Oct.13; 3675)
DM 400

ADRICHOMIUS, Christiaan
- **Ierusalem et Suburbia eius, sicut Tempore Christi Floruit.** [Cologne, 1588 or later]. 727 × 477mm. Lge. engraved double-p. plan of biblical Jerusalem from Braun & Hogenberg Civitates, in 2 sheets, joined & laid down, faint browning, F., w.a.f. (S. May 22; 260)   *Trotter.* £300
- **– Anr. Copy.** 727 × 477mm. Plan of biblical Jerusalem in 2 double-p. engraved sheets, from Braun & Hogenberg Civitates, Latin text on versos, sm. splits at lr. centre-folds without loss of engraved surface, slight margin soiling, w.a.f. (S. May 22; 261)   *Norwich.* £240
- **Situs Terrae Promisionis.** Amst., 1633 or later. 372 × 500mm. Double-p. engraved map, orientated east to the top of the sheet, partly hand-cold. in outl., German text on verso, split at centrefold without loss of engraved surface. (S. Jun.25; 6)
King. £90
- **– Anr. Edn.** Amst., Janssonius, [1658]. 375 × 495mm. Double-p. engraved map, hand-cold. in outl., elab. cold. title, figures, Dutch text on verso, rather soiled. (SG. Dec.15; 93) $250
- **– Anr. Edn.** Jansson, n.d. Ob. fo. Cold. copper engraved map, Lge. painted floral & fruit border, figure decor. (R. Oct.13; 3542)   DM 430

AINSLIE, John
- **Scotland Drawn & Engrav'd from a Series of Angles and Astronomical Observations.** L., 1789. Each sheet 600 × 540mm. Hand-cold. engraved map on 9 sheets, light soiling. (CSK. Aug.5; 18)
£150

ALLARD, Carolus
- **Exactissima Asiae Delineatio.** N.d. Ob. fo. Old cold copper engraved map, lge. figure cartouche & sm. supp. map, slightly spotted, bkd. at foot. (R. Apr.5; 3363)   DM 650
- **Nieuwe ende perfecte Caerte van het Coningryck Portugael ende Algarve.** [Amst.], ca. 1680. 450 × 562mm. Hand-cold. double-p. engraved map, orientated west to the top of the sheet, sm. stain in lr. margin. (S. Jun.25; 244).   *Ash.* £60
- **Novissima et Perfectissima Africae Descriptio.** N.d. Ob. fo. Old cold. copper engraved map, lge. figure cartouche, slightly spotted, sm. crease at foot. (R. Apr.5; 3253)   DM 900
- **Planisphaerii Coelestis Hemisphaerium Septentrionale [et] Meridionale.** Covens & Mortier, 1700. Ob. fo. Old cold. copper engraved map, 2 ll., slightly spotted, some defects. (R. Apr.5; 3142)   DM 400

ANVILLE, Jean Baptiste Bourguignon d'
- **America Septentrionalis.** Nuremb., Homann's Heirs, 1756 [or later]. 456 × 505mm. Double-p. engraved map, hand-cold. in outl., slight margin soiling. (S. Jun.25; 140)   *Faupel.* £100
- **Amérique Septentrionale.** Paris, 1746. Approx. 36 × 33 inches overall. Map, in 2 sheets, hand-cold. in outl., uncold. decor. title cartouche, decor., slightly soiled & frayed on right-hand edge. (TA. Nov.17; 85)   £100
- **– Anr. Edn.** Paris, 1746 [or later]. 435 × 870mm. (total dimensions). General map in four sheets on 3 double-p. engraved mapsheets, hand-cold. in outl.,

lge. allegorical title cartouche, sm. margin stain, faint crease. (S. Dec.1; 228)   *Nebenzahl.* £260
- **– Anr. Copy.** 435 × 870mm. Map in 4 sheets joined as 2, outl. hand-cold., impression slightly weak in places, margin stain, creasing at additional folds (1 strengthened with tape on verso). (S. Nov.1; 228)   *Burgess.* £100
- **Asia & its Islands.** L., R. Sayer, 1787 [or later]. 1122 × 1200mm. (overall). Engraved map in 4 sheets, joined as 2, cold. in wash & outl., faint offsetting & spotting. (S. Dec.13; 11)
Lassalle. £50
- **Canada Louisiane et Terres Angloises.** Paris, 1755 [or later]. 870 × 1,135mm. (total dimensions). Map in 4 double-p. engraved sheets, margin staining, slight creasing, short tear without loss of engraved surface. (S. Dec.1; 229)
Nebenzahl. £200
- **– Anr. Edn.** Paris, 1755. 34 × 45 inches. Engraved map, in 2 sheets, joined at centre seam, hand-cold. in outl., cartouche fully cold., inset map, slight wrinkling, lightly tipped onto matboard. (SPB. May 23; 21) $350
- **Carte de la Louisiane ... Dressée en Mai 1732. Publié en 1752.** [Paris], 1752 or later. 518 × 920mm. Folding engraved map, the river above Arkansas continued as an inset, sm. stain at upr. margin. (S. Dec.1; 236)   *Cartographia.* £230
- **Hémisphère Occidental [Oriental].** Paris, 1761 [or later]. 650 × 1200mm. Engraved map in twin hemispheres, in 2 sheets joined & folding, outl. hand-cold., some soiling, short tear without loss of engraved surface. (S. Nov.1; 193)   *Charles.* £75
- **A Map of South America ... with Several Improvements & Additions, & the Newest Discoveries.** 1787 [or later]. 1,080 × 1,190mm. Engraved map in 4 sheets joined as 2, outl. hand-cold., inset of Falkland Islands, elab. title-cartouche, faint offsetting. (S. Nov.1; 215)   *Frers.* £80
- **Partie Orientale du Canada.** 1776. 575 × 490mm. Hand-cold. map, cartouche, sea crudely cold. (P. Apr.12; 351)   *Ruddell.* £90

ANVILLE, J.B.B. d' & Pownall, Thomas
- **A New Map of the Whole Continent of America, Divided into North & South & West Indies, Wherein are Exactly Described the United States of North America ... Compiled from Mr. D'Anville's Maps of that Continent, ... Corrected in the Several Parts Belonging to Great Britain, from the Original Materials of Governor Pownall, M.P.** L., Robert Sayer, 1786. 520 × 1,190mm. 2 lge. double-p. engraved folding maps, hand-cold. in outl., inset map 'The Supplement to North America containing the Countries adjoining to Baffins & Hudsons Bays', & list of 'The Continent & Islands of America ... Divided & Possessed as follows ... ', very minor offsetting in places, 3-inch section of right side of 1 map soiled, with 1 repair, satisfactory margins, versos blank. (SG. Jun.7; 45) $375

ARIAS, Montano Benito
- **Tabula Terrae Canaan Abrahae Tempore et Ante-adventum Filior. Israel cum Vicinis & Finitimis Regionib.** [Amst.], 17th. C. 330 × 520mm. Double-p. engraved map, uncold., 2 sailing ships, lge. sea monster, verso blank, good margins. (SG. Jun.7; 39) $750

ARROWSMITH, Aaron
- **A Map Exhibiting all the New Discoveries in the Interior Parts of North America ...** L., Arrowsmith, 1795, with additions 1796. 35½ × 67½ inches.

Engraved map, in 3 sheets, hand-cold. in outl., overlay plt. of additional mapping west of Hudson's Bay & east of Slave Lake, slight offsetting & overall browning. (SPB. May 23; 20) $2,000
- **A Map of the United States of North America Drawn from a Number of Critical Researches.** 10 Soho Sq., L., 1 Jan. 1796 [but 1808 or later]. 1230 × 1430mm. Detailed engraved wall map, in 4 sheets, with additions to 1802, mntd. & dissected in 60 sections, wash & outl. cold. by hand, lge. cartouche, faint offsetting, folding into cont. paper s.-c. (S. Mar.6; 120)   *Quaritch.* £280
- **– Anr. Edn.** L., Arrowsmith, 1796. 48 × 56 inches. Engraved map, in 4 sheets, scenic cartouche, the whole hand-cold. in outl., slight offsetting & browning. (SPB. May 23; 29) $2,000

AUVRAY, P.L.
See— **BRUCKNER, Daniel**

BACHE, A.D.
- **Map of the Bays, Harbors & Rivers Around New York; Showing the Channels, Soundings, Lighthouses, Buoys, etc., & the Complete Topography of the Surrounding Country.** N.Y., 1866. 700 × 580mm. Hand-cold. litho. map, dampsoiled, linen-bkd., folded in 8vo-size gt.-lettered cl. covers, loose in bdg.; sigs. of Pierre C. Kane. (SG. Jun.7; 62)
$140

BARTHOLEMEW, J.
- **Dutch Possessions in South America & the West Indies. – Curacao. – Principal Dutch Colonies in the Indian Seas.** N.d. 462 × 310mm. & smaller. 3 cold. engraved maps, F. (CH. May 24; 205)   Fls. 700

BECKERINGH, Th.
- **Kaart of Landtafereel der Provincie van Groningen.** Ca. 1780. 900 × 1,120mm. Hand-cold. engraved map, slight stains, pasted on linen & folded down to 8vo. size. (VG. Dec.1; 1290)
Fls. 470

BEEK, Anna
- **Nieuwe Platte Grond van's Gravenhage.** Ca. 1690. 480 × 590mm. Engraved folding map, hand-cold. & heightened in gold, pasted on linen, margins pasted over, slight central defect. (VG. Sep.15; 1709)   Fls. 800

BELLE FOREST, F. de
- [-] **La Ville de Londres. Londinum Feracissimi Angliae Regni Metropolis.** [Paris, M. Sonnius, 1575]. 309 × 487mm. Double-p. woodcut perspective plan, copying closely state 1 of Frans Hogenberg engraved plan of 1572, publd. in 'La cosmographie universelle', faint stain, 1 fold strengthened, w.a.f. (S. May 21; 48)   *Marsden.* £200

BELLIN, Jacques Nicolas
- **Carte de la Louisiane et des Pays Voisins ... 1750.** [Paris,], 1755 or later. 478 × 613mm. Double-p. engraved map, outl. hand-cold., sm. tear at print-crease without loss of engraved surface. (S. Nov.1; 232)   *Potter.* £160
- [-] **Carte de l'Entrée de la Tamise. Avec les Bancs, Passes, Isles, et Costes Comprises entre Sandwich et Clay.** Paris, 1693. Approx. 18 × 35 inches. Map, hand-cold. in outl., 2 compass rose, rumb lines, etc. (TA. Jan.19; 101)   £50
- **– Anr. Edn.** [1766 or later]. Approx. 18 × 35 inches. Uncold. map, inset detail of the Thames from L. to the Estuary, twin compass rose, rumb

lines, etc., some light stains. (TA. Mar.15; 103)
£54

- Carte Reduite des Coste Orientales de L'Amérique Septentrionale. 1757. 480 × 900mm. Hand-cold. engraved chart, reprd. at lr. fold. (CSK. Nov.4; 25)
£200

- Partie Occidentale de la Nouvelle France ou Canada ... Paris, 1755. 18½ × 24 inches. Engraved map, hand-cold. in outl., cartouche fully cold., slight soiling, tipped onto matboard. (SPB. May 23; 8)
£750

– – **Anr. Copy.** Ob. fo. Copper engraved map, outl. cold., painted floral cartouche, lightly browned. (R. Oct.13; 3458)
DM 680

– – **Anr. Edn.** [Nuremb.], 1755 [or later]. 427 × 538mm. Double-p. engraved regional map of Great Lakes, including several fictitious islands in Lake Superior, headwaters of Mississippi & site of Chic. at 'R. et Port du Checagou', hand-cold. in outl., slight crease at centre-fold, faint rust-spot in engraved surface, w.a.f. (S. May 22; 361)
Fergusson. £325

BENNETT, John
See— SAYER, Robert & Bennett, John

BERRY, William
- The Empire of the Great Turke in Europe, Asia & Africa. [1680-1798]. 555 × 865mm. (sheet). Engraved map, hand-cold. in outl., central vertical fold, trimmed on borderline, some creasing & other defects, laid down at edges onto support sheet. (BS. Sep.21; 73)
£75

- The Mountains of the Alpes. [1680-1798]. 570 × 870mm. (sheet). Engraved map, hand-cold. in outl., central vertical fold, trimmed on borderline, stained, partly laid down on support sheet. (BS. Sep.21; 74)
£60

- The States of the Empire of the Turks in Europe ... 1683. 22 × 35 inches. Map, hand-cold. in outl., uncold. ornamental title cartouche surmounted by Royal crest & incorporating scale of distance, mntd. on support sheet (as iss.), damp-affected. (TA. Jan.19; 146)
£72

BLAEU, Cornelis
See— BLAEU, Johannes or Jan & Cornelis

BLAEU, Johannes or Jan
- Aethiopia Interior vel Exterior ... 1635. 390 × 500 mm. Line engraved map, cold. outl., Dutch text on verso. (VA. Apr.27; 572)
R 520

- Aethiopia Superior vel Interior. Ca. 1650. 500 × 300 mm. Hand-cold. map, cartouche, 2 tears in margin. (P. Jun.7; 373)
£75

- Americae nova tabula. [Amst.], ca. 1630. 15½ × 21½ inches. Hand-cold. engraved map, vigs. at top & side borders, additional inset of Greenland, sailing vessels, etc., matted, F. & G. (SPB. May 23; 22)
·$1,100

– – **Anr. Edn.** [Amst., 1630, but ca. 1650]. 410 × 550mm. Double-p. engraved general map of Americas, sm. inset of Greenland & Iceland, showing California as a peninsula, map design flanked by side borders each of 5 vigs. of costumed figures, & an upr. frieze showing 9 town views, cont. hand-cold., Dutch text on verso, w.a.f. (S. May 22; 290)
Christensen. £800

– – **Anr. Edn.** [1663]. 410 × 550mm. Engraved hand-cold. map, some light soiling, 1 crease. (CSK. Nov.4; 26)
£800

– – **Anr. Edn.** N.d. Ob. fo. Cold. copper engraved map, 2 painted cartouches, sm. supp. map, decor., 9 sm. views at head, margins brown spotted, sm. slit at right, parts of Indian figures painted over. (R. Oct.13; 3427)
DM 1,750

- Asia Noviter Delineata. [Amst., 1630, but ca. 1650]. 411 × 554mm. Double-p. engraved map of continent including Japan, the Philippines & East Indies, design flanked by side borders each of 5 vigs. illustrating costumed figures, top frieze consisting of 9 vig. town views, hand-cold. in outl., embellishments fully so, Dutch text on verso, w.a.f. (S. May 22; 422)
Alai. £480

– – **Anr. Edn.** [Amst., 1640]. 410 × 555mm. Double-p. engraved map, fully hand-cold., ships, sea monsters, animals, 9 birds-eye views of cities in horizontal panel across top, 10 costume studies in 2 vertical panels at each side, full margins, Latin

text on verso, some minor rubbing & browning. (SC. Jun.7; 74)
$600

[-] Bedfordiensis Comitatus; Anglis Bedford Shire. Buckinghamiensis Comitatus; Anglis Buckingham Shire. Ca. 1645 or later. Approx. 16½ × 21 inches. 2 orig. hand-cold. maps on 1 sheet, each with ornamental title cartouche & separate scale of distance, armorials, etc., Latin text on verso. (TA. Jul.19; 127)
£105

- Bercheria Vernacule Barkshire. Ca. 1650. 500 × 390mm. Hand-cold. map, arms, browned, F. (P. Jun.7; 379)
£50

[-] Britannia prout divisa fuit temporibus Anglo Saxonum. [Amst.], 1645 or later. 415 × 530mm. Double-p. engraved map, outl. cold., vig. side borders fully cold., Fr. text on verso. (S. Dec.1; 142)
Evans. £300

– – **Anr. Copy.** 430 × 530mm. Engraved hand-cold. map, margins trimmed, laid down on paper. (CSK. Nov.4; 4)
£150

[-] Cantabrigiensis Comitatus; Cambridge Shire. Ca. 1650. Approx. 16½ × 20½ inches. Map, hand-cold. in outl., sm. decor. title cartouche, Royal arms, many armorials, recently F. & G. (TA. Sep.15; 170)
£60

[-] Cantium vernacule Kent. [Amst.], 1645 or later. 387 × 528mm. Double-p. engraved map, Fr. text on verso. (S. Jun.25; 396)
£130

- Chili. Amst., [Blaeu, 1630]. 360 × 480mm. Double-p. engraved map, hand-cold., title, scale & Auctorial cartouches, verso blank, minor abrasion in lr. fold. (SG. Dec.15; 22)
$250

[-] Comitatus Northantonensis Vernacule Northamton Shire. Amst., ca. 1650. Approx. 15 × 20 inches. Map, hand-cold. in outl., decor. title cartouche surrounded by figures & sheep, separate scale of distance cartouche, Royal crest, armorials, minor damage to centrefold, recently F. & G. (TA. Sep.15; 171)
£75

[-] Comitatus Salopiensis Anglice Shropshire. [Amst., 1645, or later]. 383 × 501mm. Double-p. engraved map, hand-cold. in outl., Fr. text on verso, light browning. (S. Apr.9; 154)
Kidd. £55

- Cornubia. Ca. 1650. 500 × 395mm. Hand-cold. map, slightly browned arms, vig. sailing ships. (P. May 17; 457)
Pender. £130

– – **Anr. Edn.** Ca. 1660 or later. 15 × 20 inches. Map, hand-cold. in outl., ornamental title cartouche, Royal crest, several armorials, sailing ships, etc., Latin text to verso, a little soiled overall. (TA. Mar.15; 87)
£130

[-] Cumbriae; Vulgo Cumberland. Ca. 1660. Approx. 16 × 20 inches. Cont. hand-cold. map, decor. & histor. title cartouche with figures, cherubs & animals, etc., scale of distance, Royal crest, armorials, Fr. text on verso. (TA. Nov.17; 112)
£100

[-] Devonia vulgo Devon-Shire. Ca. 1660 or later. Approx. 15½ × 20 inches. Hand-cold. map, ornamental title cartouche surrounded by figures & animals, separate scale of distance, Royal crest, armorials, etc., Fr. text to verso, F. & G. (TA. Jan.19; 92)
£125

- Domino Veneto nell'Italia. [Amst., 1634, but 1662 or later]. 380 × 495mm. Double-p. engraved map, hand-cold. in outl., embellishments fully cold., no text on verso. (S. Mar.6; 130)
Brice. £55

- The East Riding of Yorkshire. 1645 or later. 15 × 20½ inches. Engraved map, hand-cold. in outl., F. & G. (CSK. Mar.9; 42)
£50

[-] Episcopatus Dunelmensis. Vulgo the Bishoprike of Durham. Ca. 1645 or later. Approx. 15 × 20 inches. Map, hand-cold., ornamental corner title cartouche incorporating figures & sheep, separate scale of distance, Royal crest, armorials, sailing ships, etc., a little browned overall, Latin text to verso. (TA. Jun.21; 120)
£80

- Essexia Comitatus. 1645 or later. 420 × 530mm. Engraved map, hand-cold. in outl., F. & G. (CSK. Dec.2; 28)
£75

– – **Anr. Edn.** [1645]. 422 × 530mm. (plt.-mark). Engraved map, hand-cold. in outl., central vertical fold, Fr. text to verso, trimmed to narrow margins, verso browned. (BS. Sep.21; 85)
£100

– – **Anr. Edn.** Ca. 1660 or later. 16½ × 20½ inches. Map, hand-cold. in outl., sm. ornamental title cartouche, separate scale of distance cartouche surmntd. by cherubs, Royal crest, armorials, Latin text on verso. (TA. Jan.19; 95)
£90

- Extrema Americae ... **Terra Nova Nova Francia.** Ca. 1650. 575 × 455mm. Hand-cold. map, vig. sailing ships, F. (P. Nov.24; 343)
Washke. £210

- Fifae Vicecomitatus – The Sherifdome of Fyfe. 1654 or later. 580 × 490mm. Engraved map, cold. in outl., heraldic arms & title cartouche, Latin text to verso, Hogarth frame, double-glazed. (PD. Dec.14; 295)
£85

- Freti Magellanici ac Novi Freti Vulgo Le Maire. N.d. Copper-engraved map, some col. offsetting, light browning. (V. Sep.29; 170)
DM 550

- Geographiae Blavianae ... Amst., 1662. Vol. VI only: 'Scotland & Ireland'. Fo. Engraved title with ptd. label, 55 engraved maps, all but 1 double-p., cont. hand-cold. thro.-out, the title & embellishments of most maps heightened in gold, contents lf. at end, dampstain affecting lr. blank margins with some softening, slight adhesion damage affecting 1 or 2 maps, generally without the browning often found in this vol., cont. gt.-panel. vell., upr. cover worn, slightly soiled. (S. Dec.1; 152)
Furno. £1,850

[-] Glamorganensis Comitatus; Vulgo Glamorganshire. [Amst.], 1645 or later. 385 × 508mm. Double-p. engraved map, hand-cold. in outl., embellishments fully cold., Latin text on verso, F. & G. (S. Mar.6; 181)
Willis. £130

- Guernsey & Jersey. [1650]. 395 × 475mm. (plt.-mark). Engraved map, hand-cold. in outl., margins, Dutch text to verso, some creasing along central vertical fold, some foxing & dampstaining. (BS. Sep.21; 106)
£95

– – **Anr. Edn.** N.d. Ob. fo. Old cold. copper engraved map, 2 painted figure cartouches, cold arms & decor., col. & text partly offset. (R. Oct.13; 3743)
DM 450

- Guiana sive Amazonum Regio. Amst., ca. 1630 or later. Approx. 14½ × 19½ inches. Map, hand-cold. in outl., ornamental title cartouche, separate scale of distance, lge. central compass rose, rhumb lines, sailing ships, etc., a little browned overall, some minor margin. dampstains. (TA. Jun.21; 122) £60

- Hampshire. Ca. 1645. 14¼ × 19¼ inches. Hand-cold. engraved map, heraldic shields & devices, F. & G. (SKC. Nov.18; 2071)
£110

[-] Hantonia sive Southantonensis Comitatus vulgo Hant-Shire. Ca. 1660 or later. Approx. 16½ × 20 inches. Map, partially hand-cold., ornamental title cartouche incorporating animals, fish, vegetables, etc., Royal crest, armorials, sailing ships, etc., Fr. text on verso, F. & G. (TA. Jan.19; 93) £95

- Hertfordia Comitatus Vernacule Hertfordshire. 1645 or later. 380 × 500mm. Engraved map, hand-cold. in outl., F. & G. (CSK. Dec.2; 27) £100

– – **Anr. Edn.** [1645]. 385 × 505mm. (plt.-mark). Engraved map, central vertical fold, Latin text to verso, some foxing. (BS. Sep.21; 86)
£110

- Insula Sacra ... **Holy Land & Farne.** [1646]. 400 × 490mm. Engraved map, hand-cold. out., title cartouche, Royal arms, text verso, F. & G. (PD. Apr.18; 158)
£65

[-] Insulae Albion et Hibernia cum Minoribus Adjacentibus. Ca. 1660 or later. Approx. 15 × 18 inches. Map, hand-cold. in outl., ornamental title cartouche, Latin text to verso, F. & double-G. (TA. Mar.15; 86)
£50

[-] Lancastria Palatinatus. Anglis Lancaster et Lancashire. Ca. 1660. Approx. 15½ × 20 inches. Cont. hand-cold. map, decor. title cartouche with figures & animals, scale of distance cartouche, Royal crest, etc., Fr. text on verso. (TA. Nov.17; 109)
£180

– – **Anr. Edn.** [1662]. Approx. 15½ × 20 inches. Cont. hand-cold. map, decor. title cartouche, surrounded by figure & animals, separate scale of distance with cherub, armorials, etc., Fr. text to verso. (TA. Sep.15; 169)
£95

- Laudelia Sive Lauderdalia ... Ca. 1654. 500 × 390mm. Engraved hand-cold. map, title & dedication cartouche, F. & G. (PD. Apr.18; 157) £50

[-] Leicestrensis Comitatus. Leicester Shire. Ca. 1645 or later. Approx. 15 × 20 inches. Map, hand-cold. in outl., sm. ornamental title cartouche, separate scale of distance with several cherubs, Royal crest, armorials, etc., browned overall, Fr. text to verso. (TA. Jun.21; 119)
£65

- Lothian & Lintitquo. N.d. 570 × 410mm. Engraved map, cold. in outl., heraldic arms & title cartouche, mntd. (PD. Dec.14; 302)
£72

BLAEU, Johannes or Jan -*Contd.*

- **Mappa Aestivarum Insularum alias Barmudas.** Amst., [1635, or later]. 400 × 535mm. Double-p. engraved map, hand-cold. in outl., embellishments fully cold., Latin text on verso, browned at upr. portion & re-margined. (S. Apr.9; 91)
Burgess. £80
- - **Anr. Edn.** L., Bassett & Chiswell, ca. 1676. 400 × 540mm. Double-p. map, from Speede's 'Theatre of the Empire of Great Britain', engraved by Abraham Goos, title cartouche in Latin & Engl., 2 scale cartouches, Engl. text on verso, some discoloration & minor repairs at fold. (SG. Dec.15; 24)
$450
- **Middle-sexia.** [1645 or later]. 390 × 410mm. Engraved hand-cold. map, F. & G. (CSK. Nov.4; 1)
£85
- - **Anr. Edn.** Ca. 1650. 410 × 390mm. Hand-cold. map, cartouche. (P. Dec.8; 444) *Sherring.* £60
- - **Anr. Edn.** Ca. 1660 or later. Approx. 15½ × 16 inches. Map, hand-cold. in outl., ornamental title cartouche incorporating figure, farm produce, etc., single armorial, Fr. text on verso. (TA. Jan.19; 94)
£65
[-] **Momonia, Hibernice Moun et Woun; Anglice Mounster.** [Amst., 1662]. 41 × 51½cm. Double-p. engraved map, hand-cold. in outl., 3 sailing ships & coat-of-arms, full margins, Spanish text on verso, light overall browning, offsetting, minor worming. (SG. Jun.7; 97)
$130
[-] **Montgomeria Comitatus et Comitatus Mervinia.** Ca. 1645 or later. Approx. 15 × 20 inches. Map, hand-cold., strapwork title cartouche, incorporating Royal & county arms, separate scale of distance with figures & cherubs, armorials, sailing ships, etc., F. & G. (TA. Jun.21; 121)
£90
- **Monumethensis Comitatus. Vernacule Monmouth Shire.** [1659]. Approx. 15 × 19½ inches. Map, cont. hand-cold., ornamental & histor. title cartouche & separate scale of distance, Royal crest & county arms, etc., Spanish text on verso. (TA. May 17; 164)
£80
[-] **Nova Belgica et Anglia Nova.** [Amst.], 1635 or later. 390 × 500mm. Double-p. engraved map, orientated west to the top, hand-cold. in outl., cartouche & other embellishments fully cold., the cartouche also heightened with gold, sm. margin wormhole, F. & G. (S. Dec.1; 238)
Lotacki-de-Veligest. £700
- **Nova et Accurata Brasiliae totius Tabula.** N.d. Ob. fo. Old cold. copper engraved map, from Visscher atlas, lge. figure cartouche, some spotting, crease on left, 3 sm. holes bkd. (R. Apr.5; 3313)
DM 560
- **Nova Regni Hispaniae Descriptio ... Anno 1605.** Amst., 1605 [or later]. 409 × 550mm. Double-p. engraved map, 4 inset views, few minor repairs, tissue-bkd., trimmed to pltmark, traces of folds. (S. Apr.9; 132)
Potter. £60
- **Nova Virginia Tabula.** [Amst.], 1630 or later]. 370 × 475mm. Double-p. engraved map of Chesapeake Bay region, orientated west to top of sheet, derived from John Smith map of 1608, inset showing Powhatan & Indian figure after John White, hand-cold., Dutch text on verso, w.a.f. (S. May 22; 374)
Vasica. £340
- - **Anr. Copy.** 370 × 475mm. Double-p. engraved map, orientated west to the top of the sheet, hand-cold. in outl., embellishments fully cold., Latin text on verso. (S. Jun.25; 153) *Schiff.* £200
- - **Anr. Edn.** Ca. 1650. 490 × 380mm. Hand-cold. map, heightened with gold, inset ill., F. & G. (P. Mar.15; 417) *Ruddell.* £260
- - **Anr. Copy.** 480 × 380mm. Uncold. map. (P. Jul.5; 398)
£160
- - **Anr. Edn.** [1667]. 375 × 480mm. Engraved map, hand-cold. in outl., Fr. text on verso. (CSK. Nov.4; 19)
£280
- **Orcadum et Schetlandiae Insularum accuratissima descriptio.** [Amst., 1654 or after]. 400 × 530mm. Double-p. engraved map, hand-cold., sailing ships, ships engaged in naval battle, sea monster, good margins, some minor rubbing, wear at fold, mntd. to backing bd. & overmat. (SG. Jun.7; 98) $110
- **Oxfordshire.** Ca. 1645. 19¼ × 23 inches. Hand-cold. engraved map, heraldic shields, astrological & scientific instruments round title, F. & G. (SKC. Nov.18; 2082)
£65

- **Oxonium Comitatus.** [Amst.], 1645 or later. 382 × 504mm. Double-p. engraved map, 16 college escutcheons in side borders, Fr. text on verso. (S. Jun.25; 405) *Kidd.* £100
- **Paraguay.** Amst., 1635 or later. 375 × 480mm. Double-p. engraved map, hand-cold. in outl., Latin text on verso. (S. Jun.25; 143) *Faupel.* £70
- **Peru.** Amst., [Blaeu, 1662]. 380 × 495mm. Double-p. engraved map, hand-cold. in outl., cold. notations, elab. title/scale cartouche, lge. compass rose, etc., Latin text on verso, minor foxing, liby. stp. in lr. margin. (SG. Dec.15; 23) $175
- **Praefecturae Paranambucae pars Borealis, una cum Praefectura de Itamarca.** [1662-65]. Approx. 16 × 21 inches. Hand-cold. map, decor. title cartouche incorporating scale of distance, decor., compass rose, etc., Latin text on verso, little browned & margin stains. (TA. Nov.17; 84)
£105
- **Provincia Oxoniensis.** [1644]. 15 × 19½ inches. Engraved map, hand-cold. in outl., Fr. text on verso, window mount. (CSK. May 4; 5)
£180
[-] **Radnoria Comitatus. Radnor Shire.** [1659]. Approx. 15 × 20 inches. Hand-cold. map, ornamental title cartouche surrounded by figure & animals, separate scale of distance, Royal crest, county arms, etc., Spanish text on verso, mntd. (TA. May 17; 166)
£60
- **Rutlandia.** Ca. 1650. 500 × 385mm. Hand-cold. map, arms, cartouche, F. (P. Nov.24; 332)
Ciditira. £60
[-] **Scotia Regnum.** N.d. 570 × 510mm. Engraved cold. map, heraldic arms & title cartouche, mntd. in Hogarth frame, under glass. (PD. Dec.14; 304)
£55
[-] **Somersettensis Comitatus. Somerset Shire.** Ca. 1645 or later. Approx. 15 × 20 inches. Old cold. map, ornamental title cartouche with figure, separate scale of distance with sheep, armorials, sailing ships, etc., Fr. text on verso, browned. (TA. Jul.19; 126)
£75
- - **Anr. Edn.** Ca. 1660. Approx. 15 × 19½ inches. Map, cont. hand-cold., ornamental title cartouche with figure, separate scale of distance, several armorials, sailing ships, etc., Latin text on verso, slightly browned overall, orig. printing crease in top left hand corner. (TA. May 17; 165)
£110
- - **Anr. Copy.** Approx. 15 × 20 inches. Uncold. map. decor. title cartouche, separate scale of distance, armorials, etc., Latin text to verso. (TA. Sep.15; 168)
£90
- - **Anr. Edn.** Ca. 1660 or later. Approx. 15 × 20 inches. Map, hand-cold. in outl., ornamental title cartouche with figure, separate scale of distance surrounded by sheep, several armorials, sailing ships, etc., some foxing. (TA. Mar.15; 88) £54
[-] **Surria vernacule Surrey.** [Amst.], 1645 or later. 382 × 500mm. Double-p. engraved map, Fr. text on verso, faint margin stain. (S. Jun.25; 416) *Kidd.* £160
- - **Anr. Edn.** 1648. 18½ × 23 inches. Hand-cold. engraved map, heraldic devices. (SKC. May 4; 1544)
£170
- - **Anr. Copy.** 16½ × 21 inches. Hand-cold. engraved map, heraldic devices, F. & G. to obverse. (SKC. Nov.18; 2085)
£140
- - **Anr. Edn.** Ca. 1650. Approx. 15 × 19½ inches. Map, decor. title cartouche, scale of distance cartouche, Royal crest, some armorials, etc., recently F. & G. (TA. Sep.15; 172)
£150
- **Suthsexia vernacule Sussex.** [Amst.], 1645 or later. 380 × 520mm. Double-p. engraved map, Fr. text on verso, faint stain in lr. margin. (S. Jun.25; 417) *Ashworth.* £130
- - **Anr. Edn.** Ca. 1650. 525 × 385mm. Hand-cold. map, arms, vig. sailing ships. (P. Apr.12; 343)
Lobo. £190
- **Tabula Magellanica qua Tierrae del Fuego.** [Amst.], n.d. 405 × 527mm. Hand-cold. engraved map, cartouche & coat-of-arms. (BBA. Aug.18; 168)
Faupel. £50
- **Terra Firma et Novum Regnum Granatense et Popayan.** Amst., [Blaeu, 1642]. 375 × 490mm. Double-p. engraved map, hand-cold. in outl., 2 lge. compass roses, Dutch text on verso, 3 full margins, some foxing, minor rubbing, top margin trimmed to plt. mark & replaced with similar paper. (SG. Jun.7; 46) $110
- **Terra Sancta quae in Sacris Terra Promissionis olim Palestina.** Amst., 1629 [but 1630 or later].

384 × 487mm. Double-p. engraved general map orientated west to top of sheet, extending from Red Sea to Sidon, hand-cold. in outl., Latin text on verso, sm. repair at lr. centrefold without loss of engraved surface, faint margin browning, w.a.f. (S. May 22; 262) *Hague.* £380
- - **Anr. Edn.** Amst., 1629 [but 1635 or later]. 380 × 497mm. Double-p. engraved map extending from Nile delta to Lebanon, showing also route of the Wanderings, hand-cold. in outl., embellishments fully so, heightened with gold, German text on verso, centrefold strengthened, w.a.f. (S. May 22; 263) *Samiramis.* £500
- **Vectis Insula.** [Amst.], 1645 or later. 386 × 500mm. Map, Fr. text on verso. (S. Jun.25; 395)
Kidd. £70
- - **Anr. Edn.** Ca. 1650. 505 × 385mm. Hand-cold. map, F. & G. (P. Mar.15; 413) *Watson.* £140
- **Venezuela.** N.d. Ob. fo. Old cold. copper engraved, map, 2 painted figure cartouches, slightly browned, especially margins. (R. Oct.13; 3501)
DM 400
- **Venezuela, cum Parte Australi Novae Andalusiae.** Amst., 1630 [but 1642 or later]. 378 × 486mm. Double-p. engraved map, outl. hand-cold., Dutch text on verso. (S. Nov.1; 221) *Burgess.* £90
[-] **Virginiae Partis Australis, et Floridae Partis Orientalis.** [Amst.], 1638 or later]. 388 × 506mm. Double-p. engraved regional map extending from Chesapeake Bay in Engl. colony of Virginia to Fr. colonies in Florida, based largely upon Hondius map of 1606, but incorporating later information in form of Irish settlement of 1621 at Newport New, hand-cold., w.a.f. (S. May 22; 373)
Marsden. £300
- - **Anr. Edn.** [Amst., 1640]. 385 × 583mm. Double-p. engraved map, hand-cold. in outl., embellishment fully cold., Latin text on verso, F. & double-G. (S. Dec.13; 5) *Anderson.* £170
- - **Anr. Edn.** [1640 or later]. 15½ × 19½ inches. Map, Latin text on verso. (CSK. Jul.6; 249) £200
- - **Anr. Edn.** [1663 or later]. 385 × 510mm. Engraved map, hand-cold. in outl., a few light dampstains on lr. margin. (CSE. Nov.4; 20) £150
[-] **Wiltonia ... Anglis Wilshire.** [Amst., 1645, but 1658 or later]. 410 × 500mm. Double-p. engraved map, hand-cold. in outl., cartouches, etc. fully cold., Spanish text on verso, faint crease at centrefold, gt. F. & double-G. (S. Mar.6; 177) *Brooks.* £110
See— **BLAEU, Willem or Guilielmus Janszoon & Johannes or Jan**
See— **VISSCHER, Nicolaus Joannes**

BLAEU, Johannes or Jan & Cornelius
- **Graecia.** [Amst., Blaeu, 1640]. 410 × 520mm. Double-p. engraved map, hand-cold. in outl., title & armorial dedication cartouches, Fr. text on verso, the whole lightly browned, minor repair on lr. fold verso. (SG. Dec.15; 58) $110
- **Russiae, vulgo Moscovia ...** [Amst., 1642]. 390 × 530mm. Engraved map, hand-cold., mostly in outl., title, coat-of-arms & scale cartouches with figures, Dutch text on verso, some separation & discoloration at fold, repairs on verso, liby. stp. (SG. Dec.15; 46) $150

BLAEU, Willem or Giulielmus Janszoon
- **Africae Nova Descriptio.** [Antw., 1630 or after]. 405 × 555mm. Double-p. engraved map, hand-cold. outl., title cartouche, vigs. at top & figures at sides. (SSA. Sep.21; 494) R 1,050
- - **Anr. Edn.** [Amst., 1630, but 1640 or later]. 411 × 556mm. Double-p. engraved map, flanked by 2 side-borders, each of 5 vigs. of costumed figures, & top frieze of 9 town views, Fr. text on verso, hand-cold., w.a.f. (S. May 22; 409)
Wood. £520
[-] **Groninga Dominim. Auctore Bartholbo Wicheringe.** Ca. 1635 or later. Approx. 15 × 19½ inches. Map, hand-cold. in outl., ornamental title cartouche surmounted by Royal coat of arms & figures, sailing ships, etc. (TA. Mar.15; 84)
£56
- **Magnae Britanniae et Hiberniae Tabula.** Amst., 1631 or later. Approx. 15½ × 20 inches. Hand-cold. map, ornamental title cartouche, separate scale of distance, inset detail of Orcades Insulae, compass rose, sailing ships, etc., Dutch text to verso, F. & double-G. (TA. Mar.15; 85)
£85
- - **Anr. Edn.** Amst., 1645. 470 × 570mm.

Engraved map, cold. outl. (SSA. Sep.21; 496)
R 220
– – **Anr. Edn.** Amst., 1645 or later. 387 × 496mm. Double-p. engraved map, hand-cold. in outl., inset, faint crease at centrefold, F. & G. (S. Mar.6; 156)
Brooks. £100
– – **Anr. Edn.** L., ca. 1662. 505 × 395mm. Hand cold. map in mount. (P. May 17; 449) *Leon.* £60

BLAEU, Willem or Guilielmus Janszoon & Johannes or Jan
– **Circulus Westphalicus sive Germaniae Inferioris.** N.d. Cold. copper-engraved map, minimal foxing. (V. Sep.29; 922)
DM 400
– **Danubius Fluvius Europae.** N.d. 410 × 960mm. Cold. copper engraved map, from 2 plts., 2 lge. painted figure cartouches, ptd. from 2 plts., some slight margin spotting. (R. Apr.6; 4391)
DM 1,200
– **Europa Recens Descripta.** [Amst., 1630 but ca. 1640]. 411 × 557mm. Double-p. engraved general map, hand-cold., showing 2 side borders of 10 vigs. of costumed figures, & upr. frieze showing 9 town views, Latin text on verso, w.a.f. (S. May 21; 191)
Christensen. £350
– – **Anr. Edn.** [Amst., 1635, or later]. 413 × 560mm. Double-p. engraved map, 2 borders each with 5 vig. ills., upr. frieze with 9 views, hand-cold., Latin text on verso, stained. (S. Apr.9; 99)
Tooley. £120
– – **Anr. Edn.** N.d. Ob. fo. Old cold. copper engraved map, painted cartouche, figure decor., browned, spotted & crumpled, several tears & faults in middle, bkd. roughly, wide margins partly defect. & strengthened. (R. Oct.13; 3591)
DM 800
– – **Anr. Copy.** Cold. copper engraved map, 1 tear reprd., slightly browned. (V. Sep.29; 152) DM 500
– **Harlemum Vernacule Haerlem.** 1649. 460 × 580mm. Engraved folding plan, from Blaeu's Town-book, Latin text on verso. (VG. Sep.15; 1695)
Fls. 500
– **Lutzenburg Ducatus.** N.d. Cold. copper-engraved map. (V. Sep.29; 245)
DM 420
– **Nassovia Comitatus.** N.d. Cold. copper-engraved map. (V. Sep.29; 688)
DM 400
– **Nova Totius Terrarum Orbis Geographica ac Hydrographica Tabula.** Amst., 1630 or later. 417 × 540mm. Double-p. engraved map on the mercator projection, hand-cold. in outl., surrounded by upr. & lr. friezes with vigs. & side borders with figures, sm. split at lr. centrefold affecting engraved surface, some faint stains, F. & G. (S. Dec.1; 215)
Wood. £1,350
– – **Anr. Copy.** 417 × 540mm. Double-p. engraved map on Mercator projection surrounded by upr. & lr. friezes incorporating vigs. representing planets & 7 wonders of the ancient world, & 2 side borders depicting seasons & 4 elements, map area hand-cold. in Engl. manner with town symbols touched in gold, sm. flaw at centre-fold, an iss. without text on verso, slight browning, w.a.f. (S. May 21; 150)
Map House. £800
– – **Anr. Edn.** Ca. 1650. Ob. fo. Old cold. copper engraved map, 4 cartouches, allegories of 4 elements & 4 seasons at side, of moon & planets at head, & below the 7 wonders of the world, 2 sm. supp. maps of pole, 3 captions, slightly browned & foxed. (R. Oct.13; 3318)
DM 6,200
[–] **Palatinatus Rheni Nova, et Accurata Descriptio.** N.p., Nicolaum Joannis Piscatore, 1652. 17½ × 21½ inches. Hand-cold. engraved map, 17 vigs., orig. hinge on verso of central vertical crease, slight adhesion defect, slight paper darkening, tipped at upr. corners to black backing sheet, F. & G. (CBA. Aug.21; 738)
$650
– **Regiones sub Polo Arctico.** N.d. Ob. fo. Old cold. map, 2 painted figure cartouches, crumpled in middle, some margin spotting & partly bkd. (R. Oct.13; 3343)
DM 500
– **Rhenus Fluviorum Europae celeberrimus.** N.d. 410 × 950mm. Cold. copper engraved map, ptd. from 2 plts., 2 lge. painted figure & heraldic maps, 10 cold. arms. (R. Apr.7; 5286)
DM 1,600
– – **Anr. Copy.** 410 × 950mm. Old cold. copper engraved map, 2 lge. painted figure & heraldic cartouches, 10 cold. arms., ptd. from 2 plts., some light browning or spotting, crumpled, folds torn &

bkd., pasted at verso to lr. margin. (R. Oct.15; 5756)
DM 1,200
[–] **Suecia, Dania, et Norvegia, Regna Europae Septentrionalis.** [Amst., 1634, but 1662, or later]. 420 × 525mm. Double-p. engraved map, Latin text on verso. (S. Apr.9; 130)
Libris. £150
– **Typus Frisiae Orientalis.** 1642 or later. 380 × 500mm. Engraved map, hand-cold. in outl., Fr. text on verso, F. & G. (CSK. Jan.13; 19)
£130
– **Tabula Islandiae. Auctore Georgio Carolo Flandro.** Amst., ca. 1630 or later. Approx. 15 × 20 inches. Map, hand-cold. in outl., ornamental title cartouche surmounted by figures, separate scale of distance, compass rose, sailing ship, etc., Latin text on verso, a little browned overall. (TA. Jan.19; 138)
£140
– – **Anr. Edn.** Amst., 1635 or later. Approx. 15 × 19½ inches. Hand-cold. map, lge. ornamental title cartouche surmounted by figures, separate scale of distance, compass rose, sailing ship, etc., Latin text on verso, overall browning. (TA. May 17; 163)
£120
– – **Anr. Edn.** Amst., ca. 1660. Approx. 15 × 20 inches. Hand-cold. map, lge. ornamental title cartouche, separate scale of distance, compass rose, sailing ship, etc., Latin text on verso, browned overall. (TA. Jul.19; 125)
£90
– **Territorium Norimbergense.** Ca. 1620. Old cold. copper engraved map, 2 old cold. & 1 sm. cold. views, minimal defects. bkd. (BR. Apr.13; 3216)
DM 500
– – **Anr. Edn.** N.d. Ob. fo. Cold. copper engraved map, 2 painted figure cartouches, cold. town plan. (R. Apr.6; 4489)
DM 500
– – **Anr. Copy.** Ob. fo. Old cold. copper engraved map, 2 painted figure cartouches & cold. town plan, some slight col. offset. (R. Oct.14; 4605) DM 400

BLASKOWITZ, Charles
– **A Topographical Chart of the Bay of Narraganset in the Province of New England** ... L., William Faden, 1777. 36 × 25 inches. Engraved map, scroll cartouche at top, listing of farms, explanatory text & dedication to Percy, Lieut.-Gen. on right-hand portion, slight trace of browning. (SPB. May 23; 12)
$950

BLOME, Richard
– **Britannia: or, A Geographical Description of the Kingdoms of England, Scotland, & Ireland.** Ill.:– W. Hollar, F. Lamb, & others, after J. Speede & others. L., 1673 or later. Fo. Full-p. plan, 50 maps, including 5 folding, 13 ll. with engraved coats of arms (12 ptd. recto & verso, the last an additional lf. not called for, ptd. recto only, with 4 additional arms & 26 blanks), Phillip Lea's plan 'The Scenography of the City of Londonderry' (1689 or later) inserted, lacks title, dedication & list of benefactors laid down or reprd., a few maps reprd., 1 or 2 with minor loss to engraved surface, outer margins of 1 folding map frayed touching engraved surface, inserted plan slightly defect. in 1 margin, 19th. C. hf. cf., worn. [Wing B 3707] (S. Dec.1; 149)
Burgess. £1,350
– **A Generall Mapp of the Isles of Great Brittaine, Designed by Monsieur Sanson** ... 1669. Approx. 16 × 20 inches. Uncold. map, ornamental title cartouche surmounted by Royal crest, with figures & fruit, etc., separate scale of distance, inset detail of the Isles of Schetland, sailing ships, slightly worn in creases, 4 wormholes. (TA. Jan.19; 102)
£80

BONNE, Rigobert
– **La Suisse divisée en ses Treize Cantons et ses Alliés.** Venise, Remondini, 1778. 515 × 710mm. Copper engraved map, outl. col., cold. rocaille cartouche & caption. (GF. Nov.17; 2787)
Sw. Frs. 360

BORDONE, Benedetto
[–] **Archipelago of Greece.** [1527]. 12 × 16 inches. Woodcut map, Italian text on verso, 1 margin slightly trimmed. (CSK. Jul.6; 164)
£60
[–] **[Candia].** [1528 or later]. 6 × 13¼ inches. Hand-cold. woodcut map, Italian text on margins & verso, hand-cold. woodcut map of Scarpanto on verso, lr. margin slightly trimmed. (CSK. May 4; 229)
£150

BOWEN, Emmanuel
[–] **An Accurate Map of the Counties of Gloucester & Monmouth, Divided into their Respective Hundreds** ... 1760 [1787]. Approx. 22 × 28 inches. Map, hand-cold. in outl., lge. uncold. historiated title cartouche, separate ornamental dedication cartouche, extensive ptd. details. (TA. Jan.19; 104)
£90
– **An Accurate Map of the County of Norfolk.** Ca. 1770. 720 × 540mm. Map, cold. in outl., cartouche. (P. Oct.20; 273)
£80
– – **Anr. Edn.** 1777. 510 × 415mm. Hand-cold. map. (P. Oct.20; 274)
£55
– **An Accurate Map of the County of Surrey.** Ca. 1760. 715 × 535mm. Hand-cold. map, cartouches, sm. tear without loss, F. & G. (P. Mar.15; 420)
Bates. £170
– **Berkshire.** 1756. 21 × 27½ inches. Engraved map, hand-cold. in outl. (CSK. May 4; 155) £60
– **Cambridgeshire.** [1765]. 28 × 20½ inches. Engraved map, hand-cold. in outl. (CSK. May 4; 154)
£65
– **The County of Lancaster.** [1764]. 27½ × 21 inches. Engraved map, hand-cold. in outl. (CSK. May 4; 151)
£80
– **The County Palatine of Chester.** [1764]. 21 × 27½ inches. Engraved map, hand-cold. in outl. (CSK. May 4; 152)
£80
– **The County of York.** [1764]. 21 × 28 inches. Engraved map, hand-cold. in outl. (CSK. May 4; 150)
£60
– **Dorset Shire, Divided into its Hundreds** ... Ca. 1760. Approx. 21½ × 27½ inches. Map, hand-cold. in outl., uncold. historiated title cartouche, extensive ptd. details, some minor margin defects. (TA. Jun.21; 116)
£68
– – **Anr.** [1764]. 21½ × 28 inches. Engraved map, hand-cold. in outl. (CSK. May 4; 156) £75
– **An Improved Map of the County of Somerset Divided into its Hundreds** ... Ca. 1760 or later. Approx. 21 × 28 inches. Map, hand-cold. in outl., lge. uncold. ornamental & historiated title cartouche, separate ornamental dedication cartouche surmounted by county arms, inset plan of Bath, extensive ptd. notes. (TA. Jan.19; 103) £85
– **Leicester & Rutland.** [1764]. 21 × 28 inches. Engraved map, hand-cold. outl. (CSK. Jul.6; 236)
£50
– **A New & Accurate Map of Turkey in Asia.** [1740-60]. 355 × 430mm. (plt.-mark). Engraved map, central vertical fold, margins. (BS. Sep.21; 69)
£55
– **A Plan of the River Lagan** ... **from Belfast to Lough Neagh** ... **Survey'd** ... 1768. 8¼ × 14 inches. Uncold. map. (GM. Dec.7; 497)
£75
– **Sussex.** Ca. 1740. 690 × 510mm. Map, cold. in outl., inset plans. (P. Sep.29; 451) *Brown.* £90

BOWEN, Emmanuel & Kitchin, Thomas
[–] **An Accurate Map of the Counties of Gloucester & Monmouth, Divided into their Respective Hundreds.** 1760. Approx. 20½ × 27 inches. Map, hand-cold. in outl., uncold. ornamental title cartouche, separate dedication cartouche, extensive ptd. details, trimmed to plt. mark, some minor margin tears; Duke of York's bkplt. on verso. (TA. Jul.19; 155)
£65
– **A New & Accurate Map of the World.** [1744]. Approx. 14 × 22 inches. Map, hand-cold. in outl. (TA. Jul.19; 154)
£90

BRADSHAW, George
– **Map & Sections of the Railways of Great Britain.** Publd. 1st. No.14 [i.e 14th Jan.?] 1839. 8vo. Lge 8vo. Lge. folding cold. map mntd. on linen, with table of gradients, orig. maroon mor. gt. case, slightly worn; dedication copy, bkplt. of James Walker, P.I.C.E. (BBA. Jan.19; 55)
Thomas. £180
– **Map of Canals situated in the Counties of Lancashire, York, Derby & Chester (the Midland Counties).** 1839. Lge. 8vo. 2 lge. cold. maps., folded & mntd. on linen, cont. cf. box lettered 'North Part'; bkplt. of James Walker, P.I.C.E. (BBA. Jan.19; 53)
Lomax. £180

BRASSIER, William
– **A Survey of Lake Champlain** ... L., Sayer & Bennett, 1776. 26½ × 19 inches. Engraved map, in 1st. state, partly hand-cold., inset map, slight

BRASSIER, William -Contd.

soiling, split at vertical fold, reprd. on verso, tipped onto mat. (SPB. May 23; 9) $850
– – **Anr. Edn.** L., Laurie & Whittle, 1794. 25½ × 19 inches. Engraved map, partly hand-cold. in outl., inset map, slight trace of offsetting & browning. (SPB. May 23; 10) $1,200

BRAUN or BRUIN, Georg & Hogenberg, Franz

[–] **Brightstowe.** Ca. 1580 or later. Approx. 13½ × 17½ inches. Uncold. town plan, sm. title cartouche, list of 15 churches in ornamental cartouche, city crest, historical figures, etc., some spotting, F. & G. (TA. Jul.19; 112) £115
[–] **Cairus, quae olim Babylon; Aegypti Maxima Urbs.** [Cologne], early 17th. C. 330 × 490mm. Double-p. engraved map, hand-cold., key to locations, Latin text on verso, some foxing, mostly in margins. (SG. Dec.15; 18) $150
[–] **Candia; La Cita de Corphu.** [1572 or later]. 14½ × 21½ inches. Engraved hand-cold. plan, Latin text on verso, several tears, slight cracking of ptd. surface. (CSK. May 4; 225) £200
– **Cantuarbury.** Late 16th. C. 430 × 290mm. Cont. hand-cold. plan, F. & G. (P. May 17; 462)
Morrison. £100
[–] **Cestria [Vulgo] Chester, Angliae Civitas.** Ca. 1570. *[Later Printing].* Approx. 12½ × 17 inches. Uncold. map, strapwork title cartouche, Royal crest, armorials, figures, etc., minor damage to centrefold, Latin text on verso. (TA. Nov.17; 113) £60
– – **Anr. Edn.** Cologne, 1581 or later. 325 × 432mm. double-p. engraved plan, embellished with escutcheons, German text on verso. (S. Jun.25; 371) £100
– **Civitas Exoniae (vulgo Excester).** 17th. C. 13 × 16¼ inches. Hand-cold. engraved bird's eye plan, from Civitates Orbis Terrarum, coats of arms, river & canal with boats & fishing nets, buildings & streets named, F., w.a.f. (LC. Mar.1; 250) £120
– **Civitates Orbis Terrarum: Chester.** Brussels & Cologne, [1573-98]. 325 × 440mm. (plt.-mark). Cold. engraved map, central vertical fold, margins, Fr. text to verso, some hairline paper splits to image, some stains, mostly marginal, F. (BS. Sep.21; 103) £60
– **Edenburgum Scotiae Metropolis.** 1572 or later. 13 3/8 × 17¾ inches. Hand-cold. map. (CE. Sep.1; 125) £135
– – **Anr. Edn.** [Cologne], 1581 or later. 343 × 450mm. Double-p. engraved hand-cold. perspective plan, Fr. text on verso, faint crease & stain at lr. centrefold. (S. Mar.6; 191) *Aberdeen.* £100
[–] **Hierosolyma.** [Cologne, 1572, or later]. 340 × 487mm. 2 perspective plans on 1 double-p. engraved sheet, fully hand-cold., Latin text on verso, sm. split lr. centre-fold reprd. with loss. (S. Apr.9; 111) *Silber.* £110
– – **Anr. Copy.** 340 × 487mm. 2 perspective plans on 1 double-p. engraved mapsheet, Latin text on verso. (S. Jun.25; 3) *Schiff.* £90
– – **Anr. Edn.** [Cologne, 1575, or later]. 330 × 415mm. Double-p. engraved perspective plan, 5 figures in foreground, Fr. text on verso, sm. split at lr. centre-fold, few faint stains. (S. Apr.9; 110) *Potter.* £150
[–] **Illustris Civitatis Conimbriae in Lustienia ... Effigies.** [Cologne], 1600 or later. 289 × 465mm. Fully cold. double-p. plan, Latin text on verso, faint browning, sm. repair touching engraved surface. (S. Dec.13; 111) *Burgess.* £50
– **Londinum Feracissimi Angliae Regni Metropolis.** [Cologne, 1572, but 1574 or later]. *2nd. State, with the Royal Exchange.* 333 × 490mm. Double-p. engraved plan in perspective, German text on verso, sm. wormholes with slight loss, light overall browning. (S. Mar.6; 168) *Ash.* £290
[–] **Moscauw.** [Cologne], 1575 or later. 349 × 490mm. Double-p. engraved cold. plan, after A. Hirschvogel, Latin text on verso, centrefold strengthened. (S. Dec.13; 49) *Crete.* £75
– – **Anr. Edn.** Ca. 1580. 490 × 355mm. Town plan. (P. May 17; 456) *Anderson.* £80
[–] **Nordovicum, Angliae civitas.** [Cologne] 1581 or later. 295 × 423mm. Double-p. engraved perspective plan after W. Cunningham, German text on verso. (S. Jun.25; 404) £50

– – **Anr. Edn.** 1588. 425 × 295mm. Hand-cold. plan. (P. Dec.8; 442) *Wilton.* £130
[–] **Venetia.** [Cologne], 1572 or later. 335 × 483mm. Fully cold. double-p. engraved plan, after Domenico delle Greche, inset below, Latin text on verso, faint browning. (S. Dec.13; 112) *Crete.* £140

BRUCKNER, Daniel

– **Canton Basel.** Ill.:– Emanuel Büchel, engraved by P.L. Auvray. Bale, 1766. 420 × 510mm. Folding copper engraved map, minimal foxing. (GF. Nov.16; 1390) Sw. Frs. 1,100

BRUIN, Georg

See— **BRAUN or BRUIN, Georg & Hogenberg, Franz**

BRY, Theodore de

– **Delineatio Promontorii, Quod Cabo de Bona Esperanca vulgo vocatur.** 1598. 140 × 170mm. Line engraved map from 'Petits Voyages', text below. (VA. Apr.27; 607) R 420

BRYANT, A.

– **The County of Gloucester from Actual Survey ...** 1824. Approx. 75 × 67 inches. Map, partially cold., uncold. vig. view of Gloucester Cathedral, browned overall, some creases, linen-bkd. (TA. Mar.15; 72) £60

BUACHE, Philippe & Jean Nicholas

– **Carte du Golphe du Mexique et des Isles Antilles.** Paris, Dezauche, 1780. 500 × 940mm. Double-p. engraved map, from 'Atlas Géographique', hand-cold. in outl., 5 compass points, earlier fold marks, some light offsetting. (SG. Dec.15; 25) $250
See— **DE L'ISLE, [J.N.] & Buache, P.**

BUCHEL, Emanuel (Ill.)

See— **BRUCKNER, Daniel**

BUNKER HILL

– **A Plan of the Action at Bunkers Hill ...** [L.], 1793. 19 × 17 inches. Engraved map, with overlay 'No. 1', extensive margins, slight traces of offsetting. (SPB. Oct.26; 1) $700

BURGHERS, M.

– **A New Map of the Terraqueous Globe according to Ancient Discoveries.** Ca. 1690. Ob. fo. Cold. copper engraved map from Wells Atlas, lge. painted arms at foot & decor. Athena, view & ship. (R. Oct.13; 3323) DM 1,200

BUSSEMACHER, J.

– **Aphrica.** Cologne, 1600 [but 1608 or later]. 210 × 295mm. Double-p. engraved map after Ortelius, outl. hand-cold., faint browning. (S. Nov.1; 200) *Potter.* £70

CANADIAN PACIFIC RAILWAY

– **Map of Manitoba, Kewaydin, British Columbia & North West Territory shewing the country traversed by the Canadian Pacific Railway.** 1883. Total dimensions 540 × 105mm. Folding litho. map, mntd. & dissected in 36 sections, folding into publisher's bds. (S. Jun.25; 135) *Quaritch.* £120

CAROLUS, G.

– **Island.** W. Blaeu, n.d. Ob. fo. Cold. copper engraved map, 2 painted figure cartouches. (R. Oct.14; 4019) DM 480
– – **Anr. Copy.** Ob. fo. Cold. copper engraved map 2 painted figure cartouches, slightly browned. (R. Oct.14; 4018) DM 400

CARTA D'UNA PARTE DELL'AMERICA Settentrionale che serve ben poter intendere le pretensioni delli Inglesi

Verona, Stamperia Vallarsi a S. Sebastiani, after 1754. 328 × 423mm. Double-p. engraved map of New England & eastern Canada. (S. Dec.1; 230) *Quaritch.* £500

CARTA TERZA GENERALE DEL'ASIA

[Flor., 1661 or later]. 457 × 370mm. Full-p. engraved sea-chart extending from Cape Mendocino to 'Iezo' & northern shores of New Guinea, w.a.f. (S. May 22; 465) *Maggs.* £280

CARTE GENERALE DE LA NOUVELLE HOLLANDE

N.d. Approx. 20 × 30 inches. Engraved map, from

account of Baudin-Peron-Freycinet expedition, some added col. (mainly of ornamental cartouches), mntd., F. & G. (KH. Nov.9; 642) Aus. $380

CARTE GENERALE DE LA TERRE NAPOLEON

N.d. Approx. 20 × 30 inches. Engraved map, from account of Baudin-Peron-Freycinet expedition, some added col., mntd., F. & G. (KH. Nov.9; 643) Aus. $450
– – **Anr. Copy.** Approx. 20 × 30 inches. 2nd. sheet, engraved map, from account of Baudin-Peron-Freycinet expedition, mntd., F. & G. (KH. Nov.9; 644) Aus. $420
– – **Anr. Copy.** Approx. 20 × 30 inches. 3rd. sheet, engraved map, from account of Baudin-Peron-Freycinet expedition, mntd., F. & G. (KH. Nov.9; 645) Aus. $280
– – **Anr. Copy.** Approx. 30 × 20 inches. 5th. sheet, engraved map, from account of Baudin-Peron-Freycinet expedition, mntd., F. & G. (KH. Nov.9; 647) Aus. $210
– – **Anr. Copy.** Approx. 20 × 30 inches. 6th. sheet, engraved map, from account of Baudin-Peron-Freycinet expedition, paper split along orig. fold (no loss), mntd., F. & G. (KH. Nov.9; 648) Aus. $170

CHATELAIN, Henri Abraham

– **Carte de l'Amérique.** Amst., 1732-39. 130 × 95mm. (total dimensions 330 × 445mm.). Inset map in double-p. description, from 'Atlas Historique', some foxing, margin repairs & creasing, liby. stp. in upr. margin. (SG. Dec.15; 27) $150
– **Carte de la Nouvelle France.** Ca. 1710. 415 × 480mm. Cold. copper engraved map, sm. cold. view at head, caption, view & plan in floral cartouche, some slight browning. (R. Oct.13; 3454) DM 850
– – **Anr. Edn.** Amst., 1719 or later. 424 × 485mm. Engraved map, insets, view. (S. Jun.25; 142) *Faupel.* £180
– **Carte de la Turquie, de l'Arabie et de la Perse.** [1720]. 415 × 535mm. (plt. mark). Engraved map, central vertical fold, margins. (BS. Sep.21; 70) £70
– **L'Empire du Japon, tiré des Cartes des Japonnois.** 1719. 360 × 440mm. Outl. cold. copper engraved map, painted arms cartouche, sm. supp. map, cartouche. (R. Oct.13; 3555) DM 620
– **Nouvelle Carte de l'Amérique Septentrionale.** Ca. 1710. Ob. fo. Outl. cold. copper engraved map, cartouche at top, 2 tables, 3 sm. bkd. holes at right. (R. Oct.13; 3484) DM 420
– – **Anr. Edn.** Ca. 1720. Approx. 19 × 24 inches. Map, hand-cold. in outl., ptd. historical geographical & genealogical details. (TA. Jun.21; 135) £115

CLEGG, Ernest

– **Map of Hampshire.** Ill.:– D. McCullough. N.p., John Waddington Ltd., ca. 1947. Lge. ob. fo. Col. litho. map on rag paper, sigd. by Dwight D. Eisenhower, cartouche, multiple vigs. (SG. Sep.29; 277) $275
– – **Anr. Edn.** Ill.:– D. McCullough. 'Tokyo', John Waddington Ltd., '1948'. Lge. ob. fo. Col. litho. map on rag paper, sigd. by Douglas MacArthur, cartouche, multiple vigs., dampstained on lr. margin. (SG. Sep.29; 278) $200
– **Map of Kent: Battle of Britain, 1940-41.** Ill.:– D. McCullough. N.p., John Waddington Ltd., ca. 1945. Lge. ob. fo. Col. litho. map on rag paper, sigd. by Churchill (under vig. design reproducing his speech of 20 Aug. 1940), Clegg, McCullough, Lord Norfolk & 2 others, cartouche, multiple vigs., some slight spotting. (SG. Sep.29; 276) $950
– **Map of Norfolk.** Ill.:– D. McCullough. N.p., John Waddington Ltd., ca. 1945. Lge. ob. fo. Col. litho. map on rag paper, sigd. by Churchill under histor. vig. design reproducing his speech of 4 Jun. 1940, cartouche, multiple vigs. (SG. Sep.29; 275) $950

COECK, G.

– **Pascaart van de Noort Zee.** 1669. Surface cold. copper engraved map, with coasts of Scotland, England, Holland, Germany, Denmark & Norway, 2 cold. cartouches, cold. wind-roses & 4 cold. arms, not North orientated, sm. margin tear bkd. (BR. Apr.13; 2884) DM 800
– **Mapa de Isla de Puerto Rico.** Madrid, 1851.

835 × 120mm. Cl. c. (DS. Mar.23; 2233)
Pts. 35,000

COLLINS, Capt. Grenville
- **Chart of Dublin Bay.** [L.], ca. 1770. 18 × 22½ inches. Uncold. map, F. (GM. Dec.7; 520) £75
- **Dartmouth.** L., ca. 1740. 565 × 450mm. Hand-cold. sea-chart. (P. May 17; 441) *Morley.* £65
- **The River of Thames from London to the Buoy of the Noare.** 1693 or later. 24 × 36 inches overall. Engraved map, on 2 sheets, hand-cold. in outl., some wear along folds, F. & G. (CSK. Mar.9; 43) £110

COLTON, Joseph H.
- **Colton's Railroad & Township Map, Western States, Compiled from the United States Surveys.** N.Y., 1855. 890 × 1,070mm. Folding engraved map, hand-cold., vigs. of St. Louis, Louisville, & Cinc., & a bison & an elk, full margins with scroll-work border, verso blank, paper thin & brittle, some tears & separation at folds, gt.-lettered leath. covers. (SG. Jun.7; 48) $150
- **Map of the United States, the British Provinces, Mexico, etc.** ... N.Y., 1849. Folding engraved map, sm. tape repair to 1 fold, 11 p. 'Particulars' in orig. cl., slightly spotted, qtr. mor. s.-c. (LH. Apr.15; 289) $800

CONDER, Lieut. C.R. & Kitchener, Lieut. (later Lord) H.H.
- **Map of Western Palestine in 26 sheets from Surveys Conducted for the Committee of the Palestine Exploration Fund ... During the Years 1872-1877.** L. [Southampton], 1880. *1st. Edn.* Various sizes. Ptd. title sheet, 26 zincographed mapsheets, laid on linen, some surface dirt, w.a.f. (S. May 22; 257) *Samiramis.* £1,100

CONDER, T.
- **A New & Correct Map of the Province of Connaught.** L., A. Hogg, ca. 1800. Approx. 12 × 8½ inches. Map, hand-cold. in outl., F. (GM. Dec.7; 515) £50

COOK, James
[–] **Chart of the NW Coast of America & NE Coast of Asia Explored in the Years 1778 & 1779.** [L., 1784]. Approx. 400 × 680mm. Double-p. engraved map, from atlas vol. of Engl. edn. of Cook's 3rd. voyage, full margins, verso blank, completely uncold., rubbed, some old creasing. (SG. Jun.7; 50) $175

CORONELLI, P. Vincenzo Maria
- **L'Africa.** Ca. 1690. Copper engraved map in 2 ll., 2 lge. figure cartouches, some spotting, tears reprd. (R. Oct.13; 3393) DM 650
- **L'Africa diuisa nelle sue Partie secondo ...** 1691. 600 × 450mm. Cold. line engraved maps, 2 sheets. (VA. Apr.27; 577) R 2,000
- **America Meridionalis.** Ca. 1695. 600 × 880mm. Cold. copper engraved map ptd. from 2 plts., 2 painted floral heraldic cartouches & figures. (R. Oct.13; 3496) DM 800
- **Archipelago [of Greece].** Ca. 1696. Each sheet 18 × 24 inches. Engraved map on 2 sheets, Italian text on verso, margins cleanly torn or reprd., 1 lr. margin trimmed. (CSK. May 4; 207) £120
- **– Anr. Copy.** 18 × 24 inches. Engraved map on 2 sheets, Italian text on verso, margins lightly stained. (CSK. Jul.6; 150) £80
- **Carta Maritima di Tutto L'Arcipelago.** [1696 or later]. 16 × 20½ inches. Engraved chart. (CSK. Jul.6; 160) £75
- **Contado D'Ollanda.** [1696]. Each sheet 18 × 24 inches. Engraved map on 2 sheets, Italian text on verso. (CSK. May 4; 181) £75
- **Corso del Reno.** Ca. 1690. 885 × 600mm. Cold. copper engraved map, 3 painted figure cartouches, ptd. from 2 plts. (R. Oct.15; 5759) DM 700
- **Ducato di Luxembourgo.** 1692. Ob. fo. Copper engraved map, 2 figure & heraldic cartouches, tear at foot bkd., margins lightly spotted. (R. Oct.13; 3674) DM 550
- **L'Europe.** Paris, J.B. Nolin, 1689. Approx. 18 × 24 inches. Map, hand-cold., in outl., uncold. ornamental title cartouche incorporating figures, a little browned, mntd. (TA. Jan.19; 139) £70
- **Golfo di Venezia.** 1688. Ob. fo. Cold. copper engraved map, 2 lge. cartouches, 22 sm. town plans,

many sm. arms, slightly spotted, partly bkd. (R. Oct.14; 4075) DM 420
- **Isola del Giapone e Penisola di Corea.** Venice, Domenico Padoani, ca. 1695. Ob. fo. Cold. copper engraved map, painted floral cartouche & sm. ill., lightly browned, some thin places strengthened. (R. Oct.13; 3553) DM 600
- **Isola di Corsica.** Ca. 1690. 460 × 610mm. Hand-cold. map, cartouches. (P. Oct.20; 291) £60
- **– Anr. Copy.** 460 × 610mm. Hand-cold. map, cartouches, text on verso. (P. Oct.20; 291a) £50
- **Isola Regno di Candia.** Ca. 1696. Overall 19 × 47½ inches. Engraved map on 2 sheets, 1 clean tear. (CSK. May 4; 209) £170
- **Isole Canarie.** N.d. Cold. copper engraved map, 3 part ill., on left coll. map, at top right lge. map of Madeira, below birds-eye-view of Funchal from sea, painted floral cartouche, elab. decor., margins slightly cockled & spotted, some sm-holes taped. (R. Apr.5; 3268) DM 400
- **Latitudo Orbis Terra cognita Antiquis.** 1690. Ob. fo. Round, copper engraved map, writing round, cartouche, arms & figures, slightly spotted. (R. Oct.13; 3325) DM 450
- **Mare del Nord.** Venice, ca. 1690. 453 × 600mm. Double-p. engraved map, elab. title cartouche, sm. tear in 1 margin without loss of engraved surface. (S. Dec.1; 239) *Faupel.* £140
- **Mare del Sud ... Mare Pacifico.** Ca. 1690. 460 × 610mm. Engraved hand-cold. map, margins lightly soiled. (CSK. Nov.4; 3) £550
- **Pianta della real Fortezza e Citta di Candia.** [1696]. 18 × 24 inches. Engraved plan, engraved plan & Italian text on verso, upr. margin slightly reprd. (CSK. May 4; 208) £110
- **Planisfero del Mondo Nuovo.** Ca. 1695. Ob. fo. Round cold. copper engraved map, figure decor. (R. Oct.13; 3428) DM 1,300
- **Planisfero del Mondo Vecchio.** Ca. 1695. Ob. fo. Round cold. copper engraved map, figure decor. & writing. (R. Oct.13; 3324) DM 600
- **Scotia.** [1696]. Each sheet 470 × 630mm. Engraved map on 2 sheets, Italian text on verso. (CSK. Dec.2; 1) £65
- **Terre Artiche.** Ca. 1695. Ob. fo. Cold. copper engraved map, painted cartouche. (R. Oct.13; 3345) DM 750
- **La Vestfalia deta Die Westpalen.** Ca. 1690. Ob. fo. Cold. copper engraved map, 2 painted figure cartouches. (R. Oct.15; 5843) DM 400

CORRECT CHART OF ST. GEORGE'S CHANNEL & THE IRISH SEA
[L.], ca. 1770. 18½ × 15 inches. Uncold. map, F. (GM. Dec.7; 516) £100

COUNTY OF MEATH
Dublin, 1837. 26 × 30 inches. Engraved folding map in 18 sections, partly hand-cold., mntd. on linen; from liby. of Luttrellstown Castle, w.a.f. (C. Sep.28; 1711) £250

COVENS, Jean
See— DELISLE, Guillaume

COVENS, Jean & Mortier, Corneille
- **L'Amérique Septentrionale.** N.p., n.d. 2 outl. cold. copper-engraved maps, browned in 2 corners. (V. Sep.29; 160) DM 750

CRUCHLEY, George F.
- **New Plan of London Improved.** L., G.F. Cruchley, ca. 1845. 530 × 1,110mm. Hand-cold. map, mntd. & dissected in 10 sections, folding into publisher's cl.-covered s.-c. (S. Dec.13; 245) *Levy.* £75

DANCKERTS, Cornelis
- **Insulae Americanae.** Amst., ca. 1680. 480 × 575mm. Double-p. engraved map, cold. in wash & outl., sm. repair at lr. centre-fold. (S. Nov.1; 224) *Burgess.* £160
- **Nieuw Aerdsch Pleyn.** N.d. Lge. fo. Outl. cold. copper engraved world map, round, painted figure cartouche, painted corner decor., cut at side to subject, sm. tear bkd., hole in lr. border. (R. Apr.5; 3129) DM 3,500

DE L'ISLE, Guillaume
- **America Meridionalis.** Augsburg, 1749 [or later]. 460 × 604mm. Double-p. fully hand-cold. engraved map, sm. wormhole at centre-fold with minimal

loss of engraved surface. (S. Nov.1; 212)
Ash. £110
- **America Septentrionalis.** T.C. Lotter, ca. 1760. 460 × 590mm. Engraved hand-cold. map. (CSK. Nov.4; 28) £350
- **– Anr. Edn.** Ca. 1776. 610 × 460mm. Hand-cold. map, cartouche. (P. Apr.12; 334) *Burgess.* £160
- **– Anr. Edn.** [Augsburg], 18th. C.?. 460 × 600mm. Double-p. engraved map, hand-cold., uncold. title cartouche with figures, scale cartouche, margins rimmed, some stains. (SG. Dec.15; 39) $200
- **L'Amérique Méridionale.** Covens & Mortier, ca. 1730. 580 × 485mm. Hand-cold. map, repairs, back strengthened. (P. Jun.7; 396) £60
- **L'Amérique Septentrionale.** P. Mortier, ca. 1708. 480 × 590mm. Engraved map, hand-cold. in outl. (CSK. Nov.4; 27) £220
- **– Anr. Edn.** Amst., 1730 or later. 450 × 580mm. Double-p. engraved map, hand-cold. in outl., lr. margin reprd. affecting engraved surface. (S. Jun.25; 141) *Faupel.* £120
- **– Anr. Edn.** Covens & Mortier, ca. 1730. Ob. fo. Copper engraved map, 2 figure cartouches, lr. margin lightly stained. (R. Oct.13; 3485) DM 620
- **l'Amérique Septentrionale; [l'Amérique Meridionale].** Amst., 1757 or later. 2 double-p. engraved maps, hand-cold. in wash & outl., slight margin soiling. (S. Dec.1; 225) *Tooley's.* £200
- **Carte d'Afrique.** Paris, 1722 [or later]. 490 × 635mm. Double-p. engraved map, hand-cold. in outl. (S. Dec.13; 19) *Ward.* £50
- **– Anr. Edn.** Covens & Mortier, ca. 1730. 635 × 525mm. Hand-cold. map, back strengthened. (P. Jun.7; 398) £60
- **Carte d'Amérique.** Paris, 1722 [or later]. 485 × 610mm. Double-p. engraved map, outl. hand-cold., without centre-fold. (S. Nov.1; 208)
Burgess. £230
- **Carte de la Louisiane et du Cours du Mississippi.** Covens & Mortier, ca. 1730. 605 × 460mm. Partly cold. map, back strengthened. (P. Jun.7; 390) £140
- **– Anr. Copy.** Ob. fo. Copper engraved old outl. cold. map, sm. supp. map. (R. Oct.13; 3502) DM 760
- **Carte de Mexique et de la Floride.** Covens & Mortier, 1722. 605 × 490mm. Hand-cold. map, a few repairs, back strengthened. (P. Jun.7; 391) £160
- **Carte du Canada ou de la Nouvelle France.** Paris, 1703. 655 × 505mm. Map, cold. in outl. (P. Oct.20; 276) £220
- **– Anr. Edn.** Paris, 1783. *Re-iss. of 1703 map.* 495 × 645mm. Double-p. engraved general map showing the Great Lakes & the headwaters of the Mississippi & Missouri systems, a re-iss. of the 1703 map with title altered to name the United States, hand-cold. in outl., w.a.f. (S. May 22; 351) *Marsden.* £180
- **– Anr. Edn.** Covens & Mortier, n.d. Ob. fo. Copper engraved map, old outl. col., figure cartouche, some slight spotting. (R. Oct.13; 3455) DM 1,000
- **Carte du Congo ...** 1730. 500 × 620mm. Line engraved map, cold. outl., F. (VA. Apr.27; 608) R 300
- **Carte du Mexique et de la Floride.** Covens & Mortier, 1722. Ob. fo. Copper engraved map, old outl. cold., 2 figurè cartouches, slightly stained at foot. (R. Oct.13; 3486) DM 700
- **L'Hemisphere Meridionale [et] Septentrionale.** Covens & Mortier, n.d. Ob. fo. 2 ll. old outl. cold. copper engraved map, minimal spotting. (R. Oct.13; 3349) DM 500
- **L'Hemisphère, les Terres, Septentrional Arctiques.** Covens & Mortier, ca. 1730. 525 × 475mm. Hand-cold. map. (P. Jun.7; 394) £95
- **Hemisphère Occidental.** Covens & Mortier, ca. 1730. 500 × 500mm. Hand-cold. map, repairs, back strengthened. (P. Jun.7; 395) £170
- **Hemisphère Oriental.** Covens & Mortier, ca. 1730. 495 × 500mm. Hand-cold. map, repairs, back strengthened. (P. Jun.7; 392) £100
- **Hemisphère Orientale [et] Occidentale.** Covens & Mortier, ca. 1740. Ob. fo. Round old outl. cold. copper engraved map, 2 ll., minimal spotting. (R. Oct.13; 3326) DM 520
- **Hemisphere pour voir les Terres. Septentrional plus distinctement Arctiques ...** Amst., R. & I.

DE L'ISLE, Guillaume -*Contd.*

Ottens, 1740 or later. Approx. 18 × 18 inches. Orig. hand-cold. map, some minor margin tears, not affecting engraved surface. (TA. Jul.19; 116)
£90

– **In Notitiam Ecclesiasticam Africae Tabula Geographica** ... Ca. 1740. 2 maps. Each 320 × 520mm. Engraved cold. maps, 1 bearing dedication to Sir Richard Temple, other with ornate engraved cartouche, ill. with whole continent of Africa, F. (PD. Aug.17; 319)
£52

– **Mappa totius Mundi.** T.C. Lotter, ca. 1760. Ob. fo. Old cold. copper engraved map in 2 hemispheres, sm. maps in upr. corners, lge. figure cartouche, some light spotting & few sm. wormholes, slightly crumpled. (R. Oct.13; 3328)
DM 550

– **Nord– u. Südgriechenland mit Kreta und den Inseln.** Covens & Mortier, n.d. Ob. fo. 2 ll. copper engraved map, old outl. col., figure cartouche. (R. Oct.13; 3775)
DM 450

– **Nova Helvetiae ... Regionum Tabula ... Sec. Commentarios. Dom. Merveilleux.** Amst., Covens & Mortier, ca. 1715. 465 × 600mm. Copper engraved map, outl. & surface col., 'Avertissement' at top left, arms at top right & lr. left. (GF. Nov.17; 2783)
Sw. Frs. 650

– **South America.** Covens & Mortier, ca. 1730. Each sheet approx. 570 × 500mm. Hand-cold. map, in 2 sheets, repairs, a few dampstains, back strengthened. (P. Jun.7; 397)
£70

DE L'ISLE, Guillaume & Buache, Philippe
– **Carte des Nouvelles Decouvertes au Nord de la Mer du Sud.** Paris, P. Buache, [1752]. *Early Iss.* 452 × 653mm. Double-p. engraved map, hand-cold. in wash & outl., faint pencil mark. (S. Dec.1; 234)   *Crete.* £420

– – **Anr. Edn.** Paris, [1780]. 455 × 640mm. Double-p. engraved map including eastern Siberia & the Northwest showing the Russian discoveries from 1723 to 1741, together with the fictitious lakes & waterbodies in western Canada, hand-cold. in outl., w.a.f. (S. May 22; 347)   *Quaritch.* £180

– **Mappemonde à l'Usage du Roy.** Paris, 1779. 440 × 670mm. Double-p. engraved double-hemispheric map, hand-cold., primarily in outl., good margins, verso blank, some tearing in margins, weak spot in lr. left corner. (SG. Jun.7; 140) $130

DEVENTER, Jacob van
See— ORTELIUS, Abraham

DE WIT, Frederick
See— WIT, Frederick de

DEUTECOM or DOETECUM, Johannes or Jan
– **Beschrijvinghe van de Zee Custen van Oost Vrieslandt, met Allen Undiepten en Bakenen.** Ca. 1584. 330 × 510mm. Folding engraved map, from Waghenaer's 'Spieghel der Zeevaart', ptd. Latin text on verso, slightly browned. (VG. Dec.1; 1271)
Fls. 1,100

– – **Anr. Edn.** 1585. *Dutch Edn.* 325 × 510mm. Old cold. copper engraved map from Wagheneer See atlas, 2 painted rollwork cartouches, decor., lr. corner & upr. blank margin strengthened. (R. Oct.13; 3379)
DM 800

– **Universi Orbis seu Terreni Globi in Plano Effigies.** Antw., 1578. 330 × 510mm. Copper engraved map, surrounded by allegories, for G. de Jodes 'Speculum Orbis Terrarum', sm. crease in upr. half with sm. margin tear bkd., some margin spotting, 2 creases & sm. wormholes at foot, bkd. in plt. margin. (R. Apr.5, 3126)
DM 14,000
See— ORTELIUS, Abraham

DEUTECOM, Johannes or Jan & Lucas von
See— JODE, G. de

DONN, Benjamin
– **The Provinces of New York, & New Jersey; With Part of Pennsylvania, & the Province of Quebec.** Sayer & Bennett, 1776. Approx. 53 × 21 inches. Map, sm. central portion shaded in green, uncold. histor. title cartouche, inset details, slightly soiled & partially split along lr. horizontal fold. (TA. May 17; 162)
£160

DOPPELMAYR, Johann Gabriel
– **Globi Coelestis in Tabula Planas Redacti.** [Nuremb.], Homann, [1742]. 495 × 590mm. Double-p. engraved chart, fully, but clumsily, hand-cold., figures & tables. (SG. Dec.15; 109) $200

DRAYTON, Michael
[–] **Middlesex.** Ca. 1620. Approx. 10 × 13 inches. Uncold. map, allegorical figures, a little browned at edges. (TA. Jan.19; 128)
£62

[–] **Oxford Shyre, Buckingham Shyre & Barck Shyre.** 1612 or 1622. Approx. 10 × 13 inches. Uncold. allegorical map, figures & animals, etc., slightly cropped along side margins. (TA. Jul.19; 188)
£60

[–] **Warwick Shyre, with Part of Stafford Shyre & Part of Lester Shyre.** 1612/13 or later. Approx. 10 × 13 inches. Uncold. allegorical map. (TA. May 17; 210)
£70

[–] – **Anr. Edn.** 1612 or 1622. Approx. 10 × 13 inches. Uncold. allegorical map, figures, animals, etc. (TA. Jul.19; 189)
£50

DRAYTON, Michael & Hole, William
– **Chesshyre.** [1612-13] or later. Approx. 10 × 13 inches. Map, uncold., allegorical, showing rivers & figures, mntd. (TA. Jun.21; 130)
£60

– **Hartford Shyre & Midlesex.** [1612-13] or later. 10 × 13 inches. Map, allegorical, uncold., showing rivers with figures & animals, etc., mntd. (TA. Jun.21; 129)
£50

DUDLEY, Sir Robert
[–] **Carta Particolare d'una parte della cota di China con l'Isola di PaKas, e altre Isole, sino alla parte piu Australe del 'Giapone.** [Flor., 1661]. 480 × 770mm. Double-p. engraved map, completely uncold., lge. compass rose, sailing ship, examples of cursive script, good margins, verso blank. (SG. Jun.7; 79)
$275

[–] **Carta Seconda Generale del'America.** [Flor., 1661 or later]. 438 × 358mm. Full-p. engraved sea-chart extending from Labrador to the Bahamas group, by way of Cape Cod, Long Island & Chesapeake Bay, w.a.f. (S. May 22; 348) *Burden.* £880

[–] **Carta Secon[d]a Generale del'Asia.** [Flor., 1661 or later]. 470 × 358mm. Full-p. engraved sea-chart including the Philippines, Celebes, the Marianas, New Guinea & part of the northern Cape York peninsula labelled 'Terra Scoperta dagl Olandesi', w.a.f. (S. May 22; 460)   *Burden.* £580

DUFOUR
– **Mapa de Galicia.** Paris, 1837. 570 × 830mm. Engraved map. (DS. Mar.23; 2172)   Pts. 36,000

DUNN, Samuel, Mathematician
– **A General Map of the World, or Terraqueous Globe with all the New Discoveries & Marginal Delineations** ... Laurie & Whittle, 1799. Approx. 41 × 48 inches. Map, in 4 joined sections, partly hand-cold. in outl., many ptd. details. (TA. Jul.19; 114)
£130

– **Scientia Terrarum et Coelorum.** Robert Sayer, 1772. Each sheet 20 × 25 inches. Engraved map, on 4 sheets, some light wear along folds, F. & G. in 2 sections. (CSK. Mar.9; 7)
£130

DURY, Andrew
See— MONTRESSOR, Capt.

DUVAL, Pierre
– **Amérique Meridionale.** Paris, 1684 [or later]. 410 × 580mm. Double-p. engraved mapsheet, comprising the South American sheet of Duval's 4 sheet world map, hand-cold. in outl., margin spotting. (S. Dec.1; 226)   *Burden.* £250

– **Carte du Royaume de Danemarq.** Ca. 1679. 545 × 410mm. Uncold. map. (P. Jan.12; 340)
Jorgensen. £60

EIMMART, Georg Christopher
– **Planisphaerium Caeleste.** [Nuremb.], Officina Homanniana, ca. 1730. 490 × 575mm. Hand-cold. double-p. engraved celestial chart in twin hemispheres, inset diagrams, slightly soiled. (S. Jun.25; 264)   *King.* £110

ELDER EXPEDITION
– **Maps to Accompany the Journal of the Elder Scientific Exploring Expedition.** N.p., n.d. 2 lge.

folding maps in orig. lettered card. case. (KH. Nov.9; 591)   Aus. $350

ELWE, Jan Barend
– **De Golf van Mexico, de Eilanden en het Omleggende Land.** Amst., 1792. 480 × 580mm. Double-p. engraved map, hand-cold., title cartouche, some spotting, lr. corners creased. (SG. Dec.15; 32)
$200

EMMIUS, U.
– **Typus Frisiae Orientalis.** Blaeuw, n.d. Cold. copper-engraved map. (V. Sep.29; 744)   DM 800

FADEN, William
– **The United States of North America: with the British Territories & Those of Spain** ... L., Faden, 1793. 20½ × 24 inches. Engraved map, partly hand-cold. in outl., vig. cartouche, extensive margins, slight discoloration. (SPB. May 23; 30) $600
See— BLASKOWITZ, Charles
See— PALMEUS, A.F.G. de
See— RATZER, Bernard
See— SAUTHIER, Claude Joseph
See— WRIGHT, Thomas
See— WRIGHT, Thomas & others

FER, Nicolas de
– **Le Cours de la Sare.** 1705. 340 × 240mm. Outl. cold. copper engraved map, caption cartouche, margins lightly foxed. (R. Oct.14; 4386)   DM 420

– **Terre Sainte Ancienne** ... Paris, 1701. 35 × 46 inches. Hand-cold. engraved map, on 4 joined sheets, matted, F. & G. (SPB. Dec.13; 480)
$1,600

FLANDRUS, G.C.
– **Tabula Islandiae.** Cold. copper-engraved map, slight browning, especially to lr. margin. (V. Sep.29; 221)   DM 420

FLINDERS, Capt. Matthew
– **Chart of Terra Australis.** 1831. East Coast Sheet 1. 25 × 21 inches. Hydrographical engraved chart, mntd. on cl., 1 sm. stain. (CSK. May 4; 184)£170

FOSSE, J.B. de la
– **Carte de France, divisée en ses Provinces, et Gouvernemens Militaires, avec toutes les principales Routes du Royaume.** Paris, 1776. 944 × 1,220mm. Engraved wall-map in 4 joined sheets, hand-cold. in outl., lge. title cartouche at lr. left, sm. repair touching 1 margin, mntd. on linen. (S. Dec.1; 244)
Quaritch. £300

FRICX, E.H.
[–] **Partie de l'Angleterre.** [Brussels, 1712, or later]. 410 × 573mm. Double-p. engraved map, partly hand-cold. in outl., faint staining, F. & G. (S. Apr.9; 149)   *Frankland.* £50

FRY, Joshua & Jefferson, Peter
– **A Map of the most Inhabited part of Virginia containing the Whole Province of Maryland with Part of Pennsylvania, New Jersey & North Carolina** ... L., Laurie & Whittle after Thomas Jeffreys, 1794. 31 × 48 inches. Engraved map, in 4 sheets, partly hand-cold. in outl., elab. scenic cartouche in lr. right-hand sheet, extensive margins, slight margin browning. (SPB. May 23; 31) $600

FULLER, Thomas
[–] **[Israel].** [Camb.], mid-17th. C. 275 × 320mm. Engraved map, to accompany 'History of the Holy War'?, hand-cold. (possibly later), coat-of-arms, dedication cartouche to Thomas Leigh, earlier creasing. (SG. Dec.15; 95) $175

GARDNER, W.
See— YEAKELL, T. & Gardner, W.

GASTALDI, G.
See— ORTELIUS, Abraham

GIBBES, Charles Drayton
– **Map of the States of California & Nevada** ... San Franc., 1878. Partially cold. folding engraved map, cl. case, with title 'Holt's Township of California & Nevada'. (LH. Apr.15; 319) $120

GIGAS, J.
– **Archiepiscopatus Coloniensis Pars Septentrionalis.** Ca. 1620. Copper-engraved map, from Atlas,

some old spotting, partly bkd. (V. Sep.30; 3026)
DM 2,600
- **Episcopatus Monasteriensis Pars Australis.** Ca. 1620. Copper engraved map, old spotting & staining, partly bkd. (V. Sep.29; 920) DM 1,200
- **Monasteriensis Episcopatus.** Blaeuw, n.d. Cold. copper engraved map. (V. Sep.29; 684) DM 520
- **Paderbornensis Episcopatus Descriptio Nova.** Blaeuw, n.d. Cold. copper-engraved map. (V. Sep.29; 749) DM 700
- **Westphalia Ducatus.** Blaeuw, n.d. Cold. copper-engraved map. (V. Sep.29; 921) DM 430

GOOS, A.
- **America.** G. Humble, 1626. Ob. fo. Copper engraved map from Speed Atlas, cartouche, sm. supp. map, 5 ills. at sides, 8 sm. views at head, extended upper margin. (R. Oct.13; 3425)
DM 2,600
- **Sueciae et Norvegiae.** 1630. 460 × 550mm. Engraved map, hand-cold. in outl., German text on verso, margins slightly trimmed. (CSK. Nov.4; 5)
£110

GOOS, Pieter
[-] **De Custen van Noorwegen, Finnmarcken, Laplandt, Spitsbergen, Ian Mayen Eylandt, Yslandt.** [Amst.], 1666 or later. 445 × 545mm. Double-p. engraved sea chart, orientated north-west to the top of the sheet, hand-cold. in outl. (S. Jun.25; 32)
Borsams Forlag. £140
[-] **Noordoost Cust van Asia.** [Amst.], 1666 or later. 446 × 545mm. Double-p. engraved sea-chart, hand-cold. in outl. (S. Jun.25; 62) *Remmington.* £150
[-] **Pas-Caart van Guinea.** [Amst.], 1666 or later. 441 × 540mm. Double-p. engraved sea-chart, hand-cold. in outl. (S. Jun.25; 82) *Schrire.* £110
- **Pascart na de Noord Zee van Texel tot de Hoofden.** N.d. 590 × 490mm. Engraved chart, cold. in outl., scroll title cartouche & devices, under glass in Hogarth frame. (PD. Dec.14; 294) £80
[-] **Paskaart van Brasil.** [Amst.], 1666 or later. 447 × 540mm. Double-p. engraved sea chart, orientated east to the top of the sheet, hand-cold. in outl. (S. Jun.25; 134) *Faupel.* £150

GORDON, William
- **An Accurate Map of the County of Bedford.** 1736. 950 × 660mm. Engraved map, in 2 sections, slightly soiled, mntd. on linen, on 2 wooden rollers. (BBA. Feb.9; 261) *Kentish.* £75

GOTTLIEB, A.
- **Americae Mappa Generalis.** Nuremberg, 1746 [or later]. 470 × 548mm. Double-p. engraved map, hand-cold. in wash & outl., repairs affecting engraved surface without serious loss, margin staining. (S. Nov.1; 209) *Ruddell.* £90

GREENE, Robert
- **A New Mapp of the World.** By Robert Greene at the Rose & Crowne in Budg Row, 1676. 440 × 552mm. Double-p. engraved map in twin hemispheres, hand-cold. in outl., surrounded by allegorical vigs., smaller insets of the North & South poles, sm. repairs & strengthening at centrefold without loss of engraved surface. (S. Dec.1; 219)
Robinson. £2,000

GREENWOOD, Christopher
- **Map of the County of Kent.** 1821. 47 × 72 inches. Hand-cold. folding engraved map, mntd. on cl., some light browning, orig. box. worn. (CSK. Jul.6; 59) £300

GREENWOOD, Christopher & John
- **A Map of the County of Sussex from an Actual Survey made in the Years 1823 & 1824.** 1825. Each section 50 × 27¾ inches. Hand-cold. engraved folding linen-bkd. map, in 3 sections, lge. vig. of Chichester Cathedral, leath. case, w.a.f. (LC. Mar.1; 278) £130
- **Map of the County of Sussex.** L., Greenwood, Pringle & Co., March 24th, 1825. 1,270 × 2,040mm. Engraved lge. scale county map, in 6 sheets, mntd. & dissected in 72 sections, lge. inset vig., some faint staining, folding into paper s.-c. (S. Mar.6; 173) *Burgess.* £150
- **Map of London.** 1830. 1,250 × 1,900mm. Folding hand-cold. engraved map, slightly soiled, mntd. on cl. (CSK. Sep.30; 111) £190

HAGEN, Christiaen van der
- **Plattegrond van Leiden.** N.d. 950 × 1,200mm. Cold. engraved map on 4 sheets, margins, 1 or 2 sm. tears, reprd., F. (CH. May 24; 225) Fls. 1,900

HAGUE, The
- **Nouveau Plan de La Haye.** The Hague, 1776. 450 × 560mm. Hand-cold. engraved plan, folds, ptd. explanation pasted on margins. (VG. Sep.15; 1710) Fls. 450

HALLEY, Edmund
- **A Chart Describing Part of the Coast of Great-Britain, from the South Foreland to Berwick.** 1701 or later. Approx. 20½ × 23 inches. Uncold. map, plain title cartouche, compass rose, rhumb lines, some minor spotting. (TA. Nov.17; 103) £60

HARENBERG, I.C.
- **Palestina in XII. Tribus Divisa, cum Terris Adiacentibus** ... Nuremb., Homannianis Heredibus, 1750. 450 × 520mm. Double-p. engraved map, main areas hand-cold., cold. title cartouche, vig., dedication cartouche & inset map. (SG. Dec.15; 96) $275
- **Palestine in XII. Tribus Divisa** [running title in French]. Nuremb., Homann's Hiers, 1750 [or later]. 452 × 530mm. Double-p. engraved map, hand-cold. in wash & outl., inset & lge. cartouche, split at centrefold reprd., margin stain. (S. Dec.13; 126) *Levy.* £60

HEATHER, William
- **Chart of the Downs & Margate Roads.** Kent, 1797. Approx. 25 × 31 inches. Map, partially cold., compass rose & extensive rhumb lines, a little browned & creased, recently F. & G. (TA. Jun.21; 95) £70

HENNET, G.
- **A Map of the County Palatine of Lancaster.** 1829. Hand-cold. folding map on linen, cf. box. (P. Sep.8; 447) *Elliott.* £60

HERISSON, E.
- **Mappe-Monde ou Globe Terrestre.** [Paris], 1836. 925 × 1,238mm. Engraved map in twin hemispheres, in 2 sheets joined, outl. hand-cold., short tear at lr. centre-fold not affecting engraved surface. (S. Nov.1; 196) *Potter.* £95

HEYMANN, I.
- **Italie Coiè Tutte le Grandi e Picciole Sovranità e Republiche d'Italia.** Trieste, Ufficio delle Poste in Trieste, [1806]. 1,085 × 1,030mm. Lge. engraved general map, in 4 sheets, mntd. & dissected, hand-cold. in outl., decor. title & key-cartouches fully cold., folding into cont. paper covered s.-c. (S. Mar.6; 129) *King.* £60

HIRSCHVOGEL, A.
See— BRAUN or BRUIN, Georg & Hogenberg, Franz

HOFFMANN, Joh.
- **Germanien oder Teutschlandes Neueste ... Geographische Charte** ... Nürnberg, ca. 1670. Cold. copper engraved map, cold arms cartouche, 5 cold. town views, cold. figure ills. in margins, tear in fold reprd. (BR. Apr.13; 2945) DM 3,600

HOGENBERG, Franz
See— BRAUN or BRUIN, Georg & Hogenberg, Franz

HOLE, William
See— DRAYTON, Michael & Hole, William
See— SAXTON, Christopher & Hole, William

HOLLAND
- **Hollandia Nova Descriptio.** Ca. 1570. 350 × 490mm. Hand-cold. engraved map by J. van Deventer from Ortelius' Theatrum, centre fold, slightly browned, F. (VG. Mar.22; 1685) Fls. 450

HOMANN, Johann Baptist
- **Archiepiscopatus et Electoratus Coloniensis ut et Duc. Iuliacensis et Montensis.** Nuremb., ca. 1720. Old cold. map, uncold arms cartouche. (HK. Nov.12; 5593) DM 440
- **Ducatus Franciae Orientalis seu Princip. et Episcopatus Herbipolensis vulgo Würtzburgensis.** Nuremb., ca. 1720. Cold. map, lge. figure cartouche, cold. outl. plan, sm. cold. view. (HK. Nov.12; 5547) DM 540
- - **Anr. Edn.** N.d. Cold. copper-engraved map. (V. Sep.29; 954) DM 700
- **Flaggen aller Seefahrende Potenzen** ... Ca. 1720. Copper engraved map, cold. in strips, ills. of 139 flags & col. guide, repairs. (BR. Apr.13; 2879) DM 450
- **Judaea sev Palestina ... Terra Sancta.** Ca. 1740. 570 × 490mm. Hand-cold. map, cartouche. (P. Dec.8; 435) £65
- **Magna Britannia.** Nuremb., 1714 or later. 490 × 580mm. Double-p. engraved map, hand-cold. in wash & outl., faint stain. (S. Jun.25; 358)
Beddows. £75
- **Nova Anglia.** Nuremb., [1716, but 1720 or later]. 484 × 570mm. Double-p. engraved regional map of Northeast extending from St John river to New Jersey, showing oversized Lake Champlain draining northward to St Lawrence, the Cape Cod peninsula as an island & with scenic cartouche depicting an Indian (inspired by de Bry) bartering with an Engl. merchant, the whole hand-cold. in wash & outl., w.a.f. (S. May 22; 365) *Ward.* £180
- - **Anr. Edn.** Ca. 1740. 585 × 495mm. Hand-cold. map, back strengthened. (P. Jul.5; 413) £140
- - **Anr. Edn.** N.d. Ob. fo. Old cold. copper engraved map, figure cartouche. (R. Oct.13; 3475) DM 500
- **Novae Hispaniae, Floridae, Novae Angliae, Carolinae, ... exhibita.** N.d. Ob. fo. Partly cold. copper engraved map, 2 figure cartouches, 2 rust holes in lr. margin bkd. (R. Oct.13; 3473) DM 650
- **Planiglobii Terrestris.** Nuremb., 1720 or later. 478 × 540mm. Double-p. engraved twin-hemispherical map, hand-cold. in outl., border of allegorical subjects, 2 inset hemispheres, slight offsetting & surface dirt. (S. Jun.25; 266) *Adamopoulos.* £300
- - **Anr. Edn.** Nuremb., ca. 1720. Cold. world map in 2 hemispheres with Northern & Southern celestial planispheres, with elements, bkd. in fold, traces of liming, sm. holes, sm. margin defects at foot, slightly soiled, lightly crumpled. (HK. May 18; 4245) DM 500
- **Potentissimae Helvetiorum Reipublicae Cantones Tredecim.** Nüremb., n.d. 470 × 560mm. Copper engraved map, old outl. col., lge. arms cartouche, 2 supp. cartouches. (GF. Nov.17; 2782)
Sw. Frs. 600
- **Principatvs et Archiepiscopatus Salisburgensis.** Nuremb., ca. 1720. Cold. map, 2 arms cartouches, allegories, etc., uncold., sm. crease in upr. margin. (HK. Nov.12; 5739) DM 500
- **Principatus et Episcopatus Eistettensis.** Nuremb., ca. 1720. Cold. map, 2 lge. cartouches & sm. views in lr. left corner not cold., some slight creases, lr. margin tear bkd. (HK. Nov.12; 5546) DM 750
- **Principatus Fuldensis in Buchonia.** Nuremb., ca. 1720. Cold. map, figure cartouche. (HK. Nov.12; 5571) DM 460
- - **Anr. Copy.** Cold. map, figure cartouche, cartouche slightly weak, some light creases. (HK. Nov.12; 5572) DM 400
- - **Anr. Edn.** N.d. Cold. copper-engraved 2-pt. map. (V. Sep.29; 543) DM 620
- **Prospect und Grundriss der Keiserl. Freyen Reichs und Ansee Stadt Hamburg.** Nuremb., ca. 1726. Cold. copper engraved map, sm. subsidiary map, decor. cartouche in lr. margin, partly cold. view, allegorical ills. at sides, cut to plt. margin, several sm. margin tears. (H. Nov.23; 398) DM 520
- **Regionis Mississipi seu Provinciae Ludovicianae ... Tabula.** Nuremb., ca. 1720. Cold. map, 2 lge. cartouches, 1 slightly faint, slightly stained in part. (HK. Nov.12; 5426) DM 500
- - **Anr. Copy.** Cold map, 2 lge. cartouches, both slightly faint. (HK. Nov.12; 5427) DM 480
- **Regni Mexicani seu Novae Hispaniae, Floridae, Nova Angliae, Carolinae, Virginiae, et Pennsylvania.** [Nuremb.?], n.d. 570 × 475mm. Map, some wear at margins. (DM. May 21; 126) $275
- **Tabula Generalis Holsatiae.** Nuremb., 1707 or later. 483 × 571mm. Double-p. engraved map, hand-cold. in wash & outl., margin stain, slight creasing. (S. Dec.13; 58) *Schuster.* £50
- **Territorii Ulmensis ... Descriptio.** N.d. Ob. fo. Old cold. copper engraved map, figure cartouche &

HOMANN, Johann Baptist -*Contd.*

sm. supp. map, partly split & bkd., margins slightly spotted. (R. Oct.14; 4448) DM 600
- **Theatrum Belli Rhenani Auspicatis Militiae Primitiis Potentissimi Roman. et Hunga. Regis Josephi I.** Nuremb., 1702. 560 × 480mm. Partly cold. copper engraved map, cartouche in top right with sm. view, cartouche at left foot & detail map. (GF. Nov.12; 1048) Sw. Frs. 400
- **Topographische Vorstellung der Neuen St. Petersburg.** Ca. 1730. 600 × 510mm. Hand-cold. town plan, cartouche. (P. Jul.26; 245) £55
- **Totius Africae Nova Repraesentatio.** Nuremberg, 1707 [but 1715 or later]. 485 × 560mm. Double-p. engraved map, hand-cold. in wash & outl. (including title-cartouche), sm. print-crease at lr. centre-fold. (S. Nov.1; 203) *Ash.* £75
- **Ukrania.** Nuremb., n.d. 472 × 570mm. Engraved map, partly hand-cold., slightly torn & soiled. (BBA. Feb.9; 262) *Lettres Slaves.* £50
- **Virginia, Marylandia et Carolina.** Nuremb., 1714 [but 1720 or later]. 480 × 575mm. Double-p. engraved map, cold. in wash & outl. (S. Nov.1; 236) *Burgess.* £170
See— LAUTENBACH, J. Chr.
See— ZOLLMANNUS, Fr.

HOMANN, Johann Baptiste, Heirs of
- **Accurater Grundriss und Prospect der Weltberühmten Hollandischen Haupt und Handels-Stadt Amsterdam.** Nürnberg, ca. 1730. 480 × 590mm. Cont. hand-cold. engraved plan, view of IJ with sailing ships below, centre fold, slight margin defects. (VG. Sep.15; 1682) Fls. 600
- **Americae Mappa Generalis.** 1746. Approx. 18½ × 22 inches. Map, partially cold., uncold. ornamental & historiated title cartouche, a little soiled. (TA. Jun.21; 133) £100
- - **Anr. Copy.** Ob. fo. Cold. copper engraved map, painted figure cartouche, slightly spotted, some thin parts & holes, mostly bkd. (R. Oct.13; 3430) DM 450
- - **Anr. Copy.** Ob. fo. Old cold. copper engraved map, painted figure cartouche, fold partly split & bkd., some foxing, margins slightly soiled. (R. Apr.5; 3289) DM 330
- **Carte des Indes Orientales.** 1748. 510 × 855mm. Old cold. copper engraved map, ptd. from 2 plts., figure cartouche, some spotting, margins stained. (R. Oct.13; 3529) DM 400
- **Circuli Sveviae Mappa.** Nuremb., 1743. 510 × 580mm. Copper engraved map with some surface col. (GF. Nov.12; 1075) Sw. Frs. 420
- **Dominia Anglorum in America Septentrionali: A. New Foundland, od. Terra Nova S. Laurentii Bay, ... B. New Engelland, New York, New Yersey und Pensilvania. C. Virginia und Maryland. D. Carolina nebst einem Theil von Florida.** [Nuremb., later 18th. C.]. 510 × 570mm. 4-pt., double-p. engraved map, hand-cold., satisfactory margins, verso blank, minor creasing, rubbing. (SG. Jun.7; 51) $130
- **Dominia Anglorum in Praecipuis Insulis Americae.** Nuremberg, 1733 or later. 493 × 560mm. 5 sm. maps showing Barbados, Jamaica, Bermuda, Antigua & St. Christopher (after H. Moll, ca. 1720) on 1 double-p. engraved sheet, outl. hand-cold., sm. repair without loss of engraved surface. (S. Nov.1; 226) *Burgess.* £110
- **Die Grafschaft Pyrmont mit d. Hanoverischen, Braunschw. u. Gr. Lippischen ... Graenzlaendern.** Nuremb., 1752. Cold. map, sm. view at top left, sm. tear at foot bkd. (HK. Nov.12; 5585) DM 410
- **Mappe-monde.** Nuremb., ca. 1750. Cont. hand-cold. map, with text, browned, reinforced in fold & margins. (VG. Dec.1; 1193) Fls. 500
- **Regionis quae est circa Londinium ...** Mid 18th C. 20 × 23 inches. Hand-cold. engraved map, F. & G. (CSK. Jul.6; 147) £60
- **Theatrum Belli ad Rhenum Superior.** 1734. Cold. copper-engraved map, 9 engraved town plans at side. (V. Sep.29; 723) DM 410
- **Urbium Londini et West-Monasterii nec non Suburbii Southwark.** Nuremb, 1736 [or later]. 510 × 1600 mm.(total dimensions). Town plan in 3 double-p. engraved sheets, extending from St. James's Park to Poplar, showing vig. ills. of Royal Exchange, Custom House, St. James's Square & St. Paul's, hand-cold., slight surface dirt, centre

folds strengthened, w.a.f. (S. May 21; 47) *Robinson.* £300
- **Venetia.** 1729. Approx. 19 × 22 inches. Map, partially cold., ornamental title cartouche, Prospect of Venice along lr. margin, sailing ships, a little soiled, some minor damage at head & foot of centrefold, F. & G. (TA. Mar.15; 73) £75
See— ANVILLE, Jean Baptiste Bourguignon d'
See— HARENBERG, J.C.
See— MAIER, T.

HONDIUS, Henricus
- **Africae Nova Tabula.** J. Jansson, n.d. Ob. fo. Cold. copper engraved map, painted cartouche, decor. (R. Oct.13; 3391) DM 600
- - **Anr. Copy.** Ob. fo. Old cold. copper engraved map, painted floral cartouche, ship & animal decor., lightly browned, sm. tear at foot to plt. margin bkd., 1 crease. (R. Apr.5; 3252) DM 420
- **America Noviter Delineata ... 1631.** [Amst.], 1631 or later. 380 × 500mm. Double-p. engraved map, hand-cold. in outl., 2 sm. insets of Greenland & the north Pole & 'Terra Australia', Latin text on verso, faint browning. (S. Dec.1; 221) *Fendrich.* £280
- **Americae Pars Meridionalis.** Amst., [1636 or later]. *Early Iss.* 460 × 545mm. Double-p. engraved map, outl. hand-cold., lge. title-cartouche with 6 Indian figures, Latin text on verso, faint browning. (S. Nov.1; 211) *Frers.* £150
- **Angliae, Scotiae et Hibernia.** Late 16th. C. Hand-cold. map, F. & G. (P. Sep.8; 474) £110
- **Asia recens summa cura delineata.** 1631. 17 × 21¾ inches. Hand-cold. engraved map, cartouches, animals on land, galleons & monsters at sea, F. (LC. Jul.5; 201) £110
- - **Anr. Edn.** [Amst.], 1631 [but 1633 or later]. 378 × 500mm. Double-p. engraved map, Fr. text on verso, sm. repair at lr. centrefold. (S. Dec.13; 8) *Burgess.* £140
- - **Anr. Edn.** [Amst., 1631, but 1636 or later]. 378 × 500mm. Double-p. engraved map, hand-cold. in outl., Latin text on verso, faint margin browning. (S. Mar.6; 146) *Burgess.* £150
- **Chorographica Tabula Lacus Lemani.** Ca. 1620. 530 × 320mm. Hand-cold. map. (P. Feb.16; 306) £70
- **Europa.** 1631. 505 × 385mm. Hand-cold. map, vig. sailing ships. (P. Apr.12; 348) *De Vine.* £110
- **Europa Exactissime Descripta.** Ca. 1630. 510 × 385mm. Hand-cold. map, fold worn, slightly browned. (P. Apr.12; 350) £85
- **Guiana sive Amazonum Regio.** Amst., [Hondius, 1633]. 375 × 490mm. Double-p. engraved map, hand-cold. in outl., mountains washed in brown, title, scale, auctorial cartouches, etc., Fr. text on verso. (SG. Dec.15; 33) $125
- **Iaponia.** 17th. C. Cold. copper-engraved map, carefully restored, offsetting. (V. Sep.29; 242) DM 400
- **India Orientalis et Insulae Adiacentes.** Jansson, n.d. Ob. fo. Cold. copper engraved map, 3 painted figure & heraldic cartouches, decor., slighly browned. (R. Oct.13; 3532) DM 400
[-] **Ins. Ceilan quae Incolis Tenarisin Dicitur.** [Amst., 1630, but 1633 or later]. 344 × 498mm. Double-p. engraved map, after Plancius, Fr. text on verso. (S. Mar.6; 148) *Potter.* £50
- **Magnae Brittaniae et Hiberniae Tabula.** Amst., 1631. Approx. 15 × 20 inches. Map, hand-cold. ornamental title cartouche with cherubs & surmounted by Royal crest, separate scale of distance, inset detail of Orcades Insulae, Engl. text on verso, slight damage to centrefold, mntd. (TA. May 17; 169) £75
- **Mappa Aestivarum Insularum, alias Barmudas.** Amst., 1633 or later. 390 × 520mm. Double-p. engraved map, outl. hand-cold., Latin text on verso, slight adhesion damage at centre-fold with loss of engraved surface. (S. Nov.1; 223) *Burgess.* £270
- **Nova Terrarum Orbis Geographica.** 1630 [but 1634 or later]. 15 × 25½ inches. Engraved hand-cold. map, Dutch text on verso, lightly soiled, several repairs, margins trimmed. (CSK. May 4; 179) £320
- **Nova Totius Terrarum Orbis Geographica ac Hydrographica Tabula.** [Amst., 1633 or later]. 380 × 540mm. Double-p. engraved map in twin hemispheres, cont. hand-cold., showing important early cartographic detail in Cape York Peninsula

region of Australia (after Jan Cartensz, 1623), also island of California, map area surrounded by allegorical vigs. of 4 elements &, in spandrels, ports. of Julius Caesar, Ptolemy, Mercator & J. Hondius, Fr. text on verso, faint discolouration at centre-fold, w.a.f. (S. May 21; 152) *Condy.* £1,200
- - **Anr. Edn.** J. Jansson, n.d. Ob. fo. Cold. copper engraved map in 2 hemispheres, medallion ports. in corners, floral decor., lge. allegories of 4 elements, sm. bkd. fault. (R. Oct.13; 3317) DM 2,800
- - **Anr. Copy.** Copper-engraved map, decor. border with ports., little old spotting, partly bkd. (V. Sep.29; 146) DM 900
- **Nova Virginiae Tabula.** Amst., ca. 1630 or later. Approx. 15 × 19½ inches. Map, hand-cold., sm. ornamental title cartouche, separate scale of distance, Royal crest, compass rose, rhumb lines, etc., Dutch text to verso. (TA. Jun.21; 134) £170
- - **Anr. Edn.** Amst., ca. 1633. Hand-cold. double-p. engraved map, inset view & cartouche, slight discoloration, matted, F. & G. (SPB. Dec.13; 489) $550
- - **Anr. Edn.** Amst., 1633 or later. *Early Iss.* 391 × 495mm. Double-p. engraved map, orientated West to top of sheet, copied from Hondius-Blaeu plt. of 1629, outl. hand-cold., embellishments fully hand-cold., Latin text on verso, sig. (S. Nov.1; 234) *Burgess.* £210
- - **Anr. Edn.** Ca. 1635. 495 × 385mm. Uncold. map, repairs, washed. (P. Jul.5; 410) £100
- - **Anr. Edn.** Jansson, n.d. Ob. fo. Cold. copper engraved map, 3 caption cartouches, figure & heraldic decor. (R. Oct.13; 3504) DM 980
[-] **Tabula Islandiae.** [Amst.], 1633 or later. 382 × 494mm. Double-p. engraved map, Fr. text on verso, sm. split reprd., faint browning. (S. Dec.13; 31) *Solnes.* £100
- **Totius Rheni Descriptio.** 1632. Ob. fo. Old cold. copper engraved map, painted figure cartouche, browned, slightly defect at foot, margins slightly spotted, some sm. holes. (R. Oct.15; 5753) DM 400
- **Typus Orbis Terrarum.** [1632]. 205 × 150mm. Hand-cold. map. (P. Apr.12; 247) *Brooks.* £65
See— MERCATOR, Gerard & Hondius, Henricus

HONDIUS, Henricus & Jansson, Jan or Johannes
- **America Noviter Delineata.** Ca. 1640. 505 × 385mm. Uncold. map, repairs. (P. Jul.5; 412) £120

HONDIUS, Jodocus
- **America.** Amst., ca. 1595 or later. 14½ × 19½ inches. Engraved hand-cold. map, vig. surrounded by strapwork cartouche in lr. left corner, decor. elements, sailing ships, etc., matted, F. & G. (SPB. Oct.26; 10) $1,100
- - **Anr. Copy.** 14½ × 19 inches. Hand-cold. engraved map, vig. of natives in strapwork cartouche at lr. left-hand corner, sailing ships, etc., overall fading, matted, F. & G. (SPB. May 23; 23) $500
- - **Anr. Edn.** Amst., [1628]. 370 × 500mm. Double-p. engraved map, fully hand-cold., sailing ships, sea monsters, Indians in canoes, exotic birds, etc., inset vig. 'Modus conficiendi et bibendi potum ... ', full margins, Fr. title ptd, on verso. (SG. Jun.7; 53) $1,300
- - **Anr. Edn.** N.d. Ob. fo. Old cold. copper engraved map, 2 painted figure cartouches, lightly browned, split bkd. (R. Apr.5; 3286) DM 1,600
- - **Anr. Copy.** Ob. fo. Old cold. copper engraved map, 2 painted figure cartouches, decor., browned, cut slightly close. (R. Oct.13; 3424) DM 1,400
[-] **America Meridionalis.** [Amst.], 1628 or later. 355 × 490mm. Cont. hand-cold. double-p. engraved map, inset, Fr. text on verso. (S. Jun.25; 148) *Faupel.* £160
[-] - **Anr. Copy.** 355 × 490mm. Hand-cold. double.-p. engraved map, inset, Fr. text on verso, faint overall browning. (S. Jun.25; 149) *Faupel.* £140
- **Asiae Nova Descriptio.** [Amst.], 1606, but 1619 or later]. 375 × 500mm. Double-p. engraved map, hand-cold. in outl., Fr. text on verso, faint overall browning. (S. Mar.6; 145) *Waterloo.* £180
- **Hispaniae Nova Descriptio.** [Amst., 1611]. 375 × 520mm. Double-p. engraved map, fully hand-cold., sailing ships, sea monsters, 2 compass roses, good margins, Fr. text on verso, all a bit rubbed, minor reinforcements on verso. (SG. Jun.7; 111) $120

[-] **Hispaniae Novae Nova Descriptio.** [Amst.], 1633 or later. 350 × 480mm. Double-p. engraved map, lge. title cartouche, sea monster & sailing vessel, the whole hand-cold. in outl. (S. Jun.25; 237)
Inskip. £70

[-] **India Orientalis.** [Amst.], 1619 or later. 350 × 480mm. Double-p. engraved map, hand-cold. in outl., Fr. text on verso, faint overall browning, margins strengthened. (S. Dec.13; 17)
Burgess. £280

– – **Anr. Edn.** [Amst.], 1628 or later. 340 × 480mm. Hand-cold. double-p. engraved map, Fr. text on verso. (S. Jun.25; 57) *Remmington.* £180

– **Nova Africae Tabula.** Amst., 1606 [but 1630]. 376 × 500mm. Double-p. engraved map, outl. hand-cold., Latin text on verso, slight browning. (S. Nov.1; 202) *Beddow.* £135

– **Nova Europae Descriptio.** Amst., [1611]. 370 × 500mm. Double-p. engraved map, hand-cold. in outl., & in light wash col., sailing ships & sea monsters, good margins, Latin text on verso, the whole rubbed, some reinforcements on verso, some worming. (SG. Jun.7; 112) $200

– **Nova Helvetiae Tabula.** Amst., [traces of erased date (1621?) in imprint, but 1630]. 411 × 530mm. Double-p. engraved map, upr. frieze of vig. views, side borders of vig. costume figures, vig. views of Basel & Zurich at lr. corners, sm. rust hole infilled, centrefold strengthened. (S. Dec.1; 252)
Israel. £1,100

[-] **Persici vel Sophorum Regni Typus.** [Amst., 1606, but 1628 or later]. 350 × 500mm. Double-p. map, engraved by P. van den Keere, hand-cold. in outl., Fr. text on verso. (S. Mar.6; 140) *Hosains.* £80

– **Tartaria.** [Amst.], 1628 or later. 344 × 495mm. Hand-cold. double-p. engraved map, Fr. text on verso. (S. Jun.25; 59) *Beddons.* £120

[-] **Virginiae Item et Floridae … Nova Descriptio.** [Amst.], 1619 or later. 340 × 490mm. Double-p. engraved map, hand-cold. in outl., Fr. text on verso, centrefold strengthened. (S. Dec.1; 237)
Robinson. £420

See— **MERCATOR, Gerard & Hondius, Jodocus**

HOOGHE, Romain de
– **Carte Maritime des Environs de Dieppe.** Amst., P. Mortier, 1693 [or later]. 588 × 475mm. Hand-cold. etched & engraved chart, 2 inset views. (S. Jun.25; 199) *Cholmeley.* £140

– **Carte Nouvelle des Costes de Bretagne.** Amst., P. Mortier, [1700 or later]. 556 × 950mm. Double-p. engraved & etched coastal chart from St Malo to Loire estuary, hand-cold., insets fully so, w.a.f. (S. May 21; 185) *Arkway.* £500

– **Carte Nouvelle des Costes de Normandie.** Amst., P. Mortier, [1700 or later]. 555 × 955mm. Double-p. engraved & etched coastal chart with insets including Le Havre, Cherbourg, Honfleur & Mont St Michel, hand-cold., w.a.f. (S. May 21; 188)
Cookson. £850

HOWELL, Reading
– **A Map of the State of Pennsylvania.** [Phila. & L.], 1792 [or later]. 36 × 63 inches. Partly hand-cold. engraved map, in 4 sheets, early state of the upr. right-hand sheet, slightly later states of the others, upr. right-hand sheet with cartouche in oval frame & above a copyright statement beginning 'District of Pennsylvania, to wit … ', a same sheet the inclusion of the Erie Triangle with 'Presqu Isle', lr. left-hand sheet with the statement 'Published 1 August, 1792 for the Author; & Sold by James Phillips … London', slight traces of offsetting & browning. (SPB. May 23; 27) $3,000

HURTER, Chr.
– **Alemannia sive Suevia Superior.** Blaeuw, n.d. Cold. copper-engraved map. (V. Sep.29; 951)
DM 470

HUTAWA, Julius
– **Map of Mexico & California … St. Louis, 1863.** *2nd. Edn.* Engraved folding map, hand-cold. in outl., orig. bds., covers lightly spotted. (LH. Apr.15; 322) $500

HUTCHINS, Thomas
– **A New Map of the Western Parts of Virginia, Pennsylvania, Maryland & North Carolina …** L., Hutchins, 1778. 35½ × 43 inches. Engraved map, in 4 sheets, joined as 1, partly hand-cold. in outl.,

slight browning & offsetting, left-hand margin slightly frayed not affecting plt. (SPB. May 23; 1) $9,000

JACOBSZ, Theunis
[-] **Pascaerte van Candia.** [1665 or later]. 15 × 20½ inches. Engraved chart, some light staining. (CSK. May 4; 205) £95

– **Pascaert van Europa.** Amst., ca. 1650. Ob. fo. Cold copper engraved map, 2 painted cartouches, ills., 7 sm. arms, reprd. & mntd., lightly spotted or browned. (R. Oct.13; 3362) DM 950

JAEGER
– **Carte de la Bavière.** N.d. Outl. cold. copper-engraved map. (V. Sep.29; 376) DM 550

JAILLOT, B.A.
– **Carte particulière des Isles de Malte du Goze et du Cuming.** Paris, 1734. [or later]. 433 × 732mm. Double-p. engraved map, orientated south-west to the top of the sheet, lge. inset plan. (S. Jun.25; 236)
Burgess. £130

JAILLOT, Hubert
– **L'Afrique.** Paris, 1692 [or later]. 540 × 880mm. Double-p. engraved map after N. Sanson, hand-cold. in outl. (S. Jun.25; 74) *Schrire.* £130

– **Le Canada ou Partie de la Nouvelle France.** Paris [but Amst.], 1696 [but 1700 or later]. 465 × 614mm. Full-p. engraved regional map of eastern Canada & the northern part of the Great Lakes, full hand-cold., heightened with gold, 3 narrow margins, w.a.f. (S. May 22; 352) *Fergusson.* £400

– **La Suisse divisée en ses Treize Cantons, ses Alliez & ses Sujets.** Amst., Pierre Mortier. n.d. 440 × 560mm. Copper engraved map, old outl. col., lge. cartouche, decor., old cold. arms borders, text & arms in upr. margin. (GF. Nov.17; 2784)
Sw. Frs. 600

See— **JANSON D'ABBEVILLE, Nicholas & Jaillot, Hubert**

JAILLOT, Hubert & Mortier, Pierre
[-] **Carte générale es des costes de L'Europe.** [Amst.], 1700 or later. 590 × 850mm. Double-p. engraved chart, hand-cold. in outl., faint offsetting. (S. Jun.25; 258) *Charles.* £100

– **Mappe-Monde Géo-Hydrographique.** 1706. 560 × 900mm. Engraved map, hand-cold. in outl., margins lightly soiled. (CSK. Oct.7; 9) £340

– – **Anr. Edn.** Amst., Covens & Mortier, ca. 1730. 980 × 590mm. Hand-cold. map, cartouche, repairs to margins & 1 crease, F. & G. (P. Jun.7; 387)
£170

JANSSON, Jan or Johannes
– **Accuratissima Brasiliae Tabula.** Amst., [later 17th. C.]. 375 × 490mm. Double-p. engraved map, hand-cold. in outl., inset vigs. & maps of 'Baya de todos os Sanctos' & 'Villa d'Olinda de Pernambuco', title cartouche flanked by Brazilian natives, sailing ships, sea monster. (SG. Jun.7; 54) $300

– – **Anr. Edn.** N.d. Ob. fo. Cold. copper engraved map, 2 painted figure cartouches, sm. plan, figures. (R. Oct.13; 3445) DM 450

[-] **Aethiopia Inferior vel Exterior.** [Amst.], 1640 or later. 380 × 500mm. Double-p. engraved map, hand-cold. in outl., embellishments fully cold., Latin text on verso, faint browning. (S. Dec.13; 21)
Ashworth. £130

– – **Anr. Edn.** Ca. 1650. Approx. 15 × 19½ inches. Hand-cold. map, ornamental title cartouche flanked by figures & incorporating scale of distance, sailing ships, animals, etc., Spanish text on verso, sm. repair to base of centrefold, not affecting engraved surface. (TA. Jul.19; 142) £115

– **America noviter delineata.** N.d. Ob. fo. Cold. copper engraved map, painted cartouche, 2 sm. supp. maps, figures, decor. (R. Oct.13; 3426)
DM 1,100

– **America Septentrionalis.** N.d. Ob. fo. Cold. copper engraved. map, 2 painted figure cantouches, decor., sm. worm trace at top bkd. (R. Oct.13; 3480) DM 1,200

– **Angliae, Scotiae, et Hiberniae.** 1621 [but later]. 350 × 500mm. Engraved map, fold reprd., F. & G. (CSK. Dec.2; 5) £180

– **Arabiae Felicis, Petraeae et Desertae Delineatio.** N.d. Cold copper engraved map, 2 painted figure

cartouches, figure decor. (R. Oct.13; 3514)
DM 750

– **Buckinghamiae Comitatus cum Bedfordiensi; vulgo Buckinghamshire & Bedfordshire.** Ca. 1650. Approx. 16 × 20 inches. Map, hand-cold. in outl., ornamental title cartouche with figures, cherubs & animals, etc., separate scale of distance, armorials, Fr. text on verso. (TA. Jul.19; 146) £90

[-] **Candia cum Insulis Aliquot Circa Graeciam.** [1636 or later]. 13½ × 19½ inches. Engraved map, Fr. text on verso, margins slightly stained. (CSK. May 4; 214) £85

– **Candia olim Creta.** [Amst.], 1645 or later. 380 × 525mm. Double-p. engraved map, German text on verso. (S. Jun.25; 198) *O'Neill.* £70

– – **Anr. Edn.** Ca. 1650. Approx. 15 × 20 inches. Uncold. map, ornamental title cartouche with figures, separate scale of distance, sailing ships, etc., Spanish text on verso, slightly browned. (TA. Jul.19; 141) £110

– **Cerectica, sive Cardianensis Comitatus. Cardigan Shire.** [1646] or later. Approx. 15 × 20 inches. Map, hand-cold., ornamental title cartouche with huntsmen & animals, separate scale of distance, Royal crest, twin compass rose, rhumb lines, sailing ships. etc., mntd. (TA. Jun.21; 127) £80

– **Chili.** Amst., [Jansson, 1647]. 370 × 480mm. Double-p. engraved map, hand-cold. in outl., mountain regions washed in light brown, sailing ships, sea monsters, faced on verso, full margins, Latin text on verso. (SG. Jun.7; 55) $120

– **China mit Japan.** N.d. Ob. fo. Cold. copper engraved map, 2 painted figure cartouches & ship decor., bkd. to plt. at bottom. (R. Apr.5; 3376)
DM 400

– **Comitatus Dorcestria. Vulgo Anglice Dorset Shire.** Amst., 1646 or later. Approx. 15 × 19½ inches. Hand-cold. map, ornamental title cartouche with animals & fruit, incorporating cherubs & armorials, separate scale of distance, 2 compass rose, sailing ships, etc., F. & G. (TA. Jul.19; 135)
£125

[-] **Comitatus Somersettensis. Somerset-Shire.** 1636-44 or later. Approx. 15 × 20 inches. Uncold. map, ornamental title cartouche, separate scale of distance, compass rose, sailing ships, etc., Dutch text on verso. (TA. Jul.19; 134) £140

[-] **Cornubia. Sive Cornwassia.** Amst., Schenk & Valk, ca. 1680 or later. Approx. 15 × 20 inches. Hand-cold. map, uncold. ornamental title cartouche with figures & animals, separate scale of distance with cherubs, several armorials, twin compass rose, rhumb lines, sailing ships, etc., some slight discoloration to centrefold, mntd. (TA. Jul.19; 137) £160

– **Devoniae Descriptio.** 1646 or later. 15 × 19½ inches. Engraved map, hand-cold. in outl., F. & G. (CSK. Mar.9; 51) £75

[-] **Ducatus Eboracensis. Anglice Yorkshire.** [1646. *1st. Edn.]*. Approx. 15 × 20 inches. Uncold. map, ornamental title cartouche with figures, separate scale of distance with figures & animals, sailing ships, etc., Latin text on verso, slightly browned. (TA. Jan.19; 98) £95

[-] **Ducatus Eboracensis pars Borealis. The North Riding of Yorkshire.** [1646. *1st. Edn.]*. Approx. 15 × 20 inches. Uncold. map, ornamental title cartouche with figures & animals, separate scale of distance, armorials with cherubs, Latin text on verso. (TA. Jan.19; 97) £80

[-] **Ducatus Eboracensis pars Occidentalis; The Westriding of Yorke Shire.** [1646]. Approx. 16½ × 20 inches. Uncold. map, ornamental title cartouche with figures & animals, separate scale of distance, Royal crest, several armorials, Latin text on verso, some minor margin dampstains. (TA. Jul.19; 136)
£100

– **Freti Magellanici ac novi Freti Vulgo Le Maire Exactissima Delineatio.** [Amst., Janssonius, 1647]. 385 × 490mm. Double-p. engraved map, hand-cold. in outl., mountains washed in brown, title & scale cartouches & key, lge. compass rose, etc., Latin text on verso. (SG. Dec.15; 37) $150

[-] **Glocestria Ducatus, cum Monumethensi Comitatu. Gloucester Shire & Monmouth Shire.** Amst., G. Valk & P. Schenk, ca. 1680. Approx. 16 × 20 inches. Hand-cold. map, ornamental title cartouche & separate scale of distance, both surrounded by figures & cherubs, etc., several armorials. (TA. Jul.19; 144) £130

JANSSON, Jan or Johannes -*Contd.*

[-] **Goa Indiae Orientalis Metropolis.** [Amst., 1657]. 330 × 460mm. Double-p. engraved map, completely uncold., key to various sites & 2 coats-of-arms, full margins, Latin text on verso, minor separations at fold. (SC. Jun.7; 80) $175

[-] **Graecia Sophiani.** Ca. 1650. Approx. 14½ × 20 inches. Uncold. map, sm. ornamental title cartouche & separate scale of distance, Fr. text on verso, slightly browned, mainly along centrefold. (TA. Jul.19; 143)   £55

[-] **Holy Iland, Garnsey, Farne Iland, & Jarsey.** [Amst.], Petrus Schenk & Gerardus Valk, ca. 1680. Approx. 16 × 19½ inches. Set of 4 maps on single sheet, each cold. with uncold. ornamental title cartouche & separate scale of distance, slightly affected by worm at head of centrefold. (TA. Mar.15; 92)   £90

– – **Anr. Copy.** Approx. 15 × 20 inches. 4-col. maps on 1 sheet, each with separate ornamental title & scale of distance, compass rose, sailing ships, etc., slightly affected by worm at head of centrefold. (TA. Jul.19; 140)   £65

– – **Anr. Edn.** Ill.:- Schenk & Valk. Amst., ca. 1710. Approx. 16 × 20 inches. 4 maps on 1 sheet, each with decor. title cartouche & separate scale of distance, compass rose, etc., slightly wormed at head of centrefold. (TA. Sep.15; 177)   £70

– **Indiae Orientalis Nova Descriptio.** Amst., 1638 or later. 390 × 510mm. Double-p. engraved map, hand-cold. in outl., Latin text on verso, faint unif. browning. (S. Dec.1; 257)   *Burden.* £230

– – **Anr. Edn.** N.d. Ob. fo. Cold. copper engraved map, 3 painted figure cartouches, browned. (R. Oct.13; 3533)   DM 450

– **Insulae Americanae in Oceano Septentrionali.** Amst., [1640 or later]. 380 × 520mm. Double-p. engraved map of Caribbean, outl. hand-cold., Latin text on verso, faint browning. (S. Nov.1; 220)   *Burgess.* £140

– – **Anr. Edn.** Amst., Janssonius, mid-17th. C. 380 × 520mm. Double-p. engraved map, hand-cold. in outl., title cartouche, etc., Dutch text on verso, very minor rubbing & browning. (SG. Dec.15; 34) $700

– – **Anr. Edn.** N.d. Ob. fo. Cold. copper engraved map, 2 painted figure cartouches. (R. Oct.13; 3438)   DM 520

– **Insulae Balearides et Pytivsae.** Ca. 1630 or later. 15 × 19½ inches. Map, hand-cold. in outl., scroll title cartouche & separate ornamental scale of distance cartouche, armorials, compass rose, rhumb lines, sailing ships, etc., a little browned overall, Dutch text to verso. (TA. Jun.21; 123)   £75

– **Lancastria Palatinus. Anglis Lancaster & Lanca-shire.** Amst., ca. 1650. Approx. 15 × 19½ inches. Uncold. map, decor. title cartouche surrounded by cherubs & horses, scale of distance cartouche, compass rose, sailing ship, etc., Dutch text on verso. (TA. Nov.17; 108)   £140

– **Leicestrensis Comitatus cum Rutlandiae. Vulgo Leicester & Rutland Shire.** Amst., [1646. *1st. Edn.].* Approx. 17 × 22 inches. Uncold. map, ornamental title cartouche & separate scale of distance, both with figures, Royal crest, armorials with cherubs, Latin text on verso, a little browned overall. (TA. Jan.19; 99)   £85

– – **Anr. Edn.** Amst., G. Valk & P. Schenk. [1646, but ca. 1700]. 434 × 540mm. Double-p. engraved map, with county towns in miniature plan form, & with graticule superimposed, hand-cold. in wash & outl., embellishments uncold., sm. flaw at upr. centrefold, light crease, F. & G. (S. Mar.6; 176)   *Clarke.* £75

– **Magellan-Strasse.** N.d. Ob. fo. Cold. copper engraved map, painted arms cartouche, 3 figure cartouches, decor. (R. Oct.13; 3462)   DM 480

– **Magnae Britanniae et Hiberniae Nova Descriptio.** Ca. 1659. 16½ × 21 inches. Engraved map, hand-cold. in outl., F. & G. (CSK. Mar.9; 50)   £75

[-] **Mar del Nort.** [Amst., Janssonius, 1650]. 435 × 560mm. Double-p. engraved map, hand-cold. in outl., scale & title cartouches surrounded by figures, etc., Latin text on verso, some darkening & offsetting. (SG. Dec.15; 38) $650

– **Middelsexiae cum Hertfordiae.** [1646 or later]. 17 × 21½ inches. Engraved map, hand-cold. outl., fold lightly browned. (CSK. Jul.6; 218)   £120

– **Nobilis Fluvius Albis. – Albis Fluvius.** Amst., 1630 or later; 1641 or later. Various sizes. 2 double-p. engraved mapsheets, Fr. text on versos, centrefold of 2nd. strengthened. (S. Dec.13; 61)   *Sennewald.* £120

– **Nortfolcia; vernacule Norfolke.** [Amst., Janssonius, 1646]. 385 × 495mm. Double-p. engraved map, hand-cold. in outl., cold. notations, title & scale cartouches, coats-of-arms, etc., Latin text on verso, lightly browned. (SG. Dec.15; 77) $120

– **Nova Belgica et Anglia Nova.** N.d. Ob. fo. Cold. copper engraved map, 2 painted figures & heraldic cartouche. (R. Oct.13; 3474)   DM 800

– **Nova et Accurata Poli Artici ... Descriptio.** N.d. Ob. fo. Cold. copper engraved map, 2 painted figure cartouches, lightly browned. (R. Oct.13; 3341)   DM 800

– **Nova Germaniae Descriptio.** Cold. copper-engraved map, decor.. offsetting. (V. Sep.29; 323)   DM 1,800

– **Nova Helvetiae Tabula.** Amst., ca. 1630 or later. Approx. 14 × 19 inches. Map, hand-cold. in outl., ornamental title cartouche, separate scale of distance, a little browned overall, German text to verso. (TA. Jun.21; 124)   £100

– **Nova Illustrissimi Ducatus Pomeraniae Tabula.** Ca. 1630 or later. Approx. 15 × 20 inches. Map, hand cold., ornamental title cartouche with figures, cherubs, fruit & crops, etc., separate scale of distance with 2 figures, armorial, compass rose, rhumb lines, sailing ships, etc., a little browned overall, Latin text to verso. (TA. Jun.21; 125)   £80

– **Nova totius Terrarum Geographica ac Hydrographica Tabula.** Ca. 1650. Ob. fo. Old cold. copper engraved map, 4 captions, allegories of 4 elements & 4 seasons at side, at top moon & planets, below 7 wonders of the world, browned, bkd. with japan paper. (R. Oct.13; 3316)   DM 2,300

[-] **Orbis Terrarum Veteribus Cogniti Typus Geographicus.** [Amst.], ca. 1650. 400 × 510mm. Double-p. engraved map, hand-cold. in outl., cold. title cartouche across upr. plt., blank cartouche in lr. plt., figures, Latin text on verso, rather browned. (SG. Dec.15; 110) $225

[-] **Oxonium Comitatus vulgo Oxford Shire.** [Amst.], Gerardus Valk & Petrus Schenk, ca. 1680. Approx. 15 × 19 inches. Map, partially cold., uncold. ornamental title cartouche surrounded by figures & incorporating scale of distance, uncold. armorials. (TA. Mar.15; 89)   £160

– **Paraguay o. Prov. de Rio de la Plata ...** N.d. Ob. fo. Cold. copper engraved map, 2 painted figure cartouches. (R. Oct.13; 3489)   DM 400

– **Pascaart vande Noort-Zee [title repeated in Latin].** Amst., 1650 or later. 435 × 553mm. Double-p. engraved chart, orientated west to the top of sheet, hand-cold. in outl., Fr. text on verso, sm. repair at centrefold. (S. Dec.13; 186)   *Schuster.* £110

– **Peru.** Amst., [Jansson, 1647]. 375 × 485mm. Double-p. engraved map, hand-cold. in outl., mountain regions washed in light brown, sailing ships & sea monsters, Latin text on verso, faced on verso, minor rubbing & creasing. (SG. Jun.7; 58) $110

– **Poli Artici ... Descriptio Novissima.** N.d. Ob. fo. Cold. copper engraved map, mntd. on Japan paper, decor. ills. in corners, browned, tears bkd., worming. (R. Oct.13; 3342)   DM 950

– **Polus Antarcticus.** [Amst.], 1641 [1645 or later]. 440 × 495mm. Double-p. engraved circular map, surrounded by vigs. of native figures, German text on verso, upr. neatline just shaved. (S. Jun.25; 30)   *Noble.* £120

– – **Anr. Edn.** N.d, Ob. fo. Round cold. copper engraved map, ills. in corners. (R. Apr.5; 3146)   DM 1,050

– – **Anr. Copy.** Ob. fo. Cold. copper engraved round map, ills., painted rollwork cartouche. (R. Oct.13; 3350)   DM 600

[-] **Principatus Walliae pars Borealis vulgo North Wales.** Amst., Schenk & Valk, ca. 1680 or later. Approx. 15½ × 20 inches. Hand-cold. map, uncold. ornamental title cartouche, separate scale of distance, armorials, compass rose, rhumb lines, sailing ships, etc., mntd. (TA. Jul.19; 139)   £63

– **Provincia Connachtiae.** Amst., ca. 1645. 15½ × 19½ inches. Hand-cold. map, F. (GM. Dec.7; 518)   £85

– – **Anr. Edn.** Amst., ca. 1660. Approx. 17 × 21

inches. Uncold. map, from the German edn. (GM. Dec.7; 500)   £50

– **Provincia Momoniae, The Province of Mounster.** Ca. 1650. Hand-cold. map, F. & G. (P. Sep.29; 463)   £65

– **Provincia Oxoniensis.** [1644]. 15 × 19½ inches. Hand-cold. engraved map, verso blank, window mount, published by Jansson in 1644 for appendix of Dutch edn. of Atlas Novus & plts. reworked for vol. IV of Atlas Novus in 1646. (CSK. May 4; 6)   £280

– **Regni Norvegiae Descriptio.** N.d. Ob. fo. Cold. copper engraved map, painted figure cartouche. (R. Oct.14; 4029)   DM 500

– **Rhenus Fluviorum Europae Celeberrimus.** N.d. Cold. copper engraved map; lge. painted figure cartouche 10 cold. arms, ptd. from 2 plts., not joined, lightly browned. (R. Oct.15; 5754)   DM 1,850

[-] **Salopiensis Comitatus cum Staffordiensi. Shropshire & Staffordshire.** Ca. 1650 or later. Approx. 15½ × 21 inches. Map, hand-cold. in outl., ornamental title cartouche with figures, separate scale of distance, armorials, cherubs, etc., Fr. text on verso, slightly browned overall. (TA. Jul.19; 145)   £60

– **Schweitzerland.** N.d. Ob. fo. Cold. copper engraved map, 4 painted figure cartouches, slightly browned, 2 corners extended. (R. Oct.13; 3963)   DM 400

[-] **Somersettensis Comitatus: Somerset Shire.** [Amst.], ca. 1680. Approx. 15 × 19½ inches. Uncold. map, ornamental title cartouche with figure & animals, separate scale of distance surmounted by cherubs, several armorials with cherubs, compass rose, 2 sailing ships, etc., lr. portion of centrefold strengthened. (TA. Mar.15; 90)   £54

– **Surrey.** L., ca. 1650. 510 × 400mm. Hand-cold. map, F. (P. Nov.24; 325)   *Green.* £150

[-] **Surria. Vernacule Surrey.** Ca. 1650. Approx. 15 × 20 inches. Uncold. map, ornamental title cartouche incorporating figures & animals, separate scale of distance with cherubs, Royal crest, armorials, etc., Latin text on verso, a little browned overall. (TA. Jan.19; 100)   £130

– – **Anr. Edn.** Amst., Schenk & Valk, ca. 1680 or later. Approx. 15 × 19½ inches. Hand-cold. map, uncold. ornamental title cartouche, separate scale of distance, Royal crest, several armorials with cherubs, etc., some slight discoloration to centrefold, mntd. (TA. Jul.19; 138)   £170

– **Suthsexia vernacule Sussex.** Ca. 1650. 510 × 385mm. Hand-cold. map, arms, cartouche. (P. Apr.12; 344)   £170

[-] **Tabula Islandiae.** [Amst.], 1636 or later. 383 × 495mm. Double-p. engraved map, hand-cold. in outl., lge. title cartouche fully cold., Latin text on verso, slight overall browning. (S. Dec.13; 32)   *Solnes.* £100

– **Tabula Magellanica, Qua Tierrae Del Fuego.** Amst., Janssonius, mid-17th. C. 410 × 530mm. Double-p. engraved map, hand-cold. in outl., title & scale cartouches, elab. armorial dedication cartouche, compass roses, etc., Latin text on verso. (SG. Dec.15; 35) $450

– – **Anr. Edn.** N.d. Ob. fo. Cold. copper engraved map, painted arms cartouche, 3 painted figure cartouches, fault bkd. (R. Apr.5; 3170)   DM 450

– **Terra Firma et Novum Regnum Granatense et. Popayan.** Amst., 1660's?. 380 × 495mm. Double-p. engraved map, hand-cold. in outl., cold. notations, title & scale cartouches, 2 lge. compass roses, lr. margin stained, Latin text on verso. (SG. Dec.15; 36) $100

– **Territorivm Francofvrtense.** Amst., ca. 1660. Old cold. map with 2 cartouches & arms, lr. margin slightly soiled, not north orientated. (HK. Nov.12; 5568)   DM 400

– **Territorium Norimbergense.** N.d. Ob. fo. 85 × 115mm. Cold. copper engraved map, 2 painted figure cartouches & cold. town plan, margins slightly spotted. (R. Oct.14; 4602)   DM 400

[-] **Virginiae Partis Australis, et Floridae Partis Orientalis ...** [Amst.,], 1699 or later. 388 × 506mm. Double-p. engraved map, outl. hand-cold., embellishments fully hand-cold., Latin text on verso, light crease. (S. Nov.1; 233)   *Burgess.* £170

[-] Wigorniensis Comitatus et Comitatus Warwicensis; nec non Coventrae Libertas. Worcester, Warwik Shire & the Liberty of Coventre. [1638]. 16 × 19½ inches. Map, hand-cold. in outl., ornamental title cartouche, Royal crest, several armorials, etc., Latin text on verso. (TA. May 17; 178) £95
See— HONDIUS, Henricus & Jansson, Jan or Johannes
See— KEERE, P. van den

JANVIER, Jean
- L'Amérique. Venice, 1762 [but 1784 or later]. 468 × 646mm. Double-p. engraved map, outl. hand-cold. (S. Nov.1; 210)　　*Mason.* £140

JANVIERE, Antide
- Mappe-Monde ou Description du Globe Terrestre ... Paris, 1762. Approx. 12 × 18 inches. Double hemisphere map, hand-cold. in outl., ornamental title cartouche, some foxing. (TA. Jul.19; 117)　£110

JEFFERSON, Peter
See— FRY, Joshua & Jefferson, Peter

JEFFERYS, Thomas
- The Coast of Caracas, Cumana, Paris & the Mouths of Rio Orinoco, with the Islands of Trinidad, Margerita, Tobago ... Robert Sayer, 1775. Approx. 19½ × 26 inches. Uncold. chart, slightly soiled, mainly along centrefold. (TA. Jul.19; 120)　£55
- The County of Bedford Surveyed Anno MDCCLXV [by J. Ainslie & T. Donald]. [1765]. *1st. Edn.* Total dimensions 184 × 115cm. Engraved map, in 8 joined sheets, hand-cold. in wash & outl., faint margin dust-soiling, mntd. on linen & rollers. (S. Jun.25; 351)　£120
- An Exact Chart of the River St. Laurence from Fort Frontenac to the Island of Anticosti. 1757 [but 1775 or later]. 591 × 945mm. Engraved map, in 2 sheets joined & folding, outl. hand-cold., 5 insets, faint offsetting. (S. Nov.1; 238)　*Burgess.* £170
- - *Anr. Edn.* 1775. Approx. 24 × 37 inches. Map, cold. in outl., uncold. ornamental title cartouche, 3 compass rose, rumb lines, etc., several minor margin defects. (TA. Mar.15; 99)　£75
See— FRY, Joshua & Jefferson, Peter

JEPPE, F.
- Map of Transvaal, or S.A. Republic & Surrounding Territories. Pretoria, 1889. 1,300 × 1,200mm. Cold. folding map, insets of Pretoria, Zoutpansberg Goldfields, Kaap Goldfields & Witwatersrand Goldfields, in orig. cl. folder. (VA. Jan.27; 207)　　　R. 310

JODE, Gerard de
- Salzburgensis Episcopatus. [Antw., 1593]. 353 × 248mm. Hand-cold. map, engraved by J. & L. van Deutecom after M. Secznagael, Latin text on verso, margin repairs just touching plt. mark. (S. Jun.25; 250)　　*Gaeta.* £220

JOHNSTON, Alex Keith
- A New Map of the North & South Part of Scotland. [Camden, 1722]. 2 hand-cold. maps, both F. & G. (P. Feb.16; 323)　£50

JORDEN, M.
See— ANTHONISZ, C. - JORDEN, M. KEERE or KAERIUS, Petrus
See— VAN DEN KEERE, Petrus, KEERE or KAERIUS, Picter or Petrus van den

KEULEN, Gerard van
- Haaven Kaart, van Eenige Voornaamste Haavens Leggende in de Middel-Landsche Zee en Archipelago. [1682 or later]. 20 × 23 inches. Engraved chart, 1 margin reprd. (CSK. May 4; 206)　£95
- Nieuwe Groote en seer Curieuse Paskaart van Geheel-Westindien. Amst., 1728 or later. 590 × 990mm. Engraved folding sea-chart, after Jan Sikkena, lge. vig. ill., slight wear (tear reprd.) at additional folds without serious loss of engraved surface. (S. Nov.1; 225)　　*Burgess.* £250
- Nieuwe Platte Paskaart van de Straat Davids. Ca. 1720. 580 × 980mm. Copper engraved map, outl. & surface cold., old cold. cartouche, old cold. supp. map, 1 defect. reprd. (BR. Apr.13; 2883)
　　　　　　　　　　　　　　　　DM 1,100
- Niewe ... Zeekaart ... Noorder Deel van Europa.

Ca. 1715. 590 × 985mm. Old cold. copper engraved map from 2 plts. (BR. Apr.13; 2885)　DM 550
- Nieuwe Paskaert van d'Oost Kust van Engelandt van Dover tot Dunwich ... Amst., ca. 1680 or later. Approx. 19½ × 23 inches. Hand-cold. chart, ornamental title cartouche with figures, incorporating scale of distance, inset detail of River Thames, twin compass rose, many rhumb lines, etc., relaid. (TA. Jul.19; 118)　£75
- Nieuwe Paskaart van Ierland en de West kust wan Engeland, Vervattende in sig. St. Joris en het Verkeerde Kanaal. Amst., [early 18th. C.]. 590 × 960mm. Double-sheet folding engraved sea chart, uncold., extensive network of rhumb lines radiating from 17 compass points, good margins, verso blank, some rubbing & soiling, particularly on verso. (SG. Jun.7; 113)　£110
- Nova Tabula Terrarum Cucan, Canara, Malabaria, Madura, & Coromandella, cum parte Septentrionali Insulae Ceylon. Amst., ca. 1725. 50 × 60cm. Double-p. engraved map, hand-cold., 5 compass roses, extensive network of rhumb lines, soundings, sailing ships, full margins, verso blank, minor stains in 1 margin. (SG. Jun.7; 83)　£100
- Pascaarte vande Norder Zeecusten van America, vande West-hoeck van Island doorde Straet Davis en Hudson, tot aen Terra Neuf. Ca. 1690. Cold. copper engraved map, 2 painted figure cartouches, minimal spotting, some sm. worm-holes & repairs to upr. margin mntd. on japan paper, sm. fault above map. (R. Oct.13; 3366)　DM 900
- Pascaert van't Eylandt Ceylon, Voordesen Taprobana, by de Inwoonders genaemt Lankaun. [Amst.], 1680 [but 1700 or later]. 510 × 595mm. Double-p. engraved sea-chart, orientated West to top of sheet. (S. Nov.1; 246)　　*Franks.* £120
- Paskaart van de Archipelagusche Eylanden. [1665]. 37½ × 23 inches. Engraved chart on 2 sheets, margins trimmed & slightly reprd. (CSK. Jul.6; 171)　£160
- Pas-kaart van de Chineesche Kust, Langs de Provincien Quantung en Fokien, als ook het Eyland Formosa. Amst., ca. 1753. 510 × 575mm. Double-p. engraved map, hand-cold. in outl., inset map of coast north of Foochow, extensive network of rhumb lines radiating from 13 compass points, soundings, uneven margins, verso blank, minor dampstaining in lr. corners; from pt. VI of the Zee-Fakel. (SG. Jun.7; 84)　£175
- Pas-Kaart vande Zee Kusten van Niew Nederland ... N.d. 510 × 580mm. 2 cold. copper engraved maps from 1 plt., painted caption cartouche, lightly browned or foxed, a few sm. wormholes, mntd. on japan paper. (R. Oct.13; 3370)　DM 1,800

KEULEN, Joannes van
See— VOOGT, C.J.

KIP, William
- Cornwall olim pars Danmoniorum. Ca. 1610 or later. Approx. 12 × 15 inches. Uncold. map, sm. strapwork title cartouche, inset detail of Launceston, Royal crest, sailing ship, etc., printing defect at head of centrefold, a little browned at edges. (TA. Mar.15; 145)　£70
See— NORDEN, John & Kip, William
See— SAXTON, Christopher & Kip, William

KITCHEN or KITCHIN, Thomas
- A New Improved Map of Hertfordshire. Ca. 1780. 665 × 540mm. Hand-cold. map, cartouche, F. & G. (P. Sep.29; 454)　　*Burgess.* £70
- A New Map of Ireland, Divided into Provinces, Counties, etc. L., 1777. 26½ × 23 inches. Map, hand-cold. in outl. (GM. Dec.7; 504)　£60
- Oxfordshire. [1764]. 28 × 21 inches. Engraved map. (CSK. May 4; 157)　£75

KITCHEN or KITCHIN, Thomas
See— BOWEN, Emmanuel & Kitchin, Thomas

KITCHENER, H.H.
See— CONDER, Lieut. C.R. & Kitchener, Lieut. (later Lord) H.H.

KITCHIN, Thomas
See— KITCHEN or KITCHIN, Thomas

KNOFF, T.H.H.
- Insulae Islandiae Delineatio. Nuremb., 1761 [or later]. 451 × 588mm. Double-p. engraved map,

hand-cold. in wash & outl. (S. Nov.1; 249)
　　　　　　　　　　　　　　　　Tonge. £130

KONIG, E.G.
- Celeberrima ac Spatiosissima Thuringiae Metropolis Erfurtum [title repeated in German]. Augsburg, M. Seutter, 1740 [or later]. 498 × 581mm. Double-p. engraved plan, hand-cold. in wash & outl., panoramic view below, right-hand margin shaved touching outer neatline. (S. Dec.13; 72)
　　　　　　　　　　　　　　　　Burgess. £65

KOOPS, M.
- Map of the River Rhine. From Mentz to Dusseldorff. 1796/97. Lge. ob. fo. Partly cold. copper engraved map, figure cartouche with aquatint, ptd. tables round, outer margin with sm. ties at head & left side. (R. Oct.15; 5764)　DM 550

LAMB, F.
[-] A Map of New England & New York. [1676]. *Bassett & Chiswell,.* 380 × 500mm. Double-p. engraved map (after Jansson 1651) extending from Maine coast to Maryland, published in final edn. of Speede's Prospect, hand-cold. in outl., sm. rusthole in engraved area infilled, Engl. text on verso, F. & double-G., w.a.f. (S. May 22; 366)
　　　　　　　　　　　　　　　　Burden. £420

LANGEVIN
- Nouvelle Carte Illustrée de l'Allemagne. Ill.:— after A. Vuillemin. Paris, Fatout,. 1860. 505 × 845mm. Outl. cold. copper engraved map, statistics at side, 11 sm. ills. (R. Oct.14; 4190)　DM 400

LA RUE, Philippe de
- Terra Promissa in Sortes Seu Tribus XII Distincta Seu Tabula ad Librum Iosue. [Amst.], ca. 1705. 410 × 535mm. Double-p. engraved map, hand-cold. in light outl., uncold. title cartouche & notations, trimmed margins, browned & foxed, tape stains on margin versos. (SG. Dec.15; 94)　$100

LAURENBERG, J.
- Mecklenburg. W. Blaeu, n.d. Ob. fo. Old cold. copper engraved map, 3 painted cartouches & cold. arms. (R. Apr.6; 4755)　DM 400

LAURIE, Robert & Whittle, James
- Africa. 1794. 1,205 × 1,050mm. Map, in 2 joined sections, cold. in outl., cantouche. (P. Oct.20; 281)　£60
- Course of the River Mississippi from the Balaise to Fort Chartres ... L., Laurie & Whittle, 1794. 43 × 14 inches. Engraved map, in 2 sheets, partly hand-cold., extensive margins, slight browning. (SPB. May 23; 11)　$600
- A New Map of the Whole Continent of America. 1794. Partly cold. map, in 2 sheets. (P. Jul.5; 393)　£120
See— BRASSIER, William
See— DUNN, Samuel, Mathematician
See— FRY, Joshua & Jefferson, Peter
See— MAXWELL, G.
See— MOUZON, Henry & others

LAUTERBACH, J. Chr.
- Nova et Accurata Territorii Vlmensis cum Domino Wainensi descr. Nuremb., Homann, ca. 1720. Old cold. map, sm. supp. map, lge. uncold. cartouche, some slight foxing, in left lr. margin light crease. (HK. Nov.12; 5522)　DM 520

LE COQ, Maj. K.L. von
[-] [Topographische Karte]. [Berlin, 1815]. Various sizes. 8 (of 22) engraved mapsheets, hand-cold. in outl., some surface dirt, 1 or 2 margins slightly frayed, linen-bkd. (S. Dec.13; 59)　*Schwedt.* £160

LE ROUGE, G.L.
- Carte des Pais Bas. Paris, 1742 [or later]. Each sheet 500 × 625mm. Lge. wall-map, in 6 double-p. engraved sheets, hand-cold. in outl., histor. title cartouche on sheet 1. (S. Jun.25; 190)
　　　　　　　　　　　　　　　　Lemmers. £160

LEWIS, Samuel
- The State of Maryland, from the best Authorities. 1795. 10¾ × 16 inches. Orig. black-&-white engraved map, removed from 1795 edn. of Mathew Carey's 'American Atlas', bearing reference to Guthrie's Geography in top margin, borders, decent

LEWIS, Samuel -*Contd.*

margins, inset at left side of Western portion of state, credit & title in plt. & at top margin, some old folds, light foxing. (HA. May 4; 20) $360

LHUYD, Humphrey
- **Angliae Regni Florentissimi Nova Descriptio.** [Antw.,], 1573 [but 1581 or later]. 378 × 469mm. Double-p. hand-cold. engraved map, as publd. in Ortelius' 'Theatrum', Fr. text on verso, sm. repair at centre-fold. (S. Nov.1; 146) *Kidd.* £170
- **-- Anr. Edn.** [Antw.], 1573 [but 1587 or later]. 380 × 469mm. Double-p. engraved map, Fr. text on verso, sm. stain. (S. Mar.6; 166) *Kidd.* £130
- **-- Anr. Edn.** [Antw.], 1573 [but 1592 or later]. 380 × 471mm. Double-p. engraved map, Latin text on verso, faint margin browning. (S. Dec.13; 188) *Burgess.* £110
- **Cambriae Typus.** [Antw.], 1573 [but 1581 or later]. 370 × 495mm. Double-p. hand-cold. engraved map, as publd. in Ortelius' 'Theatrum', Fr. text on verso, slight margin soiling. (S. Nov.1; 166) *Kidd.* £180
- **-- Anr. Edn.** Antw., [1573, but 1587 or later]. 370 × 494mm. Engraved map, many names in Latin, Welsh & Engl., Fr. text on verso. (S. Mar.6; 180) *Evans.* £210
- **-- Anr. Edn.** [Amst., J. Hondius, 1607, or later]. 350 × 493mm. Double-p. engraved map, hand-cold. in outl., Fr. text on verso. (S. Apr.9; 158) *Windsor.* £90
- **-- Anr. Edn.** Ca. 1612. 500 × 380mm. Hand-cold. map, sailing ship vig., F. & G. (P. Mar.15; 411) *Thorp.* £150
- **-- Anr. Edn.** [Amst.], 1654 or later. *Jansson Edn.* 348 × 512mm. Double-p. engraved map, hand-cold. in outl., F. & G. (S. Jun.25; 420) *Jones.* £150

LINSCHOTEN, Jan Huygen van
- **Insulae et Arcis Mocambique** ... Ca. 1595. 250 × 320mm. Line engraved map. (VA. Apr.27; 613) R 300

LOTTER, Matthew Albrecht
- **A Map of the Provinces of New-York & New-Jersey.** 1777. Each sheet 390 × 570mm. Engraved hand-cold. map on 2 sheets, margins lightly soiled. (CSK. Nov.4; 18) £200

LOTTER, Tobias Conrad
- **Recens edita novi Belgii in America Septentrionali.** Ca. 1690. 585 × 505mm. Hand-cold. map, cartouche, F. (P. Nov.24; 344) *Burgess.* £380
- **Terra Sancta sive Palaestine.** Augsburg, 1759 [or later]. 480 × 572mm. Double-p. map, engraved by M.A. Lotter after Sanson, map area cold. in wash & outl., lge. figured title-cartouche. (S. Mar.6; 139) *Westenna.* £90
- **Territorium Francofurti.** N.d. Ob. fo. Copper engraved map, old part col., lge figure & heraldic cartouche. (R. Oct.14; 4978) DM 480

LOWITZ, G.M.
- **Planiglobii Terrestris Mappa Universalis.** Nuremberg, 1746 [or later]. 450 × 525mm. Double-p. engraved map, in twin hemispheres, after Haas & Löwitz, 4 sm. hemispherical map insets, hand-cold. in wash & outl., sm. repair at centre-fold, faint browning. (S. Nov.1; 191) *Ash.* £80

LUCINI, A.F.
- **Carta Particolare dell'Isole d'Asores con l'Isola di Madera.** Ca. 1650. 460 × 740mm. Copper engraved map ptd. from 2 plts., from R. Dudley 'Arcano del Mare', decor. cartouche, lge. wind rose, cut at right to plt., light browning. (R. Oct.13; 3360) DM 650

LUFFMAN, J.
- **Somersetshire.** [1803]. Approx. 6¼ × 4 inches. Uncold. circular map with descriptive text below. (TA. Jun.21; 150) £50
- **Yorkshire [East & West Ridings].** [1803]. Approx. 6¼ × 4 inches. Uncold. circular map with descriptive text below. (TA. Jun.21; 152) £70

MAGNAE BRITANNIAE ET HIBERNIAE Nova Descriptio
17th. C. Approx. 12½ × 15 inches. Map, hand-cold. in outl., sm. decor. title cartouche, Royal crest,

inset detail of Orcades Insulae, compass rose, etc. (TA. Sep.15; 174) £80

MAIER, T.
- **Carte des Indes Orientales.** Nuremb., Homann's Heirs, 1748 [or later]. 505 × 860mm. Double-p. engraved map, hand-cold. in outl. (S. Jun.25; 56) *Remmington.* £100
- **Helvetia Tredecim Statibus Liberis quos Cantones Vocant.** Nuremb., Homann's Heirs, 1751 [or later]. 430 × 552mm. Double-p. engraved map, hand-cold. in wash & outl., slight overall browning. (S. Dec.13; 82) *Burgess.* £60

MAJER, M.J.
- **Ducatus Wurtenbergici.** Nuremb., ca. 1720. Lge. fo. Cold. 2-part map, 76 sm. arms in side margins, cartouches, 1 slightly weak. (HK. Nov.12; 5517) DM 1,500

MARTINI, Aegidius
- **Limburgensis Ducatus Nova Descriptio.** Hondius, 1603. Cold. copper-engraved map. (V. Sep.29; 332) DM 610

MARYLAND
Ca. 1790s. 6¾ × 5½ inches. Map, hand-cold. in outl., inset view of Western region, counties not delineated but simply lettered (19 counties mentioned), some cities & towns pinpointed, Wash. mentioned only as a dot, ageing in places with dark portion at top border just into print from old tape, few old folds, matted. (HA. May 4; 16) $100

MATHES, D.R.M.
- **Orbis Terrarum Typus de Integro Multis in Locis Emendatus.** Dutch, 17th. C. 290 × 510mm. Double-p. hemispheric world map, from unidentified Bible, Dutch text on verso, minor stains, edges bit chipped, some separation at earlier folds. (SG. Dec.15; 111) $950

MAXWELL, G.
- **A New Survey of the River Congo on the Coast of Africa.** R. Laurie & J. Whittle, 1795. 1,440 × 540mm. Hand-cold. engraved chart, on 2 joined sheets, slight surface dirt, laid on paper. (S. Jun.25; 80) *Kossow.* £70

MERCATOR, Gerard
- **Abissinorum Sive Pretiosi Ioannis Imperiu.** [Amst., Hondius, 1630]. 345 × 495mm. Double-p. engraved map, hand-cold. in outl., strapwork title & scale cartouches, inset map, Latin text verso. (SG. Dec.15; 19) $200
- **-- Anr. Edn.** [Amst., Hondius, 1641]. 345 × 495mm. Double-p. engraved map, hand-cold. in outl., inset map entitled 'Congi Regni in Africa Christiani Nova Descriptio', Fr. text on verso, light overall foxing & browning, some creasing at fold. map is variant described in Koeman II, Me 99A. (SG. Jun.7; 43) $100
- **Anglia, Scotia et Hibernia.** [Amst., 1609]. 330 × 410mm. Double-p. engraved map, fully hand-cold., full margins, Fr. text on verso, rubbed & age-darkened, creasing at centrefold, fold reinforced on verso. (SG. Jun.7; 114) $110
- **Asia ex Magna Orbis Terre.** [Amst., Hondius, 1613]. 38 × 47cm. Double-p. engraved map, hand-cold. in outl., sea blue-washed, elab. strapwork title cartouche, lge. sailing ship, Latin text on verso, some separation & discoloration at fold. (SG. Dec.15; 52) $225
- **Bavaria Ducatus.** Amst., H. Hondius, 1627, [but 1628, or later]. 364 × 472mm. Map, hand-cold. in outl., title-cartouche fully cold., Fr. text on verso. (S. Apr.9; 89) *Berg.* £80
- **Berghe Ducatus Marck Comitatus et Coloniensis Dioecesis.** N.d. Copper-engraved map. (V. Sep.29; 382) DM 550
- **Candia cum Insulis aliquot Circa Graeciam.** [1628 or later]. 13½ × 19½ inches. Engraved map, hand-cold. in outl., Latin text on verso, margins lightly soiled. (CSK. May 4; 231) £110
- **Dorset.** Ca. 1610. 15¼ × 17¼ inches. Map, engraved by Hondius, Dorchester street plan, F. & G. to obverse. (SKC. Nov.18; 2068) £80
- **Emden und Oldenburg.** N.d. Ob. fo. Old cold. copper engraved map, painted rollwork cartouche, sm. crumple, 2 sm. holes, margins slightly stained, sm. bkd. tear at foot. (R. Oct.14; 4778) DM 650

- **Hampshire.** 1610. 15¼ × 21¼ inches. Hand-cold. map, engraved by Hondius, Winchester town plan, heraldic devices, F. & G. (SKC. Nov.18; 2074) £110
- **Irlandiae Regnum.** [Amst., Hondius, 1609]. 345 × 470mm. Double-p. engraved map, fully hand-cold., strapwork title cartouche, Fr. text on verso, margins lightly rubbed & browned. (SG. Dec.15; 81) $300
- **-- Anr. Edn.** [Amst., Hondius, 1628]. 345 × 470mm. Double-p. engraved map, hand-cold. in outl., sea areas washed in light blue-green, good margins, Fr. text on verso, the whole a bit rubbed. (SG. Jun.7; 115) $130
- **-- Anr. Edn.** Ca. 1633. 19 × 23 inches. Hand-cold. map, Fr. text on verso, sm. hole in centre. (GM. Dec.7; 522) £160
- **-- Anr. Copy.** 19 × 23 inches. Hand-cold. map, Fr. text on verso. (GM. Dec.7; 524) £55
- **Latium nunc Campagna di Roma.** [Amst., Hondius, 1609]. 370 × 475mm. Double-p. engraved map, hand-cold. in outl., blue-green washed seas, elab. cold. title cartouche, cold. notations, Latin text on verso, repairs in lr. margin. (SG. Dec.15; 82) $150
- **Macedonia, Epirus et Achaia.** Ca. 1630's. 14 × 17 inches (plt.-mark). Double-p. engraved map, from the 1st. or 2nd. Engl. Edn. of Mercator's atlas, hand-cold. in outl., cartouche fully cold., wide margins, double-column Engl. text on verso of both ll., light ageing. (HA. Feb.24; 90) $110
- **[-] A New Description of the Shyres Lothian & Linlitquo Be. T.Pont.** [Amst., Janssonius, 1642]. 370 × 540mm. Double-p. engraved map, hand-cold. in outl., strapwork title cartouche, elab. armorial dedication cartouche, compass rose, etc., Fr. text on verso, light browning, upr. corners torn. (SG. Dec.15; 85) $150
- **[The Northern Half of Ireland].** Ca. 1633. 19 × 23 inches. Hand-cold. map, Fr. text on verso. (GM. Dec.7; 525) £140
- **[-] Paraguay, o Prov. de Rio de la Plata.** Amst., Joannes Janssonius, n.d. 370 × 475mm. Partly hand-cold. engraved map, cartouche, Engl. text on verso. (BBA. Aug.18; 173) *Faupel.* £50
- **Saltzburg Archiepiscopatus et Carinthia Ducatus.** Blaeuw, n.d. Cold. copper-engraved map, slightly foxed in margin. (V. Sep.29; 266) DM 410
- **Trier & Lutzenburg.** [Amst.], 1633 or later. 365 × 465mm. Double-p. engraved map, hand-cold. in outl., title cartouche fully cold., Fr. text on verso. (S. Jun.25; 234) *Shapiro.* £70
- **[-] Turcici Imperii Imago.** [Amst., 1619]. Double-p. engraved map, hand-cold. in outl., & in light wash col., inset port. of Sultan Mahumet, full margins, Fr. text on verso, some minor rubbing, separation at fold. (SG. Jun.7; 87) $110
- **Udrone Irlandiae in Catherlagh Baronia.** Ca. 1633. 19 × 23 inches. Hand-cold. map, Fr. text on verso. (GM. Dec.7; 526) £65
- **Ultonial Orientalis Pars.** Ca. 1633. 19 × 23 inches. Hand-cold. map, Fr. text on verso. (GM. Dec.7; 523) £55
- **[-] Universalis Tabula iuxta Ptolemaeum.** [Amst.], late 16th. C. 340 × 470mm. Cold. map, F. & G. (B. Oct.4; 826) Fls. 500
- **Warwicum ... Surria, Cantii, & Southsexia.** Ca. 1608. 370 × 470mm. Engraved hand-cold. map, some light soiling, 1 clean tear, F. & G. (CSK. Nov.4; 2) £50
- **-- Anr. Edn.** Ca. 1630. Approx. 14½ × 18½ inches. Map, hand-cold. in outl., ornamental title cartouche, Engl. text on verso, some damage to centrefold, F. & double-G. (TA. May 17; 168) £70
- **Das Wiflispurgergov. - [Argow].** [Amst., Hondius, 1628]. Approx. 360 × 470mm. Together 2 double-p. engraved maps, hand-cold. in outl., cold. notations for mountains, forests, & towns, full margins, Fr. text on versos. (SG. Jun.7; 116) $120

MERCATOR, Gerard & Hondius, Henricus
- **Chorographica Tabula Lacus Lemanni Locorumque Circumiacentium autore Iac. G. Genevensi.** Amst., 1623. Old cold map, cartouche with puttos, not north orientated, minimal spotting. (HK. Nov.12; 5762) DM 600
- **Helvetia cum Finitimis Regionibus Confoederatis.** Ca. 1610. Ob. fo. Cold. copper engraved map, 2 painted roll-work cartouches. (R. Oct.13; 3962) DM 400

– – Anr. Edn. Amst., 1623. Old cold. map, some old underlining of places, 1 with old MS. note, soiled, some creasing & 1 margin tear reprd. (HK. Nov.12; 5760) DM 520

– – Anr. Edn. N.d. 330 × 480mm. Copper engraved map, 2 rollwork cartouches, outl. col. (GF. Nov.17; 2778) Sw. Frs. 700

– Hibernia Regnum. – Hiberniae II-V Tabula. Amst., 1623. 5 maps, including coll. map, old cold., 2 maps slightly creased, 4 maps with sm. reprd. tears in lr. margin, some slight spotting, margins slightly soiled. (HK. Nov.12; 5671) DM 600

– Palatinatvs Rheni. Amst., 1623. Old cold. map, some places underlined, sm. tear bkd. at foot. (HK. Nov.12; 5597) DM 420

– Scotia, Regnum. [Amst., 1628]. 355 × 410mm. Double-p. engraved map, hand-cold. in outl., elab. strapwork title cartouche, Fr. text on verso, slightly darkened. (SG. Dec.15; 83) $200

– Scotiae Regnvm. Tab. I-III. Amst., 1623. 3 old cold. maps, rollwork cartouches, 1 map with bkd. tear, 1 map with some creasing. (HK. Nov.12; 5672) DM 650

– Zelandia Comitatus. Amst., 1623. Cold. map, old cold. cartouche, tear reprd., slightly browned. (HK. Nov.12; 5486) DM 420

MERCATOR, Gerard & Hondius, Jodocus
– America Meridionalis. 1606 or later. Approx. 14 × 19½ inches. Cont. hand-cold. map, lge. decor. strapwork cartouche surmounted by figures, separate scale of distance cartouche, inset plan, decor., Fr. text on verso, slightly wormed, mainly to lr. hf. of centrefold. (TA. Nov.17; 83) £125

– – Anr. Edn. Ill.:– Cuzco. N.d. Ob. fo. Old cold. copper engraved map, painted figure cartouche, crumpled, tear bkd., outer margins slightly spotted. (R. Oct.13; 3493) DM 630

– Iaponia. Amst., 1623. Cold. map, decor., 2 old cold. cartouches, some tears bkd., col. slightly soiled, some creases & slight spotting. (HK. Nov.12; 5452) DM 1,500

– Insulae Indiae Orientalis Praecipuae, in quibus Moluccae celeberrimae sunt. Amst., 1623. Cold. map, decor., old cold. cartouches, some tears bkd., some sm. scratches, some light spotting. (HK. Nov.12; 5440) DM 480

– Islandia. Amst., 1623. Old cold. map, rollwork cartouche, some sm. scratches, reprd. tear in lr. wide margin, 2 slight col. spots in margin. (HK. Nov.12; 5686) DM 500

– Septentrionalivm Terrarum Descriptio. Amst., 1623. Old cold. map, decor. borders, sm. island maps in 3 corners, sm. reprd. tears, creased. (HK. Nov.12; 5407) DM 850

– – Anr. Edn. N.d. Ob. fo. Old cold. round copper engraved map, floral borders, caption cartouches in corners & 3 sm. supp. maps, tears bkd. (R. Oct.13; 3340) DM 750

– Terra Sancta Quae in Sacris Terra Promissionis Palestine. [Amst., 1609]. 495 × 360mm. Uncold. map, vig. sailing ship, dampstains to lr. corners, F. (P. Nov.24; 341) Whiteson. £65

– – Anr. Edn. Amst., 1623. Cold. map, decor., old cold. cartouches, margin tears bkd., 1 cartouche spotted, some sm. foxing. (HK. Nov.12; 5462) DM 500

– – Anr. Edn. N.d. Ob. fo. Old cold. copper engraved map, 2 painted figure cartouches, lightly browned, margins foxed, partly bkd. (R. Oct.13; 3541) DM 500

– Virginiae item et Floridae Americae Provinciarum, nova Descriptio. Amst., 1623. Decor. map, old cold. cartouches, tear bkd., 2 sm. margin scratches, minimal loss to 1 cartouche, some light spotting. (HK. Nov.12; 5424) DM 900

– – Anr. Edn. [1634]. 345 × 440mm. Engraved map, hand-cold. in outl., Dutch text on verso, some light soiling. (CSK. Nov.4; 21) £320

MERCATOR, Michael
– America sive India Nova. [Amst., H. Hondius], ca. 1630. 368 × 463mm. Engraved double-p. map in circular form, 3 spendrel insets, the whole hand-cold. in outl., faint crease at centrefold, F. & G. (S. Dec.1; 227) Map House. £1,250

MERCATOR, Rumold & Georg
– Orbis Terrae compendiosa Descriptio. 1587. Ob. fo. Cold. copper engraved map in 2 hemispheres,

decor., cartouche at top, browned, margin tears reprd. (R. Oct.13; 3313) DM 1,500

MITCHELL, [J.]
– Amérique Septentrionale avec les Routes, Distances en Miles, Villages et Etablissements Francois et Anglois [title repeated in German]. Paris, [G.L.] le Rouge, 1756. 2nd. Fr. Iss. 1,240 × 1,940mm. (total dimensions). Wall-map in 8 double-p. engraved mapsheets, hand-cold. in outl., sm. margin stains not touching engraved surface, light crease in 1 sheet. (S. Dec.1; 231)
Voorhees. £2,900

MITCHELL, Samuel Augustus
– A New Map of Texas, Oregon & California with the Regions adjoining. Phila., 1846. Folding engraved map, partially cold. (Bound with:)
– Accompaniment to Mitchell's New Map ... Phila., 1846. 16mo. 46 pp. (Howes cites only 34), orig. blind– & gt.-stpd. cl., slightly worn. (LH. Apr.15; 343) $650

MOLL, Herman
– A New Chart of the Channell Between England & France ... L., early 18th. C. 450 × 580mm. Double-p. engraved map, rhumb lines from 4 compass points, margins trimmed, slightly discold. along fold, other earlier fold lines. (SG. Dec.15; 87) $140

– The North Part of Great Britain called Scotland. 1714. 620 × 1,020. 4-fold engraved semi-cold. map, engraved dedication to Bp. of Kilmore & Ardagh, title, cold. inset map of Orkney & Shetland Isles, 11 engraved views to side columns, slight tear of fold, gilded F. & G. (PD. Aug.17; 323) £160

– The South Part of Great Britain called England & Wales. 1710. 610 × 990mm. Hand-cold. map, cartouches, lists of market towns, F. & G. (P. Sep.8; 468) Stone. £95

MOLLERUS, Chr.
– Celeberrimi Flvvii Albis nova delin. Amst., 1628. Cold. map of 2 superimposed maps from 1 plt., old cold. cartouches & arms, slightly creased, slight traces of glue. (HK. Nov.12; 5564) DM 560

MONTANUS, P. [i.e. P. Van den Berg]
– A Mapp of the Cape of Good Hope, with its true situation. Ca. 1670. 280 × 360mm. Cold. line engraved map. (VA. Apr.27; 591) R 410

MONTRESSOR, Capt.
– Map of Nova Scotia or Acadia with the Island of Cape Breton & St. John's ... L., A. Dury, 1768. 39 × 54 inches. Engraved map, in 4 sheets, partly hand-cold. in outl., scenic dedication cartouche in upr. left-hand sheet, traces of offsetting & browning. (SPB. May 23; 26) $500

MORNINGTON PENINSULAR
– Map of Mornington Peninsula. Melbourne, Approx. 56 × 40 inches. Lge. folding map, in 36 sections, some col., on linen. (KH. May 1; 503)
Aus. $650

MORTIER, Corneille
See— COVENS, Jean & Mortier, Corneille
See— DELISLE, Guillaume

MORTIER, Pierre
– Théâtre de la Guerre en Espagne et en Portugal. Amst., ca. 1730. 950 × 1,190mm. Engraved wall-map in 4 joined sheets, hand-cold. in outl., elab. vig. at lr. right corner fully cold., sm. repair at 1 join with slight loss of engraved surface, mntd. on linen. (S. Dec.1; 246) Baer. £300
See— HOOGHE, R. de
See— JAILLOT, Hubert
See— JAILLOT, Hubert & Mortier, Pierre

MOSCOW
– Moskva. [1662]. 370 × 500mm. Cont. hand-cold. engraved map from Blaeu's Atlas Major, ptd. Spanish text on verso, centre fold, some margin repairs. (VG. Mar.22; 1662) Fls. 450

MOUNT, W. & Page, T.
– Virginia, Maryland, Pennsilvania, East & West New Jarsey. [1732]. 520 × 800mm. Hand-cold. engraved chart, some light soiling. (CSK. Nov.4; 24) £520

MOUZON, Henry & others
– An Accurate Map of North & South Carolina with their Indian Frontiers ... L., Laurie & Whittle, 1794. 39 × 56 inches. Engraved map, in 4 sheets, partly hand-cold. in outl., scroll cartouche in upr. left-hand sheet, 2 inset maps in lr. right-hand sheet, slight offsetting & browning. (SPB. May 23; 25) $600

MOXON, Joseph
– A Map of all the Earth and how after the Flood it was Divided among the Sons of Noah. [Amst.], ca. 1680? 325 × 460mm. Double-p. engraved map, hand-cold. in outl., 14 cold. vigs., rubbed & creased, some staining, lr. margin & creases refaced on verso. (SG. Dec.15; 101) $200

MUNSTER, Sebastian
– Africa Lybia Mozenlandt mit allen Konigreichen. [Late 16th. C.]. 10 × 13½ inches. Woodcut map, reprd. along fold & at corners. (CSK. Mar.9; 26) £70

[–] **Aphricae Tabula IIII.** [Basel], ca. 1550. 250 × 340mm. Double-p. woodcut map, hand-cold., Latin text on verso, good margins, minor rubbing & creasing along lr. edge. (SG. Jun.7; 44) $175

[–] **Asia ... showing Japan.** Ca. 1540 or later. Approx. 12 × 14 inches. Hand-cold. woodcut map, German text on verso. (TA. May 17; 176) £110

– – Anr. Edn. [Basle], 1588-1628 or later. Approx. 12½ × 14 inches. Hand-cold. woodblock map, plain corner title cartouche, German text on verso. (TA. Jul.19; 124) £100

– British Isles. Ca. 1570. 360 × 320mm. Hand-cold. woodcut map in mount, slightly discold., F. (P. Nov.24; 335) Styles. £150

– Charta Cosmographica, cum Ventorum propria Natura Operatione. Ca. 1580. Sm. fo. Woodcut map from Kosmographie, cut close, crumpled, tears bkd., some light foxing. (HK. Nov.12; 5402) DM 700

– Die Erst General Tafel. 16th. C. Sm. ob. fo. Cold. woodcut oval world map, corners decor., text on verso slightly showing thro. (R. Oct.13; 3311) DM 620

– Figura del Mondo Universale. 16th. C. Italian Edn. Sm. ob. fo. Cold. woodcut map after Ptolemaeus, decor. borders, sm. hole, margins slightly soiled. (R. Apr.5; 3125) DM 500

– Gemeine Beschreibung aller Mitnächtigen Länder. N.d. Sm. ob. fo. Cold. wood engraved map. (R. Oct.13; 3335) DM 620

– London oder Lunden die Hauptstatt in Engelland. [1598]. 355 × 250mm. Hand-cold. town plan, German text on verso. (P. Apr.12; 387)
Goodall. £150

[–] **Neüw Indian, mit vilen Anstossenden Ländern, Besunder Scythia, Parthia, Arabia, Persia, etc.** [Basel, 1540, but 1545 or later]. 255 × 341mm. Double-p. woodcut map, German text in panel on verso, tear without loss, F. & G. (S. Mar.6; 144)
Waterloo. £90

– Die Neüwen Inseln, so hinder Hispanien gegen Orient bey dem Land Indie ligen. Ca. 1550. Ob. fo. Wood cut map from Kosmographie, some light spotting, 1 sm. fault bkd. at side, slight worming reprd. (HK. Nov.12; 5420) DM 900

– – Anr. Edn. Ca. 1580. Ob. fo. Woodcut map from Kosmographie, some spotting, text on verso slightly showing through, some light stains at top. (HK. Nov.12; 5421) DM 850

[–] **Nova Graecia XXII Nova Tabula.** [1544]. 10 × 13½ inches. Woodcut map, Latin text on verso. (CSK. May 4; 230) £75

[–] **Palestine.** Ca. 1540 or later. Approx. 12 × 14 inches. Uncold. woodcut map, German text on verso, little rubbed & browned. (TA. Nov.17; 89) £92

– Ptolemaisch General Tafel, begriffend die Halbe Kugel d. Weldt. Ca. 1550. Ob. fo. Woodcut map, some slight spotting & creasing. (HK. May 18; 4244) DM 400

– – Anr. Edn. N.d. Sm. ob. fo. Cold. woodcut map, decor. border. (R. Oct.13; 3312) DM 600

[–] **Tabula Orientalis Regionis, Asiae Scilicet Extremas Complectens Terras & Regna.** [Basel, 16th. C.]. 260 × 345mm. Double-p. woodcut map, Latin text on verso, full margins, minor holes near fold. (SG. Jun.7; 89) $225

NEW MAP OF NEW ENGLAND, New York, New Jarsey, Pensilvanie, Maryland & Virginia.
John Thornton, Robert Morden & Philip Lea, [1685]. 450 × 550mm. Engraved map, hand-cold. in outl., a little light browning. (CSK. Nov.4; 22)
£550

NEW YORK CITY
– **New-York City & County Map with Vicinity entire Brooklyn, Williamsburgh, Jersey City & c.** N.Y., Charles Magnus, ca. 1855. 500 × 830mm. Litho. map, uncold., inset map of Long Island, inset of Declaration of Independence text, vignetted view of City Hall, good margins, some edge-chipping. (SG. Jun.7; 63)
$175
– **A Plan of the City of New York & its Environs to Greenwich ... John Montressor, Engineer ...** L., A. Dury, [1777]. 28 × 20 inches. Engraved map, inset view 'Chart of the Entrance to New York from Sandy Hook ... ', slight soiling. (SPB. Oct.26; 6)
$2,250
– **Plan of the City of New York in North America ...** L., Jefferys & Faden, 1776. 24 × 35 inches. Engraved map, view (8 × 35 inches) 'A South West View of the City of New York Taken from the Govenours [sic] Island ... ', a few minor tears & slight traces of soiling at folds. (SPB. Oct.26; 7)
$2,000

NOLIN, J.B. [Jnr.]
– **L'Amérique Dressée sur les Relations les plus Recentes.** Paris, 1720 or later. 1,225 × 1,425mm. Engraved wall map on 4 jointed sheets, partly hand-cold. in outl., attached border of 30 vigs., faint spotting slightly affecting appearance, imp. slightly rubbed in places, bkd. with archive tissue. (S. Dec.1; 224) *Quaritch.* £800

NORDEN, John
– **Middlesex.** N.d. 14½ × 16½ inches. Hand-cold. engraved map, title in Baroque cartouche, F. & G. (SKC. Nov.18; 2100) £50
– **Middlesex olim a Trinobantibus Habitata.** Ca. 1590 or later. Approx. 10½ × 13 inches. Uncold. map, ornamental strapwork title cartouche & separate scale of distance. (TA. Jul.19; 171) £50

NORDEN, John
See— SPEEDE, John

NORDEN, John & Hole, William
– **Hamshire Olim Pars Belgarum.** Ca. 1620 or later. Approx. 11½ × 12 inches. Uncold. map, ornamental corner title cartouche incorporating key, separate scale of distance surmounted by compass rose, laid down on linen. (TA. Jan.19; 117) £56

NORDEN, John & Kip, William
– **Hertfordiae. Comitatus a Cattifuclanis Olim Inhabitatus.** Ca. 1620 or later. Approx. 11 × 13½ inches. Map, ornamental title cartouche & separate scale of distance, laid down on linen. (TA. Jan.19; 118) £60
– **Surrey olim Sedes Regnorum.** Ca. 1610 or later. Approx. 11½ × 15 inches. Uncold. map, corner strapwork title cartouche, a little browned along centrefold. (TA. Mar.15; 147) £80
– **Sussexia Siue Southset, olim pars Regnorum.** Ca. 1610 or later. Approx. 9 × 15 inches. Map, decor. title cartouche, separate scale of distance cartouche surmounted by compass rose, Royal crest, list of Shires, etc., recently F. & G. (TA. Sep.15; 189)
£56

NORTH AMERICA
– **The British Colonies in North America.** [1785]. 345 × 342mm. Hand-cold. map. (P. Apr.12; 385) *Ruddell.* £50

NOVA SCOTIA & New England
[L.], 1625 or later. 10½ × 14 inches. Copper-plt. engraved map, from 'Purchas His Pilgrimes'. matted, F. & G. (SPB. Dec.13; 510) $950

OGILBY, John
– **The Continuation of the Extended Road from Oakeham in Rutland to Richmond Com. Ebor., together with The Road from Ferrybridge to Boroughbridge Continued to Barnard Castle in Com. Ebor.** Ca. 1675. Approx. 14½ × 18 inches. Uncold. strip road maps, ornamental title cartouche, several

compass roses, both lightly browned along centre-fold, latter with sm. tear to lr. margin, without loss. (TA. Jun.21; 112) £50
– **A New Map of the Kingdom of England & Dominion of Wales.** L., [1675]. 500 × 385mm. Hand-cold. map. (P. May 17; 437) *Thomas.* £80
[–] **Nova Terrae-Mariae Tabula.** Ca. 1671. 300 × 390mm. Engraved map, hand-cold. in outl., reprd. at lr. fold. (CSK. Nov.4; 23) £350
– **Nova Virginiae Tabula.** 1670. 360 × 300mm. Uncold. map. (P. Jul.5; 396) £140
– **Novissima et Acuratissima Barbados Descriptio.** Ca. 1670. 360 × 305mm. Uncold. map, repairs, back strengthened. (P. Jun.7; 388) £170
– **Novissima et Accuratissima Jamaicae Descriptio.** 1671. 550 × 440mm. Hand-cold. map, back strengthened. (P. Jun.7; 389) £100
– **The Road from Bristol to Banbury.** Ca. 1675 or later. Approx. 13 × 17½ inches. Hand-cold. strip road map, ornamental title cartouche incorporating Royal crest, several compass rose, F. & G. (TA. Mar.15; 93) £60
– **The Road from Exeter com. Devon to Dorchester, & from Plimouth to Dartmouth ...** [1675. 1st. Edn.]. Approx. 13 × 18 inches. Strip road map, hand-cold. in outl., central ornamental title cartouche, several compass rose, etc. (TA. Jan.19; 115) £58
– **The Road from London to New Haven.** Ca. 1675 or later. Approx. 13 × 17 inches. Hand-cold. strip road map, ornamental title cartouche incorporating Royal crest, several compass rose, F. & G. (TA. Mar.15; 95) £50
– **The Road from London to Pool.** Ca. 1675 or later. Approx. 13½ × 17½ inches. Hand-cold. strip road map, ornamental title cartouche incorporating Royal crest, several compass rose, F. & G. (TA. Mar.15; 96) £50
– **The Road from London to Southampton.** Ca. 1675 or later. Approx. 12½ MMP 8½ inches. Hand-cold. strip road map, ornamental title cartouche incorporating Royal crest & cherubs, several compass rose, F. & G. (TA. Mar.15; 94) £56

ORBIS TERRARUM TYPUS
Ca. 1720. 360 × 475mm. Cold. copper engraved world map from German Bible, in 2 hemispheres, allegorical ill. decor., 2 sm. star maps, caption at head, floral border, 1 sm. crease & spot bkd. (R. Apr.5; 3131) DM 1,500

ORDNANCE SURVEY
– **Devonshire.** L., 1809 [but 1850-55]. *Old Series or '1st. Edn.'.* 8vo. Sheets 20-27, electrotyped from 1809 Mudge plts., each mntd. & dissected in 24 sections, in cont. hf. roan gt. book-style s.-c. (S. Mar.6; 178) *Old Hall.* £100
– **The Second Part of the General Survey of England & Wales Containing the Whole of Devon.** Lieut.-Col. Mudge, Tower [of L.], 11 Oct. 1809. *1st. Edn.* Lge. fo. Engraved title, 8 double-p. map-sheets (Rodger noting 7 sheets only), in dark imps. & without piano key borders between adjoining sheets (early printing?), watermark dtd. 1801, some faint offsetting, cont. hf. russ. gt., reprd. (S. Dec.1; 147) *Ambra.* £1,050

ORTELIUS, Abraham
– **Abrahami Patriarchae Peregrinatio et Vita.** Antw., 1586 [or later]. 352 × 455mm. Hand-cold. double-p. engraved map, border incorporating 22 vigs. (S. Jun.25; 5) *Hoffbrand.* £360
– – **Anr. Edn.** N.d. Ob. fo. Old cold. copper engraved map, painted rollwork cartouche, wide border with 22 round ills. (R. Oct.13; 3540) DM 1,700
– **Aegyptus Antiqua.** [Antw.], 1584[-92]. 790 × 485mm. Engraved map in 2 jointed sheets, fully hand-cold., sm. inset, Latin text on verso, faint offsetting affecting title, slight margin browning, strengthening at folds. (S. Dec.1; 253) *Cope.* £180
– **Aevi Veteris Typus Geographicus.** N.d. Ob. fo. Old cold. copper engraved map, decor., sm. maps in corners, cartouches at top & bottom, painted rollwork cartouche beneath, sm. hole in caption reprd. (R. Oct.13; 3315) DM 400
[–] **Africae Tabula Nova.** 1570. Ob. fo. Cold. copper engraved map, painted rollwork cartouche & figure decor., margins spotted & browned. (R. Apr.5; 3251) DM 570

– – **Anr. Edn.** 1570 [1575 or later]. Approx. 15 × 20 inches. Old cold. map, strapwork title cartouche, sailing ships, sea monsters, etc., Latin text to verso, some browning, mainly to margins. (TA. Jul.19; 123) £160
– – **Anr. Edn.** N.d. Ob. fo. Old cold. copper engraved map, painted rollwork cartouche, decor., sm. col. fault. (R. Oct.13; 3389) DM 570
– **Americae sive Novi Orbis, Nova Descriptio.** 1587. Ob. fo. Old cold. copper engraved map, decor. corners, painted figure rollwork cartouche. (R. Oct.13; 3423) DM 4,200
– – **Anr. Edn.** [Antw.], ca. 1590 or later. 14½ × 19 inches. Engraved hand-cold. map, elaborate cartouche, scroll spandrels, etc., matted, slight soiling, F. & G. (SPB. Oct.26; 11) $1,600
– – **Anr. Edn.** Ca. 1640. 515 × 380mm. Hand-cold. map, repairs to margins, fold strengthened. (P. Jul.5; 417) £300
– – **Anr. Copy.** 500 × 360mm. Hand-cold. map, repairs, 1 wormhole, upr. margin trimmed. (P. Jul.5; 409) £200
– **Angliae Regni Florentissimi Nova Descriptio auctore Humfredo Lhuyd.** 1573 [but 1601]. 15 × 18½ inches. Engraved map, Latin text on verso, margins lightly stained. (CSK. May 4; 13) £100
[–] **Angliae, Scotiae et Hiberniae, sive Britannicar: Insularum Descriptio.** [Antw., 1570, but 1572 or later]. 345 × 497mm. Double-p. engraved map, Latin text on verso, sm. stain in lr. outer margin. (S. Mar.6; 153) *Kidd.* £150
– – **Anr. Edn.** [Antw.,], 1570 [but 1581 or later]. 345 × 498mm. Double-p. full col. engraved map, orientated West to top of sheet, Fr. text on verso, sm. repair at centre-fold, margin soiling. (S. Nov.1; 142) *Kidd.* £180
– – **Anr. Edn.** [Antw., 1570, 1587 or later]. 345 × 498mm. Double-p. engraved map, Fr. text on verso, faint margin stain. (S. Mar.6; 155) *Hulme.* £70
[–] **Asiae Nova Descriptio.** [Antw.], 1592 or later. 370 × 483mm. Double-p. engraved map, Latin text on verso, slight adhesion defect at centrefold with slight loss of engraved surface, sm. stains in lr. portion. (S. Dec.13; 7) *Snow.* £180
– – **Anr. Edn.** N.d. Ob. fo. Old cold. copper engraved map, painted rollwork cartouche. (R. Oct.13; 3509) DM 550
– – **Anr. Copy.** Ob. fo. Cold. copper engraved map, painted rollwork cartouche, margins foxed & browned. (R. Apr.5; 3361) DM 440
– **Brabant.** N.d. Ob. fo. Old cold. copper engraved map, 3 painted rollwork cartouches & sm. supp. map. (R. Oct.13; 3613) DM 550
– **Brandenburg.** 1588. Ob. fo. Old. cold. copper engraved map, 2 painted roll work cartouches & caption, tear bkd., some margins slightly browned. (R. Oct.14; 4673) DM 620
– **Britannicarum Insularum Typus.** 1595. Ob. fo. Old cold. copper engraved map, 3 painted rollwork cartouches, decor. (R. Oct.13; 3737) DM 420
– **Cambriae Typus.** Ca. 1579. 495 × 370mm. Hand-cold. map, hole approx 20 × 20mm. reprd. (P. Apr.12; 341) *Burgess.* £65
– – **Anr. Edn.** [Antw., 1592]. 370 × 495mm. Double-p. engraved map, hand-cold. in outl., & with light col. wash, sailing ship, sea monster, full margins, Latin text on verso, some light rubbing, minor discolouration at fold. (SG. Jun.7; 123) $110
– – **Anr. Edn.** Ca. 1595. 500 × 370mm. Cont. hand-cold. map, hole reprd. (P. Jan.12; 337) £60
– **China.** 1584. Ob. fo. Cold. copper engraved map, 3 painted figure cartouches, figure decor., sm. wormhole at foot bkd., margins foxed. (R. Apr.5; 3375) DM 670
– **China Regio Asiae.** [1585]. 3½ × 4¾ inches. Hand-cold. engraved map, Fr. text on verso, very lightly rubbed, slight text darkening. (CBA. Aug.21; 713) $160
– – **Anr. Edn.** Ill.:– J.L. de Barbuda. N.d. Ob. fo. Old cold. copper engraved map, 3 painted figure rollwork cartouches, figure decor. (R. Oct.13; 3518) DM 900
[–] **Chinae, olim Sinarum Regionis.** [Antw., 1595 or later]. 368 × 478mm. Double-p. engraved map, orientated west to top of sheet, showing China, Japan & Philippines, based on map by Luis Jorge de Barbuda (1594), Latin text on verso, faint margin discolouration, w.a.f. (S. May 22; 424) *Potter.* £240

- **Creta Iovis Magni.** [1584 or later]. 13½ × 19½ inches. Engraved map, Latin text on verso, some light staining. (CSK. May 4; 215) £130

[-] **Cypri Insulae Nova Descript.** [Antw.], 1573 [but 1595 or later]. 354 × 498mm. Double-p. map, engraved by J. van Deutecom, inset, Latin text on verso, slight unif. browning. (S. Dec.13; 121) *Burgess.* £160

-- **Anr. Edn.** [Antw., 1573]. 350 × 500mm. Double-p. engraved map, hand-cold., 3 sailing ships, inset map, 'Lemnos Insulae ... ', good margins. German text on verso, rubbed, minor foxing, discolouration at fold. (SG. Jun.7; 124) $200

-- **Anr. Edn.** [Antw.], 1603 or later. 354 × 498mm. Double-p. engraved map, engraved by J. van Deutecom, fully hand-cold., inset of Limnos, Latin text on verso, faint unif. browning. (S. Dec.1; 250) *Map House.* £250

-- **Anr. Edn.** N.d. Ob. fo. Old cold. copper engraved map, 2 painted rollwork cartouches & sm. supp. map. (R. Oct.13; 3525) DM 700

- **Cyprus.** 1573. 18 × 23 inches. Hand-cold. engraved map, title cartouche, F. & double-G. (SKC. May 4; 1522) £160

- **England.** Ill.:- after H. Lhuyd. 1573. Ob. fo. Old cold. copper engraved map, 2 painted rollwork cartouches, figure decor. (R. Oct.13; 3732) DM 430

[-] **Eryn. Hiberniae, Britannicae Insulae, Nova Descriptio, Irlandt.** Antw., 1573 [but 1581 or later]. 354 × 480mm. Double-p. hand-cold. engraved map, orientated West to top of sheet, Fr. text on verso. (S. Nov.1; 171) *Burgess.* £140

-- **Anr. Edn.** [Antw.], 1592 or later. 353 × 482mm. Double-p. engraved map, orientated west to the top of sheet, Latin text on verso, margin browning. (S. Dec.13; 194) *Burgess.* £130

- **Flandria.** N.d. Ob. fo. Oval cold. copper engraved map, decor. corners, painted rollwork cartouche & costume figures, tear at foot bkd., margins foxed. (R. Apr.5; 3481) DM 680

[-] **La Florida [&] Guastecan [&] Peruviae Auriferae Regionis Typus.** [Antw.], 1584 but 1598 or later]. 341 × 462mm. Double-p. engraved mapsheet incorporating 3 regional maps, Dutch text on verso., w.a.f. (S. May 22; 358) *Robinson.* £280

- **Florida mit Peru und Yucatan.** N.d. Ob. fo. 3 maps from 1 plt., old cold. copper engraved. (R. Oct.13; 3450) DM 1,200

[-] **Germania.** Ca. 1580 or later. Approx. 14½ × 20 inches. Map, strapwork title cartouche, separate scale of distance, lge. armorial in strapwork cartouche, Fr. text to verso. (TA. Jun.21; 132) £100

-- **Anr. Edn.** N.d. Ob. fo. Old cold. copper engraved map, 2 painted rollwork cartouches, Imp. arms, partly bkd. (R. Oct.14; 4159) DM 500

-- **Anr. Copy.** Ob. fo. Cold. copper engraved map, 2 painted rollwork cartouches & imperial arms, sm. tear at foot bkd., margins slightly spotted. (R. Apr.6; 4035) DM 440

[-] **Graeciae Universale ... descriptio.** [Antw.], 1610 or later. 365 × 515mm. Double-p. engraved map, after Gastaldi, Latin text on verso, sm. split at lr. centrefold, slight overall browning. (S. Dec.13; 116) *Moos.* £80

-- **Anr. Edn.** Late 16th. C. 14½ × 20½ inches. Engraved map, Italian text on verso, centre-fold reprd. (CSK. Jul.6; 165) £60

-- **Anr. Edn.** N.d. Ob. fo. Cold. copper engraved map, painted rollwork cartouche, margins foxed. (R. Apr.5; 3660) DM 450

- **Grossbritannien.** N.d. Ob. fo. Old cold. copper engraved map, 2 painted rollwork cartouches, cold. arms. (R. Oct.13; 3735) DM 450

[-] **Helvetiae Descriptio.** [Antw.], 1603 or later. 345 × 544mm. Double-p. engraved map, after Gilg Tschudi, [1538], orientated south to the top, fully hand-cold., Latin text on verso, faint margin browning. (S. Dec.1; 251) *Germundson.* £150

-- **Anr. Edn.** Ill.:- after A. Tschudi. N.d. Ob. fo. Old cold. copper engraved map, caption cartouche, sm. fault bkd. (R. Oct.13; 3960) DM 850

- **Hispaniae Novae ... Descriptio.** 1579. ob. fo. Cold. copper engraved map, 3 painted rollwork cartouches, margins spotted. (R. Apr.5; 3325) DM 400

-- **Anr. Edn.** [Antw.], 1579 [but 1581 or later].

348 × 506mm. Double-p. engraved map, hand-cold. in wash & outl., Fr. text on verso, faint margin soiling. (S. Nov.1; 222) *Mulder.* £60

-- **Anr. Edn.** [1606]. 345 x 500mm. Hand-cold. engraved map, Engl. text on verso. (CSK. Aug.5; 24) £130

- **Hispaniae Veteris Descriptio.** [Antw.], 1586. 475 × 560mm. Wide margin, copper engraved map, surface col., rollwork cartouche at top left with caption, at left foot, cartouche with dedication, above this privilege & date, at bottom right lge. cartouche with long geographical caption & map over, on verso description in Latin. (GF. Nov.12; 1092) *Sw. Frs.* 360

- **Hispaniolae, Cubae, Aliarumque Insularum Circumiacentium Descriptio; Culiacanae, Americae Regionis, Descriptio.** [Antw.,], 1579 [but 1592 or later]. 358 × 497mm. 2 maps on 1 double-p. engraved map-sheet, Latin text on verso, faint col. offsetting in upr. part. (S. Nov.1; 219) *Burgess.* £100

-- **Anr. Edn.** [Antw.], 1595 or later. 350 × 497mm. 2 maps on 1 double-p. engraved mapsheet, Latin text on verso, sm. repair in 1r. blank margin. (S. Dec.13; 4) *Ashworth.* £110

- **Hollandia Nova Descriptio.** Ill.:- after J.Deventer. N.d. Ob. fo. Old cold. copper engraved map, painted rollwork cartouche, cold. arms, decor. (R. Oct.13; 3638) DM 480

- **Hollandiae Antiquorum Catthorum Sedis Nova Descriptio, Auctore Iacobo A Daventria.** [Antw., late 16th. C.]. 350 × 480mm. Double-p. engraved map, hand-cold., good margins, Latin text on verso, some rubbing & discolouration, particularly at fold. (SG. Jun.7; 126) $110

- **Iaponiae Insulae Descriptio.** Ill.:- after L. Teixeira. 1595. Ob. fo. Old cold. copper engraved map, 2 painted rollwork cartouches, decor. (R. Oct.13; 3548) DM 1,000

-- **Anr. Edn.** [Antw., 1595 or later]. 485 × 355mm. Double-p. engraved map showing Japan & island of Korea (after Luis Teixera, 1595), Latin text on verso, w.a.f. (S. May 22; 426) *Bjork.* £320

- **India & Indonesia.** N.d. 18 × 22 inches. Hand-cold. engraved map, title cartouche, F. & G. (SKC. May 4; 1526) £100

[-] **Indiae Orientalis ... Typus.** [Antw.], 1570 but later]. 348 × 492mm. Double-p. engraved map showing Far East, Japan, part of North America & New Guinea, Latin text on verso, w.a.f. (S. May 22; 425) *Asian.* £200

-- **Anr. Edn.** [1595]. 14 × 19½ inches. Hand-cold. engraved map, Latin text on verso. (CSK. Jul.6; 251) £280

-- **Anr. Edn.** [Antw.], 1603 or later. 350 × 500mm. Double-p. engraved map, fully hand-cold., Latin text on verso. (S. Dec.1; 256) *Degenhardt.* £310

-- **Anr. Edn.** N.d. Ob. fo. Old cold. copper engraved map, painted rollwork cartouche, cold arms, figure decor. (R. Oct.13; 3531) DM 900

- **Insular aliquot Aegaei Maris Antiqua Descrip.** 1584. Ob. fo. Old cold. copper engraved map, surrounded by 9 sm. maps, 2 painted rollwork cartouches. (R. Oct.13; 3526) DM 400

[-] **Insularum Aliquot Maris Mediterranei Descriptio.** [Antw., 1570, but 1575 or later]. 361 × 474mm. Double-p. engraved map, fully hand-cold., Latin text on verso, few faint ink inscrs. (S. Mar.6; 132) *Brockhaus.* £100

- **Island.** N.d. Ob. fo. Old cold. copper engraved map, 3 painted rollwork cartouches, figure decor., partly bkd., some margin spotting. (R. Oct.14; 4017) DM 1,000

- **Lutzenburgensis Ducatus veriss. descript.** Ill.:- after J. Surhon. N.d. Ob. fo. Cold. copper engraved map, painted rollwork cartouche, margins spotted. (R. Oct.13; 3672) DM 400

- **Maris Pacifici, quod vulgo Mar del Zur, Descriptio.** 1589. Ob. fo. Old cold. copper engraved map, 2 painted rollwork cartouches. (R. Oct.13; 3347) DM 2,100

-- **Anr. Edn.** [Antw.], 1589 [or later]. 344 × 497mm. Double-p. engraved map, hand-cold. in outl., embellishments fully cold., ill. of Magellan's flagship 'Victoria', minor print crease, sm. repair at lr. centrefold, F. & G. (S. Dec.1; 218) *Robinson.* £650

-- **Anr. Copy.** 344 × 497mm. Double-p. engraved map, including western shores of Americas, China,

Japan & Philippines, New Guinea & Solomon Islands & ill. of Magellan's flagship, the 'Victoria', Latin text on verso, w.a.f. (S. May 22; 463) *Casten.* £540

- **Münster und Osnabrück.** Ill.:- after G. Maskop. N.d. Fo. Old cold copper engraved map, painted rollwork cartouche. (R. Oct.15; 5685) DM 850

-- **Anr. Copy.** Fo. Cold copper engraved map, painted rollwork cartouche, margins slightly spotted. (R. Apr.7; 5252) DM 500

- **Norimberg[ensis] Agri Descriptio.** 1590. Fo. Cold. copper engraved map, browned, spotted at left side. (R. Apr.6; 4487) DM 420

- **Palaestinae ... nova Descriptio.** Ill.:- after T. Stella. N.d. fo. Old cold, copper engraved map, 2 lge. painted rollwork cartouches, decor. (R. Oct.13; 3538) DM 820

- **Peregrinationis Divi Pauli Typus Corographicus.** [Antw.], early 17th. C. 355 × 505mm. Double-p. engraved map, hand-cold. in outl., cold. vigs., figures, Latin text on verso, minor separation at lr. fold. (SG. Dec.15; 102) $120

[-] **Persici sive Sophorum Regni Typus.** [Antw.], 1603 or later. 350 × 498mm. Double-p. engraved map, Latin text on verso. (S. Dec.13; 12) *Potter.* £50

- **Presbiteri Johannis, sive Abissinorum Imperii Descriptio.** [L., 1573, but 1606]. 373 × 433mm. Double-p. engraved map, hand-cold., Engl. text on verso, 2 sm. wormholes reprd. (S. Mar.6; 142) *Willis.* £80

[-] **Russiae, Moscoviae et Tartariae Descriptio.** [Antw., 1608]. 355 × 445mm. Double-p. engraved map, hand-cold. in outl., cold. notations, some vigs., Italian text on verso, unif. browning, margins reinforced on verso, some edge tears reprd. (SG. Dec.15; 53) $175

- **Salisburgensis Iurisdictionis.** [Antw., Ortelius, 1598]. 380 × 455mm. Double-p. engraved map, completely hand-cold., full margins, Fr. text on verso, some reinforcement on verso of fold & top margin, minor rubbing. (SG. Jun.7; 129) $100

- **Schlesien.** Ill.:- after M. Helwig. N.d. Ob. fo. Old cold copper engraved map, 2 painted rollwork cartouches & cold arms. (R. Oct.14; 5380) DM 450

[-] **Scotiae Tabula.** [Antw.], 1573 [but 1581 or later]. 355 × 477mm. Double-p. engraved map, orientated West to top of sheet, cold. in wash & outl., Fr. text on verso. (S. Nov.1; 168) *Pringle.* £140

-- **Anr. Edn.** [Antw., 1573, but 1587 or later]. 352 × 472mm. Double-p. engraved map, Fr. text on verso, faint margin staining. (S. Mar.6; 186) *Coulter.* £75

-- **Anr. Edn.** Ca. 1580. 470 × 355mm. Hand-cold. map. (P. Oct.20; 280) £80

-- **Anr. Edn.** [Antw.], 1592 or later. 352 × 472mm. Double-p. engraved map, orientated west to the top of sheet, Latin text on verso, sm. stain at lr. centrefold. (S. Dec.13; 193) *Potter.* £70

-- **Anr. Edn.** 1595. 480 × 360mm. Hand-cold. map. (P. Jan.12; 352) *Evans.* £50

[-] **Septentrionalium Regionum Descrip.** [Antw., 1570, but 1595 or later]. 359 × 487mm. Double-p. engraved map including Scandinavia, the British Isles, Iceland, Greenland & part of North America, Latin text on verso. w.a.f. (S. May 22; 451) *Christensen.* £300

-- **Anr. Edn.** [Antw., 1570, but ca. 1590]. 360 × 490mm. Double-p. engraved map extending from North America to Scandinavia, including Greenland, Iceland & the mythical 'Prisland', Latin text on verso, faint margin browning, w.a.f. (S. May 22; 450) *Franks.* £160

-- **Anr. Edn.** [1590 or later]. 14½ × 19½ inches. Map, Fr. text on verso, browned & reprd. (CSK. Mar.9; 28) £150

-- **Anr. Edn.** N.d. Ob. fo. Old cold. copper engraved map, painted caption cartouche, figures. (R. Oct.13; 3336) DM 1,100

- **Tartaria Typus.** N.d. Ob. fo. Old cold. copper engraved map, 2 painted rollwork cartouches. (R. Oct.13; 3550) DM 480

[-] **Tartariae sive Magni Chami Regni Typus.** Antw., 1570 [but 1581 or later]. 352 × 474mm. Map, hand-cold. in wash & outl., Fr. text on verso, margin soiling. (S. Nov.1; 239) *Mulder.* £260

-- **Anr. Edn.** [Antw., 1570 but later]. 360 ×

ORTELIUS, Abraham -*Contd.*

480mm. Double-p. engraved map showing north-eastern Asia, Japan & the American Northwest, Latin text on verso, w.a.f. (S. May 22; 345)
Franks. £180

– – **Anr. Edn.** [1595]. 14 × 18½ inches. Hand-cold. engraved map, Latin text on verso. (CSK. Jul.6; 250)   £280

[–] **Terra Sancta.** [Antw.], 1584 or later. 370 × 500mm. Hand-cold. double-p. engraved map after P. Laicksteen & C. 'sGrooten, orientated west to the top of the sheet, German text on verso, F. & double-G. (S. Jun.25; 8)   *Schiff.* £120

– – **Anr. Edn.** Ill.:– after P. Laicksteen & Ch. Schrot. ca. 1590. Ob. fo. Old cold. copper engraved map, 2 painted rollwork cartouches, figure decor., partly bkd. (R. Oct.13; 3537)   DM 650

– – **Anr. Copy.** Ob. fo. Cold. copper engraved map, 2 painted rollwork cartouches, figure decor., margins spotted. (R. Apr.5; 3394)   DM 600

– **Turcici Imperii Descriptio.** Early 17th. C. Hand-cold. map, some light foxing, F. & G. (P. Jan.12; 364)   *Burgess.* £75

– – **Anr. Edn.** N.d. Ob. fo. Old cold. copper engraved map, painted figure cartouche. (R. Oct.13; 3573)   DM 550

– **Typus Chorographicus Celebrium Locorum in Regno Iudae et Israhel.** Ill.:– after T. Stella. 1586. Ob. fo. Cold. copper engraved map, 2 painted rollwork cartouches, fold burst, sm. faults bkd. (R. Apr.5; 3393)   DM 550

– – **Anr. Edn.** [Antw.], 1586 or later. 356 × 463mm. Double-p. engraved map, hand-cold. in wash & outl., German text on verso, slight soiling. (S. Apr.9; 122)   *Tooley.* £100

– – **Anr. Edn.** Ill.:– after T. Stella. N.d. Ob. fo. Old cold. copper engraved map, 2 painted rollwork cartouches. (R. Oct.13; 3539)   DM 650

[–] **Typus Orbis Terrarum.** [Amst.], ca. 1590. 14½ × 19½ inches. Hand-cold. double-p. engraved map, Latin text on verso, matted, F. & G. (SPB. Dec.13; 512) $1,500

– – **Anr. Copy.** Ob. fo. Oval old cold. copper engraved map, decor. round, in corners quotes from Cicero & Seneca, sm. defect. through col., slightly spotted. (R. Oct.13; 3314)   DM 2,000

– – **Anr. Edn.** Ca. 1595. 490 × 360mm. Map, repair to lr. margin, fold strengthened. (P. May 17; 452)
Burgess. £580

– **Westfalen.** Ill.:– after Ch. Schrot. N.d. Ob. fo. Old cold. copper engraved map, 3 painted rollwork cartouches, slightly spotted. (R. Oct.15; 5838)
DM 800

[–] **Zelandicarum Insularum exactissima et nova descriptio.** [Antw.], 1579 or later. 335 × 468mm. Double-p. engraved map, after Jacob van Deventer, Latin text on verso. (S. Dec.13; 90) *Leycester.* £90

– – **Anr. Edn.** N.d. Ob. fo. Old cold. copper engraved map, painted rollwork cartouche, figure decor. (R. Oct.13; 3698)   DM 470

– – **Anr. Copy.** Ob. fo. Old cold. copper engraved map, torn at fold, sm. hole bkd., some col. offsetting. (R. Oct.13; 3699)   DM 420

See— **ROTENHAN, Sebastian A.**

OTTENS, Joachim

– **Novissima et Accuratissima Decem Austriacarum in Belgis Provinciarum.** N.d. Ob. fo. Cold. copper-engraved map. (V. Sep.29; 770)   DM 430

OTTENS, Reiner & Joshua

– **Totius Neobelgii Nova et Accuratissima Tabula.** Amst., ca. 1750. 460 × 530mm. Outl. cold. copper engraved map, painted figure cartouche, decor., lightly spotted, sm. thin part & hole in upr. margin strengthened. (R. Oct.13; 3478)   DM 1,800

See— **DE L'ISLE, Guillaume**
See— **WIT, Frederick de**

OVERTON, Henry

– **A New Mapp of Lincoln Shire.** 1712. 15½ × 19½ inches. Engraved map, hand-cold. outl., margins slightly soiled. (CSK. Jul.6; 213)   £60

OVERTON, John

– **Warwici Comitatis Descriptio.** 1603 [1670]. 390 × 510mm. Engraved map, hand-cold. in outl., holed with sm. loss at lr. right margin, some light soiling, close F. & G. (CSK. Jan.13; 23)   £290

OVERTON, Philip

– **Sussex.** N.d. 24 × 39 inches. Engraved map, rape divisions hand-cold., prospects of Lewes & Chichester. (SKC. Nov.18; 2096)   £160

OWEN, W.

– **Map of the Colony of Victoria, & also Exhibiting upon a Reduced Scale the Colonies, Settlements & Latest Explorations in Australia** ... 10 Nov. 1862. Approx. 37 × 55 inches. Engraved map, in 40 sections, outl. col., several sm. spots, some minor defects, laid down on linen. (KH. May 1; 544)
Aus. $550

PAGE, T.

See— **MOUNT, W. & Page, T.**

PALESTINE

– **Tabula Moderna Terre Sancte.** [Ulm, Johann Reger, 1486]. 248 × 527mm. Double-p. woodcut map of Palestine extending from Sidon to Gaza, orientated east to top of sheet, from 2nd. Ulm edn. of Ptolemy, 2nd. state with ptd. title above map area & blank verso, old hand-cold. emphasising mountain ranges, rivers, boundaries of the Twelve Tribes painted in sepia, blue & red respectively, waterbodies in lighter brown wash, sm. margin stain at upr. left corner, F. & G., w.a.f. (S. May 22; 267)
Norwich. £3,400

PALMEUS, A.F.G. de

– **A Topographical Map describing the Sovereign Principality of the Islands of Malta & Goza.** L., W. Faden, 1799 [or later]. 525 × 1,125mm. Hand-cold. engraved map, minor repair without loss of engraved surface, F. & G. (S. Jun.25; 235)
Potter. £170

PIGAFETTA, Filippo

– **[Africa, from the Mediterranean to the Cape, excluding West Africa].** 1591. 550 × 400mm. Line engraved map, ill., on 2 joined sheets, slight margins on 3 sides, some places cut close, wide margins at top, slight folds. (VA. Apr.27; 614)   R 300

PIRANESI, Giovanni Battista

– **Pianta di Roma e del Campo Marzo.** [Rome], ca. 1760. 1,210 × 700mm. Folding engraved plan, inset plan, many side notes. (S. Jun.25; 249)
Nebenzahl. £200

PLAN OF THE ATTACK OF THE FORTS CLINTON & MONTGOMERY upon Hudsons River ...

L., W. Faden, 1784. 26½ × 20 inches. Engraved hand-cold. map, slight traces of soiling. (SPB. Oct.26; 4)   £1,200

PLAN OF THE SURPRISE OF STONEY POINT

... L., W. Faden, 1784. 19¾ × 27¼ inches. Engraved hand-cold. map, slight staining at fold. (SPB. Oct.26; 5) $1,100

PLANCIUS, Petrus

– **Orbis Terrarum Typus, de Integro Multis in Locis Emendatus.** [Amst.], 1590 or later. 280 × 502mm. Double-p. engraved map in twin hemispheres engraved by Baptista van Deutecom, a version of the 1st. State, Dutch text on verso, strengthened & restored at additional folds, w.a.f. (S. May 21; 153)
Nebenzahl. £600

PLANISPHAERIUM STELLATUM

17th. C. 430 × 520mm. Hand-cold. engraved stellar map, slightly defect. at fold, F. (VG. Mar.22; 1591)
Fls. 700

PLOT, R.

[–] **Map of Staffordshire.** [Oxford], 1682 or later. 630 × 536mm. Map, engraved by J. Browne, embellished with escutcheons in borders, margins shaved (as usual), slight wear at folds. (S. Jun.25; 415)
£80

POIRSON, Jean Baptiste

– **Cours du Mississipi Comprenant la Louisiane.** [Paris], 1803. 540 × 415mm. Engraved map, hand-cold. in outl., some light foxing, earlier fold marks. (SG. Dec.15; 40) $200

POPPLE, Henry

– **Map of the British Empire in America with the French, Spanish & Hollandish Settlements.** Covens & Mortier, ca. 1740. 570 × 1,040mm. Copper engraved map, old outl. col., lge. figure cartouche & ill. in 2 ll., not joined. (R. Oct.13; 3472)   DM 1,010

– – **Anr. Edn.** Covens & Mortier, n.d. Ob. fo. Old outl. cold. copper engraved map, figure cartouche, decor., 4 sm. views, 17 town plans at side. (R. Oct.13; 3487)   DM 2,100

– **Nouvelle Carte Particulière de l'Amérique.** Covens & Mortier, ca. 1730. 570 × 1,040mm. Copper engraved old outl. cold map, in 2 ll., not joined. (R. Oct.13; 3503)   DM 2,300

PORCACCHI, Thomaso

– **Discorso Intorno alla Carta da Navigare [World].** Ca. 1572 or later. Approx. 4 × 6 inches. Uncold. map, rhumb lines. (TA. Nov.17; 96)   £58

POWNALL, Thomas

– **Generalkarte van Nordamerika samt den Westin-dischen Inseln.** [Vienna], F.A. Schrambl, 1788 [or later]. 1,018 × 1,060mm. (total dimensions). Map in 4 double-p. engraved mapsheets, hand-cold. in outl., sm. hole at centrefold of 1 sheet not affecting engraved surface. (S. Dec.1; 235) *Robinson.* £180

POWNALL, Thomas

See— **ANVILLE, J.B.D. d' & Pownall, Thomas**

PRIESTLEY, J. & Walker, John

– **Map of the Inland Navigation, Canals & Rail Roads.** Wakefield, 1830. 1,915 × 1,700mm. Lge. engraved map in 54 sections, mntd. & dissected on linen, hand-cold. in wash & outl., folding into cont. cf. gt. bookstyle s.-c. (S. Apr.9; 141)
Shirley. £160

PTOLEMAEUS, Claudius

[–] **Asia ist Dervier Theisen des Erdtrichs eims** ... Ca. 1560 or later. Approx. 12 × 14 inches. Hand-cold. woodcut map, plain title cartouche, German text on verso. (TA. Jan.19; 144)   £100

[–] **Europa nach Gelegenheit** ... Ca. 1560 or later. Approx. 12 × 14 inches. Hand-cold. woodcut map, plain title cartouche. (TA. Jan.19; 145)   £125

[–] **Generale Ptholemei.** [Strassburg, Johannes Schott, 1513 or 1520]. 445 × 569mm. Double-p. map of Ptolemaic world, 1st. publd. in this form in Waldseemüller Strassburg edn. of 1513, old hand-cold., showing Europe, Asia & Africa surrounded by heads representing 12 winds, some faint margin surface dirt, restored at centre-fold, w.a.f. (S. May 21; 157)   *Rothman.* £1,200

– **Tabulae ex Asiae; continet Indian intra Gangem Fluvium.** Early 16th. C. Ob. fo. Woodcut map, old part col., lightly spotted or browned. (R. Apr.5; 3385)   DM 500

[–] **Tabula Nova Candiae.** [1541]. 11 × 18 inches. Woodcut map, Latin text on verso. (CSK. May 4; 219)   £130

QUAD, M.

[–] **Creta iovis Magni Medio Iacet Insula Ponto.** [1600]. 9 × 12½ inches. Engraved map, Latin text on verso, browned, clean tear on lr. margin. (CSK. May 4; 220)   £160

RAMUSIO, Giovanni Battista

[–] **Terza Ostro Tavola.** [Venice, 1554, or later]. 276 × 374mm. Double-p. engraved map, centrefold restored. (S. Apr.9; 97)   *Whiteson.* £270

RAPKIN, J.

– **Thibet, Mongolia & Mandchouria.** Ill.:– H. Winkles. L., L. Printing & Publishing. 1856. 9½ × 13 inches. Engraved map, 6 sm. hand-cold. vigs. & decor. border, paper slightly darkening. (CBA. Aug.21; 834) $150

RATZER, Bernard

[–] **The Province of New Jersey Divided into East & West** ... L., William Faden, 1778. *'2nd. Edn.'.* 30½ × 22 inches. Engraved map, partly hand-cold. in outl., elab. scenic cartouche, inset table, slight browning & offsetting. (SPB. May 23; 15) $1,200

REMONDINI
See— BONNE, Rigobert

ROBERT, S.
- Carte des Grandes Routes d'Angleterre, d'Ecosse, et d'Irlande. N.d. 580 × 470mm. Engraved map, cold. in outl., pict. title cartouche, mntd. under glass in hogarth frame. (PD. Dec.14; 286) £90

ROBERT, Sr.
- Mapa de España. Paris, 1757. 560 × 490mm. Outl. cold. map. (DS. Mar.23; 2425) Pts. 20,000

ROBERT DE VAUGONDY, Gilles Robert de & Didier Robert de
See— VAUGONDY, Gilles Robert de & Didier Robert de

ROCQUE, John
- England & Wales, Drawn from the Most Accurate Surveys, Containing All the Cities, Boroughs, Market Towns & Villages. L., Sayer, [1780]. 2 lge. double-p. folding engraved sheets forming a map approx. 120 × 100cm., hand-cold. in outl., elab. pict. title cartouche, several fleets of ships, sm. inset map of the Scilly Isles, good margins, versos blank, some rubbing & offsetting, minor discolouration at some folds, a few repairs on verso. (SG. Jun.7; 134) $150
- An Exact Survey of the City & Suburbs of Dublin. L., [1756, or later]. 1,000 × 1,410mm. Lge. engraved plan in 4 sheets, engraved by A. Dury, linen mntd., browned, one sheet frayed. (S. Apr.9; 146) *Neptune.* £160

ROTENHAN, Sebastian A.
- Franciae Orientalis (vvlgo Franckenlant). Antw., Ortelius, ca. 1590. Fo. Cold. map, col. not cont., imprint slightly weak in parts. (HK. Nov.12; 5527) DM 420

RYTHER, Augustus
- Oxonia Antiqua Instaurata. [1588]. 680 × 990mm. (plt.-mark). Etched & engraved map, on 2 sheets joined together, margins, paper loss lr. right corner, some defects at edges of sheet, & some other defects, laid down on stretcher. (BS. Sep.21; 94) £160

SAMPEI, M.
- [-] Dai Nihon Zenzu. [Tokyo], before 1878. 1,800 × 2,000mm. (approx.). Lge. engraved wall-map in 2 sheets, mntd. on canvas & rollers, insets, block-cold., in Japanese, some fraying at outer margins. (S. Apr.9; 109) *Burgess.* £130

SANDRART, Joachim
- Nova Tabula Americae. Ill.:– J.B. Homann. N.d. Ob. fo. Cold. copper engraved map, 2 painted figure cartouches, decor., 3 pp. reprd., slightly spotted. (R. Oct.13; 3429) DM 1,000

SANSON D'ABBEVILLE, Nicolas
- Africa ... Paris, 1650. 390 × 550mm. Line engraved map, cold. outl. (VA. Apr.27; 595) R 180
- L'America Settentrionale. De Rossi, 1687. Ob. fo. Copper engraved map, figure cartouche. (R. Oct.13; 3482) DM 900
- L'Amérique Septentrionale. 1669. 560 × 405mm. Partly cold. map. (P. Jul.5; 411) £280
- – Anr. Edn. H. Jaillot, 1674. 550 × 875mm. Cold. copper engraved. map, ptd. from 2 plts., 2 lge. painted figure cartouches, cartouche & caption at top, col. slightly offset, lightly spotted. (R. Oct.13; 3481) DM 1,100
- [-] Carte Générale de la Caroline. Amst., [1700 or later]. 750 × 470mm. Full-p. engraved regional map incorporating detailed inset plan of Charles Town, adapted extensively from the Thornton, Morden & Lea map of [1685], fully hand-cold., heightened with gold, w.a.f. (S. May 22; 355) *Robinson.* £320
- [-] Carte Nouvelle de l'Amérique Angloise. Amst., P. Mortier, [1700 or later]. 594 × 900mm. Double-p. engraved map extending from southern Greenland to Mississippi by way of Hudson Bay, the Great Lakes, Maritime Provinces & Atlantic Seaboard, based largely on Thornton & Morden map of [1685] & showing effective Fr. control of Hudson

Bay region, the whole hand-cold., a few short symbols touched in gold, w.a.f. (S. May 22; 367) *Fergusson.* £680
- Les Isles Britanniques. Paris, 1673 [or later]. 562 × 906mm. Double-p. engraved map, hand-cold. in outl., inset showing Orkney, Shetland & Faroes, lge. cartouches uncold., sm. stain in lr. corners. (S. Nov.1; 145) *Thorp.* £85
- Iudaea, seu Terra Sancta quae Hebraeorum sive Israelitorum in suas Duodecim Tribus Divisa. Paris, 1677 [or later]. *Early Imp.* 545 × 860mm. Double-p. engraved map, outl. hand-cold., cartouches with figures of Moses, & Adam & Eve, sm. stain, faint dust-soiling, light crease at centre-fold. (S. Nov.1; 243) *Davis.* £100
- – Anr. Edn. H. Jaillot, 1691. Imp. ob. fo. Outl. cold. copper-engraved map, cartouche, some old soiling, partly bkd. (V. Sep.29; 223) DM 400
- – Anr. Edn. Amst., P. Schenk, ca. 1705. 490 × 585mm. Engraved map, from Schenk's 'Atlas Contractus', hand-cold., uncold. title & scale cartouches with figures, minor separation at centre fold, some light offsetting, liby. stp. (SG. Dec.15; 104) $100
- Mappa Mondo o vero Carta Generale del Globo Terestre. Rome, G.J. de Rossi, 1864 [or later]. 386 × 576mm. Double-p. engraved map, slight soiling. (S. Apr.9; 135) *Goldbaum.* £240
- Le Nouveau Continent ou L'Amérique. Amst., H. de Leth, ca. 1720. 520 × 490mm. Partly cold. map. (P. Dec.8; 436) *Radford.* £220
- Partie Meridionale de l'Inde en deux Presqu'Isles ... Paris, 1654. Approx. 15 × 21 inches. Map, hand-cold. in outl., uncold. ornamental title cartouche. (TA. Jun.21; 137) £70

SANSON D'ABBEVILLE, Nicolas & Jaillot, Hubert
- Archevesché et Eslectorat de Cologne. Jaillot, 1692. Outl. cold. copper-engraved map, minimal foxing. (V. Sep.30; 3030) DM 500
- Basse Partie de l'Evesche de Munster. Jaillot, 1692. Outl. cold. copper-engraved map. (V. Sep.29; 685) DM 450
- Carte des Pais situez entre la Moselle, la Saare, le Rhein, et la Basse Alsace. Iaillot, 1692. Fo. Outl. cold. copper-engraved map, slightly browned, partly bkd. (V. Sep.29; 808) DM 400
- Le Cercle de la Basse Saxe. Paris, H. Jaillot, 1676 [or later]. *Early Imp.* 553 × 888mm. Double-p. engraved map, hand-cold. in outl., light crease, faint offsetting. (S. Dec.1; 60) *Schuster.* £60
- Le Cercle de Souabe. Jaillot, 1692. Ob. fo. Outl. cold. copper engraved map, lightly browned, partly bkd. (V. Sep.29; 953) DM 400
- Le Cercle de Westphalie. Paris, 1675 [or later]. *Early Imp.* 840 × 575mm. Double-p. engraved map, outl. hand-cold., sm. wormhole at centre-fold without serious loss. (S. Nov.1; 253) *Schwedt.* £70
- – Anr. Edn. Iaillot, 1692. Fo. Outl. cold. copper engraved map, slightly browned, 1 sm. piece bkd. (V. Sep.29; 929) DM 400
- Le Cercle Eslectoral du Rhein. Jaillot, 1692. Fo. Outl. cold. copper-engraved map, lr. part lightly browned. (V. Sep.29; 768) DM 600
- Le Cours du Danvbe depuis sa Source Jusqu'à ses Embouchures. Paris, Jaillot, 1696. 600 × 1,210mm. Cold. ptd. map from 3 plts., cartouches with port., arms, etc., old col., 5 views in lr. margin, sm. detail map, multi-folded, some light spotting, some sm. holes, some scratches, slight creasing. (HK. Nov.12; 5629) DM 850
- Le Duché de Berg. Iaillot, 1692. Outl. cold. copper-engraved map. (V. Sep.29; 383) DM 850
- Haute Partie de l'Evesché de Munster. Jaillot, 1692. Outl. cold. copper engraved map, lightly browned. (V. Sep.29; 686) DM 650
- La Suisse divisée en ses Treize Cantons. Jaillot, 1693. Ob. fo. Outl. cold. copper-engraved map, 3 arms, sm. tear bkd. (V. Sep.29; 296) DM 900

SAUTHIER, Claude Joseph
- A Chorographical Map of the Provinces of New-York in North America ... L., William Faden, Jan. 1779. 72 × 54 inches. Engraved map, in 6 sheets, joined into 3, partly hand-cold. in outl., slight traces of margin browning, some slight offsetting & traces of discolouration. (SPB. May 23; 16) $1,300
- A Map of the Province of New-York ... to which is added New Jersey ... L., William Faden, 1776.

28 × 22½ inches. Engraved map, partly hand-cold., extensive margins, overall offsetting & light browning, trace of foxing. (SPB. May 23; 17) $1,100
- A Plan of the Operations of the King's Army under the Command of General Sr. William Howe, K.B. in New York & East New Jersey, against the American Forces commanded by General Washington, From the 12th of October, to the 28th of November 1776. L., William Faden, 1777. 730 × 490mm. Double-p. engraved map, hand-cold. notations for troop encampments & movements, satisfactory margins, verso blank, minor offsetting, 2 early creases, repair to 1, corner replaced. (SG. Jun.7; 67) $350
- A Topographical Map of Hudsons River. L., 1776. 790 × 530mm. Double-p. engraved tripartite map, from Faden's 'North American Atlas', hand-cold. in outl., 2 margins trimmed, slight spotting, fold marks. (SG. Dec.15; 41) $325

SAVANNAH
- Plan of the Siege of Savannah. [L., 1794]. 400 × 570mm. Engraved map, from Stedman's 'History of the ... American War', margins reprd., foxed. on verso, earlier fold marks. (SG. Dec.15; 42) $150

SAXTON, Christopher
- Anglia, Regnum. [Antw., J.B. Vrients], 1602 or 1603. 385 × 485mm. Double-p. engraved map, hand-cold. in wash & outl., lge. title cartouche & other embellishments fully cold., Spanish text on verso, sm. flaw at centrefold affecting engraved surface, F. & G. (S. Dec.1; 143) *Thulin Antik.* £230
- Cestriae. 1597. 15½ × 20½ inches. Engraved map, cont. hand-colouring in outl., some light offsetting, laid down, F. & G. (CSK. Mar.9; 23) £1,300
- The County of Hereford. Resurveyed & Enlarged [by Philip Lea]. 1665. Approx. 15 × 20 inches. Hand-cold. map, ornamental title cartouche with side figures, surmounted by Royal arms, separate scale of distance surmounted by open dividers, inset plan, armorials, etc., partially split at base of centrefold, without loss, F. & G. (TA. Jul.19; 133) £110
- Hartfordiae Comitatus Nova, Vera, ac Particularis Descriptio. Anno Dni, 1577. 1577 [or later]. 400 × 500mm. Double-p. county map engraved by Nicholas Raynolds, early hand-cold. in outl., elab. title-cartouche fully so, lr. margin cropped & restored, slight damage at centre fold affecting engraved surface, faint overall browning, F. & G. w.a.f. (S. May 21; 45) *Burgess.* £520
- – Anr. Edn. [1579]. 505 × 404mm. Cont. hand-cold. map, bunch of grapes watermark, upr. & lr. margins trimmed not affecting plt. surface, F. & G. (P. Mar.15; 418) *Burgess.* £1,500
- Lincolnshire & Nottinghamshire. Ca. 1576. 18½ × 23¼ inches. Hand-cold. engraved map, by Remigious, F. & G. (SKC. Nov.18; 2079) £280
- Mone Insulae modo Anglesey, et Caernaruan. 1578. 485 × 355mm. Cont. hand-cold. map, bunch of grapes watermark, some browning & discolouration, laid down. (P. Jun.7; 364) £420
- Montgomeri ac Merinidh. 1578. 345 × 455mm. (plt.-mark). Hand-cold. engraved map, by Remigius Hogenberg, some worming along central vertical fold, slightly stained, F. (BS. Sep.21; 102) £150
- Norfolciae Comitatus. 1574. 490 × 335mm. Engraved hand-cold. map, engraved by Cornelius Hogius, good margins, 2 wormholes, sm. hole reprd. (P. Oct.20; 271) £1,150
- Northamton Bedfordiae Cantabrigiae Huntingdoniae et Rutlandiae Comitatuum ... 1576 [or later]. 396 × 519mm. Double-p. map, probably engraved by Lenaert Terwoort, in State I (without the additional place-names & ring-fences in Bedfordshire mentioned by Tooley & detailed in Evans & Lawrence), early col., sm. flaws just affecting engraved surface at centrefold. (S. Dec.1; 148) *Burgess.* £1,050
- Oxford, Buckingham & Bark-Shire. 1690. 455 × 405mm. Hand-cold. map, inset town plan, F. & G. (P. Jan.12; 362) *Traylen.* £270
- Salopiae Comitatus, Ao. Dm. 1577. 1576 [or later]. 395 × 527 mm. Double-p. map, engraved by Remy Hogenberg, hand-cold. in outl., architectural title-cartouche & Seckford arms fully so, faint

SAXTON, Christopher -*Contd.*

offsetting, gt. F. & G., w.a.f. (S. May 21; 50)
Burgess. £440
- **Shropshire.** 1577. Hand-cold. engraved map, by Remigious, classical cartouche surmounted by heraldic device. (SKC. Nov.18; 2083) £280
- **Universi Derbiensis Comitatus Graphica Descriptio 1577.** 1577 [or later]. 393 × 480mm. Double-p. map, probably engraved by Francis Scatter, cold., cartouche, Royal & Seckford arms fully so, slight cockling at lr. margin, gt. F. & G., w.a.f. (S. May 21; 42) *Kentish*. £680
- **Warwic-Lecestriaeq ... Vera Descriptio. Ano Dni 1576.** 1576 [or later]. 395 × 327mm. Double-p. map, engraved by Lenaert Terwoort, hand-cold. in outl., cartouches, Royal & Seckford arms fully so, faint offsetting, gt. F. & G., w.a.f. (S. May 21; 53) *Kentish*. £680

SAXTON, Christopher & Hole, William
- **Eboracensis Comitatus.** 1577 [but 1579]. 21 × 29 inches overall. Engraved map, on 2 sheets, hand-cold. in outl., a few light stains on upr. margins, F. & G. (CSK. Mar.9; 37) £700
- **Eboracensis Comitatus pars Occidentalis vulgo West Riding.** 1607 or later. Approx. 10½ × 12½ inches. Uncold. map, sm. strapwork title cartouche, separate scale of distance with compass rose & surmounted by open dividers. (TA. Jul.19; 169) £50
- **Lancastriae Comitatus Palatinus olim pars Brigantum.** [1607]. Approx. 11½ × 12½ inches. Map, cont. hand-cold. in outl., ornamental strapwork title cartouche with figures, garlands of fruit, etc., separate scale of distance surmounted by open dividers, lge. compass rose, etc., Engl. text on verso, closely cropped along lr. margin. (TA. May 17; 180) £50
- - **Anr. Edn.** Ca. 1637 or later. Approx. 11½ × 12 inches. Hand-cold. map, ornamental strapwork title cartouche incorporating cherubs & fruit, etc., scale of distance surmounted by open dividers, lge. compass rose. (TA. Mar.15; 146) £55
- - **Anr. Edn.** Ca. 1680 or later. Approx. 11½ × 12 inches. Hand-cold. map, decor. title cartouche with cherubs & fruit, scale of distance surmounted by open dividers, compass rose. (TA. Nov.17; 110) £50
- **Oxoniensis.** Camden, early 16th. C. Partly cold. map, F. & G. (P. Dec.8; 417) *Hadden*. £50

SAXTON, Christopher & Kip, William
- **Dorcestriae comitatus vulgo Dorsett.** [1637]. 280 × 390mm. Engraved map, hand-cold. in outl., margins lightly stained, F. & G. (CSK. Dec.2; 12) £55

SAYER, Robert
- **Plymouth Sound, Hamoaze & Catawater, Surveyed in 1786.** 1791. Approx. 27½ × 20 inches. Uncold. map, ornamental title cartouche, compass rose, rumb lines, etc. (TA. Mar.15; 104) £62
See— JEFFERY, Thomas

SAYER, Robert & Bennett, John
- **A New & Correct Plan of the Cities of London & Westminster.** 1781. Hand-cold. plan, F. & G. (P. Sep.8; 473) *Map House*. £55
- **A New Map of the Whole Continent of America, Divided into North & South & West Indies.** 1777. Approx. 42 × 48 inches. Map, in 2 sheets, hand-cold. in outl., uncold. decor. title cartouche. (TA. Sep.15; 184) £155
- **A Plan of the Battle on Bunkers Hill.** L., 27 Nov. 1775. 593 × 475mm. Engraved map, hand-cold. in outl., inset above a 3-column panel of text entitled 'The following Description of the Action near Boston ... ', untrimmed, with deckle edges intact, a few soft creases. (CNY. May 18; 95) $1,400
See— BRASSIER, William
See— Book Section: BURGOYNE, Lieut.-Gen. John — HOWE, Visc. William — SAYER, Robert & Bennett, John, Publishers

SCHEDLER, J.
- **Karte vom Bodensee und Seiner Umgebung zum Hand- u. Reisegebrauch.** Constanz, ca. 1850. 570 × 810mm. Decor. map, margins soiled & slightly crumpled. (GF. Nov.12; 784) Sw.Frs. 500

SCHENK, Pieter
- **Africae in Mappa Geographica Delineatio.** Amst., ca. 1750. 500 × 580mm. Hand-cold. engraved map, centre fold, corners defect., F. (VG. Mar.22; 1609) Fls. 700
- **America.** Ca. 1700. Cont. cold. copper engraved map, outl. & surface cold., with North & South America, 2 cartouches. (BR. Apr.13; 2892) DM 840
- **America Septentrionalis, Novissima. America Meriodionalis, Accuratissima.** Amst., early 18th. C. 480 × 560mm. Engraved map, hand-cold., 2 uncold. title cartouches with figures, centre fold, with some breaks & repairs, title cartouches rather faint imps., liby. stp. (SG. Dec.15; 43) $350
- **Diversa Orbis Terrae Visu Incedente per Coluros Tropicorum Ambos eius Polos ...** Amst., ca. 1700. 511 × 590mm. Copper engraved world map in 2 hemispheres, cont. outl. & surface col., surrounded by sm. globes, 2 cartouches, sm. tears, middle fold & lr. margin partly bkd. (GB. Nov.3; 550) DM 1,300
- - **Anr. Copy.** Copper engraved map, cont. outl. & surface col., surrounded by 12 pole & globe maps & 2 cartouches on dark background. (BR. Apr.13; 2876) DM 1,200
- **Planisphaerium Coeleste.** Amst., ca. 1700. 487 × 562mm. Double-p. engraved map, partly hand-cold., sm. split in centrefold reprd. (S. Mar.6; 117) *Hepner*. £120

SCHENK, Pieter & Valck, Gerard
- **Haemisphaerium Australe.** Amst., ca. 1750. 430 × 510mm. Hand-cold. engraved stellar map, F. (VG. Mar.22; 1593) Fls. 450
- **Nortfolicia; Vernacule Norfoske.** Amst., ca. 1720 or later. Approx. 15 × 19 inches. Map, uncold., ornamental title cartouche with cherubs, separate scale of distance with figures & animals, armorials, etc. (TA. Jun.21; 118) £70
- **Nova et Accurata Japoniae Terrae Esonis ac Insularum adj.** N.d. Cold. copper-engraved map, slight old marks in wide margin. (V. Sep.29; 241) DM 480
- **Nova et Accurate Poli Arctici.** Ca. 1660. 525 × 415mm. Hand-cold. map. (P. Dec.8; 426) *Faupel*. £75
See— JANSSON, Jan or Johannes

SEALE, R.W.
- **Correct Chart of the Baltick or East Sea.** Ca. 1760. Ob. fo. Cold. copper engraved map for Rapin's History, painted floral cartouche & sm. supp. map, slightly spotted, sm. hole, cut. to plt. at top. (R. Oct.13; 3378) DM 440
- **Plans of the Principal Towns, Ports & Harbours in Ireland.** [L.], ca. 1770. 16 × 19½ inches. Uncold. map. F. (GM. Dec.7; 519) £80

SENEX, John
- **A New Mapp of Scotland.** L., [1721]. 570 × 470mm. Hand-cold. map, cartouche. (P. May 17; 438) *Morrison*. £80
- **A New Map of the World.** Ca. 1719. 430 × 540mm. Hand-cold. engraved map, lightly creased, 1 clean tear along margin. (CSK. Dec.2; 11) £220

SEUTTER, Georg Matthaeus
- **Africa Iuxta Navigationes et Observationes Recentissimas.** Augsburg, 1735 or later. 500 × 570mm. Double-p. engraved map, hand-cold. in wash & outl. (S. Dec.13; 20) *Cholmeley*. £110
- - **Anr. Edn.** [Augsburg], ca. 1735. 495 × 565mm. Double-p. engraved map, main areas lightly hand-cold., elab. title cartouche uncold., margins trimmed, no text on verso, rubbed, some creasing & sm. holing at cartouche. (SG. Dec.15; 21) $110
- - **Anr. Edn.** Augsburg, J.M. Probst, 1760 or later. 500 × 570mm. Double-p. engraved map, hand-cold. in wash & outl. (S. Mar.6; 141) *Beale*. £180
- **Asia cum Omnibus Imperiis Provinciis, Statibus et Insulis.** Augsburg, 1737 or later. 493 × 575mm. Double-p. engraved map, hand-cold. in wash & outl. (S. Dec.13; 10) *Burgess*. £120
- - **Anr. Edn.** Augsburg, J.M. Probst, 1760 or later. 497 × 575mm. Engraved map, hand-cold. in wash & outl. (S. Mar.6; 147) *Waterloo*. £70
- **Diversi Globi Terr-Aqvei.** Augsburg, ca. 1730. World map with both hemispheres & 8 supp. maps, some sm. splits, 2 sm. faults bkd., margins bkd.,

with repairs, some light spotting, F. (HK. Nov.12; 5405) DM 1,050
- **Holmia Celberrima Metropolis et Sedes Regia Regni Sueciae.** Augsburg, [1745, or later]. 493 × 574mm. Double-p. engraved plan, title repeated in German, 2 perspective views, plan hand-cold., stained. (S. Apr.9; 133) *Bucherkabinett*. £170
- **Nova Totius Helvetiae Tab. Geogr.** N.d. Ob. fo. Old cold. copper engraved map, 4 lge. figure cartouches, slightly spotted sm. margin tear, bkd. without loss. (R. Oct.13; 3969) DM 600
- - **Anr. Copy.** Ob. fo. Old cold. copper engraved map, 4 lge. figure cartouches, sm. tear at foot bkd., slightly spotted. (R. Apr.5; 3838) DM 500
See— KONIG, E.G.

SMITH, William 'the Anonymous Mapmaker'
[-] **Hartfordiae Comitatus Nova Descriptio.** John Overton (retaining Peter Stent's overprint), 1665 or later. 392 × 485mm. Double-p. engraved map, based on Norden's map of 1598, showing roads & giving detailed key to symbols depicted, hand-cold., sm. stain at lr. centrefold, F. & G., w.a.f. (S. May 21; 46) *Tooley*. £260
[-] **Suffolciae Comitatus Descriptio.** J. Overton, but ca. 1665 or later. 335 × 472mm. Double-p. engraved map after Christopher Saxton (1575), hand-cold. in outl., Skelton's State III, F. & G., w.a.f. (S. May 21; 51) *Hulme*. £280

SPEEDE, John
- **Africae described ...** G. Humble, 1626 [but later]. 395 × 510mm. Hand-cold. double-p. engraved map, upr. frieze of 8 town views, side borders of costumed figures, Engl. text on verso, crease at centrefold, F. & double-G. (S. Jun.25; 75) *Player*. £220
- **America with those Known Parts in that Unknowne Worlde.** Bassett & Chiswell, 1676 or later. 16 × 20½ inches. Hand-cold. engraved map, bird's eye views of towns on top border, side borders of native galleons & monsters at sea, text on reverse, a few slight holes, F., w.a.f. (LC. Mar.1; 276) £680
- **Anglesey Antiently called Mona.** R. Rea the elder & younger, 1610 [but 1662 or later]. 387 × 513mm. Double-p. engraved map, hand-cold. in outl., inset plan of Beaumaris, few minor repairs, laid down, F. & G. (S. Nov.1; 167) *Windsor*. £80
- **Barkshire Described.** 1611-12 or later. Approx. 15 × 20 inches. Hand-cold. map, central ornamental title cartouche with cherubs, compass rose, extensive view of Windsor, etc., Engl. text on verso, strengthened along centrefold, F. & double-G. (TA. Jan.19; 89) £135
- - **Anr. Edn.** Bassett & Chiswell, [1676]. 510 × 385mm. Hand-cold. map, inset of Windsor Castle, F. & G. (P. Mar.15; 421) £160
- - **Anr. Copy.** Hand-cold. map, F. & double-G. (P. Jun.7; 378) £90
- **Bedfordshire.** 1646. 390 × 510mm. Engraved map, hand-cold. in outl., some light spotting, F. & G. (CSK. Jan.13; 217) £160
- **Bermuda.** Bassett & Chiswell, [1676]. 535 × 410mm. Hand-cold. map, repairs to margin & centrefold. (P. Apr.12; 363) *Watson*. £260
- **The Bishoprick & City of Durham.** [1611]. Map, town plan, arms. F. & G. (P. Oct.20; 299) £110
- - **Anr. Copy.** Hand-cold. map, inset plan of Durham, F. & G. (P. Nov.24; 322) *Steedman*. £95
- - **Anr. Edn.** [1676]. Hand-cold. map, fold creased, margins strengthened, some stains, F. & G. (P. Sep.29; 458) *Archibald*. £80
- **Breknoke, both Shyre & Towne Described.** Bassett & Chiswell, 1610 [1676]. Approx. 15 × 20 inches. Uncold. map, ornamental strapwork title cartouche incorporating Royal arms & county crest, inset detail of Breknoke. (TA. Mar.15; 77) £70
- **Britain.** Bassett & Chiswell, [1676]. Hand-cold. map, arms, figures & scenes on side borders, F. & double-G. (P. Mar.15; 424) *Mannings*. £270
- **Buckinghamshire.** 1611 or later. 15 × 20 inches. Hand-cold. engraved map, 2 town plans, heraldic devices in architectural frames, cut. (SKC. May 4; 1529) £100
- - **Anr. Edn.** George Humble, [1627]. 15 × 20 inches. Engraved map, hand-cold. in outl., margins lightly soiled, window mount. (CSK. May 4; 9) £180

– – **Anr. Edn.** [1676]. Approx. 15 × 20 inches. Hand-cold. map, sm. title & dedication cartouches, separate scale of distance surmounted by open dividers, compass rose, inset details of Buckingham & Redding, armorials, etc., Engl. text on verso, strengthened along centrefold, a little stained, F. & double-G. (TA. Jan.19; 90) £90

– – **Anr. Copy.** Engraved map, hand-cold. outl., F. & G. (CSK. Jul.6; 209) £60

– – **Anr. Edn.** L., T. Bassett & R. Chiswell, 1676 or later. 381 × 513mm. Double-p. engraved map, inset plans, escutcheons fully cold., F. & G. (S. Mar.6; 174) *Old Hall.* £130

– **Caermarden, by Shyre & Towne Described.** Bassett & Chiswell, 1662 [1676]. Approx. 15 × 20 inches. Uncold. map, ornamental strapwork title cartouche surmounted by Royal arms with compass rose below & separate scale of distance below that, inset details of Caermarden, Engl. text to verso. (TA. Mar.15; 78) £65

– **Caernarvonshire.** 1610. 16 × 18½ inches. Hand-cold. engraved map, Caernarvon & Bangor town plans, F. & G. to obverse. (SKC. Nov.18; 2067) £60

– **Cambridgeshire.** 1611 or later. 19 × 24 inches. Hand-cold. engraved map, town plan, College coats-of-arms, Dons, etc., F. & G. (SKC. May 4; 1525) £100

– **Cardigan Shyre Described.** L., J. Sudbury & G. Humble, 1610 [but 1611 or later]. 383 × 511mm. Double-p. engraved map, with inset plan, hand-cold. in outl., embellishments fully cold., Engl. text on verso, centrefold strengthened, cut close at upr. margin, F. & G. (S. Mar.6; 183) *Export.* £70

– – **Anr. Edn.** 1610 [1676 or later]. Approx. 15 × 20 inches. Map, hand-cold. in outl., strapwork title cartouche, separate scale of distance, inset plan of Cardigan, sailing ships, sea monsters, etc., some stains to lr. margin, F. & G. (TA. Jun.21; 100) £85

– **Cornwall.** J. Sudbury & G. Humble, 1611 or later. *1st. Edn.* 382 × 511mm. Double-p. engraved map, inset view, Engl. text on verso, F. & double-G. (S. Jun.25; 372) *Ross.* £250

– – **Anr. Edn.** Sudbury & Humble, [1611]. Hand-cold. map, inset town plan, arms, some browning, F. & G. (P. Sep.29; 461) *Price.* £280

– – **Anr. Edn.** L., T. Bassett & R. Chiswell, 1610 [but 1676, or later]. 383 × 510mm. Double-p. engraved map, inset view, hand-cold. in outl., embellishments fully so, split at centre-fold, reprd., F. & G. (S. Apr.9; 144) *Welbeck.* £90

– **The Countie & Citie of Lyncolne described.** T. Bassett & R. Chiswell, 1676 or later. 385 × 512mm. Double-p. engraved map, hand-cold. in outl., inset plan, Engl. text on verso, F. & double-G. (S. Jun.25; 398) *Roberts.* £140

– **The Countie of Leinster with the Citie Dublin Described.** J. Sudbury & G. Humble, 1610. 16 × 21 inches. Engraved hand-cold. map with inset plan of Dublin, faint stain in lr. left-hand corner, Engl. text on verso, F. & G.; from liby. of Luttrellstown Castle, w.a.f. (C. Sep.28; 1720) £180

– **The Countie of Nottingham.** Sudbury & Humble, [1611]. Hand-cold. map, inset town plan, arms, F. & double-G. (P. Jun.7; 383) £90

– – **Anr. Edn.** Bassett & Chiswell, [1676]. 15 × 20 inches. Engraved map, lr. margin slightly reprd. (CSK. May 4; 144) £75

– **The Countie Palatine of Lancaster, Described & Divided into Hundreds.** Bassett & Chiswell, 1610 [but 1676]. Approx. 15 × 20 inches. Hand-cold. map, strapwork title cartouche, inset detail of Lancaster, ports., Royal arms, etc., Engl. text on verso. (TA. Nov.17; 107) £240

– – **Anr. Edn.** L., Bassett & Chiswell, 1676. Map, badly foxed, 2 sm. tears, margins stuck down to wooden frame. (P. May 17; 467) *Shaw.* £80

– – **Anr. Edn.** Henry Overton, [1713 or 1743]. Approx. 15 × 20 inches. Map, hand-cold. in outl., ornamental title cartouche, inset plan of Lancaster, several ports. of Kings & Queens, compass rose, sailing ship, etc. (TA. Mar.15; 76) £220

– – **Anr. Edn.** N.d. 16½ × 20 inches. Hand-cold. engraved map, isometric town plan & profiles of Kings & Queens, trimmed, F. & G. (SKC. May 4; 1536) £150

– **The Countie of Radnor Described & the Shyre-townes Sittuatione ... Described by Christopher**

Saxton ... Bassett & Chiswell, 1610 [1676]. Approx. 15 × 20 inches. Uncold. map, strapwork title cartouche, separate scale of distance surmounted by compass rose, Royal arms, inset plan of Radnor, Engl. text to verso. (TA. Mar.15; 79) £55

– **The Countie of Warwick.** Bassett & Chiswell, [1676]. 520 × 400mm. Hand-cold. map, 2 inset town plans. (P. Apr.12; 384) *Welloeck.* £60

– **The Countie Westmorland & Kendale the Cheif Towne Described.** L., G. Humble, 1611 or later. 387 × 520mm. Double-p. hand-cold. engraved map, inset plan, Engl. text on verso, side-margins restored, F. & G. (S. Mar.6; 185) *Welbeck.* £90

– – **Anr. Edn.** Bassett & Chiswell, [1676]. 15 × 20 inches. Engraved map, margins slightly browned. (CSK. May 4; 14) £90

– **The Countye of Monmouth.** 1610 [1613-14 or later]. Approx. 15 × 20 inches. Map, hand-cold., strapwork title cartouche surmounted by county arms, separate scale of distance, inset plan of Monmouth, sailing ship, etc., F. & G. (TA. Jun.21; 99) £85

– – **Anr. Edn.** Bassett & Chiswell, 1676 or later. 16 × 21 inches. Engraved map, title with architectonic decor., coats of arms, galleon at sea, inset plan of Monmouth, Engl. text on reverse, F. & glazed on both sides, w.a.f. (LC. Mar.1; 264) £110

– **Cumberland.** 1611. 15 × 20 inches. Engraved map, slightly soiled. (CSK. Jul.6; 207) £70

– – **Anr. Edn.** Bassett & Chiswell, [1676]. 15 × 20 inches. Engraved map, lr. fold reprd. (CSK. May 4; 15) £90

– **Darbieshire described Anno 1610.** J. Sudbury & G. Humble, 1610 [1627 or later]. 385 × 504mm. Double-p. engraved map, inset plan & view, Engl. text on verso. (S. Jun.25; 374) *Kidd.* £110

– **Denbigh Shire.** Bassett & Chiswell, [1676]. Approx. 15 × 20 inches. Uncold. map, strapwork title cartouche, scale of distance surmounted by County crest, inset plan of Denbigh, sailing ship, Neptune, sea monster, etc., Engl. text to verso. (TA. Mar.15; 82) £70

– **Devonshire with Excester Described & the Armes of such Nobles as have borne the Titles of them.** Ca. 1600. Approx. 16 × 21 inches. Cont. hand-cold. map, F. (GM. Dec.7; 510) £90

– – **Anr. Edn.** L., J. Sudbury & G. Humble. [1611]. *1st. Edn.* 376 × 508mm. Double-p. engraved map, hand-cold. in outl., inset plan, etc. fully cold., minor print-crease at centrefold without loss, gt. F. & G. (S. Mar.6; 179) *Welbeck.* £160

– – **Anr. Edn.** Roger Rea, [1662]. Hand-cold. map, inset town plan, arms, F. & G. (P. Sep.29; 460) *Burgess.* £160

– – **Anr. Edn.** Bassett & Chiswell, 1676 or later. 15¼ × 20½ inches. Title with architectonic decor., inset plan of Exeter, Royal Arms & 9 other coats of arms, text on reverse, worn at foot of central fold, F., w.a.f. (LC. Mar.1; 277) £160

– – **Anr. Copy.** Approx. 15 × 20 inches. Hand-cold. map, ornamental strapwork title cartouche, separate scale of distance surmounted by open dividers & hf. compass rose, inset plan, Royal crest, armorials, etc., Engl. text on verso, 3 minor margin repairs. (TA. Jul.19; 128) £140

– – **Anr. Edn.** Christopher Browne, ca. 1690. Hand-cold. map, inset plan, arms, no text, 2 tears in margins not affecting plt. (P. Dec.8; 441) *Burgess.* £80

– **Dorsetshyre.** 1610 [1611-12 or later]. Approx. 15 × 20 inches. Uncold. map, ornamental title cartouche, separate scale of distance, inset plan of Dorchester, armorials, sailing ships, sea monsters, etc., trimmed to border, edges strengthened. (TA. Jan.19; 87) £125

– – **Anr. Edn.** [George Humble, 1627]. 15 × 20½ inches. Engraved map, margins reprd. (CSK. May 4; 22) £95

– – **Anr. Edn.** [1676]. 15 × 20 inches. Engraved map, crudely hand-cold. outl. (CSK. Jul.6; 211) £160

– – **Anr. Edn.** 1610 [1713 or later]. Approx. 15 × 20 inches. Uncold. map, corner title cartouche, separate scale of distance, inset plan, armorials, sailing ships, sea monsters, etc., trimmed to plt. mark. (TA. May 17; 172) £145

– **Essex.** G. Humble, [1611]. Hand-cold. map, inset town plan of Colchester, arms, slight wear to lr.

fold, laid down on card, F. & G. (P. Nov.24; 321) *Haddon.* £130

– – **Anr. Edn.** Bassett & Chiswell, [1676]. 390 × 520mm. Hand-cold. engraved map, reprd. along fold, F. & G. (CSK. Dec.2; 25) £95

– **Europe.** Bassett & Chiswell, 1676. Hand-cold. map, plans & figures on 3 borders, some repairs. (P. Dec.8; 423) *Keeting.* £140

– **Flint-Shire.** Bassett & Chiswell, [1676]. Approx. 15 × 20 inches. Uncold. map, sm. strapwork title cartouche, inset plans & details of Flint, St. Asaph, & St. Winiffred's Well, compass rose, sailing ships, sea monster, etc., Engl. text to verso. (TA. Mar.15; 80) £75

– **Glamorgan Shyre.** Sudbury & Humble, [1611]. Hand-cold. map, inset town plans, F. & G. (P. Sep.29; 462) *Archibald.* £160

– – **Anr. Edn.** George Humble, [1627]. 15½ × 20 inches. Engraved map, margins reprd. (CSK. May 4; 20) £90

– – **Anr. Edn.** Bassett & Chiswell, 1610 [1676]. Approx. 15 × 20 inches. Uncold. map, ornamental strapwork title cartouche, 2 inset plans, sailing ship, sea monster, etc., Engl. text on verso, some minor damage to base of centrefold. (TA. May 17; 170) £90

– **Glocestershire.** Sudbury & Humble, [1611]. 15 × 20 inches. Engraved map, hand-cold., repair on lr. fold, F. & G. (CSK. May 4; 2) £100

– – **Anr. Edn.** [1612]. Approx. 15 × 20 inches. Uncold. map, sm. strapwork title cartouche, inset town plans of Glocester & Bristow, Royal crest, armorials, etc., Engl. text to verso, some minor restoration, F. & double-G. (TA. Sep.15; 166) £160

– – **Anr. Edn.** 1662 or later. 16 × 20 inches. Hand-cold. engraved map, 2 town plans, armorial devices & battle scene, F. & G. (SKC. May 4; 1546) £120

– **Greece.** G. Humble, 1626. Hand-cold. map, late col., in mount. (P. Apr.12; 360) *Dupont.* £90

– **Hantshire.** Sudbury & Humble, [1611]. 15 × 20 inches. Engraved map, hand-cold. in outl., lr. margins reprd., wear along fold, F. & G., w.a.f. (CSK. Mar.9; 38) £110

– – **Anr. Edn.** 1611-12 or later. Approx. 15 × 20 inches. Uncold. map, ornamental title cartouche surmounted by Royal crest, inset detail of Winchester, several armorials, a little soiled overall, a few minor margin repairs at bottom, F. & double-G. (TA. Jan.19; 85) £100

– – **Anr. Edn.** 1627. 15½ × 20½ inches. Engraved map, Winchester town plan, heraldic devices, F. & G. to obverse. (SKC. Nov.18; 2073) £80

– – **Anr. Edn.** Sudbury & Humble. [1627]. Approx. 15 × 20 inches. Uncold. map, sm. ornamental title cartouche surmounted by Royal crest, separate scale of distance, inset plan, several armorials, etc., Engl. text on verso, sm. repair to base of centrefold. (TA. Jul.19; 129) £160

– – **Anr. Edn.** Bassett & Chiswell, [1676]. 510 × 380mm. Hand-cold. map, inset town plan. (P. Apr.12; 365) *Lobo.* £220

– – **Anr. Copy.** Hand-cold. map, inset town plan, arms, wormhole, few repairs. (P. May 17; 448) *Goodall.* £140

– – **Anr. Edn.** 1676 or later. Approx. 15 × 20 inches. Map, hand-cold., plain title cartouche surmounted by Royal crest, armorials, inset plan of Winchester, etc., some minor margin tears, slightly browned along centrefold, mntd. (TA. Jun.21; 104) £135

– **Hartfordshire.** Sudbury & Humble, [1611]. 395 × 515mm. Cont. hand-cold. map, 2 inset plans, slight split in fold, F. & double-G. (P. Jun.7; 385) £220

– – **Anr. Copy.** 390 × 520mm. Engraved map, hand-cold. in outl., sm. repair to fold & lr. margin, F. & G. (CSK. Feb.10; 49) £170

– – **Anr. Edn.** [William Humble, 1646]. 390 × 510mm. Engraved map, hand-cold. in outl., fold reprd., F. & G. (CSK. Sep.16; 1) £60

– **Herefordshire.** Sudbury & Humble, [1611]. Hand-cold. map, inset plan, arms, margins & centre-fold reprd., in mount. (P. Dec.8; 431) *Morrison.* £80

– **Holy Island, Garnsey, Farne, & Jarsey.** 1610 [1611-12 or later]. Approx. 15 × 20 inches. Map, single sheet divided into 4, each with sm. title

SPEEDE, John -*Contd.*

cartouche, hand-cold., Engl. text on verso, reprd. along centrefold. (TA. Jan.19; 86)   £65
- - **Anr. Edn.** Ca. 1610. 17 × 21 inches. 4 hand-cold. engraved maps on 1 sheet, F. & G. to obverse. (SKC. Nov.18; 2104)   £50
- - **Anr. Edn.** Bassett & Chiswell, [1676]. 15 × 20½ inches. Engraved map, margins lightly browned. (CSK. May 4; 25)   £60
- **The Isle of Man.** L., [1611]. Hand-cold. map, vig. sailing ships, F. & G. (P. May 17; 468)
Smith. £160
- - **Anr. Edn.** [George Humble, 1627]. 15 × 20 inches. Engraved map, margins reprd. (CSK. May 4; 19)   £120
- - **Anr. Edn.** Henry Overton, 1610 [1713 or 1743]. Approx. 15 × 20 inches. Map, partially cold. in outl., ornamental strapwork title cartouche, separate scale of distance surmounted by open dividers, central compass rose, rumb lines, sailing ships, etc., a little browned overall, mntd. (TA. Mar.15; 75)   £115
- **Kent.** [1611]. Hand-cold. map, 2 inset town plans, arms, slightly browned, F. & G. (P. Sep.29; 459)
Burgess. £200
- - **Anr. Edn.** 1613-14 or later. Approx. 15 × 20 inches. Map, hand-cold., sm. ornamental title cartouche, inset plans of Canterbury & Rochester, Royal crest, several armorials, sailing ship, etc., centrefold reprd., Engl. text to verso, F. & double-G. (TA. Jun.21; 101)   £190
- - **Anr. Edn.** 1611 [but 1627 or later]. 380 × 508mm. Double-p. engraved map, inset plans of Canterbury & Rochester, Engl. text on verso, sm. repair at lr. centre-fold, some strengthening, faint stain, F. & double-G. (S. Nov.1; 155)
Burgess. £170
- - **Anr. Edn.** [1627-76]. 388 × 520mm. (plt.-mark). Hand-cold. engraved map, central vertical fold, margins, Engl. text to verso, F. (BS. Sep.21; 100)   £220
- - **Anr. Edn.** L., T. Bassett & R. Chiswell, 1676 or later. 381 × 507mm. Double-p. engraved map, hand-cold. in wash & outl., 2 inset plans, faint stain at lr. right corner touching engraved surface, F. & G. (S. Dec.13; 191)   *Fancy.* £190
- **The Kingdom of China.** 1626. 400 × 530mm. Engraved cold. map with cartouches of Macas Quinzay, Execution, etc. in top border, & 8 costume figures in side borders, Engl. text on verso, F. & G. (PD. Aug.17; 314)   £170
- - **Anr. Edn.** L., 1626 [1627 or later]. 395 × 510mm. Double-p. engraved map, fully hand-cold., 4 vigs. in horizontal panel across top, 8 costume studies in 2 vertical panels at each side, good margins, Engl. text on verso, some rubbing, creasing. (SG. Jun.7; 95) $600
- - **Anr. Edn.** Bassett & Chiswell, 1626 [1676]. Approx. 15½ × 20 inches. Uncold. map, decor. with figures, town plans, etc., Engl. text on verso, minor repairs, F. & double-G. (TA. Nov.17; 82)   £120
- **The Kingdome of England.** Sudbury & Humble, 1611 or later. 15¾ × 20¾ inches. Hand-cold. engraved map, figures in side borders, galleons & monsters at sea, Engl. text on verso, F. (LC. Jul.5; 231)   £190
- - **Anr. Edn.** G. Humble, [1632]. 400 × 520mm. Cont. hand-cold. map, figures on side borders, F. & double-G. (P. Mar.15; 425)   £220
- - **Anr. Edn.** Bassett & Chiswell, [1676]. 15 × 20½ inches. Engraved map, hand-cold., sm. repair at lr. fold, F. & G. (CSK. May 4; 12)   £200
- **The Kingdome of Great Britain & Ireland.** Sudbury & Humble, [1611]. 505 × 380mm. Uncold. map, 2 inset town plans, browned. (P. Apr.12; 371)
Burgess. £150
- **The Kingdome of Ireland.** L., J. Sudbury & G. Humble, 1610 [but 1612 or later]. 386 × 511mm. Double-p. engraved map, 6 vigs., margin wormholes, F. & G. (S. Mar.6; 193)   *Potter.* £180
- **The Kingdome of Persia.** 1626. Hand-cold. map, town plans & figures on 3 borders, G. (P. Jan.12; 366)   *Dupont.* £110
- - **Anr. Edn.** Bassett & Chiswell, [1676]. 15½ × 20½ inches. Engraved map. (CSK. May 4; 140)   £120
- **The Kingdome of Scotland.** J. Sudbury & G.

Humble, 1610 [1611 or later]. 382 × 510mm. Hand-cold. double-p. engraved map, 4 vigs. of costumed figures, Engl. text on verso, minor repair at lr. centrefold. (S. Jun.25; 408)   £200
- - **Anr. Edn.** Bassett & Chiswell, [1676]. 390 × 510mm. Uncold. map, figures & inset plan of Orkney, fold creased. (P. Apr.12; 369)   £140
- **Leicester.** 1610 [1611-12 or later]. Approx. 15 × 20 inches. Map, hand-cold. in outl., sm. ornamental title cartouche, separate scale of distance, Royal crest, inset detail of Leicester, compass rose, armorials, etc., Engl. text on verso, strengthened along centrefold & minor repair to each bottom corner, Hogarth-style F., double-G. (TA. Jan.19; 81) £85
- - **Anr. Edn.** L., 1610 [but 1616]. 381 × 510mm. Double-p. engraved map, inset town plan, hand-cold. in outl., Latin text, slight soiling. (S. Apr.9; 150)   *Swales.* £160
- - **Anr. Edn.** Bassett & Chiswell, [1676]. 15 × 20 inches. Engraved map. (CSK. May 4; 143)   £90
- **A Map of Jamaica & Barbados.** Bassett & Chiswell, [1676]. 390 × 500mm. Hand-cold. map, late col. (P. Apr.12; 361)   £130
- - **Anr. Copy.** 380 × 510mm. Engraved map, hand-cold. in outl. (CSK. Feb.10; 2)   £95
- **The Mape of Hungari.** 1626. 400 × 515mm. Hand-cold. map, plans & figures on 3 edges. (P. Jan.12; 349)   *Broen.* £60
- - **Anr. Edn.** George Humble, 1626 [1676]. Approx. 15 × 20 inches. Hand-cold. map, sm. ornamental title cartouche, costumed figures to each side border, 4 miniature views along top border, Engl. text on verso, mntd. (TA. May 17; 174)   £84
- **Merioneth Shire.** Bassett & Chiswell, 1610 [1676]. Approx. 15 × 20 inches. Uncold. map, strapwork title cartouche surmounted by Royal crest, separate scale of distance with open dividers & cherubs, inset plan of Harlech, sailing ships, sea monster, etc., Engl. text to verso, partially split at base of centrefold, some light stains. (TA. Mar.15; 81)   £60
- - **Anr. Edn.** Bassett & Chiswell, [1676]. 390 × 510mm. Uncold. map, inset town plan. (P. Feb.16; 311)   £50
- **Midel-Sex Described with the Most Famous Cities of London & Westminster.** George Humble, 1611 or later. 15¼ × 20¼ inches. Hand-cold. engraved map after John Norden, inset plans of L. & Westminster, views of St. Peters & St. Pauls, text on reverse, some spotting, split at foot of central fold, F., w.a.f. (LC. Mar.1; 275)   £160
- - **Anr. Edn.** [Sudbury &] Humble, [1612]. 390 × 520mm. Engraved map, 2 tears affecting blank margins. (CSK. Feb.10; 223)   £190
- - **Anr. Edn.** George Humble, [1627]. 15 × 20 inches. Engraved map, hand-cold. in outl., fold reprd., lightly soiled, window mount. (CSK. May 4; 7)   £190
- - **Anr. Copy.** 15 × 20 inches. Engraved map, hand-cold. outl., fold reprd., lightly soiled, window mount. (CSK. Jul.6; 234)   £160
- - **Anr. Edn.** Bassett & Chiswell, 1676. 510 × 390mm. Uncold. map, browned, 2 inset plans. (P. Apr.12; 370)   *Burgess.* £140
- - **Anr. Edn.** [1713 or 1743]. Approx. 15 × 20 inches. Map, hand-cold., central strapwork title cartouche incorporating scale of distance & hf. compass rose, inset plans of Westminster & L. (TA. Jun.21; 105)   £150
- - **Anr. Edn.** N.d. 16 × 21 inches. Engraved map, after Norden, Westminster & London city plans, engrs. of St. Peter's & St. Paul's. (SKC. Nov.18; 2101)   £50
- **Montgomery Shire.** 1610 [1611-16 or later]. Approx. 15 × 20 inches. Hand-cold. map, ornamental strapwork title cartouche, separate scale of distance surmounted by compass, inset plan, Engl. text on verso, F. & double-G. (TA. Jul.19; 132)   £52
- - **Anr. Edn.** Bassett & Chiswell, [1676]. Approx. 15 × 20 inches. Uncold. map, strapwork title cartouche, separate scale of distance incorporating compass rose, inset town plan of Montgomery, Engl. text to verso. (TA. Mar.15; 83)   £60
- **A New Description of Carolina.** Bassett & Chiswell, [1676]. 510 × 380mm. Uncold. map. (P. Apr.12; 364)   *Potters.* £270
- **Newe Mape of Germany.** 1626. Ob. fo. Cold.

copper engraved map, painted cartouche, 5 costume figures, 8 sm. views at top. slightly browned, sm. defects at foot bkd., margins torn & bkd., some spotting. (R. Apr.6; 4041)   DM 650
- **A Newe Mape of Poland.** L., G. Humble, 1626 [but 1627 or later]. 403 × 512mm. Double-p. engraved map, 2 side borders with 8 vigs., upr. frieze with 6 views, hand-cold., Engl. text on verso, sm. split at centre-fold without loss, faint browning. (S. Apr.9; 125)   *Nebenzahl,.* £140
- - **Anr. Edn.** N.d. Ob. fo. Cold. copper engraved map, 2 painted cartouches, 4 figures & arms at side, port. & 6 sm. views at top, lightly browned, sm. bkd. tear. (R. Oct.14; 4110)   DM 730
- **A New Mappe of the Romane Empire.** L., G. Humble, 1626. Hand-cold. map, plans & figures on 3 borders, sm. tear in margin at lr. centre fold, F. & double-G. (P. May 17; 465)   *Leon.* £130
- - **Anr. Edn.** Bassett & Chiswell, [1676]. 15½ × 20 inches. Engraved map. (CSK. May 4; 142) £95
- **A New Mape of Ye XVII Provinces of Low Germanie.** Bassett & Chiswell, 1676. Hand-cold. map, plans & figures on 3 borders, lr. margin trimmed, few sm. repairs. (P. Dec.8; 422)   *Burgess.* £90
- - **Anr. Edn.** Bassett & Chiswell, [1676]. Approx. 16 × 21 inches. Map, hand-cold. in outl., ornamental title cartouche, side borders of figures, 8 miniature views along top border, compass rose, sailing ships, etc., Engl. text to verso, strengthened along centrefold, a few minor margin repairs, mntd. (TA. Mar.15; 74)   £150
- - **Anr. Copy.** 16 × 21 inches. Engraved map, fold reprd. (CSK. May 4; 141)   £130
- **Norfolk.** Sudbury & Humble, [1611]. Hand-cold. map, inset town plan of Norwich, narrow margins. (P. Oct.20; 272)   £200
- - **Anr. Copy.** Uncold. map, inset town plan, F. & G. (P. Sep.29; 457)   *Wilton.* £130
- **The North & East Ridings of Yorkshire.** Sudbury & Humble, [1612]. 15½ × 20½ inches. Hand-cold. engraved map, fold slightly reprd., F. & G. (CSK. Mar.9; 41)   £70
- - **Anr. Edn.** [George Humble, 1627]. 15½ × 20½ inches. Engraved map, margins reprd. (CSK. May 4; 18)   £80
- **Northumberland.** Sudbury & Humble, [1611]. Hand-cold. map, inset town plan of Newcastle & Berwick, F. (P. Nov.24; 323)   *Steedman.* £95
- - **Anr. Edn.** 1610 [1626 or later]. Approx. 15 × 20 inches. Hand-cold. map, sm. ornamental title cartouche, inset plans of Barwick & Newcastle, armorials, antiquities, etc., Engl. text on verso, sm. repair at head of centrefold. (TA. Jan.19; 82)   £130
- - **Anr. Edn.** R. Rea the elder & younger, 1611 [but 1662 or later]. 383 × 506mm. Double-p. engraved map, hand-cold. in wash & outl. in early hand, inset plans of Berwick & Newcastle with ills. of Roman antiquities, slight adhesion damage at upr. centre-fold affecting engraved surface, F. & G. (S. Nov.1; 165)   *Kidd.* £90
- - **Anr. Edn.** Bassett & Chiswell, [1676]. 15 × 20 inches. Engraved map, fold lightly browned. (CSK. May 4; 16)   £85
- - **Anr. Copy.** Map, a few minor repairs to centrefold, mntd. (TA. Jan.19; 83)   £70
- **Oxfordshire.** [George Humble, 1627]. 15 × 20½ inches. Engraved map, hand-cold. in outl., some light wear along fold, window mount. (CSK. May 4; 4)   £200
- - **Anr. Copy.** Hand-cold. map, inset town plan, arms, fold slightly torn & strengthened, F. & double-G. (P. Feb.16; 319)   £120
- - **Anr. Copy.** 390 × 530mm. Engraved map, hand-cold. in outl., slight wear along fold, F. & G. (CSK. Feb.10; 46)   £80
- **Penbrokshyre described.** L., 1627 or later. 386 × 512mm. Double-p. engraved map, hand-cold. in outl., inset plans & panel showing 11 escutcheons, Engl. text on verso, some worming, laid down on paper. (S. Mar.6; 182)   *Export.* £100
- - **Anr. Edn.** Sudbury & Humble, n.d. 15 × 20 inches. Engraved map, lr. corners reprd. with loss of engraved surface, verso blank. (CSK. May 4; 21)   £70
- - **Anr. Copy.** 15 × 20 inches. Engraved map, lr. corners reprd., verso blank. (CSK. Jul.6; 233) £55

- The Province of Connaugh with the Cite of Galwaye Described. Sudbury & Humble, 1610 [1611-12]. Approx. 15 × 20 inches. Map, cont. handcold., ornamental title cartouche surmounted by Royal crest, separate scale of distance with cherubs & open dividers, inset plans, compass rose, etc., Engl. text on verso, F. & double-G. (TA. May 17; 171) £170

– – **Anr. Edn.** Sudbury & Humble, [1611]. Handcold. map, inset plan, margin & centre fold reprd., in mount. (P. Dec.8; 432) *Morley.* £55

- The Province of Mounster. Bassett & Chiswell, [1676]. 15 × 20½ inches. Engraved map. (CSK. May 4; 148) £55

- The Province of Ulster. Bassett & Chiswell, [1676]. Hand-cold. map, narrow margins, F. & G. (P. Sep.29; 456) *Lasalles.* £85

- Russia. L., T. Bassett & R. Chiswell, [1676]. 15½ × 20 inches. Map, engraved by F. Lamb, sm. cartouche, 6 vigs., all (later?) hand-cold., text on verso, margin worm defects reprd., F. & double-G. (CBA. Dec.10; 294) $200

- Rutlandshire. Sudbury & Humble, [1611]. Handcold. map, 2 inset plans, laid down on card. F. & G. (P. Feb.16; 318) £50

- Shropshyre. Bassett & Chiswell, [1676]. 15 × 20 inches. Engraved map. (CSK. May 4; 147) £85

- Somerset-Shire. Sudbury & Humble, [1611]. 385 × 515mm. Hand-cold. map, inset town plan, slight wear at lr. centre-fold, sm. tears to lr. margin. (P. Jun.7; 348) £160

– – **Anr. Edn.** Sudbury & Humble, 1611 or later. 15¼ × 20¼ inches. Engraved map, inset plan, coats-of arms, galleons at sea, Engl. text on verso, slight stain in lr. margin, sm. tear affecting inset plan, F. (LC. Jul.5; 235) £110

– – **Anr. Edn.** Sudbury & Humble, 1627 or later. 16 × 20¼ inches. Hand-cold. engraved map, inset plan, Royal arms & other coats-of-arms, galleons at sea, Engl. text on verso, slight tears at foot of fold, F. (LC. Jul.5; 234) £160

– – **Anr. Edn.** [1662]. Approx. 15 × 20 inches. Uncold. map, plain title cartouche, separate scale of distance surmounted by open dividers, inset detail of Bathe, sailing ships, etc., minor damage to bottom of centrefold, F. & G. (TA. Sep.15; 167) £140

- Spaine ... G. Humble, 1626 [1627 or later]. 412 × 520mm. Hand-cold. double-p. engraved map, upr. frieze of 9 town views, 10 side vigs. of costumed figures, Engl. text on verso. (S. Jun.25; 255) *Inskip.* £110

– – **Anr. Edn.** Bassett & Chiswell, [1676]. 15 × 21½ inches. Engraved map, hand-cold. in outl., F. & G. (CSK. May 4; 11) £95

- Stafford. Bassett & Chiswell, [1676]. 15½ × 20 inches. Engraved map. (CSK. May 4; 145) £120

– – **Anr. Edn.** Bassett & Chiswell, 1676 or later. Approx. 15 × 20 inches. Uncold. map, corner strapwork title cartouche & separate dedication cartouche, 2 inset plans, scale of distance, armorials, etc., Engl. text on verso, strengthened along centrefold. (TA. Jul.19; 131) £80

- Suffolke Described. [George Humble, 1627]. 15 × 20 inches. Engraved map, margins reprd. (CSK. May 4; 23) £80

- Surrey, Described & Divided into Hundreds. 1610 [1611-12 or later]. Approx. 15 × 20 inches. Handcold. map, ornamental title cartouche, separate scale of distance, compass rose, inset details of Richmond & Nonesuch Castles, several armorials, Engl. text on verso, very slightly soiled along centrefold, sm. repair to base, Hogarth-style F., double-G. (TA. Jan.19; 88) £185

– – **Anr. Edn.** [1611]. Hand-cold. map, arms, 2 sm. margin tears. (P. Dec.8; 424) *Hadden.* £130

– – **Anr. Copy.** 510 × 390mm. Uncold. map, browned, fold & margins strengthened, creases near centrefold, top left corner reprd. with loss of sm. part of border. (P. Apr.12; 372) *Burgess.* £70

– – **Anr. Edn.** Bassett & Chiswell, [1676]. Handcold. map, 2 inset plans, arms, fold very creased, F. & G. (P. Mar.15; 415) *Thorp.* £200

– – **Anr. Copy.** 390 × 510mm. Engraved map, handcold. in outl., fold reprd., margins lightly stained. (CSK. Oct.7; 10) £170

- Sussex. 1607. 16 × 21 inches. Hand-cold. engraved map, after Norden, Chichester street plan,

Royal arms & heraldic devices, F. & G. to obverse. (SKC. Nov.18; 2088) £150

– – **Anr. Edn.** Sudbury & Humble, [1611]. Uncold. map, town plan of Chichester, repair to lr. margin, F. & G. (P. Oct.20; 299a) £190

– – **Anr. Copy.** 17 × 22 inches. Hand-cold. map, after Norden, engraved by Hondius, town plan, heraldic devices, F. & G. (SKC. May 4; 1548) £100

– – **Anr. Edn.** L., Bassett & Chiswell, [1676]. 390 × 520mm. Hand-cold. map, inset plan, arms. (P. May 17; 435) *Goodall.* £210

– – **Anr. Copy.** 17 × 21 inches. Engraved map, after Nordern, Chichester city plan, heraldic devices. (SKC. Nov.18; 2098) £55

– – **Anr. Edn.** Henry Overton, ca. 1700 or later. Approx. 15 × 20 inches. Map, hand-cold. in outl., 'open book' title cartouche, separate scale of distance, Royal crest & several armorials, inset plan, sailing ships & sea monsters, etc., Engl. text on verso, printing defect to lr. left-hand corner. (TA. Jul.19; 130) £130

- The Turkish Empire. [1676]. 15½ × 20½ inches. Engraved map, hand-cold. outl., lr. margins lightly stained, F. & G. (CSK. Jul.6; 184) £140

- Ungarn. 1626. Ob. fo. Cold. copper engraved map, painted cartouche, 4 figures at sides, arms at top., 4 sm. views, partly lightly browned, sm. tear at foot, margin pasted. (R. Oct.14; 4149) DM 750

- Wales. J. Sudbury & G. Humble, 1610 [but 1611, or later]. 385 × 511mm. Double-p. engraved general map, side borders each incorporating 6 vig. town views, 4 smaller in map area, Engl. text on verso, the whole hand-cold., F. & double-G., w.a.f. (S. May 21; 52) *Glamert.* £280

– – **Anr. Edn.** J. Sudbury & G. Humble, 1610, [1627, or later]. 385 × 509mm. Double-p. engraved map, side borders each showing 6 inset town views, Engl. text on verso, short split at lr. centrefold without loss. (S. Jun.25; 422) £180

– – **Anr. Edn.** Bassett & Chiswell, [1676]. 15 × 20 inches. Engraved map, hand-cold. in outl., window mount. (CSK. May 4; 8) £170

– – **Anr. Edn.** L., Chiswell & Bassett, [1676 or after]. 380 × 500mm. Double-p. engraved man, later hand hand-colouring, 12 bird's-eye views of Welsh cities, in 2 vertical side panels, & 4 views of abbeys, compass rose, sailing ship, sea monsters, coats-of-arms, satisfactory margins, mntd. to backing bd. & overmat. (SG. Jun.7; 136) $225

- Warwickshire. Sudbury & Humble, [1611]. 510 × 390mm. Hand-cold. map, 2 inset town plans, arms, F. & double-G. (P. Jun.7; 375) £75

- The West Riding of Yorkeshyre. Bassett & Chiswell, 1676. Uncold. map, inset plan, washed & strengthened. (P. Dec.8; 425) *Burgess.* £55

- Wight Island. [1676] or later. Approx. 15 × 20 inches. Map, hand-cold., sm. strapwork title cartouche, separate scale of distance, inset plans of Newport & Southampton, armorials, sailing ships, etc. (TA. Jun.21; 102) £110

– – **Anr. Edn.** [1713 or 1743]. Approx. 15 × 20 inches. Map, hand-cold., sm. strapwork title cartouche, separate scale of distance, inset plans of Newport & Southampton, armorials, sailing ships, etc., a little browned overall, F. & G. (TA. Jun.21; 103) £125

– – **Anr. Edn.** H. Overton, ca. 1740. Hand-cold. map, 2 inset town plans, F. & G. (P. Jul.26; 253) £90

– – **Anr. Edn.** [1743]. Approx. 15½ × 21 inches. Hand-cold. map, sm. ornamental title cartouche, separate scale of distance, inset details of Newport & Southampton, armorials, sailing ships, etc., Hogarth-style F. (TA. Jan.19; 84) £70

- Wiltshire. Sudbury & Humble. [1611]. 515 × 395mm. Hand-cold. map, inset town plan, arms, F. & double-G. (P. Nov.24; 319) *Lintin.* £210

– – **Anr. Copy.** 510 × 385mm. Hand-cold. map, inset plans, arms. (P. Dec.8; 449) *Hadden.* £160

– – **Anr. Copy.** Hand-cold. map, inset town plan, in mount. (P. Sep.8; 469) *Sanders.* £130

– – **Anr. Edn.** H. Overton, [1743]. Hand-cold. map, inset town plan, no text on verso. (P. Mar.15; 401) £110

- Worcestershire Described. 1610 [1676]. Approx. 15 × 20 inches. Map, hand-cold. in outl., strapwork title cartouche, inset detail of Worcester, compass rose, armorials, etc., Engl. text on verso, a little

browned overall, Hogarth-style F. (TA. Jan.19; 91) £85

– – **Anr. Edn.** [1676] or later. 15 × 20 inches. Map, partially cold., strapwork cartouche, separate scale of distance surmntd. by open dividers, several armorials, inset plan of Worcester, F. & G. (TA. Jun.21; 106) £86

- Yorkshire. Bassett & Chiswell, 1676. 18½ × 20 inches. Engraved map, hand-cold. in outl., lr. margin lightly spotted. (CSK. Mar.9; 10) £100

– – **Anr. Edn.** Bassett & Chiswell, [1676]. 15 × 20 inches. Engraved map. (CSK. May 4; 146) £85

SPRENT, James

- Tasmania. L., 1859. 1700 × 1250mm. Folding hand-cold. engraved map, some light spotting, mntd. on cl., cl. folder. (CSK. Feb.24; 38) £380

STELLA, STOLTZ or STOLZ, Tileman

- Palestinae sive Totius Terrae Promissionis Nova Descriptio. [Antw., 1570 or later]. 350 × 473mm. Double-p. engraved map from Ortelius Theatrum extending from Nile delta to Beirut, showing also route of the Wanderings, 1st. state, fully hand-cold. in wash & outl., F. & G., w.a.f. (S. May 22; 266) *Samiramis.* £800

– – **Anr. Edn.** [Antw., 1579 or later]. 344 × 460mm. Double-p. engraved map extending from Nile delta to Lebanon, in post-1579 state, hand-cold., Latin text on verso, sm. repair at lr. centrefold just touching lr. neatline, faint margin browning, w.a.f. (S. May 22; 265) *Hague.* £500

– – **Anr. Edn.** [Antw., 1579, but 1587 or later]. 346 × 467mm. Double-p. engraved map extending from Nile delta to Beirut, from Ortelius's Theatrum, 2nd., post-1579 state, showing 5 sailing vessels, hand-cold. in full, Fr. text on verso, w.a.f. (S. May 22; 264) *Hague.* £400

– – **Anr. Edn.** 17th. C.? 80 × 105mm. Engraved map, hand-cold. in outl., cold. notations, Italian text on verso. (SG. Dec.15; 106) $175

TALLIS, J.

- Illustrated Plan of London & its Environs. Ca. 1850. 730 × 545mm. Hand-cold. plan, inset ills. of landmarks on 4 borders. (P. Jul.26; 241) £140

TAYLOR, Alexander

- A Map of the County Kildare. L., 1783. 25½ × 37 inches. Map, in 6 pts., uncold. engraved cartouches, etc. (GM. Dec.7; 503) £160

THORLAKSSON, G.

[-] **Islandia.** [Antw., 1589 or later]. 337 × 493mm. Double-p. engraved map, from Ortelius's Theatrum, elab. embellished with ills. of marine fauna & depiction of Hekla in full eruption, Latin text on verso, wormhole in upr. blank margin, w.a.f. (S. May 22; 452) *Tonge.* £380

TIRION, Isaac

- Nieuwe Kaart van de Kaap der Goede Hoope. 1763. 310 × 215mm. Line engraved map, outl. cold. (VA. Oct.28; 337) R 340

- Nuova Carta dell Asia ... [Venice], 1750 or before. 275 × 340mm. Map, hand-cold. in outl., title & scale cartouche, trimmed margins. (SG. Dec.15; 56) $110

TOKYO

Tokyo, [1837]. 1,320 × 1,400mm. Folding woodblock map on sheets of paper pieced to 132 × 140cm., screened cold notations for mountains & water, panels of text in Japanese, some wear & rubbing at folds, minor worming, lacks rear bd. cover. (SG. Jun.7; 96) $175

TOMBLESON, William

- Panoramic Map of the Thames & Medway. L., J. Reynolds,. n.d. Hand-cold. folding plan, linen-bkd., cl. folder. (P. Dec.8; 421) *Greenaway.* £80

TSCHUDI, Aegidius

- Helvetiae Descriptio. N.d. 340 × 450mm. Early outl. cold. map, south-orientated, surface col., lge. cartouche, Latin caption, light paper defect reprd. in lr. left corner. (GF. Nov.17; 2777) Sw. Frs. 480

THORNTON, John

- A Large Draught of New England New York & Long Island. [1685 or later]. 17½ × 22 inches. Engraved chart, hand-cold. in outl., inset chart of

THORNTON, John -*Contd.*

Boston harbour, upr. margin slightly trimmed, light browning. (CSK. May 4; 189) £480

UNITED STATES OF AMERICA
– **Il Maryland, Il Jersey Meridionale, la Delaware, e la Parte Orientale della Virginia, Carolina Settentrionale.** Ca. 1780. 12⅛ × 16¼ inches. Engraved map, hand-cold. in outl., no credit, removed from unmentioned atlas, engraved borders, title in top margin, topographical details, some text relating to Revolutionary War at right side, centrefold, extensive place notations thro.-out territory included, matted. (HA. May 4; 18) $170

VALCK, Gerard
– **Mappe-Monde Geo Hydrographique du Globe.** Amst., early 18th. C. 430 × 520mm. Double hemispheric double-p. engraved map, fully hand-cold., 2 smaller hemispheres of the Poles, satisfactory margins, verso blank, some wear at fold, minor repairs on verso. (SG. Jun.7; 144) $400
See— SCHENK, Pieter & Valck, Gerard

VALCK, Gerard & Leonhard
– **America Aurea pars Altera Mundi.** [Amst., 1690 or later]. 485 × 595mm. Double-p. engraved general map showing highly indented outl. of California island, indication of Northwest Passage running from Hudson Bay, indistinct landmass 'Terra Esonis' in northern Pacific, map area hand-cold. in wash & outl., w.a.f. (S. May 22; 293) *Cookson.* £500
– **Orbis Terrarum Nova et Accurata Tabula.** Amst., G. Valck, Ca. 1700. 470 × 580mm. Double-p. engraved map in twin hemispheres showing California as an island, Australia & New Zealand, & 'Eso' (Hokkaido) in northern Japan as a lge. peninsula of eastern Asia, the whole surrounded by elab. allegorical vigs. representing 4 continents, & 2 smaller hemispheres showing polar regions, map area hand-cold. in wash & outl., 1 or 2 faint stains affecting engraved surface, w.a.f. (S. May 21; 154) *Alai.* £1,100

VAN DEN BERG, Petrus
See— MONTANUS, P.

VAN DEN KEERE, Petrus
– **Comitatus Zutphania.** N.d. 372 × 500mm. Cold. engraved map, margins concealed by mount, central vertical fold, F. (CH. May 24; 234) Fls. 480
– **Italiae Sardiniae, Corsicae, & Confinium Regionum Nova Tabula.** Amst., 1616 [or later]. 462 × 560mm. Double-p. engraved general map, hand-cold., upr. & lr. friezes showing vig. town views of Naples, Genoa, Florence, Rome, Verona, Temeraris & Puteoloi above, & Terracina, Blitri, Templum Fragana, Venice Drepanum, Siena & Parma below, & side borders each of 4 vigs. showing male & female costume figures, traces of folds strengthened or reprd. without significant loss of engraved surface, w.a.f. (S. May 21; 206) *Maggs.* £680
[-] **Nova Germainae Descriptio.** Amst., J. Jansson, 1632 [or later]. 460 × 560mm. Hand-cold. double-p. engraved map, upr. & lr. friezes with equestrian figures & 6 (of 10) town views, side borders with costumed figures, verso blank, extensive repairs. (S. Jun.25; 219) *Menodniczansky.* £120

VANDER AA, Pieter
See— AA, Pieter van der

VAN KEULEN, Gerard
See— KEULEN, Gerard van

VAN KEULEN, Joannes
See— KEULEN, Johannes van

VAUGONDY, Gilles-Robert de
– **Mappemonde ou Description du Globe Terrestre** ... Paris, 1752. Approx. 19 × 28½ inches. Hand-cold. double hemisphere map, central ornamental title cartouche with figures & cherubs, browned at edges. (TA. Jul.19; 115) £180
– **Plan Géométrical de Paris et des ses Fauxbourgs.** 1797. 955 × 650mm. Hand-cold. town plan, F. & G. (P. Jul.26; 250) £55

VAUGONDY, Gilles Robert de & Didier Robert de
– **Partie de l'Amérique Septent. qui comprend la Nouvelle France ou le Canada.** [Paris], 1755 [or later]. 478 × 602mm. Double-p. engraved map of Maritime Provinces, incorporating a lge. detailed inset map of Great Lakes region, hand-cold. in outl., w.a.f. (S. May 22; 353) *Fergusson.* £200

VISSCHER, Nicolaus Joannis or Claes Janz
– **Antwerpen.** Amst., ca. 1680. 460 × 560mm. Cont. hand-cold. engraved map, heightened in gold, centre fold. (VG. Mar.22; 1614) Fls. 1,100
– **Asiae Nova Delineatio.** Amst., late 17th. C. 440 × 550mm. Double-p. map, hand-cold. in outl., title cartouche with figures, armorial dedication cartouche, several sm. ships, etc., few minor spots. (SG. Dec.15; 57) $140
– **Belgii Pars Meridionalis.** Amst., 1698. 475 × 550mm. Cont. hand-cold. engraved map, heightened with gold, centre fold. (VG. Mar.22; 1616) Fls. 650
– **Belgium Foederatum.** Amst., [after 1708]. 500 × 600mm. Hand-cold. folding map, from 'De Stoel des Oorlogs in de Wereld'. (VG. Sep.15; 1607) Fls. 500
– **Germania.** Amst., 1645. Map, decor. surround with costumes & views, many sm. arms cartouches, imprint slightly weak, paper remains on right-hand verso, some spots. (HK. Nov.12; 5505) DM 1,200
– **Hollandiae Pars Meridionalior, vulgo Zuyd-Holland.** Amst., [1698]. 470 × 570mm. Cont. hand-cold. engraved map, cartouche hand-cold., centre fold. (VG. Mar.22; 1798) Fls. 800
– **Indiae Orientalis.** Ca. 1680. Outl. & surface cold. copper engraved map. (BR. Apr.13; 2901) DM 480
– **Insula Ceilon olim Taprobana incolis Tenarisin et Lankawn** ... Amst., ca. 1680. Approx. 20 × 23½ inches. Hand-cold. map, ornamental title cartouche with elephant & figures, heightened with gold. (TA. Jul.19; 150) £105
– **Insulae, Americanae.** Ca. 1690. 570 × 470mm. Hand-cold. map, cartouche, decor., slightly stained. (P. Sep.8; 457) *Radford.* £160
– **Mittelamerika.** Ca. 1680. Cont. cold. copper engraved map, outl. & surface cold. (BR. Apr.13; 2894) DM 400
– **A New, Plaine & Exact Map of America.** Ill.:– after I. Blaeu. Ca. 1650. Decor. edges with figures & sm. ports. & views in upr. & lr. margin, 3 sm. holes, crumpling, some light browning or foxing. (HK. Nov.12; 5422) DM 3,600
– **Nova Totius Terrarum Orbis Geographica ac Hydrographica Tabula.** [Amst., 1649 but 1652 or later]. Double-p. engraved map on Mercator projection surrounded by upr. & lr. friezes incorporating allegories of 4 continents & equestrian miniatures of Roman emperors, 2 side borders incorporating 8 miniature vig. town views & 6 others showing regional native figures, hand-cold. in outl., faint discolouration, w.a.f. (S. May 21; 155) *Rothman.* £2,400
– – Anr. Edn. [Amst.], 1652 [or later]. Double-p. engraved map on the Mercator projection, surrounded by upr. & lr. friezes with allegories of the 4 continents & equestrian miniatures & side borders with figures & miniature vig. town views, left hand margin restored affecting engraved surface at lr. corner, slight restoration at centrefold without affecting engraved surface. (S. Dec.1; 216) *Map House.* £1,650
– **Novi Belgii Novaeque Angliae nec non partis Virginiae Tabula** ... Amst., ca. 1651. *Later iss., with Phila. added.* 457 × 550mm. Map, hand-cold. in outl., elab. cartouche with view, land mass decor. with animals, etc., cartouche & decors. fully cold., matted, F. & G. (PNY. Jun.6; 525) $1,450
– **Novissima et Accuratissima Totius Americae.** Ca. 1699. 535 × 470mm. Hand-cold. map, slightly soiled. (P. Sep.8; 458) $200
– – Anr. Edn. [Amst.], 17th. C. 440 × 550mm. Double-p. engraved map, hand-cold., dedicatory & title cartouches with figures, age-darkened & foxed in pts., few minor holes, mntd. to larger bd. (SG. Dec.15; 45) $550
– **Novissima XVII Provinciarum Tabula.** Amst., [after 1708]. 500 × 600mm. Hand-cold. folding map, from 'De Stoel des Oorlogs in de Wereld',

restored tears in margin, slightly browned in fold. (VG. Sep.15; 1604) Fls. 500
– **Orbis Terrarum Typus de Integro in Plurimis Emendatus, et Icunculis Illustratus.** [Amst., 1657 or later]. 308 × 476mm. Double-p. engraved map in twin hemispheres, fully hand-cold. & heightened with gold, showing in particular Dutch discoveries in Australia, a revised coastline at New Guinea, California as a peninsula, & route of Schouten & le Maire, the whole surrounded by allegorical figures symbolising 4 continents & 2 sm. celestial hemispherical diagrams, Dutch text on verso, faint margin stain touching lr. neatline, w.a.f. (S. May 21; 156) *Cookson.* £580
– **Planisphaerium Coeleste.** N.p., [after 1708]. 500 × 720mm. Hand-cold. folding map, from 'De Stoel des Oorlogs in de Wereld', slight offsetting, faint spots. (VG. Sep.15; 1581) Fls. 660
– **Scotiae Tabula.** Ca. 1680. 480 × 360mm. Hand-cold. map. (P. Jan.12; 351) *Stratford.* £60
– **Totius Circuli Westphalici accurate descriptio.** [Amst.], ca. 1690. 610 × 553mm. Engraved hand-cold. map on 2 joined sheets, orientated west to top of sheet, slight wear at fold affecting engraved surface. (S. Dec.13; 63) *Schuster.* £65
– **Vlakke Aard-kloot.** Amst., [after 1708]. 500 × 600mm. Hand-cold. folding map, from 'De Stoel des Oorlogs in de Wereld', defects, restored tears in margin. (VG. Sep.15; 1580) Fls. 600
– **Walcheren.** N.d. 470 × 540mm. Cold. engraved map, margins, 3 sm. tears, F. (CH. May 24; 245) Fls. 480
– **Westphaliae Circulus.** Amst., [after 1708]. 500 × 600mm. Hand-cold. folding map, from 'De Stoel des Oorlogs in de Wereld'. (VG. Sep.15; 1602) Fls. 450

VOOGT, Claes Jansz
– **Wassende Graade Kaart van de Noort Zee.** Amst., J. van Keulen, 1689 or later. 522 × 600mm. Double-p. engraved chart, orientated west to the top of sheet, hand-cold. in outl., embellishments fully cold., upr. margin shaved within neatline (as usual), bkd. with stiff paper. (S. Dec.13; 187) *Charles.* £150

WAGHENAER, Lucas Janszoon
– **Beschrijvinghe vande Zee Custen van Engelandt Tusschen Blacgneij en Scharenburch.** [1580]. 13 × 20 inches. Hand-cold. engraved chart, German text on verso, lr. margin lightly stained. (CSK. Mar.9; 11) £260
– – Anr. Edn. [Leiden, ca. 1590]. 325 × 505mm. Double-p. engraved coastal chart extending from Blakeney to Scarborough by way of King's Lynn, the Wash, the Humber estuary & Flambourough Head, hand-cold., Latin text on verso, double-glazed gt. F., w.a.f. (S. May 21; 43) *Leycester.* £150
– **Brittany.** 1588. 16 × 22 inches. Hand-cold. chart, from 'The Mariner's Mirrour', engraved by Bry, title cartouche, F. & double-G. (SKC. May 4; 1527) £120
– **Caerte der Noordt Custe va Engelandt beginnende van Robinhodes Baij tot Cocket Eijlandt.** [1586]. 13 × 20 inches. Hand-cold. engraved chart, Latin text on verso, sm. clean tear affects lr. margin. (CSK. Mar.9; 12) £260
– **Caerte van de Zee Custen van Acason en Biscaie.** Late 16th. C. *Latin Edn.* Ob. fo. Cold. copper engraved map from Seeatlas, 2 painted rollwork cartouches & decor., slightly spotted. (R. Oct.13; 3381) DM 950
– **Les Costes Marines de Biscaye entre Laredo e. S. Alana.** Late 16th. C. *Fr. Edn.* Ob. fo. Cold. copper engraved map from Seeatlas, 2 painted rollwork cartouches, & decor. (R. Oct.13; 3382) DM 850
– **Les Costes Marines de Galicie du Cap d'Aiules jusques à Ortegal.** Late 16th. C. *Fr. Edn.* Ob. fo. Cold. copper engraved map from Seeatlas, 2 painted rollwork cartouches, decor. (R. Oct.13; 3383) DM 700
– **Description des Costes Marines de Gallicie depuis le Cap de Finistère jusques à Camino.** Late 16th. C. *Fr. Edn.* Ob. fo. Cold. copper engraved map from Seeatlas, 2 painted rollwork cartouches, decor. (R. Oct.13; 3384) DM 850

WALDSEEMULLER, M.
– Tabula Noua Totius Orbis. ca. 1540. 460 ×
295mm. Uncold. map. (P. May 17; 451)
Leverton. £300

WALKER, John & Charles
– Geological Map of England, Wales & Part Scot-
land, showing the Inland Navigation of by means of
Rivers & Canals ... together With Rail Roads &
Principal Roads ... 1835. Folding engraved col.
map, linen back. s.-c. (PD. Jun.13; 172)   £65

WALKER, John
See— PRIESTLEY, J. & Walker, John

WELLS, Edward
[–] Antient Asia. – Present Asia. Ca. 1700 or later.
Approx. 15 × 20 inches. Together 2 maps, uncold.,
ornamental title cartouche, separate dedication car-
touche to William, Duke of Gloucester. (TA.
Jun.21; 143)   £60
– A New Map of Libya & Old Africa. 1701. 370 ×
495mm. Line engraved map, cold. outl. (VA.
Apr.27; 604)   R 180

WESTON, William, Engineer
– A Plan of the Line of the Proposed London &
Western Canal from Hampton Gay to Isleworth.
Ca. 1860. Approx. 20 × 58 inches. Uncold. plan,
some restoration, recently F. & G. (TA. Jul.19;
111)   £80

WIGATE, J.
– Charte of the Seas, Straits etc. thro' which HM
Sloop Furnace pass'd for discovering a Passage from
Hudson's Bay to the South Sea. L., John Bowles,
1746. 590 × 940mm. Outl. cold. copper engraved
map ptd. from 2 plts, 2 sm. supp. maps, foxed,
especially in upr. part, tears bkd., slightly crumpled.
(R. Oct.13; 3457)   DM 2,100

WILDEY, George
– A New & Correct Map of the World. Ca. 1714.
650 × 960mm. Engraved map, hand-cold. in outl.,
upr. & lr. margins trimmed & reprd., several tears
reprd., some light staining. (CSK. Dec.2; 7) £380

WIT, Frederick de
[–] Americae Meridionalis a Rio de la Plata per
Fretum Magellanicum. [Amst.], n.d. 480 × 550mm.
Hand-cold. engraved map, cartouche, text in
Latin & Dutch, slightly soiled. (BBA. Aug.18; 178)
Faupel. £120
– Anglia Regnum. Ca. 1680. 490 × 590mm. Hand-
cold. map. (P. Jan.12; 341)   *Stratford.* £65
[–] Daniae, Frisiae, Groningae et Orientalis Frisiae
Littora. Amst., R. & J. Ottens, 1745 or later. 492 ×
561mm. Hand-cold. chart, faint crease. (S. Dec.13;
38)   *Knappe.* £130
– Ducatus Slesvicensis. N.d. Cold. copper-engraved
map, minimal foxing. (V. Sep.29; 827)   DM 430
– Insula Candia. [1680]. 18½ × 22 inches.
Engraved map, hand-cold. in outl., margins slightly
stained. (CSK. May 4; 211)   £180
– – Anr. Copy. 555 × 465mm. Hand-cold. map,
inset plans, browned, back strengthened. (P. Jan.12;
329)   *Sambas.* £60
– – Anr. Edn. Early 18th. C. 18½ × 21½ inches.
Engraved map, hand-cold. outl., margins & fold
lightly stained. (CSK. Jul.6; 152)   £80
– – Anr. Edn. N.d. 16 × 20 inches. Engraved map,
margins slightly soiled. (CSK. Jul.6; 158)   £70
– Insula Candia ejusque Fortificatio. [1680 or later].
18 × 22 inches. Engraved hand-cold. map, lr.
margin lightly stained. (CSK. May 4; 232)   £150
– – Anr. Copy. 18½ × 21½ inches. Engraved map,
hand-cold. outl., margins soiled. (CSK. Jul.6; 155)
£100

– Littora Brasiliae. Pascaert van Brasil. [Amst.],
1675 or later. *Early iss., with plt. no. 21.* 480 ×
560mm. Hand-cold. double-p. engraved chart,
orientated east to the top of the sheet, lge. scenic
title cartouche at lr. centre. (S. Jun.25; 133)
Ash. £150
– – Anr. Edn. [Amst.], 1675 [but 1745 or later].
477 × 555mm. Double-p. engraved chart, orientated East to top of sheet, hand-cold. in wash &
outl., margin spotting. (S. Nov.1; 218) *Ash.* £160
[–] Magnum Mare del Zur cum Insula California.
Amst., R. & J. Ottens, [1675, but 1745]. 495 ×
570mm. Double-p. engraved sea-chart, hand-cold.,
sm. flaw at centrefold, F. & G. (S. Mar.6; 151)
Potter. £240
– Nova et Accurata Totius Africae Tabula Emendata a F. de Wit. Amst., ca. 1660. 1,210 ×
1,550mm. Engraved wall-map in 6 sheets joined,
engraved side-border vigs. showing Alexandria,
Alciers, Tunis, Oran, Elmina fort, Elmina town,
Luanda, Algiers, & Angra on left-hand side, &
Cairo, Malta, Ceuta, Tripoli, Fort Nassau, Canaria,
Sao Tome, Tangiers, & Malta on right-hand side,
ptd. text in Spanish below, mntd. on line, traces of
old col., surface dirt or discolouration, some loss of
surface, w.a.f. (S. May 22; 410)   *Rothman.* £700
– Nova Orbis Tabula, in Lucem Edita, a F. de Wit.
Amst., [1680 or later]. *State 2.* 470 × 555mm.
Double-p. engraved map in twin hemispheres,
including California as an island, New Guinea
separated from Australia, New Zealand, & with
rounded coastline of Siberia, the whole surrounded
by vig. ills. representing the 4 continents, & 2
smaller hemispheres showing polar regions, hand-
cold. in wash & outl., 1 or 2 faint marks on engraved
surface, w.a.f. (S. May 21; 151)
Map House. £1,500
– Nova Totius Angliae, Scotiae, et Hiberniae. Amst.,
ca. 1680 or later. Approx. 19 × 22 inches. Map,
hand-cold., ornamental title cartouche incorporating Royal arms & figures, armorials, etc., some
minor margin tears, hardly affecting engraved surface. (TA. Jun.21; 131)   £75
– Novissima et Accuratissima Septentrionalis ac
Meridionalis Americae Descriptio ... Amst., late
17th. C. 480 × 580mm. Engraved map, hand-cold.
in outl., title cartouches etc., margins trimmed, &
rubbed & soiled, some soiling on verso, centre
crease, some separation at fold, liby. stp. (SG.
Dec.15; 31) $600
– Occidentalior Tractus Indiarum Orientalium ...
Amst., ca. 1670. 20 × 23 inches (including margins). Hand-cold. engraved map, cartouche, 3 vigs.,
paper darkening, especially in margins, mild offsetting, 3 sm. tears, & long split in cartouche, reprd.,
verso darkened, cleaned, matted. (CBA. Aug.21;
748a) $225
– Regni Angliae ... Comprehendens Principatum
Walliae et Glocestriae. Amst., ca. 1660 or later.
Approx. 23 × 19½ inches. Map, cont. hand-cold.
in outl., decor. title cartouche surrounded by
cherubs & figures. (TA. Nov.17; 106)   £64
– Regni Daniae ... Ca. 1680. 545 × 450mm. Hand-
cold. map, arms, back strengthened. (P. Jan.12;
330)   *Jorgensen.* £60
– Scotia Regnum. Ca. 1660 or later. Approx. 23 ×
20 inches. Cont. hand-cold. map, corner tablet title
cartouche with cherub, Royal arms, sm. compass
roses, laid down. (TA. Nov.17; 105)   £54
[–] Septemtrionaliora Americae a Groenlandia, per
Freta Davidis et Hudson, ad Terram Novam. [Amst.],
1675 or later]. 488 × 566mm. Double-p. engraved
coastal chart including part of Greenland, Baffin
Land, the Ungava region & Hudson Bay, hand-
cold. in outl., cartouches fully so, w.a.f. (S. May
22; 354)   *Crete.* £300

– Tabula Indiae Orientalis. [Amst.], 1662 [but
1680]. 460 × 562mm. Double-p. engraved map,
hand-cold. in wash & outl., faint browning, upr.
margin slightly frayed. (S. Nov.1; 247)
Potter. £130
– Terra Sancta, sive Promissionis, olim Palestina
Recens Delineata. Amst., 1659 [but 1680 or later].
463 × 563mm. Double-p. engraved map after C.J.
Visscher, orientated West to top of sheet, cold. in
wash & outl., centre-fold strengthened, faint
margin browning. (S. Nov.1; 242)   *Potter.* £100
– – Anr. Edn. Amst., later 17th. C. 460 × 540mm.
Double-p. engraved map, hand-cold. in outl., inset
bird's eye view entitled 'Castrorum Populi Israelitici
... ', verso blank, full margins, some early creasing,
especially at centrefold. (SG. Jun.7; 41) $130

WOODWARD, H.P.
– Geological Sketch Map of Western Australia.
1894. Cold. folding map, on linen, orig. cl. folder.
(P. Jun.7; 365)   £75

WRIGHT, Thomas
– A New Chart of the Gulf of St. Lawrence ... L.,
William Faden, 1790. 50 × 41 inches. Engraved
chart, in 4 sheets, elab. scenic cartouche, inset
coastal views, tables & maps, wash to border, some
offsetting & slight browning. (SPB. May 23; 6)
$550

WRIGHT, Thomas & others
– A Topographical Map of the Province of New
Hampshire ... L., William Faden, 1784. 46 × 30½
inches. Engraved map, in 2 sheets, hand-cold. in
outl., extensive margins, descriptive title & advt. in
upr. sheet, slight traces of browning at folds &
margins. (SPB. May 23; 14) $4,500

WYLD, James
– Map of South Australia. Ca. 1840. 945 × 630mm.
Map, cold. in outl. (P. Sep.29; 453) *Radford.* £90
– Sketch of the Country around Montreal showing
the Villages & Military Positions. 1837. 19½ × 31
inches. Litho. map on 2 sheets, laid down on cl.,
some soiling. (CSK. Jul.6; 176)   £300

YEAKELL, Thomas & Gardner, W.
– First [–Fourth] Sheet of an Actual Topographical
Survey of the County of Sussex. L., W. Faden,
1778-83. 1,460 × 1,960mm. Engraved lge. scale
hand-cold. map, in 4 sheets, mntd. & dissected in
64 sections, some light soiling, folding into paper
s.-c. (S. Mar.6; 172)   *Cumming.* £250

YORKTOWN
– A Plan of Yorktown & Gloucester in the Province
of Virginia ... L., W. Faden, 1785. 27½ × 21
inches. Engraved map. (SPB. Oct.26; 14) $2,250

ZATTA, Antonio
– L'Impero del Giapon. Venice, 1785. 310 ×
405mm. Full-p. engraved map, outl. hand-cold.,
cartouche fully hand-cold. (S. Nov.1; 250)
Ash. £50
– Il Mappa Mondo. 1774. 425 × 295mm. Hand-
cold. map. (P. Apr.12; 353)   *Ruddell.* £70
– Mossico ovvero Nuova Spagna. 1785. 405 ×
325mm. Hand-cold. map. (P. Apr.12; 352)
Stevens. £50

ZOLLMANNUS, Fr.
– Comitatus Hanau ... ut et Büdingen et Nidda ...
Wetteravia. Nuremb., Homann, 1728. Old cold.
map with view & uncold. cartouche, lr. outer
margin bkd., slight staining at head. (HK. Nov.12;
5574)   DM 420